U.S. Army Register

(Volume III) Retired Lists

1, January 1969

Unknown

Alpha Editions

This edition published in 2020

ISBN : 9789354031397

Design and Setting By
Alpha Editions
email - alphaedis@gmail.com

DEPARTMENT OF THE ARMY
WASHINGTON, D.C.

U.S. ARMY REGISTER

VOLUME III

RETIRED LISTS

1 January 1969

Published by order of the SECRETARY OF THE ARMY

U.S. GOVERNMENT PRINTING OFFICE
WASHINGTON : 1969

For sale by the Superintendent of Documents, U.S. Government Printing Office
Washington, D.C. 20402 - Price $3.50

Distribution:

Active Army:

DCSLOG (2)
VCofS (2)
USASA (8)
ACSI (2)
DCSPER (2)
DCSOPS (6)
OPO (140)
CORC (5)
TJAG (2)
TIG (2)
CNGB (2)
CAR (2)
COA (2)
CMH (3)
CofCh (2)
TPMG (2)
CINFO (2)
CRD (2)
TSG (3)
CofEngrs (2)
Dir of Trans (2)
ACSC-E (2)
CofSptS (12)
TAG (2)
USCONARC (2)
USACDC (24)
USAMC (5)
USAECOM (17)
ARADCOM (1)
ARADCOM Rgn (1)
OS Maj Comd (2) except
  USARHAW (3)
  USARPAC (12)
MDW (2)
Armies (2) except
  1st USA (4)
  4th USA (3)
  6th USA (4)
Corps (2)
Div (1)
Bde (1)
500th MI Gp (1)
AHS (1)
CAMSTA (1)
CAMTMTS (1)
EAMTMTS (1)
WAMTMTS (1)
POE (1)
Arsenals (1)
Lab (1)
GENDEP (OS) (1)
Sup Sec GENDEP (OS) (1)
Army Dep (1)
Dep (OS) (1)
PG (1)
GH (1)
Army Hosp (1)
Centers (1)
DCA (5)
USACGSC (1)
USMA (5)
USAWC (19)
Br Svc Sch (1)
Specialist Sch (1)
Joint Sch (1)
FAOUSA (1)
TIOH, USA (1)
JBUSMC (1)
MAAG (1)
Mil Msn (1)
Units organized under following TOE:
  12-510 (1)
EACH GENERAL OFFICER ON THE RETIRED LIST (1)

NG: State AG (1).

USAR: None.

For explanation of abbreviations used, see AR 320-50.

[illegible] (2)
[illegible] (1)
[illegible]
ARADCOM [illegible]
ARADCOM [illegible] (1)
[illegible] (2) except
USARHAW (3)
USARPAC (12)
[illegible] (2)
[illegible] (2) except
[illegible] USA (4)
[illegible] USA (1)
[illegible] USA (1)
[illegible]
Reg [illegible] (1)
[illegible] Mil Gp (1)
AHS (1)
CAMSTA (1)
CAMTMTS (1)
EAMTMTS (1)
WAMTMTS (1)
POE (1)
Arsenals (1)
Lab (1)

GENDEP (OS) (1)
Sup Sec GENDEP (OS) (1)
Army Dep (1)
Dep (OS) (1)
PG (1)
GH (1)
Army Hosp (1)
Centers (1)
DCA (5)
USACGSC (1)
USMA (5)
USAWC (10)
Br Svc Sch (1)
Specialist Sch (1)
Joint Sch (1)
FAOUSA (1)
TIOH, USA (1)
JBUSMC (1)
MAAG (1)
Mil Msn (1)
Units organized under following TOE:
12–510 (1)
EACH GENERAL OFFICER ON THE RETIRED LIST (1)

[illegible] see AR 320–50.

TABLE OF CONTENTS

EXPLANATORY NOTES

SOURCE OF DATA: All data are as of 31 December 1968 and was extracted from Retired Personnel Master Tape Record maintained by U.S. Army Data Support Command, Department of the Army, Washington, D.C. 20310.

NAMES: Names appearing in the Register are limited to twenty spaces. Due to these space limitations, names appear in truncated form as entered on the Retired Personnel Master Tape Record rather than reduced to abbreviations or initials.

RETIREMENT LISTINGS: Upon Retirement from the Army, members are placed on one of the following Retired Lists. An explanation of the composition of these lists is included in the section divider page prefacing the appropriate retirement listing.

United States Army Retired List
Army of the United States Retired List
Temporary Disability Retired List
Emergency Officers Retired List

PREPARATION OF IDENTIFICATION CARDS: Detailed instructions for the preparation of DD Form 2A (Ret) (gray) (Identification Card) for retired members are contained in section V, AR 606-5.

ERRORS AND OMISSIONS: Errors in and/or omissions from the Retired Lists will be reported to The Adjutant General, ATTN: AGPF-FC, Department of the Army, Washington, D.C. 20315.

RETIREMENT CODES

CODE	EXPLANATION
1	Retired or granted retired pay for any reason, except those retired for, or granted retired pay for disability and those granted retired pay under title 10, USC, Section 1331 (formerly Title III, Act of 29 June 1948).
2	Retired for, or granted retired pay for permanent disability.
3	Granted retired pay under Title 10, USC, Section 1331 (formerly Title III, Act of 29 June 1948).

SECTION 1

UNITED STATES ARMY RETIRED LIST

The United States Army Retired List is composed of Regular Army commissioned officers and warrant officers retired under any provision of law for service, age or permanent disability.

NAME	GRADE	SVC NO	DATE RET MO YR	RET CODE
AARON ALTON E	CW4	W-0902686	0762	1
AARON MARGARET E	LTC	N-0000505	0450	1
ABBOTT DONALD I	CPT	O-0060517	1162	1
ABBOTT GLENOR P	LTC	L-0000815	0366	1
ABBOTT LYSLE I	COL	O-0034559	0552	1
ABBOTT OSCAR B	B G	O-0005748	1050	1
ABBOTT STANLEY B	LTC	O-0091730	1065	1
ABBOTT WILLIAM L	LTC	O-0039891	1061	1
ABELL JULIAN D	COL	O-0018686	0862	1
ABER JOHN E	COL	O-0023097	0363	1
ABERCROMBIE JAY A	COL	O-0020604	0359	1
ABERT GEORGE C	COL	O-0021347	0866	2
ABLETT CHARLES B	LTC	O-0067546	0868	1
ABRAHAM ROBERT	COL	O-0032427	0868	1
ABRAMOSKA HELEN M	LTC	N-0001878	0961	1
ABRAMS BERNARD W	CPT	O-0050736	1052	2
ABRAMS GEORGE F	LTC	O-0006362	0841	1
ABREVA FRANCIS E	COL	O-0079721	1068	1
ABSTON AARON A	LTC	O-0021391	1058	1
ABT ALAN B	COL	O-0060323	1167	1
ACHURY ERIK	1LT	O-0014396	1019	2
ACKERMAN STEPHEN W	COL	O-0015708	0752	1
ACKERSON DUANE W	COL	O-0045068	0666	1
ACKERT THOMAS W	COL	O-0032035	0764	1
ACKLEY CHARLES M	LTC	O-0037997	0661	1
ACKRIDGE LENORE W	CPT	L-0601616	0450	2
ACKROYD GILBERT G	COL	O-0031413	0368	1
ACTON LLOYD P	COL	O-0042667	1264	1
ADAIR ALEXANDRIA	COL	O-0007308	0552	1
ADAIR GEORGE T	COL	O-0051901	0767	1
ADAIR HUGH D	COL	O-0007452	0551	1
ADAIR PHINEAS H	2LT	O-0014588	0133	2
ADAMS ALICE L	MAJ	L-0000352	0266	2
ADAMS ANDREW J	M G	O-0018579	0667	1
ADAMS ARLYE D	LTC	O-0086981	1167	1
ADAMS ARVEL T	CW4	W-0902690	0661	1
ADAMS BILLY J	COL	O-0051933	0865	1
ADAMS BURTON R	CW4	W-0902691	0363	1
ADAMS CARL R	COL	O-0005703	0843	1
ADAMS CHARLES M JR	COL	O-0012789	0954	1
ADAMS CROLE L	CW4	W-0902692	0765	1
ADAMS DALE W	CW4	W-0902693	1066	1
ADAMS DEXTER W	LTC	O-0062247	0467	1
ADAMS DONALD L	COL	O-0031334	1066	1
ADAMS DUVAL F	COL	O-0042497	0864	1
ADAMS EDWARD F	COL	O-0015326	0954	1
ADAMS EDWARD P	CW4	W-0902694	1054	1
ADAMS EMORY S JR	COL	O-0023235	0863	1
ADAMS ERNEST C	COL	O-0020933	0464	2
ADAMS FRANK	COL	O-0051189	1060	1
ADAMS FREDERICK	COL	O-0007964	0948	1
ADAMS GEORGE E	LTC	O-0019412	0758	1
ADAMS GERARD C	COL	O-0044819	0866	1
ADAMS GILBERT N	COL	O-0018747	1062	1
ADAMS HAROLD D	LTC	O-0037281	0667	1
ADAMS HARRY J	COL	O-0043191	0866	1
ADAMS HELEN	CPT	N-0000049	1048	1
ADAMS HUBERT D	LTC	O-0079723	0464	1
ADAMS JAMES A	CW3	W-0904077	0963	1
ADAMS JAMES F	COL	O-0029968	0763	1
ADAMS JAMES Y	COL	O-0019755	0563	1
ADAMS JOHN D	LTC	O-0033147	1168	1
ADAMS JOHN H	COL	O-0028995	0758	1
ADAMS JONATHAN E JR	LTC	O-0023833	0162	1
ADAMS JOSEPH Y	LTC	O-0037529	1066	1
ADAMS L DOW	COL	O-0021203	0653	1
ADAMS LAWRENCE W	COL	O-0038608	0856	1
ADAMS LESLIE F	CW4	W-0906595	1059	1
ADAMS LEWIS R	COL	O-0039042	1268	2
ADAMS LUDLOW C	COL	O-0027337	0957	2
ADAMS MARCUS W	COL	O-0040025	0666	1
ADAMS NYAL	COL	O-0007471	0269	2
ADAMS OSCAR H	COL	O-0040131	0168	1
ADAMS PAUL D	GEN	O-0017306	1166	1
ADAMS PERCY	CPT	O-0007744	0934	1

NAME	GRADE	SVC NO	DATE RET MO YR	RET CODE
ADAMS RAY	COL	O-0051010	1154	1
ADAMS RELLIE W	COL	O-0042663	1165	1
ADAMS ROBERT H	M G	O-0019474	0766	2
ADAMS ROWLAND C	LTC	O-0076783	0664	1
ADAMS SAMUEL J	COL	O-0012583	0353	1
ADAMS THOMAS E JR	LTC	O-0055944	0564	1
ADAMS THOMAS H	MAJ	OF-0100281	0163	1
ADAMS WILLIAM	LTC	O-0042631	0963	1
ADAMSON DAVID V	LTC	O-0019096	0653	1
ADAMSON KEITH F	COL	O-0003640	0144	1
ADAMSON KENNETH F	COL	O-0083575	1065	1
ADDINGTON FRANK T	COL	O-0008061	0447	1
ADDISON HATFIELD W	LTC	L-0000025	0958	1
ADDISON JOHN W	COL	O-0044547	1265	1
ADDISON WILLIAM A	COL	O-0060111	0866	1
ADJEMIAN GEORGE R	COL	O-0023806	0168	1
ADKINS ERNEST C	COL	O-0028212	1052	2
ADKINS JOHN E JR	COL	O-0015273	0451	2
ADLER CARL J	COL	O-0003421	1151	1
ADLER CHARLES S	LTC	O-0027139	0466	1
ADLER EUGENE P	LTC	O-0029547	0754	1
ADLER GEORGE	LTC	O-0081334	0466	1
AEBISCHER LOUIS J	LTC	O-0032384	0667	1
AERNI FRANCIS J	COL	O-0031970	0968	1
AGERS HUBERT C	LTC	O-0040905	0566	1
AGNEW PIERRE A	LTC	O-0009370	1042	2
AGNEW RICHARD H	COL	O-0019956	0564	2
AGOA JOHN J	COL	O-0042205	0763	1
AGRESTA FRANCIS J	CW3	RW-0907696	0163	1
AGRESTA JAMES	LTC	O-0084582	1268	2
AGUGLIA JOHN R	LTC	O-0013477	0757	1
AHALT HENRY C	COL	O-0028886	1055	1
AHEARN CHARLES E	LTC	O-0069570	0768	1
AHEARN WALTER F	LTC	O-0018242	0557	1
AHEE JOE	COL	O-0022215	0365	1
AHERN JOHN R	LTC	O-0059918	0466	1
AHERN JOSEPH P	COL	O-0023881	0867	1
AHERN LEO J	M G	O-0002587	0946	1
AHLGREN FREDERIC F	LTC	O-0013566	0561	1
AHNFELDT ARNOLD L	COL	O-0021018	0567	1
AHRENS AMBELTEN M	LTC	O-0030026	1061	2
AIKEN ANDREA M	MAJ	L-0000328	0263	1
AIMONE JOHN J	CW4	W-0902697	1167	1
AIN MILTON	1LT	O-0068858	0159	2
AINES ANDREW A	COL	O-0043463	0467	1
AKANS JAMES E	LTC	O-0039893	0462	1
AKERMAN AMOS T	COL	O-0016060	0655	1
AKERS ELWYN N	LTC	O-0024379	0557	2
AKERS NORMAN E	COL	O-0051673	1265	1
AKERS RUSSELL F JR	COL	O-0019243	0661	2
AKIN SPENCER B	M G	O-0002918	0351	1
AKINS THOMAS W	COL	O-0040076	0167	1
ALBA BIENVENIDO	LTC	O-0016939	0855	2
ALBAN PAUL E	LTC	O-0023500	0661	1
ALBANESE ARCHIE J	LTC	O-0080536	0168	1
ALBAUGH CORNELIUS	COL	O-0040268	1262	1
ALBERGOTTI JULIAN S	COL	O-0039601	0159	1
ALBERGOTTI WILLIAM M	COL	O-0028883	1056	1
ALBERT BROOKE	CPT	O-0027944	0853	2
ALBERT JOSEPH L	COL	O-0040344	1163	1
ALBERT PAUL W	COL	O-0042507	0165	1
ALBERTIE EDWARD J	LTC	O-0040007	1263	1
ALBIN JOHN B	COL	O-0051296	0262	1
ALBRECHT ALBERT W	LTC	O-0031558	0860	2
ALBRECHT ERWIN F JR	MAJ	O-0067636	0967	1
ALBRECHT FRANK M	M G	O-0015131	0660	1
ALBRECHT LAWRENCE S	COL	O-0049937	0767	1
ALBRIGHT ARNOLD A	COL	O-0018273	0954	1
ALBRIGHT CHARLES R	COL	O-0036502	1068	1
ALBRIGHT JOHN J	COL	O-0007305	0748	2
ALBRIGHT ROY L	CW4	RW-0902158	0661	1
ALBRIGHT SHANNON D	LTC	O-0040787	0863	1
ALBRO JOHN N	LTC	O-0040217	0763	1
ALBRO ROBERT D	COL	O-0031360	1166	1
ALCORN JAMES P	COL	O-0044844	0666	1

NAME	GRADE	SVC NO	DATE RET MO YR	RET CODE
ALDENDERFER F W JR	CPT	O-0069581	0258	2
ALDRICH EDWIN W	CPT	O-0026890	0248	2
ALDRICH HARRY S	COL	O-0014467	0968	2
ALDRICH MYRTLE F	MAJ	R-0010003	0754	1
ALDRIDGE THOMAS L	MAJ	O-0058907	0864	1
ALDRUP EARL W	COL	O-0015772	0854	2
ALE[illegible] ESKIL M J	COL	O-0041452	0357	1
ALEXANDER BERTIE L	MAJ	N-0002335	0662	1
ALEXANDER [illegible] P	COL	O-0042979	0467	1
ALEXANDER DANA S	COL	O-0018114	1046	2
ALEXANDER DAVID H	LTC	O-0059956	1065	1
ALEXANDER DAVID P JR	COL	O-0049901	0564	1
ALEXANDER DONALD D	LTC	O-0028789	0753	1
ALEXANDER DOUGLAS T	LTC	O-0032927	1065	1
ALEXANDER FRANK [illegible]	COL	O-0017627	0763	1
ALEXANDER FREDERICK B	COL	O-0041949	1061	2
ALEXANDER GEORGE W	LTC	O-0034143	0962	1
ALEXANDER HENRY A	COL	O-0013565	1163	1
ALEXANDER HENRY W	CPT	O-0011185	0335	2
ALEXANDER JOSEPH D	COL	O-0050359	0957	1
ALEXANDER L [illegible] JR	COL	O-0031058	0759	1
ALEXANDER LAWRENCE H	LTC	O-0051731	0264	1
ALEXANDER MOSES	COL	O-0011821	1146	1
ALEXANDER RALPH W	LTC	O-0050373	1066	1
ALEXANDER ROBERT F	COL	O-0041912	0961	1
ALEXANDER RUSSELL W	LTC	O-0043280	1058	1
ALEXANDER SAMUEL H	COL	O-0017830	0859	1
ALEXANDER WILLIAM	COL	O-0004632	1052	2
ALFANO CHARLES [illegible]	COL	O-0025640	1266	1
ALFONTE WALLACE H	COL	O-0005441	0146	2
ALFORD JAMES M	LTC	O-0027552	0966	1
ALFORD JOHN C	LTC	O-0038839	0664	2
ALFORD TRUMAN	LTC	O-0040765	0160	1
ALFRED LEE L	COL	O-0029368	0361	1
ALFREY JIMMY	COL	O-0019859	0965	1
ALLAN CHARLES C	COL	O-0017671	0759	1
ALLARD [illegible] W	LTC	O-0027747	0950	2
ALLBEE ROGER H	COL	O-0019299	0157	1
ALLBRIGHT JAMES L	MAJ	O-0005744	0-34	2
ALLBRIGHT MARION C	LTC	O-0063678	0166	1
ALLBURY [illegible] F	COL	O-0051544	0761	1
ALLEBACH CORA [illegible]	MAJ	N-0002175	0664	1
ALLEN ARTHUR W JR	COL	O-0022074	1063	2
ALLEN BEN L	COL	O-0032103	1167	1
ALLEN CHARLES H	COL	O-0018677	0862	1
ALLEN CHESTER F	COL	O-0030060	1262	1
ALLEN EDWARD [illegible]	COL	O-0031878	0168	2
ALLEN EDWIN W JR	LTC	O-0061226	1068	1
ALLEN FRANK A JR	M G	O-0037415	1156	1
ALLEN GERTRUDE F	MAJ	N-0000251	0560	1
ALLEN GILBERT M JR	MAJ	O-0016912	0348	1
ALLEN GLENN [illegible]	COL	O-0005614	0849	1
ALLEN GLENN L JR	LTC	O-0084583	0967	1
ALLEN HAROLD E	COL	O-0037922	0964	1
ALLEN HARRY B	COL	O-0006465	0842	1
ALLEN HENRY T	COL	O-0008015	0446	2
ALLEN HUGH E	LTC	O-0043348	1065	1
ALLEN JAMES E	COL	O-0029074	0359	1
ALLEN JAMES F	LTC	O-0044955	1166	1
ALLEN JOHN [illegible]	LTC	O-0069583	0968	1
ALLEN JOHN [illegible]	MAJ	O-0020978	0345	2
ALLEN JOHN [illegible]	COL	O-0020399	0861	1
ALLEN LEVEN C	M G	O-0004760	1051	2
ALLEN MARSHALL H	COL	O-0044275	0868	1
ALLEN MARTHA [illegible]	MAJ	L-0000235	1159	1
ALLEN MEREDITH E	LTC	O-0021408	0263	1
ALLEN OLLIE J	LTC	O-0032085	0660	1
ALLEN RICHARD H	LTC	O-0050603	0967	1
ALLEN ROBERT L JR	COL	O-0010646	0753	1
ALLEN RODERICK R	M G	O-0004652	0554	1
ALLEN TERRY DE L	M G	O-0003461	0846	2
ALLEN THOMAS H	COL	O-0015865	0754	1
ALLEN WILLIAM H JR	COL	O-0018053	0660	1
ALLEN WILLIAM J JR	COL	O-0029725	0961	1
ALLEN WILLIAM M	LTC	O-0080369	0967	1

NAME	GRADE	SVC NO	DATE RET MO YR	RET CODE
ALLENDORE CARL	MAJ	O-0257989	0567	1
ALLERTON WILLIAM S	LTC	O-0059713	1067	1
ALLEY EDWARD E	COL	O-0005966	0947	2
ALLEY JOHN A JR	COL	O-0052203	0968	1
ALLEY STUART M	COL	O-0030268	1162	1
ALLGAIR JOHN A	LTC	O-0020947	0958	1
ALLGEIER ROBERT M	COL	O-0042822	1265	1
ALLIN GEORGE R JR	COL	O-0024760	0968	1
ALLISON AARON F	COL	O-0031016	1167	2
ALLISON DANIEL W	COL	O-0029071	0559	2
ALLISON HASKELL	COL	O-0007529	1046	2
ALLISON PHILIP W	COL	O-0010434	0446	1
ALLISON WALLACE M	COL	O-0010467	0848	1
ALLISON WENDELL G	CPT	O-0026657	0747	2
ALLISON WILLIAM A	LTC	O-0060176	0864	1
ALLMENDINGER VIVIAN	MAJ	N-0000052	0349	1
ALLRED WAYNE	LTC	O-0084584	0967	1
ALLRED WILLIAM M	LTC	O-0058809	0766	1
ALLWINE FRANKLIN N	COL	O-0043661	1268	1
ALM NINA	MAJ	N-0002227	0459	1
ALMAN CASPER	1LT	O-0011564	1022	2
ALMOND EDWARD M	LTG	O-0004666	0153	2
ALMOND HUGH H	LTC	O-0081943	0667	1
ALOE ROBERT C	B G	O-0016916	0657	1
ALPHIN HORACE E	COL	O-0043324	0967	1
ALSPACH RUSSELL K	B G	O-0050879	0365	1
ALSPAUGH RALPH	COL	O-0019159	0863	1
ALTEEN LEE E	CW2	W-0901477	0847	1
ALTENHOFEN MATTHEW J	LTC	O-0021054	0858	1
ALTFATHER ELLIS M	COL	O-0017816	0759	1
ALTFILISH ROMAINE S	CW4	W-0906599	0567	1
ALTHAUS KENNETH G	B G	O-0006208	0346	2
ALVAREZ THEODORE P	CPT	O-0060787	1061	1
ALVEY THOMAS W	LTC	O-0032698	0261	1
AMAZEEN CHARLES P	COL	O-0012817	0553	1
AMBRON TYRUS R	LTC	O-0032215	0467	1
AMBROSE DON C	CPT	O-0062179	0462	1
AMBROSE JOSEPH R	CW4	RW-0902672	0462	1
AMEND REBECCA V	MAJ	N-0002417	0464	1
AMES JOHN R	LTC	O-0001505	1022	1
AMES KENNETH L	COL	O-0030864	0765	1
AMICK ELLIOTT W	COL	O-0021153	0647	2
AMIS GILBERT H	MAJ	O-0038394	0761	1
AMIS LEWIS W	LTC	O-0005212	0342	2
AMIZICH AMELIA D	LTC	M-0010029	1265	1
AMLONG RANSOM G	COL	O-0015094	0753	1
AMMENWERTH BENJAMIN	LTC	O-0061963	0766	1
AMMERMAN JAMES F	B G	O-0018165	0760	1
AMMON JOHN R	CW4	W-0902708	0863	1
AMMONS BENJAMIN T	COL	O-0038692	0661	1
AMOROSO ARNOLD D	COL	O-0010777	0753	2
AMOROSO LEONARD	COL	O-0030076	0164	1
AMORY HAROLD I	COL	O-0019319	1054	2
AMOS ARTHUR K	COL	O-0020822	0665	1
ANCKER CLINTON J	CPT	O-0011145	0934	2
ANCRUM JAMES N	COL	O-0011061	0250	1
ANDERHOLM CECIL C	LTC	O-0081944	1266	1
ANDERSEN ANDREW M JR	LTC	O-0081945	0467	1
ANDERSEN ELDON B	LTC	O-0035991	1264	1
ANDERSEN HAL P	COL	O-0039920	0964	1
ANDERSEN HERMAN S	LTC	O-0031265	0866	1
ANDERSEN TOWNSEND C	COL	O-0030195	0664	1
ANDERSLAND LOUISE S	MAJ	J-0000061	0563	1
ANDERSON ALFRED G	MAJ	O-0011153	0627	2
ANDERSON ALFRED H	COL	O-0028805	0555	1
ANDERSON ANNA G	LTC	N-0000496	0548	1
ANDERSON ARTHUR J	COL	O-0033741	0162	1
ANDERSON B CONN	COL	O-0007828	0945	2
ANDERSON BERRY K	COL	O-0030384	0465	1
ANDERSON BLAINE E	COL	O-0039976	0366	2
ANDERSON BRUCE D	CW4	W-0902709	0457	1
ANDERSON CARL A	MAJ	O-0050386	1061	1
ANDERSON CARL E	COL	O-0015399	0251	1
ANDERSON CHARLES H	COL	O-0021072	1066	1
ANDERSON CHARLES W	LTC	O-0081946	1168	1

NAME	GRADE	SVC NO	DATE RET MO YR	RET CODE
ANDERSON CHESTER H	COL	0-00[illegible]0096	0164	1
ANDERSON CLARENCE L	LTC	0-0061069	0466	1
ANDERSON DAGNY V	MAJ	N-0001948	0558	1
ANDERSON DAVID L	COL	0-0025223	0167	1
ANDERSON DAVID M	LTC	0-0090538	0263	1
ANDERSON DELMAR P	COL	0-0029269	0763	1
ANDERSON ELSIE	MAJ	N-0001943	0558	1
ANDERSON ETHEL M	MAJ	N-0001548	0954	1
ANDERSON FARRELL H	LTC	0-0060157	0168	1
ANDERSON FRANCIS W	COL	0-0030354	0165	1
ANDERSON FRED G	LTC	0-0038473	0966	1
ANDERSON GEORGE H	COL	0-0014620	0753	1
ANDERSON GEORGE K	LTC	0-0035057	0764	1
ANDERSON GEORGE L	LTC	0-0031762	0163	1
ANDERSON GEORGE N	COL	0-0051379	0263	1
ANDERSON GLEN H	COL	0-0008632	0946	2
ANDERSON GORDON V	LTC	0-0047345	1164	1
ANDERSON GRANGER	COL	0-0014931	1051	2
ANDERSON JOHN B	M G	0-0003686	0646	2
ANDERSON JOHN H	COL	0-0019398	0155	1
ANDERSON JOSEPH C	COL	0-0019884	0962	1
ANDERSON KENNETH S	COL	0-0008365	0854	2
ANDERSON LAWRENCE R	COL	0-0040461	0168	1
ANDERSON LEWIS W	COL	0-0050904	0855	1
ANDERSON MILDRED J	LTC	M-0010026	0966	1
ANDERSON NORMAN A	COL	0-0031483	0861	1
ANDERSON ORVIS P	COL	0-0042727	0766	2
ANDERSON RALPH C	LTC	0-0054269	0864	1
ANDERSON RICHARD E	COL	0-0003361	0831	2
ANDERSON RICHARD H	LTC	0-0083576	0767	1
ANDERSON ROBERT I	LTC	0-0056990	0665	1
ANDERSON ROBERT N	COL	0-0021436	0666	2
ANDERSON ROBERT V	LTC	0-0067548	0767	1
ANDERSON ROLAND	COL	0-0031790	0368	1
ANDERSON TRUETT C	COL	0-0038804	1164	1
ANDERSON VIRGINIA W	LTC	N-0000372	0366	1
ANDERSON WEBSTER	M G	0-0017101	0765	1
ANDERSON WILBER K	COL	0-0043126	0866	1
ANDERSON WILLIAM H	COL	0-0056864	0164	1
ANDERSON WOODROW W	COL	0-0040220	0661	1
ANDERSSON KINGSLEY S	COL	0-0015450	0954	2
ANDERTON EDWARD C	LTC	0-0061094	1167	1
ANDING JAMES G	COL	0-0015677	0654	1
ANDINO EDUARDO	COL	0-0009820	1049	1
ANDINO JOSE A	COL	0-0024575	0766	1
ANDRAE HERBERT H	COL	0-0019546	0860	1
ANDRES CHARLES III	LTC	0-0058811	0268	1
ANDRESON PAUL S	COL	0-0030962	0761	1
ANDREW GEORGE S JR	COL	0-0034235	1268	1
ANDREWS CHARLES L	COL	0-0019363	0863	1
ANDREWS FRANK W	LTC	0-0020843	1144	2
ANDREWS JAMES D JR	COL	0-0007884	0546	2
ANDREWS JOHN A	COL	0-0007621	0651	1
ANDREWS OMAR K	LTC	0-0019702	1150	1
ANDREWS REXFORD W	MAJ	0-0017756	0246	1
ANDREWS ROBERT J	LTC	0-0063759	0767	1
ANDREWS STEPHEN E JR	LTC	0-0033976	1168	1
ANDRICK EDWIN L	COL	0-0042134	0263	1
ANDRUS BURTON C	COL	0-0006991	0452	1
ANDRUSS MALCOLM P	COL	0-0001726	0735	2
ANGEL NICHOLAS C	COL	0-0031789	0268	1
ANGEN WILLARD F	COL	0-0023596	0263	2
ANGERS DALE A	MAJ	L-0000101	1163	1
ANGERS WALTER J	COL	0-0034677	0168	1
ANGLEY JAMES A	MAJ	0-2212044	0264	2
ANGLIN WILLIAM E	LTC	0-0031464	0861	1
ANGLUIN DAVID X	COL	0-0017717	0146	2
ANGSTER ROBERT C	COL	0-0032124	0266	1
ANGWIN KEITH	LTC	0-0034741	1168	1
ANKROM URA M	MAJ	L-0000207	0155	1
ANNIN ROBERT D	COL	0-0003622	0650	1
ANSEL STURE A	COL	0-0030554	1065	1
ANSLOW RALPH O	LTC	0-0031093	0861	1
ANSON PAUL A	COL	0-0031400	0765	1
*ANTHONY ALVIN E	COL	0-0008752	1146	2
ANTHONY CAROLYN H	MAJ	L-0000290	0868	1
ANTHONY THOMAS J	LTC	0-0058813	0468	1
ANTLEY HAMPTON L	LTC	0-0031107	0756	1
ANTUZZI WILLIAM O	COL	0-0043307	1267	2
ANTRIM HAROLD F	LTC	0-0033793	0767	1
ANTRIM RALPH L JR	LTC	0-0065170	0367	1
APGAR THEODORE B	COL	0-0005556	1146	2
APOSTLE ERNEST F	LTC	OF-0103431	1168	1
APPEL EDWARD J	CPT	0-0060846	1264	1
APPLEGATE EDWARD C	MAJ	0-0014631	0938	2
APPLEGATE REX	LTC	0-0024589	0945	2
APPLETON ROLLAND D	COL	0-0081948	1268	1
ARACK GEORGE	LTC	0-0023588	0746	2
ARBUCLI JOHN R	MAJ	0-0063152	1268	1
ARCHER HARRY C	COL	0-0044792	0368	1
ARCHER HARVEY E	COL	0-0031170	0862	1
ARCHER THEODORE W	COL	0-0048383	0367	1
ARCHIBALD HAROLD G	COL	0-0007561	0847	1
ARCHIBALD HERBERT R	COL	0-0029776	0762	1
ARDREY JOHN E	COL	0-0003579	0148	1
ARFMAN JOHN F	COL	0-0042802	1163	1
ARIMA JAMES K	LTC	0-0080280	0166	1
ARLEN EDWARD L	CW4	W-0902715	1057	2
ARMES HERBERT R	CW3	W-0902716	1162	1
ARMITAGE JOHN O	COL	0-0019014	0259	1
ARMOGIDA SALVATORE	COL	0-0019741	0865	1
ARMOR MARSHALL H JR	LTC	0-0045590	0662	1
ARMS THOMAS S	B G	0-0004729	0946	2
ARMS THOMAS S JR	LTC	0-0024996	0863	1
ARMSTRONG ARMOUR S	COL	0-0044372	1166	1
ARMSTRONG CHALMERS H	COL	0-0031877	0268	1
ARMSTRONG CHARLES A	COL	0-0021375	0358	1
ARMSTRONG CHARLES R	1LT	0-0061601	0256	2
ARMSTRONG CLARE H	B G	0-0005318	0353	2
ARMSTRONG DEVERE P	COL	0-0017533	0759	1
ARMSTRONG DONALD C	B G	0-0002967	1046	1
ARMSTRONG DONALD K	COL	0-0018578	1058	1
ARMSTRONG EDWARD B	LTC	0-0032267	0864	1
ARMSTRONG ELBERT	LTC	0-0051677	1163	1
ARMSTRONG ELMER J	COL	0-0006869	0-37	1
ARMSTRONG FRANCIS T	COL	0-0003444	1046	1
ARMSTRONG FRANK H	LTC	0-0060273	0766	1
ARMSTRONG FREDERICK	COL	0-0002690	0344	1
ARMSTRONG GEORGE E	M G	0-0016548	0755	1
ARMSTRONG JOHN L	LTC	0-0028469	1167	1
ARMSTRONG JOHN R	LTC	0-0065159	0765	1
ARMSTRONG LESTER K	CW2	W-0906601	0655	1
ARMSTRONG LEWIS R	CPT	0-0011558	0934	2
ARMSTRONG MARVIL G	COL	0-0005313	0753	1
ARMSTRONG NEMESIO A	LTC	0-0059898	1262	1
ARMSTRONG RICHARD B	LTC	0-0027879	0468	1
ARMSTRONG ROBERT A	LTC	0-0081949	1067	1
ARMSTRONG ROBERT P	LTC	0-0080370	0968	1
ARMSTRONG WILLIAM H	LTC	0-0087467	1068	1
ARN ROBERT E	COL	0-0023470	0664	1
ARN ROBERT M	LTC	0-0048366	0661	1
ARNEMAN GEORGE E	COL	0-0003271	0-45	2
ARNEST RICHARD T	COL	0-0006551	1047	1
ARNETT THOMAS M	LTC	0-0020566	1047	1
ARNETT VERN R	MAJ	0-0060369	0865	1
ARNOLD ALTON V	COL	0-0041858	0361	1
ARNOLD ARCHIBALD	M G	0-0003395	0548	2
ARNOLD B O	CW3	W-0902718	0562	1
ARNOLD BERTHA G	MAJ	N-0001492	0567	1
ARNOLD BRYAN C	LTC	0-0020801	0758	1
ARNOLD EDGAR L	COL	0-0031902	0267	1
ARNOLD LESLIE A	COL	0-0030815	1066	2
ARNOLD LUTHER D	LTC	0-0022946	0964	1
ARNOLD RHODES F	COL	0-0005160	0753	2
ARNOLD RICHARD J	LTC	0-0058816	0166	1
ARNOLD ROBERT E	MAJ	0-0028313	0563	2
ARNOLD WALTER F	COL	0-0046714	0968	1
ARNOLD WILLIAM H	LTG	0-0015558	0261	2
ARNWINE HENRY B	LTC	0-0078705	0168	1
ARONSON ROLAND S	COL	0-0029206	0661	1
ARP DAVID H	COL	0-0031545	0267	1
ARROWSMITH JOHN C	M G	0-0011373	0553	1
ARSENAULT ROBERT J	LTC	0-0045217	0262	1
ARTHUR JOHN F	COL	0-0032468	0366	1
ARTHUR JOHN F JR	COL	0-0024457	0767	1
ARTHUR JOSEPH N	MAJ	0-0008755	0622	2
ARTHUR ROBERT	COL	0-0002226	0246	2
ARTHUR ROBERT E	LTC	0-0040768	1164	1
ARTISS KENNETH L	LTC	0-0057344	0864	1
ARTMAN ETHEL M	MAJ	N-0002244	0456	2
ARTMAN GEORGE	COL	0-0021342	0868	1
ARTMAN RALPH T	COL	0-0021023	0958	1
ARTZ CURTIS P	LTC	0-0057825	0856	2
ARVIN CHARLES R	LTC	0-0084577	0666	1
ARVIN PAUL D	COL	0-0080360	0867	1
ARZOLA ASDRUBAL	LTC	0-0067785	1164	1
ASBURY HAROLD D	LTC	0-0081950	0868	1
ASCHOFF JOHN F JR	LTC	0-0037856	0467	1
ASELTINE THOMAS H	MAJ	0-0088326	0166	2
ASH ALVIN	LTC	0-0028539	0165	1
ASH HUGHES L	B G	0-0031799	0168	1
ASH JAMES E	COL	0-0004037	0247	2
ASH LAURENCE W	LTC	0-0054165	0464	1
ASHBRIDGE DONALD M	COL	0-0002555	0934	2
ASHBY CLAUDE T JR	MAJ	0-0084846	0867	1
ASHBY DE GRAY H	B G	0-0003276	0147	2
ASHBY JOHN D	COL	0-0066608	1068	1
ASHBY RAYMOND C JR	COL	0-0043320	1067	1
ASHCRAFT JAMES H	LTC	0-0051658	1063	1
ASHENBRENNER PETER J	COL	0-0080371	0268	1
ASHENFELDER WILLIAM	COL	0-0040008	0764	1
ASHER OWEN S	CW4	W-0902721	1162	1
ASHFORD ALEXANDER	LTC	0-0061183	1265	1
ASHLEY MERLE W	MAJ	0-0080036	0863	1
ASHMAN ALFRED	COL	0-0019846	0764	1
ASHTON DONALD M	COL	0-0014825	0753	1
ASHWORTH EDWARD T	COL	0-0019052	0763	2
ASHWORTH ROBERT L	B G	0-0021308	0868	1
ASHWORTH TALMADGE O	COL	0-0079693	0768	1
ASKINS CHARLES	COL	0-0029852	0163	1
ASLESON ELEANOR R	LTC	N-0000056	1157	1
ASTARITA ORAZIO J	LTC	0-0061388	0768	1
ASTOR RAYMOND J	LTC	0-0050111	0266	1
ASTRELLA THEODORE F	COL	0-0042656	0266	1
ASTROSKY ANNA B	MAJ	N-0002501	0967	1
ATCHISON FRANK F	LTC	0-0058817	0766	1
ATHAN BYRON O	LTC	0-0053237	0764	1
ATHAN HAROLD W	COL	0-0052624	1268	2
ATKINS EDWIN L	COL	0-0030809	0862	2
ATKINS HERBERT R JR	CW4	W-0902722	1067	1
ATKINS JAMES L	LTC	0-0039409	1064	1
ATKINS NEILL S JR	LTC	0-0042815	0764	1
ATKINSON CHARLES E	COL	0-0006737	0246	2
ATKINSON EDWARD C	COL	0-0010131	0547	2
ATKINSON FREDERICK	B G	0-0018169	0760	1
ATKINSON JAMES W	CW4	W-0902723	0464	1
ATKINSON POLK J	COL	0-0010259	0753	1
ATLAS REYNOLD A	MAJ	0-0031894	0458	1
ATTAWAY ELMER J	COL	0-0040321	1262	1
ATWELL CLYDE L	WO1	W-0800724	1036	1
ATWELL RICHARD N	COL	0-0007293	0246	1
ATWOOD DOROTHY M	MAJ	N-0002144	0861	1
ATWOOD FRANK J	COL	0-0004686	0346	2
ATWOOD GEORGE L	COL	0-0039750	0261	2
ATWOOD WILL G JR	LTC	0-0025067	0961	1
AUBREY GEORGE A	COL	0-0023110	1265	1
AUDERER SAM	CW4	W-0902725	0561	1
AUDET CHARLES W	LTC	0-0052899	0861	1
AUERBACH ALVIN B	LTC	0-0020547	0758	1
AUGSBURGER RUSSELL H	COL	0-0024376	1066	1
AUGUR WAYLAND B	B G	0-0006659	0753	1
AUGUSTIN GEORGE A	CW4	W-0906606	1262	1
AUKBURGH RUTH O	1LT	M-0002024	0247	1
AURAND HENRY S	LTG	0-0003784	0852	1
AUSMUS DELBERT	COL	0-0007898	0846	1
AUSTIN CHARLES [illegible]	COL	0-0045239	0866	1
AUSTIN EDWARD A	COL	0-0007999	0-44	2
AUSTIN EDWARD G	COL	0-0021046	0862	1
AUSTIN EDWARD L	COL	0-0038805	0863	1
AUSTIN EDWARD W	COL	0-0051789	0866	1
AUSTIN FRANK J JR	LTC	0-0040707	1062	1
AUSTIN WALLACE	LTC	0-0032191	0367	1
AUTREY LEWELL V	LTC	0-0084587	1168	1
AVARY HUGH D	COL	0-0030838	0864	1
AVENT HUGH R	LTC	0-0003871	1022	2
AVERA WRAY B	COL	0-0012861	0553	1
AVERILL JACK F	LTC	0-0099606	0668	2
AVERY BERTRIM A	CW4	W-0902726	0257	1
AVERY HENRY H	CW4	W-0906607	0664	1
AVERY IRVING C	COL	0-0004830	0351	1
AVERY LILLIAN V	MAJ	N-0001037	1058	2
AVERY SAMUEL C	COL	0-0006825	0848	2
AVERY WILLIAM H	COL	0-0045706	0865	1
AVERY WILLIAM H JR	LTC	0-0058819	0268	1
AVERYT CLYDE R	CW3	W-0902727	0565	1
AVNER SAUL L	COL	0-0041701	0157	1
AVRETT MARION E	LTC	0-0080281	0364	1
AX CLARENCE F	LTC	0-0032198	0764	1
AXMANN MARY C	MAJ	N-0000478	0166	1
AXTELL EUGENE N	COL	0-0044281	0868	1
AXUP ROY W	COL	0-0016894	0757	1
AYCOCK ALBERT L	CW4	W-0904080	0565	1
AYCOCK ROBERT C	COL	0-0046664	0966	1
AYCOCK WILLIAM B	MAJ	0-0035051	0961	1
AYER ERNEST L	LTC	0-0006147	0242	1
AYER FRANKLIN A	LTC	0-0034199	0762	1
AYER WESLEY F	COL	0-0003156	0946	2
AYERS CARL W	LTC	0-0073436	0768	1
AYERS LOREN A	COL	0-0018561	0761	1
AYLOR JAMES L	MAJ	0-0037766	0965	1
AYNES EDITH A	MAJ	N-0000094	0456	1
AYOTTE JOHN U	COL	0-0005570	0553	1
AYRES LAURENCE T JR	COL	0-0043715	0764	2
BABBS JOHN B	COL	0-0039203	1169	1
BABCOCK C STANTON	M G	0-0016104	0661	1
BABCOCK FRANKLIN	B G	0-0002968	0846	2
BABCOCK LESLIE E JR	1LT	0-0026914	0452	2
BABER BEN L	LTC	0-0025567	0763	1
BABER BURL B	LTC	0-0051048	0757	2
BACCHIERI LUCILE B	MAJ	N-0000032	1047	1
BACHARACH THEODORE	LTC	0-0057987	0864	1
BACHE CLAUDE V	LTC	0-0061100	0966	1
BACHELOR DONALD M	LTC	0-0043723	0264	1
BACHELOR WILLIAM E	LTC	0-0094040	0666	1
BACHER ROBERT M	COL	0-0051045	0859	1
BACHMAN GEORGE A	LTC	0-0051186	1057	1
BACHMAN JOHN P	COL	0-0016970	0556	1
BACHMAN ROGER M	COL	0-0022226	0765	1
BACIOR AGNES	MAJ	N-0001530	0863	1
BACK GEORGE I	M G	0-0010267	0655	2
BACKHAUS GUS III	MAJ	0-0060714	0864	1
BACKMAN STANLEY G	COL	0-0007833	1145	2
BACKMANN CAROLINE M	MAJ	N-0002241	0960	1
BACON ELIZABETH	LTC	L-0000059	0962	1
BACON LEONARD A	MAJ	0-0085113	1166	2
BACON WILLIAM J	COL	0-0005081	0846	1
BADGER GEORGE M	B G	0-0012139	0649	1
BADGER THOMAS J	COL	0-0039981	0865	1
BADGLEY THEODORE M	LTC	0-0062975	0767	1
BAER CHARLES M	B G	0-0018718	0762	1
BAER HELENE N	LTC	L-0000003	0156	1
BAERMAN CHARLES P	COL	0-0040273	1267	1
BAETCKE BERND G	COL	0-0029497	1060	1
BAGBY CARROLL A	COL	0-0003093	0450	1
BAGGETT ELLA L	MAJ	N-0002376	1160	1
BAGLEY CHARLES T	MAJ	0-0021424	1144	2
BAGLEY JAMES C	COL	0-0080547	0867	1
BAGLEY RAY M	COL	0-0042902	1166	1
BAGNULO ALDO H	COL	0-0020550	0765	1
BAHE GORDON A	LTC	0-0023616	0246	2

NAME	GRADE	SVC NO	DATE RET MO YR	RET CODE
BAHR ROBERT C	COL	O-0019470	1160	2
BAIE JOHN J	LTC	O-0085127	0866	1
BAILEY CLARK N	COL	O-0015839	0555	1
BAILEY DONALD J	COL	O-0016174	0755	2
BAILEY EDWARD A	B G	O-0021083	0868	1
BAILEY GEORGE W JR	COL	O-0012820	0337	2
BAILEY GORDON W	LTC	O-0076848	0567	1
BAILEY HARLE G JR	LTC	O-0032167	1158	1
BAILEY IRWIN C JR	MAJ	O-0043143	0859	1
BAILEY JACK L	COL	O-0035552	1167	1
BAILEY JAMES M	COL	O-0031223	1065	1
BAILEY JAMES S	CPT	O-0014236	0620	2
BAILEY JOE	LTC	O-0069073	1268	1
BAILEY JOHN A JR	LTC	O-0040602	0962	1
BAILEY JOHN R JR	COL	O-0021136	0868	1
BAILEY JOSEPH M	CW2	W-0901259	0544	2
BAILEY KENNETH L	COL	O-0080549	1068	1
BAILEY KINCHEON H	COL	O-0015489	0253	1
BAILEY KINCHEON H JR	LTC	O-0027531	0966	1
BAILEY SAM P	CW4	W-0906611	1158	1
BAILEY WILLIAM A	COL	O-0019264	0759	1
BAILEY WILLIAM W	COL	O-0020687	0967	1
BAIN BENJAMIN B	COL	O-0007477	0347	1
BAIN JAMES G	COL	O-0017246	0758	1
BAIN JAMES JR	LTC	O-0068322	1266	1
BAIN JOE A	COL	O-0019308	0660	1
BAIR CECILE E	MAJ	N-0002232	0360	1
BAIRD ARTHUR R	COL	O-0009942	0346	2
BAIRD ELWOOD F	CPT	O-0021030	1041	2
BAIRD HARRY H	B G	O-0005789	0350	2
BAIRD OLIN J JR	CPT	O-0068075	0166	1
BAIRD RAYMOND C	COL	O-0002503	0138	1
BAIRD WILLET J	COL	O-0016499	0756	1
BAKER ARTHUR L	COL	O-0039805	0163	1
BAKER ARTHUR L	COL	O-0040456	0868	1
BAKER BARTON [illegible]	COL	O-0044222	0865	1
BAKER BILLY P	CW3	W-0902735	0560	1
BAKER DALLAS D	LTC	O-0058920	0868	1
BAKER DAVID A	LTC	O-0039971	0861	1
BAKER DENZIL L	COL	O-0043052	0567	2
BAKER DONALD A	LTC	O-1179281	0367	1
BAKER ELVERSON F	COL	O-0030183	0564	1
BAKER FORREST P	CPT	O-0005425	0622	2
BAKER HAROLD P	LTC	O-0040895	1162	1
BAKER HARRY T	COL	O-0029618	1061	1
BAKER JACK H	COL	O-0030239	0661	1
BAKER JAMES F	COL	O-0042714	0864	1
BAKER JOSEPH K	COL	O-0012168	0854	1
BAKER LEE R	CW3	W-0902738	0452	2
BAKER MARSHALL W	COL	O-0043558	0968	1
BAKER MESCAL	MAJ	N-0003109	0159	1
BAKER NINA M	LTC	N-0000594	0463	1
BAKER PAUL T	COL	O-0007490	0244	2
BAKER PHILLIP H	LTC	O-0024442	0462	2
BAKER ROBERT C	COL	O-0019427	0864	1
BAKER ROBERT L	CW2	W-0902012	0751	1
BAKER ROY C	COL	O-0029979	0863	1
BAKER RUSSELL A	COL	O-0015745	0954	1
BAKER SAMUEL E	COL	O-0042195	0764	1
BAKER THOMAS E	COL	O-0031244	0266	1
BAKER VAN R	LTC	O-0028043	0767	1
BAKER WILLIAM C JR	M G	O-0016371	0664	1
BALAS PAUL S	LTC	O-0040234	0860	1
BALCAR PAUL G	COL	O-0010060	0146	2
BALCER CHARLES I	LTC	O-0036519	0764	1
BALDINGER ORA M	COL	O-0003510	0624	2
BALDRY GEORGE A	COL	O-0030615	0654	1
BALDWIN CHARLES P	COL	O-0018624	0859	1
BALDWIN GUY W	LTC	O-0031924	0264	2
BALDWIN ORVAL J	COL	O-0019790	0962	1
BALDWIN PERRY L	COL	O-0005137	0351	1
BALDWIN RICHARD T	COL	O-0029113	0859	1
BALDWIN ROSS C	COL	O-0005137	1146	2
BALESTRA JOSEPHINE	LTC	N-0000522	1052	2
BALIKOV BERNARD	MAJ	O-0056775	0665	1

NAME	GRADE	SVC NO	DATE RET MO YR	RET CODE
BALKE FRANK T	COL	O-0038592	0355	1
BALKMAN AUSTIN F	LTC	O-0032285	0663	1
BALL ARTHUR C	LTC	O-0032070	1266	1
BALL CLINTON W	COL	O-0006294	0245	2
BALL HORACE G	MAJ	O-0013950	0720	2
BALL RAYMOND C	COL	O-0052184	0868	1
BALL RURA O	LTC	O-0028905	0455	1
BALL SPENCER F	CW4	W-0902743	0263	1
BALL WILLIAM E	COL	O-0041586	0459	1
BALLAGH ROBERT S	LTC	O-0030009	0961	1
BALLANTYNE JOHN L	COL	O-0015005	0946	2
BALLARD DEWITT	COL	O-0015425	1153	1
BALLARD JAMES L	LTC	O-0006149	1041	2
BALLARD JAMES M	CW3	W-0902745	0763	1
BALLARD JOHN A	COL	O-0007060	1042	1
BALLARD RICHARD W	CW4	W-0902746	0864	1
BALLARD ZORA M	LTC	N-0000495	1148	1
BALLENTINE JOHN F	COL	O-0039983	0865	1
BALLINGER ELDON L	LTC	O-0061202	0367	1
BALLOFF JAMES G	COL	O-0019955	0847	2
BALMER JESMOND O	B G	O-0011389	0153	2
BALOUGH JOSEPH J	MAJ	O-0990740	1157	2
BALS WILSON T	COL	O-0004743	1147	1
BALSAM ALFRED S	COL	O-0003864	1146	2
BALTZER NYLES W	COL	O-0051581	0165	1
BALTZO DOROTHY E	MAJ	N-0001442	1267	1
BAMBACE FELIX S	COL	O-0056797	0957	1
BAMBER WILLIAM H	LTC	O-0028480	0868	1
BANDLEY MARION K	LTC	O-0045222	0962	1
BANE JOHN C	COL	O-0021897	0765	1
BANE PAULL A JR	LTC	O-0032596	1059	1
BANE W FREDERIC JR	CPT	O-0088001	0366	2
BANGS ROBERT P	MAJ	O-0078710	0961	1
BANIGAN CALVIN B	LTC	O-0030376	0263	1
BANK AARON	COL	O-0028959	0258	1
BANK CARL C	B G	O-0003816	0947	1
BANKE HENRY H	LTC	O-0051832	0164	1
BANKS CHARLES H	COL	O-0022940	0468	1
BANKS CURTIS M	LTC	O-0030143	0362	2
BANKS JAMES C	CW3	W-0902748	0760	1
BANKS JOHN A JR	MAJ	O-1876393	0168	1
BANKS KEITH B	COL	O-0079695	0661	1
BANKS RETHA H	CPT	N-0002683	0264	2
BANKS RICHARD G	COL	O-0043407	1167	2
BANKUS JOHN T	COL	O-0042799	0562	1
BANNER CHARLES V	CW2	W-0901567	0148	1
BANNING EDWARD A	COL	O-0014716	0248	1
BANNISTER RAY K	COL	O-0029784	1062	1
BANNON JAMES F JR	COL	O-0031833	0368	1
BANTON HUSTON J	COL	O-0016975	0946	2
BANVILLE JAMES H	B G	O-0028921	0657	1
BARAN STANLEY JR	CPT	O-0060519	0863	1
BARBATO LEWIS	MAJ	O-0018636	0733	2
BARBER CHARLES N	MAJ	O-0052568	1050	2
BARBER DOROTHY J	MAJ	N-0002029	1058	1
BARBER HOMER G	COL	O-0022130	0666	1
BARBER JAMES T	LTC	O-0017551	0554	1
BARBER KEITH H	COL	O-0039606	0359	1
BARBER PAULINE A	MAJ	N-0000128	0361	1
BARBER REGINALD C	COL	O-0042560	0563	2
BARBER WILFRED F	LTC	O-0031693	0864	1
BARBERIE FREDERICK	LTC	O-0051050	0857	1
BARBOUR FRED A	CW4	W-0902751	1065	1
BARBOUR THOMAS E P	COL	O-0016469	0754	1
BARCLAY GORDON L	COL	O-0029691	0462	1
BARCLAY JOHN A	M G	O-0018420	0661	1
BARCO ERNEST T JR	COL	O-0033938	0263	2
BARD C ROBERT	COL	O-0018435	1158	1
BARD LILA	MAJ	L-0000227	0158	1
BARDEN ALBERT	COL	O-0012266	0753	1
BARDSLEY GEORGE H	COL	O-0011868	1044	2
BARE GEORGE H	COL	O-0012957	0354	1
BARE GEORGE S	LTC	O-0032488	1167	1
BARE WALTER E JR	COL	O-0019944	0865	2
BAREFIELD WILLIAM C	COL	O-0042763	0263	1

NAME	GRADE	SVC NO	DATE RET MO YR	RET CODE
BARISKI NICK	CW4	RW-9043759	0863	1
BARKALOW RUSSELL G	COL	O-0005997	0751	2
BARKER ERNEST E	COL	O-0009796	0648	1
BARKER GEORGE	COL	O-0004972	0753	1
BARKER GEORGE M	COL	O-0030708	0660	1
BARKER JAMES F	LTC	OF-0105321	0868	2
BARKER JAMES W II	LTC	O-0030001	0358	2
BARKER LEONARD C	LTC	O-0040213	0764	1
BARKER MARY O	LTC	N-0002476	0868	1
BARKER MARY R	MAJ	N-0002382	0761	1
BARKER MAURICE E	COL	O-0006779	0848	1
BARKER RAY W	M G	O-0003611	0247	2
BARKER STOCKBRIDG	COL	O-0018949	0566	1
BARKER TROY A	LTC	O-0042394	0762	1
BARKER WALTER E	COL	O-0022717	0166	1
BARKER WAYNE L	COL	O-0015379	1153	1
BARKIN ALBERT	COL	O-0051809	0966	1
BARKMAN WILLIAM E	LTC	O-0038899	1164	1
BARKSDALE BATTLE M	COL	O-0020719	0957	1
BARKSDALE WILLIAM E	B G	O-0029478	0157	1
BARLOW BOWMAN O	MAJ	O-0080039	0860	1
BARLOW EVERETT W	COL	O-0019724	0746	2
BARLOW JOHN F	COL	O-0020224	0758	1
BARLOW RAYMOND C	COL	O-0012379	0354	1
BARLOW RUDOLPH	COL	O-0031835	0964	1
BARNABY ADOLPH	COL	O-0039758	0262	1
BARNARD JOHN M	LTC	O-0056483	1166	1
BARNER THOMAS F	LTC	O-0041820	1158	1
BARNES DEAN W	LTC	O-0040745	1162	1
BARNES ELMER E	COL	O-0012054	0854	1
BARNES FRANCIS H	COL	O-0041601	0859	1
BARNES GEORGE L	COL	O-0029078	0359	1
BARNES GEORGE T	COL	O-0010615	0753	1
BARNES LYNN C	COL	O-0034641	0360	1
BARNES PAUL I	CW4	W-0902756	0662	1
BARNES THEODORE	COL	O-0003626	0540	2
BARNES VALENTINE	COL	O-0051434	0863	1
BARNES VERDI P	LTC	O-0017198	0565	1
BARNES WALLACE H	B G	O-0016426	0756	1
BARNES WILLIAM P JR	COL	O-0021048	0263	2
BARNES WILLIAM W	COL	O-0024425	0466	1
BARNETT ALLISON J	M G	O-0005364	1047	2
BARNETT CLARENCE C	LTC	O-0080554	0767	1
BARNETT DAVID E	COL	O-0008239	0850	1
BARNETT DAVID E JR	LTC	O-0028456	1168	1
BARNETT FRANK L	COL	O-0030489	0861	1
BARNETT HERBERT C	LTC	O-0056236	0962	1
BARNETT JAMES D	COL	O-0016234	0155	1
BARNETT JAMES W	B G	O-0004604	0649	1
BARNETT KEFF O	1LT	O-0014633	0426	2
BARNETT LACY C	MAJ	O-0094714	0467	1
BARNETT NORMAN P	COL	O-0038784	0461	1
BARNETT WILLIAM H	LTC	O-0022104	0759	1
BARNETT WILLIAM W JR	LTC	O-0046540	1065	1
BARNETTE ELLIOTT J	COL	O-0028847	0256	1
BARNEY JAMES P JR	COL	O-0012796	0152	2
BARNEY KEITH R	M G	O-0016377	0462	1
BARNEY LEONARD C	LTC	O-0037487	0862	1
BARNHART FRANK H	COL	O-0005498	0549	2
BARNHILL GERVASE L	COL	O-0076850	0968	1
BARNHIZER HARRY J	MAJ	O-0087555	0762	1
BARNITZ GERALD W	LTC	O-0060669	0868	1
BARNUM CHARLES V	CPT	O-0011632	0-35	2
BARNUM JOHN M	COL	O-0051780	0461	1
BARNUM RICHARD V	LTC	O-0036167	0763	1
BARNWELL C H JR	B G	O-0005571	0652	1
BARNWELL JOHN C	LTC	O-0080040	0669	1
BARNWELL JOHN D	COL	O-0008787	0747	2
BARON ALBERT S	COL	O-0016674	1054	1
BARON EDWIN W	COL	O-0042012	0567	2
BARONE SANDRO A	LTC	O-0080556	0567	1
BARR CHRISTINE	MAJ	N-0001642	1064	1
BARR DAVID G	M G	O-0010313	0252	2
BARR DWIGHT P	CW4	W-0902758	1057	1
BARR EARL L	COL	O-0019792	0647	2

NAME	GRADE	SVC NO	DATE RET MO YR	RET CODE
BARR EDWARD H	COL	O-0014634	0151	2
BARR JOHN	COL	O-0040148	1168	1
BARR WILLIAM H	LTC	O-0055470	0963	1
BARRATT TOM H	COL	O-0024343	0264	1
BARRELL FRANK M	COL	O-0009893	0744	2
BARRELL RICHARD	COL	O-0032104	0168	1
BARRETT CARRIE E	COL	N-0000124	0466	1
BARRETT DAVID D	COL	O-0009726	0852	1
BARRETT FRANCES M	MAJ	N-0000730	0364	1
BARRETT JOHN H	CW4	W-0904081	0159	1
BARRETT JOHN T	COL	O-0042015	0462	1
BARRETT JOHN W	LTC	O-0024448	0946	2
BARRETT LAURENCE O	LTC	O-0036652	1166	1
BARRETT LEONARD L	COL	O-0013951	0720	2
BARRETT REX M	LTC	O-0084723	0967	1
BARRETT ROSS P	CPT	O-0058824	0663	1
BARRETT RUTH	MAJ	N-0001884	1159	1
BARRETT WALTER D S	MAJ	O-0043152	0958	2
BARRETT WILLIAM P	LTC	O-0067551	0965	1
BARRICK CARROL C	COL	O-0019330	0959	1
BARRICK HARRY W	COL	O-0012345	1146	1
BARRICKLOW WILLIAM R	COL	O-0056816	0862	1
BARRIGER WILLIAM L	M G	O-0011220	0257	1
BARRINGER MICHEL L	MAJ	O-0097882	0967	2
BARRIOS WILLIE W J	LTC	O-0036748	0865	1
BARROLL MORRIS K JR	COL	O-0005241	0550	1
BARRON HELEN F	MAJ	L-0000481	0268	1
BARROW LLEWELLYN	LTC	O-0018949	0244	2
BARROWS RALPH G	COL	O-0004431	0846	1
BARRY ARTHUR F	COL	O-0023160	1165	1
BARRY CHARLES J JR	COL	O-0038713	0462	1
BARRY GEORGE W	COL	O-0039916	1064	1
BARRY JAMES P	LTC	O-0025283	0766	1
BARRY KEVIN G	LTC	O-0063478	1166	1
BARRY MARY S	MAJ	N-0000053	0751	1
BARRY ROBERT B JR	COL	O-0022674	0667	1
BARRY WILLIAM E	LTC	O-0019682	0360	1
BARSCHDORF MILTON P	COL	O-0021085	0859	1
BART WAYNE L	LTC	O-0024707	0759	1
BARTEL THOMAS B	COL	O-0022019	0746	2
BARTELMEZ THEODORE L	MAJ	O-0052051	0453	2
BARTELT ROBERT H	LTC	O-0081888	0766	1
BARTH BERLE I	MAJ	O-0091749	0567	2
BARTH GEORGE B	M G	O-0011241	1057	2
BARTH LUTHER R	COL	O-0042418	1264	1
BARTH ROBERT A	LTC	O-0005996	0636	1
BARTHLE ROBERT C	COL	O-0024246	0566	1
BARTHOLET JOHN C	COL	O-0043845	0164	1
BARTHOLF JOHN C P	B G	O-0003503	1045	2
BARTHOLOMEW HOWARD L	COL	O-0043524	0666	1
BARTHOLOMEW HOWARD W	CW2	W-0904359	0960	1
BARTHOLOMEW JAMES W	CW4	RW-0907121	1066	1
BARTHOLOW WALTER M	CW4	W-0906615	0261	2
BARTLETT FRANK E	LTC	O-0041614	0957	1
BARTLETT HARRY M	LTC	O-0039457	0765	1
BARTLETT LAURENCE W	COL	O-0012707	0749	1
BARTLETT ROY W	COL	O-0041600	0657	1
BARTLETT THOMAS R	MAJ	O-0006452	0-37	2
BARTLETT WILLIAM G	COL	O-0019047	0859	2
BARTLETT WILLIAM H	COL	O-0012695	0854	1
BARTLETT WILLIAM T	LTC	O-0042468	1162	1
BARTLEY JAMES T	LTC	O-0026649	0567	1
BARTLING CARL W	COL	O-0043091	0264	1
BARTON CHESTER T	COL	O-0029529	0261	1
BARTON DEFOREST A	LTC	O-0080558	1067	1
BARTON DENNIS L	COL	O-0023049	1168	1
BARTON DOUGLAS C	COL	O-0038829	0466	2
BARTON LEWIS B	CW3	W-0908146	0868	1
BARTON RAYMOND M	COL	O-0016185	0655	1
BARTOSIK MATTHEW J	COL	O-0052145	0762	1
BARTOW CHARLES P	LTC	O-0052310	1062	1
BARTZ RALPH F	COL	O-0016132	0244	2
BARWICK WILLIAM R	LTC	O-0061089	0168	1
BARY ROBERT S	LTC	O-0032296	0762	1
BARZYNSKI JOSEPH E	B G	O-0002082	0744	1

NAME	GRADE	SVC NO	DATE RET MO YR	RET CODE
BASHAS JAMES G	COL	0-0042454	0858	1
BASSALL JULIAN F	LTC	0-0087471	0666	1
BASH JAMES H	LTC	0-0078696	0764	1
BASILE DANIEL	COL	0-0040930	0867	1
BASS ARTHUR C	COL	0-0030292	0562	1
BASS GLENN L	COL	0-0043318	0268	1
BASS ROY M JR	LTC	0-0039125	0866	1
BASS MARSHALL B	LTC	0-0062204	0468	1
BASS ROY H JR	COL	0-0039311	1168	1
BASSETT RALPH H	COL	0-0012432	1050	1
BASSITT VASSIER G	COL	0-0019331	0865	1
BASTILLE JOSEPH A	CW4	W-0902762	0656	1
BASTION JOSEPH F	B G	0-0002805	0247	2
BASTION JOSEPH F JR	M G	0-0019162	0866	1
BATCH JOSEPH W	COL	0-0020864	0867	2
BATCHELDER HAROLD W	1LT	0-0014439	0920	2
BATCHELDER GEORGE D	COL	0-0034852	0166	1
BATCHELOR VANCE W	COL	0-0008521	1049	1
BATES GILBERT S	CW4	W-0906617	0762	1
BATES JAMES C	COL	0-0007394	0848	1
BATES JOHN F	LTC	0-0056633	0863	1
BATES PAUL L	COL	0-0029929	0563	1
BATES WILLIAM E JR	LTC	0-0059939	0767	1
BATES WILLIAM H	LTC	0-0039806	1060	1
BATHURST CHARLES R	COL	0-0012060	0554	1
BATLIN ALEXANDER	COL	0-0043927	0162	1
BATSON CURTIS C	LTC	0-0033152	1161	1
BATSON ROSCOE C	COL	0-0003104	0346	2
BATTLEY JOSEPH F	B G	0-0011288	0747	1
BATY JAMES B	LTC	0-0029141	1147	2
BAUCH ALFRED R	COL	0-0034401	0868	1
BAUCHSPIES ROLLIN L	COL	0-0017819	0959	1
BAUER ELMER H	COL	0-0043502	0768	1
BAUER FRANK L	COL	0-0026430	0663	1
BAUER RICHARD M	LTC	0-0019904	1146	2
BAUGH IRA E	CW4	W-0902764	0665	1
BAUGHMAN RICHARD A	COL	0-0060244	0268	1
BAUGHMAN VICTOR D	COL	0-0061241	0568	1
BAUGHN WILMOT T	COL	0-0040155	0761	1
BAUKNIGHT RALPH M	COL	0-0051091	0660	1
BAUM FREDERICK	LTC	0-0023385	0764	1
BAUM INEZ I	MAJ	M-0010084	0255	1
BAUMANN JULIAN H	COL	0-0016326	1155	2
BAUMER DONALD H	MAJ	0-0022987	0150	2
BAUMGARTNER JOHN W	COL	0-0043642	1168	2
BAUMGARTNER OSWALD R	CW4	W-0902765	0455	1
BAXLEY JAMES W	LTC	0-0078714	1163	1
BAXTER JAMES C	MAJ	0-0060478	0263	1
BAXTER SAMUEL F	LTC	0-0079734	0464	1
BAYA GEORGE E	COL	0-0029817	0560	1
BAYER WILLIAM L	B G	0-0016372	0756	2
BAYERLE GEORGE J JR	COL	0-0023192	0664	1
BAYLESS HARRY K	COL	0-0029104	1157	2
BAYLIS JAMES E	B G	0-0003310	1047	2
BAYLISS MILWARD W	COL	0-0041743	0763	1
BAYNE JOSEPH K	COL	0-0030913	0960	1
BAYNE ROBERT H	COL	0-0019207	0957	1
BAYOT J M	WO1	W-0800601	0733	2
BAYS HAROLD L	COL	0-0018433	0761	1
BAZE MILES J	COL	0-0041378	0155	1
BEACH BENJAMIN O	COL	0-0029505	1060	1
BEACH DWIGHT E	GEN	0-0018747	0868	1
BEACH JOHN B	LTC	0-0025978	0864	1
BEACH PRINCE O	COL	0-0058753	0868	1
BEACH WILLIAM V	COL	0-0079735	0868	1
BEADLE FRANK L	COL	0-0014996	0548	1
BEAGLE NADINE N	MAJ	N-0001711	0863	1
BEALKE JACOB W JR	COL	0-0031365	0865	1
BEALL CLAUDIUS A JR	COL	0-0039931	0564	1
BEALL EDWIN S	CPT	0-0006608	0828	2
BEALS FRANK I	MAJ	0-0014107	0508	2
BEAN EMMETT J	M G	0-0012381	0657	1
BEANE WOODROW H	CW2	W-0902371	1163	1
BEARCE HERRICK F	COL	0-0030498	0765	1
BEARD J B	LTC	0-0084450	1262	1

NAME	GRADE	SVC NO	DATE RET MO YR	RET CODE
BEARD ROBERT S	COL	0-0009412	1042	1
BEARD WILLIAM N	COL	0-0020154	0866	1
BEARDSLEY FORD M	COL	0-0040311	1268	1
BEARSS ERNEST H	COL	0-0032020	0165	1
BEASLEY CHARLES H	COL	0-0016542	0147	2
BEASLEY LOUIS J	LTC	0-0022710	0567	1
BEASLEY OSCAR H	COL	0-0018045	0859	1
BEASLEY THOMAS A	LTC	0-0065074	0566	2
BEATTIE HUNTER S	CW4	W-0902769	0467	1
BEATTIE JAMES	CW4	W-0901917	0352	1
BEATTY GEORGE L	COL	0-0019318	1057	1
BEATTY GEORGE S	COL	0-0010070	0250	1
BEATTY JOHN C	COL	0-0013952	0720	2
BEATY EDWARD K	LTC	0-0080562	1163	1
BEATY HAROLD F	COL	0-0038930	0268	1
BEATY WILLIAM F	LTC	0-0022672	0460	1
BEAUCHAMP CHARLES E	M G	0-0018238	0566	1
BEAUCHAMP ROBERT J	COL	0-0044907	0667	2
BEAUCOND CHARLES A	COL	0-0008374	0948	2
BEAUDET BERTRAND N	COL	0-0040119	1264	1
BEAUMONT LEE ROY H	LTC	0-0055170	0763	1
BEAVER FRANCIS L	COL	0-0042057	0261	1
BEAVER ROBERT I	LTC	0-0022188	0645	2
BEAZLEY CHARLES G	CW3	W-0902772	0661	1
BEAZLEY LEWIS K	CPT	0-0019397	0942	2
BECH ALBERT R	COL	0-0042585	0860	1
BECK BERNARD B	COL	0-0040481	0868	1
BECK CLARENCE E	B G	0-0021239	0268	1
BECK DONALD C	COL	0-0031329	1066	1
BECK HARRY V	LTC	0-0024210	0760	1
BECK HELEN I	MAJ	N-0002271	0563	1
BECK JOHN N	COL	0-0040258	0866	1
BECK ROBERT M JR	M G	0-0001337	0-39	1
BECK THEODOR J	CPT	0-0018622	0242	1
BECK THOMAS H	B G	0-0019164	0663	1
BECK THOMAS R	CW4	W-0902773	0764	1
BECK TRAVIS A	2LT	0-0019287	0934	2
BECK VANCEL R	COL	0-0030233	0764	1
BECKER DANIEL	MAJ	0-0006073	0436	2
BECKER HENRY C	LTC	0-0031944	0565	1
BECKER HENRY C	LTC	0-0063389	1166	1
BECKER JANE T	MAJ	N-0002051	0960	1
BECKER OLIVER G	MAJ	0-0026874	1058	2
BECKER WALTER H	COL	0-0051141	0960	1
BECKER WARD E	COL	0-0009802	0553	2
BECKER WILFRED C	LTC	0-0034839	0364	1
BECKETT ROBERT C	MAJ	0-0011671	0231	2
BECKETT THOMAS J	LTC	0-0084724	1066	1
BECKHAM JOHN B	LTC	0-0032747	0566	1
BECKJORD PHILIP R	COL	0-0031051	0960	1
BECKMAN PAUL E	LTC	0-0066135	0868	1
BECKNER JOHN D	COL	0-0030512	0754	2
BEDDOW JAMES H	COL	0-0021446	0866	1
BEDELL EDWIN A	COL	0-0039722	0661	1
BEDFORD WILLIAM H	COL	0-0043926	0267	1
BEDNAREK FRANK	COL	0-0038932	0268	1
BEE THOMAS J	LTC	0-0044437	0661	1
BEEBE JOHN E JR	COL	0-0079736	0868	1
BEEBE JOHN L	COL	0-0039970	0765	1
BEECHLEY JOHN C	LTC	0-0044115	0168	1
BEEDLE DORIS I	MAJ	N-0002235	0560	1
BEELER DONALD T	COL	0-0015437	1153	2
BEELMAN GLENN T	COL	0-0022235	0861	1
BEEMAN AARON W	B G	0-0029063	0259	1
BEER WARREN G	LTC	0-0059966	1165	1
BEERE DONALD C	COL	0-0021893	0959	1
BEERE DONALD M	COL	0-0002588	0546	2
BEESON JOHN J III	COL	0-0032013	1068	1
BEESON JOHN P	LTC	0-0024686	0767	1
BEESON WALTER L	COL	0-0031143	1263	1
BEETH HOWARD D	LTC	0-0042489	1262	1
BEETS WALTER O	COL	0-0029707	0562	1
BEEZLEY ORVA E	COL	0-0004398	1044	2
BEGANIE HENRY R	LTC	0-0088566	0967	2
BEGGS EDWIN G	COL	0-0020297	0763	1

NAME	GRADE	SVC NO	DATE RET MO YR	RET CODE
BEGGS RAYMOND W	COL	0-0019402	0363	1
BEHNKEN B T JR	LTC	0-0044052	0959	1
BEHRENS HENRY R	COL	0-0024970	0747	1
BEIDERLINDEN W A	M G	0-0019404	0655	1
BEIDLE GEORGIA V	MAJ	N-0001282	0661	1
BEIDLEMAN LAURENCE E	CW4	W-0906621	1264	1
BEIGHTLER ROBERT S	M G	0-0038581	0753	2
BEIMFOHR CASPER V	COL	0-0081858	0168	1
BEISER JOHN J	COL	0-0023025	1161	2
BEISHLINE JOHN R	B G	0-0018523	0655	1
BEITER DEAN S	COL	0-0019692	0265	1
BEITZ JAMES F	CPT	0-0097394	1066	2
BELANGER GERARD A	COL	0-0019333	1159	1
BELANGER RENALDO G	COL	0-0040109	0762	2
BELCHER JAYNIE E	CPT	N-0000051	0351	1
BELDEN ARTHUR W	LTC	0-0050950	0555	1
BELDEN HUGH	COL	0-0028819	0955	1
BELFLOWER EVA K	CPT	N-0002362	1057	2
BELIEU KENNETH E	COL	0-0032223	1055	2
BELIN HEDWIG C	LTC	L-0000136	0266	1
BELISLE MAURICE A	COL	0-0052175	0668	1
BELL ALLAN D JR	LTC	0-0081955	1168	1
BELL CLARENCE O	COL	0-0010780	0247	2
BELL CLYDE H	CW4	RW-0904092	0661	1
BELL DOVER	COL	0-0006851	0246	2
BELL EARL W	LTC	0-0027743	0765	1
BELL ELIZABETH	MAJ	L-0000015	0654	1
BELL EUGENE J JR	LTC	0-0063676	1167	1
BELL GILBERT F	LTC	0-0020917	0746	2
BELL GILMER M	COL	0-0005472	1046	2
BELL GLYNDON D	CW4	RW-0904287	0864	1
BELL J FRANKLIN	COL	0-0001687	0130	1
BELL JAMES A	LTC	0-0026452	0164	1
BELL JAMES K	COL	0-0029912	0261	1
BELL JESSE J	COL	0-0029441	0760	1
BELL JOE D	LTC	0-0063458	0765	1
BELL JOHN A	LTC	0-0033577	0764	1
BELL JOSEPH	CW4	W-0906622	0862	1
BELL MARCUS B	B G	0-0006516	1051	1
BELL MATTIE A	MAJ	N-0000694	C365	1
BELL OLIN L	COL	0-0023119	0765	1
BELL RAYMOND E	M G	0-0016897	0663	2
BELL THOMAS P	MAJ	0-0021392	0147	2
BELL URIEL L	LTC	0-0031731	1064	1
BELL WILLIAM III	LTC	0-0026934	0766	1
BELL WILLIAM W	COL	0-0079737	0868	1
BELLAMY PAUL F	COL	0-0030220	0862	1
BELLAND WALTER T	COL	0-0043450	0367	1
BELLAVANCE ARMAND L	LTC	0-0040484	C164	1
BELLICAN CHARLES P	COL	0-0019285	1054	1
BELLINGER JOHN B	COL	0-0008626	0846	2
BELLOND JACK B JR	LTC	0-0067643	0868	1
BELLONBY EMERY F	COL	0-0024441	0765	1
BELMORE RALPH W	CW3	W-0904280	0763	1
BELON RALPH G	COL	0-0043746	0261	2
BELOTE BYRON G	COL	0-0042851	0564	1
BELSER WILLIAM G JR	COL	0-0042897	0963	1
BENCH GERALD N	COL	0-0051092	0860	1
BENDA ANGELA P	MAJ	N-0002108	0768	2
BENDER LATHERINE	MAJ	M-0010024	0965	1
BENDER GEORGE F	COL	0-0016914	0857	1
BENDER PAUL C	COL	0-0047706	1065	1
BENDER THOMAS W	COL	0-0030162	0660	1
BENDFELT HARRIETT C	MAJ	L-0000083	0262	1
BENEDICT ARTHUR L	CPT	0-0009955	1032	2
BENEDICT HAROLD B	COL	0-0031566	0767	1
BENEDICT MAUDE B	LTC	N-0000197	0760	1
BENEKE ARTHUR R	LTC	0-0084542	0266	1
BENENSON ABRAM S	COL	0-0024295	0762	1
BENFORD JAMES A	COL	0-0051676	1265	1
BENGEL LAWRENCE W	COL	0-0034423	0765	1
BENGTSON THORE F	LTC	0-0018670	0650	2
BENHAM CLAUDE G	CPT	0-0005743	1128	1
BENINATE NICHOLAS A	COL	0-0059464	0567	1
BENION HARRY G	LTC	0-0020872	0565	1

NAME	GRADE	SVC NO	DATE RET MO YR	RET CODE
BENITEZ ENRIQUE M	COL	0-0004841	0451	1
BENITEZ ROBERTO F	LTC	0-0058706	1264	1
BENJAMIN DON C	LTC	0-0043070	0864	1
BENJAMIN ROBERT E	COL	0-0028887	1056	1
BENJAMIN ROY F	LTC	0-0032062	0762	1
BENKE CLYDE W	LTC	0-0076801	0868	1
BENKOSKY STEPHEN W	COL	0-0028852	0656	1
BENNER JAMES D	LTC	0-0079697	0960	1
BENNER JOHN A	LTC	0-0024203	0162	1
BENNER JOHN G	COL	0-0019571	0357	1
BENNET ALEXANDER	COL	0-0012257	1146	1
BENNETT A REGINA	LTC	N-0002407	0166	1
BENNETT ADAM J	LTC	0-0007514	0-34	2
BENNETT ALFRED F	LTC	0-0083099	0768	2
BENNETT AUSTIN W	COL	0-0022288	0147	2
BENNETT CLARENCE W	COL	0-0015618	0754	1
BENNETT CLETOS O	COL	0-0028966	0358	1
BENNETT CURTIS H	COL	0-0041821	0758	1
BENNETT EATON W	COL	0-0019604	0656	1
BENNETT ELI E	COL	0-0007557	0-43	1
BENNETT EUGENE G	COL	0-0041669	0460	1
BENNETT GEORGE W	COL	0-0021434	0255	2
BENNETT IVAN L	M G	0-0011936	0454	2
BENNETT JAMES G	LTC	0-0040400	0967	1
BENNETT JOHN C	MAJ	0-0070616	0768	2
BENNETT JOHN G	LTC	0-0029387	0758	2
BENNETT PHILIP C	2LT	0-0017593	0533	2
BENNETT VERDE W	LTC	0-0034157	0261	1
BENNETT WILLIAM C JR	COL	0-0012087	0750	1
BENNETT WILLIAM E	LTC	0-0031754	0166	1
BENNETT WILLIAM J	COL	0-0023331	0764	1
BENNETT WILMER G	COL	0-0016141	0655	1
BENNINGER MARION L	LTC	N-0001885	1262	1
BENOIT JOSEPH F	LTC	0-0051070	0455	2
BENSER ERNEST A	COL	0-0042360	0664	1
BENSON HENRY K JR	M G	0-0020331	0867	1
BENSON JENEVIEVE	MAJ	N-0002239	0860	1
BENSON JOSEPH W	COL	0-0025601	0563	1
BENSON RICHARD T	LTC	0-0052484	0868	2
BENSON ROBERT C	LTC	0-0080569	0762	1
BENSON WILMER K	COL	0-0021423	0868	1
BENT JOSEPH G JR	COL	0-0029797	1162	1
BENT WILLIAM R	LTC	0-0008063	0844	1
BENTON ARTHUR L	LTC	0-0094088	0968	1
BENTON DEWARD E	LTC	0-0033761	0160	1
BENTON ROBERT G	CW4	W-0902782	0359	1
BENTON ROBERT J	CW2	W-0902157	1147	1
BENZ HERBERT T	COL	0-0015603	0646	2
BEPLAT JAMES A	LTC	0-0043694	0866	1
BERAN KURT	LTC	0-0067644	1268	1
BERARDINELLI STEPHEN	LTC	0-0019668	1062	1
BERBERT HENRY	COL	0-0011357	0753	1
BERCAW WOODSON W JR	LTC	0-0059077	0868	1
BERENBAUM ESAI	LTC	0-0061442	0568	1
BERENDT HERBERT W	LTC	0-0031861	0466	1
BEREUTER ROBERT L	COL	0-0024451	0668	1
BERG FREDERICK	COL	0-0018412	0761	1
BERG JACOB J	LTC	0-0080571	0367	1
BERG JOSEPH P JR	LTC	0-0027211	0465	1
BERG MARY J	LTC	N-0002429	0368	1
BERGE TRYGVE O	COL	0-0030980	1164	1
BERGER MORRIS R	CW4	W-0902387	0966	2
BERGER RAYFIELD R	LTC	0-0080572	1066	1
BERGIN GERALD A	COL	0-0051722	0366	1
BERGIN WILLIAM F	M G	0-0007127	0554	2
BERGLUND HAROLD K	CW4	W-0902783	1263	1
BERGMAN ALFRED N	1LT	0-0012149	0523	2
BERGMANN JOHN A	COL	0-0042300	0164	1
BERGMANN RAY A	CW4	W-0902785	0166	1
BERGQUIST EARL C	M G	0-0016998	0859	1
BERGSAGEL RALPH M	COL	0-0079739	0868	1
BERILLA GEORGE P JR	LTC	0-0016147	0952	2
BERKEBILE ALMA J	MAJ	N-0002470	0866	1
BERLIN WALTER I	LTC	0-0080575	0368	1
BERLINER SYLVAN	COL	0-0015917	0346	2

NAME	GRADE	SVC NO	DATE RET MO YR	RET CODE
BERMAN HARRY L	COL	0-0022697	0860	1
BERNARD JOSEPH T	COL	0-0045997	1263	1
BERNARD LYLE W	COL	0-0019195	0863	1
BERNARD ROBERT J	LTC	0-0058830	1165	1
BERNAJER FLOYD V	CW4	W-0902786	0363	1
BERNER BENT E	CPT	0-0060611	0964	1
BERNHARD ALEXANDER	LTC	0-0063419	0966	1
BERNIER DONALD W	COL	0-0017911	0765	1
BERNIER JOSEPH L	M G	0-0020093	1167	2
BERNINGER ALTA	LTC	N-0000504	0452	2
BERNOCCI ROBERT J	LTC	0-0063148	0353	1
BEROL ALEXANDER	MAJ	0-0033000	0961	1
BERRIEN CLINTON S	COL	0-0011730	1048	2
BERRIGAN PAUL D	B G	0-0016741	0757	1
BERRIS MICHAEL T JR	LTC	0-0080577	0966	1
BERRY ARY C	CPT	0-0006996	0233	2
BERRY COBURN L	COL	0-0006306	0844	2
BERRY DANIEL J	COL	0-0017406	0353	2
BERRY EDWARD S	COL	0-0019119	0660	1
BERRY FLOYD L	COL	0-0038866	1166	1
BERRY FRANK E	COL	0-0084342	1067	1
BERRY FRED P	LTC	0-0080578	1064	1
BERRY HARRY W	COL	0-0042490	1264	1
BERRY JOHN A	B G	0-0013473	0661	1
BERRY JOHN E JR	MAJ	0-0031707	0552	2
BERRY JOHN L	CW4	W-0906624	1065	1
BERRY JOHN T	COL	0-0025284	0668	1
BERRY LOGAN C	COL	0-0015752	0954	1
BERRY LUCIEN S S	COL	0-0004451	0253	2
BERRY MORGAN C	COL	0-0006886	1147	2
BERRY WILBUR C	COL	0-0020410	0765	1
BERTL SAMUEL C	COL	0-0048711	1068	1
BERTRAM ROGER A	LTC	0-0025508	0863	1
BERTRAND ALOYSIUS F	LTC	0-0067552	0866	1
BERTRAND RODNEY H	CW4	W-0902787	0859	1
BERTSCH WILLIAM H JR	COL	0-0015759	0754	1
BERWALD HERBERT T	COL	0-0017831	0457	1
BESBECK LOUIS B	LTC	0-0042142	0461	1
BESS EDWARD J	CW4	W-0902788	0359	1
BESS WALTER P	B G	0-0020151	1166	1
BESSE EDWARD H	COL	0-0006312	0642	1
BESSE WARREN E	COL	0-0039989	1165	1
BESSELL WILLIAM W JR	B G	0-0012611	0665	2
BESSER WILLIAM J	LTC	0-0044039	1167	1
BESSMER EARL S	COL	0-0039324	0363	1
BESSON ROBERT	COL	0-0020771	0967	2
BEST CHARLES E	LTC	0-0058831	0667	1
BEST CLIFFORD A	COL	0-0016544	0156	1
BEST GEORGE W JR	COL	0-0025074	0468	2
BETANCES-RAMIRE CAR	LTC	0-0070524	0163	1
BETCHER ALFRED J	COL	0-0003082	0539	1
BETHART HECTOR	COL	0-0056266	1068	1
BETHEA JAMES A	M G	0-0004076	1049	2
BETHEL JOHN M	COL	0-0011203	1146	2
BETHUNE PHILIP H	B G	0-0018449	0661	1
BETHUNE SAMUEL A	LTC	0-0031502	1162	1
BETIT JOSEPH W	LTC	0-0080580	0967	1
BETTIEN RICHARD L	LTC	0-0043528	0666	1
BETTS ROBERT H	LTC	0-0050956	0449	2
BETTS THOMAS J	B G	0-0007328	0754	1
BETZOLD CURTIS W	COL	0-0019641	0164	1
BEUHLER RALPH H	1LT	0-0050729	1150	2
BEURKET RAYMOND T	COL	0-0015543	0954	2
BEVERIDGE THEODORE M	LTC	0-0081957	0666	1
BEVINGTON HOLMES H	LTC	0-0042133	1060	1
BEVINS LORETTA M	MAJ	N-0001280	0166	1
BEYER DONALD S	LTC	0-0028673	0766	1
BEYNON JAMES L	COL	0-0017605	0557	1
BIANCHI ELIZABETH	LTC	L-0000042	0261	1
BIASINI ISABELLE	MAJ	L-0000530	0867	1
BIBB JOSEPH R	COL	0-0007454	1047	1
BIBBY WILLIAM L	LTC	0-0026276	1264	1
BICKLEY RUSSELL W	LTC	0-0065474	0668	1
BIDDLE WILLIAM S	M G	0-0015180	1060	1
BIDGOOD CLARENCE	COL	0-0019777	1163	1

NAME	GRADE	SVC NO	DATE RET MO YR	RET CODE
BIDWELL BRUCE W	COL	0-0015552	0954	1
BIDWELL JAMES W	COL	0-0029508	0459	2
BIEHL PHILIP F	COL	0-0005539	0650	1
BIENVENU THOMAS F	COL	0-0030401	0363	1
BIERER BENJAMIN R	COL	0-0033722	0866	1
BIERI ALFRED C	LTC	0-0033055	1163	1
BIERI GEORGE A	COL	0-0040298	1068	2
BIERMAN DONALD L	COL	0-0023175	1064	1
BIERWIRTH WILLIAM R	1LT	0-0062245	1051	2
BIGBY WALTER A	COL	0-0010294	0153	2
BIGELOW HORACE F	M G	0-0018775	0167	1
BIGELOW MAURICE C	COL	0-0005129	0551	1
BIGGER CHESTER H	LTC	0-0024212	0962	1
BIGGS BRADLEY	LTC	0-0036892	0861	1
BIGGS RICHARD C	COL	0-0045688	0166	1
BIGGS THOMAS P	LTC	0-0063104	0666	1
BIGLEY FRANK	LTC	0-0083578	0168	1
BILBO THEODORE G JR	COL	0-0019477	0864	1
BILES GEORGE W F	COL	0-0039590	1059	1
BILHARZ DWIGHT L	LTC	0-0065952	0764	1
BILL ARTHUR T	LTC	0-0030112	0162	1
BILL DOROTHY A	MAJ	N-0002251	0961	1
BILLING DAVID O	LTC	0-0042820	1160	1
BILLINGS EDWARD R	COL	0-0039945	1163	1
BILLINGS WILLIAM H	COL	0-0030098	0859	1
BILLINGSLEY CLAUDE A	COL	0-0016620	0754	1
BILLINGSLEY JOHN D	COL	0-0017188	0968	2
BILLINGSLEY ROBERTS	COL	0-0030608	0165	1
BILLINGSLEY WALTER L	CW4	W-0906625	1163	1
BINDEMAN WILLIAM W	LTC	0-0058713	1067	1
BINDER ROBERT T	LTC	0-0089415	0967	1
BINFORD THOMAS E	COL	0-0015595	0346	2
BING JAMES F	CW3	RW-0902795	1165	1
BING RALPH C	COL	0-0015255	0854	1
BINGHAM BERNARD A	2LT	0-0014469	0919	2
BINGHAM EDWARD C JR	LTC	0-0040471	0765	1
BINGHAM EMIL S	CW4	W-0901459	1044	2
BINGHAM LEONARD L	COL	0-0015534	0754	1
BINNING MARCEL	LTC	N-0010011	0865	1
BINNS JOHN J	M G	0-0015207	1159	2
BIRCH HORACE M	CW4	W-0902796	0355	1
BIRCH THOMAS H	COL	0-0032696	0868	1
BIRCH WILSON H	LTC	0-0042816	0764	1
BIRD JOHN E	B G	0-0016179	0656	1
BIRD RAFAEL	MAJ	0-0014359	0218	2
BIRD ROBERT J	LTC	0-0032343	0664	1
BIRD VIRON E	LTC	0-0024568	1160	1
BIRDSEYE W B JR	LTC	0-0023807	0760	2
BIRKMEYER LOUIS R	CPT	0-0063576	1065	2
BIRKS HAMMOND D	B G	0-0007184	1146	2
BIRMINGHAM RICHARD L	COL	0-0004480	1045	2
BISANT OSCAR M JR	COL	0-0051387	0363	1
BISBING JOHN	COL	0-0031665	1163	1
BISBORT HAROLD E	COL	0-0029934	0862	1
BISHOP CLARENCE E	LTC	0-0080583	0667	1
BISHOP CLIFFORD D	CPT	0-0019611	0242	2
BISHOP EUGENE H	LTC	0-0041167	0865	1
BISHOP HARRY A	COL	0-0010565	0848	1
BISHOP HOEL S JR	COL	0-0009322	0954	2
BISHOP JAMES I	COL	0-0022231	0968	1
BISHOP LOREN E	COL	0-0040091	0567	1
BISHOP MARGARET N	LTC	N-0000186	0962	1
BISSELL EDWARD B	COL	0-0021360	0367	1
BISSELL JOHN T B	B G	0-0008624	0246	1
BISSELL LEFT W	1LT	0-0014364	0419	2
BISSELL PAUL V	COL	0-0041941	0162	1
BISSETT DAVID A	LTC	0-0008456	0934	2
BISSON ROGER R	CPT	0-0069861	0559	2
BITALA JOSEPH A	CW4	W-0907137	1157	1
BITNER LELAND H	LTC	0-0059570	0965	1
BITNER ROBERT E	COL	0-0017371	0254	2
BITROS MINNIE L	MAJ	N-0000691	0762	1
BITTNER JOHN H F	COL	0-0028870	0756	1
BITZEL MARGARET M	MAJ	N-0000531	1054	1
BIVENS ARTHUR L	COL	0-0042105	0163	1

NAME	GRADE	SVC NO	DATE RET MO YR	RET CODE
BIXBY HAROLD D	COL	0-0014739	0946	1
BIXBY LAWRENCE B	COL	0-0012102	0850	1
BIXBY LAWRENCE H JR	CPT	0-0025440	0648	2
BIXBY WALLACE W	CW2	W-0902900	0861	1
BIXBY WILLIS W	LTC	0-0036104	0363	1
BIXEL CHARLES P	B G	0-0016808	0757	1
BIZZELL LEE C	COL	0-0010250	0753	1
BJORK DELBERT L	COL	0-0032399	1163	1
BLACK ARTHUR H	COL	0-0038718	0662	1
BLACK ASA C	COL	0-0038894	1066	1
BLACK CLAUDE A	COL	0-0016235	0950	2
BLACK DANIEL N	COL	0-0052309	1263	1
BLACK FLORENCE S	MAJ	N-0000934	0264	1
BLACK FREDERICK	B G	0-0009719	0650	1
BLACK FREDERICK JR	LTC	0-0026796	0764	1
BLACK GARLAND C JR	LTC	0-0026105	0465	2
BLACK GEORGE W	COL	0-0032192	1265	1
BLACK GORHAM L JR	COL	0-0065111	0868	1
BLACK HAROLD	COL	0-0049373	0565	1
BLACK HENRY M	B G	0-0008596	1053	1
BLACK HERBERT D JR	LTC	0-0043223	1068	1
BLACK JAMES A	CW2	W-0900607	0446	2
BLACK JAMES G	COL	0-0039833	0363	1
BLACK JOHN W	LTC	0-0016136	0644	2
BLACK JOSEPH E	LTC	0-0039268	0966	1
BLACK PAUL J	COL	0-0016500	0756	1
BLACK PERCY G	COL	0-0005268	0340	2
BLACK PETER T L	LTC	0-0031900	1061	2
BLACK ROBERT L	COL	0-0017175	0355	1
BLACK WILLIAM E	LTC	0-0080047	0967	2
BLACKBURN WILLIAM W	LTC	0-0034244	0267	1
BLACKER KEMUEL K	COL	0-0044956	1065	1
BLACKFORD CLIFTON D	COL	0-0018205	0760	1
BLACKFORD JAMES L	MAJ	0-0058836	0563	1
BLACKLOCK WAR[illegible] T	COL	0-0032399	0965	1
BLACKMARK WILLIAM H	COL	0-0042936	0966	1
BLACKMON ROY F	COL	0-0051569	0165	1
BLACKMORE PHILIP G	B G	0-0003201	0150	1
BLACKWELL HERBERT H	COL	0-0008151	1047	1
BLACKWELL JAMES M	COL	0-0070647	0765	1
BLACKWELL JOHN R	LTC	0-0053789	0763	1
BLACKWELL LOTUS R	LTC	0-0080375	0965	1
BLADES JACK	COL	0-0033082	0560	1
BLAIN ARTHUR C	COL	0-0010644	0447	2
BLAIR ARNOLD D	LTC	0-0051477	0457	1
BLAIR EDGAR A	COL	0-0056803	0258	1
BLAIR GEORGE	COL	0-0002954	0642	1
BLAIR JOHN D	COL	0-0041736	0761	2
BLAIR JOHN H III	LTC	0-0044388	0864	1
BLAIR MELVIN R	LTC	0-0033150	1154	1
BLAIR RICHARD A	COL	0-0042858	0167	2
BLAIR ROBERT K	COL	0-0051526	1262	2
BLAIR RUSSELL	MAJ	0-0017220	0150	1
BLAIR VICTOR P	MAJ	0-0037926	1062	1
BLAIR WILLIAM P	COL	0-0012111	1146	1
BLAIR 3RD JOHN S	COL	0-0029340	1159	1
BLAKE ALLEN J	COL	0-0029229	0263	1
BLAKE CHARLES J JR	COL	0-0021122	0762	2
BLAKE DONALD G	COL	0-0031875	0565	2
BLAKE ELLIS O	COL	0-0043023	0467	1
BLAKE HOMER C	COL	0-0042959	0165	1
BLAKE HU A	COL	0-0058708	0966	1
BLAKE MARY S	LTC	L-0000078	0465	1
BLAKE STEWART P	LTC	0-0038221	0764	1
BLAKE WILLIAM R	LTC	0-0036162	0666	1
BLAKELOCK DAVID H	B G	0-0004853	0650	1
BLAKELY CARL F	COL	0-0032870	0765	1
BLAKELY CHARLES S	B G	0-0001909	0838	2
BLAKELY LARRY A	COL	0-0026426	0968	1
BLAKELY WILLIAM R	COL	0-0015398	1153	1
BLAKENEY CRESWELL G	COL	0-0014764	0854	1
BLAKENEY JAMES P	COL	0-0010000	1046	2
BLAKISTONE JOHN F	LTC	0-0042586	0863	1
BLANCETT ROLLIE N	COL	0-0021416	0264	1
BLANCHARD CHARLES C	B G	0-0011200	0854	2

NAME	GRADE	SVC NO	DATE RET MO YR	RET CODE
BLANCHARD ROBERT M	B G	0-0019282	0863	1
BLANCHARD WENDELL	COL	0-0015528	0754	1
BLANCHARD WESTON L	COL	0-0029925	0763	1
BLANCHETT LEO M JR	LTC	0-0025585	0366	1
BLANCHFIELD F A	COL	N-0000001	0947	1
BLANDFORD JAMES T JR	LTC	0-0026598	0866	1
BLANDFORD WILLIAM D	B G	0-0018990	0863	1
BLANEY GEORGE	COL	0-0006337	1046	1
BLANEY KERMIT B	COL	0-0035591	1266	1
BLANK LESLIE M	1LT	0-0014405	0120	2
BLANKENSHIP FRANCIS	COL	0-0042330	0109	1
BLANKENSHIP GEORGE H	MAJ	0-0004509	1021	2
BLANKENSHIP JACOB A	COL	0-0005975	0642	1
BLANTON EARNEST W	CW4	W-0902805	0260	1
BLANTON FRANKLIN S	LTC	0-0038634	0156	1
BLANTON WILLIAM L	COL	0-0007046	0552	2
BLASER EUGENE V	COL	0-0042364	0760	1
BLASINGAME FLOYD	COL	0-0051175	0160	1
BLASINGAME RUBY J	MAJ	N-0001064	1262	1
BLATT MARGARET E	LTC	N-0000583	0862	1
BLATT RAYMOND C	LTC	0-0006397	0939	1
BLATT RAYMOND C	LTC	0-0026186	0664	1
BLAUVELT CHARLES W	LTC	0-0020861	0353	2
BLAUVELT XAVIER F	COL	0-0003021	0-41	1
BLAZETIC GLADYS M	MAJ	N-0002064	0262	1
BLECH JEANETTE	LTC	N-0000501	1153	1
BLEDSOE CARL E	COL	0-0031592	0767	2
BLEDSOE WILLIAM P	B G	0-0008184	0646	2
BLEIMAN JUNIUS J	LTC	0-0050581	0768	1
BLENCOE GUY M	COL	0-0030245	0863	1
BLIGHT EDWARD M	COL	0-0040191	1067	2
BLISS ARTHUR	COL	0-0016134	0250	1
BLISS CHARLES J	LTC	0-0055423	0366	1
BLISS HAROLD B	COL	0-0006494	0248	2
BLITCH CLIFFORD G	COL	0-0019302	0255	1
BLIZZARD JOHN C JR	COL	0-0007581	0149	1
BLODGETT WILLIAM S	COL	0-0031438	0164	1
BLOM ARTHUR R	COL	0-0079744	0966	1
BLOMFELT OLLE G R	CW4	W-0902034	0955	1
BLOOD KENNETH T	M G	0-0003219	0248	1
BLOOD WILLIAM C	LTC	0-0078721	1066	1
BLOOMQUIST GEORGE F	COL	0-0006140	0246	2
BLOSS ARNOLD M	LTC	0-0045424	0262	1
BLOSS JACOB H	COL	0-0041416	0556	1
BLOSSMAN INEZ H	MAJ	N-0001273	0761	1
BLOUNT CHARLES E	LTC	0-0045217	1163	1
BLOUNT ROY E	B G	0-0005176	1047	2
BLOW RALPH C	CW2	W-0907453	0959	1
BLUE DANIEL L	LTC	0-0031997	0861	1
BLUE FRANK L JR	LTC	0-0017496	0955	1
BLUEMEL CLIFFORD	B G	0-0002642	1047	2
BLUM CLYDE H	CW2	W-0902381	0954	1
BLUM MILTON R	COL	0-0031695	0160	2
BLUM VERNON N	MAJ	0-0039728	0651	1
BLUME ROBERT F	LTC	0-0037024	0968	2
BLUMENFELD CHARLES H	COL	0-0029763	0962	1
BLUMENSAADT PAUL E	LTC	0-0032727	0856	1
BLUMENTHAL RALPH H	LTC	0-0029318	0662	1
BLUST RAYMOND L	LTC	0-0030671	0256	2
BLYTHE VERNON E	COL	0-0040133	0468	1
BLYTHE WILLIAM J	COL	0-0051308	0562	1
BOARDMAN CHARLES H	LTC	0-0087685	1066	1
BOARDMAN THOMAS G	LTC	0-0038665	0458	1
BOATNER HAYDON L	M G	0-0015641	1060	1
BOATNER MARK M JR	COL	0-0012050	1047	1
BOATSMAN ALFORD C	COL	0-0029588	0861	2
BOBO CARL E JR	LTC	0-0033164	1061	1
BOCHNOWSKI JOSEPH S	COL	0-0051498	0564	1
BOCK FRANK L	LTC	0-0017265	0150	2
BOCKOVEN FREDERIC T	LTC	0-0037354	0766	1
BOCKSEL ARNOLD A	CW2	W-0901770	0549	2
BODE DONALD O	COL	0-0029651	0562	1
BODE JOHN T	CPT	0-0095794	0666	2
BODEAU EDWARD	COL	0-0019008	0258	1
BODINE DONALD R	COL	0-0020238	0866	1

NAME	GRADE	SVC NO	DATE RET MO YR	RET CODE
BODINE ROY L	COL	0-0009709	1047	1
BODINE ROY L JR	COL	0-0073489	0461	2
BODIS JEANNETTE	MAJ	N-0002432	1165	1
BODNER VIC F	LTC	0-0051551	1062	1
BODNER WILLIAM C	COL	0-0051393	0463	1
BODSON GOLDIE L	MAJ	N-0001688	1267	1
BOECKMAN FRANKLIN P	COL	0-0031247	0868	1
BOEHME WERNER	CW4	W-0902242	0854	2
BOEKER RICHARD D	COL	0-0034670	0760	1
BOETTCHER ARTHUR	COL	0-0003027	1143	1
BOGAN LUCIAN D	COL	0-0005105	0247	2
BOGART THEODORE F	M G	0-0018245	0465	1
BOGER MARTHA M	MAJ	M-0010062	1265	1
BOGGAN EDGAR A	LTC	0-0059924	1265	1
BOGGS ADELBERT D	COL	0-0034569	0368	1
BOGINSKI FRANK J	CW4	W-0906626	1066	1
BOGLE JAMES G	COL	0-0052642	0267	1
BOGNER CHARLES	COL	0-0033892	0665	1
BOGNER HOWARD F	COL	0-0051370	0163	1
BOGUE JOY R	COL	0-0023990	0558	1
BOGUE WILLIAM R	LTC	0-0030470	0663	1
BOHANNON FREDERICK	COL	0-0027057	0968	1
BOHERTY PHILIP A	LTC	0-0083595	0866	1
BOHLENDER JOHN F	M G	0-0017814	1161	1
BOHN GORDON A	COL	0-0031075	0965	2
BOHN JOHN J	B G	0-0004582	0245	2
BOHNER JOHN F	CW4	W-0902389	0555	1
BOIVEAU LEON C	COL	0-0011239	0748	1
BOLAN HARRY W	COL	0-0008101	1050	1
BOLBAT WALTER J	LTC	0-0060735	0568	1
BOLDING A P JR	MAJ	0-0046764	0653	2
BOLDUC LUCIEN E	COL	0-0016137	0755	1
BOLES CATHERINE	MAJ	N-0000365	0261	1
BOLEYN JOHN C	LTC	0-0027492	0664	1
BOLEYN PAUL A	COL	0-0020903	0563	1
BOLIBAUGH ORAL B	COL	0-0004179	0450	1
BOLICK JAMES C	LTC	0-0036920	0266	1
BOLING JEAN H	COL	0-0031817-	1262	1
BOLKE FRANCIS G	LTC	0-0080591	0766	1
BOLL ARTHUR C	LTC	0-0016142	0346	2
BOLLAND GERHARD L	LTC	0-0019565	0551	2
BOLLENBECK JOSEPH W	CPT	0-0006627	0335	1
BOLLERO ANGELO D	COL	0-0039853	1063	1
BOLT JAMES L	COL	0-0011673	0753	1
BOLTE CHARLES L	GEN	0-0006908	0455	1
BOLTEN RICHARD S	MAJ	0-0021735	0743	2
BOLTON FRANK G	COL	0-0023976	1167	2
BOLTWOOD ELIZABETH	MAJ	L-0000026	1155	1
BOLTZ DELTON N	CW3	W-0906628	0456	2
BOMAR ERNEST C	COL	0-0006733	0352	2
BON DURANT JOSEPH R	COL	0-0033579	1068	2
BOND AUBREY H	COL	0-0008876	0348	2
BOND JOHN B	COL	0-0026077	0568	1
BOND JOHN R F	LTC	0-0035986	0964	1
BOND MARGARET M	MAJ	N-0001780	0968	1
BOND ROBERT M	LTC	0-0069596	0968	1
BOND THOMAS G	LTC	0-0004887	1138	1
BOND VIRGIL W	LTC	0-0042878	1058	1
BONDSHU LOWELL T	COL	0-0051670	0864	1
BONDY EDWARD W	COL	0-0005085	0247	1
BONE GEORGE A	COL	0-0081890	0868	1
BONE HOWARD C	LTC	0-0035792	0161	1
BONETTE SAMUEL J	LTC	0-0084544	1068	1
BONHAM DWIGHT D	LTC	0-0033949	0262	1
BONHAM ROSCOE	COL	0-0010767	0750	1
BONIFAY LEWIS A	COL	0-0029040	0159	1
BONNELL JOHN L JR	LTC	0-0040088	0863	1
BONNELYCKE CARL	CW4	W-0904401	1054	1
BONNER MARTHA M	LTC	L-0000097	0766	1
BONNEY FRANK E	COL	0-0003641	0644	1
BONNIWELL ALFRED E	COL	0-0042931	0267	1
BONSTEEL FRANCIS T	COL	0-0005480	0650	1
BONTA JAMES C	LTC	0-0034731	0967	1
BOOHER ELIZABETH	MAJ	N-0000264	0762	1
BOOKER PHILLIP W	COL	0-0002208	0144	1

NAME	GRADE	SVC NO	DATE RET MO YR	RET CODE
BOOKOUT HAL H	COL	0-0068179	1167	1
BOOMER EUGENE F	LTC	0-0035846	0863	1
BOON STEPHEN JR	COL	0-0006782	0646	2
BOON WALTER W	COL	0-0007642	1052	2
BOONE ABBOTT	COL	0-0002259	0-43	1
BOONE HOWARD A	COL	0-0010179	0346	2
BOONE JOSEPH W	COL	0-0015341	1150	2
BOONE MILTON O	B G	0-0008127	0548	1
BOOS FRANCIS H	COL	0-0017291	0257	1
BOOTH BENJAMIN N	COL	0-0003204	0436	2
BOOTH DONALD P	LTG	0-0016395	0262	1
BOOTH GEORGE W	CPT	0-0014265	0720	2
BOOTH JAMES R	LTC	0-0065052	0868	1
BOOTH JAMES W	COL	0-0026382	0866	1
BOOTH LANCE E	COL	0-0031755	0168	1
BOOTH MERRITT B	COL	0-0012378	0646	2
BOOTH RIVES O	LTC	0-0019967	0544	2
BOOTH ROBERT H	M G	0-0018093	0365	1
BOOTH ROBERT M	COL	0-0019964	0965	1
BORDEN JACK	LTC	0-0023306	0661	1
BORG HELGA C C	LTC	N-0000519	0248	1
BORGFELDT RICHARD N	LTC	0-0042019	1058	1
BORIN GORDON B	LTC	0-0042621	0863	1
BORK LESTER S	B G	0-0017685	0762	1
BORLEIS JOHN H A	COL	0-0018652	0859	1
BORNS CHARLES R	LTC	0-0034245	0264	1
BOROM THOMAS L	LTC	0-0050918	0454	1
BORUP PAUL C	COL	0-0018649	0657	1
BORUSKI ERNEST F	COL	0-0008292	1149	1
BOSBYSHELL JOHN H	COL	0-0030596	0163	1
BOSCO SALVATORE	CW4	RW-0906631	1161	2
BOSGIETER ERNEST W	COL	0-0041596	0559	1
BOSS PHILIPPE P	COL	0-0039960	0565	1
BOSWELL JACK	LTC	0-0025080	0763	1
BOSWELL JAMES O	B G	0-0019188	1061	1
BOSWORTH LEROY K	CW4	W-0902814	0461	1
BOTHWELL F C JR	COL	0-0020235	1046	2
BOTHWELL LYMAN D	COL	0-0051046	0859	1
BOTTOMLY R V JR	COL	0-0034071	0167	1
BOTTS JOSEPH H	COL	0-0031514	0567	1
BOTTS LUTHER B	LTC	0-0036752	0864	1
BOUCHER FRANCIS H	COL	0-0006578	0750	1
BOUCHER JEFF W	COL	0-0024173	0964	1
BOUDREAU NAPOLEON	COL	0-0005934	0548	1
BOUDREAUX RAYMOND F	COL	0-0023344	0760	1
BOUFFIER HELEN H	LTC	L-0000032	0359	1
BOURBON ROLLO P	COL	0-0008909	1047	1
BOURDEAU STEPHEN F	CW4	W-0906632	0664	1
BOURGEOIS EMILINE A	MAJ	N-0002390	0162	1
BOURQUARDEZ CHARLES	MAJ	0-0060337	1063	1
BOUTELL HORTENSE M	LTC	L-0000094	0566	1
BOUTELLE MAURICE H	LTC	0-0062126	0167	1
BOUTON ARTHUR G	LTC	0-0031306	0862	1
BOUTON IRMA V	LTC	L-0000195	0767	1
BOWDEN MARION P	LTC	0-0033104	0948	2
BOWDEN RICHARD W	COL	0-0042640	0965	1
BOWDISH JEANNE R	MAJ	R-0010121	0866	1
BOWEN ARTHUR F	LTC	0-0007778	0144	2
BOWEN CLAUDE L JR	COL	0-0019244	0863	1
BOWEN FRANCIS C	COL	0-0039682	0760	1
BOWEN FRANK S JR	M G	0-0016434	1162	1
BOWEN GENEVA N	LTC	N-0001966	1263	1
BOWEN JAMES E JR	COL	0-0015302	0452	2
BOWEN JOHN W	CPT	0-0014558	0-19	2
BOWEN JOHN W	LTC	0-0018904	1068	2
BOWEN MILLARD G JR	COL	0-0030536	1065	1
BOWEN RALPH H	COL	0-0025069	0868	1
BOWEN ROBERT B	CPT	0-0028147	0557	2
BOWEN THOMAS J	COL	0-0033333	0868	1
BOWEN WILLIAM C JR	LTC	0-0061201	0766	1
BOWEN WILLIAM S	COL	0-0001648	0642	1
BOWER HARVEY	COL	0-0019912	0965	1
BOWER JAMES C	LTC	0-0018934	0651	1
BOWER JAMES R	LTC	0-0042768	0564	1
BOWER LAURENCE R	COL	0-0016019	0952	2

NAME	GRADE	SVC NO	DATE RET MO YR	RET CODE
BOWER RALPH F	COL	0-0006610	1045	2
BOWER ROLAND E JR	COL	0-0014721	0862	1
BOWERS ALVIN T	COL	0-0016107	0755	1
BOWERS BERNA T	COL	0-0016300	0454	1
BOWERS GERALD V	1LT	0-0037602	0550	2
BOWERS MERVIN C	COL	0-0042319	0264	1
BOWERS WARNER F	COL	0-0029197	0361	1
BOWERS WILLIAM H	COL	0-0029264	0661	1
BOWERS WILLIAM S	COL	0-0038473	1262	2
BOWLBY LAWRENCE	COL	0-0045718	0766	1
BOWLER LOUIS J	COL	0-0006335	0346	2
BOWLES OTIS R	CW4	W-0902357	0958	1
BOWLING PAULINE J	LTC	N-0000578	1164	1
BOWMAN ALFRED C	COL	0-0056777	0360	1
BOWMAN CLIFFORD A	COL	0-0030728	0664	1
BOWMAN DAVID W	LTC	0-0037711	0359	1
BOWMAN FRANK C	M G	0-0012090	0656	1
BOWMAN HAROLD M JR	COL	0-0043501	0968	1
BOWMAN HOMER H	COL	0-0031700	0965	1
BOWMAN JAMES C	LTC	0-0085487	0866	2
BOWMAN JAMES F	LTC	0-0088580	0167	2
BOWMAN JAMES W	COL	0-0034813	1265	1
BOWMAN JOHN E	COL	0-0033211	0263	1
BOWMAN ORLEY D	COL	0-0010974	0146	2
BOWMAN PRESTON	CW4	W-0904400	0955	1
BOWSKY MERLE C	COL	0-0029386	0260	1
BOWYER OSCAR F	COL	0-0019934	0762	1
BOYCE JOHN C	LTC	0-0042402	0762	1
BOYCE ROBERT A JR	COL	0-0017329	0858	1
BOYCE WILLIAM M	COL	0-0079753	1165	1
BOYD ALLAN S JR	COL	0-0003278	0342	2
BOYD CHARLES W	CW3	W-0902817	0661	1
BOYD DONN T	LTC	0-0062131	0563	1
BOYD GEORGE W JR	CW3	W-0907108	0666	1
BOYD HARRY R	COL	0-0018102	0760	1
BOYD JOSEPH L	COL	0-0008783	0347	2
BOYD LAWRENCE L	COL	0-0030180	1263	1
BOYD LEONARD F	B G	0-0004811	1151	1
BOYD LOGAN W	COL	0-0010387	1052	1
BOYD MARZELLE F	COL	0-0039721	0964	1
BOYD RICHARD K	COL	0-0018548	0761	1
BOYD ROBERT P JR	COL	0-0040068	0966	1
BOYD WILLIAM F	LTC	0-0080598	1265	1
BOYD WILLIAM H	LTC	0-0037205	0468	1
BOYE FREDERIC W	B G	0-0003895	0950	1
BOYEA GERALD F	LTC	0-0037258	1268	1
BOYER EMILE J	CPT	0-0007275	0933	2
BOYER GEORGE S	LTC	0-0022297	0546	2
BOYER JOSEPH C	COL	0-0029461	0960	1
BOYER RAY Y	LTC	0-0080599	0862	1
BOYER RICHARD J	LTC	0-0037202	0966	1
BOYER SAMUEL F JR	LTC	0-0078731	1267	1
BOYKIN JAMES H	COL	0-0045838	0268	1
BOYKIN JESS G	COL	0-0008401	0245	2
BOYKIN RICHARD P	COL	0-0009247	0642	1
BOYLAN PAUL C	COL	0-0008370	0944	2
BOYLAN RUFUS	COL	0-0008045	1145	2
BOYLAN VINCENT L	COL	0-0022162	1065	1
BOYLE CONRAD L	COL	0-0015951	0954	2
BOYLE FRANK F	MAJ	0-0025326	0446	2
BOYLE GEORGE L	COL	0-0014862	1150	1
BOYLE GUY F	CW4	W-0902820	1159	1
BOYLE JOSEPH E	LTC	0-0040188	0865	1
BOYLE MARVIN	COL	0-0004539	1049	1
BOYLE ROBERT W	CW4	RW-0905714	0166	1
BOYLE RUSSELL T	COL	0-0028900	0457	1
BOYLE THADDEUS A	LTC	0-0035791	1163	1
BOYLE WILLIAM A	COL	0-0006423	0747	1
BOYLE WILLIAM J	COL	0-0021953	0867	1
BOYLES FRANCIS R	COL	0-0029803	1262	1
BOYLES SAMUEL J	COL	0-0032168	0466	1
BOYT JOHN E	COL	0-0021304	0868	1
BOZE WILBURN H	LTC	0-0065320	1067	1
BRAASCH LORAINE J	MAJ	N-0001955	0659	1
BRABSON FAY W	COL	0-0001600	0642	2

NAME	GRADE	SVC NO	DATE RET MO YR	RET CODE
BRABSON WILLIAM H JR	LTC	0-0026069	1262	1
BRACHER ALLEN N	COL	0-0019706	0955	1
BRACKEBUSCH CARL	LTC	0-0059561	0766	1
BRACKETT MORRIS E	COL	0-0025162	0862	2
BRADEN JESSIE M	LTC	N-0000062	0947	1
BRADFORD AUBREY E	COL	0-0017817	0861	1
BRADFORD DAVID F	COL	0-0016271	0637	2
BRADFORD KARL S	B G	0-0003081	1046	2
BRADFORD ROBERT W	LTC	0-0062171	0668	1
BRADISH ROBERT F	COL	0-0016955	1047	1
BRADLEY ALFORD V	LTC	0-0025259	0261	2
BRADLEY BEN W	LTC	0-0049713	1162	1
BRADLEY EARL M	LTC	0-0058219	0765	1
BRADLEY FRANCIS X	COL	0-0022740	0859	1
BRADLEY GLENN M	LTC	0-0051768	0564	1
BRADLEY JOHN A	COL	0-0035836	0763	1
BRADLEY JOHN M JR	COL	0-0042318	0758	1
BRADLEY ROBERT W	LTC	0-0080602	0767	1
BRADLEY RUBY G	COL	N-0000087	0463	1
BRADLEY RUTH W	MAJ	M-0010021	0963	1
BRADLEY WILLIAM J	B G	0-0015967	0854	2
BRADSHAW AARON JR	M G	0-0005290	0153	2
BRADSHAW JOHN F	COL	0-0054846	1168	1
BRADSHER MARIE F	MAJ	N-0000164	1059	2
BRADY BROOKNER W	COL	0-0016519	0656	2
BRADY EILEEN W	COL	N-0000091	1263	1
BRADY JOHN W	COL	0-0018627	0258	1
BRADY LAWRENCE W	COL	0-0030703	0666	1
BRADY PHILIP B	LTC	0-0028192	0868	1
BRADY ROBERT W	LTC	0-0080601	0966	1
BRADY WILLIAM I	COL	0-0012689	0151	1
BRAGALONE ALFRED A	LTC	0-0036080	0863	1
BRAGAN OTTO P	COL	0-0015754	0653	2
BRAGDON KERLIN J	COL	0-0042766	0766	1
BRAGG CLARENCE H	COL	0-0009316	0753	1
BRAID ROBERT B	COL	0-0032950	0766	2
BRALY WILLIAM C	COL	0-0007972	0147	2
BRAMBLE PHILIP H	COL	0-0033341	0767	1
BRAME WAYNE W	COL	0-0039765	0462	1
BRAMLETT HUBERT B	COL	0-0010689	0753	1
BRANCH GOODMAN S	COL	0-0051014	0259	1
BRANCH JAMES O	COL	0-0042279	0761	1
BRAND CLARENCE E	COL	0-0008432	0449	1
BRANDEWIE ROBERT A	LTC	0-0060373	0267	1
BRANDHORST HENRY W	COL	0-0011619	0548	2
BRANDIGER FREIDA A V	CPT	N-0000537	0348	1
BRANDNER CARL S	COL	0-0029442	0760	1
BRANDON THURMAN M	MAJ	0-0024754	0562	1
BRANDSTADT WAYNE G	COL	0-0018318	0853	1
BRANDT BERNICE D	MAJ	N-0002124	0360	1
BRANDT JEROME N	LTC	0-0031245	1159	1
BRANDT MARGARET M	MAJ	N-0000543	1057	1
BRANDYBERRY MARCELLA	MAJ	N-0000618	0263	1
BRANHAM CHARLES N	COL	0-0014920	0150	2
BRANIGIN JAMES E	COL	0-0053419	1265	1
BRANN HERBERT P	LTC	0-0030686	0464	1
BRANNON ERNEST M	M G	0-0012292	1054	1
BRANSON CHARLES E	MAJ	0-0030805	1057	1
BRANSON DON P	CPT	0-0007739	0934	2
BRANSON EARL V	MAJ	0-0386222	0168	1
BRANT ESTHER E	MAJ	N-0002288	0865	1
BRANT PHILIP D	COL	0-0020804	0865	1
BRANTLEY JOSEPH W	LTC	0-0030440	0563	1
BRANTON HAROLD M	LTC	0-0037345	1066	1
BRASCHER THOMAS J	COL	0-0039749	0760	1
BRASEL DONALD E	CW3	W-0902823	0961	1
BRASHEAR MARION G	CW2	W-0901554	0849	1
BRASSEL ALFRED L	LTC	0-0023420	0661	1
BRASTED FRED	COL	0-0041854	0361	1
BRATCHER BUCK	COL	0-0043409	0168	1
BRATTON DANIEL	COL	0-0006370	0248	1
BRAUD EDITH A	MAJ	N-0000724	0565	1
BRAUDE MEYER A	COL	0-0018802	0862	1
BRAUN EUGENE J	LTC	0-0037790	0966	1
BRAUN PAUL	WO1	W-0901112	0425	1

NAME	GRADE	SVC NO	DATE RET MO YR	RET CODE
BRAUN WALTER P	LTC	0-0069365	0968	1
BRAUN WALTER R	LTC	0-0060509	0564	1
BRAUNECKER MARY P	MAJ	N-0002066	0459	1
BRAUNING EDNA R	CPT	N-0000818	0459	1
BRAV ERNEST A	COL	0-0056395	0564	1
BRAVEMAN MILTON	LTC	0-0065501	0767	1
BRAYSHAW HORACE A	COL	0-0029307	0762	1
BRAZEAL LULY P	MAJ	N-0000842	0864	2
BRAZEALE EVERETT L	CW4	W-0902824	0164	1
BRAZIER KELLY L	COL	0-0039674	0555	1
BREAKEFIELD DURWARD	B G	0-0019791	1265	1
BREAKS ROBERT W	COL	0-0020273	0866	1
BREAZEALE MARY	MAJ	R-0010117	1160	1
BRECKENRIDGE JAMES O	COL	0-0039897	0464	1
BRECKINRIDGE WILLIAM	M G	0-0017210	0662	1
BRECKINS WALTER W	LTC	0-1324978	1262	1
BREDEN JOHN P	COL	0-0017135	0758	1
BREED CHARLES R	LTC	0-0065302	0968	1
BREEDLOVE MOZELLE R	MAJ	N-0002513	1267	1
BREEN EDITH K	MAJ	N-0000376	0860	1
BREEN FRANCES F	MAJ	N-0002443	0767	1
BREEN JOHN J	COL	0-0012165	0349	1
BREEN PATRICK J	COL	0-0062129	0568	1
BREITENBACH FRANK P	LTC	0-0026365	0368	1
BREITENBERG EUGENE H	CPT	0-0062819	1264	1
BREITUNG ELIZABETH	LTC	N-0001902	1064	1
BREMER ERNEST K	COL	0-0076835	0164	1
BREMKAMP LOUIS F	COL	0-0079755	0667	1
BRENEMAN RUTH F	MAJ	N-0001328	0763	1
BRENN CHARLES E	COL	0-0006263	1147	2
BRENNAN BEATRICE R	MAJ	L-0000009	1153	1
BRENNAN JAMES T	COL	0-0031183	0766	1
BRENNAN JOHN J	COL	0-0031150	0962	1
BRENNAN MARK F	COL	0-0021279	0767	1
BRENNAN PATRICK J	MAJ	0-0043756	0359	1
BRENNEMAN GARLAND E	LTC	0-0042576	0663	1
BRENNEMAN IVAN L	COL	0-0039627	0959	1
BRENNEMAN LOYD W	COL	0-0024676	0262	1
BRENNER CARL F	LTC	0-0051964	0463	1
BRENNER MATILDA R	1LT	R-0000115	1146	1
BRESLIN JOHN F	COL	0-0057525	0566	1
BRESNAHAN THOMAS F	M G	0-0007378	0348	1
BRESSLER DEAN M	LTC	0-0026909	0665	1
BRETON MARGARITA	LTC	N-0002060	1067	1
BRETT JAMES J	2LT	0-0018115	0834	2
BRETTELL JAMES A JR	LTC	0-0063600	0967	1
BREWER CARLOS	M G	0-0003539	1050	1
BREWER DWIGHT C	LTC	0-0079756	0761	1
BREWER JAMES N	COL	0-0042220	0863	1
BREWER JOHN E	LTC	0-0052741	0162	1
BREWER KENNETH A	COL	0-0018634	0861	1
BREWER MYRON L	LTC	0-0032495	1065	1
BREWER ROBERT M	COL	0-0022975	0866	1
BREWERTON HENRY R	LTC	0-0023311	0246	2
BREWSTER MARGARET E	LTC	L-0000048	1265	1
BREWSTER NATHAN	WO1	W-0901570	0242	2
BREY WILLIAM G	COL	0-0006499	0848	1
BRIAN AUDRAIN B	CPT	0-0059332	1057	2
BRIAN ADRIAN R	COL	0-0007332	0750	1
BRICE MAURICE R	LTC	0-0032557	0361	2
BRICKER L MONROE	COL	0-0007245	0649	1
BRICKMAN GEORGE A	1LT	0-0017216	0834	2
BRIDGE CARL J	CPT	0-0013949	0859	2
BRIDGER KILIE F	LTC	N-0000084	1060	1
BRIDGERS GEORGE A	COL	0-0024395	0560	2
BRIDGES BURLIN C	COL	0-0009488	0645	2
BRIDGES WILLIAM C	COL	0-0016527	0756	1
BRIDGMAN J ALLINGTO	LTC	0-0081965	1062	1
BRIDGMAN RICHARD H	COL	0-0016335	0133	2
BRIDWELL ARTHUR W	MAJ	0-0066739	0467	2
BRIEN JAMES N JR	LTC	0-0057538	0256	2
BRIER WILLIAM W	COL	0-0011062	0250	1
BRIGDEN DOUGLAS A	LTC	0-0088591	0868	1
BRIGGS DAN P	COL	0-0023169	0568	1
BRIGGS EDWIN J	COL	0-0043363	0363	1
BRIGGS GORDON W	LTC	0-0062940	0766	1
BRIGGS JOHN L	LTC	0-0058840	0866	1
BRIGGS RACHEL V	MAJ	N-0002120	0558	1
BRIGGS RICHARD F	LTC	0-0036032	1162	1
BRIGGS RUTH M	LTC	L-0000339	1264	1
BRIGGS WILLIAM A	LTC	0-0042315	0162	1
BRIGGS WINIFRED M	MAJ	N-0000992	0164	1
BRIGHTMAN JOHN Y	LTC	0-0031366	0463	2
BRILL ALBERT	MAJ	0-0010864	0337	1
BRILL HEBER C	LTC	0-0026162	0265	1
BRIMMER HOWARD W	COL	0-0012221	0753	2
BRINCKERHOFF C G JR	COL	0-0041686	0560	1
BRINDLE HARRY C	COL	0-0051380	0263	1
BRINDLEY JOHN R	COL	0-0019087	1058	1
BRINEGAR MAURINE O	LTC	L-0000531	1068	1
BRINGHAM ROBERT A	CPT	0-0014398	1019	2
BRINK JOHNNIE C	COL	0-0034658	0164	1
BRINKLEY JOSEPH S JR	COL	0-0031444	1163	1
BRINSON NOAH M	COL	0-0015663	1147	2
BRINSON ROBERT H	CPT	0-0024352	1044	2
BRINSON WILLIAM J	LTC	0-0084851	1268	1
BRISACH RAYMOND C	COL	0-0018202	0559	1
BRISACK FLOYD P	COL	0-0014740	0947	1
BRISCOE WILLIAM T	LTC	0-0054688	1165	1
BRISTER JANE G	LTC	L-0000289	0765	1
BRISTOR JOHN D	COL	0-0019710	0859	1
BRITELL CLAUDE E	COL	0-0029183	0760	1
BRITT ALBERT S JR	COL	0-0042237	0962	1
BRITT HENRY C	COL	0-0018891	0962	2
BRITT JAMES A	MAJ	0-0084592	0264	1
BRITT ROBERT C	LTC	0-0054425	0664	1
BRITT ROY E JR	CW4	W-0902826	0961	1
BRITTAIN COURTLAND	COL	0-0042341	0163	1
BRITTAIN HOMER E	CW4	W-0902827	0965	1
BRITTEN ROLAND L	LTC	0-0080609	1163	1
BRITTINGHAM A D JR	LTC	0-0039577	0356	1
BRITTINGHAM JAMES F	B G	0-0005746	0654	2
BRITTON FRANK H	M G	0-0018703	0867	1
BRITTON FRANK K	COL	0-0030532	0960	1
BRITTON GEORGE T	COL	0-0062778	0867	2
BRITTON MATTIE C	MAJ	N-0000845	0454	2
BRIZIUS CHARLES A SR	LTC	0-0059841	0667	1
BROADHURST HUGH H	COL	0-0002066	0740	1
BROADHURST ROBERT C	1LT	0-0016418	0734	2
BROBERG RICHARD A	COL	0-0021272	0766	1
BROBERG WALDEMAR S	COL	0-0012330	0454	1
BROCK JOHN A	LTC	0-0042914	1165	1
BROCK KIRK P	COL	0-0041650	0260	1
BROCK LEON A	COL	0-0041508	0858	1
BROCK MILTON E	CW3	W-0906639	1059	1
BROCKETT CHARLES K	LTC	0-0060199	0866	1
BROCKETT RAYMOND C	CW4	W-0907135	0966	2
BROCKHAUSEN FRED C	CW2	W-0901779	0646	2
BROCKMAN ERNEST F	LTC	0-0022147	0867	1
BROCKMAN SIDNEY C	COL	0-0031212	0964	1
BROCKWAY EDGAR K	CPT	0-0007814	0334	2
BRODERICK MERL L	COL	0-0008449	0753	2
BROEDLOW RUDOLPH W	COL	0-0011161	0849	1
BROGAN WILLIAM T	COL	0-0030194	0664	1
BROIDA DONALD	MAJ	0-0060641	0265	2
BROMLEY CHARLES V JR	M G	0-0015239	0356	1
BRONDSTATTER WALLACE	LTC	0-0085300	0764	1
BRONN CARL H	COL	0-0031748	0166	1
BROOK HOWARD F SR	LTC	0-0042907	1164	1
BROOKE JAMES F JR	COL	0-0017600	0250	2
BROOKENS TREVA B	MAJ	N-0002130	0360	1
BROOKES WYTHE P	LTC	0-0045447	0266	1
BROOKHART HAROLD C	COL	0-0019562	0864	1
BROOKRESON WADE Y	LTC	0-0035568	0765	1
BROOKS ALBERT O	LTC	0-0026516	0865	1
BROOKS CECIL	MAJ	0-0018313	0934	2
BROOKS DWIGHT M	LTC	0-0050004	0765	1
BROOKS EDWARD H	LTG	0-0006657	0453	1
BROOKS EDWIN F	LTC	0-0071452	0869	1
BROOKS ENGLE R JR	LTC	0-0034764	0168	1
BROOKS HAROLD F	COL	0-0018152	0760	1
BROOKS IRVING W	COL	0-0039783	0962	1
BROOKS JAMES W	LTC	0-0029736	0860	2
BROOKS JOHN A	COL	0-0003679	0946	1
BROOKS JOHN M	COL	0-0053449	0866	1
BROOKS ROLAND ST	LTC	0-0060336	0167	1
BROOKS ROY L	COL	0-0031238	0868	1
BROOKS WILLIAM A	MAJ	0-0069601	1166	1
BROOKS WILLIAM P JR	COL	0-0031654	0463	1
BROOM THAD A	B G	0-0018246	0660	1
BROPHY FRANCIS J	COL	0-0039723	0761	1
BROSSARD LOUIS F	LTC	0-0028965	1156	2
BROTHERTON RICHARD W	LTC	0-0057658	1263	1
BROTT WILLIAM F	LTC	0-0042966	0265	1
BROUN FLORENCE T	MAJ	N-0000695	0565	1
BROUN PAUL E	LTC	0-0025286	0746	2
BROWDER JEWEL F	LTC	0-0045583	0264	1
BROWER GEORGE W	COL	0-0009433	0646	2
BROWER WESLEY H	MAJ	0-0058320	0965	1
BROWN ALBERT F	M G	0-0003409	0649	1
BROWN ALLAN G	1LT	0-0059326	0353	2
BROWN ARTHUR F	COL	0-0008797	1044	1
BROWN AUBREY F JR	COL	0-0049959	0966	1
BROWN BENJAMIN C	LTC	0-0028493	0966	1
BROWN BOYD L	COL	0-0033215	0466	1
BROWN BRISBANE H	COL	0-0008279	0753	2
BROWN BURTON F	B G	0-0021113	0868	1
BROWN BYRON W	LTC	0-0039340	0763	1
BROWN CAROLUS A	COL	0-0021364	0857	1
BROWN CHARLES E	B G	0-0008042	0347	2
BROWN CHARLES F	COL	0-0017552	0661	1
BROWN CHARLES F JR	M G	0-0025845	0867	2
BROWN CHARLES P JR	COL	0-0039422	0965	1
BROWN CHARLES T	LTC	0-0057375	0355	2
BROWN DALE E	LTC	0-0080284	0757	1
BROWN DAVID F	COL	0-0017540	0859	1
BROWN DAVID W	LTC	0-0023320	0656	1
BROWN [illegible]	COL	0-0021357	0868	1
BROWN DREW E	CW4	W-0902835	0161	1
BROWN EARL J	COL	0-0039031	0767	1
BROWN EARL V	COL	0-0024044	0867	1
BROWN EDWARD A JR	B G	0-0018355	0861	2
BROWN ELI E	COL	0-0008486	0146	2
BROWN ELMER G	COL	0-0039521	0157	1
BROWN ERNEST F	LTC	0-0051929	1165	1
BROWN ERNEST L	LTC	0-0033987	0753	2
BROWN EVERETT E	B G	0-0006303	1049	2
BROWN FREDERIC J	LTC	0-0015751	0865	1
BROWN GARRY H	LTC	0-0084326	0567	1
BROWN GEORGE H	LTC	0-0048840	0864	1
BROWN GEORGE W JR	LTC	0-0058942	1066	2
BROWN GERALD F	COL	0-0019806	0861	1
BROWN GREG J	COL	0-0021793	1266	1
BROWN GUY W	LTC	0-0080612	0766	1
BROWN HALDON O	MAJ	0-0062136	0263	1
BROWN HANDY V	COL	0-0010954	1049	1
BROWN HARLEY D	COL	0-0029311	0164	2
BROWN HAROLD E	COL	0-0022888	0766	1
BROWN HAROLD M	B G	0-0020832	0267	1
BROWN HAROLD W	COL	0-0030777	0764	1
BROWN HARRY E JR	COL	0-0039930	0564	1
BROWN HARVEY E JR	COL	0-0021253	0847	2
BROWN HELEN F	LTC	N-0002558	0967	1
BROWN HERBERT E	COL	0-0021437	1064	1
BROWN HUGH G	COL	0-0042539	0365	1
BROWN HUGH M JR	LTC	0-0058843	0168	1
BROWN J TRIMBLE	COL	0-0016666	0356	1
BROWN JAMES A	COL	0-0011166	0846	1
BROWN JOHN K	COL	0-0002371	0345	2
BROWN JOHN M	LTC	0-0018453	0651	1
BROWN JOHN M JR	LTC	0-0031697	1163	1
BROWN JOSEPH E	LTC	0-0085491	0868	1
BROWN JOSEPH T	COL	0-0023969	0764	1
BROWN KATHRYN J	MAJ	N-0001370	0163	1
BROWN KITCHEN V	LTC	0-0080614	0968	2
BROWN LAURENCE C	COL	0-0020876	0767	1
BROWN LAWRENCE G	COL	0-0080376	1267	1
BROWN LEE R	MAJ	0-0039459	0664	1
BROWN LEROY C	MAJ	0-0033782	1061	1
BROWN LLOYD K	CW4	W-0906641	0160	1
BROWN MARION M	COL	0-0029806	0962	2
BROWN MASKELL E	LTC	0-0035914	1055	1
BROWN MELVIN C	COL	0-0021256	0868	1
BROWN MILLS	MAJ	0-0033487	0451	2
BROWN OLIVER B	COL	0-0041418	0656	1
BROWN PAUL M	MAJ	0-0099552	1268	1
BROWN PERCIVAL S	COL	0-0019487	0660	1
BROWN PERCY O JR	LTC	0-0037255	0658	1
BROWN PERCY H JR	COL	0-0018117	0760	1
BROWN PHILIP E	M G	0-0007073	1245	2
BROWN RICHARD K	LTC	0-0032333	0767	1
BROWN RICHARD M	MAJ	0-0061086	0367	1
BROWN RICHARD O	LTC	0-0039751	1159	1
BROWN ROBERT O	COL	0-0003608	1046	1
BROWN ROBERT O JR	COL	0-0023832	0363	2
BROWN ROBERT E	COL	0-0052098	1163	1
BROWN ROBERT Q	B G	0-0018520	0761	1
BROWN ROLAND C	COL	0-0017080	0258	1
BROWN ROTHWELL H	B G	0-0016604	1056	1
BROWN SHANNON D	COL	0-0052247	0866	1
BROWN SIDNEY G JR	COL	0-0018393	0760	1
BROWN STAUNTON L	COL	0-0019356	0358	1
BROWN STEPHEN O	COL	0-0026105	0168	1
BROWN THOMAS J	CW4	W-0904087	0755	1
BROWN TRAVIS T	B G	0-0019574	0864	1
BROWN VALLIE A	1LT	M-0000475	0844	2
BROWN VIVIAN Z	COL	0-0012034	0653	2
BROWN WALTER S	CPT	0-0014117	0809	2
BROWN WILLIAM A	LTC	0-0060815	0865	1
BROWN WILLIAM D	LTC	0-0060426	0765	1
BROWN WILLIAM E	CW4	W-0904088	1059	2
BROWN WILLIAM H	COL	0-0041552	1053	1
BROWN WILLIAM J	LTC	0-0024315	0861	1
BROWN WILLIAM L	LTC	0-0006489	0-36	2
BROWN WILLIAM M	COL	0-0031583	1167	1
BROWN WILLIAM R	MAJ	0-0069603	0367	1
BROWN WYBURN D	B G	0-0012260	0651	2
BROWNE ALLAN F	COL	0-0028831	0156	1
BROWNE BEVERLY F	B G	0-0001339	0528	1
BROWNE HARRISON C	COL	0-0002759	1146	2
BROWNE HARVEY M	LTC	0-0080051	0966	2
BROWNE HARVEY S III	COL	0-0038992	0762	1
BROWNE JOHN T	LTC	0-0040092	1062	2
BROWNE LAURENCE S	COL	0-0047086	0966	1
BROWNE ROLAND A	COL	0-0016126	1047	1
BROWNELL JAMES R	COL	0-0011764	0135	2
BROWNFIELD PAGE H	COL	0-0040395	0564	1
BROWNING FREDDIE L	LTC	0-0072827	0868	1
BROWNING HAROLD W	COL	0-0019545	0961	1
BROWNING JOHN W	COL	0-0020767	0657	1
BROWNING NEWTON F	LTC	0-0046964	0661	1
BROWNING PHILIP Y	COL	0-0021142	0565	1
BROWNING SAMUEL R	M G	0-0017081	0758	1
BROWNLEE LAURANCE H	COL	0-0017583	0859	1
BROWNLOW JOHN F JR	COL	0-0021111	0868	1
BROWNSON HAROLD N	COL	0-0043108	0862	1
BROWNYARD FRED K	LTC	0-0035279	0368	1
BROYLES HARMON E	COL	0-0029038	1156	1
BROYLES NED B	COL	0-0020289	0864	1
BRUBAKER ELBRIDGE L	COL	0-0051445	0861	1
BRUBAKER JACK H	COL	0-0083580	0766	1
BRUBAKER WILLIAM E	COL	0-0032497	0966	1
BRUBECK DAVID L	LTC	0-0080616	0165	1
BRUCE ANDREW D	LTG	0-0005857	0954	1
BRUCE BURTON B	COL	0-0019360	0660	1
BRUCE CHARLES D	COL	0-0020542	0559	1
BRUCE THOMAS R JR	COL	0-0032423	0766	1
BRUCE WALTER F	CW2	W-0902839	1161	1
BRUGH RAY K	LTC	0-0031686	1165	1
BRUCKER JOHN C	LTC	0-0030997	0266	1

NAME	GRADE	SVC NO	DATE RET MO YR	RET CODE
BRUCKER WALLACE H	M G	0-0018793	0862	1
BRUEHL PAUL E	COL	0-0032270	0868	1
BRUGGER VERNON W	LTC	0-0049966	0359	1
BRUGH ROBERT G JR	COL	0-0025009	0163	1
BRULEY HENRY L	LTC	0-0035457	0564	2
BRUMBAUGH JOHN D	CPT	0-0017351	0331	2
BRUMBY SEWELL M	COL	0-0018846	0360	1
BRUMFIEL OSCAR M	LTC	0-0023534	0760	1
BRUMMITT LEROY D	COL	0-0044087	0365	1
BRUNEAU ALFRED W	LTC	0-0023404	0660	1
BRUNI ALBERT V	COL	0-0032195	0467	1
BRUNKE WILLIAM H	COL	0-0016692	1056	1
BRUNKHORST HAROLD H	LTC	0-0058324	1267	1
BRUNNER CLARENCE D	COL	0-0029456	0960	1
BRUNO ANGEL F	COL	0-0039632	1059	1
BRUNS STOCKTON D	LTC	0-0032292	0863	1
BRUNSON MARK V	COL	0-0006231	0353	2
BRUNSON RICHARD W	LTC	0-0028615	0966	1
BRUNSVOLD RUDOLPH K	COL	0-0024201	0860	1
BRUNT WILLIAM R	CW4	W-0902675	0862	1
BRUSHER HAROLD A	COL	0-0016381	0951	2
BRUTON OGDEN L	COL	0-0029283	0661	1
BRYAN BLACKSHEAR	LTG	0-0015004	0260	1
BRYAN FREDERIC G	COL	0-0039670	0356	1
BRYAN HELEN D	MAJ	N-0001222	0467	1
BRYAN JAMES L	LTC	0-0042883	1064	1
BRYAN JUDY	MAJ	L-0000258	1159	2
BRYAN MARY C	LTC	N-0002094	0566	2
BRYAN ROBERT L	LTC	0-0041125	0165	1
BRYAN WILLIAM C	LTC	0-0034150	0161	1
BRYANT BURNELL V	COL	0-0038629	0659	1
BRYANT HAROLD F	LTC	0-0036886	0764	1
BRYANT RANDALL H	COL	0-0037195	0565	1
BRYANT ROBERT A	LTC	0-0030875	0758	2
BRYANT ROBERT L	LTC	0-0058164	0967	1
BRYANT RUBY F	COL	N-0000079	0661	1
BRYANT WILLIAM H	CW2	W-0907099	0960	1
BRYDE WALTER J	COL	0-0019825	0664	1
BRYDEN WILLIAM	M G	0-0001900	0244	1
BRYER PAUL J	COL	0-0019947	0863	1
BUCH FLOYD H	COL	0-0043500	0168	1
BUCHA PAUL A	COL	0-0031996	1064	1
BUCHAK KIRK	COL	0-0029864	0661	1
BUCHANAN DALE E	COL	0-0024759	0763	1
BUCHANAN DAVID H	M G	0-0017746	0163	1
BUCHANAN DAVID P	LTC	0-0059563	0866	1
BUCHANAN DEE C	LTC	0-0037509	1064	1
BUCHANAN EARL W	LTC	0-0036352	0767	1
BUCHANAN EVERTS R	LTC	0-0059842	1066	1
BUCHANAN JOHN K	1LT	0-0012190	0329	2
BUCHANAN JOHN D	LTC	0-0058846	1066	1
BUCHANAN MILO V	COL	0-0007219	0854	1
BUCHANAN RICHARD S	LTC	0-0071322	0167	2
BUCHANAN RUSSELL B	LTC	0-0027291	0867	1
BUCHANAN WILLIAM D	COL	0-0029594	0861	1
BUCHER JOHN C	COL	0-0051494	0464	1
BUCHWALD DONALD F	COL	0-0018599	0761	1
BUCK CARROLL D	COL	0-0001424	0640	2
BUCK CHAMPLIN F JR	COL	0-0018352	0661	1
BUCK CHARLES T	CW4	W-0902844	0455	1
BUCK DONALD G	LTC	0-0030745	0664	1
BUCK JAMES H	LTC	0-0062845	0767	1
BUCK KATHRYN V	LTC	R-0010130	0667	1
BUCK LAURENCE N	COL	0-0017657	1048	2
BUCK OLIVER F	COL	0-0084546	1068	1
BUCK WALTER A	COL	0-0015565	0653	2
BUCKALEW LOUIS W JR	LTC	0-0043462	0366	1
BUCKINGHAM JAMES S	LTC	0-0080619	0966	1
BUCKINS ALTHEA V	MAJ	N-0000055	0651	1
BUCKIUS RICHARD P	LTC	0-0070290	0368	1
BUCKLAND DANIEL P	COL	0-0012447	0753	1
BUCKLER JOHN G	CW4	W-0902345	0756	1
BUCKLER PHILLIP J	LTC	0-0037564	0166	1
BUCKLES RONALD J	LTC	0-0080620	0964	1
BUCKLEY GORDON D	LTC	0-0084347	0464	1

NAME	GRADE	SVC NO	DATE RET MO YR	RET CODE
BUCKLEY JOHN L	MAJ	0-0065288	0966	1
BUCKLEY MICHAEL JR	COL	0-0015196	0954	1
BUCKLEY THOMAS	COL	0-0052429	1165	1
BUCY ROY T	COL	0-0051188	0161	1
BUDD OTHO W JR	CPT	0-0007938	1130	1
BUDDEE RUDOLPH S	LTC	0-0088019	0967	1
BUDGE CLARE T	B G	0-0021050	0367	1
BUDGE VERNON M	COL	0-0042017	0562	2
BUDNEY CLIFFORD J	CPT	0-0059776	0663	1
BUDZ ANDREW D JR	LTC	0-0023253	0264	1
BUECHLER THEODORE E	B G	0-0008566	0753	1
BUEHLER JOHN P	COL	0-0019374	0255	1
BUEHLER VERNON M	COL	0-0053373	1267	1
BUELL GEORGE B JR	COL	0-0038599	1153	1
BUESING OLIVER R	LTC	0-0041775	1067	2
BUESS JOHN F	LTC	0-0065436	1266	1
BUFFINGTON ROLAND M	LTC	0-0041429	0551	1
BUFORD LANIER D	COL	0-0039046	0868	1
BUGHER WILLIAM A	CPT	0-0015578	1139	2
BUIE WALTER D	COL	0-0012863	0854	1
BULDAIN FRANK J	COL	0-0043495	0566	1
BULL HAROLD R	LTG	0-0003707	0752	2
BULL HENRY T	COL	0-0001608	0934	1
BULL ROBERT H	COL	0-0023424	1165	1
BULLARD ABRAHAM L	COL	0-0010027	0547	1
BULLARD FRANK M	LTC	0-0044121	0268	1
BULLARD MURRAY N	CPT	0-0062020	1057	2
BULLARD PETER C	COL	0-0003664	1152	1
BULLARD ROBERT L III	MAJ	0-0025774	0564	1
BULLARD WINIFRED W	CPT	M-0000560	0447	1
BULLIS STANLEY W	COL	0-0029182	0855	1
BULLOCK EDMUND T	COL	0-0029367	1059	1
BULLOCK RICHARD B	LTC	0-0024198	1062	1
BULLOCK WILLIAM C	M G	0-0017635	0466	1
BUMEN LOUIS G	COL	0-0029350	1059	1
BUMGARNER CHARLES H	CW4	W-0902846	1055	1
BUNCH EDD	CW3	W-0902848	0157	1
BUNCH HERBERT	WO1	W-0901090	0425	1
BUNDY HAZEL B	MAJ	L-0000075	1060	1
BUNDY JAMES A	LTC	0-0080053	0366	1
BUNGE HERWART A	CW4	W-0902849	1156	1
BUNKER RAYMOND T	COL	0-0028864	0556	1
BUNN RALPH W	COL	0-0041762	0463	1
BUNSHAW RAYMOND H	COL	0-0021024	0768	2
BUNTING GEOFFREY C	COL	0-0010357	0851	1
BUNTING LOYD D	COL	0-0011120	0551	1
BUNTON RAYMOND B	COL	0-0080622	1268	1
BUNTYN JAMES R	COL	0-0083563	1267	1
BUNTZ HOWARD E	CW3	W-0902850	0862	2
BURBACH CLAUDE F	B G	0-0016184	0556	1
BURBANK WILLIAM L	COL	0-0016186	0755	1
BURBIDGE LESTER J	COL	0-0050938	0357	1
BURCH CHARLES H	COL	0-0041914	0961	1
BURCH CHARLES T	LTC	0-0063060	0767	1
BURCH CLAUDE C	COL	0-0010365	0550	1
BURCH GEORGE D	COL	0-0042013	0462	2
BURCH JACK P	LTC	0-0045948	0765	1
BURCHAM CLYDE A	LTC	0-0015064	0847	1
BURCHELL EDWARD L	COL	0-0040251	0568	2
BURCHER HARRY E	COL	0-0039645	0258	1
BURCKES MARTIN H	LTC	0-0015491	0852	1
BURD BESSIE C	MAJ	N-0000622	0660	1
BURD HOWARD H	COL	0-0042434	0762	1
BURDGE JOHN M JR	COL	0-0016803	0757	1
BURDICK CHARLES W	CW4	W-0907130	0760	1
BURDO DOROTHY P	MAJ	N-0001651	0666	1
BURFENING JOHN W	COL	0-0022891	0368	1
BURGASSER FRANCIS X	LTC	0-0037061	0462	1
BURGER VONNA F	B G	0-0015667	0360	1
BURGESS ALBERT F JR	COL	0-0035280	0767	1
BURGESS CHARLES A JR	LTC	0-0053513	1060	1
BURGESS FRANCIS T	CPT	0-0025353	0345	2
BURGESS GEORGE P	COL	0-0012311	0854	2
BURGESS ROBERT C	LTC	0-0027551	0965	1
BURGET FRANK P	COL	0-0062120	0968	1

NAME	GRADE	SVC NO	DATE RET MO YR	RET CODE
BURGHEIM JOSEPH H	COL	0-0009114	0753	1
BURGIO JOSEPH C	MAJ	0-0085105	0161	1
BURK FRANK E	LTC	0-0063513	0868	1
BURK FRANK P	COL	0-0049569	0868	1
BURK WALTER J	COL	0-0032043	0868	1
BURKART ESHER C	COL	0-0012779	0554	1
BURKE ALVIN L	COL	0-0021148	0764	1
BURKE CARL V	COL	0-0038790	0265	1
BURKE DAVID C	COL	0-0039667	0164	1
BURKE EDWARD J	COL	0-0018857	0953	1
BURKE JAMES R	LTC	0-0080626	0967	1
BURKE JAMES T	COL	0-0034575	1268	1
BURKE MICHAEL J	LTC	0-0050375	0763	1
BURKE THOMAS W	COL	0-0031508	0567	1
BURKE WILLIAM J	COL	0-0009794	1134	2
BURKE WILLIAM J	CW3	W-0904089	0463	1
BURKETT JOSEPH F JR	LTC	0-0081368	0968	2
BURKETT LYMAN D	LTC	0-0030428	0160	2
BURKETT RAYMOND W	COL	0-0030603	0564	1
BURLESON DERWOOD E	MAJ	0-0037566	0662	1
BURLINGHAM CHARLES E	CW4	W-0902274	0862	1
BURN RICHARD C	COL	0-0034426	0865	1
BURNELL RAY L	B G	0-0004354	0248	2
BURNELL 2ND N A	M G	0-0012337	0857	2
BURNETT BURGH S	COL	0-0004162	1047	1
BURNETT EDWIN M	COL	0-0010306	0846	2
BURNETT GEORGE W	COL	0-0039499	0868	1
BURNETT HENRY H	MAJ	0-0026906	0964	1
BURNETT JOHN F	COL	0-0015204	0945	2
BURNETT JOHN W	COL	0-0042578	0761	2
BURNETT ROBERT M	COL	0-0020187	0358	1
BURNHAM MARY C	MAJ	R-0010064	0760	1
BURNS DONALD F	COL	0-0079763	0767	1
BURNS DONALD S	COL	0-0012672	0854	1
BURNS EDWARD J	LTC	0-0041709	1057	2
BURNS ELMER M	COL	0-0029499	1060	1
BURNS HELEN E	MAJ	N-0002355	0558	1
BURNS JAMES H	M G	0-0002332	1044	2
BURNS JOHN E	COL	0-0031205	0968	1
BURNS JOHN J	B G	0-0012299	0553	2
BURNS JOHN R	B G	0-0016509	0656	2
BURNS KENNETH F	LTC	0-0031210	0762	1
BURNS KENNETH P	COL	0-0025194	0367	1
BURNS PATRICK J	COL	0-0080628	0468	1
BURNS PAUL	COL	0-0038733	0163	1
BURNS RICHARD F	MAJ	0-0058121	0666	1
BURNS ROBERT E	COL	0-0016172	0848	1
BURNS ROBERT J	LTC	0-0065258	1166	1
BURNS ROBERT W	LTC	0-0052887	0164	1
BURNS SAMUEL E	COL	0-0030394	0963	1
BURNS WILLIAM H	LTC	0-0014813	0934	2
BURNSIDE WALTER	COL	0-0015208	0653	2
BURR DONALD F	1LT	0-0060824	1051	2
BURR EDWARD II	COL	0-0026009	0267	1
BURR LYNN S	LTC	0-0053788	1265	1
BURR RALPH R	COL	0-0039769	0762	2
BURR WESLEY H	COL	0-0032019	1268	1
BURRELL WALTER F	LTC	0-0024492	0262	1
BURRER JOHN D	LTC	0-0061208	0966	1
BURRESS WITHERS A	LTG	0-0004812	1154	1
BURRIS LAYTON D	LTC	0-0037413	1066	1
BURRITT GEORGE E	COL	0-0014863	0854	1
BURROWS JOHN E	COL	0-0023621	0867	1
BURROWS MARY L	LTC	N-0002152	0365	1
BURROWS ROBERT F JR	LTC	0-0025918	0866	1
BURT ERNEST H	B G	0-0004916	1046	2
BURT FARLOW	COL	0-0009752	1146	2
BURT REYNOLDS J	B G	0-0000520	1037	2
BURT REYNOLDS J JR	COL	0-0012710	0548	1
BURT ROBERT F	LTC	0-0063053	1165	1
BURT WALTER L	COL	0-0043093	0966	1
BURT WILKIE C	COL	0-0006609	0753	1
BURT WILLIAM G	MAJ	0-0009008	0240	2
BURTCHAELL JOHN W	COL	0-0023764	0766	1
BURTIS THOMAS R	CW4	W-0902854	0163	1

NAME	GRADE	SVC NO	DATE RET MO YR	RET CODE
BURTON ALBERT H	COL	0-0016067	0347	1
BURTON EMMETTE Y JR	COL	0-0020672	0867	1
BURTON ETHEL	MAJ	N-0000207	0961	1
BURTON LEWIS P	COL	0-0034567	0868	1
BURTON LLOYD P	LTC	0-0080379	0665	1
BURTS MARJORIE K	MAJ	N-0002196	1163	1
BUSBEE CHARLES M	B G	0-0003794	0753	1
BUSBEY GEORGE W	COL	0-0015639	0854	1
BUSCEMI MICHAEL O	COL	0-0073025	0161	1
BUSCH EVERETT	B G	0-0007260	0852	2
BUSER OSCAR C	COL	0-0042246	0963	1
BUSH BENJAMIN R	COL	0-0040166	0567	1
BUSH CHESTER K	COL	0-0079643	0765	1
BUSH ERNEST L	COL	0-0029843	1262	1
BUSH FRANK O	LTC	0-0047101	0261	1
BUSH GEORGE F	M G	0-0017634	0864	1
BUSH GEORGE P	COL	0-0005376	0844	2
BUSH HAL C	LTC	0-0011072	0142	1
BUSH HARRY R	COL	0-0053342	0563	2
BUSH HOWARD C	COL	0-0030205	0263	1
BUSH HUGH W JR	LTC	0-0060626	0466	1
BUSH JAMES E	COL	0-0010332	0854	1
BUSH JOSEPH K	COL	0-0014710	0651	2
BUSH KENNETH B	M G	0-0006650	0553	1
BUSH LEONARD R	LTC	0-0080630	0668	1
BUSH NEWTON G	COL	0-0009666	0753	1
BUSH STERLING C	COL	0-0043914	1162	1
BUSHNELL JAMES L	LTC	0-0050697	0568	1
BUSHNELL THEODORE L	MAJ	0-0080240	1065	2
BUSK JOSEPH P	1LT	0-0014388	1119	2
BUSSOLATI EMILE J	LTC	0-0032677	0368	1
BUSTRAAN RUTH	LTC	N-0000936	1167	2
BUTCHART JOHN N	LTC	0-0044664	0661	1
BUTCHERS RALPH J	M G	0-0017242	0764	1
BUTH WILLIAM H	LTC	0-0054312	1163	1
BUTKUS WALTER A	LTC	0-0023659	0656	2
BUTLER ALLEN S	COL	0-0030422	0565	1
BUTLER BRADFORD JR	COL	0-0031425	0766	1
BUTLER BRAXTON D	COL	0-0011422	0844	2
BUTLER DAVID C	LTC	0-0080631	0468	1
BUTLER DONALD A	MAJ	0-0059909	0164	1
BUTLER EARLE B	COL	0-0043106	0463	1
BUTLER ERNEST C	LTC	0-0035578	0865	1
BUTLER FARLEY P SR	LTC	0-0039321	0861	1
BUTLER FREDERIC B	B G	0-0012047	0453	2
BUTLER GEORGE E	COL	0-0007080	0252	2
BUTLER JAMES F	COL	0-0007292	0547	2
BUTLER JAMES J	COL	0-0030068	1263	1
BUTLER JOHN L	LTC	0-0040980	0664	1
BUTLER MIRIAM L	LTC	L-0000111	0165	1
BUTLER ROBERT G	M G	0-0017191	0759	1
BUTLER ROSE A	MAJ	N-0000590	0762	1
BUTLER STANLEY E	LTC	0-0037609	1164	1
BUTLER WARREN A	MAJ	0-0008947	1033	1
BUTNER JOHN C JR	COL	0-0007129	1151	2
BUTSCHER WINSTON	COL	0-0030599	0166	1
BUTTERFIELD JOHN L	LTC	0-0026194	0763	1
BUTTERMORE CHARLES W	COL	0-0029147	0958	1
BUTTERWORTH VIRGINIA	MAJ	N-0002278	0664	1
BUTTNER LOUIS	COL	0-0042100	1162	1
BUTTOLPH LOREN D	COL	0-0042053	0862	1
BUTTS ROBERT E	LTC	0-0032286	0364	1
BUTTS SARA C	MAJ	N-0000297	0959	1
BUYNOSKI ADAM S	COL	0-0020169	0966	1
BUYS JOSEPH H	COL	0-0029689	0462	1
BUZZETTI HELEN J	MAJ	L-0000337	0267	1
BYARS DAVID O	MAJ	0-0013932	0620	2
BYARS DAVID O JR	B G	0-0021273	0167	1
BYERS CLOVIS E	LTG	0-0012769	0659	2
BYERS LEX J	LTC	0-0063366	0666	1
BYERS RUFUS A	COL	0-0009119	0244	1
BYERS WILLIAM E	LTC	0-0057200	0968	1
BYKERK NORMAN H	COL	0-0033038	0765	1
BYNUM PIERRE D	MAJ	0-0078747	0966	1
BYNUM ROBERT M III	LTC	0-0070293	0168	1

NAME	GRADE	SVC NO	DATE RET MO YR	RET CODE
BYDRUM HENRY M	COL	0-0080380	0666	1
BYRD VELVA M	MAJ	N-0001051	0166	1
BYRD WILLIAM H JR	COL	0-0052267	0365	1
BYRNE BERNARD A	COL	0-0012404	0854	1
BYRNE ELIZABETH	MAJ	L-0000526	0468	1
BYRNE JEROME S	LTC	0-0021404	0757	1
BYRNE JOHN D	COL	0-0021937	0465	1
BYRNE MALCOLM	COL	0-0006390	0753	2
BYRNE MICHAEL J	CPT	0-0009160	0429	1
BYRNE PAUL P	LTC	0-0051433	0761	1
BYRNE ROBERT E	LTC	0-0043281	0363	1
BYRNE ROBERT J JR	LTC	0-0083581	0763	1
BYRNES LAURENCE G	LTC	0-0054163	1266	1
BYRNS ROBERT F	LTC	0-0051606	0463	1
CABANISS JELKS H JR	COL	0-0026558	0768	1
CABELL HENRY B	LTC	0-0058800	0767	1
CABREY HAZEL S	MAJ	N-0002155	0562	1
CAFARELLI ROOSEVELT	COL	0-0022265	0367	1
CAFFEE MAHLON W	LTC	0-0021769	0644	2
CAFFEY BENJAMIN F JR	B G	0-0004929	0350	1
CAGE LEE E	COL	0-0024909	0567	1
CAHILL EDWIN M	COL	0-0019141	0863	1
CAHILL GEORGE T JR	LTC	0-0076854	0966	1
CAHILL HOWARD F K	COL	0-0007978	1139	2
CAHILL VIRGINIA F	MAJ	N-0000711	0662	1
CAIN CHARLES A	COL	0-0029988	0863	1
CAIN HALL	COL	0-0021984	0647	2
CAIN JAMES W	COL	0-0026208	0868	1
CAIN LAMBERT R	COL	0-0012375	0547	2
CAIN ROBERT O	MAJ	0-0089792	1067	1
CAIN ROBERT S	COL	0-0042210	0863	1
CAIN WALTER J	LTC	0-0027696	0765	1
CAITO THOMAS P	COL	0-0037478	0468	1
CAKE JAMES M	LTC	0-0025372	0762	1
CALAHAN ROBERT H	COL	0-0040515	1168	1
CALDWELL ALBIN N	COL	0-0011625	1048	1
CALDWELL DAVID D	1LT	0-0011719	0632	2
CALDWELL GEORGE L	COL	0-0009549	0253	2
CALDWELL JACK B	COL	0-0022316	0962	1
CALDWELL JAMES A	LTC	0-0025315	0763	1
CALDWELL JOHN M	COL	0-0019313	0755	1
CALDWELL R BEVERLY	COL	0-0051185	1060	1
CALDWELL RUSS P	COL	0-0051111	1160	1
CALDWELL WILLIAM G	COL	0-0017312	0758	1
CALE FRANCES L	MAJ	N-0002033	0760	1
CALENBERG HARRY D	LTC	0-0076855	1265	1
CALHOUN WILLIAM R	M G	0-0019256	1067	1
CALL RAYMOND L	LTC	0-0060618	0468	1
CALL WILLIAM A	COL	0-0018719	0559	1
CALLAHAN DONALD M	COL	0-0034055	0265	1
CALLAHAN JAMES W	COL	0-0005435	1045	2
CALLENDER GEORGE R	B G	0-0003521	1146	2
CALLICOTT JAMES M	COL	0-0014834	0854	2
CALLINAN PATRICK M	COL	0-0080634	1168	1
CALLISON ROBERT L	COL	0-0019648	1064	1
CALLOWAY CHARLES G	M G	0-0017690	0861	1
CALMES PAUL M	LTC	0-0084827	1167	1
CALNAN FRANCIS M	MAJ	0-0084852	0868	1
CALOYA PIO W	LTC	0-0014883	0753	1
CALVERT GEORGE I	LTC	0-0030521	1063	2
CALVERT GEORGE M	COL	0-0036061	0767	1
CALVERT GEORGE N	COL	0-0043053	0966	1
CALVERT PARKER	COL	0-0020794	0948	2
CALVIN CHAUNCEY E	WO1	W-0902864	0850	2
CALVIN HARRY L	LTC	0-0011352	1043	2
CALYER PETER C	COL	0-0017116	0958	2
CAMBRE JEROME D	COL	0-0012185	0648	1
CAMERON A DONALD	COL	0-0009628	0846	1
CAMERON DONALD N	LTC	0-0024408	0962	1
CAMERON ERNEST V	COL	0-0040876	0968	1
CAMERON HENRY H	COL	0-0008206	0847	1
CAMERON JOHN H JR	CW4	W-0902865	0268	1
CAMERON RICHARD R	COL	0-0021717	0858	1
CAMERON ROBERT C	1LT	0-0015771	0934	2
CAMERON ROBERT C	COL	0-0023178	0762	1

NAME	GRADE	SVC NO	DATE RET MO YR	RET CODE
CAMERON THOMAS J	COL	0-0042804	0766	1
CAMM FRANK	B G	0-0009902	0854	1
CAMMACK NATHAN A JR	CW4	W-0902866	0968	1
CAMP ELWOOD W	COL	0-0043173	0560	1
CAMP HOWARD E	COL	0-0007226	0753	1
CAMP PIERCE H	COL	0-0010208	0845	1
CAMP THOMAS J	B G	0-0016033	1046	2
CAMPANA VICTOR W	LTC	0-0023975	0761	1
CAMPBELL ALEXANDER	COL	0-0005310	0452	2
CAMPBELL BONIFACE	M G	0-0009788	1056	1
CAMPBELL CAREY E	CPT	0-0008311	1134	1
CAMPBELL CHARLES H	LTC	0-0032031	0962	1
CAMPBELL CHARLES T	COL	0-0032180	0867	2
CAMPBELL CLARENCE S	LTC	0-0040163	0565	1
CAMPBELL CLARK S	1LT	0-0027126	1151	2
CAMPBELL DONALD	COL	0-0031122	0468	1
CAMPBELL ERNEST R	1LT	0-0014419	0220	2
CAMPBELL FRANK P	COL	0-0051129	1151	2
CAMPBELL GEORGE E	COL	0-0041437	0856	1
CAMPBELL GEORGE T JR	LTC	0-0026084	0165	2
CAMPBELL GUY L	COL	0-0032616	0768	1
CAMPBELL HARRY L	COL	0-0007143	0452	1
CAMPBELL JACK P	COL	0-0038610	0557	1
CAMPBELL JAMES B	LTC	0-0026690	0764	1
CAMPBELL JAMES R JR	1LT	0-0014376	0919	2
CAMPBELL JAMES T	COL	0-0006758	0346	1
CAMPBELL JOHN E	LTC	0-0079766	0666	1
CAMPBELL JOHN JR	COL	0-0043649	1266	1
CAMPBELL JOHN L	LTC	0-0038863	1160	1
CAMPBELL KERMIT W	LTC	0-0030690	0464	1
CAMPBELL LEVIN H JR	LTG	0-0003194	0546	1
CAMPBELL NORMAN A	COL	0-0042861	0764	1
CAMPBELL OTIS C	CW3	W-0902869	0161	1
CAMPBELL RALPH E	LTC	0-0060020	0968	1
CAMPBELL RAYMOND P	COL	0-0023861	0868	1
CAMPBELL ROBERT H	LTC	0-0026074	0864	1
CAMPBELL ROSS W	CPT	0-0027508	1051	2
CAMPBELL THOMAS E	LTC	0-0008071	0841	2
CAMPBELL VERGIL J	CW4	W-0902870	0565	1
CAMPBELL WAYNE C	LTC	0-0069615	0368	1
CAMPBELL WILLIAM A	B G	0-0006493	0248	1
CAMPBELL WILLIAM E	COL	0-0043316	1267	1
CAMPBELL WILLIAM M	COL	0-0042337	0364	1
CAMPBELL WILLIAM P	B G	0-0014886	0653	2
CAMPBELL WILLIAM R	COL	0-0040267	0868	1
CANADA CHARLES C	COL	0-0029257	0662	1
CANAN HOWARD V	COL	0-0012098	0754	1
CANARY JESSE E	COL	0-0011971	0447	1
CANBY CLARENCE P	B G	0-0017904	0662	1
CANDEE GEORGE	CW4	W-0902872	0366	1
CANDLER HARRY W	LTC	0-0018562	0651	1
CANDON MARIAN W	MAJ	N-0002381	0561	1
CANELLA CHARLES J	COL	0-0023865	0368	1
CANFIELD IRVING H	LTC	0-0063713	0268	2
CANINE CHESTER E	LTC	0-0043949	1267	1
CANINE RALPH J	LTG	0-0007154	0457	2
CANLETT FRANKLIN H	COL	0-0011991	1048	1
CANNING AUSTIN J JR	LTC	0-0026277	0364	1
CANNOLES MARGARET H	LTC	N-0001211		1
CANNON ALFRED R	COL	0-0041725	0861	1
CANNON CLINTON C JR	LTC	0-0080636	0765	1
CANNON J PARRY	LTC	0-0058852	1168	2
CANNON JOSEPH E	COL	0-0020952	0746	2
CANNON JOSEPH M JR	LTC	0-0024930	0863	1
CANNON LINDEN K JR	COL	0-0032509	0867	1
CANNON MARGARET R	MAJ	N-0002207	0365	1
CANNON ROBERT M	LTG	0-0016163	0961	2
CANON JACK Y	LTC	0-0043830	0361	1
CANSLER LOUIS	COL	0-0006580	0245	2
CANTARAL RAYMOND H	LTC	0-0080637	0467	1
CANTEY JAMES	COL	0-0030019	1063	1
CANTRELL FRED H	COL	0-0025295	0663	1
CANTY WILLIAM F	CW3	W-0907075	0357	1
CAPERS THOMAS S JR	COL	0-0032004	1068	1
CAPERTON JAMES N	COL	0-0004496	1146	1

NAME	GRADE	SVC NO	DATE RET MO YR	RET CODE
CAPITO CHARLES E	COL	0-0029568	0661	1
CAPKA THEODORE J	LTC	0-0084596	0968	2
CARABALLO RAYMOND T	COL	0-0031862	0866	1
CARAWAY FORREST	B G	0-0018466	0761	1
CARAWAY PAUL W	LTG	0-0017659	0864	2
CARBERRY EDMUND J	LTC	0-0025565	0864	1
CARBERRY FRANCIS P	COL	0-0038789	0263	1
CARBONELL ARTHUR J	COL	0-0024626	0466	1
CARDELL ROBERT L	COL	0-0018505	0661	1
CARDINELL ROBERT H	LTC	0-0056158	0367	1
CARDULLO EVERETT P	CW4	RW-0902874	0167	1
CARDWELL EUGENE F	M G	0-0038662	0862	1
CAREW THOMAS E	LTC	0-0087497	1064	1
CAREY FAY E J	COL	0-0038814	0661	1
CAREY GEORGE R	COL	0-0017597	0357	1
CAREY MERLE L	COL	0-0025586	0863	1
CARHART RICHARD B	LTC	0-0018497	1141	2
CARHARTT FORREST A	1LT	0-0027605	0347	2
CARIANO SAMUEL P	LTC	0-0084350	0564	1
CARIGNAN ROBERT E	LTC	0-0070296	0668	1
CARILIA THOMAS A	COL	0-0040115	0666	1
CARLAN ULYSSES G	COL	0-0076836	0967	1
CARLAN WILBUR C	MAJ	0-0005479	0934	2
CARLE VERNON K	CW4	W-0902172	0655	1
CARLETON DON F	B G	0-0015415	0854	1
CARLETON LINWOOD A	COL	0-0036260	1267	1
CARLISLE CARSHALL C	LTC	0-0028273	0866	1
CARLISLE GERALD	COL	0-0040324	0868	1
CARLISLE JAMES H	1LT	0-0018618	0539	2
CARLL WALTER T	LTC	0-0020106	0456	1
CARLOCK WILLARD B	COL	0-0016790	0657	1
CARLOSS ELIZABETH	LTC	R-0010065	1060	1
CARLOZZO BENEDICT A	CW3	W-0906651	1058	1
CARLQUIST PHILIP P	COL	0-0031011	0665	2
CARLSEN RICARD T	CW2	W-0901082	1146	1
CARLSON CARSTEN D	LTC	0-0080638	1163	1
CARLSON GUNNAR C	M G	0-0018515	0862	1
CARLSON GUNNARD W	COL	0-0018347	1058	1
CARLSON LEO G	COL	0-0022246	0266	1
CARLSON LUTHER M	CW3	W-0907110	1059	2
CARLSON VINCENT P	COL	0-0023694	0764	1
CARLSON WILLIAM R	COL	0-0009060	1047	2
CARLSTEN CHESTER A	COL	0-0014794	0949	2
CARLTON DONALD C	LTC	0-0067903	0967	1
CARLTON MORTON B	CPT	0-0059718	0754	2
CARMACK JOSEPH	COL	0-0018322	1046	2
CARMICHAEL R L JR	COL	0-0018176	0760	1
CARMODY JOHN J	COL	0-0051659	0865	1
CARMODY ROBERT E	COL	0-0003620	0740	1
CARN ROBERT M	LTC	0-0083564	0765	1
CARNAHAN GEORGE D	COL	0-0023007	0166	1
CARNE WILLIAM J	LTC	0-0016128	0644	2
CARNES HUGHES A	LTC	0-0043674	0863	1
CARNES JAMES J	COL	0-0015340	0854	2
CARNES NORMAN D	COL	0-0030666	0860	1
CARNES RICHARD C	LTC	0-0027321	0766	1
CARNEY HARLAND E	LTC	0-0082153	0868	1
CARNEY JONATHON D	LTC	0-0080055	1268	1
CARNEY TAYLOR E JR	COL	0-0040264	0966	1
CARNS EDWIN H J	M G	0-0017560	0765	1
CAROTHERS GLENN E	LTC	0-0010125	1041	1
CAROW THEODORE M	COL	0-0020527	0761	2
CARPEL RICHARD D	CW4	W-0906653	0565	1
CARPENTER FRANK	COL	0-0015870	0954	1
CARPENTER GEORGE R	COL	0-0051147	0461	1
CARPENTER GILES R	COL	0-0014915	0854	1
CARPENTER JACK R	LTC	0-0053450	0764	1
CARPENTER JAMES S	COL	0-0042622	0862	1
CARPENTER SIDNEY C	COL	0-0080381	1166	1
CARPENTER STANLEY J	COL	0-0041712	0460	1
CARR FRANK L	COL	0-0008608	1046	2
CARR JAMES D	CW3	W-0908077	0968	1
CARR JOHN E III	LTC	0-0066141	1266	1
CARR LOUIS F	CW4	W-0902879	0165	1
CARR ROBERT A	COL	0-0081878	1265	1

NAME	GRADE	SVC NO	DATE RET MO YR	RET CODE
CARR THOMAS W	CPT	0-0061918	1057	2
CARR WILLIAM D	MAJ	0-0060420	0364	1
CARR WILLIAM L	LTC	0-0014756	1145	1
CARRAHER RAYMOND W	COL	0-0045292	0966	1
CARRAWAY WILLIAM E	B G	0-0015144	1155	1
CARRAWAY WILLIAM R	CPT	0-0059844	0663	1
CARRELL CHARLES A	MAJ	0-0018886	0747	1
CARRIE HECTOR JR	LTC	0-0033043	0366	1
CARRIG STEPHEN J	CPT	0-0060378	0454	1
CARRIGAN JOHN A SR	COL	0-0028874	0956	1
CARRIKER JOHN H	COL	0-0005490	1049	1
CARRINGTON GEORGE C	1LT	0-0015061	0934	2
CARRITHERS FRED B	MAJ	0-0002873	0622	2
CARRITHERS TRUMAN W	CPT	0-0018079	0-42	2
CARROLL FRANCIS L	COL	0-0066615	0864	1
CARROLL JAMES B	COL	0-0015272	0954	1
CARROLL JAMES H	LTC	0-0023722	0661	1
CARROLL JAMES V	COL	0-0012119	0455	2
CARROLL JOHN E	COL	0-0041877	0861	1
CARROLL LORNE J	CW4	W-0902880	1054	1
CARROLL MURRAY L	LTC	0-0057442	0867	1
CARROLL NICHOLAS V	LTC	0-0065192	0466	1
CARROLL PAUL L	COL	0-0016502	0754	1
CARROLL PERCY J	B G	0-0004183	0946	2
CARROLL WALTER D JR	LTC	0-0079768	0765	1
CARRUTH JOHN H	COL	0-0003672	0250	1
CARSON DONALD G	COL	0-0053255	1168	2
CARSON EUGENE J	COL	0-0051446	1263	2
CARSON JAMES M	COL	0-0051626	0561	1
CARSON LANETTA I	MAJ	N-0002238	0760	1
CARSON MARION	COL	0-0008610	0853	1
CARSON THOMAS M	LTC	0-0032918	0368	1
CARTER ARTHUR P	COL	0-0029580	0861	1
CARTER CARL	CW4	W-0902881	0162	1
CARTER CLOUD G	LTC	0-0058857	1062	1
CARTER DANIEL M	LTC	0-0031406	0165	1
CARTER GEORGE E	LTC	0-0040430	0767	1
CARTER GEORGE F	COL	0-0023431	0766	1
CARTER GEORGE W JR	LTC	0-0032349	0767	1
CARTER HAMLET R JR	LTC	0-0026134	0965	1
CARTER HENRY P	COL	0-0003038	0246	2
CARTER JACK A JR	MAJ	0-0038302	1066	1
CARTER JACK H	MAJ	0-0052445	0261	1
CARTER JACK W	CW4	W-0902882	0565	1
CARTER JAMES C	COL	0-0015352	0852	2
CARTER JAMES O	COL	0-0008494	0147	2
CARTER JAMES H SR	CW4	W-0904090	0562	2
CARTER JOSEPH M	CW4	W-0902883	0155	1
CARTER LESLIE O	M G	0-0010663	1056	1
CARTER MAYNARD H	COL	0-0015077	0753	1
CARTER PAUL D	COL	0-0008416	1151	1
CARTER PHILIP R	COL	0-0029159	0559	1
CARTER ROBERT F	COL	0-0012364	1146	2
CARTER ROBERT P	MAJ	0-0063396	0367	1
CARTER SAM	LTC	0-0038955	0165	1
CARTER WILEY V	COL	0-0012204	1146	2
CARTER WILLIAM A	M G	0-0018023	0162	1
CARTER WILLIAM C	COL	0-0054761	0868	1
CARTER WILLIAM V	B G	0-0001928	0842	1
CARTTER PAUL H	CPT	0-0008995	0125	2
CARTWRIGHT LESLIE J	COL	0-0008193	0949	1
CARTY ROBERT T	LTC	0-0065188	0768	1
CARUSONE JOHN J	COL	0-0021295	0866	1
CARVER GEORGE A	M G	0-0019122	0766	1
CARVER RICHARD K	COL	0-0040039	0866	1
CARVILLE ELIZABETH	MAJ	N-0002368	0860	1
CARY HUGH T	COL	0-0018845	0862	1
CARY MILO G	COL	0-0014608	0848	1
CARY RANDOLPH J	LTC	0-0026905	0664	1
CASE CHARLES E	LTC	0-0051260	1159	1
CASE HOMER	B G	0-0007090	0854	1
CASE RICHARD	CPT	0-0019701	0442	2
CASE ROY	CW4	W-0902884	0257	1
CASE SCOTT M	COL	0-0023121	0168	2
CASEY CHARLES W	COL	0-0032356	0867	1

332-811 O - 69 - 2

NAME	GRADE	SVC NO	DATE RET MO YR	RET CODE
CASEY EDGAR L	LTC	0-0036324	1060	1
CASEY GLEN T	CW4	W-0902885	1163	1
CASEY HUGH J	M G	0-0009208	1049	2
CASEY ROBERT F	CW4	W-0904092	0964	2
CASH ALBERT W	CW4	W-0902886	0861	1
CASH JAMES H II	B G	0-0038528	1062	1
CASHMAN CHARLES J	COL	0-0019653	0157	1
CASPER RICHARD F	MAJ	0-0058331	0465	1
CASS PHIL	1LT	0-0011979	0930	2
CASSADAY GEORGE C	COL	0-0032658	1166	1
CASSEDY WILLIAM P	LTC	0-0025044	0466	1
CASSELL DONALD R	CW4	W-0902848	1164	1
CASSELL HAROLD A	LTC	0-0029956	0661	1
CASSELL LLOYD W	COL	0-0031586	1167	1
CASSERLY EDWARD A	MAJ	0-0011685	0334	2
CASSERLY MARY A	LTC	N-0001572	0568	1
CASSEVANT ALBERT F	M G	0-0018456	0160	1
CASSIBRY ROBERT C	B G	0-0023058	0867	1
CASSIDY JOHN F	B G	0-0012718	0854	1
CASSIDY ROBERT F	COL	0-0021783	0865	1
CASTERLINE JAMES I	LTC	0-0043628	0665	1
CASTLE SHIRLEY M	COL	0-0051850	0667	2
CASTO CARL S	COL	0-0032007	0464	1
CATALAN NEMESIO	CPT	0-0014884	0539	2
CATERER HORACE J	MAJ	0-0012711	0131	2
CATES TRAVIS N	CW4	W-0906655	0266	1
CATHCART WILLIAM T	COL	0-0041521	0758	1
CATHER LEO W	COL	0-0018510	0761	1
CATHRAE WILLIAM F	COL	0-0024220	0766	1
CATO RAYMOND L	COL	0-0020195	0866	1
CATRON 2ND THOMAS B	B G	0-0002597	0336	1
CATT RICHARD H	CW4	W-0902891	0867	1
CAUFIELD FRANK J	B G	0-0019515	0864	2
CAUGHRON JAMES W	COL	0-0051513	0664	2
CAUGHRON SAMUEL J JR	CW3	RW-0902676	0964	1
CAULDER BRUCE B	COL	0-0043626	0868	1
CAULDER LEROY W	LTC	0-0065122	0664	1
CAULKINS RALPH M	LTC	0-0005794	0142	1
CAUM NORMAN C	COL	0-0011803	0854	1
CAUSEY LUTHER G	COL	0-0016336	0655	2
CAUTHEN WILLIAM A	COL	0-0051257	1061	1
CAVANAGH JOHN P JR	LTC	0-0051810	0964	1
CAVE EDMUND H	MAJ	0-0059411	0262	2
CAVE JOHN W	B G	0-0018388	1060	1
CAVE RICHARD L	COL	0-0004396	1143	2
CAVELLI CHARLES JR	COL	0-0016165	0755	1
CAVENAUGH ROBERT L	COL	0-0020090	1006	1
CAVENDER CHARLES C	COL	0-0015307	0953	2
CAVENDER SAVINO W	COL	0-0031005	0567	2
CAVNESS WILLIAM D	COL	0-0023489	0168	1
CAWLFIELD PAUL A	COL	0-0030378	0862	2
CAYLE BRYCE T	CPT	0-0065189	0765	1
CAYGILL HARRY W	LTC	0-0007205	1141	1
CAYWOOD LINDSAY P	COL	0-0050898	0555	1
CAZAURANG JULIAN J	CW3	RW-0902894	1061	1
CECIL THOMAS J	MAJ	0-0002669	0927	2
CELLA ANDREW	COL	0-0052269	0962	2
CELMER THEODORE B	MAJ	0-0024066	0761	1
CEPEDA EMMANUEL S	LTC	0-0019297	0761	1
CERMACK FRANK P	CW2	W-0901122	0425	1
CEROW DONALD A	LTC	0-0057315	0968	1
CERWIN STEVEN S	COL	0-0029526	0561	1
CHABOT JOSEPH L	COL	0-0020721	0966	1
CHACE EDGAR N	MAJ	0-0018701	0-44	2
CHADBOURNE ERNEST D	LTC	0-0069879	0564	2
CHADWICK BENJAMIN F	LTC	0-0012076	0443	2
CHADWICK HAZEL C	MAJ	N-0001289	0261	1
CHADWICK MAURICE P	COL	0-0012286	0150	2
CHADWICK RALPH O	COL	0-0031280	1068	2
CHAFFEE ELMER F	COL	0-0052057	0966	1
CHAFFEE FREDERIC H	COL	0-0017524	0859	1
CHAFFIN ANDREW D JR	COL	0-0020153	0466	1
CHALGREN EDWARD JR	COL	0-0021349	0968	2
CHALLICE CHARLES JR	CPT	0-0008235	0724	2
CHAMBEPLAIN CLIFTON	COL	0-0056907	0268	1

NAME	GRADE	SVC NO	DATE RET MO YR	RET CODE
CHAMBERLAIN F R JR	COL	0-0010785	1146	1
CHAMBERLAIN HAZEL A	MAJ	N-0000554	0760	1
CHAMBERLAIN J L JR	COL	0-0016117	0755	1
CHAMBERLAIN THOMAS C	COL	0-0023145	0766	1
CHAMBERLIN F S	MAJ	N-0002032	1158	1
CHAMBERLIN STEPHEN J	LTG	0-0003397	1051	2
CHAMBERS ARTHUR K	LTC	0-0009095	0342	1
CHAMBERS BEATRICE	MAJ	N-0000107	0560	1
CHAMBERS JOHN H	LTC	0-0021323	0662	1
CHAMBERS JOHN S JR	COL	0-0025357	0967	1
CHAMBERS LAUREL L	LTC	0-0039547	0155	1
CHAMBLIN FRANCIS A	COL	0-0032255	0968	1
CHAMBLISS JOHN D	COL	0-0007551	1046	2
CHAMPENY ARTHUR S	B G	0-0008264	0753	2
CHAMPLIN HERBERT H	COL	0-0030661	0467	2
CHANCE ROBERT H	COL	0-0005618	0847	1
CHANCEY GILBERT E	CW3	W-0902896	0961	1
CHANDLER CYRIL C	COL	0-0008327	1046	2
CHANDLER DAVID J	LTC	0-0055271	0868	1
CHANDLER FITZHUGH H	COL	0-0042328	1262	1
CHANDLER HENRY	CW4	W-0902897	0560	1
CHANDLER LEROY L	CW4	W-0901667	0364	1
CHANDLER LEWELL F	CW4	W-0906656	1059	1
CHANDLER MARTIN B	COL	0-0023189	0461	2
CHANDLER MELBOURNE	LTC	0-0037486	0763	1
CHANDLER RICHARD L	MAJ	0-0074972	0968	1
CHANDLER ROBERT E	COL	0-0017559	0859	1
CHANDLER ROBERT J	MAJ	0-0021386	0547	2
CHANDLER WILLIAM E	COL	0-0018431	0661	1
CHANDLER WILLIAM L	CW3	W-0904094	1058	1
CHAPDELAINE ALBERT J	LTC	0-0051956	1163	1
CHAPLIN ROBERT T	COL	0-0009745	0753	1
CHAPMAN CARLETON G	LTC	0-0002630	1122	1
CHAPMAN CLIFFORD P	COL	0-0010191	0852	1
CHAPMAN ERNEST W	COL	0-0040704	0368	1
CHAPMAN GERALD	COL	0-0019035	0361	1
CHAPMAN GRACIE L	LT	N-0002115	0360	1
CHAPMAN JACK W	COL	0-0020616	0152	2
CHAPMAN JANET	LTC	L-0000261	0968	1
CHAPMAN LORIN P	LTC	0-0058860	0766	1
CHAPMAN OREN D	LTC	0-0040328	0464	1
CHAPMAN RAYMOND T	COL	0-0029860	0263	1
CHAPMAN ROBERT D	COL	0-0042367	1163	1
CHAPMAN WILLIAM G	CW4	W-0904095	0561	1
CHAPMAN WILLIAM MC	COL	0-0008630	0546	2
CHAPPELEAR LOUIS S	CPT	0-0020310	0841	2
CHAPPELL PAUL E	COL	0-0041968	1061	1
CHAPPUIS STEVE A	B G	0-0020899	0967	1
CHARLEBOIS GEORGE J	MAJ	0-0060767	0951	2
CHARLES ORMAN G	B G	0-0029954	0763	1
CHARLES ROLAND K JR	COL	0-0017988	0560	1
CHARLTON JESSE M JR	COL	0-0024543	0964	1
CHARTRAU DOROTHY M	LTC	N-0002099	0168	1
CHASE CHARLES H	M G	0-0019095	0868	1
CHASE EARL R	COL	0-0028811	0855	1
CHASE EDWARD D	COL	0-0030936	1264	1
CHASE JACK P	MAJ	0-0080649	1265	1
CHASE LAWRENCE R	LTC	0-0081972	0463	2
CHASE RICHARD	LTC	0-0016999	1154	1
CHASE STEPHENS F	CW4	W-0902900	0766	2
CHASE WALTER E	COL	0-0016937	0555	1
CHASE WILLIAM	COL	0-0020856	0763	1
CHASE WILLIAM C	M G	0-0004739	0255	1
CHASTAINE BEN-HUR	COL	0-0005113	1249	1
CHATFIELD MILES B	COL	0-0019404	1158	1
CHATHAM ARTHUR B	LTC	0-0031480	0465	1
CHATHAM EDWIN J	LTC	0-0052513	1266	1
CHAUFTY JOSEPH V	LTC	0-0025969	0766	1
CHAVERS MILTON	CW4	W-0906657	0864	1
CHAVEZ HELEN A	MAJ	N-0001903	1061	1
CHAVIN RAPHAEL S	B G	0-0004958	1052	1
CHAVIS NEHEMIAH	CW4	W-0902901	0159	1
CHAZAL EDWARD A	COL	0-0015791	0954	1
CHEAL RAYMOND C	LTC	0-0020845	1167	1
CHEATHAM RICHARD B	COL	0-0040124	1062	1

NAME	GRADE	SVC NO	DATE RET MO YR	RET CODE
CHECK GILBERT J	COL	0-0051936	1167	1
CHEEK ANDREW P	COL	0-0032306	1265	1
CHEEK NORFLEET R	LTC	0-0084733	0268	1
CHEEVER CHARLES [illegible]	COL	0-0014712	0448	1
CHELL PEARCE P	CW4	RW-0902405	0163	1
CHENOWETH WILLIAM C	LTC	0-0029621	1046	2
CHERNOSKY RAYMOND M	CW4	W-0902903	0862	1
CHERRY HUGH G	LTC	0-0080057	0868	1
CHERUBIN STANLEY J	COL	0-0020700	0967	1
CHESEL WALTER	CW3	W-0907111	1059	1
CHESLEY JOHN W JR	COL	0-0053264	1166	1
CHESNUT JAMES W	LTC	0-0065046	0566	1
CHESTER GEORGE A	COL	0-0016345	0155	1
CHESTER JOHN H	COL	0-0016971	1146	2
CHESTER ROBERT S	MAJ	0-0022041	1043	2
CHESTON DANIEL M III	COL	0-0019507	0763	1
CHESTON ELLIOTT B	COL	0-0031976	0467	1
CHEVES GILBERT X	M G	0-0007353	0647	1
CHEWNING CLAUDIUS C	LTC	0-0069881	1167	1
CHEYNE ARTHUR C	COL	0-0029512	0161	1
CHILD FRANK M	COL	0-0005516	1049	1
CHILD PROCTOR L	LTC	0-0067905	0767	1
CHILDERS ERNEST	LTC	0-0048416	0965	1
CHILDERS ERNEST W	CW4	W-0902904	0259	1
CHILDERS GEORGE H	CPT	0-0027035	0947	2
CHILDERS JOE E	COL	0-0031936	0364	1
CHILDRESS ALBERT W	LTC	0-0027749	0766	1
CHILDRESS CLEMENT J	CW4	W-0902298	0561	1
CHILDRESS ELLERY O	CW3	W-0902905	1159	1
CHILDRESS JOHN F	CW2	W-0902906	0151	1
CHILDRESS WILLIAM G	CW4	W-0902361	0657	1
CHILDS BOB	LTC	0-0011124	0246	1
CHILDS GEORGE W	COL	0-0020294	0755	1
CHILDS STANLEY A	CW3	W-0902907	0258	1
CHILK SAMUEL J	COL	0-0053777	0468	1
CHILSON LEE O	LTC	0-0039871	0661	1
CHILTON ALEXANDER	COL	0-0002236	0934	2
CHIMENT JOHN A	LTC	0-0027048	0664	1
CHIPMAN ALBERT O	COL	0-0004721	0846	2
CHIPMAN GUY W	COL	0-0002872	0845	2
CHIRAFISI DONALD	MAJ	0-0061409	0366	1
CHIRICO CARL F	COL	0-0029506	1060	1
CHITTENDEN ALBERT O	LTC	0-0031574	0663	1
CHLOUPEK LAURENCE F	COL	0-0044094	1166	1
CHOQUETTE LOUIS T	CW4	W-0902388	1053	1
CHORPENING CLAUDE H	M G	0-0012088	0656	1
CHORPENNING FRANK W	LTC	0-0038882	0561	1
CHRIETZBERG JAMES JR	LTC	0-0039129	0968	1
CHRIETZBERG WILLIAM	LTC	0-0080361	0365	1
CHRISMAN HAROLD F	COL	0-0015961	0750	2
CHRISTENSEN ANCHER E	LTC	0-0045271	0762	1
CHRISTENSEN ARTHUR G	COL	0-0020871	0160	1
CHRISTENSEN JOHN M	COL	0-0023856	0564	1
CHRISTENSEN NELS F	COL	0-0040100	0762	1
CHRISTIAN AVERILL L	LTC	0-0080652	1066	1
CHRISTIAN OTTO	MAJ	0-0005174	0135	2
CHRISTIAN ROBERT L	COL	0-0004609	0346	1
CHRISTIAN W H JR	COL	0-0018333	1046	2
CHRISTIANSEN JAMES G	M G	0-0012075	0954	1
CHRISTIANSON CHARLES	LTC	0-0043913	0163	1
CHRISTIANSON CHARLES	COL	0-0056824	1167	1
CHRISTIANSON DANA F	CW4	W-0902912	0360	1
CHRISTIE ALBERT F	COL	0-0004913	0248	1
CHRISTIE PAUL E	CW3	W-0906660	0963	1
CHRISTMAN ARTHUR F	CW2	W-0901535	0247	1
CHRISTMAN LOUISE O	MAJ	M-0010007	0357	1
CHRISTMAS THOMAS W E	COL	0-0016965	0157	2
CHRISTOFK ROBERT R	LTC	0-0022212	0958	1
CHRISTOL MAX S	LTC	0-0034343	0168	1
CHRISTY JAMES V	LTC	0-0025909	0865	1
CHRISTY JOSEPH T	CW3	W-0906661	0361	1
CHRONISTER EARL C	CW4	W-0906662	0664	1
CHUBBUCK JAMES B	LTC	0-0021058	0860	1
CHUCK HARRY C	COL	0-0051032	0559	1
CHURCH CORNEILLE	MAJ	0-0069619	1167	1

NAME	GRADE	SVC NO	DATE RET MO YR	RET CODE
CHURCH MITCHELL E JR	CW4	W-0902913	0966	1
CHURCHILL GEORGE A	LTC	0-0027362	0966	1
CHURCHILL JAMES M JR	COL	0-0018907	0459	2
CHURCHWELL WILLIAM H	COL	0-0041866	1160	1
CHURNEY OTTO L	COL	0-0018334	0655	1
CHUTTER ROBERT W	LTC	0-0028755	0753	1
CHYNOWETH BRADFORD G	B G	0-0003499	1047	2
CIANCHINI LUIS F	COL	0-0005553	1052	2
CIBOSKY WILLIAM	CPT	0-0083164	1066	2
CIBOTTI PHILIP P JR	LTC	0-0023309	0867	1
CINORIC ROSE H	LTC	N-0001983	1068	2
CINI ALFRED A	MAJ	0-0072013	0768	2
CIRLOT JOSEPH S	COL	0-0019311	1057	1
CISTON MICHAEL F	CW4	W-0902914	0464	1
CIZON MAX N	COL	0-0050989	0157	2
CLAFFEE ROBERT A	COL	0-0030810	0964	1
CLAGETT CHARLES T	LTC	0-0020799	0360	1
CLAINOS PETER D	COL	0-0019269	1263	2
CLAIR CHARLIE L	CW4	W-0902915	1054	1
CLANTON HENRY M	COL	0-0030771	1160	1
CLAPP EDWIN G JR	COL	0-0024914	0666	1
CLAPP MARSHALL W	LTC	0-0069882	1167	1
CLAPP STACY W JR	COL	0-0030990	0268	1
CLAPPER CHARLES L	CW4	W-0902916	0854	1
CLAPPER GERALD M	CW4	W-0902107	1064	1
CLAPPER JOHN JR	COL	0-0042835	0562	1
CLAPS LUIGI F	COL	0-0039855	0759	2
CLARDY RAY A	COL	0-0065488	1267	1
CLARK ALFRED K	COL	0-0032608	0862	1
CLARK ALICE B	LTC	N-0001870	0960	2
CLARK ALLEN B JR	CPT	0-0098637	0968	2
CLARK ALLEN F JR	B G	0-0018669	0161	1
CLARK ANNA E W	1LT	N-0000629	1047	1
CLARK CAREY A	LTC	0-0051315	0660	1
CLARK CARL V	LTC	0-0040393	1167	1
CLARK CHARLES P JR	LTC	0-0024423	0859	1
CLARK CHARLES T	COL	0-0040070	0667	2
CLARK CHESTER M II	LTC	0-0069620	0766	1
CLARK CHESTER W	M G	0-0041908	0665	1
CLARK CUYLER L JR	B G	0-0022947	0966	2
CLARK ERNEST C JR	LTC	0-0042834	0864	1
CLARK FELIE W	MAJ	M-0010002	1154	1
CLARK FRANCIS M	COL	0-0038931	0268	1
CLARK FRANK S	B G	0-0002551	1145	2
CLARK GERALD H	CPT	0-0047206	0950	2
CLARK HAROLD F	COL	0-0030040	1063	1
CLARK HARRY A	COL	0-0006141	0848	1
CLARK HOWARD L	LTC	0-0040928	0868	1
CLARK HOWARD W	COL	0-0023698	0268	1
CLARK JACK A	COL	0-0031496	0964	1
CLARK JAMES B	LTC	0-0031723	0563	1
CLARK JAMES F	COL	0-0043161	1066	1
CLARK JAMES L	COL	0-0058743	0759	1
CLARK JAMES P	LTC	0-0040342	0660	1
CLARK JAMES T	LTC	0-0033773	1065	1
CLARK JOHN B	COL	0-0032695	0968	1
CLARK JOHN E	LTC	0-0081974	0467	1
CLARK JULIUS F JR	LTC	0-0060841	0767	1
CLARK LEROY F JR	COL	0-0032863	0167	1
CLARK LESTER H	LTC	0-0042945	1164	1
CLARK MARK W	GEN	0-0005309	1053	1
CLARK MAURICE N	COL	0-0042690	1263	1
CLARK MELVIN D	COL	0-0023550	1266	1
CLARK MILTON H	COL	0-0020638	0767	1
CLARK ORVILL C	CW3	W-0902918	0859	1
CLARK PARIS W	CW4	W-0902919	0368	2
CLARK PAUL JR	COL	0-0018118	0760	1
CLARK RAYMOND L	LTC	0-0027300	0765	1
CLARK RICHARD S	LTC	0-0084598	0168	1
CLARK ROBERT F	COL	0-0023911	0867	1
CLARK ROBERT L	LTC	0-0050575	0865	1
CLARK ROBERT W	LTC	0-0026032	0764	2
CLARK ROBERT W JR	LTC	0-0003091	1122	1
CLARK STANLEY A	MAJ	0-0012932	0934	2
CLARK THEODORE S	COL	0-0039998	1265	1

NAME	GRADE	SVC NO	DATE RET MO YR	RET CODE
CLARK THOMAS A	COL	0-0002207	0642	2
CLARK THOMAS L	COL	0-0006009	1143	1
CLARK THOMAS R	LTC	0-0057148	0868	1
CLARK THOMAS R	CW3	W-0902921	0261	1
CLARK WILLIAM D	MAJ	0-0027448	0455	2
CLARK WILLIAM H	CPT	0-0014281	0920	2
CLARK WILLIAM J	LTC	0-0079773	0763	1
CLARK WILLIAM R	COL	0-0031506	0961	1
CLARK WILLIAM S	LTC	0-0021937	0347	2
CLARKE BRUCE C	GEN	0-0016068	0562	1
CLARKE CARTER W	B G	0-0011682	0854	1
CLARKE CHRISTIAN	M G	0-0018213	0163	1
CLARKE ERNEST M	COL	0-0019183	0863	1
CLARKE FRANKLIN W	COL	0-0029792	0662	1
CLARKE HOWARD P JR	LTC	0-0036505	0863	1
CLARKE JOHN	CW2	W-0901359	0343	1
CLARKE LOGAN	COL	0-0017713	0859	1
CLARKE MARGARET G	COL	N-0000745	0868	1
CLARKE TILLIE C	MAJ	N-0002354	0360	1
CLARKE WILLIAM E	CW3	W-0904097	0263	2
CLARKIN THOMAS R	COL	0-0019983	0462	1
CLARKSON HERBERT S	B G	0-0003605	0546	2
CLARY THOMAS C	LTC	0-0069621	1168	1
CLASSEY GERTRUDE M	MAJ	N-0002038	0360	1
CLATERBOS HENRY L	LTC	0-0089751	0764	1
CLAUSSEN ESTER	LTC	N-0002217	1159	1
CLAUSSEN GEORGE C	CPT	0-0015624	1039	2
CLAUSSEN JOHN S	CPT	0-0006978	0934	2
CLAUTICE EDWARD W	LTC	0-0079774	0964	1
CLAY CARMON L	COL	0-0032673	0267	1
CLAY JAMES O	COL	0-0042666	1163	1
CLAY LUCIUS DUB	GEN	0-0009318	0549	1
CLAY ROBERT P	COL	0-0016212	0755	1
CLAY ROY U	COL	0-0043072	0967	1
CLAY WILLIAM L	COL	0-0023059	0966	1
CLAYMAN DONALD C	B G	0-0020866	0765	1
CLAYPOOL CHARLES B	COL	0-0043693	1166	1
CLAYTON LAWRENCE L	COL	0-0009679	0753	1
CLAYTON REX P	COL	0-0029296	1263	1
CLEAR WARREN J	COL	0-0009753	1135	2
CLEARY EDWARD R	COL	0-0026304	1067	1
CLEARY LOUIS K	LTC	0-0054965	0663	1
CLEARY THOMAS J JR	COL	0-0023998	0868	1
CLEAVER RICHARD	CW4	W-0902923	0166	2
CLEAVES HASKELL H	COL	0-0016253	0755	1
CLEER CLYDE E	CW4	W-0906566	0756	1
CLEGG WILLIAM J JR	COL	0-0037542	0867	1
CLEGHORN RUFUS J	MAJ	0-0052767	0861	1
CLELAND JOSEPH P	M G	0-0016239	0655	1
CLELAND RALPH P	COL	0-0029178	0360	1
CLEM CARRELL A JR	LTC	0-0069470	0968	1
CLEM RHOMAN E	COL	0-0051457	1163	1
CLEM WESLEY A JR	COL	0-0052012	0568	2
CLEMA JOE A	COL	0-0043020	0367	1
CLEMENS CHESTER C	CW4	W-0902924	0565	2
CLEMENSON WENDELL L	COL	0-0006975	0-45	2
CLEMENT JOHN K	COL	0-0002992	0642	2
CLEMENT WILLIAM J JR	LTC	0-0065039	0368	2
CLEMENTS THOMAS M	COL	0-0031735	1161	2
CLENDENEN CLARENCE C	COL	0-0012725	0354	1
CLEVE EDWARD A	COL	0-0020510	0857	1
CLEVELAND ALBERT C	CPT	0-0007312	0934	2
CLEVELAND EDWIN I	LTC	0-0088631	0968	1
CLEVELAND JOHN A JR	COL	0-0019136	0657	1
CLEVELAND JOHN G	LTC	0-0026559	0467	1
CLEVELAND JOHN H	LTC	0-0059468	1165	1
CLEVELAND KATHRYN D	MAJ	L-0000061	0959	1
CLEVELAND ROBERT E	LTC	0-0036664	0764	1
CLEVERLY RICHARD D	COL	0-0021862	0866	1
CLEWELL EDGAR L	B G	0-0007081	1146	2
CLIFFE ROBERT A	COL	0-0029515	0161	1
CLIFFORD CARLETON M	COL	0-0018199	0760	1
CLIFFORD CHARLES L	COL	0-0003749	0747	1
CLIFFORD RICHARD W	LTC	0-0036761	0161	1
CLIFFORD WALTER H	COL	0-0033033	0868	1

NAME	GRADE	SVC NO	DATE RET MO YR	RET CODE
CLIFT MILDRED A	MAJ	N-0001832	0365	1
CLIFTON CHESTER V JR	M G	0-0020246	0865	1
CLIFTON JOHN R	COL	0-0030148	0464	1
CLINE EDBERT C	LTC	0-0080659	0766	1
CLINE JESSE T	CW4	W-0902926	0657	1
CLINEBELL GLENN L	COL	0-0030109	0264	1
CLIREHUGH ROBERT W	COL	0-0031833	0568	2
CLOCK RAYMOND M	COL	0-0022920	0965	1
CLORE DUNCAN D	LTC	0-0026642	0865	1
CLOUDT OTTO B JR	COL	0-0023462	0868	1
CLOUGH CASPER JR	COL	0-0021979	0767	1
CLOVIS ERNEST R	MAJ	0-0068022	0967	1
CLOW JAMES M	COL	0-0029364	1157	1
CLOW KELSO G	COL	0-0019784	0865	1
CLUME FRANCIS J	COL	0-0010756	0851	1
CLYDE GORDON F	LTC	0-0047271	1163	1
CLYMER BARBARA A	MAJ	N-0000409	0366	1
CLYMER DAVID C	COL	0-0027125	0968	1
COAN BERNARD F	MAJ	0-0078765	0664	1
COAN JACK L	COL	0-0020908	0157	2
COARD LOUISE M	MAJ	N-0001577	0964	1
COATES CHARLES E JR	LTC	0-0021746	0867	1
COATES CHARLES F	COL	0-0030433	0662	1
COATES CHARLES H	COL	0-0015710	0249	2
COATES DONALD L	COL	0-0031912	0666	1
COATES EDWARD A JR	COL	0-0004074	0149	2
COATES HARRY L	LTC	0-0010651	1041	1
COATNEY LOREN C	MAJ	0-0058340	0766	1
COATS JAMES G	COL	0-0031260	1265	1
COBALIS VINCENT J	CW3	W-0906667	0965	1
COBB ARTHUR L	LTC	0-0016845	0755	1
COBB JOSEPH F	LTC	0-0059990	1168	1
COBB LAWRENCE L	COL	0-0010300	0848	1
COBB ROBERT B	COL	0-0033025	0865	1
COBURN GEORGE C	LTC	0-0031025	1163	1
COBURN WILLIAM T	CPT	0-0050279	0263	1
COCANOUGHER EUGENE H	COL	0-0038673	0960	1
COCHEU STEPHEN D	LTC	0-0019925	0655	1
COCHICK MADELEINE	CPT	N-0000371	0948	2
COCHRAN AVERY M	COL	0-0018834	0962	2
COCHRAN JAMES H	COL	0-0021945	0564	1
COCHRAN JAMES W JR	COL	0-0089326	1266	1
COCHRAN JOHN H	COL	0-0003814	1046	1
COCHRAN LORIS R	B G	0-0018889	0862	1
COCHRAN WALTER B	LTC	0-0053411	1168	1
COCKE ALEXANDER	MAJ	0-0014214	0-19	2
COCKE JAMES W	LTC	0-0035168	0561	1
COCKE JOSEPH G	COL	0-0019658	0661	1
COCKRELL JAMES K JR	LTC	0-0024805	0864	1
COCKRILL JOHN C	LTC	0-0024730	0862	1
COCKRILL MCFARLAND	COL	0-0004938	1046	2
CODDINGTON HARVEY W	COL	0-0029316	0664	1
CODE JAMES A JR	M G	0-0005274	0346	1
CODER HAROLD E	COL	0-0018302	0655	1
CODY THOMAS J	COL	0-0017190	0355	2
COE EDWARD H	COL	0-0014759	0854	1
COE MERTON S	LTC	0-0052876	0660	1
COE WILLIAM C	1LT	0-0012637	1026	2
COELING ETHEL W	LTC	M-0010104	0267	1
COEYMAN WILLIAM M	LTC	0-0051316	0660	1
COFFEY JOSEPH I	COL	0-0021904	0860	1
COFFEY PHILIP T	CPT	0-0008121	0527	2
COFFEY ROBERT E	COL	0-0028974	0358	1
COFFEY WILLIAM D JR	COL	0-0060341	0968	1
COFFEY WILLIAM W	LTC	0-0080663	0763	2
COFFIN EDWARD C JR	COL	0-0051259	1061	1
COFFIN FRANK P	COL	0-0007981	0847	1
COFFIN RALPH B	COL	0-0038895	0964	1
COFFIN SANFORD	LTC	0-0080386	0966	1
COFFMAN GEORGE W JR	COL	0-0042293	1263	1
COFFMAN ROY F	CW4	W-0902930	0367	1
COGSWELL WILLIAM N	COL	0-0041945	1061	1
COHEN BELLE K	MAJ	M-0010059	0165	1
COHEN EPHRAIM B	LTC	0-0022781	0746	2
COHN MERRILL R	LTC	0-0058342	1268	1

NAME	GRADE	SVC NO	DATE RET MO YR	RET CODE
COHOLAN PHILIP F	COL	0-0010592	0445	2
COINER BEVERLY H	COL	0-0004720	0149	1
COKER DAVID W	CW2	W-0901666	1150	2
COKER SEARS Y	COL	0-0023697	1167	1
COLACICCO FRANK	LTC	0-0023174	1047	2
COLBY ELBRIDGE	COL	0-0008150	0848	1
COLBY JOSEPH M	B G	0-0017562	0959	1
COLE ALBERT S	CW4	W-0902931	0463	1
COLE CHARLES B JR	COL	0-0039304	0968	1
COLE EVERETT B	CW2	W-0902932	1160	1
COLE FRANK L	B G	0-0004114	0650	1
COLE GEORGE M	LTC	0-0017107	0150	1
COLE GEORGE R	LTC	0-0020842	0758	1
COLE GLENN	COL	0-0019917	0865	1
COLE HUBERT M	COL	0-0016144	0655	2
COLE JAMES P	MAJ	0-0014215	1019	2
COLE JOHN D	B G	0-0019749	0164	1
COLE JOHN L JR	CPT	0-0036092	0349	2
COLE JOHN S	LTC	0-0079700	0367	1
COLE JOHN T	B G	0-0005256	0553	1
COLE LOREN F	CPT	0-0019416	0242	2
COLE LYDON B	COL	0-0029848	0163	1
COLE NORMAN E	LTC	0-0032484	0964	1
COLE PAUL W	COL	0-0012956	0554	2
COLE RICHARD A	CPT	0-0065080	0355	2
COLE ROBERT H	COL	0-0029798	0562	1
COLE ROY W JR	COL	0-0020277	1263	1
COLE SAMUEL J	MAJ	0-0014428	0520	2
COLE THELMA L	MAJ	N-0000553	0455	1
COLEMAN BRUCE S	LTC	0-0058862	0664	1
COLEMAN BYERS H	LTC	0-0043342	1065	1
COLEMAN CHARLIE C	COL	0-0024987	0365	1
COLEMAN DARRELL D	CPT	0-5225151	0866	1
COLEMAN EUNICE S	MAJ	N-0002218	0558	1
COLEMAN HOWARD	COL	0-0029457	0858	1
COLEMAN HUBERT P	LTC	0-0042336	0462	1
COLEMAN HUGHE D	COL	0-0039848	0960	1
COLEMAN IRVING M	COL	0-0031715	1267	1
COLEMAN JAMES C JR	COL	0-0030053	1163	1
COLEMAN JAMES M	COL	0-0041582	0459	1
COLEMAN JOSEPH L	LTC	0-0024527	0960	1
COLEMAN OTTO I	CW4	W-0902373	0263	1
COLEMAN RENNIE C JR	LTC	0-0069886	1066	1
COLEMAN WALTER L	COL	0-0038738	0463	1
COLEMAN WILLIAM D	1LT	0-0014406	0120	2
COLEMAN 3RD F W	B G	0-0019216	0858	1
COLHOUN DANIEL W	MAJ	0-0005949	0226	2
COLHOUN ROSALIE D	LTC	N-0000029	0855	1
COLLADAY EDGAR B	B G	0-0002902	0846	2
COLLART JOSEPH H	COL	0-0023447	0468	2
COLLEY ERNEST J	COL	0-0081891	1268	2
COLLEY HENNING F	COL	0-0014007	0-20	1
COLLIER CLAY O	COL	0-0042928	0561	1
COLLIER H R	CW4	W-0902933	1062	2
COLLIER JAMES R	CPT	0-0062972	0652	2
COLLIER JAMES V	COL	0-0015474	0753	2
COLLIER JOHN H	LTG	0-0012388	0958	1
COLLIER JOHN H	CW4	W-0904098	0868	1
COLLIER ROBERT P	CW4	W-0902934	0160	1
COLLIER WILLIAM A	B G	0-0007598	0854	1
COLLINGS HELEN W	MAJ	N-0002848	0168	1
COLLINGS KENT J	LTC	0-0080387	0567	1
COLLINS ARTHUR H JR	LTC	0-0065500	0767	1
COLLINS CARTER	COL	0-0006959	0846	2
COLLINS CHARLES F JR	COL	0-0084043	0863	1
COLLINS CLAUDE O	LTC	0-0014907	0442	2
COLLINS ESTHER R	MAJ	N-0000570	0561	1
COLLINS GERALD J	COL	0-0029221	0961	1
COLLINS HORACE R	LTC	0-0030845	1060	2
COLLINS HUBERT W	COL	0-0008877	1047	1
COLLINS J LAWTON	GEN	0-0005247	0356	1
COLLINS JAMES F	GEN	0-0016819	0364	1
COLLINS JOHN E	LTC	0-0023116	0761	1
COLLINS JOHN S	CW4	W-0902935	0967	1
COLLINS LAWRENCE E	LTC	0-0011862	0-36	2

NAME	GRADE	SVC NO	DATE RET MO YR	RET CODE
COLLINS LEROY P	B G	0-0002203	0345	2
COLLINS MATTHEW R JR	COL	0-0033550	0962	1
COLLINS PHILIP R	LTC	0-0080666	0767	1
COLLINS RICHARD	M G	0-0029375	1264	1
COLLINS SAMUEL P	B G	0-0016444	0756	1
COLLINS WILLIAM F	LTC	0-0019698	0263	1
COLLISON CORA E	MAJ	N-0000517	0350	1
COLLISON TOM D	LTC	0-0023868	0661	1
COLMAN CHARLES C	COL	0-0041649	0260	2
COLONNA JOHN O	COL	0-0015099	0954	1
COLQUITT RAWLINS M	COL	0-0024189	1066	2
COLSON CHARLES F	B G	0-0012173	0753	1
COLT JOHN B	LTC	0-0080667	0866	2
COLTON ROGER B	M G	0-0002975	0146	2
COLVIN GEORGE T	COL	0-0030434	0565	1
COLVIN LLOYD D	LTC	0-0032853	0161	1
COLVIN REED N	LTC	0-0051190	0159	1
COLWELL LEONARD F	COL	0-0031358	0966	1
COLWELL RUSSELL M	LTC	0-0038839	1157	1
COLYER BETTY L	LTC	N-0001206	0463	1
COMELLA MARTIN S	COL	0-0031084	0161	1
COMERFORD RICHARD W	CW4	W-0902938	1265	1
COMFORT FREDERIC D	COL	0-0014714	0754	1
COMINA MARIE A	MAJ	N-0002406	1262	1
COMMERFORD LEON JR	COL	0-0040293	1068	1
COMPER JOHN B	CW4	W-0902939	0565	1
COMPTON LOUIS	COL	0-0007419	1051	1
COMPTON MARTIN A	COL	0-0021038	0758	1
COMPTON THOMAS C	COL	0-0020692	1057	1
COMPTON WILLIAM L	LTC	0-0057447	0868	1
COMSTOCK RICHARD H	COL	0-0051206	0361	1
CONABLE MORRIS E	COL	0-0007989	1046	1
CONANT PERRY E	COL	0-0021357	0865	2
CONANT RALPH E	COL	0-0065408	0367	1
CONARD ARTHUR B	COL	0-0003094	1045	1
CONDON JACK G	COL	0-0045542	0968	[illegible]
CONDON JOHN F	LTC	0-0039972	0460	2
CONDON MARGARET W	MAJ	L-0000079	0461	1
CONDY WILLIAM	COL	0-0025220	0267	1
CONE HAROLD E	COL	0-0043100	1167	1
CONE JOHN D	COL	0-0017683	0959	1
CONE MONTIE F	COL	0-0029695	0462	1
CONE SIDNEY L	COL	0-0040362	0561	2
CONER CHARLES E	LTC	0-0078643	0864	[illegible]
CONFER RODNEY R	LTC	0-0058865	1166	1
CONGDON NORMAN A	LTC	0-0017602	0246	2
CONINE JAMES C	COL	0-0030203	0666	1
CONINE ROBERT E	COL	0-0024393	1068	1
CONK ROBERT H	COL	0-0029909	[illegible]	1
CONKLIN ALVIN R	LTC	0-0084352	0661	1
CONKLIN JOHN F	B G	0-0003777	0451	1
CONLEY EDGAR T JR	B G	0-0017665	0859	2
CONLEY SAMUEL G	B G	0-0015707	1155	1
CONLEY VICTOR G	COL	0-0023276	0568	1
CONLEY WILLIAM H	COL	0-0030823	0867	1
CONLIN PAUL A	LTC	0-0042111	1060	[illegible]
CONLON MARCELLA A	MAJ	M-0010035	0360	1
CONN ARCHIE E JR	LTC	0-0063307	0763	1
CONN ARTHUR F	COL	0-0029869	0563	2
CONN CHARLES	COL	0-0032550	0966	1
CONNALLY WILLIAM P	COL	0-0017567	0857	1
CONNATSER WILLIAM T	LTC	0-0005354	0834	2
CONNAWAY CHARLES E	LTC	0-0065130	0868	1
CONNELL FLORENCE T	MAJ	N-0000337	0464	1
CONNELL JOHN F	COL	0-0011535	1046	2
CONNELL MARY B	LTC	N-0000122	[illegible]	2
CONNELLY JOHN R	MAJ	0-0065135	[illegible]	1
CONNELLY MARY F	MAJ	L-0000230	0758	1
CONNER HASKETT L	COL	0-0004181	0848	1
CONNER HASKETT L JR	COL	0-0021855	1168	1
CONNER KARL	COL	0-0031686	1167	1
CONNER LEO B	COL	0-0008617	0448	1
CONNER RAY C	COL	0-0024162	0447	2
CONNER STEVEN L	COL	0-0015122	0354	2
CONNER STEVEN L JR	LTC	0-0028432	0766	1

NAME	GRADE	SVC NO	DATE RET MO YR	RET CODE
CONNERAT WILLIAM H	COL	0-0040730	0763	1
CONNERS JOHN J	LTC	0-0030334	0961	1
CONNIFF MICHAEL J	CW2	W-0904241	0949	1
CONNOLLY DONALD H	M G	0-0002431	0248	1
CONNOLLY FRANCIS J	CW3	W-0902343	0862	1
CONNOLLY HAVILAND A	COL	0-0031575	0765	1
CONNOLLY THOMAS W	LTC	0-0058308	1165	1
CONNOR EDWARD H	COL	0-0009837	0854	1
CONNOR ELINOR J	MAJ	L-0000324	0964	1
CONNOR GEORGE H	COL	0-0011177	1152	1
CONNOR JAMES W	COL	0-0029479	1060	1
CONNOR JOHN P	COL	0-0029860	0867	1
CONNOR MARGARET E	MAJ	N-0000387	1065	1
CONNOR MARY E A	2LT	R-0001010	0845	1
CONNOR PARKER E JR	LTC	0-0023491	0863	1
CONNOR ROBERT T	COL	0-0038622	0157	1
CONNOR VORIS H	COL	0-0015405	0152	2
CONNOR WILLIAM M	B G	0-0020137	0865	1
CONNORS AMY L	MAJ	N-0000809	0266	1
CONNORS WILLIAM J	LTC	0-0091977	0965	1
CONQUEST WARD W	COL	0-0041630	1159	1
CONRAD D BRYAN	B G	0-0012226	1046	1
CONRAD GEORGE F	COL	0-0037473	0468	1
CONRAD HAROLD A	COL	0-0039654	0362	2
CONRAD VINCENT J	COL	0-0012153	0753	2
CONRAN RICHARD J	COL	0-0029820	1262	1
CONROY EDWARD T	1LT	0-0064594	1154	2
CONROY ROBERT J JR	LTC	0-0031321	0161	1
CONSTANCE PHILIP W	LTC	0-0024118	1062	1
CONSTANT SAMUEL V	COL	0-0004738	1046	2
CONWAY HAROLD J	COL	0-0014609	0854	1
CONWAY JAMES C	LTC	0-0063795	0167	1
CONWAY LEO J	COL	0-0041903	0861	1
CONWAY LEWIS W	COL	0-0037021	1067	1
CONWAY WALTER E	LTC	0-0081978	0865	1
COOEY ARCHIE W	1LT	0-0012461	1134	1
COOGAN HENRY C	CW3	W-0902944	0763	1
COOK BENJAMIN F JR	COL	0-0032801	1268	1
COOK BRAINARD S	COL	0-0018144	0160	2
COOK CHARLES H	LTC	0-0034201	0863	1
COOK CHARLES W	MAJ	0-0065968	1266	1
COOK CHARLES W	CW2	W-0901572	0647	1
COOK CLAUDE T JR	CW4	W-0906673	0768	2
COOK DAVE J	COL	0-0030051	0761	1
COOK DONALD L	COL	0-0022259	0163	1
COOK EARLE F	M G	0-0018450	0763	1
COOK EUGENE	COL	0-0030736	0664	1
COOK EVERETT L	COL	0-0008798	1146	2
COOK FREDRIC C	COL	0-0019484	0864	1
COOK GEORGE G	LTC	0-0041090	0864	1
COOK GEORGE L	LTC	0-0035450	0367	1
COOK JAMES M	CW2	W-0905135	0760	1
COOK JAMES S JR	COL	0-0043655	1268	1
COOK JAMES W	CW3	W-0902945	0261	1
COOK JOHN C	COL	0-0009091	1045	2
COOK JOHN S JR	CPT	0-0025064	0444	2
COOK JOSEPH E JR	LTC	0-0032876	0661	1
COOK LLOYD H	COL	0-0004690	0846	2
COOK MARION F	MAJ	R-0010134	1068	1
COOK MAXWELL A	LTC	0-0059846	0763	1
COOK RICHARD H	COL	0-0079779	0966	1
COOK ROBERT J	COL	0-0054922	0868	1
COOK ROBERT L	B G	0-0017675	0958	1
COOK ROBERT W	MAJ	0-0088032	0460	2
COOK TRUMAN F	COL	0-0044727	0467	1
COOK WALTER H JR	LTC	0-0025466	0964	1
COOK WALTER R	COL	0-0020112	1050	2
COOK WILLIAM B JR	LTC	0-0076861	1163	1
COOK WILLIS E	CW3	W-0906674	0660	1
COOKE FREDERICK	COL	0-0029853	0961	1
COOKE LANE B JR	LTC	0-0056257	0663	2
COOKE SAMUEL L	COL	0-0018301	0559	1
COOKE THOMAS J	LTC	0-0045043	0262	1
COOKE WILLOUGHBY	CPT	0-0009722	0521	2
COOKSEY RICHARD W	COL	0-0003908	0547	2
COOKSON GEORGE M	COL	0-0032021	0164	1
COOL WILLIAM C	COL	0-0054108	1268	1
COOLEY GEORGE M	COL	0-0083544	1068	1
COOLEY HERBERT W	LTC	0-0039773	0157	1
COOLEY JOHN H	COL	0-0014603	1048	1
COOLEY LAVELL I	COL	0-0028658	1050	2
COOLIDGE GEORGE W	B G	0-0017599	0857	1
COOLIDGE JOSEPH B	COL	0-0018570	0561	1
COOMAS RAYMOND H	COL	0-0015561	0649	1
COONEY JAMES P	M G	0-0017338	0860	1
COONLEY WILLIAM J	MAJ	0-0036724	0261	1
COONS NORMAN M	COL	0-0056078	1168	1
COONTZ JOHN B	LTC	0-0023319	0759	1
COOPER AIREL B	COL	0-0017595	0859	2
COOPER AVERY J JR	COL	0-0019107	0758	1
COOPER CHARLES F	COL	0-0008040	1049	2
COOPER CHARLES G	COL	0-0033430	1057	2
COOPER EARL M	COL	0-0034191	1160	1
COOPER EUGENE G	COL	0-0019644	0964	1
COOPER FRANKLIN B	COL	0-0067804	1065	2
COOPER GEORGE J	CW4	W-0902949	1158	1
COOPER GEORGE T	COL	0-0035983	0567	2
COOPER HARRY B JR	COL	0-0018469	0761	1
COOPER HARRY W	COL	0-0042261	0157	1
COOPER JAMES G	COL	0-0010167	0849	2
COOPER MARCUS E	COL	0-0051327	0862	1
COOPER OSBORN	LTC	0-0044135	0561	1
COOPER PAUL	COL	0-0015748	0954	2
COOPER RALPH C	M G	0-0017741	1063	1
COOPER RANDOLPH G	LTC	0-0084353	0765	1
COOPER RICHMOND J	LTC	0-0057155	0768	1
COOPER RUSSELL B	LTC	0-0028938	1055	1
COOPER WIBB E	COL	0-0002819	0946	2
COOPER WILLIAM L	COL	0-0020100	0164	1
COOPER WILLIAM L	MAJ	0-0050866	1055	2
COOPER WILLIAM R	LTC	0-0080673	0867	2
COOPERIDER HOWARD V	LTC	0-0022035	0166	1
COOTE JOHN F	LTC	0-0031596	0765	1
COOTEY JOHN L	CPT	0-0014230	0120	2
COOTS FREDERICK	LTC	0-0050995	0856	1
COPE JESSE O	LTC	0-0008948	0136	1
COPELAND EDWARD A	LTC	0-0076862	0866	1
COPELAND JOHN E	B G	0-0004775	0446	2
COPELAND ROBERT M	COL	0-0008059	0547	1
COPLEY WILLIAM M JR	LTC	0-0039114	0962	1
COPMANN CHESTER J JR	LTC	0-0046636	1268	1
CORBETT ADELBERT F	CW4	W-0902952	0858	1
CORBETT JAMES B	COL	0-0018423	0761	1
CORBETT SEWELL M	COL	0-0004081	0845	2
CORBETT STANLEY B	CW4	W-0902124	0663	1
CORBETT WILLIAM H	COL	0-0021150	0961	1
CORBIN FRANCIS J	COL	0-0033399	1262	1
CORBLY JOHN B JR	COL	0-0022944	0868	2
CORDELL BEN E	COL	0-0015455	1153	1
CORDERMAN W PRESTON	M G	0-0016387	0958	2
CORDERO MARIO	COL	0-0007527	1045	1
CORDERO VIRGIL N	COL	0-0007472	0653	1
CORDERO VIRGIL N JR	LTC	0-0060181	0768	1
CORDES CLIFFORD F JR	COL	0-0020186	0864	1
COREY HAROLD L	COL	0-0056814	0264	1
COREY JOHN B JR	COL	0-0021415	0662	2
COREY KENNETH S	CW4	W-0902953	0664	1
COREY ROBERT R	COL	0-0034006	0968	1
CORGAN FRANCIS H	LTC	0-0042885	1064	1
CORKILL WILLIAM E	COL	0-0007055	0147	2
CORLETT CHARLES H	M G	0-0003746	0546	2
CORLEY JOHN T	B G	0-0021325	1066	1
CORLIES EARL L	CW2	W-0902954	0858	1
CORMACK THOMAS B	LTC	0-0057125	0768	1
CORMIER EVERETT L	COL	0-0032923	0764	1
CORNELL BERNICE R	MAJ	N-0002303	0465	1
CORNELL GORDON O	COL	0-0051531	0862	1
CORNELL JAMES O	CW4	W-0902955	0851	1
CORNELL KENNETH W	CW4	W-0902224	1265	1
CORNELL ROBERT W	LTC	0-0080676	0565	1
CORNELL THEODORE M	COL	0-0007279	0950	1
CORNELSON ARTHUR J	COL	0-0051567	0265	1
CORNETT JACK C	COL	0-0032772	0767	1
CORNISH GEORGE R F	COL	0-0004511	1033	2
CORR JAMES	COL	0-0051082	0360	2
CORRELL LOUIS W	COL	0-0039582	0564	1
CORRELL WALTER O	LTC	0-0040122	0664	2
CORRIGAN JOHN H	COL	0-0010063	0846	2
CORSENTINO LEONARD J	LTC	0-0061461	0568	1
CORT HUGH	B G	0-0011592	0954	1
CORTESI SILVIA	MAJ	L-0000336	0857	1
CORTEZ JAMES J	LTC	0-0053277	0566	2
CORUM DABNEY R	COL	0-0017001	0655	1
CORWIN CHARLES D	LTC	0-0038834	0664	1
CORY ALLAN M	COL	0-0080390	0568	2
CORY IRA W	COL	0-0019025	0859	1
COSBY J C	CW4	W-0902456	0956	1
COSBY WARREN G	LTC	0-0065710	0667	1
COSGROVE EDWARD J	CW3	W-0902957	0760	1
COSGROVE JAMES J	COL	0-0020768	0157	2
COSGROVE SHERMAN B	COL	0-0038990	0667	1
COSNER RICHARD E JR	MAJ	0-0035933	0448	2
COSTELLO DANIEL J	LTC	0-0057579	0664	1
COSTELLO DARREL G	COL	0-0023449	0566	1
COSTELLO NORMANDO A	M G	0-0017764	0864	1
COSTELLO THOMAS A	LTC	0-0065132	0868	1
COSTIGAN CHARLES H	LTC	0-0033336	0665	1
COTA NORMAN D	M G	0-0005284	0646	2
COTHRAN FRANCIS E	CPT	0-0014999	1039	2
COTTER ANASTATIA	MAJ	R-0010171	0266	2
COTTER ARTHUR E	COL	0-0079730	0662	1
COTTER CLARENCE F	COL	0-0004924	0854	1
COTTER EDWARD J	COL	0-0018346	0644	2
COTTINGHAM LEVIN B	LTC	0-0042955	0961	1
COTTON JOHN W	COL	0-0004856	0747	1
COTULLA LOUIS F	M G	0-0029069	0359	2
COUCH BUFORD J	LTC	0-0052969	0467	1
COUCH JOSEPH R	COL	0-0023039	1147	2
COUGHLIN JOHN G	COL	0-0018898	0754	1
COUGHLIN JOSEPH V	COL	0-0006351	0444	2
COUGHLIN ROBERT F	COL	0-0012027	0753	2
COUGHLIN WILLIAM L	COL	0-0015776	0754	1
COUGILL JOHN C	COL	0-0080391	0866	1
COUK HAROLD O	CW3	W-0906676	1060	1
COULTER CHARLES S	MAJ	0-0006250	0934	2
COULTER HALVOR G	MAJ	0-0014242	0420	2
COULTER HERBERT W JR	LTC	0-0084355	1263	1
COULTER JAMES E	LTC	0-0033386	0761	1
COULTER JOHN A	MAJ	0-0024454	0660	2
COULTER JOHN A	COL	0-0033541	0766	1
COULTER JOHN B	LTG	0-0003488	0152	1
COULTER JOSEPH S	COL	0-0081892	0268	1
COUNCIL FRANCIS F	COL	0-0016969	0357	2
COUNIHAN THOMAS J	COL	0-0017183	0758	1
COUPE LAURA C	MAJ	L-0000266	0266	1
COURSER MALCOLM W	COL	0-0042211	0761	2
COURSEY RICHARD W	COL	0-0012454	0449	1
COURSON EVERETT P JR	LTC	0-0039943	0757	2
COURTNEY RALPH H	MAJ	0-0035196	0862	1
COURVOISIE THOMAS N	LTC	0-0024549	0261	1
COUTTS JAMES W	B G	0-0018875	0762	1
COVELL WILLIAM E	M G	0-0003768	0540	1
COVERDALE GARRISON B	M G	0-0017148	0863	1
COVEY WILLIAM T	LTC	0-0031100	1164	1
COVINGTON CARROLL M	COL	0-0040083	1266	1
COWAN BRYAN	COL	0-0040850	1268	1
COWAN EGBERT W V	B G	0-0011744	0554	1
COWAN GERARD C	COL	0-0018807	0862	1
COWAN KAY K	COL	0-0052217	1068	1
COWARD RAYMOND	COL	0-0051495	1163	1
COWART BYRON F	LTC	0-0052415	0464	1
COWELL EVELYN M	LTC	N-0000339	0263	1
COWEN EDWARD T	COL	0-0051042	0859	1
COWGILL CHARLES J	COL	0-0037457	1167	1
COWLES CHARLES W	COL	0-0015231	0753	1
COWLES DAVID H	COL	0-0003111	0944	2
COWLES EUGENE H	COL	0-0010470	1051	1
COWLES HARPER B	COL	0-0051515	0764	1
COWLES MILES A	B G	0-0008577	0753	2
COWLES STUART L	COL	0-0015289	0753	2
COX AMEL L	COL	0-0043971	0168	1
COX ARTHUR L	LTC	0-0065305	0568	1
COX CHARLES T	LTC	0-0036699	0367	1
COX CLAUDE F	COL	0-0012921	1146	2
COX DANA D	LTC	0-0069472	1068	1
COX EARLE E	LTC	0-0012581	0631	2
COX EDNA L	MAJ	L-0000334	0959	2
COX EMMETT W JR	LTC	0-0037200	0464	1
COX HERBERT M	MAJ	0-0016017	0142	1
COX JAMES A	CW4	W-0902962	1057	1
COX JOHN F	COL	0-0041534	0758	1
COX LAVONNE E	COL	0-0020934	0661	1
COX NOEL M	COL	0-0019883	1057	2
COX RALPH L	COL	0-0029153	0359	1
COX ROBERT W	CW4	W-0907090	0465	1
COX WALTON W	COL	0-0007442	0146	1
COX WELDON W	COL	0-0051451	1163	1
COX WILLIAM H	COL	0-0033751	1268	1
COX WILLIAM S JR	LTC	0-0031720	0548	2
COY MALCOLM L	LTC	0-0070313	0568	1
COYKENDALL FREDERICK	LTC	0-0033694	1062	1
COYNE CHRISTOPHE	COL	0-0021879	1064	1
COYNE FREDERICK	COL	0-0010941	1047	1
COZART CLARENCE A	COL	0-0020152	0864	1
COZENS GEORGE D JR	CPT	OF-0103174	0568	2
CRABB FREDERICK	COL	0-0018172	1060	1
CRABB LEONARD F	CW4	W-0902964	0355	1
CRABILL EDWIN B	COL	0-0006769	0753	2
CRADDOCK WILLIAM P	LTC	0-0037952	0565	1
CRAFT FLOYD G	LTC	0-0060627	0868	1
CRAFT JOHN B	CW4	W-0902188	0557	1
CRAFT SETH O	COL	0-0016036	0555	2
CRAGIN JOHN M	LTC	0-0062412	0867	1
CRAGUN DRESDEN J	COL	0-0015390	0849	2
CRAIG ALLAN A	COL	0-0019621	0756	1
CRAIG ALMA G	CPT	N-0001076	0353	2
CRAIG CHARLES F	B G	0-0007231	0955	2
CRAIG CLAYTON C	LTC	0-0025262	0262	1
CRAIG D MARGUERI	MAJ	N-0001898	0161	1
CRAIG DAN E	COL	0-0031879	1265	1
CRAIG DAVID W	COL	0-0004786	0153	2
CRAIG FREDERICK	CPT	0-0017795	1033	2
CRAIG HARRY W	LTC	0-0080063	0867	1
CRAIG JAMES L	COL	0-0006942	0747	1
CRAIG JAMES T	COL	0-0021248	0766	1
CRAIG JOHN E	COL	0-0024784	0668	1
CRAIG JOHN S	CPT	0-0058868	0962	1
CRAIG LOUIS A	M G	0-0003575	0552	1
CRAIG MALCOLM E	COL	0-0008123	0451	1
CRAIG MALIN JR	COL	0-0015908	0854	1
CRAIG PAUL	COL	0-0052479	0668	1
CRAIG ROBERT J	LTC	0-0081981	1066	1
CRAIG WILLIAM A	LTC	0-0043505	0860	2
CRAIG WILLIAM C	MAJ	0-0023002	0744	2
CRAIG WILLIAM H	COL	0-0007242	0854	2
CRAIN JAMES K	M G	0-0001915	0642	2
CRAIN JOY B	MAJ	N-0001954	0659	1
CRALLE MAURY S	COL	0-0017279	0758	1
CRAMER CHARLES	LTC	0-0006090	0438	2
CRAMER FREDERIC M	LTC	0-0052273	0564	1
CRAMER MYRON C	M G	0-0003010	1145	1
CRANDALL FRANCIS N	COL	0-0084822	0766	2
CRANDALL HARRY W	M G	0-0016238	0858	1
CRANDALL MURRAY B	LTC	0-0015630	1147	1
CRANDALL ROBERT G	COL	0-0017652	0859	1
CRANDALL WALTER M	COL	0-0005648	0745	1
CRANE FRANCIS S	COL	0-0039664	0762	1
CRANE FRANK A	LTC	0-0011840	1039	2
CRANE GEORGE E	COL	0-0042377	0764	2
CRANE GLENN	COL	0-0046186	0366	1

UNITED STATES ARMY RETIRED LIST

NAME	GRADE	SVC NO	DATE RET MO YR	RET CODE
CRANE HAL P JR	MAJ	0-0054794	0562	1
CRANE RICHARD Z	COL	0-0009760	0854	1
CRANE WARREN F	COL	0-0042608	0765	1
CRANE WILLIAM C	B G	0-0003538	0247	1
CRANK JAMES R	COL	0-0051346	0859	1
CRANSTON JOSEPH A	B G	0-0012465	0748	1
CRANSTON ROBERT W JR	LTC	0-0063826	1165	1
CRARY FRANCES F	2LT	M-0001208	0945	2
CRARY FRANCIS W	COL	0-0014606	0651	1
CRATCH SAMUEL C	COL	0-0008145	1144	2
CRATE GRACE A	MAJ	N-0001113	0965	1
CRAVEN VIRGIL F	COL	0-0034824	0966	1
CRAVEN WILLIAM D	LTC	0-0053969	0163	1
CRAWFORD CLAUDE L	COL	0-0020266	0164	1
CRAWFORD DONALD A	LTC	0-0037481	0665	1
CRAWFORD GROVER L JR	COL	0-0079784	0766	1
CRAWFORD HAROLD P	COL	0-0021840	0767	1
CRAWFORD JAMES B	B G	0-0003088	0646	2
CRAWFORD JAMES P	COL	0-0030906	0566	1
CRAWFORD JOHN L	B G	0-0019343	1163	2
CRAWFORD JOSEPH B	B G	0-0019215	0360	2
CRAWFORD PAUL M	COL	0-0004093	0950	1
CRAWFORD ROBERT J	LTC	0-0038315	0762	2
CRAWFORD ROBERT N	COL	0-0035353	0767	1
CRAWFORD ROBERT W	M G	0-0003667	1048	1
CRAWFORD ROSCOE C	M G	0-0003345	1149	1
CRAWFORD THOMAS M	COL	0-0012317	0854	1
CRAWLEY JOHN L JR	COL	0-0053963	0866	1
CRAZE JAMES H	LTC	0-0053279	0266	1
CREAMER JOSEPH K	COL	0-0010120	0245	2
CREAMER RAYMOND J	LTC	0-0037472	1263	1
CREASY WILLIAM M	M G	0-0016397	0858	1
CRECELIUS HERBERT F	LTC	0-0025187	0859	1
CREEK ROY E	COL	0-0039099	0867	1
CREEL BUCKNER M	LTC	0-0008460	0832	2
CREHAN JOHN P	COL	0-0009736	0844	2
CREIGHTON ROBERT R	COL	0-0042161	0762	2
CRESSMAN FREDERIC E	LTC	0-0019635	0146	2
CREUSERE MELVILLE S	COL	0-0009065	1146	2
CREWS HARRY C JR	CPT	0-0061871	0759	2
CREWS LEONARD F	COL	0-0007357	0251	2
CRIBB WILLIAM J JR	LTC	0-0060695	0265	1
CRICHLOW R W JR	M G	0-0012430	0254	2
CRIGGER HERMAN J	COL	0-0011070	0152	2
CRIGLER ELLEN G	MAJ	N-0000246	0161	1
CRIM CHARLES H	MAJ	0-0014775	0940	2
CRIM STERLING M	COL	0-0010150	1046	1
CRIMMINS JOSEPH J	COL	0-0043265	0668	1
CRISSON ROBERT C	COL	0-0036520	0968	1
CRIST WILLIAM E	B G	0-0012828	1155	2
CRISTO ANTHONY B	LTC	0-0062849	1066	1
CRISWELL HOWARD D	COL	0-0015999	0551	1
CRITTENBERGER W D	LTG	0-0003549	1052	1
CRITTENDEN EDNA F	MAJ	N-0002411	0563	1
CROCKER WILLIAM S JR	COL	0-0021074	0868	1
CROCKETT CLEMENT W	LTC	0-0020168	0346	2
CROCKETT CRESTON W	CPT	0-0060462	0563	1
CROCKETT GILMAN K	COL	0-0007381	0550	1
CROCKETT JOHN J	LTC	0-0059848	0864	1
CROFT LUCIAN C	LTC	0-0032189	0964	1
CROMBEZ MARCEL G	B G	0-0016198	0156	1
CROMELIN JOHN M	LTC	0-0020597	0758	1
CROMWELL JACK D	COL	0-0042346	0464	1
CROMWELL SAMUEL M	LTC	0-0032176	0766	1
CRON LUCIUS N	COL	0-0018411	0858	1
CRON ROBERT F JR	COL	0-0018127	0857	1
CRONIN PATRICK M	LTC	0-0040786	0863	1
CRONINGER CARL P	LTC	0-0024507	0166	1
CRONK JEFFERSON	COL	0-0030461	0463	1
CRONRATH CLETUS	CW3	W-0902968	1060	1
CROOK GERARD R	COL	0-0039713	0461	1
CROSBY CHARLES P	COL	0-0029435	0955	2
CROSBY GEORGE D	COL	0-0015512	0954	1
CROSBY GEORGE J	LTC	0-0056157	0467	1
CROSBY HENRY A	COL	0-0043102	1163	1

NAME	GRADE	SVC NO	DATE RET MO YR	RET CODE
CROSBY PAUL M	LTC	0-0060837	0966	1
CROSBY RALPH D	COL	0-0033981	0766	2
CROSBY ROGER M	COL	0-0051299	0562	1
CROSBY WILLIAM H JR	COL	0-0024639	0965	2
CROSNO GLADYS M	MAJ	N-0002056	1160	1
CROSS CLIFFORD F	LTC	0-0051733	0464	1
CROSS JACK	LTC	0-0069892	1167	1
CROSS KENNETH W	LTC	0-0035852	0864	1
CROSS WILLIAM O	CW4	W-0904242	0664	1
CROSSEN FLORA C	MAJ	N-0002397	0662	1
CROSSETT FREDERICK	LTC	0-0039963	0263	1
CROSSMAN EDWARD B	COL	0-0042428	0964	1
CROSSMAN RAYMOND S	COL	0-0032583	0566	1
CROSSON WILLIAM H JR	COL	0-0024880	0667	2
CROSSWHITE CLYDE C	LTC	0-0040750	0765	1
CROSWELL MYRTLE A	MAJ	N-0002053	1160	1
CROTEAU LIONEL J	CW2	W-0901704	0954	1
CROTTY MELVIN W	LTC	0-0026985	0965	1
CROUCH EDWARD O	LTC	0-0079785	0268	1
CROUCHER MELVILLE E	CW4	W-0906680	0767	1
CROUGH JAMES A	CPT	0-0058872	1162	1
CROW CARROLL S	CW4	W-0906682	0461	1
CROWDER JAMES H	CW4	W-0906683	0859	1
CROWELL ALBERT W	LTC	0-0052319	0167	1
CROWELL EVANS R	B G	0-0007387	0854	1
CROWELL HAROLD B	COL	0-0008201	0752	2
CROWELL THELMA	CPT	N-0000121	0459	1
CROWELL WILLIAM H JR	LTC	0-0084547	0768	1
CROWLEY ROBERT W	LTC	0-0050171	0865	1
CROWN FRANCIS J	COL	0-0023031	0766	1
CROWNOVER ROBERT L	COL	0-0042968	0764	1
CRUIKSHANK RALPH H	LTC	0-0060803	0566	1
CRUISE EDWARD E	LTC	0-0017738	0656	2
CRUM MAGDALEN I	MAJ	L-0000010	1053	1
CRUMLISH WILLIAM S	COL	0-0045536	1267	1
CRUMP FREDERIC M	LTC	0-0065530	0165	1
CRUMP IRA A	COL	0-0005250	0352	2
CRUMP WILLUS W	CW4	W-0902970	0666	1
CRUSE CHARLES F	COL	0-0056802	0655	1
CRUSE RALPH E	COL	0-0009307	0453	1
CRUZ ALFRED J	LTC	0-0090215	0868	1
CRUZAN WINSTON V	COL	0-0030981	1167	1
CRYSTAL THOMAS L	COL	0-0001946	0-42	1
CUBBISON DONALD C JR	COL	0-0019204	0759	1
CUBBISON GORDON R	LTC	0-0060234	0265	1
CUBRIA MERCEDES O	MAJ	L-0000006	0753	1
CUDE HAROLD E JR	LTC	0-0080394	0665	1
CUDLIPP RALPH L	COL	0-0008817	0346	1
CULBRETH OLIVER C	COL	0-0030429	0665	1
CULLEN JOE C	COL	0-0079786	1168	2
CULLEN MARY B	MAJ	N-0002367	1059	1
CULLEN ROBERT E	COL	0-0015700	1047	2
CULLETON JOHN R	COL	0-0012653	0652	2
CULLEY FRANK J	COL	0-0030117	1163	1
CULLINAN EDWARD J	LTC	0-0044604	0963	2
CULLINGWORTH WILLIAM	CW3	W-0902973	0963	1
CULLIS ROBERT E	COL	0-0031942	0868	2
CULLISON GEORGE B	LTC	0-0025193	0865	1
CULLY IRENE E	LTC	N-0000614	0861	1
CULMAN IONE M	CPT	N-0002280	0557	2
CULP CLARENCE M	COL	0-0004953	0852	1
CULP JAMES L	LTC	0-0045508	0866	1
CULP WILLIAM W	COL	0-0018821	0762	2
CULPEPPER GENEVA H	MAJ	N-0002121	1059	1
CULPEPPER JOSEPH T	CPT	0-0065972	0165	1
CULTON A Y	COL	0-0010164	0348	2
CULTON HUGH G	COL	0-0010325	0151	2
CUMBIE THOMAS A	LTC	0-0040542	0566	1
CUMINGS CHARLES S JR	COL	0-0025120	0667	1
CUMMING WILLIAM F	COL	0-0079701	0467	1
CUMMINGS ALEXANDER	COL	0-0008190	0651	1
CUMMINGS ANN	MAJ	L-0000322	0964	1
CUMMINGS ARTHUR B	LTC	0-0078778	0768	1
CUMMINGS EDWIN A	COL	0-0017222	0758	1
CUMMINGS EMERSON L	LTG	0-0015500	0462	1

NAME	GRADE	SVC NO	DATE RET MO YR	RET CODE
CUMMINGS HAROLD L	LTC	0-0031194	0656	1
CUMMINGS KENNETH M	CPT	0-0060526	0863	1
CUMMINGS LAWRENCE F	COL	0-0029392	0462	2
CUMMINGS RALPH B	LTC	0-0039527	1053	1
CUMMINGS S FRED JR	COL	0-0019796	0865	2
CUMPSON MERVIN	CW4	W-0902977	0866	1
CUNDIFF ELLSWORTH	LTC	0-0034847	0866	1
CUNDIFF HELEN E	MAJ	N-0001670	0763	1
CUNDIFF ISAAC W	LTC	0-0043096	0865	1
CUNDIFF VIRGINIA E	MAJ	N-0000850	0862	1
CUNDY ELSIE M	MAJ	N-0002718	1167	1
CUNIN KENNETH A	COL	0-0019481	0759	1
CUNKLE AUSTIN C	COL	0-0015303	0954	1
CUNNINGHAM ELEANOR R	MAJ	N-0002408	0763	2
CUNNINGHAM ELMO F	LTC	0-0028618	0567	1
CUNNINGHAM FRANK J	COL	0-0012145	0646	2
CUNNINGHAM HAROLD D	LTC	0-0065973	0767	1
CUNNINGHAM JOHN H	COL	0-0051325	0862	1
CUNNINGHAM JULIAN W	M G	0-0004922	0552	1
CUNNINGHAM MARTIN	COL	0-0040059	0863	1
CUNNINGHAM MELVIN F	MAJ	0-0041146	1062	1
CUNNINGHAM ROBERT K	COL	0-0037120	1168	1
CUNNINGHAM THOMAS J	COL	0-0079787	0667	1
CUNNINGHAM WILLIAM A	M G	0-0019579	0466	1
CUNNINGHAM WORTHY M	LTC	0-0045258	0262	1
CUNY CLIFFORD D	COL	0-0006437	0746	2
CUPELLO ALBERT R	COL	0-0038822	0466	1
CURHAVER CARL A	COL	0-0043296	0864	1
CUPPY MARY K	LTC	N-0000141	0461	1
CURCURO EDMOND H	CPT	0-0026229	0746	2
CURL GILBERT W	LTC	0-0023418	1060	1
CURLES CECIL M	LTC	0-0063298	0667	1
CURLEY EDWARD M	COL	0-0009477	0847	1
CURLEY RYTA M	MAJ	N-0002389	0162	1
CURLEY THOMAS W	LTC	0-0023904	0262	1
CURLL EDWIN H L	LTC	0-0049374	1264	1
CURRAN CHARLES D	1LT	0-0017091	0-35	2
CURRAN CORNELIUS	MAJ	0-0019332	1047	1
CURRAN ISABELLE R	LTC	N-0001984	0267	1
CURRAN KENTON W	CPT	0-0088640	0364	2
CURRAN ROBERT F	LTC	0-0020338	0859	1
CURREN WILLIAM F JR	COL	0-0038749	0963	1
CURRENS RONALD R	COL	0-0041916	1060	2
CURREY WALLACE H	LTC	0-0062212	0767	1
CURRIE WILLIAM R	B G	0-0017115	0758	1
CURRIER CHARLES F	COL	0-0050901	0555	1
CURRIER DON	LTC	0-0040318	0466	1
CURRIER ROGER M	COL	0-0030522	1165	1
CURRY DONALD A	MAJ	0-0046211	0863	1
CURRY JAMES A	LTC	0-0054865	1065	1
CURRY WILLIAM C	COL	0-0031677	0168	1
CURTIN EDWIN P	COL	0-0030231	0864	1
CURTIN PAUL J	LTC	0-0026361	0863	1
CURTIN RAYMOND G	COL	0-0038627	0460	1
CURTIS GUY L	COL	0-0020737	0867	1
CURTIS DONALD M	COL	0-0038837	0666	1
CURTIS HOMER K	COL	0-0051918	1167	1
CURTIS JAMES F JR	B G	0-0018109	1060	2
CURTIS JAMES W	B G	0-0007973	1048	2
CURTIS JAMES W JR	LTC	0-0067665	0168	1
CURTIS KENNETH I	B G	0-0019790	0865	1
CURTIS MILLARD S	COL	0-0010642	0352	1
CURTIS RAYMOND W	M G	0-0016784	0661	1
CURTIS ROBERT T	LTC	0-0050634	0867	1
CURTIS SARAH R	MAJ	N-0002361	0259	1
CURTISS WORTH M	LTC	0-0053305	0969	2
CUSHING CHRISTOPHE	LTC	0-0031836	0865	1
CUSHING ROBERT H JR	LTC	0-0057147	0868	1
CUSHING ROBERT L	LTC	0-0078740	0968	1
CUSHMAN HORACE O	B G	0-0006916	0153	1
CUSTIS ARTHUR B	COL	0-0008618	0852	2
CUSTIS HARRY N	LTC	0-0065027	0866	1
CUTLER STUART	B G	0-0006926	1146	2
CUTTER JAMES F	LTC	0-0079789	0865	1
CUTTINO THOMAS E	COL	0-0031397	1064	1

NAME	GRADE	SVC NO	DATE RET MO YR	RET CODE
CYGON JOSEPH R	MAJ	0-0003144	0133	2
CYPERT LONNETT H	CW4	W-0902981	0660	2
CYR ARTHUR R	COL	0-0019119	0861	1
CZAJA RUDOLPH P	COL	0-0031267	0966	1
DA COSTO STEPHEN	2LT	0-0014560	1016	2
DABNEY JOHN A	LTG	0-0016602	0961	1
DACQUISTO MICHAEL P	LTC	0-0063789	0267	1
DAEHLER RAYMOND E	COL	0-0042304	0164	1
DAGER HOLMES E	M G	0-0005013	1047	2
DAGUE ROBERT V	LTC	0-0080684	1165	1
DAHL IRWIN A	LTC	0-0043356	0965	1
DAHL LEONARD M	LTC	0-0042935	0164	1
DAHL NIELS M	LTC	0-0024466	0962	1
DAHLQUIST JOHN E	GEN	0-0007120	0256	1
DAHNKE HENRY	LTC	0-0015874	0347	1
DAHRINGER JOHN F	1LT	0-0014464	0419	2
DAILEY GERALD M	COL	0-0025249	0163	1
DAILEY JEREMIAH A	LTC	0-0058242	0159	1
DAILEY RAYMOND	COL	0-0010934	0547	1
DAILY WILLIAM D	MAJ	0-0059915	0963	1
DAINE HENRY W	COL	0-0017804	0159	1
DAKIN MYRON H	LTC	0-0025733	0764	1
DALBY ALBERT S	LTC	0-0024036	0362	1
DALE JOHN H SR	LTC	0-0076863	0866	2
DALE JOHN R	COL	0-0039857	0960	2
DALE THOMAS W	LTC	0-0058874	0367	1
DALESSANDRO JOHN	COL	0-0042510	0165	2
DALEY EDMUND L	B G	0-0002118	0942	1
DALEY ROY M	CW4	W-0902983	0763	1
DALFERES ROY L	COL	0-0010279	0753	1
DALIA GEORGE C	COL	0-0043297	1267	1
DALLMAN JAMES H	LTC	0-0027846	0268	1
DALRYMPLE ROBERT W	COL	0-0025329	0765	1
DALTO JOSEPH J	CW3	RW-0902984	0364	1
DALTON HELEN O	MAJ	N-0001886	0360	1
DALTON JAMES J	LTC	0-0040171	0366	2
DALTON JOHN J	COL	0-0042219	0763	1
DALUSKY GEORGE A	LTC	0-0087720	0868	1
DALY CORNELIUS	B G	0-0004761	1146	1
DALY EDWARD G	COL	0-0016736	0757	1
DALY JOHN C	COL	0-0004911	0151	1
DALY JOHN H	B G	0-0020284	0764	2
DALY JOHN K	COL	0-0042011	0562	1
DALZELL ROBERT C	LTC	0-0060183	0862	1
DAMAN ELI E	COL	0-0019703	1164	1
DAME HARTLEY F	COL	0-0051487	0464	1
DAMELIO GEORGE L	LTC	0-0044627	0762	1
DAMERON ERNEST C	COL	0-0032376	0168	1
DAMMER HERMAN W	COL	0-0030634	0166	1
DAMON WILLIAM F JR	COL	0-0019179	0562	1
DAMRON JAMES C	COL	0-0041793	0954	1
DAMSBO ANN M	CPT	M-0010158	1067	2
DANCAUSE PHILIP T	1LT	0-0068974	0259	2
DANEK RICHARD R	COL	0-0018617	0357	1
DANFORD ROBERT M	M G	0-0001913	0242	1
DANFORTH CARROLL F	LTC	0-0023997	0862	1
DANIEL CHARLES D	COL	0-0015668	0754	1
DANIEL CHARLES D	COL	0-0026744	1068	1
DANIEL DERRILL M	M G	0-0029500	0563	1
DANIEL MAURICE W	B G	0-0012766	0854	1
DANIEL RICHARD L	COL	0-0018329	0245	2
DANIEL ROBERT S JR	LTC	0-0028455	1066	1
DANIEL ROY E JR	COL	0-0038954	0968	1
DANIEL WILLIAM J	COL	0-0019019	0660	1
DANIELS EDWARD M	COL	0-0007589	0847	1
DANIELS HENRY F	LTC	0-0023295	0661	1
DANIELS LEONARD P	COL	0-0029550	0461	1
DANIELS LINCOLN F	COL	0-0005260	0246	1
DANIELS MADISON A	COL	0-0051019	0357	1
DANIELS ROBERT W	B G	0-0004648	0753	2
DANIELSON IDA M	LTC	N-0000010	0351	1
DANIELSON OLE W	COL	0-0021130	1047	2
DANIS JOHN J	COL	0-0018959	0248	2
DANNACHER WILLIAM H	CPT	0-0025817	1046	2
DANNEMILLER EDWARD M	LTC	0-0021822	0266	1

NAME	GRADE	SVC NO	DATE RET MO YR	RET CODE
DANNENBERG DONALD D	LTC	0-0040799	0863	1
DANNER JAMES D	LTC	0-0053384	0764	1
DANSBY CECIL [illegible]	LTC	0-0031452	0566	1
DANSBY JOHN W	COL	0-0016162	0846	2
DANTZER LAWRENCE L	LTC	0-0055602	0865	1
DANTZLER MORRIS	COL	0-0043992	0467	1
DAOUST GEORGE A JR	LTC	0-0027416	0767	1
DAPPRICH ANDREW C	LTC	0-0021040	0947	2
DARDEN JACK M	LTC	0-0060595	0466	1
DARDEN WILLIAM A JR	COL	0-0042599	0765	1
DAREZZO ALFRED J	COL	0-0021109	0168	1
DARK JOSEPH L	COL	0-0016979	1157	1
DARK ROBERT F	COL	0-0005786	0546	1
DARLING CLARENCE K	COL	0-0015645	0754	1
DARLING HOWARD N	COL	0-0055893	1268	1
DARNODY WILLIAM J	COL	0-0028904	0752	2
DARNS JOHN L JR	LTC	0-0079791	0767	1
DARVALL JOSEPH R	COL	0-0011426	1053	2
DARRAGH MATTISON A	COL	0-0042174	0463	1
DARRAH JAMES T	COL	0-0018124	0660	1
DARRAH JOHN W JR	COL	0-0019473	0463	2
DARRAH RAYMOND W	COL	0-0030029	1063	1
DARROW HOWARD W	COL	0-0031488	0866	1
DART RAYMOND D	B G	0-0008922	0750	1
DARWIN GEORGE H	COL	0-0033779	0766	1
DASCHE JAY A	COL	0-0039810	0662	1
DASHIELL GEORGE R JR	COL	0-0065529	0863	2
DAUBIN FREELAND A JR	MAJ	0-0043709	0751	2
DAUER MAXWELL	LTC	0-0031217	0161	1
DAUGHERITY RICHARD D	COL	0-0005680	0650	2
DAUGHERTY FRANCIS	COL	0-0052222	1065	1
DAUGHERTY GLEN E	LTC	0-0038980	0359	1
DAUGHERTY JOSEPH B	COL	0-0016252	0755	1
DAUGHERTY LESTER A	B G	0-0005559	0951	2
DAUGHERTY WILLIAM A	LTC	0-0027491	0866	1
DAUGHTRY BARNEY A	COL	0-0016902	0160	1
DAUGHTRY GRACE H	MAJ	N-0000545	0152	1
DAUTRICH HELEN A	MAJ	R-0010002	0355	1
DAVALL HAROLD C	COL	0-0019425	0264	1
DAVENPORT FRANK M	COL	0-0051029	0459	1
DAVENPORT HAROLD A	COL	0-0029385	0360	1
DAVENPORT MERRILL C	COL	0-0021479	0660	2
DAVENPORT WILLIAM W	COL	0-0043077	0760	1
DAVEY RALPH H JR	COL	0-0018689	0247	2
DAVIDOFF JAMES E	COL	0-0033460	0967	1
DAVIDS HOWARD G	COL	0-0000938	0934	2
DAVIDS JOHN L	COL	0-0038783	1264	1
DAVIDSON ALFRED H JR	COL	0-0039808	0762	1
DAVIDSON CECIL H	COL	0-0031560	0764	2
DAVIDSON DONALD M	1LT	0-0017369	1028	2
DAVIDSON GARRISON H	LTG	0-0016755	0564	1
DAVIDSON HENRY E JR	COL	0-0032295	1165	1
DAVIDSON LEWIS C	COL	0-0003821	1049	1
DAVIDSON MAURICE C	COL	0-0020108	0855	1
DAVIDSON ORION L	COL	0-0010358	0854	2
DAVIDSON PAUL W	LTC	0-0054119	0864	1
DAVIDSON RICHARD D	COL	0-0033262	1064	1
DAVIDSON RICHARD P	COL	0-0042785	0666	1
DAVIDSON SHIRLEY	LTC	0-0037122	0663	1
DAVIDSON WILLIAM G	COL	0-0018862	0961	2
DAVIE ROBERT C	COL	0-0040050	1058	2
DAVIES ALBERT C	COL	0-0038916	0767	1
DAVIES ELIZABETH	LTC	M-0010102	0966	1
DAVIES FRANK J	COL	0-0040126	1168	1
DAVIES ROBERTINE	MAJ	N-0001263	0865	1
DAVIS ANNA L	MAJ	N-0000732	0962	1
DAVIS BENJAMIN M	COL	0-0030282	1164	1
DAVIS BENJAMIN O	B G	0-0001217	0741	1
DAVIS BRAYTON M JR	CW4	W-0902990	0768	1
DAVIS CAROLINE	MAJ	N-0000161	1060	1
DAVIS CHARLES E	LTC	0-0060726	0268	1
DAVIS CHARLES I	COL	0-0042658	1065	1
DAVIS CHARLES J	LTC	0-0026491	0765	1
DAVIS CHARLES W	CW4	W-0904101	0263	1
DAVIS CHESTER E	COL	0-0007163	0949	2

NAME	GRADE	SVC NO	DATE RET MO YR	RET CODE
DAVIS CLAIBORNE JR	LTC	0-0037001	0764	1
DAVIS CLARENCE F JR	COL	0-0053041	0267	1
DAVIS CORRIN J	CPT	0-0028570	1052	2
DAVIS DON	COL	0-0045687	1066	1
DAVIS DONALD M	COL	0-0052410	0766	1
DAVIS DOUGLAS C	COL	0-0018985	0550	2
DAVIS EDWARD L JR	LTC	0-0034079	0761	2
DAVIS EDWARD M	LTC	0-0081987	0767	1
DAVIS ELLIS D	COL	0-0019387	0661	1
DAVIS ELLSWORTH	M G	0-0018658	1066	1
DAVIS FANNIE L	MAJ	L-0000200	0666	1
DAVIS GEORGE A	B G	0-0007078	0246	1
DAVIS GEORGE M	COL	0-0014719	0649	1
DAVIS HARRY O	MAJ	0-0003635	0722	2
DAVIS HARRY R	COL	0-0041894	0859	1
DAVIS HAWTHORNE	COL	0-0051013	0259	1
DAVIS HAZEL D	MAJ	N-0001013	0662	2
DAVIS HELEN M	LTC	R-0010004	0760	1
DAVIS HOMER L JR	COL	0-0029869	0363	1
DAVIS HOWARD H	COL	0-0006537	0753	1
DAVIS HOY D JR	COL	0-0018982	0563	1
DAVIS JAMES P	COL	0-0028895	0257	1
DAVIS JOHN	COL	0-0043012	0667	1
DAVIS JOHN F	B G	0-0003853	0552	2
DAVIS JOHN H	COL	0-0040036	0766	1
DAVIS JOHN J	COL	0-0019935	0264	2
DAVIS JOHN K	COL	0-0020408	0754	2
DAVIS JOHN M	LTC	0-0031761	0762	1
DAVIS JOHN N	COL	0-0022070	0761	1
DAVIS JOHN N	COL	0-0032808	1065	1
DAVIS JOHN W	COL	0-0016223	0755	1
DAVIS KELTON S	COL	0-0020786	0465	1
DAVIS KERMIT L	M G	0-0019386	1167	1
DAVIS LEE J	COL	0-0029623	1061	1
DAVIS LEONARD L	B G	0-0009829	1048	1
DAVIS LOREN E	LTC	0-0039444	0965	1
DAVIS MAHLON S	MAJ	0-0018095	0146	2
DAVIS MANLEY E JR	LTC	0-0058802	0466	1
DAVIS MIKE B	LTC	0-0026188	0761	1
DAVIS ORVILLE E	COL	0-0011066	0947	1
DAVIS OTTIS A SR	LTC	0-0040553	0955	1
DAVIS PAUL A JR	LTC	0-0036887	0266	1
DAVIS PAUL C	COL	0-0021141	0661	1
DAVIS PAUL C	LTC	0-0025218	0861	1
DAVIS RALPH E	LTC	0-0059813	0668	1
DAVIS RAYMOND P	LTC	0-0056400	0468	1
DAVIS RICHARD W JR	LTC	0-0027595	0866	1
DAVIS ROBERT E	LTC	0-0038307	0166	1
DAVIS ROBERT G	COL	0-0051394	0463	1
DAVIS ROBERT J	COL	0-0033886	1062	1
DAVIS ROBERT L	LTC	0-0025661	0864	1
DAVIS SAMUEL P III	LTC	0-0028393	0868	1
DAVIS SCOTT H	MAJ	0-0037432	1155	1
DAVIS THEODORE W	COL	0-0023259	0861	2
DAVIS THOMAS C	COL	0-0041981	0162	1
DAVIS THOMAS F	COL	0-0009227	1051	2
DAVIS THOMAS P	COL	0-0020380	0864	1
DAVIS THOMAS W III	COL	0-0022059	0367	1
DAVIS VICTOR A	LTC	0-0040453	0561	1
DAVIS WALTER P	CW4	RW-0902991	0964	1
DAVIS WALTER W	COL	0-0020878	0567	1
DAVIS WILLIAM	CW4	W-0906689	0764	1
DAVIS WILLIAM A	COL	0-0020198	0664	1
DAVIS WILLIAM A	LTC	0-0055935	0864	1
DAVIS WILLIAM E	LTC	0-0049241	0965	1
DAVIS WILLIAM V	COL	0-0016595	0246	2
DAVIS WILLIS H	LTC	0-0034325	0867	1
DAVISON F MCKENZIE	CPT	0-0014368	0819	2
DAVISON FRANCES M	MAJ	M-0010030	0865	1
DAVISON PAUL P	COL	0-0003660	1145	2
DAVISSON HENRY L	COL	0-0029612	0861	1
DAVITT JAMES H	LTC	0-0043490	0861	1
DAW WILLIAM J	COL	0-0012497	0946	2
DAWLEY ERNEST J	M G	0-0002843	0947	2
DAWLEY JAY P	COL	0-0021750	0866	2

NAME	GRADE	SVC NO	DATE RET MO YR	RET CODE
DAWSON ALVIN M	CW4	W-0902992	1164	1
DAWSON CLIFFORD H	LTC	0-0079023	0266	1
DAWSON CYRIL A W	COL	0-0003496	0941	2
DAWSON DALLAS O	LTC	0-0049338	1065	1
DAWSON GEORGE P JR	LTC	0-0038798	0566	1
DAWSON GORDON E	COL	0-0029587	0761	1
DAWSON HENRY B	LTC	0-0006562	0142	1
DAWSON JAMES T	COL	0-0016346	0146	2
DAWSON MILES M	B G	0-0016079	0456	1
DAWSON WALLACE H JR	COL	0-0039712	0757	1
DAY CHARLES H	COL	0-0011712	0146	2
DAY FRANCIS M	M G	0-0015614	0659	1
DAY FRANK R	LTC	0-0018325	0259	1
DAY FREDERICK	COL	0-0016760	0657	1
DAY JAMES H	COL	0-0007033	0753	1
DAY JOHN F JR	COL	0-0051502	0960	1
DAY PARKER S	COL	0-0029573	0661	2
DAY PHILIP S	LTC	0-0008571	0622	2
DAY ROBERT S	COL	0-0026490	0268	1
DAY WILLIAM H	COL	0-0020957	0759	1
DAYHUFF CHARLES H JR	COL	0-0038709	0861	1
DAYKIN ALBERT	COL	0-0042762	0566	1
DAYTON HARRY C	COL	0-0014722	0838	2
DAYTON JOHN B	LTC	0-0028049	0766	1
DE ANGELIS ANTHONY J	COL	0-0039252	0566	1
DE ARMOND GEORGE W	COL	0-0002142	1143	2
DE AUGUSTINE PETER	1LT	0-1540722	1167	2
DE BARDELEBEN DANIEL	CPT	0-0015164	0637	2
DE BELLIS ANTHONY C	LTC	0-0060862	0866	1
DE BERG OAK E	LTC	0-0042974	0664	1
DE BILL WALTER C	COL	0-0020626	0960	1
DE BRUIN CORNELIUS	CW4	W-0902230	0958	1
DE CAMARA DONALD R	LTC	0-0061108	0966	1
DE CAMARA RICHARD P	COL	0-0034399	0962	1
DE CAMP JOHN T JR	LTC	0-0026040	0765	1
DE CARLO MICHAEL R	COL	0-0042445	1164	1
DE CARO FREDERICK	CPT	0-0007915	0728	2
DE CHOW GEORGE H	COL	0-0024553	0764	1
DE COURSEY ELBERT	M G	0-0017813	0959	1
DE FRANCESCO FRED L	CPT	0-0096896	1263	2
DE FRANE GEORGIA D	MAJ	N-0000701	1068	1
DE FRATES JAMES J	LTC	0-0084734	0667	1
DE FREES LINDSAY J	COL	0-0083565	0161	1
DE GAVRE CHESTER B	B G	0-0019262	0863	1
DE GON KENNETH C	COL	0-0023676	0563	1
DE GRAFF B R	COL	0-0007594	0850	1
DE GRAFF GEORGE J	LTC	0-0049935	0467	1
DE HAAS PAUL L	COL	0-0030284	1064	1
DE HAVEN GRACE I B	MAJ	N-0000317	0562	1
DE JARNETTE JAMES T	COL	0-0042344	0464	1
DE JUSSEWICZ LOUIS	LTC	0-0006123	1038	2
DE LA VERGNE JAMES G	COL	0-0018956	0646	2
DE LANGE WALTER H	COL	0-0015096	1047	2
DE LESDERNIER L F	LTC	0-0020275	0859	1
DE LINE ALMA E	LTC	N-0000167	1262	1
DE LOACH WILBUR V	COL	0-0030449	0565	1
DE LONG JAMES C	CPT	0-0007159	0-32	2
DE LORENZO JOSEPH J	CW4	W-0902997	0461	1
DE LORIMIER ALFRED J	COL	0-0007259	0353	2
DE LORIMIER CHARLES	LTC	0-0078789	0667	1
DE MAIO MARIO	COL	0-0030399	0263	1
DE MARR JAMES D	COL	0-0042273	1163	1
DE MARS EDWARD J	COL	0-0029128	0457	1
DE MARTINO VINCENT	CW4	W-0906690	0862	1
DE MELKER BERT	COL	0-0030679	0466	1
DE MERS ROBERT J	LTC	0-0033159	0661	1
DE METROPOLIS HARRY	MAJ	0-0022021	0355	1
DE NOYA LOUIS L	COL	0-0053352	1265	1
DE PASS MORRIS B	COL	0-0010333	0854	1
DE POLLO HELEN M	MAJ	N-0002447	0267	1
DE RIEMER LOUIS M	COL	0-0017640	0859	1
DE ROHAN FREDERICK	COL	0-0004558	0453	2
DE RUSHA RICHARD A	LTC	0-0063416	1166	1
DE RUSSY RENE E JR	LTC	0-0040164	0864	1
DE SANCTIS JOHN N	LTC	0-0080069	1162	1

NAME	GRADE	SVC NO	DATE RET MO YR	RET CODE
DE SAUSSURE EDWARD H	COL	0-0010217	0446	2
DE SHAZO THOMAS E	M G	0-0016479	0560	2
DE SILVA RUDOLPH H	LTC	0-0071339	0766	1
DE VANEY CARL N	COL	0-0038770	0960	1
DE VECCHIO ROY G	COL	0-0042584	0565	1
DE WARE WILLIAM C	COL	0-0007451	0247	2
DE WEESE ROBERT E JR	LTC	0-0078790	0767	1
DE WEESE WILLIAM P	LTC	0-0084359	0966	1
DE WITT CALVIN JR	B G	0-0004459	0854	2
DE WITT FLORENCE M	MAJ	N-0001887	1059	1
DE WITT JOHN L JR	LTC	0-0029109	0557	1
DE YOUNG DANIEL	LTC	0-0038203	0363	1
DE YOUNG EDWARD M	COL	0-0020076	0661	1
DE ZAFRA CHARLES R	LTC	0-0061245	1267	2
DEAGLE EDWIN A	COL	0-0030237	0509	1
DEAHL CHARLES J JR	COL	0-0006978	0147	1
DEAKINS JOHN A	MAJ	0-0058788	0264	1
DEAN CLARENCE	1LT	0-0014989	0627	2
DEAN JAMES W	LTC	0-0031300	0768	2
DEAN JOSEPH R	COL	0-0044877	0968	1
DEAN KATHLEEN M	MAJ	N-0001596	0868	1
DEAN TERRANCE W	CW4	W-0903001	0561	1
DEAN WILLIAM A	COL	0-0046007	0267	1
DEAN WILLIAM F	M G	0-0015453	1055	1
DEANE DON L	COL	0-0020492	0357	1
DEANE HAROLD M	LTC	0-0022887	0960	1
DEANE JOHN B	COL	0-0024040	0765	1
DEANE JOHN R	M G	0-0009759	0946	1
DEANS WILLARD J	CW4	W-0906692	1068	1
DEAR RICHARD H	LTC	0-0022279	1164	1
DEAS ALSTON	COL	0-0008635	1146	1
DEASON CHARLES A	COL	0-0030601	0166	1
DEBOW DUANE L	LTC	0-0040970	0864	1
DECHANT WILSON B	LTC	0-0029173	0158	1
DECKER ARTHUR O	LTC	0-0030583	1263	1
DECKER CHARLES L	M G	0-0018549	1263	1
DECKER ELMER E	CW4	W-0902364	1058	1
DECKER GEORGE H	GEN	0-0015950	1062	1
DECKER JOSEPH F	COL	0-0029999	0863	1
DECKER KENNETH N	COL	0-0015789	0654	2
DECKER NELSON I	COL	0-0030105	0164	1
DECKER SILAS E	COL	0-0020104	0765	1
DEEKLE WILLIAM C JR	LTC	0-0026310	0961	1
DEERY HUGH A	LTC	0-0080698	0765	1
DEERY JAMES J	COL	0-0016123	0455	2
DEGENHARDT JACOB R	LTC	0-0030391	0163	1
DEGUIRE MERLIN L	B G	0-0019446	0163	1
DEHNE EDWARD J	COL	0-0051965	0966	1
DEHNE ERNST	COL	0-0056790	1065	2
DEHNER VERNON E	LTC	0-0037147	0765	2
DEIHERT RALPH C	COL	0-0012532	0845	2
DEISHER FRANCIS	LTC	0-0018852	0859	1
DEITRICK CARROLL H	M G	0-0014796	0458	1
DEL CAMPO VINCENT A	CW3	W-0903004	0765	2
DEL MAR ROLAND H	M G	0-0029917	1066	1
DEL VECCHIO MARCELLO	LTC	0-0027774	0568	1
DEL ZOPPO ROGER A	LTC	0-0039243	0762	1
DELA&CRUZ NICOMEDES	CW3	W-0907079	1059	1
DELANEY GRACE	MAJ	N-0000454	1062	1
DELANEY RICHARD	LTC	0-0023711	1162	1
DELANEY WILLIAM H	COL	0-0029590	0861	1
DELAPLANE OSCAR M	CW3	W-0903005	0661	1
DELCAMPO ANGELO R	COL	0-0018361	0456	1
DELEHANTY RUDOLPH D	CPT	0-0008605	0833	2
DELISTRATY JOHN	LTC	0-0050706	0968	1
DELMONICO LOUIS R	COL	0-0017287	0858	1
DELMORE FRED J	B G	0-0029440	0565	1
DELOSUA RAMON F	COL	0-0043713	1066	1
DELP MIRIAM A	MAJ	N-0001944	0558	1
DELUCA ARTHUR J	COL	0-0024400	0965	1
DELUCA FRANK R	MAJ	0-0058066	0854	2
DEMING DONALD A	LTC	0-0081988	0168	1
DEMITZ ROBERT S	COL	0-0021259	0657	1
DEMOREST ELSIE M	MAJ	N-0000630	0262	1
DEMPSEY ALBERT	LTC	0-0081894	0463	1

NAME	GRADE	SVC NO	DATE RET MO YR	RET CODE
DEMPSEY FREDERICK	LTC	O-0063097	0166	1
DEMPSEY JACK H	COL	O-0031766	0564	1
DEMPSTER ROBERT N	LTC	O-0080700	0767	1
DEMUTH HENRY C	COL	O-0008653	1152	1
DENBY ROLAND E	LTC	O-0034192	0368	1
DENCHFIELD ROBERT D	LTC	O-0035886	0863	1
DENHAM CHESTER	MAJ	O-0004021	1033	2
DENHAM ERNEST W JR	LTC	O-0059373	0768	2
DENHAM JOHN P	LTC	O-0074793	0868	1
DENHAM RUSSELL H	LTC	O-0054714	0867	1
DENISEVICH PETER	LTC	O-0023416	0859	1
DENISON WALCOTT	COL	O-0004035	1049	1
DENIT GUY B	M G	O-0008675	0953	2
DENNEY EARNEST J	CW4	W-0904104	0763	1
DENNIS ALBERT F	COL	O-0018052	0157	1
DENNIS ANNA K	LTC	N-0001965	1163	1
DENNIS DOMINICK C	LTC	O-0044753	0262	1
DENNIS EDWARD H	COL	O-0002973	0242	2
DENNIS NORMAN T	COL	O-0043547	0868	1
DENNISON RICHARD F	COL	O-0034040	0268	1
DENNISTON ALFRED B	M G	O-0017315	0562	1
DENNISTON ROBERT N	COL	O-0043552	0767	1
DENNO BRYCE F	COL	O-0023161	1265	2
DENNY CHARLES S	COL	O-0010102	1146	2
DENSLEY HILTON	LTC	O-0032746	0968	2
DENSON ELEY P	R G	O-0002619	0846	2
DENSON LEE A	COL	O-0012658	0954	1
DENSON PIERRE B	COL	O-0016278	0755	1
DENTREMONT ULYSSES B	CW4	W-0903008	1054	1
DERAGISCH WILLIAM J	MAJ	O-0031202	0658	1
DERBY GEORGE T	COL	O-0016744	0456	1
DERDEI JOHN B	CW4	W-0903010	1065	1
DEROSIER GERALD A	LTC	O-0079797	0965	1
DERRICK HORACE F	MAJ	O-0028626	0367	1
DERRICK JESSE D	COL	O-0008952	1047	2
DERRICK JOHN H	COL	O-0041443	1056	1
DERRYBERRY JEWELL	LTC	N-0000214	0466	1
DERZIS PETER N	COL	O-0081879	0866	1
DES ISLETS ROBERT E	COL	O-0015405	0953	2
DES PLAND LEON A JR	CPT	O-0006709	0934	2
DESCHENEAUX GEORGE	COL	O-0018902	0846	2
DESHON GEORGE E	LTC	O-0021362	0559	1
DESJARDINS LEOPOLD A	CW3	W-0908044	1168	1
DESMOND ISABELLE M	MAJ	M-0010010	0862	1
DESOBRY ELMER C	COL	O-0002395	0245	2
DESPINOSA WILLIAM J	COL	O-0015156	0753	1
DESPOSITO JOHN V	LTC	O-0024095	0761	1
DESSERT ROLLAND A	MAJ	O-0028388	0567	1
DETCHEMENDY EDWARD R	LTC	O-0045117	0865	1
DETLIE HARRY L	COL	O-0039996	1265	1
DETTREY GLENN W	LTC	O-0028546	0664	2
DEUTERMANN GEORGE J	COL	O-0016150	0847	2
DEVENBECK FLOYD C	COL	O-0015469	1253	1
DEVENDORF DONALD A	CW3	W-0903014	0457	1
DEVENS W GEORGE	LTC	O-0028008	0766	1
DEVER BERNARD A	LTC	O-0040827	0258	1
DEVEREAUX ALFRED R	COL	O-0016138	0755	1
DEVERS JACOB L	GEN	O-0002599	0949	1
DEVINE JAMES G	B G	O-0006540	0854	2
DEVINE JOHN M	M G	O-0005232	0752	1
DEVINE PATRICK H	B G	O-0031975	0766	1
DEVLIN EDWARD T	LTC	O-0051680	0164	2
DEVORE GERALD B	COL	O-0010329	0753	1
DEVORE LELAND S JR	COL	O-0032404	0965	1
DEWALT EDGAR A	CW3	W-0904244	0953	2
DEWEY GEORGE L	LTC	O-0015188	0449	1
DEWEY HOBART E	LTC	O-0039479	0666	1
DEWEY LAWRENCE R	M G	O-0015575	0361	1
DEWING ELISABETH	CW4	V-0904323	0365	1
DEWITT WILMAR W	COL	O-0014814	0153	2
DEWS OKER S	B G	O-0043079	1166	1
DEXHEIMER ROBERT	LTC	O-0032749	0165	1
DEXTER ROBERT B	COL	O-0033838	0868	1
DEY JOHN R	COL	O-0029347	1059	1
DEYO TRUMAN E	LTC	O-0024037	0262	1

NAME	GRADE	SVC NO	DATE RET MO YR	RET CODE
DEYO WILLIAM J JR	B G	O-0016449	0756	1
DEYOE ALDEN W	CW4	W-0902175	1056	1
DI GIACOMO JOSEPH	LTC	O-0040111	0763	1
DI SIMONE FRANK B	MAJ	O-0071341	06	1
DIAL RICHARD J	COL	O-0051230	0761	1
DIALS RALPH P	CW4	W-0903018	0867	1
DIAMOND IRWIN M	COL	O-0039730	0961	1
DIAZ GEORGE F	LTC	O-0078798	1166	2
DICE ROBERT I	LTC	O-0022952	0660	1
DICE WILBUR D	LTC	O-0023671	1068	1
DICHTENMUELLER HERBE	COL	O-0051706	0765	1
DICK WILLIAM W JR	LTG	O-0018384	0768	1
DICKEN KEITH O	COL	O-0043327	0562	2
DICKENS RANDOLPH C	B G	O-0020290	0866	2
DICKENSON GLENN G	COL	O-0050954	0757	1
DICKENSON ROBERT L	LTC	O-0053199	0968	2
DICKER HERMAN	LTC	O-0043154	0567	1
DICKERSON ALBERT H	COL	O-0016838	0454	1
DICKERSON JOHN O	LTC	O-0022071	0867	1
DICKERSON ROBERT B	COL	O-0040103	0766	1
DICKERSON WILLIAM R	LTC	O-0080704	0663	1
DICKEY CALVIN A L	COL	O-0028961	0158	1
DICKEY CHARLES H III	LTC	O-0044001	1067	1
DICKIE MARGARET P	MAJ	N-0001643	0666	1
DICKIE RALPH L	COL	O-0031493	0164	1
DICKINSON CHARLES W	LTC	O-0026933	0364	1
DICKINSON OLIVER A	COL	O-0002336	0142	1
DICKINSON W D JR	LTC	O-0018038	0432	2
DICKS JAMES H	LTC	O-0030043	1061	1
DICKS JOHN R	COL	O-0029982	0461	1
DICKSON DONALD D	COL	O-0032531	1167	1
DICKSON GROVA-NELL	MAJ	N-0000484	0267	1
DICKSON JEAN H	LTC	O-0036606	0465	1
DICKSON MARSHALL W	LTC	O-0042930	1062	1
DICKSON SAMUEL A	COL	O-0016219	1149	1
DIEFENDORF JOHN E	LTC	O-0040009	1163	1
DIEHL FORREST V	LTC	O-0051361	1160	1
DIEKROEGER LUELLA E	LTC	N-0001861	0466	1
DIERCKS FREDERICK	COL	O-0026599	0667	1
DIERDORFF H BEECHER	COL	O-0019347	0263	2
DIERSING MARIE B	MAJ	N-0002236	1064	1
DIES FREDERICK	LTC	O-0051067	1057	1
DIESEM WALTER F	COL	O-0043372	1267	1
DIESSNER WARREN H	COL	O-0020519	1055	1
DIESTEL CHESTER J	COL	O-0018448	0761	1
DIETERICH WILLIAM H	LTC	O-0031219	1060	1
DIETRICH JOHN P	1LT	O-0012096	0925	2
DIETRICH STERRETT E	COL	O-0058681	0964	1
DIETSCHE HELEN F	MAJ	N-0000665	0763	1
DIETZ GEORGE E	LTC	O-0018500	0859	1
DIGGS JACK F	COL	O-0076868	1066	2
DILDINE SETH C	COL	O-0010405	1046	1
DILL MACEY L	COL	O-0006352	0551	2
DILLARD DAVID S	COL	O-0022175	0367	1
DILLARD EVERETT R	CW3	W-0903021	0457	1
DILLE RICHARD T	MAJ	O-0058882	0564	1
DILLEMUTH RACHEL E	MAJ	N-0001576	0964	1
DILLER LEGRANDE A	B G	O-0015078	0954	2
DILLEY JOHN H	COL	O-0019861	0264	1
DILLEY MARION E	CW4	W-0903023	0764	2
DILLINGER W D	COL	O-0050902	0655	1
DILLON EDNA L	LTC	M-0010118	0267	1
DILLON EDWARD H	COL	O-0020552	0465	1
DILLON JOHN P	MAJ	O-0079256	0666	1
DILLON LEO J	COL	O-0008141	0651	1
DILLON LESTER R JR	LTC	O-0050228	1068	1
DILLON MACKIN R	COL	O-0030802	0966	1
DILLON WILLIAM H	LTC	O-0058883	0265	1
DILTS PETER K	MAJ	O-0023955	0262	1
DILWORTH JOEL J	COL	O-0024790	0963	1
DILWORTH JOHN R	CW4	W-0903024	0363	1
DIMOND JOHN W	CW4	W-0901221	0552	1
DINGEMAN RAY E	COL	O-0011870	0552	2
DINGLEY NELSON 30	COL	O-0005025	0851	1
DINGWALL ALLAN G JR	MAJ	O-0037249	0764	1

NAME	GRADE	SVC NO	DATE RET MO YR	RET CODE
DINKINS WILLIAM H	LTC	O-0065653	1168	1
DIRKSEN LYNN C	COL	O-0027146	0858	1
DISCH FRANK A	COL	O-0027186	0860	1
DISHMAN ADDISON V	COL	O-0018471	0761	1
DISHMAN SILAS B	COL	O-0029052	0163	1
DISMUKES JACKSON B	COL	O-0027144	0858	2
DISSINGER CHARLES F	B G	O-0007374	0853	1
DITMORE HARRY B	1LT	O-0013411	1132	2
DIVINE ROBERT F	LTC	O-0045523	0165	1
DIX JEWETT A	COL	O-0032349	1269	1
DIXON DALE D	COL	O-0038789	1163	1
DIXON FRANK H	COL	O-0003764	0150	1
DIXON FRED	COL	O-0029392	0157	1
DIXON HOUSTON T	LTC	O-0051765	0364	2
DIXON JOBIE J	COL	O-0031744	0864	1
DIXON JOHN H	COL	O-0042733	0266	2
DIXON OLIVER [illegible]	COL	O-0030494	0762	1
DIXON ONESS H JR	COL	O-0003610	1051	1
DIXON RUSSELL H	COL	O-0005775	0747	1
DIXON THOMAS V	LTC	O-0051277	0160	1
DLUGOLESKY EDMUND L	COL	O-0039727	0357	1
DOAN DONALD H	CPT	O-0014435	0620	2
DOAN HOWARD W	M G	O-0020057	0964	1
DOANE IRVIN E	COL	O-0005200	0947	2
DOANE LESLIE [illegible]	LTC	O-0023493	0664	1
DOBAK ALEXANDER	COL	O-0016703	0555	1
DOBBS OSCAR T	CW4	RW-0903027	1163	1
DOBLE JEAN	WO1	W-0800173	1129	2
DOBRINIC MATT P	LTC	O-0042785	0258	2
DOBSON JOHN W	B G	O-0021351	0867	1
DOBYNS THOMAS G	COL	O-0004789	0854	2
DOCKERY ALBERT [illegible]	COL	O-0001705	1138	1
DOCKLER CARL J	COL	O-0007605	0920	1
DOCKUM WILBUR G	COL	O-0005692	1146	2
DODD FRANCIS T	COL	O-0015306	0753	2
DODD WILLIAM A	LTC	O-0080759	0666	1
DODDS MARYELLE F	MAJ	J-0001067	0668	1
DODDS WILLIAM A	COL	O-0020815	0964	1
DODENHOFF DAVID I	COL	O-0029611	0961	1
DODENHOFF HARRY [illegible]	COL	O-0030437	0661	1
DODGE CHARLES [illegible]	LTC	O-0018072	0466	1
DODGE FREDERICK	COL	O-0012402	0451	1
DODGE HARLAND L	LTC	O-0093398	0162	1
DODGE HOWARD [illegible]	LTC	O-0051550	1159	1
DODGE ROY T	B G	O-0021468	1067	1
DODGE SARA E	MAJ	L-0000044	0558	1
DODGE WILLIAM J	CW4	W-0903028	0661	1
DODSON MINOT [illegible]	COL	O-0032660	1166	1
DOE JENS A	M G	O-0003743	0249	1
DOE ROBERT E	COL	O-0042066	0751	1
DOERFLINGER OSCAR M	COL	O-0031072	0665	1
DOERING SAM F	LTC	O-0053058	0765	1
DOERR PAUL C	COL	O-0039726	0761	1
DOGAN ADAM E	LTC	O-0030413	0463	1
DOGGETT DAVID S	COL	O-0005756	1046	2
DOHERTY DANIEL E	COL	O-0028916	0557	1
DOHERTY HAROLD A	COL	O-0014642	1052	1
DOHERTY PAUL E	COL	O-0025212	0868	1
DOHERTY STEPHEN [illegible] JR	COL	O-0084360	0968	1
DOIDGE JOHN R	LTC	O-0017235	0150	1
DOIRON HENRY [illegible]	LTC	O-0057850	1268	1
DOLAN BERNARD J JR	LTC	O-0063321	0267	1
DOLAN PATRICIA F	LTC	N-0000573	0961	1
DOLAN PHILIP [illegible]	LTC	O-0027092	0767	1
DOLEMAN EDGAR C	LTC	O-0019131	1064	2
DOLL FREDERICK	CW4	W-0903030	0357	1
DOLLAR FRED W	LTC	O-0037345	0865	1
DOLLARD EDMUND J	COL	O-0047369	1157	1
DOLLE WALTER [illegible]	COL	O-0021813	0260	1
DOLPH [illegible] CYRUS A	M G	O-0019170	1059	2
DOLSON JAMES F	COL	O-0078645	0968	1
DOMBROWSKI CHESTER	LTC	O-0031353	1064	1
DOMKE DELMAR [illegible]	COL	O-0022780	0264	1
DONAHUE DOROTHY M	LTC	N-0000621	0864	1
DONAHUE EDWARD T	COL	O-0039650	0559	1

NAME	GRADE	SVC NO	DATE RET MO YR	RET CODE
DONAHUE FRANCIS G	LTC	O-0029001	0253	2
DONAHUE JAMES H	COL	O-0008455	0148	2
DONAHUE JAMES J JR	COL	O-0076870	0966	1
DONAHUE JOHN T	CW4	W-0903032	1168	2
DONAHUE JOSEPH R	LTC	O-0043294	1062	1
DONAHUE PATRICK H	LTC	O-0034885	0666	1
DONAHUE THOMAS F	COL	O-0041435	0956	1
DONALD HERBERT P	COL	O-0052223	0868	1
DONALD SAMUEL F	MAJ	O-0022750	1147	2
DONALDSON WILLIAM R	COL	O-0022198	1167	1
DONEGAN WILLIAM E	COL	O-0011784	0149	1
DONEY CARL S	COL	O-0004456	0646	2
DONLON JAMES D JR	LTC	O-0032039	0459	1
DONNEDY MADELYN F	MAJ	N-0001220	0467	1
DONNELL THOMAS W	COL	O-0030663	0665	2
DONNELLY AUGUSTINE	COL	O-0023681	0866	1
DONNELLY EILEEN E	LTC	N-0000175	0758	1
DONNELLY HOWARD	COL	O-0003868	0347	2
DONNELLY W J JR	LTC	O-0034359	0350	2
DONOGHUE ROSE A	LTC	N-0000877	0866	1
DONOHOO ALBERT C	LTC	O-0069905	0268	1
DONOHUE JAMES M	COL	O-0019798	0863	1
DONOHUE JOSEPH P	LTC	O-0023045	1046	2
DONOVAN HAROLD F	COL	O-0026442	1168	1
DONOVAN JAMES F	LTC	O-0057546	0864	1
DONOVAN MARY E	LTC	N-0000301	1067	1
DONOVAN MARY L	MAJ	N-0002612	0365	1
DONOVAN WILLIAM N	COL	O-0021042	1163	1
DOODY KATHRYN M	MAJ	N-0003383	0666	1
DOOLEY HELEN A	MAJ	N-0002237	0660	1
DOOLEY JAMES F	LTC	O-0010342	1141	1
DOOLING HENRY C	B G	O-0004170	0747	2
DOOLITTLE GEORGE L	MAJ	O-0012723	1022	2
DOOLITTLE HOPE K	CPT	M-0000498	0747	1
DORAN CHARLES R	B G	O-0005891	0548	1
DORAN EDWARD A	COL	O-0025782	1068	1
DORAN ROY E	COL	O-0038892	0966	2
DOREN DONALD M	LTC	O-0078803	0868	1
DORENKEMPER DOROTHY	MAJ	N-0000577	1061	1
DORIS ARTHUR E	MAJ	O-0056572	1060	2
DORLAND GILBERT M	COL	O-0020132	0656	1
DORMAN PRESTON E	CW4	W-0906699	0267	1
DORN CAMILLE JO	CPT	R-0001107	0947	1
DORN FRANK	B G	O-0015278	1153	1
DORN GEORGE W	COL	O-0041979	0660	1
DORN WILLIAM C	COL	O-0036316	1148	1
DORNBLASER JOSEPH H	COL	O-00[illegible]4588	0748	1
DORNEY JOHN F JR	CW2	W-0890771	1043	2
DORRENBACHER JAMES A	CW4	W-0903033	0668	2
DORSETT ANNIE M	MAJ	N-0000225	0763	1
DORSETT HAROLD L	COL	O-0040194	1167	2
DORSEY JOHN R	CW4	W-0904106	1058	1
DORSEY RALPH M	LTC	O-0063394	0966	1
DORSEY ROBERT [illegible]	COL	O-0030100	0264	1
DORSEY WOODROW A	CW3	W-0903034	0857	1
DORST JAMES A	COL	O-0003534	0147	1
DOTY HORACE W JR	LTC	O-0057379	0860	1
DOTY KIE	COL	O-0010629	0847	1
DOTY MERCER M	LTC	O-0057221	0868	1
DOTY OTIS J	LTC	O-0062269	0867	1
DOTY RALPH E	COL	O-0016905	0157	1
DOUD HAROLD	COL	O-0016423	0754	1
DOUGAN RAMON C	COL	O-0030566	1163	1
DOUGHERTY EDWARD F	MAJ	O-0022711	0944	2
DOUGHERTY CLARENCE A	COL	O-0001564	0440	2
DOUGHERTY GEORGE F	COL	O-0051055	1059	1
DOUGHERTY GERALD A	CW2	W-0907131	0961	1
DOUGHERTY JACK [illegible]	LTC	O-0065476	0565	1
DOUGHERTY JOHN [illegible]	LTC	O-0031582	0765	1
DOUGHERTY JOSEPH S	COL	O-0008309	0754	1
DOUGLAS HARRY V	LTC	O-0042786	0564	1
DOUGLAS JAMES S	COL	O-0026625	0863	1
DOUGLAS MARION D	LTC	R-0010076	0464	1
DOUGLAS ROBERT H	COL	O-0019212	0863	1
DOUGLASS FRANCIS L	LTC	O-0024254	0965	1

NAME	GRADE	SVC NO	DATE RET MO YR	RET CODE
DOUGLASS GEORGE A	COL	0-0030296	1264	1
DOUTHITT TED F	LTC	0-0031626	1262	1
DOVENSPIKE JAY W	LTC	0-0042229	0761	1
DOW ARDEN W	COL	0-0024591	0863	1
DOW DONALD G	COL	0-0042389	0964	1
DOWD THOMAS E JR	LTC	0-0027160	0765	1
DOWDEN RICHARD L	LTC	0-0080716	0566	1
DOWDS PETER M	MAJ	0-0086082	0466	1
DOWDY JAMES H	CW4	W-0903035	0762	1
DOWELL RICHARD W	LTC	0-0039225	0562	2
DOWLESS JOSEPH D JR	COL	0-0037460	0468	1
DOWLING PAUL J	COL	0-0004867	1147	1
DOWNER JOHN W	COL	0-0001995	0642	1
DOWNER WILLIAM W	LTC	0-0034854	0861	1
DOWNING EDWARD J	LTC	0-0042655	1163	1
DOWNING ELLSWORTH	COL	0-0014986	0263	1
DOWNING GEORGE J	MAJ	0-0005550	0240	2
DOWNING LELAND A	CW3	W-0903036	0857	1
DOWNING LESLIE B	LTC	0-0012688	1047	1
DOWNING WALTER A JR	COL	0-0018991	0863	1
DOXEY THOMAS A JR	COL	0-0015978	0348	1
DOYEL ERNEST G	COL	0-0041453	0456	2
DOYLE ARTHUR L	LTC	0-0027684	0466	1
DOYLE JOHN F	COL	0-0040127	0765	1
DOYLE JOHN J S	LTC	0-0042617	0863	1
DOYLE PHILIP V	LTC	0-0018712	0949	2
DOYLE PIERCE A JR	LTC	0-0024891	0664	1
DOZIER LINWOOD G	CW4	W-0904370	0456	1
DOZIER SLATER M	COL	0-0058184	0866	1
DRAGOIU VICTORIA R	MAJ	N-0002156	0362	1
DRAHEIM JOHN H	LTC	0-0060034	0866	1
DRAIN JESSE C	B G	0-0002235	0945	1
DRAKE ALBERT F	MAJ	0-0003003	0927	2
DRAKE CHARLES C	B G	0-0003415	1046	2
DRAKE FRANK M	COL	0-0041887	0761	1
DRAKE JAMES H	COL	0-0010635	1052	2
DRAKE LELAND F	COL	0-0043894	0263	1
DRAKE MYRTIE	MAJ	N-0000837	0661	1
DRAKE THOMAS D	COL	0-0015384	0447	2
DRAKE WARREN W	LTC	0-0027727	0966	1
DRAKE WILLIAM D	COL	0-0032158	0862	2
DRAKULICH GEORGIA F	MAJ	N-0002046	0360	1
DRAPER JAMES L	COL	0-0079801	0965	1
DRAPER PHILIP H JR	M G	0-0017543	1162	1
DRAPER STUART I	COL	0-0023599	1065	2
DRAPER WILLIAM R	COL	0-0029176	0460	1
DRAVO EDWARD J	CPT	0-0026937	0647	2
DRAZEN LEONARD	COL	0-0040336	0766	1
DREISBACH ALBERT R	COL	0-0018938	1062	1
DREISS EDWARD	COL	0-0035589	0766	1
DRENNEN WILLIAM L	COL	0-0031890	0367	1
DRENNON CLARENCE B	COL	0-0083566	0767	1
DRESSELL FLORENCE A	MAJ	N-0000541	0549	1
DRESSER PAUL A	COL	0-0030037	1163	1
DRESSLER JESSE F	CPT	0-0016931	0142	1
DREWES CARL E	COL	0-0024122	0567	1
DREWRY GUY H	B G	0-0004950	0846	1
DREWS RENO E	COL	0-0043420	0268	1
DREYFUS JAMES	M G	0-0029117	0661	1
DRIGGERS CARL E	LTC	0-0005708	0-39	1
DRISCOLL ARTHUR F	LTC	0-0079802	1065	1
DRISCOLL CHARLES L	LTC	0-0017036	0450	1
DRISCOLL DANIEL M	LTC	0-0041773	0363	1
DRISCOLL MAURICE L	COL	0-0030525	1163	1
DRISKILL AUBREY C	CW3	W-0906703	0759	1
DRISKILL JOHN D	CW4	W-0903038	0860	1
DRISSEL HELEN B	LTC	L-0000507	1165	1
DRISSEL VIRGIL H	COL	0-0040010	0266	1
DRIVER COLEMAN F	CPT	0-0007612	1129	2
DROBEK THADDEUS W	LTC	0-0042453	1062	1
DROSS ALLEN F	CPT	0-0089677	1163	2
DROZD MAGDALENE	MAJ	N-0000257	0561	1
DRULEY EDWIN H	COL	0-0029476	0263	1
DRUM HEISTER H	MAJ	0-0023923	0347	2
DRUM JAMES H	COL	0-0020818	0846	2
DRUM VERNON B	LTC	0-0039318	0764	1
DRUMM BURNETT C	CPT	N-0000048	0550	1
DRUMM JUDITH M	MAJ	N-0002467	0162	2
DRUMMOND BURLEIGH B	COL	0-0051771	0766	1
DRURY FREDERICK	COL	0-0012333	0753	1
DRYE CLARENCE W	COL	0-0052413	1067	1
DRYER CHARLES W	LTC	0-0086087	1168	1
DU BOSE BURNS B JR	CW4	W-0905205	0658	1
DU HAMEL NOTLEY Y	LTC	0-0004422	0342	2
DU MOND PAUL A	COL	0-0037607	0467	2
DU MOULIN ALFRED K	COL	0-0019943	0865	1
DU RANT ROBERT N	LTC	0-0063803	0467	1
DU VAL CAMILLE H	COL	0-0041440	1056	1
DUBBELDE JOHN	COL	0-0015086	0954	1
DUBIA GILBERT P	COL	0-0039872	0164	1
DUBOIS BIRD S	COL	0-0003382	1047	2
DUBOIS HARRIS A	CPT	0-0065215	0156	2
DUBUC JOSEPH M	CW4	W-0906704	0860	1
DUBUY CARL T	COL	0-0023650	0661	1
DUCKSTAD ERIC E	MAJ	0-0023464	0445	2
DUCKWALL BERTRAM F	COL	0-0004031	0649	1
DUCKWALL RICHARD L	LTC	0-0039053	0564	1
DUCKWORTH BENTON R	LTC	0-0021934	0867	1
DUCOTE WARREN S	LTC	0-0060826	0964	1
DUDA EDWARD	COL	0-0043041	0667	1
DUDDERAR SAM K JR	LTC	0-0031764	0166	1
DUDLEY EDWARD F	LTC	0-0040374	0765	1
DUDLEY HOWARD H	MAJ	0-0018541	0946	1
DUDLEY JOHN H	B G	0-0018049	0760	1
DUDLEY ROBERT L	LTC	0-0033746	0765	1
DUDLEY WILLIAM R	COL	0-0045497	0358	2
DUDLEY WOLCOTT K	COL	0-0015799	0954	1
DUE KENNETH O	CPT	0-0024099	0445	2
DUE WILLIAM F	COL	0-0019268	1163	2
DUEHRING GEORGE C	COL	0-0018070	0460	1
DUEKER FRED E	COL	0-0032051	1060	1
DUELL CLIFFORD C	COL	0-0014645	0553	1
DUEMMEL WARREN G	LTC	0-0045004	1061	1
DUER PAMELA E	MAJ	M-0010105	1063	1
DUERR GEORGE A	COL	0-0028944	1157	1
DUERSON SAMUEL H	LTC	0-0030084	1061	1
DUFF CHARLES B	LTG	0-0018438	0866	1
DUFF FORREST W	COL	0-0043391	0462	2
DUFF ROBINSON E	M G	0-0007388	0153	2
DUFF RUSSELL G	COL	0-0014646	0555	1
DUFFILL HARRISON M	MAJ	0-0005367	0438	2
DUFFNER CARL F	COL	0-0012801	0753	1
DUFFY CATHERINE	MAJ	N-0000567	0561	2
DUFFY JACK W	LTC	0-0037349	0664	1
DUFFY JAMES R	COL	0-0052428	1267	1
DUFFY JOHN J	COL	0-0019738	0865	1
DUFRESNE GEORGE R	LTC	0-0062812	0865	1
DUFRESNE ROLAND J	CW4	W-0901591	0957	1
DUGAN AUGUSTINE	COL	0-0015610	0754	1
DUGGAN ROY H	LTC	0-0066147	0866	1
DUGGAN WALTER	LTC	0-0050053	0767	1
DUGGINS GEORGE J	MAJ	0-0058886	0663	1
DUGGINS PERCY E	COL	0-0004144	0548	2
DUHON SIMON J	CW4	W-0903039	1154	1
DUIN GERALD H	COL	0-0020148	0559	1
DUKE HENRY B	COL	0-0079803	0966	1
DUKE JAMES O	LTC	0-0060502	0867	2
DUKE JAMES T	B G	0-0006654	0653	1
DUKE RAYMOND E	COL	0-0020110	0465	1
DUKE RICHARD J	LTC	0-0089910	0968	1
DUKE ROBERT W	B G	0-0033373	1267	1
DUKE STRATFORD	CW4	R W-0903040	0561	1
DUKES DAN K JR	COL	0-0034283	0964	1
DUKES ERNEST F	COL	0-0008029	1047	1
DUKES LONZIE J	LTC	0-0058887	0367	1
DUL PETER A	LTC	0-0080720	0265	1
DULANEY JACK F	CPT	0-0025812	0847	2
DULANEY ROBERT L	M G	0-0015351	0154	1
DULAY PEDRO O	COL	0-0003236	1033	2
DULLUM DELL F	COL	0-0021011	0758	1
DUMAS ALBERT H	COL	0-0007488	0749	2
DUMAS MAMIE	MAJ	N-0000286	0160	1
DUMOND KENNETH S	LTC	0-0030748	0764	1
DUMONT FERNAND G	COL	0-0011954	1149	1
DUMPERT PAUL J	CW3	W-0903041	0859	1
DUNAWAY FINIS E	COL	0-0016085	1046	2
DUNBAR CHARLES H	CW4	W-0906706	0163	1
DUNBAR ELLEN V	MAJ	L-0000138	0364	1
DUNBAR LEE R	COL	0-0002648	0245	2
DUNBAR OLIVER C	LTC	0-0043408	0166	1
DUNCAN GEORGE T	M G	0-0018878	0867	1
DUNCAN HARRY C	LTC	0-0080400	1265	1
DUNCAN JAMES W	COL	0-0020834	0766	1
DUNCAN JOSEPH G III	COL	0-0021227	0262	1
DUNCAN MARGARET E	LTC	N-0000329	0763	1
DUNCAN WILLIAM D	COL	0-0031466	0966	1
DUNCKEL WILLIAM C	M G	0-0006676	0-45	2
DUNFORD DONALD	B G	0-0016267	1155	1
DUNHAM CHARLES E	LTC	0-0016801	0755	1
DUNHAM LEO E JR	COL	0-0022897	0761	1
DUNHAM WILLIAM H JR	COL	0-0012411	0546	2
DUNKELBERG WILBUR E	B G	0-0012206	1155	1
DUNKLE DONALD R	COL	0-0007161	0447	2
DUNLAP CLARENCE R	COL	0-0029975	0965	2
DUNLAP KNOX	COL	0-0019667	0663	2
DUNLOP ROBERT H	B G	0-0002885	0346	1
DUNLOY DEANE A	COL	0-0028825	0466	1
DUNN BEVERLY C	B G	0-0002830	0748	2
DUNN CHARLES G	B G	0-0018996	0863	2
DUNN FLOYD E	COL	0-0016261	0655	1
DUNN FRANCIS L	COL	0-0040437	0168	1
DUNN JERRY F	COL	0-0034342	0867	1
DUNN JOHN A	COL	0-0022798	0666	2
DUNN JOHN J	COL	0-0031385	0860	1
DUNN JOHN L	COL	0-0004591	1149	1
DUNN JOSEPH F	LTC	0-0024482	0268	1
DUNN MAURICE W	LTC	0-0040985	1066	1
DUNN PHILIP E	LTC	0-0050379	0962	1
DUNN SIDNEY F	COL	0-0005458	0452	2
DUNN STEPHANIC	CPT	N-0002311	0357	2
DUNN THOMAS W	LTG	0-0018157	0767	2
DUNN WELLINGTON	LTC	0-0063287	0866	1
DUNN WILLIAM P	LTC	0-0051413	0461	1
DUNNE DAVID M	COL	0-0015130	0854	1
DUNNE JOSEPH A	MAJ	0-0043200	0753	2
DUNNING MILO B	LTC	0-0009431	0538	1
DUNSTAN HENRY V	LTC	0-0040953	1165	1
DUPONT LEO E	LTC	0-0055889	0565	1
DUPREE JAMES E	COL	0-0040044	0962	1
DUPUY HENRY H	CW3	W-0903046	1058	1
DUPUY RICHARD E	COL	0-0006186	0546	1
DUPUY TREVOR N	COL	0-0021098	0758	1
DURAND PAUL	CW4	W-0903047	0666	1
DURANT BENJAMIN R	CW4	W-0903048	0963	1
DURAY JOSEPH P	LTC	0-0065257	0667	1
DURBIN PAUL J	COL	0-0052110	0268	1
DURBIN ROLLIN B	COL	0-0021244	0866	1
DURBIN WILLIAM F	COL	0-0051748	0361	1
DURDEN LEWIS M	LTC	0-0030935	1264	1
DURFEE DONALD L	COL	0-0019538	0862	1
DURFEE LOYD V	LTC	0-0008620	0841	2
DURGAN RAYMOND C	COL	0-0023527	1166	2
DURGIN CHESLEY F	COL	0-0032363	0265	2
DURHAM ERNEST E	COL	0-0035709	0962	1
DURHAM FANNY	MAJ	N-0002074	1163	1
DURHAM HOWARD W	LTC	0-0059902	0565	1
DURING FRED	COL	0-0005660	0944	1
DURNFORD JAMES A	COL	0-0011418	0250	2
DURR JOHN C	LTC	0-0028345	0966	2
DURR RICHARD H	LTC	0-0058888	0868	1
DURST RICHARD H	LTC	0-0080402	0665	1
DURST ROBERT D	COL	0-0028837	0656	1
DURYEA LYMAN C	COL	0-0057522	0158	1
DUSENBURY CARLISLE C	COL	0-0011672	0959	1
DUSENBURY RALPH W	COL	0-0002280	0445	1
DUTCHAK EUGENE M	LTC	0-0057458	0467	1
DUTTON CARL R	COL	0-0016048	0954	1
DUTTON DONALD L	COL	0-0005547	0251	1
DUTTWEILER CHARLES H	LTC	0-0079805	0464	1
DUVAL HELEN G	MAJ	N-0000348	0260	1
DUVALL ANDREW R	COL	0-0010925	1146	2
DUVALL ANDREW R JR	LTC	0-0032444	0168	1
DUVALL CLIFFORD P	LTC	0-0039270	0764	1
DUVALL EDWARD	COL	0-0041921	1061	1
DUVALL EVERETT W	COL	0-0032842	0268	2
DUVALL WALLACE L	LTC	0-0084735	1068	1
DUVALL WARD F	COL	0-0003592	0546	2
DWINELL JOHN S	COL	0-0041467	0960	2
DWORAK JOHN L	LTC	0-0025757	1167	1
DWYER JOHN R	COL	0-0042138	0463	1
DWYER PHILIP P	COL	0-0015171	0554	1
DWYRE DOUGLAS G	COL	0-0017535	0859	1
DYE EARL S JR	LTC	0-0028262	0268	1
DYE HAROLD A	COL	0-0076871	0967	1
DYEKMAN IVAN J	COL	0-0030455	0862	2
DYER ARMEL	COL	0-0042674	0862	2
DYER HAROLD F	COL	0-0043328	1164	1
DYER JAMES M	1LT	0-0069001	1156	2
DYER JOSEPH C	COL	0-0079807	0768	1
DYER KENNETH R	COL	0-0040065	1264	1
DYKE HAROLD H JR	LTC	0-0053334	0165	1
DYKE LESTER M	COL	0-0016943	0946	1
DYKES CLIFFORD E	LTC	0-0051781	0764	1
DZIUBAN STANLEY W	COL	0-0021738	0864	1
DZURKO ANNA	MAJ	N-0002200	1067	1
EAGAN WARREN C	LTC	0-0069638	0267	1
EAGER BLANCHE H	MAJ	N-0000038	0349	1
EAGER GEORGE JR	LTC	0-0036766	0965	1
EAGER HOWARD	COL	0-0003502	1046	1
EAGLE ALEXANDER	COL	0-0029910	0463	1
EAGLER VERONICA J	MAJ	N-0002265	1162	1
EAGLES WILLIAM W	M G	0-0005270	0153	1
EAKEN ANDREW J	COL	0-0040090	0467	1
EAKER ALAN B	COL	0-0043146	0667	1
EAKER FRED L	COL	0-0042223	0862	1
EAKER JOHN P	CW3	W-0903054	0461	1
EAKIN ALDEAN A	COL	0-0041994	0462	1
EALES JOHN I H	COL	0-0038751	1063	1
EALY RALPH C	CW4	W-0902150	1159	1
EANES EDWARD W	LTC	0-0029249	0860	1
EANES RICHARD H	COL	0-0009453	0949	2
EARL EDWIN O	COL	0-0029097	0457	1
EARLE HIRAM W	LTC	0-0028958	1055	1
EARLE JOHN J JR	1LT	0-0017127	0834	2
EARLES CARL T	LTC	0-0058890	1166	1
EARNEST HERBERT L	M G	0-0007282	0947	1
EASLEY BRUCE	M G	0-0017735	0562	2
EASLEY CLAUDIUS M JR	LTC	0-0035056	0564	1
EASLEY ROY W JR	LTC	0-0062631	0968	1
EASON JAMES F	COL	0-0030435	0665	1
EASON JOHN D	COL	0-0011993	1146	1
EASON RODERICK D	COL	0-0052420	0367	1
EASON SIDNEY S	LTC	0-0080403	0560	1
EAST RALPH O	CW4	W-0903055	0257	1
EASTBURN CHARLEY P	COL	0-0018203	0559	1
EASTERBROOK CHARLES	COL	0-0006130	0144	2
EASTERBROOK ERNEST F	M G	0-0018537	0667	1
EASTMOND THEODORE L	COL	0-0040013	0164	1
EASTON HARRY O	COL	0-0051822	1164	1
EASTON WILLIAM G	COL	0-0020656	0767	2
EASTWOOD HAROLD E	B G	0-0008202	0752	1
EATMAN GEORGE L	COL	0-0019548	0862	1
EATON GAIL A	LTC	0-0042268	1061	1
EATON GALEN P	COL	0-0021940	1046	2
EATON LELAND E JR	MAJ	0-0956880	0567	2
EATON RALPH P	B G	0-0015871	0854	1
EAVES ROYCE L	LTC	0-0032499	1267	1
EBBERT THEODORE H	LTC	0-0029885	0161	1
EBBS RICHARD F	COL	0-0039579	0558	1
EBEL HENRY W	COL	0-0019434	0862	2

NAME	GRADE	SVC NO	DATE RET MO YR	RET CODE
EBERHARD FRANKLIN K	COL	0-0040161	0161	1
EBERHART CLAUDE M	COL	0-0051967	0966	1
EBERLE GEORGE L	M G	0-0006613	0754	2
EBERLE SIDNEY S	COL	0-0004784	0849	1
EBERLIN RALPH	COL	0-0014222	1019	2
EBEY FRANK W	CPT	0-0019905	1047	1
EBLEN GEORGE C	LTC	0-0061195	0666	1
EBREY HENRY J JR	LTC	0-0025627	0568	1
ECHOLS ESTELA B	CPT	N-0000047	0749	1
ECHOLS LEONARD E	COL	0-0042265	0161	1
ECHOLS MARION P	COL	0-0012324	0653	2
ECK DOROTHY J	MAJ	N-0002502	1264	1
ECKERT KENNETH R	COL	0-0039196	0967	1
ECKERT NORMAN J	COL	0-0011591	0854	2
ECKHARDT RICHARD H	COL	0-0019312	0863	1
ECKLAND KENNETH F	COL	0-0032334	0765	1
ECKLES WILLIAM E	COL	0-0029450	0960	1
ECKLON LELAND C	LTC	0-0080732	0867	1
ECKMAN GEORGE R	COL	0-0051005	1058	1
ECKOLS TRUMAN O	COL	0-0043078	0464	1
ECKSTEIN PAUL A	COL	0-0040331	0266	1
EDDINS GRACE T	LTC	N-0002373	0963	1
EDDLEMAN CLYDE D	GEN	0-0015842	0462	2
EDDY ELWIN H	LTC	0-0018364	0154	1
EDDY GEORGE G	B G	0-0012108	0754	2
EDDY KENNETH A	COL	0-0029014	0958	1
EDDY ROBERT N	LTC	0-0022730	0764	1
EDELEN LARUE M	COL	0-0029445	0661	2
EDENFIELD RUTH	LTC	N-0002061	0764	1
EDENS ALLEN C JR	LTC	0-0067567	0767	1
EDENS WALTER A	COL	0-0023563	0862	1
EDGAR JAMES D	COL	0-0030635	0162	1
EDGAR THOMAS I	COL	0-0018083	0157	1
EDGE WILMER A JR	LTC	0-0038747	0553	1
EDGERLY JOHN H	LTC	0-0051684	1160	1
EDGERLY JOHN P	COL	0-0003139	0934	2
EDGERTON ERIC R	LTC	0-0043850	0667	1
EDGERTON GLEN E	M G	0-0002324	0449	2
EDINGTON JAMES E	LTC	0-0050734	0766	1
EDMAN WINIFRED L	CPT	N-0002677	1163	2
EDMOND NEIL S	COL	0-0006806	1048	1
EDMONSON EDWARD M	COL	0-0012683	0950	1
EDMONSTON RAPHAEL A	LTC	0-0017666	0245	2
EDMUNDS ARTHUR D	MAJ	0-0014431	0630	2
EDMUNDS JAMES R	COL	0-0010848	0653	2
EDMUNDS JOHN C	COL	0-0030323	0165	1
EDMUNDS KINZIE B	COL	0-0001936	0642	2
EDNIE ALFRED V	COL	0-0008157	0-45	2
EDRINGTON BETHELL JR	LTC	0-0026329	0965	1
EDSON FRANK T	COL	0-0029827	1262	1
EDSON HALLETT D	B G	0-0017541	0864	1
EDWARDS CORWIN V	LTC	0-0085159	0967	1
EDWARDS DAVID L	COL	0-0020359	0366	1
EDWARDS EARL L	COL	0-0031647	1067	1
EDWARDS EARL W	COL	0-0023502	0862	1
EDWARDS EDMUND B	COL	0-0004927	0254	1
EDWARDS EDWARD G	COL	0-0032048	1168	2
EDWARDS ELMER F	LTC	0-0080405	0667	1
EDWARDS HENRY B JR	LTC	0-0058130	0267	1
EDWARDS JAMES W	COL	0-0030274	1064	1
EDWARDS JOHN E	LTC	0-0056945	1264	1
EDWARDS JOHN W	LTC	0-0054229	0962	1
EDWARDS JULIAN B JR	1LT	0-0070695	0159	2
EDWARDS LEMUEL F	COL	0-0011284	1146	1
EDWARDS MEYER A JR	COL	0-0020702	0863	1
EDWARDS MORRIS O	B G	0-0019041	0763	1
EDWARDS PARMER W	M G	0-0016775	0760	1
EDWARDS PAUL S	COL	0-0008955	0347	2
EDWARDS PERRY	LTC	0-0030309	1162	1
EDWARDS RAYMOND F	COL	0-0006778	0548	1
EDWARDS RICHARD T	LTC	0-0005422	1041	1
EDWARDS ROBERT	MAJ	0-0012760	0442	1
EDWARDS ROBERT O	MAJ	0-0017366	1028	2
EDWARDS RUBLE R	CW3	W-0908238	0868	1
EDWARDS SAM A	COL	0-0037466	0467	1

NAME	GRADE	SVC NO	DATE RET MO YR	RET CODE
EDWARDS SHEFFIELD	COL	0-0015203	1053	1
EDWARDS SPENCER P JR	COL	0-0033990	0862	1
EDWARDS WALTON M	COL	0-0024377	1163	1
EDWARDS WILLIAM H	COL	0-0042267	0158	1
EFNOR SAM JR	COL	0-0034054	0661	1
EGAN JOHN A	COL	0-0019320	0348	2
EGAN JOHN B	COL	0-0043003	1064	1
EGAN MARGARET M	LTC	N-0002058	0164	1
EGAN ROLAND D	CW4	W-0903057	0255	1
EGAN WILLIAM J	COL	0-0007568	0-45	2
EGBERT FRANCIS J JR	CW4	W-0902380	0667	1
EGE CHARLES C	COL	0-0029102	0559	1
EGGER FLOYD C	COL	0-0052065	0167	1
EGGLESTON HOWARD K	B G	0-0030271	0166	1
EGGLESTON NORMAN E	LTC	0-0068096	1268	1
EGOZCUE EDWARD J	MAJ	0-0070330	0166	1
EHLEN EDWARD S	B G	0-0019286	0864	1
EHLERS CHRISTINE	MAJ	M-0010036	1058	1
EHRLICH KARL F	COL	0-0030858	0565	1
EICHEN HARRIS C	LTC	0-0080406	0568	1
EICHER ROGER A	COL	0-0040665	0268	1
EICHORN FREDERIC N	COL	0-0039636	0160	1
EICKHOFF ALBERT P	LTC	0-0059853	0862	1
EIDECKER EARL E	LTC	0-0084978	1268	1
EILER KEITH E	LTC	0-0026533	0565	1
EILTS ALLIE M	MAJ	N-0000589	0460	2
EINHAUS GORDON M	LTC	0-0081895	0768	1
EISENDORFF GRACE T	1LT	R-0000126	1045	2
EISENSCHMIDT CLYDE R	LTC	0-0003844	0640	2
EISIMINGER STERLING	COL	0-0040651	1167	1
EITT HERBERT F	COL	0-0032477	0966	1
EKLUND KARL F	COL	0-0020557	0467	1
EKMAN CARL N	COL	0-0022293	0561	1
EKMAN WILLIAM E	B G	0-0021190	0568	2
ELA WILLIAM E	COL	0-0041483	1057	2
ELARTH HAROLD H	LTC	0-0009032	1039	2
ELCANO MICHAEL P	LTC	0-0044142	0966	1
ELDER CHARLES J	CW3	W-0903061	0958	1
ELDER FRANK L	COL	0-0019203	0863	2
ELDER HARTWELL M	COL	0-0012576	0751	1
ELDER JAMES W	CPT	0-0019349	1141	2
ELDRACHER JOHN W	CW4	W-0903062	0568	1
ELDRED NORA P	MAJ	N-0000071	0550	1
ELDRIDGE MARY J B	MAJ	L-0000144	1066	1
ELDRIDGE RALPH S	COL	0-0023442	0968	2
ELDRIDGE WILLIAM G	COL	0-0029070	0359	1
ELEGAR AUGUSTUS G	B G	0-0018625	0560	1
ELEY WILLIAM S	COL	0-0005325	0353	2
ELGES CARL H JR	COL	0-0030511	0965	1
ELIAN ARTHUR J	LTC	0-0060946	0867	1
ELIAS PAUL	COL	0-0017546	0656	1
ELIOT AMORY V	COL	0-0008336	0753	2
ELKEY JAMES H	LTC	0-0027370	0167	1
ELKINS EDGAR A	CPT	0-0006145	1022	2
ELKINS HARRY W	COL	0-0020766	0765	1
ELKINS HORACE N JR	LTC	0-0039770	0557	1
ELKINS STEPHEN B	B G	0-0010913	0954	1
ELKINTON EDWARD	CW4	W-0903063	0657	1
ELLENBERG JULIAN S	LTC	0-0041756	0556	2
ELLERS CONWAY L	LTC	0-0039051	1064	1
ELLERSON GEOFFREY D	COL	0-0019759	0865	1
ELLERT ROBERT B	LTC	0-0059836	0166	1
ELLERY FREDERICK	B G	0-0018725	0461	1
ELLIGET DONALD A	COL	0-0019719	0963	1
ELLINGER RUTH W	MAJ	M-0001025	0163	1
ELLIOTT ALENE V	LTC	R-0010068	0461	1
ELLIOTT CHARLES B JR	COL	0-0019490	0764	1
ELLIOTT DABNEY O	B G	0-0003669	0950	1
ELLIOTT DOROTHY V	LTC	N-0002245	0464	1
ELLIOTT EDWIN E	CPT	0-0004979	0928	2
ELLIOTT ESCALUS E	COL	0-0012834	0753	2
ELLIOTT EUGENE M JR	COL	0-0051340	0962	1
ELLIOTT HAROLD S	LTC	0-0064983	1266	1
ELLIOTT IVAN W	COL	0-0031863	0364	1
ELLIOTT JAMES N	LTC	0-0050051	1163	1

NAME	GRADE	SVC NO	DATE RET MO YR	RET CODE
ELLIOTT JESSE D	COL	0-0001848	1039	1
ELLIOTT JOHN T	LTC	0-0026896	0865	1
ELLIOTT LOWELL A	COL	0-0010712	0449	1
ELLIOTT PHILIP L	COL	0-0022945	0661	1
ELLIOTT RALPH H	COL	0-0030744	1164	1
ELLIOTT RICHARD B	LTC	0-0050442	0765	1
ELLIOTT RICHARD H	CPT	0-0014420	0320	2
ELLIOTT ROBERT H	COL	0-0009324	1052	2
ELLIOTT ROBIN	LTC	L-0000064	1262	1
ELLIOTT WALLACE R JR	COL	0-0040837	0165	1
ELLIS ARTHUR M	LTC	0-0004489	1042	2
ELLIS ARTHUR P JR	LTC	0-0036150	0165	1
ELLIS BERTRAM J	COL	0-0040244	0868	2
ELLIS BURTON F	COL	0-0029033	1158	1
ELLIS DAVID J	COL	0-0063154	0966	1
ELLIS E DETREVIL	COL	0-0003831	0350	1
ELLIS EDWARD H	LTC	0-0050129	0766	1
ELLIS HAROLD B	LTC	0-0025338	0862	1
ELLIS HARRY H	COL	0-0023958	0866	1
ELLIS HARRY V	COL	0-0011945	1048	1
ELLIS HARVIE R	COL	0-0017791	0457	2
ELLIS HERBERT E	MAJ	0-0003216	0132	1
ELLIS JOAN	MAJ	L-0000331	0666	1
ELLIS LINDLEY C	LTC	0-0026849	0765	1
ELLIS MURRAY H	COL	0-0006730	0450	1
ELLIS PEARL T	LTC	N-0000016	1047	1
ELLIS RICHARD C	COL	0-0076873	0968	1
ELLIS ROBERT L	CPT	0-0095899	0968	2
ELLIS THOMAS G JR	LTC	0-0065106	0567	1
ELLIS WALTER F	COL	0-0018378	0761	1
ELLIS WILBER R	COL	0-0014652	0848	1
ELLISON HENRY B	COL	0-0011652	1047	1
ELLISON MARVIN C	COL	0-0041494	0358	1
ELLISON MILTON H	COL	0-0080739	0762	1
ELLSWORTH ROBERT A	COL	0-0015780	0146	2
ELLYETT JAMES W JR	CW3	W-0903068	0661	1
ELMES CHESTER H	COL	0-0011365	0753	1
ELMORE JOHN A	B G	0-0015823	0156	2
ELMORE ORVILLE N	CW3	W-0904246	0759	1
ELMS GEORGE G	COL	0-0012391	0854	1
ELOWER CHARLES F	CW4	W-0903070	0957	1
ELSBERRY ROBERT V	LTC	0-0023783	0761	1
ELSER FRED J	COL	0-0029557	0559	1
ELSER MAX A	COL	0-0002163	0743	1
ELTERICH JOHN A	COL	0-0029696	0462	1
ELTING JOHN R	COL	0-0079703	0468	1
ELWARD NYE K	LTC	0-0015827	0445	2
ELWOOD ERNEST A	LTC	0-0011986	1039	2
ELY LOUIS B	COL	0-0012270	1053	1
ELY ROBERT L JR	COL	0-0060211	0367	1
ELY WILLIAM J	LTG	0-0018974	0866	1
EMANUEL EMMETT H	LTC	0-0015435	1035	2
EMBRY JOHN	COL	0-0041798	0860	1
EMERSON EARL F JR	LTC	0-0057642	0867	1
EMERSON GENEVIEVE	MAJ	M-0010073	0859	1
EMERSON GOUVERNEUR	B G	0-0004048	0149	2
EMERSON KARY C	COL	0-0033991	1166	1
EMERSON MAXWELL	COL	0-0041514	0558	1
EMERY FRANK E JR	COL	0-0003837	0347	1
EMERY GUY C JR	LTC	0-0052481	0261	1
EMERY HAROLD R	COL	0-0012471	0854	1
EMERY JACK R	COL	0-0040276	0667	1
EMERY JOHN R	LTC	0-0059992	1266	1
EMIG NICKOLAUS	LTC	0-0040005	0264	1
EMMANUELLI LOUIS S	MAJ	0-0014000	0720	2
EMMONS DAVID B	COL	0-0039979	0765	1
EMOND WILFRED A	COL	0-0019642	1053	2
EMRICH ROBERT F	LTC	0-0078821	0968	1
ENDERTON HERBERT B	COL	0-0015149	0754	2
ENEBOE EDWARD S	LTC	0-0027488	0767	1
ENEY JOHN K	COL	0-0036514	1065	1
ENGDAHL FRANCIS A	CW4	W-0903074	0856	1
ENGEL HARRY J	M G	0-0039840	0568	2
ENGELHARDT EDWARD C	1LT	0-0014761	0-30	1
ENGELHART E CARL	COL	0-0012773	0850	1

NAME	GRADE	SVC NO	DATE RET MO YR	RET CODE
ENGELLAND LLOYD W	LTC	0-0032551	1159	2
ENGEMAN LEONARD E	COL	0-0029641	1161	1
ENGER EDGAR F	COL	0-0017284	0758	1
ENGERUD HAROLD	COL	0-0011716	0449	1
ENGL JOHN W	LTC	0-0044278	0868	2
ENGLAND GEORGE W JR	COL	0-0023226	0868	1
ENGLAND SANFORD P	COL	0-0023129	0862	1
ENGLEHARDT JOSEPH E	LTC	0-0033143	0461	2
ENGLEHART FRANCIS A	B G	0-0003542	0846	2
ENGLISH BURT	COL	0-0003971	0-35	1
ENGLISH JOHN T	COL	0-0021296	0168	1
ENGLISH ROBERT O JR	COL	0-0031371	1266	1
ENGSTROM GUSTAF A	COL	0-0030124	0464	1
ENNIS CHARLES	COL	0-0010336	0753	1
ENNIS ROSA E	MAJ	L-0000214	0456	1
ENNIS WILLIAM P JR	LTG	0-0016436	0962	1
ENOS WILLIAM F	LTC	0-0026819	0865	1
ENQUIST VERA A	MAJ	N-0002043	0360	1
ENSLOW PHILIP H	COL	0-0015241	0754	1
ENSRUD JOSEPH O	COL	0-0017493	0248	2
ENTWHISTLE RICHARD R	COL	0-0040198	1163	1
EPES WILLIAM J	COL	0-0012112	0854	1
EPLEY ALBERT D	LTC	0-0023250	0768	1
EPLEY GERALD G	COL	0-0018770	0762	1
EPLING FENTON G	COL	0-0006574	0145	1
EPPERLY JAMES M	M G	0-0016288	0860	2
EPPERSON ELBERT P	CPT	0-0025807	0546	2
EPPS FREDERICK	CW2	W-0901309	0345	2
EPPS GRADY D	COL	0-0014855	0744	2
EPPS LONNETTE L	MAJ	N-0000636	0161	1
EPSTEIN GERALD S	CPT	0-0028105	1054	2
ERDMAN BENJAMIN K	COL	0-0010354	0753	2
ERGAS LOUISE M	LTC	N-0002114	0857	1
ERICKSON ERIC A	COL	0-0010148	1051	1
ERICKSON JAMES L	COL	0-0033597	0168	1
ERICKSON ROBERT C	COL	0-0052177	0766	1
ERICKSON SIDNEY	B G	0-0003636	1046	2
ERICSON RICHARD A	COL	0-0012117	0854	1
ERION KENNETH W	CW4	W-0903077	0264	1
ERKENBECK VERNON J	COL	0-0019304	1157	1
ERLENBUSCH ROBERT C	COL	0-0021230	0469	1
ERLENKOTTER DAVID	LTC	0-0027350	0765	1
ERLENKOTTER ROBERT	COL	0-0019354	0760	2
ERNST ESTELLE T	MAJ	N-0000314	1059	1
ERNST JACK M	COL	0-0042371	0562	1
ERNST KENNETH F	COL	0-0018639	1159	1
ERSKINE DAVID G	COL	0-0015766	0954	1
ERSKINE JASPER N	LTC	0-0036768	0864	1
ERSPAMER FLORIAN J	LTC	0-0023242	0761	1
ERWIN LEWIS D	LTC	0-0028780	0753	2
ESCHBACH ALFRED L	COL	0-0021419	0958	1
ESCUE HODGES S	LTC	0-0063375	0867	1
ESDORN WALTER H	COL	0-0018337	0445	2
ESPELUND SELMER J	COL	0-0043416	0168	1
ESPOSITO AIDA G	MAJ	L-0000296	0760	1
ESS EARL D	LTC	0-0069915	0364	2
ESSMAN GRAYDON C	B G	0-0019242	0861	1
ESTABROOK MARCIA E	CW4	V-0904318	1164	1
ESTES CLIFFORD H	LTC	0-0065987	0867	1
ESTES GEORGE H	B G	0-0000456	1036	2
ESTES HOWELL M	COL	0-0003119	1046	2
ESTES WILLIAM B	COL	0-0051126	0158	1
ESTRADA LEON P	CPT	0-0068098	0767	2
ETCHEMENDY LEON	LTC	0-0080745	0768	1
ETHEL WILLIS G	COL	0-0031786	0268	1
ETHERIDGE WALTER L	CW4	W-0903079	1168	1
ETHERTON LOUIS M	COL	0-0039940	0862	1
ETKA DALE L	COL	0-0043898	1166	1
ETZLER CHARLES R	COL	0-0020895	0466	1
EUBANK PERRY H	COL	0-0020630	0863	1
EUBANKS C A HOLMES	COL	0-0042014	0462	1
EUBANKS FRANK C JR	MAJ	0-0062838	0567	1
EUBANKS MILDRED	MAJ	N-0022793	0264	1
EVANS ALBERT B	COL	0-0030215	0764	1
EVANS ALBERT L	COL	0-0010669	Q143	1

NAME	GRADE	SVC NO	DATE RET MO YR	RET CODE
EVANS ANDREW J	COL	0-0014356	1151	1
EVANS BELMONT S JR	LTC	0-0021811	0360	1
EVANS BILL A	LTC	0-0040714	0464	2
EVANS BILL G	LTC	0-0069642	0968	1
EVANS BRYAN	COL	0-0012133	0854	1
EVANS BRYAN JR	MAJ	0-0058497	1265	1
EVANS FRANK J	COL	0-0053630	0368	1
EVANS GILES E JR	COL	0-0020603	0660	1
EVANS GRAHAM R	COL	0-0030656	0366	1
EVANS HAZEL L	MAJ	N-0001404	0268	1
EVANS HOUSTON V	COL	0-0029011	0957	1
EVANS JACK C JR	COL	0-0023517	0468	1
EVANS JAMES H	COL	0-0017523	0859	1
EVANS JOHN D JR	COL	0-0040056	1166	1
EVANS JOHN P	COL	0-0015363	0954	1
EVANS JOHN T	COL	0-0032142	0966	1
EVANS LAWRENCE J JR	LTC	0-0038205	1268	1
EVANS LEON G	LTC	0-0052521	0465	1
EVANS LUTHER JR	COL	0-0080748	1168	1
EVANS MURRAY F	LTC	0-0031296	0468	1
EVANS RICHARD	CW4	W-0904111	1267	1
EVANS RICHARD H	COL	0-0015217	1046	2
EVANS RICHARD L	CPT	0-0025474	0346	2
EVANS ROBERT F	COL	0-0042662	0965	1
EVANS ROBERT H	LTC	0-0031628	0965	1
EVANS ROBERT N	MAJ	0-0028630	0862	2
EVANS ROY C	LTC	0-0042233	0160	1
EVANS ROY T JR	M G	0-0019140	0363	1
EVANS SYLVIA M	LTC	N-0000536	0555	2
EVANS THOMAS B	M G	0-0019174	0964	1
EVANS THOMAS N	CW3	W-0902051	0555	1
EVANS VERNON	M G	0-0003318	0153	1
EVANS WILL H	CPT	0-0007378	0229	2
EVANS WILLIAM A	COL	0-0042060	0862	2
EVANS WILLIAM E	LTC	0-0081896	0966	1
EVANS WILLIAM R	CPT	0-0051820	1066	2
EVANS WILLIAM R	CW3	W-0904247	0263	1
EVANS WILLIAM S	COL	0-0005384	0948	2
EVELAND WARREN C	COL	0-0029167	1059	1
EVENS ROBLEY D	COL	0-0039924	0161	2
EVENSON DOROTHY M	MAJ	N-0001390	1167	1
EVERETT HUGH JR	COL	0-0039573	0358	1
EVERETT WARREN S	COL	0-0019739	1263	1
EVERITT EDWARD A JR	COL	0-0006558	0450	1
EVERS CLARENCE P	COL	0-0004705	0651	1
EVERSOLE MAC C	LTC	0-0056634	0865	1
EWART JAMES A	LTC	0-0065449	0966	1
EWBANK ERNEST W JR	COL	0-0030474	1065	1
EWBANK KEITH H	COL	0-0018082	0760	1
EWELL GEORGE W	LTC	0-0001766	0-33	2
EWING CHARLES B	COL	0-0016900	0657	1
EWING FRANCIS	MAJ	N-0000069	0554	1
EWING JOHN T	COL	0-0021326	0660	1
EWING PAUL R	MAJ	0-0087511	1266	1
EWING THOMAS P	LTC	0-0033284	1060	1
EWING WALTER P	LTC	0-0042362	0862	1
EYERLY WILLIAM J	COL	0-0015628	0754	1
EYERMAN MELVIN F	COL	0-0021026	0861	1
EYLER GORDON M	COL	0-0019191	0746	2
EYSTER CHARLES H	CW3	W-0906716	1264	1
EZEKIEL RAPHAEL B	CPT	0-0017084	0242	1
FAABORG CLARENCE	CPT	0-0068100	0368	1
FABIAN KEITH R	COL	0-0024151	0764	1
FABRITIUS WILLIAM J	LTC	0-0040021	0464	1
FADE WALTER W	COL	0-0065617	1068	1
FAGIN RUSSELL D	COL	0-0042145	0363	1
FAHEY PAUL V	COL	0-0033054	0766	1
FAHRINGER EUGENE P	COL	0-0041930	0961	1
FAHS ROBERT B	LTC	0-0050824	0366	1
FAHY DONALD G	LTC	0-0061064	0766	1
FAIKS WALTER A	COL	0-0020129	0164	1
FAILING FRANK W	LTC	0-0031298	0264	1
FAILS EULA R	MAJ	N-0000412	0254	2
FAINE CYRIL E	COL	0-0017343	1053	1
FAINTER FRANCIS F	COL	0-0006360	0753	2
FAIR CECIL G	CW4	W-0903081	0165	1
FAIRBANKS EMILY	MAJ	M-0000580	0862	1
FAIRBANKS RUSSELL N	LTC	0-0040747	0662	1
FAIRBROTHER HERMAN W	COL	0-0015067	0854	1
FAIRCHILD CLARENCE G	COL	0-0040396	0563	2
FAIRCHILD JAMES M	COL	0-0030844	0165	1
FAIRCHILD JAMES R	CW3	W-0908004	0867	1
FAIRES HUNTER H JR	LTC	0-0028377	0768	1
FAIRLEY ANNA E	MAJ	N-0001304	0163	1
FAIRLEY JEFFERSON	COL	0-0052699	0968	2
FAISON THOMAS G	COL	0-0029254	1162	1
FAKE CHARLES W	LTC	0-0010225	0841	2
FALES CLARKE K	COL	0-0005330	1047	1
FALK BYRON A	COL	0-0010091	0950	1
FALK BYRON A JR	MAJ	0-0065171	0266	1
FALKE DAVID R	LTC	0-0051542	0962	1
FALKS JACK B	LTC	0-0025266	1164	1
FALLEN ARTHUR J	COL	0-0079705	0865	1
FALLIS REGINALD J	COL	0-0022256	0762	1
FALLON RUDOLPH A	LTC	0-0062225	0266	1
FANCHER PAUL S	B G	0-0018637	0658	1
FANNING CHARLES A	LTC	0-0029939	0561	1
FANNING WILLIAM E	LTC	0-0080293	1066	1
FARBER CHARLES M	B G	0-0020473	1165	1
FARBER LEO J	LTC	0-0079809	0766	1
FARGO LYNN D	COL	0-0032242	0166	2
FARIBAULT BEN M	LTC	0-0030801	0865	1
FARINACCI CHARLES J	COL	0-0020518	0960	2
FARIS CHARLES A JR	MAJ	0-0069643	1265	1
FARKASH EUGENE	LTC	0-0080750	0868	1
FARLEY CLARE F	COL	0-0025915	0368	1
FARLEY JULIUS B	LTC	0-0040226	0166	1
FARMAN ELBERT E JR	COL	0-0002595	0824	2
FARMER CLARENCE R	LTC	0-0011483	1138	1
FARMER GARLAND P	LTC	0-0068342	0266	1
FARMER HERBERT F	COL	0-0039704	0660	1
FARMER JACK M	WO1	W-0969750	0759	1
FARMER ROBERT O	LTC	0-0056280	0665	1
FARMER WESLEY E	COL	0-0051398	0463	1
FARMER WILLIAM C	COL	0-0030691	0358	1
FARNELL JOHN M	LTC	0-0034108	1267	1
FARNER HARRY J	COL	0-0008134	0748	1
FARNHAM KENNETH N	LTC	0-0080751	0667	1
FARNSWORTH EDWARD F	COL	0-0018683	0862	1
FARNSWORTH JOHN A	MAJ	0-0065612	0164	1
FARNSWORTH LOUIS D	COL	0-0019904	0863	1
FARNSWORTH THOMAS H	LTC	0-0025800	0963	1
FARNUM CHARLES W	LTC	0-0042743	0662	2
FARNUM FRANCIS H	MAJ	0-0001814	1022	2
FARNUM LAWRENCE B	COL	0-0061211	1068	1
FARR EDWARD H	COL	0-0039501	0954	1
FARRA JOHN F JR	COL	0-0017294	0545	2
FARRAND EDWARD G	M G	0-0016788	0661	1
FARRAR FRED J	LTC	0-0056838	0467	2
FARRAR WILLIAM L	COL	0-0034053	0267	1
FARRELL CARL Y	COL	0-0030628	0560	1
FARRELL CLEMENT A	COL	0-0030988	0168	1
FARRELL FRANCIS W	LTG	0-0012784	0660	1
FARRELL RAYMOND J	CPT	0-0014261	0620	2
FARRELL RICHARD J	COL	0-0025168	0866	1
FARRELL WILFRED F	LTC	0-0033950	0768	1
FARREN JAMES H	COL	0-0032670	1067	1
FARRINGTON THOMAS H	MAJ	0-0060796	0168	1
FARRIS GLENN A	COL	0-0018494	0761	1
FARRIS PHILIP A	LTC	0-0028627	0966	1
FARRIS STEPHEN C	LTC	0-0022022	0764	1
FARTHING WILLIAM E	LTC	0-0023188	0660	1
FARWICK AUGUST W	COL	0-0016276	0755	1
FATE ROBERT J	COL	0-0023010	0463	1
FAUBLE PHYLLIS H	MAJ	M-0010087	0366	1
FAULCONER JOHN W JR	LTC	0-0006679	0342	2
FAULDS JACK M	COL	0-0042581	0665	1
FAULKNER LYMAN S	COL	0-0023870	0763	1
FAUPEL RUSSELL F	CW4	W-0906719	0968	1
FAUST LACY W	CW3	W-0906720	1066	1
FAUST ROBERT J	COL	0-0040641	0965	1
FAVORITE FRANK G JR	LTC	0-0065989	0864	1
FAW JOSEPH N	COL	0-0031164	0962	1
FAY AGNES I	MAJ	N-0002012	1267	1
FAY CHARLES F JR	COL	0-0040231	0468	1
FAY JOHN A	WO1	W-0800737	0441	1
FAY JOHN E	LTC	0-0081995	0266	1
FAYLE ORIN A	LTC	0-0088260	0163	1
FEAGANS NELLIE I	LTC	N-0001547	0564	1
FEAGIN CLAUDE W	COL	0-0010820	1046	2
FEAMSTER ROBERT C	MAJ	0-0026943	0147	2
FEATHER EDWIN H	CPT	0-0016447	0239	2
FEATHERSTON IONE	MAJ	N-0000526	0148	1
FEATHERSTON WALTER C	LTC	0-0044075	1059	1
FEBIGER PAUL C	COL	0-0009761	0646	2
FECHNER WALTER W	COL	0-0031033	1167	1
FEDOR ERNEST J	COL	0-0038657	0764	1
FEEHAN JOHN P	COL	0-0030647	0366	1
FEEK WILLIAM A JR	LTC	0-0066149	0668	1
FEEMAN WILLIAM E	COL	0-0024243	1068	2
FEENEY THOMAS J	LTC	0-0084856	1168	2
FEGAN OSCAR G	COL	0-0010468	1047	1
FEHRS JOHN W	LTC	0-0027086	0865	1
FEIDT GERALD E	COL	0-0031513	0565	1
FEIGHNY ROBERT F	LTC	0-0067568	0767	1
FEIL FREDERICK	COL	0-0030379	0265	1
FEILD CONSTANCE	LTC	L-0000184	1268	1
FEINBERG PHILIP	COL	0-0038591	0155	1
FEIND EMROY E	COL	0-0028787	1051	2
FEINDEL WILLIAM B JR	COL	0-0030177	0962	1
FEJER ALBERT	CW4	W-0903084	1058	1
FELBER JOSEPH G	COL	0-0016984	1157	1
FELDMAN HERMAN	M G	0-0005724	0851	2
FELIX RUSSELL E	LTC	0-0060475	0566	1
FELIZ JAMES E	LTC	0-0043752	0764	1
FELKER LUTHER	MAJ	0-0014151	0116	2
FELL CHARLES F	COL	0-0019368	0757	1
FELLENZ LLOYD E	M G	0-0019485	0867	1
FELLENZ WALTER J	COL	0-0023055	0462	2
FELLERMAN ERWIN K	LTC	0-0080294	0961	1
FELLERS BONNER F	B G	0-0012134	1146	1
FELLOWS FRANCIS F	COL	0-0017620	0658	1
FELLOWS HAROLD C	COL	0-0004745	1051	1
FELS DOROTHY B	MAJ	N-0000169	0560	2
FELT MARION F	COL	0-0042810	0866	1
FELTON DONALD C	LTC	0-0039058	0761	1
FENN CLARENCE C	B G	0-0008049	0250	1
FENNELL MARTIN A	COL	0-0012431	0947	1
FENNON ISABEL	MAJ	N-0002371	0460	1
FENSTEMACHER EDGAR R	LTC	0-0059780	1267	2
FENTON BERNARD J	COL	0-0041755	0667	1
FENTON BRYAN C T	B G	0-0020088	0464	1
FERCHAK MICHAEL P	CW4	W-0906721	0465	1
FERENBAUGH CLAUDE B	LTG	0-0012479	0955	2
FERGASON SYDNEY C	COL	0-0006210	0753	1
FERGUSON BELVERY G	CW3	W-0908045	0868	1
FERGUSON JAMES L	COL	0-0030046	1162	1
FERGUSON KENNETH H	CW4	W-0903087	0463	1
FERGUSON LAWRENCE J	COL	0-0010154	0547	2
FERGUSON SAMUEL C	1LT	0-0072590	0659	2
FERGUSON WILLIAM M	LTC	0-0042665	0762	1
FERINGA PETER A	M G	0-0014744	0553	1
FERN VINCENT R	CPT	0-0071491	0663	2
FERNANDEZ CLAUDE E	COL	0-0030454	1164	1
FERNSTROM CARL H	COL	0-0018055	0758	1
FERONY LOUIS J	COL	0-0050979	0458	1
FERREE FLOYD W	COL	0-0007872	0937	2
FERRELL ROBERT M	COL	0-0053808	1068	1
FERRER FERDINAND	LTC	0-0062831	0868	1
FERRIN CHARLES S	B G	0-0004980	1152	1
FERRIS BENJAMIN G	B G	0-0003857	0951	1
FERRIS EDWIN H	COL	0-0019962	0649	2
FERRIS JOHN W	COL	0-0019097	0863	2
FERTIG WENDELL W	COL	0-0041406	0156	1
FETTERMAN LELAND L	LTC	0-0056856	0862	1
FICKESSEN JACK W	COL	0-0035973	0868	1
FICKETT EDWARD M	COL	0-0007216	0854	1
FICKLING RYAN W	CW2	W-0906724	0452	2
FIEDLER ARTHUR A	LTC	0-0038719	0560	1
FIEHN CHARLES W	CW4	W-0903091	0465	1
FIELD DAVID O	LTC	0-0080754	1162	1
FIELD EUGENE J	COL	0-0029830	0967	1
FIELD HARRY L JR	LTC	0-0040890	0959	2
FIELD KENNETH S	LTC	0-0036932	0863	2
FIELD LONNIE D	COL	0-0010969	0649	1
FIELD LOUIS M	COL	0-0006436	1047	2
FIELD RAYMOND F	COL	0-0042784	0566	1
FIELD REX C	CW3	W-0903092	0863	1
FIELD WILLIAM D	2LT	0-0050832	0648	2
FIELD WINSTON L	COL	0-0039869	0859	1
FIELDER JESSE W	LTC	0-0033842	0863	1
FIELDER KENDALL J	B G	0-0007450	0753	1
FIELDS ALBERT	COL	0-0011505	0447	2
FIELDS BASIL V	CPT	0-0008348	0829	1
FIELDS DARREL R	LTC	0-0062862	0468	1
FIELDS HARRY C JR	COL	0-0043592	0767	1
FIELDS JESSE A	LTC	0-0028731	0966	1
FIELDS KENNETH E	B G	0-0018957	0455	1
FIELDS WILLIAM R	COL	0-0051288	0162	1
FIGUERAS JAIME J	COL	0-0010864	0946	2
FILES MAYNARD W	LTC	0-0079811	0764	2
FILES VERNON	LTC	0-0037086	1167	1
FILIPPI FRANK A	COL	0-0030701	0566	1
FILLBRANDT ARTHUR C	LTC	0-0030520	0762	1
FILLMORE ROBERT H	COL	0-0030254	0964	1
FINAN BERNARD J	COL	0-0007890	0147	2
FINBERG IRVING W	COL	0-0042716	0863	1
FINCH CHARLES S JR	LTC	0-0061169	1163	2
FINCH JOHN E	LTC	0-0031797	0266	1
FINCH RALPH	MAJ	0-0016324	0947	1
FINCHER HERBERT A	LTC	0-0061353	0268	1
FINCHER JOE L	COL	0-0030145	1059	2
FINGARSON GEORGE E	COL	0-0007041	0854	1
FINK DONALD P	MAJ	0-0062236	0764	1
FINK JAMES L	LTC	0-0037604	1162	1
FINKE JOHN G W	LTC	0-0040037	0864	1
FINKEL JOSHUA A	COL	0-0020253	0656	1
FINKENAUR ROBERT G	COL	0-0019441	0859	1
FINKS JACK E	COL	0-0038625	0159	1
FINLAYSON HARRISON H	COL	0-0042697	0662	1
FINLEY GEORGE A	COL	0-0020136	1064	1
FINLEY GLENN S	COL	0-0007177	0854	2
FINLEY THOMAS D	M G	0-0004419	0946	2
FINN CALVIN F	LTC	0-0043413	1064	1
FINN JOHN W	COL	0-0030257	0964	1
FINN RUSSELL T	B G	0-0016237	0656	1
FINNEGAN JOHN E	COL	0-0020971	1059	1
FINNEGAN WALTER E	COL	0-0017219	0758	1
FINNEY JOHN R	MAJ	0-0024655	0453	2
FINNEY PERRY S JR	COL	0-0048263	0868	1
FIORE CAESAR F	COL	0-0019897	0157	1
FIREHOCK RAYMOND B	COL	0-0019812	0165	1
FIRNSTAHL NORMAN P	MAJ	0-0080082	1163	1
FISCHER CARL H JR	LTC	0-0027873	1068	1
FISCHER ERNEST W	COL	0-0031829	0468	1
FISCHER FRANK D	COL	0-0045412	0868	1
FISCHER HARRY O	COL	0-0029901	0562	1
FISCHER HARVEY H	LTG	0-0018832	0867	1
FISH FREDERICK	LTC	0-0080758	1066	2
FISH GROSVENOR	LTC	0-0042932	1264	1
FISH HAMILTON W	COL	0-0020592	0867	1
FISH JAMES H	COL	0-0028928	0957	1
FISHBACK JOE	COL	0-0042492	0163	1
FISHER AARON R	CW2	W-0901196	1047	2
FISHER AUSTIN G	COL	0-0020324	0656	1
FISHER CARLETON E	COL	0-0031852	0764	1
FISHER EARL E	COL	0-0029175	0260	1
FISHER HENRY A JR	LTC	0-0063274	0866	1
FISHER HENRY G	COL	0-0015357	0854	1
FISHER LUCILLE C	LTC	N-0001922	0468	1

UNITED STATES ARMY RETIRED LIST

NAME	GRADE	SVC NO	DATE RET MO YR	RET CODE
FISHER MERLE L	COL	0-0018550	0761	1
FISHER SAMUEL H	COL	0-0015835	0754	1
FISHER VINCENT J	1LT	0-0064899	0853	2
FISHER YOEMAN C	CW4	W-0903094	0961	1
FISHKIN LEON J	COL	0-0052215	1166	1
FISICHELLA NELBA A	MAJ	N-0001424	1263	2
FISK ROBERT R	LTC	0-0024614	1066	1
FISK S WALLACE	COL	0-0028945	1157	2
FISK WILLIAM	MAJ	0-0006875	0637	2
FISKE JOHN F	COL	0-0016623	1056	1
FISKE NORMAN E	COL	0-0004741	0753	1
FISKE ROBERT W	LTC	0-0080410	0968	1
FISKEN ARCHIBALD	COL	0-0006930	0948	1
FITCH ALVA R	LTG	0-0018113	0666	2
FITCH BURDETTE M	B G	0-0010718	0753	2
FITCH ELIZABETH	LTC	N-0000030	0156	1
FITCH HENRY B	COL	0-0030851	0365	1
FITE WILLIAM C II	COL	0-0021331	0165	1
FITTS WILLIAM T JR	B G	0-0011917	0754	1
FITZGERALD DOUGLAS I	COL	0-0078832	1266	1
FITZGERALD EDWARD O	LTC	0-0029870	0161	1
FITZGERALD EDWARD W	COL	0-0030495	1160	1
FITZGERALD EILEEN	LTC	N-0000575	1064	1
FITZGERALD GERALD W	COL	0-0009460	0953	2
FITZGERALD HERBERT M	COL	0-0029022	0956	1
FITZGERALD MAURICE J	COL	0-0028851	0256	1
FITZGERALD ROBERT H	CPT	0-0020676	0348	1
FITZGIBBONS JAMES J	MAJ	0-0017752	0648	1
FITZPATRICK EDWARD D	COL	0-0023288	0167	1
FITZPATRICK JOHN W	LTC	0-0050911	1153	1
FIVES PAUL E	COL	0-0032170	0467	2
FIX FLOYD S	COL	0-0050990	1152	1
FLACHSLAND NORMA M	LTC	L-0000037	0760	1
FLAGER GEORGE W	LTC	0-0053081	0867	1
FLAGG JAMES T	CW3	W-0906725	0960	1
FLAGGERT JAMES J JR	LTC	0-0063345	1266	1
FLAHAVEN WILLIAM J	MAJ	0-0040497	1161	1
FLAIG JOHN W	CW4	W-0903099	0366	1
FLAMM LEWIS L	COL	0-0042384	0864	1
FLANAGAN ELIZABETH	MAJ	N-0001046	0766	1
FLANAGAN LOIS J	MAJ	0-0024962	0846	2
FLANDERS CHARLES L	COL	0-0024006	1167	1
FLANDERS EDWARD A	COL	0-0022912	0865	1
FLANDERS WALTER C	COL	0-0081897	1268	1
FLANIGAN EDA J	MAJ	L-0000070	0660	1
FLANIGAN JOSEPH T	CW4	W-0906726	0759	1
FLANIGAN WALTER J	LTC	0-0044422	0966	1
FLANIGEN BARRINGTON	COL	0-0004504	0446	1
FLATTER FINDLAY F	LTC	0-0049941	0761	1
FLAVELLE ELIZABETH	LTC	N-0001896	1263	1
FLECKENSTEIN W A	LTC	0-0019175	0655	1
FLEET GEORGE T	CPT	0-0014297	0421	2
FLEIG RAYMOND E	LTC	0-0047197	0862	1
FLEISCHMAN GORDON K	LTC	0-0059477	0967	1
FLEMING CLARENCE A	COL	0-0051941	0168	1
FLEMING DAVID D	LTC	0-0032042	1164	1
FLEMING ELMER P JR	COL	0-0033975	1168	1
FLEMING EUGENE C JR	LTC	0-0057372	0468	1
FLEMING HERMAN R	COL	0-0029903	0557	1
FLEMING JANET M	MAJ	N-0002055	1060	1
FLEMING MARGARET C	CPT	N-0002468	0954	2
FLEMING ROBERT J JR	M G	0-0017095	0267	1
FLEMING ROBERT N	LTC	0-0050014	1265	1
FLEMING ROBERT W JR	LTC	0-0056737	0965	1
FLEMING SAM F	LTC	0-0042863	1062	1
FLEMING WILLIAM D	COL	0-0010834	0249	1
FLEMING WILLIAM J	COL	0-0028910	0657	1
FLEMING WILLIAM JR	LTC	0-0080761	0265	1
FLEMMING DAMON B	CW4	RW-0906424	1262	1
FLESCH JOSEPH M	COL	0-0031800	0767	1
FLETCHER ALLEN	COL	0-0002997	0642	1
FLETCHER DON S	LTC	0-0050476	0767	1
FLETCHER GEORGE E	COL	0-0018517	1061	1
FLETCHER JOHN W JR	LTC	0-0027813	0868	1
FLETCHER LESLIE S	COL	0-0015591	0747	2
FLETCHER MAURICE J	COL	0-0041727	0961	1
FLETCHER ROBERT H	COL	0-0002376	0337	2
FLETCHER WILLIAM T	COL	0-0010640	0750	1
FLETTE FRED J	LTC	0-0030594	1263	1
FLETTER RANDOLPH W	COL	0-0019148	0860	1
FLETTERER FLORENCE L	MAJ	N-0002428	1158	2
FLEURY VERNON G	LTC	0-0048249	0864	1
FLEWELLING JOHN D	LTC	0-0038818	0263	1
FLINCHBAUGH RALPH W	COL	0-0061071	0966	1
FLING WILLIAM J	MAJ	0-0022144	0859	1
FLINIAU FRANKLIN M	COL	0-0030263	0763	1
FLINT CHARLES W	COL	0-0043656	0965	1
FLINT GEORGE	LTC	0-0044970	0856	1
FLINT LEWIS M	COL	0-0042519	0265	1
FLINT ROBERT P	LTC	0-0040921	0664	1
FLINT WALKER H	CPT	0-0090802	0665	2
FLINT WILLARD	LTC	0-0041077	0965	1
FLINTER MARCUS H	COL	0-0061168	0264	1
FLINTJER JOHN D	LTC	0-0056920	0766	2
FLOHR REX C	CW3	W-0908086	0668	1
FLOJO CHARLES C	CPT	0-0026970	0246	2
FLOOD CLAIR V	CW4	RW-0906728	0564	1
FLOOK MARGARET H	MAJ	N-0000702	0762	1
FLORA MARVIN W	LTC	0-0034083	0565	1
FLORANCE CHARLES W	COL	0-0022119	1168	1
FLORY LESTER D	B G	0-001232[illegible]	0649	1
FLORYAN THADDEUS P	COL	0-0023249	0966	1
FLOURNOY ROBERT W JR	LTC	0-0078834	0667	1
FLOWER JAMES T III	CW3	RW-0903102	0963	1
FLOWERS MARY M	MAJ	N-0000180	0662	1
FLOYD ARTHUR	LTC	0-0007859	1141	1
FLOYD MAX R	LTC	0-0049342	0865	1
FLOYD RAY B	COL	0-0015058	0753	1
FLOYD WILLIAM T	CW2	W-0800160	1144	2
FLYNN EDMUND P	COL	0-0033350	0766	1
FLYNN JOHN R	LTC	0-0026881	0166	1
FLYNN JOSEPH V	LTC	0-0080762	0765	1
FLYNN WILLIAM J	COL	0-0041563	0159	1
FOGARTY MAXWELL B	COL	0-0042193	0663	1
FOGLE FRED M	COL	0-0005450	0250	1
FOGLEMAN PAUL V	LTC	0-0082000	1068	2
FOLEN CLIFFORD G	COL	0-0040255	1263	1
FOLEY RICHARD F	LTC	0-0080765	0866	1
FOLEY WILLIAM	COL	0-0042474	1264	1
FOLK FRANK T	COL	0-0018195	0460	1
FOLKER OLIVER F JR	CW4	W-0903104	1068	1
FOLKES JOHN G	COL	0-0051057	0959	1
FOLLANSBEE CONRAD G	COL	0-0015973	0154	1
FOLLETT CHARLES V JR	MAJ	0-0062003	0966	1
FOLLEY GEORGE M	LTC	0-0051541	0962	1
FOLLING BJARNE N	LTC	0-0052058	0464	1
FOLTS RUDOLF H	COL	0-0040784	0767	1
FOLTZ CHRISTIAN	COL	0-0005285	1047	1
FOLTZ GILBERT H	LTC	0-0050318	1066	1
FONTAINE ARCHILLE J	CW2	W-0900746	1144	1
FONTAINE RUSSELL B	COL	0-0039548	0257	1
FONVIELLE JOHN H	COL	0-0012159	0954	1
FOOKS HERBERT C	MAJ	0-0013963	0720	2
FOOKS NELSON I	COL	0-0016919	0657	1
FOOR VIRGINIA F	MAJ	N-0000735	0467	1
FOOTE DONALD C	COL	0-0038584	0753	1
FOOTE GEORGE B	COL	0-0022320	0859	1
FOOTE LOUIS H	B G	0-0017010	1157	1
FOOTE SENECA W	COL	0-0019833	0863	1
FOOTE THOMAS C	COL	0-0019488	0864	1
FORAME PETER R	LTC	0-0042866	0964	1
FORBES LAWRENCE G	COL	0-0022903	0167	1
FORBES MERWIN B	COL	0-0030097	1061	1
FORBES WILLIAM A	LTC	0-0058900	0766	1
FORCUM FORREST H	LTC	0-0051464	0562	2
FORD ARTHUR W	COL	0-0003141	0648	1
FORD BLAIR A	COL	0-0018547	0761	1
FORD ELBERT L	M G	0-0005251	1053	1
FORD HOWARD G	COL	0-0038775	1262	1
FORD JAMES S	CW4	W-0906729	0957	1
FORD JOHN A	COL	0-0024497	0965	1
FORD ROBERT L	COL	0-0038767	0858	1
FORD WILLIAM H	B G	0-0012667	0854	1
FORDE HAROLD MC	COL	0-0016409	0656	1
FORDHAM EMORY H	LTC	0-0030340	0658	2
FORDYCE ROBERT C	COL	0-0053996	0264	1
FORE LILLIAN	MAJ	N-0002054	1060	1
FOREMAN ADELE F	MAJ	N-0002164	1162	1
FOREMAN ALLEN H	COL	0-0019913	0865	1
FOREMAN HELEN K	MAJ	L-0000093	0463	1
FOREMAN TAYLOR W	COL	0-0007862	0140	1
FOREMAN WILLIAM G	LTC	0-0063106	0868	1
FORGIONE ANTHONY W	CW4	W-0903106	0861	1
FORKER WILLIAM L	LTC	0-0050125	0968	1
FORMAN DVID T	COL	0-0015590	0854	1
FORMET GARY L	CPT	0F-0105165	0768	2
FORMICA CONRAD F	CW4	W-0903107	0257	1
FORNEY DONALD M	COL	0-0038607	1150	1
FORNEY LESLIE R	COL	0-0008006	0649	1
FORREST CHARLES R	CPT	0-0010488	0328	2
FORREST FRANK G	COL	0-0022101	0364	1
FORSE WILLIAM B	COL	0-0015470	1153	1
FORSELL GEORGE T JR	LTC	0-0027376	0765	1
FORSTER GEORGE J	B G	0-0010114	0451	1
FORSTER HORACE W	COL	0-0006744	0753	1
FORSYTH ANDREW E	COL	0-0010312	0654	1
FORSYTH JAMES P	LTC	0-0024038	0668	1
FORSYTHE JOHN D	COL	0-0006636	0851	1
FORSYTHE LOIS M	COL	R-0010039	0766	1
FORT ALVIN E	LTC	0-0062163	0667	1
FORT JOHN G	COL	0-0031437	0764	1
FORTIER LOUIS J	B G	0-0006621	1050	1
FORTIN THOMAS L	COL	0-0042605	0665	1
FORTNEY CAMDEN P JR	COL	0-0032949	0863	1
FORTRESS EDWARD	COL	0-0041632	0951	1
FOSS ERLING J	COL	0-0039127	0866	1
FOSS RUSS C	LTC	0-0046767	0867	1
FOSSUM ADOLPH C	LTC	0-0050317	0764	1
FOSSUM EMBERT A	COL	0-0040210	0368	1
FOSTER ALBERT D	COL	0-0006964	0447	2
FOSTER ANDREW P JR	LTC	0-0015807	0753	1
FOSTER ANNE R	MAJ	N-0000655	1262	1
FOSTER CORA M	LTC	L-0000033	0459	1
FOSTER EUGENE M	M G	0-0006228	0551	1
FOSTER GARRAR C	COL	0-0024732	1268	2
FOSTER GAYLE H	COL	0-0079814	0868	1
FOSTER HARRY	COL	0-0006060	1049	1
FOSTER HARRY G	COL	0-0030291	0860	1
FOSTER HELEN K	MAJ	N-0001993	1167	1
FOSTER IVAN M	LTC	0-0031215	1059	1
FOSTER JAMES E	COL	0-0030256	0964	1
FOSTER JAMES K JR	LTC	0-0063161	0167	1
FOSTER JAMES W	LTC	0-0039965	0258	1
FOSTER KENNETH W	COL	0-0029376	1059	1
FOSTER MARVIN E	CW4	W-0903108	0559	1
FOSTER ROBERT J	COL	0-0003972	0944	2
FOSTER ROBERT T	COL	0-0011258	0451	1
FOSTER ROBERT T	LTC	0-0031279	1047	2
FOSTER ROBERT W JR	LTC	0-0025360	1265	1
FOSTER ROY M	COL	0-0015375	C751	2
FOSTER RUFUS C JR	CW3	W-0906730	1058	1
FOSTER VALENTINE	COL	0-0006185	0147	2
FOSTER WILLIAM B	COL	0-0008953	0353	2
FOSTER WILLIAM F	COL	0-0051016	0559	1
FOSTER WILLIAM W	COL	0-0052802	1065	2
FOUCH WILLIAM R	2LT	0-0063855	0252	2
FOUNTAIN JOHN R	COL	0-0007926	0248	1
FOUNTAIN LEE S	COL	0-0004003	0242	1
FOURT HERBERT J	LTC	0-0080769	0367	1
FOUSHEE LILLIAN F	LTC	L-0000043	0461	1
FOUST CLARENCE T	COL	0-0041860	0561	1
FOWLER CARL C	CW4	W-0901892	0955	1
FOWLER CLAYTON F	COL	0-0041553	0159	1
FOWLER DAVID M	COL	0-0015002	0554	1
FOWLER HANES M	LTC	0-0022696	0646	2
FOWLER IRA H	COL	0-0030531	0763	1
FOWLER JAMES D	COL	0-0024003	1067	1
FOWLER JOSEPH G	COL	0-0053218	0965	1
FOWLER LUCILLE I	MAJ	N-0000633	1060	1
FOWLER THOMAS G	LTC	0-0030867	0649	2
FOWLIE GLADYS D	MAJ	N-0002059	0161	1
FOWLKES B C JR	COL	0-0016087	0655	1
FOX ALONZO P	LTG	0-0008434	0757	1
FOX CHARLES K	LTC	0-0041545	0953	1
FOX GEORGE F	LTC	0-0036234	1167	1
FOX HARRY L	COL	0-0041962	1060	1
FOX JULIAN P JR	LTC	0-0051823	0164	1
FOX LAWRENCE J JR	LTC	0-0027859	0865	1
FOX RICHARD A	LTC	0-0083582	0863	1
FOX VICTOR B	LTC	0-0029896	0261	1
FOX VINCENT W	LTC	0-0051871	0661	1
FOX WILBUR J	COL	0-0009041	0746	2
FOXWORTH EDWARD M	COL	0-0042598	0665	1
FOXX JAMES E	LTC	0-0040418	1059	1
FOY LEVIE W	COL	0-0007580	0753	1
FRAILE RENE E	COL	0-0005665	0946	2
FRALISH JOHN C	COL	0-0032668	0966	1
FRAME MARSHALL W	COL	0-0019103	0863	2
FRAMPTON SIDNEY D	COL	0-0042176	0663	1
FRANASZEK JOSEPH J	LTC	0-0055447	0864	1
FRANCE GERALD D	COL	0-0004115	1045	1
FRANCIS ERNEST H	LTC	0-0040758	0866	1
FRANCIS GARNET P JR	COL	0-0030876	1065	1
FRANCIS HARRISON S	LTC	0-0052233	0266	1
FRANCIS HENRY M	LTC	0-0026715	0765	1
FRANCIS JOHN R	COL	0-0005664	1046	2
FRANCIS ROBERT	COL	0-0062122	0864	1
FRANCIS WILLIAM H	COL	0-0017693	0859	1
FRANDRUP BERNADINE	MAJ	N-0002364	0360	1
FRANK ALVA B	LTC	0-0065991	0865	1
FRANK CHARLES B	COL	0-0031153	1167	1
FRANK CLARENCE A	COL	0-0012401	1050	1
FRANK FRANCIS B	CW4	W-0903112	0563	2
FRANK FRED J	LTC	0-0054078	0867	1
FRANK HENRI F	COL	0-0046187	0465	1
FRANK JACOB	MAJ	0-0002500	0728	2
FRANK KARL C	COL	0-0015063	0753	1
FRANK LEROY P	COL	0-0085539	1068	1
FRANK SELBY H	B G	0-0003546	0851	1
FRANK SELBY M	COL	0-0032620	1161	1
FRANKE GUSTAV H JR	LTC	0-0052959	0764	1
FRANKEL HENRY	COL	0-0040178	0967	1
FRANKENBERGER SAMUEL	COL	0-0001690	0822	2
FRANKENSTEIN LEONARD	LTC	0-0054172	0662	1
FRANKLAND WALTER L	LTC	0-0028391	0766	1
FRANKLIN ALBERT G JR	B G	0-0016642	1056	1
FRANKLIN CHARLES C	COL	0-0047521	0766	1
FRANKLIN DANIEL	COL	0-0006270	0546	2
FRANKLIN EDWARD C	COL	0-0016354	0746	1
FRANKLIN ERSKINE A	COL	0-0005852	1046	1
FRANKLIN GEORGE H	LTC	0-0035175	0262	1
FRANKLIN HORACE A	LTC	0-0041618	0957	1
FRANKLIN JOHN F	COL	0-0001837	0642	1
FRANKLIN JOHN M	COL	0-0039864	1263	1
FRANKLIN JOSEPH B	COL	0-0043304	0967	1
FRANKLIN LOYCE I	MAJ	N-0002264	1162	1
FRANKLIN ROBERT B	COL	0-0019046	0863	1
FRANKLIN ROBERT B	COL	0-0049940	0868	1
FRANKLIN VICTOR A	LTC	0-0025658	0364	1
FRANKS ROBERT B	COL	0-004004[illegible]	0763	1
FRANSON PAUL D JR	COL	0-0039065	1059	1
FRASE ROBERT C	LTC	0-0038561	0867	1
FRASER FRANK G	COL	0-0016090	0655	1
FRASER HARVEY R	B G	0-0021747	0765	1
FRASER JAMES W	COL	0-0038602	0155	1
FRASER JOSEPH J	COL	0-0008444	0650	1
FRASER JOSEPH J JR	COL	0-0053292	1167	1
FRASER MILDRED L	LTC	N-0000624	1167	1
FRASER POWELL A	COL	0-0034889	0764	1
FRASER RICHARD H	LTC	0-0023080	0949	2

NAME	GRADE	SVC NO	DATE RET MO YR	RET CODE
FRASER RICHARD S	COL	0-0023595	0960	1
FRASER WILLIAM R	COL	0-0018692	0959	2
FRASIR GEORGE M	COL	0-0031596	0967	1
FRATE JOSEPH A	MAJ	0-0089331	0968	2
FRAZIER LEROY F	COL	0-0030678	1062	1
FRAZIER ROBERT L	LTC	0-0044611	0166	1
FREAKLEY EDWIN M	LTC	0-0039440	0966	1
FREAMAN JAY H	COL	0-0041458	0557	1
FREAR SETH R	MAJ	0-0026166	1046	2
FREDENDALL L R JR	LTC	0-0017235	0157	1
FREDERICK HORACE H	COL	0-0042491	0763	1
FREDERICK JOHN D	COL	0-0017453	0554	1
FREDERICK ROBERT T	M G	0-0017196	0352	2
FREDERICKS EDGAR J	COL	0-0026302	0968	1
FREDERICKS JOHN L	MAJ	0-0047721	1060	1
FREDERICKS WILLIAM	CPT	0-0012449	1022	2
FREDERICKSON ERWIN C	LTC	0-0032347	0165	1
FREDIN CATHERINE	MAJ	J-0000005	0967	1
FREDRIKSON GRAYDON F	LTC	0-0035700	0867	1
FREELAND SUMNER	LTC	0-0047401	0964	1
FREEMAN ALLEN	CW4	W-0901713	1154	2
FREEMAN DELBERT B	COL	0-0028973	0358	1
FREEMAN EDWARD V	COL	0-0011800	0749	1
FREEMAN EUGENE M	LTC	0-0040503	1161	1
FREEMAN GEORGE C	LTC	0-0044214	0762	1
FREEMAN HARLAN M	COL	0-0032407	0468	1
FREEMAN HENRY M	COL	0-0051926	1167	1
FREEMAN JAMES W	COL	0-0012202	0554	1
FREEMAN MONROE F	COL	0-0056826	0861	1
FREEMAN NORA G	LTC	N-0000500	0748	1
FREEMAN PAUL L JR	GEN	0-0017704	0767	1
FREEMAN RICHARD G	LTC	0-0033450	0362	2
FREEMAN RICHARD R	COL	0-0056187	1168	1
FREEMAN ROBERT F	COL	0-0044823	0968	1
FREER BEULAH H	2LT	R-0000569	0545	1
FREESTONE JAMES F	MAJ	0-0036937	0663	1
FREIDINGER HENRY M	COL	0-0042783	0265	1
FRENCH CHARLES A	B G	0-0003250	0248	1
FRENCH DANIEL L	LTC	0-0063850	0667	1
FRENCH EDWARD F	COL	0-0008935	0551	1
FRENCH IRMA J	MAJ	N-0001009	0162	1
FRENCH JULES K JR	COL	0-0024760	1053	1
FRENCH PAUL H	COL	0-0004783	1149	1
FRENCH SEWARD F	MAJ	0-0065994	0966	1
FRENCH STANLEY H	LTC	0-0037418	0661	1
FRENCH JEL W	COL	0-0033218	1068	1
FRENCH 3RD SANFORD W	COL	0-0023603	0760	1
FRENCK ARTHUR G	CW4	W-0903115	0762	1
FRENTZEL WILLIAM Y	B G	0-0019026	0863	1
FRESHOUR JAMES F	CW4	RW-0906733	0163	1
FRESHWATER HAROLD L	COL	0-0051739	0366	1
FREUDENDORF CHESTER	COL	0-0023303	0868	1
FREY IRENE	MAJ	N-0000603	0163	1
FRICK EDWARD H	COL	0-0031160	1267	1
FRICK JOHN E	COL	0-0042303	0164	1
FRIEDLEIN CHARLES M	MAJ	0-0085541	0668	1
FRIEDMAN WILLIAM	LTC	0-0024560	0761	1
FRIEND HAROLD C	LTC	0-0028087	1165	1
FRIEND WILLIAM A	CW4	W-0904113	1167	1
FRIERSON ANDREW A	COL	0-0015587	0949	2
FRIES JOSEPHINE	MAJ	N-0001894	0660	1
FRIES STUART G	COL	0-0019827	0865	1
FRINK ALBERT W	COL	0-0022192	0268	1
FRINK JAMES I	M G	0-0014587	0846	2
FRISBIE GILBERT A	LTC	0-0063116	0766	1
FRISBY JAMES L	CW4	W-0903116	0457	1
FRISBY VINCENT C	LTC	0-0020541	0555	1
FRISCH JOE	LTC	0-0051193	0168	1
FRISSELL DUNCAN P	COL	0-0014768	1046	2
FRITH ROBERT C	LTC	0-0014481	0863	1
FRITSVOLD MELFORD P	LTC	0-0043473	0566	1
FRITZ EDWIN G	COL	0-0051063	1059	1
FRITZ JOHN E	LTC	0-0025921	0859	1
FRITZ WILLIAM G	COL	0-0019069	0863	1
FRIZ BARBARA M	LTC	M-0010006	1262	1

NAME	GRADE	SVC NO	DATE RET MO YR	RET CODE
FRIZZELL CHARLES F	MAJ	0-0014483	0-19	2
FRIZZELL LAWRENCE C	COL	0-0004949	1046	1
FROEHLE BLAIRE A	LTC	0-0042392	0662	1
FROELICH JAMES H	LTC	0-0084365	0967	1
FROHNER EDWARD M	CW4	W-0906734	0668	1
FROLICH ALEXANDER	COL	0-0021059	0859	1
FROMER PAUL S	LTC	0-0032141	0463	1
FROMME ROBERT J	LTC	0-0039246	0767	1
FROST HUGH W	CW4	W-0903119	1164	1
FROST VIRGINIA L	MAJ	M-0010022	0966	1
FROST WILLIAM R	COL	0-0008162	0846	2
FRY CLAYTON T	LTC	0-0043904	0466	2
FRY EDMUND M	COL	0-0021431	0666	1
FRY JAMES C	M G	0-0015023	1057	1
FRY LLOYD V	COL	0-0031014	0768	1
FRYE ARTHUR H JR	B G	0-0019716	0665	1
FRYE JOHN A	COL	0-0030509	0965	1
FRYE WILLIAM J	WO1	W-0902421	1052	1
FUDGE RUSSELL O	COL	0-0030652	0762	1
FUEG JOHN W	LTC	0-0040289	1065	1
FUERST ALBERT A	CPT	0-0069650	0460	2
FUGELSO ERLING S	COL	0-0020980	0564	1
FUGER ALBERT S	COL	0-0001374	1022	1
FUGITT WILLIAM K	MAJ	0-0039346	0559	1
FULLER ANNE L	LTC	N-0000587	0565	1
FULLER ARTHUR L JR	COL	0-0018094	0960	2
FULLER CARL W	LTC	0-0031689	1165	1
FULLER CECIL H	COL	0-0040158	0366	1
FULLER HARRY S	COL	0-0010504	0-40	2
FULLER HURLEY E	COL	0-0005518	1050	2
FULLER JACK G	COL	0-0014893	0650	1
FULLER LIONEL R	LTC	0-0025380	0347	2
FULLER ROBERT G	CPT	0-0014292	1120	2
FULLER WILLIAM C	LTC	0-0028055	0666	1
FULLER WILLIAM H	COL	0-0019190	0863	1
FULLER 3RD ROBERT W	LTC	0-0019422	0246	2
FULLERTON JEANNE T	MAJ	N-0000674	0264	1
FULLERTON LEROY R	COL	0-0031690	1267	1
FULMER RICHARD P	LTC	0-0039130	0566	1
FULTON ALAN L	COL	0-0012822	0854	1
FULTON HAROLD A	COL	0-0042225	0863	1
FULTON JAMES H	COL	0-0029984	0563	1
FULTON KENNETH P	COL	0-0016938	0857	2
FULTZ ALTON L	CW4	W-0903121	0561	2
FULTZ WILLIAM S	COL	0-0031439	0267	2
FULWOOD MARTHA	MAJ	N-0000044	0150	1
FUNCHESS LINWOOD F	COL	0-0020875	0757	1
FUNK ARNOLD J	B G	0-0005580	0552	2
FUNK CARL	CW4	W-0901686	1054	1
FUNK MYRON A	COL	0-0030798	0866	1
FUNK RUSSELL D	COL	0-0042067	1062	1
FUQUA STEPHEN O JR	B G	0-0019109	0863	1
FUREY HARRY D	COL	0-0008287	0448	1
FUREY LAWRENCE M	LTC	0-0051674	1163	1
FURLONG MILDRED M	MAJ	N-0001401	0168	1
FURMAN HEZEKIAH W	LTC	0-0039464	0265	1
FURMAN MURRAY	MAJ	0-0084738	0766	1
FURPHEY ROBERT F	CW4	W-0903122	0961	1
FURPHY FOSTER L	COL	0-0020163	1163	1
FURR WILLIAM C	CPT	0-0016025	1127	2
FURRELL ALFRED W	COL	0-0042894	1266	1
FUSI BRUNA G	MAJ	N-0002182	0865	1
FUTCH JOHN M	CW4	W-0906737	0368	1
FUTCH THEODORE L	B G	0-0008572	0854	1
FUTRAL ALLEN A	COL	0-0042948	0165	2
FUTRELL ALVIN F	LTC	0-0028720	0766	1
FYE JOHN H	COL	0-0005733	0753	2
FYFE ROBERT J M JR	MAJ	0-0024432	0346	2
GABARDY ROBERT L	LTC	0-0058902	0963	1
GABY WALTER E JR	LTC	0-0034656	0667	1
GADDIS JOHN W	COL	0-0016200	0755	1
GADDIS SHELTON	COL	0-0079818	0966	1
GAFFE WILTON G	LTC	0-0030179	0162	1
GAERTNER JOHN F	COL	0-0022799	0465	1
GAFFNEY WENDELL W	LTC	0-0044235	0664	1

NAME	GRADE	SVC NO	DATE RET MO YR	RET CODE
GAFFNEY WILLIAM F	LTC	0-0051345	0960	1
GAGE FREEMAN F JR	LTC	0-0032055	1057	1
GAGE GEORGE W	COL	0-0041590	0659	1
GAGE HAROLD O	CW4	W-0903123	0657	1
GAGE PHILIP S	B G	0-0002623	0447	2
GAGE PHILIP S JR	LTC	0-0020337	0-45	2
GAGNE JAMES V JR	LTC	0-0039450	0867	1
GAGNON MILDRED S	MAJ	L-0000299	0860	1
GAHAN THEODORE P	COL	0-0038686	0461	1
GAIGE DELBERT C	MAJ	0-0074840	0168	1
GAIGE WILBER M JR	COL	0-0041538	0858	1
GAILLARD FRED F	COL	0-0010295	0653	1
GAILLARD JEANNE M	MAJ	N-0001970	0361	1
GAINES ARTHUR R	M G	0-0006261	0552	2
GAINES HAROLD W	LTC	0-0032559	0865	1
GAINES JAMES S	MAJ	0-0060655	0266	2
GAINES THOMAS E	COL	0-0041439	0956	1
GAITHER LOREN E	COL	0-0042109	1055	1
GAITHER RIDGELY	LTC	0-0015970	0562	1
GALANTI PHILIP J	COL	0-0030684	0764	1
GALBRAITH JOHN M JR	LTC	0-0033757	0261	2
GALBRAITH NICOLL F	COL	0-0011548	0450	2
GALBREAITH ROBERT B	LTC	0-0033549	0262	1
GALBREATH DURWARD H	LTC	0-0023255	0868	1
GALE CARROLL M	LTC	0-0005045	0642	1
GALL JAMES S	COL	0-0030563	0166	2
GALLAGHER FERDINAND	COL	0-0004503	0751	1
GALLAGHER JOHN L	COL	0-0017370	0246	2
GALLAGHER LEONARD A	COL	0-0007646	0947	1
GALLAGHER PHILIP E	M G	0-0011249	0257	2
GALLAGHER WILLIAM J	COL	0-0031669	0168	1
GALLEZ DOUGLAS W	LTC	0-0026594	0864	1
GALLI MARY F	LTC	N-0000011	1047	1
GALLIEN GARRY G	LTC	OF-0101240	0868	1
GALLIER ROBERT H	CPT	0-0006766	0934	2
GALLIETT HAROLD H	COL	0-0005089	0248	1
GALLION SCOTT	WO1	W-0901290	1137	1
GALLOGLY LESTER H	COL	0-0029420	0760	1
GALLOWAY DONALD H	COL	0-0015161	0754	1
GALLOWAY GERALD F	M G	0-0016043	0562	1
GALLOWAY MARIE S	LTC	N-0000511	1159	1
GALLOWAY NEAL C	LTC	0-0034158	0262	1
GALLUP WALTER F	COL	0-0018513	0861	2
GALT EDWARD A	LTC	0-0043743	0563	1
GALUSHA MORRIS F	COL	0-0043345	0261	1
GALVIN JAMES E JR	COL	0-0029263	0363	1
GALVIN MABEL	MAJ	N-0000266	0464	1
GALWEY GEOFFREY	COL	0-0035753	0146	1
GAMBLE ANDREW S	COL	0-0015801	0854	1
GAMBLE CLAUDE L	COL	0-0011292	0946	2
GAMBLE ROBERT H O	COL	0-0031203	0768	2
GAMBRILL ROBERT S	COL	0-0039716	0160	2
GAMMON JAMES P	COL	0-0006987	0552	2
GANDIA AMAURY M	COL	0-0019205	0260	1
GANO FRANK W	COL	0-0005598	0947	1
GANSCHOW ALFRED K	LTC	0-0050352	0865	1
GANT ROBERT M	COL	0-0039767	0462	2
GANTT HARRY B	COL	0-0006619	0648	2
GANTT HENRY P	COL	0-0003638	0753	1
GANZ EDWARD C JR	LTC	0-0050570	1264	1
GARAVELLI ALICE F	MAJ	N-0001468	0558	1
GARAY STEPHEN L	COL	0-0045416	0266	1
GARBALZ JOSEPH F	COL	0-0040548	0268	2
GARCIA JOSEPH G	CW2	W-0900769	0945	2
GARD HAROLD P	COL	0-0015585	0754	1
GARD ROBERT G	M G	0-0012247	1159	1
GARDEN FRANK F	LTC	0-0031742	0862	1
GARDES GEORGE W	B G	0-0024840	0756	1
GARDINER HAROLD L	MAJ	0-0002513	1022	1
GARDNER F SCOTT	COL	0-0016433	0657	1
GARDNER JAMES C	CW3	W-0904114	0864	1
GARDNER LEON L	COL	0-0016016	0549	2
GARDNER LYMAN S	COL	0-0040205	1267	1
GARDNER PAUL F	LTC	0-0038951	0563	2
GARDNER RALPH B	CW4	W-0903127	0764	1

NAME	GRADE	SVC NO	DATE RET MO YR	RET CODE
GARDNER RICHARD M	COL	0-0076877	0867	1
GARDNER ROBIN B	LTC	0-0038777	0560	1
GARDNER WAYNE B	COL	0-0041366	0735	1
GAREN ELEANOR M	MAJ	N-0001879	0559	1
GARGES PHILIP R	COL	0-0015509	0754	1
GARITTY LYLE J JR	LTC	0-0058403	0668	1
GARLAND ALBERT N	LTC	0-0082066	0968	1
GARLAND PETER W JR	COL	0-0020288	0758	1
GARN PHIL R	LTC	0-0050395	1165	1
GARNER HUGH M	LTC	0-0060219	0865	1
GARNER LLOYD M	COL	0-0009650	0653	1
GARNER ROBERT S	LTC	0-0029640	0959	2
GARNER VERNON H	CW4	W-0903129	1160	1
GARNHART GEORGE H	LTC	0-0025267	0766	1
GARNIEWSKI VICTORIA	MAJ	N-0002318	0968	2
GAROFALO RAPHAEL F	CW4	W-0901731	0163	1
GAROFALO WILLIAM E	LTC	0-0063409	0767	1
GARR ARTHUR S	LTC	0-0080782	0665	1
GARRABRANT ANDREW V	CW4	W-0907076	0268	1
GARRABRANT EVELYN D	MAJ	L-0000205	1153	1
GARRAHY JOHN	CW2	W-0903130	0562	1
GARRARD OFLZENA E	LTC	N-0001890	0263	1
GARRECHT F A JR	COL	0-0015277	1146	1
GARRETSON RALPH B	COL	0-0039835	0657	1
GARRETT FELIX R	COL	0-0060436	0968	1
GARRETT JAMES M JR	COL	0-0004920	0947	2
GARRETT JOHN K	LTC	0-0060684	0866	1
GARRETT JOSEPH B	CPT	0-0056512	0860	1
GARRETT MILLEDGE R	WO1	W-2145220	0957	1
GARRETT PHYLLIS O	MAJ	N-0001741	0766	1
GARRETT ROBERT C	B G	0-0002539	0646	2
GARRETT ROBERT W	COL	0-0023971	0667	1
GARRETT SHIRLEY O	CPT	0-0060687	0962	1
GARRIS HERBERT L	LTC	0-0032872	0267	1
GARRISON ALIDA J	LTC	N-0000012	0348	1
GARRISON CHARLES T	MAJ	0-0063246	0867	1
GARRISON LLOYD R	COL	0-0011580	1052	2
GARRISON RITCHIE	LTC	0-0030696	0464	1
GARRISON WILLIAM C	M G	0-0030144	0868	2
GARTEN MELVIN	COL	0-0048990	0868	2
GARTON EDWARD R	LTC	0-0032945	0561	1
GARTON GEORGE G	COL	0-0018138	0760	1
GARVEY DALE M	COL	0-0043910	0759	2
GARVEY DANIEL J	CPT	0-0058906	1155	2
GARVEY JAMES B	COL	0-0022095	0967	1
GARVIN CRUMP	M G	0-0012746	1058	1
GARY CEPHAS W	COL	0-0020477	0158	1
GARZA CARLOS M	LTC	0-0096971	0967	1
GASIOR EUGENE J	MAJ	0-0027802	0561	2
GASKILL ROBERT C	COL	0-0018275	0855	2
GASKINS STEVE P JR	COL	0-0026392	0562	1
GASPERINI SILVIO E	LTC	0-0023203	1066	2
GASSETT SILAS	COL	0-0031481	0267	1
GASSMAN FRED L	CW4	W-0903133	0658	2
GASTON FRANK W	CW3	W-0906739	0964	1
GASTON FREDERICK	COL	0-0020276	0866	1
GATCHELL WADE C	COL	0-0007066	1046	2
GATES ELIZABETH	MAJ	N-0002350	0558	1
GATES JACK R	LTC	0-0053457	0368	1
GATES JOHN L	LTC	0-0040539	0962	2
GATES VINCENT I	COL	0-0079820	0167	1
GATTIS MARGARET L	LTC	N-0001245	0168	1
GAUDETTE DOMINIQUE	CW4	W-0902057	1154	1
GAURNIER PAUL L	LTC	0-0061337	0967	1
GAVAN PAUL A	M G	0-0017169	0863	1
GAVIN JAMES M	LTG	0-0017676	0358	1
GAVIN JOHN A	COL	0-0018788	0960	1
GAVIN ROBERT J	LTC	0-0033807	0662	2
GAWARECKI JULIA F	LTC	N-0002273	0762	1
GAY HOBART R	LTG	0-0007323	0855	2
GAYDASH GEORGE G	COL	0-0041588	0459	1
GAYLE LESTER T JR	LTC	0-0014219	1119	2
GAYLE MARY H	MAJ	N-0002034	0360	1
GAYLE RICHARD B	LTC	0-0009740	0840	2
GAYLE SETH JR	COL	0-0017342	0757	1

NAME	GRADE	SVC NO	DATE RET MO YR	RET CODE
GAYLORD TYYNE N	MAJ	N-0001964	0960	1
GAYNOR CLEMENT J	COL	0-0008743	0248	1
GAYNOR JAMES K	COL	0-0043354	0867	2
GAYNOR WAYNE J JR	LTC	0-0035222	0463	1
GAZELLE ISA P	LTC	N-0000089	0655	1
GAZIANO SAM F	MAJ	0-0059807	0364	1
GEALTA CECIL G	COL	0-0038744	0663	1
GEAN KIRBY A	LTC	0-0025588	0966	1
GEARIN HELEN B	MAJ	R-0010000	0855	1
GEARY JOHN A	LTC	0-0017742	0-44	2
GEBBIE EARL J	LTC	0-0031361	1064	1
GEBHARDT EARL G	COL	0-0011836	1052	2
GEDDES JOHN A	COL	0-0031512	0562	1
GEE CLOUGH F	COL	0-0010263	0846	2
GEE SAMUEL E	M G	0-0019251	1067	2
GEEHAN BERNARD T	LTC	0-0079822	0868	1
GEELAN WILLIAM R	LTC	0-0040963	0864	1
GEER JOHN F	LTC	0-0063719	0868	1
GEER JOSEPH W	LTC	0-0004696	0-38	1
GEEVER ERVING F	CPT	0-0020404	0739	2
GEHMAN LESTER	MAJ	0-0014015	1020	2
GEHRING FREDERICK	LTC	0-0036462	0664	1
GEIGER EDWARD H	LTC	0-0046621	0867	1
GEIGES ELMER B JR	MAJ	0-0089211	0767	1
GEISE GERALD E	COL	0-0043167	0467	1
GELBY WALTER H	COL	0-0037560	0868	1
GELDERMANN EDWARD J	COL	0-0023803	0661	1
GEMPEL EUGENE P H	COL	0-0006706	0838	2
GENERO PETER P	LTC	0-0063063	0966	1
GENETTI EMIL J	COL	0-0026965	1161	2
GENT ANDREW J	CW4	W-0903138	1164	1
GENTILE MARGARET M	MAJ	L-0000178	0163	1
GENTRY DENNIS V JR	LTC	0-0069490	0968	1
GENUARIO LOUIS V	LTC	0-0062696	1066	2
GEORGE ALEXANDER	COL	0-0012781	0946	2
GEORGE ANNE	MAJ	N-0001908	1062	1
GEORGE CLAUDE D JR	COL	0-0031788	0266	1
GEORGE DONALD B	LTC	0-0097906	0467	1
GEORGE HORACE W JR	1LT	0-0067681	0554	2
GEORGE JOHN D	LTC	0-0030122	0162	1
GEORGE JULIAN H	COL	0-0008421	0753	1
GEORGE MAX S	COL	0-0020740	1059	1
GEORGE ROBERT J	LTC	0-0043815	0164	1
GEORGE URBAN F	COL	0-0028845	0656	1
GEORGE WILLIAM S	COL	0-0018304	0956	1
GEORGEFF BORIS	LTC	0-0082327	0968	1
GEORGES MICHAEL P	COL	0-0042242	0963	1
GEPPERT LEO J	COL	0-0026406	0664	1
GERARD PAUL T	COL	0-0030445	1065	2
GERARDO ALEXANDER	LTC	0-0028119	0868	1
GERBER AUSTIN J	LTC	0-0063175	1065	1
GERBER FRED E	COL	0-0032023	1166	1
GERDES HENRY G	COL	0-0039513	1051	2
GERE GILES H	COL	0-0051707	0366	2
GERFEN FREDERICK	LTC	0-0053165	0865	1
GERFEN ROYE P	COL	0-0007951	0846	1
GERHARDT CHARLES H	M G	0-0005259	0952	1
GERHARDT JACOB J	COL	0-0003875	1050	1
GERHARDT WILLIAM R	COL	0-0008565	0249	1
GERHART GEORGE H	COL	0-0019569	0762	1
GERIG FRANK A JR	LTC	0-0023701	0661	1
GERKEN WALTER W	COL	0-0042113	0261	1
GERLACH ALBERT G	WO1	W-0901816	0146	1
GERLACH SHIRL L	LTC	0-0063049	0263	1
GERDT JOSEPH O	COL	0-0030818	0864	1
GEROW LEE S	B G	0-0004681	0749	2
GEROW LEONARD T	GEN	0-0003151	0750	2
GERSHENOW LOUIS	COL	0-0031577	0767	1
GERSONI CHARLES S	COL	0-0056185	0365	2
GERSTNER JOHN F	COL	0-0055315	0667	1
GETCHELL WILMAH N	LTC	0-0040737	0762	1
GETTYS CHARLES W	COL	0-0015178	0954	1
GETZ AUSTIN T	COL	0-0018309	1046	2
GEWINNER MARCUS N	LTC	0-0080786	0965	1
GHORMLEY WILLIAM K	M G	0-0017674	1162	1
GIAMBELLUCA NAT	LTC	0-0044161	0468	1
GIBB JAMES W	CW4	W-0903143	0968	2
GIBBONS DONALD F	COL	0-0038724	0962	1
GIBBONS GILBERT P	COL	0-0039804	0163	1
GIBBS CHARLES H	LTC	0-0043764	0366	1
GIBBS COLEMAN T	CW3	W-0906741	0558	1
GIBBS CYRUS L	MAJ	0-0080788	0863	1
GIBBS DAVID P	M G	0-0019189	0766	1
GIBBS FREDERICK	COL	0-0029129	0557	1
GIBBS GEORGE W	COL	0-0018178	0660	1
GIBBS GERALD G	COL	0-0015637	0754	1
GIBBS JAMES J	LTC	0-0062934	0767	1
GIBNEY LOUIS G	COL	0-0005755	0753	1
GIBSON ADELNO	COL	0-0002046	0642	1
GIBSON COMET	LTC	0-0030497	0260	1
GIBSON EDWARD S	COL	0-0014913	0144	2
GIBSON ELMER P	LTC	0-0029145	0157	1
GIBSON EMERY M	LTC	0-0041604	0757	1
GIBSON ERVIN D	COL	0-0029899	0262	1
GIBSON HERBERT D	B G	0-0007152	0946	2
GIBSON HORACE C	COL	0-0020568	0657	1
GIBSON HORACE N	CPT	0-0011079	0435	2
GIBSON HOWLAND A	COL	0-0015496	0751	2
GIBSON JOHN H	COL	0-0029923	0563	1
GIBSON JOHN S	LTC	0-0053145	0868	1
GIBSON LOUIS J	CW4	W-0906742	0657	1
GIBSON RICHMOND T	COL	0-0003841	1047	1
GIBSON SAMUEL A	COL	0-0003586	0951	1
GIBSON THOMAS A JR	LTC	0-0035478	0962	1
GIBSON WILMOT L	LTC	0-0037562	0367	1
GIDDENS MITCHELL A	LTC	0-0016256	0548	2
GIDENS FLOYD E	COL	0-0030543	1265	2
GIELDSETH BETTY M	MAJ	N-0002583	0768	1
GIERLAK MICHAEL P	LTC	0-0040363	0165	2
GIES HAROLD M	CW2	W-0902009	0647	2
GIFFORD GERALD K	COL	0-0051539	0964	1
GIGGEY FREDERICK	MAJ	0-0060532	0363	1
GILBERT CHARLES L	COL	0-0029148	1158	2
GILBERT CHARLES M	COL	0-0023457	0766	1
GILBERT CLARENCE L	MAJ	0-0003244	1022	2
GILBERT DOUGLAS G	COL	0-0019202	0161	1
GILBERT HAROLD N	M G	0-0007596	1046	2
GILBERT HORACE C	CW4	W-0903148	0157	1
GILBERT JAMES R	COL	0-0051689	0962	1
GILBERT JAMES T	COL	0-0044348	0765	1
GILBERT LEONARD J	CPT	0-0027066	1050	2
GILBERT WILLIAM A	CW4	W-0903149	0962	1
GILBREATH FREDERICK	M G	0-0003086	0846	2
GILBREATH WILLIAM O	LTC	0-0059454	0464	1
GILBRETH JOSEPH H	COL	0-0007560	0546	1
GILCHRIST MALCOLM F	COL	0-0022077	0762	1
GILDART CHARLES R	COL	0-0012127	0351	2
GILDART ROBERT C	B G	0-0020703	0767	1
GILES EARL F	LTC	0-0056899	1267	1
GILES TOMMY H JR	LTC	0-0052120	0166	1
GILHART CHARLES C	2LT	0-2312157	0164	2
GILL ARLO R	LTC	0-0044983	1159	1
GILL BURGO D	LTC	0-0016347	1045	1
GILL CHARLES C	COL	0-0017840	0547	2
GILL EVERT R	CW4	W-0903150	0161	1
GILL GORDON C	COL	0-0042495	0265	1
GILL ISAAC JR	COL	0-0003739	1146	2
GILL MARIE A	MAJ	N-0001971	0461	1
GILL MARK J	LTC	0-0045784	1162	2
GILL ROBERT F	LTC	0-0009969	1041	1
GILL WILLIAM H	M G	0-0003287	0546	2
GILLAND MORRIS W	B G	0-0012066	0948	2
GILLARD MARJORIE G	MAJ	N-0000991	1263	1
GILLASPEY BRUCE N	LTC	0-0059654	1262	1
GILLEM ALVAN C JR	LTG	0-0003030	0850	1
GILLEN JOSEPH X	LTC	0-0079825	0965	1
GILLENTINE LUNCEFORD	LTC	0-0082009	1265	1
GILLENWATERS HENRY L	LTC	0-0041702	0257	1
GILLESPIE ERNEST R	COL	0-0041956	1161	1
GILLESPIE EUGENE P	COL	0-0025320	0764	1
GILLESPIE FLOYD T	COL	0-0011071	0952	2
GILLESPIE FRANCIS J	COL	0-0012215	0854	1
GILLESPIE HAROLD S	MAJ	0-0069934	0465	1
GILLESPIE JAMES D	M G	0-0016711	0357	1
GILLESPIE JOHN J	LTC	0-0032143	0267	1
GILLESPIE JOHN W JR	LTC	0-0028577	1166	2
GILLESPIE JOSEPHINE	MAJ	N-0002256	0262	1
GILLESPIE KENNETH W	COL	0-0030273	0662	2
GILLET BRUNETTA K	MAJ	M-0010019	0558	1
GILLET NORMAN D	COL	0-0011667	0854	1
GILLETTE A WARD	COL	0-0018883	0862	1
GILLETTE CHAUNCEY A	COL	0-0010039	0847	1
GILLETTE DOUGLAS H	COL	0-0003781	0253	1
GILLETTE EDWARD C JR	B G	0-0012697	0864	1
GILLETTE FRANCIS E	COL	0-0015693	0754	1
GILLETTE GEORGE W	COL	0-0005101	0148	1
GILLETTE SHELBY L	COL	0-0030727	0666	1
GILLFILLAN JAY E	COL	0-0004634	1048	2
GILLIAM ARNOLD C	COL	0-0031570	0157	1
GILLIAM WILLIE C	MAJ	N-0001472	1267	1
GILLIGAN RAMONA A	MAJ	N-0001907	0962	1
GILLIN JEROME M	MAJ	0-0065772	1168	1
GILLIS JOHN P	COL	0-0060313	1066	1
GILLIS MARCEL A	COL	0-0006810	0446	2
GILLIS NEVA G	CPT	L-0000172	0251	2
GILLIS THOMAS D	COL	0-0019864	0865	1
GILLMAN LEONARD	CW4	W-0903151	0362	2
GILLMORE WILLIAM K	LTC	0-0023432	0161	1
GILLMORE WILLIAM N	M G	0-0016196	0562	1
GILLON PAUL N	COL	0-0019048	0756	1
GILLY CLARENCE O	COL	0-0039681	0760	2
GILMAN SEYMOUR I	COL	0-0019377	0160	1
GILMAN SHELDON M	COL	0-0029624	0961	1
GILMAN TURNER W	COL	0-0031831	0661	1
GILMARTIN AUSTIN F	COL	0-0015024	0750	1
GILMER DAN	COL	0-0018876	0862	2
GILMOR ALBERT	COL	0-0001835	0841	2
GILMORE HUGH R JR	COL	0-0016555	0656	1
GILMORE ROBERT P	CW4	W-0903152	1262	1
GILMORE WILLIAM H	COL	0-0043414	0268	1
GILSON SHIRLEY M	MAJ	N-0001824	0266	1
GINGRAS ROLAND A	CW3	W-0903154	1165	1
GINGRICH HAROLD W	LTC	0-0026076	0765	1
GINN EDYTHE L	LTC	N-0001977	0861	1
GINN L HOLMES JR	B G	0-0017341	1058	2
GINN MELVIN R	MAJ	0-0005340	0622	2
GIRARD PAULINE H	LTC	N-0000218	0264	1
GIRARDE LILLIAN C	MAJ	N-0000172	0861	2
GIROUX ROSAIRE	CW4	W-0904117	0354	1
GIRTMAN JOHN C JR	COL	0-0044951	0764	1
GIST EMORY H	COL	0-0006159	0848	1
GIST HARVEY M	CW4	W-0903155	0355	1
GIVEN WILLIAM J	COL	0-0019105	.0157	1
GIVIDEN GEORGE M JR	CPT	0-0064146	0860	2
GJELSTEEN EINAR B	M G	0-0015143	0957	1
GLAB JOHN E	LTC	0-0026556	0867	1
GLACE FRANK E JR	MAJ	0-0021255	0939	2
GLADE KENNETH	LTC	0-0021181	0658	1
GLADISH ISAAC O	COL	0-0009126	0947	1
GLAFKA ALVIN R	COL	0-0041559	0259	1
GLASBRENNER HARLEY S	CW3	W-2150231	0467	1
GLASCOCK CAMBELL H	COL	0-0009141	0248	2
GLASCOCK HAROLD W JR	COL	0-0030854	0861	1
GLASEBROOK ARTHUR J	LTC	0-0045192	0667	1
GLASGOW JOSEPH M	COL	0-0012232	0550	2
GLASGOW RALPH I	B G	0-0015576	1055	1
GLASS ABRAHAM M	MAJ	0-0026780	0964	1
GLASS ALBERT J	COL	0-0029247	1163	1
GLASS ROY E	MAJ	0-0014529	0120	1
GLASSEN CHESTER E	COL	0-0033932	1163	1
GLASSER ANTHONY P	LTC	0-0059810	1066	1
GLATTERER MILTON S	COL	0-0018843	0862	1
GLAVIN EDWARD J F	COL	0-0016815	0455	1
GLEASON CHARLES C	LTC	0-0044245	0957	1
GLEASON JAMES K	LTC	0-0080794	0468	1
GLEASON THOMAS R	LTC	0-0027432	0966	1
GLEISER CHESTER A	COL	0-0031289	0965	1
GLEN GEORGE R	COL	0-0030049	1163	1
GLENDENING JAMES K	LTC	0-0026176	0164	1
GLENN CARL E	LTC	0-0050369	0765	1
GLENN DONALD W	LTC	0-0033931	0962	1
GLEW DONALD H JR	LTC	0-0059550	1065	1
GLICK ARTHUR A	LTC	0-0041444	1054	1
GLICKSON SOLOMON P	LTC	0-0054079	0464	1
GLIDDEN DOROTHY I	MAJ	M-0010155	0465	1
GLIDEWELL CALVIN E	LTC	0-0028418	0268	1
GLITHERO JOHN C	CPT	0-0007248	0227	2
GLORE JAMES	B G	0-0028758	0356	1
GLORIOD JOHN A	COL	0-0019793	0464	1
GLOVER BOB H	COL	0-0030680	0466	1
GLOVER MAYME V	MAJ	N-0002661	1068	1
GLOVER ROBERT L	CW4	W-0904118	0264	2
GLOVER WILLIAM C	COL	0-0034122	0867	1
GLUCKMAN ARCADI	COL	0-0006980	1150	1
GLYNN JOSEPH E	CW4	W-0906746	0266	1
GNAU WILLIAM D	COL	0-0043828	1163	2
GOATLEY FRANCIS J	COL	0-0051256	1161	2
GOCKER LEO L	COL	0-0007338	0446	2
GODBEY PAUL	COL	0-0030281	1164	1
GODBY GARLAND D	LTC	0-0036189	0560	1
GODFREY CARL F	LTC	0-0058410	1066	1
GODSEY DALE R	MAJ	0-0063284	0861	1
GODSHALL MELVIN W	LTC	0-0040184	0865	1
GODWIN HAROLD A JR	LTC	0-0087757	1068	1
GODWIN JAMES E	COL	0-0018768	0862	1
GODWIN NORMAN A	LTC	0-0046291	0766	1
GODWIN RENA M	MAJ	N-0000244	1163	1
GOE WILLIAM E	COL	0-0007433	1148	1
GOEBEL HERMAN P JR	COL	0-0041475	1057	1
GOEBERT ELMER C	COL	0-0006399	0746	1
GOERS WILLIAM C	LTC	0-0023487	0761	2
GOERZ PETER P	COL	0-0012095	0349	1
GOETH FREDERICK	LTC	0-0027640	0866	1
GOETHALS GEORGE R	COL	0-0013622	0819	1
GOETZ CARL	LTC	0-0031239	0367	1
GOETZ HUGO G JR	LTC	0-0039894	0662	2
GOETZ JOHN B M	COL	0-0043696	0165	1
GOFF JOHN L	COL	0-0012681	0753	2
GOFF ROBERT E	LTC	0-0081901	0761	1
GOLD WILLIAM M	COL	0-0040179	0762	2
GOLDBERG SEYMOUR L	COL	0-0079829	0966	1
GOLDBRANSON CARL E	CPT	0-0060451	0962	1
GOLDEN JOE E	COL	0-0018872	0862	1
GOLDEN WILLIAM C	COL	0-0039605	0557	1
GOLDMAN ALFRED M	MAJ	0-0005851	1039	1
GOLDRICK ROBERT N	LTC	0-0080796	0967	1
GOLDSMITH HOWARD F	LTC	0-0031946	0866	1
GOLDSMITH ROGER W	COL	0-0017163	0758	1
GOLDSTEIN JOSEPH D	COL	0-0062894	0868	2
GOLDSTEIN MANDEL N	LTC	0-0029711	0360	1
GOLDTHWAITE RALPH H	B G	0-0002562	0546	2
GOLEY BYRON H	LTC	0-0080797	0766	2
GOLLADAY EDWARD M	CW4	W-0903164	0157	1
GOLLADAY WILLIAM C	COL	0-0040897	0567	1
GOLLEHON CHARLES W	COL	0-0030918	0766	2
GOLSTON JOE R JR	LTC	0-0040657	0262	1
GOMEZ MARY L	LTC	N-0002036	0559	1
GOMOLL DAVID R	CW4	W-0906748	0364	1
GONOEK ADOLPH J	LTC	0-0044196	0468	1
GONSETH JULES E JR	COL	0-0040211	1064	1
GONTRUM RALPH W	COL	0-0051596	0862	1
GONYE AFTON M	MAJ	N-0002254	1061	1
GONZALEZ JUNE P	LTC	L-0000274	0165	1
GONZALEZ MIGUEL A	CW3	W-0906750	1056	1
GONZALEZ-RODRIG J	LTC	0-0058014	0662	1
GOOCH STACY W	COL	0-0019455	0764	1
GOOD JOHN C	1LT	0-0025346	0545	2
GOOD LARA P	CPT	0-0004977	1022	2
GOOD OTTO S	MAJ	0-0037442	.0957	1
GOODALL HENRY A	COL	0-0030977	1267	2

NAME	GRADE	SVC NO	DATE RET MO YR	RET CODE
GOODALL LESLIE D	COL	0-0030411	0965	2
GOODE ROY E	COL	0-0029921	0563	1
GOODELL FRANK Q	COL	0-0017147	0758	1
GOODELL KENNETH J	CW3	W-0906751	0459	1
GOODIN GEORGE W	CW4	W-0906752	0564	1
GOODING CLARENCE E	COL	0-0020258	0365	1
GOODLEY JOHN T	COL	0-0029566	0661	1
GOODMAN JOHN F JR	COL	0-0062997	0766	1
GOODMAN SANFORD J	COL	0-0015635	0754	1
GOODMAN THELMA B	MAJ	N-0001957	0859	1
GOODMAN THOMAS K	COL	0-0057984	1068	1
GOODMAN WILLIAM P	LTC	0-0062007	0866	1
GOODNOW JAMES L	COL	0-0031363	1266	1
GOODRICH DURWARD V	CW4	W-0903166	0864	1
GOODRICH FLORA E	MAJ	N-0002365	0760	1
GOODRICH GUINN B	COL	0-0042590	1265	1
GOODRICH MAX E	CW3	W-0906753	0964	1
GOODRICH MERLE L	LTC	0-0032693	1062	1
GOODRICH RAYMOND H	COL	0-0022911	1164	1
GOODRICH WALKER R	COL	0-0018815	0261	1
GOODRICH WALTER R	COL	0-0010172	1046	1
GOODRICK DOROTHY S	MAJ	N-0002375	0960	1
GOODRUM JACK T	CW2	W-0900380	0347	2
GOODSELL LEONARD J	COL	0-0024472	0365	1
GOODSON MELROSE C	MAJ	N-0000703	1165	1
GOODSPEED GEORGE F	MAJ	0-0060272	0165	1
GOODWIN ALBERT J	LTC	0-0042588	0663	1
GOODWIN ARTHUR C JR	COL	0-0018179	0360	1
GOODWIN JAMES B	COL	0-0030573	1065	2
GOODWIN JAMES E	COL	0-0020158	0866	1
GOODWIN JAMES E	CW2	W-0901479	0345	1
GOODWIN JAMES M	COL	0-0080799	0862	1
GOODWIN JOYCE	MAJ	N-0001284	0164	1
GOODWIN WALTER P	COL	0-0018733	0862	1
GOODWYN ALLEN A	COL	0-0011825	0653	2
GOOLER MAX H	COL	0-0015082	0754	2
GORBY ALVIN L	M G	0-0016546	0161	1
GORDANIER ROBERT S	LTC	0-0065256	0867	1
GORDER ALEXANDER	B G	0-0007213	0548	1
GORDON JAMES H	COL	0-0029227	0461	1
GORDON JAMES L	LTC	0-0039213	0767	1
GORDON LYNELL F	COL	0-0029769	0954	1
GORDON PRESTON O	LTC	0-0035828	0364	1
GORDON RANDOLPH	COL	0-0005204	0746	1
GORDON RICHARD A	COL	0-0005915	0854	1
GORDON THOMAS F	LTC	0-0023112	0761	1
GORDON WILL H	COL	0-0005827	1047	1
GORDON WILLIAM M	MAJ	0-0037430	0861	1
GORE THOMAS L	LTC	0-0004079	0-39	1
GORE WILLIAM E	LTC	0-0058911	0966	2
GORHAM FRANK W	LTC	0-0042461	1162	1
GORIUP OTHMAR F	COL	0-0029187	0960	1
GORLINSKI JOSEPH S	COL	0-0012092	0350	1
GORMAN ADAM R	CW4	RW-0903168	0764	1
GORMAN CHARLES L	COL	0-0015031	0148	1
GORMAN EMILY	COL	L-0000055	0866	1
GORMAN FRANK E	CW4	W-0907094	0660	1
GORMAN HARRY W	COL	0-0042062	0862	1
GORN JOHN W	COL	0-0022200	0764	2
GORRELL CHARLES J	LTC	0-0049942	0465	1
GORSKI ANDREW G	COL	0-0031993	1068	1
GORSKI JOSEPH	LTC	0-0079679	0766	1
GORSUCH EDWARD C	COL	0-0029740	0762	1
GORTON RUTH R	LTC	L-0000100	1063	1
GORTON WALTER T	COL	0-0008188	0847	1
GOSE ELLIOTT B	LTC	0-0016259	0944	2
GOSIGER FRED J	COL	0-0029867	0263	1
GOSS GORDON A	LTC	0-0042688	1162	1
GOSS THOMAS G	CW3	W-0906754	0962	1
GOSSETT HENRY M	LTC	0-0036941	1264	1
GOTT WILLIAM E	LTC	0-0037405	0767	1
GOTTESBUREN ROBERT E	CW3	W-0903170	0260	1
GOUGH A DEANE	COL	0-0018413	0761	1
GOUGH WESLEY P	LTC	0-0043474	0566	2
GOULD CLINTON L	COL	0-0040116	0268	1
GOULD GEORGE A	COL	0-0028968	0358	1
GOULD HAROLD A	COL	0-0080802	0965	1
GOULD HOWARD J	LTC	0-0087760	1066	1
GOULD KARL T	COL	0-0019544	0864	1
GOVERN FRANK W	COL	0-0021031	1065	1
GOWER ARTHUR W	COL	0-0006999	1148	1
GOWER WILFORD D	COL	0-0035699	1263	1
GOYETTE EDWIN M	COL	0-0020530	0257	1
GRABAN BENJAMIN H	COL	0-0010381	0750	2
GRABB ROBERT F	COL	0-0061969	0765	1
GRABER CHARLES D	LTC	0-0037555	1062	1
GRABLE GURNIA L	WO1	W-0902090	0147	2
GRAHOVE MAXWELL	COL	0-0059771	0366	1
GRACE ARTHUR B JR	LTC	0-0025498	0663	1
GRACE CHARLES O	COL	0-0009476	0753	1
GRACE JOHN O	CW4	W-0903172	0157	1
GRACE WILLIAM P JR	COL	0-0016619	0657	2
GRADY HENRY W	COL	0-0004143	0846	2
GRAEVES RAYMOND B	COL	0-0032563	0867	1
GRAF JOHN A	COL	0-0022892	0968	1
GRAF ROBERT E	LTC	0-0057083	0968	1
GRAF RUSSELL E	LTC	0-0059685	0266	1
GRAFTON FRANK L	CPT	0-0026390	0545	2
GRAHAM CLARENCE D	COL	0-0041463	0557	1
GRAHAM ELLIS C	CW4	RW-0905504	1066	1
GRAHAM EPHRAIM F JR	B G	0-0020838	0867	1
GRAHAM EUGENE S	COL	0-0041661	0360	1
GRAHAM FRANKLIN H	LTC	0-0040420	0268	1
GRAHAM GROVER C	COL	0-0006034	0947	2
GRAHAM HARROLD E	LTC	0-0037531	0568	1
GRAHAM JAMES E	B G	0-0019622	0663	1
GRAHAM JAMES W	COL	0-0024064	0767	1
GRAHAM JESSE E	COL	0-0012182	0854	2
GRAHAM RALPH W	LTC	0-0045995	0863	1
GRAHAM RAYMOND E	LTC	0-0070353	1163	1
GRAHAM ROBERT M	COL	0-0008616	1146	2
GRAHAM ROBERT O JR	COL	0-0032064	1268	1
GRAHAM ROY C L	M G	0-0004971	0952	1
GRAHAM THOMAS A JR	COL	0-0032231	0963	1
GRAHAM WALTER R	COL	0-0005020	0751	1
GRAHAM WILLIAM D	M G	0-0020067	1165	1
GRAHAM WILLIS B	CPT	0-0061873	0661	2
GRALING FRANCIS	COL	0-0015826	0754	1
GRAMZOW JOHN G	B G	0-0030735	0666	1
GRANDE IRA W	COL	0-0029503	1060	1
GRANT ANDREW R	LTC	0-0025045	0367	1
GRANT ARTHUR E	LTC	0-0064960	0667	1
GRANT CARL E	COL	0-0031653	0565	1
GRANT CHAPMAN	MAJ	0-0003646	1034	2
GRANT EDWARD J	COL	0-0038743	0761	1
GRANT GEORGE R	MAJ	0-0024980	1046	2
GRANT GILVARY P	LTC	0-0051775	0663	1
GRANT HELEN E	MAJ	N-0001835	0765	1
GRANT JOATHAN M	LTC	0-0036083	0167	1
GRANT JOSEPH A	COL	0-0004487	0651	1
GRANT LOIS K	MAJ	N-0000829	0863	1
GRANT MELVILLE F	COL	0-0014977	0854	2
GRANT PATRICIA E	LTC	L-0000181	0265	1
GRANT RUSSELL P	COL	0-0042646	0965	1
GRANT WALTER H	COL	0-0022093	0666	1
GRASS BARBARA A	MAJ	N-0000369	0165	1
GRAUER FRANKLIN H	COL	0-0057524	0962	1
GRAVER HERBERT A	LTC	0-0078858	1266	1
GRAVES ABIGAIL B	MAJ	N-0000019	0248	1
GRAVES HAROLD K	LTC	0-0059855	0964	1
GRAVES JOHN L	COL	0-0015036	0846	1
GRAVES RUPERT O	COL	0-0015794	0754	1
GRAY CLIFFORD A	CPT	0-0006088	0934	2
GRAY CLIFFORD A	COL	0-0016554	0155	2
GRAY COLUMBUS E JR	LTC	0-0059460	1068	1
GRAY DELL S	COL	0-0008765	0749	2
GRAY EUGENE W JR	COL	0-0051183	1065	1
GRAY GORDON O	COL	0-0040596	0763	1
GRAY HARVEY W	LTC	0-0060582	0267	1
GRAY IRVING	COL	0-0058738	0464	1
GRAY JOHN T	LTC	0-0037480	1162	1
GRAY LEE E	1LT	0-0012195	0934	2
GRAY MILLARD E	COL	0-0032137	1166	1
GRAY MILO I	COL	0-0041598	0559	1
GRAY NORMAN	COL	0-0040387	0368	1
GRAY PAUL JR	COL	0-0023935	0967	1
GRAY ROBERT M	COL	0-0024644	0362	1
GRAYBEAL CARL S	COL	0-0016875	0755	1
GRAYEB GEORGE A	COL	0-0016152	0655	1
GREAVES FIELDING L	LTC	0-0026656	1065	1
GREBE ALFRED A	COL	0-0020502	0655	1
GRELD EMILE J	1LT	0-0019160	0242	1
GRECO JOHN F	COL	0-0018133	1059	1
GREEAR WILLIAM H	COL	0-0017607	0859	1
GREELEY BRENDAN M	COL	0-0017740	0859	1
GREELEY LEONARD J	M G	0-0015449	0959	1
GREEN ALICE H	MAJ	N-0000876	0767	1
GREEN CARL E	COL	0-0018460	0761	1
GREEN CHARLES E	MAJ	0-0058125	1264	1
GREEN CHARLES F	COL	0-0065413	0166	1
GREEN DOROTHY E	CW4	V-0915361	0663	1
GREEN DUFF JR	COL	0-0042239	0763	1
GREEN HAZEL L JR	LTC	0-0074946	0868	1
GREEN JAMES B	COL	0-0023423	0866	1
GREEN JAMES D	LTC	0-0022182	0866	1
GREEN JAMES L	COL	0-0017074	0755	1
GREEN JAMES O III	COL	0-0023850	0865	1
GREEN JAMES W JR	B G	0-0016774	0857	1
GREEN JESSE P	COL	0-0005626	1050	1
GREEN JOHN H	COL	0-0033085	0865	1
GREEN JOHN N	COL	0-0028871	0756	1
GREEN JOSEPHINE	LTC	N-0002400	0765	1
GREEN KIRBY	COL	0-0009687	1146	1
GREEN L D	MAJ	0-0079310	0167	2
GREEN LYNELL W	COL	0-0052665	1162	1
GREEN MACK M	B G	0-0016539	0656	1
GREEN MARTIN L	COL	0-0020720	0666	1
GREEN PHILIP P	COL	0-0005400	0451	2
GREEN THOMAS C	COL	0-0050944	0457	1
GREEN THOMAS H	M G	0-0006895	1149	1
GREEN WARRNE J	LTC	0-0042898	1262	1
GREEN WINIFRED C	COL	0-0007076	1150	1
GREENBERG SAMUEL	COL	0-0041692	0656	1
GREENE ALPHONSE A	COL	0-0018400	0859	1
GREENE FRANCIS M	COL	0-0028803	0555	1
GREENE FRED W	COL	0-0038737	0656	1
GREENE JOHN N	CPT	0-0009585	0934	2
GREENE JOHN S	MAJ	0-0040514	0652	2
GREENE PHILIP S	COL	0-0020314	0157	1
GREENE RICHARDSON	COL	0-0007607	0746	1
GREENE WILLIAM H	COL	0-0042130	1262	1
GREENFIELD LOUIS	COL	0-0041926	1061	1
GREENING ORLANDO L	COL	0-0043906	0761	1
GREENLEAF HENRY M	COL	0-0020983	0858	1
GREENLEE HALFORD R	COL	0-0019801	0365	1
GREENWALD KARL C	COL	0-0003359	0240	1
GREENWELL SAMUEL A	COL	0-0007752	0143	2
GREER FIELDER P	COL	0-0018430	0761	1
GREER FRANK B	LTC	0-0033447	0262	1
GREER HARRY A	COL	0-0043685	0765	1
GREER HARRY J	CW4	W-0903177	0661	1
GREER HERMAN E	LTC	0-0080806	0965	1
GREER RICHARD S	LTC	0-0039343	0761	1
GREEVE GERALD J	COL	0-0029576	0861	1
GREGG DAVID H	COL	0-0019713	0758	1
GREGOIRE WILLIAM N	MAJ	0-0079311	1265	1
GREGORY CLYDE	LTC	0-0043044	0565	1
GREGORY FRANCIS G JR	COL	0-0031828	0267	1
GREGORY JAMES R	COL	0-0051737	0762	1
GREINER EDWIN C	COL	0-0015012	0954	1
GREINER ROBERT E	LTC	0-0038925	0562	1
GRENATA MICHAEL C	COL	0-0009304	0653	1
GRENDON ALEXANDER	COL	0-0039506	1054	1
GRENELLE EDWIN W	COL	0-0038757	0164	1
GRENIER WILLIAM T	COL	0-0030167	0464	1
GRENON JEANNETTE	LTC	N-0001002	0567	2
GRESHAM MONSEY T JR	LTC	0-0045076	0664	1
GRESHAM WENIFORD F	CW4	W-0903180	0160	1
GRETSER GEORGE R	COL	0-0019126	0863	1
GREUBEL ARVEL B	CW3	RW-0904427	1164	1
GREVERT HARRY C	LTC	0-0056077	0966	1
GRICE LETCHER D	B G	0-0008273	0753	2
GRICE THORPE C	LTC	0-0026326	0266	1
GRIDER EDGAR L	COL	0-0042112	1262	1
GRIDLEY JACK P	1LT	0-0066951	0254	2
GRIEGER ALLEN J	LTC	0-0061088	0967	1
GRIESBECK WILSON A	LTC	0-0040604	0766	1
GRIEST OLIVER F	LTC	0-0034573	1068	1
GRIEVES LOREN C JR	MAJ	0-0022143	0148	2
GRIEVES WILLIAM P	COL	0-0019742	0865	1
GRIFFIN DAVID T	COL	0-0020600	0865	1
GRIFFIN JAMES C	COL	0-0033018	0868	1
GRIFFIN JOSEPH	CW4	W-0901662	0660	1
GRIFFIN LINWOOD JR	COL	0-0043074	0767	1
GRIFFIN MARCUS S	COL	0-0019954	0865	1
GRIFFIN ROBERT J	LTC	0-0043005	0465	1
GRIFFIN THOMAS N	M G	0-0017775	0762	1
GRIFFIN WILLIAM E	COL	0-0011894	1050	1
GRIFFING LEWIS S	M G	0-0016413	0464	2
GRIFFITH FREDERICK	COL	0-0001704	0642	2
GRIFFITH GEORGE W	1LT	0-0028338	0350	2
GRIFFITH GIRVAN H	MAJ	0-0060591	0963	1
GRIFFITH HAROLD S JR	LTC	0-0023403	0559	1
GRIFFITH HENRY V	LTC	0-0069938	1067	1
GRIFFITH JACK H	COL	0-0016915	0857	2
GRIFFITH RABUN W	LTC	0-0027326	0765	1
GRIFFITH ROBERT E	LTC	0-0080811	1066	1
GRIFFITH WILLIAM H	LTC	0-0044403	0661	1
GRIGG MARTIN C	LTC	0-0030711	0464	1
GRIGGS ARCHIE J	LTC	0-0044389	0968	1
GRIGGS JOHN B	CW3	W-0906763	1060	1
GRIGGS OSCAR B	COL	0-0029315	0764	1
GRIGSBY ROBERT W	CW3	W-0903181	0862	1
GRILEY JOSEPH F	WO1	W-0901318	0138	2
GRILL HENRY S	MAJ	0-0067686	1265	1
GRIMES ALSTON	COL	0-0019252	0863	1
GRIMES ROBERT A	LTC	0-0042869	1064	1
GRIMME WALTER R	CW4	W-0902148	0364	1
GRIMMER EDWIN W	LTC	0-0005544	0342	2
GRIMSHAW CHARLES M	COL	0-0024872	0167	1
GRIMSLEY CARL E	LTC	0-0042568	0663	2
GRINER GEORGE W JR	M G	0-0007063	0846	1
GRINSTEAD JOHN B	COL	0-0017134	0858	2
GRIPPER PAUL C	COL	0-0009715	0351	1
GRISARD GUS H	LTC	0-0080095	0968	2
GRISCTI WALTER E	COL	0-0034666	0967	1
GRISSOM WILLIE M	MAJ	N-0001987	1164	1
GRISWOLD GEORGE M	COL	0-0031660	1067	1
GRISWOLD STANLEY F	COL	0-0007371	0854	2
GRIZZARD HARRY M	COL	0-0016521	0756	1
GROFF IRENE B	MAJ	L-0000316	0563	1
GROGAN GERARD J	LTC	0-0040429	1054	1
GROGAN JOHN F	COL	0-0042637	1065	1
GROGAN JOHN F	LTC	0-0065040	1068	1
GROGAN STANLEY J	COL	0-0007354	0951	1
GROH HORTENSE S	MAJ	N-0000256	0359	1
GROH MARY T	MAJ	N-0002008	0764	1
GRONBECK CHRISTIAN	COL	0-0026470	0663	1
GRONDONA RICHARD J	COL	0-0042439	1264	1
GROSE JOHN E	COL	0-0007540	0846	2
GROSECLOSE TOM S	LTC	0-0063108	1266	1
GROSJEAN DOLAS M	MAJ	L-0000027	1055	1
GROSS CHARLES A	COL	0-0030528	0364	1
GROSS CHARLES P	M G	0-0003662	1145	1
GROSS DONALD E	LTC	0-0027805	1065	1
GROSS FELIX E	COL	0-0003129	0546	2
GROSS GARDNER B	COL	0-0029859	1153	2
GROSS LESLIE M	COL	0-0038938	0468	1
GROSSMAN HARRY J	COL	0-0022786	1066	2
GROSSMAN LELAND F	2LT	0-0066405	1053	2

NAME	GRADE	SVC NO	DATE RET MO YR	RET CODE
GROTE ROBERT W	COL	0-0031717	1165	1
GROTHAUS DONALD G	B G	0-0020221	0466	1
GROTTE HELMER M	COL	0-0031622	1167	1
GROVE EDWARD A	COL	0-0020200	0363	2
GROVE LEE A	COL	0-0056187	1268	1
GROVE WILLIAM R JR	COL	0-0015185	1052	1
GROVES JASPER M	COL	0-0008305	0646	2
GROVES JOSEPH R	COL	0-0020869	1064	1
GROVES LESLIE R	LTG	0-0012043	0248	1
GROVES WILLICE E	COL	0-0030075	0760	2
GROW ROBERT W	M G	0-0004621	0153	1
GROWDON JOHN S	LTC	0-0019737	0655	1
GRUBBS ELMER W	COL	0-0020291	0866	1
GRUBBS HAYDON Y	COL	0-0016154	0755	1
GRUBBS WILLIAM E	COL	0-0018146	0760	1
GRUBE GEORGE	CW4	W-0903184	1163	1
GRUBER WILLIAM R	B G	0-0003465	0846	2
GRUBIN EDWARD L	CPT	0-0037635	1047	2
GRUENTHER ALFRED M	GEN	0-0012242	1056	2
GRUHLKEY EMORY M	CW3	W-0903185	1056	1
GRUHN ERNEST W	COL	0-0011192	0753	1
GRUNERT GEORGE	LTG	0-0001534	0745	2
GRUNERT GEORGE R	COL	0-0018859	1050	2
GRUVER GEORGE A	LTC	0-0031207	1060	1
GRZESIOW THOMAS M	CPT	0-0070355	0961	1
GUEHRING RAYMOND R	COL	0-0051723	0264	2
GUENTHER AUGUSTUS J	COL	0-0031067	0666	1
GUEST LEROY A	CPT	0-0027013	1046	2
GUEST MARION I	LTC	0-0060856	0366	1
GUEST REVELLA	MAJ	N-0000195	0163	1
GUEVARA SANTIAGO G	LTC	0-0015334	0753	1
GUICE BILLY M	LTC	0-0080815	0363	1
GUIDERA THOMAS F	COL	0-0047165	1068	2
GUILD DONALD E	LTC	0-0080816	1165	1
GUILD EUGENE R	CPT	0-0014816	1138	2
GUIMOND JOSEPH A	COL	0-0026379	0167	1
GUINAN WARREN A	LTC	0-0082018	0868	1
GUINEY PATRICK W JR	COL	0-0019066	0756	1
GUION JAMES	COL	0-0005234	0753	1
GUIRAUD RENE J A	MAJ	0-0037942	0552	2
GUISLEMAN GEORGE V	LTC	0-0039793	1060	1
GULETSKY WALTER N	LTC	0-0021309	0761	1
GULLATT DOSWELL	COL	0-0012100	0846	2
GULLICKSON HERBERT L	COL	0-0021694	0668	2
GULLION MAURICE B	COL	0-0042826	0364	1
GUNDERSON CLARENCE H	LTC	0-0018041	0758	1
GUNLOGSON ALICE	MAJ	N-0002194	0565	1
GUNN CLAUD T	COL	0-0014595	1049	1
GUNN CLEM O	COL	0-0014596	0447	2
GUNN DAMON M	COL	0-0015174	0753	1
GUNN FRANCIS C	LTC	N-0000095	0662	1
GUNN RAYMOND M	LTC	0-0065118	0668	1
GUNNER EDWIN	COL	0-0001869	0642	1
GUNNER MATTHEW J	B G	0-0003257	1046	1
GUNSTER WALTER E	COL	0-0022928	0467	1
GUNTHER CARL F	COL	0-0029193	0261	2
GURTILL COLIN K	CPT	0-0038265	0967	1
GURFEIN JOSEPH I	COL	0-0023734	0767	1
GURLEY FRANKLIN K	LTC	0-0015244	0847	1
GURNEE WILLIAM H JR	COL	0-0023974	0863	1
GURSKY ALEX R	LTC	0-0080817	0364	1
GUSHURST CLARENCE F	LTC	0-0022998	0862	1
GUSTAFSON ARTHUR W	COL	0-0051404	0163	1
GUSTIN HARRY W	CW4	W-0903188	1054	2
GUTH HENRY T	LTC	0-0032768	0268	1
GUTHRIDGE JOHN R	CW3	W-0903189	1066	1
GUTHRIE AARON S	COL	0-0050894	0555	1
GUTHRIE JAMES O	LTC	0-0031470	0958	1
GUTHRIE JOHN S	M G	0-0018228	0661	1
GUTHRIE PAUL G	COL	0-0030050	0165	1
GUTHRIE PAUL R	COL	0-0008027	1049	1
GUTHRIE RALPH R	LTC	0-0006462	0642	1
GUTHRIE RICHARD F	LTC	0-0049822	0763	1
GWALTNEY HELEN L	MAJ	N-0000210	0563	1
HAAG LUCILE M	MAJ	R-0010110	0963	1
HAAS HARRY H	COL	0-0041385	0555	1
HABERER WALTER J JR	COL	0-0052278	1265	1
HABERMAN FREDRIC W	LTC	0-0062550	0968	1
HABERMAN HOWARD F	COL	0-0040193	0164	1
HABIGER CHARLES F	CW4	W-0903190	0164	1
HACKER JOSEPH F	CW4	W-0903191	0558	1
HACKER WILLIAM C	COL	0-0038083	0968	1
HACKETT CHARLES J	COL	0-0021954	0867	1
HACKETT EDWARD J	LTC	0-0082019	0866	1
HACKETT PERRY B	LTC	0-0021443	0661	1
HACKETT ROBERT	LTG	0-0018380	0768	2
HACKETT WALLACE J	LTC	0-0023179	0561	1
HADFIELD WILLIAM A	COL	0-0029727	0662	1
HADFIELD WILLIAM A	COL	0-0029737	0662	1
HADLEY CLEO V	COL	0-0044086	1162	2
HADLEY LEO L	LTC	0-0042481	1262	1
HAEFELE JOSEPH L	COL	0-0080270	0567	1
HAFGELE IDA L	MAJ	N-0002640	0865	1
HAENISCH KATE A	MAJ	N-0000609	0663	1
HAESSLY BURDETT E	COL	0-0023016	0461	2
HAFF ALEXANDER	COL	0-0018260	1054	2
HAFF ROBERT A	CW4	W-0903192	0567	1
HAFFA ROBERT P	COL	0-0021809	0560	1
HAGAN JOHN F	COL	0-0042438	0964	2
HAGE GUNNAR H	COL	0-0029313	0464	1
HAGEDON GEORGE G	LTC	0-0027898	0966	1
HAGEN BERNARD E	COL	0-0029733	0762	1
HAGEN ROBERT P	COL	0-0021373	0966	1
HAGEN THOMAS J	COL	0-0020967	0565	2
HAGENS JOHN M	MAJ	0-0007988	1030	2
HAGERMAN CALVIN G	COL	0-0022252	1265	1
HAGERSTRAND MARTIN A	COL	0-0042957	1060	1
HAGERTY HARRY E	COL	0-0030685	0762	1
HAGERTY JAMES J JR	LTC	0-0082020	0667	1
HAGERTY WILLIAM A	COL	0-0041883	0661	1
HAGGARD EDWIN C	MAJ	0-0023081	0750	2
HAGGART ALEXANDER	COL	0-0010140	0550	2
HAGINS WILLIAM	B G	0-0004050	0448	2
HAGLER ETHEL I	MAJ	N-0002007	0864	1
HAGLER THOMAS	LTC	0-0027052	0863	1
HAGMAN CHARLES A JR	LTC	0-0063291	0366	1
HAGMAN CHARLES M	CW4	W-0903196	0263	1
HAGMAN FRANK E	COL	0-0041697	0458	1
HAGOOD JOHNSON JR	COL	0-0018452	1046	2
HAGUE JAMES E	CW4	W-0903197	0862	1
HAHN CORNMAN L	COL	0-0012063	0753	1
HAHN ERIC L	LTC	0-0065075	0165	1
HAHN LAWSON E	COL	0-0029650	0262	2
HAHN RUSSELL S	COL	0-0056815	0964	1
HAHN THOMAS M	COL	0-0038609	1056	1
HAHNEY EVERETT G	COL	0-0020185	0866	1
HAIG CHESTER R	COL	0-0003303	0247	1
HAIL CLEBERT L	COL	0-0017779	0859	1
HAILE WILLIAM G	LTC	0-0080097	0567	1
HAIN ROBERT W	COL	0-0019072	0863	1
HAINES AUBREY M	LTC	0-0087525	0866	1
HAINES HAROLD H	LTC	0-0039868	1161	1
HAINES OLIVER L	B G	0-0004670	0951	2
HAINES RALPH E	B G	0-0002891	0845	1
HAINES ROBERT G	COL	0-0029460	0960	1
HAINES ROBERT L	COL	0-0039994	1265	1
HAINES WILLIAM E	CW4	W-0903198	0457	1
HAINS PETER C III	M G	0-0015657	0561	1
HAISLIP WADE H	GEN	0-0003374	0751	1
HAKALA EDWIN W	COL	0-0021456	0758	1
HAKANSON VALERIUS	COL	0-0041371	0155	2
HALADA ROLAND J	COL	0-0042635	0662	2
HALBERT EDWARD D	COL	0-0003615	0444	1
HALDEMAN WILLIAM T	COL	0-0004992	0-45	2
HALE CARL J	CW4	W-0903199	1268	1
HALE CHARLES L	LTC	0-0071673	0968	1
HALE HARRY R	COL	0-0019828	0863	1
HALE MAURICE W	COL	0-0017333	1056	1
HALE MILTON B	COL	0-0041681	1059	1
HALE RALPH N	COL	0-0043968	0863	1
HALE ROBERT A	COL	0-0004174	0744	2
HALE WALLACE M	COL	0-0022758	1167	1
HALE WILLIAM C	LTC	0-0036124	0767	1
HALE WILLIAM H	COL	0-0022184	0265	1
HALEY JOHN J	COL	0-0079835	0167	1
HALEY T E T	COL	0-0006637	1047	1
HALEY 3RD CHARLES L	COL	0-0021226	0859	1
HALL ALLEN K	MAJ	0-0058421	0167	1
HALL ALPHUS W	LTC	0-0054490	1165	1
HALL AUGUSTUS A	COL	0-0051127	0258	1
HALL CARL L	COL	0-0030722	0763	1
HALL CHARLES A	LTC	0-0044605	1268	1
HALL CHESTER A JR	COL	0-0048018	1167	2
HALL CLAUDE H	LTC	0-0047794	0966	1
HALL DEWITT N	COL	0-0022083	0462	1
HALL EARL W	COL	0-0038698	0961	1
HALL EDNA F	MAJ	N-0002284	1264	1
HALL ETHEL E L	MAJ	N-0002399	0962	1
HALL FRANCIS G	COL	0-0018794	0262	1
HALL FREDERICK JR	COL	0-0019747	0761	1
HALL GEORGE P	LTC	0-0080826	0364	1
HALL HARRELL G	COL	0-0051580	0163	1
HALL HARRY A	COL	0-0051819	0861	1
HALL HARRY H	LTC	0-0058913	0766	1
HALL HERBERT A	B G	0-0041631	1159	1
HALL JAMES D	CW3	W-0906767	0467	2
HALL JAMES M	LTC	0-0040692	0867	1
HALL JOHN R JR	COL	0-0023576	0364	1
HALL JOSEPH S	LTC	0-0096629	0763	1
HALL LEWIS A	COL	0-0040089	0766	1
HALL RALPH	COL	0-0005488	0-44	1
HALL RICHARD E JR	COL	0-0032330	0765	1
HALL ROBERT J	COL	0-0031882	0765	1
HALL ROBERT M	LTC	0-0070358	1067	1
HALL ROBERT S	COL	0-0029174	0258	1
HALL ROY F	CPT	0-0007783	0629	1
HALL SAMUEL L	COL	0-0051594	0860	1
HALL SYLVESTER	COL	0-0040057	1062	1
HALL TURNER P JR	LTC	0-0060238	1167	1
HALL WILBUR T	LTC	0-0042908	1263	1
HALL WILLIAM C	B G	0-0018391	0463	1
HALL WILLIAM W JR	LTC	0-0028005	1167	1
HALLA CARL	COL	0-0004393	0742	1
HALLAM CLYDE M	COL	0-0011587	0554	1
HALLAREN MARY A	COL	L-0000001	0760	1
HALLDEN CHARLES H	LTC	0-0030360	0163	1
HALLINGER EARL S JR	COL	0-0069497	1067	1
HALLINGER ELMER F	LTC	0-0021212	0656	1
HALLMAN LAURA L	MAJ	N-0001636	0864	2
HALLMEYER LAWRENCE D	CW4	W-0904414	1053	1
HALLOCK DUNCAN	B G	0-0018960	0863	1
HALLOCK HOUGHTON R	COL	0-0020612	0657	1
HALLOCK RICHARD R	COL	0-0037367	0667	1
HALLOCK ROBERT F	COL	0-0015134	0854	2
HALLORAN MICHAEL E	COL	0-0007502	0854	1
HALLOWAY HARRY A	CW4	W-0902058	0656	2
HALLOWAY KENNETH E	CW4	W-0902114	0558	1
HALLOWELL MARGARET D	MAJ	L-0000233	0961	2
HALLUMS JAMES B	LTC	0-0032564	1263	1
HALONEN ALICE S	MAJ	N-0001001	0664	1
HALPIN DANIEL E	COL	0-0024957	1066	1
HALSEY FRANK W	COL	0-0009586	0446	2
HALSEY MILTON B	M G	0-0005305	0153	1
HALSTEAD FRANK	COL	0-0000698	0-26	2
HALSTEAD LESLIE H	LTC	0-0026848	0164	1
HALTER BRYAN S	COL	0-0012493	0450	1
HALTERMAN HARRY W	LTC	0-0017209	0549	1
HALTOM JOHN D	LTC	0-0020788	0445	2
HALVERSON HERMAN G	MAJ	0-0007971	1035	2
HALVORSON JOHN A	MAJ	0-0081450	0966	1
HAMBERG WILLIAM A	COL	0-0030741	0661	2
HAMBLEN ARCHELAUS	B G	0-0004731	0754	1
HAMBLIN JAMES M	LTC	0-0025127	0963	1
HAMELE LOUIS F	COL	0-0032610	0965	1
HAMERSLEY DWIGHT T	COL	0-0042159	0363	1
HAMES SARRATT T	COL	0-0015845	0953	2
HAMILL JAMES P	COL	0-0025324	0461	1
HAMILTON ADNA C	COL	0-0012480	0454	1
HAMILTON ALLAN C	COL	0-0042456	1163	1
HAMILTON ANDREW W	COL	0-0029767	0962	1
HAMILTON EARL M	COL	0-0030398	0363	1
HAMILTON EDWARD S	LTC	0-0022165	0546	2
HAMILTON FRANK C	LTC	0-0024532	0661	1
HAMILTON GLADEN R	COL	0-0020089	1152	2
HAMILTON HOMER G	COL	0-0039781	0657	1
HAMILTON J ARTHUR	COL	0-0042294	0661	1
HAMILTON JAMES R	COL	0-0014627	0854	1
HAMILTON JOHN M	COL	0-0010268	0753	1
HAMILTON LAVERSA M	1LT	M-0000434	0446	1
HAMILTON PAUL	COL	0-0016455	0656	1
HAMILTON PURLEY W JR	CW4	W-0906770	0166	2
HAMILTON RAYMOND C	COL	0-0008303	0753	1
HAMILTON STEPHEN S	COL	0-0015934	0754	1
HAMILTON STUART A JR	LTC	0-0036152	0864	1
HAMILTON WILBUR A	LTC	0-0052352	0862	1
HAMILTON WILLIAM L	LTC	0-0010031	0842	2
HAMILTON WILLIAM T	COL	0-0005777	0854	1
HAMIT HAROLD F	COL	0-0057980	0568	1
HAMLIN GUY A	LTC	0-0063740	0967	1
HAMLIN JOHN A	CW3	W-0903203	0858	2
HAMLIN JOSEPH H	COL	0-0052312	0568	1
HAMLIN WILLIAM O	M G	0-0017619	1062	2
HAMLYN ALVERA E	LTC	M-0010099	0867	1
HAMM ISSAC B	CW4	W-0902272	0865	1
HAMMACK LOUIS A	COL	0-0017696	0859	1
HAMMARLUND MABEL	LTC	N-0002057	0164	1
HAMMER JAMES F	COL	0-0024599	0967	1
HAMMER WALTER D	LTC	0-0060769	1065	1
HAMMERNESS OSCAR T	LTC	0-0039752	1059	1
HAMMERSBERG ROBERT E	COL	0-0018933	1062	1
HAMMON BERNARD C	COL	0-0020922	0266	1
HAMMOND CLAUDE G	COL	0-0005193	0646	2
HAMMOND DAVID G	COL	0-0020868	0764	1
HAMMOND ELTON F	B G	0-0012291	0854	1
HAMMOND JOHN W	COL	0-0017656	1058	1
HAMMOND THOMAS W JR	COL	0-0017622	0859	1
HAMMOND WILLIAM H JR	LTC	0-0044213	0261	1
HAMMONDS VERNON	COL	0-0051486	1061	2
HAMNER MERLE E	LTC	0-0052805	0262	1
HAMPTON MABEL E	MAJ	J-0000001	0764	1
HAMPTON MCLEAN	LTC	0-0032239	1065	1
HAMPTON WADE F	LTC	0-0043190	0666	2
HAMPTON WILLIAM A	COL	0-0018482	0761	1
HAMRICK ERASTUS N	CW4	W-0903206	0766	1
HANBURGER CHRISTIAN	COL	0-0020554	0866	1
HANCHETT FRED R JR	1LT	0-0009815	0622	2
HANCOCK DANIEL W	COL	0-0035281	0966	1
HANCOCK WILLIAM F	LTC	0-0045013	0762	1
HAND CHARLES M	COL	0-0051669	1265	1
HAND CLIFTON E	LTC	0-0080832	0966	1
HAND HARRY V	LTC	0-0005710	0342	2
HAND JAMES D	COL	0-0030328	1264	1
HAND ROBERT	LTC	0-0036415	0766	1
HAND ROBERT O	LTC	0-0032294	0765	1
HANDLEY ARTHUR L	WO1	W-0800232	1135	2
HANDLEY ARTHUR L JR	LTC	0-0026884	0865	1
HANDY THOMAS T	GEN	0-0004665	0354	1
HANEKE WILLIAM C	M G	0-0020263	1267	1
HANEY HAROLD	B G	0-0006807	0753	2
HANEY LEE W	COL	0-0014628	1146	2
HANFORD EDWARD C	COL	0-0003317	0742	2
HANFORD THOMAS B	COL	0-0029660	1061	1
HANGER JOHN W	COL	0-0039975	0465	1
HANKEL HALLAND W	LTC	0-0044049	0862	1
HANKINSON FRANK E JR	COL	0-0028884	1056	1
HANKS JAMES K	LTC	0-0042473	1162	1
HANKS LESTER	LTC	0-0030339	0163	1
HANLE WILLIAM D	CPT	0-0060348	0762	1
HANLEY JAMES E	COL	0-0039591	1058	1
HANLEY JAMES M	COL	0-0041688	0660	1

NAME	GRADE	SVC NO	DATE RET MO YR	RET CODE
HANLEY JAMES M	CW4	W-0903209	0961	1
HANLEY JOHN T	MAJ	0-0006338	0659	2
HANLEY THOMAS L	LTC	0-0078868	1068	1
HANLON JOHN H	1LT	0-0099740	0366	2
HANMER STEPHEN R	M G	0-0013348	0664	1
HANNA EDWARD J	MAJ	0-0037610	0762	1
HANNA ELIZABETH	LTC	N-0002026	0760	1
HANNA FRED S	COL	0-0038612	1057	1
HANNA GEORGE T	COL	0-0052758	0764	1
HANNA HOMER H	MAJ	0-0069499	1264	1
HANNA LLOYD M	COL	0-0009789	0148	2
HANNA LOYD J	LTC	0-0035943	0564	1
HANNA THOMAS G	COL	0-0060834	0965	1
HANNA WILLIAM G	CW4	W-0902362	0468	1
HANNAH LAUREN E	COL	0-0051358	1162	1
HANNAH PAUL V	COL	0-0024539	0368	1
HANNAH THOMAS R	COL	0-0018899	0862	1
HANNIGAN JAMES P	B G	0-0017531	0859	1
HANNIGAN KATHRYN O	LTC	N-0000150	0358	2
HANNIS HENRY F	COL	0-0012618	0750	1
HANNON ALBERT J	COL	0-0042175	0763	1
HANNON JOSEPH L	LTC	0-0059553	0468	1
HANNUM ROBERT C	LTC	0-0056048	0966	1
HANNUM WARREN T JR	COL	0-0021316	0868	1
HANNUM WILLIAM Y	COL	0-0071798	1068	1
HANSBOROUGH JOHN W	COL	0-0018376	0761	1
HANSEN EVERETT A	COL	0-0023528	0760	1
HANSEN FLOYD A	M G	0-0018767	0667	2
HANSEN GEORGE K	LTC	0-0058916	0867	1
HANSEN GEORGE R	LTC	0-0052571	0164	1
HANSEN HARRY F	COL	0-0042618	1161	2
HANSEN HERBERT C	COL	0-0070842	1065	1
HANSEN HOWARD M	LTC	0-0024554	0547	2
HANSEN IRVING S	CW4	W-0901152	0252	1
HANSEN RICHARD A	COL	0-0074943	0568	1
HANSON AJELLON F	LTC	0-0025301	0461	1
HANSON CHARLES C	COL	0-0039873	0660	1
HANSON JACK R	1LT	0-0062628	0153	2
HANSON RUSSELL H	LTC	0-0052615	0961	1
HANSON THOMAS J JR	COL	0-0005572	0445	2
HANSON WALTER S	LTC	0-0079845	0965	1
HANST KENNETH F JR	MAJ	0-0024733	0348	2
HANTZES JAMES	COL	0-0052467	0568	1
HARANT LOUIS J	LTC	0-0010461	0924	2
HARBACK HERBERT D	LTC	0-0044390	0766	1
HARBER WILLIAM V	COL	0-0039578	0658	1
HARBERT JOHN E	COL	0-0044833	0168	1
HARDAGE JOHN M	LTC	0-0067500	0967	1
HARDAGE QUENTIN R	LTC	0-0035276	0848	2
HARDAWAY EADS G	B G	0-0020955	0766	1
HARDAWAY FRANCIS P	B G	0-0002671	0448	1
HARDAWAY ROBERT M	B G	0-0004307	0848	2
HARDEE DAVID L	COL	0-0011903	1049	1
HARDEN HARRISON H JR	COL	0-0019818	1064	1
HARDENBERGH ELMER P	B G	0-0028940	1060	2
HARDENBERGH HAL	COL	0-0032740	0766	1
HARDESTY LAWRENCE H	LTC	0-0030996	0757	2
HARDICK WILLIAM L	B G	0-0013558	0661	1
HARDIMAN RALPH	COL	0-0030492	0765	1
HARDIN CLEO F	CW4	W-0903215	1268	1
HARDIN DONALD F	COL	0-0017435	0147	2
HARDIN GAEDA B	LTC	N-0000838	0264	1
HARDIN JOHN R	M G	0-0012293	0657	1
HARDIN TOLBERT F	MAJ	0-0002406	0921	2
HARDIN WILLIAM R	COL	0-0030591	0164	1
HARDING EDWIN F	M G	0-0002628	1046	1
HARDING FLOYD C	COL	0-0007404	0851	2
HARDING HENRY J P	COL	0-0015179	0954	1
HARDING HORACE	B G	0-0009530	0653	1
HARDING STANLEY L	B G	0-0032134	0666	2
HARDMAN MABEL D	MAJ	N-0000853	0163	2
HARDMAN TRACY J	LTC	0-0033907	0165	1
HARDMAN WAYNE	COL	0-0030072	1061	1
HARDWICK ARTHUR R	CW4	W-0901707	0160	1
HARDY CLARENCE W	COL	0-0017835	1153	2

NAME	GRADE	SVC NO	DATE RET MO YR	RET CODE
HARDY CONRAD P	COL	0-0011360	1052	1
HARDY DAVID F JR	MAJ	0-0069665	1064	1
HARDY EARL L	LTC	0-0027582	0766	1
HARDY HARRY R	LTC	0-0041238	0866	1
HARE RAY M	B G	0-0006943	0753	1
HARGIS THOMAS B JR	COL	0-0023076	1048	2
HARGRAVE WARREN M	LTC	0-0032071	1058	1
HARGROVE BYRON F	LTC	0-0051202	0259	1
HARGROVE EDNA	MAJ	N-0001880	0360	1
HARGUS LOWELL U	COL	0-0030315	0265	2
HARING ELLIS E	COL	0-0008122	0548	1
HARING LAURA MS	LTC	L-0000022	0658	1
HARKINS ANNA O	MAJ	N-0001416	1264	2
HARKINS BASIL A	COL	0-0051015	0359	1
HARKINS DONALD E	LTC	0-0065217	0767	1
HARKINS PAUL D	GEN	0-0017625	0864	1
HARKLEROAD DANA L	LTC	0-0051598	0463	1
HARKNESS LAWRENCE R	LTC	0-0040066	0563	1
HARLAN EDWIN F	LTC	0-0025343	0867	1
HARLAN JAMES M	LTC	0-0069667	0868	1
HARLAN JOHN F	COL	0-0050949	0557	1
HARLAN ROBERT D	LTC	0-0035861	0861	1
HARLLEE FRANCES E	LTC	L-0000532	0866	1
HARLLEE ROBERT L	LTC	0-0044146	0166	1
HARLOE BARTLEY M	COL	0-0008561	1049	1
HARLOW MARGARET H	MAJ	L-0000309	0462	1
HARMAN THELMA A	LTC	R-0010092	1167	1
HARMELING HENRY	COL	0-0007875	0846	2
HARMELING HENRY JR	LTC	0-0024843	0962	1
HARMELING JOHN T	LTC	0-0027579	0968	2
HARMON CLYDE G	CW4	W-0902409	0655	1
HARMON ERNEST N	M G	0-0005282	0248	1
HARMON WILLIAM J	CW4	W-0904122	1058	1
HARMONSON LOUIS H	CW2	W-0901911	1146	1
HARMONY JOHN W	M G	0-0015240	1059	2
HARNAR ALLEN H	COL	0-0042470	0265	1
HARNED BEN G	CW3	W-0903216	0556	1
HARNESS LESLIE J	COL	0-0023415	1166	2
HARNETT HELEN	MAJ	N-0002151	0362	1
HARNETT JOHN S	COL	0-0023094	1160	1
HARNEY CHARLES J JR	CPT	0-0049704	1147	2
HARNSTROM EDMUND V	LTC	0-0032414	0165	1
HARDUFF DONALD L	MAJ	0-0065165	0765	1
HARP CLIFFORD E	MAJ	0-0063800	0664	2
HARPER ADAM W	LTC	0-0060399	0266	1
HARPER ARTHUR MCK	M G	0-0005288	1053	2
HARPER JAMES C	LTC	0-0063379	0866	1
HARPER JAMES E	COL	0-0042404	0564	1
HARPER JOSEPH H	M G	0-0015083	1159	1
HARPER MARGARET	COL	N-0000147	1163	1
HARPER NEAL A	B G	0-0004025	0852	2
HARPER NEAL W	COL	0-0030267	0860	1
HARPER PHILIP V JR	1LT	0F-0104774	1367	2
HARPOLD HARLEY O	COL	0-0041831	0459	2
HARPOLE HUGH S	COL	0-0012528	0347	1
HARPOLE RUSSELL C	COL	0-0029023	1058	1
HARPS JOSEPH F	COL	0-0053692	0868	1
HARR EMMA T	MAJ	M-0010004	0658	2
HARRE ELMER C	LTC	0-0051977	0352	2
HARRELL CLYDE V	CW4	W-0902140	0455	1
HARRELL HENRY C	COL	0-0022307	0768	2
HARRELL JAMES L	LTC	0-0085178	0867	1
HARRELL JOE	COL	0-0018929	0256	1
HARRELSON ELMER H	COL	0-0042350	0464	1
HARRELSON JOSEPH S	COL	0-0062119	0667	1
HARRIGAN THOMAS L	LTC	0-0043538	0964	1
HARRINGTON EDWIN J	COL	0-0041587	0457	1
HARRINGTON JAMES B	LTC	0-0027455	0865	1
HARRINGTON JAMES L	LTC	0-0065221	0867	1
HARRINGTON JAMES R	LTC	0-0066158	1168	1
HARRINGTON JOHN H	COL	0-0006359	0753	1
HARRINGTON PATRICK W	COL	0-0033372	1167	1
HARRINGTON ROBERT H	LTC	0-0056543	0566	1
HARRINGTON TRACY B	COL	0-0021137	0868	1
HARRIOTT DONALD B	B G	0-0029631	0958	2

NAME	GRADE	SVC NO	DATE RET MO YR	RET CODE
HARRIS AARON E	COL	0-0019712	0656	1
HARRIS ALAN W	CW4	W-0903219	0462	2
HARRIS BENJAMIN T	B G	0-0019166	0863	1
HARRIS CECIL F	CW3	W-0904220	1060	1
HARRIS CHARLES F	COL	0-0046675	0463	1
HARRIS CHARLES W	LTC	0-0024848	0767	1
HARRIS CHARLES S	B G	0-0007244	0753	1
HARRIS EDWARD F	CW4	W-0903221	0157	1
HARRIS EDWARD M	COL	0-0017819	0961	1
HARRIS FRANKIE D	MAJ	N-0000579	1161	1
HARRIS FREDERICK	B G	0-0012750	0854	1
HARRIS HARRY P	LTC	0-0062165	0766	1
HARRIS HERBERT H	COL	0-0011817	0854	1
HARRIS HERBERT K	LTC	0-0040600	0262	1
HARRIS HUGH P	GEN	0-0018518	0365	1
HARRIS JACK P	COL	0-0044544	0963	1
HARRIS JESSE	COL	0-0011920	0249	1
HARRIS JOHN F	COL	0-0058751	0865	1
HARRIS JOHN P	COL	0-0009115	0852	1
HARRIS JOSEPH	COL	0-0012703	0451	1
HARRIS JUNE C	MAJ	N-0001182	1265	1
HARRIS KATHLEEN B	LTC	L-0000145	0263	1
HARRIS LEE V	COL	0-0010823	0854	1
HARRIS LEON W	COL	0-0080840	0866	1
HARRIS LEONARD H	MAJ	0-0063127	0467	1
HARRIS LILLIAN	LTC	L-0000096	0968	1
HARRIS MARGOT L	MAJ	L-0000243	0962	1
HARRIS MURRAY D	COL	0-0029048	1058	1
HARRIS PAUL A	COL	0-0014624	1153	2
HARRIS PETER J	COL	0-0080842	0968	1
HARRIS RICHARD E	LTC	0-0059979	0268	1
HARRIS RICHARD W	LTC	0-0062866	0768	1
HARRIS ROBERT C	COL	0-0030529	1165	1
HARRIS RONALD V	MAJ	0-0069670	0166	1
HARRIS RUSSEL D	COL	0-0039671	0460	1
HARRIS WILLIAM A	M G	0-0018976	1166	2
HARRIS WILLIAM H	B G	0-0018155	0565	1
HARRIS WILLIAM N	COL	0-0040659	0868	1
HARRIS WILLIAM W	B G	0-0018170	0460	1
HARRISON CHARLES E	LTC	0-0022953	0862	1
HARRISON DENNIS J	LTC	0-0058921	0667	1
HARRISON EDWIN H	COL	0-0015573	0854	1
HARRISON EUGENE L	B G	0-0015265	1053	1
HARRISON FRANCIS B	COL	0-0021147	0866	1
HARRISON FRANK R	COL	0-0020858	0662	1
HARRISON GEORGE P	CPT	0-0016353	1041	1
HARRISON HAROLD E	COL	0-0020078	0764	2
HARRISON JAMES H	COL	0-0046389	0868	1
HARRISON JAMES J	LTC	0-0080844	0867	1
HARRISON JOHN H	LTC	0-0040121	1161	1
HARRISON JOSEPH H	COL	0-0031396	0865	1
HARRISON MATTHEW C	COL	0-0023475	0764	1
HARRISON REGINALD W	CW4	W-0903223	0557	1
HARRISON RICHARD H	B G	0-0018409	0661	1
HARRISON ROGER R	COL	0-0003733	0446	1
HARRISON W K JR	LTG	0-0005279	0257	1
HARRISON WILLARD E	COL	0-0031892	0568	1
HARRISON WILLIAM C	LTC	0-0020091	0546	2
HARRISON WILLIAM E	COL	0-0029991	0963	1
HARROLD ARTHUR K	COL	0-0032417	0768	1
HARROLD THOMAS L	LTG	0-0016051	0661	1
HARROW JAMES A	LTC	0-0041619	0857	1
HARRUP JOHN W	LTC	0-0038136	1065	2
HARRY JOHN	COL	0-0014750	0753	1
HARSTAD LEROY D	MAJ	0-0060453	0663	1
HART ALADIN J	COL	0-0012758	0650	1
HART BERNARD A	LTC	0-0038544	0268	1
HART CATHERINE	MAJ	L-0000065	1059	1
HART CHARLES E	LTG	0-0015788	0760	1
HART HARRY L	LTC	0-0030241	0862	1
HART IRA W	LTC	0-0024808	1060	1
HART JOHN J	LTC	0-0051618	0463	1
HART JOHN L	MAJ	0-0062261	0167	1
HART JOHN M	COL	0-0034665	0867	1
HART JOHN S	CW4	W-0902363	0557	1

NAME	GRADE	SVC NO	DATE RET MO YR	RET CODE
HART RICHARD V	COL	0-0038732	1262	1
HART ROSEMARY	MAJ	L-0000311	0962	1
HART WALTER	CPT	0-0005828	0132	1
HARTEL FREDERICK	B G	0-0019254	1066	2
HARTFORD ELLIS W	CPT	0-0008112	1122	2
HARTFORD THOMAS J	M G	0-0018330	0961	1
HARTGERING JAMES B	COL	0-0049931	0664	1
HARTH JOHN F	LTC	0-0036997	0764	1
HARTLEY GLENN F	LTC	0-0084367	1067	1
HARTLEY LEROY P	COL	0-0005958	1151	2
HARTLEY MARY E	LTC	N-0001375	0467	1
HARTLINE FRANKLIN H	COL	0-0021301	0868	1
HARTMAN ALLISON R	COL	0-0017204	1053	2
HARTMAN CARL W	LTC	0-0062171	0166	1
HARTMAN DURELL B	LTC	0-0039466	0666	1
HARTMAN FRANK E	COL	0-0021346	1068	2
HARTMAN HENRY M	COL	0-0044177	0766	1
HARTMAN JACOB L	B G	0-0009551	0654	1
HARTMAN LINTON Y	LTC	0-0010008	1041	1
HARTMAN LULU J	MAJ	N-0001724	0964	1
HARTMAN NORMAN E	COL	0-0010269	0753	1
HARTMAN ROLAND F	COL	0-0041872	0561	1
HARTNESS HARLAN N	M G	0-0012269	1054	1
HARTON THOMAS G	COL	0-0042385	0364	1
HARTRIDGE THEODORE L	LTC	0-0022763	0959	1
HARTSHORN EDWIN S JR	B G	0-0018716	0862	1
HARTSOCK RAYMOND J	CW3	W-0906776	0163	1
HARTUNG HERBERT W	LTC	0-0044261	1066	1
HARVEY CLARENCE C JR	B G	0-0021076	0868	1
HARVEY CLYDE F	CW3	RW-0903226	0463	1
HARVEY DWIGHT	LTC	0-0016220	0753	1
HARVEY JAMES D	LTC	0-0069503	0968	1
HARVEY JAMES V	MAJ	0-0068012	0866	2
HARVEY JOHN B	LTC	0-0047778	0760	2
HARVEY JOHN J	LTC	0-0006241	0741	1
HARVEY MAXINE F	MAJ	N-0001425	0463	1
HARVEY MURRAY L	LTC	0-0038833	0661	1
HARVEY OLIVER C	M G	0-0038776	0866	1
HARVEY RAYMOND J	B G	0-0020116	0866	1
HARVEY ROBERT C	CPT	0-0023492	0743	2
HARVEY THOMAS H	COL	0-0018817	0862	1
HARVEY WILLIAM T	COL	0-0080846	0967	1
HARVIE CHESTER T	LTC	0-0025138	0962	1
HARWELL MACLOLM H	COL	0-0016460	0756	1
HARWOOD EDWARD C	COL	0-0012615	0137	1
HASBROUCK ROBERT W	M G	0-0008588	0947	2
HASBROUCK SHERMAN V	B G	0-0012744	0855	1
HASELMIRE NORA C	MAJ	N-0000643	0463	1
HASEMAN LEONARD L	COL	0-0022925	0366	2
HASH WILLIAM A	LTC	0-0036625	0566	1
HASKELL HAROLD G	COL	0-0030588	0862	2
HASKELL JAMES B	COL	0-0003708	0846	1
HASKELL JOSEPH F	COL	0-0018197	1146	1
HASKELL MORRIS B	LTC	0-0084317	0568	1
HASKELL ROBERT K	COL	0-0015097	0454	1
HASLAM JAMES T	MAJ	0-0033079	0162	1
HASLEY CLARENCE E	CW3	W-0907144	0264	1
HASS MARTIN F	B G	0-0015889	0754	1
HASSELBACK FREDERICK	COL	0-0022673	0865	1
HASSENFELT HAROLD E	COL	0-0022195	0760	1
HASSLOCK LOUIS W	COL	0-0005017	0348	1
HASSMAN PHILLIP E	LTC	0-0059972	0866	1
HASSON JOHN P	COL	0-0001190	0442	1
HASTING HOWARD H	COL	0-0035676	0460	1
HASTINGS ALBERT J	COL	0-0011721	1046	1
HASTINGS FREDERICK	COL	0-0031313	1168	1
HASTINGS HENRY S	LTC	0-0032830	0561	1
HASTINGS KESTER L	M G	0-0012219	0357	1
HASTINGS WILLIAM O	COL	0-0031248	0867	1
HASTINGS WILLIAM P	LTC	0-0050054	1066	1
HASWELL CLAUDE E	COL	0-0012731	0137	1
HATCH CARL H	COL	0-0029341	0764	1
HATCH FRANK E	CW4	W-0903227	0557	1
HATCH HOWARD G	CW4	W-0903228	0760	1
HATCH JAMES R	LTC	0-0061156	0868	1

UNITED STATES ARMY RETIRED LIST

NAME	GRADE	SVC NO	DATE RET MO YR	RET CODE
HATCH JOHN E	COL	0-0003073	0946	1
HATCH MCGLACHLIN	COL	0-0025578	0966	1
HATCH MELTON A	COL	0-0012136	0854	1
HATCH MERRILL G	COL	0-0033918	0268	1
HATFIELD GLENORA M	CPT	M-0000441	0348	2
HATFIELD MILLS C	COL	0-0023741	0864	2
HATFIELD RALPH H	COL	0-0039755	0362	2
HATHAWAY GAYNOR W	LTC	0-0025124	0262	1
HATHAWAY JAMES L	COL	0-0017215	0758	1
HATHAWAY LEANDER R	COL	0-0004752	0151	1
HATHAWAY PAUL	MAJ	0-0004567	0934	2
HATHAWAY WORTEN M	MAJ	0-0065652	1168	1
HATTAN ROY E	COL	0-0017563	0859	1
HATTER HARLOS V	COL	0-0032901	0868	1
HATTOX JAMES G	COL	0-0030253	1263	1
HAUCK CLARENCE J JR	M G	0-0018360	0160	1
HAUGHEY JOHN E	COL	0-0029142	0558	1
HAUSCHULTZ EARL H	COL	0-0042789	0566	2
HAUSE MABEL E	MAJ	N-0000045	1050	1
HAUSEMAN DAVID N	B G	0-0010511	0946	1
HAUSER JOHN R	LTC	0-0037946	0866	1
HAUSER ROBERT L	CW4	W-0906778	0163	2
HAUSMAN WILLIAM	COL	0-0058273	1066	1
HAVEN SAMUEL R	COL	0-0017970	0360	1
HAVEY SYLVESTER	CW2	W-0901211	0945	2
HAWES BENJAMIN W	COL	0-0019929	0347	2
HAWES GLENN A	COL	0-0042077	0861	1
HAWES HAROLD V	LTC	0-0052711	0166	1
HAWHEE GUY E	CW4	W-0903230	0258	1
HAWK EDWIN L	LTC	0-0080848	0468	1
HAWKINS ARTHUR C	CPT	0-0007171	0822	2
HAWKINS ARTHUR D	CPT	0-0015495	0132	2
HAWKINS BOYCE V	COL	0-0040233	0568	1
HAWKINS JAMES J JR	LTC	0-0045759	0763	1
HAWKINS JEAN M	MAJ	R-0010093	0963	1
HAWKINS JONATHAN D	COL	0-0016629	1154	1
HAWKINS RUSSELL L	COL	0-0019960	0865	1
HAWKINS SAMUEL F	COL	0-0003221	0142	1
HAWKINS WILSON M	M G	0-0022737	0868	1
HAWKINSON CARROLL G	LTC	0-0022318	C859	1
HAWKSWORTH F W	LTC	0-0043619	1160	2
HAWLEY HARVEY D	LTC	0-0050402	0964	1
HAWLEY ROBERT C	CPT	0-0028254	0658	2
HAWORTH VIOLET	MAJ	N-0002430	0965	1
HAWTHORNE WILLIAM B	COL	0-0016512	0756	1
HAXTHAUSEN HALLFENE	MAJ	M-0010110	0562	1
HAYCOCK CHESTER P	COL	0-0007877	1146	2
HAYCOCK WILLIAM M	COL	0-0031712	1166	1
HAYCRAFT KENNETH C	COL	0-0029704	0861	1
HAYDEL JUANITA E	MAJ	N-0001900	0761	1
HAYDEN EVERETT C	LTC	0-0017744	0749	1
HAYDEN FREDERIC L	B G	0-0012627	0955	2
HAYDEN HERBERT B	LTC	0-0013936	0620	2
HAYDEN JAMES L	COL	0-0005254	0740	2
HAYDEN JAKES M	LTC	0-0060327	0866	1
HAYDEN RAY R	MAJ	0-0065131	0164	1
HAYDEN ROBERT F	CW4	W-0903233	1263	1
HAYDEN ROBERT H	COL	0-0042356	1262	1
HAYDON PERCY S	COL	0-0006767	0948	1
HAYENGA VIRGINIA P	MAJ	N-0001976	0462	1
HAYES DAVID W	COL	0-0021214	0868	1
HAYES EDWARD S	LTC	0-0014232	0220	2
HAYES JAMES H	COL	0-0024646	0765	1
HAYES JAMES L	CW4	W-0903234	0857	1
HAYES JOHN D	LTC	0-0067694	0868	1
HAYES JOHN J	1LT	0-0059331	1053	2
HAYES JOHNNIE M	CW4	W-0903235	1158	1
HAYES KATHERINE	LTC	N-0000688	0462	1
HAYES LEO V	LTC	0-0026213	0965	1
HAYES LINCOLN R	LTC	0-0080851	0566	1
HAYES PAUL	COL	0-0017809	0559	1
HAYES PAUL W	COL	0-0030903	0361	1
HAYES ROBERT L	LTC	0-0041016	0263	1
HAYES SALLY C	LTC	N-0001231	0767	1
HAYES TAYLOR C T	LTC	0-0043542	0364	1

NAME	GRADE	SVC NO	DATE RET MO YR	RET CODE
HAYES THOMAS F	COL	0-0034738	0867	1
HAYES WAYNE A	COL	0-0020486	0167	1
HAYES WILLIAM P	COL	0-0011655	0753	1
HAYFORD BERTRAM F	M G	0-0012272	1155	1
HAYFORD 3RD WARREN	COL	0-0010347	0854	1
HAYMAN GEORGE R	COL	0-0007225	0851	2
HAYMAN GEORGE R JR	LTC	0-0026576	0865	1
HAYNE FRANK B	COL	0-0006446	1147	2
HAYNE PAUL JR	LTC	0-0039619	0657	1
HAYNES ALLEN F	COL	0-0012600	0954	1
HAYNES ASHTON M	COL	0-0018545	0761	1
HAYNES CHARLEY W	LTC	0-0043719	0764	1
HAYNES CHESTER H	LTC	0-0080854	0767	1
HAYNES EDITH S	LTC	N-0000090	0157	1
HAYNES HAROLD M	MAJ	0-0011556	0934	2
HAYNES INEZ	COL	N-0000088	0859	1
HAYNES JAMES R	1LT	0-0014360	0518	2
HAYNES LOYAL M	B G	0-0008379	0754	2
HAYNES RETURN C	MAJ	0-0063102	0964	1
HAYNES THOMAS E	COL	0-0076883	0766	1
HAYS GEORGE P	LTG	0-0007149	0453	1
HAYS MARSHALL C	LTC	0-0078872	0768	1
HAYWARD CECELIA L	MAJ	N-0001062	0662	1
HAYWARD HAROLD S	LTC	0-0051213	0459	2
HAYWORTH HELEN G	MAJ	N-0002128	0360	1
HAZEL CHARLES E	LTC	0-0039260	0363	1
HAZLEHURST MAX W	COL	0-0038723	0862	1
HAZLETT HOWARD	COL	0-0038621	1058	1
HAZLETT ROBERT T	COL	0-0039792	0461	1
HEA JAMES J	COL	0-0008661	0753	1
HEAD HAROLD S	LTC	0-0026272	0766	1
HEAD NELSON L	COL	0-0018814	0158	1
HEALD ROBERT C	COL	0-0044454	0868	2
HEALEY MICHAEL V	1LT	0-0015041	0927	2
HEALTON CURTIS E	LTC	0-0032275	0764	1
HEALY DANIEL F JR	COL	0-0015742	0954	2
HEALY JOHN H	MAJ	0-0010129	0235	2
HEALY JOHN J	LTC	0-0039707	0259	1
HEALY PATRICK J	LTC	0-0030657	0364	1
HEALY ROMEYN J JR	COL	0-0020918	0357	1
HEANEY GEORGE F JR	COL	0-0015181	0753	1
HEARD JACK W	M G	0-0002867	0946	2
HEARD OLGA S	MAJ	R-0010095	0562	1
HEARD R TOWNSEND	B G	0-0004639	1146	2
HEARD WILLIAM C	LTC	0-0069672	0767	1
HEARD WILLIAM R	COL	0-0039811	0263	1
HEARING VINCENT J	LTC	0-0050126	0466	1
HEARN ROBERT J	COL	0-0051131	0557	1
HEARN THOMAS G	M G	0-0003859	0846	2
HEARNES WARREN E	1LT	0-0028379	1049	2
HEARON VIRGIL B	CW4	W-0903236	0357	2
HEASTY CHARLES F JR	COL	0-0022665	0166	1
HEATH ALBERT	CW4	W-0906780	0760	1
HEATH BERNICE I	MAJ	N-0001385	1164	1
HEATH CALVIN A	COL	0-0024431	0660	1
HEATH LOUIS T	M G	0-0018060	0862	1
HEATH RALPH M	LTC	0-0066013	1266	1
HEATHCOTE EARL W	B G	0-0028800	0355	1
HEAVEY WILLIAM F	B G	0-0005223	0148	1
HEBERT KENNETH	CW2	W-0900978	0744	1
HECK DONALD	LTC	0-0024157	0561	1
HECK GEORGE	COL	0-0051469	1163	1
HECKEMEYER BENJAMIN	COL	0-0019930	0165	1
HECKMAN BILL A	COL	0-0080102	0368	2
HECTOR JOHN R	COL	0-0030717	0666	1
HEDDEN WILLIS A	COL	0-0006534	0345	2
HEDGES LOVEAIRE A	COL	0-0029786	1062	1
HEEP MATTHEW S JR	MAJ	0-0056981	0762	1
HEFFELFINGER HUGO W	COL	0-0046143	0966	1
HEFFERNON GEORGE A	COL	0-0029273	1159	1
HEFFNER PETE T JR	COL	0-0010319	0753	1
HEFLEBOWER ROY C	B G	0-0002770	0846	2
HEH GERARD F	CW4	W-0903238	0762	1
HEIBERG HARRISON H	COL	0-0012306	0854	1
HEIDE MARGITH H	MAJ	N-0001293	0667	1

NAME	GRADE	SVC NO	DATE RET MO YR	RET CODE
HEIDENREICH ELLSWORT	MAJ	0-0060214	0865	1
HEIDLAND ERNEST F	COL	0-0017688	0655	1
HEIDNER ALVIN A	COL	0-0041635	1159	1
HEIDT GEORGE F JR	LTC	0-0041076	0465	1
HEIL GEORGE J	LTC	0-0039109	0262	1
HEIL JOHN H JR	COL	0-0029400	0360	1
HEILFRON MILTON	COL	0-0007506	0753	1
HEIMSTEAD MERTEN K	COL	0-0020880	0266	1
HEIN FREDERICK	COL	0-0014956	0753	1
HEIN NEIL F	COL	0-0051467	0563	1
HEINE WALTER F	LTC	0-0017355	0943	2
HEINEL WALTER C	COL	0-0050947	0958	2
HEINKE SELMA F	MAJ	L-0000558	0968	1
HEINLEIN REX I JR	COL	0-0016991	1033	2
HEINRICH CHARLES T	COL	0-0029014	1167	1
HEINRICH HELEN M	MAJ	N-0000203	0661	1
HEINZ HELEN D	MAJ	N-0002065	0662	1
HEINZEL CHESTER H	CW4	W-0903239	0765	1
HEISER BENJAMIN P	B G	G-0016450	0756	1
HEISS CLARENCE L	MAJ	0-0066992	0866	1
HEISS GERSON K	B G	0-0015092	0954	2
HEISS GERSON K JR	LTC	0-0026613	0868	1
HEISS GUSTAVE M	COL	0-0018594	1146	2
HEISS JONAS S	COL	0-0051262	1061	1
HEITMAN CHARLES E JR	COL	0-0018059	0760	1
HEIWINKEL HANS W	LTC	0-0084740	0568	1
HEJNA JOHN J	LTC	0-0045033	0167	1
HELBER GEORGE Z	LTC	0-0045094	0861	1
HELD BURT	LTC	0-0019605	0245	2
HELDERMAN CHARLES F	COL	0-0031716	0168	1
HELFERS MELVIN C	LTC	0-0021359	C546	2
HELFERT PETER A	LTC	0-0032385	0962	1
HELFRICH JESSE B	LTC	0-0017792	0144	2
HELGESTAD JAMES E	COL	0-0040003	0764	1
HELIKER SHERBURNE	COL	0-0029928	0562	1
HELLER THEODORE P	LTC	0-0052389	0664	1
HELLIER EDWARD G	COL	0-0041892	0761	1
HELM MARGARET C	MAJ	N-0002401	0762	1
HELMAN HARLAN K	COL	0-0021211	0266	1
HELMICK CHARLES G	M G	0-0003606	0752	1
HELMICK GEORGE R	2LT	0-0016303	0229	2
HELMICK GLENN B	MAJ	0-0059856	1162	1
HELMS KENNETH R	LTC	0-0037023	0465	2
HELMUTH OLIVER J	COL	0-0032395	0765	2
HELSEL WILFORD P	LTC	0-0037391	0868	1
HELSLEY LLEWELLYN	LTC	0-0036900	1166	1
HELTON BURRELL W	LTC	0-0021808	0845	2
HELTON JOHN W	LTC	0-0023337	C354	2
HELTZEL WILLIAM E	COL	0-0029891	0463	1
HEMBREE TOM B	COL	0-0029789	1062	1
HEMION ROGER H	COL	0-0040075	0964	1
HEMLER DAVID W	CW2	W-0800355	1045	1
HEMMINGS HAVEN H	LTC	0-0065168	0468	1
HEMPEL JOHN H	COL	0-0042457	1160	1
HEMPERLY CECIL W	LTC	0-0080301	0865	1
HEMPLING LEONARD J	COL	0-0059784	0767	1
HENCHEY FRANCES C	LTC	N-0000023	0451	1
HENDERLY HAROLD B	LTC	0-0036065	1163	1
HENDERSON ALFRED D	COL	0-0041647	0160	1
HENDERSON BASIL W	COL	0-0046671	0966	1
HENDERSON BENEDICT A	COL	0-0039653	0463	1
HENDERSON BLAIR E	COL	0-0039813	0263	1
HENDERSON CARROLL B	COL	0-0029421	0660	1
HENDERSON CLYDE W	COL	0-0031324	0868	1
HENDERSON DONALD H	LTC	0-0027293	0866	1
HENDERSON FRED R	COL	0-0041540	1058	2
HENDERSON GLENN H	LTC	0-0069674	0867	1
HENDERSON HARRY M JR	LTC	0-0057409	1065	1
HENDERSON HARRY MC C	COL	0-0005168	0545	2
HENDERSON IVAN W	CW4	W-0906783	0959	2
HENDERSON JAMES A	CW4	W-0904314	0966	1
HENDERSON JAMES E	COL	0-0021327	1267	1
HENDERSON JOHN M JR	B G	0-0029410	0560	1
HENDERSON JOHN T	LTC	0-0069675	0968	1
HENDERSON PHILIP J	LTC	0-0016584	1043	2

NAME	GRADE	SVC NO	DATE RET MO YR	RET CODE
HENDERSON THOMAS J	COL	0-0042203	0963	1
HENDERSON WILBURN H	MAJ	0-0004423	1022	2
HENDERSON WILLIAM G	LTC	0-0037707	0961	1
HENDERSON WILLIAM H	COL	0-0045534	0168	1
HENDERSON WILLIAM W	LTC	0-0049834	0965	1
HENDLEY ROBERT C	LTC	0-0014869	1144	2
HENDRICKS CLARENCE P	LTC	0-0042302	0362	2
HENDRICKS LELIA M	LTC	M-0000605	0163	1
HENDRICKSON EDWARD H	COL	0-0023048	0968	2
HENDRICKSON HARVEY F	COL	0-0017339	0446	2
HENDRICKSON SYLVIA E	MAJ	N-0002202	1267	1
HENDRICKSON W H	LTC	0-0020345	0246	2
HENDRIX MARGUERITE	MAJ	N-0000550	G756	2
HENDRIX RALEIGH R	M G	0-0015897	0961	1
HENDRIX THOMAS L	LTC	0-0058206	0665	1
HENDRY CHARLES R	CW4	W-0904126	0762	1
HENDRY EARL	CPT	0-0009804	0231	1
HENINGER GRANT	COL	0-0011350	0246	1
HENION KARL E	COL	0-0007236	0854	1
HENLEY CHARLES M	COL	0-0020897	0746	2
HENLEY JACK J	LTC	0-0033959	0863	1
HENLINE CLAIR G	LTC	0-0045087	0262	1
HENN EDWIN A	COL	0-0005847	1051	2
HENNE CHARLES A	COL	0-0046253	0767	1
HENNEBERGER JOSIAH B	LTC	0-0004092	1042	2
HENNESSEE JOE D	LTC	0-0024897	0663	1
HENNESSEY JAMES T	COL	0-0032274	0565	1
HENNESSY HAROLD P	COL	0-0010292	0754	1
HENNESSY JAMES T	COL	0-0023148	0264	1
HENNESSY RICHARD L	COL	0-0024690	0764	1
HENNIES ELMA E	LTC	N-0000401	1065	1
HENNIG WILLIAM H	M G	0-0017122	0764	2
HENNING FRANK A JR	B G	0-0012648	0754	1
HENRY ALBERT C	LTC	0-0034497	0563	1
HENRY CHARLES H	COL	0-0007193	0844	2
HENRY CHARLES O	LTC	0-0080860	1066	1
HENRY FRANK B	COL	0-0022749	0268	2
HENRY FRANK S	B G	0-0018989	0863	2
HENRY HAROLD P	COL	0-0012589	0653	1
HENRY ISABELLA M	MAJ	L-0000302	1060	1
HENRY JAMES E	LTC	0-0088732	0965	1
HENRY LEE S JR	LTC	0-0063337	1167	1
HENRY LYLE K	COL	0-0041605	0859	1
HENRY STEPHEN G	M G	0-0005164	1046	2
HENRY STEPHEN G JR	CPT	0-0028446	0152	2
HENRY THOMAS	LTC	0-0005082	0641	1
HENRY WALTER E	WO1	W-0902152	1046	2
HENRY WILLIAM H JR	LTC	0-0063109	1267	1
HENRY WILLIAM J	COL	0-0007830	0145	2
HENRY WILLIAM J	COL	0-0021928	0767	2
HENSEL MAX G	MAJ	0-0024238	0846	2
HENSEL RAYMOND G	LTC	0-0066016	0667	1
HENSEL WILLIAM E	COL	0-0025531	0164	1
HENSEY WALTER R JR	COL	0-0014950	0854	2
HENSHAW JAMES L	LTC	0-0027357	0866	1
HENSLEY EMERY M	LTC	0-0035720	0266	1
HENSON IRA C	MAJ	0-0036423	0761	1
HENSON JACK B	CW4	W-0903245	0868	1
HENSON VIRGIL A JR	LTC	0-0087785	0668	1
HENTGES ELSIE M	MAJ	N-0000390	0662	1
HEPNER JOHN F	COL	0-0006638	1046	2
HERALD FRANCIS R	CPT	0-0019957	1042	2
HERB EDWARD G	COL	0-0018973	0655	1
HERBER DAVID	COL	0-0032689	1067	1
HERBERT BUEFORD G	LTC	0-0064986	0468	1
HERBERT FRANK JR	CPT	0-0064993	1162	1
HERBERT GEORGE F	COL	0-0010253	0753	1
HERBERT JAMES K	B G	0-0018027	0746	1
HERBERT WILLIAM D	COL	0-0003514	0440	2
HERBERTH FRANK W JR	COL	0-0029829	1262	1
HERCZ ARTHUR R	COL	0-0018566	0757	1
HERENDEEN EDWARD	COL	0-0014623	0351	1
HERGERT IONE E	MAJ	N-0002363	0360	1
HERMAN CHARLES G	COL	0-0018885	1058	2
HERMAN DEAN A	COL	0-0018563	0761	1

332-811 O - 69 - 3

NAME	GRADE	SVC NO	DATE RET MO YR	RET CODE
HERMAN FREDERICK	COL	0-0003671	0846	1
HERMAN JOHN B	COL	0-0019301	0562	2
HERMANN JOHN R	COL	0-0004876	1144	2
HERMES ELMER R	LTC	0-0069680	0867	1
HERNDON LOWE H	COL	0-0051223	0259	2
HERNDON ROBERT B	LTC	0-0051984	0366	1
HERNDON WILLIAM H	COL	0-0036636	0268	1
HERON GORDON J F	COL	0-0004728	0751	1
HERPEL FREDERICK	LTC	0-0004153	1022	2
HERR FREDERICK	COL	0-0003735	0448	1
HERREN THOMAS W	LTG	0-0007430	0757	1
HERRES HARRY L	LTC	0-0041049	0764	1
HERRICK CURTIS J	M G	0-0018538	0667	2
HERRICK HUGH N	B G	0-0007370	0144	2
HERRICK PARK B	LTC	0-0012775	1045	2
HERRIN HERBERT T	CPT	0-0062810	1158	2
HERRING WILTON A JR	LTC	0-0066017	0968	1
HERRINGTON RUSSELL M	COL	0-0005436	1147	1
HERRMANN CHARLES R	COL	0-0039779	0661	1
HERRMANN WALTER J	CW3	W-0903248	1264	1
HERROD JOHN T	COL	0-0029577	0660	1
HERRON CHARLES D	M G	0-0000777	1046	1
HERRON DONALD B	COL	0-0012696	0851	1
HERRON THOMAS M R	MAJ	0-0002293	0722	2
HERSHEY CHARLES G JR	LTC	0-0037364	1165	1
HERSHEY JACOB R	LTC	0-0030286	0762	1
HERSHEY LEWIS B	LTG	0-0006530	1046	2
HERSHEY LYLE E	COL	0-0052502	0666	1
HERSPERGER WEBB S	MAJ	0-0088099	0865	2
HERT PAUL	COL	0-0039952	0365	1
HERTE ROY J	COL	0-0016516	0756	1
HERTFORD KENNER F	M G	0-0015120	0755	1
HERVEY RAY E	CW4	W-0906788	0463	1
HERVEY STEWART D	COL	0-0007263	0547	2
HERWIG LEOPOLD J	CPT	0-0014209	1019	2
HERZER ARNO P	COL	0-0081905	1066	1
HERZIG JOHN A	LTC	0-0082022	0968	1
HESKETH WILLIAM	B G	0-0007516	0648	1
HESKETT MARCUS W	COL	0-0042218	0763	1
HESS ALFRED W	LTC	0-0020303	0946	2
HESS BUIE	COL	0-0042379	0961	2
HESS GLENN C	LTC	0-0051753	0862	1
HESS GUSTIN A	LTC	0-0040180	0762	1
HESS MILTON C	CW4	W-0903250	0864	1
HESS OLIVER A	COL	0-0004764	0452	1
HESS WALTER W JR	B G	0-0003850	0352	1
HESSELBACHER GEORGE	COL	0-0024651	1266	1
HESSIN ARTHUR L	LTC	0-0041757	1061	1
HESTER HENRY R	LTC	0-0019419	1155	1
HESTER HUGH B	B G	0-0008405	0851	1
HESTER JOHN H	M G	0-0002382	0246	2
HESTER SUE I	MAJ	N-0000442	1065	1
HESTON JOHN T	LTC	0-0052371	0665	1
HEUBERGER NEWTON J	COL	0-0035476	0566	1
HEUER HERMAN H	COL	0-0030895	0466	1
HEUSTON HAROLD W	LTC	0-0078878	0468	1
HEVENER JAMES W	MAJ	0-0037121	0459	1
HEWETT ROBERT F JR	LTC	0-0028528	0866	1
HEWETTE JAMES B	LTC	0-0044430	0761	1
HEWGLEY CLARENCE T	LTC	0-0063550	0868	1
HEWITT CLARENCE B	COL	0-0049926	0764	1
HEWITT HARRY	COL	0-0030558	0464	2
HEWITT HENRY H	LTC	0-0032827	0768	1
HEWITT MERRITT L	LTC	0-0023934	0561	1
HEWITT ROBERT A	M G	0-0018713	0867	1
HEWITT WILBUR J	MAJ	0-0063123	1266	1
HEWLETT THOMAS H	COL	0-0057932	0964	1
HEYDUCK LAWRENCE E	COL	0-0011983	1149	1
HEYER HERBERT B	COL	0-0040042	0764	1
HEYMONT IRVING	COL	0-0025040	0864	1
HEYNE DANIEL H	COL	0-0019493	0864	1
HEYWOOD FRANK A	COL	0-0005201	0553	1
HIATT ROBERT S	LTC	0-0068114	1168	1
HIATT WRIGHT	COL	0-0020139	0657	1
HIBBERD CLEMMIE L	CPT	N-0000050	0748	1
HIBBS LOUIS E	M G	0-0004426	0147	2
HIBLER CLYDE J	1LT	0-0019247	0639	2
HICKERSON ELZIE	LTC	0-0062141	0868	1
HICKEY ALBERT N	COL	0-0017000	0457	1
HICKEY DANIEL W JR	B G	0-0007544	0654	1
HICKEY JOHN D	COL	0-0052152	0468	1
HICKEY RALPH W	CPT	0-0014269	0720	2
HICKEY TERRENCE R	COL	0-0018567	0761	1
HICKEY THOMAS F	LTG	0-0010362	0458	2
HICKISCH FRANK L	LTC	0-0039686	0858	1
HICKMAN CARROLL P	LTC	0-0042564	0463	1
HICKMAN DAVID	LTC	0-0033986	1268	1
HICKMAN EDWIN G	LTC	0-0019575	0859	1
HICKMAN GEORGE W JR	M G	0-0016420	1060	1
HICKS FRED A	COL	0-0031948	0768	1
HICKS GRADY L JR	LTC	0-0038006	1167	1
HICKS LAWRENCE S	CW4	W-0903254	0165	1
HICKS PAUL S	COL	0-0032028	1168	1
HIDDLESTON EUGENE W	COL	0-0018480	0761	2
HIEBERT SAMUEL L	LTC	0-0029321	0662	1
HIERS MAURICE D	COL	0-0033715	0868	1
HIESTER DAVID W	B G	0-0020191	0467	1
HIETA CLIFFORD W	LTC	0-0078879	0668	1
HIGDON ROBERT S	COL	0-0021459	1163	1
HIGGINS CHARLES W	COL	0-0007369	1052	1
HIGGINS ELMER R	COL	0-0038755	1162	1
HIGGINS GERALD J	M G	0-0019530	0855	1
HIGGINS GREGORY L	COL	0-0021385	0868	1
HIGGINS HAROLD D	LTC	0-0023554	0660	1
HIGGINS JAMES L	COL	0-0036306	1167	1
HIGGINS JAMES W JR	COL	0-0029542	0461	1
HIGGINS JOHN G	LTC	0-0057706	0766	1
HIGGINS JOSEPH P	LTC	0-0048665	1167	1
HIGGINS MAURICE C	COL	0-0039630	1059	1
HIGGINS ROGER E	COL	0-0039867	1263	1
HIGGINS STANTON	COL	0-0009894	0546	1
HIGGINS WALTER A	LTC	0-0025112	0962	1
HIGGINS WARREN J	LTC	0-0049460	1265	2
HIGGINS WAYNE G	COL	0-0079851	0765	1
HIGGINS WILSON B	COL	0-0012624	0948	2
HIGHTOWER DAN	LTC	0-0063222	1166	1
HIGHTOWER LOUIS V	M G	0-0018502	1063	2
HIGLEY HOWARD C	COL	0-0038821	0266	1
HIGSON HERRICK	CW4	W-0903256	0668	1
HILDEBRAND HARRY B	COL	0-0005016	0746	1
HILDEBRANT CONARD	COL	0-0029902	0363	1
HILDITCH NORMAN	CPT	0-0040617	0353	2
HILDRETH RAYMOND C	COL	0-0009154	0248	1
HILL ALTON A	COL	0-0029384	0160	1
HILL BENJAMIN I	COL	0-0024791	0767	1
HILL BERNICE M	MAJ	N-0000075	1060	1
HILL CARL R	COL	0-0042101	0861	1
HILL CHARLES W	COL	0-0019430	0960	1
HILL CLIFFORD B	LTC	0-0040055	0663	1
HILL CYRIL D	COL	0-0028792	0555	1
HILL DONALD C	COL	0-0015504	0654	1
HILL EDWARD M	LTC	0-0036185	1163	1
HILL FRANCIS	B G	0-0019058	0863	1
HILL GEORGE P JR	COL	0-0019972	0865	2
HILL GUY C	COL	0-0029272	0663	1
HILL HAROLD E	LTC	0-0041142	0364	1
HILL HARRY G	LTC	0-0034106	0760	1
HILL HELEN R	MAJ	N-0000564	0361	1
HILL IRA B	COL	0-0004860	0946	2
HILL JAMES W JR	LTC	0-0080107	0264	1
HILL JESSE N	COL	0-0030702	0866	2
HILL JOHN F	CPT	0-0006400	0934	2
HILL JOHN G	B G	0-0015797	0854	1
HILL JOSEPH A	LTC	0-0061965	1065	1
HILL JOSEPH C	LTC	0-0027838	0167	1
HILL KENNETH R	LTC	0-0031898	0365	1
HILL LEROY C	LTC	0-0031874	1165	1
HILL LEVENIA E	MAJ	N-0002062	0761	2
HILL MILTON A	B G	0-0010177	1046	2
HILL PHILIP H	LTC	0-0042805	0864	1
HILL RAY C	COL	0-0002284	0839	2
HILL RAYMOND L	COL	0-0017495	1058	1
HILL RICHARD F	COL	0-0042973	0367	1
HILL ROBERT B	B G	0-0004046	1150	1
HILL ROBERT J JR	COL	0-0021933	0566	2
HILL VERNE C	COL	0-0016297	0147	1
HILL WILLIAM	COL	0-0012642	0754	1
HILL WILLIAM B	LTC	0-0058167	0767	1
HILL WILLIAM G	LTC	0-0068116	0968	1
HILL WILLIAM V	COL	0-0020482	1166	2
HILL WILLIAM W JR	COL	0-0031348	1066	1
HILLBERG LAURI J	COL	0-0018710	1058	1
HILLDRING JOHN H	M G	0-0007420	0746	2
HILLEBRAND ALVIN R	COL	0-0030586	0166	1
HILLIARD LEE H	LTC	0-0033246	0461	1
HILLMAN BURLEIGH F	COL	0-0028907	0457	1
HILLMAN CHARLES C	B G	0-0003517	0147	1
HILLS HENRY M	LTC	0-0079852	0168	1
HILLS J HUNTINGT	COL	0-0004769	0752	2
HILLYARD HARRY L	M G	0-0019524	1167	2
HILPERT ROBERT C	MAJ	0-0023446	1046	2
HILSABECK CARTER L	LTC	0-0031389	0459	1
HILSMAN EDWARD H	COL	0-0043021	0667	1
HILSMAN ROGER	COL	0-0005012	0848	2
HILTON CORSON L JR	COL	0-0024438	1167	1
HILTON KATHLYN C	MAJ	L-0000308	0462	1
HILTON WILBUR S	COL	0-0032643	1068	1
HIMES CECIL	COL	0-0020731	0967	1
HIMES DONALD S	COL	0-0030224	0864	1
HIMES WILLIAM J	COL	0-0019365	0762	1
HINCHIE JOHN C	LTC	0-0031537	0861	1
HINCKE JOHN I	COL	0-0015539	0854	1
HINCKLEY LOIS S	LTC	L-0000301	1263	1
HINDLE CLIFFORD D	COL	0-0006693	1050	1
HINDMAN EDWARD R SR	LTC	0-0059114	0468	1
HINDMAN JOHN T	CW3	W-0906792	0460	1
HINDMAN THOMAS D	LTC	0-0084842	1266	1
HINDS JOHN H	M G	0-0012106	0356	1
HINDS SIDNEY R	B G	0-0012851	0247	2
HINE DANIEL L	COL	0-0019134	0762	2
HINE HENRY C JR	COL	0-0012738	0654	1
HINES CHARLES B	COL	0-0020585	0864	1
HINES CLIFFORD C	COL	0-0042289	0164	1
HINES JOHN B	COL	0-0020606	0966	1
HINES JOHN L JR	COL	0-0016749	0552	2
HINES MARY L	MAJ	N-0001974	1061	1
HINGES NORMAN R	LTC	0-0060652	0767	1
HINMAN ELMER D	COL	0-0038633	0757	2
HINRICHS HERBERT H	LTC	0-0079665	0867	1
HINRICHS JOHN H	LTG	0-0017174	0662	1
HINSHAW FREDERICK	COL	0-0018867	0560	1
HINSON CLAUDE R	LTC	0-0051922	0964	1
HINTON ALFRED E	CW4	W-0903259	0858	2
HINTON JOE A	COL	0-0011654	1147	1
HIRSCH ALLAN S	COL	0-0038947	0668	1
HIRSCH GEORGE W	COL	0-0008580	0854	1
HIRSCH OLIVER M	COL	0-0040060	1163	1
HIRSCHHORN LLOYD E	COL	0-0043433	0167	1
HIRSHORN B J L	B G	0-0051762	0566	1
HISER CHARLES H	COL	0-0044795	1167	1
HISGEN KARL W	COL	0-0014604	0452	2
HISLE ROBERT E	LTC	0-0051476	0162	1
HITCHING JOHN L	LTC	0-0015737	0348	1
HITCHINGS DONALD L	COL	0-0052081	1067	1
HITE MERLE L	LTC	0-0038036	1165	1
HITT PARKER	COL	0-0000963	1128	1
HITTLE LESLIE L	COL	0-0015430	0954	1
HIXON CHARLES E	COL	0-0012131	1052	2
HIXSON GROVER G	CW4	W-0903260	1263	1
HJERTBERG F M I	MAJ	0-0037266	0655	2
HJORT SAMUEL C JR	CW2	W-0906794	1060	1
HLOPKO JOHN J	LTC	0-0030841	1162	1
HOAAS OLE G	COL	0-0012005	0843	2
HOADLEY DALLAS W	COL	0-0027012	0368	1
HOAG ROBERT E	COL	0-0084370	1066	1
HOAGLAND CHARLES E	LTC	0-0034645	0961	1
HOAGLAND DALE M	COL	0-0006981	0753	1
HOAGLAND ROBERT J	COL	0-0020516	0267	1
HOARD MAURICE A JR	LTC	0-0043729	0964	1
HOBBINS ELIZABETH	MAJ	N-0000569	0561	1
HOBBS ARTHUR A JR	MAJ	0-0012605	0934	2
HOBBS EDWARD C	2LT	0-0020823	0339	2
HOBBS MORRIS F	LTC	0-0031416	0163	1
HOBSON EDITH M	MAJ	R-0010042	0265	1
HOBSON HOWARD M	B G	0-0029673	0262	1
HOBSON THOMAS B JR	COL	0-0061105	0868	1
HOBSON VICTOR W JR	B G	0-0023038	1065	2
HOCHELLA MICHAEL F	LTC	0-0036480	0663	2
HOCKER RICHARD W	COL	0-0005028	1048	1
HOCKER WOODSON F	COL	0-0016879	0757	1
HODGE ROBERT D	LTC	0-0039563	1055	1
HODGES ARTHUR W	COL	0-0024437	1066	1
HODGES GENOUS S JR	LTC	0-0058926	1267	1
HODGES JOHN W	CW2	W-0901839	0849	1
HODGES JOSEPH H JR	COL	0-0020733	0766	1
HODGES MORRIS D	LTC	0-0065549	0868	1
HODGES WILLARD J JR	COL	0-0021401	0866	1
HODGSON JOHN A	COL	0-0083584	1167	1
HODNETTE LOVIC P	COL	0-0008263	0342	2
HODSON FREMONT B	B G	0-0011158	0952	2
HOEBEKE ARNOLD J	LTC	0-0023930	0861	1
HOEFFER HENRY J	B G	0-0016765	0757	1
HOEFFLER HUGH B	COL	0-0051983	0368	1
HOEFLING ADAM F	CPT	0-0067579	0166	1
HOEHNE ERVIN D K	COL	0-0039878	0164	1
HOEMAN ARTHUR J	LTC	0-0042485	0163	1
HOEY WILLIAM R	MAJ	0-0081457	0866	1
HOFF ERNEST P JR	CPT	0-0063686	0466	1
HOFF RAYMOND L	LTC	0-0025140	1062	1
HOFF STUART S	M G	0-0038766	0863	1
HOFFER EUGENE	CW3	W-0903261	0761	1
HOFFMAN ALDON M	COL	0-0042975	1065	1
HOFFMAN C W JR	LTC	0-0058243	0660	1
HOFFMAN EDWIN H	CW4	W-0901810	1054	1
HOFFMAN JACK N	LTC	0-0027459	0966	1
HOFFMAN JOHN G JR	COL	0-0031856	0163	1
HOFFMAN JOHN J JR	LTC	0-0062255	1168	1
HOFFMAN PAUL D	COL	0-0030517	0765	1
HOFFMAN RALPH W	LTC	0-0036786	0564	1
HOFFMAN RAYMOND E	CPT	0-0008329	0722	2
HOFFMAN RAYMOND F	LTC	0-0044240	0264	1
HOFFMAN ROBERT J	COL	0-0008646	0547	2
HOFFMAN ROY A	LTC	0-0026726	0866	1
HOFFMAN THEODORE F	COL	0-0019403	0864	1
HOFFMAN WILLIAM C	COL	0-0039719	0955	1
HOFFMANN KENNETH L	LTC	0-0078649	0467	1
HOFINGER LEOPOLD F	LTC	0-0044368	0165	1
HOFTO GLEN E	COL	0-0041585	0459	1
HOGAN ARTHUR H	COL	0-0018551	0159	1
HOGAN GERTRUDE F	MAJ	N-0002225	0360	1
HOGAN JAMES H	LTC	0-0037144	0764	1
HOGAN JULIAN L	LTC	0-0032178	0367	1
HOGAN MARY I	LTC	N-0002117	1160	1
HOGAN SAMUEL M	COL	0-0021094	0868	1
HOGE BENJAMIN F	COL	0-0003734	0151	1
HOGE KENNETH D	CW3	W-0906795	0563	1
HOGE KENNETH G	COL	0-0012753	0646	2
HOGE WILLIAM C	MAJ	0-0037742	1061	2
HOGE WILLIAM M	GEN	0-0004437	0155	2
HOGE WILLIAM M JR	LTC	0-0023894	1166	1
HOGLE JAMES C	COL	0-0042901	1266	1
HOHERZ MELVIN A	COL	0-0042819	0259	1
HOIN ELSIE K	MAJ	N-0002230	0559	1
HOKE WILLIAM M	COL	0-0015441	1153	1
HOKENSON CHARLES K	MAJ	0-0035615	0763	1
HOLBROOK FRANK C	M G	0-0016654	1055	1
HOLBROOK JOHN	LTC	0-0051646	0963	1
HOLBROOK W A JR	B G	0-0012177	1146	1
HOLCOMB CARL W	COL	0-0016082	0755	1
HOLCOMB CORNELIUS	COL	0-0029610	0961	1

NAME	GRADE	SVC NO	DATE RET MO YR	RET CODE
HOLCOMB JAMES F	LTC	0-0027219	0866	1
HOLCOMB JOEL P	COL	0-0046829	1265	1
HOLCOMB LESLIE P JP	LTC	0-0062761	0768	1
HOLCOMB WILLIAM L	LTC	0-0053160	0164	1
HOLCOMBE FRANK S	COL	0-0024218	0463	1
HOLCOMBE JAMES H	LTC	0-0045349	0867	1
HOLCOMBE WILLIAM H	B G	0-0003661	1046	1
HOLDEN ANNA S	LTC	N-0000507	0349	1
HOLDEN MAURICE C	COL	0-0024534	0765	1
HOLDEN NEEDHAM C JR	LTC	0-0063105	0868	1
HOLDEN OLIVER	MAJ	0-0014221	1119	2
HOLDER WILLIAM G	COL	0-0012685	0753	1
HOLDERNESS STEPHEN W	COL	0-0020157	0766	1
HOLDRIDGE HERBERT C	B G	0-0005263	0244	2
HOLDRIDGE WALTER H	COL	0-0051895	1167	1
HOLLADAY NORMAN C	MAJ	0-0038540	0865	1
HOLLAND ALICE F	MAJ	N-0002048	0460	1
HOLLAND DIXON B	COL	0-0020539	0656	1
HOLLAND DONALD B	LTC	0-0083842	1067	1
HOLLAND EDWARD C	COL	0-0031840	0468	1
HOLLAND JAMES G JR	COL	0-0024573	0967	1
HOLLAND JEREMIAH P	B G	0-0016812	0757	2
HOLLAND TEMPLE G	COL	0-0015321	0554	2
HOLLAND WILLIAM E JR	COL	0-0048873	0167	1
HOLLANDER BENNET N	LTC	0-0050693	0867	1
HOLLE CHARLES G	M G	0-0012612	1058	1
HOLLER WALKER W	COL	0-0015905	0854	1
HOLLEY JAMES E	COL	0-0017185	0758	1
HOLLEY JOSHUA L JR	LTC	0-0040612	0266	1
HOLLEY WILLIAM C	COL	0-0021433	0759	1
HOLLIFIELD WILLIAM C	LTC	0-0059671	0867	1
HOLLIMAN EARL J	COL	0-0025298	1268	1
HOLLINGER JOHN C	COL	0-0030448	0663	1
HOLLINGER JOHN JR	LTC	0-0069683	1267	1
HOLLINGER MARGARET A	LTC	N-0001962	0863	1
HOLLINGSWORTH CHARLE	LTC	0-0058075	0264	2
HOLLINGSWORTH FRANK	COL	0-0006889	0145	2
HOLLINGSWORTH P B	COL	0-0057526	0560	1
HOLLIS CHARLES F	LTC	0-0079857	0361	1
HOLLIS DWIGHT S	COL	0-0030975	0558	1
HOLLIS JEFF F	COL	0-0031528	0664	1
HOLLIS ROBERT P	M G	0-0015079	1057	1
HOLLISTER FRED M	CW4	W-0903269	0263	1
HOLLISTER PAUL G	B G	0-0029547	0461	1
HOLLOWAY KENNETH H	MAJ	0-0058441	0867	1
HOLLOWELL HARRY H	CW4	W-0902118	0964	1
HOLLY JOSEPH A	B G	0-0012360	0151	1
HOLLY LEO V	COL	0-0042420	0864	1
HOLLY OLMONT W	COL	0-0010262	1147	2
HOLM CLIFFORD P	LTC	0-0038630	0757	1
HOLM WILLIAM N	COL	0-0023282	0966	1
HOLMAN JONATHAN L	M G	0-0011226	0656	2
HOLMAN ROBERT E	COL	0-0038815	0465	1
HOLMBERG DONALD W	COL	0-0039937	1164	2
HOLMBERG GERALD W	LTC	0-0029328	0854	1
HOLMES CARL G	CPT	0-0009926	0837	2
HOLMES DON V	COL	0-0008271	1047	2
HOLMES ERNEST V	B G	0-0016100	0755	2
HOLMES HARRY C	COL	0-0029286	1163	1
HOLMES HENRY B JR	B G	0-0004656	0847	1
HOLMES JOEL G	B G	0-0005272	0852	1
HOLMES ROBERT H	COL	0-0085572	0866	1
HOLMES ROBERT M	LTC	0-0026110	0863	1
HOLMES THOMAS R	COL	0-0009702	0947	1
HOLMES WILLIAM F JR	COL	0-0020525	0746	2
HOLMES WILLIAM W	COL	0-0032247	0464	1
HOLMSTROM HELMER A	COL	0-0030382	0962	1
HOLOCHWOST GEORGE G	LTC	0-0081906	0667	1
HOLPER AMBROSE C	LTC	0-0078885	0866	1
HOLSINGER GEORGE L	COL	0-0015989	0854	1
HOLSINGER JAMES W	B G	0-0029432	0760	1
HOLST JOHN J	COL	0-0016872	0757	1
HOLT ARTHUR E	COL	0-0032326	0464	1
HOLT FRANK T	COL	0-0021908	0759	1
HOLT HAROLD G	COL	0-0006783	0151	2

NAME	GRADE	SVC NO	DATE RET MO YR	RET CODE
HOLT HARVEY S JR	COL	0-0079859	1268	1
HOLT HENRY W	COL	0-0011202	0854	1
HOLT JOHN H	LTC	0-0037814	1163	1
HOLT JOHN W	LTC	0-0041154	0561	1
HOLT OLIN P	COL	0-0043298	0961	1
HOLT ROGER H	COL	0-0029574	0661	1
HOLT RUFUS L	COL	0-0008714	0150	2
HOLT WILLIAM O	CW4	W-0903271	0657	1
HOLTER PAUL W	COL	0-0020483	1166	1
HOLTERMAN GORDON H	COL	0-0020135	0866	1
HOLTON EARL F	COL	0-0020241	0966	1
HOLTON RUSSELL G JR	LTC	0-0080421	0865	1
HOLTZ ALBERT E	COL	0-0040285	0868	1
HOLTZ WERNER	LTC	0-0032209	0661	1
HOLTZCLAW EVERST A	CW4	W-0902434	1056	1
HOLTZWORTH BERTRAM A	M G	0-0016804	0863	1
HOLYCROSS FORREST L	COL	0-0009483	1047	1
HOLZBACH HENRY E JR	LTC	0-0046861	0763	1
HOMAN SAMMIE N	COL	0-0034279	0665	1
HOMBURG ALBERT H JR	LTC	0-0035159	0166	2
HOMEWOOD JOHN W	COL	0-0015472	0151	1
HOMS JOSE M	LTC	0-0031249	0467	1
HONNEN GEORGE	M G	0-0012816	1157	1
HOOD JOHN H	COL	0-0002786	0746	1
HOOD LUND F	COL	0-0039892	0364	1
HOOD PATRICK W	MAJ	0-0031308	0458	1
HOOD RALPH E	COL	0-0032443	0260	2
HOOK GLADYS T	MAJ	R-0010017	0961	1
HOOKER HOWARD C	LTC	0-0043717	0467	1
HOOKER JOE R	LTC	0-0069684	1268	1
HOOPER ETHEL M	MAJ	L-0000253	0564	2
HOOPER PHILIP L	COL	0-0032662	0968	2
HOOPES JOSEPH V	CW4	W-0906797	0163	1
HOORN FREDERICK	COL	0-0007411	0746	1
HOOVER CHRIS O	COL	0-0037408	0764	1
HOOVER GERALD B	LTC	0-0094863	0267	1
HOOVER HALLIE E	CPT	N-0000398	1160	1
HOOVER HOLMAN O	COL	0-0030305	1264	1
HOOVER HUBERT D	M G	0-0007924	0248	1
HOOVER THOMAS H	LTC	0-0037565	0664	1
HOOVER WARREN H	COL	0-0018418	0761	1
HOPE FRANCIS M	LTC	0-0030541	0559	2
HOPKINS ARMAND	COL	0-0016083	0755	1
HOPKINS EDWARD O	COL	0-0012395	0854	1
HOPKINS GEORGE E	CW2	W-0904389	1059	1
HOPKINS JOHN	MAJ	0-0007976	0436	1
HOPKINS JOHN W JR	LTC	0-0040504	0261	1
HOPKINS MALCOLM J	MAJ	0-0032512	0148	2
HOPKINS WALTER G JR	COL	0-0033551	0366	1
HOPPENSTEIN ISAAC	COL	0-0032373	0967	1
HOPPER BRISTOW S	LTC	0-0032815	1060	1
HOPPER HAROLD W	COL	0-0080880	1166	1
HOPPOCK ELEANOR M	MAJ	N-0002377	1060	1
HOPSON BRANNON J	LTC	0-0029223	1059	1
HORAN EARL C	COL	0-0007610	0749	1
HORAN JOHN P	COL	0-0005520	0448	2
HORAN LEONA E	MAJ	N-0002431	0665	1
HORGER CHARLES A	COL	0-0007359	1046	1
HORKAN GEORGE A	M G	0-0007201	0154	2
HORLOCK FRED H	LTC	0-0080422	1065	1
HORMEL HAROLD P	CW3	W-0903275	0560	1
HORN JOHN W	CW4	W-0904127	0668	1
HORN MAURICE R	LTC	0-0059472	0968	1
HORN WILEY H	LTC	0-0031078	0862	2
HORNADAY RALPH J	LTC	0-0030423	0463	1
HORNE ELIZABETH	LTC	N-0001277	0767	2
HORNE JAMES C	COL	0-0011156	0348	1
HORNECKER HARRY E	COL	0-0029082	0459	1
HORNER ALBERT A	COL	0-0016254	0555	1
HORNER HAROLD J	CW2	W-0903276	1053	2
HORNER SAMUEL W II	COL	0-0018711	0862	1
HORNISH WILLIAM N	COL	0-0041457	0457	1
HORNISHER CHARLES J	COL	0-0026461	1163	1
HORNISHER JOSEPH J	COL	0-0017989	0158	2
HORNOR JOHN L JR	COL	0-0017726	1055	1

NAME	GRADE	SVC NO	DATE RET MO YR	RET CODE
HORDWICZ LEO S	COL	0-0080423	0565	1
HORRELL CARL O	CW4	W-0903277	1068	1
HORRIDGE JOSEPH	B G	0-0017555	0456	1
HORSTMAN SANFORD W	COL	0-0019783	0865	1
HORSTMANN JOHN W	LTC	0-0042566	0463	1
HORTON JAMES C	CW3	W-0906798	0159	1
HORTON JAMES H	LTC	0-0033609	1068	2
HORTON JOHN B	B G	0-0015150	1060	1
HORTON JOHN P	LTC	0-0042259	1061	1
HORTON PAUL J	COL	0-0002223	0934	2
HORTON ROBERT L	CW3	W-0902068	0556	1
HORTON ROY W	COL	0-0030626	0164	1
HORTON RUSSELL H	COL	0-0030125	1060	1
HORTON WILLIAM F	LTC	0-0023118	0761	1
HOSEA SILAS W	LTC	0-0015651	0753	1
HOSEMANN JOSEPH F	LTC	0-0080881	0865	1
HOSHAL QUENTIN S	LTC	0-0082029	0265	1
HOSKA LUKAS E JR	COL	0-0020717	0867	1
HOSKINS HARRY D JR	COL	0-0043846	0763	1
HOSKINS OLIVE L	WO1	W-0800013	0937	1
HOSKOT NATHANIEL	COL	0-0031379	0963	1
HOSPITAL RALPH	B G	0-0003625	0151	1
HOSS CHARLES A	COL	0-0008255	0653	1
HOSTERMAN FRANK M	COL	0-0038631	0859	1
HOSTETLER JEROME K	COL	0-0088744	1065	1
HOTALING ROBERT P	LTC	0-0062177	0863	1
HOUCK ROSE E	MAJ	N-0002141	0761	1
HOUGH CHESTER C	COL	0-0011359	0854	1
HOUGH GRANVILLE	LTC	0-0028399	0168	1
HOUGH LLOYD W	LTC	0-0023251	0464	2
HOUGHTON FRANCIS E	COL	0-0039742	1061	1
HOUGHTON RUSSELL T	COL	0-0030430	0665	2
HOUGHTON WILLIAM C	MAJ	0-0003674	0534	2
HOULE GEORGE F	LTC	0-0013629	1019	1
HOULSON KEITH H	LTC	0-0052229	1264	1
HOULT CHARLES S	COL	0-0042047	1161	2
HOUSE BARBARA M	LTC	R-0010074	0166	1
HOUSE JOHN M JR	COL	0-0029729	0762	1
HOUSE WILLIAM E	B G	0-0016406	0656	1
HOUSEMAN EVAN M	M G	0-0017307	0961	1
HOUSER HAROLD H	COL	0-0032050	1268	1
HOUSER HOUSTON P JR	COL	0-0018615	0159	1
HOUSER JACK	COL	0-0031263	0867	1
HOUSMAN WALTER S	LTC	0-0053308	0961	1
HOUSTON B Z JR	MAJ	0-0031979	1155	1
HOUSTON EMMA F	LTC	N-0001960	0463	1
HOUSTON EVA D	LTC	N-0001950	1061	1
HOUSTON PAULINE V	LTC	L-0000054	0662	1
HOVELL BERGEN B	COL	0-0023450	0662	1
HOWARD ALBERT N	CW2	W-0800264	0148	1
HOWARD CHARLES E	COL	0-0018521	0761	2
HOWARD CHARLES E	LTC	0-0030605	0164	1
HOWARD CHARLES F	COL	0-0039153	0768	1
HOWARD CHARLES F	COL	0-0017270	1047	2
HOWARD CHARLES R	LTC	0-0080109	1065	1
HOWARD CHARLES W	LTC	0-0059785	0766	1
HOWARD CLAUDE M	COL	0-0019464	0158	1
HOWARD EDWIN B	B G	0-0015361	0954	1
HOWARD FRANCIS E	B G	0-0016776	0756	2
HOWARD HARMON	LTC	0-0062180	0966	1
HOWARD HAROLD F	LTC	0-0030643	0264	1
HOWARD HERBERT H	LTC	0-0046959	1062	1
HOWARD JAMES W	COL	0-0019601	1064	2
HOWARD JOHN F	COL	0-0038695	0855	1
HOWARD JOHN G	COL	0-0012704	0954	1
HOWARD KENNETH G	LTC	0-0037550	1262	1
HOWARD LULA J	MAJ	N-0002378	0261	1
HOWARD MARTIN L	CPT	0-0007470	0722	2
HOWARD ROBERT A JR	COL	0-0017182	0758	1
HOWARD ROBERT C	COL	0-0053368	0867	1
HOWARD THEODORE O	CW4	W-0903280	1156	1
HOWARD THOMAS J	LTC	0-0033508	0660	1
HOWARD WALTER A	LTC	0-0056278	0268	2
HOWARD WARD C	COL	0-0042515	0265	2
HOWARD WILLIAM R	LTC	0-0051629	0860	1

NAME	GRADE	SVC NO	DATE RET MO YR	RET CODE
HOWARD WILLIAM R	LTC	0-0067828	0467	1
HOWARTH ALBERT E R	COL	0-0018837	0862	1
HOWE CHARLES P	COL	0-0045555	0463	1
HOWE JEROME W	MAJ	0-0003464	0424	2
HOWE PAUL C	LTC	0-0014836	0438	2
HOWELL ALBERT S JR	2LT	0-0014870	1125	2
HOWELL ALVIS M	LTC	0-0032797	0361	1
HOWELL ANN E	MAJ	N-0000985	0561	1
HOWELL CLIFFORD W	COL	0-0031462	0367	1
HOWELL EDWIN N	COL	0-0021194	0165	1
HOWELL GEORGE P	B G	0-0015291	1045	2
HOWELL HARRY R JR	COL	0-0046248	0267	1
HOWELL JOHN N	COL	0-0019840	0865	1
HOWELL LENORE P	LTC	L-0000177	1264	1
HOWELL LYLBURNE M	COL	0-0029042	1058	1
HOWELL MAURICE W	MAJ	0-0035883	0763	1
HOWELL SAMUEL W JR	LTC	0-0024989	0668	1
HOWELL WALTER E	MAJ	0-0039149	1035	2
HOWELL WILLIAM C	LTC	0-0090100	0668	1
HOWELL WILLIAM C JR	COL	0-0030085	0661	1
HOWLAND CHAUNCEY E	COL	0-0041671	0460	1
HOWLAND WILLIAM A	COL	0-0005102	1047	2
HOWZE HAMILTON H	GEN	0-0018088	0765	1
HOWZE MARION W	COL	0-0001797	0642	1
HOWZE ROBERT L JR	M G	0-0016055	0562	1
HOY CHARLES E	M G	0-0018556	0359	2
HOY CHARLES J	COL	0-0019905	1046	2
HOYLE LOUIS R	CW2	W-0901619	0451	1
HOYLE RENE DE R	M G	0-0002157	0845	2
HOYNE JOHN T	LTC	0-0029739	0860	1
HOYNE RAYMOND E	COL	0-0028804	0655	1
HUBARD RANDOLPH B	LTC	0-0017714	0150	1
HUBBARD ANNA K	MAJ	L-0000057	0659	1
HUBBARD DANIEL W	LTC	0-0060775	0967	1
HUBBARD FRANK R JR	LTC	0-0030165	1061	1
HUBBARD HARRY J	COL	0-0019459	0758	1
HUBBARD JACK A	LTC	0-0071370	0867	1
HUBBARD JEROME	COL	0-0041814	1060	1
HUBBARD JOHN R	COL	0-0009677	0942	1
HUBBARD WILLIS W	MAJ	0-0014370	0819	2
HUBBART CLARENCE G	COL	0-0029718	0662	1
HUBBELL REGINALD W	LTC	0-0012194	1041	1
HUBER DALE E	1LT	0-0019573	0241	2
HUBER TYRON E	COL	0-0056808	0568	2
HUBER WILLIAM E	LTC	0-0059088	0868	1
HUBER WILLIAM R	COL	0-0018797	0862	1
HUBERT ENRIQUE J	LTC	0-0036518	0261	1
HUCHTHAUSEN W A	COL	0-0039665	0560	2
HUCK TERENCE W	LTC	0-0036513	0868	1
HUCKABY LEWIS C	LTC	0-0078893	0868	1
HUCKINS JOHN H	LTC	0-0051290	0360	1
HUDDLESTON JAMES M	LTC	0-0025554	0866	1
HUDDON ALBERT T	CW4	W-0903284	0158	1
HUDELSON MCCLURE	LTC	0-0043371	0660	2
HUDIBURG HOWARD B	COL	0-0031741	0562	1
HUDNALL JAMES R	COL	0-0005823	0448	2
HUDSON CARROLL O	COL	0-0028785	0954	1
HUDSON CHARLES C	CW4	W-0903285	0165	1
HUDSON GEORGE B	COL	0-0011233	0753	2
HUDSON GEORGE E	COL	0-0044410	0867	1
HUDSON HEBER S	LTC	0-0065446	1167	1
HUDSON JACK F	COL	0-0042184	0463	1
HUDSON JAMES A	COL	0-0052137	0766	1
HUDSON KENNETH E	COL	0-0022278	0267	1
HUDSON LOIS E	MAJ	L-0000241	0262	1
HUDSON MAUDE A	MAJ	N-0000233	0963	1
HUEBNER CLARENCE R	LTG	0-0004552	1150	2
HUEBNER OTTO W	LTC	0-0050346	0966	1
HUETTER JOHN J	LTC	0-0063316	0962	1
HUFCUT VIRA B	MAJ	N-0002243	0261	1
HUFF JOHN S	LTC	0-0059859	0864	1
HUFF ROY P	COL	0-0014637	0347	2
HUFF RUFUS D	COL	0-0029311	1264	2
HUFF TOM	LTC	0-0058929	1162	1
HUFF WILLIAM S	COL	0-0043583	0968	2

NAME	GRADE	SVC NO	DATE RET MO YR	RET CODE
HUFFMAN LESSIE P	MAJ	N-0002228	0360	1
HUFFORD GLENN D	LTC	0-0005477	1041	1
HUFFSMITH VICTOR C	COL	0-0019539	0646	2
HUGGINS GEORGE H	CW4	W-0906801	0665	1
HUGGINS ROSCOE C	COL	0-0019451	0162	1
HUGHES BERNICE G	LTC	L-0000208	0158	1
HUGHES CLYDE F	LTC	0-0048881	0764	1
HUGHES DWIGHT	COL	0-0006594	0444	2
HUGHES FREDRICK K	LTC	0-0024471	0762	1
HUGHES GEORGE E	COL	0-0030733	0666	1
HUGHES HAROLD L	LTC	0-0080888	0263	1
HUGHES HENRY J JR	LTC	0-0027831	1165	1
HUGHES J P	LTC	0-0042745	0364	1
HUGHES JAMES E	LTC	0-0058444	0766	1
HUGHES JAMES F JR	COL	0-0033956	1067	1
HUGHES JAMES R	COL	0-0020343	1057	1
HUGHES JOHN B	COL	0-0012101	1148	1
HUGHES OLIVER W	B G	0-0014974	0854	1
HUGHES ROBERT I JR	LTC	0-0091876	0867	1
HUGHES ROBERT P	COL	0-0022769	0858	1
HUGHES THOMAS K	COL	0-0024449	1167	1
HUGHES THOMAS W L JR	MAJ	0-0062577	0765	2
HUGHES WALTER P JR	MAJ	0-0062816	0866	1
HUGHES WILLIAM N JR	COL	0-0012962	1122	1
HUHNER MYRTLE C	MAJ	N-0000042	0650	1
HULING JOHN JR	COL	0-0007587	0446	2
HULKA JOHN P SR	CW4	W-0903288	1065	1
HULL DONALD F	COL	0-0022067	0262	1
HULL JAMES M	LTC	0-0065733	0767	1
HULL JOHN B	MAJ	0-0026308	0947	2
HULL JOHN E	GEN	0-0007377	0455	1
HULL KEITH M	LTC	0-0021885	1061	1
HULPA CHARLES A	CW3	W-0906803	0859	1
HULSE ALLEN D	B G	0-0021238	0863	1
HUMBERD QUENTIN L	LTC	0-0059897	0867	1
HUME WAYNE S	COL	0-0059422	0263	1
HUMMEL ATLEE V	LTC	0-0080890	0268	1
HUMMEL JOHN F	COL	0-0042712	0266	1
HUMPHREY BEN K	MAJ	0-0023475	0546	2
HUMPHREY CHARLES V	LTC	0-0040945	0764	1
HUMPHREY CLARENCE L	LTC	0-0031609	0954	1
HUMPHREY LEON B	COL	0-0029073	0359	1
HUMPHREYS LEONARD A	LTC	0-0027467	0765	1
HUMPHREYS RUSSELL W	COL	0-0031910	0566	1
HUMPHREYS WILLIAM A	LTC	0-0028348	0766	1
HUMPHRIES TROY T	CW4	W-0903289	0760	1
HUNDLEY DANIEL H	COL	0-0015862	0654	2
HUNEYCUTT ROBERT E	COL	0-0029946	0664	1
HUNN CLIFFORD I	COL	0-0011363	0348	2
HUNNICUTT LEE V	COL	0-0008217	0546	1
HUNT ALBERT B	COL	0-0031285	1068	1
HUNT CLIFTON T	COL	0-0011909	0950	2
HUNT GEORGE A	COL	0-0007117	0546	1
HUNT GEORGE M	COL	0-0030782	0962	1
HUNT GEORGE T	MAJ	0-0036777	0161	1
HUNT HAROLD H	LTC	0-0016978	0648	1
HUNT HERMAN T JR	LTC	0-0026053	0865	1
HUNT JAY	COL	0-0032789	0168	1
HUNT JIM H	LTC	0F-0103337	0268	1
HUNT JOHN M JR	COL	0-0031089	1266	1
HUNT LEWIS A	COL	0-0039889	0364	1
HUNT ORA E	B G	0-0000450	0923	1
HUNT RICHARD J	COL	0-0019752	0862	1
HUNTER CHARLES N	COL	0-0017710	0859	1
HUNTER FLOYD W	COL	0-0004517	1146	1
HUNTER HOWARD W	COL	0-0018387	0946	2
HUNTER ROBERT C	LTC	0-0040045	0461	1
HUNTER THOMAS B	COL	0-0078791	1163	1
HUNTER W HAMILTON	COL	0-0016772	0757	1
HUNTER 3RD GEORGE W	COL	0-0029126	0355	1
HUNTINGTON ROBERT E	CW4	W-0903291	0758	1
HUNTLEY CHARLES B	COL	0-0022714	0268	1
HUNTZINGER HARVEY W	LTC	0-0070387	0867	1
HUPALO WILLIAM	COL	0-0040269	1164	1
HUPPERT GEORGE H JR	COL	0-0032277	0565	1

NAME	GRADE	SVC NO	DATE RET MO YR	RET CODE
HURD JAMES W	COL	0-0080891	0868	1
HURDIS CHARLES E	M G	0-0005229	1146	2
HURLESS BERNARD F	COL	0-0007417	0854	1
HURLEY EMERSON F	LTC	0-0031533	0856	2
HURLEY FREDERICK	COL	0-0046434	0364	1
HURLEY JOHN F	CW4	W-0903293	0658	1
HURLEY WESLEY C	LTC	0-0043319	1065	1
HURSH LAURENCE M	COL	0-0025146	0761	1
HURST CAM J JR	LTC	0-0065491	0767	1
HURST KENNETH M	COL	0-0041947	1161	1
HURST RAY H	LTC	0-0045720	0660	2
HURST RICHARD M	B G	0-0030191	1062	1
HURST ROBERT H	LTC	0-0026868	0868	1
HURT HUGH A	MAJ	0-0044210	1054	2
HURT SHIRLEY R	COL	0-0011155	0447	2
HURT WILLIAM J	COL	0-0056811	1165	1
HUSE RALPH N	COL	0-0030819	1066	1
HUSMAN DONALD L	COL	0-0032431	0766	1
HUSSEY JOHN W	LTC	0-0059999	0868	1
HUSSEY WILLIAM J	COL	0-0022205	0466	1
HUSTEAD CHARLES L JR	LTC	0-0043711	1062	2
HUSTEAD GEORGE L T	LTC	0-0079863	0165	1
HUSTEAD 2ND JAMES M	LTC	0-0024175	0660	1
HUSTON FRED R	LTC	0-0043812	0766	1
HUSTON MILBURN N	B G	0-0030612	0865	1
HUSTON ROBERT M	LTC	0-0038943	0361	1
HUTCHESON JOHN C	LTC	0-0007768	0242	1
HUTCHIN WALTER J	LTC	0-0025916	0865	1
HUTCHINS CARROLL R	COL	0-0011531	0947	1
HUTCHINS CHARLES W	LTC	0-0029714	0654	1
HUTCHINS ROBERT B	COL	0-0012407	1146	2
HUTCHINSON ARTHUR G	COL	0-0007615	0849	1
HUTCHINSON CARY B	COL	0-0015644	0954	1
HUTCHINSON D R	COL	0-0028822	0949	2
HUTCHINSON GEORGE W	LTC	0-0029744	0560	1
HUTCHINSON J W JR	1LT	0-0064117	1053	2
HUTCHINSON MELVILLE	MAJ	0-0037449	0861	1
HUTCHINSON PHILIP A	COL	0-0033200	0267	1
HUTCHINSON WILLIAM S	COL	0-0032611	0366	1
HUTCHISON CHARLES R	M G	0-0016796	0363	1
HUTCHISON JAMES H	MAJ	0-0060282	1163	1
HUTCHISON JOHN G	CW4	W-0903295	0462	1
HUTCHISON MORTIMER J	LTC	0-0034727	1061	1
HUTCHISON RUSSELL J	LTC	0-0052921	0667	1
HUTCHISON WARREN S	LTC	0-0084373	0367	1
HUTSINPILLER HERSC	LTC	0-0035487	0763	1
HUTSON JAMES C	COL	0-0004645	0845	2
HUTSON RICHARD K	COL	0-0032212	0766	1
HUTSON WILLIAM M	COL	0-0006918	1047	2
HYDE EARL A	LTC	0-0007883	1141	1
HYDE JAMES F C JR	MAJ	0-0624766	0447	2
HYDE THOMAS I	LTC	0-0080893	0468	1
HYLAND ANN T	MAJ	N-0000469	0465	1
HYLDEN MAURICE W	LTC	0-0026980	0863	1
HYMAN MARY F	MAJ	N-0001953	0859	1
HYNDMAN FLOYD M	LTC	0-0006822	0239	2
HYSSONG CLYDE L	M G	0-0008386	0749	1
HYZER PETER C	B G	0-0020589	0367	1
ICKLER JULIUS F	LTC	0-0050667	0767	1
IGERSHEIMER MILO	LTC	0-0037678	0761	1
IGO CLARENCE C	MAJ	0-0069692	0665	1
ILLIG JAMES M	B G	0-0020330	0765	1
IMHOFF JOSEPH J	COL	0-0051009	1156	1
IMLACH ELEANOR H	MAJ	N-0002711	1167	1
IMMEL JOSEPH P	WO1	W-0901421	0342	1
IMRIE MATTHEW H	COL	0-0029181	0560	1
INFOSINO LUCY M	MAJ	N-0000861	0165	1
INGE ANDREW V	COL	0-0021448	0766	1
INGEMAN MILTON J	COL	0-0042124	1262	1
INGHAM HENRY L	COL	0-0014792	1148	1
INGLES HARRY C	M G	0-0003689	0347	1
INGLIS EDWARD	LTC	0-0031964	0562	1
INGMIRE EDGAR J	COL	0-0020639	0867	1
INGOLO JOHN G	LTC	0-0003301	0837	2
INGRAHAM GORDON D	COL	0-0028848	0256	1

NAME	GRADE	SVC NO	DATE RET MO YR	RET CODE
INGRAM ALBERTA T	MAJ	N-0000391	0961	1
INGRAM FORNEY H	COL	0-0029698	0756	1
INGRAM JERRY S	1LT	0-0064219	0453	2
INGRAM LIONEL R	COL	0-0027096	0459	1
INGRAM LOUIS L	COL	0-0019492	0746	2
INGRAM RUPERT	COL	0-0051103	0960	1
INGRAM SALLIE H	MAJ	N-0001302	0666	1
INGRUM LESLIE F	CW4	W-0903299	1057	1
INMAN JAMES G	COL	0-0041734	0163	1
INMAN ROY N	CPT	0F-0114118	0868	2
INMON EBNER H	LTC	0-0008843	0540	2
INMON ERNEST G	CW3	W-0906306	0463	1
INMON THOMAS W	COL	0-0056254	0965	1
INNES JEAN W	MAJ	N-0002402	0862	1
INWOOD EUGENE R	COL	0-0020993	0654	2
IPPOLITO CHARLES J	LTC	0-0037208	1063	1
IRBY FRED B	LTC	0-0042683	1263	2
IRBY VERNON C	LTC	0-0025251	0266	2
IRBY WILLIAM B	COL	0-0031035	0866	1
IRELAND ARTHUR P	COL	0-0051543	0964	1
IRELAND THOMAS P	COL	0-0051004	1058	1
IREY NELSON S	COL	0-0030928	1165	1
IRICK EDWARD F JR	LTC	0-0060791	0667	1
IRISH RALPH G	LTC	0-0080897	0664	1
IRISH WYNOT R	COL	0-0011227	0354	1
IRONS ARTHUR L	B G	0-0016526	0857	1
IRVIN RICHARD JR	COL	0-0025118	0666	1
IRVIN ROY D	COL	0-0042104	1162	1
IRVINE ELROY S J	COL	0-0004420	1047	1
IRVINE MICHAEL M	COL	0-0018404	0761	1
IRVINE RICHARD H	LTC	0-0036705	0165	1
IRVINE WILLARD W	M G	0-0005838	0452	1
IRVING CHARLES R	CPT	0-0014223	1019	2
IRVING CLARK E	COL	0-0056286	1268	2
IRVING FREDERICK	M G	0-0005261	0854	1
IRVING GLENN C	COL	0-0043197	1168	1
IRVING HAROLD W	CW3	W-0903300	0455	1
IRVING JOHN H JR	LTC	0-0027004	0864	1
IRVING VERNIE M	MAJ	N-0001906	0862	1
IRWIN CONSTANT L	B G	0-0004757	0344	2
IRWIN GORDON C	COL	0-0005729	0847	2
IRWIN SAMUEL L	LTC	0-0031346	1064	1
ISAAC LEE	LTC	0-0080112	0866	1
ISAACSON DONALD F	LTC	0-0031965	0262	1
ISAACSON HAROLD S	COL	0-0016836	0757	1
ISACCS GEORGE	COL	0-0015959	0754	1
ISBELL HENRY W	COL	0-0009978	0947	1
ISELEY CHARLES M	COL	0-0018928	0862	1
ISEMAN JOSEPH D	COL	0-0033798	0865	1
ISENBERG CONLEY G	LTC	0-0040104	1262	2
ISH GEORGE J	LTC	0-0036102	0861	1
ISHAM CARL T	COL	0-0019856	0965	1
ISHIDA GEORGE S	MAJ	0-0078895	0265	1
ISHOY VICTOR A	COL	0-0031640	1164	1
ISKER ROHLAND A	COL	0-0007355	0546	1
ISNER ALVIS E	LTC	0-0046626	0863	1
ISON FRANK S	COL	0-0039819	0263	1
ISRAELSON JOHN A	COL	0-0080898	0765	1
ISRAELSON NATHANIEL	LTC	0-0080113	0866	1
ISRIN MICHAEL D	LTC	0-0030756	0664	1
ITSCHNER EMERSON C	LTG	0-0015516	0461	1
IULIUCCI THOMAS P	COL	0-0024848	0963	1
IVERSON VERNON L	MAJ	0-0079896	0765	1
IVES ALBERT R	COL	0-0004863	0147	2
IVES H DUDLEY	M G	0-0029509	1265	1
IVES WASHINGTON	COL	0-0015696	0954	1
IVEY RICHARD G	MAJ	0-0021116	1046	2
IVIE CARL W JR	LTC	0-0059787	0168	1
IVINS CHARLES F	COL	0-0012862	0554	1
IWANICKI WILLIAM G	CW4	W-0906807	1168	1
JABLONSKY HARVEY J	M G	0-0019390	0868	2
JACCARD PAUL A	COL	0-0016694	1054	1
JACKMAN ALBERT H	COL	0-0051402	0562	2
JACKS GORDON L	LTC	0-0049357	0266	1
JACKS SAMUEL T	COL	0-0079707	1066	1

NAME	GRADE	SVC NO	DATE RET MO YR	RET CODE
JACKSON ALBERT M	COL	0-0005854	1146	1
JACKSON ASBURY H	LTC	0-0029629	0961	2
JACKSON BURWELL B	COL	0-0034840	0868	1
JACKSON CHARLES L	COL	0-0021207	0868	1
JACKSON FRED D	COL	0-0047577	0867	1
JACKSON GAIL M	CW4	W-0903305	0466	1
JACKSON GEORGE E	LTC	0-0027821	0865	1
JACKSON GORDON E	LTC	0-0046950	0267	1
JACKSON HAL G JR	LTC	0-0088753	0966	1
JACKSON HAROLD R	B G	0-0005237	0653	1
JACKSON JAMES H	LTC	0-0031580	0560	1
JACKSON JOHN H	COL	0-0052204	1068	1
JACKSON JOHN W	COL	0-0080427	0868	1
JACKSON JOSEPH C	COL	0-0029089	0359	1
JACKSON KINGSBURY	LTC	0-0080428	0965	1
JACKSON LANGDON A JR	COL	0-0020251	0864	1
JACKSON LOUIS W	COL	0-0029474	1060	1
JACKSON M C JR	COL	0-0028820	1055	2
JACKSON MARGARET E	MAJ	N-0000918	1167	1
JACKSON MARION H	COL	0-0031629	0263	1
JACKSON NEWTON L P	CW3	W-0907123	0860	1
JACKSON NORTON	LTC	0-0040054	0862	2
JACKSON PAGE S	CPT	0-0026042	0350	2
JACKSON RALPH B	CW4	W-0906808	0563	1
JACKSON ROBERT J JR	LTC	0-0038986	0761	1
JACKSON THOMAS A	CW4	W-0906809	0368	1
JACKSON THOMAS M	CW4	W-0903307	0757	1
JACKSON WALLACE L	CPT	0-0092669	0365	2
JACKSON WENDELL T	COL	0-0057897	0966	2
JACKSON WILLIAM O	COL	0-0039628	1059	1
JACKSON WILLIAM F	COL	0-0051529	0464	1
JACO CHARLES M JR	LTC	0-0028203	0866	1
JACOBS BEN R	COL	0-0011641	0453	2
JACOBS EUGENE C	COL	0-0020499	0665	1
JACOBS FRED A	LTC	0-0041935	1059	1
JACOBS GERALD O	COL	0-0031548	1066	1
JACOBS JAMES R	MAJ	0-0003259	1022	2
JACOBS JOSEPH P	LTC	0-0069954	0968	1
JACOBS LAWRENCE P	B G	0-0031556	0466	1
JACOBS MARVIN L	COL	0-0022915	0862	1
JACOBS RICHARD C JR	COL	0-0010908	0548	1
JACOBS STANLEY E	COL	0-0052256	1064	1
JACOBS WINSTON R	MAJ	0-0058449	0168	1
JACOBSON GEORGE O	COL	0-0031703	0168	1
JACOBSON LUCY E	LTC	N-0001873	1160	1
JACOBSON SIMON	COL	0-0009577	0747	1
JACOBSON WALTER A	MAJ	0-0050473	0762	1
JACOBY ARTHUR M	COL	0-0020125	0765	1
JACOBY LESLIE E	COL	0-0012300	0753	1
JACOBY PHILIP R	LTC	0-0076262	0167	2
JACQUES DONALD M	COL	0-0050934	0157	1
JACULA PETER M	LTC	0-0028716	0767	1
JACUNSKI EDWARD W	LTC	0-0021334	1141	2
JADWIN CORNELIUS	COL	0-0011213	0948	1
JAEGER VERNON P	COL	0-0018954	0163	1
JAFFE MORTON S	COL	0-0052105	0968	2
JAGGAR JOSEPH L	COL	0-0051071	0160	1
JAGGERS JOE H	LTC	0-0072739	0868	1
JAGIELLO WALTER A	MAJ	0-0027584	0866	1
JAHNKE EDWARD J JR	COL	0-0059591	0967	1
JAKUBIAK ALICE P	1LT	M-0000799	0545	1
JAMES CHARLES A III	CPT	0-0060000	0766	1
JAMES EDWARD B	COL	0-0041549	0459	1
JAMES GEORGE W	COL	0-0030146	0364	1
JAMES GLENN A	CW4	W-0903310	0762	1
JAMES JOSEPH E JR	COL	0-0018237	0658	1
JAMES LEE B	COL	0-0025619	1163	1
JAMES OTTIS E	COL	0-0029192	1160	1
JAMES STANLEY L JR	LTC	0-0025833	0864	1
JAMES WILLARD W	LTC	0-0031167	0666	1
JAMESON ROY A	COL	0-0032072	1062	1
JAMISON R EVANGELI	LTC	N-0002009	0968	2
JAMULA CECILIA P	LTC	N-0000485	0367	1
JANAIRO MAXIMIANO	COL	0-0018098	0860	2
JANASIEWICZ THADEUS	LTC	0-0065266	0868	1

NAME	GRADE	SVC NO	DATE RET MO YR	RET CODE
JANBAZ EDWARD H	LTC	O-0081869	0868	1
JANDA EARL J	LTC	O-0066027	0867	1
JANES CLINTON W	COL	O-0038730	1160	1
JANES ERNEST L	COL	O-0031587	0767	1
JANIKULA MURIEL J	LTC	L-0000107	0268	2
JANK ARTHUR W	LTC	O-0027926	0567	1
JANKOWSKI HENDRINA	MAJ	N-0002385	0961	1
JANOF THEODORE	COL	O-0020382	0864	1
JANOUSEK NEAL F	LTC	O-0036127	0662	2
JANSEN JOSEPH F	LTC	O-0084057	1166	1
JANZ DONALD H	LTC	O-0024217	0762	1
JAPINGA ROBERT M	MAJ	O-0065142	1167	1
JARBOE JESSE J	COL	O-0030921	1265	1
JARK CARL H	LTG	O-0017556	0864	2
JARRELL JULIUS B	CW4	W-0903312	0860	1
JARRELL SHAFFER F	COL	O-0051112	1160	2
JARRETT DONALD L	LTC	O-0041845	0358	1
JARRETT JOHN A	LTC	O-0065016	0661	2
JARROLD MILTON	LTC	O-0043699	0861	1
JARVIS JOSEPH W	LTC	O-0031530	0252	2
JARVIS 3RD GEORGE M	COL	O-0050975	1057	1
JASKIERNY ARTHUR	MAJ	RW-0906811	0868	1
JASTREMSKI BRUNO	COL	O-0020526	0258	1
JAUERNIG RUSSELL R	LTC	O-0058019	0867	1
JAY HENRY D	B G	O-0004952	0948	1
JAYCOX JOHN W	MAJ	O-0022078	0658	1
JAYNE HARRIET J	MAJ	N-0000708	0261	1
JAYNES LAWRENCE C	M G	O-0010540	0853	1
JEDLOWSKI JOHN J	LTC	O-0022754	0268	1
JEFFCOTT GEORGE F	COL	O-0020077	0960	1
JEFFER KAZMIEFA A	CPT	N-0000313	0350	2
JEFFERDS JEROME S	COL	O-0052283	0964	1
JEFFERIS TOMAS C	COL	O-0031137	0467	1
JEFFERS RICHARD F	COL	O-0040165	0662	1
JEFFERSON LESLIE W	COL	O-0009767	0751	1
JEFFERSON MARIAN Y	LTC	N-0000081	0354	1
JEFFERSON WAYNE O	COL	O-0029766	0962	1
JEFFERSON WILLIAM T	CW4	W-0903314	0164	1
JEFFERY ARTHUR B	COL	O-0030201	0664	1
JEFFRES JAMES E	LTC	O-0007206	0941	2
JEFFRESS VINNIE H	COL	O-0018638	0355	2
JEFFREY ALTA R	CPT	N-0001443	0954	2
JEFFREYS ALICE C	MAJ	N-0001229	0460	1
JEFFRIES CHARLES E	LTC	O-0040208	0361	1
JEFFUS CHARLES J	COL	O-0019730	0954	1
JELLETT DAVID T	LTC	O-0019273	1054	1
JELLUM DELBERT L	LTC	O-0044478	0968	1
JENICEK JOHN A	COL	O-0057989	0967	1
JENKINS CHARLES A	COL	O-0031369	1166	1
JENKINS DONALD L	COL	O-0045935	0365	1
JENKINS EDWARD N	COL	O-0040561	1168	1
JENKINS JAMES R	LTC	O-0035054	1058	1
JENKINS JESSE S	CW3	W-0904130	0556	1
JENKINS JOHN F	COL	O-0053168	0168	1
JENKINS JOHN M JR	COL	O-0004716	1050	2
JENKINS PARK T	COL	O-0032218	0467	1
JENKINS PAUL H	COL	O-0019663	1046	2
JENKINS REUBEN E	LTG	O-0011658	0254	2
JENKINS THOMAS G	COL	O-0005760	0452	1
JENKINS WALTER E	COL	O-0005155	0753	1
JENKINS WILBUR G	COL	O-0008528	1146	2
JENKS HAROLD F	COL	O-0031691	0167	1
JENKS LOREN T	COL	O-0024356	0561	2
JENNA RUSSELL W	COL	O-0019564	0661	1
JENNA WILLIAM W	COL	O-0008642	0954	1
JENNERSON HORACE L	LTC	O-0039620	0657	1
JENNINGS CATHERINE	MAJ	N-0002125	1159	1
JENNINGS CLARENCE M	COL	O-0041643	0457	1
JENNINGS MAURICE E	COL	O-0011320	1048	1
JENNINGS RAYMOND J	LTC	O-0034120	0561	2
JENNINGS THOMAS A	COL	O-0015793	0654	1
JENNINGS WALTER F	COL	O-0014728	0854	1
JENNINGS WILLIAM E	COL	O-0019640	0961	1
JENNINGS WILLIAM E	COL	O-0039964	0962	2
JENSEN ALLEN	COL	O-0023692	0765	1
JENSEN DENMARK C	COL	O-0044694	0968	1
JENSEN DORIS F	MAJ	N-0001963	0860	1
JENSEN DOVRE C	LTC	O-0052166	0666	1
JENSEN HUBERT J	MAJ	O-0058452	0766	1
JENSEN MELVIN N	LTC	O-0045771	0863	1
JENSEN NAOMI J	LTC	N-0000080	0459	1
JENSEN OSWALD R	COL	O-0021461	0857	1
JENSEN ROLAND H	LTC	O-0053300	0763	1
JENSEN WALTER A	M G	O-0019006	0567	1
JENSEN WANDA	MAJ	N-0002123	1159	1
JENSON LLOYD K	COL	O-0059788	0265	2
JEPSON HANS G	COL	O-0029966	0563	1
JERBI FRANK C	COL	O-0052027	0965	1
JERENIMUS ROBERT D	MAJ	O-0067585	1065	1
JERVEY JAMES P JR	LTC	O-0012091	0825	2
JERVEY JOHN P	LTC	O-0049219	0865	1
JERVEY THOMAS M	COL	O-0007977	1148	2
JESPERSEN HANS C	COL	O-0010801	0546	1
JESSE WILLIAM C	COL	O-0042446	1056	2
JESSEN RAYMOND E	LTC	O-0051590	0263	1
JESURUN HAROLD M	COL	O-0026439	0767	1
JETER JOHN R	COL	O-0016342	1055	1
JETT RICHARD O	LTC	O-0027856	0367	1
JEWELL KENNETH T	CW4	W-0903317	0664	1
JEWETT JOHN J	LTC	O-0039890	0262	1
JEWETT LEONARD G	COL	O-0022236	0867	1
JEWETT RAYMOND F	CW4	W-0903318	0960	1
JEWETT RICHARD L	B G	O-0018339	0761	1
JEWKES LORUS D	MAJ	O-0061534	0868	1
JODREY DAVID B	COL	O-0043590	0968	1
JOERNS FREDERICK	LTC	O-0069699	0765	1
JOFFRAY EUGENE A	CW4	W-0903319	0461	1
JOGL JOSEPH W	COL	O-0030330	1262	1
JOHANNES HENRY C	COL	O-0006366	0945	2
JOHANSON RAYMOND R	CPT	O-0019628	0239	2
JOHANSSON ADRIAN	LTC	O-0051710	1155	1
JOHN ERNEST	COL	O-0005792	0446	2
JOHN HOWARD J	COL	O-0015802	0854	1
JOHNS DWIGHT F	B G	O-0004417	1249	1
JOHNS GLOVER S JR	COL	O-0031501	0467	1
JOHNS ONAS L	COL	O-0029323	0864	1
JOHNS WALTER E	COL	O-0017142	0946	2
JOHNSON ALBERT M	COL	O-0039858	1263	1
JOHNSON ALBERT W	COL	O-0012174	0147	1
JOHNSON ALCORN B	COL	O-0041636	1059	1
JOHNSON ALFRED B	COL	O-0003550	0548	1
JOHNSON ALICE J	MAJ	N-0000518	1149	1
JOHNSON ALLAN G W	COL	O-0023769	0868	1
JOHNSON AMOS G	LTC	O-0021363	0665	1
JOHNSON ANDREW L	LTC	O-0030934	1264	1
JOHNSON BENJAMIN E	LTC	O-0040646	0468	1
JOHNSON BERTIL A	LTC	O-0023086	1264	1
JOHNSON BERTRAM H	LTC	O-0051503	0562	1
JOHNSON BRIARD P	M G	O-0029393	1163	2
JOHNSON BRUCE H	LTC	O-0030042	1060	1
JOHNSON BURCHARD M	LTC	O-0029051	1056	1
JOHNSON CHARLES E	M G	O-0019534	1167	1
JOHNSON CHARLES F	COL	O-0008019	0849	2
JOHNSON CHARLES R JR	COL	O-0005299	0647	1
JOHNSON CHARLES S	COL	O-0007191	0753	2
JOHNSON CHARLES W	COL	O-0036315	0764	1
JOHNSON CHARLES W JR	LTC	O-0080115	1265	1
JOHNSON CLARENCE E	LTC	O-0041747	1161	1
JOHNSON CLAYTON E	LTC	O-0062244	0867	1
JOHNSON DAVID E	LTC	O-0063164	0967	1
JOHNSON DAVID T	COL	O-0012067	0753	1
JOHNSON DOUGLAS V	M G	O-0015072	0360	1
JOHNSON DWIGHT B	M G	O-0018722	0867	1
JOHNSON DWIGHT E	LTC	O-0039932	1162	2
JOHNSON EARLE A	COL	O-0008240	0353	1
JOHNSON EDNA L	MAJ	N-0001909	1062	1
JOHNSON EDWARD C	LTC	O-0030753	0664	1
JOHNSON EDWARD C	CW4	W-0904132	0564	1
JOHNSON EDWARD M	WO1	W-0800147	0137	2
JOHNSON EDWARD O JR	1LT	O-0086328	0163	2
JOHNSON EDWARD T	COL	O-0029856	0361	1
JOHNSON EDWIN H	COL	O-0005434	0753	1
JOHNSON EDWIN L	B G	O-0016158	0656	1
JOHNSON ELIZABETH	MAJ	N-0000083	0954	1
JOHNSON ELIZABETH	MAJ	N-0002692	0268	1
JOHNSON ELMER JR	LTC	O-0038799	0663	1
JOHNSON EWING C	LTC	O-0019851	1050	2
JOHNSON FINIS G	COL	O-0040067	1066	1
JOHNSON FULKEY L	LTC	O-0029431	0758	1
JOHNSON FRANCES J	LTC	M-0010031	0868	1
JOHNSON FRANK M S	COL	O-0005566	0549	2
JOHNSON GEORGE B	CW2	W-0901625	0647	1
JOHNSON GEORGE V	COL	O-0039831	0963	2
JOHNSON GORDON M	COL	O-0029406	0361	1
JOHNSON HAROLD R	COL	O-0029352	0958	1
JOHNSON HARRY W	M G	O-0016391	0161	1
JOHNSON HARRY W	LTC	O-0042821	0762	1
JOHNSON HARVEY A	COL	O-0041462	0757	1
JOHNSON HELEN V	LTC	N-0000031	0948	1
JOHNSON HENSLEY S	LTC	O-0022309	1060	1
JOHNSON HERBERT A JR	LTC	O-0033140	0257	2
JOHNSON HORACE W	1LT	O-0016625	0233	2
JOHNSON IRVIN A	COL	O-0040464	0864	1
JOHNSON JAMES A	MAJ	O-0089343	0367	1
JOHNSON JAMES E	COL	O-0043704	0667	1
JOHNSON JAMES M	COL	O-0054002	0367	2
JOHNSON JAMES R	COL	O-0020756	0867	1
JOHNSON JAMES W	LTC	O-0033387	0761	1
JOHNSON JESSE M	COL	O-0051797	0966	1
JOHNSON JOHN A JR	CW3	W-0906812	0167	1
JOHNSON JOHN E	COL	O-0039828	0463	1
JOHNSON JOHN F	LTC	O-0025538	0260	1
JOHNSON JOHN G	COL	O-0021929	0864	1
JOHNSON JOHN J	COL	O-0011865	0943	2
JOHNSON JOHN N JR	LTC	O-0007854	1041	1
JOHNSON JOHN R	COL	O-0043677	0765	2
JOHNSON JOHNNIE O	CW4	W-0903322	0757	1
JOHNSON JOSEPH L	1LT	O-0019358	0142	1
JOHNSON KENNETH C	COL	O-0044090	0467	1
JOHNSON KENNETH L	COL	O-0015416	1153	1
JOHNSON KENNETH R	COL	O-0084375	0868	2
JOHNSON LAURENCE A	LTC	O-0033361	0361	1
JOHNSON LEHMAN H JR	LTC	O-0044831	0262	1
JOHNSON LEONARD H	LTC	O-0040227	0561	1
JOHNSON LEONARD L	COL	O-0035441	0666	1
JOHNSON LEONARD M	COL	O-0015921	0754	1
JOHNSON LEONARD M	COL	O-0042329	0364	1
JOHNSON LOUIS H	LTC	O-0046097	0762	1
JOHNSON LUTHER E	LTC	O-0030535	0761	1
JOHNSON MARGARET R	LTC	L-0000066	0263	1
JOHNSON MAURICE A JR	LTC	O-0065262	0868	1
JOHNSON MILTON L	LTC	O-0042284	1061	1
JOHNSON NANCY A	MAJ	N-0000705	0161	1
JOHNSON NEAL C	B G	O-0005023	0152	1
JOHNSON RAGNAR F	COL	O-0028813	0755	1
JOHNSON RALPH K	COL	O-0042213	0763	1
JOHNSON RALPH R	LTC	O-0068018	0867	1
JOHNSON RICHARD A	LTC	O-0028145	0167	1
JOHNSON RICHARD P	COL	O-0018940	0856	1
JOHNSON ROBERT E	LTC	O-0051309	0560	1
JOHNSON ROBERT J	LTC	O-0059357	0868	1
JOHNSON ROBERT M	LTC	O-0024498	1160	1
JOHNSON ROBERT P	COL	O-0023926	0867	1
JOHNSON ROY E	CW4	W-0906815	0359	1
JOHNSON SEWALL H E	LTC	O-0028712	0766	1
JOHNSON STANLEY T	COL	O-0019743	0865	1
JOHNSON SUSIE G	MAJ	N-0002330	1264	1
JOHNSON THOMAS J	COL	O-0002374	1039	2
JOHNSON TILLMAN D	LTC	O-0022301	0859	1
JOHNSON VERNON R	COL	O-0039584	0658	1
JOHNSON VICTOR L JR	COL	O-0022013	1146	2
JOHNSON WALTER M	B G	O-0016835	0657	2
JOHNSON WALTER R	CW2	W-0901644	0748	1
JOHNSON WARREN R	COL	O-0043697	0466	1
JOHNSON WENDELL G	COL	O-0015312	0954	1
JOHNSON WESLEY L	CW4	W-0903325	0856	1
JOHNSON WILBUR M	COL	O-0030577	1265	1
JOHNSON WILHELM P	M G	O-0017229	0762	2
JOHNSON WILLIAM A JR	COL	O-0021228	0858	2
JOHNSON WILLIAM B	COL	O-0008447	0746	2
JOHNSON WILLIAM E JR	LTC	O-0061473	0868	1
JOHNSON WILLIAM G	COL	O-0038756	0464	1
JOHNSON WILLIAM H JR	COL	O-0029908	0863	2
JOHNSON WILLIAM L	COL	O-0015697	1146	2
JOHNSON WILLIAM O	MAJ	O-0005681	0131	1
JOHNSON WILLIAM T	COL	O-0011111	0247	1
JOHNSON WRIGHT H	CPT	O-0007399	0926	2
JOHNSTON CARL T	LTC	O-0087538	0565	2
JOHNSTON DANA W JR	COL	O-0019506	0864	1
JOHNSTON EDWARD S	COL	O-0004906	0744	2
JOHNSTON EUGENE C	COL	O-0012727	0954	1
JOHNSTON GEORGE W	COL	O-0031184	0568	1
JOHNSTON HAROLD L	CW3	W-0906814	0361	1
JOHNSTON JOSEPH E	COL	O-0030424	0565	1
JOHNSTON JOSEPH W	B G	O-0030462	1065	1
JOHNSTON KILBOURNE	COL	O-0017252	0650	1
JOHNSTON MARVIN V	COL	O-0043313	0962	1
JOHNSTON MONT S JR	COL	O-0053169	0463	1
JOHNSTON OSCAR R	COL	O-0012771	1051	2
JOHNSTON PAULINE V	LTC	N-0002140	0264	1
JOHNSTON ROBERT B	COL	O-0014843	0751	1
JOHNSTON ROBERT D	COL	O-0018498	0661	1
JOHNSTON ROBERT G SR	COL	O-0051033	0559	2
JOHNSTON ROBERT L	CW3	W-0906816	0756	1
JOHNSTONE JOHN C	LTC	O-0044702	1162	1
JOHNSTONE ROBERT R	WO1	W-0800032	0938	2
JOINER PHILLIP M	CW4	W-0903327	0263	1
JOINER TALLEY D	COL	O-0007569	0446	2
JOINER WILLIAM H	COL	O-0005464	0542	1
JOLLEY PAUL L	COL	O-0030764	0364	2
JOLLIFFE KATHARINE	LTC	N-0000077	1058	1
JONES ALAN W	M G	O-0005886	1245	2
JONES ARGYLE P	LTC	O-0039842	0158	1
JONES ARTHUR T	LTC	O-0021678	0758	1
JONES BERNEL	MAJ	O-0071817	1068	1
JONES BERTIL V	COL	O-0031968	1167	1
JONES BEVERLY D	COL	O-0019081	0863	1
JONES BRUCE D	COL	O-0034238	0866	1
JONES CARLTON L	LTC	O-0070393	0868	1
JONES CATESBYAPC	COL	O-0006936	1146	1
JONES CECIL R	LTC	O-0080912	0568	1
JONES CHARLES A JR	MAJ	O-0024533	0860	1
JONES CHARLES M JR	LTC	O-0025890	0765	1
JONES CHARLES P	COL	O-0012262	0946	2
JONES CHARLES R	COL	O-0005615	0946	2
JONES CHESLEY H	LTC	O-0078901	1065	2
JONES CLIFFORD	COL	O-0001805	0642	2
JONES CLIFFORD R	COL	O-0003833	0251	1
JONES CLYDE L	COL	O-0019074	0863	1
JONES DANIEL B	LTC	O-0037937	1163	1
JONES DAVID W	COL	O-0043631	1265	1
JONES DE WITT C	COL	O-0002021	0642	1
JONES DEAN H	LTC	O-0030724	0664	1
JONES DEARL F	COL	O-0048423	0968	1
JONES DOUGLAS C	LTC	O-0058454	0668	1
JONES EBEN R	COL	O-0032836	0668	1
JONES EDWIN W	LTC	O-0040530	1162	2
JONES ELIZABETH	LTC	M-0010114	0662	1
JONES EMMETT G	LTC	O-0051170	0762	1
JONES ERNEST E	LTC	O-0080122	1166	1
JONES ERNEST D	LTC	O-0069955	1068	1
JONES ERWIN A	COL	O-0041528	0758	2
JONES ERWIN B	COL	O-0036168	0667	1
JONES FRANK A	COL	O-0005187	0450	1
JONES FRED E	LTC	O-0027232	0765	1
JONES GEORGE A A	COL	O-0014845	0854	1
JONES GEORGE M	B G	O-0019965	0968	1
JONES GEORGE W	LTC	O-0031521	0862	1
JONES GILBERT C	LTC	O-0064998	1064	1
JONES GORDON A	LTC	O-0031090	0263	1

NAME	GRADE	SVC NO	DATE RET MO YR	RET CODE
JONES H CRAMPTON	COL	0-0004441	0753	1
JONES HAROLD D	COL	0-0028772	0354	1
JONES HAROLD L	LTC	0-0043337	0965	1
JONES HARRIS	B G	0-0005222	0756	2
JONES HAZEL M	MAJ	N-0000744	1165	1
JONES HENRY C	COL	0-0014745	0251	1
JONES HENRY L C	M G	0-0003168	0246	2
JONES HERBERT M	M G	0-0012251	1058	1
JONES HERMAN A JR	COL	0-0021312	1066	1
JONES HOMER H	LTC	0-0080915	0368	1
JONES HOMER W	COL	0-0012529	0747	1
JONES JENNER G	COL	0-0019603	0657	1
JONES JOHN P JR	COL	0-0030807	0866	1
JONES JOHN T	LTC	0-0030687	1060	1
JONES KENNETH C	COL	0-0042119	0657	1
JONES KENNETH P	COL	0-0029720	1058	1
JONES LAURENCE W	COL	0-0045646	0765	1
JONES LAWRENCE M	COL	0-0008578	0537	1
JONES LEE G	LTC	0-0024757	0962	1
JONES LLOYD E JR	LTC	0-0025396	0963	1
JONES LOUIS R	LTC	0-0057214	0768	1
JONES LOUIS V	COL	0-0010153	0549	1
JONES MALCOLM D	COL	0-0016435	0656	1
JONES MARCUS E	COL	0-0010291	0753	2
JONES NELSON H	LTC	0-0069703	0367	1
JONES OPAL M	MAJ	N-0002404	1262	1
JONES PEGGY G	LTC	N-0000363	1160	1
JONES RALPH E	COL	0-0002659	0939	2
JONES RAYMOND G	COL	0-0024576	0168	1
JONES REMUS L	LTC	0-0406028	0763	1
JONES RICHARD A	COL	0-0007638	0353	2
JONES RICHARD I	COL	0-0030410	0463	1
JONES RICHARD W JR	LTC	0-0051090	1058	2
JONES ROBERT D	COL	0-0080918	1166	1
JONES ROBERT E	COL	0-0002766	0546	1
JONES ROBERT J	COL	0-0028970	0357	1
JONES SHERBERT B	LTC	0-0042988	0265	1
JONES STANLEY W	M G	0-0017747	0365	2
JONES THOMAS B	COL	0-0042919	1166	1
JONES THOMAS C	LTC	0-0020065	0757	1
JONES THOMAS R	LTC	0-0019331	0153	2
JONES THOMAS S	COL	0-0052403	0962	1
JONES THORNTON E	COL	0-0030214	0764	1
JONES VIRLYN Y	LTC	0-0030739	0664	1
JONES WALTER E	CW2	W-0901295	0244	2
JONES WAYLAND JR	COL	0-0035763	0967	1
JONES WERNER F	COL	0-0028850	0356	1
JONES WILLIAM D	LTC	OF-0105719	0768	1
JONES WILLIAM M	LTC	0-0037209	0665	1
JONES WILLIAM P	CW2	W-0901337	0946	1
JONES WILLIAM P JR	COL	0-0020546	0467	1
JONES WILLIAM S	LTC	0-0029402	0458	1
JONES WILLIE H H	COL	0-0039626	1059	1
JONES WINSTON A	LTC	0-0032602	0460	2
JONES WINSTON I	COL	0-0051954	1167	1
JONES WOODFIN G	COL	0-0003712	0547	2
JONES 3RD WILLIAM C	1LT	0-0026916	0246	2
JONSON WAYNE H	LTC	0-0037484	0160	2
JOOST HORST K	COL	0-0060353	0868	1
JORDAHN ERIK W	COL	0-0044060	1065	1
JORDAN EDGAR J	LTC	0-0021943	1047	2
JORDAN EDWARD F	LTC	0-0054028	0866	1
JORDAN FRANK B	COL	0-0003617	0651	1
JORDAN HAROLD P	LTC	0-0011771	0836	1
JORDAN HERBERT A	COL	0-0038795	0660	2
JORDAN HERBERT S	COL	0-0015389	1148	1
JORDAN HOWELL H	COL	0-0016906	0157	1
JORDAN LEWIS P	COL	0-0011988	0854	1
JORDAN MARY C	LTC	N-0000987	0965	1
JORDAN MARY E	MAJ	N-0000756	0368	1
JORDAN RALPH E	COL	0-0021911	0863	2
JORDAN RICHARD H	B G	0-0001647	0740	1
JORDAN WALTER E	COL	0-0041910	1061	1
JORDAN WILLIAM H	COL	0-0020249	1047	2
JORDAN WOODROW W	LTC	0-0080431	0565	1

NAME	GRADE	SVC NO	DATE RET MO YR	RET CODE
JORGENSEN NORMAN E	MAJ	0-0097928	0968	1
JORGENSON ARTHOR L	LTC	0-0032436	0859	1
JORGENSON GEORGE H	CW2	W-0902156	0149	1
JOSEPH DONALD J	COL	0-0060027	1067	1
JOSEPH EDWIN M	LTC	0-0028522	0567	1
JOSEPH HENRY B	COL	0-0029054	0159	1
JOSEPH JOHN T	COL	0-0033756	0966	1
JOSEPH ROBERT E	COL	0-0028836	0154	1
JOSEPHSON STANTON W	COL	0-0024745	0867	1
JOSEY CLAUDE K	CPT	0-0027433	1058	2
JOSLIN WILL D	COL	0-0031816	0464	1
JOSLYN CLYDE A	LTC	0-0049893	0264	1
JOST HARRY F	COL	0-0040292	0968	1
JOYCE CLAUDE R JR	COL	0-0042426	0862	1
JOYCE MAHLEN A	COL	0-0003644	0935	2
JOYCE THOMAS F	COL	0-0010204	1052	1
JOYCE WILLIAM A	LTC	0-0020386	1144	2
JOYNER CHARLES A	MAJ	0-0038560	0766	1
JOYNER RALPH L	LTC	0-0005586	0934	2
JUDD FLORENCE E	COL	N-0000232	0968	1
JUDSON PHILIP M	LTC	0-0030516	0963	1
JUDSON ROBERT R	COL	0-0039794	0961	1
JUDSON WILLIAM J	LTC	0-0031769	0562	1
JUDY JACKSON K	COL	0-0039825	0361	1
JULIAN LEONARD J	LTC	0-0051814	1164	1
JUMP KATHERINE	COL	N-0000341	0468	1
JUNGE EDWIN B	LTC	0-0059964	0866	1
JUNGERHELD WARREN S	LTC	0-0028662	0168	1
JURASH HELEN J	LTC	N-0000528	0456	1
JURDEN DELBERT A	LTC	0-0062241	0765	1
JURGENS KENNETH E	COL	0-0043496	0864	1
JUSKALJIAN GEORGE	COL	0-0032371	0567	1
JUSTICE LONZO D	MAJ	0-0038565	0165	1
KABRICH CHARLES E	COL	0-0039856	1063	1
KACHMAN EVELYN A	MAJ	N-0000343	0463	1
KACZMAROWSKI JEROME	LTC	0-0060454	0668	1
KADICK MISHA N	COL	0-0023444	0868	1
KADROVACH DAN G	LTC	0-0037613	0163	1
KAESER WILLIAM G	LTC	0-0042685	1263	1
KAESSER HERMAN H	COL	0-0019057	0155	1
KAHN WILBUR L	LTC	0-0026631	0764	1
KAIGLER JOHNATHON	COL	0-0029721	0662	1
KAISER CLIFFORD	COL	0-0028801	0355	1
KAISER CLIFFORD F	LTC	0-0029120	0957	2
KAISER EMMA S	MAJ	N-0000224	0260	1
KAISER JAMES L	COL	0-0024085	0968	2
KAISER MAURICE E	COL	0-0019165	0863	1
KAISER ROSALYN J	LTC	L-0000053	0459	1
KAIT HARRY C	COL	0-0029532	0361	1
KALE LESTER W	COL	0-0029815	1162	1
KALEY WILLIAM E	COL	0-0041818	1160	1
KALISTA CLIFFORD J	MAJ	0-0027038	0859	2
KALLIS STEPHEN A	LTC	0-0038687	0559	2
KAMARAS JOHN G	LTC	0-0028100	1166	1
KAMINSKIE ALEX	LTC	0-0051116	1058	2
KAMISH ROBERT J	COL	0-0029295	0964	1
KAMMERAAD ANGIE C	LTC	N-0001529	0566	1
KAMMERER MALCOLM R	COL	0-0016403	0656	1
KAMP ANTHONY M JR	LTC	0-0033482	0467	2
KAMPSCHROER FELIX	COL	0-0080432	0768	2
KAMY HARRY D	COL	0-0042321	0364	1
KANAGA CLARENCE J	COL	0-0012302	0-36	2
KANE ANDREW D	COL	0-0042073	1162	2
KANE CHARLES F	COL	0-0043046	1068	1
KANE FRANK R JR	LTC	0-0079874	0966	1
KANE GEORGE W	LTC	0-0055446	0863	1
KANE HARLAND M	CW4	W-0903334	0360	1
KANE JOHN H	COL	0-0016492	0445	2
KANE LEO M	LTC	0-0024569	0965	1
KANE MICHAEL JR	COL	0-0031476	0467	1
KANE O NEILL K	COL	0-0018150	0654	2
KANE STEPHEN W	COL	0-0041754	1061	1
KANTAK GREGORY H	CW4	W-0903335	0360	1
KAPEC ANDREW J	LTC	0-0062278	0568	1
KARNS ANDRE M	LTC	0-0061974	0868	1

NAME	GRADE	SVC NO	DATE RET MO YR	RET CODE
KARNS ROBERT H	MAJ	0-0080125	0463	1
KARPEN RAYMOND J	COL	0-0041764	0764	1
KARR GUY A JR	LTC	0-0080922	1166	1
KARRER ROBERT J	COL	0-0051195	0659	2
KARRICK SAMUEL N	COL	0-0009256	0749	1
KASDORF WALTER W	LTC	0-0080723	0966	1
KASEL JOSEPH T	LTC	0-0043148	1068	1
KASPER ROBERT J	COL	0-0021084	0264	1
KASPER WILLIAM M	COL	0-0023210	0465	1
KASSE CARL M	CW4	W-0901337	0665	1
KAST KENNETH F JR	LTC	0-0062239	0968	1
KASTNER ALFRED F	B G	0-0014932	0954	1
KATES ROBERT C	LTC	0-0024787	0167	1
KATHERMAN ELLIOTT T	COL	0-0053023	0567	1
KATIN JOSEPH G	COL	0-0043758	0761	1
KATSARSKY SLAFTCHO	COL	0-0039832	0563	2
KATTNER STANLEY J	LTC	0-0080925	0568	1
KATZ HENRY J	COL	0-0020138	0766	1
KATZ PHILLIP P	LTC	0-0059957	0467	2
KATZ SIDNEY	LTC	0-0026327	0763	1
KAUFFMAN KATHREEN L	MAJ	N-0002127	0360	1
KAUFFMAN MILDRED B	MAJ	N-0002274	1063	1
KAUFFMAN ROY K	COL	0-0018598	0561	1
KAUFMAN LEE S	COL	0-0032388	0266	1
KAUFMAN PHILLIP	LTC	0-0063092	1166	2
KAWAMURA NORMAN I	1LT	0-0092596	1263	2
KAY HELEN F	MAJ	N-0002063	0162	1
KAY HERBERT J	COL	0-0080926	1268	2
KAY LETHIE L	LTC	N-0002508	1168	1
KAY PAUL J	MAJ	0-0060126	0962	1
KAYLOR JOHN P	COL	0-0016909	0757	1
KAYLOR ROY	COL	0-0016462	0656	1
KAYSER HAROLD P	COL	0-0004540	0749	1
KEAGY CHARLES O JR	CW4	W-0902088	0968	1
KEAGY ROBERT B	COL	0-0024072	0963	1
KEAN WILLIAM B	LTG	0-0012470	0954	1
KEANE SYLVESTER	CPT	0-0015172	0139	1
KEANE WALTER J	MAJ	0-0069961	1164	1
KEANE WILLIAM M	COL	0-0038702	0260	1
KEARNEY CHARLES F	COL	0-0017771	0659	2
KEARNEY LESTER A	LTC	0-0033010	0861	1
KEARNS EDWIN B JR	B G	0-0016224	0655	1
KEASEY CHARLES R	LTC	0-0038736	0261	1
KEATING FRANK A	M G	0-0005360	0850	1
KEATING FRANK W	LTC	0-0038929	1058	1
KEATING JOHN G	2LT	0-0024167	0142	2
KEATING JOHN W	B G	0-0018897	0862	2
KEATING JOSEPH W	COL	0-0019800	0465	1
KEATING MARIE A	MAJ	N-0000671	1166	1
KEATINGE JOHN H	COL	0-0007194	1149	1
KEATLEY EDWIN E	COL	0-0007019	1150	1
KEAYS DOROTHY B	MAJ	N-0002352	0558	2
KEDERICH CHARLES H	LTC	0-0043556	1062	1
KEEBAUGH DONALD R	LTC	0-0083096	0667	2
KEEFE JAMES H	LTC	0-0043634	1166	1
KEEFE JOHN L	COL	0-0029080	0359	1
KEEFE MARY E	MAJ	N-0001451	1267	1
KEEFER LOREN P	LTC	0-0038492	0368	1
KEEGAN THOMAS F JR	LTC	0-0060676	0665	1
KEEHN KENT	LTC	0-0028336	0867	1
KEELAN VIDA B	CPT	M-0010056	0955	1
KEELEY JOHN T	COL	0-0012437	1148	1
KEEN HUGH B	COL	0-0003509	0846	2
KEENAN JOHN W	CW3	W-0901630	1043	2
KEENER ERMA D	MAJ	L-0000303	1060	1
KEENER ERVIN L	COL	0-0029572	0161	1
KEENEY PAUL A	COL	0-0029143	1055	2
KEESEY CHARLES R	CW4	W-0903340	0157	1
KEETH EUGENE L	LTC	0-0034687	0464	1
KEFAUVER LLOYD A	COL	0-0003058	0946	2
KEGERREIS JOHN B	COL	0-0031242	0764	2
KEHM HAROLD D	COL	0-0015138	0854	1
KEHOE EMMETT L	COL	0-0019613	1163	1
KEHOE FRANK M	LTC	0-0043380	0764	1
KEIFER FREDERICK	LTC	0-0026927	0865	1

NAME	GRADE	SVC NO	DATE RET MO YR	RET CODE
KEILER REEVE D	LTC	0-0015857	0346	2
KEISER LAURENCE B	M G	0-0005316	0153	2
KEISH WILLIAM J	COL	0-0041885	1159	1
KEISLER DAVID S	COL	0-0032657	0465	1
KEITH CATHERINE	MAJ	N-0000662	0461	1
KEITH HUBERT W	COL	0-0009954	1046	1
KEITH JAMES F	LTC	0-0080930	0567	1
KEITHLY THOMAS G	COL	0-0041657	0260	1
KELEHER REYNOLDS R	LTC	0-0023941	0162	1
KELL ELMER A JR	COL	0-0038699	1061	1
KELLAM PAUL	COL	0-0011553	0854	1
KELLEHER EDWARD D JR	LTC	0-0099668	0868	1
KELLEHER GERALD C	B G	0-0038750	1063	1
KELLEHER JAMES E	COL	0-0025611	0767	1
KELLER ANDREW K	LTC	0-0026474	0765	1
KELLER HENRY A	COL	0-0039637	0560	1
KELLER KENNETH R	LTC	0-0033248	0762	1
KELLER MORRIS J	LTC	0-0061368	0968	1
KELLER PAUL F	COL	0-0018923	0762	2
KELLER ROBERT S	1LT	0-0061665	1153	2
KELLER WILLIAM S	LTC	0-0011957	0348	2
KELLERS FRANK	COL	0-0051432	0762	1
KELLEY DONALD C	LTC	0-0020387	1057	1
KELLEY JOSEPH J	CW4	W-0904138	0263	1
KELLEY LAURA C	MAJ	N-0000078	1055	1
KELLEY MARTIN L	CPT	0-0006028	0934	2
KELLEY PAUL A	LTC	0-0028688	1066	1
KELLEY ROBERT R	COL	0-0020984	1060	1
KELLEY SAMUEL P	LTC	0-0018187	0650	1
KELLEY THOMAS W	LTC	0-0061240	0965	1
KELLNER FRED W	LTC	0-0032358	0767	1
KELLOGG DIMITRI A	COL	0-0025433	0868	1
KELLOGG DOUGLAS S	COL	0-0016287	0455	2
KELLOGG JAMES P	LTC	0-0084048	1066	1
KELLY BURNIS M	COL	0-0019950	0955	1
KELLY CHARLEE L	LTC	L-0000024	0256	2
KELLY CLYDE	LTC	0-0007970	1033	2
KELLY DAVID C	COL	0-0006887	1048	1
KELLY EDMONDE B	COL	0-0020544	0266	1
KELLY ELBERT	MAJ	0-0015028	0336	2
KELLY ELLSWORTH	COL	0-0020488	0661	1
KELLY EVANDER F JR	COL	0-0051377	0263	1
KELLY HAROLD L JR	COL	0-0052292	0761	1
KELLY HENRY E	COL	0-0010286	0654	1
KELLY HENRY J	COL	0-0041974	0162	1
KELLY JAMES C	LTC	0-0044863	0765	1
KELLY JAMES H	CW4	W-0903343	0465	1
KELLY JOHN J	COL	0-0022185	0759	1
KELLY JOHN J JR	LTC	0-0025869	0764	1
KELLY JOHN P A	LTC	0-0022154	0458	1
KELLY JOHN S	COL	0-0019647	0557	1
KELLY JOSEPH E	1LT	0-0012002	1030	2
KELLY JOSEPH M	LTC	0-0058012	0763	1
KELLY LEM M	COL	0-0032378	0867	2
KELLY LEO F	COL	0-0050895	0255	1
KELLY MARY E	LTC	L-0000341	0867	1
KELLY PATRICK	COL	0-0008724	0644	2
KELLY PAUL B	B G	0-0012121	0551	2
KELLY PAUL C	COL	0-0012825	0934	2
KELLY PETER K	COL	0-0004703	0652	1
KELLY RALPH W	CW4	W-0903344	0466	1
KELLY ROBERT M	LTC	0-0038367	0866	1
KELLY SAMUEL G	LTC	0-0038664	0458	1
KELLY THOMAS D	LTC	0-0065420	1066	1
KELLY THOMAS J	CW2	W-0901627	0847	1
KELSEY PHILIP R	LTC	0-0080932	0165	1
KELSO MINOR L	LTC	0-0028745	0268	1
KELTNER EDGAR H	COL	0-0008241	0253	2
KELTON EDWIN C	COL	0-0003786	0244	2
KEMBLE FRANKLIN JR	COL	0-0019418	0762	1
KEMBLE JOHN W	LTC	0-0020398	0756	1
KEMM ROBERT R	LTC	0-0052139	0366	1
KEMMAN LAWRENCE H	COL	0-0038616	0556	1
KEMP DONALD C	CPT	0-0010020	0135	2
KEMP HERBERT E	LTC	0-0025742	0263	1

NAME	GRADE	SVC NO	DATE RET MO YR	RET CODE
KEMP JAMES H	COL	O-0043382	0963	1
KEMP LEILA	MAJ	N-0000379	0261	1
KEMP ROBERT B	LTC	O-0040040	0862	1
KEMP ROBERT K	LTC	O-0031344	0762	1
KEMPHER LARRY W	CW4	W-0904140	0155	2
KENDALL CHARLES B	COL	O-0004101	0152	1
KENDALL PAUL G	COL	O-0015419	0953	2
KENDALL PAUL W	LTG	O-0012199	0855	2
KENDALL QUENTIN L	COL	O-0029745	0762	1
KENDALL REX S	COL	O-0043123	0464	1
KENDALL VICTOR S JR	MAJ	O-0032521	1159	2
KENDALL WILLIAM H	COL	O-0015714	0954	2
KENDERDINE JOHN M	B G	O-0043446	1167	1
KENDRICK DOUGLAS B	M G	O-0020511	0567	1
KENDRICK ROBERT C	LTC	O-0068021	0668	2
KENDRICK WALLACE M	COL	O-0032615	0768	1
KENGLE LANSFORD F JR	LTC	O-0025975	0764	1
KENNA GEORGE W	COL	O-0084376	0666	1
KENNEDY AGNES M	MAJ	L-0000171	0264	1
KENNEDY BERNARD P	CPT	O-0014380	0-19	2
KENNEDY CHESTER E	COL	O-0024242	0264	1
KENNEDY ELMER B	COL	O-0020900	0965	1
KENNEDY GRAFTON L	COL	O-0006675	0346	1
KENNEDY GREGORY R	COL	O-0030847	0265	1
KENNEDY HAROLD P	COL	O-0046534	0767	1
KENNEDY HARRY V	CW2	W-0901353	0448	2
KENNEDY JOHN T	B G	O-0002360	0146	2
KENNEDY JOSEPH	COL	O-0005463	0246	1
KENNEDY JULIEN C	LTC	O-0057382	0264	1
KENNEDY JUSTUS C	LTC	O-0043856	0767	1
KENNEDY MARGARET K	MAJ	N-0001661	0463	1
KENNEDY NEAL D	CPT	O-0058463	0764	1
KENNEDY PAUL R	LTC	O-0035563	0664	1
KENNEDY ROBERT J	LTC	O-0050610	1166	1
KENNEDY ROBERT S	COL	O-0020780	0967	1
KENNEDY ROBERT W	LTC	O-0060729	0268	1
KENNEDY STANLEY Y JR	COL	O-0037179	0468	1
KENNETT WALTER H	COL	O-0016352	1153	1
KENNEY MAX W	CW4	W-0903349	0657	1
KENNINGTON ROBERT E	LTC	O-0023623	1161	1
KENNON BARBARA L	MAJ	R-0010100	1068	1
KENNON BLAISDELL	COL	O-0008191	0152	2
KENNON WILLIAM U	COL	O-0079876	0868	1
KENNY EUGENE A	COL	O-0018193	0760	1
KENT EDWARD F	COL	O-0020909	0263	1
KENT FRANK J	COL	O-0033087	0868	1
KENT HAROLD R	COL	O-0034103	0767	1
KENT HENRY T	COL	O-0009053	0747	2
KENT ISABEL M	MAJ	N-0001973	1061	1
KENT ROSE	COL	O-0006568	0251	1
KENWORTHY MAX R	COL	O-0076841	1268	1
KEOGH WILLIAM T	LTC	O-0033742	0861	1
KER HOWARD	M G	O-0015518	0562	1
KERANEN CHARLES M	LTC	O-0051578	0163	1
KERBER CHARLES J	CW3	W-0906828	1060	1
KERCHER FERRIS A	LTC	O-0033456	0661	1
KERIG DWAN V	LTC	O-0066172	0967	1
KERKERING JOHN H	COL	O-0020120	0765	1
KERLIN HENRY C	COL	O-0029463	1060	1
KERN THOMAS F	COL	O-0009306	0753	1
KERN TRUMAN H	COL	O-0042309	1163	1
KERN WILLIAM R	COL	O-0019566	0864	2
KERNAN MELVIN M	COL	O-0040236	0863	1
KERNAN WILLIAM F	COL	O-0006688	0844	2
KERNAN WILLIAM H	COL	O-0012891	1045	2
KERNKAMP MELVIN W	COL	O-0042923	1060	1
KERR DAVID R	COL	O-0004780	0151	1
KERR EDWIN B	MAJ	O-0027796	0759	2
KERR GEORGE M	LTC	O-0029319	0662	1
KERR GERALD L JR	LTC	O-0041033	0364	1
KERR JAMES W	LTC	O-0025417	0264	1
KERR JOHN H	CW4	W-0904143	0366	1
KERR MAURICE S	COL	O-0010973	0853	1
KERR OTTO JR	LTC	O-0063861	1068	1
KERSEY IRWIN J	LTC	O-0078912	0768	1
KERSEY SIDNEY P	LTC	O-0079877	0865	1
KERSH HENRY L	COL	O-0011579	0852	2
KERSHAW CLIFFORD G	COL	O-0010106	0148	1
KERWIN BERNARD F	LTC	O-0037567	0468	1
KESSINGER HOWARD E	B G	O-0015692	0854	1
KESSLER ROBERT H	COL	O-0020178	0466	1
KESTHELY LOUIS J	CW4	W-0906829	0464	1
KETCHAM EDWARD P JR	COL	O-0038963	1167	1
KETTLETY RAYMOND F	CW4	W-0903352	0463	1
KEUKER CHRISTOPHE	CPT	O-0096007	1067	2
KEVIN HUGH W	COL	O-0041583	0559	1
KEY GENIE	CPT	N-0000843	1157	2
KEY HERBERT L JR	LTC	O-0054858	0764	1
KEY JOHN D	LTC	O-0006484	0539	1
KEY MARY J	MAJ	L-0000004	0753	1
KEY ROBERT C	MAJ	O-0028072	0162	2
KEY WILMA H	MAJ	L-0000019	1054	1
KEYES GEORGE W	LTC	O-0065619	0667	1
KEYES LEWIS H	COL	O-0038765	0464	1
KEYES RICHARD W	COL	O-0031467	0267	1
KEYES ROY V SR	1LT	O-0017643	0638	2
KEYS EDNA M	MAJ	N-0001690	0965	1
KEYSER GEORGE V	B G	O-0012089	0354	1
KEYSER ROBERT W	LTC	O-0033355	0361	1
KIBLER EDGAR H JR	COL	O-0019039	1059	1
KIBLER GEORGE N	COL	O-0029490	0161	2
KIDD WILLIAM T	COL	O-0048216	0867	1
KIDWELL FRANCES P	MAJ	L-0000222	0857	1
KIDWELL GAYLORD B	COL	O-0012029	0553	1
KIEFER HOMER W	M G	O-0012701	0753	2
KIEFFER PIERRE V JR	COL	O-0020122	0264	1
KIEHL PAUL V	COL	O-0026397	0368	2
KIEL ARTHUR G	COL	O-0042199	0663	1
KIELSMEIER SAMUEL G	COL	O-0009596	1046	2
KIELTY JOSEPH A	LTC	O-0015669	1046	1
KIELY CLARA M	LTC	N-0000101	0263	1
KIERNAN EDWARD F	CW4	W-0903356	1268	1
KIERNAN JOSEPH F	CW4	W-0903357	0363	1
KIERSCH THEODORE A	COL	O-0024386	0761	1
KIFNER DANIEL R	LTC	O-0037530	0962	1
KIGHT HARRY D	COL	O-0056904	1167	1
KIGHT JONATHAN M	LTC	O-0044919	1167	1
KILBOURNE JOSEPH C	CPT	O-0012114	1034	2
KILBURN CHARLES S	B G	O-0005295	1146	1
KILBURN JOHN W	LTC	O-0041700	0456	1
KILCOYNE JOHN T	COL	O-0019651	0762	1
KILDAY THOMAS T	COL	O-0019288	0759	1
KILGORE FLOYD V	COL	O-0008912	0150	2
KILIAN MYRTLE M	MAJ	N-0002372	0460	1
KILLELEA WILLIAM G	LTC	O-0051174	1162	1
KILLEN WADE D	COL	O-0011131	0949	1
KILLIAN JOSEPH O	COL	O-0019370	0764	1
KILLIAN NOE C	MAJ	O-0004892	1029	2
KILLIAN WILLIAM H	LTC	O-0007500	1022	2
KILLILAE WALTER	COL	O-0025017	0968	1
KILLMAN HENRY P	LTC	O-0032538	1059	1
KILLOUGH JAMES S	LTC	O-0029697	0763	1
KILLOY DAVID H	CPT	OF-0102070	1068	2
KILPATRICK WILLARD H	COL	O-0041895	0656	1
KILROY RAYMOND F	1LT	O-0012413	0522	2
KILROY VIRGINIA K	MAJ	N-0000040	1047	1
KIMBALL CURTIS Y	COL	O-0032852	0763	1
KIMBALL MORTON W	LTC	O-0047178	1267	1
KIMBALL RALPH S	LTC	O-0003424	0138	1
KIMBALL RICHARD	COL	O-0042607	0665	1
KIMBALL ROBERT E	COL	O-0024586	0167	1
KIMBEL JOHN F	LTC	O-0026480	1165	1
KIMBRELL GORDON T	B G	O-0020851	0867	1
KIMBROUGH JAMES M JR	COL	O-0019816	0865	1
KIMM VIRGIL M	LTC	O-0016849	0252	1
KIMMEL MANNING M JR	COL	O-0003558	1044	2
KIMMELL JOHN R JR	COL	O-0019291	0554	1
KIMMET MARIE	MAJ	N-0002037	0559	1
KIMMICK LEONARD JR	LTC	O-0060558	0967	1
KIMMITT JOSEPH S	COL	O-0036343	0266	1
KIMPTON MARGARET A	LTC	L-0000211	0359	2
KIMPTON THEODORE R	COL	O-0019226	0760	1
KINARD WILLIAM H JR	COL	O-0020180	0865	1
KINBERGER ALBERT G	COL	O-0008508	0846	2
KINCAID LEONARD C	COL	O-0031732	0864	1
KINCY WILLIAM R JR	COL	O-0078916	0567	1
KIND HENRY A	COL	O-0020986	0965	1
KINDERMAN HAROLD W	MAJ	O-0010749	1036	2
KINDERVATER ERNEST A	COL	O-0005727	0649	1
KINDRED WORTH L	COL	O-0029492	0758	1
KING ARCHIBALD	COL	O-0003323	0842	1
KING ARTHUR R	MAJ	O-0024915	0846	2
KING CARY J JR	COL	O-0015574	0654	1
KING DALE M	COL	O-0033644	0660	1
KING DAVID C	CW4	W-0901805	0354	1
KING DICK A	COL	O-0030438	0863	1
KING EDGAR	B G	O-0002288	0146	1
KING EDGAR W	COL	O-0009705	0954	2
KING EDWARD H	COL	O-0030646	0267	1
KING ELNOR L	1LT	O-0056774	0451	2
KING FLORENCE H	MAJ	N-0002427	0265	1
KING FRANCIS J	LTC	O-0040265	0666	1
KING GEORGE A	COL	O-0005530	0549	2
KING GEORGE L	COL	O-0007865	0846	1
KING GLENNIS L	MAJ	O-0033661	0363	1
KING GROVER C	LTC	O-0094096	1268	1
KING HARRIET J	MAJ	N-0002732	1267	1
KING HARRISON	COL	O-0019078	0746	2
KING HARRY L JR	1LT	O-0027133	0448	2
KING HELEN E	MAJ	N-0002409	0463	1
KING J CRAIG	MAJ	O-0013320	0420	2
KING JAMES B	LTC	O-0046196	0266	1
KING JAMES I	B G	O-0018534	0160	2
KING JOHN H JR	COL	O-0020036	0755	1
KING JOHN L	CPT	O-0025358	0246	2
KING JOHN L JR	LTC	O-0031491	0465	1
KING JOSEPH C	COL	O-0002148	1142	2
KING KENDALL F	CW4	W-0903359	0365	1
KING LAURENCE T	COL	O-0030713	0566	1
KING LEMUEL G	LTC	O-0058465	0268	1
KING MARY L	LTC	N-0000321	0761	1
KING NORMAN E	LTC	O-0022287	0759	1
KING RALPH O	COL	O-0020115	0956	1
KING ROBERT A	LTC	O-0050797	0566	1
KING ROBERT W	COL	O-0051864	0365	1
KING ROGER D	LTC	O-0044600	1161	2
KING ROSEWELL H	COL	O-0028962	0158	1
KING RUTH A	LTC	L-0000534	0968	1
KING RYAN W	COL	O-0079708	1263	1
KING THEODORE T	B G	O-0028889	1056	1
KING WARREN J	LTC	O-0042850	0464	2
KING WARREN S	COL	O-0023413	1068	2
KING WILLIAM I	COL	O-0036153	0566	1
KINGHORN ALAN	LTC	O-0066175	0768	1
KINGMAN ALLEN F	B G	O-0004749	0553	1
KINGMAN ALLEN F JR	LTC	O-0057556	0265	1
KINGMAN DAN C	LTC	O-0032045	1166	1
KINKE EMIL F	COL	O-0018034	0755	1
KINLEY GORDON L	LTC	O-0065693	0768	1
KINLEY MILES A	COL	O-0051718	0166	1
KINNAIRD RUBY L	MAJ	N-0000231	0963	1
KINNE HARRY L JR	COL	O-0029583	0761	1
KINNEY FREDERICK	CW4	W-0903360	0767	2
KINNEY OLIVER G	COL	O-0032067	0661	1
KINNISON LOIS F	MAJ	N-0000245	1264	1
KINNISON PAUL	COL	O-0022581	0666	1
KINSELLA HARRY F	COL	O-0021424	1266	1
KINSEY NANCY B	MAJ	N-0002025	0360	1
KINSLER DAVID E	COL	O-0041759	0664	1
KINSLOW ALBERT V	COL	O-0030808	0966	1
KINSON RICHARD L	LTC	O-0043955	1262	1
KINTNER WILLIAM R	COL	O-0023068	0861	1
KINTZ FRANCIS P	COL	O-0018937	1058	1
KIONKA JOHN	LTC	O-0051642	0960	2
KIRBY HARRY C	LTC	O-0017105	1044	2
KIRBY LEE M	LTC	O-0022048	0862	1
KIRBY PAULINE	COL	N-0000035	0757	1
KIRBY PIERRE P	LTC	O-0060624	1164	1
KIRBY WILLIAM F	COL	O-0028906	0557	1
KIRBY-SMITH EDMUND	COL	O-0021745	0167	1
KIRCHHOFF ARTHUR A G	COL	O-0016396	0656	1
KIRCHOFF WAYNE E	COL	O-0043243	0866	1
KIRK JAMES	M G	O-0003372	0252	2
KIRK RAYMOND L	LTC	O-0087822	0467	1
KIRK RICHARD L	LTC	O-0065276	1267	1
KIRK ROBERT P	COL	O-0029710	0862	1
KIRK WARREN M	COL	O-0065674	1167	1
KIRKMAN BYRON J	CW4	W-0903363	0856	1
KIRKMAN LEWIS W	COL	O-0020066	0546	2
KIRKPATRICK BYRON M	COL	O-0024257	1268	1
KIRKPATRICK C L	COL	O-0018642	0759	1
KIRKPATRICK HARRY F	COL	O-0039807	0463	1
KIRKPATRICK MABLE	MAJ	N-0002721	0868	2
KIRKPATRICK TRAVIS M	MAJ	O-0059924	0165	1
KIRKSEY FLAYIOUS W	CPT	O-0060363	0556	2
KIRKWOOD WALTER V JR	LTC	O-0079878	0968	1
KIRPATRICK ELMER E	COL	O-0017660	1058	1
KIRSCH JOHN C	LTC	O-0063435	0768	1
KIRSNER HARRY	COL	O-0011601	1146	1
KIRSTEN ELWYN N	COL	O-0020637	0560	1
KIRTLEY EDWIN L	COL	O-0024355	1164	1
KISER SHERMAN L	COL	O-0003498	0948	1
KISER WILLIAM M	LTC	O-0028329	0866	1
KISH WILLIAM E	LTC	O-0056818	0563	1
KITCHEN LLOYD	LTC	O-0065466	1166	1
KITCHINGS BOYCE D JR	COL	O-0041565	0159	1
KITSON ALFRED P	COL	O-0010043	0147	2
KITTRELL CLARK	COL	O-0005228	1049	1
KLASING WALDEMAR J	MAJ	O-0031478	1157	1
KLEFF PIERRE A	COL	O-0039799	0960	1
KLEIN BERTHA J	MAJ	N-0000481	0762	1
KLEIN EDWARD	CW4	W-0904144	0761	1
KLEIN JOHN A	M G	O-0007536	1056	2
KLEIN JOHN H JR	MAJ	O-0058176	0966	1
KLEINMANN MORTIMER V	LTC	O-0064975	1265	1
KLEIST ERWIN H	LTC	O-0026504	1066	2
KLEMM HELEN F	MAJ	R-0010073	0462	1
KLEMP HUBERT E	COL	O-0051076	0360	1
KLEMP IRENE J	LTC	N-0000556	0361	1
KLEPINGER WALTER J	COL	O-0014839	0854	1
KLEVESAHL FRED C	LTC	O-0078920	0368	1
KLIM HENRY L	CPT	O-0060458	1163	1
KLIMA LAWRENCE J	LTC	O-0027188	0966	1
KLINCK EARL	COL	O-0028955	1057	1
KLINE EARL G	COL	O-0046466	0767	1
KLINE NICK	CW2	W-0901797	0748	1
KLINE ROBERT P	COL	O-0039780	0762	1
KLINE ROLAND A	LTC	O-0028747	0768	1
KLINETOP HOWARD A	COL	O-0039798	1262	1
KLINGAMAN MURIEL B	LTC	N-0000276	0767	1
KLINT EDMUND L	LTC	O-0042970	0263	1
KLOCK KARL T JR	COL	O-0020123	0965	2
KLOEPFER HANS E	COL	O-0006557	0146	2
KLOUS DAVID D	COL	O-0031899	0468	1
KLUGE FRED	CW4	W-0903366	0658	1
KLUNDER JOSEPH D	LTC	O-0052947	0262	1
KLUNK MARK L B	COL	O-0023273	0868	1
KNAPP ANNE E	MAJ	N-0002249	0661	1
KNAPP ERNEST C	COL	O-0038684	0660	1
KNAPP RAYMOND H	LTC	O-0042546	0261	1
KNAPP ROBERT H	LTC	O-0010234	0142	2
KNAUER JOHN G	COL	O-0006552	0653	1
KNEEPKENS JOHN A	LTC	O-0078651	0168	1
KNEISL JERRY A	MAJ	O-0060499	0963	1
KNEYSE WALTER A	COL	O-0042227	0863	1
KNICKERBOCKER BARBAR	MAJ	J-0000033	0866	1
KNICKERBOCKER MAX E	LTC	O-0041151	0764	1
KNIER ALBERT A	LTC	O-0051137	0258	1
KNIER ALOYSIUS M	LTC	O-0068368	0965	1
KNIGHT ALFRED C	LTC	O-0029684	0152	1

NAME	GRADE	SVC NO	DATE RET MO YR	RET CODE
KNIGHT ANDREW T	COL	0-0008052	0846	2
KNIGHT CHARLES C JR	LTC	0-0009073	0142	1
KNIGHT CONSTANCE	MAJ	N-0002206	0468	1
KNIGHT DANIEL H	COL	0-0014735	0-45	2
KNIGHT DARCE R	COL	0-0043487	0268	1
KNIGHT EDWIN T	COL	0-0021380	1165	1
KNIGHT GLENNA E	MAJ	L-0000220	0257	1
KNIGHT GORDON C	CW4	W-0904145	0465	2
KNIGHT JOHN J	CW4	W-0903367	0155	1
KNIGHT LONNIE W	COL	0-0030895	1165	1
KNIGHT PAUL R	COL	0-0008317	0847	1
KNIGHT REMI C	1LT	0-0014403	0120	2
KNIPE WILLIS H	LTC	0-0050829	0866	1
KNIPS ALBERTA H	MAJ	N-0000971	1061	1
KNOBELOCH WILFRED	COL	0-0042464	1264	1
KNOLL ERNEST L	LTC	0-0054304	1168	2
KNOLL WILLIAM F	LTC	0-0043535	0163	1
KNOPF STACY	COL	0-0004919	1045	2
KNORP DANIEL W	LTC	0-0070401	0968	1
KNOTT JOSEPH W	LTC	0-0031350	1064	1
KNOTT WILLIAM C	COL	0-0018922	0856	1
KNOWLES WENDELL P	COL	0-0023953	0865	1
KNOWLTON BRUCE R JR	CPT	0-0059861	0962	1
KNOWLTON HOMER C	LTC	0-0076803	0767	1
KNOWLTON JOSEPH L	COL	0-0023869	0167	1
KNOWLTON STEWART H	COL	0-0030159	0464	1
KNOX ALICE T A	MAJ	R-0010062	0558	1
KNOX CAMERON	COL	0-0031815	0461	1
KNOX JASPER N	COL	0-0018283	0946	2
KNOX JOHN C	COL	0-0050497	0753	1
KNOX OHIO	LTC	0-0030572	1163	1
KNOX WILLIAM W	LTC	0-0041558	0257	1
KNUDSEN CHARLES F SR	LTC	0-0027829	0965	1
KNUDSEN CHRISTIAN	COL	0-0012125	1046	2
KNUTSON RALPH M	CW4	W-0906835	0563	1
KNUTSON SIDNEY A	LTC	0-0036199	1062	1
KOBAYASHI THOMAS M	COL	0-0052745	1268	1
KOCH ARTHUR L	LTC	0-0006389	0838	1
KOCH BRUCE C	LTC	0-0025947	0664	1
KOCH HARLAN G	LTC	0-0028725	0766	1
KOCH OSCAR W	B G	0-0010851	0954	2
KOCH OTTO R JR	COL	0-0032074	1068	1
KOCH RALPH A	COL	0-0015830	0854	1
KOCHEVAR JOHN H	COL	0-0016867	0757	1
KOCHLI FRED JR	LTC	0-0027611	0365	1
KOECKERT WILLIAM F	MAJ	0-0069715	0865	1
KOEHN CARL J	LTC	0-0052048	0264	1
KOENIG EGMONT F	B G	0-0004700	0448	1
KOENIG WILLIAM A JR	LTC	0-0040906	0868	1
KOERBEL FREDERICK	COL	0-0010007	1048	1
KOERNER PAUL M	LTC	0-0040263	0666	2
KOERNER RUDULPH C JR	LTC	0-0052211	0163	2
KOESTER FRED W	COL	0-0009772	1047	1
KOHARI JOSEPH J	CW4	W-0903371	1168	1
KOHLER DONALD J	LTC	0-0027203	0766	1
KOHLOSS FABIUS H	COL	0-0010244	0846	2
KOHLS CARL W	COL	0-0018575	0761	1
KOHN JOSEPH P	COL	0-0005860	0753	2
KOHNSTAMM JOSEPH W	MAJ	0-0040645	1063	2
KOLB ROLAND L	COL	0-0025184	0167	1
KOLETTY JOHN W	COL	0-0040230	0763	1
KOLSTER KENNETH K	LTC	0-0032886	0457	1
KOLTVET ANNA	MAJ	N-0000119	1060	1
KONKOL RALPH E	LTC	0-0052868	0862	2
KONOPASKA ROYDEN A	COL	0-0030787	0864	2
KONOPKA URBAN S	LTC	0-0041761	0462	2
KONVICKA HENRY H	LTC	0-0088772	1067	1
KOOKEN JOHN J D	COL	0-0034743	0364	1
KOOKEN WILLIS F	COL	0-0043658	1066	1
KOON CARL C JR	CW2	W-0903373	0261	1
KOONS RAYMOND H	CW3	W-0903374	0660	1
KORCSAK ARPAD A	COL	0-0021167	1068	2
KORCSAK PETER J	COL	0-0019440	0964	2
KORF JOHN B	MAJ	0-0040812	0863	1
KORITSCHKIF CARL F	LTC	0-0080433	0762	1
KORCHEK LOUIS	CW4	W-0903376	0467	2
KORCHIN LEO	COL	0-0061173	1267	1
KOREMAN EDWARD H	COL	0-0038953	1061	1
KORNFEIND HELEN A	LTC	N-0000105	0860	1
KOSCH LEWIS F	COL	0-0006511	0947	1
KOSCHMEDER JULIA F	MAJ	N-0002307	0467	1
KOSCIELNIAK ADAM A	LTC	0-0018159	0252	1
KOSHKO JOHN R JR	LTC	0-0043974	0767	1
KOSIOREK STEPHEN T	LTC	0-0023772	0262	1
KOSMACKI LEON F	LTC	0-0024194	0967	1
KOSTER ALFRED M	COL	0-0029796	1062	2
KOSTORA LEE H	LTC	0-0031598	0264	1
KOSZEWSKI STEPHEN S	COL	0-0015654	0854	1
KOTHE HERMAN H	COL	0-0029194	0261	1
KOTICK OTTMAR F	COL	0-0028924	0757	1
KOTOWSKI EVA T	MAJ	N-0002133	0560	1
KOTTE BERNARD J	COL	0-0029172	1059	1
KOTZEBUE ALBERT L	LTC	0-0056184	0767	1
KOUNS CHARLES W	COL	0-0022129	0861	1
KOUP ELMER L	COL	0-0041999	0262	1
KOVACH FRANK Z	LTC	0-0080434	0765	1
KOVACIC EMMA C	MAJ	N-0001298	0566	1
KOVACS LESLIE B	COL	0-0051697	0266	2
KOVACS LOUIS	WO1	W-0901461	1049	1
KOVAR PAUL J	COL	0-0058240	0967	1
KOWALSKI FRANK JR	COL	0-0018086	0858	2
KOZAK EDWIN J	COL	0-0043129	1266	1
KOZIEL RICHARD J	LTC	0-0065235	0868	1
KOZIOL JEAN B	MAJ	N-0001603	0468	1
KRACHT ARTHUR N	COL	0-0020923	0861	1
KRAFFT HENRY L	COL	0-0004043	1046	1
KRAFT IDELLE D	MAJ	N-0001056	0762	1
KRAFTSCHENK DOROTHY	LTC	N-0000287	0967	1
KRAMER ARTHUR	COL	0-0020140	0657	1
KRAMER JOHN J	LTC	0-0031221	0353	2
KRAMER THEODORE JR	LTC	0-0079881	0965	2
KRAMERS JOHN T	COL	0-0033890	0766	1
KRAMOLIS MARIE C	MAJ	N-0002358	0360	1
KRAMS CORTLANDT	COL	0-0010224	0553	2
KRANYAK LOUIS W	LTC	0-0063296	0268	1
KRANZ JUSTUS W	LTC	0-0028933	0955	1
KRAUS EDWARD	COL	0-0019789	0861	1
KRAUS HANNAH	1LT	R-0000652	0146	1
KRAUS WALTER F	COL	0-0017571	0859	1
KRAUSE ALBERT S	CW4	W-0904146	0964	1
KRAUSE WILLIAM O	LTC	0-0037448	0867	1
KRAUSKOPF FREDERICK	COL	0-0057053	0866	2
KRAUSS PAUL H	COL	0-0022932	0764	1
KREBS LOGAN A	CW3	W-0906839	0356	1
KREBS ROBERT C	CW4	W-0903380	0465	1
KREGEL HERMAN J	COL	0-0038845	1264	1
KREIDBERG MARVIN A	COL	0-0022733	0163	1
KREIDEL FRANCIS A	B G	0-0039553	0657	1
KREISER OSCAR G	COL	0-0020765	0759	1
KREITZER JAMES F	LTC	0-0023096	0763	1
KREN ROBERT E	LTC	0-0028277	0867	1
KRESGE MILES W	COL	0-0007014	0247	2
KRETLOW SIDNEY P	COL	0-0050908	0954	1
KRETLOW STANLEY A	COL	0-0039708	0859	1
KREUTER ROBERT H	COL	0-0012706	0750	1
KREUTZER RICHARD B	COL	0-0025037	0666	1
KRIECHBAUM FRED M	CW4	W-0903381	0164	1
KRIEGER HOWARD G	COL	0-0065673	1267	1
KRIEGER MERVIN	LTC	0-0049000	0765	1
KRILLA MICHAEL N	CW4	W-0904147	0163	1
KROENING MARIAN F	MAJ	N-0001678	0665	1
KROHN HAROLD K	LTC	0-0042702	0861	2
KROLL MARILYN	MAJ	N-0000182	0662	1
KROMER PHILIP F JR	B G	0-0018030	0862	1
KROMETIS AUGUST A	LTC	0-0080951	0968	1
KRON JACK J	LTC	0-0045822	0262	1
KRON PHILIP H	COL	0-0010481	0842	2
KRONEMEYER SYLVIA M	MAJ	N-0000461	0761	1
KRONKE CHARLES J	LTC	0-0040371	0864	1
KROPP ARTHUR J	LTC	0-0037561	0168	2
KROYER JOHN M	LTC	0-0060039	0867	1
KRUEGER AUGUST F	CW3	W-0903383	0861	1
KRUEGER ORRIN C	COL	0-0018553	0261	1
KRUEGER PHILIP G	COL	0-0024677	0666	1
KRUEGER ROBERT H	COL	0-0015342	0455	2
KRUEGER RUSSELL C	LTC	0-0032955	0768	1
KRUEGER WALTER JR	COL	0-0018351	0361	2
KRUGER HERBERT W	COL	0-0015037	1047	1
KRUGER RICHARD O	LTC	0-0036575	0268	1
KRUGER ROBERT F	LTC	0-0082035	1066	1
KRUKAR ANDREW	CW4	W-0903384	0565	2
KRUMPERMAN LUCILE	MAJ	N-0001338	0865	1
KRUPP OSCAR	COL	0-0003221	1145	2
KRZYZOSIAK STANLEY J	CW4	W-0903386	0855	2
KUBIN MILFORD T	COL	0-0018278	0360	1
KUEFLER KENNETH T	LTC	0-0059493	1067	1
KUEHLER WALTER W	COL	0-0030731	1065	2
KUEHLKE CHRISTIAN	LTC	0-0080435	0966	1
KUENNING HOWARD F	COL	0-0042739	0766	1
KUENTZ OSCAR C	COL	0-0003752	1146	1
KUHN FRANCIS H	COL	0-0012542	0747	2
KUHN FREDOLIN W	COL	0-0051734	0364	1
KUHN LUDWIG P	COL	0-0041752	1163	1
KUHN WILLIAM A	COL	0-0031419	1064	1
KUHNS DWIGHT M	COL	0-0018294	1055	2
KUHRE LELAND B	COL	0-0016056	0755	1
KUITERT JOHN H	COL	0-0041753	1163	1
KUJAWSKI JOSEPH S	COL	0-0021276	0864	1
KULP JAMES M	LTC	0-0080436	1061	1
KUMMER WILLIAM G	CW4	W-0903387	0962	1
KUMPE EDWARD F	COL	0-0018036	1054	1
KUNA CHARLES S	COL	0-0020581	0964	1
KUNDEL TEWES	COL	0-0029037	1156	1
KUNESH FRED W	COL	0-0016768	0655	1
KUNITZ MARCELLUS	COL	0-0029642	1161	1
KUNZIG HENRY B	COL	0-0018081	0860	2
KUNZIG WILLIAM B	B G	0-0018825	0862	1
KURSTEDT HAROLD A	COL	0-0016735	1055	1
KURTH EDWARD H	COL	0-0021807	0761	1
KURTZ GUY O	B G	0-0007418	0753	1
KURTZ MYERS R	LTC	0-0079652	0867	1
KURTZ STANLEY L	CW3	RW-0906844	1062	1
KURUTZ KATHERINE	MAJ	N-0001274	1165	1
KUSEWITT JOHN B JR	LTC	0-0027495	0166	1
KUSHNER GERSEN L	LTC	0-0019420	0862	1
KUSHNER LEONARD M	CPT	0-0060818	0753	2
KUSHNER WILLIAM M	WO1	W-0800303	1129	2
KUSKE ALBERT W	CPT	0-0021001	0-42	2
KUSSMAUL WILLIAM G	COL	0-0082036	0968	1
KUSTER JOHN F	COL	0-0042419	1064	1
KUTAC AGNES F	MAJ	N-0000086	0558	1
KUTCHINSKI HENRY P	LTC	0-0026734	0465	1
KUTSCHKO EMERICK	B G	0-0011434	0846	1
KUTZ CHARLES R	COL	0-0017763	0859	1
KUTZ HARRY R	B G	0-0003066	0646	2
KUYKENDALL VIRGIL L	CW2	W-0901798	0651	1
KUZIV MICHAEL	LTC	0-0023330	0965	1
KUZNIK JOSEPH V	LTC	0-0001407	1022	1
KVAM CONRAD T	COL	0-0020467	0167	1
KYDD MARJORIE W	MAJ	N-0000324	0265	1
LA BOUNTY JACK V	LTC	0-0034422	1165	1
LA CHAUSSEE CHARLES	LTC	0-0037164	0766	1
LA COMBE JAMES L	COL	0-0031284	0266	1
LA COUR JEAN P	COL	0-0039822	0363	1
LA CROIX HAROLD J	COL	0-0010273	0844	2
LA DUE PAUL F	COL	0-0019017	0957	1
LA FARGE WILLIAM F	COL	0-0042147	0363	1
LA FLARE BENJAMIN I	LTC	0-0052159	1262	1
LA FORGE CHARLES A	COL	0-0051349	1062	1
LA FORS CLAUD O	LTC	0-0021704	1162	1
LA FRANKIE REGINALD	MAJ	0-0041163	0761	1
LA HATTE WILLIAM F	COL	0-0024206	1266	1
LA MARRE JEAN B	COL	0-0026539	1168	1
LA MEE WILLIAM S III	COL	0-0032364	0567	1
LA MONT CHARLES F	LTC	0-0079885	1162	1
LA PLANTE THERESA S	LTC	N-0001917	0665	1
LA PRAD QUENTIN C	LTC	0-0027744	0765	1
LA ROCK RALPH I	LTC	0-0028159	0766	1
LA ROSE RAYMOND J	CPT	0-0023308	0744	2
LA RUE FRANK	COL	0-0010514	0947	2
LACHANCE JOSEPH R	LTC	0-0041500	0256	1
LACHETTE MARY C	MAJ	N-0001707	0668	1
LACKAS JOHN C	COL	0-0029366	1059	1
LACKRO PAUL W JR	LTC	0-0030325	1262	1
LADD JOHN G	COL	0-0039509	1054	2
LADD MARGARET P	MAJ	M-0010115	0260	1
LAFAVER AMOS E	LTC	0-0042447	1162	1
LAFFITTE HERBERT R	COL	0-0043150	0168	1
LAGASSE FREDERICK	LTC	0-0031517	0463	1
LAGATTA ALFRED P	LTC	0-0084605	0368	1
LAGORIO ANTHONY P	COL	0-0008208	1148	1
LAHLUM ARTHUR H	COL	0-0023541	0763	1
LAHM LAWRENCE	COL	0-0024761	0764	1
LAHMER JOHN A	LTC	0-0079883	0266	1
LAHTI EDWARD H	COL	0-0021322	0662	1
LAIB ARTHUR J JR	COL	0-0043107	1167	1
LAIDLAW WALDO E	M G	0-0016414	0669	1
LAIN DALTON W	LTC	0-0040302	1166	1
LAIRD ROBERT A	LTC	0-0005565	1141	1
LAIRD WHEELER E	LTC	0-0058153	0167	1
LAITMAN MILTON A	LTC	0-0021805	0544	2
LAKE JACK F	LTC	0-0034391	1266	1
LAKE JOHN P	COL	0-0008366	0753	1
LALLY ESTELLA M	CPT	N-0000380	1051	2
LALLY LAWRENCE D	COL	0-0041674	0460	1
LAM GENE N	LTC	0-0062932	1166	1
LAMANSKY ETHEL A	LTC	N-0000041	1155	1
LAMAR HENRY C JR	LTC	0-0058950	1065	1
LAMAR JOSEPH R	COL	0-0043014	0366	1
LAMB EARNEST R	CW4	W-0906846	0564	1
LAMB OAKLEY M	LTC	0-0032751	0661	2
LAMB SAMUEL S	COL	0-0016247	1146	2
LAMBERT BENJAMIN F	MAJ	0-0041131	1061	1
LAMBERT HARRY F	COL	0-0038919	0866	2
LAMBERT HERMAN J	COL	0-0010948	0253	1
LAMBERT JOSEPH I	COL	0-0009541	1046	2
LAMBERT KENT C	COL	0-0005591	0251	2
LAMBOURNE ROBERT D	LTC	0-0057851	0667	1
LAMING PERCY H	COL	0-0042000	0262	1
LAMOND JOHN B	LTC	0-0025309	0766	1
LAMONT JAMES M	COL	0-0017226	0157	2
LAMOREUX THOMAS L	MAJ	0-0004965	1136	2
LAMOTHE FRANK E	LTC	0-0065711	0965	1
LAMPERT ERNEST R	COL	0-0080127	1268	1
LAMPERT LESTER L JR	LTC	0-0022100	0661	1
LAMUREY JUAN	CW4	W-0902070	1054	1
LANAHAN FRANCIS H	M G	0-0012735	0355	1
LANARD FRANCIS W	LTC	0-0025155	1064	1
LANCASTER ALEXANDER	COL	0-0041875	1061	1
LANCASTER HARRY R	COL	0-0030897	1058	1
LANCASTER JAMES L	CW4	W-0904148	0163	1
LANCASTER JOSEPH L	COL	0-0004779	1046	1
LANCEFIELD ROBERT L	COL	0-0018037	0959	1
LANCER THOMAS F	COL	0-0051317	0662	1
LAND CLIFTON E	CPT	0-0080254	1064	2
LAND HENRY W II	CPT	OF-0107202	1168	2
LAND JAMES D	COL	0-0030650	0865	1
LAND PETER W	WO1	W-0901049	0434	2
LAND RUFUS L	COL	0-0016392	0946	2
LANDAKER CHESTER L	COL	0-0018353	0761	2
LANDES SIDNEY W	LTC	0-0040397	0662	1
LANDIS LINCOLN	LTC	0-0027588	0965	1
LANDON DONALD C	COL	0-0030402	0565	1
LANDRESS SYLVA M	LTC	0-0084790	0266	1
LANDRUM EUGENE M JR	LTC	0-0055032	0864	1
LANDRUM JAMES E JR	M G	0-0020216	0866	1
LANDRY ERNEST S	LTC	0-0051932	0163	2
LANDRY WILMER C	COL	0-0020208	0866	1
LANDRY WILSON A JR	MAJ	0-0063378	0766	1
LANE ALBERT L	COL	0-0010178	0752	1

UNITED STATES ARMY RETIRED LIST

NAME	GRADE	SVC NO	DATE RET MO YR	RET CODE
LANE ARTHUR W	B G	O-0002056	0845	1
LANE CECILE M	MAJ	L-0000074	0261	1
LANE DANNA L	COL	O-0051520	0864	1
LANE DOUGLAS H	COL	O-0040338	0866	1
LANE HERMAN O	COL	O-0010297	0854	1
LANE JAMES W	LTC	O-0953091	0466	1
LANE SAMUEL H	LTC	O-0017322	0830	2
LANE THOMAS A	M G	O-0017075	0762	2
LANE WILLIAM T	COL	O-0021714	1163	1
LANEY JAMES R JR	COL	O-0023942	0865	1
LANG ALBERT	1LT	O-0016582	0532	2
LANG CORNELIS O	B G	O-0019734	0766	1
LANG EDMUND H	COL	O-0043006	0467	1
LANG HAROLD G	COL	O-0051600	0961	1
LANG JACK B	LTC	O-0063381	1267	1
LANG JAMES D	COL	O-0019728	0655	1
LANG NORBERT S	COL	O-0031062	0667	1
LANG RALPH W	COL	O-0023034	0764	1
LANG THELMA L	MAJ	N-0001979	1262	1
LANGBEIN LELAND H	LTC	O-0040473	0961	1
LANGDON HAZEL L	MAJ	N-0002138	1160	1
LANGDON WENDELL H	COL	O-0018101	0760	2
LANGE CHESTER E	COL	O-0030353	0165	1
LANGE WELLS B	LTC	O-0050767	0867	1
LANGENDORF WILLIAM H	LTC	O-0045551	0866	1
LANGEVIN JOSEPH L	COL	O-0012640	0554	1
LANGFORD CLARENCE A	COL	O-0021079	0568	2
LANGGUTH PAUL O	COL	O-0028923	0857	1
LANGLEY JOHN E	LTC	O-0008973	0-41	1
LANGLOIS SILAS R	COL	O-0029865	0563	2
LANGSTON CARL C	CW4	W-0903399	0259	1
LANHAM CHARLES T	M G	O-0015568	1054	1
LANKARD DELBERT W	CW4	W-0906849	1065	1
LANKENAU NORMAN H	COL	O-0018824	0552	2
LANNING HARLEY A	COL	O-0039720	0861	1
LANPHER ROLLIN A	LTC	O-0030636	0264	1
LANPHIER PAUL H	COL	O-0020949	1067	1
LANSFORD ERDIE O	COL	O-0030569	1163	1
LANSING ERNEST J	LTC	O-0063113	0766	1
LANSING SAMUEL M	COL	O-0016277	0655	1
LANTERMAN JOHN V S	COL	O-0033983	1168	2
LAPIANA VINCENT F	COL	O-0051365	1262	1
LAPSLEY WILLIAM W	M G	O-0019727	1067	1
LARCHEVEQUE RUSSELL	CW4	W-0906850	0467	1
LARDIN HARRY E	COL	O-0019494	0660	1
LAREAU GEORGE O	CW4	W-0906851	0955	1
LAREW WALTER B	B G	O-0016647	1056	1
LARK MARTHA L	MAJ	N-0002418	0464	1
LARKIN ALWYN V	COL	O-0029809	0959	1
LARKIN GEORGE T	COL	O-0023293	0765	1
LARNER THOMAS M	COL	O-0030223	0764	1
LARSEN GEORGE E	COL	O-0031550	0767	1
LARSEN JOHN W	CPT	O-0071693	0167	1
LARSON FLORIE M	MAJ	N-0002357	0858	1
LARSON GORDON P	LTC	O-0019124	0645	2
LARSON ROBERT C	COL	O-0041548	0958	1
LARSON ROBERT T	COL	O-0024506	0864	1
LARSON WERNER L	LTC	O-0029024	0956	1
LASH EUGENE L	COL	O-0042272	0866	1
LASH PERCY M JR	COL	O-0018458	0761	1
LASHER EDMUND C R	M G	O-0017624	0158	1
LASHLEY RALPH O	COL	O-0019982	0863	1
LASKOWSKY RUDOLPH	COL	O-0021243	0866	2
LASSETTER MARGARET N	MAJ	L-0000306	0761	1
LASSITER GEORGE L	LTC	O-0080957	1167	1
LASSITER JANIE L	LTC	N-0002041	0962	1
LASTAYO EDWARD H	B G	O-0012660	0853	1
LASTOVKA JOHN R	CW3	W-0901254	0247	1
LATHAM CHARLES C JR	LTC	O-0039950	0163	1
LATHEY CHARLES E	LTC	O-0081910	0261	1
LATHROP ALBA B	COL	O-0036492	0868	1
LATHROP LESLIE T	COL	O-0006642	0450	2
LATHROPE FRANCES M	LTC	L-0000021	0558	1
LATIMER FARRIS N	LTC	O-0015935	0753	1
LATIMER RAYMOND L	COL	O-0034833	0867	1
LATOU ANDREW L	CW4	W-0906852	0467	1
LATTA WILLIAM L JR	LTC	O-0023627	1268	1
LATTIN JAY D B	COL	O-0004637	0150	1
LATTIN JOHN H	COL	O-0029887	0263	1
LATZEN SAMUEL	CW4	W-0903401	0854	1
LAUBACH JAMES H	COL	O-0002278	0943	1
LAUBEN PHILIP S	COL	O-0039500	0854	1
LAUDANI ANGELO A	LTC	O-0024033	0762	1
LAUDERDALE JAMES M	LTC	O-0059552	0166	1
LAUDIERI MARIO F	LTC	O-0079887	0366	1
LAUE MARTIN W	LTC	O-0082038	1068	1
LAUER DAVID P	LTC	O-0030904	0155	2
LAUGERMAN JOHN B	COL	O-0030333	1264	1
LAUGHLIN GEORGE T	COL	O-0030723	0566	1
LAUGHLIN JOHN E	CW4	W-0906853	0657	1
LAUGHLIN THOMAS	LTC	O-0037414	0265	1
LAUGHLIN VIRGIL V	COL	O-0041059	1166	1
LAURIE PATRICK W	LTC	O-0040222	1162	1
LAURION LAWRENCE E	COL	O-0020150	0762	1
LAURSEN CHRIS N	CW4	W-0903402	0857	1
LAUTERBACH CARL G	LTC	O-0069523	1068	1
LAUTERBACH WALLACE M	COL	O-0023810	0665	1
LAUTZ EDWARD H	COL	O-0079711	0467	1
LAUX RAY J	M G	O-0042102	0967	2
LAVELL ROBERT G	LTC	O-0032080	1163	1
LAVELLEE LEO E	CW3	W-0903403	0967	1
LAVERICK BLENDA	MAJ	N-0000058	0951	1
LAVIN MARGUERITE	MAJ	N-0002071	0163	1
LAW ARTHUR G	LTC	O-0062977	0666	1
LAW CHARLES P	COL	O-0041684	0560	1
LAW WILLIAM	COL	O-0032169	0466	2
LAWES ROBERT C	LTC	O-0015571	0846	1
LAWFORD FRANK K	COL	O-0037395	0668	2
LAWLER WILLIAM H	LTC	O-0069722	0866	1
LAWLER WILLIAM J	1LT	O-0014358	0717	1
LAWLESS ROGER E J	COL	O-0080960	0767	1
LAWLEY EUGENE G JR	1LT	O-0063468	1054	2
LAWLOR JOHN D	B G	O-0019536	0864	1
LAWLOR ROBERT J	COL	O-0019036	0863	1
LAWLOR THOMAS J	COL	O-0020361	0864	1
LAWRANCE JACKSON S	COL	O-0032003	0965	1
LAWRENCE ABRAHAM M	COL	O-0008080	0644	2
LAWRENCE C W JR	COL	O-0041613	0859	1
LAWRENCE CARYL R	MAJ	N-0001242	1264	1
LAWRENCE CHARLES E	LTC	O-0052261	0367	1
LAWRENCE CHARLES S	COL	O-0014799	0949	1
LAWRENCE FRANK J	COL	O-0011133	0947	1
LAWRENCE GEORGE H	MAJ	O-0017288	1147	1
LAWRENCE JACOB H	LTC	O-0006020	0142	1
LAWRENCE JAMES R	LTC	O-0058952	0266	2
LAWRENCE LESLIE F	COL	O-0006743	0846	1
LAWRENCE MARY S	LTC	M-0010103	0962	1
LAWRENCE RAY G	LTC	O-0052606	0661	1
LAWRENCE RENN M	LTC	O-0057696	1067	1
LAWRENCE THOMAS E	LTC	O-0026835	0865	1
LAWRIE JOE S	M G	O-0020914	0667	1
LAWS WOODROW	LTC	O-0030677	0663	1
LAWSON DWIGHT	LTC	O-0018918	0643	2
LAWSON JOEL W	COL	O-0033298	0266	1
LAWSON JOSEPH F	CW3	W-0904149	0660	1
LAWSON PAUL F	LTC	O-0024529	0262	1
LAWSON RICHARD H	COL	O-0018526	0761	1
LAWSON RUTLEDGE	COL	O-0010493	0553	1
LAWSON THOMAS R	MAJ	O-0023907	0246	2
LAWSON WALTER R	COL	O-0020808	0867	1
LAWSON WAYNE E	LTC	O-0028450	1267	1
LAWTHER J PAUL	COL	O-0041937	1061	1
LAWTON ELMORE G	COL	O-0038941	0966	1
LAWTON ELVA J	MAJ	N-0001978	1062	1
LAWTON KIRKE B	M G	O-0006805	0854	2
LAWTON ROSA T	LTC	L-0000254	0967	1
LAWTON WILLIAM S	LTG	O-0014924	0560	1
LAY KENNETH E	COL	O-0022224	0764	1
LAY SYLVAN P	LTC	O-0022638	0859	1
LAYER HARLAND W	COL	O-0019643	0855	1
LAYFIELD WOODY E JR	COL	O-0023939	0165	1
LAYMAN CHARLES A	LTC	O-0049778	0865	1
LAYMAN ERNEST M JR	LTC	O-0032455	1067	1
LAYMAN RALPH E JR	LTC	O-0049996	1064	1
LAYNE CLYDE L	COL	O-0020317	0866	1
LAYTON CHARLES B	COL	O-0030729	0666	2
LAYTON VICTOR J	COL	O-0059862	0867	1
LAZAR AARON M	COL	O-0018738	0862	2
LAZZARINI LOUIS T	COL	O-0043425	0862	1
LE BLANC CLAIRE V	MAJ	N-0001851	1068	1
LE BLANC MELVIN V	LTC	O-0050690	0868	2
LE BLANC WILLIAM P	CW3	W-0903406	0961	1
LE CLAIR JOSEPH A JR	COL	O-0079888	0968	1
LE CLAIR NELSON JR	COL	O-0028797	0255	1
LE GETTE JAMES Y	COL	O-0011088	0646	1
LE GOLVAN PAUL C	COL	O-0024634	0466	1
LE MAY ROBERT W JR	LTC	O-0038236	0265	1
LE MAY ROLAND A	COL	O-0039987	0164	1
LE MONIER DONALD J	LTC	O-0080130	0767	1
LE MOON RALPH G	COL	O-0031264	0467	1
LE PENSKE F J JR	LTC	O-0039774	0660	2
LE STOURGEON PERCY E	COL	O-0014635	0753	1
LE VAN HUGH	LTC	O-0042514	1157	2
LE VIER EARL R	LTC	O-0059925	0365	1
LEACH ALICE L	MAJ	L-0000204	0953	1
LEAHY JOHN P	LTC	O-0033097	1161	1
LEAHY PAUL J	COL	O-0043267	0668	1
LEAKEY FRANK N	COL	O-0016578	0656	1
LEAR FRANK L	COL	O-0039007	1163	1
LEARNARD HENRY G JR	COL	O-0029801	0660	2
LEARY JOHN E	B G	O-0018607	0361	1
LEARY THOMAS J	COL	O-0002572	0544	1
LEAVENGOOD LEO O	LTC	O-0044938	0262	1
LEAVER FRANK Y	COL	O-0018928	0563	2
LEAVEY EDMOND H	M G	O-0008559	0649	1
LEAVEY WILLIAM J	LTC	O-0080129	0868	1
LEAVITT ALBERT M	LTC	O-0028218	0466	1
LEAVITT CHARLES A	COL	O-0051403	0563	1
LEBKICHER HARRY R	COL	O-0009995	1046	2
LECHNER ROY J	LTC	O-0060503	0768	1
LECKIE WILLIAM E	COL	O-0040296	0966	1
LEDBETTER MCWESLEY	COL	O-0051096	0860	1
LEDBETTER WILLIAM R	LTC	O-0080962	0868	1
LEDERMAN MILTON D	COL	O-0023320	1066	1
LEDFORD EDWARD B	MAJ	O-0038496	0962	1
LEDFORD LEE B JR	LTC	O-0023775	0861	1
LEDGERWOOD HOWARD G	LTC	O-0079889	0861	1
LEE ARTHUR H	COL	O-0008216	0650	1
LEE DONALD C	LTC	O-0078940	0867	1
LEE EDWARD M	COL	O-0020661	0762	1
LEE EDWIN C	COL	O-0043030	0266	1
LEE ERNEST D	COL	O-0015517	0854	2
LEE EUGENE M	COL	O-0031474	0664	1
LEE FAY W	COL	O-0014760	0247	2
LEE FLORENCE I	LTC	N-0000503	0149	1
LEE FRANK E	COL	O-0042775	0863	1
LEE FRANK M	COL	O-0014891	0850	1
LEE FREDERICK	COL	O-0039518	0955	1
LEE GAIL B	LTC	O-0033332	1060	1
LEE HARRIET S	COL	M-0010001	0360	1
LEE JOHN K JR	COL	O-0030136	0364	1
LEE JOHN L	COL	O-0051088	0660	1
LEE LEVIN L	LTC	O-0022172	0867	1
LEE LYNN C	COL	O-0023717	0765	1
LEE MARY E	MAJ	N-0002118	0360	1
LEE RAY M	COL	O-0031974	0968	1
LEE RICHARD	COL	O-0012057	0351	2
LEE RICHARD E	MAJ	O-0068126	1267	1
LEE ROBERT V	M G	O-0028882	0961	1
LEE STANTON K	CPT	O-0065719	1064	1
LEE TRUMAN	CW4	W-0904315	0766	1
LEE WAYNE H	LTC	O-0024469	1060	1
LEECH HOMAN E	COL	O-0021679	0865	1
LEECH ROBERT C	LTC	O-0040183	0364	1
LEEDHAM CHARLES L	COL	O-0017838	0855	1
LEEDY MYRON	COL	O-0014937	0348	2
LEEKA ALEC H	CW4	W-0903410	0465	1
LEEN EVELYN E	MAJ	N-0001949	0558	1
LEENEY LEWIS W	COL	O-0025206	1166	1
LEEPER BRYAN H	LTC	O-0026579	0864	1
LEER BOYD W	LTC	O-0075232	0968	1
LEER JAMES B	COL	O-0020370	0866	2
LEER JAMES M JR	LTC	O-0061204	0868	1
LEES FRANKLIN B	LTC	O-0007844	0-35	2
LEFFEL R ERNEST	COL	O-0021442	0846	2
LEFFERS RICHARD JR	COL	O-0031843	0766	1
LEGARE BEN W SR	COL	O-0039034	0866	1
LEGENDRE STEWART H	LTC	O-0042004	0260	1
LEGERE LAURENCE J	COL	O-0022937	0766	1
LEGGETT RUFUS L	LTC	O-0094609	0867	1
LEGLER MATTHEW L	LTC	O-0022114	0246	2
LEHMAN ASA M	COL	O-0004077	0149	1
LEHMAN GEORGE A	LTC	O-0030945	0563	1
LEHMAN ROBERT H	LTC	O-0079891	1266	1
LEHMANN GUS E	COL	O-0040001	0463	1
LEHNER CHARLES R	B G	O-0005740	0249	2
LEHRFELD IRVING	COL	O-0018586	0761	1
LEHTONEN REINO O	COL	O-0052532	0767	1
LEIBY KENNETH L	COL	O-0051286	0162	1
LEIDENHEIMER JOHN L	COL	O-0030795	0664	1
LEIDY MARIETTA M	CPT	N-0002269	0952	2
LEIDY ROYAL L	COL	O-0029886	1060	2
LEIGH BERT G	LTC	O-0067593	0968	1
LEIGH BEVERLY M JR	COL	O-0039917	0864	1
LEIGHTON RALPH E	COL	O-0043688	0762	1
LEIN DORENCE G	CW2	W-0902679	0257	1
LEININGER DANIEL M	LTC	O-0027992	0867	1
LEINSTER ROY L	MAJ	O-0018589	0-44	2
LEIST GEORGE F	COL	O-0020657	0963	1
LEIST WILLIAM C	MAJ	O-0060220	0164	1
LEISTER ALBERT F SR	LTC	O-0036201	0968	1
LELAND ALANSON T	COL	O-0042236	0963	1
LELAND HELENA M	MAJ	N-0000874	0965	1
LELAND LOUIS S	COL	O-0020990	1166	1
LEMA HENRY R	LTC	O-0039370	0965	1
LEMERE FRANCIS P	COL	O-0084381	1068	1
LEMKE MERRILL M	LTC	O-0061396	0868	1
LEMMON KELLY B	COL	O-0002552	0345	1
LENEKER HERBERT W	LTC	O-0078942	0968	1
LENETEN CHARLES C JR	LTC	O-0063114	0963	1
LENEY HERBER C	LTC	O-0039789	0761	2
LENHOFF RAYMOND J	CW3	W-0903415	1053	2
LENN CLAUDE R	MAJ	O-0037469	1161	2
LENNHOFF CHARLES D	LTC	O-0021882	0660	1
LENTINI ANTHONY R	LTC	O-0058479	0967	1
LENTZ BENJAMIN A	COL	O-0029401	0460	1
LENTZ CARL II	LTC	O-0021993	0866	1
LENTZ JOHN M	M G	O-0010343	0156	1
LENZ ADELINE H	MAJ	N-0000625	0160	1
LENZE GLADYS L	MAJ	N-0002224	1158	1
LENZNER EMIL	M G	O-0015810	0758	1
LEONARD AMEL T	COL	O-0015550	0654	1
LEONARD ANN M	CPT	N-0000683	0849	2
LEONARD CHARLES F JR	M G	O-0019829	0667	1
LEONARD EDGAR W	LTC	O-0037390	0561	1
LEONARD JOHN W	LTG	O-0003840	0152	1
LEONARD KATHARINE	MAJ	M-0010054	0558	1
LEONARD LAWRENCE C	COL	O-0014906	0652	2
LEONARD MARGARET W	MAJ	N-0000212	0157	1
LEONARD MARY T	MAJ	N-0002359	1058	1
LEONARD ROBERT R JR	LTC	O-0060096	0966	1
LEONARD ROBERT T	LTC	O-0080965	1066	1
LEONARD WILLIAM	CW4	W-0906861	1058	1
LEONE GEORGE E	COL	O-0018287	0960	1
LEONE LOUIS P	COL	O-0015350	0854	1
LEOPARD WALTER D	CW3	W-0903417	0863	1
LEPPING ALOYSIUS J	COL	O-0016853	0757	1
LERETTE EARLE L	COL	O-0022133	1064	1
LERNER GERALD P	COL	O-0032199	0966	1
LERNER JACK L	COL	O-0044103	0968	2

NAME	GRADE	SVC NO	DATE RET MO YR	RET CODE
LEROY CHARLES I	LTC	0-0078944	0368	1
LERRO SANTINO J	COL	0-0020540	0661	1
LESLIE ROBERT C	COL	0-0018993	0959	1
LESLIE SAMUEL H	COL	0-0001511	1022	1
LESLIE WILLIAM T	LTC	0-0069524	0866	2
LESNESKI STANLEY V	LTC	0-0032053	1166	1
LESSER LOUIS L	LTC	0-0014771	0644	2
LESSLEY GEORGIA F	LTC	N-0001869	0959	1
LESTER GRAHAM W	COL	0-0004801	0854	1
LESTER ROBERT B	CW2	W-0901783	0247	1
LEVA FRANCIS L	LTC	0-0052627	1161	1
LEVANT WILLIAM S	LTC	0-0083964	0168	1
LEVAROSEN RICHARD W	LTC	0-0080307	0267	1
LEVASSEUR ARMAND R	LTC	0-0047290	0763	1
LEVENICK MAYNARD N	COL	0-0018514	0159	2
LEVENS ARTHUR J	COL	0-0021283	0766	1
LEVESQUE PAUL M	COL	0-0037415	0868	2
LEVIE HOWARD S	COL	0-0038735	0263	1
LEVIN BEATRICE D	MAJ	L-0000018	0255	1
LEVIN EDWARD	LTC	0-0051910	0860	1
LEVIN MAURICE	COL	0-0039912	0764	1
LEVY JULIUS W	COL	0-0052466	0266	1
LEVY RICHARD M	COL	0-0004469	0450	2
LEVY RICHARD M JR	LTC	0-0023980	1165	1
LEWEY MERLE C	LTC	0-0080969	0167	1
LEWIS ALFRED E	LTC	0-0070406	0368	1
LEWIS ARDEN I	COL	0-0043360	1163	1
LEWIS BERKELEY R	COL	0-0029065	0259	1
LEWIS BLANCHE Z	MAJ	N-0000714	0566	1
LEWIS BURTON O	B G	0-0002838	0747	1
LEWIS BURTON O JR	LTC	0-0027745	0368	1
LEWIS CHARLES	COL	0-0006821	0343	1
LEWIS CHARLES	1LT	0-0018257	0-37	2
LEWIS CHARLES W	COL	0-0004005	0344	2
LEWIS CLARENCE S	COL	0-0029039	0259	1
LEWIS DAVID C	B G	0-0029735	0762	1
LEWIS DONALD L	COL	0-0030119	0264	1
LEWIS EMMETT M	LTC	0-0032866	0166	1
LEWIS EMORY A	COL	0-0019584	1162	1
LEWIS EVAN H	COL	0-0040238	1167	1
LEWIS FRENCH G	LTC	0-0033676	0868	1
LEWIS GABE W	COL	0-0042064	0761	1
LEWIS GARLAND B	COL	0-0073655	1065	1
LEWIS GEORGE G	LTC	0-0042250	1061	1
LEWIS GEORGE W	LTC	0-0038013	0862	1
LEWIS HAROLD J	LTC	0-0084321	1164	1
LEWIS HARRY J	COL	0-0019751	0762	1
LEWIS HUBERT D	COL	0-0018058	0758	1
LEWIS IVA D	MAJ	N-0001083	1163	2
LEWIS JAMES F	COL	0-0041715	1057	1
LEWIS JAMES L	COL	0-0021069	0167	1
LEWIS JESSE L	LTC	0-0024809	0459	2
LEWIS JETT W	CW4	W-0906864	0765	1
LEWIS JOHN H JR	COL	0-0012151	1048	1
LEWIS JOHN T	LTG	0-0007000	0959	1
LEWIS LEHMAN J	LTC	0-0029537	0359	1
LEWIS MARION A JR	LTC	0-0069727	0467	1
LEWIS PARRY W	COL	0-0008640	1146	1
LEWIS RALPH W	LTC	0-0020031	0843	2
LEWIS RAY C	LTC	0-0053181	0568	1
LEWIS ROBERT H	LTC	0-0037802	0465	1
LEWIS ROBERT G	CW4	W-0902377	0366	1
LEWIS THOMAS E	B G	0-0015020	0653	2
LEWIS VERNON L	COL	0-0042628	1065	1
LEWIS WALDEN S	COL	0-0014871	1049	2
LEWIS WARFIELD M	COL	0-0005242	0850	1
LEWIS WILLIAM F	COL	0-0023206	0968	1
LEWIS WILLIAM H	COL	0-0020598	0758	1
LEWIS WILLIAM P	CW4	W-0903420	0868	1
LEWITZ EDWARD W	COL	0-0045325	0665	1
LEYDECKER CHARLES E	COL	0-0019227	0863	1
LEYKO CAROLYN A	MAJ	N-0001877	0958	1
LIAKOS ELIAS F	LTC	0-0032238	1156	2
LIBASCI ALFONSO M	COL	0-0019606	0461	1
LIBBY JACK P	COL	0-0037932	0768	1
LIBERSHAL FRANCIS M	COL	0-0023471	1046	2
LICHIRIE CORNELIUS	COL	0-0018371	0761	1
LICHTENWALTER LEON	COL	0-0012850	0954	1
LICKMAN EDWIN C	LTC	0-0011897	0840	1
LICORD FRANK A	LTC	0-0079895	0465	1
LIEBE HAROLD E	COL	0-0029334	0859	1
LIEBERBERG GEORGE	COL	0-0079896	0563	1
LIEBLICH JEROME F	COL	0-0033409	1163	1
LIEDING ROBERT K	LTC	0-0080438	0865	1
LIESKE BEATA M	MAJ	N-0000361	0560	1
LIESSMAN EMERSON D	CPT	0-0019949	0242	2
LIFFITON WILLIAM T	LTC	0-0065248	0766	1
LIFSHUTZ OSCAR M	LTC	0-0052023	0865	1
LIGGETT DOYLE C	CW4	W-0902391	0457	1
LIGHT JOHN C	COL	0-0039611	0559	1
LIGHTCAP GEORGE E	COL	0-0015834	1046	2
LIGON THOMAS W	COL	0-0006656	0753	2
LIGON WALTER B	COL	0-0081912	0263	1
LIKENS ELLERY A JR	LTC	0-0079897	0565	1
LILE JOHN M	CPT	0-0007530	0233	2
LILES JAMES B	CW4	W-0903425	0762	1
LILES PAUL V S	LTC	0-0023876	0262	1
LILES ROY L	LTC	0-0058955	0766	1
LILL EUGENE M	LTC	0-0040011	0164	1
LILLARD ERMA L	MAJ	N-0002276	1263	1
LILLARD GERALD F	B G	0-0016770	0757	1
LILLY EDMUND J JR	COL	0-0007373	0753	2
LILLY GRADY F	COL	0-0036990	1267	1
LILLYMAN FRANK L	LTC	0-0032861	0968	2
LIMBACHER WALTER J	LTC	0-0067934	0368	1
LIMONCELLI DONALD D	COL	0-0042375	0664	1
LIMPUS CHARLES E JR	LTC	0-0027876	0167	1
LINCOLN RALPH A	COL	0-0016097	0755	1
LINCOLN RUSH B JR	M G	0-0018656	0265	1
LIND CARL J JR	COL	0-0029322	1059	1
LIND ELLIS R	CW2	W-0901590	0951	2
LIND HENRY D	COL	0-0020256	1060	1
LIND WILLIAM J	COL	0-0045230	0766	1
LINDAHL WILLIAM C	LTC	0-0038379	1068	1
LINDAU MARJORIE J	LTC	N-0002154	0564	2
LINDBERG PAUL S	COL	0-0052194	0968	1
LINDBLOM VICTOR E	LTC	0-0091629	0567	1
LINDEN HENNING	B G	0-0007009	0952	2
LINDEN JOHN H	COL	0-0027119	0868	1
LINDERMANN JOHN C	LTC	0-0023888	1047	2
LINDHOLM OSCAR W	CW3	W-0903427	0757	1
LINDIG EDWIN JR	LTC	0-0058776	1167	1
LINDJORD HAAKON	COL	0-0025340	0868	1
LINDMARK MARVIN L	LTC	0-0034393	0263	1
LINDNER KENNETH R	COL	0-0034650	0867	1
LINDORFF ROBERT L	MAJ	0-0072920	0863	1
LINDQUIST ALBERT A	COL	0-0041656	0360	1
LINDQUIST JOHN D	COL	0-0009614	0444	2
LINDQUIST ROY E	M G	0-0018125	0660	1
LINDSAY WALLACE W	COL	0-0038596	0858	1
LINDSAY WILLIAM B	COL	0-0061203	1068	1
LINDSEY JULIAN B	COL	0-0017772	0859	1
LINDSEY MALCOLM F	B G	0-0006914	0751	1
LINDSEY MORRIS L	LTC	0-0040935	1164	2
LINDSTROM HAROLD M	COL	0-0028932	1057	1
LINDT JOHN H	COL	0-0003379	0346	2
LINEBACK CARL M	LTC	0-0066037	0465	1
LINEBAUGH JOHN M	CPT	0-0090202	0467	2
LINEBERGER ERNEST C	LTC	0-0031297	0564	2
LINGAN WILLIAM J	LTC	0-0048851	0967	1
LINGENFELTER WILLIAM	LTC	0-0032829	0666	1
LINGER ALBERT F	1LT	0-0071219	0960	2
LINGNER FREDERICK	MAJ	0-0036387	0559	1
LININGER CLARENCE	COL	0-0001397	0642	1
LININGER JOHN B	LTC	0-0030059	1161	1
LINK LILLIAN G	CPT	N-0002644	0762	1
LINK ROGER J	LTC	0-0080974	0868	1
LINK WILLARD C	COL	0-0029028	1058	1
LINKE JEAN M	LTC	N-0001992	1168	1
LINKSWILER GILBERT F	COL	0-0016098	0655	1
LINN EDNA J	MAJ	N-0000323	0764	1
LINN LAVON P	COL	0-0030757	0966	1
LINN PHILLIP J	LTC	0-0033395	0666	1
LINN RUBY W	LTC	R-0010006	0164	1
LINN SCOTT D	COL	0-0022260	1059	1
LINN WALTER A	COL	0-0041540	0658	1
LINS HARRY W	COL	0-0009776	0749	1
LINSE FRANCIS D	LTC	0-0031858	0466	1
LINSERT HENRY	COL	0-0005540	0246	2
LINSMAN JOSEPH F	COL	0-0021476	0746	2
LINTHWAITE GEORGE F	COL	0-0029990	0963	1
LINTON WILLIAM C JR	LTC	0-0026140	1065	1
LIONAIS IRENE	MAJ	N-0001217	0264	1
LIPHAM CORINNE I	MAJ	N-0002228	1267	1
LIPINSKI JAMES B	CW4	W-0903429	0760	1
LIPOWSKI STELLA	MAJ	N-0001967	1150	1
LIPPENCOTT GEORGE H	LTC	0-0080136	0865	1
LIPPINCOTT AUBREY	COL	0-0000959	0541	2
LIPPINCOTT CLIFFORD	LTC	0-0023429	0867	1
LIPSCOMB ANDY A	B G	0-0021333	0868	1
LIPSCOMB JOHN R	LTC	0-0080977	1265	1
LIPSCOMB LAFAR JR	COL	0-0019054	0761	1
LIPSCOMB THOMAS H	M G	0-0019371	0868	1
LIPTON SAMUEL M	COL	0-0024398	0762	1
LISK BERLY F JR	COL	0-0053540	0867	1
LISK ROBERT T	LTC	0-0039957	1055	1
LISTER FRANKLIN S	COL	0-0022747	0468	1
LISTER RODERICK L	COL	0-0057753	0167	1
LISTON DAVID F	COL	0-0017820	0356	1
LITRIO JOHN J	LTC	0-0068129	0968	1
LITTELL ELMER L	B G	0-0029823	1060	1
LITTERAL EMMETT B	COL	0-0018241	1055	1
LITTLE ANDY V	MAJ	0-0019700	0646	1
LITTLE DONALD C	COL	0-0018386	0761	1
LITTLE GERALD B	LTC	0-0040554	0766	1
LITTLE MURRAY A	COL	0-0039956	0864	1
LITTLE ROGER W	LTC	0-0065220	0666	1
LITTLE WILLIAM	COL	0-0018748	0656	1
LITTLEJOHN JAMES P	COL	0-0042837	0162	2
LITTLEJOHN ROBERT M	M G	0-0003373	1046	2
LITTLETON AUGUSTINE	LTC	0-0046066	0762	1
LITTON ANDREW L	LTC	0-0080979	0167	1
LITZ WAYNE P	COL	0-0030304	0261	1
LIVERMORE FRANCIS S	LTC	0-0032203	0264	1
LIVESAY HARVEY R	COL	0-0008919	1050	1
LIVESAY WILLIAM G	M G	0-0004603	0650	1
LIVINGSTON HOYT R	LTC	0-0060228	0868	1
LIVINGSTON JOHN J	COL	0-0039714	0361	1
LIVINGSTON LEON J	COL	0-0039512	0255	1
LIWSKI FRANCIS A	COL	0-0018777	0862	1
LIZARDI LUIS R	CW4	W-0907114	0760	1
LLANA THEODORE JR	LTC	0-0059864	0368	1
LLOYD PETER J	COL	0-0007277	0753	2
LLOYD REES S	MAJ	0-0005993	0829	2
LLOYD ROBERT N	WO1	W-0904252	0849	1
LO CICERO JOSEPHINE	MAJ	N-0001296	0863	1
LOBIT WILLIAM E	COL	0-0030699	0560	1
LOCHRIE ARTHUR J	LTC	0-0028142	0667	1
LOCK EDWIN F JR	COL	0-0012064	1047	1
LOCK GREGORY J	COL	0-0051957	0566	1
LOCKE THEODORE F JR	LTC	0-0059951	0966	1
LOCKE THOMAS W	LTC	0-0053105	0964	1
LOCKE WILLIAM A	LTC	0-0029967	0256	1
LOCKE WILLIAM J	LTC	0-0040512	0862	1
LOCKETT JAMES W	COL	0-0017305	0758	1
LOCKETT JOHN	COL	0-0051292	0262	1
LOCKETT LANDON J	COL	0-0011107	0348	2
LOCKHART EUGENE E	COL	0-0020181	0866	1
LOCKHART GEORGE A	COL	0-0007622	0448	1
LOCKHART MARIE L	MAJ	N-0000295	0861	1
LOCKHART WILSON L	LTC	0-0080980	0868	1
LOCKRIDGE WILLIAM E	MAJ	OF-0102355	1268	1
LOCKSLEY NORMAN M G	COL	0-0025111	0863	1
LOCKWOOD B C JR	B G	0-0003090	0348	2
LOCKWOOD DANIEL S	COL	0-0009106	0846	1
LOCKWOOD ESTHER M	MAJ	N-0001281	1164	1
LOCKWOOD HENRY JR	CPT	0-0014372	0819	2
LOCKWOOD MULFORD C	COL	0-0038857	0768	2
LODGE EDWIN R	COL	0-0042257	0560	1
LODLE ELWOOD G	MAJ	0-0059958	0266	1
LODWELL ELMER A	COL	0-0019315	0957	1
LOOJEN GEORGE D N	M G	0-0016580	0461	1
LOE ROBERT J	LTC	0-0059960	0568	1
LOEF JOSEPH W	COL	0-0006958	1147	2
LOEWUS JAMES D	COL	0-0023205	0867	2
LOFSTRAND ALBERT F	LTC	0-0042889	1051	2
LOFTIN HAROLDE T	COL	0-0039673	0460	1
LOFTIN JOSEPH R	COL	0-0060312	0768	1
LOFTUS JAMES V	LTC	0-0042451	1162	1
LOFTUS JOSEPH F JR	LTC	0-0084645	0267	1
LOGAN PAUL P	COL	0-0009078	0446	1
LOGAN WILLIAM J	LTC	0-0024470	0860	1
LOGSDON HARLAN V	LTC	0-0044347	0560	1
LOHMAN MARTHA E	MAJ	N-0001325	0465	1
LOHR MARY G	CPT	N-0000100	0657	1
LOHRMANN AGNES B	MAJ	N-0001329	0565	1
LOHRMANN IMELDA H	MAJ	N-0001254	0565	1
LOKOTA LORETTA L	MAJ	N-0000259	0164	1
LOLLI ANDREW R	M G	0-0029844	0966	1
LOMAN MAMIE V	MAJ	N-0001014	0365	1
LONCHAR HELEN T	LTC	N-0001012	0364	1
LONDAHL JOHN F	LTC	0-0039829	0561	1
LONERO CHARLES	LTC	0-0043185	0460	1
LONG ARTHUR P	COL	0-0029287	0661	1
LONG FLOYD H	COL	0-0032889	1167	1
LONG GEORGE S	MAJ	0-0065082	1263	1
LONG HARLAN J	COL	0-0042994	0467	1
LONG HERBERT S JR	COL	0-0031985	0765	1
LONG HERNDON H	COL	0-0039759	0661	1
LONG HOMER E	COL	0-0030176	0159	2
LONG JOHN H	CW4	W-0903443	0965	1
LONG JOHNNIE E	LTC	N-0001994	0868	1
LONG MARGARET A	LTC	L-0000127	0565	1
LONG MAURICE E	COL	0-0040422	0864	1
LONG NORMAN G	LTC	0-0022759	0268	1
LONG RICHARD J	COL	0-0021175	0768	1
LONG RICHARD L	COL	0-0046931	1065	1
LONG ROBERT T	CPT	0-0056936	0449	2
LONG WILLIAM E	COL	0-0016221	0755	1
LONG WILLIAM P	CW4	W-0903445	1165	1
LONGACRE TERRANCE M	COL	0-0030047	0759	1
LONGAKER NORRIS S JR	2LT	0-0017759	0232	2
LONGANECKER C R	COL	0-0018707	1054	2
LONGBOTHAM RALPH M	LTC	0-0080985	0766	1
LONGERICH HARRY	LTC	0-0053791	0563	1
LONGINO JAMES C	COL	0-0006702	1146	1
LONGINO MERCER P	LTC	0-0024024	0764	1
LONGLEY CAM JR	COL	0-0019112	0661	1
LONGWELL WILLIAM F	MAJ	0-0015125	1041	1
LONNING STANLEY N	COL	0-0019281	0863	1
LONSINGER ROY W	LTC	0-0052192	0866	1
LOOME JAMES T	B G	0-0015584	1046	2
LOOMIS FRANCIS J	COL	0-0020551	0763	1
LOOMIS HAROLD F	B G	0-0003702	1146	2
LOOMIS JESTER M JR	COL	0-0079899	0166	1
LOONEY NEO I	COL	0-0040776	0268	1
LOOPER FLOY L	MAJ	N-0000744	0964	1
LOPER DALE F	CW4	W-0906865	1060	2
LOPER HERBERT B	M G	0-0012243	0653	2
LOPEZ FERNANDO	LTC	0-0080987	0767	1
LOPEZ HENRY F	LTC	0-0062840	0768	2
LORCH ROBERT C	LTC	0-0058957	1166	2
LORCK HORACE C	LTC	0-0036359	0864	1
LORD ERMA G	MAJ	R-0010069	0858	1
LORD HENRY E	LTC	0-0069972	1267	1
LORD ROBERT H	COL	0-0006565	0747	1
LORENCE MAX F	2LT	0-0060924	0551	2
LORENCE WALTER E	COL	0-0009317	1047	1
LORENZ ERNEST H JR	LTC	0-0023505	1159	1
LORENZ JOHN T	LTC	0-0052408	0860	1

NAME	GRADE	SVC NO	DATE RET MO YR	RET CODE
LORENZ RALPH A	COL	0-0030534	1264	2
LORENZ ROBERT M	LTC	0-0063036	1167	1
LOSCH ELMER H	CW3	W-0906866	0261	1
LOSCH JOSEPH W	COL	0-0026812	0768	1
LOSCO FIORENZO D	LTC	0-0056579	0867	1
LOSEY MELVIN D	B G	0-0042235	0863	1
LOSTEN STEVEN W	LTC	0-0048412	0764	1
LOTHROP JAMES N JR	COL	0-0026057	0768	1
LOTHROP GUY C	COL	0-0018992	0561	1
LOTOZO JAMES A	LTC	0-0023109	0362	2
LOTT DOUGLAS A	1LT	0-0027227	0350	2
LOTT LYNWOOD D	COL	0-0041796	0557	1
LOUCKS CHARLES E	M G	0-0006949	0555	1
LOUCKS MARGARET L	MAJ	N-0002050	0760	1
LOUDEN RUSSELL R	COL	0-0010159	0252	2
LOUDENSLAGER ROBERT	LTC	0-0052155	0465	1
LOUGEE LAURENCE W	COL	0-0041933	1161	2
LOUGHLIN CHARLES C	COL	0-0007734	0642	2
LOUGHMAN JACK P	LTC	0-0026282	0963	1
LOUGHRAN JOSEPH S	CPT	0-0009435	0-21	2
LOUPRET GEORGE J	COL	0-0012676	0950	2
LOVE HENRY L	LTC	0-0014653	0952	2
LOVE ROBERT B	CW4	W-0906067	1165	1
LOVE ROBERT L	COL	0-0017774	0147	2
LOVE ROBERT W	COL	0-0021062	0168	1
LOVE WALTER D	M G	0-0011506	0454	1
LOVEJOY CHARLES D	COL	0-0079900	1168	1
LOVELL HARRY F	COL	0-0042616	0559	1
LOVELL HERBERT R	LTC	0-0039253	0464	1
LOVELLY EDWARD A JR	MAJ	0-0008699	1022	2
LOVERING RICHARD S	MAJ	0-0023493	0547	2
LOVETT HILDA M	LTC	R-0010061	0558	1
LOVETT RALPH B	B G	0-0008092	0247	2
LOVETT ROBERT G	B G	0-0012062	0654	1
LOVIN HELEN B	MAJ	N-0002250	0761	1
LOVING ROGER C	LTC	0-0055885	0765	1
LOVSNES NEAL W	COL	0-0030540	1065	2
LOW HAROLD R	COL	0-0020234	0656	1
LOW JAMES L	COL	0-0030585	0166	1
LOW JOSEPH W	CW3	W-0903451	0459	1
LOWDEN CHARLES B	LTC	0-0060642	0767	1
LOWE BRYAN T	LTC	0-0070412	1068	1
LOWE ELWARD W	LTC	0-0054717	0562	1
LOWE PERCY S	COL	0-0009905	0949	2
LOWE ROBERT G	COL	0-0016800	0757	1
LOWE ROBERT L	COL	0-0042913	1165	1
LOWENSTERN SIDNEY	LTC	0-0051285	0160	1
LOWERY AUSTIN JR	COL	0-0182282	0961	2
LOWERY WILLIAM B	LTC	0-0008083	0842	2
LOWREY AUSTIN JR	COL	0-0018282	0861	1
LOWREY CHARLES A	CW3	W-0903455	0859	1
LOWRIE ELVIN S	LTC	0-0079901	1066	1
LOWRY DEXTER	LTC	0-0017628	0150	2
LOWRY EARL L	COL	0-0020992	1058	1
LOWRY EVERETT E JR	COL	0-0025799	0666	1
LOWRY LEONARD	LTC	0-0080989	0967	1
LOWRY PORTER P	COL	0-0005567	0147	2
LOWRY RICHARD	COL	0-0039725	1052	2
LOWRY ROBERT H	COL	0-0004159	0747	1
LOYD FRANK R	COL	0-0016004	0854	2
LUBBE ALBERT J	LTC	0-0012523	1044	1
LUCAS ASTOR C JR	CW4	W-0903457	0668	1
LUCAS BURTON L	COL	0-0007334	1050	1
LUCAS EDWARD D	LTC	0-0023225	0660	1
LUCAS MASON H	B G	0-0016633	1056	1
LUCAS VIRGINIA G	MAJ	N-0001551	0965	1
LUCAS WILLIAM C	COL	0-0015309	0954	1
LUCAS WILLIAM E JR	LTC	0-0004793	0142	1
LUCE DEAN	COL	0-0012389	1050	1
LUCEY GEORGE A	COL	0-0024446	0466	1
LUCHWINKO JOSEPH	CW4	W-0903458	0266	1
LUCIER ALPHONSE F JR	LTC	0-0034832	0863	1
LUCK HARRY C	COL	0-0005119	0548	2
LUCKE EMIL A	COL	0-0042331	0364	1
LUCKE WILLIAM N	LTC	0-0024430	1159	1

NAME	GRADE	SVC NO	DATE RET MO YR	RET CODE
LUCKETT JAMES S	COL	0-0018209	0760	1
LUCREE MORRIS J	COL	0-0033401	0966	1
LUDECKE FRED W	COL	0-0041898	0861	1
LUDEMAN RICHARD F	LTC	0-0022233	0759	1
LUDINGTON MARVIN W	COL	0-0029434	0860	2
LUDLAM DOUGLAS G	COL	0-0017207	0758	2
LUDWIKOSKY JOHN P	COL	0-0034228	0862	1
LUEBBERMAN HENRI A	COL	0-0016827	0549	2
LUKAS FRANK W	LTC	0-0079656	1068	1
LUKE ITTAI A	COL	0-0005541	0646	1
LUKE REGIS W	COL	0-0039859	0264	1
LUKEMAN JOHN M	COL	0-0061061	1167	1
LUKENS JAMES R	LTC	0-0063331	1265	1
LUKENS WALTER P	LTC	0-0050801	0467	1
LUKER CHARLES T	LTC	0-0038883	0161	1
LULL GEORGE F	M G	0-0003516	0446	1
LULL GEORGE F JR	COL	0-0031114	0565	1
LUM NICK	CW4	W-0906868	0466	1
LUMIA SALVATORE	LTC	0-0080991	1165	1
LUMPKIN BENJAMIN E	LTC	0-0057425	0567	1
LUMPKIN CLAUDE C JR	LTC	0-0024941	0863	1
LUMPKIN WALTER L JR	COL	0-0037615	0764	1
LUMRY RAYMOND H	COL	0-0022199	0764	1
LUNA RAYMOND C	LTC	0-0042403	0762	2
LUNCEFORD ROY L	LTC	0-0080992	0567	1
LUND GERTRUDE F	MAJ	L-0000217	0656	1
LUND JOHN B	LTC	0-0097323	0568	2
LUNDBERG FLOYD M	COL	0-0042136	0263	1
LUNDBERG GEORGE B	COL	0-0025679	0868	1
LUNDEBERG KARL R	COL	0-0017979	0454	1
LUNDQUIST CARL E	COL	0-0016889	0657	1
LUNDY IRVIN M	MAJ	0-0041000	0160	1
LUNDY JAMES T	MAJ	0-0067719	0567	1
LUNGER RICHARD T	COL	0-0025388	1262	1
LUNNEY DONALD R	1LT	0-0027110	1147	2
LUNSFORD JAMES N JR	LTC	0-0033518	0867	1
LUNTZEL ADRIAN A	CW4	W-0903460	0167	1
LUONGO HENRY L	COL	0-0016683	1056	1
LURA EDNA	LTC	M-0010034	0352	1
LUSCOMBE HAROLD B	COL	0-0018298	0356	1
LUSCOMBE JOHN B	COL	0-0012525	0946	2
LUSE ARTHUR H	COL	0-0007537	0848	2
LUSZKI WALTER A	LTC	0-0044073	1159	1
LUTES LEROY	LTG	0-0005413	0152	2
LUTES LEROY JR	COL	0-0020757	0866	1
LUTHER HENRY	COL	0-0079713	0767	1
LUTHI IRVIN L	COL	0-0038830	0566	1
LUTTRELL JAMES A	LTC	0-0036363	0863	1
LUTZ CARL G	COL	0-0043366	0264	1
LUTZ ROBERT C	LTC	0-0027359	0865	1
LUTZ ROBERT C	COL	0-0028868	0854	1
LUTZ ROBERT R	COL	0-0030767	0766	1
LUTZ WILLIAM D	LTC	0-0026018	0468	1
LUX HERBERT G	COL	0-0042212	0863	1
LYBRAND ALBERT B	CW3	W-0903461	1060	1
LYDAY CHARLES V	LTC	0-0065534	1266	1
LYDDON DONALD W	LTC	0-0026413	1052	2
LYDICK JOHN M	COL	0-0041436	0956	1
LYDLE CRAWFORD H JR	LTC	0-0052349	0859	1
LYDON JOSEPH P	LTC	0-0033853	0768	2
LYDON JOSEPHINE	LTC	R-0010123	0565	2
LYKE CLARE N	LTC	0-0024601	0262	1
LYLE CLAYTON B JR	COL	0-0040306	0767	1
LYLE JAMES B	COL	0-0032348	0865	1
LYLE JAMES W	LTC	0-0035484	0761	1
LYLE JOHN R	LTC	0-0032700	0261	1
LYLE PAUL B	LTC	0-0080993	0666	1
LYLE SHIRLEY M	MAJ	N-0000331	1059	1
LYMAN CHARLES B	B G	0-0003590	0346	1
LYMAN HARRY E	COL	0-0038903	0167	1
LYMAN IRVING R	COL	0-0024319	1064	1
LYMAN JAMES H	1LT	0-0014444	0421	2
LYMAN REGINALD P	B G	0-0014872	0854	1
LYNCH BUFORD A JR	1LT	0-0015881	0333	2
LYNCH CHARLES L	LTC	0-0057911	0766	1

NAME	GRADE	SVC NO	DATE RET MO YR	RET CODE
LYNCH FRANCIS H	1LT	0-0017748	1137	2
LYNCH FRANCIS T	MAJ	0-0056217	0863	1
LYNCH GEORGE F	M G	0-0017715	0257	1
LYNCH GEORGE P	B G	0-0016226	0556	1
LYNCH GEORGE W JR	CW4	W-0903462	0959	1
LYNCH HARRY	LTC	0-0014766	1047	1
LYNCH HUBERT J	CW4	W-0903463	0261	1
LYNCH JAMES H	B G	0-0021237	0368	2
LYNCH JAMES P	1LT	0-0026703	0546	2
LYNCH JOHN A	CPT	0-0070415	1059	2
LYNCH JOHN F	CPT	0-0014371	0819	2
LYNCH JOHN M	COL	0-0020377	0866	1
LYNCH JOHN T	COL	0-0012841	1052	1
LYNCH JOHN T	CW3	W-0903464	0957	1
LYNCH JOHN W	LTC	0-0042984	0962	1
LYNCH ROBERT J	MAJ	0-0060253	0665	1
LYNCH SUE	LTC	L-0000081	1164	1
LYNCH THOMAS D JR	MAJ	0-0080139	0361	1
LYNCH WILLIAM D	COL	0-0065081	1068	1
LYND ROY F	COL	0-0006146	0849	2
LYNDE NELSON M JR	M G	0-0017730	0364	1
LYNES DONALD L	LTC	0-0063080	0566	1
LYNN CLARK	COL	0-0001832	1138	1
LYNN CLARK JR	COL	0-0019456	0864	1
LYNN DOSS D	COL	0-0021722	0363	2
LYNN EDISON A JR	COL	0-0023085	1262	1
LYNN LAURENCE F	COL	0-0042059	0862	1
LYON ARCHIBALD	B G	0-0018682	0862	1
LYON FREDERICK	CW3	W-0903465	0558	1
LYON HAROLD C	COL	0-0041832	0161	1
LYON HENRY Y	COL	0-0005868	0753	1
LYON IRENE	MAJ	N-0002496	1168	1
LYONS CARL F	COL	0-0020824	0767	1
LYONS CATHERINE	LTC	L-0000073	1263	1
LYONS CHAUNCEY M	COL	0-0008105	0151	2
LYONS GEORGE E JR	CW4	W-0906870	0767	1
LYONS HARRY L	WO1	W-0901116	0425	1
LYONS JAMES P	COL	0-0006108	1146	1
LYONS JOHN H	LTC	0-0052079	1054	1
LYONS JOSEPH W	LTC	0-0059466	0567	1
LYTER CLINTON S	M G	0-0018291	0366	2
LYTLE JAMES R	LTC	0-0048021	0762	1
LYTLE WAYMAN H	LTC	0-0060921	1267	1
MAAS HARRY W	COL	0-0006573	0848	1
MABBOTT HAROLD C	COL	0-0006677	1047	1
MABBUTT CHARLES J	LTC	0-0007961	0934	2
MABEE RICHARD W	COL	0-0023241	1060	1
MABIE RUSSELL L	COL	0-0015626	0854	1
MABRY J P	LTC	0-0080995	0968	1
MABRY LELAND S	COL	0-0017034	0651	1
MABRY NED B	COL	0-0053148	0667	1
MABRY ROBERT A	CW4	W-0903467	0665	1
MAC ADAM LLOYD R	COL	0-0029513	1060	1
MAC ALLASTER W R	LTC	0-0051678	0157	1
MAC ARTHUR JOHN C	COL	0-0010115	0451	1
MAC ARTHUR JOHN E	MAJ	0-0040885	0162	1
MAC CONNELL T III	COL	0-0040286	0866	1
MAC DONALD ALECK F	COL	0-0022685	1065	1
MAC DONALD ALEXAND	LTC	0-0023341	0147	2
MAC DONALD ANGELINE	LTC	N-0000996	0267	1
MAC DONALD AUGUSTINE	LTC	0-0036989	0661	1
MAC DONALD FRANCIS A	LTC	0-0041082	0664	1
MAC DONALD HENRY G	CW4	W-0902089	0662	1
MAC DONALD JOHN P	LTC	0-0039368	0965	1
MAC DONALD MALCOLM E	LTC	0-0028701	0766	1
MAC DONALD MARION C	1LT	R-0000266	1146	1
MAC DONALD MELVILLE	LTC	0-0056444	1268	1
MAC DONALD STUART C	COL	0-0003854	1051	1
MAC DONALD VERNA E	MAJ	N-0002379	0261	1
MAC DONOUGH JOHN E	LTC	0-0052208	0965	1
MAC DOUGALL JAMES B	COL	0-0029335	0859	1
MAC EACHERN GEORGE A	COL	0-0038806	1065	1
MAC FARLAND JAMES C	COL	0-0080996	0868	1
MAC FARLAND JOHN J	COL	0-0018100	0260	2
MAC FEETERS DONALD W	COL	0-0025300	0268	1

NAME	GRADE	SVC NO	DATE RET MO YR	RET CODE
MAC GRAIN DONALD	COL	0-0038933	0268	1
MAC GREGOR CECIL M	COL	0-0042182	0763	1
MAC GREGOR LESTER E	COL	0-0007102	0546	1
MAC KELLAR ROSE M	MAJ	R-0010097	0868	1
MAC KELVIE JAY W	B G	0-0005476	0946	2
MAC KENZIE ALAN F S	COL	0-0028806	0655	1
MAC KENZIE ALEXAND	COL	0-0012203	0446	2
MAC KENZIE FRANK P	COL	0-0010836	0248	1
MAC KINNON WILLIAM R	COL	0-0011408	0146	2
MAC KUSICK ARTHUR L	COL	0-0042695	0962	1
MAC LACHLAN DONALD J	MAJ	0-0002238	1022	1
MAC LAUGHLIN PAUL E	LTC	0-0017332	0252	2
MAC LEAN GERTRUDE A	LTC	N-0000506	1148	1
MAC LEAN ROBERT J	LTC	0-0044042	0862	1
MAC LEOD JOHN W	COL	0-0041919	0961	1
MAC MILLAN KARL D	COL	0-0063822	0964	1
MAC MILLAN THOMAS R	MAJ	0-0037411	0861	1
MAC MORLAND EDWARD E	M G	0-0004653	0752	1
MAC NABB ALEXANDER	COL	0-0007436	0751	2
MAC NEILL FRANCIS W	LTC	0-0070416	0565	2
MAC QUEEN LAWRENCE P	COL	0-0035614	1167	1
MAC QUIGG DAVID E	LTC	0-0061174	0167	1
MAC WILLIAMS JOHN	COL	0-0012555	0546	2
MAC WILLIE DONALD M	COL	0-0030152	0464	1
MACATEE EDWARD V	COL	0-0011366	0653	1
MACE DON L	LTC	0-0021737	0257	1
MACE RALPH R	M G	0-0017578	0664	1
MACHEN EDWIN A JR	B G	0-0021284	0868	1
MACHEREY EARL J	COL	0-0019158	0763	1
MACHNICKE MAX R	LTC	0-0033465	0968	1
MACK DANIEL D JR	COL	0-0030015	1263	1
MACK HENRY W	MAJ	OF-0105472	0968	1
MACK JOHN D	COL	0-0080443	0765	1
MACK WILLIAM M	COL	0-0014866	0854	1
MACKEN JOHN J	LTC	0-0040304	1165	1
MACKENZIE GABRIEL T	COL	0-0004658	0951	2
MACKEY HAROLD V	LTC	0-0025046	0862	1
MACKIN JAMES H	COL	0-0029300	0166	2
MACKIN 3RD ROBERT N	MAJ	0-0023260	1152	2
MACKINTOSH HUGH	M G	0-0017716	0466	1
MACKINTOSH WILLIAM E	LTC	0-0051221	0250	2
MACLACHLAN WALTER L	COL	0-0050948	0657	1
MACOMBER JOHN A	LTC	0-0057965	1066	1
MACOMBER KENNETH D	COL	0-0042009	0462	1
MACON FRANCIS A JR	COL	0-0005315	0753	1
MACON ROBERT C	M G	0-0004733	0752	2
MADDALENA ARMAND S	CW4	W-0906872	1265	1
MADDEN FRANCIS J	COL	0-0046258	0668	1
MADDEN IDA K	MAJ	L-0000252	0464	1
MADDEN JOSEPH C	COL	0-0029656	0160	1
MADDEN TED J	LTC	0-0042537	0255	1
MADDING ALBERT S	LTC	0-0033680	0764	1
MADDOCKS RAY T	M G	0-0007291	0651	1
MADDOCKS THOMAS H	COL	0-0015000	0451	1
MADDOX EDWARD R	COL	0-0030036	1063	1
MADDOX GEORGE W	LTC	0-0002090	0929	2
MADDOX HALLEY G	M G	0-0012852	0259	2
MADDOX J D	CW4	W-0903471	0464	1
MADIGAN JOHN J JR	COL	0-0039538	0956	1
MADIGAN MARIE J	MAJ	L-0000069	0460	1
MAEDLER JAMES R	COL	0-0023132	0168	1
MAERDIAN FRANK R	COL	0-0017256	0758	1
MAERZ RICHARD H	LTC	0-0080444	0965	1
MAFFED MARIO A	COL	0-0043264	0268	1
MAGEE JAMES C	M G	0-0002565	0-43	1
MAGEE MERVYN M	M G	0-0018478	0667	1
MAGEE OSCAR J	LTC	0-0042158	0261	1
MAGNESS THOMAS H JR	COL	0-0051199	0261	1
MAGNOTTI JOHN F JR	LTC	0-0059200	1068	1
MAGNUSSON JOHN R	COL	0-0031432	0165	1
MAGRUDER CARTER B	GEN	0-0015155	0661	1
MAGUIRE EDWARD F	LTC	0-0030332	1262	1
MAGUIRE EDWARD J	LTC	0-0042251	0961	1
MAGUIRE HAMILTON E	B G	0-0004433	0748	1
MAGUIRE ROBERT F	COL	0-0037528	1167	1

NAME	GRADE	SVC NO	DATE RET MO YR	RET CODE
MAHAN DALE E	MAJ	0-0027642	0765	1
MAHER JOHN P JR	COL	0-0041490	1057	1
MAHER JOHN R	MAJ	0-0094432	0763	2
MAHER WILLIAM F	COL	0-0003747	0847	1
MAHONEY ARTHUR E	LTC	0-0060524	0868	1
MAHONEY ELIZABETH	LTC	N-0000499	0252	2
MAHONEY JAMES H	COL	0-0051613	0565	1
MAHONEY MARGARET E	MAJ	M-0010017	0966	1
MAHONEY WILLIAM E JR	COL	0-0023486	0861	1
MAHONEY WILLIAM J	COL	0-0018616	0754	1
MAHR RAYMOND A	COL	0-0043157	0766	1
MAIDT RONALD N	COL	0-0042513	0762	1
MAIER AARON D	LTC	0-0050559	0968	1
MAIER ROBERT J	LTC	0-0063075	0367	1
MAILHEAU ROBERT T	LTC	0-0062172	0455	2
MAIN RALPH E	LTC	0-0041200	0665	1
MAINWARING JOHN W JR	LTC	0-0030865	0561	1
MAIORANO PASQUALE P	COL	0-0042316	0264	1
MAISER NEVA B	MAJ	L-0000228	0258	1
MAISH ALEXANDER	LTC	0-0026523	0767	1
MAITA WINIFRED Z	LTC	N-0002370	0463	1
MAJ EDWARD S	LTC	0-0061360	0967	1
MAJOR BERNARD P	COL	0-0020750	0467	1
MAJOR GEORGE C	MAJ	0-0046041	0762	1
MAJORS EDWARD M	COL	0-0031971	0868	1
MAKAROUNIS ALEXANDER	CPT	0-0058962	0556	2
MAKINNEY FRED W	COL	0-0012469	0146	2
MALANKOWSKI ANTHONY	LTC	0-0030500	0363	2
MALDONADO JACK C	COL	0-0024447	0767	1
MALERBA AGNES C	MAJ	N-0001036	0366	1
MALEVICH STEVEN	COL	0-0030660	0663	1
MALEY AGNES A	COL	N-0000516	0658	2
MALIN HOWARD A	COL	0-0015821	0954	1
MALINA ANTHONY S	CW4	W-0903474	0863	1
MALING EDWIN C	COL	0-0014598	1047	1
MALISZEWSKI GEORGE M	COL	0-0020759	1067	2
MALL OSCAR A	COL	0-0031796	0767	1
MALLALIEU CHARLES F	LTC	0-0042333	0262	1
MALLETT PIERRE	B G	0-0008314	0550	1
MALLON FRANCIS B	M G	0-0003426	0946	2
MALLON JOHN B	LTC	0-0051123	1057	1
MALLONEE RICHARD C	COL	0-0008464	0854	1
MALLORY JOHN W	LTC	0-0056135	1066	1
MALLOY JOHN T	COL	0-0018576	0561	1
MALONE ALBERT C JR	LTC	0-0063275	0967	1
MALONE ARTHUR G	LTC	0-0023237	0761	1
MALONE DUANE W	LTC	0-0031479	0165	1
MALONE EUBERT H JR	LTC	0-0038253	0965	1
MALONE EVERETTE W	LTC	0-0049925	1061	1
MALONE FLORENCE C	MAJ	N-0002027	0558	1
MALONE MARIE L	LTC	L-0000198	1265	1
MALONE PATRICK M	LTC	0-0079904	0468	1
MALONE RHODA E	MAJ	N-0000364	0662	1
MALONE THOMAS R	COL	0-0029489	1160	1
MALONE WILLIAM F	LTC	0-0026044	0164	1
MALONEY ARTHUR A	COL	0-0021297	0846	2
MALONEY JAMES E JR	COL	0-0018610	0761	1
MALONEY JAMES P	LTC	0-0039556	0150	1
MALONY HARRY J	M G	0-0003385	0349	1
MALY LEWIS W	COL	0-0008755	0946	2
MAMER JAMES	1LT	0-0011559	1130	2
MANARY EUGENE D	LTC	0-0033216	0362	2
MANASCO RAYMOND O	LTC	0-0033608	0764	2
MANCUSO STEPHEN J	COL	0-0022006	0966	1
MANDEL ADRIAN D	LTC	0-0060889	0266	1
MANDELBAUM ALBERT J	COL	0-0018061	0660	2
MANDELL FRANK C	COL	0-0023234	0866	1
MANDERBACH HAROLD M	COL	0-0015984	0854	1
MANESS RALPH T	CW4	W-0906877	0560	1
MANGAN WALTER D	COL	0-0004511	0145	2
MANGES JOSEPH O	COL	0-0031055	0968	1
MANGINI MICHAEL	CW4	W-0903475	0862	1
MANGOLD HAROLD B	COL	0-0031522	0766	1
MANGONES ROBERT J	MAJ	0-0081004	0467	1
MANGUM CLAUD D	COL	0-0080446	0868	1
MANGUM ROBERT G	COL	0-0005983	1146	1
MANIFOLD MAX O	LTC	0-0060345	0868	1
MANLEY NORBERT C	LTC	0-0007820	0545	1
MANLOVE ALMON W	COL	0-0019413	0864	1
MANLY LORRAINE L	COL	0-0051373	0758	1
MANN CHARLES C	MAJ	0-0003990	0822	2
MANN HERBERT C JR	CW4	RW-0903476	0963	1
MANN HOWARD H	MAJ	0-0060259	0466	1
MANN JAMES W	LTC	0-0057497	1068	1
MANN JOHN P	CW3	W-0903478	0159	1
MANN ROBERT J	LTC	0-0027361	0766	1
MANN THOMAS L	COL	0-0022663	1267	1
MANNES CONRAD O JR	LTC	0-0032293	0459	1
MANNING EARL V	COL	0-0039941	0465	1
MANNING KENNETH T	MAJ	0-0060320	0360	1
MANNING RAMONA S	MAJ	N-0000446	0461	1
MANNING RICHARD I	LTC	0-0023439	0660	1
MANNING WALLACE A	LTC	0-0043386	1057	2
MANOV CHARLES F	COL	0-0051840	0467	2
MANRODT MANFRED P	CW4	W-0903479	0167	1
MANSAGER MERVIN E	COL	0-0041878	0661	1
MANSFIELD HERBERT V	COL	0-0080447	0861	1
MANSFIELD HERBERT W	COL	0-0018429	0761	1
MANSON PETER C	LTC	0-0023545	0660	1
MANTALAS JOHN G	CPT	0-0063064	1162	3
MANTELL LOUIS K	COL	0-0020035	0366	2
MANTER OTIS L JR	CW4	W-0906879	0566	1
MANTHEY ERWIN A	CPT	0-0006560	0134	2
MANTOR FRANCES C	LTC	N-0000813	0861	1
MANZANO NARCISO L	COL	0-0014790	0147	2
MAPES ROLAND H	COL	0-0030538	0256	1
MAPLES FREDERIC A	COL	0-0029017	1058	2
MARCH KENNETH F	COL	0-0016481	0856	1
MARCH MARY M	1LT	M-0000459	0544	1
MARCHEK CARLYLE S	COL	0-0029290	1158	1
MARCHUS DAVID E JR	LTC	0-0079636	0864	1
MARCONI SABATINE R	LTC	0-0036128	0866	1
MARCUM ROBERT D	LTC	0-0083606	0868	1
MARCUS MILTON S	COL	0-0084457	0868	1
MARCUS MORRIS H	COL	0-0014602	0954	1
MARCY ALFRED R	COL	0-0038597	0855	1
MARCY ROY W	COL	0-0031380	0763	2
MARDEN LYMAN P JR	COL	0-0040086	0562	1
MARET RAYMOND	COL	0-0063666	1066	2
MARGESON HENRY B	COL	0-0016181	0655	1
MARGETIS NICHOLAS M	CPT	0-0060112	1151	2
MARGOLIES HARRY	COL	0-0040235	0468	2
MARGOLIN OLIVER	CW3	W-0903481	0361	1
MARGRAVE CHESTER E	COL	0-0016643	0846	2
MARICLE LOUIS J	COL	0-0065055	0868	1
MARIETTA SHELLEY U	M G	0-0003290	0145	2
MARIN GERALD S	LTC	0-0081006	0868	1
MARINELLI JACK L	COL	0-0034331	0762	1
MARIS WARD H	M G	0-0006718	1152	1
MARKER HARRY J	COL	0-0051688	1265	1
MARKER RALPH E JR	LTC	0-0064337	1268	1
MARKEY EDWARD W	COL	0-0035143	0365	1
MARKEY LAWRENCE B	B G	0-0038826	0867	1
MARKHAM HARRISON S	LTC	0-0020073	0156	1
MARKHAM MICHAEL C	LTC	0-0042986	0465	1
MARKLEY HARRISON M	COL	0-0038752	1163	1
MARKLEY MARTIN A	CPT	0-0063245	1158	2
MARKOWITZ ISIDOR	COL	0-0059511	1061	1
MARKS RAYMOND A	LTC	0-0060991	0268	1
MARKS WILLARD A	CPT	0-0026728	1047	2
MARKS YOUIR M F	LTC	0-0014155	0716	2
MARKWELL DICK R	LTC	0-0065758	0967	1
MARLOW HERMAN M	LTC	0-0032606	0268	1
MARNANE THOMAS J	COL	0-0018535	0761	1
MARNOCH GABRIEL W JR	LTC	0-0081009	0968	1
MARPHIS JOSEPH C	LTC	0-0051003	0956	1
MARQUETTE WILLIAM J	COL	0-0042231	0963	1
MARR HAROLD E JR	COL	0-0020729	0867	1
MARR LLOYD M	COL	0-0031420	0467	2
MARR RICHARD S	COL	0-0015447	1153	1
MARR ROBERT A	LTC	0-0094875	0768	1
MARREN JOHN J	COL	0-0041706	0759	1
MARRERO JOHN	LTC	0-0054297	0964	1
MARRIOTT OWEN K	COL	0-0012587	0951	1
MARRIOTT RICHARD G	COL	0-0033072	0568	1
MARSDEN HENRY H JR	COL	0-0043643	1266	1
MARSH CURTIS N JR	COL	0-0079905	0766	1
MARSH EDWARD F	LTC	0-0029325	0862	1
MARSH EDWIN S	LTC	0-0031307	0765	1
MARSH HOWARD M	CW2	W-0901865	1149	1
MARSH JAMES H	COL	0-0014610	0253	1
MARSH LEON D	COL	0-0039739	0761	1
MARSH MARVIN W	COL	0-0008419	0854	1
MARSH RAYMOND	COL	0-0003798	0747	2
MARSH RAYMOND JR	LTC	0-0067720	1167	1
MARSH WILLIAM A	COL	0-0010608	1146	1
MARSHALL ALBERT B	COL	0-0052350	0962	1
MARSHALL CARLEY L	COL	0-0011765	0849	1
MARSHALL DAVID N	LTC	0-0052221	0864	1
MARSHALL EDWARD R	LTC	0-0022692	0764	1
MARSHALL ELEANOR M	LTC	M-0010040	0761	1
MARSHALL FRANCIS R	LTC	0-0058496	0768	1
MARSHALL FURMAN W	LTC	0-0042925	0662	1
MARSHALL HARRY G	CW4	W-0903483	1061	1
MARSHALL HUBERT T	COL	0-0019689	0649	2
MARSHALL IRVINE H	COL	0-0039658	1160	1
MARSHALL JAMES C	B G	0-0009316	0347	2
MARSHALL MAX L	LTC	0-0026867	0764	1
MARSHALL MORRIS L	1LT	0-0093827	0263	2
MARSHALL RICHARD	LTC	0-0052416	0160	1
MARSHALL RICHARD J	M G	0-0004635	1146	1
MARSHALL ROBERT B	COL	0-0081011	1068	1
MARSIC MARY A	MAJ	N-0001956	0558	1
MARSTON ANSON O	COL	0-0029427	0760	1
MARSTON MORRILL W	B G	0-0007126	0753	1
MARSTON OLIVER F	COL	0-0007174	0246	2
MARSZAL JOHN A	CW4	RW-0904442	0664	1
MARTAK CLYDE J	LTC	0-0054719	0763	1
MARTASIN WILLIAM N	COL	0-0044997	1166	1
MARTELINO AMADO	COL	0-0014881	0547	2
MARTENS HOWARD W	COL	0-0032324	0766	1
MARTIN ALFRED	COL	0-0023629	1165	1
MARTIN BRICE J	LTC	0-0033620	0159	2
MARTIN CHARLES H	COL	0-0011073	0749	1
MARTIN CLARENCE A	M G	0-0007007	0747	2
MARTIN CLARENCE E	CW4	W-0904155	1158	1
MARTIN CLYDE J	CW4	W-0903484	0158	1
MARTIN DANIEL J	COL	0-0015907	0946	1
MARTIN DARWIN O	COL	0-0015678	0854	1
MARTIN DAVID	LTC	0-0042947	0459	1
MARTIN EDWARD J	LTC	0-0041143	0661	1
MARTIN EMMOR G	COL	0-0016190	0847	2
MARTIN ETHEL M	MAJ	L-0000182	1264	1
MARTIN FLORENCE B	MAJ	L-0000036	0657	1
MARTIN GEORGE E	M G	0-0016802	0562	1
MARTIN HENRY F	CPT	0-0014443	0321	2
MARTIN JAMES E	MAJ	0-0081012	0364	1
MARTIN JAMES G	LTC	0-0039035	0163	1
MARTIN JAMES J	LTC	0-0081013	0864	1
MARTIN JAMES M	LTC	0-0081015	0266	1
MARTIN JAMES S	MAJ	0-0057660	0766	1
MARTIN JIM I	CPT	OF-0100907	0168	2
MARTIN JOHN	COL	0-0068321	0855	2
MARTIN JOHN A	COL	0-0024453	0661	1
MARTIN JOHN A	COL	0-0051419	0763	1
MARTIN JOHN B	LTC	0-0004563	0242	1
MARTIN JOHN T	LTC	0-0022694	1159	1
MARTIN L D KIRKWD	LTC	0-0037177	1163	1
MARTIN LEWIS T	COL	0-0030188	0762	1
MARTIN LINCOLN	COL	0-0006252	0835	2
MARTIN LORRAINE H	MAJ	N-0000351	0161	1
MARTIN LOUIS L	COL	0-0005277	0352	2
MARTIN LULUAH Y	MAJ	N-0000154	0261	1
MARTIN MARY L	MAJ	N-0000449	0364	1
MARTIN MERRITT P	LTC	0-0062215	0566	1
MARTIN MURRAY J	COL	0-0028775	0554	2
MARTIN NATHANIEL	COL	0-0019794	0857	1
MARTIN NORMAN E	COL	0-0051831	1166	1
MARTIN ORVILLE W	COL	0-0012253	1050	1
MARTIN PAUL H	COL	0-0018331	0155	1
MARTIN PAUL L	MAJ	0-0015095	0542	2
MARTIN ROBERT J	LTC	0-0062253	1166	1
MARTIN ROBERT T	LTC	0-0026641	0965	1
MARTIN ROBERT W	LTC	0-0079907	0668	1
MARTIN RONALD L	COL	0-0019428	0660	1
MARTIN SARAH N	MAJ	N-0001532	0963	1
MARTIN SIDNEY T	COL	0-0021772	0865	1
MARTIN THOMAS E	1LT	0-0014390	1119	2
MARTIN THOMAS L	B G	0-0004470	0451	1
MARTIN TRUBY C	LTC	0-0013944	0620	2
MARTIN WINFIELD L	COL	0-0020809	0665	1
MARTINEAU FREDERICK	COL	0-0042971	0864	1
MARTINEZ JOE I	LTC	0-0027446	0766	1
MARTINEZ SEVERINO JR	LTC	0-0024811	0263	1
MARTINI MARIAN E	MAJ	N-0000208	0463	1
MARTS FRED R	CW2	W-0903486	1050	2
MARTZ JOHN D JR	COL	0-0029769	0962	1
MARTZ WILLIAM V	COL	0-0019879	0862	1
MARVEL EDGAR E	LTC	0-0084871	0868	1
MARVIN GEORGE W	COL	0-0014887	0753	1
MARVIN HORACE P	COL	0-0016957	0944	2
MARWINE BEULAH L	LTC	N-0002097	1267	1
MARX GEORGE H	LTC	0-0058967	1068	2
MARX RALPH L	COL	0-0022262	0258	1
MASENGA ROBERT C	COL	0-0054101	0868	1
MASLIN FRANCIS I	COL	0-0009040	0746	1
MASLOWSKI LADISLAUS	COL	0-0021789	0567	2
MASON ALFRED L	COL	0-0004405	1138	1
MASON CHARLES H	COL	0-0016045	1147	2
MASON DON A	COL	0-0031694	0266	1
MASON EDWARD R	COL	0-0031563	0666	2
MASON GRANT W	COL	0-0030738	0665	1
MASON JOHN P	LTC	0-0044587	1262	1
MASON KERMIT R	LTC	0-0046951	0664	1
MASON MARSHALL A JR	LTC	0-0063462	1166	1
MASON RICHARD P	COL	0-0020928	0861	1
MASON STANHOPE B	M G	0-0017295	0861	1
MASON TROXELL O	LTC	0-0023522	0761	1
MASON WILLIAM H	2LT	0-0082779	0559	2
MASSARO JOSEPH	LTC	0-0015798	0753	1
MASSELLO WILLIAM JR	COL	0-0018749	0760	1
MASSENGILL PAUL	CW4	W-0902368	0560	1
MASSEY CLYDE	B G	0-0015551	0954	1
MASSEY GEORGE W	CW4	W-0903488	1165	1
MASSEY JAMES L	COL	0-0018838	0262	1
MASSEY WILLIAM R	2LT	0-0057677	0550	2
MASSINGALE JOHN T	LTC	0-0051499	0562	1
MASSOGLIA MARTIN F	COL	0-0052831	1067	1
MASTELLONE ANIELLO F	COL	0-0043115	1165	1
MASTERS GEORGE C	COL	0-0028950	1057	1
MASTERS MEREDITH D	CPT	0-0016846	0937	2
MASTON VICTOR E	COL	0-0019075	0861	1
MASTROIANNI ELLEN	MAJ	N-0002252	0961	1
MASTROLIA ANTHONY C	LTC	0-0043244	1268	1
MASTRUCCI JOSEPH P	LTC	0-0031768	0166	1
MATCHETT HENRY J	B G	0-0005503	0250	1
MATCHETTE CLAUDE H	COL	0-0031490	0467	1
MATEJKA JERRY V	M G	0-0007496	1055	1
MATERI JOSEPH T	LTC	0-0024330	0764	1
MATHE ROBERT E	B G	0-0025878	0168	1
MATHENY CHARLES W	COL	0-0024619	0762	1
MATHES EDWARD S	LTC	0-0030481	0763	1
MATHESON DAVID M	LTC	0-0021757	0667	1
MATHESON DONALD R	COL	0-0021213	0347	2
MATHESON JOHN D	COL	0-0018962	0657	1
MATHESON MARIAN M	MAJ	N-0001875	0558	1
MATHESON MARJORIE	MAJ	N-0000928	0264	1
MATHEWS CLIFFORD J	COL	0-0003736	0850	1
MATHEWS DAVID J	CW4	W-0901885	0465	1
MATHEWS DON S	LTC	0-0030121	0162	1

UNITED STATES ARMY RETIRED LIST

NAME	GRADE	SVC NO	DATE RET MO YR	RET CODE
MATHEWS ELMO S	COL	O-0017167	0658	1
MATHEWS FRANK H	COL	O-0039569	0452	2
MATHEWS JOEL L	MAJ	O-0019237	0448	2
MATHEWS LUDWIG L	CW4	RW-0903489	0262	1
MATHEWS WAYNE C	LTC	O-0070422	0667	1
MATHEWSON DAVID A JR	COL	O-0038753	1163	1
MATHEWSON ELEANOR H	MAJ	R-0000026	0463	1
MATHEWSON LEMUEL	LTG	O-0014980	0458	2
MATHEWSON NATHAN S	COL	O-0029771	0962	1
MATHIS WILLIAM H	LTC	O-0037653	0665	1
MATHOS HARRY G	COL	O-0045077	0465	1
MATHWIN ALBERT V	LTC	O-0037721	0967	1
MATLACK FRANK S	COL	O-0004171	0446	1
MATLACK TOM E	COL	O-0022238	0746	2
MATLAVAGE MATTHEW W	CW4	W-0903490	1064	1
MATLOCK HALLIE A	COL	O-0040377	0864	1
MATTE PAUL J	COL	O-0006722	0351	1
MATTER ROBERT A	COL	O-0022132	0867	1
MATTERA RALPH A	LTC	O-0066047	0368	1
MATTERNES LAWRENCE A	COL	O-0018295	0755	1
MATTESON JAMES S	LTC	O-0087847	0667	1
MATTESON MILO H	COL	O-0016127	0554	1
MATTESON ORVAL Q	COL	O-0043509	0868	1
MATTESON VICTOR E	COL	O-0083569	1268	1
MATTESON WILLIAM J	COL	O-0017100	0242	2
MATTFELDT CYLBURN O	COL	O-0006128	0934	2
MATTHAIS EDITH F	MAJ	N-0001980	0263	1
MATTHEWS CLARA M	MAJ	L-0000058	0859	1
MATTHEWS FREDERICK	COL	O-0005625	1052	1
MATTHEWS HARVIE R	COL	O-0014660	0447	2
MATTHEWS JEWETT O	LTC	O-0006492	0241	1
MATTHEWS LESLIE M	WO1	W-0800155	0642	2
MATTHEWS ROBERT A	COL	O-0046599	0968	1
MATTHEWS STANLEY L	LTC	O-0060315	0163	1
MATTHEWS WILLIS S	M G	O-0016932	0163	1
MATTHIAS NOMAN A	COL	O-0016400	0656	1
MATTICE EARL	COL	O-0015602	0854	1
MATTICE HAROLD H	LTC	O-0080143	0968	1
MATTIE EDWARD C	LTC	O-0079671	0466	2
MATTINGLY HOWARD	LTC	O-0080144	0964	1
MATTINGLY THOMAS W	B G	O-0020068	0858	1
MATTISON WILLIAM R	COL	O-0081018	0765	1
MATTOON HUGH M	COL	O-0078963	1268	1
MATTOS ANTHONY R	LTC	O-0091325	0865	1
MATUSKA WALTER H	COL	O-0029155	1058	1
MATYAS ALBERT A	COL	O-0019928	0560	1
MATZGER NEIL M	COL	O-0044539	0268	1
MAUBORGNE JOSEPH O	M G	O-0001783	0941	1
MAUGHN WILLIAM JR	COL	O-0063085	0868	1
MAUPIN CLINTON S	COL	O-0056804	0660	1
MAURER FRED D	COL	O-0029324	0864	1
MAURICE KATHRYN	MAJ	J-0000038	0265	1
MAUSERT RYERSON N	COL	O-0079913	1262	1
MAUTZ MATTHEW C	COL	O-0022729	0765	1
MAUZ HENRY H	COL	O-0029799	0461	1
MAUZY ROYALL R	LTC	O-0039984	0562	1
MAXA RUDOLPH J	LTC	O-0081019	0364	2
MAXEINER PAULINE G	MAJ	N-0000283	0860	1
MAXEY HOWARD C	LTC	O-0051955	0164	1
MAXEY PETER U	LTC	O-0051314	1052	2
MAXFIELD RALPH D	COL	O-0038683	0361	1
MAXIM CHESTER B	CW2	W-0901124	0145	2
MAXTON CORA J	LTC	N-0000509	1050	2
MAXWELL ARTHUR O	MAJ	O-0023173	0444	2
MAXWELL BENJAMIN B	LTC	O-0082048	0866	1
MAXWELL EDGIL C	CW2	W-0901522	1145	1
MAXWELL JOHN B II	COL	O-0021942	0166	1
MAXWELL JOHN W	COL	O-0039796	1162	1
MAXWELL LAVERN W	LTC	O-0059484	1165	1
MAXWELL MAMIE H	MAJ	N-0002380	0361	1
MAXWELL MARGARET A	MAJ	L-0000257	1164	1
MAXWELL PAULINE E	LTC	N-0000133	0566	1
MAXWELL ROY D	COL	O-0029265	0363	1
MAXWELL WILLIAM P	COL	O-0038636	0956	1
MAY ARTHUR G	LTC	O-0030335	0164	1

NAME	GRADE	SVC NO	DATE RET MO YR	RET CODE
MAY CHARLES R	CPT	O-0060448	0760	1
MAY DAVID D	MAJ	O-0024946	0161	2
MAY JOHN B	CW4	W-0901483	0356	1
MAY JOSEPH G	LTC	O-0032825	0467	1
MAY MARION H	LTC	O-0025576	0463	1
MAY METTICUS W	COL	O-0029394	0360	1
MAY RAY B	LTC	O-0038259	0963	1
MAY ROBERT L	COL	O-0040260	0368	2
MAY ROBERT W	COL	O-0039968	0665	1
MAY WALTER F	CW4	W-0903492	0757	1
MAYBEN JOHN W	MAJ	O-0008690	0831	2
MAYBERRY HUGH T	B G	O-0007065	1052	1
MAYER MERLE W	MAJ	O-0081020	0568	1
MAYER WILLIAM	COL	O-0006941	0152	2
MAYER WILLIAM E	LTC	O-0089897	0865	1
MAYERS THOMAS H	LTC	O-0030439	1163	2
MAYFIELD LUIE W	LTC	O-0042025	0660	1
MAYHUGH ELNA C	MAJ	R-0010132	0866	1
MAYNARD CHARLES D	COL	O-0023754	0865	1
MAYNARD STANLEY G	COL	O-0032515	0267	2
MAYNE ROBERT K	LTC	O-0067721	0767	1
MAYO ARTHUR A	CW4	W-0906886	0666	1
MAYO GEORGE	COL	O-0003913	0447	1
MAYO PAUL A	M G	O-0018621	1064	1
MAYO PERRY F	CW4	W-0903494	1262	1
MAYO RICHARD W	B G	O-0016430	0756	1
MAYO THOMAS T	1LT	O-0015483	0934	2
MAYS CHARLES W	COL	O-0008183	0452	1
MAYSON PRESTON B	COL	O-0039532	0256	2
MC ABEE FILMORE W	LTC	O-0076396	1061	1
MC ADAMS JOHN	MAJ	O-0024555	0349	2
MC AFEE BROADUS	COL	O-0029053	0159	1
MC AFEE CARLOS F	COL	O-0041629	1159	1
MC AFEE CHARLES C	WO1	W-0800049	1026	2
MC AFEE CHARLES M JR	COL	O-0020580	0161	1
MC AFEE GEORGE D	MAJ	O-0026417	0846	2
MC AFEE GLEN R	LTC	O-0063410	0765	1
MC AFEE JAMES E	CW2	W-0903496	1159	1
MC ALEAR JOHN H	COL	O-0018572	0955	1
MC ALEER WILLIAM A	COL	O-0042196	0763	1
MC ALISTER CHARLES K	COL	O-0011727	0853	2
MC ALISTER IRVINE L	MAJ	O-0014362	0319	2
MC ALLISTER CHARLES	LTC	O-0050056	0366	1
MC ALLISTER EDWIN J	COL	O-0012032	0649	1
MC ALLISTER MARTIN D	COL	O-0006808	0552	2
MC AMIS JAMES C JR	LTC	O-0060372	1165	1
MC ANDREWS BLANCHE M	MAJ	N-0000063	0759	1
MC ANENY GEORGE F	COL	O-0042075	1062	1
MC ANINCH WILLIAM T	LTC	O-0029601	0859	1
MC ANSH ANDREW T	B G	O-0038667	0560	1
MC ARDLE CHARLES E	LTC	O-0030695	1164	1
MC ARDLE JOHN F X	1LT	O-0026917	0346	2
MC ARTHUR DONALD E	LTC	O-0052892	1160	1
MC ARTOR WILLIAM S	LTC	O-0047849	0367	1
MC ATEE JOHN T	LTC	O-0056390	0168	1
MC ATEER ROBERT H	COL	O-0029072	0359	1
MC AULEY JACK A	LTC	O-0036706	0364	1
MC AULIFFE ANTHONY C	GEN	O-0012263	0556	1
MC AULIFFE JOHN H	1LT	O-0056594	0349	2
MC BANE ROBERT B	COL	O-0048890	0768	1
MC BEE MARSHELL G	COL	O-0039015	0766	1
MC BRIDE ARTHUR J	COL	O-0042870	1064	1
MC BRIDE CLYDE R	COL	O-0018424	0861	2
MC BRIDE FRANCIS G	COL	O-0033539	0966	1
MC BRIDE GLEN C	B G	O-0029004	0758	1
MC BRIDE JOHN	LTC	O-0006092	0244	2
MC BRIDE RICHARD M	LTC	O-0058071	1067	1
MC BRIDE ROBERT B	LTC	O-0037277	0664	1
MC BRIDE ROBERT B JR	B G	O-0004451	0752	1
MC BRIDE ROBERT J	COL	O-0015756	0754	1
MC BRIDE ROBERT J	COL	O-0030216	0764	1
MC BRIDE WILLIAM E	COL	O-0024587	0662	1
MC BURNEY HAROLD S	COL	O-0029248	0767	2
MC CABE EDWARD F	CW4	W-0903498	0465	1
MC CABE EDWARD R W	LTC	O-0040262	0666	1

NAME	GRADE	SVC NO	DATE RET MO YR	RET CODE
MC CABE FREDERICK	B G	O-0004553	0947	1
MC CABE ROBERT C	COL	O-0021089	1046	2
MC CABE ROBERT E	COL	O-0020269	0866	1
MC CADDON WALTER L	LTC	O-0040239	0266	1
MC CAFFERY BENJAMIN	LTC	O-0023912	0766	1
MC CAHAN WALTER D	COL	O-0028936	1157	1
MC CAIG MILTON E	MAJ	O-0062240	0762	1
MC CAIN JOSEPH D	LTC	O-0003688	0142	1
MC CAIN RUBY E	MAJ	N-0000252	0762	1
MC CALL RAY N	MAJ	O-0037381	0861	1
MC CALLUM CHARLES F	LTC	O-0051952	1265	1
MC CALLUM JAMES A	B G	O-0009466	0153	1
MC CALLY MARY J	MAJ	N-0000770	0664	1
MC CALLY MILDRED A	MAJ	N-0000771	0664	1
MC CANN CLIFTON E	CW3	W-0903500	0655	1
MC CANN JAMES H JR	COL	O-0030468	0962	1
MC CANN WILLIE H	COL	O-0042603	1065	1
MC CARLEY THOMAS R	COL	O-0011953	0551	2
MC CARTHY CHARLES W	COL	O-0016667	1156	2
MC CARTHY DONALD E	CW3	W-0903501	0957	1
MC CARTHY EDGAR A	LTC	O-0032970	0566	1
MC CARTHY EILEEN L	LTC	N-0002143	0964	1
MC CARTHY GERALD P	COL	O-0041617	1159	1
MC CARTHY JOSEPH M	COL	O-0029043	0159	1
MC CARTHY LEO J	COL	O-0007146	0348	2
MC CARTHY THOMAS D	COL	O-0020954	0660	1
MC CARTHY THOMAS F	COL	O-0010068	0250	2
MC CARTHY WALTER W	COL	O-0040062	1064	1
MC CARTHY WILLIAM J	COL	O-0011516	1052	2
MC CARTNEY DAN A	COL	O-0084389	0368	1
MC CARTY ROBERT S	LTC	O-0051970	1264	1
MC CARTY ROY C	COL	O-0020119	0866	1
MC CASKILL RALPH E	LTC	O-0020070	0843	2
MC CASLIN KERMIT J	LTC	O-0031096	0564	1
MC CATTY KENNETH	COL	O-0004691	0548	1
MC CAW ROBERT H	M G	O-0038722	0767	1
MC CHRYSTAL ARTHUR J	B G	O-0006913	0837	1
MC CLAIN DONALD M	COL	O-0042693	0861	1
MC CLAIN HARRY C	COL	O-0057697	0664	1
MC CLAIN RALPH E	LTC	O-0036661	0968	1
MC CLARY HUGH W	LTC	O-0023533	0860	1
MC CLEARY GORDON F	LTC	O-0037425	0862	1
MC CLEARY OLIVER S	LTC	O-0003095	0622	2
MC CLEARY ROBERT H	LTC	O-0041316	0164	1
MC CLEAVE ROBERT B	COL	O-0016702	1146	2
MC CLEAVE WILLIAM	COL	O-0002573	0934	2
MC CLELLAN IOLA R	LTC	N-0000278	0963	1
MC CLELLAND C B	COL	O-0017558	0859	1
MC CLELLAND CHALME	COL	O-0019011	1046	2
MC CLELLAND DON S	LTC	O-0057247	0868	1
MC CLENAGHAN ROBERT	LTC	O-0014946	0649	1
MC CLENAHAN FRANK C	LTC	O-0082053	1066	1
MC CLINTIC BROWN S	COL	O-0004145	1146	2
MC CLISH ERNEST E	LTC	O-0030432	0562	1
MC CLOSKEY JOHN A	COL	O-0036372	0165	1
MC CLOSKEY OWEN T	COL	O-0030269	1064	2
MC CLUNG EARLE J	COL	O-0004026	0751	1
MC CLURE CLINTON I	COL	O-0004967	0850	1
MC CLURE GEORGE W	COL	O-0028794	0155	1
MC CLURE MARK	M G	O-0014935	0957	2
MC CLURE MARSHALL O	LTC	O-0056767	0765	1
MC CLURE MYRON	LTC	O-0032241	0961	1
MC CLURE ROBERT B	M G	O-0010356	0554	1
MC CLUSKEY VERNA A	LTC	L-0000215	0459	1
MC COACH 3RD DAVID	COL	O-0020177	0757	1
MC COLLAM ALBERT E	LTC	O-0021748	1262	1
MC COLLUM WILLIAM B	CPT	O-0006453	0833	2
MC COMMONS DAISY M	LTC	N-0000146	0858	1
MC CONAHAY ALVA M	COL	O-0051163	0563	1
MC CONAUGHY D S	B G	O-0009738	0753	1
MC CONKEY KERNON M	LTC	O-0063384	0168	1
MC CONNELL C F	MAJ	N-0002219	0360	1
MC CONNELL CAMDEN W	COL	O-0018437	0761	1
MC CONNELL DAVID M	COL	O-0026385	0746	2
MC CONNELL EDWARD T	COL	O-0021996	1166	2

NAME	GRADE	SVC NO	DATE RET MO YR	RET CODE
MC CONNELL FRANK C	B G	O-0014873	0957	1
MC CONNELL GLENN B	COL	O-0015556	0754	1
MC CONNELL GUY G	LTC	O-0049201	0865	1
MC CONNELL JOHN A	COL	O-0079917	0368	1
MC CONNELL LEON G	COL	O-0021464	0968	2
MC CONNELL RICHARD S	COL	O-0041838	1057	1
MC CONNELL STEWART	LTC	O-0068383	0868	1
MC CONNELL VEON M	LTC	O-0051333	0860	1
MC CONNELL VIOLA B	MAJ	N-0002231	0859	1
MC CONNELL WILLIAM J	COL	O-0022052	0863	1
MC COOL EDWARD J	LTC	O-0032024	0363	1
MC CORD FRANCIS S	MAJ	N-0002388	1061	1
MC CORD JAMES H	LTC	O-0032683	1266	1
MC CORD MAX	COL	O-0052355	0868	1
MC CORD SHERWOOD J	LTC	O-0072933	0868	1
MC CORMAC BILLY M	LTC	O-0027043	0563	1
MC CORMAC WESTON A	COL	O-0030716	0566	1
MC CORMACK BETTY T	LTC	L-0000149	1165	1
MC CORMICK ALOYSIUS	COL	O-0020363	0864	1
MC CORMICK ARTHUR B	COL	O-0009576	0145	2
MC CORMICK CHARLES J	COL	O-0051083	0460	1
MC CORMICK HAROLD D	COL	O-0042765	1166	2
MC CORMICK JOHN K	B G	O-0031982	0968	1
MC CORMICK JOHN W	LTC	O-0006880	1042	2
MC CORMICK OTIS	COL	O-0015527	0754	1
MC CORMICK PATRICIA	LTC	L-0000115	0968	1
MC CORMICK ROBIN E	LTC	O-0050905	0853	1
MC CORMICK THOMAS C	COL	O-0005850	0247	2
MC CORMICK VANE E	CW4	W-0906889	1164	1
MC CORMICK WALTER L	COL	O-0010775	1047	1
MC COWEN GEORGE A	LTC	O-0065480	0567	1
MC COY EDWIN D	COL	O-0010323	0753	1
MC COY EUGENE B	LTC	O-0063089	1264	1
MC COY FRANK L	COL	O-0008325	0549	2
MC COY GEORGE W JR	COL	O-0019685	0756	1
MC COY GOLDIE M	MAJ	N-0002520	1067	1
MC COY JAMES M	LTC	O-0087558	0266	1
MC COY JOSEPH L	LTC	O-0061243	0868	1
MC COY PAUL G	LTC	O-0059501	0168	2
MC COY ROBERT G	LTC	O-0041003	0965	1
MC CRACKEN GERALD A	COL	O-0021695	0962	2
MC CRADY RICHARD T	LTC	O-0094319	1066	1
MC CRARY ARTHUR A	COL	O-0019037	0863	1
MC CRARY THOMAS A	COL	O-0019570	0165	1
MC CRARY THOMAS L	COL	O-0021258	0446	2
MC CRAVEY JAMES L	LTC	O-0060649	0464	1
MC CRAW ANNIE M	MAJ	N-0002116	0459	1
MC CREA WILLIAM S	COL	O-0020884	0664	1
MC CREARY JOHN M	LTC	O-0066180	1066	1
MC CREARY MELVIN L	COL	O-0007134	0752	2
MC CRILLIS PAUL L	COL	O-0045768	0765	1
MC CRIMMON KENNETH A	B G	O-0018336	0761	1
MC CRONE CLARENCE L	LTC	O-0071701	1168	1
MC CRONE WILLARD P	COL	O-0020548	0664	1
MC CROREY JAMES L JR	LTC	O-0022158	1064	1
MC CRORY DORSEY E	COL	O-0022683	0260	1
MC CRORY RAYMOND J	LTC	O-0037146	1165	1
MC CRUM RALPH C	LTC	O-0022643	0664	1
MC CUE EDWARD F	LTC	O-0028118	0568	1
MC CULLER LOUIS P	LTC	O-0034636	0167	1
MC CULLOUGH CHRIS	LTC	O-0040611	1168	1
MC CULLOUGH GEORGE S	COL	O-0005749	0840	2
MC CULLOUGH HOMER C	LTC	O-0018314	0855	2
MC CURDEY NEWTON F	COL	O-0015085	0954	1
MC CURDY ROBERT M	CPT	O-0008376	0622	2
MC CURDY THOMAS E	CW4	W-0903504	0964	2
MC CUTCHEN ALAN J	COL	O-0017093	0756	1
MC CUTCHEN WILMOT R	COL	O-0021744	0366	1
MC CUTCHEON HOWARD S	LTC	O-0051703	1060	1
MC DANIEL EDWARD H	M G	O-0016497	1263	1
MC DANIEL LLOYD L	COL	O-0030513	1065	1
MC DANIEL MARION E	LTC	O-0033346	0262	1
MC DANIEL MYRA L	LTC	J-0000013	0667	1
MC DANIEL OTTO L	COL	O-0011846	0753	1
MC DANIEL SEATON F	COL	O-0043098	0767	1

UNITED STATES ARMY RETIRED LIST

NAME	GRADE	SVC NO	DATE RET MO YR	RET CODE
MC DANIEL WILLIS O	LTC	0-0051900	1157	1
MC DERMOTT AUSTIN J	COL	0-0040754	1068	1
MC DIVITT JOSEPH B	COL	0-0051661	0766	1
MC DONALD AGNES C	MAJ	N-0002414	0963	1
MC DONALD CLIFFORD D	CW4	W-0903505	1054	1
MC DONALD DANIEL F	COL	0-0042884	0766	1
MC DONALD EUGENE D	COL	0-0023218	0867	1
MC DONALD HUGH	LTC	0-0028963	0156	1
MC DONALD JOHN W	COL	0-0004948	0750	1
MC DONALD JOHN W	COL	0-0029381	0260	1
MC DONALD LEE R	LTC	0-0052133	0366	1
MC DONALD LENIEL E	LTC	0-0030408	0960	1
MC DONALD LEO J	LTC	0-0017833	0248	1
MC DONALD MARY G	LTC	L-0000102	0567	2
MC DONALD MARY E	MAJ	N-0002290	0466	2
MC DONALD RAY L	1LT	0-0011560	1022	2
MC DONALD ROBERT C	COL	0-0019799	0863	1
MC DONALD THOMAS P	COL	0-0018892	1161	2
MC DONALD WILLIAM J	COL	0-0030169	0464	1
MC DONNELL HAROLD F	COL	0-0039549	0956	1
MC DONNELL PAUL J	COL	0-0004564	0647	2
MC DONNELL WILLIAM J	COL	0-0031698	0964	1
MC DONOUGH JAMES H	COL	0-0010110	0148	1
MC DONOUGH ROBERT J	LTC	0-0043591	0966	1
MC DONOUGH ROBERT K	COL	0-0016394	0656	1
MC DOWALL JOHN	COL	0-0008099	0947	2
MC DOWELL CHARLES T	LTC	0-0037309	0865	1
MC DOWELL EMERY J	CW4	W-0903506	0956	1
MC DOWELL HOWARD A	CW4	W-0903508	0868	1
MC DOWELL JAMES R	COL	0-0011605	0947	1
MC DOWELL JAMES V	COL	0-0006756	0653	2
MC DOWELL JOELLA W	MAJ	N-0000355	0361	1
MC DOWELL MARION E	LTC	0-0057399	1164	1
MC DOWELL REX MC K	B G	0-0004011	1248	1
MC DOWELL RICHARD D	COL	0-0079919	0364	2
MC DOWELL ROBERT B	LTC	0-0025980	0763	1
MC DOWELL SAMUEL T	COL	0-0030321	0365	2
MC DOWELL WILLIAM D	COL	0-0035204	1268	1
MC DUFF ROBERT J	COL	0-0028976	0658	2
MC EACHERN JOE A	LTC	0-0039907	1061	1
MC ELDOWNEY MORRIS C	LTC	0-0041719	0159	1
MC ELGIN HUGH J B	LTC	0-0001252	0221	1
MC ELHENY JOHN D	COL	0-0020170	0664	1
MC ELLIGOTT JOSEPH R	LTC	0-0031482	0365	1
MC ELROY ARVINE W	COL	0-0030093	0164	1
MC ELROY GEORGE P	COL	0-0010652	0546	2
MC ELROY JAMES F	LTC	0-0023917	1060	1
MC ELROY VIRGIL M	COL	0-0043269	0968	1
MC ELWEE FRANK D	COL	0-0025409	0867	1
MC ENTEE DUCAT	COL	0-0019932	0646	2
MC ENTEE FRANCIS A	LTC	0-0069737	1268	2
MC EVOY JOHN P	COL	0-0046774	0766	1
MC FADDEN GLENN M	COL	0-0031004	0766	1
MC FADDEN MURDOCK A	COL	0-0008517	1044	2
MC FADDEN WILLIAM C	COL	0-0012726	0954	1
MC FALL JOHN H	COL	0-0011262	0748	2
MC FALL THOMAS A	COL	0-0029215	0961	2
MC FARLAND ANDREW J	B G	0-0005086	0547	2
MC FARLAND CHARLES N	COL	0-0012280	1151	2
MC FARLAND EARL	B G	0-0002128	0743	1
MC FARLAND JAMES O	LTC	0-0053149	1263	1
MC FARLAND JOHN A	COL	0-0016489	0756	1
MC FARLAND ROBERT R	CPT	0-0060479	1265	1
MC FEELY HENRY G	COL	0-0019810	0862	1
MC FEELY HORACE F	COL	0-0038812	0963	2
MC GAHEE HORACE S	CPT	0-0060690	0365	1
MC GARR LIONEL C	LTG	0-0017225	0762	2
MC GARRAUGH RILEY F	COL	0-0009706	0854	1
MC GARY THOMAS B	LTC	0-0051540	0962	1
MC GAW EDWARD J	M G	0-0012631	0261	1
MC GAW HUGH D	COL	0-0039537	0856	1
MC GEE ARTHUR P	COL	0-0007868	0846	1
MC GEE CHARLES E	COL	0-0029241	1162	1
MC GEE GEORGE A JR	COL	0-0020806	0867	1
MC GEE JOHN H	B G	0-0018600	0861	1

NAME	GRADE	SVC NO	DATE RET MO YR	RET CODE
MC GEE WILLIAM G	LTC	0-0050855	0868	1
MC GEHEE ABNER J JR	COL	0-0015268	1038	2
MC GHAY DURWARD H	CW4	W-0903511	0557	1
MC GIFFERT STEPHEN Y	COL	0-0014865	0854	1
MC GILL DAN P JR	LTC	0-0029330	1054	1
MC GILL UPTON A	COL	0-0041659	0460	-
MC GILLIN HOWARD O	COL	0-0031743	1267	1
MC GILLIVRAY COLIN D	CW4	W-0903512	0957	1
MC GILTON HOWARD J	LTC	0-0082055	0867	1
MC GINLEY EUGENE	M G	0-0012318	1055	1
MC GINN BOYD	LTC	0-0084392	0868	1
MC GINN FLOY W	COL	0-0042127	1262	1
MC GINNESS JOHN R	LTC	0-0016242	1045	1
MC GINNIS HARRY R	CW4	W-0903513	1265	1
MC GINNIS NORMAN F	LTC	0-0069738	0868	1
MC GINNIS VELMER W	COL	0-0020059	1158	1
MC GLONE JAMES F	LTC	0-0078968	0868	1
MC GLYNN EDWARD F	CW3	W-0906893	1060	1
MC GOLDRICK FRANCIS	M G	0-0019857	0766	1
MC GONAGLE LAURENCE	LTC	0-0062938	0766	1
MC GODHAN JAMES J	LTC	0-0022753	1162	2
MC GOUGH GORDON H	LTC	0-0065041	0962	1
MC GOVERN JAMES C	MAJ	0-0004837	0934	2
MC GOVERN JOHN P	COL	0-0042391	0764	1
MC GOWAN GLENN J	COL	0-0042353	0761	1
MC GOWAN JAMES F	LTC	0-0079920	0664	1
MC GOWAN JOHN D	LTC	0-0025759	0864	1
MC GOWAN MURRAY E	COL	0-0015943	0854	1
MC GOWEN CLARENCE D	COL	0-0018605	0356	1
MC GRADY HARPER L	COL	0-0030450	0667	1
MC GRAIL THOMAS M	COL	0-0039876	0758	1
MC GRANE EDWARD J	COL	0-0024027	0466	1
MC GRATH LUTA C	LTC	L-0000226	0261	1
MC GRATH M M	MAJ	N-0000298	0559	2
MC GRATH THOMAS W	COL	0-0043322	1167	1
MC GRATH VINCENT J	COL	0-0079921	0566	1
MC GRAW JAMES E	COL	0-0015672	0649	1
MC GRAW JAMES F	COL	0-0015446	1153	1
MC GRAW LEROY E	COL	0-0010088	0446	2
MC GRAW ROBERT E	COL	0-0039107	0866	1
MC GRAYNE DONALD	COL	0-0028762	0354	2
MC GREGOR DUNCAN G	COL	0-0008594	1050	1
MC GREGOR EDWARD W	COL	0-0039096	0868	1
MC GREGOR THOMAS	COL	0-0012305	0854	1
MC GREW GORDON W	CW4	W-0903516	0658	1
MC GUCKIAN AMBROSE T	COL	0-0042725	0264	2
MC GUIGAN WILLIAM J	COL	0-0036993	0968	2
MC GUIRE JOSEPH R	LTC	0-0024138	0866	1
MC GUIRE PAUL M	LTC	0-0035705	1262	1
MC GUIRE THOMAS C	COL	0-0033296	0762	1
MC GUIRE VENCNA M	LTC	N-0002136	0960	1
MC HALE LARRY	COL	0-0005519	0546	1
MC HANEY GAILON M	COL	0-0021179	0764	1
MC HUGH HARRY O	COL	0-0015758	0954	1
MC HUGH JAMES E	COL	0-0039745	1161	1
MC HUGH JOHN J	LTC	0-0081031	1264	1
MC HUGH LOUIS J	CPT	0-0084324	1065	2
MC ILHINEY WILLIAM G	COL	0-0033005	1163	1
MC ILROY HORACE S	LTC	0-0030460	0563	1
MC ILWAIN SHIRLEY W	COL	0-0008252	0653	1
MC ILWRAITH CLARA B	MAJ	L-0000221	0257	1
MC INERNEY JAMES E B	COL	0-0015276	0554	1
MC INTIRE JOHN F	LTC	0-0082057	0967	1
MC INTOSH ALBERT E	LTC	0-0006771	0-41	1
MC INTOSH CHARLES A	COL	0-0045816	0766	1
MC INTOSH ROBERT B	LTC	0-0062006	1267	1
MC INTYRE CLARENCE A	LTC	0-0016557	0545	2
MC INTYRE EDWARD J	LTC	0-0031152	0965	1
MC INTYRE JOHN L	LTC	0-0023976	0762	1
MC INTYRE WILLIAM J	COL	0-0044171	0968	2
MC KAIG NELSON JR	COL	0-0028818	0953	1
MC KAY GRADY	CW4	W-0906894	0165	1
MC KAY HORTENSE E	LTC	N-0000110	0660	1
MC KAY JOHN T	COL	0-0011067	1144	2
MC KAY ROBERT B	COL	0-0041662	0360	1

NAME	GRADE	SVC NO	DATE RET MO YR	RET CODE
MC KAY WINFIELD R	COL	0-0008450	0351	1
MC KEAN JOHN B	LTC	0-0042502	1061	1
MC KEE BASYE C	COL	0-0029041	0159	2
MC KEE DEWEY F	LTC	0-0039254	0968	1
MC KEE EDWARD L JR	MAJ	0-0004983	0531	2
MC KEE GREGG L	COL	0-0023811	0462	1
MC KEE HENRY H	COL	0-0036190	0868	1
MC KEE JAMES	LTC	0-0060427	0668	1
MC KEE JOHN T	COL	0-0030383	0365	1
MC KEE MICHAEL R	CPT	0-0090276	1065	2
MC KEE RICHARD G	B G	0-0011217	0854	1
MC KEE RICHARD L	COL	0-0019453	0163	1
MC KEE WILLIAM A	B G	0-0031867	0468	1
MC KELVEY LOWELL E	COL	0-0030967	0761	1
MC KELVEY VINCENT T	MAJ	0-0066181	0868	1
MC KENNA JOHN P	LTC	0-0042179	0361	1
MC KENNA ROBERT A	LTC	0-0051907	0865	1
MC KENNA WARREN E	LTC	0-0081033	0968	1
MC KENNEY ALFRED E	COL	0-0011651	0754	2
MC KENZIE ALEX E	LTC	0-0039967	0663	1
MC KENZIE HENRY R	M G	0-0017623	0858	1
MC KENZIE JAMES	CW2	W-0901509	0547	1
MC KENZIE TIMOTHY H	COL	0-0039797	0260	1
MC KENZIE VERNON	COL	0-0084312	1167	1
MC KEON FRANCIS H	COL	0-0011421	0653	1
MC KEON VIRGINIA T	CPT	R-0000543	0946	1
MC KEOWN CLARENCE E	LTC	0-0031200	0766	1
MC KEOWN EUGENE P	LTC	0-0067846	0968	1
MC KERRAL HOWARD A	LTC	0-0080452	0766	2
MC KIBBEN BYRON G	COL	0-0019633	0859	1
MC KIERNAN BRIAN J	LTC	0-0078972	0368	1
MC KIERNAN FREDERICK	LTC	0-0084395	0667	1
MC KIERNAN JOHN T	LTC	0-0081036	0866	1
MC KILLIPS EDWARD J	COL	0-0040175	1167	1
MC KINLEY JAMES F JR	COL	0-0023893	0661	1
MC KINLEY KATHLEEN M	LTC	N-0000502	1148	1
MC KINNEY HARRY F	COL	0-0016888	0156	1
MC KINNEY HUGH L	LTC	0-0036986	0164	1
MC KINNEY JAMES E	LTC	0-0084648	0268	1
MC KINNEY RALPH D	COL	0-0019529	1156	1
MC KINNON JAMES L	COL	0-0015426	0649	1
MC KINNON ROBERT H	COL	0-0019590	0158	1
MC KITHAN QUINCY C	CW4	W-0905895	0460	1
MC KNIGHT ALVIE L	LTC	0-0022762	0960	1
MC KNIGHT CLYDE W	LTC	0-0029760	0760	1
MC KNIGHT JOE F	LTC	0-0017984	0350	1
MC KNIGHT JOHN T	COL	0-0032439	1168	2
MC LAIN EDWARD W	LTC	0-0020888	0165	1
MC LAMORE ROY T	COL	0-0010829	0645	2
MC LANACHAN JAMES D	LTC	0-0046037	0864	1
MC LANE ALTON O	COL	0-0038658	0755	1
MC LANE WILLIAM C	CW4	W-0903522	0164	1
MC LARREN EDMUND W	COL	0-0006662	0647	1
MC LAUCHLIN HENRY H	COL	0-0051752	0464	1
MC LAUGHLIN CHARLES	COL	0-0031639	1067	1
MC LAUGHLIN CHARLES	LTC	0-0037128	1163	1
MC LAUGHLIN CLENARD	COL	0-0000981	0642	1
MC LAUGHLIN EDWIN C	LTC	0-0044423	0661	1
MC LAUGHLIN HUGH S	LTC	0-0081914	0767	1
MC LAURIN COLIN H	CPT	0-0024493	0145	2
MC LEAN DAVID S	COL	0-0012472	1047	1
MC LEAN DONALD	COL	0-0015284	0753	1
MC LEAN EUGENE	CW2	W-0901256	0246	2
MC LELLAN DOROTHY E	MAJ	L-0000255	1062	1
MC LEMORE EPHRAIM H	COL	0-0017184	1054	2
MC LENDON ERNEST L	COL	0-0005158	1047	2
MC LENNAN DONALD G	COL	0-0019475	0864	1
MC LEOD GREGG C	LTC	0-0030674	0462	2
MC LEOD JOHN J	LTC	0-0043036	0565	1
MC MACKIN CHARLES L	LTC	0-0031511	1048	2
MC MAHAN JOHN M	CW4	W-0903526	0762	1
MC MAHON AGNES	MAJ	N-0001605	0765	1
MC MAHON BERNARD B	COL	0-0007040	0353	1
MC MAHON DENNIS J	COL	0-0019592	0862	1
MC MAHON JAMES J	COL	0-0026443	0868	2

NAME	GRADE	SVC NO	DATE RET MO YR	RET CODE
MC MAHON JOHN A	LTC	0-0054182	0164	1
MC MAHON JOHN E JR	B G	0-0003541	0950	1
MC MAHON LEO T	B G	0-0010626	0248	1
MC MAHON MONA M	MAJ	N-0002139	0261	2
MC MAHON RALPH M	COL	0-0030526	1065	1
MC MAHON WILLIAM C	M G	0-0005300	0949	1
MC MAINS J M	COL	0-0080364	0764	1
MC MAKEN EDWARD	COL	0-0030318	1264	1
MC MANAWAY FRED	COL	0-0029339	0959	1
MC MANIS THAYNE F	COL	0-0021047	0867	1
MC MANUS GEORGE H JR	COL	0-0016170	0655	1
MC MANUS HOWARD F	COL	0-0020346	0762	1
MC MANUS LUTHER M JR	LTC	0-0099923	0568	1
MC MASTER RICHARD K	MAJ	0-0016439	0342	2
MC MATH CARROLL B JR	LTC	0-0042678	0164	1
MC MATH ROBERT P	LTC	0-0060603	0968	1
MC MEEN EDWIN D	COL	0-0031109	0164	1
MC MILLAN DONALD L	COL	0-0023791	0765	1
MC MILLAN WILLIAM S	COL	0-0032703	0665	1
MC MILLIN DAN S	COL	0-0032010	0968	1
MC MILLIN JAMES M	COL	0-0012702	0753	1
MC MILLION WILLIE C	COL	0-0038668	0560	1
MC MINN JOHN H	LTC	0-0081039	0567	1
MC MORROW HUBERT A	COL	0-0006586	1047	2
MC MULLIN JAMES B	CW4	W-0906898	0868	1
MC MURDO HEW B	COL	0-0003305	1047	2
MC MURRAY CLARENCE M	COL	0-0002753	0246	2
MC MURRAY RUSSELL E	LTC	0-0029389	0358	2
MC MURTREY GAIL B	LTC	0-0046748	0962	1
MC NAIR CHARLES F	COL	0-0018383	0761	1
MC NAIR DONALD C	COL	0-0033791	0868	1
MC NAIR JOEL N	COL	0-0052075	0764	1
MC NALLY JAMES B	LTC	0-0030192	0662	1
MC NALLY JAMES D	LTC	0-0043317	0659	2
MC NALLY JOSEPH D	COL	0-0035796	0862	2
MC NAMARA ANDREW T	LTG	0-0017324	0764	1
MC NAMARA DONALD G	LTC	0-0039085	0962	1
MC NAMARA HARRY JR	COL	0-0035795	1168	2
MC NAMARA WILSON C	LTC	0-0031738	1062	1
MC NAMEE ROLAND W	COL	0-0012372	1151	1
MC NAMEE ROLAND W JR	LTC	0-0027544	0765	1
MC NARY CHARLES H	COL	0-0038742	0663	1
MC NARY QUENTIN L	LTC	0-0037212	0268	2
MC NAUGHT WARREN H	B G	0-0007582	0751	1
MC NEAL JOHN L	LTC	0-0065174	0167	1
MC NEAL JOSEPH W	MAJ	0-0014159	0716	2
MC NEAR EVAN A	COL	0-0031774	0568	2
MC NEELEY ARTHUR M	MAJ	0-0032792	0847	2
MC NEIL MURRELL B	LTC	0-0081915	1263	1
MC NEIL SAMUEL F JR	COL	0-0049354	0968	1
MC NEILL GEORGE D	CW4	W-0903527	0968	1
MC NELLIS RUSSELL	B G	0-0018935	1264	2
MC NELLY JUSTIN E	COL	0-0031026	1068	1
MC NERNEY JULES J	COL	0-0026453	0668	1
MC NICOL WALLACE N	CPT	0-0060820	0864	1
MC NINCH JOSEPH H	M G	0-0018645	0562	1
MC NINE RAYMOND W	CW3	W-0903528	1160	1
MC NITT ROBERT N	LTC	0-0065068	0860	1
MC NUTT CHARLES H	B G	0-0016751	0657	1
MC PEEK CLYDE O	1LT	0-0025026	1045	2
MC PHAIL THOMAS D	COL	0-0030613	0962	1
MC PHERON WESLEY F	COL	0-0030794	0964	1
MC PHERSON DON V	CW4	W-0903529	0662	1
MC PHERSON LEMOYNE	COL	0-0020309	0858	1
MC PHERSON ROBERT B	LTC	0-0065013	1164	1
MC PHERSON WILLIAM L	COL	0-0015464	0847	1
MC QUAIDE JOSEPH T	COL	0-0024247	0767	1
MC QUARRIE CLAUDE M	B G	0-0012830	0854	1
MC QUILLIN RAYMOND E	B G	0-0003274	0248	1
MC QUINN AUSTIN D	COL	0-0048053	0368	1
MC QUISTON MARIAN R	MAJ	N-0001567	0464	1
MC RELL DONALD W	COL	0-0029606	0961	1
MC REYNOLDS GEORGE R	COL	0-0012065	1148	1
MC SHANE JAMES E	LTC	0-0051884	0665	1
MC SHANE PATRICK I	COL	0-0020989	0856	1

NAME	GRADE	SVC NO	DATE RET MO YR	RET CODE
MC SHEEHY ROBERT J	LTC	O-0030750	0664	1
MC SHERRY FRANK J	B G	O-0007118	1046	2
MC SWAIN RICHARD G	LTC	O-0063098	0668	2
MC WATT ELIZABETH	MAJ	N-0002258	0662	1
MC WATTERS JOHN A	LTC	O-0034336	0462	1
MC WHORTER JOHN P	COL	O-0031692	0164	1
MC WILLIAMS EDWARD	COL	O-0031853	1066	1
MC WILLIAMS JOHN K	LTC	O-0032257	1061	2
MCCONKIE HOWARD S	COL	O-0017343	0459	2
MCNULTY WILLIAM A	COL	O-0018871	0862	1
MEACHAM HERBERT C	CW3	W-0903532	0163	1
MEAD A O	M G	O-0015767	0761	2
MEAD EVERETT V	LTC	O-0030317	1262	1
MEAD JOHN E	1LT	O-0019576	0342	1
MEAD WALTER P	LTC	O-0030972	0155	1
MEADE EVERARD K JR	MAJ	O-0025808	0746	2
MEADE FRANK C	B G	O-0014777	1047	1
MEADE JOHN	COL	O-0016338	1055	1
MEADE STEPHEN J	COL	O-0031834	1262	1
MEADE WARREN E	CW3	W-0903533	1155	1
MEADER GLENN S	COL	O-0028964	0158	1
MEADOR CLARK B	COL	O-0020395	0761	1
MEADOWS JAMES H	LTC	O-0090285	1168	1
MEAGHER HARVEY E	LTC	O-0031305	1265	2
MEALS ROBERT W	COL	O-0019005	0656	1
MEANS DALE E	COL	O-0018756	0762	1
MEANS WILLIAM B	COL	O-0019920	0265	1
MEANS WILLIAM E	COL	O-0018901	0862	1
MEANY WILLIAM F	COL	O-0020287	1262	1
MEARS ANNE	LTC	N-0002456	0768	1
MEASE LEONA L	MAJ	N-0001981	0363	1
MECREDY HENRY E JR	LTC	O-0045091	0865	1
MEDAKIS JOHN B	M G	O-0039554	0160	1
MEDCALF REX M	LTC	O-0084037	0768	1
MEDDING WALTER L	COL	O-0008882	0753	1
MEDDINS WALTER S	CPT	O-0058975	0664	1
MEDER LELAND G	COL	O-0017914	0260	1
MEDINNIS CHARLES L	COL	O-0022023	0868	1
MEDLEN DALTON Y	LTC	O-0411634	1064	2
MEDLEY DONAL I	LTC	O-0033165	0662	1
MEDLIN DORIS E	LTC	N-0000510	0450	1
MEDUSKY JOHN W	COL	O-0021756	1062	1
MEDWED JOHN D	COL	O-0037410	0468	1
MEEHAN CHARLES G	COL	O-0015545	0754	2
MEEHAN PATRICK H	COL	O-0051889	0767	1
MEEHAN THOMAS G	CW4	W-0902372	0757	1
MEEK CHESTER H	COL	O-0029890	1059	1
MEEK JOHN A	COL	O-0051261	1061	1
MEEK JOHN W JR	LTC	O-0063095	0966	1
MEEK STERNER ST	COL	O-0007573	0147	2
MEEKER ROLAND J	COL	O-0052185	0566	1
MEEKS DAVIS O	CPT	N-0000059	0851	2
MEEKS JOHN A	COL	O-0018735	0756	1
MEEKS KERDIS E	CW4	W-0903534	1265	1
MEEKS WILBERT D	LTC	O-0045109	0267	1
MEETHER ARTHUR J L	MAJ	O-0084460	0964	1
MEETING HERBERT JR	COL	O-0060110	0468	1
MEETZE ADAM W	B G	O-0030087	1263	1
MEGGS ERNEST L	COL	O-0035474	0267	1
MEGICA MARTIN G	COL	O-0021881	0660	1
MEGUIAR ROBERT G	COL	O-0040314	0168	1
MEHLINGER WALTER E	COL	O-0036149	0868	1
MEHNER FRANK E	LTC	O-0027122	0765	1
MEHNERT ERICH C	LTC	O-0068385	0965	1
MEHRTENS DONALD J	LTC	O-0025877	0164	1
MEIDLING GEORGE A	COL	O-0042634	0666	2
MEIER WALTER M	COL	O-0030443	0664	1
MEINECKE HENRY W	COL	O-0042722	1265	2
MEINERT FRED H	COL	O-0029851	0163	1
MEINZEN LAWRENCE L	LTC	O-0007301	0444	2
MEIS EMIL F JR	COL	O-0080454	0368	2
MEISCH HENRY W	COL	O-0011461	0946	2
MEISELL HARRY E	LTC	O-0032812	0266	1
MEISNER HELEN B	MAJ	L-0000148	1167	1
MEISS JACK M	LTC	O-0062146	0764	1

NAME	GRADE	SVC NO	DATE RET MO YR	RET CODE
MEISTER WILLIAM B	COL	O-0003288	0346	2
MELASKY HARRIS M	M G	O-0005319	0946	2
MELCHER JOHN F	LTC	O-0080455	0166	1
MELIUS DONALD C	LTC	O-0044464	0158	1
MELLETT EARLE C	LTC	O-0080456	1068	1
MELLNIK STEPHEN M	B G	O-0018754	1163	2
MELLO RALPH T	CPT	O-0058976	0358	2
MELTESEN CLARENCE R	LTC	O-0040616	0864	1
MELTON G ELIZABET	MAJ	N-0001918	0464	1
MELTON JACK R	LTC	O-0033470	0662	1
MELTON VERLE H	CW4	W-0906901	0168	1
MELVIN BENJAMIN F	LTC	O-0032585	0268	1
MENARD NOEL A	COL	O-0020835	0763	1
MENCER EDWARD A	CW3	W-0906903	0958	1
MENDELL MARTIN M	COL	O-0042082	1055	1
MENDELSON JOSEPH A	LTC	O-0009505	0934	2
MENDENHALL CLARENCE	COL	O-0012218	0146	1
MENDLER HELEN M	MAJ	M-0010153	1268	1
MENEGUS WILFRED F	COL	O-0042128	1262	1
MENGEL RALPH H II	LTC	O-0033504	0767	1
MENNIE MERLE L	COL	O-0039880	0264	1
MENOHER WILLIAM	COL	O-0018690	0955	1
MENOLD MARY V	MAJ	N-0001209	1063	1
MENTE ALVIN L JR	COL	O-0019974	0647	2
MENTZER DONALD D	CW4	W-0904253	0662	1
MENZIE JAMES T	COL	O-0006227	0948	1
MERCADER LEOPOLDO	COL	O-0002682	0-38	2
MERCADO LUIS F	COL	O-0020724	0867	1
MERCHANT EDWARD F	MAJ	O-0016687	0647	1
MERCHANT HUBERT W	COL	O-0063669	0866	1
MERCHANT MARVIN H	COL	O-0023301	0868	1
MEREDITH OWEN R	COL	O-0002363	1045	2
MEREDITH PAUL F	LTC	O-0016829	0755	1
MERGENS GEORGE C	COL	O-0015300	0954	1
MERGLER VERNON T	LTC	O-0081044	0865	1
MERIGOLD FRANK A	LTC	O-0063050	0962	1
MERIKANGAS URHO R	COL	O-0019300	0860	1
MERITT JOHN F	LTC	O-0069743	0966	1
MERKLE ERNEST A	COL	O-0015597	0954	1
MERLE LEO V JR	LTC	O-0051778	0261	1
MERRELL GEORGE O JR	LTC	O-0060812	0368	1
MERRIAM JOHN H	LTC	O-0033095	1163	1
MERRIAM LAUREN W	COL	O-0019002	0763	2
MERRIAM WHEELER G	B G	O-0030759	0766	1
MERRICK HERBERT F	CW3	W-0903541	0758	1
MERRIKEN JOHN E	LTC	O-0031253	0760	2
MERRILL ALBERTO E	COL	O-0008142	0935	2
MERRILL CHARLES C	COL	O-0010367	0346	1
MERRILL EARNEST D	COL	O-0039604	0157	1
MERRILL ELEANOR W	LTC	N-0000530	0748	2
MERRILL JOHN N	MAJ	O-0009229	1127	2
MERRILL MARIE E	MAJ	N-0000664	0864	1
MERRILL NELL W	COL	R-0010036	1054	1
MERRITT ANTHONY G	COL	O-0042255	1063	1
MERRITT CARLETON E	COL	O-0028867	0856	1
MERRITT CHARLES A	COL	O-0080459	1068	1
MERRITT WILMER R	COL	O-0012785	0753	1
MERRY LYNDON W	LTC	O-0051391	0261	1
MERRY WILLIAM T	COL	O-0000784	0-28	1
MESICK BENJAMIN S	COL	O-0015505	0854	1
MESICK JOHN	COL	O-0011207	0453	1
MESSAMORE LESLIE T	CW3	W-0903542	0859	1
MESSEC HARRY S	COL	O-0051682	0561	2
MESSER ELMER J	MAJ	O-0058977	1062	2
MESSER HERBERT G	COL	O-0011724	1046	2
MESSER MELVIN	LTC	O-0069744	1167	2
MESSERSMITH BETTY E	MAJ	N-0002142	0761	1
MESSERSMITH JOSHUA R	COL	O-0019139	0561	1
MESSNER ARTHUR E	COL	O-0030181	1162	1
MESSNER F VALINE	LTC	N-0000013	0947	1
MESZAR MARJORIE	MAJ	N-0000675	0364	1
METCALF ELSIE J	CPT	L-0000342	0865	1
METCALF FREDERIC A	COL	O-0009724	1052	1
METCALF JAMES F	COL	O-0042288	1263	1
METCALF ROBERT L JR	COL	O-0053179	0765	1

NAME	GRADE	SVC NO	DATE RET MO YR	RET CODE
METCALFE ALVIN C	LTC	O-0036809	0767	1
METCALFE CHARLES G	COL	O-0052749	0264	1
METCALFE GEORGE	LTC	O-0051637	0263	2
METCALFE SAMUEL L	COL	O-0009684	0854	1
METHENY LYAL C	B G	O-0039729	0858	1
METHVEN THERON G	COL	O-0004647	1146	2
METTS CLARENCE A JR	COL	O-0032776	1167	1
METTIE ELIZABETH	LTC	N-0000156	1164	1
METTS WALTER A JR	COL	O-0009901	0550	1
METZ MICHAEL T	LTC	O-0042071	0860	1
METZ THOMAS M	COL	O-0020696	1166	1
METZGER EARL H	B G	O-0003253	0849	1
METZGER EDWARD H	COL	O-0011729	0753	1
METZGER ELIZABETH	MAJ	L-0000095	0763	1
METZGER HOPE W	LTC	L-0000174	0868	1
MEWBORN NEEDHAM P	LTC	O-0028645	0866	1
MEWSHAW HARRY C	COL	O-0011235	0754	1
MEYER CARL W	COL	O-0016071	0655	1
MEYER CHARLES H	B G	O-0020762	0867	1
MEYER GEORGE F JR	COL	O-0031584	1167	1
MEYER HAROLD A	COL	O-0014960	0348	1
MEYER HENRY J D	B G	O-0012290	0952	2
MEYER JOHN H	COL	O-0022179	1068	2
MEYER JOHN S	CW4	W-0902379	0257	1
MEYER JULES D	LTC	O-0060014	0365	1
MEYER RICHARD D	LTG	O-0018963	1067	1
MEYER RICHARD H	LTC	O-0025872	0763	1
MEYER RICHARD J	M G	O-0019147	0268	2
MEYER ROBERT G H	COL	O-0017529	0759	1
MEYER ROBERT J	LTC	O-0069746	1265	1
MEYER THOMAS E	COL	O-0015105	0551	1
MEYER VINCENT	B G	O-0003143	1045	2
MEYER WALTER G	COL	O-0041653	0360	1
MEYER WALTER P	LTC	O-0063314	0767	1
MEYERDIRK ALVIN P	CW4	W-0906904	1164	1
MEYERS HARRY F	B G	O-0011877	0854	1
MEYERS HARRY T	COL	O-0041608	0959	1
MEYERS RUTH E	MAJ	L-0000005	0753	1
MIAL JOHN P	COL	O-0022157	1058	1
MICCIO EDWARD JR	LTC	O-0050013	0166	2
MICHAEL CLARENCE A	WO1	W-0901435	0841	1
MICHAEL GEORGE P	COL	O-0040689	1168	1
MICHAEL JAMES R	COL	O-0025609	0866	1
MICHAEL JONATHAN H	COL	O-0039594	1058	1
MICHAELIS EMILY R	MAJ	N-0001613	0465	1
MICHAELIS LEON A	COL	O-0044486	0767	1
MICHAELS CHARLES B	CW2	W-0903545	1159	1
MICHAELS CHARLES E	COL	O-0038972	1165	1
MICHAELSON FRANKLYN	LTC	O-0048532	1262	1
MICHALAK EDWARD M	1LT	O-0027191	0449	2
MICHASIOW MYRON	CW4	W-0903548	0966	1
MICHELET HOWARD E	B G	O-0021131	0868	1
MICHENER WILLIAM	COL	O-0008270	0953	1
MICKEL GEORGE E	COL	O-0038793	0265	1
MICKEL LAURENCE	COL	O-0008259	0245	2
MICKELSON EARL L	COL	O-0028923	0955	1
MICKELWAIT CLAUDE B	M G	O-0010287	0756	2
MICKLE GERALD ST	B G	O-0012350	0946	2
MIDDLEBROOKS MARVIN	COL	O-0051440	0963	1
MIDDLEKAUFF R M	CW4	W-0902014	0655	1
MIDDLETON EDWARD D	MAJ	O-0061107	0967	1
MIDDLETON EMERY D	COL	O-0030329	0163	2
MIDDLETON ETHEL W	MAJ	L-0000294	0659	1
MIDDLETON GEORGE R	COL	O-0005903	0547	2
MIDDLETON MARTER D	COL	O-0051767	0165	1
MIDDLETON SANDERS D	CPT	O-0060203	1162	1
MIDDLETON TROY H	LTG	O-0003476	0-37	1
MIDDLETON WILLIAM R	LTC	O-0030338	0960	2
MIDDLEWORTH HENRY V	COL	O-0024226	0468	2
MIDGETTE HALLAS L	CW4	W-0903549	0268	2
MIEHE WILLIAM J	COL	O-0006002	0951	2
MIESCHER WALTER H JR	LTC	O-0065017	0665	1
MIFFLIN THOMAS	COL	O-0018216	0760	1
MIGLIORA CHARLES A	CW2	W-0901721	0447	1
MIHOCH JOHN P	LTC	O-0069748	0964	1

NAME	GRADE	SVC NO	DATE RET MO YR	RET CODE
MIKETINAC ANTHONY J	LTC	O-0045671	0667	1
MIKHALEVSKY ALEXANDE	LTC	O-0038452	0268	1
MIKKELSEN HARRY E	COL	O-0020179	0757	1
MIKOWSKI FLORENCE J	MAJ	N-0001340	0365	1
MILAM JONAS C	CW3	W-0903550	1163	1
MILAN HAROLD L	COL	O-0008665	1147	1
MILAND JAMES V	COL	O-0046052	1266	1
MILBEE PAUL G	LTC	O-0061425	0768	1
MILBURN BRYAN L	M G	O-0007469	1156	1
MILBURN EUGENE	COL	O-0003978	0549	2
MILBURN WILLIAM R	LTC	O-0031599	0260	1
MILES BURTON F	COL	O-0042886	1160	1
MILES CHARLES H JR	COL	O-0019151	0158	2
MILEY JOHN D	LTC	O-0004501	0433	2
MILEY JOHN D	CPT	O-0028586	1154	2
MILEY WILLIAM M	M G	O-0011232	0755	1
MILLARD RICHARD C	LTC	O-0063356	0868	1
MILLENER GEORGE A	COL	O-0015740	0954	1
MILLER ALEXANDER	COL	O-0016769	0757	1
MILLER ALICE M	MAJ	L-0000017	0854	1
MILLER ALVA E	COL	O-0022283	0760	1
MILLER ALVIN C	COL	O-0003302	1146	2
MILLER ARLES H	COL	O-0042287	0761	1
MILLER AUSTIN A	COL	O-0019228	0461	2
MILLER BOULTON B	COL	O-0033148	1064	1
MILLER BYRON L JR	LTC	O-0037630	1067	1
MILLER CARL W	COL	O-0019740	0763	1
MILLER CAROLINE R	MAJ	N-0002374	0860	1
MILLER CHARLES F	LTC	O-0065222	0765	1
MILLER CLARENCE G	CW3	W-0904158	1159	1
MILLER DALE F	LTC	O-0084560	0466	2
MILLER DAVID F	1LT	OF-0107280	0268	2
MILLER DONALD B	COL	O-0022018	0868	1
MILLER DONALD L	MAJ	O-0084225	0868	1
MILLER DOT	MAJ	R-0010085	0760	1
MILLER EDGAR S	COL	O-0002401	0-37	1
MILLER EDNA R	LTC	L-0000038	0760	1
MILLER EDWARD C JR	COL	O-0038590	1054	1
MILLER EDWARD G	COL	O-0041633	1059	1
MILLER EDWARD M JR	COL	O-0040167	0667	2
MILLER EDWIN T	COL	O-0030006	1062	1
MILLER ELSIE K	MAJ	R-0010043	1263	1
MILLER ERNEST J SR	CW4	W-0906906	0768	1
MILLER EUGENE E	COL	O-0030156	0464	1
MILLER EUGENE L	COL	O-0011657	0450	1
MILLER EVERETT B	LTC	O-0040132	0365	1
MILLER FAUNTLEY M	LTC	O-0002283	0233	2
MILLER FRANCIS N	COL	O-0041791	0860	1
MILLER FREDERIC G	COL	O-0081052	0867	1
MILLER FREDERICK	LTC	O-0084561	0665	1
MILLER GAY E	LTC	O-0028842	0254	1
MILLER GEORGE A	B G	O-0007196	0248	2
MILLER GEORGE P	COL	O-0042475	1264	1
MILLER HARLEY N	COL	O-0053155	0768	1
MILLER HAROLD H	1LT	O-0011738	0322	2
MILLER HAROLD R	COL	O-0053967	0767	1
MILLER HAROLD T	B G	O-0012633	0654	1
MILLER HARRY W	COL	O-0016005	0754	1
MILLER HELEN E	MAJ	N-0000149	0756	1
MILLER HENRY L	COL	O-0043302	0662	1
MILLER HOMER E	COL	O-0022227	0460	2
MILLER HUBERT S	COL	O-0014664	0854	2
MILLER IVA R	MAJ	N-0001177	0863	2
MILLER JACK C	LTC	O-0023406	0864	1
MILLER JACK R	LTC	O-0057296	0868	1
MILLER JAMES A	COL	O-0040018	0760	2
MILLER JAMES B	COL	O-0030266	1064	1
MILLER JAMES B	COL	O-0084031	0667	2
MILLER JAMES F JR	MAJ	O-0019353	1138	2
MILLER JAMES R	CW4	W-0904160	0967	1
MILLER JAMES W	LTC	O-0082061	0968	1
MILLER JESSIE L	MAJ	M-0010072	0360	1
MILLER JOHN E	LTC	O-0081053	1066	1
MILLER JOHN H	LTC	O-0038010	0964	1
MILLER JOHN K	COL	O-0028890	1056	1

NAME	GRADE	SVC NO	DATE RET MO YR	RET CODE
MILLER JOHN R	CW4	W-0903553	0264	1
MILLER JOSIAH B	LTC	0-0032396	0765	1
MILLER LEE C	COL	0-0019438	0864	1
MILLER LEHMAN W	B G	0-0003773	0844	2
MILLER LELAND V	COL	0-0030235	0562	1
MILLER LEONARD C	COL	0-0024623	1065	2
MILLER LEROY	CW4	W-0904162	1060	1
MILLER LEWIS	MAJ	0-0089108	0966	1
MILLER LILLARD P	COL	0-0029511	1060	1
MILLER LOUISE	MAJ	N-0000544	0549	1
MILLER LUTHER O	M G	0-0011793	1149	1
MILLER LUTHER R	COL	0-0030737	0662	2
MILLER MABRY G	COL	0-0031486	0766	2
MILLER MARION C	COL	0-0051396	0463	1
MILLER MARY	MAJ	N-0000018	0448	1
MILLER MARY F	MAJ	N-0002014	0867	2
MILLER MAURICE L	B G	0-0004490	1150	2
MILLER MAYNARD C	COL	0-0079928	0367	1
MILLER MELVIN O	MAJ	0-0040283	0658	1
MILLER MILLARD J	LTC	0-0047804	0762	1
MILLER NORBERT C	COL	0-0038905	0163	1
MILLER OPIE G	CW4	W-0903554	0862	1
MILLER PAUL A	COL	0-0030843	0165	1
MILLER PAUL R M	COL	0-0012500	0854	2
MILLER RAYMOND G	COL	0-0011586	0753	2
MILLER ROBERT B	COL	0-0019366	0864	1
MILLER ROBERT C	COL	0-0020625	0966	1
MILLER ROBERT C	COL	0-0037409	0762	1
MILLER ROBERT D	COL	0-0041448	0257	2
MILLER ROBERT L	COL	0-0009638	1146	1
MILLER ROBERT L	COL	0-0016575	0755	1
MILLER ROBERT S	COL	0-0007959	1047	2
MILLER ROGER G	COL	0-0017798	0859	1
MILLER ROWLAN L	LTC	0-0058517	0168	1
MILLER RUSSELL J	LTC	0-0063388	0467	1
MILLER SAMUEL T	LTC	0-0031377	1055	1
MILLER SIDNEY	COL	0-0060015	0968	1
MILLER THOMAS R	COL	0-0005109	0646	1
MILLER VERLE O	COL	0-0024396	0861	1
MILLER VERNE	CPT	0-0006058	1022	2
MILLER VERNON W	WO1	W-0901006	0836	1
MILLER WALTER W	LTC	0-0065541	0464	1
MILLER WHITSIDE	LTC	0-0017790	0757	1
MILLER WILBUR O JR	LTC	0-0033126	0663	1
MILLER WILLIAM B	COL	0-0012126	0350	1
MILLER WILLIAM L	CW3	W-0904163	0457	1
MILLER 2ND ALLEN C	COL	0-0020342	0758	1
MILLER 2ND C L	LTC	0-0022149	0960	1
MILLET STEPHEN J	COL	0-0038690	0760	1
MILLHOLLAND GEORGE H	COL	0-0007150	0446	1
MILLICAN HENRY D	LTC	0-0088154	0668	1
MILLICAN RAYMOND W	COL	0-0023000	0762	1
MILLICE WILLARD F	COL	0-0015443	1046	1
MILLIGAN CAREY W	MAJ	0-0028125	0666	1
MILLIKEN CHARLES B	COL	0-0020340	0761	1
MILLIKEN WILLIAM S	LTC	0-0041017	0463	1
MILLIKIN JOHN	M G	0-0002856	0248	1
MILLIKIN JOHN JR	COL	0-0023781	0868	1
MILLNER ARNOLD C	CW4	W-0903557	0468	1
MILLS ERIC R JR	COL	0-0047272	0766	1
MILLS FRANCIS B	COL	0-0032544	1166	1
MILLS JENE E	COL	0-0023410	0267	1
MILLS MARION L	COL	0-0020038	0758	1
MILLS OLIVE E	LTC	L-0000085	0865	1
MILLS RUTH T	MAJ	N-0001580	0465	1
MILLS WILLIAM H	COL	0-0016376	0756	1
MILLS WILLIS E	MAJ	0-0014017	1020	1
MILLSON CYRIL A	COL	0-0042922	1266	1
MILLSTEIN CONAN H	LTC	0-0049920	0866	1
MILLWEE JOSEPH B	MAJ	0-0064388	0565	2
MILMORE CHARLES W	LTC	0-0026045	0767	2
MILNE WILLIAM D	COL	0-0020144	0656	1
MILNER FRANK	COL	0-0021441	1067	1
MILNER FRED C	COL	0-0007230	0552	2
MILNER JAMES W	COL	0-0023124	0367	1

NAME	GRADE	SVC NO	DATE RET MO YR	RET CODE
MILNER MORRIS E	COL	0-0041454	0357	1
MILNER WALKER W	COL	0-0018356	0758	1
MILNOR PHILIP L	MAJ	0-0002789	1022	1
MILTON THORNTON M	LTC	0-0026032	0867	1
MILVO JOHN D	CW3	RW-0907127	0664	1
MILWIT HERBERT	COL	0-0017514	0359	1
MINAHAN DANIEL J JR	COL	0-0021799	0664	1
MINAHAN JOHN E	COL	0-0022949	0868	1
MINAS FRANK A	COL	0-0019337	0147	2
MINCH HOWARD G	COL	0-0034945	1167	1
MINCKLER REX W	COL	0-0014599	0746	1
MINECCI JOSEPH P	LTC	0-0038823	0364	1
MINER EARL M	COL	0-0011656	0753	1
MINER FLORENCE Z	MAJ	N-0000672	0264	1
MINER HAROLD E	LTC	0-0043019	0565	1
MINER HAROLD W	COL	0-0051102	0960	1
MINER HOWARD A	LTC	0-0039933	1162	1
MINER JOHN W	COL	0-0009847	0350	2
MINER RALPH E	LTC	0-0023285	0660	1
MINER RUSSELL M	COL	0-0019839	0762	1
MINER RUTH S	MAJ	L-0000087	0361	1
MINERVA FRANK D	COL	0-0051962	0766	1
MINION EDWARD M	COL	0-0031601	0866	1
MINK ROBERT M	CW4	W-0906908	0660	1
MINNICH EDGAR R	COL	0-0051197	0161	1
MINOR FLOYD E	COL	0-0031668	0762	1
MINOR GEORGE H	COL	0-0020710	0246	2
MINTER JAMES M	LTC	0-0062019	0167	2
MINTON HENRY E	COL	0-0008262	1047	2
MINTON JOHN T	COL	0-0004790	0646	2
MINTON WARREN A	LTC	0-0045199	0859	1
MINTON WILLIAM	COL	0-0089263	0768	1
MIRKIN MARJORIE	MAJ	N-0000216	0560	2
MIROCHNA THADDEUS M	LTC	0-0089360	0268	1
MIRRAS PETER W	COL	0-0053684	0367	1
MISDOM HOWELL E	COL	0-0079930	1166	2
MISEVIC GEORGE W	COL	0-0051782	0366	2
MISEVIC HELEN M L	MAJ	N-0001299	0361	1
MISSAL JOSEPH B JR	LTC	0-0021247	0866	1
MITCHELL ALLAN W	COL	0-0031704	1267	1
MITCHELL BARRY H	COL	0-0079931	0765	1
MITCHELL BARTHOLOMEW	LTC	0-0078990	0868	1
MITCHELL CECIL W	CW3	W-0903558	0755	1
MITCHELL CHARLES H	COL	0-0041731	0662	1
MITCHELL CLAIR B	COL	0-0019899	0955	2
MITCHELL DONALD E	CPT	0-0088839	0763	2
MITCHELL DOUGLAS W	COL	0-0084399	0966	1
MITCHELL EARLE F	COL	0-0030272	0864	1
MITCHELL ELMO C	LTC	0-0018425	0945	2
MITCHELL EUGENE H	COL	0-0007463	0753	2
MITCHELL FRANKLIN	COL	0-0014665	0346	1
MITCHELL FRED B	LTC	0-0052633	1268	1
MITCHELL HARRIS T	LTC	0-0052670	0263	1
MITCHELL HARRY E	CPT	0-0014118	0909	2
MITCHELL HENRY C	MAJ	0-0068139	1167	1
MITCHELL HERBERT V	B G	0-0018073	0760	1
MITCHELL JAMES K	COL	0-0012647	1050	1
MITCHELL JOHN D	COL	0-0012713	0956	1
MITCHELL JOHN F	COL	0-0024405	0868	1
MITCHELL JOSEPH A JR	LTC	0-0048753	0368	1
MITCHELL JOSEPH W JR	LTC	0-0036351	0762	1
MITCHELL LAWRENCE C	COL	0-0005304	0253	2
MITCHELL OTHELDA M	MAJ	L-0000229	0558	1
MITCHELL PAUL J	COL	0-0017314	0758	1
MITCHELL RICHARD E	LTC	0-0063338	0865	1
MITCHELL RICHARD T	COL	0-0015833	0654	2
MITCHELL ROBERT F	MAJ	0-0056291	0761	1
MITCHELL STEPHEN C	LTC	0-0080151	0767	1
MITCHELL STUART M	COL	0-0029305	0264	1
MITCHELL WILLIAM L	M G	0-0012832	1055	2
MITCHELL WILLIS F	LTC	OF-0103930	1168	1
MITCHIM CHARLES F	COL	0-0020577	1061	1
MITER FRANK F	COL	0-0016477	0656	1
MITTENZWEI FRANCIS X	LTC	0-0081060	0267	1
MIXON SIDNEY T	COL	0-0034281	1168	1

NAME	GRADE	SVC NO	DATE RET MO YR	RET CODE
MIXSON ELIZABETH	LTC	N-0000533	0758	1
MIZE PAUL H	COL	0-0032335	0767	1
MIZE WILLARD H	COL	0-0030204	0764	1
MIZELL WALTER S	LTC	0-0065438	1264	1
MJAK JAMES J	COL	0-0043454	1066	1
MOATS WILTON R	COL	0-0030336	0859	1
MOBERLEY KIRK B	COL	0-0051758	0666	1
MOBLEY JAMES C	CW4	W-0906910	0767	1
MOCKBEE JAMES B	COL	0-0011035	0448	1
MODRAK HENRY H	COL	0-0065415	0266	1
MOE ANNE C	LTC	L-0000034	0559	1
MOE GEORGE R	LTC	0-0026022	0264	1
MOEHLMANN F HERBERT	COL	0-0017986	1146	2
MOELLER WILLIAM H	LTC	0-0088443	0968	1
MOFFATT CARROLL K	COL	0-0029343	0959	1
MOFFETT CHARLES W JR	CPT	0-0060807	1262	1
MOFFETT CLEWIS C	COL	0-0039909	0764	1
MOFFETT JAMES B	LTC	0-0059441	0165	1
MOFFETT OREN F	LTC	0-0080460	0966	1
MOFFITT ALFRED F JR	LTC	0-0040630	1268	2
MOHLERE EDWARD D	COL	0-0020286	0466	1
MOHN EDWARD S	CW4	W-0903561	0660	1
MOHR PHILLIP J	LTC	0-0083609	0268	1
MOHRI RALPH W	COL	0-0017985	0758	1
MOLESKY WALTER F	COL	0-0023857	0967	1
MOLITOR ERIC S	B G	0-0012115	0854	2
MOLL RICHARD A	LTC	0-0049945	0959	2
MOLLEN IRVING R	COL	0-0079933	1168	1
MOLLOHAN CECIL S	COL	0-0019309	0757	1
MOLLOY FRANCIS P	2LT	0-0016440	0527	2
MOLLOY WILLIAM T	LTC	0-0080461	0168	1
MOLYNEAUX HAROLD G	LTC	0-0056193	0465	2
MONISTON ROBERT M	COL	0-0029242	0862	1
MOMM EDWIN C	CPT	0-0018864	0947	1
MONAHAN FERGUS T	LTC	0-0065291	0268	2
MONAHAN JOHN C	B G	0-0038706	0664	1
MONCRIEF JAMES S JR	COL	0-0031623	0865	1
MONCRIEF JOHN A	COL	0-0091648	1068	2
MONETTE HELEN D	MAJ	N-0000900	0863	1
MONEYHUN JOSEPH A	LTC	0-0048065	0463	1
MONIHAN JAMES G	COL	0-0004593	0448	2
MONK JEREMIAH B JR	COL	0-0046946	0568	1
MONROE GRACE E	MAJ	N-0000563	1060	1
MONROE HAMMOND M	B G	0-0012132	0753	1
MONROE MELVIN C	LTC	0-0034552	0166	1
MONROE THOMAS H	COL	0-0003742	0446	1
MONSKE FREDA L	MAJ	N-0002135	0860	1
MONSON NELSON P	MAJ	0-0023996	1061	1
MONTAGUE ERNEST K	COL	0-0056890	1065	1
MONTAGUE MARY OD	1LT	R-0001226	0945	1
MONTAGUE THEODORE	1LT	0-0028332	0949	2
MONTESINOS MIGUEL	LTC	0-0010078	0142	1
MONTESINOS SERAFIN M	COL	0-0003197	0248	1
MONTGOMERY ALBERT E	COL	0-0057698	1262	1
MONTGOMERY AUSTIN J	B G	0-0051942	0867	1
MONTGOMERY BRIAN D	COL	0-0032529	0964	1
MONTGOMERY GUS H	COL	0-0029993	0863	1
MONTGOMERY HUNTER M	LTC	0-0059495	0468	1
MONTGOMERY JOHN H JR	COL	0-0020754	0867	1
MONTGOMERY LEE E	COL	0-0030958	0767	1
MONTGOMERY MURRAY M	COL	0-0007137	0653	1
MONTGOMERY ROBIN G	COL	0-0031525	0367	1
MONTGOMERY WALDO W	COL	0-0042890	0965	1
MONTI GILBERT A	LTC	0-0051641	0863	1
MONTILLA RAFAEL	COL	0-0051437	0863	1
MONTONDO ROBERT O	COL	0-0082064	0968	1
MONTRONE ALFRED J	COL	0-0032737	0968	1
MONTY PERCY A	LTC	0-0053945	0965	1
MOODY FLORENCE P	MAJ	L-0000116	1163	1
MOODY MARLIN S	COL	0-0028911	0557	1
MOOMAW OTHO A	LTC	0-0020905	0965	1
MOON GORDON A II	COL	0-0025214	1268	1
MOON HERBERT D	LTC	0-0084400	0663	1
MOON JACOB R	LTC	0-0015864	0448	1
MOON JAMES W	COL	0-0032540	0665	1

NAME	GRADE	SVC NO	DATE RET MO YR	RET CODE
MOON VIRGIL C	LTC	0-0061132	0568	2
MOON WILLIAM P JR	LTC	0-0031589	0765	1
MOONEY HAROLD T	COL	0-0042918	1164	1
MOONEY JAMES S	LTC	0-0003402	0828	2
MOORE ALBERT F	LTC	0-0063364	1165	1
MOORE ANDERSON T	COL	0-0009327	0854	1
MOORE ARLICE J	COL	0-0031154	0664	1
MOORE ARTHUR L	COL	0-0012429	0451	1
MOORE ARTHUR P	COL	0-0010105	0151	2
MOORE AUDREY M	MAJ	N-0002452	0267	1
MOORE BENJAMIN G	COL	0-0033158	0968	1
MOORE BIDWELL	COL	0-0023248	0166	1
MOORE BUHL	COL	0-0007329	0947	1
MOORE CECIL R	M G	0-0006669	1046	2
MOORE CHARLES E	CPT	0-0004657	0622	2
MOORE CHARLES F	LTC	0-0051837	0265	1
MOORE CHARLES H JR	COL	0-0012201	0247	2
MOORE CLARENCE A	COL	0-0050919	0756	1
MOORE CLAYTON H JR	LTC	0-0035178	1263	1
MOORE DENIS G	COL	0-0030969	1265	1
MOORE DON G	COL	0-0003982	0646	2
MOORE ELMORE P	COL	0-0051460	0259	1
MOORE EUGENE M	CW4	W-0902193	0552	1
MOORE EULESS B JR	LTC	0-0063300	0764	1
MOORE FRANK M	COL	0-0007881	1046	1
MOORE GEORGE A	COL	0-0005577	0945	2
MOORE GEORGE B	COL	0-0023904	1165	1
MOORE GEORGE B JR	COL	0-0016972	0945	2
MOORE GLADYS	MAJ	N-0000239	0461	1
MOORE HARMON D	COL	0-0051971	0267	1
MOORE HERBERT K	COL	0-0010807	0851	1
MOORE HOWARD E	MAJ	0-0025816	0864	1
MOORE J MERRIAM	COL	0-0003487	0648	1
MOORE JAMES B	CW4	W-0904165	0164	1
MOORE JAMES E	GEN	0-0015650	0763	2
MOORE JAMES F	LTC	0-0069992	0368	1
MOORE JEAN	MAJ	N-0002006	1067	1
MOORE JESSE N	LTC	0-0078993	0563	1
MOORE JOHN H	LTC	0-0065093	1167	1
MOORE JOHN J	COL	0-0031355	0766	1
MOORE JOHN M	COL	0-0012107	1146	1
MOORE JOHN M	MAJ	0-0016856	0444	2
MOORE JOHN V	LTC	0-0029093	0457	1
MOORE JOSEPH C	COL	0-0019791	0865	1
MOORE JOSEPH P	LTC	0-0050929	1154	1
MOORE JOSEPH W	COL	0-0053733	0868	1
MOORE KENNETH M	COL	0-0008558	0453	1
MOORE LESLIE S	COL	0-0051012	0259	1
MOORE LESTER B	CW4	W-0906914	1066	1
MOORE LISTER R	COL	0-0039947	1165	1
MOORE LOREN O	COL	0-0016527	1145	2
MOORE LOWELL G	LTC	0-0043539	0766	1
MOORE LOWREY R	COL	0-0029941	0462	1
MOORE NED D	M G	0-0018212	0265	1
MOORE PIERCE M	CPT	0-0069227	0861	2
MOORE PRENTICE L	COL	0-0016023	0254	2
MOORE RICHARD H	COL	0-0030721	0563	1
MOORE ROBERT B	MAJ	0-0004821	0934	2
MOORE ROBERT B	COL	0-0051294	0462	2
MOORE ROBERT E	LTC	0-0032244	1062	1
MOORE ROBERT E	LTC	0-0018781	0757	1
MOORE ROBERT F	LTC	0-0036304	1167	1
MOORE ROBERT H	MAJ	0-0065147	0765	1
MOORE ROBERT J	CW4	W-0904166	1067	1
MOORE ROBERT S	M G	0-0011911	0854	2
MOORE ROY C	COL	0-0006633	0337	1
MOORE ROY E	COL	0-0018880	0862	1
MOORE SPURGEON A	LTC	0-0038370	0966	1
MOORE STERLIN C	LTC	0-0084061	0864	1
MOORE THOMAS E	COL	0-0014867	0452	2
MOORE THOMAS N	LTC	0-0037295	0464	1
MOORE VIVIAN M	MAJ	N-0000626	0860	1
MOORE WALTER E	LTC	0-0033149	0661	1
MOORE WALTER H JR	LTC	0-0067597	1068	1
MOORE WAYNE S	COL	0-0012617	1050	1

NAME	GRADE	SVC NO	DATE RET MO YR	RET CODE	NAME	GRADE	SVC NO	DATE RET MO YR	RET CODE	NAME	GRADE	SVC NO	DATE RET MO YR	RET CODE	NAME	GRADE	SVC NO	DATE RET MO YR	RET CODE
MOORE WERNER W	COL	0-0011157	0753	2	MORRISON IDA B	MAJ	N-0001327	0465	1	MUDGETT CHARLES F JR	B G	0-0030409	0565	1	MURPHY DANIEL J	COL	0-0019776	1055	1
MOORE WILLIAM B	COL	0-0018796	0862	1	MORRISON JAMES V	CW4	W-0903573	1158	1	MUDGETT CHARLES S	COL	0-0017815	0858	1	MURPHY DANIEL N	CPT	0-0014248	0520	2
MOORE WILLIAM C	COL	0-0004899	1048	1	MORRISON JOHN A	COL	0-0020945	1163	1	MUDGETT GILMAN C	M G	0-0014766	0361	1	MURPHY DENNIS P	COL	0-0010038	1147	2
MOORE WILLIAM P	COL	0-0051052	0555	1	MORRISSEY STEPHEN B	LTC	0-0023270	0265	1	MUDGETT LOUIS F	COL	0-0031069	0866	1	MURPHY EARL J	COL	0-0016421	0656	1
MOORE WILLIAM S	COL	0-0030992	1165	1	MORROW BERTRAND	COL	0-0005301	1047	1	MUELLER EDWARD A	COL	0-0014329	1146	2	MURPHY EDWARD A	LTC	0-0004695	0442	2
MOORE WILLIAM T	COL	0-0017313	0758	1	MORROW FRANK W	COL	0-0083545	0868	2	MUELLER EDWIN L P	COL	0-0052181	0868	1	MURPHY EDWARD E	COL	0-0041634	1158	1
MOOREFIELD JESSE P	COL	0-0022244	0867	2	MORROW SAMUEL H	COL	0-0015913	0948	2	MUELLER JAMES M	LTC	0-0027121	0767	1	MURPHY EDWARD J JR	COL	0-0042061	0962	1
MOORES ZACHERY W	COL	0-0015647	0954	2	MORROW SAMUEL L JR	COL	0-0018104	0760	1	MUELLER WALDEMAR M	COL	0-0031553	1067	2	MURPHY EDWARD R	LTC	0-0052847	0166	1
MOORHEAD JAMES U	COL	0-0041957	1161	1	MORROW THOMAS D	LTC	0-0081076	0666	1	MUFFIE SAM F	COL	0-0051201	0559	1	MURPHY EILEEN K	LTC	N-0000098	0962	1
MOORING BRUCE D	COL	0-0051073	0258	1	MORSE FRANCIS H	COL	0-0012682	0854	1	MUIR JAMES B JR	COL	0-0006643	1048	1	MURPHY ERNEST V	COL	0-0031663	1067	2
MOORMAN FRANK W	M G	0-0019444	1065	1	MORSE GRANVILLE	COL	0-0015388	0846	2	MUIR JOHN E JR	LTC	0-0033754	0962	1	MURPHY FRANCIS J	LTC	0-0062156	0964	1
MOORMAN HAROLD N	COL	0-0021095	0764	1	MORSE MARY F	MAJ	N-0000860	0163	1	MUIR ROBERT P	LTC	0-0039105	0765	1	MURPHY GEORGE E	COL	0-0031047	0466	1
MOORMAN RICHARD R	COL	0-0019394	0864	2	MORSE WARREN C	COL	0-0079657	1168	1	MUIR WILLARD A	COL	0-0044774	0864	1	MURPHY JACK R	LTC	0-0051431	0761	1
MORAN JOHN J	LTC	0-0040004	1263	1	MORSE WILLIAM P	COL	0-0005106	0649	1	MULCAHY JAMES P	COL	0-0024227	0866	1	MURPHY JAMES F	CPT	0-0066185	1164	1
MORAN KATHLEEN A	2LT	R-0002170	1045	1	MORSE WOODROW W	LTC	0-0053048	0262	1	MULCAHY JULIA J	MAJ	L-0000305	0561	1	MURPHY JAMES H	COL	0-0080465	0165	1
MORAN RICHARD B	B G	0-0005399	0450	1	MORSMAN PHYLLIS J	LTC	L-0000360	0868	1	MULCAHY MICHAEL J	COL	0-0007634	1047	2	MURPHY JOHN B	M G	0-0012338	0758	2
MORAN THOMAS J	COL	0-0017266	0554	1	MORTENSEN LOUISE L	MAJ	N-0002605	1068	1	MULHERN JOHN F	COL	0-0082067	0568	1	MURPHY JOHN D	LTC	0-0027789	0867	1
MORAN TIMOTHY A	LTC	0-0032640	0268	1	MORTIMER EDWARD C	CW4	W-0903575	0165	1	MULHOLLAND RICHARD F	COL	0-0031124	0263	1	MURPHY JOHN G	COL	0-0007111	0153	1
MORAN WILLIAM J	B G	0-0029195	0266	1	MORTON CLINTON O	COL	0-0051729	0366	1	MULKEY STEVE H JR	LTC	0-0026724	0165	1	MURPHY JOHN L	COL	0-0079941	0768	2
MORAWETZ FRANCIS E	COL	0-0028947	1057	1	MORTON PAUL A	LTC	0-0062127	0563	1	MULLANE WALTER R	LTC	0-0023987	0460	1	MURPHY JOSEPH A	COL	0-0044667	0966	1
MORDECAI ALFRED	COL	0-0009513	0-44	2	MORTON WILLIAM J JR	COL	0-0015158	1033	2	MULLANEY JOHN J	COL	0-0029150	1058	1	MURPHY JOSEPH F	CW4	W-0906921	0763	1
MOREAU ARTHUR	CW4	W-0903570	0966	1	MOSCATELLI TITO G	COL	0-0017286	0758	1	MULLARKEY JAMES W	LTC	0-0033030	0164	1	MURPHY KATHRYN V	MAJ	N-0001025	1163	2
MOREE MONTESCUE	COL	0-0041834	0361	1	MOSELEY CHARLES H	COL	0-0020402	0866	1	MULLEN CARROLL C	COL	0-0051456	1163	1	MURPHY LENORE L	MAJ	N-0002131	0360	1
MOREFIELD WILLIAM J	LTC	0-0081071	0463	1	MOSELEY GEORGE V H	COL	0-0016893	0146	2	MULLEN LEMUEL T	CW4	W-0903544	0966	1	MURPHY LESLIE C	COL	0-0031021	0864	1
MORELAND HOWARD B	MAJ	0-0029466	0850	1	MOSELY SEABORN H	LTC	0-0042399	0762	1	MULLEN WARREN F	MAJ	0-0093063	0168	1	MURPHY LUTHER W	LTC	0-0043979	0865	1
MORELAND JOHN W	COL	0-0012616	0644	2	MOSEMAN MARTHA E	LTC	R-0010031	0565	1	MULLEN WILLIAM J	COL	0-0019586	0864	1	MURPHY MARGARET M	MAJ	N-0002137	0960	1
MORELOCK GEORGE L JR	LTC	0-0043960	0164	1	MOSER DEWEY F	LTC	0-0041197	0968	1	MULLENIX JOHN C	COL	0-0004605	0946	2	MURPHY PAUL E	CW4	W-0903590	0656	1
MOREMAN OTIS S JR	LTC	0-0051856	0963	1	MOSER ERNEST H	COL	0-0030960	1163	1	MULLER FRANK M	COL	0-0034715	1068	1	MURPHY PAUL W	LTC	0-0037437	1065	1
MORENO ARTURO	COL	0-0002977	1140	1	MOSES ALBERT R	LTC	0-0062235	0866	1	MULLER JOHN K	LTC	0-0024570	1060	1	MURPHY POWELL D	LTC	0-0062842	0868	1
MORGAN CHARLIE E	LTC	0-0051535	1262	2	MOSES HARRIET N	LTC	L-0000056	0762	1	MULLER MATTHAUS F	CW3	W-0904173	0861	1	MURPHY PRESTON J	COL	0-0050936	0257	1
MORGAN CLAYTON A JR	LTC	0-0049124	0565	1	MOSES JAMES R	LTC	0-0041035	0267	1	MULLER WILLIAM G	COL	0-0009161	0743	1	MURPHY ROBERT E	COL	0-0034080	0868	1
MORGAN CLAYTON R	LTC	0-0085624	0961	1	MOSES JOHN G JR	LTC	0-0025528	1166	1	MULLETT DEWITT T	COL	0-0010352	0951	2	MURPHY ROBERT V	LTC	0-0014975	0341	2
MORGAN CLYDE H	COL	0-0008587	1046	1	MOSES JOHN W	COL	0-0026170	1268	1	MULLIKEN DAVID F	LTC	0-0034949	0863	1	MURPHY THOMAS P	LTC	0-0095073	0868	1
MORGAN DALE L	COL	0-0045796	0265	1	MOSES LLOYD R	M G	0-0029362	1064	1	MULLIKIN ORVILLE W	LTC	0-0018893	1045	2	MURPHY VINCENT P	LTC	0-0042872	1158	2
MORGAN DAVID C	LTC	0-0083610	0268	1	MOSES MERILLAT	COL	0-0018421	1059	2	MULLIN WILLIAM H	LTC	0-0023015	0660	1	MURPHY WALLACE S	LTC	0-0063174	0966	1
MORGAN HENRY G JR	LTC	0-0025305	0968	1	MOSES RAYMOND G	B G	0-0004414	0549	1	MULLINIX JOSEPH P	LTC	0-0032086	0962	1	MURPHY WILLIAM D	LTC	0-0020944	1159	1
MORGAN JAMES S	COL	0-0041696	0158	1	MOSES RUSSELL L	LTC	0-0015843	0644	2	MULLINS CHARLES L JR	M G	0-0005306	0153	2	MURPHY WILLIAM E JR	COL	0-0029437	0760	1
MORGAN JOHN H	COL	0-0019871	0865	1	MOSLEY GEORGE W	COL	0-0043175	0568	1	MULLINS CLAYTON F	COL	0-0019016	0646	2	MURPHY WILLIAM F	LTC	0-0031441	0165	2
MORGAN JOHN P	LTC	0-0081072	1066	1	MOSLEY LAURA M	LTC	N-0001883	1159	1	MULLINS MABEL L	MAJ	N-0001942	0558	1	MURPHY WILLIAM M	WO1	W-0901714	1041	1
MORGAN JOHN R	CW3	W-0904168	0558	1	MOSS ALFRED H	LTC	0-0080463	0862	1	MULRONEY FRANK A	MAJ	0-0035833	0863	1	MURRAY ARTHUR M	COL	0-0021303	0868	1
MORGAN JOSEPH H	LTC	0-0051743	0464	1	MOSS JIMMIE O	LTC	L-0000179	0966	1	MULVANITY RALPH T	COL	0-0029674	0262	1	MURRAY ARTHUR R	CW4	W-0902076	0460	1
MORGAN MAURICE	COL	0-0005594	0546	2	MOSS JOE D	COL	0-0012162	0854	1	MULVANY LLOYD T	CW4	W-0903587	0661	1	MURRAY BILLIE L	LTC	L-0000084	0765	2
MORGAN RICHARD A JR	LTC	0-0077905	0268	2	MOSS MARGARET M	MAJ	N-0000054	0650	2	MULVIHILL FRANCIS K	MAJ	0-0014947	1041	1	MURRAY CHARLES M	MAJ	0-0060680	0666	1
MORGAN VERNON W	LTC	0-0045837	0966	1	MOSS ROY P	COL	0-0028838	0156	1	MUMMA HARLAN L	B G	0-0004508	0448	1	MURRAY CHARLES R	COL	0-0018792	0561	1
MORGAN WILLIAM H	LTC	0-0024660	0763	1	MOSS VAUGHN R	MAJ	0-0034144	0962	1	MUMMA JOHN K	LTC	0-0046819	0463	1	MURRAY CLARENCE F	COL	0-0009066	1145	2
MORIN MARTIN J	M G	0-0016911	0764	1	MOSSMAN ALBERT P	COL	0-0019469	0162	1	MUMMEY ROBERT M	LTC	0-0026610	1064	1	MURRAY DOROTHY H	MAJ	N-0001294	0563	1
MORLEY AUBREY R	COL	0-0029758	0862	1	MOTES PRESTON M	COL	0-0030372	0265	1	MUNCH ROBERT J	LTC	0-0045546	1268	1	MURRAY DOUGLAS C	COL	0-0024899	0667	1
MORLEY HARRISON A JR	LTC	0-0083611	0366	1	MOTISKA PAUL J JR	LTC	0-0061300	0268	1	MUNDHENK WILLIAM H	LTC	0-0038155	0968	1	MURRAY GEORGE A JR	COL	0-0034739	0868	1
MORLEY HARRY C	LTC	0-0037341	0864	1	MOTOLA MARIO V	LTC	0-0063406	0766	1	MUNDORF WILLIAM C	LTC	0-0067731	1167	1	MURRAY GEORGE J	COL	0-0020619	0360	1
MORLEY JOHN D	COL	0-0013634	0247	2	MOTT JOHN W	COL	0-0008400	0753	2	MUNDY REUBEN W	COL	0-0025063	0766	1	MURRAY GORDON C	LTC	0-0031644	0759	1
MORLEY RICHARD H	LTC	0-0065250	0268	1	MOTT WILLIAM H	CW4	W-0903579	0858	1	MUNDY ROY L	LTC	0-0069497	0165	1	MURRAY HARRY H	COL	0-0030610	0663	1
MORLOCK WALLACE J	COL	0-0013325	0457	1	MOTTER JOHN C	LTC	0-0032288	0667	1	MUNERA ANTONIO V JR	LTC	0-0049872	1165	1	MURRAY JOHN F T	COL	0-0023768	0165	1
MORREALE SAMUEL D	LTC	0-0041765	0962	1	MOTZ LESLIE L	LTC	0-0042596	0862	1	MUNFORD CHARLES A JR	MAJ	0-0050938	0462	2	MURRAY JOHN W	COL	0-0029833	0862	2
MORRELL JOHN H	COL	0-0079938	0468	1	MOUCHET WILLIAM O	COL	0-0043802	0566	1	MUNRO PERRY A	COL	0-0032940	0764	2	MURRAY ROBERT M	LTC	0-0052094	0164	1
MORRELL JOSEPH J	COL	0-0051996	1266	1	MOULTON ROBERT J	COL	0-0016665	0852	2	MUNROE DONALD A	COL	0-0084050	1067	2	MURRAY ROY A	COL	0-0042366	0564	1
MORRIS CARL E	LTC	0-0060956	1068	1	MOULTRIE MARY L	MAJ	N-0001985	0664	1	MUNSON ETHEL F	LTC	L-0000091	0366	1	MURRAY RUSSEL JR	LTC	0-0039655	0160	1
MORRIS DAVID A	COL	0-0014666	0354	1	MOUNSEY GLEN A	LTC	0-0031607	0858	1	MUNSON FREDERICK	M G	0-0016505	0756	1	MURRAY WALTER H	COL	0-0038693	0661	1
MORRIS GEORGE W	COL	0-0009076	0749	1	MOUNT CHARLES A	LTC	0-0041934	1059	1	MUNSON JACK W	LTC	0-0039349	1167	1	MURRAY WILLIAM R	CW4	W-0903592	0664	1
MORRIS HOWARD A	B G	0-0020141	0266	2	MOUNTFORD FREDERIC	COL	0-0002615	1146	1	MUNSON MERTON E	COL	0-0029519	0261	1	MURREL JOHN H	2LT	0-0018215	0924	2
MORRIS I SEWELL	M G	0-0018806	0563	1	MOURAT STEPHEN	LTC	0-0059515	0365	1	MUNSON ORVILLE O	LTC	0-0081080	0264	1	MURZYN LUCIEN A	CW4	W-0903593	0956	1
MORRIS JAMES H	LTC	0-0081074	0866	1	MOUSHEGIAN RICHARD	LTC	0-0022109	0160	2	MUNSON THOMAS V	LTC	0-0042654	1062	1	MUSCHEL LOUIS H	LTC	0-0049922	0262	1
MORRIS JOHN G JR	COL	0-0039657	0761	1	MOWBRAY JAY B	LTC	0-0024450	1059	1	MUNSTER IRENE V	LTC	L-0000110	0863	1	MUSER NORMAN F A	LTC	0-0049353	0968	2
MORRIS JOHN W	LTC	0-0080312	0963	1	MOWERY WILLIAM A	LTC	0-0051492	0462	1	MURCH GORDON F	COL	0-0031651	0864	1	MUSHAM HARRY A	MAJ	0-0003268	1022	1
MORRIS MARIE C	MAJ	N-0002234	0560	1	MOWREY FRED H	COL	0-0019687	0859	2	MURCHISON JAMES L	COL	0-0019920	1062	1	MUSHEN ROBERT L	COL	0-0043508	0963	1
MORRIS MARY C	MAJ	N-0002035	0360	1	MOYER MAYNARD G	LTC	0-0023991	1057	2	MURCHISON ROARY A	COL	0-0017908	0855	1	MUSICK LAWRENCE A	LTC	0-0031811	0164	1
MORRIS MARY S	LTC	N-0000346	0468	1	MOYERS EUGENE E	COL	0-0041938	1061	2	MURPHEY HENRY S	M G	0-0019338	1265	2	MUSICK RUSSELL G	CW4	W-0903594	0161	1
MORRIS RAYMOND C	COL	0-0079939	1063	2	MOYNAHAN GEORGE F JR	COL	0-0030210	1160	1	MURPHEY JAMES A	COL	0-0011818	1053	2	MUTH EDWIN A	COL	0-0030670	0166	2
MORRIS ROBERT C	CW4	W-0904171	1265	1	MOYNAHAN JAMES M	COL	0-0042848	1066	1	MURPHREE HAROLD C	COL	0-0068399	0168	1	MUTH MARY B	MAJ	L-0000089	1162	1
MORRIS THURMAN W	COL	0-0020315	0759	1	MOZINGO ROULE C	LTC	0-0026274	0768	1	MURPHY ALLEN M	COL	0-0028764	0354	1	MUTH ROY W	COL	0-0018180	0560	1
MORRIS WILLIAM H	LTG	0-0003102	0352	1	MOZLEY JOSEPH T	COL	0-0047611	0865	1	MURPHY ARTHUR A	LTC	0-0027951	0967	1	MUTTONI DONALD S	LTC	0-0081083	0866	1
MORRISETTE JAMES E	B G	0-0007839	0846	2	MRAZEK JAMES E	COL	0-0021268	0758	1	MURPHY ARTHUR W	LTC	0-0024156	0262	1	MUZYK ALEXANDER	COL	0-0024010	0964	1
MORRISEY JOHN C JR	LTC	0-0080462	0765	1	MRYCZKO MICHAEL M	LTC	0-0063852	0868	1	MURPHY ARTHUR P	COL	0-0052226	0665	1	MUZZY CLAUDE A	CW3	W-0902375	0856	1
MORRISON BURTON D	COL	0-0041658	0361	1	MUCCI HENRY A	COL	0-0020374	0447	2	MURPHY BINFORT W	CW4	W-0901891	0760	1	MYER FRANCIS B	COL	0-0007109	0551	1
MORRISON CHARLES E	COL	0-0012109	0548	2	MUCHA DANIEL	LTC	0-0044636	1061	1	MURPHY CLARENCE J	COL	0-0037647	0460	1	MYERS ALBERT F	LTC	0-0035239	0863	1
MORRISON DOUGLAS E	COL	0-0007555	0145	2	MUDGE BYRON R	CW4	W-0903582	1165	1	MURPHY CORNELIUS	COL	0-0023146	0766	1	MYERS CHARLES M	COL	0-0010783	0749	1

NAME	GRADE	SVC NO	DATE RET MO YR	RET CODE
MYERS COLLIN S	COL	0-0008356	0854	1
MYERS CORDELIA	LTC	J-0000062	0668	1
MYERS DONALD S	LTC	0-0057972	0964	1
MYERS FRANCIS J JR	LTC	0-0024073	0868	1
MYERS FREDERICK JR	LTC	0-0054959	0364	1
MYERS GEORGE E	COL	0-0051765	0566	1
MYERS HERBERT A	COL	0-0006131	0449	1
MYERS JAMES R	LTC	0-0022209	0865	1
MYERS LOTTIE M	MAJ	N-0002436	0168	1
MYERS PAUL E	LTC	0-0050062	0964	1
MYERS SAMUEL L	LTG	0-0017180	0463	1
MYERS SHELLY P JR	COL	0-0030157	0161	1
MYERS WILLIAM R	MAJ	0-0025513	0864	1
MYNDERSE JACOB F	COL	0-0023523	0963	1
MYRICK CHARLES M	COL	0-0029675	0559	1
NACHOD ELIZABETH	LTC	J-0000050	1167	1
NADAL CARLOS A	COL	0-0020670	0168	2
NADAL RAMONA	COL	0-0017280	0758	1
NAEGELE EUGENE L	LTC	0-0071576	0968	1
NAGLE FREDRICK W	COL	0-0020904	0967	1
NAGLE JOHN J	LTC	0-0041726	0659	1
NAHAS JACK N	COL	0-0039990	0864	1
NAIMARK MAX	COL	0-0019303	0862	2
NALER JOHN L	LTC	0-0063736	0366	1
NALLE WILLIAM	COL	0-0003410	0147	2
NANCE JOHN B	COL	0-0020663	1046	2
NAPIER HERMAN S	LTC	0-0027636	0965	1
NAPIER JACK P	COL	0-0043657	1268	1
NAPPER FRANK E	COL	0-0036416	1062	1
NASELLI GEORGE E	COL	0-0029133	1157	1
NASELROAD WINFRED C	COL	0-0035259	1068	1
NASH ALLAN B C	LTC	0-0041438	0854	1
NASH ARTHUR B JR	LTC	0-0084652	0968	1
NASH BERTRAM I	LTC	0-0040361	1057	1
NASH GROVER E	LTC	0-0036182	1064	1
NASH JAMES H	LTC	0-0026153	0567	2
NASH LEONARD C	LTC	0-0081085	0366	1
NATHAN CHARLES C	CPT	0-0006802	0722	2
NATIONS EMMETT L	COL	0-0041592	0559	1
NAUGLE PAUL T	LTC	0-0041075	0763	1
NAUMAN ARTHUR C	COL	0-0030467	0764	1
NAVAS MANUEL B	COL	0-0004840	0650	1
NAWROCKY LOUIS M	LTC	0-0030293	1062	1
NAYLOR DUNCAN N	COL	0-0038860	1268	1
NAYLOR ROBERT H	COL	0-0016739	0757	2
NAZARIO LUIS F	CW3	W-0906924	1162	1
NEAGLI CHARLES J	CW4	W-0903599	0355	1
NEAL CARROLL W	MAJ	0-0013910	0120	2
NEAL FOREST L	LTC	0-0038577	0766	1
NEAL PAUL L	B G	0-0011684	0854	1
NEAL RALPH M	COL	0-0015359	0554	1
NEALE CLAUDE L	LTC	0-0017826	0343	2
NEALON JOHN J	LTC	0-0008186	0244	2
NEARHOOD MADELINE L	MAJ	N-0000856	0861	1
NEBEL CHARLES A	COL	0-0042040	0762	1
NEDOS IVAN L	COL	0-0031268	0868	1
NEE WILLIAM F	LTC	0-0050933	1154	1
NEEDELS EDWARD V R	COL	0-0030537	1165	1
NEEL JOHN S	COL	0-0051493	0464	1
NEELY JAMES E JR	LTC	0-0040093	0465	1
NEELY ROBERT B	B G	0-0019114	0363	1
NEELY WILLIAM G	COL	0-0042538	1059	1
NEELY WILLIAM W	LTC	0-0024332	C863	1
NEES RUTH K	MAJ	N-0002643	0568	1
NEESEMAN ARTHUR C	LTC	0-0057816	0366	1
NEFF ORRIN D	LTC	0-0062189	1166	2
NEFF R WILSON	COL	0-0053439	0568	1
NEFSTEAD PAUL D	LTC	0-0069756	0168	1
NEGRON RAFAEL	LTC	0-0034115	0464	1
NEGROTTO SIDNEY H	COL	0-0006711	0151	2
NEIER THOMAS D	COL	0-0020698	0867	1
NEIL JAMES B	COL	0-0057530	0265	2
NEILL HAROLD A	LTC	0-0026271	0665	1
NEILL SAMUEL S	COL	0-0051447	0163	1
NEILSON ALEXANDER	COL	0-0009321	1049	1

NAME	GRADE	SVC NO	DATE RET MO YR	RET CODE
NEILSON HENRY	COL	0-0019588	0864	1
NEILSON ROBERT W JR	2LT	0-0026256	0544	2
NEIMAN ROBERT E JR	LTC	0-0037683	0564	1
NEIMAN WATSON E	COL	0-0031072	0763	1
NEIRBY GLADYS D	MAJ	N-0002649	0265	1
NELLI HUMBERT O	COL	0-0038586	1155	1
NELSON ANDRE H	MAJ	0-0044271	0461	1
NELSON ANDREW C	LTC	0-0038676	0150	2
NELSON ARCHIE	CW2	RW-0903601	0662	1
NELSON ARTHUR H	COL	0-0023093	0964	1
NELSON BARTIL H	CW2	RW-0904431	0564	1
NELSON CARLTON	LTC	0-0047373	0762	1
NELSON CARLTON W	COL	0-0043381	0165	1
NELSON CHRIS C	CW3	W-0904175	0852	1
NELSON CHRISTIAN	COL	0-0016910	0757	1
NELSON CLARENCE F	COL	0-0043073	0667	1
NELSON CLARENCE J	COL	0-0050942	0555	1
NELSON CURTIS D	LTC	0-0084403	0866	1
NELSON DONALD H	COL	0-0012394	0949	1
NELSON EDNA M	MAJ	N-0000604	0363	1
NELSON FLORENCE R	MAJ	N-0002173	0464	1
NELSON GUSTIN M	COL	0-0014612	0348	1
NELSON HAROLD E	COL	0-0024487	1066	1
NELSON HAROLD E M	COL	0-0029351	0759	1
NELSON HARRY J	COL	0-0020053	1065	1
NELSON HENRY H	LTC	0-0031916	0766	1
NELSON HERBERT L	COL	0-0030232	0759	1
NELSON JOHN G	COL	0-0020886	0967	1
NELSON JOSEPH W	LTC	0-0034692	0661	1
NELSON KENNETH R	MAJ	0-0020508	0243	2
NELSON KENT J	CPT	0-0011969	0839	2
NELSON KNUTE R	COL	0-0061220	1165	1
NELSON LLOYD S	LTC	0-0052325	0762	1
NELSON OLA A	COL	0-0011878	0854	1
NELSON OTTO L JR	M G	0-0015713	0346	1
NELSON PAUL B	COL	0-0016698	1056	1
NELSON POPE M	CW2	W-0902151	1047	1
NELSON RAYMOND C	LTC	0-0052775	0965	1
NELSON RAYMOND N JR	MAJ	0-0059802	0764	1
NELSON ROBERT C	LTC	0-0027124	0966	1
NELSON ROBERT S	COL	0-0020111	0655	1
NELSON RUSSELL M	COL	0-0018674	0862	1
NELSON WALLACE W	LTC	0-0065757	1267	1
NELSON WILLIAM H JR	COL	0-0031992	0567	1
NELSON WILLIAM J	MAJ	0-0058532	0968	1
NELSON WILNER N J	COL	0-0079632	0867	1
NEMEC GODFREY B	LTC	0-0028967	0256	1
NEMO RALPH	COL	0-0008362	0657	1
NEPRUD LEIF	LTC	0-0016257	0753	1
NESBITT ALLAN P	LTC	0-0052782	0967	1
NESBITT GEORGE F	CW3	W-0903603	0659	2
NESLAND MARION L	CPT	N-0000347	0448	1
NESMITH VARDELL E	COL	0-0039669	0459	1
NETHERTON THOMAS H	MAJ	0-0065552	0361	1
NETHERY DONALD M	LTC	0-0054988	1163	1
NETT JOSEPH E	LTC	0-0025804	0864	1
NETTLES WILLIAM R JR	LTC	0-0050044	0666	1
NEUBAUER WILLIAM C	COL	0-0035572	0767	1
NEUBERT BERNARD E JR	LTC	0-0049637	0563	1
NEUMANN ANNA S	MAJ	N-0002306	0467	2
NEUMANN JAMES D	COL	0-0035956	1067	1
NEUMANN RICHARD T	COL	0-0039054	0561	1
NEUMANN WILLIAM C JR	LTC	0-0044145	0468	1
NEVE JACK C	COL	0-0040893	0267	1
NEVELS ELIZABETH	MAJ	R-0010087	1262	1
NEVILLE FRED T	COL	0-0007806	0145	1
NEVIN JOHN I	LTC	0-0063804	0666	1
NEVIN STANLEY M	COL	0-0016552	0251	2
NEVINS ARTHUR S	B G	0-0007110	0846	1
NEW JAMES H	LTC	0-0043435	0266	1
NEWBY GILBERT U	COL	0-0040858	1167	1
NEWCOMB FIDELIS D	LTC	0-0022056	0959	1
NEWCOMB RALPH E	COL	0-0038727	1162	1
NEWCOMB RICHARD I	LTC	0-0042844	0864	1
NEWCOMER FRANCIS K	COL	0-0021898	0767	1

NAME	GRADE	SVC NO	DATE RET MO YR	RET CODE
NEWELL ARTHUR	LTC	0-0069533	0968	1
NEWELL CHARLES H	LTC	0-0028835	0154	1
NEWELL JOSEPH C	LTC	0-0084877	0467	1
NEWELL OLIN C	COL	0-0007507	0748	1
NEWELL ROBERT L	LTC	0-0035145	0965	1
NEWGARDEN GEORGE J	COL	0-0004500	0546	2
NEWHALL HENRY S	COL	0-0029717	0662	2
NEWMAN AUBREY S	M G	0-0016099	0360	1
NEWMAN ERMAN M	COL	0-0030173	0564	1
NEWMAN FOREST P JR	LTC	0-0080313	0766	1
NEWMAN GLENN	COL	0-0015902	0947	2
NEWMAN HAROLD H	COL	0-0038716	0862	1
NEWMAN JOHN T	COL	0-0024281	0366	1
NEWMAN MARY E	MAJ	N-0000975	0263	1
NEWMAN OLIVER P	M G	0-0015016	0658	2
NEWMAN STANLEY	LTC	0-0062965	0866	2
NEWMAN WILLIAM J	COL	0-0051635	0865	1
NEWSOM DONELL	CW4	W-0906928	0968	1
NEWSOM MARION E JR	LTC	0-0043378	1163	1
NEWTUN ARTHUR	LTC	0-0083551	1068	1
NEWTON CARLOS E JR	LTC	0-0061082	0263	1
NEWTON CARROLL T	COL	0-0020865	1163	1
NEWTON EDITH	MAJ	M-0010111	0766	1
NEWTON GEORGE D	LTC	0-0018286	0149	1
NEWTON KENNETH H	LTC	0-0042579	0961	1
NEWTON LUCILE	MAJ	N-0000134	0561	1
NEWTON ROBERT D	LTC	0-0070452	0968	1
NEWTON THOMAS J	COL	0-0042563	0565	1
NIBLACK EMMETT A	CPT	0-0011941	0138	2
NICCOLLS ROBERT S	LTC	0-0032317	0361	1
NICELY EDWARD L	LTC	0-0053251	0665	1
NICELY REBECCA M	2LT	M-0002162	1045	1
NICEWANDER DENNIS R	LTC	0-0071580	0867	1
NICHOL BYRON A	COL	0-0022286	0861	2
NICHOL ISAAC J	COL	0-0002692	0743	1
NICHOL WILLIAM W	COL	0-0018939	0662	2
NICHOLAS CHARLES P	B G	0-0016080	1067	1
NICHOLAS JACK V	COL	0-0051363	0761	1
NICHOLAS JEROME C	CW2	W-0902043	0144	2
NICHOLLS ANDREW B C	LTC	0-0031957	0866	1
NICHOLLS RUSSELL E	LTC	0-0019844	1143	2
NICHOLS CHRISTOPHE	CW4	W-0906930	0566	1
NICHOLS EARL R	COL	0-0030857	0565	1
NICHOLS GEORGE P	COL	0-0040407	0168	1
NICHOLS GEORGE W	LTC	0-0054033	0863	1
NICHOLS GLEN L	LTC	0-0058986	0962	1
NICHOLS HAROLD F	B G	0-0003076	0747	1
NICHOLS JAMES B	COL	0-0019693	0163	1
NICHOLS JOSEPH A	COL	0-0009699	0650	1
NICHOLS KENNETH O	M G	0-0017498	1053	1
NICHOLS MARK E	CW4	W-0906929	1165	1
NICHOLS MAURICE W	MAJ	0-0037532	0664	1
NICHOLS STEPHEN L	COL	0-0028844	0260	1
NICHOLS WALLACE J	COL	0-0030003	0161	1
NICK JAMES T	LTC	0-0082070	0866	1
NICKEL JOHN R	COL	0-0025553	0866	1
NICKESON DWAINE E	MAJ	OF-0105497	1268	1
NICOL DAVID J	LTC	0-0038480	0167	1
NICOLARY CARL W	LTC	0-0031226	0164	1
NICOLSON WILLIAM H	LTC	0-0030804	0762	1
NIEDERPRUEM WILLIAM	COL	0-0007893	0248	1
NIEDZIELA EDWARD	CW4	W-0903612	0465	1
NIELSEN CARL H	LTC	0-0081091	0663	1
NIELSEN EDWARD L	COL	0-0040868	1268	1
NIELSEN SVEND W	COL	0-0039753	0162	1
NIELSEN WILLARD L	COL	0-0021051	1166	1
NIELSON CHESTER O	LTC	0-0033280	1267	1
NIEMI ARVO N	COL	0-0029753	0862	1
NIGHTINGALE GARDNER	LTC	0-0081093	0265	1
NIGRO GEORGE A	MAJ	0-0059270	0465	2
NILAND WILLIAM H	COL	0-0045456	0868	1
NILES ELLERY W	COL	0-0019763	0764	1
NILES EVELYN J	MAJ	N-0001656	0166	1
NILES GIBSON	COL	0-0023938	1065	2
NILES RICHARD H	MAJ	0-0035853	0663	1

NAME	GRADE	SVC NO	DATE RET MO YR	RET CODE
NILES WALLACE E	COL	0-0014669	0949	2
NILON NILS J S	CW3	W-0903614	0664	2
NILSSON ERWIN G	COL	0-0031593	0764	1
NILSSON PAUL A	COL	0-0025274	0968	1
NISHIMURA BERT N	COL	0-0081094	1166	1
NIST CECIL W	COL	0-0015274	0454	1
NIX ASBURY L	CW4	W-0903616	0762	1
NIXDORFF JAMES B	LTC	0-0040867	0862	1
NIXON JOSEPH J	CW4	W-0902144	0255	1
NIXON PAUL	COL	0-0017912	0846	2
NIXON ROBERT T	LTC	0-0026563	0864	1
NIXON THOMAS H	COL	0-0009326	0854	2
NIXON VICTOR M	LTC	0-0047617	0767	1
NOAKE DONALD W	COL	0-0020357	0864	1
NOBLE CHARLES H	COL	0-0012383	0649	1
NOBLE DORA A	LTC	N-0000025	0349	1
NOBLE JOSEPH E JR	COL	0-0031973	0966	1
NOBLE THOMAS P	LTC	0-0060334	1068	1
NOBLE WILLIAM E	MAJ	0-0063363	1158	1
NOBLES LAWRENCE E	COL	0-0029045	1058	1
NOCE DANIEL	LTG	0-0005226	1054	2
NOCITA JOHN W	COL	0-0065045	1268	2
NOEL EDGAR A	LTC	0-0051570	1262	1
NOEL JOHN C JR	LTC	0-0031404	0462	1
NOID WILLIAM D	LTC	0-0038247	1066	1
NOLAN JAMES L	COL	0-0038689	0561	1
NOLAN WILLIAM	CW2	W-0904177	0463	2
NOLAND MARION B	LTC	0-0043603	0364	1
NOLD JAMES M	1LT	0-0062626	0753	2
NOLPH WILLIAM H	LTC	0-0081096	0568	1
NOLTE MARVIN C O	LTC	0-0036763	0267	1
NOONCASTER CLIFTON F	COL	0-0030061	1163	1
NORBY ALLEN R	MAJ	0-0065696	0962	1
NORBY THOMAS	LTC	0-0051548	0961	1
NOREEN ALBERT T	LTC	0-0060438	0464	2
NORELL JAMES A	B G	0-0039838	0763	1
NOREM ALBERT F	CW2	W-0902017	0349	1
NOREM LEROY K	LTC	0-0084749	0267	1
NORLING RALPH L	LTC	0-0032112	0266	1
NORMAN BROOKS O	COL	0-0035793	1065	1
NORMAN DANIEL P	COL	0-0015467	0954	1
NORMAN ERNEST C	COL	0-0012124	0854	1
NORMAN FRANK P JR	COL	0-0020383	1047	2
NORMAN GEORGE B	CPT	0-0026784	0747	2
NORMAN LEWIS S	COL	0-0010111	0749	1
NORMAN RANDOLPH G	COL	0-0039515	0655	1
NORMAND JOSEPH P E	CW4	W-0903625	0355	1
NORMINGTON JOSEPH M	LTC	0-0041157	0763	1
NORRIS CLOVIS B	LTC	0-0051861	0162	1
NORRIS JACK K	COL	0-0021865	0766	1
NORRIS LEON E	COL	0-0005633	0746	1
NORRIS NED T	COL	0-0020222	0866	1
NORRIS WILLARD	CW4	W-0906934	0868	1
NORRIS WILLIAM H	LTC	0-0027295	0763	1
NORTH HARRIS J	COL	0-0052158	0766	1
NORTH WILLARD L	CW4	W-0903627	0861	1
NORTH WILLIAM D	COL	0-0017345	0948	2
NORTHAM WILLIAM F	COL	0-0019547	0864	1
NORTHCROSS WM M P	COL	0-0028793	0255	1
NORTHCUTT THADEUS P	LTC	0-0040677	0863	1
NORTHEN ERNEST E JR	LTC	0-0029297	1161	1
NORTHINGTON HARTSELL	COL	0-0033275	0868	2
NORTHROP EDWARD D	COL	0-0040282	0762	1
NORTNER SYLVESTER	COL	0-0005595	0451	2
NORTON ANDERSON H	LTC	0-0008426	0934	2
NORTON AUGUSTUS	COL	0-0002668	0922	2
NORTON DOYT P	LTC	0-0065149	0868	1
NORTON RICHARD A	COL	0-0041984	0462	1
NORTON ROBERT W	CPT	0-0005771	1122	2
NORVELL FRANK C	B G	0-0019471	0864	1
NORVELL JAMES E	COL	0-0020706	0967	1
NORWOOD JAMES L	LTC	0-0044048	1059	1
NORWOOD LEONARD L JR	LTC	0-0058990	1165	1
NORWOOD WAYNE D	LTC	0-0060693	0667	1
NOSECK KENNETH A	LTC	0-0045645	0866	1

UNITED STATES ARMY RETIRED LIST

NAME	GRADE	SVC NO	DATE RET MO YR	RET CODE
NOSEK THADDEUS M	COL	0-0022934	0464	1
NOSSAMAN WARREN E	LTC	0-0025079	0466	1
NOTBOHM WILLIAM R	LTC	0-0060643	1064	1
NOTTINGHAM JONATHAN	LTC	0-0030482	0863	1
NOURSE ROBERT S	COL	0-0016484	0656	1
NOVAK THOMAS E	LTC	0-0079010	0968	1
NOVICK JEHIEL	LTC	0-0061993	1265	1
NOWE CHARLES F	COL	0-0031460	0467	1
NOYES EDWARD P	COL	0-0002674	0745	2
NOYES MELVILLE F	COL	0-0039555	0657	1
NUGENT MARCUS Y	CW2	W-0903628	0253	2
NUMAINVILLE LEON J	COL	0-0021002	0862	1
NUNGESSER WILLIAM L	COL	0-0053150	0868	1
NUNN CLIFFORD C JR	LTC	0-0060465	0767	1
NUNN DEWITT A	1LT	0-0027087	0748	2
NUNN JAMES R	CW4	W-0908018	0168	1
NUNZIATO CARL A	MAJ	0-0092763	0968	2
NUSS RUDOLPH W	COL	0-0028981	0558	1
NUSSBAUM CHARLES W	COL	0-0051281	0262	1
NUTT JAMES D	COL	0-0030164	0464	1
NUTT JOHN W	CPT	0-0076474	0262	2
NUTTER WILLIAM H	M G	0-0016095	0462	1
NUTTMAN LOUIS M	B G	0-0000484	0138	1
NYBERG ALMA M	MAJ	N-0001552	0564	1
NYE CHARLES A III	COL	0-0085058	0367	1
NYE DAVID B	COL	0-0020695	0564	1
NYE ELWOOD L	COL	0-0009444	0146	2
NYE WILBUR S	COL	0-0012797	0854	1
NYEZ WALBURGA G	MAJ	N-0001236	1064	1
NYFELER GEORGE L JR	MAJ	0-0096785	0567	2
NYGAARD JOHN P	LTC	0-0005331	0627	2
NYGARD WALTER E	LTC	0-0025669	0864	1
NYLEN ARTHUR H	COL	0-0006414	0250	1
NYPAVER MARY F	MAJ	N-0000576	0961	1
OAKES CURTISS W	LTC	0-0051471	1061	1
OAKES JAMES L	LTC	0-0051643	0264	2
OAKES JOHN C	LTG	0-0017160	0163	2
OAKLEY SAMUEL H	LTC	0-0043841	0764	1
OARTEL JOHN S	COL	0-0057039	0261	1
OATES EUGENE C JR	COL	0-0044576	0864	1
OATMAN CLYDE C JR	COL	0-0020964	0962	1
OBERG CLARA P	MAJ	N-0002024	0360	1
OBERMEYER CHARLES R	LTC	0-0044759	0862	1
OBERST DONALD A	LTC	0-0031451	0759	1
OBLER MAX	COL	0-0051287	0162	1
OBRADOVICH FRANCIS S	LTC	0-0063055	0767	1
OBRIEN DANIEL H	CW4	W-0903631	0660	1
OBRIEN EDMUND R	COL	0-0040032	0766	1
OBRIEN ELMER J	CW4	W-0906936	0466	1
OBRIEN JAMES V	LTC	0-0038230	0964	1
OBRIEN JOHN G	B G	0-0042171	0463	1
OBRIEN ROBERT A JR	COL	0-0023152	0868	1
OBRIEN ROBERT E JR	COL	0-0020313	1163	1
OBRIEN THEO W	COL	0-0006665	0846	2
OBYRNE JOHN C	COL	0-0052910	0766	1
OCHOA LOIS W	LTC	L-0000063	1262	1
OCHS WILLIAM V	COL	0-0006592	0647	1
OCONNELL AUGUSTUS B	COL	0-0005527	0752	2
OCONNELL EDWARD M	COL	0-0013563	0258	1
OCONNELL FRANCIS J	LTC	0-0030667	0364	1
OCONNELL GEOFFREY M	COL	0-0009685	0447	2
OCONNELL JAMES D	LTG	0-0014965	0459	1
OCONNELL JOHN	LTC	0-0042422	1262	2
OCONNELL JOHN D	MAJ	0-0012546	0836	1
OCONNELL THOMAS C	MAJ	0-0023994	0660	1
OCONNOR ANDREW R	LTC	0-0061103	0868	1
OCONNOR DANIEL A	M G	0-0029454	0664	1
OCONNOR EDWARD F	LTC	0-0083585	0966	1
OCONNOR EDWIN	COL	0-0003170	0747	2
OCONNOR EDWIN JR	COL	0-0023539	1064	1
OCONNOR HERBERT J	COL	0-0051654	0965	1
OCONNOR JOHN F	CW3	W-0903635	1154	1
OCONNOR JOHN J	COL	0-0052160	0864	1
OCONNOR PATRICK J	LTC	0-0028509	0268	1
OCONNOR RICHARD C	LTC	0-0062187	0368	1

NAME	GRADE	SVC NO	DATE RET MO YR	RET CODE
OCONNOR ROBERT J	COL	0-0041888	0661	1
OCONNOR THOMAS J	COL	0-0019125	0356	1
OCONNOR WALTER B	LTC	0-0051740	0364	1
OCONNOR WILLIAM W	B G	0-0016348	0656	1
ODAIR GEORGE W	CW4	W-0902376	0560	1
ODANIEL JOHN W	LTG	0-0007342	0256	1
ODAY RAY M	COL	0-0004918	0753	2
ODBERT LUCILE G	LTC	L-0000068	0363	1
ODELL DOROTHY J	MAJ	N-0000131	0461	2
ODELL EDWARD T	COL	0-0057960	1168	1
ODELL JOSEPH C	B G	0-0012439	0854	1
ODENWELLER CHARLES J	LTC	0-0018135	0558	1
ODIAM CARL E	CW2	W-0902335	0948	1
ODLE SADIEBELLE	MAJ	N-0002394	0562	1
ODOM ALTON C	LTC	0-0081101	0567	1
ODOM CLEVE C	COL	0-0008679	0647	2
ODOM HERBERT R	LTC	0-0022086	0667	1
ODOM LOUIE W	LTC	0-0065231	1067	1
ODONNELL CHARLES M	COL	0-0029010	0357	1
ODONNELL JOHN W	COL	0-0019686	0447	2
ODONNELL NEIL J	LTC	0-0027697	0868	1
ODONNELL ROBERT F	COL	0-0023228	0461	1
ODONNELL ROBERT J	COL	0-0051786	0666	2
ODOR RAYMOND W	COL	0-0012228	0647	2
ODWYER MAUREEN P	MAJ	N-0000425	0361	1
OELHAFEN WAYNE R	LTC	0-0037631	0664	1
OETTINGER VERNON S	LTC	0-0031262	1162	1
OFARRELL HUGH R	COL	0-0043888	0766	1
OFFER ROBERT D	COL	0-0021233	0968	1
OFFLEY EDWARD M	COL	0-0001398	0-37	2
OFFLEY ROBERT H	COL	0-0011205	0948	1
OFFUTT ANDREW C	MAJ	0-0025143	0449	2
OFFUTT HARRY D	B G	0-0003759	0351	2
OFFUTT RICHARD L	LTC	0-0040140	1167	1
OGDEN CHARLES L	LTC	0-0030689	0464	1
OGDEN DAVID A D	LTG	0-0012051	1057	1
OGDEN LILY M	MAJ	N-0000173	0562	1
OGDEN MILTON L	B G	0-0018687	0762	1
OGG LESTER C	COL	0-0003911	0750	2
OGILVIE JOHN M JR	COL	0-0030773	0764	1
OGILVIE KENNETH W	CW2	W-0901761	0347	1
OGLE JOSEPH A	LTC	0-0024500	0661	1
OGLE MERLE W	COL	0-0022261	0164	1
OGLESBY GEORGE R	COL	0-0019877	0555	1
OGLETREE JAMES D	COL	0-0029492	0758	1
OGRADY GEORGE L	COL	0-0029282	0963	1
OGREN OSCAR J	B G	0-0020037	0866	1
OHANLON JOSEPH P	LTC	0-0027257	0965	1
OHARA JAMES	COL	0-0019593	0862	1
OHARA LEWIS B	LTC	0-0031887	0761	1
OHEA JOHN T	LTC	0-0035486	0163	1
OHERN ROBERT S	LTC	0-0079659	1162	1
OHLSSON LENNART Y	LTC	0-0030211	0762	1
OKEEFE ARTHUR J	CPT	0-0014241	0420	2
OKEEFE KEITH T	COL	0-0030669	0865	1
OLDAKER MARION J	CW4	W-0902682	0961	1
OLDFIELD HOMER R	M G	0-0002589	1046	1
OLEARY FRANCIS X	COL	0-0040214	0268	1
OLEARY JOHN J	CW4	W-0904180	1265	1
OLHAUSEN JAMES N	COL	0-0040084	0267	1
OLIGHER HOWARD L	LTC	0-0080157	0866	1
OLIN CHARLES L	COL	0-0018190	0760	1
OLIVARES JOSE E	COL	0-0015377	0753	2
OLIVER EDWARD J	COL	0-0003238	1143	1
OLIVER GEORGE L	COL	0-0033118	1266	1
OLIVER JOHN E	COL	0-0039700	0159	2
OLIVER LUNSFORD E	M G	0-0003536	0548	1
OLIVER RICHARD H	COL	0-0043586	1166	1
OLIVER THAD S JR	LTC	0-0032553	0866	1
OLLEY CORNELIUS	CW4	W-0901829	0962	1
OLMSTEAD LOREN W	COL	0-0039721	0561	1
OLSEN EDMUND S JR	COL	0-0031071	1163	1
OLSEN HAROLD D	LTC	0-0031726	1265	1
OLSEN RAYMOND M	LTC	0-0081106	0868	1
OLSON CLARENCE D	LTC	0-0030734	1163	2

NAME	GRADE	SVC NO	DATE RET MO YR	RET CODE
OLSON CLARENCE T	COL	0-0029323	1168	1
OLSON HARDIN L	COL	0-0019110	1159	2
OLSON HARRY C	COL	0-0031399	0167	1
OLSON HARRY H	LTC	0-0081108	0866	1
OLSON JAMES C	COL	0-0060207	0968	1
OLSON JOHN E	COL	0-0022125	0867	1
OLSON MORRIS V	LTC	0-0039327	0868	1
OLSON ROY I	COL	0-0052117	0368	1
OLSON WINSTON L	COL	0-0032940	1068	1
OLSSEN MARY J	MAJ	N-0001847	1067	1
OLSZOWY FRANCES F	MAJ	N-0001061	0264	1
OMALLEY JOHN F	LTC	0-0046050	0763	1
OMANS JOHN P	MAJ	0-0024771	0147	2
OMEARA ANDREW P	GEN	0-0019062	0667	2
OMEARA EDWIN F	CW2	W-0800369	0545	2
OMOHUNDRO WILEY H	COL	0-0008545	0854	1
ONDRICK JOHN G	B G	0-0018804	0862	1
ONEAL JAMES D	LTC	0-0038018	0965	1
ONEAL WILLIAM P JR	LTC	0-0019971	0863	1
ONEIL LARRY J	COL	0-0038761	0758	1
ONEIL PAUL F	COL	0-0022902	0267	1
ONEIL THOMAS A	COL	0-0019583	0864	1
ONEILL CARROLL P	COL	0-0028505	0868	1
ONEILL EDWARD J	LTG	0-0015952	0462	2
ONEILL GEORGE P	COL	0-0015773	0555	2
ONEILL HAROLD P	CW3	RW-0903640	1066	1
ONEILL JAMES H	B G	0-0016370	0152	1
ONEILL JOHN T	COL	0-0030166	0461	1
ONEILL RICHARD J	COL	0-0033536	0967	1
OOMS HENRICUS L	CW4	W-0902263	0753	1
OPDYKE MINOTT S JR	LTC	0-0085228	1167	1
OPELLO JUNE D	MAJ	N-0002113	0666	1
OPLE RICHARD E	COL	0-0011972	0846	2
OPPENHEIMER HUGH C	LTC	0-0027568	0765	1
OPPENHIMER JOHN S	LTC	0-0036490	0766	1
OPRY GLENN C	CPT	0-0006445	1028	1
OPSAHL HAROLD E	COL	0-0061057	1162	2
ORANGE ARTHUR J	LTC	0-0051986	0459	1
ORBISON JAMES A	COL	0-0026405	0768	1
ORCUTT JOHN W	COL	0-0008520	0249	1
ORD JOHN A	COL	0-0031532	0865	1
OREAR JOHN T H	COL	0-0002890	1045	2
OREILLY AUBREY J	LTC	0-0020537	1155	1
OREILLY CHARLES A JR	COL	0-0031881	0568	1
OREILLY GEORGE T	COL	0-0040120	0664	1
OREL BURNIS	CW3	W-0906939	0261	1
ORFALEA GEORGE A	MAJ	0-0060455	0962	1
ORMES MELVIN W	COL	0-0030549	1265	1
ORMISTON EDWARD J	COL	0-0029015	1057	1
ORMSTON MERCEDES M	MAJ	L-0000108	1264	1
ORDARK DULANEY L	COL	0-0029986	0863	1
ORDJARK GERALD A	COL	0-0012130	0228	2
OROURKE DONALD C	LTC	0-0036611	1166	1
OROURKE FRANKLYN S	MAJ	0-0084243	0865	2
OROURKE PETER J	LTC	0-0038923	1163	1
ORPHAN RICHARD C	LTC	0-0026039	0863	1
ORR RAYMOND	COL	0-0006691	1147	2
ORR URIAH N	LTC	0-0053877	0263	1
ORRINGER WILLIAM D	COL	0-0023343	0966	1
ORSINGER GUNTHER	LTC	0-0014264	0620	2
ORSINGER REMINGTON	COL	0-0006625	0651	1
ORSINI CLARA E	LTC	N-0002424	0867	1
ORSINO GUY A	COL	0-0030168	0364	2
ORTEGA GEORGA A	LTC	0-0066062	0668	1
ORTH EUGENE C JR	COL	0-0019863	0464	1
ORTH GOTTLIEB L	COL	0-0020509	0859	1
ORTH RAYMOND E JR	CPT	0-0028422	0652	2
ORTH RICHARD H	COL	0-0029308	0464	1
ORTON EUGENE M	COL	0-0051844	0367	1
ORTON RAYMOND L	LTC	0-0042306	0162	1
ORTON WILLIAM R	COL	0-0003724	0545	2
OSBORNE ERIC P	COL	0-0042299	1063	1
OSBORNE HAROLD G	COL	0-0029866	0556	1
OSBORNE HUGH P	COL	0-0030151	0464	1
OSBORNE NAOMI I	MAJ	N-0001225	1063	1

NAME	GRADE	SVC NO	DATE RET MO YR	RET CODE
OSBORNE RALPH M	M G	0-0016399	1162	1
OSBORNE THEODORE M	B G	0-0015132	1047	1
OSBORNE VINCENT E	LTC	0-0033039	1062	1
OSBORNE WILLIAM L	COL	0-0032154	0166	1
OSETH INGOMAR M	COL	0-0007861	0646	2
OSHEROFF HYMAN R	COL	0-0021015	0755	1
OSMANSKI FRANK A	M G	0-0019745	0366	1
OSTENBERG FRANK T	COL	0-0016863	0757	1
OSTERHAUS LEO B	LTC	0-0084326	0964	1
OSTERHOUT FRED A JR	LTC	0-0066189	0768	1
OSTHUES HENRY E	LTC	0-0052512	0562	1
OSTNER CHARLES F	LTC	0-0024271	0661	1
OSTRANDER FORREST R	COL	0-0009169	0149	2
OSTROM CHARLES D	B G	0-0004641	0450	1
OSTROM HERBERT N	COL	0-0043614	0164	1
OSWALD DONALD C	LTC	0-0069762	1166	1
OSWALD EDWARD H	COL	0-0043330	1263	1
OSWALD MARIE A	MAJ	N-0002047	0160	1
OSWALD PAUL F	COL	0-0020160	1165	1
OSWALT JOHN W	COL	0-0046071	0763	1
OTT CHESTER W	COL	0-0018338	1145	2
OTT EDWARD R	COL	0-0050935	0257	1
OTT EDWARD S	B G	0-0007132	0247	2
OTT HAROLD G	COL	0-0016977	1057	1
OTTERBOURG CHARLES R	LTC	0-0080158	0763	2
OTTINGER CHARLES F	LTC	0-0039012	0268	1
OTTO CHARLES B	LTC	0-0088169	0667	1
OTTO SAMUEL E	COL	0-0019030	0863	1
OTTZENN HANS	COL	0-0006032	0946	2
OUIMET MARY E	MAJ	N-0001396	0468	1
OUTLAND ARLEY L	LTC	0-0044400	0661	1
OUTLAND GEORGE W	COL	0-0007035	0552	2
OUTSEN ROBERT	COL	0-0029595	0861	1
OUTWATER MURIEL	MAJ	L-0000307	0762	1
OVENSHINE RICHARD P	B G	0-0012303	0854	1
OVERALL JESSE U III	LTC	0-0046630	0966	1
OVERBY CARL H	COL	0-0030437	0665	1
OVERFELT CLIFFORD O	COL	0-0010227	0646	2
OVERHOLT EDWIN L	COL	0-0060030	1268	2
OVERSTREET SAMUEL	LTC	0-0041703	0357	2
OVERTON DANIEL	LTC	0-0027026	0566	1
OVERTON NORMAN L	LTC	0-0070461	1268	1
OWEN GLENN B	COL	0-0032725	0864	1
OWEN HENRY M JR	LTC	0-0032083	0162	1
OWEN LOUELIA	MAJ	N-0002229	0559	1
OWEN THOMAS S	LTC	0-0028544	0766	1
OWEN WILEY H	CW4	W-0903648	0561	2
OWEN WILLIAM J	COL	0-0043536	0868	2
OWEN WILLIAM V	COL	0-0041526	0658	1
OWENS ALEXANDER	B G	0-0006429	0246	2
OWENS CHARLES H	COL	0-0006957	0753	1
OWENS ELMER G	COL	0-0039181	1167	1
OWENS FREDERICK	COL	0-0043087	0661	1
OWENS GEORGE R	COL	0-0005856	0148	1
OWENS HARRY E	COL	0-0028786	1054	1
OWENS JOHN L	COL	0-0017035	1057	1
OWENS OWEN W	COL	0-0038958	1068	1
OWSLEY HOMER JR	LTC	0-0059498	0568	1
OXRIEDER RAYMOND B	COL	0-0016042	0755	1
OYSTER DALIES J	COL	0-0015456	0854	1
PACE BRICE	COL	0-0033035	0859	1
PACE GEORGE A	COL	0-0030552	0561	1
PACE GEORGE D	COL	0-0031531	0864	2
PACE GUY L	COL	0-0028826	1055	1
PACE HERBERT E	COL	0-0003016	0143	2
PACE LUCYLE M	MAJ	N-0001905	0162	1
PACE MARIE L	MAJ	N-0000066	1048	1
PACEY WILLIAM A	LTC	0-0031323	0966	1
PACHL MAX F JR	LTC	0-0062064	0968	1
PACHLER FRANCIS T	M G	0-0018488	0667	2
PACHOMSKI JOHN	LTC	0-0040252	0566	1
PACIOREK STANLEY J	MAJ	0-0033285	0863	1
PACIULLI ORLO C	LTC	0-0017427	0545	2
PACK CHARLES M	COL	0-0020378	0864	1
PACK DALLAS B	COL	0-0051517	0762	1

NAME	GRADE	SVC NO	DATE RET MO YR	RET CODE
PACKARD FLORENCE M	MAJ	L-0000239	0461	1
PADDOCK JOHN W	COL	0-0023913	0867	1
PADDOCK RALPH L JR	LTC	0-0030740	1163	1
PADDOCK ROBERT E	CW3	W-0903649	0462	1
PADEN PAUL A	COL	0-0020981	0763	1
PADGETT JERRY E	LTC	0-0081117	0567	1
PADLEY HARRY F	LTC	0-0070464	0966	1
PAETZOLD ALMA M	MAJ	N-0000886	0763	1
PAGANO GERALD	CW4	W-0903651	0365	1
PAGANO PHILOMENA	LTC	N-0000354	1163	2
PAGE BENJAMIN N	COL	0-0032530	0966	1
PAGE CECIL W JR	LTC	0-0025723	0866	1
PAGE DOUGLAS J	COL	0-0004495	0352	2
PAGE GORDON B	COL	0-0040046	0266	1
PAGE HENRY M	LTC	0-0042744	1263	1
PAGE JOHN W	COL	0-0040247	0760	1
PAGE MYRON E JR	COL	0-0021426	0868	1
PAGE REGINALD JR	COL	0-0020149	0766	1
PAGE ROBERT W JR	COL	0-0022120	0267	1
PAGE ROGER M JR	LTC	0-0029430	0758	1
PAGE SIDNEY C	COL	0-0011718	0847	2
PAGE THOMAS N	COL	0-0018300	1058	1
PAHL GAYLORD G	LTC	0-0081119	0966	1
PAICH JACK J	CW4	W-0903652	0859	1
PAIGE RALPH E	COL	0-0031023	1055	2
PAINTER DEAN E	COL	0-0022720	0868	1
PAINTER GEORGE E	LTC	0-0056813	1161	1
PAINTER MAURICE	LTC	0-0083613	1267	1
PAINTER VERE	COL	0-0008389	0146	1
PALIK THEODORE J	LTC	0-0043611	1064	1
PALIN CALIXTE A	CW4	W-0903653	0364	2
PALIZZA MAURICE J	LTC	0-0033924	1061	1
PALLISTER FRANCIS J	COL	0-0043476	0468	1
PALM EUGENE W	MAJ	0-0035643	0763	1
PALMBLAD FREDERIC H	COL	0-0034845	0968	2
PALMER CALLIE H	COL	0-0007235	1146	2
PALMER CHARLES D	GEN	0-0015519	0262	1
PALMER EDDY D	COL	0-0043224	0765	1
PALMER EDWIN S	COL	0-0030806	0864	1
PALMER EUGENE P	MAJ	0-0024245	0446	2
PALMER GEORGE W	COL	0-0015593	0754	1
PALMER GLENN H	COL	0-0015118	0854	1
PALMER HARVEY K JR	LTC	0-0015311	0753	1
PALMER HUGH A	1LT	0-0012086	0621	2
PALMER JAMES M	LTC	0-0004877	1022	2
PALMER JOHN M	COL	0-0042058	0862	1
PALMER JOHN R	LTC	0-0042758	0464	1
PALMER LESLIE F	LTC	0-0043531	0164	1
PALMER PAUL W	LTC	0-0060097	0966	1
PALMER RAYMOND D	COL	0-0015942	0854	1
PALMER ROBERT S	COL	0-0020611	0867	1
PALMER WILLISTON	GEN	0-0012246	1059	2
PALSROK JOHN	COL	0-0043722	1064	1
PAMPLIN DOUGLAS G	COL	0-0015192	0753	1
PANGBORN ELMER D	LTC	0-0010420	0142	1
PANISVICK GEORGE G	LTC	0-0089455	0367	1
PANKE ROBERT E	COL	0-0023831	0268	1
PANKER DOROTHY F	MAJ	N-0001997	1166	1
PAPA ANTHONY E	COL	0-0052294	0666	1
PAPE ROBIN B	B G	0-0015547	0654	1
PAPENFOTH WILLIAM H	COL	0-0011305	1047	2
PAPI EUGENE J	CW4	W-0901605	0556	2
PAPPAS ALLEN	COL	0-0031056	0763	2
PAPPAS CHRISTOPHE	COL	0-0051724	0366	1
PAPPAS JAMES P	COL	0-0021017	0564	1
PARASKA NICHOLAS	COL	0-0021765	0860	1
PARDUE THOMAS W	LTC	0-0028576	0966	1
PARHAM ALFRED H	LTC	0-0017304	0643	2
PARIS EDWARD J	LTC	0-0082073	0767	1
PARK EDNA K	LTC	N-0001945	0460	1
PARK HERMAN C	COL	0-0033163	0766	1
PARK RICHARD	COL	0-0002211	1143	1
PARK RICHARD JR	COL	0-0019080	0863	2
PARK ROY C S	WO1	W-0901012	1032	2
PARKER BEATRICE A	MAJ	L-0000247	0463	1

NAME	GRADE	SVC NO	DATE RET MO YR	RET CODE
PARKER BENJAMIN M	CW4	W-0903655	0165	1
PARKER DANIEL	COL	0-0019038	0762	1
PARKER DORIS L	LTC	R-0010018	0766	1
PARKER EDNA M	LTC	N-0000271	0365	1
PARKER EDWARD M	COL	0-0018349	1146	2
PARKER EDWIN P	M G	0-0003457	0153	1
PARKER ELLIOTT G	LTC	0-0037540	0559	1
PARKER GILBERT E	COL	0-0007108	0749	1
PARKER HARRY F	COL	0-0084565	1264	1
PARKER HENRY S	COL	0-0024317	0768	1
PARKER JOHN C	COL	0-0031778	1164	1
PARKER JOHN F	LTC	0-0065015	1167	1
PARKER JOHN M	COL	0-0039018	0465	1
PARKER JOHN M	LTC	0-0058992	0868	1
PARKER JOHN R	COL	0-0019735	0556	1
PARKER JOSEPH P	LTC	0-0040487	0660	1
PARKER PAUL C	CW4	W-0906941	0661	1
PARKER R L	COL	0-0031057	1162	2
PARKER REUBEN D	LTC	0-0047214	0866	1
PARKER RICHARD B	CW4	W-0902390	0864	2
PARKER RICHARD C	LTC	0-0018230	0754	1
PARKER ROBERT J	CW4	W-0903657	0256	1
PARKER ROY H	M G	0-0012565	0552	2
PARKER WILL V	COL	0-0009170	1044	2
PARKIN CHARLES M	COL	0-0005206	0350	1
PARKIN CHARLES M JR	LTC	0-0024150	0761	1
PARKINS JAMES F	LTC	0-0036855	1157	2
PARKISON PETER A	CW4	W-0901681	0555	1
PARKMAN T G JR	1LT	0-0063860	0859	2
PARKS HENRY C	CW4	RW-0903658	0963	1
PARKS JEAN L	MAJ	N-0000377	0461	1
PARKS LAVERNE A	COL	0-0021372	0868	1
PARKS LEONARD F	LTC	0-0041207	1266	1
PARKS REBECCA S	LTC	L-0000008	1156	1
PARMELEE ARCHIBALD	COL	0-0009734	0153	1
PARMELEE CLYDE D	COL	0-0007831	1045	2
PARMENTER ROBERT E	LTC	0-0062960	1267	1
PARNELLE SAMUEL W JR	COL	0-0029501	0161	1
PARR CLIFFORD E	LTC	0-0051605	0463	1
PARR IVAN W JR	COL	0-0019255	0862	1
PARR MARVIN M	LTC	0-0053681	0963	1
PARR STANLEY F	COL	0-0035524	0868	1
PARR WAYLAND H	COL	0-0017565	0358	1
PARRISH ALICE A	LTC	L-0000016	0657	1
PARRISH CHARLES P	LTC	0-0053233	1163	1
PARRY ROBERT C	COL	0-0039908	0459	1
PARSEL JANE H	MAJ	L-0000067	0259	1
PARSELL SIDNEY I	COL	0-0028937	1157	1
PARSONS ARTHUR M	COL	0-0012344	0854	1
PARSONS GEORGE F JR	LTC	0-0036095	0662	1
PARSONS HAROLD C	COL	0-0029816	1162	1
PARSONS NORMAN W	LTC	0-0030793	0762	1
PARSONS OTHAL T	LTC	0-0080162	0467	1
PARSONS RUFUS A	COL	0-0010077	0147	1
PARSONS WALTER H JR	COL	0-0039782	0862	1
PARSONS WILLIAM J	COL	0-0040228	0265	1
PARTHUM ALFRED H JR	LTC	0-0035939	0767	1
PARTIN CALVIN L	COL	0-0017636	0759	1
PARTIN EVERETT W	COL	0-0019699	1059	1
PARTLOW FRANK A	COL	0-0031099	0163	1
PARTLOW LEO L	CPT	0-0009045	1034	1
PARTRIDGE ALAN L	LTC	0-0026770	0763	1
PARTRIDGE CLARENCE E	COL	0-0002586	0846	1
PARTRIDGE DWIGHT	CPT	0-0006300	0722	2
PARTRIDGE FRANK H	M G	0-0007497	1053	1
PARTRIDGE RICHARD C	M G	0-0012630	0259	1
PARTRIDGE ROBERT B	COL	0-0020204	0465	1
PARTRIDGE STANLEY N	COL	0-0011622	0449	1
PASCAL ANDRE R	MAJ	0-0038573	0862	1
PASCHAL WALTER H	CPT	0-0017376	1138	2
PASCHALL WILLIAM D	COL	0-0015400	0654	1
PASCIAK LEONARD J	COL	0-0024765	0965	1
PASHLEY WALTER A	COL	0-0004796	0647	2
PASOLLI EMIL JR	COL	0-0028777	0754	1
PASSAILAIGUE EDWARD	COL	0-0010142	0951	2

NAME	GRADE	SVC NO	DATE RET MO YR	RET CODE
PASSARELLA P FRANCIS	COL	0-0018485	0960	2
PASSINK CLARE	COL	0-0039734	0861	1
PASSMORE JACK W	COL	0-0060144	0967	1
PASTORE JAMES A	CW4	W-0903659	1154	1
PATE BRANTLEY M JR	LTC	0-0080475	0568	1
PATE ROY H	LTC	0-0084407	0166	1
PATERICK GERALD A	LTC	0-0042853	0864	1
PATERSON KENNETH C	LTC	0-0051022	0357	1
PATERSON ROY D	1LT	0-0011198	0331	1
PATRICK BREAM C	COL	0-0018154	0146	1
PATRICK FRANCIS H	COL	0-0021235	0966	1
PATRICK LESTER P	LTC	0-0045212	1061	1
PATTEN CLARENCE W	COL	0-0035859	0468	1
PATTERSON C A	CW3	W-0903660	0956	1
PATTERSON CECIL A	LTC	0-0084408	0963	1
PATTERSON CHARLES G	COL	0-0019073	0860	1
PATTERSON DALLAS M	LTC	0-0081124	0263	1
PATTERSON DONALD R	LTC	0-0018491	0651	1
PATTERSON DOUGLAS H	COL	0-0034979	0768	2
PATTERSON EDWIN H	LTC	0-0054094	0966	1
PATTERSON FRANKLIN R	LTC	0-0038746	0661	1
PATTERSON FRED	MAJ	0-0035446	0863	1
PATTERSON JOHN A	COL	0-0081126	0968	1
PATTERSON JOHN C	COL	0-0057046	0765	1
PATTERSON LAWRENCE	LTC	0-0007571	0940	1
PATTERSON LOREN S	LTC	0-0059309	1068	1
PATTERSON RALPH M	COL	0-0021013	0355	1
PATTERSON RICHARD A	1LT	0-0028445	0550	2
PATTERSON ROBERT F	LTC	0-0028302	0865	1
PATTERSON ROBERT W	CPT	0-0007438	0634	1
PATTERSON VICTOR	CPT	0-0014377	0919	2
PATTERSON WILLIAM G	COL	0-0004494	0934	2
PATTERSON WILLIAM H	COL	0-0022110	0567	2
PATTERSON WILLIAM R	COL	0-0019933	0763	1
PATTISON DONALD I	LTC	0-0029108	0150	1
PATTISON HAL C	B G	0-0029683	0462	1
PATTON DEWEY C	CW4	W-0903662	0461	1
PATTON GORDON B	LTC	0-0024489	0767	1
PATTON HELEN H	LTC	N-0000514	0749	1
PATTON IRVIN L	CW4	W-0901687	0753	1
PATTON JOHN F	COL	0-0067949	1263	2
PATTON MAURICE V	COL	0-0008187	0552	1
PATTON TEDDY L	LTC	0-0082075	0767	1
PAUL ALBERT L	MAJ	0-0063461	1265	1
PAUL CATHERINE	CPT	N-0001040	0261	1
PAUL GERALDINE	MAJ	L-0000472	1065	1
PAUL RICHARD I	LTC	0-0036814	0866	1
PAUL THURSTON T JR	B G	0-0032243	1068	1
PAULES EARL C	COL	0-0021447	0862	1
PAULES JOHN G	LTC	0-0050681	1066	1
PAULEY JOHN L JR	COL	0-0018194	0760	1
PAULL JOSEPH K	LTC	0-0081127	0966	1
PAULLIN HOLMES G	COL	0-0007166	0753	1
PAULMANN EDWIN	LTC	0-0065010	0868	1
PAULSEN MARGARET J	CPT	N-0002974	0562	2
PAVEY KENNETH G	COL	0-0022207	0565	1
PAVIA FRANK N	LTC	0-0027791	0266	1
PAVILLARD RALPH A	CW4	W-0906944	0760	1
PAVLOVICH SYLVIA R	MAJ	N-0002028	0758	1
PAVY LAURENT D	MAJ	0-0026088	0756	2
PAWLOWSKI IRENE M	MAJ	N-0001288	1264	1
PAXSON HARRY O	B G	0-0016764	0157	1
PAXTON JOHN W	COL	0-0024199	0760	1
PAXTON ORSEN E	LTC	0-0005050	0642	1
PAYNE CHARLES G JR	LTC	0-0060637	1066	1
PAYNE CHARLES J	COL	0-0031554	0764	1
PAYNE GILBERT M	COL	0-0031713	1267	1
PAYNE IRVING P	LTC	0-0053878	0966	1
PAYNE LAURANCE B	LTC	0-0051830	1064	2
PAYNE LESLIE M	LTC	0-0043797	1264	1
PAYNE OTHO C	LTC	0-0054764	0267	1
PAYNE RUTH	LTC	N-0000529	1054	1
PAYNTER EARL F	LTC	0-0007147	0-40	1
PEABODY PAUL E	B G	0-0004912	0350	1
PEACOCK EARL G	COL	0-0043873	0565	1

NAME	GRADE	SVC NO	DATE RET MO YR	RET CODE
PEACOCK LEOLEEN I	LTC	N-0000831	1166	1
PEAIRS DOUGLAS O	LTC	0-0033479	0962	1
PEAK HOWARD W III	MAJ	0-0047981	0155	2
PEAKE ALBERT S	COL	0-0003024	0242	2
PEAKE AUGUSTA K	LTC	N-0000820	0166	1
PEAKE BEN F	COL	0-0031168	0268	1
PEALE EUGENE L	CPT	0-0060520	1263	1
PEALE JAMES N JR	COL	0-0020684	0867	1
PEALE WALTER O JR	COL	0-0020946	1267	1
PEARCE GERTRUDE C	LTC	N-0002387	1264	1
PEARCE MARTHA S	MAJ	N-0002183	0965	1
PEARCEY HAROLD W	LTC	0-0081128	1066	1
PEARS MARIA L	MAJ	N-0002040	0360	1
PEARSALL JAMES F JR	COL	0-0020774	0767	1
PEARSALL RAYMOND O	COL	0-0033548	0368	1
PEARSE MILDRED C	MAJ	N-0001951	0360	1
PEARSON FRANK J	COL	0-0007264	1151	2
PEARSON FREDERICK	COL	0-0012172	0753	2
PEARSON GENEVIEVE	MAJ	M-0001174	0463	1
PEARSON GEORGE O	COL	0-0039592	1058	1
PEARSON HAROLD J	COL	0-0042418	0864	1
PEARSON JAMES P JR	COL	0-0019157	0761	1
PEARSON MURBLE F	LTC	0-0023661	1059	1
PEARSON QUENNA A	LTC	0-0050923	0854	1
PEARSON RALPH A W	LTC	0-0004878	0637	2
PEARSON RALPH E	COL	0-0051077	0260	1
PEARSON RAYMOND W	COL	0-0003994	1046	1
PEARSON RICHARD W	COL	0-0016384	0355	1
PEARSON WILLYS H	LTC	0-0022660	0759	1
PECA PETER S	COL	0-0019392	0862	1
PECHACEK MELVIN L	MAJ	0-0081129	0762	1
PECK ALLEN L	COL	0-0020327	0866	1
PECK CLARENCE R	COL	0-0008312	0753	2
PECK LOUCELLE E	MAJ	N-0002049	0460	1
PECK MARVIN W	COL	0-0016472	0844	2
PECK MICHAEL JR	MAJ	0-0064285	0868	1
PECKHAM ELISHA O	COL	0-0031885	0965	1
PECKHAM HOWARD L	M G	0-0012058	1156	1
PECKHAM ROBERT O	LTC	0-0050740	0968	1
PECKINPAUGH EARL M	1LT	0-0010182	1029	2
PECORA FLORENCE M	LTC	N-0000359	0768	1
PECORARO ANTHONY	LTC	0-0055873	0465	2
PEDDICORD EVERETT	COL	0-0017245	0158	1
PEDDICORD LLOYD E	COL	0-0043397	0366	2
PEDERSEN MAYNARD O	LTC	0-0019842	0660	1
PEDERSEN ROBERT W	LTC	0-0030350	0961	1
PEDLEY TIMOTHY A JR	COL	0-0007160	0649	1
PEEKE CHARLES M	COL	0-0019810	0265	1
PEEL ALFRED R	LTC	0-0029245	0859	1
PEEPLES EDWARD T	COL	0-0024537	0766	1
PEEPLES RUSSELL G JR	COL	0-0036558	0968	2
PEEPLES WILLIAM M	1LT	0-0014404	0120	2
PEER GEORGE F	COL	0-0019638	0758	1
PEERENBOOM MAURICE A	COL	0-0039684	0861	2
PEERY PAUL O	1LT	0-0017141	0835	2
PEGG LOREN O	COL	0-0016754	0757	1
PEGRAM EARL F	COL	0-0042487	0761	1
PEGRAM JOHN C	COL	0-0001693	0642	1
PEIFER FRANK A	CW3	W-0906946	0462	1
PEIRCE CHRISTOPHE	COL	0-0002788	0546	1
PEIRCE GEORGE F	COL	0-0016771	0757	1
PEISEL FRANCIS J	LTC	0-0059621	1065	1
PEISINGER ROMAN J	COL	0-0041920	1160	1
PEIXOTTO JAMES M	LTC	0-0047628	0765	1
PELL KENNETH E	LTC	0-0040432	0668	2
PELL MARK G	LTC	0-0079948	0867	1
PELOSI JOHN J	COL	0-0021020	0461	2
PELTON EDWIN N SR	CW4	W-0902138	1153	1
PENAAT EDWARD F	B G	0-0029598	0963	1
PENCE DONALD C	MAJ	0-0025971	0746	2
PENCE GEORGE D	M G	0-0015629	0246	2
PENCE HARVEY J	COL	0-0043011	0466	1
PENCE JAMES H	COL	0-0016289	0548	1
PENCE WILLIAM P	B G	0-0016779	0757	1
PENDERGRAFT AMY R	LTC	N-0000028	0551	2

NAME	GRADE	SVC NO	DATE RET MO YR	RET CODE
PENDLETJN HARRY E	COL	0-0007395	1047	1
PENDLETON HENRY M	COL	0-0003829	0153	2
PENDLETON RANDOLPH T	B G	0-0003217	0849	2
PENDLETON RAYMOND L	MAJ	0-0024313	1045	2
PENDLETON RICHARD N	CW4	W-0903665	0662	1
PENDLETON ROSE A P	CPT	N-0001098	0947	1
PENDLYSHOK CHARLES A	COL	0-0021304	0368	1
PENDRAK THEODORE S	LTC	0-0070015	1166	2
PENFIELD WALTER A	LTC	0-0065707	0466	1
PENICK JACK G	LTC	0-0062218	0466	1
PENLY WILLIAM J	COL	0-0022300	1064	1
PENN FRANK A	LTC	0-0032843	1068	1
PENN WILLIAM S JR	COL	0-0019442	0762	1
PENNELL RALPH MC T	M G	0-0002150	0346	2
PENNEPACKER RUSSELL	COL	0-0052005	0662	1
PENNER RALPH S	LTC	0-0056223	0664	1
PENNIMAN CHARLES O	COL	0-0029616	0562	2
PENNINGTON ALVIE	CW3	W-0903666	0756	2
PENNINGTON EDWARD W	LTC	0-0029496	1059	1
PENNINGTON GEORGE H	CW4	W-0903667	0664	1
PENNINGTON JAMES C	COL	0-0042749	0466	1
PENNY ROBERT G	LTC	0-0059946	0967	1
PENNYPACKER LINDLEY	COL	0-0041851	0461	1
PENROD WILLIAM G	CPT	0-0060441	0962	1
PENROSE CLIFFORD E	LTC	0-0080164	1265	1
PENSINGER BARBARA H	MAJ	N-0000422	0562	2
PEOPLES ROBERT H	LTC	0-0081132	0567	1
PEOT JOSEPH J	COL	0-0031536	0567	1
PEPLOE GEORGE B	M G	0-0016246	0956	1
PEPPER KELTON L	LTC	0-0001560	0621	2
PEPPLE LOYD K	COL	0-0020262	0150	2
PERCIVAL HAZEL	LTC	N-0000696	0866	1
PEREZ WILLIAM D	COL	0-0030324	0761	1
PERHAM WENDELL W	COL	0-0028999	1058	2
PERKINS DWAIN H	CW4	W-0903668	0462	1
PERKINS HAROLD T	COL	0-0051284	0162	1
PERKINS JAMES H	MAJ	0-0082077	1267	1
PERKINS JAMES I	CPT	0-0063514	0566	1
PERKINS LEONARD G	MAJ	0-0017982	0444	2
PERKINS SALLY M	MAJ	N-0000412	0163	1
PERKINS WILLIAM F JR	COL	0-0021691	0660	1
PERLETT JOHN P	COL	0-0028956	0158	1
PERMAN JOHN E	COL	0-0016419	0756	1
PERREAULT MARSCIENE	LTC	N-0002396	0665	1
PERRICELLI VINCENT J	LTC	0-0061399	0968	1
PERRILLIAT HOWARD A	2LT	0-0016813	1031	2
PERRIN RAY S	CPT	0-0005711	0933	2
PERRIN WILLIAM K	LTC	0-0030260	0459	2
PERRY ARTHUR G	LTC	0-0052985	0864	1
PERRY BEN W	LTC	0-0035447	0362	1
PERRY BENJAMIN E	LTC	0-0037328	0866	1
PERRY DONALD S	COL	0-0004770	1047	1
PERRY EDWIN A	COL	0-0032030	0868	1
PERRY ELIZABETH	MAJ	N-0002524	0663	1
PERRY ERNEST L	COL	0-0053324	0764	1
PERRY FRED E	LTC	0-0038974	0367	1
PERRY GERALD L JR	LTC	0-0060184	0665	1
PERRY MANLEY C	COL	0-0023024	0266	1
PERRY MILLER O	B G	0-0018427	0661	1
PERRY REDDING F	COL	0-0009900	1051	1
PERRY RUSSELL V	COL	0-0015383	1153	1
PERRY THEODORE D	COL	0-0031725	1163	1
PERRY WALTER L	COL	0-0008917	0449	1
PERRY WILLIAM O JR	LTC	0-0027729	0765	1
PERRY WILLIS A	B G	0-0018131	0660	1
PERSELL ROBERT A	COL	0-0051608	0961	1
PERSHALL WILLIAM R	COL	0-0043825	1167	1
PERSIK VALENTINE	MAJ	0-0028854	0447	2
PERSON FRANK C	LTC	0-0051807	0964	1
PERSONS JOSEPH P JR	COL	0-0056776	0858	1
PERSONS WILTON B	M G	0-0007088	0649	2
PERTL MARTIN C	COL	0-0040349	0467	1
PERVIER GEORGE W	COL	0-0031736	0867	1
PERWEIN ALEXANDER	LTC	0-0012768	0548	1
PERWICH ALEXANDER	LTC	0-0028193	0967	1
PESEK JOHN M	COL	0-0015145	0954	1
PESUT ELIZABETH	MAJ	N-0000258	1058	1
PETER RICHARD H	COL	0-0029987	1263	2
PETERMAN JOHN O	COL	0-0029955	0763	1
PETERS EMANUEL P	LTC	0-0041006	1265	1
PETERS ERNEST C	COL	0-0018603	1160	2
PETERS GUSTON W	LTC	0-0035421	1058	1
PETERS JOANNA	LTC	N-0000005	0448	1
PETERS JOSEPH F	COL	0-0020075	0452	2
PETERS KENNETH A	LTC	0-0047220	0763	1
PETERS MARGUERITE	MAJ	N-0001975	0360	1
PETERS MILFRED J	COL	0-0043395	0168	1
PETERS PETER	COL	0-0039961	0565	1
PETERS ROBERT E	B G	0-0031646	0865	1
PETERSEN BYRON N	COL	0-0042734	0466	1
PETERSEN GEORGE T	COL	0-0033771	0164	1
PETERSON ARTHUR C	COL	0-0018151	0161	2
PETERSON ARTHUR C	COL	0-0042555	0565	1
PETERSON CHARLES D	COL	0-0051633	0865	1
PETERSON DONALD B	COL	0-0020535	0956	1
PETERSON EMIL J	COL	0-0015523	0754	1
PETERSON EMMETT L	LTC	0-0031138	0565	1
PETERSON GERALD	COL	0-0028912	0556	1
PETERSON IVER A	COL	0-0021105	1167	1
PETERSON JAMES D	COL	0-0030311	0664	1
PETERSON JAMES H	LTC	0-0082356	0767	1
PETERSON KENNETH H	LTC	0-0040035	0653	2
PETERSON KENNETH J	LTC	0-0031794	1262	1
PETERSON LEONARD T	COL	0-0018950	0946	1
PETERSON PAULINE F	CPT	N-0000330	1059	1
PETERSON PETER R JR	LTC	0-0047806	0667	1
PETERSON ROBERT O	COL	0-0029904	1061	1
PETERSON SAMUEL R	LTC	0-0022904	0660	1
PETERSON TED W	LTC	0-0051760	0564	1
PETERSON VIRGINIA D	2LT	R-0000891	0345	1
PETERSON WALTER L	COL	0-0018292	0655	1
PETRELLI JOHN	LTC	0-0060413	0767	1
PETRI HOWARD R	CW4	W-0901840	0157	1
PETRINI BRUNO A	COL	0-0080317	1067	1
PETROLINO JOSEPH A	COL	0-0029712	0562	1
PETRONE ROCCO A	LTC	0-0027972	0766	1
PETROS HARRY C	LTC	0-0030184	0563	1
PETTERS FREDERICK	COL	0-0003923	0346	2
PETTEY FLORENCE L	MAJ	N-0001792	0665	1
PETTIN CHARLES F	LTC	0-0083570	1165	1
PETTIS CHARLES R	COL	0-0001885	1039	1
PETTIT FRANK A	COL	0-0016092	0755	2
PETTY EDGAR L JR	LTC	0-0062249	0667	1
PETTY NORMAN E	COL	0-0033041	1268	1
PETTY TRAVIS L	COL	0-0019439	0656	1
PETZING EDWIN R	B G	0-0008463	0854	1
PEYTON HAMILTON M	COL	0-0018461	0761	1
PEYTON JOHN L	LTC	0-0029935	1157	1
PEYTON JOHN S	CW2	W-0903673	0850	1
PEYTON ROBERT E	COL	0-0018263	0957	1
PEYTON TOM L JR	LTC	0-0050117	0465	1
PEYTON WYTHE M JR	COL	0-0042830	0762	1
PFEFFER CHARLES A	COL	0-0004851	0850	1
PFEFFER CHARLES A JR	LTC	0-0020613	0247	2
PFEFFER HENRIETTA	LTC	N-0002413	0666	1
PFEFFER WILLIAM J	MAJ	0-0060593	0565	1
PFEIL ROBERT C	COL	0-0022921	0765	1
PHAIR TOM S	LTC	0-0023520	0761	1
PHARR MARION M	COL	0-0010251	0753	1
PHELAN CYRIL A	LTC	0-0003384	1022	2
PHELPS FRANKLIN E	MAJ	0-0079024	0666	1
PHELPS HARVEY W	LTC	0-0064935	0766	1
PHELPS JOSEPH V	B G	0-0012279	0549	1
PHELPS PHIL R JR	LTC	0-0026251	0864	1
PHELPS PRESTON V	COL	0-0040026	0566	1
PHELPS ROBERT H	CW4	W-0903675	0259	1
PHELPS VICTOR M	COL	0-0041455	0357	2
PHELPS WILLIAM G	LTC	0-0039369	0662	1
PHILBRICK ALTON H	CW4	W-0903676	0762	1
PHILBRICK KENNETH R	LTC	0-0031642	0965	1
PHILIPS BURTON K	COL	0-0040048	0966	1
PHILIPS DAVID F	LTC	0-0081136	0767	1
PHILLIPS ADOLPH H	COL	0-0035888	0866	1
PHILLIPS ALBERT G	COL	0-0010156	0947	1
PHILLIPS BARRY F	COL	0-0051893	0760	1
PHILLIPS EDWIN R	CW2	W-0907147	0961	1
PHILLIPS ERNEST E JR	MAJ	0-0060947	0667	1
PHILLIPS EUGENE JR	MAJ	0-0065242	0764	1
PHILLIPS HENRY G	LTC	0-0036383	0767	1
PHILLIPS HENRY J	COL	0-0031839	0568	1
PHILLIPS HENRY L	COL	0-0051249	0961	1
PHILLIPS HUDSON B	COL	0-0018653	0257	1
PHILLIPS IVAN G	LTC	0-0032941	0867	1
PHILLIPS J COULSON	LTC	0-0049712	0867	1
PHILLIPS JAMES H	M G	0-0012331	0958	2
PHILLIPS JOHN D F	B G	0-0017584	0859	1
PHILLIPS JOHN P	CW3	W-0903677	0657	1
PHILLIPS JOSEPH F	LTC	0-0030170	0360	1
PHILLIPS KATHLEEN W	LTC	N-0002458	0866	2
PHILLIPS MARY G	COL	N-0000512	0951	1
PHILLIPS MILTON B	LTC	0-0062210	0765	1
PHILLIPS MITCHELL W	COL	0-0022712	1167	1
PHILLIPS PAUL D	B G	0-0022939	0666	1
PHILLIPS RICHARD J	LTC	0-0072423	1168	1
PHILLIPS ROBENA C	LTC	N-0002150	1264	2
PHILLIPS ROBERT L JR	LTC	0-0058997	1168	1
PHILLIPS ROWELLA N	MAJ	N-0001212	1263	1
PHILLIPS STANLEY W	COL	0-0042407	0764	1
PHILLIPS WILMER S	COL	0-0004759	0753	2
PHILLOON WALLACE C	M G	0-0002611	1045	2
PHILP WILLIAM P	COL	0-0007200	0852	2
PHIPPEN WILLIAM G	LTC	0-0059581	0865	1
PHYFE HERBERT L	COL	0-0029390	0360	1
PIBURN EDWIN W JR	MAJ	0-0060380	1068	1
PIBURN HURLBERT R	LTC	0-0042500	0163	1
PICCIOTTI ROMULUS A	LTC	0-0079951	1266	1
PICCIRILLI ALBERT A	LTC	0-0060342	0661	1
PICKARD JOHN G	CPT	0-0008289	1022	2
PICKARD OLIVER J	COL	0-0019723	0765	1
PICKARD RUTH A	LTC	N-0000350	0662	1
PICKELL CLYDE V	COL	0-0031376	0861	2
PICKELS WAYNE M	COL	0-0012586	0245	2
PICKENS ARTHUR	COL	0-0006466	0842	1
PICKENS ROBERT G	MAJ	0-0026808	0865	1
PICKERING CLIFFORD E	COL	0-0010741	0946	2
PICKERING ELLIS E	COL	0-0053113	0866	1
PICKERING JAMES A	B G	0-0004444	0946	2
PICKETT BENJAMIN L	COL	0-0042099	0962	1
PICKETT CHRISTIANC	COL	0-0005552	0653	2
PICKETT CLYDE	COL	0-0005098	0946	2
PICKETT EDMUND D	LTC	0-0027723	0966	1
PICKETT GENE G	MAJ	0-0075268	0365	1
PICKETT GEORGE E	COL	0-0042131	0562	1
PICKETT JEROME	LTC	0-0005494	1141	1
PICKETT JOSEPH R	LTC	0-0079952	0262	1
PICKETT LOWELL B	LTC	0-0031336	1064	1
PICKHARDT PAUL A	COL	0-0015772	0754	1
PICKHARDT WOODROW L	COL	0-0039497	0766	1
PICKNELL MILTON O	COL	0-0041952	1161	1
PIEL MELVIN	LTC	0-0084410	0965	1
PIERCE BRUCE	LTC	0-0040200	0865	1
PIERCE CHARLES S	LTC	0-0027888	0166	1
PIERCE DONALD R	M G	0-0043332	0968	1
PIERCE HAROLD E	CW4	W-0903679	0657	1
PIERCE HARRY R	COL	0-0005302	0250	1
PIERCE HENRY J	LTC	0-0033989	0560	1
PIERCE HOSEA T	CW2	W-0901863	0646	2
PIERCE JAMES D	1LT	0-0011565	0521	2
PIERCE JAMES R	M G	0-0014979	0658	2
PIERCE JOHN A	CPT	0-0006974	1030	1
PIERCE JOHN T	B G	0-0004754	1147	2
PIERCE JOHN T III	COL	0-0038319	0268	1
PIERCE KENNETH	COL	0-0012385	1148	1
PIERCE SAMUEL JR	COL	0-0038928	0858	1
PIERCE THOMAS A	LTC	0-0079953	1166	1
PIERCE WILBUR R	COL	0-0015160	0554	1
PIERGALLINI ANNE R	MAJ	N-0001937	0965	1
PIERRE GEORGE H JR	COL	0-0032258	1168	2
PIERRE JOSEPH L	LTC	0-0084566	0766	1
PIERSON ALBERT	M G	0-0011838	0859	1
PIERSON FLORENCE B	CPT	R-0010038	0357	1
PIERSON LESLIE E	LTC	0-0087883	0265	1
PIERSON MILLARD	COL	0-0012803	0153	1
PIETSCH KENT L	CPT	OF-0101659	0868	2
PIGG ALBERT M	COL	0-0010862	0752	1
PIGOTT WILLIAM T JR	COL	0-0003467	0934	2
PIKE ROBERT P	COL	0-0042023	0662	2
PILAND OSCAR G	LTC	0-0052360	0762	1
PILEGARD ANNE K	MAJ	N-0000520	0349	1
PILET NUNEZ C	COL	0-0015931	0854	1
PILLE ROY F	COL	0-0052311	0868	1
PILLIOD DALLAS A	COL	0-0036257	0268	1
PILSBURY LAWRENCE B	MAJ	0-0009401	0934	2
PINCKNEY GLADYS H	MAJ	N-0000864	0365	1
PINE LYNN W	COL	0-0030392	0464	1
PINEAU GEORGE P	LTC	0-0080169	0968	1
PINGER FRANK W	COL	0-0008698	1051	1
PINKSTONE HUESTON L	LTC	0-0081142	0268	1
PINNELL SAMUEL W	COL	0-0025880	1267	1
PINZAN ANTHONY	WO1	W-0902217	1047	1
PIPER HARVEY O	LTC	0-0057449	0368	1
PIPIA FRANK P	LTC	0-0021720	0445	2
PIPPIN HARMON L JR	LTC	0-0040033	0664	1
PIPPIN WILLIAM I	LTC	0-0069771	1268	2
PIRAINO VINCENT J	CW4	W-0903681	0967	1
PIRAM JOSEPH S	COL	0-0019411	0864	2
PIRKEY FRANK Z	COL	0-0014601	1146	2
PIRKL JOSEPH R	LTC	0-0060898	0868	1
PIRNER HILDEGARDE	MAJ	N-0002285	0959	2
PITCHER THOMAS A	COL	0-0039607	0159	1
PITNEY MAX L	COL	0-0022721	0266	1
PITTMAN BEUFORD A	COL	0-0041913	0961	2
PITTMAN FLORA V	MAJ	N-0000367	0165	1
PITTMAN LUSFORD C	COL	0-0039586	0958	1
PITTMAN WALTER C	COL	0-0033022	1168	1
PITTS FREDERICK	COL	0-0012743	0754	1
PITTS OGENE	COL	0-0044126	0866	1
PITTS THOMAS B	MAJ	0-0053951	0861	1
PITZ OTTO G	COL	0-0003430	0346	1
PITZER JOHN H	COL	0-0015293	0648	3
PITZER JOHN M	COL	0-0026378	0664	1
PIZZATI HENRY E JR	LTC	0-0031679	0664	1
PLACE OLNEY	LTC	0-0001539	0-22	1
PLAHTE FRED L	COL	0-0029936	0663	1
PLANK CLYDE H	COL	0-0010022	0446	2
PLANK EWART G	M G	0-0012649	0549	1
PLAPP HERBERT C	COL	0-0019059	0863	2
PLAPP PAUL V	LTC	0-0043362	1065	1
PLASSMEYER JOSEPH	LTC	0-0002633	0-35	1
PLATANIA GEORGE	CW4	W-0903682	1167	1
PLATT JOHN C JR	COL	0-0004815	0753	2
PLEASANT JAMES C	LTC	0-0036059	1160	1
PLEASANTS JOHN E	COL	0-0058701	0865	1
PLEMON EVONNE L	LTC	N-0001860	1065	1
PLEMON THOMAS H JR	LTC	0-0066070	1068	1
PLEW RALPH V	COL	0-0018317	1060	1
PLICHTA FRANK	LTC	0-0040884	0863	1
PLOSHAY BERNARD J	LTC	0-0065309	0865	1
PLOWMAN FLOYD C	LTC	0-0031059	0564	1
PLUMB JOHN F	LTC	0-0059001	0167	1
PLUMMER ROOSEVELT	COL	0-0044412	0667	1
PLUNKETT OLLIE W	LTC	N-0002060	0364	1
PODBREGER HUBERT L	WO1	W-0906951	0253	2
POE JAMES E	LTC	0-0060700	0766	2
POFF ERNEST F	MAJ	0-0024020	0262	1
POGHYLA BENJAMIN H	M G	0-0030103	1066	1
POHL CLIFFORD H JR	LTC	0-0084660	0767	1
POHL FRANCIS I	LTC	0-0019065	0636	2
POHL MARION G	COL	0-0017176	0655	1
POHLY JURGEN G	LTC	0-0052934	0568	2

NAME	GRADE	SVC NO	DATE RET MO YR	RET CODE
POINDEXTER WILLIAM O	COL	0-0008207	1048	2
POINIER ARTHUR D	COL	0-0021999	0265	1
POINIER NORMAN E	COL	0-0017581	0859	1
POLAK PHILIP B	LTC	0-0027193	0866	1
POLDEN DONALD F	LTC	0-0065309	0965	1
POLICHNOWSKI HENRY J	LTC	0-0067741	0868	1
POLIFKA DONALD K	LTC	0-0060522	0366	1
POLING VERNE L	CW4	W-0906952	1268	1
POLK JOHN F	COL	0-0020859	0867	1
POLLACK JULIA R	MAJ	N-0001571	0463	1
POLLARD ARTHUR J	LTC	0-0042029	0958	2
POLLARD BERTHA F	LTC	N-0000566	0564	1
POLLARD GALE E	CW2	W-0906954	1062	1
POLLARD IRBY R	COL	0-0009497	0950	1
POLLARD JOHN S JR	LTC	0-0025291	1160	1
POLLARD MARTIN E	CW4	W-0903683	1062	2
POLLARD RICHARD J	COL	0-0042845	1066	2
POLLEY JAMES D III	LTC	0-0039036	1168	1
POLLIN GEORGE A	COL	0-0004547	1046	2
POLLITT ALLEN W	MAJ	0-0008701	0339	1
POLLOCK BYRON F	COL	0-0020925	0960	2
POLLOCK ROLLA D	COL	0-0038832	0360	1
POLLOCK WILLIAM C	COL	0-0006433	0947	2
POLOMBO FRED A	LTC	0-0042860	0964	1
POLZ ROBERT M	MAJ	0-0056431	0261	2
POMAR MIGUEL J	LTC	0-0042120	0261	1
PONDER SPEERS G	LTC	0-0041995	0460	2
PONDER WILLIAM A	CPT	0-0060589	0860	2
PONGONIS JOSEPH A	COL	0-0030301	1164	1
PONS PHILIP E	COL	0-0030621	0166	1
PONTICELLO ROSE L	MAJ	N-0002197	0765	1
POOLE CHARLES M JR	LTC	0-0089371	1167	1
POOLE THEODORE L JR	COL	0-0030606	1165	1
POOLEY NARDETH W	LTC	0-0081143	0666	1
POOR BENJAMIN W	COL	0-0041575	0459	2
POORMAN DONALD A	COL	0-0017631	0859	1
POPCKE JUNE H	MAJ	N-0001297	0566	1
POPE ARTHUR W	CPT	0-0014366	0619	2
POPE FRANCIS H	B G	0-0000543	0540	1
POPE GEORGE V W	B G	0-0007079	0754	1
POPE IDA A	MAJ	N-0001303	0666	1
POPE JOHN J	LTC	0-0031214	0663	1
POPE LEMUEL E	COL	0-0022646	1267	1
POPE LILLIE S	CPT	N-0000810	0950	1
POPE PHILLIP H	COL	0-0019115	0863	1
POPE ROBERT F	COL	0-0040672	0965	1
POPE WILLIAM P	COL	0-0031981	0664	1
POPE WILLIAM R	COL	0-0001536	0-39	1
POPLE WILLIAM H	COL	0-0043525	0868	2
POPOVICH FRANCIS J	LTC	0-0040803	0760	1
POPOWSKI MICHAEL JR	COL	0-0031633	1163	1
POPPENBURG FRANCIS F	LTC	0-0025090	1060	1
PORTE WILLIAM L	LTC	0-0023322	0946	2
PORTER ERCIL D	COL	0-0006966	0753	1
PORTER FREDERICK	COL	0-0012492	0753	2
PORTER GWINN U	COL	0-0019210	0759	1
PORTER HOBERT H	CPT	0-0063311	0463	1
PORTER HORACE L	COL	0-0009883	1149	1
PORTER JOSEPH G	LTC	0-0029520	0359	1
PORTER OLIVER F	MAJ	0-0006531	0929	2
PORTER ROY V	COL	0-0031328	0763	1
PORTER WILLIAM A JR	COL	0-0080476	0868	1
PORTER WILLIAM N	M G	0-0002763	0346	1
PORTERFIELD BEN W	MAJ	0-0020685	0344	2
PORTERFIELD HERBER	COL	0-0004064	0842	2
POSEY REBER L	MAJ	N-0001067	1063	1
POSICH LEWIS V	LTC	0-0050397	0868	1
POSPISIL JAROMIR J	COL	0-0018183	0160	2
POSSE ERNEST W	COL	0-0029989	0263	1
POST CHARLES A	COL	0-0031524	0667	1
POSTLE JOHN A	CPT	0-0070018	0459	2
POSTLETHWAIT EDWARD	COL	0-0020718	0867	1
POSTON CARL M	COL	0-0030400	1063	1
POTEAT WILLIAM D	MAJ	0-0081145	1062	1
POTEET DANIEL P	COL	0-0015089	1046	1

NAME	GRADE	SVC NO	DATE RET MO YR	RET CODE
POTHIER MATHEW V	COL	0-0019410	0655	1
POTOCHNIK ANNA M	MAJ	N-0002169	0966	1
POTTER ELEANOR M	MAJ	N-0002287	0565	1
POTTER GEORGE V	COL	0-0026434	1164	1
POTTER JOHN C JR	COL	0-0021439	0266	1
POTTER KENNETH B	COL	0-0030366	0662	2
POTTER SEYMOUR A JR	B G	0-0029937	1062	1
POTTER WALDO C	B G	0-0002231	0346	1
POTTER WILLIAM E	M G	0-0017098	0760	1
POTTER WILSON JR	COL	0-0028798	0355	1
POTTS EDWIN H	LTC	0-0031009	0563	2
POTTS FRANK G	LTC	0-0007819	0142	2
POTTS RUSSELL J	COL	0-0007241	0847	1
POUCHER CLYDE R	LTC	0-0079673	1168	1
POULSEN WALDEMAR P	1LT	0-0096134	0364	2
POUST LUTHER R	COL	0-0003435	0946	2
POUTRE CLIFFORD A	COL	0-0029371	1059	1
POVENDO NICHOLAS A	COL	0-0079956	1066	1
POWELL CHARLES J	LTC	0-0085363	0466	1
POWELL CHARNER W	COL	0-0019284	0763	1
POWELL DAVID O	MAJ	0-0057662	0967	1
POWELL DONALD F	LTC	0-0025762	1167	1
POWELL ELBERT W	LTC	0-0079032	0968	1
POWELL ELMER R	COL	0-0030414	0565	1
POWELL GEORGE M	M G	0-0019340	0266	2
POWELL GROSVENOR	COL	0-0018382	0761	1
POWELL HARRY C	LTC	0-0039336	0264	2
POWELL HERBERT B	GEN	0-0016684	0263	1
POWELL HERMAN L	CW4	W-0906958	0566	1
POWELL MALCOLM T	LTC	0-0051368	1160	1
POWELL MAURICE G	COL	0-0040259	1166	2
POWER JOSEPH L	CPT	0-0062818	1162	1
POWER MARJORIE C	LTC	L-0000218	0959	1
POWER WILLIAM J	LTC	0-0019614	0259	1
POWERS GEORGE T III	M G	0-0019137	0368	2
POWERS JAMES F	LTC	0-0039431	0564	1
POWERS JAMES W	COL	0-0083571	0766	1
POWERS JAY I	CW4	W-0903688	0963	1
POWERS JOHN L	COL	0-0020736	0865	1
POWERS LOWELL H	LTC	0-0042123	0161	1
POWERS PATRICK F	COL	0-0011659	0850	2
POWERS ROBERT A	LTC	0-0062869	0968	1
POWERS WILLIAM F	COL	0-0018672	0359	1
POWHIDA JOHN P	LTC	0-0051475	0162	1
POWLOSKI STANLEY	LTC	0-0011351	0346	1
POZERO JOE JR	CW4	W-0903689	0766	1
PRACHER JOHN R	LTC	0-0037622	0764	1
PRAHINSKI ALFRED	COL	0-0041620	1159	1
PRAHL ROBERT L	COL	0-0031555	0667	1
PRALL JOSEF A	COL	0-0051772	0666	1
PRATHER LAWRENCE H	COL	0-0031722	0663	1
PRATHER RICHARD G	M G	0-0015698	0861	1
PRATT CLARENCE W	LTC	0-0061227	0168	1
PRATT FLOYD G	COL	0-0019915	0661	1
PRATT FORD E	COL	0-0031433	0463	1
PRATT JAMES M	MAJ	0-0025135	1061	1
PRATT OWEN M	CW4	W-0903690	0163	1
PRATT RAYMOND S JR	LTC	0-0018512	0859	1
PRATT WARREN K	LTC	0-0051519	0762	1
PRAZAK GEORGE	COL	0-0018951	1062	1
PREBIL FRED C	COL	0-0079957	0764	1
PREBLE MERLE R	COL	0-0023524	0667	1
PREGALDIN CHARLES V	LTC	0-0034425	0863	1
PREISS HOLLIS J	COL	0-0081880	0967	1
PRENDERGAST JOHN D	COL	0-0040599	0665	1
PRENTICE JOSEPH C	COL	0-0031888	1266	1
PRENTISS AUGUSTIN M	B G	0-0003624	0846	1
PRENTISS LOUIS W	M G	0-0014672	0456	1
PRENTISS LOUISE M	LTC	N-0000515	0150	1
PRESSENTIN VERNON F	LTC	0-0035391	0866	2
PRESTON EDMUND R JR	LTC	0-0027525	0666	1
PRESTON LEONARD L	MAJ	0-0057430	1166	2
PRESTON MARSHALL C	LTC	0-0038893	0964	1
PRESTON ROY W	CW3	W-0903691	0756	1
PRESTON WALTER J JR	COL	0-0042388	0859	1

NAME	GRADE	SVC NO	DATE RET MO YR	RET CODE
PRESTON WILLIAM D JR	LTC	0-0032969	0764	1
PRESTON WILLIAM M	COL	0-0022099	0867	1
PRETZER EMORY A	CW3	W-0906960	0263	1
PREUTZ EDWARD A	CW4	W-0901162	0452	1
PREWITT RICHARD R	LTC	0-0044603	0860	1
PRICE ALFRED J	LTC	0-0027397	0766	1
PRICE ALFRED L	COL	0-0014994	1047	1
PRICE CARTER C	COL	0-0051018	1054	1
PRICE DAVID B	LTC	0-0043842	0864	1
PRICE DONALD L	LTC	0-0066072	0568	1
PRICE EARL M	CPT	0-0014170	0417	2
PRICE FOREST F	CW4	W-0903692	0463	1
PRICE GEORGE T	COL	0-0018647	0552	2
PRICE GEORGE W JR	MAJ	0-0087588	1166	2
PRICE HERBERT H	COL	0-0009110	0945	2
PRICE HERBERT H	LTC	0-0091153	0166	1
PRICE HERBERT H JR	LTC	0-0027825	0766	1
PRICE IDA G	LTC	N-0002353	1060	1
PRICE JAMES R	LTC	0-0087889	0868	1
PRICE JOHN W	COL	0-0083572	1066	1
PRICE MARVIN L	LTC	0-0027157	0766	1
PRICE MILTON H	LTC	0-0030518	0762	1
PRICE NEILL F	COL	0-0051841	0267	1
PRICE WALLACE W	LTC	0-0065030	1064	1
PRICE WILLIAM D	CW4	W-0903694	0766	2
PRICE XENOPHON H	COL	0-0003666	0946	2
PRICHARD CHESLEY D	LTC	0-0058562	0868	1
PRICKETT FAY B	M G	0-0004458	0453	2
PRIDDY LILLIAN F	MAJ	N-0001044	1062	1
PRIDE RONALD T	MAJ	0-0017002	0747	1
PRIDGEN CLAUDE L	COL	0-0038965	1263	1
PRIEBE WINLAW A	COL	0-0021465	1068	2
PRIEST PERRY B	COL	0-0031562	0966	2
PRIMO ADRIAN H	CW4	W-0903696	0567	1
PRINCE ALTUS E	COL	0-0025714	0667	1
PRINCE CARL M	COL	0-0029288	0855	2
PRINCE WILLIAM R	COL	0-0020219	0764	1
PRINDLE GEORGE L	COL	0-0008226	0747	1
PRINGLE HERMAN F	LTC	0-0030477	0263	2
PRIOR DAVID	LTC	0-0044304	0161	1
PRITCHARD JAMES R	COL	0-0019248	0863	1
PRITCHARD JOHN R	LTC	0-0052111	0765	1
PRITCHARD RUBY E	MAJ	N-0000690	0564	1
PRITCHARD WILLIAM C	COL	0-0029455	0960	1
PRITCHARD WILLIAM J	COL	0-0042258	1063	1
PRITCHETT HARRY H JR	COL	0-0025705	0267	1
PRIVETT FORBIE H	COL	0-0011975	0646	2
PRIVETT GEORGE P	COL	0-0015459	0954	1
PRIZER OLIVER H	COL	0-0010198	1052	1
PROBASCO NANCY A	CPT	N-0002208	1155	2
PROCTER GILBERT	COL	0-0010243	0846	2
PROCTOR MERT	COL	0-0003125	0646	1
PROCTOR WILLIAM M	LTC	0-0080171	0966	1
PROKOP JOHN J	LTC	0-0038797	0563	1
PROPST JULIAN C	LTC	0-0045943	0760	1
PROSSER CHARLES M	B G	0-0031945	0966	1
PROSSER WALTER E	M G	0-0002057	1045	2
PROSSER WILLIAM O	COL	0-0004052	0247	1
PROUTY AMOS L	CW4	W-0903698	0355	1
PROVENZANO THOMAS C	LTC	0-0028346	0766	1
PROCHA MARY F	LTC	N-0000072	0454	1
PRUETT GEORGE J	LTC	0-0037054	0268	1
PRUITT FRANCIS W	B G	0-0017812	0959	1
PRUNTY CARROLL A	COL	0-0017281	1053	2
PRUNTY THOMAS E	LTC	0-0032924	0761	1
PRYOR DELBERT A	COL	0-0018799	0660	1
PRYOR RALPH H	COL	0-0029996	0859	1
PRYST HENRY F	LTC	0-0032904	1067	1
PUCCIO DOMINICK V	LTC	0-0071857	0868	1
PUCKETT CHARLES D	MAJ	0-0026210	1061	1
PUCKETT MARTHA A	MAJ	N-0000774	1267	1
PUE EDDIE B	LTC	0-0075272	0167	1
PUGH EUNITY F E	LTC	L-0000114	0463	1
PUGH JOHN R	M G	0-0018790	0466	1
PUGH RALPH H	COL	0-0024375	0966	1

NAME	GRADE	SVC NO	DATE RET MO YR	RET CODE
PUGSLEY HELEN F	MAJ	N-0001969	0261	1
PUGSLEY MATTHEW C	COL	0-0017974	0147	2
PULASKI EDWIN J	COL	0-0041779	0765	1
PULLIAM GEORGE W JR	LTC	0-0062208	0867	1
PULSIFER ARTHUR	B G	0-0012211	0752	2
PULSIFER GEORGE JR	MAJ	0-0014006	0920	2
PULSIFER RALPH	B G	0-0015751	0945	2
PULSIFER ROBERT A	LTC	0-0068152	1068	1
PUMPELLY JAMES W	COL	0-0051384	0357	1
PUNOT WILLIE	LTC	0-0070478	1168	1
PUNSALAN LEON F	LTC	0-0042639	1163	1
PURCELL WILLIAM W	COL	0-0081881	0766	1
PURKHISER HARRY R	LTC	0-0088888	0766	1
PURKITT CLAUDE H	LTC	0-0035152	0356	2
PURKS NETA A	MAJ	N-0002356	0858	1
PURNELL EDWARD K	COL	0-0018539	0849	2
PURSALL ALFRED A	COL	0-0029491	1160	1
PURVIS ARTHUR C	COL	0-0008660	0949	2
PURVIS FRED M	CW4	W-0903703	0161	1
PUTNAM GEORGE D	LTC	0-0036328	0864	1
PUTNAM HELEN P	MAJ	N-0000171	0462	1
PUTNAM LINCOLN F	COL	0-0008712	0645	2
PUTNAM WEBSTER F	COL	0-0009831	1048	1
PUTNAM WILLIAM D	COL	0-0029605	1061	1
PYLE CLYDE S	CW3	W-0903705	0964	2
PYNES OATS A	LTC	0-0036491	1166	1
PYUEN PYUENG S	COL	0-0041976	0162	1
QUACKENBUSH ROBERT E	COL	0-0018590	0761	1
QUACKENBUSH ROBERT O	COL	0-0031317	0268	1
QUAID THOMAS D	LTC	0-0022919	0761	1
QUANDT DOUGLAS P	M G	0-0020605	0866	1
QUANTZ RAOUL J	LTC	0-0028169	0866	1
QUARANTILLO EDWARD P	COL	0-0031002	0568	1
QUARLES HUGH L	COL	0-0039614	0659	1
QUARTERMAN WILLIAM H	COL	0-0007476	0753	2
QUARTON REGINALD R	COL	0-0039663	1263	2
QUASHNOCK EMRO J	COL	0-0034321	0867	1
QUATTROCCHI FRANK S	LTC	0-0071858	1068	1
QUAVE JOSEPH	CW4	W-0907790	0864	1
QUENNEVILLE RENE O	COL	0-0039524	0356	1
QUETCHENBACK ALBERT	CW4	W-0903706	0565	1
QUICK GEORGE S	LTC	0-0044602	1167	1
QUICK JOHN T	LTC	0-0053006	1066	1
QUICKEL HERBERT L	LTC	0-0004104	0142	1
QUIGG JOHN	CW4	W-0903707	0157	1
QUIGLEY EDWARDS M	COL	0-0014673	1046	2
QUIGLEY QUENTIN S	LTC	0-0029894	0153	1
QUIGLEY RAY E	LTC	0-0006037	0340	2
QUILL JAMES B	M G	0-0017673	0962	1
QUILLIAN EUGENE L	LTC	0-0084462	0967	1
QUIMBY JAMES O JR	COL	0-0035534	0764	1
QUIN BEATRICE M	LTC	N-0000494	1047	1
QUIN HILLRIE M	LTC	0-0081923	1168	1
QUINLAN EDWARD W	LTC	0-0051617	0463	1
QUINLIN FRANK C	COL	0-0051860	1264	1
QUINN COILE A	COL	0-0030571	0264	1
QUINN DORIS M	MAJ	N-0000381	0261	1
QUINN EDWARD F JR	COL	0-0031031	0664	2
QUINN HELENA O	MAJ	R-0010066	0558	1
QUINN HORACE A	COL	0-0016820	1046	1
QUINN HOWARD W	COL	0-0018201	0650	1
QUINN JAMES F	COL	0-0031454	0267	1
QUINN LEO M	CW4	W-0903708	0368	1
QUINN MICHAEL A	COL	0-0010882	0554	2
QUINN NATHAN M	LTC	0-0042574	1062	1
QUINN RAY B	LTC	0-0036604	0864	1
QUINN WILLIAM W	LTG	0-0019283	0366	1
QUINN 3RD DANIEL W	COL	0-0017697	0846	2
QUINNELL EARLE D	COL	0-0006256	0148	2
QUINNELLY JAMES L	LTC	0-0060177	0666	1
QUINTARD ALEXANDER	COL	0-0005581	0551	1
QUINTO MYRON A	COL	0-0018210	0760	1
QUIST FREDERICK	COL	0-0052178	0867	1
RAAB HENRY JR	CW4	W-0906965	0965	1
RABER THOMAS J	COL	0-0030614	0961	1

NAME	GRADE	SVC NO	DATE RET MO YR	RET CODE
RACE ANTHONY J	LTC	0-0052163	1158	2
RACKES ADAMS E	LTC	0-0042078	0249	2
RACKHAM KARL M	LTC	0-0083586	0767	1
RACKLEFF ANGUS N	LTC	0-0030488	0763	1
RADAM DAVID	COL	0-0051736	0257	1
RADCLIFF JOSEPH A	LTC	0-0041158	0262	2
RADCLIFFE MAURICE M	COL	0-0039787	0962	1
RADEBAUGH PHYLLIS R	1LT	R-0001248	0448	1
RADER DONALD C	CW4	W-0903711	0961	1
RADER ROBERT M	LTC	0-0031523	0157	1
RADER WILLIAM F	COL	0-0031543	0667	1
RADFORD LAWRENCE C	COL	0-0021462	0662	1
RADKE MARGARET F	LTC	R-0010024	0968	1
RADKE RYLE A	COL	0-0020522	0455	2
RADLEY BARBARA M	MAJ	N-0000445	1061	1
RADLINSKI JOHN C	LTC	0-0029156	0357	2
RADZWICH EDWARD R	LTC	0-0032691	0261	1
RAFF EDSON D	COL	0-0019261	1058	1
RAFF EDWARD G	LTC	0-0032588	1164	1
RAFFERTY JOHN F	LTC	0-0051150	0659	2
RAFFERTY KATHLEEN J	1LT	R-0000862	0346	1
RAFFERTY THOMAS A	COL	0-0031793	1166	1
RAFFERTY WILLIAM A	MAJ	0-0003600	1022	2
RAGER EDWARD E	COL	0-0022116	0762	1
RAGLAND WILLIAM W	COL	0-0018344	0761	1
RAGSDALE AGNES W	MAJ	N-0001239	1064	1
RAGSDALE GERALD H	COL	0-0022217	0368	1
RAGUSE CARL W A	COL	0-0015598	0754	1
RAHMANN JOHN C	LTC	0-0066078	0767	1
RAIBL TONY J	COL	0-0051799	1061	2
RAILING JAMES M	LTC	0-0030593	1263	1
RAINES MARTIN L	COL	0-0035621	1064	1
RAINFORD WILLIAM R	COL	0-0029626	1061	1
RAINVILLE LEON H	MAJ	0-0032726	0361	1
RAJSKI LAURES B	MAJ	L-0000267	0766	1
RALEIGH ROBERT C	LTC	0-0023287	0261	1
RALEY LEROY W	LTC	0-0041733	0760	1
RALEY PERRY T	LTC	0-0031037	1266	1
RALL STATEN E	COL	0-0015410	0754	1
RALLS HOWARD L JR	LTC	0-0040186	0865	1
RALPH STEPHEN V	COL	0-0040030	0866	1
RAMEE PAUL W	COL	0-0023704	0868	1
RAMEY RUFUS S	B G	0-0006614	0453	1
RAMSAY ALLAN R	COL	0-0018915	0557	1
RAMSAY WILLIAM T	LTC	0-0056778	0657	1
RAMSBURG CHARLES E	LTC	0-0081160	0968	1
RAMSEY ALBERT L JR	1LT	0-0027996	1150	2
RAMSEY ARTHUR C	COL	0-0015497	0554	1
RAMSEY DAVID L	LTC	0-0025072	0760	1
RAMSEY DAVID M JR	COL	0-0053610	0764	1
RAMSEY FOSTER G	LTC	0-0080319	0667	1
RAMSEY GEORGE L	COL	0-0007304	0945	2
RAMSEY HARRY E	COL	0-0029191	1160	2
RAMSEY JAMES D	COL	0-0036228	0968	1
RAMSEY LLOYD A	LTC	0-0033352	0961	1
RAMSEY THOMAS H	B G	0-0009728	0150	1
RAMSEY THURMAN F	LTC	0-0051571	0760	1
RAMSHUR LOREN C	LTC	0-0078660	0968	1
RANCK JOSEPH R	B G	0-0017647	0962	2
RANCOILTA JEAN C	MAJ	N-0000253	1266	1
RAND KENAN W	COL	0-0039795	0163	2
RAND OSCAR R	COL	0-0009953	0946	2
RANDALL CHARLES W	CW4	W-0904186	1057	1
RANDALL FRANK J	COL	0-0038842	0864	1
RANDALL HAL	COL	0-0050969	1157	1
RANDALL SAMUEL J	COL	0-0003980	1044	2
RANDLE EDWIN H	B G	0-0006745	0648	1
RANDLE ROBERT B	COL	0-0052570	1067	1
RANDOLPH THOMAS J	COL	0-0015050	0746	2
RANEY JOSEPH D	COL	0-0030285	0962	1
RANKIN ALEXANDER	COL	0-0032166	0365	1
RANKIN EDWARD	LTC	0-0084664	1267	1
RANKIN FRED W JR	LTC	0-0027073	0866	1
RANKIN GEORGE H	COL	0-0032522	0267	1
RANKIN JAMES B	LTC	0-0018778	0246	2

NAME	GRADE	SVC NO	DATE RET MO YR	RET CODE
RANKIN JOHN A	COL	0-0032140	0468	1
RANKIN JOHN B	LTC	0-0040209	0963	1
RANKIN SAMUEL P	CW4	W-0902142	0762	1
RANKIN SONJA M	MAJ	L-0000321	0764	1
RANNEY DANIEL A	COL	0-0039863	1059	1
RANSICK CLARENCE E	COL	0-0040147	1268	2
RANSIER JOHN G	LTC	0-0063376	0767	1
RANSOM CHARLES H	LTC	0-0025841	0762	1
RANSOM JOHN P	LTC	0-0031140	0960	1
RANSOM PAUL L	M G	0-0004651	0548	1
RANSOM WALTER E	CW4	W-0903715	0965	1
RANSONE ALEXANDER	COL	0-0034142	1167	1
RAPALSKI ADAM J	COL	0-0041760	0966	2
RAPP ELIZABETH	MAJ	N-0002366	0360	1
RAPP PAUL C	LTC	0-0080479	0365	1
RAPSON WILLIAM F	LTC	0-0041166	1263	1
RASBACH JORIS B	COL	0-0015918	0854	1
RASCHE HERBERT H	COL	0-0051339	0862	1
RASCOE ROBERT F	CW4	W-0904276	0664	1
RASMUSON MARY L M	COL	L-0000080	0862	1
RASMUSSEN DONALD	CW4	W-0903716	0863	1
RASMUSSEN JAMES A	LTC	0-0027612	0168	1
RASMUSSEN KAI E	COL	0-0017655	0955	1
RASMUSSEN RAYMOND J	LTC	0-0059161	1068	1
RASOR SAM J	COL	0-0038769	0864	1
RASPER VINCENT W	LTC	0-0040615	1066	1
RASTETTER RICHARD J	COL	0-0023770	0664	1
RATAY JOHN P	B G	0-0006567	0846	1
RATCLIFF PATRICIA A	MAJ	N-0001795	0468	1
RATCLIFFE LAMAR C	COL	0-0019034	0763	1
RATHBONE JOHN V JR	COL	0-0042424	0561	1
RATHJE THEODORE A	COL	0-0042311	0264	1
RATHLEV ARNOLD	COL	0-0059944	0666	1
RATLIFF FRANK G	COL	0-0022637	0767	1
RATTAN WILLIAM V	COL	0-0007178	1050	1
RAU CHARLES G	COL	0-0017721	0859	1
RAUDSTEIN KNUT H	COL	0-0053611	1068	1
RAUENZAHN DANIEL A	LTC	0-0042528	0463	1
RAUKTIS HELEN O	MAJ	N-0000582	1061	1
RAULSTON JOHN W	COL	0-0020401	0862	1
RAWIE VERNON E R	COL	0-0022654	0962	1
RAWLEY ROGER A	LTC	0-0030648	0264	1
RAWLINGS JAMES G	COL	0-0033065	0163	1
RAWLINGS JOSEPH W	CPT	0-0064195	0358	2
RAWLINGS RICHARD J	LTC	0-0081164	0966	1
RAWLINGS WILLIAM W	COL	0-0042895	1062	1
RAWLINS GEORGE J	CPT	0-0011967	0235	1
RAWLINS WILLIAM A	LTC	0-0031258	0667	1
RAWLS CARLAS E	CW4	RW-0903717	0864	1
RAWLS ROBERT M	COL	0-0024675	0965	1
RAY CLAUDE F	COL	0-0051430	0863	1
RAY JEFF G	LTC	0-0031865	0566	1
RAY JIMMIE E	CW4	W-0903718	0855	1
RAY JOHN	COL	0-0021821	0868	1
RAY JOHN E	COL	0-0008384	0854	1
RAY JOHN L	LTC	0-0058570	0868	1
RAY WILLIAM J	COL	0-0026139	1267	1
RAYBURN ROBERT	LTC	0-0019295	0652	2
RAYCROFT HAROLD V	COL	0-0006815	0451	1
RAYENS CHARLES E	COL	0-0005456	0447	2
RAYHILL GILBERT L	CW4	W-0903720	0666	1
RAYLE ROY E	LTC	0-0025113	0163	1
RAYMOND ALLEN D	COL	0-0015366	0753	1
RAYMOND JULIAN E	COL	0-0012814	0954	1
RAYMOND MONTGOMERY	COL	0-0017227	0758	1
RAYMOND PHILIP H	1LT	0-0015015	1134	1
RAYMOND WILLIAM B	LTC	0-0084463	0866	1
RAYMOND 2ND C W	COL	0-0018403	0161	1
RAYNSFORD ROBERT W	COL	0-0014910	0854	1
REA EVERETT F	COL	0-0010523	1047	1
REA ROBERT P	COL	0-0019326	0854	1
READ ARTHUR J	COL	0-0084567	1267	1
READ BEVERLY C	CPT	OF-0105515	0968	2
READ BURTON Y	COL	0-0003433	0446	2
READ CLARENCE E	COL	0-0039602	0359	2

NAME	GRADE	SVC NO	DATE RET MO YR	RET CODE
READ GEORGE W JR	LTG	0-0012603	0860	2
READ JOHN W	LTC	0-0018527	0153	1
READ MAHLON M	MAJ	0-0009817	0939	2
READ ROBERT N	COL	0-0038864	0566	1
REAFLENG HARRY E	LTC	0-0036620	0960	2
REAGAN BRUCE W	LTC	0-0038975	0565	2
REAGAN THOMAS H	COL	0-0008485	1146	2
REAGAN WOODROW W	LTC	0-0043351	0962	1
REAGOR ELMER C	COL	0-0030639	0366	1
REAM ELLIS A	LTC	0-0036165	0964	1
REARDON RICHARD R	MAJ	0-0070484	1162	1
REARDON WILLIAM J	COL	0-0015631	1049	1
REBENTISCH HAMILTON	LTC	0-0044991	1167	1
REBER EDWARD C	COL	0-0017201	1055	1
REBER MILES	M G	0-0015123	1055	1
REBOVITCH MICHAEL J	CW4	W-0903721	0561	1
REDD LEMUEL B	LTC	0-0043089	0765	2
REDD THOMAS L JR	LTC	0-0035508	1264	1
REDDEN DONALD R	LTC	0-0033657	1166	1
REDDEN FREDERICK	COL	0-0018455	0859	1
REDDING FRANK J JR	COL	0-0043485	1158	1
REDDINGTON THOMAS C	LTC	0-0024401	0464	1
REDENIUS JOSEPHINE	LTC	L-0000189	0567	1
REDFIELD ROBERT S	COL	0-0030704	0566	1
REDLAND ARTHUR J	COL	0-0016947	0957	2
REDLINGER MATTHEW	MAJ	0-0024775	1148	2
REDMAN CHARLES L JR	COL	0-0032311	0566	1
REDMON WILLIAM E	CW2	W-0800037	0145	1
REDNER WALLACE J JR	LTC	0-0058767	1065	1
REDSHAW WARD F	MAJ	0-0079042	0863	1
REECE DONALD P	LTC	0-0083618	0667	1
REECE RUTH S	LTC	L-0000134	0565	1
REED ALBERT L	COL	0-0042380	0664	1
REED ARTHUR W	COL	0-0021878	0667	1
REED C WINGATE	COL	0-0011515	1049	1
REED CHARLES H	COL	0-0014948	0249	1
REED CHARLES L	COL	0-0029475	0552	2
REED CHARLES R	LTC	0-0060017	0664	1
REED CHARLES S	COL	0-0009153	0846	1
REED FRANK F	COL	0-0008583	0753	1
REED GEORGE M	COL	0-0069774	0968	1
REED HARRY E	COL	0-0011688	0753	1
REED HERBERT N	LTC	0-0051297	0360	1
REED HERMAN H	COL	0-0029081	0357	1
REED HOBART O	1LT	0-0011926	0133	2
REED JAMES W	COL	0-0035884	0967	1
REED JOHN E	LTC	0-0091495	0868	1
REED JOHN F	COL	0-0051436	0963	1
REED KATHERINE	MAJ	N-0000190	1162	1
REED KENNETH H	COL	0-0029203	0561	1
REED KENNETH O	LTC	0-0053102	0764	1
REED MELVIN W	COL	0-0029553	0561	1
REED PAUL A	COL	0-0065411	0367	1
REED PRENTISS B JR	LTC	0-0039841	0861	1
REED RALPH M	LTC	0-0022760	0867	1
REED ROBERT J	LTC	0-0060900	1263	1
REED ROBERT W	COL	0-0041597	0959	2
REED RUSSELL R	COL	0-0052162	1066	1
REED WARREN E	LTC	0-0050231	0966	1
REEDALL HAROLD M	COL	0-0010308	0246	2
REEDER JAMES R	LTC	0-0081167	0666	1
REEDER ROGER E	LTC	0-0080481	0966	1
REEDER RUSSELL P JR	COL	0-0016494	0945	2
REEDER WILLIAM O	M G	0-0008564	0153	1
REEDY LEONARD E	CW4	W-0903724	1165	1
REES ROGER S	LTC	0-0031652	0165	1
REES THOMAS H	COL	0-0003699	0651	1
REESE EMMETT C	LTC	0-0079043	0168	1
REESE FREDERICK	COL	0-0039600	0159	1
REESE ROBERT M	LTC	0-0027875	0766	1
REEVE AGATHA M	LTC	N-0000120	0856	1
REEVE ARNOLD M	LTC	0-0065453	0966	1
REEVE PARKER M	COL	0-0016390	0756	1
REEVES ANDREW P	COL	0-0006528	0353	1
REEVES ANN	MAJ	N-0000974	0263	1

NAME	GRADE	SVC NO	DATE RET MO YR	RET CODE
REEVES CHARLES P	COL	0-0043996	0964	1
REEVES JAMES H JR	COL	0-0020665	0267	1
REEVES JOSEPH R	COL	0-0021820	0465	1
REGAD EUGENE D	COL	0-0015436	1153	1
REGAN JOHN F	LTC	0-0060859	0467	1
REGAN JOHN W	LTC	0-0022783	0761	1
REGAN JOSEPH B	LTC	0-0043105	0865	1
REGAN JULIA L	LTC	L-0000035	1059	2
REGAR PHILIP W	COL	0-0040053	1162	1
REGER CHARLES K	COL	0-0020962	1267	1
REGER HAMILTON	COL	0-0030700	1163	1
REGISTER CHARLES L	COL	0-0020594	1057	1
REGISTER WILLIAM F	COL	0-0043757	1165	1
REGNIER AUGUSTUS J	COL	0-0015720	0754	1
REGNIER FRANCIS W	COL	0-0022899	0265	2
REHM DONALD H	LTC	0-0027807	0766	1
REHM GEORGE A	B G	0-0012772	0955	1
REHM HAROLD W JR	LTC	0-0066080	0767	1
REHM WILLIAM F	COL	0-0007603	0553	1
REHMANN EDWARD J	COL	0-0005060	0344	1
REHMANN EDWARD L	COL	0-0030027	1063	1
REIBER MARTIN R	COL	0-0009165	1047	2
REICHEL MICHAEL J	B G	0-0040087	0666	1
REICHELDERFER HARRY	M G	0-0007547	1156	2
REICHLE PAUL A	COL	0-0010327	0749	1
REID ALEXANDER	COL	0-0015234	1054	1
REID CLARENCE E	COL	0-0031809	0867	1
REID ELIZABETH	MAJ	N-0002077	0961	1
REID GERALD J	COL	0-0015760	0648	1
REID MARION M	LTC	0-0079964	0665	1
REID ROBERT A	LTC	0-0065718	0468	1
REID ROBERT J	LTC	0-0084412	0765	1
REID WALLACE G	MAJ	0-0060361	0761	1
REIERSON JOHN E	COL	0-0012865	0952	2
REIFF STANLEY G	COL	0-0038688	0561	1
REIFSNYDER HAROLD R	COL	0-0039881	0364	1
REILLY FRANCIS W	LTC	0-0059009	0759	2
REILLY GEORGE M	COL	0-0017758	1046	2
REILLY ROBERT S	LTC	0-0023813	0164	1
REILLY STANLEY J	LTC	0-0019654	1147	2
REIMEL STEWART E	B G	0-0007449	0246	1
REINBURG W H W	COL	0-0008606	0447	2
REINEL ANTHONY A	LTC	0-0080321	0766	1
REINERS MARIE E	MAJ	N-0000534	1148	1
REING CORNELIUS	COL	0-0029637	1161	1
REINHARDT EMIL F	M G	0-0002887	0946	2
REINHARDT GEORGE C	COL	0-0015963	0854	1
REINHARDT WILLIAM R	LTC	0-0010843	0243	2
REINHART STANLEY E	M G	0-0004421	0946	2
REINIKKA ARNOLD J	LTC	0-0062084	0167	1
REIS MARGOT	MAJ	L-0000244	0862	1
REISER LLOYD M	COL	0-0039823	0363	1
REISNER RAYMOND W	COL	0-0051656	0964	1
REISS WILLIAM J	COL	0-0030853	0267	1
REITMEIER WOODROW A	LTC	0-0055144	0867	1
REITZ GEORGE W	COL	0-0030510	1065	1
REITZ JAMES T	COL	0-0033096	0664	1
REITZEL CLAUDE E JR	COL	0-0029404	0460	1
REMFREY CURT A	LTC	0-0040169	0461	1
REMICK CHARLES E	LTC	0-0034408	0766	1
RENUS JOSEPH A	COL	0-0019275	0863	1
RENFRO CHARLES G	COL	0-0024567	0966	1
RENFRO CURTIS O	COL	0-0016248	0755	1
RENFRO JOHN W	CW3	W-0903728	0962	1
RENOLA RAYMOND	COL	0-0022971	0760	1
RENSHAW CLARENCE	B G	0-0017708	1160	1
RENSHAW SOLON B	COL	0-0009468	1152	1
RENSHAW WILLARD S	COL	0-0029426	0760	1
RENTH EDWARD J	COL	0-0006355	0651	1
REPPA ROBERT B	LTC	0-0034978	0466	1
REPPARD ROY	COL	0-0029084	0459	1
REQUARTH JACK A	COL	0-0022189	0867	1
RESCH AGNES A	LTC	N-0000009	0748	1
RESING JOSEPH W F	1LT	0-0011740	0427	2
RESLER BARCLAY T	COL	0-0042068	0862	1

NAME	GRADE	SVC NO	DATE RET MO YR	RET CODE
RESNICK SAUL M	CPT	0-0057190	0659	2
RESSEGIEU FRED F	COL	0-0020575	0358	1
RESSEGUIE GEORGE I	LTC	0-0053240	0761	1
RESSEGUIE ROY A	COL	0-0029306	0264	1
RESSIJAC LOUIS H	LTC	0-0023454	0661	1
RESTA ROBERT	WO1	W-0901021	1038	1
RETTGERS FORREST I	COL	0-0036414	1066	1
REUBEL HARRY B	COL	0-0029050	0159	1
REUSCHLEIN JOHN W	CW4	W-0904256	0858	2
REUTENAUER MARGUERIT	LTC	N-0000206	0466	1
REUTER HERBERT C	COL	0-0012776	0854	1
REVELS DELZIE C	MAJ	0-0067744	0168	1
REVIE CHARLES R	COL	0-0019369	0864	1
REYBOLD JOHN B	COL	0-0012842	0447	1
REYER GEORGE W	COL	0-0011343	0351	2
REYNOLDS ALEXANDER	1LT	0-0011811	1129	2
REYNOLDS BURKITT A	LTC	0-0030814	0964	1
REYNOLDS CARLOS F	COL	0-0029702	0354	2
REYNOLDS CHESTER A	LTC	0-0081171	0966	1
REYNOLDS EDWIN W	COL	0-0043969	0967	1
REYNOLDS EMBREE E	LTC	0-0051507	0554	1
REYNOLDS EUGENE F	LTC	0-0081173	0767	1
REYNOLDS HOUSTON C	MAJ	0-0059452	0265	1
REYNOLDS JACOB G	COL	0-0017618	0758	1
REYNOLDS JAMES H	LTC	0-0039919	0962	1
REYNOLDS JAMES H	COL	0-0042721	0963	1
REYNOLDS JOHN M	COL	0-0008347	0146	2
REYNOLDS JOSEPH E	LTC	0-0022151	0458	1
REYNOLDS LAWRENCE S	COL	0-0042982	0966	2
REYNOLDS MAURICE W	COL	0-0011539	0248	1
REYNOLDS ROBERT W	COL	0-0042638	1165	1
REYNOLDS RONALD J	LTC	0-0084667	0366	1
REYNOLDS ROYAL	B G	0-0002814	1045	2
REYNOLDS ROYAL JR	B G	0-0019238	0863	1
REYNOLDS RUSSEL B	M G	0-0008368	0849	1
REYNOLDS WYLIE S JR	LTC	0-0041094	0568	1
REYNOLDSON CHARLES L	LTC	0-0027163	1065	1
REYNOLDSON JOHN R	1LT	0-0064678	0153	2
RHEA JOHN I	COL	0-0043117	0366	1
RHEA ROBERT L	COL	0-0030327	0862	1
RHEAUME JULIANNE M	MAJ	N-0001553	0965	1
RHINE ROBERT H	COL	0-0021317	0862	1
RHINEHART CLAUDE K	COL	0-0013935	0549	2
RHOADES JOHN F	COL	0-0019375	0865	1
RHOADS HOMER E	LTC	0-0059010	0168	1
RHOADS MARK	CPT	0-0012166	0337	2
RHODERS THOMAS A JR	CW4	W-0904303	0859	1
RHODES ELSIE G	LTC	N-0000493	0448	1
RHODES LESTER F	COL	0-0012265	0649	1
RHODES RICHARD G	COL	0-0059876	1268	1
RHODES SAMUEL T	LTC	0-0056992	0868	1
RHODES WILLIAM H	LTC	0-0058154	0868	1
RHODY DEAN A	LTC	0-0030270	1062	1
RHYNE GEORGE W	COL	0-0021219	0568	1
RHYNE LLOYD T	CW3	W-0903730	1159	1
RHYNE MARION A	MAJ	L-0000210	1155	1
RIANI ALBERT	COL	0-0012093	1148	1
RIBBS EDWARD J	COL	0-0051713	0266	1
RICAMORE PHILIP W	COL	0-0010353	1046	2
RICCIARDELLI ANGELO	COL	0-0042208	0763	1
RICCIO JOSEPH A	LTC	0-0025737	1064	1
RICE ALBERT S	COL	0-0012501	0144	2
RICE CECIL P	COL	0-0042801	0866	1
RICE DELBERT F	LTC	0-0081175	0168	1
RICE EDWARD S	COL	0-0025119	1067	1
RICE FRANKLYN D	CW3	W-0903731	0763	1
RICE HERBERT E	LTC	0-0023518	0761	1
RICE HERMAN R	LTC	0-0081176	0968	1
RICE JAMES W	COL	0-0006986	0346	2
RICE JOHN A	COL	0-0043635	0968	1
RICE JOHN K	M G	0-0007183	0153	1
RICE JOHN L	COL	0-0004889	0647	1
RICE JOHN S	COL	0-0024326	0563	1
RICE KENNETH F	COL	0-0079714	0766	1
RICE VERNON W	COL	0-0030189	0662	1

NAME	GRADE	SVC NO	DATE RET MO YR	RET CODE
RICH CHARLES E	LTC	0-0070489	0768	1
RICH JOSEPH	COL	0-0020562	0846	2
RICH THAIR C	COL	0-0019631	0563	1
RICHARD ELIZABETH	CPT	N-0000953	1053	2
RICHARD JOSEPH C	MAJ	0-0024236	0144	2
RICHARDS ALBERT P	COL	0-0023194	0164	1
RICHARDS CECIL G	CW3	W-0908142	1268	1
RICHARDS DANIEL A	COL	0-0020689	0467	1
RICHARDS FRANK	COL	0-0009973	0847	2
RICHARDS FREDERICK	COL	0-0031565	0166	1
RICHARDS GEORGE J	M G	0-0003771	0153	1
RICHARDS GROVER C JR	LTC	0-0044139	0661	1
RICHARDS HARRIS T	LTC	0-0038944	0847	2
RICHARDS IRA B JR	COL	0-0022639	1065	1
RICHARDS JAMES T	COL	0-0021707	0959	1
RICHARDS RAYMOND	1LT	0-0023407	0942	1
RICHARDS WALTER L	COL	0-0005385	0547	1
RICHARDSON BERTHA D	MAJ	N-0001208	1063	1
RICHARDSON BEVERLY T	COL	0-0032864	0763	1
RICHARDSON CHESTER A	MAJ	0-0033259	1061	1
RICHARDSON EDWIN W	COL	0-0020830	0567	1
RICHARDSON FORD	COL	0-0003167	1041	1
RICHARDSON G S	MAJ	N-0002084	0261	1
RICHARDSON GEORGE M	LTC	0-0060843	1066	1
RICHARDSON HAL C JR	LTC	0-0050662	0868	1
RICHARDSON HOUSTON H	CW3	W-0903732	0857	2
RICHARDSON HOWARD B	LTC	0-0036934	0465	1
RICHARDSON JAMES	LTC	0-0023993	0262	1
RICHARDSON JAMES A	M G	0-0029906	1166	1
RICHARDSON JAMES A	COL	0-0031395	1062	1
RICHARDSON JAMES D	LTC	0-0021761	0859	1
RICHARDSON JAMES L	GEN	0-0018232	0767	1
RICHARDSON JAMES R	MAJ	0-0025491	0860	1
RICHARDSON JOHN B JR	COL	0-0019596	1062	1
RICHARDSON JOSEPH M	COL	0-0042269	1063	1
RICHARDSON JULES V	1LT	0-0019221	1041	1
RICHARDSON LEAVER	CPT	0-0014249	0520	2
RICHARDSON RICHARD L	COL	0-0044002	0866	1
RICHARDSON ROBERT E	COL	0-0080365	0568	1
RICHARDSON VELMA L	MAJ	R-0010014	1265	1
RICHARDSON W H JR	LTC	0-0019082	0653	2
RICHARDSON WILLARD D	LTC	0-0045380	0164	1
RICHEK HERBERT G	LTC	0-0040139	0861	1
RICHERT JOEL H	LTC	0-0060145	0766	1
RICHEY GRANVILLE	LTC	0-0021721	1146	2
RICHEY RALPH D JR	LTC	0-0081177	0966	1
RICHEY THOMAS B	COL	0-0059938	0968	1
RICHHART EARL A	COL	0-0029210	0662	1
RICHMOND ALBERT M	COL	0-0019678	0655	1
RICHMOND BUDD W	LTC	0-0030658	0365	1
RICHMOND CLARENCE W	COL	0-0006824	0245	1
RICHMOND HAROLD R	LTC	0-0030265	1062	1
RICHMOND JACK B	LTC	0-0043519	0965	1
RICHMOND KIMBALL R	LTC	0-0047281	0461	1
RICHMOND VAN R	LTC	0-0057531	0263	1
RICHTERS ROBERT L	LTC	0-0065109	1265	1
RICHWINE FRANCIS K	LTC	0-0066084	0367	1
RICK MARSHALL	LTC	0-0088542	0262	1
RICKARD ROY V	M G	0-0008156	1051	1
RICKENBAUGH CARL L	COL	0-0020259	0763	1
RICKERSON HOMER D	CW4	W-0906967	0567	1
RICKETTS CURTIS T	COL	0-0051438	0863	1
RICKMAN EDGAR A	LTC	0-0024796	0955	2
RICKS CHARLES L	COL	0-0043266	0868	1
RIDDICK WILLIS S JR	COL	0-0040570	0168	1
RIDDLE HASTY W	LTC	0-0037456	0860	1
RIDDLE JOHN R	LTC	0-0032745	0267	1
RIDDLEMOSER FRANCIS	CPT	0-0059014	0862	1
RIDE WALTER T JR	LTC	0-0063290	0568	2
RIDENOUR CLYDE B	CW4	W-0903734	0865	1
RIDEOUT MERLE C JR	COL	0-0060155	1266	1
RIDER ROBINSON B	COL	0-0051408	0563	1
RIDGE LAURA G	LTC	N-0000068	0156	1
RIDGE PAUL A	MAJ	0-0016590	1047	1
RIDGELL JOEL M JR	LTC	0-0030769	0764	1

NAME	GRADE	SVC NO	DATE RET MO YR	RET CODE
RIDGELY DALE H	B G	0-0017797	0859	1
RIDGWAY MATTHEW B	GEN	0-0005264	0655	1
RIDINGS EUGENE W	M G	0-0015230	0258	1
RIDLEHUBER WALTER R	COL	0-0039902	0962	1
RIDLEY CLARENCE S	M G	0-0002024	0647	1
RIEDE REINHOLD C	COL	0-0045810	0363	1
RIEGER NATHANIEL	B G	0-0051027	0459	2
RIEGLE CHARLES A	COL	0-0033325	0868	1
RIEKER MELVIN F	CW4	W-0903735	0167	1
RIEMENSCHNEIDER WALT	LTC	0-0019970	0563	2
RIENBOLT SAMUEL R	CW3	W-0903736	1058	1
RIEPE JOHN H	COL	0-0015515	0954	1
RIES ARTHUR W	COL	0-0044226	1156	1
RIGDON JONATHAN M	COL	0-0017981	0560	2
RIGDON MC DONALD	LTC	0-0028997	0656	1
RIGEL WILLIAM F	COL	0-0032894	0564	1
RIGELY GEORGE A	COL	0-0040204	1066	1
RIGG ROBERT B	COL	0-0076842	0866	1
RIGGINS LEWIS A	COL	0-0016111	0755	1
RIGGS DAN E	COL	0-0052285	0267	1
RIGGS THEODORE S	M G	0-0017076	1060	1
RILEY ELWYN A	COL	0-0040023	0666	1
RILEY FRANCIS J	CW4	W-0904189	0165	1
RILEY FRANCIS J JR	LTC	0-0096714	0766	1
RILEY GEORGE D	1LT	0-0014356	0717	2
RILEY HARRIE D W	COL	0-0008932	0547	1
RILEY HUGH W	COL	0-0018757	0946	2
RILEY JACOB L JR	COL	0-0053161	1266	1
RILEY JASPER J JR	MAJ	0-0013244	0648	1
RILEY JOHN E	LTC	0-0040465	0361	2
RILEY JOHN I	CW4	W-0903737	1163	1
RILEY JOHN R	COL	0-0038768	0762	1
RILEY KEITH L	MAJ	0-0065346	0465	2
RILEY LOWELL M	COL	0-0008654	0652	1
RILEY WILLIAM E	LTC	0-0065553	0766	1
RILEY WINIFRED G	LTC	R-0010071	1264	1
RIME MABEL L	LTC	N-0001533	1166	1
RIMLINGER JAMES L	COL	0-0081180	0968	1
RIMMER HARMON P	LTC	0-0023204	0760	1
RING WILLIAM P JR	COL	0-0029467	0960	1
RINGER MERRITT G	COL	0-0016532	1148	1
RINGGOLD CHARLES L	LTC	0-0030115	0161	1
RINGLER EARL L	COL	0-0016431	0656	1
RINGSAK ELTON W	LTC	0-0021409	0-45	2
RINGSDORF PASCHAL H	COL	0-0015287	0145	2
RINK RICHARD A	LTC	0-0064927	0667	1
RINKER CORNELIUS	COL	0-0030129	0364	2
RINQUE DONALD P	COL	0-0039874	0264	1
RIORDAN BERNARD N	COL	0-0056795	0655	1
RIORDAN CLIFFORD T	COL	0-0021318	0868	1
RIOS EDWIN T	LTC	0-0063038	1064	1
RIOUX JOSEPH G	CPT	0-0028583	0754	2
RIPLEY MICHAEL F	CW2	W-0902369	1153	1
RIPPLE RICHARD W	COL	0-0020312	0866	1
RISDEN RICHARD A	B G	0-0019278	0963	1
RISHELL CLAIR L	LTC	0-0079049	0867	1
RISHOI STANLEY O	LTC	0-0051462	1061	1
RISING HARRY N	COL	0-0008652	1052	1
RISING HARRY N JR	LTC	0-0024002	1068	2
RISLEY RICHARD G	COL	0-0032516	0868	1
RISQUE BEVERLY	COL	0-0040446	0768	1
RITCHEL CHARLES S	COL	0-0003858	0646	2
RITCHEY ANDREW W	LTC	0-0031934	0766	1
RITCHEY STERLING J	COL	0-0022771	0260	1
RITCHIE ALVA L	COL	0-0039788	1162	1
RITCHIE CHARLES A	COL	0-0029586	0761	1
RITCHIE ERNEST L	COL	0-0029957	0262	1
RITCHIE ISAAC H	COL	0-0012321	0352	2
RITCHIE PAUL J	COL	0-0038808	0965	1
RITCHIE SCOTT B	COL	0-0005255	1146	1
RITTENMAR THEO R	CW4	W-0902067	0255	1
RITTER JAMES F	COL	0-0041578	0359	1
RITTER WILLIAM L	B G	0-0007437	1050	2
RITTGERS FOREST S	COL	0-0039557	1157	1
RITTS JAMES H	LTC	0-0038720	0660	1

NAME	GRADE	SVC NO	DATE RET MO YR	RET CODE
RIVA HUMBERT L	COL	0-0026947	0661	1
RIVAS ERNEST G	COL	0-0037543	0266	1
RIVENBARK R V	COL	0-0049956	0968	1
RIVERS MAYNARD R	CW3	W-0903741	0160	2
RIVETTE DONALD F	MAJ	0-0034757	0863	1
RIXEY CHARLES O	COL	0-0039341	0866	1
RIXEY GEORGE F	B G	0-0009562	0348	1
RIZK ELIZABETH	MAJ	N-0000399	0361	1
RIZZO CORRINE C	MAJ	M-0010043	0666	1
ROACH NEAL H	LTC	0-0060689	0167	1
ROADRUCK MAX J	COL	0-0042479	0761	1
ROANE NATHAN A JR	LTC	0-0034156	0365	1
ROANE THOMAS W	COL	0-0011815	0753	2
ROBB HOLLAND L	COL	0-0004432	0753	2
ROBB JOHN E	COL	0-0042790	0666	1
ROBBE ALICE J	LTC	N-0000085	0960	1
ROBBINS ALVIN O	COL	0-0019769	0865	2
ROBBINS CHARLES	COL	0-0042512	0365	1
ROBBINS HUGH W	LTC	0-0084415	0766	1
ROBBINS ISADORE	CW4	W-0903742	0756	1
ROBBINS JACK A	LTC	0-0043543	0766	1
ROBBINS LAWRENCE A	COL	0-0051652	1165	1
ROBBINS P JR	COL	0-0017614	0859	1
ROBBINS ROBERT S	MAJ	0-0062192	0963	1
ROBBINS SIDNEY	CW4	W-0903710	0967	2
ROBBINS WALTER F	LTC	0-0056929	0665	1
ROBBINS WILLIS G	COL	0-0051081	0760	1
ROBBLEE PAUL A	COL	0-0042198	0766	1
ROBERSON GERALD L	COL	0-0019161	0657	1
ROBERSON WINFIELD S	MAJ	0-0010613	0736	1
ROBERTS BRUCE H	COL	0-0004001	1041	2
ROBERTS CECIL E	COL	0-0035232	1266	1
ROBERTS CLARENCE F	COL	0-0044612	0868	1
ROBERTS EDWIN H	B G	0-0006421	0350	1
ROBERTS ELEANOR W	MAJ	L-0000270	0167	1
ROBERTS FRANK N	M G	0-0012734	1157	2
ROBERTS FRANK W	COL	0-0039830	0962	1
ROBERTS HAYDN P	COL	0-0014678	0145	2
ROBERTS HENRY G	LTC	0-0033733	0867	1
ROBERTS HEYWARD B	LTC	0-0015544	0847	1
ROBERTS JAMES F	COL	0-0021920	0561	1
ROBERTS JOHN E	LTC	0-0057833	0865	1
ROBERTS LITTLETON	COL	0-0028991	0959	2
ROBERTS NATHAN J	B G	0-0024345	1163	1
ROBERTS PERRY J	LTC	0-0044208	0368	1
ROBERTS ROBERT V	LTC	0-0035584	0661	1
ROBERTS ROY F	COL	0-0029301	0762	1
ROBERTS SAMUEL H	LTC	0-0035553	0668	1
ROBERTS THOMAS D	COL	0-0015529	0754	1
ROBERTS WILLIAM E	COL	0-0030493	0865	1
ROBERTS WILLIAM H	COL	0-0010051	1146	2
ROBERTS WILLIAM W	LTC	0-0030264	0962	1
ROBERTSON ALAN R	CPT	OF-0103589	0268	2
ROBERTSON CHARLES E	COL	0-0051756	0566	1
ROBERTSON CLARON A	LTC	0-0057107	0868	1
ROBERTSON DANIEL S	COL	0-0009484	1046	2
ROBERTSON DAVID H	LTC	0-0080176	0665	1
ROBERTSON EMANUEL M	LTC	0-0030149	0262	1
ROBERTSON HARRY J	LTC	0-0023683	0660	1
ROBERTSON JACK L	LTC	0-0060716	0768	1
ROBERTSON JAMES C	COL	0-0081185	0568	2
ROBERTSON KENNETH C	COL	0-0031845	0167	2
ROBERTSON ROBERT R	COL	0-0051357	1162	1
ROBERTSON STERLING C	MAJ	0-0009608	0439	2
ROBERTSON SUE H	MAJ	N-0001244	0165	1
ROBERTSON WILLIAM W	COL	0-0014827	0348	1
ROBICHAUX DOUGLAS B	LTC	0-0080486	0765	1
ROBIDEAUX ROBERT J	LTC	0-0032066	0566	2
ROBINETT PAUL MC D	B G	0-0010258	0846	2
ROBINETTE A INEZ	MAJ	N-0000453	0561	1
ROBINETTE ALBERT L	LTC	0-0021892	0261	1
ROBINSON ALBERT H	COL	0-0018924	1057	1
ROBINSON ARIN F JR	MAJ	0-0058793	0464	1
ROBINSON BERNARD L	M G	0-0012652	1057	1
ROBINSON BERNARD L	LTC	0-0065325	0668	1

NAME	GRADE	SVC NO	DATE RET MO YR	RET CODE
ROBINSON CARL	MAJ	0-0012298	0837	2
ROBINSON CHARLES A	COL	0-0008280	1047	1
ROBINSON DAYTON L	COL	0-0011084	0346	2
ROBINSON DELIA D	MAJ	L-0000278	0766	2
ROBINSON EDWARD A	LTC	0-0037735	1264	1
ROBINSON EDWARD N	CW4	W-0906970	1061	1
ROBINSON ELISHA M JR	LTC	0-0029541	0767	1
ROBINSON EUGENE	MAJ	0-0013984	0720	2
ROBINSON GEORGE B	LTC	0-0023428	0758	2
ROBINSON HOWARD F	LTC	0-0063077	0267	1
ROBINSON JAMES H	COL	0-0028988	0558	1
ROBINSON JAMES R	LTC	0-0050588	0768	1
ROBINSON JODA L	LTC	0-0051857	0365	1
ROBINSON JOHN L	MAJ	0-0023929	0951	2
ROBINSON JOHN N	B G	0-0003870	0349	1
ROBINSON JOHN S	LTC	0-0038948	1266	2
ROBINSON JOSEPH S	B G	0-0011195	0850	1
ROBINSON JOSEPH W	LTC	0-0086692	0965	1
ROBINSON LEONARD G	COL	0-0031448	0766	1
ROBINSON PAUL I	M G	0-0017802	0858	1
ROBINSON RALPH D	CW4	W-0903746	0966	1
ROBINSON RAOUL L	CW4	W-0903747	1065	1
ROBINSON ROBERT B	LTC	0-0026531	0964	1
ROBINSON RUTH A	COL	J-0000045	0265	1
ROBINSON SHAYER O L	COL	0-0028902	0457	1
ROBINSON THOMAS	COL	0-0015395	0151	1
ROBINSON VICTOR L	COL	0-0012019	1146	1
ROBINSON WARREN A	COL	0-0015292	0854	1
ROBISON J SHELBURN	LTC	0-0006727	0530	2
ROBITSHEK IRVING H	LTC	0-0082087	0268	1
ROBLES FRANCIS P	COL	0-0050105	0868	2
ROBLES ORRYL S	COL	0-0007590	1143	2
ROBSON ERNESTINE	MAJ	L-0000245	1162	1
ROCHFORD ALLAN B	COL	0-0042876	1266	1
ROCHFORD CHARLES E	COL	0-0030307	0564	1
ROCK FAIRFIELD	LTC	0-0079053	0664	2
ROCKAFELLOW L HOYT	COL	0-0012369	0346	2
ROCKSTROH HENRY J	LTC	0-0056942	0864	1
ROCKWOOD CHARLES A	LTC	0-0037293	0263	1
RODDEN ROBERT M	LTC	0-0026588	0764	1
RODDY JOHN V	COL	0-0021356	0363	1
RODEHEFFER ALLEN W	LTC	0-0024602	0965	1
RODEMAN CHARLOTTE	LTC	N-0000601	0763	1
RODER CHARLES C	COL	0-0043664	1268	1
RODGERS ELTON C	MAJ	0-0065100	1064	1
RODGERS HENRY H	COL	0-0029992	0863	1
RODGERS JOHN A	COL	0-0009799	0246	1
RODGERS JOHN W	COL	0-0042764	1163	1
RODGERS LOUIE N	LTC	0-0035941	0862	2
RODGERS ROBERT C	COL	0-0029540	0461	1
RODGERS THOMAS A	COL	0-0044010	0967	1
RODGERS THOMAS F	LTC	0-0079055	0868	1
RODGERS THOMAS R	LTC	0-0043529	0766	1
RODGERS WILLIAM M	B G	0-0039812	0263	1
RODMAN FRAZER W	COL	0-0038741	0159	1
RODNEY DORSEY R	COL	0-0001817	0642	1
RODRIGUEZ MODESTO E	COL	0-0004845	0348	1
ROE THEODORE W	LTC	0-0052205	1066	1
ROE WILLIAM W JR	COL	0-0019675	0861	1
ROEBUCK THOMAS W	CPT	0-0075776	0663	2
ROEHM JOHN F	COL	0-0007218	0753	1
ROELOFS THOMAS B	COL	0-0038764	0464	1
ROEMER WILLIAM A	COL	0-0037665	0868	1
ROERIG RICHARD N	COL	0-0043180	0168	1
ROESSER JOSEPH C	LTC	0-0073481	0268	1
ROFFE A MORRELL	COL	0-0004654	1150	1
ROGERS BENTON M	LTC	0-0059020	0764	1
ROGERS CARMON A	COL	0-0019952	0657	1
ROGERS CHARLES I	MAJ	0-0036778	0562	1
ROGERS CHARLES R	LTC	0-0024967	1062	1
ROGERS DAVID B JR	LTC	0-0059341	0768	1
ROGERS DIXON C	LTC	0-0026595	0765	1
ROGERS FRED B	COL	0-0006100	0439	1
ROGERS GEORGE D	COL	0-0012409	0654	1
ROGERS GEORGE F	COL	0-0029544	0461	1

NAME	GRADE	SVC NO	DATE RET MO YR	RET CODE
ROGERS GLENN F	COL	0-0018366	0761	1
ROGERS HARRY L III	LTC	0-0026578	0466	2
ROGERS JAMES L	COL	0-0022076	0865	1
ROGERS JAMES T	COL	0-0058074	0764	2
ROGERS JESSE A JR	COL	0-0008242	0450	1
ROGERS JOHN E	COL	0-0041505	0558	1
ROGERS JOSEPH J	COL	0-0081188	1167	1
ROGERS LLOYD R	CPT	0-0006799	1030	1
ROGERS O B	LTC	0-0080322	0868	1
ROGERS PLEAS B	B G	0-0005170	0148	1
ROGERS POOLE	LTC	0-0079971	0967	1
ROGERS RALPH M	COL	0-0022943	0866	1
ROGERS RALPH W	COL	0-0012554	0248	1
ROGERS RICHARD	WO1	W-0901489	0139	2
ROGERS THEDA W	MAJ	N-0000444	0661	1
ROGERS WALTER C	MAJ	0-0005149	0833	2
ROGERS WARREN	LTC	0-0025913	0465	1
ROGERS WILLIAM C	COL	0-0031602	0967	1
ROHDE OTTO J	COL	0-0019725	0864	1
ROHR URBAN E	LTC	0-0038996	0164	1
ROJO FERNANDO S	LTC	0-0084833	0966	1
ROLAK BRUNO J	LTC	0-0046725	0862	1
ROLEY RONALD J	LTC	0-0079057	0868	1
ROLFE DOROTHY S	2LT	M-0000623	1144	1
ROLFE ONSLOW S	B G	0-0008637	0959	1
ROLLE NORMAN B	COL	0-0079715	0868	1
ROLLER HARRY G	COL	0-0018597	0757	1
ROLPH HERBERT F	LTC	0-0032091	0167	1
ROMAIN COLEMAN	COL	0-0028783	1054	1
ROMANS WARREN L	COL	0-0039150	0467	1
ROMEO NINA M	MAJ	N-0001633	1263	1
ROMINE AUBREY L	LTC	0-0061402	0863	1
ROMINE BERNADETTE	MAJ	N-0001893	0660	1
ROMLEIN JOHN W	COL	0-0020197	0966	1
RONAN CHARLES E	LTC	0-0043750	0367	1
RONDEPIERRE JEAN R	LTC	0-0061633	0868	1
ROOD JOHN W	COL	0-0052092	0266	1
ROOKER ROBERT L	MAJ	0-0026155	0662	1
ROOKER ROBERT L	CW4	W-0904190	1267	1
ROOKS DAVID L	LTC	0-0063391	0366	1
ROOKS LOWELL W	M G	0-0005602	1045	2
ROONEY FRANCIS M	LTC	0-0023147	0960	1
ROONEY THOMAS O	COL	0-0042454	1064	1
ROONEY WILLIAM S	LTC	0-0060892	0965	1
ROOS PHYLLIS	MAJ	L-0000509	0567	1
ROOS WILLIAM F	COL	0-0025982	0968	1
ROOSMA JOHN S	COL	0-0016486	0656	1
ROOT CHARLES W	CPT	0-0059950	0265	2
ROPER DANIEL W	CW4	W-0907116	0863	1
ROPER DAVID N	LTC	0-0031507	0759	1
ROPER HARRY M	M G	0-0015176	0855	1
ROPER ROBERT L	LTC	0-0042365	0162	2
ROQUE FRANCISCO	LTC	0-0063704	1165	1
RORABAUGH JAMES R	COL	0-0021445	1166	1
RORABAUGH JOHN R	CW3	W-0906971	1066	1
RORICK ALAN G	MAJ	0-0022959	1145	2
ROSADO SATURNINO	CW4	W-0902408	1054	1
ROSALER BENNIE	CW4	W-0903750	0567	1
ROSCH PAUL J	CPT	0-0074828	0259	2
ROSCOE DAVID L	COL	0-0013985	0720	2
ROSE BUEL T	COL	0-0029592	0861	1
ROSE CHARLES E	LTC	0-0035066	0461	2
ROSE MING	LTC	0-0042873	1064	1
ROSE PETER W	LTC	0-0069781	0868	1
ROSE RALPH E	LTC	0-0032079	0667	1
ROSE ROBERT R	CW3	W-0903751	0865	2
ROSE WALTER A	COL	0-0008744	0350	2
ROSE WILLIAM C	M G	0-0003155	1046	1
ROSEBAUM DWIGHT A	COL	0-0012752	0854	1
ROSELL FRED E JR	LTC	0-0024682	0761	1
ROSEN MILTON L	COL	0-0019814	0255	1
ROSENBERG KERMIT H	LTC	0-0052487	0668	1
ROSENBERG LYLE	COL	0-0015127	0846	2
ROSENGREN WALTER J	COL	0-0041392	0955	1
ROSENGREN WARREN J	MAJ	0-0062158	1055	2

NAME	GRADE	SVC NO	DATE RET MO YR	RET CODE
ROSENTHAL SADYE M	LTC	N-0000497	0748	2
ROSHTO LAWRENCE E	LTC	0-0099720	0868	1
ROSKOSKY ELSIE	MAJ	[illegible]-0010033	0554	1
ROSOFF MARTIN	LTC	0-0081191	0168	1
ROSS AARON P	LTC	0-0051794	0764	2
ROSS DAVID M N	LTC	0-0010355	0644	1
ROSS DOUGLAS M	LTC	0-0080178	0363	1
ROSS EDNA E	COL	N-0000194	0168	1
ROSS ESLIE N	CPT	0-0007016	0524	2
ROSS FRANK S	M G	0-0010213	0946	2
ROSS FRANZ H SR	COL	0-0029871	0263	1
ROSS FRED L	COL	0-0030760	0766	1
ROSS GLENN A	COL	0-0005208	1147	2
ROSS GLENN A	COL	0-0006229	1047	2
ROSS HEZEKIA J JR	LTC	0-0034112	0867	1
ROSS JAMES D	COL	0-0052442	0361	2
ROSS JOHN R JR	MAJ	0-0025688	0664	1
ROSS MARGARET C	MAJ	N-0002129	0260	1
ROSS MARY E	MAJ	N-0001947	0360	1
ROSS RALPH N	COL	0-0023315	0868	1
ROSS RAYMOND H	LTC	0-0036412	0559	1
ROSS RICHARD L	MAJ	0-0062901	0352	2
ROSS ROBERT C	COL	0-0016467	0354	2
ROSS ROSE F	MAJ	L-0000212	0959	2
ROSS THOMAS P	COL	0-0040082	0267	1
ROSS WILLIAM A	LTC	0-0039003	1067	1
ROSS WILLIAM E	LTC	0-0050151	0666	1
ROSS WILLIAM E	LTC	0-0080324	0866	1
ROSS WINFRED A	COL	0-0021395	0757	1
ROSSELL JOHN F JR	LTC	0-0024011	0262	1
ROSSER FRANCIS C	MAJ	0-0061130	1162	1
ROSSO FRANK P	LTC	0-0038820	0164	2
ROSTENBERG LEO O	COL	0-0029119	0655	2
ROTH ALMON R	LTC	0-0027355	0167	1
ROTH ANDREW W	COL	0-0028980	0458	1
ROTH ARTHUR	COL	0-0016874	0757	1
ROTH HENRY D	COL	0-0029329	0864	1
ROTH IRVING D	COL	0-0019708	0859	1
ROTH LOREN W	LTC	0-0079451	0368	2
ROTH LOUIS E	COL	0-0043387	0661	1
ROTH WENZEL C	LTC	0-0051392	0559	1
ROTHARMEL SAMUEL B	LTC	0-0051929	0964	1
ROTHBARD LEONARD	LTC	0-0054051	1263	1
ROTHERMICH ALBERT E	COL	0-0011164	0647	2
ROTHGEB CLARENCE F	COL	0-0015612	0654	1
ROTHROCK EVELYN A	MAJ	L-0000225	0258	2
ROTHSCHILD J H	B G	0-0018077	1162	1
ROTHWELL FRANCIS M	LTC	0-0064332	0968	1
ROTHWELL FRANKLIN G	COL	0-0019176	0763	1
ROTON WILLIAM F	COL	0-0023961	0967	1
ROTTSTEDT VERNON R	COL	0-0053185	0868	1
ROUGE LEON J D	COL	0-0020882	0965	1
ROUILLARD CHESTER F	LTC	0-0038598	0953	1
ROUND ROSWELL F	COL	0-0014780	0751	1
ROUNDS RAYMOND B	COL	0-0079974	0768	1
ROUNTRE BILLY J	1LT	0-0059327	0753	2
ROUNTREE DENTON C	LTC	0-0033797	0466	1
ROURKE RITA V	LTC	N-0000677	0466	2
ROUSEK CHARLES	COL	0-0044030	1065	1
ROUSSEAU JOSEPH H JR	COL	0-0012763	0555	1
ROUSSEAU VINCENT P	MAJ	0-0014394	1119	2
ROUTH CLARENCE F	LTC	0-0039875	0262	1
ROUTH DAVID B	COL	0-0019437	0862	2
ROUTHEAU EDWARD A	COL	0-0012621	0753	1
ROUTLEDGE RODHAM C	LTC	0-0040143	1165	2
ROVEGNO EUGENE S	LTC	0-0084487	0667	1
ROW LATHE B	COL	0-0003601	0647	1
ROWAN CHARLES A	COL	0-0042619	0964	1
ROWAN EDMOND M	COL	0-0018841	0562	1
ROWAN HUGH W	B G	0-0009371	0753	1
ROWAN JOHN V	COL	0-0007787	0544	1
ROWAN ROBERT L	COL	0-0031727	0767	1
ROWE GERALD W	COL	0-0035810	0767	1
ROWE GUY I	B G	0-0002754	0846	2
ROWE HAROLD C	COL	0-0029413	0560	1

NAME	GRADE	SVC NO	DATE RET MO YR	RET CODE
ROWE JOHN A	LTC	0-0008768	0-29	2
ROWLAND ARTHUR E	COL	0-0003245	0246	2
ROWLAND CHESTER A	COL	0-0015924	0754	1
ROWLAND GARLAND T	COL	0-0010245	1045	2
ROWLAND HAMPTON JR	LTC	0-0038512	0868	1
ROWLAND HENRY C JR	COL	0-0020940	1167	1
ROWLEY HOBART L	LTC	0-0081192	0868	1
ROXBURY EDWARD J JR	LTC	0-0028075	0766	1
ROY ALFRED J	CW4	W-0902683	0361	1
ROY CHRISTINE	MAJ	N-0001196	0651	2
ROY HELEN M	MAJ	L-0000092	0361	1
ROY JAMES W	COL	0-0023762	0763	1
ROY PAUL A	COL	0-0018153	0760	1
ROY THOMAS H	CW4	W-0903756	0258	1
ROYAL EVERETT C	LTC	0-0058584	1068	1
ROYALL HENRY E	COL	0-0018242	1047	2
ROYALS WALTER C	COL	0-0010991	1048	2
ROYCE CHARLES H	B G	0-0015769	1155	2
ROYCE PHILIP M	COL	0-0021814	0661	1
ROYSDON DORRANCE S	COL	0-0011135	0654	2
ROYSE FRANK	COL	0-0004828	1145	2
ROYSTER KATHRYN J	LTC	L-0000105	1067	1
ROZAMUS WALTER J	COL	0-0032892	1064	1
ROZYCKI ANNA	MAJ	N-0000835	0758	2
RUBACK JOHN C	MAJ	0-0072643	0765	1
RUBENSTEIN SEYMOUR	COL	0-0024695	1065	1
RUBIN HARVEY L	COL	0-0052006	1068	2
RUBIN MORTON A	COL	0-0039962	0565	1
RUBIN SAMUEL	COL	0-0014819	1145	2
RUBY DONALD T	COL	0-0040151	0766	1
RUBY JACK W	LTC	0-0045871	1263	1
RUCKER CHOICE R	COL	0-0031610	0865	1
RUDBERG AGNES J	MAJ	R-0010106	1166	1
RUDD DOROTHY T	MAJ	L-0000216	0556	1
RUDDLE NORMAN H	2LT	0-0063612	0453	2
RUDDY JOHN M	COL	0-0041426	0756	2
RUDE WALTER A	COL	0-0018732	0462	1
RUDELIUS ERNEST A	COL	0-0007045	0753	1
RUDISILL JOHN W	LTC	0-0031128	0767	1
RUDNICK JAMES J	1LT	0-0092849	0264	2
RUDOLPH JACK W	COL	0-0019135	0653	1
RUEDENAUER GEORGE A	CW4	W-0903758	0865	2
RUFFNER CLARK L	GEN	0-0015968	1162	1
RUFFNER DAVID L	M G	0-0006997	0653	2
RUGE HERBERT A	CW3	W-0903759	0665	1
RUGGABER JOHN C	COL	0-0028943	1057	1
RUGGLES JOHN F	M G	0-0018596	0866	1
RUHLEN GEORGE	COL	0-0002312	0-44	1
RULE DONALD O	LTC	0-0015611	0429	2
RULE MAX M	LTC	0-0041204	0865	1
RUMAGGI LOUIS J	M G	0-0014900	0659	1
RUMBOUGH WILLIAM S	M G	0-0005496	0546	1
RUMNEY MASON P JR	LTC	0-0028024	0766	1
RUMSEY IVAN C	COL	0-0019774	0963	1
RUND HENRY M	COL	0-0038606	0356	1
RUNDELL FRANCIS E	COL	0-0011228	0748	1
RUNDELL LILLA B	MAJ	N-0002392	0462	1
RUNDLE EDWARD P	CW3	W-0903760	0760	1
RUNFT HAROLD W	LTC	0-0063046	0666	1
RUNNELS JOHNNIE L	LTC	0-0069551	1068	2
RUPERT EVERETT D	CW4	W-0901871	1158	1
RUPLE CHARLES D	LTC	0-0085659	0266	1
RUPP ROBERT D	COL	0-0042103	1164	1
RUPPERT JOHN P	LTC	0-0062273	0864	1
RUSCHMEYER GERALD F	LTC	0-0062229	0768	2
RUSEK EDWARD A	LTC	0-0064283	0968	1
RUSH DONALD P	LTC	0-0062232	0968	1
RUSH PETER S	COL	0-0056793	0261	1
RUSH ROBERT I	LTC	0-0028660	0766	1
RUSHING WILLIAM J	COL	0-0040391	0368	1
RUSS SAM W	COL	0-0041555	0159	1
RUSSEL EVELYN L	MAJ	N-0000661	0463	1
RUSSELL ALBERT	CW4	W-0902378	1054	1
RUSSELL CECIL R	LTC	0-0036600	0964	1
RUSSELL CLYDE M	LTC	0-0055518	0865	1

NAME	GRADE	SVC NO	DATE RET MO YR	RET CODE
RUSSELL CLYDE R	COL	0-0032478	0168	1
RUSSELL DAN C	COL	0-0020730	0967	1
RUSSELL DEMPSEY R	LTC	0-0087905	1267	1
RUSSELL EBER O	COL	0-0029591	0861	1
RUSSELL GEORGE B	COL	0-0051913	1264	1
RUSSELL GEORGE C JR	LTC	0-0059877	0865	1
RUSSELL GEORGE R	COL	0-0041827	0161	1
RUSSELL JAMES G	LTC	0-0032580	0359	1
RUSSELL JOHN A	LTC	0-0007793	0542	2
RUSSELL JOHN T	LTC	0-0025721	0764	1
RUSSELL JOSEPH P	COL	0-0018919	0659	2
RUSSELL KATHERINE	MAJ	N-0002416	0164	1
RUSSELL LESTER F	LTC	0-0081195	0167	1
RUSSELL MELVIN R	COL	0-0021097	0868	1
RUSSELL RANDOLPH	COL	0-0006890	0847	1
RUSSELL ROBERT C	LTC	0-0024557	0347	2
RUSSELL ROGER D	LTC	0-0022797	1062	2
RUSSELL ROGER L JR	MAJ	0-0024689	0863	1
RUSSELL WALTER B JR	LTC	0-0063994	1066	2
RUSSELL WILLIAM I	COL	0-0042010	0262	1
RUSSEY JOHN W	COL	0-0007464	0753	1
RUSSI GILBERT C	COL	0-0033264	1266	1
RUSSO JEAN G	MAJ	N-0002159	0862	1
RUST CHARLES E	B G	0-0029965	0463	1
RUST JOHN H	COL	0-0020060	1158	1
RUST WILLIAM E JR	CPT	0-0025056	0244	2
RUSTEBERG EDWIN	COL	0-0019542	0864	1
RUSTEMEYER JOSEPH H	COL	0-0006056	0652	2
RUSTIGIAN BARJ A	COL	0-0031068	0566	1
RUTH HAROLD S	COL	0-0012481	0854	1
RUTHER WILLIAM J	CW3	W-0903761	0361	1
RUTHERFORD ALLAN	COL	0-0002071	0936	1
RUTHERFORD BENJAMIN	LTC	0-0080180	0866	1
RUTHERFORD DORSEY J	COL	0-0009037	0146	2
RUTHERFORD ROBERT D	LTC	0-0034355	0568	1
RUTHERMAN NILA P	MAJ	N-0000538	0451	1
RUTLEDGE BEN A	COL	0-0049950	0166	1
RUTLEDGE HUGH M	LTC	0-0032201	0667	1
RUTLEDGE PAUL W	M G	0-0007289	0456	1
RUTTE LOUIS B	COL	0-0015928	0555	1
RUTTE ROLAND J	LTC	0-0019977	0661	1
RUTTEN PAUL G	COL	0-0007871	1047	2
RUTTER WARREN C	COL	0-0012628	0949	2
RUWET VINCENT L	COL	0-0024524	1066	1
RUZEK CHARLES V JR	COL	0-0020937	1267	1
RYAN ALBERT J	COL	0-0040631	0868	1
RYAN CORNELIUS	M G	0-0007375	0757	2
RYAN EDWARD A	COL	0-0042795	1165	1
RYAN FRANCIS J	LTC	0-0056957	0964	1
RYAN GERALD J	CW3	W-0906973	0556	1
RYAN HELEN E	CW3	V-0904319	1163	1
RYAN JAMES H	CW3	W-0903763	0764	1
RYAN JOHN G	CW3	W-0904191	1066	1
RYAN JOHN L JR	LTG	0-0016451	0863	1
RYAN JOHN L JR	LTC	0-0030234	0862	1
RYAN JOSEPH S	LTC	0-0032300	0651	2
RYAN LEWIS S	COL	0-0001239	0639	1
RYAN PATRICK J	M G	0-0017363	1058	1
RYAN PHILLIP W	LTC	0-0033328	0560	1
RYAN THOMAS A	COL	0-0051795	1166	2
RYAN WILLIAM F	B G	0-0019142	0863	1
RYAN WILLIAM J	LTC	0-0009506	0542	1
RYCKAERT ELMER B	LTC	0-0079978	0662	1
RYCZEK STANISLAUS	COL	0-0019344	0644	2
RYDEN ETTA L	LTC	N-0002422	0867	1
RYDER WILLIAM T	B G	0-0020298	0566	1
RYERSON IVAN L	CW4	W-0903766	0257	1
RYKER DON W	MAJ	0-0025349	0746	2
RYLANDER CARL M	COL	0-0017337	0654	2
RYNEARSON CHARLES B	COL	0-0019722	0863	1
RYNESKA JOSEPH F	COL	0-0032017	0566	1
SAAR OTTO T	COL	0-0042033	0662	1
SABAT JULIANNA	MAJ	N-0001874	0558	1
SABATELLI THOMAS A	LTC	0-0051525	0862	1
SABINE JOHN S	COL	0-0039860	1263	1
SABINI DOMINIC J	B G	0-0005719	1046	2
SABOLYK ROBERT	COL	0-0035475	0867	1
SACERDOTE SYDNEY E	COL	0-0038920	0667	1
SACHS EDWARD I	COL	0-0018185	0760	1
SACHS MARTHA S	LTC	L-0000317	0567	1
SACKVILLE WILLIAM	COL	0-0005276	1151	1
SADLER PERCY L	B G	0-0007408	1146	1
SADLER ROBERT E	COL	0-0036522	0768	1
SAENZ RALPH	COL	0-0038762	0364	1
SAFER JOSEPH	LTC	0-0079980	0262	1
SAFFOLD EUGENE	COL	0-0043660	1266	1
SAFFORD HERMAN F	B G	0-0006692	0346	1
SAGER FLOYD C	COL	0-0009479	0548	2
SAHOLSKY BOLICK A	COL	0-0031331	0866	1
SAINE HAROLD J	LTC	0-0026291	0764	1
SAKOWSKI JOHN N	CPT	0-0061483	0954	2
SALADA REUBEN N	LTC	0-0032261	0667	1
SALGADO PETER P	COL	0-0005032	0753	1
SALING JAMES T	LTC	0-0037553	0767	1
SALISBURY HELEN M	MAJ	N-0000978	1062	2
SALISBURY HOWARD G	COL	0-0043510	0464	1
SALLEE ERNEST A	COL	0-0041523	0758	1
SALLEE JOHN T	COL	0-0005948	0246	2
SALLEY COLVIN W	COL	0-0029205	0661	1
SALLEY HENRY M	COL	0-0041430	0956	1
SALMON HENRY S JR	LTC	0-0079981	0965	1
SALMON JOHN D	COL	0-0015937	0854	1
SALTHOUSE WIRT C	LTC	0-0079982	0767	1
SALYER EVERETT G	LTC	0-0036107	0367	1
SALYER JOHN M	COL	0-0023570	0859	1
SALYERDS JAMES H	CW3	W-0903768	0562	1
SALZMAN CHARLES N	LTC	0-0079067	0867	1
SAMES HARRY B	COL	0-0042167	0463	1
SAMDUCE JAMES A	COL	0-0012666	0753	2
SAMDUCE WELLINGTON	COL	0-0015562	0954	1
SAMPLE CHARLES W	LTC	0-0023437	0859	1
SAMPLE JAMES C	LTC	0-0079068	0768	1
SAMPSON GEORGE P	M G	0-0042926	0265	1
SAMPSON JOHN H JR	COL	0-0015974	0854	1
SAMS CRAWFORD F	B G	0-0018261	0755	1
SAMS GERALD A	COL	0-0041931	0464	1
SAMS JAMES D	COL	0-0018381	1060	1
SAMS JAMES E	COL	0-0022776	0462	1
SAMS JEAN P	COL	0-0043293	1064	1
SAMS THOMAS E	COL	0-0028989	0658	1
SAMSON CHARLES P	COL	0-0022204	1265	1
SAMUEL ALLEN T JR	LTC	0-0040049	0661	1
SAMUELS ANDREW JR	COL	0-0017552	0659	1
SANDBERG WILMA K	LTC	N-0000248	0463	1
SANDEN JAMES V	COL	0-0024213	1268	1
SANDER ARNOLD R C	COL	0-0007628	0751	2
SANDERS ALLEN W JR	COL	0-0025305	0764	1
SANDERS BEN L	LTC	0-0063008	0867	1
SANDERS DONALD A	COL	0-0051489	0364	1
SANDERS EDGAR S	LTC	0-0052359	0461	1
SANDERS HENRY I	LTC	0-0042096	1060	1
SANDERS HORACE L	B G	0-0019445	0963	1
SANDERS JAMES R	WO1	W-0904192	0450	1
SANDERS LEO F	LTC	0-0089285	0665	1
SANDERS PAUL	MAJ	0-0059953	0965	1
SANDERS PAUL F	LTC	0-0053770	0866	1
SANDERS ROBERT W	LTC	0-0044296	1062	1
SANDERS SARAH L	MAJ	L-0000269	0165	1
SANDERS VERNON K	LTC	0-0025476	0562	1
SANDERS WALTER C	COL	0-0051246	0961	1
SANDERS WILBURN L	LTC	0-0084417	1167	1
SANDERS WILLIAM D JR	LTC	0-0081201	0267	1
SANDERS WILTON L	COL	0-0038794	1160	1
SANDERSON HELEN F	MAJ	N-0000220	0763	1
SANDERSON HENRY E	COL	0-0012352	0550	1
SANDERSON JOHN M	COL	0-0006710	0347	2
SANDIFER SAMUEL H	COL	0-0025158	0265	1
SANDIN RAMON A	COL	0-0039884	1263	2
SANDKAUT LOUIS G	MAJ	0-0057922	1265	1
SANDLIN JOSEPH C	COL	0-0031752	0468	2
SANDLIN TROY K	CW2	W-0902160	0945	2
SANDO RAYMOND W	COL	0-0066090	0868	2
SANDS JOSEPH N	LTC	0-0032957	0464	1
SANDS SIDNEY A	CPT	0-0006898	1022	2
SANDS THOMAS J	M G	0-0017521	0466	1
SANDUSKY RICHARD M	COL	0-0008291	0649	1
SANELLI ALFRED A	LTC	0-0060212	0765	1
SANFORD ARTHUR L JR	COL	0-0031572	0566	1
SANFORD CHARLES A	COL	0-0032857	0968	1
SANFORD GEORGE A	COL	0-0003162	1146	1
SANFORD HENRY R	COL	0-0038827	0364	1
SANFORD KENNETH H	1LT	0-0011930	0928	2
SANFORD TEDDY H	M G	0-0029893	0267	1
SANKEY THEODORE R	LTC	0-0070496	0968	1
SANKEY WILLIAM E	COL	0-0010853	0750	1
SANTORA BERT	LTC	0-0031758	0564	1
SANTOS MELECIO M	LTC	0-0014683	0753	1
SAPANOS JOHN F	CW4	W-0906978	0868	1
SAPIAGBOSCH T A	COL	0-0009805	0753	1
SAPP 3RD OSCAR L	MAJ	0-0068400	0458	2
SAR CECILIA M	LTC	N-0001876	0761	1
SARAZEN JOHN J	CPT	0-0057582	1162	1
SARGENT CHESTER E	COL	0-0010277	0150	1
SARGENT ELLWOOD W	COL	0-0039617	0559	1
SARGENT FRANK H	LTC	0-0048462	0462	2
SARGENT LOIS H	MAJ	J-0000063	0767	1
SARKESIAN SAM C	LTC	0-0064434	1068	1
SARNECKI FLORIAN P	CW4	W-0904193	1163	2
SASSE FRANCIS M	COL	0-0029807	1262	2
SATHER PETER JR	COL	0-0015867	0450	1
SATTEM IVAN	MAJ	0-0022935	0544	2
SATTERFIELD RUTH P	COL	N-0002168	0668	1
SATTERTHWAITE R W	LTC	0-0051176	1053	2
SATTERWHITE SEYMOUR	COL	0-0031431	0167	1
SAUER ANNA M	CW3	V-0921330	0465	1
SAUER EDWARD F	COL	0-0050912	1053	1
SAUER JAMES H	CW2	W-0902189	0250	1
SAUL FRANCIS W	CPT	0-0026094	1146	2
SAUL LESLIE T	MAJ	0-0004442	0-33	2
SAULNIER DOROTHY N	LTC	N-0000249	0161	1
SAULNIER STANLEY G	COL	0-0005826	0751	2
SAUNDERS CLARENCE H	CW3	W-0903772	0857	1
SAUNDERS EDWIN O	COL	0-0001530	1141	1
SAUNDERS OSWALD H	COL	0-0002915	1048	1
SAUNDERS WILLIAM S	COL	0-0031737	0668	2
SAUREL BENJAMIN W	COL	0-0042482	1264	1
SAUSER ARTHUR T	COL	0-0021379	0461	1
SAUTER IRENE M	LTC	N-0000388	0164	1
SAVACOOL EDWIN F	CW4	W-0901980	0654	1
SAVAGE LEONTINA M	MAJ	N-0002440	0466	1
SAVAGE MARY E	MAJ	L-0000052	0259	1
SAVAGE PAUL L	LTC	0-0058589	0867	1
SAVAN JULES	LTC	0-0080488	1064	1
SAWBRIDGE BEN M	M G	0-0005715	0746	1
SAWICKI STANLEY	COL	0-0018698	0762	1
SAWICKI STANLEY J	COL	0-0040215	0468	2
SAWYER ALICE V	MAJ	L-0000132	1066	1
SAWYER BICKFORD E	M G	0-0008349	0855	1
SAWYER EDWARD W	M G	0-0019918	0864	1
SAWYER HAROLD G	CW4	W-0906979	0259	1
SAWYER JOHN A	COL	0-0017177	0555	2
SAWYER TED I	COL	0-0021133	0868	1
SAX SAMUEL E	COL	0-0051267	0662	1
SAXE ROBERT K	COL	0-0043790	0965	1
SAXON MARTHA E	MAJ	L-0000272	1062	1
SAYLER HENRY B	M G	0-0003800	1149	1
SAYLOR PAUL	LTC	0-0084063	0966	1
SAYLORS JOHN H	COL	0-0031638	0967	1
SAYRE EDWIN M	COL	0-0033220	0468	1
SCALAN ENOCH J	LTC	0-0016240	0753	1
SCALES JOSEPH W	LTC	0-0079989	1165	1
SCAMEHORN RICHARD D	LTC	0-0061520	1068	1
SCANDRETT WILLIAM	COL	0-0023448	1165	2
SCANLON JOHN H	LTC	0-0033142	1061	1
SCANNON ANTHONY J	COL	0-0032393	1163	1
SCARBOROUGH LAWRENCE	COL	0-0051323	0862	1
SCARBOROUGH R F	COL	0-0041504	0358	1
SCARPITTA ANTHONY	LTC	0-0037519	0161	2
SCHABACKER GEORGE M	CPT	0-0064494	0457	2
SCHADE HOWARD G	LTC	0-0033311	0563	1
SCHAEFER CHESTER C	LTC	0-0042643	0463	1
SCHAEFER JOHN L	COL	0-0039999	0466	1
SCHAEFER PAUL B	LTC	0-0040562	0262	1
SCHAEFER WILLIAM H	COL	0-0015616	0454	1
SCHAFER WARREN	CW4	W-0903775	0461	1
SCHAFFER DONALD C	LTC	0-0038231	1163	1
SCHAFFER W HAROLD	COL	0-0015364	0853	2
SCHALL JOSEPH F	LTC	0-0065301	0866	1
SCHALLER REES F	MAJ	0-0037421	0658	1
SCHAMBER DEAN	COL	0-0020497	0259	1
SCHANER LOUIS T	LTC	0-0062200	0567	1
SCHANTZ OLIVER W	COL	0-0031795	1165	1
SCHANZE AUGUST E	COL	0-0015976	0854	1
SCHARDT BRUTON B	LTC	0-0026757	0764	1
SCHARF HENRY W	LTC	0-0040683	0862	1
SCHARRE WILLIAM F JR	LTC	0-0028085	0264	1
SCHAS WILLIAM O	COL	0-0011819	0849	1
SCHATZ JOHN P	LTC	0-0026224	1163	1
SCHAUDT ELMER M	COL	0-0051664	1165	1
SCHAUDT HOWARD P	LTC	0-0031673	0764	1
SCHAUERS CHARLES J	LTC	0-0079991	0962	1
SCHAUPP MIRIAM C	LTC	N-0000144	0962	2
SCHEEL CHARLOTTE	MAJ	N-0002445	0866	1
SCHEELE ANDREW F	COL	0-0021475	0762	1
SCHEER JAMES H	LTC	0-0037749	1264	1
SCHEIBLA HARRY D	COL	0-0010107	0547	2
SCHEID ARTHUR M	COL	0-0042812	0766	1
SCHEIDENHELM ARLENE	LTC	L-0000049	0761	1
SCHELPER ANNA K	MAJ	N-0000414	0164	1
SCHENDEL HARRY A JR	COL	0-0023526	1263	1
SCHENKEN CARLTON G	COL	0-0039609	0259	1
SCHEPP DAVID G	COL	0-0042382	0764	2
SCHERER BERNARD J	COL	0-0052147	0864	1
SCHERER HAROLD E	LTC	0-0033032	0161	2
SCHERER HARRIS F	B G	0-0012275	0854	1
SCHERER JOHN W	LTC	0-0066093	1067	1
SCHERER KARL L	COL	0-0018784	0862	1
SCHERER MARY C	LTC	N-0000026	0848	1
SCHERMERHORN JOHN G	B G	0-0020610	0767	1
SCHEUMAN WILLIAM F	COL	0-0009135	0651	2
SCHEUMANN MARCUS C	LTC	0-0066094	1268	2
SCHEURLEIN FRANK W	COL	0-0031810	0368	1
SCHEWE MARION W	B G	0-0029748	0661	1
SCHICK ROBERT	MAJ	0-0030970	0754	1
SCHIFFMAN MAURICE K	LTC	0-0031375	0561	1
SCHILD LAURA B	MAJ	N-0001652	0766	1
SCHILL GEORGE J	LTC	0-0051229	0859	1
SCHILLERSTROM MERL P	COL	0-0002638	0946	2
SCHIMMEL BERNARD H	COL	0-0079716	0667	1
SCHINDLING ROBERT C	CPT	0-0057645	0965	1
SCHINTZ THOMAS A	LTC	0-0039074	0866	1
SCHIRMER JACOB F	LTC	0-0063158	0865	1
SCHLAAK MELVIN V	COL	0-0029253	0361	1
SCHLEH WITTMER I	COL	0-0062271	1168	2
SCHLOEMER BEULAH	CPT	N-0000588	1057	1
SCHLOSBERG RICHARD T	COL	0-0010311	0748	1
SCHLOTTER WILLIAM D	COL	0-0041495	0258	1
SCHMELZ RUSSELL W	COL	0-0029353	1159	1
SCHMELZER JOHN F	COL	0-0019270	0761	1
SCHMELZLE CORNELIUS	COL	0-0031547	0767	1
SCHMICK PETER	B G	0-0018395	0161	1
SCHMID ELDON W	COL	0-0033627	0167	1
SCHMID HERBERT W	COL	0-0007907	0747	2
SCHMID WILLIAM K	LTC	0-0083620	0567	1
SCHMIDT ALVINE L	MAJ	N-0000039	0650	1
SCHMIDT GLEN L	COL	0-0028935	0955	2
SCHMIDT HOWARD H	LTC	0-0071960	0167	2
SCHMIDT HUGH F	LTC	0-0079992	0567	1
SCHMIDT JAMES K	COL	0-0021335	0868	1
SCHMIDT JOSEPH J JR	COL	0-0024672	0664	1

UNITED STATES ARMY RETIRED LIST

NAME	GRADE	SVC NO	DATE RET MO YR	RET CODE
SCHMIDT ROBERT B	LTC	0-0062966	0666	2
SCHMIDT ROBERT J	LTC	0-0041088	0865	1
SCHMIDT RONALD W	LTC	0-0080490	1062	1
SCHMIDT VIRGINIA M	MAJ	L-0000039	0857	1
SCHMIDT WALTER A	LTC	0-0038346	0866	1
SCHMIDT WILLIAM C	CW4	W-0904194	1163	1
SCHMIDT WILLIAM F	LTC	0-0042423	0862	1
SCHMIDT WILLIAM T	COL	0-0084465	0968	1
SCHMIDTKE REINHARDT	CPT	0-0019608	0242	2
SCHMITT HOWARD I	COL	0-0050987	0658	1
SCHNADER HELEN J	MAJ	N-0000834	1263	1
SCHNECKLOTH BARNEY G	LTC	0-0027756	0367	1
SCHNEIDER CARL P	LTC	0-0039688	0958	1
SCHNEIDER ELSIE E	LTC	N-0000014	0650	1
SCHNEIDER GEORGE A	CW3	W-0906981	0360	1
SCHNEIDER MILTON G	COL	0-0051639	0965	1
SCHNEIDER WALTER E	LTC	0-0038366	0764	1
SCHNEIDER WARREN J	COL	0-0056209	0968	1
SCHNEPF DONALD V	LTC	0-0050698	0167	1
SCHNITTKE RAYMOND I	COL	0-0023693	1165	1
SCHNURR HAROLD T	CW4	W-0903777	1167	1
SCHOCK ROBERT L	LTC	0-0022757	0759	2
SCHOEN WALTER A JR	LTC	0-0060737	1054	2
SCHOENBERGER SARA M	LTC	N-0000021	1047	1
SCHOENBUCHER ALBERT	COL	0-0058189	0467	1
SCHOENFELD WALTER F	COL	0-0031342	1066	1
SCHOENTHALER GEORGE	CW4	W-0903778	0754	1
SCHOLL WILLIAM P JR	COL	0-0032281	0266	1
SCHOLTZ JAMES H	CPT	0-0059349	0255	2
SCHOLZ ALLEN E	CPT	0-0064835	0159	2
SCHOMBURG AUGUST	LTG	0-0018422	0767	2
SCHONBERGER ADOLPH E	COL	0-0041461	0457	1
SCHONGALLA WILLIAM	LTC	0-0080325	1167	1
SCHONHOLZ MORRIS	COL	0-0029761	0962	1
SCHONING RICHARD H	LTC	0-0037663	0863	1
SCHOONMAKER LUCAS E	COL	0-0006687	0547	2
SCHOONOVER HARRY F	MAJ	0-0007513	0935	2
SCHOONOVER JAMES F	LTC	0-0032304	0767	1
SCHOOS ROBERT B	MAJ	0-0037375	0764	1
SCHORR DAVID P JR	B G	0-0018861	1160	1
SCHOW ROBERT A	M G	0-0012190	1058	1
SCHRADER CURTIS A	COL	0-0018760	0862	1
SCHRADER JOHN P JR	COL	0-0021818	0166	1
SCHRADER OTTO H	COL	0-0002544	1041	1
SCHRADER PAUL J	LTC	0-0062897	0864	1
SCHRANK LAWRENCE L	MAJ	0-0062861	0664	1
SCHRATZ FRANK J	CW4	W-0904195	0757	1
SCHRECENGOST H E	LTC	0-0080182	0367	1
SCHREIBER ALOUIS A	CW3	W-0903780	0857	1
SCHREIBER THOMAS S	COL	0-0057918	1167	1
SCHREIBER WILLIAM L	COL	0-0034043	1165	1
SCHREMP JOHN E	COL	0-0023709	0168	1
SCHREPEL MAURICE H	MAJ	0-0073398	0765	1
SCHRIVER ANDREW J JR	COL	0-0011132	0848	1
SCHRODER JOHN W	COL	0-0030637	0166	2
SCHRODER PETER C	COL	0-0018651	0850	1
SCHROEDER HAL L	LTC	0-0025397	0262	1
SCHROEDER JACK E	MAJ	0-0036460	1162	2
SCHROEDER NORMAN M	COL	0-0043002	0865	2
SCHROETER OSCAR A	COL	0-0051295	0462	1
SCHROY PAUL H	LTC	0-0061970	0567	1
SCHUCHMANN AMANDA	LTC	N-0002147	1064	1
SCHUCK EDWIN G	COL	0-0033606	0765	1
SCHUETZ RALPH J	COL	0-0050941	0357	1
SCHUG WILLIS E JR	LTC	0-0028039	0468	1
SCHUH MARION E	MAJ	L-0000206	1054	1
SCHUKNECHT LLOYD C	LTC	0-0081208	0564	1
SCHUKRAFT ROBERT E	COL	0-0018744	0862	1
SCHULL EDSON	COL	0-0019236	0263	1
SCHULL HERMAN W JR	COL	0-0016752	0757	1
SCHULTEN LEO E JR	COL	0-0040457	0866	1
SCHULTEN MARJORIE E	LTC	L-0000249	0866	1
SCHULTHEIS LEO J	COL	0-0029555	0561	1
SCHULTZ MARION H	COL	0-0038605	0254	1
SCHULTZ ROBERT D	MAJ	0-0079077	0567	2

NAME	GRADE	SVC NO	DATE RET MO YR	RET CODE
SCHULZ HAROLD H	COL	0-0020074	0462	1
SCHULZ ROBERT L	B G	0-0042115	0163	1
SCHUMACHER GEORGE H	COL	0-0005394	0546	2
SCHUMACHER KATHERINE	MAJ	N-0001621	1267	1
SCHUMAKER MARGARET E	2LT	R-0000304	0645	1
SCHUMM FREDERICK	LTC	0-0032479	1167	1
SCHUTT CHARLES H	LTC	0-0020107	0855	1
SCHUTZ JOHN L	COL	0-0024229	0764	1
SCHUYLER C V R	GEN	0-0014905	1059	1
SCHVANEVELDT CLYDE J	LTC	0-0084052	0865	1
SCHWAB CARL L	LTC	0-0068048	0766	1
SCHWAB JOHN S	CPT	0-0008129	0930	2
SCHWAB RAYMOND H	LTC	0-0044646	0168	1
SCHWANK BERNARD J	LTC	0-0081209	0160	1
SCHWARTZ FERDINAND	CPT	0-0059793	1062	1
SCHWARTZ PHILIP	COL	0-0014820	0753	2
SCHWARTZMAN JACK	COL	0-0040475	1167	1
SCHWARZ RICHARD A	CPT	0-0063957	0262	2
SCHWARZE HARRY M	COL	0-0010351	0652	1
SCHWARZWAELDER C A	COL	0-0006901	1146	2
SCHWATEL WILLIAM P	MAJ	0-0005819	0-34	2
SCHWEICKERT GRAHAM R	COL	0-0006787	1144	2
SCHWEIDEL KERMIT R	LTC	0-0019862	0863	1
SCHWEINLER DALE J	COL	0-0051930	1167	1
SCHWEIZER CHARLES B	COL	0-0021418	1066	1
SCHWIEN EDWIN E	B G	0-0004773	0-45	2
SCHWIND EVELYN E	MAJ	N-0002410	0463	1
SCHWING RUTH M	MAJ	N-0000099	1057	1
SCHWINGHAMER W L	COL	0-0029184	0960	2
SCIPLE CARL M	COL	0-0018745	0762	1
SCITHERS GEORGE R	COL	0-0014685	0753	1
SCOFIELD HERBERT L	M G	0-0029462	0163	1
SCOFIELD MARION E	CW4	W-0902183	0853	1
SCOFIELD NYE M	LTC	0-0023547	0661	1
SCOGGIN JAMES F JR	COL	0-0026472	0968	1
SCOLES PETER S	COL	0-0063705	0768	1
SCORDAS PAUL H	COL	0-0038914	0465	1
SCOTHORN MARION W	COL	0-0051144	1060	1
SCOTT ADRIAN	MAJ	0-0060786	1162	1
SCOTT CHARLES C	CW4	W-0906982	0464	1
SCOTT CRAIG C	MAJ	0-0063079	1163	1
SCOTT DON M	COL	0-0007023	1050	2
SCOTT DONALD H	COL	0-0029018	0958	1
SCOTT DUARD W	CW4	W-0906983	0868	1
SCOTT DWAIN L	LTC	0-0063078	1268	1
SCOTT EARL L	COL	0-0015805	0253	2
SCOTT EBBIN P JR	LTC	0-0060467	0467	1
SCOTT ECCLES H	LTC	0-0030595	0261	1
SCOTT EDMOND L	1LT	0-0083988	0461	2
SCOTT EDWARD J	CW4	W-0903783	0765	1
SCOTT EMMETT G	COL	0-0043760	0866	1
SCOTT FRANCES M	MAJ	N-0001986	1064	1
SCOTT FRANKLIN E	COL	0-0051898	0863	2
SCOTT FRED W	COL	0-0044765	1166	1
SCOTT JAMES A JR	COL	0-0020652	0767	1
SCOTT JAMES I	LTC	0-0063319	1267	1
SCOTT JAMES M	COL	0-0030822	1165	1
SCOTT JAMES M	LTC	0-0037201	0166	1
SCOTT JEAN O	COL	0-0015885	0754	2
SCOTT JESSE W	CW4	W-0904197	0459	1
SCOTT JOHN B	COL	0-0032213	0565	1
SCOTT KENNETH L	COL	0-0022121	0666	1
SCOTT LEON C	LTC	0-0018166	0946	2
SCOTT LIONEL E	COL	0-0032046	1168	1
SCOTT MARVIN R JR	COL	0-0038898	1065	1
SCOTT MAYLON E	COL	0-0008407	0953	2
SCOTT ORLANDO A	COL	0-0042187	0563	1
SCOTT OSBORNE E	LTC	0-0031188	1264	1
SCOTT PAUL T	COL	0-0030351	0165	1
SCOTT RICHARD P	B G	0-0023787	1168	1
SCOTT ROBERT S	COL	0-0043712	1066	1
SCOTT RUSSELL F JR	LTC	0-0026325	0862	1
SCOTT SAMUEL B JR	LTC	0-0036312	0764	1
SCOTT STANLEY L	M G	0-0004439	0354	1
SCOTT THOMAS M JR	LTC	0-0052544	0660	1

NAME	GRADE	SVC NO	DATE RET MO YR	RET CODE
SCOTT WALTER T	COL	0-0007340	0753	2
SCOTT WILLARD W	COL	0-0009827	1050	1
SCOTT WILLIAM J	LTC	0-0042718	0760	1
SCOTT WILLIAM R	COL	0-0001962	0642	1
SCOTT WINFIELD C	COL	0-0010624	0647	2
SCOTTGSMITH H H JR	LTC	0-0033817	0860	2
SCOVILL ELMER B	LTC	0-0035851	0966	1
SCOWDEN FRANK F	M G	0-0002863	1146	2
SCRITCHFIELD ARLYNN	CW3	W-0906984	0162	1
SCROGGS HOWARD R	COL	0-0037453	1164	1
SCROGGS JOHN P	COL	0-0021863	0766	1
SCULLEN ALLAN R	MAJ	0-0024984	0863	1
SEALE HARMON H	LTC	0-0032360	0661	1
SEALS JAMES F	COL	0-0041423	0756	1
SEAMAN JAMES B	COL	0-0020955	0657	1
SEAMAN OLEN J JR	LTC	0-0020825	0764	1
SEAMSTER DENNEY M	CW4	W-0903786	0761	1
SEARCY FRANK T	COL	0-0012819	0854	2
SEARING CARL B	CPT	0-0009637	0529	1
SEARLE VICTOR C	COL	0-0038697	0761	1
SEARLES JASPER L	COL	0-0039690	0960	1
SEARS CHARLES H	CPT	0-0007441	0926	2
SEARS FRANK S	LTC	0-0045378	0868	1
SEARS HAYDEN A	COL	0-0012839	0854	1
SEARS RALPH R	COL	0-0016269	0551	1
SEARS ROBERT	COL	0-0002632	1144	1
SEARS WALLACE R	MAJ	0-0060447	0361	1
SEATON STUART M	COL	0-0034760	0762	1
SEAVER PHILIP P	LTC	0-0021916	0959	1
SEAWARD GORDON W	COL	0-0018809	0862	1
SEAY THOMAS B	COL	0-0030862	0565	1
SEBASTIAN EDWARD P	CW3	W-0903788	0264	1
SEBELIEN BERNICE M	MAJ	N-0000242	1063	1
SEBESTA ARTHUR J	LTC	0-0025644	0864	1
SECAN FRANK D	LTC	0-0060201	1265	1
SEDBERRY GEORGE P JR	COL	0-0025415	0764	1
SEDOR ELIZABETH	MAJ	N-0001972	1161	1
SEDOR SOPHIA D	MAJ	N-0002079	0366	1
SEEBACH TIMOTHY M	2LT	0-0066390	0853	2
SEEDLOCK ROBERT F	M G	0-0020609	0268	2
SEEGER WILLIAM H	CW4	W-0903790	0561	1
SEELEY ALPHEUS H	COL	0-0026373	0368	1
SEELEY ROBERT B	LTC	0-0033436	0262	1
SEELEY SAM F	B G	0-0017344	0858	2
SEELY CHESLEY K	MAJ	0-0059025	1167	1
SEELY THEODORE A	COL	0-0016344	0355	1
SEEMAN LYLE E	M G	0-0017082	0965	2
SEESE HOMER P	1LT	0-0011549	0822	2
SEEWALD HUGHES	MAJ	0-0025381	0746	2
SEGARRA ANTULIO	COL	0-0016890	0757	1
SEIBEL PAUL	LTC	0-0036861	0962	1
SEIBERT DONALD W	LTC	0-0063413	0164	1
SEIBERT GERTRUDE C	MAJ	N-0000255	0164	1
SEIBERT LLOYD M	CW2	W-0901450	0644	2
SEID MARTIN J	CPT	0-0009450	0720	2
SEIDEMAN FRANK C	WO1	W-0800134	0740	1
SEIFERT ALBERT E	LTC	0-0024993	1163	1
SEIFERT RAYMOND A	COL	0-0052253	0865	2
SEIGLER THOMAS J JR	COL	0-0030789	1065	1
SEIPEL CLARENCE F JR	MAJ	0-0021847	0148	1
SEITZ J F R	M G	0-0017734	0466	2
SEITZMAN LEONARD H	COL	0-0060028	0867	1
SELBY ARTHUR L	COL	0-0038669	1159	1
SELBY GRANT A	LTC	0-0017906	0345	2
SELBY JOHN E	LTC	0-0005865	0341	1
SELDEN DUDLEY B	LTC	0-0051845	0260	1
SELEE RICHARDSON	COL	0-0014754	0748	1
SELEEN PAUL M	B G	0-0016139	0955	1
SELF AZILE	MAJ	N-0000228	0661	1
SELF GLADYS B	MAJ	N-0002246	0461	1
SELF SCOTT A JR	CPT	0-0084669	1061	1
SELF WILLARD	CW4	W-0903793	0364	1
SELIGMANN GUSTAV L	COL	0-0041400	0156	1
SELL RUSSELL B	COL	0-0038918	0666	1
SELLARS JACQUELINE	MAJ	N-0000931	1263	1

NAME	GRADE	SVC NO	DATE RET MO YR	RET CODE
SELLECK CLYDE A	COL	0-0002841	0447	2
SELLERS JAMES H	LTC	0-0060834	0868	1
SELLERS MELVIN B	LTC	0-0043981	0654	2
SELLERS RAYMOND W	LTC	0-0019217	0758	1
SELLERS THOMAS D	LTC	0-0065432	0667	2
SELLS CLARENCE K	LTC	0-0053600	1066	1
SELLS JOHN K	COL	0-0014770	0554	1
SELWYN ROBERT E	COL	0-0041704	0258	1
SEMBACH LEON	LTC	0-0026007	0764	1
SEMER JAMES	CW4	W-0902042	1154	1
SEMMENS CLIFTON P	COL	0-0034857	0868	1
SEMPLE CHARLES C	LTC	0-0059929	0268	1
SENAY CHARLES T	COL	0-0004699	0647	2
SENEFF GEORGE P	COL	0-0006954	1145	2
SENIOR WINFRED B	LTC	0-0056588	0567	1
SENN BURKHARDT	LTC	0-0052560	0266	1
SENN MERLE J	COL	0-0042322	0358	1
SENN MINERVA A	MAJ	N-0001813	0868	1
SEPTFONDS CHARLES E	LTC	0-0031837	0466	1
SERFAS LEE S	COL	0-0061184	0968	1
SERFASS BERNEDA A	MAJ	N-0000729	1163	1
SERFF PAUL C	COL	0-0015324	0954	1
SERGENT BYRD	COL	0-0052717	1162	1
SEROCZYNSKI HELEN M	MAJ	N-0000606	0468	1
SERREM EDWARD M	COL	0-0022090	0967	1
SESSIONS ELDRED S	LTC	0-0069789	1068	1
SESSIONS FRANK R	CPT	0-0014182	0717	2
SETCHFIELD CLARK W	CW4	W-0906986	0157	1
SETIAN ZADIG Y	LTC	0-0066095	0867	1
SETLIFFE TRUMAN H	COL	0-0024350	0763	1
SETTLE HENRY C	COL	0-0030665	0466	1
SEWALL ALEXANDER	COL	0-0016453	0656	1
SEWARD JOHN R	COL	0-0017698	0859	1
SEWELL GEORGE H	COL	0-0051595	0864	1
SEWELL TOXEY H	COL	0-0049609	1166	1
SEWELL WALTER E	COL	0-0039634	1059	1
SEXAUER LEO C	COL	0-0029251	0961	2
SEXTON LUTHER L	COL	0-0045778	1165	1
SEXTON MORRELL R	LTC	0-0034057	0366	1
SEXTON WILLIAM T	M G	0-0015777	0856	1
SEYBOLD JOHN S	M G	0-0012693	1155	1
SEYMORE DOROTHY L	LTC	N-0002268	1264	1
SEYMOUR FRED W	COL	0-0019671	1059	1
SEYMOUR WILLARD R	COL	0-0038772	0864	1
SHACTER JACOB	COL	0-0022724	0765	1
SHADE LESLIE N	LTC	0-0028698	0766	1
SHADEWALDT RUTH F	LTC	N-0000673	0367	1
SHADIE OLIVE P	MAJ	N-0000527	0750	1
SHADISH WILLIAM R	LTC	0-0071720	0766	1
SHADLE CHARLES S	B G	0-0010910	1047	2
SHADLE WILLIAM J JR	COL	0-0037262	0767	1
SHAFER HENRY L	COL	0-0028885	1056	1
SHAFER HOWARD T	LTC	0-0081882	0665	2
SHAFER WADE H	LTC	0-0027703	0767	1
SHAFFER CORNELIUS	LTC	0-0047584	0168	1
SHAFFER FORREST C	COL	0-0008581	0246	1
SHAFFER FRANCIS W	COL	0-0057896	0867	1
SHAFFER FRANK J	COL	0-0022695	0964	2
SHAFFER JARVIS K	LTC	0-0059888	1267	1
SHAFFER LEWIS N	LTC	0-0031541	0665	1
SHAFFER WILLIAM K	COL	0-0040639	0666	1
SHAFFIELD JOSEPH H	LTC	0-0060299	0268	1
SHAIMA ADOLPH L	LTC	0-0036677	0868	1
SHAKEL WILLIAM C	COL	0-0039612	0559	1
SHALER HARRISON	B G	0-0012080	0854	1
SHALLER HAROLD H	B G	0-0029657	1061	1
SHAMANSKY ANNA	MAJ	N-0000558	0459	1
SHAMBORA WILLIAM E	M G	0-0016540	0960	1
SHAMOTULSKI CHARLES	MAJ	0-0004896	0-32	2
SHANAHAN WILLIAM R	COL	0-0022950	0562	1
SHANER MILDRED M	MAJ	N-0001195	0763	1
SHANEYFELT DONALD L	COL	0-0064987	0468	1
SHANK GEORGE T	COL	0-0005138	1051	2
SHANKLE WADE L	COL	0-0028984	0558	1
SHANKS JOSEPH M	COL	0-0029061	0259	1

NAME	GRADE	SVC NO	DATE RET MO YR	RET CODE
SHANLEY PAUL M	MAJ	0-0069791	1262	2
SHANLEY THOMAS J B	COL	0-0021828	0961	1
SHANNON LELAND C	COL	0-0029346	1059	2
SHANNON ROBERT M JR	LTC	0-0024486	0861	1
SHANNONHOUSE JOHN G	COL	0-0010994	0934	2
SHAPER WILLIAM	COL	0-0081214	0968	1
SHAPIRA NORMAN I	COL	0-0060239	0866	1
SHARECK EVERETT P	LTC	0-0072987	0868	1
SHARP FELIX C JR	MAJ	0-0039057	0948	2
SHARP FREDERICK	COL	0-0008649	0237	1
SHARP HUNTER L	COL	0-0036523	1168	1
SHARP JOHN O JR	COL	0-0046693	1068	2
SHARP ROBERT	COL	0-0010121	0349	2
SHARP TURNER R	COL	0-0005645	0748	1
SHARP WALTER C JR	LTC	0-0031408	0264	1
SHARP WILLIAM B	COL	0-0010289	0447	2
SHARP WILLIAM B	LTC	0-0038645	0260	2
SHARPE EDGAR H	LTC	0-0062263	0568	1
SHARPE GRANVILLE	COL	0-0034986	0968	1
SHARPE HAROLD H	LTC	0-0043682	0962	1
SHARPE THOMAS J	COL	0-0024181	0866	2
SHARPTON BENJAMIN T	MAJ	0-0011736	1138	2
SHARRER ROBERT A	LTC	0-0022229	0867	1
SHATTUCK MILTON C	COL	0-0012835	0854	2
SHAUG JAMES J	COL	0-0051645	0964	1
SHAUGHNESSEY LEO W H	COL	0-0019458	0962	1
SHAUNESEY CHARLES A	COL	0-0023036	0868	1
SHAVALIER KENNETH	CW4	W-0903798	0367	1
SHAVER CLAUDE N	COL	0-0029333	0859	1
SHAVER ROBERT C JR	COL	0-0078614	0667	1
SHAVER ROBERT T	LTC	0-0043928	1162	1
SHAVER WILEY F JR	LTC	0-0024459	0962	1
SHAW CARL R	COL	0-0007652	0547	2
SHAW DORIS L	MAJ	N-0002433	0865	1
SHAW EUGENE A	LTC	0-0032511	0268	1
SHAW FLOYD H	CW3	W-0903800	1058	1
SHAW FRANKLIN P	M G	0-0008168	1053	1
SHAW FRANKLIN P JR	LTC	0-0025492	1064	1
SHAW HAROLD E	1LT	0-0018884	0242	1
SHAW HAROLD E	LTC	0-0058600	0868	1
SHAW HARRY J	LTC	0-0027131	0666	1
SHAW IRWIN T	LTC	0-0042679	1163	1
SHAW JOHN C	MAJ	0-0014686	1142	2
SHAW LAWRENCE E	COL	0-0016858	0356	1
SHAW LELAND B	COL	0-0028994	0658	1
SHAW MILLARD	COL	0-0042313	0164	2
SHAW PAUL A	COL	0-0042181	0563	1
SHAW STANLEY H	COL	0-0080492	1066	1
SHAW THERON	CW2	W-0903802	0954	2
SHAW VERA F	LTC	N-0000155	1162	1
SHAW VIRGIL F	COL	0-0012340	0754	1
SHAW WALTER A	COL	0-0042343	0464	1
SHAW WILLIAM G III	LTC	0-0053248	0863	1
SHAY EDWARD B	WO1	W-0800135	0438	2
SHEA DANIEL P	LTC	0-0081861	0665	1
SHEA EDWARD L	CW3	RW-0907158	0367	1
SHEA GEORGE D	M G	0-0005465	0153	1
SHEA MICHAEL C	COL	0-0008415	0854	1
SHEA PATRICK E	COL	0-0006545	0753	1
SHEALEY PERCY R	LTC	0-0031164	1165	2
SHEALY NORRIS	LTC	0-0043088	0765	1
SHEARER HUTTON A	MAJ	0-0020470	1144	2
SHEARER SPENCER F	MAJ	0-0002982	0233	2
SHEAROUSE JAMES D	COL	0-0030337	0461	1
SHEDIVETZ CLAYTON L	MAJ	0-0037514	0564	1
SHEEHAN DANIEL J	COL	0-0020929	1058	1
SHEEHAN GERARD J	LTC	0-0043221	1062	2
SHEEHAN HELEN P	LTC	J-0000046	0464	1
SHEEHAN THOMAS F	COL	0-0011428	0148	1
SHEEHY THOMAS W	LTC	0-0067614	1167	1
SHEEN CLARENCE E	COL	0-0040015	0266	2
SHEEN ERNEST T	COL	0-0029268	1055	1
SHEETS CLARENCE F JR	COL	0-0021692	1163	1
SHEETS HENRY B	COL	0-0012460	0934	. 2
SHEETZ JOSEF R	M G	0-0009720	0850	1

NAME	GRADE	SVC NO	DATE RET MO YR	RET CODE
SHEFFER GEORGE E JR	MAJ	0-0028120	0567	1
SHEFFEY JOHN P III	COL	0-0024701	1065	1
SHEFFIELD JAMES A JR	LTC	0-0088201	0765	1
SHEFFIELD L O	COL	0-0021702	0959	1
SHEFFIELD ROBERT X	LTC	0-0028734	0467	1
SHELBY RAYMOND T	LTC	0-0023504	0552	2
SHELDON GEORGE C	COL	0-0048236	0967	1
SHELL ROBERT H	COL	0-0031472	0766	1
SHELL VERNON MC	MAJ	0-0006696	0-35	2
SHELLENBERGER L C	COL	0-0020506	0655	1
SHELLEY ROYDEN R	CW4	RW-0903805	0664	1
SHELLEY SIDNEY	COL	0-0042571	0964	1
SHELLHASE LESLIE J	LTC	0-0066096	0868	1
SHELLUM ALFORD C	LTC	0-0033299	0262	1
SHELOR WARREN S	COL	0-0050994	0858	1
SHELTON CLAUDE W	MAJ	0-0014421	0320	2
SHELTON CYRUS Q	B G	0-0010784	0854	1
SHELTON FRANK W	LTC	0-0033612	0161	1
SHELTON JAMES A	LTC	0-0079994	1267	1
SHELTON JOHNNIE F	CW4	W-0903806	1163	1
SHELTON JOSEPH R JR	LTC	0-0026781	0965	1
SHELTON LOUIS H	LTC	0-0058602	0768	1
SHELTON T J	LTC	0-0038570	0464	1
SHELTON WILLIS E	COL	0-0051944	1264	1
SHEMWELL VICTOR B	COL	0-0044395	0761	1
SHEPARD GEORGE	LTC	0-0087462	0767	1
SHEPARD NORMAN C JR	LTC	0-0026654	0764	1
SHEPARD WHITFIELD	M G	0-0011908	0156	1
SHEPARD WILLIAM H	COL	0-0025110	0962	1
SHEPARDSON FRANK H	COL	0-0019068	0959	2
SHEPHERD CHARLES	COL	0-0015904	0754	1
SHEPHERD DANIEL F	COL	0-0043060	0464	1
SHEPHERD ELIZABETH	MAJ	N-0000204	0263	1
SHEPHERD GERALD O	COL	0-0031571	0762	2
SHEPHERD TYRON M	COL	0-0008021	0649	2
SHEPLER LLOYD B	LTC	0-0037445	0762	2
SHEPPARD HARVEY E	COL	0-0043086	0667	1
SHEPPARD JEROME S	MAJ	0-0060468	0562	2
SHEPPARD PAUL R E	COL	0-0004258	0646	1
SHERPECK MICHAEL L	COL	0-0021478	0865	1
SHEPPER WILLIAM L	CW4	W-0904407	0365	1
SHERBURNE T L JR	M G	0-0017293	1060	1
SHERDEN JOHN P JR	COL	0-0019901	0965	1
SHERFY ROLLAND F	CPT	0-0010067	0127	2
SHERIDAN ANDREW J	CPT	0-0088928	1067	1
SHERIDAN ARTHUR J	COL	0-0012074	1146	2
SHERIDAN JOHN W	COL	0-0043156	0666	1
SHERMAN GERALD	COL	0-0081218	0768	1
SHERMAN HARRY B	B G	0-0011243	0153	1
SHERMAN JACQUES L JR	LTC	0-0059541	0964	1
SHERMAN JOHN B	COL	0-0012160	1051	2
SHERMAN RAYMOND G	COL	0-0007609	0351	2
SHERMAN THOMAS J	CW4	W-0906988	0461	2
SHERMAN WILLIAM T	MAJ	0-0042667	0751	2
SHERRARD DAVID G	COL	0-0021345	0868	1
SHERRARD JOSEPH H	LTC	0-0040597	1065	1
SHERRARD ROBERT G JR	COL	0-0019922	0962	1
SHERRETS DONALD C	LTC	0-0044781	0662	1
SHERRILL EVAN M	CPT	0-0007413	0722	2
SHERWOOD PHILIP H	MAJ	0-0004767	0846	2
SHERWOOD ROBERT W	LTC	0-0063476	0164	1
SHEVIAK FRANK G	LTC	0-0040878	0866	1
SHEWBRIDGE EDWIN C	COL	0-0038745	0663	1
SHI JAMES O JR	LTC	0-0033230	1160	1
SHICK DALE H	LTC	0-0033412	0661	1
SHIELDS HARRY H JR	LTC	0-0054994	0866	1
SHIELDS LAWRENCE D	LTC	0-0066097	1068	1
SHIELDS MAYNARD E	CPT	0-0077198	0864	2
SHIELDS PAUL A	COL	0-0041424	0756	1
SHIERY FLOYD W	LTC	0-0051146	0259	1
SHIFLET ALBERT W	COL	0-0020507	0257	1
SHIMEK CECELIA H	MAJ	N-0002263	1062	1
SHIMONEK WILLIAM H	COL	0-0017745	0246	2
SHINKLE JOHN G	M G	0-0018979	0963	1
SHIPE BURDWELL H	COL	0-0030065	1161	1

NAME	GRADE	SVC NO	DATE RET MO YR	RET CODE
SHIPLEY ALDEN P	LTC	0-0033699	0964	1
SHIPLEY BYRON M	COL	0-0039827	0463	1
SHIPLEY WAYNE D	COL	0-0020491	0965	1
SHIPMAN KENNETH	LTC	0-0060411	0963	1
SHIPP BEVERLY A	COL	0-0008116	0748	1
SHIPSTEAD ALTON M	LTC	0-0026345	0965	1
SHIREY BURRELL P	LTC	0-0039969	0663	1
SHIREY WILLIAM M	MAJ	0-0026635	0865	1
SHIRK ROBERT V	MAJ	0-0056436	0163	1
SHIRLEY COURTNEY R	LTC	0-0059027	0366	1
SHIRLEY JACKSON E	COL	0-0033977	0861	1
SHIRLEY LOUIS H	COL	0-0029372	1059	1
SHIVE DONALD W	COL	0-0020628	0565	1
SHIVELEY CHARLES B	LTC	0-0072427	0168	1
SHIVER WILLIAM W	CW2	W-0906989	1059	1
SHJAFF ALMON L	LTC	0-0027866	0765	1
SHOCKLEY PHILIP M	COL	0-0015485	1047	2
SHOE ROBERT O	M G	0-0008119	0351	1
SHOEMAKER JOHN J	COL	0-0030133	1163	1
SHOEMAKER JOSEPH A	LTC	0-0042993	0765	1
SHOEMAKER LEO W	LTC	0-0065028	0566	1
SHOEMAKER PAUL S	COL	0-0029348	0858	2
SHOEMAKER RONALD Z	CPT	0-0072650	1265	2
SHOEMAKER SAMUEL E	COL	0-0022661	0766	1
SHOEMAKER WILLIAM S	COL	0-0039694	1160	1
SHOMION ARTHUR M	LTC	0-0040094	0365	1
SHOMO JOSEPH L	LTC	0-0061189	0165	1
SHOOK LOUIS L	COL	0-0009470	1050	1
SHOOKUS ANTHONY H	COL	0-0031772	0268	1
SHORE MOYERS S	COL	0-0029589	0861	1
SHORT AUGUSTA L	LTC	N-0000024	1054	1
SHORT DAVID S	LTC	0-0036603	1262	1
SHORT EARL R	COL	0-0031685	0863	1
SHORT JOHN J	COL	0-0024812	0767	1
SHORTALL JOHN L JR	LTC	0-0025544	0663	1
SHOWALTER WILBUR E	COL	0-0021794	0765	1
SHPAKOWSKY ADAM P	CW4	W-0903814	0566	1
SHRADER HAROLD D	COL	0-0039677	0660	1
SHREVE ARTHUR L	COL	0-0011176	1052	1
SHROEDER MELVIN W	LTC	0-0094790	1067	1
SHUEY HAROLD E	COL	0-0023640	0463	1
SHUFELT JAMES V	COL	0-0007321	0551	1
SHUFORD LOUIS A	LTC	0-0045876	0262	1
SHUFORD RICHARD H JR	LTC	0-0067756	1068	1
SHUGG ROLAND P	B G	0-0004476	0552	1
SHULER ALLEN C JR	COL	0-0031970	0563	1
SHULER WILLIAM R	M G	0-0020118	0966	2
SHULMAN FLORENCE	MAJ	L-0000319	0464	1
SHUMAN THOMAS A	MAJ	0-0063258	0868	1
SHUMARD GORDON H	LTC	0-0027497	0965	1
SHUMATE JOSEPH P	COL	0-0015537	0654	1
SHUMATE PAUL W	COL	0-0017547	0859	1
SHUMWAY LESLIE E JR	MAJ	0-0038478	0862	2
SHUNK PETER W	COL	0-0015622	0754	1
SHUPE JOSEPH B	LTC	0-0083588	0766	1
SHURE WILLIAM C	COL	0-0022751	0367	2
SHURLING JOSEPH T	CW4	W-0903816	0159	1
SHURM VERNON A	COL	0-0031436	0666	1
SHUTE BENJAMIN S	COL	0-0017097	0758	1
SHUTT EDITH L	LTC	N-0000112	1163	1
SHUTT LOGAN O	COL	0-0012441	1049	1
SIBBALD GEORGE H	COL	0-0029958	0663	1
SIBERT EDWIN L	M G	0-0011193	0154	1
SIBERT FRANKLIN C	M G	0-0003394	0646	2
SIBERT FRANKLIN R	COL	0-0020329	0460	1
SIBERT HERBERT F	COL	0-0030922	1066	1
SIBLEY ALDEN K	M G	0-0018964	0868	1
SIBLEY THOMAS N	B G	0-0021277	0868	1
SICHI WILLIAM T	COL	0-0019674	0655	1
SICKAFOOSE KEITH E	COL	0-0059138	1168	2
SICKS MARY E	MAJ	L-0000330	0766	1
SIDENSTRICKER HARRY	CW4	W-0907140	0967	1
SIDFRID LEROY O	MAJ	0-0039441	0866	1
SIDWAY RALPH W	CW4	W-0902323	1054	1
SIEBEN HERBERT U	MAJ	0-0033153	1061	1

NAME	GRADE	SVC NO	DATE RET MO YR	RET CODE
SIEBENEICHEN PAUL O	LTC	0-0034729	0961	1
SIEBER HARRY F JR	LTC	0-0054161	1163	1
SIEBERT RITA M	MAJ	N-0002425	1164	1
SIEGE ALFRED G	LTC	0-0059676	0466	1
SIEGEL CHARLES L	COL	0-0042879	0662	2
SIEGEL LEON S	LTC	0-0081220	0568	2
SIEMERS HERMAN R	COL	0-0042162	0463	1
SIEMONS PHILLIP J	CW3	W-0903818	1167	1
SIEVERS HARRY L	COL	0-0029814	0962	1
SIEVERS HENRY R	COL	0-0030298	0762	1
SIEVERS RALPH H	COL	0-0017254	0858	1
SIEVERS VERA A	LTC	L-0000020	1057	1
SIEVERS WILLIAM E	COL	0-0020299	1265	1
SIGAFOOS ROLLAND B	COL	0-0022291	0266	1
SIGERFOOS EDWARD	COL	0-0020414	0866	1
SIGHOLTZ ROBERT H	COL	0-0087614	1268	1
SIGHTLER S B JR	COL	0-0041824	1160	1
SIKES GLENN A	LTC	0-0020353	0660	1
SILBAUGH VERNE R	LTC	0-0041489	0256	1
SILBERMAN HENRY K	LTC	0-0066099	0965	1
SILCOX MARSHALL W	LTC	0-0084671	0567	1
SILER ARNOLD M	MAJ	0-0011117	0539	1
SILLIN WILLIAM F	LTC	0-0081221	1266	1
SILLS CLARENCE F	COL	0-0024463	1163	1
SILLS THOMAS H	COL	0-0028909	0557	1
SILLS TOM W	COL	0-0029949	0663	1
SILMAN JAMES B	COL	0-0035048	0861	1
SILVER MILTON B	CW2	W-0901804	0546	1
SILVER SAMUEL F	COL	0-0017770	0858	1
SILVERIA EDWIN D	CW4	W-0903822	0167	1
SILVERMAN LEO	LTC	0-0065435	1165	1
SILVERWOOD KERMIT J	COL	0-0042153	0363	1
SILVEY ROBERT M	LTC	0-0033887	0161	1
SIMENSON CLIFFORD G	COL	0-0019511	0864	1
SIMERLY RUTH N	MAJ	L-0000304	0861	1
SIMKINS TATTNALL D	LTC	0-0004440	0142	1
SIMKUS CLYDE C	COL	0-0050998	0958	1
SIMMET BERNICE C	CPT	N-0000434	1047	1
SIMMONS CHADWICK P	LTC	0-0042924	1164	2
SIMMONS ELDRIDGE C	LTC	0-0056798	1159	1
SIMMONS GEORGE M	LTC	0-0020841	0459	1
SIMMONS HOWARD H	COL	0-0039029	0866	1
SIMMONS JAMES Q JR	COL	0-0041720	0661	1
SIMMONS JOSEPH J	CW4	W-0903823	0256	1
SIMMONS TOM A JR	MAJ	0-0080326	1159	1
SIMMONS VERNON N JR	COL	0-0039063	0564	2
SIMMS RAYMOND M	CW4	W-0903824	1061	1
SIMMS WILLIAM B	COL	0-0020968	0762	2
SIMON DONALD E	LTC	0-0024776	0464	1
SIMON LESLIE E	M G	0-0015567	1155	2
SIMON LINCOLN A	COL	0-0021961	0466	1
SIMONS ROBERT E	LTC	0-0025136	0162	1
SIMPKINS MARTHA A	MAJ	N-0001265	0664	1
SIMPSON ADA M	LTC	N-0000076	0754	1
SIMPSON CHARLES L	COL	0-0020325	0864	1
SIMPSON DONALD M	COL	0-0021986	0163	1
SIMPSON EDWARD H	LTC	0-0030418	0463	1
SIMPSON GEORGE H	COL	0-0034704	1066	2
SIMPSON GEORGE L JR	LTC	0-0055818	0164	1
SIMPSON HOWARD J	LTC	0-0060987	1267	1
SIMPSON JOHN W	COL	0-0021480	0957	1
SIMPSON MARIBETH T	LTC	L-0000106	1167	1
SIMPSON RALPH T	COL	0-0029841	0859	1
SIMPSON THOMAS B	B G	0-0020902	0167	1
SIMPSON WALTER A	COL	0-0019778	0865	1
SIMPSON WILLIAM H	GEN	0-0002645	1146	2
SIMS HAROLD L	CW4	W-0906994	0955	1
SIMS JULES V	COL	0-0011147	0750	1
SIMS LEONARD H	B G	0-0008383	0854	1
SIMS MORTON D	LTC	0-0081224	1068	1
SIMS RALPH	LTC	0-0035435	1264	2
SIMS THOMAS A	LTC	0-0079086	0168	1
SINAI SAMUEL B	LTC	0-0086766	0168	1
SINCLAIR DUNCAN	COL	0-0019757	0163	2
SINCLAIR FORESTER H	LTC	0-0016834	0244	2

NAME	GRADE	SVC NO	DATE RET MO YR	RET CODE
SINCLAIR LACHLAN M	COL	0-0032369	0767	1
SINCLAIR VICTOR E	LTC	0-0020795	1057	1
SINER JOSEPH L	LTC	0-0003054	1022	2
SINGER LILLIAN	MAJ	L-0000340	0852	2
SINGER MERTON	COL	0-0021215	0165	1
SINGER PAUL L	COL	0-0006797	0453	2
SINGER RICHARD C	COL	0-0012756	0753	1
SINGLES GORDON	COL	0-0018522	0761	1
SINGLEY GEORGE T JR	LTC	0-0055928	0365	1
SINNREICH SIMON R	LTC	0-0021173	0956	1
SION EDWARD G	COL	0-0041744	0763	1
SIPES KENNETH L	COL	0-0041989	0162	2
SIPPLE BLANCHE I	LTC	N-0001204	0966	1
SIREN VINCENT W	LTC	0-0021306	0866	1
SISSON WINFIELD W	COL	0-0018096	1047	2
SITES EUGENE P	COL	0-0043526	1066	1
SITES GEORGE F JR	MAJ	0-0079089	1162	1
SITLER HENRY D	LTC	0-0081227	0566	1
SITNEK WILLIAM G	LTC	0-0040142	0164	1
SIVIGNY JOSEPH A	LTC	0-0051385	0261	1
SIZEMORE BURLEY	MAJ	0-0079090	0762	1
SJOBERG JEANETTE E	MAJ	N-0002248	0561	1
SKAGGS ROBERT N	COL	0-0039816	0158	1
SKARIK RICHARD L	LTC	0-0081229	0868	1
SKARDON BEVERLY N	COL	0-0033939	0962	1
SKEATH ELBUR J	LTC	0-0079997	0864	1
SKEEHAN RAYMOND A JR	COL	0-0067959	0967	1
SKEES HUGH S	COL	0-0079998	0565	1
SKEIBER STANLEY C	LTC	0-0080185	0865	1
SKELLS JAMES F	COL	0-0019830	0865	1
SKELLY FRANK H	COL	0-0029056	0159	1
SKELTON OSCAR G	COL	0-0003983	0946	2
SKELTON WINFRED C	B G	0-0012374	0854	2
SKENE CEDRIC M S	COL	0-0003209	0446	2
SKERRY ARTHUR W JR	2LT	0-0021162	0-40	2
SKERRY HARRY A	COL	0-0005584	1147	2
SKERRY LESLIE M	COL	0-0007313	0946	2
SKIBA SOPHIA C	MAJ	N-0000411	0662	1
SKIDMORE HERROL J	COL	0-0018664	0762	2
SKIDMORE WILBUR M	B G	0-0014440	0860	2
SKIFFINGTON EDWARD H	LTC	0-0081232	0668	1
SKILLMAN CHARLES S	COL	0-0038989	0666	1
SKINNER ASA H	COL	0-0007996	0447	1
SKINNER EDWIN C	COL	0-0050985	0658	1
SKINNER ERNEST B	COL	0-0039710	0361	1
SKINNER HARRY E	COL	0-0021425	0863	1
SKINNER JAMES H	COL	0-0019144	0559	1
SKINNER JEAN F	MAJ	N-0000572	0761	1
SKINNER LAWRENCE L	COL	0-0015325	0954	1
SKINNER ROBERT B	B G	0-0018917	1162	1
SKINNER RUSSELL	COL	0-0007533	0349	1
SKINNER THOMAS R W	COL	0-0050971	0258	1
SKINROOD NORMAN A	COL	0-0019882	0865	1
SKIPPER JOHN F	LTC	0-0033083	0861	1
SKLADAL CONRAD	LTC	0-0003631	1139	1
SKOGSBERG PAUL L	LTC	0-0062134	0664	1
SKORINA ALEXANDER	MAJ	0-0052984	0555	2
SKVARCEK ANDREW JR	CW2	W-0903826	0849	1
SLACK ADA L	MAJ	N-0002222	0360	1
SLAD HARRY A	LTC	0-0032088	0859	1
SLADE LAWRENCE	LTC	0-0008135	1141	2
SLADE TODD H	COL	0-0018789	0758	1
SLADEN FRED W JR	B G	0-0017677	0859	1
SLAGLE HALBERT J	LTC	0-0039865	0861	1
SLAPPEY EUGENE N	COL	0-0005163	1048	1
SLATE RALPH	COL	0-0005790	0746	1
SLAUGHTER DONALD F	COL	0-0022202	0965	1
SLAUGHTER JOHN E	LTC	0-0019921	0859	1
SLAUGHTER S D JR	COL	0-0029530	0361	1
SLAUGHTER WILLIS R	B G	0-0005296	0654	1
SLAWSON HARRY C	LTC	0-0055886	0865	1
SLAYDEN WILLIAM M	COL	0-0030754	0666	1
SLEDGE THEODORE J	COL	0-0005817	1044	2
SLIDER RICHARD H	LTC	0-0010309	0142	1
SLIGER IRA T JR	LTC	0-0059032	0667	1
SLIMP JACK B	COL	0-0043608	1068	1
SLISHER WELDON L	COL	0-0029787	0762	1
SLOAN EMERALD F	COL	0-0015084	1032	2
SLOAN GEORGE B	COL	0-0020821	0764	1
SLOAN HAROLD B	LTC	0-0026624	0268	2
SLOAN JOHN E	M G	0-0003018	1046	1
SLOAN WILLIAM N JR	COL	0-0024235	0767	1
SLOANE CHARLES C JR	COL	0-0016456	0756	2
SLOANE NICHOLAS J	LTC	0-0043582	0866	1
SLOAT JAMES W	COL	0-0020556	1263	1
SLOAT JESSE I	COL	0-0004054	1146	2
SLOBE ELMER L	COL	0-0042867	1066	1
SLOCUM A N JR	COL	0-0039610	0259	1
SLOCUM LECOUNT H	B G	0-0009716	0754	1
SLOSSON CHARLES F JR	WO1	W-0800156	0841	2
SLOVER ROBERT H	COL	0-0043638	1264	1
SLUMPFF CARL F	LTC	0-0084573	1262	1
SLY GEORGE W	LTC	0-0081234	1163	1
SMALL ARTHUR C	COL	0-0052214	1263	1
SMALL BALLARD B JR	LTC	0-0081235	0766	1
SMALL BRAXTON E	COL	0-0042156	0363	1
SMALLE DANIEL E	COL	0-0041576	0259	1
SMALLEY HARRY E	COL	0-0004023	0248	1
SMALLEY HOWARD N	COL	0-0020853	0867	1
SMART DONALD V	COL	0-0031597	1263	1
SMEDILE JOSEPH A	COL	0-0020942	0764	2
SMELLOW SAMUEL	COL	0-0018439	0661	1
SMIGELOW HOWARD G	COL	0-0031791	0966	1
SMILEY FRANK H	LTC	0-0037582	0862	1
SMILEY JAMES L	1LT	0-0023061	0148	1
SMILEY ROBERT F	LTC	0-0048683	1263	1
SMILEY STANLEY W	COL	0-0030160	0564	1
SMIT WALTER	COL	0-0020494	0965	1
SMITH A MARK II	COL	0-0029927	0563	1
SMITH ALBERT C	M G	0-0005265	0955	2
SMITH ALLEN T	LTC	0-0034320	0462	1
SMITH ARTHUR J JR	COL	0-0021163	0648	2
SMITH AUBURN H	COL	0-0031073	0764	1
SMITH BARTHOLOME	LTC	0-0060790	0960	2
SMITH BOYD L	COL	0-0008773	0851	2
SMITH BRADISH J	COL	0-0024049	0265	1
SMITH BYRON S	LTC	0-0043860	0767	1
SMITH C COBURN JR	B G	0-0018434	0761	1
SMITH C ELFORD	COL	0-0015074	0753	1
SMITH C ROONEY	M G	0-0016388	0857	1
SMITH CARL N	COL	0-0029105	0559	1
SMITH CAROLYN E	MAJ	R-0010089	1166	2
SMITH CECIL L	LTC	0-0023751	0759	1
SMITH CHARLES A	LTC	0-0060566	1267	1
SMITH CHARLES B	B G	0-0022113	0766	1
SMITH CHARLES C	LTC	0-0004497	1037	2
SMITH CHARLES M	LTC	0-0029199	0359	1
SMITH CHARLES R	COL	0-0011629	0548	1
SMITH CHARLES R	MAJ	0-0037608	0760	2
SMITH CHARLES W	CPT	0-0080186	1166	1
SMITH CHESTER M	LTC	0-0040993	0868	1
SMITH CLARKE S	COL	0-0000586	0624	1
SMITH CLAYTON J	MAJ	0-0060005	1265	1
SMITH CLIFFORD A	COL	0-0011424	0148	1
SMITH DALE L	COL	0-0054616	0669	1
SMITH DAN L II	COL	0-0040156	0567	1
SMITH DANA E	COL	0-0038759	0362	2
SMITH DAVID C JR	LTC	0-0043394	1264	1
SMITH DONALD H	COL	0-0016334	1055	1
SMITH DOUGLAS B	COL	0-0015699	0854	1
SMITH EDMUND C	CW4	W-0903830	0452	2
SMITH EDWIN A	COL	0-0007401	0947	1
SMITH EDWIN A	COL	0-0041459	0757	1
SMITH ELIZABETH	LTC	L-0000048	0861	1
SMITH ELLSWORTH	COL	0-0039449	0368	1
SMITH ELLSWORTH	LTC	0-0048540	0367	2
SMITH EMIL J	LTC	0-0028860	0554	1
SMITH EMMETT M	COL	0-0029161	1057	1
SMITH EMMITT D	COL	0-0042788	0564	1
SMITH ERNEST E	COL	0-0029418	0759	2
SMITH ESTELLE	MAJ	N-0002193	0465	1
SMITH ESTIL V	COL	0-0003473	0646	1
SMITH EUGENE	LTC	0-0030559	0962	1
SMITH EUGENE A	LTC	0-0008747	0440	2
SMITH FLETCHER	MAJ	0-0044638	0262	1
SMITH FLOYD V	CW4	W-0904259	0863	1
SMITH FRANCIS M	LTC	0-0023634	0859	1
SMITH FRANK A	LTC	0-0027701	0966	1
SMITH FRANK R	LTC	0-0025888	0967	1
SMITH FRANK M	COL	0-0009088	0948	1
SMITH FRANKLIN G	B G	0-0019154	0863	1
SMITH FRED C	COL	0-0038703	1161	1
SMITH FRED C	COL	0-0044457	1165	1
SMITH FREDERICK	COL	0-0051997	0157	1
SMITH GEORGE	CW4	W-0904199	1059	1
SMITH GEORGE F JR	LTC	0-0027247	0765	1
SMITH GEORGE I	COL	0-0006517	1050	1
SMITH GEORGE W	COL	0-0029013	0958	1
SMITH GLEN W	LTC	0-0038139	0866	1
SMITH GLENN K	COL	0-0020563	1066	1
SMITH GORDON K	COL	0-0029383	0260	1
SMITH GORDON K	LTC	0-0032959	0668	1
SMITH GORDON L	LTC	0-0026029	0765	1
SMITH GROVER G	LTC	0-0080001	0866	1
SMITH H REX	CW4	W-0904305	0664	1
SMITH HAROLD A	LTC	0-0031615	0660	1
SMITH HAROLD H	LTC	0-0022677	0746	2
SMITH HARRISON S	LTC	0-0068168	0868	1
SMITH HARRY L	CW3	RW-0908028	1168	1
SMITH HARRY M	LTC	0-0034041	0162	1
SMITH HARRY T	COL	0-0022001	0764	1
SMITH HARVEY H	COL	0-0010155	0252	1
SMITH HERALD H	COL	0-0032603	0368	2
SMITH HERMAN R JR	LTC	0-0033922	0766	1
SMITH HOMER A	CW4	W-0906997	0464	1
SMITH HORRELL H	LTC	0-0036562	0864	1
SMITH HULETT D	LTC	0-0081927	0167	1
SMITH IRVING JR	1LT	0-0014465	0519	2
SMITH JACK E	LTC	0-0060347	1167	1
SMITH JAMES B	LTC	0-0007508	0546	2
SMITH JAMES B	LTC	0-0051491	0462	2
SMITH JAMES H	COL	0-0065410	0566	2
SMITH JAMES P	COL	0-0030772	0266	1
SMITH JAMES W	LTC	0-0032128	0564	1
SMITH JEROME F	LTC	0-0040406	1063	2
SMITH JEROME T	COL	0-0030874	0765	1
SMITH JOHN A JR	COL	0-0010228	0349	1
SMITH JOHN A JR	LTC	0-0063843	0966	1
SMITH JOHN C	COL	0-0015656	0754	1
SMITH JOHN W	LTC	0-0010479	0729	2
SMITH JUDSON M	LTC	0-0016270	0753	1
SMITH JUNIUS P	COL	0-0017972	1053	1
SMITH KIMBALL C	COL	0-0029882	0459	2
SMITH KINGSLEY J	MAJ	0-0059034	0564	1
SMITH LELAND S	COL	0-0012799	0954	1
SMITH LEO A	COL	0-0030478	0865	1
SMITH LESLIE D	LTC	0-0033042	0863	1
SMITH LLOYD G	LTC	0-0038024	0562	1
SMITH LON H	COL	0-0018854	0762	2
SMITH LOWELL H	CPT	0-0060705	0862	1
SMITH LYNN D	B G	0-0029741	0764	1
SMITH MARK A H	COL	0-0041447	1056	1
SMITH MARK E	COL	0-0015796	0854	1
SMITH MARSHALL J	LTC	0-0080004	0966	1
SMITH MARTIN R JR	CPT	0-0059035	0663	1
SMITH MARY B	MAJ	N-0000413	0661	1
SMITH MARY I	LTC	N-0001005	1067	1
SMITH MERLE E	COL	0-0056785	0957	1
SMITH MERLE J	COL	0-0080190	0368	1
SMITH MERWIN H	COL	0-0042349	0464	1
SMITH MICHAEL G	COL	0-0012342	0547	2
SMITH MYRON D	LTC	0-0031860	0466	1
SMITH OSWALD C	LTC	0-0054531	0756	1
SMITH OSWALD H	CW4	W-0901998	1054	1
SMITH PAUL F	M G	0-0033169	0868	1
SMITH PAUL R	COL	0-0011960	0551	1
SMITH PHILIP J	COL	0-0021719	1059	1
SMITH PHILLIP B	COL	0-0030952	0862	1
SMITH PHILLIP R	COL	0-0035445	0764	1
SMITH PRESTON W	CPT	0-0009305	0-26	2
SMITH RALPH C	M G	0-0004723	1046	1
SMITH RALPH H	COL	0-0031614	1164	1
SMITH RICHARD A	LTC	0-0027490	0566	1
SMITH RICHARD O	COL	0-0029495	1160	1
SMITH RICHARD O	LTC	0-0065158	1267	1
SMITH RIDGWAY P JR	COL	0-0020243	0966	1
SMITH ROBERT O	COL	0-0019690	1046	2
SMITH ROBERT G JR	COL	0-0029804	1060	1
SMITH ROBERT L	LTC	0-0039350	0764	1
SMITH ROBERT L	LTC	0-0065129	0966	1
SMITH ROBERT M	COL	0-0015353	0847	1
SMITH ROBERT N	COL	0-0039709	0661	2
SMITH ROBERT Q JR	LTC	0-0031636	0765	1
SMITH ROLLIN H	COL	0-0031367	0166	1
SMITH ROMAN A	CW4	W-0903835	0966	1
SMITH ROY E	LTC	0-0035777	0863	1
SMITH RUSSELL B	COL	0-0019953	0863	1
SMITH RUSSELL O	COL	0-0012698	0151	1
SMITH RUTH E	CPT	N-0001152	0657	2
SMITH RUTH P	MAJ	L-0000232	0359	1
SMITH SELWYN D	COL	0-0001209	0642	2
SMITH SELWYN D JR	M G	0-0020194	0467	1
SMITH STANLEY W	LTC	0-0043042	1062	1
SMITH STEPHEN E	COL	0-0020142	0466	1
SMITH STILSON H JR	COL	0-0019480	0864	1
SMITH TERENCE J	COL	0-0039585	0857	1
SMITH THOMAS E	LTC	0-0079098	0868	1
SMITH THOMAS E W	COL	0-0033064	0365	1
SMITH TRUMAN	COL	0-0004619	0142	2
SMITH VALENTINE	COL	0-0015269	0854	2
SMITH VALLARD C	COL	0-0023543	0965	1
SMITH VERNON M	COL	0-0039993	0461	1
SMITH W DIXON	COL	0-0017085	0858	1
SMITH WALTER	MAJ	0-0013929	0620	2
SMITH WILBUR B	LTC	0-0081242	0568	2
SMITH WILLARD L	COL	0-0008048	0250	1
SMITH WILLIAM	LTC	0-0050717	0767	1
SMITH WILLIAM A	COL	0-0008674	0548	1
SMITH WILLIAM A	COL	0-0030079	1263	1
SMITH WILLIAM O	CW4	W-0904204	0760	1
SMITH WILLIAM O JR	COL	0-0029850	0163	1
SMITH WILLIAM E	CW4	W-0904205	1156	1
SMITH WILLIAM F SR	CPT	0-0074520	1062	2
SMITH WILLIAM M	CW4	W-0904268	1056	1
SMITH WILLIAM M JR	COL	0-0040724	0868	1
SMITH WILLIAM M JR	LTC	0-0080493	0867	2
SMITH WILLIAM R	LTC	0-0028562	0667	1
SMITH WILLIAM R JR	COL	0-0018661	0259	1
SMITH WILLIAM S	COL	0-0030968	0766	1
SMITH WILLIAM S	LTC	0-0038509	0963	1
SMITH WILLIAM T	COL	0-0024341	0762	1
SMITH WILLIAM W JR	COL	0-0021078	0868	1
SMITH WILLIS T	COL	0-0029518	0361	2
SMITH WOODROW M	COL	0-0022960	0762	1
SMITH WOODS B	LTC	0-0043438	0266	1
SMITHERMAN WILLIS E	COL	0-0052455	0468	1
SMITHERS FLORENCE R	MAJ	N-0002158	0862	1
SMITHSON ROBERT W	LTC	0-0063086	0168	1
SMOAK JOHN R	COL	0-0031463	0267	1
SMOAK MARION H	LTC	0-0043288	0861	1
SMOAK WILLIAM M JR	COL	0-0081857	0561	1
SMOCK STANLEY C	COL	0-0009489	0150	1
SMOLENSKI FELIX S	LTC	0-0063037	1162	1
SMOLKA JOSEPH F	CW2	W-0901033	0342	1
SMOLLER JOHN F	M G	0-0019416	0864	1
SMOTHERS WILLIAM	LTC	0-0082098	0766	1
SMOYER RAYMOND E	CPT	0-0075295	0367	1
SMYKLO ALEXANDER	CW3	W-0903837	1057	1
SMYLY JAMES W JR	COL	0-0016928	0757	1
SMYRL J T	LTC	0-0033732	0861	2

NAME	GRADE	SVC NO	DATE RET MO YR	RET CODE
SMYSER CRAIG	COL	0-0019417	0754	1
SMYSER RUDOLPH E JR	COL	0-0017090	0758	1
SMYTHE GEORGE W	M G	0-0015816	0257	2
SNAADT CORINNE E	MAJ	N-0000932	1268	1
SNAPE LONNIE	MAJ	N-0001904	1061	1
SNEDEKER EUGENE L	LTC	0-0050011	0965	1
SNEE JAMES W	COL	0-0019516	0864	1
SNELLING WALTER H	LTC	0-0026752	0765	1
SNIDER VENNE F	LTC	0-0051341	1060	1
SNIPAN GEORGE	LTC	0-0062264	0368	1
SNODGRASS EDGAR H	COL	0-0012478	0854	1
SNODGRASS JOHN W JR	LTC	0-0063477	0767	2
SNOOKS JAMES P JR	COL	0-0030011	0660	1
SNOW BEVERLY C	COL	0-0012056	1052	2
SNOW CHESTER R	LTC	0-0002483	1022	1
SNOW CLIFFORD M	COL	0-0029122	0859	1
SNOW FRANK G	CPT	0-0059879	0962	1
SNOW JAMES A	LTC	0-0060385	0864	1
SNOW ROBERT P	CW4	W-0902079	0762	1
SNOW ROBERT T	COL	0-0003417	0142	1
SNOWDEN HAZEL I	LTC	N-0001995	1163	1
SNOWDEN PAUL T	COL	0-0029811	1162	1
SNYDER AGNES P	LTC	M-0010003	0360	1
SNYDER BRADLEY J	CPT	0-0096646	0166	2
SNYDER CLIFFORD M	1LT	0-0018736	0437	2
SNYDER EMANUEL P	COL	0-0043286	0465	1
SNYDER FRANCES E	CPT	N-0002878	0762	2
SNYDER FRANK L	LTC	0-0043061	0964	1
SNYDER HARRY G	COL	0-0038854	1266	1
SNYDER HOLLICE H	LTC	0-0049998	0765	1
SNYDER HOWARD M JR	M G	0-0020213	0566	1
SNYDER HOWARD MCC	M G	0-0002412	1046	2
SNYDER IRA W JR	COL	0-0050759	0968	1
SNYDER JAMES L	M G	0-0019627	0465	1
SNYDER JAMES M	COL	0-0025036	0566	1
SNYDER MARVIN H	LTC	0-0030106	0162	1
SNYDER MYRTLE M	MAJ	N-0002446	0663	1
SNYDER OSCAR P	M G	0-0004008	1156	1
SNYDER RICHARD F	LTC	0-0039937	0660	1
SNYDER ROBERT L	COL	0-0052456	0962	1
SNYDER RUSSELL C	COL	0-0007456	0753	2
SOARES EDWARD J	COL	0-0030020	0360	1
SOCHON JOSEPH J	WO1	W-0902146	0446	1
SOCKOLOSKIE ALPHONSE	COL	0-0051945	0766	1
SOCKS HUGH J	COL	0-0039771	0762	2
SODEN ROBERT E	LTC	0-0061378	0268	1
SODERHOLM NELS L	COL	0-0006199	0851	1
SODERHOLM WALTER H	COL	0-0007203	1146	2
SODERSTROM KENNETH M	1LT	0-0019684	0-36	2
SOGARD SIDNEY S	COL	0-0041518	0758	1
SOIK NILE W	1LT	0-0027140	0648	2
SOLA GERALD C JR	MAJ	0-0069560	0468	1
SOLF WALDEMAR A	COL	0-0040145	0668	1
SOLLITTO BASIL J	LTC	0-0059796	0866	1
SOLLOHUB JULIAN V	COL	0-0020584	0567	1
SOLOMON EDWARD M	LTC	0-0032351	0766	1
SOLOMON MADDREY A	B G	0-0019194	0457	2
SOLOMON MORTON	COL	0-0051002	0858	1
SOLOMONSON LAWRENCE	2LT	0-0016318	0-29	2
SOLTZ ALICE E	MAJ	N-0000117	0958	1
SOMERS CHARLES F JR	LTC	0-0077206	1168	1
SOMERS KENNETH	COL	0-0020413	0562	1
SOMERS RICHARD	CW4	W-0903842	0859	1
SOMERVILLE DUNCAN S	COL	0-0017109	0758	1
SOMMER HARRY A	COL	0-0080192	1068	2
SOMMER HENRY J	COL	0-0029055	0159	1
SOMMERS LAWRENCE E	COL	0-0031405	0264	1
SOMMERS WILLIAM D	COL	0-0043270	0566	1
SOPER LEROY D	COL	0-0008554	1049	1
SOPRANO QUENTIN C	LTC	0-0037830	0165	1
SORBELLO ROSARIO	LTC	0-0025066	0163	1
SORENSEN LENNARD C	COL	0-0042710	1263	1
SORENSEN MARTIN O	LTC	0-0031784	0266	1
SORENSON MORRIS E	LTC	0-0031977	0858	1
SORINI CHARLOTTE	MAJ	N-0002270	0463	1
SORRELL ROY W	LTC	0-0030287	1262	1
SORRELLS JESSIE A	MAJ	N-0000600	1262	1
SORROUGH IRENE M	LTC	L-0000112	0768	1
SORUM ARNE	COL	0-0011841	0948	1
SORY CARL G	COL	0-0043670	1267	1
SOTHERN RICHARD J	COL	0-0009290	1047	1
SOTO LILA O	MAJ	N-0001990	0466	1
SOULE JOHN E	COL	0-0050960	0957	1
SOULLIERE RALPH L	CW3	W-0903843	1062	1
SOURS LILLIAN H	MAJ	N-0002682	0868	1
SOUSA JOSEPH M	LTC	0-0084673	0265	1
SOUTHARD HARRY D	COL	0-0010837	0644	2
SOUTHARD WILLIAM W	COL	0-0004167	0147	2
SOUTHERLAND JOHN T	LTC	0-0060659	1068	1
SOUTHWORTH JOHN B	CW4	W-0901547	0157	1
SOWARDS MELVIN J	LTC	0-0039473	0265	1
SOWDER JOE W	CW4	W-0903844	0358	1
SOWERS HAROLD N	LTC	0-0081248	0468	1
SOWERS KENNETH M	COL	0-0024357	0463	1
SOWERS LAWRENCE L	CW4	W-0903845	0463	1
SOX BARBARA C	MAJ	N-0002105	1267	2
SPACE FRED L	WO1	W-0800290	1037	1
SPAGNOLO JOSEPH A	LTC	0-0080495	0567	1
SPALDING BASIL D	COL	0-0004541	1145	2
SPALDING DONALD P	COL	0-0006965	0648	1
SPALDING ISAAC	B G	0-0003383	0746	2
SPALDING SIDNEY P	M G	0-0003366	0849	1
SPANGLER RICHARD S	COL	0-0018457	0761	1
SPANN CECIL E JR	COL	0-0020162	0460	1
SPANN CHARLES W	LTC	0-0027135	0865	1
SPANN CHARLES W	MAJ	0-0034695	1061	1
SPANN CLAYTON O	1LT	0-0062113	0753	2
SPANN FRANKLIN L	COL	0-0023641	0764	1
SPANN GEORGE F	COL	0-0005115	1049	1
SPANN JAMES H	LTC	0-0045979	0863	1
SPANOGLE JOHN A	1LT	0-0014422	0320	2
SPARK JOHN R	LTC	0-0051812	1058	1
SPARKS CLAUDE S JR	LTC	0-0067759	1068	2
SPARKS JOHN W	COL	0-0030900	0566	1
SPARKS MURRAY E	LTC	0-0021374	0866	1
SPAULDING EDWARD C	COL	0-0020588	0867	1
SPAULDING THOMAS M	COL	0-0002030	0136	1
SPAULDING WALTER L	COL	0-0031915	0668	2
SPAULDING WILLIAM L	COL	0-0019704	1059	1
SPEAIRS ANSE H	COL	0-0084574	1265	1
SPEAKS ROBERT J	COL	0-0034196	0367	1
SPEARS JOHN H	COL	0-0046027	1267	1
SPECIALE JOACHIM J	LTC	0-0045946	0461	1
SPECTOR SAM	LTC	0-0055037	0466	1
SPEED HORACE JR	COL	0-0012468	0951	2
SPEEDIE JOHN C	COL	0-0031730	0764	1
SPEER MILDRED	CPT	N-0002261	0459	1
SPEIDEL GEORGE S JR	B G	0-0018406	0761	1
SPEIDEL WILLIAM H	COL	0-0011074	1152	1
SPEIGELBERG FRANK J	LTC	0-0054373	0264	1
SPEIGHTS DURIS JR	LTC	0-0087924	0367	1
SPEIR WILBERT A	COL	0-0041398	0855	1
SPEIRS RONALD C	LTC	0-0035820	0464	1
SPEISER ROBIN G	COL	0-0019104	0759	1
SPELLMAN CHARLES E	COL	0-0019655	0257	1
SPELLMAN LAWRENCE E	LTC	0-0050267	0966	2
SPELLMAN SETH W JR	LTC	0-0070509	0867	2
SPENCE JUDSON C SR	LTC	0-0049771	0763	1
SPENCE RALPH W	MAJ	0-0058145	0366	1
SPENCE SOREN E	LTC	0-0085263	1268	1
SPENCE WILLIAM	B G	0-0004447	0947	1
SPENCER ANDREW	LTC	0-0036076	0366	2
SPENCER HOUCK	COL	0-0034719	0664	1
SPENCER JOHN J	LTC	0-0044248	0163	1
SPENCER THOMAS A	LTC	0-0063503	1068	2
SPENCER THOMAS C	COL	0-0002281	0644	2
SPENCER THOMAS K	1LT	0-0023327	0548	1
SPENDLOVE VENICE	MAJ	N-0001345	0367	1
SPERATI PAOLO H	COL	0-0009667	1149	1
SPERL FRANK	CW4	W-0902365	0660	1
SPERRY FREDERICK	COL	0-0051427	0863	1
SPERRY JOHN B	COL	0-0056300	1068	1
SPETTEL FRANK J	LTC	0-0014613	0948	1
SPICER CYRIL P	COL	0-0006202	1046	2
SPICER WILLIAM H	COL	0-0029719	0661	1
SPIES GAGE H	COL	0-0029419	0660	1
SPIGELMOYER ROGER W	LTC	0-0052903	0262	1
SPIKA HOWARD J	LTC	0-0037593	0666	1
SPIKER ROBERT C	LTC	0-0035972	1064	1
SPIKER THEODORE S	LTC	0-0050774	0268	1
SPILLANE JOHN H	LTC	0-0030932	0762	1
SPILLER EDWIN B	COL	0-0003445	0834	2
SPILLER OLIVER L	B G	0-0002978	0845	2
SPILLMAN LYNN	LTC	0-0050981	0456	1
SPILLMAN WILLIAM R	COL	0-0042345	0464	1
SPILLNER SIEGFRIED	COL	0-0035300	0766	1
SPINELLO MICHAEL S	LTC	0-0082101	0765	2
SPINNEY RUSSELL G	COL	0-0030054	1263	1
SPITTLER AUGUST W	COL	0-0016954	1057	2
SPITZ HARRY	LTC	0-0057378	0756	1
SPITZER JOSEPH B	LTC	0-0081252	0868	1
SPITZMILLER BOB F	LTC	0-0060188	0761	1
SPIVA FORREST R	LTC	0-0084425	1166	1
SPIVEY EVA K	MAJ	N-0001897	1160	1
SPOEDE ROBERT W	MAJ	0-0058610	0868	1
SPOHN EDWARD A	CW4	W-0903848	0365	1
SPOON THOMAS L	COL	0-0006385	0251	1
SPRAGINS ROBERT B	B G	0-0022080	0167	1
SPRAGUE FRANCIS O	LTC	0-0081253	0468	1
SPRAGUE HAROLD F	COL	0-0041940	1061	1
SPRAKE JAMES M	LTC	0-0029872	0161	1
SPRANKLE DANE D	COL	0-0042169	0961	1
SPRATT JAMES L	MAJ	0-0039233	0864	1
SPRING SIDNEY G	COL	0-0019770	0765	2
SPRINGER LOUIS F	COL	0-0079717	0567	1
SPRINGER ROBERT M	COL	0-0012422	0854	1
SPRINGER ROBERT R	COL	0-0030624	0666	1
SPRINGFIELD NORA G	LTC	L-0000062	0163	2
SPRINKLE LESTER A	COL	0-0004620	0151	2
SPROAT HARRY F	LTC	0-0057416	0266	1
SPROULL RALPH D	1LT	0-0010647	0828	2
SPRUILL VICTOR F	LTC	0-0069799	0868	1
SPURGIN WILLIAM F	COL	0-0018762	0960	1
SPURR JEROME L	LTC	0-0029398	0358	1
SPURRIER JAMES R	COL	0-0025273	0763	1
SQUIRES JOHN L JR	MAJ	0-0061539	1168	2
SQUIRES MONAS N	LTC	0-0038758	1061	1
SQUIRES WILLIAM A	COL	0-0003756	0445	2
ST CLAIR HAROLD J	COL	0-0025369	1268	1
ST HELENS BEATRICE	MAJ	L-0000040	1157	1
ST JAMES ROBERT G	COL	0-0009039	0146	2
ST JOHN CLEMENT F	M G	0-0018258	0461	1
ST JOHN FREDERICK	LTC	0-0031394	1264	1
ST JOHN FREDERICK	LTC	0-0058791	0268	1
ST JOHN RALPH P	COL	0-0039706	0161	1
ST JOHN RICHARD C	LTC	0-0043530	0862	2
ST LAWRENCE CLYDE P	CW4	W-0903850	0665	1
ST ONGE ROBERT J	LTC	0-0027844	0767	1
ST SAUVER RICHARD T	COL	0-0037658	0968	1
STAATS HARLAN H JR	CW3	W-0903851	0659	2
STABILE JOSEPH N	COL	0-0043218	0868	1
STACK ANDREW J	LTC	0-0031126	0365	1
STACK HELEN A	MAJ	N-0000104	0460	1
STACK JAMES	COL	0-0029005	0247	2
STACK MARY E	LTC	R-0010072	0165	1
STACK ROBERT I	B G	0-0007585	0753	2
STACY ROBERT S	COL	0-0031905	0868	1
STACY THOMAS J	LTC	0-0082102	0768	1
STADFIELD HAROLD R	LTC	0-0039541	1054	1
STADIG NELS F	COL	0-0005112	1047	1
STADLER JOHN H JR	B G	0-0015731	0150	1
STADTMAN CLAUD E	COL	0-0004549	0952	1
STALLENS MARTHA M	MAJ	N-0002360	1058	2
STAFFORD ALBERT T	LTC	0-0039866	1161	1
STAFFORD BEN	COL	0-0006840	1044	2
STAFFORD CHARLES E	COL	0-0010456	1046	1
STAFFORD HEZZIE W	CW3	W-0903852	1154	1
STAGG SAMUEL T III	CW4	W-0903853	1065	1
STAGLIANO FIORE J	COL	0-0016389	0656	1
STAGNER CLYDE H	CPT	0-0065183	0564	2
STAGNER JOE P	CW4	W-0903854	0860	1
STAHL JOHN A	COL	0-0039934	1264	1
STAHLER CHARLES L	LTC	0-0032197	0966	1
STAHOVICH IRINA	MAJ	N-0000833	1166	1
STAIGER THEODORE S	LTC	0-0053879	0266	1
STAKES HARRY C	LTC	0-0030775	0764	1
STALCUP BYRON B	CW4	RW-0903855	0264	1
STALEY HARRY L JR	CW4	W-0903855	0255	1
STALEY J WAYNE JR	LTC	0-0060842	0968	1
STALEY MORTIMER R	COL	0-0043620	1066	1
STALEY ROBERT B	LTC	0-0043331	0762	1
STALK THEODORE	LTC	0-0063268	0666	2
STALKER DANIEL E	LTC	0-0064959	0567	1
STAM CHARLES W	LTC	0-0081255	0966	1
STANCISKO STEPHEN E	COL	0-0011799	0954	1
STANDISH FREDERICK	LTC	0-0024981	0767	1
STANDLEE EARLE	M G	0-0016530	0457	1
STANDLEY C S JR	COL	0-0029840	1160	1
STANDLEY WILLIAM P	CW4	W-0903860	0163	1
STANFORD BLUNDEN	COL	0-0050978	0458	1
STANFORD FREDERICK	COL	0-0023812	0863	1
STANFORD WILLIAM A	COL	0-0043808	0666	1
STANGE CAROL	MAJ	M-0010058	0162	1
STANGEL LYMAN E	COL	0-0029449	0860	1
STANGLE JOSEPH H	COL	0-0021406	0962	1
STANKOVICH ALBERT A	LTC	0-0081256	0567	1
STANLEY ARTHUR W	COL	0-0008796	0742	2
STANLEY FORREST H	MAJ	0-0038545	0959	1
STANLEY HENRY C	CW4	W-0903863	1057	1
STANLEY JOHN B	COL	0-0019549	1060	1
STANLEY LESLIE W	COL	0-0038594	0655	1
STANLEY ORAMEL H	COL	0-0004080	0848	1
STANN EUGENE J	COL	0-0020573	0266	1
STANOWICZ JOSEPH J	LTC	0-0027869	0566	1
STANSILL JOHN T	LTC	0-0040738	0763	2
STANTON JULIUS D	COL	0-0019823	0757	1
STANTON RAYMUND G	COL	0-0016929	0757	1
STANTON WALTER C	COL	0-0016433	0656	1
STAPLES FRANKLIN E	MAJ	0-0065616	0563	1
STAPLES JAMES T	LTC	0-0060444	0764	1
STAPLES JOHN F	COL	0-0031967	0768	1
STAPLETON JAMES B	B G	0-0019656	0365	1
STAPLETON JOHN C	COL	0-0019878	0562	2
STAPLETON THOMAS J	LTC	0-0028285	0766	1
STAR REUBEN	LTC	0-0042920	0756	1
STARK AMELIA	MAJ	N-0000656	0263	1
STARK CHARLES R	COL	0-0028773	0354	1
STARK GILBERT J	COL	0-0042791	1162	1
STARK HARRY W	COL	0-0003437	0145	1
STARK HENRY J	COL	0-0051448	0863	1
STARK JOHN M	COL	0-0039622	0859	1
STARK NORVELL R	LTC	0-0031335	0462	1
STARK THOMAS N	COL	0-0010368	0454	1
STARKEY ARTHUR W	COL	0-0025126	0762	1
STARKEY HENRY M M	LTC	0-0027422	0666	1
STARKS LESLIE E	LTC	0-0052029	0762	1
STARNES MERVYN B	COL	0-0029188	0960	1
STARR EDWARD M	COL	0-0012427	0854	1
STARR JAMES C	COL	0-0079640	0267	1
STARR LEONARD B	MAJ	0-0088498	0766	2
STARR LESTER L	CW4	W-0903867	0962	1
STARR ROBERT S	CW4	W-0903868	0666	1
STARR RUPERT E	B G	0-0011309	0550	1
STARR WILLIAM F	COL	0-0023843	1266	1
STARRATT THOMAS R	CPT	0-0017457	0340	2
STARRETT CARL H	MAJ	0-0009941	0939	2
STATHAM HARLAN R	COL	0-0017672	1054	1
STAUB LESLIE J	COL	0-0029123	0859	1
STAUFFER ARDEN K	CW4	W-0903869	0868	1
STAUFFER CHARLES J	LTC	0-0033757	0666	1

NAME	GRADE	SVC NO	DATE RET MO YR	RET CODE
STAVER DONALD F	LTC	0-0050422	0866	1
STAVER ROBERT L	COL	0-0043650	0468	1
STAYER MORRISON C	M G	0-0002571	0746	2
STEADMAN FRANK M	COL	0-0017616	0859	1
STEARNS CUTHBERT P	B G	0-0002683	0246	2
STEARNS JOSEPH E	COL	0-0018791	0862	1
STEBBINS ALBERT K JR	COL	0-0015695	0854	1
STECK ERNEST E	LTC	0-0042490	0163	1
STECKEL GLENN A	LTC	0-0046036	0764	1
STEED OLIVER H	COL	0-0043177	1267	1
STEELE CLYDE K	LTC	0-0084676	0868	1
STEELE GORDON H	COL	0-0008175	1146	1
STEELE JOHN C	B G	0-0018668	0862	1
STEELE LOWELL R	COL	0-0025167	0765	1
STEELE MADA	MAJ	M-0010044	0464	1
STEELE PAUL	COL	0-0007509	0854	1
STEELE PRESTON	COL	0-0018729	0862	1
STEELE ROBERT L	LTC	0-0028429	0766	1
STEELE ROY H	COL	0-0041847	0361	1
STEELE RUSSELL D	LTC	0-0056800	0560	1
STEELE STANLEY F	COL	0-0020474	0759	1
STEEN ELSIE W	MAJ	M-0010109	0760	1
STEENBURGH RUTH M	MAJ	N-0002075	1060	1
STEER ARTHUR	COL	0-0057815	1267	1
STEERE JOHN A	COL	0-0006698	0947	1
STEERE THOMAS I	MAJ	0-0013988	0720	2
STEFANI LOUIS J	LTC	0-0040707	0166	1
STEFFEY WILLIAM G	LTC	0-0030404	0661	1
STEGALL OSCAR JR	LTC	0-0032014	1066	1
STEGMAIER ROBERT M	COL	0-0020725	0865	1
STEIN JOHN F	COL	0-0051538	1064	1
STEIN THOMAS F JR	LTC	0-0031411	0165	1
STEIN WILLIAM	COL	0-0063775	0465	1
STEINBACH ALOIS L	LTC	0-0048109	1166	1
STEINBACH RICHARD	M G	0-0018560	0761	2
STEINBRING MILTON E	LTC	0-0025946	0862	1
STEINER JAMES L	CW4	W-0903874	1165	1
STEINER RAYMOND B	COL	0-0051622	0165	1
STEINHARDT WALTER	CW2	W-0903875	1159	1
STEININGER DONALD H	LTC	0-0050599	1266	1
STEINKRAUSS ALBERT M	COL	0-0051843	0467	1
STEINMEYER GEORGE	COL	0-0016675	0451	1
STELMAN CHESTER P	LTC	0-0063352	1065	1
STELZENMULLER W B	COL	0-0021422	0660	1
STEMPIN HARRY J	LTC	0-0045786	0563	1
STEPCZYK FRANK	COL	0-0020051	1065	1
STEPHENS BLACKBURN	COL	0-0033060	0964	1
STEPHENS ERNEST T	CW4	W-0903877	0956	1
STEPHENS FREEMAN I	MAJ	0-0026372	C146	2
STEPHENS GEORGE R	B G	0-0027892	0261	2
STEPHENS HARVEY L	CW4	W-0902093	1162	2
STEPHENS HENRY J	CW4	W-0903878	0762	1
STEPHENS HERBERT W	MAJ	0-0069802	0765	1
STEPHENS JOHN F	COL	0-0025539	0863	1
STEPHENS JOHN J	COL	0-0031844	0568	1
STEPHENS JOSEPH W G	COL	0-0004622	0746	1
STEPHENS LEONARD E	1LT	0-0014967	0934	2
STEPHENS RICHARD W	M G	0-0015569	0658	1
STEPHENS ROY A	LTC	0-0038705	1059	1
STEPHENSON ANDREW D	COL	0-0019201	0863	1
STEPHENSON EDWARD	1LT	0-0021340	0442	2
STEPHENSON H W JR	LTC	0-0022722	1158	1
STEPHENSON HARRY W	LTC	0-0002655	1122	1
STEPHENSON HORACE G	LTC	0-0055488	0965	1
STEPHENSON JAMES D	LTC	0-0017757	1046	1
STEPPAN MARY M	LTC	N-0000113	1058	1
STERLING JOHN A	COL	0-0002693	0935	1
STERLING PHILIP C JR	LTC	0-0020848	0846	2
STERLING THOMAS M	LTC	0-0059655	0767	1
STERN BENJAMIN	COL	0-0015197	0854	1
STERN HERBERT I	COL	0-0023957	0968	1
STETEKLUH ROBERT E	LTC	0-0027575	0766	1
STEVENS ALFRED E	COL	0-0029916	1060	1
STEVENS ALFRED L	LTC	0-0051506	0562	1
STEVENS BURROWES G	COL	0-0012187	0753	1

NAME	GRADE	SVC NO	DATE RET MO YR	RET CODE
STEVENS DOUGLAS	COL	0-0038816	1265	1
STEVENS ELI	COL	0-0018235	0948	2
STEVENS GEORGE B	LTC	0-0044872	0764	1
STEVENS GEORGE R III	COL	0-0039215	0868	1
STEVENS JOHN D	B G	0-0019414	0764	1
STEVENS MILTON E	LTC	0-0025471	0868	1
STEVENS PAT M III	COL	0-0030557	1064	1
STEVENS RAY E	CW4	W-0907008	0266	1
STEVENS RICHARD D	COL	0-0028954	0556	2
STEVENS VERNUM C	COL	0-0015526	0754	1
STEVENS WILBER A	COL	0-0030365	0262	1
STEVENS WILMER B	COL	0-0037079	0868	1
STEVENSON CHARLES B	LTC	0-0060639	1168	1
STEVENSON DANIEL S	COL	0-0019696	0265	2
STEVENSON DON W	LTC	0-0034868	0763	1
STEVENSON FRANK E	COL	0-0038785	1264	1
STEVENSON HUGH W	COL	0-0017642	0859	1
STEVENSON JEROME M	LTC	0-0051897	1162	1
STEVENSON WALTER H	COL	0-0041705	0459	1
STEVENSON WILLIAM J	MAJ	0-0074856	0767	1
STEWART BLANCHE M	LTC	N-0002003	0866	1
STEWART CHARLES W	LTC	0-0032925	0261	1
STEWART CLAUDE H	COL	0-0033441	0368	1
STEWART DONALD B	LTC	0-0023028	0868	1
STEWART DONALD E	MAJ	0-0069803	1164	1
STEWART DOROTHY I	MAJ	L-0000262	0962	1
STEWART GEORGE C	M G	0-0015349	1054	1
STEWART HAROLD P	COL	0-0009780	0547	2
STEWART HARRY T	LTC	0-0027331	0166	1
STEWART HOWELL F	MAJ	0-0056571	1265	1
STEWART JAMES J JR	LTC	0-0020901	0444	2
STEWART JODIE G JR	LTC	0-0023256	0661	1
STEWART JOHN A	COL	0-0005278	0244	2
STEWART JOSEPH C	COL	0-0029662	0162	1
STEWART KEITH M	LTC	0-0027700	0867	1
STEWART LEROY J	B G	0-0014912	0451	1
STEWART MANLIUS R	LTC	0-0042503	0163	1
STEWART MARION G JR	COL	0-0030244	0864	1
STEWART MATTHEW C	COL	0-0043541	0865	1
STEWART NEIL G	COL	0-0033670	0868	1
STEWART STANLEY L	LTC	0-0042274	0160	1
STEWART THOMAS B	COL	0-0039335	0866	1
STEWART WILLIAM B	COL	0-0008766	0952	1
STEWART WILLIAM R	COL	0-0004751	1044	2
STICKNEY LOUIS S	COL	0-0007515	1048	1
STIEBEL HENRY M	COL	0-0030198	0664	1
STIEFEL ARTHUR A	LTC	0-0038934	0856	2
STIER ROBERT J	COL	0-0080008	1167	1
STIESMEYER EDWARD H	COL	0-0060741	0667	1
STIEVENART LAVERNE	MAJ	N-0000260	0560	1
STIKA ROBERT W	COL	0-0015886	0446	2
STILES LESTER W	LTC	0-0082104	0168	1
STILL ALICE E	MAJ	N-0002052	0960	1
STILL DANIEL E	COL	0-0019510	0662	1
STILL EDGAR E	LTC	0-0081260	0765	1
STILL FAYE G	MAJ	N-0000539	0449	1
STILLINGER CECIL	LTC	0-0057926	0851	2
STILLINGER OTTO R	COL	0-0010320	0744	2
STILLMAN EDMUND H	LTC	0-0006645	0142	1
STILLMAN RICHARD J	COL	0-0025038	1265	1
STILLWAUGH ELVA M	MAJ	L-0000250	1063	1
STILSON GUY D	CW4	W-0903880	1167	1
STINESS PHILIP B	COL	0-0018398	0761	1
STINSON GERALD C	MAJ	0-0061997	0364	1
STIRLING WILLIAM B	CW4	W-0903881	1059	1
STITH MARION C	COL	0-0037385	1166	1
STIVLEN SYLVIA M	MAJ	N-0001432	0664	1
STOCK MARVIN H	LTC	0-0050633	0667	1
STOCKDALE GALE E	1LT	0-0028328	0149	2
STOCKDER IREENE L	MAJ	N-0000547	0450	1
STOCKER LEE J	MAJ	0-0085115	0768	1
STOCKTON ERNEST L	COL	0-0039560	1057	1
STOCKTON HUNTER L	LTC	0-0023409	0868	1
STOCKTON JOHN B	COL	0-0026152	0867	1
STOCKTON M L JR	B G	0-0010619	0644	2

NAME	GRADE	SVC NO	DATE RET MO YR	RET CODE
STUCKTON MARSH P	LTC	0-0051769	0762	1
STOCKWELL WARREN P	LTC	0-0040438	0660	1
STODDARD AYRES W	COL	0-0043652	1168	1
STODGEL JAMES E	LTC	0-0067963	0866	1
STODTER CHARLES E	COL	0-0000505	0435	1
STODTER CHARLES S	COL	0-0016013	0954	1
STODTER JOHN H	COL	0-0015018	0654	1
STOECKERT GEORGE I	LTC	0-0036757	0467	1
STOEVER ROBERT E	COL	0-0042114	1162	1
STOKELY CARLIN C	COL	0-0002639	0446	2
STOKES MARCUS B JR	B G	0-0015613	0854	2
STOKES ORVILLE N	COL	0-0020215	1058	1
STOKES ROBERT C	LTC	0-0057887	0361	1
STOLL IRWIN C	LTC	0-0029504	0148	2
STOLL JUSTIN W	B G	0-0030483	0765	1
STOLTZ RUTH M	LTC	N-0000586	0459	1
STOLZ STEPHEN H	LTC	0-0041707	0757	1
STONE ALEXANDER	COL	0-0018076	0657	1
STONE BERNICE A	MAJ	N-0002257	0662	1
STONE DON N	CW3	W-0903885	0260	1
STONE FRED J	MAJ	0-0009108	0-34	1
STONE GUY	MAJ	0-0060213	1153	2
STONE JOEL E	LTC	0-0058165	0668	1
STONE KATRINE F	MAJ	N-0002386	0959	1
STONE LAURENCE A	COL	0-0040414	0465	1
STONE LLOYD E	MAJ	0-0027138	0561	1
STONE RAYMOND JR	COL	0-0015206	0854	1
STONE STEPHEN G JR	MAJ	0-0047960	0764	1
STONE WILLIAM S	COL	0-0018277	0654	2
STONEBACK LEE S	COL	0-0044316	0764	1
STONEKING ROBERT E	CW4	W-0903888	1165	1
STOPP JOSEPH E	LTC	0-0031693	1265	1
STORAASLI GYNTHER	COL	0-0011751	0248	1
STORKE HARRY P	LTG	0-0016468	0961	2
STORMS HARRY E	COL	0-0009725	0951	1
STORMS WILLIAM G	LTC	0-0070047	1168	1
STORRS BRUCE D	LTC	0-0061060	1065	1
STOTLAR WILLIAM G	LTC	0-0043662	0167	1
STOTT MABEL G	LTC	N-0000073	0558	1
STOUGH CHARLES S JR	LTC	0-0035187	0863	1
STOUGH PAUL A	CPT	0-0027429	1060	2
STOUT ARTHUR D	LTC	0-0031255	0161	1
STOUT CARRIE P	MAJ	N-0000889	1163	1
STOUT LOUIS M	CW4	W-0907012	0761	1
STOUT ROY A	COL	0-0008726	0949	2
STOVALL A S J JR	COL	0-0012434	0854	1
STOVER GLENN C	CW4	W-0907013	1062	1
STOVER WILLIAM J	COL	0-0031381	1266	1
STOW HAROLD E	LTC	0-0008446	0544	2
STOWBRIDGE ROBERT W	LTC	0-0036501	0362	2
STOWELL ALLEN L	COL	0-0010310	0452	2
STOWELL WILLIAM M	LTC	0-0026682	0862	1
STRADER RALPH B	COL	0-0017686	0859	2
STRADLEY SARAH C	CPT	N-0001233	0859	1
STRAIGHT CLIO E	B G	0-0024337	0661	1
STRAIN ETHEL L	CPT	N-0000811	0350	1
STRAIN JAMES F	COL	0-0008085	0850	1
STRAIN JAMES W	COL	0-0023719	0767	1
STRAND DONALD J	LTC	0-0057067	0865	1
STRANDBERG WILLIAM B	COL	0-0020579	0863	1
STRANGE HUBERT E	COL	0-0021231	0868	1
STRATFORD ELIZABETH	LTC	N-0002325	0968	1
STRATTA MAURICE D	COL	0-0081883	0768	1
STRATTON CHARLES W	COL	0-0016661	1056	1
STRATTON CHESTER M	COL	0-0030431	0565	1
STRATTON FREDERICK	LTC	0-0039544	1154	1
STRATTON JAMES H	B G	0-0012656	0749	1
STRAUB RUTH M	MAJ	N-0000166	0157	1
STRAUSS GEORGE H	LTC	0-0058618	0868	1
STRAUSS RALPH V	COL	0-0017689	1054	1
STRAWBRIDGE JOHN T	LTC	0-0040287	0165	1
STRAWN CHRISTOPHE	COL	0-0007250	1047	1
STRAYHORN KATHLEEN H	MAJ	N-0000092	0656	1
STRECKER ROBERT H	COL	0-0026853	0767	1
STREET ANCIL L	CW3	W-0907014	0262	1

NAME	GRADE	SVC NO	DATE RET MO YR	RET CODE
STREET FRANK L	COL	0-0030055	0962	1
STREET JACK B	LTC	0-0034272	0661	1
STREET JOHN C	LTC	0-0018686	1133	2
STREET ROBERT W	LTC	0-0059042	0166	1
STREETER HILWERT S	LTC	0-0020300	1057	1
STREETMAN JAMES P	LTC	0-0030086	0161	1
STREICHER FREDERICK	COL	0-0041485	1057	1
STREIT PAUL H	M G	0-0006254	0353	1
STREVIG JOHN R	LTC	0-0039656	1160	1
STRICKLAND ARTHUR T	COL	0-0044085	0266	2
STRICKLAND ERASMUS H	COL	0-0029355	0355	2
STRICKLAND HENRY E	COL	0-0016140	0755	1
STRICKLAND IDA R	MAJ	R-0010112	0365	1
STRICKLAND ROBERT P	LTC	0-0030749	1058	1
STRICKLAND WILBURN L	COL	0-0029839	0163	2
STRICKLAND Z L JR	COL	0-0024176	1064	1
STRICKLEN SIMON A	COL	0-0052136	0568	2
STRICKLER EDWARD J	COL	0-0008677	0446	2
STRIDER NICHOLAS S	COL	0-0045589	0267	1
STRIEGEL JOHN D	COL	0-0029700	0761	1
STRINGFELLOW HORACE	MAJ	0-0014195	0119	2
STRIPLING DOCK A	CW4	RW-0907015	1167	1
STRNAD JOSEPH J	COL	0-0037497	0768	1
STROBEL PHYLLIS R	MAJ	M-0010069	0565	1
STROCK ALAN M	COL	0-0023099	1162	1
STRODE JOHN T B	COL	0-0019709	0163	2
STROEDE ROGER A	LTC	0-0049045	0667	1
STROEMER RUTH M	MAJ	N-0002104	0866	1
STROHBEHN EDWARD L	COL	0-0012312	0754	1
STROHM ROBERT H	CPT	0-0065152	0265	1
STROK MICHAEL J	COL	0-0052838	0667	1
STROKER JAMES F	COL	0-0018375	0947	2
STROMBERG WOODROW W	M G	0-0020728	0268	1
STRONG CECIL H	COL	0-0022725	0366	2
STRONG EDWIN R	COL	0-0008538	0546	2
STRONG PASCHAL N	B G	0-0014904	0654	1
STRONG PAUL D	LTC	0-0007876	0342	2
STRONG ROBERT W	B G	0-0003832	0350	2
STROPES LLOYD R	LTC	0-0037629	0464	1
STROTHER KENNETH C	COL	0-0015738	0654	1
STROUBE ESTHEL O	COL	0-0041368	0954	1
STROUD JOSEPH C JR	LTC	0-0058693	0865	1
STROUD WILLIAM R	LTC	0-0028201	0966	1
STROUP DONALD F	CW4	W-0904316	0257	1
STRUBE RICHARD L	LTC	0-0082106	0567	1
STRUBLE H SPENCER	COL	0-0012953	1049	1
STRUBLE LAWRENCE A	CPT	0-0087396	0763	2
STRUNK ROBERT W	COL	0-0040581	0868	1
STRYKER WILLIAM B	COL	0-0019691	1060	1
STUART ALEXANDER	COL	0-0002307	1039	2
STUART ALEXANDER	COL	0-0019447	0762	1
STUART ARCHIBALD	M G	0-0018130	1058	1
STUART LARHETT L	B G	0-0003677	0751	1
STUART MARGARET	MAJ	R-0010084	0360	1
STUART WHITNEY D	LTC	0-0037788	1164	1
STUBBLEBINE A N JR	COL	0-0015768	0954	2
STUBBS HUGH P JR	LTC	0-0024530	0761	1
STUBBS MARSHALL	M G	0-0017706	1163	1
STUBBS WILLIAM H	COL	0-0022085	0946	2
STUCKERT JOHN M	LTC	0-0084427	1066	1
STUDER ROBERT W	COL	0-0021786	0268	1
STUDLER RENE R	COL	0-0010398	0853	1
STULL KATHERINE	MAJ	L-0000002	0753	1
STULTING HARRY W	LTC	0-0022726	0160	1
STUMP GEORGE T	COL	0-0030023	1163	1
STUMP ROBERT C	LTC	0-0023516	0861	2
STUMPF ROBERT H	COL	0-0020707	0967	1
STURDIVANT LESLIE W	MAJ	0-0058620	0966	1
STURDY WILLIAM W	COL	0-0051043	0859	1
STURGEON JOHN H	COL	0-0004095	0848	1
STURGIS SARA L	LTC	L-0000029	1058	1
STURIES CARL H	COL	0-0017192	1053	2
STURM FREDERICK	COL	0-0040185	1067	1
STURMAN J FOXHALL JR	COL	0-0012720	0753	2
STUTZMAN OLIVER G	COL	0-0032771	0467	1

NAME	GRADE	SVC NO	DATE RET MO YR	RET CODE
STOVERUD HOMER A	LTC	0-0043523	1164	1
STOWE KATHRYNE C	MAJ	N-0000296	1060	1
STYER WILHELM D	LTG	0-0004415	0447	1
STYLES SIDNEY S	CW3	W-0903894	0264	1
SUBE HERBERT P	LTC	0-0057723	0764	1
SUDDETH JAMES A	LTC	0-0055222	0865	1
SUGG DOUGLAS	COL	0-0011172	1150	2
SUGIYAMA SHIGEKI J	LTC	0-0092126	0966	1
SUGLIA ANTHONY S	LTC	0-0065108	1066	1
SULIT MARIANO S	CPT	0-0012869	0538	2
SULLIVAN ALDEN P	COL	0-0041069	0268	1
SULLIVAN ALEXANDER	COL	0-0003231	0142	1
SULLIVAN ARTHUR O	LTC	0-0030974	1162	2
SULLIVAN B H JR	COL	0-0022770	0161	1
SULLIVAN ELEANORE C	LTC	L-0000014	0257	1
SULLIVAN FRANCIS R	COL	0-0022923	0763	1
SULLIVAN GERALD J	1LT	0-0015511	0834	2
SULLIVAN JAMES J	MAJ	0-0059044	1063	1
SULLIVAN JOHN B	B G	0-0019363	0661	1
SULLIVAN JOHN J	LTC	0-0050627	0268	1
SULLIVAN JOHN M	COL	0-0030698	0766	2
SULLIVAN JOHN S	COL	0-0002271	1045	2
SULLIVAN JOSEPH P	M G	0-0005328	1053	2
SULLIVAN JOSEPH T	LTC	0-0059513	0763	2
SULLIVAN JOSEPH W	COL	0-0043260	0168	1
SULLIVAN LEO J	MAJ	0-0037027	0658	2
SULLIVAN LEON F	CPT	0-0006749	0934	2
SULLIVAN MAURICE L	COL	0-0043165	1067	2
SULLIVAN MORTIMER F	COL	0-0010660	0854	2
SULLIVAN RICHARD C	LTC	0-0084808	0867	1
SULLIVAN ROBERT E	COL	0-0043745	0268	1
SULLIVAN WILLIAM E	B G	0-0029635	0162	2
SULLIVAN WILLIAM M	LTC	0-0050750	0666	1
SULLO ERWIN E	COL	0-0042491	0265	1
SULPIZIO VIRGINIA M	MAJ	N-0001802	0665	1
SUMMA GROVER A	COL	0-0011965	0153	1
SUMMERALL C P JR	COL	0-0015726	0754	1
SUMMERALL ROBERT E	LTC	0-0039314	0968	1
SUMMERS EVELYN G	LTC	R-0010122	0667	1
SUMMERS IVERSON B	COL	0-0003830	0746	2
SUMMERS OWEN	B G	0-0008066	0647	2
SUMMERS SAMUEL J III	LTC	0-0070521	0968	1
SUMMERS WILLIAM M	COL	0-0021369	0566	2
SUMMERSETT JAMES A	LTC	0-0004882	1141	2
SUMMERSON DONALD J	LTC	0-0060747	1066	1
SUMNER EDWIN M	COL	0-0006894	0848	1
SUMNER GEORGE R	COL	0-0039689	1060	1
SUMNER HENRY K	COL	0-0002894	0544	2
SUMNICHT RUSSELL W	COL	0-0031208	0966	1
SUNDERLIN WILLIAM W	COL	0-0032678	1165	1
SUNDIN ALVAR B	COL	0-0021128	0366	1
SUNDLOF WILLIAM A	COL	0-0021236	0762	1
SUNDRE ROBERT L	LTC	0-0062950	1166	1
SUNDT DANIEL N	COL	0-0017604	0859	1
SUNDT HARALD S	COL	0-0018774	0862	1
SUNSHINE GEORGE P	LTC	0-0080497	0762	1
SUPPLE EDWARD L	COL	0-0009814	0350	1
SURBER CHARLES E	LTC	0-0032528	1057	1
SURRATT JOE F	COL	0-0019461	0661	1
SUSSMAN WILLIAM A	COL	0-0021165	0168	1
SUTHERLAND ALEXANDER	COL	0-0018609	0661	1
SUTHERLAND CHARLES F	COL	0-0007107	0146	1
SUTHERLAND FRANCES L	MAJ	N-0001735	0868	1
SUTHERLAND JOHN F	LTC	0-0030779	0764	1
SUTHERLAND KATHERINE	MAJ	L-0000286	0766	1
SUTTLE ALBERT B JR	LTC	0-0059182	0768	1
SUTTLES ERNEST A	COL	0-0016275	0255	1
SUTTON ALEXANDER JR	COL	0-0043663	1268	1
SUTTON CLYDE T JR	LTC	0-0022128	0659	1
SUTTON EARL	COL	0-0042961	0860	1
SUTTON GEORGE M	LTC	0-0035970	0363	1
SVARE CARROLL S	COL	0-0022313	0167	1
SVENSSON ERIC H F	B G	0-0017630	0859	1
SVILAR MATTHEW	LTC	0-0081270	1066	1
SWAIM ALLAN L	COL	0-0032871	0966	1

NAME	GRADE	SVC NO	DATE RET MO YR	RET CODE
SWAIN OREN	COL	0-0020176	0866	1
SWALL ROSS F	LTC	0-0037511	0464	1
SWAN ELEANOR J	MAJ	N-0001901	0861	1
SWAN THOMAS H	COL	0-0031471	0367	1
SWANGREN GORDON L	LTC	0-0059045	1168	1
SWANK MARCELL G	LTC	0-0082108	1166	2
SWANK WALTER D	COL	0-0023281	0868	1
SWANN RALPH J	LTC	0-0059046	0968	1
SWANSON BYRON A	CW3	W-0907017	0964	2
SWANSON LEONARD N	COL	0-0018936	0760	1
SWANSON RAYMOND W	COL	0-0030925	1066	1
SWANSON RUTH M	MAJ	N-0002176	0767	1
SWANTON DONOVAN	COL	0-0005314	0951	1
SWARM WILLIAM R	COL	0-0043018	0666	1
SWARTZ ALVA W	LTC	0-0025077	0962	1
SWARTZ CHARLES H	B G	0-0012798	0457	1
SWARTZ DOROTHY L	MAJ	R-0010008	0364	1
SWARTZ ROBERT N	COL	0-0035903	0664	1
SWATTA FRANK A	COL	0-0022237	0867	1
SWEANY KENNETH S	B G	0-0015251	1155	1
SWEARINGEN JOHN C	LTC	0-0034711	0365	1
SWEARINGEN SAMUEL M	LTC	0-0021381	0866	1
SWEE RICHARD J	CW4	W-0907018	0467	1
SWEEK JACK G	COL	0-0030633	0366	1
SWEENEY ANNE E	LTC	L-0000119	0266	1
SWEENEY EUGENE J	COL	0-0021254	0860	1
SWEENEY FRANCIS P	LTC	0-0081271	0667	1
SWEENEY HARDIN C	COL	0-0004569	0654	1
SWEENEY JAMES L	LTC	0-0031457	0661	1
SWEENY ANNA C	CPT	N-0000170	0648	1
SWEET FRED W JR	LTC	0-0031266	0967	1
SWEET FREDERICK	LTC	0-0038332	1068	1
SWEET JOSEPH B	B G	0-0009694	0648	1
SWEET WILLIAM H	COL	0-0006579	1047	2
SWEET WILLIAM J JR	LTC	0-0035814	0761	1
SWEETING HARRY W JR	COL	0-0019168	0863	1
SWEETLAND ROBERT H	CW4	W-0903904	0868	1
SWENSON ALICE D	MAJ	N-0000196	0461	1
SWETT DANIEL H	LTC	0-0038984	0159	1
SWICK CHARLES H	MAJ	0-0009019	0138	2
SWIDLER GEORGE J	CW4	W-0903901	0964	1
SWIFT EBEN F	COL	0-0023258	0965	1
SWIFT EDWARD V	LTC	0-0023636	0946	2
SWIFT IRA P	M G	0-0012205	0654	1
SWIFT MELVIN L	CW4	W-0902325	0156	1
SWINDLER CHARLES M	MAJ	0-0024641	1146	2
SWINDLER PERRY D	COL	0-0028827	0753	2
SWINEHART LEWIS S JR	LTC	0-0059880	0364	2
SWING JOSEPH M	LTG	0-0003801	0254	2
SWINK JESSE M	COL	0-0022315	0968	2
SWISHER ARTHUR O	COL	0-0051611	0565	2
SWITZER JOHN S	COL	0-0004747	0951	1
SWITZER WALTER E	LTC	0-0065442	0766	1
SWOFFORD JAMES L	LTC	0-0053451	0264	1
SWOGER FRANK R	COL	0-0029429	0759	1
SWOLLEY FRANK C	CW4	W-0903905	0662	2
SWOMLEY NEELY M	LTC	0-0059881	0866	1
SWOPE FRANCIS A	COL	0-0032774	0267	1
SWOPE HERMAN E	LTC	0-0080194	0566	1
SWOPE LESLIE J	LTC	0-0062216	0665	1
SYDENHAM HENRY R	B G	0-0018654	0661	1
SYDNOR WILLIAM D JR	LTC	0-0032618	0661	1
SYKES HORACE F JR	COL	0-0017494	0757	1
SYKES ORIN B	COL	0-0029003	0455	2
SYLVESTER LOREN H	MAJ	0-0062243	0763	1
SYLVESTER ROBERT W	COL	0-0051473	0164	1
SYMANOWSKI PETER P	CW4	W-0903906	0266	1
SYMBOL PAUL H	COL	0-0023452	0361	1
SYME LEANDER D	COL	0-0012334	0549	1
SYNER JAMES C	COL	0-0065462	1168	1
SYNNOTT DONALD A	LTC	0-0048542	0566	1
SYNOLDS DONALD L	CPT	0-0057670	0965	2
SYRON DARREL L	LTC	0-0025034	0764	1
SZABO JOSEPH	LTC	0-0024480	0861	2
TABER ALDEN P	B G	0-0018134	0657	1

NAME	GRADE	SVC NO	DATE RET MO YR	RET CODE
TABER HAROLD	COL	0-0050940	0256	1
TABER JOHN H	COL	0-0020987	0467	1
TABER THOMAS K	COL	0-0009775	1046	1
TABER WILLIAM A	COL	0-0005628	0545	2
TABER WILLIAM R	LTC	0-0051927	1263	1
TABSCOTT ERNEST E	COL	0-0010126	0851	2
TACK WILLIS J	COL	0-0003691	0249	1
TACKETT ORVILLE H	COL	0-0058683	0968	2
TAFT PHILIP H	LTC	0-0079116	0867	1
TAGGART OWEN H	LTC	0-0051696	0763	1
TAGGART SAMUEL J	COL	0-0041388	0755	1
TAINTOR CHARLES	MAJ	0-0003981	0224	2
TAIT ALBERT L	COL	0-0031568	1166	1
TAKAHASHI WILLIAM H	CW3	W-0904307	0564	1
TALBOT LAURENCE D	CPT	0-0011179	0137	2
TALBOT RAYMOND J	COL	0-0023608	0963	1
TALBOTT CHARLIE Y SR	COL	0-0031664	1167	1
TALLEY BENJAMIN B	B G	0-0016668	0456	1
TALLEY JOSEPHUS B JR	COL	0-0023578	0946	2
TALSMA MARTIN L	LTC	OF-0103051	0967	1
TAM DONALD R	COL	0-0043933	0968	1
TANDO KENNETH H	COL	0-0039695	1060	1
TANK CHARLES F	B G	0-0019350	1064	1
TANKERSLEY MILTON J	LTC	0-0080499	0965	1
TANKSLEY JEPTHA C	CPT	0-0026095	0147	2
TANNEHILL HELEN C	MAJ	N-0002172	0164	1
TANNER JAMES B	LTC	0-0027401	0468	2
TANNER JAMES D	COL	0-0052132	0368	1
TANNER JOHN L	LTC	0-0033683	0564	2
TANOUS PETER S	COL	0-0024067	0766	1
TANSEY PATRICK H	M G	0-0009299	0553	1
TANSEY PATRICK H JR	COL	0-0023915	1066	1
TANSEY ROBERT F	LTC	0-0027496	0166	1
TAPPER GORDON U	LTC	0-0052314	0955	2
TARANTINO FRANK S	LTC	0-0080327	0167	1
TARANTULA MICHAEL N	CW4	RW-0907020	0163	1
TARBET KENNETH D	MAJ	0-0091526	0967	2
TARBOX JAMES C	COL	0-0006776	0946	2
TARDY WALTER C	COL	0-0032532	0767	1
TARKINGTON HIRAM W	COL	0-0010618	0854	1
TARKONTON JAMES C JR	COL	0-0033283	1267	2
TARPLEY HERMAN V	LTC	0-0043121	0258	1
TARPLEY THOMAS M JR	COL	0-0017325	0457	2
TARR EUGENE S	COL	0-0042327	0864	1
TARR RAYMOND P JR	COL	0-0029358	1059	2
TARRANT JAMES E	COL	0-0028859	0458	1
TARRANT LEGARE K	B G	0-0017208	0958	2
TASKER ARTHUR N	COL	0-0002411	0838	2
TASKER HAROLD P	COL	0-0015557	0939	2
TATCH DAVID	COL	0-0031116	0666	1
TATE ALBERT	CPT	0-0014432	0620	2
TATE CLIFFORD H	COL	0-0004708	0947	1
TATE DOROTHY T	MAJ	N-0002272	0863	1
TATE FERDINAND	COL	0-0019359	0862	1
TATE FOSTER J	B G	0-0012287	0749	1
TATE JAMES E	LTC	0-0021709	0656	2
TATE JOHN C	CW3	W-0903911	0362	2
TATE NICHOLAS L	LTC	0-0038988	1058	1
TATE RALPH H	B G	0-0011949	0747	1
TATE ROY A	COL	0-0076920	0762	1
TATOM KEITH K	COL	0-0011742	0748	1
TATSCH WILLIAM D	LTC	0-0024822	0468	1
TATUM JAMES B	CPT	0-0050846	1053	2
TAUBER BERNARD L	LTC	0-0036715	1164	1
TAUSCH EGON R	COL	0-0016452	0656	1
TAVEL HENRY	COL	0-0039652	0161	1
TAWES JOHN P	LTC	0-0031357	1064	1
TAYLOR A RHJ	COL	0-0012646	0648	2
TAYLOR ANNA L	MAJ	N-0002163	1262	1
TAYLOR BARNEY C	CW4	W-0903912	0857	1
TAYLOR CLARENCE L	COL	0-0019336	0962	1
TAYLOR CLAUDE E	COL	0-0045316	0865	1
TAYLOR CLOYD V	LTC	0-0047850	1263	1
TAYLOR DANIEL R	LTC	0-0018217	0551	2
TAYLOR DAVID A	COL	0-0012156	1048	1

NAME	GRADE	SVC NO	DATE RET MO YR	RET CODE
TAYLOR EDGAR D	MAJ	0-0015024	1145	2
TAYLOR EDWARD G	MAJ	0-0014029	0121	1
TAYLOR EDWARD M	COL	0-0011388	0251	1
TAYLOR EDWARD W	COL	0-0032465	0959	1
TAYLOR ELWOOD	LTC	0-0084429	1066	1
TAYLOR FRANK F JR	COL	0-0015448	0546	1
TAYLOR GALEN M	COL	0-0012444	0947	1
TAYLOR GEORGE A	B G	0-0014992	1046	2
TAYLOR GEORGE F R	MAJ	0-0010744	0335	2
TAYLOR GLENN P	COL	0-0042387	0764	1
TAYLOR HARLAN H	COL	0-0058748	0359	1
TAYLOR HAROLD L	COL	0-0029694	0462	1
TAYLOR HAROLD W	COL	0-0039661	1063	1
TAYLOR HENRY F	COL	0-0038661	1059	1
TAYLOR HENRY P	1LT	0-0014381	0-19	2
TAYLOR INEZ A	MAJ	N-0002160	1062	1
TAYLOR JAMES	B G	0-0007262	0848	1
TAYLOR JAMES C	COL	0-0030616	0266	1
TAYLOR JAMES JR	COL	0-0021184	0767	1
TAYLOR JAMES K	COL	0-0023011	0868	1
TAYLOR JAMES S	COL	0-0019602	0451	2
TAYLOR JOHN O	COL	0-0016577	0956	2
TAYLOR KENNETH G	COL	0-0083573	0766	1
TAYLOR LLOYD W	COL	0-0031197	0862	1
TAYLOR MAXWELL D	GEN	0-0014898	0764	1
TAYLOR MILTON C	COL	0-0019867	0764	1
TAYLOR PAUL R	COL	0-0011747	1047	1
TAYLOR PERRY E	COL	0-0008128	0344	2
TAYLOR RALEIGH D	LTC	0-0076922	0466	1
TAYLOR RICHARD I	LTC	0-0036676	0767	1
TAYLOR ROBERT B	COL	0-0029903	0463	1
TAYLOR ROBERT L	COL	0-0014940	0854	1
TAYLOR ROBERT L	LTC	0-0067622	1267	1
TAYLOR ROBERT R JR	LTC	0-0031619	0865	1
TAYLOR ROY M JR	LTC	0-0039419	0763	1
TAYLOR ROYAL R	COL	0-0080195	0466	1
TAYLOR RUTH P	COL	N-0000302	1067	1
TAYLOR THOMAS F	COL	0-0003903	1149	2
TAYLOR THOMAS H	COL	0-0029931	0261	1
TAYLOR THOMAS H	CW2	W-0904363	1160	1
TAYLOR VICTOR B	LTC	0-0040130	0266	1
TAYLOR WALTER A	COL	0-0051566	1164	1
TAYLOR WENTWORTH	COL	0-0030280	1062	1
TAYLOR WILLIAM B	MAJ	0-0027077	0854	2
TAYLOR WILLIAM E	LTC	0-0063308	0168	1
TAYLOR WILLIAM JR	COL	0-0018565	0761	1
TAYLOR WILLIAM N	COL	0-0018168	0960	1
TAYNTON LEWIS C	COL	0-0034007	1265	2
TE SELLE JOHN	LTC	0-0050055	0964	1
TEABOLDT CHASE R	COL	0-0032082	1164	1
TEAGUE JACK	LTC	0-0026354	0866	1
TEAGUE MADGE M	LTC	N-0000201	0266	1
TEASLEY AGATHA B	MAJ	N-0002162	1162	1
TECCO ROBERT	CPT	0-0070525	0166	1
TECHEN EDMUND J	CW4	W-0902214	0356	1
TEDICK EUGENE	LTC	0-0059481	0264	1
TEENER DAVID R	MAJ	0-0060871	0567	1
TEESE JAMES L	MAJ	0-0063386	1066	1
TEETER EDGAR M	COL	0-0020688	0867	1
TEETERS BERNARD G	COL	0-0022081	0767	1
TEGNELL RUSSELL M	LTC	0-0042677	1163	1
TEIR WILLIAM	COL	0-0040701	0466	1
TEKSE LLOYD C	COL	0-0020062	1265	1
TELFORD CHARLES	LTC	0-0001789	1022	1
TELKE FREDERICK JR	LTC	0-0081277	0868	1
TELQUIST CLARK V	COL	0-0040443	0566	1
TEMME EUGENE J	CPT	0-0034553	0349	2
TEMPEL CARL W	M G	0-0018284	0962	2
TEMPLE CHARLES E JR	LTC	0-0047459	0863	1
TEMPLE HARRY D	COL	0-0051834	0966	1
TEMPLETON HAMILTON	COL	0-0003452	0142	1
TENCH CHARLES T	COL	0-0017502	0655	1
TENERY JOHN H	COL	0-0043172	0566	1
TENHAGEN CARL B	LTC	0-0043785	0767	1
TENNANT JOSEPH A	CW3	W-0907023	1053	1

NAME	GRADE	SVC NO	DATE RET MO YR	RET CODE
TENNANT RICHARD S	COL	0-0051474	0264	1
TENNER ARMIN L	COL	0-0041428	0856	1
TENNESSON CHARLES F	COL	0-0024190	0760	1
TENNEY CLESEN H	B G	0-0003835	1146	2
TENNIES LESLIE G	COL	0-0041715	0261	1
TERRELL HENRY JR	M G	0-0003264	0446	1
TERRELL RALPH D	COL	0-0007017	0250	2
TERRY AUGUSTUS T JR	COL	0-0031781	0765	1
TERRY CARL C	COL	0-0004693	1044	2
TERRY DUDLEY K	LTC	0-0050076	1064	1
TERRY JOHN K	CPT	0F-0105049	1068	2
TERRY MICHAEL J	MAJ	0-0099743	0868	1
TERRY WALTER C	COL	0-0081280	0868	1
TESKE THEODORE I	CW2	W-0903915	0454	1
TESNEY CLYDE C	CW4	W-0903916	0256	1
TESSEN DOROTHY A	LTC	N-0001858	0364	1
TESSMER CARL F	COL	0-0024300	0863	1
TETER LESTER W	COL	0-0051312	0562	1
TEVIS JACK M	MAJ	0-0065717	1161	1
TEWELL MOLLIE A	MAJ	N-0000333	0862	2
TEXLEY ALFRED G	COL	0-0039539	0956	1
TEXTOR JEROME D	CPT	0-0023565	0542	2
THACKERAY DONALD W	COL	0-0021265	0868	1
THACKSTON A J JR	COL	0-0016607	0856	1
THALMANN WILLIAM G	COL	0-0024303	0862	1
THAMES JOHN W	COL	0-0030768	0866	2
THAMES WILLIAM M JR	B G	0-0029846	0762	1
THAMS ROBERT W	LTC	0-0065609	0867	1
THARP LLEWELLYN	COL	0-0008062	0550	1
THARPE FELIX E	COL	0-0032204	1268	2
THATCHER MARGARET K	MAJ	N-0000973	0263	1
THAYER ALAN P	COL	0-0023087	0868	1
THAYER ELMER B	COL	0-0017156	0758	1
THAYER HENRY C	COL	0-0019754	0459	1
THEBAUD DELPHIN E	COL	0-0004612	1049	1
THEBAUD JOSEPH V	COL	0-0009074	1048	2
THEE WALTER C	COL	0-0009701	0547	1
THEILMANN ETHEL M	MAJ	M-0010055	0155	1
THEIMER JOHN E	M G	0-0017566	0765	1
THEIRING ROBERT G	COL	0-0028982	0558	1
THEISEN GEORGE L	LTC	0-0023846	0262	1
THELEN EDWARD F	COL	0-0029649	1061	1
THERRELL JOHN W	COL	0-0040899	0567	1
THERRIEN ALVIN A	LTC	0-0070527	0768	1
THETFORD JAMES A	COL	0-0038913	0866	1
THEXTON MARGARET A	MAJ	N-0001034	0366	1
THIBEAULT JAMES H	LTC	0-0069814	1068	1
THIELE CLAUDE M	B G	0-0003208	0948	2
THIELEN BERNARD	COL	0-0018782	0855	1
THIEME LEO V	LTC	0-0033561	0664	1
THIESSEN WYAN E	LTC	0-0051087	0655	2
THIGPEN HENRY S	LTC	0-0060264	0667	1
THOMA WILLIAM C	LTC	0-0063397	0766	1
THOMAS ALFRED R JR	COL	0-0006297	1048	1
THOMAS ARNOLD R	LTC	0-0023947	0661	1
THOMAS ARTHUR J	LTC	0-0035564	1059	1
THOMAS ARTHUR P	MAJ	0-0017211	0642	2
THOMAS ARTHUR R	WO1	W-0904208	0250	2
THOMAS BENJAMIN A	COL	0-0010119	0148	1
THOMAS CHARLES M	LTC	0-0081282	0861	1
THOMAS DOUGLAS P	LTC	0-0080500	0366	1
THOMAS EDWARD G	COL	0-0084432	0668	1
THOMAS ELMER G	COL	0-0005995	0642	2
THOMAS EVERT S JR	B G	0-0030107	0164	1
THOMAS FRANCIS J	CW4	W-0903919	0261	1
THOMAS GEORGE	MAJ	0-0037081	0859	1
THOMAS HARVEY G	CPT	0-0014407	0120	2
THOMAS HENRY G	COL	0-0031756	0268	2
THOMAS HENRY L	CPT	0F-0101745	0267	2
THOMAS HOMER D	COL	0-0041621	0959	1
THOMAS HUGHIE C	LTC	0-0037462	0566	1
THOMAS IKE	CW4	W-0903920	0863	1
THOMAS JAY P	COL	0-0049885	0168	1
THOMAS JESSE F	COL	0-0021135	0858	2
THOMAS JESSE JR	LTC	0-0024590	0367	1
THOMAS JESSE R	LTC	0-0036320	0966	1
THOMAS JOHN L	COL	0-0019958	0858	2
THOMAS JOHN W	CW4	W-0902046	1154	1
THOMAS JOSEPH W	LTC	0-0058015	0264	1
THOMAS KRAMER	COL	0-0004705	0346	1
THOMAS LAWRENCE M	LTC	0-0060318	1068	1
THOMAS LORRES C	LTC	0-0025930	0762	1
THOMAS LUCIUS G	COL	0-0019688	1163	1
THOMAS RALPH C	CPT	0-0007525	1034	1
THOMAS RICHARD C	COL	0-0021289	0868	2
THOMAS RICHARD G	COL	0-0023632	1059	1
THOMAS ROBERT W	CW4	W-0904391	0267	1
THOMAS RODERICK M	LTC	0-0082110	1167	1
THOMAS THEODORE G	LTC	0-0030344	0962	1
THOMAS WESLEY E	MAJ	0-0060368	0862	1
THOMAS WILLIAM A	LTC	0-0015263	1047	2
THOMAS WILLIAM A	CW3	W-0903922	0961	1
THOMAS WILLIAM E	CW4	W-0904210	1055	1
THOMAS WILLIAM G JR	CPT	0-0057144	0656	2
THOMAS WILLIAM N JR	COL	0-0007648	0653	1
THOMAS WILLIE N	COL	0-0029644	1061	1
THOMAS WILSON E	LTC	0-0082111	0867	1
THOMAS WINIFRED	MAJ	L-0000236	0260	1
THOMAS WRAY R	LTC	0-0060535	0766	1
THOMAS&STAHLE C	COL	0-0003225	0346	1
THOMASON JOEL F	COL	0-0021867	1166	1
THOMILSON MATTHEW	COL	0-0001942	0840	2
THOMMEN LOUIS A	MAJ	0-0022922	1043	2
THOMPSON ALBERT N	COL	0-0024823	0367	1
THOMPSON ALFRED F	COL	0-0081286	1068	1
THOMPSON CHESTER I	CW2	W-0902161	0146	2
THOMPSON CLARENCE A	COL	0-0033113	0765	2
THOMPSON DALE L B	COL	0-0039668	0865	1
THOMPSON DONALD F	COL	0-0020885	0866	1
THOMPSON DONALD G	LTC	0-0032844	0768	1
THOMPSON EDGAR H JR	COL	0-0020143	0966	1
THOMPSON EDWIN G	LTC	0-0081931	0766	1
THOMPSON ESTEL A	LTC	0-0029653	0956	1
THOMPSON FRANK J	COL	0-0015609	0151	1
THOMPSON FREDFRICK	COL	0-0015401	0653	1
THOMPSON FULTON G	COL	0-0050965	1057	1
THOMPSON GORDON K	CW4	W-0903923	0764	1
THOMPSON GUY D	COL	0-0005906	0854	1
THOMPSON HARRY F	B G	0-0007344	0646	1
THOMPSON HOWARD M	COL	0-0047399	1067	1
THOMPSON HUNDLEY	COL	0-0041663	0360	1
THOMPSON IDA M	MAJ	N-0000373	0261	1
THOMPSON JACK M	LTC	0-0050608	1068	1
THOMPSON JAMES B	COL	0-0036635	0968	1
THOMPSON JAMES F	MAJ	0-0084576	1065	1
THOMPSON JAMES V	B G	0-0016826	0757	2
THOMPSON JERRY V	LTC	0-0037451	1262	1
THOMPSON JOHN R	COL	0-0081289	0467	1
THOMPSON JOHN W	COL	0-0004975	0548	2
THOMPSON JOHN W	COL	0-0021067	0868	1
THOMPSON JOHN W	LTC	0-0059053	0868	1
THOMPSON JOSEPH C	COL	0-0031250	0568	1
THOMPSON LESLIE A	LTC	0-0023673	0367	1
THOMPSON LILLIAN G	LTC	N-0000015	1047	1
THOMPSON LOUIS H	COL	0-0008411	0948	1
THOMPSON MAXWELL H	COL	0-0041998	0262	1
THOMPSON MERLE R	COL	0-0017534	0557	1
THOMPSON MILLARD	COL	0-0028951	0158	1
THOMPSON MILTON O	CW4	W-0902328	1056	1
THOMPSON MILTON S	COL	0-0029125	0758	1
THOMPSON NASH O	LTC	0-0031822	1052	2
THOMPSON PAUL W	B G	0-0017506	0746	1
THOMPSON PERCY W	COL	0-0016315	0855	1
THOMPSON RICHARD C	LTC	0-0084330	0564	1
THOMPSON RICHARD M	CW4	W-0904211	0963	1
THOMPSON ROBERT G	COL	0-0023568	0160	1
THOMPSON ROBERT I	LTC	0-0085380	0968	1
THOMPSON ROBERT M	LTC	0-0043794	0564	1
THOMPSON ROBERT P	COL	0-0019098	0662	2
THOMPSON ROY JR	LTC	0-0075307	0168	1
THOMPSON SAMUEL W	COL	0-0041690	0658	1
THOMPSON SAMUEL W II	LTC	0-0056268	0267	1
THOMPSON WILLIAM J	B G	0-0017530	0859	1
THOMPSON WILLIAM L	COL	0-0011104	1151	1
THOMPSON WILLIAM V	COL	0-0019292	0157	1
THOMSON EARL F	COL	0-0014919	0854	1
THOMSON EDWARD P	COL	0-0029974	0963	1
THOMTE HUBERT D	COL	0-0022633	0966	1
THORKELSON WILLIAM L	COL	0-0022667	0460	1
THORLIN JOHN F	M G	0-0019067	0865	1
THORN WILLIAM R JR	CW4	W-0904212	0758	1
THORNBER HUBERT E	LTC	0-0041396	1053	1
THORNBURG ARTHUR M	CW3	W-0903925	1065	1
THORNE FREDERIC H	COL	0-0005922	0646	2
THORNE JOHN H	LTC	0-0036166	0868	1
THORNHILL AVERY J	CW3	W-0907024	0259	1
THORNLEY JAMES F	LTC	0-0085273	0268	1
THORNTON ALBERT L	COL	0-0031806	0761	1
THORNTON AUBREY D	LTC	0-0069816	0363	1
THORNTON JOSEPH A	COL	0-0031818	0365	1
THORNTON JOYCE A	LTC	N-0000267	0465	1
THORNTON MARGARET J	MAJ	R-0010077	0164	1
THORNTON MARGARET M	LTC	L-0000023	1058	1
THORNTON PAUL E	MAJ	0-0062815	0165	1
THORNTON VIRGIL H	LTC	0-0031503	0163	1
THORNTON WARREN G	LTC	0-0046663	0266	1
THOROUGHMAN ROY M	COL	0-0011509	0949	1
THORPE ELLIOTT R	B G	0-0011167	1149	1
THORPE FRED L	COL	0-0016935	0757	1
THORPE GEORGE M	COL	0-0040031	0766	1
THRASHER WARREN A	COL	0-0032733	0467	2
THREADGILL FRANK W	COL	0-0021019	0766	2
THREADGILL WALTON O	COL	0-0025215	0664	1
THRELKELD LAWRENCE C	MAJ	0-0051501	0354	1
THRIFT RICHARD B	COL	0-0039849	0963	1
THROCKMORTON JOHN M	COL	0-0042711	1265	1
THROCKMORTON RUSSELL	COL	0-0005140	0246	2
THROM HAVEL I	LTC	N-0000549	0550	1
THUMMEL CLAUDE B	COL	0-0002591	1045	1
THURMOND GEORGE E	LTC	0-0061585	1068	1
THURNESS ELIZABETH	LTC	N-0000436	0665	1
THURSTON BENJAMIN E	COL	0-0016408	0555	1
THURSTON CLAIR H	COL	0-0031453	0762	1
THURSTON ESTILL S	COL	0-0043469	0568	1
THURSTON MARION F JR	COL	0-0052088	0568	1
THUSS CHARLES J SR	COL	0-0067968	0166	1
THWEATT RICHMOND F	COL	0-0030766	0165	1
THYBONY WILLIAM W	COL	0-0039024	0564	1
THYING LUNSFORD	LTC	0-0081291	0968	1
TIBBETTS RALPH E	COL	0-0016156	1144	2
TIBBS RICHARD B	COL	0-0030688	0466	1
TIDLER CALVIN L	LTC	0-0081292	0665	1
TIEDE ROLAND V	COL	0-0031801	0964	1
TIEDT ELMER E	LTC	0-0019323	0646	2
TIFFANY RAYMOND H	COL	0-0020348	0866	1
TIFFANY WILLARD D	COL	0-0034230	0665	1
TIGHE JOHN R	COL	0-0009963	1146	2
TILGHMAN MAYO T	LTC	0-0051105	0359	2
TILLEY MAIDIE E	LTC	N-0000008	0349	1
TILLMAN ERLAND A	COL	0-0020941	0765	1
TILLOTSON JOHN A	LTC	0-0081294	0766	1
TILLSON JOHN C F JR	COL	0-0002657	0243	2
TILSON GEORGE E	COL	0-0051838	0666	1
TILTON KENNETH E	COL	0-0029487	0860	1
TILTON ROLLIN L	B G	0-0002664	0248	1
TIMBERLAKE EDWARD W	B G	0-0008641	0750	1
TIMBERMAN THOMAS S	M G	0-0015328	0360	1
TIMKE GEORGE H	COL	C-0020963	0866	1
TIMM EMANUEL A	LTC	0-0030619	0164	1
TIMMERMAN FREDERICK	COL	0-0063210	1068	1
TIMMES CHARLES J	M G	0-0029777	0567	1
TIMOTHY PATRICK H	B G	0-0009297	1046	2
TIMOTHY ROBERT W	COL	0-0018141	0946	1
TINARI EMANUEL J	COL	0-0080018	0168	1
TINCHER MAXWELL A	COL	0-0020798	0859	1
TINDAL WINIFRED H	MAJ	L-0000237	0360	1
TINDALL RICHARD G	B G	0-0004800	0452	2
TINGAY LYNN H	B G	0-0005970	0453	2
TINKLE EVELYN F	MAJ	N-0000199	0263	1
TIPPETT EDWARD W	COL	0-0042570	0665	1
TIPTON DOROTHY G	LTC	M-0010020	0360	1
TIPTON HENRY C	LTC	0-0032777	0461	1
TIPTON NORMAN E	COL	0-0018408	0661	1
TIPTON VERNON J	LTC	0-0065299	0668	1
TIREY JAMES H	LTC	0-0033464	0466	1
TISCH DONALD C	MAJ	0-0090555	0765	2
TISDALE WALTER M	COL	0-0018811	0162	1
TITLEY RICHARD J	LTC	0-0035982	0864	1
TITUS GEORGE F	COL	0-0038604	0356	1
TITUS REED M	LTC	0-0041879	0659	1
TITUS VIRGINIA L	MAJ	N-0000616	0657	2
TJOSTEM MARVIN L	COL	0-0030089	0164	1
TOBEY FRANK A	M G	0-0041698	1162	1
TOBEY MARY I	MAJ	N-0001039	1264	2
TOBIAS ROBERT B	COL	0-0003985	1046	1
TOBIN HOWARD C	MAJ	0-0004607	0928	1
TOBIN NORA M	LTC	N-0001872	1160	1
TODD ALAN B	B G	0-0042088	1062	1
TODD ALBERT A	COL	0-0033878	0866	1
TODD GEORGE S	CW3	RW-0903930	0864	1
TODD JAMES C	COL	0-0041972	1061	1
TODD RALPH L	LTC	0-0033696	0162	1
TODD RALPH R	LTC	0-0040242	0466	1
TODD SARAH B	LTC	L-0000259	0268	2
TODD WALTER J	LTC	0-0040491	0264	1
TODD WILLIAM A JR	COL	0-0019598	0964	1
TODD WILLIAM F	CW3	W-0904213	1066	1
TODD WILLIAM N III	LTC	0-0026846	1067	1
TODD WILLIAM N JR	COL	0-0009773	0653	2
TOFT DOUGLAS O	COL	0-0042183	0563	1
TOLAND HERBERT	CW4	W-0903931	1162	2
TOLBERT RAYMOND F	LTC	0-0031104	0855	1
TOLLEFSON HARLEY I	CW4	W-0907025	0868	1
TOLLIVER EDWARD M	COL	0-0033856	0964	1
TOLLY ROBERT J	COL	0-0031551	0367	2
TOLMAN JOHN D	COL	0-0051191	0161	1
TOLVE RALPH A	COL	0-0040027	0863	1
TOMEY WILLIAM R	COL	0-0012762	0846	2
TOMLIN JOHN W JR	LTC	0-0032249	1164	1
TOMLINSON CLARENCE M	COL	0-0014808	0248	1
TOMLINSON HUGH P	CPT	0-0061429	1064	2
TOMLINSON R H JR	COL	0-0038734	0960	1
TOMLINSON ROBERT B	COL	0-0031354	1066	1
TOMLINSON ROBERT P	LTC	0-0065545	0868	2
TOMPKINS FRANCIS P	COL	0-0011210	0747	1
TOMPKINS RAYMOND T	LTC	0-0014833	0346	2
TOMPKINS WILLIAM F	M G	0-0003780	0646	2
TONDA RICARDO D	1LT	0-0075841	1062	2
TONETTI OSCAR C	COL	0-0023864	0867	1
TONGUE ROBERT C	LTC	0-0027635	1165	1
TONNAR WILEY B	COL	0-0050955	0957	1
TOOHEY FRANCIS J	MAJ	0-0003603	0433	1
TOOLE CHARLES E	LTC	0-0083623	1167	1
TOOLE LENA A	MAJ	N-0001891	0360	1
TOOLE LESLIE E	COL	0-0007287	0753	1
TOOLEY JACK W	COL	0-0046860	0767	1
TOOMER HAROLD K	LTC	0-0040849	0662	1
TOON PHILIP B	LTC	0-0026799	0764	1
TOOTHILL EMMA A	MAJ	N-0001760	0765	1
TOPHAM DOUGLAS D	CW4	W-0903934	1055	1
TOPHAM WILLIAM O	CW2	W-0901266	1043	1
TORBETT OSCAR C	LTC	0-0055654	0767	1
TORGERSON FERNANDO G	LTC	0-0037523	0862	1
TORMEY BERNARD A	COL	0-0015266	0854	2
TORMEY DAVID M	COL	0-0059609	1068	1
TORNEY FRANCIS J	MAJ	0-0002900	1022	1
TORNSTROM CLIFFORD H	COL	0-0043138	0967	1
TOROVSKY RICHARD H	LTC	0-0015478	0844	2
TORRENCE BRYCE J	LTC	0-0081298	0364	1
TORRENCE JAMES F JR	COL	0-0015191	0954	1

332-811 O - 69 - 5

NAME	GRADE	SVC NO	DATE RET MO YR	RET CODE
TORREY JOHN D JR	B G	0-0020217	0866	1
TOSNEY JOHN L	CW4	W-0903935	0259	1
TOTH ALFRED L	LTC	0-0025587	0764	1
TOUFANJFF ANATOLY I	CW4	W-0901310	0655	1
TOURTILLOTT RAYMON	COL	0-0006932	0753	1
TOW WILLIAM M	COL	0-0010074	0350	1
TOWER JOHN V	COL	0-0015956	0854	1
TOWERS JACOB H	MAJ	0-0023883	1061	1
TOWNE CLAIR E	COL	0-0030385	0764	1
TOWNES JOHN E JR	LTC	0-0013991	0720	2
TOWNES MORTON E	B G	0-0018255	0960	2
TOWNLEY JOHN A	LTC	0-0041819	1158	1
TOWNSEND CLYDE F	COL	0-0031526	0962	1
TOWNSEND DURED F	COL	0-0031430	1066	1
TOWNSEND ELIZABETH	MAJ	M-0010077	0663	1
TOWNSEND FRANCIS M	CW2	RW-0907161	0962	1
TOWNSEND GEORGE L	COL	0-0010512	0148	1
TOWNSEND GLEN R	COL	0-0010001	0848	1
TOWNSEND HARRY F	LTC	0-0016832	0954	1
TOWNSEND HORACE E	COL	0-0030578	0765	1
TOWNSEND JAMES M	LTC	0-0036089	1267	1
TOWNSEND JAMES O	COL	0-0084433	0968	2
TOWNSEND JAMES R	B G	0-0006357	0846	1
TOWNSEND ROBERT H	COL	0-0024890	0666	1
TOWNSEND SPENCER A	COL	0-0004479	0947	1
TOWNSEND WILBUR D	LTC	0-0042562	0563	1
TOWNSLEY CLARENCE P	B G	0-0011204	0753	1
TOWNSLEY FLOYD W	LTC	0-0033953	0162	1
TOYE ALFRED E	COL	0-0041723	0261	1
TRABER OSCAR W JR	LTC	0-0028030	0667	1
TRABUE WILLIAM	COL	0-0023625	1066	1
TRACEY BEATRICE E	MAJ	N-0001952	0259	1
TRACY ALOYSIUS J	LTC	0-0041724	0859	1
TRACY DONALD	MAJ	0-0044869	0462	2
TRACY MAXWELL W	COL	0-0015691	0147	2
TRACY ORRIN A	COL	0-0031645	1167	1
TRAEGER GEORGE A	COL	0-0030746	0664	1
TRAIL HARRY E	COL	0-0030206	0461	2
TRAIN WILLIAM F	LTG	0-0018415	0667	1
TRAINER WYATTE G	COL	0-0040516	1168	1
TRAINOR ALFRED T	LTC	0-0033767	1058	2
TRAMEL HAROLD L	CW4	W-0903936	1166	1
TRAMMELL HOWARD A	LTC	0-0081300	1265	1
TRAMPE RAYMOND G	LTC	0-0042561	0661	1
TRAPNELL THOMAS J H	LTG	0-0016782	1262	1
TRAPOLINO GREGORIO	WO1	W-0901039	1040	2
TRAUB DAVID W	LTG	0-0017110	0862	1
TRAUB ROBERT	COL	0-0037450	0762	1
TRAVERS FRANCIS A	MAJ	0-0060709	1265	2
TRAVIS HARRISON G	1LT	0-0012833	0225	2
TRAVIS WILLIAM B	LTC	0-0020840	0865	1
TRAYWICK JESSIE T SR	COL	0-0015818	0954	1
TREADWAY JOSEPH E	LTC	0-0023617	0760	1
TREADWELL JOHN R	LTC	0-0027976	0367	1
TREADWELL LEWIS L	LTC	0-0053121	0262	1
TRECHTER OLIVER E G	COL	0-0005913	0854	1
TREDENICK JOHN C	COL	0-0023405	0962	1
TREDENNICK DONALD C	COL	0-0015335	0954	1
TRENEMAN ROBERT A	COL	0-0060506	0766	1
TRENHOLM DERRILL O	COL	0-0007501	0947	1
TRENHOLM JOHN H	COL	0-0037427	0666	1
TRENT JOSEPH F	COL	0-0017319	0858	1
TRETT EDWARD L	COL	0-0010402	0248	1
TREW FRANK G	COL	0-0015711	0854	1
TRIAL ERNEST T	COL	0-0030259	1164	1
TRIBE MERRILL L	B G	0-0042374	0764	1
TRICE HARLEY N	LTC	0-0019881	0948	2
TRICHEL GERVAIS W	COL	0-0012152	1146	1
TRIDEN JACK E	CW4	W-0903938	1058	2
TRIGG HARRY E	LTC	0-0060470	1066	1
TRIGG ROBERT E	LTC	0-0049819	0264	1
TRIMBLE AARON U	COL	0-0043675	1268	1
TRIMBLE FORD	COL	0-0028761	0954	1
TRIMMER JOHN C	LTC	0-0026633	0764	1
TRIMMER MILDRED L	LTC	N-0001911	0567	1

NAME	GRADE	SVC NO	DATE RET MO YR	RET CODE
TRINTER VERNON E	CPT	0-0025542	0446	2
TRIPLET WILLIAM S	COL	0-0015815	0854	1
TRIPP ROBERT C	B G	0-0018972	0863	1
TROESCHER EDWARD C	MAJ	0-0039055	0262	1
TROIANO CONSTANT A	COL	0-0022180	1164	1
TROIANO LAWRENCE V	LTC	0-0059797	0968	1
TROLAND GIRARD B	COL	0-0008562	0854	1
TROLL JOHN F	COL	0-0043029	0767	1
TRONE JOHN W	COL	0-0039523	0850	1
TROSS RALPH G	LTC	0-0050257	0964	1
TROTH JAMES R	COL	0-0042270	1163	2
TROUP MALCOLM G	COL	0-0023862	0666	1
TROUT ROBERT J	COL	0-0020347	0966	1
TROUT ROBERT L	LTC	0-0043610	0858	1
TROXEL ORLANDO C JR	M G	0-0018487	0464	1
TROXLER PAUL O	COL	0-0041693	0760	1
TRUDEAU ARTHUR G	LTG	0-0015513	0762	1
TRUDEN JAMES R	COL	0-0042248	1061	1
TRUE GERALD F	COL	0-0038773	0864	1
TRUE RICHARD O	MAJ	0-0060864	0764	1
TRULSEN HERMAN H	CW4	W-0903940	1167	2
TRULY MERRICK H	COL	0-0018614	0761	1
TRUM BERNARD F	LTC	0-0020061	0658	1
TRUMAN LOUIS W	LTG	0-0018755	0867	2
TRUMBOWER WILLIAM C	CPT	0-0005866	0133	1
TRUXES ARTHUR H	COL	0-0004726	1047	1
TRYON MERLIN O	COL	0-0038810	1065	1
TUBBS HARRY S	COL	0-0019056	1057	1
TUBBS WILLIAM R	CW4	W-0903942	0866	2
TUCK WILLIAM R	COL	0-0024444	0665	1
TUCKER ANTHONY C	COL	0-0029130	0655	1
TUCKER ARNOLD R JR	1LT	0-0026124	0746	2
TUCKER ELON B	LTC	0-0052040	0462	1
TUCKER HENRY P	COL	0-0024232	0862	1
TUCKER LA MONTE A	COL	0-0042610	0865	1
TUCKER PRESCOTT S	MAJ	0-0004061	0-33	2
TUCKER RALPH A	CW4	W-0902191	0562	2
TUCKER REUBEN H	M G	0-0019894	0863	2
TUCKER ROBERT E	COL	0-0019938	0865	1
TUCKER ROY A	LTC	0-0084434	0866	1
TUDDER ELWIN B	LTC	0-0060541	0167	1
TUDOR OSCAR B	LTC	0-0010842	0536	1
TUEBNER HARRY R	COL	0-0031624	1167	1
TUFTS SUMNER P	COL	0-0028926	0855	1
TUGGLE WILLIAM P JR	COL	0-0042093	1162	2
TULLEY DAVID H	M G	0-0016075	0461	1
TULLEY EDGAR J	COL	0-0006036	0547	1
TULLY JAMES R	LTC	0-0031352	1064	1
TULLY TERENCE J	B G	0-0012823	0854	2
TUMIN HERBERT R	COL	0-0041367	0954	1
TUNBERG CLARENCE L	LTC	0-0065680	0865	1
TUPPER FRED A	LTC	0-0065032	1264	1
TUPPER MYRON W	COL	0-0005888	1139	2
TUPPER SEVIER R	COL	0-0004827	0453	1
TURGEON BEATRICE L	MAJ	N-0002734	0565	1
TURK STANLEY J	LTC	0-0080198	0367	1
TURKKAN DOROTHY E	MAJ	N-0000935	0668	1
TURMAN JOHN R	LTC	0-0042217	0761	1
TURNAGE BENJAMIN O	M G	0-0020360	0868	1
TURNBULL FRANCIS W	LTC	0-0063112	0865	1
TURNBULL HAROLD T	COL	0-0012858	0748	1
TURNER ALEXANDER	LTC	0-0043136	0665	1
TURNER ALEXANDER	LTC	0-0051632	0461	1
TURNER ALFONSO	CW4	W-0907026	0558	1
TURNER CARL C	M G	0-0031909	1168	2
TURNER CLAUDE E	LTC	0-0050230	0865	1
TURNER CLYDE M	COL	0-0043233	0864	1
TURNER DAVID R	CW4	W-0903945	0465	1
TURNER FRANK M	MAJ	0-0084679	0859	2
TURNER FRED H	COL	0-0001527	0240	1
TURNER GLENN E JR	LTC	0-0058638	1068	1
TURNER HAROLD R	COL	0-0028752	1150	2
TURNER HARRISON F	COL	0-0019448	1146	2
TURNER HERBERT N	COL	0-0031921	1263	2
TURNER HOWARD W	COL	0-0005627	0851	1

NAME	GRADE	SVC NO	DATE RET MO YR	RET CODE
TURNER IAN F	LTC	0-0032318	0767	1
TURNER JAMES H	COL	0-0017361	1058	2
TURNER JOHN G	B G	0-0031414	0166	1
TURNER JOHN R	COL	0-0039899	1062	1
TURNER LEONARD C	LTC	0-0033952	1268	1
TURNER MILDRED S	MAJ	N-0001856	0159	1
TURNER MORDAUNT V	COL	0-0007330	0653	1
TURNER PAUL L JR	LTC	0-0019558	0744	2
TURNER ROBERT A	COL	0-0018987	0763	1
TURNER ROBERT G	COL	0-0016809	0757	1
TURNER ROBERT I	LTC	0-0079506	0868	1
TURPIN 3RD WILLIAM P	LTC	0-0018554	0344	2
TURTLE LEWIS	COL	0-0001803	0342	2
TURTON WILLIAM U	CW4	W-0902067	0256	1
TUSKEWICZ ERNEST	WO1	W-0907028	0251	2
TUTEUR CLIFFORD M	COL	0-0003243	1041	2
TUTTLE ALBERT L	LTC	0-0006330	0744	2
TUTTLE GEORGE A	COL	0-0026583	0868	1
TUTTLE JAY F	LTC	0-0057703	0364	1
TUTTLE LAWRENCE O	LTC	0-0081303	0966	1
TWICHELL HEATH	COL	0-0012078	0854	1
TWINING ELMER E	COL	0-0030662	1163	1
TWITTY WILLIAM M	MAJ	0-0059808	0464	1
TWOMBLY JOHN F III	COL	0-0023519	0764	1
TWYMAN JOSEPH H	COL	0-0018116	0760	2
TWYON DONALD E	COL	0-0032805	1068	2
TYCHSEN ANDREW C	B G	0-0008256	0653	1
TYLER ANNE A	MAJ	N-0000263	0562	2
TYLER JAMES E	COL	0-0023079	1168	1
TYLER JAMES P	CW4	W-0903946	1265	1
TYLER JOHN P III	LTC	0-0027128	0968	1
TYLER JOHN S	COL	0-0043602	0966	1
TYLER MAX C	M G	0-0001788	0944	1
TYLER MAX C	COL	0-0023809	0167	1
TYLER ORVILLE Z JR	COL	0-0018511	0859	1
TYLER WILLOUGHBY	COL	0-0031699	0966	1
TYNDALL 2ND JOHN G	LTC	0-0024014	0447	2
TYNES ACHILLES L	M G	0-0018916	1065	2
TYRALA ALFRED F	1LT	0-0026190	0845	2
TYSON ARTHUR W	COL	0-0019120	0863	1
TYSON ROBERT N	B G	0-0019594	0864	1
UCHEREK STEPHEN A	LTC	0-0031854	0861	1
UECKERT JON W	CW4	W-0903948	1065	1
UFTRING CELESTIA H	MAJ	N-0002042	1059	1
UHL FREDERICK	M G	0-0002874	0846	2
UHLMAN HAROLD R	1LT	0-0018577	0938	2
UHRBROCK HAROLD W	COL	0-0015990	0854	2
UHRHANE FRANCIS F	M G	0-0018071	0963	1
ULANS ROMAN I	COL	0-0052302	0966	1
ULLOM MADELINE M	LTC	N-0000123	0264	1
ULM OTIS M	COL	0-0023047	0959	2
ULMER JAMES C	LTC	0-0041792	0958	2
ULMER ROY C	COL	0-0041507	0356	1
ULMO HENRY W	COL	0-0010926	0942	1
ULRICH FRED R	COL	0-0035566	0868	1
ULRICH JOHN A	COL	0-0031527	0664	1
UMBACH EDNA O	LTC	N-0000007	0448	1
UMBERGER CLARENCE L	CW4	W-0907030	1054	1
UNDERCOFFER CHARLES	LTC	0-0081884	1067	1
UNDERDAHL CONRAD R	LTC	0-0033523	1167	1
UNDERHILL LEWIS K	COL	0-0003533	0646	1
UNDERWOOD CLARENCE R	COL	0-0031911	0666	1
UNDERWOOD EDGAR H	B G	0-0004768	0946	2
UNDERWOOD JEAN R	COL	0-0009230	1146	2
UNDERWOOD JOE S	COL	0-0008281	1045	2
UNDERWOOD JOHN M	LTC	0-0017621	0545	2
UNDERWOOD MILDRED R	CPT	N-0002226	0459	2
UNDERWOOD VERNON W	LTC	0-0036204	0762	1
UNDERWOOD WARREN N	COL	0-0016078	0755	1
UNDRITZ FREDERICK	COL	0-0011827	1049	1
UNGER JESS P	COL	0-0023706	0765	1
UNTERBRINK ROBERT C	CW4	W-0903949	0268	1
UNVERFERTH JOHN E	COL	0-0023499	0767	1
UPHAM JOHN S JR	LTG	0-0017178	0764	1
UPHAM ROY W	LTC	0-0065551	0167	1

NAME	GRADE	SVC NO	DATE RET MO YR	RET CODE
UPSHAW MARGARET M	MAJ	L-0000201	0753	1
UPTON RALPH R	COL	0-0024063	0565	1
URAM MICHAEL A	COL	0-0038648	0160	2
URBAN CHARLES R	LTC	0-0018490	0651	1
URBAN GEORGE	LTC	0-0080021	0962	1
URBAN JOHN G	COL	0-0021825	0759	1
URQUHART HENRY C	COL	0-0039754	0961	2
URRUTIA ENRIQUE JR	COL	0-0002976	0545	2
USCHOLD HERBERT J	CW4	W-0903951	0864	1
USERA VINCENT	COL	0-0039883	0463	2
USHER WILLIAM F	LTC	0-0055954	0865	1
USNICK EDWARD N	LTC	0-0042525	0762	1
UTKE RUSSELL D	COL	0-0028915	0657	1
UTLEY ROBERT L	COL	0-0032977	0868	1
UTTERBACK JAMES W	LTC	0-0040174	1062	2
UVAAS ISLA L	1LT	R-0000039	0846	1
VAIL BRUCE H	COL	0-0051533	0964	1
VAIL HOWARD K	MAJ	0-0016313	0644	2
VAIL ROBERT E	COL	0-0080508	1068	2
VAIL WILLIAM H JR	COL	0-0021145	0868	1
VALENCOURT CHARLES W	LTC	0-0081933	0867	1
VALENTE ABEL A	LTC	0-0041687	0658	1
VALENTE FRANK A	COL	0-0028768	0354	1
VALENTINE CHARLES H	COL	0-0016325	0955	1
VALENTINE GEORGE C	LTC	0-0050385	0165	1
VALLASTER JOHN J JR	LTC	0-0027473	0765	2
VAN ALLEN WILLIAM G	COL	0-0020931	0265	1
VAN ATTA WARD H	COL	0-0020939	1167	1
VAN AUKEN HOWARD A	COL	0-0020096	0759	2
VAN AUKEN WENDELL G	LTC	0-0026269	1068	1
VAN BAAK LOUIS H A	MAJ	N-0000127	0858	1
VAN BENSCHOTEN ELMER	COL	0-0007929	0345	2
VAN BRUNT RINALDO	M G	0-0016225	0162	2
VAN BUSKIRK ROBERT J	COL	0-000586[illegible]	0547	2
VAN COURT LLOYD P	COL	0-0038966	0865	1
VAN DE VELDE LOUIS R	LTC	0-0031895	0661	1
VAN DE VOORT LEO D	LTC	0-0039071	0965	1
VAN DELDEN KARL H	MAJ	0-0067773	0165	1
VAN DERVEER ROBERT H	MAJ	0-0083101	0965	2
VAN DERVORT EDMUND H	COL	0-0020476	1264	1
VAN DEUSEN EDWIN R	COL	0-0002636	0446	1
VAN DEUSEN EDWIN R	LTC	0-0028425	0968	1
VAN DEUSEN EDWIN S	COL	0-0007113	0547	2
VAN DEUSEN GEORGE L	M G	0-0002681	0846	1
VAN DINE WILLIAM H	COL	0-0030032	0364	2
VAN DUREN CORNELIUS	CW4	W-0907033	1165	1
VAN DUZEE FREDERIC P	COL	0-0012592	0650	1
VAN FLEET JAMES A	GEN	0-0003847	0353	1
VAN GIESON LEWIS M	COL	0-0009927	0344	1
VAN GUNDY DANIEL F	COL	0-0031938	0868	1
VAN HOOK HENRY M	COL	0-0009173	0443	2
VAN HORN JAMES H	COL	0-0001996	0642	1
VAN HORNE EDWIN J	COL	0-0016466	0647	2
VAN HOUTEN JOHN G	M G	0-0016669	0761	2
VAN HOY JOHN W JR	COL	0-0023739	1064	1
VAN INGEN JAMES C	COL	0-0007228	1049	1
VAN KEUREN EDWIN	COL	0-0050921	0656	1
VAN LAETHEM GEORGE	LTC	0-0036342	1064	1
VAN NATTA THOMAS F	M G	0-0017086	0663	1
VAN NESS ROBERT G	LTC	0-0039646	0358	1
VAN OOSTEN ADRIANUS	COL	0-0040028	0962	1
VAN ORMER HENRY P	COL	0-0019787	0865	1
VAN ORNE RONALD W	COL	0-0040725	0867	1
VAN ORNUM THURWOOD	CPT	0-0014434	0620	2
VAN ORSDEL ARTHUR D	COL	0-0041929	1061	1
VAN OSTRAND STUART O	CW4	W-0903958	0867	1
VAN RIPER IRVING K	LTC	0-0069821	0768	1
VAN SCHOICK ARTHUR W	LTC	0-0026017	0864	2
VAN SICKEL VINCENT T	LTC	0-0060257	0768	1
VAN SICKLE FLOYD E	COL	0-0041145	1068	1
VAN SICKLER DONALD R	COL	0-0038585	0954	1
VAN STUDDIFORD G	COL	0-0010230	0553	2
VAN SYCKLE DAVID L	B G	0-0016425	0656	1
VAN TUYL HARRY E	COL	0-0009501	0954	1
VAN VLIET JOHN H JR	COL	0-0020828	0859	1

NAME	GRADE	SVC NO	DATE RET MO YR	RET CODE
VAN VOLKENBURGH R H	B G	0-0003549	0250	1
VAN VOLKENBURGH ROBE	COL	0-0020758	0966	1
VAN WAGONER FRANK H	COL	0-0020095	0860	1
VAN WAGONER LOU G	B G	0-0041668	0360	1
VAN WAY CHARLES W JR	COL	0-0015757	0754	1
VAN WAY GEORGE L	COL	0-0019093	0863	1
VAN WIE GEORGE I	CW4	W-0903959	0757	1
VAN WYK HARRY	B G	0-0015555	0854	1
VANGDELVELDE R W	COL	0-0020470	0357	1
VANCE DONOVAN M	COL	0-0029360	0348	2
VANCE JOHN R	COL	0-0012301	0854	1
VANCE LEE C	COL	0-0015382	1047	1
VANCE WILLIAM W	LTC	0-0051693	1050	2
VANDENBERG OLIVER W	COL	0-0016586	0956	1
VANDENBERG ROBERT E	COL	0-0038979	0367	1
VANDER HEIDE HERB	M G	0-0017754	0662	1
VANDER-HYDEN W F	COL	0-0005248	1046	1
VANDERBOGET CARLTO	COL	0-0004522	0147	2
VANDERGRIFT KENNARD	LTC	0-0042575	0463	1
VANDERHOEF DEAN T	COL	0-0022984	0660	1
VANDERPOOL JAY D	COL	0-0034570	0667	1
VANDERSLUIS HOWARD J	B G	0-0015213	0754	1
VANDERVEER HAROLD C	B G	0-0003262	0849	1
VANDERVOORT BENJAMIN	COL	0-0022715	0846	2
VANDERVORT RALPH E	COL	0-0025337	1165	1
VANDERWOOD LENA	MAJ	N-0000057	0951	1
VANN BENNIE T SR	CW4	W-0907034	0964	1
VANN JOHN P	LTC	0-0038485	0863	1
VARDAS CONSTANTIN	COL	0-0030236	0864	1
VARHALLA ROSE F	MAJ	N-0002403	1162	1
VARNER CURTIS L	COL	0-0028779	0854	1
VASSAR PHILIP W	CW3	W-0903962	0557	1
VASSETT FRANCIS J	COL	0-0084435	1167	1
VAUGHAN CURRY N	COL	0-0031407	0465	1
VAUGHAN ELTON D	COL	0-0047395	1065	1
VAUGHAN MARY E	MAJ	N-0001669	0967	1
VAUGHAN WILLIAM W	B G	0-0003649	1146	2
VAUGHAN WINSTON H	COL	0-0020927	0857	2
VAUGHN CLIFFORD H	LTC	0-0071618	0466	1
VAUGHN FRANCIS M	LTC	0-0031567	0665	1
VAUGHN GEORGE W	COL	0-0015747	0454	1
VAUGHN JACK E	LTC	0-0080511	0167	1
VAUGHN MILDRIDGE	COL	0-0040415	0268	1
VAUGHN MOLLOY C JR	COL	0-0025393	0866	1
VAUGHT DONALD D	COL	0-0033308	0966	1
VEALE JOSEPH E	LTC	0-0021435	0866	1
VEATCH JOHN F	COL	0-0032047	1168	1
VEDDER HENRY C	LTC	0-0020999	0865	1
VELASQUEZ BEN N	COL	0-0031779	0766	1
VELIE EARL R	LTC	0-0027410	1065	1
VELO MINNIE O	MAJ	N-0000535	1047	1
VENABLE BENJAMIN W	COL	0-0007130	0946	2
VENABLE RUSSELL V	COL	0-0001934	0642	2
VER HEY HAZEL	MAJ	L-0000256	1064	1
VERDE JOE	LTC	0-0040218	1265	1
VERFUERTH VINCENT P	COL	0-0079661	1066	1
VERHONICK PHYLLIS J	LTC	N-0001800	0868	1
VERMETTE RAYMOND E	COL	0-0009746	1146	2
VERNON EUGENE H	COL	0-0015417	0946	2
VERNON WILLIAM E	CPT	0-0007255	0-28	1
VERNOR KELSO D	LTC	0-0041988	0550	2
VERSACE HUMBERT J	COL	0-0019152	0863	1
VESS JACK M	LTC	0-0048639	0455	2
VEST HUGH A	COL	0-0039692	1060	1
VEST NETTIE L	MAJ	L-0000219	1156	1
VESTAL JOHN L	CPT	0-0069823	0966	1
VESTAL MARION P	MAJ	0-0013933	0620	2
VESTAL WILLIAM M	COL	0-0017596	0859	1
VEVIA PAUL J	COL	0-0007504	1043	2
VIA LERA V	MAJ	N-0000712	0361	1
VICHULES LEO D	CPT	0-0015599	0238	2
VICKERS FRANK	CW4	W-0907035	0966	1
VICKERS JAMES E	LTC	0-0024383	0246	2
VICKERS LOUIS T	COL	0-0017244	0758	1
VICKERS-SMITH JOHN E	CW4	W-0903964	0668	1

NAME	GRADE	SVC NO	DATE RET MO YR	RET CODE
VICKOREN ANGVALD	COL	0-0019680	0265	1
VICKREY LUSTER A	COL	0-0017592	0859	1
VICTORY HOMER J	COL	0-0031826	0264	1
VICTORY THOMAS F	COL	0-0041869	0761	2
VIDA FRANK J	COL	0-0012588	0748	2
VIEDT DORIS W	MAJ	N-0000731	0160	2
VIEMAN LEWIS D	COL	0-0022201	0560	1
VIGEN OSCAR C	LTC	0-0048256	0268	1
VIGNES JOSEPH L	LTC	0-0080512	0267	1
VILHAUER JONAS A	COL	0-0032732	1168	2
VILLAMARIA AMELIA	MAJ	N-0002259	0862	1
VILLARET EUGENE	COL	0-0003695	0748	1
VILLARET GUSTAVE JR	COL	0-0007112	0552	1
VILLERE LEWIS G	COL	0-0042520	0164	1
VILLINES COLIN D	LTC	0-0063231	0865	2
VINCENT BERNARD E	CW4	W-0903965	1067	1
VINCENT CLIFTON F	CPT	0-0057440	0264	2
VINCENT EDWARD J	LTC	0-0038910	0365	1
VINCENT HOWARD	LTC	0-0065703	0268	1
VINCENT JAMES A	LTC	0-0071737	0268	1
VINCENT JOSEPH B	LTC	0-0042846	0756	2
VINCENT WILLIAM	CW4	W-0800347	0553	1
VINING OSMYN A	COL	0-0042398	0164	1
VINQUIST GLENN M	COL	0-0044867	0968	1
VINSON FRANK M JR	LTC	0-0031990	0866	1
VINSON HAROLD A	COL	0-0021711	0457	1
VINSON WILBUR H	COL	0-0010622	0753	1
VIRE HOWARD F	LTC	0-0056923	0667	1
VIRTUE CLARENCE M	COL	0-0016322	1151	2
VISSERING NORMAN H	M G	0-0041603	1162	1
VITA FRANK J	COL	0-0059664	1064	1
VITARIUS CHARLES A	LTC	0-0040544	0262	1
VITITOE VICTORIA O	MAJ	L-0000310	0562	1
VITTRUP RUSSELL L	LTG	0-0017681	0665	2
VIVAS JOSEPH R	COL	0-0022704	0559	1
VIVIAN GEORGE B	COL	0-0025272	0865	1
VIVIAN WILLIAM R	LTC	0-0031347	1064	1
VLAHOVICH FANNY E	LTC	N-0002573	0561	1
VOCKE LESTER	COL	0-0015047	0648	1
VOEGE ROY W	COL	0-0005509	1041	2
VOEGELI FRANCIS E	LTC	0-0024699	0863	1
VOEHL WILFORD E	COL	0-0019382	0864	1
VOGEL BERTHOLD	COL	0-0004871	0944	1
VOGEL EMMA E	COL	M-0010000	1151	1
VOGEL GUSTAVE H	B G	0-0012793	0854	1
VOGEL HERBERT D	B G	0-0015520	0854	1
VOGEL JOHN F	COL	0-0033585	0765	2
VOGEL LAWRENCE W	COL	0-0024661	0467	1
VOGNILD ALDEN E	LTC	0-0037080	0563	2
VOGT BRADY L JR	CPT	0-0060647	0664	1
VOGT JOHN E	MAJ	0-0079131	0263	1
VOGT ROBERT L	LTC	0-0060691	0664	1
VOINCHE MINA L	LTC	L-0000213	0359	1
VOLCKMANN RUSSELL W	B G	0-0019537	0757	2
VOLHEIM HERMAN H	LTC	0-0024593	0766	1
VOLKEL FORREST B	COL	0-0029361	0150	1
VOLKERS LOLITA M	CW3	V-0900984	0563	1
VOLLENDORFF ROBERT E	COL	0-0034398	0767	1
VOLLERTSEN ARTHUR H	COL	0-0038851	0265	1
VOLZ HEINZ H	CW4	W-0903968	0958	1
VON BENGE HERMAN H	LTC	0-0032237	0465	1
VON BURG ROBERT H	LTC	0-0035449	1264	1
VON GRENIP WALTER	CPT	0-0007614	0934	2
VON KAENEL HOWARD E	COL	0-0030527	1165	1
VON KANN CLIFTON F	M G	0-0021371	0365	1
VON KESSLER WILSON C	COL	0-0003656	0446	2
VON KOLNITZ HENRY	LTC	0-0030018	0961	1
VON SHOLLY FREDERICK	LTC	0-0080513	0166	1
VON TONGELN WALTER W	MAJ	0-0038453	0960	1
VONNAHMEN FRANCIS H	LTC	0-0061952	0767	1
VOORHEES FREDERICK	B G	0-0029374	0160	2
VOORHES MARION I	COL	0-0007077	0948	2
VOORHIS NICHOLAS R	COL	0-0038691	0961	2
VORDERMARK JONATHAN	COL	0-0025917	0766	1
VORISEK ROBERT B	LTC	0-0089158	0968	1

NAME	GRADE	SVC NO	DATE RET MO YR	RET CODE
VOTAVA MARY T	LTC	N-0000448	0567	1
VOTE RALPH B JR	LTC	0-0051818	1064	1
VOYATZIS PAUL A	COL	0-0031499	0766	1
VOYER FRANCES A	MAJ	L-0000072	0960	1
VUKOMANOVISH SAVO	CW3	W-0907037	0962	1
WACHENDORF MILES L	COL	0-0024679	0868	1
WACHTER CHRISTIAN	COL	0-0017800	0155	1
WADDELL CHARLES C	LTC	0-0080023	0767	1
WADDELL EDWARD S	LTC	0-0063068	0666	1
WADDELL HUGH B	COL	0-0012319	0154	1
WADDELL JACK L	LTC	0-0066114	0868	1
WADDELL JAMES C	COL	0-0013919	0320	2
WADDELL WILLIAM R	CW4	W-0907038	0766	1
WADDEY EDWARD P	COL	0-0008106	0151	1
WADDINGTON ROBERT B	LTC	0-0027527	0767	1
WADE DALLAS C	LTC	0-0030319	1262	1
WADE JAMES J	COL	0-0016518	0656	1
WADE RICHARD E	COL	0-0032824	0868	1
WADELTON WILLARD S	COL	0-0004714	1146	1
WADLE LOUIS J	LTC	0-0044059	0862	1
WADSWORTH LELAND JR	MAJ	0-0002272	0321	1
WAGENER MARY M	MAJ	N-0000153	0961	1
WAGGONER EDWARD F	COL	0-0042794	0763	1
WAGNER CARL N M	MAJ	0-0051225	0451	1
WAGNER DONALD L	LTC	0-0084835	0868	1
WAGNER HARRY O	CPT	0-0066592	0666	2
WAGNER HERBERT G	CW4	W-0903972	1267	1
WAGNER HERMAN H	COL	0-0008567	0651	1
WAGNER JACOB F	LTC	0-0030475	0466	1
WAGNER JOHN G	LTC	0-0051348	0557	1
WAGNER JOHN H	COL	0-0042518	0662	1
WAGNER OTTO	COL	0-0003466	0347	1
WAGNER RICHARD C	1LT	0-0064340	1152	2
WAGSTAFF DAVID JR	COL	0-0019246	0955	1
WAHL GEORGE D	B G	0-0005235	0649	1
WAHL JOHN	LTC	0-0027613	0765	1
WAID LEWIS C	LTC	0-0054314	0963	1
WAIKART WILLIAM H	LTC	0-0020504	0863	1
WAITE EILEEN M	MAJ	N-0002096	0665	1
WAITE FREDERICK	B G	0-0030358	1062	1
WAITE WILLIAM	LTC	0-0009271	0633	1
WAITS WARD B	COL	0-0040051	1163	1
WAITT ALDEN H	M G	0-0009606	0949	1
WAKEMAN PAUL M JR	CPT	0-0050500	0355	2
WAKEMAN PERCIVAL A	COL	0-0011068	0252	1
WALBRIDGE JOHN H	LTC	0-0054767	0864	1
WALBRIDGE VERN	COL	0-0015915	0854	2
WALD JOHN J	COL	0-0021804	0963	1
WALDEN JACK T	COL	0-0037422	0662	1
WALDEN JOHN F II	LTC	0-0057684	1167	1
WALDEN ROGER S	LTC	0-0041320	1066	1
WALDMAN MYRON	LTC	0-0081310	0467	1
WALDMANN CARL C	COL	0-0003447	0847	1
WALDNER STANLEY C	LTC	0-0039358	0662	1
WALDREP ALFRED C JR	LTC	0-0070057	0868	1
WALDRON MIRIAM E	MAJ	N-0001202	0965	1
WALIGORA DANIEL J	COL	0-0020055	0855	2
WALINSKI LEEROY M	CW3	W-0903974	0866	1
WALITSCHEK KURT L	COL	0-0042241	0963	1
WALK GEORGE A	COL	0-0042796	0264	2
WALKER AQUILLYA M	MAJ	N-0002435	0166	1
WALKER ARCHIE S	COL	0-0052915	0665	2
WALKER BERRISFORD	COL	0-0036195	0967	1
WALKER BOYD F	COL	0-0024998	0165	1
WALKER CHARLES P	COL	0-0019903	0157	1
WALKER CHARLES S	COL	0-0048299	0568	2
WALKER CHARLES S	CW4	W-0907039	0164	1
WALKER CLYDE W	CW4	W-0904348	0757	1
WALKER DANIEL F	LTC	0-0017727	0647	1
WALKER DELBERT F	CW4	W-0903976	0660	1
WALKER EDWARD E	MAJ	0-0005150	0132	1
WALKER ELMER H	COL	0-0019898	0159	1
WALKER FRANK E JR	COL	0-0034691	0767	1
WALKER FRED L	M G	0-0003029	0446	2
WALKER FRED L JR	COL	0-0020293	0866	1

NAME	GRADE	SVC NO	DATE RET MO YR	RET CODE
WALKER FREDERICK	LTC	0-0051655	1063	1
WALKER GEORGE C	COL	0-0035719	1068	2
WALKER GEORGE L	COL	0-0041882	0959	1
WALKER HAROLD E	1LT	0-0015414	0335	2
WALKER HERMAN A	COL	0-0037402	1267	1
WALKER ISAAC G	COL	0-0005154	0553	2
WALKER ISABELLE M	LTC	N-0000148	0964	1
WALKER J LEROY	LTC	0-0037248	1068	2
WALKER JACK K	LTC	0-0032225	1265	1
WALKER JAMES F	COL	0-0002041	1030	2
WALKER JAMES H	B G	0-0012730	0846	2
WALKER JAMES T	COL	0-0029356	1059	1
WALKER JOEL T	COL	0-0022007	0964	1
WALKER JOHN E	COL	0-0021368	1066	1
WALKER JOHN H JR	COL	0-0042857	1166	1
WALKER JOHN R	CW4	W-0904215	0967	2
WALKER KEITH A	COL	0-0062910	0166	1
WALKER LAWRENCE H JR	B G	0-0034243	0567	1
WALKER LELA A	MAJ	L-0000326	0365	1
WALKER LEONARD F	COL	0-0031344	0363	1
WALKER MARION W	COL	0-0023435	0867	1
WALKER NORVELL M	LTC	0-0034375	0367	1
WALKER PHILIP C	COL	0-0046287	0165	1
WALKER ROBERT M	LTC	0-0031740	0760	1
WALKER ROBERT T	COL	0-0031368	1066	2
WALKER ROY N	B G	0-0029112	0659	1
WALKER SAMUEL P JR	COL	0-0012179	0854	1
WALKER SIDNEY J	LTC	0-0063484	0867	1
WALKER STEPHEN M	LTC	0-0030561	1163	1
WALKER VIRGIL G	COL	0-0021700	0862	1
WALKER WELDON J	COL	0-0024307	0864	1
WALKER WILLIAM A	COL	0-0016410	0456	1
WALKER WILLIAM G	B G	0-0008073	0846	2
WALKER WILLIAM J	LTC	0-0036551	0566	1
WALKER WILLIAM L	LTC	0-0065022	0965	1
WALKOWSKI JOSEPH A	LTC	0-0051994	1159	1
WALL GEORGE R	COL	0-0040836	0867	1
WALL THOMAS F	LTC	0-0018207	0650	1
WALL THOMAS G	LTC	0-0033023	0466	1
WALLACE CHARLTON D	LTC	0-0042981	1163	1
WALLACE DAVID C	COL	0-0019715	0157	1
WALLACE EDWIN S	COL	0-0030859	0365	2
WALLACE ERNEST H	COL	0-0037552	0263	1
WALLACE EVERETT C	COL	0-0015525	0252	2
WALLACE FRANK B	CPT	0-0009063	0722	2
WALLACE JERRY G	LTC	0-0059812	1062	1
WALLACE JOHN B	LTC	0-0021680	1158	2
WALLACE JOHN K II	COL	0-0031131	0967	2
WALLACE JOSIAH A	COL	0-0006211	0545	2
WALLACE KENNETH W	COL	0-0032338	0964	1
WALLACE LEE	COL	0-0032065	1268	1
WALLACE NEIL M	COL	0-0019101	0863	1
WALLENDER ELMER F	B G	0-0005707	1249	2
WALLER ELBERT C	LTC	0-0082117	0961	1
WALLER JAMES C JR	COL	0-0050167	0968	1
WALLER JOHN L	WO1	W-0800680	0834	1
WALLER MARSHALL	LTC	0-0024758	0762	1
WALLER MARVIN E	LTC	0-0040294	1162	1
WALLER MORGAN L JR	LTC	0-0091716	0567	1
WALLEY THOMAS J	CW3	W-0908139	0668	1
WALLINGTON EDWARD C	B G	0-0003838	0251	1
WALLIS JOHN W	MAJ	0-0014186	1017	2
WALLIS LUTHER O JR	LTC	0-0026592	0867	1
WALLNER MARGARET D	MAJ	N-0002145	0861	1
WALLS NELLIE E	MAJ	N-0002070	1162	1
WALLSCHLEGER WILLIAM	LTC	0-0048250	0168	1
WALMSLEY HAROLD	B G	0-0018769	0959	1
WALO ERNEST	CW4	W-0903979	0162	1
WALPOLE JAMES R	LTC	0-0038579	1164	1
WALRATH CHARLES F	LTC	0-0036207	0764	1
WALSH ALOYSIUS J	COL	0-0051792	0866	1
WALSH ARTHUR O	COL	0-0005402	0752	2
WALSH EDWARD J	COL	0-0014697	0753	2
WALSH HAROLD J	CW4	W-0907040	0366	1
WALSH HENRY	COL	0-0041408	0256	1

NAME	GRADE	SVC NO	DATE RET MO YR	RET CODE
WALSH JOHN E	LTC	0-0033794	0863	1
WALSH JOHN X	LTC	0-0018090	0939	2
WALSH LOUIS A JR	M G	0-0019567	0366	2
WALSH MARGARET M	MAJ	N-0002420	0667	1
WALSH ORVILLE E	B G	0-0012094	0554	1
WALSH PATRICK J	COL	0-0029293	1263	1
WALSON CHARLES W	COL	0-0021267	0868	1
WALT IVAN U	COL	0-0042286	1062	1
WALTER EDWARD C	LTC	0-0031578	0765	1
WALTER EDWARD H	COL	0-0014698	0449	1
WALTER EUGENE H	COL	0-0019836	0865	1
WALTERHOUSE HARRY F	LTC	0-0051882	0962	1
WALTERS ALLIE L	CPT	0-0059056	0761	1
WALTERS EDWARD E	LTC	0-0033710	0664	1
WALTERS ELSMERE J	COL	0-0011381	0748	1
WALTERS JAMES W	COL	0-0009791	0452	1
WALTERS PAUL R	COL	0-0019050	0863	1
WALTERS WARREN E	COL	0-0024200	0766	1
WALTON ARTHUR H	COL	0-0044746	0766	1
WALTON CHARLES M	LTC	0-0009010	0242	1
WALTON CHARLES W	COL	0-0006715	0847	1
WALTON HENRY L	COL	0-0031777	0268	1
WALTON JOSEPH R	COL	0-0039821	0463	1
WALTON LEON W	COL	0-0029062	0359	1
WALTON ROBERT L	COL	0-0022734	0168	1
WALTON WILLIAM	LTC	0-0031459	0961	1
WALTZ WELCOME P	COL	0-0005429	1052	2
WALUSZ BERNARD P	CW3	W-0904437	0866	1
WALZ IVAN G	LTC	0-0028876	0954	1
WAMPLER BERT S	COL	0-0008013	0646	2
WANAMAKER WILLIAM W	B G	0-0012055	1149	1
WANDEL HUGH F	LTC	0-0045160	0859	1
WANSBORO WILLIAM P	COL	0-0021241	0868	1
WARD CHARLES P	COL	0-0019314	0863	1
WARD EDGAR R C	COL	0-0016585	0956	1
WARD FRANK	COL	0-0008041	0150	1
WARD FREDERICK	COL	0-0007566	0754	2
WARD FREDERICK	LTC	0-0039918	0962	1
WARD JUSTIN L JR	CW3	W-0903984	0956	2
WARD MARY A	MAJ	N-0000429	0561	1
WARD NATHANIEL III	COL	0-0019553	0864	1
WARD ORLANDO	M G	0-0003729	0153	1
WARD PATRICK B	LTC	0-0036239	0962	1
WARD PETER O	COL	0-0018574	0761	1
WARD ROBERT H	LTC	0-0044280	0668	1
WARD ROBERT W	M G	0-0017637	0562	2
WARD WALTER R	CW4	W-0903985	0566	1
WARD WILLIAM R	COL	0-0043262	1062	1
WARDELL DENNIS J	LTC	0-0050237	0767	1
WARDELL PATRICK G	LTC	0-0025628	0965	1
WARDEN IRVING D	COL	0-0053379	0968	1
WARDEN JOHN A	B G	0-0002473	0147	2
WARDLAW JOSEPH P	1LT	0-0014605	0428	2
WARDLOW RALPH C	LTC	0-0049516	0667	2
WARDNER WALLACE C	COL	0-0052212	1168	1
WARE JAMES V	COL	0-0004833	0951	2
WARE JOSEPH F	LTC	0-0001761	1022	2
WARE LAWRENCE R	LTC	0-0052317	0860	1
WARE WILLIAM B	LTC	0-0062114	0163	1
WARFIELD BENJAMIN M	COL	0-0020229	0864	1
WARFIELD CHARLES L	COL	0-0030590	1265	1
WARGUS EUGENE G	CW4	W-0903986	0364	1
WARING ROBERT C	LTC	0-0027721	0866	1
WARING ROBERT D	MAJ	0-0014848	1141	1
WARK JUDSON W	COL	0-0021428	0966	1
WARNER GORDON G	COL	0-0019466	0862	1
WARNER LEO V	B G	0-0008634	0854	1
WARNER OSCAR C	COL	0-0002550	1143	1
WARNER THOMAS R JR	CW4	W-0902171	1068	1
WARNER WALTER J	LTC	0-0084469	0867	1
WARNER WALTER W	COL	0-0005243	0153	1
WARNER WILLIAM A	LTC	0-0039791	0960	1
WARNKE JOHN J JR	MAJ	0-0058649	0464	2
WARNOCK ALN D	B G	0-0005162	0546	1
WARREN ARTHUR L	COL	0-0006993	0753	2

NAME	GRADE	SVC NO	DATE RET MO YR	RET CODE
WARREN CARL K JR	COL	0-0023630	0463	1
WARREN HANCEL L E	LTC	0-0065722	0868	1
WARREN JOSEPH H	COL	0-0012451	0751	2
WARREN PRATT A	LTC	0-0023412	0761	1
WARREN ROBERT B	B G	0-0019380	0864	1
WARREN ROBERT E	COL	0-0076845	0866	1
WARREN ROSS B	COL	0-0007001	0752	2
WARREN SARAH E	MAJ	N-0002322	0468	1
WARREN SHIELDS JR	COL	0-0022103	0765	1
WARREN STANLEY A	LTC	0-0045337	0864	1
WARREN VANCLEAVE	LTC	0-0024856	0263	1
WARREN WILLIAM C	LTC	0-0024852	0763	1
WARRICK FRED A	LTC	0-0081317	1167	1
WASHBURN ISRAEL B	COL	0-0029493	1058	1
WASHBURN MAURICE E	COL	0-0020475	1165	1
WASHINGTON DONALD	COL	0-0020894	0767	2
WASHINGTON WILLIAM C	COL	0-0003450	1144	2
WASKOWICZ ALOYSIUS T	COL	0-0019708	0757	1
WASSON VAL J	MAJ	0-0084836	0865	1
WASZAK EDWIN J	LTC	0-0035415	0767	1
WATERMAN BERNARD S	B G	0-0019746	0865	1
WATERMAN GLEN S	COL	0-0022239	0864	1
WATERMAN ROYCE A	CW4	W-0902366	0357	1
WATERS CHARLES H	COL	0-0020114	0666	1
WATERS DANIEL D	CPT	0-0025826	1144	2
WATERS EDWIN U O	COL	0-0009934	0145	2
WATERS GRADEN C	COL	0-0041842	1058	2
WATERS JAMES H	LTC	0-0037327	0764	1
WATERS JEROME J JR	B G	0-0005568	0551	1
WATERS JOHN F II	LTC	0-0037605	0165	1
WATERS JOHN K	GEN	0-0018481	0966	2
WATERS MARTIN J JR	COL	0-0031939	0968	1
WATERS MERVIN S	COL	0-0043533	0768	1
WATERS THOMAS L	COL	0-0012417	0854	1
WATKINS ERNEST S	LTC	0-0031028	0961	1
WATKINS MABLE A	MAJ	N-0000540	0649	1
WATKINS ORLAN R	CW4	W-0901524	0355	1
WATKINS THEODORE R	CW4	W-0904216	0166	1
WATKINS WILLIAM A	COL	0-0051237	0861	1
WATLINGTON THOMAS M	M G	0-0016780	0661	1
WATMORE DONALD J	CW4	W-0903989	0762	1
WATROUS FREDERICK	LTC	0-0015073	0846	1
WATROUS LEE R JR	COL	0-0003247	0846	2
WATRY CLARA K	MAJ	N-0000700	0664	1
WATSON ALBERT II	LTG	0-0018105	1166	1
WATSON ARTHUR A	COL	0-0041918	0561	2
WATSON ARTHUR E JR	1LT	0-0016517	1032	2
WATSON ARTHUR J	COL	0-0029730	0763	2
WATSON DONALD S	LTC	0-0028316	0766	1
WATSON DOUGLAS H	COL	0-0045908	0766	1
WATSON EDGERTON L	COL	0-0018308	0960	1
WATSON EDWIN A	LTC	0-0059469	0965	1
WATSON ERNEST C	COL	0-0029652	0861	1
WATSON FRANCIS M JR	LTC	0-0039381	0866	1
WATSON GEORGE H	LTC	0-0025740	0263	1
WATSON LEROY H	M G	0-0003896	1153	1
WATSON NUMA A	M G	0-0014968	0956	1
WATSON RALPH H	LTC	0-0042458	1062	1
WATSON RICHARD R	COL	0-0034354	1166	1
WATSON ROBERT J	LTC	0-0018092	1044	2
WATSON RONALD	LTC	0-0052459	0963	1
WATSON RUSSELL B	COL	0-0023582	0859	1
WATSON RUTH V	MAJ	N-0000416	0261	1
WATSON THOMAS R	LTC	0-0025718	0868	1
WATSON WESLEY A	CW4	W-0907044	0765	1
WATSON WHITFIELD	COL	0-0028802	0555	1
WATSON WILLIAM R	COL	0-0008354	0854	1
WATT DAVID A JR	COL	0-0017088	0758	1
WATTEN EINAR	COL	0-0044342	0466	1
WATTERS JOHN F	COL	0-0018994	0560	2
WATTERS WILLIAM E	COL	0-0015039	0753	1
WATTERSON TRAVIS K	LTC	0-0051008	1156	1
WATTS EUGENE A	COL	0-0081321	0766	1
WATTS FOSTER L	COL	0-0037569	0666	2
WATTS HARRY L JR	COL	0-0011714	0753	2

NAME	GRADE	SVC NO	DATE RET MO YR	RET CODE
WATTS JAMES K	COL	0-0030752	0566	1
WATTS ROLAND S	COL	0-0050972	1057	1
WATTS WILLIAM E	LTC	0-0040291	0966	1
WAUGH WILLIAM H JR	COL	0-0019587	0864	1
WAY DAVID W	COL	0-0032341	1167	1
WAY EVERT C	LTC	0-0032888	0663	1
WAYMAN DUANE L	CPT	0-0060472	1162	1
WAYMAN ELDEN F	LTC	0-0087461	1168	1
WAYNE ROBERT P	LTC	0-0084681	1167	1
WEADOCK THOMAS A	COL	0-0039748	0359	1
WEART DOUGLAS L	M G	0-0003774	0851	2
WEATHERBY FRANCIS E	COL	0-0005213	1048	1
WEATHERS JAMES W JR	COL	0-0026879	0868	1
WEAVER CARL A SR	COL	0-0030044	1061	1
WEAVER JAMES R	COL	0-0020278	0163	1
WEAVER JAMES W	LTC	0-0069572	0968	1
WEAVER JOHN D	COL	0-0041876	0561	1
WEAVER JOSEPH U	COL	0-0018941	1058	1
WEAVER MAYNARD B	COL	0-0032120	0264	1
WEAVER ROBERT M	MAJ	0-0067633	0665	2
WEAVER THERON D	B G	0-0007653	1052	2
WEAVER WILLIAM G	M G	0-0003413	0246	2
WEAVER WILLIAM K JR	LTC	0-0006192	1122	2
WEBB CHARLES A JR	LTC	0-0040585	0956	1
WEBB CHARLES C	LTC	0-0040620	0262	1
WEBB EDWARD C	CW4	W-0903992	0664	1
WEBB ELMER M	COL	0-0016908	0757	1
WEBB GEORGE D	COL	0-0041916	0462	2
WEBB HENDERSON JR	COL	0-0042527	0565	1
WEBB HUGH W	COL	0-0047228	1068	1
WEBB JOSEPH F JR	COL	0-0029271	0763	1
WEBB JOSEPH F	COL	0-0051001	0856	1
WEBB LESTER A	COL	0-0008451	0147	1
WEBB LYNN H	COL	0-0039946	1159	1
WEBB MAURICE E	COL	0-0030357	0663	1
WEBB MAXINE E	MAJ	N-0002267	1262	1
WEBB RALPH J	LTC	0-0065014	0766	1
WEBB RICHARD H	LTC	0-0004724	0133	2
WEBB ROBERT L	COL	0-0030207	0764	1
WEBB ROBERT M	MAJ	0-0035571	0863	1
WEBB WILLIAM H	LTC	0-0028263	1266	1
WEBBER CLARK	LTC	0-0030111	0162	1
WEBBER DONALD B	COL	0-0018392	0761	1
WEBBER IRA B	COL	0-0043375	0264	1
WEBBER REBECCA	MAJ	N-0002134	0760	2
WEBEL JAMES B	COL	0-0039463	0866	1
WEBER FREDERICK	COL	0-0018148	0760	1
WEBER JOHN H	B G	0-0018680	0762	1
WEBER JOHN P	LTC	0-0079137	0868	1
WEBER MILAN G	COL	0-0018444	0960	1
WEBER RICHARD E JR	COL	0-0019421	0864	1
WEBER ROBERT J	CPT	0-0065208	0856	2
WEBSTER AILEEN M	MAJ	L-0000293	0753	1
WEBSTER DANIEL	COL	0-0033071	0966	2
WEBSTER DONALD C	LTC	0-0081323	0567	1
WEBSTER HARRY W	LTC	0-0029294	1061	1
WEBSTER LOUIS C	COL	0-0010419	0-36	1
WEBSTER MONTGOMERY	COL	0-0021751	0667	1
WEBSTER SANFORD H	COL	0-0023222	0962	1
WEBSTER WILLIAM T	COL	0-0033858	0265	1
WECKERLING JOHN	B G	0-0011974	1054	1
WEDBUSH OTHON E	LTC	0-0055231	0966	1
WEDDELL WILLIAM A	COL	0-0016340	1055	1
WEDEMEYER ALBERT C	GEN	0-0012484	0751	1
WEED EARL D	COL	0-0009225	1046	2
WEED THOMAS J	COL	0-0010977	0852	1
WEEDON HERSCHEL R	LTC	0-0041741	0361	1
WEEGO GEORGE W	COL	0-0041484	0158	1
WEEKLEY DONALD W	CW4	W-0903994	1163	1
WEEKS BERTRAM A	COL	0-0026368	0264	1
WEEKS EUGENE L	COL	0-0024700	0868	1
WEEKS JOHN A	COL	0-0011211	0346	2
WEEKS RAYMOND W	LTC	0-0036173	0761	1
WEEKS ROBERT A	COL	0-0052011	1163	1
WEEMS MINER L	LTC	0-0040999	1163	1

NAME	GRADE	SVC NO	DATE RET MO YR	RET CODE
WEGARD VICTOR L	CW3	W-0902382	1059	1
WEGGELAND HENRY N JR	LTC	0-0059882	0866	1
WEGNER CLARENCE A	CW2	W-0901739	0247	2
WEHLE PHILIP C	M G	0-0018067	0965	2
WEHRKAMP CLETUS J	CW4	W-0903995	0463	1
WEHRLE AWTRY P	COL	0-0051017	0459	2
WEHRLE MARGARET J	LTC	L-0000240	0264	1
WEIBEL RODNEY W	LTC	0-0079139	0867	1
WEIBLE ELSIE L	LTC	L-0000320	0767	1
WEIBLE WALTER L	LTG	0-0011308	0157	1
WEIDENKOPF STANLEY J	COL	0-0041771	0165	1
WEILAND PAUL H	COL	0-0008418	0950	1
WEINBERGER HOWARD W	LTC	0-0038234	0965	1
WEINERT MCDONALD D	COL	0-0014769	0954	2
WEINERTH STUART L	LTC	0-0042620	0963	1
WEINGARTEN WILLIAM H	CPT	0-0059605	0152	2
WEINLAND ARTHUR A	LTC	0-0030123	0162	1
WEINNING ALBERT J	COL	0-0021139	0660	1
WEINSTEIN ALICE E	LTC	N-0000976	0266	1
WEINSTEIN MARVIN S	LTC	0-0028149	0766	1
WEIR GEORGE M	LTC	0-0038623	0455	1
WEIR REBA B	MAJ	N-0001881	0360	1
WEIR ROBERT W M	LTC	0-0042150	0161	1
WEIR ROY I JR	COL	0-0038874	0862	1
WEISBERG BENJAMIN	COL	0-0040085	1162	2
WEISBROD JOSEPH J	CW4	W-0907046	0163	1
WEISEMANN HEINZ	COL	0-0021956	0167	1
WEISLER JULIAN E	COL	0-0042028	0562	1
WEISMAN LOUIS G	COL	0-0009464	0753	2
WEISS ALFRED V	LTC	0-0036287	0767	1
WEISS EDWARD P	CW4	RW-0904436	0368	1
WEISSINGER WILLIAM T	COL	0-0004127	1146	2
WEISSINGER WILLIAM T	COL	0-0021154	0547	2
WEISSMAN EDWIN W	COL	0-0031559	0961	1
WEITZNER DANIEL N	CW3	W-0903997	1166	2
WELBORN JOHN C	COL	0-0018863	0859	1
WELCH GENE R	LTC	0-0024409	0261	1
WELCH GEORGE P	COL	0-0041422	0856	1
WELCH GLADYS M	MAJ	N-0002030	1058	1
WELCH GORDON B	COL	0-0004925	1146	1
WELCH JAMES C	COL	0-0012229	0251	2
WELCH JAMES C JR	LTC	0-0028367	0967	1
WELCH JOHN M	COL	0-0009204	0852	2
WELCH JOHN P	COL	0-0008055	0146	2
WELCH MARHL H	COL	0-0005972	0753	1
WELCH RAY D	COL	0-0012811	0954	1
WELD SETH L JR	B G	0-0019772	0865	1
WELDE GLENN A	COL	0-0040402	0166	1
WELLBORN C J JR	CPT	0-0050665	0155	2
WELLBORN CHARLES G	LTC	0-0065273	0966	1
WELLENDORF LEONARD E	COL	0-0029538	0664	2
WELLENREITER F L	LTC	0-0028987	0456	1
WELLER WENDELL A	COL	0-0018290	0860	1
WELLES GEORGE H	LTC	0-0024086	0965	1
WELLING ALVIN C	M G	0-0018983	0865	1
WELLS ALBERT C JR	COL	0-0019838	0861	1
WELLS CLAYTON W	COL	0-0029962	0660	2
WELLS GEORGE R	LTC	0-0008070	0142	1
WELLS GORDON M	B G	0-0006689	0947	1
WELLS HARRY M	CW4	RW-0904000	1164	1
WELLS HOWARD B	COL	0-0083591	0965	1
WELLS JAMES B	COL	0-0019554	0862	1
WELLS JAMES F	COL	0-0030654	0466	2
WELLS JESSE B	COL	0-0015580	0654	1
WELLS JOHN A	MAJ	0-0036205	0762	1
WELLS PAUL O	LTC	0-0020536	1055	1
WELLS RALPH H	LTC	0-0040014	0264	1
WELLS ROBERT B	COL	0-0024275	0568	1
WELLS THOMAS J	COL	0-0017111	0758	1
WELLS WALTER J	COL	0-0021766	0962	1
WELLS WILLIAM L	COL	0-0033641	1265	1
WELSCH ALVIN B	LTC	0-0041786	0757	1
WELSCH JERALDINE	MAJ	N-0002331	0167	1
WELSH EARL G	COL	0-0009959	1046	1
WELSH JOHN B	COL	0-0030544	1165	1

NAME	GRADE	SVC NO	DATE RET MO YR	RET CODE	NAME	GRADE	SVC NO	DATE RET MO YR	RET CODE	NAME	GRADE	SVC NO	DATE RET MO YR	RET CODE	NAME	GRADE	SVC NO	DATE RET MO YR	RET CODE
WELSH ROBERT J	COL	0-0025096	1168	1	WHEATON PAUL R	LTC	0-0027800	0666	1	WHITE ROBERT M JR	CPT	0-0028530	1059	2	WIENECKE ROBERT H	M G	0-0041569	0264	2
WELSH STUART M	COL	0-0041498	0658	2	WHEELER CECIL G	COL	0-0039520	1053	1	WHITE STEPHEN J	1LT	0-0059395	0851	2	WIENER WILLIAM M	CPT	0-0006686	0134	2
WELTMER NOYES JR	LTC	0-0080025	1067	2	WHEELER DRUID E	COL	0-0007443	1045	2	WHITE VICTOR W	COL	0-0043479	0767	1	WIERSEMA KENNETH G	COL	0-0041624	0157	2
WELTON KENNETH R	LTC	0-0042929	1264	1	WHEELER ERNEST E	MAJ	0-0060418	0967	1	WHITE WILLIAM B IV	MAJ	0-0026873	0965	1	WIEST BERNARD J	LTC	0-0066122	1267	1
WELTY REX G JR	CPT	0-0061280	0766	1	WHEELER ERNEST S	COL	0-0001373	0829	1	WHITE WILLIAM C	COL	0-0021457	0846	2	WIGGINS CHARLES B	CW4	W-0904017	0868	1
WENDEROTT MARCELLA	MAJ	N-0001548	0665	1	WHEELER EVELYN S	1LT	R-0000366	0846	1	WHITE WILLIAM D	COL	0-0004024	0950	1	WIGGINS EDWARD G	LTC	0-0036457	0463	1
WENDLE HUGH M	LTC	0-0033764	1061	1	WHEELER LESTER L	B G	0-0019951	0865	1	WHITE WILLIAM E	LTC	0-0061465	0868	1	WIGHT JERMY B	MAJ	0-0074889	0964	1
WENDORF HULEN D	COL	0-0021919	0859	1	WHEELER MARGARET H	MAJ	N-0002068	0762	1	WHITE WILLIAM F	LTC	0-0037597	0264	1	WIGHTMAN RICHARD M	COL	0-0005267	0750	1
WENDT WALTER W	COL	0-0032190	1266	1	WHEELER RAYMOND A	LTG	0-0003064	0249	1	WHITE WILLIAM N	COL	0-0011006	0854	1	WIGTON EDWARD N	1LT	0-0014402	1019	2
WENTZ ROZENE	LTC	N-0000003	0348	1	WHEELER ROBERT F	COL	0-0040872	0767	1	WHITE WILLIAM R	B G	0-0003283	0946	2	WIKEN ARENT O	COL	0-0030426	0665	2
WENZ ALBERT L	LTC	0-0065148	0968	1	WHEELER WARREN N	LTC	0-0063176	1065	1	WHITE WILLIAM R	LTC	0-0032847	0768	1	WIKLUND ANDERS O	COL	0-0044597	1168	1
WENZLAFF THEODORE C	COL	0-0016448	0655	1	WHEELIN THOMAS J	LTC	0-0038856	1262	1	WHITE WILSON E	LTC	0-0079663	0163	1	WIKOFF WILLIAM H	LTC	0-0032301	1063	1
WENZLICK GEORGE F	CW4	W-0904004	0859	1	WHELCHEL JAMES L	COL	0-0012155	0754	2	WHITEHEAD ARTHUR K	LTC	0-0043612	0863	1	WILBERT HARRY E	COL	0-0041539	1058	1
WERGELAND DAVID A	CPT	0-0092144	1166	2	WHELCHEL WILLIS W	COL	0-0016837	0757	2	WHITEHEAD JAMES R	LTC	0-0042095	1060	2	WILBUR WILLIAM H	B G	0-0003365	0347	2
WERGELAND FLOYD L	M G	0-0019599	0864	1	WHELIHAN WILLIAM P	COL	0-0019102	0863	1	WHITEHEAD SAMUEL C	CW3	W-0904015	0161	1	WILBY LANGFITT B	COL	0-0019748	0263	1
WERLEY HARRIET H	LTC	N-0001241	0264	1	WHERLEY CLYDE H	LTC	0-0030675	0759	1	WHITEHEAD THOMAS E	COL	0-0012780	0748	1	WILCOX DICK	CW4	W-0904020	0265	1
WERMUTH ANTHONY L	COL	0-0023252	1166	1	WHETSTONE RUSSELL E	COL	0-0053212	1064	1	WHITEHORNE JOSEPH W	COL	0-0025277	0167	1	WILCOX HOWARD O JR	LTC	0-0043347	0164	1
WERNER FRANKLIN A	COL	0-0033307	0268	1	WHICHER JOHN C	LTC	0-0039986	0962	1	WHITEHOUSE BENJAMIN	COL	0-0028941	1057	1	WILCOX JUDSON D	LTC	0-0030618	0761	2
WERNER RICHARD J	B G	0-0029107	0159	1	WHIPPLE HOWARD R	COL	0-0039542	0662	1	WHITELAW JOHN L	B G	0-0012357	0755	1	WILCOX LESLIE R	COL	0-0032251	0764	1
WERNGREN MARTIN S	COL	0-0039006	0266	1	WHIPPLE JOHN L	LTC	0-0043714	0164	1	WHITELEY EDWARD J	COL	0-0024627	0961	1	WILCOX PERRY O	COL	0-0010685	0446	2
WERNITZNIG EDWARD R	COL	0-0020505	1065	2	WHIPPLE SHERBURNE JR	B G	0-0019130	0863	1	WHITELEY JOSEPH H	COL	0-0009378	0447	2	WILD HENRY H	COL	0-0051064	0360	2
WERTENBERGER IRENE	MAJ	N-0000468	1163	1	WHIPPLE WILLIAM	B G	0-0018024	0760	1	WHITENTON ROBERT M	COL	0-0036114	0768	1	WILD HERMAN B	COL	0-0040333	0168	1
WERTZ GEORGE M JR	COL	0-0018357	1061	1	WHISNANT ISAAC E	LTC	0-0046983	0862	1	WHITESELL CARLIN H	COL	0-0020620	0863	1	WILDE ADNA G JR	LTC	0-0060865	1068	1
WESCOTT GEORGE B	COL	0-0007891	1133	2	WHISNER EMONS B	B G	0-0007062	0753	1	WHITESIDE DAVID O	MAJ	0-0062149	0959	2	WILDE ELIZABETH	MAJ	N-0002220	0360	1
WESKE JACK H	COL	0-0051054	0959	1	WHISTLER JOHN M	COL	0-0015104	0845	2	WHITFIELD HAROLD N	LTC	0-0041032	0868	1	WILDER CYRUS J	COL	0-0004744	0153	2
WESOLOWSKI STANLEY	LTC	0-0058655	0168	1	WHITAKER DWIGHT R	LTC	0-0084441	1163	1	WHITFIELD MORGAN A	LTC	0-0036389	0163	1	WILDER ERNEST B	LTC	0-0040271	1058	1
WESOLOWSKY CHARLES L	LTC	0-0028704	0966	1	WHITAKER ERNEST J	COL	0-0023793	0765	1	WHITFIELD ROBERT L	COL	0-0029177	0660	2	WILDER HAROLD W	LTC	0-0094969	0666	1
WESSELS THEODORE F	B G	0-0006911	0552	2	WHITAKER W R JR	COL	0-0051272	0760	1	WHITING EDWARD T	COL	0-0028855	0356	1	WILDER LYNDON S	COL	0-0056789	1060	1
WESSMILLER JOHN J	LTC	0-0054052	0862	2	WHITCOMB BEATRICE	LTC	M-0010076	0562	1	WHITING GEORGE W C	COL	0-0002484	1045	2	WILDER SAMUEL D	COL	0-0044104	1068	1
WEST BLAND	COL	0-0031378	1264	1	WHITCOMB JOHN C	COL	0-0005321	1051	1	WHITING HOWELL T	LTC	0-0088227	0968	1	WILDER WEBSTER	LTC	0-0051784	1060	1
WEST CHARLES P	COL	0-0029964	0763	1	WHITCOMB RICHARD F	LTC	0-0041531	0656	1	WHITLEY ARTHUR N	COL	0-0047359	1168	1	WILDERMAN JORDAN J	COL	0-0023092	0867	1
WEST CHARLES W	B G	0-0012774	1162	1	WHITCOMB VIRGINIE G	MAJ	N-0002240	0860	1	WHITLEY FENNER H JR	COL	0-0031106	0766	1	WILDES THOMAS	LTC	0-0040778	0962	1
WEST DARRELL W	CW3	W-0904005	0764	1	WHITE ARTHUR A	M G	0-0003900	0949	1	WHITLEY JACK R	LTC	0-0042705	0662	1	WILDEY ROBERT W	LTC	0-0052353	1167	1
WEST ETHELBERT	CW4	W-0904006	0167	1	WHITE ARTHUR E	COL	0-0019328	0656	1	WHITLEY JESSE W	LTC	0-0050070	0365	1	WILDFORSTER FRIEDRIC	LTC	0-0030346	0762	1
WEST EUGENE R	1LT	0-0014318	0805	2	WHITE ARTHUR N	MAJ	0-0004566	0622	2	WHITLOCK LESTER J	M G	0-0007138	0754	1	WILDMAN THOMAS A	MAJ	0-0017793	1041	2
WEST GEORGE C	LTC	0-0045153	0865	1	WHITE BARNEY D	COL	0-0031606	0867	1	WHITLOW ARCHIE B	LTC	0-0011916	0836	2	WILES ISAIAH A	COL	0-0022709	1266	1
WEST GUSTAVUS W	COL	0-0016146	1049	1	WHITE BOSWELL	CW4	W-0907053	0564	1	WHITMAN ELMER L	LTC	0-0029569	0659	1	WILEY EARL T JR	COL	0-0040442	0665	1
WEST JOHN A	CW4	W-0904007	0660	2	WHITE CECIL W	MAJ	0-0038208	0965	1	WHITMORE HARRY E	LTC	0-0035993	0962	1	WILEY HENRY S	CW4	W-0904221	0757	1
WEST JOHN T JR	COL	0-0030325	0366	1	WHITE CHARLES H	M G	0-0002268	0746	2	WHITMORE STANLEY F	COL	0-0052122	0168	1	WILEY IRVING B	LTC	0-0031132	0962	2
WEST LUTHER C	LTC	0-0065704	0968	1	WHITE CHARLES H JR	B G	0-0019407	0864	1	WHITNEY CARL L	COL	0-0031435	0267	1	WILEY JAMES A	COL	0-0047130	0868	1
WEST MARTHA M	MAJ	N-0001230	0764	1	WHITE CHARLES I JR	LTC	0-0059059	0267	1	WHITNEY CHARLES F	MAJ	0-0009878	0430	2	WILEY NOBLE J JR	COL	0-0017228	0758	1
WEST ROBERT J JR	COL	0-0016925	0346	2	WHITE CHARLES R	LTC	0-0066210	0868	1	WHITNEY PHILIP M	COL	0-0012448	0446	2	WILEY WILLIAM G	CW4	W-0901862	0653	1
WEST WILLIAM F	LTC	0-0058656	1168	1	WHITE CHARLES T	LTC	0-0052708	0163	1	WHITSETT WILLIAM L	COL	0-0051892	0164	1	WILHELM LELAND F	LTC	0-0048723	0967	1
WESTBROOKE JACK G	COL	0-0060518	0868	2	WHITE CLAUDE W	LTC	0-0040448	1160	1	WHITSON RAY W	COL	0-0030056	1263	1	WILHIDE GLENN C	COL	0-0028753	0653	1
WESTER RUSSELL N SR	CW4	W-0904009	0661	1	WHITE CLYDE E	LTC	0-0042700	0261	1	WHITSON ROBERT K	COL	0-0004506	1144	2	WILHOIT EDWARD	LTC	0-0031166	0155	2
WESTERMEIER JOHN T	COL	0-0018493	0861	2	WHITE DAVID C	LTC	0-0060763	1167	1	WHITT DANIEL T SR	CW4	W-0904016	1161	1	WILHOYT ELLIS E JR	B G	0-0020593	0367	1
WESTERN GEORGE F	COL	0-0076930	0166	1	WHITE DEAN	CPT	0-0084919	1165	1	WHITT RALPH L	COL	0-0080521	1167	1	WILKERSON ROBERT T	LTC	0-0079146	0968	1
WESTERVELT F B	COL	0-0018630	0860	1	WHITE DONALD G	COL	0-0012609	0448	1	WHITTAKER FRANK L	COL	0-0004766	1146	1	WILKERSON THOMAS E	CW4	W-0902685	0968	1
WESTFALL CHESTER C	LTC	0-0008204	1144	2	WHITE EDMUND D	COL	0-0029077	0459	1	WHITTAKER HORACE L	B G	0-0004791	1146	1	WILKES JOHN S	LTC	0-0030288	0959	2
WESTFALL CLARENCE R	LTC	0-0026024	0764	2	WHITE EDWARD C	COL	0-0039766	0462	1	WHITTAKER HOWARD R	B G	0-0029408	0760	2	WILKIN JOHN L	COL	0-0039847	0963	1
WESTFALL ELEANOR J	MAJ	M-0010074	0558	1	WHITE EDWARD L	COL	0-0039885	0762	1	WHITTEMORE FREDERICK	COL	0-0043255	0962	1	WILKINS ARTHUR L	LTC	0-0037438	1161	1
WESTMAN JOHN R	LTC	0-0081327	0961	2	WHITE ELI F	COL	0-0041951	1061	1	WHITTEMORE KENNETH S	COL	0-0007494	0349	1	WILKINS FRANK F	COL	0-0039731	1061	1
WESTON ALAN E	LTC	0-0026519	0764	1	WHITE EMETT R	COL	0-0031334	0966	2	WHITTEMORE PAUL B	CPT	0-0020648	0148	1	WILKINS GEORGE R	COL	0-0019750	0863	1
WESTON ORVILLE M JR	1LT	0-0061830	0951	2	WHITE FRED F	LTC	0-0033776	1268	1	WHITTEN HAROLD L	COL	0-0042954	0661	1	WILKINS LOWELL V	CW4	W-0907056	1062	1
WESTPHALINGER HENRY	M G	0-0016130	1162	1	WHITE FREDERICK	COL	0-0023326	0667	1	WHITTEN RUDOLPH G	LTC	0-0003716	0928	2	WILKINSON HARVEY W	COL	0-0017139	0347	2
WESTPHELING CHARLES	COL	0-0018533	0761	1	WHITE GEORGE E JR	COL	0-0020130	0557	1	WHITTET WILLARD A	COL	0-0029824	0252	1	WILKINSON WILLIAM C	CPT	0-0056407	1050	2
WESTRUP CHARLES M	LTC	0-0051097	0758	1	WHITE GEORGE W	B G	0-0019079	0561	1	WHITTING HENRY C	LTC	0-0044487	0862	1	WILKINSON WILLIAM E	COL	0-0020529	1155	2
WETHERBIE HAROLD B	COL	0-0041923	1160	1	WHITE GEORGE W	COL	0-0051200	0261	1	WHITTLE CALVIN L	COL	0-0015913	0757	1	WILKOWSKI ANTHONY J	MAJ	0-0052748	0550	2
WEYAND ALEXANDER	COL	0-0004510	0946	2	WHITE HILTON R	CW4	W-0904013	0763	1	WHITTON JOSEPH F JR	COL	0-0051825	0167	1	WILLARD LEROY L	MAJ	0-0063313	0863	1
WEYER DEBOLT G	CW4	W-0904010	0365	1	WHITE HOWARD S	LTC	0-0032041	0267	2	WHITWORTH MANCIL R	LTC	0-0036563	0768	1	WILLARD PAUL S	COL	0-0029541	0361	1
WEYHER THEODORE A	B G	0-0016738	0657	1	WHITE ISAAC D	GEN	0-0015080	0461	2	WHITWORTH THOMAS C	LTC	0-0035231	0965	1	WILLARD SHERMAN E	COL	0-0011089	0647	1
WHALEN HORACE K	COL	0-0018727	0462	1	WHITE JACK C	LTC	0-0040000	0962	1	WHYBARK GEORGE W	LTC	0-0006233	0838	1	WILLCOX EDWIN J	LTC	0-0025594	0766	1
WHALEY BERT K	LTC	0-0042612	0763	1	WHITE JAMES C	COL	0-0011666	0653	1	WICK ALBERT J	COL	0-0014822	1046	2	WILLEMS JOHN H	M G	0-0016176	1261	1
WHALEY EUGENE B	LTC	0-0052150	1062	2	WHITE JOHN F	LTC	0-0025507	0867	1	WICK THOMAS H	COL	0-0041689	0760	1	WILLENZICK HAROLD	COL	0-0023342	0962	1
WHARTON WILLIAM L	COL	0-0008205	0643	2	WHITE JOHN N	COL	0-0009124	1048	2	WICKENS PAUL N	COL	0-0041535	0756	1	WILLERS KARL H	LTC	0-0021671	0661	1
WHATLEY ROBERT J	LTC	0-0009944	0238	2	WHITE JOHN W	COL	0-0021319	0859	1	WICKERT HOWARD T	LTC	0-0026312	0864	1	WILLETS GEORGE D	LTC	0-0040281	0866	1
WHATLEY VACHEL D JR	COL	0-0016886	0751	2	WHITE LAWRENCE K	COL	0-0019241	0347	2	WICKEY HOWARD W	LTC	0-0030458	0663	1	WILLETT GORDON	LTC	0-0066123	0868	1
WHAYNE TOM F	COL	0-0019657	0655	1	WHITE LEE A	MAJ	0-0041061	0361	1	WICKLINE WILLIAM A	COL	0-0001496	0833	1	WILLETTE GEORGE C	COL	0-0017289	0858	1
WHEAT CLAYTON E	COL	0-0014810	0845	1	WHITE LEON A	COL	0-0010770	0546	2	WICKS ROGER M	B G	0-0012082	0550	1	WILLEY GEORGE L	LTC	0-0042408	0762	1
WHEAT LESLIE C	COL	0-0005769	0347	2	WHITE LESTER W	CW3	W-0907052	0864	1	WICKWARD ALICE C	LTC	N-0000033	0655	2	WILLEY JOHN P	B G	0-0015954	0854	1
WHEATLEY ADELINE G	MAJ	L-0000076	1060	1	WHITE LOREN H	LTC	0-0084470	0968	1	WIDENER TRAVIS F	CW4	W-0907054	1167	1	WILLEY WILFORD L	LTC	0-0038961	0664	2
WHEATLEY EDWIN T	LTC	0-0008397	0739	2	WHITE RALPH W	COL	0-0039717	0561	1	WIDMANN HOMER	COL	0-0027032	1058	1	WILLIAMS URQUHART	COL	0-0019391	0864	1
WHEATLEY ROBERT E	LTC	0-0069828	0667	2	WHITE REX H JR	COL	0-0045595	0864	1	WIDMER ALBERT W	COL	0-0041911	0961	1	WILLIAMS ALBERT S JR	COL	0-0025374	0965	1
WHEATON HARRY J	COL	0-0016598	1056	1	WHITE RICHARD A	COL	0-0040524	0968	1	WIECHMANN JOSEPH H	COL	0-0013874	0762	1	WILLIAMS ALEX N	LTC	0-0041623	0258	1
WHEATON JAMES R	COL	0-0016458	0656	1	WHITE ROBERT C	COL	0-0016851	0757	1	WIEGAND CHARLES D	COL	0-0017731	0859	1	WILLIAMS ALEX N JR	COL	0-0016810	1057	1

NAME	GRADE	SVC NO	DATE RET MO YR	RET CODE
WILLIAMS ALONZO R	MAJ	0-0041140	0864	1
WILLIAMS ANITA V	MAJ	M-0010053	0855	2
WILLIAMS ARTHUR H JR	COL	0-0043436	1167	1
WILLIAMS BASIL F	COL	0-0051025	0559	1
WILLIAMS BENJAMIN B	LTC	0-0028515	0867	1
WILLIAMS BYRON E	LTC	0-0030134	0163	2
WILLIAMS CAROL M	LTC	L-0000175	1267	1
WILLIAMS CARROLL J	COL	0-0030811	0361	1
WILLIAMS CHARLES L	COL	0-0018795	0362	2
WILLIAMS CHARLES S	COL	0-0009604	0151	1
WILLIAMS CLEON L	LTC	0-0011913	0844	2
WILLIAMS CLYDE W	CW4	W-0901886	0553	1
WILLIAMS CYRIL F	COL	0-0016982	0757	1
WILLIAMS DONALD B	COL	0-0038901	0766	1
WILLIAMS DONALD G	COL	0-0021071	0765	1
WILLIAMS EARL H	LTC	0-0020977	0346	2
WILLIAMS EDWARD T	LTG	0-0012818	0261	1
WILLIAMS EDWARD W	COL	0-0020205	0866	1
WILLIAMS ERNEST	COL	0-0007148	0553	2
WILLIAMS FREDDIE W	CPT	0-0099275	0267	2
WILLIAMS FREDERICK	LTC	0-0036227	1065	1
WILLIAMS GARDNER A	COL	0-0040301	1068	1
WILLIAMS GEORGE C	COL	0-0052146	0966	1
WILLIAMS GEORGE W	COL	0-0032077	1267	2
WILLIAMS GEORGE W SR	LTC	0-0052004	0667	1
WILLIAMS GRANT A	COL	0-0016565	1048	1
WILLIAMS HAROLD C	LTC	0-0031372	1060	1
WILLIAMS HAROLD L	LTC	0-0056984	1064	1
WILLIAMS HENRY G JR	LTC	OE-0103376	0968	1
WILLIAMS IRMA F	MAJ	N-0000830	0963	1
WILLIAMS J J B	COL	0-0005202	0846	1
WILLIAMS JAMES F JR	LTC	0-0023224	0960	1
WILLIAMS JAMES N	COL	0-0008800	0949	1
WILLIAMS JAMES W	LTC	0-0022736	0168	1
WILLIAMS JOHN A	COL	0-0042257	1063	1
WILLIAMS JOHN D	COL	0-0060446	0268	1
WILLIAMS JOHN F	COL	0-0015548	1146	2
WILLIAMS JOHN J	LTC	0-0081935	0562	2
WILLIAMS JOHN M	COL	0-0020319	0765	1
WILLIAMS JOHN P	COL	0-0042996	0467	1
WILLIAMS JOHN W	COL	0-0034107	0766	1
WILLIAMS LAURIN L	LTG	0-0008425	0657	2
WILLIAMS LEE R	COL	0-0016821	0948	1
WILLIAMS LESLIE S	COL	0-0010637	1146	2
WILLIAMS LEWIS C JR	COL	0-0040081	0266	1
WILLIAMS LEWIS H	LTC	0-0080330	0265	1
WILLIAMS LOUIS F	COL	0-0018324	0959	1
WILLIAMS MARION G	COL	0-0044841	0864	1
WILLIAMS MARION R	CW4	W-0904029	1265	1
WILLIAMS MARVIN E	LTC	0-0035386	0161	1
WILLIAMS MAUDE D	LTC	N-0001871	0860	1
WILLIAMS MYRON L	COL	0-0030622	0862	1
WILLIAMS NORMAN L	LTC	0-0026173	1063	1
WILLIAMS NORMAN P	COL	0-0008523	0753	1
WILLIAMS RAYMOND M	COL	0-0020399	0164	1
WILLIAMS RICHARD G	LTC	0-0020751	0648	1
WILLIAMS RICHARD H	COL	0-0001238	0-38	1
WILLIAMS RICHARD K	COL	0-0038174	0868	1
WILLIAMS RICHARD W	LTC	0-0047344	0861	2
WILLIAMS ROBERT C	COL	0-0040352	0466	1
WILLIAMS ROBERT C JR	COL	0-0022091	0765	1
WILLIAMS ROBERT J	LTC	0-0049162	0561	1
WILLIAMS ROBERT L JR	COL	0-0018742	0756	2
WILLIAMS ROBERT W	LTC	0-0069834	0368	1
WILLIAMS ROGER H	LTC	0-0040069	1050	2
WILLIAMS ROGER JR	COL	0-0005015	0246	1
WILLIAMS SAM S	LTC	0-0038902	1264	1
WILLIAMS SAMUEL T	LTG	0-0008472	0960	2
WILLIAMS SARAH E	LTC	N-0000508	0849	2
WILLIAMS TIMOTHY C	COL	0-0030791	0766	1
WILLIAMS TREVETT	LTC	0-0052845	0463	1
WILLIAMS WALTER H	LTC	0-0038967	1266	1
WILLIAMS WARREN R JR	COL	0-0021250	0868	1
WILLIAMS WILLIAM A	LTC	0-0032513	1167	1
WILLIAMS WILLIAM D	COL	0-0014708	0854	1
WILLIAMS WILLIAM R	LTC	0-0037675	0165	2
WILLIAMS WILLIAM S	MAJ	0-0088230	1168	1
WILLIAMS WINNIE S	MAJ	N-0001961	0560	1
WILLIAMS ZACK M	COL	0-0050966	1157	1
WILLIAMS 2ND FRANK W	MAJ	0-0024911	0148	2
WILLIAMSON CARL E	COL	0-0030178	0564	1
WILLIAMSON ELLIS V	COL	0-0012335	0550	1
WILLIAMSON JOHN	COL	0-0019900	0863	1
WILLIAMSON LEO C	LTC	0-0055065	0861	1
WILLIAMSON LYNDALL C	CPT	0-0065234	1262	2
WILLIAMSON MELVIN S	COL	0-0005687	0546	2
WILLIAMSON ROBERT L	LTC	0-0078676	1168	1
WILLIAMSON SAMUEL D	LTC	0-0039989	1063	1
WILLIAMSON WILLIAM E	COL	0-0050970	0158	1
WILLIARD WILLIS C	CW4	W-0902174	0962	1
WILLING ALEXANDER	B G	0-0038619	1162	2
WILLINGHAM CHESTER M	COL	0-0008442	0854	1
WILLINK ARTHUR	MAJ	0-0015933	0342	2
WILLIS ARTHUR N	COL	0-0014868	0552	2
WILLIS JACK E	LTC	0-0030313	0860	1
WILLIS JAMES S	B G	0-0015607	0954	1
WILLIS JAMES T	LTC	0-0020264	0657	2
WILLIS JEAN P	MAJ	0-0037283	0864	1
WILLIS JEFFERSON	COL	0-0011643	0847	2
WILLIS JOE M	LTC	0-0032854	1167	1
WILLIS LUELLA R	LTC	N-0000340	1160	1
WILLIS NICHOLAS W	COL	0-0043099	0967	1
WILLIS ORAL G	LTC	0-0018628	0345	2
WILLIS RAYMOND D	COL	0-0006106	0347	2
WILLIS WILLIAM D	COL	0-0020496	0758	1
WILLIS WINSLOW R	COL	0-0051352	1162	1
WILLISON THOMAS L	WO1	W-0901749	1042	2
WILLMANN WILLIAM C	COL	0-0081936	1068	1
WILLOUGHBY CHARLES A	M G	0-0004615	0851	2
WILLOUGHBY JESSE D	COL	0-0038787	0165	1
WILLOUGHBY WILLIAM H	COL	0-0030108	0764	1
WILLS LLOYD E	COL	0-0032060	0766	1
WILLSON ELMER J	LTC	0-0041449	0155	1
WILLSON RAY D	1LT	0-0014438	0820	2
WILLSON RICHARD T	COL	0-0015429	0555	1
WILMETH JAMES D	COL	0-0019519	0660	1
WILMOT FRED W	LTC	0-0059770	0667	1
WILSON ALBERT T	COL	0-0012574	1147	2
WILSON ARTHUR E	COL	0-0011873	0854	1
WILSON ARTHUR H JR	COL	0-0020693	0967	1
WILSON AUSTIN M JR	COL	0-0012178	0750	1
WILSON C FORREST	COL	0-0009559	0447	2
WILSON CHARLES F	CPT	0-0012363	0-33	1
WILSON CHARLES V	M G	0-0023564	0268	1
WILSON CLAIRE A	MAJ	N-0002495	0364	2
WILSON CLIFFORD C	LTC	0-0059066	1266	1
WILSON DANIEL M	COL	0-0017144	0752	2
WILSON DARRELL W	CW3	RW-0904005	0764	1
WILSON DAVID C JR	CPT	0-0058731	0452	2
WILSON DONALD B	COL	0-0051198	0261	1
WILSON DONALD C	COL	0-0030248	0964	2
WILSON DURWARD S	M G	0-0002858	0146	2
WILSON EDWARD L	COL	0-0028969	0256	1
WILSON EDWIN C	LTC	0-0060650	0966	1
WILSON ELDON R	CW4	W-0904036	1165	1
WILSON ERNEST L	MAJ	0-0008837	0724	2
WILSON ERNEST W	COL	0-0041141	1068	1
WILSON FLOYD M	MAJ	0-0058663	0368	1
WILSON FRANCIS B	LTC	0-0065737	0868	1
WILSON FRANCIS H	COL	0-0006701	0753	2
WILSON FRANCIS H JR	LTC	0-0053452	1165	1
WILSON FRANCIS J	COL	0-0014902	1046	2
WILSON FRANK B	LTC	0-0035162	0364	1
WILSON FRANKLIN L	LTC	0-0032350	0764	1
WILSON GARNETT H	COL	0-0010302	0753	1
WILSON GERALD R	LTC	0-0036338	0766	1
WILSON HAROLD D	MAJ	0-0027515	0664	1
WILSON HAROLD G	COL	0-0032370	0868	1
WILSON HAROLD G	COL	0-0041384	0756	1
WILSON HARRY L JR	MAJ	0-0023064	1144	2
WILSON JAMES K JR	B G	0-0018218	0359	1
WILSON JAMES M	COL	0-0040224	0368	1
WILSON JAMES T	COL	0-0020103	0164	2
WILSON JOHN H	B G	0-0005930	0946	2
WILSON JOHN J	MAJ	0-0070566	0467	1
WILSON JOHN L JR	COL	0-0033268	0661	1
WILSON JOHN L JR	COL	0-0039587	0758	1
WILSON JOHN M	LTC	0-0025556	0464	1
WILSON JOHN M	COL	0-0033026	0766	1
WILSON JOSEPH	CW4	W-0800357	0751	1
WILSON KERMIT J	LTC	0-0060172	0667	1
WILSON LAWRENCE M	COL	0-0038978	0968	2
WILSON LEONARD F	COL	0-0018943	1062	1
WILSON LEROY B	COL	0-0025106	0968	1
WILSON LLOYD G	LTC	0-0034685	0766	1
WILSON LOUIS A	LTC	0-0036129	0863	1
WILSON LUCILL A	CPT	N-0000394	0552	2
WILSON LYNNFORD S	COL	0-0051886	0866	1
WILSON MAX J	LTC	0-0084897	0868	1
WILSON MAYBIN H	COL	0-0010528	0851	2
WILSON MILTON E	COL	0-0012020	0149	2
WILSON MINOR K	COL	0-0041626	1059	1
WILSON MURRAY C	COL	0-0010321	1046	1
WILSON NEIL O	COL	0-0029256	0761	2
WILSON NORTON B	COL	0-0018476	0761	1
WILSON OVID O	COL	0-0015887	0954	1
WILSON PAUL F	LTC	0-0038971	0764	1
WILSON PENRHYN JR	LTC	0-0084690	0267	1
WILSON PLANTER M	LTC	0-0050884	0567	1
WILSON RALPH W	COL	0-0002963	0744	1
WILSON RAY	CW4	W-0904038	0258	1
WILSON RAYMOND J JR	COL	0-0081345	0767	1
WILSON ROBERT B	LTC	0-0039685	0958	1
WILSON ROBERT B	MAJ	0-0084691	0764	1
WILSON ROBERT F	COL	0-0039687	0960	1
WILSON RUSSELL J	COL	0-0040848	1167	2
WILSON THOMAS J	LTC	0-0087976	0168	1
WILSON VENNARD	B G	0-0007207	0653	2
WILSON WALTER K JR	LTG	0-0017512	0765	1
WILSON WELDON W	LTC	0-0032054	1166	1
WILSON WESTRAY E	COL	0-0041971	1061	2
WILSON WILBUR	COL	0-0042494	0165	1
WILSON WILLIAM E	LTC	0-0030542	1163	2
WILSON WILLIAM F	LTC	0-0089311	0668	1
WILSON WILLIAM H	LTC	0-0032820	0662	2
WILSON WILLIAM I	COL	0-0008574	0948	1
WILSON WILLIAM L	B G	0-0016950	0956	1
WILSON WILLIAM R	LTC	0-0014192	0818	2
WILSON WOODROW W	COL	0-0021755	0864	1
WILTAMUTH RALPH	COL	0-0010407	1146	2
WILTON CLIFFORD J	LTC	0-0079149	0268	1
WILTRAKIS EDWARD J	LTC	0-0051575	0163	1
WILY CHARLES	CW4	W-0904041	0968	1
WIMBERLEY JERRY M	COL	0-0025049	0966	1
WIMBERLEY NORRIS A	COL	0-0008306	1147	1
WIMER BENJAMIN R	COL	0-0017516	0557	1
WIMMER JACOB F	CW4	W-0904042	0666	2
WINCKLER RUDOLPH G	COL	0-0051399	0463	1
WINDER WAYNE M	COL	0-0034420	1264	1
WINDHAM JAMES F	LTC	0-0030651	0364	1
WINEMAN THEODORE H	LTC	0-0052354	1267	1
WINERS FREDERIC B	CPT	0-0009972	1134	2
WINFIELD IRMA H	MAJ	N-0002282	0564	1
WINFIELD RICHARD M	LTC	0-0005858	1041	1
WINFREE WESLEY C	MAJ	OF-0105876	1067	2
WING ALBERT G	COL	0-0007602	0753	1
WING FRANKLIN F JR	B G	0-0018107	0760	1
WINGET LEONARD W	COL	0-0041896	0961	1
WINGFIELD LINDSEY R	LTC	0-0016581	0748	1
WINGFIELD WILLIAM B	COL	0-0080525	1168	1
WINGO CHARLES A	COL	0-0051451	0861	1
WINGO ROLAND H	COL	0-0031098	1160	2
WINIARCZYK ANDREW W	LTC	0-0047278	0863	1
WINK ALICE R	LTC	N-0000858	1167	2
WINKLER HARRIET E	MAJ	N-0002479	0767	1
WINN DEAN F JR	LTC	0-0057959	0766	1
WINN JAMES J	COL	0-0017724	0759	1
WINN JOHN S JR	B G	0-0012140	1148	1
WINN NORMAN M	COL	0-0016567	0654	1
WINN WALTER S JR	COL	0-0012355	1146	1
WINNIE FRANKLIN E	COL	0-0041992	0462	1
WINNINGSTAD OLAF P	COL	0-0007075	0653	1
WINSLOW EDWARD	CW4	W-0904043	0658	1
WINSLOW PAUL E	LTC	0-0041721	0259	1
WINSTEAD THOMAS E	COL	0-0011649	0548	1
WINSTED JOHN B	LTC	0-0051059	1057	1
WINSTON BARLOW	COL	0-0008438	0753	2
WINSTON CHARLES S	LTC	0-0021690	0859	1
WINSTON EDWARD G	MAJ	0-0018842	0546	2
WINSTON SANFORD H	LTC	0-0062154	0564	1
WINTERMUTE JOHN S JR	LTC	0-0022039	0146	2
WINTERSTEEN JOSEPH D	COL	0-0051168	0159	1
WINTHROP EDWARD L	LTC	0-0027560	0467	1
WINTON ARTHUR V	COL	0-0008189	0452	2
WIRAK LOUIS R	COL	0-0018342	0761	1
WIRT CHARLES A	LTC	0-0025725	1163	1
WIRTZ PETER	CPT	0-0014400	1019	2
WISE CLEMENT M	CW4	W-0907061	0665	1
WISE FRANK G	LTC	0-0039678	0658	1
WISE GEORGE S	COL	0-0038589	0754	1
WISE JAMES B JR	LTC	0-0004951	0936	2
WISE JAMES E	CPT	0-0024819	0-44	2
WISE RICHARD A	LTC	0-0038171	0264	1
WISE WILLIAM A II	LTC	0-0060855	0868	1
WISE WILLIAM D JR	COL	0-0032682	0668	1
WISE 3RD SAMUEL R	MAJ	0-0057565	0554	2
WISELOGEL CHARLES O	COL	0-0016606	0447	1
WISEMAN VERA H	CPT	0-0016989	1143	1
WISHART HENRY H	COL	0-0038935	0666	1
WISS JOHN W	LTC	0-0028154	0766	1
WISSER NATHAN R	COL	0-0037522	1168	1
WITCZAK ANN M	LTC	N-0000610	0761	1
WITHERS EDWIN J	COL	0-0042921	1265	1
WITHERS LANGHORNE	LTC	0-0068062	0268	1
WITHERS WILLIAM P	COL	0-0012742	0854	1
WITMAN VINCENT B	CW4	W-0904045	0862	1
WITSELL EDWARD F	M G	0-0003455	0651	2
WITT EMITT C JR	LTC	0-0034027	0265	1
WITT GEORGE L	COL	0-0031382	0656	2
WITT ROSEMARY	MAJ	N-0001520	0865	1
WITT WILLIAM H	LTC	0-0039925	0460	2
WITTENBERG DAVID F	CW4	W-0907063	0859	1
WITTER KATHRYN G	LTC	N-0000082	0856	1
WITTER VINCENT M	COL	0-0032172	0868	1
WITTLINGER FREDERICK	LTC	0-0059069	0868	1
WITTMANN RICHARD C	COL	0-0025195	0962	1
WITTMAYER RAYMOND C	COL	0-0031631	0967	1
WOBBEKING BERNARD	COL	0-0042417	0864	1
WOERNER CHARLES A	CPT	0-0023592	0143	2
WOERNER LEO G	COL	0-0030341	0165	2
WOESTENBURG JOHN M	COL	0-0030004	0263	2
WOFFORD HOKE S	COL	0-0029480	1060	1
WOHLFEIL CARL H	LTC	0-0021907	0766	2
WOHNER JOHN H	COL	0-0023142	0868	1
WOICCAK EDWARD	CW3	W-0904047	0555	2
WOLCOTT WILLIAM J	LTC	0-0030496	0264	2
WOLD DONALD E	CW4	W-0904264	0466	1
WOLF JOHN F	COL	0-0058801	0265	1
WOLF KARL E	LTC	0-0026202	0663	1
WOLF SAMUEL S	COL	0-0038674	0960	1
WOLFE CLAUDIUS O	COL	0-0039536	0157	1
WOLFE HAROLD K	LTC	0-0031729	1265	1
WOLFE HENRY C	B G	0-0011349	0550	1
WOLFE HIRAM M III	LTC	0-0061090	0865	1
WOLFE LLOYD R	COL	0-0010117	0551	2
WOLFE RICHARD O	COL	0-0021743	0166	1
WOLFE WALTER J	COL	0-0014619	0754	1
WOLFE WALTER M	LTC	0-0057740	0865	1
WOLFE WILLIAM R	COL	0-0009457	1152	1
WOLFE YALE H	COL	0-0019415	0661	1

NAME	GRADE	SVC NO	DATE RET MO YR	RET CODE
WOLFFE PETER D	MAJ	O-0091541	0266	1
WOLFINGER ANNA M	MAJ	N-0002326	0665	1
WOLFINGER CLARENCE	LTC	O-0026831	0868	1
WOLFSON JACK C	COL	O-0040307	1268	1
WOLFSON MORTON	LTC	O-0048975	0661	1
WOLLASTON PENNOCK H	COL	O-0019854	0264	1
WOLTMON JACK W	LTC	O-0060686	0864	1
WOLVERTON DAVID R	COL	O-0007775	1043	1
WOMACK CARL D	LTC	O-0019426	0862	1
WONES EDWARD M	COL	O-0016028	0954	1
WOOD ALLEN H III	LTC	O-0028672	0766	1
WOOD BURL A	MAJ	O-0082128	0661	1
WOOD CAROLYN J	MAJ	N-0000584	0162	1
WOOD CHARLES H	COL	O-0019498	0160	1
WOOD DELMORE S	LTC	O-0004941	0934	2
WOOD ETHEL E	MAJ	N-0000887	0365	2
WOOD FRANCIS O	COL	O-0012327	0247	1
WOOD GEORGE W	LTC	O-0044203	0161	1
WOOD HARLAND G	LTC	O-0024154	0660	1
WOOD JOHN C JR	LTC	O-0052640	0868	1
WOOD JOSEPH S	CW2	W-0800348	0244	1
WOOD JULIAN C	COL	O-0041651	0460	1
WOOD LINCOLN	COL	O-0029116	0859	2
WOOD NORMAN F JR	LTC	O-0037596	0767	1
WOOD OLIVER E	LTC	O-0021998	0867	1
WOOD OLIVER S	COL	O-0002491	0942	1
WOOD PHILIP S	COL	O-0004961	0648	1
WOOD ROBERT E	B G	O-0013847	0715	1
WOOD ROBERT J	GEN	O-0018064	0965	1
WOOD ROY L	LTC	O-0059071	0867	1
WOOD STARLING W	COL	O-0080527	1066	1
WOOD STUART	COL	O-0016857	0757	2
WOOD THOMAS E	COL	O-0019483	0959	1
WOOD WALTER S	COL	O-0007474	0550	2
WOOD WAYNE L	COL	O-0051250	0961	1
WOOD WILLIAM H	B G	O-0016135	0556	1
WOODARD ANDREW J	LTC	O-0084445	0567	1
WOODARD VERNON E	COL	O-0031753	0268	1
WOODBERRY JOHN H	B G	O-0003701	0846	2
WOODBRIDGE WOODROW W	MAJ	O-0005469	0934	2
WOODBURN THOMAS B	COL	O-0007368	0951	2
WOODBURY HENRY J	COL	O-0014899	0852	2
WOODBURY JAMES A	COL	O-0042943	0267	2
WOODBURY KENNETH J	COL	O-0017601	0859	1
WOODES RAYMOND C	COL	O-0029067	0359	1
WOODLIFF CLIFFORD L	COL	O-0030796	0662	1
WOODMAN ERNEST A H	COL	O-0032822	0766	1
WOODMAN JOHN D	LTC	O-0040662	0263	1
WOODROW CHARLES E	COL	O-0032011	0364	1
WOODRUFF C E JR	COL	O-0015283	0454	2
WOODRUFF JAMES A	M G	O-0000748	0641	1
WOODRUFF OWEN E JR	COL	O-0036172	1063	2
WOODRUFF ROSCOE B	M G	O-0003819	0153	1
WOODRUFF VICTOR R	COL	O-0005684	1147	1
WOODS CAMERON F	COL	O-0042089	1162	1
WOODS CHARLES T	COL	O-0051069	1059	1
WOODS GEORGE E JR	COL	O-0041840	0161	1
WOODS JAMES R	COL	O-0035812	0767	1
WOODS JOHN J	COL	O-0022755	1067	1
WOODS KENNETH J	LTC	O-0053413	0863	1
WOODS LAWRENCE	COL	O-0006349	0150	1
WOODS LEE R JR	COL	O-0014851	0549	1
WOODS PAUL M	LTC	O-0025071	0361	1
WOODSON WILBERT T JR	LTC	O-0049358	0665	2
WOODWARD DEAN F	LTC	O-0062237	0767	1
WOODWARD ERNEST A	CW4	W-0904056	0661	1
WOODWARD HORACE M JR	COL	O-0010188	0349	1
WOODWARD NICHOLAS O	COL	O-0009704	0854	1
WOODWARD SAMUEL M	MAJ	O-0059801	1262	1
WOODWARD WILLIAM R	B G	O-0004438	1050	1
WOODWARD WILLIAM R	B G	O-0018582	1059	1
WOODWORTH GEORGE B	COL	O-0035995	0868	1
WOODYARD DONALD H	LTC	O-0051564	1162	1
WOODYARD THOMAS W JR	COL	O-0019826	0865	1
WOOLEY GEORGE F JR	B G	O-0011860	0449	1

NAME	GRADE	SVC NO	DATE RET MO YR	RET CODE
WOOLFLEY FRANCIS A	B G	O-0005699	0453	1
WOOLGAR WILLIAM A	COL	O-0017977	0454	1
WOOLLEY DONALD J	COL	O-0051478	1160	1
WOOLLEY HAROLD	COL	O-0006190	1145	2
WOOLSEY LAWRENCE S	1LT	O-0025403	0844	2
WOOTEN CHARLES A JR	LTC	O-0044599	1064	1
WOOTEN JOHN H	LTC	O-0053968	0367	1
WOOTEN SIDNEY C	M G	O-0018126	0865	1
WOOTTEN ANGUS E	LTC	O-0070572	0467	1
WORD ORVILLE C JR	COL	O-0050922	0754	1
WORKIZER BENJAMIN T	LTC	O-0020852	0944	2
WORKIZER DANIEL T	COL	O-0018608	0352	2
WORKMAN JAMES H	COL	O-0015177	0954	1
WORKS ROBERT C	COL	O-0021221	0164	1
WORLEY CHARLES E	CW3	W-0907065	1062	1
WORLEY JANE E	MAJ	N-0000303	1060	1
WORLEY THOMAS G	LTC	O-0031494	0465	2
WORRALL JOSEPH A JR	LTC	O-0067975	0866	1
WORRALL LAWRENCE P	COL	O-0007738	0642	2
WORRELL RALEIGH D	LTC	O-0032697	0468	1
WORSHAM LUDSON D	B G	O-0004428	1148	2
WORTHINGTON JAMES M	B G	O-0019797	0865	1
WORTHY WILLIAM W JR	LTC	O-0079539	1268	1
WORTMAN VOLNEY W	COL	O-0010218	0453	1
WOZNIAK STANLEY V SR	CW4	W-0907066	0165	1
WREAN JOY T	COL	O-0016871	0757	2
WRETLIND CLAYTON L	LTC	O-0060931	0168	1
WRIGHT ANDREW M	LTC	O-0018050	0546	1
WRIGHT BERTRAM S	LTC	O-0041137	0764	1
WRIGHT BRUCE E	CW4	W-0907067	0862	1
WRIGHT CHARLES E	LTC	O-0031564	0665	1
WRIGHT CHARLES R JR	COL	O-0031388	0765	1
WRIGHT CLARENCE J	CPT	O-0008748	1021	2
WRIGHT DAVID B	LTC	O-0054276	0565	1
WRIGHT EDGAR JR	COL	O-0017736	0659	1
WRIGHT EDWARD M	COL	O-0024693	0764	1
WRIGHT EDWIN K	M G	O-0015475	0955	1
WRIGHT ELWOOD M	COL	O-0031192	0668	1
WRIGHT ERNEST C	MAJ	O-0014554	0717	1
WRIGHT ERNEST C	LTC	O-0053926	0863	1
WRIGHT FREDERICK JR	COL	O-0021328	0868	1
WRIGHT JAY W	COL	O-0051916	1067	1
WRIGHT JOHN R	COL	O-0009537	1047	1
WRIGHT JOHN R JR	COL	O-0019817	0865	1
WRIGHT LESTER J	LTC	O-0037434	0362	2
WRIGHT LLOYD G	LTC	O-0065103	1267	1
WRIGHT LLOYD T	LTC	O-0092616	0767	1
WRIGHT LOWELL B	COL	O-0003918	0147	2
WRIGHT LUCIUS F JR	COL	O-0025966	0868	1
WRIGHT MARGARET M	MAJ	N-0002247	0561	2
WRIGHT ROBERT D	COL	O-0008396	0247	1
WRIGHT WILLARD L	LTC	O-0016114	0449	1
WRIGHT WILLIAM A	CW4	W-0904222	0962	1
WRIGHT WILLIAM H	LTG	O-0018129	1265	1
WRIGHT WILLIAM H	LTC	O-0059580	1065	1
WRIGHT WILLIAM M	LTC	O-0070574	0168	1
WRIGHT WILLIAM M JR	COL	O-0010433	0653	1
WRIGHTSON SAMUEL H	COL	O-0039879	0264	1
WRIGLEY JOHN H	LTC	O-0041161	1068	1
WROCKLOFF G E JR	COL	O-0015781	0954	1
WUERDINGER GERTRUDE	MAJ	N-0000385	0361	1
WUEST CHARLES H	LTC	O-0039280	0961	1
WUEST MELVIN L	CPT	O-0073939	0365	2
WUNDERLICH LEO E	CW4	W-0904059	0368	1
WUNSCH HAROLD J	MAJ	O-0092053	0468	2
WURFEL SEYMOUR W	COL	O-0029835	0860	1
WURM URBAN J	COL	O-0030971	1065	1
WURTZLER HERBERT W	COL	O-0039596	0159	1
WYAND PRESTON W	COL	O-0044363	0766	1
WYATT OTHEL	COL	O-0080027	0166	1
WYATT THOMAS C	LTC	O-0066128	0767	1
WYATT WILLIAM L	LTC	O-0032310	0764	1
WYATT WILLIAM O	COL	O-0040020	0466	1
WYCHE IRA T	M G	O-0003112	0948	2
WYCKOFF THEODORE	LTC	O-0063312	1068	2

NAME	GRADE	SVC NO	DATE RET MO YR	RET CODE
WYCOFF FRANCIS L	MAJ	O-0056391	0860	1
WYGANT ROBERT M	LTC	O-0031926	0262	1
WYMAN CHARLES L	LTC	O-0013997	0720	2
WYMAN PHILIP A	COL	O-0024854	0867	1
WYMAN THEODORE JR	COL	O-0007925	0-45	2
WYMAN WILLARD G	GEN	O-0012356	0758	1
WYMER HAROLD W	MAJ	O-0065587	1162	1
WYNNE ALBERT K	LTC	O-0081357	0567	1
WYNNE ANDREW J	COL	O-0007074	0947	1
WYNNE CONSUELO R	2LT	M-0000571	0345	1
WYNNE GEORGE C	COL	O-0011874	0653	1
WYRUCHOWSKI EDWARD P	LTC	O-0065241	1067	1
WYSS ARNOLD V	COL	O-0029788	1062	1
YAGER ROBERT H	COL	O-0022761	0565	2
YAKIMOVICZ FLORYAN L	LTC	O-0095392	1068	1
YAKSHE JOHN R	COL	O-0031820	0366	1
YALE V PAUL	MAJ	O-0022177	0147	2
YALE WESLEY W	COL	O-0014969	0854	1
YANCEY MARTHA J	MAJ	N-0002149	1161	1
YANCEY THOMAS R	M G	O-0042256	0867	1
YANKA DONALD E	COL	O-0030252	0164	1
YANTIS MYRON C	LTC	O-0038014	0766	1
YARBROUGH JAMES E	COL	O-0017348	0755	2
YARBROUGH SAMUEL K	COL	O-0019460	0764	1
YARRINGTON WILLIAM R	COL	O-0080028	0866	1
YASSEL LOUIS S	CW2	W-0901051	0642	1
YATES EAMES L	LTC	O-0050350	1163	1
YATES EDISON E	LTC	O-0039047	1167	1
YATES JULES D	LTC	O-0023127	0761	1
YATES VIRGIL T	COL	O-0052069	0866	1
YATSEVITCH GRATIAN M	COL	O-0031442	0267	1
YEAGER HAROLD R	LTC	O-0029567	0856	2
YEAGER MANFORD E	CW4	W-0907070	1262	1
YEAGER WALTER B	M G	O-0029464	0662	1
YEATON IVAN D	COL	O-0011648	0151	1
YEIK IRENE L	MAJ	N-0002383	0761	1
YEO STEWART	COL	O-0016664	0656	1
YERGER MARGUERITE	MAJ	N-0000555	1058	1
YERKS AUSTIN J JR	LTC	O-0027787	1165	1
YESSLER PAUL G	COL	O-0057027	0966	1
YEUELL DONOVAN P JR	COL	O-0023083	0660	2
YLIKOPSA GEORGE A	CW4	W-0904061	0265	2
YLINEN LYDIA R	MAJ	R-0010007	0554	1
YODER LEVERETT G	COL	O-0012048	0854	1
YODER QUENTIN F	LTC	O-0048494	1163	1
YODZIO STANLEY I	CW2	W-0901507	0543	2
YORK E T JR	1LT	O-0027018	1145	2
YORK ELTA R	MAJ	N-0001766	0668	2
YORK JERALDINE	LTC	N-0001929	1167	1
YORK JEROME B	COL	O-0025327	0764	1
YORK ROBERT E	COL	O-0012083	0753	1
YORK ROBERT H	LTG	O-0021341	0868	1
YORK WILLIAM F	CW3	W-0904062	1060	1
YORKE HAROLD W	CW3	W-0904063	0961	1
YOST CARL R	COL	O-0031542	0966	1
YOST HARVEY J	COL	O-0042277	0162	2
YOST JOSEPH B	COL	O-0020201	0866	1
YOST LOWELL A	COL	O-0039559	1057	1
YOUNG ADLAI C	COL	O-0004966	0851	1
YOUNG CHARLES G	COL	O-0020739	0967	1
YOUNG CHARLES T	COL	O-0017335	0657	1
YOUNG CLAUDE C	LTC	O-0031935	0163	1
YOUNG CLAUDE E	MAJ	O-0058792	0164	1
YOUNG CLYDE G	COL	O-0028790	0155	1
YOUNG DAVID F	LTC	O-0063091	0767	1
YOUNG DONALD A	COL	O-0006899	0847	1
YOUNG EDWARD H	COL	O-0012348	0854	2
YOUNG EDWARD P	COL	O-0028839	0256	1
YOUNG EDWARD R	1LT	O-0071899	0856	2
YOUNG ELLSWORTH	COL	O-0007483	0749	2
YOUNG ELMER W	B G	O-0016298	0859	1
YOUNG FREDERICK	COL	O-0001014	0934	1
YOUNG FREDERICK	COL	O-0018667	0653	2
YOUNG FREDERICK	LTC	O-0079157	0467	1
YOUNG GEORGE E	COL	O-0015659	0754	2

NAME	GRADE	SVC NO	DATE RET MO YR	RET CODE
YOUNG HAMILTON R	COL	O-0056786	1159	1
YOUNG JAMES	1LT	O-0064774	0554	2
YOUNG JOHN B	CW2	W-0904223	0263	1
YOUNG JOHN J	COL	O-0051172	0859	1
YOUNG MASON J	B G	O-0003788	0753	2
YOUNG MIRIAM E	LTC	N-0002081	0468	1
YOUNG NELLIE M	LTC	L-0000325	1167	1
YOUNG NORMAN B	CW4	W-0904067	1262	1
YOUNG RALPH M JR	CW3	RW-0904068	0462	1
YOUNG RANDALL M	CW4	W-0904069	0863	1
YOUNG RAYMOND F	LTC	O-0060484	0466	1
YOUNG RICHARD A JR	COL	O-0044524	0765	1
YOUNG ROBERT L	CW4	W-0904070	1065	1
YOUNG ROBERT M	LTC	O-0031891	0261	1
YOUNG ROSS	COL	O-0039001	0167	1
YOUNG SIDNEY H	MAJ	O-0005320	1036	1
YOUNG STANLEY A	COL	O-0051479	0364	1
YOUNG STEPHEN D	COL	O-0023430	0868	2
YOUNG THOMAS H	COL	O-0011479	0753	1
YOUNG WILBUR P	COL	O-0084581	0367	1
YOUNG WILLARD W	COL	O-0058739	1168	1
YOUNG WILLIAM C	COL	O-0003537	0449	1
YOUNG WILLIAM H	LTC	O-0042753	0562	1
YOUNG WILLIAM V	MAJ	O-0060604	0165	1
YOUNGBLOOD LEWIS H	LTC	O-0059967	1267	1
YOUNGBLOOD NORMAN E	B G	O-0028996	1162	1
YOUNGBLOOD ROBERT C	LTC	O-0029423	0758	1
YOUNGER MARY M	LTC	N-0000288	0263	1
YOUNT PAUL F	M G	O-0018022	0158	1
YOUNTS JAMES O JR	COL	O-0029552	0461	1
YOURTEE LEON R JR	COL	O-0044329	0968	1
YOW JOHN W	COL	O-0032361	1064	1
YUILL CHARLES W	COL	O-0005269	0447	2
YUILL HARRY F	LTC	O-0043571	0966	1
YULE RICHARD G	COL	O-0018948	0561	1
YUNCK RICHARD T	MAJ	O-0081359	0464	1
YUNKER SYLVESTER	CPT	O-0071900	0162	2
ZACHAR MARTIN JR	LTC	O-0037388	1068	1
ZACHERLE ALARICH L	COL	O-0042817	0266	1
ZACHERLE GEORGE H JR	COL	O-0030868	0661	1
ZAHRODSKY RALPH E	COL	O-0023149	0766	1
ZAIS ANNE B	LTC	N-0000227	0858	1
ZAJICEK JOHN F	COL	O-0007866	0747	2
ZAK JOSEPH T	LTC	O-0011152	0838	2
ZALESNEY NELLIE J	MAJ	N-0001536	0264	1
ZALKAN GEORGE	COL	O-0021000	1166	2
ZANCA PETER	COL	O-0051167	0763	1
ZAREMBO EDWARD B	LTC	O-0024094	1060	2
ZARESKY ALEXANDER	LTC	O-0044353	0865	1
ZARTNER BERT	MAJ	O-0067889	0266	1
ZAUMEYER LAWRENCE M	COL	O-0032906	1065	1
ZAUTNER GEORGE H	LTC	O-0005337	0542	1
ZEBROWITZ MORRIS	COL	O-0080529	0767	2
ZECCA MARIO J	COL	O-0032396	1064	1
ZEEFF DOROTHY M	MAJ	L-0000011	1053	1
ZEHNER ELERY M	COL	O-0020820	1167	2
ZEIDNER SAMUEL I	COL	O-0006104	0349	2
ZEIGLER ROBERT P	COL	O-0034726	0767	1
ZEITZ GOROCK F	CPT	O-0060352	0764	1
ZELENIK JOHN S	COL	O-0043124	0666	1
ZELL QUENTIN L	COL	O-0081361	0966	1
ZELLEFROW ALBERT E	LTC	O-0040982	0967	1
ZELLER FRANK J	COL	O-0019043	0863	1
ZELLER GEORGE A	MAJ	O-0015975	1044	1
ZELLER HENRY M	COL	O-0016843	0757	2
ZELLER JAMES R	MAJ	O-0027567	0460	2
ZEOLI RICHARD F	COL	O-0032345	0861	1
ZEPF GEORGE E	WO1	W-0901053	0941	1
ZERBEE AUGUSTINE	COL	O-0004935	0344	2
ZERZAN CHARLES J JR	LTC	O-0068065	0868	1
ZIDAP JAMES J	LTC	O-0085112	0868	1
ZIEGLER ARTHUR N	COL	O-0011886	0547	1
ZIEGLER CARL L	COL	O-0030707	0960	1
ZIEGLER ELDON F	LTC	O-0018873	1044	2
ZIELINSKI ALOYSIUS C	MAJ	O-0043162	0262	1

NAME	GRADE	SVC NO	DATE RET MO YR	RET CODE
ZIEKATH FREDERICK	M G	O-0019211	1167	1
ZIERDT JOHN G	M G	O-0020632	0767	1
ZIERINGER MATHEW P	MAJ	OF-0103790	0968	1
ZIESENHEIM JOSEPH C	LTC	O-0066130	1264	1
ZIGMUND FRANK J	MAJ	O-0059075	0862	1
ZILER WILLIAM D	COL	O-0035412	0966	1
ZILLNER DAVID	LTC	O-0026722	1064	1
ZIMMER LAYTON A	COL	O-0016688	0856	1
ZIMMERMAN ARNOLD W	CPT	O-0010101	0824	2
ZIMMERMAN GEORGE J	COL	O-0016600	0854	1
ZIMMERMAN JOHN S	COL	O-0038946	0561	1
ZIMMERMAN ROBERT H	LTC	O-0024481	0361	1
ZIMMERMAN ROBERT W	CW4	W-0904074	0168	1
ZIMMERMAN WAYNE C	M G	O-0012436	0156	1
ZIMMERMANN EDWARD A	COL	O-0029230	1266	1
ZINGALES JOSEPH A	LTC	O-0058750	0963	1
ZINNECKER GUS S	LTC	O-0042357	0562	1
ZINSER ROY F	COL	O-0030370	1064	1
ZIPF KARL A	COL	O-0039044	1166	1
ZISLIS LOUIS	LTC	O-0068066	0667	2
ZITZER FREDERICK	LTC	O-0021444	0360	1
ZITZMAN KENNETH F	B G	O-0018694	0859	1
ZIZON ANNE M	MAJ	N-0001221	0559	2
ZLOTKOWSKI EDWARD W	CW4	W-0904075	1068	1
ZOBRIST PAUL S	LTC	O-0059076	0368	1
ZOLENAS ANTHONY J JR	COL	O-0031127	0961	1
ZOLLICOFFER MARION B	LTC	O-0065184	0767	1
ZORNIG HERMANN H	COL	O-0002969	0846	2
ZUCCARDY CHARLES A	LTC	O-0064991	1066	1
ZUCKER LESTER J	LTC	O-0092056	0868	1
ZUCKERBROT IRVING	LTC	O-0036901	1064	1
ZUELZER WILHELM A	COL	O-0060730	0966	1
ZUERNER LURLINE V	MAJ	N-0001673	1067	2
ZUFELT DICK	LTC	O-0081363	0667	1
ZUMWALT CHARLES B	LTC	O-0058679	0768	1
ZUND EMIL A	LTC	O-0029168	1057	1
ZUNDEL EDWIN A	B G	O-0003792	0153	2
ZUNKER CLARA M	CPT	L-0000197	1262	1
ZUREK CHARLES M	LTC	O-0081364	1068	1
ZURTH FREDERICK	CPT	O-0065290	1060	1
ZWACK JOHN A	LTC	O-0031066	0767	1
ZWICKER RALPH W	M G	O-0016878	0560	2

SECTION 2

ARMY OF THE UNITED STATES RETIRED LIST

The Army of the United States Retired List is composed of officers other than Regular Army officers who are members and former members of the Reserve Components (Army Reserve and National Guard of the United States) and personnel who served in the Army of the United States without component, who are granted retired pay under any provision of law and retired warrant officers and enlisted personnel of the Regular Army who by reason of service in temporary commissioned grade are entitled to receive retired pay of the commissioned grade.

ARMY OF THE UNITED STATES RETIRED LIST

NAME	GRADE	SVC NO	DATE RET MO YR	RET CODE
AABERG ROBERT R	CW2	W-2103829	0945	2
AAKKEN ALVIN T	MAJ	0-0265658	1055	3
AAKKULA ANTERO	COL	0-0985345	1068	1
AAMODT ROBERT N	LTC	0-1895467	0865	1
AAMODT JOHN F JR	CPT	0-0363887	0245	2
AANONSEN HERBERT E	CPT	0-2032968	0559	1
AARNI JOHN C	LTC	0-0363335	0565	3
AARNI WILLIAM H	CPT	0-0405314	0246	2
AARON GEORGE V	CW3	W-2146987	1059	1
AARON GERALD F JR	1LT	0-2208634	1051	2
AARON JOSEPH E	1LT	0-2061587	1147	2
AARON LAWRENCE T	CW3	W-2153379	1263	1
AARON MAX C	CPT	0-2289640	0462	1
AARON NORMA B	CPT	N-0725000	1146	2
AARON STANLEY	WO1	W-2148909	0958	1
AAS ERNEST I	CPT	0-1012486	1045	2
AASEN EDWIN K	LTC	0-0351130	0962	1
AASEN MINA A	CPT	N-0700460	1046	1
AASTROM HERMAN	LTC	0-0445820	0647	1
ABANTO RIZALITO	LTC	0-1301590	0363	1
ABARE RICHARD D	CW3	RW-2206334	1068	1
ABAYA AMADEO	1LT	0-1896655	1149	1
ABBAMONTE LOUIS W	COL	0-0294494	C768	3
ABBATE ALFONSO	CPT	0-0359185	0268	3
ABBE JOHN A	LTC	0-1994376	0767	1
ABBETT JAMES W	MAJ	0-1172353	0261	1
ABBEY HARLAN I	COL	0-0221316	0962	3
ABBEY HOWARD O	CPT	0-0959067	0965	1
ABBEY JOSEPH A	MAJ	0-0333053	0146	2
ABBEY RUSSELL C	2LT	0-2035063	0345	2
ABBOTT ABBOTT O	LTC	0-1309153	0767	2
ABBOTT ALBERT W	LTC	0-0373312	1059	1
ABBOTT ALFRED A	LTC	0-1578086	0258	1
ABBOTT CARROLL S	CW3	W-2147734	0263	1
ABBOTT CHARLES G	CPT	0-1703344	0945	2
ABBOTT CLYDE B	CPT	0-1700729	1145	2
ABBOTT ELMER W	MAJ	0-0107529	1055	3
ABBOTT FLOYD A	LTC	0-0298781	0667	3
ABBOTT GEORGE E	MAJ	0-1326688	0365	1
ABBOTT HAROLD S	LTC	0-0395025	0162	1
ABBOTT HARRY P	COL	0-0219676	0265	3
ABBOTT JAMES P	COL	0-0257156	1053	2
ABBOTT JOHN B	MAJ	0-0509010	0747	2
ABBOTT JOHN C	COL	0-0186525	0753	3
ABBOTT JOHN P	1LT	0-1321983	1045	2
ABBOTT JULIA J	MAJ	N-0755199	1262	1
ABBOTT LARRY L	2LT	0-5504112	0358	2
ABBOTT LEE K	MAJ	0-1552219	0962	2
ABBOTT LOWELL W	MAJ	0-1300574	1053	2
ABBOTT MELVIN E JR	MAJ	0-1016610	0459	1
ABBOTT MICHAEL E	MAJ	0-2009381	0268	3
ABBOTT PAUL J	MAJ	0-0269089	0665	3
ABBOTT ROBERT E	CPT	0-0235860	0154	3
ABBOTT ROBERT W	1LT	0-0470541	0643	2
ABBOTT ROZELLAH	LTC	0-1105954	0268	1
ABBOTT TEMPLE W	LTC	0-0497365	0866	3
ABBOTT WALTER R	1LT	0-0406825	0345	2
ABBY ROBERT	CW2	W-2210821	0165	1
ABEE JOHN E	CPT	0-1919299	1062	1
ABEL AUGUST F	LTC	0-1182757	1262	1
ABEL CARL L	CW4	W-2144739	1268	1
ABEL DAREL M	CW3	W-2149497	0863	1
ABEL GOLDIE M	LTC	N-0724560	0761	1
ABEL HENRI E	MAJ	0-0501377	0240	2
ABEL JAMES W JR	MAJ	0-1649423	0860	1
ABEL JOHN E	CPT	0-0497118	0747	1
ABEL ORAL J	MAJ	0-1294042	1160	1
ABEL RALPH S	LTC	0-0373398	0468	3
ABEL RAYMOND L	COL	0-0100837	0556	3
ABEL ROY K	CPT	0-1648982	1059	1
ABEL SIDNEY W JR	CW3	W-2150779	0963	1
ABEL STEWART W	COL	0-0290592	0562	1
ABEL THOMAS	CPT	0-0498318	0746	1
ABEL WALTER W	LTC	0-0281774	0462	1
ABEL WILLARD E	LTC	0-0320653	0966	3

NAME	GRADE	SVC NO	DATE RET MO YR	RET CODE
ABELAIRAS ANDRES	MAJ	0-0487016	0640	1
ABELING LAWRENCE J	1LT	0-1322507	1145	2
ABELL CHARLES H	CW4	W-2109138	0967	3
ABELL FRANCIS V	MAJ	0-0503042	0557	1
ABELL HERBERT E	CPT	0-0416103	0142	2
ABELL MAURICE F	CW3	W-2143199	0567	1
ABELL WILFORD	1LT	0-1639924	0663	1
ABELLAR CELESTINO	1LT	0-1896515	0563	1
ABELON SAMSON Z	COL	0-0187897	0954	1
ABENDROTH WILLIAM H	M G	0-0245799	1055	3
ABER JESS	2LT	0-1306525	0744	2
ABER WILLIAM A	CW2	W-2173059	0747	1
ABERBACH JULIAN J	2LT	0-1316880	0344	2
ABERCROMBIE GEORGE O	CW2	W-3350266	0568	1
ABERCROMBIE LOIS	2LT	N-0744691	0145	1
ABERCROMBIE WILLARD	LTC	0-0483786	1063	1
ABERLE ALFRED L	MAJ	0-0505909	0154	1
ABERNATHY ROBERT R	MAJ	0-1640971	0966	3
ABERNATHY WILLIAM C	LTC	0-0282387	0968	3
ABERNETHY HENRY G	CPT	0-1101582	0646	2
ABERNETHY RAYMOND T	LTC	0-0329571	1166	3
ABERNETHY RICHARD	CPT	0-0438601	0453	1
ABERNETHY THOMAS J	COL	0-0100339	0955	3
ABERS BERNARD O	CPT	0-0375077	0146	2
ABERT ALBERT L	CW3	W-2206959	1265	1
ABEYTA MICHAEL G	CPT	0-0478682	1153	1
ABFALTER RUDOLPH L	MAJ	0-1043272	0868	3
ABLAN MEL	CPT	0-1896662	1064	2
ABLANEDO ARMAND L	MAJ	0-1295482	0863	1
ABLE SOTHORON K	CPT	0-0460060	0446	2
ABLER JULIUS	CPT	0-1040861	0744	2
ABNER ROBERT	CPT	0-0335226	0951	3
ABNEY JOHN D	MAJ	0-0193055	0546	2
ABNEY JOHN J	MAJ	0-0991251	0863	1
ABNEY THOMAS B	CPT	0-0476627	0750	2
ABORJAILY ASSAD N	LTC	0-1081501	0467	1
ABPLANALP ARTHUR H	LTC	0-0431104	0962	3
ABRAHAM MICHAEL K	LTC	0-1010362	0361	1
ABRAHAM WILLIAM R	MAJ	0-2014642	0767	1
ABRAHAMS FRANK A	LTC	0-0496711	0557	1
ABRAHAMS JOHN T	CW2	W-2151845	0459	1
ABRAHAMS ROLLAND S	COL	0-0221860	0950	2
ABRAHAMSON E J	2LT	N-0743392	1144	1
ABRAHAMSON GEORGE W	LTC	0-0393801	0966	1
ABRAHAMSON IRA A	COL	0-0140773	0346	2
ABRAHAMSON RAYMOND E	COL	0-0313155	1159	2
ABRAHAMSON WILLIAM R	MAJ	0-0160698	0151	3
ABRAMS BARNIE J	LTC	0-1579336	0655	2
ABRAMS EDWARD W	MAJ	0-0302238	0146	2
ABRAMS HARRY	LTC	0-0206487	0260	3
ABRAMS JOHN M	LTC	0-0270730	0155	1
ABRAMS LEONARD P	MAJ	0-0809074	0464	1
ABRAMS MAURICE	MAJ	0-1179754	0765	1
ABRAMS MAURICE J	LTC	0-0242900	1145	2
ABRAMS MELVIN L	COL	0-1684398	0268	1
ABRAMS WILLIAM C	CPT	0-0912789	0345	2
ABRAMS WILLIAM W	LTC	0-0301658	0167	3
ABRAMSON ARTHUR S	CPT	0-0492867	1046	2
ABRAMSON EMANUEL	LTC	0-0529993	0565	3
ABRAMSON JUNIUS S	1LT	0-1547219	0346	2
ABREMSKI WILLIAM J	2LT	0-0552098	0246	2
ABRON JAMES A JR	MAJ	0-1292454	0661	2
ABSHIER ROBERT E	CPT	0-1173844	0848	1
ABSHIRE ROY W	CPT	0-0541497	0946	2
ABUYEN ERNESTO	2LT	0-1896390	0748	1
ABY CHARLES W	COL	0-0260606	0965	3
ACCARDI ROY R	1LT	0-1016633	0346	2
ACCARDI VINCENT	CPT	0-0496393	1045	2
ACCIARDI ALBERT F	LTC	0-1636949	0663	2
ACCORTI PETER J	LTC	0-0084448	0468	1
ACE DREXEL M	MAJ	0-1309172	0361	1
ACEVEDO MANUEL JR	CPT	0-2263388	1162	1
ACEVEDO PLACIDO JR	CPT	0-0330882	0545	2
ACEVEDO RAMON	CW4	W-2101029	1254	1
ACHARD FRANCIS H	LTC	0-0188269	0652	3

NAME	GRADE	SVC NO	DATE RET MO YR	RET CODE
ACHAJER REED D	COL	0-0202126	0262	3
ACHENBACH JAY D	1LT	0-0244353	0664	3
ACHESON GEORGE J	LTC	0-1170616	1060	1
ACHESON ROBERT B	MAJ	0-0303279	0445	2
ACHEY KENNETH P	MAJ	0-1877154	1063	1
ACHOR JOHN R	COL	0-0407000	1164	3
ACHTERMANN ARIEL H	LTC	0-0360421	0259	1
ACKEMANN WILLIAM H	COL	0-0117655	1151	3
ACKENBOM HUGO G	CPT	0-2027492	0556	1
ACKER ALBERT L	MAJ	0-0187906	0551	3
ACKER GRANT E	CW2	W-3100496	1163	1
ACKER RALLS C JR	LTC	0-2210175	1267	1
ACKER RAYMOND	1LT	0-1032068	0746	2
ACKERLY ROBERT S	COL	0-0229682	0446	2
ACKERMAN BARTLEY E	MAJ	0-0963386	1262	1
ACKERMAN CARL J	CPT	0-0295161	0858	3
ACKERMAN DAVID M	COL	0-0271752	1264	1
ACKERMAN DON F	LTC	0-1581033	0763	1
ACKERMAN DONALD D	LTC	0-0370038	0766	3
ACKERMAN EDWARD A	LTC	0-0259147	0865	3
ACKERMAN EVERETT F	COL	0-0451623	0561	1
ACKERMAN EVERETT M	MAJ	0-1554485	0566	1
ACKERMAN FRANK L JR	LTC	0-0913170	1067	3
ACKERMAN GILBERT E	COL	0-0261635	0254	3
ACKERMAN GLENN A	CPT	0-0988044	0563	1
ACKERMAN HENRY P JR	LTC	0-1324714	0763	1
ACKERMAN HERMAN A	LTC	0-0210172	0648	3
ACKERMAN JASPER D	LTC	0-0212192	1156	3
ACKERMAN MELVIN J	LTC	0-2044373	0661	2
ACKERMAN MILTON N	CPT	0-1114899	1047	2
ACKERMAN RICHARD D	MAJ	0-0994282	0663	1
ACKERMAN RICHARD G	CW3	W-2206493	0969	1
ACKERMAN SIDNEY	CPT	0-1547666	1046	2
ACKERMAN WARREN P	WO1	W-2101355	0944	2
ACKERMANN DAVID F	LTC	0-0188792	0646	2
ACKERS LOUIE F	1LT	0-1825871	0749	2
ACKERSON CLIFTON W	LTC	0-0128091	1056	3
ACKERT WILBUR A	LTC	0-1579567	0463	1
ACKLEY AVERON C	CW2	W-2152871	0458	1
ACKLEY JAMES B	CPT	0-0166329	0249	3
ACKLEY JOHN M	MAJ	0-2036038	1060	1
ACKLEY PHILIP J	1LT	0-0390861	0844	2
ACLIN LOUIS	MAJ	0-1633043	0861	1
ACOMB ALLEN D	1LT	0-0392377	0944	2
ACOSTA ANTONIO J	CW3	W-2150923	0263	1
ACOSTA EMILIO V	CPT	0-0266952	0455	3
ACOSTA PEDRO F	1LT	0-0204286	0654	3
ACOSTA RAFAEL	COL	0-0230294	0566	3
ACOSTA-SANTINI FERNA	LTC	0-1951400	1166	1
ACREE CLARENCE R	MAJ	0-0478886	0754	1
ACREE FRANK M	MAJ	0-0480858	1045	2
ACRIVOS HAROLD N	MAJ	0-2007674	0561	2
ACTON CARL B	LTC	0-0123406	0756	3
ACTON CONRAD B	COL	0-0261181	1062	3
ACUFF CARL L	LTC	0-0272927	1266	3
ACUFF MILTON L	COL	0-0278379	1060	1
ACUFF RICHARD M	1LT	0-1327598	0447	2
ADAIR DANIEL L	MAJ	0-0482122	0651	1
ADAIR HORACE R	1LT	0-0250993	1161	3
ADAIR JAMES	CW4	W-2101310	0955	1
ADAIR JAMES T JR	LTC	0-0199739	0762	3
ADAIR JUNIUS M	MAJ	0-0365562	1159	1
ADAIR NORMAN	CPT	0-0489540	1043	2
ADAIR RUSSEL R	CW2	W-2147268	0957	1
ADAIR THOMAS F	MAJ	0-0452080	0457	1
ADAIR WILLIAM O	MAJ	0-0267247	1068	3
ADAM CHARLES W	LTC	0-2014696	0867	1
ADAM DOUGLAS G	LTC	0-0243182	1165	3
ADAM JAMES C	LTC	0-1995994	0968	1
ADAMAITIS WALTER J	MAJ	0-1650427	0961	1
ADAMCIK THOMAS J	CW3	W-2208322	0968	1
ADAMCZYK LEO J	MAJ	0-2016126	1162	1
ADAMIETZ STEVE F	MAJ	8-0974455	1161	1
ADAMO FRANK S	COL	0-0181315	0746	2
ADAMS ADAM J	CPT	0-0499562	0347	1

NAME	GRADE	SVC NO	DATE RET MO YR	RET CODE
ADAMS ALBERT H	LTC	0-0450215	0656	1
ADAMS ALFRED E	CPT	0-0384345	1045	2
ADAMS ALGERNON W	LTC	0-0264263	0151	3
ADAMS ALVIN S	COL	0-0266572	0760	1
ADAMS AMBROSE	LTC	0-1576866	0767	2
ADAMS ANDREW A	CPT	0-0476643	0456	1
ADAMS ANN A	1LT	N-0722861	0645	1
ADAMS ANTHONY B	LTC	0-0541058	0763	1
ADAMS ANTHONY O	COL	0-0126019	1048	1
ADAMS ARNEL B	COL	0-0222320	1061	3
ADAMS ARNOLD J	1LT	0-0543507	0448	2
ADAMS ARTHUR A	COL	0-0288809	0460	1
ADAMS ARTHUR A	MAJ	0-0505852	0157	1
ADAMS AUGUSTINE	1LT	0-0400780	0844	2
ADAMS B F	LTC	0-0325642	0661	1
ADAMS BERNARD H	LTC	0-1017768	1162	1
ADAMS BERT	COL	0-0456186	0266	1
ADAMS CARL C	MAJ	0-1589656	0863	1
ADAMS CARL W	1LT	0-1998626	1056	1
ADAMS CARROLL E	COL	0-0398218	0446	2
ADAMS CHARLES C	LTC	0-0170238	0851	3
ADAMS CHARLES L	COL	0-0218943	0262	3
ADAMS CHARLES L	MAJ	0-0322593	0768	3
ADAMS CHESLEY M	LTC	0-0154207	0453	3
ADAMS CLARENCE G	LTC	0-1581089	0662	1
ADAMS CLAUDE A	2LT	0-0251118	0845	1
ADAMS CLINTON L	COL	0-0281889	1068	3
ADAMS CLYDE B	LTC	0-0369182	0846	2
ADAMS CRAWFORD M	LTC	0-0252908	0665	3
ADAMS CURTIS H	COL	0-0413145	0863	1
ADAMS DALLAS C	1LT	0-1055402	1046	2
ADAMS DANIEL B	COL	0-0301363	0566	1
ADAMS DAVID J	CPT	0-2020701	0155	2
ADAMS DAVID L JR	1LT	0-2055790	1045	2
ADAMS DEAN E	MAJ	0-2208629	0668	1
ADAMS DONALD B	B G	0-0167951	0650	3
ADAMS DONALD C	LTC	0-0276107	0967	3
ADAMS DONALD K	MAJ	0-1633187	1058	1
ADAMS EARL F	MAJ	0-1996654	1159	1
ADAMS EARL P	COL	0-0301511	0766	3
ADAMS ED JR	MAJ	0-1044159	0457	2
ADAMS EDITH P	2LT	N-0743125	0946	1
ADAMS EDWARD	CW3	W-2147736	1262	1
ADAMS EDWARD E JR	LTC	0-0445457	0165	3
ADAMS EDWARD H	MAJ	0-0128789	0-52	3
ADAMS EDWARD JR	MAJ	0-1284163	0257	1
ADAMS EDWARD L	WO1	W-2140853	0550	1
ADAMS EDWARD V	LTC	0-0260956	1067	3
ADAMS EDWIN B	CPT	0-0300192	0156	3
ADAMS EDWIN G JR	1LT	0-0334046	0646	2
ADAMS ELDRED E	COL	0-0269666	0967	3
ADAMS ELIAS	MAJ	0-0240668	0965	3
ADAMS ELIZABETH	2LT	N-0764106	0845	1
ADAMS EPHRAIM	MAJ	0-0216968	0961	3
ADAMS EUGENE J	LTC	0-0304485	0148	2
ADAMS FLORENCE A	1LT	L-0402790	0945	2
ADAMS FRANCIS C	MAJ	0-0963889	0266	1
ADAMS FRANK	MAJ	0-0109643	0848	1
ADAMS FRANK C	2LT	0-1051052	0344	2
ADAMS FRANKLIN P	LTC	0-1825921	0165	1
ADAMS GEORGE A	CW2	W-2213795	0968	1
ADAMS GEORGE D	LTC	0-0451068	0457	1
ADAMS GEORGE J	LTC	0-0251380	0859	2
ADAMS GEORGE L	1LT	0-0519544	1145	2
ADAMS GEORGE M	MAJ	0-1116274	1160	1
ADAMS GEORGE R	CW3	W-2152777	0661	1
ADAMS GEORGE W	MAJ	0-0204377	0562	3
ADAMS GEORGE W	COL	0-0255288	0656	2
ADAMS HAROLD E	LTC	0-0173122	0960	3
ADAMS HAROLD P	MAJ	0-0959303	0765	1
ADAMS HARRY A	COL	0-0911403	0763	1
ADAMS HARRY G	CW4	W-2141720	0368	1
ADAMS HARTMAN R	CW3	W-2141886	0659	1
ADAMS HERKIMER E	LTC	0-0273006	0168	3
ADAMS HIBBERT J	CW2	W-2214031	0868	1

NAME	GRADE	SVC NO	DATE RET MO YR	RET CODE
ADAMS HOWARD G	LTC	0-0392673	0461	2
ADAMS HOYETI	CW2	W-2101267	0347	2
ADAMS HUGH M	WO1	W-2006771	0365	3
ADAMS ISAIAH K	2LT	0-1318505	0345	2
ADAMS JACK J	CW2	W-2151519	0561	1
ADAMS JACK R	LTC	0-0250542	0366	3
ADAMS JACK W	CPT	0-2031565	1056	1
ADAMS JAMES	LTC	0-0495260	0847	2
ADAMS JAMES C	CW3	W-2145048	0460	1
ADAMS JAMES H	1LT	0-0407158	0646	2
ADAMS JAMES H JR	MAJ	0-0363787	1044	2
ADAMS JAMES JR	LTC	0-0347806	0768	3
ADAMS JAMES M	LTC	0-1548611	0861	1
ADAMS JAMES O	CPT	0-0173209	0648	3
ADAMS JAMES S	CPT	0-1030209	0955	1
ADAMS JAMES W JR	1LT	0-1303996	1044	2
ADAMS JENNIE Y	2LT	N-0786958	1050	2
ADAMS JESSE H	MAJ	0-1297644	1061	1
ADAMS JESSE R	LTC	0-0239355	0465	3
ADAMS JIMMIE E	CPT	0-2012543	0453	2
ADAMS JOHN A	WO1	W-3156731	0968	2
ADAMS JOHN C	MAJ	0-0227308	0146	2
ADAMS JOHN J	MAJ	0-0329787	1045	2
ADAMS JOHN J	CPT	0-0959269	0160	1
ADAMS JOHN J	LTC	0-1576367	0868	3
ADAMS JOHN K	LTC	0-1546265	0764	1
ADAMS JOHN L	MAJ	0-0810183	0164	1
ADAMS JOHN P JR	LTC	0-0518857	0663	1
ADAMS JOHN Q	CPT	0-1331798	0947	2
ADAMS JOHN W	MAJ	0-1013995	0257	1
ADAMS JOHN W	CW2	W-2207006	0763	1
ADAMS JOSEPH C	CW3	W-2108477	1254	1
ADAMS JOY C	CPT	0-0173574	0758	3
ADAMS KIRK E	LTC	0-0363193	0859	1
ADAMS LANIER W	CW2	W-2145280	0460	1
ADAMS LEON L	CPT	0-0256671	1053	1
ADAMS LESLIE M	1LT	0-1017905	0845	2
ADAMS LESTER M	COL	0-0169771	0258	3
ADAMS LLOYD M	MAJ	0-1045995	0160	1
ADAMS LLOYD S	LTC	0-0152727	0553	3
ADAMS LOLA E	1LT	N-0777138	0448	1
ADAMS LONNIE B JR	LTC	0-1318265	0264	1
ADAMS MARION H	CW3	W-2147195	0962	1
ADAMS MARJORIE E	MAJ	L-1010064	0763	1
ADAMS MARY O	MAJ	N-0728238	0561	1
ADAMS MAX B	LTC	0-0240471	0363	3
ADAMS MELVIN V	CW3	W-2203649	0868	1
ADAMS MORRIS F	1LT	0-1310199	0946	2
ADAMS NORMAN H	COL	0-0280221	1055	1
ADAMS NORMAN I JR	LTC	0-0163807	0144	2
ADAMS OLIVER	CW2	W-2210140	0461	1
ADAMS ORVILLE P	CW3	W-2113359	0354	1
ADAMS OTIS O	LTC	0-1294102	1060	1
ADAMS PAUL R	LTC	0-1017431	0662	1
ADAMS PEARL S	CPT	N-0756334	0546	1
ADAMS ROBERT	CPT	0-0150254	0350	3
ADAMS ROBERT C	LTC	0-1171862	0766	1
ADAMS ROBERT C	MAJ	0-2055200	0960	1
ADAMS ROBERT F	CPT	0-1310381	0945	2
ADAMS ROBERT H	MAJ	0-1897725	0264	1
ADAMS ROBERT L	MAJ	0-1919341	0966	1
ADAMS ROBERT P	1LT	0-0452350	1044	2
ADAMS ROBERT W	LTC	0-0276019	0667	3
ADAMS ROGER R	1LT	0-2007262	0446	2
ADAMS ROY C	CW3	W-2149323	0365	1
ADAMS ROY H	LTC	0-0355254	0966	3
ADAMS ROY I JR	LTC	0-1058159	0961	1
ADAMS ROY J	MAJ	0-2050323	0361	1
ADAMS ROY W	CW3	W-2127887	0560	1
ADAMS ROYCE F	CPT	0-1289159	1151	2
ADAMS SAM H	LTC	0-0355721	1060	1
ADAMS SAM J JR	LTC	0-1292814	0761	1
ADAMS SAMUEL	1LT	0-1178265	1045	2
ADAMS SAMUEL C	1LT	0-1315517	0745	2
ADAMS SAMUEL H	2LT	0-2202784	0453	2
ADAMS SAMUEL P	LTC	0-0196498	0959	3
ADAMS SHIRLEY S	2LT	N-0736484	0342	1
ADAMS SIDNEY M	LTC	0-0310372	0666	3
ADAMS STANLEY F	LTC	0-1312449	0667	2
ADAMS STANLEY L	CPT	0-1055771	1165	2
ADAMS THOMAS F JR	CW2	W-2146649	1064	1
ADAMS THOMAS F	LTC	0-0270921	0668	3
ADAMS TYERUS F	CW4	W-2120711	1259	1
ADAMS VERNON J	MAJ	0-1825535	0763	1
ADAMS WALDO P	MAJ	0-2096982	1066	1
ADAMS WALLIS W	CW4	W-2118284	0855	1
ADAMS WALTER R JR	LTC	0-0465994	0647	2
ADAMS WARD A	MAJ	0-0242595	0152	3
ADAMS WARD W	MAJ	0-0248797	1166	3
ADAMS WELDON H	MAJ	0-0887521	0258	1
ADAMS WILBUR C	MAJ	0-0212903	0156	3
ADAMS WILEY J	COL	0-0123410	0555	3
ADAMS WILLIAM B	MAJ	0-0270491	1066	3
ADAMS WILLIAM B	MAJ	0-0370415	0550	2
ADAMS WILLIAM H	COL	0-0311363	0460	3
ADAMS WILLIAM H	COL	0-0365427	0765	1
ADAMS WILLIAM M	COL	0-0132952	0955	3
ADAMS WILLIAM O	MAJ	0-0324665	1160	1
ADAMS WILLIAM W	LTC	0-0223166	0265	3
ADAMSEN JAMES H	LTC	0-0733251	1167	1
ADAMSKI FRANK J	1LT	0-1049714	0846	2
ADAMSKI LADIMIR S	MAJ	0-0490235	0850	1
ADAMSKY JOHN	MAJ	0-0335769	0161	1
ADAMSON DOYLE E	LTC	0-0399155	0161	1
ADAMSON GEORGE D	MAJ	0-0188929	0253	3
ADAMSON GEORGE E	MAJ	0-0206646	0458	3
ADAMSON HAPPY R	CPT	0-1003436	1046	2
ADAMSON HOLTON R	LTC	0-0355030	0446	2
ADAMSON JASON	1LT	0-0108466	0540	1
ADAMSON MARVIN G	MAJ	0-0495956	1155	1
ADAMSON ORASTUS E	LTC	0-2042763	0866	1
ADAMSON OTTIS A	MAJ	0-1292409	1060	1
ADAMUCCI LOUIS A	MAJ	0-1935747	0568	1
ADATTO ALBERT	LTC	0-1641647	0862	1
ADCOCK CHARLES V	LTC	0-1542340	0361	1
ADCOCK ERNEST C	LTC	0-0444902	0653	1
ADCOCK LEE M	2LT	0-1320809	1144	2
ADCOCK MAURICE E	MAJ	0-1342063	0164	1
ADCOCK O T	CW3	W-2101357	0560	1
ADCOX GEORGE E	CPT	0-1044742	1161	2
ADCOX JOHN	CW4	W-2131440	1159	1
ADCOX WOODROW	CW2	W-2205380	0462	1
ADDEPLEY JOSEPH C JR	LTC	0-0372312	0464	1
ADDINGTON JOHN M	CW4	W-2114810	0564	1
ADDIS RUSSELL E	LTC	0-0340174	0256	1
ADDISON DONALD E	MAJ	0-0988944	1164	1
ADDISON ELVIN R	2LT	0-1326953	1145	2
ADDISON GEORGE F	LTC	0-0232422	0765	3
ADDISON JAMES F	LTC	0-0447553	0954	1
ADDISON JENNIE L	MAJ	N-0743120	0265	1
ADDISON JOHN W	CW3	W-2205743	0968	1
ADDISON WILLIAM P JR	MAJ	0-0330439	0546	2
ADDLEMAN THEODORE B	LTC	0-0277796	1063	3
ADDUCI FRANK P	CW3	W-2002549	0163	3
ADDY LESTER R	1LT	0-1299518	1045	2
ADDY ZIMRI M	1LT	0-0378920	0944	2
ADE GUY W	LTC	0-0118716	0951	3
ADE THEODORE	MAJ	0-1688620	0964	1
ADELSBERGER N R	CW2	W-2118870	1151	2
ADELSON IRVING J	MAJ	0-0535390	0868	3
ADEN IRVING J	COL	0-0279041	0959	2
ADEN WILLIAM D	MAJ	0-0945694	0865	1
ADER SAMUEL	LTC	0-0222118	0257	3
ADERHOLT CLARA E	1LT	N-0759414	1145	1
ADESKO LEON R	CW3	W-2119352	0662	1
ADEST JACOB H	MAJ	0-0496146	0346	2
ADEY EDWIN A	LTC	0-0227132	0563	3
ADIE JOHN	CW2	W-2205844	0762	1
ADIMARI FRANK J	LTC	0-1644434	0366	3
ADKINS CHARLIE H	CW3	W-2147595	0659	1
ADKINS CHARLIE R	MAJ	0-0488282	0254	1
ADKINS GLODEON	MAJ	0-1597975	0962	2
ADKINS CLYDE C	LTC	0-0327894	0164	1
ADKINS DAVID R	CPT	0-0520660	0849	1
ADKINS DONALD	CPT	0-0482385	1145	2
ADKINS EDWIN F	CW2	W-3151443	0868	1
ADKINS EUGENE S	MAJ	0-1634596	0666	1
ADKINS GEORGE Y JR	CW3	W-2212978	0168	1
ADKINS HARRY T	LTC	0-0202880	1044	2
ADKINS HUGH P	CPT	0-0469534	0345	2
ADKINS JACK O	MAJ	0-1685582	0962	1
ADKINS JAMES A	2LT	0-1013570	0245	2
ADKINS JAMES R	MAJ	0-0269387	0363	1
ADKINS JAMES E	1LT	0-0449389	0146	2
ADKINS JOSEPH E	CPT	0-0341135	0666	3
ADKINS LUTHER M	CPT	0-2023427	0556	1
ADKINS PAUL	CPT	0-1035110	1045	2
ADKINS RAYMOND	CW2	W-2143009	0455	1
ADKINS ROBERT P	CW2	W-3200284	0966	1
ADKINS VERNON	LTC	0-0271834	0268	3
ADKINS VIRGIL S	COL	0-0224734	0658	3
ADKINSON DALE W	CPT	0-0963988	0760	1
ADKINSON IVAN B	LTC	0-1284426	1163	1
ADKISON HOWARD T	LTC	0-0443524	0668	3
ADKISON NORMAN B	COL	0-0245612	0356	3
ADKISON RICHARD E	1LT	0-1293412	0945	2
ADKISSON ALFRED J	MAJ	0-0332316	0345	2
ADKISSON GLENN W	MAJ	0-1011809	1062	1
ADLAND ABE	LTC	0-0322348	0668	3
ADLER BENARD C	MAJ	0-0356490	0946	2
ADLER ERVIN A	CW3	W-2116183	0361	1
ADLER JOSEPH M	LTC	0-0265839	0668	3
ADLER JUSTIN H	MAJ	0-0493505	0646	2
ADLER LEO S	CPT	0-0483209	0146	2
ADLER WALTER	LTC	0-0215181	1156	3
ADLOW ELIJAH	COL	0-0259641	0856	3
ADMIRE ELMER F	LTC	0-1545471	0662	1
ADOLPHSON JOHN F	CPT	0-0258160	0867	3
ADRIAN GEORGE G	LTC	0-1323654	0863	1
ADRIAN JOSEPH M	MAJ	0-0970651	1165	1
ADRIAN ROBERT L	CW3	W-2152442	0467	1
ADUDDLE WILLIAM A	LTC	0-1640274	1168	1
AEBISCHER RAY P	LTC	0-1342075	0264	1
AENCHBACHER H L	CW2	W-2145929	1260	1
AERNE WALTER JR	LTC	0-1012955	0364	1
AERY LOUIS W JR	CPT	0-0786874	1164	1
AESCHLIMAN LEWIS D	MAJ	0-2263371	1162	1
AFF CHARLES E	LTC	0-1334944	0866	1
AGANSKI RUDOLPH	LTC	0-0573894	0668	1
AGAR PIUS R	1LT	0-1896432	0559	1
AGARDY LOUIS	MAJ	0-1032649	0862	2
AGATI JOHN T	CPT	0-0473344	0245	2
AGEE GLADYS L	MAJ	L-0917538	0464	1
AGEE JOE H	LTC	0-0546547	0764	2
AGEE THOMAS H	CPT	0-0568165	0760	2
AGER ARTHUR F	LTC	0-0112432	1054	3
AGER CHARLES L JR	LTC	0-0231837	1060	3
AGERS WILLIAM A	LTC	0-0331380	1167	3
AGIN PAUL L	MAJ	0-2033898	1065	1
AGNE HERBERT G	1LT	0-0517174	1146	1
AGNER JAMES E	1LT	0-1322299	0546	2
AGNEW CORNELIUS	MAJ	0-0241683	0266	3
AGNEW EDGAR T	1LT	0-0411797	0146	2
AGNEW JACK	LTC	0-1173140	0859	1
AGNEW THOMAS G	CPT	0-0382827	1144	2
AGNITSCH JOHN A	MAJ	0-1315996	0264	1
AGNOR GILMORE L	LTC	0-0174847	0359	3
AGOSTI VIRGIL R	2LT	0-1882108	1153	2
AGOSTINI GERMAN	COL	0-0191589	0862	3
AGPAOA PACIFICO O	MAJ	0-1321652	0862	2
AGPOON TOMAS P	1LT	0-0890321	0750	1
AGRELIUS ROBERT J	LTC	0-1573918	0964	1
AGRICOLA THEODORE	CPT	0-0492902	0852	1
AGSTER WILLIAM C	COL	0-0234563	0355	3
AGUAS PRUDENCIO	CPT	0-1896897	0464	1
AGUO ALFREDO	MAJ	0-1932276	0267	1
AGUERO CHARLES P	LTC	0-1184007	1264	1
AGUILAR CARLOS F	CW3	W-2151142	0762	1
AGUILAR PETER B	CW3	W-2147434	1262	1
AGUIRRE MARY E	CPT	N-2296361	1064	2
AGULE FRANK I	LTC	0-0232306	0149	1
AGUSTIN INOCENCIO	2LT	0-1896964	0762	1
AHANA KENNETH Y	MAJ	0-0955404	0862	2
AHEARN CLARENCE J	CPT	0-0128444	0753	3
AHEARN JOHN L	CPT	0-1011621	0746	2
AHERN ANDREW G JR	1LT	0-1311101	1046	2
AHERN CAROL A	1LT	N-0757721	0351	2
AHERN DANIEL K	COL	0-0249885	0367	3
AHERN JOHN F	MAJ	0-1877769	0765	1
AHERN JOHN F	COL	0-0262943	0261	1
AHERN JOHN P	COL	0-0308469	0668	3
AHERN ROBERT W	CPT	0-1293172	0446	2
AHERN WILLIAM A	CPT	0-1316518	0247	2
AHERN WILLIAM T	CPT	0-0382715	0844	2
AHL KENNETH L	COL	0-0399926	0668	3
AHLBERG ALVIN E	LTC	0-0195779	0360	3
AHLBERG JOHN K	MAJ	0-0267851	1168	3
AHLEMEYER EDWARD H	LTC	0-0345620	0262	1
AHLF ELMER G	LTC	0-0248187	0964	3
AHLSKOG IVER	MAJ	0-0169865	0958	3
AHLSTRAND FRANZ A	MAJ	0-0173642	0154	3
AHLSTROM NELS H	MAJ	0-1649427	0662	1
AHN IANTHA M	MAJ	N-0772082	0564	3
AHNMARK OSCAR P	LTC	0-0217587	1061	3
AHO EINO R	LTC	0-0873410	1267	1
AHOLA JOHN M	CW3	RW-2210756	1168	1
AHRENBECK THEO	COL	0-0266163	0164	3
AHRENS DONALD W	WO1	W-2120710	0845	2
AHRENS JOHN H	COL	0-0190496	0648	3
AHRENS WALTER E	CW2	W-2209788	0560	1
AHRENS WILLIAM	CPT	0-0495408	0944	2
AICHELE JOHN H	LTC	0-2008415	0564	1
AIDALA THOMAS F	CPT	0-0351158	0547	2
AIELLO JOSEPH T	CPT	0-1999766	0249	2
AIELLO RALPH P	MAJ	0-0397664	0256	1
AIELLO ROY G	1LT	0-1689087	1142	2
AIGNER ROBERT E	1LT	0-1323059	0846	2
AIKEN ALBERT C	LTC	0-0385914	0268	1
AIKEN HARRY W JR	MAJ	0-0303519	0768	3
AIKEN HARRY W JR	MAJ	0-4010866	1168	1
AIKEN JOHN M	1LT	0-1013235	0847	2
AIKEN RICHARD S	MAJ	0-1167717	0860	1
AIKIN SYDNEY E	MAJ	0-2037029	1163	2
AIKIN WILLIAM T	MAJ	0-1311591	1060	1
AIL IRVING I	CPT	0-0292110	0245	2
AILOR ROSCOE J	COL	0-2034835	0368	1
AILSTOCK CORNELIUS	CPT	0-0482421	0246	2
AIMONE AUGUST L	MAJ	0-1042218	0267	3
AINLAY GEORGE W SR	COL	0-0323820	1155	3
AINSWORTH H MILLER	M G	0-0104004	1154	3
AINSWORTH JACK L	CW2	W-2148376	0766	1
AINSWORTH JAMES J	LTC	0-0450082	0158	1
AIR CLEMENTS W	LTC	0-0236110	1165	3
AIRHART BOYD L	MAJ	0-0390985	0461	1
AIRIS THOMAS F	COL	0-0276628	0666	3
AIROLDI ANTHONY J	LTC	0-0354097	0246	2
AIROV SAMUEL	1LT	0-1170618	0345	2
AIRSMAN JOHN W	LTC	0-0535501	0763	1
AISENSTADT E ALBERT	COL	0-0140113	1049	3
AISHTON DONALD F	1LT	0-0452333	1044	2
AISO DANIEL I	CW3	W-2145281	1164	1
AISON EMIL L	LTC	0-0106851	0545	2
AITKEN CARROLL H	MAJ	0-0314140	0646	2
AITKEN HOWARD M	MAJ	0-0282082	0568	3
AITKEN JOHN E	2LT	0-0395252	0642	2
AITKEN MARY E	CPT	N-0736600	0847	1
AJALAT MITRY P	CPT	0-0420419	1044	2
AJEMIAN CHARLES	MAJ	0-0259840	0660	1
AKAMATSU PETER K	LTC	0-0420502	1066	1
AKE LOREN F	LTC	0-0346712	1146	2

NAME	GRADE	SVC NO	DATE RET MO YR	RET CODE
AKERS DEE F JR	CPT	0-0975442	0461	1
AKERS FRANK H	LTC	0-1317954	0960	1
AKERS FREDERICK	CPT	0-0468091	0747	1
AKERS GEORGE P	CW3	RW-2207510	0267	1
AKERS GEORGE W	LTC	0-0435624	0353	1
AKERS JAMES O	CW3	W-2146437	0962	1
AKERS KENNETH P	LTC	0-0355315	0357	1
AKERS LEONARD B	LTC	0-0450570	0858	1
AKERS MARVIN L	CPT	0-0513969	1047	2
AKERS WALTER J	LTC	0-2025502	1168	1
AKERSLOOT CHARLES	MAJ	0-4010444	0568	1
AKERSTROM OSCAR W	LTC	0-0395609	0560	1
AKEY ROBERT M	CPT	0-1767411	0850	2
AKIMOTO RALPH Y	CW3	W-2147897	0764	1
AKIMOTO THEODORE	1LT	0-1338039	1048	2
AKIN ALFRED K	COL	0-0321003	0461	1
AKIN AUBREY W	COL	0-0169690	0260	1
AKIN HENRY C P	COL	0-0142372	0648	3
AKIN KARL E	LTC	0-0059900	0168	1
AKIN KENNETH A	COL	0-0251991	0565	3
AKINS AUSTIN J	WO1	W-2119315	1046	1
AKINS CHARLES E	MAJ	0-1821527	1162	1
AKINS CLARENCE E	CW3	W-2143710	0464	1
AKINS COLUMBUS	CW3	W-2205132	0264	1
AKINS DONALD J	CPT	0-1636907	0860	1
AKINS J J	CW3	W-2124169	0661	1
AKINS KOSSIE C	LTC	0-1110985	0163	1
AKINS RACY L	LTC	0-0933325	0766	1
AKINS WALTER R	MAJ	0-0479186	1048	1
AKINS WILLIAM H	MAJ	0-1290524	1060	1
AKLEY CLARENCE V	1LT	0-0447461	0346	2
AKRIDGE CLYDE M	LTC	0-0452112	0159	1
AKRONAS ANTHONY	CW4	W-2101101	1154	1
AKSOMAITIS C J	LTC	0-1635252	0457	1
ALAIMO CARL V	LTC	0-1551997	0663	1
ALAIN THEODORE F	CW2	W-2151748	0861	1
ALAKULPPI OLAVI E	LTC	0-0985349	0168	1
ALAMEDA FRANK A	B G	0-0300304	1159	3
ALANIZ RAYMOND O	1LT	0-1312653	0267	1
ALARCON VERGILIO C	MAJ	0-0890535	0955	1
ALARIE JOHN R	MAJ	0-0401764	1047	2
ALATORRE FRANK C	MAJ	0-1338667	0563	1
ALAYON LEOPOLDO B	1LT	0-1896969	0958	1
ALBANO CAMILLO J	LTC	0-1546888	0667	3
ALBANO SALVATORE	CW2	W-2208085	0964	1
ALBAUGH KENNETH J JR	2LT	0-1323081	0844	2
ALBAUGH LYMAN P	1LT	0-1578095	0446	2
ALBEE DALE S	CPT	0-2006496	0460	1
ALBEE JAMES H	2LT	0-0298919	0262	3
ALBEE MERTON A	COL	0-0110154	0648	3
ALBEE STEPHEN JR	MAJ	0-0526858	0565	1
ALBEE THOMAS L	COL	0-0202634	0461	3
ALBER PHILLIP R	COL	0-0187778	0456	3
ALBERG GUSTAVE W	1LT	0-0395576	0145	2
ALBERI EDWIN H	MAJ	0-1283531	0147	2
ALBERS ALBERT H	CPT	0-1914334	0243	1
ALBERS CLARENCE F	COL	0-0140774	0257	3
ALBERS RAYMOND H	LTC	0-0289538	0758	1
ALBERSHARDT HARRY F	MAJ	0-0206429	0555	3
ALBERSON HUGH T	MAJ	0-1641203	0767	1
ALBERSTADT NORMAN N	CPT	0-1718485	0850	2
ALBERT ALLEN C	LTC	0-0245503	0562	3
ALBERT BENJAMIN B	COL	0-0174726	0254	1
ALBERT CARL B	COL	0-0281522	0668	3
ALBERT CARL H	CW4	W-2150146	0369	1
ALBERT FRED E	LTC	0-1330228	0268	1
ALBERT OWEN S J	COL	0-0214315	0564	3
ALBERTELLI QUINTO J	CW3	W-2150669	1258	1
ALBERTI ALBERTO	MAJ	0-0263594	0246	1
ALBERTINE CAMELL	MAJ	0-0471716	0448	1
ALBERTINI ALBERT F	1LT	0-1993815	1146	2
ALBERTINI CONNELL	LTC	0-0290222	0757	3
ALBERTIS PAUL H	MAJ	0-0225703	0664	3
ALBERTO MELECIO P	1LT	0-2032266	0150	1
ALBERTS WILLIAM	COL	0-0181384	0655	3
ALBERTSON FRANK P	CPT	0-0358744	0545	2
ALBERTY RALPH F	CW3	W-2211762	1268	1
ALBIG WILLIAM B	MAJ	0-1575663	0561	1
ALBIN LEON	COL	0-0398839	1059	1
ALBUSTA FRANK M	LTC	0-0384008	0765	3
ALBRECHT CARL W	LTC	0-0263965	0166	3
ALBRECHT CONRAD E	COL	0-0294342	0765	3
ALBRECHT DENVER D	MAJ	0-1308898	0866	1
ALBRECHT GERALD D	LTC	0-0400009	0145	2
ALBRECHT JOHN S	CPT	0-1288489	0444	2
ALBRECHT RALEIGH P	MAJ	0-1309488	0563	3
ALBRECHT WILLIAM H	LTC	0-1012176	0862	1
ALBRECHT WILLIAM JR	MAJ	0-0140089	0257	3
ALBREN EDWARD J	CPT	0-1171028	0547	2
ALBRICK EDGAR J	LTC	0-0450568	0364	1
ALBRIGHT BLANCHE C	MAJ	N-0728982	0766	1
ALBRIGHT DONALD E	1LT	0-1315258	0545	2
ALBRIGHT DONALD G	MAJ	0-2305750	0766	1
ALBRIGHT EVERETT W	2LT	0-2027062	0157	1
ALBRIGHT GEORGE O	WO1	W-2143828	0367	3
ALBRIGHT GEORGE R	MAJ	0-1585405	1058	1
ALBRIGHT LAWRENCE M	CW3	W-2105819	0860	1
ALBRIGHT MILES W	LTC	0-0476846	0857	3
ALBRIGHT OTIS K	LTC	0-0213693	0663	3
ALBRIGHT WILLIAM V	LTC	0-0285831	0764	3
ALBRITTON ARTHUR M	CW3	W-3150282	0168	1
ALBRITTON EMORY C	MAJ	0-0993286	0965	1
ALBRO LLOYD W	MAJ	0-0990354	0465	1
ALBRO RAYMOND L	MAJ	0-0988081	1266	1
ALBUCKER SAM	2LT	0-1314576	0545	2
ALCANTARA MICHAEL	1LT	0-1897013	0966	1
ALCINI ROY F	1LT	0-1179001	0945	2
ALCOCER RALPH R	CPT	0-2006441	0761	2
ALCOE EDGAR L	1LT	0-1316978	0845	2
ALCORN WILLIAM L	MAJ	0-0295312	0346	2
ALCOZE JOHNNIE W	CW3	W-2149746	1260	1
ALDEN BERNHARD W	LTC	0-0267202	0868	3
ALDEN WILBUR L	CW2	W-2150046	1161	1
ALDERDYCE JOHN C	LTC	0-0128267	1044	2
ALDERFER ISADORE C	CPT	0-0382662	1145	2
ALDERMAN GORDON L	LTC	0-0479536	0962	1
ALDERMAN MARTHE B	MAJ	N-0724332	0561	1
ALDERMAN NORMAN E	CPT	0-1706025	0448	2
ALDERMAN OSCAR D	MAJ	0-0979351	1163	1
ALDERMAN WALTER A	CPT	0-0968899	0662	1
ALDERMAN WILLIAM R	MAJ	0-1304845	1060	1
ALDERTON JAMES R	COL	0-0384081	0661	2
ALDINGER DANIEL T	LTC	0-1332122	1068	1
ALDRICH FREDERIC D	LTC	0-0245579	0446	2
ALDRICH FREDERICK	MAJ	0-2210324	0167	1
ALDRICH HARLEY J JR	MAJ	0-1181610	1165	2
ALDRICH HUGO C	LTC	0-0382585	1060	1
ALDRICH LEON J	MAJ	0-1922663	0364	1
ALDRICH LLOYD L	CPT	0-0318014	0852	2
ALDRICH MERLYN A	COL	0-0305649	1068	3
ALDRICH RALPH L	LTC	0-1036890	1163	1
ALDRICH STANLEY B	LTC	0-1100925	0658	1
ALDRICH THEODORE B	CPT	0-0924936	0645	2
ALDRICH WARREN H	COL	0-0118753	1051	2
ALDRIDGE CLYDE S	MAJ	N-0735831	0563	2
ALDRIDGE EARL W	MAJ	0-1306216	1059	1
ALDRIDGE ELIZABETH	2LT	N-0700163	0837	1
ALDRIDGE EUGENE V JR	MAJ	0-4043516	0668	2
ALDRIDGE IRA L	MAJ	0-0140446	0551	3
ALDRIDGE JAMES E	CW3	W-2205563	0766	1
ALDRIDGE JOHN S	1LT	0-1914107	0920	1
ALDRIDGE JOSEPH R	CW3	W-2144390	0557	1
ALDRIDGE RICHARD D	LTC	0-1285568	0756	2
ALE CLARENCE K	CPT	0-0520234	0945	2
ALEFF KENNETH G	LTC	0-0330956	0263	1
ALENIK IRVING	2LT	0-1596563	0145	2
ALEO ANTONIO	MAJ	0-1116985	1060	1
ALESHIRE CLIFFORD W	MAJ	0-1548614	1058	2
ALEWINE MARION H	CPT	0-0488386	1046	2
ALEX MILLARD A	LTC	0-1545114	0162	1
ALEX STEPHAN H	CPT	0-0944226	0951	2
ALEXANDER A F J	2LT	0-1062802	0146	2
ALEXANDER ALBERT P	LTC	0-1551782	0757	1
ALEXANDER ALBERT W	LTC	0-0348720	0962	1
ALEXANDER ALEC	CPT	0-1034625	0947	2
ALEXANDER ALFRED L	MAJ	0-0445068	0849	1
ALEXANDER ANTHONY	CW3	W-2153127	0263	1
ALEXANDER ARTHUR A	COL	0-0237603	0854	3
ALEXANDER ARTHUR G	COL	0-0222143	1162	3
ALEXANDER ARTHUR P	MAJ	0-0120663	0853	3
ALEXANDER ARTHUR S	CPT	0-0367386	1042	2
ALEXANDER BENJAMIN K	CPT	0-1312859	0450	2
ALEXANDER BRYCE	LTC	0-0319638	0157	1
ALEXANDER CHARLES F	1LT	0-1290356	0444	2
ALEXANDER CHARLES E	MAJ	0-2016269	0761	1
ALEXANDER CHARLES H	COL	0-0453798	0565	1
ALEXANDER CHARLES M	MAJ	0-0497503	1152	1
ALEXANDER CHARLES N	LTC	0-0266674	0168	3
ALEXANDER CLEON H	LTC	0-1636911	0164	1
ALEXANDER CLIFFORD	CW2	W-2144451	0562	1
ALEXANDER DONALD L	MAJ	0-0553996	0258	1
ALEXANDER DUANE F	LTC	0-1686424	0962	1
ALEXANDER EARLE L	MAJ	0-0268155	1058	3
ALEXANDER EDWARD	1LT	0-0185221	0630	1
ALEXANDER EDWARD A	1LT	0-1055517	0946	2
ALEXANDER EDWARD I	CPT	0-1922586	1162	1
ALEXANDER ERNEST	CPT	0-0483112	0849	1
ALEXANDER EUGENE	CW2	W-2209866	0166	1
ALEXANDER EVERETT G	LTC	0-1167718	0461	1
ALEXANDER FARRIS O	MAJ	0-2017793	1263	1
ALEXANDER FLOYD E	LTC	0-1325958	1062	1
ALEXANDER FLOYD P	LTC	0-0211363	0762	1
ALEXANDER FRANK JR	CW3	W-2110828	0456	1
ALEXANDER FRED N	CW4	W-2129330	1264	2
ALEXANDER GAIL H	CW2	W-2211884	0168	1
ALEXANDER GARY E	MAJ	0-1185529	0657	1
ALEXANDER GEORGE C	LTC	0-0278729	1168	3
ALEXANDER GEORGE R	MAJ	0-0947550	0868	1
ALEXANDER GEORGE W	1LT	0-1895293	0845	2
ALEXANDER GRANT H	LTC	0-0455609	0865	1
ALEXANDER HAROLD J	MAJ	0-0902068	1045	2
ALEXANDER HAROLD J	2LT	0-1323082	1044	2
ALEXANDER HARRY F	MAJ	0-0976925	0562	1
ALEXANDER HARRY W	COL	0-0463511	0762	3
ALEXANDER HARVEY A	CPT	0-2262723	1060	2
ALEXANDER HERMAN D	1LT	0-1317934	0845	2
ALEXANDER HILDA C	2LT	N-0764024	0745	1
ALEXANDER J W	CPT	0-0487568	0350	2
ALEXANDER JAMES C	CPT	0-1297556	0255	1
ALEXANDER JAMES E	CPT	0-0958208	0459	1
ALEXANDER JAMES F	CPT	0-2262523	1062	1
ALEXANDER JAMES N	MAJ	0-2206281	1265	1
ALEXANDER JEAN W	CPT	0-1799321	1154	1
ALEXANDER JOE S	1LT	0-1297955	0945	2
ALEXANDER JOSEPH B	LTC	0-1051967	0565	1
ALEXANDER JOSEPH W	COL	0-0238430	1162	3
ALEXANDER JOSEPH T	CPT	0-0929650	1052	2
ALEXANDER LASSAR	CPT	0-0318232	0546	2
ALEXANDER LEONARD C	CPT	0-0484918	1144	2
ALEXANDER LEROY T	CW4	W-2113364	1058	2
ALEXANDER LESLIE H	CPT	0-2041438	0364	1
ALEXANDER LESTER D	2LT	0-2026885	0360	1
ALEXANDER LEWIS E	MAJ	0-1337760	1164	1
ALEXANDER LYLE G	CW3	W-2150368	0559	1
ALEXANDER MARTIN P	MAJ	0-2040850	0364	1
ALEXANDER MARVIN T	1LT	0-1063026	0346	2
ALEXANDER MARY F	MAJ	N-0763944	0468	1
ALEXANDER MAURICE S	LTC	0-1100834	0461	1
ALEXANDER MELVILLE W	1LT	0-0308649	0744	2
ALEXANDER MORRIS O	MAJ	0-2015011	0661	1
ALEXANDER NEWTON W	COL	0-0100159	0857	3
ALEXANDER ORLANDO C	MAJ	0-2029190	1268	1
ALEXANDER PAUL C	CPT	0-1290872	0145	2
ALEXANDER PYRON L JR	CW2	W-2214555	0968	1
ALEXANDER RALPH G	MAJ	0-0923701	0 0	2
ALEXANDER RAYMOND H	MAJ	0-0181129	0648	3
ALEXANDER RENA J	MAJ	N-0727701	1163	1
ALEXANDER RICHARD	LTC	0-0328538	1062	1
ALEXANDER RICHARD L	LTC	0-0274260	0348	2
ALEXANDER ROBERT A	LTC	0-1280102	0866	1
ALEXANDER ROBERT F	LTC	0-0271446	0166	3
ALEXANDER ROBERT G	LTC	0-0497209	1162	1
ALEXANDER ROBERT M	LTC	0-0287011	0260	1
ALEXANDER RUTH G	2LT	N-0775112	0145	1
ALEXANDER SAMUEL C	MAJ	0-1101055	1160	1
ALEXANDER SMITH K	LTC	0-1302101	0962	1
ALEXANDER SPENCER L	MAJ	0-0444321	0463	1
ALEXANDER THEODORE C	CW2	W-3250217	0767	1
ALEXANDER THOMAS B	LTC	0-0322451	1164	3
ALEXANDER THOMAS L	COL	0-0187486	0253	3
ALEXANDER THOMAS L	LTC	0-1166034	1162	1
ALEXANDER THOMAS L	MAJ	0-1822849	1264	1
ALEXANDER VINCENT A	2LT	0-1327486	0346	2
ALEXANDER WILLIAM M	CPT	0-1736243	1048	2
ALEXANDER WILLIAM P	CW4	W-2004246	0765	1
ALEXANDER WILLIE C	CW3	W-2148159	0464	1
ALEXANDER WILSON C	LTC	0-0888374	0267	3
ALEXANDER WRISTON C	CPT	0-1914108	0326	1
ALEXANDER YOUNG C	1LT	0-0212494	0857	3
ALEXICK EDWARD J	CPT	0-0494847	1049	1
ALFANO SYLVESTER	1LT	0-1310200	0645	2
ALFAR FRANCISCO	1LT	0-1896691	0450	1
ALFONSO CARL D	CPT	0-1296627	1045	2
ALFONSO JOSEPH O	CW4	W-2004209	0965	1
ALFORD CARL G	MAJ	0-2263505	0863	1
ALFORD CLIFTON JR	MAJ	0-1885513	1066	1
ALFORD COLEMAN E	LTC	0-0916842	0366	3
ALFORD DEAN C	MAJ	0-1030743	0261	1
ALFORD HENRY H	COL	0-0238297	0365	3
ALFORD KENNETH H	MAJ	0-1060337	0465	1
ALFORD LEROY	CW3	W-2203271	0562	1
ALFORD PEARCE	CW3	W-2117955	1055	1
ALFORD ROBERT B	COL	0-0296193	0568	3
ALFORD ROY A	COL	0-0407690	0556	3
ALFORD WILLIAM L	MAJ	0-0757146	0266	1
ALFORQUE PORFIRIO	CPT	0-0890546	0656	1
ALGAROTTI ROBERT A	MAJ	0-0450783	0764	1
ALGAZY EDWIN R	2LT	0-1044744	0645	2
ALGEO HAROLD L	COL	0-0117966	1149	3
ALGER CHARLES M	LTC	0-1302472	0866	1
ALGER DUANE L	CW3	W-2144082	1165	1
ALGER JAMES A	LTC	0-1310201	0668	3
ALGER JOHN	MAJ	0-0230894	0560	1
ALGER RUSSELL W	CW4	W-2151675	0868	1
ALGIE CECIL L	1LT	0-1591561	1159	1
ALGOOD REUBEN C	LTC	0-0340094	0162	1
ALGUIRE ADDISON D	COL	0-0142506	0157	3
ALICEA JUAN	MAJ	0-0980817	0961	1
ALICKI JOHN A	MAJ	0-1303076	0157	1
ALIFF CONRAD L G	CW2	W-2148426	0458	1
ALINE ROBERT F	MAJ	0-2046634	0857	2
ALISCH EMIL	COL	0-0265591	0268	3
ALISON JEFFERSON JR	LTC	0-0261155	0966	3
ALIX FRANCIS	MAJ	0-1170619	0656	1
ALKIM ALPHONSE F	CW4	W-2110495	0661	1
ALKIRE CHARLES P	LTC	0-1284980	1164	1
ALKIRE DALE V	LTC	0-1340971	0268	2
ALKIRE EDWARD M	COL	0-0263066	0467	3
ALKIRE EINFRED C	MAJ	0-1177263	1265	1
ALL FRED H	COL	0-0169510	0456	3
ALLABOUGH DAVID B	LTC	0-0302206	0348	3
ALLAIN CARL N	MAJ	0-0967640	0963	1
ALLAN ANDREW A	MAJ	0-0295919	0561	1
ALLAN HELEN V	1LT	N-0721601	0546	1
ALLAN WILLIAM	LTC	0-1001062	0169	1
ALLAN WILLIAM D	LTC	0-1284805	0656	1
ALLARD DWIGHT W	LTC	0-1579831	1166	1
ALLARD GERALD D	LTC	0-0231131	1264	3
ALLARD GORDON E	CPT	0-0452713	0454	1
ALLARD ROBERT D	LTC	0-1288346	1060	1

NAME	GRADE	SVC NO	DATE RET MO YR	RET CODE
ALLARD WAYNE E	CPT	0-2004312	0853	2
ALLARDICE GEORGE M	CPT	0-1042471	0546	2
ALLBAUGH ONEA D	CW2	W-2001788	0665	1
ALLBEE EARL R	COL	0-0505325	0164	3
ALLBEE RUTH E	MAJ	L-1010511	0868	1
ALLBRIGHT JAMES J JR	LTC	0-1166879	1060	1
ALLBRIGHT PAUL H	CPT	0-0486980	0244	2
ALLBRIGHT WILLIAM J	MAJ	0-1114027	0658	1
ALLBRITTON BENJAMIN	LTC	0-0229614	0765	3
ALLCORN HUGH J	1LT	0-1294592	0745	2
ALLCORN LUTHER H JR	CPT	0-0294181	0345	2
ALLDREDGE BEDFORD H	LTC	0-0325736	0662	3
ALLEE RALPH E	MAJ	0-0402196	0154	2
ALLEGRA JAMES J	LTC	0-0506602	0263	1
ALLEGRA MICHAEL	MAJ	0-2212087	0262	1
ALLEGRETTI ANTHONY J	COL	0-0312619	1267	3
ALLEMAN CHARLES H	MAJ	0-2025949	0265	1
ALLEMAN MABEL C	MAJ	N-0725779	0164	3
ALLEMEIER RALPH F	MAJ	0-1587047	0963	1
ALLEMEIER RALPH W	CW4	W-2102601	0859	1
ALLEN ALBERT A	MAJ	0-0245625	1163	3
ALLEN ALBERT L	CPT	0-0140091	0952	3
ALLEN ALBERT R	1LT	0-0539787	0146	2
ALLEN ALLEN L	LTC	0-1533242	1161	2
ALLEN ALVA J	CPT	0-0287332	1056	3
ALLEN ALVIN H	CW4	W-2145283	0856	1
ALLEN ANDRA W	MAJ	0-1323752	0164	1
ALLEN ARLISS C	LTC	0-0262981	0461	3
ALLEN ARTHUR F	COL	0-0228350	0460	3
ALLEN BEATRICE E	1LT	N-0722990	0346	2
ALLEN BERNARD F	LTC	0-1035224	0164	1
ALLEN BERNARD G	MAJ	0-0372704	0246	2
ALLEN BERTRAN L	MAJ	0-1585407	0662	1
ALLEN CHARLES D	CPT	0-0360098	1143	2
ALLEN CHARLES D	CPT	0-0890384	0853	2
ALLEN CHARLES E	LTC	0-0371420	1060	1
ALLEN CHARLES E	1LT	0-0450226	0146	2
ALLEN CHARLES E	LTC	0-1555936	0565	1
ALLEN CHARLES E	CW2	W-2152665	0560	1
ALLEN CHARLES H	MAJ	0-0959213	0567	1
ALLEN CHARLES L	LTC	0-1046709	0761	1
ALLEN CHARLES W	COL	0-0214814	1162	3
ALLEN CHARLES W	MAJ	0-1303998	1163	1
ALLEN CHESTER E	CPT	0-1342357	0261	1
ALLEN CHESTER R	LTC	0-1031617	0662	1
ALLEN CLAIR K	CPT	0-0144867	1153	3
ALLEN CLAUDE W	MAJ	0-0963458	0562	1
ALLEN CLEARDE	WO1	W-2146142	1151	2
ALLEN CLIFFORD	LTC	0-1311959	0962	1
ALLEN CLINTON L SR	MAJ	0-5301570	0268	1
ALLEN DANIEL A	CW2	W-2145378	0556	1
ALLEN DONALD E	LTC	0-0375459	0660	1
ALLEN DOUGLAS J	CW4	W-2147029	0668	1
ALLEN DOUGLAS L	CW4	W-2153330	0259	1
ALLEN DWIGHT D	CW3	W-2203423	0465	1
ALLEN EDGAR W	LTC	0-1623034	1062	1
ALLEN EDWARD L JR	MAJ	0-2102988	0167	1
ALLEN EDWIN B	MAJ	0-0230295	0758	3
ALLEN ELBERT T	LTC	0-0213850	0464	3
ALLEN ELIZABETH	2LT	N-0729530	1045	1
ALLEN ELLEN R	CPT	N-0745532	0856	2
ALLEN EMERSON R	MAJ	0-0967011	0964	1
ALLEN ERNEST H	WO1	W-2109229	0750	1
ALLEN ESTEL L	MAJ	0-1100413	0161	1
ALLEN ESTHER L	2LT	N-0722663	1143	1
ALLEN EUGENE D	LTC	0-0450444	0655	1
ALLEN EVELIN J	CPT	N-0773059	0446	1
ALLEN FORREST R	CW2	W-2150720	0859	1
ALLEN FRANCIS W	COL	0-0264733	1067	3
ALLEN FRANK C JR	LTC	0-0232337	0565	3
ALLEN FRANK H	CPT	0-0224799	0847	1
ALLEN FRANK L	LTC	0-0262652	0760	3
ALLEN FRANK M JR	CW3	W-2151505	0267	1
ALLEN FURMAN	LTC	0-1012065	0965	1
ALLEN G I	LTC	0-0212079	0368	3

NAME	GRADE	SVC NO	DATE RET MO YR	RET CODE
ALLEN GEORGE E	LTC	0-1798544	1164	1
ALLEN GEORGE G	MAJ	0-2262729	0763	1
ALLEN GEORGE S	MAJ	0-0445838	0551	1
ALLEN GEORGE W JR	MAJ	0-0962177	0462	1
ALLEN GLEN V	MAJ	0-0310425	0867	3
ALLEN GLENN J	LTC	0-0260511	0856	2
ALLEN GUY R	CW2	W-2215673	0968	1
ALLEN HARLAN K	LTC	0-0322395	0567	3
ALLEN HAROLD E	LTC	0-1645304	0163	1
ALLEN HAROLD E	CPT	0-2263030	0561	1
ALLEN HAROLD M	MAJ	0-0957519	0867	1
ALLEN HAROLD V	LTC	0-0419320	0259	1
ALLEN HAROLD W	COL	0-0312761	0251	1
ALLEN HARRY	LTC	0-1104701	0157	1
ALLEN HARRY A	LTC	0-0261034	1067	3
ALLEN HARRY D	LTC	0-0118454	0954	3
ALLEN HECTOR L	LTC	0-1103493	1262	1
ALLEN HERBERT W	CPT	0-0197574	0846	2
ALLEN HERBERT W	LTC	0-1534419	0769	3
ALLEN HERMAN C	CPT	0-0359529	1043	2
ALLEN HILTON J	MAJ	0-2008365	1064	1
ALLEN HUBERT L	2LT	0-1996441	1045	2
ALLEN IDA M	MAJ	R-0000739	0763	1
ALLEN IVAN C	MAJ	0-1823684	0461	1
ALLEN IVAN J	LTC	0-0397769	0361	1
ALLEN IVOR H	CW3	W-2151869	0463	1
ALLEN JACK G	COL	0-0278601	0665	3
ALLEN JAMES E	MAJ	0-1894487	0955	1
ALLEN JAMES G	1LT	0-1321008	1045	2
ALLEN JAMES H	COL	0-0202149	0353	3
ALLEN JAMES H JR	CPT	0-2264117	0660	2
ALLEN JAMES J	1LT	0-0340127	1145	2
ALLEN JAMES N	CPT	0-0237839	0863	3
ALLEN JAMES R	LTC	0-0169350	0159	3
ALLEN JAMES W	LTC	0-2203746	0765	1
ALLEN JIMMIE C	LTC	0-1635555	0160	1
ALLEN JOHN D	MAJ	0-2028409	0264	1
ALLEN JOHN G JR	MAJ	0-0256698	0144	2
ALLEN JOHN H	COL	0-0103883	1053	3
ALLEN JOHN H JR	1LT	0-1011006	1143	2
ALLEN JOHN H JR	MAJ	0-1294593	1060	1
ALLEN JOHN J	LTC	0-1821952	0661	1
ALLEN JOHN L	MAJ	0-5301938	0668	1
ALLEN JOHN R	LTC	0-0333631	0561	1
ALLEN JOHN W	1LT	0-0520872	0449	2
ALLEN JOSEPH	WO1	W-2147418	0555	1
ALLEN JOSEPH B	LTC	0-1314918	1062	1
ALLEN JOSEPH W	1LT	0-1640165	0645	2
ALLEN KENNETH O	COL	0-0113362	0550	3
ALLEN KENNETH G	COL	0-0170099	0460	3
ALLEN KENNETH G	MAJ	0-1055518	1266	3
ALLEN LAWRENCE B	LTC	0-0397363	1161	1
ALLEN LAWRENCE J JR	1LT	0-0416072	1045	2
ALLEN LAYTON E	LTC	0-0345317	1167	3
ALLEN LEE M	COL	0-0134415	0755	3
ALLEN LEONARD B JR	1LT	0-0537251	0646	2
ALLEN LEONARD F	MAJ	0-1889848	0866	1
ALLEN LEONARD R	MAJ	0-0266946	0667	3
ALLEN LEWIS O	MAJ	0-2262951	1163	1
ALLEN LLOYD C	LTC	0-0278831	0867	3
ALLEN LLOYD D	1LT	0-2001847	1047	2
ALLEN LOUIS A JR	LTC	0-0278790	0862	1
ALLEN LOUIS D	CW2	W-2152816	1257	1
ALLEN LULA M	1LT	N-0773912	0646	1
ALLEN LYLE B	CW3	W-2147240	0566	1
ALLEN LYNN	1LT	0-0449391	0445	2
ALLEN MARGARET H	MAJ	N-0741690	1167	1
ALLEN MARY D	2LT	N-0741006	0645	1
ALLEN MARY S	2LT	N-0703075	0942	1
ALLEN MELVIN F	CW3	W-2146796	0263	1
ALLEN MILLARD R	LTC	0-1179759	1067	1
ALLEN MYRON M	CW4	W-2135224	1059	1
ALLEN NORMAN	1LT	0-1642595	1145	2
ALLEN NUEL H	MAJ	0-0955628	0962	1
ALLEN ODIE K	MAJ	0-2042981	0863	1

NAME	GRADE	SVC NO	DATE RET MO YR	RET CODE
ALLEN OLA L	LTC	0-0278446	0255	2
ALLEN OLIVE T	CPT	M-0000499	0146	1
ALLEN ORLO B	MAJ	0-1304703	0959	1
ALLEN OSCAR J JR	LTC	0-0269553	0146	2
ALLEN OTTO H	MAJ	0-0521310	0953	1
ALLEN OZNI E	LTC	0-0485707	1054	1
ALLEN PAUL A	LTC	0-0236820	0266	3
ALLEN PAUL J	CPT	0-1333160	0758	1
ALLEN PAUL L	CPT	0-1549202	0654	1
ALLEN PAUL W	LTC	0-0356951	0960	1
ALLEN PHILIP A	MAJ	0-0538792	0665	1
ALLEN RALPH B	LTC	0-0178355	0160	3
ALLEN RALPH C	COL	0-0128749	1152	3
ALLEN RAY C	COL	0-0267268	0447	2
ALLEN RAY L	LTC	0-0411441	0861	1
ALLEN RAYMOND	LTC	0-0346740	0660	1
ALLEN RAYMOND R	MAJ	0-1045702	0366	1
ALLEN RAYMOND S	CW2	W-2147436	0662	1
ALLEN RICHARD E JR	LTC	0-1339501	0568	1
ALLEN RICHARD F	MAJ	0-0259670	1163	3
ALLEN RICHARD H	LTC	0-0420856	0960	1
ALLEN RICHARD L	1LT	0-0351210	0545	2
ALLEN RICHARD L JR	LTC	0-1340611	0968	1
ALLEN ROBERT A	COL	0-0370166	0968	3
ALLEN ROBERT B	COL	0-0330519	1167	3
ALLEN ROBERT C	LTC	0-1336855	0968	1
ALLEN ROBERT D	CPT	0-1299514	0750	2
ALLEN ROBERT D	CW2	W-2143020	0562	1
ALLEN ROBERT E	COL	0-0237666	0260	3
ALLEN ROBERT H JR	LTC	0-1056622	0163	1
ALLEN ROBERT L	LTC	0-0283118	1267	3
ALLEN ROBERT M	1LT	0-0476644	0157	1
ALLEN ROBERT N	CPT	0-0393565	0146	2
ALLEN ROBERT P	MAJ	0-2049165	1155	1
ALLEN ROBERT S	1LT	0-0445412	0644	2
ALLEN ROBERT S	COL	0-0481033	1046	2
ALLEN ROSCOE L	LTC	0-0274435	0859	3
ALLEN ROSS J	1LT	0-1580567	1144	2
ALLEN ROY C	MAJ	0-1642289	0357	1
ALLEN RUSSELL B	CPT	0-0493576	0259	1
ALLEN SIDNEY F	MAJ	0-1998398	0155	1
ALLEN SIMEON L	WO1	W-2120718	0445	2
ALLEN STANLEY C	LTC	0-1046335	0865	1
ALLEN STUART V	MAJ	0-1308259	0462	1
ALLEN THOMAS A	MAJ	0-0148926	0547	2
ALLEN THOMAS C N	MAJ	0-0224215	1058	3
ALLEN THOMAS L	COL	0-0152439	0358	3
ALLEN TOM J	LTC	0-0103498	0648	3
ALLEN ULYSESS W	CW2	W-2208188	0965	1
ALLEN VERNON E	CW3	W-2143759	0957	1
ALLEN VIRGIE	1LT	N-0734503	1045	1
ALLEN WADE W	MAJ	0-2011087	0260	1
ALLEN WALTER C	CW2	W-2147104	0461	1
ALLEN WALTER P	CPT	0-0987998	0562	2
ALLEN WARREN	COL	0-0120537	0756	3
ALLEN WARREN E	MAJ	0-1335373	0962	1
ALLEN WARREN G	LTC	0-1104035	1155	1
ALLEN WAYNE H	MAJ	0-1994556	0860	1
ALLEN WAYNE R	M G	0-0171232	0159	3
ALLEN WILBERT H	1LT	0-1165991	1262	2
ALLEN WILLARD J	CW4	W-2111716	0958	1
ALLEN WILLIAM E	CPT	0-1320005	0546	2
ALLEN WILLIAM H	COL	0-0223875	1066	3
ALLEN WILLIAM H	CW3	W-2206034	1067	1
ALLEN WILLIAM M	CPT	0-0212291	1062	3
ALLEN WILLIAM W	LTC	0-0489662	0256	1
ALLENSWORTH EVERETT	CPT	0-1003463	0666	1
ALLENTUCK SAMUEL	MAJ	0-0496597	1045	2
ALLERS WILLIAM D	MAJ	0-1821305	0347	2
ALLERTON PERRY	LTC	0-0215115	0657	3
ALLESEE MARVIN E	MAJ	0-0271604	0844	2
ALLEY FRANK M	CW4	W-2144419	1168	1
ALLEY FRANK D JR	LTC	0-0142171	0744	2
ALLEY HAROLD E	LTC	0-0232929	0362	3
ALLEY HERMAN L	LTC	0-1167719	0862	1

NAME	GRADE	SVC NO	DATE RET MO YR	RET CODE
ALLEY JOHN M	MAJ	0-0968444	0261	1
ALLEY LEON A	COL	0-0226369	1052	3
ALLEY LOFTON H	LTC	0-0410926	0161	1
ALLEY ROBERT G	LTC	0-1542580	1061	1
ALLEY THELMA L	CW3	V-2215659	0265	1
ALLEY WILLIAM P	MAJ	0-1290179	0865	1
ALLGEYER WILLIAM	2LT	0-1299515	0365	2
ALLGIRE ARCHIE C JR	MAJ	0-0361372	0960	1
ALLGOOD JOHN L	LTC	0-1292953	0657	1
ALLGOOD TOMMY L	MAJ	0-0490600	0856	1
ALLI JOSEPH H	COL	0-0482461	0449	3
ALLICON PHILLIP A	LTC	0-1284806	0261	1
ALLIE HENRY P	CPT	0-0982694	0162	1
ALLIN CHARLES W	1LT	0-1325847	0446	2
ALLINGHAM DAVID J	LTC	0-1283532	1165	1
ALLIS JOHN A	CPT	0-0239718	0864	3
ALLISON ALEXANDER JR	MAJ	0-0360688	1044	2
ALLISON CHARLES H	LTC	0-1002565	1262	1
ALLISON CHARLES R JR	COL	0-0297190	1167	3
ALLISON DALE O	MAJ	0-0224775	0663	3
ALLISON DONALD G	CPT	0-0192920	1162	3
ALLISON EDGAR C	CPT	0-0511872	0151	1
ALLISON HOMER B	CW2	W-2206012	0962	1
ALLISON HOWELL K	CW2	W-2119759	0350	1
ALLISON JAMES G JR	CW2	W-2141178	0561	1
ALLISON JAMES H JR	LTC	0-0273033	0766	3
ALLISON JAMES R	1LT	0-1551561	1045	2
ALLISON KENNETH E	2LT	0-1321730	0644	2
ALLISON KENNETH M	MAJ	0-2032946	0862	1
ALLISON NOAH D	B G	0-0278182	0259	3
ALLISON PAUL W	LTC	0-0496793	0462	1
ALLISON RODGERS W	LTC	0-0382961	0257	1
ALLISON SAMUEL C	LTC	0-0384115	0157	1
ALLISON WILLIAM B	CW2	W-2143703	0559	1
ALLMAN JAMES R	CPT	0-0360354	0563	3
ALLMAN JOSEPH R	CW3	W-2152922	1264	1
ALLMAN MORRIS	LTC	0-0885088	0254	2
ALLMAN SYDNEY J	LTC	0-0321937	0167	3
ALLNUTT ERNEST C JR	LTC	0-0451069	0646	2
ALLOTT THOMAS J	CPT	0-0430671	1047	2
ALLOU CHARLES A	LTC	0-1321276	0267	3
ALLOWAY FRANK L	LTC	0-0182512	0945	2
ALLPHIN CHARLES W	LTC	0-0245329	0152	3
ALLREAD DEWEY JR	LTC	0-1290359	0163	1
ALLRED ANTHON V	LTC	0-2210207	1067	1
ALLRED ELLA M	MAJ	N-0735555	0163	2
ALLRED JOE O	1LT	0-1109786	1045	2
ALLRED PAUL C	MAJ	0-2262864	0762	1
ALLRED ROBIN J	1LT	0-0548082	1145	2
ALLRED VINCENT C	COL	0-0330123	0866	3
ALLRED WILLIAM H	CW2	W-2210814	0363	1
ALLSOP MILDRED A	1LT	N-0759993	0246	1
ALLSTEAD EDITH M	2LT	N-0784705	1044	1
ALLUMS MARVIN M	MAJ	0-2204454	0566	1
ALLWINE ROBERT E JR	MAJ	0-1917769	0665	1
ALLYN CHESTER	CPT	0-0298408	0958	3
ALLYN WILLIAM P	COL	0-0103196	0556	3
ALLYNE ARTHUR B	LTC	0-0234401	0664	1
ALLYNE ROLLIN F	COL	0-1574951	0665	3
ALMAS SAM	CW2	W-2151319	0560	1
ALMASSY LOUIS	CPT	0-1321472	1047	2
ALMASSY THOMAS G	CPT	0-1551559	0646	2
ALMEDA CHARLES	CW2	W-2142311	1260	1
ALMES GEORGE A	LTC	0-0135059	0346	2
ALMOND PHILIP C	MAJ	0-2015654	0664	1
ALMQUIST ALLEN F JR	LTC	0-1176534	0367	1
ALMQUIST CARL T	LTC	0-0289963	0855	3
ALMQUIST JOSEPH H JR	1LT	0-1323393	0146	2
ALMSTEAD GEORGE M	MAJ	0-0949216	1163	1
ALMY BENJAMIN F JR	CW3	W-2145784	1062	1
ALNUTT THOMAS L	LTC	0-0213389	1063	3
ALOISE SALVATORE	MAJ	0-1308457	0964	1
ALONZO ANTHONY L	MAJ	0-1037958	0363	1
ALONZO GERALD J	MAJ	0-0377153	0346	2
ALPAUGH STANLEY H	MAJ	0-1294247	0161	1

NAME	GRADE	SVC NO	DATE RET MO YR	RET CODE
ALPER IRWIN I	COL	0-0230450	0362	3
ALPERN MYER	LTC	0-0272339	0568	3
ALPERT HERBERT R	1LT	0-1104705	0251	2
ALPERT IRVING F	LTC	0-0394060	1067	3
ALPERT PAUL	1LT	0-1168997	0545	2
ALPS BAYARD G	MAJ	0-0180841	1152	3
ALS WILFRID P	MAJ	0-0199774	1157	3
ALSAKER ROBERT S	LTC	0-1179002	0868	1
ALSBERGE EDWARD W	LTC	0-0268030	0265	3
ALSBURY DENNIS P	CPT	0-2019543	1053	2
ALSBURY ROMAINE T	MAJ	0-1302934	0261	1
ALSHULER ROBERT E	1LT	0-0444751	0745	2
ALSPACH JERRY V	CPT	0-0939666	0158	1
ALSTERLUND C W JR	1LT	0-0435932	1045	2
ALSTON ARVILLE B	CPT	0-4006519	0167	1
ALSTON CHARLES N	MAJ	0-0176081	0549	3
ALSTON FRANK G	COL	0-0207735	1263	3
ALSTON WILLIAM K	COL	0-0176424	0756	3
ALSTROM JOHN T JR	MAJ	0-0381333	0252	2
ALSUP CECIL B	CW2	W-2105082	0946	2
ALSUP JEPTHA O	MAJ	0-2262571	1068	1
ALSWORTH WILKINSON	LTC	0-0931661	0666	1
ALT GRACE E	LTC	N-0724122	0864	3
ALT LOUIS M	COL	0-0271884	0768	3
ALT WALTER F	COL	0-0237611	0456	3
ALTAFFER HARRY C	LTC	0-0233687	1060	3
ALTENBURG CARL W	MAJ	0-1944856	0864	1
ALTENBURG SAMUEL L	MAJ	0-2020508	0264	1
ALTENDORF EDWARD L	MAJ	0-0230666	0562	3
ALTERI ANTHONY M	MAJ	0-1332908	0559	1
ALTERMAN ROBERT H	CPT	0-1689962	1045	2
ALTERMATT RAYMOND C	LTC	0-0181413	0755	3
ALTHAUS JOHN W A	COL	0-0327234	1263	3
ALTHOFF ELEANOR R	2LT	N-0771702	0844	1
ALTHOUSE RAYMOND R	LTC	0-0251813	0566	3
ALTIERI JAMES J	CPT	0-2055876	0154	2
ALTIERI ROBERT	COL	0-0382748	0868	3
ALTIMUS FREDERICK	CW2	W-2213199	0168	1
ALTMAN ELLIS F	COL	0-0115649	0449	3
ALTMAN FRANK A	MAJ	0-0234037	0357	3
ALTMAN GEORGE H	LTC	0-0465995	0562	1
ALTMAN JACOB	LTC	0-0321494	0446	2
ALTMAN LEON J	CPT	0-0511843	1146	2
ALTMAN MARTIN	2LT	0-1339596	0846	2
ALTMAN MARY R	1LT	N-0772103	0246	1
ALTMAN MILTON H	CPT	0-1573009	0245	2
ALTMAN RICHARD	COL	0-0277085	1264	3
ALTMAN WILLIAM T	MAJ	0-2097023	0866	1
ALTMANSBERGER R H	CW2	W-2114801	0746	1
ALTMEYER FRANK N	CW2	W-2152939	1061	1
ALTNOW GERALD H	LTC	0-0326176	0562	3
ALTOSE ALEXANDER	LTC	0-0360485	0546	2
ALTSHULER LOUIS N	COL	0-0482980	0864	1
ALTSTAETTER FREDERIC	LTC	0-0301548	0567	3
ALTUS NATHAN	WO1	W-2115286	0347	2
ALVAREZ FERNANDO L	MAJ	0-1301592	0763	1
ALVAREZ JAMES J JR	2LT	0-0536618	0845	2
ALVAREZ JOSE M	MAJ	0-1288669	1060	1
ALVAREZ LUIS A	MAJ	0-2055296	1154	1
ALVAREZ MIGUEL A	CPT	0-1303285	0561	1
ALVATOR JAMES E	LTC	0-1181525	1163	1
ALVERSON ROBERT M	LTC	0-0257664	1266	3
ALVERSON WILLIAM G	CPT	0-1294596	0647	2
ALVES HENRY A	1LT	0-0357929	0844	2
ALVES VIRGINIA H	2LT	N-0720360	0943	1
ALVESTAD VERNON L	WO1	W-2112282	0463	1
ALVEY HASKEL D	2LT	0-0996787	1052	2
ALVIAR FREDERICK	MAJ	0-1326689	0264	1
ALVIN ALBERT	MAJ	0-1308901	0266	1
ALVIS AUBREY	CPT	0-0517564	0250	1
ALVIS ELMO H	COL	0-0340503	0862	1
ALVIS ROBERT L	MAJ	0-1950533	0664	1
ALWARD SHELBY C	MAJ	0-1645357	0761	1
ALWINE VIRGINIA E	1LT	N-0797234	0147	1
ALYEA COURTLAND	CW4	W-2003506	0764	3

NAME	GRADE	SVC NO	DATE RET MO YR	RET CODE
ALZMANN HENRY F	MAJ	0-1017580	0661	1
AMADIO JOHN A	LTC	0-1559871	1166	1
AMAGUIN JOSE	2LT	0-1896627	0950	1
AMAKER JOHN B	LTC	0-1288670	1062	1
AMAN PAUL W	LTC	0-1053456	0661	1
AMANN ANDREW C	CPT	0-0235576	0352	3
AMANN RALPH J	CPT	0-0452338	0646	2
AMANTI JEROME J	LTC	0-0265909	0262	1
AMARAL CLARENCE L	MAJ	0-1301761	0960	1
AMARINE ROBERT E	CPT	0-2014665	0862	1
AMARO JAMES P	LTC	0-1315757	0366	1
AMASON MARY J	MAJ	N-0734593	0367	1
AMASON MATTIE M	CPT	N-0726002	0247	1
AMASON WARREN H	LTC	0-0310285	1160	2
AMATO JAMES P	LTC	0-0261329	1066	3
AMATO JOSEPH J	1LT	0-1041285	1047	2
AMATO LOUIS L	CPT	0-0361148	1145	2
AMATO PINO C	1LT	0-1036827	0545	2
AMATO SAM L	LTC	0-1176238	0766	1
AMATO VINCENT J	COL	0-0228313	0655	3
AMATO VINCENT L	1LT	0-1062958	0645	2
AMBERG JOHN A	COL	0-0234144	1064	3
AMBLER ALFRED C	CPT	0-0298176	0543	2
AMBLER CHARLES W JR	LTC	0-0248343	0866	3
AMBLER ROBERT T	CW2	W-2146560	1154	1
AMBOS ARNOLD M	1LT	0-1319593	1052	2
AMBRAZ SIMON P	LTC	0-0198368	1149	3
AMBRAZAVITCH MICHAEL	LTC	0-1178684	0368	1
AMBRE RALPH A	LTC	0-1052235	0962	1
AMBROSE EDMOND G	LTC	0-0333982	0167	3
AMBROSE FELIX J	CW2	W-2143744	0563	1
AMBROSE IKE H JR	MAJ	0-0425658	0959	1
AMBROSE JEFFERSON	LTC	0-0252053	0466	3
AMBROSE JOHN M C	1LT	0-1313185	1145	2
AMBROSE JULIAN	1LT	0-0524713	0745	2
AMBROSE PAUL M	MAJ	0-1286756	0760	1
AMBROSIANO N R	CPT	0-0424010	1045	2
AMBROSOME JOSEPH P	1LT	0-0527733	1145	2
AMBUEHL LEO JR	CW3	W-2143475	0166	1
AMBURGEY GLENNIS A	LTC	0-2202812	0767	1
AMDUR HYMAN B	COL	0-0362690	0463	3
AMEEL ROSE E	MAJ	N-0772444	0464	1
AMEEN SAIAD W	MAJ	0-1587288	0663	1
AMELUNKE ALVIN E	1LT	0-1702999	1145	2
AMEN MARK	COL	0-0276253	0455	1
AMEND DAVID H	CPT	0-1326598	0547	2
AMEND EDWARD C	CW2	W-2109799	0545	2
AMENDE JAMES K	LTC	0-1040336	0962	1
AMENDOLA FREDERICK	MAJ	0-0445477	0743	2
AMENT MERTON J	LTC	0-0236268	1162	3
AMENT RICHARD G	CW3	W-2208355	1068	1
AMER ELI L	LTC	0-0335436	0857	2
AMERINE PAULINE E	2LT	N-0763269	0144	1
AMERMAN RICHARD H	MAJ	0-0948279	1067	3
AMERMAN WALTER G	CPT	0-1307632	0146	2
AMES EDWARD S	CPT	0-0185383	1143	2
AMES ERNEST D	LTC	0-0277652	0263	1
AMES FRANCIS H	CW4	W-2122181	0460	1
AMES HAROLD F	COL	0-0178472	0857	1
AMES HAROLD W	LTC	0-1181816	0163	1
AMES HENRY P	MAJ	0-0260445	1050	3
AMES JEWEL E	WO1	W-2148685	1159	2
AMES JOHN L JR	COL	0-0148696	0755	3
AMES JOHN M	CW3	W-2147907	0262	1
AMES JOHN S	LTC	0-2014742	0768	1
AMES JOHN T	MAJ	0-0259047	1267	3
AMES LOUIS F	MAJ	0-1325194	1061	1
AMES MAY K	CPT	N-0700115	1044	1
AMES RALPH H JR	LTC	0-0415739	0657	1
AMES ROY M	LTC	0-0168691	0957	3
AMES THOMAS T	WO1	W-2131966	0745	2
AMEY HARRY E	LTC	0-0243368	0466	3
AMICK JAMES F	CPT	0-0243731	0856	3
AMICK MELVIN M	LTC	0-1300907	0766	1
AMIDON ROGER E	LTC	0-0252212	0565	3

NAME	GRADE	SVC NO	DATE RET MO YR	RET CODE
AMIRAL HIRAM H	LTC	0-0126193	0950	3
AMLIE PAUL J	1LT	0-0385994	0343	2
AMLING RAYMOND O	CPT	0-0510185	0246	2
AMMEL LOUIS J	LTC	0-0277161	0765	3
AMMON DAVID A	MAJ	0-1036828	0256	2
AMMON GEORGE F JR	LTC	0-1325623	0468	1
AMMON GEORGE L	LTC	0-0302023	0545	2
AMMONS JAMES A	CW3	W-2147615	0862	1
AMMONS RAYMOND F	CW2	W-2212961	1068	1
AMMONS TELLER	LTC	0-0167464	1055	3
AMODEI FRANK V	CW3	W-2103838	0860	1
AMODIO GUODIE P	CW3	W-2143254	0660	1
AMON THEODORE M	CPT	0-1321565	0655	1
AMOS ELBERT V SR	MAJ	0-1550308	0561	1
AMOS EVERETT M	LTC	0-0357729	0660	1
AMOS FREDERICK	MAJ	0-0250131	0446	2
AMOS OSCAR G	COL	0-0115567	0158	3
AMOS RICHARD T	LTC	0-1283988	1162	1
AMOS ROBERT E	LTC	0-1292986	0961	1
AMOS ROBERT F	LTC	0-1286415	0657	1
AMOS THOMAS G	MAJ	0-0198363	0948	3
AMOTT LAWRENCE G	LTC	0-0283695	1166	3
AMRHEIN LEO F	CPT	0-0553610	0346	2
AMSLER HILDRED S	LTC	0-0304707	0361	1
AMSLER OTTO L	COL	0-0118478	1053	3
AMSPACHER GEORGE L	MAJ	0-2000956	1265	1
AMSTER ADOLPH B	1LT	0-0540311	0845	2
AMSTER HENRY	1LT	0-0545945	1147	2
AMSTER MILTON W	COL	0-0296980	1068	3
AMSTERDAM JULIUS	CPT	0-0547087	0945	2
AMUNDS GEORGE R	MAJ	0-0238819	0955	3
AMUNDSEN ARNOLD L	COL	0-1104314	0268	1
AMUNDSEN EARL	LTC	0-1015338	0361	1
AMUNDSON EDWIN M	LTC	0-1822937	0767	1
AMUNRUD ARNOL A	LTC	0-0313157	1161	1
AMY ARMANDO	1LT	0-0954374	1154	2
AMY HENRY J	COL	0-0100856	0555	3
AMY MARY W	2LT	N-0764004	1044	1
AMY ROBERT N	CW3	W-2146212	1160	1
AMY RUPERT	LTC	0-0404337	0760	1
ANASCO HILARION	1LT	0-0890547	0150	1
ANASTASAS HENRY O	LTC	0-0262568	1167	3
ANCHEL DAVID	CPT	0-1689310	0746	2
ANCHETA CARLOS F	MAJ	0-1316979	0263	1
ANCHICKS CARL S	MAJ	0-0169172	0761	3
ANCHORS GARNER B JR	CPT	0-0306341	0245	2
ANDEL HENRY L	1LT	0-0537788	1045	2
ANDERLITCH FRANK	LTC	0-0271147	0968	3
ANDERMANN HENRY W	LTC	0-0381777	0166	1
ANDERS CHARLES H	MAJ	0-2010745	0163	1
ANDERS EMET P	LTC	0-0838023	0167	1
ANDERS FRANKLIN D	LTC	0-0337596	0347	2
ANDERS HARLEY D	2LT	0-1303442	0744	2
ANDERS STERLING H	LTC	0-0273939	0267	3
ANDERS VERION Z	CPT	0-0258049	0546	2
ANDERSEN ALFRED O	LTC	0-0481974	0466	1
ANDERSEN ANDREW L	MAJ	0-1048270	0260	1
ANDERSEN CYRIL C	MAJ	0-1010793	0148	2
ANDERSEN ELMER P	MAJ	0-1634784	0758	1
ANDERSEN HAROLD G	COL	0-0218499	0651	3
ANDERSEN HOMER N	LTC	0-0450719	0758	1
ANDERSEN IRVIN C	LTC	0-0443767	0663	1
ANDERSEN JOHN S	COL	0-0420158	0961	1
ANDERSEN LESLIE	1LT	0-1291384	1256	1
ANDERSEN LEW M	CW3	W-2141104	0662	1
ANDERSEN OSCAR W	LTC	0-1080338	1262	1
ANDERSEN RALPH M	LTC	0-0474498	1063	3
ANDERSEN RICHARD M	LTC	0-1798768	0867	1
ANDERSEN WILHELM A	COL	0-0164438	0754	3
ANDERSON ALAN F	CPT	0-1116072	0846	2
ANDERSON ALBERT M	CW3	W-2142799	1059	1
ANDERSON ALBERT S	MAJ	0-0959521	1164	1
ANDERSON ALBERTA M	2LT	N-0724624	1043	1
ANDERSON ALFRED O	1LT	0-0109261	0131	1
ANDERSON ALFRED L	CW4	W-2001725	1058	3

NAME	GRADE	SVC NO	DATE RET MO YR	RET CODE
ANDERSON ALFRED W	CPT	0-0484175	0844	2
ANDERSON ALLEN O	LTC	0-0408991	0567	1
ANDERSON ALVAH W	MAJ	0-1281846	0561	1
ANDERSON ALVIN J	MAJ	0-1913286	0268	1
ANDERSON ANDERS T	CPT	0-1306687	0546	2
ANDERSON ARNETT S	COL	0-0221831	0656	1
ANDERSON ARTHUR C	LTC	0-0231965	1058	3
ANDERSON ARTHUR O	CPT	0-0911405	0544	2
ANDERSON ARTHUR D	2LT	0-1573011	0843	2
ANDERSON ARTHUR E	CW3	W-2209048	0168	1
ANDERSON ARTHUR G	LTC	0-0258399	0957	1
ANDERSON ARVAL L	COL	0-0225342	1062	3
ANDERSON B F JR	LTC	0-0354454	1060	1
ANDERSON BARNOT A	COL	0-0126999	1049	3
ANDERSON BARROLL E	COL	0-0269567	0958	3
ANDERSON BEAUFORD T	1LT	0-2103120	0952	2
ANDERSON BRYANT B	LTC	0-0286552	1067	3
ANDERSON BUEHREN O	CW2	W-2146302	0765	1
ANDERSON CAPL A	LTC	0-0140108	0948	3
ANDERSON CARL A	LTC	0-0270919	0565	3
ANDERSON CAPL E	LTC	0-0235974	0159	3
ANDERSON CARL E	COL	0-0261330	0565	3
ANDERSON CARL E	COL	0-0331057	0866	3
ANDERSON CARL E	CPT	0-0481718	0547	2
ANDERSON CARL E	CW3	W-3150591	0468	1
ANDERSON CARL F	COL	0-0287866	1062	3
ANDERSON CARL G	LTC	0-0327168	0459	1
ANDERSON CARL R	MAJ	0-1331461	0561	1
ANDERSON CARL S	1LT	0-1312112	0945	2
ANDERSON CARL T	CW2	W-2119589	1048	1
ANDERSON CHARLES A	COL	0-0167095	0654	3
ANDERSON CHARLES A	LTC	0-0314914	1210	1
ANDERSON CHARLES C	MAJ	0-4006835	0667	1
ANDERSON CHARLES E	COL	0-0348456	0660	1
ANDERSON CHARLES L	MAJ	0-0362349	0743	2
ANDERSON CHARLES L	COL	0-0437179	0965	1
ANDERSON CHARLES W	CW3	W-2206494	0468	1
ANDERSON CHARLIE R	LTC	0-0498172	0256	1
ANDERSON CHESTER R	1LT	0-0545570	0846	2
ANDERSON CLARENCE C	LTC	0-0285441	0566	3
ANDERSON CLARENCE F	LTC	0-0445094	1162	3
ANDERSON CLARENCE M	CW3	W-2205469	0566	1
ANDERSON CLARENCE W	CPT	0-0209352	0557	3
ANDERSON CLAUDE C	LTC	0-1548974	0266	1
ANDERSON CLAYTON H	MAJ	0-1554849	0161	1
ANDERSON CLIFTON E	LTC	0-1575679	1266	1
ANDERSON CLINTON M	CW3	W-2144681	1165	1
ANDERSON CLYDE J	WO1	W-2115599	0645	2
ANDERSON COLEMAN M	MAJ	0-0206519	0461	3
ANDERSON CONRAD	CPT	0-0445067	0949	1
ANDERSON CURTIS E	LTC	0-0918336	0265	3
ANDERSON DAVID S	LTC	0-0425943	0856	2
ANDERSON DAVID V	CPT	0-1948140	0656	2
ANDERSON DON C	MAJ	0-0126955	0944	2
ANDERSON DONALD C	CPT	0-0438426	1046	2
ANDERSON DONALD P	CPT	0-0364254	0746	2
ANDERSON DONALD R	CW3	W-2150905	1062	1
ANDERSON DONALD W	MAJ	0-1685652	0861	2
ANDERSON DORIS L	CPT	M-0000444	0545	1
ANDERSON EARL J	MAJ	0-2019268	1060	1
ANDERSON EARL L	MAJ	0-0289970	0747	2
ANDERSON EARL T	CPT	0-1061608	0547	2
ANDERSON EDGAR N	MAJ	0-1175026	1060	1
ANDERSON EDNA L	1LT	N-0732892	0845	1
ANDERSON EDWARD	CPT	0-0992619	0162	1
ANDERSON EDWARD A	CPT	0-1119023	1052	2
ANDERSON EDWARD F	COL	0-0265113	0964	3
ANDERSON EDWARD H	1LT	0-0995123	1052	2
ANDERSON EDWARD M	LTC	0-1535856	0767	1
ANDERSON EDWARD P	CPT	0-0257473	1056	3
ANDERSON EDWIN C	CW2	W-2112234	0249	1
ANDERSON EDWIN S	MAJ	0-0967316	1061	1
ANDERSON ELBERT B	MAJ	0-0271607	0445	2
ANDERSON ELDON C	CPT	0-2289642	0562	1
ANDERSON ELLIOTT V	MAJ	0-0285383	0766	3

ARMY OF THE UNITED STATES RETIRED LIST

NAME	GRADE	SVC NO	DATE RET MO YR	RET CODE
ANDERSON ELLSWORTH H	CW3	W-2141856	1058	1
ANDERSON ELMER A	CW4	W-2146634	0861	1
ANDERSON EMIL S	CPT	0-1296631	0447	2
ANDERSON EMMETT C	LTC	0-0336997	1264	3
ANDERSON ERNEST	CW2	W-2102606	0445	2
ANDERSON EUGENE C	1LT	0-0280274	0545	2
ANDERSON EUGENE L	CW2	W-2113034	0960	1
ANDERSON HARRIS S	CW3	W-2205665	0167	1
ANDERSON FLOYD V	LTC	0-1293881	0861	1
ANDERSON FRANK A	LTC	0-0247219	0662	2
ANDERSON FRANK C JR	CPT	0-1030321	0446	2
ANDERSON FRANK G	COL	0-0150305	1051	3
ANDERSON FRANKLIN K	CW2	W-2152399	1063	1
ANDERSON FRED R	CW3	W-2205617	0164	1
ANDERSON FREDERICK	MAJ	0-0193274	0145	2
ANDERSON FREDERICK	LTC	0-0307234	0360	3
ANDERSON GARLAND O	1LT	0-1289191	0646	2
ANDERSON GEORGE	CPT	0-0464178	0444	2
ANDERSON GEORGE	MAJ	0-1540679	0862	1
ANDERSON GEORGE A	LTC	0-0563476	1264	1
ANDERSON GEORGE K P	CW3	W-2149199	0163	1
ANDERSON GEORGE P	LTC	0-0206577	0657	3
ANDERSON GEORGE R	CPT	0-0197744	0562	3
ANDERSON GEORGE R	LTC	0-0249357	0863	3
ANDERSON GEORGE R	MAJ	0-0285946	0550	2
ANDERSON GEORGE R	MAJ	0-0976584	0662	1
ANDERSON GEORGE S	MAJ	0-0517800	0457	1
ANDERSON GEORGE W	1LT	0-1015282	0346	2
ANDERSON GLASSELL B	2LT	0-0488701	1043	1
ANDERSON GLEN R	CPT	0-1825107	0462	1
ANDERSON GRANT S	LTC	0-0246621	1266	3
ANDERSON GUSTAVE JR	CW3	W-2147461	0964	1
ANDERSON GUY R	1LT	0-0410158	0246	2
ANDERSON HAL N	1LT	0-1300909	1145	2
ANDERSON HAMPTON	B G	0-0243475	1150	3
ANDERSON HANS M	MAJ	0-0154077	1050	3
ANDERSON HARAMONT N	LTC	0-0120499	0648	3
ANDERSON HARLAN B	1LT	0-1764857	1046	2
ANDERSON HARLEY	CW3	W-2145603	1062	1
ANDERSON HAROLD	MAJ	0-0120498	0456	3
ANDERSON HAROLD J	COL	0-0120497	0752	2
ANDERSON HAROLD L	MAJ	0-1313944	0266	1
ANDERSON HAROLD W	COL	0-1289366	0561	1
ANDERSON HARRY W	COL	0-0187089	1050	3
ANDERSON HARRY W	COL	0-0276373	1167	3
ANDERSON HARVEY K	CW2	W-3430157	0467	1
ANDERSON HELEN G	2LT	N-0773845	0246	1
ANDERSON HENRY	CPT	0-0508161	1047	1
ANDERSON HENRY C	LTC	0-0201175	0758	3
ANDERSON HENRY D	1LT	0-1182050	0546	2
ANDERSON HENRY G	LTC	0-0328256	0161	1
ANDERSON HENRY W	LTC	0-0321651	1056	3
ANDERSON HERBERT H	LTC	0-0260155	0266	3
ANDERSON HOLGER V	CPT	0-1062463	0346	2
ANDERSON HOLLY L	MAJ	0-0189259	0357	3
ANDERSON HOWARD J	CPT	0-0274856	0445	2
ANDERSON HUGH C JR	MAJ	0-1594676	0165	1
ANDERSON IRVING B	LTC	0-0383038	0267	1
ANDERSON ISAAC M	LTC	0-0519565	0663	3
ANDERSON IVAN A	WO1	W-2117537	0246	2
ANDERSON JACK J	1LT	0-1177266	0646	2
ANDERSON JACK W	LTC	0-2034491	1267	1
ANDERSON JAMES A	CPT	0-1114828	0963	1
ANDERSON JAMES C	CPT	0-1012940	0352	2
ANDERSON JAMES C	CPT	0-2018273	0261	1
ANDERSON JAMES C	MAJ	0-2262570	1067	1
ANDERSON JAMES E SR	CW3	W-2144092	0562	1
ANDERSON JAMES H	MAJ	0-0237152	0664	3
ANDERSON JAMES L	1LT	0-1304654	0545	2
ANDERSON JAMES O	CPT	0-0518270	1147	2
ANDERSON JEFFERSON	CPT	0-0498795	0446	2
ANDERSON JIMMY E	CW4	W-2141902	0862	1
ANDERSON JOE R	MAJ	0-0975959	0562	1
ANDERSON JOHN A	CPT	0-1056278	0447	2
ANDERSON JOHN A	MAJ	0-1185390	0457	1

NAME	GRADE	SVC NO	DATE RET MO YR	RET CODE
ANDERSON JOHN A	LTC	0-1636922	0562	1
ANDERSON JOHN A	MAJ	0-2208003	0165	1
ANDERSON JOHN B	CPT	0-0540731	0847	2
ANDERSON JOHN D JR	MAJ	0-0257186	0666	3
ANDERSON JOHN E	LTC	0-1636923	0664	1
ANDERSON JOHN E	WO1	W-2147562	1263	1
ANDERSON JOHN G	LTC	0-0286402	0968	3
ANDERSON JOHN G	LTC	0-0290316	0567	3
ANDERSON JOHN I	LTC	0-1100002	0860	1
ANDERSON JOHN J	CPT	0-0450228	0249	1
ANDERSON JOHN K	LTC	0-0450219	0658	1
ANDERSON JOHN L	COL	0-0181053	0649	3
ANDERSON JOHN L	LTC	0-0507976	0766	2
ANDERSON JOHN P	LTC	0-0959825	1068	1
ANDERSON JOHN R JR	1LT	0-1107078	0745	2
ANDERSON JOHN W	LTC	0-1553944	0464	1
ANDERSON JOSEPH	1LT	0-0486075	0449	2
ANDERSON JOSEPH	CW4	W-2113906	1154	1
ANDERSON JOSEPH H	MAJ	0-1325853	0261	1
ANDERSON JOSEPH W	MAJ	0-0166596	0750	2
ANDERSON JOSEPH W	1LT	0-1185710	1045	2
ANDERSON JUSTIN V G	CPT	0-0148912	0748	3
ANDERSON KARL G	MAJ	0-1179272	1062	1
ANDERSON KATHERINE	1LT	N-0764840	0650	2
ANDERSON KENNETH C	CPT	0-1285872	0559	1
ANDERSON KENNETH K	WO1	W-2106493	0552	2
ANDERSON KENNETH O	CPT	0-1030767	1047	2
ANDERSON KENNETH W	CW4	W-2111991	0966	3
ANDERSON KENT E	2LT	0-0887618	0146	2
ANDERSON KERMIT O	MAJ	0-2010787	0762	1
ANDERSON LAWRENCE B	LTC	0-0347336	0455	1
ANDERSON LAWRENCE R	CPT	0-1180791	0252	2
ANDERSON LEIF	COL	0-0254027	1265	3
ANDERSON LELAND R	CW2	W-2205111	0761	1
ANDERSON LELAND Z	1LT	0-0341601	0666	3
ANDERSON LEO	CW3	W-2153236	0762	1
ANDERSON LEO D	MAJ	0-2018631	0959	1
ANDERSON LEONARD J	WO1	W-2147967	1053	1
ANDERSON LEONARD T	CPT	0-0514043	0547	1
ANDERSON LEROY A	CPT	0-2096673	0763	1
ANDERSON LEROY H	M G	0-0239452	0366	3
ANDERSON LEROY R	MAJ	0-1170625	0161	1
ANDERSON LESLIE I	CPT	0-0963385	0261	1
ANDERSON LEWIS M	COL	0-0337938	1265	3
ANDERSON LILLY A	2LT	N-0700144	1038	1
ANDERSON LLOYD	2LT	0-1284446	0644	2
ANDERSON LLOYD E	LTC	0-0888339	0166	1
ANDERSON LLOYD H	CPT	0-0981892	0760	1
ANDERSON LLOYD L	CW3	W-2205768	0765	1
ANDERSON LOUIS A	MAJ	0-1000080	0655	1
ANDERSON LOTHER B	MAJ	0-1321277	0659	2
ANDERSON LYLE S	LTC	0-0981851	0668	1
ANDERSON LYMAN C	LTC	0-1314140	0866	3
ANDERSON MARGOT M	1LT	N-0720602	0646	1
ANDERSON MARTHA S	LTC	L-1010073	1267	1
ANDERSON MARTIN V	CPT	0-0461221	0264	1
ANDERSON MARY J	CPT	L-0115641	0346	2
ANDERSON MAURICE	COL	0-0148703	0855	3
ANDERSON MAURICE F	LTC	0-0316875	0661	1
ANDERSON MAURICE T	LTC	0-0473359	1146	2
ANDERSON MELCHOIR G	LTC	0-0332403	1159	2
ANDERSON MELVIN B	1LT	0-1178685	0144	2
ANDERSON MELVIN F	LTC	0-0208915	0956	3
ANDERSON MERTON S	CPT	0-1307788	1145	2
ANDERSON MILFORD X	COL	0-0350073	0547	2
ANDERSON MILLARD T	WO1	W-2142330	0659	1
ANDERSON MILNOR B	1LT	0-0392163	1043	2
ANDERSON NATHAN W	MAJ	0-0366587	0752	2
ANDERSON NELS A	COL	0-0121306	0852	3
ANDERSON NEVIN B	COL	0-0274254	1154	3
ANDERSON NONNIE	MAJ	N-0786016	0765	1
ANDERSON NORMA J	1LT	N-0731014	0548	1
ANDERSON NORMAN E	LTC	0-1287643	0161	1
ANDERSON NORMAN I	COL	0-1184343	0868	1
ANDERSON OLIVER C	1LT	0-1032187	0846	2

NAME	GRADE	SVC NO	DATE RET MO YR	RET CODE
ANDERSON ORRIN F	LTC	0-0324513	1162	3
ANDERSON ORVILLE P	CW2	W-3440042	0768	1
ANDERSON OSCAR H	LTC	0-0298892	1165	1
ANDERSON OSCAR S	CW2	W-2101377	0953	1
ANDERSON OTIS C	2LT	0-1310667	0245	2
ANDERSON PAUL A	1LT	0-1587691	1263	1
ANDERSON PAUL E	MAJ	0-0387004	0960	1
ANDERSON PAUL E	CPT	0-1010543	0245	2
ANDERSON PAUL F	LTC	0-1573712	0865	1
ANDERSON PAUL V	LTC	0-0245368	0967	3
ANDERSON PAUL W	CPT	0-0251472	0353	3
ANDERSON PERCEVILLE	MAJ	0-1923600	0368	1
ANDERSON PETER M	LTC	0-0339298	0462	1
ANDERSON PHILIP	CPT	0-1702755	0157	1
ANDERSON PHILIP S	MAJ	0-0248370	1066	3
ANDERSON POWELL A	LTC	0-1010876	0361	1
ANDERSON RALPH H	LTC	0-1114032	0262	1
ANDERSON RALPH O	LTC	0-1546338	0662	1
ANDERSON RALPH W	1LT	0-1822559	0246	2
ANDERSON RAY F	1LT	0-1303444	0945	2
ANDERSON RAYMOND A	CW4	W-2114651	1163	1
ANDERSON RAYMOND E	1LT	0-1032092	0246	2
ANDERSON RAYMOND F	CPT	0-0302065	0145	2
ANDERSON RAYMOND J	COL	0-0286731	0868	3
ANDERSON RAYMOND W	WO1	W-2146720	1053	1
ANDERSON RAYNA L	MAJ	L-0704403	0463	1
ANDERSON RAYNARD E	1LT	0-1284447	0145	2
ANDERSON RAYNOR E	COL	0-0193968	0761	3
ANDERSON REX N	COL	0-0246235	1066	3
ANDERSON RICHARD C	LTC	0-1338543	0565	2
ANDERSON RICHARD D	MAJ	0-0290670	0665	3
ANDERSON RICHARD D	CW4	W-2111651	1166	1
ANDERSON RICHARD F	COL	0-0177189	0546	2
ANDERSON RICHARD M	2LT	0-1056623	0244	2
ANDERSON ROBERT	LTC	0-0339780	0450	2
ANDERSON ROBERT A	COL	0-0272203	0468	3
ANDERSON ROBERT B	COL	0-0404740	0258	1
ANDERSON ROBERT C	LTC	0-0381332	0461	1
ANDERSON ROBERT D	MAJ	0-1876256	0667	1
ANDERSON ROBERT D	MAJ	0-2287135	1067	1
ANDERSON ROBERT E	LTC	0-1285691	0661	1
ANDERSON ROBERT F	1LT	0-1824388	1151	2
ANDERSON ROBERT J	1LT	0-1181818	1146	2
ANDERSON ROBERT J	CW4	RW-2143640	0965	1
ANDERSON ROBERT L	CPT	0-1293517	1045	2
ANDERSON ROBERT M	LTC	0-0452158	1157	2
ANDERSON ROBERT R	CPT	0-0132925	0345	2
ANDERSON ROBERT R	MAJ	0-1010852	0846	2
ANDERSON ROBERT R	MAJ	0-1918955	0264	1
ANDERSON ROBERT S	1LT	0-2021075	0352	2
ANDERSON ROBERT S	CW3	W-2148245	1062	1
ANDERSON ROBERT T	2LT	0-0269390	0466	3
ANDERSON ROBERT W	MAJ	0-0228628	0146	2
ANDERSON ROGER L	CW2	W-2210941	1064	1
ANDERSON ROY E	LTC	0-1634801	0162	1
ANDERSON ROY W	MAJ	0-1559289	0563	1
ANDERSON RUDOLPH D	CPT	0-1823079	1046	2
ANDERSON RUSSELL H	COL	0-0136982	0658	3
ANDERSON RUSSELL V	LTC	0-1287813	1058	1
ANDERSON RUTH	1LT	N-0720567	0846	1
ANDERSON RUTH C	LTC	N-0700381	0946	1
ANDERSON SAMUEL E	LTC	0-1185793	0363	1
ANDERSON SAMUEL P	LTC	0-0270492	1067	3
ANDERSON SIDNEY F	LTC	0-1288636	1061	1
ANDERSON THEODORE H	LTC	0-0250937	0167	3
ANDERSON THEOPHILUS	MAJ	0-1181528	0265	1
ANDERSON THOMAS F	LTC	0-0267653	1168	3
ANDERSON THOMAS F	CPT	0-0975660	0762	1
ANDERSON THOMAS L.	1LT	0-1333298	1048	2
ANDERSON THOMAS P	LTC	0-0282390	0368	3
ANDERSON THOMAS R	MAJ	0-1920237	0766	1
ANDERSON THOR S	COL	0-0385132	1160	1
ANDERSON THRAVES L	1LT	0-1106520	0746	2
ANDERSON VERNON J	LTC	0-0299354	0962	3
ANDERSON VERNON T	COL	0-0263880	1046	2

NAME	GRADE	SVC NO	DATE RET MO YR	RET CODE
ANDERSON VICTOR F	LTC	0-0357896	0366	1
ANDERSON WADE M	2LT	0-0364079	0543	2
ANDERSON WALLACE G	MAJ	0-0255892	1045	2
ANDERSON WALLACE W	1LT	0-0536621	1045	2
ANDERSON WALLACE W	1LT	0-1173532	0946	2
ANDERSON WALTER A	MAJ	0-0192614	1047	1
ANDERSON WALTER A	LTC	0-0367614	0565	3
ANDERSON WALTER C	CPT	0-0421964	0644	2
ANDERSON WALTER L	B G	0-0232594	1053	3
ANDERSON WALTER R	CW2	W-2101017	0250	1
ANDERSON WALTER W	COL	0-0304113	1264	3
ANDERSON WENDELL B	LTC	0-0379666	0547	2
ANDERSON WESLEY H	CW3	W-2148427	0862	1
ANDERSON WILBERT O	CPT	0-1291212	1060	1
ANDERSON WILLARD	LTC	0-0339701	0767	1
ANDERSON WILLIAM A	MAJ	0-1288672	0860	1
ANDERSON WILLIAM A	MAJ	0-1798104	1060	1
ANDERSON WILLIAM A	WO1	W-2134503	0448	1
ANDERSON WILLIAM B	LTC	0-0150299	0546	2
ANDERSON WILLIAM B	MAJ	0-1573702	0954	1
ANDERSON WILLIAM C	CPT	0-1103037	0863	1
ANDERSON WILLIAM C	CPT	0-1173533	0545	2
ANDERSON WILLIAM D	COL	0-0321936	0666	3
ANDERSON WILLIAM D	LTC	0-1642202	1066	1
ANDERSON WILLIAM E	COL	0-0124534	1054	3
ANDERSON WILLIAM E	LTC	0-1109789	0862	1
ANDERSON WILLIAM F	LTC	0-0506628	0657	1
ANDERSON WILLIAM H	LTC	0-1283188	0963	1
ANDERSON WILLIAM H	2LT	0-1303445	0345	2
ANDERSON WILLIAM H	CPT	0-1689884	0446	2
ANDERSON WILLIAM J	LTC	0-0462546	0768	1
ANDERSON WILLIAM J	MAJ	0-1289530	0662	1
ANDERSON WILLIAM L	LTC	0-1580027	0962	1
ANDERSON WILLIAM L	MAJ	0-1694233	0645	2
ANDERSON WILLIAM M	1LT	0-0315514	0846	2
ANDERSON WILLIAM N	COL	0-0261892	0468	3
ANDERSON ZANE L	MAJ	0-1010412	0758	2
ANDES ERNEST W	COL	0-0166248	0648	3
ANDES JAMES O	COL	0-0224859	1159	3
ANDES MARCELINO	1LT	0-1896882	0655	2
ANDIE JOHN R	MAJ	0-0223681	0564	3
ANDING GILBERT	CPT	0-1299567	0447	1
ANDO TOMOMI	MAJ	0-0957167	0867	1
ANDORA JUAN P	1LT	0-0890442	1048	1
ANDRAE ARTHUR C	LTC	0-0390239	0968	3
ANDRAE WILLIAM E	LTC	0-1685005	0567	1
ANDRAIN MILTON D	LTC	0-0224932	1159	3
ANDRAKE JOHN	LTC	0-1947628	0766	1
ANDRAKE JOHN C	LTC	0-0150449	0454	3
ANDRASIK JOSEPH JR	LTC	0-0374307	0764	1
ANDRE DAVID L	LTC	0-0409994	0663	1
ANDRE EARL P	CW3	W-2203372	0763	1
ANDRE HARVEY M	MAJ	0-1687310	0546	2
ANDRE ROBERT J	MAJ	0-2011787	0163	1
ANDRE ROY D	LTC	0-0317561	0959	3
ANDRE WILLIAM M	CPT	0-0470919	0944	2
ANDREAS JOSEPH	LTC	0-1583887	0461	1
ANDREAS STEPHEN G	LTC	0-1301762	1262	1
ANDREASON NORMAN M	CPT	0-0278865	0857	3
ANDREASSEN EINAR C	COL	0-0266556	0152	3
ANDREE RICHARD J	CW2	W-2211821	0167	1
ANDREEN CARL O	LTC	0-0418786	1265	1
ANDREEN RUTH H	MAJ	N-0736826	1061	1
ANDREN KARL A	CPT	0-0338691	1045	2
ANDREOLI LOUIS	CW2	W-2142800	1052	2
ANDRES EDWARD J	MAJ	0-2288507	0767	1
ANDRESANO ROCCO J	CPT	0-1535120	0845	2
ANDRESEN ROSEMARY A	CPT	N-0771399	1047	1
ANDRESON WILLIAM H	2LT	0-1013988	1045	2
ANDRESS JESSE	MAJ	0-0501249	0157	2
ANDREUS FRANK C	CPT	0-0314477	0944	2
ANDREW FRED W	1LT	0-1340613	0449	2
ANDREW JOE C	CW4	W-2145948	0568	1
ANDREW WILLIAM JR	WO1	W-2142747	0356	1
ANDREWS ALFRED C	LTC	0-0344645	0347	2

NAME	GRADE	SVC NO	DATE RET MO YR	RET CODE
ANDREWS ARTHUR D	LTC	0-1171433	0367	1
ANDREWS AVANEAL E	2LT	N-0734122	1043	1
ANDREWS BENJAMIN D	CW2	W-2144983	0559	1
ANDREWS BILL L	LTC	0-0247307	0863	3
ANDREWS CARL W	CPT	0-1824555	1157	1
ANDREWS CHARLES	MAJ	0-1640189	0854	1
ANDREWS CHARLES F	CPT	0-0484764	1158	2
ANDREWS CHARLES H	COL	0-0185560	0859	1
ANDREWS CHARLES L	MAJ	0-0979156	0563	1
ANDREWS CLIFFORD T	LTC	0-0496860	0356	1
ANDREWS CLYDE L	CW3	W-2144899	0264	1
ANDREWS D LEE	CPT	0-0190307	0244	2
ANDREWS EARLE E	CPT	0-0124220	0749	3
ANDREWS ELMER	LTC	0-0241243	0764	3
ANDREWS EVERETT G	LTC	0-0530568	0763	1
ANDREWS FABIAN R	MAJ	0-1002571	0861	2
ANDREWS FLOYD S	LTC	0-0202451	0558	3
ANDREWS FRANCIS F	CW3	W-2148586	0962	1
ANDREWS FRANCIS J	COL	0-0162791	0265	3
ANDREWS FRED F	MAJ	0-0404032	1046	2
ANDREWS GEORGE A JR	CW2	W-2206320	1163	1
ANDREWS GEORGE C	MAJ	0-1306529	0161	1
ANDREWS GEORGE T	LTC	0-0260305	0668	3
ANDREWS GORDON G	LTC	0-1284262	0561	1
ANDREWS GRAHAM H	CPT	0-1341932	0959	1
ANDREWS HAL J	COL	0-0909716	0167	3
ANDREWS HARRY S	CW4	W-2002817	0658	3
ANDREWS HAYWARD	MAJ	0-0339114	0646	2
ANDREWS HERBERT G JR	2LT	0-1541660	0246	2
ANDREWS HUBERT L	CPT	0-0450220	1054	1
ANDREWS HUBERT T	MAJ	0-0234540	1052	3
ANDREWS HUNTER C	MAJ	0-2036419	0455	1
ANDREWS JACK B	LTC	0-1542905	0967	1
ANDREWS JACK E	LTC	0-1824394	0163	1
ANDREWS JACK R	LTC	0-1944861	0964	1
ANDREWS JAMES	COL	0-0163896	0256	3
ANDREWS JAMES C	LTC	0-0171131	0157	3
ANDREWS JAMES M JR	LTC	0-0974955	0962	1
ANDREWS JAMES W	COL	0-0209387	0456	3
ANDREWS JOHN C	CPT	0-0554715	0747	2
ANDREWS JOHN J	MAJ	0-1308445	0761	1
ANDREWS JOHN N	B G	0-0150451	0356	3
ANDREWS JON F	MAJ	0-1556367	1061	1
ANDREWS JOSEPH V	2LT	0-1169413	0145	2
ANDREWS LEWIE M	CW3	W-2152817	0468	1
ANDREWS LEWIS F	CW4	W-2142092	0166	1
ANDREWS LOMAX	MAJ	0-1321393	0661	1
ANDREWS LUTHER B	CPT	0-1173143	1059	1
ANDREWS MARTIN D JR	2LT	0-0479084	0245	2
ANDREWS MICHAEL F	CPT	0-0353802	0652	1
ANDREWS MILES S	CPT	0-0257381	0168	3
ANDREWS PATRICK H	MAJ	0-0347262	1163	1
ANDREWS RALPH C	LTC	0-1821528	0664	1
ANDREWS ROBERT F	MAJ	0-2025363	0965	1
ANDREWS ROBERT H	1LT	0-1165223	0144	2
ANDREWS ROBERT K	COL	0-0347874	1065	3
ANDREWS ROBERT O	CW2	W-2211964	0946	1
ANDREWS ROBERT P	LTC	0-1030637	0261	2
ANDREWS ROBERT S	CW4	W-2152291	1057	1
ANDREWS SAMUEL M	1LT	0-1051467	1147	2
ANDREWS SYDNEY P	CW2	W-2151395	0962	1
ANDREWS TALCOTT D	LTC	0-0545445	0167	1
ANDREWS TEDFORD G	CPT	0-0284200	1064	3
ANDREWS THOMAS L	LTC	0-2262930	1068	1
ANDREWS WALTER F	LTC	0-0388990	0860	2
ANDREWS WARD B	1LT	0-1284263	0145	2
ANDREWS WILLIAM C	LTC	0-1041704	0457	1
ANDREWS WILLIAM H	LTC	0-1688556	1168	2
ANDREWS WILLIAM M	CW2	W-2101241	1046	2
ANDREWS WILSON E	LTC	0-0372890	0867	1
ANDREWSEN WALTER D	LTC	0-1102603	0561	1
ANDRIDGE RICHARD S	1LT	0-1174211	0845	2
ANDRIST HARLAND F	LTC	0-1580577	0267	1
ANDROSKI WILLIAM A	CPT	0-1283893	0446	2
ANDROSKO FRANK J	MAJ	0-1300254	0159	1

NAME	GRADE	SVC NO	DATE RET MO YR	RET CODE
ANDRULONIS VICTOR J	CW2	W-2110429	0855	1
ANDRUS CHARLES H	COL	0-0463490	0850	2
ANDRUS CLINTON F	CW2	W-2143857	0458	2
ANDRUS EDWARD O	LTC	0-0289731	0160	1
ANDRUSS WALTER E	LTC	0-0425227	0561	1
ANDRZEJEWSKI HENRY R	MAJ	0-0819081	0464	2
ANESI RICHARD A	1LT	0-1179004	0659	1
ANESTOS TASH P	LTC	0-0384014	0461	1
ANETRINI VALENTINO	CW2	W-2211990	0468	1
ANGEL FRED D	LTC	0-1171434	0867	1
ANGEL NICHOLAS C	MAJ	0-1100387	0746	2
ANGEL NORMAN B	CPT	0-1919100	1262	1
ANGELES GODOFREDO	COL	0-1897082	0267	1
ANGELI ORLANDO JR	CW3	W-2129732	0461	1
ANGELICH MARY E	MAJ	N-0773782	0864	1
ANGELIDES NICHOLAS	LTC	0-0383361	0360	1
ANGELILLIS PAUL	CPT	0-0264178	0458	3
ANGELL LESTER W	LTC	0-0972548	0866	3
ANGELL THEODORE F	LTC	0-0196149	0861	3
ANGELO ARTIE L	MAJ	0-0957249	1264	1
ANGELO EDWARD	CW2	W-2119910	0346	2
ANGELO MICHAEL D	CPT	0-2020510	1058	1
ANGELO WALTER L	MAJ	0-0232083	0646	2
ANGELOFF ELIA	MAJ	0-0970053	0565	1
ANGELOFF WILLIAM	CW2	W-2149374	0659	2
ANGER ROBERT T	LTC	0-1585444	1263	1
ANGERMAN CLYDE W	LTC	0-1541441	0866	1
ANGEVINE WENDELL E	LTC	0-1951598	0368	1
ANGLAND THOMAS A	CPT	0-0494995	0945	2
ANGLE DON L	MAJ	0-1003924	0358	1
ANGLE RAYMOND O	LTC	0-0386570	0265	3
ANGLEMAN LOUIS W	LTC	0-1587813	0862	2
ANGLEMYER JAMES L	LTC	0-1633272	0363	1
ANGLETON JAMES H	LTC	0-0117023	0246	2
ANGLEY ROLAND C	CW3	W-2151782	0162	1
ANGLIM EDWARD M	CPT	0-0397088	0746	2
ANGLIN WILLIAM H	MAJ	0-0939698	0763	1
ANGONE ANTHONY C	MAJ	0-1937823	0366	1
ANGSTADT RAYMOND W	CPT	0-1100422	0851	1
ANGSTREICH HERBERT S	CPT	0-0452260	0445	2
ANGUS ALEXANDER	LTC	0-0439478	0954	1
ANGUS HERSHEL E	LTC	0-0336109	0967	3
ANHALT HOWARD A	CPT	0-1104710	0446	2
ANJO OLIVER H	MAJ	0-2210027	0564	1
ANKELEIN WILLIAM J	MAJ	0-0286685	0344	2
ANKER HARRY	CPT	0-0493403	1144	2
ANKNEY GEORGE R	1LT	0-1111763	0147	2
ANKNEY ROBERT D	1LT	0-2085592	0452	2
ANKRUM HOMER R	LTC	0-1691731	0164	1
ANLOFF GARRY J JR	LTC	0-0269779	0360	1
ANNAS HOWARD G	COL	0-0333220	0358	1
ANNEN EDWIN H	CW2	W-3150606	0367	1
ANNESE JOSEPH J	CPT	0-1715112	0448	2
ANNINOS JOHN P	LTC	0-0506902	0263	1
ANNIS ORAL J	CW4	W-2122937	0167	2
ANNONI ALBERT E	WO1	W-2148873	0154	1
ANSBRO FRANCIS	CPT	0-0306792	1148	1
ANSCHICKS LOUISE M	CPT	N-0701940	0746	1
ANSEAUME CHARLES R	CPT	0-0953762	0559	1
ANSEL BOE G	LTC	0-0323350	0664	1
ANSELL LAWRENCE S	2LT	0-2201149	0952	2
ANSELMO PETER	MAJ	0-0493873	0648	1
ANSKE LEANDER H	LTC	0-0407509	1160	1
ANSLEY JOSIAH C	LTC	0-0280691	1266	3
ANSLEY OSCAR L	1LT	0-1035639	1045	2
ANSLEY WILLIAM T	LTC	0-1540658	0361	1
ANSLOAN GEORGE E	MAJ	0-1335875	0361	1
ANSLOW RALPH J	CPT	0-1822659	1148	2
ANSPACH HARRY S	2LT	0-2015013	0653	1
ANSPACH RAYMOND L	MAJ	0-0438272	0250	1
ANSPON ALWIN W	CPT	0-0299494	1044	2
ANSTED DAVID T	CPT	0-0310134	0458	1
ANSWINI RITA L	MAJ	N-0759864	0166	1
ANTAL FRANCIS R	CW2	W-3430410	0768	1
ANTANG ALFED O	1LT	0-1896628	0561	1

NAME	GRADE	SVC NO	DATE RET MO YR	RET CODE
ANTE SALVADOR P	CPT	0-1896768	0158	1
ANTELL GUNNARD J	CPT	0-0511948	0447	2
ANTELL HENRIK	COL	0-0166599	1055	3
ANTENUCCI MARIO M	LTC	0-0324609	0563	3
ANTES DONALD E	COL	0-0227497	1164	3
ANTHONY ALBERT J	LTC	0-0171997	1054	3
ANTHONY DELPHINE M	2LT	N-0760423	0745	1
ANTHONY EUGENE H	MAJ	0-0373425	0147	2
ANTHONY FLOYD L	LTC	0-0271861	1266	3
ANTHONY FRED M	CW2	W-2101387	0446	2
ANTHONY GEORGE L	CW4	W-2112238	1057	1
ANTHONY HAROLD H	1LT	0-1179766	0258	1
ANTHONY HENRY D	MAJ	0-0269490	0668	3
ANTHONY HENRY S JR	1LT	0-0436179	0445	2
ANTHONY HERBERT L	LTC	0-1688750	0468	2
ANTHONY JAMES C	COL	0-0213910	0563	3
ANTHONY JAMES T	1LT	0-1287116	1043	2
ANTHONY JOSEPH G	1LT	0-1048272	0744	2
ANTHONY KELLY R	LTC	0-1546081	1062	2
ANTHONY MICHAEL L	1LT	0-1309199	0445	2
ANTHONY PERRY E	WO1	W-2143670	0853	1
ANTHONY RALPH W	MAJ	0-2020375	0361	1
ANTHONY ROBERT B	LTC	0-0359534	0367	3
ANTHONY TAYLOR C	LTC	0-0449178	0965	1
ANTHONY THOMAS C JR	MAJ	0-0306667	0744	2
ANTHONY THOMAS E	LTC	0-0291263	0768	3
ANTHONY VICTOR A	LTC	0-1036720	0562	1
ANTHONY WILLIAM H	LTC	0-1171372	1066	1
ANTHONY WILLIAM W	MAJ	0-2263655	0265	1
ANTIGNAT RAYMOND F	MAJ	0-1591573	0163	1
ANTOINETTE JOHN L	CW2	W-2210883	0666	1
ANTOL LOUIS JR	COL	0-0343170	0466	1
ANTOLINE SAMUEL	CPT	0-0181640	1060	3
ANTON GEORGE F	MAJ	0-0196927	0652	3
ANTON MICHAEL C	MAJ	0-0397522	0846	2
ANTON PHILIP A	CPT	0-0509975	0347	1
ANTONACCI-MICHAEL H	LTC	0-0254879	0862	3
ANTONAKOS T	MAJ	0-0331530	0745	2
ANTONCHICK JOHN	LTC	0-0355354	0947	2
ANTONELLI ROBERT J	LTC	0-0396191	0448	2
ANTONITIS JOSEPH J	2LT	0-0453129	0544	2
ANTONSEN STANLEY P	MAJ	0-1542496	1266	1
ANTONUCCI JOSEPH A	1LT	0-1303518	1144	2
ANUSKEWICZ WILLIAM J	COL	0-0275425	0368	3
ANZALONE ANTHONY V	LTC	0-1575683	0859	1
ANZELMO SAM S	LTC	0-1596570	0263	1
APABLASA SALVADOR C	LTC	0-0269780	0865	3
APEL ARNO M	MAJ	0-1876457	1066	1
APFFEL CORNELIUS	LTC	0-0378906	0166	3
APGAR HARRY E JR	LTC	0-1283894	0164	1
APGAR JOHN A	CW4	W-2142215	0559	1
APGAR STERLING E	COL	0-0505443	0246	2
APLER JOHN H	WO1	W-2119635	0150	1
APOLLONY JOHN C	LTC	0-1638927	0862	1
APONE DOMINICK P	MAJ	0-1947899	1262	1
APONTE ALFREDO	CPT	0-0252437	1061	3
APONTE FRANCISCO	2LT	0-1799683	0865	2
APOSTOLON GEORGE	CW2	W-2150039	0263	1
APOSTOLOS TIMOTHY	2LT	0-0922786	0145	2
APPEL HENRY	COL	0-0241378	0166	3
APPEL HENRY F	CW4	W-2117536	0361	1
APPELGATE JOSEPH M	COL	0-0389918	0563	3
APPELL LEONARD A	CPT	0-1283534	1045	2
APPELMAN GUSTAVE B	COL	0-0146326	0649	3
APPIARIUS JOHN C	LTC	0-0221847	0754	3
APPIARIUS WALTER P	LTC	0-0221596	0761	3
APPLE CHARLES O	MAJ	0-0207019	1048	3
APPLE HARRY	LTC	0-1286416	0961	1
APPLE HOWARD D	CPT	0-0416065	1144	2
APPLE OSBORNE F	LTC	0-0353105	0361	1
APPLEBAUM LEON B	LTC	0-0272962	0867	3
APPLEBY ALVA S	CPT	0-0474389	0645	2
APPLEBY J JR	1LT	0-1555502	0446	2
APPLEGARTH A R JR	CPT	0-0346376	0146	2
APPLEGATE DANIEL W	LTC	0-0304166	0267	3

NAME	GRADE	SVC NO	DATE RET MO YR	RET CODE
APPLEGATE DELBERT P	LTC	0-1636934	0361	1
APPLEGATE EDNA H	2LT	N-0735280	0844	1
APPLEGATE JOHN	LTC	0-1280271	0160	1
APPLEGATE LINDSAY M	LTC	0-0208842	0459	1
APPLEGATE ROBERT W	CW2	W-2143859	0261	1
APPLEGATE RODNEY W	MAJ	0-1013706	0161	1
APPLEMAN RUSSELL E	LTC	0-0488692	1055	1
APPLER HAROLD M	1LT	0-0514295	1045	2
APPLETON F R JR	LTC	0-0142229	0648	3
APPLETON WILLIAM C	LTC	0-0378472	1062	1
APPLETON WILLIAM E	LTC	0-0195937	0462	3
APPLEWHITE AUSTIN H	MAJ	0-0488484	0447	2
APPLEWHITE WARREN G	MAJ	0-0554977	0463	1
APPLEYARD THOMAS J	CW2	W-3440112	0768	1
APPLING GRADY S	2LT	0-0152555	0456	3
APPLING HARRY D	MAJ	0-1289194	0464	2
APPLING ROBERT K	MAJ	0-1100858	0260	1
APPOLD DOROTHY M	1LT	N-0731422	0746	1
APRIL LEO M	1LT	0-1317866	1145	2
APRILL LIONEL J	1LT	0-1312396	0347	2
APT SAMUEL	LTC	0-0311153	1164	3
APTED CLARK H	COL	0-0182562	0754	3
APTER HARRY	CPT	0-0419536	0545	2
APTER LEONARD	MAJ	0-0682687	0363	1
AQUINO ANTONINO G	CPT	0-1640652	0661	3
AQUINO ENRIQUE J	CPT	0-1324126	0762	1
AQUINO JOSE S	1LT	0-1896405	1061	1
AQUINO RAYMUNDO	1LT	0-1896391	0659	1
ARAM SHIRLEY O	1LT	L-0502276	0645	2
ARANSON FLORENCE S	1LT	N-0755536	0847	1
ARANT FRANK S	LTC	0-0228723	0864	3
ARANT PHILIP W	LTC	0-1041497	1264	1
ARANT WILLIAMS E	CPT	0-0244819	0766	3
ARAUJO JUAN	LTC	0-0155649	1055	3
ARAUJO URBAN J	CW3	W-2150693	1064	1
ARBOGAST EDWARD P	MAJ	0-1998433	0564	1
ARBOGAST JACK G	MAJ	0-0400148	0546	2
ARBOGAST LOUIS W	LTC	0-0464576	1059	3
ARBOGAST NORVILLE E	1LT	0-0524623	1045	2
ARBOUR LOUIS P	CW3	W-2103848	0160	1
ARBUCKLE ALEXANDER	COL	0-0213710	0162	3
ARBUCKLE ERNEST V	MAJ	0-0131522	0352	3
ARBUCKLE HOWARD B JR	COL	0-0248318	0566	3
ARBURDA JOSEPH M	LTC	0-0104230	0155	3
ARBURY HOWARD H	B G	0-0255103	0966	3
ARBUTHNOT WILLIAM B	MAJ	0-0238577	0366	3
ARCANA PETER S	LTC	0-1041077	0461	1
ARCAY LUIS	CPT	0-0203296	0849	1
ARCENEAUX CLESMAY J	CPT	0-0260604	1164	3
ARCENEAUX MILTON J	CW3	W-2145955	0962	1
ARCHAMBAULT JACK C	LTC	0-0395310	0457	1
ARCHAMBEAU GRANT E	1LT	0-1822763	0646	2
ARCHER BRUCE F JR	MAJ	0-1556238	0162	1
ARCHER GAYLEN	MAJ	0-1553022	1265	2
ARCHER HARRY D	CPT	0-0416188	0748	2
ARCHER HARRY E	MAJ	0-0957692	0866	1
ARCHER HOWARD L	COL	0-0174552	0854	3
ARCHER HOWARD L	1LT	0-0407567	0446	2
ARCHER JAMES B	CPT	0-1822092	0360	1
ARCHER RALPH J	MAJ	0-0585012	1062	1
ARCHER RICHARD F JR	MAJ	0-1826036	0464	1
ARCHER ROBERT B	CPT	0-0197253	1162	3
ARCHER ROBERT C	MAJ	0-0348919	0256	2
ARCHER ROY J	LTC	0-1587814	0962	1
ARCHER VERNON W	CPT	0-1114829	0765	1
ARCHER WILLIAM W JR	MAJ	0-0180641	0762	3
ARCHIBALD GEORGE H	LTC	0-1634073	0864	1
ARCHIBALD RAY F	LTC	0-0358060	0568	3
ARCHIBALD ROBERT J	LTC	0-0384421	0557	1
ARCHIBALD THOMAS R	COL	0-0159940	0546	2
ARCHULETA JAMES M	CPT	0-2210030	0967	1
ARCINO FRANCISCO	CPT	0-1896629	0360	2
ARCISZ JOSEPH J	1LT	0-1048273	1144	2
ARCULEER JOHN H	LTC	0-1822926	1163	1
ARD MYRTLE E	1LT	N-0752967	0953	2

332-811 O - 69 - 6

NAME	GRADE	SVC NO	DATE RET MO YR	RET CODE
ARDILL FRANCES E	MAJ	N-0728254	0668	3
ARDISON ROBERT J	MAJ	O-0294309	0952	2
ARDUSER HELEN M	LTC	M-0010097	0368	1
AREIAS RACHEL F	1LT	N-0783343	0746	1
ARELLANO ARSENIO Y	LTC	O-1301594	0766	3
ARELLANO JACOB	CW3	W-2209165	0968	1
ARENA ARTHUR A	LTC	O-1575686	0262	2
ARENA JOHN W	CW2	W-2145542	1265	1
ARENAS FELIPE G	2LT	O-1896354	1150	2
ARENDS G WILLIAM	CPT	O-1821306	1046	2
ARENDS JESSE E M	LTC	O-1557406	0668	3
ARENGO RAFAEL A	CPT	O-1896760	0859	1
ARENSON ARTHUR N	LTC	O-0382172	1064	3
ARENZ ARNOLD H F	LTC	O-1330617	0665	1
ARENZ ARTHUR H	COL	O-0242530	0457	1
ARENZ MARK B	1LT	O-2031856	0448	2
ARFORD CARROLL W	LTC	O-0284439	0565	3
ARGETSINGER DICK W	LTC	O-1105966	1262	1
ARGETSINGER L W JR	LTC	O-0207354	0650	3
ARGILLA JOSEPH	COL	O-0265836	0346	2
ARGO CLYDE R	MAJ	O-1173144	0161	1
ARGO ROBERT	LTC	O-0248853	0566	3
ARGUE ALEXANDER JR	MAJ	O-0474212	0657	2
ARGUE ANSON J	LTC	O-0324409	0660	1
ARGUE HORACE R	MAJ	O-0302816	0567	3
ARGYRIS CHRIS A	CPT	O-1290181	0445	2
ARIAIL DAVID W	COL	O-0316647	0864	1
ARIAS ARMANDO	MAJ	O-1324386	0963	1
ARIENS MONROE J	MAJ	O-0331390	0962	1
ARIETA ROBERT J	CW3	W-3350139	0668	1
ARIOLA DOMINIC S	CPT	O-0496054	0446	2
ARIS DEMETRIADE	1LT	O-0475153	1044	2
ARKET WILLIAM F	CW4	RW-2124466	1164	1
ARKIN MORRIS	1LT	O-1640674	0845	2
ARKUS ELLIS	COL	O-0279815	0561	1
ARLAUD CARL F	LTC	O-0404436	0861	1
ARLEDGE ELZEY J	CW3	W-2103850	0160	1
ARLEIN MYRON S	MAJ	O-0369004	0845	2
ARMAGOST PETER H	LTC	O-1171436	0367	1
ARMAN ROBERT C	CPT	O-1297475	0854	2
ARMAND JOSEPH J	CPT	O-0495738	1051	1
ARMANDO MICHAEL	CW2	W-2149495	0359	1
ARMANN LOUIS L	CPT	O-0480088	0145	2
ARMBRECHT LOUIS B	MAJ	O-0223440	0954	3
ARMBRUSTER WILLIAM M	CPT	O-0265699	1155	3
ARMELLINO JOHN R	MAJ	O-0442775	1046	2
ARMENTROUT CARL D	LTC	O-1298012	1165	2
ARMENTROUT W W	CPT	O-1000199	0346	2
ARMER ALVIN L	CPT	O-0400574	0145	2
ARMIGER JESSE I	CW3	W-2148364	0664	1
ARMIJO FRANCIS C	CPT	O-0982002	1060	1
ARMIJO RICHARD A	CW2	W-2149898	0266	1
ARMINGTON ROBERT L	CPT	O-0447659	0146	2
ARMINTROUT FOREST C	CPT	O-1821530	0654	1
ARMISTEAD BEVERLY A	COL	O-0230440	0365	3
ARMISTEAD GRADY B JR	1LT	O-5241913	0268	2
ARMISTEAD WIRT M JR	COL	O-0203469	0863	3
ARMITAGE SAMUEL P	CPT	O-1175924	0868	3
ARMON AARON H	CPT	O-0136902	0648	3
ARMON THEODORE	CW2	W-2143524	0559	1
ARMOUR JOSEPH C	LTC	O-2002074	0762	1
ARMOUR PHIL B	LTC	O-1559290	1165	1
ARMOUR RICHARD W	COL	O-0244378	0866	3
ARMSTEAD JAMES H	WO1	W-2149659	0460	1
ARMSTRONG ALBERT B	LTC	O-2033728	0868	1
ARMSTRONG ALBERT E	LTC	O-0120418	0854	3
ARMSTRONG ANDREW C	CPT	O-1101314	0962	1
ARMSTRONG BENNIE	LTC	O-1314358	0263	1
ARMSTRONG CHARLES T	CW4	W-2142216	0559	2
ARMSTRONG CHARLES W	MAJ	O-0239453	0765	3
ARMSTRONG DOUGLAS A	CPT	O-1336025	0763	1
ARMSTRONG EARL F	LTC	O-0250740	0156	3
ARMSTRONG EDMOND G	MAJ	O-0378481	0561	2
ARMSTRONG EDWIN K	1LT	O-1057667	1046	2
ARMSTRONG EDWIN W	LTC	O-0249774	1154	3
ARMSTRONG ELMER S	COL	O-0108028	0754	3
ARMSTRONG EMMET E	LTC	O-0217630	0856	3
ARMSTRONG EUGENE A	LTC	O-1578118	1060	1
ARMSTRONG FORREST R	COL	O-0301255	1159	1
ARMSTRONG FRED W	CPT	O-1596251	0159	2
ARMSTRONG GEORGE A	MAJ	O-1948387	1263	1
ARMSTRONG GEORGE E	LTC	O-0065598	0368	2
ARMSTRONG GEORGE J	MAJ	O-0284579	0953	2
ARMSTRONG GEORGE W	2LT	O-1016714	0944	2
ARMSTRONG HAROLD E	CPT	O-0450221	1264	1
ARMSTRONG HENRY P	LTC	O-0268629	0852	3
ARMSTRONG HERBERT L	COL	O-0161803	1052	2
ARMSTRONG HERBERT T	LTC	O-1030887	0762	1
ARMSTRONG JACK H	CPT	O-1935549	0966	1
ARMSTRONG JAMES B	CPT	O-1168156	0948	2
ARMSTRONG JAMES B	1LT	O-1323511	0446	2
ARMSTRONG JAMES F	COL	O-0184635	0257	3
ARMSTRONG JAMES F JR	LTC	O-0343935	0567	1
ARMSTRONG JAMES S	LTC	O-0267712	1067	3
ARMSTRONG JESSIE C	CPT	O-0200185	0558	1
ARMSTRONG JOHN E	MAJ	O-0229597	1262	3
ARMSTRONG JOHN H	MAJ	O-2039646	0661	1
ARMSTRONG JOHN O	MAJ	O-0311104	0668	3
ARMSTRONG JOHN R	MAJ	O-0242777	0465	3
ARMSTRONG JOSEPH E	LTC	O-1633318	0962	1
ARMSTRONG JOSEPH R	MAJ	O-1946428	0256	1
ARMSTRONG KENNETH L	MAJ	O-0311362	0540	2
ARMSTRONG KENNETH W	MAJ	O-1941500	1266	1
ARMSTRONG LEE ROY W	COL	O-0966576	0664	3
ARMSTRONG LEROY JR	CPT	O-1111819	0362	2
ARMSTRONG LESLIE R	LTC	O-0289600	0164	3
ARMSTRONG LUTHER L	CPT	O-0509406	0653	1
ARMSTRONG MICHAEL A	LTC	O-0266118	0262	3
ARMSTRONG MICHAEL E	MAJ	O-2017797	0662	1
ARMSTRONG NOAH	MAJ	O-1285873	1060	1
ARMSTRONG NOEL	2LT	O-1170627	0843	2
ARMSTRONG NORMAN H	CPT	O-1050162	0846	2
ARMSTRONG R M JR	CPT	O-1061084	0555	2
ARMSTRONG RALPH A	LTC	O-0115063	0356	3
ARMSTRONG RALPH N	LTC	O-1280519	0261	1
ARMSTRONG RAYMOND E	CPT	O-0183276	0254	3
ARMSTRONG RAYMOND I	CPT	O-1287644	0345	2
ARMSTRONG RICHARD C	1LT	O-1924937	0353	2
ARMSTRONG ROBERT A	COL	O-0271843	1068	3
ARMSTRONG ROBERT J	CW3	W-2203278	0365	1
ARMSTRONG ROBERT L	CW2	W-2211425	0966	1
ARMSTRONG ROBERT N	CW2	W-2149146	0959	1
ARMSTRONG ROBERT R	LTC	O-1314359	0763	1
ARMSTRONG ROLLIN S	LTC	O-0272101	0445	2
ARMSTRONG RUTH E	1LT	N-0768161	0146	1
ARMSTRONG THOMAS R	MAJ	O-2015807	1060	1
ARMSTRONG WILLIAM D	1LT	O-1176539	1145	2
ARMSTRONG WILLIAM H	MAJ	O-2026890	0157	1
ARMSTRONG WILLIAM T	LTC	O-0518046	0967	3
ARMUS HARRY P	LTC	O-1573998	1067	3
ARNAU LOUIS J	CW2	W-2101063	0649	1
ARNBERG ROBERT A	MAJ	O-0958095	0868	1
ARNBRECHT ELMER F	COL	O-0228816	0658	1
ARNDT GEORGE W	CW4	W-2104954	1056	1
ARNDT PAUL JR	MAJ	O-0300780	0847	1
ARNDT THEODORE A	B G	O-0257062	1163	3
ARNEBERG JOHN R	MAJ	O-0996961	0767	1
ARNER ERNEST S	1LT	O-1053457	0546	2
ARNER WELDON C	1LT	O-1307492	1045	2
ARNERT CARL M	WO1	W-2144091	0852	2
ARNESON CHARLES W	1LT	O-1326066	1145	2
ARNESON PAUL E	COL	O-0267916	1166	3
ARNEST HOWARD L	CPT	O-0455092	1148	2
ARNETT CLYDE E	LTC	O-0373613	0866	1
ARNETT HAROLD I	CPT	O-0154727	1053	3
ARNETT MARION L	MAJ	O-0966307	0663	1
ARNETT NOBLE L	MAJ	O-0397002	0346	2
ARNETT WILLIAM T	LTC	O-0248399	1065	3
ARNETTE RICHARD W	CW3	W-2141121	0453	1
ARNHOLD WILLIAM J	CW3	W-2151134	0365	2
ARNHOLS DANIEL	LTC	O-1280881	1061	1
ARNIM VICTOR T	MAJ	O-0216725	0663	3
ARNN EDWARD T	CPT	O-0466092	1046	2
ARNN ISAAC I	1LT	O-0925569	0445	2
ARNOLD BENJAMIN W	LTC	O-0246877	0948	3
ARNOLD BILLY B	CW2	W-2212891	0968	1
ARNOLD CARL D	LTC	O-1036830	0261	1
ARNOLD CAROL E	CW3	W-2144900	0166	1
ARNOLD CHARLES E	LTC	O-1289674	1052	1
ARNOLD CHARLES F	LTC	O-0319265	1060	1
ARNOLD CHARLES J	LTC	O-1549422	0861	1
ARNOLD CHARLES W	CPT	O-0405690	0361	1
ARNOLD CHARLEY D	MAJ	O-1557245	0848	2
ARNOLD CLARENCE W	CW3	W-2152111	0365	1
ARNOLD CLEATIS A	CPT	O-2042971	0958	1
ARNOLD CLIFFORD F	LTC	O-0206145	0962	3
ARNOLD DAVID S	LTC	O-0442432	0562	1
ARNOLD DOUGLAS W	MAJ	O-0943008	0561	1
ARNOLD DOZIER P	LTC	O-1038216	0567	1
ARNOLD EDWARD P	COL	O-0293833	0265	1
ARNOLD EDWIN P	LTC	O-0383974	0360	2
ARNOLD EDWIN W	CW2	W-2152598	0359	1
ARNOLD ELMER C	CPT	O-0376703	0246	2
ARNOLD EMMETT L	MAJ	O-0185972	1149	3
ARNOLD ERNEST J	MAJ	O-1683972	0757	1
ARNOLD EVERETT A	LTC	O-0213870	1163	3
ARNOLD FERRIS L	LTC	O-0210025	1045	2
ARNOLD FLOYD S	COL	O-0162283	0958	3
ARNOLD FRANK J	LTC	O-0405383	0960	2
ARNOLD FRANK R	CPT	O-0107734	1042	2
ARNOLD FRAZER	COL	O-0105732	0648	3
ARNOLD GEORGE A	LTC	O-0239017	0365	3
ARNOLD GILBERT C	COL	O-0229505	0565	3
ARNOLD GLEN I	MAJ	O-2015685	0559	1
ARNOLD GORDON L JR	1LT	O-1308448	1045	2
ARNOLD GRACE M	1LT	N-0741626	1045	1
ARNOLD HAROLD J	LTC	O-0439106	0848	1
ARNOLD HENRY C	CPT	O-2017170	0657	1
ARNOLD HORACE L	MAJ	O-0268438	0467	3
ARNOLD IGOR S	CPT	O-2026974	0554	2
ARNOLD JACK L	CW2	W-3430615	1168	1
ARNOLD JAMES G JR	LTC	O-1118856	0766	1
ARNOLD JAMES M	COL	O-0241348	0566	3
ARNOLD JAMES W	MAJ	O-0266356	0968	3
ARNOLD JOE M	LTC	O-1169844	0267	2
ARNOLD JOHN G JR	CPT	O-0368629	1044	2
ARNOLD JOHN T	1LT	O-1047858	0745	2
ARNOLD JOHN W	LTC	O-0118762	1059	3
ARNOLD JOHN W	CW4	W-2151202	0868	1
ARNOLD JOSEPH M	MAJ	O-0243722	0462	3
ARNOLD JULEAN JR	LTC	O-0343701	0246	2
ARNOLD JULIA M	MAJ	N-0798892	0266	1
ARNOLD LAWRENCE E	LTC	O-0359726	0860	1
ARNOLD LOY L	CW2	W-2215480	1067	1
ARNOLD LYDIA	MAJ	N-0742385	1164	3
ARNOLD OPAL H	2LT	N-0765375	0346	1
ARNOLD OTIS M	1LT	O-1283358	0945	2
ARNOLD PETER J	CPT	O-5325206	0168	2
ARNOLD RALPH L	CPT	O-0520081	0245	2
ARNOLD RAY	1LT	O-1318852	0147	2
ARNOLD RICHARD E	COL	O-0287996	0665	3
ARNOLD RICHARD L	1LT	O-1308289	1045	2
ARNOLD RICHARD L	CW2	W-2152841	0563	1
ARNOLD ROBERT H	LTC	O-1640722	1058	1
ARNOLD ROBERT J	LTC	O-1040339	0461	1
ARNOLD ROBERT L	CPT	O-1031365	0648	2
ARNOLD ROBERT S	MAJ	O-0980826	0567	1
ARNOLD STANLEY D	MAJ	O-0261006	1267	3
ARNOLD STEWART H	LTC	O-1558773	0765	1
ARNOLD TOM A	COL	O-0450027	1066	1
ARNOLD WALTER R	LTC	O-0370826	0267	3
ARNOLD WALTER T	1LT	O-1634042	0245	2
ARNOLD WILLARD D	LTC	O-0228629	0365	3
ARNOLD WILLIAM C	MAJ	O-0294429	0367	3
ARNOLD WILLIAM D	CW2	W-3430132	1066	1
ARNOLD WILLIAM M	MAJ	O-1636893	1057	1
ARNOLD WYATT A JR	LTC	O-2046364	1262	1
ARNOLDY ELVIN O	MAJ	O-2036494	0457	1
ARNONE FRANCIS A	CW2	W-2146650	0959	1
ARNONE LOUIS F	LTC	O-0338507	1264	3
ARNTZ CLARENCE A	MAJ	O-0325745	0545	2
ARON FRED W	LTC	O-1101195	1060	1
ARONOFF SOLOMON	1LT	O-1014912	0646	2
ARONS HARRY	CPT	O-1692216	0346	2
ARONS NATHAN	LTC	O-0439920	0849	1
ARONSON EARLE	COL	O-0234742	1165	3
ARONSON SAMUEL S	2LT	O-0439109	0945	2
AROWESTY JOHN	1LT	O-1179007	0746	2
ARPKE CALVIN A	CPT	O-0226514	0945	2
ARPKE ROBERT S	CPT	O-1171037	1146	2
ARPS MERVIN W JR	LTC	O-0557986	0965	1
ARRADAZA MAR G	1LT	O-1896902	1063	2
ARRANTS CLAIR L	MAJ	O-1310204	0661	1
ARRAS MARGUERITE	1LT	N-0794345	1047	1
ARREDONDO FERDINAND	LTC	O-0301960	0568	3
ARRIGO JOSEPH	LTC	O-1581492	0862	1
ARRIVAS SERAFIN B	1LT	O-1896973	1052	1
ARRONET HERBERT A	COL	O-0126892	0349	3
ARROWOOD RUFUS D	CW2	W-2149200	0858	1
ARROWSMITH GEORGE M	LTC	O-0232900	0648	3
ARROYAS JOHN G	CPT	O-1799563	0457	1
ARROYO ALFONSO S	CPT	O-0514895	0246	2
ARROYO AUGUSTO	MAJ	O-1315760	0257	1
ARROYO-SANCHEZ JOSE	CPT	O-1887867	0868	1
ARSENAULT JAMES E	CW2	W-2206138	1163	1
ARTAMONOFF GEORGE L	COL	O-0240754	0562	3
ARTANDI TIBOR	1LT	O-0927477	1045	2
ARTASERSE GEORGE V	CPT	O-1692121	0445	2
ARTELL STEPHEN S	CPT	O-2055145	1054	1
ARTER JOHN B	COL	O-0507812	1162	3
ARTER THEODORE	COL	O-0204909	1054	3
ARTHER HUGH	CW3	W-2146461	1059	1
ARTHIN SAMUEL H	CW3	W-2148099	0664	1
ARTHUR CARLTON M	CPT	O-0231287	0959	3
ARTHUR DANIEL B	MAJ	O-1296971	0362	2
ARTHUR DONALD J	CPT	O-1331132	0152	2
ARTHUR EDWARD J	1LT	O-0335920	1054	3
ARTHUR FREDERICK	MAJ	O-0411012	0565	1
ARTHUR HAROLD J	MAJ	O-0300762	0364	3
ARTHUR HARRY M	B G	O-0148758	1059	3
ARTHUR HENRY G	MAJ	O-1640183	0256	1
ARTHUR JACK	MAJ	O-0993070	0968	1
ARTHUR JOHN D	LTC	O-1323655	0962	1
ARTHUR PERRY M	CW3	W-2149827	0164	1
ARTHUR RALPH W	COL	O-0451070	0460	1
ARTHUR ROBERT C	LTC	O-0304808	0547	2
ARTHUR STEVE JR	1LT	O-1181629	0945	2
ARTHURS JOHN F JR	COL	O-0244224	0765	3
ARTICOLA VICTOR J	CPT	O-1001507	1059	1
ARTIS SAUL S	CPT	O-0432344	0245	2
ARTLEY MILTON J	1LT	O-0456329	0744	2
ARTMAN DONALD H	LTC	O-0926501	0965	3
ARTS JOSEPH B	LTC	O-0468061	1265	3
ARTZ NORMAN P	2LT	O-2055970	0753	1
ARVIDSON ROBERT R	MAJ	O-0497373	0557	1
ARVIN EDWARD B	MAJ	O-1323272	0463	1
ARWOOD FRANCIS M JR	LTC	O-0335120	0763	1
ASAI GEORGE N	MAJ	O-1335375	1264	1
ASAY FRANK F	2LT	O-2048833	0745	2
ASBELL DON C	LTC	O-1296972	1264	2
ASBELL ERNEST	MAJ	O-0265675	0447	2
ASBELL OSCAR O	MAJ	O-0269915	0468	3
ASBRIDGE ERNEST	MAJ	O-0450026	1151	1
ASBURY FRANCIS JR	MAJ	O-1035302	0168	3
ASBURY KEITH W	CW3	W-2209392	1068	1
ASBURY MARJORIE H	1LT	N-0755872	0845	1
ASBURY ROY W	MAJ	O-0464223	0647	1
ASBURY ROY W JR	MAJ	O-2005267	0764	1
ASCHE LEROY T	CPT	O-0132400	1048	3
ASCHWALD HOWARD B	MAJ	O-1334077	1161	1

NAME	GRADE	SVC NO	DATE RET MO YR	RET CODE
ASCOLI LAWRENCE	COL	0-0400104	0160	1
ASEL NORMAN D	1LT	0-0472163	1146	2
ASH DWIGHT A	1LT	0-1113047	1044	2
ASH EDWARD T	CW3	W-2122130	1060	1
ASH FRANCIS G	B G	0-0154915	1153	3
ASH HENRY P	LTC	0-0124408	0256	3
ASH JAMES H	MAJ	0-0965959	1161	1
ASH MAURICE L JR	LTC	0-0253561	0265	3
ASH ROBERT T JR	LTC	0-2055471	0768	1
ASHBACHER VERNON L	MAJ	0-1686273	0459	1
ASHBAUGH JAMES O	CW2	W-2152077	1055	1
ASHBRIDGE WHITNEY	COL	0-0229797	1264	3
ASHBY CARROLL A	CPT	0-1877126	0462	1
ASHBY CARROLL B	CPT	0-0349498	0446	2
ASHBY DANIEL M	CW2	W-2210908	0867	1
ASHBY FRANK G	LTC	0-0419031	0865	1
ASHBY JESSE W	2LT	0-0400322	0445	2
ASHBY MILTON L	CW3	W-2145003	1062	2
ASHBY RICHARD C	LTC	0-1319160	1064	1
ASHBY ROBERT K	LTC	0-1011259	0364	1
ASHCRAFT RAYMOND J	CW4	W-2120699	1154	1
ASHCRAFT ROY L JR	1LT	0-1293518	0844	2
ASHDOWN SAMUEL G	COL	0-0361016	0257	1
ASHE JOHN R	MAJ	0-0371171	0868	3
ASHE JOSEPH P	CW2	W-2102617	1043	2
ASHE RICHARD B	COL	0-0103173	0356	3
ASHE SILAS M P	1LT	0-0444258	1044	2
ASHELFORD RUTH A	MAJ	N-0774237	0165	1
ASHER CARL A	CPT	0-0483690	1046	2
ASHER JEFFERSON JR	1LT	0-1047429	0448	2
ASHER JOHN T	MAJ	0-1288675	1060	1
ASHER JOHN W	1LT	0-0403270	0446	2
ASHERMAN DAVID G	MAJ	0-0454550	0548	2
ASHEY CLARENCE O	1LT	0-0493016	0561	1
ASHFORD EARNEST B	1LT	0-0358574	0347	2
ASHFORD ELLIOTT F	MAJ	0-0490168	0157	1
ASHLEY ALVIN F	LTC	0-2263731	0868	1
ASHLEY CARL E	MAJ	0-0961542	0863	2
ASHLEY CHARLES M	COL	0-0352019	0563	1
ASHLEY FLOY L	CPT	0-0254907	0145	2
ASHLEY FRANCIS S	LTC	0-0249737	0565	3
ASHLEY GEORGE E	1LT	0-1321137	1045	2
ASHLEY HALLAR B	1LT	0-1327799	0147	2
ASHLEY HARLEY R	CW3	W-2148307	0765	1
ASHLEY IRA J	MAJ	0-4010375	0866	1
ASHLEY JERALD M	LTC	0-0150192	0648	3
ASHLEY JOE E	MAJ	0-0990107	0664	1
ASHLEY LEROY D	CW3	W-2147152	0964	1
ASHLEY MARK B	MAJ	0-0197611	0841	2
ASHLEY RAYMOND W	CW4	W-2135377	0760	1
ASHLEY ROBERT A	CPT	0-1948445	1055	1
ASHLEY SIDNEY J	1LT	0-0886904	0446	2
ASHLEY THOMAS D	MAJ	0-1823104	0762	1
ASHLEY WILLIAM F	MAJ	0-1696298	0963	1
ASHLOCK DONALD M	COL	0-0219043	0362	3
ASHMEAD ANITA H	MAJ	L-0300308	0263	1
ASHMORE CHARLES W	MAJ	0-0501755	0149	1
ASHMORE HUGIE	WO1	W-2141181	0552	2
ASHMORE PAUL R	CPT	0-1019312	0961	1
ASHMORE SHERMAN H	CPT	0-0396834	0947	2
ASHMORE SIDNEY A	MAJ	0-1173146	0755	1
ASHTON HAROLD D	MAJ	0-0124763	1044	2
ASHTON HERBERT H	MAJ	0-0275125	0957	3
ASHTON JEROME	MAJ	0-1102608	0859	1
ASHTON JOHN J	COL	0-0289203	0762	3
ASHTON MARY W	1LT	N-0734039	1047	1
ASHTON MERTON E	MAJ	0-0524555	1058	3
ASHTON STUART T	LTC	0-1171440	1168	1
ASHURST EMORY B	CW2	W-2211029	0164	1
ASHWORTH GEORGE F	COL	0-0336700	0668	3
ASHWORTH JAMES	MAJ	0-0225301	0957	3
ASHWORTH JAMES L	MAJ	0-2262342	0865	1
ASHWORTH JOHN A JR	CPT	0-0397186	0147	2
ASHWORTH KENT T	1LT	0-1950944	0558	1
ASHWORTH MAYNARD R	LTC	0-0146978	1044	2
ASHWORTH NORMAN H	LTC	0-0441651	0768	3
ASKER EARL H	CPT	0-0456013	1046	2
ASKEW HUGH	COL	0-0171198	0456	3
ASKEW JOE B	CW2	W-2111537	1145	2
ASKEW JOHN E	1LT	0-1011443	0846	2
ASKEW PORTER L	CPT	0-0886367	0448	2
ASKEW RALPH O SR	CPT	0-1823923	1162	1
ASKINS CHARLES M	1LT	0-1304994	0746	2
ASKINS JOHN K	1LT	0-1010684	1145	2
ASKINS LYNN O	MAJ	0-0811308	0767	1
ASLIN HARRY C	LTC	0-1056970	0468	1
ASLUND CHARLES B	2LT	0-1636938	0943	2
ASMAN HAROLD G	MAJ	0-0240888	0563	3
ASMAN HENRY B	MAJ	0-1685107	0146	2
ASMUS LEWIS O	LTC	0-0171725	0556	3
ASMUS LORAINE	1LT	0-1010747	0347	1
ASON STANLEY	COL	0-0528238	0963	3
ASP NOGI A	COL	0-0259856	1264	3
ASP STANLEY	MAJ	0-0109082	0649	3
ASPDEN WILLIAM U	LTC	0-1797414	1160	1
ASPINALL MURRAY C	LTC	0-0331827	0158	3
ASPIRAS JOHN O	CW2	W-2144056	0762	1
ASPNES GARNET S	LTC	0-0347187	0267	3
ASSEFF EMMETT G	2LT	0-1583760	1045	2
ASSELIN EDWARD O	MAJ	0-0262677	0346	2
ASSIRAN PHILIP J	CPT	0-1796018	1146	2
ASSMUS EDWARD A	LTC	0-1323897	0762	1
ASTBURY CHARLES	LTC	0-0277190	0161	3
ASTIN JOHN O	CW2	W-2146698	0454	2
ASTING NEIL J	LTC	0-0374852	0360	1
ASTLER DEWITT G	CPT	0-0499706	0645	2
ASTON LOUIE C	COL	0-0250276	1263	3
ASTOR HARRY W	LTC	0-1011412	0562	1
ASTRAB HARRY A	LTC	0-1172363	0662	1
ASTRUP MARK H	LTC	0-0430120	1261	3
ASUMA THOMAS V	CPT	0-2273272	0759	2
ATANASIO JOSEPH F	MAJ	0-0531738	0946	2
ATCHESON BELLFIELD	CPT	0-1684519	0245	2
ATCHINSON ARCHIE T	1LT	0-1574189	0552	1
ATCHISON ARTHUR L	LTC	0-0287096	0461	3
ATCHISON DICK E	CPT	0-1298783	0548	2
ATCHISON EDWARD R	LTC	0-0202437	0763	3
ATCHISON ELLIS C	LTC	0-1634942	1160	1
ATCHISON JAMES H	CPT	0-0487880	1046	1
ATEN FRANK N	CPT	0-1821553	0753	1
ATEN JAY B JR	1LT	0-1596253	0146	2
ATEN JOHN A	CPT	0-2017634	1059	1
ATEN LOUIS H	MAJ	0-0382739	0259	1
ATES ELLIS R	LTC	0-0400319	0663	1
ATHANASON NICHOLAS A	COL	0-0219847	0756	1
ATHAY ROLAND M JR	CPT	0-0451933	0246	2
ATHERTON DONALD H	LTC	0-0204726	0648	3
ATHERTON DONALD J	CW3	W-2142801	1160	1
ATHERTON JAMES P	CPT	0-0237840	0964	3
ATHERTON THOMAS H	COL	0-0179247	0648	3
ATHEY JAMES R	CPT	0-2028660	0263	1
ATHY GREGG B	MAJ	0-1700286	0546	2
ATILES-CRESPO RAFAEL	CPT	0-1924109	0863	1
ATKESON THOMAS Z	CPT	0-0370343	0845	2
ATKINS ADMIRAL	CW3	W-2139804	0156	1
ATKINS CHARLES B	LTC	0-0295716	0565	3
ATKINS CLIFFORD F	LTC	0-0481131	0167	1
ATKINS CLINTON O	CW3	W-2145570	0359	1
ATKINS FRANK A	LTC	0-0248509	0167	3
ATKINS HARROLD C	CPT	0-0337016	0564	3
ATKINS JOE F	CPT	0-0497968	0746	2
ATKINS JOHN C	1LT	0-2036877	0264	1
ATKINS JOHN E	CPT	0-0971213	0961	1
ATKINS JOHN L	COL	0-0243555	0766	3
ATKINS KENNETH W	1LT	0-1317364	1145	2
ATKINS LOIS P	2LT	N-0743664	0944	1
ATKINS LOUIS H	CPT	0-0982680	1062	1
ATKINS MONTIVILLE	LTC	0-1304325	0762	1
ATKINS NORMAN D	LTC	0-0283356	0754	3
ATKINS PERRY C	CPT	0-1685705	0864	1
ATKINS ROBERT C	MAJ	0-0276316	0250	1
ATKINS THOMAS T	COL	0-0246315	0863	3
ATKINS WILLIAM D	CPT	0-2023954	0157	1
ATKINSON ALFRED O	COL	0-0353615	0463	1
ATKINSON ANN M	1LT	N-0744622	1046	1
ATKINSON BILLY	1LT	0-1284265	0945	2
ATKINSON CHARLES H	CPT	0-0150286	1159	3
ATKINSON CHARLES M	CPT	0-1110038	0953	1
ATKINSON CHARLES M	CW4	W-2114335	0659	1
ATKINSON CHRISTOPHE	MAJ	0-0271108	0369	3
ATKINSON DANIEL D	CPT	0-0176944	0555	3
ATKINSON DONALD E	LTC	0-1032267	0666	1
ATKINSON ERNEST P	1LT	0-1591905	0965	3
ATKINSON FREDDIE R	CPT	0-0327859	1044	2
ATKINSON GEORGE M	1LT	0-0179303	0355	3
ATKINSON GILBERT S	LTC	0-0395223	0766	3
ATKINSON HAROLD E	1LT	0-1011133	0945	2
ATKINSON HAROLD J	LTC	0-0131902	1052	3
ATKINSON HARRY G	LTC	0-0183309	1150	3
ATKINSON HERBERT E	MAJ	0-0281197	0968	3
ATKINSON HOWARD T	CPT	0-0504771	0447	1
ATKINSON JACK	MAJ	0-0981552	1263	1
ATKINSON JOHN A	MAJ	0-0254514	1163	3
ATKINSON JOHN B	LTC	0-1107212	1166	1
ATKINSON JOHN H	1LT	0-0381594	0945	2
ATKINSON JOSEPH E	MAJ	0-0978934	0262	1
ATKINSON LUTHER D	WO1	W-2119148	0856	1
ATKINSON LUTHER J	MAJ	0-1342033	0967	1
ATKINSON MARVIN E	CW3	W-2005656	0666	1
ATKINSON ROBERT L	CPT	0-0447436	0248	2
ATKINSON ROBERT L	CW2	W-2205600	0662	1
ATKINSON ROBERT M	COL	0-0256711	0967	3
ATKINSON THOMAS P	LTC	0-0191430	1044	2
ATKINSON WALTER	COL	0-0249677	0165	3
ATKINSON WALTER G JR	MAJ	0-2005300	0860	1
ATKINSON WILLIAM J	COL	0-0235393	0859	3
ATKISON WILLIAM L	LTC	0-0252394	1146	2
ATLAS ANDOR H	CPT	0-0273393	0445	2
ATLAS CHARLES	2LT	0-1055775	0644	2
ATMAR LAURA B	CPT	N-0734678	1050	2
ATON THOMAS L	MAJ	0-2006400	1060	1
ATTARIAN EDWARD J	1LT	0-0464233	0145	2
ATTAWAY JAMES R	MAJ	0-1919429	1265	1
ATTAYA HENRY F JR	LTC	0-0354099	0463	1
ATTEBERRY DAVID G	LTC	0-0453131	0457	1
ATTEBERRY EMMETT M	MAJ	0-1294413	0960	1
ATTEBERRY HARRY M	1LT	0-1303830	1044	2
ATTEBERY JOHN J	LTC	0-0451823	0666	1
ATTEBURY EVERETT G	CPT	0-1821531	0146	2
ATTERBURY HENRY S	MAJ	0-1291758	0857	1
ATTICK WILLIAM F	MAJ	0-0970237	0263	1
ATTRIDGE FRANCIS L	MAJ	0-0486548	1047	2
ATTRIDGE PATRICK J	1LT	0-1925593	0354	2
ATTRIDGE ROBERT D	MAJ	0-1052659	1164	1
ATWATER MONTGOMERY	CPT	0-1300259	0945	2
ATWELL CHARLES F	LTC	0-0397206	0660	1
ATWELL HARRY B	CW3	W-2151697	1163	1
ATWELL RAYMOND B	LTC	0-0438850	0146	2
ATWOOD ARLICE G	MAJ	0-4043286	0567	1
ATWOOD JOSEPH	MAJ	0-0186511	1155	3
ATWOOD NORMAN C	COL	0-0214225	0163	3
ATWOOD ROBERT B	MAJ	0-0111740	0445	2
ATWOOD VERNON S	MAJ	0-0454334	0157	1
AUBREY GORDON K	MAJ	0-1318243	0257	1
AUBREY SAM B	1LT	0-0527770	1145	2
AUBURN HORACE T	LTC	0-0142453	1059	3
AUCHARD ROBERT R	2LT	0-1032501	0445	2
AUCHARD VIRGIL M	LTC	0-0221261	0645	2
AUD HERSCHEL B	2LT	0-0359294	0646	2
AUDA ANTHONY J	CPT	0-1302752	1047	2
AUDET NORMAN A	CW3	W-2145284	0361	1
AUDETTE PAUL J	1LT	0-0517092	1145	2
AUDETTE ROLAND D	CW3	W-2149007	0365	1
AUE CARLTON F	LTC	0-2036528	0465	2
AUERBACH CAESAR J	LTC	0-0504799	0563	3
AUERBACH EDWIN H	CPT	0-0233637	0146	2
AUERBACH EMIL E JR	MAJ	0-0264719	0565	3
AUERBACH MILTON G	CPT	0-0915306	0546	2
AUFDEMORTE M T JR	MAJ	0-1030542	0448	2
AUFFINGER G H JR	COL	0-0183639	0258	3
AUGENSTINE HELEN F	2LT	N-0733549	0644	1
AUGER CLARENCE A	CW2	W-2149317	1057	2
AUGER LEONARD S	LTC	0-1576893	0563	1
AUGUR ROBERT F	CPT	0-0301982	0546	2
AUGUST ALFRED F	COL	0-0347711	0668	3
AUGUST LOIS V	LTC	0-0354619	1147	2
AUGUSTAUSKAS ANTHONY	LTC	0-1284626	1153	1
AUGUSTINE CHARLES J	CW4	W-2113666	0958	1
AUGUSTINE JOHN	1LT	0-0887663	0857	1
AUGUSTINE LOUIS	CW2	W-2154660	1057	1
AUGUSTINE WALTER I	CPT	0-0535215	0945	2
AUGUSTINE WILLIAM H	2LT	0-1308450	1044	2
AUGUSTINE WILLIAM J	CPT	0-0450787	0254	1
AUGUSTINOS PETER	MAJ	0-1047859	0657	1
AUGUSTYNOWICZ WALTER	CW3	W-2207243	1067	1
AUGUSTYNOWSKI E M	CPT	0-1293520	1049	2
AUK JULIA R	CW3	V-0313502	1164	1
AULD FRED G JR	CW2	W-2152786	0161	1
AULD ORRIN C	LTC	0-0262496	1266	3
AULDS HAROLD	CW2	W-2150889	1160	1
AULETTA ANTHONY J	LTC	0-0460153	0765	1
AULICK CARL H	B G	0-0260430	0665	3
AULMANN HERMAN F JR	1LT	0-0455949	0346	2
AULT DONALD V	MAJ	0-0967199	0563	1
AULT GLENN S	COL	0-0142216	0446	2
AULTMAN DWIGHT E II	COL	0-0181401	0262	3
AULTMAN ROBERT A	CW4	W-2117225	0960	1
AUMEND JEAN E	1LT	N-0728805	0251	2
AUMILLER FERD R	LTC	0-1552630	0264	1
AUMULLER EDWIN C	MAJ	0-1545045	1063	1
AUNGST FOSTER W	COL	0-0343491	0360	1
AUNGST RUSSELL J	LTC	0-2039242	0168	1
AURAND PAUL B	LTC	0-0341629	0463	1
AURE GARMON O	LTC	0-1184616	0766	1
AURELIO HONORIO V	CPT	0-0395564	0964	1
AURELIO SALVATORE	LTC	0-1685683	0467	1
AURELIUS LAWRENCE E	LTC	0-0217586	0656	3
AUREN WALTER I	CW4	W-2101393	0455	1
AURINGER FRANK J	CPT	0-1575697	1046	1
AURIT SAMUEL	LTC	0-0047925	0764	1
AUSAN FREDERICK	MAJ	0-1031885	0461	1
AUSAN JAMES V	LTC	0-1297649	0862	1
AUSANKA ALGERT F	2LT	0-0412287	0545	2
AUSBROOKS WILBUR D	CW3	W-2149190	1064	1
AUSHERMAN HAROLD P	LTC	0-0122848	0258	3
AUSLAND JOHN E	MAJ	0-0418525	0345	2
AUST ROBERT A	MAJ	0-1686628	0462	1
AUSTELL MICHAEL H	COL	0-0140215	0555	2
AUSTILL FREEMAN J	LTC	0-1944865	0960	1
AUSTILL WILLIAM E	COL	0-0337302	0961	1
AUSTIN ANDREW Y	MAJ	0-0290164	0760	1
AUSTIN ARCHIE C	LTC	0-2035280	0766	1
AUSTIN CARROLL F	CPT	0-0246307	0744	1
AUSTIN CHARLES D	LTC	0-0490065	0359	3
AUSTIN DALE J	LTC	0-0400604	0146	2
AUSTIN EDWARD K	LTC	0-0292447	0367	3
AUSTIN FINIS H	LTC	0-0425149	0767	3
AUSTIN FRANK B	MAJ	0-1634997	0958	1
AUSTIN FREDERICK	B G	0-0252501	0467	3
AUSTIN GEORGE W	1LT	0-1551345	0547	2
AUSTIN HAROLD D	LTC	0-0182373	0153	3
AUSTIN IRA W	2LT	0-0887604	0246	2
AUSTIN IVAN O	LTC	0-0318263	0459	3
AUSTIN JESSIE L	1LT	N-0736689	0246	1
AUSTIN JOHN B	MAJ	0-0346920	0268	3
AUSTIN JOHN G	MAJ	0-0419921	0555	1
AUSTIN JOHN W JR	MAJ	0-0311954	0145	2
AUSTIN KATHLEEN M	1LT	N-0755557	0147	1
AUSTIN KAYLOR E	LTC	0-1573017	1160	1
AUSTIN LELAND A	COL	0-0222041	1058	1

NAME	GRADE	SVC NO	DATE RET MO YR	RET CODE	NAME	GRADE	SVC NO	DATE RET MO YR	RET CODE	NAME	GRADE	SVC NO	DATE RET MO YR	RET CODE	NAME	GRADE	SVC NO	DATE RET MO YR	RET CODE
AUSTIN LESLIE H	MAJ	0-1644299	0761	1	AXELSON JOHN M	CPT	0-0316040	0845	2	BABBS CHARLES F	MAJ	0-0215219	0765	2	BACON ERNEST L	LTC	0-0249712	1067	1
AUSTIN LOUIS H	MAJ	0-1001509	0262	3	AXELSON OSCAR A	COL	0-0256857	1151	2	BABCOCK DANIEL W	COL	0-0269340	0664	3	BACON EUGENE F	LTC	[illegible]	0161	1
AUSTIN MARSHALL H	LTC	0-0170766	0960	1	AXLERUD ASHER A	MAJ	0-0331608	0665	3	BABCOCK EARL C	CPT	0-0475225	0949	1	BACON FORSYTH	COL	[illegible]	[illegible]	2
AUSTIN NATHANIEL	1LT	0-1292634	1044	2	AXTELL CLYDE R JR	CPT	0-1104718	0553	2	BABCOCK JAMES O	LTC	0-0521504	0347	2	BACON FREEMAN E	LTC	0-0225700	[illegible]	3
AUSTIN OTTO C	COL	0-0310071	0166	3	AXTMAN STUART E	MAJ	0-1310383	0168	3	BABCOCK LAWRENCE A	COL	0-2200174	0168	3	BACON HENRY C	LTC	0-1556535	1163	1
AUSTIN PATRICK J	CW4	W-2031874	1058	3	AXVALL CHESTER C	MAJ	0-0254724	1165	3	BABCOCK LEON F	LTC	0-1581410	0464	1	BACON HENRY F	COL	0-0324414	0967	3
AUSTIN PERRY L	MAJ	0-0401765	1163	1	AYALIN HILARION S	2LT	0-1896968	0857	1	BABCOCK ROBERT A	CPT	0-1284989	0646	2	BACON HENRY S	MAJ	0-0124098	0257	3
AUSTIN RALPH F	MAJ	0-0430154	1057	2	AYARS ALVIN F	CW2	W-3430440	1167	1	BABCOCK ROBERT F	MAJ	0-1831151	1167	1	BACON HOWARD P	LTC	0-0168034	0549	3
AUSTIN ROBERT O	LTC	0-0299978	1155	3	AYARS HERBERT M	CW2	W-3420027	0968	1	BABCOCK ROBERT L	MAJ	0-1294414	1160	1	BACON JAMES R	MAJ	0-1085698	0162	3
AUSTIN SAMUEL L	COL	0-0106761	1058	3	AYBAR JOSE A	COL	0-0240001	0764	2	BABCOCK SAMUEL A	LTC	0-2046876	1166	2	BACON JOHN A	COL	0-0272259	1266	1
AUSTIN WILLIAM B	LTC	0-1136559	0266	3	AYCOCK BENNETT	COL	0-0299391	1057	2	BABCOCK WILBUR F	1LT	0-0175987	0753	3	BACON JOHN R	MAJ	0-0342149	0546	2
AUSTIN WILLIAM D	CW3	W-2205935	0468	1	AYCOCK CHARLES H	LTC	0-0277164	0245	2	BABEL PHILIP F	MAJ	0-0508672	0463	1	BACON ROBERT R	LTC	0-1281292	0466	1
AUSTIN WILLIAM P	1LT	0-1106560	1145	2	AYCOCK EDNA M	LTC	N-0702984	0547	1	BABERS FRANK H	COL	0-0228845	0764	3	BACON RONALD K	CPT	0-1010981	1157	2
AUSTIN WILLIAM R	LTC	0-0814215	0368	1	AYDELOTTE W W JR	1LT	0-1308584	0845	2	BABERS JOHN R	CW2	W-2215665	1167	1	BACON THOMAS F	1LT	0-0493777	1158	1
AUSTIN WILLIAM R	1LT	0-1823654	0346	2	AYDLETT FRED W	MAJ	0-0451201	0253	1	BABES FRED J	LTC	0-1550537	0361	1	BACOS JOHN M	CPT	0-0544609	1067	2
AUSTRAW JAMES L	COL	0-0248553	0866	3	AYER CLARENCE F	LTC	0-0333934	0868	3	BABIARZ FRANK W	1LT	0-0934796	0162	2	BACZEK MARY A	2LT	N-0753366	0845	
AUTARO EUGENE J	1LT	0-0383749	0841	2	AYER CORNELIA W	LTC	N-0736232	0461	1	BABIN ANDREW JR	LTC	0-1179279	0761	1	BADE ERNEST E	MAJ	0-0443901	0756	1
AUTEN MAURICE L	1LT	0-1313075	0345	2	AYER JASPER H	LTC	0-0362882	1061	1	BABISH FRANK F	LTC	0-1062659	0466	1	BADEEN LOUIS J	1LT	0-1775634	0945	2
AUTRAND VERNON L SR	MAJ	0-1301083	0961	1	AYER ROBERT G	1LT	0-0447206	0745	2	BABJACK DENNIS B	CW2	W-3100539	0966	2	BADELA ADAM	MAJ	0-1553214	0962	1
AUTREY ERNEST R	COL	0-0443781	0453	1	AYER WARDNER D	COL	0-0199374	0648	3	BABKIEWICH JOSEPH W	1LT	0-1297666	0746	2	BADEN DAVID O	CPT	0-0553958	0966	2
AUTRY JOSEPH F	CW3	W-2145085	0960	1	AYERS CHARLES F JR	CW4	W-2205316	1166	1	BABLER MARY A	1LT	N-0743548	0347	1	BADENHOOR AUGUST G	LTC	0-0233569	0865	3
AUTRY MARIE M	MAJ	0-1580584	1155	1	AYERS CLAUDE G	CW4	W-2114635	0464	3	BABLER OSCAR E	CPT	0-0520577	1045	2	BADER FRANCIS A	LTC	0-0446946	0165	1
AUTRY ROY	CPT	0-0499345	0646	2	AYERS EDWARD G	MAJ	0-0366432	1045	2	BABOVEC BENJAMIN S	LTC	0-1115174	1263	2	BADER GILBERT F	MAJ	0-0967552	0761	1
AUTRY WILLIAM J	CW3	W-2152818	0166	1	AYERS HAROLD R	CW2	W-2121111	0651	2	BABSON JOHN C	COL	0-0157490	1162	3	BADER PHILIP	CW3	W-2152154	1162	1
AUVIL DANIEL M	LTC	0-2000007	0563	1	AYERS HOWARD	COL	0-0195224	0859	3	BABYOCK NICHOLAS	1LT	0-1037799	0847	2	BADEY WILLIAM	COL	0-1043559	0966	1
AUZAT EMILE T	CW4	W-2120830	0762	1	AYERS KENNETH L	MAJ	0-1313042	1160	1	BACCAY CLARK	1LT	0-1896680	0759	1	BADGER CLAYTON I	CW3	W-2145355	0964	1
AVAKIAN RUPEN G	CPT	0-0462263	0946	2	AYERS ROBERT S	LTC	0-1289855	0463	1	BACCO ANTHONY J	2LT	0-1053354	1144	2	BADGER DARWIN H	CPT	0-1844953	0459	1
AVANS JOSEPH JR	CPT	0-2016828	1155	2	AYERS SEABORN A	COL	0-0214927	0856	3	BACCUS EDWIN V	LTC	0-2055822	1161	1	BADGER DONALD W	1LT	0-2211126	0653	2
AVANT ELIZABETH	2LT	N-0702513	1039	1	AYERS SPILLMAN L	CPT	0-1290182	0747	1	BACH AUSTIN W	LTC	0-0545870	0964	1	BADGER EDWARD B	COL	0-0309824	0746	2
AVEDON HERBERT	LTC	0-1642350	1266	3	AYERS WILLARD C	LTC	0-0261269	1061	1	BACH HOLGER C	LTC	0-0295270	0468	3	BADGER GEORGE S	LTC	0-0257037	1267	3
AVENDANO NUMA P	COL	0-0226352	0162	3	AYLESWORTH HOWARD C	LTC	0-2272725	0862	1	BACH JULIUS I	MAJ	0-0250950	1166	3	BADGER HARRY S	1LT	0-1650153	0947	2
AVERA BERTIE L	LTC	0-0176399	1158	3	AYLING RICHARD C	1LT	0-1170273	1145	2	BACH KENNETH J	LTC	0-0515798	0766	1	BADGER MARION H	LTC	0-0260954	0362	3
AVERA DOUGLAS J	CPT	0-1298337	0364	1	AYLOR JOHN M	LTC	0-0409978	0157	1	BACH ROLAND F	CPT	0-1956510	1066	2	BADGER WALTER E	LTC	0-0393628	0960	1
AVERELL ANSON M	LTC	0-0270396	0467	3	AYLWARD FRANCIS T	MAJ	0-2000045	1060	1	BACH WILLIAM J	MAJ	0-1558998	0763	1	BADGER WALTER L	LTC	0-0275090	1164	3
AVERILL BERYL R	LTC	0-0268669	1165	3	AYMAT OCTAVIO	LTC	0-0386939	1060	1	BACHAR PAUL W	2LT	0-1116199	1044	2	BADGER WALTER M	LTC	0-0370989	1265	3
AVERILL EDWARD R	LTC	0-1334806	0766	1	AYNES ERMAN E	CPT	0-2000446	0957	1	BACHAR PERRY H	LTC	0-0490116	1047	1	BADGETT CHARLES B	MAJ	0-2204072	0766	1
AVERILL ERNEST P	CW4	W-2131494	1060	1	AYNSLEY JAMES S	CW2	W-2109439	0647	1	BACHAUD JEAN C	MAJ	0-2036849	0966	1	BADGETT LLOYD J	MAJ	0-0402708	0463	1
AVERILL JOHN M	CW3	W-2146615	0565	1	AYOTTE PAUL J	CPT	0-1171039	1146	2	BACHE BENJAMIN A	LTC	0-0332400	0657	1	BADGETT WALTER H	COL	0-0260953	0167	3
AVERILL ROBERT B	CPT	0-1043853	0147	2	AYOUB EDWARD J	2LT	0-1291137	0745	2	BACHELLER WESLEY M	MAJ	0-0267117	0966	3	BADGLEY FOREST R	LTC	0-1056029	0267	1
AVERILL WILLIAM S	LTC	0-0148016	0-53	3	AYOUB WILLIAM J	LTC	0-1294770	0267	1	BACHELLOR WILLIAM S	MAJ	0-0972805	0765	2	BADGLEY JOHN L	MAJ	0-1692938	1161	1
AVERITT JAMES B	LTC	0-0274340	0545	2	AYRE DAVID JR	1LT	0-0300881	0646	2	BACHENHEIMER RICHARD	1LT	0-0927940	1046	2	BADIN FRED P	MAJ	0-1553949	0860	1
AVERKA CHARLES P	LTC	0-0385988	0546	2	AYRE RICHARD H	COL	0-0173533	0260	3	BACHISON ANDREW H	MAJ	0-1845139	0358	1	BADO JOHN T	1LT	0-0991356	0453	2
AVERY ALPHONSO C	CPT	0-1304849	0748	2	AYRES ALAN A	MAJ	0-1949694	0262	1	BACHMAN ARTHUR D	1LT	0-2044548	0146	2	BADOVINAC JOHN D	MAJ	0-1641136	0455	1
AVERY CHARLIE J	1LT	0-1546892	0346	2	AYRES CHARLES U JR	MAJ	0-0963056	0165	1	BACHMAN GEORGE D	LTC	0-0964307	0768	1	BADOVINUS CHARLOTTE	1LT	N-0775058	0446	1
AVERY CLIFFORD O	MAJ	0-0214634	1262	3	AYRES DENNIS A	LTC	0-1047013	0864	1	BACHMAN OSCAR G	LTC	0-0149743	0151	3	BADT MORRIS B	COL	0-0150294	0648	3
AVERY CLYDE K	CW2	W-2142802	0462	1	AYRES EDWARD P	COL	0-0189864	1053	3	BACHMANN EDWARD R	MAJ	0-0270076	0368	3	BADURA DONALD R	1LT	0-1298000	1045	2
AVERY DUNCAN C	MAJ	N-0701619	0947	1	AYTES GLENN R	COL	0-0324655	1161	1	BACHMANN JOHN J	LTC	0-2200426	1267	1	BAEBLER ARTHUR H JR	1LT	0-0541854	0847	2
AVERY EARLE S	LTC	0-0358149	1262	1	AZBELL SILAS C	1LT	0-0494076	0149	1	BACHMEIER IGNATIUS	CPT	0-1844980	0657	1	BAEHR FRED W	LTC	0-0376274	0555	1
AVERY FLOYD E	CW2	W-3430604	1168	1	AZEVEDO JOHN V	LTC	0-0488902	0966	1	BACHMIRSKI STANLEY M	CW2	W-2206182	0862	1	BAELLA RAFAEL A	LTC	0-0266882	0367	3
AVERY GEORGE W	MAJ	0-2000973	0165	1	AZOFF SAMUEL	1LT	0-1725592	0246	2	BACHRACH CARL M JR	CPT	0-0456687	0246	2	BAENZIGER ALBERT F	MAJ	0-1080341	0762	1
AVERY HAROLD	CW4	W-2142403	1164	1	AZZOPARDI JOHN	MAJ	0-0996608	0664	1	BACHTELER WILLIAM F	CW2	W-2147727	0765	1	BAER FRANK A	MAJ	0-0920670	1044	2
AVERY JAMES C	MAJ	0-0136970	0153	3	BAAJE HENRY	MAJ	0-1643632	1061	1	BACHTELL LEO M	1LT	0-1058165	0852	1	BAER GEORGE W	CW2	W-2120143	0546	1
AVERY JAMES O	MAJ	0-1104474	0859	1	BAAR FRANCES J	2LT	N-0702676	1035	1	BACK GEORGE A	CPT	0-1333299	0961	1	BAER HAROLD K	LTC	0-1557740	1068	2
AVERY JOHN C	COL	0-0272548	0867	3	BAAS EDWARD C	MAJ	0-1300911	1060	1	BACK HARLEY R	CW3	W-2153237	0565	1	BAER HARRY	1LT	0-1038409	0346	2
AVERY MARION D	COL	0-0168134	0358	3	BABACY FRANK W	WO1	W-2109694	0248	1	BACK JOHN F	LTC	0-0451206	0865	1	BAER JOSEPH C	LTC	0-1041289	0363	1
AVERY MAURICE C	MAJ	0-2028770	0967	2	BABALONIS ANTHONY J	CW2	W-2141923	0756	1	BACK KENNETH	CPT	0-0452291	0551	2	BAER ROBERT D	LTC	0-0411167	0162	1
AVERY NATHAN C	MAJ	0-0198816	0253	3	BABB CLYDE A	LTC	0-0283860	0267	3	BACK LEO W	CW3	W-2206338	1165	1	BAER ROBERT M	CPT	0-4031384	0567	1
AVERY RAYMOND A	MAJ	0-0289532	0867	3	BABB DOY H	CW4	W-2146213	1058	1	BACK SAMUEL H	COL	0-0327476	0263	3	BAER ROBERT O	MAJ	0-0500666	0850	2
AVERY ROSCOE E	LTC	0-0492501	1145	2	BABB EARL F	LTC	0-1307636	0964	1	BACKER JOHN H	LTC	0-1997750	1162	3	BAER VICTOR	LTC	0-0324016	0245	2
AVERY ROY H	MAJ	0-1171877	1163	1	BABB GEORGE A	CW3	W-2141184	0262	1	BACKER MAX B	CPT	0-0341190	0345	2	BAER VINCENT T	CW2	W-2210009	0564	1
AVERY VESTAL C	COL	0-0391416	0660	1	BABB HENRY R	MAJ	0-0203450	0361	3	BACKES CHARLES C	LTC	0-0152565	0648	3	BAER WALTER	CW3	W-2149419	1064	1
AVERY VIVIEN H	1LT	N-0751035	0846	1	BABB HOMER H	CPT	0-1944907	1045	2	BACKES HARRY M	CPT	0-0493624	0957	1	BAER WALTER A	LTC	0-0244040	0460	1
AVILES EMILIO F	CPT	0-0888084	1048	2	BABB LEO D	MAJ	0-1040866	0457	1	BACKES JAMES M	COL	0-0304809	0153	2	BAERGEN JOHN	LTC	0-0518399	0363	1
AVILLA FRANK A	1LT	0-1118156	0447	2	BABB MORRIS	1LT	0-0526605	0648	1	BACKLUND ELMER F	MAJ	0-0424233	0768	3	BAES JEROME L	MAJ	0-2033628	0561	1
AVIN EDWARD	CW3	W-2144293	0964	1	BABBEY STEVE A	CW3	W-2144043	0956	1	BACKSTROM BERT H	LTC	0-0332146	0260	1	BAEZ RAMON E	CW2	W-2151642	1060	1
AVISON GORDON W JR	MAJ	0-0938720	0264	2	BABBIT WORTH B	CPT	0-1322847	0246	2	BACKUS DANA C	COL	0-0924388	0367	3	BAGAAN FREDDIE	2LT	0-1896484	0254	1
AVON ROBERT	LTC	0-1331802	0267	1	BABBITT DEANE F	LTC	0-0548142	0268	3	BACKUS HAROLD B	MAJ	0-1014458	0658	2	BAGACINA FELIX M	CPT	0-1896828	0159	1
AVRIETT BYRON A	LTC	0-2044596	0155	2	BABBITT FRANK K SR	MAJ	0-1798902	0760	1	BACKUS WAYNE E	CPT	0-0237821	0346	2	BAGANZ HERBERT M	CPT	0-0120055	0658	3
AVRIETT ROBERT J	MAJ	0-1329668	1161	1	BABBITT FREDERIC M	CPT	0-0214327	0663	3	BACOCH JOHN JR	1LT	0-1690943	1147	2	BAGARIA JAMES C	2LT	0-1314582	0245	2
AVVEDUTI LOUIS	2LT	0-2008651	0348	2	BABBITT FREDERICK	WO1	W-2132762	0458	1	BACON ALLEN F	LTC	0-0299784	0146	2	BAGBY HERBERT W	CW3	RW-2144254	0463	1
AWBREY DON C	CPT	0-1543320	0645	2	BABBITT JAMES T	LTC	0-0287320	1161	1	BACON BERNARD J	CW2	W-2210707	0866	1	BAGBY JOHN	COL	0-0226051	1061	3
AWBREY LLOYD L	LTC	0-0308503	0765	3	BABBITT JOHN H	MAJ	0-4010794	1166	1	BACON CLARENCE B	LTC	0-1288676	0561	1	BAGBY LAWRENCE E	WO1	W-2115384	0945	2
AWE LESTER A	1LT	0-1301921	1046	2	BABBITT PAUL L	COL	0-0359826	0461	1	BACON DAVID F	MAJ	0-2202791	0568	1	BAGBY ROBERT T	LTC	0-1104476	1065	1
AWTRY JOHN H	COL	0-0914101	0353	2	BABBITT THEODORE	COL	0-0136923	0257	3	BACON EARL W	COL	0-0108783	0946	1	BAGBY WILLIAM R	MAJ	0-1644773	1060	1
AXBERG NELS	WO1	W-2123062	0852	1	BABBITZ ALBERT L	LTC	0-0310140	0665	3	BACON ELBRIDGE JR	COL	0-0324170	0560	1	BAGDONIS ALPHONSE J	MAJ	0-1177858	0761	1

NAME	GRADE	SVC NO	DATE RET MO YR	RET CODE
BAGGARLY JAMES R JR	MAJ	0-0291548	0668	3
BAGGERLY VAUGHN H	MAJ	0-1645133	1264	1
BAGGETT ALLEN T JR	CW3	W-2000807	0166	3
BAGGETT BOYD J	LTC	0-0265427	1060	3
BAGGETT KENNETH J	LTC	0-0338097	0666	1
BAGGETT LEO	CPT	0-1014208	0960	1
BAGGETT MARION L	MAJ	0-0384798	0761	1
BAGGETT STOKES E	CPT	0-1293351	0746	2
BAGGETT WARREN C	CPT	0-0269018	1059	1
BAGGETT WILBUR C	MAJ	0-0877348	1065	1
BAGGETT ZULA B	MAJ	N-0765610	0655	1
BAGLEY ALBERT G	COL	0-0104281	1051	3
BAGLEY CECIL C	COL	0-0187958	0748	3
BAGLEY DUANE W	MAJ	0-1291387	0161	1
BAGLEY EARL S	MAJ	0-0991351	0366	1
BAGLEY FERNALD S	LTC	0-0299294	1158	1
BAGLEY HARRY E	CPT	0-0493763	0745	2
BAGLEY HOWARD L	CPT	0-0463460	0152	1
BAGLEY JAMES H	LTC	0-0262025	1058	3
BAGLEY JAMES P JR	1LT	0-1949048	0547	2
BAGLEY JAMES W	CW3	W-2142804	0661	1
BAGLEY JOHN H JR	LTC	0-0348173	1060	1
BAGLEY JOHN P	MAJ	0-1280459	1047	2
BAGLEY LEO W	COL	0-0384166	0754	1
BAGLEY MASON R	LTC	0-0375461	0859	1
BAGLEY RICHARD H	LTC	0-0312160	0563	3
BAGLEY RICHARD D	CPT	0-0486485	0448	2
BAGLEY ROBERT A	LTC	0-0295992	0368	3
BAGLEY RUTH C	2LT	N-0752700	0445	1
BAGLEY THOMAS D	CPT	0-1300119	0646	2
BAGLEY THOMAS J	MAJ	0-0486390	0756	1
BAGLEY TOM B	MAJ	0-0283213	0644	2
BAGLIEY SAMUEL	LTC	0-0237519	0145	2
BAGNALL ELMER R	LTC	0-0325390	0657	3
BAGNALL GEORGE F	MAJ	0-0334939	0568	3
BAGNALL HARRY W	LTC	0-0142206	0644	2
BAGNELL DOUGLAS R	LTC	0-0267816	1059	3
BAGWELL JAMES H	MAJ	0-1031051	0262	1
BAGWELL JAMES R	CPT	0-1011081	0357	1
BAHME NATHAN	LTC	0-0316454	0261	1
BAHNER ALBERT R	MAJ	0-1998115	0163	1
BAHNSON FRANCIS H	CPT	0-1550740	0764	1
BAHORIC ALBERT J	LTC	0-1178692	0465	1
BAHR LELAND D	CW4	W-2108247	1262	2
BAHRKE CHESTER M	CW2	W-2147909	0461	1
BAIAS SAM	1LT	0-1305707	0644	2
BAICH STEVE	WO1	W-2135052	1154	2
BAICZER ABRAHAM I	LTC	0-0530323	1266	3
BAIER EDWARD A	COL	0-0247004	1163	3
BAIER FRANK E	MAJ	0-0443929	0847	1
BAIER VICTOR H	1LT	0-1012738	1045	2
BAILES ELBERT L JR	LTC	0-0359155	0366	3
BAILES LEONARD W	MAJ	0-0301201	1160	1
BAILES RUSSELL G	CPT	0-1308452	1146	2
BAILEY ALBERT O	CW4	W-2002244	0965	1
BAILEY ALFRED H	COL	0-0170308	0847	1
BAILEY ARDITH BEL	1LT	N-0788603	1045	1
BAILEY ARTHUR F	CPT	0-0384117	0760	1
BAILEY BENJAMIN E	LTC	0-1340615	0866	1
BAILEY BENJAMIN P JR	LTC	0-0191355	0163	3
BAILEY CHARLES C	CPT	0-0482985	0447	1
BAILEY CHARLES C	MAJ	0-0492828	0746	1
BAILEY CHARLES D	1LT	0-1103498	1145	2
BAILEY CHARLES M JR	CW2	W-2147212	1162	1
BAILEY CHARLES T	MAJ	0-0957584	1061	1
BAILEY CLARENCE L JR	MAJ	0-1328870	0866	1
BAILEY CLARK A	1LT	0-1944926	1044	2
BAILEY CLIFFORD H	MAJ	0-1692928	1162	1
BAILEY CLINTON B	WO1	W-2126177	0445	2
BAILEY DAVID M	MAJ	0-0507673	0854	1
BAILEY EDWARD B	CPT	0-1290875	0346	2
BAILEY EDWARD L	1LT	0-0375716	1043	2
BAILEY ELDON L	COL	0-0218668	0661	3
BAILEY ELLSWORTH	LTC	0-0452056	1164	1
BAILEY ELMA L	1LT	N-0729873	0346	1

NAME	GRADE	SVC NO	DATE RET MO YR	RET CODE
BAILEY ERNEST D	CW3	W-2147337	0764	1
BAILEY ERNEST M	LTC	0-0377939	0454	2
BAILEY ERNEST M	LTC	0-0453983	0762	1
BAILEY EUGENE A	1LT	0-1305370	0645	2
BAILEY EVERARD A	CPT	0-0225491	0864	3
BAILEY EVERETT C	MAJ	0-1594692	1164	1
BAILEY FLORENCE A	2LT	N-0734575	1145	1
BAILEY FORD G	MAJ	0-2262327	1263	1
BAILEY FRANCIS M JR	CPT	0-0249782	1046	2
BAILEY FRED T JR	MAJ	0-0287483	0148	2
BAILEY GEORGE D	MAJ	0-1014051	0166	1
BAILEY GEORGE G	MAJ	0-0312904	0367	3
BAILEY GEORGE H	2LT	0-0888337	1044	2
BAILEY GEORGE W	CPT	0-0975231	0761	1
BAILEY GILBERT J	CW2	W-2108863	0552	1
BAILEY GLENN A	1LT	0-2007221	0453	1
BAILEY GLENN G	LTC	0-1588416	0357	1
BAILEY GUY G	MAJ	0-0204815	0553	3
BAILEY HAROLD A	MAJ	0-0259459	0367	3
BAILEY HAROLD P	CW4	W-2001568	0862	3
BAILEY HARRY C	COL	0-0195866	0362	3
BAILEY HENRY C	MAJ	0-1823253	0562	1
BAILEY HENRY V JR	LTC	0-1286587	0161	1
BAILEY HERBERT	2LT	0-2262034	0752	2
BAILEY HEYWARD C	LTC	0-0201065	0763	3
BAILEY HORACE E	2LT	0-1062660	0345	2
BAILEY HUGH E	MAJ	0-0212500	0761	3
BAILEY JACK W	MAJ	0-1877070	0766	1
BAILEY JACKSON W	CPT	0-0432347	1145	2
BAILEY JAMES L	CW2	W-2208953	0663	1
BAILEY JAMES D	CPT	0-0461332	0345	2
BAILEY JAMES O	CW3	W-2148428	0960	1
BAILEY JAMES P	LTC	0-0228473	1160	3
BAILEY JAMES T	CPT	0-0204050	1048	1
BAILEY JAMES V	MAJ	0-0479440	1153	2
BAILEY JESSE L	LTC	0-0331039	0265	3
BAILEY JEWELL F	1LT	N-0763667	0546	1
BAILEY JOHN E	MAJ	0-0376495	1045	2
BAILEY JOHN E	CPT	0-1030114	0447	1
BAILEY JOHN W	1LT	0-4005401	0856	2
BAILEY JOSEPH V	LTC	0-2210206	0168	1
BAILEY JOSEPH W	MAJ	0-0297623	0944	2
BAILEY LEONARD E	LTC	0-1291378	0366	3
BAILEY LEONARD J SR	CW3	W-2210646	1068	1
BAILEY LEONARD V	LTC	0-1308083	1162	1
BAILEY LESTER H	LTC	0-0200582	0460	3
BAILEY LEWIS G	CW4	W-2117906	0659	1
BAILEY LLOYD U	COL	0-0192922	0862	3
BAILEY MARVIN W	LTC	0-2210276	0868	1
BAILEY MCDONALD	LTC	0-0479003	0157	1
BAILEY MORRIS H	WO1	W-2145710	0957	1
BAILEY MURIEL	CW3	V-0208653	0964	1
BAILEY NOEL R	CPT	0-0501285	0546	2
BAILEY ORVILLE R	CPT	0-0973840	0263	1
BAILEY OSCAR A	LTC	0-1291053	1165	1
BAILEY OTTO C	MAJ	0-4021546	0867	1
BAILEY PARK W	COL	0-0242216	0361	3
BAILEY PAUL H	1LT	0-1310043	1147	2
BAILEY PAUL S	CPT	0-0225052	0349	3
BAILEY PETER C	CW3	W-2147279	0263	1
BAILEY RALPH C	COL	0-0264984	0865	3
BAILEY ROBERT A	1LT	0-0542186	0346	2
BAILEY ROBERT C	LTC	0-0379958	0760	1
BAILEY ROBERT C	LTC	0-1341066	0167	1
BAILEY ROBERT L	MAJ	0-2211010	0367	1
BAILEY ROBERT N	2LT	0-1109798	0945	2
BAILEY ROBERT V JR	CPT	0-1313857	0647	2
BAILEY ROY W	COL	0-0102725	0152	3
BAILEY SAMUEL W	1LT	0-0419324	0146	2
BAILEY THERON P	CPT	0-0195894	0262	3
BAILEY THOMAS	CPT	0-2039441	0863	1
BAILEY VERNON F	MAJ	0-1948127	0561	1
BAILEY WALTER A	MAJ	0-2042106	0368	1
BAILEY WAYNE C	B G	0-0231317	1167	3
BAILEY WILLIAM A	LTC	0-1038803	0866	2

NAME	GRADE	SVC NO	DATE RET MO YR	RET CODE
BAILEY WILLIAM E	MAJ	0-2208422	0666	1
BAILEY WILLIAM H	MAJ	0-0310052	0646	2
BAILEY WILLIAM J	LTC	0-1547873	0265	1
BAILEY WILLIAM N	COL	0-0264147	0763	3
BAILEY WILLIAM S	B G	0-0103209	1159	3
BAILEY WILLIAM S JR	LTC	0-0138919	1058	3
BAILEY WILSON L	LTC	0-1297301	1164	1
BAILIN JACOB B	LTC	0-0311719	0763	3
BAILIN MEYER M	LTC	0-4007690	0755	2
BAILLARGEON RAYMOND	CW2	W-2214515	0767	1
BAILLIE EDWARD P	MAJ	0-0242999	0863	3
BAILLIE HAROLD D	LTC	0-1555503	0168	2
BAILLIE MILTON C	MAJ	0-0277503	0550	2
BAILLOD YVONNE A	CPT	L-0408109	0348	2
BAILLY RANDOLPH M	CPT	0-0548025	0447	2
BAILY LOUIS W	LTC	0-0248166	0164	3
BAIM CLARENCE	WO1	W-2147346	0457	2
BAIN ARCHIE G	CW2	W-2150698	0258	2
BAIN CLARENCE H	LTC	0-1011103	0161	1
BAIN GEOFFREY C	COL	0-0313430	0262	1
BAIN GERALD E	LTC	0-1307354	0761	1
BAIN WESLEY T	MAJ	0-1302580	0557	1
BAINE CLYDE D	CPT	0-0259631	0566	3
BAINER FRANK A	CW2	W-2153238	0160	1
BAINES JESSE F	CW2	W-2146956	0461	1
BAINES THOMAS R	LTC	0-0397658	0261	1
BAINS ERSKINE	COL	0-0144535	0648	3
BAIR CLINTON F	CW3	W-2152426	0462	1
BAIR EUGENE B	MAJ	0-1284843	0159	1
BAIR GEORGE E	LTC	0-1575703	0361	1
BAIR HAROLD H	MAJ	0-1924552	0768	1
BAIR LEIGHTON M	CW3	W-2112706	0858	1
BAIR LESTER W	CW4	W-2101450	0658	1
BAIR SCOTT W	LTC	0-0722805	0968	1
BAIRD ALBERT C	LTC	0-1551787	1061	1
BAIRD ALONZO E	LTC	0-0376930	1263	1
BAIRD ALTON T	LTC	0-1113088	0665	1
BAIRD BENJAMIN D	CPT	0-0517895	1054	1
BAIRD BERTRAM O	CPT	0-1922745	0867	1
BAIRD CHARLES D JR	COL	0-0299751	1068	3
BAIRD CHARLES T	2LT	0-1308414	0944	2
BAIRD CLETUS H JR	CW3	W-2149660	0763	1
BAIRD CUD T JR	LTC	0-0194257	0552	3
BAIRD EARL F	LTC	0-1012427	0256	1
BAIRD EMMA M	LTC	L-0800109	0368	1
BAIRD EUGENE F	LTC	0-0308989	1055	1
BAIRD FOSTER R	CW3	W-2141506	0761	1
BAIRD GILBERT R	LTC	0-0306815	0762	1
BAIRD GLENN E	COL	0-0275774	0968	3
BAIRD HENRY	LTC	0-1795753	0463	1
BAIRD HUGH JR	LTC	0-0375073	0267	3
BAIRD JAMES C	CPT	0-1592798	1145	2
BAIRD JAMES E	LTC	0-0148601	0755	3
BAIRD JOHN E	COL	0-0189461	0351	3
BAIRD JOHN R	LTC	0-0214545	0763	3
BAIRD JONATHAN L	LTC	0-1541287	0761	1
BAIRD KENNETH W	LTC	0-0391407	0865	3
BAIRD PAUL E	LTC	0-0332112	0763	3
BAIRD RALPH W	LTC	0-0205652	1063	3
BAIRD RAYMOND D	CPT	0-0243067	0865	3
BAIRD RENNIE W	CPT	0-0249783	0166	3
BAIRD ROBERT C	2LT	0-1306960	1044	2
BAIRD RUTH B	CPT	N-0788601	1047	1
BAIRD WILLIAM D	LTC	0-0256856	0566	3
BAIRD WILLIAM F	CPT	0-1595360	0646	2
BAISDEN ARTHER M	MAJ	0-0362972	0861	1
BAISLEY THOMAS M	LTC	0-0439577	0366	1
BAIZ RAYMOND J	MAJ	0-1062661	0662	1
BAJ CASIMIR J	LTC	0-1795844	0565	1
BAJANDAS JOSE A	MAJ	0-1308291	1160	1
BAJORIN B J	MAJ	0-0517447	0454	1
BAJUK JOSEPH M	LTC	0-0919611	0664	1
BAKALIAN ARAM	LTC	0-1110914	0762	2
BAKASY ANDREW V	1LT	0-1296942	0956	1
BAKELESS JOHN E	COL	0-0126528	1054	3

NAME	GRADE	SVC NO	DATE RET MO YR	RET CODE
BAKEN PALMER M	LTC	0-0336117	0254	3
BAKER ADOLPH	1LT	0-0373038	0146	2
BAKER ALBERT S	COL	0-0200830	0459	3
BAKER ALBERT U	MAJ	0-1557741	1160	1
BAKER ALFRED P	LTC	0-0335959	0663	3
BAKER ALONZO O	CPT	0-0307680	0648	1
BAKER ANDERSON L	CW2	W-2149485	0261	1
BAKER ANDREW D	LTC	0-0356281	0965	3
BAKER ANDREW Z	1LT	0-1037391	0646	2
BAKER ANSON P	CPT	0-1053904	0347	2
BAKER ARTHUR A	MAJ	0-0977424	1262	1
BAKER ARTHUR D	LTC	0-0506201	0854	1
BAKER ARTHUR R	LTC	0-0492217	0345	2
BAKER BERNARD	1LT	0-1306365	1045	2
BAKER BERTRAM	LTC	0-0204238	1054	1
BAKER CECIL B	MAJ	0-2040680	0357	1
BAKER CHARLES A	CPT	0-0217369	0464	3
BAKER CHARLES D	COL	0-0169615	0361	3
BAKER CHARLES H	CW2	W-2108408	0761	1
BAKER CHARLES J	MAJ	0-0171823	1052	3
BAKER CHARLES L	LTC	0-1113553	0267	1
BAKER CHARLES M	CW2	W-2143861	1166	1
BAKER CLIFFORD V	CPT	0-1333407	0662	1
BAKER DALE R	CW3	W-2203524	1264	2
BAKER DASYL F	2LT	0-2262393		2
BAKER DONALD J	LTC	0-0436251	0357	1
BAKER DOUGLAS S	MAJ	0-1633008	1162	1
BAKER DUMOND H	CW3	W-2002789	0860	3
BAKER E E	1LT	0-1299836	1045	2
BAKER EDGAR A	LTC	0-1324803	0863	1
BAKER EDGAR F	CPT	0-1283644	0851	1
BAKER EDWARD D	LTC	0-1322616	1262	1
BAKER EDWARD F	LTC	0-1303448	0261	1
BAKER ELLIS B III	COL	0-0481184	1068	3
BAKER ELMER L	MAJ	0-0498137	0654	1
BAKER ERLINE	2LT	N-0735863	0645	1
BAKER ERNEST H	LTC	0-1183804	0263	1
BAKER ERNEST J	CPT	0-0226113	0956	3
BAKER EVELYN E	MAJ	N-0773098	1167	1
BAKER EZRA E	WO1	W-2118091	0255	1
BAKER FLAVEY E	LTC	0-1171879	1161	1
BAKER FORDYCE W	MAJ	0-1573025	1145	2
BAKER FRANK E	1LT	0-0538590	0745	2
BAKER FRED C	LTC	0-0315873	0266	3
BAKER FRED H	LTC	0-1177274	1063	1
BAKER FRED P	LTC	0-0298789	0759	1
BAKER FREDERICK	CW2	W-3200271	0366	1
BAKER FURMAN J JR	1LT	0-0549410	0147	2
BAKER GEORGE	LTC	0-1922851	0267	3
BAKER GEORGE A	LTC	0-0315515	0963	3
BAKER GEORGE A	MAJ	0-1040087	0158	1
BAKER GEORGE F	MAJ	0-0319461	0955	1
BAKER GEORGE H	MAJ	0-0265525	0845	1
BAKER GEORGE H	COL	0-0334654	0661	3
BAKER GEORGE V	COL	0-0189190	1054	2
BAKER GEORGE W	LTC	0-0468436	0366	3
BAKER GEORGE W	LTC	0-0900223	0563	3
BAKER GERTRUDE C	2LT	N-0794938	0946	1
BAKER GLEN	LTC	0-1043598	0961	1
BAKER HARL W	LTC	0-2011508	0668	2
BAKER HAROLD J	LTC	0-0281919	1065	3
BAKER HARRY A	1LT	0-0489170	1043	2
BAKER HARRY E	CPT	0-0490675	1049	1
BAKER HARRY L JR	LTC	0-0245785	0565	3
BAKER HARRY S	MAJ	0-0470575	0660	1
BAKER HARRY S JR	1LT	0-1286057	1044	2
BAKER HENRY C JR	COL	0-0259194	1166	3
BAKER HENRY P	CW3	W-2016492	1060	1
BAKER HOMER D	LTC	0-0502575	0464	3
BAKER HUGH C	LTC	0-1044446	0563	1
BAKER IRVIN H	LTC	0-1010422	0361	1
BAKER JACK C	COL	0-0286063	0865	3
BAKER JACK U	CW4	W-2146214	1160	1
BAKER JAMES A	COL	0-0361122	0766	3
BAKER JAMES E	CPT	0-1291561	0646	2

NAME	GRADE	SVC NO	DATE RET MO YR	RET CODE
BAKER JAMES F	MAJ	0-0384506	0963	1
BAKER JAMES F JR	CPT	0-4005457	1063	1
BAKER JAMES G	LTC	0-0209465	1159	1
BAKER JAMES H	LTC	0-0343241	0264	1
BAKER JAMES J	1LT	0-1301085	1045	2
BAKER JAMES L	COL	0-0302066	1055	1
BAKER JAMES L	CW3	W-2150548	0664	1
BAKER JAMES N	CW3	RW-2143049	1061	1
BAKER JAMES T	LTC	0-1015625	1162	1
BAKER JAMES W	1LT	0-0385746	1044	2
BAKER JAMES W	LTC	0-1049722	1065	3
BAKER JEAN L	MAJ	0-0981292	1063	1
BAKER JERRY	1LT	0-0491940	0847	1
BAKER JOHN A JR	MAJ	0-2018094	0168	2
BAKER JOHN B	COL	0-0194158	0657	3
BAKER JOHN E	CPT	0-2006552	0960	1
BAKER JOHN J	LTC	0-0369286	0862	1
BAKER JOHN M	LTC	0-0192392	0755	3
BAKER JOHN M JR	COL	0-0233229	0365	3
BAKER JOHN P	CW3	W-2152784	0465	1
BAKER JOHN W	1LT	0-1318853	1045	2
BAKER JOSEPH A	LTC	0-0401655	0860	1
BAKER JOSEPH D	LTC	0-0163885	0852	3
BAKER JOSEPH F	2LT	0-1329669	0748	2
BAKER JOSEPH H	CPT	0-0120302	1056	3
BAKER JOSEPH W	LTC	0-0386370	0460	1
BAKER JOSEPH W	CPT	0-1304660	1045	2
BAKER KENNETH D	1LT	0-1302754	0945	2
BAKER KENNETH R	LTC	0-0211337	1059	3
BAKER KIMBALL A	CPT	0-0509418	0145	2
BAKER LAWRENCE L	COL	0-0244958	0164	3
BAKER LEE H	CW3	W-2143601	0562	1
BAKER LEON H	LTC	0-0452213	0761	1
BAKER LINVILLE A	COL	0-1035144	0668	3
BAKER LYLE E	MAJ	0-1172739	0464	1
BAKER MARCUS	2LT	0-1583456	0944	2
BAKER MARCUS F	CW3	W-2146215	1060	1
BAKER MARION V	LTC	0-0405403	0865	1
BAKER MAURICE H JR	2LT	0-1301923	0245	2
BAKER MCGAIL C	CW2	RW-2207005	0364	1
BAKER MELVIN C	LTC	0-1175931	0767	1
BAKER MILES B	2LT	0-1318855	0544	2
BAKER MORGAN W	CPT	0-0494836	1044	2
BAKER MOSES	1LT	0-0493939	0146	1
BAKER NED B	LTC	0-0551236	1266	1
BAKER NEIL C	LTC	0-1586416	1163	2
BAKER NELSON C	LTC	0-0453400	0561	1
BAKER NICHOLAS J	LTC	0-0979809	0268	1
BAKER NORMAN	CW3	W-2141185	0763	1
BAKER NORMAN J	COL	0-0250430	0167	3
BAKER ORLEN E	MAJ	0-0505097	0548	2
BAKER OTHA L	1LT	0-1169348	0750	1
BAKER PAUL D	LTC	0-1634360	0861	1
BAKER PAUL E	MAJ	0-1002861	0260	1
BAKER PAUL H	LTC	0-0171993	0852	2
BAKER PAUL J	1LT	0-1315997	0946	2
BAKER PERLEY D	LTC	0-0152213	0557	3
BAKER PHILIP I	COL	0-0284379	0554	3
BAKER PHILLIP F	1LT	0-1308907	0745	2
BAKER RALPH R	MAJ	0-0206536	0447	1
BAKER RALPH S	COL	0-0251400	1163	3
BAKER RALPH W	LTC	0-0156086	0953	3
BAKER RAYMOND A	MAJ	0-2018814	0163	1
BAKER RAYMOND E	CW3	W-2206121	1166	1
BAKER RAYMOND F	LTC	0-0406931	1054	1
BAKER RICHARD H	MAJ	0-0309032	0246	2
BAKER RICHARD K	CW3	W-2208470	1168	1
BAKER RILEY E	2LT	0-1336318	0446	2
BAKER ROBERT	CW3	W-2129192	0659	1
BAKER ROBERT B	MAJ	0-0215534	0257	1
BAKER ROBERT C	LTC	0-0354894	0647	2
BAKER ROBERT L	MAJ	0-1824469	0361	1
BAKER ROBERT W	LTC	0-0418930	1162	1
BAKER ROBERT W	LTC	0-1019683	1265	1
BAKER ROBERT W	LTC	0-1059738	1165	1

NAME	GRADE	SVC NO	DATE RET MO YR	RET CODE
BAKER ROGER K	MAJ	0-1923707	0668	1
BAKER ROSCOE D	LTC	0-0146579	1053	3
BAKER ROSCOE G	MAJ	0-1332664	0764	1
BAKER ROY H	CPT	0-0156733	1054	3
BAKER RUFUS B	2LT	0-0386217	0442	2
BAKER RUSSELL A	LTC	0-1108459	0168	1
BAKER RUSSELL G	B G	0-0291797	0165	3
BAKER RUSSELL L	LTC	0-0124056	0152	3
BAKER SEWARD J	CPT	0-1717517	0549	2
BAKER SILAS K	COL	0-0176754	0462	3
BAKER STEWART J	LTC	0-0387163	0860	1
BAKER THELMA M	1LT	N-0735003	0346	1
BAKER THEODORE M	MAJ	0-0488939	1055	1
BAKER THEODORE R JR	1LT	0-2005948	0566	2
BAKER THOMAS A SR	COL	0-0277801	1160	3
BAKER THOMAS H	CW3	W-2146501	0763	1
BAKER TRACY	LTC	0-0182592	0549	3
BAKER VAUGHN O	COL	0-0154781	0456	3
BAKER WARREN J	LTC	0-0259345	0467	3
BAKER WILLARD	MAJ	0-1583907	0361	1
BAKER WILLARD C	MAJ	0-1106566	0764	2
BAKER WILLIAM	LTC	0-0103272	0158	1
BAKER WILLIAM A	COL	0-0312444	0954	2
BAKER WILLIAM C	LTC	0-0338288	0761	1
BAKER WILLIAM D	MAJ	0-1635286	0348	2
BAKER WILLIAM F	1LT	0-0974545	1058	1
BAKER WILLIAM H	LTC	0-1169008	0261	1
BAKER WILLIAM M	CW3	W-2206980	0768	1
BAKER WILLIAM O	COL	0-0370189	0461	1
BAKER WILLIAM W	2LT	0-0525343	1044	2
BAKER WINFRED H	CPT	0-1105976	0364	1
BAKER WINSTON A	CW2	W-2208854	0465	1
BAKER WOODROW W	CPT	0-1548349	0450	2
BAKER WRIGHT G	LTC	0-0144532	0551	3
BAKEY RUSSELL F	LTC	0-0391537	1163	1
BAKKE NORMAN M	LTC	0-0404269	1060	1
BAKKE WILLIS M	CW2	W-2208911	0466	1
BAKKEN WALTER	MAJ	0-0255760	0758	1
BAKKER JAMES R	CPT	0-1320224	0846	2
BAKKIE MILTON R	LTC	0-1637015	0459	3
BAKONIS JOSEPH A	1LT	0-1798827	0546	2
BAKY JOHN A	CPT	0-1795845	0468	3
BALACANO SERGE	1LT	0-2027079	1148	1
BALAFAS ANGELO J	LTC	0-2017943	0768	1
BALANGA PAULY A	CPT	0-1896551	1059	1
BALASQUIDE MIGUEL A	LTC	0-0278006	0162	3
BALBARIN RUPERTO B	1LT	0-2030127	0864	1
BALBO MARY J	MAJ	N-0725768	0465	1
BALBONI HENRY F	CPT	0-1298169	1047	2
BALCAEN RAOUL G JR	LTC	0-1633462	1060	1
BALCAVAGE PAUL A	CPT	0-1920218	1163	1
BALCER FRANK A JR	MAJ	0-0191688	1049	3
BALCESZAK LIGE M	CPT	0-1289676	0148	1
BALCH ERNEST H	COL	0-0236974	1058	3
BALCH GLENN O	COL	0-0286138	0163	3
BALCHINAS BRUNO R	MAJ	0-1183659	0965	1
BALCIUS JOSEPH J	1LT	0-2006348	0847	2
BALCK LARS F O	LTC	0-0276383	0161	1
BALCOM E RODNEY	CPT	0-0547451	0566	1
BALCOMBE DEWEY W	MAJ	0-0978176	1263	1
BALCONI JOSEPH A	LTC	0-1115628	0768	3
BALDASSARI CARLO	LTC	0-0307418	0567	3
BALDES JOHN R	LTC	0-0301498	1053	1
BALDOCK CARROLL M	LTC	0-0260734	1064	3
BALDOCK RAWLEY M	LTC	0-0162645	0461	3
BALDRA FRED M	2LT	0-1549656	0743	2
BALDRIDGE ROBERT L	LTC	0-0288503	1166	3
BALDRIDGE ROY	LTC	0-0508019	0368	3
BALDWIN ARTHUR B	CPT	0-0364129	0560	3
BALDWIN BERTRAM G	LTC	0-0353443	0468	3
BALDWIN BUN JR	CPT	0-1173862	0846	2
BALDWIN BYRON O	LTC	0-1289536	0860	1
BALDWIN C B	LTC	0-1294771	0163	1
BALDWIN CLARENCE J	COL	0-0283694	1064	3
BALDWIN EARL E	LTC	0-1288678	0961	1

NAME	GRADE	SVC NO	DATE RET MO YR	RET CODE
BALDWIN EDWARD T	LTC	0-0450701	0760	1
BALDWIN EDWIN A	MAJ	0-0196156	0956	3
BALDWIN ELBERT B	CPT	0-1999257	0156	1
BALDWIN FRANCIS M	COL	0-0303012	1160	3
BALDWIN FRED W	LTC	0-0114033	0157	3
BALDWIN FREDERIC K	MAJ	0-1573721	0147	2
BALDWIN GEORGE M	MAJ	0-0304170	0145	2
BALDWIN GEORGE P	LTC	0-0450790	0261	1
BALDWIN IRVING R	LTC	0-1703248	0363	2
BALDWIN JACK A	CPT	0-1333751	0358	1
BALDWIN JAMES E	LTC	0-1636959	1060	1
BALDWIN JAMES L	CW2	W-2113426	0352	1
BALDWIN JOHN D C	LTC	0-0315833	1060	1
BALDWIN JOHN F	1LT	0-1016589	0545	2
BALDWIN JOHN H	CW3	W-2145285	0561	1
BALDWIN JOSEPH	CW2	W-2109523	1046	2
BALDWIN LAURA E	MAJ	N-0727894	0465	1
BALDWIN MARION C L	LTC	0-0377344	0846	2
BALDWIN PAUL H	1LT	0-1541929	0345	2
BALDWIN RALPH R	1LT	0-1044447	1045	2
BALDWIN RICHARD O	LTC	0-0783491	0667	1
BALDWIN RICHARD S	1LT	0-1012267	1045	2
BALDWIN ROBERT B	1LT	0-0152994	0856	3
BALDWIN ROBERT C	MAJ	0-1062736	0663	1
BALDWIN RUSSELL J	LTC	0-0144568	0958	3
BALDWIN RUTH H	LTC	N-0742709	0862	1
BALDWIN THOMAS E	2LT	0-2000574	0446	2
BALDWIN VIRGIL H P	LTC	0-0266510	0261	3
BALDWIN WILLARD G	LTC	0-1184345	1066	1
BALDWIN WILLIAM B JR	CW3	W-2148085	0861	1
BALDWIN WILLIAM R JR	CPT	0-1553950	0447	2
BALDY JOHN S	CW3	W-2145901	0761	1
BALE CLARENCE W	LTC	0-0310415	0557	1
BALE WILBER O	LTC	0-1580595	0961	1
BALENT LOUIS L	MAJ	0-0979802	1162	1
BALERVIEZ MICHAEL P	LTC	0-1555168	0466	1
BALES BARNETT L	LTC	0-1167306	1165	2
BALES CHARLES A	LTC	0-0262353	0866	3
BALES CHARLES E	CW4	W-2203285	0868	1
BALES CHESTER L	2LT	0-0506068	0753	1
BALFOUR CHARLES H JR	MAJ	0-0154632	0560	3
BALFOUR CHARLES L	CPT	0-1552436	0647	2
BALFOUR FRANK H JR	MAJ	0-0422360	0167	1
BALGROSKY STEVEN A	MAJ	0-1047868	0447	2
BALICKI HENRY S	MAJ	0-1306222	0961	1
BALIN ALBERT P	2LT	0-1797071	0944	2
BALINT RUTH L	2LT	N-0790906	0946	1
BALK VILAS D	MAJ	0-0674274	1263	1
BALKCOM MARSHALL W	LTC	0-1552632	0661	1
BALKEMA RAYMOND P	LTC	0-0334710	0760	3
BALKWELL LEROY G	1LT	0-1297985	1043	2
BALL ALLAN M	LTC	0-0266309	0454	3
BALL BENJAMIN W	CW2	W-2103860	0448	2
BALL BILLY E	CW3	W-3150380	0967	1
BALL CLAUDE	1LT	0-1821807	0460	1
BALL CLYDE S	CW2	W-2147937	1059	1
BALL DONALD R	CW3	W-2205873	0865	1
BALL EDGAR A	CW2	W-2151740	0659	1
BALL EUGENE N	MAJ	0-1946090	0363	1
BALL FRANKLIN P	MAJ	0-0489767	0646	2
BALL FRED S JR	MAJ	0-0366588	0458	2
BALL GEORGE A	1LT	0-0491689	0653	1
BALL GEORGE H	LTC	0-0397112	1159	1
BALL HARRY R	CPT	0-0247161	0453	3
BALL HOMER L	CW4	W-2117948	0756	1
BALL JAMES	1LT	0-2262147	0157	1
BALL JAMES A	LTC	0-1304486	0761	1
BALL JAMES D	LTC	0-0215015	0459	3
BALL JAMES H	LTC	0-0258638	0668	3
BALL JAMES H JR	LTC	0-1101321	0463	1
BALL JAMES S	1LT	0-0467837	0146	2
BALL JOHN F	CW3	W-2105529	0862	1
BALL JOHN S JR	MAJ	0-1179772	0662	1
BALL JOHNNIE J	CW4	W-2118161	0959	1
BALL LAURA M	LTC	N-0751278	1167	1

NAME	GRADE	SVC NO	DATE RET MO YR	RET CODE
BALL LAWRENCE C	COL	0-0311247	0655	1
BALL LESLIE K	COL	0-0244506	0866	3
BALL LIONEL C	LTC	0-0266552	1267	3
BALL MELVIN B SR	1LT	0-1103503	0662	1
BALL MILLARD J	MAJ	0-0494079	0854	1
BALL OLIVER V	CPT	0-1290876	0546	2
BALL PRENTIS E	LTC	0-1533251	0661	1
BALL RICHARD D	MAJ	0-1308757	0865	1
BALL ROBERT O	MAJ	0-1182054	0761	1
BALL ROBERT P	LTC	0-0212035	1045	2
BALL ROBERT W	COL	0-0313066	0161	3
BALL THEODORE B	CPT	0-1544183	0357	1
BALL THEODORE M	LTC	0-0226534	0557	1
BALL THOMAS L	LTC	0-1304326	1262	1
BALL URBAN H	1LT	0-0301309	0647	2
BALL WILLIAM C	MAJ	0-0284730	0968	3
BALL WILLIAM L	COL	0-0290530	0962	3
BALL WILLIAM L	MAJ	0-0955142	0562	1
BALL WILLIAM N	MAJ	0-1116564	1059	1
BALL WOODROW W	MAJ	0-1017174	0161	1
BALLAGH JAMES C J	LTC	0-0184062	0858	3
BALLAM CYRIL J	CPT	0-0251643	1047	2
BALLANCE JAMES L	CW3	W-2148377	0562	1
BALLAND SAMUEL B	COL	0-0136831	0648	3
BALLANTINE JOHN J	CPT	0-0438826	0363	1
BALLANTINE LAURENCE	MAJ	0-0438851	0961	2
BALLANTYNE STANLEY E	LTC	0-2033815	1068	1
BALLARD CAROL B	CPT	0-0414551	0645	2
BALLARD CLAUDE H	LTC	0-0384648	0867	3
BALLARD CLAUDE T	LTC	0-0212519	0561	3
BALLARD FRANCIS J	CW4	W-2110187	0960	1
BALLARD FRED E	CW3	W-2149924	0263	1
BALLARD GEORGE W	LTC	0-0347590	0162	3
BALLARD HAZEL G	1LT	N-0762681	1048	2
BALLARD LAWRENCE E	MAJ	0-0257666	1166	3
BALLARD LAWRENCE O	1LT	0-1120557	1265	2
BALLARD LEE R	CPT	0-1038257	0261	1
BALLARD LEVI	COL	0-0183165	1062	3
BALLARD LOCKETT F	1LT	0-1171881	1045	2
BALLARD MARY E	MAJ	N-0751226	0462	2
BALLARD MILTON E	LTC	0-1637614	0563	1
BALLARD RAYMOND H	CPT	0-0990662	0758	2
BALLARD RICHARD W	MAJ	0-0510626	0146	2
BALLARD ROBERT M JR	LTC	0-0418263	1061	1
BALLARD RULON J	COL	0-0286877	0757	2
BALLARD ULYSSES G	CPT	0-1100434	0548	1
BALLARD WALTER	CPT	0-0486154	0647	1
BALLARD WILLIAM H	LTC	0-1184980	1262	1
BALLAS JOSEPH E	CW4	W-2145300	1166	1
BALLENGER RICHARD S	MAJ	0-0452208	0147	2
BALLENTINE K W	1LT	0-0381976	1044	2
BALLEW EVELYN M	CPT	L-0801316	0248	2
BALLEW JOE B	CPT	0-4031050	1065	1
BALLEW JOSEPH H	B G	0-0183226	0648	3
BALLEW THOMAS M	MAJ	0-1877756	0867	1
BALLF HAROLD P	COL	0-0236850	0662	3
BALLF HARRY A	COL	0-0236851	0662	3
BALLI ALFRED	CW2	W-3250189	1163	1
BALLIET CHARLES A	CW2	W-2142487	0255	1
BALLIET J PALMER	MAJ	0-2009724	0164	1
BALLIET KENNETH E	COL	0-0162424	1054	1
BALLIET THOMAS G	LTC	0-0393761	0760	1
BALLIN MICHAEL	CPT	0-0333566	0246	2
BALLINGER ERNE L	CPT	0-0261935	0850	2
BALLINGER LEWIS F	MAJ	0-1180109	1060	1
BALLINGER RODNEY P	MAJ	0-2012696	1062	1
BALLMENT HAROLD F	LTC	0-0488624	0259	1
BALLMER EMERSON A	MAJ	0-0299804	1066	3
BALLON CHARLES	LTC	0-0918098	1045	2
BALLOU ALFRED F	LTC	0-0944664	1166	1
BALLOU CHARLES B	LTC	0-0354922	0546	2
BALLOU EDGAR W	1LT	0-1308454	0148	2
BALLOU WILLIAM H	MAJ	0-1573029	0568	3
BALLOUGH WILMANS K	COL	0-0115223	0256	3
BALLYK PETER	CW4	W-2139609	0358	1

NAME	GRADE	SVC NO	DATE RET MO YR	RET CODE
BALME CHARLES H	2LT	0-1947966	0146	2
BALMORES SILVINO R	1LT	0-1896905	1059	1
BALMOS WILBUR H	COL	0-0259049	0465	3
BALOGH STEPHEN F	LTC	0-0403873	0766	3
BALONA MARGARET B	CPT	N-0751252	0260	2
BALSAMO JOSEPH J	CPT	0-0499044	1045	2
BALSER JOSEPH F	MAJ	0-2200403	0565	1
BALSIS JOSEPH C	MAJ	0-0967831	0363	1
BALSLEY KENNETH P	LTC	0-1047017	0262	1
BALSLEY WILLIAM G	LTC	0-0295515	0767	3
BALSTERS ROBERT O	2LT	0-1178405	0444	2
BALTES GERARD W	WO1	W-2006595	0165	2
BALTES JAMES C	CW3	W-2147987	0460	1
BALTIER MICHAEL A	CPT	0-0969096	1161	1
BALTRUCKI EDMUND V	MAJ	0-0499176	0546	2
BALTZ EDWARD C	CW2	W-2205417	0861	1
BALTZ MARY C	MAJ	N-0779092	1063	1
BALTZ WILSON M	1LT	0-0482903	0944	2
BAMBERG EDMUND F	WO1	W-2131720	1046	2
BAMBERG GEORGE W	1LT	0-0226796	1063	3
BAMBERG ROBERT K	LTC	0-0431103	0663	1
BAMBERGER HENRY F	LTC	0-0235501	0554	3
BAMBERY JOHN T	CPT	0-1575709	0356	1
BAMBRICK EUGENE P	1LT	0-2006180	0746	2
BAME HARRY	CPT	0-0506823	0646	2
BAMFORD ARTHUR J JR	MAJ	0-0357932	0446	2
BAMFORD FREDERICK	1LT	0-2200076	0752	2
BAMFORD MALCOLM	MAJ	0-0982989	0867	1
BAMFORD WARREN H	LTC	0-0279793	1164	3
BANARES LINO B	1LT	0-2027040	1050	2
BANAS ANTHONY T	CPT	0-1176877	1161	2
BANASZAK SYLVESTER	CPT	0-0386536	0845	2
BANATAJ BEN B	1LT	0-2027436	0450	1
BANCROFT HENRY K	COL	0-0217592	0563	3
BANCROFT LINCOLN JR	MAJ	0-1598309	0267	3
BANCROFT MARK W	MAJ	0-2052428	1165	3
BANCROFT RAYMOND E	MAJ	0-0295544	0663	3
BANDEL ALEXANDER	CPT	0-0975114	0260	1
BANDEL KENNETH W	LTC	0-0338545	0667	3
BANDIK MICHAEL G	1LT	0-1038600	0946	2
BANDURA ANTON J	CPT	0-0159789	0154	3
BANDY ADELE M	MAJ	N-0741041	1267	1
BANDY CLYDE B	MAJ	0-1641200	0365	1
BANDY JOE A	MAJ	0-2289766	1067	1
BANE ALFRED W	LTC	0-1045014	0563	1
BANE ERNEST J	CW4	W-2146108	1168	1
BANE VERNON K	MAJ	0-1919144	0767	1
BANEN DAVID M	COL	0-0333667	0764	3
BANEY HAZEL S	2LT	N-0756050	0245	1
BANG ANTHON H	2LT	0-1305180	0445	2
BANG HANS	CW4	RW-2145234	0267	1
BANG JACOB	LTC	0-0248798	0464	3
BANGEMAN JOHN D	CPT	0-0366883	0545	2
BANGERT DONALD V	MAJ	0-1045015	1045	2
BANGERT ELGIN T	LTC	0-0319234	1168	3
BANGHART ROBERT M	2LT	0-1303450	0844	2
BANGO HAROLD J	COL	0-0234751	0754	1
BANGS GERALD C	CW2	W-2211799	0964	1
BANGS HARRY E	LTC	0-0907882	0865	3
BANGSBOLL LEIF	LTC	0-1957738	0563	1
BANICK VINCENT W	LTC	0-0326777	0545	2
BANIGAN GEORGE E	LTC	0-1944389	0359	1
BANISTER ELLIS L	MAJ	0-2055281	0561	1
BANISTER SAMUEL B	CPT	0-1922689	0462	1
BANISTER WELLMAN R	LTC	0-1541817	0361	1
BANK THEODORE P	COL	0-0142645	1057	3
BANKER WALTER E JR	LTC	0-1334081	0565	1
BANKERD LINCOLN E	LTC	0-0337393	0967	3
BANKERT CHARLES W	MAJ	0-0333153	0645	2
BANKES CLYDE W	LTC	0-1035191	0462	1
BANKHEAD MELVIN J	LTC	0-0269363	0845	2
BANKO JOHN P	MAJ	0-0332594	0961	1
BANKOWSKI JOHN R	CW3	W-2146779	1163	1
BANKS A B	LTC	0-0334589	0258	1
BANKS ALBERT C	CW3	W-2149192	0266	1
BANKS CHARLES E	CW2	W-2214367	0867	1
BANKS EARL R	CW4	W-2143098	0163	1
BANKS EDWIN B	COL	0-0422968	0967	1
BANKS EITEL F	MAJ	0-1685825	0268	1
BANKS ELMER E	MAJ	0-1550103	0757	1
BANKS ELWYN P	CW3	W-2152187	0164	2
BANKS EMIL	CW2	W-2205649	1163	1
BANKS FRED M	LTC	0-0209378	0453	3
BANKS GEORGE W	LTC	0-0381882	0360	1
BANKS GERALD F	LTC	0-0351207	0246	2
BANKS HERBERT W	LTC	0-2028468	1068	1
BANKS JAMES H	COL	0-0924622	0467	3
BANKS JAMES O	LTC	0-0286456	0564	3
BANKS JOHN F	MAJ	0-0259625	0166	3
BANKS JOHN H	CW2	W-2109490	0557	1
BANKS JOHN L	CPT	0-0504356	0857	1
BANKS KARL W	LTC	0-1544624	1060	1
BANKS OWEN G	WO1	W-2114369	0246	2
BANKS RAYMOND A	LTC	0-1285174	0563	1
BANKS RICHARD	2LT	0-1297303	1158	1
BANKS ROBERT L	CPT	MN-2289417	0761	2
BANKS ROLAND W	MAJ	0-0283746	0846	2
BANKS ROY G	LTC	0-0223697	0461	3
BANKS RUPERT J	COL	0-1798771	1268	3
BANKS SUMNER B	LTC	0-0274545	0565	3
BANKS WILLIAM E	MAJ	0-4031052	0867	1
BANKS WILLIAM F	2LT	0-1325733	0445	2
BANKS WILLIAM H	2LT	0-1013634	0245	2
BANKS WILLIAM M	CPT	0-0404215	0544	2
BANKS WILLIAM W	CPT	0-0435878	0647	2
BANKSTON BARNEY	MAJ	0-0450419	0654	1
BANKSTON BUFORD B	CW4	W-2119532	0355	1
BANKSTON H R	CPT	0-1184765	0865	3
BANNAN JAMES F	CW2	W-2203633	0660	1
BANNER FREDERICK	2LT	0-1166891	0445	2
BANNER JULIUS D	CW3	W-2148402	0561	1
BANNERMAN ROBERT B	CPT	0-1574381	1054	1
BANNICK JOHN H	COL	0-0326070	0363	1
BANNING ANDREW C	LTC	0-1056292	0768	3
BANNING FLOYD M	MAJ	0-2019698	0461	1
BANNING JOHN W	CPT	0-0511814	0548	1
BANNING ROBERT J	CPT	0-2036351	0957	1
BANNISTER HOWARD W	COL	0-0281706	0468	3
BANNISTER JAMES	MAJ	0-1799449	0764	1
BANNISTER L G JR	2LT	0-1061051	0345	2
BANNISTER WILLIAM P	COL	0-1057955	0768	2
BANNON CORNELIUS	LTC	0-0492641	0954	2
BANNON EDWARD J	COL	0-1010019	0765	1
BANNON JAMES E	CPT	0-1313950	0947	2
BANOV ISADORE L	CPT	0-0259148	1065	3
BANOVITCH CARL A	2LT	0-1013613	0145	2
BANOWETZ LEONARD F	1LT	0-1168157	1045	2
BANQUER JACOB E	COL	0-0173984	0146	2
BANSBACK CHARLES L	CPT	0-0223861	0162	3
BANTA FRANK L	LTC	0-0510039	1054	1
BANTA NEIL W	1LT	0-0491547	1144	2
BANTHAM HARRY C JR	LTC	0-2200608	0966	1
BANTIN CARL	CW3	W-2150233	0565	1
BANTON HARTLEY L	1LT	0-0413646	1044	2
BANTON JAMES A	LTC	0-0239388	1064	3
BANZET FRANK B	LTC	0-1302542	0467	3
BAR EDWARD	LTC	0-1175031	1064	2
BARABE CLIFFORD A JR	LTC	0-0327810	1044	2
BARABE EMILE L	LTC	0-1014441	0962	1
BARAGER KENNETH M	COL	0-0112127	0753	2
BARALE GEORGE	WO1	W-2149100	1160	1
BARAN ADALBERT P	MAJ	0-0980562	0263	1
BARANOWSKI GEORGE J	LTC	0-0330189	0461	1
BARANOWSKI HENRY S	WO1	W-2151800	0158	1
BARANOWSKI RAYMOND C	LTC	0-1845382	0464	1
BARANSKI ROBERT J	CPT	0-4020903	1265	1
BARAT ERNEST	CW2	W-2147968	0556	1
BARAT LEON J	1LT	0-2025781	1149	1
BARATA VENTURA M	LTC	0-1169417	1060	1
BARATTA JOSEPH J	LTC	0-0366940	1059	1
BARATTINO EMANUEL J	LTC	0-1797418	0865	1
BARAY ROBERT R	CPT	0-0447973	0945	2
BARB PAUL F	MAJ	0-1685534	1163	1
BARBANO ALFRED J	CPT	0-0369562	0845	2
BARBATO ANGELO J	MAJ	0-0990306	0164	2
BARBATO NICHOLAS J	1LT	0-1302919	1144	2
BARBE HAROLD C	MAJ	0-1944391	0762	1
BARBEAU ARTHUR A	LTC	0-1284809	0665	1
BARBEE BILLIE M	LTC	0-1297478	0962	1
BARBEE ERNEST G	CW2	W-2146033	0659	1
BARBEE ISADORE R	CPT	0-4074379	0168	1
BARBEE JAMES E	LTC	0-0283993	0766	3
BARBEE RAY C	LTC	0-1040341	0858	1
BARBER ALVIN B	CW4	W-2144394	1263	1
BARBER BEN F	CPT	0-1114038	0252	2
BARBER CHARLES W	MAJ	0-1106571	1066	1
BARBER CLIFFORD A	CW2	W-3430284	1167	1
BARBER DARRELL C	CW4	W-2106099	0758	1
BARBER DEANE C	MAJ	0-0444073	1053	1
BARBER DELOSS H	COL	0-0121149	0446	2
BARBER EDGAR W	LTC	0-0446210	0246	2
BARBER FRED D	COL	0-0291914	0868	3
BARBER GEORGE C	LTC	0-0498639	0860	1
BARBER GLENN F	CPT	0-1280149	0848	2
BARBER HAROLD L	MAJ	0-1922656	0765	1
BARBER HERBERT W	2LT	0-1545568	0844	2
BARBER HUGH T JR	1LT	0-0551951	0745	2
BARBER JAMES E	COL	0-0373107	1262	1
BARBER JAMES M	CPT	0-0981016	0662	1
BARBER JOSEPH W	CPT	0-0482248	0246	2
BARBER LEE H	WO1	W-2142947	0355	1
BARBER LEONARD D	LTC	0-1299178	0161	1
BARBER LOUIS F	LTC	0-0358820	0860	1
BARBER ROY M	CPT	0-2034070	0661	1
BARBER RUSSEL O	1LT	0-1172742	0645	2
BARBER RUTH J	MAJ	N-0779254	1263	1
BARBER THOMAS W	CW2	W-3430238	0968	1
BARBER WILLIAM A	2LT	0-0450420	0243	2
BARBER WILLIAM A	CPT	0-0477490	1046	1
BARBERA HAROLD J	LTC	0-2017491	0967	1
BARBERA HARRY J	MAJ	0-0395787	0350	2
BARBIE JOHN N	CPT	0-2051588	0757	2
BARBIER EVELYN	MAJ	N-0722370	0661	1
BARBOSA EUGENIO	MAJ	0-1315764	0761	1
BARBOSA GILBERTO	MAJ	0-0965370	1060	1
BARBOUR CHARLES H	MAJ	0-1011424	0857	1
BARBOUR DOUGLAS I	LTC	0-1636967	0162	1
BARBOUR EDMUND N	CPT	0-0530724	0346	2
BARBOUR FRANK P JR	LTC	0-0821197	0768	1
BARBOUR GEORGE E	CPT	0-1688167	1045	2
BARBOUR JOSEPH L	CPT	0-1899419	0660	1
BARBOUR LUTHER H	CPT	0-0208923	0353	3
BARBOUR LUTHER T JR	LTC	0-1290185	0161	1
BARBOUR MABEL M	MAJ	N-0741057	0560	2
BARBOUR MADELINE	MAJ	L-1020103	1168	1
BARBOUR NATHAN P	COL	0-0205474	0648	3
BARBOUR PAUL P	MAJ	0-1329557	0966	1
BARBOUR RICHARD H	CPT	0-1012460	0848	2
BARBOUR ROSCOE W	LTC	0-0255821	1062	3
BARBUTO ROCCO J	LTC	0-1016117	0366	1
BARCH RALPH R	LTC	0-1643137	1161	1
BARCHAN STANLEY S	COL	0-0183062	0356	3
BARCHARD FRANK V	COL	0-0273886	0165	3
BARCK WILLIAM F	COL	0-0132666	0648	3
BARCLAY CHARLES H	LTC	0-0291546	0461	2
BARCLAY DAVID W	MAJ	0-0255009	1044	2
BARCLAY ELTON W	MAJ	0-1995364	0756	1
BARCLAY MORTON J	CW4	W-2147928	0667	1
BARCLAY ROBERT F	LTC	0-1308292	0664	1
BARCLAY WALTER P	LTC	0-0298545	0762	3
BARCLAY WALTER T	CPT	0-0385698	1145	2
BARCLIFT PAUL H	CW3	W-2211083	1068	1
BARCO NORMA L	LTC	N-0726022	1060	1
BARCUS WILLIAM O	MAJ	0-0236500	0557	3
BARD DONALD I	MAJ	0-0969251	0966	1
BARD ERNEST K	2LT	0-2266243	0453	2
BARD JAMES T	LTC	0-0506031	0367	3
BARD SOLI	CW2	W-2105042	1145	2
BARDEN ALBERT	COL	0-0148064	0449	3
BARDEN ARNOLD L	CW3	W-2144011	0761	2
BARDEN LAWRENCE C	LTC	0-0313251	0568	3
BARDEN WILLIAM R	MAJ	0-0484814	1053	1
BARDES HERBERT C	1LT	0-0504853	0645	2
BARDES HOWARD G	LTC	0-0340730	0658	2
BARDES WILLIAM H	LTC	0-0286119	0663	3
BARDIN LEO W	LTC	0-0235382	0164	3
BARDIN OLLIE A	CPT	0-2046293	1050	2
BARDON BENNIE F	1LT	0-1822225	0544	2
BARDONNER WILMER J	LTC	0-0251927	0566	3
BARDWELL HARMON A	MAJ	0-0234807	0862	3
BARDWELL JOHN S	LTC	0-0454982	0961	2
BARDWELL MARJORIE S	2LT	N-0793865	0446	1
BARE ARNOLD W	WO1	W-2143829	0252	2
BARE HENRY M	LTC	0-0286201	0547	1
BARE LUCIEN K	2LT	0-1333919	0146	2
BAREFOOT EVERETTE A	CW3	W-2151806	0764	1
BAREFORD HAROLD S	MAJ	0-0132918	0454	3
BARENDSE ROBERT M	LTC	0-0452206	0465	1
BARERA ADLO	CW3	W-2150740	0865	1
BARFELL LLOYD M	CW2	W-2150063	0959	2
BARFIELD CEPHUS	CW3	W-2131999	0765	1
BARFIELD ELWOOD M	CW2	W-2144110	0559	1
BARFIELD JAMES J	COL	0-0128669	0946	2
BARFIELD LEONARD W	CPT	0-0980911	1158	1
BARFOOT DANIEL F	MAJ	0-0404154	0546	2
BARG RAYMOND J	LTC	0-1290186	0647	2
BARGAS JOSEPH E	COL	0-0287979	1162	3
BARGE ROBERT H JR	1LT	0-2020513	0352	2
BARGER ABRAHAM C	1LT	0-0438519	0645	2
BARGER ALPHONSO S	MAJ	0-0900276	0646	2
BARGER CHARLES M	MAJ	0-0998316	0265	1
BARGER JOSEPH M	LTC	0-0258096	0966	3
BARGERON RICHARD L	MAJ	0-0312613	0147	2
BARGERON WILLIAM R	CPT	0-1341319	0864	1
BARGLEBAUGH W M	2LT	0-1018813	0645	2
BARGMAN SAUL H	COL	0-0190119	0862	3
BARHAM CLIFFORD S	CPT	0-0974552	0161	2
BARHAM HUGH F	MAJ	0-0517247	0466	1
BARHAM THOMAS E JR	1LT	0-0322069	0745	2
BARHAM WILLIAM L	1LT	0-0550872	0346	2
BARIBAULT GEORGE J	CPT	0-0245078	0344	2
BARICUATRO ZACARIAS	CW3	W-2150539	0166	1
BARIL JOSEPH F	MAJ	0-0496906	0454	1
BARIL JOSEPH F R	LTC	0-1573030	0655	1
BARIL JOSEPH M R	MAJ	0-1011417	1058	1
BARINGER HENRY J	MAJ	0-1317469	0865	1
BARINGER RAYMOND A	LTC	0-1167308	1062	1
BARISH LOUIS	LTC	0-0544536	0966	2
BARISKI ALEXANDER	CPT	0-1701445	0158	1
BARK FREDERICK	CPT	0-1081686	1055	1
BARK HURDMAN W	LTC	0-0259099	0759	3
BARKALON F S JR	LTC	0-0329669	0546	2
BARKAS WILLIAM	CPT	0-0472614	0245	2
BARKDOLL IVAN H	MAJ	0-0263769	1267	3
BARKEEN WALLACE I	LTC	0-0390987	1060	1
BARKELL JACK R	CPT	0-1339424	0254	2
BARKER A C JR	CPT	0-0452790	0145	2
BARKER ALBERT B	MAJ	0-1635887	0466	1
BARKER ALBERT R	LTC	0-1642008	0666	1
BARKER ALMAN J	MAJ	0-0943411	0264	1
BARKER ARTHUR W	LTC	0-2046881	1065	1
BARKER BERTRAM T	MAJ	0-1575808	0854	1
BARKER CARLETON J	COL	0-0251050	0159	3
BARKER CHARLES F JR	1LT	0-1287646	0146	2
BARKER CLARENCE O	COL	0-0224241	1147	2
BARKER CLARENCE D	MAJ	0-0266306	0958	3
BARKER CLARK A	COL	0-0281808	0457	1
BARKER DON A	LTC	0-0235173	0859	2
BARKER DOUGLAS P	MAJ	0-1924901	0965	1
BARKER ERNIE L	CW4	W-2115799	0964	1

NAME	GRADE	SVC NO	DATE RET MO YR	RET CODE
BARKER GEORGE T	MAJ	0-0191411	1159	3
BARKER GERALD J	LTC	0-1642011	0964	1
BARKER HAROLD B	MAJ	0-1322302	0961	1
BARKER HAROLD S	COL	0-0336517	0963	3
BARKER JAMES T	CW2	W-2141188	0861	1
BARKER JOSEPH W	LTC	0-0223627	0751	3
BARKER KARL M	MAJ	0-1634450	0357	1
BARKER KENNETH	LTC	0-1116825	0368	1
BARKER KENNETH A JR	CPT	0-0425643	1044	2
BARKER LEAVITT R	MAJ	0-0123671	1052	3
BARKER LEE A	MAJ	0-0344633	0457	1
BARKER MARVIN T	CW2	RW-2142128	0364	1
BARKER MELVYN A	CPT	0-0291473	0748	2
BARKER NEAL H	LTC	0-0489623	0363	2
BARKER NORMAN C	2LT	0-1326450	1145	2
BARKER PRINCE P	LTC	0-0263945	0158	3
BARKER ROBERT C	LTC	0-0313639	1263	3
BARKER ROY F	LTC	0-0301328	0146	2
BARKER STANLEY G	LTC	0-0126236	0648	3
BARKER VALENTINE	MAJ	0-1283192	0361	1
BARKER WALTER B	LTC	0-1102757	0455	1
BARKER WAYNE G	LTC	0-1645198	1165	1
BARKER WILBURN N	CW3	W-2146183	0265	1
BARKER WILLIAM A	MAJ	0-0987646	0167	1
BARKER WILLIAM H	LTC	0-1284991	1060	1
BARKER WILLIAM L	LTC	0-0661693	1165	1
BARKER WILLIAM R	CW4	W-2124188	1154	1
BARKER WILLIAM S	2LT	0-1317870	1044	2
BARKER WITT H	LTC	0-1170275	0961	1
BARKLEY BRACKETT	CW3	W-2149748	0961	1
BARKLEY CLAUDE L	COL	0-0171738	0455	3
BARKLEY HILLARD R	MAJ	0-1324390	0960	1
BARKLEY JOHN	COL	0-0253806	1061	3
BARKLEY JOHN B	CPT	0-0523901	1048	1
BARKLEY JOHN W	CPT	0-1587100	0957	1
BARKLEY JOSEPH H	MAJ	0-1551160	1066	2
BARKLEY THOMAS J	MAJ	0-1687868	0546	2
BARKLEY WILLIAM E	WO1	W-2116056	0859	1
BARKMAN HARRY F	CPT	0-0364809	0547	2
BARKMAN WILLIAM E	LTC	0-0189260	0158	3
BARKOVIC STEVE A	MAJ	0-1308753	0857	1
BARKSDALE DAN C	CW2	W-2152137	0557	1
BARKSDALE GARLAND R	MAJ	0-0498257	0346	2
BARKSDALE JELKS	CPT	0-0247239	1061	3
BARKSDALE SHULAR A	CW2	RW-2147404	1061	1
BARKUS FREDERICK	MAJ	0-0258015	0168	3
BARKUS ROBERT A SR	CW2	W-2212902	0867	1
BARLAND NORVIS M	CPT	0-0304708	0859	1
BARLETTA MARY A	CPT	M-0000693	1047	1
BARLEY ARTHUR W	1LT	0-0310707	0445	2
BARLEY HAROLD S	CW4	W-2002277	0865	1
BARLEY JOHN J	CPT	0-1945752	0446	2
BARLOCK ROBERT J	LTC	0-0415111	0861	1
BARLOW EDWARD L	LTC	0-0189851	0349	3
BARLOW LEE A	CW2	W-2209280	0264	1
BARLOW PAUL J	CPT	0-0522742	0245	2
BARLOW ROSCOE B	CW3	W-2145705	0361	1
BARLOW VINCENT J	CPT	0-0291109	1267	3
BARLOW WILLIAM C	MAJ	0-0151473	0157	1
BARLOW WILLIAM H	CPT	0-1165813	0546	2
BARMORE CHARLES B	MAJ	0-0259126	1264	3
BARNA DANIEL	CW3	W-2143289	0660	1
BARNAK FRANK J	CW2	W-2154860	1263	1
BARNARD DONALD E	LTC	0-1017504	0265	1
BARNARD ERNEST J	CPT	0-0378861	0144	2
BARNARD EUGENE A	1LT	0-1552840	0545	2
BARNARD HARVIE	CPT	0-0223658	0246	2
BARNARD JAMES C	CW2	W-2214497	1068	1
BARNARD MAX C	LTC	0-1995211	0361	1
BARNARD MORGAN C JR	CW2	W-3430560	0568	1
BARNARD MORTON J	LTC	0-0230305	0465	3
BARNARD PAUL D	MAJ	0-0163229	0354	3
BARNARD VIRGIL D	COL	0-0171875	1151	3
BARNARD WILLIAM H	LTC	0-0238243	0865	3
BARNARD WILLIAM R	1LT	0-1322670	1045	2

NAME	GRADE	SVC NO	DATE RET MO YR	RET CODE
BARNEBURY HARVEY B	MAJ	0-0395198	0547	2
BARNER ELWOOD M	MAJ	0-0261844	0268	3
BARNES ADEN L	MAJ	0-1949050	1162	1
BARNES ADRIAN D	MAJ	0-0215074	0563	3
BARNES ALBERT E	LTC	0-0115788	0555	3
BARNES ALEXANDER	LTC	0-0242275	1159	3
BARNES ALLAN C	MAJ	0-1687184	0145	2
BARNES ALLEN E JR	CPT	0-1103505	0546	2
BARNES ALTON F	MAJ	0-0291391	1267	1
BARNES ARTHUR L	MAJ	0-1932359	0667	1
BARNES ASA	COL	0-0299595	0464	3
BARNES BENJAMIN F	MAJ	0-0506920	0645	2
BARNES BRUCE F	CPT	0-1945894	0157	1
BARNES BURRELL S	MAJ	0-0426655	0956	1
BARNES CARLTON J	MAJ	0-1326969	0457	1
BARNES CAROL T	LTC	0-0980039	1168	1
BARNES CECIL J	LTC	0-0311384	0263	3
BARNES CHARLES E	CW4	W-2142435	0359	1
BARNES CLARENCE E	COL	0-0227256	0468	3
BARNES CLARK N	MAJ	0-1308455	0147	2
BARNES CYRIL A	LTC	0-0476213	0656	1
BARNES DAVID G JR	LTC	0-0450716	0958	1
BARNES DEBBY E	CW2	W-2206630	0264	1
BARNES DELBERT P	MAJ	0-0331122	0245	2
BARNES DOUGLAS	LTC	0-1555660	0764	3
BARNES EDDIE W	2LT	0-1018588	0445	2
BARNES EDWARD M	MAJ	0-0273395	1065	1
BARNES EDWIN A	COL	0-0204360	0154	3
BARNES FERRIS F	LTC	0-0306303	0661	1
BARNES FLOYD H	MAJ	0-1168546	0964	1
BARNES GEORGE G	LTC	0-0531820	0767	1
BARNES HAL B JR	CPT	0-1312076	0847	2
BARNES HAROLD E	LTC	0-0519261	0666	1
BARNES HAROLD J	1LT	0-1041960	0 5	2
BARNES HERBERT W	CW2	W-2209861	1164	1
BARNES HUBERT D	COL	0-0267294	1062	3
BARNES ISOBEL C	MAJ	N-0737654	1162	1
BARNES JAMES A	LTC	0-0264266	0360	3
BARNES JAMES A	CPT	0-1701594	0547	2
BARNES JAMES A	CW3	W-2142129	0559	1
BARNES JAMES E	CW3	W-2144646	0364	1
BARNES JESSE E	CW3	W-2152923	1159	1
BARNES JESSE F	MAJ	0-1322848	1262	2
BARNES JOHN T JR	MAJ	0-2096536	0565	1
BARNES LAWRENCE A	LTC	0-1012125	0866	1
BARNES LYLE E	MAJ	0-0942947	0662	1
BARNES MARGARET L	2LT	N-0767377	0145	1
BARNES MATTHEW J	CPT	0-1171042	0954	2
BARNES NELSON N	CPT	0-0395868	0345	2
BARNES NORMAN P	COL	0-0378019	0460	1
BARNES OTIS A	LTC	0-0190647	0644	2
BARNES PAUL N	MAJ	0-0273118	0860	3
BARNES QUINTON E	MAJ	0-0491954	0661	1
BARNES RAYMOND C	MAJ	0-0177349	0345	2
BARNES REUBEN R	MAJ	0-2262472	0364	1
BARNES RICHARD A	2LT	0-1551791	0943	2
BARNES RICHARD W	LTC	0-0270362	1262	3
BARNES ROBERT A	LTC	0-1534667	0565	1
BARNES ROBERT H	1LT	0-1113559	0944	2
BARNES ROBERT I	CPT	0-1578139	0546	2
BARNES ROBERT T	LTC	0-0362196	1163	1
BARNES ROBERT V	MAJ	0-0239449	0164	3
BARNES ROY H	LTC	0-1030116	0355	1
BARNES ROY M	MAJ	0-0257021	0765	3
BARNES RUSSELL H	MAJ	0-0385710	0146	2
BARNES SAMUEL E	MAJ	0-1893553	0767	2
BARNES SETH S	COL	0-0347803	0167	3
BARNES TERRY A	CPT	0-0496252	0546	1
BARNES VERNON H	LTC	0-0244626	1060	3
BARNES VIRGIL K	MAJ	0-4010692	0867	1
BARNES WALTER L	LTC	0-0425612	0464	1
BARNES WALTER W	2LT	0-1318988	1145	2
BARNES WEBSTER R	2LT	0-2023627	0257	1
BARNES WILLARD O	MAJ	0-0466934	0854	1
BARNES WILLIAM B	2LT	0-0467400	0845	2

NAME	GRADE	SVC NO	DATE RET MO YR	RET CODE
BARNES WILLIAM E	LTC	0-0256617	1051	1
BARNES WILLIAM E	MAJ	0-0486368	0947	1
BARNES WILLIAM H	COL	0-0340879	1262	1
BARNES WILLIAM J JR	MAJ	0-0330438	0344	2
BARNES WILLIAM L	CW3	W-2152078	1263	1
BARNES WILLIAM M	CPT	0-0315024	0643	2
BARNES WILLIAM S	COL	0-0371056	0364	1
BARNETSON ALFREDA B	2LT	N-0722076	0744	1
BARNETT ABE	1LT	0-1014099	0848	2
BARNETT BILLIE A	CW3	W-2124532	0656	1
BARNETT CHARLES M	CPT	0-1292457	0847	2
BARNETT CHARLEY R	CW3	W-2144390	1159	1
BARNETT DAN C	CPT	0-0524933	0248	2
BARNETT DOLPH	LTC	0-0182938	0522	3
BARNETT DOYLE E	MAJ	0-1685594	0864	1
BARNETT EARCELL R	CW3	W-2148365	0664	1
BARNETT EMMETT K	LTC	0-0450024	0361	1
BARNETT FRANK E	CW4	W-2114631	0659	1
BARNETT FRANKLIN	1LT	0-0321650	0745	2
BARNETT GENE H	MAJ	0-1306345	0361	1
BARNETT GORDON P	MAJ	0-0500204	0246	2
BARNETT HENRY E JR	CW2	W-2216766	0768	1
BARNETT HERBERT	LTC	0-1291389	0164	1
BARNETT HERBERT N	LTC	0-0152039	0648	3
BARNETT HERMAN H	1LT	0-1001510	0851	2
BARNETT IRVING H	CPT	0-1692197	0145	2
BARNETT JAMES C	COL	0-0185919	0156	3
BARNETT JAMES E	MAJ	0-1014736	0463	1
BARNETT JAMES G	LTC	0-0337013	0560	1
BARNETT JAMES S	CW2	W-2213117	0967	1
BARNETT JAMES W	MAJ	0-0452382	1159	1
BARNETT JESSIE F	CW3	W-2147389	0163	1
BARNETT JOSEPH S JR	COL	0-0159281	0952	3
BARNETT LARRY E	1LT	0-5337847	1268	2
BARNETT LOUIS L	CPT	0-1686901	1043	2
BARNETT MARION B	LTC	0-0195547	0663	3
BARNETT MAX K	LTC	0-1636883	0367	3
BARNETT MORTON L	1LT	0-0485506	0245	2
BARNETT OVAL C	CPT	0-0497810	0449	1
BARNETT PAUL G JR	1LT	0-0555668	1046	2
BARNETT PAUL L	CW4	W-2149282	0168	1
BARNETT PAUL W	1LT	0-1306196	0157	1
BARNETT RALPH T	CW2	W-2150038	0561	1
BARNETT RAYMOND R	MAJ	0-1878198	0965	1
BARNETT RICHARD B	1LT	0-1889790	0554	2
BARNETT RICHARD G	CW3	W-2142217	1062	1
BARNETT ROY L	CPT	0-1018744	1047	2
BARNETT RUSSELL F	LTC	0-1321280	0866	1
BARNETT WILLIAM F	CPT	0-0353093	1045	2
BARNETT WILLIAM K	LTC	0-0154976	0955	3
BARNETT WILLIAM R	CPT	0-0483404	0652	1
BARNEY ALFRED F	LTC	0-1293887	0164	1
BARNEY CHAUNCEY E	CPT	0-1314869	0846	2
BARNEY FRANK L	1LT	0-0126532	0252	3
BARNEY JAMES G	MAJ	0-0101939	0629	1
BARNEY JOHN A	LTC	0-0435004	0764	1
BARNEY JOSEPH	MAJ	0-0496970	0347	2
BARNEY WILLIAM V	MAJ	0-0203562	1055	3
BARNHARDT GEORGE B	1LT	0-0190621	0655	3
BARNHART CHARLES F	LTC	0-1300746	0865	1
BARNHART DESTER A	CW4	W-2127574	0863	2
BARNHART JOSEPH H	MAJ	0-1541848	0446	2
BARNHART ROBERT A	CW2	W-2149894	0862	1
BARNHILL JACK V JR	CW4	W-2144637	0768	1
BARNHILL JAMES F	LTC	0-0370500	0361	1
BARNHILL PAUL P	LTC	0-1281140	1164	1
BARNHILL ROBERT J	LTC	0-1171883	0368	3
BARNHOUSE WILLIAM C	LTC	0-0926719	1264	1
BARNI ROY	2LT	0-1054471	1144	2
BARNO MICHAEL F	CW3	W-2144965	0659	1
BARNS BENJAMIN E	1LT	0-0280338	0943	1
BARNSBEE ALEXANDER	LTC	0-1636972	0763	1
BARNSLEY DAN R	COL	0-0233148	0756	3
BARNUM EDWARD F	LTC	0-0493976	0856	2
BARNUM FRANK L	LTC	0-0225443	0146	2

NAME	GRADE	SVC NO	DATE RET MO YR	RET CODE
BARNWELL DANIEL J	LTC	0-1040090	0866	1
BARNWELL J B	CPT	0-0966698	0866	1
BARNWELL JAMES R JR	LTC	0-0281996	0245	2
BARNWELL WILLIAM H	CW4	W-2148308	1168	1
BARNY FREDERICK	2LT	0-0175298	0960	3
BARON CHARLES	COL	0-0383316	1067	3
BARON CHARLOTTE	2LT	N-0737754	0944	1
BARON HARRY	WO1	W-2145310	1065	2
BARONDES DORCAS A	CPT	N-0783934	0863	1
BARONE AMICO J	MAJ	0-0224161	0359	3
BARONE FRANCIS A	LTC	0-0249679	0262	3
BARONE NICHOLAS L	LTC	0-0196645	0247	2
BAROTT KENNETH J	MAJ	0-0967119	0264	1
BAROWSKI EDWARD W	CW4	W-2103865	0659	1
BARR ALBERT R	CW4	W-2004927	0965	1
BARR ALEXANDER	COL	0-0195027	0961	3
BARR ANDREW	COL	0-0176447	0661	3
BARR ARTHUR W	LTC	0-1301241	0562	1
BARR BASIL O	LTC	0-0138839	1154	3
BARR BOWMAN T	LTC	0-1641850	0666	1
BARR CHARLES I JR	MAJ	0-0424536	0462	1
BARR CLIFFORD J	1LT	0-1822300	1045	2
BARR CLIFFORD N	CW2	W-2152413	1060	1
BARR CLINAL E	2LT	0-0401439	0543	2
BARR FRANCIS E	COL	0-0302606	0657	1
BARR FRANK E	COL	0-0165123	1051	3
BARR FRANK W	LTC	0-0948306	1268	2
BARR FREDERICK	MAJ	0-1165853	0661	1
BARR HARRY G	LTC	0-0251900	1164	3
BARR HENRY H	MAJ	0-0248069	1145	2
BARR HILDA M	1LT	N-0737208	0646	2
BARR HOWARD M	CW3	W-2148403	0960	1
BARR JAMES L	CW2	W-2151645	0164	1
BARR JOHN B	LTC	0-0475840	1057	1
BARR JOHN T	LTC	0-0483823	0458	3
BARR JOHN W	LTC	0-0069854	0368	2
BARR JOSEPH L	MAJ	0-0497801	1047	1
BARR MARSHALL D	COL	0-0216553	1059	1
BARR OLIVER F	LTC	0-1184894	0657	1
BARR RAYMOND C	CW3	W-2145042	0964	1
BARR RICHARD A	1LT	0-0537841	0945	2
BARR ROBERT C	CPT	0-0393760	0945	2
BARR ROBERT N	COL	0-0263452	1062	3
BARR WALTER J	MAJ	0-1169854	0665	1
BARR WARREN D	LTC	0-1795754	0862	1
BARR WILLARD D	COL	0-0292238	0465	3
BARR WILLIAM F	MAJ	0-0315822	0164	3
BARR WINSTON H	CPT	0-1586421	0852	2
BARRACLOUGH H H	CPT	0-0124225	0745	2
BARRACLOUGH JOHN E	WO1	W-2128295	0745	2
BARRANCO ANTHONY J	CPT	0-0484068	0446	2
BARRANTE HENRY A	LTC	0-1294956	0962	1
BARRATT LEROY T	CPT	0-0346362	0661	3
BARRELL HARVEY W	COL	0-0373193	0764	1
BARREN RALPH G	LTC	0-1106574	0465	1
BARREN ROBERT J	MAJ	0-1031053	0166	1
BARRENTINE JAMES R	CPT	0-1167733	1165	1
BARRERA CAL R	CW3	W-2148587	0963	1
BARRERA MARK	1LT	0-1896809	0250	1
BARRESI FRANK L	LTC	0-1643186	1167	2
BARRESI PETER A	2LT	0-1798637	0351	2
BARRET JOHN T	LTC	0-1554504	1163	3
BARRETT BERNARD	1LT	0-0567205	1044	2
BARRETT CLARENCE L	CPT	0-0497688	1047	1
BARRETT CLINTON O	LTC	0-0175545	0760	3
BARRETT DANIEL W	CPT	0-0330874	0648	3
BARRETT DEXTER R	CPT	0-0382643	0647	2
BARRETT DONALD E	LTC	0-0349076	0267	3
BARRETT EARL H	CW3	W-2146651	1262	1
BARRETT EDWARD J	LTC	0-0514569	0268	1
BARRETT FRED O	COL	0-0250431	1166	3
BARRETT FRED L	CPT	0-0223881	1164	3
BARRETT FREDERICK	LTC	0-1822660	0164	1
BARRETT GEORGE F	CPT	0-1177725	0349	2
BARRETT HELEN R	2LT	N-0795823	0146	1

NAME	GRADE	SVC NO	DATE RET MO YR	RET CODE
BARRETT HIRAM E	1LT	0-0339097	0544	2
BARRETT HOWARD F	1LT	0-2048841	1045	2
BARRETT JAMES	1LT	0-1996538	0360	1
BARRETT JAMES A	MAJ	0-0784665	0464	1
BARRETT JAMES C	MAJ	0-1575719	0355	2
BARRETT JAMES F	LTC	0-1032191	0763	1
BARRETT JOHN A	CW3	W-2001855	0866	3
BARRETT JOSEPH W	LTC	0-1055212	0365	1
BARRETT JULIAN B	MAJ	0-0259720	1054	3
BARRETT KENNETH W	MAJ	0-2021470	1066	1
BARRETT ORION D	CW3	W-2205835	0866	1
BARRETT PATRICK J	LTC	0-0929398	0165	1
BARRETT PETER T	MAJ	0-2032082	0564	1
BARRETT RALPH M S	COL	0-0248233	0162	3
BARRETT ROBIN M JR	LTC	0-2033831	0868	1
BARRETT ROGER M	1LT	0-0264185	1046	1
BARRETT ROLAND C	COL	0-0219212	0556	3
BARRETT RUTH R	MAJ	N-0783228	0968	3
BARRETT THELMA A	MAJ	N-0744373	1162	1
BARRETT WILLIAM G	B G	0-0182445	0758	3
BARRETT WILLIAM G	LTC	0-2020919	0768	1
BARRETT WILLIAM H	CW3	W-3150481	0568	1
BARRETT WILLIAM T	COL	0-0195602	1060	3
BARRETTE CECIL F	COL	0-0922214	0265	3
BARRETTO ANITA T	2LT	N-0735389	0145	1
BARRIAGE ARCHIE R	1LT	0-0452303	1144	2
BARRICK CHARLES L	LTC	0-1113561	0366	1
BARRICK DALE L	LTC	0-0267013	0462	1
BARRICK MILFORD D	LTC	0-0334717	1059	1
BARRICKLOW JOHN D	COL	0-0272438	0268	3
BARRIE CHARLES F	LTC	0-1845016	0764	1
BARRIE FERDINAND	LTC	0-1576909	0361	1
BARRIER GEORGE L	LTC	0-0292319	0467	3
BARRIGA JULIO	1LT	0-1896799	0150	1
BARRINEAU JAMES A	LTC	0-0283075	0968	3
BARRINGTON PAUL S	MAJ	0-1030328	0964	1
BARRINGTON ROBERT B	CW2	W-2146303	0158	1
BARRINGTON VAN M	CW3	W-2142748	1060	1
BARRIOS-SANCHEZ FRAN	CW2	W-2205377	0661	1
BARRON CLARENCE B	COL	0-0220602	0564	3
BARRON EDWARD C	CPT	0-1647765	0361	1
BARRON ELBERT M	COL	0-0217679	0646	2
BARRON ERIC S	COL	0-0241526	0457	3
BARRON FLOYD T	LTC	0-1175936	1162	1
BARRON GAINES J	COL	0-0282954	0560	3
BARRON ROBERT E	COL	0-0242028	0162	3
BARRON ROUBLE C	MAJ	0-0283201	0948	2
BARRON STEPHEN F	COL	0-0111953	0648	3
BARRON WILLIAM F	LTC	0-0959259	0467	1
BARRON&NARCISO G	CPT	0-0306420	0345	2
BARRONIAN RICHARD	CPT	0-1169547	0446	2
BARRONTON JOHN C	CPT	0-1331254	0751	2
BARRONTON LESTER C	LTC	0-0487088	0746	1
BARROS RUSSELL D	COL	0-0298071	0460	1
BARROW CLAUDE A	2LT	0-1180415	1145	2
BARROW DOUGLAS A	CPT	0-1289858	0758	1
BARROW EMMETT W JR	LTC	0-1052252	1164	1
BARROW HERBERT A	COL	0-0222042	0661	3
BARROW VIRGINIA	2LT	N-0726487	0144	1
BARROW 2ND F R	LTC	0-0155024	1045	2
BARROWS BARNEY	MAJ	0-0290960	1047	3
BARROWS BRADFORD S	MAJ	0-1017764	0761	2
BARROWS EDWARD R	COL	0-0265062	0768	2
BARROWS GEORGE A	MAJ	0-1583674	0159	1
BARROWS HARRY	LTC	0-0225125	0149	3
BARROWS MAX W	LTC	0-0170103	0160	3
BARROWS PAUL	MAJ	0-1821533	0264	1
BARROWS RAYMOND R	LTC	0-0378496	0165	3
BARROWS RICHARD P	LTC	0-0265063	0965	3
BARROWS RICHARD S	CPT	0-2262155	1060	1
BARROWS WILLIAM M JR	LTC	0-0262983	0468	3
BARRY ABERT D	LTC	0-0353700	0566	1
BARRY AMBROSE C	CW2	W-2153174	0961	1
BARRY BERNARD V	LTC	0-1101325	0762	1
BARRY CALVIN E	B G	0-0271325	0158	3

NAME	GRADE	SVC NO	DATE RET MO YR	RET CODE
BARRY CHARLES R	MAJ	0-0991317	0366	1
BARRY DANIEL T	CPT	0-1635921	0759	2
BARRY DONALD J	CPT	0-1302758	0164	1
BARRY EDGAR L	CPT	0-2262355	1060	1
BARRY ELMO A	MAJ	0-0132849	1049	3
BARRY FRANCIS M	LTC	0-0394375	0468	3
BARRY FRANK E	CPT	0-0493614	0254	1
BARRY HAROLD A	LTC	0-1046348	0967	1
BARRY HENRY F	LTC	0-0242603	0757	3
BARRY JEROME S	2LT	0-2265902	0953	2
BARRY JOHN F	CW3	W-2149058	0367	1
BARRY JOHN J JR	1LT	0-1317472	0547	2
BARRY JOHN W	COL	0-0201480	0656	3
BARRY LYMAN F	MAJ	0-0171207	0461	3
BARRY ROBERT E	LTC	0-1594017	0763	1
BARRY THOMAS A	LTC	0-0414994	0763	1
BARRY THOMAS E	LTC	0-0384324	0767	3
BARRY THOMAS F	COL	0-0368699	0668	3
BARRY WILLIAM F	CPT	0-1053907	0447	2
BARSALOU ELIZABETH	MAJ	N-0761187	0963	1
BARSANTI GABRIEL W	CPT	0-0317002	1046	1
BARSCH DONALD W	CW3	W-2202650	0868	3
BARSI SAMUEL A	CW2	W-2146182	0559	1
BARSTIS ALBERT	LTC	0-0372051	0557	1
BARSTOW THOMAS T	COL	0-0262920	1057	3
BARSZCZ EDWARD J	LTC	0-1285354	0757	1
BARTA EDWARD J	COL	0-0238183	1059	3
BARTA EDWARD J	LTC	0-0397016	0663	1
BARTE GEORGE R	1LT	0-0262354	0651	2
BARTECCHI HENRY A	MAJ	0-2032091	0865	1
BARTELL DON J	LTC	0-0233037	0364	1
BARTELL JACK	MAJ	0-0359127	0646	2
BARTELLONI LOUIS	COL	0-0199859	0147	1
BARTELS HARRY H	CPT	0-0395745	0945	2
BARTELS JOHN C	COL	0-0274769	1165	3
BARTELT PAUL E	CW2	W-2208850	1164	1
BARTELT WILLIAM F	LTC	0-0183884	0647	2
BARTGIS JAMES E JR	COL	0-0330807	1165	3
BARTH ARTHUR W JR	1LT	0-1643837	0445	2
BARTH EDWARD J	CPT	0-1019520	0158	1
BARTH GEORGE H	LTC	0-1945919	0763	1
BARTH LEE D	COL	0-0286199	1160	1
BARTH TODD M	MAJ	0-1999356	1162	1
BARTHA NICHOLSA P	CPT	0-1689791	1044	2
BARTHEL ELMER W	1LT	0-2008412	1045	2
BARTHELME GENE A	MAJ	0-1182116	0556	1
BARTHELOW ADAM J	MAJ	0-0380515	0663	2
BARTHLOW CHARLES W	CPT	0-0420189	0646	2
BARTHOLME FRANCES M	MAJ	N-0800094	0765	1
BARTHOLOMAY EUGENE C	MAJ	0-2263064	0364	1
BARTHOLOMEW ALBERT S	LTC	0-1335728	0964	1
BARTHOLOMEW CARROLL	MAJ	0-2204034	0766	1
BARTHOLOMEW CECIL E	LTC	0-0349918	1059	2
BARTHOLOMEW CLAIR J	LTC	0-0254741	0863	3
BARTHOLOMEW HERBERT	LTC	0-0246422	0763	3
BARTHOLOMEW LEE	CW3	W-2205057	1266	1
BARTHOLOMEW O T	1LT	0-1590982	0654	1
BARTHOLOMEW RALPH J	CW2	W-2147472	0963	1
BARTHOLOMEW ROBERT F	1LT	0-0967948	1052	2
BARTHOLOMEW WILLIAM	MAJ	0-1876322	0364	1
BARTICK PHILIP R	CW2	W-2146004	0360	1
BARTIZEK ALBERT	CPT	0-1059997	0546	2
BARTKUS EDWARD P	MAJ	0-0407759	0445	2
BARTLE FRANCIS C	COL	0-0370087	0764	1
BARTLES CLAUDE L	MAJ	0-0959441	1164	1
BARTLESON RICHARD J	CPT	0-1686736	0863	1
BARTLETT ASA	LTC	0-0298763	0758	3
BARTLETT BERNICE B	CPT	N-0761093	1147	1
BARTLETT CHARLES E	LTC	0-0245935	1066	3
BARTLETT CHARLES M	LTC	0-1036038	1163	1
BARTLETT CHARLES O	CW2	W-2144244	0360	1
BARTLETT CLIFFORD O	MAJ	0-4005876	1067	1
BARTLETT DAVID E	1LT	0-1017375	1145	2
BARTLETT DOUGLAS P	MAJ	0-1322197	0559	2
BARTLETT EBEN B JR	COL	0-0366695	0563	1

NAME	GRADE	SVC NO	DATE RET MO YR	RET CODE
BARTLETT FRANK	MAJ	0-2206415	1066	1
BARTLETT GENE R	CPT	0-1644956	0857	1
BARTLETT GEORGE G JR	COL	0-1045336	0562	1
BARTLETT GEORGE H	LTC	0-1038025	1162	2
BARTLETT HENRY H	LTC	0-0300799	1061	3
BARTLETT HENRY L	COL	0-0264155	1147	2
BARTLETT ISABEL E	CW3	V-0400970	0265	1
BARTLETT JOHN E	COL	0-0402391	1061	1
BARTLETT JOHN L	COL	0-0159285	0252	3
BARTLETT JOSEPH B	2LT	0-0909864	0244	2
BARTLETT LEE F JR	1LT	0-1002760	0845	2
BARTLETT LELAND O	LTC	0-0213258	0447	2
BARTLETT MERLIN D	CPT	0-1178408	0858	1
BARTLETT ROBERT L	LTC	0-1643867	0865	3
BARTLETT WALTER M	COL	0-0329845	0254	2
BARTLETT WILLIAM J	MAJ	0-1170641	0461	1
BARTLETT WILLIAM P	MAJ	0-0285258	1164	3
BARTLETT WOODROW J	LTC	0-1640275	0765	1
BARTLEY ANTHONY R	CW3	W-2142218	0559	1
BARTLEY CHARLES P	CPT	0-0390199	1145	2
BARTLEY CLAUD E	MAJ	0-2018979	1159	1
BARTLEY CORNELIUS	MAJ	0-1885675	1066	1
BARTLEY EDWARD W	COL	0-0178249	0162	3
BARTLEY JOHN A JR	CPT	0-0424342	0745	2
BARTLEY JOSEPH F	1LT	0-1297640	1044	2
BARTLEY JOSEPH L	LTC	0-1582638	0463	1
BARTLEY SAMUEL H	CPT	0-1951530	0263	1
BARTLEY THOMAS A	MAJ	0-0425537	1054	2
BARTLEY WALTER L	LTC	0-1994562	0163	1
BARTLEY WILLIAM E	CPT	0-0425221	0546	2
BARTLEY WILLIAM S	COL	0-0135235	1054	3
BARTNESS ADOLPH C	LTC	0-0272609	0155	1
BARTNIK HANS K	CW2	W-2142445	0455	2
BARTO EDWARD E	LTC	0-0401516	0662	1
BARTO JACK	CPT	0-0979373	1160	1
BARTO JASPER	LTC	0-1000010	0759	1
BARTO JOSEPH C JR	LTC	0-1917719	0968	1
BARTOLEC SYLVESTE	1LT	0-0506208	0453	1
BARTOLI EVO A	CW2	W-3430495	0768	1
BARTOLINI ALFREDO	CW3	W-2207513	0267	1
BARTON BYRON	LTC	0-0479032	1156	1
BARTON CECIL L	CPT	0-0203329	1059	3
BARTON CHARLES W	LTC	0-0314051	1162	3
BARTON CORNELIUS	LTC	0-1543136	0661	1
BARTON GEOFFREY A	LTC	0-1047434	0762	1
BARTON GEORGE A	CW3	W-2150170	0463	1
BARTON GEORGE H	LTC	0-0313874	1064	3
BARTON HARRY M JR	LTC	0-1035517	0365	1
BARTON HOWARD A	1LT	0-0312394	1045	2
BARTON JAMES E	CPT	0-0360157	0345	2
BARTON JEAN O	CPT	L-1010340	0964	1
BARTON JERRY W	MAJ	0-2055222	0361	1
BARTON JESS S	CPT	0-1289371	0645	2
BARTON JOHN V	LTC	0-0414960	0961	1
BARTON LAURENCE G	LTC	0-0123401	1055	3
BARTON LELAND H	LTC	0-0274532	0957	3
BARTON LOYD K	CW4	W-2103869	0860	2
BARTON RANDALL W	COL	0-0299686	0459	1
BARTON ROBERT T JR	COL	0-0171824	1051	3
BARTON ROGER A	LTC	0-0369874	0164	3
BARTON THEODORE A	1LT	0-1844619	1145	2
BARTON WADE G JR	LTC	0-1913425	0668	1
BARTON WARREN D	1LT	0-0394030	0644	2
BARTON WILLIAM O	LTC	0-1946656	0667	1
BARTONI DONALD A	LTC	0-1284811	0264	1
BARTOSIK THOMAS J	MAJ	0-1120737	1063	1
BARTOSZWICZ H C	1LT	0-1304998	0645	2
BARTRAM WILLIAM J JR	CPT	0-1726775	1047	2
BARTSCH EDWARD J	WO1	W-2108409	1048	1
BARTSCH FRANCIS R	CPT	0-0362122	0346	2
BARTZ AMOS D	CPT	0-1171451	0747	2
BARVIAN FRANCES A	1LT	N-0756557	0347	1
BARWICK CHARLES L	CW3	W-2151036	0261	1
BARWICK LEON S	LTC	0-0472128	0954	1
BARWICK LIDE R	MAJ	0-1936694	0567	1

NAME	GRADE	SVC NO	DATE RET MO YR	RET CODE
BASARA STELLA M	MAJ	N-0722240	0162	1
BASCO DAMASO K	1LT	0-0369415	0550	2
BASCO JOSEPH O	1LT	0-0890543	0159	1
BASFORD ALVIN T	LTC	0-0205867	1063	3
BASH JOHN JR	CW3	W-2153102	0862	1
BASHAM ELDON O	LTC	0-0836074	0368	1
BASHAM RAY	LTC	0-1633056	0166	3
BASHAM TRUMAN H	MAJ	0-0887666	0161	1
BASHAW WILLIAM N	LTC	0-0259490	1064	3
BASHISTA FRIEDA	1LT	N-0720323	1045	1
BASHORE KENNETH M	CW3	W-2148899	0765	1
BASILIERE DONALD E	CW2	W-2148703	0762	1
BASILLIO ATANACIO	2LT	0-0890496	1150	1
BASINSKI DANIEL H	CPT	0-0533824	0246	2
BASKETT EDGAR S	MAJ	0-0130010	1049	3
BASKETT JOHN L	LTC	0-0181769	0862	3
BASKETT JOHN W	1LT	0-0548297	0546	2
BASKETT MELVIN C	MAJ	0-1686599	1263	1
BASKIN LOUIS J	CPT	0-1690041	0844	2
BASKIN THOMAS C	MAJ	0-1946658	1265	2
BASKINS DONALD E	LTC	0-0454322	1062	1
BASLER BESSYE S	MAJ	N-0764087	1263	1
BASNER WILLARD J	MAJ	0-1018520	0863	1
BASNETT ESTEL W	CW4	W-2110555	1157	1
BASOM MERLE D	LTC	0-1296977	1060	1
BASON WILLIAM A	MAJ	0-0405398	0262	1
BASORA DEFILLO J	LTC	0-0251503	0763	3
BASORE BERNIECE M	MAJ	N-0735581	1166	3
BASS ANDREW J	LTC	0-0367227	0761	1
BASS BENNETT R	CW3	W-2151365	1060	1
BASS BRUCE C	LTC	0-0315025	0868	3
BASS ELMER D	CW2	W-2141183	0756	1
BASS HENRY C	1LT	0-1635548	1045	2
BASS JAMES W	COL	0-0214852	0760	3
BASS LEROY R	LTC	0-1325544	0667	1
BASS MERVIN A	1LT	0-0557074	0447	2
BASS NOAH W	CPT	0-1107275	0954	1
BASS PAUL W	MAJ	0-1941387	1267	1
BASS SILAS W	LTC	0-0288526	0565	1
BASS WILLIAM A	MAJ	0-1576910	0761	1
BASS WILLIAM E	CPT	0-1596577	0658	2
BASSAKIDES GEORGE J	CW2	W-3430047	0166	1
BASSE HUGH	MAJ	0-1797420	0756	1
BASSEN EDWARD J	LTC	0-0439519	0346	2
BASSETT CHARLES F	LTC	0-0197726	0157	3
BASSETT DAVID M	MAJ	0-0263028	0546	2
BASSETT EDYTHE M	CPT	N-0798228	0468	3
BASSETT EUGENE W	LTC	0-0344114	0565	3
BASSETT FRANK E	CW2	W-2000107	0656	3
BASSETT HERBERT	MAJ	0-1173865	0257	1
BASSETT JAMES E JR	CPT	0-0439943	1262	1
BASSETT JOHN L D	2LT	0-0511081	0344	2
BASSETT RALPH H JR	MAJ	0-1559140	1163	1
BASSETT SANFORD S	CW4	W-2102634	0955	1
BASSETT WILLIAM H JR	LTC	0-0111232	0157	3
BASSETTI HENRY	LTC	0-1030006	1060	1
BASSFORD GEORGE E	1LT	0-0209236	0659	3
BASSHAM OLLIS	CPT	0-1795846	0849	1
BASSHAM WILLIAM L	MAJ	0-2039388	1163	1
BASSICH CYRIL JR	LTC	0-1183015	0267	1
BASSINOR BEN L	LTC	0-0330495	0368	3
BASSO JAMES	MAJ	0-1579365	0164	1
BAST ALBERT J JR	LTC	0-1897723	1067	1
BASTABLE CHARLES M	CPT	0-0503401	0945	2
BASTENDORF WILLIAM L	1LT	0-0539892	0146	2
BASTEYNZ ACHILLE	MAJ	0-1913510	1047	1
BASTIAN CHARLES W JR	CPT	0-0394312	0868	1
BASTIAN KATHRYN V	MAJ	N-0742772	0767	2
BASTIAN THOMAS C	MAJ	0-0525609	0746	2
BASTIDA JOHN C	CPT	0-1108468	0246	2
BASTILLE ALBERT J	1LT	0-1324693	0746	2
BASTIN HARRY D	MAJ	0-1589046	0257	1
BASTINGS MARCEL S	CW3	W-2109987	1060	1
BASTNAGEL GEORGE H	CPT	0-0375138	1049	1
BASTNAGEL RAYMOND	CPT	0-0887668	0756	1

NAME	GRADE	SVC NO	DATE RET MO YR	RET CODE
BASYE CARL B	MAJ	0-0279658	0560	3
BASYE JOHN S	MAJ	0-1329673	0561	1
BATALIA DONALD C	CPT	0-1844529	0861	1
BATCHELDER GEORGE F	CW4	W-2002275	0368	3
BATCHELDER JAMES H	LTC	0-0376155	0961	1
BATCHELDER ROLAND C	COL	0-0199934	0655	1
BATCHELOR JOHN J	LTC	0-0264140	0555	3
BATCHELOR ROBERT E	CPT	0-0332596	0942	2
BATCHELOR VIRGIL R	MAJ	0-1546317	0746	2
BATCHELOR W P JR	LTC	0-0201411	0461	3
BATDORF RICHARD O	LTC	0-0288931	0466	3
BATE ERNEST I	COL	0-0217711	0748	2
BATEMAN DAVID H	LTC	0-1167736	1166	2
BATEMAN DICK S	WO1	W-2122941	1050	1
BATEMAN HAROLD C	LTC	0-0212544	0462	3
BATEMAN MARIE C	2LT	N-0724363	0945	1
BATEMAN NEEDHAM R	COL	0-0290096	0765	3
BATEMAN WILLIAM C	LTC	0-0265874	0346	2
BATEMAN WILLIAM T	LTC	0-0503497	0157	1
BATES A C JR	COL	0-1111480	0468	1
BATES A E GRIFFI	LTC	0-0301926	0367	3
BATES ALFRED F	MAJ	0-1544820	0760	1
BATES ARTHUR B	LTC	0-0174555	0157	3
BATES CHARLES F	CW2	W-2150344	0861	2
BATES CHARLES JR	CW2	W-3350352	0567	1
BATES CHARLES R	1LT	0-0382048	0556	1
BATES CHARLIE M	MAJ	0-0485896	0250	1
BATES CLIFTON E	CPT	0-0240509	0341	2
BATES CREED F	LTC	0-0163616	0254	3
BATES DUANE H	2LT	0-1339032	0746	2
BATES EDWARD R	MAJ	0-1797592	0161	1
BATES ERNEST A	CPT	0-4031059	0468	1
BATES EUGENE	CPT	0-1574312	1050	2
BATES GEORGE H	1LT	0-1301414	0944	2
BATES HAROLD A	1LT	0-1544378	1146	2
BATES HAROLD L	MAJ	0-1108470	0463	1
BATES JAMES L	MAJ	0-1015257	0658	1
BATES JAMES R	LTC	0-1637066	0964	1
BATES JESSE O	MAJ	0-1294774	1059	1
BATES JOHN F	1LT	0-2296230	0150	3
BATES JOHN L	COL	0-0331347	0658	1
BATES JOSEPH O	MAJ	0-1252820	0960	1
BATES JOSEPH D JR	LTC	0-0225409	0963	3
BATES KENNETH E	LTC	0-1533007	0457	1
BATES LYNN R	LTC	0-1635551	0761	1
BATES OSCAR L	LTC	0-0259586	1165	3
BATES PERRY N	CW2	W-2143653	1053	1
BATES PERVIS M	LTC	0-1313190	0967	1
BATES RALPH L	MAJ	0-0482381	1066	3
BATES RALPH R	CPT	0-0339783	1045	2
BATES RAYMOND B	MAJ	0-0223691	0357	3
BATES REXFORD B	CPT	0-1798547	0547	2
BATES ROBERT F	COL	0-0243892	0646	2
BATES ROBERT H JR	MAJ	0-2037450	0763	1
BATES ROBERT S	LTC	0-0332865	0660	2
BATES TED R	LTC	0-1591584	0163	1
BATES THOMAS E	LTC	0-0188061	1050	3
BATES WILLIAM L	COL	0-0220855	0555	3
BATH PAUL L	CPT	0-1581020	0645	2
BATHEN JOHN P	1LT	0-4062599	0758	2
BATHORN JAMES J	CW2	W-2143183	1053	2
BATOK STANISLAW	MAJ	0-2288098	0667	1
BATOON CORNELIO	2LT	0-2032113	0150	1
BATOT MILTON J	CPT	0-0220776	0963	3
BATSFORD THEODORE H	MAJ	0-1044750	0261	1
BATSON CARROLL C	LTC	0-0208243	0252	3
BATSON CLYDE M	CPT	0-0489296	1045	2
BATSON FRANK E	COL	0-0240254	1063	3
BATSON HOWARD E	LTC	0-0264360	0566	3
BATSON WILLIAM K	1LT	0-1014519	0645	2
BATT LOUIS	CPT	0-1045664	0751	2
BATT ROBERT	MAJ	0-1312276	0665	1
BATTAFARANO M F	1LT	0-1583155	0245	2
BATTAGLIA ANGELO J	MAJ	0-0190281	1060	3
BATTELL FRANCES J	1LT	N-0786649	0353	2
BATTEN DOUGLASS H	CPT	0-0475929	1045	2
BATTEN JOHN L	1LT	0-1294068	0944	2
BATTENSLAG FRED G	LTC	0-0223073	0862	1
BATTERSBY MARK W	LTC	0-0372697	0146	2
BATTERSON JOHN E	LTC	0-0475841	0862	1
BATTERTON ROBERT V	COL	0-0309691	0661	3
BATTESTIN CHARLIE E	2LT	0-1010635	0745	2
BATTIGE CARL C	COL	0-0296452	0765	3
BATTISSON JOSEPH T	1LT	0-1994533	0350	1
BATTISTA JOSEPH E	COL	0-1280321	0968	1
BATTISTA WILLIAM L	MAJ	0-0414485	0960	2
BATTLE DORSEY JR	CW2	W-2206517	0563	1
BATTLE FOSTER L	CPT	0-1035193	0146	2
BATTLE HILTON L	MAJ	0-0347313	0361	1
BATTLES FREODL	LTC	0-0265859	1056	3
BATTON HOMER W	CW2	W-2142318	0755	1
BATTS VANCE C	MAJ	0-4043455	0367	1
BATTY ARTHUR B	LTC	0-0205017	1059	1
BATZ HERBERT	MAJ	0-1102144	0653	1
BAUCHLEY MICHAEL JR	CPT	0-1332459	0655	1
BAUCK LELAND	1LT	0-0285460	1144	2
BAUCUM RALPH L	LTC	0-1316723	0263	1
BAUDE WALTER A	COL	0-0170401	0347	2
BAUDOIN JOSEPH C	LTC	0-0412028	0761	1
BAUDOUINE TEX G	LTC	0-0259635	0560	1
BAUER ALBERT H	LTC	0-0308627	1165	3
BAUER CHARLES B	CPT	0-0402874	0945	2
BAUER DEWITT C	COL	0-0266550	1058	3
BAUER EDWARD O JR	LTC	0-1798107	0667	3
BAUER FRANK J	MAJ	0-0386160	0457	1
BAUER HARRY C	CPT	0-1914014	1134	1
BAUER JOHN G	LTC	0-0969701	0668	3
BAUER KENNETH N	1LT	0-1544858	0145	2
BAUER MARY N	MAJ	N-0796114	0466	1
BAUER MILTON E	CW3	W-2145230	0661	1
BAUER PAUL O	CW4	W-2103872	1057	1
BAUER RALPH C	COL	0-0182605	0956	3
BAUER ROSCOE W	COL	0-0198181	0860	3
BAUER WALTER P	CW2	W-2142386	0157	1
BAUER WILLIAM C	COL	0-0324816	0766	3
BAUER WILLIAM JR	CPT	0-0201279	1054	3
BAUER WILLIAM M	CPT	0-0136942	0749	2
BAUER WILLIAM R	LTC	0-0327483	0559	1
BAUERS WILLIAM	LTC	0-0544468	0465	2
BAUGH CHARLES H	CW2	W-3350360	0267	1
BAUGH DANIEL R	COL	0-0175641	0855	1
BAUGH DONALD P	MAJ	0-0945400	0967	1
BAUGH JAMES F B JR	MAJ	0-0262932	1167	3
BAUGH JAMES P	MAJ	0-0997419	1168	1
BAUGH JOHN W	MAJ	0-0334030	0861	1
BAUGH JOSEPH R	MAJ	0-0345559	0563	1
BAUGH LESTER I	MAJ	0-5701482	0867	1
BAUGH ROBERT H	MAJ	0-0238263	0266	3
BAUGH WILFORD A JR	MAJ	0-1339340	0465	1
BAUGHER THOMAS J	LTC	0-1019046	0758	1
BAUGHMAN JIM T	LTC	0-0337677	0366	3
BAUGHMAN NEO F	MAJ	0-1647869	0361	1
BAUGHMAN ROBERT W	CPT	0-0515602	0347	2
BAUGHN EARLE H	MAJ	0-1794896	0461	1
BAUGHN MILTON H JR	LTC	0-0271229	0964	1
BAUM ALDEN H	LTC	0-0235163	0255	3
BAUM CLYDE C	LTC	0-0451072	0457	1
BAUM EDWIN K	COL	0-0170067	0360	3
BAUM HOWARD A	MAJ	0-0322133	0763	3
BAUM JOHN P	COL	0-0195343	0262	3
BAUM JOHN W	1LT	0-1299668	1045	2
BAUM LEE E	MAJ	0-0310688	1066	3
BAUM LYNN T	2LT	N-0764133	1045	1
BAUM ROBERT	LTC	0-0330835	1060	2
BAUM VICTOR	CPT	0-0438750	1145	2
BAUM WILLIAM W	2LT	0-2017637	0851	2
BAUMAN ALBERT E JR	LTC	0-1169013	1061	1
BAUMAN AVON	LTC	0-0354515	1159	1
BAUMAN CHARLES U	COL	0-0146400	0756	3
BAUMAN DARWIN T	LTC	0-0302084	0746	2
BAUMAN ERNEST N	B G	0-0262926	1056	3
BAUMAN OTTO F	WO1	W-2111366	0451	2
BAUMAN ROBERT O	MAJ	0-1331591	0762	1
BAUMAN WALTER J	CPT	0-2208509	1164	1
BAUMANN BERNARD F	MAJ	0-1036987	0968	3
BAUMANN BERNARD J	MAJ	0-1959190	0460	1
BAUMANN CARL A	MAJ	0-0144481	1054	3
BAUMANN CHARLES H	CPT	0-1821231	0545	2
BAUMANN CHARLES J SR	LTC	0-0155100	0356	3
BAUMANN FRANZ	CPT	0-1702874	0146	2
BAUMANN HUBERT F	MAJ	0-1579367	0658	1
BAUMBACH ERNEST J	MAJ	0-1844898	0464	3
BAUMEISTER FRED S	CPT	0-1180806	0663	1
BAUMEISTER T A JR	1LT	0-0466469	1045	2
BAUMGARDNER ARTHUR	LTC	0-2040681	0860	1
BAUMGARDNER HOMER T	MAJ	0-1330774	0563	1
BAUMGARDNER JOSEPH H	CPT	0-1287460	0563	1
BAUMGARDNER KENNETH	LTC	0-1316001	0866	1
BAUMGARDNER PEARLY L	CPT	0-0330824	0442	2
BAUMGART HANS	CW4	W-2108673	0359	1
BAUMGART SYLVESTER	LTC	0-0434974	1166	2
BAUMGARTEN GEORGE G	MAJ	0-0949191	0562	1
BAUMGARTEN JOHN H	LTC	0-0358063	1165	3
BAUMGARTNER DORST F	MAJ	0-0259491	0867	3
BAUMGARTNER GEORGE R	1LT	0-1057675	0146	2
BAUMGARTNER IRA P	CPT	0-0142902	0957	3
BAUMGARTNER JOHN R	CW2	W-2214739	0668	1
BAUMGARTNER RUPERT P	CPT	0-0248344	0145	2
BAUMGARTNER WALTER J	LTC	0-0277241	0861	3
BAUMOEHL ABRAHAM	CPT	0-0494712	0246	2
BAUSCHARD HAROLD C	MAJ	0-0908977	0345	2
BAUSER MARGARET L	2LT	N-0757465	0947	1
BAUSS HARVEY C	LTC	0-0306454	0168	3
BAUTISTA FRANK B	1LT	0-1896383	0952	1
BAUTISTA GUILLERMO	1LT	0-2030659	0464	1
BAVAGNOLI WILLIAM A	1LT	0-1926961	0554	2
BAVARA CAMILLE M	MAJ	N-0745198	0368	3
BAVARIA ERNEST A	MAJ	0-0967012	1163	1
BAVER JAMES M	1LT	0-0363567	1045	2
BAVOUSET JAMES S	1LT	0-1031465	0245	2
BAXLEY ALBERT N	CW2	W-2211401	0964	2
BAXTER ARTHUR	LTC	0-2289512	0767	1
BAXTER AUGUST C	LTC	0-1285881	0867	1
BAXTER CHARLES E	COL	0-0341602	0767	1
BAXTER CHARLES E JR	COL	0-0251097	1067	3
BAXTER COY L	MAJ	0-1014337	0158	1
BAXTER DONALD E	MAJ	0-1844542	1164	1
BAXTER EARL E	MAJ	0-0972587	0265	1
BAXTER EVERETT L	MAJ	0-1553025	0466	1
BAXTER GEORGE B	LTC	0-0136976	1049	3
BAXTER GEORGE H	LTC	0-0393219	1060	1
BAXTER JACK	MAJ	0-1183467	1262	1
BAXTER JAMES A	MAJ	0-0731794	0363	1
BAXTER JOHN G	COL	0-0307495	1160	1
BAXTER JOSEPH	LTC	0-0360011	0860	1
BAXTER LEVON G	MAJ	0-1184983	0461	1
BAXTER OWEN I	MAJ	0-1306223	1058	1
BAXTER RAY L	MAJ	0-0949792	0762	1
BAXTER RAYFIELD W	CPT	0-0319605	0245	2
BAXTER ROBERT E	CPT	0-1317473	0446	2
BAXTER ROSCOE	COL	0-0362837	1063	1
BAXTER ROY J	1LT	0-2035915	0245	2
BAXTER STUART A	COL	0-0166064	0546	2
BAXTER THOMAS P	CPT	0-0987612	0768	3
BAXTER THOMAS R	CPT	0-2023551	0346	2
BAXTER WILLIAM C	COL	0-0173679	0162	3
BAY EDWARD S	WO1	W-2146073	0254	1
BAY WILLIAM J	LTC	0-0277206	0568	3
BAYE FIRMIN J JR	CW4	W-2207723	0968	2
BAYER ANTHONY R	COL	0-0359741	0966	1
BAYER EDWARD	CPT	0-1329787	0358	1
BAYER FREDERICK	LTC	0-0364898	0147	2
BAYER HENRY J	MAJ	0-0978989	1061	1
BAYER MICHAEL	CPT	0-0450222	0357	1
BAYER ROBERT L	CW3	W-2145711	0165	1
BAYERS ARTHUR J	CPT	0-0181374	0455	3
BAYERS DONALD R	COL	0-0273497	1168	3
BAYLES DONALD D	2LT	0-1583926	0245	2
BAYLES WAYNE W	MAJ	0-1295490	0462	1
BAYLESS BILLY B	LTC	0-1168165	0863	1
BAYLESS REX S	LTC	0-0386809	0662	1
BAYLESS WILLIAM B	1LT	0-1030544	0946	2
BAYLEY ERNEST R	MAJ	0-0132156	0555	3
BAYLEY RUSSELL J	CPT	0-0467439	0647	2
BAYLIFF BERT R	1LT	0-0958274	0653	2
BAYLISS JAMES C	LTC	0-0407385	0863	1
BAYLISS ORVAL H	LTC	0-1641243	0862	1
BAYLISS WILLIAM R	COL	0-0343394	0765	2
BAYLOR JACK	MAJ	0-1036640	0946	2
BAYLOR WILLIAM A	CW3	W-3150695	1168	1
BAYMON PORTER L	CPT	0-1688310	0862	1
BAYMOR MICHAEL	COL	0-0374850	0561	1
BAYNARD LUDLOW B	MAJ	0-0282252	0867	3
BAYNE JAMES W JR	CW4	W-2122309	0759	1
BAYNE JOHN M	LTC	0-0333422	0668	3
BAYNE ROBERT O	CW2	W-2208451	0667	1
BAYNE&JONES STANHOPE	B G	0-0170753	1049	3
BAYSEK ALFRED J	MAJ	0-1825366	0461	1
BAYSINGER HOWARD E	MAJ	0-0303584	0747	2
BAYTEL LOUIS JR	1LT	0-1182507	0146	2
BAZARD WALTER S	MAJ	0-0142564	1153	3
BAZEMORE JAMES M	LTC	0-1689877	0648	2
BAZYLDO STANLEY JR	MAJ	0-1329310	0461	1
BAZZANO JOHN J	CPT	0-0369225	1045	2
BEABER CHRIS	LTC	0-1552007	0166	1
BEACH ARVID K	CW2	W-2207534	0564	1
BEACH BENJAMIN S	COL	0-0299915	0260	3
BEACH BURNETT B	LTC	0-1290364	1057	1
BEACH EARL E	LTC	0-1169015	1163	1
BEACH EUGENE H	CPT	0-0462550	1049	2
BEACH FRANCES C	CPT	N-0767281	0547	1
BEACH GEORGE A	LTC	0-0196429	0662	3
BEACH GEORGE I	WO1	W-2109623	0165	3
BEACH GILBERT A	MAJ	0-1116045	0262	2
BEACH GORDON L	COL	0-0250449	0858	1
BEACH IRVING F	LTC	0-0261169	0559	3
BEACH NORMAN A	LTC	0-0250360	0265	3
BEACH PERRY A	CPT	0-0178105	0955	3
BEACH RALPH P	CW2	W-2123043	0450	1
BEACH ROY E	1LT	0-0347349	0444	2
BEACH WILBER E	COL	0-0266051	1156	3
BEACH WILLIAM J	MAJ	0-1324821	0863	1
BEACH WILLIAM M	2LT	0-1321603	0344	2
BEACHAM PHILIP D	CW4	W-2144716	0768	1
BEACHBOARD THOMAS W	MAJ	0-0953639	0464	1
BEACHLEY FRANK A	1LT	0-0310829	0346	2
BEACHNAW DONALD C	CW3	W-2205964	0266	1
BEACOM JAMES E JR	MAJ	0-1284083	0546	2
BEAGLE HARRY	MAJ	0-1303451	0357	1
BEAGLE HARVEY L	WO1	W-2102639	0544	2
BEAHM ANDREW H	LTC	0-0428987	0763	3
BEAHM ARTHUR N	CW2	W-2114817	0150	1
BEAHM CARROLL R JR	MAJ	0-0495583	1062	1
BEAKLEY FELTON T	2LT	0-2055853	0745	2
BEAKLEY JULIAN	COL	0-0286390	0464	3
BEAL CHARLES E	LTC	0-2033654	0168	1
BEAL FREDERICK	CPT	0-0909828	0946	2
BEAL GEORGE C	CW3	W-2152030	0263	1
BEAL GORDON L	LTC	0-0383630	0361	1
BEAL PETER L	CPT	0-0440259	1045	2
BEAL ROBERT P	LTC	0-0287850	0868	3
BEALAND EDWIN P	CPT	0-1119783	0161	1
BEALE ALTON A	MAJ	0-0450697	0248	2
BEALE HARRY C	1LT	0-2021211	0752	2
BEALE JESSE M	LTC	0-1576915	1263	1
BEALE JOHN A	CPT	0-0384039	1045	2
BEALE LEO A	LTC	0-0468597	0448	1
BEALE LOUIS R	MAJ	0-0230109	1264	3
BEALE ROBERT C	MAJ	0-0975182	0363	1
BEALE RUDOLPH W	MAJ	0-4021214	0467	1

NAME	GRADE	SVC NO	DATE RET MO YR	RET CODE
BEALE WARREN J	LTC	O-0400930	1061	1
BEALE WILLIAM A	MAJ	O-0496670	0154	2
BEALL BURTCH W	LTC	O-0142533	1148	3
BEALL CARL F	MAJ	O-0192309	0255	2
BEALL DAVID C	LTC	O-0240745	0665	3
BEALL EVERETT L	MAJ	O-1635992	0261	1
BEALL EWELL C	LTC	O-0468595	0964	3
BEALL IRVING A	MAJ	O-0263744	1060	3
BEALL JAMES F JR	MAJ	O-0262548	0366	3
BEALL JOHN A	M G	O-0019907	0268	2
BEALL ROBERT W	LTC	O-0114794	1155	3
BEALL THORNTON	LTC	O-0533679	1163	3
BEALL WILBUR W	MAJ	O-2267804	0668	1
BEALS GEORGE W	COL	O-0322288	1045	2
BEALS RUSSELL M	LTC	O-0395013	0360	1
BEAM BURTON T	LTC	O-0451210	0160	1
BEAM GEORGE M	LTC	O-0371777	0457	1
BEAM MARION J	CPT	O-0360496	0146	2
BEAM RICHARD L	MAJ	O-1688642	0665	1
BEAM SIM F	COL	O-0294791	1067	3
BEAM WILLIAM S	CW3	W-3200164	1068	1
BEAMAN CHARLES D	CPT	O-1295982	0946	2
BEAMAN JOSEPH J	LTC	O-1558633	0763	1
BEAMAN MARVIN L	MAJ	O-1293182	0255	2
BEAMAN SHERMAN	1LT	O-0280662	0168	3
BEAMER CHARLES R	MAJ	O-0411759	1160	1
BEAMER HENRY R JR	COL	O-0197734	0459	3
BEAMISH HAROLD L	COL	O-0172128	0160	3
BEAMS ALBERT I	LTC	O-1168549	0557	1
BEAN ABE K	1LT	O-1590987	1051	2
BEAN CHARLES L	COL	O-0270219	0162	3
BEAN CHARLES R	COL	O-0186832	0160	3
BEAN EARL C	MAJ	O-0226115	1044	2
BEAN EVERETT F	CPT	O-1045020	0258	1
BEAN GEORGE E	MAJ	O-1294964	0561	1
BEAN GOLDING M	LTC	O-0408157	0763	1
BEAN JOHN J	CPT	O-1057349	0258	1
BEAN K CHARLES	COL	O-0155095	0648	3
BEAN LORENZO A	2LT	O-1589683	0444	2
BEAN RALPH W	LTC	O-0124576	0648	3
BEAN RICHARD A	COL	O-0210566	0259	3
BEAN ROBERT A	MAJ	O-1339247	0960	1
BEAN RUBIE K	CPT	O-0264630	1167	3
BEAN SIMON A	MAJ	O-0262610	0463	3
BEAN THERON W	COL	O-3230042	1062	3
BEAN WILLARD F	COL	O-0249869	0367	3
BEAN WILLIAM E	MAJ	O-0973149	0455	1
BEAN WYONT B	COL	O-0277404	1265	3
BEANE BURL B	2LT	O-1324930	0645	2
BEANE NORMAN G	CPT	O-1080242	1047	2
BEANS ALVA R	CPT	O-0359193	0346	2
BEANS YANDELL S	COL	O-0219680	0858	3
BEANSTOCK SAM	CPT	O-0370784	0445	2
BEAR CHARLES E	LTC	O-0245776	0954	1
BEAR HENRY H	LTC	O-0520676	0166	3
BEAR HERBERT K	COL	O-0103046	0648	3
BEAR JENNINGS R	CPT	O-0495248	0445	1
BEAR MANFORD C	CPT	O-0400702	0845	2
BEAR WILLIAM P	LTC	O-0116318	0648	3
BEARCE BOYDEN	MAJ	O-1593934	1058	1
BEARD ALVIN H	1LT	O-1535487	0451	2
BEARD BERNARD H	LTC	O-1576916	1264	1
BEARD CLETUS F	LTC	O-0450793	0656	1
BEARD CLYDE A	LTC	O-1688401	1268	1
BEARD FRED	MAJ	O-0142495	0753	3
BEARD FRED L	LTC	O-0327695	0446	2
BEARD HENRY J	MAJ	O-2018819	0165	1
BEARD HOWARD B	LTC	O-0397224	0664	3
BEARD IRA L	LTC	O-1173966	0662	1
BEARD IRVIN E	CW2	W-2214531	1268	1
BEARD JAMES F	1LT	O-1995368	0936	2
BEARD JESSE F	CPT	O-0967802	1160	1
BEARD JOHN M	LTC	O-0132115	0455	3
BEARD LAMBERT A	COL	O-0192978	0648	3
BEARD LAWSON R	MAJ	O-0450059	0960	1

NAME	GRADE	SVC NO	DATE RET MO YR	RET CODE
BEARD NORMAN E	LTC	O-0407266	0854	1
BEARD ROBERT H	1LT	O-0293634	1046	2
BEARD ROBERT M	CPT	O-1549213	0164	1
BEARDEN ALVA G	LTC	O-1036838	1062	3
BEARDEN EUGENE I	CW2	W-3100514	0267	1
BEARDEN GARTH C	CW2	W-2147938	0955	1
BEARDEN J C	LTC	O-1016957	0463	1
BEARDEN JOHNNY L	MAJ	O-1286591	1057	1
BEARDEN NORMAN C	LTC	O-1104488	1265	1
BEARDEN RUFUS P	CW2	W-2205943	0663	1
BEARDEN WILLIAM R	MAJ	O-2030983	0964	1
BEARDMORE CHARLES C	1LT	O-0346933	0743	2
BEARDSLEE CHARLES G	LTC	O-0450575	1067	1
BEARDSLEE LEONARD L	COL	O-0210251	0746	2
BEARDSLEE VIRGIL K	1LT	O-1184770	1045	2
BEARDSLEY CHARLES H	COL	O-0230317	0864	3
BEARDSLEY HENRY S	COL	O-0261940	0655	3
BEARDSLEY MARVIN P	1LT	O-1300265	0158	1
BEARDSLEY ROBERT E	CW4	W-2142020	1268	1
BEARE JAMES D	CW2	W-2143562	0357	1
BEARLEY WILBER P	LTC	O-1695602	0966	1
BEARMAN EDWIN R	CW4	W-2143648	0167	1
BEARMAN EUGENE J	CPT	O-0447579	0146	2
BEARON MAX	CPT	O-0251579	0167	3
BEAROR OLIVER W	LTC	O-1635556	1061	1
BEARR RICHARD J	LTC	O-1280462	0860	1
BEARSCOVE KARL O	MAJ	O-0411366	0847	2
BEARSON BERNARD B	1LT	O-1895968	0945	2
BEARUP ROSS H	LTC	O-1332566	1165	1
BEASLEY CHARLES M	MAJ	O-2018983	0762	1
BEASLEY CHARLIE R	MAJ	O-0965200	0563	1
BEASLEY CLAUDE G JR	MAJ	O-2016456	1062	1
BEASLEY CLOYD O	MAJ	O-0179209	0155	3
BEASLEY JAKE W	1LT	O-1180808	0245	2
BEASLEY JOE C	1LT	O-0238597	0663	3
BEASLEY JOHN G	MAJ	O-1318007	1158	1
BEASLEY JOHNEY W	CW2	W-2151110	0157	1
BEASLEY JOSEPH L	MAJ	O-0963298	0563	1
BEASLEY LEE H	1LT	O-1796564	1046	2
BEASLEY LOUIS S	MAJ	O-1287461	1268	1
BEASLEY MARVIN J	MAJ	O-0984749	0865	1
BEASLEY ROBERT T	2LT	O-0334330	0543	2
BEASLEY SAM C	MAJ	O-1285357	0955	1
BEASLEY THEODORE L	LTC	O-1299842	0461	1
BEASLEY THOMAS G	CW3	W-2152000	1061	1
BEASLEY WILLIAM N	CW3	W-3400026	1168	1
BEASLEY WILLIAM O	LTC	O-0916979	1162	1
BEASON JOHN T	LTC	O-0248975	0466	3
BEASTEY LEWIS	2LT	O-1323517	1144	2
BEASTON ALICE L	2LT	N-0784012	0945	1
BEATH JOHN R	CW4	W-2103663	0357	1
BEATON DONALD F	1LT	O-1822522	1146	2
BEATSON JOHN B	COL	O-0361850	1163	1
BEATTIE CHESTER M JR	MAJ	O-1534915	0656	1
BEATTIE JAMES F	1LT	O-1011533	0846	2
BEATTIE JOHN C	LTC	O-0146785	0850	3
BEATTIE LUCILLE M	2LT	N-0755150	0744	1
BEATTIE ROBERT W	CW4	W-2142623	0563	1
BEATTIE WALTER O	LTC	O-0235981	0963	3
BEATTY CHARLES	1LT	O-1640316	0867	3
BEATTY CHARLES G	CPT	O-1017794	1047	2
BEATTY DALE T	MAJ	O-1894620	0265	2
BEATTY FRANCIS J	COL	O-0171017	0853	3
BEATTY RICHARD F JR	CPT	O-0963992	0663	1
BEATTY ROBERT E	CW2	W-2208499	1066	1
BEATTY ROBERT L	LTC	O-0243421	0859	1
BEATTY THOMAS E	LTC	O-0979087	0769	1
BEATTY VIVIAN B	CPT	N-0735808	0355	2
BEATY HERCHEL N	1LT	O-1184984	1057	1
BEATY JOSEPH M	CW2	W-2214812	0969	1
BEATY LESTER C	CW4	W-2145035	0764	1
BEATY ROBERT E JR	1LT	O-0520727	0246	2
BEATY THOMAS C	MAJ	O-1013322	0848	2
BEAU HENRY R	CPT	O-1878683	1063	2
BEAUBIEN JOHN W	MAJ	O-2016449	0163	1

NAME	GRADE	SVC NO	DATE RET MO YR	RET CODE
BEAUBIEN WILLIAM L	MAJ	O-1303620	0554	1
BEAUCHAMP E W JR	LTC	O-0396207	1060	1
BEAUCHAMP GLENN A	LTC	O-1257141	0466	1
BEAUCHAMP HUBERT C	MAJ	O-1172748	0954	1
BEAUCHAMP JAMES D	CPT	O-0510826	0761	1
BEAUCHAMP JAMES W	CW2	W-2203377	1157	1
BEAUCHAMP MARK L	CPT	O-0498552	0745	2
BEAUCHAMP ROBERT E	COL	O-0218843	0858	2
BEAUCHAMP S J	LTC	O-0168865	1060	3
BEAUCHAMP THOMAS O	CW4	W-2109358	1054	1
BEAUCHAMP WILLIAM	LTC	O-1114363	0367	1
BEAUCHEMIN JOSEPH P	CW3	W-2143249	0861	1
BEAUDET CECELIA A	CPT	N-0752296	1047	1
BEAUDET GRUSCH C JR	CPT	O-1107792	0547	2
BEAUDET ROBERT J	MAJ	O-1922550	0768	1
BEAUDETTE GERALD J C	MAJ	O-2009235	1057	1
BEAUDIN THEODORE J	MAJ	O-1633612	1058	1
BEAUDOIN EUCLIDE P	CPT	O-1316004	0847	2
BEAUDOIN ROBERT L	MAJ	O-1282399	1060	1
BEAUDRY AIMIE H	LTC	O-1107284	0663	1
BEAUDRY EUGENE J	CW3	W-2207227	1165	2
BEAUDRY RICHARD C	LTC	O-0942351	0866	1
BEAUFORD FRANKIE F	CW2	W-2144741	0559	1
BEAULAC JOHN J	CPT	O-0331249	0666	3
BEAULIEU ANTHONY A	CW4	W-2143220	0266	1
BEAULIEU DELTON C	COL	O-0155090	0359	3
BEAULIEU JAMES E	LTC	O-0274488	1060	1
BEAULIEU PHILIP F	MAJ	O-0407899	0561	1
BEAULIEU WILLIAM	1LT	O-1914912	0948	1
BEAUMONT FRED H	LTC	O-0249822	1264	3
BEAUMONT WILLIAM D	MAJ	O-0290283	1060	1
BEAUPARLANT JAMES H	LTC	O-1994565	0962	1
BEAUPERTHUY LOUIS F	CPT	O-4006382	1063	2
BEAUPRE AUGUSTUS J	COL	O-0124575	0954	3
BEAUREGARD JOSEPH A	LTC	O-1633621	0258	1
BEAUREGARD JOSEPH A	MAJ	O-2011766	0666	1
BEAUREGARD PRESTON M	LTC	O-0238226	0358	3
BEAUREGARD RALPH E	CW2	W-2211463	0167	1
BEAUVAIS WILLIAM E	MAJ	O-0923681	1048	2
BEAVER ALFRED T	LTC	O-0385215	1061	1
BEAVER DAVID	1LT	O-1114045	0146	2
BEAVER HERMAN P	CPT	O-2036531	0752	2
BEAVER JOHN D	LTC	O-0379544	0560	1
BEAVER JOHN T JR	LTC	O-1685015	0868	1
BEAVER JOSEPH N	LTC	O-1280115	0958	1
BEAVER WILLIAM C	LTC	O-0424489	0746	2
BEAVERS DON L	LTC	O-0339461	0660	1
BEAVERS GEORGE F	CPT	O-0192068	0758	3
BEAVERS INMAN L	1LT	O-1243527	0446	2
BEAVERS VERNON E	MAJ	O-2011775	0163	1
BEAVERS VONJAL D	LTC	O-0396862	0360	1
BEAVERS WILLIAM R	COL	O-0281198	0261	2
BEAZLEY ALEXANDER JR	MAJ	O-0310897	1068	3
BEBEE ELVIE I	CPT	N-0797228	1047	1
BEBENSEE FRED D SR	LTC	O-0363452	1054	1
BEBLER CLELL W	LTC	O-1047430	0167	1
BECCO LAWRENCE A	CW4	W-2114753	1068	1
BECHARAS GEORGE S JR	1LT	O-0517490	0446	2
BECHEL CHARLES R	LTC	O-1040092	0261	1
BECHEN VERNON T	MAJ	O-2036512	0163	1
BECHER JOHN D	LTC	O-2040722	0464	1
BECHER JOHN S	MAJ	O-0309669	0768	3
BECHET ALEXANDER	COL	O-0479811	0560	3
BECHT FREDERICK	CPT	O-1333167	0360	1
BECHT GRACE M	MAJ	N-0720578	0765	3
BECHTEL HAROLD A	CPT	O-0257005	0358	3
BECHTEL JACK C	MAJ	O-1923524	0565	1
BECHTEL JOHN M	LTC	O-1578151	0763	1
BECHTEL VICTOR J JR	MAJ	O-2018097	0762	1
BECHTELHEIMER ALICE	MAJ	N-0776334	0264	1
BECHTELL HOMER F	1LT	O-1925277	0554	2
BECHTLE EUGENE W	1LT	O-1324240	1145	2
BECHTOL JOHN L	1LT	O-1091137	0860	1
BECHTOL LAUREN L	COL	O-0297200	0768	3
BECHTOLD EDWIN J	MAJ	O-2049457	0762	1

NAME	GRADE	SVC NO	DATE RET MO YR	RET CODE
BECHTOLD HERBERT K	CW3	W-2152758	0563	1
BECK ALICE M	1LT	N-0784088	0148	1
BECK ARTHUR C	MAJ	O-0142857	1055	2
BECK BERT L	CW4	W-2101419	0358	1
BECK BJORN D	LTC	O-0244976	0966	3
BECK CLARENCE A	1LT	O-2055150	0753	1
BECK CLAYTON M	MAJ	O-1044450	1164	1
BECK DANIEL H	COL	O-0449560	0447	2
BECK DONALD W	1LT	O-0401613	0146	2
BECK EDWARD J	LTC	O-0337516	0562	1
BECK FLOYD A	LTC	O-1547877	0966	3
BECK FRANK E	CPT	O-0336684	0645	2
BECK GEORGE T	LTC	O-0266226	0868	3
BECK GILBERT	MAJ	O-0369978	0246	2
BECK HAROLD J	MAJ	O-0326735	0146	2
BECK HARRY L	CPT	O-0109129	0640	1
BECK HENRY H	CPT	O-0225074	0747	1
BECK HERMAN C JR	CPT	O-1580610	1047	2
BECK HERMAN L	LTC	O-2051043	1265	2
BECK JESSE A	COL	O-0255287	0351	2
BECK JOE T	LTC	O-1321988	0662	1
BECK JOHN F	LTC	O-0420117	0454	1
BECK KONRAD C JR	COL	O-0205524	0959	1
BECK L D	1LT	O-0511475	0743	2
BECK MALCOLM D	MAJ	O-1048279	0467	3
BECK MERRILL G	COL	O-0183406	1051	2
BECK MOXLEY L	LTC	O-0228176	0663	3
BECK PAUL R	CW2	W-2216451	0968	1
BECK ROBERT A	1LT	O-0464619	0745	2
BECK ROLAND L	MAJ	O-0981737	0565	1
BECK THEODORE S	MAJ	O-1053492	0165	3
BECK THOSS R	COL	O-0309434	0261	1
BECK WALTER D	MAJ	O-2017801	0762	1
BECK WESLEY W	CPT	O-0943764	1151	2
BECK WILLIAM A	LTC	O-0400432	0667	1
BECK WILLIAM H JR	COL	O-0234311	1058	3
BECK WILSON	CW2	W-2145320	0960	1
BECKAGE PAUL	MAJ	O-1044452	1158	1
BECKEMEYER KARL D	MAJ	O-1003184	0457	1
BECKENHAUER R W	1LT	O-1174223	0945	2
BECKER ALBERT H	LTC	O-2200102	0268	1
BECKER ARNOLD B	LTC	O-0303406	0461	1
BECKER BENJAMIN	LTC	O-0273800	0261	1
BECKER BRUCE A	CPT	O-4067345	1058	2
BECKER CARL H	LTC	O-2040775	0265	1
BECKER DAVID J	LTC	O-0294551	1058	1
BECKER EDA F	LTC	N-0771259	0668	1
BECKER ELMER W	COL	O-0202054	0362	1
BECKER EUGENE S	1LT	O-1322619	0845	2
BECKER FREDERICK	COL	O-0406995	0469	1
BECKER GEORGE A	CW2	W-2102641	0951	1
BECKER GEORGE J	MAJ	O-1534916	1166	3
BECKER HARLEY L	LTC	O-1550315	0559	1
BECKER HAROLD H	CW2	W-2209353	0162	1
BECKER HARRY F	COL	O-0199392	0246	2
BECKER HARRY G	COL	O-0322088	1165	3
BECKER HOWARD J	MAJ	O-1924071	0266	1
BECKER JOHN H	MAJ	O-2026346	0165	1
BECKER JOHN R	1LT	O-1286944	1044	2
BECKER JOSEPH G	LTC	O-0253672	0748	2
BECKER JULIUS R JR	COL	O-0253219	1057	3
BECKER LEONARD S	LTC	O-0397149	0862	1
BECKER PHILIP	LTC	O-1636008	0867	3
BECKER PHILIP A	MAJ	O-0363912	0759	2
BECKER REINHARD	COL	O-0270567	1068	3
BECKER ROBERT C	MAJ	O-1947636	1265	1
BECKER ROBERT J	MAJ	O-1798832	1263	1
BECKER ROBERT L	CW2	W-3200428	0668	2
BECKER ROLLIN F	COL	O-0319376	0446	2
BECKER SAMUEL	2LT	O-1296315	0644	2
BECKER SELDEN G	CPT	O-1342149	0261	1
BECKER WEST	LTC	O-0336338	0461	1
BECKER WILBERT R	MAJ	O-1558376	0157	1
BECKER WILLIAM C	COL	O-0203141	0655	1
BECKERMAN WILLIAM	CPT	O-0477331	0450	1

NAME	GRADE	SVC NO	DATE RET MO YR	RET CODE
BECKERT JOHN E	CPT	0-0320148	0445	2
BECKETT FRANCIS E	LTC	0-1113099	0365	1
BECKETT GERALD E	MAJ	0-0969805	1061	1
BECKETT HERBERT M	MAJ	0-1949701	0765	3
BECKETT IRVING P	MAJ	0-0175822	0745	2
BECKETT JOHN A	LTC	0-0462245	0965	3
BECKETT JOHN G	CW3	W-2203292	0962	1
BECKETT NEIL S	1LT	0-1302568	0946	2
BECKETT NICHOLAS S	COL	0-0253658	0660	3
BECKETT RICHARD L	CPT	0-1041710	1046	2
BECKETT WILLIAM H	CW4	W-2144351	1059	1
BECKHAM BENJAMIN M	LTC	0-0250580	0945	2
BECKHAM JAMES H	CPT	0-0963930	1060	1
BECKHAM LONA L	CPT	0-1166434	0448	1
BECKHAM MALCOLM F	COL	0-0337033	0157	1
BECKHAM ROBERT O	CPT	0-1174226	0763	1
BECKHAM THOMAS M	CPT	0-1047875	0866	1
BECKHAM WILLIE S	LTC	0-0245644	0662	1
BECKLEN ALICE A	LTC	N-0700172	1045	1
BECKLEY HARRY A	LTC	0-0302375	0659	3
BECKLEY LEO H	COL	0-0236865	0864	3
BECKLUND WALTER A	LTC	0-1636014	0363	1
BECKMAN ALBERT J	1LT	0-0121466	0453	3
BECKMAN CARL H	1LT	0-0549200	0146	2
BECKMAN CLETUS F	1LT	0-4028016	0358	2
BECKMAN DILL D	COL	0-0268974	0566	3
BECKMAN ELMER P	2LT	0-1030641	0744	2
BECKMAN FRED L	CPT	0-1825754	1046	2
BECKMAN FREDERIC R	COL	0-0325132	0960	1
BECKMAN JACK	CW2	W-2141903	0755	1
BECKMAN PAUL L	LTC	0-1823819	0962	1
BECKMANN GEORGE G	CPT	0-0178053	0157	3
BECKNELL ROBERT G	LTC	0-1051478	1062	1
BECKNER ROBERT R	CW2	W-2150892	0360	1
BECKNO JOHN	MAJ	0-0451074	0958	1
BECKORD DONALD C A	MAJ	0-0234925	1065	3
BECKSTED G ELEANOR	MAJ	N-0755671	0463	1
BECKSTROM ALLAN O	CPT	0-0424191	0245	2
BECKWITH CARL A	MAJ	0-0394590	1263	1
BECKWITH CHARLES E	2LT	0-1547878	1143	2
BECKWITH HAROLD C	LTC	0-1578154	C764	2
BECKWITH MILLEDGE M	COL	0-0272050	0658	1
BECKWITH NANCY K	2LT	N-0762002	0545	1
BECKWITH RAYMOND W	CW3	W-2152173	0564	1
BECKWITH ROBERT L	MAJ	0-0391909	1045	2
BECKWITH SUTHERLAND	LTC	0-0116001	1050	3
BECKWITH THEODORE I	MAJ	0-0229595	1162	3
BECKWITH WARREN E	CW3	W-2144403	0460	1
BECQUE WILLIAM	2LT	0-1035589	0344	2
BECTON THOMAS H	LTC	0-1287650	0767	1
BECTON WENDELL R	LTC	0-0917744	0565	3
BEDA STEPHEN W	LTC	0-0362704	0949	2
BEDARD LAWRENCE R	1LT	0-1322874	0246	2
BEDAYAN KEERKOP	MAJ	0-1545076	0657	1
BEDDINGFIELD WALTER	MAJ	0-0958178	0262	1
BEDELL ARCHER W	MAJ	0-0223690	0648	3
BEDELL FOREST L	MAJ	0-0227996	0164	3
BEDELL GEORGE W	LTC	0-1062328	0967	1
BEDELL HARRY P	LTC	0-0196163	0760	3
BEDELL JOHN A	CPT	0-1316122	0247	2
BEDELL JOHN R	COL	0-0136943	0354	1
BEDELL M JOSEPHIN	CPT	N-0720145	0846	2
BEDELL MATTHEW G	LTC	0-1104049	0156	1
BEDELL ROBERT J	COL	0-0272437	0868	3
BEDENBAUGH B H	MAJ	0-1798432	0656	1
BEDER MARVIN L	1LT	0-0512002	0845	2
BEDESSEM PHILIP M	COL	0-0325405	0451	3
BEDFORD ALFRED C JR	CPT	0-1011333	0545	2
BEDFORD ARCHIE G	2LT	0-0431547	1043	2
BEDFORD GEORGE J	LTC	0-0223156	1064	3
BEDFORD GORMAN L	LTC	0-1633657	0461	1
BEDFORD HUGH R	LTC	0-0451487	0954	1
BEDFORD JOSEPH S	LTC	0-0309270	0762	1
BEDFORD WILLIAM H JR	CPT	0-0463835	1146	2
BEDNARZ HENRY	LTC	0-1555345	0763	1

NAME	GRADE	SVC NO	DATE RET MO YR	RET CODE
BEDNARZ JOSEPH P P	MAJ	0-1336864	0563	1
BEDRICK DAVID N	1LT	0-1551352	0745	2
BEDSOLE NED	CW3	W-2143611	0660	1
BEDSOLE QUINCY L SR	CW4	W-2004297	1067	1
BEDWELL LYMAN C	LTC	0-1894550	0162	1
BEDZIS BENJAMIN	LTC	0-1308415	0261	1
BEE CARL E	COL	0-0286101	1152	2
BEEBE ALBERT H	LTC	0-0432507	0767	1
BEEBE EUGENE H	MAJ	0-1301766	0867	3
BEEBE FRANCES J	1LT	N-0787350	0146	2
BEEBE FRANCIS A	LTC	0-0220006	0650	3
BEEBE FRANK O	MAJ	0-0278904	0667	3
BEEBE JERVIS S	CW3	W-2210737	0768	1
BEEBE RAYMOND L	CW3	W-2007442	0865	1
BEEBE REVERE H	LTC	0-0221290	0759	3
BEEBE THOMAS G	MAJ	0-0229536	1161	3
BEECH CHARLES W	MAJ	0-0249776	0554	3
BEECH CLIFFORD L	MAJ	0-1581024	0264	1
BEECH FRED P	MAJ	0-1104489	0660	1
BEECH JOHNSTONE	MAJ	0-0499933	1047	2
BEECH SIDNEY C	MAJ	0-1291939	0561	1
BEECH WILLIAM K	CW3	W-2145958	0760	1
BEECHER VERNE L	CW4	W-2144483	1060	1
BEECHERL LOUIS A	MAJ	0-0152990	0654	3
BEECHINOR ROBERT M	COL	0-0384446	0764	1
BEECHLER JOHN G	1LT	0-1879006	0354	2
BEEDY STANTON L	CW3	W-2205966	0865	1
BEEKMAN FREDERIC	MAJ	0-0469873	0847	2
BEEKMAN WILLIAM N	LTC	0-0323541	0662	1
BEELER CARL G	CW3	W-2206431	0265	1
BEELER CHARLES F	MAJ	0-0142400	0558	3
BEELER HENRY S	COL	0-0286503	0268	3
BEELER HERBERT	LTC	0-0160496	1055	3
BEELMAN EMIL W	LTC	0-0180153	0561	3
BEEM FRANK C	CPT	0-0487858	0757	1
BEEM JACOB J	MAJ	0-0326183	1265	3
BEEM RICHARD C	LTC	0-0257556	0464	3
BEEMAN ALBERT E	CW4	W-2143302	1266	1
BEEMAN FRED	LTC	0-0230996	0758	3
BEEMAN JAMES E	CW3	W-3150316	0568	1
BEEMAN JOHN A	COL	0-0250746	0567	3
BEEMAN LALLY	LTC	0-1823969	0962	1
BEEMAN ROBERT L	CPT	0-1292458	0247	2
BEEMER WILLIAM H	CPT	0-1320014	0662	1
BEENE JONATHAN J	MAJ	0-1342238	0764	1
BEER ANTON C	LTC	0-0370094	0965	1
BEER GEORGE R	MAJ	0-1283711	1065	1
BEER RALPH D	LTC	0-1001727	1166	2
BEER WILLIAM C JR	LTC	0-1047022	0366	3
BEERE HARRY W	CW4	W-2120026	0659	1
BEERMAN HERMAN P	LTC	0-0286486	1056	3
BEERMAN MAX	LTC	0-0173370	0645	2
BEERS BARNET W	COL	0-0120516	0856	2
BEERS CARL K	MAJ	0-1996333	0261	1
BEERS DRYDEN N	MAJ	0-0247606	0566	3
BEERS INEZ F	MAJ	N-0725841	1067	1
BEERS JAMES F	LTC	0-1C80509	0859	1
BEERS JOHN H	CPT	0-0379336	0945	2
BEERS RICHARD H	CPT	0-0537882	0847	2
BEERY CHARLES E	CW3	W-2211086	1168	1
BEERY CLARENCE H JR	LTC	0-0387251	1062	1
BEERY EDWIN N	COL	0-0325016	0246	2
BEERY MARVIN D	MAJ	0-0263243	0367	3
BEERY WALLACE C SR	CPT	0-2014550	0766	1
BEESMER JOHN F	MAJ	0-1338549	0464	1
BEESON BILLY G	LTC	0-0536435	1264	1
BEESON EARL A	CPT	0-0498696	0254	1
BEESON JOHN R	1LT	0-0960363	1052	2
BEESON MARK T	MAJ	0-1013894	0662	1
BEESTON WILLIAM H	1LT	0-1292283	0845	2
BEETHAM ROLAND M JR	CPT	0-1012266	0545	2
BEETLE MELVIN W	MAJ	0-1103059	0762	1
BEETS FREEMAN H	1LT	0-1062122	1045	2
BEEVES EARL J	CPT	0-1640209	0257	1
BEGBIE JAMES W	MAJ	0-0291121	0346	2

NAME	GRADE	SVC NO	DATE RET MO YR	RET CODE
BEGEMAN MYRON L	LTC	0-0158160	0953	3
BEGGEHLY ANDREW F	1LT	0-1317612	1145	2
BEGGS CHARLES G	LTC	0-0248900	0965	3
BEGGS ELMORE C	LTC	0-0269492	0568	3
BEGGS GEORGE H	1LT	0-1293528	0645	2
BEGGS JOHN A	CPT	0-0793977	1054	2
BEGGS RICHARD J	CW2	W-2143171	0457	1
BEGIEN ROBERT S	COL	0-0308589	0564	3
BEGLEY MARCUS F	2LT	0-1591591	0544	2
BEGLEY RICHARD R	CW2	W-2142131	0656	1
BEGNAUD MELVIN	MAJ	0-2055479	1160	1
BEGOVICH JOHN C	2LT	0-2055253	1045	2
BEHAN WILLIAM E SR	MAJ	0-1688633	0163	2
BEHEE PAUL	CW3	W-2118194	0262	1
BEHLE CALVIN A	COL	0-0487245	0467	1
BEHLING HARVEY W	MAJ	0-0888195	0364	1
BEHLKE WILLIAM O	CPT	0-0118421	0858	2
BEHNE FRANK J	CPT	0-1310674	0257	1
BEHNISCH ERWIN A	LTC	0-0154981	0444	2
BEHNKE DONALD A	MAJ	0-2032863	1062	1
BEHNKE DONALD W	CPT	0-0372749	0544	2
BEHNKE EWALD	MAJ	0-0510299	0153	1
BEHNKE RUSSELL D	CW2	W-2147722	0261	1
BEHNY HAROLD C	1LT	0-2020783	1151	2
BEHR ALEXANDER	CPT	0-1307182	0148	2
BEHR KENNETH P	CPT	0-0123302	0556	3
BEHRENBERG WILLIAM C	LTC	0-0354674	1060	1
BEHREND ALBERT	COL	0-0336774	0967	3
BEHREND WILMER R	LTC	0-1053048	0263	1
BEHRENS CHARLES N	LTC	0-0240133	0949	3
BEHRENS CYRIL	1LT	0-1334673	1056	1
BEHRENS DAVID R	CW3	W-2103664	1054	1
BEHRENS HERMAN W	CW3	W-2200103	0666	3
BEHRENS WILLIAM G	LTC	0-0219859	0648	3
BEHRING CARL F	MAJ	0-0188218	0153	3
BEHRLE FRANK C JR	MAJ	0-0253725	0447	2
BEHRMAN ABRAHAM S	COL	0-0212187	1052	3
BEHRNS JOHN L	COL	0-0205704	0858	1
BEICHEK BORIS B	1LT	0-1633066	0347	2
BEICIUNAS PETER	CPT	0-0481756	0447	1
BEIDECK RUDOLPH R	MAJ	0-1583436	0261	1
BEIDLE JAMES C	CPT	0-1317873	1061	1
BEIDLER JOHN	LTC	0-0418690	1053	1
BEIER GAYLORD E	LTC	0-1286061	1063	1
BEIERSCHMITT ROBERT	LTC	0-1295151	0562	1
BEIGHLEY FRANK H	CPT	0-0984116	0462	1
BEIGHLEY HAZEL F	2LT	N-0734833	0345	1
BEILING WAYNE A	MAJ	0-0450403	0258	1
BEILSMITH LOWELL H	MAJ	0-1061057	1061	1
BEIN SOLOMON S	MAJ	0-0321965	0146	2
BEINECKE ALVIN A	LTC	0-1573035	0566	1
BEINECKE CHARLES R	MAJ	0-0955406	0363	1
BEINSTEIN JOSEPH	CPT	0-0506266	0246	2
BEIRIGER WALTER F	MAJ	0-0312896	1162	3
BEIRNE JOHN F A	COL	0-0287462	0161	3
BEIRSTEIN SAMUEL S	MAJ	0-1689814	0444	2
BEISEL CLIFFORD L	CW4	W-2101428	0659	1
BEISEL JOHN E	2LT	0-1307345	1144	2
BEISHEIM JOHN W	LTC	0-1115869	0265	3
BEISLER HAROLD A	LTC	0-0206614	0360	3
BEISTEL ARTHUR F	MAJ	0-0351258	0863	1
BEISTEL HENRY F	COL	0-0280287	0767	3
BEISTLE DONALD D	MAJ	0-0402659	0161	2
BEITIA-SALAND COSME	1LT	0-0155726	0255	3
BEITLER CLAUDE T	CW3	W-2151783	0863	1
BEITLER JACK F	CW3	W-2153239	0467	1
BEJACH LOIS D	MAJ	0-0150578	0648	3
BEJASA GREGORIO D	1LT	0-1896278	0950	2
BEK RICHARD C	LTC	0-2036289	0667	1
BEKERIS LOUIS J	1LT	0-1646544	0745	2
BEKIER HENRY J	CPT	0-0532986	1048	2
BEKOWITZ SOLOMAN	CPT	0-1945951	1047	1
BELAIR EDWARD P	1LT	0-0393607	0145	2
BELAND OAKLEY B	COL	0-0325246	1165	3
BELANGER ALFRED V	MAJ	0-1044754	0261	1

NAME	GRADE	SVC NO	DATE RET MO YR	RET CODE
BELANGER FRANCIS J	CW3	W-2143866	0762	1
BELANGER IRVING J	CPT	0-0106492	0758	3
BELANGER LEONARD S	1LT	0-0489296	0745	2
BELANGER LEWIS A	1LT	0-0375870	1045	2
BELANGER PHILIP A	CW3	W-2209822	0968	1
BELASCO PHILIP	MAJ	0-2053829	0854	1
BELAWICH LEO B	1LT	0-1327922	0547	2
BELBA ISADORE M	LTC	0-1998367	0566	1
BELCH JAMES E	CPT	0-1333414	0557	1
BELCHER BASCOM A	LTC	0-0248131	1067	3
BELCHER CLIFFORD L	MAJ	0-0963739	0864	1
BELCHER EARL S	LTC	0-1575730	0253	2
BELCHER ORVAL	MAJ	0-2025362	0859	1
BELCHER TAYLOR	LTC	0-0140424	0648	3
BELCHER VERA H	2LT	N-0764131	0146	1
BELCOVSKY ADOLPH	MAJ	0-0480885	0647	1
BELDEN DARWIN J	2LT	0-1558115	0645	2
BELET WILMER F	MAJ	0-0991102	0963	1
BELGARD CECIL C	LTC	0-0250337	0164	3
BELGRADE NATHAN B	MAJ	0-0320911	1058	1
BELICOSE RALPH J	CW4	W-2102643	0859	1
BELIE ROBERT A	CW2	W-2208528	1161	1
BELILES PERLE	1LT	0-1686150	0349	1
BELITSKY FRANK C	LTC	0-1175038	0763	1
BELIVEAU EUGENE H	LTC	0-1289372	1055	1
BELK CLARENCE L	WO1	W-2120323	0855	1
BELK SAMUEL E	CPT	0-1323798	1146	2
BELKNAP CLIFFORD B	CPT	0-0486529	0445	2
BELKNAP FLORENCE M	LTC	L-0125022	0962	1
BELKNAP HOBART D	COL	0-0215798	0157	3
BELKNAPP JAMIESON R	LTC	0-0272510	0259	3
BELKOV SYLVIN	CPT	0-0385231	1144	2
BELKOVICZ JOHN A	1LT	0-1049725	1146	2
BELKY WILLIAM H	LTC	0-1799224	0761	1
BELL ALBERT J	1LT	0-1596265	0446	2
BELL ARTHUR H	LTC	0-0219479	0357	3
BELL ARTHUR R	CW2	W-2143017	0456	1
BELL ARTHUR S	COL	0-0155108	0546	2
BELL ARVIN	LTC	0-1173160	0665	1
BELL BANKS H	LTC	0-0271447	1067	3
BELL BENJAMIN	LTC	0-1047437	0761	1
BELL BERNARD D	2LT	0-1290366	0445	2
BELL BESSIE S	1LT	N-0700020	1033	1
BELL BILL	LTC	0-1643465	0963	1
BELL BRYAN JR	1LT	0-1313366	0845	2
BELL BYARD	MAJ	0-1640353	0562	1
BELL CARL	CPT	0-0300610	0754	3
BELL CHARLES E JR	COL	0-0282580	0768	3
BELL CHARLES L	COL	0-0266304	1061	3
BELL CHARLES L	MAJ	0-1011584	0547	2
BELL CHARLES R	1LT	0-1179293	1045	2
BELL CHESTER E	1LT	0-1284454	0745	2
BELL CLARENCE V	MAJ	0-0226310	0461	3
BELL CLYDE C JR	1LT	0-0408158	0246	2
BELL CLYDE R	1LT	0-1573809	0248	2
BELL COOPER C	MAJ	0-1110367	1160	1
BELL DEWITT	1LT	0-2205719	1153	2
BELL DONALD A	LTC	0-1342235	0967	1
BELL DOROTHY M	MAJ	N-0772238	0767	2
BELL EDGAR V H	COL	0-0180702	0559	3
BELL EDGAR W	LTC	0-2049177	0863	1
BELL EDITH M	MAJ	L-1010009	0763	1
BELL EDWARD C	CPT	0-0301385	0648	3
BELL ERNEST L JR	LTC	0-0206259	0460	3
BELL ERNEST T	CW3	W-2147245	0265	1
BELL EUGENE H	LTC	0-0245576	0863	3
BELL EUGENE M	MAJ	0-0437470	0848	1
BELL FOSTER F	CPT	0-2009573	0557	1
BELL FRANC W	CPT	0-1844863	0755	1
BELL FRED O	CW3	W-2203424	0466	1
BELL GEORGE M J	MAJ	0-1342038	0262	1
BELL GEORGE R	COL	0-0916829	1167	3
BELL GEORGE R	1LT	0-2055191	0546	1
BELL GLENN C JR	MAJ	0-1306751	0759	1
BELL GORDON F	MAJ	0-1284634	0346	2

NAME	GRADE	SVC NO	DATE RET MO YR	RET CODE
BELL GRADY J JR	CPT	0-0377782	0346	2
BELL HARRY B	CW3	W-2145101	0361	1
BELL HARVEY E JR	MAJ	0-0380588	1146	2
BELL HENRY G	MAJ	0-0330345	1044	2
BELL HENRY N JR	CPT	0-0216728	0262	3
BELL HOWARD K	CW3	W-2151923	0263	1
BELL IRVING	1LT	0-1323799	1045	2
BELL JACK H	WO1	W-2148516	0656	1
BELL JAMES E	CW2	W-2144939	1263	1
BELL JAMES H	CPT	0-2010735	0958	2
BELL JAMES I	MAJ	0-0229294	0660	3
BELL JEAN N	LTC	0-0256986	1167	3
BELL JESS W	CW2	W-2132324	0262	2
BELL JOE W	CPT	0-1290706	1158	1
BELL JOHN E	CPT	0-1303291	1061	1
BELL JOHN R	MAJ	0-1633068	0757	1
BELL JOHN S	MAJ	0-0325173	0544	2
BELL JOHN T	LTC	0-0221255	1055	3
BELL JOHN T	LTC	0-0336145	0160	1
BELL JOSEPH	LTC	0-1300267	0561	1
BELL JOSEPH A	CW4	W-2143477	1162	1
BELL KENNETH D	CW3	W-2153334	0266	1
BELL LACY H	LTC	0-0320476	0267	3
BELL LADDIE P	CW3	W-2143680	0560	1
BELL LEON B	CPT	0-1062366	0453	2
BELL LEON H	MAJ	0-1919208	0567	1
BELL LEONARD	LTC	0-1796407	0566	1
BELL LEROY A	1LT	0-1032365	0147	2
BELL LLOYD M	1LT	0-1296638	1043	2
BELL LUTHER F	COL	0-0295066	0968	3
BELL MARY E	2LT	N-0729444	0146	1
BELL PAUL B	M G	0-0215450	0362	3
BELL PAUL G	COL	0-0253330	0647	2
BELL PERCY B	LTC	0-0918730	0763	3
BELL RALPH M	LTC	0-0402485	0146	2
BELL RAYMOND J	MAJ	0-0887598	0954	1
BELL RILEY L	MAJ	0-0979128	0766	2
BELL ROBERT	MAJ	0-0262138	0846	2
BELL ROBERT C	CPT	0-1878863	0666	1
BELL ROBERT E	CW2	W-3440020	0267	1
BELL ROBERT J	MAJ	0-1100872	0846	2
BELL ROBERT R	CPT	0-1109137	0846	2
BELL ROY	MAJ	0-1885916	1266	1
BELL SIDNEY A	CPT	0-0401536	0545	2
BELL SIDNEY C	CPT	0-1283007	0148	2
BELL SPURGEON	LTC	0-0184927	0648	3
BELL STUART C	LTC	0-0296859	1067	3
BELL THOMAS D	CW3	W-2206653	1268	1
BELL VIRGIL R	MAJ	0-1101730	0167	1
BELL VIRGIL W	CW3	W-2149784	0456	1
BELL WALLACE A JR	MAJ	0-1298345	1060	1
BELL WALTER M	LTC	0-0250086	1266	3
BELL WALTER W	MAJ	0-0985828	0568	1
BELL WARREN J	MAJ	0-1552636	1055	1
BELL WILBURN K	CPT	0-0340128	0145	2
BELL WILLIAM G	LTC	0-1031383	1062	1
BELL WILLIAM H	COL	0-0205969	1061	3
BELL WILLIAM H	LTC	0-0997482	1267	1
BELL WILLIAM H	CW3	RW-2142537	0162	1
BELL WILLIAM K	1LT	0-0912817	1143	2
BELL WILLIAM P	COL	0-0247026	0665	3
BELL WILLIAM T JR	COL	0-0419125	0666	1
BELL WILMER U	COL	0-0268865	1167	3
BELLAH JAMES M	LTC	0-1166006	0759	1
BELLAH JAMES W	COL	0-0219868	1059	3
BELLAMY JESSE P	COL	0-0177755	0958	3
BELLAMY JOHN A	LTC	0-0287615	0346	2
BELLAN JOHN M	MAJ	0-0254902	0552	3
BELLANTUONI JOSEPH	CPT	0-2055305	0156	1
BELLAS WILLIAM J	CW2	W-2152261	0264	1
BELLASSAI ANTHONY	MAJ	0-2287670	0667	1
BELLEFONTAINE JOHN P	CW2	W-2207331	1164	1
BELLEGANTE LOUIS	MAJ	0-0252613	1062	3
BELLEMAN WILLIAM I	CW3	W-2148954	0266	1
BELLEMARE ARTHUR J	CW3	W-2151921	0161	1

NAME	GRADE	SVC NO	DATE RET MO YR	RET CODE
BELLER CHARLES H	WO1	W-2151409	0257	1
BELLER EARL J	LTC	0-0501538	0954	1
BELLES JOHN H	LTC	0-0415425	0958	1
BELLES VIRGIE M	MAJ	N-0797765	0765	1
BELLEVILLE R C III	COL	0-0179724	0458	3
BELLIEU LED H	LTC	0-0513431	0863	2
BELLINGER FREDERICK	COL	0-0309358	0964	3
BELLINO VINCENT	MAJ	0-0957255	1163	1
BELLINY DANIEL S	2LT	0-1311966	0145	2
BELLIS LEON R	1LT	0-1585159	0145	2
BELLMAN MARTIN L	CW4	W-2108954	0655	1
BELLOCCHI ROBERT R	CPT	0-1294418	1145	2
BELLOIR ROBERT G	LTC	0-1286945	1058	1
BELLOMY OTTO E	1LT	0-1104493	0146	2
BELLOWS HAROLD S	MAJ	0-0981439	1263	1
BELLOWS LESLIE R	MAJ	0-1293184	0558	1
BELLOWS PAUL R	LTC	0-0900885	0745	2
BELLUCCI LAWRENCE T	1LT	0-1280545	0745	2
BELLUCCI VINCENT	LTC	0-0919360	0363	1
BELLUSCI FRANK P	LTC	0-1638076	0766	1
BELMONT GAIL H	MAJ	0-2033183	0661	1
BELMONT MORRISON H	MAJ	0-1693481	0346	2
BELMONT PHILIP F	LTC	0-0532807	0861	1
BELMONT ROBERT	LTC	0-1055778	0866	1
BELNAP HOWARD K	LTC	0-0285944	0346	2
BELOT GUSTAVE H	CW4	W-2114475	0459	1
BELOTE GEORGE E JR	1LT	0-0355134	0644	2
BELOTE LEM Y	LTC	0-1101332	0960	1
BELOW WILLIAM M	MAJ	0-0197813	0953	3
BELSCHWENDER ROBERT	CW3	W-2152941	0764	1
BELSER IRVINE F	COL	0-0108975	0150	3
BELSER RICHARD B	LTC	0-0305405	0248	2
BELSHAW MARSHALL E	MAJ	0-0225445	0765	3
BELSHER HORACE E	COL	0-0245388	0565	3
BELSKY WILLIAM E	LTC	0-1550107	1062	1
BELSON MORVALE O	MAJ	0-1324241	0356	1
BELT CARL D	COL	0-0344542	0763	1
BELT WARREN H	LTC	0-1534210	0468	1
BELT WILLIAM G	LTC	0-2055454	1162	1
BELTEN CHARLES D	MAJ	0-2096469	0466	1
BELTON GWILYM I	MAJ	0-1051869	0364	1
BELTRAN EVANS B	1LT	0-2027444	0552	1
BELTRAN LUDOVICO	1LT	0-2031846	1060	1
BELTZ JACK N	LTC	0-1016562	0366	1
BELVEL PAUL W	CPT	0-0538710	0455	2
BELZ JOSEPH A	COL	0-0321360	1267	3
BELZER MEYER S	COL	0-0285420	0168	3
BEMIS CLARA L	2LT	N-0700166	1033	1
BEMIS HOWARD C	MAJ	0-0276862	0661	3
BEMIS LEELIN A	MAJ	0-0178793	0261	3
BEMIS RUSSELL B	LTC	0-1109138	0766	1
BENACK WILLIAM B	1LT	0-1318641	1045	2
BENASSI NORINE M	CPT	N-0783098	0946	1
BENBOW EDGAR V	MAJ	0-0479192	0944	2
BENBOW SPENCER D	LTC	0-0261785	0866	3
BENBURY LEMUEL S	CPT	0-0286490	0267	3
BENCH BERNARD M	LTC	0-0259702	0966	3
BENCH WILLIAM F	LTC	0-0201169	0745	2
BENCIVENNI RAOUL W	LTC	0-0371787	0561	1
BENDELL ALFRED S JR	COL	0-0918584	0566	3
BENDER ALFRED J JR	LTC	0-0909346	0663	1
BENDER CLEBURNE S	LTC	0-0197328	0959	1
BENDER EARL	LTC	0-0194581	0453	3
BENDER ELMER P	CW3	W-2102646	0954	2
BENDER FOREST P	MAJ	0-0263486	1058	3
BENDER FRED	LTC	0-0120365	1054	3
BENDER FREDERICK	CPT	0-1942261	0665	2
BENCER GEORGE	CPT	0-1649696	0856	1
BENDER GLEN A	CW3	W-2212577	0968	2
BENDER GLENNON F	1LT	0-1544347	1046	2
BENDER HARRY W	CPT	0-1013795	0854	1
BENDER HENRY A	MAJ	0-1765205	1047	2
BENDER JAMES W	COL	0-0297342	0861	1
BENDER JOHN R	LTC	0-0404663	0164	1
BENDER LLOYD C	LTC	0-1174772	0266	3

NAME	GRADE	SVC NO	DATE RET MO YR	RET CODE
BENDER MATTHEW F	MAJ	0-1633859	0246	2
BENDER MICHAEL N	CPT	0-1689687	0645	2
BENDER NORMAN J	MAJ	0-0201840	0360	1
BENDER PAUL J	2LT	0-1182777	1144	2
BENDER ROBERT J	CW3	RW-2143460	0562	1
BENDER ROBERT O	CW4	W-2102648	1154	1
BENDER ROY M	LTC	0-0253114	1052	2
BENDER WILLIAM H	COL	0-0241394	0461	3
BENDER WILLIAM R	MAJ	0-1949596	0666	1
BENDERSON NATHAN	1LT	0-0921004	0645	2
BENDKOWSKI DOROTHY M	MAJ	N-0745550	0764	1
BENDL ROBERT F	MAJ	0-1919424	1166	1
BENEDETTI BART P	LTC	0-2208541	0268	1
BENEDETTO ELMO F	1LT	0-2046888	0945	2
BENEDICT ALFONSO J	MAJ	0-0385697	0864	1
BENEDICT BRUCE W	CPT	0-0379996	0744	2
BENEDICT CHARLES A	MAJ	0-2096814	0265	1
BENEDICT DANIEL W	COL	0-1280103	0964	1
BENEDICT DONALD D	CPT	0-0364845	0845	2
BENEDICT EDWARD E	1LT	0-0505596	1044	2
BENEDICT HELEN G	CPT	N-0731137	1047	1
BENEDICT HOWARD W JR	2LT	0-1323900	0645	2
BENEDICT ROBERT D	LTC	0-1950577	0164	1
BENEDICT ROBERT M	MAJ	0-0452367	0661	1
BENEDOSSO VICTORIA T	2LT	N-0753083	0446	1
BENEFIEL JENNIE P	CPT	N-0729924	0652	2
BENEFIEL WILEY R	CW4	W-2111112	0659	1
BENEFIELD FREDERICK	CW3	W-2146495	0766	1
BENEGAR ARCHIE S	LTC	0-0394293	1060	1
BENET GEORGE	COL	0-0212066	0748	3
BENEVELLI ALEXANDER	CW3	W-2144839	0962	1
BENEVENTI JOHN R	CPT	0-0411147	1047	2
BENEZECH EDWARD P	LTC	0-0186188	0954	3
BENFORD FRANK S	CPT	0-1042232	1160	1
BENFORD GEORGE H	MAJ	0-1923625	0665	1
BENFORD MILTON A	LTC	0-0461469	1164	1
BENGE DAVID W	MAJ	0-1019289	0359	1
BENGE MARTHA F	CPT	N-0728933	0350	2
BENHAM LELAND F	CW4	W-2112016	0960	1
BENHAM SARAH M	MAJ	L-0202689	0463	1
BENHAM SPERRY S	MAJ	0-1037037	0863	1
BENINI FLAVIO	CPT	0-1109139	0546	2
BENIOFF BEN	COL	0-0169145	0860	3
BENIT DUDLEY J	COL	0-0396342	0763	1
BENJAMIN DAYTON L JR	2LT	0-1112560	1143	2
BENJAMIN FRANCIS J	MAJ	0-1114049	0860	1
BENJAMIN HAROLD G	COL	0-0342449	0867	3
BENJAMIN HARRY	MAJ	0-2046639	1055	1
BENJAMIN IRVING	1LT	0-0495591	1145	2
BENJAMIN JASON	CW4	W-2114766	0157	1
BENJAMIN JULIEN E	COL	0-0142844	1050	3
BENJAMIN KENNETH R	COL	0-0348393	0959	1
BENJAMIN LESTER V	CPT	0-0126652	1053	3
BENJAMIN MILTON	CPT	0-0489084	0944	2
BENJAMIN WILLIAM E	CPT	0-0194531	1044	2
BENKE RALPH L SR	MAJ	0-1020065	1166	1
BENKENDORF DONNA V	CPT	0-0474395	1145	2
BENN BENJAMIN	CW2	W-2102651	0857	1
BENNEFELD LESTER O	CW4	W-2152016	0760	1
BENNER CHRISTIANA	2LT	N-0735753	0445	1
BENNER FREDERICK	LTC	0-0262011	0563	3
BENNER HARRY L	CPT	0-0313111	1059	3
BENNER HULBERT H	CPT	0-1683487	0658	1
BENNER MEARL S	MAJ	0-1304666	0161	1
BENNER STANFORD R	LTC	0-0888584	1160	1
BENNERS JOHN S	CW3	W-2152103	0762	1
BENNETT ADOLPH J	CPT	0-1058438	0347	2
BENNETT ALBERT M	LTC	0-0305212	0347	2
BENNETT ALVIN E	WO1	W-2141711	0958	1
BENNETT ALVORD A	CW2	W-2214474	0468	1
BENNETT ARCHIE	1LT	0-1698839	0845	2
BENNETT ARDEN L	LTC	0-0366931	1158	1
BENNETT ARTHUR A	MAJ	0-1642092	0158	2
BENNETT BENJAMIN H	LTC	0-1101333	1060	1
BENNETT BERT W	CPT	0-1016029	0756	1

NAME	GRADE	SVC NO	DATE RET MO YR	RET CODE
BENNETT BYRON A	MAJ	0-0255345	0446	2
BENNETT CAROLINE E	1LT	N-0700600	0444	1
BENNETT CHARLES E	CPT	0-1300916	0147	2
BENNETT CHARLES W	MAJ	0-1168170	0763	1
BENNETT CHESLEY J	COL	0-0454606	0868	2
BENNETT CHESTER N	LTC	0-0258713	0167	3
BENNETT CLARENCE H	CPT	0-0986284	1060	1
BENNETT CLAYTON C	1LT	0-1323997	0346	2
BENNETT CLYDE P	LTC	0-1795848	0862	1
BENNETT DAVID L	2LT	0-1303454	1144	2
BENNETT DENVER R	MAJ	0-1294256	0660	1
BENNETT DONALD H	LTC	0-0447843	0254	1
BENNETT EDWARD J	CW3	W-2145232	0862	1
BENNETT ERNEST R	1LT	0-1183240	0346	2
BENNETT EUGENE O	COL	0-0201988	1044	2
BENNETT EUGENE L	MAJ	0-0988893	0466	1
BENNETT EVERETT H	MAJ	0-1890385	1066	1
BENNETT FLOYD K	LTC	0-1175040	0962	2
BENNETT FOREMAN R	LTC	0-0238487	0466	3
BENNETT FRANK M JR	LTC	0-0692267	0363	1
BENNETT FRANK R	MAJ	0-1318953	0955	1
BENNETT FREDERICK	LTC	0-0336339	0960	1
BENNETT GEOFFREY W	COL	0-0318456	0806	3
BENNETT GEORGE B	COL	0-0264235	0165	3
BENNETT GEORGE E	LTC	0-0428456	1061	1
BENNETT GLENN L	LTC	0-0262106	0767	3
BENNETT GORDON C	MAJ	0-2021037	0765	1
BENNETT HAROLD T	CPT	0-0489916	0253	1
BENNETT HARRY J	LTC	0-0232730	0964	3
BENNETT HARRY W	CPT	0-0493174	0257	1
BENNETT HORACE M	LTC	0-0913115	0565	3
BENNETT HOWARD H	CW3	W-3150721	1068	1
BENNETT HUBERT	CPT	0-0484072	1047	1
BENNETT IRA F	COL	0-0124335	0848	3
BENNETT IRA L	CPT	0-1080599	1057	1
BENNETT JACK	LTC	0-0947083	0967	1
BENNETT JACOB C JR	LTC	0-1341391	0667	1
BENNETT JAMES B	COL	0-0309960	0257	1
BENNETT JAMES C	1LT	0-1286947	1046	2
BENNETT JAMES G	LTC	0-0286013	0665	3
BENNETT JAMES H	LTC	0-0420695	0561	1
BENNETT JAMES R	MAJ	0-2262731	0863	1
BENNETT JEWEL E	CPT	0-0996458	0164	1
BENNETT JOE D JR	CPT	0-1825599	0559	2
BENNETT JOE H	CPT	0-0978957	1060	1
BENNETT JOHN B	LTC	0-0229717	0355	3
BENNETT JOHN H	COL	0-0142738	0355	3
BENNETT JOHN R	LTC	0-0554021	0763	1
BENNETT JOSEPH E	MAJ	0-0116945	0648	3
BENNETT JOSEPH M	MAJ	0-1312485	0361	1
BENNETT JOSEPH R	LTC	0-0226664	0860	3
BENNETT JUANITA L	MAJ	N-0759247	1162	1
BENNETT KENNETH C	CPT	0-2023590	1057	1
BENNETT KENNETH M	LTC	0-1295983	0961	1
BENNETT LENSEY B	MAJ	0-1925574	0867	1
BENNETT LOYD V	CPT	0-0498266	0154	1
BENNETT MARVIN D	LTC	0-1635571	0661	1
BENNETT MATHEW E	CW2	W-3151314	0168	1
BENNETT MAX B	MAJ	0-1651913	0165	1
BENNETT OLIVER P	COL	0-0172709	1152	3
BENNETT PAULINE M	CPT	N-0728979	0847	1
BENNETT RAYMOND E	LTC	0-0369778	1061	1
BENNETT RICHARD E	COL	0-0286550	0362	3
BENNETT RICHARD S	MAJ	0-1058176	0761	1
BENNETT ROBERT A	MAJ	0-0433301	0962	1
BENNETT ROBERT F	COL	0-0194532	0357	3
BENNETT ROBERT L	CPT	0-1534211	1162	1
BENNETT ROBERT N	MAJ	0-1637008	0260	1
BENNETT ROBERT S	1LT	0-1102134	1045	2
BENNETT ROWLAND K	COL	0-0160814	1054	3
BENNETT RUSSELL C	CPT	0-0258161	1066	3
BENNETT RUSSELL E	LTC	0-0976409	0268	1
BENNETT SAMUEL L	MAJ	0-0975175	1262	1
BENNETT SANFORD A	CPT	0-0369958	0243	2
BENNETT SPENCER W	MAJ	0-1644718	0658	1

NAME	GRADE	SVC NO	DATE RET MO YR	RET CODE
BENNETT THOMAS E	LTC	0-0340227	0858	1
BENNETT THOMAS H	1LT	0-1312269	0645	2
BENNETT THOMAS W JR	MAJ	0-1058722	0165	1
BENNETT TRUMAN L	MAJ	0-1061315	0955	1
BENNETT WALTER W K	COL	0-0247516	1166	1
BENNETT WILFRED C	1LT	0-1013342	1144	2
BENNETT WILLIAM B	CPT	0-1637009	0355	1
BENNETT WILLIAM E	LTC	0-0268765	0868	1
BENNETT WILLIAM L	LTC	0-0318055	0146	2
BENNETT WILLIAM L	LTC	0-1286772	0860	1
BENNETT WILLIAM T	LTC	0-0218442	0164	3
BENNETTS EARL E	LTC	0-1634521	1161	1
BENNEY JOHN N	LTC	0-0193851	0263	3
BENNING WILLARD E	LTC	0-0278558	1048	1
BENNINGER HERBERT P	CPT	0-0969308	0861	1
BENNINGTON CLAUDE F	MAJ	0-1797422	0663	1
BENNINGTON JOSEPH R	MAJ	0-0403965	0546	2
BENNIS JOSEPH F	CPT	0-1295153	0856	1
BENOIT GILBERT A	MAJ	0-0507936	0945	2
BENOIT JOSEPH J	COL	0-0176766	1061	3
BENOIT RAYMOND L	MAJ	0-1544999	1061	2
BENREY IRWIN I	COL	0-0528633	0468	3
BENS RICHARD A	LTC	0-0451212	0462	1
BENSCOTER DANIEL B	LTC	0-0168216	1059	3
BENSER NORMA R	2LT	N-0768676	0846	1
BENSHOOF JULIAN L	MAJ	0-0183571	1164	3
BENSKY ABRAHAM	1LT	0-0496807	0648	1
BENSLEY HARRY R	MAJ	0-0411584	0963	1
BENSON ALLEN G	COL	0-0261610	0856	3
BENSON ARTHUR E	MAJ	0-0231017	0463	3
BENSON CARL	LTC	0-0168085	0660	3
BENSON CARL F	MAJ	0-1950842	1064	1
BENSON CARL S	CPT	0-0503944	1144	2
BENSON CHARLES M	LTC	0-0450795	0554	1
BENSON CLARENCE M	CW3	W-2150772	1060	1
BENSON DAVIS A	MAJ	0-1687288	1046	2
BENSON EDWARD E	COL	0-0144821	0654	3
BENSON FRANCIS M	LTC	0-0261183	0660	3
BENSON FRANK L	COL	0-0943765	0364	3
BENSON FRANK R P	MAJ	0-1291061	0560	2
BENSON GEORGE B	COL	0-0311058	1062	3
BENSON GEORGE C S	COL	0-0266951	0268	3
BENSON GEORGE M	CW3	W-2124583	0263	1
BENSON GERHARD R	LTC	0-1795850	0966	1
BENSON HOWARD F	CPT	0-1580885	0247	2
BENSON JAMES C	LTC	0-1896216	0461	1
BENSON JAMES P	MAJ	0-0497742	1053	1
BENSON JEANETTE M	2LT	N-0732326	1044	1
BENSON JESSE M	MAJ	0-0503276	0246	2
BENSON JOHN K	CW2	W-2217239	0968	1
BENSON JOHN D	1LT	0-1043566	0444	2
BENSON JOHN W	CW3	W-2152333	0561	1
BENSON LEO C	MAJ	0-1893746	0366	1
BENSON LEROY I	CW2	W-2208773	0564	2
BENSON LOUIS F	LTC	0-0301961	1057	3
BENSON MURRAY	COL	0-0275067	1164	3
BENSON NOLON J	MAJ	0-0960824	0262	1
BENSON OLIN E	CW4	W-2132165	1163	2
BENSON OLIVER G	COL	0-0309965	1065	3
BENSON PAUL F	LTC	0-1294682	0764	1
BENSON PAUL R	MAJ	0-0323682	0667	3
BENSON RAYMOND T	COL	0-0203848	0854	3
BENSON ROBERT G	LTC	0-0282929	1156	3
BENSON ROBERT H	CW2	W-2114790	0147	1
BENSON SAMUEL L	LTC	0-0248192	0465	3
BENSON STERLING O	1LT	0-1926347	0554	2
BENSON THURSTON E	MAJ	0-0288279	1063	3
BENSON VERNON W	CPT	0-0452239	1263	1
BENSON WALTER P	MAJ	0-2056270	0567	3
BENSON WESLEY T	CPT	0-0284808	1144	2
BENSON WILLIAM F	LTC	0-0159268	1043	2
BENSON WILLIAM V JR	MAJ	0-0559591	1163	1
BENT CARL D	CPT	0-1301597	0248	2
BENT EVERETT A	CW3	W-2145352	0861	1
BENT HARVEY G	CPT	0-0331451	1048	2

NAME	GRADE	SVC NO	DATE RET MO YR	RET CODE
BENTER JOSEPH V	1LT	0-1553589	0146	2
BENTIVOGLIO ISADORE	CW2	W-2150081	0959	1
BENTLEY ALBERT D	COL	0-0325768	0162	3
BENTLEY DEWEY E	MAJ	0-1014855	0859	1
BENTLEY EDWARD L	CPT	0-0394620	0147	2
BENTLEY FREDERICK	MAJ	0-1296160	0261	1
BENTLEY GEORGE	LTC	0-0480357	0662	3
BENTLEY GEORGE T	LTC	0-0104036	0544	2
BENTLEY HARLAND D	CPT	0-0379433	0745	2
BENTLEY HOWARD H	COL	0-0184211	0858	3
BENTLEY LUCILLE R	2LT	N-0702360	0535	1
BENTLEY MARY E	2LT	N-0727076	1044	1
BENTLEY MARY M	CPT	N-0737375	0757	2
BENTLEY ORVILLE G	MAJ	0-0444148	0546	2
BENTLEY ROBERT A L	LTC	0-0395065	0368	3
BENTLEY ROBERT F	MAJ	0-2004131	1268	1
BENTLEY ROBERT H	MAJ	0-2283921	0266	1
BENTLEY RODEN K	MAJ	0-2033780	0664	1
BENTLEY ULLA M JR	CW2	W-2149689	0960	1
BENTLEY WILLIAM C	LTC	0-1304490	0467	1
BENTLEY WILLIAM E JR	LTC	0-0349811	0959	1
BENTON BENJAMIN J	LTC	0-1325625	0163	1
BENTON CHARLES B	LTC	0-0261629	0845	2
BENTON DARRELL W	2LT	0-1293702	0245	2
BENTON EARL B	MAJ	0-0209022	1058	3
BENTON EMORY G	WO1	W-2145383	1158	1
BENTON EVERETT L	MAJ	0-0242427	0151	2
BENTON FOREST T	COL	0-0258355	1267	3
BENTON HARWOOD O	COL	0-0122168	1154	3
BENTON HERBERT A	LTC	0-1111489	0562	1
BENTON HOWARD E	1LT	0-1546656	0959	1
BENTON ISHMAEL C	MAJ	0-1651932	1160	1
BENTON JAY A	LTC	0-1575732	0261	1
BENTON MARION L	CPT	0-0518491	0648	1
BENTON RICHARD L	CW2	W-2214719	0968	1
BENTON RICHARDSON	COL	0-1304665	0462	1
BENTON ROBERT A	LTC	0-0292432	0166	3
BENTON ROBERT H	1LT	0-1109141	0944	2
BENTON ROBERT R	CPT	0-0981832	0860	1
BENTON THOMAS L	LTC	0-1110371	0167	1
BENTON WILLIAM C	LTC	0-0244162	0664	3
BENTSON MARTIN	CPT	0-1053485	0267	3
BENTSON WILLIAM A	MAJ	0-0958494	0963	1
BENTY HERBERT A	1LT	0-1301769	0547	2
BENTZ FRED F	MAJ	0-1544814	1060	1
BENZ HAROLD J	1LT	0-0336617	0843	2
BENZ JOHN G JR	2LT	0-1330898	0346	2
BENZ MORRIS	LTC	0-0295035	0246	2
BENZA FRANK C	CPT	0-1690270	0246	2
BENZICK ALLEN B	2LT	0-1060003	1044	2
BENZIGER ALICE C	1LT	L-0201545	0246	2
BERANIA MELCHOR P	2LT	0-1897007	1048	2
BERARD ALBERT J	1LT	0-0128833	0648	3
BERARD MARSHALL A	LTC	0-0435720	0155	1
BERARD WILBUR J JR	1LT	0-1013924	0545	2
BERARDELLI JOSEPH H	CW3	W-2109197	0261	1
BERARDI JAMES B	COL	0-0339828	0161	3
BERARDI RALPH J	MAJ	0-1302930	0960	1
BERASLEY MICHAEL	MAJ	0-1030118	1051	1
BERBERIAN HERACH M	LTC	0-0441979	1067	1
BERBIGLIA NICKOLA JR	MAJ	0-0372825	1060	1
BERCAW WOODSON W	CPT	0-0107912	0556	3
BERCH THOMAS H	LTC	0-0124963	1154	3
BERCHENKO FRANK	MAJ	0-0348791	1045	2
BERCKMAN ERNEST C	MAJ	0-0389821	0662	1
BERCOT KATHRYN W	2LT	N-0759900	0445	1
BERDEEN THOMPSON N	MAJ	0-0264516	0667	3
BERDIN ELADIO N	1LT	0-0182561	0257	3
BERDON LOUIS J	CPT	0-0311733	0145	2
BERENATO FRANK L	LTC	0-1638179	0461	1
BERENDSEN HENRY E	MAJ	0-1315768	1160	1
BERENDSEN LLOYD H	CPT	0-0112445	1045	2
BERENDT ELMORE F	COL	0-0216733	1063	3
BERESFORD CHARLES	MAJ	0-1941358	0766	1
BERESFORD G F	MAJ	0-0424534	0547	2

NAME	GRADE	SVC NO	DATE RET MO YR	RET CODE
BERESWILL WILLIAM	MAJ	0-1335882	0662	1
BERETTA JOHN W	COL	0-0185317	0359	3
BERG ALF M	MAJ	0-1920127	0765	1
BERG ANNA M	MAJ	N-0762722	1264	1
BERG ARNOLD	LTC	0-0256672	0267	3
BERG CHARLES R	CW3	W-2106439	1154	1
BERG DEL MONTE	MAJ	0-0354194	0160	1
BERG DUANE P	MAJ	0-2265847	0365	1
BERG ESTHER	MAJ	N-0777413	0465	1
BERG HOWARD A	LTC	0-1057354	1062	1
BERG HOWARD W	MAJ	0-0302470	1045	2
BERG JACK	MAJ	0-0327003	0346	2
BERG JACK E	MAJ	0-1550745	0663	1
BERG JANIS M	1LT	N-0795315	0347	1
BERG LAWRENCE E	MAJ	0-0484865	0846	2
BERG LAWRENCE P	MAJ	0-1315897	1162	1
BERG LLOYD G	MAJ	0-0971535	0865	1
BERG MILTON E	LTC	0-0479450	0667	1
BERG NILS O	MAJ	0-2007477	0860	1
BERG PETER	WO1	W-2100033	1057	3
BERG PHILLIP E	COL	0-0344548	0868	3
BERG ROBERT A	CPT	0-0955410	0361	1
BERG ROBERT J	MAJ	0-0467333	0648	1
BERG ROBERT O	MAJ	0-0289378	0656	3
BERG ROLLAND H	CW3	W-2145120	0961	1
BERG THEODORE	MAJ	0-0461631	0346	2
BERG WALTER T	LTC	0-0227255	0846	2
BERG WILLIAM A	MAJ	0-0406855	0147	2
BERGAMINI HERBERT M	COL	0-0136526	0350	3
BERGAN CARL A	LTC	0-0262757	0265	3
BERGAN MARTIN P	LTC	0-0330540	0468	3
BERGE ADOLPH K	LTC	0-1574572	1162	1
BERGEN CHANDLER W	LTC	0-1289537	0163	1
BERGEN HERBERT L	MAJ	0-1557595	1263	1
BERGEN RAPHAEL J	LTC	0-1796409	0661	1
BERGEN WILLIS	LTC	0-0235245	1046	2
BERGENDAHL HAROLD A	CPT	0-0500308	0745	2
BERGER ALEXANDER	LTC	0-1051483	0566	2
BERGER ARMISTEAD	MAJ	0-1542487	0658	1
BERGER ARTHUR J	LTC	0-0239183	0157	3
BERGER CHARLES J	1LT	0-0556180	0746	2
BERGER DAVID Z	CPT	0-0486270	1145	2
BERGER EMANUEL	LTC	0-0323261	0263	3
BERGER ENGELBERT	LTC	0-0333912	0561	1
BERGER FRANKLIN W	CW2	W-2131369	1051	1
BERGER GEORGE C JR	LTC	0-1283010	0763	1
BERGER GEORGE J	MAJ	0-0965428	1162	1
BERGER HERMAN W JR	1LT	0-0351094	0444	2
BERGER MAROLF B	MAJ	0-0363678	1045	2
BERGER MAURICE	MAJ	0-0201491	1045	2
BERGER MERTON M	CPT	0-1181540	0862	1
BERGER ROBERT	MAJ	0-1641334	1064	1
BERGER ROGER	LTC	0-0251736	0264	3
BERGER THEODORE	CPT	0-1302583	0556	2
BERGER VINCENT P	LTC	0-0280631	0667	3
BERGER WILLIAM J	CPT	0-1081264	0258	1
BERGERON KENNETH T	CPT	0-1100442	0146	2
BERGERON PAUL E	CPT	0-1174776	0147	2
BERGFELDER WILLIAM E	LTC	0-0382195	0768	3
BERGHEIMER ALFRED	MAJ	0-1328002	0262	1
BERGIN JOHN J	1LT	0-1298346	0353	2
BERGIN LOUIS H	CW4	W-2141192	1064	1
BERGIN SAMUEL A	MAJ	0-1576925	0763	1
BERGIN WILLIAM A	CW3	W-2109273	0356	2
BERGLUND CHARLES W	MAJ	0-0328458	0562	3
BERGLUND ELMER A	LTC	0-0261005	0367	3
BERGLUND FERN L	1LT	N-0733417	1045	1
BERGLUND HARRY G	LTC	0-0234921	0846	2
BERGLUND LEONARD B	MAJ	0-1307498	0163	1
BERGLUND ROBERT M	MAJ	0-2280059	0966	1
BERGMAN HAROLD O	CPT	0-1000084	1145	2
BERGMAN JAMES A	MAJ	0-1180417	0163	1
BERGMAN KENNETH E	CW3	W-2148704	0961	1
BERGMAN ROBERT	1LT	0-1292114	1044	2
BERGMANN JEROME W	CPT	0-0496281	0845	2

NAME	GRADE	SVC NO	DATE RET MO YR	RET CODE
BERGMANN JOHN C	MAJ	0-0309708	0944	2
BERGMANN PAUL F	1LT	0-1294071	0352	2
BERGMANN ROBERT F	LTC	0-0288530	0560	1
BERGMANN RUSSELL A	LTC	0-1011757	0164	1
BERGNER ELROY G	WO1	W-2139820	0352	2
BERGQUIST F W	LTC	0-0241742	0356	3
BERGQUIST IVOR W	CW2	W-2205639	0863	1
BERGQUIST WALTER J	COL	0-0237219	0857	3
BERGSCHNEIDER F F	CPT	0-1169022	1160	1
BERGSCHNEIDER J G	1LT	0-1107292	0945	2
BERGSTEN ROBERT E	MAJ	0-0452785	0456	1
BERGSTROM M A	1LT	N-0752373	0248	2
BERGSTROM VINCENT A	LTC	0-0307636	0462	1
BERGUP FIN A	CPT	0-0464196	0250	1
BERHALTER JOSEPH J	COL	0-0281295	0668	3
BERICK JAMES	CPT	0-1044760	0446	2
BERISFORD JOSEPH S	CPT	0-1914346	0332	2
BERK BRUCE W	MAJ	0-2019977	1164	1
BERK HARRY B	2LT	0-0315697	1142	2
BERK JACK E	MAJ	0-0345491	0246	2
BERK JOHN F	LTC	0-1302939	0766	1
BERK RICHARD B	1LT	0-0546699	0646	2
BERKE LOUIS J	MAJ	0-0263030	0764	3
BERKE THOMAS J	CPT	0-0211590	1055	3
BERKEBILE FRED D	MAJ	0-0506052	0847	2
BERKEBILE ROBERT R	MAJ	0-1186802	0664	1
BERKELEY CHARLES C	LTC	0-0280339	0367	1
BERKENFIELD ROY K	LTC	0-0243428	0767	3
BERKHEIMER WILLIAM J	CPT	0-0483298	0646	2
BERKIN HARRY L	LTC	0-1699822	0368	3
BERKOVE ALFRED B	COL	0-0287660	0864	3
BERKOVITZ EDWARD	1LT	0-1039456	1045	2
BERKOWICK BENJAMIN M	MAJ	0-2262616	1062	1
BERKOWITZ GEORGE	LTC	0-0486199	0568	3
BERKOWITZ GEORGE	1LT	0-1012476	1045	2
BERKOWITZ MARVIN	CPT	0-1718222	0146	2
BERKQUIST ROBERT H	1LT	0-1290534	0244	2
BERKSHIRE EARL D	MAJ	0-4074234	0468	1
BERKSON SUZANNE D	2LT	N-0787296	1144	1
BERKY EUGENE R	LTC	0-1016987	1162	1
BERL JESSE	MAJ	0-1689808	0946	2
BERLE CHARLES H	COL	0-0136542	0159	3
BERLEME GEORGE H	2LT	0-1645507	0744	2
BERLEY BONNIE	1LT	0-1996336	0860	1
BERLIN CHARLES H	MAJ	0-2011940	1062	1
BERLIN FREDERICK	MAJ	0-0398136	0246	2
BERLIN MILTON D	LTC	0-0298541	1165	3
BERLINE JAMES H	1LT	0-1305712	0146	2
BERLINER ORVAL S	MAJ	0-1578166	0761	1
BERLOVE DONALD L	1LT	0-1018983	0146	2
BERLOVE IRA J	LTC	0-0478399	1145	2
BERMAN HARRY	1LT	0-0530325	1045	2
BERMAN JAMES D	1LT	0-1319166	1145	2
BERMAN LOUIS	CPT	0-0479815	0547	2
BERMAN PERITZ S	1LT	0-1184985	1045	2
BERMAN REUBEN	LTC	0-0297556	0368	3
BERMAN SAMUEL S	CPT	0-0486538	1045	2
BERMAN SANFORD A	CPT	0-0308156	0645	2
BERMAN SOL A	CPT	0-0419769	0344	2
BERMAN WILLIAM	COL	0-0128961	0354	2
BERMEL CHARLES J	COL	0-0422838	1168	2
BERMINGHAM FRANKLIN	LTC	0-1061619	0168	1
BERNARD ALBERT L	LTC	0-1796565	0862	1
BERNARD BARBARA H	2LT	N-0729081	0745	1
BERNARD EDWARD	LTC	0-0298935	0161	1
BERNARD HENRY D JR	CPT	0-1299181	0754	2
BERNARD JUNIOR J	MAJ	0-1535726	1061	1
BERNARD LOUIS	MAJ	0-1589696	0359	1
BERNARD LOUIS B	LTC	0-1797026	1263	1
BERNARD PROSPER G	CPT	0-0246737	0644	2
BERNARD WILLIAM J	MAJ	0-2018639	0863	1
BERNARDI EUGENE R	LTC	0-0258483	1059	3
BERNARDIC JOHN L	MAJ	0-1321990	0257	1
BERNARDIN JOSEPH B	COL	0-0161156	0659	3
BERNARDO CARMELO J	LTC	0-0960826	1166	1

NAME	GRADE	SVC NO	DATE RET MO YR	RET CODE
BERNARDONI BERNARDO	LTC	O-0231677	0763	3
BERNATZ GRETCHEN B	1LT	N-0733098	0845	1
BERNAUER NICHOLAS J	CPT	O-1169023	0346	2
BERNAYS HELEN M	1LT	N-0732828	0746	1
BERNAYS MURRAY C	COL	O-0506039	1145	2
BERNDSEN ALBERT J	MAJ	O-2096472	0266	1
BERNE FREDERICK	1LT	O-1292115	1045	2
BERNE-ALLEN ALLAN	LTC	O-0226506	0962	3
BERNER ERIC P	MAJ	O-2028830	0356	1
BERNER JACK L	1LT	O-1101335	0245	2
BERNER LYLE C	MAJ	O-2319363	0867	1
BERNHAGEN JAMES D	1LT	O-1301415	1045	2
BERNHARD CARL W	MAJ	O-0248591	0367	3
BERNHARD JULIUS A	LTC	O-1321142	1162	1
BERNHARD ROBERT E	CPT	O-0352537	0146	2
BERNHARD STEVE J	MAJ	O-2016330	0564	1
BERNHARDT CHARLES J	CW3	W-2152573	0762	1
BERNHARDT DONALD R	CPT	O-1714834	0947	2
BERNHARDT FRANZ E	LTC	O-1174231	1064	1
BERNHARDT HERMAN	COL	O-0332950	0368	3
BERNHARDT RALPH H	CW2	W-2214902	1066	1
BERNHARDT WILLIAM J	MAJ	O-2007930	0161	1
BERNHART ROBERT C	CW2	W-2214591	0866	1
BERNHEIM BERTHOL M	1LT	O-1580629	0546	2
BERNHEIM JACK W	LTC	O-1895987	1162	1
BERNICK FRANK M	CW2	W-2212922	0467	1
BERNIER DENNIS D	MAJ	O-0318209	0645	2
BERNIER JOSEPH L A	CPT	O-2024243	0353	1
BERNING JOSEPH E	LTC	O-1293531	0465	3
BERNING LAWRENCE H	MAJ	O-0300326	0854	1
BERNOTAS JOHN J	MAJ	O-2019414	0263	1
BERNS CHARLES	COL	O-0245693	0462	3
BERNSDORFF FLETCHER	LTC	O-0246943	0463	3
BERNSHAUSEN FRITZ	MAJ	O-1925560	0766	1
BERNSTEIN DAVID	MAJ	O-0332951	0146	2
BERNSTEIN DAVID	CPT	O-0918211	1055	2
BERNSTEIN DAVID	1LT	O-1796213	0146	2
BERNSTEIN ETHAN	1LT	O-1291766	0346	2
BERNSTEIN JOSEPH J	LTC	O-0258956	0267	3
BERNSTEIN LEO H T	LTC	O-0483931	0263	2
BERNSTEIN ROBERT	LTC	O-0444638	0667	1
BERNSTEIN WILLIAM H	CPT	O-1683874	0845	2
BERNT DANIEL M JR	MAJ	O-0916058	1045	2
BERNTHAL HERBERT T	1LT	O-0512011	1143	2
BERNUCCI KATHRYN T	CPT	N-0724626	1044	1
BEROUNSKY ADOLPH L	1LT	O-1018018	0646	2
BERRENT SAMUEL G	LTC	O-0224959	1263	3
BERRET THOMAS J	CW2	W-2144511	1154	1
BERRETH CLARENCE J	LTC	O-0735511	0166	1
BERRIER CECIL G	MAJ	O-0968268	0863	1
BERRIER WILLIS H	MAJ	O-0277081	0260	3
BERRINGTON ZEMA W	MAJ	O-0167257	0347	1
BERRIOS JOSE R	COL	O-0108228	1053	1
BERRIOS-DIAZ TOMAS	1LT	O-0450848	0346	2
BERRISH FRANK	LTC	O-2033700	0268	1
BERRY ARTHUR P	CW3	W-2142908	1159	1
BERRY CARL S	CW3	W-3150221	0368	1
BERRY CARL W	MAJ	O-0171425	0946	2
BERRY CAUSA E	LTC	O-1304329	1263	1
BERRY CECIL	CPT	O-0490953	0247	1
BERRY CHARLES M	CPT	O-1104747	0346	2
BERRY CHARLES P	MAJ	O-0970383	0664	1
BERRY CLIFFORD E	MAJ	O-1169024	0161	1
BERRY CONWARD R	COL	O-0365967	0761	1
BERRY DEE	COL	O-0212922	0853	3
BERRY DELTA B	MAJ	O-0971004	1163	1
BERRY DENZIL J	CPT	O-1051873	0847	2
BERRY DONALD E	MAJ	O-1688420	0862	1
BERRY EDWARD J	MAJ	O-1283011	0348	2
BERRY EDWARD W	COL	O-0244768	0762	3
BERRY ELIZABETH	2LT	N-0766667	1047	1
BERRY EUGENE J	COL	O-0187629	1148	3
BERRY EUGENE V	MAJ	O-2000508	0765	1
BERRY FERRIS M	COL	O-0345362	0564	1
BERRY FRANCIS W JR	LTC	O-0155200	0157	3

NAME	GRADE	SVC NO	DATE RET MO YR	RET CODE
BERRY FRANK B	B G	O-0166083	0552	3
BERRY FRANKLIN H	COL	O-0219393	0664	3
BERRY FREDERICK	MAJ	O-0353117	0946	2
BERRY GASSIWAY H	MAJ	O-1797423	0461	1
BERRY GEORGE G	COL	O-0276675	0363	3
BERRY GEORGE S JR	LTC	O-0166629	1057	3
BERRY HAROLD E	LTC	O-0332172	0160	1
BERRY IDA E	MAJ	N-0724523	0661	1
BERRY JACK T	LTC	O-1825618	1162	1
BERRY JAMES B	MAJ	O-1296801	0161	1
BERRY JAMES B JR	COL	O-0361784	0960	1
BERRY JAMES F	LTC	O-0918273	1264	3
BERRY JAMES L	MAJ	O-0254446	0166	3
BERRY JAMES M	LTC	O-0237112	0464	3
BERRY JAMES R	1LT	O-0416377	1045	2
BERRY JOHN C	MAJ	O-1876416	0665	1
BERRY JOHN F	CPT	O-1877767	0162	1
BERRY JOHN G	COL	O-0294690	0367	3
BERRY JOHN L	COL	O-0262679	0460	3
BERRY JOHN L	1LT	O-1179722	0947	2
BERRY JOHN T	LTC	O-0736952	1067	1
BERRY JOSEPH	LTC	O-1821667	1063	1
BERRY JOSEPH B	LTC	O-1327704	1167	1
BERRY KENNETH D	CPT	O-1011504	1059	2
BERRY LELAND P	LTC	O-0239988	0863	3
BERRY LESLIE A	CW4	W-2127889	0957	1
BERRY LESTER	LTC	O-0469561	0247	1
BERRY LEWIS W	1LT	O-1311967	0845	2
BERRY MACK P	LTC	O-1119645	0966	1
BERRY MARY E	LTC	N-0792311	1069	1
BERRY NORMAN E	CW3	W-2208542	0167	1
BERRY OTHMAR B	MAJ	O-0914045	0146	2
BERRY PAUL	CW3	W-2127363	0157	1
BERRY PAUL J	CW3	W-2208642	1068	1
BERRY PAUL N	MAJ	O-0447479	1046	2
BERRY PAUL W	LTC	O-1045342	0768	3
BERRY RALPH U	MAJ	O-0353827	1145	2
BERRY REBECCA J	MAJ	N-0721440	1265	2
BERRY ROBERT E	LTC	O-1587123	0365	1
BERRY ROBERT H	2LT	O-1176253	0445	2
BERRY ROBERT L	1LT	O-2051942	1045	2
BERRY ROBERT L	CW4	RW-2005054	1267	1
BERRY ROBERT M JR	MAJ	O-1342362	0459	1
BERRY ROCKWOOD N	CPT	O-0413662	0245	2
BERRY WALLACE D	LTC	O-0369597	0167	3
BERRY WILLIAM A	MAJ	O-1922518	0967	1
BERRY WILLIAM B	MAJ	O-2021257	0666	1
BERRY WILLIAM J	2LT	O-0329903	0364	3
BERRY WILLIAM L	COL	O-0250332	0666	3
BERRYHILL RALPH D	MAJ	O-2055128	0760	1
BERRYMAN MARY W	1LT	N-0779173	0446	1
BERRYMAN WALDO B JR	COL	O-0287847	0463	1
BERSEY ARTHUR T	MAJ	O-0241529	0265	3
BERSHAD MILTON	MAJ	O-0241379	1265	3
BERSON ARTHUR I	MAJ	O-0246034	0260	2
BERSON JOSEPH	MAJ	O-0984292	0764	2
BERTACCINI ALBERT G	LTC	O-0446558	1168	1
BERTAGNOLI ROBERT W	LTC	O-1637292	0861	1
BERTELS GLENN G	LTC	O-0325164	0660	3
BERTELSEN HENRY C	MAJ	O-0126951	0648	3
BERTELSMAN PATRICK E	CPT	O-0998178	1062	1
BERTHELSEN NELS M	MAJ	O-1554320	0460	1
BERTHELSEN WALTER L	LTC	O-0668044	0466	1
BERTINO FRED	LTC	O-0375390	1067	3
BERTOLET ALBERT G	CW4	W-2141974	0265	1
BERTRAM HENRY E	CW3	W-2143867	0662	1
BERTRAND CHARLES H	LTC	O-0347672	0367	3
BERTRAND GERARD A	LTC	O-1533012	0265	2
BERTRAND JAY	COL	O-0260947	1066	3
BERTRAND JOHN W	MAJ	O-1557120	0961	1
BERTSCH LEO	LTC	O-0906103	0162	1
BERTSCH PIUS A	CPT	O-2049472	0746	2
BERTUGLI RUDOLPH	CW4	W-2141195	1066	1
BERTULIS SIMON J	1LT	O-1303647	0246	2
BERTZ HENRY	LTC	O-0164388	0546	1

NAME	GRADE	SVC NO	DATE RET MO YR	RET CODE
BERUBE JOSEPH A P	MAJ	O-1587035	1164	1
BERWICK JOHN F	CW3	W-2141196	0862	1
BERZELIUS CARL E	LTC	O-0252214	1265	3
BERZINEC GEORGE G	1LT	O-0551230	0745	2
BERZOFF SYDNEY D	2LT	O-1944625	0244	2
BESANCENEY CHARLES E	LTC	O-0322055	0967	3
BESCHENBOSSEL A W	LTC	O-0236619	0954	3
BESCHENBOSSEL HARLO	COL	O-0255007	0667	3
BESECKER CLIFFORD A	MAJ	O-0519283	0853	2
BESENDORF GEORGE J	CPT	O-0215367	1153	3
BESHARA JOHN J	LTC	O-0235112	0758	3
BESHERS THOMAS M	MAJ	O-2007511	1162	1
BESLY CLAY A	COL	O-1168554	0261	1
BESNAH ALBERT N	LTC	O-0152959	0648	3
BESNIER WILLIAM C	MAJ	O-2006974	0857	1
BESS GORDON	MAJ	O-0324390	0646	2
BESS GORDON W	MAJ	O-1040497	0859	1
BESS JOHN E JR	LTC	O-1549888	0662	1
BESS WALDO R	LTC	O-0347414	0660	1
BESSELIEVRE ALLEN M	CPT	O-2043037	0646	2
BESSEN ROBERT E	CW3	W-2206294	1165	1
BESSENT EARL L	CPT	O-1923534	1162	1
BESSETTE ANITA E	MAJ	N-0799277	0765	1
BESSETTE LOUIS J	CPT	O-0239803	0753	3
BESSETTE ROLAND J	MAJ	O-0989010	1262	1
BESSEY ROY F	LTC	O-0111743	0949	3
BESSLER ALBERT D	LTC	O-1170651	0862	1
BESSMAN LEONARD M	LTC	O-0454641	0668	3
BESSUNGER THEODORE N	CPT	O-0920716	1045	2
BEST AUGUSTIE P	CPT	O-0492497	0547	2
BEST DALE D	LTC	O-1038741	0164	1
BEST DEAN	CW4	RW-2144726	1168	1
BEST GEORGE H	LTC	O-0244161	0864	3
BEST GEORGE R	CPT	O-2033667	0665	2
BEST HENRY L	LTC	O-0241910	0952	3
BEST HERBURN L	1LT	O-1313545	0845	2
BEST HOWARD	MAJ	O-0207063	0648	3
BEST JANET C	2LT	N-0784323	0845	1
BEST JEWEL G	CPT	O-0497979	0459	1
BEST JOHN L	COL	O-0193618	0459	1
BEST LEALON L	CPT	O-2262202	0261	1
BEST LEE J	LTC	O-0202836	0955	3
BEST LEONIDAS W	MAJ	O-1176255	0861	1
BEST MELVIN R	LTC	O-1101736	0861	1
BEST NOLAN R	1LT	O-1549640	0444	2
BEST OSCAR V	LTC	O-0247733	0253	3
BEST RICHARD E	MAJ	O-2036352	0959	1
BEST RICHARD J	LTC	O-1102153	1161	1
BEST RICHARD R	MAJ	O-1114050	1060	1
BEST ROBERT M	CW3	W-2210645	0669	1
BEST ROY L	2LT	O-1308586	1143	2
BEST RUSSELL C	2LT	O-1107803	0944	2
BEST TORREY L	CPT	O-1596464	0661	1
BEST WALTER E	LTC	O-0265275	0267	3
BEST WILLIAM	MAJ	O-0200750	0349	3
BEST WILLIAM T	2LT	O-1305882	0444	2
BESTE BENJAMIN F	CW2	W-2115813	1154	1
BESTENBOSTEL ANNE L	2LT	N-0720034	0544	1
BESTICK JAMES E	CW3	W-2114663	0461	1
BESTOR GEORGE C	MAJ	O-0194890	0862	3
BESWICK WILLIAM L	COL	O-0224225	0253	2
BETANCOURT ARTHUR	CPT	O-1341742	0958	1
BETHANCOURT WILTZ J	COL	O-0423624	1161	1
BETHARD ALVIN J	MAJ	O-0310686	0347	2
BETHARD MYRON G	CW3	W-2206336	1265	1
BETHEA CORA E	CPT	N-0762364	0848	2
BETHEA ROBERT J	CW2	W-2148465	0657	2
BETHEL CHARLES E	CW3	W-2206662	0466	1
BETHEL LENSON	LTC	O-0205488	1057	3
BETHEL MILLIGAN	MAJ	O-0238488	1162	3
BETHEL WILLIAM H JR	MAJ	O-0963140	0366	1
BETHERS CARL E	LTC	O-0290937	0446	2
BETHKE CLARENCE E	LTC	O-1633669	1161	1
BETHMAN JOHN J	LTC	O-0377987	0256	1
BETIT CLARENCE L	LTC	O-1010036	1165	1

NAME	GRADE	SVC NO	DATE RET MO YR	RET CODE
BETKA ROBERT D	LTC	O-0975185	0268	1
BETKER CHRIS J	MAJ	O-0334580	0344	2
BETRUS THOMAS A	MAJ	O-1120624	0664	1
BETSON CASPER F SR	2LT	O-0425161	0245	2
BETT GEORGE F	MAJ	O-1646069	0762	1
BETTELHEIM BERNARD K	COL	O-0227763	0964	3
BETTENDORF HENRY J	MAJ	O-1287820	0558	1
BETTENDORF HENRY L	LTC	O-1321871	0268	3
BETTERLY JOHN A	COL	O-0251814	0266	3
BETTERLY WARREN A	MAJ	O-0144697	1047	2
BETTERS WILLIAM H JR	MAJ	O-1298487	0861	1
BETTGE HENRY M	LTC	O-0342918	0766	3
BETTI ALDER P	CPT	O-0959304	0261	1
BETTINGER JOHN	WO1	W-2102657	0345	2
BETTINGER JOHN C JR	1LT	O-0537952	0448	2
BETTINGER MAURICE E	COL	O-0249594	0657	1
BETTOLI FRANK S	2LT	O-1054910	0645	2
BETTONEY LAURICE A	1LT	N-0735052	0346	1
BETTS CHARLES E	1LT	O-0284839	1043	2
BETTS EDWIN J	MAJ	O-1295157	0157	1
BETTS HARRY H	MAJ	O-0225140	0265	3
BETTS JOHN H	MAJ	O-0300018	0968	3
BETTS JOHN W	CPT	O-1305001	0646	2
BETTS JOSEPH L	MAJ	O-0118714	0255	3
BETTS RICHARD H	LTC	O-1824910	0864	1
BETTS ROBERT A	LTC	O-0214263	0663	3
BETTS WILLIAM G	CW2	W-2110109	0945	2
BETZ GEORGE E	MAJ	O-0483976	0862	3
BETZ JOHN F	MAJ	O-0965519	0965	1
BETZER BOYCE F	COL	O-0298412	0564	3
BETZNER ROBERT O	LTC	O-0474420	1065	3
BEUCLER WILLIAM G	MAJ	O-0231018	0450	3
BEUTEL WILLIAM C	LTC	O-1169800	1266	1
BEUTTEL WILLIAM W	CPT	O-0514272	1048	2
BEVANS ROSCOE E	CW3	W-2143908	1067	1
BEVEL HAROLD W	MAJ	O-1918879	0463	1
BEVEL ROY E	MAJ	O-0322429	0648	1
BEVENS WRAY	LTC	O-0954560	0667	3
BEVER JAMES M	1LT	O-0501734	0147	2
BEVERAGE BOYD M JR	CW2	W-2150671	0760	1
BEVERAGE KEITH D	MAJ	O-1018515	0261	1
BEVERIDGE WILLIAM M	COL	O-0190607	0746	2
BEVERLEY JOHN H	MAJ	O-2031847	0766	1
BEVERLEY WILLIAM JR	CPT	O-0269422	0166	3
BEVERLY GRANT E	COL	O-0229530	0564	3
BEVERLY JOSEPH L JR	CW3	W-3150424	0867	1
BEVERLY RICHARD C	CPT	O-0293446	1167	3
BEVERS BILL	LTC	O-0964322	1068	2
BEVILACQUA FRANK	1LT	O-0485213	1043	2
BEVILL JOHN L	1LT	O-1112020	0346	2
BEVILLE HUGH M JR	LTC	O-0263473	0568	3
BEVINGTON CLIFFORD R	LTC	O-0254455	0464	3
BEVINS JAMES R	MAJ	O-0948345	0863	1
BEVIS HARRY L	CPT	O-1180816	0456	2
BEVIS ROBERT E	1LT	O-0341615	1145	2
BEWIE EDWARD F	LTC	O-0364448	0258	2
BEWLEY JESSE W	CPT	O-0794481	0262	1
BEWLEY LOYAL V	COL	O-0231666	1058	3
BEWSHER ELEANOR W	CPT	N-0744040	0747	1
BEY BARNETT E	MAJ	O-0291838	0444	2
BEY FLORENCE L	CPT	R-0000271	0347	1
BEYATT EUGENE R	MAJ	O-0121642	0951	3
BEYDLER EARL S	MAJ	O-1824564	0761	2
BEYER CARL W	LTC	O-1795755	0262	1
BEYER ERWIN P	COL	O-0201544	0959	1
BEYER FRANCIS D SR	LTC	O-0278537	1053	3
BEYER GEORGE W	1LT	O-1797075	0564	1
BEYER GEORGE W A	LTC	O-0346821	0758	1
BEYER JAMES S	LTC	O-1100446	0367	1
BEYER ROBERT W	LTC	O-0322957	0260	1
BEYERLEIN RAYMOND H	1LT	O-2279415	1151	3
BEYERS CLIFFORD F	B G	O-0267530	0265	3
BEYERS JOHN A	LTC	O-1548642	0763	1
BEYERS ROBERT A	1LT	O-1825277	0947	2
BEYERS WILLIAM F JR	CW2	W-3151989	0167	2

NAME	GRADE	SVC NO	DATE RET MO YR	RET CODE
BEYENSDORFER FRED A	LTC	0-0274441	1158	3
BEYL IRVIN A	LTC	0-1704024	1165	1
BEYMER CLYDE E	1LT	0-0889998	0247	2
BEYRER EDNA M	CPT	N-0700042	0740	1
BEZ JOHN A	LTC	0-1055781	1262	1
BEZIAT ROBERT L	LTC	0-0371342	0560	1
BEZLER ELEANOR J	1LT	N-0759342	1045	1
BEZOCHA ROBERT G	1LT	0-1165708	0144	2
BEZY EDWIN H	MAJ	0-1542842	0157	2
BIAFORA JOSEPH R	1LT	0-0446966	0345	2
BIAFORE SAM F	MAJ	0-1283712	0549	1
BIANCHI ANTHONY J	MAJ	0-1824412	0361	1
BIANCHI EMILIO R	LTC	0-1550109	1062	1
BIANCHI JOSEPH J	LTC	0-1041968	0264	1
BIANCO AUGUST J	LTC	0-0203013	0846	1
BIANCO FRANCIS R	CPT	0-1305529	1046	2
BIANCO FRANK D	COL	0-0185981	0556	3
BIAS DORSEY V	CPT	0-0495776	1262	2
BIAS WETZEL L	CPT	0-0980560	1060	1
BIASELLA HUMBERT F	COL	0-0336886	0760	1
BIBB ARTHUR JR	1LT	0-0525921	0944	2
BIBB EUGENE S	COL	0-0144077	0150	3
BIBB EVERETT I	LTC	0-0262498	0657	1
BIBBINS EDWARD A	CPT	0-0395549	0653	1
BIBICH NICK	MAJ	0-2096630	0464	1
BIBLE EDWARD M	MAJ	0-1335733	0765	1
BICE CARL N	CW2	W-2212785	1268	1
BICE WALTER M	MAJ	0-1583946	0557	2
BICHKO ANDREW C	1LT	0-1695739	0159	1
BICKEL JOHN A	COL	0-0144486	0649	3
BICKETT ROBERT J	1LT	0-1016978	0146	2
BICKHAM CHARLES E	LTC	0-0177546	0661	3
BICKING JOHN W	LTC	0-1553223	0667	3
BICKLE LORENE A	2LT	N-0735392	0145	1
BICKLEY WILLIAM G JR	MAJ	0-0405161	0760	1
BICKMORE EUGENE G	MAJ	0-2007703	0765	1
BICKNELL GEORGE W	LTC	0-0275524	1265	3
BICKNELL RAY A	MAJ	0-1688484	0664	1
BICKNELL ROBERT L	1LT	0-0887449	0845	2
BICKSTON HAROLD B	CPT	0-0998773	0263	1
BIDART MARIE A	1LT	N-0736518	1045	1
BIDDIEX HAROLD L	2LT	0-1318911	0645	2
BIDDLE CLAYTON R	MAJ	0-1317749	0465	1
BIDDLE JAMES C	LTC	0-1575751	0662	1
BIDDLE JUANITA F	LTC	L-0900707	0964	1
BIDDLE KENNETH J	MAJ	0-1182065	1265	1
BIDDLE NICHOLAS	COL	0-0144488	0545	2
BIDDLE OSCAR L	LTC	0-0213689	1263	3
BIDDLE RUSSELL A	CW3	W-2147728	0964	1
BIDDLE SAM H	MAJ	0-1930984	0765	1
BIDDLE WALTER I	LTC	0-0448892	0762	3
BIDLACK CECIL S	CPT	0-0213296	0863	3
BIDLE PAUL J	LTC	0-0343055	0258	1
BIDUS LEO M	COL	0-0322215	1154	2
BIDWELL HAROLD F	LTC	0-0115640	0653	3
BIDWELL PAUL W	COL	0-0246597	0648	3
BIDWELL RAY B	CW3	W-2210815	0667	1
BIDWELL RAYMOND H	MAJ	0-1167742	0547	2
BIDWELL ROBERT L	LTC	0-0451077	0461	1
BIEBER BRUCE	MAJ	0-0230697	1048	1
BIEBER CHARLES V	COL	0-0324382	0365	3
BIEBER HAROLD J	LTC	0-1174502	0465	1
BIEBER HYMAN	2LT	0-1913525	0624	1
BIEBER JAMES B	CPT	0-2262208	0161	1
BIEBER MELVIN H	MAJ	0-2001069	0762	1
BIEBESHEIMER EDWARD	LTC	0-0203279	0959	3
BIEBLE LESLIE J	CPT	0-1549219	1160	2
BIEDA WALTER P	MAJ	0-1799090	0960	1
BIEDERMAN RICHARD E	MAJ	0-1011679	0347	2
BIEDLER ASHBY L	MAJ	0-0140878	0757	3
BIEDRZYCKI LEO J	1LT	0-1298174	0645	2
BIEG HENRY C	COL	0-0180925	0661	3
BIEGANSKI EDMUND	CPT	0-1591593	0459	1
BIEHL DAWSON D	CW2	W-2210043	0564	1
BIEHL JAMES A	LTC	0-0273906	1264	3

NAME	GRADE	SVC NO	DATE RET MO YR	RET CODE
BIEHLER KARL F	LTC	0-0114089	1055	3
BIEHN FLORENCE D	LTC	0-0221157	0662	3
BIEL VINCENT F	CPT	0-1694344	1144	2
BIELAK RAYMOND L	LTC	0-0424189	0564	1
BIELAWSKI HILARY S	MAJ	0-2030843	0463	1
BIELEFELDT ROY A	CW3	W-2147080	0862	1
BIELFELDT CLAIRE J	1LT	N-0772573	0646	1
BIELSKI ROBERT H	1LT	0-2049473	0546	2
BIELSS AUGUST C	MAJ	0-0399156	0163	2
BIELUCKI CHESTER B	MAJ	0-1576933	1160	1
BIEMER PAUL I	CPT	RW-0902792	1062	1
BIENEMAN ROBERT E	MAJ	0-0452029	0551	1
BIER ROBERT A	COL	0-0212248	0959	3
BIERBAUER JOSEPH M	LTC	0-1293704	0868	3
BIERBAUM CARL J	CW4	W-2152142	1268	1
BIERBAUM LEWIS J	MAJ	0-1030952	1056	1
BIERBOWER C G JR	LTC	0-1548353	1060	1
BIERBOWER PARK P	CW3	W-2147437	1162	2
BIERER BION B	COL	0-0256670	1058	3
BIERKAN HOWARD E	MAJ	0-1573729	1145	2
BIERKORTTE GEORGE R	LTC	0-1113583	0867	1
BIERLEY DAVID H	1LT	0-1296639	0945	2
BIERLY ROBERT L	LTC	0-0556371	0866	1
BIERMAN GEORGE F	CPT	0-1557252	0646	2
BIERMAN GEORGE W	MAJ	0-1547235	0766	1
BIERMAN HARRY J	MAJ	0-0110229	0657	3
BIERMAN PHILIP W	COL	0-0265081	0267	3
BIERNAT JOHN J	1LT	0-1556841	0646	2
BIERNAT ROBERT L	2LT	0-2006413	0247	2
BIERNOFF JOSEPH	CPT	0-0331694	0144	2
BIERSTADT FRANCIS E	COL	0-0286429	0556	3
BIERSTEKER N O	LTC	0-0338847	0161	1
BIERY JAMES H	LTC	0-1080004	0361	1
BIESE JOSEPH J	CPT	0-1014621	0549	2
BIESEMEYER HAROLD L	1LT	0-1322305	1145	2
BIESEMEYER HERBERT J	1LT	0-0332363	0844	2
BIEVER PHILIP M	LTC	0-0363120	0661	1
BIFANO SALVATORE	MAJ	0-1303097	0258	1
BIGART WILLIAM D	LTC	0-0926385	1065	3
BIGELOW ALBERT S	LTC	0-0181175	0648	3
BIGELOW ALLEN C	COL	0-0181860	0554	3
BIGELOW EDWARD B	LTC	0-0179422	0648	3
BIGELOW HARRY J	CPT	0-1012681	0846	2
BIGELOW LOUIS E	MAJ	0-1104754	0357	1
BIGELOW MAURICE H	COL	0-0919939	1163	3
BIGELOW ROBERT A	LTC	0-1305374	0167	1
BIGELOW ROBERT W	CW3	W-2207559	1067	1
BIGELOW WILLIAM F	COL	0-0124291	0360	3
BIGGAM RUSSELL F JR	1LT	0-1873328	0754	2
BIGGAR FRANK W JR	2LT	0-1287991	0543	2
BIGGAR WALTER T	LTC	0-0126423	0356	3
BIGGER CLARENCE V	COL	0-0277267	0959	3
BIGGER ERWIN B	LTC	0-0402126	0363	1
BIGGER WALTER K	MAJ	0-1080513	0854	1
BIGGERS WILLIAM G	1LT	0-1944402	0445	2
BIGGERSTAFF GEORGE W	LTC	0-0300279	0659	3
BIGGERSTAFF W H	COL	0-0381862	1054	1
BIGGINS PHILIP F	MAJ	0-0482013	0759	1
BIGGS ANSON W	1LT	0-0514580	0745	2
BIGGS DAN T SR	LTC	0-1283013	1265	1
BIGGS GEORGE T	CPT	0-0430692	1044	2
BIGGS HAROLD W	LTC	0-1580633	0564	3
BIGGS HORACE F	MAJ	0-0467334	0847	2
BIGGS JACK U	CW2	W-2150270	0163	1
BIGGS JAMES E JR	2LT	0-0550653	1145	2
BIGGS JOSEPH P JR	MAJ	0-0396336	0960	1
BIGGS LAWRENCE W	MAJ	0-0452160	0658	1
BIGGS RAYMOND L	WO1	T-0193159	1065	2
BIGGS ROBERT C	MAJ	0-0121643	0845	2
BIGHAM DOYLE B	CPT	0-0953986	1060	1
BIGHAM HUGHEY W JR	LTC	0-1300440	0366	2
BIGHAM ROCKWELL V	MAJ	0-1014170	0366	1
BIGLER EARL A	MAJ	0-0188320	0350	1
BIGLER LYNN E	CPT	0-0321536	1043	2
BIGLER THOMAS J	MAJ	0-2263096	0665	1

NAME	GRADE	SVC NO	DATE RET MO YR	RET CODE
BIGLER THURMAN P	CW2	W-2149008	1160	1
BIGLIN WALLACE W	COL	0-0270002	0365	3
BIGLIN WELLMAN W	MAJ	0-1889823	0766	1
BIGNELL ARTHUR T	WO1	W-2103847	0857	1
BIGNELL SAMUEL E	COL	0-0298702	0457	1
BIHLMEYER EARL W	LTC	0-0361955	0862	1
BIHLMIRE JAMES M	1LT	0-1303098	1045	2
BIHN ROBERT M	1LT	0-0338233	0844	2
BIKLE CHARLES E JR	MAJ	0-0332696	0747	2
BILBO THOMAS J	LTC	0-1040179	0562	2
BILDERBACK FRANK	MAJ	0-1895921	0557	1
BILELLO JOSEPH W	COL	0-0291368	0163	1
BILES ALFRED F	LTC	0-0157009	0154	3
BILES DERWOOD C	LTC	0-1011034	0860	1
BILES GEORGE L	1LT	0-1687866	0543	2
BILES RANDALL H	MAJ	0-1113104	1162	1
BILES THOMAS H	LTC	0-0330889	0360	3
BILEWICZ ROGER L	LTC	0-0386927	0857	1
BILGER ARTHUR S II	LTC	0-0451555	0567	1
BILGER CECIL R	COL	0-0375833	0361	1
BILGER CHARLES E	CW2	W-2211146	0666	1
BILGER WALTER G	LTC	0-0334118	0762	1
BILINOVICH LOUIS P	1LT	0-1181541	0145	2
BILINS STEPHEN M	LTC	0-1549889	0763	1
BILIOKE ALBERT C	COL	0-0234994	0562	3
BILKS PATRICK S	CPT	0-0225230	1047	1
BILLA DORIS J	1LT	N-0790353	0946	2
BILLADO REGINALD J	COL	0-0404297	1264	1
BILLBE MERRILL O	LTC	0-0477264	1057	1
BILLER LOREN H	CPT	0-0977253	0462	1
BILLETER FRANK J	COL	0-0210640	0451	3
BILLETT HARRY H	CPT	0-0242924	1163	3
BILLETT RUSSELL A	COL	0-0142122	0758	3
BILLGER GERALD T	MAJ	0-0686967	0561	1
BILLIGMEIER ELMER C	CPT	0-1581032	0251	2
BILLIGMEIER RUBEN	CPT	0-1575752	0749	1
BILLINGER ELMER F	MAJ	0-2263151	0364	1
BILLINGER ROBERT H	CW2	W-2146217	0562	1
BILLINGS DONALD K	LTC	0-0146372	1045	2
BILLINGS HARRY G	COL	0-0226247	1062	3
BILLINGS HENRY J	CW3	W-2149284	1060	1
BILLINGS HOWARD J	LTC	0-0269091	0268	3
BILLINGS JOHN R	LTC	0-1303650	0166	1
BILLINGS RUFUS K	CW2	W-2101004	0253	2
BILLINGS THOMAS J JR	CPT	0-1286427	0746	2
BILLINGS WENDELL R	CW4	W-2105349	0866	1
BILLINGSLEY ROYCE	CPT	0-1701301	1045	2
BILLINGSLEY HARRISON	CPT	0-0109719	0540	2
BILLINGSLEY JOHN C	COL	0-0295566	1068	3
BILLINGTON C A	1LT	0-2046294	1148	1
BILLINGTON KENNETH	CPT	0-0546023	0364	1
BILLINGTON SIMPSON I	MAJ	0-1291220	0457	1
BILLION CHARLES E	COL	0-0249616	0966	3
BILLIPP RUDOLPH A	LTC	0-0240486	0762	2
BILLMAN CALVIN J	1LT	0-1307793	1044	2
BILLMAN HARLAN F	CPT	0-1311474	0947	2
BILLMAN HERBERT C	CPT	0-1702976	0747	2
BILLMAN LEROY S	CPT	0-0280605	0145	2
BILLMIRE GARRETT O	LTC	0-0312255	0964	3
BILLS CLYDE A JR	COL	0-0913495	1062	1
BILLS KENNETH G	CPT	0-0404216	0144	2
BILLS REED G	1LT	0-1167743	0345	2
BILLS WELTON B	MAJ	0-1593457	0161	1
BILLUPS CRISTOPHER	LTC	0-0245951	0446	2
BILLUPS RUDOLPH R	COL	0-0475793	0265	3
BILLUPS WILLIAM D	MAJ	0-1686631	1162	1
BILLY MICHAEL	CPT	0-1585846	0554	2
BILLY SCHLICHT	2LT	0-2006051	0146	2
BILODEAU EDWARD G	MAJ	0-0927524	0666	3
BILOUS WILLIAM H	LTC	0-1945757	0859	1
BILOWICH TED	1LT	0-1060361	0460	1
BILTZ FREDERICK	COL	0-0273262	0852	3
BILTZ PAUL M	MAJ	0-0990078	0668	1
BILYEU DICK	CW2	W-2145989	0861	1
BINCKLEY MILTON J	COL	0-0217619	0262	3

NAME	GRADE	SVC NO	DATE RET MO YR	RET CODE
BINCO MICHAEL P	MAJ	0-0181461	1146	1
BINDA STANLEY J	CPT	0-0423703	0846	2
BINDER HERBERT	CPT	0-1716248	1054	2
BINDER JOHN A	MAJ	0-0408918	0760	1
BINDER LEON	LTC	0-1100019	0256	1
BINDER ROBERT D	1LT	0-0522583	0945	2
BINDER SAMUEL H	LTC	0-0358239	0160	1
BINDIG CHARLES H	MAJ	0-0205204	1157	3
BINDNER JOSEPH T	LTC	0-0922944	0664	3
BINDON LEONARD W	LTC	0-0307186	0346	2
BINFORD JOHN K	CPT	0-0979979	1160	1
BINGAMAN ROBERT L	MAJ	0-0959747	0564	1
BINGEN JOHN R	CPT	0-1826143	0252	2
BINGERT FRANK P	CW4	W-2129758	0858	1
BINGHAM DALE E	CPT	0-0305547	0945	2
BINGHAM DWIGHT W	LTC	0-0373616	1060	1
BINGHAM ERNEST S	MAJ	0-1951531	0561	1
BINGHAM GEORGE G JR	LTC	0-0383689	1265	2
BINGHAM GEORGE W	CPT	0-0144968	0349	3
BINGHAM GLENN F	CPT	0-0180644	0544	1
BINGHAM HOLLAND W	CW2	W-2143869	0563	1
BINGHAM JAMES F	CW2	W-2101023	0244	1
BINGHAM PAUL J	MAJ	0-2263337	0565	1
BINGHAM RALPH E	CPT	0-1918920	0661	1
BINGHAM SIDNEY H	COL	0-0477781	1245	2
BINGHAM STUART A	LTC	0-0217449	0863	3
BINK JACK G	1LT	0-1181542	0966	1
BINKERD WILFRED W	1LT	0-1590287	0945	2
BINKLEY ALBERT L	1LT	0-1794761	0245	2
BINKLEY DAVID V	LTC	0-0266378	1059	3
BINKLEY HOWARD L	2LT	0-0549412	1045	2
BINKLEY JOHN E JR	1LT	0-0949128	0552	2
BINKLEY WILLIAM R	COL	0-0299967	0263	1
BINKO JOSEPH A JR	MAJ	0-1686634	0565	1
BINKOSKI JOSEPH J	1LT	0-2000954	1052	2
BINNALL MARGARET H	2LT	N-0721169	1044	1
BINNEY HORACE	CPT	0-0252566	0448	2
BINNION JOHN E	1LT	0-1578171	1044	2
BINNS JAMES F	MAJ	0-0476550	0346	2
BINNS OTWAY P	COL	0-0325115	0662	1
BINSWANGER LEWIS W	WO1	W-2147063	0860	2
BINTNER MATTHEW S	MAJ	0-2262700	1162	1
BINZER HERMAN S	LTC	0-0247077	0264	3
BION BENJAMIN L	CPT	0-0217082	1061	3
BIONDI EUGENE	LTC	0-1017494	0862	1
BIONDO THOMAS	LTC	0-0228205	0261	3
BIPPUS HAROLD M	WO1	W-2127770	0355	1
BIRCH BASIL G	MAJ	0-0403600	1267	3
BIRCH DARRELL J	COL	0-1293892	0868	1
BIRCH HAROLD H	LTC	0-0422186	1060	1
BIRCH HOWARD L	MAJ	0-1800128	0565	1
BIRCH MELVIN R	MAJ	0-2007670	0661	1
BIRCHER JOHN E	LTC	0-1326888	0366	1
BIRCHESS STEVE S	LTC	0-0493793	1054	1
BIRCHFIELD MILLARD F	CW2	W-2150536	0858	1
BIRCKHEAD EDWARD F	CPT	0-1051487	0254	2
BIRCUMSHAW JOHN H	1LT	0-1324719	1045	2
BIRD ALBERT R	LTC	0-0179860	1050	3
BIRD BYRON	COL	0-0178080	0848	3
BIRD CHARLES L	MAJ	0-0371278	0251	1
BIRD EDWARD E	LTC	0-1541723	0860	1
BIRD EDWARD W	COL	0-0400179	0746	2
BIRD ERNA D	1LT	N-0736727	0654	2
BIRD EUGENE K	LTC	0-2033122	1266	1
BIRD FRANK	CPT	0-1283196	0746	2
BIRD JAMES H	1LT	0-0518949	0553	1
BIRD JESUS J	1LT	0-1301090	0557	1
BIRD JOHN D	LTC	0-1578172	1060	1
BIRD JOHN R	COL	0-0298356	0766	3
BIRD WHITTIER S	COL	0-0172025	1158	3
BIRD WILLIAM A	COL	0-0280648	1164	3
BIRDSALL CHARLES H	LTC	0-1553224	1067	1
BIRDSELL JOHN J	LTC	0-1796746	0764	1
BIROSONG CLAUD T	MAJ	0-1574586	0359	1
BIROSONG ROY I	CW2	W-2144723	1061	1

NAME	GRADE	SVC NO	DATE RET MO YR	RET CODE
BIRDSONG THOMAS B	COL	0-0184289	1054	3
BIRDSONG WITHERS G	COL	0-0299104	0561	1
BIRELY JOHN H	MAJ	0-0101925	0654	3
BIRGE ARTHUR B	CPT	0-1291395	1045	2
BIRGE JACKSON P	LTC	0-0486345	0846	2
BIRKBY VINCENT C	CW4	W-2144708	0259	1
BIRKEDAHL LEROY	MAJ	0-1688604	1163	2
BIRKENESS RALPH T	COL	0-0268584	0855	3
BIRKES CLEVE R	CW2	W-2147578	0359	1
BIRKHIMER DOW J	LTC	0-0417482	0861	1
BIRKHIMER ROBERT P	MAJ	0-1303455	1055	1
BIRKINSHA HARRY E	MAJ	0-0994695	0864	1
BIRKNER ARCHIE G	LTC	0-0416862	0563	1
BIRKNER JACK W	1LT	0-1915796	0354	2
BIRKNER JOHN F	LTC	0-0495657	0465	1
BIRKS JOHN G	MAJ	0-0475277	0747	1
BIRMINGHAM CALVIN W	CPT	0-2212064	0361	2
BIRNBACH CHARLES	2LT	0-4006656	0654	2
BIRNBAUM GEORGE L	LTC	0-0256324	0662	3
BIRNBAUM NATHAN	COL	0-0901502	0867	3
BIRNEY DAVID T	LTC	0-0274855	0554	1
BIRNEY GEORGE H	LTC	0-0542236	0965	1
BIRNLEY FRANCIS W	MAJ	0-0385978	0661	1
BIROC DENNIS W	MAJ	0-1295817	0563	1
BIRON DONALD R	MAJ	0-0234732	0855	3
BIRON ERNEST M	MAJ	0-0319843	0555	3
BIRON PAUL E	LTC	0-1687950	0846	2
BIRRA ALFRED F	LTC	0-1104506	1161	1
BIRREN MURRELL H	MAJ	0-0206086	0544	2
BISAILLON ROLAND C	CW4	W-2105871	0565	1
BISBEE JAMES R	LTC	0-1280033	0468	2
BISBING LEWIS H	MAJ	0-1001090	1055	1
BISCHOFF ERIC E	COL	0-0420287	0562	1
BISCHOFF GEORGE H	CPT	0-0374535	0644	2
BISCHOFF MARIE S	1LT	N-0729127	0745	1
BISCOE JOHN S	LTC	0-0250582	1165	3
BISCOE STANLEY J	MAJ	0-0369902	0966	3
BISENIUS CHARLES F	COL	0-0216321	0560	3
BISER FRANK M	1LT	0-0488891	0648	1
BISH SETH G	CW4	W-2142458	0564	1
BISHARD ELMORE H	CPT	0-1184354	0146	2
BISHER GEORGE M	CPT	0-0178974	0854	3
BISHER WILLIAM	LTC	0-0222483	0260	3
BISHOFF ROBERT G	MAJ	0-1917752	0965	1
BISHOP ALFRED W	CW3	W-2002838	0967	3
BISHOP ALVIN L	CW2	W-2153240	0160	1
BISHOP ANDREW M JR	LTC	0-0254284	0764	3
BISHOP ANDREW R	1LT	0-1178711	0945	2
BISHOP BILLY G	MAJ	0-0959305	0862	1
BISHOP BOBBY L	MAJ	0-4045776	1168	1
BISHOP CECIL V	CW2	W-2142809	1060	1
BISHOP CHARLES W	CPT	0-0272549	1045	2
BISHOP CHARLIE L	CPT	0-2262852	0461	1
BISHOP CLARENCE	2LT	0-1999064	0157	1
BISHOP CLIFFORD	MAJ	0-1310676	0957	1
BISHOP DELBERT S	MAJ	0-2014822	0766	1
BISHOP DONALD H JR	CW3	W-2205426	1266	1
BISHOP ELDRIDGE L	1LT	0-1824271	1265	1
BISHOP ERRETT	LTC	0-0202641	0644	2
BISHOP ETHELBERT	2LT	0-1039156	0146	2
BISHOP GAYLORD M	COL	0-1030954	0968	1
BISHOP GLEN O	LTC	0-0381175	0464	3
BISHOP HAROLD C	CPT	0-1294420	0546	2
BISHOP HARRY D	COL	0-0324967	0256	3
BISHOP JACK W	LTC	0-1342236	1067	1
BISHOP JOHN J SR	MAJ	0-0973430	0263	1
BISHOP JOHN W	MAJ	0-1533735	0854	1
BISHOP JOSEPH I	LTC	0-0472317	0560	3
BISHOP LUCILLE A	MAJ	N-0763961	1063	1
BISHOP LYNN R	MAJ	0-1923666	0167	1
BISHOP MARTHA B	2LT	N-0785210	0945	1
BISHOP MATTHEW F	LTC	0-1000709	0554	2
BISHOP OLIVE	1LT	N-0755250	1145	1
BISHOP PAUL R JR	CPT	0-1578173	0744	2
BISHOP PHILIP E	MAJ	0-1103063	0764	1

NAME	GRADE	SVC NO	DATE RET MO YR	RET CODE
BISHOP PRESTON R	COL	0-0228836	0864	3
BISHOP RALPH C	COL	0-0136993	1051	3
BISHOP RAYMOND	MAJ	0-2026263	0858	1
BISHOP ROBERT A	1LT	0-1642180	0445	2
BISHOP ROBERT L	MAJ	0-0398121	0561	2
BISHOP THOMAS J	COL	0-0292279	1159	1
BISHOP WALTER G	LTC	0-0264593	0957	3
BISHOP WALTER T	1LT	0-1010106	0445	2
BISHOP WENDELL C	2LT	0-1550544	1044	2
BISHOP WILLIAM A	COL	0-0289979	0565	3
BISHOP WILLIAM A JR	LTC	0-0327237	0346	2
BISHOP WILLIAM C JR	LTC	0-0028428	0867	1
BISHOP WILLIAM D	MAJ	0-0244655	1064	3
BISHOP WILLIAM D	MAJ	0-1179724	0161	2
BISHOP WILLIAM J	MAJ	0-2021254	1167	1
BISHOP WILLIAM J	CW2	W-2212896	0768	1
BISNOFF IRVIN	COL	0-0267909	0555	1
BISNOFF WILLIAM H	COL	0-0231241	0462	3
BISON THEODORE R	CPT	0-0193685	0560	3
BISS EDWARD C	CPT	0-0486397	1044	2
BISSELL EDWARD H	LTC	0-0312975	0359	1
BISSELL FLOYD H JR	CW2	W-2146829	0261	1
BISSELL HARRY B	COL	0-0115544	0150	3
BISSELL INEZ M	MAJ	N-0737766	1164	3
BISSELL NORMAN F	COL	0-0909426	0864	3
BISSET DAVID JR	LTC	0-0326333	0565	1
BISSON REGINALD A	COL	0-0273337	0568	3
BISSON ROLAND P	LTC	0-0900061	0765	3
BISTANY VICTOR	MAJ	0-1287124	0361	1
BISTLINE CLARENCE H	COL	0-0285268	0467	3
BISTRITZ WILLIAM P	CW4	W-2105645	0866	1
BISZANT GEORGE P	MAJ	0-0508570	0853	3
BITLER EDWIN F	LTC	0-0206140	0463	3
BITLER RALPH M	COL	0-0255908	0358	1
BITNER HAROLD M	1LT	0-1821536	0844	2
BITTAKER LEROY F	CW4	W-2203296	0667	1
BITTENBENDER W P	MAJ	0-0359646	1146	2
BITTER REUBEN H	LTC	0-0224696	1055	3
BITTING NORMAN C	CW2	W-2117064	0860	1
BITTING WINFIELD W	CW4	W-2116131	0968	1
BITTINGER JOHN V	1LT	0-0322964	1066	3
BITTINGER WILLIAM	1LT	0-0154897	0558	3
BITTLE DELBERT	CPT	0-0445604	0848	1
BITTLE GERALD F	COL	0-0178719	0547	2
BITTLE RUSSELL	MAJ	0-1919851	0468	1
BITTMAN EDWARD S	LTC	0-0121282	0253	3
BITTNER JOHN T JR	MAJ	0-1594725	0959	1
BITTNER NORMAN W	LTC	0-1100021	0457	1
BITTRICH LOUIS E	CPT	0-0382896	0949	1
BITTS CLARENCE A	MAJ	0-0260473	0466	3
BITZEL RENO	CPT	0-0323758	0745	2
BIVENS WOODROW B	CW2	RW-2143268	0661	1
BIVERT RAYMOND E	LTC	0-0227254	1062	3
BIVINGS YANCEY H JR	LTC	0-0453301	0961	1
BIVINS BRACK A	LTC	0-1011113	0265	1
BIVINS EDWARD A	CW4	W-2006336	0364	2
BIVINS JACK L	1LT	0-1283898	1147	2
BIVINS THOMAS E	CPT	0-0535260	0247	2
BIVINS THOMAS O	MAJ	0-2041667	0766	1
BIXBY FRANK H	CPT	0-0529696	0844	2
BIXBY FRANK J	MAJ	0-1548646	0959	1
BIXLER ETHEL G	LTC	N-0760383	0268	3
BIXLER HENRY E	MAJ	0-1103518	0565	3
BIXLER RAY	MAJ	0-1327601	0164	1
BIXLER SALLY K	2LT	N-0725389	0344	1
BIXLER WILLIAM T	LTC	0-0417639	0863	1
BIZJAK WILLIAM J	LTC	0-1052675	0766	1
BIZZARO TONY	MAJ	0-1317476	0448	2
BIZZELL WILLIAM S	LTC	0-0162779	0961	3
BJERKE HELEN M	MAJ	R-0000246	1067	1
BJERKE JEROY E	1LT	0-1587132	0944	2
BJERKE MARY K	2LT	N-0787398	0645	1
BJERKE MERLIN W	CW3	W-2147844	1063	1
BJERRE FOLMAR I	MAJ	0-0217596	0362	3
BJORGUM ROBERT T	1LT	0-1310556	1045	2

NAME	GRADE	SVC NO	DATE RET MO YR	RET CODE
BJORKE RULF O	1LT	0-0889893	0952	2
BJORKLUND ARNOLD L	1LT	0-1287993	0345	2
BJORKLUND EUGENE D	LTC	0-1548354	1162	1
BJORKLUND FLOYD H	MAJ	0-1040012	0258	1
BJORKLUND JESSE W	LTC	0-2050728	0863	1
BJORNBERG HARRY K	MAJ	0-1326374	0559	1
BJUGSTAD WILMER G	MAJ	0-1056041	1066	1
BLABER LEO B SR	1LT	0-1281818	1045	2
BLACH IVAN K	2LT	0-0523483	0145	2
BLACHER ALBERT F	2LT	0-1323999	1044	2
BLACK ALBERT W	1LT	0-1692596	0553	2
BLACK ALLEN B	MAJ	0-0444632	1148	2
BLACK ARTHUR K	LTC	0-0254310	0345	2
BLACK BRUCE H	LTC	0-1103064	0467	1
BLACK CARL W	LTC	0-0242829	1045	2
BLACK CHARLES H	MAJ	0-1877795	1063	1
BLACK CHARLES L	LTC	0-1174779	0864	1
BLACK CLARENCE R	1LT	0-2035571	0958	1
BLACK CLAYTON D	LTC	0-1100022	0860	1
BLACK DALL L	LTC	0-1114051	0864	1
BLACK DAVID H	2LT	0-1285696	0645	2
BLACK EDWARD L	LTC	0-0250088	1166	3
BLACK ELBERT C JR	CPT	0-0393007	0846	2
BLACK ELI	LTC	0-0417834	0856	1
BLACK ERNEST S	CPT	0-0504502	0655	1
BLACK GANES	LTC	0-1542533	0866	1
BLACK GLENN A	1LT	0-2000803	0846	2
BLACK GLENN R	COL	0-0248718	1166	3
BLACK HENRY M	COL	0-0259095	0667	3
BLACK HOWARD R	CPT	0-1015871	0959	2
BLACK HUGH E	CPT	0-0116614	0643	2
BLACK IRENE D	CPT	N-0773625	1047	1
BLACK JAMES A	COL	0-0192581	1055	3
BLACK JAMES G	MAJ	0-1554136	0263	1
BLACK JAMES R JR	MAJ	0-0259630	1264	3
BLACK JOHN L	CW2	W-2147290	0861	2
BLACK LEAHMAN C	LTC	0-1055552	0663	1
BLACK LONNIE M	CPT	0-1032323	0349	2
BLACK MERVIN T	CW3	W-2143871	1162	1
BLACK MINNIE M	LTC	N-0700723	0946	1
BLACK ORMOND D	LTC	0-0228178	0265	3
BLACK OTTIS E	MAJ	0-1895468	1157	1
BLACK PETER F	CPT	0-0405017	0845	2
BLACK PETER P	LTC	0-0450596	0954	1
BLACK RAYMOND	LTC	0-0481955	0553	2
BLACK RAYMOND H	LTC	0-2036354	0662	1
BLACK ROBERT W JR	LTC	0-0233372	0164	3
BLACK RUDY	MAJ	0-1310515	0862	1
BLACK SCOTT U	CPT	0-1179300	0756	1
BLACK SIDNEY M	CW2	W-2152446	0959	1
BLACK THOMAS B	CW3	W-2124095	1058	1
BLACK THOMAS E JR	CPT	0-0397442	1145	2
BLACK THOMAS R	COL	0-0439464	1061	3
BLACK WALTER J	LTC	0-0887554	0468	1
BLACK WILLIAM B	MAJ	0-0327444	0447	2
BLACK WILLIAM E	LTC	0-0251667	0565	3
BLACK WILLIAM E	COL	0-0282633	1065	3
BLACK WILLIAM J JR	LTC	0-0298145	1052	3
BLACK WILLIAM W	LTC	0-1167745	0865	1
BLACKBURN ASA O	MAJ	0-1885441	0767	1
BLACKBURN BOBBY L	MAJ	0-4011014	0867	1
BLACKBURN CARL C	CW3	W-2211062	1068	1
BLACKBURN CHARLES W	LTC	0-0294800	0166	3
BLACKBURN CLARENCE B	CW2	W-2152819	0364	1
BLACKBURN CLARENCE V	CW2	W-2150968	0659	1
BLACKBURN CLARK K	WO1	W-2114496	1164	2
BLACKBURN EDWARD D	CPT	0-0272260	0168	3
BLACKBURN ESTES M	COL	0-0331596		3
BLACKBURN EUNICE R	CPT	N-0773866	0247	1
BLACKBURN FRANK C	MAJ	0-0278015	0664	3
BLACKBURN GEORGE T	1LT	0-0549271	1047	2
BLACKBURN GLEN S	CPT	0-1031879	0861	1
BLACKBURN HARRY C	MAJ	0-1289683	0263	2
BLACKBURN HARRY F	LTC	0-1015640	0863	1
BLACKBURN JAMES H	CPT	0-1031466	0857	2

NAME	GRADE	SVC NO	DATE RET MO YR	RET CODE
BLACKBURN JAMES K	CPT	0-1297305	1046	2
BLACKBURN JOHN S	CW3	W-2120780	0855	1
BLACKBURN LEROY E	CW2	W-2141198	0260	1
BLACKBURN REBECCA P	CPT	N-0724119	0646	1
BLACKBURN ROBERT C	MAJ	0-0409342	0646	2
BLACKBURN ROBERT H	COL	0-0425728	1268	1
BLACKBURN ROY V	MAJ	0-0291701	0962	1
BLACKBURN THOMAS R	1LT	0-1012072	0444	2
BLACKBURN TRACY R	1LT	0-1599104	1053	2
BLACKBURN WALTER R	1LT	0-0396718	0845	2
BLACKBURN WILLIAM L	1LT	0-0961370	0253	2
BLACKETT RAYMOND G	MAJ	0-0473044	0452	1
BLACKEY LAWRENCE L	CW3	RW-2209213	0168	1
BLACKEY PHILIP R	LTC	0-1794763	0564	1
BLACKFORD ALBERT W	1LT	0-1284997	1145	7
BLACKFORD JOE F	MAJ	0-1049729	0160	1
BLACKFORD R F	MAJ	0-0243281	0750	3
BLACKISTONE ZACHARIA	COL	0-0368673	0868	3
BLACKLEDGE VICTOR R	LTC	0-0169742	0760	3
BLACKLEY LAWRENCE R	MAJ	0-2021096	0566	1
BLACKLIDGE GLENN R	MAJ	0-1640442	0160	2
BLACKMAN CARLE L	MAJ	0-1584164	0460	1
BLACKMAN HAROLD J	LTC	0-0181414	0457	3
BLACKMAN JAY V	COL	0-0179532	1051	2
BLACKMER BENJAMIN A	MAJ	0-1287652	0648	2
BLACKMER VIRGINIA H	CPT	L-0900770	0549	2
BLACKMORE EDWARD G	CW4	W-2130710	0157	1
BLACKMORE KENNETH B	CPT	0-2263713	1162	1
BLACKMORE NORMAN H	MAJ	0-2008338	0657	1
BLACKNELL CLYDE S	CW2	W-3200391	0868	1
BLACKORBAY BRADIE P	1LT	0-0510470	1046	1
BLACKSHARE EVERPIT O	LTC	0-1051879	0467	3
BLACKSHEAR WILLIAM S	LTC	0-0150495	0253	3
BLACKSTOCK LEO G	COL	0-0348409	1059	3
BLACKWELDER LEROY J	LTC	0-1111497	0361	1
BLACKWELL CHARLES L	WO1	W-2108622	0847	2
BLACKWELL EUGENE B	LTC	0-1341141	0665	1
BLACKWELL FRANK Y	LTC	0-0163542	0353	3
BLACKWELL GEORGE C	MAJ	0-1327602	0161	1
BLACKWELL GEORGE W	CPT	0-1921094	0353	2
BLACKWELL HARRELSON	MAJ	0-0969737	0662	1
BLACKWELL JAMES E	MAJ	0-0315566	1064	1
BLACKWELL JAMES L	CPT	0-0560642	0762	1
BLACKWELL JOHN C	CPT	0-2262983	0463	1
BLACKWELL LELAND P	MAJ	0-0963404	0168	1
BLACKWELL LOWELL L	LTC	0-0426055	1054	1
BLACKWELL MARVIN E	MAJ	0-2204068	1165	1
BLACKWELL NOAH M	CW4	W-2129619	0361	1
BLACKWELL PAUL	MAJ	0-1919895	0767	1
BLACKWELL RICHARD C	COL	0-0243688	0463	3
BLACKWELL SYLVESTER	COL	0-0245183	1062	3
BLACKWELL TED R	CPT	0-0503554	1058	1
BLACKWELL WALTER E	LTC	0-0261576	0667	3
BLACKWELL WILLIAM H	MAJ	0-4007115	1165	1
BLACKWOOD BOB T	MAJ	0-1116204	0663	2
BLACKWOOD CHARLES J	LTC	0-0102686	0756	3
BLACKWOOD CHARLES M	COL	0-0224727	0864	3
BLACKWOOD DEWEY	MAJ	0-0351082	1043	2
BLACKWOOD HERMAN W	COL	0-0277179	1067	3
BLACKWOOD JAMES P	CPT	0-2007771	1148	2
BLACKWOOD WILLIAM F	1LT	0-0521814	0146	2
BLACKWOOD WILLIAM H	MAJ	0-1881730	0866	1
BLADEN WILFORD A	LTC	0-2203402	0768	1
BLAETTLER PETER M	CPT	0-0415413	0545	2
BLAGDEN CRAWFORD	1LT	0-1308780	0945	2
BLAHA JOSEPH JR	COL	0-1100451	1067	3
BLAHNIK ROMAULO J	2LT	0-1307794	0945	2
BLAIN ROGER L	MAJ	0-1550546	0963	1
BLAIN THOMAS B	1LT	0-0338965	0642	2
BLAINE BELFORD C	CPT	0-0338497	0246	2
BLAINE FREDERICK	MAJ	0-2200212	0566	1
BLAINE RONALD L	CPT	0-0970823	1168	1
BLAINE WILLIAM J	CPT	0-1291769	0253	2
BLAIR ARLO	CW3	W-2142923	0462	1
BLAIR CHARLES J JR	COL	0-0250583	1166	3

332-811 O - 69 - 7

NAME	GRADE	SVC NO	DATE RET MO YR	RET CODE
BLAIR CRITTENDEN	COL	0-0315108	0968	3
BLAIR ELMER N	MAJ	0-1300921	1061	1
BLAIR EUGENE F	MAJ	0-1575755	0766	1
BLAIR FORREST L	1LT	0-0473768	1043	2
BLAIR FRED O JR	CPT	0-2262353	1060	1
BLAIR GEORGE S	COL	0-0163590	1048	3
BLAIR GORDON T	LTC	0-0279910	0368	3
BLAIR HAROLD D	LTC	0-0278917	0460	3
BLAIR HERBERT M	CPT	0-1687261	0845	2
BLAIR HOWARD M	LTC	0-0321156	0362	3
BLAIR JAMES L	LTC	0-1574200	1061	1
BLAIR JAMES L	CW3	W-2147285	0666	1
BLAIR JOHN G	LTC	0-0261372	0462	1
BLAIR JOSEPH R	1LT	0-1822524	1045	2
BLAIR LESLIE M	CPT	0-1101336	0862	1
BLAIR LESTER M	MAJ	0-0158602	0648	3
BLAIR MATTHEW D	COL	0-0931890	1268	1
BLAIR ORVILLE R	LTC	0-0236093	1163	3
BLAIR PAUL M	COL	0-0249401	0667	3
BLAIR PHILIP W	MAJ	0-0500345	1053	1
BLAIR RALPH H	2LT	0-1913528	1144	1
BLAIR RAY R	CPT	0-1895773	0147	2
BLAIR ROBERT C	COL	0-0205035	0661	3
BLAIR ROBERT M	LTC	0-1046726	0864	1
BLAIR RUSSELL T	MAJ	0-1311366	1057	1
BLAIR TROY	MAJ	0-1102358	0159	1
BLAIR VERNON N	CW3	W-2141904	0659	1
BLAIR VERNON W	COL	0-0335059	0159	3
BLAIR VICTOR J	CW3	W-2149646	0766	1
BLAIR WILLIAM F	MAJ	0-0299807	0261	3
BLAIR WILLIAM J	LTC	0-0321512	0159	1
BLAIS ARMAND	LTC	0-0312391	0954	2
BLAISDELL FRANK G	MAJ	0-0100792	0751	3
BLAISDRE HAROLD	2LT	0-1308088	0645	2
BLAKE BERTRAM C	CW3	W-2208907	0567	1
BLAKE CLYDE M	LTC	0-0122414	0648	3
BLAKE CONNIE P	CPT	0-0224819	0254	2
BLAKE DAVID A	2LT	0-0423182	0545	2
BLAKE EDWARD H	COL	0-0256925	0368	3
BLAKE EDWARD K	CW2	W-2124237	0762	2
BLAKE ELWOOD C	CPT	0-0966400	0160	2
BLAKE ERNEST B	CPT	0-0213540	0453	2
BLAKE EVELYN M	2LT	N-0727229	1044	1
BLAKE FOREST P	1LT	0-1313336	0146	2
BLAKE FOSTER C	LTC	0-0451078	1155	1
BLAKE FRANK A JR	MAJ	0-1296982	0861	1
BLAKE FRANK O	LTC	0-0234136	0656	3
BLAKE JAMES A	LTC	0-0223874	0859	1
BLAKE JAMES F	CPT	0-2289643	0860	1
BLAKE JAMES H	CW3	W-2207639	1068	1
BLAKE JOHN V	LTC	0-0293948	0864	3
BLAKE JOSEPH E	CW2	W-2143232	1262	1
BLAKE JOSEPH M	CW4	W-2142687	0963	1
BLAKE JUNIOUS L	CW2	W-2141199	1062	1
BLAKE MILTON J	COL	0-0347707	1265	3
BLAKE RALPH J JR	LTC	0-1846247	1162	1
BLAKE THOMAS W	MAJ	0-0946106	0864	1
BLAKE WALTER C	LTC	0-1633078	0960	1
BLAKE WALTER M	LTC	0-0364580	0361	1
BLAKE WILLIAM G JR	LTC	0-0405968	0163	1
BLAKELEY LUTHER D	MAJ	0-0292400	0656	2
BLAKELY CHARLES B	CPT	0-0507080	0357	1
BLAKELY EUGENE J JR	COL	0-0172594	1057	3
BLAKELY FRANK E	LTC	0-2050730	0967	1
BLAKELY HOWARD M	MAJ	0-1284088	0860	1
BLAKELY HUGH J	LTC	0-1845386	0564	1
BLAKELY PAUL G	MAJ	0-0414133	1145	2
BLAKELY RICHARD N	MAJ	0-2102920	0167	1
BLAKELY ROBERT W	MAJ	0-0466471	0765	1
BLAKENEY LEWIS H	LTC	0-0213467	1263	1
BLAKER JOHN W	MAJ	0-1295494	0361	1
BLAKESLEE ARNOLD B	CPT	0-1013976	0547	2
BLAKESLEE ERNEST L	CPT	0-0451217	0256	1
BLAKESLEE F O	CW2	W-2146187	0957	1
BLAKESLEE ROBERT B	MAJ	0-0334461	0146	2

NAME	GRADE	SVC NO	DATE RET MO YR	RET CODE
BLAKEWAY WILLIAM R	CW4	W-2151759	0566	1
BLAKEY TOM	MAJ	0-1327804	1161	1
BLAKLEY JAMES C	CW3	W-2152002	0957	1
BLALOCK JAMES H	MAJ	0-1300441	0954	1
BLALOCK JOHN F JR	CPT	0-0359564	0545	2
BLALOCK JOSEPH G	CPT	0-0967797	0357	2
BLAN OLLIE L	MAJ	0-0102513	0556	3
BLANAR ROBERT R	COL	0-0159269	0857	3
BLANC JOHN R	MAJ	0-1341621	0865	1
BLANCHARD ALBERT C	LTC	0-0394865	0267	3
BLANCHARD ARTHUR J	CW2	W-2206379	0763	1
BLANCHARD BASIL B	MAJ	0-1061064	0363	1
BLANCHARD DELIA F	2LT	N-0726644	0745	1
BLANCHARD ELWYN W	LTC	0-0341405	0546	2
BLANCHARD EMIL A	MAJ	0-0252395	0157	3
BLANCHARD ERNEST L	CPT	0-0271529	1066	3
BLANCHARD HAROLD J	CW2	W-2102662	0657	1
BLANCHARD JAMES C JR	1LT	0-1015609	0945	2
BLANCHARD JAMES F JR	CW3	W-2141905	0463	1
BLANCHARD JAMES L	2LT	0-1050184	0345	2
BLANCHARD LAWRENCE K	COL	0-0230947	1163	3
BLANCHARD LEO J	LTC	0-0181396	0746	2
BLANCHARD MELVIN H	LTC	0-2047925	0166	1
BLANCHARD ROBERT D	MAJ	0-0272115	0768	3
BLANCHARD TALMADGE L	CW3	W-3150483	0968	1
BLANCHARD WAYNE M	MAJ	0-0422265	0652	2
BLANCHARD WILLIE J	CW3	W-2150784	0764	1
BLANCHE LESTER M	CPT	0-0267840	0566	3
BLANCHETTE JOSEPH R	CPT	0-0976471	0461	2
BLANCHETTE LEON O	CW3	W-2152842	0463	1
BLANCHETTE NAPOLEON	1LT	0-0383253	0144	2
BLANCK WILLIAM R	CW3	RW-2145384	1164	1
BLANCO JOSE R	1LT	0-0156774	0147	2
BLAND BLANCHARD	MAJ	0-0400752	0646	2
BLAND EUGENE H	COL	0-0286560	1266	3
BLAND GEORGE H	CPT	0-1169029	1046	2
BLAND GEORGE W	LTC	0-0271764	0265	3
BLAND IRVIN J	MAJ	0-0467782	0748	1
BLAND LONNIE C	CW3	W-2141201	0466	1
BLAND ROBERT T JR	MAJ	0-0449087	0846	2
BLANDFORD EARL F	1LT	0-1897740	0753	1
BLANDFORD ROBERT S	COL	0-0174483	0362	3
BLANDIN RAY W JR	MAJ	0-1312872	0860	1
BLANDING ALBERT H	M G	0-0222742	0648	3
BLANDING DONALD M JR	MAJ	0-0250089	0165	3
BLANDING THOMAS L	LTC	0-0502796	0868	3
BLANEY FRED H	CPT	0-0372647	0346	2
BLANEY LAMSON	MAJ	0-0504163	0746	2
BLANFORD DAVID W	MAJ	0-4074360	1167	1
BLANFORD HOWARD L	LTC	0-2050731	1167	1
BLANK DAVID A	CPT	0-0482436	1147	1
BLANK HARRY C	CPT	0-0171406	0554	3
BLANK HOMER C	CPT	0-0961188	1262	1
BLANK JULIUS M	COL	0-0137112	0545	2
BLANK ROBERT E	LTC	0-1550112	1067	1
BLANK WILLIAM J	COL	0-0305210	0466	3
BLANKENBAKER GEORGE	CPT	0-0509587	0967	1
BLANKENBECKLER G K	LTC	0-0275062	0944	2
BLANKENBECLER L C	CPT	0-1640236	1158	1
BLANKENBURG LEON D	MAJ	0-1924123	0868	1
BLANKENBURG RUDOLPH	COL	0-0240819	0365	3
BLANKENSHIP ARTHUR C	MAJ	0-1283014	0446	2
BLANKENSHIP BASIL R	MAJ	0-0976994	0665	2
BLANKENSHIP EDD	CW3	W-2145375	0857	1
BLANKENSHIP EDWARD W	CW4	W-2144129	1164	1
BLANKENSHIP FRED V	CW2	W-2207494	0963	1
BLANKENSHIP JOE P	CW3	W-2209563	1168	1
BLANKENSHIP MICKEY D	1LT	0-1296802	0445	2
BLANKENSHIP OCIE V	LTC	0-0248863	0366	3
BLANKENSHIP OWEN	MAJ	0-1644300	0559	1
BLANKENSHIP PAUL E	MAJ	0-1168175	0656	1
BLANKENSHIP ROY A	CW2	W-2215980	0668	1
BLANKENSHIP SHIRLEY	WO1	W-2128400	1051	2
BLANKENSHIP WADE A	1LT	0-1794901	0245	2
BLANKLEY CLIFTON T	MAJ	0-0237262	1063	3

NAME	GRADE	SVC NO	DATE RET MO YR	RET CODE
BLANKLEY HAROLD W	MAJ	0-1643536	0258	1
BLANKS CLAYTON P	CW2	W-2147790	0961	1
BLANKS ISAAC C	CW3	W-2148198	0563	1
BLANKS RICHARD P	COL	0-1284637	0561	1
BLANN CLIFFORD L	1LT	0-1310769	1045	2
BLANTON ARTHUR	LTC	0-0450772	0557	1
BLANTON DENNIS M JR	MAJ	0-1298419	0563	1
BLANTON DORIS M	CPT	L-1010311	0966	1
BLANTON MARY E	2LT	N-0727900	1045	1
BLANTON ROBERT J	1LT	0-0507112	0446	2
BLASCO ALBERT	LTC	0-1637033	0865	1
BLASDEL CHARLES F	LTC	0-0450422	0655	1
BLASE ANDREW	COL	0-0382076	0663	2
BLASEN ROBERT E	LTC	0-0304144	0445	2
BLASER EUGENE S	CPT	0-2009627	0749	2
BLASER IDA A	1LT	N-0772729	0146	1
BLASER JOHN T	CW2	W-2150656	0860	1
BLASINGAME AMOS	CW2	W-2108714	0762	1
BLASIUS FRANK M	MAJ	0-0317964	0960	1
BLASKO HELEN C	MAJ	N-0761524	1068	3
BLASKO RUDOLPH	MAJ	0-1285359	0657	1
BLASS LOUIS JR	MAJ	0-0178203	0347	2
BLATCH JOSEPH H	1LT	0-0413883	1045	2
BLATCHFORD LAWRENCE	CPT	0-1310388	1267	3
BLATT DANIEL F	MAJ	0-2262295	1163	1
BLATT DONALD C	LTC	0-1184774	1167	1
BLATT DONALD H	1LT	0-0546808	0247	2
BLATT SAMUEL F	LTC	0-0453231	0365	3
BLATTER ERWIN H	COL	0-0195716	0357	2
BLAU ELMER W	COL	0-0246421	0566	3
BLAUSTEIN MAURICE	MAJ	0-0230397	1043	1
BLAUSTEIN MORTON L	MAJ	0-0982162	0564	1
BLAUVELT ARTHUR F	LTC	0-0227176	1064	3
BLAUVELT JOHN D	MAJ	0-0264354	0468	3
BLAUVELT JOSEPH W	WO1	W-2148837	1263	2
BLAUVELT ROBERT T	LTC	0-0920834	1266	3
BLAWJER CHANCE D	LTC	0-0299687	0765	3
BLAYLOCK FLOYD M	MAJ	0-1550547	0954	1
BLAYLOCK ROBERT G	COL	0-0909999	0862	1
BLAYNEY LINDSEY	LTC	0-0150487	0648	3
BLAZER FRANK	LTC	0-1284276	0459	1
BLAZETIC JOHN P	MAJ	0-0534913	0457	1
BLAZI MICHAEL C	CW3	W-2151335	0768	1
BLAZY LOUIS J JR	CW3	W-2211447	0468	1
BLEAKLEY ELLIS F JR	2LT	0-0493037	0545	2
BLEASDALE JOHN W	MAJ	0-0195437	0657	3
BLECH JOSEPH	CPT	0-0182161	0945	2
BLECHA ARTHUR E	CW2	W-2150361	0661	1
BLEDSOE EVERETT J	MAJ	0-0496919	1152	1
BLEDSOE HENRY JR	CPT	0-1116687	0447	2
BLEDSOE JAMES P	CW2	W-2210972	0166	1
BLEDSOE RALEIGH C	CPT	0-1786382	0747	2
BLEDSOE ROBERT F	CW2	W-2142132	0657	1
BLEDSOE TRIS L	COL	0-0372641	0660	1
BLEIBERG JACOB	CPT	0-0465682	0645	2
BLEICE HERBERT M	WO1	W-2129245	0146	2
BLEICH JACK K	LTC	0-0256339	0967	3
BLEICHFELD SAMUEL	COL	0-0250258	0563	3
BLEIL LOUIS T	CPT	0-1103522	0462	1
BLEIL WALTER C	MAJ	0-0189334	0648	3
BLEKAITIS VETO	COL	0-0401452	1060	1
BLENDER THOMAS K	LTC	0-0265937	0667	3
BLENKLE VICTOR A	LTC	0-0219328	0160	3
BLESER LOUIS W	MAJ	0-0269016	0644	2
BLESS GEORGE F	MAJ	0-0967058	0265	1
BLESSING JACK W	LTC	0-0318495	0552	2
BLESSING REX C	1LT	0-0291216	1145	1
BLESSINGER RAYMOND J	1LT	0-1299982	0945	2
BLETHEN ARNOLD P	LTC	0-1104763	0962	1
BLETT ERNEST H	MAJ	0-0310399	1068	1
BLETTE JOHN JR	LTC	0-0294007	0260	1
BLEVANS JACK A	LTC	0-0287851	1265	3
BLEVINS JOHN M	CPT	0-0418729	0361	1
BLEVINS JOSEPH C	MAJ	0-0983702	0865	1
BLEVINS LESTER W	LTC	0-1331259	1265	2

NAME	GRADE	SVC NO	DATE RET MO YR	RET CODE
BLEVINS PAUL W	1LT	0-2005571	0555	1
BLEVINS WILLIAM F	CW3	W-2152366	0765	2
BLEW MICHAEL J	COL	0-0118537	1151	3
BLEWITT JOHN J	CPT	0-0918076	0244	2
BLEZA FELICISIMO	2LT	0-1897014	0847	1
BLICKLE FREDERICK	LTC	0-2001704	1163	1
BLIED LEO J	COL	0-0181466	1053	3
BLIEM EMILE G	COL	0-0276572	0260	3
BLIGH ROGER J	LTC	0-1176886	0964	1
BLIND MILDRED M	CPT	N-0724274	0758	2
BLINKENBERG HAROLD G	LTC	0-0255230	0859	1
BLINKHORN GEORGE R	MAJ	0-0260491	0466	3
BLINSKEY JOHN	CPT	0-2046645	0757	1
BLISH MORRIS J	MAJ	0-0179419	0153	3
BLISS ARTHUR G	COL	0-0253918	1061	1
BLISS EDWARD G	COL	0-0171900	0752	3
BLISS GUSTAVE E	CW3	W-3150576	1068	1
BLISS HOWARD C	MAJ	0-0334120	0862	1
BLISS JOHN N	CW3	W-2146613	1063	1
BLISS PERCIVAL M	COL	0-0257995	0267	3
BLISS RALPH P	LTC	0-1341938	0468	1
BLISS RAYMOND W JR	1LT	0-0385792	0446	2
BLISS ROBERT J	MAJ	0-0381668	0246	2
BLISS WALTER S	MAJ	0-0455855	0346	2
BLISS WILLIAM C	COL	0-0130984	0453	3
BLISS WILLIAM H	LTC	0-0909542	0862	1
BLISS WILLIAM R	CW4	W-2145605	0667	1
BLISS ZENAS R	COL	0-0195832	0358	3
BLITCH HARVEY L	CPT	0-0256614	1165	3
BLITCHINGTON JOHN A	MAJ	0-0351856	1062	1
BLITZER MARTIN	MAJ	0-0979206	0862	1
BLIZZARD JOE W	LTC	0-1040877	0763	1
BLOCH EDMUND C	COL	0-0382301	1047	2
BLOCH RALPH H	MAJ	0-1582804	0563	1
BLOCH WILLIAM JR	LTC	0-0171803	0452	3
BLOCHER ARCH C JR	1LT	0-1308781	0246	2
BLOCHER SAMUEL J	COL	0-0200703	0154	2
BLOCK ABRAHAM M	1LT	0-1014339	0946	2
BLOCK ARENO W	1LT	0-2036462	0446	2
BLOCK DONALD J	2LT	0-1178713	0145	2
BLOCK EDWARD	1LT	0-1012467	0346	2
BLOCK EDWARD L	MAJ	0-0272880	0968	3
BLOCK GEORGE F	CPT	0-0121332	0354	3
BLOCK HARRY	MAJ	0-0103973	0953	3
BLOCK JOHN H JR	CW2	W-2209296	0563	1
BLOCK MARTIN N	LTC	0-0301423	0462	1
BLOCK MARY B	CPT	N-0755145	0146	1
BLOCK PAUL L	2LT	0-1180820	1144	2
BLOCKER DANIEL J JR	LTC	0-1290189	0166	1
BLOCKER TOM B	COL	0-0177183	0353	3
BLODGETT ALOYSIUS L	CPT	0-0315703	0364	3
BLODGETT FORREST C	LTC	0-1120740	0868	1
BLODGETT HAROLD E	LTC	0-0128915	1053	3
BLODGETT JAMES A	LTC	0-0366225	1060	1
BLODGETT JUAN J	CW2	W-2144733	0265	2
BLODGETT RILEY	1LT	0-1167321	1044	2
BLODGETT STANTON B	CPT	0-0316059	1044	2
BLODGETT WALTER R	LTC	0-1586445	0864	1
BLOECHL FRANK J	LTC	0-0337105	1166	3
BLOEMENDAAL GERRIT J	MAJ	0-0227111	0160	3
BLOHM JACK	LTC	0-1174782	1160	1
BLOHM JOHN O	CPT	0-1052264	0864	1
BLOIR EDWARD	COL	0-0256723	1058	3
BLOIS ELLSWORTH	LTC	0-0915168	0964	1
BLOK JAMES	CPT	0-0345949	0260	3
BLOM JAY D	CW3	W-2213715	0168	1
BLOM ROBERT W	1LT	0-1016287	0546	2
BLOMBERG EARL H	1LT	0-1031998	0146	2
BLOMELEY LLOYD E	CW3	W-2152112	0364	1
BLOMME CHARLES R	COL	0-0278567	0460	1
BLOMQUIST ALLEN R	CPT	0-0298783	0944	2
BLOMQUIST CLAYTON A	1LT	0-1035067	0645	2
BLOMQUIST REINHOLD F	CPT	0-1642212	0657	1
BLOMQUIST RICHARD N	1LT	0-1325260	0545	2
BLOMQUIST VERNON B	CPT	0-1004420	0860	2

NAME	GRADE	SVC NO	DATE RET MO YR	RET CODE
BLONDELL VERNON J	COL	0-0190200	0460	3
BLONDER ERWIN H	1LT	0-0524094	1045	2
BLOOD LEE H	1LT	0-1289684	0864	1
BLOOD MARGARET M	1LT	N-0741705	0645	1
BLOODWORTH JOSEPH A	CW2	W-2145264	0862	1
BLOOM BONI V	LTC	0-0303048	0868	3
BLOOM CHARLES M	1LT	0-1327924	0452	2
BLOOM D GEORGE	MAJ	0-0493928	1145	2
BLOOM EDWARD I	CPT	0-1695860	1144	2
BLOOM EDWIN J	1LT	0-0317557	0445	2
BLOOM EVERETT C	LTC	0-1115497	0163	1
BLOOM EVERETT O	LTC	0-0248800	1159	3
BLOOM FRANCIS J	LTC	0-1587136	0664	1
BLOOM FRANK	COL	0-0469826	0152	3
BLOOM FRANK H	MAJ	0-4001275	1267	1
BLOOM GEORGE A JR	MAJ	0-2034091	0965	1
BLOOM GEORGE F	CW4	W-2147030	0768	1
BLOOM HENRY C	2LT	0-1312102	0161	1
BLOOM HERBERT M	LTC	0-0389848	0462	1
BLOOM JAMES F	LTC	0-1117106	0866	1
BLOOM JEANETTE	1LT	N-0722964	0945	1
BLOOM LEWIS H	MAJ	0-1289034	0457	2
BLOOM SAMUEL M	MAJ	0-0344720	1146	2
BLOOM SAUL S	LTC	0-0289874	0261	3
BLOOMENTHAL JOHN	1LT	0-0369355	0143	2
BLOOMFIELD CHESTER L	CPT	0-1317263	1045	2
BLOOMFIELD JOHN O JR	CW2	W-2143711	0260	1
BLOOMFIELD JOHN W	LTC	0-2009653	0965	1
BLOOMROSE RHODA V	2LT	N-0753526	1045	1
BLORE RICHARD E	LTC	0-0217781	0157	1
BLOSE LEWIS N	LTC	0-1585179	0763	1
BLOSE PAUL W	MAJ	0-1167747	0557	1
BLOSJO ROLAND V	LTC	0-1574591	0264	1
BLOSS LORIMOR P	1LT	0-0975187	0156	1
BLOSSER GUY C	LTC	0-0294526	0560	1
BLOSSOM GEORGE L	COL	0-0173340	0454	3
BLOTZER JOHN W	COL	0-0417619	0867	1
BLOUGH ELMER	1LT	0-0495371	0746	1
BLOUGH GEORGE G	2LT	0-1644322	0844	2
BLOUGH ROBERT J	MAJ	0-1176888	1147	2
BLOUNT ALLEN T	COL	0-0290620	0162	3
BLOUNT BARBARA	MAJ	N-0795228	1262	1
BLOUNT BRADFORD G	2LT	0-0542966	1144	2
BLOUNT LEWIS C	LTC	0-0250842	0260	3
BLOUNT LORENZO	1LT	0-1287821	0845	2
BLOWE WILLIAM O	MAJ	0-0425739	0462	1
BLOWER BRUCE G	2LT	0-5001966	0360	2
BLOWERS RALPH F	MAJ	0-1108419	0265	3
BLOWERS RAYMOND F	CPT	0-5301579	0568	1
BLOWERS TOM H	LTC	0-0300142	0364	1
BLOYS WILLIAM B	CW3	W-2143010	0360	1
BLOZE DANIEL M	2LT	0-1797237	0144	2
BLUE ARTHUR C	CPT	0-0969794	1058	1
BLUE FORREST M	CPT	0-1168562	0960	1
BLUE HAROLD J	CW2	W-2214716	1268	1
BLUE JULIAN H	MAJ	0-0273917	0759	3
BLUEJACKET DONALD D	LTC	0-2026348	0864	1
BLUETT JOHN H	WO1	W-2150302	1053	1
BLUHM FRITZ	CPT	0-0337222	0656	1
BLUHM HENRY C	LTC	0-1104511	0563	1
BLUHM HERBERT W	LTC	0-0210468	0559	1
BLUM ANDREW J	MAJ	0-1301093	0862	2
BLUM BEATRICE S	1LT	N-0723416	0346	1
BLUM CHARLES J	MAJ	0-0180961	1161	3
BLUM CHARLES J	COL	0-0324067	0265	1
BLUM FRANK J	MAJ	0-0311620	0860	1
BLUM HARRY S JR	1LT	0-1305003	0745	2
BLUM HARVEY R	CW4	W-2108815	1055	1
BLUM HERMAN R	MAJ	0-2018822	1265	2
BLUM HOWARD H	LTC	0-1894998	0667	1
BLUM JOSEPH F	COL	0-0295663	1167	2
BLUM JULIUS F	CW2	W-2211729	1156	1
BLUM MAX	CPT	0-1944878	1146	2
BLUM MERLE D	MAJ	0-1048288	0863	1
BLUM MORRIS	CPT	0-0511324	1045	2

NAME	GRADE	SVC NO	DATE RET MO YR	RET CODE
BLUM RUDOLPH A	LTC	0-0248450	0964	3
BLUM SIDNEY	LTC	0-1052265	0967	1
BLUM WALTER P	COL	0-0355809	0966	1
BLUMBERG SIDNEY H	CPT	0-0349046	0143	2
BLUME ARTHUR J	CPT	0-0232936	0364	3
BLUMENFELD IRVING	CPT	0-0400723	0346	2
BLUMENSAADT NORMAN S	LTC	0-0358062	1060	1
BLUMENSHINE HUGH M	1LT	0-1118848	1051	2
BLUMENSTEIN EDWARD J	MAJ	0-1100878	0462	1
BLUMENTHAL JACK	CW3	W-2151045	0964	1
BLUMER HOWARD D	1LT	0-0416379	1045	2
BLUMER MAK A	LTC	0-0543867	0247	2
BLUMHAGEN ROBERT F	MAJ	0-1297662	0461	1
BLUMSTEIN ALBERT	CPT	0-0335899	1163	3
BLUNK ADLAI S	CPT	0-0123281	1052	3
BLUNK ROBERT A	CW2	W-3151436	1168	1
BLUNT ALAN R	CW2	W-2208645	0760	1
BLUNT ARTHUR E	1LT	0-1287126	0446	2
BLUNT WILLIAM J	CW2	W-2143427	1063	1
BLUNTZER WOODROW K	LTC	0-1556091	0664	1
BLUSH RUSSELL F	LTC	0-1595941	1066	2
BLUST CHARLES W	CPT	0-1168177	0857	1
BLUTEAU KENNETH R	LTC	0-1284998	0760	1
BLY ALBERT O	1LT	0-1031227	0844	2
BLY HARRY R	CW3	W-2150313	0562	1
BLY SYLVESTER	LTC	0-1040879	0363	1
BLYCKER LAWRENCE R	LTC	0-0507529	0555	1
BLYSKAL STANLEY	CPT	0-0490197	0455	2
BLYSTONE WILLIAM P	CW3	W-2206689	0766	1
BLYTH ROBERT P	CW2	W-2150336	1059	2
BLYTHE HARVEY C	CW3	W-2101456	1057	1
BOAG JOHN M	LTC	0-0230240	0752	2
BOAKS RAYMOND J	CPT	0-0504971	0549	2
BOAL GEORGE L	MAJ	0-0969448	1164	1
BOAL HOWARD W	1LT	0-0126340	0252	3
BOAN VURLYNE F	2LT	N-0720891	0744	1
BOARD JOHN S	CPT	0-0236725	0265	3
BOARDMAN DONALD R	LTC	0-0089034	0468	1
BOARDMAN EDWARD J	LTC	0-1285885	0760	1
BOARDMAN GEORGE F	LTC	0-0914417	0665	3
BOARDMAN JOSEPH A	MAJ	0-0977706	0563	1
BOARDMAN ROBERT P	LTC	0-0154836	0649	3
BOARDMAN THOMAS H	CPT	0-0265824	0158	3
BOATMAN RALPH A	LTC	0-0481187	1057	1
BOATNER YANDELL	1LT	0-1179303	0946	2
BOATRIGHT CHARLES C	LTC	0-0208528	0246	2
BOATRIGHT HENRY B	CW2	W-3200437	1167	1
BOATRIGHT LEAMON D	MAJ	0-1534679	0257	1
BOATRIGHT MELVIN C	CPT	0-1042765	0647	2
BOATWRIGHT GRIMES A	1LT	0-1303456	0446	2
BOATWRIGHT JOHN H	1LT	0-1178416	0346	2
BOATWRIGHT JOHN R JR	LTC	0-1292997	0561	2
BOATWRIGHT JUNICUS T	LTC	0-1181826	0967	1
BOAZ RALPH A	LTC	0-0335232	0459	1
BOAZ THOMAS Z	LTC	0-0504355	1054	1
BOBB DONALD B	CW3	W-2143148	0858	1
BOBB LAWRENCE W	CW2	W-2113000	0450	1
BOBB ROBERT C	LTC	0-1011645	1060	1
BOBB WALLACE D	1LT	0-1824592	0746	2
BOBBITT HUBERT B	MAJ	0-1945996	0357	1
BOBBITT ROY R	CPT	0-0144023	0145	2
BOBBITT THOMAS A	CW2	W-2153223	0960	1
BOBER MARY F	2LT	N-0797536	0447	1
BOBERG DONALD E	CPT	0-1177291	0346	2
BOBERG RAYMOND W	LTC	0-0168599	0666	3
BOBERTZ CHARLES R	2LT	0-1327324	0745	2
BOBES SOLOMON S	COL	0-0313387	0268	3
BOBINGER WILLIAM H	LTC	0-0909508	1065	3
BOBKO ERNEST J	LTC	0-1293533	0961	1
BOBO CARL V	MAJ	0-0505427	0656	1
BOBO WILLIAM A	LTC	0-1014591	0462	1
BOBROW AARON H	CPT	0-1844499	1045	2
BOBROW LEON B	CPT	0-0470308	0146	2
BOBST FRANCIS	CW2	W-2149326	0359	1
BOCCELLA HENRY J	MAJ	0-0974624	0165	1

NAME	GRADE	SVC NO	DATE RET MO YR	RET CODE
BOCCELLI JOHN S	CW3	W-2149009	0666	1
BOCCHINO ELIOT J	LTC	0-0377876	0760	1
BOCCIERI JAMES N	MAJ	0-2006536	0263	1
BOCELATO JOSEPH A	LTC	0-1550968	0762	3
BOCH ALBERT P	1LT	0-1557568	0745	2
BOCH HARRIS E	COL	0-0322210	0868	3
BOCHAT MILTON W	MAJ	0-0309654	1046	2
BOCK ABE	COL	0-0255188	0867	3
BOCK CHARLES H	COL	0-0310407	1050	1
BOCK DONALD P	CW2	W-2213429	0168	1
BOCK GEORGE	CW2	W-2117591	1048	1
BOCK HARRY E JR	LTC	0-0395172	1060	1
BOCK JOHN J	LTC	0-1846111	0665	3
BOCK JOSEPH J	MAJ	0-0390026	1262	1
BOCKMAN ALFRED P	MAJ	0-1173163	0461	1
BOCKMAN MACK	WO1	W-2150570	1068	1
BOCKMON ROBERT W	COL	0-0289473	0660	1
BOCKOVEN JOHN S	CPT	0-0436712	0446	2
BOCKOVEN MILTON E	MAJ	0-1597369	0161	1
BOCKSEL RAYMOND A	CPT	0-0973378	1051	2
BOCKSTAHLER LOUIS A	LTC	0-1337131	0166	1
BOCKTING BERNARD H	CW3	W-2152695	0463	1
BOCKWITH JOHN C	2LT	0-1037397	0545	2
BOCOCK GORDON B	LTC	0-1014398	1166	3
BOCOOK JAMES S	CW2	W-2152760	0662	1
BODAK MICHAEL C	CPT	0-1286597	0147	2
BODAL EMIL K	LTC	0-0233064	1164	3
BODANSKY OSCAR	LTC	0-0494407	1046	2
BODDA ROBERT N	LTC	0-1637041	0863	1
BODDEN HARRIS L	LTC	0-0557357	0767	1
BODE JOSEPH H	MAJ	0-2034388	0861	2
BODEKER MARGARET P	COL	N-0744590	0768	3
BODELL DALE	MAJ	0-1301400	0358	1
BODELL WILLIAM J	LTC	0-0455324	0455	1
BODEN THOMAS H	LTC	0-0346797	0762	3
BODENHAMER FORREST S	MAJ	0-0276632	1067	3
BODENHAMER GEORGIA S	MAJ	N-0776094	0966	1
BODENHAMER MILTON F	LTC	0-1013939	0863	1
BODENHAMER RICHARD C	LTC	0-0150381	0254	1
BODENHAMER VIRGIL A	CW3	W-2209675	1168	1
BODGE BASIL L	CPT	0-2038900	0655	1
BODIAN MARTIN	CPT	0-0351473	0446	2
BODINE GEORGE C JR	1LT	0-1102141	0745	2
BODINE HAROLD W	LTC	0-1290190	1066	2
BODINE LILLIAN B	1LT	N-0757610	0947	1
BODINE WILLIAM B	LTC	0-1636210	0562	1
BODKIN CHESTER C	CPT	0-1062665	0348	2
BODKIN JOHN P	MAJ	0-1080918	0267	1
BODLEY DONALD C	1LT	0-0418000	1043	2
BODNAR JOHN A	2LT	0-1308243	1144	2
BODNAR LESLIE M	CPT	0-0533623	1047	2
BODNAR STEPHEN	LTC	0-0450799	0959	1
BODVER MITCHELL	MAJ	0-0223353	0549	1
BODON GEORGE R	MAJ	0-0515845	1145	2
BODY LOWELL H	MAJ	0-0252773	1160	1
BODY RALPH L	LTC	0-0215264	0363	3
BODY RAYMOND F	MAJ	0-0209797	0851	3
BOE LESTER L	1LT	0-0217554	1263	3
BOE ORVIL M	CW4	W-2142749	0566	1
BOE ROLF T	2LT	0-1171057	0343	2
BOEBEL EARL F	COL	0-0289764	0165	1
BOECKH EVERARD H	LTC	0-0165786	0853	3
BOECKMAN RICHARD J	MAJ	0-1552234	0564	1
BOEDECKER HARRY W	1LT	0-0415028	1044	2
BOEFER GUSTAV F	CPT	0-0157455	1062	3
BOEGE RAYMOND A	COL	0-0268102	0868	3
BOEGLI WILBUR J	LTC	0-0373191	0457	1
BOEH DANIEL H	CPT	0-0484025	0146	2
BOEHLER CARL H	CPT	0-0520080	0346	2
BOEHM BENNIE H	LTC	0-1293360	0361	1
BOEHM EDWARD	1LT	0-1168565	0646	2
BOEHM HANS E	LTC	0-1304687	0962	1
BOEHM LAWRENCE W	CPT	0-1922780	0968	1
BOEHM ROBERT C	CPT	0-0402182	1044	2
BOEHME DONALD W	MAJ	0-0404420	1047	2

NAME	GRADE	SVC NO	DATE RET MO YR	RET CODE
BOEHME WERNER	MAJ	0-1596384	0157	1
BOEHNE BRUCE G	1LT	0-4022417	0562	2
BOEHNKE EMIL C	COL	0-0219902	0746	1
BOEHRINGER MILDRED	2LT	N-0768857	0745	1
BOEKEL WILLIAM A	COL	0-0114152	0854	3
BOEKER WILLIAM E	CPT	0-1322878	1152	2
BOELLHOFF LAWRENCE E	CPT	0-2291703	1267	1
BOELTER AUGUST A	MAJ	0-1552844	0253	2
BOELTER RICHARD W	MAJ	0-5301580	0867	1
BOEMANNS HERMAN J	MAJ	0-1168566	1163	1
BOEPPLE GRAF A	LTC	0-1591601	0265	1
BOERBON ROBERT F	CW3	W-2126727	0760	1
BOERLAGE PETER J	MAJ	0-1799820	0167	1
BOERNER FRED H	CW3	W-2102667	1154	1
BOERSTLER FRANCIS W	CPT	0-0468435	0962	1
BOERTH WALTER H	CPT	0-0236656	0165	3
BOERTLEIN JULIUS P	1LT	0-1635596	1044	2
BOERUM ROBERT M JR	2LT	0-1053913	0344	2
BOES JOHN J	MAJ	0-0967309	0265	1
BOES JOSEPH H	1LT	0-1286066	0645	2
BOESCH JOHN C JR	LTC	0-0341206	0346	2
BOESE CLARENCE I	1LT	0-0375408	0142	2
BOESE HARVEY A	LTC	0-0330100	0657	1
BOESEL JACOB W	CPT	0-1284638	0146	2
BOESEL PAUL G	1LT	0-1054184	1145	2
BOESKE HOWARD E	1LT	0-2000002	0747	2
BOESLUND NORMAN N	1LT	0-1313069	0245	2
BOESSER ROBERT C	1LT	0-1185672	0752	2
BOESSNECK MAX	MAJ	0-0480862	0653	1
BOETTCHER ANDREW J	CPT	0-0968375	0857	1
BOETTCHER ARNOLD A	COL	0-0275224	0162	3
BOETTCHER ERVIN W	COL	0-0885038	0866	3
BOETTIGER HANS F	MAJ	0-0469283	1057	2
BOFF GORDON F	CPT	0-0452111	1058	1
BOFF ROBERT J	MAJ	0-1330377	1064	1
BOFTO EINO A	MAJ	0-0293924	0667	3
BOGAN DAVID E	LTC	0-1036860	1165	1
BOGAN ELAINE E	2LT	N-0733969	0845	1
BOGAN JAMES J JR	CW3	W-2150767	0765	1
BOGAN JOHN J	COL	0-0300424	1067	3
BOGAN LEE M	LTC	0-0299392	0668	3
BOGAN LEOLA A C	1LT	N-0722608	0746	2
BOGAN TOLLIE	CW2	W-2146179	0557	1
BOGAR STEPHEN A	MAJ	0-0282044	0166	3
BOGARD THOMAS A	CPT	0-1001512	0946	2
BOGARDUS GEORGE M	CPT	0-1696558	0845	2
BOGART GEORGE D	CW2	W-2148199	0356	1
BOGART JAMES W	LTC	0-1051882	1167	1
BOGART JAMES W	MAJ	0-2006205	0762	1
BOGART WALTER J	LTC	0-1637045	1162	1
BOGASKI EDMUND	LTC	0-0518522	1054	1
BOGATIN ROBERT S	1LT	0-0550032	0746	2
BOGDAN WESLEY S	LTC	0-1307185	0662	1
BOGEN BEN	MAJ	0-0345295	0446	2
BOGEN JOHN F	CW3	W-2004618	0667	1
BOGER DANIEL J	COL	0-0294694	0958	3
BOGER GEORGE H JR	MAJ	0-1112030	1163	1
BOGER JOHN D	COL	0-0146652	0349	3
BOGER REINHARDT	LTC	0-1015082	0666	1
BOGERT DONALD C	CPT	0-1310214	0946	2
BOGERT GEORGE E	LTC	0-2262746	1168	1
BOGES DAVID P	CPT	0-1930920	0565	1
BOGGESS CARTER T	LTC	0-0377877	0766	1
BOGGESS HARRY R	MAJ	0-1997368	0560	1
BOGGESS ROUGH A	MAJ	0-1325626	0164	1
BOGGIANO CHANCE F JR	LTC	0-0353192	0663	1
BOGGS CLARENCE E	COL	0-0116517	0648	3
BOGGS CLYDE S	LTC	0-0522296	0667	3
BOGGS DONALD G	CPT	0-1895323	0348	2
BOGGS JAMES F	COL	0-0298951	0160	3
BOGGS KENNETH L	LTC	0-0277052	1057	1
BOGGS LEAMON	CW2	W-2214901	1066	1
BOGGS LYNN	CPT	0-1913561	0428	1
BOGGS ROBERT K	LTC	0-0948725	0568	1
BOGGS ROY A	CW3	W-3150284	0767	1

NAME	GRADE	SVC NO	DATE RET MO YR	RET CODE	NAME	GRADE	SVC NO	DATE RET MO YR	RET CODE	NAME	GRADE	SVC NO	DATE RET MO YR	RET CODE	NAME	GRADE	SVC NO	DATE RET MO YR	RET CODE
BOGGS ROY L	CPT	O-1823391	0562	1	BOJUS JOHN	LTC	O-0350832	0761	1	BOLTON CARLTON M	1LT	O-1640491	0647	2	BONEY JOHN C	CPT	O-0924609	0446	2
BOGGS 3RD GEORGE	1LT	O-0493716	0346	2	BOKAMPER JESSE W	CPT	O-0973837	1060	1	BOLTON CHANNING M	COL	O-0213912	0563	3	BONFIGLIO JOSEPH	LTC	O-1285697	1062	1
BOGH ROY E	COL	O-1043029	0866	1	BOLAND CARL D JR	CPT	O-1646727	0847	2	BOLTON FREDERICK	CW4	W-2129466	0668	1	BONFIGLIO JOSEPH H	1LT	O-0123475	1053	3
BOGIA ROLAND A	COL	O-0276995	0768	3	BOLAND CLEMENT R	1LT	O-1725011	0248	2	BOLTON HAROLD M	CPT	O-1179789	0747	2	BONFORTE JOHN	LTC	O-0167237	1158	3
BOGIE WILLIAM P	COL	O-0269873	0868	3	BOLAND EDWARD L	MAJ	O-0340720	0750	1	BOLTON HOWARD F	CW2	W-2210323	1062	1	BONGARD CALVIN L	CW3	W-2150235	0165	1
BOGLE CLYDE F	CPT	O-1292118	0946	2	BOLAND FRANCIS F JR	M G	O-0233853	0965	3	BOLTON JAMES J	CPT	O-0276232	0146	1	BONHAM BYRON M JR	LTC	O-1292825	0265	1
BOGLE EUGENE R	COL	O-0148419	0849	3	BOLAND JAMES G	MAJ	O-0382571	0855	1	BOLTON JOHN C	COL	O-0335873	1160	1	BONHAM CLAUDE D	MAJ	O-0484066	0445	2
BOGLE JAMES A	MAJ	O-0994770	0267	1	BOLAND JAMES J	LTC	O-1559882	0466	1	BOLTON LAWSON T	WO1	W-2143931	0855	1	BONHAM DONALD H	CW4	W-2145211	0668	1
BOGLE JAMES P	LTC	O-0560657	0159	1	BOLAND JOHN P	LTC	O-0308256	1267	3	BOLTON LEE B	LTC	O-0265539	0363	1	BONHAM JAMES H	CPT	O-1019035	0747	2
BOGLE JOHN H	LTC	O-0460723	0557	1	BOLAND JOSEPH B	MAJ	O-0962775	1162	2	BOLTON LENWARD J	LTC	O-0321911	1053	1	BONHAM WILLIAM A	CPT	O-1174507	0259	1
BOGLE JOSEPH B	COL	O-0276647	0657	3	BOLAND JOSEPH J	CPT	O-1684256	0844	2	BOLTON LEONARD T	LTC	O-1183243	1162	1	BONICH CATHERINE	2LT	N-0783651	1045	1
BOGLE RALPH H	LTC	O-0246276	0557	1	BOLAND PATRICIA R	1LT	N-0729980	0946	1	BOLTON LONNIE D	MAJ	O-1113112	0168	3	BONICORO LOUIS	CW3	W-2149424	0964	1
BOGLE ROBERT G	LTC	O-0260946	0967	3	BOLAND WILLIAM L	COL	O-0288771	1054	1	BOLTON RAYMOND E	MAJ	O-1575769	0457	1	BONIFACE JOHN A	CPT	O-1031056	0248	2
BOGOSEWSKI ZYGMUND	CW3	W-2147081	1162	1	BOLAND WILLIAM V	CPT	O-0358103	0246	2	BOLTON WILBUR M	COL	O-0227311	0558	3	BONIFAY SAMUEL A	CPT	O-0228727	1061	3
BOGOSEWSKI ZYGMUND	CW3	W-2147091	1162	1	BOLANTE AGAPITO	CW2	RW-2147405	0262	1	BOLTON WILLIAM F JR	CW3	W-2211426	1168	1	BONILLA TOMAS	CPT	O-0217530	1047	2
BOHAN JOHN J	CPT	O-1949615	1156	1	BOLATIN GEORGE	CPT	O-1939271	0955	2	BOLTZ THOMAS F	CW2	W-2208302	0363	1	BONILLA TOMAS F	MAJ	O-0371125	0760	1
BOHAN PETER J	CW4	W-2142688	0164	1	BOLDIZAR JOSEPH A	CPT	O-1320091	0863	1	BOLTZ THOMAS F	MAJ	O-1291399	0662	1	BONIN ARTHUR L	WO1	W-2142815	1152	1
BOHAN ROBERT J	MAJ	O-1169430	0566	1	BOLDIZSAR JULIUS S	LTC	O-0888219	0465	1	BOLVIN RALPH E	CPT	O-1634540	0557	1	BONINE WILLIAM J	CPT	O-0229672	1056	3
BOHANAN DONALD E	MAJ	O-0991406	0668	1	BOLDT STEPHEN C	COL	O-0172378	0758	1	BOLYARD CHARLES A	CPT	O-1309500	0547	2	BONINI JOHN B	CPT	O-1284278	0152	1
BOHANNA GLENN A	LTC	O-0225695	1064	3	BOLDT WALDEMAR H	LTC	O-0490920	0446	2	BOMAR PORTER H	LTC	O-0213967	0563	3	BONJEAN AMERICO F	CPT	O-0251018	0148	2
BOHANNAN CHARLES T	LTC	O-2034493	0761	1	BOLDUAN NILS W	MAJ	O-1690137	0246	2	BOMBARD GLENDON A	1LT	O-1327087	0746	2	BONK JOHN A	MAJ	O-1641450	1146	2
BOHANNAN CLARK C	LTC	O-0450017	0960	1	BOLDUC ANTONIO J	LTC	O-1044456	0966	1	BOMGARDNER MERRILL L	LTC	O-1010670	1060	1	BONKOSKY STEPHEN W	LTC	O-1897768	0668	1
BOHANNAN ROBERT C	COL	O-0176016	0257	3	BOLE DAVID C JR	1LT	O-1280047	1044	2	BOMMARITO JOSEPH A	CPT	O-1944406	0845	2	BONKOWSKI JOHN S	MAJ	O-1594050	0556	2
BOHANNON EDWARD J	LTC	O-0375129	0462	1	BOLE JOHN C	COL	O-0225712	0463	3	BOMSTAD ROLAND G	CPT	O-0525945	1144	2	BONNAVILLE JOHN E	CW2	W-2145073	0357	1
BOHANNON JAMES R	CW3	W-2150282	0363	1	BOLEKY EDWARD J JR	MAJ	O-0384976	1046	2	BONA ARTHUR P	LTC	O-1114850	0563	2	BONNEAU CHARLES R	CPT	O-0383563	0357	1
BOHANNON JOHNNIE L	MAJ	O-4006657	1066	1	BOLEN HARRY L	M G	O-0185986	0256	3	BONANNO JOSEPH J	CPT	O-0404620	1044	2	BONNELL FLOYD E	LTC	O-1167748	0162	1
BOHANNON RALPH M	LTC	O-0239213	1163	3	BOLENDER LYLE S	LTC	O-1319918	[illegible]	1	BONAPARTE MARTIN	CW2	W-2147031	1162	1	BONNELL RALPH T	LTC	O-0218667	0256	3
BOHANNON RALPH W	LTC	O-0450241	1054	1	BOLER GLEN	CPT	O-0958927	1160	1	BONAR HAROLD F	LTC	O-0148383	0252	3	BONNELL THOMAS C	MAJ	O-0301702	0468	3
BOHANNON THOMAS F	LTC	O-0420423	0262	1	BOLER JOHN P	1LT	O-1596273	1045	2	BONAVENTURA CHARLES	MAJ	O-1314429	0761	1	BONNELL WILLIAM K	COL	O-0156592	0355	3
BOHANON WOODROW W	1LT	O-0336433	0845	2	BOLES BOBBY P	CW2	W-2207953	0465	1	BONCODIN EULALIO	2LT	O-1896380	0348	1	BONNELL WILLIAM L	CW3	W-2149327	1060	1
BOHOAN JOHN J	MAJ	O-2002230	0262	1	BOLES CARSIE L	WO1	W-2108424	0147	1	BOND ARTHUR L	MAJ	O-1589067	0960	1	BONNER CHESTER C	MAJ	O-0271603	0648	3
BOHIN HARRY JR	MAJ	O-2021186	0566	1	BOLES EDWARD N	CW2	W-2210141	0465	1	BOND BENJAMIN B	MAJ	O-1583961	0165	1	BONNER DAN H	MAJ	O-2018103	0864	1
BOHIN TOM W	CPT	O-0489991	1061	1	BOLES JANE L	1LT	N-0767782	0646	1	BOND CHANNING A	CPT	O-1649253	0557	1	BONNER DOUGLAS W	LTC	O-1168568	0568	1
BOHLENDER WILLIAM E	LTC	O-0181766	0956	3	BOLES RICHARD	WO1	W-2127984	1052	1	BOND CHARLES A	LTC	O-0239401	0662	3	BONNER EDWIN D	LTC	O-0461768	0954	1
BOHLER GEORGE M	MAJ	O-0146741	1146	2	BOLEWSKI JOSEPH M	MAJ	O-1824417	1060	1	BOND CICERO B	COL	O-0167690	0555	3	BONNER EUGENE C	CW3	W-2152309	0162	1
BOHLER JAMES E	MAJ	O-1038540	0661	1	BOLEY HAROLD C	COL	O-0271009	0867	3	BOND CLIFFORD H	MAJ	O-1284639	1060	2	BONNER FRANCIS C	CPT	O-0477214	1145	2
BOHLKEN JAMES D	LTC	O-1100880	0563	1	BOLGER ALFRED F	MAJ	O-0235509	0954	1	BOND DONALD H	MAJ	O-0271528	0845	2	BONNER JAY W	CW3	W-2115855	0155	1
BOHM ALBERT	CPT	O-1115190	0945	2	BOLGER ROBERT E	LTC	O-0069863	0468	1	BOND DONALD J	LTC	O-0303523	0662	1	BONNER JOHN V	1LT	O-1583985	0745	2
BOHM GEORGE M	CPT	O-1636211	0846	2	BOLICK CLARENCE P	COL	O-0174447	0456	3	BOND DOW G	MAJ	O-0405201	0747	2	BONNER JOHN W	COL	O-0318553	0862	3
BOHMER RUDOLPH J	LTC	O-0910608	1062	1	BOLICK SAM P	1LT	O-1104769	0245	2	BOND EDWARD C	CPT	O-0996094	0859	1	BONNER MOFFATT G	LTC	O-0221629	0762	3
BOHN GUY F	MAJ	O-1703936	0559	1	BOLIN ARVIO H	LTC	O-1011469	0761	1	BOND EDWARD W P	COL	O-0190937	0648	3	BONNER ROBERT A	MAJ	O-1325367	0667	1
BOHN ISHMAEL J	CW2	W-2209674	0967	1	BOLING VICTOR L	LTC	O-0376800	0160	1	BOND EUGENE A	COL	O-0114179	0550	3	BONNER WILLIAM M	CW4	W-2004506	0168	3
BOHN J RUSSELL	COL	O-0282632	0668	3	BOLINGER CHARLES R	CPT	O-1000207	1053	1	BOND FLOYD D	LTC	O-0228120	0165	3	BONNET CHRISTOPHE	MAJ	O-0392960	0261	1
BOHN JOSEPH F	MAJ	O-0969594	0664	1	BOLINGER HIMES W	LTC	O-2046551	0268	1	BOND GEORGE A JR	COL	O-0295771	1046	2	BONNETT LEON	1LT	O-1589712	1045	2
BOHN MATHIAS	CPT	O-1185567	0756	1	BOLINGER JOHN J	CW2	W-2146145	0962	2	BOND GEORGE D	LTC	O-0370954	0864	1	BONNETTE JAMES L	MAJ	O-1578183	0757	1
BOHN RICHARD G	COL	O-1100881	0368	1	BOLIVER THOMAS E	LTC	O-0171010	0953	3	BOND GLENN F	CW3	W-2147369	0663	1	BONNETTE ROLAND H	CPT	O-0261036	1066	3
BOHN WILLIAM	CPT	O-0504072	1052	2	BOLKAN PETER	MAJ	O-0173689	1162	2	BOND HENRY G	1LT	O-1016824	0845	2	BONNEY CHARLES J	MAJ	O-0364280	0360	1
BOHN WILLIAM F	LTC	O-1017593	1167	1	BOLL IOLA S	2LT	N-0744542	0845	1	BOND JAMES	CPT	O-0268597	1146	2	BONNEY HARRY L JR	MAJ	O-1583991	0264	1
BOHNENBLUST CLARENCE	LTC	O-0238797	0566	3	BOLL JOHN H	CPT	O-0966095	0157	1	BOND JUANITA R	MAJ	L-1010288	0264	1	BONNING CHARLES W	MAJ	O-1283900	0261	1
BOHNER RAY H	CW4	W-2102669	0659	1	BOLLAG LAWRENCE M	LTC	O-0920700	0467	3	BOND LEE F	LTC	O-0395570	0261	1	BONNINGTON JAMES A	COL	O-0249277	1060	3
BOHNERT ALFRED F	LTC	O-0338269	0364	1	BOLLAND JAMES W	CPT	O-1044178	0947	2	BOND LEROY	MAJ	O-2000026	0963	2	BONNIWELL CHARLES M	CPT	O-0426529	0746	2
BOHNERT FRANCIS C	MAJ	O-2208703	0465	1	BOLLENBACHER JAMES T	CPT	O-0265228	0562	3	BOND MYRON D	CW4	W-2144167	0565	1	BONNYCASTLE ARTHUR C	COL	O-0302356	1068	1
BOHNETT LEO F JR	1LT	O-1286950	1045	2	BOLLER EDWARD P	MAJ	O-0290784	1067	3	BOND RIDGELY B JR	B G	O-0237069	0765	3	BONSALL THOMAS F	COL	O-0308506	0560	3
BOHORFOUSH JOSEPH G	COL	O-0361755	0168	3	BOLLES ELLSWORTH	LTC	O-1306231	0162	1	BOND STANLEY L	1LT	O-1693479	0145	2	BONTEMPS BENJAMIN W	MAJ	O-1633683	0660	1
BOHR JOHN F	MAJ	O-1633680	1059	1	BOLLETTIERI P J	1LT	O-0551425	0147	2	BOND THOMAS M	COL	O-0281646	0561	1	BONUCCI LINO	LTC	O-0417429	0266	1
BOHREN DONALD E	2LT	O-4058909	0656	2	BOLLINE FLAVIUS C	LTC	O-0350307	1167	3	BOND THOMAS W	CPT	O-1580660	0459	1	BONURA ROCCO F SR	LTC	O-0518199	0563	1
BOHREN ROBERT F JR	MAJ	O-1889673	1265	2	BOLLINGER CHARLES M	MAJ	O-0504864	1154	1	BOND URBAN S	LTC	O-0660716	0267	1	BONUS ROMAN A	MAJ	O-0934799	0763	1
BOHRER MAX	CPT	O-0922117	0545	2	BOLLINGER RAYMOND P	LTC	O-1328875	0767	1	BOND WILMER K	LTC	O-0146454	1056	3	BONVILLAIN JOSEPH A	CW4	W-2113409	0268	3
BOIAN GENTRY P	CPT	O-0290760	1066	3	BOLLMAN CLIFFORD R	CPT	O-0280262	0146	2	BONDE ODILO N	CPT	O-2009647	0260	1	BONZER WILLIAM A	LTC	O-1824974	1263	1
BOIAN HAROLD L	LTC	O-2018990	1265	1	BOLLMAN HENRY F	MAJ	O-1170657	0964	2	BONDI JOSEPH	CPT	O-0972511	1060	1	BOO CLINTON R	LTC	O-0233952	1057	3
BOICE ROBERT C	LTC	O-0242288	1065	3	BOLLUM EDWIN H	1LT	O-0265778	0655	3	BONDI JOSEPH B	MAJ	O-0460648	0750	2	BOOGE JOHN L	CPT	O-0302014	0262	1
BOICE ROBERT R	LTC	O-0318578	0968	3	BOLLWEG GEORGE C	MAJ	O-0477362	0154	1	BONDS FEASTER W	2LT	O-1178075	0144	2	BOOKER LYNN H	CW2	W-2143832	0660	1
BOICH JOSEPH A	LTC	O-1101338	0861	1	BOLOGNA ANGELO R	CPT	O-1689402	0845	2	BONDS SAMUEL T	LTC	O-1035422	1163	1	BOOKER MILTON R	CPT	O-1945760	1059	3
BOICHOT DONALE F	COL	O-0320119	0457	1	BOLON HARRY C	MAJ	O-0258130	0765	3	BONDURANT JOHN F	MAJ	O-0415101	0346	2	BOOKHAMER JOSEPH A	LTC	O-0382539	0561	1
BOID JOHN C	1LT	O-0371816	0245	2	BOLSON JESSE A	MAJ	O-1011836	0661	1	BONDY DONALD H	2LT	O-1175645	0345	2	BOOKWALTER GEORGE R	COL	O-0142890	0852	3
BOIES HARRIETTE	2LT	N-0723597	0546	1	BOLSTAD HAROLD J	CW3	W-2141514	0865	1	BONE MAURICE C	MAJ	O-1175051	1160	1	BOOLE JAMES D JR	LTC	O-0888317	0857	1
BOIES WILBER H	1LT	O-1323905	0545	2	BOLT HARRY F	COL	O-0118749	0259	3	BONE NORFLEET G	CPT	O-0184170	1032	2	BOOLOOKAS NICHOLAS H	1LT	O-1574595	0246	2
BOIES WILTON R	MAJ	O-0993115	0465	1	BOLT JACK W	MAJ	O-1170289	0258	1	BONE WINSTEAD P JR	CPT	O-0501228	0144	2	BOOMER RICHARD J	COL	O-1042243	1268	1
BOILEAU 3RD WALLIS	1LT	O-0378637	0745	2	BOLT LEWIS G	COL	O-0357727	0660	1	BONEBRAKE JOSEPH R	LTC	O-0376026	0465	1	BOON CHARLES B	LTC	O-0478130	1263	3
BOILES DAMON J	LTC	O-1046020	0960	1	BOLTE CHARLES G	CW2	W-2142624	0161	1	BONER GEORGE T	CW3	W-2135983	1062	1	BOONE CHARLES L	MAJ	O-2206400	0367	1
BOISCLAIR HERMAN H	MAJ	O-0192311	1061	3	BOLTE KATHRYN M	CPT	L-0702026	0747	2	BONESS OSCAR I	MAJ	O-1583981	1162	1	BOONE CLARENCE A	LTC	O-0259629	0463	3
BOISVERT GEORGE A	MAJ	O-0966035	0764	1	BOLTER HARRY G	MAJ	O-1546910	0762	1	BONESTELL DEAN	LTC	O-0455097	1061	1	BOONE DANA H	LTC	O-0200206	0757	3
BOISVERT JOSEPH A	MAJ	O-1018031	0762	1	BOLTINGHOUSE TOMMY B	MAJ	O-1334087	0761	2	BONETTI ALBERT C	1LT	O-2046897	1145	2	BOONE DANIEL F	COL	O-0221957	0864	3
BOITANO JOHN E	MAJ	O-1637046	0361	1	BOLTON ARNOLD E	CW2	W-3200469	0268	1	BONEY EDWIN W	LTC	O-0104375	0954	3	BOONE DANIEL H	CPT	O-2028867	0156	1
BOIVIN DOROTHY C	2LT	N-0722752	0745	1	BOLTON ARTHUR K	CPT	O-0535356	1146	2	BONEY JOHN B JR	CPT	O-1647121	0247	2	BOONE DANIEL L	CPT	O-1342237	1057	2

NAME	GRADE	SVC NO	DATE RET MO YR	RET CODE	NAME	GRADE	SVC NO	DATE RET MO YR	RET CODE	NAME	GRADE	SVC NO	DATE RET MO YR	RET CODE	NAME	GRADE	SVC NO	DATE RET MO YR	RET CODE
BOONE JEFFERSON	MAJ	0-1043872	0858	1	BORDERS RAY M	LTC	0-1312185	0165	1	BOSAK JOHN B	LTC	0-1556399	0967	1	BOTHWELL JAMES H	LTC	0-0208212	0861	3
BOONE LEO E	CPT	0-1109822	0646	2	BORDERS WILLIAM A	COL	0-0222335	0964	3	BOSCH EDMUND A	LTC	0-0288978	0861	3	BOTNICK ABRAHAM J	LTC	0-1172386	0466	1
BOONE RALPH L	CW2	W-2204093	0562	1	BORDEWICH JOHN P	2LT	0-1015813	0245	2	BOSCH HENRY M	CW3	W-2143606	1063	1	BOTSFORD GERALD F	LTC	0-0206177	0556	3
BOONE RANKIN R	COL	0-0229398	0960	3	BORDLEY ARTHUR W	MAJ	0-1039212	1061	1	BOSCHER HARRY W	MAJ	0-1043873	0561	1	BOTSFORD HARTLEY W	1LT	0-1323524	1145	2
BOONE SAM W	LTC	0-0567376	0862	1	BORDONARO ANTHONY C	CW2	W-2103897	0944	2	BOSCHKE WILLIAM R	2LT	0-1048291	1044	2	BOTSFORD NORMAN L JR	LTC	0-0430473	0563	1
BOONE SAMUEL C	CPT	0-0168678	0258	3	BORDONARO JAMES J	CW3	W-2203635	0463	1	BOSCO EDWARD J	LTC	0-1547883	0867	1	BOTT EDWARD	MAJ	0-1323525	0357	1
BOONE WILLIAM E	COL	0-0199358	0755	2	BOREK JOHN W	1LT	0-1823824	0145	2	BOSEN HERBERT A	1LT	0-1936237	0755	2	BOTTEMILLER HARLEY L	MAJ	0-2265310	0965	1
BOONE WILLIAM S JR	MAJ	0-0668885	1163	1	BOREL DOLZEY	CW3	W-2113728	0555	1	BOSENBERG CHARLES F	CPT	0-0338392	0345	2	BOTTEMILLER HAROLD E	LTC	0-0345231	0446	2
BOONSTRA SAMUEL P	MAJ	0-0119732	0648	3	BORELL ELDON W	LTC	0-0419609	1164	3	BOSFIELD HUGH H	CPT	0-0265908	0265	3	BOTTING LEONARD P	COL	0-0172678	0657	3
BOOP NORWOOD F	LTC	0-2037620	0768	2	BORELL ROBERT W	LTC	0-1116827	1167	1	BOSHART MELVIN W	CW4	W-2119506	0762	1	BOTTOM NORMAN R	LTC	0-0255869	1062	1
BOORAS THOMAS J	MAJ	0-2200327	0766	1	BOREN CLAUD W	MAJ	0-1300444	0856	1	BOSHOFF WILLIAM H	COL	0-0466828	0251	2	BOTTOMLEY CORNELIUS	MAJ	0-0383327	0556	2
BOOROM OWEN D	COL	0-0489965	0360	2	BOREN DEAN A	MAJ	0-1182521	0160	1	BOSINIO LOUIS L	CW3	W-2152188	0563	1	BOTTOMLEY HOWARD E	LTC	0-0347009	0860	1
BOORSTEIN LOUIS S	1LT	0-1543787	0146	2	BOREN EDGAR H	LTC	0-0371305	0560	1	BOSKEY LOESER M	COL	0-0241686	0266	3	BOTTOMS CHARLES B	COL	0-0206722	1263	3
BOOSA JOHN R	MAJ	0-0264602	0646	2	BOREN JOHN O	LTC	0-0312354	0758	3	BOSKY WALTER F	LTC	0-0351823	0260	1	BOTTOMS DELMAS A SR	MAJ	0-1585195	0168	3
BOOSE HOWARD R JR	COL	0-0376925	0261	1	BOREN LESTER R	CPT	0-0489369	1050	1	BOSKY ZIGMOND M	CPT	0-1573058	0645	2	BOTTOMS IRA G	CPT	0-0374578	1047	2
BOOSE LLOYD	COL	0-0165769	0955	3	BORENTZ DORA K	1LT	N-0728622	1045	1	BOSLEY BEATRICE M	LTC	N-0734346	0961	2	BOTTOMS WILMER R	LTC	0-0525504	0264	1
BOOT SAMUEL K	LTC	0-1545187	0467	1	BORER WILLIAM J	CPT	0-0529484	0346	2	BOSLEY CHARLES H	LTC	0-0406732	0361	1	BOTTONI DOMINIC J	1LT	0-1047890	0944	2
BOOTH AUGUST M	COL	0-0269795	0264	1	BORESCH URBAN W	COL	0-0392227	0760	1	BOSLEY DONALD G	LTC	0-2262425	0868	1	BOTTORFF JAMES C	LTC	0-1031788	0862	2
BOOTH BENJAMIN J	LTC	0-1111502	0863	1	BORESON EVELYN N	CPT	N-0773100	0746	1	BOSLEY JAMES L	1LT	0-1285886	0558	3	BOTTORFF MARCUS G	LTC	0-1326377	0363	1
BOOTH BRUCE G	COL	0-0211148	0360	3	BORGATTI RAOUL F	1LT	0-1060016	0447	2	BOSLEY JOHN D	CPT	0-0492137	0347	1	BOTTS PETE	CW3	W-2145386	0760	1
BOOTH CECIL V	CW4	W-2122649	0255	1	BORGELT PERSHING H	CPT	0-0467166	1046	2	BOSMA CHARLES E	CPT	0-0523355	0546	2	BOTTS ROBERT C	CPT	0-0466908	0645	2
BOOTH EDWIN L	MAJ	0-1798552	0860	1	BORGEN LLOYD O	LTC	0-1168179	0864	1	BOSMA THEODORA C	LTC	L-0502131	0766	3	BOUCHARD HOWARD S	LTC	0-0264033	1143	2
BOOTH EDWIN S	LTC	0-0250507	0747	2	BORGENS CLARENCE	LTC	0-1329316	1062	1	BOSOLD ROBERT F	CW3	W-2145131	0561	1	BOUCHARD PAUL E	CPT	0-1308782	0862	1
BOOTH FREDERICK	MAJ	0-0378452	1045	2	BORGER WILMER F	MAJ	0-2035686	1060	1	BOSS GERALD S	CW3	W-2148275	0163	1	BOUCHARD PAUL H	LTC	0-2010445	0861	1
BOOTH GILBERT	MAJ	0-1540698	0860	1	BORGESON CARL A	COL	0-0207567	1263	3	BOSSARD SAMUEL L	LTC	0-0228065	0849	3	BOUCHARD RAYMOND E	LTC	0-1041972	0765	1
BOOTH HAROLD R	COL	0-0114180	1054	1	BORGESON GEORGE F	MAJ	0-0650804	0667	3	BOSSART DAVID H	MAJ	0-0559037	0658	1	BOUCHER GEORGE H	LTC	0-0315561	0366	1
BOOTH JOHN C JR	CPT	0-0241488	0564	1	BORGIA ANTHONY W	LTC	0-1637392	0862	1	BOSSE EDWARD V	LTC	0-0379205	0760	1	BOUCHER HAROLD E	MAJ	0-0285523	0468	3
BOOTH JOHN L	1LT	0-1323891	0346	2	BORICAN CHARLES H JR	MAJ	0-0247460	1162	1	BOSSERT EUSEBIUS	1LT	0-2006046	0452	2	BOUCHER HARRY J	MAJ	0-1328965	1059	1
BOOTH MALCOLM C	CPT	0-0305408	0447	2	BORIE HENRY P	MAJ	0-0322919	1160	3	BOSSERT LESTER	CW4	W-2110124	0959	1	BOUCHER VERNON A	MAJ	0-0144433	0748	3
BOOTH MAYNARD B	LTC	0-0395521	1160	1	BORING CLYDE O	LTC	0-1596276	0966	2	BOSSICK ANDY	WO1	W-2115661	0347	1	BOUCHEREAU DONALD P	1LT	0-1168180	1045	2
BOOTH ORAIN G	MAJ	0-0267018	0155	1	BORING HAROLD	CW3	W-2141202	0461	2	BOSSIDY REYNOLD J	COL	0-0379045	0662	2	BOUCHEY WILFRID J	LTC	0-0402651	0565	3
BOOTH PAUL M	COL	0-0327750	0560	1	BORING JOHN S	LTC	0-0573983	0961	1	BOSSINGHAM EARL N	LTC	0-0318260	0966	3	BOUCK PERCY	COL	0-0111721	0854	1
BOOTH RICHARD G	LTC	0-2203302	0868	1	BORIS WALTER	CW3	W-2143412	0862	1	BOSSLER GERTRUDE J	LTC	N-0758266	1168	1	BOUDEMAN FREDERICK	CPT	0-1031229	0847	2
BOOTH ROBERT G	MAJ	0-1598747	1262	1	BORISS MARION E	LTC	0-0228662	0265	3	BOSSON DONAL C	1LT	0-0550430	0446	2	BOUDINOT HENRY M	LTC	0-0347315	0355	2
BOOTH ROBERT L	MAJ	0-1926469	1267	1	BORK LEROY V	2LT	0-1998097	0646	2	BOSSON HENRY	2LT	0-0187904	1161	1	BOUDREAU BERNICE	MAJ	N-0721754	1162	1
BOOTH WALTER G	1LT	0-1308090	0845	2	BORKIN EMILIA V	1LT	N-0755013	0745	1	BOSTEDO KATHRYN F	CPT	N-0744442	0353	2	BOUDREAU FLOYD T	CPT	0-0495767	0145	2
BOOTH WAYNE F JR	1LT	0-1107306	0345	2	BORKOWSKI ADAM A	LTC	0-2017190	1267	1	BOSTER VERN	LTC	0-0383476	0557	1	BOUDREAUX ARCHIE F	CW2	W-2101154	0246	2
BOOTH WILLIAM P	1LT	0-1315135	0745	2	BORKSTROM THEODORE W	1LT	0-1580548	0646	1	BOSTIC JOHN H	COL	0-0355189	1161	1	BOUDREAUX JULES A	CPT	0-0404321	1045	2
BOOTHBY AUSTIN L	CW3	W-2148486	0166	1	BORLAND WALLACE C JR	MAJ	0-0978953	0967	1	BOSTICK ARTHUR C JR	1LT	0-0398141	1043	2	BOUDREAUX LOUIS E	MAJ	0-1018243	0461	1
BOOTHE HOWARD P	2LT	0-1578185	0944	2	BORLAND WHITNEY M	LTC	0-1110939	1265	3	BOSTICK BENJAMIN	LTC	0-0302283	1043	2	BOUEY DONALD E	1LT	0-1325196	1045	2
BOOTHE LAWRENCE L	CW4	W-2144843	0864	1	BORLING WILLIAM	MAJ	0-1949268	1068	1	BOSTICK HARRY W	LTC	0-1046362	0258	1	BOUFFARD CHARLES J	MAJ	0-0257109	1160	3
BOOTHE RUBY E	2LT	N-0700238	0936	1	BORMAN WILLIAM R	MAJ	0-1885197	0864	1	BOSTICK JOSEPH E	LTC	0-0383943	0261	1	BOUFFARD HENRI J	LTC	0-1549433	0466	1
BOOTON LAWRENCE J	CW3	W-2004168	0559	3	BORN RICHARD W	1LT	0-1288687	0146	2	BOSTICK MACON L	CPT	0-2012352	0861	1	BOUFFARD ULPIC J	LTC	0-0188085	1156	3
BOOZE THOMAS W	CPT	0-1881409	0365	1	BORNDAHL RICHARD I	LTC	0-0338260	0660	1	BOSTICK ORBIE	LTC	0-0293977	1044	2	BOUGARD JOSEPH G	WO1	W-2149804	1153	1
BOOZER GEORGE W JR	CPT	0-0403672	0646	2	BORNE ANNE	CPT	L-0201406	1047	2	BOSTICK SAMUEL M	MAJ	0-1758775	0461	1	BOUGHNER DUNCAN S	MAJ	0-1041973	0361	1
BOOZER MATTHEW F	CPT	0-0315517	0345	2	BORNEMAN ESTHER B	MAJ	N-0726918	0462	1	BOSTICK SIDNEY F	COL	0-0266448	1053	2	BOUGHTON CHARLES A	MAJ	0-1593467	0464	1
BOOZER WILLIAM L	MAJ	0-0174364	0961	1	BORNEMAN JOHN K	COL	0-0266084	0450	2	BOSTOCK GEORGE M	COL	0-0140131	1056	3	BOUGHTON WELBY E	2LT	0-0398734	0344	2
BOPP JAMES	MAJ	0-0277471	0865	1	BORNEMEIER WALTER C	MAJ	0-0174683	0561	3	BOSTON DAVID	1LT	0-1544240	1144	2	BOUGHTON WILLIAM H	COL	0-0243886	0356	3
BORAH HARRY A	LTC	0-0237173	0362	1	BORNHOFFT HENRY J JR	CPT	0-0528393	0747	2	BOSTON DONALD W	LTC	0-1636302	0861	2	BOUK JUNIOR F	2LT	0-1318643	1043	2
BORAL HENRY	CPT	0-0495539	0849	2	BORNHOLDT JOHN N	COL	0-0342327	0866	1	BOSTON GEORGE A	MAJ	0-1822526	1161	1	BOUKNIGHT FRANK C	CPT	0-0270765	0268	3
BORAN GEORGE H	COL	0-0360972	0161	1	BORNKESSEL JULIUS G	LTC	0-0384018	0960	1	BOSTON HOWARD B	MAJ	0-0955149	0864	1	BOUKNIGHT WILLIAM R	COL	0-0520010	0567	3
BORASCH EDWARD J	CW3	W-3150392	1167	1	BORNMAN CASPER S	LTC	0-1051492	0962	1	BOSTON JOHN A	LTC	0-0192874	0749	3	BOULAIS FREDERICK	MAJ	0-1332670	0161	1
BORCHERDT JACK A	CPT	0-1293836	1145	2	BORNMAN JAMES A	LTC	0-0451824	1060	1	BOSTWICK WILLIAM C	CPT	0-0553424	1047	2	BOULDEN HENRY W JR	MAJ	0-1951643	0166	1
BORCHERS RAYMOND W	LTC	0-0303312	0568	3	BORNSCHEUER WILLIAM	LTC	0-1054916	0165	1	BOSWELL ANDREW V	MAJ	0-0247446	0353	3	BOULDEN MARION P	COL	0-0118806	1057	3
BORCHERS ROBERT R	CPT	0-0328310	0644	2	BORNSTEIN LEON M	1LT	0-1846252	0445	2	BOSWELL AUBREY	CPT	0-0333408	0346	2	BOULDIN ALLEN H	LTC	0-1101342	1058	1
BORCHERT ERNEST F	CPT	0-0170807	0954	3	BORONDA RICHARD C	LTC	0-1058445	0868	3	BOSWELL CARL A	MAJ	0-0304144	1068	3	BOULDIN CHARLES E	CPT	0-1642944	0355	1
BORCHERT JOSEPH J	COL	0-0297890	0359	1	BOROP LYLE E	1LT	0-1170290	0446	2	BOSWELL CHARLES A	CPT	0-1292645	0446	2	BOULDIN EDWARD J	CPT	0-1321146	1047	2
BORCHERT MAX A	MAJ	0-0256184	0249	1	BOROS WILLIAM K	CPT	0-0539508	0546	2	BOSWELL CLARENCE H	LTC	0-0472263	0146	2	BOULDIN WILLIAM R	CPT	0-1287129	0246	2
BORCK CHARLES A	WO1	W-2114628	0366	1	BOROUGHS WILLIAM J	LTC	0-0362217	1166	3	BOSWELL HENRY D	MAJ	0-1634990	1163	2	BOULER WALTER T	LTC	0-1012066	0962	1
BORCK JOHN F	LTC	0-0997701	0468	1	BOROWITZ FRANK P	LTC	0-0980121	0266	1	BOSWELL JAMES M	CW3	W-2149988	1062	1	BOULEY ARTHUR G	CW4	W-2101106	0259	1
BORCUK PETER J	LTC	0-1319171	0763	1	BOROWSKI ANTHONY	LTC	0-0498195	0557	1	BOSWELL JOHN W	LTC	0-1951003	0167	1	BOULLEMET MARSEILLE	MAJ	0-0228872	0155	3
BORDE HARRY J	1LT	0-0464377	0144	2	BOROWSKI JOHN D	LTC	0-0369156	0861	1	BOSWELL KENNETH B	MAJ	0-0367783	0761	1	BOULLION KENNETH L	LTC	0-1284089	0258	1
BORDEN DANIEL L	COL	0-0186593	0648	3	BORREGO ALBERTO M	1LT	0-0290651	1160	3	BOSWELL LESTER R	2LT	0-1822097	0550	1	BOULTER ROBERT E	COL	0-0378621	0866	3
BORDEN FRANK	MAJ	0-1574202	0460	1	BORRELIZ ANTONIO	CW2	W-2210425	0766	1	BOSWELL WILLIAM H	1LT	0-0511869	0145	2	BOULTON ALBERT F	LTC	0-0271397	0967	3
BORDEN GARLAND A	LTC	0-1171910	0661	1	BORRELL GERALD J	CW2	W-2143833	0559	1	BOSWELL WILLIAM P	MAJ	0-1302264	0661	1	BOULTON JOHN W	2LT	0-0436842	1045	2
BORDEN HOXSEY J	LTC	0-0278268	0466	1	BORRES MICHAEL G	MAJ	0-1341940	1263	1	BOSWELL WILSON S	MAJ	0-0450016	0854	1	BOULWARE CHARLIE L	CW2	W-2145700	0659	1
BORDEN NATHANIEL	COL	0-0241874	1054	1	BORROR CARSON M	LTC	0-0239231	1163	3	BOSWORTH JULIAN E	CW4	W-2142222	1265	1	BOULWARE JOHN P	CPT	0-0497223	0148	1
BORDEN RALPH L	CW4	W-2122316	1267	1	BORROR DOROTHEA A	MAJ	L-1010820	0968	1	BOSZE FRANCIS G	CW3	W-2206894	0468	2	BOUNDS JESSE C	1LT	0-0286424	0160	2
BORDEN ROBERT B	LTC	0-1551029	0163	1	BORROWMAN JOHN K	COL	0-0258115	0767	3	BOTDORF CHARLES F JR	LTC	0-1116355	1164	1	BOUNDS JOHN A	LTC	0-1589715	0167	1
BORDEN WALTER J	LTC	0-1039180	0161	1	BORSHER IRVING P	CPT	0-0539075	0847	2	BOTDORF FREDERICK	CW2	W-2143872	0166	1	BOUNDS SIDNEY V	MAJ	0-1296163	0961	1
BORDER CHARLES R	LTC	0-0369388	0967	1	BORTIRI MAXIMUS	1LT	0-0538863	1144	2	BOTELER LANHAM L	LTC	0-1114555	1165	1	BOUQUET WILFRED J	MAJ	0-1895481	1068	3
BORDER TONOKA H	1LT	0-1031999	0552	2	BORTNER LESTER E	CW2	W-2146627	1154	1	BOTELHO BENJAMIN	CW4	W-2002060	1060	3	BOUR LAWRENCE J	LTC	0-0408743	0861	1
BORDER WILLARD C	LTC	0-1302586	0162	1	BORUM VERNON L	LTC	0-0176353	0361	3	BOTERF CHESTER A	LTC	0-0482364	0563	1	BOURDEAU HERBERT F	LTC	0-0451630	0959	1
BORDERS COLEMAN P	LTC	0-1113114	1061	1	BORUSZAK NATHAN	COL	0-0189302	1262	3	BOTHE CHRISTOPHE	CPT	0-0319607	1045	2	BOURDON WILLIAM R	LTC	0-0128111	1155	3
BORDERS HUEY T	LTC	0-0298985	0166	1	BOSA JOSEPH R	LTC	0-0304030	0260	1	BOTHWELL FLORA H	CPT	N-0731424	0747	2	BOURGEOIS LAWRENCE J	MAJ	0-1580667	0160	1

NAME	GRADE	SVC NO	DATE RET MO YR	RET CODE	NAME	GRADE	SVC NO	DATE RET MO YR	RET CODE	NAME	GRADE	SVC NO	DATE RET MO YR	RET CODE	NAME	GRADE	SVC NO	DATE RET MO YR	RET CODE
BOURGEOIS MARCEL G	LTC	0-1647969	0264	1	BOWEN WILLIAM C	COL	0-0191754	1162	3	BOWLES JOSEPH M	2LT	0-1541118	0344	2	BOY GRACE N	CPT	N-0737653	0246	1
BOURGOIN CARMIN M	MAJ	L-0221270	0164	1	BOWER BERNARD W	1LT	0-0535765	1045	2	BOWLES VICTOR D	2LT	0-2046902	0245	2	BOYACK ARCHIE R	COL	0-0268986	0161	1
BOURISSEAU DALE S	2LT	0-1311471	1144	2	BOWER CECIL L	LTC	0-0163573	1156	3	BOWLEY RAY A	CW3	W-2152367	0763	1	BOYCE BINGHAM	COL	0-0225875	1060	1
BOURKE EDWARD	LTC	0-1166442	0457	1	BOWER CHARLES W	MAJ	0-1050190	0164	1	BOWLIN ALLAN K	LTC	0-0262925	0665	3	BOYCE CARL B	LTC	0-1798435	0962	1
BOURKE JOHN D	1LT	0-1324100	0446	2	BOWER EDWARD C	LTC	0-0233227	0762	3	BOWLIN CLEO S	LTC	0-1581666	1062	1	BOYCE DAVID C	MAJ	0-0977308	1262	1
BOURKE THOMAS C	COL	0-0130259	0653	3	BOWER FRED L	MAJ	0-0281416	0446	2	BOWLIN DONALD W	CW2	W-2147563	1159	1	BOYCE DAVID K	MAJ	0-1646784	1060	1
BOURLAND PHILIP E M	LTC	0-0337842	1060	1	BOWER HAROLD C	2LT	0-1182780	0745	2	BOWLIN FOREST W	2LT	0-1014420	0645	2	BOYCE HENRY W	COL	0-0107859	0648	3
BOURLAND SAM H	CW3	W-2147226	0862	1	BOWER JACK W	CW2	W-2209862	0663	1	BOWLIN FRANCIS R	COL	0-0291073	0559	1	BOYCE HUGH S	LTC	0-2034623	0466	1
BOURNE ELDRED G	CW3	W-2153344	0966	1	BOWER JOHN L	2LT	0-1181828	0944	2	BOWLIN WILLIAM D	MAJ	0-1109325	0663	1	BOYCE LARRY J	W01	W-2110921	0945	2
BOURNE GORDON M	MAJ	0-0974079	1067	1	BOWER LEWIS C	MAJ	0-1282357	0962	1	BOWLING ROBERT H	1LT	0-1285366	0546	2	BOYCE LLOYD L	LTC	0-0180015	0561	3
BOURNE ROBERT F	LTC	0-0342860	0746	2	BOWER LOYS F	LTC	0-0243010	0157	3	BOWLING SILAS B	CW3	W-2148276	0864	1	BOYCOTT CECIL M	COL	0-0171340	0956	3
BOURNE ROBERT L	CPT	0-1300751	0747	2	BOWER RICHARD F	CPT	0-0483222	0946	2	BOWLING TRULY T	MAJ	0-0503398	0755	1	BOYD ALBERT G	CW4	W-2148830	1268	1
BOURNS PAUL M	LTC	0-0387089	1163	3	BOWER WAYNE E	CW3	W-2150599	0365	1	BOWMAN BEATRICE	MAJ	L-0602965	0467	1	BOYD ALLEN W	CW2	W-2151612	0762	1
BOURQUE JOSEPH A A	CW2	RW-2210907	1165	1	BOWERMAN RALPH L	COL	0-0189953	0158	3	BOWMAN BRADLEY L	LTC	0-0315436	0958	2	BOYD ARTHUR L	LTC	0-1341500	0967	1
BOURQUIN RALPH H	MAJ	0-2026471	0261	1	BOWERMAN THOMAS J	LTC	0-1796412	0261	1	BOWMAN CLAIR F	LTC	0-0245952	0760	3	BOYD BERL	LTC	0-0184596	0356	3
BOUSCHOR CHARLES F	CPT	0-0490507	1145	2	BOWERMASTER FRED C	LTC	0-0414174	0667	3	BOWMAN CLARENCE	CW3	W-2205364	1066	1	BOYD BILLIE R	MAJ	0-1317068	0761	1
BOUSE THERMAN	LTC	0-1581541	0565	1	BOWERMASTER JAMES W	1LT	0-1541580	1053	2	BOWMAN CLARENCE W	W01	W-2151834	0255	1	BOYD BUFORD F	COL	0-0256619	1165	3
BOUSH GILBERT W	COL	0-0228018	0361	3	BOWERS ALBERT V	COL	0-0249564	0865	3	BOWMAN DORIS E	CPT	N-0742773	0448	1	BOYD CARTER	1LT	0-0392964	0544	2
BOUSQUET WILLIAM C	CW2	W-2143523	0953	1	BOWERS BENJAMIN E	CW3	W-2150602	0659	1	BOWMAN EDWIN C	MAJ	0-1851544	0755	2	BOYD CHARLES C	LTC	0-1318859	0566	3
BOUSQUIN SYLVIO L	LTC	0-0351472	0757	1	BOWERS BYRON D	LTC	0-0274990	0156	3	BOWMAN FRANK S JR	MAJ	0-1560337	0763	1	BOYD CHARLES W	CW2	W-2213174	1268	1
BOUST EDWARD B	LTC	0-0204391	0960	1	BOWERS CARL E	MAJ	0-1037953	0761	1	BOWMAN GEORGE H	LTC	0-0346618	0961	1	BOYD CLYDE C JR	CW2	W-2149318	0461	1
BOUTILIER FRANKLIN M	MAJ	0-1335225	0967	1	BOWERS CHARLES E	MAJ	0-0972296	1064	1	BOWMAN GORDON D	1LT	0-0250585	0366	3	BOYD COLLIN J	LTC	0-0284145	1060	1
BOUTIN JOHN A	MAJ	0-0947299	0663	1	BOWERS CLAUDE T	M G	0-0183291	0859	3	BOWMAN HAROLD M	MAJ	0-1937448	1266	1	BOYD DALE E	1LT	0-0447698	0246	2
BOUTON JAY H	LTC	0-0268670	0646	2	BOWERS EATON J III	MAJ	0-0407223	1160	1	BOWMAN HARVEY F JR	LTC	0-1295988	0765	1	BOYD DAVID J JR	CW2	RW-2144613	0163	1
BOUTON JOHN W	LTC	0-0295769	1267	3	BOWERS EDWARD G	2LT	0-0108779	0545	1	BOWMAN HENRY C	MAJ	0-0121333	0556	3	BOYD DEMPSTER A	CW3	W-2150557	1164	1
BOUTON VERNON W	MAJ	0-2016248	0457	1	BOWERS EDWARD W	LTC	0-0409997	0560	1	BOWMAN HOWARD F	LTC	0-0218097	0952	3	BOYD DON C	CW2	W-2213899	1167	1
BOUTTE CLARENCE P	LTC	0-0282255	0467	3	BOWERS EUGENE D	MAJ	0-1342151	1066	1	BOWMAN HOWARD F	MAJ	0-0888601	0257	1	BOYD DUDLEY Q	LTC	0-0929726	0665	1
BOUTWELL GENE A	1LT	0-1234641	0544	2	BOWERS F A I SR	CPT	0-0195616	0660	3	BOWMAN IRA G	CW4	W-2005868	0663	1	BOYD DWIGHT I	LTC	0-0586553	0862	1
BOUTWELL JAMES R	CW2	W-2210938	0568	1	BOWERS FRANKLIN E	2LT	0-1301248	0745	2	BOWMAN JACOB	CPT	0-0199391	0363	3	BOYD EDGAR F JR	LTC	0-0509602	0567	1
BOUTWELL WILLIAM F	MAJ	0-0309614	0868	3	BOWERS GAH T	CPT	0-0265119	0943	2	BOWMAN JAMES C	LTC	0-1292826	0968	1	BOYD EMMETT T	CPT	0-0974980	0956	2
BOUVIER THOMAS J	MAJ	0-0357898	0767	3	BOWERS HAROLD D	MAJ	0-0380790	0546	2	BOWMAN JAMES H	MAJ	0-1821541	0761	1	BOYD ENNIS E	MAJ	0-1552236	0557	1
BOVE EMIL	MAJ	0-1691184	0745	2	BOWERS J B JR	LTC	0-0269537	0463	1	BOWMAN JAMES P	CW3	W-2205796	0167	1	BOYD FRANK K	LTC	0-0279249	0453	3
BOVINO VICTOR J	LTC	0-1282317	1167	1	BOWERS JACK G	CW2	W-2148026	0761	1	BOWMAN JANET S	MAJ	N-0754548	0765	1	BOYD GEORGE W	CPT	0-0175650	0757	3
BOWAB ANTHONY J	MAJ	0-0103282	1058	3	BOWERS JESSE W	COL	0-0231465	0648	3	BOWMAN JOHN D	1LT	0-1015114	0146	2	BOYD GRAYDON F	CPT	0-1182910	0359	1
BOWDEN AMBROSE H	CPT	0-0233072	1067	3	BOWERS JOHN A	COL	0-0212638	1263	3	BOWMAN JOSEPH J	LTC	0-0349209	0267	3	BOYD HAROLD L	LTC	0-0239604	1062	3
BOWDEN CLIFTON M	LTC	0-0271221	1067	3	BOWERS JOHN A	2LT	0-1019285	0745	2	BOWMAN KENNETH D	2LT	0-1321283	0245	2	BOYD HOWARD	1LT	0-0375311	1145	2
BOWDEN FRANK J	LTC	0-0375405	0758	3	BOWERS JOHN E	1LT	0-1100884	0459	1	BOWMAN LAKIN A	1LT	0-0402016	0244	2	BOYD HOWARD R	1LT	0-1285180	0446	2
BOWDEN HAYGOOD S	LTC	0-0329494	0465	3	BOWERS JOSEPH J	MAJ	0-1549893	0357	1	BOWMAN LAWRENCE R	2LT	0-1587145	0144	2	BOYD JAMES	COL	0-0236154	0165	3
BOWDEN HERMAN R	W01	W-2150809	0861	1	BOWERS JOSEPH M	MAJ	0-1169433	0161	1	BOWMAN LELAND E	CPT	0-1288689	0246	2	BOYD JAMES C	1LT	0-1287654	0145	2
BOWDEN HOWARD W	LTC	0-1312271	0261	1	BOWERS LAWRENCE J	MAJ	0-1030334	0456	1	BOWMAN MARTIN	CPT	0-1058201	0747	2	BOYD JAMES H	MAJ	0-2005421	0461	1
BOWDEN JOHN W	COL	0-0352722	0851	1	BOWERS LEOLA O	CPT	N-0792560	0956	2	BOWMAN MAUDE	LTC	N-0700039	0846	1	BOYD JAMES M	LTC	0-0227675	0563	3
BOWDEN JOHN W JR	MAJ	0-1115192	0857	1	BOWERS LOWELL F	COL	0-0118809	0355	3	BOWMAN MILTON S	COL	0-0162224	0946	2	BOYD JAMES R	COL	0-0279151	0952	3
BOWDEN MURRAY C	MAJ	0-0986768	0865	1	BOWERS RALPH K	MAJ	0-0203780	0145	2	BOWMAN OLIN F	CW3	W-2147277	1262	1	BOYD JOHN C	COL	0-0338141	0662	1
BOWDEN RICHARD	CW3	W-2205660	0568	1	BOWERS RICHARD G	1LT	0-0501757	0445	2	BOWMAN RAYMOND X	LTC	0-1172769	0863	1	BOYD JOHN L	MAJ	0-2033307	1061	1
BOWDEN THOMAS N JR	CW2	W-2147739	0756	1	BOWERS RICHARD W	MAJ	0-1574737	0460	1	BOWMAN ROBERT L	1LT	0-0256152	0857	3	BOYD JOHN S	CPT	0-1312400	1052	2
BOWDEN TROY C	CPT	0-2026574	0857	1	BOWERS ROBERT F	CW3	W-2147123	0162	1	BOWMAN SAMUEL A	LTC	0-0382345	0161	1	BOYD JOHN W	MAJ	0-0124266	0853	3
BOWDEN WALTER H	COL	0-0395769	0862	1	BOWERS ROBERT J	CPT	0-0481954	0148	1	BOWMAN SAMUEL H	MAJ	0-0146443	0555	3	BOYD JOSEPH G	W01	W-2110673	0862	1
BOWDISH ARVINE C	CPT	0-0900310	1043	2	BOWERS RUSSELL S	MAJ	0-0213571	0549	3	BOWMAN TINSLEY	1LT	0-0255487	1160	3	BOYD LESLIE C	LTC	0-1178417	1262	2
BOWDLE HARVEY C	LTC	0-0453406	0665	1	BOWERS WARREN B	2LT	0-1299361	0544	2	BOWMAN VERNON D	LTC	0-0452481	0461	1	BOYD MARIE A	1LT	N-0724346	0345	2
BOWE FRANKLIN G	W01	W-2105384	0758	2	BOWERS WILLIAM H JR	LTC	0-0197068	0758	3	BOWMAN WESLEY W	COL	0-0221028	0160	3	BOYD MARIE K	MAJ	N-0722801	0162	1
BOWE NATHANIEL	LTC	0-1637415	0868	1	BOWERS WILLIAM L	CPT	0-0495740	0647	1	BOWMAN WHEELER G	CPT	0-2036042	0861	1	BOYD MARY	1LT	N-0735358	0345	1
BOWEN CARL D	COL	0-0104770	1040	1	BOWERS ZELOTIS B	1LT	0-1288506	0545	2	BOWMAN WILLIAM	MAJ	0-0186504	0931	1	BOYD MARY G	1LT	N-0737568	0845	1
BOWEN CLARENCE W	LTC	0-0317443	0157	3	BOWERSOCK JOHN O	LTC	0-0446194	0262	1	BOWMAN WILLIAM B	1LT	0-1305130	0161	2	BOYD MAX W	MAJ	0-0971963	0763	1
BOWEN CLIFFORD JR	LTC	0-1175054	1160	1	BOWES ALMON N	COL	0-0146762	1155	3	BOWMAN WILLIAM M	MAJ	0-0522308	0460	2	BOYD NOEIS F	CW2	W-2143873	0461	2
BOWEN E A	CPT	0-1288698	0546	2	BOWES JOHN G	COL	0-0330575	1163	3	BOWMAN WILLIAM T	1LT	0-1826145	1145	2	BOYD PAUL S	COL	0-0953900	1067	3
BOWEN EMERY J	CPT	0-0221839	0349	3	BOWIE CLYDE F	MAJ	0-1683859	0246	2	BOWMASTER CHARLES B	W01	W-2112119	0444	2	BOYD PHILLIPS L	B G	0-0230117	0165	3
BOWEN FLOYD L	CW4	W-2117006	0161	1	BOWIE DWAIN T	LTC	0-0329216	0861	1	BOWNS JAMES S	LTC	0-1640249	0168	1	BOYD RALPH G	B G	0-0203104	1161	3
BOWEN GLENN R	COL	0-0351354	0764	1	BOWIE ELEAZAR R	COL	0-0121290	0349	3	BOWRON JAMES E	COL	0-0103169	0253	3	BOYD RALPH W	CW3	W-2205058	0364	1
BOWEN HAROLD F	LTC	0-0911782	1062	1	BOWIE RALPH W	LTC	0-0254979	0867	3	BOWSER GEORGE M	LTC	0-0220014	1263	3	BOYD RANDOLPH W	LTC	0-0269494	0560	1
BOWEN HAROLD H	LTC	0-0277027	0664	3	BOWIE WILLIAM R	MAJ	0-1560404	0863	1	BOWSER GLEN	CPT	0-2032978	0267	1	BOYD RAYMOND K	2LT	0-1304627	0144	2
BOWEN HARRY E	LTC	0-0491600	0455	2	BOWIN LYNN L	COL	0-0327153	1165	1	BOWSER HARRY F JR	CPT	0-1040350	0660	1	BOYD ROBERT H JR	1LT	0-1926344	1054	2
BOWEN HUBERT F JR	CPT	0-1169033	0546	2	BOWINGTON ELMER W	MAJ	0-1013646	0858	1	BOWSER ROBERT M	LTC	0-0293357	0866	3	BOYD ROBERT E	CW3	W-2152992	1061	1
BOWEN ISAIAH F	LTC	0-0201342	0757	3	BOWKER IRVING A	1LT	0-1333923	1056	2	BOWSHER PAUL L	LTC	0-0359691	0960	1	BOYD ROBERT P	CPT	0-1692238	0146	2
BOWEN JACK	MAJ	0-1293361	0661	1	BOWLAND FRANK Y JR	LTC	0-0424188	0765	1	BOWSTEAD LEONARD A	2LT	0-0353223	0245	2	BOYD RUDOLPH	CW2	W-2147994	0360	1
BOWEN JOEL H	MAJ	0-0276539	0964	3	BOWLBY JAMES D	LTC	0-1948697	0665	2	BOWYER CHARLES S JR	MAJ	0-0962457	0967	1	BOYD RUTH	MAJ	R-0000773	0160	1
BOWEN JOHN J	LTC	0-1556539	0367	1	BOWLBY JOHN G	CW3	W-2149690	0363	1	BOWYER DALE E	1LT	0-0543128	0146	2	BOYD RUTH G	1LT	N-0787097	0346	1
BOWEN JOHN P	MAJ	0-1549434	0366	1	BOWLER DANIEL A	CPT	0-1114380	0147	2	BOWYER DELMAR M	CW3	W-2144569	1059	1	BOYD SPURGEON C	LTC	0-1548016	1263	1
BOWEN KENNETH F	CPT	0-0255822	1058	3	BOWLER FRANCIS H	CPT	0-0124267	0259	3	BOWYER MILFORD B	1LT	0-1313371	1045	2	BOYD THOMAS H JR	1LT	0-0328142	0344	2
BOWEN ORVAL W	LTC	0-0484218	0863	1	BOWLER JOSEPH L	MAJ	0-0944658	0562	1	BOWYER RALPH W	LTC	0-0323978	0168	3	BOYD THOMAS L	CPT	0-0291884	0844	2
BOWEN PHILIP M	CW3	W-2144227	0461	1	BOWLER ROBERT V	COL	0-0294619	0647	2	BOWYER WESLEY C	CPT	0-1300123	0348	2	BOYD THOMAS W	MAJ	0-1014810	0761	1
BOWEN RAYMOND J	CPT	0-1691270	0545	2	BOWLES ARTHUR L	W01	W-2146870	0157	1	BOWZER CHARLES E	MAJ	0-0980488	1168	1	BOYD THURMAN L	LTC	0-1058192	1162	1
BOWEN RICHARD A II	COL	0-0231931	0559	1	BOWLES CECIL C	1LT	0-0919735	0245	2	BOX HERMAN F	CPT	0-1303266	0760	1	BOYD TILLMAN F	COL	0-0250041	0947	2
BOWEN ROBERT F JR	1LT	0-0425625	1045	2	BOWLES GEORGE M	LTC	0-0322775	0459	1	BOX VIRGIL M	LTC	0-1575776	0562	1	BOYD WARLAND F	CPT	0-1591683	0146	2
BOWEN ROBERT W	CW2	W-2213129	0467	1	BOWLES GEORGE R JR	1LT	0-0965057	0858	2	BOX WILLIAM G	CW3	W-2205411	1065	1	BOYD WESTON A	CW3	W-2149203	0961	1
BOWEN WHEELER B	MAJ	0-0452290	0557	1	BOWLES HERSHEL D	CPT	0-0499526	0847	1	BOXER LEO M	LTC	0-0408494	0646	2	BOYD WILLIAM C	LTC	0-0405788	0665	1

NAME	GRADE	SVC NO	DATE RET MO YR	RET CODE
BOYD WILLIAM C	MAJ	O-0237357	0464	3
BOYDEN WILLIAM F	MAJ	O-0126292	0450	2
BOYEN WILLIAM A	COL	O-0373051	0166	1
BOYER BENJAMIN F	COL	O-0238364	1064	3
BOYER CHARLES M	COL	O-0148831	0648	3
BOYER CLARENCE L	COL	O-0142755	0154	3
BOYER EDGAR J	2LT	O-0395080	0745	2
BOYER FRED A	LTC	O-0535712	0561	3
BOYER GEORGE C	LTC	O-0389822	0247	2
BOYER GEORGE H	LTC	O-0156961	0648	3
BOYER GERALD D	COL	O-0254128	0559	3
BOYER GROVER A	MAJ	O-0189412	0648	3
BOYER HOWARD E	COL	O-0218680	1062	3
BOYER JACK K	MAJ	O-0398138	0748	2
BOYER JAMES N	LTC	O-1543482	0661	1
BOYER JOHN A	MAJ	O-1548359	0157	1
BOYER JOHN F	LTC	O-1047033	1167	3
BOYER JOHN S JR	MAJ	O-0256422	1067	3
BOYER LESLIE W	LTC	O-0324770	0567	3
BOYER LESTER L	MAJ	O-1547547	0258	1
BOYER LLOYD L	COL	O-0290358	0966	3
BOYER MERIL A	LTC	O-0277229	0957	3
BOYER OTHA W	MAJ	O-0200795	0855	3
BOYER PAUL N	MAJ	O-1919179	1066	1
BOYER ROBERT M	1LT	O-0446912	0146	2
BOYER ROBERT R	1LT	O-1293194	0844	2
BOYER ROSWELL R	COL	O-0223124	1055	1
BOYER WILLIAM O	MAJ	O-1047463	0762	1
BOYER WILLIAM M	LTC	O-0120774	0858	3
BOYERS PAULINE J	MAJ	N-0767919	1263	1
BOYES BEDFORD W	COL	O-0174387	1052	3
BOYES JAMES G	1LT	O-0109824	1041	1
BOYETTE HARDY A	CPT	O-0968270	0159	1
BOYKIN BREVARD	LTC	O-0245024	0561	3
BOYKIN CECIL A	LTC	O-1000086	1161	1
BOYKIN HERMAN N	1LT	O-1043876	1045	2
BOYKIN SAMUEL	MAJ	O-0473521	0446	2
BOYKIN STARLEY N JR	COL	O-0260944	0248	2
BOYLAN JAMES W	CPT	O-0503022	1046	1
BOYLAN PAUL C JR	LTC	O-1118551	0867	1
BOYLAN ROBERT F	1LT	O-1013144	1045	2
BOYLAN WILLIAM J	CW4	W-2002612	0267	1
BOYLE BERNARD	LTC	O-1552237	0466	3
BOYLE CHARLES F	MAJ	O-1101749	1047	2
BOYLE EDWARD W	LTC	O-0405860	0860	1
BOYLE FRANCIS P	CPT	O-0889762	0856	1
BOYLE FRANK J JR	WO1	W-2127822	0645	2
BOYLE IRVING C	CPT	O-0415801	0948	1
BOYLE JAMES H	CPT	O-0132811	0315	1
BOYLE JAMES L JR	1LT	O-1056989	1045	2
BOYLE JOHN C	CW3	W-2141150	1163	1
BOYLE JOHN W	LTC	O-1299363	0165	2
BOYLE JOSEPH A JR	1LT	O-0498990	0944	2
BOYLE JOSEPH R	CPT	O-0472789	0247	2
BOYLE LEO M	M G	O-0266202	0859	3
BOYLE MICHAEL J	MAJ	O-0903249	1045	2
BOYLE MURAT	1LT	O-1010942	0345	2
BOYLE PATRICK J	LTC	O-0148815	0150	3
BOYLE PAUL E	CW3	W-2144004	1056	1
BOYLE PHILIP F	LTC	O-1945250	0361	1
BOYLE THOMAS F	MAJ	O-0902831	0944	2
BOYLE WILLIAM E	2LT	O-0527680	1144	2
BOYLEN ERNEST L	MAJ	O-0231264	0445	2
BOYLES ALBERT E	CW3	W-2150199	0563	1
BOYLES DALE K	MAJ	O-0297368	1068	3
BOYLES EDWARD E	MAJ	O-1299673	0258	1
BOYLES FRANK B	CPT	O-1046731	0545	2
BOYLES FRED M	MAJ	O-0360921	0544	2
BOYLES JAMES L	CPT	O-2263458	1061	1
BOYLES RAYMOND F	MAJ	O-1302945	0556	1
BOYLES ROLLIN C	COL	O-0312046	0763	3
BOYNTON CHARLES I	COL	O-0173911	0850	3
BOYNTON EDGAR B	LTC	O-0154920	0459	3
BOYNTON HENRY B	COL	O-0154917	0459	3
BOYNTON HENRY G	MAJ	O-2292486	0168	1

NAME	GRADE	SVC NO	DATE RET MO YR	RET CODE
BOYNTON JAMES W	LTC	O-0225537	1057	3
BOYNTON LEONIE C	MAJ	L-0903116	0466	3
BOYNTON MALCOLM B	COL	O-0124265	1154	3
BOYNTON MELVILLE S	CPT	O-0410689	1157	2
BOYNTON RALPH E	COL	O-0300716	0161	1
BOYNTON WYMAN P	COL	O-0287982	1068	3
BOYS RALPH W	LTC	O-0383115	0267	1
BOYSON EDWARD W	MAJ	O-1935532	0465	1
BOYSON GLORIA D	1LT	N-0754980	0848	2
BOYSON WILLIAM A	COL	O-0247250	0954	3
BOYT SAMUEL W	MAJ	O-0411009	0559	1
BOYTIN MICHAEL	CW4	W-2148839	1068	1
BOZADA ALFONSO M	CPT	O-1329208	1047	2
BOZAROT MARION L	COL	O-0276824	0260	1
BOZARTH ESTEL A	COL	O-0375012	0657	1
BOZE JOSEPH M	MAJ	O-0200064	0562	3
BOZEMAN DAVID M	MAJ	O-1062801	0566	1
BOZICEVICH JOSEPH R	LTC	O-1330706	0466	1
BOZIGIAN HAIG	LTC	O-0416117	0346	2
BOZORTH HARRY S III	MAJ	O-2038888	1061	2
BOZORTH ROBERT E	LTC	O-1304007	0962	1
BOZZO AUGUST R	CPT	O-1296644	0746	2
BRAACK JOY W	LTC	O-0245701	0653	1
BRAASCH WALTER C	LTC	O-1557634	0865	3
BRAATEN INGVALD T	LTC	O-0186519	0754	3
BRAATHEN MELVIN A	2LT	O-2007433	0647	1
BRABANT ROBERT P	CW4	W-2142302	0865	1
BRABEC ROBERT	LTC	O-2034720	0761	1
BRABENEC JOHN J JR	MAJ	O-1167324	0257	1
BRABHAM WILLIAM R	MAJ	O-0579820	1060	1
BRABNER-SMITH JOHN W	COL	O-0368922	0763	3
BRABON RALPH M	CW2	W-2215811	1267	1
BRABSON WILLIAM A	2LT	O-1300753	1043	2
BRACALELLO WILLIAM A	CW2	W-2142355	0659	1
BRACEWELL WILLIAM D	MAJ	O-1917822	1165	1
BRACEY KENNETH R	LTC	O-0477621	0261	2
BRACKEN CARL F	1LT	O-0322829	0344	2
BRACKENS PERCY	CW4	W-2105935	0156	2
BRACKETT CECIL F O	LTC	O-0298139	0565	3
BRACKETT EDWARD F	LTC	O-1302109	1062	1
BRACKETT FREDERICK	LTC	O-0286862	0760	1
BRACKETT GERALD C	MAJ	O-1576954	0154	1
BRACKETT MAX A	COL	O-0242184	0463	3
BRACKETT ROBERT M	LTC	O-1553229	0763	1
BRACY JOHN C	LTC	O-1298181	0962	1
BRADBERRY JOHN W JR	MAJ	O-1058447	0667	1
BRADBURY FRANK A	LTC	O-0384845	0261	1
BRADBURY GEORGE E	MAJ	O-2200126	0765	1
BRADBURY GEORGE L	MAJ	O-1305717	0358	2
BRADBURY HORACE C	COL	O-0335428	0664	1
BRADBURY JOHN F	LTC	O-1100027	1060	1
BRADBURY MAURICE J	COL	O-0224401	0263	3
BRADD PHILBIN M	MAJ	O-0585962	0955	1
BRADDOCK JOSEPH M	CPT	O-0252983	0455	3
BRADDOCK WILLIAM A	1LT	O-0497415	0455	1
BRADDOCK WILLIAM H	COL	O-0183735	0849	3
BRADDY JAMES A	MAJ	O-0983052	0765	1
BRADEN CLYDE F	CPT	O-0272363	0153	3
BRADEN CLYDE H C	MAJ	O-0275136	1060	1
BRADEN JOHN W	LTC	O-1553599	1267	1
BRADEN LAWRENCE A	MAJ	O-0301973	0245	2
BRADEN RALPH A	MAJ	O-0402070	0946	2
BRADEN ROBERT C	LTC	O-1035670	1263	1
BRADER LELAND C	MAJ	O-1591005	0663	1
BRADER LORAN J	MAJ	O-1552021	0264	1
BRADEY ELMER J	MAJ	O-1053063	0860	2
BRADFIELD EARL F	LTC	O-0195662	0945	2
BRADFIELD HENRY F	CPT	O-0974700	0263	1
BRADFIELD MAX E	MAJ	O-0364544	1052	2
BRADFIELD ROBERT W	COL	O-1107310	1168	1
BRADFORD BRAIN K	CPT	O-0467543	1147	2
BRADFORD BYRON B	LTC	O-0350320	0561	1
BRADFORD CARLTON D	1LT	O-1285888	1046	2
BRADFORD CHESTER	1LT	O-1316373	1145	2
BRADFORD DON C	CW4	W-2144783	0867	1

NAME	GRADE	SVC NO	DATE RET MO YR	RET CODE
BRADFORD G I JR	LTC	NO-0491575	0157	1
BRADFORD GARLAND B	LTC	O-1299674	0964	1
BRADFORD HARRY A	CPT	O-0105625	0648	3
BRADFORD JOSEPH F	CW4	W-2109234	0256	1
BRADFORD LLOYD L	LTC	O-0204543	0256	3
BRADFORD MARY P	1LT	N-0789542	1047	1
BRADFORD WILLIAM S	MAJ	O-1172771	0761	2
BRADFORD ZELDA F	MAJ	N-0763768	0165	3
BRADIN BENJAMIN M	LTC	O-1059721	0960	1
BRADIN JOHN P JR	MAJ	O-1942308	0868	3
BRADISH JOHN A	LTC	O-0284157	0566	3
BRADLEY BERNARD W	COL	O-0248604	1164	3
BRADLEY CARMON J	MAJ	O-0493663	0256	1
BRADLEY CECIL U SR	COL	O-0177215	1059	3
BRADLEY CHARLES F	CW3	W-2144845	0562	1
BRADLEY CHARLES I	LTC	O-1796263	0656	1
BRADLEY CHARLES W	2LT	O-1913554	1143	1
BRADLEY CHARLIE A	CW4	W-2143835	0457	1
BRADLEY CLARENCE W	LTC	O-0477278	0157	1
BRADLEY CLAUDE L	LTC	O-0918956	0167	3
BRADLEY CLAY C	1LT	O-0164035	0646	2
BRADLEY EARL G	CW2	W-2215053	1166	1
BRADLEY EARL K	LTC	O-0530722	0466	3
BRADLEY EDWARD D	CPT	O-0146685	0648	3
BRADLEY GLENN P	2LT	O-0529810	0945	2
BRADLEY GORDON W	LTC	O-0443022	0856	1
BRADLEY HARRY F	COL	O-0154583	0954	3
BRADLEY HOMER C	CW3	W-2207495	0466	1
BRADLEY ISAAC M	LTC	O-0425178	0756	1
BRADLEY JACK JR	CPT	O-0288637	0848	1
BRADLEY JAMES A	LTC	O-0204969	0762	3
BRADLEY JAMES F	MAJ	O-0394754	0547	2
BRADLEY JAMES M	LTC	O-1576957	1265	1
BRADLEY JAMES W	MAJ	O-0972976	0563	1
BRADLEY JOHN A	MAJ	O-1315775	1060	1
BRADLEY JOHN C JR	COL	O-0341714	0563	1
BRADLEY JOHN E	LTC	O-0259997	1262	2
BRADLEY JOHN J	LTC	O-0415705	0661	1
BRADLEY JOSEPH A	LTC	O-1276647	1160	1
BRADLEY JOSEPHINE	1LT	N-0732617	0446	1
BRADLEY MARION H	CPT	O-0351924	0446	1
BRADLEY MARION R JR	MAJ	O-1919092	1267	1
BRADLEY MARSHALL E	LTC	O-0411973	0562	2
BRADLEY MARVIN C	COL	O-0174330	0855	3
BRADLEY NOAH C	1LT	O-0150406	0155	3
BRADLEY ODELL	CW3	W-2209982	0768	1
BRADLEY OSBORN W JR	1LT	O-1320417	0546	2
BRADLEY PAUL F	LTC	O-0921770	0363	2
BRADLEY PHIL F	CW4	W-2146159	0267	1
BRADLEY RICHARD	CW3	W-2205339	0265	1
BRADLEY RICHARD J	MAJ	O-1647396	0853	1
BRADLEY ROGER T	MAJ	O-1293534	0366	1
BRADLEY ROLAND H	COL	O-0194790	0657	3
BRADLEY ROY	COL	O-0332523	0752	3
BRADLEY RUFUS A	CPT	O-2263386	1266	1
BRADLEY SAM J	COL	O-1283539	0163	1
BRADLEY STANLEY A	LTC	O-0436447	0663	1
BRADLEY THOMAS M	COL	O-0205329	0755	3
BRADLEY VICTOR W	CPT	O-1010041	0959	1
BRADLEY VOLNEY F	COL	O-0205179	0155	3
BRADLEY WALTER G	WO1	W-2109660	0145	2
BRADLEY WILBUR W	1LT	O-0920288	0245	2
BRADLEY WILLIAM F	LTC	O-1950954	1167	1
BRADLEY WILLIAM O	LTC	O-0904592	0762	1
BRADLEY WILLIAM R JR	CW3	W-2145388	0662	1
BRADLEY WILLIAM W	CPT	O-1011062	0361	1
BRADLEY ZITA A	1LT	N-0788827	0450	2
BRADLUK DONALD G	MAJ	O-0969700	1064	1
BRADMAN JOHN	LTC	O-0383892	1162	1
BRADS ANDREW V	MAJ	O-1546294	1160	1
BRADSHAW ARNOLD F	CPT	O-1292287	0446	2
BRADSHAW ARNOLD W	1LT	O-1317221	1046	2
BRADSHAW ARTHUR L	LTC	O-0940730	0166	1
BRADSHAW AUBREY O JR	1LT	O-1319716	0246	2
BRADSHAW CHARLES W	CW2	W-2105482	0862	3

NAME	GRADE	SVC NO	DATE RET MO YR	RET CODE
BRADSHAW DELBERT L	MAJ	O-0965921	1262	1
BRADSHAW FREDERICK	COL	O-0321316	0964	3
BRADSHAW HENRY C	LTC	O-1116049	0265	1
BRADSHAW JAMES P	LTC	O-1053499	0965	1
BRADSHAW JESSE N	LTC	O-1001517	0257	1
BRADSHAW JOSEPH F	MAJ	O-2029693	1159	1
BRADSHAW PALMER M	MAJ	O-1003483	0568	3
BRADSHAW THOMAS F	CPT	O-1042246	0447	2
BRADSHAW WILLIAM W	LTC	O-0287137	0266	3
BRADSHAW WOODROW C	LTC	O-0455649	0261	1
BRADT EDWARD T	LTC	O-0244590	1045	2
BRADY BENJAMIN G	LTC	O-1015209	1263	1
BRADY BERNARD J	COL	O-0421721	0967	1
BRADY BRUCE M JR	MAJ	O-1994387	0866	1
BRADY CALVIN O	CW2	W-3430108	0665	1
BRADY CARL M	LTC	O-1327499	0364	2
BRADY CHARLES E	LTC	O-0272633	0363	3
BRADY CHARLES P	CPT	O-1049422	0246	2
BRADY DAVID C	MAJ	O-0277248	0463	3
BRADY DONALD L	MAJ	O-1014203	0761	1
BRADY EDWARD C	MAJ	O-1573063	0747	2
BRADY ELMER J	LTC	O-1585202	0760	3
BRADY GEORGE D	CPT	O-1050192	0246	2
BRADY GEORGE S	COL	O-0110406	0648	3
BRADY GEORGE W	CW2	RW-2151035	1163	1
BRADY HARTSEL J	MAJ	O-0948701	0364	1
BRADY HERBERT P	CPT	O-1116205	0263	1
BRADY HUGH H	LTC	O-0487841	1062	1
BRADY HUGH W	LTC	O-1178077	1062	1
BRADY JACK E	MAJ	O-0953641	0661	1
BRADY JAMES F	LTC	O-1323801	0566	1
BRADY JAMES F	MAJ	O-1685654	0565	1
BRADY JAMES H	2LT	O-0157480	0941	1
BRADY JOHN F	MAJ	O-1031865	1146	2
BRADY JOHN F	1LT	O-1168573	1144	2
BRADY JOHN F JR	1LT	O-1304333	1045	2
BRADY JOHN J JR	LTC	O-2017499	0967	1
BRADY JOHN M	COL	O-0464884	0568	3
BRADY JOHN T	MAJ	O-0977129	1161	1
BRADY JOSEPH R	1LT	O-1309503	1145	2
BRADY JOSEPH T	MAJ	O-1542912	0557	1
BRADY KYLE F	1LT	O-1297833	1045	2
BRADY LESTER C JR	LTC	O-0415071	1060	1
BRADY MALCOLM J	CPT	O-1040500	0667	3
BRADY PATRICK J	LTC	O-1647052	0364	1
BRADY RANDLE J	LTC	O-0266151	0563	3
BRADY ROBERT F JR	LTC	O-2033731	1168	1
BRADY THOMAS F	CW2	W-2214677	1267	1
BRADY THOMAS F SR	MAJ	O-1560008	1265	1
BRADY VESTER G	MAJ	O-0419683	1045	2
BRADY WALTER F	CW3	W-2152447	0164	1
BRADY WILLIAM A	CPT	O-0418818	1046	2
BRAENDLE WILLIAM E	LTC	O-2035212	1054	1
BRAGAN JAMES A	MAJ	O-0461478	0446	2
BRAGAN LAWRENCE	CW4	W-2124546	0659	1
BRAGDON GEORGE O	MAJ	O-0188236	0648	3
BRAGDON ROY M SR	2LT	O-0198647	0155	3
BRAGG CALVIN A	CW4	W-2112070	1154	1
BRAGG CHARLES O	CPT	O-2017644	0157	1
BRAGG GENE T	CPT	O-1937569	0466	1
BRAGG GORDON F	COL	O-0322706	0558	1
BRAGG HAROLD W	MAJ	O-0475765	0747	1
BRAGG JAMES G	CPT	O-0354579	0444	2
BRAGG JAMES H	1LT	O-0531998	0346	2
BRAGG JAMES H	LTC	O-1556848	0663	1
BRAGUNIER R BOWIE	LTC	O-0902067	0964	3
BRAHAM JAMES C	LTC	O-1317878	1162	1
BRAHMST GEORGE W	LTC	O-0248557	0861	3
BRAID WILLIAM D	1LT	O-0518709	1045	2
BRAIKER HAROLD R	CPT	O-1013211	0846	2
BRAIN MARION S	1LT	N-0727163	1045	1
BRAIN THOMAS	COL	O-0178639	0357	3
BRAINARD CARROLL D	CW2	W-2209166	0962	1
BRAINARD DWIGHT A	MAJ	O-0236826	0864	3
BRAINARD FRANCIS D	LTC	O-0242489	0962	3

NAME	GRADE	SVC NO	DATE RET MO YR	RET CODE
BRAINARD STANLEY L	LTC	0-0303524	0261	1
BRAINARD WARREN M	CW4	W-2118278	1058	1
BRAINERD GARETH N	COL	0-0342330	0463	3
BRAISTED HARRY P	CW4	W-2003407	1060	3
BRAITHWAITE ROBERT J	CW2	W-2109511	0761	1
BRAITMAN MAX	1LT	0-0344379	1143	2
BRAKE FRED E	CPT	0-0258253	0855	2
BRAKE GEORGE E	MAJ	0-1550972	0760	3
BRAKE JOHN W	CPT	0-1635615	0746	2
BRAKE OTIS	CPT	0-2005552	1157	1
BRAKE RAYMOND C	LTC	0-1283369	0656	2
BRAKE WILLIAM C	MAJ	0-0281199	0467	3
BRAKE WILLIAM P	MAJ	0-0946413	0962	1
BRAKKEN BOYD B	CPT	0-1575780	0554	1
BRALY BYRON D	CPT	0-1999142	0762	2
BRALY LONNIE B	MAJ	0-2007639	0960	1
BRAMAN LIMER C	LTC	0-0244812	0964	3
BRAMBLE ALBERT L JR	CPT	0-0174385	0460	3
BRAMBLE RUSSELL B	LTC	0-0252271	0264	1
BRAMBLETT MARY C	MAJ	N-0742004	1052	2
BRAMBLETT RAPHE J	1LT	0-1318558	0945	2
BRAME DONALD E	MAJ	0-1934745	0968	1
BRAME FELIX J	MAJ	0-1626334	0553	1
BRAME JAMES Y JR	LTC	0-0259145	0568	3
BRAME WEBB	MAJ	0-0130291	0648	3
BRAME WILLIAM K	COL	0-0250654	1064	3
BRAMEIER CHARLES L	CW3	W-2203528	1066	1
BRAMI RUSSELL M	MAJ	0-2262844	0763	2
BRAMLETTE JOYCE O	CW2	W-2150639	0960	1
BRAMLEYHENRY D	MAJ	0-1310562	0963	1
BRAMLITT HUGH W	CW2	W-2149425	0860	1
BRAMMER DOUGLAS H	2LT	0-0507975	0844	2
BRAMMER FRED F	LTC	0-0230869	1150	3
BRAMMER HAROLD I	1LT	0-0539225	1146	2
BRAMSON EDWIN M	1LT	0-0558768	0348	2
BRAMSON JACK	LTC	0-1548652	0566	1
BRANAM FRED G	CW2	W-2150083	1058	1
BRANAMAN WILLIAM S	1LT	0-0528664	1146	2
BRANAN JOHN H	CPT	0-0406003	0146	2
BRANAN WILLIAM JR	COL	0-0287548	0468	3
BRANAUM EUGENE M	COL	0-0182563	0252	3
BRANCACCIO A A	CPT	0-2017191	0257	1
BRANCFIELD LEO N	LTC	0-0422418	0462	3
BRANCH DANIEL B	MAJ	0-0250850	1267	3
BRANCH EDWARD B	CW3	W-3150202	1166	1
BRANCH HOUSTON JR	CW2	W-2211691	0367	1
BRANCH JAMES E	COL	0-0248662	0866	3
BRANCH JESSE J	MAJ	0-2001755	0368	1
BRANCH JOSEPH H	CW2	W-2152262	0262	1
BRANCH JULIAN D	MAJ	0-1552022	0967	3
BRANCH NORMAN B	LTC	0-0334999	0166	3
BRANCH OLIVE S	2LT	N-0759125	0544	1
BRANCH ROBERT K	CW3	W-2146891	0363	1
BRANCH WILLIAM M	CPT	0-0306550	0344	2
BRANCHCOMB VESTER R	1LT	0-0250468	1162	3
BRANCO SALVATORE	MAJ	0-4006023	0765	1
BRAND ALEX M	MAJ	0-1289596	0461	1
BRAND ELIAS B	LTC	0-0325213	0863	1
BRAND HARRISON JR	COL	0-0103807	0851	3
BRAND HERBERT B	M G	0-0916491	0966	3
BRAND JOHN R	LTC	0-0361418	0667	1
BRAND JOHN W	MAJ	0-1104059	0759	1
BRAND LEONARD J	MAJ	0-1548018	0556	1
BRAND MARGARET E	MAJ	N-0764951	0468	1
BRAND WILLIAM A	MAJ	0-4005766	0967	1
BRAND WILLIAM T	LTC	0-1580676	0364	1
BRANDARIZ CARLOS A	MAJ	0-1308297	1060	1
BRANDEIS ERVINE J	LTC	0-0210653	0756	3
BRANDEJSKY FRANK	1LT	0-0212823	1058	3
BRANDELL JOHN F	MAJ	0-2102971	1268	1
BRANDENBERGER E F	MAJ	0-1012528	0859	2
BRANDENBURG EDWIN W	CPT	0-0451501	0446	2
BRANDENBURG F H	CPT	0-0438076	0146	2
BRANDENBURG HOWARD	LTC	0-1547549	0168	1
BRANDENBURG PARK H	LTC	0-0511565	1060	2

NAME	GRADE	SVC NO	DATE RET MO YR	RET CODE
BRANDENBURG W G	CPT	0-1290889	1047	2
BRANDENBURG WALTER	CW3	W-2153341	1062	1
BRANDENBURG WILLIAM	LTC	0-0353095	1046	2
BRANDENHOFF HOWARD N	LTC	0-1166443	0358	1
BRANDES KONRAD G	CW4	W-2141087	0664	1
BRANDLEY PETER H	2LT	0-0925136	0445	2
BRANDLEY WILLIAM H	MAJ	0-0260985	1063	3
BRANDLY ROLAND L	COL	0-0353193	1161	1
BRANDMILL DINSMORE	LTC	0-0216952	0763	3
BRANDON CHARLES B	1LT	0-0445791	1045	2
BRANDON DAVID R	COL	0-0242144	1057	3
BRANDON ENZER L	LTC	0-0286328	0457	3
BRANDON JAMES W SR	LTC	0-0351084	0966	1
BRANDON LELAND B	MAJ	0-0192695	1062	3
BRANDON LOREN E	CW3	W-2143378	0762	1
BRANDON WILLIAM P	CPT	0-0170830	1161	3
BRANDOW ROBERT O	LTC	0-1001956	0866	1
BRANDS WILLIAM H	LTC	0-1041510	0567	1
BRANDT ALFRED P	1LT	0-1825830	1145	2
BRANDT CHARLES J	COL	0-0287795	1060	1
BRANDT EDWIN	LTC	0-0290698	1164	2
BRANDT IRVING O	1LT	0-1183248	0945	2
BRANDT JOHN J	CW3	W-2203350	0967	1
BRANDT JUSTIN	1LT	0-0464625	0146	2
BRANDT LEWIS F JR	2LT	0-1327706	0945	2
BRANDT LLOYD H	CPT	0-0496969	1052	1
BRANDT MULFORD M	COL	0-0254578	1065	3
BRANDT ONEIL F	2LT	0-0382505	0653	1
BRANDT ROGER H	1LT	0-1106010	1043	2
BRANDVOLD FLORENCE C	MAJ	N-0776427	0364	1
BRANDYBURG FULTON C	WO1	W-2106554	0445	2
BRANEN FRED B	CPT	0-1114384	1053	1
BRANFORD WILLIAM J	LTC	0-1545077	0964	1
BRANHAM DONALD S	COL	0-0197978	0448	2
BRANICK WILLIAM G	MAJ	0-1103076	0857	1
BRANIGAN DANIEL A	MAJ	0-0169412	0647	2
BRANIGAN EDWARD S JR	B G	0-0325381	0468	3
BRANIGAN THOMAS L	MAJ	0-1016936	0662	1
BRANIN CHARLES E	MAJ	0-0142610	0654	3
BRANISEL JOHN JR	2LT	0-1111511	0346	2
BRANN WILLIAM T	CPT	0-0223900	1152	1
BRANNAM FINIS C	CW3	W-2146897	1058	1
BRANNAN JACK D	CPT	0-0980876	1060	1
BRANNAN ROBERT E JR	LTC	0-1171465	0766	1
BRANNEN JO A	MAJ	N-0726615	1066	1
BRANNEN MALCOLM D	LTC	0-0292262	0462	1
BRANNEN WILLIAM A	CPT	0-0510788	0653	1
BRANNER GEORGE L	MAJ	0-0180147	1154	3
BRANNIGAN FRANK	LTC	0-0136589	1155	3
BRANNOCK WILLIAM R	CPT	0-0555958	1147	2
BRANNON ATHOS W	LTC	0-1299675	0861	1
BRANNON EARL P	LTC	0-0302308	0968	3
BRANNON GEORGE M	CPT	0-0394409	0145	2
BRANNON HERBERT A	MAJ	0-1031387	0358	1
BRANNON J BRUCE JR	CW3	W-2151808	0265	1
BRANNON JAMES G	MAJ	0-1877914	0765	1
BRANNON PAUL F	2LT	0-1308417	0545	2
BRANNON WILLIAM C	LTC	0-0455613	0559	1
BRANNON WILLIAM H	LTC	0-1998453	0862	1
BRANON JOHN C	2LT	0-1307932	1044	2
BRANSCOMB RUSSELL	1LT	0-2263490	0461	1
BRANSCOMBE JAMES H	MAJ	0-0969816	1062	1
BRANSFORD HORTON W	MAJ	0-1048297	1166	1
BRANSFORD THOMAS L	LTC	0-0909276	0264	3
BRANSON ALBERT S	COL	0-0258329	1163	3
BRANSON CHARLES A	1LT	0-1314250	1147	2
BRANSON EUGENE H	CW2	W-2148429	0755	2
BRANSON LOUNSBURY	COL	0-0306842	0663	1
BRANSON MARION A	MAJ	0-0170567	0855	3
BRANSON ROBERT S	LTC	0-1641491	0363	1
BRANSON WILLIAM A	MAJ	0-1292288	1057	1
BRANSTAD WILLIAM	COL	0-0273480	0967	3
BRANSTETTER ROY	LTC	0-0108567	0347	1
BRANT ARTHUR A	CW2	W-2151761	0356	2
BRANT DONALD R	LTC	0-0336589	0760	1

NAME	GRADE	SVC NO	DATE RET MO YR	RET CODE
BRANT FLORENCE M	2LT	N-0753041	0446	1
BRANT FREDERICK	LTC	0-0494842	0760	3
BRANT IRVIN L	CPT	0-0341077	1045	2
BRANT PAUL B	WO1	W-2128538	0746	2
BRANT SANDI	CPT	L-1010012	1054	2
BRANT WILBUR J	1LT	0-0966752	0754	2
BRANTLEY ED JR	MAJ	0-2204028	0166	1
BRANTLEY JOE K	COL	0-0103346	1051	3
BRANTLEY RICHARD V	CPT	0-1877796	0663	1
BRANTLEY ROBERT H	LTC	0-0372306	0866	3
BRANTON CHARLES H	CW2	W-2143022	1055	2
BRANTON CHARLES K	LTC	0-0404600	1060	1
BRANTON DALTON F	CW3	W-2151157	0863	1
BRANUM ARTHUR M	CPT	0-0885984	0146	2
BRANUM MARVIN L	MAJ	0-0994085	0566	1
BRANUM ORRIS F	CW3	W-2146565	0764	1
BRANYAN ALBERT G	COL	0-0358802	0968	3
BRANYAN CHARLES D	COL	0-0393605	0666	1
BRANYON WADE L	CPT	0-0973915	1160	1
BRARMANN EDWARD F	CPT	0-0351739	0745	2
BRAS PEDRO J	LTC	0-0155794	0556	3
BRASE WESLEY C	WO1	W-2131333	0263	1
BRASELTON ROSCOE	MAJ	0-0450404	0157	1
BRASH EDMOND J	1LT	0-1325861	1145	2
BRASHAW ERNEST H	CW3	W-2206496	0568	1
BRASHEAR FENTON W	MAJ	0-1559002	1262	1
BRASHEAR GOLDMAN T	LTC	0-0452022	0160	1
BRASHEAR ILO L	MAJ	0-0469339	0456	1
BRASHEAR JAMES L JR	LTC	0-1169870	0764	1
BRASHEARS GEORGE L	LTC	0-0376389	0162	1
BRASINGTON DALTON K	LTC	0-0271105	1068	3
BRASSELL RAY O	MAJ	0-1288850	0855	1
BRASSFIELD JOSEPH D	LTC	0-1330903	0467	1
BRASSIL JOHN	2LT	0-0164561	0039	1
BRASWELL CLOVIS L	CPT	0-1299366	0546	2
BRASWELL ERNEST	CW3	W-2143357	0462	2
BRASWELL JAMES L	1LT	0-2262711	1154	2
BRASWELL VERNON S	MAJ	0-1174237	0861	1
BRATCHELL HAROLD T	CPT	0-0491209	0662	1
BRATCHER ROBERT E	MAJ	0-1592631	0764	1
BRATLAND ADLER H	MAJ	0-1683434	0666	1
BRATTEBO NORMAN B	2LT	0-1315021	0843	2
BRATTIN WILLIAM C	MAJ	0-0228321	0663	3
BRATTLOF KENNETH W	2LT	0-1308262	0545	2
BRATTON ARGALUS B	LTC	0-0233935	1046	1
BRATTON NEIL A JR	1LT	0-1314431	0148	2
BRATTON PAUL E	MAJ	0-1796754	0657	1
BRAUCH JOSEPH E	CW3	W-2153120	0562	1
BRAUCHER JOHN L JR	1LT	0-1320275	0845	2
BRAUCHT GLEN B JR	1LT	0-1062470	0951	2
BRAUD WESTON M	LTC	0-1633091	0166	1
BRAUER ALBERT G	LTC	0-0363123	0463	1
BRAUER ALVIN P	CPT	0-0302358	0646	2
BRAUER EARLE W	CPT	0-0478029	0147	2
BRAUER EDWARD L	MAJ	0-0966169	0461	1
BRAUER EUGENE H	2LT	0-1324816	0345	2
BRAUER HARRY M	1LT	0-0466717	0846	2
BRAUER JOHN C	COL	0-0256443	1065	3
BRAUER ROBERT W	LTC	0-0463525	0158	1
BRAUN ALBERT F	MAJ	0-0966560	1062	1
BRAUN ALBERT W	LTC	0-0134329	1149	3
BRAUN ELMER H	LTC	0-0308667	1059	3
BRAUN ERIC J	LTC	0-0301303	1157	1
BRAUN ROBERT J	MAJ	0-1112582	1063	1
BRAUN ROLAND R	MAJ	0-0277079	0444	2
BRAUN WILLIAM E	LTC	0-0484213	1167	3
BRAUNECKER AUGUST J	MAJ	0-1695601	0958	1
BRAUNER FREDERICK	MAJ	0-1637073	0161	1
BRAUNS JOHN W	COL	0-0196689	0962	3
BRAUNSCHWEIGER OTTO	1LT	0-1315022	1146	2
BRAUNSTEIN ALBERT L	CPT	0-0482305	0145	2
BRAUNSTEIN ELIHU B	LTC	0-1166675	1167	1
BRAUNSTEIN LEONARD	CPT	0-0357673	1146	2
BRAUNWARTH WILLIAM W	LTC	0-0263124	0643	2
BRAUSA PAUL V	LTC	0-0307833	0562	1

NAME	GRADE	SVC NO	DATE RET MO YR	RET CODE
BRAUSCH RAYMOND A	LTC	0-1948700	0565	1
BRAUTMAN ALVIN W	1LT	0-1012243	0646	2
BRAVERMAN LOUIS	MAJ	0-0484356	0349	1
BRAVOS GEORGE J	COL	0-0183018	0858	1
BRAWNER SELMA M	COL	N-0731302	1163	1
BRAXLEY SAMUEL E	MAJ	0-0427915	0263	1
BRAXTON DAVID	CW3	W-2150065	1063	1
BRAY ANN	MAJ	L-0514231	0863	1
BRAY BOBBY J	MAJ	0-1878231	0168	1
BRAY CECIL H	MAJ	0-1324000	0960	1
BRAY DILLARD W	MAJ	0-0196681	0561	3
BRAY ELMER A	CPT	0-0360551	1060	1
BRAY FRANCIS O	CW4	W-2145512	0968	1
BRAY FRANCIS G	LTC	0-0246662	0366	3
BRAY GEORGE	MAJ	0-1574604	1154	1
BRAY HAROLD P	MAJ	0-0420953	0446	2
BRAY JOHN C	MAJ	0-0463952	0647	2
BRAY LELAND D	LTC	0-2263369	0868	1
BRAY WILLARD F	CPT	0-0258636	1267	3
BRAY WILLIAM F	CW2	W-2147269	1057	1
BRAY WILLIAM H	COL	0-0220952	0355	3
BRAY WILLIAM M	CPT	0-1573066	1045	2
BRAY WILLIAM P	COL	0-0266987	0955	3
BRAYDEN ROBERT A	CW2	W-2150281	1161	1
BRAYE WILLIAM E	CW3	W-2148346	1262	1
BRAYFIELD RALPH S	CW2	W-2143875	1158	1
BRAYMAN HERBERT H JR	CW4	W-2119448	0159	1
BRAYTON JEAN H	CPT	0-0225828	1161	3
BRAYTON PAUL F	LTC	0-0270574	0967	3
BRAZDA FRANK F	MAJ	0-0924668	1047	2
BRAZEALE HERBERT P	MAJ	0-2262614	0663	2
BRAZEAU ALFRED L	MAJ	0-1340257	1065	2
BRAZEE GEORGE T	LTC	0-0425910	0468	3
BRAZELL FLOYD F	LTC	0-1109154	1160	1
BRAZEN FRANK J	MAJ	0-0423110	1047	2
BRAZIER MELVIN L	MAJ	0-0278315	0366	3
BRAZIL THOMAS R	MAJ	0-1920357	1166	1
BRAZIL WILLIAM R	MAJ	0-0451505	0358	1
BREACH REGINALD A	LTC	0-0502043	0866	3
BREADON HUBERT R	LTC	0-0224806	1051	1
BREADY FREDERICK	CPT	0-2046343	0551	2
BREAKIRON HARRY T	MAJ	0-1063134	0163	1
BREARLEY JOSEPH W	LTC	0-0286569	0954	1
BREARLEY RALPH A	CPT	0-0521863	0146	1
BREARTY CHARLES R	LTC	0-0173852	0562	3
BREARTY FRANCIS W	CPT	0-0487029	0750	1
BREASHEARS WILLIAM F	MAJ	0-1334252	1263	1
BREATCHEL EDMUND O	1LT	0-1591008	0347	2
BREAUD C S JR	LTC	0-1580682	1160	1
BREAULT FRANK H	CW2	W-2144875	0463	1
BREAUX ALLEN C	MAJ	0-1641498	0860	1
BREAUX ROY C	CPT	0-1283016	0945	2
BREAUX WALTER J	CPT	0-0247295	0744	2
BREAZEALE T C JR	1LT	0-0460079	0346	2
BREBNER CHARLES E	COL	0-0284440	0958	1
BRECHBIEL FRANK W	CPT	0-0564896	0663	1
BRECHER CHARLES	LTC	0-1796036	0963	1
BRECHT JOHN W	1LT	0-1048298	0245	2
BRECHTEL DAVID W	MAJ	0-1280309	0857	1
BRECK ROGER S	LTC	0-0240814	0365	3
BRECKENRIDGE J G JR	1LT	0-1304607	1045	2
BRECKENRIDGE LEWIS R	CW3	W-2142224	0860	1
BRECKINRIDGE ETHELBE	MAJ	0-2005232	0662	1
BREDAEL FRED B	1LT	0-0403999	0446	2
BREDBENNER AMBROSE M	MAJ	0-0278351	0761	3
BREDIN RYERSON A	LTC	0-0297346	1065	3
BREECE JAMES M	MAJ	0-0972319	0662	1
BREEDEN BERRY C	CPT	0-1324243	1264	2
BREEDEN CHARLES U	MAJ	0-0509288	0846	2
BREEDEN PERCY L	2LT	0-1824122	0844	2
BREEDEN ROBERT F	MAJ	0-2288722	0268	1
BREEDEN SAM L	MAJ	0-0159157	1058	3
BREEDING CHARLES F	MAJ	0-1945264	1060	1
BREEDING CHARLES S	COL	0-0282559	0864	3
BREEDING DAVID N	LTC	0-0358862	0367	3

NAME	GRADE	SVC NO	DATE RET MO YR	RET CODE
BREEDING HOWARD M	CW3	RW-2152369	1165	1
BREEDING WILLIAM C	CPT	0-0969873	0462	1
BREEDLOVE CONNER M	CPT	0-0197512	0655	3
BREEDLOVE GEORGE E	CW2	W-2214363	0767	1
BREEDLOVE JOHN C	LTC	0-0311829	0960	1
BREEDLOVE ROBERT E	CW3	W-2141934	0763	1
BREEDON DANIEL F	MAJ	0-1044185	0557	1
BREELAND GLENN E	CPT	0-2032907	0157	1
BREEN CORNELIUS	COL	0-1240712	0668	1
BREEN GERALD E	MAJ	0-0259001	0963	3
BREEN GLADYS M	1LT	N-0720820	1045	1
BREEN HARRY P	LTC	0-0274891	1164	3
BREEN JOHN D	CPT	0-2033188	0463	1
BREEN JOSEPH A	1LT	0-2292030	1149	3
BREEN JOSEPH M	LTC	0-0487867	0954	2
BREEN MARVIN	LTC	0-1169036	0567	3
BREEN MAURICE	1LT	0-1110396	1147	2
BREEN ROBERT H	LTC	0-1172389	1165	1
BREEN ROBERT W	COL	0-0257629	0668	3
BREEN THOMAS	CPT	0-0331295	0457	3
BREEN WILLIAM H JR	COL	0-0452384	0166	1
BREESE EDWARDS W	COL	0-0271103	0968	3
BREESE JOE W	CPT	0-2263717	0163	2
BREESE RALPH M	LTC	0-0485638	0657	1
BREESE THURLOW W	MAJ	0-1283540	0765	1
BREEZE THOMAS H JR	CPT	0-1042496	0248	2
BREEZLEY HENRY F	LTC	0-1548361	0558	1
BREEZLEY MARY B	1LT	N-0761031	0546	1
BREFCZYNSKI JOHN H	CW2	W-2208380	0962	1
BREGAN JOSEPH F	CW3	W-2208851	0167	1
BREGER SAMUEL	LTC	0-0331656	0965	3
BREGNARD ADRIAN L	LTC	0-0321695	0960	1
BREHAUT BURTON L	2LT	0-1313690	1044	2
BREHENY GEORGE R	CW3	W-2121104	1054	1
BREHM ARTHUR G	MAJ	0-1924818	1268	1
BREHM CLIFFORD A	CPT	0-1589078	1162	2
BREHM RUSSELL A	CW2	W-2214590	0856	1
BREHM WILLIS H	LTC	0-1643582	0168	1
BREIDENBACH AMELIA L	2LT	N-0728576	0844	1
BREIDENBAUGH HENRY C	LTC	0-1844689	1065	3
BREIDSTER WALDEMAR F	M G	0-0221917	0760	3
BREILING OTTMAR A	LTC	0-0309646	0965	3
BREITEGAN GREGG O	LTC	0-0809090	0263	1
BREITENBACH R J	CPT	0-0103000	1147	2
BREITENBERG HARRY J	MAJ	0-1020526	0765	1
BREITENSTEIN JOHN J	CPT	0-1039605	0557	1
BREITFELLER JOSEPH C	CPT	0-1016973	0857	1
BREITHAUPT HOWARD M	LTC	0-1039544	0863	1
BREITLING GERALD E	LTC	0-0281896	0956	2
BREITMAN HARRY B	CPT	0-0233659	1043	2
BREITSMAN WILLIS J	WO1	W-2110551	0456	3
BREITWIESER CARL H	COL	0-0152440	0757	3
BREIZ FLORENTINO	2LT	0-0193249	1150	1
BREKKE MARTIN H	2LT	0-1327927	1145	2
BRELAND HENRY T	MAJ	0-2023916	0164	1
BRELAND JAMES E	LTC	0-0250965	1063	3
BRELL JAMES	CW2	W-2112147	0746	1
BREM JACOB	COL	0-0285742	1164	3
BREMEL GERHARD W	CW2	W-2144316	0560	1
BREMER AUGUST W	LTC	0-0456041	1061	1
BREMER FRED H	LTC	0-1895962	1266	3
BREMER HENRY M	LTC	0-0316442	0464	3
BREMER VIRGIL I	CW3	W-2149345	0263	1
BREMER WILLIAM R	LTC	0-1296480	1153	1
BREMERMAN F J	COL	0-0463647	0157	1
BREMERMAN FRANK E	CW2	W-2148311	0358	2
BREMSER EDWARD F	LTC	0-0245033	0760	3
BRENAHAN CHARLES	LTC	0-0280996	0746	2
BRENAN ALBERT	LTC	0-1542185	0457	1
BRENCE FRANK F	CPT	0-0296041	0544	2
BRENCHLEY GEORGE A	LTC	0-1589080	1062	1
BRENDEL ADOLPH P	CPT	0-0376558	0745	2
BRENDLE ROY C	MAJ	0-1289539	0457	1
BRENDZA JOSEPH V	LTC	0-0964973	0268	1
BRENER LAZARO S	CPT	0-0542366	1045	2

NAME	GRADE	SVC NO	DATE RET MO YR	RET CODE
BRENGEL DEXTER	LTC	0-1647075	0768	3
BRENINGER ALFRED H	LTC	0-1283716	1057	1
BRENN GERALD C	1LT	0-1325548	1145	2
BRENN HARRY A	COL	0-0212413	0663	3
BRENNAN ALAN H	1LT	0-2014799	0165	2
BRENNAN DANIEL J	CW3	W-2131805	0365	1
BRENNAN EDWARD F	LTC	0-1169434	1167	1
BRENNAN EDWARD J	CPT	0-1295332	0347	2
BRENNAN FELIX J	LTC	0-0349487	0668	3
BRENNAN FREDERICK	LTC	0-0359230	1055	3
BRENNAN JACK J	CW2	W-2150587	0361	1
BRENNAN JAMES D	LTC	0-1015053	0964	1
BRENNAN JOHN A	MAJ	0-1167334	0952	2
BRENNAN JOHN R	1LT	0-1590343	0146	2
BRENNAN JOHN T	LTC	0-1103077	0861	1
BRENNAN JOHN V	CPT	0-1297151	0647	2
BRENNAN JOSEPH	CPT	0-0497834	0849	1
BRENNAN JOSEPH G	CPT	0-1106012	0246	2
BRENNAN JOSEPH R	CW4	W-2141762	1268	2
BRENNAN LEO W	CW4	W-2143208	0965	1
BRENNAN NORMAN G	LTC	0-0287815	0367	3
BRENNAN RAYMOND F	WO1	W-2123176	0447	2
BRENNAN ROBERT E	LTC	0-1107314	0861	1
BRENNAN VERONICA F	MAJ	N-0787215	0168	3
BRENNAN WILLIAM	CPT	0-2008163	0756	1
BRENNAN WILLIAM C	MAJ	0-0491551	0557	2
BRENNECKE FRANCIS C	COL	0-0205865	0463	3
BRENNEKE CHARLES H	COL	0-0263976	0346	2
BRENNEMAN FLOYD E	LTC	0-1556093	1060	1
BRENNEMAN GERALD E	LTC	0-1330778	0568	2
BRENNEMAN ROBERT C	LTC	0-1113598	0265	1
BRENNEN HAROLD L	MAJ	0-0477494	0250	1
BRENNER GILBERT	MAJ	0-0348709	0165	1
BRENNER HARRY F JR	CPT	0-1533740	0550	1
BRENNER HUDSON D	MAJ	0-1014898	0859	1
BRENNER JOEL J	MAJ	0-0418242	0246	2
BRENNER LEON S	CPT	0-0493776	0245	2
BRENNER PAUL J	CPT	0-1310975	0268	1
BRENNER RICHARD J	LTC	0-0453141	0761	1
BRENNER THEODORE H	MAJ	0-2002233	1160	1
BRENNY MARTIN J	CPT	0-0452520	0145	2
BRENT EDWARD F JR	MAJ	0-0328956	0265	3
BRENT ROBERT A	CPT	0-0522757	0446	2
BRENTANO AUGUST	MAJ	0-0202261	0460	3
BRENTON ELMER	LTC	0-0162754	0757	3
BRENTS WALKER A	LTC	0-0282830	1056	3
BREON CHARLES C	CW4	W-2147147	0768	1
BRERETON JOHN F	CPT	0-0306654	0451	1
BRERETON JOHN V	MAJ	0-0287721	1262	3
BRESCKA RUDOLPH S	MAJ	0-0233238	0461	3
BRESHEARS JAMES O	CW3	W-2153380	1163	1
BRESKE CHARLES C	CW4	W-2146576	1167	1
BRESLER ROBERT F	1LT	0-1042248	0346	2
BRESLIN EDWARD F	MAJ	0-0963529	0265	1
BRESLIN HUGH J JR	MAJ	0-1181546	0862	1
BRESLIN JAMES	LTC	0-0131851	0648	3
BRESNAHAN JOHN F	LTC	0-0102758	0346	2
BRESNICK SAMUEL	1LT	0-0359433	0245	2
BRESSAN ROBERT C	2LT	0-1115195	0645	2
BRESSETT FLORENCE L	CPT	N-0802018	1065	1
BRESSINCK EDWARD F	MAJ	0-0450243	0158	1
BRESSLER RICHARD E	MAJ	0-2263514	1066	1
BRESSLER SYDNEY	COL	0-0331745	0567	3
BRETANA ERNESTO	MAJ	0-0983917	0663	1
BRETH JAMES E	COL	0-0173712	0563	3
BRETON CLIFFORD F	CW4	W-2101474	0861	1
BRETON GUSTAVO A	CW2	W-2145132	0959	1
BRETON JOSEPH E	CPT	0-2002408	0858	1
BRETON PIERRE L	CPT	0-0505335	1144	2
BRETSCHNEIDER ARTHUR	CW3	W-2145390	0865	1
BRETT GEORGE P JR	MAJ	0-0101696	0556	3
BRETT JOHN J	CW3	W-2152668	0563	1
BRETT THOMAS J	LTC	0-0450224	0357	1
BRETTON WILLIAM J	2LT	0-0838907	1145	1
BRETZ ANDREW JR	LTC	0-0416511	0961	1

NAME	GRADE	SVC NO	DATE RET MO YR	RET CODE
BRETZ BENJAMIN P	LTC	0-0294106	0767	3
BRETZ RUSS E	CPT	0-0971775	0958	1
BRETZER HERMAN	LTC	0-1000034	0657	1
BRETZKE LOUIS F	LTC	0-0267000	0851	3
BREUER ALFRED	CPT	0-0328857	0445	2
BREUER ARTHUR N	CPT	0-0507156	1045	2
BREUER WYLIE E	LTC	0-0328030	0347	2
BREVDA HARRY	MAJ	0-0330145	0245	2
BREVIG HJALMAR I	CPT	0-0494297	1263	1
BREVIK ROBERT T	1LT	0-0414661	1145	2
BREWER ALLEN L	COL	0-1035205	1064	1
BREWER ANGUS M	MAJ	0-2033322	0361	1
BREWER ARTHUR S	LTC	0-0507436	1263	3
BREWER BEACHER H	MAJ	0-1312272	0954	1
BREWER BOBBY J	MAJ	0-1581044	1060	1
BREWER CHARLES H	MAJ	0-0948970	0963	1
BREWER CHESTER D	COL	0-0308546	0261	1
BREWER CLEO H SR	CPT	0-1292290	1160	1
BREWER DANIEL F	LTC	0-0347529	0460	1
BREWER DAVID L	LTC	0-0511211	0954	2
BREWER DEAN E	MAJ	0-1637077	0264	1
BREWER EDWARD G	WO1	W-2109994	0953	1
BREWER ELTO H	WO1	W-2117862	0762	2
BREWER FRANK J	CW4	W-2110657	0655	1
BREWER GARLAND S	CW3	W-2151918	0663	1
BREWER GEORGE A JR	COL	0-0225014	0262	3
BREWER GEORGE E	MAJ	0-1798438	1061	1
BREWER HAROLD A	CPT	0-1702253	0264	1
BREWER HAROLD G	LTC	0-0146377	0257	3
BREWER HAROLD W	CW4	W-2109094	0758	1
BREWER HERCHELL E	CW4	W-2144165	1265	1
BREWER HOWELL	COL	0-0171412	0648	3
BREWER IRA V JR	MAJ	0-2016389	0663	1
BREWER JAMES A JR	CPT	0-4074364	0968	1
BREWER JAMES C	MAJ	0-1550118	0761	1
BREWER JOHN F	LTC	0-0360077	1154	3
BREWER JOHN H	LTC	0-0390991	0962	1
BREWER JOSEPH C JR	1LT	0-1091463	1046	2
BREWER JUNIOR J	CW2	W-3350237	1068	1
BREWER KAY M	CW2	W-2107225	0267	1
BREWER MARJORIE J	CPT	N-0728043	0246	1
BREWER MARK	1LT	0-1797774	0358	1
BREWER ROBERT E	1LT	0-0504388	0653	1
BREWER ROBERT N	LTC	0-1552023	0466	1
BREWER ROY L	COL	0-0316654	0662	1
BREWER RUBEN N	CPT	0-0489144	0251	1
BREWER THEODORE R	LTC	0-0349527	1154	3
BREWER VIRGIL D	WO1	W-2122940	0857	1
BREWER WESLEY B	2LT	0-1051047	0945	2
BREWER WILL	LTC	0-0285938	1267	3
BREWER WILLIAM A	CW3	W-2146007	0966	1
BREWER WILLIAM C	LTC	0-0185774	0156	3
BREWER WILLIAM H	CW2	W-3350451	1268	1
BREWER WILLIAM L	WO1	W-2145391	1056	1
BREWER WILLIAM M	COL	0-0251177	1262	3
BREWER WILLIAM S	CPT	0-1170294	0461	1
BREWINGTON ALLEN G	MAJ	0-0976215	0861	1
BREWRINK JAMES L	COL	0-0236372	0166	3
BREWSTER EDWARD S	LTC	0-0321194	1067	3
BREWSTER JOHN D	COL	0-0198894	0146	2
BREWSTER PHILIP H	LTC	0-0259492	0145	2
BREWSTER RICHARD T	LTC	0-0320117	0966	3
BREWTON MURRAY P	1LT	0-0434593	0947	2
BREWTON WILLIAM S	1LT	0-0419819	0845	2
BREX CHARLES J JR	1LT	0-1534684	0345	2
BREZEE FREDERICK	MAJ	0-1693833	0656	1
BREZIN DAVID	CPT	0-0371116	0346	2
BREZINA EDDIE B	CW3	W-2104648	0859	1
BREZNICKY JOSEPH J	CW3	W-2142135	0864	1
BRIA ALBERT J	CW3	W-2152513	0263	1
BRIANS NORMAN E	WO1	W-2122210	1047	2
BRICE ARTHUR T	COL	0-0167877	0952	3
BRICE JAMES P	COL	0-0504275	0466	3
BRICE MARSHALL M	COL	0-0205284	0858	3
BRICE WILLIAM A	COL	0-0173576	0162	3

NAME	GRADE	SVC NO	DATE RET MO YR	RET CODE
BRICK EDWARD J	1LT	0-0541815	0445	2
BRICK JOHN J	MAJ	0-1691005	1045	2
BRICK JOHN P	CPT	0-0414176	0845	2
BRICKEN WILLIAM M	MAJ	0-0402608	0657	1
BRICKER ERNEST L	WO1	W-2121976	0252	2
BRICKER GARY R	LTC	0-0322712	1054	1
BRICKER HAROLD S	2LT	0-2012010	0763	2
BRICKER PETER D	MAJ	0-0230807	1064	3
BRICKER THOMAS G	LTC	0-0362935	1059	1
BRICKETTO EDWARD J	1LT	0-1951544	0151	2
BRICKEY CLARE R	CW2	RW-2142402	0462	1
BRICKHOUSE GREGORY L	LTC	0-1103529	0363	1
BRICKMAN LLOYD F	CPT	0-2050736	1059	1
BRIDENSTINE FRANCIS	LTC	0-0447645	0962	2
BRIDGE CARL F	1LT	0-1319258	0546	2
BRIDGEFORTH WILLIAM	WO1	W-2129579	0446	2
BRIDGERS SAMSON K	CPT	0-0265776	1156	3
BRIDGES ARCHIE	CW3	W-2150625	0163	1
BRIDGES CLARA E	2LT	N-0764640	1145	1
BRIDGES IRA B	MAJ	0-0461561	1048	1
BRIDGES JAMES E	CPT	0-0267207	0263	1
BRIDGES JAMES P	MAJ	0-0377641	0844	2
BRIDGES JIMMIE H	MAJ	0-1010994	0948	2
BRIDGES JOHN T	CW2	W-2206882	0263	1
BRIDGES JOSEPH H	CPT	0-1579421	0157	1
BRIDGES JOSEPH L	MAJ	0-1056048	0862	1
BRIDGES MELVIN W	MAJ	0-0119092	0649	3
BRIDGES RICHARD B	LTC	0-1691931	0864	1
BRIDGES ROBERT H	CPT	0-0375851	0346	2
BRIDGES ROBERT L	CW3	W-2149872	0359	2
BRIDGES ROBINSON E	LTC	0-1598005	0765	1
BRIDGES ROLSTYN O	LTC	0-0144962	0151	3
BRIDGES STANLEY B	1LT	0-1844410	1045	2
BRIDGES WILLIAM C	MAJ	0-0976536	1161	1
BRIDGHAM SAMUEL W	COL	0-1690163	0765	3
BRIDWELL CHARLES G	CPT	0-0437849	0647	1
BRIDWELL ERNEST A	LTC	0-1591610	0766	1
BRIDWELL WILLIAM E	MAJ	0-0210753	0648	3
BRIEHL MARK R	CW2	W-2210968	0763	1
BRIEL FRED W	MAJ	0-0344479	1047	2
BRIENZA PAUL J	CPT	0-0394380	0345	2
BRIER GLEASON L	LTC	0-0195220	0962	3
BRIER HUBERT L	LTC	0-0253567	0667	3
BRIER JOHN C	COL	0-0284920	0546	2
BRIER MORRIS	1LT	0-2043121	1045	2
BRIERLY JAY B JR	LTC	0-2289413	0568	1
BRIERY CLIFFORD C	COL	0-0205909	0857	3
BRIGANTE LAWRENCE J	CPT	0-0498524	0346	1
BRIGEMAN RICHARD W	MAJ	0-1635623	0361	1
BRIGGMAN ROGERS C	1LT	0-2004049	0954	2
BRIGGS ALBERT F	LTC	0-0261500	0263	3
BRIGGS CHARLES B	LTC	0-0290685	1267	3
BRIGGS CHARLES W	LTC	0-0107685	0648	3
BRIGGS CLARK A	CPT	0-0167606	0853	3
BRIGGS ELMER H	MAJ	0-2028550	1164	1
BRIGGS GEORGE R	MAJ	0-0152831	0854	3
BRIGGS GLOW D	LTC	0-1315414	0757	1
BRIGGS JOHN C	MAJ	0-1030223	0660	1
BRIGGS LAWRENCE R	1LT	0-1020009	1052	2
BRIGGS LEROY F	MAJ	0-0219143	0648	3
BRIGGS MARK R	MAJ	0-0395215	0547	2
BRIGGS MARVIN L JR	LTC	0-0370071	0363	1
BRIGGS PAUL H	MAJ	0-0257654	0745	2
BRIGGS PERLEY J	MAJ	0-0996167	1268	1
BRIGGS RALPH O	COL	0-0275763	0453	3
BRIGGS RAYMOND C	LTC	0-0240174	1165	3
BRIGGS THOMAS E	COL	0-0223942	0146	2
BRIGHAM EARNEST	CPT	0-1312510	0647	2
BRIGHAM EUGENE V	LTC	0-1181830	0258	1
BRIGHAM HERMAN C	LTC	0-0142494	1159	1
BRIGHAM LINCOLN F	MAJ	0-2208308	1067	1
BRIGHAM ROBERT A	MAJ	0-0315188	0544	2
BRIGHT CLYDE	CW2	W-2120062	1153	1
BRIGHT EVERETT W	LTC	0-0177763	0860	3
BRIGHT GEORGE H JR	CPT	0-0422146	0246	2

NAME	GRADE	SVC NO	DATE RET MO YR	RET CODE
BRIGHT GRANT T	LTC	0-0191548	0247	1
BRIGHT HARRY R	LTC	0-0450244	0657	1
BRIGHT HENRY C	MAJ	0-0363607	0257	1
BRIGHT HOMER L	2LT	0-2015604	0958	1
BRIGHT J T	CPT	0-1550549	0648	1
BRIGHT JAMES L	1LT	0-0495122	0548	1
BRIGHT JOHN E	CPT	0-1051049	0148	2
BRIGHT MARVIN L	CW2	W-2146318	0757	1
BRIGHT MERLE E	MAJ	0-1297152	1159	1
BRIGHT RICHARD	CW3	W-2147942	0861	1
BRIGHT WILLIAM E	LTC	0-0360902	0465	3
BRIGHTBILL RODGER D	1LT	0-0553761	0546	2
BRIGHTBILL ROLLIN M	LTC	0-0289987	1059	1
BRIGHTMAN JULIAN N	CPT	0-0511851	0947	1
BRIGHTWELL W G	CW3	W-2153016	0661	1
BRIGIDA GAETANO A	LTC	0-1039417	0167	1
BRIGNON RALPH O JR	MAJ	0-2265723	0165	1
BRILES ESTHER K	MAJ	L-0403164	0751	2
BRILEY FINOS O	COL	0-0286425	0760	1
BRILEY FRED L	CW3	W-2144659	0560	1
BRILEY KARL G	CW3	W-2148707	0665	1
BRILL CLINTON H	COL	0-0175436	0-53	3
BRILLANTE ORLANDO E	MAJ	0-1875130	0564	1
BRIM BYRON A	LTC	0-1291572	0261	1
BRIMBERRY JOHN H	COL	0-0109470	0146	2
BRIMLEY RALPH F W	LTC	0-1559303	0168	3
BRIMMER FORREST F	MAJ	0-0350865	0246	2
BRIMMER WILLIAM C	MAJ	0-0432947	0161	1
BRINCKMANN EDWIN L	COL	0-0345882	0266	3
BRINDLEY SEARCY W	LTC	0-0469132	1054	1
BRINEGAR DENISVILLE	CW3	W-2211516	0968	1
BRINGHURST EDMOND L	1LT	0-0262928	0754	3
BRINGLE CLARENCE E	CW2	W-2120829	1145	2
BRINING JOHN R	MAJ	0-1552024	1065	1
BRINK ARTHUR R	MAJ	0-1302590	1163	1
BRINK JAY F	MAJ	0-0148859	0852	3
BRINK LEE V	LTC	0-1327411	0266	1
BRINKE ROBERT P	MAJ	C-1295823	0765	1
BRINKER CLARENCE T	MAJ	0-0239329	0761	3
BRINKER VIRGEL C	CW3	W-2151327	0764	1
BRINKERHOFF ARTHUR D	CW3	W-2142093	0756	1
BRINKERHOFF HENRY S	CW2	W-2215266	0368	1
BRINKERHOFF OLIVER J	MAJ	0-1554689	0557	1
BRINKERHOFF ROBERT	LTC	0-0236812	0263	1
BRINKERHOFF ROY A	CPT	0-0492378	0851	1
BRINKHOUS KENNETH M	COL	0-0295870	0668	3
BRINKLEY ALBERT H	CPT	0-0544576	0747	2
BRINKLEY GEORGE A	CPT	0-0907122	0745	2
BRINKLEY GEORGE W	LTC	0-1823976	0766	1
BRINKLEY JIMMIE T	CW2	W-2107540	0146	2
BRINKLEY WILLIS J	1LT	0-1080516	1155	1
BRINKMAN EMIL F	LTC	0-0227640	0656	1
BRINKMAN GERARD J	LTC	0-0323828	1265	3
BRINKMAN ROLLAND V	1LT	0-1322764	0247	2
BRINKMEYER JOHN E	LTC	0-0167015	1147	2
BRINKWART HUGO JR	LTC	0-1047458	0656	1
BRINKWORTH BEN	LTC	0-1951644	0467	1
BRINSFIELD JENNINGS	LTC	0-1175653	1266	1
BRINSMEAD HENRY	MAJ	0-1166235	0760	1
BRINSON CONNIE H JR	MAJ	0-0933438	0365	2
BRINSON ELMER J	WO1	W-2142419	0653	1
BRIODY THOMAS J	1LT	0-1284282	0745	2
BRION CLAY W	COL	0-0359834	0759	1
BRIONES DOMINADOR	1LT	0-0395565	1162	2
BRIOR JOHN E	CPT	0-0502980	1156	1
BRISBANE JULIUS S	MAJ	0-1637082	0562	1
BRISBEN WESLEY W	LTC	0-2045067	0563	1
BRISBINE DAWES F	COL	0-0195791	0346	2
BRISBINE TOM R JR	1LT	0-5514750	0466	2
BRISBOIS GERALD C	WO1	W-2119444	1145	2
BRISCO ELMER F	CW3	W-2144216	0663	1
BRISCOE EVELYN B	LTC	L-0800013	0163	1
BRISCOE GEORGE W	MAJ	0-1104466	0358	1
BRISCOE HENRY J	CPT	0-1573068	0159	1
BRISCOE PIERCE W	LTC	0-1325715	0766	1
BRISCOE WILLIAM A	COL	0-0191614	0355	3
BRISENTINE ROBERT A	CW2	W-3430054	1265	1
BRISK MICHAEL M	MAJ	0-2032589	0762	1
BRISKIN SAMUEL J	LTC	0-0398826	0743	2
BRISSETTE ALPHONSE L	MAJ	0-0948201	0166	1
BRISSON HERVEY R	MAJ	0-1552025	0563	1
BRISTER BENSON E	CPT	0-1318341	1062	1
BRISTER JAMES H	LTC	0-1168578	0962	1
BRISTER MARVIN C	MAJ	0-0453142	0546	2
BRISTO CLOIS E	LTC	0-1106015	0762	1
BRISTOL LELAND A	CW2	W-2101480	1148	2
BRISTOL ROBERT A	CPT	0-0363019	1044	2
BRISTOL WALTER L	LTC	0-0357883	0966	3
BRISTOW DON L	CPT	0-1560406	0855	2
BRISTOW JOHN A	LTC	0-1114391	1164	3
BRISTOW WALTER J	LTC	0-0169481	0952	3
BRISTOW WILLIAM A	LTC	0-1104787	1157	2
BRITAIN ERIC R	CPT	0-0162066	0653	3
BRITCHEY JEROME M	LTC	0-0349295	0846	2
BRITE BYRON H	LTC	0-1173173	0363	1
BRITE CHARLES R	1LT	0-1107827	0845	2
BRITO JOHN A	LTC	0-0480655	0157	1
BRITT CECIL A	CPT	0-1690809	1057	1
BRITT EARL F	MAJ	0-0310152	0168	3
BRITT EDWARD J	CW3	W-2151315	1063	1
BRITT GERALD L	CW4	W-2121199	0456	1
BRITT JAMES J III	MAJ	0-1182523	0361	1
BRITT JOEL A	MAJ	0-1037414	0960	1
BRITT MAURICE L	CPT	0-0410196	1044	2
BRITT PAUL B	LTC	0-0132123	0157	3
BRITT REDDIN	MAJ	0-0480599	0346	2
BRITT ROBERT W	LTC	0-1182524	0166	1
BRITT THOMAS W	1LT	0-1182496	0557	2
BRITT WILLIAM D JR	MAJ	0-0213837	0264	3
BRITTAIN CECIL	CW2	W-2205105	0161	1
BRITTAIN CHARLES C	CPT	0-1541475	0256	2
BRITTAIN FREDERICK	LTC	0-1051050	0462	1
BRITTAIN HAROLD M	LTC	0-0221999	0847	2
BRITTAIN JOHN R	LTC	0-0280433	0860	3
BRITTAIN RICHARD G	CW2	W-3400084	0968	1
BRITTAIN WALTER	CW3	W-2152785	1167	1
BRITTAIN WILLIAM C	MAJ	0-0235731	1146	2
BRITTEN CHARLES H	LTC	0-0298594	1156	1
BRITTEN WILLIAM F	COL	0-0148163	0-53	3
BRITTENHAM EDWARD O	MAJ	0-2014540	0163	1
BRITTINGHAM ELMER A	MAJ	0-0300237	0867	3
BRITTINGHAM F A	CW3	W-2148336	1058	1
BRITTINGHAM GEORGE L	COL	0-0220637	0657	1
BRITTINGHAM HARRY A	2LT	0-0293053	0842	2
BRITTINGHAM LOUIS W	LTC	0-0197453	0761	3
BRITTO GEORGE R	LTC	0-1303655	1060	1
BRITTON ALTON C	LTC	0-0172703	0656	3
BRITTON CLARK V	MAJ	0-0301494	1162	3
BRITTON CLYDE V	LTC	0-1287298	1060	2
BRITTON DUDLEY J	LTC	0-0450560	0958	1
BRITTON EMMA L	LTC	N-0731265	1262	2
BRITTON ERNEST G	LTC	0-1174239	0961	1
BRITTON GLENN W	MAJ	0-0192261	0-49	3
BRITTON IRVING E	CW4	W-2208803	0868	1
BRITTON JACK A	MAJ	0-1922647	0765	1
BRITTON JAMES G	COL	0-0916437	0566	3
BRITTON JAMES W	MAJ	0-1683064	1044	2
BRITTON KIRBY L	MAJ	0-0962559	1262	1
BRITTON RAYMOND M	LTC	0-0364069	1045	2
BRITTON ROBERT S	CPT	0-1583978	1155	2
BRITTON WILLIAM F	LTC	0-1184991	0162	1
BRITTON WILLIAM P	LTC	0-1798242	0467	3
BRITTON WILLIAM S	CPT	0-0323915	0456	1
BRITTS CHESTER L	CW2	W-2103912	1045	2
BRIX JAMES A	CPT	0-0322645	1143	2
BRIZEE ROBERT E	LTC	0-0779773	1165	1
BRIZZOLARA CHARLES M	CPT	0-0407217	0246	2
BRIZZOLARA LOUIS A	CW3	W-2152501	1064	1
BROAD BERTRAM C	LTC	0-0260836	0468	3
BROAD FAY E	MAJ	0-0118433	0444	2
BROAD GARDNER S	MAJ	0-0328601	0245	2
BROADAWAY JERRY L	CW3	W-2152031	0864	1
BROADBENT EVERETT F	LTC	0-0226346	0963	3
BROADDUS JACKSON A	CPT	0-0281434	0167	3
BROADDUS MALCOLM D	LTC	0-1300593	0762	1
BROADDUS MURRAY F	LTC	0-0323564	1144	2
BROADDUS RUSSELL G	COL	0-0314980	0866	1
BROADDUS THORBURN B	LTC	0-1310054	0665	1
BROADDUS WILLIAM L	2LT	0-4049351	0857	2
BROADHEAD WILLIAM C	LTC	0-0322962	0648	3
BROADHURST EDWARD C	MAJ	0-1575789	1061	1
BROADHURST LANSING E	LTC	0-1589083	0763	1
BROADHURST THOMAS I	MAJ	0-1878020	0667	1
BROADSTON LEONARD L	CW3	W-2146190	0961	1
BROADWELL ROLLAND E	LTC	0-1101346	0565	1
BROBST CHARLES R	MAJ	0-0474993	1159	1
BROBST GEORGE W JR	LTC	0-1318756	0666	1
BROCK DARWIN A	COL	0-0453556	0667	1
BROCK DONALD L	LTC	0-0261880	0465	3
BROCK FRANK P	COL	0-0250777	0267	3
BROCK HOWELL E	LTC	0-1171921	1165	1
BROCK JAMES L JR	MAJ	0-0282221	1268	3
BROCK JOHN M	MAJ	0-1599144	1262	1
BROCK LEWIS D	LTC	0-1171063	1061	1
BROCK LLOYD S	CW3	W-2004804	0967	1
BROCK ROBERT L	CW3	W-2151089	0157	1
BROCK ROGERS E	CW2	W-2108314	0846	1
BROCK RONALD C	M G	0-0242225	0759	3
BROCK WALLACE W	CPT	0-1306371	0661	1
BROCK WALTER S	1LT	0-0255791	0444	2
BROCK WILLIAM C	CPT	0-0290664	0767	3
BROCK WILLIAM E	MAJ	0-0964091	0565	1
BROCKDORFF BEVERLY	LTC	0-1112048	0563	1
BROCKERT KENNETH E	CPT	0-2036293	0657	1
BROCKETT HILLAS B	LTC	0-0447963	0954	1
BROCKETT STANLEY M	CW2	W-2215074	0767	1
BROCKIE JOHN M JR	COL	0-0277251	0360	1
BROCKLEHURST R A	COL	0-0174521	0954	3
BROCKMAN CHARLES J	COL	0-0209360	0757	3
BROCKMAN EARL H	CPT	0-0116593	1052	3
BROCKMAN HARRY D	LTC	0-0216939	0163	3
BROCKMAN RAYMOND P	MAJ	0-0253182	0363	3
BROCKMAN ROBERT C	MAJ	0-1637086	0863	1
BROCKO JOHN B	COL	0-0313253	0568	3
BROCKSIEPER CLARENCE	MAJ	0-1062471	0461	1
BROCKWAY ARTHUR J	LTC	0-1290196	0457	1
BROCKWAY GEORGE B	LTC	0-1114393	0764	1
BROCKWAY RONALD S	LTC	0-0450761	1162	1
BROCKWAY RUTH H	CPT	N-0784621	0847	2
BROCOPP HERMAN A	COL	0-0136185	0356	3
BRODBECK JAMES A	CPT	0-1304334	0647	2
BRODER ARNOLD	1LT	0-1044464	0346	2
BRODER SIMON	LTC	0-0312397	0164	3
BRODERICK CHARLES J	LTC	0-0438745	0662	1
BRODERICK CROCKETT B	LTC	0-0321609	1266	3
BRODERICK DAVID F	CW2	W-2114205	1145	2
BRODERICK FRED W	COL	0-0245228	0160	1
BRODERICK JOHN M	CPT	0-1306054	0548	2
BRODERICK THOMAS C	CPT	0-0389242	0245	2
BRODERICK WILLIAM J	1LT	0-1295333	0146	2
BRODEUR JOSEPH R	LTC	0-0267707	0450	3
BRODIE ARTHUR M	LTC	0-1333928	0167	1
BRODIE DONALD W	CPT	0-1684508	0245	2
BRODIE DUDLEY D	COL	0-0120524	0255	3
BRODIE JOHN T	LTC	0-0399938	0663	1
BRODKIN HENRY A	COL	0-0207258	0361	3
BRODKORB WALTER J	1LT	0-0160145	0455	3
BRODMAN HERBERT W	1LT	0-0471098	0749	1
BRODMAN KEEVE	MAJ	0-0244885	0444	2
BRODNAX MARION J	MAJ	0-0170258	1060	3
BRODRICK FRANK W	LTC	0-0150380	1045	2
BRODRICK GEORGE W	CW2	W-2142493	0856	1
BRODSKY ALEXANDER	1LT	0-0472333	0845	2
BRODY ALFRED W	CPT	0-0460731	1050	2
BRODY ARTHUR P	COL	0-0410462	1062	1
BRODY HERMAN	MAJ	0-0168550	1044	2
BRODY JAMES F	MAJ	0-0565881	0966	1
BRODY JOSEPH	CPT	0-1689403	0643	2
BRODY JOSEPH	1LT	0-1994389	0240	2
BRODY NATHANIEL	2LT	0-1314750	0645	2
BRODY WILLIAM	MAJ	0-0481997	0146	2
BRODZINSKY JACOB	MAJ	0-1109827	0567	1
BROE VARLEY F	MAJ	0-1310336	0862	1
BROEHM WALTER J	LTC	0-0183772	0847	2
BROFF MAURICE H	MAJ	0-0229100	1054	3
BROGAN RICHARD N	MAJ	0-5405118	0568	1
BROGAN WILLIAM A JR	MAJ	0-1062472	0461	1
BROGDON LELAND R	CPT	0-0495815	0750	1
BROILES JAMES O	CPT	0-1307501	0654	1
BROILLET EUGENE H	MAJ	0-1046465	0160	1
BROITMAN JACK	WO1	W-2105408	0946	2
BROKAW CHARLES E	COL	0-0170201	1158	3
BROKAW JOHN D	LTC	0-1015265	1062	1
BROKAW MAX V	LTC	0-0347639	0657	1
BROKAW STUART F	LTC	0-0220422	1051	3
BROKAW WILLIAM H	MAJ	0-0972067	0164	1
BROLIN EDWARD R	LTC	0-0270144	1066	3
BROLINE ELINOR L	1LT	N-0776581	0347	1
BROM JACOB M	LTC	0-1035106	0364	1
BROMBLE EDWARD W	MAJ	0-0958098	1162	1
BROMLEY ROBERT D	MAJ	0-0523043	0657	1
BROMLEY W K JR	CPT	0-0528753	1046	2
BROMS GUSTAVE A	LTC	0-0289478	0764	3
BROMSER PAUL F	MAJ	0-1823399	0261	1
BRONER RUSSELL A	LTC	0-0373366	0460	1
BRONISZ MATTHEW S	MAJ	0-0413907	1062	1
BRONNENBERG EDGAR M	LTC	0-1320096	0763	1
BRONNENBERG WILLIAM	MAJ	0-1543300	0761	1
BRONNER LEONARD E	LTC	0-2001024	0564	1
BRONNER NELLIS B JR	CPT	0-0455346	1144	2
BRONSON HARRY S	LTC	0-0167542	0645	2
BRONSON IRWIN P	CW3	W-2205400	0966	1
BRONSON SIDNEY W	1LT	0-0267982	0650	1
BROOK OCONO	2LT	0-1112050	0545	2
BROOK R J	CW2	W-2152727	0861	1
BROOKE ARTHUR C JR	LTC	0-1081391	0962	1
BROOKE DONALD C	CW2	W-3430029	0666	1
BROOKE ROYAL G	COL	0-0307703	0867	3
BROOKE TYLER S	2LT	0-0467000	0745	2
BROOKENS NORMAN J	CW3	W-2206864	0167	1
BROOKER GORDON L	CPT	0-1112051	1047	2
BROOKES NORMA	2LT	N-0731297	0244	1
BROOKFIELD WILLIAM L	LTC	0-0262485	0368	3
BROOKHART SMITH W	COL	0-0508524	1165	3
BROOKMAN STUART W	CW2	W-2214423	0866	1
BROOKMAN WILLIAM E	LTC	0-0411008	0760	1
BROOKNER JACK A	MAJ	0-1036875	0266	1
BROOKS ALBERT C JR	LTC	0-2014601	0668	1
BROOKS ALBERT H	CPT	0-1291066	104N	2
BROOKS ALEXANDER	2LT	0-2006182	0146	2
BROOKS ALVIN L	CPT	0-2028882	0161	2
BROOKS ANDREW J JR	CPT	0-0372294	0565	1
BROOKS ARTHUR B JR	2LT	0-1051898	0445	2
BROOKS BERNARD J	1LT	0-1285371	1045	2
BROOKS CARL R	CPT	0-1931867	0962	1
BROOKS CHARLES A	CPT	0-1301249	0352	2
BROOKS CHARLES H	CW4	W-2119343	0557	1
BROOKS CLOYCE H	LTC	0-1104791	1060	1
BROOKS CURTIS A	MAJ	0-0446018	0546	2
BROOKS DALE L	MAJ	0-1016536	0361	1
BROOKS DAVID E	LTC	0-1308092	0663	1
BROOKS DAVID M	CPT	0-1696080	1043	2
BROOKS DONALD F	CW2	W-2113388	1061	1
BROOKS EARL B	LTC	0-0219260	0648	3
BROOKS EARL T	CPT	0-0299296	0867	3
BROOKS EARLE C	LTC	0-1584080	0663	1
BROOKS EDGAR D	LTC	0-0454995	1162	1
BROOKS EDWARD H	1LT	0-0445627	0945	2
BROOKS ELTON G	1LT	0-2212003	0567	1
BROOKS EUGENE A	MAJ	0-1183251	0960	1

ARMY OF THE UNITED STATES RETIRED LIST

NAME	GRADE	SVC NO	DATE RET MO YR	RET CODE
BROOKS EUGENE F	CPT	0-0504720	0446	2
BROOKS FRANK B JR	MAJ	0-1336476	0864	2
BROOKS FRANK N	MAJ	0-2006538	0860	1
BROOKS GARMON W	CW3	W-2151382	0966	1
BROOKS GEORGE L	CW4	W-2102694	0357	1
BROOKS GEORGE W JR	COL	0-0277250	0766	3
BROOKS GILBERT	LTC	0-0320489	0666	3
BROOKS GILMON D	CW3	W-2147216	0366	1
BROOKS GLENN F	LTC	0-0364891	0556	1
BROOKS GRADY S	B G	0-0248317	0766	3
BROOKS HENRY L	LTC	0-1337605	1165	1
BROOKS HERBERT H	2LT	0-1823828	1044	2
BROOKS HERBERT J	CPT	0-0488834	0155	2
BROOKS HERBERT O	CW3	W-2142285	1058	1
BROOKS HERROLD E	COL	0-0179518	0163	3
BROOKS HOWARD R	1LT	0-0493083	0147	1
BROOKS JAMES B	MAJ	0-0406641	0447	2
BROOKS JAMES H	LTC	0-0932110	0665	3
BROOKS JOE E	CW3	W-2147740	0863	2
BROOKS JOHN E	COL	0-0309218	1158	3
BROOKS JOHN J	LTC	0-1944413	0463	1
BROOKS JOHN K	1LT	0-1061635	0945	2
BROOKS JOHN R	CPT	0-0407968	0246	2
BROOKS JOHN R	MAJ	0-2263013	0264	1
BROOKS JOHN S	MAJ	0-1293538	1160	1
BROOKS JOHN W	CPT	0-1010853	0144	2
BROOKS JOHNNY Y	LTC	0-1182782	1162	1
BROOKS LYLE A	CPT	0-0195345	1062	3
BROOKS MATTHEW L	LTC	0-1317145	1162	1
BROOKS MAXWELL	2LT	0-1012662	0651	2
BROOKS MORTON P	COL	0-0294943	0864	1
BROOKS PAUL R	COL	0-0268087	0564	3
BROOKS PAUL R	CW3	W-2143837	1167	1
BROOKS PERRY R	MAJ	0-1950607	0264	1
BROOKS PHILIP M	CPT	0-0493415	0648	1
BROOKS RALPH D	LTC	0-0187204	0648	3
BROOKS RAYFORD L	LTC	0-2204403	0868	1
BROOKS RAYMOND A	LTC	0-0425809	1162	3
BROOKS ROBERT	WO1	W-2124108	1146	1
BROOKS ROBERT A	CW2	W-3430058	1267	1
BROOKS ROBERT G	MAJ	0-1587753	1065	1
BROOKS ROBERT G	CW2	W-2122501	0753	2
BROOKS ROBERT G	WO1	W-2146757	0555	1
BROOKS ROBERT N	MAJ	0-1644470	1060	1
BROOKS RODNEY C	LTC	0-1165269	1165	1
BROOKS ROLAND	CPT	0-0160048	0153	3
BROOKS ROY I	COL	0-0308103	0759	1
BROOKS RUSSELL O	LTC	0-0275480	0467	3
BROOKS SAMMIE W	MAJ	0-2212009	0662	1
BROOKS STANLEY M	CW2	W-2147267	0464	1
BROOKS T F JR	LTC	0-1056974	0768	1
BROOKS THOMAS G	CW4	W-2121961	0662	1
BROOKS TROY N	LTC	0-0989815	0868	1
BROOKS VERNON P	MAJ	0-2024231	0856	1
BROOKS WALTER H	CPT	0-0263315	0363	3
BROOKS WILFRED E	CW4	W-2142627	0968	1
BROOKS WILLARD A	MAJ	0-1646810	0557	1
BROOKS WILLARD R	2LT	0-1822232	1143	2
BROOKS WILLIAM F	CW2	W-2152858	0256	1
BROOKS WILLIAM V	1LT	0-1295825	1145	2
BROOKS WILLIS P	LTC	0-2263035	0468	1
BROOKS WINFORD R	MAJ	0-1919353	0664	1
BROOKS WINSTON R	LTC	0-1598322	0462	1
BROOKS WINSTON S	LTC	0-0397079	0860	1
BROOKS WOODROW W	CPT	0-0496251	0253	2
BROOM CHARLES G	CPT	0-1926470	1164	1
BROOM DAVID	CPT	0-0528486	1050	1
BROOM EDWARD C	CW3	W-2149147	0364	1
BROOMALL FRED A	CPT	0-0171301	0542	1
BROOMALL SAMUEL C	MAJ	0-1558557	1162	1
BROOME JEROME C	LTC	0-0910355	0367	3
BROOMFIELD ROBERT E	LTC	0-1043581	0760	1
BROPHY ALLEN O	LTC	0-0181956	1149	3
BROPHY EANES R	CPT	0-0507655	1052	2
BROPHY EDWARD A	MAJ	0-1994823	1062	3

NAME	GRADE	SVC NO	DATE RET MO YR	RET CODE
BROPHY JAMES D	LTC	0-0328916	0860	1
BROPHY JOSEPH F	1LT	0-0226226	0850	3
BROPHY WILLIAM S JR	LTC	0-1548171	0267	1
BRORSEN JOHN J	MAJ	0-2211574	0967	1
BROSAMER JOHN J	CPT	0-1051500	1062	1
BROSE CARL E	LTC	0-0237147	0757	1
BROSHEAR JOHNNY W	MAJ	0-1822351	0561	1
BROSIN HENRY W	COL	0-0231426	0864	3
BROSIUS CHARLES C	MAJ	0-1688802	0466	1
BROSKE ABE	MAJ	0-0184671	1056	3
BROSKIE MARION L	2LT	N-0752474	0345	1
BROSKLEY STANLEY R	LTC	0-1170667	0868	1
BROSNAN PATRICK J	CPT	0-5331708	1168	2
BROSOKAS VICTOR P	LTC	0-0388976	0346	2
BROST BERNARD A	CPT	0-1560179	0865	1
BROSTEK ALEXANDER	LTC	0-0301001	0747	2
BROTEMARKLE W A	1LT	0-1050194	0452	2
BROTHER GEORGE M	COL	0-0332486	1167	3
BROTHERS DONALD E	LTC	0-1913419	0368	1
BROTHERS HARRISON S	COL	0-0245815	0266	3
BROTHERS JOSEPH L	WO1	W-2114494	0344	2
BROTHERS MAURICE F	COL	0-0194942	0660	3
BROTHERS WILLIAM W	COL	0-0189122	0146	2
BROTHERTON DONALD R	MAJ	0-0973512	0164	1
BROTHERTON HENRY A	LTC	0-1553780	0563	2
BROTHERTON HOLMAN A	LTC	0-0519647	1263	1
BROTHERTON JAMES R	LTC	0-0347168	0258	1
BROTHERTON KENNETH E	MAJ	0-0479036	0350	1
BROTHERTON WILLIAM W	COL	0-0220791	0164	3
BROTMAN GERALD	LTC	0-1081201	0667	1
BROUGH HARRY R	LTC	0-0290902	0162	3
BROUGHAM JAMES P JR	MAJ	0-1310802	0257	1
BROUGHER COOPER JR	LTC	0-0362102	0266	3
BROUGHER GEORGE B	LTC	0-1150127	0965	3
BROUGHMAN WARNER A	CPT	0-0389459	0346	2
BROUS CHRIS J	CPT	0-0450693	1045	2
BROUSSARD CHARLES C	LTC	0-0328259	0165	1
BROUSSARD DENIS	LTC	0-0481566	0857	1
BROUSSEAU LOUIS O	LTC	0-0262067	0866	3
BROWDER EDWARD M JR	COL	0-0236155	0266	3
BROWDER JESSE S	MAJ	0-0443898	1148	1
BROWER BESSIE L	MAJ	N-0779009	0765	1
BROWER DANIEL R JR	COL	0-0248691	0465	3
BROWERS HOWARD W	CW3	W-2141206	1059	1
BROWN A W	MAJ	0-1692933	0563	1
BROWN AARON C	COL	0-0410800	0667	1
BROWN ABE A	LTC	0-0148269	0954	3
BROWN ABRAHAM	MAJ	0-1588457	1267	3
BROWN ALAN	LTC	0-0314336	0266	3
BROWN ALANSON D JR	MAJ	0-1825129	1063	1
BROWN ALBERT E	2LT	0-1552848	0345	2
BROWN ALBERT L	CPT	0-0205370	0859	3
BROWN ALBERT L JR	MAJ	0-1553959	0864	1
BROWN ALBERT N	MAJ	0-0240143	0747	2
BROWN ALBERT S	MAJ	0-0969476	0465	1
BROWN ALFRED G	COL	0-0114468	0750	3
BROWN ALFRED W	1LT	0-1305375	1147	2
BROWN ALLAN H	MAJ	0-0138326	0845	2
BROWN ALLEN E	CW2	W-2102695	0558	1
BROWN ALMER G	CW3	W-2203634	0763	1
BROWN ALONZO L	MAJ	0-1048696	1162	1
BROWN ALSA P	LTC	0-0284950	0560	3
BROWN ALTON A	MAJ	0-2262990	0865	1
BROWN ANDREW J	MAJ	0-1290540	1163	1
BROWN ANN S	1LT	N-0759933	0246	1
BROWN ARCHIE E	CPT	0-0470760	0645	2
BROWN ARDEN E	CPT	0-1913288	0967	1
BROWN ARNOLD L	MAJ	0-1296318	0658	1
BROWN ARRY L	LTC	0-0310288	1166	3
BROWN ARTHUR	CPT	0-0134887	0157	3
BROWN ARTHUR C JR	1LT	0-2262582	0859	2
BROWN ARTHUR D	COL	0-0904286	1168	3
BROWN ARTHUR F	1LT	0-1285890	1145	2
BROWN ARTHUR G JR	MAJ	0-2032937	0862	1
BROWN ARTHUR W	2LT	0-1292928	0145	2

NAME	GRADE	SVC NO	DATE RET MO YR	RET CODE
BROWN AUDREY R	CW4	W-2143165	0559	1
BROWN AUSY P	COL	0-0368781	0660	1
BROWN BEE H	MAJ	0-1322881	0859	1
BROWN BENJAMIN F	LTC	0-1313713	1066	1
BROWN BERNARD A	COL	0-0256766	0655	3
BROWN BERNARD N	LTC	0-1018994	1066	1
BROWN BOBBIE E	CPT	0-2053899	0350	2
BROWN BOYCE R	MAJ	0-1117371	0262	1
BROWN BRYAN L	LTC	0-0276297	0567	3
BROWN BURRELL G	LTC	0-1697491	0158	1
BROWN BYRON F	LTC	0-0212967	0860	3
BROWN CALVIN R	CW2	W-2210179	0364	1
BROWN CAMERON	LTC	0-0369922	0246	2
BROWN CAMPBELL H	LTC	0-0401532	1049	1
BROWN CAREY H	COL	0-0276742	0648	3
BROWN CARL H SR	MAJ	0-1080604	0561	1
BROWN CARL L	CPT	0-0978086	1060	1
BROWN CARL R	CPT	0-0329595	0446	2
BROWN CARLOS L	CPT	0-0155740	0757	3
BROWN CATHARINE	1LT	L-0601502	0245	2
BROWN CECIL E	COL	0-0338746	0561	1
BROWN CECIL J	LTC	0-1040886	0264	1
BROWN CHARLES A	LTC	0-1301250	1065	1
BROWN CHARLES A	CW2	W-3100523	0167	1
BROWN CHARLES B	MAJ	0-1046367	1264	1
BROWN CHARLES C	WO1	W-1440606	0656	3
BROWN CHARLES D	LTC	0-0345704	0958	3
BROWN CHARLES E JR	MAJ	0-1109159	1061	1
BROWN CHARLES G	MAJ	0-1180763	0760	1
BROWN CHARLES H	MAJ	0-0379816	0246	2
BROWN CHARLES J	MAJ	0-0925023	0944	2
BROWN CHARLES L	CW4	W-2102696	0255	1
BROWN CHARLES M	LTC	0-0404367	0453	2
BROWN CHARLES M	LTC	0-1080689	1266	1
BROWN CHARLES M	LTC	0-1314590	0166	1
BROWN CHARLES S	CW4	W-2122989	1060	1
BROWN CHARLIE	CPT	0-0481710	0547	1
BROWN CHARLTON A	1LT	0-0400486	0442	2
BROWN CHESTER H	MAJ	0-2212001	0165	1
BROWN CHESTER T	LTC	0-0231573	1157	1
BROWN CLAIRE A	2LT	N-0742192	0745	1
BROWN CLAUDE P	LTC	0-0146350	1149	3
BROWN CLIFFORD A	CPT	0-1046026	1165	1
BROWN CLIFFORD A	MAJ	0-1894451	0961	1
BROWN CLIFFORD F	CW2	W-2114839	0455	2
BROWN CLIFFORD N	LTC	0-1533265	0753	1
BROWN CLIFTON O	CW3	W-2148786	0966	1
BROWN CLINTON H	MAJ	0-2208113	1165	1
BROWN CLYDE JR	CPT	0-0382126	0646	2
BROWN COATS	CW3	W-2149426	1065	1
BROWN COLEMAN T	LTC	0-0181119	0152	3
BROWN COURTNEY P	COL	0-0243994	1264	3
BROWN CURTIS P	LTC	0-1320380	1063	1
BROWN DAVID F K	CW3	W-2147495	0762	1
BROWN DAVID O	LTC	0-0501649	0657	1
BROWN DAVID W	CW3	W-2145628	0166	1
BROWN DECATER	LTC	0-0885510	0854	1
BROWN DEWAYNE G	1LT	0-1823978	0157	1
BROWN DONALD A	COL	0-0181651	0161	1
BROWN DONALD A	CPT	0-0376935	0146	2
BROWN DONALD E	COL	0-1594731	1068	1
BROWN DONALD R	1LT	0-1893809	1056	2
BROWN DONALD W	1LT	0-0405175	0743	2
BROWN DOUGLAS A	CW2	W-2214361	0966	1
BROWN EARL	LTC	0-1553781	0862	1
BROWN EARL J	1LT	0-1319321	0448	2
BROWN EARL S	LTC	0-1080178	0661	1
BROWN EARLE H	CPT	0-1287469	1146	2
BROWN EDGAR L	MAJ	0-0975470	0763	1
BROWN EDGAR T	CPT	0-1821672	0749	2
BROWN EDMUND H	CPT	0-0338771	0468	3
BROWN EDWARD	CW4	W-2132164	0656	1
BROWN EDWARD A	LTC	0-1046378	1165	3
BROWN EDWARD A	LTC	0-1949154	0365	1
BROWN EDWARD C	LTC	0-0507468	0768	1

NAME	GRADE	SVC NO	DATE RET MO YR	RET CODE
BROWN EDWARD E	CW2	W-2209014	0961	1
BROWN EDWARD F	MAJ	0-1307798	0261	1
BROWN EDWARD M	COL	0-0164412	0153	3
BROWN EDWARD S	CPT	0-0405550	0146	2
BROWN EDWIN E	MAJ	0-1283017	0358	2
BROWN EDWIN H	MAJ	0-1894909	0167	1
BROWN EDWIN S	CW4	W-2113669	1262	1
BROWN ELVIE C	CW2	W-2109227	1044	2
BROWN EMIL	LTC	0-0115141	0255	3
BROWN EMMETT	CPT	0-0148927	0150	3
BROWN ERNEST A	CW3	W-2151885	1062	1
BROWN ERNEST J	CW4	W-2101486	0158	1
BROWN ERNEST L	CPT	0-1581559	0256	1
BROWN ERNEST M	COL	0-0307194	0468	3
BROWN EUGENE C	CPT	0-0307754	0346	2
BROWN EUGENE J	CPT	0-0914674	0346	2
BROWN EUGENE L JR	MAJ	0-0116372	0648	3
BROWN EUGENE S	LTC	0-1106018	0465	1
BROWN FELIX B	MAJ	0-0468145	1145	2
BROWN FLETCHER H	CPT	0-1951039	1057	2
BROWN FLOYD O	1LT	0-1845329	1145	2
BROWN FLOYD L	LTC	0-0228728	0658	1
BROWN FLOYD S	CW4	W-2127548	0652	1
BROWN FLOYD W	COL	0-0286462	0648	1
BROWN FORREST D	COL	0-0319479	0960	1
BROWN FRANCES M	MAJ	N-0729820	0663	1
BROWN FRANCIS G	MAJ	0-0962620	0263	1
BROWN FRANK	CW2	W-2115687	0451	1
BROWN FRANK A	LTC	0-0217282	1263	3
BROWN FRANK J	CPT	0-0496935	0429	2
BROWN FRANK L	LTC	0-0450579	0457	1
BROWN FRANK M	COL	0-0188318	0257	3
BROWN FRANK M JR	CPT	0-0890107	0447	2
BROWN FRED L	1LT	0-1173886	0147	2
BROWN FREDERIC B	CPT	0-0289845	0866	3
BROWN FREDERICK	MAJ	0-0971749	0763	1
BROWN FREDERICK	WO1	W-2115152	0747	2
BROWN FREDRICK J	CW3	W-2148074	0765	1
BROWN GALE C	CPT	R-0000083	0946	1
BROWN GALE L	1LT	0-1111516	0846	2
BROWN GARDNER W	MAJ	0-0276949	1145	2
BROWN GARNHART T	CPT	0-0693843	0252	2
BROWN GEORGE	COL	0-0328152	1061	1
BROWN GEORGE	CPT	0-0471637	0655	1
BROWN GEORGE A	LTC	0-0439640	1157	1
BROWN GEORGE A JR	LTC	0-1326234	0868	1
BROWN GEORGE B	LTC	0-0183238	1047	2
BROWN GEORGE B	CPT	0-0385492	0145	2
BROWN GEORGE C	LTC	0-0205800	0158	3
BROWN GEORGE C	MAJ	0-0305426	0445	2
BROWN GEORGE C	LTC	0-1031388	0557	1
BROWN GEORGE E	MAJ	0-0976347	0563	1
BROWN GEORGE H	MAJ	0-1874909	1065	1
BROWN GEORGE L	COL	0-0255870	0562	3
BROWN GEORGE S	COL	0-0144316	0754	3
BROWN GEORGE S	MAJ	0-0298158	1045	2
BROWN GEORGE W	1LT	0-1047453	1047	2
BROWN GERALD E	LTC	0-2050416	0364	1
BROWN GILBERT L	CPT	0-1015802	0446	2
BROWN GLENN J	1LT	0-0391530	0144	2
BROWN GLENN W	MAJ	0-1031156	0562	1
BROWN GRACE D	MAJ	L-0704036	0955	2
BROWN HARLAN C	MAJ	0-0257092	0266	3
BROWN HARLEY L	LTC	0-1331370	0267	1
BROWN HARLEY M	MAJ	0-1312273	0761	1
BROWN HAROLD A	1LT	0-2008608	0847	2
BROWN HAROLD A JR	CPT	0-0926414	0153	2
BROWN HAROLD E JR	LTC	0-0548971	1067	1
BROWN HAROLD G	LTC	0-0276640	1059	3
BROWN HAROLD H	MAJ	0-0447990	0647	1
BROWN HAROLD J	MAJ	0-0235967	0166	3
BROWN HAROLD O	LTC	0-0286530	0745	2
BROWN HARRISON E	LTC	0-0921365	0667	3
BROWN HARRY B	CPT	0-0229656	0554	3
BROWN HARRY E	COL	0-0239288	0865	3

NAME	GRADE	SVC NO	DATE RET MO YR	RET CODE
BROWN HARRY F	CPT	0-0442587	0346	2
BROWN HARRY I	1LT	0-0403795	0958	1
BROWN HARRY L JR	MAJ	0-1545500	0661	1
BROWN HARRY R	MAJ	0-0280089	0962	3
BROWN HARRY W	MAJ	0-0296622	0945	2
BROWN HARRY W JR	CPT	0-0317250	0644	2
BROWN HARVEY N	LTC	0-0105877	0259	3
BROWN HARVEY W JR	CW3	W-2205407	0168	1
BROWN HENRY N	CW3	W-2154662	0559	1
BROWN HENRY P	CPT	0-1168187	0745	2
BROWN HERBERT E	MAJ	0-0268642	0744	2
BROWN HERBERT E	W01	W-2125039	0546	2
BROWN HERBERT J	CPT	0-1573748	1046	2
BROWN HERBERT M	COL	0-0268900	0668	3
BROWN HERMAN	CW4	W-2146420	0768	2
BROWN HERMAN W	CW3	W-2210944	0968	1
BROWN HOLT S	LTC	0-0482493	0255	2
BROWN HOMER A	MAJ	0-1547243	1262	1
BROWN HOMER B	CPT	0-0413742	0348	2
BROWN HORACE O	COL	0-0201728	1160	3
BROWN HOUSTON A	COL	0-0284648	0967	3
BROWN HOWARD F	COL	0-0403968	0667	1
BROWN HOWARD L	MAJ	0-0144307	1057	3
BROWN HOWARD S	CPT	0-0488752	0450	1
BROWN HOWARD T	CPT	0-0395428	1045	2
BROWN HOWARD W	LTC	0-0291849	0660	1
BROWN HUBERT V	CW2	RW-2152820	0263	1
BROWN JACK E	CPT	0-1296988	0947	2
BROWN JACK M	1LT	0-0340734	0444	2
BROWN JACK W	MAJ	0-1298655	0557	1
BROWN JACOBS A	1LT	0-1032692	0945	2
BROWN JAMES A	LTC	0-0342779	0662	1
BROWN JAMES A	MAJ	0-1179313	0156	2
BROWN JAMES B	COL	0-0177023	0546	2
BROWN JAMES F	MAJ	0-0262444	0567	3
BROWN JAMES E	MAJ	0-4010991	0667	1
BROWN JAMES E	CW2	W-2149329	0362	2
BROWN JAMES G	CPT	0-0341761	1045	2
BROWN JAMES G	MAJ	0-1824420	1051	2
BROWN JAMES H	CPT	0-0219430	0754	3
BROWN JAMES H	CW2	W-2147930	0363	1
BROWN JAMES JR	1LT	0-1114397	0645	2
BROWN JAMES M	1LT	0-0373427	0845	2
BROWN JAMES M	MAJ	0-1913403	1264	1
BROWN JAMES N	LTC	0-0269761	0967	3
BROWN JAMES S	CPT	0-0449188	0746	2
BROWN JAMES T	COL	0-0226891	1264	3
BROWN JAMES W	MAJ	0-0516573	1163	1
BROWN JAMES W	LTC	0-1587154	0665	1
BROWN JASON L	CW2	0-1321698	1057	1
BROWN JEFF G JR	CPT	0-1937081	0865	1
BROWN JESS W	W01	W-2112849	0458	1
BROWN JESSE C	LTC	0-1328879	1265	1
BROWN JESSE F	COL	0-0101100	0648	3
BROWN JESSE H	LTC	0-0281200	0267	3
BROWN JESSIE F	MAJ	N-0752934	0864	1
BROWN JOHN A	LTC	0-0152648	0356	3
BROWN JOHN B	LTC	0-0509008	1166	3
BROWN JOHN E	MAJ	0-0450691	0460	1
BROWN JOHN E	CPT	0-0485646	0146	2
BROWN JOHN E JR	LTC	0-0335893	0263	3
BROWN JOHN H	LTC	0-0121708	0952	3
BROWN JOHN H	CPT	0-0450073	1145	2
BROWN JOHN H	CPT	0-0493406	0549	1
BROWN JOHN H	1LT	0-1291406	1144	2
BROWN JOHN H	CW3	W-2151874	0164	2
BROWN JOHN H	CW2	W-3156426	1168	2
BROWN JOHN J	COL	0-0249438	0465	3
BROWN JOHN J	CPT	0-0314189	0743	2
BROWN JOHN L	CPT	0-0108608	0852	3
BROWN JOHN M	MAJ	0-1894168	0968	1
BROWN JOHN N	2LT	0-2313275	0261	3
BROWN JOHN R	MAJ	0-1011361	0461	1
BROWN JOHN S	LTC	0-0268321	1166	3
BROWN JOHN T	CPT	0-1313958	1048	2
BROWN JOHN W	MAJ	0-0250058	1262	1
BROWN JOHN W	CPT	0-0383264	1044	2
BROWN JOSEPH W	LTC	0-1574615	0665	1
BROWN JOSEPH W	MAJ	0-1646822	0760	1
BROWN KARL J	CW2	W-2142037	1056	1
BROWN KELLY	CW3	W-2205754	0866	1
BROWN KENNETH A	LTC	0-1798976	0167	3
BROWN KENNETH C	COL	0-0118949	0755	3
BROWN KENNETH F	LTC	0-1177304	0263	1
BROWN KENNETH H	MAJ	0-0394266	0346	2
BROWN KENNETH R	LTC	0-0217823	0364	3
BROWN KENNETH W	CPT	0-1318277	0246	2
BROWN KENNETH W	CW3	W-2147426	0666	1
BROWN LAURENCE H	LTC	0-0176337	0659	3
BROWN LAURENCE R	LTC	0-0210563	1262	3
BROWN LAWRENCE E	MAJ	0-1845151	1051	1
BROWN LAWRENCE E	CW3	W-2203647	0864	1
BROWN LAWRENCE T	LTC	0-0113280	0854	3
BROWN LEO F	MAJ	0-1045400	0163	1
BROWN LEON G	COL	0-0261953	0661	3
BROWN LESTER A	LTC	0-1011084	0456	1
BROWN LESTER C	LTC	0-1894884	0960	1
BROWN LEWIS D	CPT	0-1945091	1047	2
BROWN LLOYD C	LTC	0-0360656	1064	1
BROWN LLOYD E	MAJ	0-0290042	0854	1
BROWN LLOYD M	MAJ	0-1640266		1
BROWN LONNIE V	CW2	W-2151047	0466	2
BROWN LOUCKS B	COL	0-0179349	0848	3
BROWN LOUIS J	CW2	W-2107957	0762	1
BROWN LYMAN E	MAJ	0-0399993	0155	1
BROWN MAE L	MAJ	N-0797488	0665	1
BROWN MAE S	MAJ	N-0796787	1068	3
BROWN MAJOR D	MAJ	0-2023354	1060	1
BROWN MALCOLM Z	LTC	0-0408923	1061	1
BROWN MARCELLUS	1LT	0-1319376	0646	2
BROWN MARGARET A	1LT	N-0741249	0546	1
BROWN MARIEM F	2LT	N-0787998	0844	1
BROWN MARION E	1LT	0-1106019	0745	2
BROWN MARY G	1LT	N-0761744	0247	1
BROWN MAX H	COL	0-0466962	0762	2
BROWN MCGREGOR E	CPT	0-0193166	0645	2
BROWN MCKINLEY	CW2	W-2142136	0656	1
BROWN MELVIN C	CW2	W-2151506	0461	1
BROWN MERLE H	MAJ	0-1549899	0157	1
BROWN MERLE S	MAJ	0-2021282	0364	1
BROWN MERTON F	CW3	W-2149976	0961	1
BROWN MICHAEL J	LTC	0-1180826	0866	1
BROWN MILON I	1LT	0-1315903	0645	2
BROWN MILTON A	1LT	0-1180827	0845	2
BROWN MILTON L	CW2	W-2150298	0761	1
BROWN MINOT J	LTC	0-0184476	0648	3
BROWN MORRIS B	MAJ	0-0205227	1045	2
BROWN NATHAN A JR	COL	0-1765917	0761	3
BROWN NEELY R	LTC	0-1185838	0264	1
BROWN NOEL C	COL	0-0351697	1161	1
BROWN NORMAN C	COL	0-0280302	0657	3
BROWN NORMAN E	LTC	0-1286956	1060	1
BROWN OMAR O	COL	0-0234670	0967	3
BROWN OSBORN H	CPT	0-0477489	1158	1
BROWN OSCAR R	LTC	0-1533019	0857	1
BROWN PAUL C	LTC	0-0450014	0255	1
BROWN PAUL E	LTC	0-0265795	0863	3
BROWN PAUL G	CW2	W-2205280	1056	2
BROWN PAUL R	2LT	0-0228324	0366	3
BROWN PHILIP G	COL	0-0344790	0361	1
BROWN PHILIP H	LTC	0-1001959	0862	1
BROWN QUINTON C	CW3	W-2147041	1266	1
BROWN RALPH	CPT	0-1289000	1045	2
BROWN RALPH C	LTC	0-0264974	0865	3
BROWN RALPH S JR	CW2	W-2146740	1060	1
BROWN RAY A	CPT	0-0507953	0446	1
BROWN RAYFORD F	CPT	0-1185383	0758	1
BROWN RAYMOND A	COL	0-0177181	0648	3
BROWN RAYMOND D	MAJ	0-2017501	0858	1
BROWN RAYMOND J	COL	0-0265647	1266	3
BROWN RAYMOND W	MAJ	0-1013934	1263	1
BROWN REMBERT H	CW3	W-2150879	0663	1
BROWN REX G	LTC	0-0924858	0468	3
BROWN RICHARD C	1LT	0-1285701	1045	2
BROWN RICHARD F	LTC	0-0329429	0163	1
BROWN RICHARD E	LTC	0-1320819	1165	1
BROWN RICHARD G	MAJ	0-1110959	0251	2
BROWN RICHARD G	CPT	0-1919234	0363	1
BROWN RICHARD L	1LT	0-1169875	1045	2
BROWN RICHARD P	MAJ	0-1321320	0363	1
BROWN RICHARD T	MAJ	0-0439632	0446	1
BROWN RICHARD W	LTC	0-1175391	0163	1
BROWN ROBERT A	1LT	0-0796075	1052	2
BROWN ROBERT B	CPT	0-0971826	0363	2
BROWN ROBERT C	COL	0-0234765	0558	3
BROWN ROBERT C JR	LTC	0-1640268	0863	1
BROWN ROBERT E	1LT	0-0148950	0363	3
BROWN ROBERT E	COL	0-0247461	0364	3
BROWN ROBERT F	LTC	0-1016677	0865	1
BROWN ROBERT E	CW2	W-2147319	1160	1
BROWN ROBERT F	LTC	0-1052274	0267	1
BROWN ROBERT H	LTC	0-1186565	0466	1
BROWN ROBERT J	2LT	0-1584107	1144	2
BROWN ROBERT L	MAJ	0-1342239	1166	2
BROWN ROBERT L JR	COL	0-0319865	0162	1
BROWN ROBERT L JR	LTC	0-1171066	0161	1
BROWN ROBERT L JR	MAJ	0-1999219	0861	1
BROWN ROBERT L JR	MAJ	0-2262388	0166	1
BROWN ROBERT M	LTC	0-0413249	0861	1
BROWN ROBERT M	MAJ	0-1651580	0963	1
BROWN ROBERT O	MAJ	0-1882290	1067	1
BROWN ROBERT W	COL	0-0274312	0760	1
BROWN ROBISON JR	MAJ	0-0222333	0864	3
BROWN ROSEN T	1LT	0-1913512	0337	1
BROWN ROSS C	LTC	0-0144065	0457	3
BROWN ROSS C	LTC	0-1010604	0663	1
BROWN ROWLAND S	COL	0-0144834	0746	2
BROWN ROY	MAJ	0-0472324	0148	1
BROWN ROY C	MAJ	0-1120000	0664	1
BROWN ROY C	CPT	0-1285185	0946	2
BROWN ROY O	LTC	0-0183877	0948	3
BROWN ROY E	2LT	0-2016347	1047	1
BROWN ROY F	LTC	0-1305537	0962	1
BROWN ROY W	1LT	0-1754786	0847	2
BROWN ROYAL L	MAJ	0-0466340	1047	2
BROWN RUTH M	1LT	N-0776212	1145	1
BROWN SAMUEL	MAJ	0-1011353	1161	2
BROWN SAMUEL A JR	LTC	0-0241975	1054	3
BROWN SAMUEL A JR	2LT	0-1948095	0546	2
BROWN SAMUEL C	MAJ	0-0200058	1059	3
BROWN SAMUEL S	CPT	0-0916274	0845	2
BROWN SANFORD P	LTC	0-0185920	0355	3
BROWN SARA M	MAJ	N-0765370	0465	1
BROWN SCRIBNER J	MAJ	0-1339041	1165	1
BROWN SELLERS B JR	LTC	0-2006313	0467	1
BROWN SHELDON	1LT	0-0385144	0845	2
BROWN SIDNEY A	CW4	W-2108890	0968	1
BROWN SIDNEY S	1LT	0-1585218	0460	1
BROWN SILAS D	MAJ	0-1919050	0964	1
BROWN SIMON	2LT	0-1324502	0545	2
BROWN SPENCER A	LTC	0-0282870	0163	3
BROWN STANLEY B	CPT	0-0395041	0560	1
BROWN STANLEY G	1LT	0-1289038	0445	2
BROWN STANLEY J	CPT	0-0499612	0156	1
BROWN STEPHEN L	LTC	0-1168583	0962	1
BROWN STEWART S	MAJ	0-0270431	0767	3
BROWN STUART O	COL	0-0207717	0755	3
BROWN THELMA A	CPT	N-0805027	0560	2
BROWN THEODORE D	CW3	W-2103914	0855	1
BROWN THEODORE R	CPT	0-0253103	0647	2
BROWN THOMAS	CPT	0-0485800	1047	1
BROWN THOMAS A	LTC	0-0239327	0657	1
BROWN THOMAS E	LTC	0-1054953	0166	1
BROWN THOMAS G	LTC	0-0918662	0346	2
BROWN THOMAS H	1LT	0-0378517	0245	2
BROWN THOMAS L	LTC	0-0232623	0360	3
BROWN THOMAS L	MAJ	0-2036045	0461	1
BROWN THOMAS M	LTC	0-0289896	0158	3
BROWN THOMAS M	LTC	0-1640270	1162	1
BROWN THOMAS M	MAJ	0-1640271	1160	1
BROWN THOMAS M	CW2	RW-2152429	0358	1
BROWN THOMAS P	LTC	0-0267634	0362	3
BROWN THURSTON O	MAJ	0-0192372	1162	3
BROWN VERNER D	COL	0-0351995	0267	3
BROWN VERNON M	LTC	0-0401792	0161	1
BROWN VERNON P	MAJ	0-0486077	0356	1
BROWN VERNON S	LTC	0-0256832	1064	3
BROWN VICTOR C	2LT	0-2035520	1044	2
BROWN VIRGIL A	MAJ	0-0324754	1267	3
BROWN VIVIAN C	MAJ	0-1051887	0157	1
BROWN WALKER T	MAJ	0-0372320	0867	3
BROWN WALTER A	LTC	0-1543277	0268	1
BROWN WALTER C	COL	0-0250589	0567	3
BROWN WALTER E	MAJ	0-1541762	0557	1
BROWN WALTER H	MAJ	0-0349612	0868	3
BROWN WALTER J	MAJ	0-1636453	0956	1
BROWN WALTER L	LTC	0-0378511	0967	3
BROWN WALTER T JR	CPT	0-2036628	0859	1
BROWN WARREN P	LTC	0-0299745	1051	2
BROWN WASHINGTON	LTC	0-0354220	0467	3
BROWN WENDELL W	LTC	0-0268533	0264	3
BROWN WILBUR A	CPT	0-1183029	0861	1
BROWN WILEY W JR	CPT	0-1578213	0966	2
BROWN WILFRED S	CPT	0-0356045	0467	1
BROWN WILLARD H	MAJ	0-1170296	0761	1
BROWN WILLARD H JR	2LT	0-4004740	1056	2
BROWN WILLARD J	MAJ	0-0121139	0-52	3
BROWN WILLIAM A	COL	0-0124053	0355	3
BROWN WILLIAM A	LTC	0-1797428	1065	2
BROWN WILLIAM C	2LT	0-1799936	0754	2
BROWN WILLIAM E	MAJ	0-0164427	0346	1
BROWN WILLIAM E	MAJ	0-1281088	0354	2
BROWN WILLIAM F	LTC	0-1060023	0363	1
BROWN WILLIAM G	MAJ	0-1166918	0258	1
BROWN WILLIAM H	MAJ	0-0196249	1042	2
BROWN WILLIAM H	LTC	0-0199550	1160	3
BROWN WILLIAM H	CPT	0-1050180	0467	1
BROWN WILLIAM H	1LT	0-2005667	1045	2
BROWN WILLIAM H	MAJ	0-2206113	0363	2
BROWN WILLIAM H	CW3	W-2142120	0664	1
BROWN WILLIAM H	CW3	W-2209648	1067	1
BROWN WILLIAM J	COL	0-0253838	0265	3
BROWN WILLIAM J	MAJ	0-1637496	0163	1
BROWN WILLIAM L	W01	W-2135097	0756	1
BROWN WILLIAM L	CW2	W-2206961	0661	1
BROWN WILLIAM M	LTC	0-1288000	0856	1
BROWN WILLIAM N	LTC	0-0290332	0465	1
BROWN WILLIAM S	LTC	0-1583990	0161	1
BROWN WILLIAM T	COL	0-0291245	0555	1
BROWN WILLIAM V	CW3	W-2123074	1167	2
BROWN WINSTON W	CW2	W-2143700	0657	1
BROWN WOODROW W	MAJ	0-1180132	0664	1
BROWNBACK RUSSELL J	CPT	0-0146735	1053	3
BROWNCHWEIG SIDNEY B	MAJ	0-1634566	1154	2
BROWNE ARTHUR S	MAJ	0-0126232	0156	3
BROWNE CARTER E	MAJ	0-1341504	0266	1
BROWNE GEORGE W	MAJ	0-0162506	0359	1
BROWNE HAROLD L	1LT	0-0498522	1045	2
BROWNE JOHN E	1LT	0-1703808	0645	2
BROWNE JOSEPH S	CPT	0-1917690	0162	1
BROWNE NORMAN E	LTC	0-1297670	0561	1
BROWNE RANDOLPH M	LTC	0-0301156	0661	1
BROWNE RICHARD E	1LT	0-1291943	0950	2
BROWNE RICHARD H	CPT	0-0184583	0154	3
BROWNE ROBERT W	LTC	0-1547552	1067	1
BROWNE THOMAS P	MAJ	0-0134379	0648	3
BROWNE THOMAS W	1LT	0-1035678	0644	2
BROWNE WILFRED R	MAJ	0-0188726	0252	3
BROWNE WILLIAM E	1LT	0-1104530	0645	2
BROWNE WILLIAM F	1LT	0-1634567	0944	2

ARMY OF THE UNITED STATES RETIRED LIST

NAME	GRADE	SVC NO	DATE RET MO YR	RET CODE
BROWNE WILLIAM G	LTC	0-0132029	0648	3
BROWNE WILLIAM H	COL	0-0253877	0247	2
BROWNELL ALBERT W	2LT	0-1325198	0745	2
BROWNELL EDWARD F	LTC	0-0217598	0460	3
BROWNELL GEORGE R	LTC	0-0215323	0160	3
BROWNELL GEORGE T	LTC	0-0269274	0167	3
BROWNELL HAROLD C	COL	0-0195219	0660	3
BROWNELL PAUL G	MAJ	0-0359107	0545	2
BROWNELL RALPH E	CW2	W-2214903	1167	1
BROWNELL VINCENT E	LTC	0-1103081	0865	1
BROWNELLER KENNETH E	LTC	0-1294426	1160	1
BROWNEWELL THELMA L	1LT	N-0728703	0447	1
BROWNFIELD A O JR	CPT	0-0462444	0247	2
BROWNFIELD BAYNE S	LTC	0-1058202	0167	1
BROWNFIELD SOPHRON	2LT	N-0729968	1045	1
BROWNING ANTHONY	CPT	0-0209344	0146	2
BROWNING CECIL O	1LT	0-0352093	0644	2
BROWNING CLARENCE E	1LT	0-1305005	0756	2
BROWNING CLIFFORD F	LTC	0-0342456	0251	2
BROWNING CLIFTON M	CPT	0-0385158	0749	1
BROWNING FLOYD C	MAJ	0-1297671	0367	1
BROWNING FLOYD W	COL	0-0230483	0553	2
BROWNING FRANK M	COL	0-0150008	1057	3
BROWNING HERBERT H	MAJ	0-0972800	1057	1
BROWNING HOMER F	LTC	0-0279252	1066	3
BROWNING JAMES L	CPT	0-0468014	0943	2
BROWNING JAMES L	LTC	0-1001960	0668	3
BROWNING JOHN J	CPT	0-1305538	0847	2
BROWNING JOHN R	COL	0-0235533	1165	3
BROWNING JOHN W	MAJ	0-1635635	0561	1
BROWNING LORA R	MAJ	N-0769666	1065	2
BROWNING LUTHER R	MAJ	0-0972508	1163	1
BROWNING MARTIN	LTC	0-1284819	0757	1
BROWNING ROBERT C	COL	0-0902476	0568	1
BROWNING ROLAND S	CPT	0-0473027	1045	2
BROWNING SAMUEL S	MAJ	0-1171469	0661	1
BROWNING WILLIAM L	COL	0-0233937	0965	3
BROWNING WILLIAM L	CPT	0-1011653	0268	3
BROWNLEE HENRY	1LT	0-1179314	1044	2
BROWNLEE JOHN H	1LT	0-0374136	0943	2
BROWNLEE JOHN H	MAJ	0-1104531	1055	1
BROWNLEE RICHARD H	1LT	0-1310566	0447	2
BROWNLEE WILLIAM J	LTC	0-1180133	0862	1
BROWNLOW JAMES C	LTC	0-1645042	0365	2
BROWNRIDGE GEORGE W	LTC	0-0309915	0865	3
BROWNRIDGE WILLIAM T	LTC	0-0291710	1068	3
BROWNSCOMBE TWILA B	CPT	N-0761278	0846	1
BROWNTON WESLEY F	LTC	0-0333869	0868	3
BROWNYER BURT W	MAJ	0-1637104	0466	1
BROXTON FREDERICK	CW4	W-2146051	1068	1
BROXTON GEORGE F	CW2	W-2149662	0559	1
BROYLES DUDLEY H	LTC	0-1329444	0768	1
BROYLES EDWARD S	MAJ	0-0969433	0162	2
BROYLES GILMER P	MAJ	0-1170668	0660	1
BROYLES HENRY F	MAJ	0-0215559	0862	3
BROYLES JAMES N	1LT	0-1298656	0146	2
BROYLES LENA L	1LT	N-0733476	0745	1
BRU VIVIAN B	LTC	0-1548366	1066	1
BRUAW EUGENE H	1LT	0-1304496	0257	1
BRUBAKER ERNEST E	LTC	0-0197086	0363	3
BRUBAKER JOSEPH M	CPT	0-0508307	0952	1
BRUBAKER RALPH W	LTC	0-1575796	1061	1
BRUCCOLERI BART	MAJ	0-0969688	0964	1
BRUCE ALBERT W	LTC	0-0217878	0863	3
BRUCE ALFRED D	MAJ	0-2023550	0657	1
BRUCE BYRON S	COL	0-0102443	0648	3
BRUCE CAROLINE H	LTC	N-0702482	0847	2
BRUCE CHARLES F	LTC	0-0889129	0562	1
BRUCE CLARENCE W	MAJ	0-0376550	0560	1
BRUCE DONALD A	MAJ	0-0346083	1266	3
BRUCE EVERETT C	MAJ	0-0218909	0263	3
BRUCE HAROLD D	LTC	0-1576973	0157	1
BRUCE HARRY G	LTC	0-0321187	1068	3
BRUCE HENRY A	COL	0-0254856	0661	3
BRUCE JOHN E	LTC	0-0252623	0965	3

NAME	GRADE	SVC NO	DATE RET MO YR	RET CODE
BRUCE JOHN M	MAJ	0-0969477	0163	1
BRUCE JOSEPH F	MAJ	0-2036629	0762	1
BRUCE MARGARET E	2LT	N-0784356	1044	1
BRUCE PETER P	CPT	0-0338753	0445	2
BRUCE RALPH	WO1	W-2127561	0949	1
BRUCE RICHARD J	MAJ	0-0223027	1046	1
BRUCE ROBERT A	CW2	W-3100262	0764	1
BRUCE ROBERT H	CPT	0-1393894	1061	2
BRUCE ROBERT L	MAJ	0-0959281	0862	1
BRUCE ROBERT S	LTC	0-1293899	0364	1
BRUCE THOMAS E	MAJ	0-1031297	0657	1
BRUCE THOMAS K	MAJ	0-1999850	1061	1
BRUCE THOMAS M JR	1LT	0-1322517	0545	2
BRUCE WESLEY D JR	MAJ	0-2204152	1065	2
BRUCE WILBUR C	MAJ	0-1020244	0265	1
BRUCE WILLIAM J	LTC	0-1053509	0165	1
BRUCE WILLIAM R	1LT	0-1919227	0367	2
BRUCK CARL R	MAJ	0-0447892	0254	2
BRUCKER HERBERT	MAJ	0-2045272	1160	1
BRUCKNER MAX D	LTC	0-1115199	0763	1
BRUDER MILDRED H	1LT	N-0703976	0246	1
BRUDERER PAUL J	MAJ	0-0482277	0147	2
BRUDNOY HARRY G	COL	0-0326266	0868	3
BRUE LEIF J	LTC	0-0397172	0457	1
BRUE LEO K	MAJ	0-1310803	0259	1
BRUEDIGAM MARVIN J	LTC	0-0287034	0762	1
BRUEGGEMEIER CARL F	LTC	0-0487907	1067	3
BRUEHL GEORGE J	1LT	0-1317754	1046	2
BRUEHL WILLIAM D	MAJ	0-0253534	0566	3
BRUER JOE C	MAJ	0-1936361	0966	1
BRUETT WILLIAM F	LTC	0-0162985	0249	3
BRUFF THOMAS B	MAJ	0-2020388	0762	1
BRUFFY LAWRENCE E JR	2LT	0-1185265	0545	2
BRUGGEMAN ELMER H	CPT	0-0471644	0663	1
BRUGGER ERNEST J	COL	0-0277103	1154	1
BRUGGERE WILLIAM H	MAJ	0-0130154	0944	2
BRUGH STANLEY G	LTC	0-1169876	0463	1
BRUHN ARTHUR K	CW2	W-2142949	0157	1
BRUHN HERMAN L	LTC	0-1100464	0958	2
BRUHY JAMES R	CPT	0-0966525	1161	1
BRULLE WILLIAM M	LTC	0-0299673	0560	1
BRUMAGIM ROBERT S	LTC	0-0295906	0168	3
BRUMBACK HENRY M	1LT	0-0390317	0742	2
BRUMBAUGH ALOYSIUS M	M G	0-0225777	1161	3
BRUMBAUGH DAVID M	MAJ	0-1301938	1060	1
BRUMBAUGH ETHEL M	1LT	N-0761651	0746	1
BRUMBAUGH HARRY C	COL	0-0165468	0648	3
BRUMBAUGH JOHN C	LTC	0-0211544	0847	1
BRUMBERGER ALFRED	LTC	0-0136765	0648	3
BRUMBY PAUL B	MAJ	0-0543568	0546	2
BRUMER RUSSELL L	MAJ	0-2018831	0762	1
BRUMET CHESTER C	CPT	0-2020880	0859	1
BRUMFIELD ARTHUR W	1LT	0-0482422	0466	1
BRUMFIELD DAVID W	CW2	W-2145002	0359	1
BRUMFIELD MELBOURNE	1LT	0-1287299	0946	2
BRUMHALL JOHN H	MAJ	0-0167988	0149	3
BRUML LEONARD F	CPT	0-0339176	0441	2
BRUMLEY PAUL E	MAJ	0-1046027	0163	1
BRUMMITT GEORGE P	CW3	W-2203426	0666	1
BRUNACCI ALFRED W	CPT	0-0262216	0243	2
BRUNACCI GUY J	LTC	0-1114401	0367	1
BRUNDAGE ALBERT E	COL	0-0146674	0-52	3
BRUNDAGE ARTHUR E	CPT	0-0250322	0648	3
BRUNDAGE FRANK C	LTC	0-2048232	0457	1
BRUNDAGE LYLE D	LTC	0-0253026	0763	3
BRUNDICK LEROY	COL	0-0267174	1057	3
BRUNDICK WILLIAM T	COL	0-0245940	0450	3
BRUNEAU PATRICIA	2LT	N-0784454	0445	1
BRUNELLE LOUIS W	1LT	0-1310056	0253	2
BRUNER CHARLES A	MAJ	0-0501255	1048	1
BRUNER DORSEY W	LTC	0-0357658	0167	3
BRUNER DOYLE B	MAJ	0-0974541	0563	1
BRUNER GEORGE D	COL	0-0379441	0761	1
BRUNER GEORGE E	MAJ	0-1821819	0361	1
BRUNER HUGH H SR	LTC	0-0356814	1265	3

NAME	GRADE	SVC NO	DATE RET MO YR	RET CODE
BRUNER JULIAN M	LTC	0-0255346	0161	3
BRUNER ROBERT C	MAJ	0-1183668	0460	2
BRUNET HENRI B	LTC	0-0285479	1068	3
BRUNET LAWRENCE J	CPT	0-1001739	0357	1
BRUNET PAUL G	CPT	0-0423826	1145	2
BRUNETTE VIOLET L	1LT	N-0786937	1047	1
BRUNETTI VERA W	1LT	N-0760603	1145	1
BRUNEY RAYMOND R	LTC	0-1001961	1061	2
BRUNGER ERNEST G	COL	0-0275925	0860	3
BRUNHAVER GEORGE D	LTC	0-1845883	1064	1
BRUNI UBALD P	CW3	W-2151741	0863	1
BRUNICK MARVIN T	LTC	0-2035574	0161	1
BRUNJES MARTIN JR	CPT	0-1166022	0863	1
BRUNK EUGENE L	LTC	0-0943414	0666	1
BRUNKE HERMAN	LTC	0-0288280	1262	1
BRUNKOW ALMON F	1LT	0-2010695	0847	2
BRUNKOW PAUL H	MAJ	0-1103536	0665	1
BRUNNER FRANK E	LTC	0-0504465	0747	2
BRUNNER JOSEPH A	LTC	0-0292275	1061	1
BRUNNER MICHAEL C	COL	0-0217000	1059	3
BRUNNER ROBERT L	MAJ	0-0266290	0157	3
BRUNNER ROBERT L	1LT	0-0545538	0862	2
BRUNO ANTHONY J	LTC	0-0422217	1057	2
BRUNO DAVID C	LTC	0-1289393	1263	1
BRUNO HENRY A	MAJ	0-1302922	0762	1
BRUNO JAMES R	1LT	0-1324455	0446	2
BRUNO JOSEPH J	COL	0-0359146	0467	3
BRUNO PAUL M	LTC	0-1292293	0661	1
BRUNO RALPH	1LT	0-1052278	0245	2
BRUNO ROBERT G	LTC	0-0288113	0465	3
BRUNO RUDOLPH	MAJ	0-0373129	0157	1
BRUNOW MARCEL F J	COL	0-0163831	1153	1
BRUNS HENRY	CPT	0-1172779	0761	1
BRUNSON GAIL E	CW2	W-2101483	0947	1
BRUNSON GEORGE W JR	MAJ	0-0372691	1146	2
BRUNSON HAROLD F	CW3	W-2152448	1163	1
BRUNSON WADE W JR	CPT	0-0344119	0646	2
BRUNSON WILLIAM L	1LT	0-0460081	1144	2
BRUNSTEIN EDWARD J	CW4	W-2146210	0868	1
BRUNSVOLD KENNEY T	COL	0-0211367	1054	1
BRUNSVOLD RICHARD T	CPT	0-1951580	0157	1
BRUNSWICK LEO J	LTC	0-1585219	0868	3
BRUNT ROBERT C	CW2	W-2205149	0561	1
BRUNTON JAMES	1LT	0-1179739	1145	2
BRUNTON LIONEL J	COL	0-0233982	1055	3
BRUSCHWEIN HAROLD F	CPT	0-0374513	1044	2
BRUSH ALFRED P	CW3	W-2141836	0262	1
BRUSH EDWARD N	LTC	0-0223253	0864	3
BRUSH GEORGE M	CPT	0-0322940	1061	1
BRUSH HERBERT S JR	1LT	0-0383766	0245	2
BRUSH OLIVER G	CPT	0-0196072	0554	3
BRUSH ROBERT J	CPT	0-1593478	0861	2
BRUSH WILLIAM F	CW3	W-2148840	0661	1
BRUSH WILLIAM H	LTC	0-2019280	0968	1
BRUSKI EUGENE A	MAJ	0-1185329	0764	1
BRUSSELL ALBERT S	B G	0-0307587	0668	3
BRUSSELL SOLOMON	LTC	0-1036455	0268	3
BRUSSOW KARL W	CW3	W-2142817	0261	1
BRUSTAD MARVIN O	CPT	0-0254816	0846	2
BRUSTKERN VERN J	LTC	0-0332557	1059	3
BRUSTMAN WILLIAM F	LTC	0-1323532	0364	1
BRUTON CARROL T	COL	0-0440653	0747	2
BRUTON JOHN B	1LT	0-0418931	0551	2
BRUTON THOMAS W	COL	0-0213891	1062	3
BRUTON WALTER S	1LT	0-2055419	0454	2
BRYAN ALBERT L	LTC	0-0384120	1166	3
BRYAN ARTHUR H	MAJ	0-0211377	0345	2
BRYAN CLARENCE P	MAJ	0-0275293	0350	2
BRYAN CORVAN S	LTC	0-0250207	0556	1
BRYAN DAVID C JR	1LT	0-0460082	0845	2
BRYAN DELBERT L	MAJ	0-0708642	0663	1
BRYAN EDWARD C	CPT	0-0486552	0646	2
BRYAN EDWIN H JR	LTC	0-0235071	0758	3
BRYAN EUGENE R	CW3	W-2152799	0463	1
BRYAN FLOYD R	COL	0-0168137	1060	3

NAME	GRADE	SVC NO	DATE RET MO YR	RET CODE
BRYAN FRANK D	LTC	0-1584110	0767	1
BRYAN GORDON H	1LT	0-1310397	0646	2
BRYAN H ROSS	LTC	0-0308566	0961	1
BRYAN HARRISON R	LTC	0-0189588	0256	3
BRYAN JAMES W	CPT	0-2212036	0960	1
BRYAN JOHN C	MAJ	0-0499627	0157	1
BRYAN JOHN W	LTC	0-0308745	1163	3
BRYAN JOHN W	MAJ	0-1297155	0361	1
BRYAN JOSEPH D	LTC	0-0100866	0758	3
BRYAN JULIUS C	LTC	0-0279971	1151	2
BRYAN JUNIOR L	CW2	W-2152599	0161	1
BRYAN LESTER W	COL	0-0324378	0855	3
BRYAN LUCRETIA M	CPT	N-0704009	0761	1
BRYAN PINK E	CPT	0-0490415	1047	1
BRYAN ROBERT C	2LT	0-1103083	0745	2
BRYAN ROBERT E	MAJ	0-0386402	0653	1
BRYAN ROBERT L JR	CPT	0-1012311	1047	2
BRYAN WILBUR F	COL	0-0279055	0665	3
BRYAN WILLIE E	LTC	0-0368240	0661	1
BRYANT ALFRED A	COL	0-0164989	1061	3
BRYANT ANDREW T	1LT	0-0890317	1047	1
BRYANT BARNARD M	CW3	W-2144157	0363	1
BRYANT CARROLL M	2LT	0-1018505	1044	2
BRYANT CHARLES G	CPT	0-1685255	0945	2
BRYANT CHARLES J	LTC	0-0282585	1067	3
BRYANT CLARENCE M	LTC	0-1822530	0261	1
BRYANT EARL R	LTC	0-0262508	0360	3
BRYANT EDGAR M	CW2	W-2142094	0355	1
BRYANT ELVIN J	MAJ	0-1543101	0463	1
BRYANT GEORGE C	LTC	0-1293540	0461	1
BRYANT GEORGE W	MAJ	0-1951678	0962	1
BRYANT GORDON L	MAJ	0-0259360	0267	3
BRYANT GUY C	CW4	W-2115467	1262	1
BRYANT HERBERT E	MAJ	0-0441951	0157	1
BRYANT HERBERT L	LTC	0-1324750	0263	1
BRYANT JAMES A	COL	0-0337654	1062	3
BRYANT JAMES B	CW2	W-3400059	1168	1
BRYANT JAMES R	LTC	0-1558123	0568	1
BRYANT JOAN N	1LT	N-0789820	0946	1
BRYANT JOHN L	MAJ	0-0966561	0862	1
BRYANT JOHN L JR	LTC	0-0983700	0868	1
BRYANT JOHN M	MAJ	0-0486247	1147	1
BRYANT KENNETH A	LTC	0-0367229	1046	2
BRYANT LEON S	MAJ	0-0152811	0349	3
BRYANT LESLIE L	COL	0-0348218	0954	2
BRYANT MALCOLM M	MAJ	0-0243191	0759	1
BRYANT MARION G	1LT	0-1581564	0445	2
BRYANT MARK F	LTC	0-0307291	0264	3
BRYANT MAURICE F	CPT	0-1702353	0344	2
BRYANT NILES JR	COL	0-0144227	0653	3
BRYANT PHINEAS B	1LT	0-0212556	0863	3
BRYANT PINKEY A JR	CW3	W-2152062	0464	1
BRYANT RICHARD H	MAJ	0-0390491	0246	2
BRYANT ROGER O	CW3	W-2151854	0464	1
BRYANT RUSSELL A	MAJ	0-0258131	0666	3
BRYANT SAMUEL P	LTC	0-0347733	0860	1
BRYANT SIDNEY H	MAJ	0-1922523	0465	1
BRYANT THOMAS D	LTC	0-1109833	0457	2
BRYANT THOMAS F	1LT	0-1110964	0346	2
BRYANT THOMAS R	MAJ	0-1643066	0765	1
BRYANT VICTOR W	LTC	0-0277242	0167	3
BRYANT VIRGIL O	COL	0-1575800	0761	1
BRYANT WALTER T	MAJ	0-1305006	0354	2
BRYANT WELCH C	LTC	0-1031869	1161	1
BRYANT WILLARD A	MAJ	0-0501508	0953	1
BRYANT WILLIAM C	MAJ	0-0296050	0746	2
BRYANT WILLIAM C	CPT	0-0361786	0945	2
BRYANT WILLIAM C	CW3	W-2211084	0666	1
BRYANT WILLIAM J SR	CW3	W-2152032	0263	1
BRYANT WOODROW W	LTC	0-0316280	1053	2
BRYCE CHARLES H	MAJ	0-1917739	0864	1
BRYCE HAROLD E	CW4	W-2003367	1163	3
BRYCE HUGH M	MAJ	0-1896044	0861	1
BRYCE JAMES	1LT	0-1298990	0545	2
BRYDAHL IRVING L	1LT	0-1649680	0346	2

NAME	GRADE	SVC NO	DATE RET MO YR	RET CODE
BRYDEN JOHN E	MAJ	0-0501101	0768	3
BRYER BENJAMIN F	LTC	0-0356581	0646	2
BRYGIDYR JULIAN	CPT	0-1080179	0465	1
BRYHN CORNELL B	LTC	0-1287831	0261	1
BRYLA ADAM E	1LT	0-1317484	0747	2
BRYLA JOHN A	CPT	0-1544990	0358	1
BRYLA JOSEPH J	MAJ	0-1691384	0846	2
BRYLES MURPHY C	CW4	W-2132757	0761	1
BRYMER THOMAS H	CPT	0-1104798	1060	1
BRYNER LEON K	LTC	0-0368562	0766	3
BRYNIARSKI ALBERT J	CW2	W-2142818	1054	1
BRYSON JESSE D	CW4	W-2115899	0659	1
BRYSON JOHN V	CPT	0-0301974	0446	2
BRYSON LEO A	MAJ	0-0210274	0454	3
BRYSON RICHARD C	LTC	0-0399628	1060	2
BRYSON WILLIAM F	2LT	0-1018541	0545	2
BRYSON WILLIAM J JR	LTC	0-0217409	0763	1
BRZEZINSKI STANLEY B	1LT	0-0491640	0157	1
BRZOSKA ARTHUR J	LTC	0-0842185	0768	1
BSTANDIG PAUL J	LTC	0-2049487	1262	1
BUBA RAYMOND W	CW2	W-2142370	0357	1
BUBB RICHARD F	MAJ	0-1169442	0361	2
BUBERNAK SAMUEL	CW3	W-3150696	0868	1
BUBLITZ KATHERINE	CPT	N-0751288	0646	1
BUBOLZ DANFORD J	1LT	0-1013249	0146	2
BUCALDY SIMON P	2LT	0-1896663	1055	1
BUCCIARELLI JOSEPH	CW3	W-2147150	0865	1
BUCCIARELLI TONY	1LT	0-0483687	0444	1
BUCEK CHESTER A	1LT	0-1013635	C645	2
BUCEK ROY E	1LT	0-0465333	1145	2
BUCHAN HENRY M	MAJ	0-1167760	0861	1
BUCHAN WILLIAM M	1LT	0-1104066	1144	2
BUCHANAN ALFRED K	COL	0-0303753	0263	1
BUCHANAN BILLY C	MAJ	0-1685685	0165	1
BUCHANAN CHARLES W	CPT	0-0431094	0246	2
BUCHANAN DURANT T	CPT	0-1580695	0760	1
BUCHANAN ELIC L	CW2	W-2207535	1262	2
BUCHANAN ELMER R	MAJ	0-2035070	1065	1
BUCHANAN FELIX G	LTC	0-2043027	1266	1
BUCHANAN FRANCIS J	CPT	0-1295505	0647	2
BUCHANAN FRANK B JR	COL	0-1584111	1264	1
BUCHANAN FRANK C	CW2	W-2217097	0968	1
BUCHANAN FRANKLIN B	MAJ	0-0505877	0351	2
BUCHANAN GENE W	MAJ	0-0453265	0361	1
BUCHANAN GEORGE W	LTC	0-0205422	0762	3
BUCHANAN GRAHAM C	COL	0-0216735	1262	3
BUCHANAN HALL	MAJ	0-0265781	0656	3
BUCHANAN HENRY D	LTC	0-0255537	0648	3
BUCHANAN HERBERT S	MAJ	0-1647240	0858	1
BUCHANAN HERBERT T	COL	0-0923158	0266	3
BUCHANAN HEYDON W	COL	0-0321472	0952	2
BUCHANAN JACK W	2LT	0-2049498	1044	2
BUCHANAN JAMES A JR	MAJ	0-0174404	1056	3
BUCHANAN JAMES B	COL	0-0146715	0254	2
BUCHANAN JESSE F	LTC	0-0236373	0564	3
BUCHANAN JOHN C	LTC	0-1018728	0265	1
BUCHANAN LEIL O	LTC	0-0243549	0566	3
BUCHANAN LESLIE	LTC	0-0326185	0647	2
BUCHANAN PAUL W	CPT	0-1324104	1047	2
BUCHANAN ROBERT C	LTC	0-2200532	1167	1
BUCHANAN ROBERT W	MAJ	0-0551565	0366	1
BUCHANAN ROY	MAJ	0-1591025	0957	1
BUCHANAN SAMMY W	2LT	0-1179740	0344	2
BUCHANAN SPENCER J	B G	0-0231626	0463	3
BUCHANAN TERRENCE O	LTC	0-1342156	0968	1
BUCHANAN VIVA G	MAJ	N-0775743	1163	1
BUCHANAN W G JR	MAJ	0-0327905	0946	2
BUCHBINDER MURRAY W	COL	0-0290868	0665	3
BUCHEN BAYARD K	2LT	0-1797947	0145	2
BUCHER LEE	MAJ	0-0945731	0567	3
BUCHER WALTER J	CPT	0-0240020	0545	2
BUCHHOLZ JAMES W	MAJ	0-1922595	0963	1
BUCHHOLZ MILTON E	MAJ	0-1556983	0459	2
BUCHHOLZ OSCAR T	LTC	0-1283904	0166	1
BUCHHOLZ RICHARD H	MAJ	0-1824570	0861	1
BUCHHOLZ RICHARD S	LTC	0-1644499	0859	1
BUCHHOLZ WILLIAM F	LTC	0-0236326	0465	3
BUCHHOLZ WILLIAM F	1LT	0-1285892	0845	2
BUCHLER LLOYD G	COL	0-0247169	0167	3
BUCHMAN ROBERT A	MAJ	0-1019784	0765	1
BUCHNER RICHARD E	1LT	0-0246189	1043	2
BUCHNER RICHARD J	1LT	0-0337364	0645	2
BUCHSBAUM IRWIN	CPT	0-0330733	0444	2
BUCHSBAUM JOHN H	LTC	0-0583087	1063	2
BUCK BURTON B	CW2	W-2214592	0767	1
BUCK CAMELLUS W	MAJ	0-0988908	0865	1
BUCK CHARLES	1LT	0-1914093	0530	1
BUCK DONALD G	2LT	0-1052696	0944	2
BUCK EARLE H JR	MAJ	0-1326453	0765	1
BUCK EDWARD M	CW3	W-2149183	1264	1
BUCK FAY B	CW2	W-2214557	0568	1
BUCK FREDERIC C	LTC	0-1534224	0161	1
BUCK FREDERICK	MAJ	0-2009553	0156	1
BUCK GEORGE A	LTC	0-0461237	1263	1
BUCK GEORGE L JR	LTC	0-0368144	1147	2
BUCK HARPER P	LTC	0-0905890	1165	3
BUCK HENRY G	COL	0-0324089	0453	1
BUCK HIRAM H JR	LTC	0-1533506	0864	1
BUCK HOWARD F	LTC	0-0296492	0567	3
BUCK HOWARD H	CW2	W-2106482	0353	1
BUCK JAMES C	MAJ	0-1298815	1158	2
BUCK JAMES D	LTC	0-1175657	0662	1
BUCK JAMES H	LTC	0-1646274	0562	1
BUCK JOHN D	COL	0-0179291	0648	3
BUCK JOHN S	LTC	0-0253930	0857	3
BUCK KEITH D	MAJ	0-0461873	0662	1
BUCK MARSHALL G	COL	0-0309188	0357	3
BUCK MICHAEL M	CPT	0-1315905	0747	2
BUCK ORLAND D	LTC	0-0305000	1160	1
BUCK PEER A	LTC	0-2055826	1160	1
BUCK SAMUEL L	LTC	0-0443899	0154	1
BUCK SHELBURNE	LTC	0-0405799	0465	3
BUCK THOMAS E	LTC	0-1692931	1263	1
BUCK WERMER	CPT	0-1314876	0847	2
BUCK WILLIAM G	1LT	0-5505313	0662	2
BUCKALEW JAY R	CW3	W-2147885	0662	1
BUCKBEE CLIFFORD R	LTC	0-0324772	1262	1
BUCKBEE MILTON R	CW4	W-2144940	0567	1
BUCKHALT H J	CW2	W-3150174	0962	2
BUCKHAULTS JULIUS E	CW3	W-2108570	0960	1
BUCKHOLT BENNETT B	CW4	W-2144252	0366	1
BUCKHOLTS WALTER H	COL	0-0264271	1163	3
BUCKHOLTZ IRA E	LTC	0-0319193	0666	3
BUCKHOUT EGBERT C	MAJ	0-0793056	0867	1
BUCKI WALTER O	COL	0-1175395	0968	3
BUCKINGHAM BURDETTE	COL	0-0291529	0967	3
BUCKINGHAM CHARLES H	LTC	0-0347243	0466	3
BUCKINGHAM CHARLES W	MAJ	0-0195301	0155	3
BUCKINGHAM EDWARD B	LTC	0-0484748	0363	1
BUCKIUS WILLIAM H	LTC	0-1330150	1266	1
BUCKLAND CHARLES D	COL	0-0487981	0554	1
BUCKLAND FLOYD H	LTC	0-0298179	0765	3
BUCKLAND FREDERICK	1LT	0-0532268	0247	2
BUCKLAND JAMES A	MAJ	0-2040861	0261	1
BUCKLER GEORGE F	CPT	0-1594071	0447	2
BUCKLER JOE T	CW4	W-2148017	1267	1
BUCKLES HARRY A	2LT	0-1012490	1144	2
BUCKLES LOUIS M	CPT	0-1019462	1056	1
BUCKLES PAUL K	LTC	0-0231504	0856	3
BUCKLES ROSCOE C	COL	0-0390668	0860	1
BUCKLEY ANTHONY	CW2	W-2150924	0662	1
BUCKLEY ARNOLD F	LTC	0-1300447	0262	1
BUCKLEY ARTHUR E	LTC	0-0377843	0863	1
BUCKLEY CHARLES A	MAJ	0-0502787	0954	1
BUCKLEY CHARLES C	COL	0-0319496	0267	3
BUCKLEY CHARLES H	MAJ	0-1169879	0960	1
BUCKLEY EARL E	CPT	0-0411421	0949	2
BUCKLEY EDWARD M	1LT	0-1062473	0462	2
BUCKLEY FRANCIS X	LTC	0-1101758	1062	2
BUCKLEY FREEMAN C	LTC	0-0250966	0663	3
BUCKLEY GERALD T	LTC	0-2012566	1167	1
BUCKLEY HELEN F	CPT	N-0722698	0446	1
BUCKLEY HOWARD	CW3	W-2150601	0163	1
BUCKLEY JACK C	CPT	0-2025480	0258	1
BUCKLEY JACK E	LTC	0-0170302	0658	3
BUCKLEY JOHN L	LTC	0-1059383	0366	1
BUCKLEY JONATHAN F	LTC	0-1579441	0761	1
BUCKLEY LOUIS E	MAJ	0-0111422	0746	2
BUCKLEY PATRICK H	COL	0-0507317	0656	2
BUCKLEY ROBERT B	CPT	0-1011411	1045	2
BUCKLEY VERLIN J	CW3	W-2147939	0862	1
BUCKLEY WALTER L	LTC	0-0425616	0866	1
BUCKLEY WILLIAM F	MAJ	0-2037621	1062	1
BUCKLEY WILLIAM H	COL	0-1289204	0566	1
BUCKLIN JOHN W	MAJ	0-0475356	0159	2
BUCKMAN ALEX	MAJ	0-0450249	0758	1
BUCKMAN MORRIS F	1LT	0-0512848	1045	2
BUCKNELL ROMEO H JR	MAJ	0-1330151	0663	1
BUCKNER ARLEY V	CPT	0-0507869	0350	2
BUCKNER CHARLES G	CPT	0-0197938	0557	3
BUCKNER FREDERICK	1LT	0-1314435	0845	2
BUCKNER HERBERT G	CW4	W-2005143	0868	1
BUCKNER JESSE J	CW2	W-2213076	0767	1
BUCKNER LESLIE M	MAJ	0-1693455	1045	2
BUCKNER LEWIS H	CW3	W-2114123	0461	1
BUCKNER LOUIS D JR	CW3	W-2145336	0665	1
BUCKNER LOUIS R	LTC	0-1285374	0165	1
BUCKNER ROBERT C	LTC	0-0255694	0363	3
BUCKNER WILLIAM B JR	LTC	0-2288860	0962	1
BUCKNER WILLIS L	MAJ	0-1293198	0555	1
BUCKO JOHN P	CPT	0-1110965	0762	1
BUCKOVINSKY ANDREW T	CPT	0-0890200	0651	2
BUCKSPAN HAROLD	LTC	0-1306970	1163	1
BUCKTHAL ALBERT E	CPT	0-1796414	0646	2
BUCKWALD RUDOLPH A	CPT	0-0306151	0345	2
BUCKWALTER CHARLES K	LTC	0-0415395	1157	1
BUCKWALTER FRANKLIN	LTC	0-1642354	0366	3
BUCKWALTER JOHN B	CW2	W-2114995	C746	1
BUCKWALTER ROY R	LTC	0-0826874	0568	1
BUCY LAWRENCE W	LTC	0-1642358	1155	1
BUCY ROBERT E	CW2	W-2148898	0859	1
BUCY WILLIAM F JR	1LT	0-0519356	0747	2
BUCZEK JOHN	LTC	0-1017060	0962	1
BUCZKOWSKI FELIX J	LTC	0-1948869	0264	1
BUCZKOWSKI HARRY E	CPT	0-0510289	0749	2
BUDAHN EDSEL R	COL	0-1166922	0866	1
BUDATZ EARL	LTC	0-1293900	0761	1
BUDD ARTHUR D	MAJ	0-1311351	0367	1
BUDD CECIL G	2LT	0-1181556	0844	2
BUDD CHARLES C	COL	0-0148957	0450	2
BUDD CHARLES W	CW3	W-2154663	1262	1
BUDD RAYMOND E	2LT	0-1594738	0758	3
BUDDENHAGEN C G JR	MAJ	0-1637118	0460	1
BUDDIN CECIL E	CPT	0-1013653	1145	2
BUDERER GEORGE L JR	MAJ	0-0294729	1147	1
BUDET-FERRER ANTONIO	MAJ	0-0946612	1267	1
BUDGE BRUCE C	LTC	0-0312678	1146	2
BUDLONG THOMAS F	MAJ	0-1650395	0161	1
BUDNER SIMON	LTC	0-0290541	1046	2
BUDNY STANLEY J	CW2	W-2139464	0656	1
BUDNY WALLACE C	2LT	0-1110967	0445	2
BUDWAY EMIL	CW3	W-2152925	1162	1
BUDZ LOUIS R	CPT	0-2000125	0947	2
BUDZIK WALTER M	MAJ	0-0470442	0846	2
BUECHE CLEMENT A	1LT	0-1596597	1045	2
BUECHE FRANK	LTC	0-0259401	0867	3
BUECHLER ARTHUR J	LTC	0-1101349	0566	1
BUECHLER JOHN H JR	LTC	0-0455873	0866	1
BUECHNER FREDERICK	LTC	0-0232425	1045	2
BUEHL LOUIS H JR	LTC	0-0242745	0960	3
BUEHLER CARL W	MAJ	0-0204947	0156	3
BUEHRER KENNETH E	MAJ	0-1922978	0667	1
BUEHRER ROLLAND F	CPT	0-1285704	0246	2
BUELL CHARLOTTE	1LT	N-0726863	1145	1
BUELL FRANCES G	MAJ	L-0402015	0164	3
BUELL RAYMON C	COL	0-0490768	0547	2
BUELL VERNON C	MAJ	0-1289687	1060	1
BUENAFE EMMANUEL V	1LT	0-1896846	0266	1
BUENING BERNARD R	LTC	0-0506236	0-53	1
BUENTELLO ANTONIO JR	CW3	W-2144858	0666	1
BUERGE MYRON W	MAJ	0-1105291	0867	3
BUERGER OTTO M	MAJ	0-0199441	1058	3
BUERKE JAMES L	WO1	W-2112227	0553	1
BUERKI WILLIAM C	MAJ	0-0508649	0764	1
BUERKLE JOHN G	COL	0-0242058	0852	3
BUESING JUSTUS D	COL	0-1575803	0868	1
BUETTELL ERNEST O	LTC	0-0152986	0651	3
BUETTNER HENRY F	COL	0-0221734	0347	2
BUEZO SALOMON	MAJ	0-0291236	0462	3
BUFANO JAMES T	LTC	0-2019982	0267	1
BUFFALANO FRANK A	LTC	0-1044770	1161	1
BUFFINGTON C P JR	MAJ	0-1542590	0460	1
BUFFINGTON CALE W	MAJ	0-0992921	0867	1
BUFFINGTON FRANCIS S	CPT	0-0368684	1044	2
BUFFINGTON RALPH M	LTC	0-0252076	0367	3
BUFFINGTON THOMAS T	LTC	0-1168587	0166	3
BUFFKIN JOHN F JR	LTC	0-1286781	0960	1
BUFFO MICHAEL H	LTC	0-0919857	1262	1
BUFFONE JAMES V	CW4	W-2122033	0959	1
BUFFUM JAMES T	LTC	0-0265130	0868	3
BUFFUM WILLIAM R	CW3	W-2152787	0963	1
BUFORD CECIL M	MAJ	0-0476385	0154	1
BUGAY LEE A	1LT	0-1059384	0945	2
BUGBEE JAMES T	COL	0-0251931	0566	3
BUGCOYNE MARVIN K	MAJ	0-4014419	0368	1
BUGEL JOHN JR	WO1	W-2123543	1060	1
BUGEL JOSEPH	LTC	0-1289866	1057	1
BUGENHAGEN HELENE T	MAJ	N-0763980	0968	1
BUHISAN ANGELITO T	CPT	0-0890485	0868	1
BUHL BERNICE M	2LT	N-0773812	1045	1
BUHL LEON E	1LT	0-1320821	1144	2
BUHLER ALLEN C	2LT	0-2017346	1145	2
BUHR LOUIS H	LTC	0-0329764	0868	3
BUHRMAN MAC B	2LT	0-0200945	0246	2
BUIE HERMAN F	2LT	0-1540668	0945	2
BUIE NEIL D	COL	0-0253515	1163	3
BUIE NEILL D	LTC	0-0325027	0361	1
BUIRGE RAYMOND E	CPT	0-0326278	0945	2
BUISCH ARTHUR F	CW2	W-2210732	0663	1
BUJAC JAMES N	LTC	0-0150553	1057	3
BUJNOWSKI ANTHONY	1LT	0-0169076	0859	1
BUKACEK FRANK J	LTC	0-0905754	0363	3
BUKANTZ SAMUEL C	CPT	0-0425807	0146	2
BUKEY NORMAN J	COL	0-0244159	0763	3
BUKOVEC HELEN A	2LT	N-0737595	0645	1
BUKOVITZ STEVE L	LTC	0-0423722	1060	1
BUKOWSKI BERNARD V	1LT	0-1032577	1146	2
BUKOWSKI PHILIP S	2LT	0-0235079	0254	3
BUKSA EDWARD M	MAJ	0-1688465	0463	1
BULAT JOHN	CW4	W-2108885	0959	1
BULAWAN JUSTIN A	CPT	0-2027258	1049	1
BULGER JAMES E	MAJ	0-1822233	0465	3
BULILAN BIENVENIDO	1LT	0-2031860	0766	2
BULL CHARLES B	MAJ	0-0212493	0345	2
BULL DONALD E	MAJ	0-1339043	0764	1
BULL FREDERICK	LTC	0-0272553	0767	3
BULL FREDERICK	CW3	W-2151847	0662	1
BULL HORATIO W	1LT	0-0924437	1145	2
BULL HOWARD E	MAJ	0-0369348	0945	2
BULL ROGER L	1LT	0-0460084	0145	2
BULL THERON W	MAJ	0-1587051	0755	1
BULL WILLIAM B	CW4	W-2218218	1160	1
BULL WILLIE M	MAJ	0-0972000	1262	1
BULLA LOUIE L	CPT	0-2005945	1060	1
BULLARD CECIL G	LTC	0-1015321	0864	1
BULLARD CLARENCE P	MAJ	0-1174516	1055	1
BULLARD DAVID E	CPT	0-1642368	1059	1
BULLARD DORDTHY N	1LT	N-0727628	1145	1
BULLARD LEONARD M	CPT	0-1297311	0156	1
BULLARD LUCILE G	1LT	N-0789852	0645	1

NAME	GRADE	SVC NO	DATE RET MO YR	RET CODE
BULLARD MERLIN A	LTC	0-1555180	0967	1
BULLARD NORMAN R	CPT	0-0334748	0355	2
BULLARD RAY E	MAJ	0-0330767	0246	2
BULLARD WALTER F	MAJ	0-2020252	1060	1
BULLARD WILLIAM R JR	LTC	0-0455345	0960	1
BULLEN SAMUEL R	MAJ	0-1698512	0663	1
BULLENS RICHARD S	CPT	0-1326204	0847	2
BULLINER FREDERICK	LTC	0-2209563	0868	1
BULLINGTON WILLIAM T	CW3	W-2141208	0360	1
BULLION JAMES P	COL	0-0431349	1064	1
BULLIS HAROLD E	COL	0-0155516	0748	3
BULLIS PERRY D	MAJ	0-2008259	0960	1
BULLMAN BUFORD D	MAJ	0-2010351	0863	1
BULLOCK BOYD W	LTC	0-0169405	1160	3
BULLOCK CHARLES L	LTC	0-0202723	1055	3
BULLOCK DEAN A	LTC	0-0465245	1162	1
BULLOCK EDWARD D	MAJ	0-1060724	1059	1
BULLOCK EDWARD S	LTC	0-0195384	0162	3
BULLOCK ELDON D	CPT	0-2102724	1268	2
BULLOCK ELMORE C	MAJ	0-0357899	0146	2
BULLOCK GALE V	MAJ	0-1047468	1059	1
BULLOCK HAYWOOD W	MAJ	0-0488436	0358	1
BULLOCK JACK M	1LT	0-1915722	0554	2
BULLOCK JOHN E	LTC	0-0165388		2
BULLOCK JOHN R	CPT	0-1304167	0647	2
BULLOCK JOSEPH B	1LT	0-2055332	0346	2
BULLOCK LOREN J	LTC	0-0942991	1165	1
BULLOCK MARSHALL E	MAJ	0-0503264	1051	2
BULLOCK MARVIN C	CW3	W-2103923	0659	1
BULLOCK ORLINZA A	CW2	W-2153653	0560	1
BULLOCK ROBERT H	CPT	0-1291577	0753	2
BULLS JERALD C	CPT	0-1307191	0860	1
BULLUCK HEBER A	LTC	0-0502688	0656	1
BULMAN GUY	CW3	W-2145792	0263	1
BUMGARDNER EDGAR	MAJ	0-0471097	0854	1
BUMGARNER FRANK E	LTC	0-0242656	0756	3
BUMGARNER GEORGE W	MAJ	0-1648862	0157	1
BUMGARNER JOHN R	MAJ	0-0381108	1046	2
BUMP SAMUEL C	LTC	0-0333535	0546	2
BUMP WILBUR T	MAJ	0-1324003	0459	1
BUMPAS CHARLES E	CW2	W-2145673	0960	1
BUMPUS ALTA M	1LT	N-0742383	0146	1
BUMSTEAD CHARLES M	LTC	0-1001523	0866	3
BUNCE HOMER T	MAJ	0-0244613	0866	3
BUNCH ALMER	CW4	W-2146438	0766	1
BUNCH CHARLES S	MAJ	0-0215305	0662	3
BUNCH JOEL F	MAJ	0-1999344	0563	1
BUNCH HERMAN L	LTC	0-0250400	0954	1
BUNCH JOHN B	MAJ	0-1186880	0765	1
BUNCH LEONARD	CW3	W-2143386	1263	1
BUNCH LVERNON	CPT	0-0268705	1054	3
BUNCH WILFORD W	CPT	0-0497640	1146	1
BUNCHMAN FLOYD M	1LT	0-0289040	1147	2
BUNDA JOSE	1LT	0-1896553	0762	1
BUNDARA WEJAY S	LTC	0-0361073	0361	1
BUNDICK EDWARD H	MAJ	0-0988997	0467	1
BUNDLIE HAROLD W	CW2	W-2108222	1045	2
BUNDO GEORGE R	CPT	0-1300272	0561	1
BUNDRANT JOHN W	1LT	0-0111366	0648	3
BUNDREN HERMAN R	WO1	W-2107917	0649	1
BUNDRICK HERMAN W	MAJ	0-1011158	1046	2
BUNDY ALMON S	1LT	0-1310216	0446	2
BUNDY GEORGE H	CPT	0-1321096	0146	2
BUNDY JAMES W	CW3	W-2143312	0959	1
BUNDY JOHN W	MAJ	0-0887350	1054	1
BUNDY ROY	LTC	0-2046548	1161	2
BUNGAY ROBERT H	COL	0-0266848	0368	3
BUNGE WERNER D	MAJ	0-0100743	0159	3
BUNIS HENRY J	MAJ	0-1107834	0661	1
BUNKER EVANS C	LTC	0-0312871	0865	3
BUNKER NORMAN F	1LT	0-1026772	0146	2
BUNKER RUSSELL S	COL	0-0235720	0663	3
BUNKER THEODORE	MAJ	0-0188439	0157	3
BUNKER WILLIAM D	MAJ	0-2009682	0658	1
BUNKIN IRVING A	CPT	0-0512302	0145	2

NAME	GRADE	SVC NO	DATE RET MO YR	RET CODE
BUNKLEY THOMAS H	CPT	0-1298816	0161	1
BUNN ELDON H	MAJ	0-0963179	0261	2
BUNN FRANK R	MAJ	0-1330264	0959	1
BUNN MARSHALL R	MAJ	0-1821820	0166	1
BUNN SARAH W	MAJ	N-0722210	1165	1
BUNN SHERMAN F	LTC	0-2037484	0368	1
BUNN THOMAS G	MAJ	0-1301750	0557	1
BUNNELL ALBERT C	LTC	0-2036616	0562	1
BUNNELL GEORGE G JR	CW2	W-2211028	1263	1
BUNNELL HAROLD R	CW3	W-2205528	0267	1
BUNNELL LEE M	WO1	W-2101497	1047	1
BUNNER CHARLES M	CW3	W-2143551	0662	1
BUNTING LELAND K	1LT	0-1322885	0745	2
BUNTING LOUIS G	CPT	0-0468602	0745	2
BUNTING RICHARD P	CW3	W-2205167	1166	1
BUNTING STONEHAM E	CW3	W-2141518	0960	1
BUNTING WILLISTON	MAJ	0-0381900	1045	2
BUNTON GEORGE R	LTC	0-0247955	1166	3
BUNTON HARRY H	LTC	0-1300757	0664	3
BUNTROCK ARNO W	1LT	0-1588463	0547	2
BUNTROCK WALTER F	LTC	0-0285874	0464	3
BUNTS KENNETH R	CW3	W-2208511	0367	1
BUNYAN ROBERT D	LTC	0-0229911	1164	3
BUNYON EDMUND F	COL	0-0244818	1262	3
BURACK PHILIP I	LTC	0-0267968	0660	3
BURANDT HAROLD F	MAJ	0-1102171	0461	1
BURANT ALEXANDER	MAJ	0-0471242	0746	2
BURBA JOSEPH C	CPT	0-5301506	1268	1
BURBA JOSEPH W	COL	0-0245423	0160	3
BURBACH ERWIN E	LTC	0-0315121	1060	1
BURBANK DANIEL J	MAJ	0-1877759	0166	1
BURBANK NATT B	LTC	0-0217957	0164	3
BURBANK PETER	2LT	0-1823260	0845	2
BURBECK ROBERT T	CW4	W-2144380	1060	1
BURBINE THOMAS J	CW2	RW-2148233	1061	1
BURBRIDGE ALBERT D	CW2	W-2141712	0760	1
BURBY NORMAN V	CW2	W-2152337	0765	1
BURCELL ROBERT W	2LT	0-2024226	0945	2
BURCH ALVIN F	LTC	0-0513432	0263	1
BURCH ANDREW J	COL	0-0115128	0660	1
BURCH CHARLES A	1LT	0-0535062	0346	2
BURCH CLARK W	LTC	0-0354629	1067	3
BURCH EDWARD H	LTC	0-0235352	0451	2
BURCH FELIX C	CW2	W-2109503	0154	1
BURCH GEORGE L	LTC	0-1114060	0966	3
BURCH JAY C	CPT	0-1335231	0465	1
BURCH JOHN A JR	1LT	0-1994729	0646	2
BURCH LEO L	MAJ	0-1102646	0754	1
BURCH LYMAN Y	LTC	0-0303979	1264	1
BURCH RAYMOND E	1LT	0-1298657	1045	2
BURCH RICHARD E	COL	0-0910869	0962	1
BURCH WOODROW W JR	CPT	0-2324010	0868	2
BURCHARD HENRY H	LTC	0-0323800	0960	3
BURCHARD SENECA B	MAJ	0-0469497	1158	2
BURCHARD THOMAS C	CPT	0-0212311	0444	2
BURCHELL ROBERT J	COL	0-0123447	0955	2
BURCHETT GEORGE P	CPT	0-0955471	1160	1
BURCHETT HARRY P	MAJ	0-2012787	0857	1
BURCHFIELD EVALYN G	MAJ	N-0722259	1263	3
BURCIN STEVE	CPT	0-1012843	0846	2
BURCK GEORGE D	CW3	W-2206737	0365	1
BURCKHARD FRANK A	CPT	0-1010292	1264	2
BURCKHARTT VIOLET M	LTC	L-0700111	1262	1
BURD EDWARD D	CPT	0-1324505	0946	2
BURD WILLIAM L	CPT	0-0987188	1060	1
BURDAN JACK H	CW4	W-2119485	1054	1
BURDEN GEORGE L	LTC	0-0270722	1168	3
BURDEN JOHN A	COL	0-0344796	0947	2
BURDEN RUSSELL B	MAJ	0-0503713	0847	1
BURDEN WILLIAM H	LTC	0-0253128	0765	3
BURDESS ROBERT L	MAJ	0-1106027	0562	1
BURDETT JAMES B	CW3	W-2108927	0557	2
BURDETTE CLAUDE M	LTC	0-0261325	0667	3
BURDETTE HAROLD E	LTC	0-1046030	1061	1
BURDETTE JAMES A	CW3	W-2151138	1164	1

NAME	GRADE	SVC NO	DATE RET MO YR	RET CODE
BURDETTE JAMES W	COL	0-0210770	0768	3
BURDETTE LEVI C	CW4	W-2143515	1066	1
BURDIC RURIC L	MAJ	0-0204984	0556	3
BURDICK ARTHUR A	1LT	0-1012180	1045	2
BURDICK FRANCIS D	MAJ	0-0368246	0947	2
BURDICK FRANK A	LTC	0-0985386	0668	1
BURDICK FREMONT R	LTC	0-0493565	1164	1
BURDICK HARVEY L	1LT	0-1755241	0146	2
BURDICK LAWRENCE T	COL	0-0259615	0468	3
BURDICK MARSHAL A	MAJ	0-1688419	0861	1
BURDICK RALPH M	CW4	W-0904405	0558	1
BURDICK RAYMOND B	MAJ	0-0237466	0464	3
BURDICK WALLACE I	2LT	0-1301102	0145	2
BURDIN EDWARD F	LTC	0-0917125	0365	3
BURDISH JOHN P	MAJ	0-1297487	0463	1
BURELBACH ARTHUR L	LTC	0-0264809	0162	1
BUREM HENRY S	CPT	0-0475419	1145	2
BUREN WOLCOTT E	LTC	0-0252274	0159	3
BURESH LUMIR F	CPT	0-0313232	0345	2
BURFETE JAMES A	1LT	0-1295168	0446	2
BURFORD DAVID R	LTC	0-0397832	0862	1
BURFORD JAMES L	MAJ	0-0977582	0962	1
BURFORD JOHN C	LTC	0-0532491	1063	1
BURFORD OSCAR W	LTC	0-0379238	0561	1
BURG MORRIS H	MAJ	0-1596279	0657	1
BURGAMY RAYMOND E	MAJ	0-1306373	0660	1
BURGAN ATHAL E	MAJ	0-1303102	0159	1
BURGDOFER EVAN	CW2	W-2118285	1046	1
BURGE COLLIN M	CPT	0-0274611	0761	1
BURGE LOUIS C	MAJ	0-1291227	0261	1
BURGE NELSON J	COL	0-0380278	0662	1
BURGE PAUL	COL	0-0266315	0167	3
BURGE WILLIAM R	MAJ	0-1555799	0860	1
BURGER CLARENCE J	CPT	0-1297156	0367	3
BURGER ELVIN H JR	MAJ	0-1688503	1268	1
BURGER HAROLD	LTC	0-0324041	0446	2
BURGER LAWRENCE J	LTC	0-1080691	0960	1
BURGER LYLE D	MAJ	0-1931525	0566	1
BURGER PAUL S	LTC	0-0451219	0457	1
BURGER STANLEY M	1LT	0-5338221	0768	2
BURGERT ROBERT H	MAJ	0-1049749	0361	1
BURGES MARVIN J	CW2	W-2149285	1159	1
BURGES PHILIP W	COL	0-0178095	0355	2
BURGESON FLOYD M	COL	0-0318457	0468	3
BURGESON JOHN C	MAJ	0-0300760	1058	2
BURGESS ALBERT H	2LT	0-1293901	0845	2
BURGESS CHARLES L	1LT	0-0918891	1043	2
BURGESS CLAYTON A	CPT	0-1337134	0756	2
BURGESS CLYDE C	CPT	0-1933927	0166	1
BURGESS EDWARD P	CW3	W-2148841	0467	1
BURGESS FRANK V	CPT	0-0501341	0351	2
BURGESS GEORGE D	1LT	0-1587864	0546	2
BURGESS HARRY D	CW2	W-2005377	0755	2
BURGESS JAMES	LTC	0-0490474	1057	2
BURGESS JAMES G	LTC	0-1055230	0765	1
BURGESS JAMES R JR	MAJ	0-1169444	0962	1
BURGESS JOHN F	LTC	0-1556097	0263	1
BURGESS JOHN S JR	LTC	0-0238400	0264	3
BURGESS JOSEPH G	MAJ	0-1296478	1164	1
BURGESS JOSEPH J	LTC	0-0438734	0964	3
BURGESS LAURENCE E	COL	0-0197235	0361	3
BURGESS LUTHER G JR	MAJ	0-0979140	0665	1
BURGESS NOAH	MAJ	0-0345200	1052	2
BURGESS RAYMOND N	LTC	0-0246289	0745	2
BURGESS RAYMOND R	2LT	0-1055234	0845	2
BURGESS RICHARD F	1LT	0-1104068	0244	2
BURGESS ROBERT A	MAJ	0-1922682	0967	1
BURGESS ROBERT I	MAJ	0-1633719	1162	1
BURGESS ROY E	MAJ	0-0338182	0447	2
BURGESS STANLEY K	LTC	0-0267321	0150	3
BURGESS VIRGIL W	MAJ	0-0366094	0167	3
BURGESS WILBUR H	COL	0-0350773	1060	1
BURGESS WILBUR T	LTC	0-0292873	0667	3
BURGESS WILLIAM F	CPT	0-1031906	1053	1
BURGESS WILLIAM K	LTC	0-1306973	0461	1

NAME	GRADE	SVC NO	DATE RET MO YR	RET CODE
BURGESS WILLIAM M	CW2	W-2148496	0862	1
BURGESS WILLIAM O	CW4	W-2103925	0758	1
BURGESS WILLIS M	MAJ	0-2042813	0453	1
BURGETT ELDON J	LTC	0-1635648	0863	1
BURGETT GEORGE M	LTC	0-0322293	1160	1
BURGHARDT WALTER F	MAJ	0-1011166	0557	1
BURGHARDT WILLIAM C	LTC	0-0451912	0164	1
BURGIN ASBURY F JR	LTC	0-1635649	0662	1
BURGLAND FREDERICK	CPT	0-0262080	0743	2
BURGLUND WILFRED P	LTC	0-0284533	0468	3
BURGMEIER WILLIAM O	MAJ	0-1554870	1060	1
BURGNER ROBERT W	LTC	0-1167343	1265	1
BURGOON GARREL	LTC	0-0269473	0760	3
BURGOON PAUL L	MAJ	0-1550763	0561	2
BURGOS CANDIDO S	CPT	0-0191335	0648	3
BURGOS ELADIO A	MAJ	0-1301606	0660	1
BURGOS JOSE A	MAJ	0-1329085	0164	1
BURGOSEMACIAS RAFAEL	CPT	0-0155756	1054	3
BURGUSON EDWIN F	LTC	0-0261574	1066	3
BURHANS ROBERT D	COL	0-0354646	0161	1
BURHOE ROBERT D	1LT	0-1047907	0752	2
BURIAN CHARLES M	1LT	0-1181557	0446	2
BURINGRUD WENDELL E	MAJ	0-0963000	0664	1
BURK CLYDE J	LTC	0-0325037	0647	2
BURK E CHARLES	2LT	0-1545582	0844	2
BURK EUGENE C	MAJ	0-1290543	0662	2
BURK FREAR	MAJ	0-0191773	0660	3
BURK JOSEPH E	CPT	0-0468020	0346	2
BURK LEROY R	LTC	0-0946178	1067	2
BURK PAUL J	CPT	0-0492049	1046	1
BURK THOMAS C	MAJ	0-1846396	0257	3
BURKART RICHARD G	2LT	0-1166449	0844	2
BURKE ALLEN T	LTC	0-0449586	0862	1
BURKE ANDREW A JR	MAJ	0-1548665	0554	2
BURKE ANDREW J	COL	0-0244860	0764	3
BURKE ARCHIE	MAJ	0-0486001	0854	1
BURKE ARTHUR L	MAJ	0-2025123	0163	1
BURKE AUDREY A	1LT	N-0776819	0946	1
BURKE BARNEY F	MAJ	0-1292470	0266	1
BURKE CHARLES E	CPT	0-0475029	0553	2
BURKE CHARLES M	MAJ	0-1637580	0263	1
BURKE CLARE M	2LT	N-0789565	0545	1
BURKE CLYDE L	LTC	0-0588285	1267	3
BURKE CRANE D	1LT	0-5405651	0663	2
BURKE DONALD	1LT	0-0552034	1145	2
BURKE DONALD E	MAJ	0-2263701	1265	1
BURKE DONALD J	LTC	0-0887943	0867	1
BURKE EDMUND J	CPT	0-2001759	0766	1
BURKE FRED	LTC	0-1291228	0760	1
BURKE GERARD J	MAJ	0-0386722	0762	1
BURKE HAROLD D	LTC	0-0481695	0163	1
BURKE HARRY C JR	MAJ	0-2017955	0863	1
BURKE HUBERT D	COL	0-0341064	0268	3
BURKE HUGH E	COL	0-0252120	1264	3
BURKE IRENE M	1LT	N-0789011	1045	1
BURKE JACKSON O	LTC	0-0521007	0947	1
BURKE JACOB R	LTC	0-1283205	0160	1
BURKE JAMES A	CPT	0-1578221	1161	2
BURKE JAMES C JR	LTC	0-1315557	0967	1
BURKE JAMES E	CPT	0-2288097	0168	1
BURKE JAMES H	MAJ	0-0323403	1047	1
BURKE JAMES L	MAJ	0-1644542	0357	1
BURKE JAMES M	MAJ	0-1325187	0763	2
BURKE JOHN C	LTC	0-0264092	0764	3
BURKE JOHN D	COL	0-0244270	0657	1
BURKE JOHN E	LTC	0-0391811	0660	1
BURKE JOHN J	CW2	W-2144163	1161	2
BURKE JOSEPH F	LTC	0-0346893	0358	2
BURKE JOSEPH M	LTC	0-0290320	0754	1
BURKE MARTYN L	MAJ	0-1031540	0162	1
BURKE MAURICE J	CPT	0-2035623	1059	1
BURKE MAXWELL F	MAJ	0-0254503	0964	3
BURKE MERVYN F	COL	0-0212141	1059	3
BURKE MICHAEL	2LT	0-2008463	0157	1
BURKE PATRICK H	CW2	W-3430608	1068	1

NAME	GRADE	SVC NO	DATE RET MO YR	RET CODE
BURKE PAUL F	CPT	0-0488471	0944	2
BURKE PERCY H	LTC	0-0906602	0764	1
BURKE PHILIP T	MAJ	0-0954337	0963	1
BURKE RALPH E	MAJ	0-2049491	0561	1
BURKE RALPH W	CPT	0-1175335	0547	2
BURKE RAYMOND J	LTC	0-0455954	0756	1
BURKE RICHARD	COL	0-0278691	0867	3
BURKE RICHARD M	LTC	0-2043079	1266	1
BURKE ROBERT J	CW4	W-2122302	0962	1
BURKE ROBERT P	2LT	0-1545502	0645	2
BURKE ROLLAND J	1LT	0-0464469	1045	2
BURKE STERLING C	COL	0-0206532	0961	3
BURKE THOMAS F	COL	0-0282364	1147	2
BURKE THOMAS F	MAJ	0-0969738	1161	1
BURKE THOMAS F	2LT	0-1533511	1043	2
BURKE THOMAS F	CW4	W-2119968	0459	1
BURKE THOMAS J	MAJ	0-0972048	0363	2
BURKE VINCENT W	LTC	0-1584152	1166	1
BURKE WAYNE H	1LT	0-0499506	0955	2
BURKE WILBUR C	COL	0-0334986	0268	3
BURKE WILLIAM H	1LT	0-1824713	1045	2
BURKE WILLIAM V	CPT	0-0409043	0146	2
BURKE 3RD JAMES F	CW3	W-2114155	0756	1
BURKENBINE REESE A	CW3	W-2150807	0565	1
BURKERT CLIFFORD R	MAJ	0-1535662	1163	1
BURKERT HARRY J	LTC	0-0518629	0763	3
BURKES ROBERT A	MAJ	0-0300026	1059	2
BURKET CHALMER O	LTC	0-0982446	0268	1
BURKET JAMES W	MAJ	0-1321486	0161	1
BURKET PHILIP A	COL	0-0276679	1056	2
BURKET RAY S	MAJ	0-0305494	0846	2
BURKETT EVELYN G	2LT	N-0725055	1044	1
BURKETT HAROLD G	LTC	0-0348844	0161	1
BURKETT JEROME E	MAJ	0-2001061	0263	1
BURKETT RAY W	MAJ	0-1318863	0860	1
BURKEY PAUL F	CPT	0-0227715	0564	3
BURKGREN MARVIN C	LTC	0-1000526	0961	1
BURKHALTER LEONARD L	CPT	0-0148433	0648	3
BURKHARDT HARRY A	LTC	0-1054198	0967	1
BURKHARDT HENRY S	MAJ	0-0220973	0853	3
BURKHARDT PHYLLIS T	MAJ	L-0200602	0555	2
BURKHART JAMES W	MAJ	0-0328829	0245	2
BURKHART JOHN T	CPT	0-1031791	1048	2
BURKHART JOSEPH H	LTC	0-0382440	1165	3
BURKHART MERLE R	COL	0-0146804	0153	3
BURKHART PEYTON H	1LT	0-1168589	0845	2
BURKHART THOMAS F	MAJ	0-0347240	0957	1
BURKHEAD MERVIN D	LTC	0-1557695	1164	1
BURKHOLDER JAMES A	LTC	0-0237296	1163	3
BURKHOLDER LLOYD A	LTC	0-1324097	1162	1
BURKHOLDER RICHARD O	MAJ	0-1342046	1060	1
BURKHOUSE FRANK X	MAJ	0-1999522	0757	1
BURKITT HENRY R	MAJ	0-0238684	0367	3
BURKITT JOEL L	LTC	0-0217191	1059	3
BURKLAND RICHARD L	MAJ	0-0315392	0744	2
BURKLE RALPH E	CW3	W-2119078	1151	2
BURKLEY JOSEPH A	LTC	0-2056689	0463	1
BURKS BARNEY	CPT	0-1580706	1046	2
BURKS FRANK J	COL	0-0211002	0756	3
BURKS FRANK M	LTC	0-1947395	0868	3
BURKS GEORGE S	CPT	0-1290373	0146	2
BURKS JOHN B	WO1	W-2110259	1044	2
BURKS JULIAN	CPT	0-1100897	1046	2
BURKS ROY	LTC	0-0325375	1266	3
BURKS WILLIAM P	LTC	0-0247508	0957	1
BURL HARRY V	MAJ	0-0448334	1046	2
BURLA WILLIAM O	LTC	0-1317367	0363	3
BURLEIGH GEORGE N	COL	0-0325378	0865	3
BURLEIGH JOSEPH P	MAJ	0-1037421	0962	1
BURLESON JOE W	COL	0-0308774	0660	1
BURLESON PERCY L	CW3	W-2146130	0559	1
BURLEY DEXTER V	CW3	W-2145323	0265	2
BURLEY ROBERT D	MAJ	0-0356261	0645	2
BURLING FRANCIS P	CW2	W-2109918	0744	2
BURLINGAME ANSON H	1LT	0-1319719	0944	2

NAME	GRADE	SVC NO	DATE RET MO YR	RET CODE
BURLINGAME CHARLES R	LTC	0-0245948	0653	3
BURLINGAME ELLMONT L	LTC	0-1322420	0764	1
BURLINGAME F W	CPT	0-0104357	0849	3
BURLINGAME GARNET J	MAJ	0-0246157	0244	2
BURLINGAME IVAN H	CW2	W-2146357	1154	1
BURMAN CHARLES H	LTC	0-1533978	0860	1
BURMAN JAMES A	MAJ	0-0988069	0864	1
BURMAN JOHN H	COL	0-0406380	0165	1
BURMAN MANNY	MAJ	0-0498417	0147	1
BURMEISTER HARRY K	LTC	0-0895677	0166	3
BURMESTER WILLIAM L	LTC	0-1636565	0760	1
BURNA GEORGE E	LTC	0-0349387	0262	2
BURNAP COURTNEY N	MAJ	0-0975966	0962	1
BURNAUGH CHARLES R	MAJ	0-0498177	0557	1
BURNELL HARRY T	LTC	0-1168195	0963	1
BURNELLE LOWELL F	LTC	0-0308157	0862	3
BURNER JACOB O JR	CPT	0-1701130	0146	2
BURNES JOSEPH A	CPT	0-0498089	1148	1
BURNES RALPH O	LTC	0-1998299	0866	1
BURNETT ALEXANDER	LTC	0-1645063	0263	1
BURNETT ALFRED S	MAJ	0-1286784	0161	1
BURNETT ALMER C	COL	0-0152155	1044	2
BURNETT ASTOR O JR	CPT	0-1701431	0146	2
BURNETT BERRY H	COL	0-0140626	0648	3
BURNETT CHARLES A	LTC	0-0249127	0167	3
BURNETT CHARLES H	LTC	0-0138878	0548	2
BURNETT CLARENCE F	LTC	0-0304229	0557	1
BURNETT DONALD E	LTC	0-2009406	1267	2
BURNETT ELDON E	1LT	0-1011893	0157	1
BURNETT FRANCIS G	LTC	0-0250092	0667	3
BURNETT FRANCIS K	LTC	0-0132054	1151	3
BURNETT FRANK L	CW2	W-2151133	0562	1
BURNETT GLYNN N	CW3	W-2148106	0757	1
BURNETT HAL A JR	LTC	0-1047470	0766	1
BURNETT HUGH B	COL	0-0326127	0867	3
BURNETT I D	MAJ	0-1685538	0662	1
BURNETT JAMES E	MAJ	0-2262859	1165	1
BURNETT JAMES F	CW3	W-2206801	1266	1
BURNETT JOE	MAJ	0-1591622	0655	1
BURNETT KENNETH H	MAJ	0-0276085	1168	3
BURNETT MARK L	1LT	0-1017782	0945	2
BURNETT THOMAS C	COL	0-0287439	0458	3
BURNETT THOMAS K	LTC	0-1546783	0266	2
BURNETT THOMAS M	1LT	0-1914019	1043	1
BURNETTE ALBERT F	LTC	0-1174517	1055	1
BURNETTE FRANK C	CPT	0-1055231	1047	2
BURNETTE JAMES C	CPT	0-1844548	1052	2
BURNETTE MARSHALL J	LTC	0-0493619	0856	1
BURNETTE ROY L	CW4	W-2141211	0366	1
BURNETTE TALMADGE L	CPT	0-1283373	0745	2
BURNETTE WILLIAM B	CW4	W-2147053	0664	1
BURNEY WILLIAM F	COL	0-0198304	0953	3
BURNHAM ALAN B	COL	0-0259852	0958	3
BURNHAM ARCHER L	LTC	0-0130910	0648	3
BURNHAM ARTHUR L	LTC	0-0468670	0161	1
BURNHAM CHESTER W	CPT	0-0299212	0545	2
BURNHAM CLYDE R	1LT	0-0395821	0544	2
BURNHAM FRANK J	MAJ	0-1997970	0761	1
BURNHAM HAYNES G	2LT	0-2018287	0346	2
BURNHAM HERBERT W	MAJ	0-0230056	0663	3
BURNHAM LEE H	COL	0-0364800	0561	1
BURNHAM LEON	LTC	0-0523568	0265	3
BURNHAM PERCY C	LTC	0-0447785	0454	2
BURNHAM PHILIP C JR	CPT	0-0372460	0746	2
BURNHAM ROY E JR	CW3	W-2206306	0966	1
BURNIE WILLIAM T	CPT	0-0910579	0646	2
BURNIER AUGUST E	MAJ	0-1315478	1146	2
BURNLEY JAMES O	LTC	0-1104071	0766	1
BURNOTES WALTER A	CPT	0-0481507	0548	1
BURNS ALBERT S	LTC	0-0238643	0365	3
BURNS ARTHUR S	COL	0-0157689	1056	3
BURNS BRENDAN A	M G	0-0188865	0257	3
BURNS BURTON F	MAJ	0-0265947	0258	3
BURNS CHARLES P	LTC	0-0415426	0267	3
BURNS COLEMAN C	CPT	0-0481005	0445	2

NAME	GRADE	SVC NO	DATE RET MO YR	RET CODE
BURNS CORNELIUS	CW2	W-3430465	1068	1
BURNS DARNCE B	COL	0-0332393	0954	3
BURNS DELBERT W	1LT	0-1030129	1144	2
BURNS EARLE F	CW4	W-2145630	0868	1
BURNS EDGAR M	COL	0-0284342	0267	3
BURNS EDWARD	COL	0-0188634	1054	3
BURNS EDWARD J	MAJ	0-1294973	1060	1
BURNS ELIZABETH	CPT	N-0757093	0755	2
BURNS ELLSWORTH	COL	0-0450810	0167	1
BURNS ELLUS C	MAJ	0-1299987	0860	1
BURNS FELIX J	LTC	0-1643098	1066	1
BURNS FRANCIS H	LTC	0-0470764	0554	1
BURNS FRANK G	LTC	0-0219616	0559	3
BURNS FRANK H	LTC	0-1575809	0264	1
BURNS FRANK R	MAJ	0-0394298	0960	1
BURNS FRED M	COL	0-0442615	1154	1
BURNS FREDERICK JR	CPT	0-0269275	0944	2
BURNS GEORGE A	LTC	0-0393852	0457	1
BURNS GEORGE C	MAJ	0-0255131	0758	3
BURNS GERALD E	MAJ	0-1015459	0363	1
BURNS GERALD F	MAJ	0-0985684	0164	1
BURNS HARRY A	LTC	0-0166134	1060	3
BURNS HARRY K	1LT	0-1292122	0745	2
BURNS HUGH J	CPT	0-0481902	0546	2
BURNS JAMES C	LTC	0-0312555	0461	3
BURNS JAMES F	CPT	0-1011627	0946	2
BURNS JAMES J	MAJ	0-0242450	0565	3
BURNS JESSICA O	1LT	N-0726004	0347	2
BURNS JOHN A	LTC	0-1323534	0962	1
BURNS JOHN F	LTC	0-1012433	0565	1
BURNS JOHN H	CW3	W-2210010	0168	1
BURNS JOHN J	1LT	0-0417214	1144	2
BURNS JOHN M	CPT	0-1166452	0647	2
BURNS JOHN M	MAJ	0-1585230	0368	3
BURNS JOHN R	LTC	0-1176273	0762	1
BURNS JOHN W	MAJ	0-2210124	0665	1
BURNS JOSEPH	CPT	0-0343493	0644	2
BURNS JOSEPH E	LTC	0-0306416	0762	1
BURNS KELCIE H	CW2	W-2148908	1060	1
BURNS KENNETH B	LTC	0-0168293	1158	1
BURNS LAURENCE W	CPT	0-0338116	0544	2
BURNS LAWRENCE R	1LT	0-1286785	1145	2
BURNS LEE H	LTC	0-0447209	0962	1
BURNS LENTHO	CPT	0-1288930	0447	2
BURNS MARSDON S	LTC	0-0475717	0267	3
BURNS MARVIN P	CPT	0-0200047	0756	1
BURNS MARY A	1LT	N-0724023	0246	1
BURNS MATTHEW A JR	1LT	0-1319720	1045	2
BURNS NELSON C	LTC	0-0916685	1047	2
BURNS ORAN F	COL	0-0354709	0966	1
BURNS PATRICK J	CW2	W-3150551	0567	1
BURNS PAUL J	LTC	0-1107836	0464	1
BURNS RALPH M	MAJ	0-1551582	1062	1
BURNS RAYMOND M	MAJ	0-1297488	1160	1
BURNS ROBERT F	MAJ	0-2017347	0863	1
BURNS ROBERT F	MAJ	0-0193728	1157	3
BURNS ROBERT H	1LT	0-1284647	1145	2
BURNS ROBERT J	CW4	W-2105110	0358	1
BURNS ROBERT J JR	LTC	0-1645072	0764	1
BURNS ROBERT M	2LT	0-1056996	1044	2
BURNS ROBERT W	CPT	0-0385546	0268	3
BURNS ROBERT W	LTC	0-1634579	0859	1
BURNS RUSSELL	LTC	0-0158528	0152	3
BURNS SAMMIE	LTC	0-1574010	0863	1
BURNS SAMUEL S	MAJ	0-1285541	1062	1
BURNS SOPHY M	CPT	N-0700017	0239	1
BURNS TERENCE F	CPT	0-0544199	1145	2
BURNS THOMAS	2LT	0-1913572	0838	1
BURNS THOMAS J	1LT	0-0540641	0546	2
BURNS THOMAS M JR	2LT	0-1295661	1044	2
BURNS VERNON P	MAJ	0-0366741	0547	2
BURNS WALTER J	1LT	0-0847401	1046	2
BURNS WALTER W JR	1LT	0-0464630	0845	2
BURNS WILLIAM C	COL	0-0283642	0146	2
BURNS WILLIAM H	CW2	RW-2208375	0463	1

NAME	GRADE	SVC NO	DATE RET MO YR	RET CODE
BURNS ZED H	MAJ	0-0237890	1263	3
BURNSIDE HOWARD W M	2LT	0-0492608	0643	2
BURNSIDE VIRGIL J	CW2	W-2153021	0959	1
BURNSTEIN IRVING M	1LT	0-1894452	0646	2
BURPEE GERALD N	CPT	0-1109839	0961	1
BURPEE HARRY W	MAJ	0-1633723	0557	1
BURPITT JAMES W	LTC	0-0165093	0357	2
BURPO PAUL W	MAJ	0-2047582	0760	1
BURPO ROBERT C	MAJ	0-0965239	0862	1
BURR ALAN C	MAJ	0-1997375	1162	1
BURR ALBERT H	CPT	0-0533666	0746	2
BURR DAVID F	MAJ	0-0130470	0648	3
BURR DEPORTER	CW4	W-2126967	1155	1
BURR EDWIN M	CPT	0-0204545	0154	3
BURR GEORGE D	COL	0-0102253	1158	3
BURR HUGH	CPT	0-1167346	0946	2
BURR KENNETH D	LTC	0-1575811	1054	1
BURR ROLLIN D	CPT	0-0252381	0863	3
BURR ROSCOE C	LTC	0-0502836	0666	3
BURR SAMUEL E	LTC	0-0247375	1057	3
BURRAGE ROBERT H	COL	0-0126597	0352	3
BURRELL ETHELBERT	MAJ	0-0108150	1043	1
BURRELL FREDERICK	1LT	0-1541697	1145	2
BURRELL JACK B	CW2	W-2149805	0859	1
BURRELL MATTHEW J	LTC	0-0255100	1160	3
BURRIER LEON F	CPT	0-0189972	0554	3
BURRIL CHARLES F	MAJ	0-0154497	0456	3
BURRILL DON H	CW3	W-2152740	0863	1
BURRILL GERALD M	1LT	0-0538714	1145	2
BURRIS ERLTON W	CPT	0-2012738	0257	1
BURRIS GARLAND F	2LT	0-1018246	0145	2
BURRIS LEVI A	CW3	W-2148200	1066	1
BURRIS LUIS M	LTC	0-0453373	1063	1
BURRIS MYRA V	1LT	N-0734025	0246	1
BURRIS ORVAL F	WO1	W-2146358	0964	1
BURRIS THOMAS T	MAJ	0-1305888	0859	1
BURRISS CLIFTON A	COL	0-0193072	1062	3
BURRISS KENNETH K	LTC	0-0282087	0168	3
BURRISS VIRGIL E	MAJ	0-0160358	0655	3
BURRISS WALTER F	COL	0-0214470	0264	3
BURRITT DONALD J	CW4	W-2214514	0868	1
BURRITT JOHN M	MAJ	0-0235236	0245	2
BURROUGHS ARTHUR T	LTC	0-1318410	0867	3
BURROUGHS DONALD L	MAJ	0-0990704	0266	1
BURROUGHS EARL T	1LT	0-0493175	0152	1
BURROUGHS EDGAR S JR	LTC	0-1287472	1066	1
BURROUGHS JAMES A	LTC	0-0227872	0164	3
BURROUGHS JOHN D	2LT	0-0557655	1145	2
BURROUGHS LISLE	COL	0-0124641	0559	3
BURROUGHS WALTER L	LTC	0-0203457	0961	3
BURROUGHS WILLIAM D	MAJ	0-1014211	0463	1
BURROWES HILLIER M	MAJ	0-0173795	0648	3
BURROWES ROBERT W	LTC	0-1297674	1266	1
BURROWS CARLOS W	MAJ	0-1290893	1057	2
BURROWS CHARLES A	LTC	0-0228531	1043	2
BURROWS DOUGLAS J	MAJ	0-1296480	0958	1
BURROWS HENRY	CPT	0-0253533	0966	3
BURROWS JOHN O	LTC	0-0221939	1160	3
BURROWS JOHN R	CPT	0-0508884	0446	2
BURROWS JOSEPH S	MAJ	0-0300935	0760	1
BURROWS LEON S	CW3	W-2143469	0664	1
BURROWS ROBERT B	LTC	0-0525552	1167	3
BURROWS STANLEY R	CPT	0-1585231	1046	2
BURROWS WALLER T	CPT	0-0257630	0860	3
BURRUS RUFUS B	COL	0-0253920	0560	3
BURSE DAVID A	CW3	W-2006984	0766	3
BURSELL WILLIAM R	MAJ	0-1998464	0961	1
BURSET MIGUEL A	COL	0-0382380	0761	1
BURSIEK RALPH C	LTC	0-0288660	1266	3
BURSLEY HARRY C	LTC	0-0268633	0859	3
BURSON CHARLES H	MAJ	0-2205896	1263	1
BURSON CURTIS E	MAJ	0-0354804	1045	2
BURSON JAMES C	MAJ	0-0233458	1148	1
BURSTEIN MAX W	CPT	0-0479826	0847	2
BURSTEIN THEODORE	COL	0-0164734	0244	2

NAME	GRADE	SVC NO	DATE RET MO YR	RET CODE
BURSTEN HAROLD R	CPT	0-1933719	0661	2
BURT ANDREW G JR	LTC	0-1633724	0363	1
BURT CLARENCE D	CW4	W-2112553	0461	1
BURT DANIEL C	LTC	0-1037422	0562	1
BURT ELEANOR M	LTC	L-0701241	0668	1
BURT GEORGE	MAJ	0-1935616	1268	1
BURT HERSEY F	CPT	0-0222130	1161	3
BURT JAMES B	CPT	0-1302427	1047	2
BURT KENNETH L	MAJ	0-2035521	0760	1
BURT RALPH B	CPT	0-0310903	0546	2
BURT ROBERT D	CPT	0-2014641	1067	1
BURT ROWELL F	CPT	0-1175396	0446	2
BURT ROY A	COL	0-0184703	1052	3
BURT RUSSELL E	LTC	0-0252689	1059	1
BURTCH LYMAN C	LTC	0-1297489	0455	1
BURTH ALBERT E	CW3	W-3150608	0968	1
BURTIS DONALD N	CW4	W-2009779	0368	3
BURTIS KENNETH C	LTC	0-0184804	1162	3
BURTNER CALVIN R	LTC	0-0197819	0355	1
BURTNETT MERVIN	CPT	0-1107331	0561	1
BURTON ALBERT L JR	CW3	W-2150138	0467	1
BURTON ALVA A	1LT	0-0496979	0150	[illegible]
BURTON CECIL J	LTC	0-1685545	1065	1
BURTON CHARLES V	LTC	0-1319128	1162	1
BURTON CHESLEY E	CW2	W-2003643	1167	3
BURTON CLARK D	1LT	0-0416144	0245	2
BURTON CLYDE A	MAJ	0-1030226	0761	1
BURTON DAVID G	LTC	0-1060027	0962	1
BURTON EDWARD K	LTC	0-1947471	1066	1
BURTON EMERY H	CPT	0-0166713	0753	3
BURTON HAROLD J	LTC	0-0912318	1062	1
BURTON HARRY	COL	0-0121426	0746	2
BURTON JOSEPH C	COL	0-0189286	0555	3
BURTON JOSEPH D	1LT	0-0115100	1052	3
BURTON KENNETH W	CW4	W-2206690	0166	1
BURTON LAWRENCE F	LTC	0-1032514	1264	1
BURTON LEON E	LTC	0-1180299	1061	1
BURTON LLOYD	LTC	0-0481038	0157	1
BURTON LLOYD F	LTC	0-0484333	1055	1
BURTON LOUIS W JR	MAJ	0-2019283	0765	1
BURTON MARION J	CPT	0-0906592	0145	2
BURTON MELVIN F	1LT	0-1316142	0446	2
BURTON RAYMOND M	CPT	0-0507059	0745	2
BURTON RICHARD A	LTC	0-1173177	0361	1
BURTON ROBERT A	CPT	0-0266313	1053	3
BURTON ROBERT A JR	COL	0-0425305	1263	3
BURTON ROBERT B	MAJ	0-0418443	0757	2
BURTON ROBERT H	MAJ	0-2265315	0764	1
BURTON ROYCE F	LTC	0-1635654	1163	1
BURTON THOMAS L	1LT	0-1300125	0852	2
BURTON WILFRED C	COL	0-1053928	0767	1
BURTON WILLIAM A	LTC	0-1647429	0367	1
BURTON WILLIAM H	1LT	0-0284571	0855	3
BURTON WILLIAM P	CPT	0-0498676	0745	2
BURTYK CHARLES W JR	COL	0-1286434	0868	1
BURUD WILLIAM N	LTC	0-1292123	0764	1
BURUM GARNETT M	MAJ	0-0516893	0260	1
BURWASSER JOSEPH	MAJ	0-0983944	1061	1
BURWELL JAMES W	LTC	0-1175061	0762	1
BURWINKLE WILLIAM M	CPT	0-1288176	0862	2
BURY COLIN J JR	1LT	0-0867490	0146	2
BURY LOYD A	COL	0-0297909	0666	3
BURY STANLEY	CW3	W-2142334	0161	1
BURZ ALEXANDER	LTC	0-1304677	1066	1
BUSBY ALBERT	MAJ	0-0976348	0765	1
BUSBY BALLARD G	LTC	0-1179037	0468	3
BUSBY HUGH C	LTC	0-0417066	0861	1
BUSBY LONNIE L	CW3	W-2144701	0760	1
BUSBY OSCAR M III	MAJ	0-1595403	1162	1
BUSBY PAUL H	CPT	0-0401458	0345	2
BUSBY SCOTT J	MAJ	0-1051063	1059	1
BUSBY YANCY L JR	MAJ	0-1579450	0261	1
BUSCALL DAVID C JR	MAJ	0-0404331	0166	3
BUSCH CHARLES A	LTC	0-1307149	0863	1
BUSCH HENRY W	CPT	0-0443932	0648	1

NAME	GRADE	SVC NO	DATE RET MO YR	RET CODE
BUSCH PHYLLIS M	CPT	N-0721688	1047	1
BUSCH RAY O	COL	0-0384458	0262	1
BUSCH WILLIAM F	MAJ	0-0329559	0567	3
BUSCHER CLEMENT E	MAJ	0-0376734	0445	2
BUSCHER KENNETH L	COL	0-0352643	0466	1
BUSCHKAMPER EDWARD	COL	0-0383326	0660	1
BUSCHMAN MELVIN C	1LT	0-0538103	0146	2
BUSER BERNARD P	CPT	0-1178430	0646	2
BUSER VERONICA H	MAJ	N-0732765	1062	1
BUSEY JOHN F JR	COL	0-0309417	0367	3
BUSH ANGUS M	CW3	W-2144346	1165	1
BUSH ARTHUR D	MAJ	0-0270213	0247	2
BUSH BREWSTER C	LTC	0-1533746	1066	1
BUSH CHARLES C JR	LTC	0-0168569	0660	3
BUSH CHARLES H	CW2	W-2110623	1044	2
BUSH CHARLES L	MAJ	0-0163086	0653	1
BUSH DONALD E	CW2	W-2213497	0267	1
BUSH DONALD P	LTC	0-0286543	0167	3
BUSH EDWARD L	1LT	0-0442278	0346	2
BUSH GERALD A	CPT	0-0400021	0945	2
BUSH HARLAND L	1LT	0-1325472	0556	1
BUSH HERMAN A	1LT	0-1320822	0445	2
BUSH HOUSTON L JR	2LT	0-1171933	0745	2
BUSH JEPTHA H	MAJ	0-0257431	0947	1
BUSH JOE M	MAJ	0-0237029	0166	3
BUSH JOSEPH V	1LT	0-1013034	0846	2
BUSH JULIUS L	MAJ	0-1589096	0763	2
BUSH KENNETH W	1LT	0-1325551	0 46	2
BUSH LAWRENCE G	1LT	0-0183947	0559	3
BUSH MARION F	MAJ	0-1556550	0562	1
BUSH MARSHALL E	B G	0-0298635	0867	3
BUSH MARVIN E	1LT	0-0320477	1044	2
BUSH MORGAN M	MAJ	0-1533979	0565	1
BUSH OTTIS B	CPT	0-0259992	0844	2
BUSH PAUL J	MAJ	0-1306974	0365	1
BUSH RALPH B	CPT	0-0373550	0245	2
BUSH RAYMOND B	COL	0-0231213	0959	3
BUSH RICHARD A	LTC	0-0357888	0167	3
BUSH RICHARD M	LTC	0-0911806	1067	3
BUSH RICHARD S	MAJ	0-0455155	0362	2
BUSH ROBERT N	CPT	0-1017368	0846	2
BUSH RUDOLPH M	COL	0-0240844	0162	1
BUSH S M JR	1LT	0-0538973	0346	2
BUSH SARGENT	CPT	0-0521005	0346	2
BUSH WEAVER L	LTC	0-0278697	0760	1
BUSHAW DELMON R H	CW3	W-2145396	1060	1
BUSHEK EMIL F	MAJ	0-1798440	0964	1
BUSHELL DORIS M	1LT	L-0909109	0644	2
BUSHERY LAWRENCE J	2LT	0-1291945	1144	2
BUSHEY DALE R	MAJ	0-1647266	0363	1
BUSHEY GEORGE O	CW2	W-2203632	0866	1
BUSHEY GORDON G	LTC	0-0215303	0158	1
BUSHEY HOWARD W	LTC	0-0372646	0263	1
BUSHEY JOHN M	LTC	0-0296294	0661	1
BUSHIE GORDON J	CW4	W-2004965	0865	1
BUSHMAN CHARLES S	COL	0-0121428	0656	3
BUSHNELL BYRON	COL	0-0116354	0355	3
BUSHNELL JOHN S	MAJ	0-1119390	0865	1
BUSHNELL LOUIS A M	LTC	0-0103695	0449	3
BUSHNELL THOMAS M JR	MAJ	0-0448333	0662	1
BUSHNELL WATROUS F	MAJ	0-0267873	0460	3
BUSHNELL WILFRED A	MAJ	0-0276415	0461	2
BUSHNER STANLEY	LTC	0-0504676	0661	1
BUSHOUSE ARTHUR A	MAJ	0-0888550	0757	1
BUSHOUSE WILLIAM J	CW4	W-2144271	0161	1
BUSHYHEAD JACK	CPT	0-1284822	0850	2
BUSI JOSEPH H	MAJ	0-0888299	0660	1
BUSKE HERMAN F	WO1	W-2106788	1146	1
BUSKETT BRUCE D	MAJ	0-2053918	0756	1
BUSKIRK HAROLD F	1LT	0-2002239	0448	2
BUSKIRK JAMES H	LTC	0-0224949	0246	2
BUSKIRK WINFRED C	LTC	0-1049093	0368	3
BUSKNESS CARL O	CW2	W-2112741	0360	1
BUSKY ALBERT H	CPT	0-0213628	0862	3
BUSO WALTER	1LT	0-1299195	0645	2

NAME	GRADE	SVC NO	DATE RET MO YR	RET CODE
BUSS JOE	1LT	0-1167762	1043	2
BUSS JOHN F JR	LTC	0-0957585	1267	1
BUSS JOHN R	LTC	0-0238877	0764	3
BUSSE HERMAN A	CPT	0-2262818	0466	2
BUSSE OTTO C	LTC	0-0203744	1049	3
BUSSEN OLIVER J	LTC	0-1554744	1263	1
BUSSEY ARTHUR S	LTC	0-1333778	0967	1
BUSSEY CHARLES M	LTC	0-0804548	0366	1
BUSSEY DONALD S	COL	0-1299512	0567	2
BUSSEY FREDERICK	CPT	0-0322209	0546	2
BUSSEY GRANVILLE	COL	0-0347378	0864	1
BUSSEY HUGH D	CW3	W-2149332	0264	1
BUSSEY ROBERT H	LTC	0-0455598	0661	1
BUSSEY WILLARD D	MAJ	0-1575815	0661	1
BUSSON JAMES C	MAJ	0-0970928	0268	1
BUSTARD WILLIAM W	CPT	0-1013997	0446	2
BUSTER THOMAS J	1LT	0-0509169	1147	1
BUSWELL BRENTON D	LTC	0-1556693	0168	1
BUSWELL CLARK J	MAJ	0-0257130	0867	3
BUSWELL DEWEY L	CPT	0-1541189	0864	1
BUSWELL EDWARD H	CW2	W-2113915	0557	1
BUSZTA JOSEPH J	2LT	0-1038927	0445	2
BUTCAVAGE ANTHONY J	MAJ	0-0972307	0665	1
BUTCH EDMUND R	LTC	0-0405085	0861	1
BUTCH LEO J	LTC	0-1102650	0763	1
BUTCH MICHAEL A	1LT	0-1036461	0945	2
BUTCHER DASH G	CW3	W-2145793	1164	1
BUTCHER DAVE F	LTC	0-0432858	0563	1
BUTCHER EDWARD T	MAJ	0-1312275	0562	1
BUTCHER ELMER H	MAJ	0-0356457	0162	2
BUTCHER EUGENE T	MAJ	0-0279591	1059	3
BUTCHER GEORGE J	CW3	W-2008989	0268	3
BUTCHER HOWARD L	CW4	W-2144866	0866	1
BUTCHER JAMES P	MAJ	0-0201760	1046	2
BUTCHER MARVIN L	LTC	0-0958610	0968	1
BUTCHER MARY D	MAJ	N-0773887	0964	1
BUTCHER ORVILLE K	LTC	0-1324140	0363	1
BUTCHER WILLIAM E	LTC	0-1310976	1067	1
BUTCHER WILLIAM E	1LT	0-1318382	0945	2
BUTEAU FREEMAN H	CW4	W-2102715	0859	1
BUTHERUS HENRY	LTC	0-0310426	1157	1
BUTHORN WILLIAM F	1LT	0-0294223	0844	2
BUTIN PAUL	MAJ	0-1913505	1141	1
BUTKAS ALBERT A	MAJ	0-0397953	0946	2
BUTLER ALANSON H	MAJ	0-0424799	1160	1
BUTLER ALBERT M	COL	0-0335220	0962	1
BUTLER ANNIE F	MAJ	N-0757037	1067	3
BUTLER ARLIN S	CPT	N-0727799	0746	1
BUTLER BETTY I	MAJ	L-1010232	0863	1
BUTLER BURLIE C	CPT	0-0508318	0646	1
BUTLER BYRON N	LTC	0-0259499	0467	3
BUTLER CARL H	CPT	0-0171845	0653	3
BUTLER CARMON D	1LT	0-0200065	1055	3
BUTLER CHARLES A	COL	0-1641624	0155	1
BUTLER CHARLES E	LTC	0-0243226	1163	3
BUTLER CHARLES O	COL	0-0163672	0557	3
BUTLER CHARLES P	LTC	0-0370978	0260	1
BUTLER CHARLES W	CW2	W-2005142	0853	2
BUTLER CLETUS H	CPT	0-1317617	1062	1
BUTLER DAVID S	MAJ	0-0331348	0263	1
BUTLER DERUYTER A	LTC	0-0256999	0760	3
BUTLER DONALD R	CW2	W-2108494	1046	1
BUTLER EDWARD F	LTC	0-0300975	1052	2
BUTLER EDWARD F	MAJ	0-0490578	1145	2
BUTLER EDWARD R	1LT	0-1549235	0346	2
BUTLER ELLIS H	LTC	0-0511577	0266	3
BUTLER ELWYN H	MAJ	0-1800170	0665	1
BUTLER ETHAN F	LTC	0-0157979	0-53	3
BUTLER EUGENE B	LTC	0-0114127	0856	3
BUTLER EUGENE P	MAJ	0-1109170	0564	1
BUTLER EVERETT L	COL	0-0474142	0767	3
BUTLER FRANKLIN C	COL	0-0235354	0355	3
BUTLER FRED	1LT	0-0438273	1044	2
BUTLER FRED W	LTC	0-0958601	0868	3
BUTLER GEORGE H	B G	0-0186922	0558	3

NAME	GRADE	SVC NO	DATE RET MO YR	RET CODE
BUTLER GEORGE K	CPT	0-0322835	1045	2
BUTLER GRADY W	LTC	0-0354741	0856	1
BUTLER GRANT R	CW2	W-2152884	0162	1
BUTLER HAROLD A	LTC	0-0338469	1162	1
BUTLER HAROLD K	CW2	W-2118678	0454	1
BUTLER HAROLD R	1LT	0-0420026	0944	2
BUTLER HARRY	MAJ	0-0219920	0648	3
BUTLER HARRY G	LTC	0-0213621	0662	3
BUTLER HARVIE N	LTC	0-1305889	0264	1
BUTLER HENRY W	COL	0-0120530	0158	3
BUTLER HERBERT E	2LT	0-1328790	0546	2
BUTLER HERBERT H	COL	0-0335709	1166	3
BUTLER JACK D	1LT	0-0328260	0345	2
BUTLER JAMES E	COL	0-0255024	0757	1
BUTLER JAMES F	LTC	0-1545675	0661	1
BUTLER JAMES H	1LT	0-1324616	0647	2
BUTLER JAMES L	LTC	0-0306013	0560	1
BUTLER JAMES M	LTC	0-0405501	0847	2
BUTLER JAMES M	CW4	W-2143118	0263	1
BUTLER JAMES O	MAJ	0-0246824	1054	3
BUTLER JAMES R	LTC	0-1977376	0968	1
BUTLER JAMES W	CW2	W-2145039	0457	2
BUTLER JAMES W JR	CW3	W-2146760	0265	1
BUTLER JIMMIE L	MAJ	0-2051068	0261	1
BUTLER JOHN E	CW3	W-2141212	0762	1
BUTLER JOHN J	MAJ	0-1100468	1061	1
BUTLER JOHN J	CPT	0-1301608	0863	1
BUTLER JOHN L	MAJ	0-0974517	1262	1
BUTLER JOHN O	CW3	W-2143462	0262	1
BUTLER JOSEPH F	LTC	0-0451221	0657	1
BUTLER JOSEPH F	LTC	0-0475552	1047	2
BUTLER KING S	LTC	0-0398131	0560	1
BUTLER LAUREL E	COL	0-0241817	0859	1
BUTLER LEO S	CW3	W-3200189	1068	1
BUTLER LEONARD A	CW2	W-2145397	0456	1
BUTLER LUTHER B JR	1LT	0-2006894	0147	2
BUTLER MELVIN	CPT	0-1923536	0264	1
BUTLER RAYMOND K	LTC	0-0214106	1059	3
BUTLER RAYMOND T	2LT	0-2055093	1144	2
BUTLER ROBERT C	LTC	0-0114876	1162	1
BUTLER ROBERT J	LTC	0-0435264	0662	1
BUTLER ROBERT W	COL	0-0373313	0761	1
BUTLER ROSS D	MAJ	0-1796987	0965	1
BUTLER ROWLAND A	MAJ	0-0337410	1165	3
BUTLER ROY L	COL	0-0278870	1147	2
BUTLER SAM W	CPT	0-0480887	0346	1
BUTLER SUSANN K	MAJ	N-0757718	0966	1
BUTLER THOMAS F	CW4	W-2136645	0261	1
BUTLER VAUGHN V	CPT	0-0920547	1048	2
BUTLER WILLIAM E	1LT	0-0331226	0945	2
BUTLER WILLIAM F	CPT	0-0177288	0450	3
BUTLER WILLIS D	LTC	0-0142785	0145	2
BUTMAN BURTON B	MAJ	0-0365408	0546	2
BUTNER CORNELIUS	LTC	0-1107839	0663	1
BUTNER HUGH F	CPT	0-0306345	0345	2
BUTT ARTHUR J JR	CPT	0-0383673	0544	2
BUTT CECIL G	CPT	0-0993432	0653	2
BUTT CLIFFORD W	COL	0-0175381	1264	3
BUTT EUPHEMIA L	1LT	N-0752963	0546	1
BUTT HERBERT H	COL	0-0479678	0157	2
BUTT MARSHALL W JR	MAJ	0-1924772	0468	1
BUTT RICHARD L JR	COL	0-0336856	1265	1
BUTT WILLIAM	WO1	W-2115956	0344	1
BUTTE CHARLES D	LTC	0-2029549	0367	1
BUTTERFIELD C L	1LT	0-0342316	0445	2
BUTTERFIELD EARL	CW4	W-2005676	1068	1
BUTTERFIELD LELAND W	LTC	0-0328921	1165	3
BUTTERFIELD MAX H	CPT	0-0265823	0246	2
BUTTERFIELD RUTH E	1LT	L-0115175	0745	2
BUTTERS BLAINE W	LTC	0-1580715	1061	2
BUTTERS FORREST H	CW4	W-2101512	0559	1
BUTTERS MANLY G	CPT	0-1697864	0745	2
BUTTERS WILLIAM F	LTC	0-0337407	1045	2
BUTTERSTEIN A F	2LT	0-0447700	1044	2
BUTTERWORTH JAMES E	COL	0-0103853	0855	3

332-811 O - 69 - 8

NAME	GRADE	SVC NO	DATE RET MO YR	RET CODE
BUTTERWORTH WALTON B	LTC	0-0196712	0459	3
BUTTGEN GEORGE A	MAJ	0-0967410	1061	1
BUTTLER JOHN F	CPT	0-1310569	1046	2
BUTTOLPH MILAN D	LTC	0-0256388	0846	2
BUTTON ALLEN M	LTC	0-0197492	0847	1
BUTTON FRANK P	MAJ	0-0200439	0857	3
BUTTON JAMES G	CPT	0-1637135	0558	1
BUTTON OSWALD W	MAJ	0-0959706	0661	1
BUTTON RONALD E	COL	0-0118810	1055	3
BUTTON WILLIAM B	LTC	0-0383861	0262	1
BUTTREY LINTON J	MAJ	0-0407113	0654	1
BUTTS CHARLES G	CPT	0-1004743	0647	2
BUTTS DAVID T JR	MAJ	0-0361741	0562	2
BUTTS JACKSON K	CW3	W-2206208	0667	1
BUTTS PAUL E	LTC	0-1318758	0267	1
BUTTS RALPH F	MAJ	0-1923501	1262	2
BUTTS SAMUEL T SR	CPT	0-1582927	0758	1
BUTTS WALTER	1LT	0-0492158	0744	1
BUTZKE EDWARD W	COL	0-0254686	0865	3
BUVENS RICHARD H	LTC	0-0162113	0145	2
BUWEN FREDERICK	CPT	0-0908333	0745	2
BUX ALBERT C	MAJ	0-0227815	0-50	3
BUXTON ARNOLD H	MAJ	0-1865989	1068	1
BUXTON JOHN A	LTC	0-0161202	0157	3
BUXTON JOHN E	LTC	0-0169405	0752	3
BUYAK MITCHELL V	MAJ	0-0310512	1062	3
BUYS WILLIAM C	LTC	0-1110971	0464	1
BUYZE DANIEL	LTC	0-0360159	1061	1
BUZA ALFRED J	CW3	W-2145229	0862	1
BUZARD JOHN H	LTC	0-1105299	1067	1
BUZASH ALBERT S	LTC	0-0405814	0459	1
BUZZARD DONALD H	LTC	0-1010335	0561	1
BYALL WILLIAM F	MAJ	0-1917751	0565	1
BYARD RAYMOND J	MAJ	0-1920284	0426	1
BYARS CLARENCE F	CW2	W-2146938	0356	1
BYARS JOSEPH R	LTC	0-0334533	0762	3
BYARS RICHARD C	LTC	0-0261037	1066	3
BYARS ROBERT A	MAJ	0-0259585	0867	3
BYARS ROBERT D	1LT	0-2018835	0851	2
BYARS WARNER S	CPT	0-1543734	1047	2
BYAS CARL W	MAJ	0-0452019	0957	1
BYASSEE MARSHALL C	MAJ	0-0967270	0464	1
BYBEE CLEAOUS	CW3	W-2144641	0367	2
BYBEE JOE T	CW2	W-2149663	1262	1
BYBEE JOHN W	LTC	0-1294430	0262	1
BYCZYNSKI STANLEY J	CPT	0-0965857	1160	1
BYE SIGURD E	LTC	0-0243033	1160	3
BYE STANLEY F	MAJ	0-0244752	1044	2
BYE WILLIAM R	CPT	0-1822234	1045	2
BYER CALVIN	MAJ	0-1686817	0166	1
BYER RUSSELL R	CPT	0-0138849	0657	3
BYERLEY WENDELL C	MAJ	0-2023958	0663	1
BYERLY FENTON H	CPT	0-1798441	0257	1
BYERLY GEORGE F JR	LTC	0-1287135	0161	1
BYERLY MATTHEW W	MAJ	0-0336132	0960	1
BYERS ALONZO C	LTC	0-0501440	0158	1
BYERS ANDREW	MAJ	0-0948502	1066	1
BYERS BENJAMIN H	LTC	0-0148868	0757	3
BYERS CARLOS L	MAJ	0-1036894	0461	1
BYERS DAVID F	LTC	0-1315264	0963	1
BYERS GEORGE	LTC	0-0170001	0753	3
BYERS HANS	CPT	0-2020523	0559	1
BYERS JASON H	LTC	0-0290942	0460	3
BYERS LAWRENCE W	COL	0-0169786	0657	1
BYERS MELVIN W	CW3	W-2150333	0164	1
BYERS RAYMOND A	COL	0-0243238	0558	3
BYERS ROBERT W	CW3	W-2209049	0966	1
BYERS ROLAND C	LTC	0-1171935	1262	1
BYKLE LAURA C	MAJ	N-0772431	1063	1
BYLAND WARREN T	MAJ	0-1301105	0764	1
BYLER RALPH J	COL	0-0318638	0246	2
BYLES HOWARD T	COL	0-0187175	0852	3
BYLES ROBERT E	LTC	0-0349174	0451	2
BYNUM HARTWELL T	COL	0-0267306	0858	3
BYNUM HENRY W	MAJ	0-0377680	1061	1
BYNUM JIMMIE D	MAJ	0-1688317	0164	1
BYNUM THOMAS W SR	LTC	0-0246261	0351	3
BYNUM WILLIAM L	LTC	0-0352705	0660	1
BYRAM CHARLES R	LTC	0-0439326	1053	3
BYRAM HERMAN E	MAJ	0-1302949	0464	1
BYRAM RUTH E	1LT	N-0785595	0947	1
BYRD ADRAIN	LTC	0-1178727	0755	1
BYRD CECIL C JR	MAJ	0-0968681	0862	1
BYRD CLAYTON R	1LT	0-0955228	0952	2
BYRD COHEN B	COL	0-0410926	1061	1
BYRD DANIEL B	B G	0-0185002	1048	3
BYRD DAVID C	COL	0-0238264	0166	3
BYRD DAVID L	CW3	W-2211783	1268	1
BYRD FELTON L	LTC	0-1049095	0858	1
BYRD GEORGE M	LTC	0-0270494	0766	3
BYRD HARDEN B	LTC	0-0348993	0657	1
BYRD HARVEY B	1LT	0-0340969	0845	2
BYRD HAZEL L	COL	0-0304497	0559	1
BYRD JAMES E	MAJ	0-2006101	0766	1
BYRD JESSE L	COL	0-0198514	0251	3
BYRD JIMMY P JR	CW3	W-2207102	0766	1
BYRD JOHN C	LTC	0-0372321	0768	3
BYRD KURT	CPT	0-0956823	0257	2
BYRD LARKIN A JR	MAJ	0-1328791	1262	1
BYRD LIONEL P	MAJ	0-0953925	1061	1
BYRD LUCAS M JR	MAJ	0-0501767	0847	2
BYRD NELLIE B	MAJ	N-0727347	0846	1
BYRD PAUL E	LTC	0-0404271	0263	1
BYRD SAM	1LT	0-0488677	0650	1
BYRD SAM	MAJ	0-2046302	0954	1
BYRD SMITH T	2LT	0-1286435	0345	2
BYRD WILLIAM H	1LT	0-0491309	0146	2
BYRNE CLEMENT A	LTC	0-1573087	0157	1
BYRNE EDWARD G	CW2	W-2130873	0953	1
BYRNE EDWIN S	1LT	0-0414846	0450	2
BYRNE GERARD N	COL	0-0254282	0266	3
BYRNE JOHN F	LTC	0-1946450	0263	1
BYRNE JOHN J	CPT	0-1324004	0446	2
BYRNE JOHN P	MAJ	0-1579453	0465	1
BYRNE JOSEPH S	LTC	0-0497162	0862	1
BYRNE MARK R	MAJ	0-0485184	0561	2
BYRNE MICHAEL	LTC	0-1291944	0363	1
BYRNE PAUL C	COL	0-0194842	0961	3
BYRNE RICHARD J	COL	0-0395777	0761	1
BYRNE ROBERT A	LTC	0-1533512	0962	1
BYRNE STEPHEN B	MAJ	0-1950963	1162	2
BYRNE THOMAS F	COL	0-0102103	0266	3
BYRNE THOMAS P	1LT	0-5023859	0867	2
BYRNE WILLIAM F JR	MAJ	0-0368227	0346	2
BYRNE WILLIAM J	CPT	0-1573704	0456	1
BYRNES ALBERT E	CPT	0-1635660	0358	1
BYRNES ARTHUR A	CPT	0-1100470	0164	1
BYRNES GARRETT J	COL	0-0321225	0467	3
BYRNES GEORGE J	MAJ	0-0955545	0566	1
BYRNES JAMES L JR	1LT	0-0349740	1147	2
BYRNES JOHN P	1LT	0-1326354	0346	2
BYRNES JOSEPH B	MAJ	0-1043587	0560	1
BYRNES ROBERT J	CW3	W-2151198	0864	1
BYRNES THOMAS F	MAJ	0-1061329	0862	2
BYROM CASSIE N	2LT	N-0744546	0544	1
BYRON ALEXANDER	CPT	0-0124297	0150	3
BYRON CHARLES E	LTC	0-1293545	0561	1
BYRON CHRIS	1LT	0-0957991	0852	2
BYRON EDWARD S	COL	0-0210770	0-49	3
BYRON ELMER H	CW2	W-2148107	0662	1
BYRON FRANK J	LTC	0-1994395	1162	1
BYRON JOHN E	CPT	0-1289041	0954	1
BYRON WILLIAM E	1LT	0-1949223	0552	2
BYRUM GEORGE R JR	LTC	0-0213848	0747	2
BYRUM WILLIAM W	MAJ	0-1103543	1060	1
BYSINGER WALLACE G	LTC	0-1635662	0868	1
BYSTRAK PAUL	MAJ	0-0977286	1263	1
BYTHER PAUL F	LTC	0-0354042	0163	1
BYUS JOHN JR	LTC	0-0374754	1060	1
BYWATERS JAMES H	LTC	0-0262986	1067	3
BYWATERS RICHARD E	LTC	0-1826413	0763	1
BYZEK STEPHEN J	CPT	0-2055520	0959	1
BZOULA EDWARD B	CPT	0-1596602	0447	2
CABABAAN PABLO	1LT	0-1896567	0450	1
CABALLERO JOSE O	1LT	0-2030125	1050	2
CABANILLAS JUAN	MAJ	0-0934244	0765	1
CABANISS LEM JR	LTC	0-0966116	1266	1
CABANISS MARION I	CPT	0-1312748	1046	2
CABANISS WILLIAM L	COL	0-0293176	0546	2
CABAZA JOSE E	LTC	0-1030958	0468	1
CABBAGE VICTOR	2LT	0-1914017	1043	1
CABELL RANDOLPH M	COL	0-0189318	1155	3
CABIAO PROTACIO	1LT	0-2032075	1052	1
CABIL JUAN	1LT	0-0170615	0648	1
CABLE PAUL E	CW3	W-2146220	0162	2
CABLES GRACE M C	LTC	R-0001040	1165	3
CABOT RUSSELL C	LTC	0-0267432	1165	3
CABRER AGUSTIN	2LT	0-1081464	1045	2
CABRERA CHARLES T	LTC	0-0187263	0961	3
CABRERA DAGO	CW2	W-2143905	0667	1
CABRERA JUAN R	1LT	0-0527493	1045	2
CABRINHA ANTHONY M	LTC	0-0348171	0961	1
CABUNTALA STEVE	2LT	0-2031894	0652	1
CACCAMISE FRANCIS J	CW3	W-2142998	0959	1
CACCHIOTTI RALPH R	MAJ	0-1046032	1060	1
CACCIATO RICHARD C	LTC	0-0935273	0767	1
CACCIATORE DONALD E	CW2	W-2110608	0861	1
CACERES RALPH K	CPT	0-0450811	0547	2
CACHILLI FRED H	MAJ	0-1290545	0161	1
CADDELL CLYDE M	2LT	0-1311976	0445	2
CADDELL JAMES B JR	1LT	0-0535907	1045	2
CADDES ELMER E	LTC	0-0313537	0965	1
CADDINGTON WARD W	LTC	0-0231597	0945	2
CADDLE JOHN	LTC	0-0366365	0561	2
CADDY EDWARD W JR	MAJ	0-1554146	0961	1
CADE GEORGE F	MAJ	0-1550339	0364	1
CADE WILLIAM H	2LT	0-0553493	1045	2
CADIGAN ROBERT S	LTC	0-0426069	0664	1
CADIGAN WILLIAM J	MAJ	0-1110408	0962	1
CADLE RUSSELL H	MAJ	0-1913336	1166	1
CADMAN EUGENE F	LTC	0-0202985	0256	3
CADOGAN LARRY J	MAJ	0-1545644	0467	3
CADORET MARCEL A	1LT	0-0503255	0745	2
CADUNGUG DELFIN C	2LT	0-2032076	1048	1
CADWALADER HENRY	CPT	0-0340410	0744	2
CADWALLADER CHARLES	LTC	0-0144961	0951	3
CADWALLADER EDGAR C	CPT	0-1595407	0346	2
CADWELL CAROL V	COL	0-0150855	1054	1
CADWELL JOHN H	MAJ	0-0450253	0955	1
CADWELL VERN L	CPT	0-0173490	1145	2
CADY DUANE L	COL	0-0335065	0246	2
CADY FRED A	1LT	0-1301943	1157	1
CADY LAWRENCE R	LTC	0-1031542	0658	1
CADY LEE O	COL	0-0168429	1056	3
CADY MAX W	MAJ	0-0355693	0151	2
CAENEN EDWARD L	LTC	0-0280961	0368	3
CAESAR GORDON M	CPT	0-1288177	0846	2
CAFARO SECONDO R	MAJ	0-0349741	0745	2
CAFFERTY JAMES C	LTC	0-2021172	1168	1
CAFFEY ROBERT C	MAJ	0-0347416	0847	2
CAFFO LOUIS L	CPT	0-0492302	0752	1
CAFFREY CHARLES E	MAJ	0-0534773	0448	2
CAFFREY CHARLES G	LTC	0-0375830	0364	3
CAFFREY DAVID R	LTC	0-1322203	0363	2
CAFFREY EDWIN J	MAJ	0-2056899	0766	1
CAFFREY GERALD C	1LT	0-2007423	0648	2
CAFFREY JAMES A	LTC	0-0246167	1160	3
CAFFREY JOSEPH G	CW2	W-2208321	0864	1
CAFFREY ROBERT J	LTC	0-1549441	0267	1
CAFONE JULIO J	CPT	0-1823835	1152	2
CAGANN ARNOLD R	MAJ	0-1174519	0962	1
CAGE ARNETT	CW3	W-2151378	0366	1
CAGGIULA VINCENT L	CPT	0-0351770	0346	2
CAGLE CHARLES O	MAJ	0-1016731	0747	2
CAGLE DARRELL J	CW4	W-2120969	0364	2
CAGLE JAMES M	CW4	W-2129268	0562	1
CAGLE JOHN F	COL	0-0516221	0368	1
CAGLE PAUL M	MAJ	0-1919273	1264	1
CAGNONI GUIDO J	1LT	0-0345939	0544	2
CAGULADA LEONARDO	2LT	0-1896850	0151	2
CAHILL EDWARD A	LTC	0-0385138	1267	3
CAHILL EDWARD H	MAJ	0-0106904	1044	2
CAHILL EDWIN D	CPT	0-1169450	0849	2
CAHILL HENRY F	LTC	0-1180142	0563	1
CAHILL JAMES T	CPT	0-0374958	0346	2
CAHILL JOHN B	CW4	W-2003740	0567	1
CAHILL ROBERT R	MAJ	0-1799239	0263	1
CAHILL STANLEY E	2LT	0-1118555	1045	2
CAHILL THOMAS F	CPT	0-1287302	1047	2
CAHILL THOMAS H JR	LTC	0-0188990	0755	3
CAHILL VINCENT E	CPT	0-1049429	0866	1
CAHOON AUGUST T	CPT	0-0361753	1145	2
CAHOUN WILLIAM B JR	MAJ	0-1593486	0168	3
CAHOY ANDY L	CPT	0-0283567	0246	2
CAIN ALVA N	LTC	0-0449577	0562	3
CAIN BEDFORD R	MAJ	0-1057000	0464	3
CAIN CLESSON C JR	MAJ	0-0968208	1062	2
CAIN DANIEL E	CW2	W-2149883	0758	2
CAIN FRANK O JR	1LT	0-0554497	0646	2
CAIN FREDERICK	COL	0-0244924	0562	3
CAIN GEORGE E	MAJ	0-0983241	0562	1
CAIN GLADYS C	MAJ	N-0751617	0867	1
CAIN HERVEY C	CPT	0-0496774	0646	2
CAIN JAMES S	LTC	0-2055885	1060	1
CAIN JOHN J	MAJ	0-0366731	0847	2
CAIN JOHN S	MAJ	0-0344674	0147	2
CAIN MEMORY H	COL	0-0232299	0147	2
CAIN RAY E	LTC	0-1321288	0862	1
CAIN ROBERT C	MAJ	0-1323210	1067	3
CAIN ROLLIE W	1LT	0-1056655	0346	2
CAIN THOMAS E	LTC	0-0371462	0257	1
CAIN THOMAS R	1LT	0-0409095	0644	2
CAIN VINCENT C	MAJ	0-4009552	0766	1
CAIN WARREN E	LTC	0-0360608	0960	1
CAIN WILLIAM D	1LT	0-0543225	0846	2
CAIN WILLIAM F	MAJ	0-1041306	0462	2
CAINE IRVING	CPT	0-0471948	0445	2
CAINE JOSEPH P	CW3	W-2205275	0866	1
CAINE TRACY M	LTC	0-1062914	0767	1
CAINES THOMAS I	CPT	0-2039429	0557	1
CAIRNS JAMES C	B G	0-0285315	0968	3
CAIRNS MONIVAL A	LTC	0-0401962	0760	1
CAIRNS PAUL M	COL	0-0221610	0657	3
CAIRNS ROBERT T	MAJ	0-0125816	0746	2
CAIRNS VERNON T	COL	0-0362015	0268	3
CAIRY SCOTT A	LTC	0-0275662	0349	3
CAITHNESS JOHN H	COL	0-1822101	1268	1
CAIVANO JAMES J	1LT	0-1292127	0146	2
CAKALIC ELINT M	LTC	0-0318271	1059	1
CAKE CHARLES	CPT	0-0508654	1046	2
CALABRESE DINO O	CPT	0-0419544	0146	2
CALABRESE EDWARD S	MAJ	0-0344965	0246	2
CALABRO EUGENE R	CW4	W-2005141	0968	1
CALAHAN RICHARD A	CW3	W-2143282	1262	1
CALAMARI JOHN J	LTC	0-0305979	0767	3
CALAMBRO ALFREDO A	CPT	0-1896758	0359	1
CALAPINI URBANO E	2LT	0-2030128	1050	1
CALARCO CARMINE L	LTC	0-0960910	0468	3
CALARCO LOUIS O	COL	0-0410022	1065	1
CALAWAY GEORGE A	MAJ	0-0292401	1145	2
CALBOS FRANK	1LT	0-1821821	0946	2
CALCI HENRY V	1LT	0-1705374	1044	2
CALDER JOSEPH H	LTC	0-1313566	1163	1
CALDER NATHAN A	CPT	0-1308596	0746	2
CALDERON RAMON F	CPT	0-2020924	0260	1
CALDERONE JOSEPH J	CW3	W-2147950	0561	1
CALDERWOOD HOWARD N	LTC	0-0211463	0648	3
CALDERWOOD JOSEPH B	CW4	W-2110119	1057	1
CALDWELL ADRIAN B	LTC	0-1305159	0562	1
CALDWELL ALBERT B	1LT	0-1310977	0645	2

NAME	GRADE	SVC NO	DATE RET MO YR	RET CODE
CALDWELL ALBERT L	MAJ	0-1017811	0161	1
CALDWELL ALLEN R JR	1LT	0-2043089	0446	2
CALDWELL ARNOLD E	CPT	0-1284651	0645	2
CALDWELL BEVERLY C	MAJ	0-0237098	1146	2
CALDWELL BULEY H III	LTC	0-2014599	0168	1
CALDWELL BYRON L	LTC	0-1585237	0766	3
CALDWELL CARL E	2LT	0-1049430	0945	2
CALDWELL CHARLES C	COL	0-0217778	0463	3
CALDWELL CHARLES I	MAJ	0-2034500	0262	1
CALDWELL CHARLIE	CPT	0-0166821	0652	3
CALDWELL CLOYD T	COL	0-0266527	0657	1
CALDWELL EARL	MAJ	0-1110972	1159	1
CALDWELL EDWARD G	LTC	0-2046303	1166	1
CALDWELL FREDERICK	CPT	0-0436952	0246	2
CALDWELL GEORGE D	COL	0-0125218	0551	3
CALDWELL GEORGE H	CPT	0-1174520	0550	2
CALDWELL GEORGE H	CW3	W-2209528	0868	2
CALDWELL HAMMOND D	LTC	0-0288780	0756	1
CALDWELL HAROLD G	CW3	W-2134090	0562	1
CALDWELL HAZLITT B	LTC	0-0165727	0455	3
CALDWELL HERMAN V	1LT	0-0965520	0962	1
CALDWELL HOWARD S	MAJ	0-0248374	1266	3
CALDWELL HUGH M	MAJ	0-1324313	0453	1
CALDWELL JAMES	MAJ	0-1913436	0565	1
CALDWELL JAMES E	CPT	0-0370929	0765	2
CALDWELL JAMES H	CW2	W-2150895	0562	1
CALDWELL JOE R	LTC	0-2037529	0868	1
CALDWELL JOHN A	LTC	0-1581790	1162	2
CALDWELL JOHN F	CPT	0-0268860	0849	1
CALDWELL JOHN E JR	MAJ	0-1341852	0865	2
CALDWELL JOHN H	LTC	0-1109843	0763	1
CALDWELL JULIUS A	CPT	0-0339930	0146	2
CALDWELL LANGSTON H	LTC	0-0544283	0463	1
CALDWELL LEONARD A	CW3	W-2144002	1263	1
CALDWELL LESTER R	MAJ	0-1947183	0156	1
CALDWELL MELVIN H	CW3	W-2207607	0166	1
CALDWELL MILLARD F	LTC	0-0450208	0557	1
CALDWELL MILTON V	CPT	0-0474079	0745	2
CALDWELL RALPH D	MAJ	0-0264373	0943	2
CALDWELL RALPH W	LTC	0-0323920	1162	1
CALDWELL RALPH W	CW3	W-2153242	0863	1
CALDWELL RICHARD H	MAJ	0-0271186	0168	3
CALDWELL ROBERT C	2LT	0-1112600	1044	2
CALDWELL ROBERT E L	CW3	W-2120775	1057	1
CALDWELL ROBERT M	1LT	0-1058465	1045	2
CALDWELL ROSS	CPT	0-0336597	1045	2
CALDWELL SHERRILL C	2LT	0-1547558	0445	2
CALDWELL THOMAS B	LTC	0-0229052	0864	3
CALDWELL TROY G	CPT	0-0493515	0746	1
CALDWELL VERNON	MAJ	0-1545823	0561	1
CALDWELL VIOLETTE N	2LT	N-0736768	0844	1
CALDWELL VIRGIL E	COL	0-0136361	0856	3
CALDWELL WILLIAM E	LTC	0-0245901	0245	2
CALDWELL WILLIAM H	CW3	W-2142040	0257	1
CALDWELL WILLIAM R	LTC	0-0493169	0855	1
CALDWELL WINSTON F	LTC	0-0366846	0264	1
CALE LUTHER T	LTC	0-0228729	0864	3
CALE RICHARD C	LTC	0-0336415	1064	3
CALEB ROBERT S	COL	0-1580717	0661	1
CALEF RALPH F	1LT	0-1577245	0745	2
CALENDER ALLIE O	LTC	0-1557701	0566	1
CALERO AMILCAR R	MAJ	0-0962999	1063	1
CALESTINI JOSEPH C	CW4	W-2103932	0859	1
CALFEE LEE D	MAJ	0-1894956	0961	2
CALFEE RICHARD A	MAJ	0-2051425	1262	1
CALFEE WILLIAM A	LTC	0-1299711	1161	1
CALGOY PABLO C	1LT	0-0355420	1059	1
CALHOUN ALFORD E	COL	0-0323112	0664	1
CALHOUN ALISTAIR A	MAJ	0-2049495	0865	2
CALHOUN CHARLES E	LTC	0-1325553	0665	1
CALHOUN CHARLES H JR	LTC	0-0363284	0860	1
CALHOUN CHARLES L	MAJ	0-0236413	0758	3
CALHOUN EDWARD H	CPT	0-1302271	0949	1
CALHOUN FORREST JR	1LT	0-1933668	0554	2
CALHOUN GRIFF C	MAJ	0-0486507	0253	1
CALHOUN JACK	CPT	0-0409632	0146	2
CALHOUN JESSE E	MAJ	0-0434724	0347	2
CALHOUN JOHN N	LTC.	0-1533271	0164	3
CALHOUN PAUL R	LTC	0-2044318	0662	1
CALHOUN ROBERT S	1LT	0-1323256	0548	1
CALHOUN SAMUEL	MAJ	0-1311115	0560	1
CALHOUN SHELLACE T	LTC	0-1309212	0867	1
CALHOUN THOMAS	MAJ	0-0231888	0648	3
CALHOUN WESLEY P	CW2	W-2208449	0165	1
CALIFF JOHN W	LTC	0-0220384	0560	3
CALIGUIRI FRANCIS F	LTC	0-1184467	0263	1
CALISCH MERRIL H	MAJ	0-0706565	0765	1
CALKIN FREDERICK	LTC	0-0125817	0754	3
CALKIN GEORGE R	LTC	0-1051894	0563	1
CALKIN RALPH F	LTC	0-0341614	0260	1
CALKINS DELOS S	LTC	0-0284042	0661	1
CALKINS HARRY R	COL	0-0287444	0946	2
CALKINS JAMES E	LTC	0-0384430	0960	1
CALKINS JOHN D JR	LTC	0-1949063	0766	1
CALKINS JOHN U JR	M G	0-0114357	1149	3
CALKINS LUTHER S	LTC	0-1640750	0363	1
CALKINS MYRON L	1LT	0-0263484	1043	2
CALL CHAUNCY C	CPT	0-0271564	0647	2
CALL CORNELIUS	2LT	0-2011076	0747	2
CALL FREDERICK	MAJ	0-1556254	1163	1
CALL JOSEPH B JR	1LT	0-1296319	0745	2
CALL LUTHER P JR	COL	0-0125819	0258	3
CALL THOMAS D	LTC	0-0366567	1160	1
CALL 3RD LUTHER P	CPT	0-0975668	0858	2
CALLAGHAN ELLEN K	1LT	N-0787540	1146	1
CALLAGHAN EUGENE J	LTC	0-0450813	1060	2
CALLAGHAN GEORGE J	LTC	0-0453714	1153	1
CALLAGHAN HAROLD F	MAJ	0-1823401	1165	2
CALLAGHAN HENRY E	MAJ	0-2014472	0264	1
CALLAGHAN PATRICK E	LTC	0-1556551	1162	1
CALLAGHAN RICHARD P	MAJ	0-1315908	1063	1
CALLAGHAN ROBERT E	1LT	0-0544606	0646	2
CALLAHAM EDWARD J	1LT	0-1287833	0647	2
CALLAHAM JAMES F	COL	0-0260318	0767	3
CALLAHAN CHARLES F	2LT	0-1824631	0744	2
CALLAHAN DEWEY H	CPT	0-0984921	0559	1
CALLAHAN FRANCIS B	LTC	0-1797245	0766	1
CALLAHAN FRANCIS P	LTC	0-1286958	0361	1
CALLAHAN FRANK E JR	LTC	0-0340098	0446	2
CALLAHAN FRANK J	1LT	0-1324456	104N	2
CALLAHAN GABRIEL P	CW4	W-2143107	0865	2
CALLAHAN GEORGE	1LT	0-0886318	0251	2
CALLAHAN HAROLD H	MAJ	0-0966310	0763	1
CALLAHAN HELENA M	MAJ	L-0115751	0363	1
CALLAHAN HORACE N	LTC	0-0336538	0346	2
CALLAHAN HUBERT A	MAJ	0-0984717	0766	1
CALLAHAN JAMES D	MAJ	0-0288511	0267	3
CALLAHAN JAMES E	LTC	0-0229603	0265	3
CALLAHAN JEAN G	MAJ	0-0298690	0266	2
CALLAHAN JOHN A	MAJ	0-1176911	0964	2
CALLAHAN JOHN D	CW3	RW-2142095	0263	1
CALLAHAN JOHN J JR	CW3	W-2144229	0564	1
CALLAHAN JOHN R	CW4	W-2109238	0652	1
CALLAHAN NOEL	LTC	0-0293135	1064	1
CALLAHAN REGIS F	CW4	W-2145990	0668	1
CALLAHAN RICHARD D	CW3	W-2150792	0966	1
CALLAHAN RICHARD L	MAJ	0-0974978	1163	1
CALLAHAN THOMAS J	LTC	0-0390706	1160	1
CALLAHAN WILLIAM C	CW2	W-2150114	0356	1
CALLAHAN WILLIAM J	MAJ	0-0302373	0348	1
CALLAHAN WILLIAM R	LTC	0-0407650	0261	1
CALLAN RAYMOND E	MAJ	0-1685651	0865	1
CALLANAN JOHN J	COL	0-0279797	0463	3
CALLANAN WILLIAM A	COL	0-0255935	1164	3
CALLANDER ADELBERT R	LTC	0-0273164	1058	3
CALLAWAY BRANTLEY B	LTC	0-0473228	0548	1
CALLAWAY GEORGE H	LTC	0-0979303	0763	1
CALLAWAY HERBERT M	1LT	0-0258711	0366	3
CALLAWAY HOMER A	LTC	0-0200744	0355	3
CALLAWAY KERMIT H	LTC	0-0250157	1059	1
CALLAWAY OSWALD F	CPT	0-2262787	0963	1
CALLAWAY SAMUEL M	CPT	0-0959307	1060	1
CALLAWAY THOMAS W	CPT	0-1324254	0558	1
CALLEN JAMES M	CPT	0-0490017	0354	1
CALLENBERGER JAMES D	CW2	W-2148709	0160	1
CALLENDER WILLIAM R	COL	0-0222342	0965	3
CALLERY JAMES B	LTC	0-2035624	0861	1
CALLIER STRATTON F	LTC	0-1293720	0960	2
CALLIER THOMAS P	1LT	0-0509854	1045	2
CALLIHAN AEVID A	MAJ	N-0735716	0665	3
CALLIHAN CHAMPION M	2LT	0-1309909	1144	2
CALLIHAN CHARLES W	MAJ	0-1924766	0565	1
CALLIS JOSEPH E	LTC	0-1550979	0368	1
CALLIS OTIS W	LTC	0-1001312	0762	1
CALLIS RUSSELL S	LTC	0-1110410	0461	1
CALLISON EUGENE H	LTC	0-0171575	1161	3
CALLOW HERBERT T	CPT	0-0211433	0858	3
CALLOWAY LAWRENCE H	COL	0-0250967	1065	3
CALLOWAY RICHARD H	LTC	0-0384690	0461	1
CALLOWAY ROBERT F	CW3	RW-2149750	0263	1
CALLOWAY VICTOR L	MAJ	0-2265361	1266	1
CALM ELY	1LT	0-1856630	0249	1
CALNAN JAMES T	LTC	0-1796917	0765	1
CALUS SPERO W	MAJ	0-0963816	0761	1
CALPIN CATHERINE	2LT	N-0762380	0645	1
CALPIN MICHAEL J	LTC	0-1303661	0363	1
CALPO MAURICIO	1LT	0-1876417	0654	1
CALTON RALPH N	1LT	0-1579460	0945	2
CALUGAS JOSE	CPT	0-1896617	0457	1
CALVANESE IDEAL M	LTC	0-1585241	0862	1
CALVARY PAUL R	MAJ	0-1171076	0859	1
CALVERLEY CHARLES E	MAJ	0-0285480	0864	3
CALVERT BINNIE F	1LT	N-0700853	1134	1
CALVERT CECIL	CPT	0-0166409	1146	2
CALVERT FLORENCE	2LT	N-0700100	0938	1
CALVERT GEORGE H	LTC	0-0228227	0764	3
CALVERT JACK F	LTC	0-1581579	0568	1
CALVERT LAWRENCE R	CPT	0-0324640	0157	1
CALVERT MICHAEL J	CPT	0-0130717	0954	3
CALVERT NORVAL K	CPT	0-1304016	0346	2
CALVERT PHILLIP E	CPT	0-1317880	0347	2
CALVERT RALPH C	1LT	0-1054508	0246	2
CALVERT ROBERT W	CPT	0-1110973	0556	2
CALVERT WILLIAM H	CW3	W-2142488	0161	1
CALVERT WILLIAM P	CW2	W-2152350	0859	1
CALVIN ASA E	MAJ	0-0298405	0862	3
CALVIN ELMER B	LTC	0-0195544	0761	3
CALWAY JAMES N	MAJ	0-1542497	1162	1
CALZA PETER	COL	0-0344311	0156	1
CAMACHO HAROLD J	CW4	RW-2144579	1168	1
CAMACHO MIGUEL A	1LT	0-0410457	0743	2
CAMBELL CHARLES K	MAJ	0-1635666	1060	1
CAMBLIN JOHN W	1LT	0-2032971	0760	1
CAMBRE GERARD I	COL	0-0272504	0764	3
CAMERA VERGIL C	CW3	W-2205767	1068	1
CAMERON ANDREW L	LTC	0-0249129	0666	3
CAMERON ARNOLD C JR	COL	0-0157196	0762	3
CAMERON CHARLES F	1LT	0-1556696	0745	2
CAMERON CLARENCE P	MAJ	0-1688091	0146	2
CAMERON DAVID A JR	MAJ	0-2034080	0966	2
CAMERON DORT A	1LT	0-0393545	1143	2
CAMERON EUSTACE R	CPT	0-1107337	0948	2
CAMERON FRANCES S	MAJ	L-0408198	0865	1
CAMERON FRANCIS	CW3	W-2128123	0661	2
CAMERON GERALD J	MAJ	0-1286305	0861	2
CAMERON HENRY M	LTC	0-0300431	0760	3
CAMERON JACK H	LTC	0-0477070	0256	1
CAMERON JOHN K	CPT	0-0405215	0745	2
CAMERON NEIL J	MAJ	0-1878052	0866	1
CAMERON NORMAN	CW3	W-2142951	0857	1
CAMERON RALPH H	COL	0-0265696	1152	3
CAMERON RALPH J	MAJ	0-0221750	0350	1
CAMERON RICHARD D	MAJ	0-1558368	0462	1
CAMERON ROBERT D	CW4	W-2110714	0664	3
CAMERON WILLIAM E JR	2LT	0-0926513	0146	2
CAMERON WILLIAM L	MAJ	0-1179320	0767	1
CAMERON WILLIAM P	MAJ	0-0292410	0648	3
CAMERON WILLIAM T	LTC	0-0244633	1056	3
CAMERUCI GLENN F	1LT	0-1284653	0745	2
CAMINER GERALD E	CW4	W-2136563	1164	1
CAMMACK OWEN F	MAJ	0-0901720	0246	2
CAMMACK RALPH I	MAJ	0-1289385	0563	1
CAMMACK WILLIAM R	2LT	0-0404183	0144	2
CAMP BERNARD L	CW2	W-2145074	0753	2
CAMP FRANK JR	CW2	W-2207101	0461	1
CAMP GEORGE M JR	CPT	0-2005447	1057	2
CAMP JAMES F	MAJ	0-2204431	1167	1
CAMP JOSEPH J	MAJ	0-1014832	0460	1
CAMP LEWIS L	LTC	0-0904172	1065	3
CAMP MARSHALL F	MAJ	0-0246071	0966	3
CAMP MAURICE A	MAJ	0-1950270	0262	1
CAMP MERWIN J	LTC	0-0292567	0662	1
CAMP ORVILLE S	LTC	0-0423006	0860	1
CAMP RALPH M	1LT	0-1018066	0846	2
CAMP ROBERT L	CW3	W-2142225	0564	1
CAMP THOMAS F	CPT	0-0314027	0847	1
CAMPAGNA JOSEPH R	LTC	0-1172792	0767	2
CAMPAGNA SEBASTIAN	2LT	0-0361721	0444	2
CAMPAIN JOHN W	MAJ	0-0279154	1065	3
CAMPANILE MICHAEL	1LT	0-1056313	0845	2
CAMPBELL ALAN B	CPT	0-0292313	0668	3
CAMPBELL ALEXANDER	COL	0-0159968	0652	3
CAMPBELL ALFRED R	MAJ	0-1038931	0557	1
CAMPBELL ALLAN	LTC	0-0257514	0157	1
CAMPBELL ALLIE H	CW3	W-3150512	1067	1
CAMPBELL ANGUS L	COL	0-0201593	0356	2
CAMPBELL ARNOLD	MAJ	0-1581841	0367	3
CAMPBELL ARTHUR E	COL	0-0157114	1052	3
CAMPBELL BOBBIE D	CW3	W-2113410	0157	2
CAMPBELL BOBBY R	LTC	0-0527112	1267	1
CAMPBELL BOWEN	LTC	0-0196594	0462	3
CAMPBELL BRUCE B JR	1LT	0-0382744	0745	2
CAMPBELL BRUCE W JR	MAJ	0-0359177	0745	2
CAMPBELL BUFORD J	CW4	W-2116156	0664	1
CAMPBELL BURDETTE F	1LT	0-1299847	0945	2
CAMPBELL CALVIN C	COL	0-1100472	0761	1
CAMPBELL CARL	CW4	W-2123107	0666	1
CAMPBELL CARL C	LTC	0-1055549	0468	1
CAMPBELL CHANDLER E	LTC	0-1015239	0666	1
CAMPBELL CHARLES E	1LT	0-0443987	1045	2
CAMPBELL CHARLES E	LTC	0-1640298	1166	1
CAMPBELL CHARLES H	COL	0-0183196	1053	1
CAMPBELL CHARLES K	MAJ	0-0177257	0157	3
CAMPBELL CHARLES M	1LT	0-0460089	0246	2
CAMPBELL CHARLES M	CPT	0-1321287	0363	1
CAMPBELL CHARLES S	CPT	0-1702568	0944	2
CAMPBELL CHARLES S	CW3	W-2206784	0267	1
CAMPBELL CHARLES W	MAJ	0-0278643	0757	3
CAMPBELL CHARLES W	CPT	0-0399183	0644	2
CAMPBELL CLARENCE N	CPT	0-0507058	0245	2
CAMPBELL CLARK L	CPT	0-1165713	1158	1
CAMPBELL COLEMAN E	LTC	0-0276161	1068	3
CAMPBELL COLIN A	MAJ	0-0140178	0755	3
CAMPBELL COLIN C	LTC	0-0234463	0857	2
CAMPBELL DANIEL J	LTC	0-0190417	1148	3
CAMPBELL DAVID E	MAJ	0-2262969	0562	1
CAMPBELL DAVID F	LTC	0-1100902	0161	1
CAMPBELL DAVID H	2LT	0-1308470	0945	2
CAMPBELL DAY H	COL	0-0168140	0959	3
CAMPBELL DELVAN R	CW3	W-2151195	0166	1
CAMPBELL DONALD J	CW3	W-2205605	1268	1
CAMPBELL DONALD R	CW2	W-2207450	0463	1
CAMPBELL EARL M	LTC	0-0464795	0662	1
CAMPBELL EDITH B	2LT	N-0762024	0944	1
CAMPBELL EDITH M F	2LT	N-0755369	0944	1
CAMPBELL EDNA C	MAJ	N-0723451	1264	3
CAMPBELL EDWARD B	LTC	0-1100474	1160	1
CAMPBELL EDWARD C	LTC	0-1172793	0258	1
CAMPBELL EDWIN C	LTC	0-2002414	1168	1
CAMPBELL EDWIN W	1LT	0-1556552	0646	2

NAME	GRADE	SVC NO	DATE RET MO YR	RET CODE
CAMPBELL ELVIS S	LTC	0-0196036	0361	3
CAMPBELL EUGENE D	WO1	W-2150115	0657	1
CAMPBELL FLOYD A	CW2	W-2206325	0862	1
CAMPBELL FORDYCE E	LTC	0-0195074	1054	1
CAMPBELL FRANCIS H	LTC	0-1176257	0765	1
CAMPBELL FRANCIS J	WO1	W-2110023	0948	1
CAMPBELL FRANK H	CPT	0-2150766	1057	1
CAMPBELL FRANK H	CPT	RO-2150766	1057	1
CAMPBELL FRANK J	LTC	0-0337015	1159	1
CAMPBELL FRANK S JR	MAJ	0-2029644	0465	1
CAMPBELL FRED H	CPT	0-0105647	0155	3
CAMPBELL GEORGE A	1LT	0-0544230	1145	2
CAMPBELL GEORGE J	MAJ	0-0383599	0859	1
CAMPBELL GEORGE J	MAJ	0-2203318	0569	1
CAMPBELL GEORGE J	CW2	W-2117172	1046	2
CAMPBELL GEORGE L	CW2	W-2145715	0461	1
CAMPBELL GEORGE W JR	CW2	W-2214904	1167	1
CAMPBELL GERALD D	LTC	0-0294819	0355	1
CAMPBELL GERTRUDE M	CPT	N-0729031	0948	2
CAMPBELL GLEN W	LTC	0-0207185	0656	3
CAMPBELL GORDON W	MAJ	0-1319760	0561	1
CAMPBELL GORDON W	MAJ	0-1899451	1264	1
CAMPBELL GRAHAM G	LTC	0-0134191	0553	3
CAMPBELL GUY E	LTC	0-1234824	0260	1
CAMPBELL HAROLD R	CW4	W-2145122	0666	1
CAMPBELL HARRY M	LTC	0-0219918	0257	3
CAMPBELL HENRY C	COL	0-0115893	0446	2
CAMPBELL HERBERT D	CW2	W-2114991	1044	2
CAMPBELL HOLMES	MAJ	0-0244620	0259	2
CAMPBELL HOWARD N	1LT	0-1012983	0551	2
CAMPBELL HOWELL H	1LT	0-1320505	0346	2
CAMPBELL HUGH B	LTC	0-0367510	0264	1
CAMPBELL JACK H	CPT	0-1995062	1051	2
CAMPBELL JAMES	CPT	0-2057010	0162	1
CAMPBELL JAMES A JR	LTC	0-0249130	0766	3
CAMPBELL JAMES D	COL	0-0243258	1154	1
CAMPBELL JAMES E	MAJ	0-1798444	0967	1
CAMPBELL JAMES G	LTC	0-1114932	0668	1
CAMPBELL JAMES J	MAJ	0-0254398	0964	3
CAMPBELL JAMES J	LTC	0-0313493	0663	3
CAMPBELL JAMES JR	LTC	0-1115386	0264	1
CAMPBELL JAMES M	MAJ	0-0513975	0437	1
CAMPBELL JAMES S	CPT	0-0944651	0860	1
CAMPBELL JAMES S	LTC	0-1588601	1262	1
CAMPBELL JAMES V	1LT	0-1298352	1045	2
CAMPBELL JAMES W	CW3	W-2207208	0867	1
CAMPBELL JOE C	1LT	0-0485658	0255	1
CAMPBELL JOHN	COL	0-0243514	0664	3
CAMPBELL JOHN E	1LT	0-1328114	1046	2
CAMPBELL JOHN F	CW2	W-2151809	0359	1
CAMPBELL JOHN G	2LT	0-0425866	0443	2
CAMPBELL JOHN H	LTC	0-0382000	0761	1
CAMPBELL JOHN JR	MAJ	0-2203031	0767	1
CAMPBELL JOHN M	1LT	0-0535905	1045	2
CAMPBELL JOHN N	1LT	0-0165681	0952	3
CAMPBELL JOHN P	COL	0-0115894	0648	3
CAMPBELL JOHN P	LTC	0-1169047	0561	1
CAMPBELL JOHN W JR	CW3	W-2146656	1065	1
CAMPBELL JOSEPH B	COL	0-0917810	0468	3
CAMPBELL JOSEPH L	COL	0-0332746	0368	3
CAMPBELL JOSEPH P	1LT	0-0400443	0244	2
CAMPBELL JULIA M	2LT	N-0726533	0444	1
CAMPBELL JUNIOR R	CW3	W-2147744	1264	2
CAMPBELL KENNETH A	LTC	0-0408829	0645	2
CAMPBELL KENNETH B	CW3	W-2149102	0265	1
CAMPBELL KENNETH M	CW3	W-2151762	1068	2
CAMPBELL LAURIE P	MAJ	0-0423151	0149	2
CAMPBELL LAWRENCE J	LTC	0-0222427	0864	3
CAMPBELL LELAND E	CPT	0-0388511	0346	2
CAMPBELL LELAND JR	MAJ	0-0778719	0656	2
CAMPBELL LOUIS J	MAJ	0-0889617	0457	1
CAMPBELL MARION B	CW2	W-2143604	0656	1
CAMPBELL MARION L	LTC	0-0348975	1163	3
CAMPBELL MAVER J	MAJ	0-0271903	0366	3
CAMPBELL MAX E	CW3	W-2203658	0767	1

NAME	GRADE	SVC NO	DATE RET MO YR	RET CODE
CAMPBELL MERLE F	MAJ	0-1051505	1262	1
CAMPBELL MONTGOMERY	LTC	0-0203344	1058	3
CAMPBELL MURDOCK A	B G	0-0186286	0952	3
CAMPBELL NELLIE O	2LT	N-0734614	1043	1
CAMPBELL OREN E	MAJ	0-0243872	0666	3
CAMPBELL PAUL L	LTC	0-0499813	0155	1
CAMPBELL PLEASANT P	CPT	0-1297158	0850	1
CAMPBELL RALPH L	LTC	0-0273521	0467	3
CAMPBELL RAY C	MAJ	0-0921003	0763	1
CAMPBELL RICHARD E	LTC	0-1044487	0863	1
CAMPBELL RICHARD H	LTC	0-0125205	0853	3
CAMPBELL RICHARD J	LTC	0-0919615	0568	3
CAMPBELL RICHARD O	MAJ	0-0321197	0448	2
CAMPBELL ROBERT A	WO1	W-2101514	0845	2
CAMPBELL ROBERT H	MAJ	0-2017199	0164	1
CAMPBELL ROBERT J	LTC	0-1295990	0662	1
CAMPBELL ROBERT M	COL	0-0232139	0260	3
CAMPBELL ROBERT T	CW3	W-2142820	0261	1
CAMPBELL ROBERT W	CPT	0-0549388	0747	2
CAMPBELL ROBERT W	LTC	0-1312277	0161	1
CAMPBELL ROLLEN F	LTC	0-1594082	0767	1
CAMPBELL RUSSELL A	MAJ	0-0401877	0860	1
CAMPBELL SAMUEL T JR	LTC	0-1316381	0666	1
CAMPBELL STEWART T	CW3	W-2145269	1065	1
CAMPBELL THEODORE	CW2	W-2101515	0350	1
CAMPBELL THEODORE	CW4	W-2144282	0161	1
CAMPBELL THEODORE M	MAJ	0-0510226	0546	2
CAMPBELL THERMAN L	CW2	W-2146691	0956	1
CAMPBELL THOMAS E	LTC	0-1042780	1161	1
CAMPBELL THOMAS G	MAJ	0-1553967	0565	1
CAMPBELL THOMAS H	MAJ	0-0385686	0760	1
CAMPBELL THOMAS J	MAJ	0-0469341	0452	2
CAMPBELL WALLACE J	CPT	0-0394267	0444	2
CAMPBELL WALTER F	LTC	0-0922274	0961	3
CAMPBELL WILBUR L	CW3	W-2205385	0868	1
CAMPBELL WILLIAM C	LTC	0-0250121	0966	3
CAMPBELL WILLIAM E	COL	0-0160696	0354	2
CAMPBELL WILLIAM H	CPT	0-2288112	1262	1
CAMPBELL WILLIAM J	CPT	0-0915152	0445	2
CAMPBELL WILLIAM J	CPT	0-1306378	0550	2
CAMPBELL WILLIAM N	CW3	W-2148842	0662	1
CAMPBELL WILLIE W	1LT	0-1013087	0358	1
CAMPBELL WINSTON E	CW3	W-2149250	0265	1
CAMPEAU JOHN	CW4	W-2200034	0368	3
CAMPER DEWEY C	CW3	W-2141215	1165	1
CAMPER HARRY G JR	CPT	0-0517378	1046	2
CAMPER WILLIAM L JR	MAJ	0-1290547	1060	1
CAMPFIELD ALLAN B	COL	0-0142359	1154	3
CAMPFIELD ARTHUR M	CPT	0-0350050	0745	2
CAMPION ALBERT E	LTC	0-0276272	0967	3
CAMPISANO JOSEPH T	LTC	0-0302443	0666	3
CAMPISI ORLANDO A	MAJ	0-2262660	0566	1
CAMPLAN CHARLES W	CPT	0-0276097	0767	3
CAMPO DOMINIC	CPT	0-1897739	1158	1
CAMPO JOHN A	CW3	W-2146148	0468	1
CAMPOBELLO SAMUEL	1LT	0-1062568	1045	2
CAMPRINI RODERICK P	LTC	0-1312375	0263	1
CAMUNEZ ARTHUR D	LTC	0-1313202	0762	1
CAMUTI LOUIS J	CPT	0-0140563	0853	3
CAMY LEON H	COL	0-0240337	0549	3
CANADA JAMES E	CPT	0-0172724	0648	3
CANADA JOHN B	COL	0-0259867	0867	3
CANADA JOHN R	MAJ	0-1108536	0363	2
CANADA JOHN R	CW3	W-2148784	1065	1
CANADA SAMUEL L	LTC	0-0947274	0866	3
CANADAY WILLIS L	MAJ	0-1876726	0666	1
CANALE ANTHONY J	1LT	0-5326853	1067	2
CANANT DENNIS C	LTC	0-2210044	1267	1
CANANT ERMER O	MAJ	0-2262856	1163	1
CANAS ENRIQUE J	CW3	W-2144702	0161	1
CANCELLARE ANTHONY D	LTC	0-0333094	0860	1
CANCIGLIA ALPHONSE	MAJ	0-0959097	0962	1
CANCIO LEONARDO D	1LT	0-2027039	1151	1
CANDELARIO JOSE M	2LT	0-1573756	0743	2
CANDLER ROBERT G JR	LTC	0-1014690	1167	1

NAME	GRADE	SVC NO	DATE RET MO YR	RET CODE
CANDLER WILLIAM W	2LT	0-1304858	1044	2
CANDY JOE E	LTC	0-1166925	0161	2
CANE DONALD B	LTC	0-1623734	0657	1
CANELLOS PETER J	LTC	0-1048710	1061	1
CANET ROSE P	2LT	N-0763770	0145	1
CANFIELD BRUCE H	MAJ	0-0307588	1145	2
CANFIELD DONALD T	1LT	0-0120389	0955	3
CANFIELD GEORGE H	COL	0-0103796	0648	3
CANFIELD HENRY P	MAJ	0-0186478	0556	3
CANFIELD JOHN J	CPT	0-1695271	0746	2
CANFIELD MORRIS H	MAJ	0-1183297	1164	1
CANGELOSI IGNAZIO F	MAJ	0-1688412	0762	1
CANGER ANDREW J	2LT	0-1016997	0945	2
CANHA ALVIN A	CW3	W-2110718	1060	1
CANIFF THOMAS F	CW2	W-2116015	0648	1
CANILAO LUPO	1LT	0-1896903	0452	2
CANINO&JIMENEZ V M	LTC	0-1924308	C958	2
CANIPELLI EDWARD	CPT	0-0331242	0145	2
CANLETT FRANKLIN H	1LT	0-2103072	0162	2
CANN ALFRED H JR	LTC	0-1180443	0166	1
CANN HOWARD L	LTC	0-0385640	1163	1
CANN JOSEPH R	CPT	0-1699962	0858	1
CANNADY ELLEN B	2LT	N-0743893	1044	1
CANNAN EDWIN J	LTC	0-0450097	1059	2
CANNEFAX WARREN M	MAJ	0-1649722	0555	1
CANNEY BERNARD J	CPT	0-1284654	0647	2
CANNICOTT WILLIAM	COL	0-0266089	0268	3
CANNING CHARLES F	CW3	W-3000207	1266	1
CANNING ROBERT A	MAJ	0-0232666	0463	3
CANNON EARL O	1LT	0-0905829	0645	2
CANNON ANGUS B	1LT	0-0279402	0461	1
CANNON CECIL L	MAJ	0-1292300	0759	1
CANNON CHARLES E	LTC	0-1103090	0862	1
CANNON ESPEY F	MAJ	0-0345394	1045	2
CANNON FRANK W	MAJ	0-0243193	0851	3
CANNON GEORGE E P	MAJ	0-1799939	0463	1
CANNON GEORGE M	MAJ	0-0109166	1130	1
CANNON HARVEY P	MAJ	0-1051068	0657	1
CANNON JACK D	MAJ	0-1649723	1064	1
CANNON JAMES P	MAJ	0-0237956	0165	3
CANNON JOE F	LTC	0-0447757	1155	1
CANNON JOHN B	COL	0-0200174	0358	3
CANNON JOHN E	LTC	0-1309344	0962	1
CANNON JOHN J	MAJ	0-0908902	0468	3
CANNON JOHN P	CW3	W-2127106	0656	1
CANNON JOSEPH F	LTC	0-1289386	0366	1
CANNON JOSEPH H	CPT	0-0360804	1143	2
CANNON JOSEPH M	CPT	0-0108821	1027	1
CANNON MALCOLM F	CW4	W-2141217	0465	1
CANNON MALLORY K JR	LTC	0-0215954	1262	3
CANNON OLIN B JR	CPT	0-0460090	0146	2
CANNON RAYMOND J JR	MAJ	0-0375991	0146	2
CANNON ROBERT J	CPT	0-1340261	1168	2
CANON CLEO R	CW2	W-2147208	0662	1
CANON PERCY W	CPT	0-1918962	0668	2
CANONICA GEORGE	LTC	0-1554873	0765	1
CANOVA ENRIQUE C	COL	0-0235001	1056	3
CANRIGHT WARREN W	1LT	0-0430265	0547	2
CANTACESSI PAT	LTC	0-0970267	0964	1
CANTAGO LUCIO	1LT	0-0890480	0548	1
CANTAGO REGINO	2LT	0-2031879	0159	1
CANTERBURY SHERMAN C	LTC	0-0345195	0266	1
CANTILLON THOMAS P	1LT	0-1293202	1046	2
CANTLEY CHARLES E	MAJ	0-0493813	0157	1
CANTLEY CHARLES E JR	MAJ	0-0987825	0265	1
CANTLEY EUGENE H	MAJ	0-1578236	0859	1
CANTLEY HOMER H	MAJ	0-0971355	0662	1
CANTLEY NORMAN J	LTC	0-0325076	0761	1
CANTLEY ROGER H	CPT	0-1999210	0646	2
CANTNER HARRY E	LTC	0-0191606	0648	3
CANTONI PETE J	1LT	0-2048241	0645	2
CANTOR JESSE E	LTC	0-0519174	1045	2
CANTOR MORTIMER J	LTC	0-0325167	1046	2
CANTOR PHILIP E	COL	0-0488955	0266	3
CANTORE THOMAS A	MAJ	0-2033077	0463	1

NAME	GRADE	SVC NO	DATE RET MO YR	RET CODE
CANTRALL EVANS F	CPT	0-0118338	0648	3
CANTRELL ALLEN W	CPT	0-2032972	0764	1
CANTRELL BOYD T	MAJ	0-1582655	0965	1
CANTRELL DAVID M	CW3	W-2148687	1060	1
CANTRELL JACK G	CW2	W-2209577	0263	1
CANTRELL JAMES A	CW2	W-3200169	0764	1
CANTRELL JAMES C	MAJ	0-1341400	1165	1
CANTRELL LEONARD E	LTC	0-0676019	1166	1
CANTRELL LIGE L	CPT	0-0360654	0944	2
CANTRELL LYNDELL O	CW2	W-2146738	1059	1
CANTRELL OSCAR C	1LT	0-0887450	0556	1
CANTRELL RALPH E	LTC	0-0503011	0555	1
CANTRELL ROBERT B	MAJ	0-0399724	0862	1
CANTRELL THOMAS A	MAJ	0-0317971	0246	2
CANTRELL WARREN G	MAJ	0-1180444	1267	1
CANTRELL WILFRED O	CW3	W-2146706	0961	1
CANTRELL WILLIAM A	CPT	0-2026529	0154	1
CANTRELL WILLIAM P	CPT	0-1321744	0754	2
CANTRILL EVERETT R	MAJ	0-0975815	1155	1
CANTWELL CALVIN A	1LT	0-1175966	0645	2
CANTWELL JAMES F	M G	0-0396657	0968	3
CANTWELL JAMES W	MAJ	0-0303255	0244	2
CANTWELL JOHN J JR	2LT	0-1822956	0645	2
CANTWELL ORVILLE D	LTC	0-0243448	0963	3
CANTWELL ROBERT C	MAJ	0-2033626	0261	1
CANTY LEONARD C	1LT	0-0308982	0647	2
CANUP CLYDE W	CW3	W-2206456	0468	1
CANUTESON ELMORE C	CPT	0-0266492	1265	3
CANZANO JOSEPH	MAJ	0-0885732	0156	1
CAPARINO BRUNO	1LT	0-2030575	1049	1
CAPASSO ALEXANDER	MAJ	0-0352729	0260	1
CAPASSO SALVATORE	LTC	0-0403197	0860	1
CAPE GURNEE	1LT	0-1013252	0546	2
CAPE JOSEPH R	CW3	W-2150890	0263	1
CAPELLE WILMER B	CPT	0-1291230	0452	2
CAPEN EDGAR A	CPT	0-0163940	1044	2
CAPERS HAROLD H	COL	0-0204559	0854	1
CAPERS ROBERT A	CPT	0-1301945	0347	2
CAPERTON LUCIEN M	MAJ	0-0304343	0745	2
CAPILDUTO ISAAC E	CPT	0-0353731	0545	2
CAPITELL ROBERT W	1LT	0-0396588	0344	2
CAPKA ADOLPH J	LTC	0-1703854	1263	1
CAPLAN CHARLES C	CPT	0-0537200	1045	2
CAPLAN LESLIE	MAJ	0-0413434	0746	2
CAPLE GEORGE H JR	LTC	0-0299266	0857	1
CAPLE JOHN A JR	CW3	W-2153349	0466	1
CAPLE RALPH G	LTC	0-1950643	0764	1
CAPLES ROBERT O	CPT	0-0481554	0345	2
CAPLES WILLIS H	LTC	0-0556902	0365	1
CAPLIN BERNARD	WO1	W-2121109	1144	2
CAPLINGER HAROLD S	COL	0-0264190	1060	3
CAPO MILFORD T	1LT	0-0417299	0945	2
CAPO RAFAEL	LTC	0-0279050	1065	3
CAPONE EDMUND P	COL	0-0225410	0564	3
CAPONEGRO ALFRED B	1LT	0-2041155	0552	2
CAPOZZI HENRY L	1LT	0-1102656	0146	2
CAPP GEORGE R	COL	0-0162771	0946	2
CAPPELEN JOHN J JR	MAJ	0-0998291	1262	1
CAPPELETTI LAWRENCE	MAJ	0-1998387	1060	1
CAPPELLETTI JOSEPH M	LTC	0-0450814	0759	1
CAPPER ARTHUR M	LTC	0-0201376	0763	1
CAPPER RANDOLPH B	MAJ	0-1587166	1060	1
CAPPS GARY F	LTC	0-1637150	0167	1
CAPPS JESSE L	CPT	0-0495247	0759	1
CAPPS RICHARD B	LTC	0-0386360	0346	2
CAPPS RODNEY D	LTC	0-0334655	0761	1
CAPPS TED	MAJ	0-1323285	0157	1
CAPPS WILLIAM B	MAJ	0-0328729	0754	2
CAPPS WILLIAM T JR	2LT	0-1295826	0544	2
CAPPUCCIO FRANK S	WO1	W-2126259	0745	2
CAPPY ANDREW L	LTC	0-1535146	0161	1
CAPRARO SALVATORE	1LT	0-0496218	0644	2
CAPRIELIAN LEON R	1LT	0-1166242	0745	2
CAPRIO MICHAEL J	1LT	0-1575829	1060	2
CAPRON ARTHUR D	LTC	0-1920281	1168	1

NAME	GRADE	SVC NO	DATE RET MO YR	RET CODE
CAPROON DOUGLAS M	2LT	0-5310853	0761	2
CAPSHAW LAWSON M	MAJ	0-2009292	0860	1
CAPSHAW ROY E JR	MAJ	0-1286789	0459	1
CAPSTICK DONALD R	LTC	0-1557129	1262	1
CAPTAIN GEORGE F	CW2	W-2209211	1264	1
CAPUANO ANDREW	CPT	0-1319599	0946	2
CAPUCILLE HENRY G	LTC	0-1998420	0712	1
CAPUTO MICHAEL L	1LT	0-1544539	0347	2
CAPUTO PETER A	MAJ	0-1895277	1054	2
CARAMAT RAFAEL	1LT	0-1896722	0951	1
CARANTO ERIBERTO	MAJ	0-1896462	0267	1
CARARIE ANTHONY	LTC	0-1166926	0861	1
CARAVAN ANTHONY	CW3	W-2144786	0563	1
CARAVATI CHARLES M	LTC	0-0481994	0646	2
CARAWAY JEWELL H	CW3	W-2150006	0264	1
CARAWAY LUTHER D	MAJ	0-4010214	0866	2
CARBALLO ABIGAIL	1LT	0-4028375	0857	2
CARBALLO DOMINADOR	1LT	0-1896611	1062	1
CARBAUGH KENNETH W	CPT	0-0291134	0945	2
CARBAUGH JOYCE A	CPT	0-0955451	0559	1
CARBERRY JAMES F	LTC	0-1017793	0965	1
CARBERRY WILLIAM F	CW2	W-2210665	0367	1
CARBIA MARIO	MAJ	0-0395353	0153	1
CARBIN JOHN P JR	LTC	0-1290897	0265	3
CARBIS WAYNE F	LTC	0-0159008	0756	3
CARBONE ALFONSO R	MAJ	0-1795361	1157	1
CARBONE FRANK A	MAJ	0-1637151	0161	1
CARBRINHA ANTHONY M	LTC	0-0343171	0860	1
CARBRY VINCENT N	CPT	0-0189903	0856	3
CARCHIDI GEORGE M	CW3	W-2149404	0865	1
CARCIONE LAWRENCE C	MAJ	0-1382541	0768	3
CARD ALBERT H	MAJ	0-1040988	0468	3
CARD JACK H	1LT	0-1821678	0745	2
CARD LLOYD S	CW4	W-2102727	0357	1
CARD THOMAS B	COL	0-0147154	0955	3
CARD WILLIAM R	CPT	0-1799779	0962	2
CARDAMON ALBERT J	LTC	0-0401482	0265	1
CARDE MANUEL [illegible]	CPT	0-0167385	0654	3
CARDELLA JAMES A	CW3	W-2147237	0463	1
CARDEN ALVA E SR	CPT	0-0233358	0357	1
CARDEN BLYTHE R L	COL	0-0195812	0960	3
CARDER ALVA L	CPT	0-0246217	0649	3
CARDER FRANK R	MAJ	0-0444959	0148	1
CARDER NATHANIEL	COL	0-0266138	0453	3
CARDER WESLEY S JR	2LT	0-2010805	0945	2
CARDILLO LUCA F	LTC	0-0395352	0560	1
CARDINAL EUGENE C	CW3	W-2145381	0860	1
CARDLE GEORGE E	LTC	0-0486915	0165	3
CARDONA VICTOR	MAJ	0-0274202	1166	3
CARDONE MICHAEL A	CW3	W-2152801	0762	1
CARDONE SAMUEL M	LTC	0-0299613	1067	3
CARDOTT WAYNE Y	MAJ	0-0265590	0267	1
CARDOZA HOWARD H	1LT	0-1177318	0551	2
CARDOZA HUGH L	COL	0-0357549	1165	1
CARDWELL ARDENTER B	MAJ	0-1012124	1055	1
CARDWELL CECIL L	MAJ	0-1281395	0555	1
CARDWELL CLIFTON G	MAJ	0-2036851	1060	1
CARDWELL CLYDE W	CPT	0-0234103	1264	3
CARDWELL FOSTER M	1LT	0-1796575	0944	2
CARDWELL JOHN F	CPT	0-0112896	0352	3
CARDWELL NICHOLAS	1LT	0-0491813	1046	1
CARDWELL OTIS P	CPT	0-1000921	0764	1
CARDWELL PERCY L	LTC	0-0179599	0354	3
CAREL MORRIS W	MAJ	0-0977372	0562	1
CAREL RALPH A	CPT	0-1588444	0657	1
CAREW JOHN H	1LT	0-1017345	0346	2
CAREW JOHN J	COL	0-0126433	0345	2
CAREW LAWRENCE F	COL	0-0234272	0246	2
CAREY ALFRED J	MAJ	0-0495992	0157	1
CAREY CHARLOTTE	1LT	0-1103551	1045	2
CAREY EDWARD J	LTC	0-0232531	0163	3
CAREY FRANK J	COL	0-0165389	0452	3
CAREY GLENN W	COL	0-0171565	0542	2
CAREY HARRY H	LTC	0-0175988	0648	3
CAREY JAMES	CPT	0-1299682	0459	1

NAME	GRADE	SVC NO	DATE RET MO YR	RET CODE
CAREY JAMES E	1LT	0-1011130	0945	2
CAREY JAMES F	LTC	0-0229821	0465	3
CAREY JAMES H	LTC	0-0443645	0365	1
CAREY JAMES T	MAJ	0-1796231	0657	1
CAREY JOHN A	2LT	0-1325373	0345	2
CAREY JOHN F JR	CW4	W-2203346	1268	1
CAREY JOHN J JR	1LT	0-1304859	1045	2
CAREY JOSEPH M	CW2	W-2206666	0262	1
CAREY LAURENCE M	CPT	0-0902242	0745	2
CAREY LEO A	CPT	0-0489270	1146	2
CAREY MARC R	CPT	0-0167818	1155	3
CAREY NELSON B	LTC	0-1042511	0263	1
CAREY PERRY E	CPT	0-2026964	0757	1
CAREY THOMAS G	COL	0-0325545	1060	1
CAREY WILLIAM L	CPT	0-0361903	0244	2
CAREY WILLIAM M	CPT	0-1105307	0461	1
CAREY WILLIAM M	LTC	0-1115517	0368	1
CAREY WILLIAM N	COL	0-0165788	0648	3
CAREY WILLIAM T	MAJ	0-2040783	0660	2
CARFAGNO JOSEPH J	MAJ	0-1585751	0958	1
CARFANO FRANCIS A	2LT	0-0439867	1042	2
CARFIELD WILLIAM E	MAJ	0-1917720	0264	1
CARGEN JOHN B	1LT	0-0528394	1145	2
CARGILE C B JR	CW3	W-2149841	0965	1
CARGILL DEXTER A	LTC	0-0272532	0758	3
CARGILL GEORGE S JR	MAJ	0-0227598	1164	3
CARGILL WILLIAM JR	CPT	0-1042781	1060	1
CARHARTT FORREST M	COL	0-0114232	0257	3
CARICH JOE	MAJ	0-0478521	1045	1
CARIDEO BIAGIO A	LTC	0-0273291	0667	3
CARIE JAMES J	MAJ	0-2265191	0167	1
CARIGLIA MICHAEL W	LTC	0-0503750	1262	1
CARINI JIM	LTC	0-0489146	0456	2
CARIS JOHN A	CW3	W-2203646	0964	1
CARKEEK STANLEY N	LTC	0-0326167	0146	2
CARL DANIEL E	LTC	0-0484552	1051	1
CARL FLOYD C	COL	0-0103260	1145	2
CARL FRED W	CW2	W-2109510	0647	1
CARL GEORGE A	CW4	W-2001822	1161	3
CARL HARRY F	CPT	0-1170675	1047	2
CARL RAYMOND A	CPT	0-1049137	0467	3
CARL ROY G	MAJ	0-0247249	0160	3
CARL RUSSELL R	CPT	0-1573098	0446	2
CARLAW ROBERT H	1LT	0-1576295	0245	2
CARLENO ALBERT F	LTC	0-0498691	0655	1
CARLETON ALBION M	MAJ	0-1180146	0261	2
CARLETON CHARLES D	COL	0-0182940	0159	3
CARLETON GEORGE	LTC	0-0286910	0157	3
CARLETON GEORGE A	LTC	0-1108538	0862	1
CARLETON HARRY F	1LT	0-1061645	0146	2
CARLETON HOWARD JR	LTC	0-0166011	0447	2
CARLETON MILDRED L	1LT	N-0721617	0346	1
CARLIER JOHN W	MAJ	0-0311155	1165	3
CARLILE NORMAN A H	LTC	0-0315334	1264	1
CARLIN EDWARD L	CW4	W-2149412	1168	1
CARLIN LOUIS	CPT	0-0533659	0447	2
CARLIN RAYMOND C	MAJ	0-0408151	0950	2
CARLISLE DOROTHY N	2LT	N-0775265	0145	2
CARLISLE FLOYD L	LTC	0-0221666	0156	3
CARLISLE FRANK R	LTC	0-1325075	0263	1
CARLISLE GLENN P	CPT	0-0315421	0758	2
CARLISLE HAROLD E	LTC	0-1107846	1161	2
CARLISLE JOHN S	LTC	0-0300626	0957	1
CARLISLE JOHN T	LTC	0-0169009	1060	3
CARLISLE JOSEPH Y	CW4	W-2113398	0366	3
CARLISLE RICHARD M	LTC	0-0365439	0265	3
CARLISLE ROBERT J	1LT	0-1319104	0945	2
CARLL FREDERICK	CW3	W-3150460	0967	1
CARLO ANGEL L	CPT	0-1301779	0860	1
CARLO JOSEPH F	1LT	0-0335042	0145	2
CARLO MICHAEL	MAJ	0-0286823	0847	1
CARLOCK HENRY A	LTC	0-0236114	1045	2
CARLOCK HORACE V	MAJ	0-0395543	0462	1
CARLOCK MARION F	MAJ	0-0268165	0566	3
CARLOCK NEIL S	LTC	0-0312663	0646	2

NAME	GRADE	SVC NO	DATE RET MO YR	RET CODE
CARLOCK ROBERT H	CPT	0-1324507	0247	2
CARLOS WILLIAM	CW3	W-2145192	1062	1
CARLOVITCH FRANK	WO1	W-2148665	0655	1
CARLOW FRANK L	2LT	0-2010464	0167	3
CARLSEN CHARLES E	LTC	0-1307367	0466	1
CARLSEN EMANUEL	LTC	0-0468863	0163	1
CARLSEN WILLIS E	MAJ	0-1315458	0862	1
CARLSON ALBERT D	LTC	0-0243876	0262	3
CARLSON ALF R	MAJ	0-0503293	0450	1
CARLSON ARTHUR J	LTC	0-0192152	0457	1
CARLSON ARTHUR W	MAJ	0-1579469	0557	1
CARLSON BERNICE A	2LT	N-0742870	1044	1
CARLSON CARL A	LTC	0-0195144	0162	3
CARLSON CARL A	LTC	0-0303119	0855	3
CARLSON CARL A	MAJ	0-0966491	1262	1
CARLSON CARL E	CW2	W-2205063	0468	3
CARLSON CARL O L	1LT	0-0413886	1144	2
CARLSON CHARLES P	LTC	0-0359045	0760	1
CARLSON CLARENCE W	LTC	0-0316874	0161	1
CARLSON CONRAD T	MAJ	0-2262992	0264	1
CARLSON CORINNE C	1LT	N-0744718	0845	1
CARLSON DALE W	MAJ	0-1309923	0865	1
CARLSON DOLPHINE H	CW4	W-2113910	0157	1
CARLSON EARL P	CW3	W-2150349	1065	1
CARLSON EDWIN D	LTC	0-0276143	1059	1
CARLSON ERNEST J	CPT	0-1285377	1045	2
CARLSON GEORGE C	LTC	0-0411511	0965	3
CARLSON GEORGE D	LTC	0-0456219	0461	1
CARLSON GLENN D	COL	0-0250791	0562	3
CARLSON GUSTAF M	MAJ	0-1105308	0967	3
CARLSON HENNING G	LTC	0-0242802	1153	3
CARLSON HERBERT A	MAJ	0-1333601	0461	1
CARLSON HERBERT F	CPT	0-1307193	0446	2
CARLSON JOHN A	LTC	0-1283210	0562	1
CARLSON JOHN F	MAJ	0-1799423	0961	1
CARLSON LEONARD J	LTC	0-0144086	0-49	1
CARLSON LEONARD W	LTC	0-1646909	0367	2
CARLSON LESLIE R	CW2	W-2211370	0967	1
CARLSON LLOYD T	CW2	W-2141219	1060	2
CARLSON LLOYD V	MAJ	0-1110412	0666	2
CARLSON MAURICE JR	MAJ	0-0980963	0368	1
CARLSON MAURICE L	1LT	0-0510533	0945	2
CARLSON MCKINLEY S	LTC	0-0212357	0761	3
CARLSON NORMAN V	COL	0-0283113	0364	3
CARLSON PAAVO D	COL	0-0306506	1266	1
CARLSON RALPH E	LTC	0-0201955	1162	3
CARLSON RAYMOND A	LTC	0-0948457	1267	1
CARLSON RAYMOND F	LTC	0-0126926	1150	3
CARLSON RICHARD	MAJ	0-1335744	0865	1
CARLSON ROBERT B	LTC	0-1341511	1168	1
CARLSON ROBERT H	CPT	0-0451429	0346	2
CARLSON ROBERT H	CW3	W-2153113	0566	1
CARLSON ROBERT L	COL	0-0304919	0565	1
CARLSON ROBERT V	CW2	W-2144499	0960	1
CARLSON ROGER K	2LT	0-0975353	0953	2
CARLSON ROY F	LTC	0-1183430	0661	1
CARLSON SIDNEY A	CPT	0-0276616	1264	1
CARLSON SIGFRID F	COL	0-0351200	0162	1
CARLSON THEODORE D	CPT	0-0519992	0345	2
CARLSON TILFORD F	1LT	0-0245607	0961	1
CARLSON VERNON W	LTC	0-0544702	1167	1
CARLSON WINSTON L	MAJ	0-1823402	1263	1
CARLSTROM CHARLES H	MAJ	0-0289337	0767	3
CARLTON CHARLES W JR	LTC	0-0186837	0762	3
CARLTON DUANE R	MAJ	0-0175245	0560	3
CARLTON GEORGE C	CPT	0-0509534	0357	1
CARLTON GEORGE S	CW2	W-2214655	1166	1
CARLTON HARRY N	LTC	0-0294712	0968	3
CARLTON RAY F	MAJ	0-1100906	1151	1
CARLTON RICHARD W	LTC	0-1030314	1264	1
CARLTON THAD M SR	CPT	0-0477473	0648	2
CARLTON TULLIE H	LTC	0-0182954	1155	3
CARLTON WILLIAM R JR	COL	0-0414915	0767	1
CARLTON WILLIAM H	CW2	W-2205945	0960	1
CARLYLE CHARLES E	LTC	0-1533275	0860	1

NAME	GRADE	SVC NO	DATE RET MO YR	RET CODE
CARMACK CRAIG S	LTC	0-0237332	0366	3
CARMACK GEORGE G	CW4	W-2141522	0868	1
CARMACK JESSE	CPT	0-0443897	0944	1
CARMACK LLOYD D	LTC	0-2014705	0168	1
CARMACK VERBA W	MAJ	0-0203761	0557	3
CARMAN CHARLES K	1LT	0-2028825	0750	1
CARMAN CHARLES M	1LT	0-0324062	1045	2
CARMAN DAVID B	2LT	0-1112072	0744	2
CARMAN DONALD L	MAJ	0-1010763	1047	2
CARMAN ROBERT M	CPT	0-1650461	0158	1
CARMEAN CHARLES C	MAJ	0-1633737	1161	1
CARMEL DAVID B	WO1	W-2128360	0545	2
CARMER CLARENCE W	1LT	0-0967311	1158	1
CARMER RALPH P	MAJ	0-0988112	0865	1
CARMICAL WILLIAM K	CW3	W-2149427	0367	1
CARMICHAEL EDWARD L	B G	0-0256012	1064	3
CARMICHAEL ELBERT E	LTC	0-0268211	1059	1
CARMICHAEL FRANCIS A	MAJ	0-0406625	0146	2
CARMICHAEL GEORGE W	CPT	0-0983441	0762	1
CARMICHAEL HOWARD E	MAJ	0-0183223	0648	3
CARMICHAEL HUBERT L	MAJ	0-2075529	0166	2
CARMICHAEL KENNETH C	MAJ	0-1923597	0465	1
CARMICHAEL MABEL M	MAJ	N-0720651	0468	3
CARMICHAEL THOMAS N	CPT	0-0440407	0246	2
CARMICHAEL TURNER F	CPT	0-2262664	1165	1
CARMICHAEL WHITFIELD	CW4	W-2152079	1268	1
CARMICHAEL WILLIAM A	COL	0-0154303	0648	3
CARMICHAEL WILLIAM C	LTC	0-0995557	1068	1
CARMICHAEL WILLIAM H	CPT	0-0389697	0844	2
CARMICHAEL WILSON H	MAJ	0-0955096	0968	1
CARMICHEAL WILLIAM A	LTC	0-1289544	0559	1
CARMODY DENNIS M	1LT	0-0419349	0544	2
CARMODY JOHN V	CPT	0-0488620	0650	1
CARNAGEY ERMAN P	MAJ	0-1686757	1165	1
CARNAGHAN RAYMOND S	CW4	W-2002355	0163	1
CARNAHAN ANDREW B	LTC	0-0415812	0561	1
CARNAHAN CLARENCE	CPT	0-0490447	0948	1
CARNAHAN HUGH L	COL	0-0122016	0251	3
CARNAHAN PAUL M	CPT	0-0218942	1056	3
CARNAHAN ROBERT S	CPT	0-0257131	0160	3
CARNAHAN WILLIAM G	1LT	0-0300631	0145	2
CARNAN CHARLES W JR	MAJ	0-0470163	1045	2
CARNE NORBERT O	CPT	0-1932329	0765	1
CARNER LESLIE	MAJ	0-0108572	1136	1
CARNER WILFORD R	LTC	0-0488923	1054	2
CARNES AVERY W	CPT	0-1032615	0156	1
CARNES CHARLES N	1LT	0-0497236	0246	2
CARNES CHARLES W	COL	0-0391298	0165	1
CARNES WILLIAM T	1LT	0-1297835	1045	2
CARNESALE PETER L	COL	0-0388930	0468	3
CARNETT CHARLES D	MAJ	0-0263994	0753	3
CARNETT RAYMOND R	COL	0-0275087	0768	3
CARNEY CHARLES A	COL	0-0241002	0158	1
CARNEY CHARLES P JR	MAJ	0-1298354	0346	2
CARNEY ELIZABETH	MAJ	N-0760080	0466	1
CARNEY HARRY P	COL	0-0276321	1263	3
CARNEY HENRY J	LTC	0-0245768	1059	3
CARNEY JAMES H	LTC	0-1552034	1162	1
CARNEY JEAN	LTC	0-1650462	0368	1
CARNEY JOHN E	CW4	W-2110734	0758	1
CARNEY JOHN G JR	LTC	0-1590364	0862	1
CARNEY JOHN J	CPT	0-0924539	0745	2
CARNEY JOHN P	1LT	0-1316529	0845	2
CARNEY LAWRENCE B	LTC	0-0273610	0767	3
CARNEY LEONARD E	CW2	W-2145794	1160	1
CARNEY LEROY F	LTC	0-1114889	1067	1
CARNEY MARY L	2LT	N-0700830	0239	1
CARNEY SIDNEY	CPT	0-1169889	0446	2
CARNEY STANIS P	LTC	0-0510339	0557	2
CARNEY THOMAS M	1LT	0-1312103	0945	2
CARNEY WILLIAM	1LT	0-0178737	0241	1
CARNEY WILLIAM P	WO1	W-2105564	0146	2
CARNEY WILLIAM T	LTC	0-1038735	0364	2
CARNINE DONALD M	LTC	0-1822358	0661	1
CARNS ANDY M	LTC	0-1104076	0360	1

NAME	GRADE	SVC NO	DATE RET MO YR	RET CODE
CARNS WILLIAM A	CPT	0-1913581	1023	1
CAROL HAROLD L	2LT	0-1013007	1043	2
CAROLAN FRANCIS J	LTC	0-0310710	1068	3
CAROLIN JOHN V	LTC	0-1031470	1262	1
CARON JOSEPH C	CPT	0-0521273	1146	1
CARON JOSEPH R	CPT	0-1573760	0256	1
CAROTHERS ARTHUR W	LTC	0-1554874	0765	2
CAROTHERS PAUL L	WO1	W-2128325	1044	2
CAROTHERS VICTOR L	CPT	0-0267728	0656	3
CARP EDWARD M	MAJ	0-1341630	0363	1
CARP EDWIN W	2LT	0-1306240	0645	2
CARP FRED	COL	0-0218472	0748	3
CARP PETER F	MAJ	0-1104077	0264	1
CARPENTER ALVA C	COL	0-0290429	0262	3
CARPENTER CHARLES L	MAJ	0-1702256	1165	1
CARPENTER CHARLES M	LTC	0-0312540	0146	2
CARPENTER CHESTER F	LTC	0-2018481	0764	1
CARPENTER CLAIR F	1LT	0-1291413	0345	2
CARPENTER CLERON J	1LT	0-1297678	0 46	2
CARPENTER DELBERT O	LTC	0-1049433	0863	1
CARPENTER EDWIN H	MAJ	0-1881159	1267	1
CARPENTER EDWIN J	COL	0-0300589	0859	1
CARPENTER ELLIOTT JR	CPT	0-1016118	0746	2
CARPENTER ELMER W	2LT	0-0889618	0968	3
CARPENTER EMMETT M	LTC	0-0430158	1264	3
CARPENTER FINLEY B	1LT	0-1310808	1046	2
CARPENTER FLAVE J	LTC	0-1691936	0266	1
CARPENTER FRANCIS W	MAJ	0-0255328	0867	3
CARPENTER FRANK G	2LT	0-0463904	0444	2
CARPENTER FRANKLIN E	COL	0-0377163	0868	1
CARPENTER G Y JR	MAJ	0-0467679	0547	2
CARPENTER GEORGE K	LTC	0-0491892	1145	2
CARPENTER GEORGE L	1LT	0-1390172	1058	3
CARPENTER GILBERT B	LTC	0-1545815	1064	1
CARPENTER GROVER N	LTC	0-1595417	0367	1
CARPENTER HOWARD J	LTC	0-0483866	0458	2
CARPENTER HOWARD S	WO1	W-2114333	1043	2
CARPENTER HUGH	LTC	0-0924983	0364	3
CARPENTER JACK D	MAJ	0-1296168	1159	1
CARPENTER JAMES H	LTC	0-0346782	0660	1
CARPENTER JAMES J	MAJ	0-1107340	0956	2
CARPENTER JAMES J	CW3	W-2143440	0257	1
CARPENTER JAMES L	MAJ	0-0488297	0950	1
CARPENTER JOAN G	1LT	N-0768969	1147	1
CARPENTER JOHN C JR	1LT	0-0446422	0646	2
CARPENTER JOSEPH D	1LT	0-1019125	1062	2
CARPENTER KENNETH C	1LT	0-0492915	0153	1
CARPENTER KENNETH L	MAJ	0-0975887	1163	1
CARPENTER LAWRENCE F	CPT	0-0282178	0346	2
CARPENTER LESLIE B	LTC	0-0218170	0856	3
CARPENTER LYLE F	CW3	W-2147199	0266	1
CARPENTER MALCOLM Y	LTC	0-0266067	0756	3
CARPENTER MARY L	1LT	N-0734251	1047	1
CARPENTER MAURICE P	1LT	0-1304173	0346	2
CARPENTER MELVIN M	1LT	0-1307653	0546	2
CARPENTER ORVILLE F	MAJ	0-0441789	0448	2
CARPENTER PHILIP A	MAJ	0-1301429	0361	1
CARPENTER RALPH E	LTC	0-2018482	1163	1
CARPENTER RALPH G	MAJ	0-1308207	0859	1
CARPENTER RAYMOND C	MAJ	0-1798114	0157	1
CARPENTER REED L	MAJ	0-1306701	0954	2
CARPENTER RICHARD T	MAJ	0-0369847	0968	3
CARPENTER ROBERT D	CW3	W-2144404	0862	1
CARPENTER ROBERT R	LTC	0-1573761	0157	1
CARPENTER ROLAND E	1LT	0-1328119	0646	2
CARPENTER ROY R	LTC	0-1060387	0462	1
CARPENTER WALTER N	LTC	0-1286606	0966	1
CARPENTER WARNER H	CW2	W-2209740	0863	1
CARPENTER WILBUR B	MAJ	0-0219633	0947	1
CARPENTER WILLIAM J	MAJ	0-1640834	0767	1
CARPENTER WILLIAM J	MAJ	0-1949503	1262	1
CARPENTER WILLIAM R	LTC	0-0268641	0263	3
CARPENTER WILLIAM R	LTC	0-0387079	0461	1
CARPER HAROLD O	LTC	0-1894777	0361	1
CARPER JOHN H	LTC	0-0436263	0368	3

NAME	GRADE	SVC NO	DATE RET MO YR	RET CODE
CARPER ROBERT J	LTC	0-0107605	0153	3
CARPLES EDMOND N	MAJ	0-0109526	1155	3
CARPPI WALTER L	MAJ	0-0370313	0561	1
CARR ALFRED L	LTC	0-0115834	0756	3
CARR BERNARD	MAJ	0-0491216	0347	1
CARR CHARLES A	MAJ	0-0263485	0457	3
CARR CHESTER M	LTC	0-0451086	0854	1
CARR CLARENCE R	COL	0-0260108	1166	3
CARR CLAUDE J	1LT	0-1995557	0846	2
CARR CLINTON C	LTC	0-0401791	0763	1
CARR EDWARD A JR	CPT	0-1704914	1147	2
CARR EDWARD J	CW4	W-2127932	1058	1
CARR EDWIN O	LTC	0-2014614	0868	1
CARR FOSTER A	CPT	0-1648573	0356	2
CARR FRANCIS J	MAJ	0-1294618	0461	1
CARR FRANK O	LTC	0-0493874	0557	1
CARR FREDERIC C	CW3	W-2143230	1263	2
CARR GEORGE P	LTC	0-1106040	0463	1
CARR GEORGE W	MAJ	0-0126320	0547	2
CARR GUY F	MAJ	0-0373428	0346	2
CARR ISAAC N	LTC	0-0205660	0252	3
CARR JACK O	CPT	0-0460233	0945	2
CARR JAMES M	COL	0-0215827	0158	3
CARR JAMES W	CW3	W-2142137	0863	1
CARR JESSIE E	CW3	W-2121386	0856	1
CARR JOHN R	LTC	0-0349141	0960	2
CARR JOSEPH E	LTC	0-2049195	1162	1
CARR KENNETH P	CW4	W-2115608	1267	3
CARR LELAND E	LTC	0-0359589	0861	1
CARR LEMAR B	2LT	0-1998633	0945	2
CARR MILTON L	LTC	0-0452544	0561	2
CARR PHILLIP R	CPT	0-0972485	0562	1
CARR RALPH W JR	LTC	0-1014256	0866	1
CARR RAYMOND H	MAJ	0-2030526	0167	1
CARR RAYMOND O	MAJ	0-1081123	0156	1
CARR REX V	MAJ	0-0377256	0648	2
CARR RHEA	LTC	N-0741197	0165	3
CARR RICHARD B	MAJ	0-1885612	0865	1
CARR ROBERT W	MAJ	0-1307194	0863	1
CARR ROGER W	MAJ	0-2023326	1061	1
CARR SAM B JR	LTC	0-1169452	0162	1
CARR SEYMOUR J	CPT	0-4014174	1054	2
CARR SHIRLEY N JR	CW3	W-2145400	0561	1
CARR STEPHEN J	MAJ	0-0288972	1150	1
CARR THAD	CPT	0-0409382	0245	2
CARR THOMAS A	LTC	0-0150176	0857	3
CARR THOMAS J	CPT	0-1018842	1147	2
CARR WALTER L	LTC	0-1549680	0363	1
CARR WESLEY	1LT	0-1284290	0445	2
CARR WILLIAM F	1LT	0-0301953	0657	3
CARR WILLIAM H	CW4	W-2148491	0168	1
CARR WILLIAM P	LTC	0-1307195	0259	1
CARR WILLIAM R	LTC	0-0196824	1162	3
CARRABINO JOSEPH F	MAJ	0-0954058	1165	1
CARRAGHER TIMOTHY A	CW4	W-2118106	0155	1
CARRAWAY THOMAS L JR	1LT	0-0544173	0447	2
CARRELL ELMER N	LTC	0-0274860	0268	3
CARRELL STEPHEN E	CPT	0-0251081	1062	3
CARRELL VIRCEL R	CW2	W-2209274	0661	1
CARRERAS WILFRED C	MAJ	0-0502430	1046	2
CARRICK HAROLD T	CPT	0-0219935	0844	2
CARRICO ALFRED W	2LT	0-0503340	0644	2
CARRICO ANDREW III	1LT	0-1010859	1045	2
CARRICO DONALD G	CW3	W-2210321	0568	1
CARRICO FRANK G	COL	0-0163875	0754	3
CARRICO JOHN L	WO1	W-2126079	0545	2
CARRICO MELVILLE D	1LT	0-0108891	0633	1
CARRIER CLIFFORD C	1LT	0-1030646	1046	2
CARRIER ERNEST H	CPT	0-2043292	0556	1
CARRIER JOHN S	LTC	0-0333935	0750	2
CARRIER JOHN X	LTC	0-1176573	0667	1
CARRIER LUVERN J	CPT	0-0331981	0144	2
CARRIER NELL D	MAJ	N-0726111	0764	1
CARRIER ROLAND R	CPT	0-1332230	1059	2
CARRIER WILLIAM H	LTC	0-0183089	1055	3

NAME	GRADE	SVC NO	DATE RET MO YR	RET CODE
CARRIERE EDGAR	1LT	0-2025952	0652	1
CARRIERE EDWARD F	COL	0-0248513	0565	3
CARRIG JOHN T JR	MAJ	0-1684974	1164	1
CARRIGAN MARY L S	2LT	N-0723119	1044	1
CARRIGER HERMAN D	1LT	0-1286791	0745	2
CARRIKER WALTER W	LTC	0-0337251	1146	2
CARRINGTON H K	CPT	0-0267161	0945	2
CARRINGTON HENRY P	CPT	0-0352502	1061	1
CARRINGTON LEON J	LTC	0-0298611	0560	2
CARRINGTON PAUL W	LTC	0-1180447	0565	3
CARRION JOSEPH S	MAJ	0-1283375	1054	1
CARRIVEAU EDWARD T	CPT	0-1297317	0556	1
CARROLL ADDISON B	CPT	0-1035693	1068	2
CARROLL ALFRED E	MAJ	0-1919043	1263	1
CARROLL BARNEY A	LTC	0-1633740	1065	1
CARROLL BERNICE	1LT	N-0730801	0446	1
CARROLL BERRY W JR	LTC	0-1046388	1064	1
CARROLL CARL W	MAJ	0-4074586	0768	1
CARROLL CHARLES	COL	0-0212391	0857	1
CARROLL CHARLES L	MAJ	0-1800064	1062	1
CARROLL CHARLES P	LTC	0-0282964	0263	2
CARROLL CHARLES T	MAJ	0-0381448	0246	2
CARROLL CLIFFORD C	MAJ	0-0150757	0753	3
CARROLL DELMAR B	LTC	0-0362830	0760	1
CARROLL DOYLE D	MAJ	0-0379100	0661	1
CARROLL EDWARD A	LTC	0-0921879	1166	3
CARROLL EDWARD B	LTC	0-0225094	0458	3
CARROLL EDWARD D	LTC	0-1172795	1165	1
CARROLL EDWARD J	MAJ	0-1004746	0557	1
CARROLL EDWARD J	1LT	0-1109184	0845	2
CARROLL ELMO O	LTC	0-2017351	1160	1
CARROLL ERVIN J	MAJ	0-0383996	0958	1
CARROLL EVAN W SR	CPT	0-0163356	0559	3
CARROLL FINLEY M	1LT	0-0332507	1068	3
CARROLL FRANCIS B	COL	0-0264666	0962	1
CARROLL FRANK S	LTC	0-0286562	0360	3
CARROLL GEORGE E	MAJ	0-1684950	0862	1
CARROLL GEORGE P	LTC	0-0136928	1149	3
CARROLL HAROLD J	MAJ	0-1054203	1064	1
CARROLL HARRY M	COL	0-0191732	0351	3
CARROLL HARRY W	MAJ	0-1037429	0263	1
CARROLL HOMER D	CW3	W-2141837	0860	1
CARROLL JABEZ F JR	1LT	0-1119161	0948	2
CARROLL JACK P	1LT	0-1307940	0147	2
CARROLL JAMES A	MAJ	0-0217344	1045	2
CARROLL JAMES F	LTC	0-0276021	1267	3
CARROLL JAMES J	LTC	0-0330470	0261	2
CARROLL JAMES W	LTC	0-2262989	0468	1
CARROLL JASPER G	1LT	0-2018840	1057	1
CARROLL JOHN	CW2	W-2145328	1160	1
CARROLL JOHN E JR	LTC	0-0177281	0562	3
CARROLL JOHN F	1LT	0-2034936	0452	2
CARROLL JOHN J JR	CPT	0-1166685	0768	2
CARROLL JOHN W	CPT	0-1165006	0546	2
CARROLL JOSEPH A	MAJ	0-0265746	0747	1
CARROLL JOSEPH J	MAJ	0-2025149	0563	1
CARROLL KENNETH L	1LT	0-1876452	0956	2
CARROLL KENT F	2LT	0-5701772	0259	2
CARROLL LAWRENCE W	CPT	0-0482470	0257	1
CARROLL LEONARD B	MAJ	0-0271877	0868	3
CARROLL LEONARD N	1LT	0-1110980	0246	2
CARROLL LEONARD S	COL	0-0292341	1155	1
CARROLL MACK M	CW3	W-2143395	0659	1
CARROLL MICHAEL L	CW3	W-2143712	0160	1
CARROLL OWEN J	LTC	0-1324141	1065	1
CARROLL PAUL F	1LT	0-1325971	0546	2
CARROLL PETER J	1LT	0-0557702	0546	2
CARROLL PHILLIP H	CPT	0-0412189	0945	2
CARROLL ROBERT F	LTC	0-0481182	0759	1
CARROLL ROBERT F JR	1LT	0-1308601	0745	2
CARROLL ROBERT H	CPT	0-1325865	1158	1
CARROLL ROBERT J	MAJ	0-1540853	1162	1
CARROLL ROGER C	LTC	0-0264044	0759	1
CARROLL ROLLY	CPT	0-1937997	0363	1
CARROLL SANFORD A	COL	0-0236833	1060	3

NAME	GRADE	SVC NO	DATE RET MO YR	RET CODE
CARROLL SHELBY T	CW3	W-2149762	0761	1
CARROLL THADDEUS L	LTC	0-0281986	0868	3
CARROLL THOMAS F	LTC	0-0101020	0757	3
CARROLL VINCENT A	COL	0-0148806	0552	3
CARROLL WALKER K	COL	0-1100479	0163	2
CARROLL WALTER B	LTC	0-1329800	0268	1
CARROLL WESLEY W	CW2	W-2148108	0459	1
CARROLL WILLIAM F	CPT	0-0501756	0248	1
CARROLL WILLIAM G	1LT	0-1015369	0146	2
CARROLL WILLIAM R	M G	0-0246570	0456	3
CARROLL WILLIAM R	1LT	0-0924932	1145	2
CARROLL WINTON A J	MAJ	0-1014648	1059	1
CARROLLO JOHN J	LTC	0-0310209	1162	1
CARRON HECTOR M	MAJ	0-0174032	0150	3
CARROTHERS JOHN W	COL	0-0167282	0758	3
CARROUM OMER D	LTC	0-1284825	0761	1
CARROW WILFRED J	MAJ	0-1325374	1060	1
CARROZA ORLANDO W	MAJ	0-1335511	0863	1
CARRUTH HUGH B	LTC	0-0359382	1267	3
CARRUTH JAMES E	LTC	0-1104552	0158	1
CARRUTHERS GORDON E	1LT	0-2047591	0446	2
CARRUTHERS HECTOR K	MAJ	0-1058750	1059	2
CARRUTHERS J T JR	COL	0-0479653	0167	3
CARSCH HARRY	CW3	W-2149010	1065	1
CARSE STEWART L	LTC	0-0372147	1055	1
CARSKADEN LEWIS J	CPT	0-0157218	0954	3
CARSLEY ALBERT E	LTC	0-1300597	1264	1
CARSON ARCHIE K	CW3	W-2149039	0964	1
CARSON BAYLIS R JR	MAJ	0-0374109	0862	1
CARSON CARYL C	MAJ	0-0175135	1060	3
CARSON DAVID M	LTC	0-0407391	0562	1
CARSON DOUGLAS B	MAJ	0-1292833	0350	1
CARSON EARL J	2LT	0-0454299	1043	2
CARSON EDWARD C	CW3	W-2147137	0165	1
CARSON HARLIN C	CPT	0-0485400	0554	1
CARSON JAMES K	CW4	W-2110114	1155	1
CARSON JOHN L	MAJ	0-1924956	0861	2
CARSON KARL J	LTC	0-1170808	0764	1
CARSON PAT	MAJ	0-1111538	0963	1
CARSON REX W	WO1	W-2127037	0646	1
CARSON RICHARD L	MAJ	0-1331015	1064	1
CARSON ROBERT G	CW2	W-2143476	0865	1
CARSON ROBERT H	MAJ	0-1926060	0868	1
CARSON ROBERT J	COL	0-0159178	1152	3
CARSON ROBERT L	MAJ	0-1173898	0461	1
CARSON THOMAS F	MAJ	0-0218860	0658	3
CARSON WILLIAM L	LTC	0-1293716	0358	1
CARSTARPHEN JACK	COL	0-1551816	0267	1
CARSTENS HENRY R	COL	0-0162798	1048	3
CARSWELL RONALD W JR	CW2	W-2212849	0267	1
CARSWELL WILLIAM D	LTC	0-0348737	0863	1
CARTE CARL R	CW3	W-2118159	0959	1
CARTER ADGER M	COL	0-0259210	0860	1
CARTER ALBERT C	COL	0-0237910	1263	3
CARTER ALFONSA C	CW3	W-2210144	0268	1
CARTER ALFRED H	CPT	0-0446423	0653	2
CARTER ALFRED M	LTC	0-2032093	0668	1
CARTER ARCEMUS	LTC	0-0109273	0337	1
CARTER ARTHUR	CPT	0-0518411	0546	2
CARTER ARTHUR B	CW3	W-2147351	1164	1
CARTER AUBURN H SR	CPT	0-0167807	0858	3
CARTER BOOKER W	LTC	0-1322204	0463	2
CARTER BRADLEY J	CPT	0-0275393	0355	3
CARTER BRYANT E	COL	0-0293814	0361	1
CARTER CHARLES	CPT	0-0191682	0452	3
CARTER CHARLES A	LTC	0-1102659	1162	1
CARTER CHARLES C	LTC	0-1589113	0761	1
CARTER CHARLES H	2LT	0-1180842	0645	2
CARTER CHARLES J	MAJ	0-1167765	1060	1
CARTER CHARLES L SR	CPT	0-0255914	0757	3
CARTER CHARLES M	CPT	0-1920308	0662	1
CARTER CHARLES R	LTC	0-1315558	0961	1
CARTER CHARLES R	MAJ	0-1649257	1164	1
CARTER CHARLES W	COL	0-0476804	0863	1
CARTER CHARLIE W	CPT	0-0152532	0754	3

NAME	GRADE	SVC NO	DATE RET MO YR	RET CODE
CARTER CHESTER	CPT	0-0248366	0365	3
CARTER CLARENCE J	CW3	W-3150750	1268	1
CARTER CLAUDE E	COL	0-0319749	1061	3
CARTER DAVID L	MAJ	0-4074667	0868	1
CARTER DELL E	MAJ	0-1303810	0262	1
CARTER DONALD F	COL	0-0540128	0665	1
CARTER DOUGLAS E	CW3	W-2109046	0155	1
CARTER EARL	MAJ	0-0483615	0347	2
CARTER EDWARD E	MAJ	0-1175068	0957	1
CARTER ELIZABETH	1LT	N-0744864	0345	1
CARTER ELLERBE W	B G	0-0204334	0648	3
CARTER EVELYN M	2LT	N-0758343	0546	1
CARTER FRANK L	1LT	0-0189443	0836	1
CARTER GARRARD E	1LT	0-1591041	0745	2
CARTER GEORGE A JR	2LT	0-1175398	0745	2
CARTER GEORGE F	CPT	0-0492601	0145	2
CARTER GEORGE F	CW2	W-2127986	0547	2
CARTER GEORGE R	CW2	W-2147093	0861	1
CARTER GEORGE W	LTC	0-0227395	1163	3
CARTER GORDON L	COL	0-0123847	0453	3
CARTER HAROLD L	LTC	0-0267752	0551	1
CARTER HARRY B	LTC	0-0301632	0767	3
CARTER HENRY E JR	1LT	0-0556525	0846	2
CARTER HORACE W	COL	0-0212222	0352	2
CARTER IVAN L	LTC	0-0297322	0454	3
CARTER J FLOYD	LTC	0-1004551	0962	1
CARTER J P	CW4	W-2145796	0968	1
CARTER JACKSON	CPT	0-0270772	0867	1
CARTER JACOB M JR	MAJ	0-0100448	1155	1
CARTER JAMES C JR	1LT	0-1316011	0845	2
CARTER JAMES E	LTC	0-0932874	1066	3
CARTER JAMES H	MAJ	0-0272077	0345	2
CARTER JAMES N JR	LTC	0-2020709	0766	1
CARTER JAMES P	LTC	0-1293204	1058	1
CARTER JAMES T	MAJ	0-1318513	1059	1
CARTER JERAL E	MAJ	0-0996674	0364	1
CARTER JESSE S	CPT	0-0186985	0627	1
CARTER JOE T	CPT	0-1844595	0746	2
CARTER JOHN C	1LT	0-0277275	0857	3
CARTER JOHN C	LTC	0-0370812	0556	1
CARTER JOHN C	CW2	W-2212744	1168	2
CARTER JOHN G	CPT	0-0359223	0447	2
CARTER JOHN H	COL	0-0276104	0346	2
CARTER JOHN H	COL	0-0410471	0460	1
CARTER JOHN J	CW4	W-2136751	0263	1
CARTER JOHN S	LTC	0-0217343	0755	3
CARTER JULIAN H	MAJ	0-0374761	0563	3
CARTER KARL R	CW4	W-2131289	0659	1
CARTER KENNETH A	CW4	W-2107953	0659	1
CARTER KENNETH L	CW3	W-2144902	0960	1
CARTER LAWRENCE D	LTC	0-1580726	0863	1
CARTER LEROY M	1LT	0-1298659	1059	1
CARTER LLOYD W	MAJ	0-1922588	0963	1
CARTER LUCIAN C	MAJ	0-0492700	0146	2
CARTER MAJEL S	2LT	N-0769858	0446	1
CARTER MARGUERITE	1LT	N-0731728	0746	1
CARTER MARTIN S	MAJ	0-1306784	0860	1
CARTER MARY F	MAJ	N-0783500	1067	3
CARTER MELVILLE G	CPT	0-1305547	0147	2
CARTER MILTON P	MAJ	0-0300170	0663	3
CARTER NATHANIEL	MAJ	0-2262496	0363	1
CARTER NOAH J	2LT	0-2000503	0845	2
CARTER NUMA R	MAJ	0-0181991	1152	3
CARTER OWEN H	COL	0-0334313	0854	1
CARTER PAYSON O	MAJ	0-0924217	0846	2
CARTER RAYMOND F	CPT	0-0418684	0446	2
CARTER RICHARD E	MAJ	0-0301935	0564	3
CARTER RICHARD T	CW2	W-2142451	0758	1
CARTER ROBERT T	MAJ	0-1054204	0364	1
CARTER ROLLA N	MAJ	0-0175530	1160	3
CARTER ROLLAND D	CPT	0-1324143	0661	1
CARTER RONALD P	COL	0-0370782	0863	3
CARTER RUTH A	MAJ	N-0802138	0965	1
CARTER RUTH F	1LT	N-0790453	0746	1
CARTER SANFORD J	LTC	0-0420374	0861	1

NAME	GRADE	SVC NO	DATE RET MO YR	RET CODE
CARTER SHERWOOD J	LTC	0-0960102	0667	1
CARTER THOMAS B	LTC	0-0203915	0648	3
CARTER THOMAS M	COL	0-0115875	0648	3
CARTER THOMAS N	LTC	0-1303301	0163	1
CARTER TONY L JR	COL	0-0279246	1057	3
CARTER VERNON L	CPT	0-1105319	1046	2
CARTER VICTOR S	LTC	0-0385758	0346	2
CARTER VILLA	LTC	0-0450557	0257	1
CARTER WICKHAM R JR	MAJ	0-0354518	1046	2
CARTER WILLIAM A	LTC	0-0289074	0762	1
CARTER WILLIAM C	MAJ	0-0244374	0757	3
CARTER WILLIAM M JR	MAJ	0-0391652	0645	2
CARTER WILLIAM L	MAJ	0-1031063	0662	1
CARTER WILLIAM P JR	LTC	0-1596289	0965	1
CARTER WILLIAM R	LTC	0-0293459	0960	1
CARTER WILLIS JR	MAJ	0-1822359	0361	1
CARTER WOODROW W	LTC	0-1304338	0967	1
CARTER WYNN W	CPT	0-0327811	0144	2
CARTER ZINA R	MAJ	0-0306308	0862	1
CARTHEW IRVING G	MAJ	0-1308096	0762	1
CARTIER LOUIS F	1LT	0-1844596	0346	2
CARTLEDGE JAMES C	MAJ	0-1288854	1163	1
CARTMELL WILLIAM T	CPT	0-2262927	1067	1
CARTO DAVID S	2LT	0-1640840	0345	2
CARTON JOSEPH D	LTC	0-0245279	1264	3
CARTWRIGHT CHARLES B	MAJ	0-1314756	1060	1
CARTWRIGHT CHARLES R	LTC	0-0401396	0461	1
CARTWRIGHT CLARENCE	CPT	0-1414618	0446	1
CARTWRIGHT GENE H	CPT	0-1132928	0559	1
CARTWRIGHT GEORGE O	CPT	0-0495303	0747	1
CARTWRIGHT GEORGE T	MAJ	0-1291584	0360	1
CARTWRIGHT H A JR	CW3	W-2205044	0566	1
CARTWRIGHT HERBERT L	LTC	0-2020786	0166	1
CARTWRIGHT JAMES J	CPT	0-0291077	0857	3
CARTWRIGHT JOHN E	MAJ	0-1684981	0164	1
CARTWRIGHT KENNETH R	MAJ	0-2262835	0363	1
CARTWRIGHT MALCOLM F	MAJ	0-0970104	0766	1
CARTWRIGHT MYRTLE L	2LT	N-0733045	0445	1
CARTWRIGHT SAM F	1LT	0-1304020	0745	2
CARTWRIGHT WILLIAM O	COL	0-0203914	0947	2
CARTY CHARLES H	LTC	0-0399735	1160	1
CARTY GERALD J	1LT	0-1183032	1045	2
CARUGNO FRANK J	MAJ	0-0888949	0657	1
CARUS VICTOR	2LT	0-1550983	0845	2
CARUSO GEORGE A	MAJ	0-0235485	0258	3
CARUSO JOHN J	CPT	0-1690637	1045	2
CARUTHERS FRANK E	CPT	0-0471611	1058	1
CARVELL EATHEL C	CW3	W-2149286	0162	2
CARVER ARTHUR W	CW3	W-2144222	1262	1
CARVER CHARLES C	CW2	W-2114726	1164	3
CARVER CLARENCE D	MAJ	0-1581874	0765	3
CARVER DERL D	CW4	W-2125835	0659	1
CARVER HENRY V JR	CW3	W-2142741	0762	1
CARVER JAMES L	CW3	W-2152200	0564	1
CARVER KATHRYN F	1LT	N-0723048	1044	1
CARVER KENNETH F	CPT	0-0921820	0345	2
CARVER ROBERT L	MAJ	0-1919911	0467	1
CARVER WILLIAM H	LTC	0-1552245	0965	1
CARVILL JACK	1LT	0-0370344	1142	2
CARWILE ADDISON B	COL	0-0148807	1056	3
CARWILE JACK F	LTC	0-0109143	0646	1
CARY CARROLL E	LTC	0-1172404	1263	1
CARY HENRY B	COL	0-0410107	1057	1
CARY LOUIS A	MAJ	0-0211135	0354	3
CARY MAX E	LTC	0-1313495	0964	1
CARY WILLIAM F	1LT	0-0375835	1145	2
CASADA MARGARET V	MAJ	L-0605290	0767	1
CASADA MILTON T	2LT	0-1320427	0460	1
CASADY EDWIN L	CPT	0-1287809	1047	2
CASALE CARLO C	COL	0-0413949	0465	1
CASALE CHARLES E	COL	0-0257400	0358	3
CASAS GUILLERMO	CW2	W-2151636	0860	1
CASAUS CARLOS H JR	LTC	0-1053517	1062	1
CASAZZA CHARLES J	MAJ	0-1327812	0756	1
CASAZZAR EDWARD G	CPT	0-0462267	0546	2

NAME	GRADE	SVC NO	DATE RET MO YR	RET CODE
CASCIO CARL W	LTC	0-1010598	0657	1
CASDORPH ROY A	CPT	0-2262437	1060	1
CASE ALBERT N	1LT	0-1286244	1045	2
CASE BEN F	CPT	0-0483983	0243	1
CASE BERNARD	COL	0-0194876	0959	3
CASE CHARLIE	1LT	0-0488673	0545	2
CASE DAVID L	LTC	0-1040191	0261	1
CASE ELMER J	1LT	0-1546279	0448	2
CASE GEORGE I JR	CPT	0-1324508	0668	3
CASE HAROLD T	CPT	0-0525944	0346	2
CASE HERSCHEL F	MAJ	0-0132012	1056	3
CASE HERSHEL C	LTC	0-0417237	1160	1
CASE JAMES R	LTC	0-0110145	1154	3
CASE KENNETH T	COL	0-0248874	0463	3
CASE LAWRENCE C	COL	0-0335454	0659	3
CASE LUTHER G	COL	0-0309384	0954	1
CASE MILTON L	MAJ	0-1824577	0262	1
CASE OLIVER L	MAJ	0-0430186	0157	1
CASE REX R	1LT	0-2009607	0753	1
CASE ROBERT J	2LT	0-5705909	1061	2
CASE ROY E	COL	0-0244693	1058	3
CASE WILLIAM L	LTC	0-2034839	0167	2
CASEBEER GAYLE M	MAJ	0-1015991	0361	1
CASEBEER JAMES R	MAJ	0-1593147	0657	1
CASELLA ANTHONY P	CW4	W-2152017	1168	1
CASELLAS ROZAS F N	1LT	0-1326891	0453	2
CASELLI ORLANDO J	CPT	0-0346178	1044	2
CASERIO CHARLES C	LTC	0-1100480	0962	1
CASEY ALOYSIUS J	LTC	0-0233957	1162	3
CASEY CLARE C	LTC	0-0908057	1167	3
CASEY EDWARD J JR	LTC	0-1557823	0361	1
CASEY EDWIN W	LTC	0-0554365	1064	1
CASEY GEORGE W	MAJ	0-1104715	0761	1
CASEY HERBERT O JR	MAJ	0-1017863	1163	1
CASEY JAMES E	COL	0-0300239	0566	3
CASEY JAMES J	LTC	0-0396693	0463	1
CASEY JAMES J	LTC	0-1995572	1168	1
CASEY JAMES W	MAJ	0-0325143	0762	1
CASEY JOHN F	LTC	0-1284468	0157	1
CASEY JOHN J	CPT	0-0512409	0645	2
CASEY JOHN J	CW4	W-2108664	0464	1
CASEY JOHN P	1LT	0-1016323	0346	2
CASEY JOHN P	CW2	W-2146446	0559	1
CASEY JOHN V	1LT	0-1182537	0246	2
CASEY JOHN W	COL	0-0289076	0160	1
CASEY JOSEPH A	LTC	0-0492901	1055	1
CASEY LEE V	COL	0-0195810	0254	3
CASEY MARY A	1LT	N-0770001	0347	2
CASEY POWELL A	LTC	0-0281301	1265	3
CASEY ROBERT F	CW3	W-2141525	1060	1
CASEY STEPHEN R	LTC	0-1325268	0367	1
CASEY TIMOTHY C	MAJ	0-2027375	0560	1
CASEY WALTER A	MAJ	0-0531978	0565	1
CASEY WILFRED	CW4	W-2139485	0556	1
CASEY WILLIAM C	LTC	0-1578249	0657	1
CASEY WILLIAM K	LTC	0-1312833	0361	1
CASEY WILLIAM L	COL	0-0125187	0953	3
CASH ARNOLD B	MAJ	0-0220598	0345	2
CASH HAROLD F	LTC	0-1080836	0367	1
CASH PHILIP G	1LT	0-1058755	0546	2
CASH RALEIGH M	LTC	0-1703765	0358	1
CASH WALTER A	1LT	0-1321880	0146	2
CASH WARREN P	LTC	0-0227223	0565	3
CASH WILLIAM T	WO1	W-2124725	0650	2
CASH WILLIE F	CW3	W-2144867	0561	1
CASHIN DONALD F	1LT	0-0472307	0952	1
CASHION JOHN H	LTC	0-0462239	1064	1
CASHION MERRELL C	MAJ	0-1293908	0363	1
CASHMAN HARRY	MAJ	0-0978529	0167	1
CASHON IDA O	MAJ	N-0735434	1067	1
CASIANO-NAZARIO FERM	MAJ	0-4031039	0866	1
CASIMIR JOHN	1LT	0-1000094	1043	2
CASIMO ANTHONY J	CPT	0-1180147	0446	2
CASKEY EDWARD A	LTC	0-0904102	0251	2
CASKEY NEAL L	LTC	0-0407024	0460	1

NAME	GRADE	SVC NO	DATE RET MO YR	RET CODE
CASKEY WILLIAM P	MAJ	0-0490731	0556	1
CASNER JOHN R JR	1LT	0-0534850	0846	2
CASNER LEETA L	1LT	0-1321488	0146	2
CASNER LEWIS E	MAJ	0-1183484	0359	2
CASO ANTHONY R	CW4	W-2007044	0468	1
CASON CLAUDE E	LTC	0-1311739	0261	1
CASON ELBERT H	CPT	0-0440873	0945	2
CASON FRANCIS L	LTC	0-1341746	0768	1
CASON JOSEPH H	MAJ	0-1304021	0161	1
CASON WILLIS S	MAJ	0-0377355	0746	2
CASPER ANDREW F	COL	0-0171780	1060	3
CASPER CHARLES R	LTC	0-0888551	1060	1
CASPER RAYMOND E	MAJ	0-0202697	0747	2
CASPER RAYMOND E JR	1LT	0-0329837	1043	2
CASPERSON PETER C	COL	0-1296484	0967	1
CASS ROGER L	MAJ	0-1300598	0557	1
CASSADA JAMES C	MAJ	0-2000075	0464	1
CASSADY CHARLES A	LTC	0-0228803	0455	3
CASSADY MILBURNE C	MAJ	0-2263022	0463	1
CASSADY THOMAS C	LTC	0-0314369	0660	1
CASSANO JAMES	LTC	0-0286189	0968	3
CASSARO ANGELO J	MAJ	0-1054936	0664	1
CASSAVANT THEODORE W	CPT	0-0144041	0356	3
CASSAVECCHIA WALTERE	CW3	W-2147456	0763	1
CASSCELLS SAMUEL R	CPT	0-0477283	0946	2
CASSEGRAND JOHN A JR	CW2	W-2211102	0765	1
CASSEL JONATHON F	MAJ	0-1533985	0957	1
CASSELBERRY WILLIAM	CPT	0-0990214	0763	1
CASSELL BENJAMIN F	COL	0-0407012	0267	3
CASSELL CHARLES G	COL	0-0302301	0358	1
CASSELL HARRIS	LTC	0-0556161	0963	1
CASSELL PAUL E	CPT	0-1310979	0846	2
CASSELL ROBERT S	LTC	0-0349803	0661	2
CASSELL THOMAS G	LTC	0-0471764	0153	1
CASSELL WILLIAM H JR	CW3	W-2141220	1060	1
CASSELLA PETER A	CPT	0-0327462	0146	2
CASSELMAN BERT W	LTC	0-0284727	1146	2
CASSELMAN LAWRENCE	CPT	0-1101772	1045	2
CASSETT GEORGE	LTC	0-0223851	0262	3
CASSETT WILLIAM C	MAJ	0-1549239	0158	1
CASSIDY ALBERT D	LTC	0-1101773	0761	1
CASSIDY ARTHUR E	LTC	0-0212112	0447	2
CASSIDY GLENN E	LTC	0-0332266	0268	3
CASSIDY IRWIN F	CPT	0-0910133	0766	2
CASSIDY JAMES J	LTC	0-1297680	0664	1
CASSIDY JAMES J	CPT	0-2041003	0648	2
CASSIDY JOHN P	MAJ	0-0966157	0265	1
CASSIDY JOSEPH P	CPT	0-1012494	0346	2
CASSIDY LEONARD P JR	LTC	0-0676745	0163	1
CASSIDY LEWIS E	LTC	0-2294003	0765	1
CASSIDY LOUIS G	CPT	0-1945772	0347	2
CASSIDY MARGARET A	LTC	L-1010539	0668	1
CASSIDY MARGARET A	MAJ	N-0755704	0467	3
CASSIDY MARIE G	2LT	N-0722359	1043	1
CASSIDY MARK M	LTC	0-1945552	0860	1
CASSIDY MARY F	LTC	L-0202588	1066	3
CASSIDY RICHARD P	LTC	0-0965643	1067	1
CASSIDY WILEY L	MAJ	0-1298355	0563	1
CASSINELLI W J JR	CPT	0-1301948	1045	2
CASSITY GEORGE W	LTC	0-0248294	0563	3
CASSITY RICHARD P	1LT	0-2263384	0957	2
CASSON HILLMAN C	CW2	W-2118158	0756	2
CASSON JOHN E	LTC	0-1304022	0962	1
CASTAGNETO FRANK C	COL	0-0338380	0864	2
CASTANARES SALVADOR	LTC	0-0473721	0446	2
CASTEEL BLAINE B	LTC	0-1592073	1262	1
CASTELL JOHN H	MAJ	0-0388252	0446	2
CASTELLA CHARLES C	LTC	0-0225163	1264	3
CASTER MAYNARD F	LTC	0-0384096	1062	1
CASTETTER CHARLES H	CW4	W-2142494	0657	1
CASTILLE SIMON	COL	0-0234762	1165	3
CASTILLO JOSE A	COL	0-0290344	0660	1
CASTILLO JOSE M	CPT	0-0507883	0544	2
CASTILLO RALPH	LTC	0-1575839	1060	1
CASTLE CLARENCE F	LTC	0-0252907	1166	3

NAME	GRADE	SVC NO	DATE RET MO YR	RET CODE
CASTLE DON R	LTC	0-1321611	1063	1
CASTLE ELEANOR M	1LT	N-0720312	1044	1
CASTLE JOE F	LTC	0-1046037	1066	1
CASTLE KENDALL R JR	CPT	0-0235229	0561	3
CASTLE PHILLIP A	MAJ	0-0239518	1264	3
CASTLE ROBERT W	COL	0-0230213	0863	3
CASTLE WILLIAM R JR	LTC	0-0179425	0457	3
CASTLEBERRY GUY	MAJ	0-0182523	0743	2
CASTLEBERRY HARRALL	MAJ	0-1306243	1163	1
CASTLEBERRY L M	CPT	0-0550349	0547	2
CASTLEBERRY W M	1LT	0-0502578	1044	2
CASTLEMAN WILLIAM L	1LT	0-1010165	1145	2
CASTLEN JOHN C	COL	0-0425217	0966	1
CASTLES RICHARD P	LTC	0-1581930	0662	2
CASTNER EARL L	LTC	0-0219632	1058	3
CASTNER LEWIS JR	MAJ	0-0979343	1262	2
CASTON BENJAMIN F	LTC	0-0453387	0859	1
CASTON CHARLES W SR	CPT	0-1593496	0746	2
CASTONGUAY ROLAND G	MAJ	0-0925161	0148	2
CASTOR TULLUS R	CW4	W-2007999	0866	1
CASTORINA ALFRED R	MAJ	0-1108546	1060	1
CASTRIANNI SAM J	CW2	W-2150200	0261	1
CASTRILLO JACINTO	COL	0-0269840	0964	3
CASTRO ALFONSO A	LTC	0-1313496	0161	2
CASTRO EDWARD F	MAJ	0-0452512	0761	2
CASTRO TEODORO	1LT	0-1896677	0764	1
CASWELL ALAN R	LTC	0-2034812	0865	1
CASWELL ARTHUR D	LTC	0-0212866	0658	3
CASWELL GILBERT F	CPT	0-1796577	0548	2
CASWELL PAUL E	LTC	0-0329191	0767	3
CASWELL RALPH A	LTC	0-0381963	0462	1
CASWELL RAY	LTC	0-0405882	0560	1
CATALAN GUILLERMO	MAJ	0-1947976	1162	1
CATALANO ANTHONY C	CPT	0-0228586	0546	2
CATALANO BASIL B	CW3	W-3150319	0867	1
CATALANO EDWARD W	MAJ	0-0486594	0848	2
CATALANO SALVATORE	MAJ	0-1542427	0361	1
CATALDI ANTONIO A	MAJ	0-1874398	0867	1
CATALINE LEROY A	2LT	0-1824132	1044	2
CATANIA DANIEL	1LT	0-1797779	0348	1
CATANIA GUIDO R	MAJ	0-1046038	0562	1
CATANIA JOSEPH J II	MAJ	0-1599023	0962	1
CATE CARROLL W	CW4	W-2143299	1068	1
CATE CHARLES V	LTC	0-0938010	1266	1
CATE CLIFTON J	LTC	0-0322384	1058	3
CATE HARRY R	CW2	W-2146205	0659	1
CATE HUGH C	MAJ	0-0169240	1158	3
CATE PETER M	CW2	W-2210712	1266	1
CATE ROBERT C	CW3	W-2144178	0561	1
CATELLI CECILE M	MAJ	N-0793188	0865	3
CATENA JAMES J	CW3	W-2144048	0466	1
CATERSON RODMAN P	MAJ	0-1050587	1164	3
CATES DAVID A	1LT	0-1182344	0245	2
CATES EDWIN H	COL	0-0239607	1265	3
CATES HOWARD C	LTC	0-0314703	0668	3
CATES JOE M	LTC	0-0441927	1046	2
CATES JOHN H JR	LTC	0-0249463	0159	1
CATES ROBERT G JR	MAJ	0-0378911	1044	2
CATHCART GWEN P B	MAJ	L-2289820	0868	1
CATHELL WILLIAM T	MAJ	0-2030426	0366	1
CATHERMAN DONALD L	LTC	0-0367489	0563	1
CATHERMAN GUY W JR	LTC	0-1684959	0367	1
CATHEY A M JR	2LT	0-1318761	1044	2
CATHEY CARL H	COL	0-0298039	0558	3
CATHEY CLYDE W	1LT	0-1544509	1045	2
CATHEY CORNELIUS	COL	0-0262727	0568	3
CATHEY FRANCIS E	LTC	0-1043294	0267	1
CATHEY HARRIS H	LTC	0-1325269	1262	1
CATHEY JAMES W	LTC	0-0239433	0366	3
CATHEY JOSEPH G	COL	0-0289257	0564	1
CATHEY WALTER K	COL	0-0299425	1060	1
CATHEY WILLIAM A	MAJ	0-0248319	1065	3
CATINO DOMINIC	CW4	W-2148711	1068	1
CATIZONI DOMINIC V	2LT	0-1313497	1044	2
CATLETT HAROLD G	LTC	0-1586479	0461	1
CATLETT JAMES G	COL	0-0115309	0256	3
CATLETT JAMES T	LTC	0-0144660	0158	3
CATLETT ROBERT L	CW2	W-2154103	0961	1
CATLIN HAMILTON R	CPT	0-0390092	1045	2
CATLIN VIRGIL G	LTC	0-0379591	0962	1
CATLIN WILLARD E	COL	0-0240408	0965	3
CATO ALLEN E	MAJ	0-0314062	0854	1
CATO EARL L	CW3	W-3200248	1268	1
CATO JOHN R	LTC	0-0903967	0868	3
CATO REBECCA	MAJ	L-0903026	1163	3
CATON RUSSELL J	COL	0-0179275	0951	3
CATON WILLIAM R	CW2	W-2146179	1060	1
CATOR RICHARD D	CPT	0-1877901	1162	1
CATRAMBONE DOMINIC R	CW3	W-2148201	0167	1
CATRELL FREDERICK	LTC	0-1315266	0868	2
CATRON ROBERT T	MAJ	0-0308528	0964	3
CATTANACH CHARLES G	MAJ	0-0994419	0566	1
CATTANACH GILBERT J	MAJ	0-1796758	0563	1
CATTANACH LACHLAN M	MAJ	0-0501189	0246	2
CATTARUZZA ROBERT	MAJ	0-1699957	0662	1
CATTELL WILLIAM R	LTC	0-0372308	1067	3
CATTILINI EDWARD E	COL	0-0256611	0758	1
CATTS GEORGE W	CPT	0-0132019	1253	3
CAUBLE DALE W	1LT	0-1548374	1144	2
CAUCH JACK K	MAJ	0-2018290	0960	1
CAUCHON HERVE P	CPT	0-0187787	0149	3
CAUDILL CECIL	CW4	W-2151000	0868	1
CAUDILL RAYMOND	LTC	0-0885815	0954	1
CAUDILL WILLIAM S	WO1	W-2115447	0150	1
CAUDLE REUBEN D	CPT	0-0243400	0554	3
CAUDLE ROBERT G JR	CPT	0-1996704	0660	1
CAUDLE ROY C	CPT	0-0994737	1057	2
CAUGER ARTHUR V JR	MAJ	0-1637169	1060	1
CAUGHELL RALPH J	MAJ	0-2017811	0865	1
CAUGHLAN ARTHUR B	LTC	0-0252997	1155	2
CAUGHMAN ROBERT H	LTC	0-1633111	0162	1
CAULDER BARBARA F	1LT	N-0703975	0645	1
CAULEY ANTHONY	CPT	0-0972275	1061	1
CAULFIELD CHARLIE F	LTC	0-1550556	1057	1
CAULFIELD THOMAS E	2LT	0-0446425	0544	2
CAULK CARL D	CW3	W-2153340	1264	1
CAULKINS DANIEL P	COL	0-0136086	0757	3
CAULKINS JOHN P	CW3	W-2208472	1167	1
CAUM RICHARD H	CW3	W-2143676	1066	1
CAUMARTIN HUGH T	MAJ	0-0466261	0646	2
CAUSEY CHARLES D	LTC	0-1844624	0863	1
CAUSEY CHARLES M	2LT	0-1913575	0545	1
CAUSEY CHARLES M	CW2	W-2149428	0966	1
CAUSEY CHARLES O	2LT	0-0425288	1144	2
CAUSEY EDGAR	CPT	0-0885706	0550	1
CAUSEY JACK W	MAJ	0-1172406	1159	1
CAUSEY LILY F	CPT	N-0724818	0846	1
CAUTHEN IRBY B JR	1LT	0-1540564	0646	2
CAUTHEN JOHNNY M	CPT	0-0358955	1061	1
CAUTHEN WILBUR L	MAJ	0-1324824	0565	1
CAUTHEN WILLIAM C	COL	0-0239994	0960	3
CAUTHORN THOMAS E	MAJ	0-0415821	0347	2
CAVAGNARO MARGARET A	CPT	N-0759719	0846	1
CAVALCANTE JAMES J	CW3	W-2147249	0363	1
CAVALIER EUGENE H	CPT	0-0801244	1158	1
CAVALIER JOSEPH V	MAJ	0-0423109	1066	3
CAVALIERE VINCENT J	CPT	0-0443294	0946	2
CAVALIERI JULIA	CPT	N-0756989	1046	1
CAVALLO ANTHONY M	CPT	0-0359559	1045	2
CAVANAGH BERNARD B	MAJ	0-0235833	0145	2
CAVANAGH JAMES M	MAJ	0-4006139	0568	2
CAVANAGH JOHN M	LTC	0-1016537	0962	1
CAVANAUGH DORA P	CPT	N-0702486	1044	1
CAVANAUGH EDWARD W	CW2	W-2144550	1164	1
CAVANAUGH JOHN H JR	CW2	W-2207496	1164	1
CAVANAUGH JOHN P	2LT	0-1298995	1046	2
CAVANAUGH JOHN P	2LT	0-1322422	1144	2
CAVANAUGH JOSEPH P	2LT	0-1110982	0744	2
CAVANAUGH MICHAEL A	COL	0-1015294	0168	2
CAVANAUGH PAUL W	CPT	0-0550270	1046	2
CAVANAUGH WILLIAM D	CW3	W-2144578	0662	2
CAVANESS WALTON R	2LT	0-1017951	0944	2
CAVANOR FRANK T	COL	0-0130232	0648	3
CAVAZOS IGNACIO SR	CW2	W-2209457	0961	1
CAVE FRANKLIN	LTC	0-1640887	0466	3
CAVE GLENN E	LTC	0-0411934	0960	1
CAVE JACK	MAJ	0-2039392	1160	1
CAVE JOHN E	CPT	0-1794779	0761	1
CAVE LESLIE C	COL	0-0265631	1262	3
CAVE RICHARD F	MAJ	0-1031302	0163	1
CAVE WILLIAM R	MAJ	0-0985148	1067	1
CAVEN DONALD W	LTC	0-0144952	0648	3
CAVEN WALTER T	1LT	0-1319177	0146	2
CAVENAUGH DAVID E	CPT	0-0399377	1144	2
CAVENDER MARVIN L	MAJ	0-2014792	1165	1
CAVENESS JAMES R	CW2	W-2147598	0662	1
CAVER EUGENE L	CPT	0-1573764	1057	1
CAVERLY JOHN R	LTC	0-1548026	1062	1
CAVERLY ROBERT P	CPT	0-1587878	0356	1
CAVIN DELMER L	CPT	0-1169453	0145	2
CAVIN WALTER M	LTC	0-0320789	0255	3
CAVINESS DONALD G	CPT	0-0885737	0863	1
CAVINESS FRED P	LTC	0-0343488	1266	3
CAVINESS JAMES M	COL	0-0178278	1045	2
CAVINS JAMES H	COL	0-0313067	0160	1
CAWELTI JOHN R	MAJ	0-1598813	0964	1
CAWLEY AMOS	CPT	0-0497850	0350	1
CAWLEY ANN C	1LT	N-0786461	0552	2
CAWLEY EDWARD P	MAJ	0-1686917	0645	2
CAWLEY THOMAS A	LTC	0-1010006	0861	2
CAWOOD FRANCIS L	COL	0-0354357	1266	1
CAWTHON CHARLES R	COL	0-0407674	0764	1
CAWTHON KING W	CW2	W-2103946	0352	1
CAWTHORNE TEMPLAR S	COL	0-0199928	0461	3
CAWTHRON LEO JR	COL	0-1172407	0966	1
CAYCE WALTER B	COL	0-0150741	1156	3
CAYER JOSEPH C	LTC	0-1637171	0462	1
CAYLOR ED L	LTC	0-1040676	1060	1
CAYLOR HUGH L	CPT	0-0209926	1047	2
CAYTON HENRY W	COL	0-0268889	0259	3
CAYWOOD GEORGE T	LTC	0-1289692	0757	1
CAZEAUX JOHN R JR	2LT	0-2008117	0246	2
CAZEL MAURICE H	MAJ	0-1001749	0163	1
CEAGLSKE BOYCE O	LTC	0-1552246	1262	1
CEASE ROBERT W	2LT	0-1323912	0345	2
CEASE WILLIAM M JR	CW4	W-2127208	0168	1
CEBEL JOHN	MAJ	0-0374612	0255	1
CEBROWSKI CASIMIR C	1LT	0-1317489	0247	2
CECAN BENJAMIN R	2LT	0-0395794	0942	2
CECCHINI LOUIS A	COL	0-0450009	0567	1
CECIL CLARENCE C	MAJ	0-0218503	0253	3
CECIL ERNEST H	MAJ	0-0410745	1266	3
CECIL GEORGE H	MAJ	0-1641153	0960	1
CECIL JANET R	2LT	N-0703246	1040	1
CECIL JOHN L	LTC	0-1169052	0964	1
CECIL RICHARD F	MAJ	0-0315520	0946	2
CECIL ROY L	LTC	0-0182750	0648	3
CECIL SYLVESTER	LTC	0-0295221	0259	1
CECIL WAYNE A	LTC	0-1107854	1164	1
CECIL WILLIAM H	MAJ	0-0257671	0167	3
CECKA JAMES T	LTC	0-1293717	0165	1
CEDERBORG SAMUEL L	LTC	0-2052294	0167	3
CEDERVALL ANTON A	CPT	0-0934800	0656	2
CEGLAREK WALLACE J	CPT	0-1108568	0647	2
CEI PETER G	LTC	0-0337204	0647	2
CEJKA OLIVER J	LTC	0-0329593	0962	1
CELANI ALFRED J	MAJ	0-2263282	0167	1
CELANI FLORINDO J	COL	0-0339063	0164	1
CELAYA LAURA F	MAJ	N-0737930	0865	1
CELEY J B	1LT	0-1337273	0661	1
CELIS DOMINGO	1LT	0-1896633	0149	2
CELKO JOSEPH F	CW3	W-2146001	0867	1
CELLA EDWARD L	MAJ	0-0338261	0362	2
CELLA FRANK E	CW2	W-2118141	0647	1
CELLIO LEWIS W	COL	0-0318327	0646	2
CELY TOM R	CPT	0-0356804	0245	2
CENIZA FLORENTINO	CPT	0-1896624	0559	1
CENSNER JOHN J	CW4	W-2124110	1059	2
CENTER FRANCIS C	1LT	0-1294976	0646	2
CENTRE DAVID	1LT	0-1314880	0146	2
CENTRONE PATRICK A	CPT	0-0352923	1045	2
CERALDI BERNARD A	CPT	0-0463729	0547	2
CERASOLI ANTHONY N	LTC	0-1795765	0261	1
CERECEDO JAVIER H	COL	0-0274377	0153	3
CERESI ANTHONY A	LTC	0-1283548	0561	1
CEREZO CARMELO	MAJ	0-0184640	0257	3
CERNAGHAN ALBERT L	MAJ	0-0165967	1150	3
CERNY CHARLES W JR	LTC	0-0377943	0868	3
CERNY JEROME J	LTC	0-0116380	0648	3
CERNY JERRY	CW4	W-2106939	1055	1
CERNY JOSEPH	LTC	0-0261409	0766	3
CERTAIN JACK	CPT	0-1285190	1048	2
CERVANTES ANTHONY V	1LT	0-0356887	1264	1
CERVERA SEVERO J	CW3	W-2147274	1063	1
CERVOLA JOHN	MAJ	0-1328465	0263	1
CERVONE ISADORE C	1LT	0-0177911	0654	3
CERVONI WALTER A	CPT	0-0976379	0552	2
CERWINS JOSEPH M	COL	0-0369845	1164	3
CERWONKA FRANCIS W	MAJ	0-1950653	1164	1
CESAR CHARLES	MAJ	0-1633747	0258	1
CESKE WALLACE G	CPT	0-2034523	0866	1
CESSAR MATTHEW A	1LT	0-1185212	0346	2
CESTERO HERMAN J	LTC	0-0405148	0566	3
CETRULO PETER X	MAJ	0-2002054	1062	1
CEVAAL JOHN	MAJ	0-2024518	0660	1
CEWE LEROY G	MAJ	0-1017736	0762	1
CEY WILLIAM J	CW2	W-2203258	0562	1
CHABERT ALFRED A	LTC	0-0254531	0367	3
CHABOT ALBERT L	LTC	0-0237209	0358	1
CHABOT FELIX J	LTC	0-1533520	1063	1
CHABOT LOREN J	1LT	0-0425978	0345	2
CHACE MYRON D	COL	0-0464526	0257	3
CHACEY DANIEL K	COL	0-0506305	0166	3
CHACEY JOUETT A	LTC	0-0242015	0965	3
CHACON JOSE	CPT	0-0292323	0553	1
CHADDICK ELMER H	WO1	W-2131614	0146	2
CHADDLER WARREN D	LTC	0-1285383	0768	3
CHADSEY MERLIN J	LTC	0-0274593	0960	3
CHADWELL JAMES A	CW4	W-2141222	1267	1
CHADWELL RIXEY C	LTC	0-1580738	0861	1
CHADWICK ARTHUR C JR	CPT	0-1300274	1046	2
CHADWICK FLOYD S JR	MAJ	0-2017812	1159	1
CHADWICK FLOYD S SR	2LT	0-1913597	0244	1
CHADWICK JANET K	2LT	N-0736605	0943	1
CHADWICK JOHN S	LTC	0-0262758	1066	3
CHADWICK KERMIT V	LTC	0-0299178	0445	2
CHADWICK RUSSELL H	1LT	0-1101374	1045	2
CHADWICK STURGIS E	LTC	0-0246700	0366	3
CHADWICK WILLIE J	LTC	0-1303664	1054	1
CHADWICK WINFIELD S	MAJ	0-0401303	0561	1
CHAFFEE LEROY E	MAJ	0-1036903	0860	1
CHAFFEE THALIA A	CPT	N-0730596	0946	1
CHAFFEUR JOHN J	LTC	0-1999345	0763	1
CHAFFIN WENDEL T	LTC	0-0261616	0567	3
CHAFFIN WILLIAM A	MAJ	0-0574185	1055	1
CHAFIN WILLIAM V	LTC	0-0273102	1263	3
CHAGAMI RONALD T	CW3	W-2141069	0562	1
CHAILLE JAMES L	COL	0-0254303	0666	3
CHAILLE JOSEPH H	COL	0-0239434	0265	3
CHAIN BENJAMIN H JR	CW2	W-2149103	0861	2
CHAIN JOHN S	LTC	0-0246433	0265	3
CHAIRES WILLIAM R	MAJ	0-1646952	0160	1
CHAISSON GILBERT J	COL	0-0456022	0965	1
CHAIT MATTHEW W	LTC	0-0288109	0260	2
CHAIT ROBERT A	MAJ	0-0493946	0746	2
CHAKUROA GEORGE J	CW3	W-2206648	0468	1
CHALFANT JAMES R	1LT	0-1317071	0845	2
CHALFIN SAMUEL L	CPT	0-1689009	1044	2
CHALIAN ALEXANDER	MAJ	0-0356519	0463	3
CHALKER JOHN O SR	CW3	W-2145797	0561	2

NAME	GRADE	SVC NO	DATE RET MO YR	RET CODE
CHALKER MARION L JR	LTC	0-0965910	0868	1
CHALKLEY BEN R SR	CPT	0-1307370	0266	1
CHALKLEY JUDSON I	CPT	0-0418612	0845	2
CHALKLEY MARJORIE G	MAJ	N-0723599	0962	1
CHALLAN JOHN A	MAJ	0-1175072	0757	1
CHALLENNER ANSEL P	LTC	0-0223670	1064	3
CHALLEY CLYDE	CPT	0-0236645	0963	3
CHALLIN ROBERT C	WO1	W-2108384	0464	2
CHALLMAN SAMUEL A	COL	0-0263450	0264	3
CHALMERS FRANKLIN S	COL	0-0118589	0252	3
CHALMERS GEORGE W	LTC	0-1019314	0862	1
CHAMBERLAIN ALMA	LTC	0-1173899	0762	1
CHAMBERLAIN CULVER B	1LT	0-0914019	0845	2
CHAMBERLAIN DON E	LTC	0-0138148	0648	3
CHAMBERLAIN EDWARD M	LTC	0-1635684	0962	1
CHAMBERLAIN ERVIN W	LTC	0-0175716	0443	2
CHAMBERLAIN F G	LTC	0-0150831	0648	3
CHAMBERLAIN FRANCIS	MAJ	0-1647211	0565	2
CHAMBERLAIN GEORGE L	1LT	0-1541210	0744	2
CHAMBERLAIN GEORGE M	MAJ	0-1689675	0467	1
CHAMBERLAIN GORDON W	LTC	0-1301950	1064	1
CHAMBERLAIN H G	1LT	0-1173900	0445	2
CHAMBERLAIN HARRY E	1LT	0-0437385	0957	1
CHAMBERLAIN HARRY F	CW2	W-2109954	0547	1
CHAMBERLAIN HOLCOMBE	MAJ	0-0908747	1145	2
CHAMBERLAIN JAMES R	LTC	0-2049502	0562	1
CHAMBERLAIN JOSEPH V	LTC	0-0302144	0945	2
CHAMBERLAIN LLOYD A	CW3	W-2206828	0965	1
CHAMBERLAIN LOUIS J	LTC	0-0887469	0563	1
CHAMBERLAIN MARIO C	LTC	0-0270419	1061	1
CHAMBERLAIN PHILIP L	LTC	0-1917863	1168	1
CHAMBERLAIN ROBERT L	CPT	0-0868611	0851	2
CHAMBERLAIN W H	COL	0-0238613	0951	3
CHAMBERLAIN WARD	1LT	0-1323106	0747	2
CHAMBERLAIN WILLIAM	CW2	W-2210409	1264	2
CHAMBERLIN ARTHUR J	CW4	W-2003160	0667	3
CHAMBERLIN FRANCIS A	1LT	0-0376597	0144	2
CHAMBERLIN HENRY R	MAJ	0-0467680	0263	1
CHAMBERLIN ROBERT M	CW3	W-2144101	1266	1
CHAMBERLIN ROBERT N	LTC	0-0286831	1060	3
CHAMBERLIN ROBERT W	B G	0-0279810	0660	3
CHAMBERLIN WILLIAM F	COL	0-0307335	0965	1
CHAMBERS ALAN R	CPT	0-0331422	0246	2
CHAMBERS ALBERT L	CPT	0-1303594	0546	2
CHAMBERS ANITA M	MAJ	N-0730062	0463	3
CHAMBERS ARTHUR D	MAJ	0-2017354	0863	1
CHAMBERS BAYARD S	LTC	0-0299133	0765	3
CHAMBERS BURGESS D	LTC	0-1010025	1060	1
CHAMBERS CHESTER H	COL	0-0169166	1046	2
CHAMBERS EDWIN P	COL	0-0316445	0259	3
CHAMBERS ELWOOD W	CW2	W-2152993	0360	1
CHAMBERS GORDON H	COL	0-0254701	0846	2
CHAMBERS HEWITT W	MAJ	0-0106120	0952	3
CHAMBERS JAMES D	1LT	0-1759828	0157	1
CHAMBERS JAMES S	LTC	0-1032072	1062	1
CHAMBERS JAMES T	1LT	0-0174354	1060	3
CHAMBERS JOHN A	COL	0-0251918	0459	3
CHAMBERS JOHN C	LTC	0-0342602	0968	3
CHAMBERS JOHN F	LTC	0-1313964	0467	1
CHAMBERS JOHN S	MAJ	0-0254082	0357	3
CHAMBERS JOHN T	COL	0-0276919	0158	3
CHAMBERS JOHN T	CPT	0-0397657	0761	2
CHAMBERS MARTIN M	MAJ	0-1115210	0561	1
CHAMBERS MARVIN A	CPT	0-1895261	1057	1
CHAMBERS MAX E	MAJ	0-2203408	1165	1
CHAMBERS PETER F	LTC	0-1030134	0262	3
CHAMBERS RALPH H	LTC	0-0500867	0457	2
CHAMBERS REX K	CW3	W-3150262	1068	1
CHAMBERS ROBERT L	MAJ	0-0146472	0254	3
CHAMBERS ROBERT P	LTC	0-0288811	0865	3
CHAMBERS ROBERT W	LTC	0-1542382	0962	1
CHAMBERS RUSSEL	CPT	0-0497881	0157	1
CHAMBERS STANLEY L	MAJ	0-0388954	0561	1
CHAMBERS THOMAS F	CPT	0-0501766	0851	1
CHAMBERS THOMAS L	CPT	0-0482005	0746	2

NAME	GRADE	SVC NO	DATE RET MO YR	RET CODE
CHAMBERS TUFFY J	MAJ	0-1341256	0766	1
CHAMBERS WAYNE A	LTC	0-0506655	0447	2
CHAMBERS WILLARD E	LTC	0-1302429	0266	1
CHAMBERS WILLIAM L	CPT	0-0266944	0658	3
CHAMBERS WOODFIN C	LTC	0-0425472	0966	3
CHAMBERS WYLIE C	2LT	0-1308473	0445	2
CHAMBLISS JAMES R	LTC	0-0238599	0862	3
CHAMBLISS WILLIAM C	CW3	W-2206009	1068	1
CHAMBREAU WILLIAM J	WO1	W-2133086	0945	2
CHAMNESS JOSEPH C	MAJ	0-1637174	0559	1
CHAMNESS LEO L	LTC	0-0257919	0368	3
CHAMPAGNE ANDRE	1LT	0-1043590	1155	1
CHAMPAGNE EDWARD E	MAJ	0-0972915	1160	1
CHAMPAGNE NORMAND H	CW2	W-2152371	1060	1
CHAMPAGNE ROLAND J	LTC	0-0421885	0366	1
CHAMPION ATWELL E	1LT	0-1314882	0545	2
CHAMPION GLENN R	LTC	0-0261331	0267	3
CHAMPION ROBERT L	MAJ	0-1936387	0966	1
CHAMPION WILLIAM H	MAJ	0-1119964	1063	1
CHAMPLIN DOUGLASS D	MAJ	0-0980964	1262	1
CHAMPLIN NATHANIEL	2LT	0-1112075	1044	2
CHAMPLIN NICHOLAS D	LTC	0-0310881	1166	3
CHAMPNEY GUY W H	LTC	0-0284931	0868	3
CHAMPOUILLON JOSEPH	MAJ	0-2021604	0167	1
CHAMPOUX FRANCIS L	LTC	0-1311981	0166	1
CHAN ROBERT J	LTC	0-1321994	0661	1
CHANCE HARRY C	CW2	W-2145287	0454	1
CHANCE S ETHEL	CPT	N-0724739	0646	1
CHANCE VERNON L	MAJ	0-1017844	0665	1
CHANCE WALTER R	LTC	0-0353500	1059	1
CHANCE WARD L	1LT	0-1684973	0752	2
CHANCE WAYNE A	LTC	0-1115523	0764	1
CHANCELLOR WILFORD J	LTC	0-1285382	0954	1
CHANCELLOR WILLIAM W	CPT	0-1114883	0261	1
CHANCEY NATHAN	MAJ	0-0275287	0666	3
CHANOLER ALBERT	LTC	0-1286962	0954	1
CHANOLER ALBERT M JR	MAJ	0-1167358	1146	2
CHANOLER ARTHUR J	2LT	0-2204042	0656	2
CHANOLER ASA N	MAJ	0-4011111	1263	1
CHANOLER CARL C	LTC	0-1551373	0662	1
CHANOLER CARL F	LTC	0-0412376	0167	1
CHANOLER CARLTON P	CPT	0-0364566	0346	2
CHANOLER CLINTON B	MAJ	0-0486905	0948	2
CHANOLER COVY B	CW2	W-2146131	1155	1
CHANOLER EARL F	2LT	0-0554417	0845	2
CHANOLER EARL R	LTC	0-0281674	1263	3
CHANOLER EDWARD R	CPT	0-1051515	1153	2
CHANOLER EDWIN M	CW3	W-2149104	0864	1
CHANOLER EKILLIS M	LTC	0-1057011	1262	1
CHANOLER ELI C	LTC	0-1112617	0862	1
CHANOLER EUGENE	2LT	0-1289693	0145	2
CHANOLER GEORGE A	LTC	0-0154047	0155	3
CHANOLER GEORGE A	MAJ	0-0219158	0955	3
CHANOLER GRAHAM L	MAJ	0-0372639	0862	3
CHANOLER HAROLD M	CW4	W-2114306	0257	1
CHANOLER HORTON L	COL	0-0130618	0558	3
CHANOLER JAMES C	LTC	0-0294432	0959	2
CHANOLER JOE F	MAJ	0-2009416	0661	1
CHANOLER JOHN A	MAJ	0-1044194	0358	1
CHANOLER JOHN H	MAJ	0-2028373	1167	1
CHANOLER LEROY	CPT	0-0477947	1045	2
CHANOLER LOUIS J	LTC	0-0349551	0946	2
CHANOLER NOREEN C	1LT	N-0774412	0547	1
CHANOLER PATRICK M	CW3	W-2146322	0565	1
CHANOLER RALPH E	MAJ	0-1030230	0859	1
CHANOLER RAY J SR	MAJ	0-2263711	0266	1
CHANOLER ROBERT L	MAJ	0-0292092	0846	2
CHANOLER SIDNEY P	LTC	0-0154676	0854	3
CHANOLER STEPHEN J	MAJ	0-2011918	0959	1
CHANOLER VERNON M	LTC	0-0281089	0467	3
CHANOLER WALTER B	MAJ	0-0415578	0958	1
CHANOLER WALTER C	2LT	0-1171083	0743	2
CHANOLER WILLARD C	LTC	0-0168538	0144	2
CHANOLER WILLARD J	CPT	0-0356212	0646	2
CHANOLER WILLIAM H	CW2	W-2152885	1059	2

NAME	GRADE	SVC NO	DATE RET MO YR	RET CODE
CHANDLER WOODROW W	CPT	*0-2017009	0657	1
CHANEY ALBERT A	MAJ	0-4006356	0167	1
CHANEY EDWIN C	LTC	0-0450819	0456	1
CHANEY GEORGE L	CPT	0-1055559	0647	2
CHANEY HAROLD W	CPT	0-2029829	1058	1
CHANEY JAMES H	CPT	0-0850140	0148	2
CHANEY JOSEPH B	CW2	W-2203309	0761	1
CHANEY LUTHER M	LTC	0-1281724	0261	1
CHANG JAMES T M	MAJ	0-0249592	1159	1
CHANLEY HERMAN S	MAJ	0-1686318	0563	1
CHANNEY STEPHEN	LTC	0-0545784	0365	1
CHANNON HIRAM B	CPT	0-0130619	0854	3
CHANOSKI JOHN F	MAJ	0-1299373	0958	1
CHANOWSKI JOHN P	2LT	0-2002248	0546	2
CHANT HAROLD S	LTC	0-0223707	0157	3
CHANTRY ARTHUR S W	CPT	0-0509151	1047	2
CHAPA FRANK L	COL	0-0159185	0957	3
CHAPA MANUEL U	MAJ	0-4024749	0267	2
CHAPHE CARROLL G	LTC	0-0548563	1065	1
CHAPIN EARL L	1LT	0-1594425	0845	2
CHAPIN GERALD G	1LT	0-1169598	1045	2
CHAPIN JOHN L	1LT	0-1047063	0145	2
CHAPIN NORMAN G	MAJ	0-2010679	1265	1
CHAPIN STANLEY D	MAJ	0-0146422	0553	3
CHAPIN THEODORE	CPT	0-0368466	1244	2
CHAPIN THOMAS C	LTC	0-0450688	0468	3
CHAPIN WILLIAM B	CW3	W-2147936	0962	1
CHAPIN WILLIAM H	LTC	0-1553236	0563	1
CHAPIN WINONA M	1LT	N-0720140	0946	1
CHAPIN 3RD EDWARD Y	1LT	0-0528759	0146	2
CHAPLAIN JOHN R	CPT	0-0298968	0645	2
CHAPLESKY MARION P	CPT	0-2033528	0260	1
CHAPLIN EARNEST C	LTC	0-1533753	1066	1
CHAPLIN RALPH S	MAJ	0-2009389	1264	1
CHAPLIN ROBERT L	MAJ	0-0308397	0462	1
CHAPLIN ROBERT M	CPT	0-1322423	0856	2
CHAPLIN THOMAS S	MAJ	0-0956348	0568	1
CHAPLINSKI ANTHONY	CPT	0-1950129	1159	1
CHAPLINSKI CHARLES W	MAJ	0-1100046	0257	1
CHAPMAN ALBERT	COL	0-0217008	0264	3
CHAPMAN ALFRED S	CW3	W-2113380	0662	1
CHAPMAN ARTHUR B JR	COL	0-0498009	1062	1
CHAPMAN ARTHUR J	MAJ	0-0254545	0266	3
CHAPMAN BRADY B	1LT	0-1821548	0750	1
CHAPMAN CAREY E	LTC	0-0176160	0557	1
CHAPMAN CECIL W	LTC	0-0301086	0347	2
CHAPMAN CHANEY	LTC	0-2024325	0962	1
CHAPMAN CHARLES F	CW2	W-2118126	0645	2
CHAPMAN CHARLES G	LTC	0-0298192	0165	3
CHAPMAN CLARENCE L	COL	0-0373429	0867	1
CHAPMAN CLARK R JR	2LT	0-1179811	0445	2
CHAPMAN CLYDE V	LTC	0-0386819	1257	1
CHAPMAN DORENE	CPT	N-0792315	0257	2
CHAPMAN DENMAN S	LTC	0-0324542	1065	1
CHAPMAN DONALD L	LTC	0-0319641	0856	2
CHAPMAN DONALD M SR	LTC	0-0290399	0455	1
CHAPMAN EARL H	COL	0-0105456	0756	3
CHAPMAN FORREST M	MAJ	0-1297497	0746	2
CHAPMAN FRANK B	COL	0-0136075	0349	3
CHAPMAN FREDERICK	LTC	0-2015057	1167	1
CHAPMAN GEORGE A	LTC	0-0285109	0263	1
CHAPMAN GERALD E	1LT	0-0550574	0246	2
CHAPMAN GERALD L	LTC	0-0124608	0454	3
CHAPMAN GORDON B	CPT	0-0287219	0345	2
CHAPMAN HAROLD L	CPT	0-1168193	1152	1
CHAPMAN HAROLD O W	LTC	0-0921129	0265	3
CHAPMAN HERBERT L	CPT	0-0483211	0247	1
CHAPMAN HESTER	MAJ	N-0736913	0467	1
CHAPMAN HOWARD K JR	MAJ	0-0239336	1064	3
CHAPMAN JAMES E	1LT	0-1036904	0345	2
CHAPMAN JAMES L	COL	0-0100573	1149	3
CHAPMAN JAMES R	LTC	0-0495817	0762	1
CHAPMAN JEFF M	CPT	0-0415670	0152	2
CHAPMAN JOHN C	MAJ	0-0348256	0546	2
CHAPMAN JOHN G	CW2	W-2112920	0746	2

NAME	GRADE	SVC NO	DATE RET MO YR	RET CODE
CHAPMAN LAWRENCE W	LTC	0-1175399	0862	2
CHAPMAN LEICESTER	LTC	0-0190127	0654	3
CHAPMAN LLOYD	LTC	0-1114417	0966	1
CHAPMAN LOIS O	2LT	N-0736402	0545	1
CHAPMAN MARION O	CW2	W-2149189	1160	1
CHAPMAN MARY	1LT	N-0755663	1147	1
CHAPMAN MIKE W	CW4	W-2142437	1065	1
CHAPMAN RAYMOND C	MAJ	0-1183827	0661	1
CHAPMAN RAYMOND H	CW3	W-3150461	0368	1
CHAPMAN RICHARD H	LTC	0-0452116	0856	1
CHAPMAN RICHARD J	MAJ	0-0478267	0154	1
CHAPMAN RICHARD W	LTC	0-0956349	1167	1
CHAPMAN ROBERT B	CW2	W-2207539	0166	1
CHAPMAN STANLEY	CPT	0-1175969	0450	2
CHAPMAN THOMAS L	MAJ	0-0958750	0163	1
CHAPMAN THOMAS S	LTC	0-0242151	1265	3
CHAPMAN WILLIAM C	CW4	W-2142821	0856	1
CHAPMAN WILLIAM H	LTC	0-1556985	1060	1
CHAPMAN WOODROW W	LTC	0-1556700	0266	1
CHAPNICK HENRY	LTC	0-1687103	1046	2
CHAPNICK RONALD	CPT	0-4046952	0962	2
CHAPPEL DONALD M JR	1LT	0-1296169	0347	2
CHAPPELEAR JOHN R	CW2	W-2148843	0960	1
CHAPPELL ALFRED H	LTC	0-1293371	1158	1
CHAPPELL CARL W	WO1	W-2106235	1045	2
CHAPPELL CLAUD H	MAJ	0-1685133	0745	2
CHAPPELL CLINTON C	CPT	0-0519315	0745	2
CHAPPELL DANIEL H	LTC	0-0211598	0161	3
CHAPPELL EDWIN J	MAJ	0-1685012	1164	1
CHAPPELL JAMES R	MAJ	0-1170311	0959	1
CHAPPELL JOHN L	CPT	0-2035241	0863	2
CHAPPELL JOHN M	LTC	0-0463586	0652	2
CHAPPELL WILLIAM B	MAJ	0-1293911	0461	1
CHAPPLE WILLIAM E	CPT	0-0413425	0346	2
CHAPUT EDWARD L	MAJ	0-1638869	0859	1
CHAPUT LOUIS J JR	LTC	0-1542846	0561	1
CHAPUT OMER T	COL	0-0365453	0960	1
CHAJUETTE LAWRENCE T	LTC	0-0307862	0162	1
CHARBONNEAU ALBERT D	MAJ	0-4021040	0868	1
CHARBONNEAU LOUIS H	B G	0-0142965	0157	3
CHARDON CARLOS F	COL	0-0256034	1067	3
CHARETTE NORMAN A	CW3	W-2146223	0161	1
CHARETTE REGINALD W	LTC	0-1056316	0266	1
CHARITON RAYMOND C	MAJ	0-1540854	0761	1
CHARLES EARLE H	MAJ	0-0289640	0146	2
CHARLES HARRY M	LTC	0-1107341	1163	1
CHARLES MICHAEL P	CPT	0-1101375	0549	2
CHARLES RALPH	LTC	0-0176885	0562	3
CHARLES WILLIAM	COL	0-0355783	0367	2
CHARLES WILLIAM S	LTC	0-1183035	0868	1
CHARLESTON ELIZ M	2LT	N-0721139	0344	1
CHARLESWORTH JOHN R	CW4	W-2000317	0765	1
CHARLET REINHART F	1LT	0-0377023	0445	2
CHARLTON ARTHUR J	MAJ	0-0918715	0863	1
CHARLTON JOHN B	LTC	0-0949325	0968	2
CHARLTON NELSON	MAJ	0-2036359	1262	1
CHARLTON ROBERT D	M G	0-0235009	0560	3
CHARLTON RUSSELL C	COL	0-0205558	1059	3
CHARNECO RAFAEL	LTC	0-0199348	0663	3
CHARON EDWARD J	LTC	0-1581952	1162	1
CHARON GEORGE	CW3	W-2147663	0966	1
CHARRIEZ GILBERTO O	CPT	0-0970810	1061	1
CHARTIER CURTIS R	CW2	RW-2210143	1264	1
CHARTOCK WILLIAM	LTC	0-0274623	0360	1
CHARTRAND HELENE E	1LT	N-0721268	0246	1
CHARTRES GERARD	2LT	0-0464866	0744	2
CHARVAT ROSE C	1LT	N-0700419	0941	1
CHASE ALDEN	CW3	W-2206649	1266	1
CHASE ARCHIE P	MAJ	0-1052291	1262	1
CHASE ARTHUR R	LTC	0-1015721	0264	1
CHASE BENJAMIN O	MAJ	0-0917954	0258	2
CHASE BERNICE M	LTC	N-0720146	0461	1
CHASE BURTON K	MAJ	0-1183928	0668	3
CHASE CARL	CW4	W-2139465	0862	1
CHASE CARL E	MAJ	0-0252835	0262	3

ARMY OF THE UNITED STATES RETIRED LIST

NAME	GRADE	SVC NO	DATE RET MO YR	RET CODE
CHASE CHARLES F	LTC	0-0241023	0364	3
CHASE CLIFFORD A	COL	0-0511085	0965	3
CHASE DAVID W	CPT	0-1048313	0463	1
CHASE DONALD L	CW3	W-2209355	0668	1
CHASE DURWARD C	CPT	0-0312199	0153	2
CHASE EDMUND P	MAJ	0-0188766	0454	3
CHASE ELIZABETH	2LT	L-0116068	1044	2
CHASE EUGENE B	LTC	0-0301057	0361	3
CHASE EUGENE L	CW3	RW-2142325	0662	1
CHASE FRED M	LTC	0-0244869	0966	3
CHASE FREDERICK	CPT	0-0419292	0946	2
CHASE GLENN	CW3	W-2142822	1062	1
CHASE HARLAN F	COL	0-0218422	0459	3
CHASE HOWARD H	MAJ	0-0272273	0659	1
CHASE HURLEY W	LTC	0-0334396	0958	1
CHASE HYMAN Y	COL	0-0212557	0960	1
CHASE IRENE F	2LT	N-0720256	0144	1
CHASE JACK M	CPT	0-1106642	0146	2
CHASE JACKSON B	MAJ	0-0193266	0950	3
CHASE JAMES JR	CPT	0-1937237	1164	1
CHASE JEAN L	LTC	0-1168200	0161	1
CHASE LEONARD J	LTC	0-0417328	0161	1
CHASE LESTER J	LTC	0-0298059	0559	1
CHASE LOUIS S	MAJ	0-0499966	0346	2
CHASE LUCIUS P	COL	0-0178374	0262	3
CHASE MELVIN C	CW2	W-2118320	0953	1
CHASE NATHANIEL JR	CPT	0-2016848	0461	1
CHASE PARAN F	CW3	W-2152202	0466	1
CHASE RICHARD G	1LT	0-1292834	1044	2
CHASE ROBERT L	LTC	0-0455040	0859	1
CHASE ROSS	COL	0-0167352	0558	3
CHASE S BRUCE	COL	0-0242449	0466	3
CHASE SAMUEL L	LTC	0-0412498	0466	3
CHASE STODDARD B	COL	0-0311455	0261	1
CHASE VOLNEY A	MAJ	0-0173954	0860	3
CHASE WILLIAM A	CPT	0-0379663	0346	2
CHASE WILLIAM D	LTC	0-0176231	0759	3
CHASE WILLIAM M	COL	0-0154340	0551	2
CHASEN HAROLD	1LT	0-1080520	0745	2
CHASEN PHILIP	1LT	0-1307507	0545	2
CHASEN WILLIAM H	COL	0-0361118	0667	3
CHASNOFF JULIUS	COL	0-0247246	0862	3
CHASSE EDWARD D	2LT	0-1304862	0245	2
CHASSE MERIL J	CW3	W-2145798	0462	1
CHASSY GILBERT H	CPT	0-0381074	1145	2
CHAST ANN	2LT	N-0758083	0945	1
CHASTAIN FRED A	LTC	0-0443895	0756	1
CHASTAIN JOHN F	CPT	0-0261615	0564	3
CHASTAIN JOHN T	CW2	W-2145153	0958	1
CHASTAIN KENNETH L	MAJ	0-1259850	0547	2
CHASTAIN MYRA E	MAJ	L-0403293	0263	1
CHASTAIN WALTER R	LTC	0-0258709	0565	3
CHASTAIN WILLIS L	MAJ	0-1535150	1054	1
CHASTEN STEPHEN M	MAJ	0-0488789	1151	2
CHASWOOD ERNEST E	WO1	W-2126914	0846	1
CHASZAZ ELIZABETH	CPT	N-0729415	0946	1
CHATELAIN HARRY	WO1	W-2115686	0647	1
CHATELLE JOSEPH S	CW2	W-2151070	0963	1
CHATFIELD LEE W	LTC	0-0258286	0745	2
CHATHAM JOHN W	MAJ	0-1694382	0246	2
CHATHAM ROY L	LTC	0-0415851	0461	1
CHATIGNY ADRIAN G	MAJ	0-2101756	0966	1
CHATLAIN DEAN F	1LT	0-0453496	0244	2
CHATLAIN JOHN K	2LT	0-2006828	1045	2
CHATLEY ROBERT I	MAJ	0-0234360	0247	1
CHATLIN MORRIS	CPT	0-0922520	0945	2
CHATMAN CHARLIE L	CW3	W-2146989	1068	1
CHATMAN RICHARD C JR	CW2	W-2207656	1061	1
CHATMON THOMAS H JR	CPT	0-0183839	0454	3
CHATNVET BARTHELEM	CPT	0-2029625	0158	1
CHATTAWAY ERNEST H	MAJ	0-1550344	0561	1
CHATTERTON FLOYD F	CW2	W-2210137	0167	1
CHATTERTON FRANCIS C	MAJ	0-0245745	0757	3
CHAUDOIN ELIOT O	LTC	0-0197275	0261	3
CHAUDOIR WILLIAM	CPT	0-0492474	1054	1
CHAUNCEY PHILLIP T	1LT	0-4034421	0262	2
CHAUSSE LOUIS F	CPT	0-1052292	1164	1
CHAUVIN HUGH J	CW3	W-2205914	0966	1
CHAVARRIA CORENA R	CPT	N-0759619	0147	1
CHAVERS SIDNEY L	LTC	0-1046040	1068	1
CHAVES CEFERINO	2LT	0-1897030	0249	1
CHAVES ELMER R	1LT	0-1825855	1068	1
CHAVET WALTER A	LTC	0-0451228	0960	1
CHAVEZ ANTHONY T JR	CPT	0-0384790	0945	2
CHAVEZ JOSEPH E	LTC	0-0450623	1160	1
CHAVEZ LEO	CPT	0-0978128	1062	1
CHAVIS DENNIE JR	LTC	0-0451312	0960	1
CHAVIS WILLIAM B	2LT	0-1645609	1044	2
CHAVKIN RALPH	MAJ	0-0455657	0546	2
CHAYES CHARLES M	CPT	0-0487601	0945	2
CHAYES EDWARD	COL	0-0115804	0554	3
CHEADLE EDWIN K	COL	0-0136814	0855	3
CHEADLE JOHN A	LTC	0-0205389	0863	3
CHEANEY DENNIS F	COL	0-0284016	0368	3
CHEANEY FRANK H	MAJ	0-0237281	0662	3
CHEARY ELDON L	MAJ	0-1885152	1066	1
CHEATHAM ALBERT B	MAJ	0-1186262	0964	1
CHEATHAM CADER W	COL	0-0216167	1162	3
CHEATHAM GEORGE L	CW4	W-2119266	1160	1
CHEATHAM GUY C	MAJ	0-0225082	0245	2
CHEATHAM JAMES C	LTC	0-0190751	0163	3
CHEATHAM LEWIS W	LTC	0-1581962	0566	1
CHEATHAM ORME E	LTC	0-0264523	1167	3
CHEATHAM WILLIAM E	COL	0-0266584	1162	1
CHEATWOOD HERMAN A	CW4	W-2108458	0860	1
CHECKIE FABIAN L	LTC	0-1796578	0660	1
CHEDERQUIST ELMER C	LTC	0-1555523	1162	1
CHEDESTER FRANK M	LTC	0-0244870	0866	3
CHEDESTER MYRON O	LTC	0-0406773	0661	1
CHEDESTER RICHARD F	CPT	0-1323538	0446	2
CHEEK ISAAC E	LTC	0-1000724	1158	1
CHEEK JAMES E	LTC	0-0400102	0760	1
CHEEK LEE A JR	CPT	0-4006445	0667	1
CHEEK RICHARD C	CW2	W-2119675	1045	2
CHEEK RUBYE J	MAJ	N-0726878	0347	1
CHEEK VERNON E	CPT	0-0402511	0756	1
CHEEK VICTOR L	MAJ	0-0267751	0868	3
CHEEK WILLIAM W	LTC	0-1174528	1263	1
CHEELEY GRANVILLE	MAJ	0-0320627	1045	2
CHEESMAN BURT	1LT	0-0164802	0242	1
CHEESMAN LEROY V	MAJ	0-2053935	0655	1
CHEEZEM ROBERT L	CW4	W-2005682	1166	1
CHEEZUM THOMAS R	CW4	W-2108901	0758	1
CHEKEL MARTIN A	CW3	W-2132184	0557	1
CHELEDEN JOHN J	MAJ	0-0294345	0846	2
CHELLEW EDWARD M	COL	0-0177691	0860	3
CHELLIS RUEL B	COL	0-0162388	0556	3
CHEMA THOMAS	LTC	0-2294014	0965	1
CHEN JAMES E	MAJ	0-1895944	0765	1
CHENERY CHARLES E	LTC	0-0903124	0654	2
CHENERY HUBERT L	COL	0-0430349	1162	3
CHENEVERT ALAN H	LTC	0-0544924	1068	1
CHENEY ARTHUR M JR	MAJ	0-0330462	1066	3
CHENEY BENJAMIN E	COL	0-0112508	1155	3
CHENEY CURTIS V	LTC	0-1080094	0466	1
CHENEY ERVIN F	2LT	0-0333719	0444	2
CHENEY GILBERT D	LTC	0-1341257	0968	1
CHENEY ISAAC P JR	CPT	0-0549897	0362	2
CHENEY JOHN P JR	MAJ	0-1056664	0266	1
CHENEY LAURENCE R	LTC	0-0241151	1062	3
CHENEY LEIGH H	CPT	0-4046892	0268	1
CHENEY LINWOOD G	1LT	0-1044195	0645	2
CHENEY RUSSELL S	LTC	0-0296974	0362	3
CHENEY WILLIAM D	CPT	0-0393396	0446	2
CHENOWETH C C	MAJ	0-1844948	0361	2
CHENOWETH MARY N	MAJ	N-0742394	0766	1
CHERAKIN BEN	LTC	0-0292550	0650	3
CHERBONNIER ANDRE V	LTC	0-0925568	0160	3
CHERNE MILTON P	LTC	0-1688819	0168	1
CHERNEY HYMAN	MAJ	0-2012651	0461	1
CHERNOW HOWARD H	CPT	0-1786191	0348	2
CHEROKE GEORGE	MAJ	0-0579858	0565	1
CHERRIE GEORGE M	MAJ	0-0188998	0157	3
CHERRINGTON ROBERT B	1LT	0-1055243	0745	2
CHERRINGTON VIRGIL A	LTC	0-0502365	0265	3
CHERRON PETER	LTC	0-1647569	0962	1
CHERRY ALFRED E	MAJ	0-0887658	0657	1
CHERRY CHARLES C	LTC	0-1285547	0761	1
CHERRY CHARLES M	2LT	0-1055244	0645	2
CHERRY CHARLES S	LTC	0-0450425	1057	1
CHERRY DITTMAR P	1LT	0-1043895	0344	2
CHERRY EDMOND B	CW3	W-2142751	1060	1
CHERRY ELTON K	LTC	0-0921296	0557	2
CHERRY FRANK I	COL	0-0150756	0-49	3
CHERRY JEFF F	MAJ	0-1884203	0867	1
CHERRY JERRY P	CPT	0-1185970	0258	1
CHERRY JIM E	MAJ	0-1314732	1060	1
CHERRY JOHN E	MAJ	0-1798448	0756	1
CHERRY JOSEPH A	LTC	0-1015046	0164	1
CHERUBINI AMERIGO J	MAJ	0-1533521	1055	1
CHESBRO IVAN A	COL	0-0119089	0651	3
CHESCHEIR GEORGE M	COL	0-0189716	0849	3
CHESHIRE CLAYTON H	CW4	W-2006195	1167	3
CHESHIRE GODFREY	COL	0-0181901	0153	3
CHESHIRE JOSEPH B	LTC	0-0229153	0562	3
CHESHIRE WILLIAM A	LTC	0-0323620	1266	3
CHESIRE JAMES C JR	MAJ	0-1177734	0461	1
CHESKI WILLIAM A	MAJ	0-0493177	0952	1
CHESKO JOSEPH W	1LT	0-1050593	104N	2
CHESLER MAURICE P	2LT	0-1587883	0144	2
CHESLEY CATHERINE	1LT	N-0772147	0346	1
CHESLEY PHILIP B	MAJ	0-2020925	0663	1
CHESLEY WILLIAM C	1LT	0-1289045	0644	2
CHESLOCK THEODORE J	MAJ	0-1937167	0466	1
CHESMORE CARLTON R	LTC	0-0245898	1166	3
CHESNOVSKY OTTO C	LTC	0-1120643	0468	1
CHESNUT DONALD C JR	MAJ	0-1882025	1267	1
CHESNUTT JAMES G	COL	0-0906935	0667	3
CHESROW EUGENE J	COL	0-0115306	0153	3
CHESROW FRANK W	COL	0-0258680	0463	3
CHESS METKIN	CPT	0-0536967	0346	2
CHESSER FRED H	MAJ	0-1115212	0954	1
CHESSER GERALD T	1LT	0-5338393	0668	2
CHESSER JAMES A JR	1LT	0-1182082	1045	2
CHESSER JAMES L	1LT	0-0499480	0351	1
CHESSER LEWIS F	MAJ	0-1646350	0157	1
CHESSHIRE DOUGLAS	CPT	0-1542297	0661	1
CHESSMAN CHARLES JR	CPT	0-1018652	0846	2
CHESSMAN WALTER E JR	1LT	0-0426750	0246	2
CHESTER ALBERT W	CPT	0-1633117	1146	2
CHESTER ARTHUR M	LTC	0-0196485	1054	1
CHESTER CHARLES W	CW4	W-2115718	0365	2
CHESTER LEWIS S III	1LT	0-0395383	0161	2
CHESTERMAN ALBERT F	1LT	0-0922317	0245	2
CHESTERTON ALLAN B	CPT	0-0241266	0960	3
CHESTNUT JOHN S	CPT	0-0177738	0560	3
CHESTNUTWOOD JACK B	MAJ	0-1544001	0863	1
CHESTNUTWOOD ROBERT	1LT	0-0410378	0744	2
CHETNIK ANTHONY J	1LT	0-1292477	1044	2
CHETTLE EARL V	MAJ	0-0260020	0965	3
CHEVALIER ALAIN A	LTC	0-1037588	0864	1
CHEVALIER FRANK C	COL	0-0918459	0263	3
CHEVALIER WILLIAM M	CPT	0-0505139	0447	2
CHEVERIE JAMES P	MAJ	0-1926844	0167	1
CHEVES FOREST A	CPT	0-0889461	0457	1
CHEW HERBERT W	LTC	0-1004747	0368	3
CHEW LUN K	CPT	0-0320525	1045	2
CHEWNING REGINALD D	CW4	W-2127497	0157	1
CHEWNING ROBERT E JR	MAJ	0-0249785	0966	3
CHEWNING WILLIAM T	2LT	0-1324879	0445	2
CHEYNE LESTER J	MAJ	0-0447853	0451	2
CHEYNE WILLIAM	LTC	0-2036360	0762	2
CHEYNEY RUSSELL G	1LT	0-1308474	0945	2
CHEYNEY WALDRON J	COL	0-0105631	0345	2
CHEYRION LOUIS J	1LT	0-1281809	1047	1
CHEZEM HAROLD R	LTC	0-1312835	1162	1
CHEZMAR JULIUS	LTC	0-1542699	0561	1
CHIANESE CAJETAN T	COL	0-0169198	0959	3
CHIARAMONTE JULIO	LTC	0-0348151	0161	1
CHIARELLA ANTHONY D	LTC	0-1012254	0268	1
CHIARELLI PETER F	MAJ	0-2010569	0868	3
CHICATELLI JACOB J	CPT	0-1323238	0546	2
CHICAZOLA MELVIN A	LTC	0-1104560	0464	2
CHICHWAK LUCILLE C	1LT	N-0725556	0446	1
CHICK LAMONT C	CPT	0-0236175	0258	2
CHICK LANGSTON F	CW2	W-2209354	1262	1
CHICK VIRGIL C	MAJ	0-4006603	0968	1
CHICKERING F L	CW4	W-2108242	1059	1
CHICKERING M N	CPT	L-0105077	1054	2
CHICLES CHRIS	LTC	0-1922649	1168	1
CHICO LUIS A	LTC	0-0229044	0265	3
CHIDESTER CLARKE W	LTC	0-0341071	1059	1
CHIDESTER GEORGE F	2LT	0-2016866	0746	2
CHIEFFALO FRANK J	LTC	0-1578259	0967	1
CHIER REUBEN O	CPT	0-0338426	1045	2
CHIESA ALDO C	LTC	0-0287230	0463	3
CHILBERG GEORGE E	LTC	0-1544327	0667	2
CHILCOTE EARL H	CPT	0-1042783	0854	1
CHILD BARBARA J	MAJ	L-1010078	0865	1
CHILD HARRY M	LTC	0-1107857	0661	1
CHILD ROBERT W	COL	0-0173982	0158	3
CHILDE JOHN W JR	1LT	0-1313570	0645	2
CHILDERS ARLIE M	MAJ	0-0969432	0867	1
CHILDERS CALVIN C	CW3	W-2205814	0764	2
CHILDERS CHESTER W	MAJ	0-1542402	0157	1
CHILDERS DOROTHY T	MAJ	L-0900013	0565	1
CHILDERS EARL G	LTC	0-0388122	0760	1
CHILDERS FITZHUGH L	MAJ	0-0510348	0147	1
CHILDERS GEORGE T	LTC	0-0385461	0663	1
CHILDERS JACK S	MAJ	0-1703058	0461	1
CHILDERS JAMES E	LTC	0-1012375	0968	1
CHILDERS JUNIOR A	MAJ	0-2005493	0361	1
CHILDERS RAYMOND L	2LT	0-1049103	0844	2
CHILDERS WARREN P	CPT	0-1637182	0952	2
CHILDRES JAMES B	LTC	0-0505393	0155	1
CHILDRESS CREED T	CW2	W-2150660	0559	1
CHILDRESS DENNIS R	2LT	0-1585272	0544	2
CHILDRESS EASOM G	CW2	W-2211144	1068	1
CHILDRESS HERSCHEL M	CW2	W-2214801	0968	1
CHILDRESS HUGH J	MAJ	0-0277209	0653	3
CHILDRESS J T	2LT	0-1999222	0446	2
CHILDRESS LEWIS E	LTC	0-1554520	1166	1
CHILDRESS PAUL E	WO1	W-2150922	1154	1
CHILDRESS RAYMOND E	CPT	0-0281984	0768	3
CHILDRESS ROBERT C	LTC	0-0288178	0266	3
CHILDS DOMINIC J III	MAJ	0-1031233	1160	1
CHILDS EDWARD P JR	LTC	0-0189317	0556	3
CHILDS ERNEST W JR	MAJ	0-0221060	0568	3
CHILDS GEORGE L	MAJ	0-0287059	0468	3
CHILDS J H	CPT	0-1305011	0947	2
CHILDS JAMES N	1LT	0-1058473	0446	2
CHILDS JEANNE G	MAJ	L-0501178	0163	1
CHILDS JOHN P	2LT	0-1053086	0745	2
CHILDS LAWRENCE D	WO1	W-2150769	0155	1
CHILDS LINCOLN B	CPT	0-0422647	0344	2
CHILDS ORRICK A	LTC	0-1825592	0661	1
CHILDS RALPH F SR	MAJ	0-1000332	0961	1
CHILDS RALPH S	COL	0-0246801	0959	3
CHILDS ROBERT F	LTC	0-1296997	0463	1
CHILDS THOMAS M	COL	0-0134213	0-51	3
CHILES HENRY L	CPT	0-2001130	0155	1
CHILES VERNON E	1LT	0-1304863	0845	2
CHILMAN FRANCIS R	1LT	0-1012956	0744	2
CHILSON CHARLES G	CW2	W-2147848	0860	1
CHILSON FRANCIS A	COL	0-0318792	0860	1
CHILSON GEORGE H	CPT	0-2671338	1060	1
CHILSON VIRGAL R	COL	0-0311448	0262	1
CHILTON CARL E	MAJ	0-1050594	0159	1
CHILTON ELMORE F	LTC	0-0885544	0758	2
CHILTON FRANK	LTC	0-0375005	0155	1

NAME	GRADE	SVC NO	DATE RET MO YR	RET CODE
CHILTON LLOYD	MAJ	0-2024103	0161	1
CHILTON PAUL G	LTC	0-1042784	1162	1
CHIMINIELLO DOMINIC	COL	0-0308309	0166	1
CHIN WOODROW Y	MAJ	0-0974976	0663	1
CHINDAHL ANITA G	CPT	N-0727992	0547	1
CHINENE JON J	1LT	0-2046476	1047	2
CHING TAI TONG	CPT	0-0507662	0745	2
CHINKES STANLEY	MAJ	0-0958677	0663	1
CHINLUND JOSEPH F	1LT	0-0466747	1146	2
CHINN KEITH R	COL	0-0288424	0563	3
CHINOWTH CHARLES C	CW2	W-2126894	0145	2
CHINSKE RICHARD W	MAJ	0-2016588	1060	1
CHINWORTH JOHN L	CPT	0-0979767	0361	1
CHIODO SANTO F	LTC	0-0451229	1262	1
CHIOTAKIS VACILIOS A	LTC	0-1174249	0467	1
CHIPLEY EHRLICH L	LTC	0-0305410	0562	1
CHIPMAN ALBERT B	MAJ	0-0184857	1055	3
CHIPMAN ALBERT B JR	1LT	0-0538397	0945	2
CHIPPEAUX HARRY L	MAJ	0-1119915	0461	1
CHIRICO ANTHONY R	MAJ	0-1946685	1164	1
CHIRIGOTIS F F	LTC	0-1013071	0261	1
CHIRON ALBERT E	MAJ	0-0491244	0546	2
CHIROS JIMMY	1LT	0-1183829	0946	2
CHISAMORE EARL F	LTC	0-0312267	0868	3
CHISHOLM ELMER F	LTC	0-0234797	1263	3
CHISHOLM GORDON A	1LT	0-1288703	0545	2
CHISHOLM JOSEPH D	MAJ	0-0114287	0455	3
CHISHOLM LAWRENCE W	1LT	0-1587734	0654	1
CHISHOLM WILLIAM G	LTC	0-0392509	1264	1
CHISHOLM WILLIAM H	CPT	0-0230808	0448	2
CHISMAN THOMAS D	CW3	W-2141838	0958	1
CHISMAR FRANK E	MAJ	0-0471641	0257	1
CHISMIRE FRANK E	MAJ	0-1291587	0561	1
CHITTENDEN HERBERT M	LTC	0-0340826	0562	1
CHITTENDEN MILES C	LTC	0-0112801	0955	3
CHITTICK CLAIRE R	LTC	0-1306704	0856	1
CHITTICK GERVAISE S	COL	0-0903369	0662	1
CHITTICK HARRY A	LTC	0-0293577	0263	3
CHITTICK HARRY S JR	LTC	0-0399870	0959	1
CHITTICK MARTIN B	COL	0-0100258	0452	3
CHITTIM JAMES M	LTC	0-0197975	0762	3
CHITTY CHARITA M	CPT	N-0763935	0747	1
CHITWOOD ALBERT E	MAJ	0-1047918	0761	1
CHITWOOD GLENN W	MAJ	0-1822105	1157	1
CHITWOOD JULIUS R	MAJ	0-0447123	0346	2
CHITWOOD PAUL W	CW3	W-2117378	0560	1
CHIVERAL JAMES C	LTC	0-1302774	0767	3
CHIVINGTON FREDERICK	LTC	0-1111547	0163	1
CHLADEK ARTHUR L	LTC	0-0246596	0366	3
CHLAPOWSKI THEODORE	MAJ	0-0981145	0265	1
CHLEVIN B J JR	2LT	0-1050211	1144	2
CHLOUPEK CARL C	LTC	0-2289439	1166	1
CHMIELEWSKI JANE T	1LT	N-0720455	1046	1
CHMIELEWSKI SIGMUND	MAJ	0-1176280	1057	1
CHO DAVID	MAJ	0-0977723	0763	1
CHO SAMUEL	CW3	W-2144179	0666	1
CHOATE BENJAMIN D	COL	0-0257236	0648	3
CHOATE HAROLD J	COL	0-0321782	0867	3
CHOATE JAMES F	1LT	0-0489756	0347	1
CHOATE JAMES F	MAJ	0-1919128	1263	1
CHOATE JOHN F	COL	0-0174426	1153	3
CHOATE REGINALD C	CW4	W-2147513	1164	1
CHOFFREY MARIO J	LTC	0-1947553	0463	1
CHOINSKI WALTER F	COL	0-0246915	0558	1
CHOJECKI CHESTER J	LTC	0-1638874	0663	1
CHOJNACKI ANDREW F	CW3	W-2144568	0662	1
CHOLLAK JOSEPH P	CPT	0-0423442	0346	2
CHOMEAU HENRI	MAJ	0-0242706	0160	3
CHOMJACK JOHN	CW2	W-2117034	0447	2
CHOMKO PAUL	1LT	0-1291415	0844	2
CHOMOS STEVE V	LTC	0-1646359	0666	1
CHONG KIM-FAN	LTC	0-0270480	0162	1
CHONG PAUL	CW3	W-2151052	0563	1
CHONKO LILLIAN H	1LT	N-0725498	0246	2
CHOPP WILLIAM R	1LT	0-1767158	0245	2
CHOPSON EDWIN W	COL	0-0243625	0766	3
CHOQUETTE GRACE A	1LT	N-0756263	1145	1
CHORNYAK HELEN M	COL	N-0755305	0163	1
CHORNYAK JOHN	COL	0-0225878	0661	3
CHOTAS MATTHEW E	COL	0-0317045	1060	1
CHOUINARD ARTHUR C	MAJ	0-1924578	0561	1
CHOW GEORGE	COL	0-1555026	0263	2
CHOWENHILL CHARLES F	LTC	0-0921981	0563	3
CHOWNING RICHARD L	LTC	0-1295668	1061	2
CHOWNING WILLIAM B	CPT	0-0949793	1159	1
CHRANE ROBERT N	CPT	0-0969796	1060	1
CHREST JOHN F	LTC	0-0911808	0265	1
CHRIMES THEODORE D	MAJ	0-0202262	0846	2
CHRISLEY JOHN R	CW3	W-2126176	0457	1
CHRISMAN CECIL M	WO1	W-2149691	0765	2
CHRISMAN ROBERT R	LTC	0-0211187	1063	3
CHRISMAN WILLIAM G	CPT	0-0260646	1267	3
CHRISSINGER HORACE B	LTC	0-0281293	0668	3
CHRISTEN RUSSELL C	MAJ	0-1950654	1064	1
CHRISTENSEN ALAN W	LTC	0-0243971	1164	3
CHRISTENSEN ALLEN O	CW3	W-2136684	1262	1
CHRISTENSEN ANDREW J	LTC	0-1635693	0463	1
CHRISTENSEN ARLET C	CPT	0-0279720	0747	2
CHRISTENSEN BURT P	CPT	0-0419153	0346	2
CHRISTENSEN CAROL M	2LT	N-0775987	0345	1
CHRISTENSEN CHRIST J	1LT	0-1886633	0658	2
CHRISTENSEN DONALD W	LTC	0-0986289	0868	1
CHRISTENSEN EARL D	1LT	0-1305388	0345	2
CHRISTENSEN EARL E	1LT	0-2036535	0545	2
CHRISTENSEN EDWARD	LTC	0-1294434	0761	1
CHRISTENSEN ELLIS G	COL	0-0280507	0656	3
CHRISTENSEN FRANK P	COL	0-0216096	0953	1
CHRISTENSEN FRED G	LTC	0-1587176	1167	1
CHRISTENSEN HALDOW E	LTC	0-0255480	0246	2
CHRISTENSEN HANS K	CPT	0-1766950	1047	2
CHRISTENSEN HOLGER	CPT	0-0494322	0351	1
CHRISTENSEN HUGH W	1LT	0-1785321	0645	2
CHRISTENSEN JENS	CPT	0-1913590	0836	1
CHRISTENSEN JOHN B	LTC	0-0232887	1164	3
CHRISTENSEN LESTER C	CPT	0-2262728	0361	1
CHRISTENSEN LESTER F	MAJ	0-1586762	0660	1
CHRISTENSEN LINCOLN	CW3	W-2149808	0867	1
CHRISTENSEN MELVIN	CW2	W-3100555	0567	1
CHRISTENSEN MILTON J	MAJ	0-5301848	0868	1
CHRISTENSEN NOAL A	LTC	0-1338922	0866	1
CHRISTENSEN PAUL E	CPT	0-0363126	0246	2
CHRISTENSEN PETER A	LTC	0-0204635	0756	3
CHRISTENSEN R W	CPT	0-0488964	0246	2
CHRISTENSEN REX	MAJ	0-1634612	1160	1
CHRISTENSEN ROBERT	CW3	W-2147388	1062	1
CHRISTENSEN RUSSELL	LTC	0-0273522	0868	3
CHRISTENSEN VAGN H	LTC	0-0306441	0867	3
CHRISTENSEN VIGGO	COL	0-0185784	0546	2
CHRISTENSEN WIGGO	MAJ	0-1546157	0960	1
CHRISTENSEN WILLIAM	CPT	0-1051908	0159	1
CHRISTENSEN WILLIAM	1LT	0-5514636	0164	2
CHRISTENSEN WOODROW	CPT	0-1294266	0657	1
CHRISTENSON ALBERT W	LTC	0-0209532	0345	2
CHRISTENSON CONRAD W	CPT	0-0480356	0446	2
CHRISTENSON EARL O	LTC	0-0110007	1155	1
CHRISTENSON HAROLD E	1LT	0-1295339	1146	2
CHRISTENSON JEWELL C	LTC	0-0336544	0867	3
CHRISTENSON JOHN C W	CW3	W-2150335	1162	1
CHRISTENSON ROBERT L	LTC	0-1545067	0667	1
CHRISTIAN ALBERT O	2LT	0-0958647	0451	2
CHRISTIAN BEATRICE M	1LT	N-0702500	1146	1
CHRISTIAN DEXTER J	CW3	W-2143884	1160	1
CHRISTIAN EARL H	LTC	0-0223567	0760	3
CHRISTIAN GEORGE W	CPT	0-0332959	0944	2
CHRISTIAN GLEN H	LTC	0-0514108	0762	1
CHRISTIAN HENRY A	COL	0-0239704	0546	2
CHRISTIAN HOWARD J	1LT	0-1635695	0146	2
CHRISTIAN JACK	LTC	0-0219884	0856	3
CHRISTIAN JAMES T	1LT	0-1109197	0745	2
CHRISTIAN JOHN D	MAJ	0-1692548	0960	1
CHRISTIAN JOHN M	1LT	0-1080838	0246	2
CHRISTIAN JOSEPH L	1LT	0-1003895	0857	1
CHRISTIAN LOUIS C JR	MAJ	0-0451839	0647	2
CHRISTIAN MILTON B	LTC	0-1549908	0219	1
CHRISTIAN NICHOLAS J	2LT	0-1108552	0345	2
CHRISTIAN RUSSELL O	CW3	W-2143066	0357	1
CHRISTIAN WILLIAM F	LTC	0-0357000	1267	1
CHRISTIAN WILLIAM G	CPT	0-1106644	0255	1
CHRISTIAN WILLIAM L	LTC	0-0207332	1263	3
CHRISTIANS CRYSTAL R	1LT	N-0742095	0946	1
CHRISTIANS JEROME J	LTC	0-0310427	0767	3
CHRISTIANSEN ALFRE	MAJ	0-1541781	0356	1
CHRISTIANSEN ARNE C	LTC	0-1313571	0268	1
CHRISTIANSEN ARTHU	1LT	0-0298540	0845	2
CHRISTIANSEN ARTHUR	MAJ	0-1297839	0565	1
CHRISTIANSEN CARL R	CPT	0-0983191	1264	1
CHRISTIANSEN EMIL G	LTC	0-0389878	0363	1
CHRISTIANSEN ERNES	2LT	0-1015615	1044	2
CHRISTIANSEN GEORGE	LTC	0-1014723	1061	1
CHRISTIANSEN GEORGE	MAJ	0-1692647	0860	1
CHRISTIANSEN LAWRENC	MAJ	0-1334767	0862	1
CHRISTIANSEN ROBERT	1LT	0-0988194	0858	1
CHRISTIANSEN VERNO	MAJ	0-1593238	0960	1
CHRISTIANSEN WALTER	MAJ	0-1324146	0364	2
CHRISTIANSON HAROLD	COL	0-0297506	0968	3
CHRISTIANSON KENNETH	CPT	0-0447525	0946	2
CHRISTIE CLARENCE M	LTC	0-0269674	0467	3
CHRISTIE EVELYN M	MAJ	N-0721964	1267	3
CHRISTIE GEORGE P	CW2	W-3200261	0268	1
CHRISTIE GEORGE T JR	LTC	0-1309516	0764	3
CHRISTIE GOTTLIEB C	CW2	W-2149664	0260	1
CHRISTIE HAROLD R	LTC	0-0248770	0565	3
CHRISTIE ROBERT E	MAJ	0-0384663	0868	3
CHRISTIE ROBERT M	LTC	0-0299031	0862	1
CHRISTIE ROBERT S	CPT	0-0220611	0660	3
CHRISTIE THOMAS M	MAJ	0-1014201	0167	2
CHRISTINA ANTHONY A	CPT	0-1288855	1157	1
CHRISTINE JAMES H	WO1	W-2118404	0848	1
CHRISTINE MILLER C	LTC	0-0446281	1160	2
CHRISTINE PAUL D	CW3	W-2152508	0762	1
CHRISTJOHN GLADYS R	2LT	N-0775665	1044	1
CHRISTL ERNEST M	MAJ	0-1041311	0146	2
CHRISTMAN ARTHUR V	CPT	0-1291952	0146	2
CHRISTMAN JOSEPH S	MAJ	0-0920461	1046	2
CHRISTMAN ROBERT J	1LT	0-2005340	0248	2
CHRISTMAS ELLIS H	CW3	W-2206847	0266	1
CHRISTMAS FRANK M	LTC	0-1283913	0961	1
CHRISTMAS JOE C	MAJ	0-0977849	0463	1
CHRISTNER EUGENE B	CW3	W-2150156	0764	1
CHRISTOFFERSON HARLE	LTC	0-1036470	0662	1
CHRISTOPH CHARLES J	MAJ	0-1175075	0261	1
CHRISTOPHER ALVA J	LTC	0-1542821	1162	1
CHRISTOPHER ARTHUR C	LTC	0-0312811	1065	3
CHRISTOPHER DANIEL R	CW2	W-2141839	0756	1
CHRISTOPHER GLEN J	MAJ	0-1650469	0761	1
CHRISTOPHER JOHN	MAJ	0-1289121	0454	1
CHRISTOPHER JOHN O	LTC	0-1548177	0164	1
CHRISTOPHER LEON D	LTC	0-1334417	0864	1
CHRISTOPHER MILLARD	MAJ	0-2263448	0965	1
CHRISTOPHER SIDNEY L	CW2	W-2144162	0659	1
CHRISTOPHERSON CLIFF	LTC	0-0311038	0360	3
CHRISTOPHERSON GORDO	MAJ	0-0962892	0461	1
CHRISTOPHERSON OLAF	LTC	0-0330492	1064	1
CHRISTY GALE D	MAJ	0-1174530	0361	1
CHRISTY JOHN G	COL	0-0256819	0757	3
CHRISTY KENNETH R	LTC	0-0347606	0465	3
CHRISTY ROBERT J	MAJ	0-1100485	0566	2
CHRISTY THOMAS N	1LT	0-0440617	0446	2
CHRISWELL FRED O	LTC	0-0450582	0754	1
CHROMCIK BESSIE O	2LT	N-0792876	0751	2
CHRONI EDWARD	CW2	W-2152821	0757	1
CHRONIS LEONIDAS M	LTC	0-0313490	0961	3
CHRONQUIST GEORGE C	CPT	0-0484339	1143	2
CHRYSLER CLAYTON D	LTC	0-0236805	1057	3
CHRYST STANLEY T	MAJ	0-0488715	0753	1
CHRZAN WALTER S	1LT	0-1318651	0248	1
CHUBAK WILLIAM J	MAJ	0-0450622	0455	1
CHUBB GEORGE F	CW3	W-2150040	0166	1
CHUBBUCK CHARLES D	COL	0-0258476	0268	3
CHUBBUCK FRANK M	CPT	0-0128927	0648	3
CHUM ANDREWS S JR	MAJ	0-1114887	0660	2
CHUMBLEY CHARLES M	LTC	0-1541239	0457	1
CHUMLEY SILAS E	LTC	0-1913426	0368	1
CHUN ARTHUR B	COL	0-0343577	0762	2
CHUN RICHARD S	MAJ	0-0953945	0862	1
CHUN-MING ARCHER	LTC	0-0308700	0548	2
CHUNG DAVID	MAJ	0-1340157	0765	1
CHUNG HENRY H	LTC	0-0322272	1065	3
CHUNG WAH N	1LT	0-0378070	0446	2
CHUNN FLOYD H	LTC	0-0315418	0858	3
CHUNN FRANCIS A	CPT	0-1032196	0258	1
CHUNN THOMAS H	2LT	0-0346754	0542	2
CHUPINSKY PETER	MAJ	0-1587178	0567	1
CHUPAN DOROTHY	1LT	N-0785680	1046	1
CHURCH ARCHIE W JR	LTC	0-1316383	0865	1
CHURCH CARL N	MAJ	0-0981591	0866	1
CHURCH CHARLES O JR	CW2	W-2143261	0666	1
CHURCH CLAUDE H.	COL	0-0200642	0648	3
CHURCH ELVIN H	CPT	0-0146537	0257	3
CHURCH GEORGE B JR	LTC	0-0322549	0859	1
CHURCH GERALD L	COL	0-0288207	0155	1
CHURCH GUY N JR	LTC	0-0398278	0263	1
CHURCH HARRY J	2LT	0-1104084	0445	2
CHURCH JACOB H	MAJ	0-1173187	1058	1
CHURCH JAMES A	LTC	0-0888263	1160	1
CHURCH JOHN A	2LT	0-0468511	0745	2
CHURCH JOSEPH H	COL	0-0248168	0463	3
CHURCH KENNETH W	CPT	0-0300082	1162	3
CHURCH MERTON F	LTC	0-0329610	0261	1
CHURCH ORVILLE T	LTC	0-0116144	0557	3
CHURCH RALPH C	CW4	W-2000324	1060	2
CHURCH RAYMOND B	MAJ	0-2055381	0656	1
CHURCH RICHARD L	MAJ	0-1926845	1168	1
CHURCH SAMUEL A	2LT	0-1550134	0643	2
CHURCH SANFORD E	LTC	0-0102910	0648	3
CHURCH WAYNE G	COL	0-0210727	0160	3
CHURCH WILLIAM K	MAJ	0-1281971	0262	1
CHURCHBOURNE HENRY	MAJ	0-1183038	0259	2
CHURCHILL CHARLES O	LTC	0-0471669	0668	3
CHURCHILL DAVID R	LTC	0-1683453	1167	1
CHURCHILL HELEN K	CPT	N-0787471	0246	2
CHURCHILL MARJORIE P	MAJ	L-1000893	0664	1
CHURCHILL RALPH O	LTC	0-0340543	0764	1
CHURCHILL RICHARD T	CPT	0-0533422	1047	2
CHURCHILL RILEY V	CW2	W-2211382	1266	1
CHURCHILL WALTER P	MAJ	0-0142663	1049	3
CHURCHMAN DONALD B	LTC	0-1634615	1165	1
CHURCHMAN HENRY C	LTC	0-0122316	1055	3
CHURCHWELL SAMUEL B	MAJ	0-0253814	1054	3
CHYNOWETH JOHN H	CPT	0-1947185	0462	1
CHYNOWETH WILLIAM R	LTC	0-0183567	0648	3
CI MARCONE WILLIAM A	MAJ	0-1949507	0561	1
CIAGLO MICHAEL J	1LT	0-1172411	0346	2
CIAMPA RALPH P	CPT	0-0499649	1044	2
CIAMPA UBALDI J	CW2	W-2111600	0350	2
CIANI RAYMOND R	CW2	W-3000286	0966	1
CIANOS MICHAEL	LTC	0-1298662	0564	1
CIARALDI AMERICO S	LTC	0-1589757	1167	1
CIARLO JOHN W JR	MAJ	0-2263028	1164	1
CIBOROWSKI MITCHELL	LTC	0-1039902	0862	1
CIBULA ALVIN M	COL	0-0256320	1067	3
CIBULSKI FRED C	MAJ	0-1042516	0954	1
CICCARELLI LAWRENCE	MAJ	0-0980818	0264	1
CICCIOLLO DOMINICK N	CW3	W-2145337	1061	1
CICCIU ANGELO	LTC	0-1177736	0166	1
CICCOLI MICHAEL J	LTC	0-1292659	0261	1
CICCONE ALEX M	LTC	0-1107861	1163	1
CICCOTELLI DOMINIC R	CW4	W-2147714	0766	1
CICERCHIA IOLANDA M	LTC	N-0721609	0767	1
CICHANSKI WILLIAM J	LTC	0-0411005	0766	1

NAME	GRADE	SVC NO	DATE RET MO YR	RET CODE
CICHY JOSEPH J	CW4	W-2141977	1265	1
CICOLANI RENO R	CW4	W-2117879	1266	3
CICONE GADDIO J	MAJ	O-1011832	1147	2
CIELINSKI EDWARD	LTC	O-1288856	0657	1
CIESIELSKI FRANCIS	LTC	O-0933326	0266	1
CIEZAK HENRY F	MAJ	O-1644667	1062	1
CIFORELLI BART L	LTC	O-1013443	1265	3
CIHOS CARL	CPT	O-1308208	0452	1
CIKA PETER	LTC	O-1101784	1267	1
CILINO STEPHEN	LTC	O-1047922	0565	1
CILLEY GEORGE E	LTC	O-0336143	0460	1
CILLIS VINCENT A	LTC	O-1948104	0167	3
CIMINO JOSEPH N	CW3	W-2152203	1157	1
CIMINO VINCENT JR	MAJ	O-1686247	0563	1
CINAK THEODORE J	LTC	O-0319379	0968	3
CINCOTTI JOHN J	COL	O-0370798	0168	3
CINI JULIAN A	MAJ	O-0976180	1165	1
CINQ-MARS PAUL R	LTC	O-0342446	0363	1
CINQUANTA FIORINO A	LTC	O-0782170	1167	1
CIOCHETTI HANNIBAL S	LTC	O-0164102	0552	1
CIOLA DOMINICK P	2LT	O-1185397	0545	2
CIPPES ISAAC B	MAJ	O-0237678	1043	2
CIPRIANO JOSEPH J	CW3	W-2147339	0265	1
CIPRIANO XAVIER V	LTC	O-0556666	0966	1
CIRELLI MARIO G	CPT	O-0534991	0446	2
CIRIACKS RUBEN H	LTC	O-1055248	1263	1
CIRILLO JOSEPH	MAJ	O-1595424	1060	1
CIROCCO CARMEL J	1LT	O-1553610	0645	2
CIROLIA PHILIP J	1LT	O-0553204	0146	2
CISCO JOSEPH A	MAJ	O-1313340	0955	1
CISEWSKI LAMBERT E	1LT	O-1291234	1144	2
CISZEK JULIUS G	CPT	O-1053521	0558	1
CISZEWSKI JOSEPH	CPT	O-0450709	1056	1
CITO ALBERT V	LTC	O-0326051	0360	1
CITRON ROBERT R	CPT	O-0337616	0645	2
CITRON WILLIAM M	MAJ	O-0478888	0344	2
CIUCHTA JOHN T	CW3	W-2151763	1062	1
CIULIK JOSEPH D	1LT	O-0931275	0346	2
CIVALIER JOSEPH J	CPT	O-1306064	0146	2
CIVELLO ANTHONY R	MAJ	O-1554521	0661	1
CIVICK RICHARD J	MAJ	O-0965346	0167	1
CIVIDANES MANUEL	MAJ	O-1315788	0461	1
CIVIK FRANK C	1LT	O-1798449	0848	1
CIVILLE LEWIS A	COL	O-1308101	0968	1
CIVITELLA CAESAR J	MAJ	O-1918864	0964	1
CIZAN CLIFFORD L	MAJ	O-0976798	1063	1
CIZEK MELVIN A	LTC	O-1059740	0763	1
CLAASSEN RALPH I	LTC	O-0283509	0268	3
CLABAUGH RICHARD P	2LT	O-1053522	0344	2
CLABAUGH SAMUEL F	COL	O-0265446	0352	3
CLABEAUX HARRY W	CW2	W-2144903	1162	1
CLABO PETER	2LT	O-0422850	0442	2
CLAFF LESLIE A	COL	O-0530863	1064	3
CLAFFEY JAMES S	LTC	O-1822237	0766	1
CLAFLIN FREDERICK	LTC	O-0379751	0463	1
CLAGETT DARRELL M	MAJ	O-1173562	0258	1
CLAGETT DONALD P	1LT	O-1284473	0944	2
CLAGETT JOHN F	MAJ	O-0177622	0561	3
CLAGETT THOMAS B	LTC	O-1293011	1263	1
CLAGG JESSE E	MAJ	O-1541733	0157	1
CLAGGETT RICHARD F	1LT	O-1637727	0846	2
CLAGGETT THOMAS O	LTC	O-0308624	0864	3
CLAGHORN CLIFFORD H	LTC	O-0277269	1150	3
CLAGUE JOHN P	LTC	O-0244578	0861	3
CLAIBORNE JOHN W JR	COL	O-0295481	0768	3
CLAIN MARVIN B JR	MAJ	O-1554877	0661	1
CLAINS GERARD J	LTC	O-1290554	0461	1
CLAIR CARL W	CPT	O-1590377	0346	2
CLAIR MARIE T	1LT	L-0120188	1050	2
CLAIRE GUY S	COL	O-0306823	0856	3
CLAITOR DAVID E	2LT	O-1037956	1044	2
CLAMPET JAMES R	LTC	O-0456542	0656	2
CLAMUCHA ANASTASIO	1LT	O-1896695	0151	2
CLANCY ANNA K	2LT	N-0700781	1036	1
CLANCY CLYDE O	COL	O-0310513	0963	1

NAME	GRADE	SVC NO	DATE RET MO YR	RET CODE
CLANCY JOHN L	CW2	W-2150201	0761	1
CLANCY LOUIS J	LTC	O-1797781	0268	1
CLANCY THADDEUS	CPT	O-0183569	0762	3
CLANCY THOMAS G	LTC	O-1948566	1266	1
CLANCY WILLIAM H	CPT	O-0172135	0155	3
CLANTON ALBERT C	CPT	O-1032145	0657	1
CLANTON DAVID L	LTC	O-1030135	0764	1
CLANTON THOMAS K	CW2	W-2105769	1147	2
CLAPHAM AUGUST J	CW3	W-2148577	1162	1
CLAPP ERNEST	1LT	O-0109074	0335	1
CLAPP EUGENE O	CW2	W-2144876	1055	1
CLAPP HARVEY R JR	CPT	O-0247527	0266	3
CLAPP LAURENCE W	CW2	W-2209167	0762	1
CLAPP LESTER L	MAJ	O-0217678	1057	3
CLAPP RALPH X	1LT	O-1313207	1055	1
CLAPP ROGER F	LTC	O-0260225	0867	3
CLAPP TILLMAN L	1LT	O-0977620	0859	1
CLAPP WILEY M	2LT	O-1913606	0336	1
CLAPP WINTHROP S	COL	O-0221525	1047	2
CLAPP 3RD RUSSELL A	2LT	O-0535591	0446	2
CLAPPER HUBBARD G	MAJ	O-1296488	1060	1
CLAPPER NEAL E	MAJ	O-0504279	0753	1
CLAPPER WILLARD C	LTC	O-1581599	0664	1
CLAPPISON CHARLES D	1LT	O-0492460	0946	2
CLARDY CARL D	CPT	O-0271233	0747	2
CLARE JOHN W	MAJ	O-1305730	0865	1
CLARE JOSEPH E	LTC	O-1638876	0666	3
CLARE JOSEPH F	COL	O-1080923	1068	1
CLARE LELAND T	1LT	O-0391124	0644	2
CLARE THOMAS H	1LT	O-1058474	1047	2
CLARENS HARRY F	LTC	O-1296998	0363	1
CLAREY JOHN C	LTC	O-2055099	0263	1
CLARICK MILDRED S	1LT	N-0751603	0146	2
CLARIDGE FREDERICK	LTC	O-0177316	0459	3
CLARK ALBERT C	MAJ	O-0272843	0367	3
CLARK ALBERT P	CPT	O-2200012	0555	2
CLARK ALFRED V	LTC	O-1053524	0865	1
CLARK ALLEN B	LTC	O-0416242	1062	1
CLARK ALLEN R	CPT	O-0375912	0746	2
CLARK ALVIN E	LTC	O-0374810	0766	1
CLARK ALVIN W	LTC	O-0196398	0862	3
CLARK ARCHIE D JR	MAJ	O-0398001	0567	1
CLARK ARCHIE E	COL	O-0498188	0761	2
CLARK ARTHUR B JR	1LT	O-0441254	0745	2
CLARK ARTHUR F	CPT	O-2030433	1062	1
CLARK ARTHUR H	LTC	O-0291066	0445	2
CLARK ARTHUR W JR	MAJ	O-1104562	0364	1
CLARK AUBREY H	CPT	O-1298194	0447	2
CLARK AUREL R	LTC	O-0410123	0754	1
CLARK BENJAMIN F	COL	O-0308088	0566	3
CLARK BILLY C	MAJ	O-0386208	0257	2
CLARK BRADFORD A	CPT	O-0298052	0845	2
CLARK BROADUS	CW2	W-2151095	1057	1
CLARK CARROLL H	LTC	O-0232382	1057	3
CLARK CHARLES A	MAJ	O-0505228	0550	1
CLARK CHARLES C	LTC	O-0481948	0366	1
CLARK CHARLES C	MAJ	O-1287665	0160	1
CLARK CHARLES C JR	LTC	O-1293551	0468	1
CLARK CHARLES D	COL	O-0201707	0661	3
CLARK CHARLES E	COL	O-0144653	0252	3
CLARK CHARLES G	LTC	O-0338072	0555	3
CLARK CHARLES I	COL	O-0196442	0253	3
CLARK CHARLES K	CW2	W-2206930	1063	1
CLARK CHARLES L	MAJ	O-0288225	1067	3
CLARK CHARLES L JR	LTC	O-0300788	1164	1
CLARK CHARLES N	MAJ	O-1106055	0563	1
CLARK CHARLES T	MAJ	O-1031795	0161	1
CLARK CHESTER A	COL	O-0199426	1148	1
CLARK CHESTER E	MAJ	O-2263349	1264	1
CLARK CLAUDE C	LTC	O-0266443	0160	1
CLARK CLEMENT W JR	LTC	O-0414900	0561	1
CLARK CLIFTON T	CW4	W-2107881	0659	1
CLARK CLYDE L	LTC	O-0250749	0167	3
CLARK CORBETT W	MAJ	O-0981312	1061	1
CLARK DANIEL J	MAJ	O-0551547	0963	1

NAME	GRADE	SVC NO	DATE RET MO YR	RET CODE
CLARK DANIEL R	COL	O-0456541	0561	1
CLARK DELMAR R	WO1	W-2143761	0662	1
CLARK DILBERT	MAJ	O-2263038	1164	1
CLARK DON B	LTC	O-2035665	0667	1
CLARK DONALD L	MAJ	O-0972824	1162	1
CLARK DONALD M	CW2	W-2150651	0662	1
CLARK DOYLE H	COL	O-0340638	0466	3
CLARK DUDLEY B	LTC	O-0471956	0157	1
CLARK DUDLEY C	MAJ	O-0580620	0468	3
CLARK DUNLAP C	COL	O-0115910	1156	3
CLARK EARL B	LTC	O-0113974	0648	3
CLARK EDITH M	MAJ	N-0730865	1067	1
CLARK EDMUND W	MAJ	O-0966143	1262	1
CLARK EDWARD	CPT	O-1318015	0547	2
CLARK EDWARD A	1LT	O-0527734	0646	2
CLARK EDWARD F	COL	O-0205961	0155	1
CLARK EDWARD J	CPT	O-1323539	1053	1
CLARK EDWARD O JR	COL	O-0126302	1158	3
CLARK ELDRED S	CW3	W-2143886	1162	2
CLARK ELLWOOD	CW4	W-2133008	0263	1
CLARK ELMER F	LTC	O-1100913	0758	1
CLARK EMERSON	CW4	W-2122829	0754	1
CLARK ERNEST M	LTC	O-0225866	0864	3
CLARK ERROL O	LTC	O-0964193	0168	1
CLARK ESTHER P	2LT	N-0702396	0733	1
CLARK EUGENE F	LTC	O-0362279	0945	2
CLARK EUGENE S JR	COL	O-0290853	0159	3
CLARK FLOYD H	LTC	O-1640933	0967	1
CLARK FRANK S	LTC	O-0309994	0559	3
CLARK FRANK W	CPT	O-0968850	0759	1
CLARK FRANKLIN D	CW3	W-2144237	0661	1
CLARK FRED G	COL	O-0234487	0754	3
CLARK FRED G	CW2	W-2143596	1056	1
CLARK FRED H	LTC	O-0193543	0555	3
CLARK FRED P	COL	O-0175054	0255	3
CLARK GEOFFREY	COL	O-0316999	0553	1
CLARK GEORGE A	CPT	O-0123276	0156	3
CLARK GEORGE A JR	MAJ	O-2051615	0563	1
CLARK GEORGE D	CW2	W-2214888	1166	1
CLARK GEORGE E	LTC	O-0376765	0161	2
CLARK GEORGE E	MAJ	O-0415102	1060	1
CLARK GEORGE J	MAJ	O-0370232	0944	2
CLARK GEORGE M	MAJ	O-2019851	0463	1
CLARK GEORGE P	LTC	O-0320604	0861	1
CLARK GEORGE P	CPT	O-1303463	0958	1
CLARK GEORGE P	1LT	O-2055439	0860	1
CLARK GEORGE W	CPT	O-1018239	0862	1
CLARK GLEN	MAJ	O-2000968	0959	1
CLARK GLEN L	MAJ	O-0224661	0761	3
CLARK GLEN R	LTC	O-1115528	0962	1
CLARK GORDON C	CW2	RW-2143599	0561	1
CLARK HAROLD A	CW2	W-2150739	0157	1
CLARK HAROLD H	CPT	O-0381979	0354	2
CLARK HARRY B	CPT	O-0238080	0250	3
CLARK HARRY B	CPT	O-0495134	0347	2
CLARK HARRY E	MAJ	O-0174998	0353	2
CLARK HARRY K	COL	O-0140395	0951	3
CLARK HASKELL G	MAJ	O-1318016	0767	3
CLARK HENRY M	LTC	O-0192179	0753	3
CLARK HENRY M	CW4	W-2145987	1068	1
CLARK HERBERT D	COL	O-1002592	0968	1
CLARK HOWARD B	MAJ	O-1633125	0160	1
CLARK HUGH D JR	CPT	O-1754909	1045	2
CLARK IRVING T	LTC	O-0284917	0666	3
CLARK JACK A	LTC	O-0889302	0263	1
CLARK JACK A	MAJ	O-1290207	0261	1
CLARK JACK L	CW4	W-2147680	0868	1
CLARK JACK P	LTC	O-0260812	0446	2
CLARK JACK R	MAJ	O-1052721	0558	1
CLARK JAMES A	LTC	O-0288429	1067	3
CLARK JAMES A	MAJ	O-1295509	0459	1
CLARK JAMES A JR	CPT	O-0427909	0346	2
CLARK JAMES C	1LT	O-1307944	1145	2
CLARK JAMES E	1LT	O-0506130	0445	2
CLARK JAMES E	MAJ	O-1925160	1166	1

NAME	GRADE	SVC NO	DATE RET MO YR	RET CODE
CLARK JAMES F	CW2	W-2212624	0768	1
CLARK JAMES E JR	LTC	O-1316619	1167	2
CLARK JAMES F	COL	O-0311779	0668	3
CLARK JAMES L	CW2	W-2141778	0554	1
CLARK JAMES R	CPT	O-1171490	1065	1
CLARK JAMES R	LTC	O-1542974	0264	1
CLARK JAMES W	1LT	O-1326740	0248	2
CLARK JESSE B	MAJ	O-0251101	0660	3
CLARK JOE	1LT	O-1996652	0747	2
CLARK JOE W	CW3	W-2142096	0762	1
CLARK JOHN A	1LT	O-1002593	0546	2
CLARK JOHN B	LTC	O-0351998	0163	1
CLARK JOHN E	LTC	O-0391524	0868	3
CLARK JOHN H	MAJ	O-0249412	0562	3
CLARK JOHN H	MAJ	O-1599106	0763	1
CLARK JOHN J	LTC	O-0938545	0468	1
CLARK JOHN N	COL	O-0197339	1161	3
CLARK JOHN P	MAJ	O-0907549	0146	2
CLARK JOHN R	MAJ	O-0142743	0650	3
CLARK JOHN R	LTC	O-0414898	1265	3
CLARK JOHN S	COL	O-0248627	0267	3
CLARK JOHN S	CPT	O-1323108	1046	2
CLARK JOHN S	LTC	O-1339613	0967	1
CLARK JOHN S	CPT	O-1998095	0955	1
CLARK JOHN T	MAJ	O-1633757	0453	2
CLARK JOHN W JR	LTC	O-0965373	0768	1
CLARK JOSEPH	CW4	W-2111342	1054	2
CLARK JOSEPH E	LTC	O-1575862	0565	1
CLARK JOSEPH G	LTC	O-0305107	0668	3
CLARK KENNETH	LTC	O-0444045	0751	2
CLARK KENNETH B	CPT	O-0222966	0444	2
CLARK LAWRENCE B	LTC	O-1167362	0261	1
CLARK LAWRENCE B	MAJ	O-1312664	0657	2
CLARK LAWRENCE C	CW2	W-2126226	0659	1
CLARK LAWRENCE F	COL	O-0246021	0754	3
CLARK LEROY K	MAJ	O-0475021	0347	1
CLARK LEX L	MAJ	O-0966364	0763	1
CLARK LINCOLN E	LTC	O-0387078	1060	1
CLARK LOIS L	CW4	V-0911145	0767	1
CLARK LOREN D	CPT	O-1324605	0947	2
CLARK LOUIS S	MAJ	O-2017813	0363	1
CLARK LOWELL L	LTC	O-0311740	0763	3
CLARK LUCIEN B	MAJ	O-2051623	0561	1
CLARK LYMAN J	COL	O-0401708	0760	3
CLARK MACK JR	MAJ	O-1105339	0965	1
CLARK MAJOR	LTC	O-1171088	0960	1
CLARK MANLEY W	LTC	O-1305896	0164	1
CLARK MARVIN C	COL	O-0193709	0162	3
CLARK MAURICE E	MAJ	O-0203476	0545	2
CLARK MAX A	LTC	O-2080330	0867	1
CLARK MERTON J	CPT	O-0296047	0345	2
CLARK MICHAEL I	LTC	O-2014461	0466	1
CLARK NATHANIEL	LTC	O-1107865	1064	1
CLARK NEIL M	MAJ	O-0402067	0746	2
CLARK NEWTON	1LT	O-0162704	0959	3
CLARK NORMAN E	MAJ	O-1822364	0962	1
CLARK OMER W	MAJ	O-0138770	0648	3
CLARK ORIE J	MAJ	O-1303249	0161	1
CLARK ORVAL C	MAJ	O-1998390	1154	1
CLARK OTMAR A	CW4	W-2004400	0866	1
CLARK PAUL	MAJ	O-0497855	0155	1
CLARK PAUL D	COL	O-0230925	1061	3
CLARK PAUL M	COL	O-0125343	0454	2
CLARK PHILO D	MAJ	O-0174161	0463	1
CLARK PORTER A JR	MAJ	O-1171948	0261	1
CLARK RALPH C	CPT	O-2025488	0859	1
CLARK RALPH E	MAJ	O-2103027	0168	1
CLARK RALPH W	LTC	O-0192466	0648	3
CLARK RAY O	LTC	O-1298026	1055	1
CLARK RAYMOND	MAJ	O-1108555	0560	1
CLARK RAYMOND J	LTC	O-0113570	0855	3
CLARK REX T	MAJ	O-2011201	1262	1
CLARK RICHARD A	MAJ	O-1553792	1062	1
CLARK RICHARD H	MAJ	O-0408832	0562	1
CLARK RICHARD H	MAJ	O-0981896	0962	1

NAME	GRADE	SVC NO	DATE RET MO YR	RET CODE	NAME	GRADE	SVC NO	DATE RET MO YR	RET CODE	NAME	GRADE	SVC NO	DATE RET MO YR	RET CODE	NAME	GRADE	SVC NO	DATE RET MO YR	RET CODE
CLARK RICHARD T	MAJ	0-0497490	0755	1	CLARKE GEORGE M JR	LTC	0-0284815	0368	3	CLAY GEORGE M	CW4	W-2102762	1154	1	CLEM PAUL W	LTC	0-1328672	0168	1
CLARK RIDGWAY J II	LTC	0-1055290	1062	1	CLARKE GEORGE W	1LT	0-1116762	0746	2	CLAY GROVER C	MAJ	0-0130935	0253	3	CLEM ROBERT G	COL	0-0273566	0360	3
CLARK ROBERT C	CPT	0-1324307	0751	2	CLARKE GERARD T	1LT	0-0416145	0445	2	CLAY HASKELL	CW3	W-2144963	0962	1	CLEM WILLIAM A	LTC	0-1995226	1167	1
CLARK ROBERT E	LTC	0-0241799	0567	3	CLARKE JAMES E	LTC	0-0310482	0760	3	CLAY LILLIAN [illegible]	LTC	N-0743890	0468	2	CLEMANS CHARLES C	LTC	0-0304461	1063	3
CLARK ROBERT E	COL	0-0910154	0568	3	CLARKE JAMES T	LTC	0-0199453	0961	3	CLAY MORRISON F	MAJ	0-1053940	1060	1	CLEMENS JOHN E	CPT	0-0497129	0948	1
CLARK ROBERT F	CPT	0-2001211	0548	2	CLARKE JOHN J	LTC	0-0209933	0556	3	CLAY PAUL V	MAJ	0-0156723	1150	3	CLEMENS PAUL E	LTC	0-0248098	0954	2
CLARK ROBERT F	1LT	0-2211115	0655	2	CLARKE JOSEPH G	CPT	0-0172629	0754	3	CLAY ROGER A	CPT	0-1593500	0863	1	CLEMENS PAUL J	CW4	W-2001776	0356	3
CLARK ROBERT H	1LT	0-12[illegible]345	0146	2	CLARKE JOSEPH V	1LT	0-0920545	0746	2	CLAY SHERMAN	MAJ	0-1701758	0357	1	CLEMENS PAUL M	MAJ	0-1293552	0562	1
CLARK ROBERT K	CPT	0-0451740	0246	2	CLARKE MAURICE L	MAJ	0-0190381	0761	3	CLAY UEL E	CW3	W-2150294	1263	1	CLEMENS Q VAN	CPT	0-0189610	0556	3
CLARK ROBERT K	CPT	0-1577437	0356	1	CLARKE NEWELL W	LTC	0-0261788	1166	3	CLAY WESLEY B	CPT	0-0285605	1045	2	CLEMENS REUBEN B	1LT	0-1290899	0246	2
CLARK ROBERT L	LTC	0-1287349	0563	1	CLARKE NILES A	MAJ	0-0337714	1067	3	CLAY WILLIAM A JR	LTC	0-1342243	1168	1	CLEMENS ROBERT E	2LT	0-1013658	1043	2
CLARK ROBERT L	CW2	W-2151736	0158	1	CLARKE PERRY A	1LT	0-0377749	1059	1	CLAY WILLIAM M	MAJ	0-2206266	1266	1	CLEMENS SIEGFRIED	LTC	0-1100918	1160	1
CLARK ROBERT P	CPT	0-1324511	0746	2	CLARKE RILEY H	MAJ	0-1342367	0162	1	CLAYBOURN GLEN L	LTC	0-0238668	0462	3	CLEMENT ALBERT V	MAJ	0-2263759	0964	1
CLARK ROBERT W	CW3	W-2148716	0764	1	CLARKE SAMUEL J JR	CW2	W-2150558	1263	1	CLAYBOURN JOY H	LTC	0-1683319	0468	1	CLEMENT ANDREW W	COL	0-0203133	0861	3
CLARK ROGER W	LTC	0-1301952	0264	1	CLARKE VAN A	LTC	0-0144084	1145	2	CLAYDON MAURICE	MAJ	0-0978236	1061	1	CLEMENT BAXTER L	CPT	0-0498677	1045	2
CLARK ROSCOE	CW4	W-2149495	0968	1	CLARKE WATTS R	MAJ	0-0278199	0958	3	CLAYMAN SIGMUND J	MAJ	0-0384964	0747	2	CLEMENT CURTIS D	LTC	0-0322981	1266	3
CLARK ROSCOE E	LTC	0-1046097	0767	1	CLARKE WILLIAM J	MAJ	0-1300602	0557	1	CLAYPOOL BURRISS E	LTC	0-0222689	0964	3	CLEMENT ELEANOR M	1LT	N-0753024	0648	1
CLARK ROY B	LTC	0-0238991	1165	3	CLARKE WILLIAM L	LTC	0-1311045	0865	1	CLAYPOOL CHARLES W	MAJ	0-4006027	0267	1	CLEMENT FRANKLIN C	1LT	0-1302432	0758	2
CLARK ROY D	CPT	0-1011800	1147	2	CLARKIN FRANCIS J	LTC	0-0343389	0268	3	CLAYPOOL JOSEPH S	MAJ	0-0499151	0550	1	CLEMENT JAMES H	CPT	0-0411093	0345	2
CLARK RUSSELL E	MAJ	0-0222893	1054	3	CLARKIN WILLIAM L JR	LTC	0-0966625	0768	1	CLAYSON GEMAR	LTC	0-1167778	1262	1	CLEMENT JAMES R	LTC	0-1316713	0267	1
CLARK RUSSELL N	LTC	0-1797783	0667	1	CLARKSON DALE F	CW2	W-2205646	0661	1	CLAYSON LESTER V	MAJ	0-0503374	0161	1	CLEMENT LAWRENCE M	CPT	0-1686237	0268	2
CLARK STANLEY J	1LT	0-0924116	0744	2	CLARKSON EDWARD D	MAJ	0-0155662	0344	2	CLAYTON BERT V	MAJ	0-0214866	0649	3	CLEMENT LAWRENCE P	2LT	0-1799614	0759	1
CLARK STERLING H	LTC	0-0233079	0762	3	CLARKSON EDWARD H JR	LTC	0-0264261	0953	3	CLAYTON CURTIS F	CW3	W-2203879	0365	2	CLEMENT RAYMOND I JR	LTC	0-0387381	0762	1
CLARK STRUTHER J	MAJ	0-1845404	0450	2	CLARKSON MILAN E	CW3	W-2146916	0763	1	CLAYTON HAROLD O	CPT	0-0114704	0657	3	CLEMENT ROBERT W	CPT	0-0990765	0461	1
CLARK THADDEUS J	MAJ	0-0495801	0157	1	CLARKSON SAMUEL O	CPT	0-0239304	0665	3	CLAYTON HARRY A	CPT	0-0322477	1165	3	CLEMENT ROY C	CW2	W-2105642	0260	1
CLARK THEODORE F	2LT	0-1549124	0245	2	CLARNO JOSEPH S	1LT	0-0492169	0244	2	CLAYTON J [illegible]	CPT	0-2011642	0657	1	CLEMENT WALTER B	CPT	0-0324761	0245	2
CLARK THOMAS C	CW2	W-2210042	0660	1	CLARY HORACE E JR	LTC	0-0415852	126[illegible]	1	CLAYTON JOEL W	COL	0-0116216	0157	3	CLEMENTE LEONARD J	LTC	0-0301633	0364	3
CLARK THOMAS F	MAJ	0-1553420	0365	1	CLARY JAMES O	CW3	W-2106337	1057	1	CLAYTON JOHN D	LTC	0-0445007	0252	1	CLEMENTS ARNOLD	CW3	W-2145075	0956	1
CLARK THOMAS W	CPT	0-0434799	0346	2	CLARY JOHN G	CW3	W-2143466	1160	1	CLAYTON JOHN JR	1LT	0-1315521	1045	2	CLEMENTS EDWARD S	CPT	0-1318448	0455	2
CLARK VICTOR L	LTC	0-0243333	0757	1	CLARY WILLIAM R	CPT	0-0359062	1060	3	CLAYTON MICHAEL P	MAJ	0-2010429	1062	1	CLEMENTS JAMES P	CPT	0-0415715	0447	2
CLARK VIRGIL E	1LT	0-1311487	0845	2	CLASPILL BERTRAM A	MAJ	0-0275371	0447	1	CLAYTON NEPHI W	CW2	W-2107858	0246	2	CLEMENTS JOHN P	MAJ	0-0990619	0964	1
CLARK VIRGIL W	LTC	0-0451460	1054	1	CLASSEN CLIFFORD J	CW2	W-3430540	1268	1	CLAYTON RAYMOND C	CW3	W-2207583	0267	1	CLEMENTS KENNETH	CPT	0-0359484	0648	2
CLARK WALTER C	CW2	W-2212626	1267	1	CLASSEN EDWIN C	WO1	W-2124080	1044	2	CLAYTON ROBERT F	MAJ	0-2037664	0962	1	CLEMENTS LEWIS M	CW4	W-2141228	0560	1
CLARK WALTER K	MAJ	0-1877180	0765	2	CLAUDE WILLIAM T	1LT	0-0109411	1059	3	CLAYTON ROBERT S	MAJ	0-1180455	0859	1	CLEMENTS MOSES R	MAJ	0-1049440	1264	1
CLARK WALTER N JR	MAJ	0-0308569	0745	2	CLAUDIO JOSE F	CPT	0-1876311	0462	1	CLAYTON SAMUEL	MAJ	0-0500674	0446	2	CLEMENTS QUILLIAN O	MAJ	0-2263454	0766	1
CLARK WALTER W	CW3	W-2266704	1068	1	CLAUDIO LEONARDO D	1LT	0-0890549	0155	1	CLAYTON SAMUEL S	CPT	0-0420113	0862	1	CLEMENTS ROBERT E	CW2	W-2209787	1265	1
CLARK WARREN E	MAJ	0-1823263	1163	1	CLAUER LESTER J	LTC	0-1016468	1165	1	CLAYTON WILLIAM N	LTC	0-0454545	0661	1	CLEMENTS WILLIAM C	MAJ	0-0973622	0563	1
CLARK WARREN W	CW4	W-2136687	0766	1	CLAUNCH EMMETT S JR	1LT	0-1590378	0745	2	CLAYTOR ALTON B	CPT	0-0227260	0664	3	CLEMINSON HALDANE JR	COL	0-0230302	1064	3
CLARK WILFORD L	CW2	W-2145154	0659	1	CLAUNCH GEORGE W	CW2	W-2145401	1158	1	CLAYTOR FRANK W	CPT	0-0401308	0645	2	CLEMMENSEN PAUL V	MAJ	0-1591055	1162	1
CLARK WILL H	COL	0-0258865	0964	3	CLAUNCH JAMES E	MAJ	0-1922696	0567	1	CLAYTOR JOHN B JR	MAJ	0-0404529	0746	2	CLEMMER JOHN S	CPT	0-2035075	1146	2
CLARK WILLARD D	LTC	0-0296497	1157	1	CLAUNCH THOMAS H	COL	0-0322868	1060	1	CLEAR CLINTON B	CPT	0-1171491	0367	3	CLEMMER LEWIS M	CPT	0-1304688	0148	2
CLARK WILLARD E	MAJ	0-0459415	0657	1	CLAUS EVERETT C	COL	0-0312224	0660	3	CLEARY ALVA F	LTC	0-0400242	0954	1	CLEMMONS LAWRENCE T	CPT	0-0972272	1060	1
CLARK WILLIAM A	CPT	0-1313958	0446	2	CLAUSEL CALVIN L JR	1LT	0-0479223	0946	2	CLEARY DANIEL J JR	LTC	0-1320303	1163	1	CLEMONS CLETES V	CW3	W-2142694	0758	1
CLARK WILLIAM B	CW2	W-3350234	0766	1	CLAUSEN ARTHUR D	MAJ	0-0169403	0659	3	CLEARY DAVID E	LTC	0-0403599	0760	1	CLEMONS GEORGE E	CW2	W-2210438	1061	1
CLARK WILLIAM C	MAJ	0-1307402	0561	1	CLAUSEN ERVIN H	COL	0-0100383	1149	3	CLEARY FRANCIS J	CPT	0-1302114	0846	2	CLEMONS HARRISON L	COL	0-0155065	0846	2
CLARK WILLIAM F	MAJ	0-0889039	0264	1	CLAUSEN GEORGE E	MAJ	0-0331799	0746	2	CLEARY FRED K	LTC	0-1686754	1067	1	CLEMONS JAMES	CW2	W-2151359	1159	1
CLARK WILLIAM G	LTC	0-1533756	1061	1	CLAUSEN GILBERT H	CW3	W-2207657	1168	1	CLEARY HOWARD F	LTC	0-1641168	0962	1	CLEMONS RAYMOND J	MAJ	0-1698181	1159	1
CLARK WILLIAM G	LTC	0-1557261	0664	1	CLAUSEN RALPH T	2LT	0-0517527	0545	2	CLEARY JOHN D	CW3	W-2206498	1265	1	CLEMONS WILLIAM L	LTC	0-1825595	0163	1
CLARK WILLIAM H	LTC	0-1821680	0962	1	CLAUSEN WILLIAM H	LTC	0-0516577	0967	1	CLEARY RICHARD N	CW4	W-2148717	0968	1	CLENDENIN RICHARD M	COL	0-0323305	0763	1
CLARK WILLIAM M	CPT	0-1586493	0954	2	CLAUSING GERALD A	LTC	0-1052712	0666	1	CLEARY THOMAS D	LTC	0-1003696	0663	1	CLENDENNING MELVIN H	CW3	W-2153343	0465	1
CLARK WILLIAM P	LTC	0-0289748	0252	2	CLAUSON MARVIN A	CW2	W-2208817	0963	1	CLEARY THOMAS F	CPT	0-1108558	0164	1	CLEPPE JOHN B	CW2	W-2203710	1060	1
CLARK WILLIAM R	LTC	0-0912914	0767	3	CLAUSS FRANCIS L	CW2	W-2002710	0263	3	CLEARY TIMOTHY	LTC	0-0264848	0657	1	CLERICO LOUIS R JR	1LT	0-1298027	0245	2
CLARK WILLIAM R	MAJ	0-0970514	0964	1	CLAUSS FREDERICK	1LT	0-1638881	0646	2	CLEAVER GEORGE A	COL	0-0279613	1061	1	CLESS GEORGE H	LTC	0-0243465	0146	2
CLARK WILLIAM T	MAJ	0-1053541	1066	1	CLAUSSEN GLEN O	LTC	0-1103102	0767	1	CLEAVER HAROLD J	CPT	0-1120533	0263	2	CLESS RALPH S JR	1LT	0-1284103	1044	2
CLARK WILLIAM T	2LT	0-1323291	0245	2	CLAUSSEN HARLEY M	LTC	0-2037225	1063	1	CLEAVER OSCAR P	COL	0-0912368	0265	3	CLEVELAND ANSON H	MAJ	0-2035296	0363	1
CLARK WILLIAM W	LTC	0-0234225	0466	3	CLAUTICE JOSEPH W	LTC	0-0286591	0167	3	CLEAVER THAYER	LTC	0-0225749	1163	3	CLEVELAND CHARLES N	MAJ	0-1111550	0954	1
CLARK WILLIAM W	2LT	0-0403437	1042	2	CLAVEL THOMAS S	1LT	0-1896510	0853	1	CLEAVER WILLIAM K	COL	0-0346405	0168	3	CLEVELAND EDWARD K	LTC	0-0289108	0557	1
CLARK WILLIE V	WO1	W-2110956	0566	3	CLAVIN CHARLES B	COL	0-0211697	0959	3	CLEAVES MARK B	MAJ	0-0453423	0762	1	CLEVELAND GEORGE R	MAJ	0-1175668	0857	1
CLARK WINDFIELD	CW2	W-2151075	0664	1	CLAWSER SAMUEL M JR	LTC	0-0453659	1061	1	CLEAVES RICHARD H	MAJ	0-1303268	1063	1	CLEVELAND HENRY E	CPT	0-0198252	0744	2
CLARKE ALAN K	LTC	0-0415186	1166	1	CLAWSON ARTHUR L	CPT	0-1541698	0755	1	CLECKLER FRANK S	COL	0-0190862	0454	3	CLEVELAND JOSEPH S	CW4	W-2113271	0161	1
CLARKE ALFRED N JR	1LT	0-0454093	1045	2	CLAWSON CLARENCE A	MAJ	0-0980080	0362	2	CLECKLER WILLIAM F	LTC	0-0185417	1155	3	CLEVELAND MATHER	COL	0-0205765	0949	3
CLARKE ANDREW F	LTC	0-0260968	0862	3	CLAWSON EDWARD J	MAJ	0-0494539	0455	1	CLEGG JACK A	LTC	0-0927130	0667	1	CLEVELAND RALPH L JR	1LT	0-1325376	1145	2
CLARKE ARCHIE	CW3	W-2147020	0659	1	CLAWSON GORDON L	COL	0-0299004	0757	3	CLEGG JAMES A	1LT	0-1573117	0644	2	CLEVELAND REESE	CPT	0-0192038	0160	3
CLARKE BERNARD L	LTC	0-1798119	1060	1	CLAWSON GREAR O JR	LTC	0-0483591	0764	1	CLEGG JOHN P	MAJ	0-0104731	0154	3	CLEVELAND STEWART E	MAJ	0-1105345	0861	1
CLARKE BRUCE E	COL	0-0160404	0950	3	CLAWSON HENRY A	CPT	0-0109769	0241	2	CLEGG KERMIT D	1LT	0-1318515	1045	2	CLEVELAND WILLIAM C	1LT	0-0390063	1044	2
CLARKE CHARLES J	CPT	0-0177816	0753	3	CLAWSON IRWIN	LTC	0-0187234	0152	3	CLEGG ROBERT J	1LT	0-0577148	1052	1	CLEVELAND WILLIAM J	LTC	0-1170319	0966	1
CLARKE CLAUDE R	MAJ	0-0109052	0627	1	CLAWSON SAMUEL M	LTC	0-0489846	0555	1	CLEGG SAM E	LTC	0-0420086	0860	1	CLEVENGER TRUMAN I	CPT	0-0445450	1143	1
CLARKE CREIGHTON	MAJ	0-1035222	0466	1	CLAWSON THOMAS A JR	COL	0-0244565	0247	2	CLEGG WILLIAM B	LTC	0-0255515	0954	3	CLEVERDON HERBERT S	LTC	0-0126456	0648	3
CLARKE CYRUS A	MAJ	0-0490998	0146	2	CLAXTON GEORGE P	MAJ	0-2007479	0860	1	CLEGHORN DAVID F	CW3	W-2143655	0163	1	CLEVIDENCE GILBERT H	LTC	0-0264073	0557	3
CLARKE EDWARD S	MAJ	0-2019433	0762	1	CLAXTON LAWRENCE L	CPT	0-1175078	0349	1	CLELAND GAIL	COL	0-0126315	0755	3	CLEW MAURICE	CPT	0-0174977	0958	3
CLARKE ELIJAH S	LTC	0-1947658	1167	3	CLAY ALTON M	LTC	0-0395061	1266	3	CLELAND JOHN V	CW2	W-2118772	0647	1	CLEW WILLIAM J	CPT	0-0902852	0343	2
CLARKE FRANCIS J	1LT	0-1295175	1045	2	CLAY BOYD V	CW2	W-2147397	1059	1	CLELAND JOSEPH M	CPT	0-5323436	1268	2	CLEWELL WILLIAM L	LTC	0-0964468	0464	3
CLARKE GEORGE H	MAJ	0-1336879	0366	1	CLAY CECIL	CW2	W-2153243	0659	1	CLELAND WILLIAM A	CW3	W-2141527	0659	1	CLEWETT FRANK S	COL	0-0384585	0359	1
CLARKE GEORGE J	WO1	W-2114237	0755	1	CLAY EDMOND G	2LT	0-1578270	0746	2	CLEM CLAUDE A	MAJ	0-0304827	0968	3	CLEWIS HOWARD R	COL	0-0355216	1066	3
CLARKE GEORGE L	COL	0-0170681	0758	3	CLAY EUGENE H	MAJ	0-1108556	0657	1	CLEM JOHN T JR	MAJ	0-1332674	0264	1	CLEWORTH EARL W	LTC	0-0311339	0262	1

NAME	GRADE	SVC NO	DATE RET MO YR	RET CODE
CLEWS WILLIAM R	CW2	W-2114270	0847	1
CLICK ALBERT F	MAJ	0-0401968	0753	2
CLICK ROBERT H	CPT	0-0453511	0845	2
CLICK ROBERT O	1LT	0-1325867	0450	2
CLIFF WILLIAM L	1LT	0-1824712	0346	2
CLIFFE EDWIN E	LTC	0-0349240	1266	3
CLIFFE HARRY L	CPT	0-1289695	0455	1
CLIFFE WILLIAM R	1LT	0-1309654	0146	2
CLIFFORD ALDEN F	LTC	0-0450621	1160	1
CLIFFORD BERNARD D	MAJ	0-0382218	0957	1
CLIFFORD CHARLES F	LTC	0-0349227	1061	1
CLIFFORD COOPER	CW3	W-2152088	0363	1
CLIFFORD DANIEL	CW4	W-2006120	0764	3
CLIFFORD DENNIS J	CPT	0-1054943	0358	1
CLIFFORD PAUL J	LTC	0-1821973	0364	1
CLIFFORD SEWARD V	LTC	0-0102129	0559	3
CLIFFORD WESTELL J	LTC	0-1640946	1166	1
CLIFFORD WILLIAM H	LTC	0-1105347	1068	3
CLIFFORD WILLIAM V	CPT	0-0452152	1145	2
CLIFT CHARLES G	CPT	0-1312406	0546	2
CLIFT GRAYDON H	MAJ	0-1318017	1266	1
CLIFT HUBERT P	LTC	0-0963608	0963	1
CLIFT JAMES B	LTC	0-0331589	0662	1
CLIFT JOHN D	LTC	0-1115530	1060	1
CLIFT MAURICE G	COL	0-0334335	0960	1
CLIFT STANTON H	CW2	W-2144690	0361	1
CLIFTON CLIFFORD H	LTC	0-1796923	1263	1
CLIFTON DAVID A	2LT	0-2263750	0654	2
CLIFTON EDWARD E	MAJ	0-1584052	1161	1
CLIFTON EDWARD F	1LT	0-0419103	0344	2
CLIFTON FRANK R	1LT	0-0447925	0944	2
CLIFTON GEORGE M	CPT	0-0488371	0547	1
CLIFTON HARVEY B	COL	0-0319860	0457	1
CLIFTON JOHN H JR	1LT	0-1580760	0152	2
CLIFTON MCCORMICK	CW4	W-2107529	0462	1
CLIFTON RAYMOND K	2LT	0-1107866	0745	2
CLIFTON ROY F	LTC	0-0325374	0866	3
CLIFTON WARD B	CW2	W-2212627	0367	1
CLIFTON WILLIAM C	CPT	0-1332675	0157	1
CLIMIE ROBERT L	MAJ	0-2037782	0860	1
CLIMO HENRY J	COL	0-0436878	0665	3
CLINARD ALLIE L	CPT	0-1920001	1061	1
CLINE BURTON V	LTC	0-1015331	0862	1
CLINE DELBERT H	CW3	W-2144551	0562	1
CLINE FREDERICK	LTC	0-0927645	0567	3
CLINE GEORGE H	LTC	0-0229966	0763	3
CLINE HARRY G JR	MAJ	0-2046332	0657	1
CLINE HERBERT N	LTC	0-1999842	0564	1
CLINE J EDWARD	LTC	0-1173563	0463	1
CLINE JAMES D	COL	0-0451846	0960	1
CLINE LESTER L	MAJ	0-0325803	0546	2
CLINE LOUIS W	LTC	0-0173532	0158	3
CLINE MILTON D	2LT	0-2035297	0444	2
CLINE MINNIE L	MAJ	L-0803051	1268	2
CLINE PAUL A	1LT	0-1047441	1144	2
CLINE RUSSELL E	CPT	0-0493213	1047	1
CLINE WESLEY M	CW4	W-2147684	0968	1
CLINE WILLIAM H	LTC	0-1534234	1061	1
CLINE WILLIAM J	COL	0-0178048	0656	1
CLINE WILLIAM P	LTC	0-0256002	1050	3
CLINESMITH JAMES M	LTC	0-1324512	1165	1
CLINGER EARL A	CPT	0-0412749	0961	2
CLINITE FLOYD E	LTC	0-0150444	0648	3
CLINK JACK J	MAJ	0-0391884	0945	2
CLINKINBEARD JOHN E	1LT	0-0393048	0945	2
CLINKSCALES RUBEN	1LT	0-0398766	0448	2
CLINTON CLEO S	MAJ	0-0331598	0362	3
CLINTON EDGAR T	CPT	0-0248694	1066	3
CLINTON GERTRUDE T	2LT	N-0720166	0744	1
CLINTON MICHAEL F	1LT	0-0925522	0845	2
CLINTON PAUL R	2LT	0-1309911	0245	2
CLINTON WESTCOTT	MAJ	0-1334829	0467	1
CLINTON WILLIAM H	MAJ	0-0249387	0466	3
CLINTON WILLIAM P	LTC	0-0300942	1163	1
CLIPPARD JAMES H	COL	0-0261326	0446	2
CLIPPINGER FRED B	CW4	W-2115110	0557	1
CLISBY KEITH M	COL	0-0315319	1065	3
CLISE FLOYD W JR	1LT	0-1299853	0246	2
CLISSOLD WALTER C	CPT	0-1166939	0944	2
CLISSON WILLIAM H	LTC	0-0404791	0860	1
CLODE HAROLD G	LTC	0-0365782	1060	1
CLODFELDER JAMES E	CW2	W-2146324	0463	1
CLOHOSEY BERNARD M	CPT	0-0493821	1049	1
CLONINGER FLOYD R	MAJ	0-1292133	0258	2
CLONINGER JOHN M	MAJ	0-0970844	0664	1
CLONTS JAMES F	CW4	W-2142319	0859	1
CLOORE HAROLD A	LTC	0-0284923	0460	1
CLOPINE RAYMOND L	CW4	W-2119238	0763	1
CLOPPER PAUL W	COL	0-0116282	0347	2
CLOPTON ROBERT H	LTC	0-2010924	1262	2
CLOPTON WILLIAM H	MAJ	0-1171090	0961	1
CLOR ALFRED L	CPT	0-1584529	0559	1
CLORE WALTER L	CPT	0-0505601	0546	2
CLOROFILLA ALFRED	1LT	0-0493160	0644	2
CLOSE ANN C	CPT	N-0725189	0746	1
CLOSE GERALD V	LTC	0-0162782	0755	3
CLOSE WILLIAM K	LTC	0-0318962	0263	3
CLOSSON ALVIN W	CW3	W-2146580	1262	1
CLOSSON JOHN L	MAJ	0-0887460	1154	1
CLOSTERMAN JOHN H	CW3	W-2152509	1063	1
CLOTFELTER ROY L	MAJ	0-1333314	0760	1
CLOTHAKIS CONSTANTIN	CPT	0-1080095	0463	1
CLOTHIER JOHN D JR	MAJ	0-0921980	0449	2
CLOTHIER LYLE B	MAJ	0-0272791	0457	3
CLOUD ARTHUR O JR	1LT	0-0456218	0245	2
CLOUD DONALD G	CW2	W-2210742	0865	1
CLOUD FREDERICK	MAJ	0-1287480	0459	1
CLOUD MASON C JR	CPT	0-1289545	0747	2
CLOUD MILTON H	LTC	0-0193242	0758	3
CLOUD RALPH M	CPT	0-1336880	0258	2
CLOUD SAMUEL E	CW2	W-2114193	0945	2
CLOUDT WALTER O JR	2LT	0-0392732	1041	2
CLOUDT WERNER H	MAJ	0-0980115	0461	1
CLOUGH ARTHUR M	LTC	0-0175753	0156	3
CLOUGH KENNETH M	MAJ	0-0229688	0762	3
CLOUGH LAWRENCE A	LTC	0-1175669	0461	1
CLOUSE CHARLES F	2LT	0-1297321	1143	2
CLOUSE HOWARD T	LTC	0-1575866	0563	1
CLOUSE WINFRED S	CW2	W-2145800	0658	1
CLOUSER SYLVIA M	CPT	N-0760847	0750	2
CLOUTIER ALBERT J	CPT	0-0486236	1047	1
CLOUTIER GEORGE A JR	MAJ	0-0179904	0454	3
CLOUTIER JOHN P	CW3	W-2145718	0760	1
CLOVER GLENN C	MAJ	0-1080352	1061	1
CLOW MELVIN L	LTC	0-0298519	0362	3
CLOWARD THOMAS M	LTC	0-0244546	0161	3
CLOWER ERNEST E	CW2	W-2207059	0760	1
CLOWER JAMES I	LTC	0-0174479	0160	3
CLOWES DUDLEY W	LTC	0-0444540	0767	1
CLOWNEY FRANK S JR	1LT	0-1182800	1044	2
CLOYD DAVID N	LTC	0-0970831	0368	1
CLOYD WILLIAM C	CW3	W-2206967	0366	1
CLUBA JOSEPH J JR	MAJ	0-2211824	1065	1
CLUCAS PHILIP D	1LT	0-1320430	0147	2
CLUCK HOMER E	1LT	0-1292134	0344	2
CLULEY FREDERICK	1LT	0-1337395	0850	2
CLURE DOUGLAS M	LTC	0-1323292	0962	1
CLUTCHKER JOSEPH M	LTC	0-0445266	0156	1
CLUTE GLEN C	LTC	0-1574646	0766	1
CLUTTER PAT C JR	CPT	0-0394556	0544	2
CLUTTER ROBERT D	CW3	W-2206734	0166	1
CLUTTER WADE D	MAJ	0-1584536	1265	1
CLYATT CLARENCE L JR	2LT	0-1055809	0545	2
CLYATT JOHN L	LTC	0-0354519	1159	1
CLYBURN ROYCE E	CW3	W-2205102	0864	1
CLYBURN WILLIAM P	MAJ	0-0260299	0967	3
CLYDE ALFRED M	CPT	0-0358752	0244	2
CLYDE THOMAS J	MAJ	0-0293117	0566	1
CLYDE WYLIE L	COL	0-0277709	1066	3
CLYMER CLARENCE D	WO1	W-2120962	1045	2
CLYMER JAMES M	LTC	0-1013216	0968	3
CLYMER MERYLE M	CPT	L-0900137	0845	2
CLYMER SAMUEL H	LTC	0-1585285	0563	1
CLYNE IRVING M	LTC	0-0336000	0646	2
CLYNES RICHARD J	LTC	0-0162680	0157	3
COAKES WILLIAM A	MAJ	0-0262913	0967	3
COAKLEY ANTHONY H	LTC	0-0397300	0763	1
COAKLEY BERTHA I	2LT	N-0722928	0145	1
COAKLEY FRANCIS H	LTC	0-0414297	0761	1
COAKLEY GEORGE F	LTC	0-0414298	0661	1
COAKLEY JOSEPH P	MAJ	0-1331268	1159	2
COALSON JAMES W	CW2	W-2141529	0261	1
COAN HERMAN S	CW2	W-2153022	0258	1
COANE RALPH W	B G	0-0209500	0346	2
COATE HAROLD D	LTC	0-0132425	0648	3
COATES AUSTIN M	CPT	0-0167094	0555	3
COATES B N JR	1LT	0-0515370	1145	2
COATES EVERETT W	LTC	0-0236706	0648	3
COATES LESLIE F	LTC	0-0338317	0161	1
COATES LESLIE R	CPT	0-1306200	0767	3
COATES MARVIN D	LTC	0-1282188	1066	1
COATES PALGRAVE H	CPT	0-1114420	0646	2
COATES ROBERT B	LTC	0-1582664	0966	1
COATS CHARLES E	CPT	0-1822238	0247	2
COATS JAMES M	CW2	W-2147723	0965	1
COATS MARVIN	CW3	W-2142825	0659	1
COATS MAURICE E	LTC	0-1109208	0467	1
COATS NORRIS W	CPT	0-0198862	0563	3
COATSWORTH JAMES T	COL	0-0335373	1063	3
COBAIN BURLE G	CW2	W-2149742	1160	1
COBB ADOLPHUS D JR	1LT	0-1589127	1045	2
COBB ANDREW G JR	CW2	W-2210776	1064	1
COBB ARLON G	1LT	0-2005318	0562	1
COBB CECIL H	MAJ	0-1640951	0358	1
COBB CHARLES S JR	COL	0-0253904	1267	3
COBB DONALD M	MAJ	0-0282936	0268	3
COBB DONALD W	CPT	0-1635704	1056	1
COBB EDWARD G	LTC	0-1555673	0561	1
COBB EUGENE S JR	CPT	0-0410377	0648	2
COBB FARRAR M	LTC	0-0218001	0462	3
COBB GEORGE E	MAJ	0-0322982	0257	3
COBB HOWELL D	LTC	0-1311741	0665	1
COBB HOWELL E	LTC	0-0905724	0963	3
COBB IRVIN S	CPT	0-1291591	0246	2
COBB IVOREY	MAJ	0-1314994	0862	1
COBB JULIA M	1LT	N-0758628	0546	1
COBB KELLEY B	MAJ	0-1181205	0560	1
COBB LUTHER F JR	COL	0-0275271	0560	1
COBB MARION N	CW2	W-3200420	0267	1
COBB NELSON L	MAJ	0-1286965	1164	3
COBB NORMAN S	MAJ	0-1290033	0365	1
COBB ROBERT F	LTC	0-1010211	0866	1
COBB WATSON B	CW2	W-2200907	0668	3
COBB WILLIAM B	COL	0-0232640	1054	3
COBB WILLIAM H	COL	0-0919765	1064	3
COBB WILLIAM R	CW3	W-2146191	0461	1
COBB WILLIE R	LTC	0-0510824	0655	1
COBBE CHARLES T	CPT	0-0318794	0962	1
COBBLE LYNNE M	CW2	W-2205618	0661	1
COBBS RICHARD H	MAJ	0-0214298	0963	3
COBEAN GEORGE G JR	CPT	0-0322422	0446	2
COBERG WALLACE H	MAJ	0-1051081	0561	1
COBIS JOSEPH F	MAJ	0-1878786	0167	1
COBLE EDWIN E	CPT	0-0366034	0644	2
COBLE MAX W	LTC	0-0265099	1266	3
COBLE OLIVER D	LTC	0-0150147	0858	3
COBLENTZ RALPH E	LTC	0-0271875	0566	3
COBLENTZ SIEGFRIED	COL	0-0209944	0154	3
COBLYN GEORGE H	MAJ	0-1303302	0461	1
COBO EDWARD A	CW2	W-2151919	0359	1
COBURN ANDERSON N	CPT	0-1291416	0459	1
COBURN BERNARD P	LTC	0-0392022	1060	1
COBURN CLARENCE D	LTC	0-0450827	1157	1
COBURN GEORGE J	CPT	0-0188843	0951	3
COBURN GEORGE J	1LT	0-1298028	1145	2
COBURN GLEN E	MAJ	0-1014419	1057	1
COBURN NICHOLAS W	COL	0-0232694	0465	3
COBURN PATRICK J	MAJ	0-2262345	0861	1
COBURN RALPH H	MAJ	0-0148577	0952	3
COBURN THEODORE J	CPT	0-0493343	0546	2
COBURN TRUMAN J	MAJ	0-2047952	0257	1
COCCA JOHN G	1LT	0-0334407	0442	2
COCCARI JAMES	LTC	0-1334259	0867	1
COCCIA NANCY D	1LT	N-5520445	0168	2
COCHARD EDMOND J	LTC	0-1114421	0467	1
COCHRAN ALBERT L	COL	0-0909557	0668	3
COCHRAN ALLEN J JR	CW3	W-2142512	0560	1
COCHRAN ARDYTH E	LTC	0-1167780	0263	1
COCHRAN CLARENCE	COL	0-0263221	1147	2
COCHRAN CLAUD H	CW3	W-2149751	0863	1
COCHRAN COLLINS C	CW3	W-2149287	0263	1
COCHRAN EDWIN C	CW2	W-3430170	0367	1
COCHRAN ELMO D	2LT	0-2008421	1147	2
COCHRAN GEORGE H	COL	0-0118497	1150	3
COCHRAN GEORGE H	LTC	0-0197223	0463	3
COCHRAN GEORGE M	CPT	0-0478121	0645	2
COCHRAN JACK W	MAJ	0-1013291	0663	1
COCHRAN JAY M	CW4	W-2141713	1065	1
COCHRAN JOEL L	LTC	0-0233582	0760	3
COCHRAN JOHN	CW3	W-2152189	0263	1
COCHRAN JOHN B JR	MAJ	0-1119865	0165	1
COCHRAN JOHN J	MAJ	0-2012467	1065	1
COCHRAN JOHN W	LTC	0-0282408	1168	3
COCHRAN LAWRENCE J	MAJ	0-0448147	0858	3
COCHRAN LESLIE	1LT	0-2042910	1145	2
COCHRAN LESTER D	MAJ	0-0497104	1047	2
COCHRAN LYLE A	CW3	W-2205664	0566	1
COCHRAN LYLE E	CPT	0-1297841	0457	1
COCHRAN LYNN F	LTC	0-1298828	0766	1
COCHRAN NEIL M	COL	0-0331055	0165	3
COCHRAN PRICE C	LTC	0-0279614	1059	2
COCHRAN RAYMOND J	MAJ	0-0430273	0163	1
COCHRAN RICHARD C	MAJ	0-1045377	1160	1
COCHRAN ROBERT S	COL	0-0266612	0968	3
COCHRAN SAM L JR	MAJ	0-0887402	0862	1
COCHRAN WALLACE J	LTC	0-0335292	0461	1
COCHRAN WILLIAM M	1LT	0-1039285	0850	2
COCHRANE BURTON C	LTC	0-0110163	0952	3
COCHRANE GEORGE M	1LT	0-1555957	1245	2
COCHRANE ROBERT B	LTC	0-0276372	1167	3
COCHRANE ROY	COL	0-0885009	1157	1
COCHRANE WILLIAM J	COL	0-1032198	0266	1
COCHRUN CLARENCE L	1LT	0-1001971	0445	2
COCHRUN EDGAR R	COL	0-0175905	0950	3
COCKE ERLE JR	MAJ	0-0441300	0247	2
COCKE PHILIP ST	COL	0-0885058	0464	1
COCKEFAIR GEORGE A	COL	0-0211751	0364	3
COCKERELL LONNIE L	CPT	0-1052715	0964	2
COCKERHAM DENVER H	CW2	W-2149139	0859	1
COCKEY MARY M	1LT	N-0742244	0845	1
COCKFIELD CHARLES D	LTC	0-0322724	1162	1
COCKRELL ELDRIDGE H	LTC	0-1103107	0261	1
COCKRELL HAROLD B	CPT	0-1289696	1057	1
COCKRELL HENRY B	MAJ	0-0271132	0648	3
COCKRELL THOMAS J	LTC	0-0169110	1060	3
COCKRELL WAYNE L	LTC	0-0202057	0463	3
COCKRUM HERBERT L	1LT	0-1559312	1046	2
COCO THEODORE A	CPT	0-1107868	0451	2
COCRERILL DONALD R	CW4	W-0904240	0659	1
CODD LEO A	COL	0-0205117	0455	3
CODDINGTON DAVID L	COL	0-0225717	0564	3
CODDINGTON ROY H	CPT	0-0460725	0461	1
CODE RALPH J JR	CPT	0-0365917	0945	2
CODER CLIFFORD F	CW2	W-3440000	1163	1
CODER HARRY F	COL	0-0411762	0865	1
CODIN KENNETH	1LT	0-0518928	0145	2
CODNER STANISLAUS	COL	0-0445066	0854	1
CODY BERNARD P	LTC	0-0223209	0347	2
CODY CHARLES L	MAJ	0-1170321	0463	1
CODY ERNEST H	CPT	0-0379963	0251	2

ARMY OF THE UNITED STATES RETIRED LIST

NAME	GRADE	SVC NO	DATE RET MO YR	RET CODE
CODY FLOYD W	LTC	0-0478522	1154	1
CODY GEORGE L	COL	0-0252440	0864	3
CODY RICHARD R	2LT	0-1294622	0244	2
CODY RICHARD S	1LT	0-1305392	0945	2
COE CHARLES A JR	LTC	0-1701473	1263	1
COE CHARLES V	CW3	W-2142579	0158	1
COE HAROLD A	2LT	0-2000657	0246	2
COE HEARK D	CW3	W-2148312	0557	1
COE KENNETH C	LTC	0-0451230	0656	1
COE KENNETH S	WO1	W-2147601	0660	2
COE NOBLE M	COL	0-0194915	1051	3
COE ROBERT E	MAJ	0-1010320	0663	1
COE THOMAS H JR	LTC	0-0924246	0847	2
COE WARREN T	CPT	0-0378514	1045	2
COEN JOHN J	MAJ	0-1637203	0664	2
COEN KENDALL W	MAJ	0-1588479	0460	1
COEN WALTER L	WO1	W-2109925	0655	1
COERS DAVID H	CPT	0-0152936	0649	3
COERS DAVID H JR	LTC	0-1341748	1066	1
COEY GROVER E	MAJ	0-1994405	1161	1
COFER CHARLES A	MAJ	0-1172415	1060	1
COFER CHARLES L	CPT	0-1581605	0945	2
COFER CHARLES R	MAJ	0-0983320	0364	1
COFER HEKSTON H	CPT	0-2262793	0461	1
COFER HORACE J	LTC	0-1288860	1155	1
COFER LOUIS C	CPT	0-0479149	1144	2
COFER WAYNE H	MAJ	0-1179447	0462	1
COFFEE DAN E	CPT	0-0452592	0845	2
COFFEE RUSSELL F	CPT	0-1294088	0267	2
COFFEE VIRGIL O	MAJ	0-1544123	0156	1
COFFEEN KENNETH	CW4	W-2143100	0862	1
COFFEY CLARENCE W	1LT	0-0492156	1047	1
COFFEY EDWARD L	MAJ	0-1587533	1060	1
COFFEY EILEEN F	MAJ	N-0730198	0268	1
COFFEY ELMER J	MAJ	0-0455395	0657	1
COFFEY JOHN J	CW4	W-2004214	1063	3
COFFEY JOHN L	MAJ	0-0222900	0258	3
COFFEY JOHN M	LTC	0-1994580	1061	1
COFFEY RALPH E	MAJ	0-0269964	0246	2
COFFEY SPENCER F	CPT	0-0475238	0650	1
COFFEY THOMAS G	CPT	0-1823983	0161	1
COFFEY ULYSSES M	MAJ	0-1032638	1157	2
COFFEY WALTER A	CW2	W-2146197	1157	1
COFFIE JAMES	CW3	W-2140910	1162	1
COFFIE JAMES	CW3	W-2150910	0659	1
COFFIN EDWARD J	LTC	0-1299375	1060	1
COFFIN HAROLD W	COL	0-0181699	1051	3
COFFIN JAMES H	CPT	0-0460928	1265	1
COFFIN PAUL A	1LT	0-1821551	1043	2
COFFIN RAYMOND D	LTC	0-1112621	0763	1
COFFIN ROBERT T	1LT	0-1324984	0745	2
COFFIN WILLIAM H	COL	0-1833884	0268	3
COFFMAN ALBERT W	CPT	0-1541340	0460	1
COFFMAN ALDINE J	CPT	0-0260702	1067	3
COFFMAN BURNESS L	LTC	0-0244731	1064	3
COFFMAN CARL C JR	2LT	0-1300604	1144	2
COFFMAN CHARLES A	CW4	W-2146493	1063	1
COFFMAN CLARENCE A	CW2	W-2211065	0965	1
COFFMAN CLARENCE E	CPT	0-1011604	0247	2
COFFMAN EARL R	MAJ	0-1031297	0263	1
COFFMAN HERSCHEL T	CPT	0-0885724	1046	1
COFFMAN JACK C	LTC	0-1120742	0168	1
COFFMAN JACOB E	1LT	0-1104569	0344	2
COFFMAN JENNINGS B	CPT	0-0370413	0859	1
COFFMAN TROY	MAJ	0-0172456	0245	2
COFFMAN WILLIS A	MAJ	0-0440740	0444	2
COGAN JAMES R	1LT	0-1683332	0543	3
COGAN JOSEPH P	LTC	0-0145664	1058	3
COGAN LEO J	MAJ	0-0320233	0145	2
COGAN RICHARD H	2LT	0-1313909	0445	2
COGAR RUSSELL A	LTC	0-1183491	0267	1
COGBILL JOHN V JR	CW2	W-2205746	0463	1
COGDALL THOMAS F	LTC	0-0334876	0547	2
COGDELL JAMES F	COL	0-0234845	1053	3
COGDILL RAY J	CW3	W-2145110	0959	1
COGER JOHN W	CW3	W-2141230	0461	1
COGGESHALL HOWARD L	CW2	W-2214899	1266	1
COGGHILL FRANCIS R	MAJ	0-0287489	0546	2
COGGIN EARLE R	MAJ	0-0343504	0760	1
COGGIN JOSEPH H	1LT	0-0143633	0632	1
COGGIN LA DEITRIC	MAJ	0-1580768	0466	1
COGGINS CYRIL W	MAJ	0-1037725	0658	2
COGHLAN CECIL L	LTC	0-1307657	0564	1
COGHLAN JOHN E	MAJ	0-1041314	1263	1
COGLEY FERNANDO JR	LTC	0-0450106	1263	2
COGLIATI DENNIS J	CPT	0-1824732	0261	1
COGSWELL DANIEL D	CW3	W-2148249	0964	1
COGSWELL MASON J	2LT	0-0374441	0641	2
COGSWELL RICHARD B	2LT	0-2006491	0845	2
COGSWELL WILLIAM C	LTC	0-0451231	0157	1
COHAN S HOWARD	LTC	0-0230865	0746	2
COHANE ARTHUR J	CPT	0-0527921	1045	2
COHEE GLENN D	CPT	0-1297162	0854	1
COHEN ABRAHAM B	LTC	0-0189956	0754	3
COHEN ABRAHAM J	MAJ	0-0979610	0466	1
COHEN ALBERT	CW3	W-2203298	0862	1
COHEN ALEXANDER	LTC	0-0535221	0657	1
COHEN ASHER Z	COL	0-0158252	0856	3
COHEN BEATRICE R	2LT	N-0720425	0745	1
COHEN BERNARD	CW2	W-2142482	0856	1
COHEN CLARENCE H	COL	0-0176291	0246	2
COHEN DAVID D	LTC	0-0301845	0967	3
COHEN ELMER A	CPT	0-0384194	1145	2
COHEN GEORGE M	MAJ	0-0351310	0450	2
COHEN HAROLD	CPT	0-0399839	0245	2
COHEN HAROLD W	MAJ	0-0335001	1146	2
COHEN HARRY	MAJ	0-0189869	0157	1
COHEN HERBERT	1LT	0-0521199	0346	2
COHEN HERBERT J	LTC	0-0264445	0267	3
COHEN HOWARD T	1LT	0-1874932	0654	2
COHEN JACK B	LTC	0-0461886	0647	2
COHEN JASPER N	MAJ	0-1112089	1059	1
COHEN LEE	MAJ	0-0109163	0330	1
COHEN LEO	CPT	0-0230662	1162	3
COHEN LEO	LTC	0-0307525	1055	1
COHEN LEON	CPT	0-1286967	0346	2
COHEN LEONARD A	MAJ	0-1638889	0259	1
COHEN LOUIS M	CPT	0-1945556	0647	2
COHEN MANUEL W	CPT	0-1308791	0246	2
COHEN MORRIS	MAJ	0-0476728	0264	1
COHEN MORRIS	1LT	0-1103109	0346	2
COHEN MORRIS C	CPT	0-1001115	0148	2
COHEN MOSES	MAJ	0-0477735	0845	2
COHEN MYER	MAJ	0-1289213	1156	1
COHEN NATHAN	CPT	0-0285412	0645	2
COHEN NATHAN N	MAJ	0-1691285	1146	2
COHEN NORMAN	CPT	0-0399980	0546	2
COHEN PHILIP	CPT	0-0498455	1057	1
COHEN RICHARD M	1LT	0-1579496	0745	2
COHEN SAMUEL	LTC	0-0509168	1054	1
COHEN SAMUEL	2LT	0-1643840	1045	2
COHEN SAMUEL A	COL	0-0101151	0753	3
COHEN SAMUEL H	LTC	0-0195962	0346	2
COHEN SHELDON G	CPT	0-0464563	0547	2
COHEN SIDNEY H	1LT	0-1311352	0445	2
COHEN STANLEY	MAJ	0-2055369	0158	2
COHEN WALLACE W	CPT	0-1015481	0448	2
COHEN WILLIAM	LTC	0-0292661	0966	3
COHEN WILLIAM R	COL	0-0232302	1059	3
COHEN YALE H	CPT	0-0452875	1145	2
COHN BERNARD R	LTC	0-0405151	0268	1
COHN BYRON S	CPT	0-0179381	0956	2
COHN EDWARD P	MAJ	0-1533029	0546	2
COHN GEORGE M	LTC	0-1311684	0363	1
COHN MELVIN J	CW3	W-2149175	1060	1
COHN RALPH	CPT	0-0126439	1052	3
COHN ROBERT D	LTC	0-1582667	1061	1
COHN SIDNEY	1LT	0-1320508	0645	2
COHOON GILBERT D	MAJ	0-1308209	1263	1
COHOON WILLIAM H	COL	0-0323355	0957	1
COIA GEORGE J	CPT	0-0484329	0551	1
COIL ARTHUR L	CPT	0-1310434	0246	2
COIL GEORGE J	1LT	0-1581608	0545	2
COIL MILFORD [illegible]	CW2	W-2115958	0846	1
COILE KATHLEEN R	1LT	N-0741004	1045	1
COIN CHARLES W	MAJ	0-1701674	0361	1
COINER DAVID T	LTC	0-0363729	0161	1
COING EDWARD E	LTC	0-1895591	0765	3
COIRO JOHN F	CW2	W-2145965	0655	1
COKAY OLIVER [illegible]	LTC	0-0233471	0167	3
COKELEY WILLIAM L	1LT	0-0534286	0147	2
COKER FRANK C	MAJ	0-0420101	0946	2
COKER HAYDEN C JR	MAJ	0-1100923	0660	1
COKER JAMES R	MAJ	0-1179344	1160	1
COKER JOHN B	2LT	0-1324316	1045	2
COKER JOHN H	CPT	0-2262376	0461	1
COKER MARION L	CW3	W-2207209	1166	1
COKER PAUL F	COL	0-1031394	0666	1
COLACINO JOHN [illegible]	MAJ	0-1825382	0361	2
COLALUCA ROBERT D	LTC	0-1919036	1268	1
COLANE VINCENT R	MAJ	0-1043595	0767	1
COLANGELO [illegible]	MAJ	0-0507025	0247	2
COLAVITA HENRY J	LTC	0-0283015	1059	1
COLBERT CLIFFORD J	LTC	0-0368675	0867	3
COLBERT HEINZ C	CW2	W-3430479	0668	1
COLBERT HERSCHEL M	COL	0-0130454	1051	3
COLBERT JACK A	LTC	0-1312407	0662	1
COLBERT JACK L	LTC	0-0347594	0847	2
COLBERT JAMES R	CPT	0-1177349	0358	1
COLBERT LOUIS M	CPT	0-0506955	1055	1
COLBERT MAURICE R	LTC	0-0114742	0653	3
COLBERT RALEIGH F	CPT	0-1993479	1047	2
COLBERT ROBERT M	COL	0-0258801	0854	3
COLBERT SEYMOUR	CW3	W-2149062	1163	1
COLBORN JOHN W	LTC	0-0240662	0460	3
COLBURN EDWARD	2LT	0-1913615	0243	1
COLBURN JOHN W	CW3	W-2209131	0168	2
COLBURN WILLIAM R	CW2	W-2117543	0150	1
COLBY DEBORAH	MAJ	N-0757847	1265	3
COLBY J JESS	2LT	0-1012664	1045	2
COLBY JOHN H	MAJ	0-0297797	0364	1
COLBY MELVIN M	MAJ	0-1822544	0965	1
COLBY PAUL W	LTC	0-0121122	1054	3
COLBY SANFORD L	CW3	W-2147342	0656	1
COLBY THOMAS W	COL	0-0259156	0767	3
COLBY WALTER W	2LT	0-1107350	0545	2
COLBY WARD A	CPT	0-1914134	0746	2
COLCLASURE WYETT H	CPT	0-0367080	0445	2
COLDREN IRA D	COL	0-0215268	0462	3
COLDREN JOHN A	MAJ	0-0225498	0460	3
COLDREN LEON F	MAJ	0-1175080	0258	1
COLDSNOW LESLIE P	LTC	0-0254765	0965	3
COLE ALBERT G	LTC	0-1011574	0763	1
COLE ALBERT P	1LT	0-0311516	0967	3
COLE ARIS W	MAJ	0-1331377	0363	1
COLE ARTHUR L	MAJ	0-0496863	1146	1
COLE AUSTIN F	CPT	0-1176236	0163	1
COLE BERYL A	MAJ	N-0774384	1063	3
COLE BRYAN T	LTC	0-0402178	1068	3
COLE CHARLES A	LTC	0-0182613	1048	2
COLE CHARLES C	LTC	0-0363378	0964	1
COLE CHARLES E	CPT	0-1640960	0358	1
COLE CHARLES R	MAJ	0-1825903	0163	1
COLE CHARLES T	1LT	0-5225768	0867	1
COLE CHESTER J	MAJ	0-1598962	0462	1
COLE CLIFTON	CW2	W-2151017	0761	1
COLE COLLEN E	CPT	0-2043587	1045	2
COLE DANIEL M JR	CW2	W-2147250	0462	1
COLE DELBERT L	MAJ	0-1641176	0664	2
COLE DEWEY	CW4	W-2101535	1154	1
COLE DONALD F	COL	0-1686410	0566	3
COLE DONALD N	LTC	0-1577029	0168	1
COLE EARL E	LTC	0-0243217	0462	3
COLE ELIZABETH	2LT	N-0721519	0445	1
COLE ELMER	MAJ	0-1307659	0262	1
COLE ERNEST J	CPT	0-0181783	0648	3
COLE FELIX J JR	CW3	W-2207658	0866	1
COLE FRANCIS J	CW3	W-2150503	0564	1
COLE FRANK J	CW4	W-2147931	0768	1
COLE FRANKE L	1LT	0-1317885	0446	2
COLE GEORGE D	CPT	0-1101788	0768	3
COLE GRANVILLE	CW3	W-2206535	0868	1
COLE HADEN J	CW2	W-2144721	0758	1
COLE HAROLD C	CPT	0-0552218	0347	2
COLE HAROLD J	COL	0-0246891	1266	3
COLE HAROLD L	CW2	W-2430081	0666	1
COLE HARRY	MAJ	0-0446137	0447	1
COLE HAZEN W	1LT	0-0940753	0749	2
COLE HERBERT E	MAJ	0-0452507	1066	1
COLE HERBERT L	CW3	W-2139557	1055	1
COLE HORACE R	LTC	0-1114890	0365	1
COLE HOWARD R	LTC	0-1288708	0660	1
COLE HUGHIE B	CW3	W-2206576	0665	1
COLE JACK C	1LT	0-0349465	1043	2
COLE JAMES A	LTC	0-1586338	0462	1
COLE JAMES B	LTC	0-0180200	0757	3
COLE JAMES B	LTC	0-0408183	0161	1
COLE JAMES U	1LT	0-2010762	0860	1
COLE JEFFRIES G	MAJ	0-0263031	0764	3
COLE JENNINGS B	WO1	W-2106991	0447	2
COLE JESSE J	MAJ	0-1030748	1055	1
COLE JOE N	COL	0-0288990	0557	1
COLE JOHN C	1LT	0-5318330	0963	2
COLE JOHN C JR	LTC	0-1040199	0566	1
COLE JOHN J	LTC	0-1548695	0463	1
COLE JOHN M	LTC	0-0372004	1059	1
COLE JOHN W	MAJ	0-0450569	0946	2
COLE JOHN W	1LT	0-0965672	0652	2
COLE JOSEPH F	COL	0-0243345	0766	3
COLE JOSEPH G	CPT	0-0499773	0645	2
COLE JOSEPH G	CPT	0-1690169	1045	2
COLE KENNETH J	LTC	0-0174284	0161	3
COLE LAWRENCE A	LTC	0-1645200	1167	1
COLE LAWRENCE R	COL	0-0233785	0659	3
COLE LEIN L JR	COL	0-0288921	0566	3
COLE LOYAL J	MAJ	0-1633763	0258	1
COLE MAC	1LT	0-2046341	0945	2
COLE MARION C	1LT	0-1052301	0945	2
COLE MARTIN K	LTC	0-1285710	0764	1
COLE MARTIN G	CPT	0-0290842	0864	3
COLE MILTON J	COL	0-0414899	1264	3
COLE NATHANIEL	LTC	0-0262646	0446	2
COLE NEWELL C	1LT	0-0275257	0945	2
COLE OSCAR F	LTC	0-0469253	0645	2
COLE PAUL M	CW3	W-2145614	0463	1
COLE RALEIGH J	CPT	0-0456674	1148	1
COLE RALPH C	CPT	0-1303078	1047	2
COLE RALPH D	MAJ	0-1844633	0951	2
COLE RALPH F	COL	0-0226831	0265	3
COLE RAYMOND A	LTC	0-0415409	0660	1
COLE RICHARD G	LTC	0-0335540	0557	1
COLE RICHARD H	CPT	0-0365971	1045	2
COLE RICHARD J	1LT	0-1114423	0445	2
COLE RICHARD S	LTC	0-0291144	0858	3
COLE ROBERT E	MAJ	0-1294089	0763	1
COLE ROBERT F	LTC	0-0367404	1246	2
COLE ROBERT J	MAJ	0-0355670	0853	2
COLE ROBERT K	CW4	W-2106920	0859	1
COLE ROBERT S	MAJ	0-1663871	1060	1
COLE ROSS R	LTC	0-0155676	0643	3
COLE ROY C	1LT	0-1016190	0545	2
COLE RUFUS L JR	MAJ	0-2263088	0364	1
COLE RUSSELL A	CPT	0-0365770	0644	2
COLE SCOTT	1LT	0-1295831	0545	2
COLE STANLEY W	CW4	W-2141531	1055	1
COLE THELMA M	2LT	N-0737060	0744	1
COLE THOMAS J	MAJ	0-1293210	1157	1
COLE TOM E	COL	0-0323339	0662	1
COLE WILLIAM A	CPT	0-0494795	0447	1
COLEBANK WILLIAM F	CW4	W-2115397	0656	1

NAME	GRADE	SVC NO	DATE RET MO YR	RET CODE
COLEBANK WILLIAM W	CPT	0-0954590	1160	1
COLEBORN JOSEPH L JR	MAJ	0-1647363	0263	1
COLEGROVE JACOB B	LTC	0-0253350	1045	2
COLEGROVE WESTLEY	LTC	0-0507826	0855	1
COLEHOUR MORRIS S	MAJ	0-0224254	0965	3
COLEMAN ALFRED I	MAJ	0-2014687	0266	1
COLEMAN BILLY J	MAJ	0-2206401	0165	1
COLEMAN CARL H	COL	0-0357728	0260	1
COLEMAN CARL C	LTC	0-0884903	0760	1
COLEMAN CHARLES S	CW3	W-2149828	0764	1
COLEMAN CHAUNCEY E	1LT	0-1282059	0653	1
COLEMAN CLARENCE M	MAJ	0-0463172	1146	2
COLEMAN CLARENCE N	COL	0-0420496	1162	2
COLEMAN CRANSTON R	MAJ	0-1574647	0761	1
COLEMAN DANIEL L	MAJ	0-0360205	1060	1
COLEMAN DAVID J JR	LTC	0-0376394	0866	1
COLEMAN DELREY	COL	0-0196961	0262	3
COLEMAN DONALD F	MAJ	0-1936778	0568	1
COLEMAN EDMOND A	CPT	0-5318477	0866	2
COLEMAN EDMUND A JR	MAJ	0-1116833	0663	2
COLEMAN EUGENE	2LT	0-2011581	0546	2
COLEMAN FLEMSTEAD	COL	0-0370187	0368	3
COLEMAN FLOYD E	CPT	0-1703800	0157	1
COLEMAN FLOYD M	CPT	0-0493879	0753	1
COLEMAN FRANCIS F	LTC	0-0207403	1063	3
COLEMAN FREDERICK	LTC	0-1010433	0461	1
COLEMAN GEORGE J	LTC	0-1050603	1263	1
COLEMAN GERALD G	1LT	0-2034504	0855	1
COLEMAN HENRY	CW3	W-2203337	0764	1
COLEMAN HENRY C	LTC	0-0226432	0764	3
COLEMAN HENRY G	1LT	0-1684725	0145	2
COLEMAN HENRY H	LTC	0-0338445	0764	3
COLEMAN HENRY N	COL	0-0104016	0648	3
COLEMAN HERBERT L	LTC	0-1291236	0666	1
COLEMAN HOWARD S	CW2	W-2152080	0664	1
COLEMAN JAMES	1LT	0-0971755	0865	2
COLEMAN JAMES B	CW2	W-2125278	0752	1
COLEMAN JAMES F	LTC	0-0901062	0545	2
COLEMAN JAMES F	MAJ	0-1311842	0446	2
COLEMAN JAMES P	MAJ	0-1336040	0963	1
COLEMAN JAMES T	1LT	0-1797785	0161	1
COLEMAN JAMES W	LTC	0-0177916	0854	2
COLEMAN JOE R S	MAJ	0-1304638	1060	1
COLEMAN JOHN F	COL	0-0256251	0667	3
COLEMAN JOHN G	2LT	0-1314445	0545	2
COLEMAN JOHN J	MAJ	0-1315793	1060	1
COLEMAN JOHN L	CPT	0-1289393	0763	1
COLEMAN JOHN R	LTC	0-0399878	1059	1
COLEMAN JOSEPH F	CPT	0-0150837	0345	2
COLEMAN JUANITA V	CPT	N-0755308	0746	1
COLEMAN KENNETH G	MAJ	0-0250174	0362	3
COLEMAN KIRBY L	2LT	0-1319182	0545	2
COLEMAN LEONARD S	CW4	W-2109693	0562	1
COLEMAN LEWIS C	LTC	0-0164403	0144	1
COLEMAN LEWIS C JR	LTC	0-0338518	0956	1
COLEMAN MADIE L	MAJ	N-0763971	1063	1
COLEMAN MICHAEL J	LTC	0-0267074	0654	3
COLEMAN ORAN S	LTC	0-0577172	0662	1
COLEMAN PHILIP F	LTC	0-0323809	0867	3
COLEMAN RAEPHEL V	1LT	0-1032419	0945	2
COLEMAN RAYMOND M	CW2	W-2147515	0663	1
COLEMAN ROBERT A	1LT	0-1573124	0364	1
COLEMAN ROBERT R	CPT	0-0310005	0545	2
COLEMAN ROBIN R	MAJ	0-0478621	1046	1
COLEMAN ROY B	LTC	0-1104572	0363	1
COLEMAN SAM J	CPT	0-0325795	0344	2
COLEMAN SAMUEL	LTC	0-0453092	0961	1
COLEMAN STAFFORD L	1LT	0-0257866	0267	3
COLEMAN STUART T	MAJ	0-0166404	0652	3
COLEMAN THEODORE F	COL	0-1003494	0566	3
COLEMAN THOMAS P	LTC	0-1291419	1162	1
COLEMAN THOMAS V JR	MAJ	0-1041737	0657	2
COLEMAN WARREN C	MAJ	0-1321157	0862	1
COLEMAN WILBUR R	MAJ	0-1299996	0161	1
COLEMAN WOOD P	LTC	0-0238493	0560	3

NAME	GRADE	SVC NO	DATE RET MO YR	RET CODE
COLEN JOSEPH E	CPT	0-0536646	1047	2
COLES FRANCIS A	LTC	0-0247664	0467	3
COLES FREDERICK	MAJ	0-1322312	0163	1
COLES GORDON L	CW4	W-2207387	0968	1
COLES JULIAN G	MAJ	0-2262386	1262	1
COLES PHILIP J	LTC	0-1799572	0958	1
COLES RUSSELL A JR	CW3	W-2144768	0663	1
COLETTA MARTIN M	MAJ	0-0403394	0945	2
COLETTI DONALD	CPT	0-4074248	1267	1
COLETTO GEORGE G	MAJ	0-1114424	0162	1
COLEY ALBERT J	MAJ	0-1650894	1060	1
COLEY BERT R	CW2	W-2211638	0765	1
COLEY CLARENCE W	WO1	W-2149011	0853	1
COLEY LESLIE G	COL	0-0274316	0155	3
COLFORD LEONE M	2LT	N-0730361	1044	1
COLFORD ROBERT W	LTC	0-1306553	0462	1
COLGAN ROCHESTER	LTC	0-0964702	1066	3
COLGAN WILLIAM H	CPT	0-0136835	0950	3
COLGIN CLARENCE H	LTC	0-0409529	1062	1
COLGLAZIER JACK E	1LT	0-1313209	0845	2
COLGLAZIER ROBERT W	LTG	0-0223635	0266	1
COLGLAZIER WALDO W	LTC	0-1994735	0161	1
COLHARD FRED T	MAJ	0-1056670	0360	2
COLIN IRVING	2LT	0-1643251	0245	2
COLIO EDISON P	LTC	0-0354520	0567	1
COLISON CHARLES W	COL	0-0444193	0765	3
COLLAER NICK D	CPT	0-0114017	0456	3
COLLAR CHARLES L	2LT	0-1179819	0245	2
COLLAR HENRY N	1LT	0-2046466	0845	2
COLLARD JOHN A	CPT	0-0971540	0361	1
COLLAZO FRANCISCO	MAJ	0-2263321	1265	2
COLLAZO JOSE A	CW3	W-2147627	0761	1
COLLAZO SANTIAGO	CW3	W-2147645	1060	1
COLLEARY JOHN C	CPT	0-0528497	0450	2
COLLESTER GAYNOR P	1LT	0-1289047	0145	2
COLLETT THEODORE J	1LT	0-0481621	0753	1
COLLETTE EDNA M	MAJ	N-0761302	1265	1
COLLETTE PATRICK W	CW3	W-2153075	0463	1
COLLETTI JOHN T JR	CPT	0-1923506	0262	1
COLLEY ARTHUR T	LTC	0-0271771	1065	3
COLLEY DWIGHT T	COL	0-0166222	0556	3
COLLEY JOHN	CW2	W-2110113	0553	1
COLLEY MAX D	CW3	W-2210960	0968	1
COLLEY RALPH C	MAJ	0-0949732	0464	1
COLLEY TOLBY J	MAJ	0-0527019	0854	1
COLLEY WILLIAM B	LTC	0-1281112	1262	1
COLLIER ARCHER C	CPT	0-1798912	0754	1
COLLIER CALHOUN C	CPT	0-1295178	0248	2
COLLIER CHARLES F	COL	0-0230964	0762	3
COLLIER ERNEST J	1LT	0-1315142	1052	2
COLLIER ERNEST M	CPT	0-0195596	1143	2
COLLIER EVELYN O	MAJ	N-0736147	0361	1
COLLIER EVERETT R	CW3	W-2203274	0962	1
COLLIER GEORGE R	CPT	0-0514920	0547	2
COLLIER GERALD	MAJ	0-1118558	0663	1
COLLIER HAROLD L	LTC	0-0244285	0960	3
COLLIER HERMAN C	LTC	0-0271616	0359	1
COLLIER JAMES C	1LT	0-1010126	0655	2
COLLIER LEONARD L	LTC	0-1547252	1262	1
COLLIER PAUL R	MAJ	0-0201790	0763	3
COLLIER RAYMOND F	LTC	0-0262519	0160	1
COLLIER ROBERT	CPT	0-0493057	1047	2
COLLIER ROBERT B	COL	0-0307337	0166	1
COLLIER SAMUEL H	CPT	0-0275695	0648	3
COLLIER SOL R	CPT	0-1052304	1046	2
COLLIER THOMAS H	1LT	0-0497812	0148	1
COLLIER VINCENT R	MAJ	0-1946691	0663	1
COLLIER WILLIAM C	MAJ	0-0918701	0652	2
COLLIER WYNN A	CPT	0-1107353	0568	3
COLLIGAN JOHN W	LTC	0-1581610	0667	1
COLLIGAN LAWRENCE H	CPT	0-0964953	0661	1
COLLIGEN JAMES	2LT	0-1698001	0643	2
COLLIGNON RAMOLA R	2LT	N-0776100	0645	1
COLLIN JONAS F II	LTC	0-1299205	0761	1
COLLING JOHN G	MAJ	0-1284296	0546	2

NAME	GRADE	SVC NO	DATE RET MO YR	RET CODE
COLLINGE GEORGE R	CW3	RW-3150286	0968	1
COLLINGS ALFRED W	CPT	0-0342849	0345	2
COLLINGS JOHN B	COL	0-0351999	0662	1
COLLINGS WILLIAM J	CPT	0-1317494	0847	2
COLLINGWOOD HAROLD D	COL	0-0276634	0858	3
COLLINS ADAM	LTC	0-1306982	0761	1
COLLINS ANDREW E	CW1	W-2143576	0659	1
COLLINS ANNE K	1LT	N-0789195	0746	1
COLLINS ANNE M	1LT	N-0721507	0745	1
COLLINS ARNOLD JR	LTC	0-2017015	0168	1
COLLINS ARVIL B	CW2	W-2207140	1161	1
COLLINS ASA W	LTC	0-0284777	0360	3
COLLINS BERNHARD B	LTC	0-0314373	0359	1
COLLINS BILLINGS J	1LT	0-2035874	1145	2
COLLINS BRIEN T	CPT	0-5418709	1268	2
COLLINS BURR W	MAJ	0-1107354	1166	2
COLLINS CARL F	MAJ	0-0498783	0354	1
COLLINS CHARLES D	COL	0-0461824	0965	1
COLLINS CHARLES N	MAJ	0-0480265	0954	1
COLLINS CHARLES R	1LT	0-1030344	1045	2
COLLINS CLARE D	LTC	0-1950321	1265	2
COLLINS CLARENCE L	CW3	W-2144754	1262	1
COLLINS DALE D	1LT	0-1315272	0146	2
COLLINS DAVID W	2LT	0-0537254	0845	2
COLLINS DOROTHIE E	CPT	N-0741344	1148	2
COLLINS EDNA M	LTC	N-0767217	0963	2
COLLINS EDWARD H	CPT	0-1640321	0355	2
COLLINS EDWARD V	CPT	0-0452035	1146	2
COLLINS ELIJAH A JR	LTC	0-1109211	0962	1
COLLINS ERNEST L	CPT	0-1290559	0964	3
COLLINS EUGENE L	MAJ	0-1920315	0266	1
COLLINS EVERETT T JR	2LT	0-0465084	0944	2
COLLINS FLOYD	CPT	0-0229447	0947	1
COLLINS FLOYD M	1LT	0-2055048	1146	2
COLLINS FRANCIS E	1LT	0-1014161	0746	2
COLLINS FRANCIS X	CW4	W-2142826	0165	1
COLLINS FRANK B	MAJ	0-0298350	0247	2
COLLINS GEORGE B	LTC	0-1287145	1060	1
COLLINS GEORGE F	MAJ	0-1327333	0561	1
COLLINS GEORGE H	LTC	0-0108049	0745	2
COLLINS GEORGE H	2LT	0-1879119	0762	2
COLLINS GEORGE H	LTC	0-1994886	1067	1
COLLINS GEORGE W	LTC	0-0386042	1055	1
COLLINS HAROLD V	LTC	0-0416557	1060	1
COLLINS HELEN K	2LT	N-0720465	0445	1
COLLINS HENRY	CW2	W-2145402	0460	1
COLLINS HENRY H	COL	0-0365781	0567	3
COLLINS HOWARD	LTC	0-1633765	0460	1
COLLINS HOWARD B	CPT	0-0428298	1045	2
COLLINS HUGH C	MAJ	0-1058211	0762	1
COLLINS J B	CW4	W-2113397	1055	1
COLLINS JAMES A	CW2	W-3400066	0968	1
COLLINS JAMES D	1LT	0-1846405	0846	2
COLLINS JAMES G	LTC	0-0181325	1159	3
COLLINS JAMES M	MAJ	0-1106066	0661	1
COLLINS JAMES P	CW2	W-2141800	1057	1
COLLINS JASON J	LTC	0-0335638	0665	3
COLLINS JEFFERSON	LTC	0-0408182	0962	1
COLLINS JOHN B	MAJ	0-2025606	0960	1
COLLINS JOHN C	LTC	0-0302867	0263	3
COLLINS JOHN G	LTC	0-1548031	1063	1
COLLINS JOHN W	1LT	0-0409492	1044	2
COLLINS JOHN W	1LT	0-1822858	0346	2
COLLINS JOSEPH A JR	CW3	RW-2144895	0263	1
COLLINS JOSEPH T	CW4	W-2116074	0456	1
COLLINS JOSEPH T	CW2	W-2142358	0X59	1
COLLINS KENNETH C	MAJ	0-1949811	0963	1
COLLINS LAFAYETTE	MAJ	0-0967133	0764	1
COLLINS LAFIECE D	LTC	0-0336764	0457	2
COLLINS LAWRENCE	COL	0-0114204	0958	3
COLLINS LEHMAN R	CPT	0-0294777	0762	1
COLLINS LEIGH G	CPT	0-0356676	1043	2
COLLINS LELAND G	MAJ	0-0968870	0668	1
COLLINS LLOYD E	LTC	0-0287172	0759	3
COLLINS MELVIN P	MAJ	0-1877950	0864	1

NAME	GRADE	SVC NO	DATE RET MO YR	RET CODE
COLLINS OTHO H	LTC	0-0402572	0762	2
COLLINS RALPH H	LTC	0-0463631	0454	1
COLLINS RALPH T	LTC	0-0297684	0568	3
COLLINS RAYMOND D	CPT	0-1289214	1145	2
COLLINS RAYMOND E	LTC	0-0918298	0266	3
COLLINS RAYMOND L	CPT	0-0949811	0860	1
COLLINS RICHARD H	LTC	0-2274612	0563	1
COLLINS ROBERT F	COL	0-0253024	0566	3
COLLINS ROBERT S	LTC	0-1548184	1054	1
COLLINS ROBERT W	LTC	0-1167367	0263	1
COLLINS RUPERT G	LTC	0-0290590	0462	1
COLLINS SHERWOOD E	LTC	0-0314485	0947	2
COLLINS SIDNEY H JR	COL	0-1945776	1263	3
COLLINS THOMAS A JR	CW2	W-2151017	0163	1
COLLINS THOMAS E	LTC	0-0500889	0555	2
COLLINS THOMAS H	1LT	0-0110926	1045	2
COLLINS THOMAS L	LTC	0-1558128	0165	1
COLLINS VIRGIL T	MAJ	0-2011892	1163	1
COLLINS WALTER H	CW3	W-2152802	0864	1
COLLINS WILLIAM	MAJ	0-2301007	0864	1
COLLINS WILLIAM E	MAJ	0-0311847	1167	3
COLLINS WILLIAM E	LTC	0-1638899	1066	1
COLLINS WILLIAM J	LTC	0-1117069	0767	1
COLLINS WILLIAM J	LTC	0-1314258	0867	3
COLLINS WILLIAM J	CPT	0-1317887	0946	2
COLLINS WILLIAM L	LTC	0-0246956	0266	3
COLLINS WILLIAM L	CPT	0-2204314	0954	2
COLLINS WILLIAM N	1LT	0-1548699	0844	2
COLLINS WILLIAM S	MAJ	0-0116183	0748	3
COLLINS WILLIAM S	MAJ	0-1175403	0555	1
COLLINS WILSON R	LTC	0-0295396	1068	3
COLLINSWORTH GORDON	CPT	0-0463299	0646	2
COLLISON BERNARD O	CPT	0-1917533	0462	1
COLLISTER LOREN O	CW3	W-2143133	0161	1
COLLITON ELLSWORTH	1LT	0-1041317	1145	2
COLLIVER JESSE Y	CPT	0-1577032	1058	1
COLLMAN ROLAND J	2LT	0-1303852	0345	2
COLLOM CHARLES R	CPT	0-1047484	0446	2
COLLOM HAROLD L	COL	0-0235573	0561	3
COLLOPY JAMES S	MAJ	0-1291078	0364	1
COLLOTON FRANCIS T	CPT	0-0159731	0453	3
COLLUM THEODORE J	LTC	0-0384009	0854	1
COLLUMS JIM K	LTC	0-1641833	0962	1
COLLUP GEORGE W	CPT	0-1318135	1046	2
COLMAN CHARLES K	CW2	W-2215388	0767	1
COLMAN HOMER J	LTC	0-0358918	0560	1
COLMAN WILLIAM A	CPT	0-1552256	0246	2
COLMER MEYER J	CPT	0-0491690	0546	2
COLN CHESTER C	MAJ	0-0947730	1066	1
COLO FRANCIS W	MAJ	0-1054947	0960	1
COLOM JOSE E	COL	0-0174221	0249	3
COLOMB FRANCIS D	MAJ	0-1936957	0168	1
COLOMBEL C E JR	1LT	0-1017942	1145	2
COLOMBO JAMES A	2LT	0-0975986	0764	2
COLOMBO JAMES A	CW2	W-2207064	0561	1
COLOMBO RAYMOND L	CW3	W-2145193	0764	1
COLON BELEN D	MAJ	N-0755538	0264	3
COLON VENANCIO	MAJ	0-0368631	0259	2
COLON-MALDONADO EFRA	MAJ	0-1063140	0765	1
COLONNA BENJAMIN A	LTC	0-0146517	1154	3
COLONNA DELIO	LTC	0-1106067	0157	1
COLORIO ANTHONY J	MAJ	0-0966087	1264	2
COLOSIMO JOSEPH	CW2	W-2109176	0965	1
COLOVOS NICHOLAS F	1LT	0-0548289	0845	2
COLOZZI CARL A	LTC	0-1181844	0767	2
COLSON ALEX G	CW2	W-2115697	0555	1
COLSON GARDNER	1LT	0-1325150	1046	2
COLSON GUY L	MAJ	0-0269193	0459	1
COLSON OLIVER K	LTC	0-1322313	1065	1
COLSTON CHARLES L	CW2	W-2152621	1060	1
COLT LEBARON C	LTC	0-0232847	0446	2
COLTON DONALD A	MAJ	0-1640324	1059	1
COLTON JOSEPH D	CW2	W-3100502	0868	1
COLTON JOSEPH O	CW2	WW-3100502	0868	1
COLTRIN DONALD C	MAJ	0-0198469	0457	3

NAME	GRADE	SVC NO	DATE RET MO YR	RET CODE
COLUMBIA FRANK L	LTC	0-0456530	1164	1
COLOMBO EUGENE	CW2	W-2206963	0261	1
COLUMBUS LEO M	1LT	0-0523059	0844	2
COLUMNA VICENTE D	MAJ	0-1896492	0861	1
COLUSSI LOUIS A	1LT	0-0377025	0544	2
COLVARD FREELAND A	LTC	0-0225167	0460	3
COLVERT THOMAS C	CW2	W-2148919	1055	1
COLVIN ARTHUR H	LTC	0-1285712	0460	1
COLVIN CHARLES B	CPT	0-1315557	1058	1
COLVIN ERNEST F	LTC	0-0105484	0554	3
COLVIN EUTA M	1LT	0-1735681	0146	2
COLVIN JAMES A	MAJ	0-1342051	0966	1
COLVIN JAMES E	LTC	0-1010819	0867	1
COLVIN KATHERINE	1LT	N-0744022	0345	1
COLVIN ROBERT R	WO1	W-2116498	0743	2
COLVIN WILLIAM J	CPT	0-0535150	0746	2
COLWELL CLARK M	CW2	W-2149204	1262	2
COLWELL EVERETT L	LTC	0-0126388	1152	3
COLWELL HANFORD T	LTC	0-0495998	0364	1
COLWELL MARTIN A	CW2	W-2144840	0157	1
COLWELL RALPH W	LTC	0-0481391	0457	1
COLWELL ROBERT F	CW2	W-2134341	0648	2
COLYER CHARLES F	LTC	0-0402513	0258	1
COLYER DAVID J	COL	0-0130923	0854	3
COLYER WILLIAM N	LTC	0-0375207	0557	1
COMAN HOWARD J	MAJ	0-0968085	0763	1
COMBATALADE EDMOND A	LTC	0-0252672	0965	3
COMBEL GEORGE H	COL	0-0286587	0866	3
COMBEL OSBORNE P	LTC	0-1635713	0960	1
COMBES ERNEST L	LTC	0-0533161	0868	3
COMBES GEORGE J	WO1	W-2146009	0653	1
COMBES J DERAISME	LTC	0-0138055	0251	3
COMBES PROCTACIO	1LT	0-1896435	1168	1
COMBS ALONZO F	CPT	0-2036380	1159	1
COMBS CHARLIE A	CW3	W-2152502	0662	1
COMBS CLYDE M	MAJ	0-1560411	0860	1
COMBS CORNELIUS	LTC	0-0904922	0148	2
COMBS EMANUEL JR	COL	0-0439189	0563	1
COMBS GEORGE E	LTC	0-1290379	0161	1
COMBS HAROLD O	2LT	0-1287242	0944	2
COMBS HENRY H	1LT	0-2000862	1147	1
COMBS HERBERT L JR	LTC	0-1633766	1262	1
COMBS HERMAN L	COL	0-0297735	0868	3
COMBS HORACE E	LTC	0-2012216	0266	1
COMBS ISHMAEL T	WO1	W-2151160	0157	1
COMBS JAMES	CW4	W-2147572	1268	1
COMBS JOHN A	MAJ	0-0445465	0853	2
COMBS JOHN P	1LT	0-1010395	0446	2
COMBS KERMIT S	LTC	0-0502506	1057	2
COMBS OLIVER B	LTC	0-0207587	0955	1
COMBS PALLAS C	CPT	0-1577034	1051	1
COMBS PAUL P	1LT	0-0324551	0549	2
COMBS RAYMOND W	COL	0-0114205	0753	3
COMBS SAMUEL R	COL	0-1641839	0868	1
COMBS SYDNEY S	MAJ	0-0387993	0346	2
COMBS THEODORE C	COL	0-0253303	0866	3
COMBS WATSON G	LTC	0-1825391	0263	1
COMBS ZENAS P	LTC	0-0224406	0761	3
COMEALL EDWARD J	2LT	0-1044493	0243	2
COMEAU EVANGELINE	CPT	N-0722240	0447	1
COMEAU LEAH A	MAJ	N-0752873	1066	3
COMEAU WILBERT F	CW3	W-2209608	1268	2
COMER BARTHOLOME	MAJ	0-0463230	0346	2
COMER BRAUDIS A	MAJ	0-1936645	1267	1
COMER CHESTER J	LTC	0-0235872	0465	3
COMER EDWARD	COL	0-1317498	1168	1
COMER EVERETT B	COL	0-0244925	0946	2
COMER HARRY L	MAJ	0-0468539	1047	1
COMER READIE	CPT	0-0437469	0144	1
COMER THOMAS P	CPT	0-0452490	0446	2
COMER VIRGIL	CPT	0-0289338	1045	2
COMERFORD EDWARD R J	LTC	0-1103115	1162	1
COMERFORD MARTIN AJ	MAJ	0-0298023	1160	1
COMES FABIAN M	CPT	0-1308305	1052	1
COMESKY HARRY A	LTC	0-0285893	1066	3

NAME	GRADE	SVC NO	DATE RET MO YR	RET CODE
COMEY EVERETT L	CW3	W-2146917	0561	2
COMEY LYMAN E	LTC	0-0275707	0260	3
COMFORT EDWIN G H	LTC	0-0274274	0967	3
COMFORT JOSEPH A	CPT	0-0461512	0545	2
COMFORT PRINCE F	CPT	0-1047075	0468	3
COMINGS JAMES H	COL	0-0374201	0157	1
COMISKY BENEDICT J	MAJ	0-1846676	0464	1
COMLEY CHARLOTTE	MAJ	N-0760069	0968	3
COMMINS GEORGE J	CPT	0-2263213	0762	1
COMMINS SAUL	CPT	0-1691054	0146	2
COMMONS CHARLES H JR	CPT	0-0248696	0866	3
COMNES GREGORY A	LTC	0-1289049	1060	1
COMO MARTHA B	MAJ	N-0726007	0966	1
COMPARETTE HOMER L	MAJ	0-0382422	0448	2
COMPETENTE MAXIMONO	2LT	0-1896438	0648	1
COMPTON DON E	1LT	0-1637813	1045	2
COMPTON EDWARD A	COL	0-0333294	0860	3
COMPTON EVELAND C	MAJ	0-0376395	0448	2
COMPTON GEORGE W	1LT	0-0414299	0145	2
COMPTON HARRY O	COL	0-0227449	1163	3
COMPTON JOHN B	LTC	0-0341218	0359	2
COMPTON JOSEPH R	LTC	0-0910195	0668	3
COMPTON MAURICE W	LTC	0-0310455	0168	3
COMPTON MORGAN L	CPT	0-2000467	1046	2
COMPTON MUTT L	MAJ	0-1534456	1060	2
COMPTON OERY	MAJ	0-1582339	1063	1
COMPTON ROBERT J	MAJ	0-0309031	0363	3
COMPTON SHERMAN W	CPT	0-0494560	1053	1
COMPTON WILLIAM F	2LT	0-1913608	0935	1
COMRIE RUSSELL M	LTC	0-0374514	0759	1
COMROE IRVING H	LTC	0-0309583	1063	3
COMSTOCK CARL R JR	CPT	0-0469597	0345	2
COMSTOCK DONALD R	CW2	W-2148086	0860	1
COMSTOCK JOSEPH B JR	LTC	0-0988027	0868	1
COMSTOCK OLIVER O	LTC	0-0275871	0460	3
COMSTOCK RAYMOND C	MAJ	0-0483258	1153	1
COMSTOCK ROBERT F	MAJ	0-1637819	0759	1
COMUNTZIS MARCUS G	CPT	0-0447058	1045	2
COMYACK GEORGE W	CW2	W-2209458	1263	1
CONA ANTHONY T	1LT	0-1017176	0646	2
CONAN NEAL J JR	1LT	0-0464565	1045	2
CONANT LEWIS T	MAJ	0-1951582	0960	1
CONANT LYNNE	1LT	0-0263788	0143	2
CONARD EUGENE S	MAJ	0-1101386	0759	1
CONARD HARRY M	CW3	W-2153185	0164	2
CONARD HORACE V	LTC	0-1533758	0362	3
CONARD WILLIAM E	LTC	0-1050605	0665	1
CONARROE MILFORD T	CW2	W-2216034	0768	1
CONARTON MICHAEL D	CPT	0-5301850	0468	1
CONARTY EARL C	1LT	0-1303111	1045	2
CONARY GEORGE W	CPT	0-0128311	1055	3
CONATSER MAX C	LTC	0-1640325	0462	1
CONATSER TROY F	CW3	W-2143023	1058	1
CONAWAY CHARLES M	MAJ	0-0171080	0958	3
CONAWAY RALPH C	CW2	W-2102776	0248	2
CONBOY JAMES E	CW3	RW-2210958	0868	1
CONBOY JOHN J	LTC	0-0991184	1068	1
CONBOY JOHN W P	LTC	0-1113149	0567	1
CONBOY RAY	CPT	0-0498436	0746	2
CONCAGH JOSEPH P	1LT	0-1650817	0647	2
CONCANNON JAMES M	1LT	0-0446828	0446	2
CONCAR MARY B	1LT	N-0767998	0846	1
CONCORDIA JOHN D	MAJ	0-1302777	0158	1
CONDAN WILLIAM H	1LT	0-0982101	1060	1
CONDELL WILLIAM J	COL	0-0265950	0456	3
CONDER FRANCIS E	COL	0-0179883	0860	1
CONDICT STEPHEN H	MAJ	0-1797605	0762	1
CONDIT CHARLES P JR	MAJ	0-1186076	0866	1
CONDIT HERBERT J	LTC	0-1534944	0767	1
CONDIT JOHN V	CPT	0-1283027	0550	
CONDIT WILLIAM H	WO1	W-2121449	1045	2
CONDON DEAN L	LTC	0-0314838	0861	1
CONDON EDWARD J	MAJ	0-0304027	0167	3
CONDON EDWARD V	COL	0-0209458	1153	3
CONDON ELLIOTT B	COL	0-0333179	1066	3

NAME	GRADE	SVC NO	DATE RET MO YR	RET CODE
CONDON HERBERT T JR	LTC	0-0351330	1062	1
CONDON JAMES L	1LT	0-2008796	0256	2
CONDON JOHN	1LT	0-1017190	0745	2
CONDON JOSEPH M	LTC	0-0907151	0265	3
CONDON KELLISON T	LTC	0-0916566	1063	3
CONDON RICHARD P	WO1	W-2122001	1053	1
CONDON WILLIAM G	LTC	0-1944649	0164	1
CONDON WILLIAM H	1LT	0-1301955	0245	2
CONDON WILLIAM J	1LT	0-1645658	0545	2
CONDON WILLIAM M	LTC	0-0405150	1060	1
CONDON WILLIAM T	MAJ	0-0515520	1168	3
CONDRAY WILLIAM W	CPT	0-0257189	1267	3
CONDREY DWIGHT L	1LT	0-2262083	0963	2
CONDRICK MAURICE P	1LT	0-0210926	0250	3
CONDRON HARRY D	1LT	0-1315440	1145	2
CONDY HUGH K	LTC	0-1288710	0960	2
CONE ANTHONY D	CPT	0-0478184	1048	1
CONE HUTCHINSON JR	LTC	0-0324193	1065	2
CONE JAMES P	WO1	W-2125495	1143	2
CONE RALPH N	LTC	0-1647281	0867	1
CONE ROY G	1LT	0-1114429	1262	1
CONE WILLIAM W	LTC	0-0198552	0761	3
CONEFREY FRANK A	MAJ	0-0243032	0857	3
CONEIN LUCIEN E	LTC	0-1322769	1061	1
CONELLEY WILLIAM R	MAJ	0-1341355	1166	1
CONELLY CHESTER L	CPT	0-0363701	0944	2
CONELLY RAYMOND J	COL	0-0298550	1060	1
CONELLY THOMAS J	2LT	0-2005373	1267	2
CONERLY CECIL F	CPT	0-0323360	0344	2
CONERLY MAXWELL R	MAJ	0-2262432	0861	1
CONERLY SEDRIC E	MAJ	0-1080010	1054	1
CONEY DUDLEY F	COL	0-1015596	0165	1
CONEY JOHN D	COL	0-0297801	1161	1
CONEY JOHN S	CPT	0-0484330	0745	1
CONEY RICHARD H	MAJ	0-1994736	0862	1
CONEYBEER ROBERT T	LTC	0-1061206	0361	1
CONFEHR WILMER D	LTC	0-1895934	0767	3
CONFER ELMA I	MAJ	N-0724711	0464	1
CONFER WILLIAM R	MAJ	0-0887357	0756	1
CONGDON CHARLES C	CPT	0-1757031	0847	2
CONGDON JOHN	2LT	0-1300763	1144	2
CONGDON LEON A	MAJ	0-0142681	0554	3
CONGDON PAUL E	COL	0-0335455	0667	3
CONGER ALWYN C	CPT	0-0887446	0255	2
CONGLETON DEWEY S	MAJ	0-0245505	0244	2
CONINE HUBERT F	CPT	0-0237893	0946	2
CONISKI FRANK T	LTC	0-1309218	0862	1
CONKEL LLOYD J	LTC	0-0216502	1147	2
CONKELL FRANK JR	CW4	W-2110137	0265	1
CONKIN CHARLES A	CW2	W-2152503	0861	1
CONKLE JOHN D	LTC	0-1821825	0261	1
CONKLIN ALBERT R	COL	0-0287947	0560	1
CONKLIN CHARLES M	MAJ	0-1633138	0956	1
CONKLIN CLARENCE E	LTC	0-0284654	0964	3
CONKLIN DEANE L	1LT	0-0144018	0254	3
CONKLIN EDWARD M JR	COL	0-0317520	0854	2
CONKLIN FRANK J	CW3	W-2145735	0965	1
CONKLIN GORDON C	LTC	0-1315561	1168	1
CONKLIN HARRY I	LTC	0-0309081	0962	3
CONKLIN JAMES S	MAJ	0-1690890	0263	1
CONKLIN LEROY R	LTC	0-1302604	0866	1
CONKLIN MARY C	1LT	N-0754786	1048	2
CONKLIN ROSCOE R	MAJ	0-1686227	0158	1
CONKLING SAMUEL R	CPT	0-1637219	0452	2
CONLAN DAVID N	1LT	0-0915859	0445	2
CONLAN WILLIAM P	LTC	0-0255450	0466	3
CONLEY BENJAMIN F JR	CW4	W-2147158	1168	2
CONLEY DON B	LTC	0-0321900	0747	2
CONLEY EARL G	1LT	0-1041997	0844	2
CONLEY EDWARD J	1LT	0-1031546	1150	1
CONLEY EDWARD R	MAJ	0-0507977	0654	1
CONLEY FRANK G G	MAJ	0-0316986	0267	3
CONLEY GEORGE E	LTC	0-1103117	0661	1
CONLEY HARLAN L	1LT	0-1324085	1045	2
CONLEY IRVING L	MAJ	0-1634626	0261	1

NAME	GRADE	SVC NO	DATE RET MO YR	RET CODE
CONLEY JAMES E	1LT	0-1999824	0846	2
CONLEY JOSEPH G	COL	0-0286588	0962	3
CONLEY LELAND H	LTC	0-0920741	0267	3
CONLEY MARGARET J	MAJ	N-0742444	0862	2
CONLEY PAUL B	1LT	0-1286246	0546	2
CONLEY PETER	CW3	W-2145882	0159	1
CONLEY RAYMOND F	MAJ	0-2265052	0267	1
CONLEY ROBERT L	LTC	0-1115534	0168	1
CONLEY RUSSELL E	CPT	0-0267467	0757	3
CONLEY THOMAS W	CW2	W-2111680	0653	1
CONLEY WILLIAM R	CPT	0-5518006	0265	2
CONLEY WILLIAM S	CW2	W-2144859	0758	1
CONLIN ALVIN B	CPT	0-1312128	1060	1
CONLIN CHARLES A	COL	0-0317150	0966	1
CONLIN FRANK A	LTC	0-0177639	1157	3
CONLIN JOHN P	MAJ	0-0357806	0946	2
CONLIN JOHN T	MAJ	0-1104097	0748	2
CONLIN RICHARD G	LTC	0-1104576	0864	1
CONLIN THOMAS J	COL	0-0322171	0760	1
CONLON ARTHUR B	CPT	0-2044294	0460	1
CONLON THOMAS P	LTC	0-0401470	1060	1
CONLON WILLIAM F	LTC	0-0487093	0856	1
CONLOW JOHN J	1LT	0-1318867	1045	2
CONLYN PEARSON C	COL	0-0254617	0165	3
CONLYN WILLIAM J JR	CPT	0-0348303	1045	2
CONN KERMIT N	MAJ	0-1300130	0258	1
CONN LUCILLE T	MAJ	N-0765935	0767	1
CONN MILTON H	1LT	0-1795863	0944	2
CONN ROBBINS L	COL	0-0100445	0754	3
CONN SOLOMON J	LTC	0-1108576	0658	1
CONN WILLIAM M	1LT	0-1558843	0257	1
CONNALLY CHARLES E	CW3	W-2145864	0659	1
CONNALLY DUDLEY B	MAJ	0-0226793	0563	3
CONNALLY LYNTON E	CPT	0-2208303	0358	2
CONNARN JOHN P	CPT	0-0414143	0547	2
CONNELL CECIL H	COL	0-0336954	0363	3
CONNELL EDWIN M	COL	0-0378900	1060	1
CONNELL GEORGE B	CW2	W-2119340	1045	2
CONNELL HENRY L	LTC	0-0228845	0363	3
CONNELL JAMES B	1LT	0-0506670	0246	2
CONNELL JAMES K	LTC	0-0296567	0167	3
CONNELL NORMAN G	CPT	0-0414300	0864	2
CONNELL PAUL	CPT	0-0498228	1047	2
CONNELL WILBUR L	MAJ	0-0246559	0658	3
CONNELL WILLIAM R	LTC	0-1878844	1268	1
CONNELLAN GERALD V	MAJ	0-1645214	0460	1
CONNELLY ALLEN N	CPT	0-0266991	0847	2
CONNELLY FRANCIS J	MAJ	0-0348978	0346	2
CONNELLY FRANCIS M	LTC	0-1051083	1167	1
CONNELLY IRETON G	MAJ	0-0230660	1162	3
CONNELLY JAMES G	MAJ	0-1332932	0864	1
CONNELLY JOHN B	LTC	0-0369930	0660	1
CONNELLY JOHN K	COL	0-0337388	0961	1
CONNELLY ROBERT J	MAJ	0-2033203	0662	1
CONNELLY ROSE F	1LT	N-0751161	0745	1
CONNELLY THOMAS E	CPT	0-1303673	0746	2
CONNER BERTIS A JR	CPT	0-0708658	0147	2
CONNER CARROLL L	CW2	W-2151668	0659	1
CONNER CHARLES E	COL	0-0179246	0346	2
CONNER DAVID J	MAJ	0-0959309	1162	1
CONNER DONALD E	LTC	0-0455815	0160	1
CONNER EDGAR G	MAJ	0-1285199	0860	1
CONNER ELI T	LTC	0-0284918	1065	3
CONNER FRANK E	2LT	0-0317999	0659	3
CONNER HAROLD A	MAJ	0-2018846	0562	1
CONNER HARRY R	1LT	0-1315910	0747	2
CONNER HENRY F	LTC	0-0273523	0566	3
CONNER HOWARD W	2LT	0-1288711	0151	2
CONNER HOWARD W	CW2	RW-2209677	0966	1
CONNER IRA M	CPT	0-0297137	0547	2
CONNER IRIA C	1LT	0-2212016	0556	1
CONNER JAMES T	CW2	W-2148718	0656	1
CONNER JESSE H	1LT	0-0435913	1145	2
CONNER JOHN W	MAJ	0-0483566	0754	2
CONNER JOSEPH R	CW3	W-2143135	0358	1

332-811 O - 69 - 9

NAME	GRADE	SVC NO	DATE RET MO YR	RET CODE	NAME	GRADE	SVC NO	DATE RET MO YR	RET CODE	NAME	GRADE	SVC NO	DATE RET MO YR	RET CODE	NAME	GRADE	SVC NO	DATE RET MO YR	RET CODE
CONNER KENNETH H	MAJ	0-0325729	0566	3	CONOVER WOLFERT D	CPT	0-0163755	1055	1	CONWAY JOHN F	1LT	0-1301439	0146	2	COOK JAMES T	COL	0-0227760	1064	3
CONNER LLOYD W	MAJ	0-1548702	0561	1	CONRACE JOSEPH E C	MAJ	0-0189103	0256	3	CONWAY JOHN F	CPT	0-1684299	1044	2	COOK JAMES V	1LT	0-1062479	0747	2
CONNER LOWELL L	CPT	0-0257900	0649	3	CONRAD ALLISON A	COL	0-0327559	1058	1	CONWAY JOHN R	2LT	0-1329806	0945	2	COOK JAMES W	B G	0-0298148	0159	3
CONNER MEREDITH	1LT	0-1310813	0945	2	CONRAD ARTHUR J	CW4	W-2117921	0659	1	CONWAY JOHN V	CPT	0-0122460	1152	3	COOK JAMES W	MAJ	0-1844379	0558	1
CONNER OTTO R JR	LTC	0-0439212	0955	1	CONRAD BERNARD R	1LT	0-0526646	0647	2	CONWAY JOSEPH M	LTC	0-0424522	0365	1	COOK JOHN A JR	1LT	0-2049208	0350	2
CONNER PHILIP H	LTC	0-1403499	1060	1	CONRAD CHESTER R	MAJ	0-1112628	0261	1	CONWAY MALACHI J	LTC	0-0433964	0363	1	COOK JOHN B	MAJ	0-1821684	1054	1
CONNER RANDAL E	CW2	W-2150810	1161	2	CONRAD DODA	CPT	0-1691533	0347	2	CONWAY MARK E	COL	0-0270692	1165	3	COOK JOHN C	COL	0-0329674	0559	1
CONNER ROY E	1LT	0-0544024	0346	2	CONRAD EDWARD	1LT	0-1291239	1055	1	CONWAY RAYMOND F	2LT	0-1822370	1043	2	COOK JOHN C	LTC	0-1637838	0960	1
CONNER SIDNEY J	CPT	0-0286706	0346	2	CONRAD FRANK H	LTC	0-0184829	0862	3	CONWAY RICHARD H	MAJ	0-1339515	1164	1	COOK JOHN G	LTC	0-1010872	0156	1
CONNER WORTH L	LTC	0-1080183	0961	1	CONRAD HARLAN C	MAJ	0-0308742	0148	1	CONWAY ROBERT H	MAJ	0-1640975	0764	1	COOK JOHN J	LTC	0-0284279	0757	1
CONNERAT EDWIN S	LTC	0-0297551	0368	3	CONRAD HAROLD C	LTC	0-0359386	0647	2	CONWAY WILLIAM A	CPT	0-0453653	0844	2	COOK JOHN M	LTC	0-0403681	0346	2
CONNERLEY MELVIN H	CW4	W-2131445	0761	1	CONRAD HOWARD E	1LT	0-0408406	1045	2	CONWELL ROBERT W	CW3	W-2151609	0163	1	COOK JOHN S	CPT	0-0522366	0151	1
CONNERS DANIEL J JR	1LT	0-1012234	1046	2	CONRAD HUGH N	1LT	0-0888364	0264	3	CONWELL STANTON A	MAJ	0-0205206	0962	1	COOK JOSEPH L	LTC	0-0198959	1150	3
CONNERS EDWARD D	CPT	0-1294787	1165	1	CONRAD JAMES H	CW3	W-2206327	0166	1	CONWELL WILLIAM A	COL	0-0259758	0668	3	COOK JOSEPH W	LTC	0-0480995	0355	1
CONNERS PAUL R	CW2	W-2206083	0963	1	CONRAD JAMES L	COL	0-0183985	1060	3	CONYERS CHRISTOPHE	LTC	0-0170256	0759	3	COOK JOSEPH W	1LT	0-1308478	1146	2
CONNERS VINCENT P	MAJ	0-1691749	0763	1	CONRAD JAMES P	1LT	0-1635717	0345	2	CONYERS EDWARD	1LT	0-0109923	0632	1	COOK LAMAR H	1LT	0-1554882	0366	2
CONNERTH SARA	2LT	N-0700826	0536	1	CONRAD JAMES R	CW3	W-2146686	1059	1	CONYERS LUDGER B JR	MAJ	0-1061343	0564	1	COOK LAURENCE	2LT	0-1031395	1045	2
CONNERY JOSEPH W	CW4	W-2005843	0908	3	CONRAD JOHN E	LTC	0-0269613	0868	3	CONZETT DONALD C	COL	0-0224796	0159	3	COOK LAWRENCE E	CPT	0-0114028	0646	2
CONNERY RICHARD F	COL	0-0217671	0960	3	CONRAD JOSEPH E	2LT	0-1823986	1044	2	COOGAN BERNARD L	LTC	0-1555526	1062	1	COOK LAWRENCE R	CW2	W-2153654	0560	1
CONNICK JAMES P	LTC	0-0219108	1061	3	CONRAD LEON H	CW4	W-2102778	1157	1	COOK ADAM E	LTC	0-0502205	0256	1	COOK LELAND M	LTC	0-0450265	0357	1
CONNICK ROBERT F	1LT	0-1287307	1145	2	CONRAD OLIVER H	MAJ	0-1047485	0667	1	COOK ALBERT B JR	LTC	0-0178788	1161	3	COOK LEO H	MAJ	0-0504258	0158	1
CONNIFF JOHN J	CPT	0-1109862	1146	2	CONRAD OMAR G	CPT	0-1542181	0346	2	COOK ALONZO E	MAJ	0-2262171	0862	1	COOK LEONARD J	1LT	0-0525002	0745	2
CONNINGTON CHARLES S	MAJ	0-0201348	0863	3	CONRAD ROBERT L	CPT	0-0376955	0446	2	COOK ARIE D	CW2	W-2151065	0857	1	COOK LEXIE W	CPT	0-1294269	0549	2
CONNOLLY BERNARD	1LT	0-0444707	1045	2	CONRAD STANLEY T	CW2	W-2150556	0260	1	COOK ARNOLD A	LTC	0-0487353	0266	3	COOK LINDSLEY F	CPT	0-1010506	0246	2
CONNOLLY BERNARD F	LTC	0-0419084	0961	1	CONRAD WARD E	LTC	0-0267905	0165	3	COOK BILLIE G	CW4	W-2148314	0767	1	COOK LYLE E	COL	0-0301020	1168	3
CONNOLLY BERNARD T	CW3	W-2119581	0655	1	CONRAD WILBER D	MAJ	0-1822369	1155	2	COOK BYRON J	LTC	0-0238745	0566	3	COOK MADISON E	MAJ	0-0475736	0154	1
CONNOLLY CHARLES R	LTC	0-0254089	0762	3	CONRADI CHARLES R	2LT	0-2001667	0758	2	COOK CALLIE N	MAJ	0-1284105	1060	1	COOK MARIO V	CPT	0-0398164	0144	2
CONNOLLY GEORGE A	COL	0-0255259	0867	3	CONRATH ROBERT E	COL	0-0264544	0768	3	COOK CARL H	CPT	0-0390709	0445	2	COOK MAXWELL W	MAJ	0-0361042	0168	3
CONNOLLY JAMES J JR	MAJ	0-0909335	0862	2	CONREY ELDEN E JR	LTC	0-0268221	1068	3	COOK CARROLL K	CPT	0-0472402	0645	2	COOK MELVIN S	MAJ	0-1582104	0961	1
CONNOLLY JAMES R	1LT	0-1310226	0446	2	CONROD ROBERT L	LTC	0-0126228	0257	3	COOK CHARLES	CW4	W-2111209	0455	1	COOK MILTON	MAJ	0-0234336	1065	3
CONNOLLY JOHN P	1LT	0-1799104	0246	2	CONROW JOSEPH M	LTC	0-0284655	0667	3	COOK CHARLES E	LTC	0-0182965	0962	3	COOK MYRON D	COL	0-1166035	0461	1
CONNOLLY JOSEPH J	MAJ	0-1110426	0366	1	CONROY CHARLES W	MAJ	0-0974232	0165	1	COOK CHESTER L	CW2	RW-3150238	0466	1	COOK NATHANIEL	CW2	W-2145856	0257	1
CONNOLLY LEO M	1LT	0-0282536	0568	3	CONROY GEORGE R	LTC	0-1287147	0364	1	COOK CLARENCE C JR	CPT	0-0350421	0646	2	COOK OLIN L	MAJ	0-0954743	1161	1
CONNOLLY LEONARD W	LTC	0-0185389	0951	3	CONROY HARRY A	COL	0-0255076	1148	3	COOK CLAYBOURNE	WO1	W-2149040	0160	1	COOK OSSIAN L	LTC	0-0117769	0354	3
CONNOLLY REDMOND J	COL	0-0255066	0660	1	CONROY JOSEPH F	COL	0-0331875	0760	1	COOK CLIFFORD B	CPT	0-2055883	0758	1	COOK OTIS S	CW3	W-2146132	0558	1
CONNOLLY ROBERT D JR	LTC	0-1633139	0563	1	CONROY LESLIE J	LTC	0-0472152	0954	1	COOK CLIFFORD J JR	MAJ	0-0969387	0365	1	COOK OTTO G	LTC	0-0194064	1049	3
CONNOLLY ROBERT M	COL	0-0319372	1060	1	CONROY RALPH J	LTC	0-0565081	0564	1	COOK DARREL O	WO1	W-2112265	0348	1	COOK OWEN E	2LT	0-1826259	0145	2
CONNOLLY THOMAS F	MAJ	0-1578294	0561	1	CONROY TERESA B	MAJ	N-0761041	0657	1	COOK DAVID W	CPT	0-1287483	1147	2	COOK PATRICK J	2LT	0-1304181	0746	2
CONNOLLY THOMAS H	MAJ	0-1175980	0661	1	CONROY WALTER R	MAJ	0-1019778	1161	1	COOK DEAN J	CW2	W-2211735	0167	1	COOK PAUL D	MAJ	0-1184027	0356	1
CONNOLLY THOMAS N	MAJ	0-2030145	1161	1	CONROY WILLIAM R	LTC	0-1017850	0862	1	COOK DENNIS S	MAJ	0-0399324	0645	2	COOK PAUL F	MAJ	0-0517788	0556	1
CONNOLLY W A JR	LTC	0-0329480	1160	1	CONSER FRANK M	MAJ	0-0436223	0946	2	COOK DON W	LTC	0-0308708	1060	1	COOK PAUL I	MAJ	0-0537146	0363	1
CONNOR BOBBY D	LTC	0-2042108	1168	1	CONSIDINE FLORENCE R	MAJ	0-1177345	1163	1	COOK DONALD F	CPT	0-0972939	1062	1	COOK PHILIP M	LTC	0-0330370	0459	1
CONNOR BRIAN K	1LT	0-0916704	0944	2	CONSIDINE LORETTA M	1LT	N-0771906	0646	2	COOK DONALD J	1LT	0-0534870	1045	2	COOK RALPH J	CW4	W-2144292	0367	1
CONNOR CLAUDE	CPT	0-0495341	0147	1	CONSIDINE ROY J	CPT	0-1821826	0547	2	COOK DONALD M	LTC	0-0128314	1153	3	COOK RAYMOND O	MAJ	0-0296699	0362	3
CONNOR DONALD G	LTC	0-1175083	0763	1	CONSTABLE EVERETT R	CW2	W-2142828	0862	2	COOK EDWIN W	CPT	0-1283215	0147	2	COOK RICHARD	M G	0-0107835	0658	3
CONNOR EDWARD F	1LT	0-1325632	1045	2	CONSTABLE FRANCIS W	LTC	0-0200873	0756	3	COOK EMORY J	LTC	0-0289844	1066	3	COOK RICHARD L	LTC	0-0404590	1160	1
CONNOR FRANCIS J	LTC	0-1822536	0563	1	CONSTANT JOE R	LTC	0-1640328	1066	1	COOK ERNEST T	CPT	0-0495918	1147	2	COOK RICHARD L	MAJ	0-1286971	0960	1
CONNOR HERBERT D	MAJ	0-1169069	0860	1	CONSTANTINE JAMES	LTC	0-1011550	0656	1	COOK FRANK	CPT	0-0491449	0350	2	COOK ROBERT B	LTC	0-0439267	0967	1
CONNOR JAMES F	CW2	W-2213442	0967	1	CONSTANTINE JAMES T	CW3	W-2005258	1264	3	COOK FREDDIE	CW3	W-2143485	1162	1	COOK ROBERT B	LTC	0-1119477	1068	1
CONNOR JAMES F	LTC	0-0394059	1164	1	CONSTANTINE WALTER J	LTC	0-0418789	0563	1	COOK FREDERICK JR	MAJ	0-0278476	0468	3	COOK ROBERT L	CW3	W-2208234	1066	2
CONNOR JAMES T	COL	0-0385243	0965	3	CONTANT CHARLES F	LTC	0-0421249	0860	1	COOK GEORGE A	CW4	W-2001611	0666	3	COOK ROBERT R	LTC	0-1166036	0461	1
CONNOR JOHN G JR	2LT	0-5007891	0761	2	CONTAPAY FLORENTINO	1LT	0-1896618	0357	1	COOK GEORGE S	M G	0-0251434	0966	3	COOK ROBERT W	LTC	0-0476214	0155	1
CONNOR JOHN J	MAJ	0-1535410	0657	2	CONTE ANGELO J	LTC	0-0378678	1060	1	COOK GEORGE W	MAJ	0-0202683	0757	3	COOK ROGER A	MAJ	0-0154345	1054	3
CONNOR JOHN M	CPT	0-0259377	0367	3	CONTE JOSEPH	CPT	0-1591065	0961	1	COOK GERALD C	COL	0-0450216	0764	1	COOK ROLAND E	MAJ	0-0706702	0961	1
CONNOR JOHN M	COL	0-0321714	0646	2	CONTE PETER A	MAJ	0-1550768	0157	1	COOK GILBERT W	CPT	0-1885925	0366	1	COOK ROY H	LTC	0-1326255	1162	1
CONNOR JOHN W	MAJ	0-0338393	1145	2	CONTI ALBERT	MAJ	0-4026387	1068	2	COOK GORDON W	COL	0-0035454	0268	2	COOK RUSSELL D	COL	0-0367035	0964	1
CONNOR JOSEPH	MAJ	0-1298502	0563	1	CONTI AUGUSTO W	LTC	0-1549918	1263	1	COOK GRIFFITH E JR	LTC	0-0448583	0557	1	COOK RUSSELL E	CPT	0-0394966	0747	2
CONNOR JOSEPH R	CW3	W-3150237	0168	1	CONTI DOMINIC L	CPT	0-1311983	0946	2	COOK HARRY A	LTC	0-0301333	0764	3	COOK SHIRLEY S	LTC	0-0424484	0557	1
CONNOR MARGARET M	2LT	N-0757648	0345	1	CONTI EDWARD J	LTC	0-1796581	0861	1	COOK HARRY J JR	MAJ	0-2287137	0166	1	COOK STEWART G	LTC	0-0562763	0466	3
CONNOR MYLES J	COL	0-0182391	0253	2	CONTOS DESPINA C	CPT	N-0784195	0247	1	COOK HARVEY R	MAJ	0-0175299	0961	3	COOK THEODORE H JR	LTC	0-1544827	1064	1
CONNOR PRESTON B JR	CPT	0-0146880	0756	3	CONTRAROS GEORGE J	CW3	W-2143260	0660	1	COOK HELEN A	1LT	N-0703899	0446	1	COOK THEODORE J	COL	0-0322984	0957	1
CONNOR ROBERT J	LTC	0-1170686	0664	1	CONTRERAS JOSE T	1LT	0-1896635	0655	1	COOK HENRY G	LTC	0-1584696	0467	3	COOK THOMAS F	CPT	0-1300278	1060	1
CONNOR RODNEY V	1LT	0-0971167	1153	2	CONTRERAS PEDRO J	LTC	0-1030867	0768	1	COOK HENRY R	MAJ	0-0397533	0361	1	COOK THOMAS J B	CW3	W-2146703	0864	1
CONNOR SAMUEL W	COL	0-0220108	0549	3	CONTROULIS THOMAS	CW3	W-2146170	0260	1	COOK HERMAN W	COL	0-0173413	0361	3	COOK TIM O	COL	0-0263796	1164	3
CONNOR STANLEY P	LTC	0-0376766	0759	1	CONVERSE DUANE B	1LT	0-1290209	0245	2	COOK HORACE D	CW4	W-2008728	0268	3	COOK WALTER G	CW4	W-2201047	1066	3
CONNOR THOMAS J	LTC	0-1041604	1163	1	CONVERSE GEORGE L	LTC	0-0291438	0759	1	COOK HUGH D JR	2LT	0-1589133	0945	2	COOK WALTER R	MAJ	0-1917775	0563	1
CONNOR WILLIAM H	CW3	W-2149159	0563	1	CONVERSE JASON H	LTC	0-0253023	0865	3	COOK IVAN M	CW2	W-2152670	0561	1	COOK WAYNE R	LTC	0-0319129	0147	2
CONNOR WILLIAM J	MAJ	0-1280187	0758	2	CONVERY FREDRICK R	MAJ	0-0275487	1263	3	COOK JACK C	LTC	0-1175084	0865	1	COOK WENDELL B	MAJ	0-0279016	0664	3
CONNOR WILLIAM J	MAJ	0-1341856	0561	1	CONWAY BERNARD E	COL	0-0265759	0360	1	COOK JAMES A	MAJ	0-0282411	0367	3	COOK WILLIAM B	LTC	0-0206632	1048	3
CONNOR WILLIAM T	LTC	0-1796580	0763	1	CONWAY CHARLES J	WO1	W-2141533	0457	1	COOK JAMES B	CW3	W-2205177	0565	1	COOK WILLIAM B	MAJ	0-0245391	1264	3
CONNORS GERALD T	MAJ	0-0463341	0854	1	CONWAY EDWARD H	LTC	0-0386858	1160	1	COOK JAMES D	LTC	0-1303269	0962	1	COOK WILLIAM B	LTC	0-1552463	0767	1
CONNORS HUGH M	COL	0-0229175	0859	3	CONWAY FRANKLIN M	LTC	0-2033792	1268	1	COOK JAMES E JR	COL	0-0262569	0368	3	COOK WILLIAM E	CPT	0-1304182	0847	2
CONNORS LAWRENCE P	LTC	0-1290903	0960	1	CONWAY FRAZIER M	MAJ	0-1185781	0461	1	COOK JAMES J	1LT	0-1016059	1147	2	COOK WILLIAM G	COL	0-0275468	0365	3
CONNORS PANSY E	CW2	V-2211887	0866	1	CONWAY JAMES	CW3	W-2143887	0263	1	COOK JAMES L	MAJ	0-1913366	0965	1	COOK WILLIAM G	2LT	0-1641877	0944	2
CONOVER ARLIE B	MAJ	0-0235930	0648	3	CONWAY JOHN A	LTC	0-0249919	0765	3	COOK JAMES K	LTC	0-0294837	1267	3	COOK WILLIAM H	MAJ	0-1102428	1059	1

NAME	GRADE	SVC NO	DATE RET MO YR	RET CODE
COOK WILLIAM H	LTC	0-1534704	0468	3
COOK WILLIAM K	LTC	0-1302275	0662	1
COOK WILLIAM R	CPT	0-0887451	0348	2
COOKE BRONSON F	LTC	0-0278138	0858	1
COOKE BURDETTE F	CPT	0-2029657	1056	1
COOKE DON A	MAJ	0-0279518	0358	3
COOKE EDWIN T	COL	0-0198868	0251	3
COOKE ELLIS A	LTC	0-1578299	1061	2
COOKE ERNEST C	MAJ	0-0963352	0165	1
COOKE HORACE G	LTC	0-1179822	0263	1
COOKE JAMES J	COL	0-0337465	0463	3
COOKE JOSEPH E	CPT	0-2288504	0863	1
COOKE JOSEPH L	LTC	0-0287983	0168	3
COOKE JOSEPH W	LTC	0-0251892	0166	3
COOKE JOSEPH R	COL	0-0100239	0753	1
COOKE LANE A	CPT	0-0966438	0161	1
COOKE LANE B	COL	0-0150563	1047	2
COOKE LEONARD C	COL	0-0316938	0560	1
COOKE OSCAR	MAJ	0-0277260	0863	3
COOKE PAUL B	MAJ	0-0975285	0751	1
COOKE RAFE	CW3	W-2115507	0356	1
COOKE RAYMOND W	MAJ	0-0511018	1047	2
COOKE ROBERT A	CPT	0-0917581	0744	2
COOKE SAMUEL H	LTC	0-0223604	0560	3
COOKE THOMAS P	MAJ	0-0287274	0858	1
COOKE TOLBERT A	CPT	0-0244625	0250	1
COOKE WILLIAM C	LTC	0-0455662	0168	3
COOKE WOODROW P	LTC	0-1647479	0365	1
COOKERLY VAN	COL	0-0150560	1047	2
COOKINGHAM THOMAS A	LTC	0-0436057	0962	1
COOKSEY DONALD W	MAJ	0-2033250	0765	1
COOKSLEY RICHARD E	CPT	0-1540943	0860	1
COOKSTON RAYMOND E	LTC	0-0909861	0467	3
COOL VALENTINE	MAJ	0-2262712	0663	1
COOLE HAROLD I	MAJ	0-2017360	0663	1
COOLEY ARTHUR E	LTC	0-0284411	0657	1
COOLEY CHARLES W	1LT	0-1755711	0946	2
COOLEY DANIEL S	CW3	W-2150920	0965	1
COOLEY FLOYD C	MAJ	0-0204394	0156	3
COOLEY FRED A	LTC	0-0150920	1049	3
COOLEY HARRY A	CW3	W-2104560	1053	1
COOLEY HENRY	CW2	W-2145541	0161	1
COOLEY MARVIN G	MAJ	0-1001318	1155	1
COOLEY NORMAN E	MAJ	0-2023740	0867	1
COOLEY ORRIN K	1LT	0-1321020	1045	2
COOLEY PAUL S	CW2	W-2204454	0165	1
COOLEY RAY N	COL	0-0164819	0155	1
COOLEY RAYMOND H	LTC	0-0325730	0268	3
COOLEY RICHARD S	MAJ	0-0515519	1145	2
COOLEY THOMAS H	MAJ	0-0118568	0944	2
COOLEY THOMAS F	CPT	0-0270082	0754	2
COOLEY WARREN H	LTC	0-1041003	0464	1
COOLICAN MICHAEL J	LTC	0-0355807	1167	3
COOLICK JOHN	COL	0-0910539	0165	1
COOLIDGE FLOYD G	CPT	0-0163619	0150	3
COOLIDGE HAROLD J	MAJ	0-0925143	1045	2
COOLIDGE LYLE C	LTC	0-0450832	1157	1
COOMBE JOHN V	LTC	0-0272716	0968	3
COOMBE OWEN L	CPT	0-3416677	1145	2
COOMBS ALBERT H JR	1LT	0-1041112	0348	2
COOMBS FRANCIS B	MAJ	0-1020090	0862	1
COOMBS FREDERICK	COL	0-0325427	0865	3
COOMBS PERCY L	LTC	0-0337117	0867	1
COOMBS RICHARD B	COL	0-0080672	0168	1
COOMBS WOODROW W	1LT	0-2007694	1046	2
COOMER JOSEPH A	MAJ	0-1686673	0766	1
COOMES JAMES A JR	LTC	0-1045053	0563	1
COON HARRY W	LTC	0-0290027	0261	3
COON SIDNEY E	CPT	0-1283726	0646	2
COON WALTER B	1LT	0-0410453	1043	2
COON WILLIAM E	CPT	0-2007226	1062	3
COON WILLIAM L	COL	0-0330421	1066	3
COONE GERALD E	MAJ	0-0219713	1044	2
COONE MARGARET J	MAJ	L-0120113	0967	1
COONE K V	LTC	0-2289751	0568	1

NAME	GRADE	SVC NO	DATE RET MO YR	RET CODE
COONEN RAYMOND T	2LT	0-2007354	1045	2
COONER ETHERIDGE	MAJ	0-1647368	1163	1
COONEY JOHN J	CW3	W-2203339	0164	1
COONEY JOHN R	2LT	0-1057020	0145	2
COONEY LEO A	MAJ	0-0297054	0753	3
COONEY WILLIAM H	LTC	0-0218573	0760	3
COONLEY DEAN F	COL	0-0192051	0966	2
COONRADT HAROLD L	MAJ	0-1554700	0161	1
COONS BRADD B	LTC	0-2014328	0962	1
COONS EARL B	LTC	0-1823266	0365	1
COONS ELLEN F	2LT	N-0741567	0145	1
COONS ROYAL E	CPT	0-1174541	0446	2
COOP EDNA	MAJ	N-0784493	1264	3
COOP NELCE L	LTC	0-0492338	1054	1
COOPE ROBERT L	2LT	0-0959729	0751	2
COOPER ADOLPH H	MAJ	0-1339969	0766	1
COOPER ALBERT H	LTC	0-0324341	1266	3
COOPER ANTHONY F	CW3	W-2147904	1163	1
COOPER BASIL P	LTC	0-0213916	0664	3
COOPER BEAUFORD O	LTC	0-0103940	1056	3
COOPER BEMUS F	LTC	0-0922324	1167	3
COOPER BRADLEY M	COL	0-0271373	1168	3
COOPER BRENT V	MAJ	0-1886606	1067	1
COOPER CARL	WO1	W-2147652	0354	1
COOPER CARL F	CPT	0-0420136	0144	2
COOPER CARROLL G	LTC	0-0372416	1160	1
COOPER CECIL A	1LT	0-0960000	0361	2
COOPER CECIL P	CW2	W-2146902	0963	1
COOPER CHARLES A	CPT	0-1320433	0247	2
COOPER CHARLIE G	CW3	W-2205383	1162	1
COOPER CLARENCE C	LTC	0-1113153	0662	1
COOPER CURTIS	LTC	0-0403436	0156	1
COOPER DONALD R	2LT	0-1822965	0645	2
COOPER EDWARD	1LT	0-1303469	1045	2
COOPER EDWARD H	CW3	W-2103967	0259	1
COOPER ELTON R	MAJ	0-0210192	0164	3
COOPER EMMETT JR	CPT	0-0293764	0246	2
COOPER EVERETT R	LTC	0-1014305	0757	1
COOPER FRANCIS M	LTC	0-0962430	0667	3
COOPER GEORGE L	LTC	0-0243325	1065	3
COOPER GEORGE T	CPT	0-0256981	0764	3
COOPER GERALD E	LTC	0-0359852	0166	3
COOPER GERALD W	MAJ	0-0981390	0463	1
COOPER HAROLD L	MAJ	0-0488807	1049	1
COOPER HARRY F	COL	0-0195474	0560	3
COOPER HENRY R	LTC	0-1041316	0861	1
COOPER HERSTON M	MAJ	0-0241256	0245	2
COOPER HUGH P	MAJ	0-0232330	0765	3
COOPER IRVIN E	LTC	0-0106810	0457	3
COOPER IVAN J	LTC	0-1037444	0161	1
COOPER JACK L	1LT	0-5533605	0968	2
COOPER JAMES C	COL	0-0205195	1053	3
COOPER JAMES H	LTC	0-0336819	1055	2
COOPER JAMES H	LTC	0-0673402	1066	1
COOPER JAMES F	CW2	W-2144111	1160	1
COOPER JOHN R	LTC	0-0215942	1263	3
COOPER JOHN H B	LTC	0-0232339	0765	3
COOPER JOHN F	MAJ	0-0964411	0261	1
COOPER JOHN O	LTC	0-0199056	0757	1
COOPER JOHN P	MAJ	0-0279747	0768	3
COOPER JOHN V	1LT	0-1080271	0344	2
COOPER JOHN W JR	LTC	0-0246826	0563	3
COOPER JOSEPH B	2LT	0-1598346	0147	1
COOPER JOSEPH H	MAJ	0-0115691	0854	3
COOPER LEE	1LT	0-2008648	1154	1
COOPER LEON C	CW2	RW-2147877	0461	1
COOPER LEONARD S	CPT	0-1317495	0448	2
COOPER LESLIE M	LTC	0-0455661	0864	1
COOPER LOUIS A	LTC	0-0334439	0466	3
COOPER LOWELL M	MAJ	0-0966142	0665	1
COOPER LUTHER S	CPT	0-0494231	1048	1
COOPER MARK F	CW2	W-2105771	0547	2
COOPER MARTIN W	LTC	0-1289549	0557	1
COOPER MAURICE Z	COL	0-0290534	0368	3
COOPER MELBOURNE	MAJ	0-0472517	1143	2

NAME	GRADE	SVC NO	DATE RET MO YR	RET CODE
COOPER MICHAEL	CPT	0-1757790	0546	2
COOPER MURRAY I	CPT	0-1036240	0646	2
COOPER NATHAN J	1LT	0-0441995	1045	2
COOPER NEWSOM	COL	0-0254034	0267	3
COOPER NORMAN P	2LT	0-1305734	1044	2
COOPER NORMAN W	LTC	0-2037046	0263	1
COOPER OBIE W	MAJ	0-1703768	0360	1
COOPER OMER C	LTC	0-0282834	0164	3
COOPER OSWALD	CPT	0-0470938	0945	2
COOPER PAUL D	LTC	0-0296895	0658	2
COOPER RALPH C	MAJ	0-1893627	0667	1
COOPER RALPH W JR	B G	0-0266469	1165	3
COOPER RICHARD E	CPT	0-1012896	0450	2
COOPER RICHARD W	COL	0-0237470	1061	3
COOPER ROBERT C	CW2	W-2144354	0560	1
COOPER ROBERT R	LTC	0-0549712	1265	1
COOPER RUFUS A	LTC	0-0534582	1164	1
COOPER SCOTT	LTC	0-1281145	1262	1
COOPER STANLEY W	CW2	W-2146830	0261	1
COOPER THOMAS E	CW3	W-2206030	0668	1
COOPER WALTER E	CPT	0-0477798	1048	1
COOPER WILLIAM	MAJ	0-0471116	1145	2
COOPER WILLIAM B	LTC	0-0417128	0562	1
COOPER WILLIAM H JR	CPT	0-0450112	0945	2
COOPER WILLIAM J	1LT	0-1549686	0246	2
COOPER WILLIAM R	MAJ	0-1933851	1164	1
COOPER WILLIAM T	LTC	0-1294436	0965	1
COOPER WILLIAM W	CW3	W-2006433	0468	3
COOPER WINFORD H	WO1	W-2108977	1160	1
COOPER WINSTON E	1LT	0-0510166	1151	2
COOPER WYLIE	LTC	0-0450266	1063	1
COOPER ZELIS	1LT	0-0557225	0846	2
COOPER 3RD JAMES S	MAJ	0-2036297	0960	1
COOPMAN WILLIAM C	CW4	W-2136639	1061	1
COOTS CLYDE	CW2	W-2147278	0460	1
COOVER ROBERT E	CW3	W-2203628	1163	1
COPADIS NICHOLAS G	1LT	0-2200923	0352	2
COPE ALFRED E	CW2	W-2142453	0561	1
COPE CYRIL H	2LT	0-0910323	0545	2
COPE MORIS F	CPT	0-0930060	0654	2
COPE JAMES F	CW4	W-2142696	0163	1
COPE LEE H	COL	0-0332852	0962	3
COPE OLLE B	LTC	0-1038946	0565	1
COPELAND EDGAR P	MAJ	0-2262721	0961	1
COPELAND CAROL W	CPT	0-0323586	1045	2
COPELAND CHARLES A	MAJ	0-1997510	0661	1
COPELAND CLYDE	LTC	0-1591086	0568	1
COPELAND ELBRIDGE	MAJ	0-2019434	0465	1
COPELAND FRED M	MAJ	0-0227250	0760	1
COPELAND HAROLD B	CW3	W-2152033	1064	1
COPELAND HAROLD E	CW4	W-2106995	0665	1
COPELAND INA L	MAJ	N-0702078	0347	1
COPELAND JAMES C	MAJ	0-1031304	0762	1
COPELAND JAMES M	LTC	0-0282407	1068	3
COPELAND JOHN D JR	LTC	0-0264531	0560	1
COPELAND JOHN W	MAJ	0-0247955	0245	2
COPELAND JOHN W	COL	0-0247269	0167	3
COPELAND KENNETH L	MAJ	0-1104582	0165	1
COPELAND LEE P	CW3	W-2207448	0363	1
COPELAND L[illegible] R	LTC	0-0252574	0163	1
COPELAND MARY E	CPT	N-0744697	0636	1
COPELAND MAURICE E	MAJ	0-1634774	1054	1
COPELAND RAYMOND E	LTC	0-0139765	1045	2
COPELAND RICHARD T	MAJ	0-0371610	0462	1
COPELAND ROBERT E	LTC	0-2096650	1068	1
COPELAND ROYAL S	COL	0-0290405	0751	1
COPELAND RUSSELL W	CW3	W-2102782	0256	1
COPELAND SHERMAN A	LTC	0-0323636	1162	1
COPELLO FLORENCE H	MAJ	N-0722683	0264	1
COPENHAVER L L JR	MAJ	0-1294091	1148	2
COPENING FRANK L JR	LTC	0-0333671	0665	3
COPHUS LOUIS L	MAJ	0-2263411	0568	1
COPLAN BENJAMIN J	CPT	0-0255215	0158	3
COPLEN JOHN W	COL	0-0163149	0161	3
COPLEY ANDREW R	CPT	0-0346539	0946	2

NAME	GRADE	SVC NO	DATE RET MO YR	RET CODE
COPP ANDREW J JR	COL	0-0104498	0648	3
COPP CHARLES A	LTC	0-0169342	0745	2
COPP CLARENCE W	CW3	W-2152104	0566	1
COPP FULTON W	LTC	0-0196345	0662	3
COPPAGE JOHN K	COL	0-0909559	1064	1
COPPAGE ORIS E	MAJ	0-1535411	0760	1
COPPARD VICTOR I	COL	0-0288624	0759	3
COPPERS NEIL T	1LT	0-0472745	0545	2
COPPINO DOMINICK	MAJ	0-1703046	1265	1
COPPLE HARRY A	CW2	W-2149692	1157	1
COPPOCK EVERETT H	MAJ	0-1825659	0361	1
COPPOCK PAUL W	LTC	0-1018248	0267	1
COPPOLA LOUISE	2LT	N-0756731	0944	1
COPPS JAMES F	MAJ	0-0411474	0561	1
CORAY JEROME B	COL	0-0508438	1165	3
CORB MARCEL	2LT	0-0986806	0352	2
CORBALEY LAURENCE H	MAJ	0-0187297	0554	3
CORBE HUBERT A	LTC	0-0906987	0962	3
CORBETT EDWIN J	LTC	0-1591654	0967	3
CORBETT ELSIE H	CPT	N-0772377	0446	1
CORBETT FRANCIS J	1LT	0-2040729	0845	2
CORBETT GEORGE C JR	LTC	0-0247637	0566	3
CORBETT JAMES J JR	LTC	0-1015035	1162	1
CORBETT JOHN F	LTC	0-1553613	1166	1
CORBETT KENNETH M	COL	0-0274041	0465	3
CORBETT MARGARET M	2LT	N-0735574	0345	1
CORBETT PAUL F	LTC	0-0405982	1264	3
CORBETT PURCELL W	WO1	W-2139978	1145	2
CORBETT ROBERT J	CPT	0-1933830	0954	2
CORBETT WILLIAM A	CPT	0-0523960	0346	2
CORBETT WILLIAM J	MAJ	0-1170687	0565	1
CORBIN DAMON F	CPT	0-0235341	0845	2
CORBIN FREDERICK	MAJ	0-2045176	0565	1
CORBIN JOHN R	1LT	0-1291726	0346	2
CORBIN JULES	WO1	W-2149245	1154	1
CORBIN PAUL E	MAJ	0-1289550	0560	1
CORBIN THOMAS J	COL	0-0262152	0562	3
CORBIN VIRGIL M	LTC	0-0236853	0664	3
CORBITT CLAUDE E	1LT	0-0548212	0646	2
CORBITT JAMES S	COL	0-0283980	0868	3
CORBOFF JOHN J	CW3	W-2205360	0963	2
CORBOY JOSEPH V	1LT	0-1585302	1045	2
CORBY GEORGE B	MAJ	0-0138321	1055	3
CORBY HARRY G	LTC	0-0123259	0655	3
CORBY JOHN F JR	LTC	0-1169906	0463	1
CORBY RALPH F	LTC	0-0300623	1160	1
CORBY ROY A	LTC	0-0240032	0366	3
CORCORAN EDWARD J JR	1LT	0-1598029	1065	3
CORCORAN EDWARD M	MAJ	0-0992606	1264	1
CORCORAN GEORGE T	LTC	0-0297997	0760	1
CORCORAN JEROME J	MAJ	0-0942338	1165	1
CORCORAN JOHN R	LTC	0-0450833	1162	1
CORCORAN JOHN S	LTC	0-0353450	0865	3
CORCORAN JOSEPH A	LTC	0-0489402	1162	1
CORCORAN JOSEPH J	CW3	W-2148109	0565	1
CORCORAN LAURENCE M	LTC	0-0370045	0163	1
CORCORAN WILLIAM J	MAJ	0-1320305	0359	1
CORCOS LEON F	LTC	0-1585770	0764	1
CORD WILLIAM C	COL	0-0276083	0567	3
CORDEAN AUGUST F	LTC	0-1315796	0762	1
CORDELL CARRIE M	1LT	N-0770039	0547	1
CORDELL HEWERL	CW3	W-2143380	0963	1
CORDELL JOE W	1LT	0-0462822	0546	2
CORDELL JOHN W	MAJ	0-2047956	1267	1
CORDELL RAYMOND L	CPT	0-0979311	0562	1
CORDEN FREDERICK	LTC	0-1100499	0961	1
CORDER CLINTON M	CPT	0-1580796	0654	1
CORDER FRANK H	CPT	0-0394557	0245	2
CORDER WILLIAM A	CW3	W-2003678	1161	3
CORDER WILLIAM M	MAJ	0-0325756	0344	2
CORDERO ANTERO M	MAJ	0-1896811	0461	1
CORDERO FERDINAND	COL	0-0338363	0868	3
CORDES JIM C	1LT	0-0411245	0845	2
CORDES RAYMOND L	MAJ	0-0395249	0263	1
CORDES WALTER F	LTC	0-1577045	0559	2

NAME	GRADE	SVC NO	DATE RET MO YR	RET CODE
CORDICK CHARLES F	MAJ	0-2054917	0657	1
CORDIER VICTOR H	LTC	0-0361754	0963	1
CORDINGLY EDWIN H	LTC	0-0268078	0857	3
CORDON CHARLES G	LTC	0-2035527	0166	1
CORDOVA ANTHONY C	MAJ	0-2056506	0765	1
CORDOVA JOHN B	MAJ	0-0969095	1162	1
CORDOVA RALPH	CW4	W-2214793	0868	1
CORDOVES WILFREDO	1LT	0-0386108	1045	2
CORDREY GEORGE F	LTC	0-0287647	0466	3
CORDREY KEITH F	LTC	0-0298737	0668	3
CORDREY MELVIN J	LTC	0-1587716	1162	1
CORDTZ JOHN H	CW4	W-2141534	0968	1
CORDY BERNARD C JR	MAJ	0-2034099	1168	1
CORE ARTHUR D	COL	0-1573826	0968	1
CORE CARROLL B	MAJ	0-0257426	0956	3
CORE EARL F	1LT	0-0406179	0244	2
CORE EDWIN R	CPT	0-1689664	0645	2
COREY ALEXANDER	COL	0-0272917	1064	3
COREY GEORGE H	LTC	0-1100931	0360	2
COREY JOLE F	LTC	0-0250482	0957	3
COREY KENNETH F	CW3	W-2142140	0359	1
COREY WILLIAM C JR	LTC	0-0542207	1063	1
CORFF MEYER	COL	0-0253288	1264	3
CORIDEN MARY H	CPT	N-0736489	0347	1
CORIGLIANO MATTHEW J	2LT	0-1031305	0245	2
CORKER NEWMAN	COL	0-0247797	0267	3
CORKHILL ROBERT K	1LT	0-1165717	0646	2
CORL ROBERT M	COL	0-0359673	0962	1
CORLESS JACK W	2LT	0-1313524	0945	2
CORLESS LEE M	COL	0-0269279	0965	3
CORLETT DONALD D	COL	0-0238482	1157	3
CORLEY BRUCE W	CW3	W-2141840	0659	1
CORLEY CHARLES G	MAJ	0-1586508	0661	1
CORLEY JAMES F	CW2	W-3000091	0864	2
CORLEY KARL C	LTC	0-0294502	1166	3
CORLEY KARL P	CW3	W-2202247	0968	3
CORLEY PUMP	CPT	0-2262320	1162	1
CORLEY SAMUEL P	LTC	0-0248992	1162	1
CORLEY THOMAS J	MAJ	0-0362929	0961	1
CORLEY WILLIAM D	MAJ	0-1042529	0561	1
CORLIES MARIE H	2LT	N-0771119	0345	1
CORMACK JOSEPH M	LTC	0-0213137	0853	3
CORMAN MILLARD B	CPT	0-0510760	1048	1
CORMIER GUSTAV J	LTC	0-1109871	0266	1
CORMIER HENRY L	CPT	0-1312283	0746	2
CORMIER ULYSSE	LTC	0-0310488	0366	3
CORN EDWARD W	MAJ	0-0353841	0247	2
CORN FORREST A	MAJ	0-0475785	1044	2
CORN HORACE E	LTC	0-0226433	0564	3
CORN JAMES F	COL	0-0129126	1054	3
CORN RITA M	MAJ	N-0727112	0562	1
CORNABY LESLIE H	COL	0-0245604	1061	3
CORNAIRE RAYMOND F	LTC	0-1998389	0462	1
CORNEIL MARION G	MAJ	0-0931317	0263	1
CORNEIL ROBERT F JR	LTC	0-0954949	1167	1
CORNEL JOHN M	1LT	0-2030660	0555	1
CORNELISON HAROLD R	MAJ	0-0430406	0246	2
CORNELISON HARRY H	CW2	W-2143286	1059	1
CORNELISON JACK C	MAJ	0-1335126	0263	1
CORNELIUS GEORGE F	LTC	0-0324310	0565	3
CORNELIUS GEORGE W	MAJ	0-1053092	0264	1
CORNELIUS JONATHAN P	LTC	0-0361546	0246	2
CORNELIUS KENNETH C	CPT	0-0454347	1045	2
CORNELIUS LOWELL	MAJ	0-2025384	0462	1
CORNELIUS MARK F	CPT	0-2262571	0861	1
CORNELIUS REX	CW2	W-2142506	1062	1
CORNELIUS ROBERT J	CW2	W-3150189	1265	1
CORNELIUS VERNON Y	COL	0-0407743	1168	1
CORNELIUS WARREN C	1LT	0-1294789	0545	2
CORNELL DALE D	CPT	0-0948969	1061	1
CORNELL GLENN H	COL	0-0239232	0765	3
CORNELL HARRY L	LTC	0-1284429	0355	1
CORNELL HENRY W	COL	0-1100055	1264	3
CORNELL IRVING B	MAJ	0-2294555	1166	1
CORNELL JAMES H	CPT	0-0378620	0845	2
CORNELL KENNETH W	LTC	0-1012080	0565	1
CORNELL MARK W	CW3	W-2207679	0666	1
CORNELL RAY F	1LT	0-1301112	0751	1
CORNELL RICHARD P	1LT	0-0299841	0946	2
CORNELL WALTER S	COL	0-0150002	0648	3
CORNELL WILLIAM W	MAJ	0-0280468	0264	3
CORNELL WILLIS E	LTC	0-1796234	0663	1
CORNER RICHARD JR	MAJ	0-0404583	0467	3
CORNETSKY ANTHONY F	LTC	0-1318964	0763	1
CORNETT ALAN G	LTC	0-0436902	0662	1
CORNETT BUSTER	LTC	0-0347339	0256	1
CORNETT CHARLES	LTC	0-1312667	0958	1
CORNETT EDNA MAY L	2LT	N-0700496	0439	2
CORNETT JESSE J	LTC	0-0107911	1144	2
CORNILLIE ISABELLE J	2LT	N-0801434	0946	1
CORNING BENJAMIN R	2LT	0-0502750	0944	2
CORNING GEORGE F	CPT	0-0477734	0446	2
CORNISH BRUCE B	1LT	0-1925314	0354	2
CORNISH CABELL C	COL	0-0144640	0658	3
CORNISH RUTH K	2LT	N-0720813	1044	1
CORNISH WILLIAM M	CW2	W-2145203	1153	2
CORNS JOSEPH B	LTC	0-0238496	0365	3
CORNWALL OSCAR L	MAJ	0-0116280	0150	3
CORNWALL PAUL W	CW3	W-2152451	0461	1
CORNWELL EUGENE W K	LTC	0-0857328	1266	1
CORNWELL FRANCIS E	LTC	0-0406121	0460	1
CORNWELL JOHN B JR	CPT	0-0537383	0846	2
CORNWELL OZNI H	COL	0-0189475	0753	3
CORNWELL WALTER J	CPT	0-0322173	1157	1
CORNWELL WILLIAM D	COL	0-0252079	0367	3
CORP JAMES H	CPT	0-0271336	1045	2
CORPENING ALBERT N	COL	0-0320631	1059	3
CORPORAN FREDERICK	LTC	0-0860100	0461	1
CORPUZ ROMUALDO O	2LT	0-0182935	0251	3
CORR JOSEPH J JR	LTC	0-1045382	0766	1
CORR WILLIAM P	COL	0-0213954	0360	3
CORRAN ROBERT L	LTC	0-0749811	0565	1
CORRE MAMERTO C	1LT	0-0890335	0258	1
CORREAL THOMAS R	LTC	0-1110429	1262	1
CORREALE WILLIAM H	LTC	0-0196483	1160	3
CORREIA EDMUND G	LTC	0-1573131	0758	1
CORRELL CHARLES L	MAJ	0-2009721	1060	1
CORRELL ERVIN T	CW3	W-2127848	1059	1
CORRELL FRANKLIN E	1LT	0-0325653	0945	2
CORRELL GERALD M	LTC	0-1037221	1161	1
CORRELL IRVIN H	MAJ	0-0934349	0965	1
CORRELL JIM E	WO1	W-2113846	0748	2
CORRELL JOSEPH T	CW3	W-2126178	1154	1
CORRELL MELVIN W	1LT	0-0468480	0745	2
CORRICK CONNELL O	MAJ	0-1300280	0365	3
CORRIGAN BURTON E	MAJ	0-1080841	0962	1
CORRIGAN EDWARD	2LT	0-0535594	0446	2
CORRIGAN ELAINE B	MAJ	N-0721251	0263	3
CORRIGAN GEORGE F	MAJ	0-2200339	1267	1
CORRIGAN HARVEY W	CPT	0-1584713	0747	2
CORRIGAN IRVING J	CW2	W-2150496	1060	1
CORRIGAN JAMES J	1LT	0-0191322	0758	3
CORRIGAN PAUL	MAJ	0-0329452	1045	2
CORRIGAN ROBERT E	LTC	0-0415951	1059	1
CORRIGAN ROBERT N	CPT	0-2045219	0246	2
CORRIGAN THOMAS J	MAJ	0-1638916	0562	1
CORRIN BROWNLEE S	MAJ	0-0464356	0847	2
CORRIN WILLIAM H	MAJ	0-1110430	0356	1
CORRINGTON LEWIS N	LTC	0-1016673	0165	1
CORRY JAMES W	CW2	W-2147625	0659	1
CORRY TED H	B G	0-0280166	0668	3
CORSA RICHARD T	LTC	0-0962685	0168	1
CORSAUT EVELYN H	2LT	N-0773896	0945	1
CORSER GEORGE E	LTC	0-0484551	1054	1
CORSER JOHN B JR	LTC	0-0244680	0766	3
CORSETTI MANUEL R	MAJ	0-1304352	0158	1
CORSO LEON	COL	0-0404852	0366	1
CORSO PHILIP J	LTC	0-1047930	0363	1
CORSON CLARENCE O JR	CW3	W-2206499	0167	1
CORSON DAVID R	COL	0-0230459	0962	3
CORSON FRED J	LTC	0-0384548	0660	1
CORSON ROY W	LTC	0-0234960	0744	2
CORSON WILLIAM	CPT	0-0306442	1045	2
CORTESE JOHN	MAJ	0-2018653	0662	1
CORTESI GINO J	CW2	W-2215588	1268	1
CORTEZ ALVINO	MAJ	0-5301740	0468	1
CORTHELL MARK A JR	CW4	W-2118521	1058	1
CORTRIGHT TOM	1LT	0-1290560	0545	2
CORTS GEORGE F	CPT	0-0456158	0146	2
CORUM JAMES E	MAJ	0-0944223	0565	1
CORWIN EMANUEL M	CPT	0-0285864	0543	2
CORWIN GERALD A	LTC	0-1036100	0966	1
CORWIN LEROY R	LTC	0-0148039	1055	3
CORWIN RICHARD W	LTC	0-0359553	0660	1
CORWIN THOMAS P	MAJ	0-1110431	0447	2
CORY ARTHUR M	COL	0-0287218	0767	3
CORY MARK E JR	COL	0-0314293	0563	2
CORY MAX E	MAJ	0-1766491	0946	2
CORY RUSSELL M	1LT	0-1313973	1145	2
CORYELL RALPH L	LTC	0-0221195	0961	3
CORZATT CHARLES W	MAJ	0-0985451	0665	1
CORZINE TROY B	1LT	0-1290904	0744	2
COSBY CARL H	LTC	0-0383501	0657	1
COSBY EARL F	COL	0-0287329	0764	3
COSBY FRANK B	COL	0-0180405	0847	2
COSBY GEORGE H JR	B G	0-0167827	0661	3
COSBY RUFUS V	MAJ	0-0949877	0252	1
COSCH FREDERICK	LTC	0-1594873	1266	3
COSDEN GILBERT C	LTC	0-0343937	0261	3
COSENTINO FRANK F	MAJ	0-4051166	0967	1
COSENTINO GAETANO T	MAJ	0-0958690	0764	1
COSENTINO OSCAR	CW2	W-2209302	0966	1
COSEY VICTOR J	CW2	W-2205619	0860	2
COSGRAY HAROLD H	COL	0-0510424	0266	3
COSGROVE EDNA S	MAJ	N-0756580	0463	1
COSGROVE EMMET F	1LT	0-1640337	0249	2
COSGROVE FRANCIS N	CPT	0-1177348	0546	2
COSGROVE RICHARD A	LTC	0-0292499	1066	3
COSHEY JOHN R	CPT	0-0182446	0957	3
COSHOW GEORGE H	LTC	0-0214030	0563	3
COSHUN WILLIAM E	LTC	0-0398337	0161	1
COSKEY JACK W	CPT	0-1100933	1145	2
COSLETT CHARLES F	CW2	W-2150172	0457	1
COSLICK THOMAS L	1LT	0-1634638	1159	1
COSLOW HAROLD H	LTC	0-0347850	0261	1
COSMAN EARL R	MAJ	0-2262840	0663	1
COSMEN FRANCIS G	COL	0-0256526	0246	2
COSNER ROBERT L	MAJ	0-2005320	0155	1
COSNER TROY L	CW3	W-2145412	0465	2
COSPER GORDON B	2LT	0-1167789	0745	2
COSPER JOHN H	COL	0-0161789	0954	2
COSS HARRY E	CPT	0-1288010	0246	2
COSSEY WOODROW V	CPT	0-0966122	1059	1
COSSICK WILLIAM	LTC	0-1306816	0863	1
COSSIDENTI JOSEPH G	CPT	0-4031451	0268	1
COSSON CLARENCE	LTC	0-0323043	0566	3
COST CARL S	LTC	0-0178344	0552	3
COST EGBERT J	CPT	0-1017941	0462	1
COST JOHN W	LTC	0-0318165	1164	3
COSTA ALBERTA M	2LT	N-0761130	0546	2
COSTA ARTHUR J	CW2	W-2152034	0556	1
COSTA JUANITA	LTC	N-0743356	0862	1
COSTA JUNE E	1LT	N-0795856	0947	1
COSTA MICHAEL M	CW2	W-2145246	0461	1
COSTA STERGE A	LTC	0-1949624	0266	1
COSTABILE VINCENT	CPT	0-0500451	0844	2
COSTALES VINCENT E	MAJ	0-1306707	0762	1
COSTANTINO JOSEPH S	MAJ	0-1638907	0960	1
COSTANZA HARRY J	CPT	0-0290909	0145	2
COSTANZA VINCENT E	1LT	0-1019341	0446	2
COSTAR SANTE P	LTC	0-1318138	1167	1
COSTELLO ALPHONSUS	MAJ	0-1555189	1061	1
COSTELLO CHARLES E	CPT	0-1552861	0847	2
COSTELLO EDWARD E	CW4	W-2141235	0365	1
COSTELLO EDWARD J	LTC	0-1165602	0265	1
COSTELLO JAMES B	COL	0-0917158	0257	2
COSTELLO JOHN H	WO1	W-2109507	0649	2
COSTELLO JOHN J	MAJ	0-0981229	0663	1
COSTELLO JOHN J	CW2	W-2213131	0567	1
COSTELLO PAUL J	CW4	W-2113850	1060	1
COSTELLO PHILIP J L	LTC	0-1846409	1066	3
COSTELLO REGIS L	CW4	W-2002965	0668	1
COSTELLO SAMUEL J	LTC	0-1180156	0867	1
COSTELLO THOMAS J	1LT	0-1647798	0546	2
COSTER HERBERT S	LTC	0-0261294	0468	3
COSTES JOSE P	1LT	0-1896465	0860	1
COSTIGAN DANIEL J	2LT	0-0442276	1044	2
COSTIGAN HAROLD F	CPT	0-0366159	0247	2
COSTLEY ROBERT A	LTC	0-0910992	0963	3
COSTLOW WILLIAM H	LTC	0-0154132	0556	3
COSTOLO HAL P	LTC	0-0174832	0662	1
COSTON JAMES M	CPT	0-0278458	0445	2
COSTON MARY M	MAJ	L-0402413	0167	3
COSTON RALLS M	LTC	0-0195604	1162	3
COSTON TONY	CPT	0-1913620	0525	1
COTA ROBERT V	LTC	0-1035229	1060	1
COTE GEORGE R	LTC	0-1893896	0968	1
COTE JOSEPH F	CW2	W-2209576	0361	1
COTE LEO J	MAJ	0-1575883	0661	1
COTE WILLIAM L	1LT	0-0972823	1058	1
COTET TROJAN I	2LT	0-1579512	0546	2
COTHAO WILLIAM Z	CPT	0-0414599	0246	2
COTHAM WILLIAM O JR	MAJ	0-1104103	0760	2
COTHES JOHN C	MAJ	0-0497171	1052	1
COTHRAN BEN J	COL	0-0290028	0468	3
COTHRAN DONALD F	LTC	0-1288361	0761	1
COTHRAN ROBERT L	CW4	W-2150495	0864	1
COTNAM SIDNEY E	COL	0-0201315	0752	3
COTNER HERMAN F	LTC	0-0270958	0860	3
COTNER RAYMOND E JR	MAJ	0-2027020	1061	1
COTRONEO SALVATORE	1LT	0-1101392	0745	2
COTSENMOYER LLOYD G	MAJ	0-2015471	0666	1
COTSONIS DENUS A	MAJ	0-1341750	0961	1
COTTEN CHARLES G	MAJ	0-0159273	0551	3
COTTEN RAYMOND D	MAJ	0-0972019	0263	1
COTTER AMBROSE J	LTC	0-1846127	0966	3
COTTER CHARLES E	MAJ	0-2263311	1061	1
COTTER DANIEL S	COL	0-0242156	0465	3
COTTER HOWARD J	1LT	0-1796763	1044	2
COTTER JOHN	COL	0-0370658	1061	3
COTTER JOHN F	MAJ	0-0518947	0646	2
COTTER MICHAEL F	MAJ	0-1293556	0264	1
COTTER PAUL M	CPT	0-1298504	0146	2
COTTER WALTER H	MAJ	0-1821828	0361	1
COTTER WILLIAM H	1LT	0-1895037	0255	3
COTTER WILLIAM J	COL	0-1318868	0468	3
COTTER WILLIAM M	WO1	W-2115280	0748	1
COTTINGHAM BROMO T	LTC	0-0463572	0752	1
COTTINGHAM HARRY H	COL	0-0330599	0864	1
COTTINGHAM JAMES S	LTC	0-0313075	0964	3
COTTINGHAM WORTH M	2LT	0-0277262	1064	3
COTTLE NORMAN G	MAJ	0-0490237	1053	1
COTTON ARTHUR J	CW3	W-2210936	1168	1
COTTON CHANDLER	MAJ	0-1294092	0662	1
COTTON GEORGE C	LTC	0-1557132	1262	1
COTTON JAMES	CW2	W-2141237	1054	1
COTTON JAMES M	MAJ	0-1635729	0161	1
COTTON JOHN V	MAJ	0-1044203	0764	1
COTTON LEWIS P	CPT	0-1285202	1046	2
COTTON LOUIS H	LTC	0-0346404	1063	2
COTTON RAY E	COL	0-0165125	0851	3
COTTON WILLIAM D	LTC	0-0229623	0546	2
COTTON WILLIAM E	1LT	0-0375381	0245	2
COTTRELL ALVIN R	LTC	0-0176259	1056	3
COTTRELL CHARLES D	LTC	0-0493082	1154	1
COTTRELL HARRY R	1LT	0-0219085	0344	2
COTTRELL TURNER R	LTC	0-0222677	0660	3
COTTRELL WILLIAM W	CPT	0-1635730	0457	1
COTTRILL FRANK A JR	1LT	0-1310072	1045	2
COTTS CLIFFORD H	COL	0-0157044	0855	2

NAME	GRADE	SVC NO	DATE RET MO YR	RET CODE
COTY PAUL M	CPT	O-1285388	0346	2
COUCH DAVID M	1LT	O-5331404	0968	2
COUCH FRANK V B	COL	O-0322971	0660	1
COUCH FRANKLIN L	LTC	O-0124526	0352	3
COUCH GEORGE H F	1LT	O-1291261	0845	2
COUCH INEZ	MAJ	N-0764932	0567	1
COUCH JAMES O	2LT	O-0257457	0956	3
COUCH JAMES R	CPT	O-0988491	0761	1
COUCH MELVIN J	MAJ	O-2000028	1060	1
COUCH RAYMOND R	LTC	O-0915860	1064	1
COUCH STERLING S	MAJ	O-0999033	0867	1
COUCH WELDON M	LTC	O-0328643	0159	1
COUCHMAN HOMER	COL	O-0263480	0952	2
COUCHMAN JOHN P	MAJ	O-1183047	1064	1
COUDRAY WYMAN F	COL	O-0207099	0247	2
COUGHER THOMAS E	CW4	W-2147674	0859	1
COUGHLAN VERNON H	LTC	O-0303437	1162	3
COUGHLIN DANIEL P	1LT	O-1797092	0545	2
COUGHLIN DANIEL T	MAJ	O-1319055	0361	1
COUGHLIN EDWARD J	COL	O-0483716	0566	3
COUGHLIN JOHN F	MAJ	O-2019558	1162	1
COUGHLIN JOHN M	LTC	O-0337030	1168	3
COUGHLIN LLOYD E	CW3	W-2152510	0265	1
COUGHLIN THOMAS P	MAJ	O-2006281	0365	1
COUGILL MILDRED N	MAJ	N-0772676	0963	1
COUGLE RAYMOND W	CPT	O-0450836	1061	1
COUK CLAUDE A	WO1	W-2123945	1044	2
COULAM DONALD M	CW4	W-2141536	0562	1
COULS WALTER F	WO1	W-2144905	0161	2
COULSON ARTHUR G	COL	O-0227036	0963	3
COULSON EUGENE M	2LT	O-1293724	0844	2
COULSON GEORGE H	LTC	O-0315452	0661	1
COULTER CHAN F	COL	O-0221082	1061	3
COULTER JACK W	LTC	O-1285916	0361	1
COULTER JOHN J	MAJ	O-0433015	0452	1
COULTER ROBERT	MAJ	O-1037740	0762	1
COULTER WILLIAM E	LTC	O-0364911	1054	1
COUNCIL CONWAY H	1LT	O-1039916	1150	2
COUNTERMAN HAROLD J	CW2	W-2151722	0665	1
COUNTRYMAN ROBERT N	MAJ	O-0343394	0648	3
COUNTS ERNEST L	2LT	O-2006350	0653	2
COUNTS MYRTLE I	2LT	N-0733700	0145	1
COUPE FREDERICK	CW4	W-2101560	0157	1
COUPENS JOSEPH P	MAJ	O-2262175	1061	1
COUPERUS THELMA	1LT	N-0776204	1046	1
COUPLAND RICHARD H	LTC	O-1685787	1067	1
COURAGE MAXWELL B	LTC	O-0430410	0966	1
COURAIN ROBERT C	LTC	O-1579309	0164	1
COURIER MONTE R	CPT	O-0276765	1067	3
COURNOYER WILFRED W	CPT	O-0504915	1156	1
COURSEY MAURICE E	LTC	O-0450427	0557	1
COURSON PRENTISS	B G	O-1173570	1168	3
COURT EVELYN H	1LT	L-0110001	0845	2
COURT JAMES W	CPT	O-1301113	0946	2
COURTEMANCHE HENRY P	MAJ	O-1100059	1053	2
COURTENAY BENTLEY	COL	O-0922370	1263	3
COURTEWAY CHARLES H	WO1	W-2128423	0254	1
COURTENAY JUSTIN A	COL	O-0168722	0360	3
COURTLAND ROGER	MAJ	O-0305838	0546	2
COURTNEY CHESTER C	CPT	O-0150935	1150	3
COURTNEY FRANCIS V	CPT	O-0338001	0146	2
COURTNEY HELEN P	2LT	N-0724606	0944	1
COURTNEY JOHN P	CPT	O-1994887	0346	2
COURTNEY LLOYD M	LTC	O-0515399	0763	1
COURTNEY LYNN C	LTC	O-0331729	0664	3
COURTNEY NEWTON S	MAJ	O-0267795	0649	2
COURTNEY OSCEOLA S	CPT	O-1004094	0451	1
COURTNEY SAMUEL F	MAJ	O-0935061	0264	1
COURTNEY WILLIAM M	CPT	O-1102680	0956	1
COURTRIGHT ROBERT G	LTC	O-1014415	0763	1
COURTS EDWARD L	1LT	O-0347482	0144	2
COURVOISIER WILLIAM	CW2	W-2102789	0647	1
COURY PHILIP A	LTC	O-1591072	0668	3
COUSINEAU IRVIN E	CPT	O-1553614	1157	2
COUSINS BERNARD F	CW3	W-2143218	0767	1

NAME	GRADE	SVC NO	DATE RET MO YR	RET CODE
COUSINS HENRY W	MAJ	O-1016723	0364	2
COUSINS MORRIS W	LTC	O-0226614	0564	3
COUSINS RICHARD F	CPT	O-0928436	1162	1
COUSINS ROBERT D	CPT	O-2019854	0360	1
COUSINS WALLACE I	LTC	O-0162348	1060	3
COUSINS WAYNE A	LTC	O-1170329	0961	2
COUTO ANTONIO	CPT	O-0505958	0348	1
COUTURE FRANK S	1LT	O-1101394	0947	2
COUTURE JAMES E	MAJ	O-1321102	1262	1
COUTURE JOSEPH R	CPT	O-1313210	1158	1
COUTURIER EUGENE A	CW3	W-2147421	0966	1
COUVILLION YELDE	MAJ	O-0199410	1037	1
COUVILLON ANTHONY R	MAJ	O-2033582	0260	1
COVAN EDWARD L	MAJ	O-1798453	0656	1
COVAULT CHARLES W	LTC	O-1595976	0765	1
COVE JOSEPH E	COL	O-0312417	0262	3
COVEL HAROLD O	2LT	O-1701676	0646	2
COVELL CRANSTON E	LTC	O-1041320	0261	1
COVELL ROBERT L	CPT	O-1302952	0546	2
COVELL SHELDON M	LTC	O-0273524	0866	3
COVELL STILLMAN D	LTC	O-0309605	0960	1
COVENEY JOHN A	MAJ	O-1302116	0662	1
COVENY JOHN R	MAJ	O-1637233	0961	1
COVERDALE RALPH T	MAJ	O-0110001	0255	3
COVERDELL VERN A	COL	O-0294862	1157	3
COVERT GEORGE W	COL	O-0532608	0364	3
COVERT GLENN D	LTC	O-1299854	0361	1
COVERT GRIFFIN J	MAJ	O-1824433	0562	1
COVEY ALLAN D	LTC	O-0996653	1263	1
COVINGTON ALBERT W	LTC	O-0506788	0366	3
COVINGTON AUBREY Y	COL	O-0339573	0466	3
COVINGTON B W JR	LTC	O-0306422	1160	1
COVINGTON D BRIAN	1LT	O-1294271	0346	2
COVINGTON DAVID L	CPT	O-0954310	0764	1
COVINGTON ELIAS W	CPT	O-0964961	0262	1
COVINGTON FEN H	MAJ	O-0385741	0346	2
COVINGTON GUY M	LTC	O-2028434	1168	1
COVINGTON HENRY L	LTC	O-1171502	0266	1
COVINGTON JAMES M	MAJ	O-0224100	1049	1
COVINGTON ROBERT E	LTC	O-0259456	0561	1
COVINGTON ROBERT L	CW3	W-2143651	0764	1
COVOTSOS CONSTANTIN	MAJ	O-2032069	0160	1
COWAN ADRIAN C	CPT	O-0498528	0545	2
COWAN AUDRA M	CPT	O-1306246	1046	2
COWAN JAMES H	MAJ	O-0324194	0245	2
COWAN JOHN B	CPT	O-0252161	1160	3
COWAN JOHN D	COL	O-0244991	0461	3
COWAN JOHN J JR	LTC	O-1325275	1167	3
COWAN JOSEPH H	CPT	O-0498122	1045	2
COWAN KENNETH P	MAJ	O-1010857	1046	2
COWAN WALTER F	MAJ	O-1112632	1061	1
COWAN WILLIAM R	LTC	O-1574219	0862	1
COWAND JESSE R	MAJ	O-0272081	0247	2
COWARD ALGIER D	CW3	W-2141238	0159	1
COWARD AUBREY J	1LT	O-2005326	0761	1
COWARD GEORGE S JR	CW3	W-2152452	0365	1
COWARD JESSE M	CPT	O-0430294	0646	2
COWARD RICHARD W	COL	O-0177497	1146	2
COWART CLARENCE H	COL	O-0300438	0463	3
COWART JAMES F	CW3	W-2149333	1163	1
COWART JOHN H	MAJ	O-2262853	0264	1
COWART LEROY	LTC	O-0118448	0550	2
COWART O HIRAM	LTC	O-0285794	0961	3
COWART WALTER J	CPT	O-0259503	0266	3
COWDEN GERALD F	2LT	O-1879122	0453	2
COWDEN HARRY L	LTC	O-0229728	0161	3
COWDEN WILLIAM E	COL	O-0312707	1154	1
COWDREY CHARLES M	LTC	O-0308297	0960	1
COWELL ALVA R	1LT	O-0213700	1063	3
COWELL DAVID H	LTC	O-1051088	0567	1
COWELL WINFIELD S	CW4	W-2147745	0964	1
COWEN HENRY P	LTC	O-1061659	0662	1
COWEN HERMAN R	LTC	O-0211155	0264	3
COWGILL JOHN B	MAJ	O-1046057	0461	1
COWGILL NORMAN H	MAJ	O-1312668	0161	1

NAME	GRADE	SVC NO	DATE RET MO YR	RET CODE
COWGILL PAUL K	LTC	O-1554702	0966	1
COWGILL THURSTON	CPT	A-0516857	1147	2
COWGILL WILLIAM P	1LT	O-0526474	0346	2
COWHERD WILLIAM C	CPT	O-0179734	0153	3
COWHIG JOHN J	1LT	O-0496764	1157	1
COWIE ALAN K	CW2	W-3430597	0968	1
COWIE ROBERT L	MAJ	O-1043303	0664	1
COWLES CONNIE M JR	1LT	O-2002064	0147	2
COWLES PHILIP C	LTC	O-0391273	1167	3
COWLES WALTER G	COL	O-0356739	0466	3
COWLEY EDWARD C	MAJ	O-0948840	0865	1
COWLEY JAMES E	LTC	O-1015212	0463	1
COWLEY JOHN H	CPT	O-1296000	1045	2
COWLEY LEONARD M	COL	O-0185078	0359	3
COWLEY WESLEY H	COL	O-0358970	0368	3
COWLEY WILLIAM F	LTC	O-0314376	0746	2
COWLING ALONZO N	CW3	W-2144024	0660	1
COWLING DEWEY JR	1LT	O-1174110	0745	2
COWMAN FORREST M	LTC	O-0291454	0662	1
COWNE WILLIAM A	LTC	O-0314974	0862	1
COWSERT LEX H	LTC	O-0910665	0862	1
COX ALBERT J	COL	O-0112219	0648	3
COX ALBERT H	MAJ	O-0232549	0252	3
COX ALLEN H	MAJ	O-0150617	0555	3
COX ARTHUR A	CPT	O-0948659	0361	2
COX ARTHUR J	MAJ	O-0995627	1164	1
COX BENJAMIN J	MAJ	O-1585312	0461	1
COX BESSIE A	2LT	N-0735606	0345	1
COX BRISCOE C	LTC	O-1309348	0862	1
COX BURNS C	COL	O-0189960	0955	3
COX BURWELL H	WO1	W-2149743	1066	1
COX CARL A	CW2	W-2208914	0466	1
COX CHARLES B	LTC	O-0273363	0766	3
COX CHARLES C	COL	O-0260195	1167	3
COX CHARLES F	MAJ	O-4070655	1168	1
COX CHARLES M	1LT	O-0445088	1060	1
COX CLARENCE L	LTC	O-0291079	0346	2
COX DANIEL M	2LT	O-0462632	0544	2
COX DELBERT	LTC	O-1290385	0161	1
COX DEMMIE H	COL	O-0216765	0162	3
COX EARL M	1LT	O-0972484	0760	1
COX EARL R	LTC	O-1181849	1165	1
COX EDGAR C	CPT	O-0451236	1049	1
COX EDGAR E JR	1LT	O-1295334	0846	2
COX EDWARD A	MAJ	O-2026004	0762	1
COX EDWIN	COL	O-0221851	1062	3
COX EDWIN W	CPT	O-1691714	0857	2
COX ELDRIDGE H	COL	O-1577052	1165	1
COX ELMER L	LTC	O-0463397	0763	1
COX EMMETT M JR	LTC	O-0975776	0368	1
COX ERIC E	LTC	O-0180367	0254	3
COX EUGENE E	LTC	O-1171505	0561	1
COX FRANCES R	1LT	N-0720923	0146	1
COX FRANK A	LTC	O-1113155	0365	1
COX FRANKLIN	CPT	O-0400600	0844	2
COX FREDERIC R	CPT	O-0182911	0653	3
COX GEDDES M JR	CPT	O-1020078	1167	1
COX GEORGE	CPT	O-0375333	0146	2
COX GEORGE C	COL	O-0136953	1147	2
COX GEORGE E	1LT	O-0540335	1046	2
COX GEORGE E	1LT	O-1014359	1046	2
COX GEORGE W JR	CW3	RW-2207419	1067	1
COX GERALD R	LTC	O-0339232	0246	2
COX GORDON L	CW4	W-2149728	1068	1
COX HAROLD S	CW2	W-2205467	0563	1
COX HAROLD S	CW3	W-2205476	0164	1
COX HARRY E	MAJ	O-0323594	0159	1
COX HENRY C	LTC	O-0247914	1163	3
COX HENRY E	COL	O-0140172	0357	3
COX HENRY E	MAJ	O-1334976	0865	1
COX HERBERT A JR	LTC	O-1824962	0864	1
COX HERBERT J	1LT	O-1547258	0146	2
COX HERMAN G JR	LTC	O-0260964	0645	2
COX HOBART C	CPT	O-1330162	0464	1
COX HOLLACE E	MAJ	O-0175848	0160	3

NAME	GRADE	SVC NO	DATE RET MO YR	RET CODE
COX HOMER J JR	CW3	W-2152372	0365	1
COX HUBERT L	CW4	W-2143840	1266	1
COX HUGH D	CW3	W-2111767	1154	1
COX HUGH J	B G	O-0244422	0859	3
COX IRVEN M	COL	O-0215126	0946	2
COX IRVIN L	CPT	O-2033631	1156	1
COX JAMES B JR	CPT	O-0337675	0146	2
COX JAMES C	MAJ	O-2271532	0367	1
COX JAMES D	MAJ	O-2262824	0365	1
COX JAMES R	CPT	O-0250026	0663	3
COX JAMES S	CW3	W-2152310	0365	1
COX JAMES W JR	MAJ	O-1913493	0366	1
COX JOE R	MAJ	O-1177749	0463	1
COX JOHN A	CPT	O-0363734	0346	2
COX JOHN A	MAJ	O-0365124	0346	2
COX JOHN J	LTC	O-0350281	0668	3
COX JOHN P JR	LTC	O-1044789	0763	1
COX JOHN T	MAJ	O-2020791	0663	1
COX JOSEPH C	LTC	O-0293460	0351	2
COX JOSEPH D	CPT	O-0483312	1147	2
COX JOSEPH F	COL	O-0214665	0462	3
COX JOSEPH E JR	LTC	O-1550992	0367	3
COX JOSEPH H	MAJ	O-0392697	0750	2
COX JOSEPH R	CW4	W-2144338	0967	1
COX LAWRENCE H	COL	O-0198411	0352	3
COX LENUAL D	CPT	O-0533008	1048	2
COX LEON L	MAJ	O-0198123	0648	3
COX LEONARD R	WO1	W-2150202	0754	1
COX LEONE M	2LT	N-0783020	1045	1
COX LLOYD J	MAJ	O-1283917	0447	2
COX LOGAN W	LTC	O-1295513	0462	1
COX LOUIE C	MAJ	O-0403556	0565	1
COX LOUIE C	CW4	W-2143184	1068	1
COX MARGARET L	1LT	N-0756909	1045	1
COX MARVIN W	CW2	W-2208107	0962	1
COX MARY L	2LT	N-0729027	0844	1
COX MELVIN R	LTC	O-0440736	0951	1
COX MICHAEL J	MAJ	O-0532817	0446	2
COX NOEL O G	CW3	W-2206482	0568	2
COX NORMAN E	WO1	W-2107891	0446	2
COX NORWOOD L	WO1	W-2146226	0159	2
COX OBERT T	1LT	O-0291179	0542	2
COX OLIVER S JR	CPT	O-2010610	1065	1
COX OMAR L	CPT	O-0492052	0149	1
COX OSBORNE S	LTC	O-0365868	0767	1
COX PHILIP J	1LT	O-0517900	0444	2
COX ROBERT L	COL	O-0156078	1156	3
COX ROBERT M	1LT	O-0496672	0946	1
COX ROBERT W	LTC	O-1994739	0865	1
COX ROWLAND E	MAJ	O-0970235	0267	1
COX ROY L	1LT	O-0969451	0551	2
COX ROY M	2LT	O-1080526	0245	2
COX ROY W	LTC	O-0195109	0252	3
COX RUBYE T	2LT	N-0764042	0847	1
COX SAMUEL V	LTC	O-1035442	0863	1
COX SARA S	1LT	N-0764307	0745	1
COX SHULER P	MAJ	O-0331223	0363	1
COX THOMAS E	MAJ	O-1582173	0554	2
COX THOMAS M	2LT	O-2035078	0644	2
COX TOM C	CPT	O-0890133	1047	2
COX VERNON G	MAJ	O-0159161	0855	3
COX WALTER H	CW3	W-2005435	0652	2
COX WARREN H	CPT	O-1541932	1044	2
COX WILBUR L	MAJ	O-1886196	0465	1
COX WILLARD M	CW3	W-2149817	0563	1
COX WILLIAM D	LTC	O-0227261	0265	3
COX WILLIAM F	CW2	W-2005326	0961	2
COX WILLIAM F JR	1LT	O-1118866	0547	2
COX WILLIAM J	MAJ	O-4031047	1068	1
COX WILLIAM R	CPT	O-0236315	0253	3
COX WILLIAM R	MAJ	O-0581545	0457	1
COX WILLIAM R SR	CW2	W-2149288	1059	1
COX WILLIAM S	MAJ	O-1637873	0258	1
COX 4TH THOMAS B	1LT	O-1646482	1145	2
COXE DWIGHT E	CW2	W-2142515	0160	1

NAME	GRADE	SVC NO	DATE RET MO YR	RET CODE
COKE ROBERT E	LTC	0-0423175	0262	2
COKE WILLIAM C	CW2	W-3440351	1168	1
COKEY MYNATT F	2LT	0-1296326	0844	2
COKWELL JAMES M	CW3	W-2143738	0367	1
COY WILLIAM S JR	LTC	0-1325634	0868	3
COYKENDALL FAYETTE L	MAJ	0-0247429	0843	2
COYLE DELLA M	CPT	N-0737858	0449	2
COYLE EDWARD J	CW2	W-2214794	1168	1
COYLE FRANCIS J JR	MAJ	0-2021166	0662	2
COYLE JOHN E	LTC	0-1295304	0366	1
COYLE JOHN J	MAJ	0-1061560	0357	1
COYLE JOHN J	CW3	W-3200132	0668	1
COYLE JOHN W	CPT	0-1297688	0746	2
COYLE LOUELLA	1LT	N-0730730	0849	2
COYLE MICHAEL	CPT	0-1913617	0621	1
COYLE WILBUR F JR	LTC	0-0207405	1263	3
COYLE WILLIAM G	MAJ	0-0967408	1265	1
COYLE WILLIAM H	LTC	0-0271189	1067	3
COYNE CHARLES A	CPT	0-1289551	0461	1
COYNE CLARENCE W	LTC	0-0386807	0966	1
COYNE EDWARD J	LTC	0-0288789	0646	2
COYNE FLOYD P	LTC	0-1292368	1065	1
COYNE JOHN W JR	CPT	0-0369215	1045	2
COYNE THOMAS J	CPT	0-1043907	1153	1
COYNE VINCENT P	BG	0-0236410	0562	3
COYNER JOHN S	LTC	0-0281366	0968	3
COZART JESSE C	CW3	W-2206122	1165	1
COZART WILLIAM A	CPT	0-1303856	0146	2
COZENS BRADBURY R	CPT	0-1052725	0562	1
COZINE HENRY J	LTC	0-1637974	0856	1
COZINE WILLIAM R	CPT	0-0901935	0946	2
COZORT WILLIAM M	MAJ	0-1177352	0157	1
COZZATI BRUNO J	LTC	0-2025750	1064	1
CRABB LLOYD A JR	CPT	0-0540742	0846	2
CRABBE LELAND E	CW3	W-2144435	0164	1
CRABBS FAYE L	2LT	0-2289327	0355	3
CRABILL CAUMUS F	LTC	0-1649261	0667	1
CRABLE JACK B	MAJ	0-1556707	1162	1
CRABTREE CLARENCE	LTC	0-1305017	0166	1
CRABTREE DON R	MAJ	0-1917637	0663	1
CRABTREE DWIGHT E	MAJ	0-0293591	0757	3
CRABTREE EDWIN	1LT	0-0964036	1057	1
CRABTREE ERNEST B	CW3	W-2144044	0960	1
CRABTREE HOWARD W	CW3	W-2152236	0665	1
CRABTREE JOHN W	LTC	0-1101336	0666	1
CRABTREE MATTHEW L	COL	0-0266557	1058	3
CRABTREE PAUL E	CW3	W-2210317	0766	1
CRABTREE SAMUEL J	CPT	0-2024247	0458	2
CRABTREE VERNON D	CPT	0-0970533	0761	1
CRACKEL GEORGE E	LTC	0-1290720	0461	1
CRACRAFT MCLURE	COL	0-0315106	0163	1
CRADDICK CLARENCE F	MAJ	0-0156076	0752	3
CRADDOCK FRANCIS B	MAJ	0-0297301	0947	2
CRADDOCK GEORGE J	2LT	0-1053095	0545	2
CRADDOCK IRA	CPT	0-0450005	0753	1
CRADDOCK ROBERT R	LTC	0-0291076	0562	1
CRADDOCK HALLEY H	1LT	0-1014349	0248	2
CRAFT CHARLES W	LTC	0-1300283	0966	1
CRAFT GEORGE W	LTC	0-0260492	0266	3
CRAFT RONALD M	LTC	0-1824363	0965	1
CRAFTON DENNIS H	LTC	0-1331378	1067	1
CRAFTON GERALD T	1LT	0-1703009	0760	1
CRAFTS CLAYTON F	LTC	0-0292094	0161	3
CRAGER JOSEPH L	COL	0-1167794	0161	1
CRAGG JOHN B	MAJ	0-1038568	0463	1
CRAGG WALTER	1LT	0-1301441	1145	2
CRAGG WILBUR W	MAJ	0-0180715	1149	3
CRAGHEAD MELVIN W	LTC	0-0415961	0863	1
CRAGIN ROBERT B	LTC	0-0193710	0346	2
CRAGO FELIX H	MAJ	0-0359430	0446	2
CRAGUN HENRY O	COL	0-0308800	1263	3
CRAIG ALBERT	LTC	0-1643904	1061	1
CRAIG ALLAN C	CW3	W-2151688	0567	1
CRAIG ASHTON M	CW3	W-2152886	0960	1
CRAIG BENJAMIN K	1LT	0-1289216	0844	2

NAME	GRADE	SVC NO	DATE RET MO YR	RET CODE
CRAIG BERTIE F	COL	0-0322720	0954	1
CRAIG CECIL P SR	CPT	0-1172425	1062	2
CRAIG CHARLES	CPT	0-0164460	0627	1
CRAIG CHARLES R JR	CPT	0-1926603	1163	1
CRAIG CHASTEEN B	MAJ	0-1296328	0957	1
CRAIG DAVID K	LTC	0-0467337	0767	1
CRAIG DAVID M	COL	0-0249272	1058	1
CRAIG DONALD E	1LT	0-0534261	0746	2
CRAIG DONALD F	MAJ	0-1546940	1162	1
CRAIG DONALD J	MAJ	0-1013919	1265	1
CRAIG EDWARD W	LTC	0-0332192	0460	1
CRAIG ELMER C	1LT	0-0485298	0844	2
CRAIG HARRY M	COL	0-0250539	1261	1
CRAIG HARRY N JR	LTC	0-1797959	0364	1
CRAIG HERBERT B	LTC	0-0140187	0451	2
CRAIG HOMER G	MAJ	0-1047933	0164	1
CRAIG JAMES	MAJ	0-1036923	0562	1
CRAIG JAMES A	MAJ	0-0351086	0660	1
CRAIG JAMES A JR	LTC	0-1285555	0546	2
CRAIG JAMES L JR	COL	0-0316415	0563	1
CRAIG JAMES R	MAJ	0-0452322	0660	1
CRAIG LAWRENCE W	MAJ	0-1311616	0457	1
CRAIG LEE E	CPT	0-0503712	0146	2
CRAIG LESLIE L	CPT	0-0924744	0744	2
CRAIG MALCOLM H	CW2	W-2205990	1163	1
CRAIG MAX W	MAJ	0-0487811	0854	1
CRAIG ORAN W	1LT	0-0397517	0345	2
CRAIG PHILIP C	LTC	0-1573830	0861	1
CRAIG REGINALD S	COL	0-0297500	0457	3
CRAIG RICHARD J	CW3	W-2148920	0263	1
CRAIG ROBERT	CW3	W-2146852	1262	1
CRAIG ROBERT E	CW3	W-2149105	0964	1
CRAIG ROBERT J	COL	0-0263226	1264	3
CRAIG ROBERT K	COL	0-1101397	1168	1
CRAIG ROBERT M	CPT	0-1323542	0452	2
CRAIG ROLLIN B	MAJ	0-1556404	1163	2
CRAIG RONALD W	CW4	W-2105119	0359	1
CRAIG ROWLAND T	MAJ	0-0409330	0662	2
CRAIG SAMUEL F	LTC	0-0225529	1163	3
CRAIG SIDNEY C	CW3	W-2147646	0163	1
CRAIG THOMAS H	1LT	0-0504172	0147	1
CRAIG THOMAS K	MAJ	0-2262305	0763	1
CRAIG WILLIAM H	1LT	0-0420334	1046	2
CRAIG WILLIAM H	MAJ	0-1574663	1165	1
CRAIG WINIFRED S	MAJ	N-0768231	0866	1
CRAIGHILL EDLEY	COL	0-0335063	0754	3
CRAIGO RICHARD L	COL	0-0279816	0564	3
CRAIN ALFRED P	MAJ	0-0399750	0444	2
CRAIN BERNARD C	CPT	0-0355261	0446	2
CRAIN CHARLES N	MAJ	0-0493744	1054	1
CRAIN HALL S	COL	0-0202070	0955	3
CRAIN L D	LTC	0-0229346	0847	2
CRAIN MARVIN E	CW3	W-2142753	0661	1
CRAIN RAY	CPT	0-1320509	1046	2
CRAIN ROBERT F JR	CPT	0-4011025	0660	2
CRAIN TAFT F	CW2	W-2151156	1060	2
CRAIN VERNON J	CW2	W-2151801	0461	1
CRAIN WILLIAM H	1LT	0-0538887	1046	2
CRAIN WILLIAM H	CPT	0-0948728	0161	1
CRAINE NORBERT L	MAJ	0-0482643	0250	1
CRALL HERBERT D	COL	0-0235629	0147	2
CRALLE JEFFERSON	COL	0-0911508	0757	2
CRAM GEORGE D	LTC	0-0204400	0651	3
CRAMER ARTHUR F	CPT	0-0261983	1167	3
CRAMER CARL H	MAJ	0-0450428	0756	1
CRAMER CHARLES W	COL	0-0179712	0147	2
CRAMER EARL D	MAJ	0-0468867	0246	2
CRAMER FREDERICK	MAJ	0-0339308	0165	1
CRAMER HOWARD A	LTC	0-0207467	0152	3
CRAMER HOWARD K	CW4	W-2001943	0563	3
CRAMER JOHN A JR	MAJ	0-1872284	0668	1
CRAMER JOHN R	LTC	0-1042049	0262	1
CRAMER JOHN W	COL	0-0242037	0256	3
CRAMER JOHN W JR	CW2	W-2152453	0161	1
CRAMER LEW W M	CPT	0-1844775	1057	2

NAME	GRADE	SVC NO	DATE RET MO YR	RET CODE
CRAMER MERRITT	MAJ	0-0476937	0154	1
CRAMER NEIL F	LTC	0-0889241	0860	1
CRAMER WALTER B	COL	0-0134092	0552	2
CRAMER WILLIS A	1LT	0-1794786	0245	2
CRAMPTON ALEXANDER	MAJ	0-0421201	0345	2
CRAMPTON EARLE W	CPT	0-0167393	0955	3
CRAMPTON ROGER B	CW2	W-2215593	0868	1
CRAMSIE KENNETH J	COL	0-0238103	0760	1
CRANAGE JOSEPH L	MAJ	0-0383782	0663	1
CRANDALL AUSTIN R	MAJ	0-1337815	0467	1
CRANDALL DONALD L	LTC	0-1289699	0366	1
CRANDALL EUGENE F	LTC	0-1042003	0762	1
CRANDALL EVERETT F	MAJ	0-1324220	1263	1
CRANDALL FRANK B	MAJ	0-0198826	1043	2
CRANDALL GEORGE A	COL	0-0261467	0966	3
CRANDALL HUBERT E	CPT	0-0348191	0344	2
CRANDALL JESSE L	LTC	0-0275124	0956	3
CRANDALL KERN C	COL	0-0148897	1156	3
CRANDALL RICHARD	LTC	0-1061349	0464	1
CRANDALL ROBERT A	MAJ	0-0272794	0566	3
CRANDELL CHARLES A	CW3	W-2136029	1060	1
CRANDELL MALCOLM S	MAJ	0-2029139	1262	1
CRANDELL OLIN H	CPT	0-0274328	0962	3
CRANDELL WILLIAM R	CW2	W-2148202	0459	1
CRANE ALLEN B	COL	0-0150038	0453	3
CRANE CHARLES T	1LT	0-2209101	0952	2
CRANE CLYDE C JR	1LT	0-1113650	0644	2
CRANE COY A	MAJ	0-0994251	0365	1
CRANE DEWEY L	CW4	W-2144945	0567	1
CRANE DONALD R	LTC	0-1036487	0162	1
CRANE FRANK S	LTC	0-1795769	0261	1
CRANE FRED E	CPT	0-1000037	0946	2
CRANE GEORGE F	LTC	0-0320884	0446	2
CRANE GEORGE H JR	1LT	0-1303676	0447	2
CRANE HENRY M	CPT	0-0887403	0546	2
CRANE HERMAN T JR	MAJ	0-0704828	1060	1
CRANE JAMES L	LTC	0-0324195	1052	2
CRANE JOHN W	MAJ	0-0397226	0463	1
CRANE JOHN W	MAJ	0-1951078	0762	1
CRANE LAWRENCE M	LTC	0-1294439	0266	1
CRANE NORMAN T	LTC	0-1692149	0146	2
CRANE RICHARD D	CW3	W-2149869	1064	1
CRANE TERRILL	LTC	0-0262570	0765	3
CRANE WILLIAM H	1LT	0-0535870	1145	2
CRANEY EDWARD B	LTC	0-1294626	0462	1
CRANFIELD REGINALD E	CPT	0-1320107	0346	2
CRANFILL HARVEY L	LTC	0-1051919	1062	1
CRANFORD JAMES R	LTC	0-0325470	0760	1
CRANFORD PAUL H	CPT	0-0546027	0663	2
CRANGLE EDWARD C	1LT	0-1999193	0247	2
CRANK CHARLES R	CW3	W-2122911	0859	1
CRANK MELVIN N	LTC	0-1309882	0760	1
CRANK RAWSER P	MAJ	0-0499857	0246	2
CRANKSHAW DAUNE W	LTC	0-0128967	0546	2
CRANKSHAW EDWARD D	MAJ	0-1535876	0164	1
CRANMER EUGENE W	CPT	0-0501090	0747	1
CRANMER RAYMOND H	MAJ	0-0497278	1150	2
CRANNA WILLIAM B	CW4	W-2126826	1263	1
CRANO JOHN A	1LT	0-1107369	0644	2
CRANSHAW WILLIAM	MAJ	0-0400745	1048	2
CRANSTON DONALD J	CPT	0-0207446	0253	3
CRANWELL JOHN P	LTC	0-0331482	0564	3
CRAPO EDWARD	COL	0-0164471	0146	1
CRAPO ISAAC A	COL	0-0187598	0650	3
CRAPSON CARMON L	MAJ	0-2032275	0664	1
CRARY ELISHA A	COL	0-0281006	0765	3
CRASNOW SAMUEL S	LTC	0-1557432	0368	1
CRASS CLINTON W	CPT	0-0295669	0747	2
CRATHERN CHARLES F	LTC	0-0471073	0147	2
CRAVATAS JOSEPH H	LTC	0-0265910	0165	3
CRAVEN C L	CW4	W-2135338	1155	1
CRAVEN HAROLD E	COL	0-1304349	0865	1
CRAVEN JOHN C	LTC	0-0959871	1067	1
CRAVEN LAWRENCE A	CW4	W-2145123	0660	1
CRAVEN ROBERT W	COL	0-0190507	1053	1

NAME	GRADE	SVC NO	DATE RET MO YR	RET CODE
CRAVEN WAYNE L	MAJ	0-0969704	1167	1
CRAVENS CHARLES	CPT	0-2011618	0663	1
CRAVENS IRA D	CPT	0-1183676	0846	2
CRAVENS JAMES J	MAJ	0-1177752	1062	1
CRAVENS MILDRED R	1LT	N-0702455	1042	1
CRAVER RICHARD L	LTC	0-0450429	0357	1
CRAVIS ROBERT M	1LT	0-1280813	1045	2
CRAWFORD ALBERT E	COL	0-0255502	0557	3
CRAWFORD ANDY W	COL	0-0275777	0364	3
CRAWFORD BENJAMIN B	MAJ	0-2000723	1160	1
CRAWFORD CHARLES D	LTC	0-1285205	0861	1
CRAWFORD CHARLES J	LTC	0-0297835	1061	2
CRAWFORD CHESTER H	LTC	0-1314449	0665	1
CRAWFORD CHESTER H	CW4	W-2115882	1057	1
CRAWFORD CLYDE L	WO1	W-2146228	0958	1
CRAWFORD DAVID J	MAJ	0-1306247	0161	1
CRAWFORD DAVID M	CW3	W-2152908	0162	1
CRAWFORD DONALD D	LTC	0-0175697	0652	3
CRAWFORD DONALD D	COL	0-0315234	0859	1
CRAWFORD EARL W	1LT	0-2040788	0645	2
CRAWFORD EDWARD W	COL	0-0366437	0961	1
CRAWFORD ELZIE L	CPT	0-1297845	0954	1
CRAWFORD FLOYD W	1LT	0-1638923	1145	2
CRAWFORD FRANK W	COL	0-0174604	0359	3
CRAWFORD FRED B	LTC	0-0157394	1154	3
CRAWFORD GARRETT O	MAJ	0-1342160	0365	1
CRAWFORD GEORGE W	LTC	0-0260012	1166	3
CRAWFORD GEORGE W	CW2	W-2207727	1263	1
CRAWFORD GLEN C JR	1LT	0-1015125	1045	2
CRAWFORD GLEN M	1LT	0-1294094	1045	2
CRAWFORD GLENN D	COL	0-0214144	0456	3
CRAWFORD HARRY E	CPT	0-0184889	0344	2
CRAWFORD HERMAN H	CW3	W-2141907	0261	1
CRAWFORD IAN C	2LT	0-1556403	1243	2
CRAWFORD JAMES C	LTC	0-0984069	0768	1
CRAWFORD JAMES N	LTC	0-0174289	0454	3
CRAWFORD JAMES R	WO1	W-2103687	0745	1
CRAWFORD JAMES T	LTC	0-1944426	0667	1
CRAWFORD JESSIE E	MAJ	N-0702333	1060	1
CRAWFORD JOHN C JR	LTC	0-1042532	0961	1
CRAWFORD JOHN D	CPT	0-1704917	0648	2
CRAWFORD JOHN E	CPT	0-0105623	0145	2
CRAWFORD JOHN N	CW2	W-2208815	1164	1
CRAWFORD JOHN P	CW4	W-2143641	0268	1
CRAWFORD JOHN T	COL	0-0237752	0962	3
CRAWFORD JOSEPH C	LTC	0-0191987	0462	3
CRAWFORD JOSEPH H	COL	0-0311190	0465	3
CRAWFORD KENNETH	MAJ	0-1824587	0163	1
CRAWFORD KENNETH E	CPT	0-1297500	1161	2
CRAWFORD LEO F	LTC	0-1288011	0859	1
CRAWFORD LETCHER	LTC	0-1313974	0463	1
CRAWFORD LINDSAY J	LTC	0-1643345	1066	3
CRAWFORD LLOYD C	COL	0-0285553	1161	2
CRAWFORD MARSHALL F	LTC	0-1036928	0267	1
CRAWFORD MAYNARD C	MAJ	0-0234826	0643	2
CRAWFORD OTTO M	MAJ	0-1011382	0757	1
CRAWFORD RALPH C	LTC	0-0294239	0446	2
CRAWFORD RANSOME H	CW4	W-2114336	0257	1
CRAWFORD RAY	WO1	W-2215389	0465	1
CRAWFORD RICHARD F	2LT	0-0419957	0145	2
CRAWFORD RICHARD G	LTC	0-0463004	0857	1
CRAWFORD RICHARD G	LTC	0-0974615	1068	2
CRAWFORD ROBERT E	CPT	0-0488223	0247	1
CRAWFORD ROBERT H	LTC	0-0325820	0747	2
CRAWFORD ROBERT M	CW3	W-2144612	0261	1
CRAWFORD ROBERT P	LTC	0-1324985	0263	1
CRAWFORD RONALD	LTC	0-0335040	0168	3
CRAWFORD SAMUEL T A	LTC	0-0332912	0860	2
CRAWFORD THEODORE B	LTC	0-1179824	1168	2
CRAWFORD THOMAS B	MAJ	0-0225830	0365	3
CRAWFORD THOMAS K	MAJ	0-1928184	0267	1
CRAWFORD VERNE O	CPT	0-2033569	0462	1
CRAWFORD WALTER A	MAJ	0-0271351	1160	1
CRAWFORD WALTER C	MAJ	0-0259890	0566	3
CRAWFORD WILLIAM H	COL	0-0273860	0156	3

NAME	GRADE	SVC NO	DATE RET MO YR	RET CODE
CRAWFORD WILLIAM H	CPT	O-1001532	0146	2
CRAWFORD WILLIAM L	LTC	O-2042774	1054	1
CRAWFORD WILLIAM W	LTC	O-0323841	1056	3
CRAWFORD WM C	WO1	W-2106060	0444	2
CRAWLEY HAROLD G	LTC	O-1107881	0862	2
CRAWLEY HORACE L	MAJ	O-2102618	1167	1
CRAWLEY LESLIE L SR	LTC	O-1293032	1161	1
CRAWLEY MANUEL F	1LT	O-1554114	0348	2
CRAWLEY NELSON W	1LT	O-1825156	1045	2
CRAYNE BRUCE A	LTC	O-0246443	0360	1
CRAYS CHARLES G	CW3	W-2144425	1063	1
CREA ANTHONY W	MAJ	O-0302527	0468	3
CREAGHE JOHN S	1LT	O-1325827	1145	2
CREAL WILLIAM R	MAJ	O-0341456	1145	2
CREAMER FORREST W	LTC	O-0252809	0960	2
CREAMER GEORGE W	CPT	O-0394996	0147	2
CREAMER JOHN S	CW2	W-2151773	0262	1
CREAN JULIAN J	1LT	O-0457819	1159	1
CREARY WILLIAM C	LTC	O-0228964	0663	1
CREASEY CHARLES W	CPT	O-0450704	1057	1
CREASEY GEORGE S JR	MAJ	O-0245242	0860	3
CREASON LYNN A	1LT	O-1165170	0444	2
CREATI JOSEPH A	LTC	O-1252819	0656	2
CRECELIUS OWEN L	COL	O-0221208	0955	3
CRECY WARREN G H	MAJ	O-2011754	0165	2
CREDE WILLIAM A	COL	O-0142394	0648	3
CREECH CLARENCE M	COL	O-0310248	0463	3
CREECH JOHN R	CPT	O-2019296	0161	1
CREECH WALTER D JR	LTC	O-1170692	0467	3
CREECH WHITLEY	WO1	W-2122267	0553	1
CREED RITA M	1LT	N-0721453	0847	1
CREEDON FRANCIS D	LTC	O-0204937	0359	2
CREEGAN MARGARET M	CPT	N-0741022	0355	2
CREEGAN MATTHEW T	CPT	O-1948572	0759	1
CREEGAN THOMAS F	LTC	O-0450687	0765	1
CREEK HARRY J	CPT	O-1877357	0762	1
CREEKMUR ARNOLD J	CW2	W-2154664	1160	1
CREEL ANDRUS	MAJ	O-0971321	0468	1
CREEL BOYCE L	MAJ	N-0735955	0364	1
CREEL E T JR	CPT	O-1542341	0667	2
CREEL JAMES C	LTC	O-0247360	0558	1
CREEL LAWRENCE F JR	1LT	O-0399506	0445	[illegible]
CREEL NORVEL [illegible]	MAJ	O-1056578	0258	1
CREELEY MATTHEW W	CW2	W-2205499	1165	1
CREELY ANDREW J	MAJ	O-0124503	0455	3
CREESY CLYDE K	LTC	O-0111641	0954	3
CREGG JAMES L	LTC	O-0277857	0365	3
CREGO CLYDE A	LTC	O-1582227	1061	2
CREIGH CARL W	LTC	O-0920556	0153	1
CREIGHTON GEORGE W	LTC	O-2018554	0765	1
CREIGHTON LUTHER J	LTC	O-0325373	0367	3
CREIGHTON WALLACE E	CW2	W-2102797	0147	1
CREIGHTON W S SR	CW2	W-2152976	0161	1
CREIGHTON WILBUR F	MAJ	O-0233736	1266	3
CREITH WILLIAM L	CW3	W-2149446	0464	1
CRELLIN STANLEY R	CW4	W-2002415	0264	1
CRENSHAW CALVIN L	CW4	W-2150901	0765	1
CRENSHAW CARLTON	MAJ	O-0237160	0465	3
CRENSHAW LEONARD C	CW3	W-2208255	0568	1
CRENSHAW WILLIAM J	2LT	O-0538514	0545	2
CREPACK GEORGE	CW4	W-2131251	0559	1
CREPEAU CHARLES R	LTC	O-1291781	0861	2
CRESCENTA WILLIAM G	LTC	O-1544943	1065	3
CRESON ROBERT F	LTC	O-1341518	0767	1
CRESPO DEMETRIO	LTC	O-0230270	0156	3
CRESS CHARLES W	CW2	W-2146166	0760	1
CRESS HOWARD F	COL	O-0224271	0656	3
CRESS JAMES B	MG	O-0139031	0151	2
CRESS ROBERT E	CPT	O-0354685	0446	2
CRESSE HENRY A	MAJ	O-0265510	0954	3
CRESSEND JOHN B	2LT	O-1053548	0251	2
CRESSLER HARRY S	COL	O-0234783	1157	1
CRESSMAN HOWARD A	COL	O-0263125	1067	3
CRESSMAN KERMIT I	MAJ	O-2043209	1061	1
CRESSY ROBERT N	MAJ	O-1580809	0364	1

NAME	GRADE	SVC NO	DATE RET MO YR	RET CODE
CRESTA GORI M	2LT	O-1054522	0944	2
CRETIN THEODORE D	MAJ	O-1688766	0265	1
CRETTON CLAYTON E	CW2	W-2215229	0766	1
CREVAR NICHOLAS	LTC	O-2042860	0367	1
CREVELING GUY L	CW2	RW-2209620	0166	1
CREVELT JAMES R	MAJ	O-0455673	0961	1
CREVENSTEN DANIEL C	LTC	O-1945336	0563	1
CREW ROBERT S	LTC	O-0316372	1068	3
CREW WOODROW W	CW2	W-2152105	1157	1
CREWDSON ROYSTON	LTC	O-0293642	0866	3
CREWE JAMES A	COL	O-0367440	1060	1
CREWES SIDNEY L	CPT	O-0330275	0145	2
CREWS BOBBY E E	CPT	O-4006661	1066	1
CREWS CHARLES F	CPT	O-1919025	0254	2
CREWS DARIUS J	MAJ	O-0406905	1060	1
CREWS FRANK D	CPT	O-1325479	0547	2
CREWS HOWARD J	CW3	W-2203631	1063	1
CREWS JAMES R	CW3	W-2141239	0760	1
CREWS LYTLE F	CPT	O-0180563	0455	3
CREWS NORMAN C	MAJ	O-0259504	1066	3
CREWS PHILLIP W	1LT	O-5209024	1162	2
CREWS RALPH W	MAJ	O-0483740	0162	1
CREWS RUFUS	LTC	O-0370829	1066	3
CREWS WILLIAM H	LTC	O-1055567	0263	2
CRIBBINS JOSEPH P	LTC	O-1030967	0766	1
CRIBBS EDWARD S	LTC	O-1895791	0766	1
CRICH JACK M	CW2	W-2153306	0660	1
CRICH WALTER H	COL	O-0325396	0852	2
CRICHFIELD MARLUS R	LTC	O-0289719	1057	3
CRICHTON DAVID E	MAJ	O-1324757	1060	1
CRICKMORE ISAAC C	MAJ	O-1302606	1165	1
CRIDER FRANK B	COL	O-0220902	0162	3
CRIDER HUBERT P	LTC	O-1579520	0763	1
CRIDER WILLIAM V JR	LTC	O-1050618	0566	1
CRIFASI PHILIP G	MAJ	O-1179694	1064	1
CRIGER RALPH D	LTC	O-0327538	0666	3
CRIGGER HARRY G	2LT	O-1186378	0950	2
CRIGHTON JOHN C	LTC	O-1945108	0164	3
CRIGLER THOMAS H	CPT	O-0234407	0262	3
CRILE HERMAN R	MAJ	O-0179668	0145	2
CRILEY FRANK W	CPT	O-1014034	0252	2
CRILL GEORGE H	CPT	O-0366396	1045	2
CRIM ERNEST M	CPT	O-0495925	1059	1
CRIM JOSEPH W	LTC	O-0290798	0148	2
CRIMMINS JAMES F	LTC	O-1698041	0961	1
CRIMMINS JOHN P	LTC	O-1112635	0961	1
CRINKLEY JOHN W	LTC	O-0237432	0864	3
CRIPE HERBERT W	LTC	O-0349602	0462	3
CRIPPS GEORGE W	LTC	O-1041322	0655	1
CRIPPS JACK N	CW2	W-2142754	0957	1
CRIQUI HERBERT L	2LT	O-1533528	1043	2
CRISE WILLIAM F	LTC	O-1114081	0763	1
CRISFIELD JACK C	MAJ	O-1289553	1061	1
CRISLIP GENE	LTC	O-1339520	1165	1
CRISMAN GERALD W	1LT	O-1036488	1045	2
CRISMAN SEWELL W JR	LTC	O-0324910	0246	2
CRISMON LEO J	2LT	O-1316991	1143	2
CRISOSTOMO SERRY S	CW3	W-2150960	1066	1
CRISP CHARLES F	CW2	W-2144986	0657	1
CRISP JESSE M	1LT	O-1645726	0845	2
CRISP LAURENCE H	LTC	O-0958444	0968	1
CRISP THOMAS F	1LT	O-1048730	0945	2
CRISPIN WILFRED T	LTC	O-2055371	1162	1
CRISSEY GILBERT W	LTC	O-0165060	0750	3
CRISSMAN ALONZO S	CPT	O-0365857	0645	2
CRISSMAN LEEROY A	1LT	O-2037204	0846	2
CRIST ALLARD D	1LT	O-1309524	0744	2
CRIST FRANCIS M JR	MAJ	O-0383997	0958	1
CRIST GUY D	LTC	O-0544815	0668	1
CRIST JERRY O	COL	O-0347135	0847	2
CRIST JOSEPH A	COL	O-0266431	1057	3
CRIST MILTON B	LTC	O-0468650	1263	3
CRISTE ANITA F	2LT	N-0726058	0244	1
CRISTOFENE FELIX F	CPT	O-0111244	0656	3
CRISWELL ARTHUR J	LTC	O-0578425	0968	1

NAME	GRADE	SVC NO	DATE RET MO YR	RET CODE
CRITCHFIELD THEODORE	MAJ	O-4074252	1267	1
CRITCHLOW GEORGE C	MAJ	O-0291243	0657	1
CRITES CHARLES R	MAJ	O-2263335	0865	1
CRITTENDEN BRUCE S	2LT	O-1119164	1045	2
CRITTENDEN CHARLES E	1LT	O-1554794	0545	2
CROAD ROBERT G	LTC	O-1114867	1265	1
CROAK LEE M	MAJ	O-1641100	0258	1
CROAN MELVIN	COL	O-0127279	0648	3
CROAN MELVIN L	1LT	O-1995395	0647	2
CROAS PAUL R	WO1	W-2114612	1150	2
CROASDALE EMMETT F	CW3	W-2153278	1262	1
CROCHETIERE NORMAN P	1LT	O-1324009	0248	2
CROCKATT GEORGE W	COL	O-0144623	1051	3
CROCKER ALFRED	MAJ	O-0271236	0365	3
CROCKER ALVIN F	LTC	O-0250971	1058	1
CROCKER ATHEL W	LTC	O-1285714	0661	1
CROCKER FRANCES O	1LT	N-0742257	1145	2
CROCKER JOHN W	LTC	O-0454608	0257	1
CROCKER JOSEPH R JR	LTC	O-0279507	1161	1
CROCKER LYMAN E	MAJ	O-1110434	0960	1
CROCKER RADFORD L	MAJ	O-1341858	0761	1
CROCKER REGINALD E	LTC	O-1117251	1167	1
CROCKER RICHARD P	1LT	O-0493914	0347	2
CROCKER THOMAS O	CW3	W-2151422	0867	1
CROCKER WALTER C JR	COL	O-0155044	1058	3
CROCKER WILLIAM B	LTC	O-0444630	0862	1
CROCKER ZENAS 3D	1LT	O-1338325	0252	2
CROCKETT CHARLES B	COL	O-0444313	0767	1
CROCKETT CHARLES N	CPT	O-0202735	0456	3
CROCKETT DANIEL	MAJ	O-0205668	0555	3
CROCKETT DAVY R	CPT	O-1111004	0166	2
CROCKETT DORSEY L	1LT	O-0973024	0263	2
CROCKETT EDWARD O	CPT	O-0257721	0745	2
CROCKETT JOHN H	CPT	O-0363824	0646	2
CROCKETT JOHN R JR	CPT	O-1327834	1046	2
CROCKETT JOHN W	COL	O-0300304	0767	3
CROCKETT THOMAS P	1LT	O-1302277	0746	2
CROCKETT WILLIAM O	CW2	W-2124712	0265	2
CROCKETT WILLIAM L	CW3	W-2103982	0455	1
CROCKFORD F H	MAJ	O-1100507	0760	1
CROFOOT BRAINERD D	MAJ	O-1553445	0565	1
CROFOOT DEWEY V	MAJ	O-2023773	0265	1
CROFOOT GEORGE W	MAJ	O-0444284	0542	2
CROFOOT JACK F	LTC	O-0245130	0966	3
CROFT BLISS H	LTC	O-0944727	1067	1
CROFT GORDON Y	LTC	O-0162409	0943	2
CROFT HARRY P	COL	O-0191937	0857	3
CROFT NATHANIEL	1LT	O-0556382	0245	2
CROFT SAMPSON A	MAJ	O-0364935	0947	2
CROFT VIVIAN L	MAJ	O-0781528	0164	1
CROFTON GEORGE R	LTC	O-0233079	0845	2
CROKE ALLAN B	CW2	W-2147462	0262	1
CROKEN HOWARD K	1LT	O-1644795	1053	1
CROKER BYRON P	2LT	O-1996886	0645	2
CROLL ALFRED W	LTC	O-0285571	0650	1
CROLL FORREST R	LTC	O-0177538	0549	3
CROLL RAYMOND H	COL	O-0228565	0664	3
CROMB VERNON F	CPT	O-1824284	0560	2
CROMELIN JULIAN T	MAJ	O-0219964	1063	3
CROMER FRANK X	CW2	W-2151002	0461	1
CROMER HOWARD E	LTC	O-1637903	0267	1
CROMER WALTER A	CPT	O-0260557	1143	2
CROMLISH VIRGIL	1LT	O-1317972	1047	1
CROMMETT RALPH L	LTC	O-2057572	0667	1
CROMWELL JAMES O	LTC	O-0309370	0465	1
CROMWELL RAYMOND F	1LT	O-1032699	0446	2
CROMWELL WILLIAM O	LTC	O-0337385	0459	1
CRON FREDERICK	LTC	O-0247279	0966	3
CRON GEORGE F	CW3	W-2148921	0764	1
CRONAN CHARLES J	LTC	O-0123564	0955	3
CRONAN FRANCIS W	LTC	O-0185365	0159	3
CRONAN FRANK X	1LT	O-2027437	0546	2
CRONAJER LEO A	MAJ	O-0571377	0964	1
CRONE CHARLES F	COL	O-0273576	1059	1
CRONE GEORGE K	CPT	O-1057715	1145	2

NAME	GRADE	SVC NO	DATE RET MO YR	RET CODE
CRONE JOHN B	MAJ	O-0118948	0754	3
CRONHEIM KURT P	CPT	O-0510494	1045	2
CRONIA JAMES O	MAJ	O-2021049	0364	1
CRONIC HENRY T	LTC	O-2015513	0168	1
CRONIN ARTHUR F	1LT	O-1316970	0845	2
CRONIN BERNARD M JR	LTC	O-1037452	0864	1
CRONIN DANIEL P	CPT	O-1303270	0246	2
CRONIN DENIS J	MAJ	O-0155150	0748	3
CRONIN JAMES J	COL	O-0922351	0765	3
CRONIN JOHN A	MAJ	O-2000905	0660	1
CRONIN JOHN F	LTC	O-0296621	0747	2
CRONIN JOHN F	MAJ	O-2239381	0963	1
CRONIN JOHN L	CPT	O-1295514	0446	2
CRONIN JOSEPH M JR	1LT	O-0544235	0746	2
CRONIN KENNETH J	MAJ	O-2046588	1060	1
CRONIN LOUIS E	CPT	O-2026902	0855	1
CRONIN MARGARET M	LTC	N-0743396	0667	3
CRONIN MARY L	MAJ	N-0720201	0467	1
CRONIN MICHAEL E	CW2	W-2116280	0255	1
CRONIN PATRICK L	COL	O-0266888	1057	3
CRONIN ROBERT A	LTC	O-1109880	0764	1
CRONIN ROBERT O	MAJ	O-4005937	0866	1
CRONK JAMES R	CW4	W-2144604	0856	1
CRONK NORMAN H	LTC	O-0403321	1160	1
CRONK ROSE A	CPT	N-0722432	1047	1
CRONKHITE EDWARD J	LTC	O-1637243	0562	1
CROOK ARHA V	MAJ	O-0262030	0758	3
CROOK EVAN J	MAJ	O-0277393	0558	3
CROOK JOHN M	LTC	O-0426858	0766	1
CROOK KERMIT G	1LT	O-1036930	0546	2
CROOK WELTON J	COL	O-0242716	1051	3
CROOK WILLIAM H	MAJ	O-1101796	1060	1
CROOK WILLIAM V	1LT	O-0288549	0266	3
CROOKER HAROLD L	2LT	O-1297503	1044	2
CROOKS EDGAR D	COL	O-1100508	0655	1
CROOKS GEORGE C	COL	O-0279325	0265	3
CROOKS THOMAS O	MAJ	O-1298667	0361	1
CROOKS WILLIAM T	CW3	W-2141539	1061	1
CROOKSTON WILLIAM A	LTC	O-0106319	0352	3
CROON OSCAR G	1LT	O-0532102	1045	2
CROPP FORREST L	COL	O-0232673	1160	3
CROPP GARNET O	1LT	O-0505421	1058	1
CROPP HERBERT H	CPT	O-1574221	1044	2
CROPP RICHARD	LTC	O-0274437	1163	3
CROPPER PAUL E	CW3	W-2149840	0763	1
CROSBIE WILLIAM H	2LT	O-1318518	0944	2
CROSBY BRADFORD D	CW2	W-2134765	1154	1
CROSBY ELMER L	CW4	W-2107919	1054	1
CROSBY ERNEST G JR	CPT	O-2262381	0461	1
CROSBY GARTH M	CPT	O-1184188	0268	1
CROSBY GEORGE C	LTC	O-0923712	0966	3
CROSBY JOSEPH C	LTC	O-0489410	0855	1
CROSBY JOSEPH W	CW3	W-2148688	0664	1
CROSBY MANFORD E JR	COL	O-0324838	1166	1
CROSBY RALPH M	CPT	O-0490456	0445	2
CROSBY RAWLAND P	CW2	W-2151396	0262	2
CROSBY RAYMOND J	LTC	O-2048885	1166	2
CROSBY THOMAS F	2LT	O-1031708	0545	2
CROSBY THOMAS L	CW4	W-2142755	1168	1
CROSBY THOMAS W	LTC	O-0300509	0868	3
CROSBY WILL G	COL	O-0100291	0648	3
CROSKEY RALPH S	LTC	O-0150282	0652	3
CROSLEY CHARLES E	CW3	W-2152373	1064	1
CROSLIN CLYDE E	1LT	O-0932514	1046	2
CROSMAN CHARLES H	1LT	O-1535427	0845	2
CROSMAN RICHARD J	CW3	W-2210970	0868	1
CROSS ALFRED L	CW2	W-2108143	1046	2
CROSS ALLEN S	CPT	O-0330391	1045	2
CROSS CHARLES R	1LT	O-1287671	0547	2
CROSS CHARLES H	LTC	O-1551593	1262	1
CROSS CLINTON L	CW2	W-2146601	0958	1
CROSS CLYDE C	MAJ	O-1824144	1057	1
CROSS EDWIN S	MAJ	O-1296330	0847	2
CROSS FRANK M	CPT	O-2047961	0546	2
CROSS GEORGE C	MAJ	O-0489674	0747	2

NAME	GRADE	SVC NO	DATE RET MO YR	RET CODE	NAME	GRADE	SVC NO	DATE RET MO YR	RET CODE	NAME	GRADE	SVC NO	DATE RET MO YR	RET CODE	NAME	GRADE	SVC NO	DATE RET MO YR	RET CODE
CROSS GERALD [illegible]	2LT	0-1541390	1163	2	CROW JOHN H	MAJ	0-1300608	1060	1	CRUXTON AMOS [illegible]	CW2	W-2144379	0660	1	CUCCIA EDWARD	MAJ	0-1947329	1066	1
CROSS GERALD [illegible]	LTC	0-0350737	0462	3	CROW LAWRENCE M	MAJ	0-0365188	0846	2	CRUXTON JOHN M	MAJ	0-1019779	0259	1	CUCCINIELLO DOMINIC S	CPT	0-1311619	0946	2
CROSS HAYWARD A	LTC	0-0427240	0562	1	CROW MILTON F	CPT	0-0407020	0645	2	CROZIER COURTENAY	COL	0-0115747	1154	3	CUCCITI ANTHONY C	MAJ	0-0976113	0966	1
CROSS HERMAN V	MAJ	0-0238978	0149	1	CROW RALPH L	1LT	0-0190765	0945	2	CROZIER EDGAR R	MAJ	0-0971754	1262	1	CUCK WILLIAM [illegible]	LTC	0-0238608	0866	3
CROSS JAY	1LT	0-1027436	1167	1	CROW RAYMOND W	2LT	0-1010968	0543	2	CRUCE WILLIAM R	LTC	0-1921415	0163	1	CUDDINA JOHN W	1LT	0-1039932	0758	1
CROSS [illegible] J	CPT	0-1175677	1064	1	CROW ROBERT H	CPT	0-0271067	0543	2	CRUDGELEY ARNOLD D	LTC	0-1580816	1061	1	CUDMORE THOMAS J	MAJ	0-1107886	1162	1
CROSS LEONARD L	COL	0-0381227	0257	1	CROW SAM C	1LT	0-0446022	0146	2	CRUEY RAY L	1LT	0-0469949	0566	2	CUE HOWARD T	LTC	0-0398947	0955	1
CROSS LEWIS A	LTC	0-0147468	0250	3	CROW WALTER C	MAJ	0-1994409	0160	1	CRUEY WOODLAND V	COL	0-0263571	0665	3	CUE LESLIE [illegible]	CPT	0-0945576	0555	2
CROSS MELVIN A	MAJ	0-2034507	0557	1	CROW WENDELL H	CPT	0-0366124	0944	2	CRUGNALE CARL A	CW2	W-2210499	0264	1	CUEBAS RAFAEL	1LT	0-0164115	0547	1
CROSS MILO J	2LT	0-2053833	0345	2	CROW WILFRED M	CPT	0-0367618	0246	2	CRUICKSHANK JAMES H	LTC	0-1283590	0865	1	CUERDA TOMAS	LTC	0-0339649	1162	3
CROSS PATRICK E	LTC	0-2263208	1068	1	CROW WILLIAM J	COL	0-0221226	0262	3	CRUICKSHANK JOHN P	COL	0-0167526	0960	3	CUERVO MABEL S	MAJ	N-0724136	0266	3
CROSS RALPH E	MAJ	0-0279866	1053	1	CROWDER ARDEN H	LTC	0-0241890	1059	1	CRUICKSHANK KENNETH	MAJ	0-0280761	0766	3	CUEVAS ALBERT J	LTC	0-0198313	0648	2
CROSS RALPH F	CPT	0-1735992	0446	2	CROWDER JOHN F JR	MAJ	0-1644809	0757	1	CRUIKSHANK DONALD B	LTC	0-0272340	1158	3	CUEVAS DOMINGO	CPT	0-0519622	1151	1
CROSS RALPH H	LTC	0-1062534	0564	1	CROWDER KARL A	CPT	0-1322525	0466	2	CRUISE ROBERT H	LTC	0-1010915	0261	1	CUEVAS-BAEZ FRANK	LTC	0-1062565	0666	1
CROSS RICHARD A	MAJ	0-1295556	1058	1	CROWDER NILE D	1LT	0-1300769	0855	2	CRUIT GEORGE F	WO1	W-2126793	0445	2	CUFF HAROLD J	CW3	W-2143671	0263	1
CROSS ROBERT F	LTC	0-0423451	0662	3	CROWDER RICHARD S	COL	0-0242861	0257	1	CRULL JOHN J	LTC	0-0299502	0358	1	CUFFEE CLARENCE J	2LT	0-4002120	0954	2
CROSS ROSCOE	COL	0-0194709	0546	2	CROWDER ROBERT E	CW3	W-2209903	0668	1	CRULL OSCAR O	CPT	0-0484332	0556	1	CUFFNEY WILLIAM P	MAJ	0-2047286	0358	1
CROSS THEARON M	CW3	W-3150365	0667	1	CROWDER ROBERT P JR	CPT	0-0971083	0659	2	CRUM CARROLL M	LTC	0-0248199	0662	1	CUITE THOMAS J	LTC	0-1096341	1148	2
CROSS WILLIAM H	MAJ	0-1324759	1062	1	CROWDER WANDA M	MAJ	N-0760261	1163	1	CRUM EDWARD M	1LT	0-1757259	0146	2	CULBERSON GEORGE F	CW4	W-2141240	0462	1
CROSS WILLIAM M JR	LTC	0-1300457	0765	1	CROWDER WILLIAM R	2LT	0-2016858	0446	2	CRUM GEORGE F	CPT	0-0317170	0745	2	CULBERT JAMES N	CW3	W-2150027	1064	1
CROSS WILLIAM P	LTC	0-0272940	0168	3	CROWDUS ROBERT P	COL	0-0228124	0764	3	CRUM JAMES H	CW3	W-2209823	1167	1	CULBERT OTTO L	MAJ	0-0281776	0265	3
CROSS WILLIAM R	CPT	0-0203421	0648	3	CROWE ALVIN L	LTC	0-0257796	0567	3	CRUM JAMES W	COL	0-0114985	0948	3	CULBERT VINCENT J	MAJ	0-0973205	1064	2
CROSSEN JOHN R	LTC	0-0331254	1264	3	CROWE DAVID B	LTC	0-1169074	1061	1	CRUM MORRIS G	CW2	W-2124174	0964	1	CULBERTSON CARL C	2LT	0-1595447	0561	2
CROSSETT JESSE H	LTC	0-0177118	0853	3	CROWE FRANK H	CPT	0-0383525	1045	2	CRUM WILLIAM P	COL	0-0237608	1050	3	CULBERTSON CHARLES L	CPT	0-1314562	0449	2
CROSSLAND ROBERT J	MAJ	0-1923526	0764	1	CROWE FRANK I	MAJ	0-0982067	0663	1	CRUM WOODROW W	LTC	0-1043308	0567	1	CULBERTSON JOHN H	MAJ	0-1176694	0664	2
CROSSLEY CHARLES H	MAJ	0-1913494	0366	1	CROWE HUBERT L	CW3	W-2205539	0567	1	CRUMB FRANCIS P	LTC	0-1100062	0757	1	CULBERTSON GREIF M	MAJ	0-2017517	0659	1
CROSSLEY SPENCER	MAJ	0-0916989	0847	2	CROWE JOHN D	CW2	W-2210905	0665	1	CRUMBAKER CHARLES H	CW3	W-2122325	0657	1	CULBERTSON PAUL M	LTC	0-0225626	0763	3
CROSSLEY WALTER C	LTC	0-0240060	0466	3	CROWE JOHN W	MAJ	0-0185508	0337	1	CRUMBLISS JOSEPH P	MAJ	0-1289473	0851	1	CULBERTSON RALPH F	CW3	W-2212867	0169	1
CROSSLIN MACK F	MAJ	0-0970014	0463	1	CROWE JOSEPH E	WO1	W-2123195	1045	2	CRUME HUGH L	1LT	0-1109219	0949	2	CULBERTSON ROBERT F	2LT	0-1324396	1044	2
CROSSMAN GILBERT C	LTC	0-0250912	0166	3	CROWELL DAN L	1LT	0-1821830	0163	2	CRUME WOODROW W	2LT	0-0395369	0443	2	CULBERTSON RONALD D	LTC	0-0287326	0446	2
CROSSMAN LESTER E	CW4	W-2103984	0555	1	CROWELL DONALD C	LTC	0-0347556	0467	3	CRUMLEY GRADY M	CW4	W-2148250	0958	1	CULBERTSON WEST	COL	0-0267015	0355	3
CROSSMAN MORTON	CPT	0-0263811	0845	2	CROWELL DOUGLAS O	CW2	W-2206800	1060	1	CRUMLEY HENRY C	LTC	0-0291575	1145	2	CULBERTSON WILLIAM L	LTC	0-1648239	0166	1
CROSSMAN RAYMOND M	MAJ	0-0453115	0946	2	CROWELL GEORGE A	CPT	0-2204414	1168	1	CRUMLEY JACK W	CPT	0-1062431	0747	2	CULBRETH CECIL H	2LT	0-1581635	1159	1
CROSSMAN ROBERT L	LTC	0-1558425	0764	2	CROWELL GEORGE K	LTC	0-0261022	0268	3	CRUMLEY JAMES L	MAJ	0-0295164	1264	1	CULBRETH DOUGLAS F	CPT	0-0385744	0660	1
CROSSON RAYMOND L	MAJ	0-0132071	0753	3	CROWELL HAMILTON T	COL	0-1643372	0765	1	CRUMM CLIFTON J	LTC	0-0474411	0557	1	CULBRETH PAUL	CW2	W-2214807	0866	1
CROSTHWAITE LAURENCE	LTC	0-0260035	0863	3	CROWELL HAROLD L	1LT	0-1313574	1145	2	CRUMMETT CLOVIS V	MAJ	0-1646491	0163	1	CULCLASURE DAVID F	MAJ	0-1893941	0368	1
CROTHERS FLOYD F	CW3	W-2143431	0561	1	CROWELL HAROLD W	CPT	0-0287212	0462	1	CRUMP ORLANDUS	CW2	W-2152699	0762	1	CULHANE NICHOLAS J	CPT	0-1107375	0762	1
CROTHERS JAMES A	B G	0-0189362	0753	3	CROWELL HARRIS C	LTC	0-1311489	0665	1	CRUMP THOMAS E	LTC	0-0150584	0648	3	CULKIN KENNETH B	LTC	0-1300000	0861	1
CROTTS HYLTON K	LTC	0-0296270	0868	3	CROWELL HENRY R JR	LTC	0-0195387	0862	3	CRUMP WARREN [illegible]	LTC	0-0273928	0758	3	CULL EDLINE C	CPT	L-0501176	0753	2
CROTTY DANIEL	2LT	0-2008742	0950	1	CROWELL RUPERT J	LTC	0-0140166	0456	3	CRUMPACKER DANIEL L	LTC	0-0337170	0763	1	CULLAR JOHN W	CPT	0-1299006	0860	2
CROTTY FRANCIS C	COL	0-0285078	1266	3	CROWELL WILLIAM B	LTC	0-0414717	0563	1	CRUMPTON SIDNEY R	COL	0-0293549	0162	1	CULLATHER BERNARD O	MAJ	0-1032618	0557	1
CROUCH ADAM L	LTC	0-1163616	1166	1	CROWELL WILLIAM L	CW3	W-2145461	0860	1	CRUMRINE WILLIAM H	CPT	0-1304183	0747	2	CULLEN ERNEST D	2LT	0-2012237	1056	1
CROUCH CHARLES P	LTC	0-0493305	0366	2	CROWIE ROBERT C	2LT	0-1560344	0347	2	CRUPE ROBERT I	CW4	W-2125201	0261	1	CULLEN FREDERICK	CW3	W-3150514	0467	1
CROUCH EARL	LTC	0-0914762	0468	3	CROWL ELMER F	MAJ	0-2006687	1064	1	CRUPI ALBERT J	LTC	0-1316319	1067	1	CULLEN HARRY F	1LT	0-1293016	0245	2
CROUCH EDWARD P	COL	0-0211019	1263	3	CROWLEY ALLEN P	MAJ	0-0354712	0646	2	CRUSE GORDON L	CPT	0-1822776	1045	2	CULLEN JOHN B JR	MAJ	0-1641209	0960	1
CROUCH EDWIN H	LTC	0-2021078	0668	1	CROWLEY ANNA J	MAJ	N-0700113	0246	1	CRUSE KENNETH	WO1	W-2143399	1053	2	CULLEN JOSEPH D	MAJ	0-1926250	0167	1
CROUCH HENRY W	LTC	0-0168952	0360	3	CROWLEY ARTHUR J JR	MAJ	0-1308109	0260	1	CRUSE LENN B	MAJ	0-1643373	0967	3	CULLEN JOSEPH F	LTC	0-1165721	0557	1
CROUCH JOHN F	CPT	0-1886141	1268	1	CROWLEY FRANCIS	LTC	0-0242335	0358	1	CRUSH RAYMOND R	MAJ	0-0500291	0348	2	CULLEN MARY A	2LT	N-0744656	0645	1
CROUCH LLOYD C	COL	0-0150056	0949	3	CROWLEY JACK A	COL	0-0172799	0251	3	CRUSIE CLYDE F	MAJ	0-1794737	0161	1	CULLEN MICHAEL R	MAJ	0-1184799	0562	1
CROUCH LOUIS C	COL	0-0279774	0464	1	CROWLEY JAMES A JR	LTC	0-1647376	0865	1	CRUSOE CLAUDE C	CPT	0-0103188	0648	3	CULLEN PAUL H	COL	0-0314377	0360	1
CROUCH ROBERT O	LTC	0-0305557	0168	3	CROWLEY JARVIN G	LTC	0-1643922	0763	1	CRUTCHER JAMES W	LTC	0-2052775	0368	3	CULLEN RICHARD N	CW2	W-3150610	0665	1
CROUCH THEODORE	CPT	0-0450696	1149	2	CROWLEY JOHN F	CPT	0-1693806	0468	3	CRUTCHER JOHN S	2LT	0-1012399	0745	2	CULLEN RICHARD S	CW3	W-2146947	0866	1
CROUCH VERNON F	CW3	W-2111361	1155	1	CROWLEY JOHN RICHA	WO1	W-2123177	1046	2	CRUTCHER JOHN S JR	COL	0-0262972	0165	3	CULLEN ROBERT D	MAJ	0-1550353	0958	1
CROUCH WILBUR S	LTC	0-0233339	0166	3	CROWLEY JOSEPH P	COL	0-0277297	0462	2	CRUTCHFIELD G M	1LT	0-0971811	0858	1	CULLEN THOMAS P	LTC	0-0277293	0264	3
CROUSE FRANKLIN D	CPT	0-0453912	0157	1	CROWLEY LEO V	LTC	0-0544765	0564	1	CRUTCHFIELD JACK M	CPT	L-0912156	0548	2	CULLEN WILLIAM J	LTC	0-0100413	0648	3
CROUSE IRVING I	COL	0-0499220	0360	3	CROWLEY LILLIAN C	MAJ	L-0118688	0568	3	CRUTCHFIELD JAMES G	COL	0-0170385	0546	2	CULLENS STEVE M	LTC	0-0411004	0147	2
CROUSE JOHN C	LTC	0-0294392	0667	3	CROWLEY MARION A	MAJ	L-1010081	1068	1	CRUTCHFIELD JAMES M	LTC	0-1010109	1166	1	CULLER HARRY G	CPT	0-0379715	0345	2
CROUSE JOHN C JR	MAJ	0-1996648	0465	1	CROWLEY MARY A	CPT	N-0722545	0947	1	CRUTCHFIELD JOSEPH M	LTC	0-0349535	1059	1	CULLEY FRANK L	COL	0-0250972	0264	3
CROUSE MARION W	COL	0-0391054	0257	1	CROWLEY MELVIN F	MAJ	0-0962309	0763	1	CRUTCHFIELD OWEN S	MAJ	0-1057395	0463	1	CULLEY OTTO	CW4	W-2142472	0766	1
CROUSE NEWT K	MAJ	0-0362918	0445	2	CROWLEY THOMAS N	LTC	0-0206496	1055	3	CRUTCHFIELD WILLIAM	LTC	0-1030352	0861	1	CULLEY TOM R	1LT	0-1018629	0146	2
CROUSE WILEY H	1LT	0-1578318	0746	2	CROWLEY WILLIAM J	LTC	0-1036490	0366	3	CRUZ ANTONIO A	1LT	0-1896532	0656	1	CULLIFER LUTHER E JR	CPT	0-0970832	0764	2
CROUSER CLAUDE S	LTC	0-0246707	0158	3	CROWLEY WILLIAM J JR	MAJ	0-0994622	1266	1	CRUZ JOSE L	MAJ	0-1294299	0661	1	CULLIGAN JOSEPH M	1LT	0-1308794	0745	2
CROVATTO LOUIS F	WO1	W-2110572	0744	2	CROWLEY WILLIAM S	MAJ	0-0992368	0663	1	CRUZ LORENZO H	LTC	0-0302453	0960	1	CULLIMORE DOUGLAS	MAJ	0-0995383	0566	1
CROVO EDMUND P	MAJ	0-2009380	0464	1	CROWLIE JOHN B	1LT	0-0965934	0453	2	CRUZE ARTHUR D	MAJ	0-0975188	0163	1	CULLINAN GEORGE L	CW3	W-2144449	0865	1
CROVO EDWARD P	MAJ	0-2011680	0463	1	CROWLY JOSEPH H	LTC	0-0290406	1053	3	CRUZE WENDELL W	COL	0-0272900	1167	3	CULLINAN HENRY J	MAJ	0-0938978	0762	1
CROW CLARENCE T	CW2	W-2209241	1061	1	CROWN JOHN R	COL	0-0914100	1267	3	CRYER CLIFFORD T	CPT	0-0212425	0453	3	CULLINAN KENNETH J	1LT	0-1645254	0845	2
CROW CLIFFORD C	1LT	0-0520787	0644	2	CROWN SAMUEL	LTC	0-0266168	0352	3	CRYER MARRION M	CW2	W-2102401	0944	2	CULLINANE HENRY J	CPT	0-1585320	0261	1
CROW DEE W	CW2	W-2208191	1162	1	CROWNOVER AUSTIN A	CPT	0-0342162	1046	2	CRYMES THOMAS P	COL	0-0235831	0254	3	CULLINGTON ALICE M	MAJ	N-0738023	1062	1
CROW FRANK G	LTC	0-0233119	0865	3	CROWNOVER HERMAN A	LTC	0-1309526	0868	3	CRYNOCK PETER D	1LT	0-1697079	0244	2	CULLISON CARL C	MAJ	0-0262738	0961	3
CROW FRANK M	COL	0-0334339	0761	1	CROWSON JAMES C	COL	0-0199898	0150	3	CSERGIE LOUIS	LTC	0-0924904	0964	1	CULLITON ANNIE C	1LT	N-0722763	0145	1
CROW HARRY S	LTC	0-0214553	0457	3	CROWSON JOHN F	1LT	0-1015475	1046	2	CUADRADO ANGEL R	MAJ	0-0995997	0653	2	CULLOM EUGENE H	CW3	W-2152887	0959	1
CROW HERSCELL M	1LT	0-1323229	0446	2	CROWTHER ADDISON C	LTC	0-0376813	1160	1	CUANANG CELESTINO	1LT	0-1896475	0864	2	CULLOTON EDWARD L	1LT	0-1320436	0446	2
CROW HORACE E JR	1LT	0-0394245	0145	2	CROWTHER ALBERT B	B G	0-0308510	0958	3	CUBBAGE LELAND F	LTC	0-1946704	0662	1	CULLUM JAMES B JR	COL	0-0224446	1060	3
CROW HOWARD R	WO1	W-2210336	1059	3	CROWTHER FREDERICK	COL	0-0236854	0166	3	CUBBAGE RANSOM R	COL	0-0295597	0465	1	CULLY RALPH H	MAJ	0-0214649	0648	3
CROW JAMES W	LTC	0-0364140	0760	1	CROWTHER ROBERT W	LTC	0-0203436	0463	3	CUBBERLEY JAMES D	LTC	0-0518322	0667	1	CULLYFORD JAMES S	LTC	0-0337155	1066	3

NAME	GRADE	SVC NO	DATE RET MO YR	RET CODE
CULNAN EDGAR P	MAJ	O-0112151	0648	3
CULP ALLEN J	MAJ	O-1298507	0664	1
CULP ARNOLD D	MAJ	O-1936647	0666	1
CULP BENJAMIN B	CPT	O-0325655	0746	2
CULP CLETUS C JR	MAJ	O-22044[illegible]2	0963	1
CULP EDWIN K	LTC	O-0234300	1263	3
CULP WILLARD F	LTC	O-1584733	0862	1
CULPEPPER CHARLES R	COL	O-0396635	1165	3
CULPEPPER DOUGLAS O	MAJ	O-1280920	1058	1
CULPEPPER JAMES R	CW2	W-3430605	1168	1
CULPEPPER PHIL L	CPT	O-1307516	0446	2
CULPEPPER WILLIAM F	CPT	O-0969305	0557	1
CULVER FRANK L	CPT	O-1014152	0563	1
CULVER FRANK P JR	COL	O-0154749	0949	3
CULVER ROBERT W	1LT	O-1165949	0844	2
CULVER THOMAS P	1LT	O-1542208	1153	2
CULVERHOUSE ROBERT E	MAJ	O-1923538	1063	1
CUMARELAS JOHN	MAJ	O-0494982	0746	1
CUMB RAYMOND F	MAJ	O-2017664	0960	1
CUMBERLAND DUANE K	LTC	O-0337561	1054	1
CUMBEY WILLIAM W	LTC	O-1030138	0557	1
CUMBOW ROBERT M	MAJ	O-0977506	0564	1
CUMBY KENT	LTC	O-1003213	0962	1
CUMISKEY FRANK	LTC	O-0492376	0849	1
CUMMING BRUCE H	MAJ	O-0957406	0666	1
CUMMING GORDON F	LTC	O-0413409	0863	1
CUMMING JAMES G	LTC	O-0122561	0548	3
CUMMING JOSEPH R	COL	O-0254292	1266	3
CUMMING RICHARD C	COL	O-0252451	1162	3
CUMMINGS ARTHUR T	LTC	O-1645259	0267	1
CUMMINGS BILL	CPT	O-2024158	0759	1
CUMMINGS CHARLES L	LTC	O-2049981	0564	1
CUMMINGS CHARLES W	COL	O-0279857	0560	3
CUMMINGS CHARLES W	MAJ	O-1824145	0266	1
CUMMINGS CLARENCE L	CW4	W-2145379	1267	2
CUMMINGS CLARENCE S	MAJ	O-0423447	0756	1
CUMMINGS DAVID L	CW2	W-2214712	0567	1
CUMMINGS EDWARD H	MAJ	O-1015719	0363	1
CUMMINGS ELDRIDGE M	LTC	O-0383366	0960	1
CUMMINGS FRED A	MAJ	O-2012366	0164	1
CUMMINGS FREDERICK	MAJ	O-1300609	0561	1
CUMMINGS GEORGE B	LTC	O-1535742	0557	1
CUMMINGS GEORGE E	CPT	O-0492400	1159	1
CUMMINGS HUBERT G	COL	O-1042079	1267	1
CUMMINGS JACK	CPT	O-0123500	0654	3
CUMMINGS JAMES R	CPT	O-1165835	0446	2
CUMMINGS JAMES H	WO1	W-2128290	1145	2
CUMMINGS JOE V	MAJ	O-1635744	0960	1
CUMMINGS JOHN C	CW2	W-2152454	0260	1
CUMMINGS JOHN F	MAJ	O-1014796	0562	1
CUMMINGS JOHN J	MAJ	O-0124516	0648	3
CUMMINGS JOHN L	LTC	O-0230573	0761	3
CUMMINGS JOHN P	CPT	O-0920339	1046	2
CUMMINGS JOSEPH H	LTC	O-0255055	1066	3
CUMMINGS LEIGHTON W	CPT	O-0180972	0360	3
CUMMINGS LEO F	CPT	O-2262132	1060	1
CUMMINGS LEONARD D	COL	O-0276957	0560	1
CUMMINGS MELVILLE F	2LT	O-0473694	0545	2
CUMMINGS MICHAEL P	CW3	W-2148011	1262	1
CUMMINGS RAYMOND H	LTC	O-1018034	1068	1
CUMMINGS RICHARD W	MAJ	O-0220354	1159	3
CUMMINGS STANLEY L	MAJ	O-1594097	0563	1
CUMMINGS TAFT	MAJ	O-0505391	0556	1
CUMMINGS THOMAS F	COL	O-1895707	0665	3
CUMMINGS VINCENT P	LTC	O-0360954	0666	3
CUMMINGS WALTER A	1LT	O-1294794	0446	2
CUMMINGS WILMER F	LTC	O-0499464	0556	3
CUMMINS EARL M	CPT	O-0522938	0646	2
CUMMINS GERALD J	MAJ	O-1011633	0564	3
CUMMINS HALDANE C	CPT	O-1703187	0146	2
CUMMINS JAMES F JR	2LT	O-0466786	0445	2
CUMMINS JOHN F	CW3	W-2207456	0867	1
CUMMINS KENNETH G	LTC	O-0292361	0667	3
CUMMISKEY JOHN T	MAJ	O-0321159	1166	3
CUNDELL ARTHUR B	MAJ	O-0150854	0648	3
CUNDIFF CARL H	COL	O-0447827	0863	3
CUNDIFF CLARE R	MAJ	O-0286049	0548	1
CUNDIFF PAUL L	LTC	O-0321678	0660	1
CUNDIFF ROY	CPT	O-0364165	0346	2
CUNDIFF WILGUS B	CPT	O-1110439	1045	2
CUNEO RAYMOND F	2LT	O-1185357	0645	2
CUNJAK FRANKLIN J	CPT	O-1695251	0445	2
CUNNEEN LEONARD J	CPT	O-2023885	0761	1
CUNNINGHAM ALBERT	MAJ	O-1920066	1066	1
CUNNINGHAM ANDREW W	1LT	O-1056682	1244	2
CUNNINGHAM ARTHUR O	CPT	O-0299179	1160	1
CUNNINGHAM AUDREY W	MAJ	O-0940776	0960	1
CUNNINGHAM BERNARD W	CPT	O-0243216	0962	3
CUNNINGHAM BILLY H	LTC	O-1935929	1168	1
CUNNINGHAM CALHOUN O	LTC	O-0188590	1061	3
CUNNINGHAM CHARLES	COL	O-0281312	1064	3
CUNNINGHAM CHARLES C	LTC	O-2019994	0867	1
CUNNINGHAM CHARLES J	1LT	O-1287150	0446	2
CUNNINGHAM CHARLES J	LTC	O-1822538	0364	1
CUNNINGHAM CHARLES W	CPT	O-0171622	0545	2
CUNNINGHAM CLARK M	CPT	O-0335255	0245	2
CUNNINGHAM DANIEL L	MAJ	O-2042729	0965	1
CUNNINGHAM DAVID C	1LT	O-1549692	1262	1
CUNNINGHAM DENNIS R	LTC	O-1175679	0564	1
CUNNINGHAM DONALD S	CPT	O-5301510	0864	2
CUNNINGHAM EDMOND	COL	O-0192834	0560	3
CUNNINGHAM ELIJAH W	MAJ	O-1796242	0762	1
CUNNINGHAM EMORY B	CW2	W-2146825	0956	1
CUNNINGHAM FINIS A	CPT	O-0493024	0450	2
CUNNINGHAM FRANCIS	1LT	O-1018159	1045	2
CUNNINGHAM FRED I	CW2	W-3200342	1166	1
CUNNINGHAM FREDRIC	2LT	O-1014971	0445	2
CUNNINGHAM GEORGE L	LTC	O-0226389	1064	3
CUNNINGHAM GEORGE M	MAJ	O-0259835	1267	3
CUNNINGHAM GEORGE W	1LT	O-1104596	1147	2
CUNNINGHAM GORDON L	LTC	O-1635747	1266	1
CUNNINGHAM HAROLD L	LTC	O-0453094	0261	1
CUNNINGHAM HARRY R	MAJ	O-1596519	0164	1
CUNNINGHAM HENRY K	MAJ	O-0167050	0756	3
CUNNINGHAM HENRY L	CPT	O-1018769	0454	2
CUNNINGHAM HERBERT B	MAJ	O-1303251	1058	2
CUNNINGHAM HUGH J	COL	O-0150281	0555	3
CUNNINGHAM HUSTON P	LTC	O-0365910	0263	3
CUNNINGHAM JACK	MAJ	O-1342164	0962	1
CUNNINGHAM JACK C	CPT	O-1311581	0747	2
CUNNINGHAM JACQUES A	LTC	O-2041090	1062	1
CUNNINGHAM JAMES A	COL	O-0111196	0950	3
CUNNINGHAM JAMES A	CW2	W-2145134	0858	1
CUNNINGHAM JAMES C	COL	O-0229410	0763	3
CUNNINGHAM JAMES E	CPT	O-1702366	0744	2
CUNNINGHAM JAMES M	LTC	O-0287625	0564	3
CUNNINGHAM JAMES M	CPT	O-0508189	0846	2
CUNNINGHAM JAMES P	LTC	O-1286252	0865	1
CUNNINGHAM JOHN E JR	CPT	O-1304351	0146	2
CUNNINGHAM JOHN F	1LT	O-1307517	0644	2
CUNNINGHAM JOHN J	CPT	O-0888269	1046	2
CUNNINGHAM JOHN J	CW3	W-2147281	0662	1
CUNNINGHAM JOHN K	COL	O-0277284	1266	3
CUNNINGHAM JOHN L	LTC	O-0352620	0346	2
CUNNINGHAM JOHN L	LTC	O-1168619	0763	1
CUNNINGHAM JOHN O	MAJ	O-1172824	0762	1
CUNNINGHAM JOHN P	MAJ	O-1997962	0163	1
CUNNINGHAM JOHN R	MAJ	O-1100511	0961	1
CUNNINGHAM JOHN W	LTC	O-0496400	0655	1
CUNNINGHAM JOSEPH B	MAJ	O-0349125	0561	1
CUNNINGHAM JOSEPH H	MAJ	O-1640354	0160	1
CUNNINGHAM LAFAYETTE	LTC	O-0270588	1060	1
CUNNINGHAM LAWRENCE	MAJ	O-1018446	0263	1
CUNNINGHAM LEROY	LTC	O-0447298	1165	1
CUNNINGHAM MARY F	2LT	N-0703522	0944	1
CUNNINGHAM MILFORD A	CW2	W-2214296	0768	1
CUNNINGHAM MILTON E	CW3	W-2148487	0569	1
CUNNINGHAM NOBLE O	LTC	O-1637249	1163	1
CUNNINGHAM OWEN	MAJ	O-0243511	0860	3
CUNNINGHAM PHILLIP J	LTC	O-1688563	0168	1
CUNNINGHAM RALPH F	LTC	O-1001119	0865	1
CUNNINGHAM RAYMOND J	COL	O-0117798	1056	3
CUNNINGHAM RICHARD T	CW3	W-2147538	0665	1
CUNNINGHAM ROBERT D	MAJ	O-0192183	1056	3
CUNNINGHAM ROBERT F	LTC	O-0260119	0666	3
CUNNINGHAM ROBERT M	CPT	O-2300857	0765	1
CUNNINGHAM ROBERT R	1LT	O-2000175	0146	2
CUNNINGHAM ROBERT S	LTC	O-0341959	0267	3
CUNNINGHAM ROBERT T	COL	O-0207409	0961	3
CUNNINGHAM ROY D	1LT	O-1015917	0151	2
CUNNINGHAM ROY W	MAJ	O-2202212	0166	1
CUNNINGHAM RUSSELL E	MAJ	O-1882432	1267	1
CUNNINGHAM THOMAS J	COL	O-0234500	1065	3
CUNNINGHAM THOMAS P	MAJ	O-1649116	0161	1
CUNNINGHAM THOMAS S	1LT	O-1255344	0645	2
CUNNINGHAM VAN H	LTC	O-0157557	1049	1
CUNNINGHAM WALTER H	LTC	O-1317893	0962	1
CUNNINGHAM WILLIAM A	MAJ	O-1999200	1060	1
CUNNINGHAM WILLIAM H	1LT	O-2007102	0947	2
CUNNINGHAM WILLIAM L	CW3	W-2207680	0167	1
CUNNINGTON EARL C	LTC	O-2047609	1167	1
CUNYUS PAUL A	COL	O-0238501	0965	3
CUNZEMAN PAUL W	CW4	W-2141541	0964	1
CUOZZO SALVATORE	MAJ	O-1339849	0164	1
CUPIT ELMER H	CW2	W-2150540	0661	1
CUPIT WILLIAM F	CW2	W-2145965	0566	1
CUPOLI CHARLES	CPT	O-1917733	0765	2
CUPP DONALD E	CPT	O-0519328	0345	2
CUPP HORACE R	COL	O-0312105	1063	3
CUPP WENDELL L	LTC	O-0450413	1054	1
CUPP WILLIAM D	MAJ	O-2262743	0963	1
CUPPLES REUBEN O	LTC	O-0450838	0757	1
CUPPS CECIL C JR	LTC	O-1061666	0463	1
CUPRYS FERDINAND	MAJ	O-1116216	0956	1
CURCIO LOUISE T	MAJ	N-0752115	1265	3
CURCIO MICHAEL S	CW4	W-2111364	1056	1
CURCIO ROCCO A	CW3	W-2152006	0765	1
CURD JOHN T	LTC	O-0339351	0361	1
CURD PAUL	CPT	O-0957604	0361	2
CURETON EDMUND H	MAJ	O-0232129	0563	3
CURETON EVERARD F JR	1LT	O-1286799	1143	2
CURETON HUGH R	CPT	O-0318180	0559	3
CURFMAN RALPH H	LTC	O-1288713	0261	1
CURIE ROBERT V	CPT	O-0455924	1043	2
CURIT LOUIS I	MAJ	O-0990264	1064	1
CURL FRED A	LTC	O-0334664	0765	3
CURL JAMES P	MAJ	O-0472654	0351	1
CURL LOUIS J JR	MAJ	O-1292139	0946	2
CURL VINCENT L	LTC	O-0470047	0754	1
CURLEY ARTHUR L	CW3	W-2108023	0256	1
CURLEY BERNARD J	MAJ	O-1547249	0761	1
CURLEY DONALD W	LTC	O-1296662	1263	1
CURLEY LEO J	MAJ	O-0526409	0957	2
CURLEY WILFRED J	LTC	O-1797261	0658	1
CURLL RAYMOND A	MAJ	O-1794918	1060	2
CURNUTT SIDNEY K	MAJ	O-1540399	0661	1
CURO HAROLD W	1LT	O-0374189	0467	3
CURRAN BOB L	MAJ	O-0973913	0164	1
CURRAN CHARLES L	LTC	O-0455007	0865	3
CURRAN DANIEL J	LTC	O-0322404	1149	3
CURRAN EDWARD J JR	LTC	O-2263083	0968	1
CURRAN ELIZABETH	1LT	N-0731878	0646	1
CURRAN GEORGE A	1LT	O-0360172	0644	2
CURRAN GEORGE F	1LT	O-0427547	0645	2
CURRAN JAMES J	CPT	O-1307807	0255	2
CURRAN JOHN C	LTC	O-0495200	0859	1
CURRAN JOHN F	MAJ	O-0235129	0455	3
CURRAN JOHN J	2LT	O-0446735	0143	2
CURRAN JOHN J JR	MAJ	O-1324245	0967	3
CURRAN JOHN K	CPT	O-1182806	1058	1
CURRAN JOHN M	1LT	O-1181956	1060	2
CURRAN LOUIS F	1LT	O-1785794	0844	2
CURRAN MICHAEL F	1LT	O-2011078	0948	2
CURRAN MORRIS T	LTC	O-0271497	1066	3
CURRAN PATRICK H	1LT	O-1874404	0952	2
CURRAN PHILIP J	MAJ	O-1637252	0462	1
CURRAN WILLIAM P	LTC	O-0473756	1054	1
CURRAY JACK L	LTC	O-1056684	1262	1
CURRELL RALPH W	2LT	O-1179353	0545	2
CURREN FREDERICK	LTC	O-0211326	0850	3
CURRENCE DONALD R	1LT	O-1925385	0959	2
CURRENCE HOMER C	LTC	O-1116836	0264	1
CURRENT ANDREW M	1LT	O-0367761	1043	2
CURRENT FRANCIS B	CPT	O-0406444	0348	2
CURREY CLARENCE A	CW3	W-2142071	0463	1
CURREY JOHN R	COL	O-0176207	1059	3
CURREY NEIL P	1LT	O-1031066	1145	2
CURRIE JAMES W	LTC	O-0931964	0766	3
CURRIE RALPH H	1LT	O-0510031	0753	1
CURRIE WILLIAM B	COL	O-0242572	1062	3
CURRIE WILSIE A	LTC	O-0923848	0767	3
CURRIER DALLAS O	CPT	O-0888850	1048	2
CURRIER DONALD E	COL	O-0245107	1152	3
CURRIER FRANK T	MAJ	O-1287152	1264	1
CURRIER GREGORY F	MAJ	O-0481802	0356	1
CURRIER JOSEPH W	CPT	O-0464864	1045	2
CURRIER LELAND L	LTC	O-0215071	0664	3
CURRIER RUSSELL E	MAJ	O-1050619	1064	1
CURRIN FLEMING B JR	LTC	O-1588504	0961	1
CURRIN VIRGIL D	LTC	O-1055568	0565	3
CURRY AL J JR	1LT	O-1106077	1145	2
CURRY ALEXANDER JR	CW2	W-2214921	0167	1
CURRY CORNIE B JR	MAJ	O-2263582	1167	1
CURRY DON C	LTC	O-0448891	1059	3
CURRY DONALD G	MAJ	O-1876335	0866	1
CURRY FLOYD A	LTC	O-0374857	0868	3
CURRY FLOYD L	CW4	W-2146770	0156	1
CURRY FRANK C	LTC	O-0379215	0447	2
CURRY GEORGE T	CPT	O-0385600	0746	2
CURRY HAROLD R	CW3	W-2119300	0659	1
CURRY HILLARY J JR	CW3	W-2146959	0962	1
CURRY HUGH J	LTC	O-0937878	0764	1
CURRY JAMES D JR	1LT	O-1107376	1045	2
CURRY JAMES L	CW2	W-2003380	1146	1
CURRY JAMES R	MAJ	O-1533041	1263	1
CURRY JOHN H	2LT	O-1638935	0345	2
CURRY JOHN M	2LT	O-2036365	0645	2
CURRY JOHN W	1LT	O-0525004	1145	2
CURRY KENNETH E	LTC	O-1308312	0667	1
CURRY LASSIE	2LT	N-0767432	0439	2
CURRY MICHAEL E	LTC	O-0289209	1160	2
CURRY MORRIS J	CPT	O-1295345	1046	2
CURRY PAUL E	CW3	W-2207047	0868	1
CURRY RAY H	CPT	O-1589145	0662	1
CURRY ROBERT E	CW2	W-2150246	0761	1
CURRY ROBERT T	MAJ	O-1885715	0868	1
CURRY ULYSSES S	MAJ	O-1002191	0655	1
CURRY VEARL M	LTC	O-1316020	1067	3
CURRY VIRGIL O	LTC	O-0237474	0466	3
CURRY WILLIAM M	CW3	W-2150847	1263	1
CURTES JOHN G	CPT	O-1548385	1055	1
CURTICE NORMAN B	MAJ	O-0108023	1155	3
CURTIN EDWARD N	2LT	O-1309668	1044	2
CURTIN ELDON R	1LT	O-1794916	1044	2
CURTIN ELMER P	LTC	O-0305653	0457	1
CURTIN JOSEPH S	LTC	O-1030870	1060	1
CURTIN JOSEPH T	MAJ	O-0158132	0749	3
CURTIN LAWRENCE R	CW3	W-2146150	0263	1
CURTIN MICHAEL F	LTC	O-2044397	1162	1
CURTIS ARTHUR W	COL	O-0903616	1166	3
CURTIS BENJAMIN C	LTC	O-1103122	0361	1
CURTIS BERNARD L	LTC	O-0464429	0954	1
CURTIS CHARLES C JR	COL	O-0260172	0746	2
CURTIS CLARENCE E JR	COL	O-0298246	0564	3
CURTIS CLARENCE R	MAJ	O-1316621	0264	1
CURTIS CLARK C	MAJ	O-0202202	0462	3
CURTIS CLAUDE F JR	LTC	O-1324516	0163	1
CURTIS DONALD L	MAJ	O-1533763	0459	1
CURTIS DONALD S	MAJ	O-0277291	0363	3
CURTIS DONALD W	MAJ	O-2033885	0264	1

NAME	GRADE	SVC NO	DATE RET MO YR	RET CODE
[illegible]	MAJ	[illegible]	[illegible]	1
CURTIS [illegible]	[illegible]	[illegible]	[illegible]	1
[illegible]	MAJ	[illegible]	1063	1
[illegible]	[illegible]	[illegible]	0645	2
[illegible]	COL	[illegible]	1151	1
[illegible]	[illegible]	[illegible]	1261	3
[illegible]	CPT	[illegible]	[illegible]	3
CURTIS [illegible]	[illegible]	[illegible]	[illegible]	1
[illegible]	[illegible]	W-214[illegible]	[illegible]	2
[illegible]	[illegible]	[illegible]	[illegible]	1
CURTIS [illegible]	COL	[illegible]	1055	3
CURTIS [illegible]	MAJ	[illegible]	[illegible]	3
CURTIS [illegible]	MAJ	[illegible]	1158	3
CURTIS [illegible]	[illegible]	W-2149846	0361	1
CURTIS [illegible]	COL	[illegible]	0855	3
CURTIS [illegible]	MAJ	[illegible]	1162	2
CURTIS MERRILL J	LTC	[illegible]	1054	3
CURTIS [illegible]	1LT	[illegible]	0347	2
CURTIS [illegible]	COL	[illegible]	0766	3
CURTIS OWEN A	MAJ	0-0156045	0756	3
CURTIS REUBEN F	COL	0-0262460	0666	3
CURTIS ROBERT F	1LT	0-1011326	0945	2
CURTIS ROBERT J	COL	0-0474530	0668	1
CURTIS ROBERT MC	1LT	0-0345716	1144	2
CURTIS ROBERT R	LTC	0-0948203	0868	1
CURTIS ROBERT W	MAJ	0-2262252	0364	1
CURTIS ROSS F	MAJ	0-1307377	0863	1
CURTIS RUSSELL J	CPT	0-0406371	1046	2
CURTIS RUSSELL W	LTC	0-0121081	0452	3
CURTIS SELVIE J	COL	0-0300642	0547	2
CURTIS THEODORE F JR	COL	0-0254348	1158	1
CURTIS VERL M	CW2	W-2111340	1058	1
CURTIS VERNON C	LTC	0-0322886	0560	3
CURTIS WALKER L	CPT	0-0441314	0945	2
CURTIS WILLIAM F JR	LTC	0-0240363	0166	3
CURTIS WILLIAM L	CPT	0-4005775	0566	1
CURTIS WILLIAM L	WO1	W-2151784	0164	1
CURTIS WILLIAM M	CW4	W-2205399	0167	1
CURTIS WILLMOTTE	LTC	0-0406307	1060	1
CURTISS CLAUDE D	COL	0-0183804	0455	3
CURTISS ROBERT R	LTC	0-0263242	0266	3
CURTISS ROBERT H	MAJ	0-1633788	0357	1
CURTIUS BENJAMIN L	CW3	W-2143428	0663	1
CURTNER MYRON L	COL	0-0214367	0749	3
CURTS CHARLES W	1LT	0-1179927	0847	2
CURTS HOLROYD R	MAJ	0-1100066	0647	2
CURZON MYRON W	MAJ	0-1894625	0546	2
CUSAC WILLIAM M JR	CW3	W-2205072	0568	1
CUSACK JOHN P JR	CPT	0-1315036	0646	2
CUSACK WILLIAM P	1LT	0-1258670	0244	2
CUSANELLI CARL F	LTC	0-1296495	1060	1
CUSATO SYLVANUS F	CPT	0-1551382	0468	3
CUSHING ANTHONY	MAJ	0-1195966	0863	1
CUSHING CARL F	CW2	W-2110121	1052	2
CUSHING EMORY C	COL	0-0175235	0450	2
CUSHING EUGENE G	MG	0-0286447	0965	3
CUSHING JOSEPH	COL	0-0349677	0660	1
CUSHING LLOYD W	LTC	0-0419425	1062	1
CUSHMAN ALLERTON	COL	0-0265242	0967	3
CUSHMAN EDWIN P	COL	0-0275995	0867	3
CUSHMAN JOSEPH W	MAJ	0-1305735	0657	1
CUSHMAN ROBERT H	LTC	0-1641211	0566	1
CUSHMAN ROBERT P	1LT	0-0362963	0246	2
CUSHNER JOHN W	CPT	0-1305736	0346	2
CUSICK BART C JR	MAJ	0-1108596	0265	1
CUSICK JOHN	MAJ	0-1044791	1157	1
CUSICK JOSEPH W	1LT	0-1039301	1056	1
CUSTER BRUCE C W	COL	0-0247445	0659	2
CUSTER CHALMERS R	MAJ	0-1643389	1060	1
CUSTER CHARLES A	COL	0-0277290	0961	1
CUSTER GEORGE W	LTC	0-0242157	0245	2
CUSTER HUBERT O	2LT	0-2005443	0246	2
CUSTER MARVIN B	COL	0-0455675	0862	1
CUSTIS EARL R	COL	0-0155311	0947	2
CUSTIS WARREN L	CW3	W-3150347	0968	1

NAME	GRADE	SVC NO	DATE RET MO YR	RET CODE
[illegible] LEONARD F	MAJ	0-4021261	1168	1
[illegible] JOHN A	COL	0-0154314	0648	3
CUTHBERT CLARENCE T	COL	0-0298077	0365	2
CUTHBERT DONALD A	COL	0-0276375	0167	3
CUTHBERT JAMES J JR	MAJ	0-0178761	0844	2
CUTHBERT RICHARD F	2LT	0-2036052	0445	2
CUTHBERTSON C L	CPT	0-1555192	0259	1
CUTHBERTSON WILLIAM	CW4	W-2148228	0667	2
CUTLER ALLEN G	2LT	0-1310580	0945	2
CUTLER CHESTER B	COL	0-0256629	0960	3
CUTLER DAVID	WO1	W-2122293	0147	1
CUTLER HARRY S	MAJ	0-0115335	0355	3
CUTLER IRVING	CPT	0-1299535	0159	1
CUTLER LEO J	1LT	0-0369554	1143	2
CUTLER MORTON T	MAJ	0-2047964	0964	1
CUTLER NORMAN R	1LT	0-1010998	1045	2
CUTLER QUENTIN R	CW2	W-2205667	0361	1
CUTLER RAYMOND H	LTC	0-1296822	0167	1
CUTLER SAMUEL	LTC	0-0209232	1163	3
CUTLER THORNTON L	COL	0-0124511	0555	3
CUTRER JAMES F	2LT	0-1303861	0445	2
CUTRER LEWIS W JR	2LT	0-4033959	0956	2
CUTSHALL LEONARD L	COL	0-0216453	1263	3
CUTSHALL LEONARD W	MAJ	0-0397698	0561	1
CUTTER HAROLD C	LTC	0-0271400	0868	3
CUTTER HENRY T JR	LTC	0-1329329	0465	1
CUTTER LEON E	CPT	0-0165611	0653	3
CUTTER LLOYD A	LTC	0-0237183	0465	3
CUTTIN LUIGI W	CW2	W-2104990	0943	2
CUTTING ROBERT F	1LT	0-0961764	1152	2
CUTTS ALFICE V	CW4	W-2148076	1068	1
CUTTS EVERETT T	CW2	RW-2146188	0263	1
CUTTS FRANCIS W	LTC	0-1057028	1167	1
CUTTS WARREN G JR	2LT	0-0539214	0245	2
CUVIELLO JOSEPH M	LTC	0-0309671	1166	3
COZICK ROBERT A	COL	0-0036311	0468	1
CWALINSKI EDWARD J	CW3	W-2110769	0659	1
CYPRET CLELLA O	CPT	0-0479220	0659	1
CYR EUCLID J	1LT	0-1168622	1145	2
CYR HUBERT G	CW4	W-2101580	1154	1
CYR LUCIEN	1LT	0-1946941	0556	1
CYRIER BERNARD A	CPT	0-1313155	0447	2
CZACH MARY A	MAJ	N-0731473	0566	1
CZAJKOWSKI JOHN J	2LT	0-1015853	0845	2
CZAJKOWSKI WALTER S	LTC	0-0451521	0557	1
CZAPLA EDWIN H	LTC	0-0450742	0557	1
CZAPLA WALTER A	CPT	0-2017022	0266	2
CZAPRAN WALTER P	LTC	0-1058965	0764	1
CZARKOWSKI HARRY S	CW3	W-2150295	1262	1
CZARNIK RAYMOND T	LTC	0-1039302	0167	1
CZARNY KASMIR R	LTC	0-1039106	0163	1
CZECHOWICZ MARTIN C	LTC	0-0419936	0965	1
CZEKANSKI ALPHONSE J	CW3	RW-2152021	0168	1
CZERNIEJEWSKI R C	CPT	0-0888853	0746	2
CZERNY WILLIAM	LTC	0-1052310	0763	1
CZERSKI EDWARD	LTC	0-1637255	0557	1
CZUHAJEWSKI FRANK J	MAJ	0-1315275	0566	1
CZWALINA PAUL F	CW3	W-2147022	0860	1
D ARCANGELO JOSEPH C	CW4	W-2006605	0168	3
DA PRATO RAYMOND E	LTC	0-0438844	0764	1
DABB WAYNE C	1LT	0-0811324	1055	2
DABBS RALPH T	LTC	0-0065244	1167	1
DABERRY JOHN D	CW2	W-2150018	1160	2
DABLER HARRY L	MAJ	0-0270223	0752	3
DABNEY WALTER H	LTC	0-0267438	1162	1
DABOV ANTONY	MAJ	0-1043602	0861	1
DABRAVALSKAS JOHN P	MAJ	0-1557831	1066	1
DABROWSKI STANLEY J	1LT	0-1298360	0361	1
DACH RICHARD J	CPT	0-0485321	1145	2
DACHMAN BERNARD	2LT	0-1002403	0444	2
DACK MERLE F	CW3	W-2141242	0363	1
DACKLIN PAUL H	MAJ	0-1337402	0161	1
DADA THEODORE A	1LT	0-0467446	0645	2
DADDATO FRANK J	CW2	W-2151785	1162	1
DADDOW ELWOOD G	LTC	0-1332625	0161	1

NAME	GRADE	SVC NO	DATE RET MO YR	RET CODE
DA[illegible] MATTH[illegible]	MAJ	[illegible]	1061	1
DA[illegible] JAMES	CPT	[illegible]	0644	2
DAFFERN CLYDE [illegible]	WO1	W-211[illegible]	[illegible]	1
DAFFERN MARGARET M	1LT	N-0736717	0253	2
DAFFERN PHILLIP L	CPT	0-0355110	0745	2
DAGENHART QUENTIN S	2LT	0-1296823	1144	2
DAGGETT [illegible] H	CPT	0-1244301	1053	1
DAGGETT [illegible]	MAJ	0-1542434	0157	1
DAGGETT LYLE [illegible]	MAJ	0-1692578	0358	1
DAGGETT RUSS[illegible]	CW3	W-2126791	0856	2
DAGNALL JAMES D	LTC	0-1106081	0562	1
DAGNEY ISABELLA F	2LT	N-0703767	0844	1
DAGOSTINO ANGELO A	MAJ	0-2051432	0361	1
DAGOSTINO COSMO	LTC	0-1550145	0768	3
DAGOSTINO RALPH	WO1	W-2122188	1148	1
DAGOUJN PEDRO	2LT	0-1896443	0465	1
DAGWORTHY JOHN H	CPT	0-0916499	0766	3
DAHL ARNOLD C	1LT	0-0285500	0945	2
DAHL ARTHUR G	COL	0-0231408	0761	3
DAHL ARVID P	LTC	0-0375760	0860	1
DAHL EARL B	LTC	0-0252297	0465	3
DAHL HERBERT A	1LT	0-1140158	0647	2
DAHL JACK V	2LT	0-1823945	0545	2
DAHL JOHN K	LTC	0-2034510	0265	1
DAHL JOHN S	MAJ	0-0887582	1266	1
DAHL JOSEPH V	1LT	0-1300288	1045	2
DAHL LAWRENCE K	1LT	0-1533764	1059	1
DAHL OWEN L	1LT	0-2055267	0748	2
DAHL RICHARD S	MAJ	0-1291427	1265	1
DAHL WILLIAM E	LTC	0-0238104	0263	3
DAHLBERG GEORGE P	1LT	0-0918700	0944	2
DAHLBERG LENEK V	CW2	W-2152763	0761	1
DAHLEN DUANE C	MAJ	0-0942992	0163	1
DAHLGREN ARNOLD W	LTC	0-1797263		1
DAHLGREN DALE A	MAJ	0-0354713	1050	2
DAHLIN LE ROY F	CPT	0-0325971	1045	2
DAHLIN ROY E	LTC	0-0280784	0568	3
DAHLIN TORALF A	CW3	W-2152944	0364	1
DAHLKE OTTO H	LTC	0-0410994	1063	1
DAHLMAN ORRIN J	MAJ	0-1030462	1157	1
DAHLQUIST LAWRENCE V	CW2	W-2151404	0758	1
DAHLSTROM CARROL A	CPT	0-0322998	0145	2
DAHMEN CHARLES A	LTC	0-0400014	1166	1
DAHMEN DANIEL J	1LT	0-1823416	0246	2
DAHN ROBERT C	MAJ	0-1877899	0767	1
DAHRLING BRUCE E	LTC	0-0364905	1263	1
DAIB WALTER C	LTC	0-0405380	0464	3
DAIGER JOHN G	LTC	0-0124726	0456	3
DAIGLE ALBERT J	MAJ	0-1556859	0854	1
DAIGLE ALBERT P	LTC	0-1001536	0658	1
DAIGLE DEBORAH	1LT	N-0720849	0346	1
DAIGLE HORACE E	CW2	W-2151211	0959	1
DAIGLE JOHN P	1LT	0-1339850	0752	2
DAIGLE PAUL J	LTC	0-0316223	0161	1
DAIGLE RICHARD J	LTC	0-0472379	0151	2
DAIGLE ROYDEN F JR	LTC	0-1171967	0666	1
DAILEY EDMOND R	CPT	0-0289695	0745	2
DAILEY ELLEN F	2LT	N-0722168	1043	1
DAILEY ERNEST W	1LT	0-1304036	1047	2
DAILEY JOSEPH M	1LT	0-0490393	0143	2
DAILEY MARION H	1LT	N-0776685	0945	1
DAILEY MARK D	MAJ	0-1589147	0857	2
DAILEY ROBERT C	LTC	0-1548387	0861	1
DAILEY WILLIAM G	MAJ	0-1947476	0161	1
DAILEY WILLIAM J	MAJ	0-0944673	0462	1
DAILY ALLEN H SR	CW3	W-2010379	0958	3
DAILY CLARENCE H	1LT	0-1302660	0745	2
DAILY GEORGE S	MAJ	0-2026573	0263	1
DAILY HENRY R JR	LTC	0-1547579	0166	1
DAILY RICHARD	COL	0-0201881	0856	3
DAILY ROBERT R	1LT	0-2025398	1060	1
DAILY VICTOR L	2LT	0-1310412	0943	2
DAINA MORDECAI M	LTC	0-0926988	1065	2
DAINES DELBERT A	CW3	W-2145409	1062	1
DAINES HAZEN B	LTC	0-0322294	0546	2

NAME	GRADE	SVC NO	DATE RET MO YR	RET CODE
DAI[illegible] CECIL L	CW3	W-2152965	1265	1
DAI[illegible] HENRY J	CPT	0-1174550	0448	2
DA[illegible] CARMEN F	MAJ	0-1821689	0653	2
DAKAN FRANK P	COL	0-1101799	0366	1
DAKE BENJAMIN F III	MAJ	0-1120525	0665	1
DAKE JOHN P JR	MAJ	0-1686737	0765	1
DALATON MARK S	1LT	0-1896479	0466	1
DALBEY MANLEY A	COL	0-1577067	1165	1
DALBOTTEN INGEBORG M	2LT	N-0701832	0933	1
DALBY CHRIS N	CW3	W-2138251	1160	1
DALBY HERBERT W	LTC	0-0320065	0362	1
DALBY RAYMOND E	CPT	0-2041006	0546	1
DALE ADRIAN S	CPT	0-0510520	0953	1
DALE BORIS C	LTC	0-0792003	1065	1
DALE CHARLES S	CPT	0-1283918	0546	2
DALE CLARENCE M	CPT	0-0213114	0457	3
DALE EDWARD J	MAJ	0-1285560	0361	1
DALE ELMER C	LTC	0-0362300	0368	3
DALE GEORGE H	LTC	0-0175953	0648	3
DALE JAMES A	MAJ	0-1120617	0663	1
DALE JOE BOB	MAJ	0-2103020	0265	1
DALE RAYMOND	MAJ	0-2055824	0257	1
DALE REX R JR	2LT	0-1338318	0446	2
DALE ROBERT J	MAJ	0-1548036	0161	1
DALE WILLIAM V	LTC	0-1548037	0268	1
DALEMBERTE CLINTON H	LTC	0-1533534	0365	1
DALEN ROSCOE E	MAJ	0-1641115	0363	1
DALES BERTRAM R JR	COL	0-0370504	0964	1
DALESSANDRO O T	1LT	0-1016317	1052	2
DALESSIO JOSEPH A	CPT	0-0487031	0644	2
DALESSIO WAGNER J	LTC	0-0262179	0567	3
DALEY ADALENE F	1LT	N-0730291	0646	1
DALEY ARTHUR S	LTC	0-0322657	0968	3
DALEY CHARLES S	CPT	0-1304505	0446	2
DALEY FORREST W	MAJ	0-0294664	1267	3
DALEY FRANCIS G	MAJ	0-0546553	0166	1
DALEY HARRY P	CW3	RW-2143892	1068	1
DALEY JAMES P	CW2	W-2214619	1166	1
DALEY JEREMIAH	LTC	0-1283730	0557	1
DALEY PATRICK	CW2	W-2129709	0561	1
DALEY ROLAND B	CPT	0-0191320	0153	3
DALEY THOMAS F	LTC	0-0551043	0864	1
DALEY WALTER E	LTC	0-1308111	0557	1
DALEY WILLIAM	CPT	0-0333025	0648	3
DALGLIESH GEORGE E	LTC	0-0413928	0862	1
DALIN WILLIAM Z	LTC	0-0558329	0768	3
DALIPE JUAN	MAJ	0-0200848	0849	1
DALKE CLAYTON G	LTC	0-2035804	1160	1
DALKE RICHARD L	CW4	RW-2141243	1062	1
DALL CHARLES W	LTC	0-0101788	0648	3
DALL NORMAN E	1LT	0-0885441	0450	1
DALLAIRE ERNEST A	LTC	0-1553243	0462	1
DALLAS ALLEN K	LTC	0-2274769	0563	1
DALLAS BERTRAM J	MAJ	0-1294097	0164	1
DALLAS DOROTHY M	1LT	N-0722249	0346	1
DALLAS EUGENE D	LTC	0-1307206	0368	3
DALLAS MAURICE H	CPT	0-0241861	1164	3
DALLAS RUSSELL L	MAJ	0-0227396	1144	2
DALLEMAND GEORGE E	MAJ	0-0285033	0868	3
DALLENBACH JOHN C	COL	0-0108553	0648	3
DALLENBACH KARL M	LTC	0-0159733	0648	3
DALMAO JOSEPH	1LT	0-1896861	0351	2
DALMAS VICTOR P JR	LTC	0-0445785	0268	1
DALO PEDRO E	CW3	W-2147227	0465	2
DALRYMPLE DONALD I	LTC	0-1293213	0556	1
DALRYMPLE LAWRENCE A	CPT	0-0338186	0862	2
DALRYMPLE LESTER R	LTC	0-1179050	0662	1
DALRYMPLE ROBERT A	MAJ	0-1999879	0364	1
DALTON ALVIN J	CPT	0-0976488	0261	1
DALTON CHARLES F	CPT	0-2005616	0157	1
DALTON CHARLES W	CPT	0-0494099	0255	1
DALTON EDWARD J	MAJ	0-1913482	0962	1
DALTON ELBERT	CPT	0-0461454	0246	2
DALTON FRANCIS P	CW2	W-2113927	0644	2
DALTON HAROLD J	CW3	W-2145268	0363	1

NAME	GRADE	SVC NO	DATE RET MO YR	RET CODE
DALTON HELEN L	1LT	N-0795519	0547	1
DALTON JACK	CW2	W-2122299	0749	1
DALTON JOHN B	MAJ	0-0244470	0154	3
DALTON JOHN S	1LT	0-0449495	1143	2
DALTON JOHN T	LTC	0-1562672	0368	1
DALTON JOHN T JR	2LT	0-1999819	0351	2
DALTON JOHN W	1LT	0-1177951	0546	2
DALTON KENNETH W	COL	0-0297636	0460	1
DALTON LILLIAN E	1LT	N-0727083	0247	1
DALTON LUKE F	MAJ	0-0290202	1061	2
DALTON MARSHALL A	LTC	0-0425251	0561	1
DALTON ROBERT J	LTC	0-0295246	1263	3
DALTON THEODORE J	LTC	0-0338853	0757	1
DALTON THOMAS J	CW4	W-2106352	0862	1
DALTON WILLIAM A	CPT	0-2262498	0857	1
DALTON WILLIAM H	CPT	0-1056686	1256	2
DALTRY RAYMOND E	LTC	0-1318288	0763	1
DALWAY BENJAMIN C	MAJ	0-0379203	0245	2
DALY ANDREW	LTC	0-1825087	1154	1
DALY CHARLES B	LTC	0-0973470	0766	3
DALY DENIS A	LTC	0-0193433	0648	3
DALY FRANK A	1LT	0-0358726	0848	1
DALY FREDERICK	MAJ	0-1081061	0860	1
DALY HARRIET C	MAJ	N-0799473	0466	1
DALY HARRY A	LTC	0-0512351	0850	2
DALY JAMES E	COL	0-0109809	0347	1
DALY JAMES G	CPT	0-0269760	0765	3
DALY JAMES J	LTC	0-1638936	0762	1
DALY JAMES V	LTC	0-0463570	0657	1
DALY JAMES V	MAJ	0-1845697	0660	1
DALY JAMES W	CPT	0-0366538	0147	2
DALY JOHN A	LTC	0-1004098	1164	1
DALY JOHN F	MAJ	0-0234911	0646	2
DALY JOHN L	LTC	0-0293946	1265	3
DALY JOHN O	CW3	W-2206979	0665	1
DALY JOHN W	LTC	0-0304804	0161	1
DALY LAWRENCE R	MAJ	0-1177356	0765	1
DALY LELAND J	LTC	0-1168625	0562	1
DALY MICHAEL J	CPT	0-1692630	0846	2
DALY OSWALD G	LTC	0-0125622	0754	3
DALY PAUL G	COL	0-0149189	1052	2
DALY PETER F	MAJ	0-0434550	0345	2
DALY THOMAS A	MAJ	0-0273747	0847	1
DALY WILBUR T JR	LTC	0-0403225	1060	1
DALY WILLIAM H	CPT	0-0888289	0546	2
DALY WILLIAM J	2LT	0-1114446	0744	2
DALY WILLIAM J	LTC	0-1165173	0361	1
DALZELL JAMES E	CPT	0-1651782	0556	1
DALZELL JOHN A	MAJ	0-1332937	1162	1
DAM CYRUS K	COL	0-0248451	0865	3
DAMAN CHARLES R	COL	0-0292501	0267	3
DAMATO JOSEPH M	CW3	W-2148509	0163	1
DAMBROSIO ANTONIO J	LTC	0-0992380	0268	1
DAME FRANK E	MAJ	0-0285110	0467	3
DAME MARY B	1LT	N-0775489	0548	1
DAME MORENCY R	LTC	0-1314451	1163	1
DAME RAYMOND E	MAJ	0-0455491	0147	2
DAMEN EDWARD M	LTC	0-0450839	0457	1
DAMER THOMAS T	1LT	0-1547580	0547	2
DAMERON JAMES H	CW2	W-2214606	0667	1
DAMERON THOMAS H	COL	0-0192414	0555	3
DAMERON WILLIAM G	LTC	0-0242158	0961	3
DAMEWOOD OSIE C	COL	0-0223241	0256	3
DAMEWOOD WALTER W	LTC	0-0260631	0766	3
DAMGEN EDWARD G	LTC	0-1550769	1061	1
DAMIANI COLUMBUS J	1LT	0-0436472	0955	1
DAMIANI JULES V JR	1LT	0-1322116	1145	2
DAMIANS PHILIP A	1LT	0-0410486	0845	2
DAMICO ANGELO F	LTC	0-1945110	0465	3
DAMICO ARTHUR	MAJ	0-0420182	0146	2
DAMICO FRANK J	2LT	0-1049123	1043	2
DAMICO JOSEPH P	MAJ	0-1327115	0464	1
DAMICO WILLIAM P	LTC	0-1054527	1165	1
DAMIENS JOSEPH N	MAJ	0-0257182	0145	2
DAMISH ADOLPH	MAJ	0-2017213	1159	1

NAME	GRADE	SVC NO	DATE RET MO YR	RET CODE
DANKOWITCH MICHAEL	LTC	0-1308483	0361	1
DANMAN RAYMOND F	1LT	0-1644835	0445	2
DAMME WILLIAM H	LTC	0-0238894	0246	2
DAMMEN ARNOLD H	LTC	0-0296083	1067	3
DAMON CHARLES P	LTC	0-0372347	0763	1
DAMON RALPH B	LTC	0-0378428	0656	1
DAMOND JOSEPH L	LTC	0-0234603	0957	3
DAMORE ANTHONY M	1LT	0-1323296	0551	2
DAMORE JOSEPH E	CPT	0-0921487	0645	2
DAMORE ROY	LTC	0-1036499	0563	1
DAMOTH CHARLES E	MAJ	0-1285561	0664	1
DAMPIER CHARLES E	MAJ	0-1313010	0959	1
DAMREN JOHN E	CW3	W-2145765	0863	1
DAMRON SIDNEY E	CPT	0-0475063	0646	2
DAMRON WILBUR T	MAJ	0-0984508	0765	1
DAMROW ARTHUR E	LTC	0-0269655	0763	3
DANA CECIL P	LTC	0-0475137	1068	3
DANA RICHARD A	COL	0-0423622	0160	1
DANAHER RICHARD J	MAJ	0-1949517	1066	1
DANCE CLAUDE A	COL	0-0171499	0961	3
DANCE EUGENE A	LTC	0-1290725	0666	1
DANCE WILLIAM G	LTC	0-0402115	0266	1
DANCHERTSEN JOHN D	CPT	0-0291896	0752	2
DANCULOVICH GEORGE N	1LT	0-1286973	1045	2
DANDO EDWARD C	LTC	0-0420466	1160	1
DANDO ROBERT R JR	LTC	0-0399456	1060	1
DANDRETO JOSEPH	MAJ	0-1691515	1054	1
DANDRIDGE WILLIAM M	MAJ	0-1332938	0765	.
DANDY IRVING E	CPT	0-0977223	0161	1
DANE CLARENCE B	MAJ	0-0260444	1062	2
DANE RALPH N	LTC	0-0419319	0961	1
DANE SIDNEY P	MAJ	0-1313343	0161	1
DANEKER CHARLES R JR	MAJ	0-0338957	0844	2
DANEKER JOHN L	COL	0-0144469	0855	3
DANENHOUR GEORGE B	MAJ	0-2262398	0562	1
DANER VALENTINA	2LT	N-0725829	1143	1
DANFORD BEECHER	CPT	0-0166621	0648	3
DANFORD CHARLES A	CW3	W-2203487	0865	1
DANFORD ROBERT W	MAJ	0-1647520	0861	1
DANFORTH DWIGHT A	LTC	0-0902868	0665	3
DANFORTH E C B JR	B G	0-0234688	0854	2
DANFORTH GEORGE	LTC	0-0314839	0668	3
DANFORTH LESTER F	LTC	0-0260134	1066	3
DANGELO ANTHONY E	COL	0-0241922	0560	3
DANGELO ANTHONY T	MAJ	0-1999092	0465	1
DANGELO JOHN P	CW2	W-2206029	0763	1
DANGELO VINCENT	MAJ	0-1186636	0765	1
DANGELONE ANTHONY JJ	CW3	W-2147283	1262	1
DANGLER RALPH B	LTC	0-1589783	0665	3
DANGREMOND LEROY M G	LTC	0-0165386	0346	2
DANHOUR GEORGE S	MAJ	0-0142792	0242	2
DANICO MARION L	2LT	N-0754946	0946	1
DANIEL ANDREWS F	WO1	W-2106967	0746	2
DANIEL CAMERON D	CW2	W-2144806	1056	1
DANIEL CORNELIUS	CW3	W-2207705	0668	1
DANIEL ELIJAH W	CW2	W-2121955	0346	2
DANIEL ELLIS J	LTC	0-1325188	1267	3
DANIEL EMMETT W	1LT	0-2003153	0758	2
DANIEL ERNEST H JR	COL	0-0259961	0368	3
DANIEL FLOYD F	MAJ	0-0388729	0348	2
DANIEL HAROLD C	1LT	0-0555874	0546	2
DANIEL HENRY S	MAJ	0-0257355	0667	3
DANIEL HERBERT H	CW2	W-2149208	0861	1
DANIEL HERBERT L	MAJ	0-2263309	0765	1
DANIEL HUGH M	MAJ	0-0401406	0944	2
DANIEL JAMES G	LTC	0-0297435	0157	2
DANIEL JAMES H	LTC	0-0299395	0368	3
DANIEL JAMES M	MAJ	0-1844494	0658	1
DANIEL KENNETH J	LTC	0-0283570	1045	2
DANIEL LANDON G	LTC	0-0162874	0757	3
DANIEL LOUIE S	CPT	0-1693088	0246	2
DANIEL MASON B	LTC	0-1598033	0568	3
DANIEL NIK J	1LT	0-2262335	0953	2
DANIEL ORVAL	MAJ	0-1996597	0860	1
DANIEL PENTECOST	CW2	W-2119450	0546	1

NAME	GRADE	SVC NO	DATE RET MO YR	RET CODE
DANIEL RAYMOND J	LTC	0-1301442	1267	3
DANIEL RICHARD R	MAJ	0-1183679	0261	1
DANIEL ROBERT L	1LT	0-0336167	0158	3
DANIEL WELDON O	CW4	W-2123164	1264	1
DANIEL WILLIAM H	MAJ	0-1799709	1262	1
DANIELEK JAN SR	CW2	W-2142144	0457	1
DANIELEWICZ EDWARD J	CPT	0-1322133	0148	2
DANIELL JOHN T	LTC	0-0279746	0660	1
DANIELL SMITH C	MAJ	0-0201237	0849	3
DANIELLO ANTHONY A	MAJ	0-1994584	0657	2
DANIELS ANTHONY J	MAJ	0-0420501	0961	1
DANIELS ARTHUR C	MAJ	0-0486021	0445	2
DANIELS CECIL E JR	LTC	0-1341637	1167	1
DANIELS CHARLES E	MAJ	0-1300133	0854	2
DANIELS ERNEST W	LTC	0-1172828	0466	1
DANIELS EUGENE	MAJ	0-1549925	1054	1
DANIELS EUGENE B SR	LTC	0-0335512	0861	3
DANIELS FRANK JR	CW3	W-2205745	1165	1
DANIELS GILBERT	LTC	0-0482671	0457	1
DANIELS HARRISON W	1LT	0-1306069	0446	2
DANIELS HARRY B JR	MAJ	0-0387235	0646	2
DANIELS HERMAN E	CPT	0-0389399	0446	2
DANIELS HILLIARD SR	CW3	W-2145051	0263	1
DANIELS HOWARD	1LT	0-1173916	1045	2
DANIELS HOWARD A	MAJ	0-1547265	0959	1
DANIELS HOWARD B	CW2	W-2212858	0868	1
DANIELS IRENE H	CPT	N-0795855	0555	2
DANIELS JAMES N	MAJ	0-1547267	0964	2
DANIELS JOHN H JR	LTC	0-1293019	0463	1
DANIELS JOHN T	MAJ	0-1304038	0159	1
DANIELS JOHN T	CW3	W-2150237	0164	1
DANIELS KENNETH W	MAJ	0-1924820	0866	1
DANIELS LEROY H	WO1	W-2143193	0663	1
DANIELS OREL M	CPT	0-2018307	0360	1
DANIELS PAUL B	COL	0-0321524	0661	2
DANIELS PAUL B	MAJ	0-1897732	0361	1
DANIELS PERCY E	MAJ	0-0247143	0262	3
DANIELS RAYMOND O	CW3	W-2149041	0368	1
DANIELS REUBEN H	LTC	0-0203842	1046	1
DANIELS ROBERT P	LTC	0-0333281	0268	3
DANIELS WALTER L	LTC	0-0255014	0457	3
DANIELS WILLIAM J	MAJ	0-1688479	1065	1
DANIELSON BERT L	MAJ	0-0967897	1060	1
DANIELSON ERNEST L	LTC	0-0162398	1044	2
DANIELSON LINNEA A	MAJ	N-0777537	1161	2
DANIELSON PAUL E	CPT	0-1306388	0048	2
DANIELSON RAYMOND W	MAJ	0-0248271	0265	3
DANIELSON RUEBEN J	CW4	W-2143509	0762	1
DANILAVEZ ROBERT L	MAJ	0-0968484	0668	1
DANITZ ANSELM L	CPT	0-0258279	1044	2
DANKS GENE H	MAJ	0-0922067	1045	2
DANLEY JOSEPH C	COL	0-0247153	0457	1
DANLEY PRINCE H JR	MAJ	0-1551187	0556	1
DANN ARTHUR G	CPT	0-4005082	1165	1
DANN CLIFFORD H	LTC	0-1311125	1061	1
DANN ROSCOE E JR	MAJ	0-2202804	0466	1
DANNENMUELLER ELMER	CW4	W-2008170	0566	3
DANNER ELLIS	LTC	0-0259430	0467	3
DANNER EUGENE B	LTC	0-1055823	0563	1
DANNER JOHN O	CW3	W-2211138	1168	1
DANNER LEROY M	LTC	0-1573834	0865	1
DANNER LYMAN E	WO1	W-2130779	0962	1
DANNER REX W	CW2	W-2119540	0665	1
DANNIS LOUIS W	1LT	0-0403322	0646	2
DANO BASIL W	LTC	0-1546942	0962	2
DANROT HENRY C	LTC	0-0297157	0868	3
DANSBY BRADLEY L	LTC	0-0237361	1265	3
DANSER DAVID F	COL	0-0366696	0468	1
DANSER ROBERT C	LTC	0-0403217	1157	1
DANSON PAUL A	LTC	0-0217267	1160	1
DANTON RITA P	MAJ	L-1010212	0365	1
DANTONIO RINALDO N	CW2	W-2148847	0963	1
DANTZLER DANIEL B	CPT	0-0496156	0345	2
DANTZLER EDWARD A JR	LTC	0-0904258	1067	2
DANZENBAKER JOHN D	LTC	0-1296180	0964	1

NAME	GRADE	SVC NO	DATE RET MO YR	RET CODE
DANZI RICHARD A	LTC	0-1822375	0746	2
DANZIGER DANIEL	LTC	0-0212857	0737	1
DARBE RAY E	CW3	W-2207630	0467	1
DARBY JEWELL E	MAJ	N-0735511	0663	1
DARBY JOHNIE T	LTC	0-1297690	0960	1
DARBY NORMAN D	LTC	0-1107892	0362	1
DARCANGELIS A F	CPT	0-1586470	0347	2
DARCHE LEO J	CW4	W-2102809	0859	1
DARCY ARTHUR E H	CPT	0-0265069	0455	3
DARCY HELEN K	1LT	N-0787034	1046	1
DARDEN ARNOLD W	CPT	0-1323544	0348	2
DARDEN DANIEL M	2LT	0-1318259	0245	2
DARDEN EDWIN H	CPT	0-0450841	1143	2
DARDEN JAMES W	LTC	0-0398206	0561	1
DARE AFTON	LTC	0-1179829	0664	1
DARE BEATRICE M	LTC	N-0701180	0446	1
DARE EDWARD	MAJ	0-0191347	0653	3
DARE EDWIN C	CW3	W-2149878	0564	1
DARGAN WALTER C	CPT	0-0248996	0946	2
DARGUSCH CARLTON S	B G	0-0246180	0947	2
DARISON HENRY E	LTC	0-1111013	0567	3
DARK CARLETON W	LTC	0-0157089	0857	3
DARK FOY E	LTC	0-1341754	0767	1
DARKE FRANCIS J	COL	0-0291764	0547	2
DARKE WILLIAM J	LTC	0-0384130	0468	3
DARKER EVELYN A	MAJ	N-0769177	0365	2
DARKEY GUY F	MAJ	0-0461812	0846	1
DARKOW ALWIN J	LTC	0-0263385	0862	1
DARLEY WILLIAM H	MAJ	0-0395509	0860	1
DARLING BRICE H	CPT	0-1310688	1046	2
DARLING BRUCE B	2LT	0-1012832	1044	2
DARLING BYRON P	MAJ	0-1049459	1155	1
DARLING CLINTON S	MAJ	0-0117178	0865	1
DARLING FRANCIS W	COL	0-0265108	0966	3
DARLING GERALD S	LTC	0-0359644	0366	3
DARLING JOSEPH W	COL	0-0900258	0668	3
DARLING MAYO A	COL	0-0172647	0358	3
DARLING RICHARD W	1LT	0-1002897	0746	2
DARLING WILFRED D	COL	0-0297594	1067	3
DARLING WILLIAM V	CPT	0-0321473	0747	2
DARLINGTON BURLEY H	CPT	0-0498158	1048	1
DARLINGTON HARRY D	COL	0-0255142	0365	3
DARLINGTON JOHN E	LTC	0-1106672	1266	3
DARMAND ROSCOE C	LTC	0-0209809	1052	3
DARMER EDWILL F	1LT	0-0483071	0345	2
DARMOPRAY MICHAEL	MAJ	0-0150171	0856	3
DARNALL JAMES W	LTC	0-0486003	0554	1
DARNELL DONALD F	MAJ	0-1338065	0268	1
DARNELL FRANK J JR	CW3	W-2209833	1168	1
DARNELL GRADY P	CPT	0-0973557	0361	1
DARNELL ORVAL D	1LT	0-1923030	1053	2
DARNELL RALPH R	LTC	0-1166467	0556	1
DARNELL THOMAS F	MAJ	0-1633790	0954	1
DARNELL WILLIAM B	MAJ	0-0482469	1144	1
DARNER FLOYD W	MAJ	0-2262310	0563	1
DARNER OTIS L	MAJ	0-0348630	0759	3
DARR WILLIAM H	CPT	0-0486132	0852	1
DARRACOTT HALVOR T	COL	0-0391615	1062	1
DARRAGH SCUDDER H	LTC	0-0525619	0965	3
DARRAH BOBBY J	MAJ	0-1935627	0368	1
DARRIGO JOSEPH	CPT	0-1325278	0451	2
DARRIN WILLIAM A	1LT	0-1317894	0446	2
DARROUGH GLENN E	LTC	0-1637258	1163	1
DARROUGH JOHN W	COL	0-0214672	0364	3
DARROUGH WILLIAM J	LTC	0-0233129	0955	3
DARROW ALBERT	MAJ	0-0499263	1051	1
DARROW ROBERT C	1LT	0-1180160	0945	2
DARROW RUSSELL E	MAJ	0-1534465	0357	1
DARST GEORGE I	MAJ	0-1184479	0664	1
DART JOHN	COL	0-0205781	0446	2
DARTENAY LEO P	LTC	0-1557438	1160	1
DARTEZ JOHN E	2LT	0-1795867	1159	2
DARVER ALBERT	LTC	0-0387328	0568	3
DASDORF JOHN H	LTC	0-0494887	1261	3
DASHIELL SAMUEL C	MAJ	0-1111565	1265	1

NAME	GRADE	SVC NO	DATE RET MO YR	RET CODE	NAME	GRADE	SVC NO	DATE RET MO YR	RET CODE	NAME	GRADE	SVC NO	DATE RET MO YR	RET CODE	NAME	GRADE	SVC NO	DATE RET MO YR	RET CODE
DASHIELL WILLARD H	MAJ	0-0402536	0661	1	DAVID ALEXANDER	MAJ	0-1334114	1263	1	DAVIES RONALD N	LTC	0-0226763	0165	3	DAVIS CLYDE	CW3	W-2144971	0563	2
DASHNER RICHARD W	MAJ	0-0422625	1058	1	DAVID CHARLES F	CPT	0-0493933	0753	1	DAVIES RUSSELL G	CPT	0-1169477	0846	2	DAVIS CLYDE F	MAJ	0-1642784	0557	1
DASINGER ANTON	1LT	0-0393448	0145	2	DAVID EDWARD F	LTC	0-0297740	1045	2	DAVIES SAM L	LTC	0-0342728	0859	1	DAVIS CLYDE J JR	MAJ	0-1595027	0963	1
DASSE PIERRE E	CW4	W-2006456	0366	1	DAVID FREDERICK	LTC	0-1826041	0363	1	DAVIES SAMUEL O	LTC	0-0260446	0544	2	DAVIS CLYDE M	MAJ	0-1285211	0263	2
DASTOLI ANGELO N	CW3	W-2151690	0956	1	DAVID HERMAN O	MAJ	0-0198724	1153	3	DAVIES STANLEY J	MAJ	0-1046762	0159	1	DAVIS CURTIS C	MAJ	0-0497910	0157	1
DATSON JOHN	COL	0-0338253	0551	3	DAVID JAMES R	LTC	0-0283070	0768	3	DAVIES STEWART H	COL	0-1302953	1168	1	DAVIS CURTIS C	WO1	W-2105928	1045	2
DATTILO JOHN C	LTC	0-2036167	0164	1	DAVID LAWRENCE P	MAJ	0-0994888	1065	1	DAVIES THOMAS	LTC	0-2055891	0557	1	DAVIS DALE	MAJ	0-2336479	0564	1
DAUBENFELD ALFRED	LTC	0-0360144	0262	1	DAVID LEON T	COL	0-0201780	0061	3	DAVIES WILLIAM	LTC	0-1302435	0366	1	DAVIS DAMON	1LT	0-2053903	1051	1
DAUBENSPECK LOUIS A	CW2	W-2208531	1060	1	DAVID MARSHALL S	LTC	0-0265200	0166	3	DAVIES WILLIAM A	1LT	0-1548479	0246	2	DAVIS DANIEL	CPT	0-0425709	1045	2
DAUBENSPECK WAYNE M	COL	0-0346775	1264	3	DAVID ROBERT E	LTC	0-1012836	0766	1	DAVIES WILLIAM C	CW3	W-2112562	0660	1	DAVIS DAVID F	WO1	W-2106684	0346	2
DAUBER ELMER C	CW3	W-2144755	0162	1	DAVID ROSE	2LT	N-0190592	0746	1	DAVIES WILLIAM J	CPT	0-1299343	0147	2	DAVIS DAVID O	LTC	0-0246799	0866	3
DAUDELIN FREDERICK	CW4	W-2153144	1060	1	DAVIDS THAD	1LT	0-0337625	1044	2	DAVILA BENIGNO	MAJ	0-0227751	0365	3	DAVIS DELMAR J	CW3	W-2153167	0764	1
DAUDELIN JOE A	COL	0-0336127	1061	2	DAVIDSON ALTA F	1LT	N-0703757	0446	1	DAVILA FERNANDO T	MAJ	0-1329677	0763	1	DAVIS DELROY R	MAJ	0-0443250	0847	2
DAUDELIN NORMAN A	MAJ	0-0987407	0663	1	DAVIDSON ARCHIE B	LTC	0-1287312	0263	1	DAVILA LUIS A	CPT	0-2263291	0761	1	DAVIS DENVER E	1LT	0-0523304	0246	2
DAUE ARNOLD K	MAJ	0-2036368	0760	1	DAVIDSON BENJAMIN F	CW2	W-2144832	1060	1	DAVILA RAFAEL	1LT	0-0167773	1052	3	DAVIS DEVON A	LTC	0-0510646	0566	3
DAUGETTE CLARENCE W	COL	0-0326457	1063	3	DAVIDSON C G	1LT	0-1113657	1145	2	DAVILA RUDOLPH B	1LT	0-1692556	0550	2	DAVIS DEWITT D	LTC	0-0220909	0764	3
DAUGHERTY CARY S	COL	0-0237033	0765	3	DAVIDSON CHARLES Y	LTC	0-0376242	0156	1	DAVIN HARRISON L	LTC	0-0489792	1164	3	DAVIS DONALD A	2LT	0-0299280	0544	2
DAUGHERTY DURWOOD A	LTC	0-1289309	0557	1	DAVIDSON ELI L	CW2	W-2143894	0861	1	DAVIS ADDISON C	1LT	0-0374363	0844	2	DAVIS DONALD A	CPT	0-1287674	0345	2
DAUGHERTY FRED N	LTC	0-0279348	0657	3	DAVIDSON ERNEST C	MAJ	0-1695712	1159	1	DAVIS ALBERT H C JR	MAJ	0-1335630	0761	1	DAVIS DONALD D	MAJ	0-0905913	0446	2
DAUGHERTY HENRY S	LTC	0-0300320	0162	1	DAVIDSON EUGENE W	1LT	0-0420523	0545	2	DAVIS ALBERT H	MAJ	0-0228847	1262	3	DAVIS DONALD S	MAJ	0-1919199	1166	1
DAUGHERTY HERSCHEL	MAJ	0-0981499	1265	2	DAVIDSON HAROLD V	CPT	0-0917747	0145	2	DAVIS ALBERT M	2LT	0-2034512	0545	2	DAVIS EARL	LTC	0-0399043	0557	1
DAUGHERTY HUGH D	CPT	0-1573149	1045	2	DAVIDSON HARRY O	LTC	0-1107894	1060	1	DAVIS ALBERT R	CPT	0-0150423	0854	3	DAVIS EARL J JR	MAJ	0-1637897	0960	1
DAUGHERTY LEE F	LTC	0-0499535	0960	1	DAVIDSON HEBERT	COL	0-0240079	0662	3	DAVIS ALLEN K	LTC	0-0207451	1056	1	DAVIS EARL L	MAJ	0-2262148	0761	2
DAUGHERTY LYLE S	LTC	0-0340520	1159	1	DAVIDSON HENRY E	LTC	0-0317171	1067	3	DAVIS ALLIE E	CW4	W-2111195	0356	1	DAVIS EDGAR C	MAJ	0-0496922	0747	1
DAUGHERTY TEMPLE J	MAJ	0-1030011	0261	1	DAVIDSON HYATT L	LTC	0-0375913	1062	1	DAVIS ALVIN D	MAJ	0-1885368	1265	1	DAVIS EDISON L	MAJ	0-1175412	0962	1
DAUGHERTY THOMAS J	MAJ	0-1956570	1060	1	DAVIDSON IRVING E	CW2	W-2214501	0766	1	DAVIS ALVIN L	CPT	0-1053553	0460	2	DAVIS EDISON O	COL	0-0244990	0360	3
DAUGHTON KILMER F	CPT	0-0437949	0863	1	DAVIDSON JAMES E JR	COL	0-0312108	0759	1	DAVIS AMOS R JR	1LT	0-0327573	0545	2	DAVIS EDMOND H SR	CW2	W-2141245	0653	1
DAUGHTREY LYMAN C	MAJ	0-0197342	0263	3	DAVIDSON JAMES V JR	1LT	0-1546943	1045	2	DAVIS ANDREW A	MAJ	0-0181882	0255	3	DAVIS EDWARD F	CPT	0-2262782	1160	2
DAUGHTRY EDWARD F	CW3	W-2143942	0659	1	DAVIDSON JESSE M	COL	0-0255927	0556	3	DAVIS ANNA M	1LT	N-0769453	0348	1	DAVIS EDWARD H	LTC	0-0182585	0954	3
DAUGUSTINE ANTHONY P	MAJ	0-1100941	0760	1	DAVIDSON JEWEL L	1LT	0-1177357	0745	2	DAVIS ANNIE J G	MAJ	N-0751791	1267	3	DAVIS EDWARD J	CPT	0-0486761	0853	1
DAUGUSTINO PATRICK	CPT	0-2046562	0250	1	DAVIDSON JOHN L	LTC	0-1288714	1060	1	DAVIS ARDIE K	MAJ	0-2025495	1059	1	DAVIS EDWARD J	1LT	0-2302258	1257	1
DAUME KENNETH P	1LT	0-0470588	0345	2	DAVIDSON JOHN P	1LT	0-0421394	0946	2	DAVIS ARNOLD K	1LT	0-1647359	0246	2	DAVIS EDWIN A	LTC	0-0354192	0463	3
DAUN ARTHUR L	MAJ	0-1553245	0657	1	DAVIDSON JUSTUS S	MAJ	0-0173239	0855	3	DAVIS ARTHUR A	1LT	0-0179628	0360	3	DAVIS EDWIN F	CPT	0-1292484	0459	1
DAUNIS JOHN F	MAJ	0-0512477	0646	2	DAVIDSON LESTER E	CW3	W-2148252	0761	1	DAVIS ARTHUR C	WO1	W-2129690	0645	2	DAVIS ELLSWORTH	COL	0-0359641	0165	1
DAUPHIN LESTER R	MAJ	0-2042964	1058	1	DAVIDSON LILLIAN M	2LT	N-0777301	0446	1	DAVIS ARTHUR D	LTC	0-0489370	1055	1	DAVIS ELMER E	MAJ	0-1644846	0268	1
DAUS ARCHIE H	MAJ	0-1692932	1058	1	DAVIDSON MARGARET M	2LT	N-0737438	0744	1	DAVIS ARTHUR L	1LT	0-1103585	0547	2	DAVIS ELMER K	MAJ	0-0238774	0265	3
DAUS MILTON J	MAJ	0-0258657	0945	2	DAVIDSON MARION	1LT	0-2046396	1145	1	DAVIS AUBREY A	LTC	0-0964527	0868	1	DAVIS EMMETT R	CPT	0-2044287	0900	1
DAUSEY FRANK W	LTC	0-1047493	0165	1	DAVIDSON MURRAY P	LTC	0-0275503	0766	3	DAVIS BAXTER C	LTC	0-0353502	1145	2	DAVIS ENOCH A JR	LTC	0-0226618	0760	3
DAUWAY ALFONSO	CPT	0-0169316	0559	3	DAVIDSON NORMAN H	MAJ	0-0144716	0354	3	DAVIS BEN	CW4	W-2140901	0168	1	DAVIS ERNEST G	LTC	0-0320023	0260	3
DAVANZO CHARLES S	CPT	0-0331541	1045	2	DAVIDSON OLE K	MAJ	0-0278531	0554	3	DAVIS BEN M	MAJ	0-0155014	0155	3	DAVIS ERVILLE A	CW2	W-2144908	0162	1
DAVEE CHARLES W	1LT	0-0971937	1152	2	DAVIDSON ROYCE L	MAJ	0-0973555	1064	1	DAVIS BENJAMIN F	CPT	0-0167927	0558	3	DAVIS EUGENE C JR	LTC	0-2292323	0768	2
DAVENPORT ARTHUR I	LTC	0-0234348	0765	3	DAVIDSON SAMUEL L	COL	0-0162543	1149	1	DAVIS BERNARD P	LTC	0-2042970	1067	3	DAVIS EVERETT E	MAJ	0-1336490	0762	1
DAVENPORT ARTHUR R	MAJ	0-0961661	1163	1	DAVIDSON TEDDY B	CW2	W-2212572	1065	1	DAVIS BOWIE W	1LT	0-1304039	1045	2	DAVIS FENIMORE E	COL	0-0335605	1165	3
DAVENPORT CHARLES F	2LT	0-1306248	0245	2	DAVIDSON W S JR	LTC	0-0265450	0452	3	DAVIS BRUCE A	MAJ	0-1686579	0662	1	DAVIS FITZGERALD	LTC	0-0348411	1167	3
DAVENPORT CHESTER L	LTC	0-0348610	1262	2	DAVIDSON WESLEY H	LTC	0-1304870	0961	1	DAVIS BURTON F	1LT	0-1314261	0845	2	DAVIS FLOYD E	LTC	0-1322979	0263	1
DAVENPORT CLARA H	2LT	N-0764934	0446	1	DAVIDSON WILLIAM S	LTC	0-0484260	0665	1	DAVIS CALEB	MAJ	0-1703015	0258	1	DAVIS FRANCIS E	COL	0-0257430	1067	3
DAVENPORT CLINTON M	MAJ	0-2103039	0964	1	DAVIDSON WILLIAM T	LTC	0-1592758	0767	3	DAVIS CARL F	CPT	0-0461673	0944	2	DAVIS FRANCIS M	CW3	W-3430045	0868	1
DAVENPORT DARYL R	MAJ	0-0954673	0465	1	DAVIE GEORGE A	MAJ	0-0464450	1054	1	DAVIS CARL R	LTC	0-0248112	1050	2	DAVIS FRANCIS W	COL	0-0263000	0168	3
DAVENPORT DORSEY H	LTC	0-0290285	0264	3	DAVIE JAMES C	LTC	0-0309804	0462	3	DAVIS CARROL F	CW4	W-2122946	1054	1	DAVIS FRANCIS W	COL	0-0275021	0660	1
DAVENPORT DUANE T	CPT	0-2317127	1268	1	DAVIE PAUL J	LTC	0-1310815	0862	1	DAVIS CARROLL R	MAJ	0-0157720	0145	2	DAVIS FRANK A	CPT	0-1319725	0847	2
DAVENPORT EDGAR E	MAJ	0-0961924	0965	1	DAVIE WARREN C	1LT	0-1637261	0845	2	DAVIS CARY A	1LT	0-0208249	0253	3	DAVIS FRANK F	MAJ	0-0374717	0146	2
DAVENPORT EDWARD I	LTC	0-0400911	0760	1	DAVIES ADELAIDE A	MAJ	N-0756489	0563	1	DAVIS CATHERINE	MAJ	N-0737039	0464	3	DAVIS FRANK H	CPT	0-0487501	0945	2
DAVENPORT ESTELLE E	MAJ	L-2291711	1067	1	DAVIES ALAN A	CPT	0-1177758	0847	2	DAVIS CECIL A JR	LTC	0-2035080	0865	1	DAVIS FRANK M	MAJ	0-0405152	0166	3
DAVENPORT HAROLD O	MAJ	0-0310161	1059	1	DAVIES BRINLEY R	1LT	0-0272679	0168	3	DAVIS CHARLES C	CW2	W-2153664	1061	1	DAVIS FRANK R	CPT	0-0493626	0950	1
DAVENPORT J C	LTC	0-1633152	0160	1	DAVIES CHARLES W JR	MAJ	0-1042540	0860	1	DAVIS CHARLES O	LTC	0-0215527	1061	3	DAVIS FRANK W	CW3	W-2147647	0160	1
DAVENPORT JAMES M	COL	0-0358076	0865	2	DAVIES CLARENCE E	COL	0-0134089	0351	3	DAVIS CHARLES D	MAJ	0-2262384	0463	1	DAVIS FRANKLIN C	LTC	0-0245234	1059	1
DAVENPORT JOE S	WO1	W-2147340	0858	1	DAVIES CLYDE T	LTC	0-0197493	1160	1	DAVIS CHARLES E	LTC	0-0297250	0459	1	DAVIS FRANKLIN C	LTC	0-0291926	0964	1
DAVENPORT JOHN S	LTC	0-0487018	1062	1	DAVIES DAVID G	CPT	0-0227383	0564	3	DAVIS CHARLES E	LTC	0-0382975	0660	1	DAVIS FREDERICK	MAJ	0-1294273	0161	1
DAVENPORT JOSEPH R	CPT	0-0164183	0836	1	DAVIES DAVID J	CPT	0-1030554	0361	1	DAVIS CHARLES E	1LT	0-1014454	0744	2	DAVIS FREDERICK	1LT	0-1800093	0151	2
DAVENPORT LEO P	CPT	0-1032425	0261	1	DAVIES DAVID M	MAJ	0-1925899	0667	1	DAVIS CHARLES E	LTC	0-1309045	0562	2	DAVIS GEORGE A	MAJ	0-1688605	1165	1
DAVENPORT MARSHALL R	1LT	0-1011172	1046	2	DAVIES EUGENE C	LTC	0-0308947	0660	1	DAVIS CHARLES F	MAJ	0-2265726	0368	1	DAVIS GEORGE C	LTC	0-0183485	0449	3
DAVENPORT MERLE E	1LT	0-1307670	0651	2	DAVIES GEORGE N	LTC	0-0411033	0757	1	DAVIS CHARLES F	CW2	W-2213454	1167	1	DAVIS GEORGE D	CPT	0-0267293	0147	1
DAVENPORT NORMAN E	LTC	0-1173579	0662	1	DAVIES GEORGE R II	COL	0-1038679	0268	1	DAVIS CHARLES F	2LT	0-0978454	0352	2	DAVIS GEORGE H	COL	0-0307826	0167	3
DAVENPORT RALPH H	LTC	0-0567830	0864	1	DAVIES HARRY H	LTC	0-0253625	0561	3	DAVIS CHARLES H	CW4	W-2144907	0168	1	DAVIS GEORGE M	COL	0-0193961	1060	1
DAVENPORT ROBERT F	MAJ	0-1686693	0465	1	DAVIES HOMER G	MAJ	0-0138709	0648	3	DAVIS CHARLES H	CW3	W-2150982	0566	1	DAVIS GEORGE M	CPT	0-1312751	0148	2
DAVENPORT ROY C	LTC	0-0508710	0846	2	DAVIES IVOR J	COL	0-0499026	1065	3	DAVIS CHARLES J	LTC	0-0248088	0846	2	DAVIS GEORGE P	MAJ	0-0258645	0567	3
DAVENPORT ROY L	MAJ	0-2212058	0265	1	DAVIES JAMES E	MAJ	0-1036939	0461	2	DAVIS CHARLES L	MAJ	0-0225051	1057	3	DAVIS GEORGE W	MAJ	0-0982905	0164	1
DAVES MAX E	MAJ	0-0565154	0256	1	DAVIES JOHN R	MAJ	0-0997098	1163	1	DAVIS CHARLES M	COL	0-0184468	0439	2	DAVIS GERALD E	LTC	0-1702833	1146	2
DAVES ROBERT W	LTC	0-1798458	1161	1	DAVIES LAURENCE E	CW2	W-2113120	0460	1	DAVIS CHARLES W	CW4	W-2101591	1054	1	DAVIS GESNA B JR	MAJ	0-0992922	0166	1
DAVEY DONALD A	1LT	0-1295840	0645	2	DAVIES PURCELL R	CPT	0-0244801	1159	3	DAVIS CHARLIE	LTC	0-0464453	0258	1	DAVIS GLEN F	LTC	0-0559719	1065	1
DAVEY EDWARD J	CPT	0-1692946	0946	2	DAVIES RAY J	LTC	0-0455587	1059	1	DAVIS CHESTER P	LTC	0-1321376	1166	1	DAVIS GRIFFIN L	LTC	0-0450843	0258	1
DAVEY KENNETH V	LTC	0-1100942	1057	1	DAVIES RICHARD P	CW3	W-2143437	0561	1	DAVIS CLARENCE C	COL	0-0245380	0766	3	DAVIS GROVER C	LTC	0-0104968	0648	3
DAVEY RUSSELL B	LTC	0-1106674	0168	1	DAVIES ROBERT P	1LT	0-1637262	0252	2	DAVIS CLAUDE L	1LT	0-0490732	0447	1	DAVIS GUILLETT G JR	LTC	0-0203089	0264	3
DAVEY THOMAS N	CW4	W-2146743	0564	1	DAVIES ROBERT R	MAJ	0-1650818	1159	1	DAVIS CLAUDE W	LTC	0-0299274	0164	3	DAVIS HAROLD C	LTC	0-0164999	1159	3
DAVIA DAVID W	CW3	W-2142497	0859	1	DAVIES RONALD E	MAJ	0-1895008	0662	1	DAVIS CLEO G	1LT	0-0446024	1045	2	DAVIS HAROLD E	CW2	W-3100592	0668	1

NAME	GRADE	SVC NO	DATE RET MO YR	RET CODE	NAME	GRADE	SVC NO	DATE RET MO YR	RET CODE	NAME	GRADE	SVC NO	DATE RET MO YR	RET CODE	NAME	GRADE	SVC NO	DATE RET MO YR	RET CODE
DAVIS HAROLD F	LTC	0-0158668	1151	3	DAVIS JOHN E	LTC	0-1307520	1047	2	DAVIS PAUL L	CW2	W-2101305	1047	1	DAVIS WILLIAM G	LTC	0-0276137	1053	2
DAVIS HAROLD L	COL	0-0359292	0468	3	DAVIS JOHN F	COL	0-1543251	0868	2	DAVIS PAUL M	LTC	0-0267081	0857	3	DAVIS WILLIAM G	CPT	0-0333985	0763	3
DAVIS HAROLD L	CPT	0-0497641	0748	1	DAVIS JOHN K	LTC	0-1003216	0168	3	DAVIS PAUL M	MAJ	0-0527787	0663	1	DAVIS WILLIAM G	MAJ	0-0885031	0956	1
DAVIS HAROLD L	LTC	0-1587915	0962	1	DAVIS JOHN L	MAJ	0-1585336	0264	1	DAVIS PAUL R	MAJ	0-0171599	0262	3	DAVIS WILLIAM G	1LT	0-1797967	0944	2
DAVIS HARRY C	LTC	0-0456336	1059	1	DAVIS JOHN M	MAJ	0-0400213	0662	1	DAVIS PAUL V	LTC	0-0204492	0354	3	DAVIS WILLIAM G	CW2	W-2213316	0867	1
DAVIS HARRY F	LTC	0-0928438	1167	1	DAVIS JOHN M	CPT	0-0404419	0154	2	DAVIS PAUL V	CPT	0-0962556	0459	1	DAVIS WILLIAM H	LTC	0-1302783	0766	1
DAVIS HARRY G	MAJ	0-2096727	0963	1	DAVIS JOHN P	MAJ	0-0316373	0446	2	DAVIS PAUL W	LTC	0-0294583	1059	1	DAVIS WILLIAM H	CW3	W-2206520	0166	1
DAVIS HARRY L	MAJ	0-0109617	1047	1	DAVIS JOHN P	MAJ	0-1284672	0548	2	DAVIS PERK L	MAJ	0-0497213	0546	2	DAVIS WILLIAM J	LTC	0-0117786	0245	2
DAVIS HARRY L	LTC	0-0197898	0665	1	DAVIS JOHN P	CW3	W-2144036	0564	1	DAVIS PETER F	MAJ	0-1643974	1157	1	DAVIS WILLIAM J	CPT	0-0548029	0547	2
DAVIS HARRY L JR	MAJ	0-1036500	0862	1	DAVIS JOHN R	LTC	0-0383617	1264	3	DAVIS QUENTIN P	COL	0-0257622	0168	3	DAVIS WILLIAM J	1LT	0-1101402	1045	2
DAVIS HARRY O	LTC	0-1328239	0767	1	DAVIS JOHN R	1LT	0-0399025	0743	2	DAVIS RALEIGH H	MAJ	0-1551190	0865	1	DAVIS WILLIAM J	1LT	0-4006879	0856	2
DAVIS HARRY V	LTC	0-1049791	0962	1	DAVIS JOHN R	LTC	0-1110450	1060	1	DAVIS RALPH M	MAJ	0-0342379	1045	2	DAVIS WILLIAM J JR	2LT	0-1328577	0945	2
DAVIS HARRY W	LTC	0-2018659	0868	1	DAVIS JOHN S	LTC	0-0287913	0762	3	DAVIS RANDALL B	MAJ	0-1330794	0967	1	DAVIS WILLIAM L	CW2	W-2149789	0756	1
DAVIS HAYWOOD M	CPT	0-0498010	0845	2	DAVIS JOHN S	2LT	0-0374065	1041	2	DAVIS RAY L	COL	0-0418102	1060	1	DAVIS WILLIAM M	LTC	0-0504891	0161	1
DAVIS HENLEY H	MAJ	0-0271214	0566	3	DAVIS JOHN S	COL	0-0918672	0667	3	DAVIS RAY M	CPT	0-0210708	0645	2	DAVIS WILLIAM M	1LT	0-0955165	1053	2
DAVIS HENRY T	1LT	0-1315280	0945	2	DAVIS JOHN T	LTC	0-0308748	0563	1	DAVIS RAY M	WO1	W-2127967	0567	2	DAVIS WILLIAM M JR	LTC	0-1181862	1062	1
DAVIS HERSCHEL F	CPT	0-0228162	1157	3	DAVIS JOHN V	MAJ	0-0684494	0865	1	DAVIS RAYMOND A	CPT	0-1182811	0961	1	DAVIS WILLIAM O	CPT	0-1590403	0161	2
DAVIS HOMER M	MAJ	0-0192690	0860	3	DAVIS JOHN W	LTC	0-0256769	1041	2	DAVIS REECE D	MAJ	0-0970532	0464	1	DAVIS WILLIAM R	CPT	0-0465657	0646	2
DAVIS HORACE B	CW3	W-2101593	0955	1	DAVIS JOHN W	LTC	0-0454735	0463	1	DAVIS REED T	CW3	W-2146762	0663	1	DAVIS WILLIAM S	CW2	W-2209383	0266	1
DAVIS HOWARD B	CPT	0-0105958	1054	1	DAVIS JOHN W	CPT	0-1308796	0246	2	DAVIS RICHARD B	MAJ	0-2016122	0563	1	DAVIS WILLIAM T	LTC	0-0387322	0767	3
DAVIS HOWARD F	CPT	0-0397821	0862	1	DAVIS JOHN W	MAJ	0-2025465	1068	1	DAVIS RICHARD E	LTC	0-1179830	0264	1	DAVIS WILLIAM W	COL	0-0322164	0663	1
DAVIS HOWARD P	MAJ	0-0304103	0253	3	DAVIS JOHNNIE E	CPT	0-1996700	0757	1	DAVIS RICHARD H JR	MAJ	0-2005449	0860	1	DAVIS WILLIE F	CW4	W-2132990	0960	1
DAVIS HOWARD S	1LT	0-0496865	0858	1	DAVIS JOSEPHINE	MAJ	N-0700665	1146	1	DAVIS RICHARD L	COL	0-0213229	0763	3	DAVIS WILLIE S	LTC	0-2204055	0768	1
DAVIS HOWELL A JR	MAJ	0-0498614	0557	1	DAVIS JOSHUA W	COL	0-0208140	1056	3	DAVIS RICHARD M	LTC	0-0451588	0261	1	DAVIS WILLSON	LTC	0-0253364	0267	3
DAVIS HUBERT L	CPT	0-2014561	0763	1	DAVIS JULIAN W	COL	0-0281980	1068	3	DAVIS RICHARD S	1LT	0-5423945	0468	2	DAVIS WILSON S	MAJ	0-1321571	1160	2
DAVIS HUBERT V	LTC	0-0173376	1058	3	DAVIS KARL P	MAJ	0-0112224	0255	3	DAVIS RICHARD W	1LT	0-0529766	0146	2	DAVIS WOODARD B	CW3	W-2145802	0462	1
DAVIS HUDSON T	CPT	0-0520932	0357	3	DAVIS KENNETH E	MAJ	0-2289141	0960	1	DAVIS ROBERT A	LTC	0-0887366	0564	1	DAVIS WORTH C	MAJ	0-0966414	0964	1
DAVIS HUGH D	MAJ	0-0420277	0747	2	DAVIS KENNETH G	WO1	W-2152115	1054	2	DAVIS ROBERT F	LTC	0-0984475	0767	1	DAVISON ALLEN P	CPT	0-1281146	1062	1
DAVIS HUGH F	COL	0-0332404	0954	1	DAVIS KYLE F	COL	0-0423327	0962	1	DAVIS ROBERT H	CPT	0-1799621	0258	1	DAVISON BURNS H	CPT	0-0119471	1158	3
DAVIS HUGH O	COL	0-0245651	0959	3	DAVIS LAURENCE R	MAJ	0-1542456	0658	1	DAVIS ROBERT J	CPT	0-5419757	1268	2	DAVISON CHARLES H	1LT	0-0747764	0646	2
DAVIS HUGO M	CPT	0-0275977	0948	1	DAVIS LAWRENCE B	1LT	0-1044792	0345	2	DAVIS ROBERT L	LTC	0-0174834	0362	3	DAVISON CHRISTINE	MAJ	N-0702015	0366	3
DAVIS IRVIN C JR	LTC	0-1297169	0459	1	DAVIS LAWRENCE C	LTC	0-0496683	0466	3	DAVIS ROBERT L	CW2	W-2148399	1059	1	DAVISON DAVID J	2LT	0-5206670	0160	2
DAVIS IRVING	MAJ	0-0317628	0447	2	DAVIS LAWRENCE E	LTC	0-1102690	1065	1	DAVIS ROBERT M	MAJ	0-1305473	0861	1	DAVISON DONALD L	LTC	0-1585340	0662	1
DAVIS J C	MAJ	0-1823125	0361	1	DAVIS LAWRENCE J	1LT	0-0493807	0246	2	DAVIS ROCKWELL A	LTC	0-0225959	0760	3	DAVISON EDWARD H	MAJ	0-0251344	1165	3
DAVIS JACK I	COL	0-0301288	1160	1	DAVIS LEO W	LTC	0-0165723	0655	3	DAVIS ROGER F	CW2	W-2111172	0549	1	DAVISON FLOYD A	LTC	0-0178600	1061	3
DAVIS JACK R	LTC	0-1108603	0962	1	DAVIS LEON M	CPT	0-1920228	0463	1	DAVIS ROSEMARY F	1LT	N-0773520	1046	1	DAVISON JOSEPH A	LTC	0-1540761	1267	1
DAVIS JACK W	1LT	0-2034705	0545	2	DAVIS LEON N	CPT	0-0321879	0546	2	DAVIS ROSS P	CW4	W-2145258	1067	1	DAVISON KENNETH A	LTC	0-0355738	0959	1
DAVIS JACK W	CW3	W-2145410	0657	1	DAVIS LEONARD E	CPT	0-1637991	1058	1	DAVIS ROY A	LTC	0-0450206	0557	1	DAVISON LEE F	CW3	W-3150203	0868	1
DAVIS JAMES A	LTC	0-1633794	0660	1	DAVIS LESLIE F	CPT	0-0226824	0764	3	DAVIS ROY JR	LTC	0-0422331	0961	1	DAVISON LEON R	MAJ	0-1280223	0354	1
DAVIS JAMES D	CW2	W-2145991	1060	1	DAVIS LESTER L	1LT	0-0206143	1054	3	DAVIS SAMUEL L	LTC	0-0284797	0448	2	DAVISON TREADWELL	MAJ	0-0419444	0146	2
DAVIS JAMES E	MAJ	0-0259108	0945	2	DAVIS LESTER W	LTC	0-1324759	0967	1	DAVIS SHERWOOD S	1LT	0-0469667	0844	2	DAVISON WARREN P	MAJ	0-0388465	1045	2
DAVIS JAMES E	MAJ	0-0371150	0964	1	DAVIS LLOYD E	MAJ	0-2035805	0657	1	DAVIS SIDNEY S	COL	0-0326715	0760	1	DAVISON WILLIAM C	1LT	0-0397741	0245	2
DAVIS JAMES F	MAJ	0-0500393	0863	1	DAVIS LONARD N	CW2	W-2214512	0767	1	DAVIS STANLEY F	1LT	0-1702997	1145	2	DAVISSON CLAUDE R	CPT	0-0546636	0247	2
DAVIS JAMES F	LTC	0-1323545	0268	1	DAVIS LORANZIA E	MAJ	0-1300136	0661	1	DAVIS STANLEY V	1LT	0-1015300	1045	2	DAVISSON JOHN E	LTC	0-0225511	0460	1
DAVIS JAMES F	CW3	W-2147886	0563	1	DAVIS LOUIS G	1LT	0-1309917	1145	2	DAVIS STEVE G	COL	0-1165342	0850	2	DAVISSON RUSSELL W	MAJ	0-2006888	1165	1
DAVIS JAMES F JR	LTC	0-0379440	1264	1	DAVIS MACK A	CW3	W-2237728	0267	1	DAVIS SYLVIA	CPT	L-0204378	1046	2	DAVOLL WILLIAM C	MAJ	0-0373246	0760	1
DAVIS JAMES H	CPT	0-0497972	0353	1	DAVIS MAJOR B	CW2	W-2144447	1160	1	DAVIS TANDY L	CPT	0-1293215	0161	1	DAVOUST NORBERT J	CPT	0-1100072	0346	2
DAVIS JAMES H	LTC	0-0917369	1150	2	DAVIS MAMIE D	CPT	N-0763592	0747	1	DAVIS TEX	LTC	0-0441648	0954	1	DAVY MARTIN E	LTC	0-0309924	0759	1
DAVIS JAMES H	MAJ	0-2019561	0466	1	DAVIS MARION B	LTC	0-0382314	0466	3	DAVIS THEODORE F	CW3	W-2147763	1060	1	DAWE EDWARD J	MAJ	0-0374428	1046	2
DAVIS JAMES H	CPT	0-2032446	0457	1	DAVIS MARTIN L	LTC	0-0336888	0663	1	DAVIS THEODORE R	CW3	W-2212208	1068	1	DAWES CHARLES C	COL	0-0166510	0359	3
DAVIS JAMES J	LTC	0-1555534	0657	1	DAVIS MAURICE JR	CPT	0-1825402	1262	1	DAVIS THOMAS E	LTC	0-0672577	0867	1	DAWES HENRY C	CPT	0-1577079	0149	1
DAVIS JAMES K	LTC	0-1015929	0559	1	DAVIS MAYRON J	CW2	W-3151359	1067	1	DAVIS THOMAS F	MAJ	0-1004459	0650	2	DAWES RICHARD M	CPT	0-0285707	0665	3
DAVIS JAMES L	COL	0-0277799	0566	1	DAVIS MC LAIN SR	1LT	0-0988597	1058	1	DAVIS THOMAS H	LTC	0-0244487	0859	3	DAWLEY CHARLES R	COL	0-0128309	0257	3
DAVIS JAMES L	MAJ	0-0477655	1146	2	DAVIS MELVILLE D	LTC	0-0277298	0960	3	DAVIS THOMAS H	1LT	0-0291197	0167	3	DAWS REX T	MAJ	0-0297846	0144	2
DAVIS JAMES L JR	LTC	0-0415808	0161	1	DAVIS MICHAEL	CW3	W-2148922	0863	1	DAVIS THOMAS J	LTC	0-1168528	0760	1	DAWSEY WILLIAM C	MAJ	0-0379248	1150	2
DAVIS JAMES M	MAJ	0-0355720	0662	1	DAVIS MILDRED E	MAJ	N-0742477	0848	2	DAVIS TOMMYE H	MAJ	N-0727336	1263	3	DAWSON ALVA D	COL	0-0223424	1164	1
DAVIS JAMES T	CW2	W-2141246	1159	1	DAVIS MILES M	CPT	0-1574410	0146	2	DAVIS VANN B	CPT	0-0342055	0645	2	DAWSON ARCH A	CPT	0-0304989	1045	2
DAVIS JAMES W	COL	0-0265116	0459	1	DAVIS MILFORD C	WO1	W-2206827	0956	2	DAVIS VERNON F	LTC	0-1323670	0265	1	DAWSON ARCHIE L	CPT	0-2008032	0656	1
DAVIS JAMES W	COL	0-0376799	0265	1	DAVIS MILLARD Q	MAJ	0-1285391	0864	1	DAVIS VERNON T	1LT	0-1635760	0857	1	DAWSON CHARLES D	CPT	0-1651733	0860	1
DAVIS JAMES W	MAJ	0-1693132	0963	1	DAVIS MONTAGUE E	MAJ	0-1899398	1060	1	DAVIS VIRGIL F	1LT	0-0268862	0745	2	DAWSON CHARLES L	WO1	W-2115514	0247	1
DAVIS JAMES W	CW3	W-2147180	0966	1	DAVIS MURRAY H JR	CPT	0-0262843	0664	3	DAVIS VORIS R	1LT	0-1822176	1145	2	DAWSON CHARLES O	COL	0-0262988	0167	3
DAVIS JAY D	MAJ	0-0972290	0661	1	DAVIS NATHAN H	1LT	0-2025896	0955	1	DAVIS W A	1LT	0-1283219	0845	2	DAWSON CHARLES P	WO1	W-2122422	0846	1
DAVIS JAY M	LTC	0-0259211	1264	2	DAVIS NEIL W	1LT	0-0368448	1144	2	DAVIS WALTER A	LTC	0-0555769	0767	1	DAWSON CHESTER C	B G	0-0319742	1068	3
DAVIS JAY R	CW4	W-2146427	0967	1	DAVIS NELL M	MAJ	N-0730219	0465	3	DAVIS WALTER C	CPT	0-0574369	0152	2	DAWSON CLAUD L	MAJ	0-0489547	0552	1
DAVIS JENNIE G	MAJ	N-0723394	0263	1	DAVIS NELSON F	2LT	0-1304871	0145	2	DAVIS WALTER G	MAJ	0-1306390	0359	1	DAWSON DARREL W	CW2	W-2147600	0365	1
DAVIS JESSE C	LTC	0-0226194	0862	3	DAVIS NOAH S JR	LTC	0-0242091	0346	2	DAVIS WARREN R JR	CW4	W-2150275	0168	1	DAWSON DUDLEY T	COL	0-0203513	0648	3
DAVIS JESSE T	LTC	0-0234122	0765	3	DAVIS NORMAN H JR	COL	0-0236511	0266	3	DAVIS WAYNE F	MAJ	0-1920149	0465	1	DAWSON EDWARD	CPT	0-0509180	1046	1
DAVIS JIM	LTC	0-0967906	0168	1	DAVIS NORMAN S	CPT	0-0504304	0445	2	DAVIS WENDELL T	CW2	W-2109855	1043	2	DAWSON EDWARD S JR	MAJ	0-0146740	0648	3
DAVIS JOAN E	MAJ	N-0781324	1063	1	DAVIS OCTAVIUS C	LTC	0-0384319	0660	1	DAVIS WILBUR P	MAJ	0-0277303	0858	3	DAWSON ELMER A	MAJ	0-0336540	1064	3
DAVIS JOE E	COL	0-0336049	1156	3	DAVIS OLE C	LTC	0-1036115	1163	1	DAVIS WILLIAM A	LTC	0-1323546	0263	1	DAWSON FRANCIS M	CW4	W-2151754	1168	1
DAVIS JOE S	CW3	W-2145466	0262	1	DAVIS OLIVER E	CW2	W-2208753	0264	1	DAVIS WILLIAM E	MAJ	0-0245661	0953	3	DAWSON FRANCIS W	COL	0-0400036	1168	1
DAVIS JOHN B	MAJ	0-1014065	0860	1	DAVIS ORVILLE R	LTC	0-0197494	1060	3	DAVIS WILLIAM F	1LT	0-1174317	1044	2	DAWSON FREDRICK	MAJ	0-0996491	1164	1
DAVIS JOHN C	LTC	0-0201365	1144	2	DAVIS OSCAR L	MAJ	0-0510298	0955	1	DAVIS WILLIAM F	CPT	0-1946025	0447	1	DAWSON GEOFFREY S	CW2	W-2112141	1058	1
DAVIS JOHN C	MAJ	0-1080777	0460	1	DAVIS PAUL A	MAJ	0-1043320	0161	1	DAVIS WILLIAM F	CW2	W-2152018	1156	1	DAWSON GEORGE I	COL	0-0265919	0453	3
DAVIS JOHN E	CPT	0-0110132	0551	3	DAVIS PAUL G	CPT	0-1057719	0567	3	DAVIS WILLIAM G	COL	0-0240362	0263	1	DAWSON GEORGE P	MAJ	0-0946802	1067	1

NAME	GRADE	SVC NO	DATE RET MO YR	RET CODE
DAWSON GEORGE W	CPT	0-0128710	0668	3
DAWSON HARWIN	CPT	0-1631155	0361	1
DAWSON JACK W	MAJ	0-1587205	0957	1
DAWSON JAMES E	MAJ	0-1944913	0962	1
DAWSON JEROME W	CPT	0-2037224	0747	2
DAWSON LOUIS S JR	COL	0-0221961	1045	2
DAWSON MERLE R	COL	0-0923554	0864	1
DAWSON MILLARD E	CW2	W-2209330	0664	1
DAWSON PAT W	LTC	0-0336300	0664	3
DAWSON REX H	MAJ	0-1824269	0661	1
DAWSON RICHARD	MAJ	0-0987541	1066	1
DAWSON ROBERT H	COL	0-0269466	0768	3
DAWSON ROBERT L	MAJ	0-0517112	0156	2
DAWSON ROBERTA R	1LT	L-0900831	1145	2
DAWSON RUSSELL H	LTC	0-1165343	0164	1
DAWSON THOMAS H	CPT	0-1796244	0849	1
DAWSON THURMAN E	MAJ	0-0382749	0146	2
DAWSON WILLIAM A	MAJ	0-0310463	1144	2
DAY ALANSON R	MAJ	0-1309046	0947	2
DAY ALFRED L	COL	0-0136537	0346	2
DAY ALFRED K JR	LTC	0-1104602	0962	1
DAY CHARLES H	LTC	0-1062351	0667	1
DAY CHARLES W	CPT	0-0969390	0862	1
DAY CHARLIE F	2LT	0-1304874	0944	2
DAY CLAYTON F	CW3	W-2210974	0663	1
DAY DAINE L	LTC	0-0330642	1065	1
DAY DANIEL E	LTC	0-0422885	0261	2
DAY EDNA S	1LT	N-0731221	0546	1
DAY EDWARD H	MAJ	0-0489393	0954	1
DAY EKNNETH F	LTC	0-0392311	0460	1
DAY EVAN B	MAJ	0-1056073	0163	1
DAY GEORGE E	CW3	W-2207157	0367	1
DAY GEORGE H	LTC	0-0986892	0767	1
DAY HAL B	CPT	0-2000117	0761	1
DAY HARRY I	2LT	0-0281277	1064	3
DAY HOWARD L	LTC	0-0926915	0968	3
DAY JOHN F	CW3	W-3100304	0968	1
DAY JOHN G	2LT	0-1081552	0265	3
DAY JOHN J	MAJ	0-0338453	0267	3
DAY JOHN S	LTC	0-1316940	1159	1
DAY LAWRENCE F	CW4	W-2112038	0461	3
DAY LEONARD R	LTC	0-0394989	0756	1
DAY LEWIS A	LTC	0-0177313	0161	3
DAY MARION W	LTC	0-0290688	0446	2
DAY MYRON G	CW2	W-2205783	0960	1
DAY OSWALD N	CPT	0-0101682	1051	3
DAY OWENS L	CPT	0-0352356	0445	2
DAY ROBERT L	MAJ	0-2046943	0665	1
DAY ROBERT E	COL	0-0910386	0967	3
DAY ROGER D	COL	0-0212622	1160	3
DAY RUTH B	2LT	N-0751127	0545	1
DAY THOMAS L	CPT	0-0934091	0152	2
DAY THOMAS R	MAJ	0-1015286	0759	1
DAY THOMAS W	MAJ	0-1283922	0267	3
DAY WALTER L	LTC	0-0441089	0154	1
DAY WALTER W	CPT	0-2262618	0261	1
DAY WESSELS H	LTC	0-2033001	0266	1
DAY WILBUR	1LT	0-0451239	0245	2
DAY WILLIAM P	COL	0-0184920	0652	3
DAY WILLIAM R	CW3	W-2208005	0868	1
DAY WILLIAM W	MAJ	0-1573152	0457	1
DAY WILLIAM Z	CW4	W-2147746	0957	1
DAYE KHLAR J	MAJ	0-1319403	0161	1
DAYLEY JOHN W III	CPT	0-1062919	0753	2
DAYNES GERALD P	CPT	0-0265893	0145	2
DAYSH HARRISON J	1LT	0-1298362	0745	2
DAYTON EUGENE K	1LT	0-1318769	0545	2
DAYTON PERCY H	LTC	0-0509186	0761	1
DAYTON WILLIAM J	CW3	W-2142389	1160	1
DAYTON WILLIAM R	COL	0-0333295	1061	1
DAZE DAVID J	2LT	0-1692600	0845	2
DAZEY WILLIAM B	2LT	0-2012325	0346	2
DE AGLE ELWELL T	LTC	0-1635763	0960	1
DE ANDREA ALFONSO R	CW4	W-2003921	1065	1
DE ANGELIS ALFRED	LTC	0-1292665	0959	1

NAME	GRADE	SVC NO	DATE RET MO YR	RET CODE
DE ANGELIS FREDERICK	LTC	0-0199180	0263	3
DE ANGELIS MICHAEL L	LTC	0-1314263	0261	1
DE ANGELO JOHN A	MAJ	0-0502704	1054	1
DE ANTONIO LOUIS	LTC	0-1823126	0262	1
DE ARMAN CHARLES R	LTC	0-0258519	0368	3
DE ARMAS LOUIS H	2LT	0-1288020	0245	2
DE ARMOND ALBERT M	COL	0-0245748	0159	3
DE ARMOND EBEN A	MAJ	0-0425879	0547	2
DE ARMOND GRAVES L	LTC	0-0360622	0261	1
DE ARMOND JOE S	MAJ	0-1295518	0561	1
DE ARMOND PAUL D	1LT	0-5239752	0668	2
DE AVEIRO CHARLES F	2LT	0-1324724	0645	2
DE BACKER RAYMOND H	CW2	W-2152764	0561	1
DE BAGGIS JOHN H	CPT	0-1549694	0947	2
DE BARBIERI THOMAS F	LTC	0-1542832	0661	1
DE BARD CARL O	M G	0-0288794	0864	3
DE BARRY JULIA	1LT	N-0741198	0246	1
DE BAST LEROY R	MAJ	0-1315916	1068	3
DE BAT LUCILE A	CPT	L-0303858	1047	2
DE BELLEVUE CASSIUS	LTC	0-0482146	0566	3
DE BERNARDI L A	2LT	0-1036502	0245	2
DE BEVOISE CHARLES P	LTC	0-1011022	0164	1
DE BIASE JOHN D	1LT	0-1180869	0746	2
DE BLOIS RENE L	COL	0-0282807	0160	1
DE BOE FREEMAN C	LTC	0-0362705	0267	3
DE BOEF CLARENCE P	2LT	0-0888238	0444	2
DE BOER ARLEN M	MAJ	0-1282395	0562	1
DE BOER GUY W	CPT	0-1686998	0346	2
DE BOER RALPH E	1LT	0-1324518	0846	2
DE BOILE BENJAMIN S	MAJ	0-0119639	0249	3
DE BOIS WALTER	MAJ	0-0447965	0153	2
DE BOLT FRANCIS M	CPT	0-1703417	0465	1
DE BOLT PAUL L	LTC	0-1544052	0660	1
DE BONI LAWRENCE M	CW3	W-2144510	1163	1
DE BORD MARSHALL E	MAJ	0-0150602	0251	3
DE BORD PAUL S	CPT	0-0554172	1060	1
DE BOURKE JOHN M	MAJ	0-2263595	1164	1
DE BOWER RICHARD M	LTC	0-0259053	0867	3
DE BOY WILLIAM H	LTC	0-0366038	0966	1
DE BRABANDER PROSPER	MAJ	0-1341951	1262	1
DE BROHL EDWARD C	CPT	0-1040517	0760	1
DE BROHL PAUL K	MAJ	0-1285907	0945	2
DE BRULER DOUGLAS A	1LT	0-1894621	0744	2
DE BOSK FRED G	COL	0-0281598	0965	3
DE BUSK HARRY L	LTC	0-0492409	0457	1
DE BOYS WILLIAM E	LTC	0-0259865	0767	3
DE CAIR JESSE R JR	LTC	0-1186637	1266	1
DE CAIRIO ALFONZO	1LT	0-0291556	0546	2
DE CAMP ALLEN L	COL	0-0316374	1068	3
DE CAMP CLARENCE A	LTC	0-0103508	0648	3
DE CARLO JESS	MAJ	0-0496327	0456	1
DE CARLO JOSEPH B	CW4	W-2144366	0766	2
DE CARLO MAURICE	CPT	0-0493885	1053	1
DE CARLO VINCENT J	WO1	W-2127206	0955	1
DE CAROLIS FREDERICK	LTC	0-0346817	0968	3
DE CASTLE MASON V	LTC	0-0310007	0768	3
DE CESARIS ALFRED F	LTC	0-0280505	0867	3
DE CHARLEROY ALBERT	LTC	0-0394271	0867	1
DE CHARLES ROGER Y	1LT	0-1175990	0745	2
DE CHOW GEORGEEN H	1LT	N-0801234	0947	1
DE CHRISTOFARO JOHN	COL	0-0303389	0768	3
DE CLEENE CLARENCE B	MAJ	0-2208027	0762	1
DE CLUE CLYDE R	CW3	W-2147252	1165	1
DE CORY CLAUDE C	LTC	0-0391355	0560	1
DE COSTANZO NICHOLAS	LTC	0-1335756	0366	1
DE CRISTOFORO W H E	CPT	0-0388921	1060	1
DE CRISTOFORO WALTER	LTC	0-0450844	0663	1
DE DIEGO MANUEL	CPT	0-0404792	0745	2
DE DOMENICO JOHN T	1LT	0-1010356	0945	2
DE FALCO MICHAEL	CW3	W-2150321	0165	1
DE FEEN MICHAEL A	MAJ	0-1290727	1157	1
DE FINA MICHAEL V	CPT	0-0347284	0966	3
DE FLON LOUISE A	1LT	N-0737528	0646	1
DE FLORIA ANTHONY G	1LT	0-1637280	0345	2
DE FLORIN HENRY E	LTC	0-0395530	0868	1

NAME	GRADE	SVC NO	DATE RET MO YR	RET CODE
DE FORD DON D	COL	0-0250178	0964	1
DE FORD LELAND E	CPT	0-0982593	0962	1
DE FORD LESTER J	CPT	0-0184555	0951	3
DE FOREST EARLE W	LTC	0-0359532	0563	3
DE FOREST RALPH E	CPT	0-1755785	0248	2
DE FORGE JOHN D	LTC	0-0834143	0868	1
DE FOY WALTER F	COL	0-0323796	0560	1
DE FRAIN RAY L	MAJ	0-1822265	0159	2
DE FRANCO MARY R	MAJ	N-0756912	1063	1
DE FRANCO RUTH O	1LT	N-0742214	0546	2
DE FREES JOHN H JR	MAJ	0-1878852	0466	1
DE FREEST JAMES W	LTC	0-1316993	0561	2
DE GARMO IVAN M	MAJ	0-1591087	0262	1
DE GARMO JAMES M	LTC	0-0406806	0463	1
DE GIACOMO FRANK	COL	0-0285035	0661	2
DE GLAS JACQUES G	CW3	W-2211085	0868	1
DE GRACIE JAMES F	LTC	0-1316021	0568	3
DE GRAFF FARRIS E	MAJ	0-1286452	1057	1
DE GRAM JOHN C	CW3	W-2145615	0761	1
DE GRANGE JUSTIN H	LTC	0-0475270	0251	1
DE GRAW KENNETH F	COL	0-0216508	0363	3
DE GRAZIA EUGENE J	CPT	0-1684574	0545	2
DE GREGORIO ANTHONY	CW4	W-2143491	0564	2
DE GREGORIO JOSEPH J	MAJ	0-2212028	0763	1
DE GREY SIDNEY	1LT	0-0278642	1041	2
DE GROAT JAMES R	MAJ	0-0546599	0966	3
DE GROFF CHARLES F	COL	0-0323997	1166	3
DE GROOT FRANKLIN T	MAJ	0-1796587	1160	1
DE GROOT LAWRENCE R	LTC	0-0910402	0962	1
DE GROVE JOHN M	1LT	0-2016450	1046	2
DE GUINZBOURG VICTOR	LTC	0-1692515	0365	3
DE GUZMAN GERMAN C	1LT	0-2030661	0150	2
DE GUZMAN JOSE J	CPT	0-0278133	0860	3
DE HART LOWELL M	LTC	0-0204481	0959	3
DE HAVEN CLARENCE T	COL	0-0268867	0167	3
DE HAVEN JACOB G	LTC	0-0505432	0963	1
DE HAVEN ROLAND E	WO1	W-2106649	0854	1
DE HAVEN WILLIAM D	COL	0-0237034	0363	3
DE HAVEN WILLIAM E	CPT	0-0269859	0545	2
DE HOFF EMMETT	MAJ	0-1101405	0254	1
DE HORN RONALD F	LTC	0-0313160	0656	1
DE HORSEY REEL D B	LTC	0-1641988	0765	1
DE JARNETTE DAVID L	MAJ	0-0259127	0767	3
DE JARNETTE JAMES L	LTC	0-0239405	0764	3
DE JARNETTE LEWIS W	COL	0-0284066	0968	3
DE JARNETTE WILLIAM	COL	0-0220036	0764	3
DE JESS ARTURO	LTC	0-0953689	1268	1
DE JESUS JOSE	1LT	0-1896486	0962	1
DE JESUS VINCENTE	CW3	W-2213341	1167	2
DE JONGE ALFRED P W	COL	0-0243318	0648	3
DE KASER RICHARD J	1LT	0-1178454	1146	2
DE KAY ORMONDE	LTC	0-0173314	1160	3
DE KENO RICHARD L	CW3	W-2145674	1063	1
DE KEYSER ERNEST	MAJ	0-1635770	0856	1
DE KLOTZ FRED W	COL	0-0216937	0561	3
DE KROYFF RICHARD D	LTC	0-0213813	0361	3
DE LA MATER J A JR	LTC	0-0252741	1047	2
DE LA PENA MIGUE	LTC	0-1303119	0467	1
DE LACY CLIFFORD H	CPT	0-1310818	0448	2
DE LAITE DONALD K	CW4	W-2004330	1068	1
DE LAMARTER RICHARD	LTC	0-1551598	1263	1
DE LAMATER WALTER A	B G	0-0142906	0648	3
DE LANLEY ZEB V	MAJ	0-0370749	0260	1
DE LANO MELVIN F	MAJ	0-2051436	1262	1
DE LANO PAUL K	1LT	0-1290729	0845	2
DE LANE JAMES K	MAJ	0-1638031	1265	1
DE LANEY CHARLES S	CPT	0-1176303	1046	2
DE LANEY THERON B	CW3	W-2145768	1162	1
DE LANEY VIRGIL L	MAJ	0-1185359	1160	1
DE LAP DAVID F	COL	0-0242740	1150	3
DE LAPPE GEORGE R	MAJ	0-2041093	0561	1
DE LARM FREDERICK	LTC	0-0362103	0664	3
DE LASHMET CARL A	LTC	0-1013850	1163	1
DE LAUNE WYBRA S	1LT	0-1293380	0745	2
DE LAURA VINCENT J	1LT	0-1315038	0945	2

NAME	GRADE	SVC NO	DATE RET MO YR	RET CODE
DE LAUTER LLOYD W	LTC	0-1543124	1068	3
DE LECLUSE EDMOND H	MAJ	0-1584912	0650	2
DE LEE MERINE	LTC	0-0115722	1059	3
DE LEO GAN A	1LT	0-1287315	1145	2
DE LEO FELIX R	CPT	0-0444612	0546	2
DE LEON EDWARD F	LTC	0-0452359	0957	1
DE LEON EUGENE P	MAJ	0-1301621	0560	1
DE LISO HENRY G	CPT	0-0469251	1044	2
DE LISSOVOY VLADIMIR	CPT	0-0426659	0345	2
DE LIT CLEMENT	CPT	0-1689490	0246	2
DE LOACH JAMES F	MAJ	0-4006202	0868	1
DE LOACH JAMES W	LTC	0-1286255	1060	1
DE LOACH SAM C	LTC	0-1944659	1057	1
DE LOACH SERRE D	LTC	0-0219392	1161	1
DE LOGE WILFRED T	CPT	0-1287156	1045	2
DE LONG CLEO W	MAJ	0-1107387	0561	1
DE LONG HOWARD M	LTC	0-1289557	0666	1
DE LONG JOHN	LTC	0-0962144	1068	3
DE LONG ROBERT D	CPT	0-0556595	1147	2
DE LONG WALTER C	MAJ	0-0372095	1153	1
DE LONG WALTER J	COL	0-0176195	0358	3
DE LONG WILLIAM J	MAJ	0-1923795	0568	1
DE LOS RIOS LEO B	LTC	0-0904917	1266	3
DE LOZIER LEON S	1LT	0-1013875	0747	1
DE LUCA FRANK P	CPT	0-1690135	0445	2
DE LUCA JOHN V	LTC	0-1546745	1262	1
DE LUCA NICHOLAS J	2LT	0-2040733	0744	2
DE LUCCIA EMIL R	LTC	0-0241181	1064	3
DE MACKIEWICZ J H	LTC	0-0251741	0660	3
DE MAINE HENRY M JR	CPT	0-1057405	0651	2
DE MAIO ARMAND	MAJ	0-1322900	0260	1
DE MARANVILLE KENDAL	WO1	W-3156763	0468	2
DE MARCAY GEORGE A	LTC	0-1045391	0662	1
DE MARCO JOSEPH	LTC	0-1293022	0661	1
DE MARCO LOUIS R	MAJ	0-1299708	0562	1
DE MARCO MATTHEW	MAJ	0-0957568	1062	1
DE MARIO CHARLES A	CW2	W-2209815	0765	1
DE MARIO DAVID	1LT	0-1317278	0247	2
DE MARS ROBERT E	CPT	0-0966817	0363	1
DE MARTINO JAMES V	LTC	0-0275627	0551	2
DE MASSE THEODORE E	LTC	0-1577090	1161	1
DE MATTEO IGNATIUS M	CPT	0-0422087	0345	2
DE MELO ANGELO	CPT	0-0473043	0450	1
DE MENT RUSSELL D	MAJ	0-1337551	0864	1
DE MERCHANT CHESTER	CW2	W-2146962	0762	1
DE MERELL GEORGE S	LTC	0-0162171	0753	3
DE MERITT EDWIN W	CPT	0-1049797	0955	1
DE MERRITT ARTHUR L	MAJ	0-0533658	1054	1
DE MERSE ARTHUR E	LTC	0-0378057	1161	1
DE MEULENAERE JOHN C	CPT	0-0381024	0346	2
DE MEY MAURICE	MAJ	0-2263535	1264	1
DE MILIA ALFRED F	CPT	0-0483936	0345	2
DE MILLE LYNN V	MAJ	0-1176932	0360	1
DE MILLER EDGAR A	MAJ	0-0228358	1262	1
DE MONO GERALD G	CW2	W-2105427	1160	1
DE MONE CHARLES J	LTC	0-0426052	0465	1
DE MONTFORT HAROLD	1LT	0-0312076	1163	3
DE MOOR LEONARD	LTC	0-0485775	1262	3
DE MOORE EUGENE W	LTC	0-0312250	0650	2
DE MOTT ARTHUR E	MAJ	0-0184881	0952	3
DE MOTT HARRY B	CPT	0-2032248	0563	1
DE MOTTE THEODORE M	LTC	0-1556713	0165	3
DE MUN OLIVER M	CW3	W-2145937	0157	1
DE MUTH EDGAR F	COL	0-0208086	1262	3
DE NEAU ROY E	CPT	0-0242120	0245	2
DE PALMA JOSEPH P JR	CPT	0-0966123	0960	1
DE PALO WILLIAM A	LTC	0-0344432	0661	1
DE PANO NATHANIEL	1LT	0-1897054	0659	2
DE PASQUALE FRANCIS	COL	0-0230759	0961	3
DE PASQUALE GEORGE L	LTC	0-0253854	0562	3
DE PASS MAURICE M	LTC	0-1040696	0666	1
DE PAUL ARTHUR	1LT	0-1051538	0445	2
DE PAUL ERNEST F	LTC	0-1045393	0766	1
DE PAUW WILBUR O	LTC	0-1637289	0667	1
DE PETRILLO VICTOR H	LTC	0-1081695	1165	1

NAME	GRADE	SVC NO	DATE RET MO YR	RET CODE
DE PIERRE BRANTON A	MAJ	0-1337940	0963	1
DE PIETRO JAMES A	CW3	W-2147187	0464	1
DE PINTO DOMINIC A	CPT	0-1821459	0245	2
DE PRIEST ERNEST O	CPT	0-0530495	0849	1
DE PRIMO JOSEPH G	LTC	0-1177364	1264	1
DE PRIZIO CARL J	LTC	0-0253070		2
DE PUMPO LESTER J	LTC	0-1544759	0964	1
DE QUOY ALFRED W	COL	0-0369341	0167	1
DE RAMUS INEZ	1LT	N-0734060	0947	1
DE RAMUS JUDSON D	COL	0-0184482	0656	3
DE RENNE ALFRED L	CPT	0-1283387	1046	2
DE RITA JOSEPH	COL	0-0307079	0260	1
DE ROCHE JOHN E	LTC	0-1010053	0366	1
DE ROCHE JOSEPH F	CPT	0-0498185	0357	1
DE ROO CLEMENT O	MAJ	0-0427682	0856	1
DE RUDDE RUDOLPH	CPT	0-0363637	0546	2
DE RODN LOUIS JR	CPT	0-0382541	0446	2
DE ROSA FRANK T	CW3	W-2205710	0865	1
DE ROSA HENRY T	MAJ	0-1553431	0462	1
DE ROSA JOHN J	LTC	0-0339033	0747	2
DE ROSA JOHN J JR	LTC	0-0447286	0662	1
DE ROSA MICHAEL	LTC	0-1552265	1060	1
DE ROSA NICHOLAS J	CPT	0-0480940	0750	1
DE ROSIA JOHN J	MAJ	0-1327823	0862	2
DE ROSSET WILLIAM G	LTC	0-0124791	0648	3
DE SALVO WILLIAM J	COL	0-1301270	0768	1
DE SANDERS NEIL J JR	CPT	0-0375198	0845	2
DE SANDRE ARRIGO	LTC	0-0210984	1055	3
DE SANTIAGO ISAAC	2LT	0-0309086	0444	2
DE SCHWEINITZ LAWREN	MAJ	0-2033124	0660	1
DE SELMS WILBUR C	CPT	0-1000346	0550	1
DE SICO PHILIP A	COL	0-0256603	1165	3
DE SIMONE CARMELO E	LTC	0-1041332	0466	1
DE SIMONE S V	1LT	0-0554922	1146	2
DE SOUCEY EDWARD H	LTC	0-1015396	0366	1
DE SPAIN BETTY L	1LT	N-0733194	0146	1
DE SPAIN LAWRENCE M	CW2	W-2150738	0562	1
DE STAEL NORBERT T	MAJ	0-1695633	0661	1
DE STASIO BARTHOLOME	LTC	0-1101810	1262	1
DE TARNOWSKY ALEXIS	MAJ	0-0222694	0964	3
DE TEMPLE FRANKLIN H	CW3	W-2205597	1266	1
DE TONNANCOURT W	2LT	0-0164363	0648	3
DE TOSKEY PAUL B	MAJ	0-1324929	0662	1
DE VALL LOUIS D	MAJ	0-1297006	0862	1
DE VALL ROGER A	MAJ	0-0948350	1262	1
DE VAN WILLIAM T JR	1LT	0-1825445	0146	2
DE VANE HYBERT T	MAJ	0-1298199	0159	2
DE VEAU LEON R	WO1	W-2120945	0861	2
DE VEAUX WALTER S	MAJ	0-0965983	0861	1
DE VERA DAMASO M	MAJ	0-1896355	0267	1
DE VERTER PAUL L	MAJ	0-0119986	0654	3
DE VILLE ODELL E	LTC	0-0328269	0267	3
DE VINCENT CHESTER J	LTC	0-1796049	1065	1
DE VINE PEARL H	MAJ	N-0775704	0168	3
DE VIRGILIO LOUIS F	MAJ	0-1003504	0261	1
DE VITO LOUIS J	LTC	0-2018857	0868	1
DE VITT EDWARD J	2LT	0-1179368	0445	2
DE VLAMING GEORGE W	MAJ	0-0375857	0461	1
DE VOE GEORGE M	LTC	0-0319949	0664	3
DE VOE JAY J	LTC	0-0169142	0660	3
DE VOR HAROLD V	MAJ	0-0252768	0565	3
DE VORE JANIE M	MAJ	N-0762732	1164	1
DE VORE JEROME L	LTC	0-1081471	0862	1
DE VORE ROBERT L	CW4	W-2152909	0368	1
DE VOSS JAMES T	COL	0-0351360	0561	1
DE VRIES JOHN A	LTC	0-0269825	0765	3
DE WALD JOY H	MAJ	0-1049802	0761	1
DE WALL WALTER R	CW3	W-2146823	0961	1
DE WALT GORDON V	WO1	W-2146326	0153	2
DE WAR LLOYD K	MAJ	0-1013196	0561	1
DE WEERD JAMES A	CPT	0-0520591	0945	2
DE WEES EDWARD C JR	LTC	0-0279758	0868	3
DE WEESE CALVIN S	MAJ	0-0502189	0744	2
DE WEESE JAMES A	CPT	0-0184586	0758	3
DE WEIN HAROLD J W	1LT	0-0371757	1262	2

NAME	GRADE	SVC NO	DATE RET MO YR	RET CODE
DE WEY PAUL	LTC	0-1175415	0762	1
DE WITT DENNIS M	MAJ	0-0286171	0767	3
DE WITT EIRVIN M JR	MAJ	0-1885255	0867	1
DE WITT GEORGE L	MAJ	0-2010822	1262	1
DE WITT HOY S	LTC	0-2021139	0268	1
DE WITT LEONARD A	WO1	W-2121139	0546	2
DE WITT LEONARD C JR	LTC	0-2036639	1267	1
DE WITT PAUL A	LTC	0-0407784	0668	1
DE WITT ROSCOE H	LTC	0-0234920	0660	3
DE WITT VIRGIL B	CPT	0-0249837	0461	3
DE WOLF ANSON B	LTC	0-0174026	1061	3
DE WOLF HOWARD P	CPT	0-1913611	0338	1
DE WOLF LEWIS M	COL	0-0274912	1264	3
DE WOLFE THOMAS A	CPT	0-0383360	0241	2
DE WOODY GERALD M	CPT	0-0312327	0246	2
DE WOODY HUGH G	CPT	0-1303309	0248	2
DE YONG LOUIS W	LTC	0-0195711	0762	3
DE YOUNG KENNETH D	LTC	0-0310700	1159	1
DE YOUNG ROBERT M	MAJ	0-2016157	0164	1
DE&LA&CONCEPCIO A	CPT	0-1896409	0857	1
DE&LA&CRUZ JEREMIAS	2LT	0-1896584	0348	2
DE&ST&AUBIN VICTOR E	1LT	0-1297852	0646	2
DE-LOS-ANGELES F E	1LT	0-0172708	1147	1
DEABLER WALTER E	LTC	0-1281418	0463	1
DEACON JOSEPH F	MAJ	0-1111567	1060	1
DEACON MILTON L	LTC	0-1635762	0562	1
DEACY EDWARD Q	LTC	0-0949394	1067	1
DEADY WILLIAM W	COL	0-0192464	0457	3
DEAKINS JOHN W JR	MAJ	0-1012787	0566	2
DEAL CLAUDE V	LTC	0-0485827	0466	3
DEAL DANIEL W	1LT	0-1175094	0546	2
DEAL HAROLD L	CW4	W-2004015	0768	1
DEAL RAYMOND E	CW3	W-2146644	0360	1
DEAL ROBERT S	CW2	W-2145629	0461	1
DEAL STANLEY V	1LT	0-0509545	0354	1
DEAL WILLIAM E SR	CPT	0-0267441	1047	2
DEAMUD WILDER S	MAJ	0-1289703	0860	1
DEAN ARCHIBALD	MAJ	0-1288019	0666	1
DEAN ARTHUR G	MAJ	0-0300658	0668	3
DEAN AVIS T	1LT	N-0733730	0546	1
DEAN BUFORD W JR	CPT	0-1637275	0346	2
DEAN CECIL R	MAJ	0-0205020	1061	3
DEAN CHARLES J	CW3	W-2141249	1159	1
DEAN CLARENCE	CW4	W-2127949	0659	1
DEAN EDWARD F	1LT	0-1166696	0147	2
DEAN EDWIN L	MAJ	0-0269932	0668	3
DEAN ELMER W	LTC	0-1284834	1057	1
DEAN EVERETT	MAJ	0-0319743	0447	1
DEAN FRANKLIN A	CW2	W-2145304	1059	1
DEAN GEORGE L	CPT	0-0988028	0261	1
DEAN GEORGE M	COL	0-0195665	1261	3
DEAN GERALD C	COL	0-0533792	1167	1
DEAN GERTRUDE M	MAJ	N-0794749	0465	1
DEAN GRACE M	1LT	N-0701440	0643	1
DEAN GUY F	CPT	0-0451559	0357	1
DEAN HAROLD D	MAJ	0-1183498	0859	1
DEAN HAROLD S	COL	0-0276497	0847	2
DEAN HERBERT P	B G	0-0144649	0648	3
DEAN JAMES M JR	1LT	0-0385071	1145	2
DEAN JAMES T	LTC	0-0487671	0157	1
DEAN JOEL L	LTC	0-0250095	0567	3
DEAN JOHN P	COL	0-0113820	0751	3
DEAN JOHN R JR	LTC	0-1950683	1266	3
DEAN JOHN W	MAJ	0-0964918	0163	1
DEAN JOSEPH E	LTC	0-0494722	0459	1
DEAN LEONARD M	1LT	0-0405517	0248	2
DEAN LEWIS W	WO1	W-2127944	1044	2
DEAN LLOYD A	CPT	0-0219521	0855	3
DEAN LUTHER J	LTC	0-1822678	0764	1
DEAN MATTHEW B	MAJ	0-2032129	0858	1
DEAN MERLIN F	MAJ	0-1300772	0854	2
DEAN NORMAN D	COL	0-0178888	1046	2
DEAN OLIN	CPT	0-1578344	0958	1
DEAN PATRICK C	LTC	0-1574412	0561	1
DEAN PAUL R	LTC	0-1553061	0268	1

NAME	GRADE	SVC NO	DATE RET MO YR	RET CODE
DEAN RALPH M	LTC	0-0189712	1058	3
DEAN ROBERT	MAJ	0-1165845	1162	1
DEAN ROBERT C	B G	0-0327502	0164	3
DEAN ROBERT C	CW3	W-2209566	0568	2
DEAN ROBERT D	MAJ	0-0249140	1265	3
DEAN ROBERT P	MAJ	0-1299537	0156	1
DEAN STANLEY E	MAJ	0-1171515	1166	1
DEAN THOMAS J	MAJ	0-0298099	0263	3
DEAN VERNICE E	CW4	W-2146448	1163	2
DEAN VIRGIL F	CPT	0-0920247	0745	2
DEAN WALLACE E	1LT	0-1306565	1045	2
DEAN WESLEY H	MAJ	0-1945112	0863	3
DEAN WILLIAM W JR	LTC	0-1633799	0563	1
DEAN WILSON H JR	MAJ	0-0965126	0263	1
DEANE GEORGE J	CW3	W-2150583	0263	1
DEANE GLENN E	LTC	0-1321104	0962	1
DEANE JOHN J	COL	0-0185004	0154	1
DEANE LESTER C	CPT	0-0990989	0759	2
DEANE WILLIAM V	CW4	W-2141925	0459	1
DEANER ARCHER S	1LT	0-0461546	0645	2
DEANER JAMES F	CPT	0-0996665	0562	1
DEANS GLEN C	MAJ	0-1002198	1058	1
DEANS KENNETH V	LTC	0-0311210	1159	1
DEANS SYLVESTER	MAJ	0-1000343	0247	2
DEANS WILLIAM F	MAJ	0-0961017	0965	1
DEAR CHARLES B	MAJ	0-0332611	0967	3
DEARBORN DONALD H	CPT	0-1999043	0247	2
DEARDORFF RAYMOND A	LTC	0-1290389	0165	3
DEARIE WALTER E	CW2	W-2150110	0662	1
DEARMOND GEORGE W JR	1LT	0-0465866	0145	2
DEARTH JAMES A	MAJ	0-1296826	0547	2
DEARTH JAMES S	LTC	0-2034875	0864	1
DEARTH ROBERT D	LTC	0-1166469	0661	1
DEASE JOSEPH M	2LT	0-1045061	1144	2
DEASON MARY C	1LT	L-0402470	0546	2
DEASON THOMAS B	CW3	W-2206536	1166	1
DEASY RICHARD M	MAJ	0-1999918	0363	1
DEATH RICHARD C	CW2	W-2146824	0561	1
DEATHERAGE CARL	CPT	0-0498268	0254	1
DEATHERAGE HUBERT D	MAJ	0-2005282	1163	1
DEATHERAGE LEON F	CW3	W-2146755	0161	1
DEATHERAGE WILLIAM R	MAJ	0-0254854	0554	3
DEATON ANDY N	LTC	0-0252992	0760	3
DEATON GEORGE V	LTC	0-1573154	0555	1
DEATON JAMES E	MAJ	0-1686640	0165	1
DEATON JAMES T	LTC	0-1637276	1060	1
DEATSCH ROBERT W	CW4	W-2108994	1265	1
DEAVOURS AUBREY W	CPT	0-1292487	0653	1
DEAVY JOHN	CPT	0-0191903	0221	1
DEBALD HARRY G	LTC	0-0920074	0665	3
DEBAR MAURICE	LTC	0-0325755	0463	3
DEBATES RALPH F	WO1	W-2116688	0744	2
DEBELAK WILLIAM F	MAJ	0-0343026	0746	2
DEBES DALE A	LTC	0-0364702	1154	1
DEBEJOISE PAUL	COL	0-0141239	0145	2
DEBIAS FRANK J	1LT	0-1292488	0645	2
DEBO WILLIAM	1LT	0-1822541	0345	2
DEBOER CLARENCE J	CPT	0-1686990	0346	2
DEBOLT LAWRENCE G	LTC	0-1690899	0268	1
DEBORD LEONARD D	1LT	0-1115547	0448	2
DEBRECHT JOSEPH C	1LT	0-1303117	0647	2
DEBROECK CARL E	CPT	0-1303118	0345	2
DEC JOHN J	MAJ	0-1693965	0563	1
DECAMP WILSON H	MAJ	0-0262124	0468	3
DECESARE CARL R	CPT	0-0889359	1058	1
DECESARE FRANK J	CPT	0-0489945	0845	2
DECHANT EDWARD G	MAJ	0-1574348	0154	1
DECHON JOHN F	LTC	0-2014703	1167	1
DECHRISTOFORO ARTHUR	CPT	0-1689584	0145	2
DECK HENRY R	LTC	0-1534950	0764	1
DECK LEON C R	1LT	0-1587919	0351	2
DECK LUCIUS L	LTC	0-0227263	0957	3
DECK WALTER V JR	LTC	0-1294510	0663	1
DECKARD DEWEY	CPT	0-0225040	0349	1
DECKARD LAWRENCE	CW2	W-3430131	0968	1

NAME	GRADE	SVC NO	DATE RET MO YR	RET CODE
DECKARD PAUL D	LTC	0-0262755	0368	3
DECKARD PERCY E	LTC	0-0146834	0648	3
DECKER ALFRED F	LTC	0-1040693	0963	1
DECKER ALPHONSE J	MAJ	0-1822117	0161	1
DECKER ALPINE N	CW3	W-2152636	0665	1
DECKER ARNOLD F	CW2	W-2212261	0864	2
DECKER ARTHUR	LTC	0-1300137	1265	1
DECKER CARL F	LTC	0-0318655	0661	1
DECKER CHARLES	CPT	0-0285792	0757	3
DECKER CHARLES A	COL	0-0272210	1067	3
DECKER CLIFFORD F JR	MAJ	0-0967740	0363	1
DECKER CLIFFORD N	LTC	0-0380319	1160	1
DECKER DOYLE V	CPT	0-2027264	0551	2
DECKER ERVIN A	CW2	W-2212122	0866	1
DECKER FORREST E	LTC	0-1294799	0961	1
DECKER FORREST E	CW2	W-2207393	0861	1
DECKER FREDERICK	CPT	0-0164047	0545	2
DECKER FREDERICK	LTC	0-0497542	0457	1
DECKER FREDERICK	MAJ	0-1017898	0865	1
DECKER HARRY S	MAJ	0-0490637	0754	2
DECKER HOLLIS A	CPT	0-0518259	0452	2
DECKER LEROY S	MAJ	0-1686614	0264	1
DECKER LESLIE E	CW4	W-2151301	0961	1
DECKER RALPH JR	1LT	0-1032272	0751	2
DECKER RUDOLPH F	CPT	0-0130316	0648	3
DECKER RYNOLD E	LTC	0-1700992	0668	3
DECKER WILLIAM T	MAJ	0-1311621	0461	2
DECKERT ARTHUR A	MAJ	0-2021021	0968	1
DECLERT ALBERT T	LTC	0-1555370	0163	1
DECLET CEFERINO	MAJ	0-2263294	0563	1
DEDAKIS NICHOLAS G	COL	0-0265422	1067	3
DEDEAUX EUGENE J	MAJ	0-1643468	0462	1
DEDECKER ADRIAN F JR	CPT	0-1286450	0247	2
DEDERER HERMAN M	MAJ	0-0205193	0556	3
DEDI CHARLES A	COL	0-0358539	0960	1
DEDITZ FRANK L	CPT	0-0484553	0348	2
DEDMON JESSE D JR	CPT	0-0291474	1044	2
DEDMON ROBERT C	CPT	0-1030355	0348	1
DEDMON ROY L	LTC	0-1030140	0766	1
DEDRICK WILLIAM T	1LT	0-0444542	0344	2
DEE ORVILLE F	LTC	0-1054532	0167	3
DEE SIDNEY E	CPT	0-0365178	0344	2
DEE WINFIELD S	LTC	0-0905592	1065	3
DEEBACH RALPH M	2LT	0-1118562	0457	1
DEEDS CLAUDE F	CW3	W-2151774	0565	1
DEEDS FRANK E	MAJ	0-1120313	0663	1
DEEDS FRANK H JR	2LT	0-2010806	0646	2
DEEDY EDWARD J	MAJ	0-0526206	0456	1
DEEG MILES F	1LT	0-1341952	0953	2
DEEGAN ROBERT J	CPT	0-1314394	0346	2
DEELEY JOSEPH M	COL	0-0267563	0264	3
DEELSTRA NICHOLAS J	LTC	0-1314453	1161	1
DEEMER CHARLES F	MAJ	0-0975298	0766	1
DEEMING GEORGE S	LTC	0-1108612	0166	1
DEEMS HAROLD E	LTC	0-0405210	0661	1
DEEMS IRWIN W	CW4	W-2114315	1160	1
DEEMS MYERS B	LTC	0-0278326	0566	3
DEEPE GEORGE S	LTC	0-1944657	0465	1
DEER THOMAS O	CW4	W-2104666	0859	1
DEER WILBER L	CW3	W-2147297	0465	1
DEERE WILLIAM R	WO1	W-2121204	0753	1
DEERING ROSS F	CW3	W-2148162	0263	1
DEERING WILLIAM A	LTC	0-1182812	0263	1
DEES RAYMOND J	LTC	0-0499856	0462	2
DEESE WALTER E	CPT	0-1101404	0747	2
DEETER EMMETT	COL	0-0298667	0564	3
DEETER MORTON L	MAJ	0-0399089	1151	2
DEETZ HENRY H	CPT	0-2019718	0958	1
DEFANDORF JAMES H	COL	0-0178688	0452	3
DEFFEYES THEODORE E	CPT	0-0488272	1049	1
DEFORD JOHN E	MAJ	0-0185320	0648	3
DEFOREST OFRIN L JR	CW2	W-2215387	0768	1
DEFOURNEAUX RENE J	MAJ	0-0887913	0265	1
DEFREES WILLIAM A	MAJ	0-0985648	0767	1
DEFUNIAK HERBERT R	MAJ	0-0450119	0164	1

NAME	GRADE	SVC NO	DATE RET MO YR	RET CODE
DEGER [illegible]	COL	0-0[illegible]	1152	3
DEGLES GEORGE	MAJ	0-1436498	1065	1
DEGN SADIE A [illegible]	2LT	N-073[illegible]	1044	1
DEGNAN JOHN M	MAJ	0-1030722	0567	1
DEGNER CARL [illegible] JR	LTC	0-[illegible]	0367	3
DEGOEY JOHN [illegible]	2LT	0-1996604	0945	2
DEGON VINCENT M	MAJ	0-1399040	0865	1
DEGONY [illegible] FREDERICK	CW2	W-2153157	1159	1
DEGOOD ALBERT [illegible]	CW3	W-2142953	0758	1
DEGRAW JOSEPH I	LTC	0-0451382	0356	1
DEGURSE JEAN B	2LT	N-0730713	0644	1
DEGUTIS EDWARD J	LTC	0-1395345	1060	1
DEHNER WALTER J	LTC	0-0175594	0462	3
DEIBERT FRANKLIN L	LTC	0-1040604	0264	1
DEISLER HARRY M	LTC	0-0299759	1265	3
DEIGNAN FRANCIS W	1LT	0-0452723	1144	2
DEIMLER JOHN L	COL	0-0296271	1068	3
DEINES DAVID F	LTC	0-0240372	0759	1
DEIS HENRY M	CW4	W-2002837	1262	3
DEIS JOHN R	CPT	0-1329929	1068	3
DEISS GWENDOLYN	CPT	N-0702850	0147	1
DEITCH EDWARD A	MAJ	0-1050228	1063	1
DEITCH LOUIS	2LT	0-1298674	1044	2
DEITERS FRIEDHELM	CW3	W-2148565	1164	1
DEITZ THAD B	CW2	W-2142422	0856	1
DEITZ WILLIAM C	1LT	0-1303472	1048	1
DEJAIFFE RAYMOND	MAJ	0-0261841	0268	3
DEKALANDS ROBERT W	2LT	0-2019857	0950	2
DEKIS CONSTANTIN	1LT	0-1319467	0745	2
DEKKER CLARENCE F	LTC	0-1342325	0567	1
DEKKER JOHN L	LTC	0-1175933	0666	1
DEKTOR ABRAM A	LTC	0-0309256	0765	3
DEL BENE FRANCIS J	LTC	0-1294560	0462	1
DEL BENE JOSEPH A	LTC	0-1104120	0563	1
DEL BIAGGIO AMIL	CPT	0-0966894	0860	1
DEL CORRO IBARRA G	MAJ	0-1896381	0861	1
DEL CORSO ANDREW A	LTC	0-2043001	0767	1
DEL COETO RENATO A	MAJ	0-1181224	0165	3
DEL ETOILE NORBERT	CW4	W-2120061	1159	1
DEL GIORGIO F M	1LT	0-1826130	1145	2
DEL GOBBO VINCENT J	CW2	W-2143231	0859	1
DEL HOMME ELMER E	LTC	0-0230976	0464	3
DEL PORTE JACK B	MAJ	0-1342249	0767	1
DEL PRETE EUGENE	LTC	0-1558134	0163	1
DEL REGNO LAWRENCE	MAJ	0-1111575	0764	1
DEL ROSARIO A	2LT	0-1896672	0757	1
DEL ROSARIO AMBROCCO	LTC	0-0496050	0354	1
DEL ROSARIO C	MAJ	0-1288365	0860	1
DEL TORO JOSE E	COL	0-0195797	1062	3
DEL TORO UBALDO	COL	0-0191567	0662	3
DEL VALLE ANTONIO	MAJ	0-1317224	1060	1
DEL-CHICCA SILVIO	CPT	0-0515967	0445	2
DELA CRUZ JOSE	1LT	0-0890323	1149	1
DELA CRUZ VICTORIANO	2LT	0-1896871	0150	1
DELACCRUZ LESCUM	CPT	0-2027361	0958	2
DELAFIELD JOSEPH L	CPT	0-0911611	0346	2
DELAHAY B T JR	2LT	0-1825844	0945	2
DELAMAIN FREDERIC W	COL	0-0383470	0568	3
DELAMATER GEORGE L	MAJ	0-1120537	1265	1
DELAMETER CHARLES M	LTC	0-0377027	0859	1
DELANO FRANCIS R	LTC	0-0214761	1262	3
DELANEY CARROLL S	1LT	0-1014784	1145	2
DELANEY CLAUDE R	MAJ	0-2037048	0263	1
DELANEY DANIEL T	LTC	0-0451663	0361	1
DELANEY FRANCES T	CPT	N-0756816	0347	1
DELANEY FRIEDA L	1LT	N-0779164	0845	1
DELANEY HARVEY R	CW4	W-2141947	0257	1
DELANEY JAMES A	LTC	0-0484998	0460	3
DELANEY JOSEPH H	MAJ	0-1951550	0364	1
DELANEY MARGARET A	1LT	N-0754429	0247	1
DELANEY NORMAN J	CW2	W-2144769	0657	1
DELANEY RALPH A	LTC	0-0397134	0262	1
DELANEY THOMAS F	MAJ	0-0983906	0364	1
DELANEY THOMAS J	CW4	W-2142303	0859	1
DELANEY WILLIAM E	CW2	W-2205737	0864	1

NAME	GRADE	SVC NO	DATE RET MO YR	RET CODE
DELANEY WILLIAM H	2LT	0-0271315	1154	3
DELANEY WILLIAM J JR	LTC	0-0417736	0461	1
DELANEY WILLIAM L	CPT	0-0309237	1159	3
DELAND FRANK B	B G	0-0110597	1050	3
DELANO JOHN W	CPT	0-1875744	0957	2
DELANO NORMAN	CW3	W-2144877	0564	1
DELANY GERALD M	CPT	0-1174819	0350	2
DELAUNAY ARTHUR J	MAJ	0-0444379	1044	2
DELAUNE RICHARD K	LTC	0-0531094	1267	1
DELEGRAM EMILE J JR	MAJ	0-1315804	1160	1
DELERUYELLE F J	2LT	0-2039597	0148	1
DELESHA LAVERN L	CPT	0-2289438	1162	1
DELFINI MANLIO T	LTC	0-0272959	1168	3
DELFS HAMILTON O	1LT	0-1307951	1046	2
DELGADO ENRIQUE	2LT	0-0362563	1142	2
DELGREGO ARTHUR L	LTC	0-0272452	0646	2
DELHORNE ROOSEVELT	LTC	0-0452334	0463	1
DELIA ANTHONY JR	LTC	0-0309867	0963	3
DELIA JOSEPH L	CW2	W-2208647	0665	1
DELIA PIERRE J	MAJ	0-0326244	0467	3
DELICH PETER F	WO1	W-2130709	0645	2
DELISCU FRANCOIS	COL	0-0164542	1154	2
DELIZ JOHN F	MAJ	0-1688448	0163	1
DELK JOHN L	MAJ	0-0963778	0266	2
DELK JOHN W	LTC	0-0483998	0555	1
DELK LUCIUS	LTC	0-0292592	1167	3
DELL LEWIS B	CW3	W-2130751	0457	1
DELL WALTER J	LTC	0-0223772	0655	3
DELL-OMD JOHN L	LTC	0-1996891	0568	1
DELLA ROCCA ANTH	COL	0-0242357	0262	3
DELLA&ROCCA RENATO J	1LT	0-1310076	0546	2
DELLA-PENNA CARLE	1LT	0-1315917	0348	2
DELLAGO JOSEPH L	CW4	W-2143375	0967	1
DELLAPORT NORMAN	2LT	0-1329571	0945	2
DELLAVIA CINZIO	LTC	0-0321064	0768	3
DELLEPIANE HENRY L	LTC	0-0224076	0863	3
DELLERA JOSEPH L	MAJ	0-0101533	1057	3
DELLERT HOWARD C	COL	0-0397842	0958	1
DELLGREN CARL A	LTC	0-0282371	0861	1
DELLI-CARPINI DOMENI	LTC	0-0586606	0766	1
DELLIGATTI HENRY J	2LT	0-1998523	0846	2
DELLITT FRANK R	1LT	0-1061670	0346	2
DELMAGE SHERMAN H	MAJ	0-0969633	0465	1
DELMO ANTONIO	CPT	0-1587757	0755	1
DELMONICO JAMES R	CPT	0-1824438	1046	2
DELO PERRY A	LTC	0-0465660	0745	2
DELONG WILLARD K	CW3	W-2209816	1167	1
DELOREY DONALD W	CPT	0-1308314	0447	2
DELOREY JOHN R	MAJ	0-2033572	1059	1
DELP JOHN P	MAJ	0-1302280	1062	1
DELPINO ROBERT A	LTC	0-0515924	0765	1
DELSON LEON	MAJ	0-0184003	1156	3
DEMA JOHN J	CW2	W-2111538	1058	1
DEMAREST JAMES V	COL	0-0137232	0449	3
DEMARS ARTHUR J	MAJ	0-0235111	0668	3
DEMBERGER JAMES T	MAJ	0-0949056	1062	1
DEMBOSKI HENRY	LTC	0-0291375	0868	3
DEMBOSKY ANTHONY E	CW4	W-0901887	0752	1
DEMCHO NICK M	1LT	0-1313984	1145	2
DEMCHOK ANDREW J	LTC	0-1306708	0862	1
DEMENT JAMES W JR	COL	0-0284252	0868	3
DEMENT RICHARD F	WO1	W-2112245	0650	1
DEMERANVILLE M I	CPT	0-1287316	0353	2
DEMERS ALBERT G	CW4	W-2115250	1054	1
DEMERS JACKSON J	CPT	0-1040695	1045	2
DEMERS LEON M	CPT	0-1169480	0561	1
DEMERS ROLAND R	MAJ	0-1179366	1165	1
DEMERS WILLIAM G	CPT	0-0385100	0146	2
DEMERY ROBERT L	CW3	W-2205477	0667	1
DEMETER MIKE	MAJ	0-2263412	1062	1
DEMETRAS LEO	2LT	0-1020046	0946	2
DEMICK FRANK W	LTC	0-1059762	0863	1
DEMICO JOSEPH H	CW4	W-2119750	0564	1
DEMING ALLEN C	LTC	0-1634669	1067	1
DEMING CLIFTON L	LTC	0-1554350	0363	1

NAME	GRADE	SVC NO	DATE RET MO YR	RET CODE
DEMING CURTIS C	2LT	0-1016301	0446	2
DEMINGS CHARLES S	CW4	W-2115916	0463	1
DEMINT THOMAS W	COL	0-0299765	1156	2
DEMIK FRANCIS S	LTC	0-1283039	0961	1
DEMITRIADES CONSTANT	MAJ	0-1060410	1262	1
DEMKO WILLIAM	CW3	W-2147468	0163	1
DEMLING MARTIN A	CW4	W-2142559	0567	1
DEMLOW ROBERT F	1LT	0-1294131	1048	2
DEMMEL CLYDE F	LTC	0-0407756	1067	3
DEMMERS HENRY	1LT	0-0420188	0249	1
DEMO EDWARD L	CW2	W-2153246	0561	1
DEMO JOHN J	CPT	0-0338466	0245	2
DEMOS ALEXANDER	LTC	0-1176600	0261	1
DEMOUY MARSHALL E	CW3	W-2209527	0967	1
DEMPSEY ALFRED J SR	MAJ	0-1314603	0145	1
DEMPSEY EDWARD F	LTC	0-0240921	0464	3
DEMPSEY HARRY J	MAJ	0-1578352	0661	1
DEMPSEY HENRY V JR	MAJ	0-1335906	0764	1
DEMPSEY JACOB P	2LT	0-0108325	0836	1
DEMPSEY JAMES C	COL	0-0255023	1051	2
DEMPSEY JOHN F	LTC	0-0373203	0752	1
DEMPSEY JOHN P	MAJ	0-1589157	0261	1
DEMPSEY JOHN T	WO1	W-2141841	0952	2
DEMPSEY JOHN T JR	1LT	0-1286094	1044	2
DEMPSEY LAWRENCE J	CPT	0-0461182	0850	1
DEMPSEY PERCY F	WO1	W-2113533	0350	2
DEMPSEY RALPH P	MAJ	0-2011723	0161	1
DEMPSEY S ELIZABET	1LT	N-0744437	1046	1
DEMPSEY WILLARD F JR	MAJ	0-4030895	0168	1
DEMPSEY WILLARD M	2LT	0-0863195	0545	2
DEMPSTER CLYDE B	COL	0-0199693	1153	3
DEMPSTER LESLIE J	CPT	0-0499532	0747	1
DEMSKI RAYMOND W	LTC	0-1104607	1165	1
DEMSKY THEODORE C	CPT	0-0537559	0550	1
DEMULLING JOSEPH J	CW2	W-3200130	0566	1
DEMUTH VICTOR J	CPT	0-1011983	1144	2
DEN BOER CORNE	1LT	N-0744566	0846	1
DEN-OUDEN CHRISTIAN	LTC	0-0350152	0554	2
DENARO RUSSELL G	MAJ	0-2049787	1263	1
DENAS JOSEPH M	LTC	0-1173585	0263	1
DENAULT HERBERT M	MAJ	0-0405158	0760	1
DENBEAU JOSEPH M	LTC	0-0371322	0260	1
DENBY OTIS E	MAJ	0-0547513	0564	1
DENEEN ARTHUR B JR	1LT	0-1292145	0645	2
DENFIP MYRTLE M	MAJ	N-0702296	1062	1
DENHAM CECIL W	CW3	W-2119756	0757	1
DENHAM CHARLIE A	CPT	0-1996596	0656	1
DENHAM THOMAS J	MAJ	0-0282955	0144	2
DENHARD CHRISTOPHE	LTC	0-1051102	0567	1
DENICK WILLIAM A	LTC	0-1647841	0962	1
DENIS JEAN B	LTC	0-0270767	0246	2
DENISE FRANK L	LTC	0-0280041	0357	1
DENISENKO IVAN	MAJ	0-5405006	1268	1
DENISON BURKE B	LTC	0-0361215	0868	3
DENISON IRA J	2LT	0-1300292	0345	2
DENISON NELLIE M	MAJ	N-0700777	0346	1
DENISON WILLIAM R	MAJ	0-0211550	1058	3
DENISON WILLIAM R	CPT	0-0322311	0648	3
DENISSEN CLETUS M	CW2	W-2212542	0668	1
DENISTON DEAN T	CPT	0-1287844	1046	2
DENIT LEO A	COL	0-0189222	0355	3
DENKENBERGER JAMES V	MAJ	0-1306392	0960	1
DENLER WARREN A	MAJ	0-0443751	0962	1
DENLINGER EARLE R	LTC	0-0322254	0966	3
DENMAN JAN D	LTC	0-0291184	0267	3
DENMAN JOHN L	1LT	0-0378868	1144	2
DENMAN OLL O	WO1	W-2109272	0945	2
DENMAN RICHARD E	CW2	W-2151932	1057	1
DENMAN ROGER S	MAJ	0-0231368	0660	3
DENMAN WAYNE L	MAJ	0-0243265	0263	3
DENMAN WILLIAM F JR	1LT	0-0481799	0343	2
DENMARK HARRY A	2LT	0-1642794	0954	1
DENNARD BILLY C	2LT	0-1292843	1165	2
DENNELL ALFRED R	CPT	0-1313578	0347	2
DENNEY CHARLES A	MAJ	0-2204434	0666	1

NAME	GRADE	SVC NO	DATE RET MO YR	RET CODE
DENNEY WILLIAM F	CW2	W-2145136	0758	1
DENNEY WILLIAM [illegible]	COL	0-0124661	0254	3
DENNER ROBERT E	1LT	0-0437428	0349	2
DENNETT FRANCIS J	CW4	W-2126820	1166	1
DENNEY CARL P	CPT	0-1178755	1053	1
DENNEY EDWIN R	MAJ	0-0965317	1163	1
DENNEY HUGH H	1LT	0-0507228	0457	1
DENNEY JOHN E	LTC	0-1310690	0862	1
DENNEY JUDD W	LTC	0-0552223	0967	1
DENNEY THOMAS V	LTC	0-1058491	0765	2
DENNEY WELLS H	LTC	0-0248070	0265	3
DENNIN JOHN H	LTC	0-0338600	0562	1
DENNING STANLEY P	CW3	RW-2206053	1065	1
DENNING WALTER S	COL	0-0262688	0963	3
DENNIS ANDREW O	MAJ	0-0502219	0547	2
DENNIS BENJAMIN F	CPT	0-1689804	0845	2
DENNIS BERTHA E	2LT	N-0759315	1044	1
DENNIS CAREY	LTC	0-0275594	0961	3
DENNIS CARL A	MAJ	0-1325189	0157	1
DENNIS CARL R	LTC	0-2288237	0867	1
DENNIS CAROL M	1LT	0-0274803	0744	2
DENNIS CHARLES E	LTC	0-1332152	0966	1
DENNIS EDWARD W	LTC	0-1055575	1262	1
DENNIS EVERETT S	CPT	0-0372748	0268	3
DENNIS FREDERICK	COL	0-0182090	0854	1
DENNIS GUY G	CPT	0-0328501	1144	2
DENNIS JAMES A	LTC	0-1101806	0360	1
DENNIS JAMES A	CPT	0-1551385	0562	1
DENNIS JAMES A	1LT	0-2049219	0350	2
DENNIS JERRY T JR	1LT	0-0441526	0944	2
DENNIS LEONARD R	LTC	0-1691893	0967	1
DENNIS LORANCE L	COL	0-0383692	0861	2
DENNIS MARTHA R	MAJ	L-1010043	0167	1
DENNIS MILTON L	LTC	0-0900616	1046	2
DENNIS ORVILLE T	1LT	0-2008583	0951	1
DENNIS RAYMOND H	CW4	W-2142341	1264	1
DENNIS SIDNEY M	1LT	0-0491002	1053	1
DENNIS WALTER H	CPT	0-1697975	0346	2
DENNIS WALTER J JR	COL	0-0263628	0268	3
DENNIS WALTER R	MAJ	0-0369610	0745	2
DENNIS WILLIAM F	LTC	0-0450845	0257	1
DENNISON JAY G JR	2LT	0-1293926	0345	2
DENNISON LAWRENCE E	MAJ	0-0490962	1058	1
DENNISON VEACHEL A	CPT	0-1011578	0448	1
DENNISTON GEORGE C	LTC	0-0243631	0766	3
DENNY CHARLES A	MAJ	0-1578354	0450	2
DENNY CHARLES H	LTC	0-1530855	0667	3
DENNY DONALD P	MAJ	0-0266665	0868	3
DENNY EDWARD R JR	LTC	0-0460101	0862	1
DENNY IRA F	CW2	W-2111083	0145	2
DENNY JASPER N	CPT	0-0231512	1148	3
DENNY JOHN L	MAJ	0-0172961	0258	3
DENNY JOHN W	MAJ	0-0495312	0149	1
DENNY ROBERT M	LTC	0-1013921	0366	1
DENNY THOMAS	LTC	0-0253512	0359	3
DENNY WILLIAM M	MAJ	0-0404647	0847	2
DENSLOW WILLIAM R	CPT	0-0353198	0445	2
DENSMORE LEONARD O	COL	0-0181447	0956	3
DENSMORE RALPH A	COL	0-0169990	1055	3
DENT BRUCE	CW3	W-2142632	0361	1
DENT CARLOS E	WO1	W-2149668	0255	1
DENT DOROTHEA M	2LT	N-0741588	0845	1
DENT MARY B	1LT	N-0726920	0845	1
DENT PAUL L	MAJ	0-1685130	0845	2
DENT PERRY E	CW2	W-2148138	1159	1
DENT RAYMOND A	MAJ	0-1011138	0361	1
DENT TOWNSEND E	CPT	0-0264204	0346	2
DENTON CHARLES T	LTC	0-1114449	1061	1
DENTON CHARLES W	CPT	0-1579553	0145	2
DENTON DOROTHY A	2LT	N-0763394	0345	1
DENTON GORDON B	CPT	0-0416525	0261	1
DENTON JOHN R	MAJ	0-0267368	0968	3
DENTON LEWIS E	MAJ	0-0356033	1061	2
DENTON MILLIS O	MAJ	0-1646553	1062	1
DENTON MONROE A	1LT	0-0320281	0743	2

NAME	GRADE	SVC NO	DATE RET MO YR	RET CODE
DENTON ORRIN	LTC	0-0496584	0457	1
DENTON OWEN G	MAJ	0-0378701	0455	1
DENTON SAMUEL A JR	MAJ	0-1923598	0965	1
DENTON SAMUEL A SR	LTC	0-0184720	0750	1
DENTON SAMUEL T	LTC	0-0499731	0654	1
DENTON SHELBY T	MAJ	0-0500530	0547	2
DENTON WALTER F	CPT	0-0497988	0154	2
DENTON WILLIAM I	LTC	0-0216220	0963	3
DENTON WILLIAM M	1LT	0-1661363	0158	1
DENTREMONT JAMES E	LTC	0-1548725	1062	1
DENUNZIO VINCENT L	CPT	0-0175395	0545	2
DENVIR JAMES F	1LT	0-1311988	0547	2
DENZER RAYMOND	LTC	0-1036949	1166	1
DEO CLAUDE J	1LT	0-0888954	0146	2
DEOBALD HARVEY J	LTC	0-0259442	0667	3
DEONIER WILLIAM C	LTC	0-0342319	1157	2
DEPEW HARLEY V	WO1	W-2128489	0145	2
DEPIERRO FRANK T	1LT	0-0436871	1044	2
DEPLER ROBERT E	MAJ	0-1117393	0765	1
DEPP DONALD S	CPT	0-0380368	0146	2
DEPPE ROBERT E	MAJ	0-0386998	0665	1
DEPPEN GEORGE D	MAJ	0-1166041	1163	1
DEPPENSMITH LLOYD F	MAJ	0-1559440	0960	1
DEPRE RICHARD A	CW3	W-2141252	0156	1
DEPREZ ALEXANDER	MAJ	0-1327119	0764	1
DEPT WILLIAM J	1LT	0-0493165	0556	1
DEPTULA FELIX A	1LT	0-0497112	0251	1
DEPTULA VINCENT	MAJ	0-1035148	0554	1
DEPUGLIA JOSEPH A	CPT	0-1797447	1058	1
DEQUAINE OWEN J	CW2	W-2214838	0966	1
DER MUTT WILLI	MAJ	0-0194596	0563	3
DERAS MARTIN W	1LT	0-1946472	0946	2
DERBER WARD H	1LT	0-1319141	1045	2
DERBES EARL M	LTC	0-0219918	0664	3
DERBIN CHARLES A	CW3	W-2152156	0363	1
DERBLICK MICHAEL	2LT	0-2030567	1047	1
DERBONNE JOHN K	LTC	0-1104124	1060	1
DERBY ALBERT C	CW4	W-2141253	1062	1
DERBY HENRY S	COL	0-0267562	0457	3
DERBY HENRY V	LTC	0-0261772	0862	3
DERBY HOWARD E	COL	0-0265780	0661	3
DERBY RAY L	LTC	0-0235915	0758	3
DERBY RICHARD G	MAJ	0-1845134	0564	1
DERBY STANLEY F	MAJ	0-0720808	0465	1
DERBY WILLIAM P	MAJ	0-0474437	0452	1
DERENZO AURELIO G	CPT	0-0929095	0646	2
DERGE RICHARD H	MAJ	0-1579555	0455	2
DERHAM EDGAR M	CPT	0-0220829	0446	2
DERIEUX WILLIAM T	1LT	0-2204948	0654	2
DERINGER MAJORIE A	MAJ	N-0728753	0463	1
DERIS GEORGE F JR	1LT	0-1170705	0246	2
DERKSEN WILLIAM J	MAJ	0-0296850	0546	2
DERMONT JOHN G	1LT	0-4001705	1155	2
DEROCHE ALCIDE W	CW4	W-2006456	0668	3
DEROSA JOHN E	1LT	0-1283041	0944	2
DEROSA MILTON A	2LT	0-1306710	0145	2
DEROSIER GEORGE H	1LT	0-1300138	0354	1
DEROY JUDITH M	1LT	N-0784138	0146	1
DERPA CHARLES B	MAJ	0-2047622	1057	2
DERRICK CEPHAS P	LTC	0-0222243	0657	3
DERRICK CHARLES D	MAJ	0-0451540	0559	1
DERRICK CHARLES W	COL	0-0255840	0967	3
DERRICK JOHN N	CW2	W-2152264	0464	2
DERRICK WILLIAM F	LTC	0-0393799	1068	3
DERRICO ARMAND J	MAJ	0-0325594	0646	2
DERRY EUGENE F	CW2	W-2143895	0755	1
DERRY JOHN A	COL	0-0262333	0667	3
DERRYBERRY I D	CPT	0-1018207	0346	2
DERSCHEID LYLE A	1LT	0-0522520	0446	2
DERTZO JOHN	LTC	0-0388325	1162	1
DERUS LEROY P	2LT	0-1013427	0344	2
DERUSSO LOUIS J	CPT	0-0167244	0257	3
DERVEY RAYMOND J	MAJ	0-0360473	0945	2
DERWIN JAMES J JR	WO1	W-2132769	0545	2
DERY ALEXANDER	CW4	W-2002182	0757	3
DES CHAMPS CLAUDIUS	COL	0-0243497	0766	3
DES JARDINS NORMAND	MAJ	0-1554533	0264	1
DES LAURIERS LAURENC	LTC	0-1548727	1062	1
DES PREZ FRANCES E	MAJ	M-0002395	0368	3
DESA-SOTO LUIS	LTC	0-0968190	0368	1
DESANTIS LOUIS J	LTC	0-1306568	0962	1
DESAUTEL EDWARD	CPT	0-1179367	0361	1
DESCHENES HOMER	LTC	0-0497682	0554	2
DESCHNER FABIAN S	CPT	0-0261639	1264	3
DESERANO CHARLES E	MAJ	0-1106091	1054	1
DESFORGE WILLIAM V	1LT	0-0885765	1145	2
DESGUIN PAUL F	1LT	0-0450847	0349	1
DESHAIES GEORGE J	MAJ	0-1016684	0662	1
DESHANE ELMA A	2LT	N-0736053	1042	1
DESIST SAMUEL	MAJ	0-0980842	0664	1
DESJARDINE LOUIS P	MAJ	0-0255807	0944	2
DESJARDINS WILFRED A	CW3	W-2110079	0160	1
DESKIEWICZ T M	CW4	W-2144710	0960	1
DESKINS LILBURN S	CPT	0-1014759	0965	1
DESKO MICHAEL D	LTC	0-1283388	0656	1
DESLANDES ELLERY D	CW2	W-2209454	0264	1
DESMOND GORDON B	MAJ	0-0942608	0155	2
DESMOND JOHN T	1LT	0-0435614	1043	2
DESMOND THOMAS J	COL	0-0265316	0465	3
DESMOND WALTER C	CW4	W-2119747	0862	1
DESNOYER ROY M	CPT	0-1597417	0253	2
DESONIE JAMES J SR	LTC	0-0354425	0566	3
DESONIER ROLAND P	LTC	0-0257530	0562	1
DESPAIN CHARLES	2LT	0-1048330	0351	2
DESPRES LEONARD A	CPT	0-0527310	1045	2
DESROCHERS EDWARD J	CW3	W-2145786	0861	1
DESROCHERS JEAN B	LTC	0-0491712	0546	2
DESROCHES ALCIDE	COL	0-0484261	0956	1
DESROSIERS ROMEO J	CPT	0-1056689	0459	1
DESSEN SAMUEL	MAJ	0-1684272	0446	2
DESSNER BURTON	LTC	0-0975646	1267	1
DESSUREAU DONALD A	LTC	0-1553432	0764	1
DESSUREAULT M J	CW2	W-2102834	0654	1
DESSUREAULT ROBERT L	2LT	0-1637293	1043	2
DESTEFANO JOSEPH	MAJ	0-1289876	0651	2
DESUTA FRANK J	LTC	0-0957569	0763	1
DESUYO AMBROSIO	1LT	0-2032077	0449	1
DETERRA JOSEPH B JR	1LT	0-0977387	1264	2
DETERS JACK	CW2	W-2205882	1160	1
DETERT CHARLES W	LTC	0-1333188	1264	1
DETIMER HENRY C	CW3	W-2152265	0264	1
DETLEFSEN BERNARD W	CPT	0-1119561	0561	1
DETLEFSEN MARVIN J	CPT	0-1112649	0257	1
DETLOR GEORGE F	MAJ	0-1100949	0368	3
DETRICK MERLE H	WO1	W-2111090	0950	1
DETRICK ROY M	2LT	0-1691716	1045	2
DETRIE ARTHUR	MAJ	0-0906372	0746	2
DETROIT LANCELOT L	CPT	0-0486541	0453	1
DETTELBACK GEORGE	LTC	0-0246818	0366	3
DETTMANN RALPH W	CPT	0-1697689	0446	2
DETTMER HERMAN W	LTC	0-0256022	0967	3
DETTMER MARTIN W	LTC	0-1048331	0367	1
DETTMER STANLEY	LTC	0-0265252	0667	3
DETWEILER ERWIN E	CPT	0-0982057	1060	1
DETWILER HARRY L	LTC	0-0238644	0364	3
DETWILER HARVEY C	MAJ	0-0508630	0450	2
DETWILER ROBERT H	MAJ	0-0490892	0146	2
DETWILER SAMUEL S	MAJ	0-1001987	0765	3
DETWILLER ALBERT K	COL	0-0199153	0648	3
DEU PREE CHARLES L	CPT	0-1057720	0446	2
DEUEL JOHN V	CPT	0-0100749	0959	3
DEUEL ROBERT L	1LT	0-1533539	0851	2
DEUELL ROBERT G	LTC	0-1300140	0263	1
DEUGAN LESTER A	CPT	0-1533769	0156	1
DEUGAW LLOYD	MAJ	0-0968074	0759	1
DEUPREE JACK D	LTC	0-1308315	0762	1
DEURLOO HENRY W	COL	0-0345096	1168	3
DEUTCH MAX	LTC	0-0227882	0765	3
DEUTER CARL	COL	0-0283195	0955	2
DEUTSCH ALBERT C	MAJ	0-0156770	0154	3
DEUTSCH ALBERT C	COL	0-0193161	1061	3
DEUTSCH BERNARD B	CPT	0-0488340	0146	2
DEUTSCH HAROLD	MAJ	0-0254951	0351	2
DEUTSCH LAWRENCE M	2LT	0-1644906	0845	2
DEUTSCH MARTIN J	LTC	0-0274447	0367	3
DEUTSCH NICHOLAS J	LTC	0-1287317	0667	1
DEUTSCHER EDWIN J	1LT	0-5005159	0364	2
DEUTSCHLE JOSEPH S	LTC	0-0246503	0446	2
DEUTSCHMAN REYNOLD P	MAJ	0-0545636	1146	2
DEVALL ARCHIBALD	COL	0-0155657	1055	2
DEVALL SAMUEL S	COL	0-0195088	1156	3
DEVANY EUGENE P	1LT	0-1109892	0346	2
DEVENDORF CURTIS L	COL	0-0294692	1263	3
DEVENPORT RUSSELL J	CW2	W-2150818	0463	2
DEVER RALPH F	LTC	0-0236456	0465	3
DEVERALL ROBERT L	CPT	0-0338210	0865	3
DEVEREUX RICHARD A	COL	0-0296831	0266	3
DEVERS ARVIN S JR	MAJ	0-1011049	0763	1
DEVERY GERALD P	1LT	0-1799653	1045	2
DEVICK ALVIN O	2LT	0-0378632	1142	2
DEVINE ANNA M	CW3	V-0800023	1265	1
DEVINE CRAIG W	CW4	W-2201186	0766	3
DEVINE DAVID	CW2	W-2215179	0567	1
DEVINE DONALD Q	CPT	0-1585358	0547	2
DEVINE GEORGE J	CW2	W-2204795	0968	3
DEVINE HAROLD A	MAJ	0-0202562	0158	3
DEVINE JAMES H	1LT	0-1823127	1046	2
DEVINE JOHN J	LTC	0-0229592	0964	3
DEVINE JOSEPH C	LTC	0-0288791	0165	3
DEVINE RICHARD C	2LT	0-1180165	0845	2
DEVINE RICHARD J	MAJ	0-1038593	0968	3
DEVINE ROBERT M	CW3	RW-2143213	0962	1
DEVINE RUTH T	1LT	N-0784389	0446	1
DEVINE THEODORE M	LTC	0-1184370	0767	1
DEVINE WILLIAM J	MAJ	0-0485673	0245	2
DEVINEY RUTH M	MAJ	N-0736444	0264	1
DEVIS DONALD A	LTC	0-1585359	0766	1
DEVLIN ALLAN W	MAJ	0-1821833	0662	1
DEVLIN CHARLES N	CPT	0-1015842	1145	2
DEVLIN EDWARD T	COL	0-0301790	0968	3
DEVLIN GEORGE W	CW4	W-2001967	0358	3
DEVLIN JAMES W	LTC	0-1590406	1062	1
DEVLIN JOSEPH H	1LT	0-1311123	0546	1
DEVLIN JOSEPH J	CPT	0-1111576	0363	1
DEVLIN LAURANCE F	COL	0-0256080	0459	3
DEVLIN LAWRENCE F	LTC	0-0253466	0545	2
DEVLIN RAYMOND P	LTC	0-1050647	0762	1
DEVLIN THOMAS J	MAJ	0-0247438	1266	3
DEVOE CLIFTON B	CPT	0-2017822	0257	1
DEVOL DANA R	MAJ	0-1109136	0267	3
DEVOL HOWARD C	CW2	W-2207536	0464	1
DEVONALD 2ND DAVID H	1LT	0-0539125	0845	2
DEVORE DALE T	MAJ	0-0292073	1145	2
DEVRIES HENRY P	LTC	0-0912346	1044	2
DEW PERRY T	CPT	0-1181864	1065	1
DEW ROBERT J JR	2LT	0-0556940	0346	2
DEWALT DAVID E	CPT	0-5416122	0168	2
DEWALT HENRY J	CPT	0-0507816	0247	1
DEWAR DONALD B	MAJ	0-1112651	0964	1
DEWAR JOHN K	CW4	RW-2141814	0268	1
DEWART BENJAMIN B	LTC	0-0128568	1150	3
DEWEL CHARLES H	COL	0-0245026	1065	3
DEWELL AZOR M	CW4	W-2005960	0968	1
DEWEY ALBERT T	CPT	0-0116141	0650	3
DEWEY BLAIR H	LTC	0-2211248	0767	1
DEWEY CHARLES C	MAJ	0-0318320	1052	1
DEWEY CHARLES H	MAJ	0-0186968	0648	3
DEWEY CHARLES W	LTC	0-0236355	1051	3
DEWEY DONALD W	CPT	0-2018136	0558	1
DEWEY FRANKLIN H	LTC	0-0259973	0568	3
DEWEY GEORGE	LTC	0-0251860	0345	2
DEWEY GEORGE A	LTC	0-1646584	1063	2
DEWEY GEORGE B	CPT	0-1012402	0353	1
DEWEY WILLIAM H	LTC	0-0364454	1064	1
DEWEY WILLIAM JR	MAJ	0-1633158	0646	2
DEWHIRST ROBERT B	CPT	0-4051052	0858	2
DEWHIRST VICTOR E	2LT	0-2006508	0546	2
DEWHURST DAVID H	CPT	0-0150605	1049	3
DEWHURST LAWRENCE	MAJ	0-1584133	0457	1
DEWITT FREDERICK	CPT	0-0261630	0448	2
DEWITT HENRY	2LT	0-2029433	1147	1
DEWS ELI M	MAJ	0-0347156	0756	1
DEWS JACK	MAJ	0-0206349	1052	3
DEWS SAMUEL C	COL	0-0336845	0165	3
DEWSNAP STANLEY	MAJ	0-0124872	1149	3
DEXTER ALLAN L	COL	0-0162523	0852	3
DEXTER FRANK	CPT	0-1913941	1029	1
DEXTER FREDERICK	CW3	W-2153317	0263	1
DEXTER HARRY A	LTC	0-2055317	1167	1
DEXTER HENRY V JR	MAJ	0-1328578	0561	1
DEXTER ROBERT V	LTC	0-0517523	0463	1
DEXTER RODNEY S	MAJ	0-0394208	1160	1
DEXTER THEODORE J	CW3	W-2208006	0668	1
DEXTER WALDO H	CW4	W-2152874	1068	1
DEXTON HENRY A	MAJ	0-1038547	0657	1
DEY FLOYD M	MAJ	0-1924683	1266	1
DEYARMOND GEORGE E	LTC	0-0256205	1059	3
DEYESO FREDERICK	LTC	0-1798460	0666	1
DEYO HARRY N	COL	0-0215193	1052	3
DEYO RALPH F	CW2	W-2147748	0157	1
DEZULOVICH STEVE A	LTC	0-1554351	0761	1
DI BENEDETTE ANNE M	CPT	N-0724068	0650	2
DI BERTO ENIO O	MAJ	0-1290040	1160	1
DI BIANCO PASCHAL F	LTC	0-0359657	0766	1
DI BRIZZI THOMAS G	MAJ	0-0170689	1043	2
DI CAPRIO ALFRED J	MAJ	0-1644916	0668	3
DI CAPRIO JOSEPH M	CPT	0-1922206	0659	2
DI CARLO GAETANO J	LTC	0-2001795	1165	1
DI CARLO PHILIP A	MAJ	0-0886902	0363	1
DI CRISTINA EDUARDO	LTC	0-0369175	0660	1
DI CRISTINA HUMBERT	LTC	0-0196742	1160	3
DI DOMENICO DONALD V	CW3	W-2145265	0663	1
DI FABION PAUL J	CW3	W-2150945	0765	1
DI GANGI MARION R	MAJ	0-0368574	0246	2
DI GIACOMO FRANK	COL	0-0314556	0167	3
DI GIGLIA JOHN A	CPT	0-0489259	0544	2
DI GIOVANNI JOSEPH C	MAJ	0-2017671	1163	1
DI GIROLOMO FRANK E	MAJ	0-1014497	0465	1
DI GUISEPPI ERNEST	CW4	W-2153189	0466	1
DI LEO MICHAEL B	CPT	0-0524710	0645	2
DI LORENZO SAVERIO F	MAJ	0-0954060	1163	1
DI LORENZO VINCENT	MAJ	0-1289878	1157	2
DI MARCO JOHN J	CPT	0-1298040	0161	1
DI MARINO NICHOLAS J	LTC	0-1594798	0660	1
DI MASCIO CHARLES J	LTC	0-1104612	0862	1
DI MATTIA ARTHUR A	CW3	W-2146953	1163	1
DI MEO SAVERIO	COL	0-0288824		2
DI MONDA LEOPOLDO JR	CW2	W-2210139	0265	1
DI MUZIO ANGELO A	CW2	W-2147548	0460	2
DI NARDO BENJAMIN L	LTC	0-1018647	0267	1
DI NITTO RAYMOND J	CW2	W-2214625	0868	1
DI PALMA ANELLO	1LT	0-1582681	0561	1
DI PASQUALE ROSATIO	CW3	W-2144238	1162	1
DI PIETRO JOSEPH A	LTC	0-0193566	0354	3
DI PIETRO LIETO P	MAJ	0-1116334	0763	1
DI RESTA GENE J	CW3	W-2147387	0962	1
DI SALLE RICHARD C	LTC	0-1541887	0962	1
DI SANTIS FRED J	WO1	W-2123175	0958	2
DI YORIO JOSEPH V	2LT	0-1018017	0244	2
DI ZEREGA PHILIP V	LTC	0-1111030	0167	3
DIAKOFF ALEXANDER	CW3	RW-2144310	1064	1
DIAL LEE J JR	LTC	0-1683451	0766	1
DIAL MATTHEW P JR	CPT	0-1291511	0446	2
DIAL PAUL E	1LT	0-1293219	1045	2
DIAL RUTH E	MAJ	N-0744347	0568	3
DIAMANT ALFRED	1LT	0-1016844	0645	2
DIAMOND ABRAHAM I	MAJ	0-0501179	1045	2
DIAMOND ABRAHAM J	MAJ	0-0500030	0447	2
DIAMOND ALBERT	CPT	0-1633159	0555	1
DIAMOND BENJAMIN C	1LT	0-0493674	0844	2

332-811 O - 69 - 10

NAME	GRADE	SVC NO	DATE RET MO YR	RET CODE
DIAMOND FRANK B	2LT	0-0547938	0945	2
DIAMOND FRANK J	LTC	0-1322626	0263	2
DIAMOND HERBERT D	MAJ	0-1636898	0360	1
DIAMOND JOSEPH	COL	0-0355762	0467	3
DIAMOND LOUIS L	MAJ	0-1289220	0160	1
DIAMOND SIDNEY	CPT	0-0358742	0667	3
DIAMOND SOLOMON	1LT	0-1062486	0347	2
DIAS [illegible]	1LT	0-0489836	0749	1
DIAS DOUGLAS E	LTC	0-0225942	0954	3
DIASIO JOSEPH S	COL	0-0254948	0361	3
DIAZ CARLOS G	MAJ	0-2283398	1262	1
DIAZ FLORENCIO	1LT	0-1896909	0764	1
DIAZ-BERRIOS CARLOS	CW4	W-2151632	1168	1
DIAZ-BETANCOURT ENRI	MAJ	0-1329103	0763	1
DIBBLE EDWARD C	1LT	0-1634676	1055	1
DIBBLE GEORGE B	LTC	0-0402145	0162	3
DIBBLE GEORGE E	CW4	W-2102836	0756	1
DIBBLE HAROLD A	MAJ	0-1946949	0657	1
DIBBLE LEROY	CPT	0-4004222	0166	2
DICE FRANCIS R	LTC	0-0274432	0864	3
DICK ALFRED B	LTC	0-0254371	0755	1
DICK ALLAN E	COL	0-0265906	0860	3
DICK ARTHUR C	LTC	0-0276022	0367	3
DICK ARTHUR J	LTC	0-1081646	0466	1
DICK DALLAS	MAJ	0-1289705	0855	1
DICK DAVID W	COL	0-0397358	1062	1
DICK EWART G	CPT	0-0488808	0944	2
DICK GEORGE A	CPT	0-1165846	1046	2
DICK JAMES	LTC	0-0362109	0163	1
DICK JAMES E	COL	0-0393827	1068	1
DICK JOHN F	LTC	0-0514141	1067	3
DICK KENNETH R JR	MAJ	0-1685739	1165	1
DICK ROY B	LTC	0-1055266	0868	3
DICK RUSSELL G	LTC	0-0385675	0660	1
DICK VERNON S	LTC	0-1685944	1046	2
DICK WALTER A JR	MAJ	0-0528534	0353	2
DICK WILLARD J	CW2	W-2209582	0564	1
DICKAS ROBERT B	LTC	0-0101113	1144	2
DICKASON RALPH B	LTC	0-0305194	1267	3
DICKENS GASTON L	MAJ	0-0349128	0245	2
DICKENS PITTS B	MAJ	0-1183271	0860	1
DICKENS ROBERT P	1LT	0-1309323	0645	2
DICKENS WILLIAM P	CPT	0-0187467	0256	3
DICKENSHEETS PAUL F	CPT	0-0193163	1055	3
DICKENSON HARRY	LTC	0-0491503	0954	1
DICKERMAN WILSON K	LTC	0-0339933	0759	1
DICKERSON BENJAMIN W	1LT	0-0389020	0845	2
DICKERSON BURL F	CW3	W-2146327	0863	1
DICKERSON GEORGE W	MAJ	0-0164080	1139	1
DICKERSON GERALD T	LTC	0-0084976	0268	1
DICKERSON HENRY W	COL	0-0102963	0859	3
DICKERSON JAMES W	LTC	0-1234837	1064	1
DICKERSON JIM F	MAJ	0-0966492	0963	1
DICKERSON JOHN E	CW4	W-2102837	0858	1
DICKERSON MADELINE L	1LT	N-0773002	0546	1
DICKERSON PAUL S	LTC	0-1180872	0367	1
DICKERSON ROBERT C	LTC	0-1302614	0660	1
DICKERSON ROBERT V	1LT	0-0455654	0547	2
DICKERSON THOMAS W	MAJ	0-1314108	1263	1
DICKERSON WENDELL H	LTC	0-0405523	0560	1
DICKEY ALBERT B	LTC	0-0971111	0852	2
DICKEY BERGIN V	COL	0-0360244	0563	1
DICKEY DEAN R	LTC	0-0323965	0456	3
DICKEY ELIZABETH	1LT	N-0762991	0548	1
DICKEY EUGENE C SR	LTC	0-0374860	0369	3
DICKEY GEORGE F	LTC	0-0266773	0247	2
DICKEY HAROLD	1LT	0-1307207	0146	2
DICKEY HARRY L	LTC	0-0282958	0965	3
DICKEY IVAN N	CPT	0-0467549	1148	1
DICKEY JACK D A	MAJ	0-1541827	1163	1
DICKEY JOSEPH B	MAJ	0-0506375	0452	2
DICKEY OTTO P	WO1	W-2126268	0452	1
DICKEY PHILIP A	COL	0-0188685	0852	3
DICKEY THOMAS E	MAJ	0-1185217	0563	1
DICKEY WALTER L JR	CPT	0-0994504	0361	1
DICKEY WAYNE S	CPT	0-0965885	1061	1
DICKHOFF CARL W	1LT	0-0407482	0145	2
DICKIE ALEXANDER	LTC	0-0247653	1165	3
DICKINSON ALBERT E	1LT	0-2210376	0353	2
DICKINSON ARNOLD W	2LT	0-1300616	0344	2
DICKINSON CHESTER J	LTC	0-0272853	0341	2
DICKINSON DAVID L	LTC	0-1052324	0262	1
DICKINSON DONALD C	LTC	0-0309678	0859	1
DICKINSON DONALD P	MAJ	0-0836741	1065	1
DICKINSON EDWARD B	1LT	0-1647892	0955	1
DICKINSON EDWARD P	LTC	0-0248495	0367	3
DICKINSON GEORGE F	CPT	0-1117394	1146	2
DICKINSON HAROLD G	CW3	W-2151299	0658	1
DICKINSON HARRY D	1LT	0-1293024	0945	2
DICKINSON JAMES O	CW3	W-2212543	0268	1
DICKINSON JAMES H	LTC	0-0302127	0166	3
DICKINSON JESSE E	CPT	0-1553986	0155	1
DICKINSON KENNETH J	1LT	0-0334848	0744	2
DICKINSON MARSHALL C	MAJ	0-1180167	0956	1
DICKINSON NONNIE F	CW4	W-2143644	0166	1
DICKINSON ROBERT E	MAJ	0-1318520	0560	1
DICKINSON THEODORE M	LTC	0-0241310	1065	3
DICKINSON W C	LTC	0-0372800	1060	1
DICKINSON WILLIAM J	CW3	W-2147210	1065	1
DICKISON ANDREW J	CPT	0-1922646	0162	1
DICKISON LOREN W	MAJ	0-1920226	1163	1
DICKISON WILBERT	WO1	W-2122271	0248	1
DICKS ARTHUR E	LTC	0-1633161	0368	3
DICKS EDWARD A	CW4	W-2121182	0464	1
DICKS MAXWELL E	MAJ	0-0993924	0466	1
DICKSON BENJAMIN A	COL	0-0184469	1045	2
DICKSON BYRON R	MAJ	0-1046768	0962	1
DICKSON CHARLES M	COL	0-0447766	1047	2
DICKSON DONALD R	CPT	0-1061136	1165	1
DICKSON EDWARD B	1LT	0-1647992	0955	1
DICKSON ELAINE R	MAJ	L-0202209	1266	3
DICKSON GEORGE A	CPT	0-1691942	0867	1
DICKSON GEORGE G	MAJ	0-0309002	1145	2
DICKSON GEORGE L	CPT	0-1824733	0662	2
DICKSON HARRY	2LT	0-1555810	0445	2
DICKSON IBER B JR	LTC	0-1316862	1162	1
DICKSON JACK P	CPT	0-1574685	1059	1
DICKSON JAMES D	LTC	0-0298901	0168	3
DICKSON JAMES D	CPT	0-1884166	1262	1
DICKSON JAMES H	1LT	0-0150516	0652	3
DICKSON JAMES T	LTC	0-1178457	0565	1
DICKSON JOHN	CPT	0-0497046	0464	3
DICKSON JOHN R	LTC	0-1593947	0168	1
DICKSON PAUL	COL	0-0265507	0956	1
DICKSON RICHARD S	LTC	0-1014014	0665	1
DICKSON ROBERT B	MAJ	0-0138562	0648	3
DICKSON ROBERT C	WO1	W-2132706	0945	2
DICKSON ROBERT H	LTC	0-0103032	0649	3
DICKSON WILLIAM A	LTC	0-1319607	0565	1
DICKSON WILLIAM K	COL	0-0138612	0555	3
DICKSON WILLIAM M	CPT	0-2262970	0257	1
DICKSON WILLIAM T	1LT	0-1316390	0246	2
DICUS GEORGE L	CPT	0-1116219	0450	2
DIDERRICK MARY K	2LT	N-0733567	0745	1
DIDUCH MICHAEL J	1LT	0-1318771	0646	2
DIEBELS WILLIAM J JR	1LT	0-5301598	0859	2
DIEBOLT JAMES L	CW2	W-2205834	1162	1
DIEDIKER VICTOR W	LTC	0-0392136	1160	2
DIEDRICH WILLIAM C	LTC	0-0254895	0567	3
DIEDRICHS MARTIN A	MAJ	0-0382401	0154	1
DIEFENBACH GEORGE H	LTC	0-0286242	0947	2
DIEFENBACH WILLARD E	MAJ	0-2019300	0363	1
DIEFENDORF RANDALL A	2LT	0-0392821	0344	2
DIEFENDORF RICHARD O	CPT	0-0510022	0845	2
DIEHL ALFRED I	CW3	W-2143672	0168	1
DIEHL AUGUST P	MAJ	0-0177947	0445	2
DIEHL BRUCE E	MAJ	0-0432945	0266	1
DIEHL CHARLES E	LTC	0-0394925	0658	2
DIEHL CONDA H	LTC	0-0277525	0263	3
DIEHL EDWARD L	2LT	0-0554724	0645	2
DIEHL FRANK A	2LT	0-1645330	0745	2
DIEHL GEORGE W	CPT	0-1103596	0861	1
DIEHL HARRY A	MAJ	0-0423203	0557	1
DIEHL MAURICE	COL	0-0221033	0962	3
DIEHL PAUL J	MAJ	0-1103597	1151	2
DIEHL RAY E	COL	0-0209409	1155	3
DIEHL RAYMOND L	LTC	0-1011845	0164	1
DIEHL WALLACE J	1LT	0-1301447	1145	2
DIEHL WINIFRED F	MAJ	N-0725230	0464	3
DIEHOLD JAMES A	MAJ	0-2037123	1162	1
DIEM JACOB	MAJ	0-1796591	1155	1
DIEMER DONALD K	1LT	0-2035133	0147	2
DIENER JOHN E	LTC	0-0544779	1168	1
DIENST CARL A	MAJ	0-0275061	0859	3
DIENST CHARLES F	LTC	0-0115869	0648	3
DIER CLIFFORD L	B G	0-0246655	0664	3
DIER STEPHEN C	COL	0-0381926	1057	3
DIERCKS FRED H	LTC	0-0060890	1167	2
DIERKES PAUL A	LTC	0-0450121	0161	1
DIESEL HALBERT M	MAJ	0-1557439	1060	1
DIETER EDWARD J	LTC	0-0298502	0660	3
DIETER GEORGE H	COL	0-0152241	0648	3
DIETER LOUISE C	MAJ	N-0736257	0563	2
DIETERICH ALVAH M	1LT	0-1046411	0146	2
DIETERICH WARREN C	CW3	W-2120762	0760	1
DIETERMAN JOHN R	MAJ	0-1643495	0965	1
DIETLE JACK F	LTC	0-1171118	1160	1
DIETRICH BENNY S	1LT	0-1174559	0346	2
DIETRICH ELEANOR J	2LT	N-0723934	0845	1
DIETRICH LEO A	LTC	0-1647895	0361	1
DIETRICH ROBERT E	MAJ	0-2266365	1166	1
DIETSCH EMIL F JR	1LT	0-1582301	0245	2
DIETTRICH ROGER B	LTC	0-1995080	1162	1
DIETZ CARL I	CPT	0-0196683	1158	3
DIETZ CLARENCE C	CW2	W-2142756	0259	1
DIETZ FRED A	CPT	0-0107926	0848	3
DIETZ FREDERICK	MAJ	0-1280038	1055	1
DIETZ JOHN L	LTC	0-1641994	1267	1
DIETZ JOSEPH A JR	CW3	W-2143246	0962	1
DIETZ LOUIS H	LTC	0-1328130	1263	1
DIETZ NICHOLAS JR	LTC	0-0338569	0161	3
DIETZ NORBERT W	MAJ	0-0962251	0464	1
DIETZ PHIL G	MAJ	0-1012575	1047	2
DIETZ RAYMOND W	CW2	W-2141255	0460	1
DIETZE VICTOR E	MAJ	0-1703760	0450	2
DIFFEE GUY E	CW2	W-2151835	0857	1
DIFFENDERFER H C	1LT	0-1012190	0247	2
DIFFENDERFER HARRY S	LTC	0-0281288	0961	3
DIFFIN JOHN C	MAJ	0-0516339	0646	2
DIFFLEY THOMAS L	LTC	0-1184034	1063	1
DIGEORGE IGNATIUS J	1LT	0-1293025	0945	2
DIGGES ALEX P JR	MAJ	0-1101409	0561	1
DIGGINS VERNON T	MAJ	0-2262556	0465	1
DIGGS ARTHUR E	COL	0-0180120	0756	3
DIGGS JOHN C	LTC	0-0209509	0648	3
DIGGS JOHN W	COL	0-0359919	0456	3
DIGGS RAYMOND A	LTC	0-0304322	0561	1
DIGIACOMO WILLIAM H	CPT	0-0547104	1045	2
DIGIONI LOUIS C	MAJ	0-1109896	0662	1
DIGMAN RITA A	1LT	N-0751147	0846	1
DIHM HENRY A	LTC	0-0116139	0153	3
DILBURN ERNEST L	WO1	W-2120701	0458	1
DILDINE JOHN W	CPT	0-0495375	1262	1
DILDINE WILLIAM F	LTC	0-0280266	0359	1
DILIONE ROBERT R	CPT	0-2034075	1061	1
DILKS KENNETH E	LTC	0-0410771	0960	1
DILL CHARLES C JR	LTC	0-1586537	0461	1
DILL DONALD G	CW3	W-2109862	1055	1
DILL ERNEST W	CPT	0-1169486	1061	1
DILL FRANCIS W	LTC	0-1553067	0661	1
DILL JERRY L	CW3	W-2203308	0566	1
DILL LESTER C	MAJ	0-1541002	0854	1
DILL WALTER J JR	LTC	0-0256559	0966	3
DILL WILLIAM G JR	MAJ	0-1641239	0667	1
DILL WILLIAM H	MAJ	0-2021245	0567	1
DILLAHEY WALTER R	LTC	0-0907864	1061	3
DILLAMONT CHESTER A	LTC	0-1822246	0966	1
DILLARD HARDY C	COL	0-0440753	1162	3
DILLARD HENRY D	CPT	0-0395345	1043	2
DILLARD JAMES M	MAJ	0-1944663	0763	1
DILLARD JAMES R	COL	0-0253528	1060	3
DILLARD RALPH E JR	LTC	0-1799258	0968	1
DILLARD WALTER S	CW3	W-2152138	0365	1
DILLAWAY GEORGE L JR	COL	0-0167528	0655	2
DILLE HENRY W	LTC	0-0390686	0760	1
DILLEHAY JAMES G	LTC	0-1573163	0363	1
DILLENBACK FRANK H	MAJ	0-0123371	0245	2
DILLENBECK WILLIAM H	LTC	0-0304934	0363	3
DILLER EVERELL W	COL	0-0216278	1066	3
DILLER JOHN C	COL	0-0150609	0555	3
DILLERY JOSEPH L	CPT	0-0273775	0545	2
DILLESHAW HOWARD D	CW3	W-2148253	0163	1
DILLEY CHESTER A	CPT	0-2053819	0554	1
DILLEY DONALD J	MAJ	0-1821692	0660	1
DILLINGHAM ALLAN M	2LT	0-1633163	0647	2
DILLINGHAM HAROLD S	B G	0-0315416	0565	3
DILLINGHAM PAUL W	COL	0-0200926	1058	1
DILLIPLANE CHARLES M	LTC	0-1946474	1265	1
DILLMAN CLIFTON J JR	CPT	0-1547587	0746	2
DILLMAN DON W	MAJ	0-0980274	0762	1
DILLMAN MELVIN A	COL	0-0410711	0866	3
DILLON ALVIN JR	MAJ	0-2014497	1165	1
DILLON ANGELA J	CPT	N-0737001	0346	1
DILLON ASAHEL S	COL	0-0184196	1153	3
DILLON CARSON L	CPT	0-0975294	0461	1
DILLON CLYDE J	MAJ	0-0682693	1055	2
DILLON EDWARD JR	LTC	0-0181850	0758	3
DILLON GARLAND S	LTC	0-1309699	0964	1
DILLON GEORGE E JR	CPT	0-1997520	0367	2
DILLON HARRY D	LTC	0-0983384	0468	1
DILLON HENRY S	MAJ	0-1292147	0264	1
DILLON HOWARD E	CW2	W-2150805	0158	1
DILLON JACK J	LTC	0-1102533	1058	1
DILLON JAMES M	CPT	0-0305330	0145	2
DILLON JAMES R	LTC	0-0305432	0859	1
DILLON JOHN	LTC	0-1581662	0668	3
DILLON JOHN F	MAJ	0-1176305	0263	1
DILLON JOHN F	COL	0-1581093	1263	1
DILLON JOHN F JR	1LT	0-0383066	1045	2
DILLON JOHN R	CPT	0-0161722	1153	3
DILLON JOHN R JR	MAJ	0-0248409	0766	3
DILLON JOHN V	LTC	0-2049957	0868	1
DILLON LESTER R	LTC	0-0189920	0656	3
DILLON LLOYD H	LTC	0-0185654	1057	3
DILLON MARGARET F	CPT	N-0733151	0747	1
DILLON RALPH R	LTC	0-1551194	0767	1
DILLON STUART P	LTC	0-0197965	0360	3
DILLON WALTER	CPT	0-2011589	0853	1
DILLON WILLIAM E	CW3	W-2206521	0368	1
DILLON WILLIAM G	1LT	0-0527232	0945	2
DILLOW TROY D	CPT	0-0571473	0153	2
DILLS ROWLAND H	MAJ	0-1544053	0762	1
DILMAN FRANK	CPT	0-0496788	0849	1
DILWITH LEWIS M	CPT	0-1301448	0147	2
DILWORTH FRANCIS H	LTC	0-0269783	0565	3
DIMARIA NICHOLAS	CPT	0-0484671	0445	2
DIMARIA VINCENT	2LT	0-1062160	1144	2
DIMENNA PAT	1LT	0-1298200	0944	2
DIMIT CHARLES H JR	CW2	W-3250354	0866	1
DIMLING JOHN N JR	1LT	0-1286803	0146	2
DIMMICK EDGAR L	MAJ	0-1689007	0752	2
DIMMICK HENRY S	LTC	0-0170197	1160	3
DIMMITT JOHN W	CW3	W-2211631	1268	1
DIMOND KENNETH R	MAJ	0-1937633	1267	1
DINAN KATHLEE M	2LT	N-0702674	1036	1
DINEEN ALOYSIOUS	MAJ	0-0253666	0648	3
DINEEN JOHN J	LTC	0-0300737	1056	3
DINEEN MICHAEL L	CW2	W-2214731	1167	1
DINEEN THOMAS P	MAJ	0-0938044	0363	1
DINELEY RICHARD L	CPT	0-0444678	0862	1

NAME	GRADE	SVC NO	DATE RET MO YR	RET CODE
DINES CHARLES H	CW3	W-2211494	1068	1
DINGEE JOHN F	1LT	0-1320311	0645	2
DINGER JAMES F	MAJ	0-1518310	0468	3
DINGER JULIUS J	CPT	0-1574698	1046	2
DINGES GEORGE J	COL	0-0235780	1164	3
DINGES LINUS A	CPT	0-0445287	1147	2
DINGMAN BERNARD G	LTC	0-0258288	1267	3
DINGS PARLEY M	LTC	0-0311753	0767	1
DINGUS WILLIAM V	CW3	W-2209015	0968	1
DINGWALL KENNETH M	2LT	0-0150434	0455	3
DINKEL ALFRED J	LTC	0-1573165	0252	2
DINKELKAMP ARNOLD J	LTC	0-1035243	0663	1
DINKELSPIEL EDWARD A	MAJ	0-0264615	0645	2
DINNERMAN MURRAY	CW2	W-2214698	1068	1
DINNERVILLE R F	2LT	0-1038598	1144	2
DINNING WILLIAM L	COL	0-0259508	0867	3
DINNIS OSCAR F	CPT	0-0166870	0256	3
DINSE MABEL	MAJ	N-0736728	1065	3
DINSMOOR CARLTON G	LTC	0-0246735	0866	3
DINSMORE ALBERT L	CPT	0-1649428	0356	2
DINSMORE ALDEN C	CPT	0-0388717	0244	2
DINSMORE GEORGE R	LTC	0-0272654	1264	3
DINSMORE JOSEPH S	LTC	0-0266072	0955	3
DINSMORE THOMAS D	LTC	0-0548260	0664	1
DINSMORE WAYNE A	LTC	0-1036123	0261	1
DINSTBIR JOHN F	CPT	0-1296667	1067	2
DINTEMAN WERNER	LTC	0-0361664	0459	2
DINWIDDIE CHARLES R	COL	0-0152576	0754	3
DINWIDDIE JACK D	LTC	0-0254460	1263	3
DINWIDDIE JOEL W	1LT	0-0492791	0347	2
DIOGSON CONRAD V	1LT	0-1896471	0559	1
DIOKNO MELCHOR V	MAJ	0-2026763	0257	1
DION DOROTHEA G	2LT	N-0741765	1144	1
DION POLYDORE E	CPT	0-0399095	0157	1
DIONNE ARTHUR D	CPT	0-2017029	0358	1
DIONNE JOSEPH A	LTC	0-0481499	1155	1
DIONOLO THOMAS	LTC	0-1298607	0462	1
DIOTT THEODORE J	LTC	0-1306711	0658	2
DIPPO FRANK H	CPT	0-0204517	1151	3
DIPPO WILLIAM G	MAJ	0-1376719	0664	1
DIPPOLITO JOSEPH H	LTC	0-0364078	0865	1
DIRDEN DON S	1LT	0-1638961	1045	2
DIRESTA ANTHONY T	LTC	0-0963780	0868	1
DIRKS EDWARD F	LTC	0-0213255	0764	3
DIRRIM PAUL F	CPT	0-0981971	0261	1
DISBROW HARRY L	2LT	0-1329517	0844	2
DISCH JOHN L	2LT	0-1326827	0546	2
DISCOE HENRY	CW4	W-2129877	1054	1
DISEKER ELLIS G	LTC	0-0249141	0363	3
DISHAROON JOHN C	LTC	0-0510777	0464	1
DISHONG WILLIAM W	MAJ	0-0269505	0568	3
DISICK SOLOMON	MAJ	0-0331209	0845	2
DISKO MICHAEL	1LT	0-0388731	1045	2
DISLER ELLIOTT E	1LT	0-1319266	0945	2
DISMORE ALBERT B	MAJ	0-0233215	0847	2
DISMORE RAY A	MAJ	0-0475909	0947	1
DISMUKE GRACE M	CPT	N-0763524	0654	2
DISMUKE HENRY S	1LT	0-1010822	1151	2
DISNEY CYRIL C	LTC	0-1167395	0262	1
DISNEY ROBERT	COL	0-0237301	0455	3
DISNEY STANLEY F	MAJ	0-0513303	0147	2
DISPENZA SEBASTIAN	MAJ	0-0348382	0360	1
DISSEL THAYER W	LTC	0-0978073	0768	1
DISSER RALPH K	LTC	0-1286096	0455	1
DISSINGER ARTHUR H	LTC	0-1552659	0161	1
DISSPAIN ED	MAJ	0-1103136	0554	1
DISSTON HARRY	COL	0-0149374	1059	3
DISTELHORST FRED M	COL	0-0172975	0252	3
DITATA DOMENICK	COL	0-0331814	0754	3
DITMAN MARTHA E	MAJ	N-0760060	0368	1
DITTHERNER VAN F	LTC	0-0401419	0566	2
DITTERT JESSE J	1LT	0-1303583	0945	2
DITTES PHILIP C	MAJ	0-0479557	0165	3
DITTMANN EARL F	CPT	0-0372566	0645	2
DITTMAR GUSTAVE C	COL	0-0131195	0955	3

NAME	GRADE	SVC NO	DATE RET MO YR	RET CODE
DITTMAR MAX C	CW3	W-2151865	0363	1
DITTMAR RUSSELL E	COL	0-0224865	1059	1
DITTMAR RUSSELL W	CPT	0-0969736	1165	1
DITTMER CHARLES H	MAJ	0-0193353	0648	3
DITTMER JOHN S	COL	0-1030143	1163	1
DITTRICH FRANK	LTC	0-1058978	1065	1
DITTRICH KARL W	COL	0-0381571	0663	1
DITZEL WILLIAM E JR	LTC	0-1331161	0767	1
DITZLER JOHN H	CW3	W-3150426	0768	1
DIUGUID JOHN W	LTC	0-0231096	1163	3
DIVELBISS WILLIS	CW2	W-2203474	0762	2
DIVELEY REX L	COL	0-0201482	0156	3
DIVELY JOHN M	LTC	0-0472154	0557	1
DIVELY SHIRLEY F	MAJ	0-0956567	0963	1
DIVEN DANIEL C	MAJ	0-1917756	0665	1
DIVERS JESSE W	CW3	W-2143073	0664	1
DIVICH STEVE M	LTC	0-0317860	0146	2
DIVINE BERNICE M	1LT	N-0776516	1045	1
DIVINE JOHN E	1LT	0-1281836	0546	2
DIX HAROLD L	CPT	0-0969735	0161	1
DIXON AGES G	LTC	0-1342369	0767	1
DIXON ALTON W	CW2	W-2206286	1262	2
DIXON BERNEST L	MAJ	0-0268505	0268	3
DIXON BRYAN R	1LT	0-1342169	0752	2
DIXON CALVERT R	1LT	0-1573792	1045	2
DIXON CHARLES R	CW2	W-2212218	1066	1
DIXON COLIN A	MAJ	0-0279473	0157	3
DIXON DON S	1LT	0-1647537	1045	2
DIXON DON W	COL	0-0343066	0264	1
DIXON FLOYD N	LTC	0-1309700	0962	1
DIXON FLOYD V	MAJ	0-0242602	0262	3
DIXON FRANK J	LTC	0-1320443	1262	1
DIXON FRANK L	MAJ	0-0265493	1146	2
DIXON GEORGE M	CW2	W-2206095	0961	1
DIXON GILBERT W	MAJ	0-0243186	0245	2
DIXON HARLOW C	CPT	0-0287267	0845	2
DIXON HAROLD	CW2	W-2143227	1053	1
DIXON HOSEA J	MAJ	0-0200207	1044	2
DIXON JAMES A	LTC	0-0347640	0157	1
DIXON JESSE T	1LT	0-0487945	1047	1
DIXON JOHNNIE M	2LT	0-0409643	0643	2
DIXON JOSEPH C	CW2	W-2213031	0968	1
DIXON JOSIE G	1LT	N-0726343	0146	1
DIXON KENNETH J	MAJ	0-2016336	0366	3
DIXON LEE G	WO1	W-2115849	0646	1
DIXON LEONARD S	2LT	0-0514264	0345	2
DIXON LOIS E	1LT	N-0724827	0646	1
DIXON MARVIN H	COL	0-0205567	1163	3
DIXON MOSE E	CPT	0-1298676	0257	1
DIXON PAUL H	LTC	0-1175998	1065	1
DIXON PERRY M	LTC	0-0285833	1054	1
DIXON ROD P	2LT	0-1597394	0346	2
DIXON ROLAND B	CPT	0-1300943	0662	1
DIXON ROY F	MAJ	0-0304118	0446	2
DIXON SAMUEL C	MAJ	0-1994751	1055	2
DIXON SHERWOOD	COL	0-0119005	0656	3
DIXON THOMAS E	MAJ	0-0289989	1154	1
DIXON THOMAS S	MAJ	0-1919103	1266	1
DIXON TYLER F	LTC	0-0452600	0846	2
DIXON WALTER R	LTC	0-0315419	0860	3
DIXON WILLARD L	CW3	W-2147163	0664	1
DIXON WILLIAM R JR	LTC	0-1000349	0167	3
DIXON WILLIAM R	LTC	0-0452270	0161	1
DIXON WILLIAM R	MAJ	0-1318654	1162	1
DIXON WORDEN F	LTC	0-1650065	1162	1
DIXON ZANDA B	CPT	N-0743817	1160	1
DIXSON I J JR	CPT	0-0970670	1060	1
DIXSON MONROE P	2LT	0-1292490	1044	2
DIXSON ROY H	CW3	W-2205950	0867	1
DJERNES ENTAR	MAJ	0-1301449	0464	1
DJIOVANIDIS JOHN C	2LT	0-1047093	0745	2
DLUGOSH LEONARD C	CW3	W-2150203	1263	1
DLUGOSZ STANLEY	1LT	0-2055102	1046	2
DMOHOWSKI ANTHONY	1LT	0-1182097	1145	2
DMUCHOWSKI ARTHUR M	1LT	0-1334555	0649	2

NAME	GRADE	SVC NO	DATE RET MO YR	RET CODE
DOAK ALEXANDER	MAJ	0-1581663	0862	1
DOAK JOHN W	LTC	0-0285564	0562	1
DOAN MARTIN L	MAJ	0-2263484	1264	1
DOAN RAYMOND A	1LT	0-1794920	1045	2
DOAN ROBERT M	MAJ	0-1120051	1062	1
DOAN ROLAND E	LTC	0-0104452	0152	1
DOANE DWIGHT L	MAJ	0-5301599	0867	1
DOANE ELLIS B	CPT	0-2042828	1051	1
DOANE FRANCIS H	LTC	0-0226254	1046	2
DOANE JOHN E	LTC	0-1063119	0262	1
DOANE RALPH L	MAJ	0-1341645	0568	1
DOAR LEROY H	LTC	0-0193307	0455	2
DOBAK RAYNOLD S	LTC	0-0885621	1062	1
DOBBER STANLEY	1LT	0-1051933	0455	1
DOBBIE HARRY S	LTC	0-1594141	1061	1
DOBBIE JAMES N JR	LTC	0-1945786	1162	1
DOBBIN JOSEPH G	MAJ	0-1292149	0854	1
DOBBIN LOUISE	MAJ	N-0743726	1162	1
DOBBINS CLAUDE F	CPT	0-1554712	0446	2
DOBBINS ERNEST F	LTC	0-0292948	0859	1
DOBBINS FRANK P	COL	0-0481441	1160	3
DOBBINS JACK P	1LT	0-1823575	0845	2
DOBBINS ROBERT E	CW4	W-2142390	1068	1
DOBBINS THOMAS	COL	0-0102452	0648	3
DOBBINS WALTER E JR	COL	0-0221555	0556	1
DOBBINS WILLIAM F	MAJ	0-0980673	0366	1
DOBBS BENJAMIN C	1LT	0-1374099	0945	2
DOBBS CHARLES H	COL	0-0239798	0759	3
DOBBS TOMMIE F	CPT	0-0535754	0157	1
DOBBS WILLIAM A	COL	0-0347197	0163	1
DOBBS WILLIAM H	MAJ	0-0506134	0255	1
DOBBS WILLIAM M	CPT	0-0284963	0946	2
DOBBYN HARRY W	LTC	0-0361015	0760	3
DOBER HARRY C	MAJ	0-1335759	0964	1
DOBIE CLYDE A	CW3	W-2203648	0665	1
DOBILES JOHN G	1LT	0-0497575	0550	1
DOBKIN ARTHUR	MAJ	0-0308186	0945	2
DOBLE HENRY P JR	MAJ	0-1342252	0667	1
DOBLE WILLIAM A JR	COL	0-0204145	0854	3
DOBLE WILTON B	WO1	W-2006563	0768	3
DOBLER GEORGE O	LTC	0-0413396	0763	1
DOBRESK SAMUEL	LTC	0-1599156	1167	1
DOBRICK HERBERT R	CPT	0-0481145	0853	1
DOBRINDT CARL H	2LT	0-0529625	0744	2
DOBROLET GREGORY	MAJ	0-1535159	0463	2
DOBRY JAMES	MAJ	0-1103137	0646	2
DOBRZYNSKY CHARLOT	1LT	N-0720810	0646	1
DOBSON CATHERINE	CPT	N-0752964	0148	1
DOBSON CECIL R	MAJ	0-0237971	1263	3
DOBSON CHARLES W	LTC	0-0454046	0361	1
DOBSON LAWRENCE	LTC	0-1166047	0457	1
DOBSON ROBERT J B	1LT	0-1056337	1146	2
DOBYNS DONALD L	CW2	W-2213362	0468	1
DOCHARTY MARGARET E	CPT	N-0793739	0847	1
DOCHERTY SADIE M	MAJ	N-0757623	0464	3
DOCHNEY JAMES J	CPT	0-1593542	0663	1
DOCK PAUL T	1LT	0-1533048	0245	2
DOCKA CLARENCE W	LTC	0-0276186	0466	3
DOCKAL LLOYD J	COL	0-0275420	1162	3
DOCKHAM RALPH A	CW3	W-2150689	0962	1
DOCKSTADER L A	CPT	0-0162100	1044	2
DOCKTER JACK G	MAJ	0-0494300	0357	1
DOCKUM OSCAR L	COL	0-0169108	1160	3
DODD A L	WO1	W-2127386	1047	2
DODD ABBY M	LTC	0-0278357	0646	2
DODD ALFRED H	MAJ	0-0493221	1054	1
DODD BENTLEY H	1LT	0-1011335	1044	2
DODD CARL H	MAJ	0-2262354	0765	1
DODD CHARLES E	CPT	0-1541498	0645	2
DODD EDWIN N	LTC	0-1573837	0253	1
DODD GEORGE K	CPT	0-0100651	1055	3
DODD GORDON B	CW4	W-2131623	0355	2
DODD HARRY J	MAJ	0-1295343	0361	1
DODD JOHN L	CW3	W-2205410	0366	2
DODD KENNETH H	LTC	0-1594403	1062	1

NAME	GRADE	SVC NO	DATE RET MO YR	RET CODE
DODD LEWIS J	CPT	0-2017823	1160	1
DODD RAY H	1LT	0-1292318	1145	2
DODD STEPHEN F	LTC	0-0058372	1167	1
DODD WILBURN C	CPT	0-0164279	1133	2
DODD WILLIAM A	CPT	0-0512527	0745	2
DODD WILLIAM L	CPT	0-2025874	0757	1
DODDRIDGE THOMAS W	CPT	0-1844674	0547	2
DODDS ARTHUR D	LTC	0-0322130	0259	1
DODDS GERALD C	MAJ	0-0451095	0157	1
DODDS HORTON C	LTC	0-1584143	0764	1
DODDS JOHN F	MAJ	0-0516569	0667	1
DODDS JOHN H	LTC	0-0276428	1053	3
DODDS RUSSELL W	COL	0-0194035	0760	1
DODDS VERA L	1LT	N-0733085	0646	1
DODDS WILLIAM G	MAJ	0-1633164	0445	2
DODEL WALTER W	1LT	0-1172435	1045	2
DODGE ALBERT D	COL	0-0235131	0865	3
DODGE CLARENCE P	1LT	0-0259989	1045	2
DODGE CLAYTON E	MAJ	0-1886107	0267	1
DODGE DONALD J	CPT	0-1291087	1144	2
DODGE FRANK M	1LT	0-0509115	1146	1
DODGE GEORGE W	LTC	0-0393603	1059	1
DODGE HARRY W JR	LTC	0-1546335	1162	1
DODGE ISRAEL P	MAJ	0-0221612	0954	3
DODGE JOSEPH A	COL	0-0465919	0365	1
DODGE LAURENCE S	1LT	0-0105300	1055	1
DODGE LEONARD A	CW2	W-2105061	0845	2
DODGE LYNN W	MAJ	0-0267959	0246	2
DODGE PHILIP R	COL	0-0265581	0160	3
DODGE ROBERT H	LTC	0-1331273	0267	2
DODGE ROBERT I JR	COL	0-0250160	1167	3
DODGE ROBERT N	CW3	W-2204972	0763	1
DODGE WARREN M JR	MAJ	0-0498420	0944	2
DODGE WILLIAM H	LTC	0-0278854	0267	3
DODGE WILLIAM H	LTC	0-1183057	0867	1
DODGE WILLIAM P	MAJ	0-0148319	0664	1
DODGE WILLIS B	2LT	0-2020123	0951	2
DODGE WINTHROP A	CW3	W-2104005	0768	1
DODGEN ALBERT J	LTC	0-0511360	0859	1
DODGEN FLORENCE D	LTC	0-2295345	0365	2
DODGEN THOMAS B JR	MAJ	0-1823274	0866	1
DODGION RAYMOND E	CW3	W-2143762	0460	1
DODSON FURLON G	MAJ	0-0193730	0859	1
DODSON JAMES A	CW2	W-2210520	1166	1
DODSON JOHN T	1LT	0-1585370	0844	2
DODSON LAVERE A	LTC	0-0507217	0663	3
DODSON LEONARD F	1LT	0-0449199	0546	2
DODSON ROGER S	CW2	W-2150307	0662	1
DODSON ROLAND S	MAJ	0-0278265	0759	3
DODSON WALTER S	1LT	0-1295135	0345	2
DODSON WILLARD F	COL	0-0174148	1059	3
DODSON WILLIAM C	CW2	W-2143763	0663	1
DOOT WAYNE O	MAJ	0-1685648	0765	1
DOEBLIN ROBERT E	MAJ	0-1293026	1162	1
DOEDEN LESTER J	2LT	0-1015142	0645	2
DOEGE ARTHUR J	LTC	0-0349791	0660	[illegible]
DOELLINGER HERMAN C	COL	0-0296639	0450	3
DOERGES CLEON C	MAJ	0-2011776	0759	1
DOERING ANNE M	LTC	L-0800451	0467	[illegible]
DOERING CHARLES E	CW2	W-2150300	0661	[illegible]
DOERNBACH WILLIAM	CPT	0-2023686	0555	[illegible]
DOERR DAVID	CPT	0-1821835	1046	[illegible]
DOERR JEAN P	LTC	0-0416469	1163	[illegible]
DOERR NELSON E	MAJ	0-1181594	0465	3
DOERRMAN RICHARD M	MAJ	0-1917874	0660	1
DOERTY WALTER L	COL	0-0246922	0555	[illegible]
DOESBURG CHARLES E	LTC	0-2035977	0860	[illegible]
DOETTERL FRANK A	MAJ	0-0221442	0861	[illegible]
DOFF AARON	CPT	0-1310583	0966	[illegible]
DOFFLEMEYER NORMAN C	MAJ	0-2007971	0153	[illegible]
DOGGETT BENJAMIN F	1LT	0-0433820	1050	[illegible]
DOGGETT WALTER L	1LT	0-1007412	0949	2
DOGGETTE JORDAN O	CPT	0-1303806	1046	[illegible]
DOHERTY DONALD R	MAJ	0-1119480	0162	[illegible]
DOHERTY EDWARD F	MAJ	0-1047094	0463	1

NAME	GRADE	SVC NO	DATE RET MO YR	RET CODE
DOHERTY FRANCIS D	LTC	0-1642304	0767	1
DOHERTY JACK	LTC	0-1165950	0462	1
DOHERTY MICHAEL	2LT	0-2010700	0751	1
DOHERTY OWEN F	LTC	0-1045769	1067	1
DOHERTY PATRICK L	LTC	0-1533101	0164	1
DOHERTY RAYMOND F	WO1	W-2129923	1057	1
DOHERTY VINCENT H	MAJ	0-1922552	0365	1
DOHERTY WILLIAM J	WO1	W-2144789	0858	1
DOHERTY WILLIAM R	MAJ	0-0376743	0746	3
DOHLSTROM GEORGE F	LTC	0-0981868	0468	1
DOHME JOHN F	2LT	0-1016578	1144	2
DOHN FRANCIS A	MAJ	0-1638366	0358	2
DOHR RAYMOND F	LTC	0-0227594	1161	3
DOHRMANN JACK F	LTC	0-0227515	0467	3
DOHT GERALD W	CPT	0-5322378	0968	2
DOHY ALEXANDER	CW3	W-2152374	0563	1
DOIDGE HAROLD I	MAJ	0-2079344	0464	1
DOIG EDWIN A	LTC	0-0192014	0358	3
DOIL RALPH D	MAJ	0-2263074	0264	1
DOKE LOWELL V	1LT	0-1031307	0846	2
DOLAN BENJAMIN R	CPT	0-0171747	0457	3
DOLAN CHESTER A JR	MAJ	0-0913657	1045	2
DOLAN DANIEL F	CW4	W-2143024	1164	1
DOLAN EDWARD S	LTC	0-1647400	0766	3
DOLAN FRANCIS S	COL	0-0475385	0459	2
DOLAN GEORGE H	MAJ	0-1557271	0964	1
DOLAN GERALD	MAJ	0-0315394	0144	2
DOLAN JAMES H	1LT	0-0955079	0452	2
DOLAN JOHN	LTC	0-1994898	1163	1
DOLAN JOHN E JR	MAJ	0-0223264	1045	2
DOLAN JOHN J	CPT	0-0341763	0445	2
DOLAN JOSEPH C	COL	0-0228092	0466	3
DOLAN KENNETH J	MAJ	0-0302646	0346	2
DOLAN LEONARD J	LTC	0-1170711	0967	1
DOLAN LESLIE C	LTC	0-1647542	0164	3
DOLAN MICHAEL J	LTC	0-1284839	0764	1
DOLAN PATRICK T	CPT	0-0369484	0546	2
DOLAN PETER E	COL	0-0202334	0261	3
DOLAN RONALD S	CW3	W-2145413	0760	1
DOLAN WILLIE L	WO1	W-2152994	0654	2
DOLBEARE RICHARD	LTC	0-0277412	1063	3
DOLBEE WALTER J JR	MAJ	0-0559034	0961	1
DOLBIER JOHN L	1LT	0-1112116	0757	1
DOLCE JOSEPH R	COL	0-0284818	0468	3
DOLCE MATTHEW L	MAJ	0-1647545	0357	1
DOLE DAVID H	MAJ	0-1168623	1267	3
DOLE LILLAN O	MAJ	N-0753490	0868	1
DOLE ROBERT J	CPT	0-1327518	0748	2
DOLEJSI FRANK C	MAJ	0-1302439	0258	1
DOLES ALVIN D	CW2	W-2117079	0653	1
DOLES EMMETT A	CPT	0-0482231	0345	2
DOLEZAL HENRY	MAJ	0-0232627	0265	3
DOLGOPOL RICHARD Z	1LT	0-1937060	0448	2
DOLIBER EARL L JR	CW3	W-2205454	0766	1
DOLL CECIL T	COL	0-0915315	0965	3
DOLL CLARENCE E JR	MAJ	0-0309293	1059	1
DOLL CLIFFORD K	WO1	W-2127700	1061	2
DOLL FRANK A	LTC	0-0522593	0568	1
DOLL WILLIAM E	MAJ	0-1922517	0565	1
DOLLAR CARMEL T	MAJ	0-1309148	0657	1
DOLLAR JAMES W	LTC	0-1322683	0962	1
DOLLAR LOUISE	CPT	N-0727762	1047	1
DOLLAR MAUREE E	MAJ	0-1796935	0959	1
DOLLINGER ROBERT F	2LT	0-1113172	0244	2
DOLLIVER HAROLD W	MAJ	0-1683943	0462	1
DOLLOFF HORACE A	CW4	W-2111834	0962	1
DOLMAGE GEORGE H	CPT	0-0499402	0145	2
DOLMAN HAROLD R	1LT	0-0428934	0345	2
DOLOZIK ANTHONY S	1LT	0-1823851	0347	2
DOLPH IVAR E	COL	0-0342225	0963	3
DOLSEY HERBERT S	LTC	0-1044209	1060	1
DOLSON IRMA A	MAJ	N-0736143	0765	1
DOLTON HENRY J	COL	0-0216803	0258	1
DOLVEN FRANK M	MAJ	0-0438573	1156	3
DOMAIGE DOMMAIRE L	CPT	0-0300162	0147	2

NAME	GRADE	SVC NO	DATE RET MO YR	RET CODE
DOMAN ADOLPH C	MAJ	0-1292491	1061	1
DOMAN THURMAN S	COL	0-0298093	0360	1
DOMANSKI VINCENT P	CW2	W-2212025	0767	1
DOMBEK WALTER J	MAJ	0-2035246	0658	1
DOMBROSKI FRANK A	MAJ	0-1994589	0865	1
DOMBROSKI STANLEY T	2LT	0-1823275	0245	2
DOMBROWSKI EUGENE L	CW3	W-2152430	0462	1
DOMBROWSKI FRANCIS	1LT	0-0449625	1145	2
DOMBROWSKI HENRY F	MAJ	0-1102698	0457	1
DOMENIL RALPH E	CW3	W-2205712	0767	1
DOMER WILLIAM G	WO1	W-2108442	0347	1
DOMINA DONALD E	COL	0-1534002	0868	2
DOMINE GENARO L	1LT	0-1896658	0667	1
DOMINGO DANIEL J	MAJ	0-1587930	0658	1
DOMINGOES FRANK A JR	MAJ	0-1997992	0761	1
DOMINGUEZ ALBERTO M	CPT	0-0402279	0945	2
DOMINGUEZ EDWARD SRA	1LT	0-1896759	0354	1
DOMINGUEZ ELISEO	CPT	0-1914341	1130	2
DOMINGUEZ JOSE R	MAJ	0-1326490	0561	1
DOMINGUEZ WILLIAM	CPT	0-2262638	0261	1
DOMINICK LEO H	LTC	0-0166411	0952	3
DOMINICK LOUIS	MAJ	0-1174827	0258	1
DOMINICK WILLIAM A	COL	0-0240088	0565	3
DOMINIQUE CHARLES J	COL	0-0084361	1267	1
DOMINO THOMAS	CPT	0-0968070	0959	1
DOMME EDWARD J	2LT	0-1015182	0245	2
DOMMER JOSEPH T	LTC	0-1186942	0768	1
DOMMERT HOWARD F	MAJ	0-0966041	1061	1
DOMOKOS ALEX P	MAJ	0-2024129	0655	1
DOMOTOR JOSEPH J	CPT	0-1013470	0759	1
DOMS ALBERT R	LTC	0-0313206	0467	3
DON LEAVY ALPH	LTC	0-1578379	0961	1
DON-BATALLA ROBERT	1LT	0-1896445	1062	1
DONADIO SALVATORE	MAJ	0-1286982	0457	1
DONAGHY DONALD J	CW2	W-2111577	1045	2
DONAGHY GEORGE E	LTC	0-0335945	1266	3
DONAGHY WILLIAM R	LTC	0-0511618	0563	1
DONAH DONALD A	CW2	W-2146231	0856	1
DONAHEY RAYMOND E	CPT	0-0213113	0145	2
DONAHO EDDIE L	CPT	0-0981836	0661	2
DONAHOE JOHN P JR	CPT	0-0423376	0746	2
DONAHUE EDWARD L	CW4	W-2150504	1060	1
DONAHUE FRANK J	LTC	0-1060075	0465	3
DONAHUE HAROLD C	1LT	0-1317897	1045	2
DONAHUE HARRY F	LTC	0-0244961	0560	3
DONAHUE HARRY G	MAJ	0-1645796	0661	1
DONAHUE JOHN E	LTC	0-2046950	0967	2
DONAHUE JOHN P	1LT	0-1018039	0446	2
DONAHUE JOSEPH J	COL	0-0155398	1055	3
DONAHUE JOSEPH K	LTC	0-1043317	0761	1
DONAHUE JOSEPH P	LTC	0-1001321	0465	1
DONAHUE NINA E V	CPT	L-0115004	0455	2
DONAHUE ROBERT J	MAJ	0-2006446	0962	2
DONAHUE ROBERT V	LTC	0-1645344	0865	1
DONAHUE THEODORE R	LTC	0-1042795	1166	1
DONAHUE THOMAS F	CPT	0-2046617	1154	1
DONAHUE TIMOTHY M	CPT	0-0156073	0253	3
DONAHUE TIMOTHY S	MAJ	0-1633168	1057	1
DONALD H WEBSTER	LTC	0-0297315	0766	3
DONALD JEANETTE E	2LT	N-0801421	0947	1
DONALD JOHN	1LT	0-1184037	0446	2
DONALD WILLIAM S	LTC	0-1176601	0562	2
DONALDS JOHN G	CW2	W-2215897	0468	1
DONALDSON BEATRICE	1LT	N-0737724	0945	1
DONALDSON CALVIN L	LTC	0-0312366	0661	3
DONALDSON GEORGE	CPT	0-1635790	0747	1
DONALDSON GEORGE H	MAJ	0-1165281	0346	2
DONALDSON GEORGE M	LTC	0-0287511	0957	1
DONALDSON HAROLD A	COL	0-0479361	1064	3
DONALDSON HAROLD B	COL	0-0310552	0661	1
DONALDSON JAMES W	MAJ	0-0404601	1047	2
DONALDSON JOHN J	MAJ	0-0969391	0464	1
DONALDSON LEE F	LTC	0-1579571	0966	1
DONALDSON MAX A	MAJ	0-0359640	1265	3
DONALDSON RAE A	COL	0-0354109	0661	1

NAME	GRADE	SVC NO	DATE RET MO YR	RET CODE
DONALDSON ROBERT B	LTC	0-1171123	0462	1
DONALDSON ROBERT E	MAJ	0-0208651	0231	2
DONALDSON SIDNEY S	MAJ	0-0372341	0962	1
DONALDSON VERNON H	LTC	0-0269280	0966	3
DONALDSON WAYNE R	MAJ	0-0224521	1054	3
DONALDSON WILLIAM C	COL	0-0265943	0657	3
DONALDSON WILLIAM F	MAJ	0-0187930	0947	1
DONALDSON WOODROW E	LTC	0-0459968	0955	2
DONAT ANTHONY J	LTC	0-0370852	0957	1
DONATH ROBERT T	MAJ	0-1933589	0167	1
DONATY ROBERT L	MAJ	0-1301450	0363	1
DONAVIN KIRKWOOD M	MAJ	0-0909171	0267	1
DONCHECK REMUS A	CPT	0-0437695	0646	2
DONEGAN JOHN J	MAJ	0-2037539	0563	1
DONEGAN THOMAS D	LTC	0-1321891	0265	1
DONELAN STEPHEN F	LTC	0-2016082	1167	1
DONELAN THOMAS E	LTC	0-0241290	0255	3
DONELSON DAVID K	COL	0-0275137	1158	1
DONELSON ROYAL M	CW3	W-2207210	0466	1
DONELSON SAMUEL JR	1LT	0-0209265	0160	3
DONERY MARY A	MAJ	N-0732413	1064	3
DONEY RICHARD J	MAJ	0-0392769	0845	2
DONG CHARLES	LTC	0-1054540	0361	2
DONHAJSER STEWART E	LTC	0-0305906	0661	1
DONIGAN BERGE P	LTC	0-0361412	1064	3
DONIGAN ROBERT L	COL	0-0263634	0463	3
DONIGAN WILLIAM R	LTC	0-0272708	0565	3
DONIVAN LEO H JR	CPT	0-0316659	0245	2
DONKLE MELVIN C	COL	0-0196099	0562	3
DONLAY WILLARD J	1LT	0-1640397	0545	2
DONLEVY JAMES H	CPT	0-1056339	0147	2
DONLEY DAVID F	LTC	0-0229409	0662	3
DONLEY DONALD	LTC	0-0214108	0258	3
DONLEY DONALD J	CPT	0-1304697	0357	1
DONLEY JOHN C	CPT	0-1283045	1045	2
DONLEY RALPH M	MAJ	0-0992979	0268	2
DONLEY ROBERT M	WO1	W-2127901	0451	2
DONLEY WILLIAM J	MAJ	0-1116371	0858	1
DONLIN CLYDE J	MAJ	0-1922520	0168	1
DONLIN DONALD J	1LT	0-0515669	0545	2
DONLON JOSEPH E	1LT	0-1318290	0146	2
DONLON MARGARET M	2LT	N-0793385	0946	1
DONNAL JOHN C JR	MAJ	0-0192888	0362	3
DONNELL HENRY J	COL	0-0300977	1160	3
DONNELL JOHN B	LTC	0-0339839	0346	2
DONNELLAN JOSEPH J	CPT	0-0200210	0455	3
DONNELLY ANDREW J JR	MAJ	0-2032595	0561	1
DONNELLY ANDREW S	LTC	0-2040990	0657	1
DONNELLY ARTHUR E	MAJ	0-0901680	0562	1
DONNELLY CATHERINE	2LT	N-0729272	0546	1
DONNELLY CHARLES H	COL	0-0287435	0956	3
DONNELLY CLARENCE S	COL	0-0279213	0255	3
DONNELLY DESMOND B	1LT	0-1045399	0646	2
DONNELLY DONALD F	LTC	0-1569169	0667	1
DONNELLY EDWARD D	CPT	0-1081129	1146	2
DONNELLY EDWIN L	MAJ	0-1301793	0561	1
DONNELLY ELIZABETH	2LT	N-0787131	0944	1
DONNELLY EMMET F	LTC	0-1551833	0862	1
DONNELLY FRANK H	CPT	0-0360458	1167	3
DONNELLY FRANK J	LTC	0-1063141	0461	1
DONNELLY GEORGE F	MAJ	0-1038591	0266	1
DONNELLY HARRY G	CW3	W-2205711	0868	1
DONNELLY JAMES J	MAJ	0-1046426	0561	2
DONNELLY JOHN E	LTC	0-0262691	0368	3
DONNELLY JOHN J	LTC	0-0204772	0153	3
DONNELLY JOSEPH E	LTC	0-1638103	1162	1
DONNELLY PETER E	COL	0-0286835	0764	3
DONNELLY RICHARD E	CPT	0-1797450	0759	2
DONNELLY ROBERT E	MAJ	0-0931409	0363	1
DONNELLY ROBERT H	LTC	0-1844968	0566	3
DONNELLY ROBERT J	COL	0-0265260	0868	3
DONNELLY THOMAS J	1LT	0-1319727	1045	2
DONNELLY W H JR	CPT	0-1176602	0648	2
DONNELLY WALTER P	LTC	0-1305165	1166	3
DONNELLY WILLIAM A	CPT	0-0466257	0246	2

NAME	GRADE	SVC NO	DATE RET MO YR	RET CODE
DONNER WILBUR S	LTC	0-0219965	1059	3
DONNER WILLIAM C	MAJ	0-1931180	0867	1
DONNIGAN CLARKE F	LTC	0-0176600	0758	3
DONGERIS NICHOLAS	MAJ	0-1647401	0762	1
DONOHO ELSMER E	CPT	0-1185270	0260	2
DONOHOE GUY F	CPT	0-0128803	0648	3
DONOHOE MARY F	1LT	N-0787645	0647	1
DONOHOE PATRICK	CPT	0-1176310	0454	2
DONOHOO DAVID O	COL	0-0136963	0648	3
DONOHUE EMMETT A	1LT	0-1037666	0360	1
DONOHUE JAMES J	CW2	W-2147824	0560	1
DONOHUE JOSEPH T JR	MAJ	0-1697929	0660	1
DONOHUE RITA G	1LT	N-0741737	1145	1
DONOHUE ROBERT F	1LT	0-0347031	0446	2
DONOHUE THOMAS A	LTC	0-0407414	0266	1
DONOHUE WALTER P	LTC	0-0493550	0161	1
DONOHUE WILLIAM M	LTC	0-1944664	0662	1
DONOVAN ALICE M	CPT	N-0756868	0945	1
DONOVAN BILLY B	MAJ	0-2262975	0567	1
DONOVAN EUGENE M	LTC	0-0248805	0458	1
DONOVAN FRANCIS	MAJ	0-0185393	0148	1
DONOVAN FRANCIS J	CPT	0-1557835	1060	2
DONOVAN GEORGE F	LTC	0-0223766	0258	3
DONOVAN GORDON J	MAJ	0-1325281	0261	1
DONOVAN HOWARD P	LTC	0-2044494	0655	1
DONOVAN JAMES H	CW4	W-2141891	1066	1
DONOVAN JAMES R	COL	0-0451096	0457	1
DONOVAN JEROME V	LTC	0-1644933	1164	1
DONOVAN JESSE F	MAJ	0-1550577	0661	1
DONOVAN JOHN J	COL	0-0204798	0154	1
DONOVAN JOSEPH M	LTC	0-0915437	0365	3
DONOVAN JOSEPH W	LTC	0-0420030	0963	1
DONOVAN MIKE C	LTC	0-0287624	0660	1
DONOVAN MORTIMER W	LTC	0-0261949	0662	3
DONOVAN TIMOTHY J	1LT	0-1913299	0353	2
DONOVAN WILBUR L	1LT	0-1283389	0444	2
DONOVAN WILLIAM A	MAJ	0-1546788	0860	1
DONOVAN WILLIAM J JR	CPT	0-1106097	0147	2
DONOWSKI STANLEY W	MAJ	0-1683458	0560	1
DONSKY JOSEPH J	MAJ	0-2049958	1163	1
DONZIGER IRVING S	1LT	0-0526281	0945	2
DOOB FREDERICK	CPT	0-0472718	0245	2
DOODY WILLIAM F	LTC	0-1797796	0562	1
DOOHALUK ALFONZO J	MAJ	0-2041435	0866	1
DOOLEN ARTHUR H	MAJ	0-0226520	1051	2
DOOLEY ALBERT J	LTC	0-0243573	0265	3
DOOLEY BEN H	CW3	W-2146858	0565	1
DOOLEY DONALD W	LTC	0-1000548	0657	1
DOOLEY HERBERT J	LTC	0-0266675	0845	2
DOOLEY JAMES C	LTC	0-0322503	1057	1
DOOLEY JAMES L	1LT	0-1593545	0146	2
DOOLEY JIMMIE	LTC	0-0336301	0468	3
DOOLEY JOHN D	CW3	W-2151810	1263	1
DOOLEY JOHN J	CW3	W-2004434	0967	1
DOOLEY JOHN R	LTC	0-1311129	0763	1
DOOLEY JOSEPH M	CPT	0-1168223	0247	2
DOOLEY LEONARD	MAJ	0-2288009	0160	1
DOOLEY LESLIE W	CPT	0-0434863	1145	2
DOOLEY MERLE H	2LT	0-1824441	1044	2
DOOLEY THOMAS F	MAJ	0-2006577	0165	1
DOOLEY WALTER M	CW3	W-2122249	1060	1
DOOLEY WILLIAM L	COL	0-0209942	0846	2
DOOLIN ROBERT F	LTC	0-1648382	0364	1
DOOLITTLE CLARENCE	CPT	0-0246987	0350	2
DOOLITTLE DOUGLAS	2LT	0-1185540	1045	2
DOOLITTLE DWIGHT F	CPT	0-0259429	0867	3
DOOLITTLE ROBERT L	LTC	0-1822973	0361	1
DOOLITTLE SPIVEY N	2LT	0-1014427	1043	2
DOOLITTLE WILLIAM M	LTC	0-0247544	1166	3
DOONAN STEPHEN P	CPT	0-2262379	1265	1
DOONEIEF ALFRED S	LTC	0-0384651	0146	2
DOOP RALPH F	1LT	0-1171980	0645	2
DOOSE DONALD L	1LT	0-1053563	0446	2
DOPONA JOHN C	CW2	W-2147750	0764	1
DORAN ARTHUR F	LTC	0-0452506	0258	1

NAME	GRADE	SVC NO	DATE RET MO YR	RET CODE
DORAN EDWIN	LTC	0-1104622	0662	1
DORAN FLOYD J	COL	0-0277350	1064	3
DORAN GEORGE W	LTC	0-0404389	0363	1
DORAN HARRY G JR	1LT	0-1175589	0945	2
DORAN JAMES J	1LT	0-1117119	0466	1
DORAN JOHN RALPH	COL	0-0174450	1047	2
DORAN JOHN J	LTC	0-0268125	1266	3
DORAN JOHN P	LTC	0-0300756	0161	1
DORAN JOHN W	LTC	0-0257033	1267	3
DORAN JOSEPH A	1LT	0-0368252	0945	2
DORAN PATRICK H	LTC	0-0301872	0364	3
DORAN PHILLIP J	CW2	W-2214470	0866	1
DORAN RALPH F	1LT	0-2000653	0159	1
DORAN ROBERT A	LTC	0-1994592	1263	1
DORAN ROBERT A	CW2	W-2211427	1167	1
DORAN WILLIAM P	CW2	W-2142633	0854	1
DORAN WILLIAM T	1LT	0-0010391	0337	2
DORATO LAWRENCE F	COL	0-0267453	0458	3
DORAZIO JOHN J	LTC	0-1011135	1163	1
DORBANDT JAMES L	COL	0-0346649	0555	3
DORBRITZ WILLIAM C	MAJ	0-0171007	0356	3
DORE ELIZABETH	2LT	N-0700688	0737	1
DORE FRANK L	CW4	W-2148203	0467	1
DORE ROBERT A	2LT	0-1324153	0544	2
DORECIAK JOHN J	LTC	0-1540937	0167	1
DOREK GEORGE F	1LT	0-2262708	1167	1
DOREY LESTER E	MAJ	0-1685661	1063	1
DORF VICTOR	MAJ	0-0380865	1045	2
DORFMAN SAUL S	COL	0-0193611	0365	3
DORIA LOUIS C	CPT	0-1300005	0646	2
DORIE EDMOND L	LTC	0-1575922	1167	3
DORIGAN JAMES T	1LT	0-0402066	1144	2
DORIN CHARLES G	CPT	0-0331809	0864	3
DORIN WILLIAM H JR	LTC	0-0245583	0360	1
DORING GEORGE E	MAJ	0-1295185	0658	1
DORMAN DALE R	MAJ	0-0976212	0765	1
DORMAN GERALD O	COL	0-0404715	1263	3
DORMAN JOHN A	MAJ	0-1913272	0863	1
DORMAN LINSLEY R	LTC	0-1314457	0763	2
DORMAN WALTER F	1LT	0-2012360	0253	2
DORMER THOMAS L	MAJ	0-1325204	1060	1
DORMINEY JACK C	CW3	W-2147047	0466	1
DORMINEY WOODROW W	CW3	W-2143602	1058	1
DORN EDWIN	MAJ	0-0278746	0265	3
DORN FREDERICK JR	2LT	0-1169639	1044	2
DORN HAROLD C	1LT	0-1324248	0845	2
DORN RICHARD W	CPT	0-0452015	0657	1
DORN WALTER E JR	LTC	0-1341862	0967	1
DORNBLATT BERNHARD M	LTC	0-0192280	1262	3
DORNEY JOHN H	2LT	0-2036369	0345	2
DORNEY MARION C	COL	0-0346131	0866	1
DORNSIFE EUGENE L	LTC	0-1642009	0866	1
DOROBIALA HENRY	CW4	W-2144745	1165	1
DORR EDGAR F	LTC	0-0301906	0764	1
DORR THOMAS W	CPT	0-1756180	0649	2
DORRANCE JAMES I	LTC	0-1327124	0268	2
DORRE REYNOLD S	MAJ	0-0384640	0647	2
DORRIS HERBERT E	MAJ	0-0165685	1049	3
DORRIS LEWIS R	MAJ	0-1015316	0160	1
DORRITY THOMAS G	CPT	0-0438728	0546	2
DORROH GEORGE D	LTC	0-0335269	0345	2
DORROH GLENN O	COL	0-0298135	0461	3
DORROUGH THOMAS A JR	LTC	0-1080846	0463	1
DORSETT FRANCIS M	CPT	0-0405534	0261	2
DORSETT LESTER	CW3	W-2206275	1265	1
DORSETT NELLIE C	2LT	N-0704041	1144	2
DORSETT RICHARD H	MAJ	0-2044302	1158	2
DORSETT WILLIAM R	CW3	W-2141258	0661	1
DORSEY EDWARD V	1LT	0-1327721	0546	2
DORSEY FRED J	LTC	0-1578387	0462	1
DORSEY HORACE T	CPT	0-1550366	0954	1
DORSEY JAMES M	1LT	0-1316391	1145	2
DORSEY JOSEPH R	CPT	0-0452451	1045	2
DORSEY THOMAS B	LTC	0-2006727	0768	1
DORSEY WILLIAM H	LTC	0-0177223	1160	3

NAME	GRADE	SVC NO	DATE RET MO YR	RET CODE
DORSEY WILLIAM H	LTC	0-0263765	0766	3
DORSEY WILLIAM P	LTC	0-0905341	1168	3
DORSEY WOODROW E	2LT	0-0465511	1043	2
DORSHOW SAMUEL A	2LT	0-0887593	0845	2
DORST CLARENCE L	COL	0-0284868	1166	3
DORST HOWARD E	COL	0-0300270	1064	3
DORSTE GEORGE C	CPT	0-1056694	0657	1
DORT HELEN C	1LT	N-0720713	0746	1
DORTCH LEONARD J	MAJ	0-1919466	0164	1
DORTON HOWARD E	MAJ	0-0446138	0346	2
DORTON JAMES H	CW2	W-2149483	0562	1
DORTORT ISADORE	LTC	0-0237576	0464	3
DORULA WALTER S	2LT	0-1309178	0945	2
DORWART FREDERIC G	LTC	0-0144589	0853	3
DORWART WILLIAM V	LTC	0-0368892	0268	3
DORY DELBERT A	CW2	W-3200165	0963	1
DORY REX G	MAJ	0-0196684	0162	3
DOSCHER ALBERT H	CW3	W-2143511	0665	1
DOSS ALTON	CPT	0-0485096	0355	1
DOSS ESTLE H	LTC	0-2011494	1066	1
DOSS HAROLD C	CW2	W-2210901	0965	1
DOSS JAMES W	CW2	W-2141842	1055	1
DOSS ROBERT L	2LT	0-1183273	0145	2
DOSS WILLIAM R SR	LTC	0-1342254	1266	1
DOSS WINTHA T	CW2	W-2152417	0560	1
DOSS WYATT C JR	MAJ	0-2033666	1163	1
DOSSETT JOHN A	WO1	W-2149431	1154	2
DOSSETT ROBERT C	MAJ	0-0222240	1051	2
DOSSMAN PIERRE M	LTC	0-0887472	0963	1
DOSTALL DOUGLAS J	MAJ	0-1559167	0763	2
DOSTER CARLTON A	LTC	0-0332661	0668	3
DOSTER HIRAM H	1LT	0-1058500	0853	1
DOSTER JIM B	CW3	W-2119510	1160	1
DOSTER PAUL C JR	MAJ	0-1060078	0162	1
DOSTIE JOSEPH F	LTC	0-0393522	0762	1
DOTEN HENRY L	LTC	0-0174384	0159	3
DOTEN ROBERT K	LTC	0-0241153	0166	3
DOTSON ARTHUR J	CPT	0-0384310	1265	2
DOTSON EARL J	LTC	0-1634684	1163	1
DOTSON GERALD W	CPT	0-1822974	0662	1
DOTSON JOHN C	LTC	0-0482007	0746	1
DOTSON LEONARD	CPT	0-0424454	0943	2
DOTSON LLOYD J	CPT	0-0557683	0253	2
DOTSON ORVILLE R	WO1	W-2123214	0152	2
DOTSON RAYMOND S JR	MAJ	0-1575924	0960	1
DOTTERER HAROLD A	MAJ	0-1917847	1063	1
DOTTEN DUNCAN A	2LT	0-1061101	0145	2
DOTTS NEIL T	1LT	0-2030412	0754	2
DOTY CHESTER R	LTC	0-1642806	0464	1
DOTY EDOUARD R	COL	0-0312822	0561	3
DOTY HAROLD G	COL	0-0287734	0763	1
DOTY HENRY F	COL	0-0207926	0658	3
DOTY HERBERT K	CPT	0-1117014	0361	1
DOTY IRVING W	LTC	0-0916143	1166	3
DOTY IRWIN T	LTC	0-0252822	1165	3
DOTY JESSE B JR	1LT	0-0354046	1046	2
DOTY JOHN H	CW2	W-2107495	0647	2
DOTY LUTHER L JR	CPT	0-1292844	1145	2
DOTY LYLE E	LTC	0-1104130	0863	1
DOTY NORMAN J	2LT	0-1947704	1046	1
DOTY REGINALD J	LTC	0-0906383	0460	3
DOTY REGINALD J JR	CW3	W-2208649	0867	1
DOTY RUSSELL E	LTC	0-0289455	0167	3
DOUBERLY ROSCOE	CW3	W-2142146	1057	1
DOUBLET HAROLD J	LTC	0-1018814	1067	1
DOUBT MARY O	1LT	R-0000213	0346	2
DOUCET EDWIN J	1LT	0-1999477	0753	1
DOUCET LILLIAN N	1LT	N-0754555	0251	2
DOUCET ROBERT J	CPT	0-1296007	0860	1
DOUCET WILLS J	MAJ	0-0497054	0657	1
DOUCETT FRANCIS M	LTC	0-0320337	0860	1
DOUCETT RAYMOND G JR	LTC	0-0452615	0158	1
DOUCETTE JOSEPH J	MAJ	0-2037540	0861	1
DOUCETTE MYRON E	COL	0-0218254	1162	3
DOUD ALFRED H	B G	0-0266144	1164	3

NAME	GRADE	SVC NO	DATE RET MO YR	RET CODE
DOUDNA IRVIN J	LTC	0-2051106	1267	1
DOUDS HAROLD L	LTC	0-0[illegible]17572	1066	3
DOUDS PAULINE R	2LT	N-0754297	1144	1
DOUGALL JAMES L	CPT	0-0217025	0460	3
DOUGAN AULTON R	LTC	0-0331820	0945	2
DOUGAN CLARENCE R	CPT	0-1587759	0366	1
DOUGAN STEWART I	MAJ	0-1341863	0463	1
DOUGHERTY BUFORD T	CPT	0-1004756	0450	1
DOUGHERTY CHARLES F	COL	0-0102461	0649	3
DOUGHERTY CLYDE E	M G	0-0150855	0462	3
DOUGHERTY DANIEL V	CPT	0-0357834	1143	2
DOUGHERTY EDWARD A	LTC	0-1776436	0664	1
DOUGHERTY EDWARD D	LTC	0-1011444	0464	1
DOUGHERTY FRANK R	CPT	0-0279191	0745	2
DOUGHERTY HARRY S	CPT	0-1058782	0263	1
DOUGHERTY HUGH L	COL	0-0256749	0259	3
DOUGHERTY JAMES F	1LT	0-1311557	0645	2
DOUGHERTY JAMES J	1LT	0-1560873	0944	2
DOUGHERTY JOHN A	CW2	W-2147501	1064	1
DOUGHERTY JOHN P	LTC	0-1634689	0562	1
DOUGHERTY KENNETH D	MAJ	0-1598041	0962	1
DOUGHERTY MARY A	CW3	W-2151058	0959	2
DOUGHERTY R W F	MAJ	0-1578389	0859	1
DOUGHERTY RICHARD S	LTC	0-1322430	0365	1
DOUGHERTY ROBERT L	COL	0-0312733	0663	3
DOUGHERTY ROBERT W	LTC	0-0344751	0364	3
DOUGHERTY SALLY C	1LT	N-0723025	0246	1
DOUGHERTY VIRGINIA	1LT	N-0779751	0352	2
DOUGHERTY W B JR	1LT	0-0409644	0545	2
DOUGHERTY WILLIAM C	MAJ	0-1115558	0559	1
DOUGHERTY WILLIAM H	LTC	0-1014262	0967	1
DOUGHERTY WILLIAM L	CPT	0-1591382	0358	1
DOUGHTIE HOWARD J	CPT	0-0246745	0744	2
DOUGHTIE JAMES D	MAJ	0-0888205	0954	1
DOUGHTON HOWARD F	MAJ	0-0367102	0647	2
DOUGHTY SEVERN R JR	2LT	0-1169641	0744	2
DOUGHTY WILLIAM D JR	LTC	0-0262439	0962	3
DOUGLAS ALLEN M	CPT	0-1642807	0548	2
DOUGLAS CHARLES L	LTC	0-0324315	0755	3
DOUGLAS DONALD R	CW2	W-2110849	0546	2
DOUGLAS EDMUND T	MAJ	0-0116236	1049	3
DOUGLAS ELMER A	CW3	W-2150308	0860	1
DOUGLAS FRANCIS H	MAJ	0-2203317	0568	1
DOUGLAS FRANK E	CPT	0-1256500	0446	2
DOUGLAS FRANK W	CPT	0-0277094	0549	2
DOUGLAS GLENN R	LTC	0-0231424	0563	3
DOUGLAS GORDON W	CPT	0-0368467	0645	2
DOUGLAS HARRY V	CPT	0-0359142	1044	2
DOUGLAS HENRY C	MAJ	0-1547923	1263	1
DOUGLAS IRVIN N	LTC	0-0347553	0466	3
DOUGLAS JAMES W	CW2	W-2210479	0265	1
DOUGLAS JESSE S	COL	0-0281504	1160	2
DOUGLAS JOHN M	CPT	0-1100954	1044	2
DOUGLAS JOHN R JR	MAJ	0-1119482	0861	1
DOUGLAS JULIAN L	LTC	0-0207604	0751	2
DOUGLAS LEE I	CW4	W-2000619	1062	1
DOUGLAS LEON O	CPT	0-1306394	0548	2
DOUGLAS LESTER E	CW3	W-2149385	0364	1
DOUGLAS MARVIN B	COL	0-0293138	0860	2
DOUGLAS RALPH	CW4	W-2114819	0657	1
DOUGLAS REYNOLDS E	LTC	0-0259143	0465	3
DOUGLAS ROBERT M	LTC	0-1876989	1168	1
DOUGLAS ROBERT L	CW2	W-2203293	0861	1
DOUGLAS ROBERT M	1LT	0-1313580	0446	2
DOUGLAS WALLACE S	COL	0-0169714	0261	3
DOUGLAS WILLIAM A	CW2	W-2149854	0561	1
DOUGLAS WILLIAM C JR	1LT	0-0445128	0244	2
DOUGLASS DAVID R	COL	0-0281305	0452	3
DOUGLASS FRANK S	1LT	0-1845557	0146	2
DOUGLASS HAROLD E	LTC	0-0451856	0665	1
DOUGLASS HARRY S	LTC	0-0171461	0650	3
DOUGLASS HENRY S	MAJ	0-0235101	1044	2
DOUGLASS JOHN M	1LT	0-0511448	1143	2
DOUGLASS LOUIS R	LTC	0-0181875	0648	3
DOUGLASS MADELYN A	MAJ	N-0721611	0468	1

NAME	GRADE	SVC NO	DATE RET MO YR	RET CODE
DOUGLASS RAYMOND W	LTC	0-0300116	0268	3
DOUGLASS ROBERT M	COL	0-0128015	1157	3
DOUGLASS TRUMAN L	1LT	0-0499846	0154	2
DOUGLASS WILLIAM R	LTC	0-1549698	0767	1
DOUGOVITO CARL J	LTC	0-0280007	0957	1
DOUM ALBERT O	MAJ	0-1796437	0258	1
DOUR WILLIAM W	LTC	0-1044800	0267	1
DOURESS PHILIP C	1LT	0-1173589	0945	2
DOURLET NESTOR J	LTC	0-0567934	0365	1
DOUTHIT HAROLD C	LTC	0-1012014	0467	1
DOUTHIT JIMMY W	CW2	W-2211667	0468	1
DOUTHITT CHARLES L	LTC	0-1054543	0762	1
DOUTHITT JOHN	CPT	0-1599157	1262	1
DOUTHITT MERTON H	1LT	0-0417433	0444	2
DOUTHITT MERTON J	LTC	0-0117140	1153	3
DOUTNEY WILLIAM W	LTC	0-0240476	0561	3
DOUVIER GREGOR J	LTC	0-1300619	0867	1
DOUYOTAS WALTER F	MAJ	0-1638972	0358	1
DOVAL ARMANDO	LTC	0-0262227	1064	3
DOVALOSKY CHARLES R	LTC	0-0175568	1160	3
DOVE ALBERT C	LTC	0-0452546	1159	1
DOVE FREDERICK	MAJ	0-1052755	0760	1
DOVE JACK E	CPT	0-0861577	1167	2
DOVE JOHN C	LTC	0-0425215	1163	1
DOVER CARL L	CPT	0-2000996	0861	1
DOVER EARL L	MAJ	0-0959315	0562	1
DOVER GEORGE J JR	LTC	0-0349801	0961	1
DOVER HILL J	LTC	0-2205291	0868	1
DOVERS GEORGE W	MAJ	0-1553071	0356	1
DOVEY GORDON L	1LT	0-0418799	1045	2
DOVEY HOWARD	CPT	0-0448157	1047	1
DOVHOLUK PAUL	CPT	0-0887963	0448	2
DOW EUGENE W	LTC	0-0784864	0868	1
DOW HOWARD B	LTC	0-1542628	0860	1
DOW JEREMIAH G	CPT	0-1080276	0847	2
DOW ORWIN F	MAJ	0-0154245	0857	3
DOW RAYMOND W	LTC	0-0489813	0445	2
DOW WENDALL W	MAJ	0-1948731	0164	1
DOW WILLIAM C	COL	0-1297511	0664	1
DOWD FRANCIS C	CW2	W-3400123	0968	1
DOWD HELEN F	CPT	N-0732718	1046	1
DOWD HOMER F	LTC	0-0205212	1163	3
DOWD JAMES H	CPT	0-0411577	0446	2
DOWD JAMES J	2LT	0-2017523	1045	2
DOWD JOHN J	MAJ	0-1545420	1157	1
DOWD JOHN T	MAJ	0-0314420	0658	1
DOWD LAWRENCE V JR	LTC	0-0972672	0867	1
DOWD MORRIS O	CPT	0-1701260	1144	2
DOWD WILLIAM S	LTC	0-1543329	0662	2
DOWDELL FRANCIS W	MAJ	0-1321702	0268	2
DOWDELL HERMAN L	2LT	0-0984843	0352	2
DOWDELL JAMES L	COL	0-0395362	1068	3
DOWDEN ALVIN C	1LT	0-1185868	0550	2
DOWDEN JOHN F	CPT	0-0476449	0347	1
DOWDEN RUSSELL H SR	WO1	W-2150342	0160	2
DOWDEY GEORGE H	LTC	0-1108628	0568	1
DOWDLE HUGH J	MAJ	0-0282420	0146	2
DOWDY LEON	MAJ	0-2262367	0862	1
DOWELL GEORGE L	CW2	W-2209242	0661	1
DOWELL LORENZO	CPT	0-0498626	1046	1
DOWELL WILBUR E	CW3	W-2104012	0853	1
DOWELL WILLIAM F	LTC	0-0534333	0663	1
DOWEN ROBERT H	CPT	0-0262335	0346	2
DOWGILLO ALEXANDER	MAJ	0-1080848	1157	1
DOWIS WELDON M	LTC	0-0241967	0360	1
DOWLER FRANK H III	COL	0-0371463	0860	1
DOWLING BERNARD J	1LT	0-0972258	0453	2
DOWLING CHARLES E	LTC	0-0289140	0254	1
DOWLING CHARLES R	LTC	0-1798132	0562	1
DOWLING DOLORES I	1LT	N-0728901	0846	1
DOWLING DONALD A	CW2	W-3430041	1164	1
DOWLING GEORGE E	LTC	0-1100083	0959	1
DOWLING GEORGE H	CPT	0-0590682	0454	2
DOWLING GORDON R	2LT	0-0207150	0363	3
DOWLING HENRY A	CW3	W-2149334	1268	1

NAME	GRADE	SVC NO	DATE RET MO YR	RET CODE
DOWLING JOSEPH H	LTC	0-0460141	1060	1
DOWLING JOSEPH P	MAJ	0-0971911	1163	1
DOWLING MOYE L JR	2LT	[illegible]	1044	2
DOWLING REGINALD J	COL	0-0274421	1162	3
DOWLING SAMUEL F	LTC	0-2203341	0767	1
DOWNER HARRY M	LTC	0-0360942	0957	1
DOWNEY CORNELIUS	1LT	0-1046374	0946	2
DOWNEY DOROTHY F	2LT	N-0743673	0943	1
DOWNEY ARLIE L	LTC	0-0199557	1053	2
DOWNEY AUGUSTUS J	LTC	0-1574580	0764	1
DOWNEY BENJAMIN A	CPT	0-2042733	0257	1
DOWNEY DAVID H	MAJ	0-1698497	1165	1
DOWNEY DONALD L	MAJ	0-1337154	0161	1
DOWNEY EARL E	LTC	0-0411360	0863	1
DOWNEY EDWARD F	1LT	0-1019002	0252	2
DOWNEY GILBERT L	2LT	0-1925904	0253	2
DOWNEY JACK W	LTC	0-0450433	0358	1
DOWNEY JAMES H	CPT	0-1044213	0852	2
DOWNEY JAMES H	1LT	0-1294480	1145	2
DOWNEY JAMES R JR	MAJ	0-0498385	0655	1
DOWNEY JOHN A	MAJ	0-1644084	0361	1
DOWNEY JOHN J JR	COL	0-0384228	0860	1
DOWNEY JOSEPH F	CPT	0-1080782	1047	2
DOWNEY MICHAEL J	MAJ	0-2263967	0667	1
DOWNEY MILFORD R	LTC	0-2200323	0468	1
DOWNEY OLIVER F	LTC	0-1111584	0967	1
DOWNEY REGINALD J	CPT	0-0225799	0263	3
DOWNEY ROBERT J	MAJ	0-1342060	1264	1
DOWNEY THOMAS A	MAJ	0-2035035	0662	1
DOWNEY TOM K	LTC	0-1549256	0163	1
DOWNEY WILLEM	CPT	0-1896574	0359	1
DOWNEY WILLIAM F	CW2	W-2151524	1157	1
DOWNING EARL L	COL	0-0179271	1154	1
DOWNING JAMES M	1LT	0-1573168	0345	2
DOWNING JOHN M	LTC	0-0258569	0865	3
DOWNING JOHN R	LTC	0-0294485	0767	3
DOWNING KENNETH C	COL	0-0222925	0760	3
DOWNING LELAND R	MAJ	0-1543593	1060	1
DOWNING ROLAND F	MAJ	0-1044802	0861	1
DOWNING SARAH P	CPT	N-0760727	0946	1
DOWNING THEODORE A	LTC	0-0268212	0364	3
DOWNING THEODORE O	MAJ	0-0294445	0368	3
DOWNING WILLIAM E	CPT	0-0245274	1047	2
DOWNING WILLIAM L	LTC	0-0266721	0764	1
DOWNS CHARLES R	LTC	0-1172440	1267	3
DOWNS CLARENCE R	LTC	0-0418201	0266	3
DOWNS EDWARD J JR	CPT	0-1061038	0547	2
DOWNS FREDERICK JR	COL	0-0195508	0960	3
DOWNS HAROLD T	MAJ	0-0252648	0561	3
DOWNS JAMES C	MAJ	0-1577109	0146	2
DOWNS JAMES C	MAJ	0-2263767	1164	1
DOWNS JOSEPH J	1LT	0-2049225	0146	2
DOWNS JOSEPH R	CW4	W-2144390	0764	1
DOWNS THERESA M	CPT	N-0732170	1146	1
DOWNS WILLIAM W	2LT	0-2035807	0345	2
DOWS SAMUEL R	COL	0-0184044	0656	3
DOWTY JOHN A	CW3	W-2142934	1057	1
DOXSIE GERALD P	CPT	0-0333650	0662	1
DOYING WILLIAM W	CW3	W-2145867	1162	1
DOYLE ALBERT F	LTC	0-0321290	0265	3
DOYLE ALICE F	LTC	N-0720462	1263	1
DOYLE CURTIS W	CPT	0-2026214	0456	1
DOYLE DANIEL G	LTC	0-0251054	0562	1
DOYLE EUGENE T	MAJ	0-0994007	1165	1
DOYLE FRANCIS	MAJ	0-4005425	1267	1
DOYLE FRANK	2LT	0-1030971	0345	2
DOYLE GODFREY W	LTC	0-1053111	0366	1
DOYLE GREGORY J	MAJ	0-0326083	0744	2
DOYLE HERSHEL L	WO1	W-2124772	1044	2
DOYLE HUGH	LTC	0-0109756	1047	2
DOYLE JACOBS H	MAJ	0-0233577	0944	2
DOYLE JAMES A	COL	0-0236421	0651	3
DOYLE JAMES I	COL	0-0244575	0955	3
DOYLE JAMES M M	MAJ	0-1540887	0168	1
DOYLE JAMES W	CPT	0-0125780	0945	2

NAME	GRADE	SVC NO	DATE RET MO YR	RET CODE
DOYLE JAMES W	MAJ	0-0959316	0764	1
DOYLE JERRY E	1LT	0-2205230	0453	2
DOYLE JOHN A JR	LTC	0-0421855	0163	1
DOYLE JOHN C	COL	0-0138594	0258	3
DOYLE JOHN F	CW2	W-2207007	0364	1
DOYLE JOHN J	MAJ	0-1882033	0967	1
DOYLE JOHN M	LTC	0-0262366	0266	3
DOYLE JOSEPH A	LTC	0-1645353	1163	1
DOYLE JOSEPH H	COL	0-1042796	0763	1
DOYLE JOSEPH T	1LT	0-0448522	1045	2
DOYLE JUSTIN G	COL	0-0205111	0360	1
DOYLE KATHLEEN M	CPT	N-0723045	0746	1
DOYLE LAURENCE F	1LT	0-1019238	1045	2
DOYLE LEWIS W	LTC	0-1698096	1160	1
DOYLE LILLIAN	2LT	N-0700493	0834	1
DOYLE MARY C	MAJ	N-0752710	0464	1
DOYLE ROBERT	MAJ	0-0959031	0162	2
DOYLE WALTER J	LTC	0-0317970	0763	1
DOYLE WILLIAM C	MAJ	0-0960618	0763	1
DOYLE WILLIAM H	MAJ	0-0314193	0146	2
DOYLE WILLIAM H	WO1	W-2117923	1053	1
DOYLE WILLIAM J	1LT	0-1913650	1138	1
DOYLE WILLIAM M	COL	0-0370133	0267	1
DOYLE WILLIAM-OA	LTC	0-1573796	1161	1
DOYLE WILSON E	LTC	0-1300621	0462	1
DOYON ALBERT B	LTC	0-0399316	0864	1
DOZE CHARLES A	CPT	0-1281604	0667	1
DOZIER DAVID T	LTC	0-1177778	0566	1
DOZIER JAMES B JR	1LT	0-1059770	1046	2
DOZIER MARCELLUS	MAJ	0-1553801	1054	1
DOZIER MINNIE L	2LT	N-0742816	1144	1
DOZIER MORRIS	CW3	W-2143844	1162	1
DRABIC JOHN J	MAJ	0-1011275	0557	1
DRACHMAN FRANK E	1LT	0-1889126	0554	2
DRACK RUTH O	MAJ	N-0724310	0561	1
DRAEGER EMERY H	LTC	0-0504779	0754	1
DRAGANZA JOHN G	LTC	0-1103607	0465	1
DRAGISITY GEORGE	LTC	0-1329335	1267	1
DRAGNEFF NICHOLAS W	COL	0-0379990	0954	1
DRAGNETT WILLIAM V	LTC	0-0312173	0159	3
DRAGO GEORGE R	CPT	0-1300006	1045	2
DRAGO PAOLO	MAJ	0-1920163	0366	1
DRAGOTJ ELY	MAJ	0-1185572	0863	2
DRAGOMANI LEO A	LTC	0-2033062	0166	1
DRAGON JOHN	CPT	0-1338573	0254	1
DRAGOO CHARLES M	LTC	0-0211862	0364	3
DRAGOO DON H	LTC	0-0380055	1262	1
DRAGOO RUSSELL N	MAJ	0-1640404	0359	1
DRAGSTEDT CARL A JR	MAJ	0-0935434	0564	1
DRAHEIM WILLIAM A	COL	0-0246210	1058	3
DRAIN FREDERICK	LTC	0-1797267	0662	1
DRAIN JAMES F A	MAJ	0-0387165	0852	2
DRAIN MILTON J	MAJ	0-0350142	0762	2
DRAINE OLIVER W	CPT	0-0390054	1046	2
DRAIZAR PAUL H	2LT	0-1179840	1044	2
DRAKE ALLEN H	CPT	0-1596310	0965	2
DRAKE ANTHONY F	CW3	W-2146742	0157	1
DRAKE ARTHUR	MAJ	0-0295104	0666	3
DRAKE CHARLES A	COL	0-0155790	0554	3
DRAKE CLEATUS R	LTC	0-0239763	0565	3
DRAKE DAVID H JR	1LT	0-1320613	1145	2
DRAKE DAYTON D	LTC	0-0475805	0762	1
DRAKE DONALD W	LTC	0-1112661	0567	1
DRAKE EMERSON R	CPT	0-1824442	1046	2
DRAKE GARLAND L	MAJ	0-0297992	0568	3
DRAKE HARRIS H	MAJ	0-0415189	0246	2
DRAKE HARRY C	1LT	0-1291439	0645	2
DRAKE HERMAN R	CW4	W-2124176	1059	1
DRAKE HORACE B	MAJ	0-0248998	0966	3
DRAKE HORACE L	CPT	0-0517279	1044	2
DRAKE JAMES F	CPT	0-0499816	0547	1
DRAKE JAMES R	CPT	0-0176983	0557	3
DRAKE JOHN T	CW4	W-2107996	1159	1
DRAKE JOSH M JR	1LT	0-1319268	0246	2
DRAKE LEO G	LTC	0-0277413	1261	3

NAME	GRADE	SVC NO	DATE RET MO YR	RET CODE
DRAKE LINCOLN C	LTC	0-1104134	0761	1
DRAKE RAYMOND J	LTC	0-0352004	0462	1
DRAKE RICHARD N	MAJ	0-0472640	0353	1
DRAKE ROBERT J	CPT	0-0455540	0346	2
DRAKE RODGER E	MAJ	0-1893271	0467	1
DRAKE SIMEON F	CPT	0-0497531	0751	1
DRAKE THEODORE T	LTC	0-0334657	0448	2
DRAKE THOMAS A	CW2	W-2143899	0558	1
DRAKE WARREN A	LTC	0-0451272	1262	1
DRAKE WILLIAM J	1LT	0-2005674	0347	2
DRAKULICH ELI	MAJ	0-1551834	0861	1
DRALLE ROBERT B	MAJ	0-1825526	0661	1
DRANE LESLIE R	COL	0-0269111	0668	1
DRANSFIELD GEORGE W	CW4	W-2120057	1064	1
DRAPER ANDREW J	LTC	0-1597001	0463	1
DRAPER CONSTANCE	1LT	N-0737922	1045	1
DRAPER DONALD E	MAJ	0-1285397	1054	1
DRAPER GEORGE L	MAJ	0-1638133	1058	1
DRAPER HOWARD A	LTC	0-1102705	0859	1
DRAPER JOHN I	CW3	W-2205436	1163	1
DRAPER JOHN W	MAJ	0-0498846	1045	2
DRAPER PAUL J	LTC	0-1637325	1167	3
DRAPER ROBERT A	CPT	0-2262926	0664	1
DRAPER ROBERT C	CW2	W-2213503	0267	1
DRAPER WILLARD T	1LT	0-1321496	0945	2
DRAPER WILLIAM H JR	MG	0-0148333	0756	3
DRAPES STANLEY E	MAJ	0-0403626	0960	1
DRASHEFF GEORGE	LTC	0-1037468	0565	1
DRASHPIL ALEX V	LTC	0-1796053	0464	1
DRATH FRANCIS S	COL	0-0222669	0462	1
DRATH WILFRED H	LTC	0-1055269	0266	1
DRAUGHON ROBERT W	COL	0-0256378	0160	3
DRAUTZ RUDOLPH A	CPT	0-1999373	0255	1
DRAVES NORMAN M	LTC	0-1165384	0455	1
DRAWBAUGH VICTOR R	CPT	0-0319722	1045	2
DRAWDY HOWELL E JR	CW2	W-2146011	0659	1
DRAY GENE E	MAJ	0-0981651	0266	1
DRAYER CALVIN S	LTC	0-0285205	0766	3
DRAYER JOSEPH H	CPT	0-0257341	0751	3
DRAYTON DOUGLAS C	LTC	0-0205109	0562	3
DROA ROBERT J	MAJ	0-0437496	0365	1
DRDLA STANLEY	LTC	0-0346530	0468	3
DREBBER BERNARD S	MAJ	0-1337154	0663	1
DREDGE THOMAS E SR	COL	0-0257234	1062	3
DREGER RICHARD W	CPT	0-1553435	0546	2
DREGSETH IRVING B	1LT	0-1308118	1145	2
DREHER FRANCIS T	CW4	W-2117133	0659	1
DREIFUS CARL T	MAJ	0-0279164	0362	3
DREILING RICHARD J	CPT	0-0264525	0445	2
DREIS FRANK	CPT	0-0472746	0345	2
DREIS LEROY L	LTC	0-1143277	0561	1
DREISBACH HERBERT P	CPT	0-0235277	1164	3
DREISBACH ROBERT F	LTC	0-0485121	1156	1
DRENAN JOHN M	CPT	0-0430164	0342	1
DRENNAN LEONARD JR	1LT	0-0445657	1145	2
DRENNEN CHARLES N	LTC	0-0233361	1163	3
DRENZEK ALFRED	LTC	0-1299016	0762	1
DRESBACH HOWARD T	LTC	0-0196808	0462	3
DRESBACH RICHARD F	COL	0-0295398	1162	1
DRESBACK WILLIAM W	1LT	0-5213052	0663	2
DRESCHER WALTER	LTC	0-1949744	1163	1
DRESSEL MARTHA M	1LT	N-0725489	0246	1
DRESSER GREY	LTC	0-0394854	0760	1
DRESSER HOLLAND L	LTC	0-0275711	0263	1
DRESSER WILDER L	COL	0-0212470	1162	3
DRESSLER RAYMOND H	LTC	0-0251013	0246	2
DRESSOR WILFRED D	LTC	0-0279541	0161	3
DRESTE JOHN P	CW2	W-3100433	0167	1
DREVER CRAWFORD H	MAJ	0-1822976	0361	1
DREVNJ SANDER A	1LT	0-1176313	1045	2
DREW ARTHUR G	LTC	0-0451589	0255	1
DREW BERNARD J	COL	0-0361342	1057	1
DREW CHARLES A	CPT	0-1293738	0648	2
DREW DONALD W	MAJ	0-0228396	0464	3
DREW FRANCIS J	MAJ	0-1551605	0361	1

NAME	GRADE	SVC NO	DATE RET MO YR	RET CODE
DREW FREDERICK	LTC	0-0249870	0266	3
DREW HARLEY R	MAJ	0-0974472	0165	1
DREW HAROLD F	COL	0-0271314	0457	3
DREW HAROLD G	CPT	0-0251751	0862	3
DREW JACK	LTC	0-0179566	0454	3
DREW JACK S	CW4	W-2147996	1164	2
DREW JAMES B	LTC	0-0279287	0463	3
DREW JOHN J	CPT	0-0508165	1147	1
DREW JOHN L	COL	0-0172074	0946	2
DREW MICHAEL C	CW2	W-2147377	0562	1
DREW RAYMOND J	CW2	W-2148701	0359	1
DREW SAMUEL M JR	MAJ	0-1038121	0361	1
DREWERY FRED C	LTC	0-1035748	0267	1
DREWES HENRY F	COL	0-0280783	0867	3
DREWRY LYMAN A	MAJ	0-0293508	0368	3
DREWS WILLIAM E	1LT	0-0335429	0445	2
DREXEL CONRAD G	COL	0-0257259	0154	1
DREXLER BERNARD	CPT	0-0333662	1145	2
DREXLER ERIC H	MAJ	0-0364588	0166	3
DREYDOPPEL AARON	CPT	0-0398168	0368	3
DREYER ALBERT	LTC	0-0256305	0165	3
DREYER CARL W	MAJ	0-2202647	1167	1
DREYER CHARLES H	COL	0-0253538	0361	3
DREYER DAVID L	CW2	W-2142099	0359	1
DREYER EDWARD T	MAJ	0-1299217	0156	1
DREYER ROBERT D	CPT	0-1298042	0346	2
DREYER RODERICK G	CPT	0-1313082	0647	2
DREYER WAYNE J	MAJ	0-1047503	0364	1
DREYFOUS FELIX J	MAJ	0-0911173	0146	2
DREYFUS JOSEPH C JR	MAJ	0-0241451	0345	2
DREZMAL ALENE	LTC	L-0704017	1155	2
DRIER CHARLES H JR	LTC	0-0521349	0463	1
DRIES JOSEPH A	LTC	0-0885865	0358	1
DRIESBACH JOHN D	CW3	W-2207492	1166	1
DRIGGERS JULIAN K	CPT	0-0504857	1047	1
DRIGGERS LEE R	CW2	W-2000402	0465	3
DRIGGERS VAUGHAN W	LTC	0-0215494	1063	3
DRIGGS DALE M	CPT	0-0970266	0461	1
DRIGGS EDWIN D	LTC	0-0267820	1067	3
DRIGGS FRANCIS H	MAJ	0-1549257	0960	2
DRINKWATER DOROTHY L	2LT	N-0742854	1044	1
DRISCHEL FRANK G	COL	0-0332657	1160	3
DRISCOLL CHARLES D	1LT	0-1050638	0944	2
DRISCOLL ELBERT A	CPT	0-0301552	0957	1
DRISCOLL HAROLD F	CW4	W-2007762	0566	3
DRISCOLL J T M T	1LT	0-0916137	0945	2
DRISCOLL JOHN F	LTC	0-1105397	0265	3
DRISCOLL KEITH F	LTC	0-0254029	0146	2
DRISCOLL ROBERT H	COL	0-0327598	0946	2
DRISCOLL ROBERT J	CW3	W-2144722	0663	1
DRISCOLL THERON W	MAJ	0-2038148	0463	1
DRISCOLL THOMAS O	LTC	0-0275111	0246	2
DRISCOLL WILLIAM J	CPT	0-2009792	0664	1
DRISKELL DELBERT W	CPT	0-1115901	0446	2
DRISKELL EZRA H	CW2	W-2209050	0863	1
DRISKELL HERMAN L	MAJ	0-0253360	1048	3
DRISKELL JOHN C	LTC	0-0270712	0767	3
DRISKELL JOSEPH L	COL	0-0284940	1158	1
DRISKI VINCENT P	1LT	0-1998325	0955	1
DRISLANE JAMES J	MAJ	0-1578397	0445	2
DRISSEL ODN J	LTC	0-1332240	0968	1
DRITTENBASS ALBERT R	2LT	0-0923006	1144	2
DRIVER ALTON C	CW3	W-2113369	0660	1
DRIVER DON	CPT	0-0477791	0148	1
DRIVER JOHN B	LTC	0-1316666	0864	1
DRIVER LOUIS F JR	LTC	0-0241745	0265	3
DRIVER PAUL R	CW2	W-2101635	0647	1
DRIVER ROBERT S	LTC	0-0112888	1053	2
DRNEK JOHN F	CW2	W-2151638	1156	1
DROBA PATRICIA L	2LT	N-0768758	1145	1
DROBEK OLGA M	MAJ	N-0742607	0767	1
DROBEK PETER J	1LT	0-0890173	0560	1
DROHNIS DAVID D	LTC	0-0180956	0758	3
DROEGE EDWARD H	COL	0-0248239	0260	3
DROEGEMUELLER W H	LTC	0-0395816	1045	2

NAME	GRADE	SVC NO	DATE RET MO YR	RET CODE
DROESBECK CAMIEL L	1LT	O-1304037	0459	1
DROGAN JOHN J	1LT	O-0468229	0247	1
DROGE WILLIAM R	LTC	O-0180804	1145	2
DROHAN THOMAS W	CPT	O-0370946	0247	2
DROHAN WILLIAM F	1LT	O-1314764	1145	2
DROKE HOWARD H	CW2	W-2151015	0657	1
DROLET RAYMOND A	MAJ	O-0473373	1056	1
DROLLINGER GABRIEL E	MAJ	O-0258081	1067	3
DROMMOND MAX E	COL	O-0222356	0358	3
DROMS FRANK A	LTC	O-0190713	0251	3
DRON JOHN A	MAJ	O-0110606	0953	3
DRONBERGER CHARLES S	LTC	O-0375886	1159	1
DROSE EDWIN M	MAJ	O-4005183	0968	1
DROSS HERBERT C	WO1	W-2128165	0357	1
DROSS MARION J	LTC	O-1320513	0467	3
DROSTE ELMER H	COL	O-0218641	0655	3
DROSTE HAROLD N	LTC	O-0292014	0768	3
DROUIN FRANK H	CPT	O-0973507	0460	1
DROWN CLARENCE H	MAJ	O-0319409	0545	2
DROWNS WILLIAM A	COL	O-0322115	0257	1
DROZD WALTER T	MAJ	O-2056921	0563	1
DROZESKI EDWARD H	CW3	W-2148527	0965	1
DRUBA ROYAL E	LTC	O-2042745	1159	1
DRUCKER ARTHUR	LTC	O-0866923	0865	1
DRUEN RALPH I	CW2	W-2206300	0563	1
DRUET ARTHUR L	1LT	O-2053913	0554	1
DRUM CLIFFORD H	LTC	O-1585383	1066	3
DRUM GEORGE	LTC	O-0298543	0657	1
DRUM THOMAS J	CPT	O-0359692	1143	2
DRUMM BYRON M	MAJ	O-1924567	0865	1
DRUMMOND ADDISON P	COL	O-0259120	0367	3
DRUMMOND ALFRED A	LTC	O-0146897	1056	3
DRUMMOND FREDERICK	LTC	O-0358214	1163	3
DRUMMOND JAMES	MAJ	O-2027754	1161	1
DRUMMOND JOSEPH R	CPT	O-0280471	0645	2
DRUMMOND MANCE F	LTC	O-1110465	0967	3
DRUMMOND PALMER R	MAJ	O-0239302	0845	2
DRUMMOND RAY C	CW4	W-2004226	1265	1
DRUMMY WILLIAM F	CPT	O-1794794	0445	2
DRUPIEWSKI JOSEPH	CW4	W-2003930	1060	3
DRURY BILL C	1LT	O-1304048	1045	2
DRURY CECIL M	LTC	O-0401832	0966	3
DRURY CHARLES W	MAJ	O-0243320	0160	3
DRURY EDWARD A	MAJ	O-1935749	0366	1
DRURY FORREST J	COL	O-0189680	0648	1
DRURY FREDERIC F JR	COL	O-0326705	0960	3
DRURY GEORGE A	LTC	O-0176008	0955	3
DRURY PERCIVAL P	LTC	O-0159314	0856	3
DRURY WILLIAM W	LTC	O-1069081	0766	1
DRUSCHEL ALBERT E	LTC	O-1062811	1268	1
DRUSS ABE K	LTC	O-1594133	0966	3
DRUYOR FRANK A	LTC	O-1184805	0868	1
DRY ELMER J	MAJ	O-0119069	1145	2
DRY RALPH L	MAJ	O-0347758	1044	2
DRYDALE WILLIAM T	MAJ	O-1322138	0760	2
DRYDEN BEN	CW3	W-2147077	0361	1
DRYDEN DEAN W	MAJ	O-0514154	0158	2
DRYDEN JACK T	2LT	O-2000519	0656	1
DRYDEN JACK T	2LT	O-2000559	0656	1
DRYDEN JOHN F	CPT	O-1044503	0855	1
DRYDEN JOHN R	COL	O-0237475	1064	3
DRYDEN SHERMAN L	MAJ	O-0571515	0151	2
DRYDEN VANCE H	CW4	W-2150204	1168	2
DRYER ADOLPH	1LT	O-1305219	0346	2
DRYER ARNOLD JR	MAJ	O-1015723	0164	1
DRYER GENE F	2LT	O-1995411	0944	2
DRYER JAMES C JR	LTC	O-0298231	0664	3
DRYER OLIN G	LTC	O-0132527	0652	3
DRYMON BRANDT C	MAJ	O-1016821	1060	1
DRYSDALE GEORGE H	MAJ	O-0278493	1056	3
DRYSDALE WALTER S JR	LTC	O-0327499	0356	2
DU BOIS BENJAMIN G	COL	O-0116480	0648	3
DU BOIS EARL D	COL	O-0215780	0858	3
DU BOIS FRANK A	LTC	O-1299863	0765	1
DU BOIS MARY E	1LT	N-0759594	0346	1

NAME	GRADE	SVC NO	DATE RET MO YR	RET CODE
DU BOIS ROBERT H	MAJ	O-0961930	0468	1
DU BOIS ROBERT S	COL	O-0208072	0951	3
DU BOIS WILLIAM O	CW3	W-2146232	0661	1
DU BOSE CHARLES G	LTC	O-0315522	0161	1
DU BOSE FRANK H	LTC	O-0256571	0465	3
DU BOSE WITTICH C	LTC	O-1047504	0468	3
DU CHARME BENJAMIN J	2LT	O-0571519	1052	1
DU CONGE EDWIN J	CPT	O-1592786	0160	2
DU FLOCQ EUGENE W	MAJ	O-0239782	0965	3
DU FRANE FRANCIS A	CW3	W-2142147	0960	1
DU MOULIN JULIA P	2LT	N-0720854	0547	1
DU PONT GEORGE J	MAJ	O-1178130	0765	1
DU PRE OSCAR L	COL	O-0231324	0565	3
DU PUIS ROBERT C	LTC	O-1310176	1061	1
DU PUIS ROBERT H	WO1	W-2106599	1044	2
DU PUY ELBERT N	COL	O-0254792	1164	3
DU RANT HARRY N	CPT	O-1919484	1263	1
DU RETTE CECIL A	MAJ	O-0189042	0355	3
DU TREMBLE LAURIEN R	CPT	O-1293732	0661	1
DU VAL HENRY W JR	1LT	O-1017161	1045	2
DU VALL EARL W	CW3	W-2207388	0661	1
DU VALL HERMAN C	LTC	O-0436250	0457	1
DU VALL THOMAS B	CW4	RW-2142836	0264	1
DU VARNEY EDWARD J	MAJ	O-1886462	1164	1
DUANE FRANCIS K	CPT	O-1322316	0147	2
DUANE STEPHEN A	COL	O-0136331	0257	3
DUARTE MANUEL J JR	CW2	W-2209567	1064	1
DUBBERLEY JOHN A	CPT	O-0379249	0348	2
DUBBS WILLIAM B	MAJ	O-1544051	0763	1
DUBE PAUL H	MAJ	O-0481894	0146	2
DUBES RUSSELL F	LTC	O-1647857	1067	1
DUBIN ABE	LTC	O-1845028	0566	3
DUBINSKI WILLIAM A	LTC	O-1284481	0854	1
DUBLIN SOLOMON	2LT	O-1177779	0944	2
DUBNICKA JOSEPH A	CPT	O-1185332	0746	2
DUBOIS EDWARD F	MAJ	O-2032287	1262	2
DUBOIS ETHELYN C	1LT	N-0727575	1045	1
DUBOIS JACK G	LTC	O-0231869	1263	3
DUBOIS WILLIAM H	MAJ	O-0271438	0168	3
DUBOSE ROBERT N	CPT	O-0339100	0944	2
DUBRISKE RAYMOND A	LTC	O-1577118	0961	1
DUBSON REUBEN F	LTC	O-0482407	0756	1
DUBUC JOSEPH A	LTC	O-1080099	0666	1
DUBUCLET WALTER M	MAJ	O-1799115	0462	1
DUCEY FREDERICK	MAJ	O-0169924	0355	3
DUCHAINE GEORGE E	LTC	O-1642018	0966	1
DUCHAINE JULIEN G F	CPT	O-0451273	0864	1
DUCHAJ JOHN H	LTC	O-1327127	0563	1
DUCHARM DARRELL L	LTC	O-0308404	0268	3
DUCHARME JOSEPH D E	LTC	O-0481416	0754	1
DUCHARME RAYMOND J	CW4	W-2102856	0157	1
DUCHEK JOSEPH D	LTC	O-0510067	0467	1
DUCHIEN WESLEY L	LTC	O-0485882	0753	1
DUCK WILLIAM F	MAJ	O-2202785	0268	1
DUCKER HAROLD R	MAJ	O-1335255	0164	1
DUCKETT ODEN B	CPT	O-0923935	0745	2
DUCKETT PIERCE F	CPT	O-0450123	0258	1
DUCKMAN JOHN A	MAJ	O-1012013	0366	3
DUCKWITZ ALBERT H	CPT	O-1822119	0863	1
DUCKWORTH CARL L	LTC	O-0453337	1146	2
DUCKWORTH DOROTHY C	2LT	N-0794798	0846	1
DUCKWORTH ERNEST G	CW4	W-2143410	0959	1
DUCKWORTH GEORGE H	CPT	O-2262158	0960	1
DUCKWORTH GEORGE J	MAJ	O-0384832	1047	2
DUCKWORTH GLENN O	CPT	O-0504286	1055	1
DUCKWORTH GRADY C	CW4	W-2141065	0368	1
DUCKWORTH HARRY R SR	CW4	W-2144661	0668	1
DUCKWORTH JAMES C JR	CW3	W-2145416	1059	2
DUCKWORTH JOHN C	COL	O-0271127	0667	3
DUCKWORTH LEWIS F JR	1LT	O-0442859	1044	2
DUCKWORTH PHILLIP B	MAJ	O-1049812	0261	1
DUCKWORTH VIRGINIA	2LT	N-0784783	0945	1
DUCLON WARREN E	CPT	O-0551434	0547	2
DUCLOS CYRILLE A	CPT	O-1311495	0347	2
DUCOTE HAROLD A	1LT	O-1047100	0745	2

NAME	GRADE	SVC NO	DATE RET MO YR	RET CODE
DUCOTE HARRY J JR	CW3	W-2146233	0762	1
DUDA ALBIN J	2LT	O-0337268	1044	2
DUDA GEORGE	MAJ	O-0450683	0356	1
DUDA MICHAEL	MAJ	O-1321109	1159	1
DUDAS STEPHEN	CPT	O-0975770	0857	1
DUDDING WILLIAM C	MAJ	O-2026069	0860	1
DUDDY JOSEPH J	WO1	W-2106109	1148	1
DUDE LUDWIG	MAJ	O-1001992	0860	1
DUDEK ALEXANDER	2LT	O-5925000	0161	2
DUDEK ROMAN F	CW2	W-2203376	0963	1
DUDISH ANDREW C	1LT	O-0524684	1145	2
DUDLEY ARTHUR L	MAJ	O-0945810	0266	1
DUDLEY CHARLES W	LTC	O-1542997	0163	1
DUDLEY FRANK G	MAJ	O-0490639	0956	1
DUDLEY GORDON C	1LT	O-1111587	0846	2
DUDLEY HARRY D	CPT	O-0214675	0557	3
DUDLEY HARVARD E	LTC	O-1540562	0562	1
DUDLEY HENRY H	CPT	O-0130193	0251	3
DUDLEY JACK B	MAJ	O-0439365	0849	1
DUDLEY PAUL W	COL	O-0281532	0168	3
DUDLEY RICHARD C	MAJ	O-0260594	0567	3
DUDLEY RICHARD S	2LT	O-2012079	0946	2
DUDLEY WILFRED	1LT	O-1640409	1043	2
DUDLEY WILLIAM R	CW2	W-2214439	0866	1
DUDMAN WILLIAM R	MAJ	O-0444519	0250	1
DUDONIS JOSEPH J	CPT	O-2055106	0156	1
DUDREY PHYLLIS G	1LT	N-0776050	1045	1
DUDYK PAUL P	CPT	O-1936899	0357	1
DUDZIEC BERNICE A	MAJ	N-0755068	1068	1
DUDZINSKI VINCENT R	CW3	W-2151631	0364	1
DUEHRING ROBERT A	1LT	O-5346726	1068	2
DUELL EVERETT A	LTC	O-0136727	1151	2
DUELL HOWARD S	1LT	O-0114802	0755	3
DUELL RONALD H	LTC	O-1172439	0766	1
DUENOW RICHARD H	LTC	O-1010042	0157	1
DUER ROBERT K	MAJ	O-1116713	1066	1
DUERNER LEWIS W	COL	O-0298331	1054	2
DUESER FRANK J	MAJ	O-1171520	0461	1
DUFF CARL L	COL	O-0905938	0863	1
DUFF LEONARD A	COL	O-0347855	1052	2
DUFF OSCAR A	2LT	O-1299864	0844	2
DUFF PETER J	COL	O-0420540	0756	1
DUFF SYBIL K	MAJ	N-0743833	0865	1
DUFF THOMAS M	COL	O-0276832	0855	3
DUFF WILLIAM	1LT	O-1691602	0745	2
DUFFEY CATHERINE	CPT	N-0700591	0245	1
DUFFEY EARLE L	LTC	O-0841050	0868	1
DUFFIE HAROLD R	B G	O-0126221	1054	3
DUFFIE JOHN M	MAJ	O-0243335	0960	3
DUFFIELD CLYDE W	LTC	O-0382986	0862	1
DUFFIELD DORRENCE T	LTC	O-1295846	0968	2
DUFFIELD JAMES I	LTC	O-1338204	1167	1
DUFFIELD JOHN R	LTC	O-0269801	0768	3
DUFFIELD JOHN M	LTC	O-0365405	0657	1
DUFFIELD KEITH R	MAJ	O-0975498	0961	1
DUFFIN DANIEL J	CPT	O-0903832	1044	2
DUFFIN EDSON C	MAJ	O-1548198	0161	1
DUFFY ADAM V	CPT	O-1535448	0146	2
DUFFY ALBERT W	CW3	W-2102857	0156	1
DUFFY BERNARD J JR	MAJ	O-1587224	0161	1
DUFFY EDWARD F JR	CPT	O-0245964	0753	3
DUFFY FRANCIS K	LTC	O-0100252	0844	2
DUFFY FRANCIS X	CW4	W-2005197	1066	3
DUFFY HAROLD E	LTC	O-0452588	0960	1
DUFFY JAMES A	MAJ	O-2203010	0567	1
DUFFY JAMES J	LTC	O-1116373	1162	1
DUFFY JAMES M	1LT	O-1549700	0146	2
DUFFY JAMES W SR	LTC	O-0177503	0156	3
DUFFY JOHN H	1LT	O-1284303	0644	2
DUFFY JOHN J	CPT	O-0243043	0648	3
DUFFY JOHN J	CPT	O-0499377	1044	2
DUFFY JOHN P	MAJ	O-1799259	0561	2
DUFFY JOSEPH D	1LT	O-0387579	0245	2
DUFFY LAMBERT F	1LT	O-1549258	1145	2
DUFFY MARGARET G	MAJ	L-0610747	1163	1

NAME	GRADE	SVC NO	DATE RET MO YR	RET CODE
DUFFY PAUL J	WO1	W-2125910	0146	2
DUFFY ROBERT A JR	WO1	W-2144174	0367	2
DUFFY ROBERT N	MAJ	O-1286985	1059	1
DUFFY WILLIAM E	LTC	O-0410009	1060	1
DUFFY WILLIAM R	LTC	O-1299218	0764	1
DUFOE FABBIAN G JR	LTC	O-1181231	0666	1
DUFORD ROBERT E	CW2	W-3250469	1168	1
DUFORT LEO W	MAJ	O-0239667	0862	3
DUFRESNE ALFRED A	CW2	W-2143494	1154	1
DUFRESNE CARYL A	LTC	O-0379825	0566	1
DUFRESNE RAYMOND J	CW3	W-2144287	0267	1
DUGAN EDWARD C	1LT	O-0467178	0945	2
DUGAN EDWARD E	2LT	O-1178768	0245	2
DUGAN EDWARD S	CW3	W-2205609	0668	1
DUGAN FRANK C	LTC	O-0123495	0648	3
DUGAN JOHN J	LTC	O-0183402	0954	3
DUGAN JOIE A	1LT	N-0790040	1046	1
DUGAN KASTANTER	CPT	O-1283391	0458	1
DUGAN LESTER J	LTC	O-0328471	0268	3
DUGAN RICHARD F	COL	O-0203374	0560	3
DUGAN THOMAS M	CPT	O-1726372	0549	2
DUGAN WALTER J	1LT	O-1289224	0246	2
DUGART ROBERT E	CW3	W-2152928	0467	1
DUGAS FRANK J	2LT	O-0922726	0344	2
DUGAS GUSTAVE H JR	MAJ	O-1796438	0761	1
DUGAS HENRY J	CW2	W-2123932	0360	1
DUGAS PAUL P	MAJ	O-1101417	1266	3
DUGAS RONALD R	LTC	O-2263327	0968	1
DUGGAN CHARLES W	CPT	O-1317767	0748	2
DUGGAN CLIFTON D	CW3	W-2143846	0461	2
DUGGAN CORNELIUS	CW4	W-2003205	1157	3
DUGGAN FRANCIS L	LTC	O-0319886	0756	2
DUGGAN JAMES E	CPT	O-1995242	0746	2
DUGGAN JOHN J	CW4	W-2125166	0867	3
DUGGAN JOHN S	1LT	O-1104626	0546	2
DUGGAN SAMUEL F	LTC	O-1101418	0762	1
DUGGAN WALTER L	CW3	W-2148960	0764	1
DUGGAY WILLIAM C	MAJ	O-0955788	0467	1
DUGGER JOHN	CPT	O-1633177	0248	1
DUGGER VIRGINIA N	2LT	N-0735896	0345	1
DUGHI PETER A	CPT	O-1308616	0147	2
DUGINGER LYNN C	CPT	O-1290017	1145	2
DUHANT ELIZABETH	2LT	N-0775127	0545	1
DUHART ROY S	COL	O-0340290	0359	1
DUHE HENRY M	CPT	O-0417905	0446	2
DUHL ARTHUR L	LTC	O-0518320	0868	1
DUHM WALTER T	MAJ	O-0430088	0546	2
DUHON WOODROW W	1LT	O-1825213	0745	2
DUISMAN JOE	CW4	W-2110200	0957	1
DUKAS ALEXANDER	LTC	O-1323299	0564	1
DUKE CHARLES L	LTC	O-0452521	0761	1
DUKE DURWARD A	MAJ	O-0986624	0163	2
DUKE FRANCIS	LTC	O-0906954	0466	3
DUKE FRANKLIN L	MAJ	O-2288515	0867	1
DUKE GRADY E	MAJ	O-1913405	0864	2
DUKE JOHN P	COL	O-0150396	0457	3
DUKE OSCAR	CPT	O-0503010	0952	1
DUKE PHILLIP W	MAJ	O-0159033	0648	3
DUKE RALPH L	LTC	O-1685031	0367	1
DUKE SPOTTSWOOD	COL	O-0154656	0554	3
DUKE THOMAS H JR	MAJ	O-1633178	0760	1
DUKE WILLIAM R	CPT	O-1642817	0353	1
DUKEHART GRAHAM	MAJ	O-0302350	0465	3
DUKELOW BURTON M	CW3	W-2148248	0165	1
DUKES EULA F	2LT	N-0761327	0245	1
DUKES JOHN D	LTC	O-0206953	1158	3
DUKES ROBERT J	LTC	O-0281979	0662	1
DUKES SAMUEL J	CW2	W-2214618	0868	1
DUKES WILSON E	MAJ	O-1998417	1154	1
DUKESHAR WILLIAM E	CW3	W-2203499	0167	1
DULAN ELVA L J	2LT	N-0724860	0544	1
DULANEY MARLAND D	MAJ	O-2021092	1064	1
DULANEY ROBERT A	CW3	W-3150264	0667	1
DULBERGER HOWARD	CPT	O-1013436	0946	2
DULEY FRANK P	MAJ	O-1036957	0461	1

NAME	GRADE	SVC NO	DATE RET MO YR	RET CODE	NAME	GRADE	SVC NO	DATE RET MO YR	RET CODE	NAME	GRADE	SVC NO	DATE RET MO YR	RET CODE	NAME	GRADE	SVC NO	DATE RET MO YR	RET CODE
DULIAN CLIFFORD V	CPT	0-1584149	1044	2	DUNCAN HAROLD F	MAJ	0-1580887	0858	1	DUNHAM RICHARD B	CPT	0-0511094	0646	2	DUNN EDWARD	MAJ	0-1692536	0561	1
DULIN BYRON W	CW4	W-2002344	0867	3	DUNCAN HARRY L	COL	0-0165433	0648	3	DUNHAM ROBERT J	LTC	0-0265613	0861	3	DUNN EDWARD C	M G	0-0020245	0368	1
DULIN CHARLES	CPT	0-0941429	0161	1	DUNCAN HENRY T	COL	0-0231114	0863	3	DUNHAM RUPERT F	LTC	0-0327213	0458	1	DUNN ELMORE	2LT	0-1913658	0444	1
DULIN GEORGE W	MAJ	0-0212745	0364	3	DUNCAN HERBERT L	MAJ	0-0995144	0663	1	DUNHAM RUSSELL C	MAJ	0-0146877	1049	3	DUNN ELVIS	1LT	0-2024283	1047	2
DULIN HOWARD L	MAJ	0-0474248	0849	1	DUNCAN HIRAM A JR	MAJ	0-2036641	0661	1	DUNHAM WALTER A	1LT	0-0535310	0949	1	DUNN ESTHER M	CPT	N-0767645	0754	2
DULIN RAMSEY W JR	1LT	0-1130958	0246	2	DUNCAN HORACE L	LTC	0-0405927	0960	2	DUNHAM WILLIAM C	LTC	0-1647861	0463	2	DUNN HAROLD W	LTC	0-0325376	0946	2
DULIN [illegible] JOHN W	MAJ	0-0435191	0949	2	DUNCAN JAMES	1LT	0-2027290	1152	2	DUNHAM WILLIAM F	CW2	W-2145543	0461	1	DUNN HOWARD J	MAJ	0-1313052	1155	1
DULINA ANDREW S	MAJ	0-0900831	1167	2	DUNCAN JAMES B	COL	0-1287496	0263	2	DUNHAM WILLIAM H	COL	0-0253409	0161	3	DUNN HUGH P	LTC	0-0215037	0861	3
DULING [illegible]	CW3	W-2203297	0661	1	DUNCAN JOE	MAJ	0-1174834	0154	1	DUNKEL LEONARD N	B G	0-0178133	0459	3	DUNN JACK	COL	0-0308633	0268	3
DULING EARL P	MAJ	0-1002616	0758	1	DUNCAN JOHN A	1LT	0-2033309	0952	2	DUNKEN HALWEN A	COL	0-0323543	1068	3	DUNN JAMES A	MAJ	0-1175691	1155	1
DULL CHARLES F JR	LTC	0-1581670	1065	1	DUNCAN JOHN H	LTC	0-0317675	0759	1	DUNKIN GLEN W	CPT	0-1284110	0658	1	DUNN JAMES D	LTC	0-0505176	0661	1
DULL DOROTHY A	2LT	N-0797454	1047	1	DUNCAN JOHN C SR	MAJ	0-1950155	0463	2	DUNKIN LEON M	CW3	W-2147702	1262	1	DUNN JAMES N JR	CPT	0-0495652	0350	2
DULL FRANCIS J	MAJ	0-0956697	0265	1	DUNCAN JOHN V	MAJ	0-0974614	0667	1	DUNKIN SAMUEL J	LTC	0-0205190	0860	3	DUNN JAMES W	MAJ	0-0509793	0155	1
DULL HAZEL [illegible]	1LT	N-0727295	0246	1	DUNCAN JOSEPH D	CW3	W-2141843	1162	1	DUNKLE CYRUS G	MAJ	0-0222505	0561	3	DUNN JAMES W	LTC	0-1643511	1264	1
DULL LLOYD W	LTC	0-1049815	1265	1	DUNCAN JOSHUA M	CW2	W-2214905	0968	1	DUNKLE GLENN M	MAJ	0-0296012	1267	3	DUNN JEFF S	MAJ	0-0281094	1058	1
DULLEA MAURICE B	MAJ	0-1925353	0864	2	DUNCAN MADISON M	COL	0-0250659	0361	1	DUNKLE SIMON R	COL	0-0194620	1062	3	DUNN JOHN P	1LT	0-0202385	1154	3
DULLENTY ADOLPH L JR	LTC	0-0380523	0147	2	DUNCAN MARY E	1LT	N-0765509	0847	1	DUNKLEE CARL [illegible]	LTC	0-0219134	1055	3	DUNN JOHN R	CW4	W-2148291	0368	1
DULONEY CURTIS V	CW3	RW-2145305	0361	1	DUNCAN MARY V	MAJ	N-0741943	0762	1	DUNKLEE THOMAS E	CW2	W-3200434	0767	1	DUNN JOSEPH B	LTC	0-1168229	0258	1
DULSKI STANLEY J	LTC	0-1844679	0561	1	DUNCAN ORAN W	COL	0-0238746	0562	3	DUNKLEY FRANK	B G	0-0240437	0557	3	DUNN JOSEPH F	CW3	W-2206341	0268	2
DULUDE STEPHEN E	MAJ	0-1824294	0462	1	DUNCAN PAUL JR	MAJ	0-1947684	0567	3	DUNKLIN VOLNEY L	MAJ	0-0311282	0246	2	DUNN JOSEPH L	1LT	0-0244736	0260	3
DUMAINE ALBERT L	2LT	0-0108353	0532	1	DUNCAN RALPH A	CPT	0-0508718	0245	2	DUNLAP BRADY	MAJ	0-1051941	0959	1	DUNN JOSEPH M	COL	0-1080532	1168	1
DUMAINE JOHN H	LTC	0-1294106	0860	1	DUNCAN RALPH E	CPT	0-0116487	0251	3	DUNLAP CLAUDE E JR	COL	0-0410764	0161	1	DUNN JULIA L	1LT	N-0730144	0746	1
DUMANDAN TIM [illegible]	1LT	0-1846729	0561	1	DUNCAN RALPH G	LTC	0-0325842	0860	1	DUNLAP EDWARD L	LTC	0-0168808	0658	3	DUNN LEO F	LTC	0-0245408	1062	3
DUMANDIS HAROLD G	COL	0-0275204	0367	3	DUNCAN RALPH M	CPT	0-2288111	0563	1	DUNLAP FREDERICK	LTC	0-0383123	0147	2	DUNN MARY C	MAJ	N-0744195	0865	1
DUMANSKE MORRIS F	MAJ	0-1579590	1160	1	DUNCAN RAYMOND L	MAJ	0-0503354	0549	1	DUNLAP GEORGE R	CW3	W-2141260	0760	1	DUNN PAUL C	1LT	0-1032077	1152	2
DUMAS ANDREW L	LTC	0-1011399	0961	1	DUNCAN RICHARD E	MAJ	0-1923633	1066	1	DUNLAP GORDON C	CW2	W-2146641	0557	1	DUNN PAUL C JR	LTC	0-1042551	1262	1
DUMAS EDGAR J	CW3	W-2152116	0659	1	DUNCAN ROBERT G	CW3	W-2143272	0962	1	DUNLAP HAROLD J	COL	0-0281572	0664	3	DUNN PHILLIP L	LTC	0-1633183	0661	1
DUMBRIGUE ALEXANDER	MAJ	0-1924905	0966	1	DUNCAN ROBERT P	CW4	W-2133199	0559	1	DUNLAP HERBERT P	COL	0-0217408	0563	3	DUNN RAYMOND C	MAJ	0-2017975	0762	1
DUMEY ARNOLD I	LTC	0-0921391	1266	3	DUNCAN ROBERT S	1LT	0-0249142	1266	3	DUNLAP JAMES D	COL	0-0101252	0256	3	DUNN RICHARD D	LTC	0-0431992	0564	1
DUMIC JOE	LTC	0-0451097	0155	1	DUNCAN ROBERT T	2LT	0-1559904	1146	2	DUNLAP JOHN A	COL	0-0325757	0968	3	DUNN ROBERT H	MAJ	0-2026665	0963	1
DUMLAO MIGUEL P	MAJ	0-1896416	1058	1	DUNCAN ROY O	MAJ	0-1320514	0564	1	DUNLAP JOSEPH H JR	LTC	0-1821983	0866	1	DUNN ROBERT J	CW4	W-2111849	0655	1
DUMMER RUTH L	1LT	N-0731432	0845	1	DUNCAN RUDOLPH L	COL	0-0219079	0755	3	DUNLAP KINLOCH F JR	LTC	0-0252863	1266	3	DUNN ROBERT L	1LT	0-1047507	1057	1
DUMONT WOODROW M	MAJ	0-0364593	1045	2	DUNCAN RUSSELL T	MAJ	0-1917823	1165	2	DUNLAP MERRITT S	LTC	0-0274723	0966	3	DUNN ROBERT R	2LT	0-1011536	0144	2
DUMSER GERALD T	LTC	0-1549701	0263	1	DUNCAN SCOTT M	LTC	0-0126837	0653	3	DUNLAP RALPH F	CPT	0-2011344	0562	1	DUNN ROY F	LTC	0-0293001	0466	3
DUNAVANT GEORGE A	COL	0-0401077	0463	1	DUNCAN THEODORE R	CW3	W-2145104	0159	1	DUNLAP RICHARD D	MAJ	0-1174283	0753	1	DUNN RUSSELL M	CW3	W-2152788	1166	1
DUNAWAY AUGUSTUS	LTC	0-0164110	0254	3	DUNCAN WILBUR H	MAJ	0-0201880	1157	3	DUNLAP ROBERT B	CPT	0-0361126	1065	1	DUNN SAMUEL C	LTC	0-0313468	1167	3
DUNAWAY MARION E	1LT	N-0742017	0445	1	DUNCAN WILLIAM A	MAJ	0-1060082	0860	1	DUNLAP ROBERT C	MAJ	0-0220242	0857	3	DUNN SAMUEL T	CPT	0-0347647	0964	1
DUNAWAY MARSHALL W	MAJ	0-1176941	1262	1	DUNCAN WILLIAM B	2LT	0-0713655	0246	2	DUNLAP STEPHEN E	CPT	0-1726921	1046	2	DUNN STANLEY	CPT	0-1011714	0846	2
DUNBAR ARTHUR B	MAJ	0-0190499	0757	3	DUNCAN WILLIAM C JR	CPT	0-1553074	0960	1	DUNLAP WALLACE W	MAJ	0-0129175	0655	1	DUNN THOMAS B	1LT	0-2055394	1044	2
DUNBAR CLARENCE F	COL	0-0192761	0648	3	DUNCAN WILLIAM L	MAJ	0-1638147	1167	1	DUNLAP WALTER H	LTC	0-0353142	0963	1	DUNN THOMAS J	MAJ	0-0188404	0759	3
DUNBAR ERNEST J	WO1	W-2149594	0455	1	DUNCAN WILLIAM O	CW3	W-2210777	1168	1	DUNLAP WALTER T	CPT	0-1324830	0949	2	DUNN THOMAS J	1LT	0-1825459	0964	1
DUNBAR FREDERICK	CW3	W-2145884	0862	2	DUNCAN WILLIE Y	LTC	0-0182186	0653	3	DUNLAP WILBUR	CW3	W-2124232	0561	1	DUNN WALTER F JR	LTC	0-1101817	0363	1
DUNBAR GERALD C	MAJ	0-0225997	1162	3	DUNCANSON JAY O	LTC	0-1037969	0967	1	DUNLAP WILLIAM A	1LT	0-0551020	0646	2	DUNN WARREN A	CPT	0-1176606	1059	1
DUNBAR HANSON D	LTC	0-1587226	0265	3	DUNCANSON WILLIAM M	MAJ	0-0175486	1147	2	DUNLAP WILLIAM C	MAJ	C-2226188	0866	1	DUNN WILLIAM A	LTC	0-1587939	0766	1
DUNBAR HARVEY L	2LT	0-1017956	0545	2	DUNCKEL RALPH L	COL	0-0215940	0549	2	DUNLAP WILLIAM M	LTC	0-0152045	0955	3	DUNN WILLIAM F JR	LTC	0-1080620	0763	1
DUNBAR JOHN C	COL	0-0218231	1153	3	DUNCKLEE HENRY W	2LT	0-0492814	0555	1	DUNLAP ZAC K	1LT	0-0372348	1045	2	DUNN WILLIAM M	COL	0-0183724	0648	3
DUNBAR PAUL A	CPT	0-0246781	0265	3	DUNCOMBE H S JR	COL	0-0144626	0356	3	DUNLEAVY JAMES J	1LT	0-0501495	0747	2	DUNN WILLIAM M SR	LTC	0-1585077	0666	1
DUNBAR QUINTIN R JR	CW3	W-2206537	0967	1	DUNDA NICHOLAS	CPT	0-1180879	1163	1	DUNLEAVY ROY R	LTC	0-0399245	0261	1	DUNN WILLIAM P	CW3	W-2144432	1165	1
DUNBAR ROBERT A	MAJ	0-1633181	0756	1	DUNDAS HARRY R	MAJ	0-0470504	0945	2	DUNLEVEY DAVID B	LTC	0-0334130	0746	2	DUNN WILSON H	COL	0-0302364	0163	3
DUNBAR WALLACE H JR	CW3	W-2147330	0464	1	DUNDAS JACK S	LTC	0-1634699	0865	1	DUNMAN DOUGLAS W	CW3	W-2145747	0265	1	DUNNAHOO JACK R	MAJ	0-1306076	1160	1
DUNBAR WALTER B	LTC	0-0329561	0368	3	DUNDAS JAMES E	MAJ	0-1341646	0663	1	DUNMAR HAROLD	MAJ	0-2063998	0164	1	DUNNAM MILFORD A	CW2	W-2150007	1060	1
DUNBAR WILBUR R	CW4	W-2002118	0756	3	DUNEGAN FRANCIS E	2LT	0-1321463	0945	2	DUNMORE FRANCIS E	MAJ	0-4026450	1165	1	DUNNE CHARLES J JR	LTC	0-0502156	1262	1
DUNBAR WILLIAM F JR	1LT	0-1061943	0546	2	DUNFEE JAMES F	CPT	0-0504609	0447	1	DUNN ALBERT A	COL	0-0157531	1052	2	DUNNE EDWARD J	2LT	0-1697945	0744	2
DUNCAN ANDREW	CPT	0-0109167	1026	1	DUNFORD FREDERICK	MAJ	0-1113180	0661	1	DUNN ALBERT D	CW2	W-2145178	1060	1	DUNNE JOHN J	CPT	0-0321202	0768	3
DUNCAN ANDREW J	1LT	0-0274957	0845	2	DUNFORD JUNIUS E	LTC	0-0154246	0545	2	DUNN ALBERT W	1LT	0-0885748	0859	1	DUNNE JOSEPH J	1LT	0-1292156	1045	2
DUNCAN AUBREY T	1LT	0-1548199	1157	1	DUNG PURDESON O	MAJ	0-0961956	1164	1	DUNN ALFRED D	MAJ	0-1015939	0760	1	DUNNELL CHARLES A JR	LTC	0-0456035	0261	1
DUNCAN AUBURN B	2LT	0-0556581	1044	2	DUNGAN DAVID V	CW4	W-2118287	0959	1	DUNN ALLEN W	COL	0-0261218	0468	3	DUNNIGAN CATHERINE	MAJ	N-0788525	0963	1
DUNCAN CARL O	COL	0-1633182	0853	1	DUNGEE JOHN R	CPT	0-0460209	1046	2	DUNN ANDERSON R JR	MAJ	0-0401878	0444	2	DUNNING BARBARA T	1LT	N-0790370	0546	1
DUNCAN CHARLES A	MAJ	0-1297334	0960	1	DUNGEY LEONARD A	CW4	W-2114139	0661	1	DUNN ANDREW M	COL	0-0348514	0859	1	DUNNING CHESTER H	COL	0-0052421	0368	1
DUNCAN CHARLES A	MAJ	0-2035217	0955	1	DUNGEY LYNN E	MAJ	0-2039473	0163	1	DUNN ARLO M	CPT	0-0314921	0646	2	DUNNING ELLIS G	LTC	0-0296631	0667	3
DUNCAN CHARLES M JR	LTC	0-0405858	0860	1	DUNGEY PERSHING M	CW3	W-2206039	1267	1	DUNN ARTHUR E	2LT	0-1797617	1044	2	DUNNING FLOYD S	COL	0-0277389	0560	1
DUNCAN CLYDE W	CPT	0-1324991	0258	1	DUNHAM CARL C	LTC	0-0411002	0663	1	DUNN ARTHUR M	CPT	0-1293030	0547	2	DUNNING JACK R	CPT	0-1923539	0463	1
DUNCAN DANIEL E	COL	0-1288522	0367	1	DUNHAM CARL E	LTC	0-0342630	1058	3	DUNN BYRON E	LTC	0-0233241	1264	3	DUNNING JAMES E	COL	0-0352990	1266	1
DUNCAN DONALD F	MAJ	0-0554189	0863	1	DUNHAM DAN S	1LT	0-1825335	0850	2	DUNN CECIL G	COL	0-0275937	0364	3	DUNNING JAMES J	MAJ	0-0334073	1144	2
DUNCAN DONALD W	CPT	0-1317080	0766	1	DUNHAM EVERETT C	LTC	0-1051940	0963	1	DUNN CHARLES A	MAJ	0-1000357	1162	1	DUNNING LESTER T	MAJ	0-0360934	0568	3
DUNCAN DURMAN L	LTC	0-0305380	0560	3	DUNHAM FRED A	COL	0-0220388	1059	3	DUNN CHARLES C	MAJ	0-2262873	1062	1	DUNNING THURLOW R	COL	0-0226516	0957	3
DUNCAN EARL L	MAJ	0-1170721	0561	1	DUNHAM GEORGE F	CPT	0-0261790	0244	2	DUNN CHARLES C	CW3	W-2147794	0366	1	DUNNINGTON EARL V JR	CW3	W-2111770	0261	1
DUNCAN EMORY L	MAJ	0-4006285	0367	1	DUNHAM HOWARD R	LTC	0-0360301	0460	1	DUNN CHARLES F	MAJ	0-0171782	0652	3	DUNNINGTON RAYMOND E	COL	0-0248170	1266	3
DUNCAN EUGENE F	MAJ	0-0308531	0163	1	DUNHAM JAMES F	1LT	0-0265137	0146	2	DUNN CLARENCE A	LTC	0-0281520	0451	1	DUNPHEY PATRICIA E	2LT	N-0758564	0945	1
DUNCAN FRED	MAJ	0-1299865	0866	1	DUNHAM JAMES F	MAJ	0-1288873	1155	1	DUNN D Y	LTC	0-0125252	0652	3	DUNPHY ALBERT C	COL	0-0171022	0457	3
DUNCAN FRED J	LTC	0-0360148	0154	1	DUNHAM JAMES W	LTC	0-0266317	0868	3	DUNN DARWIN A	MAJ	0-0324123	0746	2	DUNPHY CHARLES H	LTC	0-0317209	0246	2
DUNCAN GEORGE A	LTC	0-1688244	0564	2	DUNHAM JOSEPH F	CPT	0-0443474	0846	1	DUNN DARWIN C	MAJ	0-1168649	1056	1	DUNPHY CYRIL F	MAJ	0-0372806	0245	2
DUNCAN GEORGE H	MAJ	0-0271850	0962	1	DUNHAM LEWIS L	LTC	0-1342255	0666	1	DUNN DAVID F	MAJ	0-2263706	0868	1	DUNPHY JOHN T	LTC	0-1337409	1162	1
DUNCAN GEORGIA C	MAJ	N-0726438	1267	3	DUNHAM PAUL A	CW2	W-2144731	0660	1	DUNN DAVID J	1LT	0-1306924	1045	2	DUNSHEE DONALD T	MAJ	0-0252218	1063	3
DUNCAN HAROLD B	LTC	0-0209590	0960	3	DUNHAM RAYMOND L	CW3	W-2203711	0767	1	DUNN DONALD J	2LT	0-1184195	0944	2	DUNSMOOR ELMER E	CW2	W-3430217	1066	1

NAME	GRADE	SVC NO	DATE RET MO YR	RET CODE
DUNSMORE MURRAY K	LTC	O-0332774	0146	2
DUNSMORE RICHARD E	COL	O-1011998	0966	2
DUNSON NEIL B	MAJ	O-1169087	0164	1
DUNSTAN EDGAR M	COL	O-0257226	0462	3
DUNTON WALLACE A JR	COL	O-0209922	0454	3
DUNWIDDIE ROBERT B	LTC	O-0738120	0562	1
DUNWOODY JAY W	MAJ	O-1646648	1163	1
DUNWOODY LEONARD L	LTC	O-0319633	0357	2
DUNWOODY WILLIAM K	COL	O-0301862	1168	3
DUPAS CAMILE J	MAJ	O-1285218	0260	1
DUPEE EDWARD L	MAJ	O-0964228	1264	1
DUPERE RAYMOND J	MAJ	O-0984942	0264	1
DUPES HENRY O	MAJ	O-0961880	0166	1
DUPIN PAUL E	MAJ	O-1556567	0466	1
DUPLANTIS JUSTIN A	2LT	O-1300144	1144	2
DUPLIS WILLIAM E	2LT	O-1311992	0544	2
DUPONT GEORGE H JR	1LT	O-1634704	0345	2
DUPONT LOUIS J	CW3	W-2151194	0861	1
DUPRAS LEO A	LTC	O-1310586	0867	1
DUPRE LEO A	COL	O-0123601	0856	3
DUPREE DONALD J	LTC	O-0454204	1160	1
DUPREE LESTER F	1LT	O-0890389	0147	2
DUPREE LEWIS J	COL	O-0134439	0152	3
DUPREE SCOTT W	MAJ	O-0450584	0461	1
DUPRES MARION R	LTC	O-0224077	0961	3
DUPREY FLOYD J	CW4	W-2143245	0959	1
DUPUIS ARTHUR N	MAJ	O-1119054	0860	1
DUPUIS CHARLES C	LTC	O-1585395	0461	1
DUPUIS PAUL H	LTC	O-1290570	0761	1
DUPUY HELEN C	CPT	M-0000679	0948	2
DUQUETTE HENRY B	MAJ	O-0271371	0445	2
DUQUETTE HERBERT E	MAJ	O-0188440	1057	3
DURALL BEN O	MAJ	O-1698454	1163	1
DURAN ALBERT F	LTC	O-0228522	0365	3
DURAN JOHN	CPT	O-1927483	0360	2
DURAN JOHN A	MAJ	O-1919467	0165	1
DURAND CLIFFORD	MAJ	O-1944439	0661	1
DURAND PAUL J	CPT	O-1293699	0448	2
DURAND WILLIAM R	COL	O-0182973	0861	3
DURANT EDWARD J	LTC	O-2046473	0954	1
DURANT ROBERT J	LTC	O-0904741	0662	1
DURANTE VICTOR L	CW3	W-2152804	0567	1
DURBIN CLIFFORD J	LTC	O-0249290	1166	3
DURBIN EDGAR JR	1LT	O-5329787	1067	2
DURBIN GLENN P	MAJ	O-1647721	1165	1
DURBIN HARVEY	CW2	W-2144883	0260	1
DURBIN JOSEPH P	1LT	O-1292849	0146	2
DURBIN MARCELLUS	LTC	O-0392225	0265	3
DURBIN ROBERT F SR	COL	O-0119018	0457	3
DURBROW ROBERT T	LTC	O-0293056	0568	3
DURDEN JOHN D JR	1LT	O-0445762	0245	2
DURDEN WILLIAM W	CW2	W-2121246	0848	1
DUREE CHARLES P JR	CPT	O-1922249	0445	2
DURELL HOWARD J	CPT	O-1798657	0861	1
DURETZ JACK	2LT	O-1322686	0245	2
DUREY THANE M	LTC	O-0146126	0858	3
DURFEE CHARLES W	1LT	O-1292850	0447	2
DURFEE DAVID W	MAJ	O-1796055	0759	1
DURFEY HARRY L	LTC	O-1309231	0468	2
DURFLINGER WILLARD L	MAJ	O-0252767	0462	3
DURFOR WALTER	MAJ	O-1165851	0161	1
DURGAN HERBERT L	1LT	O-0379644	0546	2
DURGIN SIDNEY L	CPT	O-0956915	0762	1
DURHAM ADAM W	MAJ	O-1283717	0159	1
DURHAM CHARLES T	MAJ	O-1309353	0657	1
DURHAM FELIPE	MAJ	O-1686271	0361	1
DURHAM GAIL N	MAJ	O-4010451	1168	1
DURHAM GRADY C	LTC	O-0313390	0567	3
DURHAM GUY	LTC	O-0078911	0268	1
DURHAM ISAIAH D JR	CPT	O-0452882	0544	2
DURHAM JAMES F	MAJ	O-0164196	0739	1
DURHAM JAMES C JR	MAJ	O-0994746	0966	2
DURHAM JOHN F	CW2	W-2210574	1163	1
DURHAM JOSEPH P	2LT	O-2206085	0951	2
DURHAM LEWIS F	CW3	W-2146041	0166	1

NAME	GRADE	SVC NO	DATE RET MO YR	RET CODE
DURHAM MAX J	LTC	O-0262529	0266	3
DURHAM MILLARD G	LTC	O-1207381	0757	1
DURHAM OSCAR L	CW2	W-2151042	1062	1
DURHAM WILLIAM C	LTC	O-0418202	0161	1
DURHAM WILLIAM M	2LT	O-1638172	0943	2
DURIE ROTH C	2LT	O-0475406	1060	1
DURIO GEORGIANNA	MAJ	L-1010555	0265	2
DURKEE DANIEL R	MAJ	O-0953626	0365	1
DURKEE HARRY D	CPT	O-0552163	0747	2
DURKEE MELVIN S	COL	O-0322845	0767	3
DURKEE RALPH H	COL	O-0159278	1048	3
DURKEE RICHARD W	CPT	O-1325809	0255	2
DURKIN HOWARD J	1LT	O-1644113	0645	2
DURKIN PATRICK J	MAJ	O-1285911	0162	1
DURKIN PATRICK J JR	WO1	W-2146424	0260	1
DURKIN ROBERT A	MAJ	O-0988668	0867	1
DURKIN ROBERT W	1LT	O-1335908	0847	2
DURKIN WILLIAM V	LTC	O-0451397	0757	1
DURNELL HOMER A	LTC	O-0423486	0164	1
DURNIN JAMES N	CW2	W-2214051	0768	1
DUROCHER NORMAN L	LTC	O-2282483	0269	1
DURR GORDON V	LTC	O-0255757	0165	3
DURRANT WILLIAM L JR	LTC	O-0060858	0768	1
DURRETT HAROLD O	COL	O-0292450	0267	3
DURRETT JAMES B	1LT	O-1053569	1145	2
DURRETT WILLIAM B	MAJ	O-0939667	0262	1
DURSCHNITT SAMUEL	COL	O-0238074	1061	1
DURST GEORGE G	COL	O-0270788	0846	2
DURUZ WILLIS P	COL	O-0112605	0256	3
DURYEA WILBUR E	LTC	O-0235093	0166	3
DUSCHECK ROLAND P	1LT	O-1327612	0945	2
DUSELL WILLIAM H	1LT	O-0840418	0252	2
DUSENBERRY ROBERT W	CPT	O-0288551	0668	3
DUSHKO JOHN JR	2LT	O-1176319	0644	2
DUSINBERRE PETER O J	1LT	O-0536725	0446	2
DUSK GEORGE M	LTC	O-0302985	0563	3
DUSOLO PAUL E	MAJ	O-1923663	1167	1
DUSSAULT HORACE J	LTC	O-2036240	0967	1
DUSSAULT LAWRENCE H	LTC	O-0420100	0355	1
DUSTIN HERMAN E	MAJ	O-0150595	0155	3
DUSTIN LAUREN L	MAJ	O-1300625	0557	1
DUTASSY CHAPMAN	MAJ	O-1633822	0761	1
DUTCHER BURTT D	1LT	O-1642822	0546	2
DUTCHER HAROLD W	COL	O-0136408	0648	2
DUTCHER HENRY G	LTC	O-0926814	0563	1
DUTCHER JAMES T	MAJ	O-1014634	1264	1
DUTCHER SIDNEY H	CW3	W-2143720	0763	1
DUTCHESS DON D	CPT	O-2034087	0163	1
DUTKANYCH ANDREW	MAJ	O-0331389	0662	1
DUTKOWSKI CLARENCE H	2LT	O-1030759	0745	2
DUTO HENRY R	1LT	O-0289809	0549	2
DUTREAU CHARLES W	MAJ	O-1036958	0260	1
DUTRO JOHN A	LTC	O-0363563	0868	3
DUTT LORIS M	LTC	O-0264374	0364	3
DUTTENHOFER C S	COL	O-0182255	0954	3
DUTTENHOFER FRANCIS	MAJ	O-0411794	0346	2
DUTTON ARNOLD S	LTC	O-1310587	0266	1
DUTTON BILL L	LTC	O-2210189	1168	1
DUTTON CALVIN P	MAJ	O-2033573	0365	1
DUTTON GEORGE L	LTC	O-0144621	0544	2
DUTTON JAMES P	CW2	W-2149888	0161	1
DUTTON MARVIN R	MAJ	O-1081001	0868	3
DUTTON RALPH A	COL	O-0229142	0859	1
DUTTON SHELLEY E	COL	O-0191490	0659	3
DUTZ DEWITT C	COL	O-0243753	0660	3
DUVA EDWARD A	MAJ	O-0347724	1165	3
DUVA NICHOLAS	LTC	O-1693855	0966	1
DUVAL CLAIBORNE	COL	O-0156771	1153	3
DUVAL CLAUDE	MAJ	O-0505746	0949	1
DUVAL ROBERT G	CPT	O-0986863	1060	1
DUVALL CHARLES T	MAJ	O-1644282	0160	1
DUVALL RUFUS G	1LT	O-2010372	0951	2
DUVALLY JOSEPH B	CW2	W-2212929	0368	1
DUVEL ALBERT W	LTC	O-0214639	0763	3
DUVOS LOUIS C	MAJ	O-1288874	0762	1

NAME	GRADE	SVC NO	DATE RET MO YR	RET CODE
DUXBURY MAYNARD C	MAJ	O-0213082	1145	2
DUYSEN CARL D	MAJ	O-1577122	0454	1
DUZAN JAMES T	CW4	W-2117228	0962	1
DVOJACKY SYLVIA	1LT	N-0757058	0246	1
DVORAK ANTON E	CW3	W-2131794	1061	1
DVORSHAK ALVIN F	CW4	W-2102863	1056	1
DWIGHT FRANCIS M	MAJ	O-0138733	0956	3
DWIRE REGINALD B	LTC	O-0506469	0163	1
DWORAK ARTHUR F	MAJ	O-0246636	1265	3
DWORK KERMIT G	MAJ	O-1690709	0646	2
DWORKIN MAX M	CPT	O-0335240	1044	2
DWORKIN SAUL	CPT	O-0344944	1045	2
DWYER ELMER W	1LT	O-0220787	0865	3
DWYER FRANK A JR	COL	O-0079806	0568	1
DWYER FRANK H	LTC	O-1306571	0662	1
DWYER FREDERICK	CPT	O-0246774	0454	1
DWYER GERARD F	2LT	O-2043052	0445	2
DWYER GUSTAVE R	CPT	O-0917432	0847	2
DWYER HARRY S	MAJ	O-0146397	0745	2
DWYER JAMES E JR	MAJ	O-1062581	0465	1
DWYER JAMES J	MAJ	O-1320445	0159	1
DWYER JAMES J JR	MAJ	O-2000843	1162	1
DWYER JAMES P	1LT	O-1546034	0445	2
DWYER JEREMIAH H	LTC	O-0552700	1266	1
DWYER JOHN P	MAJ	O-1546767	0854	1
DWYER JOSEPH F	COL	O-0348199	0546	[illegible]
DWYER JOSEPH J	1LT	O-1315672	0346	2
DWYER JOSEPH P	CPT	O-0239650	0551	3
DWYER KENNETH J	MAJ	O-2014491	0464	1
DWYER LEO X	1LT	O-1599808	0146	2
DWYER RAYMOND F	MAJ	O-1116997	0261	1
DWYER VICTOR H	CW2	W-2209996	0865	1
DWYER WAYNE F	LTC	O-1149937	0161	1
DWYER WILLIAM J	LTC	O-1311086	0461	1
DWYER WILLIAM J	WO1	W-2128442	0146	2
DWYER WILLIAM R	LTC	O-0344931	0747	1
DYAKON MICHAEL	1LT	O-1822251	1145	2
DYAR LLOYD W	CPT	O-0967242	1061	1
DYAS JAMES H	CPT	O-0984426	0461	2
DYCUS JOHN E	CW2	W-2005555	0765	3
DYDEK FRANCIS J	MAJ	O-0974727	0567	1
DYE DALE H	LTC	O-1821695	0262	1
DYE DARWIN L	MAJ	O-2288699	1168	2
DYE DONALD W	COL	O-0215029	0164	3
DYE ELMER E	LTC	O-0253529	0462	3
DYE EMMETT C	MAJ	O-0152551	0857	3
DYE GEORGE F	CW3	W-2149335	1262	1
DYE HAMPTON	LTC	O-0910441	0563	3
DYE HAROLD A	CPT	O-0385491	0344	2
DYE HOMER A JR	CPT	O-0190509	0553	3
DYE ROBERT K	MAJ	O-2098650	0764	1
DYE TANNER C	LTC	O-0184212	0856	3
DYE WILLIAM F	LTC	O-0378739	0764	1
DYER ALLAN G	MAJ	O-1047104	0662	1
DYER BERNARD J	MAJ	O-1297696	1061	1
DYER EDGAR N	MAJ	O-0320350	0453	2
DYER EDYTHE M	LTC	N-0736920	0964	1
DYER ELGIN F	MAJ	O-0110642	1150	3
DYER EMMETT R	CW4	W-2118307	0553	1
DYER FRANCES G	1LT	N-0768348	0746	1
DYER GEORGE R	LTC	O-0299236	0964	3
DYER HAROLD D	LTC	O-2018494	0766	1
DYER HARRY M	CW3	W-2210047	0268	1
DYER JOHN E JR	MAJ	O-1541391	0758	1
DYER JOHN W	MAJ	O-0499286	0662	1
DYER JOSEPH A	MAJ	O-0275509	0546	1
DYER LARRY C	CW2	W-2150662	0566	2
DYER LOWELL	1LT	O-1312294	0845	2
DYER ROBERT A	MAJ	O-2262819	0665	1
DYER VERNON W	2LT	O-1540594	0347	2
DYER VOLNEY A	CPT	O-0323915	1166	3
DYER WILLIAM S	MAJ	O-2262821	0864	1
DYER WILLIS C	MAJ	O-0934560	0464	1
DYERS ORVILLE	COL	O-0419218	1045	2
DYESS CARLTON W	CW4	W-2101645	0659	1

NAME	GRADE	SVC NO	DATE RET MO YR	RET CODE
DYGERT VINCENT D	LTC	O-1302789	0562	1
DYHRMANN FRED P	COL	O-0411000	1262	2
DYKE MARTIN T	LTC	O-0114056	0945	2
DYKE THEODORE	1LT	O-0435657	0145	2
DYKE WALTER J	MAJ	O-1647412	0563	1
DYKEMA RUTH D	2LT	N-0774483	0546	1
DYKEMAN CARL F	CPT	O-0372323	0549	1
DYKEMAN DANIEL W	1LT	O-1107924	0945	2
DYKEMAN RICHARD B	CPT	O-0448346	0647	2
DYKES ALONZO JR	1LT	O-1290221	1067	3
DYKES CLAUDE B	LTC	O-1035454	1161	1
DYKES FRANKLIN B	1LT	O-0509990	0958	1
DYKES JAMES M	LTC	O-0340171	1265	3
DYKES LEONARD R	COL	O-0103934	0850	3
DYKES WALTER W JR	MAJ	O-1913396	1066	1
DYROFF EDMUND	MAJ	O-2012719	0855	1
DYROFF WILLIAM H	LTC	O-1284841	1048	2
DYSART GRADY L	WO1	W-2123178	0153	1
DYSART MAURICE S	LTC	O-0419978	0860	1
DYSART PALMER	CPT	O-0490661	0145	2
DYSON GEORGE T	MAJ	O-1703818	0557	1
DYSON JOHN D	LTC	O-0387099	0646	2
DYSON JOHN M	LTC	O-0220586	0563	3
DYSON RICHARD	COL	O-0229626	0161	3
DYSON WILLIAM A	CPT	O-2040772	0365	3
DYSTRA RAYMOND J	MAJ	O-2262534	1166	1
DZAMBA JOHN R	1LT	O-0391325	1044	2
DZIADUL ADAM C	LTC	O-2040795	0563	1
DZIADULA LOUIS	CPT	O-0488739	0251	1
DZIUK JOSEPH E	WO1	W-2118244	0648	1
DZURY OLGA	MAJ	N-0755300	0164	1
EABY WILLIAM D JR	CW3	W-2144580	0261	1
EACHUS CLIFFORD E	CW3	W-2149193	0863	1
EACHUS OLIVE H	MAJ	N-0756160	0463	1
EADDY BARBARA	1LT	N-0762588	1047	1
EADDY CARROLL M	1LT	O-0414318	0746	2
EADDY LIVINGSTON	CPT	O-0414314	0146	2
EADE CHARLES E	LTC	O-1950339	0964	1
EADES ERIC	LTC	O-0150377	0658	3
EADES OLIVER B	CW3	RW-2147192	0961	1
EADS CHILON E	CW2	W-2150737	0655	1
EADS FORREST B	MAJ	O-1013886	1160	1
EADS JACK D	CW2	W-2210481	0761	1
EADS ROBERT L	MAJ	O-0980509	0965	1
EAGAN CHARLES C	MAJ	O-0146179	0356	3
EAGAN ROBERT W	MAJ	O-1895394	1067	2
EAGER ELWOOD B	MAJ	O-1171985	0660	1
EAGER SHERMAN W	LTC	O-0119021	0648	3
EAGLE MYRON B	LTC	O-0252404	0965	3
EAGLE WILLIAM J	1LT	O-0244559	0753	3
EAGON HERBERT B	BG	O-0266977	0868	3
EAKER ARTHUR T	LTC	O-0166939	0756	3
EAKER DOYLE H	CW3	W-2141262	1262	1
EAKER LAMONT J	LTC	O-0280298	1059	3
EAKINS RAY C	MAJ	O-0577429	1060	1
EALES KEITH	1LT	O-1047952	0345	2
EALY ELFRIEDA W	CPT	N-0772226	0347	1
EAMES WILLIS H	LTC	O-0918310	0868	3
EARDLEY CATHERINE	CPT	N-0772077	0448	1
EARDLEY JOHN K	CPT	O-0253472	1044	2
EARDLEY SAMUEL	2LT	O-1306826	1045	2
EARGLE ROY E	MAJ	O-0497368	0149	1
EARHART CHARLES E	LTC	O-0334600	0146	2
EARHART DANIEL E	LTC	O-1635622	0864	1
EARHART HUGH T	CW2	W-2152843	0666	1
EARL DALE E	CW4	W-2145721	0566	1
EARL DUNCAN D	WO1	W-2108069	0161	3
EARL EDWARD L	WO1	W-2105938	0149	1
EARL JAMES R JR	MAJ	O-1119699	0962	1
EARL LLOYD B	LTC	O-0340568	0647	2
EARL N CLARKSON JR	LTC	O-0901946	0744	2
EARL ROBERT J	MAJ	O-4002899	0567	1
EARL TONY H JR	CW3	W-2151513	0766	1
EARL VINCENT D	MAJ	O-1645394	1159	1
EARL WAYNE A	MAJ	O-1550581	1157	2

NAME	GRADE	SVC NO	DATE RET MO YR	RET CODE
EARL WOODROW B	CPT	[illegible]	0466	2
EARLE FRANK H	LTC	0-0262331	0568	1
EARLE FREDERICK	WO1	W-2110744	0147	1
EARLE GEORGE W	CPT	0-0971692	1160	1
EARLE MILTON H JR	LTC	0-0181580	1266	1
EARLE PRINCE	CPT	0-1306753	0945	2
EARLE RICHARD B	LTC	0-0306106	0462	1
EARLE WALLACE H	LTC	0-0355416	0661	1
EARLE WILLIAM A	CW3	W-2208963	0567	1
EARLEY HAROLD [illegible]	LTC	0-1162406	0261	2
EARLEY JANE S	2LT	N-0731307	1144	1
EARLEY JOHN B	LTC	0-0364553	0863	1
EARLIN LOUIS	LTC	0-0180765	0656	3
EARLL THEODORE B	LTC	0-0371584	0462	1
EARLY ALBERT C	MAJ	0-1016670	0862	1
EARLY CHARLES D	1LT	0-0907544	0345	2
EARLY EDWIN Y	CPT	0-1644413	0146	2
EARLY JOHN A	COL	0-1010100	0561	1
EARLY JOHN M	1LT	0-0173141	0744	2
EARLY ROBERT	CW3	W-2122819	0261	1
EARLY STEPHEN T JR	1LT	0-1325392	1145	2
EARNEST JAMES W	CW3	W-2101647	0354	1
EARNEY CHARLES F JR	CPT	0-1000744	0658	1
EARNHEART RICHARD L	COL	0-0236903	0765	3
EARNSHAW CHARLES W	COL	0-0272543	0968	3
EARP CARLYLE R	MAJ	0-0171085	0251	3
EARP JULIAN B	CPT	0-2262755	1061	1
EARP RALPH N SR	COL	0-0213394	0563	3
EASBY JOHN P	COL	0-0177754	0855	1
EASLER CARVIN H	LTC	0-0506114	0559	1
EASLER WILBUR C	MAJ	0-1918704	0565	1
EASLEY BERNICE	MAJ	N-0761213	1164	1
EASLEY CHARLES L	LTC	0-1019774	0166	1
EASLEY DAVE L	CW3	W-2207958	0666	1
EASLEY DAVID C JR	LTC	0-0277584	0264	3
EASLEY ELDON A	MAJ	0-1185489	0657	1
EASLEY JAMES L	1LT	0-1173225	1148	2
EASLEY JAMES P	LTC	0-0138135	1048	3
EASLEY JOHN R	LTC	0-1584168	0462	1
EASLEY MARION D	CW2	W-2149277	0660	1
EASLEY PURVIS F	CW3	W-2147719	1263	1
EASLEY RAY K	LTC	0-0104303	0458	3
EASLEY ROY W	B G	0-0172501	0251	3
EASLEY SMILEY T	CW3	W-2147038	0163	1
EASON ALTON W	CW2	W-2104675	0645	2
EASON CHESLEY A	CW3	W-2146113	1161	1
EASON EARL D	WO1	W-2004350	1067	3
EASON GEORGE W	LTC	0-0363829	1060	2
EASON HENRY N	LTC	0-0223705	0543	2
EASON MILTON C	CPT	0-0289316	0966	3
EASON TALMADGE D	CPT	0-2039548	1157	1
EASON WALTER T	CPT	0-0451970	0952	2
EASSON GRAEME S	LTC	0-0200425	0655	3
EASSON WILLIAM C	COL	0-0235257	0659	3
EAST ALTON M	CPT	0-0920221	0547	2
EAST EDGAR L	CPT	0-1287159	1143	2
EAST GARLAND M	1LT	0-0166850	0855	3
EAST HERMAN M	CPT	0-0354999	0962	1
EAST PAUL G	MAJ	0-1190478	0363	1
EAST RICHARD F	COL	0-0415443	0168	1
EAST ROBERT V	CW2	W-2116818	0546	2
EAST ROLAND L	LTC	0-0397231	1160	1
EASTER CHARLES H	MAJ	0-0281203	1166	3
EASTER CARTER G	CPT	0-1309707	0555	1
EASTERDAY DAVID M	COL	0-0367790	0161	1
EASTERDAY KENNETH	MAJ	0-1684993	0765	1
EASTERDAY VANBUREN	CPT	0-0969823	0861	1
EASTERLING ALBERT C	MAJ	0-0963152	0667	3
EASTERLING CELCIS	1LT	0-1589108	0146	2
EASTERLING GEORGE R	MAJ	0-0274165	1165	3
EASTERLING MARCUS C	LTC	0-0271178	0347	2
EASTERLING ORAL B	2LT	N-0726204	0445	1
EASTERLING ROBERT Q	COL	0-1000106	0762	1
EASTERLING WALTER O	LTC	0-1702201	0146	2
EASTHAM COWAN C JR	LTC	0-1330529	0267	1
EASTHAM RAMON G	CPT	0-1342067	1160	1
EASTHAM WILLIAM B	CW2	W-2144132	0552	2
EASTIN VERNON K	LTC	0-1010007	0461	1
EASTLAND FREDERIC R	LTC	0-0282899	0262	3
EASTLAND GEORGE A	CPT	0-0977628	0162	1
EASTLAND WALTON E	CW2	W-2105888	0648	1
EASTMAN ALBERT E	MAJ	0-1178773	0764	1
EASTMAN ARTHUR F	CPT	0-0192431	0263	3
EASTMAN CHARLES A	MAJ	0-1334988	1059	1
EASTMAN CYRUS O	LTC	0-0300775	0766	3
EASTMAN ERIC I	LTC	0-0402052	0361	1
EASTMAN GORDON E	CW3	W-2149289	0663	1
EASTMAN JAMES M	CW2	W-2144103	0958	1
EASTMAN ORAN S	MAJ	0-1685701	0663	1
EASTMAN RAY	MAJ	0-0500000	0354	2
EASTMAN RUSSELL V	COL	0-0174251	0258	3
EASTMAN SEELEY H	LTC	0-1055273	0167	1
EASTMAN WALTER F	1LT	0-1293933	0246	2
EASTMAN WILLIAM A JR	1LT	0-1325588	0246	2
EASTMAN WILLIAM E	MAJ	0-0494552	0347	2
EASTMEAD JOSEPH H	MAJ	0-2294697	0663	1
EASTON GEORGE D	MAJ	0-1876400	0867	1
EASTON JANE M	CPT	N-0722371	0646	1
EASTON JOHN V	LTC	0-0274143	1167	3
EASTON JOHN W	COL	0-0225721	0664	3
EASTON MYRON N	1LT	0-1166474	1055	1
EASTON OSCAR E JR	LTC	0-1587942	1061	1
EASTON RALPH L	MAJ	0-1011148	0462	1
EASTON WALTER J	COL	0-0308641	0357	3
EASTRIDGE BENJAMIN R	CPT	0-1321759	0147	2
EASTWOLD JOHN D	MAJ	0-0154115	0347	2
EASTWOOD FRANCIS J	MAJ	0-1543939	0964	1
EASTWOOD HENRY C	1LT	0-1822546	0847	2
EATIN LOUIS	MAJ	0-1578427	0768	3
EATON ALLEN L	CW3	W-2152339	0563	1
EATON ARTHUR F	MAJ	0-5301957	0268	2
EATON GEORGE E	COL	0-0323370	1153	1
EATON GEORGE S	1LT	0-1541353	0245	2
EATON GEORGE W JR	CW2	W-2143157	0860	1
EATON HARRY E	COL	0-0365921	0864	1
EATON HARVEY D JR	LTC	0-0188315	1152	3
EATON HOMER O JR	M G	0-0201691	0862	3
EATON HUGH M	MAJ	0-1011030	0660	1
EATON JACK	LTC	0-1581678	0457	1
EATON JAMES A	MAJ	0-1642029	1058	2
EATON JAMES W	LTC	0-0464222	0154	1
EATON JOSEPH S	LTC	0-0321974	0168	3
EATON LINDSEY F	LTC	0-0452200	0361	1
EATON MILDRED C	1LT	L-0909135	0645	2
EATON PETER J	LTC	0-1285027	1060	1
EATON RICHARD E	LTC	0-0394783	0461	1
EATON RICHARD J	LTC	0-0165737	0351	3
EATON RICHARD O	LTC	0-0309077	0967	3
EATON ROBERT L	CW3	W-2143409	0659	1
EATON WALTER J	MAJ	0-0223422	0353	3
EATON WILFRED P	COL	0-0273289	0268	3
EATON WILLIAM M	CW2	W-2105998	0345	2
EAVENSON JOHN H	WO1	W-2109883	1045	2
EAVES LLOYD L	CW2	W-2152948	0360	1
EAVES ROBBY M	MAJ	0-1642030	1058	1
EAVEY HARRY B	CW3	W-2143504	0566	1
EAZARSKY THOMAS E	LTC	0-0980629	0563	1
EBAUGH DONALD O	CW2	W-2148315	1060	1
EBAUGH PAUL L JR	1LT	0-1061944	1145	2
EBBECKE GEORGE V	CPT	0-1303074	0259	1
EBBELER PAUL O	CPT	0-0349910	1065	3
EBBERT CARL S	1LT	0-1080850	0458	1
EBBERT CHARLES A	MAJ	0-0304035	0452	2
EBBITT JOSEPH M	COL	0-1002207	0765	1
EBECK CHARLES F	MAJ	0-1052334	0661	2
EBEL ALFRED	COL	0-0361048	0567	3
EBEL HENRY N	MAJ	0-1081699	0463	1
EBELING JAMES C	MAJ	0-0495916	0657	1
EBER LESSER	1LT	0-2040936	1045	2
EBERHARD CLARENCE J	CW4	W-2123199	0356	1
EBERHARD JOHN L	MAJ	0-0979241	0662	1
EBERHARDT DONALD L	MAJ	0-2030505	0468	1
EBERHARDT ELMER L B	MAJ	0-0111332	0753	3
EBERHARDT HARRY G	MAJ	0-1311748	0461	1
EBERHARDT HIRAM C JR	MAJ	0-1301122	0961	1
EBERHARDT JOHN J	MAJ	0-1284842	0949	2
EBERHARDT MARTIN W	CW3	W-2143198	0254	1
EBERHARDT ROBERT S	CW3	W-2154665	0562	1
EBERHART JOHN H	LTC	0-0194038	0756	3
EBERHART ROBERT O	1LT	0-1861886	0353	2
EBERHART VINCENT R	MAJ	0-1874711	1065	1
EBERLE HERMAN J	MAJ	0-0977258	1263	1
EBERLEIN CARL A	MAJ	0-1317153	1062	1
EBERLEIN CHARLES L	WO1	W-2127814	0645	2
EBERLEIN WILLIAM	MAJ	0-0100713	0256	3
EBERLY CHARLES W	LTC	0-1650511	0465	1
EBERLY GEORGE D	CPT	0-0323518	0445	2
EBERLY JACOB Y	MAJ	0-0201256	0153	2
EBERSOLE F LESLIE	COL	0-0275646	0446	2
EBERSOLE ROBERT P	CPT	0-0539531	0547	2
EBERSTEIN JULIUS S	COL	0-0398873	0965	3
EBERT CLAUDE S	CPT	0-0919179	0345	2
EBERT LOUIS	MAJ	0-0313214	1044	2
EBERT RALPH L	CW2	RW-2203549	0264	1
EBERT ROBERT D	2LT	0-0442724	0743	2
EBERT ROBERT V	LTC	0-2046957	0263	1
EBERT WILMA A	LTC	N-0792321	0968	1
EBERTS FRANCIS W	MAJ	0-1106111	0762	1
EBERTS RALPH T JR	1LT	0-1547283	0546	2
EBETINO MICHAEL T	LTC	0-2015426	0767	1
EBNER CHARLES F JR	CW3	W-2143136	0564	1
EBRIGHT ALBERT P	COL	0-0171377	1061	3
EBY CYRUS K	CPT	0-1920182	1164	1
EBY LOUIS R	MAJ	0-0293589	1051	3
ECCARD ALICE T	1LT	N-0755525	0845	1
ECCARD JOHN M	1LT	0-2047633	1145	2
ECCLES FRANK	COL	0-0361182	0556	1
ECCLESTON THOMAS A	LTC	0-1041337	0461	1
ECHANDI FRANCISCO	MAJ	0-1329105	1164	1
ECHOLS CHARLES L	2LT	0-1824833	0345	2
ECHOLS CLYDE F	2LT	0-1300626	0543	2
ECHOLS EUGENE S	LTC	0-0911505	1047	2
ECHOLS GEORGE P	CW2	W-2145537	0857	1
ECHOLS JOSEPH L	LTC	0-1296502	0563	1
ECHTERHOFF HARRY R	LTC	0-1699803	0446	2
ECK ELDEN	CW4	W-2001850	0966	3
ECK HERMAN JR	CPT	0-2262499	0656	1
ECK PAUL J	CW2	W-2145022	0157	1
ECK STANLEY E	1LT	0-1581679	0246	2
ECKAM ANNA L	2LT	N-0700185	0637	1
ECKARD CHESTER R	CPT	0-1031634	0346	2
ECKARD GEORGE W	MAJ	0-1645542	1060	1
ECKARDS THEODORE M	LTC	0-1042280	1162	1
ECKBERG ORVILLE E	LTC	0-1683305	1164	1
ECKBURG JOHN T	1LT	0-1292492	0847	2
ECKDALL FRANK F	LTC	0-0300585	0667	3
ECKE ROBERT S	LTC	0-0438083	0546	2
ECKELS CHARLES W	LTC	0-1645543	0268	1
ECKELS JACK C	CPT	0-0967602	0657	1
ECKENFELS WILBUR C	CPT	0-1339150	0165	2
ECKER CHARLES T	WO1	W-2101281	0844	2
ECKER FRANK A	CW4	W-2125193	0968	2
ECKER JOSEPH J JR	MAJ	0-0396854	0446	2
ECKER RAY E	LTC	0-0405162	0660	1
ECKERMAN DANIEL W	COL	0-0301414	0958	3
ECKERT ALBERT R	CW3	W-2145156	1062	1
ECKERT CHARLES J	1LT	0-1303125	0850	2
ECKERT HENRY G JR	1LT	0-0538086	1045	2
ECKERT JOHN C	LTC	0-0276371	0359	3
ECKERT RALPH G	LTC	0-1283227	0567	3
ECKERT ROBERT A	LTC	0-1115248	0264	1
ECKERT ROBERT W	1LT	0-1311381	0845	2
ECKERT THOMAS A	MAJ	0-1040213	0157	1
ECKFELDT ROGER W	M G	0-0177191	1051	3
ECKHART ARTHUR G	COL	0-0302678	1064	3
ECKHOFF EARL F	CPT	0-0490425	1053	1
ECKHOFF WILLIAM R	MAJ	0-1297176	0261	1
ECKHOUTE RENE V	CW2	W-2118027	0645	2
ECKLER JAMES A	WO1	W-2106779	0965	2
ECKLEY RALPH F	CW2	W-2207386	0761	1
ECKMAN IRVING I	CPT	0-1690580	0946	2
ECKMAN PAUL R	MAJ	0-2001672	0859	1
ECKMANN CLAUS	CW4	W-2145053	0157	1
ECKSTEIN ALBERT	LTC	0-0363481	0768	3
ECKSTEIN DELBERT C	CW3	W-2142757	0861	1
ECKSTEIN HARRY	1LT	0-0289250	0962	3
ECKSTEIN PHILIP C	CPT	0-5508488	1263	2
ECKWALL ARVID O	MAJ	0-0497367	0956	1
ECOFF ALFRED H JR	CPT	0-1184811	0747	2
ECOFF JAY M	CW3	W-2205602	0859	1
ECOFF ROBERT W	LTC	0-1284113	0657	1
ECUYER ELMER O	MAJ	0-0916753	0646	2
EDBERG HOWARD L	LTC	0-1821696	0261	1
EDDEN JAMES A	LTC	0-0524476	0658	2
EDDINGER ADOLPH G	1LT	0-0150358	0755	3
EDDY ALLEN C	CPT	0-0956691	0159	1
EDDY DAVID W	LTC	0-0322994	0353	3
EDDY EMERSON W	CPT	0-0231933	0864	3
EDDY GEORGE R	CW2	W-3100259	0562	1
EDDY GEORGE W	COL	0-1057046	1268	2
EDDY JOHN B	CPT	0-0453259	0144	2
EDDY JOHN L	COL	0-0121528	0255	3
EDDY LAURENCE W	COL	0-0162619	0560	3
EDDY LEVI C	COL	0-0198297	0647	2
EDDY MILTON A	LTC	0-1172442	0361	1
EDDY ROBERT A	MAJ	0-0262054	0356	3
EDDY ROBERT D	LTC	0-0164366	0154	3
EDDY ROGER W	MAJ	0-1291790	0946	2
EDDY SAMUEL G	COL	0-0283950	0858	1
EDDY THOMAS H	LTC	0-0243734	1053	3
EDDY WALDO O	MAJ	0-0384102	0559	1
EDDY WILLIAM H	CW2	W-3400055	1267	1
EDE ALBERT B	COL	0-0208024	0353	3
EDEBURN PAUL W	CPT	0-0256055	0654	3
EDEL ARLYEEN E	CPT	N-0756142	1046	1
EDELE FRED L	MAJ	0-0154038	1049	3
EDELEN JOSEPH F	CPT	0-1289055	0745	2
EDELEN STEPHEN W	LTC	0-1012333	1264	1
EDELL NATHAN G	CPT	0-0447353	1045	2
EDELMAN BERNARD L	CPT	0-0230306	0164	3
EDELMAN MAURICE	LTC	0-0888465	0353	1
EDELSON EDMOND K	CPT	0-0367391	0144	2
EDELSON MARSHALL	CPT	0-4073403	0961	2
EDELSTEIN LEWIS	CW4	W-2103697	0659	1
EDELSTEIN MONROE M	CPT	0-1689645	0544	2
EDENFIELD ROBERT A	MAJ	0-1288877	0747	2
EDENFIELD ROY P	LTC	0-1030466	0666	1
EDENS ELVERT M	COL	0-1114911	0365	1
EDENS ORVILL E	1LT	0-0980557	0857	1
EDER FRED M	LTC	0-0226955	1164	3
EDER HELEN M C	CPT	N-0724510	0161	2
EDER HERBERT R	LTC	0-1175697	0163	1
EDER STEVE J	1LT	0-1042553	1044	2
EDERLE WILLIAM C	WO1	W-2148647	0363	1
EDFORS HUGO W	CPT	0-1058989	0752	2
EDGAR CLIFFORD M	MAJ	0-1826379	0557	1
EDGAR FRANK M JR	LTC	0-2026501	0566	1
EDGAR GERALD N	MAJ	0-1325205	0764	1
EDGAR HAROLD L	MAJ	0-0229861	0258	3
EDGAR JACKIE F	MAJ	0-1341764	0163	1
EDGAR JOHN L	LTC	0-0481323	0767	3
EDGAR JOSEPH H	LTC	0-2051894	1167	3
EDGAR LAWRENCE E	MAJ	0-1586553	0557	1
EDGAR LYLE W	MAJ	0-0490062	1055	1
EDGAR RALPH G	LTC	0-1295692	0264	1
EDGAR RICHARD N	CPT	0-1037365	1145	2
EDGAR ROBERT C	COL	0-0258257	0759	1
EDGAR THOMAS C	MAJ	0-1011152	0147	2
EDGAR WILLIAM A	COL	0-0386408	1054	1
EDGAR WILLIAM C	LTC	0-0185149	0157	3

NAME	GRADE	SVC NO	DATE RET MO YR	RET CODE
EDGAR WILLIAM H	1LT	O-1303477	0447	2
EDGCOMB ROY H	CW4	W-2121253	0157	1
EDGE CORNELIUS	LTC	O-1060096	0967	1
EDGE JOHN B	1LT	O-1043614	0146	2
EDGE JOHN W	CPT	O-1046077	0746	2
EDGE WILLIAM N JR	2LT	O-0992531	0352	2
EDGERLY JOHN P	MAJ	O-1575940	0163	1
EDGERTON C E JR	LTC	O-0125248	1054	3
EDGERTON ERNEST B	LTC	O-0233993	1162	3
EDGERTON IRVING A	LTC	O-0360920	0464	3
EDGERTON KARL A	COL	O-0174291	0359	2
EDGEWORTH HARVEY F	CPT	O-1312894	1145	2
EDGEWORTH R H JR	MAJ	O-2024151	0157	1
EDGING BOYD P	CW2	W-2207091	0864	2
EDGINGTON DONALD W	MAJ	O-1336048	0960	1
EDGINGTON OLGA M	LTC	N-0729029	1062	1
EDGLEY ALFRED B	LTC	O-1878875	1168	1
EDGMON JON T	LTC	O-1320717	0666	1
EDGMON WARD F	1LT	O-0399975	0344	2
EDGREN ROBERT D	LTC	O-0262181	0368	3
EDHOLM LAWRENCE	LTC	O-1114466	0568	1
EDINGTON ALFRED A	COL	O-0241992	1054	1
EDINGTON FRANK G	COL	O-0283464	0768	3
EDINGTON HELEN H	MAJ	N-0802155	1065	1
EDLAVITCH MARY W	MAJ	N-0742317	0767	3
EDLESTON ROBERT W	CW3	W-2145544	0863	1
EDLIN GUY	CPT	O-1101920	0448	2
EDLUND RICHARD E	CPT	O-0947710	0863	[illegible]
EDMARK RICHARD D	LTC	O-1010163	0762	1
EDMINSTER ROBERT M	CPT	O-1113571	0660	1
EDMISTEN EDWARD E	MAJ	O-2262444	1164	1
EDMISTON EDWARD J	MAJ	O-0895700	0457	1
EDMISTON FRED W	COL	O-0225258	1044	2
EDMISTON LEWIS L	LTC	O-1101821	0866	1
EDMISTON WALTER A	LTC	O-0331569	1264	3
EDMONDS ALONZO L	LTC	O-0287104	1165	3
EDMONDS CHARLES D	LTC	O-1090728	0765	1
EDMONDS CHARLES P	LTC	O-2212079	1168	1
EDMONDS EUGENE H	MAJ	O-1331523	0663	1
EDMONDS HOWARD L	LTC	O-1541750	1164	1
EDMONDS JAMES E	M G	O-0125247	0648	3
EDMONDS N E	CW2	W-2149860	0365	1
EDMONDS RAYMOND	LTC	O-0545267	1154	1
EDMONDS ROBERT F	COL	O-0392042	0355	1
EDMONDS ROBERT F	MAJ	O-0995718	0966	1
EDMONDS WILLIAM S	2LT	O-1324249	1044	2
EDMONDSON C S H	COL	O-0216309	0258	3
EDMONDSON FRANK M	2LT	O-1321694	0744	2
EDMONDSON FRAZOR T	MAJ	O-0246884	0964	3
EDMONDSON HERBERT R	LTC	O-0273097	0868	3
EDMONDSON JOHN W	1LT	O-1547285	0964	3
EDMONSON ROBERT	MAJ	O-1824445	0561	1
EDMONSTON ALBERT E	LTC	O-1573177	0660	1
EDMONSTON ALEXANDER	COL	O-0199371	0563	3
EDMONSTON CHARLES M	MAJ	O-1106112	1157	1
EDMONSTON WEBSTER V	CW2	W-2151347	0460	2
EDMUNDS CHARLES R	CPT	O-0325976	0159	3
EDNEY CHARLES H	LTC	O-1575941	1061	1
EDRINGTON JOHN B	CW2	W-2152498	1062	1
EDRINGTON JOHN W	1LT	O-1294997	1045	2
EDRIS EDWIN N	LTC	O-0283083	1160	1
EDSALL CLARENCE A	1LT	O-1322535	1045	2
EDSALL JAMES B	MAJ	O-1323645	0461	1
EDSON CARROLL A	COL	O-0121087	1051	3
EDSON EDSON A	LTC	O-0241360	1265	3
EDSON JOHN C	MAJ	O-0191744	0263	3
EDSON MARIE L	MAJ	N-0730534	1051	1
EDSON RALPH A	LTC	O-0310987	0659	3
EDSON SAMUEL S	COL	O-0251807	0666	3
EDSON WENDELL T	COL	O-0499881	0158	1
EDSTROM VIRGIL E	CW4	W-2117160	0860	1
EDWARDES LIONEL C	MAJ	O-0445054	0550	1
EDWARDS ALBERT A	CPT	O-0266794	0855	3
EDWARDS ALEX H JR	MAJ	O-1057414	0768	3
EDWARDS ALFRED C	LTC	O-0341618	0765	1

NAME	GRADE	SVC NO	DATE RET MO YR	RET CODE
EDWARDS ALFRED H	2LT	O-2003970	0254	2
EDWARDS ALLEN	MAJ	O-1336896	1161	1
EDWARDS ALMON J JR	CW4	W-2147013	0268	1
EDWARDS ALTON B	CPT	O-0482771	0146	2
EDWARDS AROL L	MAJ	O-2027287	0861	1
EDWARDS AULDON G	1LT	O-1305745	0146	2
EDWARDS BARNEY H	MAJ	O-0203568	0247	2
EDWARDS CHARLES F	CPT	O-1294109	0346	2
EDWARDS CHARLES H	COL	O-0182236	1057	3
EDWARDS CLARENCE	CW2	W-2151875	0761	1
EDWARDS CLARENCE W	MAJ	O-1304510	0261	1
EDWARDS CLARK	LTC	O-0467279	0862	1
EDWARDS CLIFFORD R	CW2	W-2206295	0365	1
EDWARDS CYRUS L	MAJ	O-0216718	0360	3
EDWARDS DAN M	1LT	O-0518824	0445	2
EDWARDS DAN T	LTC	O-0299305	0868	3
EDWARDS DAVE W	MAJ	O-1047106	0861	1
EDWARDS DENNIS W A	LTC	O-1180480	0854	1
EDWARDS EDWARD C	1LT	O-1289226	0944	2
EDWARDS EDWIN A	CW4	W-2114941	0360	1
EDWARDS ELMER W	LTC	O-1697883	1160	1
EDWARDS ELZIE F	1LT	O-1547597	0346	2
EDWARDS ERNEST A	MAJ	O-1032753	1161	1
EDWARDS ERNEST E	MAJ	O-0496864	0154	1
EDWARDS ERNEST P	COL	O-0261396	0754	1
EDWARDS F D JR	1LT	O-1172443	0246	2
EDWARDS FORREST W	COL	O-0290775	0953	3
EDWARDS FRANCIS R	MAJ	O-0246939	0847	2
EDWARDS FRANK J	CW3	W-2150723	0662	1
EDWARDS GEORGE A	CW4	W-2108157	0659	1
EDWARDS GEORGE F	MAJ	O-1549179	0859	1
EDWARDS GEORGE N	LTC	O-1588540	1264	1
EDWARDS GEORGE W	CW3	W-2152208	0468	3
EDWARDS GEORGE W JR	CPT	O-1289403	0748	2
EDWARDS GILBERT H	LTC	O-0229998	0264	3
EDWARDS GUY D	LTC	O-0222593	0948	3
EDWARDS HAROLD A	CW2	W-2147971	0160	1
EDWARDS HARRY A	LTC	O-0265277	0365	3
EDWARDS HELENE R	2LT	N-0755650	0845	1
EDWARDS HUGH F	CPT	O-0449155	0145	2
EDWARDS HUGH J	LTC	O-0405902	0660	1
EDWARDS J R	LTC	O-0452881	0364	1
EDWARDS JACK D	MAJ	O-2263196	0662	1
EDWARDS JACK G	CW3	W-2145105	0762	1
EDWARDS JAMES B	CW4	W-2142699	0168	1
EDWARDS JAMES E	CPT	O-1822781	1060	1
EDWARDS JAMES H	1LT	O-1292853	0546	2
EDWARDS JAMES H	CPT	O-2000739	0457	1
EDWARDS JAMES H JR	LTC	O-1944673	1161	1
EDWARDS JAMES R JR	CW2	W-2203527	0963	1
EDWARDS JAMES S JR	MAJ	O-0371222	1045	2
EDWARDS JAMES T	CW4	W-2003032	1068	1
EDWARDS JAMES W	CW3	RW-2152035	0265	1
EDWARDS JANE B	1LT	N-0755951	0945	1
EDWARDS JESSE W	1LT	O-1107401	0645	2
EDWARDS JOE F	CPT	O-2000946	0666	1
EDWARDS JOEL H	CW4	W-2113510	0760	1
EDWARDS JOHN G	COL	O-0155358	0953	1
EDWARDS JOHN H	MAJ	O-0403545	0646	2
EDWARDS JOHN W	MAJ	O-1286457	0859	1
EDWARDS JOHNSON P	COL	O-0235024	0661	3
EDWARDS KENNETH J JR	LTC	O-0519254	0666	1
EDWARDS KENNETH R	CPT	O-0504547	0547	2
EDWARDS L ROBERT J	COL	O-0199541	1150	3
EDWARDS LAWRENCE	MAJ	O-4031054	0568	1
EDWARDS LEGRONDE	LTC	O-1109265	0662	1
EDWARDS LELAND W	MAJ	O-2014580	1264	1
EDWARDS LEON F	CW3	W-2143214	0861	1
EDWARDS LOUIE F	MAJ	O-1877835	1267	1
EDWARDS MANLEY W	CPT	O-0228344	1165	3
EDWARDS MARIAN R G	2LT	N-0755954	1044	1
EDWARDS MILES C	CW4	W-2141264	1268	1
EDWARDS NORMAN	MAJ	O-2263158	1162	1
EDWARDS NORMAN B	M G	O-0019936	0168	1
EDWARDS NORMAN E	COL	O-0246054	0953	3

NAME	GRADE	SVC NO	DATE RET MO YR	RET CODE
EDWARDS OOIS J	CW2	W-2147156	0357	1
EDWARDS OLLIE W	1LT	O-2212000	0958	1
EDWARDS PAUL L	LTC	O-0485120	0665	1
EDWARDS PERCY B	CW2	W-2143716	0861	1
EDWARDS POMEROY	1LT	O-0124899	0553	3
EDWARDS RALPH P	LTC	O-0241471	1057	3
EDWARDS REESE E	MAJ	O-1103615	1061	1
EDWARDS REXFORD C	CPT	O-0253300	0145	2
EDWARDS RICHARD R	CPT	O-0965600	0359	1
EDWARDS ROBERT A	MAJ	O-1342256	0862	1
EDWARDS ROBERT O SR	CW3	W-2203885	0767	1
EDWARDS ROBERT P	COL	O-0439491	0167	3
EDWARDS ROBERT W	COL	O-1308618	0867	1
EDWARDS ROY W	LTC	O-1114467	1262	1
EDWARDS SHERWOOD C	MAJ	O-0259998	0946	2
EDWARDS SMITH	LTC	O-1100964	0663	1
EDWARDS SOLOMON C	LTC	O-0257656	1062	1
EDWARDS STANLEY	COL	O-0197962	0355	3
EDWARDS T M JR	CPT	O-1106704	1045	2
EDWARDS THOMAS L	LTC	O-0243038	1059	3
EDWARDS THOMAS M	CPT	O-0369292	0543	2
EDWARDS THOMAS W	CPT	O-0239340	1045	2
EDWARDS W G M	LTC	O-1845710	1158	3
EDWARDS WALTER C	CW4	W-2114217	1160	1
EDWARDS WALTER R	CPT	O-1797800	0763	1
EDWARDS WALTON L	LTC	O-1178775	0363	1
EDWARDS WARREN C	1LT	O-1300627	0646	2
EDWARDS WILBUR P SR	MAJ	O-1341765	0662	1
EDWARDS WILLIAM A	LTC	O-0271015	0563	3
EDWARDS WILLIAM A	LTC	O-0351514	0758	1
EDWARDS WILLIAM H	MAJ	O-0242969	0963	3
EDWARDS WILLIAM R	CW3	W-2143430	0956	1
EDWARDS WILLIAM W	LTC	O-1293568	0465	1
EDWARDS WOODROW W	WO1	W-2132077	0656	1
EELLS EARNEST E	LTC	O-0156250	1152	3
EFFINGER VICTOR W	MAJ	O-1536401	0962	1
EFFORD JOHN T	COL	O-0301202	1063	3
EFFROS DAVID V	CPT	O-0332871	0645	2
EFFRON MORTON	CPT	O-0424504	0246	2
EGAL HENRY J	LTC	O-1549932	0164	1
EGALKA MORRIS	CPT	O-1705270	0646	2
EGAN DONALD H	LTC	O-0388466	0761	1
EGAN EDWARD C	LTC	O-0299653	0958	3
EGAN EDWARD J	CPT	O-0531550	0645	2
EGAN ELIZABETH	1LT	N-0724357	1045	1
EGAN HORACE F JR	LTC	O-0310937	1052	1
EGAN JAMES D	CPT	O-1926835	1146	2
EGAN JAMES J	LTC	O-0413625	0363	3
EGAN JAMES J	MAJ	O-1846421	0963	1
EGAN JOHN J	MAJ	O-1597422	1068	3
EGAN THOMAS J	CPT	O-0359133	0947	1
EGBERT CLARENCE H	1LT	O-0435198	1045	2
EGBERT HAROLD S	LTC	O-1344674	0655	1
EGBERT HENRY D	MAJ	O-0409000	0547	2
EGBERT WALTER W	LTC	O-2042953	0564	1
EGDAHL LAWRENCE R	LTC	O-0298601	0963	3
EGELER IVAN P	LTC	O-1578417	0962	1
EGERER EDMONT A	MAJ	O-0102457	0545	2
EGERT CHESTER W	MAJ	O-0517333	1055	2
EGGAN FREDERICK	LTC	O-1950341	1156	1
EGGEN JOHN W	CW3	W-2204977	0266	1
EGGEN KARL M	COL	O-0263365	0466	3
EGGEN MILTON P	MAJ	O-0478754	0549	1
EGGER ALPHONSE J	LTC	O-1102714	0465	1
EGGERMAN WENDELL F	LTC	O-1525623	0865	1
EGGERS JULES H	CPT	O-1577127	1149	1
EGGERS RUTH H	CPT	N-0900079	0358	2
EGGERT ARTHUR P	CW2	W-3430161	0163	1
EGGERT HOWARD L	2LT	O-1323313	1144	2
EGGERT JAY P	1LT	O-1035752	1145	2
EGGIMAN FRED	CPT	O-0496790	0948	1
EGGIMANN EMIL L	COL	O-0451536	1065	1
EGGLER ALVIN F	CPT	O-1846278	0546	2
EGGLESTON ANNA L	1LT	N-0761926	0946	1
EGGLESTON GEORGE L	LTC	O-0181476	0462	3

NAME	GRADE	SVC NO	DATE RET MO YR	RET CODE
EGGLESTON HERBERT C	MAJ	O-0181429	0154	3
EGGLESTON HOMER L	CW4	W-2123030	1062	1
EGGLESTON KENNETH L	LTC	O-1325637	1267	1
EGGLESTON ROBERT T	LTC	O-0318098	0363	3
EGGLETON LEO J	CPT	O-0147202	0842	2
EGGUM DONALD J	MAJ	O-0975062	0365	1
EGLESTON NATHANIEL	B G	O-0242017	0648	3
EGLOFF GEORGE J	CPT	O-0465012	0754	1
EGNER RAYMOND A	COL	O-0256064	0958	3
EGOLF OSCAR T	LTC	O-0299504	0468	3
EHARDT HENRY	CPT	O-2036424	0851	1
EHINGER JOHN	COL	O-0169673	0750	3
EHLEN GEORGE H	2LT	O-0397179	0742	2
EHLENFELDT VERNON B	MAJ	O-0974091	0165	1
EHLER ERNEST W	LTC	O-0972975	0765	1
EHLER PAUL	CW2	W-2211946	0368	1
EHLERS ANTOINETTE	2LT	N-0724062	0145	2
EHLERS EDWARD C	MAJ	O-1799944	1061	1
EHLERS HARRY C	LTC	O-0452016	0361	1
EHLERS WALDO H	LTC	O-0248205	0962	3
EHLERT CHARLES O	COL	O-0309902	0566	3
EHLERT RAYMOND A	1LT	O-1304880	0446	2
EHLIN WILLIAM	2LT	O-1288878	0944	2
EHMKE ROBERT C	MAJ	O-1589809	0863	1
EHMSEN WALTER C	CW2	W-2151693	0861	1
EHNI JACOB	CPT	O-2010984	0755	1
EHREN ELMER A	1LT	O-0372987	0144	2
EHREN JOHN A	LTC	O-0193599	0959	3
EHRENBURG OTTO	LTC	O-0284154	1266	3
EHRESMANN STANLEY S	LTC	O-0450835	0756	1
EHRET DONALD M	WO1	W-2114617	0244	2
EHRET LESTER A	MAJ	O-0968140	0557	2
EHRGOTT WINSTON W	LTC	O-0241647	1061	3
EHRHARDT MARTIN W	CW3	W-2152995	0665	1
EHRHART EUGENE J	COL	O-0506966	0664	3
EHRHART GEORGE H	1LT	O-5338814	0968	2
EHRLICH DAVID	LTC	O-0324925	0460	1
EHRLICH DAVID H	COL	O-0286676	1068	3
EHRLICH GERALD	2LT	O-1329582	0645	2
EHRLICH HERMAN	MAJ	O-1689639	1145	2
EHRLICH MILTON	M G	O-0293592	0868	3
EHRMANN CHARLES H	LTC	O-1107928	1162	1
EHRSAM HARLEY A	2LT	O-0918407	1143	2
EHRSTEIN MARY B	1LT	N-0758136	0248	1
EIBER HAROLD P	MAJ	O-0492670	0246	2
EICHBAUM JOSEPH H	CPT	O-1647865	0947	2
EICHELBERGER JOHN C	CPT	O-1582679	0460	1
EICHELBERGER R A	MAJ	O-1584175	1060	1
EICHEN MARVIN A	1LT	O-1012343	0845	2
EICHENBERG HERMANN R	COL	O-0276982	0864	3
EICHENBERGER EARL R	LTC	O-0949748	0167	1
EICHENBERGER GENE R	2LT	O-0393746	0143	2
EICHER GLEN O	LTC	O-0971732	0568	1
EICHERS ARMUND J	CW2	W-2214554	0867	1
EICHHOLTZ VERNER F	LTC	O-0300236	0147	2
EICHHORN ADRIAN A	MAJ	O-1020405	0463	1
EICHHORN DAVID M	LTC	O-0482124	0266	3
EICHHORN LEROY A	CW2	W-2152157	0161	1
EICHINGER JACK W JR	COL	O-0226940	1064	3
EICHLER ARTHUR L	LTC	O-0348515	1165	3
EICHLER THOMAS C	LTC	O-0352744	0461	1
EICHLING ROBERT E	MAJ	O-1925218	0161	1
EICHORN RUDOLPH W	LTC	O-1169500	0566	1
EICKENHORST WALTER E	CW2	W-2101053	1146	2
EICKHOFF DAVID L	LTC	O-1053122	1062	1
EICKHOFF FREDERICK	MAJ	O-1010490	1047	2
EIDEM HERMAN P	LTC	O-2208585	0268	1
EIDMAN ARTHUR JR	2LT	O-1323675	1045	2
EIDY ADAM	MAJ	O-1058890	0360	1
EIFERT EUGENE C	2LT	O-1594816	0844	2
EIFERT SYLVESTER	LTC	O-0331799	0954	1
EIFFERT CECIL H	MAJ	O-0335310	1045	2
EIFLER CARL F	COL	O-0288691	0947	2
EIGABROADT EARL E	CPT	O-0970153	0161	1
EIGELBACH RICHARD B	LTC	O-0308437	0355	1

NAME	GRADE	SVC NO	DATE RET MO YR	RET CODE
EISNER EMMETT H	CW2	W-2145346	0660	1
EISNER ARTHUR F	1LT	0-1032771	0446	2
EISENBERRY ROBERT W	CPT	0-1209479	0959	2
EISENBERRY RUDOLPH L	COL	0-0255432	1165	3
EILAND LEVY F JR	MAJ	0-0944397	1064	1
EILERS DONALD E	MAJ	0-1037494	1059	1
EILERS BALDWIN E	LTC	0-0212601	0462	3
EILERT CHARLES T	LTC	0-1593390	1061	2
EILERT WILLIAM J	LTC	0-0337237	0846	2
EILERTSEN JOHN [illegible]	LTC	0-0158346	0648	3
EIMERMAN [illegible] J	CPT	N-0741361	1146	1
EIMERS JAY R	MAJ	0-1845562	1146	2
EINBECK ARTHUR H	CPT	0-0163711	0959	3
EINBECK AUGUST C	LTC	0-0337934	0661	1
EINHALT CARL R	LTC	0-0244157	0465	3
EININGER ROBERT K JR	LTC	0-0254619	0465	3
EINSTEIN ALFRED	2LT	0-1307213	0544	2
EINKNECHT IRA S	2LT	0-0131273	0361	1
EISEL JOSEPH B	MAJ	0-0243378	0663	3
EISELE EDWARD J	LTC	0-0277427	0247	2
EISELE PAUL L	LTC	0-0331241	0962	3
EISELT AUDREY A	1LT	N-0731587	0448	1
EISEN IRWIN H	MAJ	0-1545341	0765	1
EISEN JACOB	LTC	0-0290247	0261	3
EISEN JAY E	LTC	0-1799508	1165	1
EISEN NANCY J	MAJ	N-0757175	0866	1
EISENBARTH WILLIAM F	CW2	W-2122843	1059	1
EISENBERG BEN C	MAJ	0-0302558	0646	2
EISENBERG DAVID S	LTC	0-0303932	1167	3
EISENBERG ELI	CPT	0-1690553	0246	2
EISENBERG NATHAN P	CPT	0-0331741	1045	2
EISENBERG RANKIN H	CPT	0-1298842	1047	2
EISENBERG SOL	2LT	0-1691751	0545	2
EISENBERG STUART J	1LT	0-0441864	0645	2
EISENBERGER ROBERT R	CPT	0-2032974	0759	1
EISENHART MARION S	LTC	0-1298517	0361	1
EISENHAUER ADAM J	LTC	0-0393429	1159	1
EISENHAUER BOIES J	LTC	0-1642034	1062	1
EISENHAUER JOHN H	CPT	0-0490171	0148	2
EISENHAUER ROBERT F	LTC	0-1950159	0763	1
EISENHOWER FRANK L	CPT	0-1111677	0148	2
EISENHOWER ROY F	CW2	RW-2207262	0762	1
EISENHUT JOHN	1LT	0-1301123	0145	2
EISENMAN FRANCIS J	MAJ	0-0175077	0623	1
EISENSMITH ISADORE [illegible]	MAJ	0-1597230	1262	1
EISENSTAEDT WERNER F	COL	0-0430258	0667	1
EISENSTARK JULIUS	1LT	0-0541256	0945	2
EISENSTEIN EDWARD	CPT	0-1684332	0545	2
EISFELLER ROBERT C	CPT	0-0502571	0946	1
EISMAN SAMUEL N	CPT	0-1342327	1159	1
EISON FREDERIC J	LTC	0-0260342	0846	2
EISON ROY P	CPT	0-0294592	1045	2
EISS FRANK J	CPT	0-1166477	0745	2
EISSNER HARRY C	CPT	0-1035754	0750	2
EKBLAD EUGENE H	LTC	0-1001125	0960	1
EKDAHL SIGURD	LTC	0-0150658	0648	3
EKE REGINALD	1LT	0-1633012	0846	1
EKLUND CARL W	MAJ	0-0420300	0867	3
EKMAN GEORGE A	1LT	0-0176341	1043	1
EKONEN RALPH C	MAJ	0-2287022	0968	1
EKROT EDWIN H	1LT	0-1245221	0951	1
EKSTRAND LOYD J	MAJ	0-1109269	0763	1
EKSTROM ALTON C	MAJ	0-1173594	0959	1
ELA CLAYTON M	LTC	0-0237542	1057	1
ELAM CHARLES R JR	LTC	0-0270024	0461	1
ELAM EDWARD F	MAJ	0-1923584	0664	1
ELAM HARRY M	LTC	0-1325206	0966	1
ELAN MORRIS	1LT	0-1042556	0944	2
ELBEL JAMES A	MAJ	0-1595998	0262	1
ELBRADER WILLIAM C	LTC	0-0403591	0665	1
ELD VINCENT P	MAJ	0-1173936	1062	1
ELDEN HAROLD	LTC	0-0266779	0468	3
ELDER ARCHIBALD	LTC	0-0354205	1160	1
ELDER EARL F	MAJ	0-2263242	0765	1
ELDER FRANCIS B	COL	0-0353740	0566	3
ELDER FRANK R	LTC	0-0473230	0157	1
ELDER HAROLD H	LTC	0-0277428	0164	3
ELDER HUBERT B	COL	0-0213721	0761	3
ELDER MILES M	MAJ	0-0221340	1151	3
ELDER NEIL M	LTC	0-0392498	0264	1
ELDER RALPH E	CW2	W-2152491	0761	1
ELDER RAYMOND W	LTC	0-1548202	0368	1
ELDER ROBERT P	1LT	0-1535636	0347	2
ELDER RUFUS H	LTC	0-0228699	1161	3
ELDER SMITH L	LTC	0-0405834	0650	1
ELDER THOMAS C	LTC	0-0302482	0162	3
ELDER THOMAS H	CW3	W-2148690	0164	1
ELDER THOMAS J	COL	0-0295041	0166	1
ELDER WILLIAM H	CW4	W-2152070	0868	1
ELDER 3RD GEORGE W	1LT	0-0546703	0550	2
ELDERDICE HUGH L	COL	0-0124901	1055	3
ELDERS JAMES F	1LT	0-0508034	0746	1
ELDRACHER JOSEPH J	MAJ	0-0977385	0962	1
ELDRED ARTHUR C	LTC	0-0294189	0167	3
ELDRED PERCY D	LTC	0-0240556	0763	3
ELDRED ROBERT C	CPT	0-1174566	0246	2
ELDREDGE CHARLES J	1LT	0-1284115	0446	2
ELDREDGE JAMES C	CW2	W-2101656	1046	1
ELDRIDGE ALBERT C	MAJ	0-1861665	0763	1
ELDRIDGE ALLAN F	LTC	0-0308652	0660	3
ELDRIDGE BRUCE S	LTC	0-0353810	0562	1
ELDRIDGE DAVID H	LTC	0-0480875	0668	3
ELDRIDGE EMORY M	CPT	0-1996552	0556	1
ELDRIDGE ERNEST B	MAJ	0-0175922	0246	2
ELDRIDGE GEORGE B	CPT	0-1303693	0155	2
ELDRIDGE HARRY F	LTC	0-0176311	0157	3
ELDRIDGE IRVING C	MAJ	0-0237734	0562	3
ELDRIDGE JAMES C	2LT	0-1913674	1130	1
ELDRIDGE LEO B	2LT	0-2262988	0852	2
ELDRIDGE WILLIE J	2LT	0-0426911	1143	2
ELERICK KERN	CPT	0-0290317	1044	2
ELEVELD SIDNEY Z	COL	0-0185895	0648	3
ELFERT BERNARD G	LTC	0-2204106	0966	1
ELGART JACOB M	LTC	0-1553990	1067	3
ELGIN CARL C	LTC	0-1314115	0263	1
ELGIN JAMES C	CPT	0-0381367	0645	2
ELGIN LOREN M	MAJ	0-0574973	0763	1
ELIA VIRGINIA P	LTC	N-0728407	1168	1
ELIAS CYRIL C	2LT	0-0901511	0246	2
ELIAS ELMER J	MAJ	0-0250382	1164	3
ELIAS GEORGE A	MAJ	0-1308316	0558	1
ELIAS MICHAEL A	LTC	0-1593970	0867	1
ELIAS MIGUEL G	MAJ	0-0492508	1043	2
ELIASON EVERETT J	LTC	0-0177696	0461	3
ELIASON NEWEL G	LTC	0-0270910	0968	3
ELIASSEN EVERETT D	CPT	0-1306255	0947	2
ELIASSON HILDA E	MAJ	N-0738047	0867	3
ELIOT JOHN A	MAJ	0-0272618	1044	2
ELK KENNETH M	MAJ	0-1642832	0166	1
ELKIN RAYMOND F	COL	0-0113551	0552	3
ELKIND MURRAY C	MAJ	0-1176323	0968	3
ELKINS ESTEL	LTC	0-1284484	0164	2
ELKINS JAMES W	1LT	0-1920286	0658	2
ELKINS OSCAR M	LTC	0-0231407	0463	3
ELKINS THEODORE O	CW3	W-2142758	1162	1
ELKINS VERNON E	CPT	0-1691494	0954	1
ELKINS WALTER E	MAJ	0-1923540	0868	1
ELLARD GEORGE E	MAJ	0-0235250	0958	3
ELLAS RICHARD G	LTC	0-0966082	0968	1
ELLE KURT D	CW4	W-2136619	0263	1
ELLEDGE DANIEL W	LTC	0-0972900	0368	1
ELLEDGE EDWIN L	LTC	0-0967565	0668	1
ELLEDGE ELDON W	MAJ	0-0473382	0347	1
ELLEDGE EPHRAIM H	CW2	W-2148254	0555	1
ELLEDGE GEORGE R	MAJ	0-0501631	0359	2
ELLEDGE HORACE C	CW2	W-2149943	0361	1
ELLEDGE JOHN A	LTC	0-1042282	0566	1
ELLENBAST HENRY L	CW4	W-2111468	0266	2
ELLENBERGER DAVID T	CW2	W-2211088	0165	1
ELLENBERGER WILLIAM	COL	0-0335517	0268	3
ELLENBURG CHARLES I	CW2	W-3151323	0267	1
ELLENBURG ROBERT F	MAJ	0-0519725	1151	2
ELLER CLEMIN J	CW3	W-2145559	0460	1
ELLER DAVID A	CW2	W-2210431	0366	1
ELLER EDMUND P	1LT	0-1322776	0946	2
ELLER ELBERT H	LTC	0-0391352	0361	1
ELLER FLOYD E	COL	0-0186660	0953	3
ELLER HERMAN H	WO1	W-2121157	1049	1
ELLER JOHN H	LTC	0-1038602	0963	1
ELLERBE CONGRESS W	MAJ	0-1164073	0346	2
ELLERBE HENRY I	COL	0-0150789	0144	2
ELLERBE THOMAS H	LTC	0-0471425	0257	1
ELLERY ARTHUR D	1LT	0-0467264	0845	2
ELLETT ASA	CW2	W-3150646	0264	2
ELLETT HOMER C	MAJ	0-0438887	0662	1
ELLEY CHARLES R	CPT	0-2208460	0567	1
ELLIBRITT SYLVESTER	1LT	0-1287692	0346	2
ELLIGET EDWIN J	CPT	0-0377306	0744	2
ELLING CARL M	1LT	0-0354714	0146	2
ELLINGER JUNIOR J	2LT	0-1297513	0644	2
ELLINGER MAURICE R	MAJ	0-1100967	0765	1
ELLINGSWORTH C W	CW3	W-2141267	0557	1
ELLINGSWORTH WILLIAM	MAJ	0-1924131	0364	1
ELLINGTON CLAUDE	MAJ	0-0448302	1140	2
ELLINGTON GILMER	CW2	W-2210519	0165	1
ELLINGTON JOE W	LTC	0-0279133	0364	3
ELLINGTON JOHN C	WO1	W-2147579	1159	1
ELLINGTON RAPLE C	CPT	0-0339881	0146	2
ELLINGTON WILLIAM T	LTC	0-1305028	1267	1
ELLIOT CARLISLE I	LTC	0-1550586	0766	1
ELLIOT CHARLES	CW4	W-2141552	1060	1
ELLIOT CHARLES W	COL	0-0493060	1160	1
ELLIOT CHESTER S	LTC	0-0176630	0649	3
ELLIOT PAUL F	MAJ	0-1338325	0663	1
ELLIOT PERCY J	LTC	0-0220406	0656	3
ELLIOTT BASS P	1LT	0-1335406	0352	2
ELLIOTT CARL A SR	1LT	0-1305747	0944	2
ELLIOTT CARROLL W	COL	0-0224921	1163	3
ELLIOTT CECIL A	1LT	0-1285402	0444	2
ELLIOTT CLARENCE L	2LT	0-0452879	1143	2
ELLIOTT CLARENCE N	LTC	0-0885081	0551	1
ELLIOTT CLAUD	CPT	0-1318969	1166	3
ELLIOTT DALE N	CW4	W-2142545	1162	1
ELLIOTT DANIEL O	CW3	W-2147260	0863	1
ELLIOTT DAVID D	MAJ	0-0132027	0159	3
ELLIOTT DONALD C	COL	0-0451276	1068	1
ELLIOTT DONALD F	COL	0-0334000	0865	3
ELLIOTT EDWARD B	MAJ	0-0359454	0858	1
ELLIOTT EDWARD C	MAJ	0-0351586	1044	2
ELLIOTT EDWARD J	CW2	W-2151125	0856	1
ELLIOTT EDWARD M	LTC	0-0205313	1053	3
ELLIOTT EDWIN	LTC	0-0451964	0364	1
ELLIOTT ENNIS B	CPT	0-1649421	0954	1
ELLIOTT ERNEST C	LTC	0-0969409	0868	1
ELLIOTT ERNEST O	LTC	0-0268459	1052	2
ELLIOTT EWING W	COL	0-0374987	1067	3
ELLIOTT GEORGE E JR	MAJ	0-2044606	0760	1
ELLIOTT GEORGE H	MAJ	0-1999372	0857	1
ELLIOTT GEORGE W	LTC	0-0417832	0967	3
ELLIOTT GILBERT M	COL	0-0311917	0662	3
ELLIOTT GRANT R	LTC	0-0281601	0361	3
ELLIOTT HAROLD F	MAJ	0-1003721	0757	1
ELLIOTT HARRY R	1LT	0-0542333	1045	2
ELLIOTT HAYES	MAJ	0-2034607	0257	1
ELLIOTT HENRY	MAJ	0-1642036	0756	1
ELLIOTT HENRY F	2LT	0-1319695	0445	2
ELLIOTT HENRY W	CPT	0-1047473	0263	1
ELLIOTT HERBERT J	LTC	0-0368663	0466	3
ELLIOTT HOMER	CW3	W-2209941	1267	1
ELLIOTT HOMER H	COL	0-0312911	0460	3
ELLIOTT HOWARD J	MAJ	0-0320197	1159	3
ELLIOTT HOWARD P JR	MAJ	0-2034513	0861	1
ELLIOTT IVAN A	LTC	0-0118734	1149	3
ELLIOTT JACK R	MAJ	0-1100968	1060	1
ELLIOTT JAMES A	LTC	0-0268762	0866	3
ELLIOTT JAMES E	2LT	0-1106709	0544	2
ELLIOTT JAMES R	CPT	0-2027430	0948	1
ELLIOTT JIMMY I	CPT	0-2265392	0744	1
ELLIOTT JOHN A	2LT	0-1106116	0744	2
ELLIOTT JOHN C	LTC	0-0419341	0560	1
ELLIOTT JOHN F	WO1	W-2129592	1050	1
ELLIOTT JOHN P	MAJ	0-1550781	0860	1
ELLIOTT JOHN W	CPT	0-0164885	1147	2
ELLIOTT JOSEPH	CPT	0-0501284	0649	1
ELLIOTT JOSEPH	WO1	W-2122415	0748	1
ELLIOTT JULIAN C	MAJ	0-1643077	0345	2
ELLIOTT KENNETH C	MAJ	0-0355505	1163	1
ELLIOTT MAX B	2LT	0-1541507	1045	2
ELLIOTT NATHANIEL	LTC	0-0179605	0558	1
ELLIOTT NORRIS G	CW4	W-2145245	0168	1
ELLIOTT PAYTON F	1LT	0-1312295	0747	2
ELLIOTT RALPH A	COL	0-0435393	0566	3
ELLIOTT ROBERT E	CPT	0-1283744	0152	2
ELLIOTT ROBERT F	MAJ	0-2263445	0444	1
ELLIOTT ROBERT J	COL	0-1165284	0965	2
ELLIOTT RODNEY S	CPT	0-0416080	0446	2
ELLIOTT RUSSELL	CPT	0-0244995	0359	3
ELLIOTT RUTHEILEEN	1LT	N-0799388	1047	1
ELLIOTT SAM G	COL	0-0244798	1159	1
ELLIOTT SAMUEL E	1LT	0-1012689	1147	2
ELLIOTT SHELDEN O	MG	0-0519660	0766	3
ELLIOTT SIDNEY L	MAJ	0-1997211	0762	1
ELLIOTT VIRGIL H	LTC	0-0327746	0561	1
ELLIOTT WALLACE W	COL	0-0331777	0865	3
ELLIOTT WALTER F	LTC	0-1293736	1163	1
ELLIOTT WILLIAM C	LTC	0-0273960	0768	3
ELLIOTT WILLIAM E	COL	0-0254106	1165	1
ELLIOTT WILLIAM E	LTC	0-0276877	1165	3
ELLIOTT WILLIAM R	CPT	0-1580903	0759	2
ELLIS ALBERT	MAJ	0-0284303	1166	3
ELLIS ALFRED O	LTC	0-1049140	0859	1
ELLIS ALLEN J	CPT	0-1042017	0357	1
ELLIS ARTHUR A	CPT	0-0465248	0646	2
ELLIS BARRY L	CW2	W-3151829	1068	2
ELLIS BENJAMIN T	LTC	0-0351587	0365	2
ELLIS CARL F	CPT	0-1646708	0557	1
ELLIS CARLTON B	MAJ	0-0491243	0147	2
ELLIS CASSIUS M	LTC	0-0505543	1163	1
ELLIS CHARLES A	COL	0-0181368	0246	2
ELLIS CHARLES L JR	CPT	0-0328403	0545	2
ELLIS CHARLES O	CW3	W-2142759	0659	1
ELLIS CHARLES R	CPT	0-2008542	1062	1
ELLIS CLARENCE R	CPT	0-1056704	0858	1
ELLIS CLYDE L	LTC	0-0910492	0262	3
ELLIS DAN B	1LT	0-1018888	0747	2
ELLIS DAVID E	CW2	W-2151174	0159	1
ELLIS DEE R	LTC	0-0123899	0357	3
ELLIS DONALD D	2LT	0-1012831	0144	2
ELLIS EARL M	LTC	0-0248434	0355	1
ELLIS EDWARD M	2LT	0-1642833	0444	2
ELLIS FORREST W	CW2	W-2209351	0163	1
ELLIS GERALD H	LTC	0-1297514	0461	1
ELLIS GLENN A	LTC	0-0420288	0463	1
ELLIS GRENVILLE	MAJ	0-0241640	0666	3
ELLIS HARRY N	CPT	0-0964315	0160	1
ELLIS HERBERT L	CW4	W-2152844	1168	1
ELLIS HILLERY M	CW4	W-2146114	1164	1
ELLIS HUBERT H	LTC	0-1297338	0161	1
ELLIS HUGH B	MAJ	0-0257680	1044	2
ELLIS HUGH W	MAJ	0-0281900	0968	3
ELLIS JAMES V	CPT	0-1290224	0849	1
ELLIS JOHN R JR	LTC	0-0366485	0959	1
ELLIS KENNETH K	LTC	0-0227901	0264	3
ELLIS KENNETH L	LTC	0-1109914	0363	1
ELLIS LAVERNE E	MAJ	0-1634720	0158	1
ELLIS LAWRENCE W	MAJ	0-0889070	1063	1
ELLIS LEO F	LTC	0-1338326	0468	1
ELLIS LEONARD F	CW3	W-3430101	1268	1
ELLIS LEONARD G	MAJ	0-0483163	1046	2
ELLIS LEWIS C	MAJ	0-0402864	0660	1

NAME	GRADE	SVC NO	DATE RET MO YR	RET CODE
ELLIS MARCUS O	CW3	W-2152504	0864	1
ELLIS MARGUERITE	CPT	N-0751556	0549	2
ELLIS MILDRED C	2LT	N-0702444	0542	1
ELLIS MORRISS W	1LT	O-1010193	0944	2
ELLIS NATHAN W	LTC	O-0211683	1163	3
ELLIS NORMAN	CPT	O-0504714	1046	1
ELLIS NORMAN H	CW2	W-2151354	0762	1
ELLIS RAYMOND A	1LT	O-0489982	0554	1
ELLIS RICHARD T	CW3	W-2203469	1168	1
ELLIS ROBERT C	MAJ	O-0206939	0553	3
ELLIS ROBERT E	MAJ	O-0142705	1152	3
ELLIS ROGER S	LTC	O-0208006	1263	3
ELLIS RONALD F	CPT	O-1047958	0358	1
ELLIS RUBY J	1LT	N-0761572	0846	1
ELLIS RUNNELL R	LTC	O-1633830	0357	1
ELLIS THEO H	1LT	O-0367235	0245	2
ELLIS THEODORE	LTC	O-1546966	0667	1
ELLIS THURMAN L	LTC	O-0402746	0660	1
ELLIS VIRGIL	CPT	O-1341865	0766	1
ELLIS WILLIAM A	MAJ	O-1649764	0762	1
ELLIS WILLIAM H	1LT	O-1055291	0761	2
ELLIS WILLIS T	COL	O-0239642	0360	1
ELLISON ALEXANDER	COL	O-0136921	0850	3
ELLISON ALFRED M	LTC	O-0510439	0668	3
ELLISON CARROLL	CPT	O-0461823	1155	1
ELLISON CHARLES D	MAJ	O-1334557	0859	1
ELLISON DOROTHY M	MAJ	M-0000734	0666	1
ELLISON EDMOND C	CW2	W-2141935	0861	1
ELLISON FRANK S	LTC	O-0337277	0760	2
ELLISON HAROLD A	COL	O-0912303	0864	1
ELLISON HARRY E	CPT	O-1797269	0154	2
ELLISON IRVING J	CPT	O-1298843	0660	2
ELLISON JOHN G B	1LT	O-1304192	1045	2
ELLISON KENNETH E	LTC	O-0315498	0247	2
ELLISON LARRY R	1LT	O-5224263	0167	2
ELLISON MARLON L	LTC	O-0374654	0360	1
ELLISON NELSON M	LTC	O-0254574	0965	3
ELLISON NORMAN B	LTC	O-0256739	1054	3
ELLISON RALPH L	MAJ	O-1118714	0264	1
ELLISON RAYMOND D	LTC	O-1577134	1062	1
ELLISON REUBEN Y	LTC	O-0257731	1267	3
ELLISON ROY L	CPT	O-1576852	1154	1
ELLISON STANLEY H	COL	O-0133973	0156	3
ELLISTON FRED A	LTC	O-0239641	1064	1
ELLMS EDGAR H	LTC	O-0245556	0354	3
ELLOIAN IRA P	CW4	W-2143244	0767	1
ELLOWITCH SHELDON H	1LT	O-0392325	1145	2
ELLSWORTH ALLEN F	2LT	O-1176950	0345	2
ELLSWORTH DE VON	LTC	O-0358727	1063	3
ELLSWORTH ELMAN K	LTC	O-0401510	0364	1
ELLSWORTH EUGENE	WO1	W-2126424	1046	1
ELLSWORTH JAMES F	CPT	O-1302795	0347	2
ELLSWORTH JOE K	MAJ	O-0267521	1165	3
ELLSWORTH LEONARD K	COL	O-0234974	0360	1
ELLSWORTH RAY D	CPT	O-1307529	0257	1
ELLSWORTH RICHARD J	LTC	O-0962295	1168	1
ELLSWORTH THEODORE O	COL	O-0502527	1065	3
ELLWANGER CLARA F	1LT	N-0701224	0135	1
ELLWOOD RICHARD M	CPT	O-1919154	0564	2
ELLZEY ROBERT C	LTC	O-1010540	0357	1
ELMAN MEYER J	LTC	O-0333931	0465	3
ELMBLAD VICTOR A	MAJ	O-0184627	1055	3
ELMEN PAUL H	MAJ	O-0528067	0646	2
ELMER ALBERT W	1LT	O-1306574	1145	2
ELMER CATHERINE	MAJ	N-0727918	0767	1
ELMES WILLIAM T	COL	O-0225978	0764	3
ELMGREN FLOYD E	MAJ	O-0335200	0949	1
ELMGREN LLOYD E	MAJ	O-2014987	0367	1
ELMORE ARTHUR J	MAJ	O-0450138	0657	1
ELMORE CLIFFORD L	CW2	W-2214784	0867	1
ELMORE HERBERT R	LTC	O-0522201	0457	1
ELMORE WILLIAM F	CW2	W-2143317	1060	1
ELMSTRUM CLARENCE L	LTC	O-0474623	0766	3
ELOTT MILAN F	LTC	O-2036298	0664	1
ELROD FRED S	2LT	O-1004315	0444	2

NAME	GRADE	SVC NO	DATE RET MO YR	RET CODE
ELROD JOHN O	MAJ	O-1998425	1160	1
ELROD ORVILLE E	CW2	W-2146133	0629	1
ELROD WELDON	MAJ	O-1825663	0766	1
ELSAM HAROLD G	COL	O-0435368	0462	3
ELSBERG WILLIAM	1LT	O-1014823	1045	2
ELSEA CARL A	LTC	O-0292729	1264	3
ELSEE WALTER B	1LT	O-1043615	0446	2
ELSEN VERNON H	1LT	O-1318528	1045	2
ELSER ROBERT M	CPT	O-1575952	0962	1
ELSHIRE JACK L	CW3	W-2116099	0561	1
ELSHOF HENRY	1LT	O-1289885	0745	2
ELSIFOR FLOYD D	COL	O-0369763	0661	1
ELSLER RICHARD J JR	LTC	O-0285180	0465	3
ELSOM RUSSELL L	LTC	O-0155292	0456	3
ELSON EDWARD L R	COL	O-0276662	0167	3
ELSON JULIUS	CPT	O-0544198	1045	2
ELSON MAURICE	1LT	O-1302619	1045	2
ELSTON HARRY S	MAJ	O-1103152	0546	2
ELSTON NORMAN E	MAJ	O-2084110	0563	1
ELSWEILER JOHN A	LTC	O-1041544	0461	1
ELTON CAREY F	CW2	W-2000401	0648	3
ELTON CHARLES E	LTC	O-1297399	0957	1
ELTON NORMAN W	COL	O-0122465	0757	2
ELTZROTH RICHARD T	CPT	O-1081600	0964	1
ELVIDGE BESSIE R	MAJ	N-0797162	0666	1
ELVIN ALMA G	2LT	N-0735455	0144	1
ELVIN NORRIS C	CPT	O-1690001	1145	2
ELWELL J STEWART JR	1LT	O-0323272	0145	2
ELWELL LEO D	LTC	O-0370335	0747	2
ELWIN JOHN	LTC	O-0191521	0761	3
ELWOOD LAVERN	CPT	O-0487878	0449	1
ELY CARLTON G	CPT	O-1304882	0446	2
ELY CHARLES B	LTC	O-0214193	1163	3
ELY CHARLES T	1LT	O-0386303	0245	2
ELY CHARLES W	MAJ	O-0971773	1163	1
ELY EIRVIN F	1LT	O-1003227	0945	2
ELY GEORGE C	1LT	O-1946722	1146	2
ELY GERALD F	LTC	O-0317743	0758	1
ELY HIRAM B	COL	O-0425123	0854	2
ELY HUDSON P	LTC	O-0476295	0155	2
ELY JAMES F	LTC	O-0337939	1167	3
ELY JAMES H JR	COL	O-0306015	0665	3
ELY JOE T	LTC	O-1635840	0766	1
ELY JOSEPH C	CPT	O-1573182	0745	2
ELY JUNIOR R	LTC	O-0497509	0657	1
ELY KINGSTON G	1LT	O-1320828	0946	2
ELY NATHANIEL	COL	O-0219732	0563	3
ELY RAY	LTC	O-0262616	1165	3
ELY WILLIAM B	CPT	O-0313014	0146	2
ELYO MICHAEL	CW3	W-2151899	0563	1
ELZEA JOHN W	LTC	O-0268345	1266	3
EMANUEL EUGENE J	MAJ	O-1824447	0963	1
EMANUEL JAMES W	MAJ	O-0963466	0860	1
EMARD ALFRED J	LTC	O-0298738	0461	1
EMBACH HAROLD B	LTC	O-0104744	0648	3
EMBODY CALVIN F	CPT	O-0445145	0446	2
EMBREE ELISHA O	COL	O-0150803	1147	2
EMBREE RAY O	COL	O-0274028	0859	1
EMBREE THOMAS R	CW3	W-2142701	0559	1
EMBREY CECIL L	CW3	W-2146234	1157	1
EMBREY LEMUEL J	CPT	O-0371438	0447	2
EMBRY SHERRILL E	1LT	O-0415314	0344	2
EMBURY MELVIN W	COL	O-0264790	0563	3
EMBURY ROY V	CW2	W-2154871	1058	2
EMDE JOHN M	COL	O-0172468	0153	3
EMDE RAYMOND J	CW4	W-2206760	0561	3
EMEIS RICHARD E	LTC	O-0300227	0765	3
EMELIA ALFREDO R	2LT	O-1896825	1050	2
EMENEKER CHARLIE	CW2	W-2148407	0757	1
EMENHISER LEE K	COL	O-0307238	0167	3
EMERICK CHARLES E	CW3	W-2144150	1059	1
EMERICK DAVE D	CPT	O-4063743	0667	1
EMERSON ALLEN M	LTC	O-0195259	1059	3
EMERSON ALLMON C	LTC	O-1171527	0262	1
EMERSON BURTON L	LTC	O-0313853	1161	3

NAME	GRADE	SVC NO	DATE RET MO YR	RET CODE
EMERSON CALDWELL G	LTC	O-0267005	1262	2
EMERSON CHARLES F	LTC	O-0320235	1167	3
EMERSON DONAHUE L	LTC	O-0165545	0647	1
EMERSON ELMER W	CW3	W-2152845	0464	1
EMERSON FRANK H	LTC	O-0358173	0664	1
EMERSON GEORGE F	MAJ	O-1686073	1046	2
EMERSON HAROLD S	CPT	O-0227161	1264	3
EMERSON JAMES H	MAJ	O-0684505	0766	1
EMERSON JAMES L	CPT	O-1010107	1062	2
EMERSON JAMES R	LTC	O-0401912	1160	1
EMERSON MACK	MAJ	O-0439152	0245	2
EMERSON PAUL J	CW2	W-2210666	0765	1
EMERSON RICHARD S	CW4	W-2001940	1067	3
EMERSON TOM W	CPT	O-1101424	1160	1
EMERSON WILLIAM D	MAJ	O-1548401	0859	1
EMERSON WILLIAM H	COL	O-0189310	0453	3
EMERSON WINIFORD F	LTC	O-1178776	0663	1
EMERY ARLO A	COL	O-0180288	0350	3
EMERY CECIL K	LTC	O-0322443	1167	3
EMERY CLYDE A	LTC	O-0333861	0564	3
EMERY CLYDE J	CW3	W-2153382	0565	1
EMERY DAVID G	MAJ	O-1020039	0761	1
EMERY DUNCAN M	LTC	O-1300300	0763	1
EMERY EARL E	LTC	O-1041756	0361	1
EMERY EDWIN L	1LT	O-1896006	1153	1
EMERY GEORGE W	1LT	O-1295188	0643	2
EMERY GEORGE W	WO1	W-2006204	0766	3
EMERY HARVEY F	1LT	O-0451277	0952	1
EMERY HERBERT T	MAJ	O-0266166	0459	3
EMERY JAMES I	LTC	O-1049821	1064	1
EMERY JOHN F	1LT	O-1176324	0656	1
EMERY JOSEPH JR	LTC	O-1578424	0565	1
EMERY JOSEPH S	LTC	O-0451591	0158	1
EMERY MARGARET F	1LT	N-0721040	0246	2
EMERY MARY S	CPT	N-0700769	0345	1
EMERY MYRON C	MAJ	O-1553258	0763	1
EMERY WALTER A	CPT	O-0482899	0448	2
EMERY WALTER T JR	MAJ	O-1103153	1064	2
EMHARDT FREDERICK	1LT	O-1290575	1046	2
EMIG CATHERINE	LTC	L-0215416	1062	1
EMIGH HARRY G JR	1LT	O-0958486	0452	2
EMM JOHN S	1LT	O-1326081	0152	2
EMMA FRANK	CW3	W-2211436	0868	1
EMMA GERARD J	1LT	O-1581686	0645	2
EMMANUEL KARL F	COL	O-0115685	0750	3
EMMANUEL MAX D	COL	O-0187947	0356	3
EMMANUELLI JUAN R	CPT	O-0255126	0244	2
EMME ARTHUR H JR	LTC	O-1059778	1062	1
EMMECK LEROY S	1LT	O-1049757	0545	2
EMMERICH LAWRENCE H	CPT	O-1306396	1046	2
EMMERLING FRANK	CPT	O-0579921	0760	1
EMMERLING HERBERT J	2LT	O-1299867	0944	2
EMMERLING JOHN F	LTC	O-0269632	0246	2
EMMERSON ARTHUR	COL	O-0100813	0955	2
EMMERSON WILLIAM F	CPT	O-0949401	0361	1
EMMETT NED C	MAJ	O-1031635	1165	1
EMMONS CLARK W	LTC	O-1549705	0461	1
EMMONS CLAUDE D	CPT	O-0409732	0346	2
EMMONS DEIGHTON K	2LT	O-1925396	0853	2
EMMONS MARION C	1LT	N-0703061	0946	1
EMMONS RALPH L	CPT	O-1320829	0846	2
EMOND ALFRED G	LTC	O-2050036	1067	1
EMOND DANIEL L	MAJ	O-0238391	0655	3
EMORY MORRIS S	2LT	O-1327941	1045	2
EMPEY HOMER R	LTC	O-2048286	1164	1
EMPFIELD WARREN A	CW2	W-2152036	0561	1
EMRICH JACOB A	LTC	O-1581687	1262	1
EMRY ALBERT JR	MAJ	O-0967197	1162	1
EMRY JESS C	MAJ	O-0372509	1045	2
EMSHOFF LEE ROY H	CPT	O-1341866	1157	2
EMSLIE WILLIAM R	MAJ	O-1535707	0864	1
ENARSON RUTH E	1LT	N-0737669	1146	1
ENBODY CLARENCE	LTC	O-1177785	0462	1
ENCK FRANK E	LTC	O-0225585	0261	3
ENDE CARL F	COL	O-0168954	0459	3

NAME	GRADE	SVC NO	DATE RET MO YR	RET CODE
ENDEBROCK JOHN C JR	MAJ	O-0254808	0165	3
ENDERLIN LEON W	MAJ	O-1547286	0161	1
ENDERS GORDON B	COL	O-0426988	0461	1
ENDERS MILDRED P	CPT	N-0724107	1146	1
ENDERUD WILLIAM L	LTC	O-0230044	0863	3
ENDICOTT JOSEPH A	LTC	O-1115567	0264	1
ENDICOTT RICHARD C	LTC	O-0209063	0547	2
ENDICOTT STEWART G	1LT	O-0401064	1044	2
ENDLER HAROLD A	LTC	O-0586633	0164	1
ENDLING REINHOLD A	MAJ	O-1845032	1053	1
ENDO ICHIRO	LTC	O-1899431	0768	1
ENDSLEY CLARENCE F	LTC	O-1548049	0357	1
ENDSLEY JAMES H	CPT	O-1794926	0247	2
ENEMARK ROY O	LTC	O-0451278	1067	2
ENFIELD JOHN B JR	LTC	O-1584182	0968	3
ENFINGER ALLEN V	MAJ	O-1081131	0858	1
ENG ERNEST K H	LTC	O-1596318	1162	1
ENG JOE	MAJ	O-4032312	0967	2
ENG SAMUEL Y	MAJ	O-0447790	0346	2
ENGARD MASON S	LTC	O-1030761	0162	1
ENGARDIO JOHN J	1LT	O-1177380	1045	2
ENGART HENRY S	CPT	O-0264906	0467	3
ENGBERG JOHN A	COL	O-0315360	1053	1
ENGBERG ROBERT W	LTC	O-0065104	0168	1
ENGDAHL HAROLD W	CPT	O-0970219	1061	1
ENGDAHL THEODORE N	CPT	O-1700706	0446	2
ENGEBRETSON M E	CPT	N-0703806	0546	1
ENGEL ANDREW H	LTC	O-1030144	0863	2
ENGEL BERNARD J	CW3	W-2104029	1159	1
ENGEL CARLTON B	CPT	O-0279545	1159	3
ENGEL CLINTON M	LTC	O-0443410	1054	1
ENGEL EDMUND J	CPT	O-0108131	0545	2
ENGEL EDWARD F	COL	O-0318058	0368	3
ENGEL HANS	LTC	O-1035149	0655	1
ENGEL KENNETH E	MAJ	O-0216720	1063	3
ENGEL RALPH E	LTC	O-0375428	0665	3
ENGEL RICHARD B	COL	O-0378184	0960	1
ENGEL WILBUR W	LTC	O-0318297	0967	3
ENGELBECK RANALD B	COL	O-0221966	0964	3
ENGELHARD WARD H SR	MAJ	O-1821988	0962	1
ENGELHARDT CHARLES W	MAJ	O-0965794	0563	1
ENGELHARDT RONALD	1LT	O-1049141	0945	2
ENGELMAN EDWARD	LTC	O-0432915	1162	1
ENGELMAN JACK S	LTC	O-0499255	1267	3
ENGELMANN WILLIAM G	LTC	O-1296190	0261	1
ENGELS JAMES E	CW2	W-2151821	1059	1
ENGELS VIRGINIA I	MAJ	L-1010016	1166	1
ENGELS WILLIAM N	LTC	O-0340293	0746	2
ENGEN MILLARD O	COL	O-1291609	0868	1
ENGER EARLE M	MAJ	O-0372594	0364	3
ENGER JAMES A	LTC	O-1543503	0462	1
ENGER WILLIAM T	COL	O-0192044	0657	3
ENGERT LLOYD S	LTC	O-1280112	0447	2
ENGESATH HENRY B	COL	O-0909181	1062	3
ENGESSER GERALD W	CW4	W-2114558	0366	1
ENGLAND CHARLES F	COL	O-0337440	0364	2
ENGLAND COURTNEY L	CW2	W-2217237	0968	1
ENGLAND JOE C	MAJ	O-0870740	0961	1
ENGLAND JOHN E	LTC	O-0214240	0463	3
ENGLAND JOHN J	CW3	W-2211675	1268	1
ENGLAND JOHN M JR	MAJ	O-1282383	0965	1
ENGLAND RICHARD A	MAJ	O-1012612	0260	1
ENGLAND WARREN	MAJ	O-1575954	1059	1
ENGLE ADELINE R	2LT	N-0759365	0444	1
ENGLE CARL J	LTC	O-0319844	0747	2
ENGLE DONALD F	MAJ	O-1031477	0161	1
ENGLE ELDON B	LTC	O-0228789	1057	3
ENGLE FANNIE W	2LT	N-0759003	0945	1
ENGLE HARRY	CW2	W-2143154	0960	1
ENGLE HARRY O	CPT	O-0275926	0951	3
ENGLE HERMAN L	CW2	W-3200287	0866	1
ENGLE ROBERT C	LTC	O-0412565	0268	1
ENGLE ROBERT J	MAJ	O-1688756	0465	1
ENGLE STOKES K	LTC	O-1641271	0960	1
ENGLEBERG JOHN J	CPT	O-0968813	0262	1

NAME	GRADE	SVC NO	DATE RET MO YR	RET CODE
ENGLEHART LLOYD H JR	1LT	[illegible]	1154	[illegible]
[illegible]	MAJ	[illegible]	0663	1
ENGLEHARDT ERNEST C	LTC	[illegible]	0557	1
ENGLEMAN SAMUEL	MAJ	[illegible]	0261	1
ENGLER GEORGE F	CPT	[illegible]	0446	2
ENGLER LUDWIG R	COL	0-0901767	0768	3
ENGLERT WALTER F	LTC	0-0461770	1054	1
ENGLES FRANK	2LT	0-1945571	1145	2
ENGLEY THOMAS W	LTC	0-1635843	0663	1
ENGLISH BILLY J	CW3	W-2206502	0267	1
ENGLISH CLAUDE H	CW4	W-2145905	0859	1
ENGLISH DONALD L	LTC	0-1288720	0161	1
ENGLISH DORIS J	2LT	N-0790789	0445	1
ENGLISH EDWARD D	1LT	0-2035305	0152	2
ENGLISH EDWARD H	MAJ	0-1114115	0346	2
ENGLISH EDWARD L	MAJ	0-1685682	0363	1
ENGLISH ELIHU A	WO1	W-2112263	1043	2
ENGLISH EVERETT W	MAJ	0-1044504	1047	2
ENGLISH FITZHUGH N	MAJ	0-1293389	0963	1
ENGLISH FRANK C	LTC	0-0451495	1060	1
ENGLISH JAMES H	MAJ	0-0189334	0552	3
ENGLISH JESSE D JR	MAJ	0-2033141	0262	1
ENGLISH JOHN	WO1	W-2122716	0862	2
ENGLISH LEWIS K	1LT	0-1035112	0246	2
ENGLISH MILLARD C	LTC	0-1287684	0361	1
ENGLISH ROBERT C	1LT	0-1111047	0645	2
ENGLISH ROY C	WO1	W-2145266	0455	1
ENGLISH SAMUEL R	CPT	0-0132610	0648	3
ENGLISH THOMAS M	LTC	0-0378114	0567	3
ENGLISH TRACY L	LTC	0-0350778	0252	2
ENGLISH WILLIAM C	CPT	0-0389050	0761	1
ENGLISH WILLIAM D	MAJ	0-0259858	0266	3
ENGLUND ADELL A	CPT	0-0906384	0644	2
ENGLUND DEWITT W	1LT	0-0473347	0544	2
ENGQUIST MARVIN J	COL	0-0412586	0463	1
ENGRAM VANCE B	2LT	0-1695727	1045	2
ENGS ROBERT N	CPT	0-2203411	0864	1
ENGSTROM DALE M	LTC	0-1289886	0861	1
ENGSTROM PAUL V	COL	0-0222570	0757	3
ENGWELL LAVERN T	MAJ	0-2019303	0363	1
ENICH MITCHELL	MAJ	0-1822256	0561	1
ENLOE NEWMAN W	MAJ	0-0281283	0667	3
ENLOE THOMAS A	LTC	0-0482370	0761	1
ENLOW RALPH W	CW3	W-2145932	0160	1
ENNEN GORDON R	1LT	0-1317154	0146	2
ENNES CHARLES F	MAJ	0-2266367	1167	1
ENNIS CLARENCE H	COL	0-0394232	0960	1
ENNIS HILLIS H	LTC	0-0407586	0460	1
ENNIS JAMES P	1LT	0-0366706	1042	2
ENNIS RAYMOND G	MAJ	0-1293563	1262	1
ENNIS WILLIAM T	LTC	0-0212727	1057	1
ENOCH JOHN K	MAJ	0-0972901	0464	2
ENOCHS CARROLL A	CPT	0-0213993	0962	3
ENOCHS JOHN	CPT	0-0154123	0648	3
ENRIGHT CORNELIUS	COL	0-0242383	0764	3
ENRIGHT HAROLD F	MAJ	0-0236220	0547	2
ENRIGHT THOMAS F	1LT	0-1322406	0246	2
ENRIQUEZ VICTOR M	CPT	0-0222555	0555	3
ENSEL LEE W	COL	0-0913178	0764	3
ENSIGN DAVID T	LTC	0-0479563	0567	3
ENSIGN EDWIN W	MAJ	0-0288527	1043	2
ENSINGER LEAH M	LTC	N-0760987	0863	1
ENSLEN GEORGE E	MAJ	0-2273344	0368	1
ENSLEN W M JR	MAJ	0-0245357	1057	3
ENSLEY SHERMAN W	MAJ	0-1336778	0565	1
ENSLOW RIDLEY M	LTC	0-0168566	1159	3
ENSMANN BERNARD	LTC	0-0310465	0968	3
ENSMINGER HARRISON	MAJ	0-0326077	0660	1
ENSMINGER LEONARD A	1LT	0-1017062	0146	2
ENSMINGER PHILIP R	CW4	W-2108840	1164	1
ENSMINGER RAMAN V	MAJ	0-1051119	0763	1
ENSMINGER WILLIAM	MAJ	0-2036501	0462	1
ENSWORTH GLENN E	CPT	0-1300781	0859	1
ENTERLINE HENRY M	LTC	0-0168607	0261	3
ENTREKIN HERSHEL P	MAJ	0-1920204	0668	1

NAME	GRADE	SVC NO	DATE RET MO YR	RET CODE
ENTREKIN WILLIAM W	MAJ	0-2017381	0961	1
ENTRINGER JOSEPH H	COL	0-0186963	0554	3
ENTZMINGER WILLIAM C	MAJ	0-0163079	0255	3
ENTZMINGER WILLIAM C	MAJ	0-1589812	0862	1
ENWALL HAYFORD D	COL	0-0332979	0865	3
ENYEART ROGER T	CW2	W-2207263	0662	1
ENZOR ALLEN A	MAJ	0-0420261	0846	2
EOVALDI WILLIAM J	LTC	0-0307895	1068	3
EPAMINONDA JOHN G	LTC	0-0382573	0664	3
EPP FREDERIC D	LTC	0-0405722	0268	3
EPPARD JOHN C	COL	0-0900165	0268	3
EPPERSON DIMPSTER E	COL	0-0366606	0165	1
EPPERSON GLENN I	COL	0-0260539	0457	1
EPPERSON JACK E	LTC	0-1337158	1068	1
EPPERSON JAMES E	CPT	0-0389707	0645	2
EPPERSON JESSE V	2LT	0-2000092	0146	2
EPPERSON JOHN I	2LT	0-1080362	0944	2
EPPERSON LESTER Y	1LT	0-1913672	0738	1
EPPERSON LLOYD A	MAJ	0-0975299	1064	1
EPPERSON MANUEL H	MAJ	0-0990769	0464	1
EPPINGER JOSUA JR	LTC	0-0290235	1162	3
EPPLER JAMES E	MAJ	0-1691530	0655	1
EPPLER JOSEPH M	MAJ	0-0160679	0449	3
EPPLER RUDOLF	MAJ	0-1179064	0457	1
EPPLEY GEARY F	COL	0-0112612	1055	3
EPPRIGHT CHARLES L	CW3	W-2206949	0966	1
EPPS ALFRED G	CW3	W-2148721	0563	1
EPPS CALVIN	CPT	0-0108257	1137	1
EPPS CHARLES K	LTC	0-0250097	1057	1
EPPS OLIVER C	CPT	0-1945123	0646	2
EPPS SAMUEL H	LTC	0-0990761	0768	1
EPSARO AUSTIN F	LTC	0-0542653	0265	1
EPSOM GEORGE A	LTC	0-1796595	1264	1
EPSTEEN CASPER M	LTC	0-0446241	1045	2
EPSTEIN ABRAHAM	MAJ	0-2016869	0363	2
EPSTEIN ARNOLD	MAJ	0-0172177	0157	3
EPSTEIN BENJAMIN	1LT	0-1639005	0252	1
EPSTEIN LOUIS	CW4	W-2112233	0355	1
EPSTEIN PHILIP G	1LT	0-1109275	0246	2
EPSTEIN SIDNEY S	MAJ	0-0500416	0446	2
EPTING ELMER E	MAJ	0-0282423	0947	2
EPTING SYLVIAN W	1LT	0-0390515	1145	2
EPTING THOMAS H	1LT	0-0373432	1044	2
EPTON JOHN W	COL	0-0284786	0566	3
EPTON T L	1LT	0-0947921	1151	2
ERARD EDGAR B JR	CPT	0-0397118	0146	2
ERB CLARENCE L	CW3	W-2152209	0963	1
ERB GEORGE W	LTC	0-1299545	0462	1
ERB JOHN W	CPT	0-0191500	0651	2
ERBE OSCAR F	CW4	W-2122115	1062	1
ERBES ALBERT C	LTC	0-2034672	0860	1
ERBST OTTO C	MAJ	0-1303127	0159	1
ERBY JOHN W	1LT	0-5338628	0768	2
ERCKMAN CHARLES D	LTC	0-0482838	0868	3
ERD GEORGIA H	MAJ	N-0774051	0165	1
ERDEI BEATRICE A	1LT	N-0772175	0448	2
ERDEL GEORGE T	1LT	0-1302956	0646	2
ERDESKY JOSEPH L	LTC	0-2008529	0965	1
ERDLEY ANNA F	1LT	N-0761089	0745	1
ERDMAN ALEXANDER	LTC	0-2032597	0167	1
ERDMAN ERVIN E	MAJ	0-0999035	0566	1
ERDMAN GEORGE B	CPT	0-1316395	1057	1
ERDMAN ROBERT C	CW3	W-2209293	0868	1
ERDMAN WILLIAM K	LTC	0-0918587	0747	2
ERDMANN ARTHUR C	MAJ	0-1010606	0247	2
ERDMANN EDWARD A JR	MAJ	0-1300301	0564	1
ERDMANN LOUIS E	LTC	0-0273482	0266	3
ERDMANN ROBERT E	LTC	0-2007507	1163	1
ERDMANN ROY G	CPT	0-1014022	0146	2
ERDOFY MAXWELL E	COL	0-0159943	1045	2
ERFURT HENRY F	MAJ	0-1051551	1057	1
ERGLE THEORDORE	LTC	0-0274272	1157	1
ERGOOD ALLEN M	CPT	0-0180249	1057	3
ERHARDT CHRIS	LTC	0-2082991	0868	1
ERHARDT FRANCIS J	LTC	0-1284307	0563	1

NAME	GRADE	SVC NO	DATE RET MO YR	RET CODE
ERHART FRANK P	COL	0-0182156	1151	3
ERHART HERMAN A	COL	0-0208409	0554	3
ERICHSEN FRANK P	LTC	[illegible]	1068	3
ERICKSEN ERLING	CW2	[illegible]	1060	1
ERICKSEN PAUL O	LTC	0-2014904	0263	2
ERICKSEN ROBERT E	CPT	[illegible]	0944	2
ERICKSON ALBERT F	LTC	0-0359655	1164	3
ERICKSON ALVIN	LTC	0-0349750	0665	3
ERICKSON CARL G	CPT	0-0174849	1155	3
ERICKSON CLARENCE P	LTC	0-0244975	1046	2
ERICKSON DWIGHT A	1LT	0-1050245	0445	2
ERICKSON EARL N	MAJ	0-1688425	0864	1
ERICKSON EDGAR C	M G	0-0171317	0559	1
ERICKSON EDWARD T JR	1LT	0-1302918	0346	2
ERICKSON EINAR A	LTC	0-0299121	0457	1
ERICKSON ERNST	LTC	0-0919692	0263	3
ERICKSON FLOYD C	LTC	0-1060764	0967	1
ERICKSON GENE C	LTC	0-1284308	0166	1
ERICKSON HARRY	COL	0-0164437	0749	2
ERICKSON HENRY T	MAJ	0-0271827	1067	3
ERICKSON JOHN F	CW4	W-2145420	0261	1
ERICKSON JOHN R	COL	0-0411753	0166	3
ERICKSON JOHN W	1LT	0-0920344	0545	2
ERICKSON KARL F	LTC	0-0253213	0157	3
ERICKSON KENNETH D	CW3	W-2211405	0568	1
ERICKSON LEONARD A	1LT	0-1109276	0365	3
ERICKSON LEONARD C	LTC	0-0285501	0568	3
ERICKSON LILLY W	MAJ	N-0744074	0568	3
ERICKSON OWEN M	LTC	0-0273483	0268	3
ERICKSON PETER A	LTC	0-1288372	0561	1
ERICKSON RALPH L	LTC	0-0348080	0460	3
ERICKSON REIDAR A	CW4	W-2143270	0967	2
ERICKSON RICHARD A	LTC	0-1184816	0962	1
ERICKSON RICHARD J	CW3	W-2149064	1162	1
ERICKSON ROBERT	LTC	0-0290381	0457	1
ERICKSON ROBERT C	1LT	0-1325207	0246	2
ERICKSON THORSTEN A	LTC	0-1166257	0159	1
ERICKSON VANCE C	LTC	0-1310825	0668	3
ERICKSON VICTOR H	MAJ	0-1923513	0865	1
ERICKSON WARREN D JR	LTC	0-1548756	0461	1
ERICKSON WILLIAM M	LTC	0-1315288	0962	1
ERICSON EVERETT F	CPT	0-1298520	0247	2
ERICSON JOSEPH H JR	MAJ	0-0527014	0557	2
ERICSON VINCENT H	CW3	W-2205962	0965	1
ERICSSON ADAM E	MAJ	0-0225365	0148	2
ERICSSON ARTHUR J	COL	0-0244419	1049	3
ERIE DEWITT W	LTC	0-0235655	0346	2
ERIKSEN ERIK	MAJ	0-1291968	0454	2
ERIKSEN NORMAN G	MAJ	0-2001735	0366	1
ERIKSON ALDEN F	LTC	0-0170195	1059	3
ERIKSON CARL A	WO1	W-2124703	1044	2
ERIKSON HERBERT B	CPT	0-0502825	1045	2
ERIKSSON NILES L	LTC	0-0331060	0761	1
ERISMAN ROBERT E	CPT	0-0355881	0545	2
ERKES MARION J	MAJ	0-0493273	1055	1
ERKKILA JACK	LTC	0-0294666	0667	3
ERKKILA MARTHA M	MAJ	N-0759158	0866	2
ERLE HAROLD	MAJ	0-0450414	0555	1
ERLE LUTHER M	MAJ	0-1644302	0861	1
ERMELBAUER CARL	CPT	0-1325186	0347	2
ERMENTROUT ROBERT A	LTC	0-0253610	0559	1
ERMERT CARL L	LTC	0-0423374	0658	1
ERMLER PETER J	CPT	0-0300890	0962	3
ERNESS LEE G	CPT	0-1594150	0262	1
ERNEST EDWARD F	MAJ	0-0486107	1152	1
ERNEST HENRY B	CPT	0-1575956	0350	2
ERNEST STANLEY S	MAJ	0-1341867	0864	1
ERNESTI ROGER	CPT	0-0345768	0146	2
ERNSER JOHN J	MAJ	0-1312896	0365	1
ERNST CLAUDE A	MAJ	0-1635847	1160	1
ERNST FRED G	2LT	0-1109277	0845	2
ERNST GEORGE	MAJ	0-1951392	0263	1
ERNST MANFRIO P	LTC	0-1184379	0862	1
ERNST RAY A	CPT	0-5534957	0368	2
ERNST VICTOR L	LTC	0-0324090	0761	3

NAME	GRADE	SVC NO	DATE RET MO YR	RET CODE
ERNSTEIN ARTHUR	LTC	[illegible]	[illegible]	3
ERNSTING WILLIAM JR	CPT	[illegible]	0745	2
ERNYEI WILLIAM	CW3	[illegible]	0163	1
ERON HOBART V JR	CPT	[illegible]	0160	1
ERRICKSON FRED M	MAJ	[illegible]	1262	2
ERRINGTON ROBERT M	LTC	0-0165167	0455	3
ERSAY EMIL F	LTC	0-0302587	1266	3
ERSKINE ALEXANDER	MAJ	0-0195568	0662	3
ERSKINE FRANK G	MAJ	0-0318314	0566	3
ERSKINE GEORGE P	CPT	0-1544068	0968	3
ERSKINE HENRY F	CPT	0-1297638	0446	2
ERSKINE JOHN G	1LT	0-1010911	1045	2
ERSKINE ROBERT K	LTC	0-0194892	1061	3
ERTL CLARENCE F	CPT	0-1304512	0161	1
ERTWINE DOYLE C	WO1	W-2121992	0958	1
ERVIN ALVIN P JR	LTC	0-1558264	0766	1
ERVIN DARBY D	LTC	0-1322321	1262	1
ERVIN FRED M	WO1	W-2125751	1145	2
ERVIN GLADYS C	CPT	N-0737330	0947	1
ERVIN ROBERT T JR	COL	0-0209036	0462	3
ERWIN ANNE H	MAJ	N-0788979	1065	1
ERWIN BEYRL C	MAJ	0-0310995	0545	2
ERWIN EARL	LTC	0-0167923	1059	3
ERWIN ESTHER R	MAJ	N-0800214	0865	1
ERWIN HOWARD	MAJ	0-1648447	0759	1
ERWIN HUGH	CPT	0-0442375	0545	2
ERWIN JEFFERSON	CPT	0-2262313	1060	1
ERWIN JOHN T	MAJ	0-2016870	0162	2
ERWIN ROGER J	CPT	0-0450274	0244	2
ERWIN ROY C	MAJ	0-1288881	0258	1
ERWIN WALLACE F	MAJ	0-0285926	0468	3
ERYAVEC MARTIN F	CW4	W-2121279	0659	1
ESAACSON RICHARD L	CPT	0-1046779	0657	1
ESAIAS JOHN R	COL	0-0222010	0648	3
ESATOW THEODORE R	CPT	0-0395717	0549	2
ESBERG ARTHUR B	CPT	0-0282928	0967	2
ESCAMOS JOHNNY	1LT	0-0179409	0250	1
ESCH CHARLES A	MAJ	0-1288032	0754	1
ESCH ROLLAND O	CW2	W-2145960	0559	1
ESCH ROYAL L	CPT	0-0473101	0853	1
ESCHBACH ROBERT E	LTC	0-0439954	0468	1
ESCHENBACHER A W	MAJ	0-1545394	0460	1
ESCOE LINDSY J	CPT	0-0477023	0445	2
ESCUDERO EDMUNDO	COL	0-0313914	0960	1
ESCUE CHARLES W JR	MAJ	0-1182822	1264	2
ESDERTS WILLIAM J	CW2	W-3430123	0966	1
ESENWEIN AUGUST JR	MAJ	0-1647965	0960	1
ESH LELAND D	LTC	0-0290920	0762	1
ESHELMAN CLARENCE F	CPT	0-1018053	0557	1
ESKELSEN RUEL M	LTC	0-0247148	1053	3
ESKOFF JOHN	MAJ	0-1173236	0358	2
ESKRIDGE CHARLES E	CW2	W-2143326	0159	1
ESLINGER WALLACE V	LTC	0-0353729	0754	1
ESMOND WILLIAM O	CPT	0-0414567	0645	2
ESPARAS MANUEL M	CPT	0-1896826	0859	2
ESPARZA ARTURO G	CW3	W-2147662	0862	1
ESPARZA MANUEL M	2LT	0-2055271	0645	2
ESPELIEN ERICK E	MAJ	0-0167101	0648	3
ESPEN JOHN M JR	LTC	0-1186535	0866	1
ESPENSCHADE PARK W	LTC	0-0239851	0166	3
ESPENSHADE PAUL S	LTC	0-0447770	1052	2
ESPERSEN RUBEN W	COL	0-0263448	0962	3
ESPEY HELEN E	MAJ	L-1010017	1264	1
ESPEY JAMES C	1LT	0-0112254	0344	2
ESPINOSA AURELIO M	LTC	0-0907331	0667	3
ESPINOSA MARIO A	CW3	W-2146759	0461	1
ESPOSITO ALFENSE R	CW4	W-2003896	0368	3
ESPOSITO ANDREW R	LTC	0-0321608	0768	3
ESPOSITO EVA E	1LT	N-0735399	0146	1
ESPOSITO JOSEPH F	MAJ	0-1534475	1061	2
ESPY GOODMAN B JR	LTC	0-0259130	0167	3
ESSAM DUANE R	MAJ	0-0391097	0854	2
ESSECK RUDOLPH B	1LT	0-1298682	0551	2
ESSER GILBERT F	LTC	0-0337558	0956	3
ESSEX GEORGE T JR	LTC	0-1061382	1263	1

NAME	GRADE	SVC NO	DATE RET MO YR	RET CODE
ESSEX MARTIN J	1LT	0-1821989	0846	1
ESSEX WILLIAM	MAJ	0-1997523	0765	2
ESSRIG ROSE B	2LT	N-0758899	0346	1
ESTABROOK VIVIAN A	CW3	V-0104057	1263	1
ESTARIS MATEO	1LT	0-1896785	0250	1
ESTAVILLE LAWRENCE E	1LT	0-1017086	1045	2
ESTEL ADOLPH T JR	CPT	0-0407538	0247	2
ESTELL JAMES W	CW3	W-2129941	0766	2
ESTER JESSE M	1LT	0-1593560	1057	1
ESTERLY ARTHUR H	MAJ	0-0139610	0150	3
ESTES AUBREY C	CPT	0-0478190	1147	2
ESTES CHILTON J	CPT	0-0298067	1045	2
ESTES CLIFF M	CPT	0-0383609	0146	2
ESTES EDGAR S JR	LTC	0-0241794	0566	3
ESTES EUGENE J	CW3	W-2205446	0563	1
ESTES EZRA W	MAJ	0-0888525	0753	1
ESTES FRED K	COL	0-0199927	0258	3
ESTES HAROLD E	LTC	0-0970105	0868	1
ESTES HORACE C	CPT	0-1289404	0762	1
ESTES L PARLIN	LTC	0-1597351	0568	3
ESTES ROBERT M	MAJ	0-0367499	0156	1
ESTES VERNON P JR	LTC	0-2006757	1268	1
ESTES WARD M	LTC	0-0253007	0460	3
ESTES WELDON L	CPT	0-2273273	0758	2
ESTEVES BUENAVENTU	LTC	0-1326987	0568	1
ESTEVEZ MANUEL M	LTC	0-1326047	0563	1
ESTEY WILLIAM H	LTC	0-0439452	1264	1
ESTOCK JOHN A	LTC	0-1580907	0261	1
ESTOK FRANK W	MAJ	0-1186000	0465	1
ESTORGE LEONARD	CPT	0-0337093	0546	2
ESTRADA MATEO J	MAJ	0-1890618	1068	2
ESTRADA THOMAS E	LTC	0-2033605	0167	1
ESTRIDGE DONALD G	CW3	W-3430317	0668	1
ESTRIDGE ROY W	CPT	0-0919889	1144	2
ESTRIDGE THOMAS W	CPT	0-0950980	0164	2
ESTUS ROBERT C	1LT	0-1797107	0246	2
ESTY LUCILLE M	1LT	N-0722664	1145	1
ESZES JOSEPH P	LTC	0-1558137	0865	1
ETHERIDGE FRANK W	CW3	W-2149616	0263	1
ETHERIDGE J T	MAJ	0-1642841	0358	1
ETHERIDGE WILLIAM C	CW2	W-2204983	0463	1
ETHERTON RAY E	CW2	W-2148961	0261	1
ETHINGTON IVAN C	1LT	0-1114917	0445	2
ETHINGTON WILLIAM M	MAJ	0-1923585	1164	1
ETHREDGE JACK R	MAJ	0-1877765	0765	1
ETHRIDGE JAMES C	1LT	0-0905111	1144	2
ETHRIDGE JOHN A	CW3	W-2209964	1267	1
ETHRIDGE KENNETH M	CPT	0-1326541	0164	1
ETHRIDGE QUINN	MAJ	0-1996473	0465	1
ETINGOFF WILLIAM	CW2	W-2144534	1154	1
ETNIRE LEONARD H	CPT	0-1936961	0365	1
ETTENGER MORRIS S	CPT	0-1695938	0146	2
ETTER EDWARD F	LTC	0-0237735	0861	3
ETTER FORREST S	LTC	0-0245580	1145	2
ETTER HALL	LTC	0-0103435	0648	3
ETTER HAROLD K	CW2	W-2150806	0163	1
ETTER HELEN M	MAJ	N-0778679	0865	1
ETTER JOE W	LTC	0-0158792	0959	3
ETTER LEWIS E	LTC	0-0237798	0261	3
ETTINGER ARTHUR	CPT	0-0275152	0666	3
ETTINGER JEROME	1LT	0-1746822	0345	2
ETTINGER ROBERT C W	1LT	0-1320830	0348	2
ETZ EDWARD C	1LT	0-0520882	0545	2
ETZEL BERNARD A	1LT	0-0530045	0146	2
ETZWEILER ALBERT R	MAJ	0-0185024	1149	3
EUBANK CHARLES G	COL	0-0174262	0961	3
EUBANK DICK B	1LT	0-0286365	0645	2
EUBANK GEORGE B	MAJ	0-2007000	0267	1
EUBANK HENRY H	2LT	0-1317155	1045	2
EUBANK JAMES M	CW2	W-2149696	0161	1
EUBANK JARRELL M	MAJ	0-0506353	0567	2
EUBANK WILLIAM B	COL	0-0268815	0367	3
EUBANK WILLIAM H	CW2	W-2212209	0957	1
EUBANKS BURNIE L JR	CW3	W-2144294	1060	1
EUBANKS HERMAN T	COL	0-0255041	1265	3

NAME	GRADE	SVC NO	DATE RET MO YR	RET CODE
EUBANKS JOHN W JR	CW2	W-3151465	1268	1
EUBANKS MARTIN E	LTC	0-0451593	0358	1
EUCHNER PERRY C	COL	0-0160785	0452	3
EUDY CHARLIE W	LTC	0-0493620	0155	1
EUDY RAY J	CW3	W-2208343	0568	1
EUELL DANIEL W SR	1LT	0-0199906	0367	3
EUKEL DONALD D	CW3	RW-2207986	0766	1
EULER HENRY J	LTC	0-0140008	1051	3
EULER POLAND A	1LT	0-0494657	1045	2
EULLER RICHARD B	COL	0-0300982	0867	3
EUM DANIEL D S	MAJ	0-4009474	0268	1
EUNICE DONALD A	CPT	0-1998653	1053	2
EURE JAMES C	LTC	0-1592803	0566	1
EURE OTHO A	MAJ	0-0520316	0746	2
EURE WILLIAM J	CW2	W-2146776	1060	1
EUSTACE CHARLES C	MAJ	0-0269170	0867	3
EUSTACE VIRGIL R	CPT	0-1000751	0946	2
EUSTIS WILLIAM J	CW3	W-2206647	0468	1
EUSTROM HARVEY H	LTC	0-0177436	1047	2
EUTEMARK FRANK	MAJ	0-0947116	1165	2
EUTIZE WALTER J	MAJ	0-1111598	1162	1
EVANCHO ANDREW	CW2	W-2149319	0261	1
EVANOER DAN L	MAJ	0-0332194	0555	3
EVANGELISTA PETER J	CW2	W-2142634	0959	1
EVANICSKO MICHAEL	MAJ	0-1646735	0261	1
EVANOFF EVAN D	CW2	W-2215001	0868	1
EVANOSKI JOSEPH	1LT	0-1018118	0246	2
EVANS ABEL W	1LT	0-1299391	0546	2
EVANS ARLEIGH U	LTC	0-0295696	1061	1
EVANS ARTHUR E	CPT	0-0249925	0645	2
EVANS ARTHUR P	LTC	0-0306350	0160	1
EVANS BENJAMIN F	COL	0-0174337	0648	3
EVANS BERT M	1LT	0-1119294	0550	2
EVANS BILLIE R	MAJ	N-0780335	0666	1
EVANS BILLY K	CW3	W-2203886	1268	1
EVANS BLANCHE	MAJ	N-0759506	0163	1
EVANS C J JR	LTC	0-0146167	0159	3
EVANS CARLOS B	1LT	0-1305903	0645	2
EVANS CARVEL S	COL	0-0319357	0266	3
EVANS CECIL F	LTC	0-0214875	0958	3
EVANS CHARLES R	1LT	0-1012116	0945	2
EVANS CLARENCE B	CPT	0-0490715	0160	2
EVANS CLARENCE W	LTC	0-0285367	0668	3
EVANS CLIFFORD V	MAJ	0-1642843	0168	1
EVANS DANIEL	MAJ	0-1040216	0161	1
EVANS DARYL G	1LT	0-1558265	0346	2
EVANS DAVID B	CW3	W-2147247	0563	1
EVANS DAVID C	CW3	W-2144842	0662	1
EVANS DAVID J	MAJ	0-0235075	0960	3
EVANS DAVID J JR	MAJ	0-1167826	1060	1
EVANS DAVID L	LTC	0-1703769	0361	1
EVANS DAVID W	COL	0-0347260	0266	1
EVANS DEAN P	1LT	0-0146131	1054	3
EVANS DON G	LTC	0-0223408	0150	3
EVANS DORIS Y	1LT	N-0723456	0546	1
EVANS DOYLE H	CW3	W-2205759	0365	1
EVANS EARL N	CW3	W-2151830	1063	1
EVANS EDGAR	1LT	0-1301972	0644	2
EVANS EDWARD A	B G	0-0122172	0955	3
EVANS EDWARD P	LTC	0-1102231	1163	1
EVANS EDWARD V JR	CPT	0-1283745	1046	2
EVANS ELDEN E	LTC	0-0402858	0161	1
EVANS ELDON E	CPT	0-0354408	1145	2
EVANS ELEANOR J	MAJ	N-0800007	0765	1
EVANS ERNEST A	LTC	0-0289454	0658	3
EVANS EUGENE L	CW4	W-2144528	1068	1
EVANS EVERETTE C	CPT	0-0972069	1061	1
EVANS FERDINAND	COL	0-0404920	0366	1
EVANS FRED C	LTC	0-0451279	0358	1
EVANS FREDERICK	LTC	0-0270147	0268	3
EVANS FREDERICK	LTC	0-1691503	1168	3
EVANS GEORGE F	LTC	0-1287686	1059	1
EVANS GEORGE G	LTC	0-0451099	0958	2
EVANS GEORGE J	LTC	0-0146608	0653	3
EVANS GEORGE M	CPT	0-0265898	0445	2

NAME	GRADE	SVC NO	DATE RET MO YR	RET CODE
EVANS GEORGE O	LTC	0-0226768	0360	3
EVANS GEORGE S	MAJ	0*1593562	0960	1
EVANS GEORGE T	MAJ	0-0387306	0346	2
EVANS GEORGE V	MAJ	0-1845372	0559	1
EVANS GERALD W	1LT	0-1534724	0746	2
EVANS GOLDEN F	LTC	0-1000938	1158	1
EVANS GORDON F	1LT	0-0285657	0343	2
EVANS HARDIE M	CW2	W-2141268	0257	1
EVANS HARLEY W	CW2	W-2211118	0864	1
EVANS HAROLD A	MAJ	0-2001821	1164	1
EVANS HAROLD J	CW3	W-2109639	0357	1
EVANS HARRY A	WO1	W-2108939	0251	2
EVANS HARRY B JR	CPT	0-0397364	1147	2
EVANS HARRY D	CW3	W-2211438	0766	1
EVANS HENRY C	M G	0-0124891	0957	3
EVANS HENRY M	LTC	0-0181038	0254	3
EVANS HILARY W	WO1	W-2133221	0754	1
EVANS HORACE L	2LT	0-2048614	0245	2
EVANS HOWARD C	LTC	0-0393794	1167	3
EVANS HUGH F	COL	0-0308498	0161	3
EVANS J T	1LT	0-0548293	0446	2
EVANS JAMES	LTC	0-0404230	0859	1
EVANS JAMES C	CPT	0-1692612	0358	1
EVANS JAMES H	1LT	0-0414321	0943	2
EVANS JOHN B	COL	0-0259166	1046	2
EVANS JOHN E	LTC	0-0262751	0557	1
EVANS JOHN H JR	LTC	0-1172448	0762	1
EVANS JOHN R	LTC	0-0255997	0166	3
EVANS JOHN T	LTC	0-0238424	0865	3
EVANS JOHN W	MAJ	0-0255059	0867	3
EVANS JOHN W	1LT	0-0326759	0547	2
EVANS JON P	COL	0-0052010	0567	1
EVANS KENNETH B	LTC	0-1106718	0461	1
EVANS KENNETH K	LTC	0-0347953	1060	1
EVANS LEE	CPT	0-0305331	0744	2
EVANS LEONARD	MAJ	0-1644201	0461	1
EVANS LEONARD L	MAJ	0-0213836	0763	3
EVANS LESLIE L	B G	0-0246332	0659	3
EVANS LESTER J	LTC	0-0316975	0746	2
EVANS LESTER K	MAJ	0-1100974	0557	1
EVANS LINTON H JR	LTC	0-1037479	0361	1
EVANS LLOYD A	CPT	0-0230625	1060	3
EVANS LLOYD E	1LT	0-1308938	1145	2
EVANS LONDON JR	CPT	0-4009441	1265	1
EVANS LOUIE G	CW3	W-2146127	0162	1
EVANS MARCELLUS SR	CPT	0-1041141	0568	2
EVANS MAX C	MAJ	0-1541159	0559	1
EVANS MELTON L	CW3	W-2150285	0161	1
EVANS MELVIN T	CW2	W-2206921	0264	1
EVANS MORGAN Z	MAJ	0-1634730	1060	1
EVANS NEAL T	COL	0-0232787	1164	3
EVANS NILE	COL	0-0460368	0353	2
EVANS OBIE F	CW4	W-2146561	0165	1
EVANS ORAL B	CPT	0-1322010	1058	1
EVANS ORVILLE T	CPT	0-1685138	1145	2
EVANS OSCAR	MAJ	0-1031636	0365	1
EVANS OWEN C	CPT	0-0981005	0852	2
EVANS PAUL	2LT	0-1300949	1043	2
EVANS PAUL B	LTC	0-0288307	0762	1
EVANS PAUL C	CPT	0-1010725	0954	1
EVANS PAUL J	LTC	0-1691786	0763	1
EVANS PAUL R	1LT	0-1000040	0354	2
EVANS PAUL R	MAJ	0-1552663	0555	1
EVANS PERCY W	COL	0-0115979	0848	3
EVANS PHILLIP I	MAJ	0-1298846	0661	1
EVANS RAYMOND W	1LT	0-1304362	1045	2
EVANS RICHARD H	CPT	0-0362568	0745	2
EVANS RICHARD J	MAJ	0-0574543	0560	1
EVANS RICHARD W	LTC	0-1177381	0966	1
EVANS RICHARD W JR	COL	0-0285236	0846	2
EVANS ROBERT A	MAJ	0-1645827	0361	1
EVANS ROBERT B	LTC	0-2030408	0868	1
EVANS ROBERT C	LTC	0-1010953	1263	1
EVANS ROBLEY D	1LT	0-1895308	0745	2
EVANS RONALD M	CPT	0-1035114	0346	2

NAME	GRADE	SVC NO	DATE RET MO YR	RET CODE
EVANS ROY D	WO1	W-2127562	0948	1
EVANS RUTH	2LT	N-0724690	0644	1
EVANS SAMUEL C	LTC	0-1002211	0968	3
EVANS STANLEY G	LTC	0-1946042	0264	1
EVANS STUART	LTC	0-0286015	0467	3
EVANS STUART A	CPT	0-1168655	1052	2
EVANS THOMAS	MAJ	0-1592806	1067	3
EVANS THOMAS A	CPT	0-0333628	0356	3
EVANS THOMAS H	COL	0-0261219	0566	3
EVANS THOMAS H	LTC	0-1168656	1167	1
EVANS THOMAS J	MAJ	0-2020002	0263	1
EVANS THOMAS M	MAJ	0-0107287	0656	3
EVANS TREVOR	MAJ	0-1306954	0161	1
EVANS VAUGHN M	LTC	0-1946243	0962	1
EVANS VAUHGN D	MAJ	0-1297699	0364	1
EVANS VIRGIL O	CPT	0-1287687	1060	1
EVANS WALKER W	LTC	0-0378141	0661	1
EVANS WALTER L	MAJ	0-1726621	1050	2
EVANS WAYNE L	LTC	0-0323179	0865	2
EVANS WILLIAM A	LTC	0-0368677	0361	1
EVANS WILLIAM A JR	1LT	0-1995086	1145	2
EVANS WILLIAM D	MAJ	0-0181923	0862	3
EVANS WILLIAM F	CPT	0-0983063	0263	2
EVANS WILLIAM R	MAJ	0-1014440	0356	1
EVANS WILLIAM W	CPT	0-0504871	0546	2
EVANTS JOE F	CW2	W-2206289	1163	1
EVARTS FORREST S	CW3	W-2153183	1064	1
EVARTS SAMUEL W	1LT	0-0142643	0150	3
EVE ROBERT R	CW3	W-2149763	0761	1
EVEDON ROBERT A	1LT	0-1916844	1052	2
EVELAND THOMAS C	LTC	0-0338826	1160	1
EVELAND WILLIAM	LTC	0-0253060	1050	1
EVENBURGH RALPH L	LTC	0-0240268	0259	3
EVENS ALVEN	CW2	W-2109334	1053	2
EVENS WARREN M	2LT	0-1322011	0445	2
EVENSEN NORMAN	CW4	W-2144668	0660	1
EVENSON EDWIN F	LTC	0-0256525	0859	3
EVENSON FRED E	CPT	0-2262297	1160	1
EVEREST FOLSOM	COL	0-0180304	0446	2
EVERETT ADRIAN J	LTC	0-1635849	0765	1
EVERETT BILL B	MAJ	0-1293391	0263	1
EVERETT BURTON N	LTC	0-0334054	0854	1
EVERETT CECIL R	COL	0-0146604	0456	3
EVERETT DON W	LTC	0-1170728	0265	1
EVERETT EARL B	LTC	0-1301460	1164	1
EVERETT GOODMAN C	MAJ	0-1544315	0559	1
EVERETT HAROLD R	MAJ	0-0989116	0166	1
EVERETT JOHN A	MAJ	0-1555202	0457	2
EVERETT JOHN W	COL	0-0168798	0360	3
EVERETT LEROY	COL	0-0331168	0660	1
EVERETT LEWIS J	LTC	0-1109920	1162	1
EVERETT MERLE L	CPT	0-1178781	0968	3
EVERETT MYRON A	LTC	0-1102233	0954	1
EVERETT PERCY E	CW2	W-2102885	1148	1
EVERETT PERLEY L	COL	0-0289822	1160	1
EVERETT ROBERT L	CPT	0-0486248	0549	1
EVERETT VAUGHN B	LTC	0-0212296	0564	3
EVERETT WILLIAM E	MAJ	0-4074597	1168	1
EVERETT WILLIAM E	CW2	W-2211617	0468	1
EVERETT WILLIAM J	CW3	W-2203344	0664	1
EVERETT WILLIAM R	MAJ	0-0402367	0646	2
EVERETT WILLIAM S	COL	0-0225063	0864	3
EVERHART EDGAR S	COL	0-0174822	0648	3
EVERHART WILLIAM G	1LT	0-0925440	1145	2
EVERITT DONALD B	CW3	W-2147752	0762	1
EVERITT VERNON C	MAJ	0-0272341	0468	3
EVERLY RAYMOND H	MAJ	0-1100976	0862	1
EVERS FRANCIS O	LTC	0-1298649	0261	1
EVERS JOHN	MAJ	0-1575295	1054	1
EVERSOLE EDWIN A	MAJ	0-2262145	0662	1
EVERSOLE FRANK P JR	LTC	0-1010839	0164	1
EVERSOLE JOSEPH JR	LTC	0-1574712	1163	1
EVERSOLE WILLIAM F	1LT	0-0326003	0944	2
EVERSON CLYDE W	MAJ	0-0994974	0464	1
EVERSON ROBERT F	LTC	0-1321111	1167	1

NAME	GRADE	SVC NO	DATE RET MO YR	RET CODE
EVERT FLORENCE M	MAJ	N-0700703	0646	1
EVERT GERTRUDE S	MAJ	N-0700704	1055	1
EVERT ROBERT W	MAJ	0-1944597	1055	1
EVETTS JAMES R	LTC	0-0917450	1045	2
EVEY JOHN M	MAJ	0-0176245	0648	3
EVILSIZER LESTER J	2LT	0-0126663	0157	3
EVINGER FLOYD H	MAJ	0-0107317	0644	2
EVJY MARTIN	COL	0-0225638	1262	3
EVRARD SERVAIS L	LTC	0-0172032	0254	3
EWALD DONALD F	LTC	0-0222369	0646	1
EWALT LELAND G	LTC	0-0321163	1265	3
EWALT THEODORE A	LTC	0-1695687	0561	1
EWAN JOHN R	1LT	0-0400225	0642	2
EWART RYLAND K	LTC	0-0374029	0663	2
EWASKIO HARRY	1LT	0-0448112	0944	2
EWBANK GENE M	MAJ	0-0862737	0758	1
EWBANK JOHN M	LTC	0-0300809	0366	3
EWBANK ROBERT E	COL	0-0334569	0968	3
EWERS SCOTT H	LTC	0-0296943	1165	3
EWING CHARLES G	LTC	0-0387667	0566	1
EWING CHESNEY G	LTC	0-0245103	1056	3
EWING CLARKE E	COL	0-0253951	0156	3
EWING DONALD E	MAJ	0-1598556	0962	1
EWING DOROTHY A	MAJ	N-0769526	1166	1
EWING EARLE F	COL	0-0110470	1055	1
EWING HARRIET F	1LT	N-0760463	0146	1
EWING HARRY C	MAJ	0-1946044	1054	1
EWING HOWARD F	COL	0-0337144	0664	1
EWING JAMES C	2LT	0-0206534	0156	3
EWING JAMES W	COL	0-0259916	0847	2
EWING JEWEL W	LTC	0-0351565	0568	1
EWING JOHN W	LTC	0-1948453	0966	2
EWING MARLIN R	CPT	0-0986940	0553	2
EWING MARTHA A	CPT	N-0702793	0147	1
EWING RALPH B	2LT	0-1946244	1144	2
EWING RAYMOND D	CPT	0-2055345	0546	2
EWING ROBERT E	CPT	0-0515513	0451	2
EWING ROY L	MAJ	0-0486135	0158	1
EWING THOMAS G	1LT	0-0497056	0646	2
EWING WILLIAM A	MAJ	0-1544229	0557	1
EWING WILLIAM H	MAJ	0-1588991	0466	1
EWING WILLIAM W	CW2	W-2146236	1160	1
EWING WYLIE B	1LT	0-0156079	1150	3
EWOLDT LEON H	CW4	W-2148152	0667	2
EWRY RALPH H	COL	0-0214465	0155	3
EWTON FRANCIS R	1LT	0-0376239	0344	2
EXLEY JOSEPH M	CPT	0-0324386	0954	3
EXLINE MAX R	MAJ	0-1686374	0556	1
EXNER JOSEPH H	CW2	W-2119594	1048	1
EXNER WILLARD H	CW2	W-2152455	0659	1
EXTON WALTER J	2LT	0-1300350	1144	2
EXUM CHARLES E	MAJ	0-0976490	0165	1
EXUM JAMES V	WO1	W-2108976	0551	1
EY JOHN A JR	LTC	0-1701694	0164	1
EY LEO F	MAJ	0-0144122	0146	2
EYCLESHYMER HAROLD D	LTC	0-0299506	0565	3
EYER PHILIP F	MAJ	0-1635852	0457	1
EYESTONE RAYMOND T	COL	0-0438054	0658	1
EYHERABIDE STEPHEN P	1LT	0-1297862	0745	2
EYLE GEORGE W	LTC	0-1642844	0867	2
EYLER HARRY E JR	LTC	0-0293777	0866	3
EYMER CLARENCE M	COL	0-0196296	0346	2
EYRE FRANK R	COL	0-0451661	0768	3
EYRE HARLAN A	MAJ	0-1581120	1264	1
EYRICH ALBERT A	MAJ	0-1102720	0964	3
EYSTER JAMES A	MAJ	0-0148010	0156	3
EYSTER RICHARD W	2LT	0-1302287	0144	2
EZELL KINCHELOE	LTC	0-0300390	0762	2
EZZARD WILLIAM T	LTC	0-0315215	0167	1
EZZELL ALVIN C	CW3	W-2152524	0763	1
EZZELL JAMES M	CPT	0-1185616	0160	2
EZZELL LAURISTON	CPT	0-1693008	0346	2
FAASSE ADRIAN	MAJ	0-0468452	0946	2
FABE[illegible] SALEM	CPT	0-0398473	0744	2
FABEL DONALD C	COL	0-0144379	0857	3

NAME	GRADE	SVC NO	DATE RET MO YR	RET CODE
FABER BENJAMIN L	1LT	0-0434868	1045	2
FABER EDWIN J	LTC	0-0232682	0762	3
FABER JOHN E JR	MAJ	0-0490968	1045	2
FABER WILLIAM H	MAJ	0-0975287	1061	1
FABERT MARVIN C	LTC	0-1031479	1263	1
FABIAN EMIL M	MAJ	0-0115980	1145	2
FABIAN EUGENE R	MAJ	0-1533310	1055	1
FABIAN ISAAC P	CW3	RW-2146973	0966	1
FABIAN JOSEPH A	MAJ	0-2212049	0463	1
FABIAN MARY J	MAJ	L-0200504	0865	3
FABINSKY WALTER R	CW3	W-2148204	1267	1
FABLINGER WILLIAM D	CPT	0-1322213	0147	2
FABRIC FRED	1LT	0-0938169	0348	2
FABRICK JOHN	LTC	0-0529235	0866	1
FABRIZE ANGELO C	CW4	W-2117196	0355	1
FACE ALBERT R	1LT	0-0410598	1043	2
FACENDA ALBERT J	CW4	W-2120295	0262	3
FACER GRANT T	1LT	0-0550579	0446	2
FACEY FRED W JR	LTC	0-0902370	1266	3
FACKENTHAEL ALLAN H	WO1	W-2104037	1044	2
FACKERELL ALVIN P	CW3	W-2152176	1162	1
FACKLER JOHN M JR	1LT	0-0330146	0542	2
FACKO ROBERT F	LTC	0-0493371	0765	1
FACTEAU HENRY H	MAJ	0-0136053	0550	3
FADDEN VERNON J	LTC	0-0455895	0361	2
FADDIS CHARLES I	COL	0-0187211	0650	3
FADDIS CLIFFORD B	MAJ	0-0353166	0759	2
FADER CHARLES	CPT	0-0503359	0145	2
FADLEY KENNETH L	CPT	0-0505004	0548	1
FAES JESSE G	COL	0-0130201	0454	3
FAETH HENRY J	MAJ	0-1341528	0962	1
FAGAN JOHN J JR	LTC	0-2036857	0468	3
FAGAN LEMUEL T	COL	0-0357368	0863	3
FAGAN QUENTIN E	CW3	W-2152492	0165	1
FAGAN ROBERT F	2LT	0-1054559	0345	2
FAGAN WALTER F	LTC	0-1016387	0962	1
FAGERBERG EVERT C	1LT	0-1640433	0346	2
FAGGARD LIONEL E	MAJ	0-1552062	0860	1
FAGNANT PROSPER A	MAJ	0-0583754	0661	1
FAGUET BENJAMIN B	CPT	0-0533150	0546	2
FAHEY BERNARD D	MAJ	0-2025641	0461	1
FAHEY DANIEL C JR	COL	0-0247716	1266	3
FAHEY GEORGE L	MAJ	0-0505527	0647	2
FAHEY JOHN J	COL	0-0385525	0360	1
FAHEY JOSEPH M	LTC	0-1894973	0365	3
FAHI MARTIN A	LTC	0-1318292	0563	1
FAHL JAMES C	COL	0-0522403	0868	3
FAHLEY ANTON N	CPT	0-1913670	0336	1
FAHNERT CURTIS E	MAJ	0-0160363	0354	3
FAHRES MARCELLUS	LTC	0-0267595	0168	3
FAHRINGER VICTOR T	COL	0-0158915	0646	2
FAHRION LOUIS E	LTC	0-0189104	0951	3
FAIL JAMES F JR	MAJ	0-1798570	1160	1
FAILLACE GAETANO	MAJ	0-2030375	1264	1
FAILOR RALPH M	CPT	0-0382895	0246	2
FAIN BYRON R	1LT	0-0527373	1045	2
FAIN JAMES T JR	LTC	0-0250063	0467	3
FAIN STANSELL H	CPT	0-0407350	1146	2
FAIR CHARLES H	LTC	0-0395085	0854	1
FAIR CLIFTON D	CW2	W-3430478	0167	1
FAIR FISHER A	LTC	0-2030655	0368	1
FAIR HAROLD	LTC	0-0442950	1150	1
FAIR HARRY	LTC	0-0954168	0667	1
FAIR JOSEPH K	MAJ	0-0108482	1036	1
FAIR ORSON F	1LT	0-1316634	0446	2
FAIR ROBERT J	LTC	0-1280818	0663	2
FAIR THEODORE	LTC	0-1017273	1266	1
FAIRBANKS CLIFTON A	COL	0-0287363	0667	3
FAIRBANKS LESTER L	LTC	0-1557839	0561	1
FAIRBANKS LYNN N	LTC	0-0321062	0365	3
FAIRBANKS RUSSELL	MAJ	0-1308802	0761	2
FAIRBANKS WESTON E	MAJ	0-2007585	0761	1
FAIRCHILD DUWAIN H	MAJ	0-1640435	0858	2
FAIRCHILD GEORGE W	COL	0-0138773	1151	3
FAIRCHILD JACKSON K	COL	0-0187028	0449	3

NAME	GRADE	SVC NO	DATE RET MO YR	RET CODE
FAIRCHILD ORLO R	CW3	W-2147972	0763	1
FAIRCHILD TED	1LT	0-1589820	1266	2
FAIRCHILD WILLIAM H	COL	0-0454625	0761	1
FAIRCLOTH MIRIAM C	MAJ	N-0784471	1167	3
FAIRES THOMAS F	MAJ	0-0252082	0646	2
FAIRFAX HARRY	CW2	W-2112073	0350	2
FAIRFIELD WILLIAM A	MAJ	0-0224999	1044	2
FAIRMAN CHARLES	COL	0-0118642	0757	3
FAIRWEATHER ELWYN B	MAJ	0-2049236	0163	1
FAIRWEATHER PATRICK	MAJ	0-0486676	0964	3
FAITH CHARLES M	LTC	0-1295854	1166	1
FAITZ EVERETT K	CPT	0-0298193	1163	3
FAJARDO AURELIO G	1LT	0-1856571	0149	1
FAKE GORDEN C	CPT	0-1284690	0545	2
FALANDERS EDWARD W	CPT	0-0152093	0250	3
FALASCA LAWRENCE J	LTC	0-1943588	1262	1
FALATEK JOHN J	MAJ	0-0932577	0567	3
FALBE JOHN J SR	MAJ	0-1591706	0357	1
FALCK HAROLD E	LTC	0-1294284	0961	1
FALCON DAVIS F	LTC	0-0328273	0160	1
FALCON SIMON F JR	LTC	0-0275088	0954	1
FALCONER JAMES E	2LT	0-1178784	0445	2
FALCONER LEONARD J	CPT	0-1885817	1065	1
FALEN AUGUST C	MAJ	0-1288725	0660	1
FALISE ALPHONSE	LTC	0-0138810	0254	3
FALK ALBION J	CPT	0-0488259	0847	3
FALK ARTHUR E	MAJ	0-1845881	0951	2
FALK BERNARD S	MAJ	0-1114920	1262	1
FALK DONALD A	LTC	0-0297058	0262	3
FALK MILTON	LTC	0-0307712	0966	1
FALKE THEODORE W	1LT	0-0490713	0543	2
FALKENAU ROBERT M	COL	0-0136601	0344	2
FALKENBERG GEORGE	1LT	0-0169400	1054	3
FALKENBURY ROBERT D	LTC	0-1300467	0964	1
FALKENRATH JOHN A	1LT	0-0452018	0646	2
FALKENSTINE ALLAN	LTC	0-0162950	0357	3
FALKENSTRØM ARTHUR L	MAJ	0-1337286	1061	1
FALKNER JAMES E SR	MAJ	0-1341870	0764	1
FALKNER MURRAY C	MAJ	0-0263713	0659	3
FALKNER WILLIAM J	LTC	0-0391611	0561	1
FALKOVIC FRANK O	MAJ	0-1100978	0761	1
FALKOVICH MARK F	LTC	0-0384163	0557	1
FALL JELLVON K	COL	0-1645559	0968	1
FALLAT HOMER J	LTC	0-0235370	0662	3
FALLEUR JULIEN G	COL	0-0260463	0465	3
FALLIN EDMUND R	LTC	0-2010597	0566	1
FALLIN EDWARD D	MAJ	0-2035307	0263	1
FALLIS FRANK H	CW2	W-2147217	1164	1
FALLON JOHN W	LTC	0-1292856	0961	1
FALLON WILLIAM H	LTC	0-0199713	1053	3
FALLS LLOYD W	2LT	0-1319188	0645	2
FALLS RAYMOND O	COL	0-0319618	1060	3
FALSEY EDWARD T	1LT	0-0529722	0646	2
FALSTICK CLEMENT J	CW2	W-2142761	0766	1
FALTINOW TOM J	MAJ	0-1038609	1162	1
FALVEY ARTHUR W	CPT	0-0130986	0252	3
FALZGRAF BENJIMAN A	LTC	0-0364166	0557	1
FALZONE CHARLES V	CW3	W-2147829	1062	1
FAMBROUGH JAMES M	COL	0-0216188	1062	3
FAMIGLIETTI ANTHONY	LTC	0-0311400	0668	3
FAMULARO NICHOLAS A	MAJ	0-0367477	0446	2
FANCHALSKY ELIZABETH	MAJ	N-0725765	0967	1
FANCHER HARVEY A	MAJ	0-0108656	0733	1
FANCHER HOWARD W	CW3	W-2143453	1060	2
FANDLE FRANK J	CPT	0-0108339	0250	1
FANEUF MARJORIE E	1LT	N-0721239	0546	1
FANGEROW WILLIAM E	LTC	0-0468655	0348	2
FANJOY ALLAN C	1LT	0-2204607	0853	2
FANJOY BERTHA J	MAJ	N-0756315	1065	1
FANKBONER WILSON M	CPT	0-1170358	0347	2
FANN BILLY M	CPT	0-2011098	0462	2
FANN WILLIAM F	CW4	W-2110606	0659	1
FANNIN ROBERT	MAJ	0-0980197	0163	1
FANNIN STELLA J	2LT	N-0735390	0645	1
FANNIN WILLIAM C	MAJ	0-0488415	0954	1

NAME	GRADE	SVC NO	DATE RET MO YR	RET CODE
FANNING HOMER E	LTC	0-0269802	1263	3
FANNING JAMES C	LTC	0-0227584	1262	3
FANNING JOHN H	CPT	0-0110769	0213	1
FANNING MARY C	MAJ	R-0002281	0464	2
FANNING MERLE J	CW2	W-2214885	1166	1
FANNON WALTER C	1LT	0-1295002	0846	2
FANSLER EDWARD	MAJ	0-0499514	0157	1
FANSLER LYMAN C	MAJ	0-0979003	0167	1
FANT GLENN F	COL	0-0331752	0865	1
FANT HANDY B	COL	0-0208159	1263	3
FANT SHERMAN B	MAJ	0-1924775	0766	1
FANTAUZZI JOSE	CW4	W-2114068	0557	1
FANTINI WALTER J	LTC	0-1582316	0768	3
FANTOM ERNEST B	CPT	0-0174334	1054	3
FANUCCHI ANNA R	1LT	N-0728814	0246	1
FARACI CHARLES J	MAJ	0-2266426	0368	1
FARACI FRANK J	MAJ	0-2029088	0563	1
FARAGHER JOHN H	1LT	0-1018426	0945	2
FARBER CHARLES F	LTC	0-1053127	0667	1
FARBER JACK E	CPT	0-1283228	0546	2
FARBER LOU J	COL	0-0224984	1054	3
FARDAHL NELS	LTC	0-0297580	0764	1
FARDEN BERNARD N	COL	0-0251148	0660	1
FARELL JOSEPH H	MAJ	0-1922585	0764	1
FARGO CHARLES C	COL	0-0245810	0559	1
FARGO JAMES C	LTC	0-0188006	0648	3
FARGO MARY M	1LT	N-0725321	0546	2
FARGO WARREN C	COL	0-0237215	0450	3
FARGO WELLS	COL	0-0186674	1160	1
FARGUSSON RALPH M	MAJ	0-2212033	0962	1
FARHAT MAYNARD M	MAJ	0-0356679	1145	2
FARIA JUAN L	MAJ	0-0294534	0962	3
FARIEL WILLIAM O	CW2	W-2213540	0766	2
FARINA VINCENT F	MAJ	0-0453102	0945	2
FARINACCI MAURICE G	CPT	0-0343724	0745	2
FARINATO JOHN J	2LT	0-1999975	0246	2
FARINGTON IRWIN E	MAJ	0-0186643	1157	3
FARINHOLT WILLIAM W	LTC	0-0269460	1067	3
FARIS EDITH	2LT	N-0727042	0444	1
FARIS THOMAS M	COL	0-0193125	1159	3
FARKAS ARCHIE J	WO1	W-2115264	0854	1
FARLAND GEORGE A	CW3	W-2151811	0862	1
FARLEMAN MERWYN G	LTC	0-0253013	0566	3
FARLER FRED S	CPT	0-0509924	0947	2
FARLEY ALBERT W JR	LTC	0-1080443	0562	1
FARLEY ARTHUR B	MAJ	0-0949978	0661	1
FARLEY FRANCIS A	LTC	0-1299018	0763	3
FARLEY FRANCIS J	MAJ	0-1285404	1061	1
FARLEY FRANK H	MAJ	0-0484817	0354	1
FARLEY FREDERICK	MAJ	0-1598557	0962	1
FARLEY GRACE E	LTC	N-0756631	0266	3
FARLEY JOHN C	1LT	0-0928063	0645	2
FARLEY JOHN L	COL	0-0174058	0452	3
FARLEY JOSEPH J	COL	0-0275583	0859	1
FARLEY MATTHEW B	MAJ	0-0474060	0647	1
FARLEY PAUL J	COL	0-0134488	0456	3
FARLEY SAMUEL N	LTC	0-0901922	0265	3
FARLEY THOMAS J	CPT	0-1322012	0952	2
FARLEY THOMAS J	2LT	0-1590443	0244	2
FARLEY WIRT P	LTC	0-0319685	0853	1
FARMER ANTHONY X	WO1	W-2147480	0454	2
FARMER CHARLES D	MAJ	0-2256315	1167	1
FARMER CHARLIE H	CPT	0-0258486	0546	1
FARMER DONALD W	LTC	0-0990962	0868	2
FARMER EDWARD S	MAJ	0-1284309	0457	1
FARMER FRED E JR	CW3	W-2205756	0767	1
FARMER GARY P	LTC	0-1109282	1060	1
FARMER GEORGE A	LTC	0-1336052	0964	1
FARMER GEORGE R	CPT	0-0157234	1145	2
FARMER HENRY C	MAJ	0-0972489	0965	1
FARMER HOLLY S	CPT	0-0523542	0553	2
FARMER HOWARD	CPT	0-0372281	1146	2
FARMER JACK J	MAJ	0-1105417	0157	1
FARMER JAMES E	LTC	0-1043622	0264	1
FARMER JAMES L	LTC	0-0385629	0557	1

NAME	GRADE	SVC NO	DATE RET MO YR	RET CODE
FARMER JAMES R	CPT	0-1551202	1045	2
FARMER JAMES W	LTC	0-1030764	0463	1
FARMER JOHN G JR	LTC	0-0341902	0959	1
FARMER JOHN H	CW2	W-2143070	0255	1
FARMER JOHN H	CW4	W-2143637	0756	1
FARMER MAURICE A	2LT	0-1946726	1046	2
FARMER MURRAY W	CPT	0-0411862	0845	2
FARMER TRAVER H	MAJ	0-2262123	0661	1
FARMER VERE L	COL	0-0275076	0157	3
FARMER WALTER A	1LT	0-1995027	0646	2
FARMER WILLIAM A	LTC	0-0226445	0364	3
FARMER WILLIAM F	MAJ	0-0256593	1054	3
FARMER WILLIAM G	CPT	0-0438347	0849	1
FARMER YEWELL M	LTC	0-1011043	0760	1
FARNELL ERIC C	LTC	0-1596003	0662	1
FARNER FRED H	LTC	0-0970531	0868	1
FARNER KENNETH T	CPT	0-0306563	1144	2
FARNESS ORIN J	LTC	0-0322118	0247	2
FARNEY EMIL J	CPT	0-1110475	0657	1
FARNHAM JOHN A	LTC	0-1585168	0967	3
FARNHAM RAYMOND K	COL	0-0462074	0946	2
FARNHAM VERNON D	CW4	W-2205506	1266	1
FARNSLEY MURRY J	LTC	0-1111052	0862	1
FARNSWORTH CLAYTON B	CPT	0-1319190	0946	2
FARNSWORTH DENNY K	LTC	0-0331352	0968	1
FARNSWORTH JOSEPH B	LTC	0-0358044	0662	1
FARNSWORTH L M	CPT	0-0312372	1047	1
FARNSWORTH ORA L	COL	0-0444318	1053	1
FARNSWORTH RICHARD C	1LT	0-1080444	0645	2
FARNSWORTH W L	1LT	0-0494894	1044	2
FARNSWORTH WALLACE W	MAJ	0-1313084	0365	1
FARO HARRY	CW2	W-2118328	0347	1
FARQUHAR GEORGE A	COL	0-0242122	0665	3
FARQUHAR GUY L	1LT	0-0116037	0457	3
FARQUHAR JOSEPH W	MAJ	0-1319611	0957	1
FARQUHAR WILLIAM R	LTC	0-1176012	0562	1
FARR BURLLE R	COL	0-0291786	1267	3
FARR DAVID J	LTC	0-1548053	0168	1
FARR GEORGE W	CPT	0-5328247	0968	2
FARR HENRY L	LTC	0-0287065	0265	3
FARR KENNETH H	LTC	0-1596563	0268	1
FARR LEONARD W	1LT	0-1169948	0145	2
FARR RICHARD S	COL	0-0159150	0550	3
FARR STEPHEN A	LTC	0-1117601	0463	1
FARR WILLIAM JR	LTC	0-1102235	0358	2
FARRA JOHN S	LTC	0-1040917	0954	1
FARRAGUT LOYALL D	LTC	0-0312130	0447	2
FARRALO HARRY E	MAJ	0-1322983	0658	1
FARRAR ANDREW J	MAJ	0-1011680	0160	1
FARRAR CHRISTY M	MAJ	0-0107198	0648	3
FARRAR CLAYTON P	1LT	0-1175704	0347	2
FARRAR EMMONS B	MAJ	0-0182201	0352	3
FARRAR MARION L	LTC	0-1303696	0562	1
FARRAR RALPH W	COL	0-0226261	0863	3
FARRAR ROBERT G	MAJ	0-0990751	0867	1
FARREL THOMAS P	CPT	0-0255193	1046	1
FARRELL ALBERT M	CPT	0-1102236	1046	2
FARRELL ANDREW F	MAJ	0-0188655	0553	2
FARRELL BARBARA A	MAJ	L-1010051	0668	1
FARRELL EDWARD J	WO1	W-2111811	1262	3
FARRELL ERNEST R	LTC	0-0488156	0154	1
FARRELL ERWIN D	LTC	0-1317604	0865	1
FARRELL EUGENE J	LTC	0-0303935	0865	3
FARRELL FRANK J	1LT	0-0303391	1042	2
FARRELL HENRY F	1LT	0-1290734	0446	2
FARRELL HUGH P	LTC	0-0918923	1059	2
FARRELL JAMES M	LTC	0-0966565	0868	1
FARRELL JAMES W	MAJ	0-1175112	0165	1
FARRELL JEROME	LTC	0-0220537	0361	3
FARRELL JOHN P	CW3	W-2151634	0864	1
FARRELL JOSEPH F	MAJ	0-1013132	1061	1
FARRELL JOSEPH F	MAJ	0-1546970	1159	1
FARRELL LEE J JR	LTC	0-0379594	0365	1
FARRELL LUTHER K	CPT	0-1304513	0664	1
FARRELL MARK A	CPT	0-0476978	0746	2
FARRELL NEIL K	MAJ	0-1923620	1165	2
FARRELL PHILIP V	CPT	0-0371489	0246	2
FARRELL RAYMOND G	MAJ	0-2018667	0463	2
FARRELL ROBERT G	LTC	0-0913473	0856	1
FARRELL ROBERT S	MAJ	0-1341650	0961	1
FARRELL ROLAND J	LTC	0-0426770	0565	1
FARRELL ROY W	MAJ	0-0502047	0147	2
FARRELL THOMAS J JR	LTC	0-0450858	0762	1
FARRELL WALTER J	MAJ	0-0503836	1047	2
FARRELL WILLIAM E	CPT	0-2014535	0660	1
FARRELL WILLIAM J	MAJ	0-0179839	0658	3
FARREN ERNEST G	LTC	0-1010110	0565	1
FARREN JOHN J JR	COL	0-0365605	0868	1
FARRENS BEVERLY P	MAJ	0-2030222	1159	1
FARRER THOMAS J	CPT	0-0918791	0644	2
FARRIMOND JAMES W	COL	0-0244637	0866	3
FARRINGTON A A JR	MAJ	0-1057055	0161	1
FARRINGTON ALAN M	LTC	0-0499041	0157	1
FARRINGTON CARL S	1LT	0-0537819	0946	2
FARRINGTON CHARLIE L	CPT	0-1286808	0747	2
FARRINGTON HOWARD E	1LT	0-1579630	0653	1
FARRINGTON JAMES T	MAJ	0-1298522	0863	1
FARRINGTON JAMES W	CPT	0-0323490	0457	1
FARRINGTON JOSEPH O	LTC	0-0468634	0646	2
FARRINGTON PAUL JR	CW3	W-2142072	0358	1
FARRIOR ALAN R	MAJ	0-0586637	0863	1
FARRIS BRUCE V O	LTC	0-1574716	1264	1
FARRIS CARROL M	CW3	W-3430028	0868	1
FARRIS CHARLES H	COL	0-0125214	1153	3
FARRIS FRANK H	MAJ	0-1285224	0846	2
FARRIS GARVIN B	COL	0-0287791	1047	2
FARRIS HOUSTON S	LTC	0-0309320	0456	2
FARRIS JESSE H	LTC	0-0281098	1266	3
FARRIS JOHN I	LTC	0-0389829	0463	1
FARRIS JOHN J	CPT	0-1736653	1050	2
FARRIS JOSEPH A	CPT	0-0429479	0646	2
FARRIS THAD L	LTC	0-1183512	1064	1
FARRISH FERDINAND	MAJ	0-1178137	0663	1
FARRISH THOMAS O	COL	0-0278806	0455	1
FARROW JOE B	MAJ	0-0959266	0563	1
FARROW JOE L	LTC	0-1175431	0862	1
FARROW JOE T	CW3	W-2141269	0165	1
FARRY LAWRENCE W	CPT	0-1323301	0747	2
FARSON WILBUR E	COL	0-0143685	0453	3
FARTHING ARTHUR C	COL	0-0274346	0867	3
FARTHING JACK A	COL	0-0370179	1068	3
FARVER WARREN L	CPT	0-0183247	1148	3
FARWELL DAVID J	COL	0-0331696	0667	3
FARWELL RUDOLPH G	MAJ	0-1924077	0763	1
FARWIG WILLIS O	2LT	0-1038973	0445	2
FASANO DOMENIC T	CW2	W-3430542	0967	1
FASCE EGI V	LTC	0-0236271	1062	3
FASIG HAMPTON P	COL	0-0371901	0768	1
FASSETT HIRAM B JR	LTC	0-0245351	0350	3
FASSETT WILLIAM E	CPT	0-1300782	0454	2
FASSLER SALLY	2LT	N-0703265	0744	2
FASSNACHT PAUL L	MAJ	0-1643539	0463	1
FASTAIA MARTIN J	LTC	0-1302620	0363	1
FASTENBERG LOUIS J	1LT	0-1315152	0958	2
FATE LESTON R	CPT	0-0286069	1066	3
FATH LAURENCE M	LTC	0-1284486	1054	1
FATINA JOE J	1LT	0-1697906	0245	2
FATKIN GEORGE A	CW2	W-2108315	0460	3
FATORA JOHN A	MAJ	0-1120316	0163	1
FATULA ESTER J	MAJ	N-0799588	1267	1
FATULA JOHN JR	MAJ	0-1877110	0765	1
FAUBER EARL B	LTC	0-1100537	1161	1
FAUBER JOHN E	COL	0-0263178	0465	3
FAUBER ROBERT S	CPT	0-1923586	1262	1
FAUBERT VICTOR T	MAJ	0-0974055	0162	1
FAUBION ERNEST E	CW4	W-2105247	0461	1
FAUBLE DOUGLAS G	CW3	W-2002804	0568	3
FAUCETT JACK H	LTC	0-0280933	1068	3
FAUCETTE GEORGE R	COL	0-1000041	0761	1
FAUCHER RAYMOND E	MAJ	0-1913364	0465	1
FAUCHEUX CLANCY J	MAJ	0-1686641	0468	1
FAUCON IVAN V	MAJ	0-0987910	0565	1
FAUGHT COLONEL H	LTC	0-0348573	1160	1
FAULCONER E L SR	COL	0-0189349	1058	3
FAULCONER JAMES N	LTC	0-0255244	1045	2
FAULDS JOHN W	COL	0-0163991	0753	3
FAULHABER GEORGE B	MAJ	0-1058996	1263	1
FAULK ARCHIE L	COL	0-0174499	0246	2
FAULK EVERETTE W	COL	0-0331414	1063	3
FAULK HARRY M	CW2	W-2215149	0967	1
FAULK WILEY C	LTC	0-0451101	1060	1
FAULKENBERRY M W	1LT	N-0763918	1045	1
FAULKINGHAM RICHARD	MAJ	0-1341767	0865	1
FAULKNER ACE E	LTC	0-0308907	0355	2
FAULKNER CLARENCE R	MAJ	0-0370959	0867	3
FAULKNER CLINTON E	MAJ	0-0319272	0258	1
FAULKNER DAVID P	LTC	0-0277342	0567	3
FAULKNER DEWEY	CPT	0-0182733	0945	2
FAULKNER EDMUND B	2LT	0-1310589	0545	2
FAULKNER HOWARD G	COL	0-0202744	1055	1
FAULKNER JAMES D	LTC	0-0170799	0658	3
FAULKNER LIONEL E	LTC	0-0251898	0961	3
FAULKNER LOUIE L	CW4	W-2121218	0660	1
FAULKNER TRUEMAN E	MAJ	0-0217624	0157	3
FAULKS GLENN O	MAJ	0-0971337	0561	1
FAULLING BISHOP T	CW3	W-3200153	1068	1
FAULS DOROTHY M	MAJ	L-0604503	1063	1
FAULVE MARCELO	1LT	0-0890487	0849	1
FAUNTLEROY LORENZO B	CW3	W-2129822	0863	1
FAUP JEAN H	LTC	0-1288726	0761	1
FAUROT BILLIE C	MAJ	0-2251443	1167	1
FAUROT EARL E	MAJ	0-1167829	1057	1
FAUS ROBERT R	COL	0-0199978	1157	3
FAUSEL EVERETT G	LTC	0-0213627	1061	3
FAUSEL WALTER F	CPT	0-0261869	0544	2
FAUSET MERL J	LTC	0-0254699	0351	1
FAUSKE EINAR P	CW3	W-2147699	0964	1
FAUSSET DUANE S	MAJ	0-1185617	0160	1
FAUST ALMA V	2LT	N-0775595	0645	1
FAUST CARLTON L	LTC	0-0196780	0162	3
FAUST ELEANOR S	CPT	N-0794630	0454	2
FAUST JOHN E	MAJ	0-0517246	0457	1
FAUX JAMES B	LTC	0-1554365	0162	1
FAVATA FRANCIS M	MAJ	0-0258013	0765	3
FAVERMAN BARNET	LTC	0-1052341	0467	1
FAVINGER BOB F	LTC	0-2033725	0668	1
FAVINGER CALVIN F	LTC	0-0321566	0862	3
FAVORITE RALPH S	MAJ	0-1111604	0859	1
FAVRE ILSE M	2LT	N-0737040	0445	1
FAVRE JOHN L	MAJ	0-0935366	1063	2
FAVREAU FRANK E	LTC	0-0377906	1057	1
FAVREAU WALDO S	LTC	0-0902781	0367	3
FAWCETT EDWARD G	1LT	0-1031076	1044	2
FAWCETT HARRY O	COL	0-0325163	1060	1
FAWCETT JOHN R JR	LTC	0-0415978	0664	1
FAWCETT PAUL W	LTC	0-0304909	0757	2
FAWCETT ROBERT A	CPT	0-1596321	0360	1
FAWCETT THEODORE L	2LT	0-1822122	1143	2
FAXON ALFRED A JR	LTC	0-0361523	0667	3
FAXON HENRY H	MAJ	0-0399190	0745	2
FAY ELMER R SR	CPT	0-0488048	1044	2
FAY EUGENE E	MAJ	0-1540839	0664	1
FAY JOSEPH G	CW2	W-2144054	0358	1
FAY PATRICK B	COL	0-0333123	0559	3
FAY STANLEY A	LTC	0-0222227	1060	3
FAY THOMAS H	1LT	0-1312754	1057	1
FAY WILLIAM H	CW2	W-2152955	0563	1
FAYE EYVIND M	LTC	0-0236585	0166	3
FAYETTE NELSON C	CW3	W-2142762	0461	1
FAYLE LESLIE F	LTC	0-0256284	1262	3
FAYLE PERCY R	CPT	0-0379011	1045	2
FAYNE WILLIAM C	CPT	0-0454793	0559	1
FAYNE WILLIAM J	LTC	0-0470756	1147	1
FAYTLE ORIEL F	CPT	0-1574717	0246	2
FAZAKERLEY F J	LTC	0-0268130	0758	3
FAZENBAKER EDGAR L	MAJ	0-1180179	1062	1
FAZENDIN ROGER A	1LT	0-0414574	0545	2
FAZIO HARRIET P	1LT	N-0728240	1145	1
FAZIO JOSEPH	CW2	W-2000607	0247	2
FEAGAN KENNETH M	MAJ	0-0288221	0964	3
FEAGANS WILLIAM C	LTC	0-1578446	1060	1
FEAGIN JOHN L	LTC	0-0237853	1165	3
FEAGIN OSCAR R	CPT	0-1310924	0849	2
FEAGLER DALTON G	CPT	0-0948792	0261	1
FEAGLES ROBERT W	CPT	0-0518826	0847	2
FEARING ALBERT H	LTC	0-0212471	0160	3
FEARING ARTHUR N	LTC	0-0371730	0466	1
FEARING OLIN K	MAJ	0-0245522	1155	3
FEARN ODELL E	MAJ	0-1650084	0660	1
FEASER ROBERT G	CW2	W-2118999	1047	1
FEAST HARRY C L	COL	0-0203302	0455	3
FEASTER BURNES L	MAJ	0-0116085	1058	3
FEASTER ORION O	LTC	0-0106052	0453	3
FEATHER ARTHUR C JR	CW2	W-2153190	0460	1
FEATHER JOHN W	2LT	0-0201373	1158	3
FEATHER RAYMOND O	MAJ	0-0215130	0463	3
FEATHERSTON ERNEST M	MAJ	0-0302220	0966	3
FEATHERSTON GEORGE O	MAJ	0-1541578	0457	1
FEATHERSTON THOMAS	1LT	0-0521151	1145	2
FEATHERSTONE FRED E	LTC	0-0418190	0462	1
FEATHERSTONE RALPH O	MAJ	0-0986825	1163	1
FEAY ROBERT W	LTC	0-0565325	0263	1
FEAZEL WILLIAM J	LTC	0-0448211	0150	1
FECHTER WILLIAM J JR	LTC	0-0450859	0657	1
FECTEAU ROLAND G	2LT	0-2006090	0268	1
FEDENETS ANDREW	MAJ	0-1175433	0755	1
FEDER EDWARD P	MAJ	0-0239477	1045	2
FEDERICK JOSEPH C	CPT	0-0500636	0445	2
FEDERICO JOSEPH L	CPT	0-1797803	0846	2
FEDERLIN FERDINAND	MAJ	0-0402445	0456	1
FEDERSPIEL JOHN A	CW4	W-2115549	0659	1
FEDOR GEORGE	LTC	0-1796256	0361	1
FEDORCHAK STEVE L	MAJ	0-1106723	1163	1
FEDOSI ALEC L	MAJ	0-1166977	0954	1
FEDOSIUK GEORGE S	LTC	0-0335259	0468	3
FEE ALBERT A	CPT	0-1300010	0963	1
FEE ROBERT J	CPT	0-0134477	0648	3
FEELEY EDWARD J JR	MAJ	0-1796257	0261	1
FEELEY MICHAEL J	CPT	0-2287676	0765	2
FEEMSTER KENNETH L	1LT	0-2262896	1052	2
FEENAN JAMES J	CPT	0-0525497	0348	1
FEENER LESTER C	MAJ	0-0474006	0646	2
FEENEY ALFRED L	MAJ	0-0525634	0754	1
FEENEY BARTHOLOME	MAJ	0-1039338	0958	1
FEENEY CHARLES F	MAJ	0-1106724	1262	1
FEENEY ELTON O	LTC	0-0125212	0960	3
FEENEY IRENE C	MAJ	N-0752254	1163	1
FEENEY JOHN F A	MAJ	0-0219338	1054	3
FEENEY RICHARD T	LTC	0-1290401	0661	1
FEENEY ROBERT F	CW3	W-2152590	1263	1
FEENEY WILLIAM E	CPT	0-1015354	0368	2
FEESE ARTHUR J	WO1	W-2151999	0158	1
FEGAN JAMES J	MAJ	0-1169101	0861	1
FEGER GEORGE S H JR	MAJ	0-0392011	0562	1
FEGLEY PAUL M	COL	0-0294731	0365	3
FEHLANDT PHILIP R	LTC	0-0497680	1060	3
FEHLANDT THEODORE F	MAJ	0-0235238	1165	3
FEHLMAN ROSS G	LTC	0-0235669	0160	3
FEHNER KENNETH C	MAJ	0-1316029	0266	1
FEHRENBACHER FRANK J	MAJ	0-0116088	1153	3
FEICHTINGER JOHN R	CPT	0-1106726	1145	2
FEIERABEND OTTO W	CPT	0-0290017	0867	3
FEIERLEIN OTTO F	LTC	0-1287850	0667	1
FEIGEL CLAYTON SR	CW2	W-2101285	1053	2
FEIGHERY EDWARD P	CW2	W-2147487	0663	1
FEIGIN EMANUEL V	MAJ	0-0335819	0646	2
FEILD MAURICE A	LTC	0-1297018	1264	1
FEILD SAM C	1LT	0-1994758	0645	2
FEILEN JOHN T	1LT	0-1316030	0348	2
FEIMER THEODORE J	LTC	0-0358085	0156	1

332-811 O - 69 - 11

ARMY OF THE UNITED STATES RETIRED LIST

NAME	GRADE	SVC NO	DATE RET MO YR	RET CODE	NAME	GRADE	SVC NO	DATE RET MO YR	RET CODE	NAME	GRADE	SVC NO	DATE RET MO YR	RET CODE	NAME	GRADE	SVC NO	DATE RET MO YR	RET CODE
FEIN EDWARD E	CW4	W-2120929	1065	2	FELSTEAD CHARLES F	COL	0-0302380	0163	3	FERBER GERHARDT H	CPT	0-0482540	0243	2	FERGUSON WADE O JR	LTC	0-1103158	0262	1
FEIN MAURICE	CPT	0-0429735	0245	[illegible]	FELT STANTON W	1LT	0-1585686	0147	2	FERBER SAMUEL J	MAJ	0-0492777	0246	2	FERGUSON WADE H	LTC	0-0281204	0864	3
FEINBERG BERNARD S	CPT	0-1533779	0546	2	FELT WILLIAM A	LTC	0-1037483	0862	1	FERDERBER CHARLES J	COL	0-2050470	0868	1	FERGUSON WILLIAM G	LTC	0-1540640	1167	1
FEINBERG HARRY	CPT	0-0439435	0745	2	FELTENBERGER A L	1LT	0-0157549	0535	1	FERDERBER WILLIAM	LTC	0-0302975	1061	3	FERGUSON WILLIAM H	MAJ	0-1185942	0161	1
FEINBERG IRWIN	LTC	0-1167568	0965	1	FELTER RANDALL H	LTC	0-0376468	0460	1	FERDINAND HAROLD W	MAJ	0-1333528	1265	1	FERGUSON WILLIAM R	MAJ	0-0247919	1166	3
FEINBERG RAYMOND	CPT	0-1647871	1262	1	FELTMAN JAMES D	MAJ	0-2288299	0661	1	FEREBEE EDWARD S	LTC	0-0234459	0865	3	FERGUSSON CECIL O	COL	0-0171625	0556	3
FEINBERG SEYMOUR O	1LT	0-0441149	0245	2	FELTMAN REUBEN	MAJ	0-0273187	0546	2	FERGUSON ALBERT E	LTC	0-0186037	0654	3	FERHINHOFF THEODORE	LTC	0-0213724	0963	3
FEINDEL HOWARD W	LTC	0-0305603	1060	1	FELTNER BILL JR	LTC	0-1824003	0661	1	FERGUSON ALEXANDER	LTC	0-1596644	0667	3	FERLA SALVATORE	CPT	0-0488656	1146	2
FEINER EDWARD J	MAJ	0-0205060	1162	3	FELTON HAROLD V	CPT	0-1309237	0346	2	FERGUSON ALFRED H	LTC	0-0226852	0666	3	FERNALD GORDON H	LTC	0-0104201	0649	3
FEINSTEIN ISIDORE I	CPT	0-1324514	1166	2	FELTON PHILIP K	LTC	0-0453442	0259	1	FERGUSON ALONZO G	LTC	0-0187855	1055	3	FERNANDES ARTHUR M	MAJ	0-0888510	0853	1
FEITELL ARTHUR	MAJ	0-0345522	0346	2	FELTS BUFORD B	WO1	W-2114661	1061	1	FERGUSON ALVIN L	CPT	0-0970838	0762	1	FERNANDES JUDITH M	2LT	N-0901766	1054	2
FEITIG LOUIS R	CPT	0-1290053	0647	2	FELTS CARL B	CW2	W-2101675	0949	1	FERGUSON ARTHUR W	LTC	0-0162239	0958	3	FERNANDES ROBERT J	1LT	0-0425321	0646	2
FEJDASZ JOSEPH F	CW2	W-2142584	0454	1	FELTS CLIFFORD F	CW2	W-2141273	0157	1	FERGUSON BEN F	CPT	0-0374460	0944	2	FERNANDES VERNON R G	COL	0-1105099	1168	1
FEKETE ALFRED E	MAJ	0-0479651	0453	2	FELTS EUGENE A	CPT	0-2046397	0149	2	FERGUSON BILLY A	WO1	W-2126368	0345	2	FERNANDEZ CHARLES R	LTC	0-0328274	0861	2
FEKETY STEPHEN	MAJ	0-0885713	0657	1	FELTS HEBER H	CPT	0-0391053	1045	2	FERGUSON BYRON F	MAJ	0-1178789	0667	1	FERNANDEZ EDWARD F	MAJ	0-2027344	0154	1
FELBER JULIUS J JR	MAJ	0-2021110	0363	1	FELTS JAMES K	MAJ	0-0248666	0664	3	FERGUSON CAROLYN E	MAJ	N-0725548	0767	1	FERNANDEZ EUGENE	1LT	0-1896814	0557	1
FELBER STEPHEN	CW3	W-2141272	0159	1	FELTS JOHN R JR	CW3	W-2144134	0867	1	FERGUSON CHARLES A	LTC	0-1297702	0161	1	FERNANDEZ F L JR	MAJ	0-1320028	1155	1
FELBER THOMAS F	CW2	W-2127794	1046	1	FELTY GEORGE M	2LT	0-1016566	0145	2	FERGUSON CHARLES E	2LT	0-1825908	0445	2	FERNANDEZ F O	2LT	0-1896573	1147	2
FELCYN ROMAN O	2LT	0-1579633	1045	2	FELTY JAMES K	LTC	0-1308940	0263	2	FERGUSON CHARLIE W	CPT	0-1543407	0954	1	FERNANDEZ FELIPE A	CPT	0-1896856	0767	1
FELD ALBERT E	CPT	0-1578450	0446	2	FELTY WILLIAM E	LTC	0-1014575	0258	1	FERGUSON CLARENCE F	CPT	0-0488675	0650	1	FERNANDEZ JOHN S	CW4	W-2115860	1055	1
FELD ALLAN H	COL	0-1036139	0968	1	FELZ JAMES J	CPT	0-1797805	1046	2	FERGUSON CLIFFORD W	MAJ	0-0176563	0346	2	FERNANDEZ JUAN R	1LT	0-0396833	0545	2
FELD EDWARD L	MAJ	0-0244207	0265	3	FELZMAN JOHN H D C	CPT	0-1578454	0865	1	FERGUSON CLYDE W	WO1	W-2145127	0752	2	FERNANDEZ MARIO R	CPT	0-1797454	0761	1
FELD HARRY E	LTC	0-1556574	0367	1	FENDER HARRY G	1LT	0-0404450	0845	2	FERGUSON COMADORA M	CPT	0-0378801	1046	2	FERNANDEZ MIGUEL A	LTC	0-1301628	0264	1
FELDBUSH RICHARD L	MAJ	0-0967375	0464	1	FENDER RAY H	MAJ	0-0568110	0664	1	FERGUSON D H C JR	MAJ	0-0422417	0346	2	FERNANDEZ RAMON M	2LT	0-1896340	0550	2
FELDER DAVID J	MAJ	0-2263267	0463	1	FENDRICH MANNING	CPT	0-0321652	1045	2	FERGUSON DANIEL L	1LT	0-1796773	0968	1	FERNANDEZ VICTOR M	MAJ	0-0962218	0163	1
FELDHACKER C J	MAJ	0-1288211	0457	1	FENDRICK JOSEPH H	MAJ	0-0493950	1054	1	FERGUSON DONALD V	MAJ	0-0493062	0347	2	FERNER CHARLES R	LTC	0-1118369	0467	1
FELDHAUS JAMES G	LTC	0-0249717	0266	3	FENIG EDWARD	COL	0-1298371	1267	1	FERGUSON EARL A	MAJ	0-1541530	0862	2	FERNS JOHN H	MAJ	0-0272860	0868	3
FELDHUSEN FRANK H	CPT	0-1634738	0446	2	FENIGSON PHILIP M	WO1	W-2106633	0745	2	FERGUSON EDWARD F	LTC	0-0181575	1161	3	FERO JACOB	MAJ	0-0545566	0764	1
FELDMAN ARNOLD H	COL	0-0285529	0863	3	FENIMORE EARL R	CW3	W-2145179	0161	2	FERGUSON EDWARD O	CW4	W-2005844	0767	1	FERRANDINA A F JR	1LT	0-1698186	0546	2
FELDMAN BENJAMIN W	MAJ	0-0275431	0967	3	FENLEY JOHN H JR	CW2	W-2142678	1054	1	FERGUSON EMANUEL R	CPT	0-0533822	0745	2	FERRANDINO ROSARIO F	CW3	RW-2152493	1264	1
FELDMAN DANIEL	2LT	0-1307809	0545	2	FENN ALVA L	COL	0-0190501	0762	3	FERGUSON ERNEST L JR	1LT	0-1043336	0644	2	FERRANDO JOHN W	CW2	W-2208708	1265	1
FELDMAN DANIEL J	MAJ	0-0442921	0846	2	FENN EDWARD P	LTC	0-0232874	0962	3	FERGUSON FRANK H	MAJ	0-0246731	0859	3	FERRARA ANTHONY	2LT	0-1052765	0245	2
FELDMAN HAROLD B	LTC	0-1590445	0664	1	FENN FRED H	COL	0-0248521	1164	3	FERGUSON GEORGE X	MAJ	0-1294641	1060	1	FERRARA DOMINICK	LTC	0-0451530	0457	1
FELDMAN HAROLD H	1LT	0-0336098	0844	2	FENN HARLIN L	LTC	0-0275988	0760	2	FERGUSON GERALDINE	CPT	N-0702085	0646	1	FERRARESE CHARLES J	LTC	0-1599127	1067	1
FELDMAN HARRY H	CPT	0-0374269	0446	2	FENN JACK B	1LT	0-0418200	0544	2	FERGUSON GLEN E	CW3	RW-2151715	1065	1	FERRARI ALBERT N	LTC	0-1894928	1062	1
FELDMAN HERBERT	1LT	0-1013912	0448	2	FENN MANNIE	1LT	0-1315572	0546	2	FERGUSON HAROLD L	1LT	0-0955858	0352	2	FERRARI FRANK L	MAJ	0-1049829	0167	1
FELDMAN IRWIN R	1LT	0-1885830	0454	2	FENN WALLACE J	MAJ	0-1850711	0668	3	FERGUSON HAYDEN R	2LT	0-1691759	0452	2	FERRARI LEWIS J	2LT	0-0373198	0445	2
FELDMAN JACK	1LT	0-2017040	0747	2	FENNELL ALEXANDER	MAJ	0-1924083	1264	1	FERGUSON HAZEL M	1LT	L-0800636	0845	2	FERRARO ANTHONY	MAJ	0-4010430	0568	1
FELDMAN JEROME	MAJ	0-1043938	1165	1	FENNELL CHARLES H	CW3	W-2146831	1262	1	FERGUSON HENRY A	LTC	0-0170110	1160	3	FERRARO GERALD J	MAJ	0-1319191	0864	1
FELDMAN MARY L	2LT	N-0741842	0844	2	FENNELL JAMES	MAJ	0-0300605	1046	1	FERGUSON J NEILE	LTC	0-1634743	0862	1	FERRARO LOUIS	CW4	W-2120155	0968	1
FELDMAN MAX	MAJ	0-0360469	0346	2	FENNELL JAMES	CW4	W-2115852	0257	1	FERGUSON JACK L	CW2	W-2212923	0167	1	FERREE ALBERT A	MAJ	0-0445000	1157	1
FELDMAN SEYMOUR	MAJ	0-1821990	0562	1	FENNELL JAMES F	LTC	0-0480888	0859	1	FERGUSON JAMES A	MAJ	0-1535893	1160	1	FERREIRA AUGUSTO	WO1	W-2135575	0646	2
FELDMANN GERALD C	MAJ	0-2033896	0764	1	FENNELL JAMES F	1LT	0-1294116	0246	2	FERGUSON JAMES D	CW3	W-2207684	0467	1	FERREIRA JOSEPH	CW2	W-2153250	0462	1
FELDMILLER WILLIAM H	LTC	0-0281658	1158	3	FENNELL JAMES M	MAJ	0-0497882	0752	2	FERGUSON JAMES H JR	CPT	0-0422034	0945	2	FERRELL CHARLES D	CPT	0-0523822	0753	2
FELDNER GEORGE D	LTC	0-0224109	0960	3	FENNELL JOSEPH W	2LT	0-1887608	0160	2	FERGUSON JAMES R	MAJ	0-0517262	0549	1	FERRELL CURTIS L JR	COL	0-1550163	1266	1
FELDSHUH ALFRED M	MAJ	0-0267670	0146	2	FENNELL WILLIAM F	COL	0-0313094	1057	1	FERGUSON JAMES R	1LT	0-1998434	0546	2	FERRELL GEORGE H	2LT	0-0407785	0444	2
FELDSTEIN WILLIAM	CPT	0-1592809	1263	1	FENNER HENRY C JR	1LT	0-0326500	0745	2	FERGUSON JAMES W JR	CW2	W-2210230	0466	1	FERRELL JAMES C	2LT	0-1310698	1044	2
FELESKI PAUL E	CW4	W-2146851	0960	1	FENNER JOHN E	LTC	0-1633850	0764	1	FERGUSON JOHN A	1LT	0-1557142	1146	2	FERRELL JOE R	1LT	0-1010556	0244	2
FELICE JAMES C	LTC	0-1287500	1165	1	FENNER REX N	CPT	0-1176956	1046	2	FERGUSON JOHN C	LTC	0-0250855	1164	3	FERRELL LEE A	MAJ	0-1592813	1160	1
FELICIANO FERDINAND	LTC	0-0487850	1154	1	FENNESSEY FRANCIS P	CW3	W-2146692	0560	1	FERGUSON JOHN E	WO1	W-2148348	0653	1	FERRELL PALMORE A	COL	0-0390338	1262	1
FELICIANO GEORGE	MAJ	0-4006266	0567	1	FENNO JOHN C	CPT	0-0334813	0946	2	FERGUSON JOHN G	LTC	0-0282427	0568	3	FERRELL RICHARD S	MAJ	0-2036906	0661	1
FELICIOTTI DOMINIC	LTC	0-1287163	0863	1	FENNO WILLIAM A	CW4	W-2144445	0966	1	FERGUSON JOHN L	COL	0-0162558	0858	3	FERRELL SETH JR	CPT	0-1875124	0462	1
FELIX EDWARD A	WO1	W-2123422	0454	1	FENSCH CLARA M	CPT	N-0702048	0846	1	FERGUSON KARL F	MAJ	0-1999040	0866	1	FERRELL THOMAS E JR	CPT	0-1699814	1143	2
FELIX PAUL S	CPT	0-0446508	0944	2	FENSKE HERBERT O	MAJ	0-1329576	1161	1	FERGUSON KEITH W	MAJ	0-0888429	1263	1	FERRELL WILFORD L	LTC	0-0472326	0855	1
FELIX ROBERT L	MAJ	0-0964107	0865	1	FENSTER LOUIS Z	1LT	0-1174849	0945	2	FERGUSON L J JR	CW2	W-2211794	0766	1	FERREN EARLE N	MAJ	0-0977588	0166	1
FELIX WARREN T	LTC	0-0285999	0161	1	FENSTER ROBERT	1LT	0-1799122	0863	2	FERGUSON LAURA B	1LT	N-0728583	0846	1	FERRER ALFRED JR	MAJ	0-0406108	0859	1
FELIX WOODROW D	MAJ	0-0409488	1060	1	FENSTERMACHER EDWARD	1LT	0-0270708	0259	3	FERGUSON LAWRENCE P	LTC	0-1063034	1168	1	FERRERA MELVIN R	MAJ	0-2210166	0663	1
FELIZ EDWARD F	LTC	0-1637401	1262	1	FENSTERMACHER H G	1LT	0-1297180	0145	2	FERGUSON LORY F	CPT	0-0311119	0944	2	FERRERO MARTIN R	1LT	0-1822980	1146	2
FELKER JAMES V	CW2	W-2148848	1159	1	FENSTERMACHER W A	LTC	0-0398418	0945	2	FERGUSON LOUIS F	LTC	0-0475962	0255	1	FERRESE RALPH W	LTC	0-1291093	0261	1
FELKER STANLEY Y	CPT	0-1594205	0957	1	FENSTERMAKER J C	MAJ	0-2046968	0359	1	FERGUSON MELVIN S	CW3	W-2106558	0966	2	FERRICK JAMES H	COL	0-0259743	0367	3
FELL GEORGE K	MAJ	0-0342056	0859	1	FENT ANSEL L	LTC	0-1285564	1159	1	FERGUSON MOSES D	CW3	W-2149985	1164	1	FERRICK JOHN V	MAJ	0-1003920	0657	2
FELL RANALD H	LTC	0-0262793	0563	3	FENTON DEAN W	LTC	0-0282911	1067	3	FERGUSON NORMAN W	CW3	W-2153277	1164	1	FERRIE JOHN A	MAJ	0-1017392	0962	1
FELLENGER PAUL M	LTC	0-0288439	0961	3	FENTON FREDERIC C	LTC	0-0266828	0868	3	FERGUSON PAUL F	MAJ	0-0245190	0154	3	FERRIER WILLIAM W	LTC	0-0289904	0644	2
FELLER ROSS P	CW2	W-2207486	0959	1	FENTON HARRY M	LTC	0-0251739	0553	2	FERGUSON ROBERT L	CW2	W-2114211	0553	1	FERRILL OLIVER J	LTC	0-0444896	0852	2
FELLERMAN HENRY S	MAJ	0-0971482	0862	1	FENTON JAMES R	1LT	0-0245658	0355	3	FERGUSON ROBERT M	1LT	0-1882038	0159	2	FERRIS ALFRED A	LTC	0-1337830	1168	3
FELLERS ALBERT G	MAJ	0-0980640	0763	1	FENTON JOSEPH W	CPT	0-0494826	1046	2	FERGUSON ROBERT R	MAJ	0-4010561	0768	1	FERRIS ASSAD G	MAJ	0-0482622	0943	2
FELLMAN LEON	CPT	0-0254270	0445	2	FENTON LEE M	CW3	W-2152293	1263	1	FERGUSON ROBERT S	COL	0-0410119	1266	1	FERRIS BERNHARDT	LTC	0-0248410	0466	3
FELLMAN 2ND WILLIAM	LTC	0-0322317	0446	2	FENTON MATTHEW C JR	LTC	0-0180389	0845	2	FERGUSON ROSCOE C	MAJ	0-0163278	0650	3	FERRIS CHARLES B	B G	0-0213192	0464	3
FELLON HAROLD C	CW3	W-2206638	1165	1	FENTRESS FRANCIS P	CW3	W-2143632	0768	1	FERGUSON RUSSELL P	LTC	0-1295527	0867	2	FERRIS JAMES A	MAJ	0-0495499	0555	1
FELLOWS CARL H	MAJ	0-0144382	0554	1	FENTRESS ROBERT B	LTC	0-0148905	0950	3	FERGUSON SAMUEL H	CPT	0-0363233	0257	1	FERRIS JOHN W	LTC	0-2017526	0361	1
FELLOWS CLIFFORD H	CPT	0-1645526	1050	2	FENTRISS CHESTER R	CPT	0-1649272	0460	1	FERGUSON SIDNEY J	LTC	0-0176209	0556	1	FERRIS RICHARD D	LTC	0-1081003	0267	1
FELLOWS DEAN C	LTC	0-1168659	0168	1	FENWICK GEORGE B	MAJ	0-0272093	0466	3	FERGUSON SYRL K	CW2	W-2117354	0848	1	FERRIS ROBERT M	MAJ	0-1554357	0361	1
FELLOWS FRANK C	MAJ	0-0307805	0448	2	FENWICK HARRY D	CW3	W-2143489	0560	1	FERGUSON THOMAS L	LTC	0-0451745	0444	2	FERRIS ROY H	2LT	0-0442464	1044	2
FELMUS LAURENCE B	CPT	0-1690651	1145	2	FENWICK OPAL T	MAJ	L-0701599	0463	1	FERGUSON VERNON A	1LT	0-1295528	1044	2	FERRIS 3RD ROYAL A	CPT	0-1010367	0345	2
FELS EUGENE E	LTC	0-1822259	1164	1	FENWRICK GIL	CW2	W-2142474	1056	1	FERGUSON W LOAR	LTC	0-0264880	0264	3	FERRO BENEDICT O	MAJ	0-1180890	0157	1

NAME	GRADE	SVC NO	DATE RET MO YR	RET CODE
FERRO SALVATORE	CPT	0-0438839	1146	2
FERRON EARL	1LT	0-1639027	0645	2
FERRY DENNIS J	CW3	W-3150490	1068	1
FERRY JOHN J	CPT	0-0530934	1146	2
FERRY JOSEPH	CW2	W-2141555	1054	1
FERRY MILES JR	MAJ	0-1895080	0647	2
FERRY THEODORE S	LTC	0-0840798	1068	1
FERSHTMAN MAX B	CPT	0-1690498	0247	2
FERSTER NORMAN A	LTC	0-0474455	0366	3
FERTE JOHN G JR	CPT	0-0338292	1145	2
FERTIG CHARLES A	COL	0-0130208	0652	3
FERTIG JAMES C	1LT	0-1315675	0746	2
FERTITTA CENA V	CPT	0-0194474	0245	2
FERTITTA SAM K	1LT	0-0403980	0245	2
FESS FREDERICK	LTC	0-1302924	0661	1
FESSELMEYER ROBERT W	MAJ	0-0390021	0647	2
FESSLER GUENEVERE	1LT	N-0755275	0846	1
FESSLER HAROLD A	MAJ	0-1559911	1264	1
FEST THEODORE L	CW4	W-2122039	0858	1
FESTA CARMINE P	CPT	0-1314462	0247	2
FESTNER FRANCIS J	CPT	0-0194004	0654	3
FESTNER THOMAS E	1LT	0-1315047	0346	2
FETCHKO GEORGE	CW4	W-2117357	1155	1
FETGATTER HANEY C	CW2	W-2206785	1263	1
FETSCO PETER M	CPT	0-1294588	0347	1
FETTE WILLIAM F	CW3	W-2206460	1066	1
FETTER IVAN R	LTC	0-1634747	0162	1
FETTERHOFF HAROLD L	MAJ	0-1643542	0367	1
FETTERHOFF W M	MAJ	0-1579636	0547	2
FETTERMAN CLINTON F	LTC	0-1107944	0661	1
FETTERMAN JOSEPH	MAJ	0-0501662	0944	2
FETTERMAN ULYSSES G	LTC	0-0445459	0954	1
FETTERS DARWIN K	MAJ	0-1311384	1266	1
FETTY LILLIAN I	2LT	N-0729399	1044	1
FETZER CHARLES K JR	1LT	0-1165854	1045	2
FETZER EARL W	MAJ	0-1043001	0159	1
FETZER FRANCIS G	1LT	0-0507097	1045	2
FETZER JAMES J	CW2	W-2148166	0955	1
FEUERLICHT HENRY D	LTC	0-0181347	0856	3
FEUERMAN ZOLTON	MAJ	0-1948736	0564	1
FEULNER LOUIS H	MAJ	0-1315419	1063	1
FEUSTEL WILLIAM F	LTC	0-0146266	0352	2
FEWSMITH JOSEPH JR	1LT	0-1178790	0146	2
FEWSTER JAMES F JR	COL	0-1575972	1262	1
FEXY GEORGE D	LTC	0-0241183	0364	3
FEY HOMER D	LTC	0-0250754	0165	3
FEYLER WARREN D	COL	0-0242996	0366	3
FIALA GARTH A	MAJ	0-0167617	0255	3
FIALA ROBERT	1LT	0-0885598	0346	2
FIANDACA PATSY M JR	COL	0-0368512	0766	1
FIANO JOSEPH	CW3	W-2151372	0962	1
FICALORE VINCENT J	CW2	W-2141274	0259	1
FICHTER EMIL	MAJ	0-0184078	0849	3
FICHTER WILLIAM H	MAJ	0-1596645	0658	1
FICK ALBERT F	LTC	0-1544552	0763	1
FICK CHARLES B	1LT	0-1300012	0356	1
FICK JOHN H	MAJ	0-0298146	0567	3
FICKE CHARLES W	COL	0-0223759	1264	3
FICKESSEN W R JR	LTC	0-1280741	0261	1
FICKETT RICHARD N	LTC	0-0280569	0166	3
FICKLEN HOLMES	CPT	0-0322032	0645	2
FICO GERALD J	LTC	0-1030101	0962	1
FIDDES RITA H	1LT	N-0720853	0346	1
FIDLER WILLIS R	1LT	0-0927788	0247	2
FIDLOW HARRY	LTC	0-0377940	0960	1
FIEBIG HARRY A	2LT	0-0217072	0355	3
FIEDLER ROBERT W	CW2	W-2205963	0763	1
FIEJDASZ STANISLAW	CW2	W-2152652	0659	1
FIEL VICENTE	1LT	0-0890481	0550	1
FIELD ALMONT E	CW2	W-2143900	1060	1
FIELD ARTHUR W	COL	0-0269575	1061	3
FIELD CROSBY	COL	0-0138854	0349	3
FIELD DONALD E	CPT	0-1098792	0862	2
FIELD DWIGHT	MAJ	0-0518374	0561	3
FIELD EMMETT W	CW4	W-2110564	0659	1

NAME	GRADE	SVC NO	DATE RET MO YR	RET CODE
FIELD ERNEST L	1LT	0-0396624	0445	2
FIELD EUGENE B	CW3	W-2203657	0864	1
FIELD FRANCIS C	1LT	0-0439489	0845	2
FIELD FRED H	COL	0-0235926	1262	3
FIELD GERTRUDE L	2LT	N-0700280	0734	1
FIELD GORDON	LTC	0-0070335	1167	2
FIELD GUY O	MAJ	0-0167991	0648	3
FIELD HAROLD W	LTC	0-0529664	0368	3
FIELD HENRY D	MAJ	0-0520814	1154	1
FIELD JOHN L	CPT	0-0912863	0944	2
FIELD JOHN M III	LTC	0-1056360	1268	1
FIELD JOHN W JR	1LT	0-1799437	0646	2
FIELD LACHLAN M	LTC	0-0372500	0661	1
FIELD LYMAN E	1LT	0-1544905	0245	2
FIELD MARSHALL N	1LT	0-1292162	0346	2
FIELD MARY E	1LT	N-0775219	0846	1
FIELD RICHARD D	MAJ	0-0290210	0665	3
FIELD RICHARD M	MAJ	0-0979585	1066	1
FIELD ROBERT G	MAJ	0-0480904	1052	2
FIELD ROBERT J	CW2	W-2145106	0763	1
FIELD THEODORE S	1LT	0-1173239	0845	2
FIELD THOMAS G	CPT	0-1105424	0547	1
FIELD VIRGIL F	COL	0-0470144	0455	1
FIELD WILLARD E	LTC	0-1057057	0264	1
FIELDER DANIEL W	COL	0-0345943	0259	1
FIELDER ROBERT A	LTC	0-0441621	0667	1
FIELDER WILLIAM R	1LT	0-1044511	0346	2
FIELDING JAMES M JR	COL	0-0322434	0467	3
FIELDING JOSEPH F	1LT	0-0399351	0244	2
FIELDING JOSEPH H	1LT	0-1642051	0561	1
FIELDING TEMPLE H	MAJ	0-0374072	0645	2
FIELDS ALLEN	CPT	0-0360785	1044	2
FIELDS CLARENCE O	CPT	0-0486508	0647	1
FIELDS DONALD I	1LT	0-5244787	0868	2
FIELDS ERNEST	MAJ	0-0496107	1047	2
FIELDS GEORGE G	MAJ	0-1317383	0955	1
FIELDS H MAXWELL	CPT	0-0502232	0445	2
FIELDS HAROLD N	COL	0-0256756	1167	3
FIELDS ISAAC P	CW2	W-2208546	0461	1
FIELDS JOE E	MAJ	0-2024266	0562	1
FIELDS JOEL B	LTC	0-0374238	0159	2
FIELDS JOHN R	CW3	W-2150077	0465	1
FIELDS JOSEPH A	LTC	0-1338329	0766	1
FIELDS LEON	COL	0-0302147	0563	3
FIELDS LEONARD B	MAJ	0-1046431	0361	1
FIELDS LLOYD C	CW2	W-2151111	1062	1
FIELDS MELVIN F	LTC	0-1169512	0960	1
FIELDS NORMAN E	CW2	W-2147530	1160	1
FIELDS RICHARD A	CW4	W-2146238	0368	1
FIELDS ROSE M	MAJ	N-0722405	0661	1
FIELDS SAMUEL A	CW3	W-2210000	0468	2
FIELDS SANFORD W	CW2	W-3440033	1067	1
FIELDS SIDNEY	1LT	0-1589191	1045	2
FIELDS SINCLAIR	CW2	W-2208064	1162	2
FIELDS STANLEY E	MAJ	0-0414147	0366	1
FIELDS THOMAS B	CW3	W-2209275	0767	1
FIELDS WENDELL C	COL	0-0306693	0359	1
FIELDS ZANE W	MAJ	0-1693122	0164	1
FIEMAN PHILIP	CPT	0-0460799	1143	2
FIENHAGE WILFRED J	CW3	W-2122262	0856	1
FIERING ABRAHAM M	MAJ	0-1692015	1045	2
FIERRAVANTI TERESA M	2LT	N-0754536	0946	1
FIERS WALTER H JR	CPT	0-0452995	0245	2
FIES ROBERT L	1LT	0-2203579	0952	2
FIESELER LOUIS O	MAJ	0-1328683	1160	1
FIESTER JOSEPH W	CPT	0-1686385	0657	1
FIFE FRANK H	LTC	0-1289567	1061	1
FIFE HARRY M	CPT	0-0332932	0568	3
FIFE HENRY P	1LT	0-0164455	1044	1
FIFE JACK W	1LT	0-0410770	0446	2
FIFE PORTWOOD	LTC	0-0338207	0454	1
FIFE ROBERT G	1LT	0-0396264	0244	2
FIFIELD GERALD F	LTC	0-0407351	1166	1
FIFIELD GILBERT L	CW3	W-2148367	1262	1
FIGEL GEORGE E	LTC	0-2041144	0267	1

NAME	GRADE	SVC NO	DATE RET MO YR	RET CODE
FIGLER SEYMOUR J	1LT	0-1303485	1145	2
FIGLEY RAY T	MAJ	0-0269804	0968	3
FIGUERAS JOSE	LTC	0-0161876	0553	3
FIGUEROA ARCADIO	MAJ	0-0156041	0353	3
FIGUEROA PASTOR	CW2	W-2113900	0246	2
FIGUEROA VICTOR A	LTC	0-0388405	0660	1
FIGUEROA-RIVERA RUBE	CPT	0-2034213	0962	2
FIGUEROA-SANTAN EMI	MAJ	0-2034212	0667	1
FIKE HAROLD E	LTC	0-0336714	0662	1
FIKE JAMES H	LTC	0-0210648	0255	3
FIKE WALTER B	WO1	W-2113745	0550	1
FIKENTSCHER ARTHUR	LTC	0-1052343	1062	1
FILAK JOHN J	1LT	0-2003531	0453	2
FILAN JOSEPH S	CPT	0-0452106	0943	2
FILBECK RAYMOND H	2LT	0-1015052	0152	1
FILBERT EARL J	CW3	W-2147215	0864	1
FILBERT JOHN A	LTC	0-1293034	0866	1
FILE KENNETH L SR	LTC	0-1553081	0868	1
FILES ALONZO A	LTC	0-0150894	0252	3
FILES CHESTER A	B G	0-0297695	0351	3
FILES WILLIAM A	1LT	0-0281868	0967	3
FILES WILLIAM S	LTC	0-1644319	0562	1
FILIBERTI GEORGE J	LTC	0-0326504	0262	3
FILIBERTO ANTHONY E	COL	0-0360584	0368	3
FILIPCZYK BOLESLAW C	CW3	W-2203342	1162	1
FILIPI EDWARD F	MAJ	0-0258280	0146	2
FILIPIAK JOHN J	LTC	0-0400082	0556	1
FILIPOVICH CARLO W	LTC	0-1110478	0764	1
FILIPPINI ALBERT R	WO1	W-3000324	1162	2
FILIPPONE JOSEPH	CW2	W-2107920	0152	2
FILIPSKI JOSEPH	CW2	W-2102895	0254	1
FILKINS WARREN O	CPT	0-0489054	0147	2
FILL LEON	CPT	0-0505126	0146	2
FILLE ARTHUR D	LTC	0-0348130	0546	2
FILLER WALTER S	LTC	0-0285168	1061	1
FILLER WILLIAM R	MAJ	0-1844979	1055	2
FILLEY CLARENCE E	CW3	W-2142042	1161	1
FILLIETTAZ CHARLES M	COL	0-0243642	0649	2
FILLINGHAM RALPH H	MAJ	0-0326202	1264	3
FILLMAN EDWARD R	MAJ	0-1046789	0859	1
FILLMAN GEORGE	LTC	0-1112685	0861	1
FILLMAN JAMES C	CPT	0-1688421	1168	1
FILLMER HENRY A	LTC	0-0415371	0761	1
FILLMORE JAMES R	1LT	0-1284311	0744	2
FILLMORE ROBERT L	2LT	0-0554851	1145	2
FILOCCO MARIO A	CPT	0-0961570	0560	1
FILTEAU CLIFFORD E	CW2	W-2142956	0556	1
FILTER CHESTER	1LT	0-0346156	0843	2
FILUCCI JOHN	MAJ	0-4030804	0767	1
FILZER NATHAN	MAJ	0-1635872	1067	3
FINA PASCAL A JR	1LT	0-0977580	0960	1
FINAN JOHN J	LTC	0-1289059	0660	1
FINCH BENJAMIN C	LTC	0-2263024	0468	1
FINCH CHARLES S	COL	0-0395756	0462	1
FINCH DONALD F	CPT	0-2289548	1167	1
FINCH ELMER L	MAJ	0-0902904	0847	2
FINCH ERNEST O JR	LTC	0-0232056	0660	3
FINCH FRANK	CW3	W-2104047	0959	1
FINCH FRANK C	LTC	0-0169941	1059	3
FINCH JAMES S	CW4	W-2147190	1268	1
FINCH KENNETH G	1LT	0-1185042	0446	2
FINCH ROGER A	1LT	0-1257704	0146	2
FINCH WILLIAM T	WO1	W-2128009	0546	2
FINCHER ROBERT C JR	CPT	0-1736682	1047	2
FINCHER WARREN C	CW2	W-2144911	0760	1
FINCHER WILLIAM H	LTC	0-0241669	0564	3
FINCK ROBERT F	LTC	0-1797808	0361	1
FINCKE FRANK A JR	2LT	0-1176620	0144	2
FINCLE LOUIS P	LTC	0-0286622	0664	3
FINDEL SOLOMON	CPT	0-0526102	0846	2
FINDERUP ELMER P	1LT	0-1290404	0545	2
FINDLAY JAMES C	WO1	W-2143300	0153	2
FINDLAY R G JR	LTC	0-0348381	1046	2
FINDLAY ROBERT T	COL	0-0213002	1061	3
FINDLAY WALTER G	2LT	0-5710005	0965	2

NAME	GRADE	SVC NO	DATE RET MO YR	RET CODE
FINDLEY EVERETT E JR	CPT	0-1643710	0846	2
FINDLEY JACKSON A	COL	0-0350006	1057	1
FINDLEY JAMES E	MAJ	0-1645244	0461	1
FINDLEY LUKE W	B G	0-0288773	0267	3
FINDLEY MERYL G	CPT	0-0333826	0166	3
FINDLEY SEAB H JR	2LT	0-1299020	0943	2
FINDLEY VIVIAN L	2LT	N-0760390	0345	1
FINE HENRY	WO1	W-2139924	0345	2
FINE HENRY R	COL	0-0287641	0662	3
FINE JAMES P	CW3	W-2209295	0866	1
FINE JOSEPH	CPT	0-0167008	0865	3
FINE MERTON R	CW2	W-3150554	0865	1
FINE MORTIMER C	LTC	0-0273193	0467	3
FINE PAUL R	LTC	0-0497244	1162	1
FINE SIDNEY A	LTC	0-1168664	1265	1
FINE WILLIAM T	LTC	0-0393571	1266	1
FINEGAN CHARLES P	LTC	0-0480019	0853	1
FINEREN WILLIAM W JR	LTC	0-0914956	0963	3
FINGER HARVEY N	COL	0-1577159	0357	1
FINGERHUT WALTER C	LTC	0-1285406	0757	1
FINIELS RICHARD D	MAJ	0-1946051	0163	1
FINIGAN JOHN B	LTC	0-0386029	0560	1
FINK AUGUST O	LTC	0-0159456	1049	3
FINK EDWIN H	LTC	0-0252686	0158	3
FINK FREDERICK	LTC	0-0241883	0246	2
FINK GEORGE	MAJ	0-0262154	0545	2
FINK HENRIETTA	1LT	N-0788823	1045	1
FINK HERBERT C	CW3	W-2147849	0464	1
FINK IRA S	MAJ	0-0414248	0547	2
FINK JOSEPH	CPT	0-0386307	1145	2
FINK LEROY M	LTC	0-0162196	0355	3
FINK RICHARD S	CW4	W-2004476	0865	1
FINK SOL P	COL	0-0136513	0358	3
FINK THEODORE H	LTC	0-0210570	1061	3
FINKEL JASON M	1LT	0-1182571	0146	2
FINKEL MAXWELL E	LTC	0-0276327	0567	3
FINKELMAN NATHAN	MAJ	0-1573200	0857	1
FINKELMAN SAMUEL	LTC	0-1542338	1262	1
FINKELSON JOHN M JR	MAJ	0-0307526	0645	2
FINKELSTEIN DAVID	CPT	0-1695765	0146	2
FINKELSTEIN LEON	CW4	W-2120194	0760	1
FINKLE BEVERLY A	COL	0-1165014	1268	1
FINKLE FREDERICK	CPT	0-0275075	0653	1
FINKLE JAMES D	LTC	0-1053597	0962	1
FINKLE JOHN R	COL	0-0173687	0161	3
FINKS RAYMOND T	COL	0-0275582	1055	3
FINKS WILLIAM R	LTC	0-1533313	0757	1
FINLAY ANDREW M	2LT	0-0425736	0944	2
FINLAY WILLIAM D	LTC	0-1823716	0866	1
FINLAYSON DOUGLAS W	COL	0-0409886	1160	1
FINLAYSON FRANK E	1LT	0-1102242	0146	2
FINLAYSON ROBERT V	CPT	0-0889204	0559	1
FINLEY DEAN H	LTC	0-0303891	0960	1
FINLEY FRED L	CPT	0-0955807	0661	1
FINLEY GEORGE R	CPT	0-0360346	0462	2
FINLEY GEORGE V	MAJ	0-0225121	0454	3
FINLEY GORDON B	LTC	0-0272164	0868	3
FINLEY HARRISON C	CPT	0-0222871	1046	1
FINLEY MARK	LTC	0-0297439	0867	3
FINLEY MERLE F	LTC	0-1283052	0557	1
FINLEY OWEN J JR	2LT	0-0527152	0545	2
FINLEY SETH D	LTC	0-1320517	1262	1
FINLEY VICTOR G	LTC	0-1170735	0467	1
FINLEY WALTER C	MAJ	0-0305678	0944	2
FINLEY WILLARD L	LTC	0-0234070	1057	3
FINLEY WILLIS W	LTC	0-0152644	0555	3
FINN AIDAN A	1LT	0-1038616	1145	2
FINN BERNARD J	CW3	W-2204915	1067	3
FINN CLEMENT E	LTC	0-0373256	1061	2
FINN DUANE L	MAJ	0-0988639	1164	1
FINN FRANK M	LTC	0-1308127	0866	1
FINN GEORGE J JR	1LT	0-1303486	0145	2
FINN JAMES J	LTC	0-1102243	0561	1
FINN JOHN L	LTC	0-0995010	0567	2
FINN MAURICE D	COL	0-0904181	0367	3

NAME	GRADE	SVC NO	DATE RET MO YR	RET CODE
FINN PHILLIP S JR	LTC	0-0270791	0546	2
FINN SILAS M	LTC	0-0188094	0260	3
FINN THOMAS H	COL	0-0267560	1063	3
FINN WALTON C	LTC	0-0279762	0664	3
FINNEGAN ARTHUR M	LTC	0-0932656	0765	1
FINNEGAN DAVID F	MAJ	0-1951472	1060	1
FINNEGAN EDWARD B	LTC	0-2046604	0258	1
FINNEGAN JOHN J	MAJ	0-0968686	1162	1
FINNEGAN LEONARD J	LTC	0-1796444	1161	1
FINNEGAN MARGARET J	CW3	V-8200410	0364	1
FINNEGAN MILES J	LTC	0-0239178	1160	3
FINNEGAN RICHARD A	MAJ	0-1306516	0962	1
FINNEGAN RICHARD A	1LT	0-1311385	1045	2
FINNEGAN RUSSELL M	LTC	0-1113202	0761	1
FINNEGAN ZENUS F	LTC	0-0505148	1154	1
FINNELL GALEN F	CW2	W-2113676	0849	1
FINNELL JAMES K	1LT	0-1302960	1145	2
FINNELL JOHN W	LTC	0-1001554	0166	1
FINNELL WOOLSEY JR	COL	0-0250414	0766	3
FINNEMORE MERTON G	WO1	W-2152957	0853	1
FINNERAN EUGENE D	CW2	W-3430517	0868	1
FINNERTY CHARLES H	CPT	0-0922979	0844	2
FINNERTY JAMES H	MAJ	0-0307562	1059	3
FINNERTY WILLIAM J	2LT	0-1999398	0965	2
FINNEY JAMES C	MAJ	0-0307260	1045	2
FINNEY NORMAN C	COL	0-0308426	0160	1
FINNEY PHILIP A	LTC	0-1638383	1065	1
FINNEY RAY L	LTC	0-0421810	1061	1
FINNEY THEODORE H	CW2	W-2144644	0863	1
FINNIGAN DONALD C	MAJ	0-0990814	0165	1
FINNIN RICHARD H	CPT	0-4074807	0862	2
FINNING EDWARD D	MAJ	0-1297516	1054	1
FINSTER ROY R	MAJ	0-0367435	0467	3
FINT MELVIN J	CPT	0-1559016	0159	1
FINT RENEX J	LTC	0-1577163	0960	1
FINTON ALMON L	MAJ	0-1920268	0264	1
FIORE ANTOINETTE	2LT	N-0703435	0443	1
FIORE HENRY R	LTC	0-1180493	1062	1
FIORE MICHAEL N	LTC	0-1043337	1262	1
FIORELLA PASQUALE J	CPT	0-0266026	0557	3
FIORI GEORGE	MAJ	0-2262483	0862	1
FIPPS ELMER F	1LT	0-1109286	1045	2
FIREBAUGH ALBERT E	COL	0-0331411	0963	3
FIRESTONE IRWIN	LTC	0-1061110	1267	3
FIRESTONE MILTON H	MAJ	0-0480833	1145	2
FIRPO JOHN J	LTC	0-0380768	0146	2
FIRSHT PETER H	LTC	0-0288158	0568	3
FIRTH WILLIAM F	COL	0-0252170	1048	3
FISCHBACH CLIFTON M	COL	0-1656600	0962	1
FISCHBACK ALEXANDER	LTC	0-0260807	1167	3
FISCHER ALBERT C	MAJ	0-1117604	0860	1
FISCHER ANTHONY C	1LT	0-1322630	0648	2
FISCHER CARL H	MAJ	0-0480264	0752	1
FISCHER CARL L	MAJ	0-1302622	0765	1
FISCHER CARL S	COL	0-0326179	0168	3
FISCHER DONALD R	CPT	0-1018658	1063	1
FISCHER EARL F	CPT	0-0356955	1048	2
FISCHER EUGENE A	MAJ	0-0283042	0961	3
FISCHER FRANK E	LTC	0-0233560	0865	3
FISCHER HERBERT M	CW4	W-2135096	1060	1
FISCHER JOHN H	CPT	0-1633209	0745	2
FISCHER JOHN J	MAJ	0-5405056	1067	1
FISCHER LAWRENCE R	1LT	0-1579645	0545	2
FISCHER LEONARD H	MAJ	0-1015495	0265	1
FISCHER LOUIS	CPT	0-0450860	0248	2
FISCHER LYNN J	1LT	0-1328135	0846	2
FISCHER MARY H	CPT	N-0733063	1047	1
FISCHER MEYER	1LT	0-0353140	0246	2
FISCHER MORTON	LTC	0-0202570	0863	3
FISCHER MURIEL F	2LT	N-0730497	1042	1
FISCHER PERRY F	MAJ	0-0971503	0262	1
FISCHER RAY C	MAJ	0-0370568	1068	3
FISCHER VICTORIA M	MAJ	N-0731733	1064	1
FISCHER WERNER	LTC	0-1100985	0765	3
FISCHER WILBUR H	LTC	0-0510023	1058	1
FISCHESSER CHARLES P	MAJ	0-1103630	0461	1
FISCHLE EDWARD J	MAJ	0-2036982	0161	1
FISCHLE EDWARD K	LTC	0-1297347	0662	1
FISCHLER JOSEPH	MAJ	0-1644256	0266	1
FISCUS ETHEL M	2LT	N-0735738	0445	1
FISCUS LLOYD	1LT	0-0195448	0556	3
FISCUS MILLARD W	MAJ	0-1595329	0565	3
FISET LEWIS H	MAJ	0-0452525	1046	2
FISH DAVID J	MAJ	0-0469359	0146	2
FISH DONALD D	CPT	0-1011538	0347	2
FISH ELBRIDGE G	LTC	0-0422591	0464	1
FISH FREDERICK	LTC	0-0266988	0146	2
FISH GORDON T	LTC	0-0165919	0546	2
FISH HAMILTON	COL	0-0168979	1048	3
FISH ISAAC W	CW2	W-2205611	0363	1
FISH JACK C	LTC	0-0341193	0666	3
FISH JAMES E	COL	0-0178358	1061	3
FISH LELLIE W	LTC	0-1303319	0454	1
FISH LESTER W	COL	0-0270461	0859	3
FISH RICHARD D	MAJ	0-0370981	0562	1
FISH VIRGIL D	COL	0-0272138	0567	3
FISH WALDO H JR	B G	0-0282806	1168	3
FISH WILLIAM D	1LT	0-1081647	0246	2
FISH WILLIAM P	LTC	0-2048293	1167	1
FISHBACK AMOS M	MAJ	0-0332209	0860	1
FISHBACK DAVID B	CPT	0-0504865	0744	2
FISHBACK JOHN S	LTC	0-0175062	1045	2
FISHBACK LOUIS F JR	MAJ	0-0243480	0959	3
FISHBACK WILLIAM M	2LT	0-1320031	1045	2
FISHBURN RANDOLPH E	LTC	0-0407560	0661	1
FISHBURNE FRANCIS J	COL	0-0237977	0165	3
FISHEL DONALD R	CW4	W-2144154	0565	1
FISHER ABE A	CPT	0-1693779	0246	2
FISHER ALFRED S	CW3	W-2147587	0862	1
FISHER ALLAN G	MAJ	0-0188136	0552	3
FISHER ARTHUR F	COL	0-0246246	0747	2
FISHER BERNARD	CPT	0-0320727	0344	2
FISHER BILLY W	CW3	W-2144620	0965	1
FISHER BYRON G	MAJ	0-1321169	0361	2
FISHER CARL J	CPT	0-0440495	1144	2
FISHER CHARLES	LTC	0-0403871	0761	1
FISHER CHARLES A	CPT	0-0318566	0245	2
FISHER CHARLES E	LTC	0-1551615	0962	2
FISHER CHARLES E	1LT	0-1646163	1160	1
FISHER CHARLES H JR	1LT	0-1015174	0145	2
FISHER CHARLES L	WO1	W-2113901	0147	1
FISHER CHARLES L JR	MAJ	0-1169107	1067	3
FISHER CHARLES R	COL	0-0123484	0648	3
FISHER CHESTER E	MAJ	0-0990348	0862	1
FISHER CLYDE E	COL	0-0178829	0255	3
FISHER DALE R	1LT	0-0555909	0648	2
FISHER DELPHIA F JR	LTC	0-0331595	0265	3
FISHER DONALD D	LTC	0-0477033	0457	1
FISHER DONALD R	MAJ	0-0956942	0163	1
FISHER EDWARD	MAJ	0-0419039	0846	2
FISHER ELIZABETH	MAJ	N-0741303	0863	1
FISHER ERNEST L	CPT	0-1648017	0856	1
FISHER EUGENE L A	LTC	0-0481878	0754	2
FISHER EUGENE V	MAJ	0-0269510	0966	3
FISHER FRANCIS P	LTC	0-0251502	1147	2
FISHER FRANK F	MAJ	0-0271866	0967	3
FISHER FRANK R	1LT	0-1323304	0456	1
FISHER GEORGE	LTC	0-0411052	0761	1
FISHER GEORGE E	CPT	0-1183065	1045	2
FISHER GEORGE F	MAJ	0-1585212	0161	3
FISHER GEORGE W	COL	0-0248561	1065	3
FISHER GERALD C	LTC	0-1338936	0968	1
FISHER GERALD F	MAJ	0-2026976	0562	1
FISHER GWYNDOLYN	CPT	N-0727199	1146	1
FISHER HAROLD B	LTC	0-0251943	0859	1
FISHER HAROLD E	COL	0-0212600	1262	3
FISHER HAROLD R	MAJ	0-0946887	1064	1
FISHER HENRY R	LTC	0-0286746	0665	3
FISHER HENRY T	MAJ	0-0133942	0955	3
FISHER HERMAN P	LTC	0-0249643	0966	3
FISHER HOWARD A	CPT	0-1597434	0657	1
FISHER HOWARD S JR	LTC	0-0261142	0567	3
FISHER HYMAN	LTC	0-0256820	0263	3
FISHER HYMAN S	MAJ	0-1695686	0465	1
FISHER JACK D	LTC	0-0276617	0364	3
FISHER JACK D	MAJ	0-1922660	0366	1
FISHER JAMES L	MAJ	0-1590456	0663	1
FISHER JAMES R	COL	0-0234335	1067	3
FISHER JOHN	2LT	0-1914423	0749	1
FISHER JOHN H	LTC	0-1337289	0665	1
FISHER JOHN P	LTC	0-0290016	0167	3
FISHER JOHN W	MAJ	0-0186245	1048	3
FISHER JOSEPH S	1LT	0-1041066	0754	1
FISHER KATHERINE	2LT	N-0762690	0945	2
FISHER KEITH E	LTC	0-2051125	0868	2
FISHER KENNETH M	CW4	W-2108488	0358	1
FISHER KENNETH W	MAJ	0-0887624	0957	1
FISHER LEO W	CPT	0-0451965	0146	2
FISHER LLOYD A	MAJ	0-0300651	1163	3
FISHER LLOYD W	LTC	0-1290922	0560	1
FISHER MARY H	1LT	N-0759660	0745	1
FISHER MAX B	1LT	0-1310084	0846	2
FISHER MILTON R	LTC	0-0298174	0850	3
FISHER MORGAN C	WO1	W-2126320	0645	2
FISHER PAUL F	1LT	0-0497576	0447	1
FISHER PEARL C	LTC	N-0700798	0145	1
FISHER RAYMOND	MAJ	0-1047962	1165	1
FISHER RAYMOND A	CW4	W-2101686	0959	1
FISHER RAYMOND F	LTC	0-0337868	0763	1
FISHER RET H	CW2	W-2104938	1044	2
FISHER ROBERT A	LTC	0-0107554	1155	3
FISHER ROBERT H	LTC	0-1030029	0364	1
FISHER ROBERT S	1LT	0-1014674	0945	2
FISHER SAMUEL	CPT	0-0110091	0648	3
FISHER SEWALL	LTC	0-0308301	0861	1
FISHER SEYMOUR	COL	0-0323743	0567	3
FISHER THEODORE E	CPT	0-0245959	0843	2
FISHER VINCENT L	CPT	0-1281686	1146	2
FISHER WALTER A	LTC	0-0303506	0662	1
FISHER WESLEY C	LTC	0-1320382	0667	1
FISHER WILBERT D JR	COL	0-1104151	0866	1
FISHER WILLIAM C	COL	0-0158932	0753	2
FISHER WILLIAM C	LTC	0-0293513	0267	3
FISHER WILLIAM H	LTC	0-0228850	0962	3
FISHER WILLIAM H JR	CW3	W-2200558	0965	3
FISHER WILLIAM JR	MAJ	0-0259511	1267	3
FISHMAN MORRIS	CPT	0-0490724	0246	2
FISHPAW ELI I	LTC	0-1171140	1162	1
FISK DURWARD C	LTC	0-0408958	0461	1
FISK EARL A	MAJ	0-0988992	1062	1
FISK FRANK W	MAJ	0-0453505	0764	1
FISK GORDON A	1LT	0-0412208	0846	2
FISK HARRY H	LTC	0-0154122	0255	3
FISK HERBERT B	LTC	0-0445669	0964	3
FISK JOHN L	LTC	0-0289331	0659	1
FISKE DAVID L	MAJ	0-0161350	0758	3
FISKE EDWARD R JR	MAJ	0-0250909	0366	3
FISKE LEIGH G	CPT	0-1703178	0745	2
FISKE MAHLON F	LTC	0-0321475	1066	3
FISKE WILLIAM M	COL	0-0203517	1058	1
FISSEL GEORGE C	1LT	0-1326989	0746	2
FISSELL JOHN	LTC	0-0408089	0862	3
FISTER FRED M JR	COL	0-0257681	0466	3
FITCH ALBERT W JR	LTC	0-0664555	0262	1
FITCH CLIFTON L	CW4	W-2145279	0468	1
FITCH CODY W	2LT	0-1593952	0460	2
FITCH CURRY F	CW3	W-2150952	0566	1
FITCH EDWARD W	CW2	W-2145180	0358	1
FITCH FRANCIS B JR	LTC	0-0918150	1266	3
FITCH FRANKLIN G	2LT	0-1180182	1045	2
FITCH HANFORD M	2LT	0-1054361	1044	2
FITCH JAMES C	COL	0-0212131	0264	3
FITCH JAMES H JR	CW2	W-2210106	0464	2
FITCH JAMES L	CW3	W-3150597	0468	1
FITCH JAMES P	1LT	0-0501133	0944	2
FITCH JOSEPH R	LTC	0-1058510	0868	1
FITCH LEE F	MAJ	0-0320538	1067	3
FITCH WILLIAM E	CW2	W-2214887	1167	1
FITCH WILLIAM L	LTC	0-1311752	1165	1
FITCHETT HELEN M	MAJ	N-0797421	0566	1
FITCHHORN RAY E	CW3	W-2205546	1065	1
FITCHIE ROBERT G JR	LTC	0-0307725	0668	3
FITE HARRISON F	MAJ	0-2262283	0162	1
FITE HIRAM E	MAJ	0-0313892	1267	3
FITE HUGH S	LTC	0-0310886	0663	1
FITE RANDOLPH V	COL	0-0381254	0757	1
FITE WILBER L	MAJ	0-0388558	1045	2
FITES EDWARD A	MAJ	0-2291672	0464	1
FITES ROBERT E	CPT	0-1544050	0346	2
FITKIN WILLIAM W	COL	0-0210549	0754	3
FITTING CHARLES L	CW2	W-2210024	1265	1
FITTS JAMES O	CW3	W-2151681	0663	1
FITTS PRYOR W	LTC	0-0265318	1064	3
FITTS RALPH L	LTC	0-0162368	1060	3
FITTS SAMUEL	CW3	W-2149752	0564	1
FITZ HARRIS RIC	MAJ	0-1289060	1060	1
FITZ SAMUEL B	CW2	W-2143328	0257	1
FITZ&GIBBON GEORGE W	1LT	0-1310430	0246	2
FITZ&GIBBON JAMES E	LTC	0-0103034	1056	3
FITZ-GIBBON GEORGE E	LTC	0-0121767	0648	3
FITZ-HUGH BERNICE R	2LT	N-0742432	0545	1
FITZGERALD CHARLES N	LTC	0-1799438	0767	1
FITZGERALD CHARLES R	COL	0-0206816	1048	3
FITZGERALD DERMOT T	2LT	0-2016875	1061	1
FITZGERALD DONALD E	MAJ	0-2262674	0566	1
FITZGERALD DONALD J	MAJ	0-2035085	0161	1
FITZGERALD EDWARD J	LTC	0-0258106	1064	3
FITZGERALD EDWARD J	CPT	0-0528916	0846	2
FITZGERALD EDWARD N	LTC	0-0386379	0760	1
FITZGERALD EUGENE J	MAJ	0-1315676	1160	1
FITZGERALD FRANCIS A	2LT	0-1111611	0145	2
FITZGERALD FRANCIS R	MAJ	0-1014210	1058	1
FITZGERALD FREDERICK	CW4	W-2142547	0863	1
FITZGERALD GERALD P	CW3	RW-2152623	0464	1
FITZGERALD GLENN L	MAJ	0-0226011	1161	3
FITZGERALD HOWARD A	MAJ	0-1114120	0758	1
FITZGERALD J MARION	LTC	0-0298330	1063	3
FITZGERALD J P	1LT	0-1173607	0744	2
FITZGERALD JAMES L	MAJ	0-0320809	0465	3
FITZGERALD JOHN F	MAJ	0-0228404	1052	3
FITZGERALD JOHN J	B G	0-0290834	0865	3
FITZGERALD JOHN W	MAJ	0-0548286	0867	3
FITZGERALD JOSEPH C	COL	0-0263329	0965	3
FITZGERALD LESTER F	CPT	0-1948457	0857	1
FITZGERALD LOREN P	LTC	0-0888355	0261	1
FITZGERALD MARION J	MAJ	N-0736684	0459	2
FITZGERALD MATTHEW D	CW2	W-3440129	0968	2
FITZGERALD NORMAN E	MAJ	0-1548769	1060	1
FITZGERALD PAUL J	CPT	0-0503897	1147	1
FITZGERALD RALPH J	CW3	W-2146832	1061	1
FITZGERALD RICHARD	WO1	W-2147384	1158	1
FITZGERALD RICHARD H	1LT	0-1825462	0745	2
FITZGERALD RICHARD J	1LT	0-0411076	0344	2
FITZGERALD ROBERT M	MAJ	0-1947697	1058	2
FITZGERALD THOMAS D	CW3	W-2152605	0467	1
FITZGERALD THOMAS F	MAJ	0-0188808	0551	3
FITZGERALD WADE E	MAJ	0-0443941	0646	1
FITZGERALD WAYNE D	CW2	W-2104053	0164	1
FITZGERALD WILLIAM E	MAJ	0-1553082	1056	1
FITZGERALD WILLIAM J	MAJ	0-1013874	0963	1
FITZGIBBONS THOMAS C	LTC	0-1552667	0962	2
FITZGIBBONS TIM L	MAJ	0-1327830	0661	1
FITZHUGH ANDREW F	MAJ	0-0330935	0347	2
FITZHUGH EDWARD B	MAJ	0-2033635	0661	2
FITZHUGH SAMUEL A	1LT	0-1058511	0646	2
FITZMAURICE F E	LTC	0-0309979	0359	1
FITZPATRICK CLYDE	CW2	W-2143901	0159	1
FITZPATRICK DAVID A	MAJ	0-1647884	1058	1
FITZPATRICK EDWARD J	MAJ	0-0155132	0355	3
FITZPATRICK EDWIN A	LTC	0-0193021	0146	2

ARMY OF THE UNITED STATES RETIRED LIST

NAME	GRADE	SVC NO	DATE RET MO YR	RET CODE
FITZPATRICK F X	CPT	0-0477687	0546	2
FITZPATRICK FRANCIS	LTC	0-0254424	0766	3
FITZPATRICK FRANK R	LTC	0-0383610	1164	3
FITZPATRICK GORDON J	MAJ	0-1643547	0861	1
FITZPATRICK HAMILTON	LTC	0-0303566	0866	3
FITZPATRICK JAMES B	WO1	W-2116222	0244	2
FITZPATRICK JAMES O	2LT	0-2043211	0745	2
FITZPATRICK JAMES I	LTC	0-0383464	0860	1
FITZPATRICK JOHN D	CPT	0-1040380	0246	2
FITZPATRICK JOHN J	LTC	0-0212439	0562	3
FITZPATRICK JOHN J	LTC	0-0336864	0661	1
FITZPATRICK JOHN J	MAJ	0-1040525	1164	3
FITZPATRICK JOHN J	1LT	0-2041638	0554	2
FITZPATRICK LYLE J	COL	0-0300496	0559	1
FITZPATRICK PATRICK	MAJ	0-1946249	1262	1
FITZPATRICK ROBERT W	COL	0-0441611	1154	1
FITZPATRICK THOMAS A	COL	0-0184765	0147	2
FITZPATRICK THOMAS S	MAJ	0-1553631	0462	2
FITZPATRICK WILLIAM	LTC	0-0291255	0547	2
FITZSIMMONS JOHN P	MAJ	0-0447616	1145	2
FITZSIMMONS RICHARD	LTC	0-1060096	0263	2
FITZSIMMONS WALLACE	LTC	0-1541316	0661	1
FITZSIMONS ARCHIE L	LTC	0-0256049	1061	3
FITZWATER ROGER P	LTC	0-0451388	0954	1
FITZWILSON DEANE P	MAJ	0-1947870	0961	1
FIVEHOUSE NEAL R	CW2	W-2212118	0866	1
FIVES WILLIAM B	LTC	0-2055444	0967	1
FIX ALFRED E	LTC	0-0411607	1060	1
FIX JOSEPH E	COL	0-0173782	0857	3
FIX LESLIE N JR	MAJ	0-2096457	0565	1
FIXEL ROWLAND W	COL	0-0167941	0648	3
FJERSTAD KENNETH H	CW3	W-2210037	0668	1
FLACH GEORGE L	MAJ	0-0245222	1152	3
FLACH JOSEPH B	LTC	0-0212427	0951	3
FLAGEL FRANK F	LTC	0-0198149	1048	1
FLAGG JAMES H	LTC	0-1924994	1168	1
FLAGG MARGARET C	2LT	N-0774630	0446	1
FLAGG MILDRED W	CPT	N-0743630	0647	1
FLAGG RAYMOND P	2LT	0-0392304	0243	2
FLAGG SEWELL L	CPT	0-0279070	0954	3
FLAGG STANLEY E	LTC	0-0162525	1044	2
FLAGG WILLARD G	LTC	0-0248667	0766	3
FLAHERTY EDWARD B	LTC	0-0371402	0646	2
FLAHERTY EILEEN V	LTC	N-0720526	0766	2
FLAHERTY JAMES J	1LT	0-1534968	1145	2
FLAHERTY JOHN J	LTC	0-1579468	0761	1
FLAHERTY JOHN L	LTC	0-2043002	0263	1
FLAHERTY JOSEPH R	LTC	0-0410422	1262	1
FLAHERTY MATTHEW J	LTC	0-1050255	0563	1
FLAHERTY R G JR	LTC	0-0450275	0955	1
FLAHERTY WALTER T	1LT	0-0525505	0645	2
FLAHIVE JOHN D	MAJ	0-0958441	0166	1
FLAHIVE JOHN P	2LT	0-0239200	1042	2
FLAHIVE ROBERT E	MAJ	0-1120276	0264	1
FLAIG FRANK J	CPT	0-1296350	0347	2
FLAIM RUDOLPH A	MAJ	0-1322538	0759	1
FLAITZ JAMES R	CW3	W-2146467	0461	2
FLAMER MORTIMER	MAJ	0-0523131	0246	2
FLAMION LEO P	CPT	0-0253858	0658	3
FLAMM LEO M	1LT	0-0451542	1056	1
FLANAGAN CHARLES C	MAJ	0-0963512	0166	1
FLANAGAN CHARLES P	MAJ	0-2034516	0663	1
FLANAGAN DANIEL	LTC	0-1541843	1162	1
FLANAGAN FREDERICK	CW2	W-2151907	0361	1
FLANAGAN HARRY A	CPT	0-2032990	0959	2
FLANAGAN HARRY D	2LT	0-1551619	1044	2
FLANAGAN JAMES B	LTC	0-0528367	0863	2
FLANAGAN JAMES L JR	MAJ	0-0965793	0366	1
FLANAGAN JIM M	CW2	W-2117855	0646	2
FLANAGAN JOHN D	CPT	0-1111058	0966	1
FLANAGAN JOSEPH E	CW3	W-2151371	1063	1
FLANAGAN JOSEPH P	CW4	W-2009156	0567	3
FLANAGAN LAWRENCE M	MAJ	0-1332248	0664	1
FLANAGAN MILDRED H	2LT	N-0758000	0844	1
FLANAGAN PAUL R	LTC	0-0454283	1066	2

NAME	GRADE	SVC NO	DATE RET MO YR	RET CODE
FLANAGIN MARVIN M	COL	0-0410691	0567	3
FLANAKIN HUBERT A	LTC	0-0921945	0365	3
FLANAKIN JEWELL B	2LT	N-0726372	0643	1
FLANARY JOHN	1LT	0-0495004	0945	2
FLANDERS CHARLES R	CW3	W-2152624	0463	1
FLANDERS EVERETT M	MAJ	0-1540715	0657	1
FLANDERS HERBERT P	MAJ	0-0294385	0845	2
FLANDERS RAY T	CW3	W-2147706	0563	1
FLANDERS WILLIAM E	MAJ	0-1594079	0863	1
FLANDRO ARTHUR L	COL	0-0209052	0752	3
FLANIGAN ANGELA C	MAJ	N-0755078	0666	1
FLANIGAN DEWAYNE P	LTC	0-1318971	0668	2
FLANIGAN JAMES P	CPT	0-1997076	0855	2
FLANIGAN PAUL T	2LT	0-0357804	0843	2
FLANIGAN RICHARD A	2LT	0-1998331	0545	2
FLANIGAN THOMAS J	1LT	0-0549631	0646	2
FLANIGAN WALTER L	LTC	0-1037980	0268	1
FLANIGAN WILLIAM M	B G	0-0265698	0354	3
FLANNIGAN CLAUD B	LTC	0-0491553	1155	1
FLANNIGAN ROBERT W	1LT	0-0449514	0745	2
FLANSBURG DALE M	CW2	W-2150676	0461	1
FLAPAN MAXWELL	LTC	0-0261236	0666	3
FLASCHNER IRA	CPT	0-0416664	0246	2
FLASH HOWARD S	CPT	0-1294811	0664	1
FLATLEY JOHN W	CPT	0-0423688	0346	2
FLATT ROBERT LIN	2LT	0-1319193	0551	2
FLATTLEY THOMAS M JR	LTC	0-0386318	1060	2
FLAUGHER THOMAS E	MAJ	0-1051956	0960	1
FLECHER JOHN	CW3	W-2109149	0756	1
FLECK BERNARD	WO1	W-2120000	0245	2
FLECK LEROY S	LTC	0-0177175	0161	3
FLECK WILLIAM C	LTC	0-0489340	0568	3
FLEEGE HERBERT W	1LT	0-0390005	0744	2
FLEEGLER SAUL M	CPT	0-0355896	0246	2
FLEEK DELBERT I	MAJ	0-1010562	0847	1
FLEEK NELSON	2LT	0-1031170	0845	2
FLEES FRANK J	1LT	0-1305406	1145	2
FLEET GLADYS M	CPT	N-0764350	1052	2
FLEETWOOD RAYMOND	CPT	0-0454753	1153	1
FLEGAL CLAUDE P	CPT	0-0922076	0847	2
FLEGEL DAYLE F	MAJ	0-0410110	0361	1
FLEISCH JOHN J	LTC	0-0290901	0968	3
FLEISCH THOMAS O	MAJ	0-0981181	1167	2
FLEISCHAKER WILLIAM	LTC	0-1895662	1162	1
FLEISCHER EDWARD J	COL	0-0388185	0968	3
FLEISCHER IRVING S	LTC	0-0498764	1061	1
FLEISCHER JOSEPH	COL	0-0304042	0866	3
FLEISCHER JOSEPH K	MAJ	0-0962343	0763	1
FLEISCHER MILTON L	CPT	0-1114475	0661	1
FLEISCHMAN ANDREW	LTC	0-2019576	0366	1
FLEISCHMAN ARTHUR E	MAJ	0-0284834	0665	3
FLEISCHMAN FORREST G	COL	0-0344840	0661	1
FLEISHER ARLENE A	MAJ	N-0755074	1067	1
FLEITZ BENJAMIN F	MAJ	0-0148842	1054	3
FLEMENS NORRIS L	CPT	0-2007236	0957	1
FLEMING ANTHONY	COL	0-0274994	0562	1
FLEMING BALLARD	MAJ	0-2042140	0166	1
FLEMING CARL S	1LT	0-0495624	0550	2
FLEMING CHARLES A	MAJ	0-0469767	0747	1
FLEMING CHARLES C	MAJ	0-1313868	0166	1
FLEMING CHRISTOPHE	CW3	W-2143221	0959	1
FLEMING CLYDE	MAJ	0-2263200	0166	1
FLEMING DALE H	CPT	0-0973589	1161	1
FLEMING DANIEL D	CW3	W-2142942	0159	1
FLEMING DAVIDSON M	MAJ	0-0174824	0648	3
FLEMING EARL L	LTC	0-1280435	0360	1
FLEMING EDMOND C	MAJ	0-0309162	1053	3
FLEMING GEORGE A	MAJ	0-0953672	0862	1
FLEMING JAMES C	LTC	0-0238508	0662	3
FLEMING JAMES F	CPT	0-0338961	0146	2
FLEMING JAMES L	MAJ	0-1307215	0962	1
FLEMING JAMES T	LTC	0-0257682	0167	3
FLEMING JOHN	1LT	0-2002807	0954	2
FLEMING JOHN C	COL	0-0233512	0560	3
FLEMING JOHN E	CPT	0-1690960	0762	1

NAME	GRADE	SVC NO	DATE RET MO YR	RET CODE
FLEMING JOHN H	1LT	0-1322399	1046	2
FLEMING JOSEPH	CPT	0-1104154	1145	2
FLEMING JOSEPH H	LTC	0-0903827	0958	3
FLEMING KARL J	2LT	0-1646166	0244	2
FLEMING KATHLEEN P	MAJ	N-0720273	0661	1
FLEMING MAURICE C	1LT	0-0387964	0342	2
FLEMING OMER J	CPT	0-1699980	0466	1
FLEMING PAUL O JR	MAJ	0-0982985	0168	1
FLEMING RALPH O	CW2	RW-2209867	0464	1
FLEMING RAYMOND H	M G	0-0165022	0253	2
FLEMING RAYMOND L	MAJ	0-1041343	1061	1
FLEMING REX	MAJ	0-0301218	0859	3
FLEMING RICHARD W	CPT	0-1584216	0446	2
FLEMING ROBERT J	CPT	0-1746695	0147	2
FLEMING ROBERT L	MAJ	0-1116774	0860	1
FLEMING SALVADOR	WO1	W-2123722	0757	1
FLEMING SAMUEL C JR	CW2	W-2147309	0764	1
FLEMING THOMAS T	MAJ	0-2035247	1160	1
FLEMING WALTER J	CPT	0-1301465	1048	2
FLEMING WILLIAM H	COL	0-0282429	0566	3
FLEMING WILLIAM M	CPT	0-0478547	1060	1
FLEMING WILLIAM M	LTC	0-2016499	0165	1
FLEMINGS MILTON B	LTC	0-1547934	0263	1
FLEMMING CHARLES W	CW4	W-2141276	0962	1
FLEMMING JOHN K	COL	0-0225136	0360	2
FLENNERY MANLEY J	LTC	0-0957740	0968	1
FLESCH LAWRENCE H	WO1	W-2108208	0946	1
FLESHER WILLIAM J	CPT	0-1103162	0561	1
FLETCHER ARCHIBALD	COL	0-0490514	0465	1
FLETCHER ARTHUR L	LTC	0-0101336	0648	3
FLETCHER CHARLES H	MAJ	0-0442003	1046	2
FLETCHER CHARLES J	LTC	0-1169958	0359	1
FLETCHER CHARLES M	CW3	W-2145332	0663	1
FLETCHER CHARLES R	LTC	0-1317510	0464	1
FLETCHER CHARLES V	COL	0-0298773	0259	3
FLETCHER CHARLES W	LTC	0-0353605	0468	3
FLETCHER CLAUDE C	COL	0-0126882	0954	3
FLETCHER DANIEL L	1LT	0-1309656	1045	2
FLETCHER DOZIER	LTC	0-1167837	0963	1
FLETCHER EDWARD A	1LT	0-1042563	0145	2
FLETCHER ELGIE C	LTC	0-1319938	0165	1
FLETCHER ELLSWORTH	1LT	0-0510341	0446	2
FLETCHER GERALD E	CW4	W-2141926	0764	2
FLETCHER HARRY M	CPT	0-0497898	0644	2
FLETCHER HARRY M	CW3	W-2153080	0365	1
FLETCHER HILBERT E	LTC	0-0478719	0265	3
FLETCHER JAMES H	MAJ	0-0411981	0761	1
FLETCHER JEANNE M	2LT	N-0722262	1044	1
FLETCHER JESS F	CPT	0-0488856	0645	2
FLETCHER JESSE H	LTC	0-1310085	0462	1
FLETCHER JOHN G	LTC	0-0226890	1264	3
FLETCHER JOHN V	CW2	W-2150339	1162	1
FLETCHER JOHN W	LTC	0-0126802	0748	3
FLETCHER JOSEPH F	CW3	W-2148349	0263	1
FLETCHER KENNETH L	1LT	0-0474936	1045	2
FLETCHER LA VERNE M	COL	0-0290434	0164	3
FLETCHER LEWIS A	LTC	0-0377794	0661	1
FLETCHER LOUIS W	LTC	0-0237870	0262	3
FLETCHER MARVIN H	LTC	0-1555208	0962	1
FLETCHER MILLARD M	LTC	0-1174572	0662	1
FLETCHER NANNIE B	CPT	N-0763845	0161	2
FLETCHER OSCAR E	CPT	0-1170368	0960	1
FLETCHER ROBERT O	CPT	0-0408082	0146	2
FLETCHER RODNEY	MAJ	0-2077785	0465	1
FLETCHER SAMUEL M	LTC	0-0270678	1055	1
FLETCHER THOMAS H JR	CPT	0-0402965	1263	1
FLETCHER WALTER C	CPT	0-1103631	0646	2
FLETCHER WALTER M	2LT	0-2001668	0546	2
FLETCHER WILLIAM F	LTC	0-0221292	0961	3
FLETT WILLIAM C	CPT	0-1061111	0347	2
FLEURY EDGAR	MAJ	0-2023875	1060	1
FLEURY JOHN B	2LT	0-0888461	1044	2
FLEWELLEN ROBERT H	1LT	0-1283402	1044	2
FLEWELLING MAX S	MAJ	0-0217188	0956	3
FLEWELLING MILTON F	MAJ	0-0525684	0547	2

NAME	GRADE	SVC NO	DATE RET MO YR	RET CODE
FLEXSENHAR WILLIAM J	LTC	0-1179067	0968	1
FLEXSER EDWIN L	CW4	W-2126015	0867	1
FLICK FRANK C	LTC	0-0182695	1048	1
FLICK JOHN L	1LT	0-1298043	0146	2
FLICK LAWRENCE G	COL	0-0187137	0654	2
FLICK ROBERT L	WO1	W-2121771	0743	2
FLICKINGER ELMER E	LTC	0-1284122	1160	1
FLICKINGER LLOYD H	LTC	0-0235816	0364	3
FLICKINGER MALCOLM W	LTC	0-0370967	0965	1
FLIEGELMAN MAURICE T	MAJ	0-0381224	0346	2
FLIEGER JOHN H	MAJ	0-1635884	0756	1
FLINCHUM JAMES M	WO1	W-2147755	1162	1
FLINDERS DAVID C	CPT	0-1172859	0261	1
FLINN CHARLES O	LTC	0-1297705	0566	1
FLINN GEORGE W	LTC	0-1031078	1265	1
FLINN RICHARD D JR	LTC	0-0260011	0567	3
FLINT CARL	MAJ	0-0861580	0764	1
FLINT CURTIS E	COL	0-1167421	0866	1
FLINT DONALD C	MAJ	0-0337127	0546	2
FLINT EARL P	2LT	0-0538272	0745	2
FLINT RAYMOND W	MAJ	0-0167698	0151	3
FLINT ROBERT J	CPT	0-1012030	0350	2
FLINT ROBERT N	LTC	0-0904810	0364	1
FLINTOSH JOSEPH	MAJ	0-0471639	0952	2
FLIPPO BETTYE P	MAJ	N-0724319	0948	2
FLOCCO THOMAS O	LTC	0-0398875	1266	3
FLOCKEN FRED B	LTC	0-0232539	0763	3
FLOCKS MAYER	CPT	0-0300968	0745	2
FLOM ANDREW M	MAJ	0-2015852	0262	1
FLOM CARL A	COL	0-0268006	0766	3
FLOM MERVIN O	LTC	0-0159369	0758	3
FLOOD ALBERT O	COL	0-0292542	0146	2
FLOOD ARNOLD O	LTC	0-2049889	1266	1
FLOOD ARTHUR P	COL	0-0915225	0362	3
FLOOD CLARENCE D	CPT	0-1045732	0550	1
FLOOD CLYDE E	CPT	0-0317832	0345	2
FLOOD EDWARD J	LTC	0-0919124	0266	3
FLOOD GERALD J	CW2	W-2146750	0662	1
FLOOD MARGARET E	2LT	N-0796945	0747	1
FLOOD MATTHEW J	WO1	W-2148469	0356	1
FLOOD ORMOND K	CPT	0-0168089	0146	2
FLOOD RAYMOND J	CW2	W-2120985	0852	2
FLOOD ROGER A	COL	0-0107883	0553	2
FLOOD WILLIAM J	WO1	W-2115255	0345	2
FLOOK HARRY E	LTC	0-0126800	0646	2
FLOOK KENNETH G	LTC	0-0450862	0457	1
FLOOR ALBERT C	LTC	0-1558429	1063	1
FLORA HARRY O	CW4	W-2143991	1056	1
FLORENCE VICTOR G	CW4	W-2109861	0955	1
FLORES ARTHUR	CW2	W-2212742	0867	1
FLORES FLORO M	1LT	0-1896556	0350	2
FLORES FRANK S	LTC	0-0316893	0668	3
FLORES JUSTINO	CPT	0-0980805	1161	1
FLORES NESTOR J	CW2	W-2214733	0568	1
FLORES PABLO J	CW3	W-2147659	0663	1
FLOREY JAMES R	2LT	0-0409734	0344	2
FLOREY THEODORE C	LTC	0-0402983	0660	1
FLORIDIS GREGORY G	COL	0-0321257	0566	3
FLORIMONT FRED S	LTC	0-0911697	0157	2
FLORKE HARRY W	CW3	W-3100525	0267	1
FLORO LAWRENCE A	LTC	0-0264327	0957	2
FLORY GAYLORD G	1LT	0-1172003	1045	2
FLORY HAROLD R	CW3	W-2148722	0966	1
FLORY JOHN W	LTC	0-1300784	0865	3
FLORY KEITH N	LTC	0-0321518	0768	3
FLORY OLIVER E	LTC	0-0298885	1067	3
FLORY ROBERT D	LTC	0-0132105	0653	3
FLOURNOY DAVID M III	LTC	0-0254510	0666	3
FLOURNOY ROBERT E L	1LT	0-1019047	0845	2
FLOWER JAMES F JR	1LT	0-1017690	1147	2
FLOWERS BENJAMIN D	LTC	0-1172860	0163	1
FLOWERS DAVE	COL	0-0304718	1047	2
FLOWERS FARRAND	LTC	0-0261093	0167	3
FLOWERS FRED G	CPT	0-1172454	0246	2
FLOWERS JACK M	MAJ	0-0971470	0766	1

NAME	GRADE	SVC NO	DATE RET MO YR	RET CODE
FLOWERS JOHN F	LTC	0-0256437	0461	3
FLOYD ALBERT J JR	LTC	0-0388993	0363	1
FLOYD CHARLES J	LTC	0-1010584	0457	1
FLOYD CYRIL F	COL	0-0257443	0757	1
FLOYD ENGLISH H	MAJ	0-0258726	0667	3
FLOYD EVERETT E	LTC	0-0224279	0160	1
FLOYD GEAVE	CW2	W-2212736	1265	1
FLOYD GEORGE W	MAJ	0-0414323	0847	2
FLOYD HAMILTON	LTC	0-0219930	0664	3
FLOYD HAROLD P	MAJ	0-1541836	0957	1
FLOYD HENRY C	COL	0-0234159	0146	2
FLOYD HENRY [illegible]	1LT	0-0974671	0363	2
FLOYD HILTON L	1LT	0-1685626	1052	2
FLOYD JOE R	COL	0-0324510	0546	2
FLOYD JOHN C	2LT	0-1112693	1143	2
FLOYD MARCUS L	CW2	W-2208440	1162	1
FLOYD MONROE	1LT	0-2045300	0654	1
FLOYD PAUL H SR	MAJ	0-0201123	0559	3
FLOYD RAY	LTC	0-1165729	0561	1
FLOYD RICHARD T	MAJ	0-0291756	0967	3
FLOYD WALTER R	MAJ	0-0425420	0662	1
FLOYD WALTER R	LTC	0-1544083	0157	1
FLOYD WILFRED F	COL	0-1584218	0868	1
FLOYD WILLIAM E	MAJ	0-0300049	0465	2
FLOYD WILLIAM M	1LT	0-0503109	1044	2
FLOYD WILLIAM M	2LT	0-0537261	0245	2
FLOYD WILLIAM T	CW4	W-2124179	0761	1
FLUELKIGER FREDRICK	MAJ	0-5301753	0268	1
FLUES ABRAM G	COL	0-0902712	0963	3
FLUHARTY JUNIOR J	CPT	0-1922966	0666	2
FLUKE NORRIS W	1LT	0-1547295	0547	2
FLUSCHE FREDRICK A	1LT	0-1176961	0545	2
FLY AUSTIN	COL	0-0279378	0456	2
FLYNN ARTHUR J	MAJ	0-1081473	0357	1
FLYNN CALLUM J	CW2	W-3150431	0268	1
FLYNN CATHERINE	MAJ	N-0721060	0367	1
FLYNN CHELMER L	LTC	0-0341188	0564	1
FLYNN DENEEAR W	LTC	0-0450277	1057	1
FLYNN DONALD R	CPT	0-0287760	0545	2
FLYNN EDWARD J	1LT	0-0532089	0546	2
FLYNN EDWIN R	LTC	0-1333198	1168	1
FLYNN GEORGE A	CW3	W-2205738	0867	1
FLYNN GRADY J JR	LTC	0-0397768	0662	1
FLYNN HAROLD O	LTC	0-0431362	0459	1
FLYNN JAMES F	1LT	0-0887561	1154	1
FLYNN JAMES F	CPT	0-1044819	0450	2
FLYNN JAMES W	1LT	0-1295697	0447	2
FLYNN JOHN E	CW3	W-2141817	0462	1
FLYNN JOHN J	CPT	0-1030976	0746	2
FLYNN JOHN J	LTC	0-1580947	0763	1
FLYNN JOSEPH W	CPT	0-1166986	0257	1
FLYNN KATHERINE	MAJ	N-0757910	0364	1
FLYNN LELAND C JR	LTC	0-1186742	1267	1
FLYNN LESTER M	MAJ	0-0739175	0262	2
FLYNN MARIE D	2LT	L-0805638	1144	2
FLYNN MATTHEW A	LTC	0-0108989	0845	2
FLYNN PETER F	LTC	0-1341530	1066	1
FLYNN RAYFORD D	LTC	0-1056716	0867	1
FLYNN RICHARD T	COL	0-0261238	1057	3
FLYNN ROBERT M	LTC	0-1301978	0954	1
FLYNN THOMAS F	2LT	0-1949097	0346	2
FLYNN THOMAS J	MAJ	0-0358449	0465	3
FLYNN THOMAS L	LTC	0-0335453	0965	3
FLYNN THOMAS P	COL	0-0366126	1162	1
FLYNN VENCINO A	LTC	0-0324278	1265	3
FLYNN VINCENT P	CPT	0-4074685	1168	1
FLYNN WALTER J	LTC	0-0394891	0460	1
FLYNN WALTER J	CPT	0-0414741	0445	2
FLYNN WALTER W	LTC	0-0298075	0767	3
FLYNN WILLIAM A	CPT	0-0941979	0459	1
FLYNN WILLIAM E JR	LTC	0-1115581	0561	1
FLYNN WILLIAM F	MAJ	0-2021230	1163	1
FLYNN WILLIAM L	CPT	0-1919134	0964	1
FLYNT JASON C	CW2	W-2145172	0356	1
FOARD ROBERT A	CPT	0-0184564	0252	3

NAME	GRADE	SVC NO	DATE RET MO YR	RET CODE
FOBES ALFRED WEN	CPT	0-0359670	1051	2
FOBES RAMON O	LTC	0-0223989	1262	1
FOCHT WILLIS F	MAJ	0-1014367	1047	2
FODDRA ALBERT A	CPT	0-0494393	1145	2
FODY EUGENE J	CPT	0-0948688	0666	1
FOE DONALD W	1LT	0-1172004	0246	2
FOEGLE ROBERT E	2LT	0-1913678	0442	1
FOEHRENBACH FRANK A	LTC	0-0302543	1065	3
FOEHSER ARTHUR W	LTC	0-1055851	1066	1
FOELEY ROGER R	MAJ	0-1107954	0462	1
FOELKER FRANK B	CPT	0-1287689	1159	1
FOERCH JOSEPH H JR	LTC	0-1637429	0361	1
FOERCH WILLIAM G	MAJ	0-0203625	0554	3
FOERSTER ERROL J	LTC	0-0235432	0159	3
FOERSTER HERVEY A	COL	0-0246052	1263	3
FOERSTER WILLIAM J	LTC	0-0278338	0660	3
FOERY FRANK R	LTC	0-1573203	0464	1
FOGARTY CLARENCE J	LTC	0-1011136	0461	1
FOGARTY DANIEL T	LTC	0-1822550	0464	1
FOGARTY HARRY B	MAJ	0-0148110	0651	3
FOGARTY JAMES S	CPT	0-0949572	1060	1
FOGARTY JOHN P	MAJ	0-1182824	0560	1
FOGARTY PHILIP E	1LT	0-0426843	0346	2
FOGARTY RICHARD E	LTC	0-1103165	1057	1
FOGARTY THOMAS C	LTC	0-1896186	0966	1
FOGARTY WILLIAM S	MAJ	0-2027815	1265	1
FOGEL ARTHUR A	CPT	0-1945130	1046	2
FOGEL HAROLD	2LT	0-1317593	1043	2
FOGEL LEO B	CW4	W-2005703	0568	1
FOGEL ROY U	LTC	0-1165611	0258	1
FOGEL RUBEN H	LTC	0-1171143	1065	3
FOGERTY WILLIAM W	MAJ	0-4004923	0668	2
FOGG ALLSTON H	COL	0-0272640	0565	3
FOGG CHARLES E	COL	0-0289282	0847	2
FOGG CHARLES H	LTC	0-0507611	0566	1
FOGG SAMUEL H	2LT	0-1573204	0852	1
FOGG SUMNER S	LTC	0-0162073	0648	3
FOGG WILLIAM A	COL	0-0469505	1068	3
FOGLEMAN ELWOOD L	LTC	0-0461179	0462	1
FOGLEMAN HOMER T	2LT	0-2009924	0648	1
FOGLEMAN JOSEPH O	WO1	W-2126989	0947	2
FOGLER EDWARD N	COL	0-1010794	0961	1
FOGLI THOMAS W	2LT	0-2001064	0146	2
FOGO ALDEN E	CPT	0-1755879	0847	2
FOGUS WAYNE W	MAJ	0-4005429	1268	1
FOIZIE EARL W	LTC	0-0186514	1054	3
FOLAROS ARTHUR M	LTC	0-1594841	0563	1
FOLB HENRY	CPT	0-0495913	1045	2
FOLDEN PETER T	LTC	0-0262663	1064	3
FOLEY CECIL W	1LT	0-1013773	0359	1
FOLEY CHARLES E	COL	0-0360602	1165	3
FOLEY DAVID	CW3	W-2141556	0358	1
FOLEY FRANCES R	MAJ	N-0736414	0266	1
FOLEY FRANCIS J	MAJ	0-0437844	0646	2
FOLEY FRANCIS W	LTC	0-1049154	0264	1
FOLEY FRANCIS X	LTC	0-1058512	1165	3
FOLEY FREDERICK	MAJ	0-1300631	0862	1
FOLEY FREDERICK JR	MAJ	0-2263188	0666	1
FOLEY GEORGE E JR	MAJ	0-2103059	1064	1
FOLEY HENRY J	COL	0-0885518	0354	1
FOLEY JAMES M	COL	0-0265619	0264	3
FOLEY JAMES M JR	COL	0-0192723	0561	3
FOLEY JOHN C	LTC	0-1585457	0762	1
FOLEY JOHN G	CW3	W-2205688	0268	1
FOLEY JOHN L	CPT	0-0124840	0435	1
FOLEY JOHN P	CPT	0-1286108	0247	2
FOLEY JOHN P	LTC	0-1287332	0361	1
FOLEY JOHN P	CW2	W-2214438	0867	1
FOLEY JOHN T	2LT	0-1333956	0246	2
FOLEY LAWRENCE E	MAJ	0-1822788	1063	2
FOLEY LEONARD V	CPT	0-0400023	1144	2
FOLEY MAURICE J	LTC	0-0263615	1056	3
FOLEY OLLIE L	CW2	W-2125928	0853	1
FOLEY PATRICK H	1LT	0-1646167	0546	2
FOLEY ROBERT J	COL	0-0299855	0164	3

NAME	GRADE	SVC NO	DATE RET MO YR	RET CODE
FOLEY WILLIAM H	2LT	0-2263526	0353	2
FOLEY WILLIAM J	LTC	0-0287638	0767	3
FOLEY WILLIAM V	CPT	0-1678404	0555	1
FOLGER JOSEPH W	LTC	0-1100541	0364	1
FOLIO JOSEPH R	LTC	0-1108664	0268	1
FOLK BRUCE W	CW4	W-2114128	0358	1
FOLK FREDERICK	CPT	0-2288302	0562	1
FOLK JOHN J	LTC	0-0480880	0964	2
FOLK THOMAS A	CPT	0-0227681	0944	2
FOLK WILLIAM H	CPT	0-1696435	1045	2
FOLKERTS ORVILLE C	LTC	0-1824847	0868	1
FOLKINS FLOYD L	COL	0-0426098	1164	1
FOLKMAN STANLEY M	LTC	0-0281494	0564	1
FOLKOFF CASPAR	LTC	0-0464331	0146	2
FOLLETT CHARLES D	1LT	0-0520250	1046	2
FOLLETT ELLSWORTH	CW2	W-2101292	0845	2
FOLLETT LESLIE C	LTC	0-0252697	1159	3
FOLLETTE ROGER L	LTC	0-1994909	0560	1
FOLLIS GEORGE M	2LT	0-0108675	0136	1
FOLLMAN CHARLES C	LTC	0-1038377	0767	1
FOLLMER WILLARD R	MAJ	0-0416081	0146	2
FOLRATH LAIRD O	MAJ	0-0299683	0563	3
FOLSOM EDWIN W	LTC	0-0200799	0263	3
FOLSOM HARRY L	1LT	0-0197316	0648	3
FOLSOM M B	CPT	0-1169514	0746	2
FOLTA ALFRED J	CW2	W-2107594	0145	2
FOLTS DAVID K	CPT	0-0254060	1147	2
FOLTZ WENDELL A	1LT	0-1314463	0647	2
FOLTZER WILLIAM O JR	2LT	0-1286110	0445	2
FOLWELL PAUL A	CPT	0-1047963	0659	1
FONDA EDWARD S	LTC	0-0128058	1053	2
FONDREN JAMES C	CW3	W-2009830	1066	3
FONG CLIFTON	CPT	0-1921702	0652	2
FONG THEODORE C	COL	0-0197781	0760	3
FONGER BERNARD A	MAJ	0-0986208	1062	1
FONS AUGUST M	LTC	0-1059451	0465	1
FONT CHARLES D	LTC	0-0980765	0967	3
FONT GILBERTO M	LTC	0-0198206	0163	3
FONT MANUEL	COL	0-0187488	0948	3
FONT RAMON JR	MAJ	0-0154940	0361	3
FONT WILLIAM A	COL	0-0191893	1062	3
FONTAINE LEWIS E	LTC	0-0484318	0367	3
FONTAINE PIERRE W	CW4	W-2148432	0468	1
FONTAINE RAYMOND V	LTC	0-1013389	0261	1
FONTAINE WILFRED H	CPT	0-1633857	0257	1
FONTANELLA RICHARD J	1LT	0-1328348	1147	2
FONTECCHIO THOMAS E	1LT	0-1290925	0445	2
FONTENOT LAWRENCE J	MAJ	0-4014553	1168	1
FONTENOT NASEN J	CW3	W-2149044	1061	1
FONTENOT STEWART F	CW2	W-2112571	0748	1
FONTRON JOHN F JR	LTC	0-0507337	0164	3
FONZI NICHOLAS J	CW2	W-2149908	0860	1
FOOS JOHN L	CPT	0-2040693	0647	2
FOOSE FRANCIS I	1LT	0-1304531	0845	2
FOOTE BERNIE F	WO1	W-2008889	0254	3
FOOTE BOYD H	MAJ	0-2014701	1068	1
FOOTE FRANCIS C	MAJ	0-0128304	0354	3
FOOTE FRANKLIN M	COL	0-0337416	0568	3
FOOTE GEORGE C JR	LTC	0-1647642	1263	1
FOOTE GEORGE F	MAJ	0-0209819	0944	2
FOOTE GLEN L	LTC	0-0450438	0657	1
FOOTE GLENN M	CW4	W-2148433	0868	1
FOOTE JAMES E	MAJ	0-0298845	0364	3
FOOTE RILEY F	1LT	0-1165577	0146	2
FOOTE WILLIAM A	LTC	0-0285561	0859	2
FOOTE WILLIAM G	MAJ	0-1923720	1167	1
FOOTE WILLIS B	MAJ	0-0262977	1047	2
FOPPE ANDREW J	CPT	0-1013425	0347	2
FORAKER CLARENCE M	LTC	0-0329097	0266	3
FORAN JAMES L	CW4	W-2148622	0662	1
FORBES CHARLES H	MAJ	0-2033194	0964	1
FORBES CLARENCE L	LTC	0-1684975	0967	1
FORBES GERALD W	LTC	0-1169517	1163	1
FORBES JACK R	LTC	0-1169518	1165	1
FORBES JACK W	CW3	W-2205838	0965	1

NAME	GRADE	SVC NO	DATE RET MO YR	RET CODE
FORBES JAMES	2LT	0-1826266	0945	2
FORBES JOSEPH P	LTC	0-1585835	0366	3
FORBES LAUREN G	1LT	0-0972986	0657	1
FORBES LOUIS M	1LT	0-0198749	0253	3
FORBES LOWELL L	LTC	0-0101929	0154	3
FORBES MARRELL A	MAJ	0-0399717	0146	2
FORBES RICHARD W	CPT	0-0357274	0644	2
FORBES ROBERT W	COL	0-0154443	0557	3
FORBES THOMAS A	CPT	0-0168988	0344	2
FORBES WILLIAM H JR	MAJ	0-0474405	1047	1
FORBUSH CLIFTON H	COL	0-0177033	0857	3
FORBUSH EARL A	MAJ	0-1746168	1064	1
FORCHETTE DONALD G	MAJ	0-0995642	0265	1
FORCIER FRANCIS F	CW3	W-2150796	0659	1
FORCIER LOWELL A	CW3	W-2142795	0764	2
FORD ALEXANDER	CPT	0-0164456	0536	1
FORD ALICE M	1LT	N-0725486	0745	1
FORD ANDREW F	CW3	W-2211589	1168	1
FORD ANDREW J	1LT	0-1796600	1145	2
FORD AUGDIL L	CPT	0-0468152	0444	2
FORD AZEL G	MAJ	0-0678217	0565	1
FORD BOBBIE B	LTC	0-0403524	1160	1
FORD CARL J	CPT	0-2263152	1062	1
FORD CARL L	CPT	0-1115258	0452	2
FORD CARLETON R	COL	0-0268927	0567	3
FORD CHARLES H	CPT	0-1002217	0458	1
FORD CLOVIS B	CPT	0-1289230	0246	2
FORD DALE M	MAJ	0-1035771	0262	1
FORD DANIEL W	CPT	0-1305563	0446	2
FORD DAVID A	WO1	W-2108355	0551	2
FORD DOUGLAS C	CPT	0-0515331	0347	1
FORD DUANE B	MAJ	0-1933438	0567	1
FORD EDGAR	LTC	0-0332936	1159	1
FORD EDWARD L	CPT	0-1047122	0962	3
FORD EDWARD M	LTC	0-0400717	0664	1
FORD EDWARD P	CPT	0-0173912	1044	2
FORD EDWIN F	MAJ	0-1935440	0767	1
FORD EDWIN R JR	LTC	0-1318531	0961	1
FORD ELBERT G	WO1	W-2106214	0160	1
FORD ERNEST H	MAJ	0-2016059	0163	1
FORD FRANK G	2LT	0-1303130	1144	2
FORD FREDERICK	CW2	W-2000812	1044	2
FORD GEORGE B	LTC	0-0486004	0256	1
FORD GEORGE J	LTC	0-0450863	0258	1
FORD GEORGE L	COL	0-0404999	0961	1
FORD GEORGE R	2LT	0-2001780	1059	2
FORD GEORGE U	LTC	0-0383261	0559	1
FORD HANSFORD D	LTC	0-0396847	1165	1
FORD HARRY S	CPT	0-0410089	1046	2
FORD HENRY H	CW3	W-2144180	0659	1
FORD HOWARD D	1LT	0-1058251	0646	2
FORD HOWARD G	WO1	W-2113538	1044	2
FORD HUBERT	MAJ	0-0975942	1167	1
FORD HUGH G	CW2	W-2143343	0462	1
FORD JAMES J	COL	0-0406192	1068	1
FORD JAMES T	LTC	0-0475906	0947	1
FORD JAMES W	LTC	0-0189846	0351	3
FORD JOHN A	MAJ	0-1283232	0261	1
FORD JOHN D	CW3	W-2145033	0962	1
FORD JOHN H	1LT	0-2205264	0154	2
FORD JOHN J	CPT	0-0480310	0949	1
FORD JOHN N	MAJ	0-1338937	0865	1
FORD JOHN R JR	MAJ	0-1339979	0765	1
FORD JOSEPH A JR	MAJ	0-0356113	0363	1
FORD JOSEPH C	MAJ	0-0233885	0345	2
FORD JOSEPH C	1LT	0-0451449	0844	2
FORD LEO W	CPT	0-0527793	0949	2
FORD LEONARD H	LTC	0-0102148	0648	3
FORD LEONARD M	LTC	0-2263281	1068	1
FORD LESTER A	CW2	W-2145128	0659	1
FORD LUTHER E	MAJ	0-1177392	0960	1
FORD MABEL M	2LT	N-0700171	1138	1
FORD MARY	2LT	N-0700168	0840	1
FORD MARY J	MAJ	N-0731689	0163	1
FORD NORMAN A	2LT	0-0443986	0544	2

NAME	GRADE	SVC NO	DATE RET MO YR	RET CODE
FORD PAUL F	COL	0-0289855	0360	1
FORD PERKINS	CPT	0-0415676	0850	1
FORD RALPH F	2LT	0-1291616	1044	2
FORD RAY W	CPT	0-0497040	0350	1
FORD RAYMOND F	COL	0-0259513	0867	3
FORD RAYMOND D	COL	0-0174149	0461	3
FORD RICHARD	CW3	W-2151061	0267	1
FORD RICHARD G	LTC	0-0371112	0265	1
FORD ROBERT E	CPT	0-1038378	0246	2
FORD ROBERT E	1LT	0-2000624	1147	2
FORD ROBERT L	MAJ	0-1030240	0854	1
FORD ROBERT M A	LTC	0-1056365	0363	1
FORD ROBERT R	CW4	W-2141557	0559	1
FORD ROBERT W	LTC	0-1287505	0861	1
FORD ROY J	LTC	0-0270338	0868	3
FORD STANLEY B	CPT	0-0451710	0546	2
FORD STEPHEN K	LTC	0-0260213	1264	3
FORD WARREN A	LTC	0-0104266	1059	3
FORD WILLARD B	MAJ	0-2042966	0762	1
FORD WILLIAM E	CPT	0-1286991	1047	2
FORD WILLIAM G JR	CW3	W-2147509	0463	1
FORD WILLIAM H	MAJ	0-0258503	0158	3
FORD ZARVIS T	1LT	0-0414324	0844	2
FORDE ALBERT L	MAJ	0-0280405	0467	3
FORDHAM ADOLPH E	2LT	0-1051127	0245	2
FORDHAM HENRY B	CPT	0-2025991	1058	1
FORDYCE WENDELL L	CPT	0-2263734	0662	1
FORDYCE WILLIAM L	1LT	0-1013315	0761	2
FORE CHARLES H	LTC	0-0373423	0163	1
FORE CLYDE A	CPT	0-2014607	0756	2
FORE HOWARD I	MAJ	0-1289062	0158	1
FOREE ROBERT W	CW2	W-2108586	1045	2
FOREHAND RICHARD L	MAJ	0-1292328	0157	1
FOREMAN ALBERT S	LTC	0-0459060	0467	3
FOREMAN ARTHUR B	LTC	0-0115935	0549	3
FOREMAN CLEMONS W	CPT	0-0102145	1055	3
FOREMAN GRAYSON A	CPT	0-0494120	0854	1
FOREMAN H H	1LT	0-2006060	0450	2
FOREMAN HARRY A	LTC	0-0209805	0164	3
FOREMAN JAMES N	LTC	0-0363342	0361	1
FOREMAN JOHN	COL	0-0200303	0459	3
FOREMAN LEONARD	CPT	0-0885712	0853	1
FOREMAN RICHARD G	CPT	0-4010970	0667	1
FOREMAN ROBERT D	MAJ	0-1685628	0864	1
FOREMAN ROBERT W	MAJ	0-0346196	1156	2
FOREMAN WALLACE G	LTC	0-0294775	0160	1
FOREMAN WILLIAM C	LTC	0-0359679	0766	1
FORESMAN HAROLD A	LTC	0-0361156	0163	3
FORESMAN HENRY J	CPT	0-0412794	0645	2
FOREST GEORGE F	CPT	0-1555041	0346	2
FORESTA ANGELO	CW2	W-2134771	0163	1
FORESTER ROBERT J	1LT	0-0502598	1045	2
FORGASON JACK P	COL	0-0348615	0460	3
FORGIONE PASCAL D	LTC	0-0360618	0567	3
FORINASH KYLE	MAJ	0-2262184	1062	1
FORKS LOUIS J	LTC	0-1050664	0662	1
FORLAND ARTHUR E	CW3	W-2150638	1264	1
FORMALEJO BERNARDINO	1LT	0-1896531	0650	1
FORMAN DAVID W	MAJ	0-0989500	0968	1
FORMAN EDWARD	1LT	0-0432916	1046	2
FORMAN EVELYN K	MAJ	N-0721431	1262	1
FORMAN IRENE S	2LT	N-0727517	1044	1
FORMAN JACOB	LTC	0-1692308	0968	3
FORMAN JAMES E	CPT	0-0419675	0745	2
FORMAN JOHN G	CPT	0-0447081	1046	2
FORMAN JOSEPH	CPT	0-1589837	0647	2
FORMAN MAURICE R	MAJ	0-0915116	1145	2
FORMAN ROBERT C	LTC	0-0339217	0162	1
FORMAN SEYMOUR	2LT	0-1054992	0745	2
FORMAN THEODORE M	MAJ	0-0212502	0861	3
FORMANACK ANGELA M	MAJ	N-0732811	1167	1
FORMHALS HARRY B	MAJ	0-0182284	1153	3
FORMSMA ROBERT J	2LT	0-1050665	0843	2
FORNASH LUKE JR	1LT	0-2041011	0945	2
FORNEA GENE F	CW2	W-2101695	0153	1

NAME	GRADE	SVC NO	DATE RET MO YR	RET CODE
FORNELIUS CARL F	CPT	0-0495006	0448	2
FORNELL JOSEPH E	CPT	0-1552668	1045	2
FORNES HINTON E	LTC	0-1556414	0862	2
FORNEY DAVID H	CPT	0-1030559	0149	2
FORNEY HARRY R	COL	0-0150731	1055	3
FORNEY JOHN E	LTC	0-1112696	0661	1
FORNEY JOSEPH T	MAJ	0-1290226	0165	1
FORNEY LEON E	MAJ	0-1575316	0357	1
FORNEY RICHARD M	LTC	0-1598377	0464	1
FORNOF THEODORE W	CPT	0-1937501	0764	1
FORNOF WILBERT H	1LT	0-1172007	0146	2
FORONDA CRESCENCIO	2LT	0-1896605	0457	1
FORQUER WARREN K	CW3	W-2144299	1061	1
FORREN KENNETH P	MAJ	0-1890404	1068	1
FORREST ARTHUR A	MAJ	0-1012947	0163	2
FORREST EUGENE B	LTC	0-0205835	0956	3
FORREST J D	1LT	0-1303699	0446	2
FORREST JAMES R	1LT	0-0454057	1047	2
FORREST JAMES R	2LT	0-0536232	0444	2
FORREST JOHN W	1LT	0-1691930	1146	2
FORREST KENNETH B	LTC	0-1639039	0762	1
FORREST MYRTLE I	MAJ	N-0777936	0465	1
FORREST NOLA G	LTC	N-0701473	0946	1
FORREST RAYMOND E	MAJ	0-0350768	0246	2
FORREST ROBERT C JR	CW4	W-2111759	1161	1
FORREST SAMUEL G	MAJ	0-0477284	0242	1
FORRESTAL WILLIAM T	CPT	0-1184383	0547	2
FORRESTER EDWIN C	CPT	0-1173947	0647	2
FORRESTER ELLIS L	MAJ	0-0320624	0968	3
FORRESTER JEPTY L	CW4	W-2145677	1066	1
FORRETT JOHN G	MAJ	0-4074272	0468	1
FORRY THOMAS P	2LT	0-0900073	0542	2
FORRY WALTER E	COL	0-0299879	0363	3
FORSBERG CARL E	LTC	0-0360549	1164	1
FORSBURG OSCAR W	CPT	0-0164908	1053	3
FORSEE JOHN S JR	CW4	W-2142636	0368	1
FORSGREN FRED A	LTC	0-1010173	0263	1
FORSHA KENNETH D	MAJ	0-1015555	0861	1
FORSHAW WALTER H JR	CPT	0-1057733	0868	3
FORSLUND CARL A	LTC	0-1822125	1266	1
FORSMAN HUGH K	COL	0-0173844	1161	3
FORSSELL WILLIAM R	CPT	0-0276320	0257	3
FORST GEORGE H	COL	0-0170784	0948	1
FORSTNER DOROTHY I	CPT	N-0783376	1046	1
FORSYTH CHARLES L	CPT	0-0435721	0846	2
FORSYTH EARL N	LTC	0-0290148	0557	1
FORSYTH LYLE B	COL	0-0307572	0968	3
FORSYTHE BELMONT	LTC	0-2292056	0866	1
FORSYTHE EMMETT C	MAJ	0-0144166	0256	3
FORSYTHE ERWIN F	LTC	0-0451952	0860	2
FORSYTHE FRANK W	COL	0-0333358	1054	3
FORSYTHE HERBERT L	LTC	0-0976795	0368	1
FORSYTHE JAMES V	CW3	W-2141801	0159	1
FORSYTHE LESTER D	2LT	0-0385099	1067	3
FORSYTHE ROBERT J	MAJ	0-0978135	0462	1
FORT ERNEST A	LTC	0-0204821	1063	3
FORT GLEN A	LTC	0-0921360	1062	1
FORT JAMES A JR	LTC	0-0169049	0760	3
FORT WAYNE W	LTC	0-0506940	0164	1
FORTE SALVATORE	CW2	W-2213113	1167	1
FORTENBERRY HARRY E	CPT	0-1041549	0561	1
FORTENBERRY JASPER H	CPT	0-0924952	0348	2
FORTES CLAUDIO	2LT	0-0890531	0248	1
FORTH FRANK F	1LT	0-0989963	1152	2
FORTH JOHN T JR	MAJ	0-1640459	0762	2
FORTIER ELMO A	LTC	0-1548774	0262	2
FORTIER ROMAINE M	MAJ	0-1646172	0856	1
FORTIER ROY M	LTC	0-0176508	1149	3
FORTIN CLARENCE C	MAJ	0-2019446	0263	1
FORTNER CARL	CPT	0-2044567	1053	1
FORTNER EDWARD F	MAJ	0-1172008	1158	1
FORTNER WILL M	1LT	0-1294118	0945	2
FORTNEY ARTHUR C	COL	0-0278668	0263	3
FORTNEY KENNETH R	MAJ	0-0252653	1066	3
FORTSON EUGENE P JR	LTC	0-0295072	1166	3

NAME	GRADE	SVC NO	DATE RET MO YR	RET CODE
FORTUNA PETER P	1LT	0-0528400	0545	2
FORTUNA VALENTINE	1LT	0-1331488	0348	2
FORTUNATO JOSEPH W	1LT	0-1119182	0946	2
FORTUNATO NICHOLAS A	COL	0-1305751	1165	1
FORTUNATO SAMUEL J	CPT	0-0345498	0845	2
FORTUNE DANIEL L	MAJ	0-0947159	0764	1
FORTUNE JOHN H	1LT	0-2036731	0355	1
FORTUNE MARVIN B	CPT	0-1047123	0747	2
FORTUNOFF SAUL	COL	0-1689037	0365	3
FORWARD DONALD O	LTC	0-0244566	0955	3
FORWARD FLETCHER C	LTC	0-0301591	1160	1
FORYS WALTER M	LTC	0-0442550	0459	1
FOSBURGH DAVID L	MAJ	0-0271369	0167	3
FOSDICK JACK B	1LT	0-1321501	0945	2
FOSEID OSCAR F	MAJ	0-0519793	0547	2
FOSHEE BEVERLY C	MAJ	0-0970485	0668	1
FOSHEE CLYDE H	MAJ	0-0273818	1045	2
FOSKO JOHN J JR	1LT	0-1535637	0246	2
FOSS ALVIN E	LTC	0-0124842	0851	3
FOSS DAVID F	CPT	0-0523168	0948	2
FOSS DONALD L	LTC	0-1534484	0163	1
FOSS LAURISTON	COL	0-1100989	1163	1
FOSS REGINALD E	COL	0-0214958	0648	3
FOSS SHELDON H	MAJ	0-2033954	0465	1
FOSS SIMON A	LTC	0-0121652	1053	3
FOSSE MAURICE J	MAJ	0-1315049	0468	1
FOSSEL JULIUS D	2LT	0-1329697	1045	2
FOSSETT HARRY J JR	2LT	0-1109296	1044	2
FOSSON JOHN W	1LT	0-1581716	1048	2
FOSTER ALBERT P	CW3	W-2144789	0761	1
FOSTER ALBERT W	CPT	0-1579658	0455	1
FOSTER ANNE C	MAJ	N-0756906	0663	1
FOSTER BEDFORD F	LTC	0-0275422	0965	3
FOSTER BILLY H	1LT	0-1294119	0347	2
FOSTER CECIL C	LTC	0-0887625	0463	1
FOSTER CHARLES C	MAJ	0-0314147	1046	2
FOSTER CHARLES D	LTC	0-0270918	1167	3
FOSTER CHARLES F	MAJ	0-2007016	1262	1
FOSTER CHARLES G	CPT	0-0550452	1046	2
FOSTER CHARLES M	MAJ	0-1104665	1266	1
FOSTER CLARENCE B	LTC	0-0297470	0866	3
FOSTER CLIFFORD D	CW3	W-2126244	0762	1
FOSTER DAVID A	CPT	0-0290444	1045	2
FOSTER DONALD L	MAJ	0-1172863	0861	1
FOSTER DOYLE E	LTC	0-1294120	1263	1
FOSTER DWIGHT K	COL	0-0221420	0556	3
FOSTER EARL D	COL	0-0326181	0863	3
FOSTER EARL D	MAJ	0-1307391	0164	1
FOSTER EARL H	CPT	0-2262553	0864	1
FOSTER EDGAR M	1LT	0-0888230	0545	2
FOSTER EDWARD B	CPT	0-0283954	0246	2
FOSTER EDWARD T	COL	0-0276916	1064	3
FOSTER EDWIN B	MAJ	0-0262241	0568	3
FOSTER EDWIN T	MAJ	0-0490575	1262	1
FOSTER ELBERT F	LTC	0-0371577	0866	3
FOSTER ETHELBERT	MAJ	0-0112555	0950	3
FOSTER EUGENE C	MAJ	0-0172945	0247	1
FOSTER FRANKLYN H	CW3	W-2106297	1160	1
FOSTER FRED	CPT	0-0396923	0146	2
FOSTER GEORGE L	LTC	0-0289265	1165	1
FOSTER GEORGE L	LTC	0-0495334	0155	1
FOSTER GEORGE M	CPT	0-1042023	0346	2
FOSTER GEORGE R	MAJ	0-1545924	0660	1
FOSTER GILBERT J	LTC	0-0304651	0360	1
FOSTER GLENN A	MAJ	0-0339646	0547	2
FOSTER GUY W	MAJ	0-0496907	0154	1
FOSTER HARRY M	MAJ	0-0478380	0242	1
FOSTER HARRY W	MAJ	0-0212742	0563	3
FOSTER HART G	COL	0-0123331	0950	3
FOSTER HENRY	CW4	W-2106549	0358	1
FOSTER HUBERT E	CPT	0-0193488	0544	2
FOSTER JACK W	CPT	0-1080020	0261	1
FOSTER JAMES B JR	COL	0-0419161	0861	1
FOSTER JAMES R	MAJ	0-0949262	0562	1
FOSTER JAMES R	MAJ	0-1016551	0961	1

NAME	GRADE	SVC NO	DATE RET MO YR	RET CODE
FOSTER JAMES T	CW2	W-2142086	0463	2
FOSTER JOHN C	LTC	0-0268153	1059	1
FOSTER JOHN E	LTC	0-0423446	0961	3
FOSTER JOHN L	MAJ	0-1039349	0562	1
FOSTER JOHN R	MAJ	0-2001723	1262	1
FOSTER JOHN S	LTC	0-0910808	0667	3
FOSTER JOSEPH T	CPT	0-1797456	1047	2
FOSTER JULIAN S	MAJ	0-0976881	0865	1
FOSTER KATHERINE	1LT	N-0763856	1145	1
FOSTER KENNETH D	LTC	0-1112698	1064	1
FOSTER LAURENCE G	MAJ	0-0487992	0759	1
FOSTER LAWRENCE G	LTC	0-0261298	0566	1
FOSTER LEMUEL L JR	1LT	0-1582693	0747	2
FOSTER LEON M	LTC	0-0346519	0562	1
FOSTER LEROY F	1LT	0-1312532	1045	2
FOSTER LEWIS E JR	LTC	0-1102245	0267	1
FOSTER LOREN N	CW3	W-3150367	0667	1
FOSTER MALCOLM L	CPT	0-0361929	0645	2
FOSTER MARSHALL P	CW3	W-2207961	1067	1
FOSTER MAX W	MAJ	0-1171146	0155	1
FOSTER MAXWELL S JR	LTC	0-0337928	0560	1
FOSTER MILO P	MAJ	0-1114480	1262	1
FOSTER MILTON M	1LT	0-0499245	0643	2
FOSTER MOSES A	LTC	0-0315595	0650	2
FOSTER NORMAN J	MAJ	0-2055984	0764	1
FOSTER NORMANS	1LT	0-1017338	1046	2
FOSTER PAUL	CPT	0-0490054	0347	1
FOSTER PAUL	CW3	W-2142375	0557	1
FOSTER PAUL G	LTC	0-0358292	0450	2
FOSTER PAUL L	MAJ	0-0187696	0151	1
FOSTER PAUL W JR	CW2	W-2115842	0155	1
FOSTER RALPH D	LTC	0-0203768	1048	2
FOSTER ROBERT A	LTC	0-0500377	0657	1
FOSTER ROBERT A	1LT	0-1017394	0446	2
FOSTER ROBERT C	LTC	0-0495778	1267	2
FOSTER ROBERT G	MAJ	0-1104159	0862	1
FOSTER ROBERT M	MAJ	0-0109040	0745	1
FOSTER ROGER H	CW4	W-2141277	0966	1
FOSTER ROGER M	WO1	W-2119484	0960	2
FOSTER SAMUEL F	LTC	0-1169961	1067	1
FOSTER SAMUEL W	LTC	0-2046491	0356	1
FOSTER SYBIL G	1LT	N-0726710	0745	1
FOSTER SYDNEY E	LTC	0-0259026	1065	3
FOSTER THEODORE P	LTC	0-1577179	1263	2
FOSTER THOMAS G	LTC	0-2200127	1267	1
FOSTER THOMAS J	MAJ	0-1646175	0655	1
FOSTER WALTER L	CW2	*W-2148279	0964	1
FOSTER WALTER W	1LT	0-0509592	0546	2
FOSTER WILLIAM B	LTC	0-0360650	0760	1
FOSTER WILLIAM D	MAJ	0-0420790	1065	3
FOSTER WILLIAM G	LTC	0-0285749	0558	3
FOSTER WILLIAM H	CW4	W-2142573	0865	1
FOSTER WILLIAM M	MAJ	0-0270792	0268	3
FOSTER WILLIAM S	MAJ	0-2015741	0263	1
FOSTER WILLIAM W	CW3	W-2152824	0364	1
FOSTER WINSLOW	COL	0-0222331	0360	3
FOTI SAMUEL J	LTC	0-1701699	0767	1
FOUCHS LAWRENCE E	COL	0-0181218	1059	1
FOULK ELDEN K	MAJ	0-2019578	0365	1
FOULK FRANK H	CPT	0-0488860	0747	2
FOULKE CARTER W	1LT	0-0536593	0146	2
FOULKE GEORGE A	LTC	0-0357997	1056	3
FOULKE PHILIP A	MAJ	0-1019316	0366	1
FOULKES HARVEY B	LTC	0-0130636	1155	1
FOULKS ERNEST E	COL	0-0228921	0963	3
FOULSTONE ROWLAND M	MAJ	0-1014011	0461	1
FOUNTAIN FLOYD G	CPT	0-1173948	0448	2
FOUNTAIN GEORGE L	LTC	0-0548503	1064	1
FOUNTAIN JESS W	1LT	0-1822871	0456	1
FOUNTAIN JOHN R	MAJ	0-0345188	1167	3
FOUNTAIN RAY C	M G	0-0121655	0954	3
FOUNTAIN RISDEN L	LTC	0-1010405	0561	1
FOUNTAINE ALFRED J	CW4	W-2102900	0559	1
FOUNTAINE ROBERT H	MAJ	0-2005592	1165	1
FOURACRE WILLIS A	MAJ	0-1295006	1047	2

NAME	GRADE	SVC NO	DATE RET MO YR	RET CODE
FOURCMAN ROY H	LTC	0-0255112	0555	3
FOURNIER ALPHONSE J	MAJ	0-0456889	0357	1
FOURNIER CHARLES A	LTC	0-0744946	0567	1
FOURNIER JOSEPH A	LTC	0-1031927	0965	2
FOURNIER LEROY	CPT	0-0111061	0854	1
FOURNIER LOUIS B	MAJ	0-0291441	0163	1
FOURNIER PAUL C	CPT	0-2337288	1168	2
FOURNIER ROLAND P	COL	0-0436623	0657	1
FOURNIER VINCENT G	MAJ	0-1645577	1064	1
FOURQUREAN CROMWELL N	LTC	0-0344222	1065	1
FOUSE DONALD W	MAJ	0-0341084	0146	2
FOUSHEE LEWIS P	LTC	0-0924493	0467	3
FOUSHEE SCHLESINGE	LTC	0-0304685	1064	3
FOUST ALAN S	LTC	0-0271124	0768	3
FOUST BILLY	MAJ	0-1171530	0566	1
FOUST JOHN W	LTC	0-1821992	0663	1
FOUST PERRY F	MAJ	0-0405536	0961	1
FOUT JAMES F JR	LTC	0-1032081	0862	1
FOUTCH QUINTON W	LTC	0-0272129	1165	3
FOUTS ANDREW S	MAJ	0-0400767	1145	2
FOUTS HAROLD J	CPT	0-0910623	1043	2
FOWLE PHYLLIS L	LTC	L-0703018	0468	3
FOWLER BUTLER B JR	CPT	0-0409736	0145	2
FOWLER CECIL C	LTC	0-0450738	1055	1
FOWLER CECIL W	LTC	0-1299686	0361	1
FOWLER CHARLES E	CPT	0-1290228	0457	1
FOWLER CHARLES R	1LT	0-0527795	0546	2
FOWLER CHARLES P	CPT	0-1181888	0657	1
FOWLER CLARENCE A	CW2	W-2115724	1053	2
FOWLER CLARENCE W	1LT	0-1683312	0145	2
FOWLER CLYDE F	LTC	0-0921302	0363	1
FOWLER DARRELL	CPT	0-0255563	0345	2
FOWLER DELOS	MAJ	0-0175449	0456	3
FOWLER DONALD G	CW3	W-2151428	0666	1
FOWLER FORREST L	MAJ	0-1341088	0764	1
FOWLER FRANK X	LTC	0-1340448	0168	1
FOWLER GEORGE D	CPT	0-2263719	1262	1
FOWLER GEORGE W JR	CW3	W-2146833	1264	1
FOWLER GILL	MAJ	0-0451596	1059	1
FOWLER GORDON C	LTC	0-0196186	0163	3
FOWLER GRACE H	MAJ	N-0700653	0346	1
FOWLER GRACE R	2LT	N-0731931	0644	1
FOWLER HARMON L	COL	0-0113287	0648	3
FOWLER HARRY R	COL	0-0167229	1155	3
FOWLER HENRY F	WO1	W-2149290	1054	1
FOWLER HENRY G	COL	0-0253899	0247	2
FOWLER HERBERT H	CW3	W-2146239	0862	1
FOWLER HERMAN W	CPT	0-1030472	0156	1
FOWLER HUBERT B	MAJ	0-0501045	1054	1
FOWLER JAMES C	LTC	0-1108667	0862	1
FOWLER JAMES E	MAJ	0-0983946	0267	1
FOWLER JAMES F	CPT	0-1325884	0446	2
FOWLER JAMES H	2LT	0-0194344	0225	1
FOWLER JAY G	LTC	0-1641295	0867	3
FOWLER JESSE L	CW4	W-2108172	0960	1
FOWLER JOHN E	MAJ	0-1686748	0968	1
FOWLER JOHN F	LTC	0-1031401	0561	1
FOWLER JOHN L	CPT	0-0486109	0448	1
FOWLER JOHN M	LTC	0-0306967	0460	1
FOWLER JOHN P	MAJ	0-1684944	0564	1
FOWLER JOHN R	CPT	0-0450199	0960	1
FOWLER JOSEPH D	CPT	0-0449793	0846	2
FOWLER JOSEPH H JR	WO1	W-2152210	0160	2
FOWLER LEO K	MAJ	0-0328119	1150	2
FOWLER LESTER D	LTC	0-2023386	0764	1
FOWLER MARION B	COL	0-0171554	0656	3
FOWLER MARION S	CPT	0-0301679	0146	2
FOWLER MAURICE R	LTC	0-0428308	0162	1
FOWLER PAUL I	MAJ	0-1114481	0565	2
FOWLER PAUL L	COL	0-0362004	0247	2
FOWLER ROBERT H	MAJ	0-0426209	0443	2
FOWLER ROBERT M	COL	0-0384792	0560	1
FOWLER ROBERT T	MAJ	0-2021219	0665	1
FOWLER ROLAND K	CPT	0-0484982	0549	1
FOWLER SID R	MAJ	0-2055148	1055	1

NAME	GRADE	SVC NO	DATE RET MO YR	RET CODE
FOWLER STEPHEN	LTC	0-0389992	0366	1
FOWLER STEPHEN A	1LT	0-2279323	1163	2
FOWLER THOMAS A	CW2	W-2208306	1065	1
FOWLER WALTER H	LTC	0-0292943	0263	1
FOWLER WALTER H	MAJ	0-0974550	0361	1
FOWLER WILLIAM H	COL	0-0270339	1059	1
FOWLES LESLIE O	LTC	0-0330128	0145	2
FOWLIE ERVINE A	1LT	0-1796775	0557	1
FOWLKES JAMES H	CW2	W-2144535	0163	2
FOWLKES REXFORD R	CW3	W-2151179	0664	1
FOWLKES RICHARD S	LTC	0-1041345	0166	3
FOWLKES ROBERT J	MAJ	0-0154769	0155	3
FOWLKS EVERILL W	COL	0-0492457	0467	3
FOWSER MARK F	MAJ	0-1176019	0861	1
FOWSER WILLIAM C	MAJ	0-2200540	0764	1
FOX ALDEN E	2LT	0-0407882	0446	2
FOX ANNA S	LTC	N-0771593	1268	1
FOX ANNIE G	MAJ	N-0700454	1045	1
FOX ARTHUR C	LTC	0-0165106	0445	1
FOX ARTHUR W	MAJ	0-0235500	0856	3
FOX BUEL K	LTC	0-0503181	0954	1
FOX C LYN	M G	0-0154765	1156	3
FOX CARL J	LTC	0-0109572	0937	1
FOX CHARLES O	LTC	0-0412121	1162	1
FOX CHARLES F	1LT	0-0511989	0347	1
FOX CHARLES W	MAJ	0-0987376	1263	1
FOX CLIFFORD E	MAJ	0-0451843	0359	1
FOX DANIEL K	2LT	0-1055852	1044	2
FOX DEAN C	CW3	W-2148962	0465	1
FOX DON H JR	CW2	W-2214331	0667	1
FOX DONALD A	LTC	0-0549929	0767	1
FOX EARL L	1LT	0-1317772	0158	2
FOX EDWARD J	1LT	0-1116775	0447	2
FOX EDWARD V	CW2	W-2117016	0245	2
FOX ELMER M	LTC	0-1294645	0561	1
FOX ERNEST F	LTC	0-0229494	1162	3
FOX ERNEST L	MAJ	0-2263287	0662	1
FOX EVERETT R	CW4	W-2214113	0968	1
FOX FRANCIS A	MAJ	0-1550592	0855	1
FOX FRANCIS E	MAJ	0-1945133	0566	1
FOX FRANCIS T	2LT	0-1321112	0444	2
FOX FRANCIS V	MAJ	0-2049555	0861	1
FOX FREDERICK	COL	0-0122607	0554	3
FOX FREDERICK	MAJ	0-0320052	0963	3
FOX FREDERICK JR	COL	0-1283750	1266	1
FOX GEORGE J	CW2	W-2210015	0161	1
FOX GERTRUDE T	1LT	N-0737155	1045	1
FOX HARRY L	1LT	0-1689728	1043	2
FOX ISAAC B	1LT	0-2012428	0748	1
FOX JACK	LTC	0-0887439	0166	1
FOX JAMES B	1LT	0-1640462	0146	2
FOX JAMES E	MAJ	0-1926036	0568	1
FOX JAMES H	LTC	0-0186646	0648	3
FOX JERVIE P JR	MAJ	0-0962479	1263	1
FOX JOHN F	2LT	0-1589619	0744	2
FOX JOHN F	LTC	0-1686286	0768	1
FOX JOHN G	MAJ	0-0200982	1055	3
FOX JOHN J	CW3	W-2145274	0765	1
FOX JOSEPH H	LTC	0-0271538	0168	3
FOX JOSEPH P	LTC	0-1330640	0966	1
FOX KENNETH E	1LT	0-1011433	0945	2
FOX LAWRENCE B	WO1	W-2121408	0744	2
FOX LAWRENCE J	MAJ	0-0196908	1053	3
FOX LESTER I	MAJ	0-0368002	0946	2
FOX LEWIS B	2LT	0-1032012	0845	2
FOX LOUIS	MAJ	0-1697908	0745	2
FOX MAURICE P	CW2	W-2209104	0765	1
FOX MYEE F	2LT	N-0742408	0346	1
FOX NATHAN S	MAJ	0-0331679	0945	2
FOX NEWTON F	CW4	W-2145138	0960	1
FOX NOEL B	COL	0-0100379	0648	3
FOX RAYMOND C	CPT	0-1040922	0459	1
FOX RICHARD J	MAJ	0-0450864	0253	1
FOX RICHARD O	LTC	0-1312138	0266	1
FOX RICHARD W	CW3	W-2117208	0163	1

NAME	GRADE	SVC NO	DATE RET MO YR	RET CODE
FOX ROBERT A	WO1	W-2120115	0960	2
FOX ROBERT L	COL	0-0902190	0567	3
FOX ROBERT M	LTC	0-0325920	0467	3
FOX ROYAL G	MAJ	0-0276541	1158	3
FOX SHELDON	CPT	0-0474786	0745	2
FOX SINCLAIRE	CW4	W-2101702	0859	1
FOX THEODORE P	CPT	0-0969293	0860	1
FOX THOMAS O	LTC	0-1288884	0662	1
FOX THOMAS P	B G	0-0230823	0463	3
FOX THOMAS P	CW4	W-2104685	0568	1
FOX VERNON A	CW3	W-2151786	0564	1
FOX WAYNE A	MAJ	0-0247652	0165	3
FOX WILLIAM H	MAJ	0-0340103	0762	1
FOX WILLIAM L	1LT	0-1303131	1044	2
FOX WILLIAM L	1LT	0-1821847	0246	2
FOX WILLIAM M	MAJ	0-0182450	0861	1
FOX WILLIAM M	CPT	0-0333799	0145	2
FOX WILLIAM M	LTC	0-1948135	0866	1
FOX WOODSON W	COL	0-1172865	0567	1
FOXWORTH LEWIS H	CPT	0-0494842	1047	1
FOY ALBERT J	LTC	0-0266938	0865	3
FOY GEORGE L	COL	0-0140017	0958	1
FOY JAMES J	CW2	W-2216096	0568	1
FOY NELSON E	MAJ	0-1309180	0864	1
FOY ROBERT E	LTC	0-1640463	0761	1
FOYE EDWARD O	MAJ	0-0147190	1045	2
FOYE KATHLEEN A	MAJ	L-0204280	0563	1
FOYLE CHARLES M JR	LTC	0-1046439	0462	1
FOYLE JOHN J	MAJ	0-1081409	1164	3
FOZ FREDRIC	MAJ	0-1896444	0661	1
FRADKIN IRVIN M	CPT	0-0495485	0446	2
FRADKIN JOSEPH	CPT	0-1541249	0346	2
FRADY CLARK K	1LT	0-1182363	1045	2
FRADY CLYDE H	CPT	0-0911415	1145	2
FRADY JAMES F	CW2	W-2205513	1264	1
FRADY PORTER R	MAJ	0-1590924	1266	1
FRAGGE STANLEY L	MAJ	0-1062813	1162	1
FRAIN JAMES F	1LT	0-1049839	0146	2
FRAINT SAUL	MAJ	0-1100991	0347	2
FRAIZER WAYNE D	LTC	0-1291254	0661	1
FRAKE CHESTER D	COL	0-0236328	1157	1
FRAKER HAROLD E	LTC	0-0451986	1165	1
FRAKES WILLIAM P	1LT	0-0422240	1044	2
FRALEY DANIEL W	CPT	0-0173979		1
FRALEY FLETCHER W	CPT	0-1703052	0759	1
FRALEY RAYMOND W JR	CPT	0-0954171	1058	1
FRALEY WILLIAM J JR	LTC	0-1106737	0267	1
FRALICK LAWRENCE R	MAJ	0-2028683	1065	1
FRAMBACH ARTHUR A	LTC	0-0185324	0853	3
FRAME JAMES W	LTC	0-0291465	0151	2
FRAME WILLIAM F	COL	0-0220711	0560	1
FRAMER DOROTHY M	MAJ	N-0733173	0962	1
FRAMPTON CHARLES R	1LT	0-0467715	1044	2
FRAMSON SELMA B	1LT	N-0762906	1047	1
FRANCAVILLA ANTHONY	MAJ	0-0991711	0364	1
FRANCAZI BRUNO A	LTC	0-2038800	1067	1
FRANCE DOUGLAS C	COL	0-0189015	1053	3
FRANCE JOHN J	MAJ	0-0265557	0364	3
FRANCE LEWIS J	CPT	0-0393843	1061	1
FRANCE MILLARD R	CPT	0-1995596	0759	1
FRANCE ORVIL K	CW2	W-2145429	1157	1
FRANCE WILLIAM L	LTC	0-1318151	0366	1
FRANCES CHARLES A	LTC	0-0412659	0162	1
FRANCES WALLACE J	CW3	W-2142763	0659	1
FRANCHER HAROLD A	LTC	0-1291970	1160	1
FRANCHERE CHETWYND M	MAJ	0-0121786	0552	3
FRANCHINA CHARLES A	1LT	0-0449041	0246	2
FRANCHINA CHARLES T	LTC	0-1555687	0363	1
FRANCIS ALFRED W JR	1LT	0-0265611	0364	3
FRANCIS CLYDE D	CPT	0-1635903	0157	1
FRANCIS CRUSOE	CPT	0-1286467	0645	2
FRANCIS DONALD S	1LT	0-1558485	0646	2
FRANCIS FABIAN G	CPT	0-1534969	1050	2
FRANCIS FRANK	MAJ	0-0191915	1148	1
FRANCIS FRANK V	CPT	0-1799044	0357	1

NAME	GRADE	SVC NO	DATE RET MO YR	RET CODE
FRANCIS FRED M	LTC	0-1321821	0966	3
FRANCIS GILBERT J	MAJ	0-0469503	0761	3
FRANCIS HARRY A	CW2	W-2149889	0861	1
FRANCIS HARRY B	LTC	0-0212720	1060	3
FRANCIS HERBERT H	LTC	0-0906647	0864	1
FRANCIS JOHN G	CPT	0-0497684	1146	1
FRANCIS JOHN J	1LT	0-0490869	0544	1
FRANCIS JOHN L	CW3	W-2119342	1164	1
FRANCIS JOSEPH	CW3	W-2141279	0860	1
FRANCIS LAWRENCE S	CW2	W-2145055	0658	1
FRANCIS LEO J	MAJ	0-1307532	0256	1
FRANCIS LEWIS E	MAJ	0-1176021	1263	1
FRANCIS MARGARET E	MAJ	N-0726244	1064	3
FRANCIS MARION E	LTC	0-1102728	0461	1
FRANCIS MELVIN C	LTC	0-1011793	1065	1
FRANCIS MORRIS E	LTC	0-1293233	0861	1
FRANCIS MORRIS J	CPT	0-0481725	0354	1
FRANCIS OLIVER J	LTC	0-1293575	0663	1
FRANCIS RAYMOND J	LTC	0-1110487	0967	1
FRANCIS RICHARD A	2LT	0-1300700	0459	1
FRANCIS SILVIO M	LTC	0-1050864	0962	1
FRANCIS THOMAS L	LTC	0-0252591	0365	3
FRANCIS URBAN L	LTC	0-1294121	0561	1
FRANCIS VINCENT O	COL	0-0346595	1262	3
FRANCIS WILLIAM H	LTC	0-0237854	0361	3
FRANCISCO FELIPE	1LT	0-1897022	1166	1
FRANCISCO FRANK F	MAJ	0-1116661	1262	1
FRANCISCO GEORGE L	1LT	0-1012134	0945	2
FRANCISCO WINSTON S	MAJ	0-0885893	0854	1
FRANCK HERBERT A	LTC	0-0334964	0662	1
FRANCK WALTER W	LTC	0-1595508	0363	1
FRANCKE ROY L	MAJ	0-0358994	0462	1
FRANCO BIAGIO	CPT	0-0343888	1045	2
FRANCO ERWIN J	CPT	0-1031240	0757	1
FRANCO JAMES W	LTC	0-1316501	0765	1
FRANCO LOUIS L	COL	0-0290228	0465	3
FRANCOIS JOSEPH L	CPT	0-0275991	0661	3
FRANCONA ANTHONY	CPT	0-0332005	1043	2
FRANCONE JOSEPH L	1LT	0-1103166	0349	2
FRANDEN NED W	CPT	0-1578481	0645	2
FRANDLER MONROE	CPT	0-0380400	0945	2
FRANDSEN DANA C	CPT	0-1283576	0646	2
FRANDSEN EARL F	CPT	0-1285407	1147	2
FRANEK ANTHONY A	2LT	0-1308320	0145	2
FRANGEDAKIS PANOALEO	LTC	0-1105440	0467	3
FRANGIE JAMES J	MAJ	0-1899371	0163	1
FRANGOS MICHAEL W	1LT	0-1875366	0355	2
FRANK ARNOLD F W	LTC	0-0543005	0965	1
FRANK BENJIMAN H	MAJ	0-0232043	0154	1
FRANK CHARLES P	CPT	0-1177800	0547	2
FRANK DAVID	LTC	0-0346321	0861	1
FRANK DAVID W	CPT	0-4030940	0666	1
FRANK EGON	WO1	W-2124121	0846	2
FRANK FLOYD	CW4	W-2005872	0468	1
FRANK FREDERICK	WO1	W-2131346	0859	3
FRANK GEORGE F	MAJ	0-1636879	0660	1
FRANK GEORGE W	MAJ	0-0361614	1045	2
FRANK HAROLD W	LTC	0-0497672	0167	3
FRANK HARRY C JR	LTC	0-1002920	0267	1
FRANK HOWARD	CPT	0-0384463	0146	2
FRANK ISRAEL R	COL	0-0297899	0865	3
FRANK JAMES E	M G	0-0268106	1168	3
FRANK JAMES L	LTC	0-1755183	0259	2
FRANK JOHN L	2LT	0-2047315	0245	2
FRANK JOHN M	LTC	0-1112155	1162	1
FRANK JOHN T	CW2	W-2207537	0661	1
FRANK JOSEPH P	1LT	0-0517753	0550	1
FRANK KENNETH L	CPT	0-0420524	1045	2
FRANK LOUIS W	LTC	0-0517574	0362	3
FRANK NATHAN	CPT	0-1692102	0346	2
FRANK PAUL J	1LT	0-1285408	1045	2
FRANK PAUL S	LTC	0-0177619	1160	3
FRANK PHILIP N	1LT	0-1061294	0845	2
FRANK SAMUEL S	LTC	0-0330180	1066	3
FRANK TONY C	COL	0-0479293	1153	1

NAME	GRADE	SVC NO	DATE RET MO YR	RET CODE
FRANK WILLIAM B	LTC	0-0239353	0961	1
FRANK WILLIAM H	1LT	0-0239000	0355	3
FRANK WILLIAM M	MAJ	0-0243506	0666	3
FRANK WILLIAM R	1LT	0-2027779	0955	1
FRANK WILLIAM W	CW2	W-2209094	0560	1
FRANKE EDWARD F	LTC	0-1102247	0363	1
FRANKE HARRISON L	MAJ	0-1578483	0366	1
FRANKE THOMAS W	WO1	W-2153024	1055	2
FRANKE WILLIAM J	CPT	0-1693392	0346	2
FRANKE WILLIAM M	CW3	W-2143318	0662	1
FRANKEL HERBERT G	MAJ	0-0144232	0655	3
FRANKEL ISRAEL	CPT	0-0401415	0246	2
FRANKEL THEODORE	CPT	0-1305035	0248	2
FRANKEN PAUL L	CPT	0-0418302	1145	2
FRANKENBERGER J B	LTC	0-0195445	1053	3
FRANKENBURG FRANCIS	MAJ	0-1557147	0663	2
FRANKENBURGER M C	MAJ	0-1291797	0460	1
FRANKENFIELD JOHN J	CW3	W-2143075	0659	1
FRANKENFIELD KENNETH	MAJ	0-1053132	0961	1
FRANKENSTEIN KENNETH	MAJ	0-0312660	0967	3
FRANKHOUSER M L	2LT	N-0725330	0145	1
FRANKIE VALENTINE	CW3	W-2144915	0866	1
FRANKINA SAMUEL N	MAJ	0-2262357	0664	1
FRANKL ERNEST A W	LTC	0-0342972	0865	3
FRANKL STEPHEN JR	LTC	0-1311755	0866	1
FRANKLAND ROBERT E	M G	0-0277098	0364	3
FRANKLAND WALTER L	COL	0-0251710	0456	3
FRANKLIN ALFRED A	1LT	0-0385885	1042	2
FRANKLIN ARTHUR	2LT	0-1285918	1143	2
FRANKLIN ARTHUR L	CW4	W-2101706	1055	1
FRANKLIN BENJAMIN	CW4	W-2116042	0255	2
FRANKLIN BILLIE J	CW2	W-2210355	0168	1
FRANKLIN BURTIS	2LT	0-1044360	0145	2
FRANKLIN CARL W	MAJ	0-2204402	1265	1
FRANKLIN CHESTER V	1LT	0-1692524	0647	2
FRANKLIN CLAUD L JR	CW4	W-2147872	0264	2
FRANKLIN EDMOND L	CW4	W-2146014	0760	1
FRANKLIN EDWIN J	MAJ	0-1303701	0264	1
FRANKLIN ELSIE L	CPT	0-0237627	0261	3
FRANKLIN ELMER E	WO1	W-2119790	0154	1
FRANKLIN EMERSON	CPT	0-0967014	1060	1
FRANKLIN FREDRIC B	LTC	0-1319614	0962	1
FRANKLIN GEORGE H	LTC	0-1295860	0361	1
FRANKLIN GUSTAVE K	COL	0-0166708	0648	3
FRANKLIN JAMES C	LTC	0-0555685	0168	3
FRANKLIN JAMES D	CPT	0-1641299	0860	1
FRANKLIN JAMES W	MAJ	0-1799725	1262	1
FRANKLIN JEFF L	CW2	W-2210167	0863	1
FRANKLIN JENNINGS R	CW2	W-2144175	0461	2
FRANKLIN JOHN D	MAJ	0-1299210	0361	1
FRANKLIN JOHN H	CW2	W-2150728	0462	1
FRANKLIN JOHN S	MAJ	0-0416431	1061	3
FRANKLIN LAWSON D	MAJ	0-0435386	1062	1
FRANKLIN LESLIE	LTC	0-0261775	0859	3
FRANKLIN LESLIE R	CPT	0-1062175	0657	1
FRANKLIN MARY H	1LT	N-0763251	0145	1
FRANKLIN OLIN S	CW4	W-2117431	0858	1
FRANKLIN ORLAND A	2LT	0-1317773	0844	2
FRANKLIN RALPH H	LTC	0-0326461	0753	1
FRANKLIN RAYMOND	CPT	0-0514172	0346	1
FRANKLIN RAYMOND J	LTC	0-0383421	0768	3
FRANKLIN ROBERT A	CPT	0-0548744	0446	2
FRANKLIN ROBERT B	MAJ	0-2017727	0168	1
FRANKLIN ROBERT J	2LT	0-1591720	1044	2
FRANKLIN ROBERT S	1LT	0-1010567	0944	2
FRANKLIN THOMAS C	LTC	0-1950349	0866	1
FRANKLIN VERNAL H	MAJ	0-2288099	0667	1
FRANKLIN WILLIAM A	1LT	0-1165731	0246	2
FRANKLIN WILLIAM G	MAJ	0-1918313	1263	1
FRANKLYN EARL S	MAJ	0-0436962	0947	1
FRANKS ANDREW G	COL	0-0257150	0767	3
FRANKS BILLIE P	MAJ	L-0602017	1059	2
FRANKS CHARLES H	CW3	W-2150362	0163	1
FRANKS GARRET D	CW3	W-2206538	0866	1
FRANKS JOSEPH A	LTC	0-1186205	0968	1
FRANKS MILFORD R	MAJ	0-1877941	0567	1
FRANKS ROBERT H JR	MAJ	0-1314363	1062	1
FRANKS VICTOR L	MAJ	0-2208735	0966	1
FRANKVILLE DOMINICK	LTC	0-0395039	0562	1
FRANSCIONI FRANCIS T	MAJ	0-1913475	1168	1
FRANSEIN ELDON E	MAJ	0-0947371	0864	1
FRANSISCO FLOYD L	LTC	0-1574044	1060	1
FRANTZ CHARLES H	LTC	0-0320410	0744	2
FRANTZ DONALD E	1LT	0-1012151	0146	2
FRANTZ HARRISON S	1LT	0-1016588	1046	2
FRANTZ KARL L	LTC	0-1048778	0465	1
FRANTZ WILLIAM A	LTC	0-0174918	0651	3
FRANTZICH RICHARD H	MAJ	0-0404371	0661	2
FRANZ EDWIN F	LTC	0-0905703	0567	3
FRANZ LEO F	LTC	0-1577188	0657	1
FRANZ PAUL W	CW2	W-2101708	0149	2
FRANZ WALTER D	LTC	0-0445064	0349	1
FRANZEN IVAR P	1LT	0-1644967	0355	1
FRANZEN JAMES G	MAJ	0-1012170	0561	1
FRANZEN ROY O	LTC	0-0221934	0864	3
FRAPPIER JOSEPH F	CPT	0-0172188	0158	3
FRAPS JOSEPH A	LTC	0-0229732	0164	3
FRARY WILLARD E	CPT	0-1640465	0358	1
FRASER ANDREW S	CPT	0-0379864	0346	2
FRASER CARL A	LTC	0-0230548	0764	3
FRASER DEAN B	MAJ	0-0128057	0950	3
FRASER DONALD K	MAJ	0-2000567	0665	1
FRASER DONALD M	LTC	0-1106739	0762	1
FRASER DONALD R	MAJ	0-0231336	0665	3
FRASER DUNCAN F	MAJ	0-0429289	0557	1
FRASER FRANK E	M G	0-0222901	0958	3
FRASER HAROLD L	1LT	0-0390867	0646	2
FRASER HARRY C	LTC	0-0464521	0147	1
FRASER HUGH W	LTC	0-1013473	0366	1
FRASER JAMES G	LTC	0-0356933	0667	3
FRASER JAMES W	COL	0-0165792	1156	3
FRASER JOHN A	LTC	0-1283577	1163	3
FRASER JOHN W	1LT	0-1296356	0944	2
FRASER JOSEPH B	M G	0-0247121	0856	3
FRASER LEO H	LTC	0-0546797	0768	2
FRASER LLOYD D	LTC	0-0272950	0967	3
FRASER REGINALD S	CPT	0-0188493	0954	3
FRASER RONALD N	MAJ	0-0957023	0768	1
FRASER SHERMAN C	LTC	0-0487567	1146	2
FRASER THOMAS C	1LT	0-0437741	0645	2
FRASER WILLIAM M	MAJ	0-0553468	0865	1
FRASIER GWENDOLYN	LTC	0-1548779	0759	1
FRASIER RODERICK J	MAJ	0-2032881	0261	1
FRASL ETHEL J	2LT	N-0797347	1046	1
FRATICELLI EDDIE	MAJ	0-2033634	0261	1
FRATIS ELWOOD J	COL	0-0236538	0466	3
FRAVEL JESSE S	LTC	0-1553997	0663	1
FRAY LOREN M	1LT	0-0530482	1144	2
FRAYER WILSON A	1LT	0-2019307	1047	2
FRAZE CHARLES C	LTC	0-0403540	0368	3
FRAZEE LOWELL B	CW4	W-2141559	0864	1
FRAZEE MARGARET L	LTC	N-0703602	1264	1
FRAZER DONALD O	CPT	0-0983948	0557	1
FRAZER GEORGE P	LTC	0-0259958	0368	3
FRAZER PERCY W	MAJ	0-0259957	0966	3
FRAZIER BENJAMIN W	MAJ	0-0409965	0864	3
FRAZIER CECIL E	LTC	0-1697827	0561	1
FRAZIER DALE	CPT	0-0500893	0350	1
FRAZIER DANIEL H	CW3	W-2151424	0662	1
FRAZIER DERWOOD E	MAJ	0-0984411	0863	2
FRAZIER EARLY H	MAJ	0-0293403	0246	2
FRAZIER EDWIN	WO1	W-2154666	0956	1
FRAZIER FRANK A	MAJ	0-0370416	1155	2
FRAZIER GAEL M	LTC	0-1320938	1262	1
FRAZIER GEORGE F	CPT	0-0922430	1045	2
FRAZIER JAMES E	LTC	0-1293035	1167	1
FRAZIER JAMES E	CW3	W-2142586	1162	1
FRAZIER JAMES O	LTC	0-1115584	1262	1
FRAZIER JOHN	CW4	W-2115751	1154	1
FRAZIER JOHN M	LTC	0-0318085	0760	3
FRAZIER JULIUS D	LTC	0-0417602	0960	1
FRAZIER KENNETH H	CW4	W-2106897	1060	1
FRAZIER MURRAY	LTC	0-0383800	1160	1
FRAZIER NOAH L	CW3	W-2205720	0865	1
FRAZIER OSCAR H	LTC	0-0169180	0760	3
FRAZIER RAYMOND L	WO1	W-2146134	0853	1
FRAZIER RICHARD D	CW4	W-2151376	0968	1
FRAZIER ROBERT S	MAJ	0-4009146	1067	1
FRAZIER SHERVERT H	LTC	0-0322693	0646	2
FRAZIER STANLEY P	MAJ	0-1937600	0668	1
FRAZIER THOMAS A	B G	0-0375140	0945	2
FRAZIER WILLIAM R	LTC	0-0302068	1147	2
FRAZIER WILLIE R	CW2	W-2149432	0762	1
FRAZIN ALFRED B	LTC	0-0916346	0167	2
FRAZIN BERNARD	LTC	0-0309638	0167	3
FRAZIOR DAVID M	COL	0-0222230	0964	3
FRAZY CESIRA A	CPT	M-0000779	0757	1
FREANEY WILLIAM J	LTC	0-0117870	1151	3
FREAK HARRY J	MAJ	0-1294814	1060	1
FREAS LILLIAN	MAJ	N-0723782	0960	2
FRECHETTE DONALD L	1LT	0-1331830	0347	2
FRECKLETON EARLE F	1LT	0-1289893	1045	2
FREDA ARMAND A	MAJ	0-0259376	0467	3
FREDA CESERE R	MAJ	0-2020935	0363	1
FREDEEN HARLAN L	CPT	0-0400048	0544	2
FREDEMAN FRANK H	LTC	0-0101681	0844	2
FREDEN GUNNAR D	LTC	0-0301512	0766	3
FREDENBURG DAVID L	LTC	0-0154792	0552	1
FREDERIC EDGAR H	MAJ	0-0272071	0968	3
FREDERICK A E	LTC	0-0154053	0648	3
FREDERICK ALBERT R	COL	0-0259514	0867	3
FREDERICK ALVIN E	MAJ	0-2263331	0666	1
FREDERICK DAILEY F	MAJ	0-1951684	0868	1
FREDERICK DONALD R	CPT	0-1019140	0346	2
FREDERICK ELMER F	LTC	0-0276839	0560	3
FREDERICK FRANCIS D	MAJ	0-0990152	0764	1
FREDERICK GEORGE F	LTC	0-0927620	0463	3
FREDERICK JAMES M	MAJ	0-0705677	0564	1
FREDERICK JOHN A	MAJ	0-1305161	0263	1
FREDERICK JOHN H	LTC	0-0183440	0652	3
FREDERICK LEO L	1LT	0-1574426	1047	2
FREDERICK ROBERT R	LTC	0-0214784	0462	3
FREDERICK ROSCOE	2LT	0-1185870	1045	2
FREDERICK THOMAS J	CPT	0-0290471	1163	3
FREDERICK WILLIAM G	COL	0-0290371	1056	3
FREDERICKS BORIS	LTC	0-1000118	1160	1
FREDERICKS PARKER JR	LTC	0-1106144	0867	1
FREDERICKS ROBERT F	CPT	0-0404069	0246	2
FREDERICKSEN PETER A	COL	0-0179024	0446	2
FREDETTE WARREN H	MAJ	0-1874901	0365	1
FREDIANI JACK F	MAJ	0-2102836	0764	1
FREDIN HUGH R	MAJ	0-2033690	0967	1
FREDIN JOHN E	COL	0-0225144	0961	1
FREDINE ALLAN R	COL	0-0513861	1163	1
FREDLUND THEODORE F	CW3	W-2007369	0265	1
FREDLUND VICTOR J	MAJ	0-1292681	0465	1
FREDREGILL JASPER I	LTC	0-0333701	0265	3
FREDRICK ANNA M	1LT	N-0771032	0845	1
FREDRICKS ERVIN Z	LTC	0-0292433	0662	3
FREDRICKS WILLIAM H	LTC	0-0325388	0365	3
FREDRICKSEN WILLIS L	MAJ	0-1547298	1060	1
FREDRICKSON CLYDE H	COL	0-0197979	0458	3
FREDRICKSON THEODORE	CW3	W-2110619	0659	1
FREE HELEN P	2LT	N-0733997	0945	1
FREE JOHN H	1LT	0-2037145	0666	1
FREEBLE THOMAS V	LTC	0-0142674	0758	3
FREEBORN ROBERT S	CPT	0-1325386	0846	2
FREEBURG ROBERT P	CW3	W-3430059	1168	2
FREEBURN HERBERT D	CW4	W-2127175	0259	1
FREED OLOF E	CPT	0-1018560	0854	1
FREEDMAN ALFRED	1LT	0-1321704	0947	2
FREEDMAN ARNOLD M	LTC	0-1310089	0862	1
FREEDMAN DAVID	CPT	0-0486414	0146	2
FREEDMAN DAVID T	MAJ	0-1640468	0547	2
FREEDMAN GEORGE	COL	0-0400769	0768	1
FREEDMAN HARRY L	LTC	0-0253075	0160	3
FREEDMAN LEO	LTC	0-0191515	0562	3
FREEDMAN MILTON	1LT	0-1282102	1153	1
FREEDMAN ROBERT I	MAJ	0-1997081	1263	1
FREEDMAN SAMUEL A	CPT	0-1895050	0652	2
FREEDMAN STANLEY S	CPT	0-0335894	0146	2
FREEL WILFRED I	LTC	0-0213704	0663	3
FREELAND FREDERICK	LTC	0-1638475	1064	2
FREELAND NEWTON F	CW4	W-2129351	0756	1
FREELAND WALTER K	LTC	0-0397145	0461	1
FREELING RICHARD N	1LT	0-0439882	0845	2
FREELS FRANK H	LTC	0-1182828	0762	1
FREEMAN ALAN C	CPT	0-0924341	0154	2
FREEMAN ALBERT	CPT	0-0419746	1046	1
FREEMAN ALBERT S	LTC	0-1285033	0461	1
FREEMAN ALLYNE F	LTC	0-0138133	1154	2
FREEMAN ANNE D	1LT	N-0755217	0546	1
FREEMAN ARTHUR N	CPT	0-1290926	0347	2
FREEMAN CAROL J	LTC	0-0375209	0961	1
FREEMAN CHARLEY H	COL	0-0336781	0162	3
FREEMAN CLARENCE S	COL	0-0367100	1262	1
FREEMAN CLAUDE L	1LT	0-1310090	0148	2
FREEMAN CLIFFORD W	LTC	0-0406002	0560	1
FREEMAN CONRAD J	COL	0-0224719	1051	3
FREEMAN CURTIS W JR	LTC	0-1330056	0966	1
FREEMAN EARL K	CPT	0-0331567	0444	2
FREEMAN ED W	MAJ	0-1884184	0967	1
FREEMAN EDGAR I	CPT	0-0223057	1052	3
FREEMAN EDITH	2LT	N-0722244	0145	1
FREEMAN EDWARD H	CPT	0-0144408	0547	2
FREEMAN ERNEST	MAJ	0-0250153	0653	3
FREEMAN EUGENE C	1LT	0-0497857	0550	1
FREEMAN GEORGE W	1LT	0-0299593	0566	3
FREEMAN GERALD M	LTC	0-1001133	1160	1
FREEMAN GREGORY J	COL	0-0284397	0852	1
FREEMAN HAL W	CPT	0-0446116	0746	1
FREEMAN HAROLD E	1LT	0-1533554	0945	2
FREEMAN HARRY C	2LT	0-0992207	0452	2
FREEMAN HELEN L	1LT	N-0730639	0546	1
FREEMAN HERBERT C	CPT	0-0361615	0745	2
FREEMAN HOWARD L	LTC	0-0243570	1165	3
FREEMAN IRA	LTC	0-0158794	0249	3
FREEMAN JACK	1LT	0-1000119	0949	1
FREEMAN JACOB R	MAJ	0-0325873	1061	1
FREEMAN JAMES E	MAJ	0-0206714	0947	1
FREEMAN JAMES N	CW3	W-2146875	0762	1
FREEMAN JAMES W	2LT	0-1053602	0845	2
FREEMAN JOHN C	MAJ	0-1950982	1263	1
FREEMAN JONES M	COL	0-0101928	0655	3
FREEMAN JOSEPH L	WO1	W-2152312	1159	1
FREEMAN JOSEPH W	MAJ	0-0266023	0556	3
FREEMAN KENNETH J	CW3	W-3200146	0968	1
FREEMAN LESLIE V	CPT	0-0167550	0853	3
FREEMAN LOUIS C JR	COL	0-0236963	1265	3
FREEMAN LUTHER T	1LT	0-0889613	0957	1
FREEMAN LYNN A	LTC	0-2017389	0966	1
FREEMAN MARCOS	MAJ	0-0185241	0344	2
FREEMAN MARTIN I JR	LTC	0-0386632	0263	1
FREEMAN MARY F	LTC	N-0765434	0368	1
FREEMAN MERLE E	1LT	0-1061692	1146	2
FREEMAN ORVILLE E	MAJ	0-0904061	0367	3
FREEMAN RALPH C	MAJ	0-0969472	0964	1
FREEMAN RALPH C JR	MAJ	0-0987474	1162	1
FREEMAN RALPH W	LTC	0-0271007	0568	3
FREEMAN RAY M	COL	0-0322892	0661	3
FREEMAN RICHARD C	LTC	0-0297739	0567	3
FREEMAN RICHARD W	2LT	0-5875131	0962	2
FREEMAN RITA P	1LT	N-0751032	1045	1
FREEMAN ROBERT A	CW4	W-2113675	1157	1
FREEMAN ROBERT B	MAJ	0-1821993	0561	1
FREEMAN ROBERT L	CPT	0-0450198	0845	2
FREEMAN ROBERT S	MAJ	0-2097100	0164	1
FREEMAN ROGER A	CW4	W-2120288	0559	1
FREEMAN SUSAN E	CPT	N-0724383	0745	1
FREEMAN WALDO O	COL	0-0321037	0666	1

NAME	GRADE	SVC NO	DATE RET MO YR	RET CODE
FREEMAN WALTER F	COL	0-0496790	0860	1
FREEMAN WILLIAM A	LTC	0-0175396	1060	1
FREEMAN WILLIAM L	2LT	0-0246313	0357	3
FREEMAN WILLIAM E	LTC	0-1171541	0561	1
FREEMAN WILLIAM H	MAJ	0-1305911	1165	3
FREER GEORGE G	COL	0-0256421	0560	3
FREER LOUIS B	LTC	0-0211285	0648	3
FREER WAYNE T	LTC	0-2208608	0268	1
FREER WILLARD O	CPT	0-1640469	0157	1
FREESE CARLETON T	CW2	W-2110601	1154	1
FREESE CHARLES A	CW3	W-2120073	0960	1
FREESLAND JOSEPH E	LTC	0-0340618	1062	1
FREEZE GEORGE G JR	CW2	W-2150205	0955	1
FREGEAU LAWRENCE R	CW3	W-2147155	1163	1
FREGOE HARRY B	CPT	0-0531204	0946	2
FREGOSI ALBERT	COL	0-0272905	0660	2
FREIBAND CARL A	LTC	0-0327777	0163	1
FREID JOSEPH A	1LT	0-0669030	0245	2
FREIDEN JOSEPH N	CPT	0-0474364	0945	2
FREIDKIN MARVIN J	CPT	0-0265643	1045	2
FREIHUBE ROBERT C JR	MAJ	0-0312604	0560	1
FREITAG MAC A	COL	0-0247486	0259	3
FREITAG ROY A	LTC	0-1011392	0961	1
FREITAS EDWARD W	CPT	0-2032318	0160	1
FREITCHEN LEROY C	CW3	W-2150994	0865	1
FRELIGH WILLIAM P	LTC	0-0563039	0663	1
FREMSTAD LISTON J	MAJ	0-0415778	0561	2
FRENCH ARCHIE	MAJ	0-0327385	0746	2
FRENCH ARLYN R	COL	0-0216587	0464	3
FRENCH CHARLES L	MAJ	0-1258046	0162	1
FRENCH CHARLES W	CPT	0-1302626	0558	1
FRENCH DANIEL C	1LT	0-0373068	0146	2
FRENCH DEWITT H JR	CPT	0-1540721	1159	1
FRENCH DUDLEY L	LTC	0-1001796	0566	3
FRENCH EDWARD A	COL	0-0406644	1068	1
FRENCH EUGENIE G	MAJ	N-0752412	1263	1
FRENCH GEORGE R	1LT	0-0536726	1045	2
FRENCH GEORGE S	MAJ	0-2038135	1161	1
FRENCH GEORGE T	CW2	W-2203340	0262	1
FRENCH GEORGE W JR	LTC	0-1100107	1163	1
FRENCH HOMER M	MAJ	0-0138654	1158	3
FRENCH IRVINE	2LT	0-0144229	1153	3
FRENCH ISAAC S	MAJ	0-2017984	0865	1
FRENCH JOHN A	MAJ	0-0249740	0765	3
FRENCH JOHN A	1LT	0-1011170	0461	1
FRENCH JOHN L	CW3	W-2104067	1051	2
FRENCH JOHN P	CPT	0-0904996	0344	2
FRENCH KEITH A	LTC	0-0467186	0764	1
FRENCH LORNE	LTC	0-0443687	1047	2
FRENCH MARCUS R	MAJ	0-0980815	0563	1
FRENCH PAUL J	CW3	W-2147211	0962	1
FRENCH RALPH W	MAJ	0-0165184	0548	1
FRENCH RAY W	2LT	0-1304369	0644	2
FRENCH RICHARD E	LTC	0-0152131	0645	2
FRENCH RICHARD P	CW4	W-2105290	0860	1
FRENCH ROBERT M	CPT	0-0312004	1146	1
FRENCH ROLLIE L	MAJ	0-0272856	0759	1
FRENCH SHIRLEY S JR	1LT	0-1315420	1045	2
FRENCH STEPHEN F	COL	0-0118628	0154	3
FRENCH TRAVIS A	LTC	0-1826320	1068	1
FRENCH VERLAND A	MAJ	0-1949319	0468	3
FRENCH VERNON L	MAJ	0-1110488	0961	1
FRENCH WALKER M	LTC	0-1108671	0167	3
FRENCH WILL C	CPT	0-0259936	0850	2
FRENCH WILLIAM C	LTC	0-1168675	1166	1
FRENCH WILLIAM C	LTC	0-2020936	1068	1
FRENCH WILLIAM T	CPT	0-1914353	1046	2
FRENCHER JOSEPH	MAJ	0-1016782	0457	1
FRENCK GARDEN	MAJ	0-1639047	0966	3
FRENKEL GEORGE L	MAJ	0-0552533	0664	1
FRENNA LEO C	COL	0-0167682	0555	3
FREPPEL PAUL L	LTC	0-1555965	0167	3
FRERICHS JOHN D	LTC	0-0350027	0167	3
FRESE GEORGE H	CPT	0-0226227	0955	2
FRESF WILLIAM O	LTC	0-0311674	0960	1

NAME	GRADE	SVC NO	DATE RET MO YR	RET CODE
FRESHLEY LOWELL C	2LT	0-1177399	0345	2
FRESHNOCK JAMES H	CW4	W-2144671	0168	1
FRESHOUR LARKIN W	LTC	0-1288729	0760	1
FRET JOSE A	2LT	0-0222463	0844	2
FRETER JOHN M	2LT	0-1327832	0146	2
FRETER KAY F	LTC	0-0931411	0563	1
FRETHEM ALLEN A	CPT	0-1766214	1049	2
FRETUEG KENNETH D	1LT	0-0577603	0860	2
FRETZ JOHN C	LTC	0-0219365	0160	3
FREUDENBERG WALTER	LTC	0-1299392	0563	1
FREUND JACK A	CPT	0-1311875	0347	2
FREUND PHIL W	LTC	0-0333371	0454	1
FREVELE ALBERT R	MAJ	0-0428605	0553	2
FREVERT WILLIAM	2LT	0-1035199	0544	2
FREW ARCHIE JR	CPT	0-0966108	1060	1
FREWIN NORMAN H	MAJ	0-1103641	1266	1
FREY ARTHUR J	COL	0-0157661	1157	3
FREY ARTHUR J JR	MAJ	0-1295008	0258	1
FREY ARTHUR M	LTC	0-0362045	0959	1
FREY EDWIN F	MAJ	0-0519133	1053	1
FREY FREDERICK	COL	0-0138981	0654	3
FREY HAROLD M	LTC	0-0258446	1165	3
FREY HARRY J	LTC	0-0140054	0954	3
FREY HOWARD C JR	CW2	W-2208861	0559	1
FREY MARCY	COL	0-0311492	0165	3
FREY RAYMOND T	2LT	0-1100544	0843	2
FREY RICHARD D SR	CW3	W-2150703	0267	1
FREY ROBERT F	LTC	0-0375479	0460	1
FREY WALTER J	CW2	W-2141282	0656	1
FREY WILLIAM C	MAJ	0-0409003	0646	2
FREY WILLIAM N	LTC	0-0523242	0365	1
FREYDER LEO F	COL	0-0271822	0166	3
FREYER JOSEPH	MAJ	0-1579663	0868	3
FREYERMUTH JAMES R	COL	0-0262373	0267	3
FREYERMUTH OTT G JR	CPT	0-0443334	1045	2
FREYMUTH HARRY W	MAJ	0-1003106	0163	1
FREYTAG ROBERT E	MAJ	0-0542117	0962	1
FREYTAG ROBERT J	MAJ	0-2262786	0463	2
FRIANT STUART T	COL	0-0186345	0447	2
FRIAR HERBERT H	LTC	0-1585470	0161	1
FRIBANCE AUSTIN E	MAJ	0-0273288	0867	3
FRIBERG ROBERT A	MAJ	0-0482043	0646	2
FRIBERG WALTER R	LTC	0-0302096	0268	3
FRIBLEY EARL F	CPT	0-0118643	1064	3
FRICH GEORGE H JR	1LT	0-0265278	1044	2
FRICK CHARLES H	LTC	0-0144920	0648	3
FRICK CLARENCE F	MAJ	0-2263504	0665	1
FRICK DONALD S	CW2	W-3430049	0966	1
FRICK HARVEY L	CPT	0-0505715	0146	2
FRICK JOHN P	COL	0-0205855	0559	3
FRICK RALPH J	LTC	0-1170739	0261	1
FRICK RAYMOND R	MAJ	0-0257749	0546	2
FRICK RUPERT G	CPT	0-1825183	0957	1
FRICK WALTER H	LTC	0-0171447	0856	3
FRICKE HARRY C	1LT	0-0534889	0745	2
FRICKE JOHN W	1LT	0-1331279	0452	2
FRICKE LOWELL J	LTC	0-0468844	0964	1
FRICKER NORMAN K	MAJ	0-1293936	0662	2
FRIDAY EDWARD R	CPT	0-1290928	0346	2
FRIDAY JOE	MAJ	0-1920223	0264	1
FRIDAY JOHN D	COL	0-0171088	0760	1
FRIDAY RICHARD W	2LT	0-1996911	1145	2
FRIDELL MYRON D	MAJ	0-1686649	0964	1
FRIDIE DAVID H	1LT	0-2002879	0355	2
FRIDINGER WILLIAM T	1LT	0-0439821	0744	2
FRIDLEY JESSE R	COL	0-0150049	0648	3
FRIDRICH RICHARD L	MAJ	0-0179077	1056	3
FRIED GEORGE W	LTC	0-0235918	0855	3
FRIED HAROLD V	CPT	0-0247922	1165	3
FRIED JACOB V	MAJ	0-0574644	0762	1
FRIED JOSEPH A	CPT	0-1299394	0347	2
FRIED SAMUEL A	LTC	0-1004581	1264	3
FRIEDAH HAROLD F	CPT	0-1165859	0447	2
FRIEDBERG KARL M	LTC	0-1553446	0762	1
FRIEDENTHAL ADOLPH L	LTC	0-0112552	0557	3

NAME	GRADE	SVC NO	DATE RET MO YR	RET CODE
FRIEDENTHAL RALPH F	LTC	0-0289531	0347	1
FRIEDENWALD AARON	LTC	0-0397823	0261	1
FRIEDERS CARL F	MAJ	0-0953671	0862	1
FRIEDFELD LOUIS	CPT	0-0500834	0444	2
FRIEDLAENDER ALEX S	MAJ	0-0351474	0843	2
FRIEDLAND GRACE P	1LT	N-0724521	0946	1
FRIEDLANDER JACKSON	MAJ	0-0430257	0446	2
FRIEDLANDER K R	MAJ	0-0257392	1055	3
FRIEDLI GOTTFRIED	1LT	0-1182930	1045	2
FRIEDMAN ALEXANDER	MAJ	0-0507642	0846	2
FRIEDMAN ARTHUR H	MAJ	0-1014572	0168	3
FRIEDMAN BERNARD E	1LT	0-1295530	1146	2
FRIEDMAN CHARLES	CPT	0-0533633	0546	2
FRIEDMAN CHARLES F	LTC	0-0423493	0361	1
FRIEDMAN EGON E	LTC	0-1017676	1264	1
FRIEDMAN FRANK	LTC	0-0503038	0857	1
FRIEDMAN HAROLD B	LTC	0-0254268	1164	3
FRIEDMAN HARRY	1LT	0-1013194	1145	2
FRIEDMAN HARRY	CPT	0-1690295	0346	2
FRIEDMAN HENRY T	1LT	0-0489226	0245	2
FRIEDMAN HERBERT S	MAJ	0-0344284	0146	2
FRIEDMAN IRVING I	1LT	0-1014213	0346	2
FRIEDMAN MILTON J	MAJ	0-1584231	0446	2
FRIEDMAN PAUL S	CPT	0-0361551	0345	2
FRIEDMAN ROBERT L	CPT	0-0449539	1145	2
FRIEDMAN SAUL	2LT	0-1798253	0644	2
FRIEDMAN WILLIAM F	LTC	0-0166764	0951	3
FRIEDRICH DONALD F	MAJ	0-2263119	1065	1
FRIEDRICH HELEN E	MAJ	L-0203873	0663	1
FRIEDRICHS VICTOR	MAJ	0-0100200	0853	3
FRIEFELD NATHAN	MAJ	0-0508871	0446	2
FRIEL JOHN J	1LT	0-2017390	0958	1
FRIEL RAYMOND P	CW3	W-2205839	1166	1
FRIEND FREDERICK	MAJ	0-1288038	0854	1
FRIEND HILBERT E	1LT	0-1014260	0146	2
FRIEND JAMES W	COL	0-0314382	1162	1
FRIEND LESTER D	LTC	0-0198231	0758	3
FRIENDLY EDWIN S JR	CPT	0-0493717	0146	2
FRIERSON LUTHER	LTC	0-0473387	0954	1
FRIERSON PETE H	CPT	0-0462639	1144	2
FRIES DONALD F	MAJ	0-1926491	0864	1
FRIES HAROLD J	CPT	0-1112705	0246	2
FRIES JOSEPH B	CW2	W-2205843	1060	2
FRIES ROBERT G	CW3	W-2001606	0266	3
FRIES WALTER B JR	CPT	0-1312298	0547	2
FRIES WEYNAND J	COL	0-0371279	0966	2
FRIESE ROBERT E	MAJ	0-1590475	0856	1
FRIESEL DAVID	COL	0-0444437	0853	1
FRIESEN WALTER C	CW2	W-3400396	0467	1
FRIESS HAROLD M	CPT	0-1285919	0346	2
FRIESZ LEONARD O	COL	0-0358172	0764	1
FRIGO LIONEL O	LTC	0-1293576	0561	2
FRILEY CHARLES E JR	MAJ	0-0337674	0845	2
FRILOT MATTHEW W	1LT	0-1302424	0145	2
FRINAK JOHN M	LTC	0-0405920	1060	1
FRINCHI LOUIS D	MAJ	0-1998347	1062	1
FRINDELL HAROLD M	COL	0-0363319	1163	1
FRINKS CHARLES P	MAJ	0-1920305	1166	1
FRIPP EDGAR W	MAJ	0-1535581	0958	1
FRISBEE CHARLES V	LTC	0-0298731	0760	1
FRISBIE WILLIAM E	1LT	0-1914354	0538	2
FRISBY JACK D	MAJ	0-0289383	0444	2
FRISBY RALPH F	1LT	0-1325210	0448	2
FRISCH ARNOLD R	1LT	0-1314615	0447	2
FRISCH GEORGE A	LTC	0-0152615	0648	3
FRISCH ISAAC J	COL	0-0242778	0250	3
FRISCH JOSEPH	CPT	0-0509144	1145	2
FRISCHKNECHT REED L	2LT	0-1826078	0644	2
FRISHKEY FRANK	MAJ	0-0961085	0167	1
FRISHKEY NICK	CPT	0-0954840	0157	2
FRISOLI GAETON M	CW3	W-2209489	1068	1
FRISTOE FRANK H	LTC	0-0911615	1265	3
FRISTOE KENNETH W	LTC	0-0516331	0563	1
FRITH CLIFFORD F	MAJ	0-0268713	0446	2
FRITH GILBERT R	COL	0-0343743	0763	3

NAME	GRADE	SVC NO	DATE RET MO YR	RET CODE
FRITH ROBERT L	1LT	0-1004583	0146	2
FRITON WILLIS L	MAJ	0-1922756	0368	1
FRITSCH CARL F	COL	0-0159891	0256	3
FRITSCH HENRY F JR	2LT	0-0554910	0246	2
FRITSCH JAKE R	CPT	0-0515376	0447	2
FRITSCH WILLIAM N	CPT	0-0235518	1059	3
FRITSCHE FREDERICK	CPT	0-0263519	0461	3
FRITSCHE JOHN P	CPT	0-0596042	0350	2
FRITSCHEL HERBERT F	COL	0-0175702	0655	3
FRITTS HARRY I	COL	0-0135031	0456	3
FRITTS MELVIN V	LTC	0-1286630	0757	1
FRITZ DANA R	2LT	0-1015107	0345	2
FRITZ FRANK J	MAJ	0-2055117	0457	1
FRITZ GEORGE	2LT	0-0451622	0154	2
FRITZ JOHN F	LTC	0-0192027	1152	3
FRITZ LAWRENCE F	CW4	W-2141775	0968	1
FRITZ LAWRENCE J	2LT	0-1573853	0144	2
FRITZ SAMUEL F	LTC	0-0410377	0760	1
FRITZ WILLIAM D	COL	0-0220646	0363	3
FRITZ WILLIAM G	2LT	0-1301231	0445	2
FRITZ WILLIAM R	2LT	0-1049481	0644	2
FRITZE WALTER W	LTC	0-1322688	0163	1
FRITZEN CLAUS A	CPT	0-1313233	0848	2
FRIZ WILLARD C	LTC	0-0303986	1264	1
FRIZELL LEWIS	LTC	0-0452107	1054	1
FRIZELL LEWIS E	CPT	0-2009225	0261	1
FRIZZELL EDWARD R	CPT	0-0101825	0648	3
FRIZZELL ROY E	1LT	0-2001134	0746	2
FRIZZELL TEDROW B	CPT	0-0371070	0750	1
FRIZZELLE REGINALD E	COL	0-0332135	0460	1
FROBERGER GEORGE A J	CPT	0-0184141	0656	3
FROCK EARL M	CW4	W-2136738	1165	1
FROEDE A O SR	LTC	0-0244496	0157	3
FROEHLICH THEODORE W	CW3	W-2141283	0760	1
FROELICH ARCHIE W	LTC	0-0107034	0254	3
FROEMEL EUGENE E	MAJ	0-1548787	0461	1
FROERER CARL	CPT	0-0506843	0344	2
FROGNER LESTER S	LTC	0-0326281	0763	3
FROHARDT DAVID E	MAJ	0-0522599	1266	1
FROHMAN HOWARD L	1LT	0-0449555	1144	2
FROHMAN IRVING G	COL	0-0186368	1262	3
FROHMAN LOUIS H	COL	0-0159856	0753	3
FROHNHOEFER FRANK	CW3	W-2147999	0264	1
FROL ANTHONY B	LTC	0-0080776	0468	1
FROMAN AMNA L	LTC	0-0248122	0365	3
FROMAN PAUL L	LTC	0-0920868	1057	3
FROME MANUEL M	1LT	0-1302803	0345	2
FROMENT HOWARD H	MAJ	0-1018559	0263	1
FROMER CHARLES L	MAJ	0-2268774	0963	1
FROMHART ROBERT E	LTC	0-2043280	0966	1
FROMM CHESTER E	CPT	0-0973464	0263	1
FROMM JOHN D	CW3	W-2105917	0852	2
FROMM JOHN D	LTC	0-1589845	1060	1
FROMMHAGEN F C	COL	0-0277989	1154	3
FROMUTH HERMAN C	LTC	0-0232357	0654	3
FRONAUER HENRY J	CPT	0-0939006	0464	1
FRONCILLO RENATO	MAJ	0-0347881	0146	2
FRONCZAK FLORIAN F	MAJ	0-0307937	0367	3
FRONK JOHN M	COL	0-0204016	0260	1
FRONK ROBERT A	LTC	0-0280801	0367	3
FRONTERA ENRIQUE	LTC	0-0402466	1165	1
FROOMAN MAURICE	WO1	W-2128177	1045	2
FROSH VOLLIE E	CPT	0-1166715	0546	2
FROST CAROL E	CPT	0-4030907	1066	1
FROST CHARLES G	MAJ	0-0126348	0648	3
FROST DAYTON H	COL	0-0527143	1163	3
FROST EARL G	LTC	0-0388910	1055	1
FROST EARLE R	CPT	0-0144004	0758	3
FROST FRANK A	LTC	0-0111373	0648	3
FROST JACK T	MAJ	0-1317082	0664	1
FROST JAMES F	LTC	0-1644971	1163	1
FROST JAY C	CPT	0-2289183	1164	1
FROST JOE M	1LT	0-1180185	0346	2
FROST JOHN F JR	LTC	0-0918628	0362	3
FROST KENNETH D	MAJ	0-0967026	.0263	1

NAME	GRADE	SVC NO	DATE RET MO YR	RET CODE
FROST KENNETH E	1LT	0-2004145	1055	2
FROST MERVIN J	CW3	W-2149211	1061	1
FROST MILLARD I	COL	0-0254541	1060	3
FROST NOEL C	CPT	0-1998100	0754	2
FROST OREN S	CPT	0-0383297	0745	2
FROST RAYMOND F	LTC	0-0289152	1263	1
FROST RICHARD M	LTC	0-0918341	0168	3
FROST ROBERT J	LTC	0-0422232	0661	2
FROST ROBERT L	CW3	W-2203364	0365	1
FROST ROY L	1LT	0-1306262	0845	2
FROST WINSTON R	LTC	0-1555548	1162	1
FROUNFELKER FRANK A	MAJ	0-0379516	0265	3
FROYD ERWIN A	COL	0-0103318	0648	3
FROYD PAUL C	1LT	0-1302634	0546	2
FRUECHTENICHT G H	CPT	0-0205397	1161	3
FRUEHWALD RAYMOND M	CPT	0-1319942	0647	2
FRUIN CHARLES E	LTC	0-0297444	0565	3
FRUIN EMMETT G	LTC	0-0259426	0767	3
FRUIN MABEL E	2LT	N-0779278	0446	1
FRUIT CLYDE W	LTC	0-0259819	1266	3
FRUMKES GEORGE	COL	0-0488350	0446	2
FRUSCELLA SALVATORE	MAJ	0-0324331	1263	1
FRUTCHEY RUSSELL W	LTC	0-0323676	0361	3
FRUZAN RALPH M	CPT	0-1056619	0161	1
FRY ARTHUR E	COL	0-0473090	0968	3
FRY ARTHUR H	CW4	W-2109829	1154	1
FRY ARTHUR W	LTC	0-0326502	1060	1
FRY CHARLES A JR	LTC	0-1101833	0755	1
FRY CHARLES V	LTC	0-0235121	0864	3
FRY FRANKLYN D	LTC	0-0360928	1159	3
FRY HARVEY D	MAJ	0-0387369	1146	2
FRY JOHN A	LTC	0-0239037	0861	3
FRY JOHN W	COL	0-0321899	1047	2
FRY KENNETH L	LTC	0-0354246	0462	1
FRY LEONARD H	LTC	0-1642074	0868	3
FRY LEROY H	CPT	0-1882176	0264	1
FRY RICHARD E	COL	0-0267513	1267	3
FRY ROBERT W	MAJ	0-1923602	0566	1
FRY THOMAS C	LTC	0-0384200	0360	1
FRY WALTER J	LTC	0-0467111	0668	3
FRY WARREN N	LTC	0-1327616	0566	1
FRY WILLIAM H	LTC	0-1312535	0961	1
FRYAR JOHN H	CW2	W-2147912	1058	1
FRYDAY ALVORD C	2LT	0-1301288	0843	2
FRYDENLUND BERTHA A	1LT	N-0732654	0645	1
FRYE ALEX A	MAJ	0-1293752	0858	1
FRYE AUSTIN P	MAJ	0-0232884	0163	3
FRYE CHARLES L	2LT	0-1295534	0844	2
FRYE DELMAR D	MAJ	0-1290229	0561	1
FRYE HARRY JR	CW3	W-2206599	1166	1
FRYE HERBERT H	LTC	0-0942984	0961	1
FRYE JOHN H	COL	0-0202125	0262	3
FRYE JOSEPH W	LTC	0-0289264	0762	3
FRYE LUCIUS C	CW3	W-2153377	0865	1
FRYE MARCUS M	LTC	0-0230846	0359	1
FRYE ROBERT C	MAJ	0-0996492	0363	1
FRYE SHELDON B	LTC	0-1106745	0266	3
FRYER CHARLES W	CPT	0-2008351	0948	2
FRYER DOROTHY J	MAJ	N-0736589	0862	1
FRYER GORDON L	MAJ	0-1541124	0261	1
FRYER HERBERT F	CW4	W-2152958	1262	1
FRYER OSCAR G	MAJ	0-0188611	0156	3
FRYER SAMUEL R	CPT	0-1701759	0346	2
FRYKHOLM LLOYD D	2LT	0-0348063	0963	3
FRYKHOLM VERNON L	LTC	0-1284125	0663	1
FRYKLAND BASIL N	LTC	0-0251869	0959	3
FRYMIRE ALTON P	2LT	0-1165860	1045	2
FRYOU EUGENE J JR	CW2	W-2148378	1059	1
FRYXELL JOHN	MAJ	0-1649273	0958	1
FUCCI CHARLES P	CW3	W-2143580	1162	1
FUCHS ARTHUR L	MAJ	0-0159276	0354	3
FUCHS EDMUND H	WO1	W-2117546	1049	1
FUCHS FREDERICK	MAJ	0-0341767	0744	2
FUCHS HENRY	CPT	0-0919558	1163	2
FUCHS JAMES R	1LT	0-0556916	0446	2
FUCHS JOHN J	MAJ	0-1926260	1167	1
FUDGE ROBERT C	CW2	W-2209234	0767	1
FUDOLO JOHN H	LTC	0-1947707	1067	1
FUECKER FRED M	COL	0-0154055	0355	3
FUENTES JOSE	LTC	0-0265443	1050	1
FUERTES RAFAEL R	1LT	0-0370820	0144	2
FUGATE DOUGLAS B	LTC	0-0246340	0966	3
FUGATE GLENN	CW4	W-2101209	0961	1
FUGATE ROBERT S	LTC	0-0410735	1160	1
FUGE WILFRED W	COL	0-0353741	1265	3
FUGICH JOHN	CW2	W-2144005	1056	1
FUGIT PRICE W	CPT	0-1290930	0247	2
FUGITT HOWARD D	LTC	0-1556878	1262	1
FUGLESTAD CARL L	LTC	0-1688560	1268	1
FUHR EARL W	LTC	0-0166154	1152	3
FUHR MASON W	CPT	0-0918598	0446	2
FUHRMANN JOHN M	1LT	0-1296195	0845	2
FUKUCHI STANLEY T	CPT	0-0943000	0158	2
FUKUMOTO MASASHI	CW4	W-2133701	0767	1
FULBRIGHT WORTH C	COL	0-0279211	0557	1
FULCHER MALCOLM W	MAJ	0-1684926	0762	1
FULENWIDER JOHN O JR	CPT	0-0359584	0845	2
FULFORD WILLIAM H JR	COL	0-0366757	1067	2
FULGHAM FRANK E	LTC	0-0278863	1265	3
FULGHAM FRANK M	CPT	0-1307004	0746	2
FULK EDWIN E	CPT	0-0975286	0258	1
FULK HUBERT A	LTC	0-0302453	1060	1
FULK WILLIAM W	MAJ	0-0423372	0859	2
FULKERSON JACK M	2LT	0-0531101	0345	2
FULKERSON THOMAS B	LTC	0-0251704	0566	3
FULKERSON WELDON M	CW2	W-2117142	0657	1
FULKS HENRY	CPT	0-0120820	1050	3
FULLAM THOMAS J JR	LTC	0-1533059	0468	2
FULLBRIGHT BESSIE V	LTC	N-0741927	0662	1
FULLBRIGHT MILDRED	2LT	N-0726652	1045	1
FULLBRIGHT PRESTON E	CW3	W-2151003	1157	1
FULLEN LILBURN S	LTC	0-0480157	0357	1
FULLENWIDER LEO	CW2	W-2147449	1060	1
FULLENWIDER RAY H	CPT	0-0243728	0249	3
FULLER ALBERT W	CPT	0-0279182	0544	2
FULLER ALFRED E JR	MAJ	0-0949689	1162	1
FULLER ALONZOE H	WO1	W-2108670	1045	2
FULLER ANDREW J	LTC	0-0314855	0260	3
FULLER ARTHUR C	LTC	0-0241207	0561	1
FULLER ARTHUR H	COL	0-0242601	1155	3
FULLER BASIL B	MAJ	0-1920121	0167	1
FULLER BENJAMIN F	CPT	0-0498427	0547	1
FULLER BERNARD B	LTC	0-0273028	0957	3
FULLER CLARENCE H	MAJ	0-1332051	0365	1
FULLER CLIFFORD R	LTC	0-2007610	1161	2
FULLER DELBERT O	COL	0-0171586	0455	3
FULLER DONALD W	MAJ	0-0337120	0551	2
FULLER DORSEY R	LTC	0-1056720	0767	1
FULLER EDWARD F	CPT	0-0486720	1043	2
FULLER ELMER E JR	CPT	0-1112706	1046	2
FULLER ELMER G	LTC	0-0144347	0845	2
FULLER ERNEST T	CW2	W-2112104	0749	1
FULLER FRANK W	LTC	0-0165636	0259	3
FULLER FRED	2LT	0-0108492	0341	1
FULLER GEORGE G	MAJ	0-0170755	1048	3
FULLER GEORGE S	LTC	0-0238428	0566	3
FULLER GRAYDON E	COL	0-1101834	1062	1
FULLER HAROLD B	CW2	W-2150126	0959	2
FULLER HAROLD F	MAJ	0-1335140	1263	1
FULLER HARRY C	CPT	0-0491979	0757	1
FULLER HENRY M	MAJ	0-1297183	1058	1
FULLER HERBERT W	LTC	0-1634779	0266	1
FULLER HOWARD E	B G	0-0130484	0946	2
FULLER IRWIN L	LTC	0-0291967	1162	1
FULLER J BURNS	CPT	0-0148885	1052	3
FULLER JACK P	1LT	0-0409654	1045	2
FULLER JAMES M	LTC	0-1104164	0261	1
FULLER JAMES N	LTC	0-0215349	1059	3
FULLER JOHN E	LTC	0-0405395	1160	1
FULLER JOHN G	LTC	0-1296357	0861	1
FULLER JOHN JR	LTC	0-0240805	1262	3
FULLER JOHN L	CW3	W-2145723	0663	1
FULLER JOSEPH W JR	LTC	0-0296104	0766	3
FULLER KATHERINE	CPT	L-0609658	0351	2
FULLER LEONARD H	COL	0-0333505	0860	1
FULLER LIVONIA W	LTC	0-0282962	0962	3
FULLER MCKINLEY L	CW2	W-2117916	1147	1
FULLER MELVIN L SR	CPT	0-0966482	0161	1
FULLER MELVYN W	LTC	0-1634780	0463	1
FULLER MORRIS G	MAJ	0-0187826	1056	3
FULLER MYRON C JR	MAJ	0-1599162	0266	1
FULLER ORVILLE M	LTC	0-1112707	0962	1
FULLER PAUL M	COL	0-1686860	1160	3
FULLER RAYMOND N	2LT	0-1030561	1146	2
FULLER RICHARD O	LTC	0-0525382	0864	1
FULLER ROBERT A	LTC	0-0313876	1162	1
FULLER ROBERT A	LTC	0-1104165	0662	1
FULLER ROBERT C	LTC	0-0314045	0261	1
FULLER ROBERT W	CPT	0-2033971	0461	1
FULLER SPURGEON O	1LT	0-1308808	0545	2
FULLER THOMAS	B G	0-0248411	1066	3
FULLER VERNON E	MAJ	0-0262555	0664	3
FULLER WALTER C	LTC	0-0256541	0163	3
FULLER WAYNE E	CPT	0-1313995	0748	2
FULLER WAYNE P	MAJ	0-0888220	1065	2
FULLER WESLEY E	LTC	0-1106147	1265	1
FULLER WILLIAM J	CW3	W-2205391	0666	1
FULLER WILLIAM M	LTC	0-1062847	0968	1
FULLER WILLIAM P	CPT	0-0488812	0154	1
FULLER WILLIS	LTC	0-0258574	0266	3
FULLERTON ALBERT L	MAJ	0-0364164	0147	2
FULLERTON DOYLE	MAJ	0-1174859	0961	1
FULLERTON HUGH T	COL	0-0285727	0560	3
FULLERTON PAUL A	MAJ	0-0361659	0455	1
FULLERTON 3RD ROBERT	COL	0-0356666	0946	2
FULLILOVE EMMA S	1LT	N-0793971	0951	2
FULLMER CYRIL D	CPT	0-0469531	1147	2
FULMER JAMES L	LTC	0-0337579	0960	3
FULMER WILLIAM A	LTC	0-0172088	0559	3
FULP ORVILLE D SR	LTC	0-1002922	0962	1
FULTON ALFRED	MAJ	0-0505342	1154	1
FULTON DONALD M	MAJ	0-1169968	0361	1
FULTON EDWIN B	CW3	W-2149292	0562	1
FULTON ETHAN A	CPT	0-2285438	1155	3
FULTON HAROLD J	CPT	0-0211982	1058	3
FULTON HARRIET V	1LT	N-0773275	0746	1
FULTON HENRY M	1LT	0-0347681	0442	2
FULTON JOHN D	CPT	0-1920277	0564	1
FULTON OLIVER B	MAJ	0-0266795	1160	1
FULTON ROBERT L	CW3	W-2122481	0659	1
FULTON ROBERT M	LTC	0-0905063	0762	1
FULTON ROBERT W	WO1	W-2107842	0845	2
FULTON THOMPSON R	CPT	0-0507881	0254	1
FULTON WILLIAM R	LTC	0-0224886	0555	3
FULTZ ARTHUR D	MAJ	0-0949988	0662	1
FULTZ T LYSTON	LTC	0-0915086	1162	3
FUMAROLA NANCY J	1LT	N-0767736	0746	1
FUMICH VALENTINE	LTC	0-1633871	0965	1
FUNCHES WILLIAM W JR	LTC	0-2026317	0868	1
FUNCHESS JESSE B	MAJ	0-0250976	1044	2
FUNDA FERDINAND	LTC	0-0274196	1051	1
FUNDERBURG GEORGE W	1LT	0-1293235	0747	2
FUNDERBURG L W	MAJ	0-0494508	0651	2
FUNDERBURK ROBERT W	MAJ	0-2036175	1061	1
FUNDERBURK WILBUR H	LTC	0-0232628	1063	3
FUNK BRIANT C	CW3	W-2206408	0967	1
FUNK CHARLES W	CW2	W-2143195	0955	1
FUNK DONALD A	LTC	0-1318931	0766	1
FUNK DONALD S	CPT	0-0215218	0162	3
FUNK DOROTHY M	2LT	N-0780057	1145	1
FUNK GARLAND E	1LT	0-0507746	1051	2
FUNK GENE D	CW3	W-2143187	0664	1
FUNK HAROLD I	LTC	0-1796453	0361	1
FUNK HARRY W	CW2	W-2113269	1146	1
FUNK IAN C	CPT	0-0469458	0646	2
FUNK IVERS L	MAJ	0-0383463	0460	1
FUNK JACK A	MAJ	0-0984520	0863	2
FUNK JAMES C	1LT	0-0538271	0946	2
FUNK JOHN	CPT	0-0349472	0544	2
FUNK JOHN S	CW2	W-2102917	0853	1
FUNK JOSEPH W	CPT	0-0413610	0646	2
FUNK MELVIN C	CW4	W-2141561	0861	1
FUNK NEIL E	COL	0-0205770	0648	3
FUNK WHARTON T	COL	0-0309253	1063	3
FUNKE EIMO G	LTC	0-0208171	1056	3
FUNKHOUSER CECIL R	CW2	W-2142587	1155	2
FUNSTON JOHN H	LTC	0-1584235	0862	1
FUQUA EALEY T	CW4	W-2101721	1154	1
FUQUA HARRY T	CW3	W-2150207	0962	1
FUQUA JACK R	MAJ	0-1543420	0257	1
FUQUA JOHN B	CW4	W-2101309	0758	1
FUQUA JOHN T JR	CW3	W-2206640	1165	1
FUQUA PAUL H	CPT	0-0150713	0648	3
FUQUARY HENRY W	CW3	W-2142638	1058	1
FURAY JOHN B	COL	0-0264230	0768	3
FURBEE RAYMOND H	LTC	0-1325154	0563	1
FURBER CHARLES L	COL	0-0184779	0648	3
FURBER EDITH H	CPT	L-0400511	1045	2
FURBERSHAW WALTER L	COL	0-0182893	0648	3
FURBISH CHESTER A	COL	0-0266646	0157	2
FURBUSH ERVING A	MAJ	0-0260227	0967	3
FURCHES CLAYTON S	LTC	0-0213264	0164	3
FURCHES DOUTHIT L	LTC	0-1038989	0664	1
FURGISON RICHARD P	CW2	W-2214349	1068	1
FURGIUELE PETER M	LTC	0-0364227	0762	1
FURHMEISTER ERNEST L	LTC	0-1544568	1062	1
FURIN ANNA L	CPT	N-0769325	1054	2
FURLO FRANK A	CPT	0-1316401	1265	1
FURLONG C E JR	CPT	0-0971978	1060	1
FURLONG DANIEL J	LTC	0-0436319	1267	2
FURLONG GERARD D	MAJ	0-1643565	0158	1
FURLONG HAROLD A	COL	0-0158405	0955	3
FURLOUGH ARTHUR W JR	MAJ	0-0990533	0264	1
FURMAN EDITH L	1LT	N-0765416	1047	1
FURMAN NORMAN	1LT	0-1313085	0946	2
FURMAN SOLI	WO1	W-2129498	1145	2
FURMAN WALTER A	MAJ	0-1639054	0263	1
FURNER EDWARD M JR	CPT	0-1031081	1161	2
FURNISH EDWARD S	COL	0-0166273	1055	3
FURNISH VILLIE B	1LT	0-0199825	1035	1
FURNISS CLINTON C	MAJ	0-0388952	0461	1
FURR CARL J	COL	0-0278934	1063	3
FURR WILLIAM H	MAJ	0-1994603	0265	1
FURRY EMMERT E	LTC	0-0450868	0656	1
FURSE STEPHEN S	COL	0-0256086	0465	3
FURST ALAN S	LTC	0-1581138	1061	1
FURST ANTHONY R	1LT	0-0408723	1046	2
FURST HAROLD A	LTC	0-0270404	0246	2
FURST JACQUES	MAJ	0-1699503	0665	2
FURSTENAU THEODORE C	CPT	0-1543348	0356	1
FURTADO JOSEPH F	CPT	0-1303603	0655	1
FURUKAWA JAMWS M	MAJ	0-0958191	0966	1
FUS BERNICE G	1LT	N-0730519	0646	1
FUSARO CLARENCE A	1LT	0-1042813	1045	2
FUSCO JEREMIAH N	LTC	0-1330174	0167	1
FUSELIER ALLEN J	1LT	0-1945801	0745	2
FUSELIER BURLEY P	MAJ	0-2024382	0464	1
FUSHIMI CARL N	MAJ	0-2096460	0268	1
FUSNER BRUCE	LTC	0-1183291	0768	2
FUSS CARL R JR	MAJ	0-0987405	0566	1
FUSS LEO J	CW2	W-2207138	0262	1
FUSSELL GEORGE W	MAJ	0-0970863	0264	1
FUSSELL HAROLD R	2LT	0-1063020	1044	2
FUSSELL JAMES B-	CPT	0-0489267	0457	1
FUSSELL JAMES R	LTC	0-1173250	0861	1
FUSSELMAN EARL O	CPT	0-1574047	1044	2
FUTCH HUBERT K	MAJ	0-2017682	0864	1
FUTTERMAN JACOB	CPT	0-0286169	1067	3
FYFFE BILLY L	MAJ	0-0994506	0364	1
FYFFE JOHN H	MAJ	0-1541401	0247	2

NAME	GRADE	SVC NO	DATE RET MO YR	RET CODE
FYKE FRANK L	LTC	0-1698082	1060	1
FYOCK FLOYD C	CW4	W-2003628	0565	3
FYRNYS EDWARD L	MAJ	0-0319704	0965	1
GAA DONALD C	LTC	0-0289951	1263	3
GAALAAS ALBAN F	COL	0-0282836	0147	2
GAALKEN JOSEPH M	MAJ	0-1592529	0668	3
GABA HOWARD R	CPT	0-0500080	0146	2
GABARDI ALBERT I	1LT	0-1944683	0944	2
GABARRON GINES A	LTC	0-0391131	0860	1
GABBARD EDWARD H	MAJ	0-0409875	0165	1
GABBARD JAKE R	MAJ	0-1290406	0847	2
GABBERT JOHN R	LTC	0-0339293	0460	1
GABEL BENJAMIN G	CW3	W-2205615	1265	1
GABEL FRANCIS S	COL	0-0284930	0658	1
GABEL GUS	LTC	0-1030660	0161	1
GABEL KURT	MAJ	0-1905383	0266	1
GABELMAN L G SR	MAJ	0-0161809	0648	3
GABERLEIN RAYMOND W	CW3	W-2148614	1164	1
GABERT LAWRENCE W	COL	0-0336839	0167	3
GABLE ELMER W	MAJ	0-0333311	1064	3
GABLE FRANK F	CPT	0-0397138	1060	1
GABLE HULETTE R	MAJ	0-0279174	0662	3
GABLE JACK M	1LT	0-1311877	0645	2
GABLE JOSEPH W	COL	0-0171037	0456	3
GABLE LINWOOD M	COL	0-0164887	1051	2
GABLE NUNIE W	COL	0-0234277	1159	3
GABLER LOUIS	MAJ	0-0887420	1054	1
GABORSKY GODFREY V	LTC	0-0427370	0960	1
GABRIEL ALFREDO B	MAJ	0-1896539	0263	1
GABRIEL CARMEN M	1LT	0-1119194	0747	2
GABRIEL CHARLES H	MAJ	0-0450196	0348	2
GABRIEL FRANCIS X	MAJ	0-0960946	0868	1
GABRIEL FRANK G	1LT	0-0440485	0345	2
GABRIEL JAMES C	COL	0-0220083	0455	1
GABRIEL JOHN DONAL	2LT	0-2018870	0351	2
GABRIEL NICHOLAS J	CPT	0-0413958	0346	2
GABRIEL WALTER A	CPT	0-0233766	0965	3
GABRINGER NORBERT J	2LT	0-1594848	0245	2
GABRYSCH CLAUDE J	1LT	0-1171015	0648	2
GACHAR AUGUST	CPT	0-0494134	0954	1
GACHES ROBERT A L	MAJ	0-2018500	0763	1
GACHET FRED	MAJ	0-0290914	0546	2
GACHETTE HEZEKIAH	CW2	W-2144305	1162	1
GACHNIK ANTON J	1LT	0-1798467	0659	1
GACKOWSKI VERN A	CPT	0-1524720	0952	1
GADBERRY LUTHER C	MAJ	0-0144751	0555	3
GADD RICHARD H	CPT	0-1641962	0457	1
GADD ROBERT F JR	LTC	0-0336227	1066	3
GADD WILLIAM J	MAJ	0-2262312	0364	1
GADDE EDWARD JR	LTC	0-0552010	0568	1
GADDIS ARDEN M	1LT	0-1822872	0268	2
GADDIS GLEN D	1LT	0-0290809	0347	2
GADDY ERNEST C	CW3	W-2116127	0753	2
GADE MELVILLE B	LTC	0-0905526	1265	3
GADES FRED H JR	2LT	0-0530004	0845	2
GADEHOLTZ FRITZ A H	COL	0-0266797	0963	3
GADU ANTONIO L	COL	0-0181252	1051	1
GAEBLER EUGENE F	LTC	0-0174498	1152	3
GAEDKE EDWARD C	CW3	W-2210715	0968	1
GAER WILLIAM C	CW4	W-2102918	0659	1
GAETZKE EUGENE V	CPT	0-1686784	1166	2
GAFEANEY ROBERT T	2LT	0-1300542	0545	2
GAFFEY EARL	MAJ	0-1296509	1054	1
GAFFIN CARLOS A	LTC	0-0344737	0168	3
GAFFNEY F G JR	CW2	W-2152341	0960	1
GAFFNEY JAMES J JR	LTC	0-0357736	1045	2
GAFFNEY JOSEPH M	LTC	0-1640475	0763	1
GAFFNEY LAWRENCE	1LT	0-1324015	1145	2
GAFFNEY RAYMOND A	MAJ	0-2263000	0164	1
GAFFNEY WALTER K	1LT	0-0507067	0249	1
GAFFNEY WILLIAM R	LTC	0-1002923	0662	1
GAFFORD CHARLES W	2LT	0-1031242	0451	2
GAFFORD VIRGIL S	COL	0-0211040	0552	3
GAGE EARL J	CPT	0-0488602	0246	2
GAGE EDGAR W	MAJ	0-0100507	1151	3

NAME	GRADE	SVC NO	DATE RET MO YR	RET CODE
GAGE JOHN B	CPT	0-0452172	0746	2
GAGE JOSEPH M	LTC	0-1047976	1061	1
GAGE MORRIS V	MAJ	0-1996462	0958	1
GAGE ROBERT F	LTC	0-1306083	0363	1
GAGE WILLIAM JR	CW3	W-2146367	0559	1
GAGE WILLIAM L	COL	0-0261894	0466	3
GAGHAGEN HOWARD R	LTC	0-0150039	1057	1
GAGIN JOHN D	LTC	0-0953636	0468	1
GAGLIANO ANTHONY J	LTC	0-0381262	1060	1
GAGLIANO NICK G	LTC	0-1552882	0566	1
GAGNE ARMAND E J	MAJ	0-1701164	1167	1
GAGNE EMILE R	CW2	W-2105030	0250	1
GAGNEA JOHN	CW3	W-2211620	0968	1
GAGNER FREDERICK	MAJ	0-1553634	0367	1
GAGNON ARISTIDE	CW2	W-2120760	0352	1
GAGNON CLAYTON E	LTC	0-0401648	0661	1
GAGNON DAVID C	CPT	0-1016111	0647	2
GAGNON HOWARD A	MAJ	0-1293236	0461	1
GAGNON LORENZO A	LTC	0-0319415	1158	1
GAGNON MARIE J	2LT	N-0754446	0247	1
GAGNON NELSON C	MAJ	0-1081701	0762	1
GAGNON OMER A	MAJ	0-0973467	0662	1
GAGNON RAOUL A	CW2	W-2000105	0261	2
GAGNON VICTOR W	CPT	0-2200341	0757	2
GAHAGAN WALTER H JR	MAJ	0-0917360	0945	2
GAHAN WILLIAM J	LTC	0-0445873	0867	1
GAHNZ ELMER F	LTC	0-0276349	0363	3
GAHRING WILLIAM R	MAJ	0-0142998	0645	2
GAIBLE BENJAMIN J	2LT	0-1291976	0544	2
GAIDE JOHN F	MAJ	0-1540881	0564	1
GAIDOSICK HAROLD G	LTC	0-0907625	1046	2
GAILLARD DAVID S	COL	0-0174224	0150	3
GAILLARD ELLEN L	MAJ	N-0763922	0365	1
GAILUS RAUL P	1LT	0-1541905	0145	2
GAILY WALTER JR	CW3	W-2148963	0262	1
GAIN MICHAEL L	MAJ	0-0975985	1162	1
GAINES BERNARD R	LTC	0-0348078	0450	2
GAINES CATHERINE	2LT	L-1000406	1045	2
GAINES CHARLES J SR	MAJ	0-0983554	0862	1
GAINES CLARENCE L	1LT	0-1307961	0146	2
GAINES DONALD L	COL	0-0357552	0466	3
GAINES FRANK	LTC	0-0304841	0161	1
GAINES FRANK P	COL	0-0260345	0168	3
GAINES HARRY W	CPT	0-0178161	0854	3
GAINES HERMAN L	LTC	0-0169039	0261	3
GAINES KENNETH L	2LT	0-2212069	0252	2
GAINES LARRY	LTC	0-0266263	0155	2
GAINES RABUN M	MAJ	0-0450542	0457	1
GAINES ROBERT E	CPT	0-1307962	0646	2
GAINES SARAH F	MAJ	N-0726404	0566	1
GAINES THOMAS R	LTC	0-0499304	0346	2
GAINES VIRGIL J	CPT	0-1176344	1145	2
GAINES WILLARD M	COL	0-0233697	1159	1
GAINES WILLIAM J	MAJ	0-0967862	0466	1
GAINES WILLIAM M	CW2	W-2107936	1151	1
GAINEY DAVID F	MAJ	0-1650875	1162	1
GAINEY FRANCIS J	CPT	0-0451489	0365	1
GAINEY NOEL R	CW2	W-2141285	0855	1
GAINEY REDMON R	1LT	0-1016119	0146	2
GAINEY TILLMAN W	CW3	W-2210200	0168	1
GAINOR EDWARD P	MAJ	0-2288258	0667	1
GAIRING JOHN A	LTC	0-0255074	0867	3
GAIPLOFF LESTER	MAJ	0-0958150	0366	1
GAIS ELMER S	COL	0-0442919	0746	2
GAITHER EDGAR	LTC	0-0419813	0563	1
GAITHER JAMES F JR	1LT	0-0497015	1045	2
GAITHER JAMES L	LTC	0-0066151	0268	1
GAITHER RALPH W	LTC	0-1286270	0764	1
GAITHER ROSCOE B	LTC	0-0292757	0954	3
GAITHER THOMAS R	LTC	0-0215975	0762	3
GAKEY JACK L	CW4	W-2150555	0562	1
GALAMBOS LOUIS	MAJ	0-1650101	1263	1
GALANG RICARDO C	LTC	0-0515082	0267	3
GALANIS HARRY W	LTC	0-1647899	0165	1
GALANTE DOMINICK A	LTC	0-1081213	0667	1

NAME	GRADE	SVC NO	DATE RET MO YR	RET CODE
GALANTE PETER J	COL	0-0326093	1266	3
GALAWAY JOHN A JR	LTC	0-1597264	0862	1
GALBRAITH ALEXANDRIA	1LT	0-0453440	0644	2
GALBRAITH HOWARD J	MAJ	0-0272861	0667	3
GALBRAITH JOHN F	LTC	0-0256899	1267	3
GALBRAITH JOHN H	2LT	0-1044924	1043	2
GALBRAITH JOHN R	MAJ	0-0236625	0458	3
GALBRAITH JOSEPH M	LTC	0-0397191	0660	1
GALBRAITH LAWRENCE C	COL	0-0148671	0948	3
GALBRAITH LEO L	MAJ	0-0229769	0164	3
GALBREATH CHARLES S	MAJ	0-0372084	0745	2
GALBREATH JOHN C	LTC	0-0227398	0962	3
GALBREATH LOYAL T	LTC	0-0248641	0566	3
GALBREATH PAUL JR	MAJ	0-1290175	0163	2
GALBRUNER HOMER C	COL	0-0144637	0857	3
GALE BERNARD G	CPT	0-1594179	0561	1
GALE CHARLES H	CW3	W-2148532	0659	1
GALE DAVID M	LTC	0-1533784	0361	1
GALE JON S	LTC	0-1049164	1061	1
GALE HOWARD C	LTC	0-1648063	1262	1
GALE JAMES M	COL	0-0456469	0767	1
GALE MILES W	CPT	0-1295777	1047	2
GALE STANLEY H	2LT	0-1060099	0245	2
GALE THOMAS L	MAJ	0-1002924	0858	1
GALE WALTER C	CPT	0-0309889	0245	2
GALE WALTER R	1LT	0-1327728	0450	2
GALE WILLIAM P	LTC	0-0416089	0650	2
GALEAZZI LEO J	2LT	0-1590479	0151	2
GALER ROBERT F	LTC	0-0392177	0165	1
GALES ARTHUR M	CW2	W-2147905	0761	1
GALES RICHARD C	COL	0-1011147	0367	1
GALFOND ALLEN W	LTC	0-2020280	1067	1
GALIANO MICHAEL C	B G	0-0269138	0666	3
GALIFFA WARREN V	MAJ	0-1120149	0164	1
GALIGHER THOMAS W	COL	0-0257523	0566	3
GALIN ARTHUR H	MAJ	0-2037374	0168	1
GALINDRE DANIEL B	2LT	0-5429636	0668	2
GALIPEAU DURIUS P	MAJ	0-0964360	0865	1
GALITELD PETER D	CW3	W-2144736	1166	1
GALL ANDREW L	LTC	0-1322632	0961	1
GALL EDWIN A	2LT	0-1313589	0245	2
GALL EWALD A	LTC	0-0163832	0953	3
GALL JOHN	LTC	0-1176633	0562	1
GALLACHER A J	CW2	W-2153191	0161	1
GALLAGHER ALICE H	MAJ	N-0700779	1146	1
GALLAGHER ANTHONY B	MAJ	0-1169116	0261	1
GALLAGHER ARTHUR R	COL	0-0319759	0767	3
GALLAGHER C E	CPT	0-0443390	0951	2
GALLAGHER C J H	1LT	0-0921330	0844	2
GALLAGHER DANIEL P	COL	0-1102136	0765	1
GALLAGHER DONALD J	MAJ	0-0963623	0466	1
GALLAGHER EDWARD	LTC	0-1796068	0766	3
GALLAGHER EDWARD F	LTC	0-0109712	0648	2
GALLAGHER EDWARD W	CW2	W-2146899	0463	1
GALLAGHER FRANCIS J	MAJ	0-0138093	0648	3
GALLAGHER FRANCIS J	1LT	0-2011676	0248	2
GALLAGHER FRANK	CPT	0-0488953	1044	2
GALLAGHER FRED R	CPT	0-1305566	0947	2
GALLAGHER HARRY L	LTC	0-0450736	0457	1
GALLAGHER HIRAM	MAJ	0-0312932	0546	2
GALLAGHER HOWARD J J	2LT	0-2037281	0546	2
GALLAGHER HUGH F	1LT	0-2049247	0846	2
GALLAGHER HUGH T	1LT	0-1580977	0744	2
GALLAGHER IRVING F	CPT	0-1588349	1046	2
GALLAGHER JAMES B	1LT	0-1011435	1045	2
GALLAGHER JAMES F	1LT	0-1697981	0763	1
GALLAGHER JAMES J	LTC	0-1061401	0166	1
GALLAGHER JAMES R	LTC	0-0522744	1055	1
GALLAGHER JAMES S	COL	0-0174034	0653	3
GALLAGHER JAMES T	LTC	0-1049483	0765	1
GALLAGHER JAMES T	CW2	W-2151787	0661	1
GALLAGHER JAMES W	CPT	0-2033625	0357	1
GALLAGHER JOHN J	2LT	0-0887354	0245	2
GALLAGHER JOHN J	CPT	0-1913686	1020	1
GALLAGHER JOSEPH G	LTC	0-1185790	0964	1

NAME	GRADE	SVC NO	DATE RET MO YR	RET CODE
GALLAGHER KENNETH N	LTC	0-2049800	0762	1
GALLAGHER LAVERGNE A	CW4	W-2141562	1058	1
GALLAGHER LAWRENCE J	CPT	0-2020413	0861	2
GALLAGHER M T	CPT	N-0760303	0846	1
GALLAGHER MARTIN L	MAJ	0-0446994	1045	2
GALLAGHER MICHAEL J	LTC	0-0454058	1165	1
GALLAGHER PAUL	COL	0-0218280	0248	2
GALLAGHER PAUL L	MAJ	0-1303134	0463	1
GALLAGHER PHILIP N	LTC	0-0297775	0957	1
GALLAGHER ROBERT	2LT	0-1298381	0957	1
GALLAGHER ROBERT F	LTC	0-1328686	0167	1
GALLAGHER T J JR	1LT	0-1057094	0247	2
GALLAGHER THOMAS F	MAJ	0-4009811	0866	1
GALLAGHER THOMAS H	LTC	0-1291454	0566	1
GALLAGHER THOMAS J	1LT	0-1102565	0344	2
GALLAGHER WILLIAM	MAJ	0-0203210	1045	2
GALLAGHER WILLIAM F	LTC	0-0244098	0461	3
GALLAGHER WILLIAM F	1LT	0-2035420	1145	2
GALLAGHER WILLIAM G	CW2	W-2146507	0557	1
GALLAGHER WILLIAM J	LTC	0-1173956	0765	2
GALLAHER ELMER L	CW2	W-2150088	0363	1
GALLAMORE ROBERT E	1LT	0-2064200	0259	2
GALLAND MICHAEL R	1LT	0-0342991	1041	2
GALLANT EDWARD J	CPT	0-2033591	0857	1
GALLANT FRANCIS X	LTC	0-0409334	0860	1
GALLANT GEORGE W	MAJ	0-1109308	0265	1
GALLANT JOHN H	LTC	0-1635907	1058	1
GALLANT JOSEPH A	CW3	W-2144547	0162	1
GALLANT JOSEPH H	CPT	0-1299225	1263	1
GALLANT STEVEN H	LTC	0-1115590	0363	1
GALLARDO FRED F	2LT	0-1896763	0955	1
GALLARDO HORTENSE M	1LT	N-0735341	0247	1
GALLARDO ROBERT	LTC	0-2262267	0768	1
GALLAUDET JOHN B	CPT	0-0910949	0845	2
GALLAWAY MICHAEL J	LTC	0-1594850	0768	1
GALLAWAY ROBERT L	COL	0-1580978	0868	2
GALLEGOS CAESAR A	CW3	W-2109270	0745	2
GALLEGOS CARLOS V	LTC	0-0257361	0663	3
GALLENA JOSEPH A	LTC	0-0441998	0965	1
GALLERD RAMON	2LT	0-1896699	1157	1
GALLERT EARL W	MAJ	0-1032707	0764	1
GALLET LARRY	CPT	0-1042028	0146	2
GALLETTE HENRY A	MAJ	0-0279451	0855	3
GALLIGAN JOHN H	LTC	0-1642887	1167	1
GALLIHER DAVID	LTC	0-1053137	0768	1
GALLIK JOSEPH J	LTC	0-0288569	0857	1
GALLINA JOSEPH D	LTC	0-1175441	0960	2
GALLINOTO MICHAEL R	LTC	0-1043635	0164	1
GALLION RALPH C	CW4	W-2148114	0564	1
GALLIONE FREDERIC W	LTC	0-0288485	0464	3
GALLIVAN JOHN D III	LTC	0-0865304	0264	1
GALLMAN ALVIN	MAJ	0-2030827	1059	1
GALLMAN HARRY E	LTC	0-1296314	0761	1
GALLMAN JOSEPH E	MAJ	0-0214937	0961	3
GALLO JOHN	WO1	W-2120033	0958	1
GALLO SALVATORE JR	MAJ	0-0571726	1060	1
GALLO WILLIAM H	CPT	0-1114492	1163	1
GALLOF JACK	MAJ	0-4021800	1165	1
GALLOGLY LAWRENCE V	MAJ	0-1319272	0964	1
GALLOTTE WILLARD A	LTC	0-0301592	0462	3
GALLOWAY ARTHUR L	LTC	0-1549273	0861	1
GALLOWAY DON I	CW2	W-2101722	0347	1
GALLOWAY ENGLAND L	MAJ	0-2262696	0961	1
GALLOWAY ERNEST W	LTC	0-0264844	0663	3
GALLOWAY FRANK R	LTC	0-0404360	0646	2
GALLOWAY HARVEY J JR	MAJ	0-0975085	1155	2
GALLOWAY JAMES L	LTC	0-1550378	0657	1
GALLOWAY JOHN H	COL	0-0905301	1062	3
GALLOWAY JOSEPH S	1LT	0-1283407	0744	2
GALLOWAY PAUL W	CW2	RW-2152638	0961	1
GALLOWAY RAY L	1LT	0-2016356	0349	2
GALLOWAY ROBERT E	MAJ	0-0900703	0359	1
GALLOWAY VERNON H	CW3	W-2144379	0557	1
GALLOWAY WALTER G	MAJ	0-0311007	1044	2
GALLOWAY WARREN P SR	LTC	0-1341961	0967	1

NAME	GRADE	SVC NO	DATE RET MO YR	RET CODE
GALLOWAY WILLIAM H	CPT	0-1643570	0946	2
GALLOWAY WILLIAM S	1LT	0-1116662	0746	2
GALLUCCIO ANTHONY C	MAJ	0-0242358	1045	2
GALLUP EARLE H	MAJ	0-1315421	0965	1
GALO GEORGE JR	2LT	0-1305037	0944	2
GALOT JOHN J	CPT	0-0498899	0949	1
GALPERIN LEON	LTC	0-1171153	1161	1
GALPIN ROBERT E	MAJ	0-2023894	0759	1
GALSTER BERNARD L	1LT	0-1323825	1046	2
GALT HENRY T	LTC	0-0222353	0964	3
GALUSAKA ANDREW J	MAJ	0-1548795	1157	1
GALUSKA EDWARD L	CW3	W-2150912	0265	1
GALVAN ALONZO M	CW4	W-2109056	1054	1
GALVAN ANTONIO J	MAJ	0-2030994	0764	1
GALVIN JOHN R	2LT	0-1331386	0346	2
GALVIN PAUL J	MAJ	0-1308502	0767	3
GALVIN WILLIAM J	COL	0-0105776	0757	3
GALWAY RICHARD E	LTC	0-0347043	0265	1
GALYEAN DUBLIN SR	LTC	0-0306567	0968	3
GALYEN RICHARD L	CW3	W-2147873	1064	1
GALYON WALTER O	LTC	0-1595515	0766	1
GAMACHE PAUL L	LTC	0-1016069	0463	1
GAMACHE ROMEO J	COL	0-0426506	0964	1
GAMALK CHARLES A	CW2	W-3100529	0167	1
GAMARA NORBERT J	1LT	0-0923302	1044	2
GAMAS HORACE F	MAJ	0-2035421	1160	1
GAMBA JOSEPH	CPT	0-0491601	0844	2
GAMBEE JAMES J	COL	0-0261957	0164	3
GAMBERT CHARLES A	1LT	0-0930835	0547	2
GAMBERT LAWRENCE	CPT	0-0378840	1044	2
GAMBILL JOSEPH F	CPT	0-2041100	0547	2
GAMBILL MELBURN H	LTC	0-1328024	1262	1
GAMBINO RALPH R	CW2	W-2210738	0566	1
GAMBLE ALEXANDER	CPT	0-1310094	0348	2
GAMBLE CHARLES F	LTC	0-0917032	0467	3
GAMBLE DAVID S	LTC	0-0380397	1054	1
GAMBLE FRED R	1LT	0-1316286	1045	2
GAMBLE SAMUEL H	LTC	0-0238646	0465	3
GAMBLE SHELBY V	CPT	0-0109714	0844	2
GAMBLE WILLIAM A	MAJ	0-0177589	0654	3
GAMBLE WILLIAM D	CW4	W-2144050	0868	1
GAMBLE WILLIAM F	MAJ	0-0792905	0864	1
GAMBOA EARNESTO A	CPT	0-1878770	1163	1
GAMBOA GEORGE T	1LT	0-1896653	0349	1
GAMBRELL JAMES H	LTC	0-0416093	0866	1
GAMBRELL RAY N	MAJ	0-0358121	0752	2
GAMBRELL ROBERT L	LTC	0-1292501	0964	1
GAMEL ALFRED L	COL	0-0450640	0267	1
GAMEL JAMES B	LTC	0-1296846	1166	1
GAMES WILLIAM J	LTC	0-2020014	0666	1
GAMM STANFORD T	1LT	0-1553635	0845	2
GAMMIE THOMAS G	LTC	0-0142259	1152	3
GAMMILL EVAN D	LTC	0-0450281	1057	1
GAMMILL LEE C	COL	0-0194428	0858	3
GAMMILL VINCENT M	1LT	0-1581727	0645	2
GAMMINO JOSEPH	WO1	W-2119896	0348	1
GAMMON EDWARD A	MAJ	0-1179861	0860	1
GAMMON FRANCIS D	CPT	0-0275632	0661	3
GAMMON FRANK M	CW2	W-2142746	0259	1
GAMMON ROBERT W	1LT	0-1998711	0945	2
GAMWELL RICHARD L	MAJ	0-0383544	0745	2
GANDY CHARLES V	LTC	0-1548796	0461	1
GANDY THOMAS A JR	LTC	0-0401092	0764	1
GANE JOHN W	LTC	0-0488204	0363	1
GANEAU WILFRID F	LTC	0-1295864	0565	1
GANELLAS CONSTANTIN	CPT	0-0286913	0962	3
GANER GEORGE J	LTC	0-0354766	0463	1
GANEY JEROME	CW3	W-2207586	0766	1
GANG CARLOS D	LTC	0-1553813	0862	1
GANGE HAROLD H	LTC	0-0250550	0665	3
GANGNATH IRVIN T	CW3	W-2142703	0761	1
GANIO GINO	1LT	0-1012268	0746	2
GANN BRENT L	CPT	0-1283581	1147	2
GANN HENRY	MAJ	0-1689484	0146	2
GANN RUFUS I	MAJ	0-1325083	0561	1
GANN WILLIAM C	CW3	RW-2146329	0465	1
GANNARELLI JAMES	CW3	W-2205420	0464	1
GANNON EDWIN T	CW3	W-2150793	1262	1
GANNON EUGENE R	1LT	0-1172458	0746	2
GANNON FRANCIS E	MAJ	0-2009540	0668	3
GANNON JOHN E	LTC	0-0502095	0163	1
GANNON JOHN F	MAJ	0-0234673	0348	2
GANNON JOHN J	2LT	0-0224861	1165	3
GANNON JOHN P	MAJ	0-0930712	1262	1
GANNON JOSEPH J	LTC	0-1637479	0962	1
GANNON RALPH A	CPT	0-0297730	0867	3
GANNON ROBERT L	LTC	0-1947993	1064	1
GANNON THOMAS F JR	MAJ	0-2009698	1060	1
GANNON THOMAS P	LTC	0-1300017	0761	1
GANNON WENDELL C	LTC	0-0420887	1265	1
GANNON WILLIAM J	CPT	0-0408495	0446	2
GANO HERMAN D	CW2	W-2211120	1166	1
GANOUS BONNIE T	1LT	0-1301129	0246	2
GANOW GLEN Q	LTC	0-1169971	1061	1
GANS EDWARD J	CPT	0-1036991	0656	1
GANSEL ROBERT W	MAJ	0-1599085	0963	1
GANT WILLIAM T	MAJ	0-0969392	0865	1
GANTENBEIN CALVIN E	COL	0-0309393	1166	3
GANTENBEIN EARL D	CPT	0-0407268	0346	2
GANTER LEWIS E	MAJ	0-1633232	0466	1
GANTOS ALEX L	CW2	W-2209840	0561	1
GANTT BOB	CPT	0-0228668	0344	2
GANTT FRANK E	LTC	0-0352994	1266	1
GANTT GEORGE B	LTC	0-0335960	1263	3
GANTT HOUSTON H	MAJ	0-2011789	1060	1
GANTZ CHARLES E	CPT	0-1944450	0357	1
GANTZ MAURICE H	MAJ	0-0299813	0145	2
GANZ CARL D	LTC	0-0211981	0351	3
GAPINSKI WESLEY	1LT	0-0888571	0760	1
GARABEDIAN VAUGHAN	1LT	0-0401391	0945	2
GARAMELLA MICHAEL A	1LT	0-1040716	0945	2
GARBARINI URSULA B	2LT	L-0200199	0744	2
GARBARINO VICTOR J	COL	0-0171767	1059	1
GARBE JOE A	COL	0-1588573	0864	1
GARBER ALFRED E	LTC	0-0116941	0552	3
GARBER EDWARD E	MAJ	0-1776271	0646	2
GARBER HOWARD A	LTC	0-0293404	1167	3
GARBER JACOB S	CPT	0-1689514	1045	2
GARBER JARED Y	LTC	0-0309905	1167	3
GARBER JOSEPH	LTC	0-0296277	1066	3
GARBER LYNN L	MAJ	L-0401565	0563	1
GARBER MITCHEL W	1LT	0-1117861	0146	2
GARBER PAUL E	CPT	0-2263359	0262	1
GARBOW PHILIP	WO1	W-2148447	1053	1
GARBUTT CHESTER H	MAJ	0-0183781	0760	3
GARCELON RAYMOND H	LTC	0-1633874	0261	1
GARCHIE RICHARD	CPT	0-1920310	1264	1
GARCIA AUGUSTO M	MAJ	0-0242797	0156	3
GARCIA BINO F	LTC	0-1587989	0665	1
GARCIA EDWARD V	COL	0-0173369	0947	2
GARCIA FELIX	MAJ	0-1031642	0860	1
GARCIA GERARD L JR	CW3	W-2208431	0868	1
GARCIA GREGORIO N	LTC	0-1574427	1054	1
GARCIA HECTOR D	MAJ	0-1541895	0259	1
GARCIA HERMAN	MAJ	0-1795031	1060	1
GARCIA JOSE	CPT	0-0250736	0145	2
GARCIA MIGUEL A	1LT	0-0450182	1145	2
GARCIA NICK D	MAJ	0-2006516	1262	1
GARCIA OBALDO	MAJ	0-1046808	0956	1
GARCIA RAFAEL A	CPT	0-0371330	1160	1
GARCIA ROBERTO R	MAJ	0-4031302	0867	1
GARCIA SADY	MAJ	0-2263319	1061	1
GARCINA GEORGE M	1LT	0-0396551	1044	2
GARD JOHN I	MAJ	0-0451104	0657	1
GARD RAYMOND A	CW2	W-2147066	0459	1
GARD WILLIAM H	MAJ	0-1036992	0661	1
GARDELLA LEROY	MAJ	0-1699965	0663	1
GARDEN ALLAN C	LTC	0-0118650	1044	2
GARDEN HENRY B	MAJ	0-0175770	0360	3
GARDEN HENRY J	MAJ	0-1591735	0862	1
GARDENIER CHARLES K	LTC	0-0565405	0561	2
GARDENIER ROBERT C	LTC	0-1340548	0667	1
GARDINER ELMER W	LTC	0-1011556	0866	1
GARDINER ESTHER S	2LT	N-0745088	1043	1
GARDINER EVERETT E	LTC	0-0404662	0865	3
GARDINER GEORGE W	COL	0-0194699	1055	1
GARDINER HAROLD F	WO1	W-2112584	1147	1
GARDINER HAROLD W	COL	0-0210080	0463	3
GARDINER JAMES F W	LTC	0-0457693	0762	1
GARDINER JOHN F	LTC	0-0107035	0747	2
GARDINER WILLIAM P	WO1	W-2145181	0853	2
GARDNER AGNES R	LTC	N-0741199	0162	1
GARDNER ALLAN M	CPT	0-0290542	0465	2
GARDNER ALMA H	LTC	0-0287840	0368	3
GARDNER ANNETTE A	CPT	N-0762561	1154	2
GARDNER ARCHIE T	MAJ	0-0493272	0554	1
GARDNER BENNIE R	CW3	W-2207206	1068	1
GARDNER CHARLES F	MAJ	0-1946058	0550	2
GARDNER CHARLES H	B G	0-0273050	0967	3
GARDNER CLINTON G	1LT	0-0444549	1146	2
GARDNER DAVID D	1LT	0-1824299	1045	2
GARDNER DONALD B JR	CW4	W-2113283	0659	1
GARDNER DONALD L	MAJ	0-1257349	0560	1
GARDNER EARLE F	LTC	0-1184050	1062	1
GARDNER EDGAR W	WO1	W-2109221	0147	2
GARDNER EDWIN L	1LT	0-1319943	1045	2
GARDNER ELDON C	1LT	0-1319273	1045	2
GARDNER EUGENE	MAJ	0-0990521	0365	1
GARDNER FRANK F	CPT	0-0970535	1161	1
GARDNER FRANK H JR	1LT	0-0954783	1152	2
GARDNER FRANKLIN T	LTC	0-0277457	0545	2
GARDNER FRED V	MAJ	0-0293029	0767	3
GARDNER FREDERICK	LTC	0-0386747	0463	1
GARDNER GEORGE F	1LT	0-1014813	1145	2
GARDNER GEORGE W	MAJ	0-1313392	0862	1
GARDNER HARRISON W	MAJ	0-0221677	0149	3
GARDNER HARRY R	LTC	0-1031807	0461	1
GARDNER HAZEL M	MAJ	N-0799010	0665	1
GARDNER HOWARD K	COL	0-0213846	0362	3
GARDNER HUGH H	LTC	0-1321300	0766	3
GARDNER JAMES D	LTC	0-0382474	0368	3
GARDNER JESS L	CPT	0-1019144	0947	2
GARDNER JESSE E	MAJ	0-1582932	0463	1
GARDNER JOHN J	CPT	0-1010575	0158	1
GARDNER JOHN L	LTC	0-1685725	0967	1
GARDNER JOHN N	1LT	0-0352056	0744	2
GARDNER JOHN P JR	LTC	0-1265738	0862	1
GARDNER JOSEPH M	2LT	0-1281157	0645	2
GARDNER KENNETH S	CW2	W-2151724	0762	1
GARDNER KENNETH W	LTC	0-0225595	0961	3
GARDNER LAMAR W	CPT	0-0265535	0146	2
GARDNER LEE H	CPT	0-0402910	0161	1
GARDNER LOUISE H	2LT	N-0767536	0744	1
GARDNER MADISON D	MAJ	0-2055279	1163	1
GARDNER MAN O	CPT	0-0202061	0863	3
GARDNER MICHAEL C	CPT	0-1894768	0161	2
GARDNER MILO S	LTC	0-0360427	0556	1
GARDNER MOFFAT A	MAJ	0-1340178	0263	1
GARDNER NORD A	LTC	0-0935348	0766	1
GARDNER ORVILLE K	LTC	0-0904141	0163	1
GARDNER PAUL H	CPT	0-0248890	0865	3
GARDNER ROBERT	MAJ	0-2262365	1163	1
GARDNER ROBERT A	LTC	0-0271404	0667	3
GARDNER ROBERT E	LTC	0-0217424	0551	3
GARDNER ROBERT P	LTC	0-0260518	1060	1
GARDNER ROBERT W	CPT	0-0512903	0346	2
GARDNER ROY E	MAJ	0-0221515	0955	3
GARDNER SIDNEY M	MAJ	0-0323625	0746	2
GARDNER WARREN F	CPT	0-0450343	1146	1
GARDNER WESTON D	CPT	0-0470064	0845	2
GARDNER WILLIAM A	MAJ	0-0414327	1047	2
GARDNER WILLIAM B	MAJ	0-0444333	0447	1
GARDNER WILLIAM C	CPT	0-1051153	1055	1
GARDNER WILLIAM F	2LT	0-0504854	0845	2
GARDNER WILLIAM H	LTC	0-0546538	0863	1
GARDNER WILLIAM J	1LT	0-0890399	0849	1
GARDNER WILLIAM L	LTC	0-0250100	0146	2
GARDNER WILLIAM M	CPT	0-0185472	0747	2
GARDNER WILLIAM M	LTC	0-1055300	1162	1
GARDNER WILLIAM R	CW2	W-2107890	1053	1
GAROZINA EDWARD J	CW3	W-2145961	0664	1
GARE JOHN P	LTC	0-0332509	0765	3
GAREN JOSEPH F	MAJ	0-0252416	0467	3
GAREY ALVA E	COL	0-0154723	0648	3
GAREY GERARD S	CPT	0-0455407	0545	2
GAREY PHILIP	COL	0-0242064	1046	2
GARFIELD JAMES S	COL	0-0163794	0356	3
GARFIELD MELVIN G	1LT	0-1556722	0146	2
GARFIELD MORRIS	MAJ	0-0332401	0157	1
GARFIELD SEYMOUR E	CPT	0-1586590	0858	1
GARFIELD WARREN E	LTC	0-2090014	1267	1
GARGAN MICHAEL T	CW2	W-2152046	0656	1
GARGAND HENRY N	1LT	0-1014072	1045	2
GARGARD ISADORE A	LTC	0-1574234	0163	1
GARGUILO ALFRED V	2LT	0-1301467	0245	2
GARGUREVICH LUKE T	CW2	W-2148292	0463	1
GARIBALDI LINN D	COL	0-0268031	0766	3
GARICK LAWRENCE T	CPT	0-0377373	0546	2
GARIEPY GEORGE H JR	LTC	0-0454612	0960	2
GARIGAN THOMAS P JR	CPT	0-1104674	0662	1
GARILLI HERBERT J	CPT	0-0317679	0745	2
GARINGER TRUMAN D	LTC	0-0257247	0751	3
GARLAND CYRUS G	MAJ	0-2020937	1162	1
GARLAND EDMUND S	COL	0-0263902	0155	3
GARLAND HOWARD Y	CW3	W-2149433	0465	1
GARLAND KENNETH D	CW2	W-3200139	0363	1
GARLAND MALVIN M	CPT	0-1100996	1046	2
GARLAND MAX L	MAJ	0-1165292	0557	1
GARLAND MYRTLE E	1LT	N-0726029	0846	1
GARLAND PAUL P	CW4	W-2114721	0764	3
GARLAND TEA	1LT	0-2006439	0456	1
GARLAND WILLIAM F	CW2	W-2147756	0158	1
GARLAND WILLIAM H	2LT	0-1081474	0645	2
GARLINGER JOHN H	2LT	0-1169972	0144	2
GARLOCK EUGENE N	CW3	W-2146730	1060	1
GARLOCK FRED C	LTC	0-0253021	0665	3
GARLOCK JOHN B	LTC	0-1580984	0361	1
GARLOCK LEON M	MAJ	0-0973239	0463	1
GARLOCK SCHELLER L	MAJ	0-2000680	0561	1
GARMAN ROBERT L	CPT	0-0985575	1262	1
GARMENT EDWARD M	LTC	0-0369265	0166	3
GARMON HARRY H	LTC	0-0902124	0664	3
GARNAR THOMAS E	MAJ	0-0160581	1050	3
GARNEAU GASTON D	MAJ	0-1300787	0466	3
GARNER ARTHUR L	COL	0-0333679	1053	1
GARNER BLAINE W	1LT	0-1824450	1045	2
GARNER CARL	CW4	W-2101724	0259	1
GARNER CARL W	CW2	W-2213732	1168	1
GARNER ERNEST JR	MAJ	0-1120398	1263	1
GARNER GEORGE E	LTC	0-1036994	0762	1
GARNER GEORGE F JR	1LT	0-1637484	1048	2
GARNER GERVAIS J	COL	0-0405169	0848	2
GARNER HARRISON L	COL	0-0156793	0648	3
GARNER INGRAM B JR	LTC	0-1592209	0365	1
GARNER JACK G	LTC	0-1302451	0467	1
GARNER JAMES A	MAJ	0-0414328	1046	2
GARNER JAMES A	CW3	W-2206523	1267	1
GARNER JAMES A	CW3	W-2207564	0166	1
GARNER JAMES D	LTC	0-0497991	0756	1
GARNER JAMES G	1LT	0-1291455	0346	2
GARNER JESSE A	MAJ	0-1297022	1060	1
GARNER JESSE P	CPT	0-0492339	1053	1
GARNER JOHN E	LTC	0-0916854	1162	1
GARNER JOHN J	COL	0-0242264	0954	3
GARNER LAWTON F	COL	0-0240272	1161	1
GARNER PASCAL G	MAJ	0-0490577	0154	1
GARNER PAUL N	LTC	0-1167429	0364	1
GARNER PORTER S JR	1LT	0-0558276	0846	2
GARNER RICHARD E	MAJ	0-1935023	0966	1
GARNER RUTH L	LTC	N-0785428	0868	1

NAME	GRADE	SVC NO	DATE RET MO YR	RET CODE
GARNER SAMUEL B	LTC	O-0261309	0267	3
GARNER W H	LTC	O-0452038	0860	1
GARNER WILLIAM H	CPT	O-1286753	0645	2
GARNER WILLIAM M	CPT	O-1284316	0745	2
GARNETT JAMES W	CW3	W-2149949	0364	1
GARNETT RAYMOND H	COL	O-1014765	0768	1
GARNETT ROBERT J JR	1LT	O-1312536	0161	2
GARNHAM CHARLES W	CPT	O-1306263	1047	2
GARR MORRIS H	WO1	W-2149899	1051	1
GARRAHRANT WILLIAM A	CPT	O-1013305	0963	1
GARRARD LEON A	1LT	O-4029307	0656	2
GARRARD LEONARD S	CPT	O-0282052	0668	3
GARRED BERNARD L JR	LTC	O-2028577	1268	1
GARRETSON KENNETH C	LTC	O-2028687	1168	1
GARRETSON WILTON B	LTC	O-0293996	0662	1
GARRETT BECKHAM	CPT	O-0270740	0366	3
GARRETT BENJAMIN G	MAJ	O-0236755	0365	3
GARRETT BILL H	LTC	O-0959299	0967	1
GARRETT CHARLES A	1LT	O-2206749	0753	2
GARRETT CHARLES B	MAJ	O-0266606	0259	3
GARRETT CHARLES S	LTC	O-0111959	0246	2
GARRETT CHARLES W	CPT	O-2013983	0756	2
GARRETT CURTIS	MAJ	O-1890237	1068	1
GARRETT DAVID R R	MAJ	O-0159515	0357	1
GARRETT EDGAR E	CPT	O-1320835	1047	2
GARRETT EMIL G	LTC	O-1103646	0366	1
GARRETT FELIX B	CW2	W-3150931	0766	1
GARRETT FRANKLIN H	MAJ	O-0267192	0556	3
GARRETT FREDERICK	CPT	O-1639064	0657	1
GARRETT GEORGE C	LTC	O-0428639	0662	1
GARRETT GEORGE E	LTC	O-0442110	0963	3
GARRETT GEORGE E	1LT	O-2262427	1058	1
GARRETT GEORGE E C	LTC	O-0125752	1052	3
GARRETT GORDON H	LTC	O-0256021	1067	3
GARRETT HARRY W	MAJ	O-1878961	0267	1
GARRETT HERBERT K	MAJ	O-1103175	0853	2
GARRETT HOMER F	LTC	O-0383047	0762	1
GARRETT HUGH W	MAJ	O-1286471	0159	1
GARRETT JAMES E	LTC	O-0226620	0646	2
GARRETT JESSE H	LTC	O-0205339	1154	3
GARRETT JOHN B	1LT	O-0498432	0645	2
GARRETT LEN J	LTC	O-1546988	1162	1
GARRETT MAHLON C	CPT	O-0231069	0463	3
GARRETT MARVIN D	MAJ	O-2067447	0660	1
GARRETT MORRIS G	LTC	O-1234648	1165	3
GARRETT ROBERT W	LTC	O-0251705	0966	3
GARRETT ROY C	CPT	O-0365225	0144	2
GARRETT SEXTUS D	MAJ	O-0477937	0744	2
GARRETT STEINER D JR	1LT	O-0522926	1045	2
GARRETT VERN T	CW3	W-2146241	1062	1
GARRETT WILLARD M	MAJ	O-1302452	0264	2
GARRIGH ALBIN A	CW3	W-2152376	1163	1
GARRICK DAVID	MAJ	O-0319874	1044	2
GARRICK DAVID	CW4	W-2134418	0959	1
GARRICK KATHERINE	2LT	N-0732644	0343	1
GARRIGAN GEORGE A	LTC	O-0155085	0654	3
GARRIGAN ROBERT E	LTC	O-0516798	0367	3
GARRIOTT COLBY I	CW2	W-2144602	0558	1
GARRIOTT MILTON H	CW3	W-3200421	0768	1
GARRISON ADELINE	2LT	N-0732458	1043	1
GARRISON CHARLES J	CPT	O-1756070	1160	1
GARRISON DAVID M	1LT	O-1116951	0665	2
GARRISON DAVID M JR	CPT	O-1166068	0146	2
GARRISON DONAL D	CW2	W-2214622	0667	1
GARRISON DONALD L	1LT	O-1301468	1046	2
GARRISON DWIGHT	COL	O-0103221	0955	3
GARRISON EDWARD B	1LT	O-0969908	0153	2
GARRISON EDWIN F SR	CW3	W-2141563	0860	1
GARRISON H R	CPT	O-1584242	0757	1
GARRISON HALSEY E	LTC	O-0286635	1054	3
GARRISON HARRY J	1LT	O-1290585	0745	2
GARRISON JAMES E	CW4	W-2003444	0266	1
GARRISON JOHN J JR	LTC	O-0233118	0865	3
GARRISON JOHN O	LTC	O-1284493	0161	1
GARRISON JOHN W	CW2	W-3350453	1068	1
GARRISON JOSEPH O	COL	O-0194996	0259	3
GARRISON NOLAND R	CPT	O-0915206	0348	2
GARRISON RAYMOND W	CPT	O-2263246	0962	1
GARRISON ROBERT H	COL	O-0247352	0267	3
GARRISON SAMUEL T	CPT	O-0491008	0845	2
GARRISON WALLACE R	LTC	O-1169529	0764	1
GARRISON WENDELL L	MAJ	O-0397778	0554	2
GARRISON X LEWELL	MAJ	O-0358686	0544	2
GARRITY EDWARD C	CW4	W-2144868	1068	1
GARROD THEODORE R	MAJ	O-1102735	0157	1
GARROTTO JOSEPH P	LTC	O-1291257	1163	1
GARSETT JOHN M	CPT	O-1587990	0147	2
GARSON BARNETT	1LT	O-1586591	1045	2
GARSON JOHN	MAJ	O-1798468	0859	1
GARST RUTH R	MAJ	L-0400690	0163	1
GARSTAD EARL A	CW3	W-2141848	0258	1
GARTEN CHARLES E	MAJ	O-0488711	0155	1
GARTEN GERALD W	COL	O-0242079	0159	1
GARTH JAMES H JR	MAJ	O-2019582	1160	1
GARTLAND ARTHUR V	1LT	O-1112163	0246	2
GARTLAND JAMES B	CW3	W-2144748	0960	1
GARTLAND JAMES M	CPT	O-1646191	1146	2
GARTMAN EDWARD	COL	O-0486405	1067	2
GARTNER FRED W	LTC	O-0242447	0663	3
GARTNER LEONARD G	LTC	O-0203615	0648	3
GARTON FLOYD E	LTC	O-0263795	1162	3
GARTON WILLIAM H	LTC	O-0336348	0463	2
GARTZKE GRAHAM O	CPT	O-0364902	0544	2
GARTZKE OPAL M	2LT	N-0733712	0345	1
GARVER ARTHUR S	LTC	O-0451105	1057	1
GARVER CARTER O	LTC	O-0245114	1246	1
GARVER CLYDE V	CPT	O-2012475	0658	1
GARVER HAROLD W	1LT	O-1286472	0448	2
GARVER JOHN T	LTC	O-1000566	0856	1
GARVER LESLIE A	MAJ	O-2262760	0163	1
GARVEY ARTHUR R	COL	O-0124950	0856	3
GARVEY DONN E	CPT	O-1285923	0745	2
GARVEY JOHN C	MAJ	O-1030662	0259	2
GARVEY JOHN W	MAJ	O-0512207	0657	1
GARVEY MARGARET A	MAJ	N-0761326	1163	2
GARVEY RAYMOND E JR	LTC	O-1111069	0962	1
GARVEY RAYMOND T JR	LTC	O-1543908	0961	1
GARVEY ROBERT J P	CPT	O-1114498	0746	2
GARVEY THOMAS A	1LT	O-1294454	0145	2
GARVEY VICTOR D	CW2	W-2150942	0659	1
GARVEY WILLIS A	CPT	O-0182097	1054	3
GARVILLE ARMANDO J	1LT	O-1054580	1046	2
GARVIN ALBERT E	LTC	O-0222073	0449	3
GARVIN ARTHUR R	MAJ	O-0375918	0263	1
GARVIN JAMES E	MAJ	O-0990700	1264	1
GARVIN JAMES J	MAJ	O-0255129	0559	3
GARVIN JAMES M	1LT	O-1031243	0945	2
GARVIN PAUL C	1LT	O-1287691	0145	2
GARVIN WILLIAM C JR	1LT	O-0493876	0953	1
GARVIS HAROLD G	LTC	O-0264077	0462	3
GARWICK KENNETH S	CW4	W-2108296	0960	1
GARWICK NORA P	MAJ	N-0743354	0668	2
GARWOOD HAROLD W	LTC	O-0185939	0754	3
GARWOOD PAUL S	LTC	O-0247635	1166	3
GARY DONALD A	LTC	O-0963192	0768	1
GARY GORDON S	COL	O-0335737	0760	1
GARY HENRY G	CPT	O-1113698	0246	2
GARY JAMES R	1LT	O-1287692	0645	2
GARY JOSEPH E	LTC	O-0367749	1062	1
GARY KATHERINE	LTC	N-0759255	0863	3
GARY MICHAEL J	MAJ	O-1307535	0860	1
GARY THOMAS H	CPT	O-0378197	1045	2
GARZA ARTHUR	MAJ	O-1684948	0764	1
GARZA ISMAEL H JR	CPT	O-1547303	1047	2
GARZA JOE L	CW3	W-2146330	1262	1
GARZARELLI RICHARD L	LTC	O-1295196	0566	1
GASATAYA FREDERICK	2LT	O-1896546	0362	1
GASCHEN MONROE L	LTC	O-1552068	1061	1
GASIOROWSKI THOMAS	LTC	O-0338134	1049	1
GASKE JOHN M	LTC	O-0405460	0862	1
GASKE MARION M	1LT	N-0758467	1046	1
GASKILL EARNEST R	CPT	O-1995256	0550	1
GASKILL HAROLD E	LTC	O-0268714	1266	3
GASKILL JAMES E	MAJ	O-0971821	0963	1
GASKILL JOHN H	1LT	O-0299747	0942	2
GASKILL PETER C	LTC	O-0508290	0164	3
GASKIN HUBERT S JR	CPT	O-2033256	0763	1
GASKIN HUBERT W	CW3	W-2147795	1061	1
GASKINS DOUGLAS A	CW2	W-2112277	0750	1
GASKINS ORVILLE A	CW3	W-2146711	0162	1
GASKO JOSEPH J	CW4	W-2147425	1158	1
GASMAN ERLING	MAJ	O-0278776	1058	3
GASPER FRANK J	LTC	O-1934207	0666	2
GASS CHARLES J	CW4	W-2149336	0868	1
GASS ROBERT H	MAJ	O-1103647	0259	1
GASS VIRGIL J	LTC	O-0406810	0164	1
GASSEL JACOB	2LT	O-1914189	1048	1
GASSER JOHN R	LTC	O-0255195	1145	2
GASSERT LEE F	LTC	O-1010127	1264	1
GASSIE DONALD V	COL	O-0919273	0267	3
GAST GARRETT A	2LT	O-1317515	0344	2
GAST OTTO W	CPT	O-0404312	0746	2
GASTAUER WAHLERS H	CPT	O-1032434	0148	2
GASTON DANIEL J	COL	O-0354917	0568	1
GASTON HENRY J	LTC	O-0334464	0566	3
GASTON HUGH W	MAJ	O-0252036	1066	3
GASTON JAMES A	COL	O-0030138	1159	1
GASTON LAMAR D	LTC	O-0238025	0265	3
GASTON MARVIN C	MAJ	O-2208465	0467	1
GASTON RUTHERFORD	2LT	O-2025869	0847	2
GATCH GORDON G	LTC	O-1312907	0664	1
GATCHELL CHARLES W	1LT	O-1585488	1045	2
GATELEY FRANK R	CW2	W-2131972	1065	1
GATELY JOHN E	MAJ	O-1685018	1066	1
GATELY THOMAS C	CPT	O-0334308	0745	2
GATEMAN MURRAY H	1LT	O-0499337	0543	2
GATES CHESTER M	LTC	O-0341954	0262	1
GATES CLARENCE G	MAJ	O-0967269	0565	1
GATES DELBERT C	LTC	O-1313394	0763	1
GATES DONALD C	LTC	O-0273910	0545	2
GATES EUGENE F	2LT	O-1301981	1043	2
GATES FRANCIS K	CPT	O-0320879	0246	2
GATES FRANKLIN F	MAJ	O-1304890	1062	1
GATES GEORGE D	CW2	W-2151355	0761	1
GATES GEORGE D JR	LTC	O-1559562	1167	1
GATES GLEN E	MAJ	O-0169739	1058	3
GATES HARVEY E	MAJ	O-2030643	0768	3
GATES IRA E	CPT	O-1913688	0617	1
GATES JACK C	CPT	O-1290587	0546	2
GATES JAMES L	1LT	O-1308943	0451	2
GATES JOHN J	COL	O-0307450	0146	2
GATES JOSEPH	LTC	O-0378523	0960	1
GATES JUNIOR D	MAJ	O-1923544	1264	1
GATES LLOYD R	COL	O-0249374	1263	3
GATES MARCIA L	1LT	N-0730145	0246	1
GATES REGINALD S	MAJ	O-0493639	1155	1
GATES ROBERT E	CW2	W-2210660	0463	1
GATES RYERSON D III	CPT	O-0464360	1162	1
GATES STANLEY M	LTC	O-0252735	0150	3
GATES THURMOND P	LTC	O-0280661	1151	2
GATES WILBUR JR	CPT	O-2042001	0162	1
GATES WILLIAM G	CW2	W-3430476	1167	1
GATES WILLIAM O	CW2	W-2141979	0953	1
GATEWOOD WILLIAM M	CW4	W-2118288	1054	1
GATHRIGHT EMMETTE F	1LT	O-1328808	0946	2
GATLEY EVERETT J	MAJ	O-2028578	0268	1
GATLEY WILLIAM P	COL	O-0322450	1159	3
GATLIN CARL E	COL	O-0231809	1061	3
GATLIN GRADY T	LTC	O-0488854	0557	1
GATLIN LEE B	MAJ	O-1549274	0161	1
GATLIN OLLIE M	LTC	O-1045435	0664	1
GATLIN ORRIN W	CPT	O-0515070	1147	2
GATLING JOHN	MAJ	O-0495789	0147	2
GATLING MERBORNE P	LTC	O-0173131	1161	3
GATON ALBERT W	MAJ	O-0902446	1045	2
GATSKE CARL H	LTC	O-0393743	1060	1
GATT FREDERICK	CW2	W-2101727	0456	1
GATTAS FRED A	CPT	O-1756428	0948	2
GATTMAN LOUIS W	MAJ	O-0115403	0756	3
GATWOOD MILLARD F	CW3	W-2208166	0666	1
GATZ THOMAS	CW3	W-2206674	0765	1
GATZKE CARL W	LTC	O-0439600	0862	1
GAU HENRY L	LTC	O-0319758	1159	3
GAUBERT DENIS J	LTC	O-1924998	1168	1
GAUDET AUGUSTINE	MAJ	O-0451285	0658	1
GAUDET PERLEY I	CW3	W-2142155	0564	1
GAUDIERI JOSEPH L	1LT	O-0267002	0845	2
GAUDREAU CHILSON P	MAJ	O-2020135	0959	1
GAUDREAU EUGENE L	LTC	O-0493321	0657	1
GAUDREAU ROBERT C	MAJ	O-0535731	0546	2
GAUDRY F J	CW2	W-2214829	0768	1
GAUDY WILLIAM T	COL	O-0447349	1264	1
GAUGER PAUL C JR	COL	O-0358244	0863	1
GAUGHAN ELMER M	CPT	O-0355752	0144	2
GAUGHAN MARY A	MAJ	N-0744438	0366	3
GAUGHAN WILLIAM G	LTC	O-0455060	0762	1
GAUKEL JOSEPH A JR	2LT	O-1581733	0544	2
GAULD GEORGE I	CPT	O-0400533	0943	2
GAULDING KARL J JR	2LT	O-1304517	0144	2
GAULE STEPHEN E	LTC	O-0268640	0654	3
GAULKE ALVIN T	MAJ	O-0313882	0265	3
GAULKE EDWARD E	MAJ	O-0949104	0163	1
GAULT BENJAMIN J	LTC	O-0936716	0660	1
GAULT CHARLES B	LTC	O-1533787	0761	1
GAULT J F	1LT	O-1998327	0557	1
GAULT JACK C	COL	O-0244796	1152	1
GAULT VACTOR J	1LT	O-1996625	1057	1
GAUMER ARDIS V	1LT	N-0760467	0646	1
GAUMER DAVID C	MAJ	O-2035469	1158	1
GAUMER EDMUND L	MAJ	O-0193495	0261	3
GAUMNITZ FREDERICK	LTC	O-0148365	0154	3
GAUNT HARRY	LTC	O-1556422	1063	1
GAUNTT JAMES O	LTC	O-0465203	0567	1
GAUNTT JAMES R	COL	O-0407587	0968	1
GAUSE FREEMAN M	MAJ	O-1045098	1162	1
GAUSE WILLIAM L	MAJ	O-1633879	1054	1
GAUSMAN WILLIAM C	CPT	O-0302888	0345	2
GAUSTAD JOHN W	MAJ	O-0450869	0146	2
GAUTHIER ARCHIE P	COL	O-0387677	1061	1
GAUTHIER BLUMES	1LT	O-1290588	0145	2
GAUTHIER FREDERICK	LTC	O-1167431	0561	1
GAUTHIER GEORGE A	MAJ	O-0319201	0465	3
GAUTHIER VERNESE M	CPT	N-0721653	0449	2
GAUTHREAUX ERVIN M	1LT	O-0888909	0345	2
GAUTSCHI WILLIAM I	CPT	O-0886212	1045	2
GAVA AUGUST JR	CW3	W-2148000	0763	1
GAVARINSKI FRANK J	1LT	O-1166069	1045	2
GAVIGAN JOHN J	CPT	O-1685178	1045	2
GAVIN CHARLES G	CPT	O-1291259	0346	2
GAVIN JOHN C	CPT	O-0375030	0145	2
GAVIN JOHN J	MAJ	O-0480749	0854	1
GAVIN JOHN R	2LT	O-1936221	0362	2
GAVIN MARY	LTC	N-0700063	0844	1
GAVIN RICHARD P	LTC	O-1322143	0266	1
GAVIN WILLIAM A	LTC	O-0171144	0858	1
GAVULA MICHAEL	LTC	O-2034944	0862	1
GAW ROBERT A	COL	O-0264956	0457	1
GAWENKA EVA	MAJ	N-0777541	1265	1
GAWKOWSKI PAUL	LTC	O-1181259	0163	1
GAWLAS FREDERICK	1LT	O-1303136	0345	2
GAWNE CHARLES B	CPT	O-1821420	0446	2
GAY ALDEN	MAJ	O-2009432	1061	1
GAY BRYAN W	MAJ	O-0969583	0263	1
GAY CHARLES HE JR	CPT	O-0925669	0847	2
GAY ELLERY C	LTC	O-0313177	0863	3
GAY ELMER D	COL	O-0290536	0167	3
GAY HERBERT	MAJ	O-0949044	0762	1
GAY JACK R	LTC	O-1297351	1061	1
GAY JAMES J	CPT	O-0528873	1046	2
GAY JAMES O	LTC	O-1338944	0267	1

NAME	GRADE	SVC NO	DATE RET MO YR	RET CODE
GAY JAMES W	MAJ	0-1822263	0657	1
GAY JOE A	LTC	0-0320623	0864	3
GAY MABELLE A	2LT	N-0751029	0444	1
GAY OTIS F	LTC	0-0461626	1146	2
GAY THOMAS H JR	1LT	0-1825665	0246	2
GAY TOMMIE L	CPT	0-1300018	1047	2
GAY TRAVIS R	LTC	0-1949969	1067	1
GAY WILLIAM S	MAJ	0-0250603	0245	2
GAYDON EMZY W JR	1LT	0-0415558	1046	2
GAYDOSH LOUIS W	CPT	0-0294195	0267	3
GAYHART LLOYD W	CW2	W-2144055	0963	1
GAYLE JAMES O	LTC	0-0214727	0264	3
GAYLES JOHN L	MAJ	0-0426219	1060	1
GAYLOR ROSCOE D	COL	0-0232859	0964	3
GAYLORD CARL W	CPT	0-2056090	0867	1
GAYLORD GEORGE H	LTC	0-1825528	0166	1
GAYLORD LEON J	CPT	0-1634788	0858	1
GAYLORD MORRIS L	LTC	0-1540552	0868	1
GAYNE ARTHUR G	LTC	0-1030366	0856	1
GAYNIER WILLIAM N	2LT	0-0539899	0645	2
GAYNIN HENRY T	CPT	0-1690364	0845	2
GAYNOR DAVID R	1LT	0-1310999	0745	2
GAYNOR ELIZABETH	1LT	N-0721001	0346	1
GAYNOR GEORGE G	LTC	0-1017143	0562	1
GAYNOR HELEN A	LTC	L-0500009	0265	1
GAYNOR JOHN F JR	1LT	0-1016230	1145	2
GAYNOR PAUL F	LTC	0-0423108	1047	2
GAYNOR ROBERT M	LTC	0-0326696	1246	2
GAYNOR WAYNE J	MAJ	0-1895549	0664	1
GEAKE FRANCIS JR	CW2	W-2152827	0261	1
GEANEY JOHN J	1LT	0-1041767	0266	1
GEAR AUBREY C	CW2	W-2150667	0557	1
GEAR LELAND C	MAJ	0-1311386	1263	1
GEAR RICHARD H	COL	0-0488698	1064	1
GEAREN WALTER O	LTC	0-0170666	0257	3
GEARHART CARL P	MAJ	0-0484835	0647	2
GEARHART CHARLES H	COL	0-0274076	0361	3
GEARHART IRA D	CW4	W-2126123	0164	1
GEARHART JACK L	MAJ	0-0734334	0961	1
GEARHART RODMAN	1LT	0-1019249	0946	2
GEARING MILTON J	COL	0-0206863	0648	3
GEARING WILLIAM H	LTC	0-0453248	0263	1
GEARY JOSEPH W JR	CPT	0-0154949	0653	3
GEARY LEO A	CPT	0-1287513	0545	2
GEARY LEO P	LTC	0-0280476	0767	3
GEARY WILSON	CPT	0-0313539	0145	2
GEASE JOHN H JR	LTC	0-1574758	0764	1
GEB FREDERICK JR	COL	0-1649782	0868	1
GEBBEN ALBERT	CW4	W-2143906	0765	1
GEBHARDT CHARLES A	MAJ	0-0264187	0147	1
GEBHARDT EDWIN P	LTC	0-1795789	0568	1
GEBHARDT EUGENE L	1LT	0-1294123	0145	2
GEBHARDT HARRISON W	LTC	0-0255538	1055	3
GEBHARDT KARL F	LTC	0-0275448	0462	3
GEBHART J D	LTC	0-1579681	1160	1
GEBHART JOHN F	LTC	0-0245487	0866	3
GEBHART MARK M	LTC	0-1000366	1054	1
GEBHART PEARL E	CW3	W-2148852	0264	1
GECIK MICHAEL G	LTC	0-1559915	0965	1
GECKLER JOHN H	CPT	0-0492148	0246	2
GEDDES GEORGE F	LTC	0-1944945	0165	1
GEDDES PAUL F SR	CW2	W-2148536	0659	1
GEDDES ROBERT W	MAJ	0-0326458	1266	3
GEDDES WILLIAM L	MAJ	0-0410795	1165	1
GEDDIE ROWLAND H	LTC	0-0921519	1065	3
GEDDINGS EUGENE N	MAJ	0-0254300	0666	3
GEDDINGS JOHN C	MAJ	0-1542711	1055	1
GEDEIST HOWARD S	LTC	0-0336593	1062	1
GEDRICH EDWARD	MAJ	0-1292867	0348	2
GEDULDIG CHARLES C	COL	0-1000122	0561	1
GEE CHARLES J	COL	0-0346676	0663	1
GEE CLAY H	CW2	W-2147543	0560	1
GEE EDWARD W	CPT	0-1306085	1153	2
GEE GRANT	LTC	0-0336412	0859	3
GEE JAMES A	CW2	W-2209923	0264	1

NAME	GRADE	SVC NO	DATE RET MO YR	RET CODE
GEE JAMES G	COL	0-0164263	0547	2
GEEDING WALTER E JR	CW4	W-2005841	0868	1
GEER EDWARD W JR	COL	0-0402749	0860	1
GEER ELIHU	COL	0-0202045	0862	3
GEER FRANK	CW3	W-2102925	0459	1
GEER ROBERT C	LTC	0-2005967	0266	1
GEER WILLIAM C	MAJ	0-4014277	0267	1
GEERLINGS LEE T	MAJ	0-0421718	1263	1
GEERS PAUL E	CPT	0-1307343	0747	2
GEERTSEMA JOHN G	CPT	0-1011600	0151	2
GEESEMAN GORDON E	2LT	0-0541046	0145	2
GEESEY SCOTT S	LTC	0-0271377	0868	3
GEESLER FRED M	1LT	0-0278477	0546	2
GEESLIN WILLIAM F	COL	0-0250575	0655	3
GEEVER FRANCES B	2LT	N-0700476	0938	1
GEFFEN LOUIS	LTC	0-0359175	1264	3
GEFFERT ALVIN O	MAJ	0-0290939	0146	2
GEFFNER DAVID G	LTC	0-0300913	0468	3
GEFOROS ELMER B	LTC	0-0399872	0960	1
GEGAN JOHN B	COL	0-0170192	0760	3
GEGECKAS DOROTHY T	2LT	N-0724629	0544	1
GEGESKY BENJAMIN W	MAJ	0-1637489	0264	1
GEHM EDWIN A	LTC	0-2055810	0155	1
GEHM ROBERT J	MAJ	0-2262308	1062	1
GEHMAN MIRIAM P	MAJ	N-0742864	0667	1
GEHR LAWRENCE A	CPT	0-0451447	0860	1
GEHR MIRES C	MAJ	0-0256660	0564	3
GEHRI EMIL F	LTC	0-0331719	0468	3
GEHRIG VICTOR J JR	1LT	0-1180508	1045	2
GEHRING HARRY G	CW2	W-2213305	0967	1
GEHRING HERMAN F JR	1LT	0-1032208	0545	2
GEHRMANN AUGUST J	MAJ	0-1541696	0757	3
GEHRMANN FRED G	MAJ	0-4005433	1068	1
GEIGENMULLER WARNER	LTC	0-0512180	1066	3
GEIGER CLARENCE E	COL	0-0230033	0465	3
GEIGER ELBERT C	MAJ	0-0313391	0945	2
GEIGER HORACE W	MAJ	0-2051642	0866	1
GEIGER JOHN	1LT	0-0493508	0544	2
GEIGER ORVILLE T	LTC	0-1551408	0464	1
GEIGER WILLIAM D	MAJ	0-0132808	0648	3
GEIGLEIN JOHN C	COL	0-0406664	0163	1
GEIGLEY JOHN D	MAJ	0-1031403	0858	1
GEIKLER JOHN A	COL	0-0197167	0461	3
GEIMER EMIL J	LTC	0-1178807	0962	1
GEIS ROBERT J	MAJ	0-0506855	0653	3
GEIS ROBERT W	MAJ	0-0296513	1053	2
GEISE CHARLES B	1LT	0-0132981	0953	3
GEISE DANIEL E	1LT	0-1117013	1056	1
GEISEL JOHN G	MAJ	0-0326882	1159	1
GEISELMAN ROBERT C	COL	0-0176486	1161	3
GEISENDORFER W C	CW2	W-2122913	0847	1
GEISER ELEANORE T	LTC	L-0200261	0765	1
GEISER FRANK E	MAJ	0-0177179	0550	3
GEISER JOHN E	COL	0-0247668	0160	1
GEISER ROBERT F	CW3	W-2206867	0567	1
GEISINGER EDWIN S	1LT	0-1080103	1045	2
GEISINGER LESLIE H	MAJ	0-0300473	0462	1
GEISLER ANDREW L	LTC	0-0452058	0358	1
GEISLER ARTHUR M	COL	0-0113187	0855	3
GEISLER RAYMOND J	MAJ	0-1299230	0661	1
GEISLER WILLIAM H	CPT	0-0489534	0645	2
GEISSINGER CARL B	LTC	0-1047131	0461	1
GEIST WILBUR F	MAJ	0-0395264	0258	1
GEIWITZ HERBERT J	LTC	0-0313194	0960	3
GELABERT LORENZO JR	2LT	0-0411582	1142	2
GELARDI ANTHONY	LTC	0-0377981	0862	1
GELBER JULIUS	CPT	0-0419694	0246	2
GELBER LOUIS J	MAJ	0-0466523	0545	2
GELDART WILLIAM A	CPT	0-0413999	0444	2
GELDER EDWARD L JR	LTC	0-1111624	1265	1
GELDER JOHN Q	LTC	0-1107427	1065	1
GELETA LEO A	MAJ	0-2019730	0765	1
GELFAND DANIEL E	CPT	0-0439344	1147	2
GELFOND JOHN J	1LT	0-1319380	1145	2
GELINA HOWARD M	CPT	0-1633233	0560	1

NAME	GRADE	SVC NO	DATE RET MO YR	RET CODE
GELINI ELMO E	1LT	0-1325885	1046	2
GELLER GEORGE B	LTC	0-0211417	0 46	2
GELLER MORRIS	CPT	0-1685891	0446	2
GELLER MORTON J	CPT	0-0440199	1045	2
GELLER PHILIP F	CPT	0-1293237	0146	2
GELLER PHILIP S	MAJ	0-0302036	0646	2
GELLER RALPH L	2LT	0-2034416	0444	2
GELLER ROBERT H	1LT	0-1647453	0646	2
GELMAN MURRAY C	MAJ	0-0363248	0645	2
GELNETT RAYMOND F	LTC	0-0284733	0768	3
GELONECK WILLIAM K	CPT	0-1580992	0254	1
GELSTHORPE FRANCIS O	LTC	0-1594231	0665	2
GELSTON WARREN W	MAJ	0-0996087	0165	1
GELTMACHER HARRY R	LTC	0-0279667	0662	1
GELTZ CHARLES G	MAJ	0-0166476	0256	3
GELUSHIA WARREN G	2LT	0-1823285	0944	2
GELWICK ARTHUR B	LTC	0-0131761	1048	3
GELWICK ROBERT A	LTC	0-0465137	0762	1
GEMINIANI MARIO	LTC	0-0326460	0346	2
GEMMELL JAMES D	LTC	0-0352365	0161	1
GENARO JOSEPH F	LTC	0-2044283	0167	2
GENCO JASPER J	CW3	W-2152959	0464	1
GENDREAU ERNEST E J	1LT	0-1100114	1146	2
GENERALES C A	1LT	0-1705515	0647	2
GENERAUX CARNIE A	CPT	0-0925190	1044	2
GENEREAU EDMUND F	CPT	0-1994431	0646	2
GENEREUX WALTER J	CW2	W-2152606	0266	1
GENG CHARLES F	COL	0-0336505	0958	3
GENGELBACH ROBERT D	LTC	0-0349736	0963	3
GENIN FRANCIS G	CPT	0-0493707	0645	2
GENNETT KENNETH A	CPT	0-0427927	0866	3
GENOVAR ROBERT L	CPT	0-0403608	0145	2
GENOVESE JOSEPH	LTC	0-0571765	0862	1
GENOVESE SEBASTIAN	1LT	0-0470274	0446	2
GENRE EMILE J	COL	0-1102740	0464	1
GENSCHAW WALTER W JR	LTC	0-1320836	1262	1
GENSON PAUL E	CW3	W-2101730	0456	1
GENT WARREN D	COL	0-0208591	0648	3
GENTER JOSEPH H	MAJ	0-0978665	1161	1
GENTES CHARLES E	MAJ	0-0308358	1262	1
GENTHON RENE M	COL	0-0134701	0154	3
GENTILE DOMINICK P	1LT	0-1289408	1045	2
GENTILE GEORGE	MAJ	0-1595521	0861	1
GENTILE JOSEPH P	2LT	0-1557286	0445	2
GENTILE ROY J	MAJ	0-1307220	0864	1
GENTILICH JOHN S	COL	0-0314767	0868	3
GENTINE PAUL W	CW3	W-2125853	0557	1
GENTLE JAMES C	COL	0-0296048	0864	3
GENTLE JAMES E	LTC	0-0451950	1060	1
GENTLE PAUL D	CPT	0-2037547	0854	1
GENTNER JOHN M	COL	0-0166960	0451	2
GENTON MAURICE F	MAJ	0-0556578	0663	1
GENTRY ALBERT B	MAJ	0-2204418	1163	1
GENTRY CHARLES E	COL	0-0329967	1060	3
GENTRY CHARLES J JR	LTC	0-1342329	0464	1
GENTRY COY W	1LT	0-0256350	0642	2
GENTRY GERRY M	MAJ	0-1536175	1063	1
GENTRY HARRY L	MAJ	0-0467188	0346	2
GENTRY HERBERT C	1LT	0-0405390	1046	2
GENTRY JACK C	LTC	0-1284128	1263	1
GENTRY JOE C	MAJ	0-2211498	0766	1
GENTRY JOHN F	MAJ	0-1030245	0547	1
GENTRY JULIUS A	CPT	0-0495783	0746	1
GENTRY LAWRENCE L	CW2	W-2101087	1147	1
GENTRY MARION M	MAJ	0-1282376	0860	1
GENTRY ORVILLE L	LTC	0-0885079	0555	1
GENTRY THOMAS E	MAJ	0-0152820	0756	3
GENTRY THOMAS F	COL	0-0251165	0167	3
GENTRY WILLIAM N	LTC	0-0920108	0668	3
GENTRY WILLIAM R	MAJ	0-0224642	0157	3
GENTRY WILLIAM R	LTC	0-0997241	1163	1
GENTRY WILLIAM R	CPT	0-2026506	0457	1
GENTZKOW MYLES J	1LT	0-0517662	0346	2
GENUA JOHN A	MAJ	0-1310593	1061	1
GENUNG JOEL M	LTC	0-0358379	0960	1

NAME	GRADE	SVC NO	DATE RET MO YR	RET CODE
GEOFFRION RAYMOND J	LTC	0-1171157	0866	1
GEOGHEGAN JOSEPH F	LTC	0-2011395	0264	1
GEOGHEGAN JOSEPH M	COL	0-0294855	0868	3
GEOHAGAN JAMES M	1LT	0-1648122	0346	2
GEORGE ALBERT	CPT	0-0982304	1061	1
GEORGE ALLAN	CPT	0-1017148	0667	2
GEORGE ALLEN M	CW3	W-2141287	0560	1
GEORGE ANNA L	CPT	N-0700051	0545	1
GEORGE ANTHONY R	MAJ	0-0341331	1046	2
GEORGE ARTHUR G	LTC	0-0131759	0149	3
GEORGE ATHOL W	LTC	0-0451106	0756	1
GEORGE CHARLES A	MAJ	0-1313735	0462	2
GEORGE CHARLES M	LTC	0-1316716	0661	2
GEORGE CHARLES W	MAJ	0-1010618	0261	1
GEORGE CHRISTIAN	LTC	0-1289409	0761	1
GEORGE CLAIR L	MAJ	0-1035260	1158	1
GEORGE CLARENCE J	COL	0-1576012	0264	2
GEORGE DAVID E	LTC	0-0407452	0455	1
GEORGE DEWEY J	MAJ	0-1316287	0862	1
GEORGE DON R	MAJ	0-1557847	0261	1
GEORGE EDMUND T	CPT	0-0513858	0750	1
GEORGE EDWARD C	1LT	0-1315679	0946	2
GEORGE ELMER C	MAJ	0-2028877	0864	1
GEORGE FRANCIS W	CW4	W-2141564	0568	1
GEORGE FRANK A	COL	0-0247128	1163	3
GEORGE GUSTAVE	LTC	0-0207174	1263	3
GEORGE HARRY C	MAJ	0-1824452	1060	1
GEORGE HARRY M	CW2	W-3200439	0368	1
GEORGE HERBERT E	LTC	0-0307673	1061	3
GEORGE JAMES H	CW2	W-2143660	0653	2
GEORGE JAMES V	MAJ	0-0885612	0350	2
GEORGE JAMES W	LTC	0-2049560	0861	1
GEORGE JESSE M	LTC	0-0176982	1061	3
GEORGE JESSE R	CW4	W-2104085	0859	1
GEORGE JOHN J	MAJ	0-0947016	1165	1
GEORGE JOHN L	2LT	0-1302805	0145	2
GEORGE JOSEPH P	1LT	0-1295010	0246	2
GEORGE LLOYD E	1LT	0-0537182	0845	2
GEORGE MARTIN A SR	CPT	0-0297849	0544	2
GEORGE RALPH A	LTC	0-1334451	0367	1
GEORGE RALPH K	CPT	0-2265131	1262	1
GEORGE RAMON T	LTC	0-2274645	1063	1
GEORGE ROBERT C	MAJ	0-1876299	0367	1
GEORGE ROBERT E	CW2	W-2208362	1064	1
GEORGE ROLLAND E	COL	0-0248283	1057	3
GEORGE SIDNEY L	LTC	0-2040694	0766	1
GEORGE STUART M	LTC	0-0270949	0966	3
GEORGE TAFT L	1LT	0-1999052	0146	2
GEORGE TERRELL B	CPT	0-0486891	1145	2
GEORGE THOMAS A	COL	0-1285742	0467	1
GEORGE THOMAS J	CW2	W-2205353	1059	2
GEORGE WELTON L	WO1	W-2117029	0453	1
GEORGES JAMES	CW2	W-2147460	0363	1
GEORGES STANLEY	MAJ	0-1118895	0364	1
GEORGESKI ANTHONY J	LTC	0-0307517	0862	3
GEORGIA HAROLD B JR	2LT	0-1323120	1044	2
GEOUGE DON E DON E /	CW3	W-2209841	1268	1
GEPHART MESEKE O	MAJ	0-0190563	0760	3
GEPHART STANTON L	LTC	0-1543724	1060	1
GERACI PHILIP C	LTC	0-1578511	1060	1
GERALDO EUGENE	CW2	W-3400074	0768	1
GERARD DARWIN P	LTC	0-1182838	0559	2
GERARD JAMES N	2LT	0-0949899	0652	2
GERARD JAMES W II	COL	0-1577220	0161	1
GERARD PAUL	LTC	0-0497797	0954	1
GERARD RAPHAEL C	COL	0-0246187	1263	3
GERARD STANLEY R	LTC	0-0402502	1060	1
GERARD WILLIAM F	LTC	0-1298853	0461	1
GERARD WILLIAM J	MAJ	0-1167854	0261	1
GERATY THOMAS H	MAJ	0-0359247	0346	2
GERBER ERNEST	LTC	0-0276965	0959	3
GERBER GALEN G	MAJ	0-1332253	0164	1
GERBER JACK H	MAJ	0-1182839	1265	1
GERBER JASPER E	MAJ	0-0278453	0959	1
GERDES NORMAN J	LTC	0-0416248	1060	2

NAME	GRADE	SVC NO	DATE RET MO YR	RET CODE
GERDING PAUL P	COL	0-0161194	1155	3
GERECKE ELMER G	CW3	W-2210575	0968	1
GERENT ARTHUR J	CPT	0-1299898	1046	2
GERETY JOHN H	COL	0-0270173	0959	3
GERFEN CARL A	COL	0-0272730	1266	3
GERFEN HERBERT E	COL	0-0276723	1162	1
GERGELY JOHN P	CPT	0-2262699	0361	1
GERHARDSTEIN LEO H	MAJ	0-1599163	1052	1
GERHART AMELIA M	2LT	N-0759738	0444	1
GERICKE OTTO L	COL	0-0308439	0867	3
GERIG FRED L	LTC	0-0358610	0962	1
GERING GEORGE G	CPT	0-1689574	0346	2
GERIS JOSEPH D	MAJ	0-1922714	1066	1
GERKE FREDERICK	LTC	0-0349269	1046	2
GERKEN FRED E	LTC	0-0911334	0965	1
GERKEN FRED J	LTC	0-1310240	1262	2
GERKEN HENRY A	MAJ	0-0215944	0763	3
GERKEN RICHARD L	1LT	0-0416090	1144	2
GERKIN GEORGE E	LTC	0-0425897	0860	1
GERL JOHN G	MAJ	0-1322903	0960	1
GERLACH JOSEPH F	MAJ	0-1286994	1057	1
GERLACH RICHARD P	MAJ	0-1647455	0759	1
GERLETT JOHN P	CW3	W-2147830	1164	1
GERLOCK FRANK G JR	CPT	0-0973312	0261	3
GERMAIN EDWARD L	1LT	0-2000051	1046	2
GERMAIN RAYMOND J	MAJ	0-0272186	0246	2
GERMAK MICHAEL J	1LT	0-1633234	0645	2
GERMAN AMBROSE H	CW2	W-2149034	0566	1
GERMAN DAVID P	MAJ	0-0509430	0346	2
GERMAN EDGAR P	LTC	0-0392678	0246	2
GERMAN FORREST A	1LT	0-2040875	0746	2
GERMAN FRANK C	COL	0-0183703	0855	3
GERMAN RALPH H	CW3	W-2152342	0258	1
GERMAN WALTER A	LTC	0-0277895	0966	3
GERMANE DOMINIC G	WO1	W-2129903	1059	1
GERMANN EDWARD H	LTC	0-2008135	0764	1
GERNAND CARL F	MAJ	0-2032581	0763	1
GERNER CHARLES S	LTC	0-1822557	0665	3
GERNER LOUIS J	LTC	0-1043639	1163	1
GERNHART JACK C	MAJ	0-1117135	0465	1
GERNON RICHARD W SR	CPT	0-0404630	0261	2
GERNON WILLIAM	MAJ	0-0400253	0646	2
GERO RALPH L	LTC	0-1287335	0864	1
GEROMANOS LEON A JR	CPT	0-0969543	0661	1
GEROMETTA EMANUEL	CPT	0-1183858	0154	1
GEROULO JUSTIN J	MAJ	0-2007446	0463	1
GEROW BENJAMIN R	CPT	0-2017686	0365	1
GEROW LUDWIG C	MAJ	0-0347683	0251	2
GERRARD HUBERT J	1LT	0-1597105	0949	2
GERRELLS TRAVIS A	LTC	0-0403571	1160	1
GERREN EMMET A	2LT	0-1914156	0746	1
GERREY ELTON E	MAJ	0-0320193	0668	3
GERRICK BERNARD H	WO1	W-2118858	0945	2
GERRIE PAUL H	1LT	0-1101842	0444	2
GERSHENSON LOUIS	CW2	W-2000215	0648	3
GERSHON GORDON M	LTC	0-0389438	0760	1
GERSHON SOL	LTC	0-0461298	0566	3
GERSON ALEX D	CPT	0-1693625	0446	2
GERST ROBERT J	LTC	0-1649784	1068	1
GERSTEIN MICHAEL	1LT	0-1292868	0345	2
GERSTEN FELIX	MAJ	0-1549477	0960	1
GERSTEN JULIUS	LTC	0-0244469	1144	2
GERSTEN MAX	MAJ	0-1642090	1263	1
GERSTEN ROY	MAJ	0-0970658	0563	1
GERSTIN STANLEY	LTC	0-0911643	0768	3
GERTH HENRY C	MAJ	0-1170747	0463	1
GERTH IRVIN W	LTC	0-0312633	0556	1
GERTIE STAN G	LTC	0-0253813	0663	3
GERTZ ROBERT E	LTC	0-0395201	0750	2
GERVAIS NARCISSE	MAJ	0-0245870	0759	2
GERVIG CHARLES M	1LT	0-0541108	0646	2
GERVIN LEON M	CPT	0-2036374	0461	2
GERWIG JOHN H	MAJ	0-0416476	0547	2
GERY EUGENE A	2LT	0-1291977	0745	2
GERYE WALTER A	COL	0-0135319	0648	3
GESIN WALTER G	MAJ	0-0961705	0864	1
GESKER MITCHELL E	CPT	0-1895747	0151	2
GESREGEN ROBERT H	LTC	0-1591745	0562	1
GESS JERROLD P	COL	0-0338030	1164	3
GESS PAUL M	MAJ	0-1544777	0859	1
GESSER CARL	MAJ	0-0343808	0447	2
GEST JOHN F	LTC	0-0212776	0551	3
GESTER WALTER H	CW2	W-2109723	0947	2
GESTRING JOHN F	COL	0-0233786	1147	2
GETCHELL MARY L	MAJ	N-0761351	1163	1
GETCHELL RALPH A	COL	0-0173482	1158	3
GETCHELL RALPH W JR	1LT	0-1047132	0145	2
GETSINGER BOARDMAN G	MAJ	0-0148744	1156	3
GETSINGER JOHN G	1LT	0-0394435	1045	2
GETTER KERIN P	CW3	W-2110764	0956	1
GETTMAN HENRY	MAJ	0-1291622	0963	1
GETTNER FRANK E	LTC	0-2036732	0464	1
GETTSY WILLIAM J	MAJ	0-1937176	0867	1
GETTY CHARLES W	LTC	0-1000123	1060	1
GETTY CHESTER C	CPT	0-2262479	0758	1
GETTY GEORGE L	COL	0-0354996	0266	1
GETTY RICHARD W	LTC	0-0122942	1149	3
GETZE ROLAND	CPT	0-0325585	1043	2
GETZINGER PHILIP L	COL	0-0352031	0764	1
GETZOFF CYRUS G	1LT	0-1321623	1145	2
GEURTS JEROME R	LTC	0-1924963	1068	1
GEUSS EMIL W	MAJ	0-0475023	1052	1
GEVARTER HERMAN J	1LT	0-1318781	0146	2
GEVEDON OMER C	MAJ	0-1115596	1262	1
GEVERS CARL M	COL	0-0101940	1052	3
GEWINNER RAYMOND J	CPT	0-1303139	1045	2
GEYER CZERNEY D	CPT	0-0478745	0848	2
GEYER ELWOOD W	LTC	0-0272346	0968	3
GEYER WALTER R	CPT	0-0313932	0246	2
GEZELMAN RALPH L	COL	0-0268199	0756	2
GFROERER KENNETH J	MAJ	0-0276333	0268	3
GHAN WILLIAM C	MAJ	0-0493076	0952	2
GHELARDI ANTHONY F	COL	0-0185708	1055	3
GHENT GEORGE W	MAJ	0-1647727	0662	1
GHENT IRA W	LTC	0-0368097	0367	1
GHENT WILLIAM F	LTC	0-1322144	0865	1
GHER RALPH G	LTC	0-0102175	0154	3
GHERARDI GUY J	1LT	0-1312393	0845	2
GHEZZI ANTHONY L	CPT	0-1823432	1046	2
GHINI GUIDO	MAJ	0-2037190	1264	1
GHIOTTO ANTHONY C	CW4	W-2145225	0166	1
GHIZ EDWARD M	COL	0-0342820	0463	1
GHOLSTON LAFAYETTE	1LT	0-0446740	0445	2
GHOLZ LORETTA E	1LT	N-0759757	0146	1
GIACOBBE WADIE	MAJ	0-1313395	1058	1
GIACOBBI SAMUEL N	CPT	0-2009992	0456	1
GIACOMAZZI RICHARD P	MAJ	0-1799729	0766	1
GIACOMINI ANTONIO J	LTC	0-0493244	0766	3
GIACOMO CASPER W	CPT	0-1324835	0847	2
GIAMMALVO FRANCESCO	MAJ	0-1281281	0459	1
GIAMMARCO DANTE A	LTC	0-1061403	1263	1
GIANDOMENICO FRANK A	COL	0-0144556	1155	3
GIANELLI A E JR	MAJ	0-1297353	1047	2
GIANFRANCESCO H B	CPT	0-0469478	1147	2
GIANNAKIS JOHN	CW3	W-2152960	0965	1
GIANNARIS JOHN	CPT	0-1322908	0146	2
GIANNETTI ARNOLD S	MAJ	0-1640486	0568	3
GIANNI JOSEPH A	2LT	0-1112719	0946	2
GIARDINA ANTHONY L	MAJ	0-0250386	0865	3
GIARLA THOMAS C	MAJ	0-0365471	0650	2
GIARTH WILLIAM C	LTC	0-0247022	0646	2
GIATTINA ANGELINE	2LT	N-0754870	0147	1
GIBANICA SAMUEL	MAJ	0-0454384	1056	1
GIBB ADDISON R	COL	0-0222672	0258	3
GIBBARD CECIL O	1LT	0-1172023	0945	2
GIBBARD JOHN W	LTC	0-2010527	1068	1
GIBBARD RODNEY H	1LT	0-0948758	0255	2
GIBBENS CHARLES A	MAJ	0-1295703	1160	1
GIBBINS KENNETH A	CW2	W-2145415	0856	1
GIBBLE HOWARD L	CW3	W-2144848	1060	1
GIBBON JOHN H JR	LTC	0-0399220	0246	2
GIBBONS CHARLES E	LTC	0-2053936	0256	1
GIBBONS CHARLES G	1LT	0-0316159	0845	2
GIBBONS CHARLES W	LTC	0-0450060	0455	1
GIBBONS DONALD L	CW3	W-2152037	0364	1
GIBBONS HARRIS A	1LT	0-0293278	0344	2
GIBBONS JAMES N	1LT	0-0441566	1145	2
GIBBONS JAMES R	CW3	W-2142381	0864	1
GIBBONS JOHN B JR	COL	0-0270376	0260	1
GIBBONS JOHN F JR	COL	0-0273684	1267	3
GIBBONS JOHN T	MAJ	0-0171133	0945	2
GIBBONS LEO W	MAJ	0-0326482	0955	2
GIBBONS LEONARD L	CW2	W-2150637	0459	1
GIBBONS MAURICE C	LTC	0-1043958	0562	1
GIBBONS MURRAY F	COL	0-0144925	0251	3
GIBBONS ROBERT G	LTC	0-0346339	0961	3
GIBBONS ROBERT G	LTC	0-0346826	0758	1
GIBBONS WILLIAM E	COL	0-0310967	0666	1
GIBBONS WILLIAM J JR	1LT	0-2203401	0658	2
GIBBS CHARLES W	COL	0-0408155	0861	1
GIBBS CLARENCE R	COL	0-0386843	0960	1
GIBBS DONALD R	CPT	0-0501308	1045	2
GIBBS DOUGLAS C	CPT	0-0312632	1146	2
GIBBS EDWIN M	COL	0-0257445	1156	3
GIBBS ERVIN F	LTC	0-1822987	0868	3
GIBBS EVERETT R	MAJ	0-0969811	0261	1
GIBBS GRADY B	CW2	W-2147757	0761	1
GIBBS HOWARD W	MAJ	0-1588586	0861	1
GIBBS JACK	MAJ	0-0450637	0167	3
GIBBS JAMES B	LTC	0-0372602	1163	3
GIBBS JAMES L	CPT	0-1055859	0846	2
GIBBS JAMES M	MAJ	0-1108680	0761	1
GIBBS JOE B	WO1	W-2129182	0152	1
GIBBS JOHN L JR	MAJ	0-2040876	1164	1
GIBBS JOHN S	COL	0-0295839	1057	1
GIBBS JOHN W	CPT	0-0155121	0146	2
GIBBS KENNETH C	LTC	0-1105451	0662	1
GIBBS MARSHALL G	MAJ	0-0284521	0868	3
GIBBS PAUL J	CPT	0-0375368	1046	2
GIBBS RALPH	MAJ	0-0890308	1155	1
GIBBS ROYCE L	MAJ	0-1298528	1263	1
GIBBS SEYMOUR	LTC	0-1584255	1158	1
GIBBS THOMAS R	2LT	0-1058522	0844	2
GIBBS WILLIAM D	CPT	0-1894095	0167	1
GIBBS WILLIAM H	1LT	0-0299095	0962	3
GIBBS WILLIAM J	CW3	W-2207988	0168	1
GIBERSON DONALD K	1LT	0-1316894	0146	2
GIBERT GEORGE S	CW3	W-2108432	0758	1
GIBLER JOHN W	MAJ	0-0301693	0747	2
GIBNEY JAMES J	1LT	0-0109693	1134	1
GIBNEY MATTHEW J JR	LTC	0-0318117	0864	1
GIBOULEAU M M	2LT	N-0787475	0345	1
GIBSON ALMA	1LT	N-0720168	0946	1
GIBSON ARTHUR L JR	CW4	W-2118116	0559	1
GIBSON BOAS E	CPT	0-0112917	0654	3
GIBSON BOYD M JR	CW2	W-2152218	1262	1
GIBSON CECIL C	LTC	0-0451980	0455	1
GIBSON CHARLES B	MAJ	0-1294293	0563	2
GIBSON CHARLES C	1LT	0-1014949	0546	2
GIBSON CHARLES H	CW3	W-3150582	1167	1
GIBSON CHARLES M	COL	0-0339617	0461	1
GIBSON CHARLES M	1LT	0-0571772	0965	3
GIBSON CHARLES V	LTC	0-0505256	1067	3
GIBSON CLAIR R	MAJ	0-2020285	0164	1
GIBSON CLARENCE M	CPT	0-1700585	0345	2
GIBSON CLYDE W	LTC	0-0298977	0160	1
GIBSON DALE E	LTC	0-1686241	0468	1
GIBSON DAVID O	MAJ	0-0178507	1154	3
GIBSON DONALD L	MAJ	0-1882044	0867	1
GIBSON DONNE E SR	MAJ	0-2056135	0954	1
GIBSON EARL S	LTC	0-0192405	0363	3
GIBSON EARLE A	MAJ	0-0308600	0846	2
GIBSON EDMOND J	CPT	0-0341235	1145	2
GIBSON ELI W	CPT	0-2037913	1060	1
GIBSON ELMER H	LTC	0-0263693	0855	3
GIBSON EMILY	2LT	N-0700241	0538	1
GIBSON ERNEST V	MAJ	0-1307009	0961	1
GIBSON ERNEST W	COL	0-0175884	0461	3
GIBSON FLOYD D	LTC	0-0196695	0460	3
GIBSON FORD	MAJ	0-0510327	0348	2
GIBSON FOREST S	MAJ	0-0999616	0662	1
GIBSON FRANK A	CW3	W-2151166	0764	1
GIBSON FRANK H	CW4	W-2105877	0561	3
GIBSON GAYNOR A	LTC	0-1651744	0763	1
GIBSON GEORGE W	COL	0-0264324	0467	3
GIBSON GIFFORD G	MAJ	0-0454470	1166	1
GIBSON GLEN F	MAJ	0-2036648	0960	1
GIBSON GORDON J	MAJ	0-1107433	0761	1
GIBSON HAROLD C	MAJ	0-0241870	0350	2
GIBSON HAROLD L	MAJ	0-1693107	1062	1
GIBSON HERMAN N	CW3	W-2144724	1262	1
GIBSON JACK S	CW3	W-2207632	0766	2
GIBSON JACK W	CPT	0-0453039	1045	2
GIBSON JAMES A	MAJ	0-1639077	0361	1
GIBSON JAMES E	MAJ	0-0410204	0448	2
GIBSON JAMES T	CW2	W-2113300	0646	2
GIBSON JOHN C	CPT	0-1995440	0847	2
GIBSON JOHN D	CPT	0-0389633	1045	2
GIBSON JOHN R	MAJ	0-0453246	0346	2
GIBSON JOHN S	MAJ	0-2025917	0561	1
GIBSON JOSEPH F	COL	0-0333128	0157	3
GIBSON LEE P	LTC	0-0410091	0765	1
GIBSON LEO P	CW3	W-2141288	0459	1
GIBSON LLOYD L	CW4	W-2128809	0662	3
GIBSON LOYD D	LTC	0-0414199	0957	1
GIBSON MABRY H	MAJ	0-1294457	0659	1
GIBSON MARION E	MAJ	0-1335270	0464	1
GIBSON MARY A	MAJ	N-0724740	0861	1
GIBSON MOSES S	CPT	0-1798469	0657	1
GIBSON OTHAR W	CW4	W-2142343	1065	1
GIBSON PAUL L II	MAJ	0-1300635	0161	1
GIBSON PERRY JR	CW2	W-2152577	0761	1
GIBSON RAY S	CPT	0-1846437	0746	2
GIBSON REGINALD W JR	MAJ	0-1178811	1161	1
GIBSON RICHARD G	1LT	0-1311293	0945	2
GIBSON RICHARD G JR	CPT	0-1058808	0847	2
GIBSON ROBERT A	MAJ	0-0154612	0454	3
GIBSON ROBERT M	LTC	0-1166070	0265	2
GIBSON ROLAND B	CPT	0-1885674	0664	1
GIBSON ROY C	MAJ	0-2033144	0165	1
GIBSON SAMUEL H	COL	0-0178546	1052	2
GIBSON TERRY A	MAJ	0-1111072	0259	2
GIBSON TYLER W	CW3	W-2144340	0363	1
GIBSON VERL H	LTC	0-1325387	0661	1
GIBSON WARREN T	CPT	0-0492938	0746	1
GIBSON WHITE E JR	COL	0-0322668	0868	3
GIBSON WILLIAM L	MAJ	0-2029648	0164	1
GIBSON WILLIE C	MAJ	0-2212097	0962	1
GICA THOMAS	1LT	0-1896946	0458	1
GIDDENS JESSIE O	MAJ	0-2263217	0962	1
GIDDINGS ALBERT A	LTC	0-1303706	0367	1
GIDDINGS CLYDE H	COL	0-0238296	1045	2
GIDUSKO ANDREW M	MAJ	0-0965384	0661	1
GIDWITZ VICTOR E	CPT	0-0425706	0246	2
GIEBNER FLORA M	2LT	N-0723413	1044	1
GIEFER IRA	MAJ	0-0825148	0765	1
GIEGER MACK	LTC	0-1012677	1265	1
GIELLE FREDERICK	1LT	0-1321302	0345	2
GIELOW HOWARD J	CPT	0-1304713	0246	2
GIENTY EDWARD K	COL	0-0271366	0968	3
GIER EUGENE F	LTC	0-0119879	0650	3
GIER JACOB B	CPT	0-0336377	1145	2
GIERAS RICHARD	MAJ	0-0964206	1262	1
GIERE CARL N	CPT	0-0333749	0542	2
GIERE JOSEPH C	MAJ	0-0535516	0246	2
GIERISCH WILLIAM C	LTC	0-1165500	0361	1
GIERKE GEORGE E	CPT	0-1641318	0268	3
GIERMAN GEORGE T	CW2	W-2142452	0953	1
GIES WILLIAM A	LTC	0-0288132	0158	1
GIESE DOUGLAS H	MAJ	0-0436868	0647	2

NAME	GRADE	SVC NO	DATE RET MO YR	RET CODE
GIESE OSCAR A	MAJ	0-0494234	0154	1
GIESECKE LEONARD F	MAJ	0-0346658	0446	2
GIESECKE RAYMOND H	LTC	0-1845888	0866	1
GIESELMANN PAUL E	COL	0-0216233	0662	3
GIESEMANN JOSEPH	CPT	0-0446438	0653	2
GIESEN ARTHUR P	COL	0-0251688	1166	3
GIESER ALBERT F	MAJ	0-1894105	0166	1
GIESEY ALVIN F	MAJ	0-0275074	0658	3
GIESLER GARNETT J	LTC	0-0291552	0751	2
GIEZENTANNER ARCHIE	LTC	0-1052354	1065	3
GIEZENTANNER M N	MAJ	0-0269805	0161	1
GIFFE GEORGE M	LTC	0-0255269	0767	3
GIFFIN ARCH K	LTC	0-1001567	0766	3
GIFFIN JAMES L	MAJ	0-0131461	0856	3
GIFFORD ALLEN G	MAJ	0-0490087	1047	2
GIFFORD BILL	1LT	0-1031486	0556	1
GIFFORD BYRON G	LTC	0-0322680	0564	1
GIFFORD CHARLES C	CPT	0-2001695	0967	3
GIFFORD CHARLES F	CPT	0-0259662	1167	3
GIFFORD GEORGE H	LTC	0-0136625	0648	3
GIFFORD GEORGE T	COL	0-0256679	0167	3
GIFFORD JAMES A	MAJ	0-0986770	0366	2
GIFFORD JOHN P	CPT	0-1037497	1266	2
GIFFORD LESLIE A	MAJ	0-0400878	0546	2
GIFFORD MILLARD H	LTC	0-1255538	1061	1
GIFFORD STEPHEN J JR	MAJ	0-1107975	0761	1
GIGANDET FRANCIS V	MAJ	0-0349880	0154	1
GIGANDET JOSEPH H	MAJ	0-1042575	0860	1
GIGGI ALPHONSE	LTC	0-1290742	1060	1
GIGLEVITCH VLADIMAR	1LT	0-0554916	1045	2
GIGLIA TONY R JR	CPT	0-0469103	0547	2
GIGLIO EDWARD	CW3	W-2147940	0464	1
GIGLIOTTI VINCENT W	1LT	0-1997780	0746	2
GIGLIO WILLIAM F	CPT	0-0818654		2
GIGNILLIAT ARTHUR M	LTC	0-0249990	1264	3
GIGRAY JACK C	MAJ	0-0951640	1164	1
GIGUERE ALFRED J JR	LTC	0-1597013	0163	1
GIGUERE LOUIS N	1LT	0-1794934	0961	2
GIITTER LEO F	COL	0-0288861	0160	1
GIL DE LAMADRID JOSE	CPT	0-1924142	0363	1
GIL JOSE H	MAJ	0-1283060	0352	2
GILBERT ALBERT	LTC	0-1037987	1064	1
GILBERT ALBERT A	CPT	0-1179864	0957	1
GILBERT ALBERT E	LTC	0-0347644	1161	3
GILBERT ALLEN L	CW3	W-2203265	0466	1
GILBERT ARTHUR S	2LT	0-1037000	0845	2
GILBERT BURTON R	COL	0-0277508	0760	1
GILBERT CHARLES E	LTC	0-0334814	0365	1
GILBERT DOUGLAS	CPT	0-1330811	0757	2
GILBERT EARL E	1LT	0-1549278	0546	2
GILBERT ELI	LTC	0-0421526	1068	3
GILBERT ELMER W	COL	0-0324752	0565	3
GILBERT FRANCIS B	CPT	0-1314034	0368	1
GILBERT FRANCIS M	MAJ	0-0221815	0158	3
GILBERT FRANK A	LTC	0-0170427	0460	3
GILBERT GAYLORD S	COL	0-0119408	0854	3
GILBERT GEORGE A	MAJ	0-0413019	0447	1
GILBERT GERALD E	LTC	0-0335871	0358	1
GILBERT GERALD F	COL	0-0173811	0853	3
GILBERT HARRY N	1LT	0-2026216	0952	2
GILBERT JOE M	MAJ	0-1924581	0466	1
GILBERT JOHN A	LTC	0-1290743	0962	1
GILBERT JOHN A	1LT	0-1305416	0445	2
GILBERT JOHN H	LTC	0-1180911	0861	1
GILBERT JOSEPH J	COL	0-0285737	0967	3
GILBERT KENNETH V	CPT	0-0194852	1047	1
GILBERT LEO	COL	0-0495298	0153	1
GILBERT LEROY C	COL	0-0254547	0563	3
GILBERT MATTHEW H	CPT	0-0352947	1046	2
GILBERT MELVIN B	MAJ	0-1165733	0656	1
GILBERT MILTON D	2LT	0-1106167	1044	2
GILBERT MORGAN M	MAJ	0-0240117	0265	3
GILBERT OWEN G	CPT	0-1312001	0847	2
GILBERT RAYMOND C	MAJ	0-0276211	0462	3
GILBERT RAYMOND P	CW4	W-2141567	0961	1
GILBERT RICHARD N	MAJ	0-1913303	0968	1
GILBERT RICHARD P	LTC	0-1543121	0861	1
GILBERT ROBERT F	MAJ	0-1641643	0363	1
GILBERT ROBERT M	CW3	W-2147609	0763	1
GILBERT SNOWDEN	1LT	0-0494334	0857	1
GILBERT STANLEY S	LTC	0-0328082	0866	3
GILBERT THOMAS H JR	LTC	0-1014818	0966	2
GILBERT VAUGHN G	MAJ	0-1685649	0862	1
GILBERT VINCENT C	LTC	0-0320889	0546	2
GILBERT WALTER JR	1LT	0-1325722	1046	2
GILBERT WALTER L JR	2LT	0-0550770	0645	2
GILBERT WALTER W	CW2	W-2143311	0557	1
GILBERT WARD T	LTC	0-1550799	0464	1
GILBERT WARREN E	MAJ	0-0274588	0158	3
GILBERT WILLIAM E	LTC	0-1594865	1162	1
GILBERT WILLIAM J	MAJ	0-1119702	1163	1
GILBERT WILLIS G	CW2	W-2119977	0946	1
GILBERTSON ARNOLD R	LTC	0-0266446	0566	3
GILBERTSON GERALD O	CPT	0-1183690	1164	1
GILBERTSON OSCAR F	COL	0-0236189	0164	3
GILBERTSON RALPH O	COL	0-0253639	0557	1
GILBOY JOHN P JR	CPT	0-0456664	0944	2
GILBRIDE LESLIE J	LTC	0-0204613	0556	3
GILCHRIST CHARLES A	LTC	0-1166271	0467	2
GILCHRIST FREDERIC	COL	0-0144769	0353	3
GILCHRIST HUGH A	LTC	0-0383127	0762	1
GILCHRIST PHILIP J	LTC	0-0972621	1068	1
GILCHRIST RICHARD W	LTC	0-0309096	0861	2
GILCHRIST ROBERT B.	CW3	W-2001925	1167	3
GILCHRIST ROBERT T	LTC	0-0278030	0964	3
GILDEA VADA M	2LT	N-0732722	0743	1
GILDEN BERNARD B	COL	0-0290176	0265	3
GILDEN CHARLES T JR	COL	0-0148121	1055	3
GILDER ALBERT C	LTC	0-2285752	1267	1
GILDER CLYDE P	CW4	W-2102937	0455	1
GILDER JACKSON H	CPT	0-1645991	0864	1
GILDERSLEEVE HAROLD	LTC	0-1556285	1167	1
GILDERSLEEVE WILLIAM	COL	0-0301035	0663	3
GILE RICHARD E	LTC	0-0960389	1067	1
GILES GLADYS A	CPT	N-0702481	0346	1
GILES HOBERT L	2LT	0-0301700	0944	2
GILES JIMMIE	LTC	0-2017835	0866	1
GILES MALCOLM R JR	2LT	0-0475994	0644	2
GILES MALLIE T	1LT	0-0499061	0449	1
GILES MARGARET J	LTC	N-0783882	0863	1
GILES NORMAN R	WO1	W-2104093	1143	2
GILES WALTER V	COL	0-0287185	0658	3
GILES WILFRED	MAJ	0-1312002	0161	1
GILES WILLIAM T	1LT	0-1002430	0544	2
GILFILLAN A H	COL	0-0266512	0546	2
GILFORD IRVING	CW3	W-2119798	0662	1
GILFOY EDWIN G	1LT	0-1824608	0153	2
GILHOOLY WILLIAM P	MAJ	0-1048371	0161	1
GILKES WILLIAM J	CPT	0-4074812	0867	1
GILKESON VINCENT S	CPT	0-1112173	0662	1
GILL ANNETTE S	1LT	N-0722582	0549	2
GILL BERNICE E	MAJ	0-0270376	0766	3
GILL CHARLES A	LTC	0-1299727	0561	1
GILL CHARLES D	CW3	W-2140634	0461	1
GILL CHARLES H	CPT	0-0922155	0445	2
GILL EARL K	COL	0-0259574	0262	3
GILL EDWARD V	CPT	0-1587995	0262	1
GILL EUGENE L	CPT	0-1597107	0667	3
GILL FREDERIC G	MAJ	0-1051145	0862	1
GILL HERMAN C	LTC	0-0405489	0968	3
GILL JAMES	MAJ	0-0109676	0648	3
GILL JAMES L JR	MAJ	0-1935343	0467	1
GILL JOHN D	WO1	W-2115696	0146	2
GILL JOHN J	1LT	0-1324404	0850	2
GILL JOHN W	LTC	0-0229397	1264	3
GILL LAWRENCE H	CPT	0-1585499	0647	2
GILL LOUIS J	COL	0-0309282	0668	3
GILL M B	MAJ	N-0787866	1167	3
GILL MACLEAN J	CPT	0-0466639	0545	2
GILL MATTHEW J	CPT	0-1686864	0645	2
GILL MONROE W	LTC	0-0456271	0868	3
GILL NORMAN	CW3	W-2148001	1059	1
GILL OLIVER C	CPT	0-4009813	1061	2
GILL ROBERT F	CW2	W-2149109	0661	1
GILL VINCENT M	LTC	0-1598395	1163	1
GILL WALTER L	1LT	0-0507430	1045	2
GILL WILLARD H	CPT	0-0349567	1267	3
GILL WILLIAM L	MAJ	0-0326459	0666	3
GILLAM CLAUDE E	CPT	0-0510215	0146	2
GILLAM FLOYD E	CW3	W-2146054	0264	1
GILLAM FRANK D	LTC	0-0921379	0163	3
GILLAM FRED JR	CPT	0-0352997	0446	2
GILLAM WILLIAM S	1LT	0-0386432	1045	2
GILLAN REAMER G	MAJ	0-0264400	0254	3
GILLAND EVERETT L	LTC	0-0326829	0163	1
GILLANDER ALEXANDER	MAJ	0-0467011	0268	3
GILLARD ARTHUR F	LTC	0-0288989	0968	3
GILLARD THOMAS W	COL	0-0101966	0953	3
GILLASPIE ROBERT A	LTC	0-1329110	1066	1
GILLASPIE TREVELYA	MAJ	0-0201341	0652	3
GILLELAND PALMER A	CW2	W-3200294	0265	1
GILLEN CHARLES R	LTC	0-1052355	0767	1
GILLEN EDWARD L	MAJ	0-1042297	0865	2
GILLEN JOHN R	1LT	0-1994916	1045	2
GILLEN MARION T JR	MAJ	0-0993447	0965	2
GILLEN WILLIAM C	MAJ	0-1582994	1163	1
GILLENS CHARLES H	LTC	0-1166071	1158	1
GILLENWATER ANDREW J	WO1	W-2110206	0358	1
GILLENWATER KENT L	LTC	0-0515310	0954	1
GILLENWATER WILLIAM	CW2	W-2152910	0361	1
GILLERAN THOMAS A	1LT	0-1552070	0646	2
GILLESPIE BRYCE	CPT	0-1043959	1160	1
GILLESPIE CHARLES B	MAJ	0-1996494	0859	1
GILLESPIE DANIEL	CW2	W-2210480	0262	1
GILLESPIE DAVID A	MAJ	0-0242423	0247	2
GILLESPIE DONALD L	1LT	0-1331493	0447	2
GILLESPIE EDWIN P	MAJ	0-1037499	0662	1
GILLESPIE EMERSON	MAJ	0-0495280	1145	2
GILLESPIE GLENN W JR	CW3	W-2151306	0767	1
GILLESPIE HARRY	MAJ	0-0386231	0546	2
GILLESPIE HARRY A	WO1	W-2123708	0845	2
GILLESPIE JAMES D JR	CPT	0-0443305	0147	2
GILLESPIE JAMES J	COL	0-0354218	0646	2
GILLESPIE JOHN D	LTC	0-0388361	0164	1
GILLESPIE JOSEPH E	MAJ	0-1937838	0765	1
GILLESPIE JULIA B	MAJ	N-0726351	0661	1
GILLESPIE LAWRENCE C	WO1	W-2149791	0762	2
GILLESPIE MAX H	CW2	W-2148471	0558	1
GILLESPIE NORMAN E	LTC	0-0265138	0860	3
GILLESPIE RICHARD L	COL	0-0245821	0267	3
GILLESPIE ROBERT J	COL	0-0501229	0465	3
GILLESPIE ROBERT V	CW3	W-2149972	0766	1
GILLESPIE THOMAS M L	1LT	0-1643586	0946	2
GILLESPIE VICTOR P	COL	0-0245713	0765	3
GILLESPIE WILLIAM J	LTC	0-1302574	0562	1
GILLETTE EDWARD	COL	0-0183903	1055	3
GILLETTE GEORGE H	CPT	0-0254855	0244	2
GILLETTE GEORGE V	LTC	0-1171158	0667	1
GILLETTE GLENN	LTC	0-0321834	0867	3
GILLETTE JOSEPH A	CW4	W-2117949	1059	1
GILLETTE JOSEPH R	COL	0-0237916	0965	3
GILLETTE MYRON R	LTC	0-0122579	1054	3
GILLETTE PERCIVAL W	COL	0-0187882	1054	3
GILLEY WILLARD S	CPT	0-0520888	0647	2
GILLHAM WILLIAM T	LTC	0-0272207	1068	3
GILLIAM CLUFFIE C	MAJ	0-0293141	0266	3
GILLIAM ROYCE B	CW2	W-2152379	0261	1
GILLICH PETER	MAJ	0-0439185	0147	1
GILLIE HENRY F	MAJ	0-0305896	0847	2
GILLIES LEROY D	1LT	0-1913689	0532	1
GILLIES ROBERT C	LTC	0-0338478	0262	3
GILLIGAN CARL M	1LT	0-1881428	0554	2
GILLIGAN DEVERN R	LTC	0-0298630	1263	1
GILLIGAN ELEANOR J	1LT	N-0788089	0546	1
GILLIGAN JOHN W	MAJ	0-0379204	0546	2
GILLIGAN THOMAS F	LTC	0-0204993	0360	3
GILLILAND ANNIE W	1LT	N-0765877	1147	1
GILLILAND CURTIS R	LTC	0-1597462	1068	1
GILLILAND DONALD C	MAJ	0-0969812	0264	1
GILLILAND JOHN O JR	MAJ	0-2033771	1265	1
GILLILAND ROBERT W	1LT	0-2263039	0454	2
GILLILAND WAYNE R	CW3	W-2141568	0660	1
GILLINGHAM C E	1LT	0-1638677	0246	2
GILLINGHAM CHARLES R	LTC	0-0312774	0657	1
GILLINGHAM GEORGE O	LTC	0-0100518	1054	3
GILLIS ANDREW J	CW2	W-2146874	0561	1
GILLIS CHARLES F	CW2	W-2104094	0545	2
GILLIS CHARLIE L	MAJ	0-1647942	0661	1
GILLIS GEORGE L	CW2	W-2118149	1046	1
GILLIS GLEN	MAJ	0-1183860	0258	1
GILLIS LESLIE JR JR	1LT	0-0259914	0967	3
GILLIS RICHARD O	LTC	0-0450441	0357	1
GILLMAN ELBERT O	CW2	W-3150909	0965	1
GILLMORE LLOYD J	CW4	W-2124355	0961	1
GILLOCK OLIVER P	MAJ	0-0314491	0346	2
GILLOTTE TONY	1LT	0-0497686	0947	1
GILLS JOSEPH A	CPT	0-0250661	0766	3
GILLULY GEORGE K	MAJ	0-1037500	0561	1
GILLY PAUL A	LTC	0-1166997	1060	1
GILLY WILFRED G	MAJ	0-1166998	0261	1
GILMAN HAROLD D	MAJ	0-0192655	0656	3
GILMAN HARRIS H	1LT	0-1315053	1145	2
GILMAN HORTON P	CPT	0-1311879	0146	2
GILMAN JOHN S	CW2	W-2146867	0463	1
GILMAN JOSEPH	MAJ	0-0493790	0246	2
GILMAN JOSEPH R	LTC	0-0326693	0754	3
GILMAN MATTIE L	MAJ	N-0773121	0264	1
GILMAN RICHARD M	1LT	0-1014861	0945	2
GILMARTIN JAMES JR	CW3	W-2151788	0162	1
GILMER JAMES M	LTC	0-0271023	1058	3
GILMER LAWRENCE D	LTC	0-0255409	0866	3
GILMER MELVIN A	MAJ	0-1951570	1064	2
GILMOR OWINNELL	CPT	0-0326496	0944	2
GILMORE CARL E	LTC	0-0268015	1264	3
GILMORE CHARLES E	2LT	0-1322018	0545	2
GILMORE CHARLES H	COL	0-0472783	0668	1
GILMORE CLIFFORD E	CW3	W-2142796	1057	1
GILMORE FRANK	LTC	0-0312035	0665	3
GILMORE GAYLORD H	LTC	0-0407240	0661	1
GILMORE GERALD E	LTC	0-1317775	0563	1
GILMORE GLENN R	1LT	0-0888335	0145	2
GILMORE GORDON S	LTC	0-0247844	1156	3
GILMORE JOSEPH O	LTC	0-0314629	0160	1
GILMORE MARK A	1LT	0-1042817	0145	2
GILMORE RICHARD A	1LT	0-1179865	0146	2
GILMORE ROBERT B	CPT	0-1797985	0264	1
GILMORE SHELDON C	MAJ	0-0300753	1065	3
GILMORE THOMAS H	2LT	0-1697998	1044	2
GILMORE THOMAS P	COL	0-0172612	0254	3
GILMORE WALTER E	CW3	W-2142840	0760	1
GILMORE WILLIAM E	MAJ	0-1324765	0462	1
GILMORE WINFRED T	2LT	0-1574239	0343	2
GILMOUR GEEN	CPT	0-0275414	0561	3
GILPATRICK GEORGE E	CW4	W-2008098	1057	3
GILPATRICK JAMES M	MAJ	0-0219840	0556	3
GILPIN VERNON T	LTC	0-1583002	1061	1
GILRAY GRANT N	2LT	0-1318423	1044	2
GILREATH DALE F	MAJ	0-1322440	0857	1
GILROY EDWARD F	LTC	0-0254585	0764	3
GILROY JOHN E	MAJ	0-1303815	0864	1
GILROY ROBERT J	LTC	0-1320626	1162	1
GILROY VINCENT J	MAJ	0-0377964	0351	2
GILSDORF ARTHUR F	LTC	0-0286761	0360	3
GILSDORF GEORGE S	LTC	0-1637508	0563	1
GILSDORF RONALD B	CW3	W-3150351	1068	1
GILSDORFF HOWARD H	MAJ	0-0217863	0862	3
GILSON JOHN A	CW3	W-2151643	0864	1
GILSON SAMUEL B	CW3	W-2209870	1168	1
GILSON THOMAS L	MAJ	0-1935444	0865	1
GILSTEIN CYRUS S	2LT	0-1044227	0251	2

332-811 O - 69 - 12

NAME	GRADE	SVC NO	DATE RET MO YR	RET CODE
GILSTRAP LEE F	LTC	0-0252500	0645	2
GIMBLIN BERT H	LTC	0-0277462	0967	3
GIMESKY JOSEPH T	MAJ	0-2101869	0767	1
GIMPEL RICHARD W	LTC	0-1039157	0662	2
GINDELE CARL W	LTC	0-0384677	0662	1
GINDER NORINE D	MAJ	J-0101152	0366	1
GINETTE PAOKO A	LTC	0-1317005	1068	3
GINGELL THOMAS R	LTC	0-1111626	0862	1
GINGERICH MARION C	LTC	0-0359053	0367	3
GINGERY LEWIS W	LTC	0-1030474	0861	1
GINGLES ERNEST F	CW4	W-2147225	0566	1
GINGRAS GEORGE J	MAJ	0-1291101	0861	1
GINGRICH KENNETH T	MAJ	0-1284129	0561	1
GINGRICH LEROY D	CPT	0-1823434	0861	1
GINITHAN FRED	1LT	0-1686519	0259	1
GINN HARRY L	LTC	0-1300309	0560	1
GINN WILLIAM	COL	0-0316612	0367	2
GINN WILLIAM E	1LT	0-0285774	0351	3
GINNATY JOHN R	LTC	0-0263403	0265	3
GINSBERG ISADORE I	MAJ	0-0331193	0447	2
GINSBERG NATHAN N	MAJ	0-0250387	0664	3
GINSBERG STEWART T	COL	0-0320411	0556	3
GINSBURG ABRAHAM S	1LT	0-1638699	0745	2
GINSBURGH A S	LTC	0-0231297	0645	2
GINTER JOHN W	LTC	0-1594264	0961	1
GINTER MALAESKA M	LTC	0-0248173	0566	3
GINTHER FRANCIS C	LTC	0-1297522	1055	2
GINTHER FRED C	MAJ	0-0504357	0157	1
GINZLER ARTHUR M	COL	0-0486318	0868	3
GIOGLIO FRED A	MAJ	0-0417821	0966	3
GIORDANO NICHOLAS	LTC	0-1103654	0963	1
GIORDANO OSCAR R	MAJ	0-0954627	0965	1
GIORDANO SANTO J	WO1	W-2002350	1167	3
GIORLANDO CHARLES V	LTC	0-0301129	0460	1
GIOSCIA NICOLAI	MAJ	0-0493316	0547	2
GIOVETTI ALBERT	LTC	0-2007654	0564	1
GIOVINE LOUIS J	MAJ	0-1645993	0161	1
GIPPLE WILL C	CW2	W-2144656	1060	1
GIPSON CURTIS A	COL	0-0232334	0260	3
GIPSON JAMES M	COL	0-0905158	0365	3
GIPSON JAMES T	CW3	W-2143855	0260	1
GIPSON THOMAS E	CPT	0-0974370	0359	2
GIPSON WILLIAM H	CPT	0-0980892	0261	1
GIRAND CHARLES F	LTC	0-0284019	0967	3
GIRARD ARMAND E	CW3	W-2147973	1061	1
GIRARD CHESTER H	MAJ	0-2050800	0266	3
GIRARD EARL A	LTC	0-0384924	0467	3
GIRARD HAROLD H	LTC	0-0267701	0860	3
GIRARD MAURICE P JR	MAJ	0-2036907	0462	1
GIRARD WILLIAM	LTC	0-0286696	1062	3
GIRARDEAU MARVIN D	LTC	0-0174820	0658	3
GIRARDI GUY	CW2	W-3430214	0567	1
GIRARD LYLE O	CW4	W-2143710	0567	1
GIRLINGHOUSE GUS N	COL	0-0180779	0558	3
GIRON PASCUAL M	CPT	0-0230057	0148	1
GIROUARD T J JR	LTC	0-2032603	0866	1
GIROUX ALBERT	CPT	0-1048372	0157	1
GIROUX LUCIUS A	MAJ	0-0424826	0447	2
GIROUX PAUL N	MAJ	0-1015314	0867	1
GIROUX ROBERT O	1LT	0-1102742	0944	2
GIRSTANTAS WALTER A	LTC	0-1000568	0961	1
GISH HENRY G	CPT	0-1593592	0355	1
GISH HERBERT D	COL	0-0334895	0658	3
GISH WILBUR A	LTC	0-0342383	0268	3
GISONDI FRANK A	MAJ	0-1587763	0561	1
GISSE FRED H	CPT	0-1015346	1047	2
GISSELL CLIFFORD J	CPT	0-1000949	0858	1
GITLIN HERMAN	CPT	0-1300475	0646	2
GITLIN SAUL	COL	0-0320654	1058	1
GITTELSON HERMAN	1LT	0-1015380	0445	2
GITTINGS BEN L	2LT	0-0329225	1142	2
GITTLEMAN HAROLD	LTC	0-1995094	0760	1
GIULIANO ANNIELLIO	LTC	0-0425419	0462	1
GIUNFOLI WILLIAM M	2LT	0-1288374	0444	2
GIVAN FRANK M JR	MAJ	0-1995604	0964	1

NAME	GRADE	SVC NO	DATE RET MO YR	RET CODE
GIVAN GEORGE P	CW3	W-2141909	0659	1
GIVEN ARTHUR G	LTC	0-0359347	0661	1
GIVEN GEORGE L	CW3	W-2147128	0363	1
GIVENS FRANKLIN L	CW2	W-3430491	1068	1
GIVENS JAMES T JR	CW3	W-2143782	0666	1
GIVENS JOHN W	LTC	0-1174576	0264	1
GIVENS MALCOLM E	1LT	0-2201531	0753	2
GIVENS MARCEL	CW3	W-2147832	0564	1
GIVENS MITCHELL S	LTC	0-2047333	0267	2
GIVENS WILLIS R	COL	0-0239323	0556	1
GIVENTER EDWARD	LTC	0-1045089	0865	3
GIVHAN JOHN B	1LT	0-5314983	1064	2
GIVOTOFF HYMAN	MAJ	0-0359197	0467	3
GIZA JOSEPH J JR	MAJ	0-0987838	0564	1
GIZZI ERNEST P	LTC	0-0371600	0260	1
GIZZI FREDERIC J	MAJ	0-0309343	0668	3
GIZZI TULLIO J	LTC	0-1584265	0967	1
GLAAB LAWRENCE H	LTC	0-1183862	0267	1
GLACEL EDWIN W JR	LTC	0-1590137	0163	1
GLACKIN JAMES A	LTC	0-0450194	0157	1
GLADDEN EMORY T	1LT	0-0315602	0346	2
GLADDEN MARTHA L	MAJ	N-0737319	1264	1
GLADDING PHILIP E	MAJ	0-0978977	0462	1
GLADIN CHANDLER B	LTC	0-0227588	0464	3
GLADING EUGENE J	LTC	0-1639078	0563	1
GLADNEY JAMES F JR	LTC	0-0419859	1047	2
GLADSON JAMES F	LTC	0-1298049	0657	1
GLADSTONE GEORGE L	LTC	0-0269156	0758	1
GLADWIN CHARLES C	MAJ	0-1047535	0565	1
GLADYS JOHN A	MAJ	0-1012242	0765	1
GLADYS STANLEY J	CPT	0-0890083	0756	2
GLADZIK FERDINAND JR	LTC	0-0224213	1264	3
GLAESNER ROBERT D	CPT	0-1687121	0246	2
GLAISTER HENRY R	LTC	0-0293058	0761	1
GLAMORE JAMES H	CPT	0-1321303	0246	2
GLANCEY JAMES W	MAJ	0-1913273	0766	1
GLANCY EDWARD B	CW3	W-3150556	1267	1
GLANCY LLOYD L	CPT	0-1637509	0747	1
GLANTZ ROBERT	LTC	0-1294294	0960	1
GLANZ WILLIAM H	COL	0-0247765	0961	1
GLASCO PERCY L	1LT	0-1040926	1144	2
GLASCOCK CHARLES L	LTC	0-1547309	0761	2
GLASCOCK FRANCIS R	CPT	0-0362216	0562	1
GLASE JOHN T	COL	0-0264570	0368	3
GLASER HERBERT R	LTC	0-0906735	1067	3
GLASER LELAND F	LTC	0-0311193	0446	2
GLASER LEO	CPT	0-1578519	0947	2
GLASGOW CHARLES C JR	LTC	0-1997220	1268	1
GLASGOW JOHN E	CW3	W-2152380	0565	1
GLASGOW RALPH H	CPT	0-0982782	0657	1
GLASGOW WILLIAM M	CPT	0-0155278	0648	3
GLASGOW WILLIAM R	CPT	0-0218622	0261	3
GLASGOW WILLIS H	CPT	0-0506821	1048	1
GLASHEEN GEORGE L	COL	0-0506844	1065	3
GLASIER EDWIN L	LTC	0-0114454	0450	3
GLASPEL CYRIL J	LTC	0-0136101	0353	3
GLASS CHARLES R	LTC	0-0425322	0161	1
GLASS DOSSIE B	MAJ	0-0588789	1062	1
GLASS GARNET C	CPT	0-2005953	0647	2
GLASS HARLEY G	LTC	0-1330539	0368	1
GLASS JAMES F	MAJ	0-1011079	0862	1
GLASS MERTON L	MAJ	0-1037504	0155	2
GLASS NORMAN C JR	CPT	0-0409966	0145	2
GLASS THOMAS E	LTC	0-1014692	0560	1
GLASS THOMAS E	1LT	0-1301291	0845	2
GLASS VERNON F	CW2	W-2114727	0846	1
GLASSBURNER FRED R J	CPT	0-0361778	1045	2
GLASSCOCK EARL C	COL	0-0348298	0660	1
GLASSCOCK MARGARET M	LTC	L-0800001	0767	3
GLASSEN CLIFFORD W	CPT	0-1284494	1145	2
GLASSER BENJAMIN F	MAJ	0-1688151	0147	2
GLASSER HYMIE	1LT	0-1321403	1047	2
GLASSER JOSEPH G	2LT	0-1997713	1145	2
GLASSER JULIUS M	LTC	0-0211257	0346	2
GLASSER ROBERT	MAJ	0-1294820	0967	3

NAME	GRADE	SVC NO	DATE RET MO YR	RET CODE
GLASSFORD DAVID M	LTC	0-0342120	0767	3
GLASSMAN JAMES	LTC	0-1044527	0465	3
GLASSMOYER ROBERT S	LTC	0-0976261	0768	1
GLASSNER WILLIAM	LTC	0-0281595	0853	3
GLASTON MAX M	MAJ	0-1037004	0465	3
GLATHART CLIFFORD E	LTC	0-1573857	1057	2
GLATT RALPH A	COL	0-0241994	0854	3
GLAUBMAN WILLIAM A	1LT	0-0386586	0843	2
GLAUSER WILLIAM H	CPT	0-0493393	1048	1
GLAVE CHARLES W	MAJ	0-1686340	0566	1
GLAVES ALEXANDER	CPT	0-1635934	0957	1
GLAZE EDWARD L	1LT	0-1327139	0452	2
GLAZER ARNOLD M	CW3	W-2205604	0868	1
GLAZER FRED	1LT	0-1169126	0545	2
GLAZIER FRANK X	CW2	W-2141569	0253	2
GLAZIER HERBERT F	1LT	0-1825910	1145	2
GLAZIER SAMUEL	COL	0-0163240	1060	3
GLEADLE RUSSELL H	1LT	0-1794802	0944	2
GLEASNER LEO H JR	MAJ	0-0989219	0767	1
GLEASON DANIEL	LTC	0-1314598	0962	1
GLEASON GEORGE M	MAJ	0-2262271	0264	2
GLEASON GUS M JR	LTC	0-4001962	1155	2
GLEASON JAMES A	COL	0-0249665	0365	3
GLEASON JAMES V	CPT	0-1301472	0850	2
GLEASON JOEL W JR	CW4	W-2102940	0659	1
GLEASON JOHN C	LTC	0-0965951	1068	1
GLEASON JOSEPH F	MAJ	0-0949337	0865	1
GLEASON PERCY M	LTC	0-0174922	0648	3
GLEASON ROBERT E	CPT	0-0263979	1054	3
GLEASON ROBERT M	MAJ	0-2102972	1063	1
GLEASON THOMAS J	LTC	0-1171161	0267	1
GLEASON WALLACE A	COL	0-0263447	0764	3
GLEASON WALTER J	COL	0-0284957	1162	3
GLEASON WILLIAM C	LTC	0-2017836	0766	1
GLEASON WILLIAM L	CPT	0-0117687	1259	3
GLEESON ANDREW A	MAJ	0-0903557	0365	1
GLEESON EDITH M	1LT	N-0796782	1047	1
GLEFFE WILLIAM F	1LT	0-2009794	0761	1
GLEICHAUF WILLIAM R	CW4	W-2143229	0567	1
GLEICHER SOL H	1LT	0-1306265	0446	2
GLEICHMANN WILLIAM L	LTC	0-0975308	0968	1
GLEIM EDNA A	CPT	J-0101150	0661	2
GLEISBERG WILLIAM R	MAJ	0-1553999	0656	1
GLEITSMAN ERNEST W	CW2	W-2209693	0866	2
GLEMSER ROBERT	CPT	0-0986155	0661	1
GLEN JOHN R	LTC	0-0248132	0966	3
GLENDENING DALE O	MAJ	0-1823725	0561	1
GLENDENING WILLIAM A	1LT	0-1320451	0757	1
GLENDY ROBERT F	LTC	0-0213896	1062	3
GLENN CARL J	1LT	0-1573232	0145	2
GLENN DELVIN C	MAJ	0-0955443	0463	1
GLENN EDWARD R	MAJ	0-0495981	0446	2
GLENN EDWARD H	MAJ	0-0148616	0857	3
GLENN EUGENE B	COL	0-0310748	0467	3
GLENN FRANCIS A	LTC	0-0274454	1045	2
GLENN FRANK J	MAJ	0-1104681	1068	3
GLENN HARRY F	CW3	W-2210041	0168	1
GLENN HARRY J JR	CPT	0-0366436	0847	2
GLENN HENRY L	COL	0-0162411	0861	3
GLENN JAMES L	LTC	0-1165502	0265	1
GLENN JAMES M	CPT	0-2006631	0157	1
GLENN JOSEPH S	CPT	0-0489890	1147	2
GLENN JOSEPH W JR	CPT	0-0726675	0463	3
GLENN LORETTA B	CPT	N-0724880	0448	1
GLENN MARSHALL W	CPT	0-0314686	0646	2
GLENN MARTIN R	COL	0-0361541	0166	3
GLENN OTIS R	MAJ	0-0486581	0451	1
GLENN PAUL F	MAJ	0-1060105	0166	1
GLENN RAY	MAJ	0-1060101	0860	1
GLENN RICHARD C	MAJ	0-1644363	1060	1
GLENN ROBERT	LTC	0-0239521	0564	3
GLENN ROBERT L	MAJ	0-0419291	0346	2
GLENN SAMUEL A	1LT	0-1032624	0859	1
GLENN THOMAS C	MAJ	0-1557157	0364	1
GLENN WESLEY A	LTC	0-1634799	0761	2

NAME	GRADE	SVC NO	DATE RET MO YR	RET CODE
GLENN WILLIAM T	MAJ	0-2035319	0663	1
GLENNAN JOHN F JR	LTC	0-0451474	0958	1
GLENNAN KENNETH A	MAJ	0-2028580	1066	1
GLENNEY JULIUS G	CPT	0-0316567	0545	2
GLENNON JOHN J	CPT	0-1321912	0646	2
GLEOGGLER FRED J	LTC	0-0202382	0453	3
GLERUM CORNELIUS JR	CPT	0-1169127	0647	2
GLERUM LAURENCE D	LTC	0-0253017	0567	3
GLESSNER FRANK J	LTC	0-2018155	0167	1
GLESSNER PAUL E	CW3	RW-2209631	1069	1
GLESSNER RUDOLF I	LTC	0-1305760	0465	1
GLEW GEORGE W	LTC	0-1556584	0761	1
GLEYE PAUL H	LTC	0-2008185	1067	1
GLICK ALBERT	2LT	0-1997085	1051	2
GLICK BERNARD W	CPT	0-0312038	0346	2
GLICK MARIE	2LT	N-0742689	0844	1
GLICKFELD WILLIAM	LTC	0-0453041	0746	2
GLICKMAN LEO G	MAJ	0-0235169	1159	3
GLIDDEN BURNETT E	MAJ	0-2007662	0361	1
GLIDDEN GORDON G	LTC	0-0234913	0765	3
GLIDDEN HAROLD L	CPT	0-1165865	0946	2
GLIDDEN HERBERT H	COL	0-0123639	0258	1
GLIDDEN HOWARD F	MAJ	0-1643591	0263	1
GLIDER JOSEPH	1LT	0-1297884	0246	2
GLIDEWELL JAMES B	MAJ	0-0897566	0361	1
GLINES VICTOR L	COL	0-0235276	1055	3
GLINSKI EDWARD J	LTC	0-0457629	0847	1
GLISAN ANDREW R	CW3	W-2152828	0361	1
GLISCH HARRY S	COL	0-0278637	0165	3
GLISH JOSEPH A	CW2	W-2120777	0547	1
GLISSON CHARLES J	CPT	0-1044829	0356	1
GLISSON JAMES R	LTC	0-1554367	0764	1
GLISSON MARION L	WO1	W-2101749	1053	1
GLOANINGER CHARLIE E	LTC	0-0282407	0168	3
GLOBUS ROBERT	CPT	0-0241654	0760	3
GLOCK ROBERT W	COL	0-0410816	0265	1
GLODELL LEROY M	COL	0-0292049	0760	1
GLOGOJVCSAN RUDOLF	MAJ	0-1640489	0757	1
GLOMB LOUIS G	CW3	W-2150940	0667	1
GLOMINSKI JOHN A	MAJ	0-0128372	0648	3
GLOMSKI ARTHUR R	CW2	W-2143852	0261	1
GLOSSOP MARVON	COL	0-1315297	0966	1
GLOTZBACH CLIFFORD W	LTC	0-0384335	1266	3
GLOVATZKY WADIN J	MAJ	0-1702356	0348	2
GLOVER ALFRED L	1LT	0-1320939	1145	2
GLOVER CHARLES C	CW3	W-2153128	0563	1
GLOVER HERBERT C	2LT	0-1176974	0544	2
GLOVER JOHN C	CW2	W-2147606	0762	1
GLOVER JOSEPH A	LTC	0-0255393	0260	2
GLOVER KENNETH	MAJ	0-2045160	0165	1
GLOVER MERLE M	MAJ	0-0516938	0649	1
GLOVER PAUL G	LTC	0-0527148	1166	1
GLOVER RALPH C	COL	0-0333022	0865	3
GLOVER ROY A JR	LTC	0-1588482	0762	2
GLOVER WELLINGTON	COL	0-0234431	0257	1
GLOVER WILLIAM P	LTC	0-0492526	0765	1
GLOVER WILLIAM S	MAJ	0-2263127	0962	1
GLOWACKI CLARENCE A	1LT	0-0388283	1145	2
GLOZER NORMAN L	MAJ	0-1080934	0962	1
GLUCH JOHN J JR	LTC	0-1045438	0463	1
GLUCHOWSKI FRANK W	LTC	0-1321175	1162	1
GLUCK ALVIN H	MAJ	0-1185490	0258	1
GLUCK EDWARD	COL	0-0239172	0357	3
GLUCK HAROLD	2LT	0-1306266	0244	2
GLUCK OSCAR W	LTC	0-0384150	0467	3
GLUCKHERTZ THOMAS E	CW3	W-2144210	0261	1
GLUMP FRANK	MAJ	0-1945588	0760	2
GLUNTZ EDWIN C	COL	0-0271024	0158	2
GLYMPH JAMES L	COL	0-1293241	0868	1
GLYNN FORREST B	LTC	0-0451107	0163	1
GLYNN HAZEL E	MAJ	L-0602912	0363	1
GLYNN JOHN L	COL	0-0371425	0258	1
GLYNN JOSEPH P	LTC	0-1944455	0463	1
GLYNN ROBERT F	MAJ	0-1293582	0361	1
GLYNN THOMAS J	CPT	0-0454087	0256	1

NAME	GRADE	SVC NO	DATE RET MO YR	RET CODE
GLYNNE LAVINIA J	2LT	N-0722634	1042	1
GMEINER LOREN L	COL	O-0246176	0454	2
GMYR BRONISLAW	CPT	O-1903885	0662	1
GNADT WILLIAM H	MAJ	O-1688414	0863	1
GNIADEK MARY M	MAJ	N-0751007	1164	1
GNIFFKE PAUL G	LTC	O-1306087	1265	1
GNUS MARIE	1LT	N-0761226	0446	1
GOAD SIDNEY E	MAJ	O-0252803	0866	3
GOATES FLOYD W	COL	O-0150783	0157	1
GOATES JOHN R	MAJ	O-1557851	0663	1
GOATLEY DURAND R	LTC	O-1010087	0757	1
GOBAR KENNETH W	LTC	O-1035079	0557	1
GOBLE ARTHUR L	CW2	W-2101751	0448	1
GOBLE CHESTER W	M G	O-0100210	0255	3
GOBLE NEIL T	CPT	O-0318803	1044	2
GOBLE ROBERT F	MAJ	O-1923603	1164	1
GOBLE ROBERT J	CPT	O-0338515	0446	2
GOBLE WILLIAM H	1LT	O-1019179	0446	2
GOBRECHT WALTER R	1LT	O-0522458	1043	2
GOCHENAUR FRED M	LTC	O-1641328	0565	1
GOCHENOUR JOHN C	LTC	O-1949327	0565	1
GOCHENOUR OBED L JR	MAJ	O-1648160	0657	1
GOCHNAUER OSCAR R	MAJ	O-0272374	0961	3
GOCHNOUR FLOYD E	LTC	O-0319229	0560	2
GOCHNOUR ROSCOE J	MAJ	O-2042688	0155	1
GODBER JOHN T	MAJ	O-1589854	0962	1
GODBEY MERLE H	MAJ	O-0373740	0346	2
GODBOUT JOHN R	MAJ	O-1554369	0356	1
GODBOUT MEDRIC M	WO1	W-2131964	0847	2
GODDARD BERNARD L	MAJ	O-0885085	1058	1
GODDARD CHARLES H	MAJ	O-0346892	0547	2
GODDARD GEORGE	CPT	O-1037006	0962	1
GODDARD HARRY F	LTC	O-0331602	0467	3
GODDARD JAMES E	COL	O-0251320	0966	3
GODDARD JAMES H	LTC	O-0293713	1047	2
GODDARD JOHN B	CPT	O-1323424	0846	2
GODDARD JOHN L	COL	O-0269784	0968	3
GODDARD LAWRENCE L	LTC	O-1297524	1162	1
GODDARD LEWIS C	1LT	O-1895765	0646	1
GODDARD WILLIAM B	COL	O-0209216	0858	3
GODDARD WILLIAM L SR	LTC	O-0453439	0261	1
GODDEN ROSCOE H	MAJ	O-0363246	0557	1
GODFREY ALBERT J	LTC	O-0199503	0459	1
GODFREY ANSEL B	M G	O-0163566	1160	3
GODFREY CECIL H	COL	O-0216324	0863	3
GODFREY CLARENCE M	LTC	O-0503421	0364	3
GODFREY GEORGE H	LTC	O-0277909	0761	3
GODFREY JOHN F	CW3	W-2152505	0264	1
GODFREY THOMAS R	LTC	O-0296852	0668	3
GODFREY THORNTON H	CPT	O-0988211	1160	1
GODFREY WILLIAM C	COL	O-0134992	0551	3
GODFREY XELIS W	LTC	O-0923973	0962	3
GODIN GEORGE V H	1LT	O-0466336	0746	2
GODING LLOYD A	CPT	O-0355265	0346	2
GODLEWSKI LEO A	CW3	W-2144045	0163	1
GODLEY JOSEPH	MAJ	O-0184608	0845	2
GODLEY ROBERT E	CPT	O-0488776	0945	2
GODLEY VES W	LTC	O-0256822	1044	2
GODSEY HAROLD H	LTC	O-0284254	0868	3
GODSEY HOWARD E JR	CW2	W-2152627	1064	1
GODSMAN PAUL J	LTC	O-0408705	1064	1
GODSMAN SIDNEY P	COL	O-0239076	0950	3
GODSTREY HERBERT H	WO1	W-2145638	0654	1
GODWIN ALBERT S	CW3	W-2106194	1154	1
GODWIN DALE M	LTC	O-0298291	1062	3
GODWIN EARL J	CW3	W-2145772	0162	1
GODWIN GERALD S	CPT	O-1322329	0148	2
GODWIN GROVER	LTC	O-0132226	1057	3
GODWIN HARRY E	1LT	O-1826271	1144	2
GODWIN HOLLIS E	MAJ	O-1171555	0256	1
GODWIN JAMES A	LTC	O-0328524	0661	1
GODWIN JIMMIE J	COL	O-0187471	1056	3
GODWIN JOHN J	CW2	W-2147629	1057	1
GODWIN PAUL H	CPT	O-1640490	1056	1
GODWIN TULLIS M	1LT	O-0407840	0144	2

NAME	GRADE	SVC NO	DATE RET MO YR	RET CODE
GOODWIN WILLIAM O	CW3	W-2151610	1060	1
GOE GEORGE W JR	CW4	W-2146795	0868	1
GOEBEL RALPH N	CPT	O-0175719	0557	3
GOECKER LOUIS E	LTC	O-0178918	1055	3
GOEDDE VICTOR H	LTC	O-0166980	1057	3
GOEDEN LOUISE E	MAJ	L-0600306	0267	3
GOEDHART ROBERT G	2LT	O-0367169	0245	2
GOEDIKE JOHN G	COL	O-0152369	0648	3
GOEHRING RUFUS C	MAJ	O-0286654	1163	3
GOEN NEIL M	CPT	O-0506381	0555	3
GOERING GEORGE B	LTC	O-1011917	0766	1
GOERING WILLIAM H	LTC	O-0258981	0862	3
GOERISCH ROBERT W	MAJ	O-1031554	0256	1
GOESKE JOHN W	CW4	W-2142157	0961	1
GOESSENS LEONEL	MAJ	O-1338704	0666	1
GOETH CARL F	MAJ	O-0345155	1045	2
GOETHEL LOUIS N	LTC	O-0300215	0560	1
GOETTE JOSEPH A	MAJ	O-1281947	0166	1
GOETZ ALBERTA M	MAJ	N-0798983	0665	1
GOETZ CHARLES M	MAJ	O-1101845	0861	1
GOETZ FRED A	MAJ	O-1686320	0758	1
GOETZ JOHN A	CPT	O-0298822	0144	2
GOETZ PAUL D	LTC	O-1173258	0466	2
GOETZ PHILLIP R	COL	O-0426265	0546	2
GOETZ ROBERT F	CPT	O-0474843	1047	2
GOETZ WILLIAM L JR	MAJ	O-1330301	0163	1
GOETZKE GEORGE D	LTC	O-0916236	0862	1
GOEWEY JAMES H	LTC	O-0528599	1160	2
GOFF ABE M	COL	O-0173019	0160	3
GOFF ALLSTON S	MAJ	O-0282531	1045	2
GOFF CARLES N	LTC	O-1288043	0761	1
GOFF DIXWELL	LTC	O-0297954	1165	3
GOFF DONALD H	CPT	O-0417234	0947	2
GOFF EDDIE G SR	WO1	W-2153251	0958	2
GOFF FREDERICK	CPT	O-0257190	0344	2
GOFF LEE B JR	LTC	O-0247485	0656	3
GOFF LOUIS E	MAJ	O-1823288	0365	1
GOFF LYMAN E	2LT	O-1315054	1044	2
GOFF MARSHALL A	LTC	O-0154333	0545	2
GOFF PAUL	CPT	O-0450285	0761	1
GOFF ROBERT R	1LT	O-1315577	1145	2
GOFF VIRGIL R	MAJ	O-1876716	1263	1
GOFF WILLIAM J	MAJ	O-0941966	0161	1
GOFFAR ANNA K	MAJ	L-1010022	0766	1
GOFORTH DELBERT J	CW3	W-2141570	0859	1
GOFORTH HARRY J	1LT	O-1291804	0845	2
GOFOURTH THEODORE T	MAJ	O-1341774	0861	1
GOGATS JOHN C	CW4	W-2117386	0659	1
GOGGANS ELMER F	MAJ	O-0443980	0246	1
GOGGANS EMORY L JR	LTC	O-0452293	0562	1
GOGGANS OSCAR F JR	MAJ	O-1004590	0758	1
GOGGIN DANIEL F	CW4	W-2106010	0762	2
GOGGIN JOSEPH F	CPT	O-1283585	1045	2
GOGGIN ROY F	COL	O-0234412	0160	3
GOGGIN THOMAS W	LTC	O-0410732	1060	1
GOGLIA EDWARD G	1LT	O-0396637	0352	2
GOGLIO ALEXANDER	1LT	O-1061704	0447	2
GOGOLA BENJAMIN J	LTC	O-0415581	0461	1
GOGOLA MITCHELL A	CW4	W-2114168	0263	1
GOGUEN ARTHUR A J	LTC	O-0295097	0666	3
GOGUEN LEO A	MAJ	O-1014857	1060	1
GOHMERT EDWARD H	LTC	O-0201992	0860	3
GOHN ESTEL E	LTC	O-1635943	1060	1
GOHS FRANK J	CW4	W-2123216	0662	1
GOIN OTIS S	CW3	W-2143854	0163	1
GOING CHARLES F	COL	O-0265914	0152	3
GOINS RICHARD W	MAJ	O-1297525	0658	1
GOLAR LEWIS L	CPT	O-0199559	0648	1
GOLAR LOUIS L	CPT	O-0454730	0162	1
GOLBA SOPHIE K	MAJ	N-0722856	0964	2
GOLBEY FRANK A	LTC	O-0402961	0147	2
GOLBY LLOYD R	CPT	O-0887508	0648	2
GOLD ALEX E	CPT	O-0313688	0246	2
GOLD CLARENCE B JR	MAJ	O-1115600	0860	1
GOLD MORRIS A	MAJ	O-0336330	0346	2

NAME	GRADE	SVC NO	DATE RET MO YR	RET CODE
GOLDA PETER A	WO1	W-2146744	0255	1
GOLDBACH FRANCIS H	2LT	O-1637522	0645	2
GOLDBECK BEN T JR	CPT	O-1164689	1044	2
GOLDBERG BENJAMIN A	1LT	O-0364125	0444	2
GOLDBERG GEORGE	CW3	W-2150913	0964	1
GOLDBERG IRWIN	1LT	O-0278217	0944	2
GOLDBERG ISADORE	MAJ	O-0499871	0954	1
GOLDBERG LEON	LTC	O-0279928	0546	2
GOLDBERG LOUISE E	MAJ	N-0725262	0866	1
GOLDBERG NORMAN L	CPT	O-0510389	0545	2
GOLDBERG SAMUEL L	MAJ	O-0497896	0347	2
GOLDBERG STANLEY S	MAJ	O-0469313	0446	2
GOLDBERGER MAXWELL	COL	O-0140750	0250	3
GOLDBLATT LOUIS L	LTC	O-0167589	0648	3
GOLDBLATT MEYER G	CW2	W-2209926	0767	1
GOLDBLOOM LAWRENCE J	LTC	O-1945140	0867	3
GOLDBURG NORMAN M	MAJ	O-0319814	0762	3
GOLDEN ABRAHAM	COL	O-0100485	0654	2
GOLDEN ARTHUR	CPT	O-1549947	0668	3
GOLDEN BEVERLY J	2LT	N-0777086	1045	1
GOLDEN ERNEST F	COL	O-0423107	0866	1
GOLDEN GEORGE J	1LT	O-1287338	1045	2
GOLDEN GERARD W	CPT	O-1556881	0746	2
GOLDEN GILBERT A	1LT	O-1045749	1046	2
GOLDEN HENRY J JR	2LT	O-1046102	0544	2
GOLDEN HERMAN B	MAJ	O-2046580	0756	1
GOLDEN JOHN R	LTC	O-0519280	1067	3
GOLDEN JULIUS	COL	O-0321435	0765	3
GOLDEN MARVIN L	MAJ	O-1895775	0460	3
GOLDEN PAUL F	MAJ	O-2096670	0865	1
GOLDEN PAUL M	CPT	O-2039459	0457	1
GOLDEN ROBERT F	CPT	O-0356620	0446	2
GOLDEN THEODORE S	MAJ	O-0497963	0546	2
GOLDEN WAYNE H	MAJ	O-1342175	1060	1
GOLDEN WILLIAM T	LTC	O-1179413	0867	1
GOLDENBERG AUBREY H	CPT	O-0984701	0457	1
GOLDENBOGEN ROBERT L	2LT	O-1577238	1043	2
GOLDENER DONALD	MAJ	O-4030733	0367	1
GOLDENSOHN ELI S	CPT	O-0389237	0644	2
GOLDER JULIUS B	MAJ	O-1931973	1068	2
GOLDER THOMAS F	CW4	W-2144991	0456	1
GOLDEY CLARENCE W	LTC	O-2014584	0168	1
GOLDFARB HERMAN	CPT	O-1103181	0646	2
GOLDFARB JOSEPH S	1LT	O-0500124	0644	2
GOLDFARB MORRIS	MAJ	O-1995426	0963	2
GOLDFARB OSCAR	1LT	O-1534496	0146	2
GOLDIAN JOSEPH M	MAJ	O-1170750	1159	1
GOLDIN ABRAHAM W	1LT	O-1591753	1051	2
GOLDIN JOHN M	MAJ	O-0171722	0753	3
GOLDIN LEO N	MAJ	O-0502961	0346	2
GOLDING HAROLD B	CPT	O-0224132	1144	2
GOLDING HOWARD B	1LT	O-1310357	0845	2
GOLDMAN EPHRAIM J	CPT	O-0496604	0845	2
GOLDMAN ERNEST N	LTC	O-0104773	0556	3
GOLDMAN FRANKLIN J	MAJ	O-0253262	1164	3
GOLDMAN GEORGE	COL	O-0282995	0456	3
GOLDMAN HARRY	CPT	O-0886867	0856	1
GOLDMAN HERMAN L	LTC	O-1016127	0767	1
GOLDMAN IRVING	1LT	O-1995607	0746	2
GOLDMAN IRVING R	MAJ	O-0397115	0346	2
GOLDMAN LEONARD N	1LT	O-1322020	1045	2
GOLDMAN MARCUS S	COL	O-0231570	0554	3
GOLDMAN MARTIN I	LTC	O-1824301	0766	1
GOLDMAN MAX	MAJ	O-0344923	0345	2
GOLDMAN MAX R	CPT	O-0487810	0245	2
GOLDMAN MEYER N	CW2	W-2000301	0349	3
GOLDMAN NATHAN C	CPT	O-0921386	0244	2
GOLDMAN ROBERT	1LT	O-1324767	0345	2
GOLDMAN SIDNEY S	LTC	O-0227106	1162	3
GOLDMAN SYLVAN R	CW3	W-2151903	0864	1
GOLDMAN THOMAS D	LTC	O-1114945	0767	3
GOLDMAN WILLIAM H	CW3	W-2207733	0568	1
GOLDNER ROBERT B	1LT	O-0493568	1045	2
GOLDSBERRY JOHN J	LTC	O-0313087	0962	3
GOLDSBERRY WILLIAM M	CPT	O-0193258	0747	1

NAME	GRADE	SVC NO	DATE RET MO YR	RET CODE
GOLDSBY JOE C	LTC	O-0255515	0267	3
GOLDSCHMIDT HENRY G	LTC	O-0122845	1055	3
GOLDSMITH ARTHUR L	CPT	O-0411356	0944	2
GOLDSMITH CLARENCE A	1LT	O-0499489	1047	1
GOLDSMITH FRED J	LTC	O-1038644	0867	1
GOLDSMITH GORDON D	MAJ	O-1922609	0166	1
GOLDSMITH HENRY C	LTC	O-0138918	1156	3
GOLDSMITH IRWIN R	CPT	O-0311844	0743	2
GOLDSMITH MYRON B	MAJ	O-0218536	0854	3
GOLDSMITH RICHARD L	MAJ	O-0410874	1049	1
GOLDSMITH ROBERT F	LTC	O-0395037	0760	2
GOLDSMITH SAM	LTC	O-0461642	0254	1
GOLDSMITH WILLIAM E	CPT	O-0223826	0957	3
GOLDSTEIN ARTHUR H	COL	O-0207404	0360	1
GOLDSTEIN DAVID	1LT	O-1534264	0845	2
GOLDSTEIN DAVID M	MAJ	O-0356433	0546	2
GOLDSTEIN GEORGE	LTC	O-0296847	0263	3
GOLDSTEIN HENRY	CPT	O-0230766	1162	3
GOLDSTEIN HOWARD J	CPT	O-1695821	0546	2
GOLDSTEIN JOSEPH	MAJ	O-0167519	0544	2
GOLDSTEIN MILTON	CW2	W-2104099	1046	1
GOLDSTEIN PHILIP	COL	O-0245051	1157	3
GOLDSTEIN QUENTEN E	MAJ	O-1338451	1265	1
GOLDSTEIN SAMPSON	LTC	O-0209636	1058	3
GOLDSTON WILLIAM M	COL	O-0202419	0254	3
GOLDT HENRY B	CPT	O-0357701	0146	2
GOLDTHWAITE DONALD E	1LT	O-1291102	0144	2
GOLDTRAP ROBERT L	1LT	O-4031229	0162	2
GOLDY CHARLES B	MAJ	O-1541871	0858	1
GOLEMAN OCIE A	LTC	O-0489059	0557	1
GOLEMON HAPPY W	MAJ	O-0258522	0266	3
GOLER HAROLD K	LTC	O-0296901	0546	2
GOLEY WILLARD C	COL	O-0244760	0358	3
GOLIDAY FRANKLIN E	CW3	W-2143909	0461	1
GOLIGHTLY HAROLD E	CW3	W-2149874	0964	1
GOLISCH CLARENCE F	COL	O-0336047	0265	3
GOLKOPF WILLIAM A	1LT	O-1051147	1144	2
GOLKOWSKI ADELINE S	MAJ	N-0788420	0167	3
GOLL JOHN N	1LT	O-0448341	0945	2
GOLL MOKIE F	LTC	O-0301902	1059	3
GOLLA NICK	CPT	O-1896521	0559	1
GOLLER CHARLES G	CW4	W-2110290	0960	1
GOLLINGS FRANK J	COL	O-0364177	0967	3
GOLLNICK ALBERT H	MAJ	O-2009805	0359	1
GOLLOB HAROLD T	LTC	O-2035315	0767	1
GOLLUB MORRIS	MAJ	O-1590495	1060	2
GOLOJUCH FRANK J	1LT	O-1316490	1045	2
GOLSAN JOSEPH L	LTC	O-0378805	0146	2
GOLSAN WILLARD R	COL	O-0176812	0961	3
GOLTIAO HERMINIO	CPT	O-2027441	1158	1
GOLTMAN JOHN T	LTC	O-0268263	1262	3
GOLTZ SANFORD C	1LT	O-1549950	0246	2
GOLTZENE HOMER H	LTC	O-0183265	0356	3
GOLUBOW SAMUEL	CPT	O-0241381	0564	3
GOMAN CLIFFORD R	MAJ	O-0452141	1158	1
GOMBER HENRY A JR	MAJ	O-1291979	1060	1
GOMBERG CHARLES A	CPT	O-0921127	0463	1
GOMBERG JACK B	1LT	O-0527482	1045	2
GOMBOSH ARTHUR J	MAJ	O-2002279	0761	1
GOMEZ ABRAHAM	LTC	O-0444110	0563	1
GOMEZ ANTONIO F	CW2	W-3440057	0868	1
GOMEZ BENJAMIN E	CPT	O-1039295	0547	2
GOMEZ HENRY W	LTC	O-1301913	0860	1
GOMEZ JOHN L	MAJ	O-1115601	0163	1
GOMEZ MARGARET M	1LT	N-0757972	0847	1
GOMEZ-CINTRON RAMON	CPT	O-0109083	0530	1
GOMIEN SCOTT	CPT	O-0216983	0254	3
GOMMESEN JACK	LTC	O-1181612	0364	1
GOMOLCHAK LEO A	MAJ	O-4009028	0366	1
GOMOLL OSCAR F	CPT	O-0494394	0346	2
GOMON HORACE	LTC	O-0238898	1262	3
GOMON LYLE G	LTC	O-0253317	0462	3
GOMSAK PETER O	MAJ	O-0275913	0364	3
GONDA JOSEPH A JR	2LT	O-1594868	0244	2
GONDEK FRANK	WO1	W-2120680	0246	2

NAME	GRADE	SVC NO	DATE RET MO YR	RET CODE
GONDERMAN LAMAR F	CW3	W-2145141	0562	1
GONDRAN ALBERT O	1LT	0-2207467	0553	2
GONEAU ERNEST B	CW3	W-2144869	0861	1
GONEAU FLORENCE M	MAJ	N-0753059	1268	1
GONSALVES ADA M	MAJ	N-0729825	0568	3
GONSALVES FRANK B	WO1	W-2121809	1151	1
GONYO WILLIAM C	CPT	0-0970210	0960	1
GONZALES EXEQUIEL	1LT	0-0282960	0953	1
GONZALES LEO J	CW2	W-2150663	0861	1
GONZALES LISANDRO F	LTC	0-0359030	0658	1
GONZALES MOSES	CW2	W-2152459	0760	1
GONZALES PABLO F	CPT	0-1896679	0559	1
GONZALES RALPH J	CW3	W-2204588	1167	1
GONZALES REGINALD R	CW3	W-2146834	1061	1
GONZALEZ ANDRES C JR	1LT	0-1541156	1043	2
GONZALEZ ANGEL G	CPT	0-0502914	0944	2
GONZALEZ ERNESTO	LTC	0-0229046	0265	3
GONZALEZ HIGINIO JR	CPT	0-0980712	0962	2
GONZALEZ ISHMAEL G	MAJ	0-2263333	0466	2
GONZALEZ JAIME	MAJ	0-0102156	0245	1
GONZALEZ JUAN	1LT	0-0263643	1047	1
GONZALEZ JUAN O JR	MAJ	0-0408303	0148	2
GONZALEZ LAWRENCE N	LTC	0-0273330	0968	3
GONZALEZ MAXIMO	LTC	0-0203229	0660	1
GONZALEZ ORVIS L	MAJ	0-0132890	1052	3
GONZALEZ REINALDO F	CPT	0-2033199	0762	2
GONZALEZ VICTOR	MAJ	0-1333625	0762	1
GONZALEZ-GARCIA AMER	MAJ	0-0960677	0368	1
GONZALEZ-JULIA GILBE	MAJ	0-0334520	0661	1
GONZALEZ-MORALE FER	CW3	W-2147630	0962	1
GONZALEZ-RAMIRE LUI	COL	0-0310451	1063	3
GONZALVES GORDON B	CPT	0-0936633	1059	2
GOOCH CHRISTOPHE JR	LTC	0-1958118	1267	1
GOOCH CLIFFORD A	1LT	0-0405418	0445	2
GOOCH ELMER	1LT	0-1102263	0245	2
GOOCH GORDON H	MAJ	0-1897753	0164	1
GOOCH PAUL A	LTC	0-1321505	1066	1
GOOCH RAYMOND A	CW2	W-2110237	0947	2
GOOD BRUCE A	COL	0-0322822	0968	3
GOOD CLIFTON H	MAJ	0-0286291	0246	2
GOOD CLYDE L	CPT	0-0512318	0466	3
GOOD DEAN K	LTC	0-0464845	0655	1
GOOD GEORGE W	CW3	W-2148449	0464	1
GOOD GILBERT C	2LT	0-1309715	0844	2
GOOD JOSEPH	MAJ	0-2011218	1160	1
GOOD MARVIN A	CPT	0-0397093	0644	2
GOOD PAUL E	MAJ	0-1283587	0959	1
GOOD RALPH C	CW3	W-2147657	1262	1
GOOD ROBERT N	CPT	0-0358405	0762	2
GOOD STANLEY J	LTC	0-0448462	0546	2
GOOD WALTER R	CPT	0-0535373	0646	2
GOOD WEALTY W	LTC	0-0348174	0968	3
GOODALE ROY F	CPT	0-0163090	0652	3
GOODALE THOMAS E	MAJ	0-0213489	0364	3
GOODALL FRANK A JR	LTC	0-1055305	0463	1
GOODALL ROBERT M	COL	0-0190297	1055	3
GOODBODY HENRY R	CPT	0-0509999	1044	2
GOODBOLD THOMAS G	LTC	0-1307010	0762	1
GOODBOUT ELENORE E	MAJ	N-0758980	0665	1
GOODBREAD WALTER L	MAJ	0-1296021	0258	1
GOODCHILD HOWARD H	CPT	0-1647910	1060	1
GOODE ALFRED L	MAJ	0-2103054	1064	2
GOODE ARCHIE E	CPT	0-0358258	1044	2
GOODE EDWARD A	2LT	0-0395276	0542	2
GOODE EDWIN F	1LT	0-1303329	0750	2
GOODE JAMES C	LTC	0-1179078	0262	1
GOODE JEWELL M	CW3	W-2148409	1263	1
GOODE LEMUEL	1LT	0-0447030	0945	2
GOODE SAMUEL W	MAJ	0-1686789	0165	1
GOODE THOMAS H	MAJ	0-1913404	0865	2
GOODE WALTER L	MAJ	0-0218356	0546	2
GOODE WAYNE T	2LT	0-1999798	1045	2
GOODE WILLIAM	LTC	0-0452564	1165	1
GOODE WILLIAM G	LTC	0-0885056	0864	3
GOODELL HERBERT A	CPT	0-0273365	0967	3

NAME	GRADE	SVC NO	DATE RET MO YR	RET CODE
GOODELL HERMON U	LTC	0-0273366	0967	3
GOODELL LORENA M	MAJ	N-0744928	0668	1
GOODELL PAUL E	LTC	0-0326643	0260	3
GOODELL ROLLAND J	COL	0-0233794	0266	3
GOODELL STEWART A	CW2	W-2142548	1155	1
GOODEN JAMES H	LTC	0-1637529	0163	1
GOODENOUGH FRED H	MAJ	0-0405526	0660	1
GOODENOUGH NELSON B	CPT	0-0132200	0454	3
GOODENOW EDWIN R	COL	0-0336073	0756	1
GOODEVE JOHN G	LTC	0-0419750	0463	1
GOODFELLOW CAREY W	2LT	0-1557938	0944	2
GOODFELLOW JOHN J	COL	0-0568334	0767	1
GOODFELLOW MILLARD P	COL	0-0199214	0552	3
GOODFRIED MILTON S	LTC	0-0248040	0763	3
GOODFRIEND ARTHUR	LTC	0-0286300	0767	3
GOODHART ELLA M	2LT	N-0700515	0735	1
GOODHART JACOB A	CPT	0-1821158	0845	2
GOODHART RAYMOND C	LTC	0-0110301	0346	2
GOODHEW JOHN W JR	LTC	0-0309976	1066	3
GOODIN WALTER R	2LT	0-1646202	0944	2
GOODIN WILLIAM L	MAJ	0-1786131	0548	2
GOODINE AMELIA I	1LT	N-0700035	0837	1
GOODING CALLIS C	CW2	W-2214916	0868	1
GOODING HUGH T	CPT	0-0306568	0844	2
GOODING ROBERT	CPT	0-1312841	1046	2
GOODLETT LLOYD	CPT	0-2036477	0754	1
GOODLETT WILLIAM D	CW4	W-2147009	0164	1
GOODLOE GAIL F	MAJ	0-1823587	0968	3
GOODLOE HENRY B	LTC	0-0165273	0648	3
GOODMAN ARTHUR J	1LT	0-1060782	0746	2
GOODMAN ARTHUR L	CPT	0-1167863	1147	2
GOODMAN AUSTIN	WO1	W-2125303	0253	1
GOODMAN BARNETT G	MAJ	0-0341370	0646	2
GOODMAN CALVIN B	MAJ	0-0314344	0447	1
GOODMAN CLARENCE E	MAJ	0-0465204	0165	1
GOODMAN DAVID R	MAJ	0-0992935	1165	1
GOODMAN EDWARD	CPT	0-0331565	1045	2
GOODMAN ERNEST L JR	CW3	W-2151041	1063	1
GOODMAN ETTA R	2LT	N-0736580	0745	1
GOODMAN GEORGE E	CW2	W-2143765	0359	1
GOODMAN GEORGE R	MAJ	0-2049254	0559	1
GOODMAN GERTRUDE F	2LT	N-0783584	0245	1
GOODMAN JACK	LTC	0-1585514	1262	1
GOODMAN JACK A	LTC	0-0240958	0464	3
GOODMAN LESTER B	CW3	W-3150267	0868	1
GOODMAN MARGARET P	1LT	N-0731202	1245	2
GOODMAN MAX J	LTC	0-0273457	0568	3
GOODMAN MERVILLE L	LTC	0-0344650	0957	1
GOODMAN MILTON J	COL	0-0360143	0346	2
GOODMAN NORBERT C	MAJ	0-1885700	1168	1
GOODMAN RICHARD W	CPT	0-1303140	1147	2
GOODMAN ROSCOE	MAJ	0-0181469	0449	1
GOODMAN SAMUEL	LTC	0-1634807	1262	1
GOODMAN SHELDON H	LTC	0-0222645	0257	3
GOODMAN SIDNEY	CPT	0-0490085	0445	2
GOODMAN STELLA H	CPT	N-0757540	0758	2
GOODMAN TRUMAN C	MAJ	0-1554370	0661	1
GOODMAN WILLIAM	1LT	0-1184056	0367	2
GOODMAN WILLIAM A	LTC	0-1316039	1065	1
GOODMAN WINIFRED E	MAJ	L-0204055	0966	3
GOODMANN CHARLES J	1LT	0-1016838	0945	2
GOODNIGHT CURTIS S	MAJ	0-1877305	0266	1
GOODNIGHT HULEN V	CW3	W-2150736	0559	2
GOODNOUGH CLEON W	LTC	0-0308977	0258	3
GOODNOUGH ROBERT C	MAJ	0-1165734	0459	1
GOODPASTER HOLMAN E	2LT	0-0286482	0866	3
GOODPASTURE CHARLES	MAJ	0-0466690	0762	1
GOODRICH ARTHUR F	MAJ	0-0275217	0360	3
GOODRICH DONALD E	CPT	0-0399862	0647	2
GOODRICH GAWIN L	CW3	W-2132763	0162	1
GOODRICH GEORGE A	CW3	W-2149753	0358	1
GOODRICH GEORGE M	COL	0-0242348	0851	3
GOODRICH GEORGE R	LTC	0-1101010	0261	1
GOODRICH HAROLD P	CPT	0-0573197	1162	1
GOODRICH HARVEY B	1LT	0-1588006	0646	2

NAME	GRADE	SVC NO	DATE RET MO YR	RET CODE
GOODRICH JAMES L	CPT	0-09249[illegible]	0146	2
GOODRICH LEWIS F	COL	0-0143753	1045	2
GOODRICH LOUIS R	COL	0-0216110	0959	3
GOODRICH RAYMOND A	LTC	0-1579701	1166	1
GOODRICH SAMUEL J	CW3	W-2144987	0761	1
GOODRICH SHELDON G	CW2	W-2213468	1168	1
GOODRICK CARL H	LTC	0-0320726	0857	2
GOODRIDGE GEORGE L	COL	0-0124739	0156	3
GOODRUM RALPH C	MAJ	0-2036509	1265	1
GOODRUM WILLIAM H	MAJ	0-1103621	0964	1
GOODSON DORRIS M	CW2	W-2104907	0746	2
GOODSON JAMES R	2LT	0-0545755	1045	2
GOODSON OSCAR L	LTC	0-1292311	0164	1
GOODSON PAUL G	MAJ	0-1031555	0556	1
GOODSON ROBERT E	CPT	0-0242933	0354	3
GOODSPEED HOWARD A	LTC	0-0190914	0749	3
GOODSPEED JOHN W	1LT	0-0910685	1143	2
GOODWATER LEROY W	MAJ	0-0136567	0856	3
GOODWIN ARTHUR F	CW3	W-2152093	0965	1
GOODWIN CHARLES L	MAJ	0-0304061	0647	2
GOODWIN CHARLES W	COL	0-0204424	0759	1
GOODWIN CHESTER F	LTC	0-2042809	0261	1
GOODWIN CLINTON T	LTC	0-1011155	0266	3
GOODWIN DANIEL P	LTC	0-0140768	0553	3
GOODWIN DURWARD T	LTC	0-0480144	0367	3
GOODWIN EDWARD L	LTC	0-0913180	0266	3
GOODWIN EDWIN A	LTC	0-0249871	1065	3
GOODWIN ELIZABETH	MAJ	N-0730459	0766	1
GOODWIN ELVIN C	LTC	0-1550388	0762	1
GOODWIN FRANCIS D	COL	0-0279129	0563	1
GOODWIN GEORGE F	COL	0-0271865	1167	3
GOODWIN GEORGE H	COL	0-0290459	0367	3
GOODWIN GEORGE V	2LT	0-1825111	1145	2
GOODWIN HENRY C	CPT	0-1058525	0453	1
GOODWIN HOMER L	COL	0-0279814	0259	3
GOODWIN HUGH W	2LT	0-0547257	0546	2
GOODWIN JACK F	MAJ	0-2262219	0966	1
GOODWIN JAMES F	CPT	0-1107984	1046	2
GOODWIN JOHN W	CPT	0-2203019	0557	2
GOODWIN LEMUEL R	MAJ	0-0955843	0963	1
GOODWIN LEO JR	MAJ	0-0336964	0146	2
GOODWIN LOREN H	COL	0-0269050	0166	3
GOODWIN MAC N	CW2	W-2146331	0259	1
GOODWIN NORMAN E	MAJ	0-0402588	0661	1
GOODWIN NORMAN W	LTC	0-1174579	1061	1
GOODWIN OTIS C	CW3	W-2150068	0564	1
GOODWIN POWELL JR	CW2	W-2210856	0167	1
GOODWIN RANDOLPH	MAJ	0-2030993	0565	1
GOODWIN ROBERT M	1LT	0-0373079	0143	2
GOODWIN ROY L	COL	0-0255146	1067	3
GOODWIN WALTER I	MAJ	0-2210448	0764	1
GOODWIN WILLIAM I	COL	0-0124738	0256	3
GOODWIN WILLIAM M	COL	0-0263950	1059	3
GOODWIN WILLIAM M	CPT	0-0513247	0246	1
GOODWIN WILLIAM R	CPT	0-0253635	0444	2
GOODWIN WILLIAM V	MAJ	0-1693142	0965	1
GOODWIN WILLIAM W	1LT	0-1306837	0545	2
GOODWYN CHARLES A	LTC	0-0278187	0946	2
GOODYEAR AUGUSTUS S	COL	0-0165991	0547	2
GOODYEAR EMIL S	MAJ	0-0496416	0945	2
GOOGE JAMES P	COL	0-0269092	0968	3
GOOGE PAUL H	COL	0-0115405	0956	3
GOOGINS DANFORTH M	MAJ	0-0271365	0365	3
GOOLMAN GEORGE V	LTC	0-1298217	0767	1
GOOLRICK W K JR	MAJ	0-0438144	1047	2
GOOLSBY CHARLES E	LTC	0-1588596	1162	1
GOOLSBY LACY R	CPT	0-1588008	0355	1
GOOLSBY LONNIE L	LTC	0-1012903	1061	1
GOOLSBY MINA E	MAJ	N-0727300	1268	1
GOOLSBY ROBERT R	MAJ	0-0917963	0863	2
GOOMBS FRANK B	CW2	W-2210006	0966	1
GOON THEODORE J	1LT	0-1312543	1145	2
GOORLEY JOHN T	LTC	0-0327231	0467	3
GOOTNICK ABRAHAM	CPT	0-0346966	0246	2
GOOZEE WILLIAM W	CPT	0-0985924	0361	1

NAME	GRADE	SVC NO	DATE RET MO YR	RET CODE
GOPCEVIC RADE P	1LT	0-1296849	1054	1
GORANSON ROBERT A	LTC	0-1306838	0264	1
GORBEA RAFAEL	MAJ	0-1285231	0960	1
GORBY WILLIAM R	CW4	W-2151154	1267	1
GORDEN DONALD L	MAJ	0-1592228	0255	1
GORDIN GORDON SR	CW2	W-2144112	0657	1
GORDINER RALPH H	CW2	W-2147114	0661	1
GORDINIER TRUMAN W	LTC	0-1182370	0263	1
GORDON ALGERNON C	1LT	0-2003852	0853	2
GORDON ALVIN H	1LT	0-1303712	0960	1
GORDON BERTHA M	CPT	N-0759276	0846	1
GORDON CHARLES	MAJ	0-0501691	1047	1
GORDON CHARLES B JR	CW2	W-2144446	0465	1
GORDON CHARLES C	CPT	0-0987057	0257	2
GORDON CHARLES S	MAJ	0-1322441	0159	1
GORDON CHARLES W	COL	0-0222103	0158	3
GORDON CHESTER B	CW3	W-2150173	1061	1
GORDON CLARY D	CW3	W-2143792	0659	1
GORDON CLYDE W	CPT	0-0194099	0755	3
GORDON DONALD L	MAJ	0-1936107	0566	1
GORDON EARL O JR	LTC	0-1946738	0665	2
GORDON EDWARD S	MAJ	0-0286555	0646	2
GORDON EDWARD W JR	MAJ	0-1645607	0161	1
GORDON FRANK L	CPT	0-1590497	0446	2
GORDON FREDERICK	LTC	0-0451110	0856	1
GORDON GERALD L	MAJ	0-0281252	0768	3
GORDON GERALD M	LTC	0-2035220	0568	1
GORDON GILES D	LTC	0-1548420	0661	1
GORDON HAROLD L	LTC	0-0425898	1060	1
GORDON HARRY D	2LT	0-0389469	0343	2
GORDON HARRY H	CW2	W-2143910	0764	1
GORDON HENRY A	LTC	0-1056381	1264	1
GORDON HOWARD L	CW2	W-2101123	0251	1
GORDON IVAN A SR	CW2	W-2105920	1048	2
GORDON JAMES	CPT	0-1689692	0246	2
GORDON JAMES	CW2	W-2111204	1061	2
GORDON JAMES A	MAJ	0-2035093	0861	1
GORDON JAMES M	CPT	0-0485276	1044	2
GORDON JAMES W	LTC	0-1546575	0163	1
GORDON JESSE	CW2	W-2145076	0157	1
GORDON JOSEPH R JR	LTC	0-1016892	1162	1
GORDON KATHRYN W	MAJ	N-0724832	1061	1
GORDON MARION B	CPT	0-0990654	0661	1
GORDON MARK H	LTC	0-1167443	0763	1
GORDON MAURICE	CPT	0-0925487	0745	2
GORDON MORTON	2LT	0-1080786	0445	2
GORDON MURDOC A	CW3	W-2142790	1160	1
GORDON NATHAN G	CPT	0-0369516	1045	2
GORDON OREN S	MAJ	0-2012748	0559	1
GORDON OTHELLO	LTC	0-1110509	0968	3
GORDON PAUL H	LTC	0-2010565	0562	1
GORDON PETER	MAJ	0-2039549	0363	1
GORDON PHILIP	LTC	0-1550806	0267	1
GORDON RICHARD	WO1	W-2106507	0447	1
GORDON RICHARD C	MAJ	0-1104687	1055	1
GORDON RICHARD H	MAJ	0-0962387	1060	1
GORDON ROBERT A	LTC	0-0503873	0257	1
GORDON ROBERT R	LTC	0-0175093	0162	3
GORDON ROY T	CPT	0-1103656	0262	2
GORDON ROYAL G	CW3	W-2144730	1263	1
GORDON SAMUEL A JR	COL	0-0247399	0754	2
GORDON SAMUEL J	MAJ	0-1588597	0660	1
GORDON SAMUEL M	LTC	0-0235698	0958	3
GORDON SIDNEY U	MAJ	0-1598971	0263	1
GORDON STANLEY B	MAJ	0-1339352	0265	1
GORDON THEODORA A	CW4	W-2101016	1055	1
GORDON THOMAS C	WO1	W-2120681	0459	1
GORDON VIRGIL C	COL	0-0207502	0159	3
GORDON WALLACE H	CPT	0-0444151	1046	2
GORDON WALTER L	1LT	0-1174300	1044	2
GORDON WALTER S	LTC	0-0484495	1264	3
GORDON WILLIAM H JR	1LT	0-1646203	0546	2
GORDON WILLIAM J	MAJ	0-0271510	0963	3
GORDON WILLIAM V	LTC	0-1549951	0462	1
GORDON WILSON	LTC	0-1323121	0163	1

NAME	GRADE	SVC NO	DATE RET MO YR	RET CODE
GORDY RAYMOND E	CW3	W-2149338	0264	1
GORDY SAMUEL T	MAJ	0-0494692	0845	2
GORE AARON M	CPT	0-0495625	0250	1
GORE ALFRED JR	LTC	0-1920042	1168	1
GORE FRANK R	CW3	W-2108537	0163	1
GORE HILDRETH C	CPT	0-0494988	0447	1
GORE LAWRENCE L	CPT	0-0280874	0960	3
GORE MAHLON L	LTC	0-0225357	1056	3
GORE MELVIN I	1LT	0-1319089	0146	2
GORE RAYMOND S	CW3	W-2135056	0154	1
GORE ROY C	MAJ	0-0119897	0754	3
GORE WILLIAM A	LTC	0-0279670	0646	2
GORE WOODROW	MAJ	0-1822129	0261	2
GORECKI FRANK	CW3	W-2142100	0461	1
GOREHAM JAMES N	LTC	0-1174580	0763	1
GORELICK ALBERT P	MAJ	0-0979160	0562	1
GOREN SIDNEY M	CPT	0-0478551	0845	2
GOREY GEORGE F	COL	0-0118673	0654	3
GORGENSEN WILLIAM H	CW3	W-2141290	1262	1
GORGODIAN HENRY	COL	0-0264200	1046	2
GORHAM CHARLES S	MAJ	0-0113083	0452	3
GORHAM FORDYCE	MAJ	0-1283940	0446	2
GORHAM FRANCIS J	LTC	0-0522966	0464	1
GORHAM JOSEPH	CPT	0-1644371	0947	2
GORIN NORMAN	CW4	W-2144327	0967	1
GORING CHARLES	MAJ	0-1315422	0954	1
GORING HAROLD J	CW4	W-2141765	0764	1
GORING JACK F	MAJ	0-0490897	0644	2
GORK L HENRY	COL	0-0708577	0652	3
GORMAN ANGELINE L	1LT	N-0700070	1039	2
GORMAN CORNELIUS	COL	0-0252490	0167	3
GORMAN DAVID	MAJ	0-0409877	0946	2
GORMAN DAVID B	LTC	0-0285716	0244	2
GORMAN DAVID H	MAJ	0-0158151	0648	3
GORMAN ELMER R	LTC	0-1036163	0367	1
GORMAN FRANCIS J	CPT	0-1289068	0946	2
GORMAN FRANK H	CPT	0-1063065	1147	2
GORMAN GERARD	LTC	0-1578532	0868	3
GORMAN GERARD F	CPT	0-1533790	1046	2
GORMAN HENRY A	MAJ	0-0149222	0948	3
GORMAN HOWARD A	LTC	0-1573249	0364	1
GORMAN J FRANCIS	LTC	0-0417883	0962	1
GORMAN JAMES E	LTC	0-1339631	0966	1
GORMAN JOHN A	LTC	0-0175253	0858	3
GORMAN JOHN B	CPT	0-1318663	0446	2
GORMAN JOHN J	MAJ	0-1686775	0663	1
GORMAN JOHN J	CW3	W-2206868	1167	1
GORMAN JOHN M	1LT	0-0453465	0944	2
GORMAN JOHN W	COL	0-0565466	0868	1
GORMAN JOSEPH P	LTC	0-0394914	1161	1
GORMAN LAURENCE G	LTC	0-0249282	0262	3
GORMAN LEONARD J	CPT	0-1541595	1044	2
GORMAN LESLIE F	CPT	0-0344204	0854	1
GORMAN PETER J	CW3	W-2149110	0466	1
GORMAN THOMAS	LTC	0-1012136	1165	1
GORMAN WILLIAM A	LTC	0-1114946	0563	1
GORMAN WILLIAM J	LTC	0-0266623	0868	3
GORMELY JOHN E	LTC	0-1174868	0164	1
GORMLEY DANIEL J JR	MAJ	0-2205200	1067	1
GORMLEY HARRY	MAJ	0-0265324	1053	3
GORMLEY WILLIAM J	2LT	0-1692626	0447	2
GORMLIE GEORGE F	LTC	0-0383912	0161	1
GORMSEN ALFRED N	COL	0-0253410	0864	3
GORMSEN NORMAN E	CPT	0-0390029	0645	2
GORNTO MILLSON R	MAJ	0-0333973	0258	1
GORRELL REX W	CW2	W-2106274	0750	2
GORRELL RUSSELL D	CW2	W-2151204	1268	2
GORRILL ATHOL R	LTC	0-0150619	1053	3
GORRILL GALEN A	LTC	0-0244585	0258	3
GORRY MICHAEL F	2LT	0-0970987	0452	2
GORSCH RUDOLPH V	COL	0-0172530	0545	2
GORSKI THADDEUS M	MAJ	0-0237786	0546	2
GORSKY JACK A	CW2	W-2151027	0766	2
GORSLINE EARL E JR	CW4	W-2122614	1067	3
GORSUCH CHARLES B	CPT	0-0522883	0746	2

NAME	GRADE	SVC NO	DATE RET MO YR	RET CODE
GORSUCH ROBERT D	CW3	W-2146773	0666	1
GORTER RUSSELL T	CPT	0-2287870	0260	1
GORTON ALDEN D	LTC	0-0432417	0562	1
GORTON ANNA M A	1LT	L-0210159	0947	2
GORTON DONALD G	COL	0-0268295	1065	3
GORTON ELLIS H	LTC	0-0176765	0262	3
GORUM JAMES R	CW3	W-2144948	0463	1
GORWODA KARL F	MAJ	0-1643602	1060	1
GOSCH GEORGE JR	LTC	0-0297981	0866	3
GOSCH LENERT C	CPT	0-0294960	0344	2
GOSCIEWSKI ANTONI K	1LT	0-0233393	0847	1
GOSE EARLE M	CPT	0-0504175	1053	1
GOSHKO JOHN M	1LT	0-4035943	1162	2
GOSHORN EDWARD B	LTC	0-0510412	1154	3
GOSHORN FRANK R	1LT	0-1112729	0246	2
GOSLEE CHARLES F	LTC	0-1798665	0762	1
GOSLIN HAROLD W	CW4	W-2105060	0560	1
GOSMAN WILLIAM M	LTC	0-0309598	0463	1
GOSNELL JESSE L	CPT	0-2011269	0257	1
GOSNELL JOHN D	MAJ	0-0503352	0156	1
GOSORN LOUIS M	COL	0-0323238	0855	2
GOSS HAROLD L	B G	0-0201505	0750	3
GOSS JAMES H	CPT	0-1308764	0747	2
GOSS LAWRENCE H JR	MAJ	0-1937101	0668	1
GOSS LEO E	CPT	0-1300022	0954	2
GOSS MARSHALL J	COL	0-0230147	0360	3
GOSS THEODORE C	MAJ	0-1175444	0355	2
GOSS VERNON V	1LT	0-0384067	1045	2
GOSSARD PETER D	2LT	0-0536502	1045	2
GOSSARD SYLVESTER	CW3	W-2143634	0164	1
GOSSE ANTHONY C	2LT	0-1545602	0845	2
GOSSEN CHARLES G	CW3	W-2147392	0565	1
GOSSEN ROBERT C	1LT	0-1546865	1146	2
GOSSERT GEORGE C	CPT	0-0946693	1062	1
GOSSETT EVERETT J	CW3	W-3150519	1168	1
GOSSETT GEORGE M	LTC	0-0921396	0158	2
GOSSETT JAMES C	MAJ	0-2025629	0761	1
GOSSETT JOHN A	MAJ	0-0326710	0468	3
GOSSIAUX JOSEPH A	1LT	0-0885643	0953	1
GOSSMAN ALBERT J JR	2LT	0-2010680	0346	2
GOSWICK M S	CW4	W-2149857	0168	2
GOTAAS HAROLD B	COL	0-0242819	1066	3
GOTAY EMETERIO	COL	0-0156743	0352	3
GOTERA MARTIN	2LT	0-1896684	0248	2
GOTHAM FRED C	MAJ	0-1646204	0461	1
GOTHARD JOHN W	CPT	0-1597016	0547	2
GOTHIA MACK J JR	CW2	W-2211731	0666	1
GOTHOLD DAVID J	COL	0-0203239	1044	2
GOTT LEONARD K	MAJ	0-1044228	0859	1
GOTTARDI CARL E	LTC	0-1913300	1068	1
GOTTER FRED B	LTC	0-1323560	1163	1
GOTTESMAN JOSEPH L	MAJ	0-0494216	0446	2
GOTTFREDSON DAVID	COL	0-0233589	0644	2
GOTTFRIED CHARLES J	MAJ	0-0307613	0146	2
GOTTLIEB MEYER P	LTC	0-0298685	0166	3
GOTTLOB JANET A	MAJ	N-0779249	1263	1
GOTTSACKER HAROLD A	1LT	0-1321115	0845	2
GOTTSCHALK ALBERT O	CPT	0-0296181	0447	2
GOTTSCHALK JERE L	CPT	0-1322331	0747	2
GOTTSCHALK WALTER R	LTC	0-0279023	0667	3
GOTTSCHALL IRVIN B	CW3	W-2206590	0468	2
GOTTSCHALL ROBERT	LTC	0-1634813	1163	1
GOTZIAN HENRY L	LTC	0-1551215	0862	1
GOUCH CHESTER L	MAJ	0-1695748	0258	1
GOUCHER CHARLES A JR	MAJ	0-1015103	0161	1
GOUDEMOND ANTHONIE J	MAJ	0-1104176	1057	1
GOUDEY KEITH H	1LT	0-0476570	0545	2
GOUDREAU LEODORE	CW4	W-2113434	0959	1
GOUGEON EDWARD P	MAJ	0-2263058	0465	1
GOUGH EDWARD A	CPT	0-0199817	0648	3
GOUGH JAMES A	1LT	0-1031556	0144	2
GOUGH JAMES F JR	1LT	0-1592866	1046	2
GOUGH KENNETH E	MAJ	0-0969507	1267	1
GOUGH WILLIAM G	LTC	0-0103228	0656	3
GOUGHER ROSE L	MAJ	N-0725865	0867	1

NAME	GRADE	SVC NO	DATE RET MO YR	RET CODE
GOUGUET LOUIS J E	LTC	0-0102984	0648	3
GOULARD LOWELL J	MAJ	0-1293941	1146	2
GOULARTE JOSEPH C	LTC	0-1040727	0665	1
GOULD ADRIAN G	COL	0-0209448	1052	3
GOULD CHARLES K	COL	0-0298119	0764	3
GOULD EDWARD A	COL	0-0222107	1046	2
GOULD EDWARD J	MAJ	0-2200113	1065	1
GOULD ERNEST E	CPT	0-0212871	0264	3
GOULD FRANK E	MAJ	0-0181426	0654	3
GOULD FRANK F	1LT	0-1283941	0546	2
GOULD FRED W	CW3	W-3200309	1266	1
GOULD HAROLD S	COL	0-0297957	1060	1
GOULD JEDEDIAH	CPT	0-0375194	0352	1
GOULD JERROLD	LTC	0-0349711	1262	1
GOULD JOHN A	MAJ	0-1062679	0765	1
GOULD JOHN D	1LT	0-1080107	1045	2
GOULD JOHN E	CPT	0-0351148	1044	2
GOULD JOHN J	CPT	0-0545759	1045	2
GOULD JOHN W	2LT	0-1016212	0844	2
GOULD KINGDON J	2LT	0-2009589	0247	2
GOULD LEGRAND A	CPT	0-1303879	1045	2
GOULD RALPH C	CPT	0-1167446	0461	1
GOULD RALPH P	COL	0-0237144	0265	3
GOULD RICHARD G	CPT	0-0530597	0846	2
GOULD RUSSELL L	CPT	0-0343320	1044	2
GOULD VERNON G	LTC	0-0188814	0554	3
GOULD WILFRED E	LTC	0-0217801	1061	3
GOULD WILLIAM J JR	1LT	0-1646206	0450	1
GOULDING MELVIN K	LTC	0-1999326	0868	1
GOULDING VICTOR H	1LT	0-1101458	0845	2
GOULET BERTRAND L	MAJ	0-0194659	0650	3
GOULET ROBERT J	MAJ	0-1175721	0664	1
GOULET STEPHEN C	CW4	W-2144279	0168	1
GOULSBY THEODORE	COL	0-0224019	0952	3
GOURD BERNARD M	CW2	W-2150883	0661	1
GOURGUES HAROLD W	COL	0-0282267	0457	1
GOURLEY JAMES L	CW2	W-2150898	0764	1
GOURLEY REX S	CPT	0-1049175	0845	2
GOUTIEREZ JAMES A	CW4	W-2152020	1167	1
GOVE GEORGE M	CPT	0-0253686	0653	3
GOVER ARTHUR F	LTC	0-1642117	1066	3
GOVER JESSE	MAJ	0-0111660	0648	3
GOW FRANCES R	2LT	N-0726512	1145	1
GOW RALPH F	COL	0-0236244	0463	3
GOWAN JAMES F	MAJ	0-0974673	1265	1
GOWANS ALBERT S	WO1	W-2119847	1047	2
GOWEN EDWARD J	1LT	0-1039649	0446	2
GOWEN FREDERICK	CW3	W-2115841	0457	1
GOWEN HARRY W	1LT	0-4032495	0757	2
GOWEN MAX F	1LT	0-1318535	0546	2
GOWER JOE R	MAJ	0-1032347	1265	1
GOWER WALTER R	MAJ	0-0243059	0864	3
GOWIN VIVIAN W	MAJ	N-0744929	0665	1
GOWKA WALTER W	2LT	0-1106172	0144	2
GOWLAND JOSEPH S	CPT	0-0918386	0246	2
GOYCOCHEA ALLAN G	CPT	0-5304112	0666	2
GOYETTE LINUS F G	COL	0-0374053	0667	3
GOZA RUFUS J	MAJ	0-0253654	0444	2
GRAB JOHN A	LTC	0-0154326	0755	3
GRABER EDWARD A	MAJ	0-0309231	0647	2
GRABER FRANK H	WO1	W-2130695	0147	1
GRABER LOUIS C	MAJ	0-1697764	0546	2
GRABERT EDWARD T	1LT	0-0931956	0346	2
GRABFIELD G PHILIP	COL	0-0163556	1045	2
GRABIAK GEORGE W	COL	0-0526972	0864	3
GRABICKI JOSEPH F	CW3	W-2142392	0758	1
GRABILL JOSEPH A	CPT	0-0458720	0546	2
GRABLE CARL F	CW3	W-2144203	0261	1
GRABOWSKI HENRY	LTC	0-1080860	0262	1
GRABSKI EDWARD J	CW3	W-2207588	0868	1
GRACE ANGUS O	CPT	0-1683863	0845	2
GRACE CHARLES W JR	MAJ	0-1031557	1058	1
GRACE CORNELIUS	CPT	0-1299556	0246	2
GRACE GEORGE B	LTC	0-0415859	0863	1
GRACE GEORGE L	LTC	0-1553454	1262	1

NAME	GRADE	SVC NO	DATE RET MO YR	RET CODE
GRACE GEORGE T	CW4	W-2128853	0557	1
GRACE HUBERT C	CW3	W-2112169	1154	1
GRACE LUCILLE A	1LT	N-0703666	0245	1
GRACE WILLIAM G	MAJ	0-1180193	0465	1
GRACE WILLIAM P JR	COL	0-0269827	1068	3
GRACE WILLIAM S	1LT	0-1047986	0447	2
GRACIE EDWIN F	LTC	0-0452527	1060	1
GRACIE RAYMOND	CW3	W-2203267	0565	1
GRACY BRAINARD B	CPT	0-1166495	1046	2
GRACYK EDWIN C	2LT	0-1822130	0944	2
GRADALL GLEN P	CPT	0-0473963	0450	1
GRADO JOHN SR	MAJ	0-0497384	0949	1
GRADWELL GEORGE H	MAJ	0-1014977	0761	1
GRADY EDWARD F	LTC	0-0401447	1160	1
GRADY GLEN E	LTC	0-0477747	0966	1
GRADY JAMES W	CPT	0-0333150	0146	2
GRADY JOHN E	MAJ	0-0277451	1163	3
GRADY JOHN F	LTC	0-0292249	0654	1
GRADY JOHN W	COL	0-0378189	1160	1
GRADY PAUL J	COL	0-0326200	1060	3
GRADY ROBERT V	LTC	0-1296683	1061	1
GRADY WILLIAM H	MAJ	0-1685504	1263	1
GRADY WILLIAM J	CPT	0-1053147	0246	2
GRAEBENER JOHN P	COL	0-0346127	0961	1
GRAEBER DON F	2LT	0-2055903	0845	2
GRAEBER JOHN N	LTC	0-1052787	0268	3
GRAEF FREDERICK JR	COL	0-0318024	0758	2
GRAEFF GEORGE R	LTC	0-1043968	1265	1
GRAEN LLOYD G	CW3	W-2149068	0263	1
GRAETZ MARION	LTC	0-0354842	0766	3
GRAF ERNEST W	MAJ	0-0206077	1046	1
GRAF FRANK J	COL	0-0225221	1166	2
GRAF GLENN F	LTC	0-0228567	0162	3
GRAF JEROME A	CPT	0-0236829	1063	3
GRAF LLOYD J	1LT	0-2010337	0346	2
GRAF ROBERT W	MAJ	0-1335273	1164	1
GRAFF EDWARD F	1LT	0-1304519	0646	2
GRAFF EDWARD S	MAJ	0-1691140	0146	2
GRAFF HUGH A	LTC	0-0240274	1264	3
GRAFF LESTER A	CW2	W-2212951	0867	1
GRAFF RUTH R	2LT	N-0721877	0645	1
GRAFFAGNINO PETER C	MAJ	0-0425300	1046	2
GRAFFAM CHARLES A	LTC	0-0316828	1047	2
GRAFFILE FORREST I	CW3	W-2141927	0763	1
GRAFFLIN ARTHUR C	CPT	0-0472392	0644	2
GRAFFUM ROBERT T	MAJ	0-1922507	0365	1
GRAFTON CLEALON V	LTC	0-0213140	0450	2
GRAFTON ELDON C	LTC	0-0224966	1061	3
GRAFTON WILLIAM D	2LT	0-1038042	1044	2
GRAGARD EVERETT JR	CPT	0-1543105	0845	2
GRAGG JACK E	MAJ	0-0271136	0368	3
GRAHAM CHARLES A SR	2LT	0-2013989	0267	3
GRAHAM ANTHONY M	LTC	0-1288045	0463	1
GRAHAM ASA J	CW4	W-2001805	0855	3
GRAHAM BENJAMIN H	MAJ	0-1634815	0457	1
GRAHAM BERT F JR	CPT	0-0968260	0361	1
GRAHAM BERT W	1LT	0-1994609	0146	2
GRAHAM CHARLES H	LTC	0-0273936	1065	2
GRAHAM CLYDE H	MAJ	0-0290060	0962	3
GRAHAM CLYDE L	2LT	0-0278856	0851	3
GRAHAM DALE M	CW3	W-2209273	0568	1
GRAHAM DARL H	CW3	W-2142232	0259	1
GRAHAM DAVID	LTC	0-1172878	0664	1
GRAHAM DAVID F	LTC	0-1109960	0365	2
GRAHAM DORRIS C	LTC	0-0223685	0763	3
GRAHAM DOUGLAS R	1LT	0-0956091	1053	2
GRAHAM DRENNAN C	1LT	0-1796078	0758	1
GRAHAM EDWARD E	CPT	0-0275437	0854	1
GRAHAM ELIOT S	LTC	0-0291530	0868	3
GRAHAM ELIZABETH	MAJ	L-0400521	0565	3
GRAHAM ELMER C	CPT	0-2037974	0963	2
GRAHAM EUGENE F	1LT	0-1550389	0844	2
GRAHAM EULOS E	1LT	0-0976864	0357	1
GRAHAM EZRA E	LTC	0-0277055	0449	1
GRAHAM FRANK D	LTC	0-1995095	0159	1

NAME	GRADE	SVC NO	DATE RET MO YR	RET CODE
GRAHAM FRANK K	1LT	0-1032082	0945	2
GRAHAM FRED L	COL	0-0245497	1262	3
GRAHAM GEORGE A	1LT	0-0412922	0642	2
GRAHAM GEORGE A JR	LTC	0-0353393	1162	1
GRAHAM HAROLD G	CPT	0-0250606	0762	3
GRAHAM HAROLD M	LTC	0-0162764	0648	3
GRAHAM HAROLD W	CW3	W-2207566	0167	1
GRAHAM HARRY L	CPT	0-0474461	0347	2
GRAHAM HENRY S	MAJ	0-0222282	1053	3
GRAHAM HERSHAL M	MAJ	0-1336637	0561	1
GRAHAM HOWARD O	COL	0-0119591	0151	3
GRAHAM HURLIS V	MAJ	0-0966819	0961	1
GRAHAM JAMES M	MAJ	0-0122816	0250	3
GRAHAM JAMES M	LTC	0-1634817	1155	1
GRAHAM JAMES R	CW3	W-2211388	0868	1
GRAHAM JAMES W	LTC	0-1597453	0763	1
GRAHAM JIMMIE	1LT	0-0994682	1054	2
GRAHAM JOHN F	LTC	0-0252713	1162	3
GRAHAM JOSEPH JR	1LT	0-0416018	0246	2
GRAHAM JOSEPH K	MAJ	0-0973838	0163	1
GRAHAM JOSEPH M	CW3	W-2141571	0762	1
GRAHAM JOSEPH N	MAJ	0-1314004	0258	1
GRAHAM JOY M	CPT	0-0216642	0164	3
GRAHAM JULIAN O	LTC	0-0175022	0458	3
GRAHAM LAWRENCE M	COL	0-0102195	0648	3
GRAHAM LEE W JR	LTC	0-2033822	0268	1
GRAHAM LLOYD O	COL	0-0294445	1267	3
GRAHAM LLOYD L	LTC	0-1110514	0868	3
GRAHAM LOIS D	CPT	N-0788681	0447	1
GRAHAM LYLE G	CW2	W-2111674	0547	2
GRAHAM MARGARET	MAJ	N-0737187	0662	1
GRAHAM MARY C	1LT	R-0000638	0346	1
GRAHAM NORVAL M	1LT	0-1311883	0845	2
GRAHAM RALPH F	COL	0-0345891	0860	1
GRAHAM RALPH M	MAJ	0-0194943	1162	3
GRAHAM RICHARD S	MAJ	0-1300436	0247	2
GRAHAM RICHARD W	LTC	0-0964394	0761	1
GRAHAM ROBERT B	LTC	0-2006062	0663	1
GRAHAM ROBERT C	LTC	0-0275336	0544	2
GRAHAM ROBERT C	LTC	0-0288417	1166	3
GRAHAM ROBERT H	MAJ	0-0155681	0548	2
GRAHAM RONALD M	CW2	W-2146765	0961	1
GRAHAM RUFUS F	LTC	0-0111636	0648	3
GRAHAM SIMON N	LTC	0-0293554	1163	2
GRAHAM THOMAS F	CPT	0-0541139	1147	2
GRAHAM THOMAS L	MAJ	0-0221158	1058	3
GRAHAM THOMAS P	MAJ	0-0183322	0647	2
GRAHAM WALTER C	LTC	0-0330260	0946	2
GRAHAM WESLEY J	1LT	0-2007651	1153	1
GRAHAM WILLIAM F	1LT	0-1177812	0246	2
GRAHAM WILLIAM L	CPT	0-0979208	1160	1
GRAHAM WILLIAM M	MAJ	0-0990451	1163	1
GRAHAM WILLIAM T JR	1LT	0-0452704	0844	2
GRAHEK FRANK E	CW2	W-2145885	1055	1
GRAHL CHARLES H	B G	0-0234562	0960	1
GRAHL MAURICE R	WO1	W-2102950	1044	2
GRAHLFS ARMIN L	LTC	0-0178014	0650	1
GRAHLMAN JOSEPH S	MAJ	0-0262034	0267	3
GRAHN CLARENCE A	LTC	0-0248593	1263	3
GRAHN PETER M JR	LTC	0-0405714	0860	1
GRALAK VICTOR H	CPT	0-0358187	0145	2
GRALINSKI ALFRED	CPT	0-1289899	0355	1
GRAM RALPH L	LTC	0-0343477	0260	1
GRAM WILLIAM D	CW2	W-2144399	0461	1
GRAMATA GEORGE	1LT	0-0509322	0554	2
GRAMBORT EVERETT A	COL	0-0359736	0361	1
GRAMER WILLIAM L	COL	0-0260681	0166	3
GRAMLICH FRANCIS J	MAJ	0-2005406	0959	1
GRAMLICH WILLIAM	MAJ	0-0373297	0253	1
GRAMLIGH WILBUR A	LTC	0-0466399	1267	2
GRAMLING CHARLES A	LTC	0-0262205	0462	3
GRAMLING ROY M JR	LTC	0-0390536	0454	2
GRAMM HAROLD	MAJ	0-0959408	0465	1
GRAMMAR GLIDEWELL	MAJ	0-1644377	0159	1
GRAMMER GEORGE W	CPT	0-2018873	0857	1

NAME	GRADE	SVC NO	DATE RET MO YR	RET CODE
GRAMMER WAYMON D	CPT	0-1822991	0158	1
GRAMMONT WILLARD C	CW2	W-2144240	0658	1
GRAMONT RAYMOND J	MAJ	0-0450874	1059	1
GRAMPIETRO ROBERT F	1LT	0-1289854	0352	2
GRAMS JOSEPH	1LT	0-2006955	0846	2
GRAMSTAD JIM	MAJ	0-1874622	0865	1
GRAMSTORFF THEODORE	COL	0-0258197	0962	3
GRAN CONRAD L	COL	0-0263402	0463	3
GRANADE JAMES N JR	LTC	0-0354523	0859	1
GRANADE JOE C	WO1	W-2121844	1045	2
GRANBACKA ALEXANDER	CPT	0-0233030	0347	1
GRANBERG MARTHA G	MAJ	N-0722112	1065	1
GRANBERRY HAROLD E	LTC	0-0301726	0260	3
GRANDE GERARD F	LTC	0-1555819	1162	1
GRANDE JAMES L	CPT	0-2007263	0758	1
GRANDE NICHOLAS	CW2	W-2145436	0460	1
GRANDEA ANDRES G	1LT	0-2027388	0353	1
GRANDJEAN WALTER I	COL	0-1281570	1168	1
GRANDSTROM JOHN L	MAJ	0-1542209	0760	1
GRANDY LAURENS B	MAJ	0-1824302	0261	1
GRANECKI WALTER Z	LTC	0-1106173	0162	1
GRANFIELD EUGENE G	MAJ	0-1045757	0546	2
GRANGER AVERY L	MAJ	0-1116963	0163	1
GRANGER DAVID E	CW2	W-2109424	0148	1
GRANGER EARLE G	COL	0-0263843	0146	2
GRANGER EUGENE A	LTC	0-1175134	0762	1
GRANGER HOWARD C	CW3	W-2142841	1158	1
GRANGER ROBERT H	CW2	W-2208805	0965	1
GRANING MARTIN C	1LT	0-1547314	0446	2
GRANITO DANTE	CW3	W-2141291	0257	1
GRANNIS JOHN A	CPT	0-2102800	1262	1
GRANNIS ROBERT L	MAJ	0-1826411	1162	1
GRANO MARIO	CPT	0-2041102	0747	2
GRANQUIST KARL J	1LT	0-0312308	0645	2
GRANRATH CLARENCE W	MAJ	0-2212038	0865	1
GRANRUD WALTER H	LTC	0-0425279	0161	1
GRANSON NICHOLAS	LTC	0-1284010	1262	1
GRANT ALEXANDER	MAJ	0-2053830	0565	1
GRANT ANGUS G	MAJ	0-0491022	0145	2
GRANT ANTHONY H	MAJ	0-2033054	0662	1
GRANT ARTHUR B	COL	0-0239659	0163	3
GRANT ARTHUR F	CPT	0-1703823	0449	1
GRANT ARTHUR T	2LT	0-1642912	0944	2
GRANT ARVIN W	LTC	0-0325402	1065	3
GRANT BEN E	COL	0-0234887	0255	3
GRANT BEN R	CW3	W-2146541	1064	1
GRANT BENSON	LTC	0-1050684	1162	1
GRANT BYRON W	CPT	0-1001350	0246	2
GRANT CHARLES C	COL	0-0308106	0566	1
GRANT CLYDE E	COL	0-0290217	0568	3
GRANT DAVID	MAJ	0-2033571	0561	1
GRANT DONALD I	MAJ	0-1050715	0960	1
GRANT EARLY T	2LT	0-0263858	0355	3
GRANT EDWARD C	LTC	0-0395183	0960	1
GRANT ERNEST H	MAJ	0-0241267	1057	3
GRANT FRANCIS J	CW3	W-2146057	0162	1
GRANT FRANKLIN E	1LT	0-1336371	0950	2
GRANT FRED S JR	LTC	0-0262477	0565	3
GRANT FREDERICK	LTC	0-0372476	0460	2
GRANT GEORGE O	CPT	0-1012603	0657	1
GRANT GILBERT R	CPT	0-1052364	1045	2
GRANT GLEN D	MAJ	0-0446990	0660	1
GRANT GORDON H	CW3	W-2141292	0562	1
GRANT GORDON P	MAJ	0-0306789	1266	3
GRANT HAROLD C	1LT	0-0969165	0254	2
GRANT HAROLD D	CW3	W-2148147	0761	2
GRANT HAROLD O	CW4	W-2000726	0768	3
GRANT HARRY	CW2	W-2150186	0663	1
GRANT HENRY B	CPT	0-0462714	0146	2
GRANT HOWARD E	MAJ	0-1016322	0260	1
GRANT JAMES A	COL	0-0102832	0648	3
GRANT JAMES A G JR	CPT	0-0563150	0464	2
GRANT JAMES W	LTC	0-0382747	0859	1
GRANT JOHN E	1LT	0-1882452	0554	2
GRANT JOHN H	1LT	0-2049255	0746	2

NAME	GRADE	SVC NO	DATE RET MO YR	RET CODE
GRANT JOHN N	CPT	0-0337629	0754	3
GRANT JOHN W	COL	0-0918906	1064	3
GRANT JOSEPH V JR	CW2	W-2144453	0561	1
GRANT LUTHER J	CPT	0-1894490	0147	2
GRANT MILTON N	LTC	0-1586618	0866	3
GRANT PAUL F	CW2	W-2147893	0457	1
GRANT PETER H	MAJ	0-0995581	0766	1
GRANT RAYMOND J	CPT	0-0358184	1043	2
GRANT RICHARD B JR	LTC	0-0290658	0545	2
GRANT ROBERT F	MAJ	0-1642121	0264	1
GRANT VIRGIL V	LTC	0-1582233	0263	1
GRANTHAM ALBA M	1LT	0-0462642	0344	2
GRANTHAM HENRY H	LTC	0-1311642	0466	1
GRANTHAM ROY E	LTC	0-0305719	0267	3
GRANTZ IRWIN A	LTC	0-0278614	0459	3
GRANVILLE GEORGE G	CW4	W-2145182	0566	1
GRANVILLE JOHN C	1LT	0-1173624	0146	2
GRAPATIN JOHN W	LTC	0-0435526	1067	3
GRAPEK HARVEY L	1LT	0-1051151	1045	2
GRAPES HOWARD F	CW3	W-2149837	0866	1
GRAPP HAROLD H	CW2	W-2142842	0356	1
GRASS EDWARDS J	COL	0-0238970	0757	3
GRASS MELVIN F	1LT	0-1795893	0445	2
GRASS PHILIP M	MAJ	0-2033957	0862	1
GRASS SAMUEL	CPT	0-0500752	1045	2
GRASSEY CHARLES	CPT	0-0145945	0249	3
GRASSL JOHN E	COL	0-0256228	0260	1
GRASSO LEONARD	2LT	T-0224371	1143	2
GRASSO MICHAEL L	CPT	0-0289715	0762	3
GRATER VINCENT M	1LT	0-0924037	0346	2
GRATHWOL JOHN D	WO1	W-2132829	0747	2
GRATRICK WILFORD D	COL	0-0322438	0764	1
GRATZER GEORGE M	CPT	0-5709778	0968	2
GRAU BRYSON L	MAJ	0-1292332	0857	1
GRAU LESTER A	LTC	0-1049177	0665	1
GRAUBERGER RAYMOND W	CW3	W-2211107	0268	1
GRAUEL JOHN E	CPT	0-1745394	0649	2
GRAVATT BASIL E	LTC	0-0268786	0764	3
GRAVATT JAMES H	CW3	W-2144746	0562	1
GRAVATT VERGIL O	MAJ	0-1797460	0360	3
GRAVEL JOSEPH M	WO1	W-2111447	0450	2
GRAVEL PAUL M	2LT	0-0440895	0145	2
GRAVELDINGER BERT	MAJ	0-0142823	0648	3
GRAVELIE ALBERT T	CPT	0-1995266	0947	2
GRAVELY LOUIS O JR	M G	0-0249412	1267	3
GRAVENSTEIN EDWIN L	MAJ	0-0993073	0765	1
GRAVER FREDERICK	LTC	0-0241100	0463	3
GRAVES BEN S JR	CPT	0-1048790	0645	2
GRAVES CHARLES W	LTC	0-1823730	0167	1
GRAVES CLAUDE T	LTC	0-1165736	0358	1
GRAVES DONALD G	LTC	0-0219160	0563	3
GRAVES ELMER C	CPT	0-1015061	1060	1
GRAVES EVERETT C	CW2	W-2214753	1066	1
GRAVES HENRY R	CPT	0-1286999	0245	2
GRAVES JACK O	MAJ	0-1633899	0261	1
GRAVES JAMES W	CPT	0-0411579	1051	2
GRAVES JEFFERSON	COL	0-0112283	0648	3
GRAVES KENNETH K	1LT	0-0554315	1045	2
GRAVES KERMIT R	CPT	0-1114950	1168	1
GRAVES LAMAR F	LTC	0-1845998	0656	2
GRAVES LLOYD R	MAJ	0-1290622	1057	1
GRAVES MARVIN H	LTC	0-0293050	0265	3
GRAVES PAUL H	CW3	W-2146058	0661	1
GRAVES PERCY E	LTC	0-0309513	0257	3
GRAVES RALPH I	LTC	0-0111658	0648	3
GRAVES RAYFORD P	COL	0-0285410	0465	1
GRAVES RAYMOND C	LTC	0-1169986	0959	1
GRAVES RICHARD R	MAJ	0-2272272	0767	1
GRAVES ROBERT N	MAJ	0-0314319	1060	3
GRAVES THEODORE J	LTC	0-2206111	1267	1
GRAVES WILLIAM L	CPT	0-0304694	0245	2
GRAVES WYMAN A JR	WO1	T-0010371	0965	2
GRAVIN NORMAN R	LTC	0-0323038	0966	3
GRAVIS JOHN B	CPT	0-0491667	1043	2
GRAVLEY JACOB W	MAJ	0-1292169	1046	2

NAME	GRADE	SVC NO	DATE RET MO YR	RET CODE
GRAVLIN ARTHUR M	LTC	0-1639094	0566	1
GRAW SIDNEY	MAJ	0-0942975	1060	1
GRAW WILLIAM K	LTC	0-0557363	0964	1
GRAY ANDREW S	CPT	0-0218624	0755	3
GRAY ARLINGTON	CPT	0-1172035	0946	2
GRAY ARTHUR L	2LT	0-1285743	0645	2
GRAY ARTHUR M	LTC	0-0466618	0365	2
GRAY ARTHUR R	CPT	0-1289573	0157	1
GRAY BASIL C	MAJ	0-0494232	0846	2
GRAY BENNETT G JR	LTC	0-0289552	0560	1
GRAY BERNADETTE	2LT	N-0700761	0139	1
GRAY BERNARD C	2LT	0-1310708	0345	2
GRAY CARROLL	COL	0-0105888	0754	3
GRAY CECIL L	CW3	W-2203522	0965	1
GRAY CHARLES H	CW4	W-2148338	0567	1
GRAY CHARLES T	CW3	W-2112002	1160	1
GRAY CHARLES W	MAJ	0-0447686	0346	2
GRAY CLARENCE D	CPT	0-0330517	0944	2
GRAY CORNELIUS	MAJ	0-0994609	0768	1
GRAY DANIEL A	CW2	W-2149726	0955	1
GRAY DAVID A	CPT	0-0441954	0346	2
GRAY DONALD D	LTC	0-0962159	0563	1
GRAY DONALD G	LTC	0-1031940	0463	1
GRAY DOUGLAS T JR	MAJ	0-0408410	1146	2
GRAY EDGAR M	1LT	0-1824303	1045	2
GRAY ELDON A	CW2	W-2133565	0960	2
GRAY ERNEST R JR	COL	0-0363031	0160	1
GRAY FRANK H	LTC	0-0287610	0661	2
GRAY FRED	CPT	0-1314468	1045	2
GRAY FREDERICK	WO1	W-2126863	1045	2
GRAY GEORGE A	LTC	0-0228264	0658	3
GRAY GEORGE A JR	2LT	0-0887712	0945	2
GRAY GEORGE F	LTC	0-0335092	1165	3
GRAY GEORGE E	CPT	0-1017352	1062	1
GRAY GLEN O	CW3	W-2147220	0163	1
GRAY GORDON M	WO1	W-2151320	1165	1
GRAY HARRISON	CPT	0-0487073	1149	1
GRAY HERBERT C	COL	0-0205709	1061	3
GRAY HILLARD E	MAJ	0-1017393	1060	1
GRAY HOMER W	MAJ	0-0371130	0860	1
GRAY HOWARD F	1LT	0-1322916	1045	2
GRAY HOWARD R	CW3	W-2205451	0465	1
GRAY HOWARD W	LTC	0-1103657	0665	1
GRAY IRWIN H	MAJ	0-0484762	0548	2
GRAY JACK E	LTC	0-0303864	0867	3
GRAY JACK K	LTC	0-1168257	0459	1
GRAY JAMES	CPT	0-0292236	0347	1
GRAY JAMES A	LTC	0-0290921	1160	1
GRAY JAMES B	COL	0-0284088	0961	1
GRAY JAMES D	LTC	0-0165195	0648	3
GRAY JAMES W	CPT	0-0490220	1046	2
GRAY JEAN M	COL	0-0289625	1058	1
GRAY JERRY C	LTC	0-1103658	0962	1
GRAY JOHN C	2LT	0-1913699	0144	1
GRAY JOHN C R	CW3	W-2205862	0665	1
GRAY JOHN O	MAJ	0-1578543	0668	3
GRAY JOHN E	LTC	0-0300301	0360	1
GRAY JOHN G	LTC	0-1579714	0868	3
GRAY JOHN H	LTC	0-0244130	0565	3
GRAY JOHN H	MAJ	0-1633900	1059	1
GRAY JOHN M	MAJ	0-2209645	1068	1
GRAY JOHN T	LTC	0-0196309	0446	2
GRAY JOHN T	1LT	0-0408177	0944	2
GRAY JOHN W	LTC	0-1101461	0165	1
GRAY JOSEPH A	MAJ	0-0172879	0849	3
GRAY JOSEPH R	MAJ	0-0395889	0647	2
GRAY KAY N	CW3	W-2147138	0166	1
GRAY KENNETH S	LTC	0-0298651	0666	3
GRAY KENNETH W	MAJ	0-1312004	0255	2
GRAY MARJORIE	1LT	N-0742566	0146	1
GRAY ORVILLE G	CW3	W-2210377	0167	1
GRAY OSCAR W	COL	0-0290958	0364	1
GRAY PAUL T	1LT	0-1323827	0645	2
GRAY RALPH J	MAJ	0-1587287	0161	1
GRAY RALPH W	LTC	0-0450619	0857	1

ARMY OF THE UNITED STATES RETIRED LIST

NAME	GRADE	SVC NO	DATE RET MO YR	RET CODE
GRAY RAYMOND G	MAJ	0-2049256	0466	1
GRAY RAYMOND S	CW3	W-2146854	0964	1
GRAY REGIS L	2LT	0-1307153	0145	2
GRAY RICHARD E	CW3	RW-2207735	1166	1
GRAY RICHARD T	LTC	0-0909948	0267	3
GRAY ROBERT C	MAJ	0-2262806	0965	1
GRAY ROBERT E	MAJ	0-0142822	0952	3
GRAY ROBERT E JR	CW4	W-2146662	0868	1
GRAY ROBERT H	LTC	0-1043348	0965	1
GRAY ROBERT N	WO1	W-2128344	0844	2
GRAY ROBERT R	CPT	0-1557456	0863	1
GRAY ROBERT S	LTC	0-1535905	0668	1
GRAY ROBERT W	LTC	0-1290746	0658	2
GRAY ROBINSON A	MAJ	0-2005336	0461	1
GRAY ROLLIE L	MAJ	0-0229922	1063	3
GRAY ROY E	MAJ	0-1317628	0558	1
GRAY RUSSELL A	LTC	0-0230905	0962	1
GRAY RUSSELL E	LTC	0-1293584	0862	1
GRAY THOMAS M	COL	0-0338637	0867	3
GRAY VAUGHN T	CPT	0-0217697	0156	3
GRAY VELMA L	2LT	N-0789104	1044	1
GRAY VICTOR A	LTC	0-0403924	0660	1
GRAY VICTOR C	LTC	0-1106175	0261	1
GRAY WALDO G	LTC	0-1294827	0664	1
GRAY WALTER J	WO1	W-2150305	1052	2
GRAY WAYNE W	LTC	0-0322666	0964	3
GRAY WILLIAM A	MAJ	0-0359248	0245	2
GRAY WILLIAM A	CPT	0-0385084	0246	2
GRAY WILLIAM B	LTC	0-0762314	0463	1
GRAY WILLIAM R JR	CPT	0-0378728	0450	2
GRAY WILLIAM G	CPT	0-1579716	0646	2
GRAYBEAL JESSE B	CPT	0-0903877	0746	2
GRAYBILL HENRY M JR	CPT	0-1280178	0845	2
GRAYBILL HERBERT A	1LT	0-1320627	0945	2
GRAYBILL JOHN W	CPT	0-1080544	1055	1
GRAYBILL WAYNE A	2LT	0-1326088	0645	2
GRAYDON CHARLES K	COL	0-0273657	0765	1
GRAYLESS PAUL N	CW4	W-2002954	0268	3
GRAYSON ARTHUR M	LTC	0-0222595	0556	3
GRAYSON JOHN F	MAJ	0-0366271	0946	2
GRAYSON LINCOLN R	LTC	0-0326466	0767	3
GRAYSON LUTHER	2LT	0-2055169	0245	2
GRAYSON REX H	MAJ	0-0498451	0155	1
GRAYSON ROY D	LTC	0-0486834	1043	2
GRAYSON STEWART M II	COL	0-0407673	0466	2
GRAZIANO MARIE E	1LT	N-0761999	1146	1
GRAZIER CHARLES S	LTC	0-1100564	1166	1
GRAZIER HOBART E	CPT	0-1286637	1047	2
GRBINICH FRANK	MAJ	0-0975059	0964	1
GREANEY RICHARD T	MAJ	0-1120112	0663	1
GREANY ANNE M	CPT	N-0901873	0662	2
GREASER EVERETT M	LTC	0-1640497	0164	1
GREASON SAMUEL	COL	0-0107929	0648	3
GREATHOUSE ALBERT T	COL	0-0265392	0463	3
GREATHOUSE CECIL E	CPT	0-1896022	0854	1
GREATHOUSE CHARLES I	LTC	0-0397914	0762	1
GREATHOUSE CICERO B	MAJ	0-0494233	0157	1
GREATHOUSE EVERETT F	1LT	0-2012267	0657	1
GREATHOUSE GERALD W	COL	0-0300025	0868	3
GREATHOUSE HERMAN	MAJ	0-0967195	0763	1
GREATHOUSE VERNON	CW3	W-2144009	1057	1
GREAVES DONALD L	MAJ	0-1303714	0259	1
GREAVES THOMAS G JR	CPT	0-0378648	0945	2
GREAVES VINCENT L	COL	0-0332513	0366	3
GREAVY WALTER G	COL	0-0378307	0764	3
GREB MILLARD J	LTC	0-0224763	1154	2
GREBE FRANK D	COL	0-0383678	0461	1
GREBINGER CHARLES J	LTC	0-1012578	0661	1
GRECO FRANK	LTC	0-0406856	0560	1
GRECO SEBASTIAN	MAJ	0-0310136	0646	2
GRECSEK ERNEST R	CPT	0-0254098	0564	3
GREDINGER LAWRENCE M	COL	0-0205027	1162	3
GREEK ANGELO	CW2	W-2207403	0562	1
GREELEY JOHN B JR	LTC	0-0325748	1154	2
GREELEY LOYAL L	LTC	0-0155248	0753	3
GREELISH JOSEPH E	1LT	0-0170637	0641	1
GREEMAN GERALD B	MAJ	0-0360326	0747	2
GREEN ABRAHAM L	CPT	0-0497967	1044	2
GREEN ALBERT B	MAJ	0-1180194	1163	1
GREEN ALLEN E	LTC	0-0417603	0363	2
GREEN ALOYS J	CPT	0-1544114	1046	2
GREEN ALVIS G	MAJ	0-0367172	0146	2
GREEN ARCHIBALD	LTC	0-0279531	0653	3
GREEN ARTHUR L	CW2	W-2150930	1161	1
GREEN BENTON H	CW2	W-2119507	1061	1
GREEN BERNARD W	MAJ	0-1114517	0760	1
GREEN BOYNTON M	MAJ	0-0229029	0851	3
GREEN CARL E	LTC	0-0428191	0363	1
GREEN CARL R	LTC	0-0248413	1165	3
GREEN CARL V	MAJ	0-0365385	0859	2
GREEN CECIL C	CW2	W-2208607	0465	1
GREEN CHARLES A	LTC	0-0231538	0260	3
GREEN CHARLES C	MAJ	0-1111637	1262	1
GREEN CHARLES J	LTC	0-0298587	0262	3
GREEN CLARENCE J	LTC	0-0148230	0648	3
GREEN CLAUDE E	2LT	0-1881905	0753	2
GREEN CLELLAN H	CPT	0-1186412	0860	1
GREEN CURTIS E	CPT	0-2032901	0859	1
GREEN CYRIL C	COL	0-0368647	1163	1
GREEN DAVID	CW2	W-2148914	0361	1
GREEN DAVID G	CW2	W-2104106	0451	2
GREEN DONNA G	CPT	N-0733569	1046	1
GREEN DUANE M	CPT	0-0513939	1047	2
GREEN EDWARD C	LTC	0-1167866	1262	1
GREEN EDWARD J	MAJ	0-1331173	0263	1
GREEN EDWARD L	CW2	W-2152962	1262	1
GREEN EDWARD W	CW3	W-2102954	0257	1
GREEN EDWIN B	COL	0-0240222	0665	3
GREEN EMANUEL	1LT	0-0518182	0345	2
GREEN ERNEST J	MAJ	0-1294654	0166	1
GREEN EUGENE	CPT	0-1297189	0267	1
GREEN FOREST T	LTC	0-0237630	1064	3
GREEN FRANK E	LTC	0-0320221	0561	1
GREEN FRANK M JR	LTC	0-0386164	0661	1
GREEN FRED M	LTC	0-0234472	0447	2
GREEN GEORGE C	COL	0-0218076	0662	3
GREEN GEORGE D	LTC	0-0246346	0460	3
GREEN GEORGE M JR	LTC	0-0313398	1267	3
GREEN GLENN M	COL	0-0247866	0665	3
GREEN GRANT S	COL	0-0264558	0365	1
GREEN GUY B	CPT	0-0493168	1056	1
GREEN HAMPTON L	COL	0-0269907	1058	1
GREEN HAROLD	CW2	W-2126787	0545	2
GREEN HAROLD D	LTC	0-0298290	0762	3
GREEN HARRISON H	LTC	0-0919222	0168	3
GREEN HARRY F	CPT	0-1062501	0757	1
GREEN HARRY S	COL	0-0279571	0557	1
GREEN HARVEY D	CW4	W-2102955	0359	1
GREEN HENRY P	LTC	0-0271681	0868	3
GREEN HENRY W	CPT	0-0331583	1145	2
GREEN HORACE E	MAJ	0-0483919	0462	1
GREEN HORACE F	CW4	W-2144185	0764	2
GREEN HOWARD M	CW3	W-2118108	1154	1
GREEN HUGH W	MAJ	0-0266529	0953	3
GREEN JACK P	MAJ	0-0236934	0445	2
GREEN JACOB M	1LT	0-0528825	1052	1
GREEN JAMES A	LTC	0-1643610	0962	1
GREEN JAMES C	CPT	0-0508329	0246	2
GREEN JAMES E	MAJ	0-2025780	0164	1
GREEN JAMES H	MAJ	0-0979832	1061	1
GREEN JAMES L	2LT	0-0407930	1041	2
GREEN JAMES P	MAJ	0-1944694	0548	2
GREEN JAMES R	LTC	0-0342844	0961	1
GREEN JAMES W	CPT	0-1051976	0557	1
GREEN JOE H	LTC	0-0119516	0159	3
GREEN JOE S	LTC	0-0226821	1162	3
GREEN JOHN A	CPT	0-0217477	0757	3
GREEN JOHN A	CPT	0-2007705	0747	2
GREEN JOHN C	MAJ	0-0183216	1054	3
GREEN JOHN W	LTC	0-0209019	0449	3
GREEN JOSEPH R	MAJ	0-1291267	0163	1
GREEN JOSEPH S	LTC	0-0487285	0563	3
GREEN JUDD V	LTC	0-0450299	0758	1
GREEN LAWRENCE E	CW3	RW-2208882	0467	1
GREEN LAYTON H	LTC	0-1288535	0765	1
GREEN LE ROY V	COL	0-0287833	1168	3
GREEN LENARD J	MAJ	0-1826384	0358	1
GREEN LEONARD D	1LT	0-0958312	0954	2
GREEN LEROY	CPT	0-1550393	0156	1
GREEN LINWOOD O	LTC	0-0447359	0957	1
GREEN LLOYD G	LTC	0-0414731	1054	1
GREEN LOUIS S	MAJ	0-0243054	0363	3
GREEN MANUEL	CPT	0-0517567	0146	2
GREEN MARIN W	LTC	0-2055146	1055	1
GREEN MARTIN D JR	1LT	0-0924682	1143	2
GREEN MAURICE C	LTC	0-1037512	0566	1
GREEN MELVIN C	MAJ	0-1117430	0962	1
GREEN MONROE H	LTC	0-1689220	0646	2
GREEN MONROE S	2LT	0-1055338	1044	2
GREEN MYRON J	LTC	0-0294388	0561	1
GREEN NOAH A JR	MAJ	0-2019314	1160	1
GREEN ORVIE L	COL	0-0346643	0367	3
GREEN PAUL P	WO1	W-2148236	0157	1
GREEN RAYMOND	LTC	0-2204142	0868	1
GREEN RAYMOND B	MAJ	0-1688754	1064	1
GREEN RICHARD F	MAJ	0-0225726	0162	3
GREEN RICHARD I	MAJ	0-1106178	0662	1
GREEN ROBERT B	2LT	0-1633901	0443	2
GREEN ROBERT C	CPT	0-1913698	0546	1
GREEN ROBERT E	CW3	W-2144158	0861	1
GREEN ROBERT E	CW3	W-2209490	0867	1
GREEN ROBERT H	1LT	0-1290413	0546	2
GREEN ROBERT M	MAJ	0-1002637	0960	1
GREEN ROBERT T	CW3	W-2152314	0464	1
GREEN ROBERT W	1LT	0-1826079	1045	2
GREEN ROY	COL	0-0222729	1055	3
GREEN ROY A	M G	0-0226513	0557	3
GREEN ROY A	MAJ	0-0490171	0557	1
GREEN ROY F	MAJ	0-1300159	1160	1
GREEN SAMUEL	CPT	0-1304895	0146	2
GREEN SAMUEL G	COL	0-0183191	0250	3
GREEN SAMUEL T	MAJ	0-1107990	0761	1
GREEN SIGMUND	2LT	0-1589234	0844	2
GREEN THOMAS F	LTC	0-0401110	0861	1
GREEN THOMAS W	LTC	0-1058529	0265	1
GREEN VANZEL	MAJ	0-1646018	0756	1
GREEN VESTA D	1LT	N-0763931	0745	1
GREEN VIRGIL C	LTC	0-1305575	0765	1
GREEN WALLACE F	1LT	0-1055905	1045	2
GREEN WALTER E	CPT	0-1320628	0946	2
GREEN WARREN H	MAJ	0-1108693	0160	1
GREEN WARREN W	CPT	0-0492802	0944	2
GREEN WAVERLY S	CPT	0-1311385	0646	2
GREEN WILBUR V	MAJ	0-1923573	1063	1
GREEN WILLIAM F	COL	0-0224988	0164	3
GREEN WILLIAM J	LTC	0-1300023	1062	1
GREEN WILLIAM O	COL	0-0253569	1166	3
GREEN WILLIAM P	1LT	0-0447288	1046	2
GREEN WILLIAM S	LTC	0-0236182	0461	3
GREEN WILLIAM V	CPT	0-1041157	0959	1
GREENALL CHARLES H	COL	0-0900306	0352	2
GREENAWALT CLYDE W	LTC	0-0347434	0459	3
GREENAWALT EZMA F	MAJ	N-0724842	1066	1
GREENAWALT HOWARD A	LTC	0-1320523	0661	1
GREENAWAY ROBERT E	CW3	W-2152549	1060	1
GREENBAUM EDWARD S	B G	0-0132915	0254	3
GREENBERG ABRAHAM	COL	0-0301947	0168	3
GREENBERG ANNA K	1LT	N-0723800	0746	1
GREENBERG BENJAMIN	1LT	0-0534417	0146	2
GREENBERG CHARLES	MAJ	0-0491079	1053	1
GREENBERG FRANK J	LTC	0-1587290	1162	1
GREENBERG HARRY A	LTC	0-2043102	1154	1
GREENBERG HERBERT	CPT	0-1175723	0246	2
GREENBERG HERBERT A	CPT	0-0526123	1145	2
GREENBERG HERBERT H	MAJ	0-0982830	0168	3
GREENBERG MAX	MAJ	0-0312467	0366	3
GREENBERG MEYER	LTC	0-0321355	0565	3
GREENBERG MORRIS W	COL	0-0316987	0767	3
GREENBERG NORMAN S	LTC	0-1577251	0765	1
GREENBERG ORRIN	CPT	0-0273197	0845	2
GREENBLATT LOUIS T	CPT	0-1555693	0456	2
GREENBROOK REGINAL	CPT	0-1320725	1047	2
GREENBUSH WILLIAM E	CW2	W-2104107	0560	1
GREENE ALLYN W	LTC	0-1641342	1065	3
GREENE BENJAMIN B	MAJ	0-0213557	1057	3
GREENE CARROLL F	MAJ	0-1946269	0357	2
GREENE CHARLES E	CW2	W-2152381	0761	1
GREENE CHARLES F	LTC	0-0352924	0953	1
GREENE CHARLES M	CW3	W-2206006	1066	1
GREENE CLARENCE E	LTC	0-0361490	0263	3
GREENE CLIFTON S	CPT	0-1591764	1146	2
GREENE DENMAN H	MAJ	0-1533793	0557	1
GREENE DONALD W	LTC	0-1536259	0268	1
GREENE DOUGLASS	LTC	0-1582830	0865	1
GREENE DUDLEY W	LTC	0-0430722	0861	2
GREENE EARL F	LTC	0-0451602	0763	1
GREENE EARL T	1LT	0-0488862	0745	1
GREENE EDDWARD C	WO1	W-2119717	0546	2
GREENE EDWARD W	MAJ	0-1633902	1059	1
GREENE EUGENE E	MAJ	0-0272070	0164	3
GREENE GERALD	COL	0-0302030	0865	3
GREENE GLEN H	WO1	W-3430759	0467	2
GREENE GRANTLAND	CPT	0-0208647	1048	3
GREENE GUTHRIE R	LTC	0-2035422	0264	1
GREENE HARLEY B	1LT	0-1643611	0745	2
GREENE HERMAN L	WO1	W-2109377	0445	2
GREENE HOWARD G	MAJ	0-0549469	0865	1
GREENE IDA E	LTC	N-0744859	0768	1
GREENE JAMES O	1LT	0-1307224	0944	2
GREENE JAMES S JR	COL	0-0023137	0868	1
GREENE JAMES T	1LT	0-0324313	0342	2
GREENE JOBE L JR	CW2	W-2143661	0657	1
GREENE JOHN D	MAJ	0-0163371	0347	2
GREENE JOHN H	CPT	0-0409992	0345	2
GREENE JOSEPH F	LTC	0-0305999	0764	1
GREENE JOSEPH L	CPT	0-0332636	0146	2
GREENE JUSTIN L	MAJ	0-0511311	1045	2
GREENE KENNETH A	CW2	W-2147000	0563	1
GREENE KENNETH D	LTC	0-0243808	1163	3
GREENE KENNETH J	MAJ	0-0986876	0463	1
GREENE LAWRENCE W	LTC	0-0395765	1062	1
GREENE LAWRENCE W	COL	0-0529912	1264	3
GREENE LENWOOD	CW2	W-2142491	0157	1
GREENE LEON G	CW3	W-2149890	0363	1
GREENE LESTER M	MAJ	0-0233399	0765	3
GREENE LLEWELLYN	LTC	0-1101464	1266	3
GREENE LLOYD B	MAJ	0-0403245	1053	3
GREENE LUTHER W	COL	0-0168305	1060	3
GREENE MARCELLUS	CPT	0-1050685	0257	1
GREENE MARION G	2LT	0-1310026	0245	2
GREENE MAURICE L	LTC	0-0224333	1159	3
GREENE MAURICE W	CPT	0-0999003	1062	1
GREENE MICHAEL I	CPT	0-1552681	1162	1
GREENE NATHANIEL	1LT	0-0517960	1144	2
GREENE NELSON G	LTC	0-0918886	0157	2
GREENE PAUL C	LTC	0-0198380	0454	3
GREENE PETER P	CW3	W-2145437	0861	1
GREENE PORTER C	LTC	0-0252903	0365	3
GREENE RALPH E	1LT	0-0469193	0745	2
GREENE RAY P	LTC	0-1826412	1062	1
GREENE RAYMOND A	CW3	W-2145752	0760	1
GREENE ROBERT	LTC	0-0329557	0767	3
GREENE ROBERT A	MAJ	0-0276318	0544	2
GREENE ROBERT C	COL	0-0299297	1061	1
GREENE ROY W	1LT	0-2000560	0448	2
GREENE THEODORE W	CPT	0-1533567	0247	2
GREENE VERNON F	LTC	0-0331258	1165	3
GREENE VICTOR M JR	MAJ	0-1702270	1066	1
GREENE WALLACE J	LTC	0-0239411	0961	3
GREENE WARREN F	MAJ	0-0179211	0863	1

NAME	GRADE	SVC NO	DATE RET MO YR	RET CODE
GREENE WELCH H	CPT	0-0343744	0945	2
GREENE WILBUR M	CPT	0-4074599	0967	1
GREENE WILLIAM B	CPT	0-1290593	0546	2
GREENE WILLIAM D	CPT	0-1926740	0166	1
GREENE WILLIAM D	CW3	W-2148965	1263	1
GREENE WILLIAM H	1LT	0-0538196	0945	2
GREENE WILLIAM P	MAJ	0-1297890	1267	1
GREENE WILLIAM T	CPT	0-0448433	1146	1
GREENE WILLIAM W	MAJ	0-0285209	1145	2
GREENE WILSON P	2LT	0-1318783	0945	2
GREENE WINSTON W	CW4	W-2145438	0568	1
GREENE WINTHROP S	LTC	0-0102010	0551	3
GREENER GLENN L	COL	0-1011097	0564	1
GREENFIELD ALFRED R	CPT	0-0423663	0546	2
GREENFIELD GEORGE A	MAJ	0-1030151	0558	1
GREENFIELD HERMAN L	CW2	W-2108029	0444	2
GREENFIELD LEONARD R	COL	0-0235677	0546	2
GREENFIELD SAMUEL J	1LT	0-0225853	1164	3
GREENHAGEN MILTON E	LTC	0-1043645	1061	1
GREENHALGH ROBERT A	LTC	0-1642124	1263	1
GREENHAW HERMAN H	MAJ	0-0305720	0845	2
GREENHAW LEONARD F	1LT	0-0426672	0645	2
GREENHILL NOBLE F	MAJ	0-0523733	0644	2
GREENHILL SOLOMON	LTC	0-0292226	0665	3
GREENHOUSE MAXWELL N	CPT	0-1918011	0953	2
GREENHUT FREDERICK	MAJ	0-0201736	1043	2
GREENIA LAWRENCE J	MAJ	0-2055142	0960	1
GREENING ELDRIDGE A	CW3	W-2141293	0162	1
GREENING JAMES A	CW2	W-2146910	0661	1
GREENING THOMAS R	1LT	0-1176644	0745	2
GREENLAW RAYMOND H	LTC	0-2046991	0866	1
GREENLAW WALTER R	MAJ	0-1047543	0561	1
GREENLEE HAROLD E	COL	0-0274633	1061	3
GREENLEE JOSEPH C	MAJ	0-0980321	0468	1
GREENLEE RAE	MAJ	0-2283754	0764	2
GREENLEE RICHARD W	LTC	0-0488481	1154	1
GREENLEE WILLIAM G	CW2	W-2149919	0965	1
GREENLEES DOROTHY E	1LT	N-0775967	1045	1
GREENLEY CHARLES W	CW2	W-2210001	0564	2
GREENOUGH FREDERICK	2LT	0-1175725	0144	2
GREENSTEIN GEORGE H	MAJ	0-0438795	0446	2
GREENUP CHARLES N	LTC	0-0381878	0265	3
GREENWALD AARON T	LTC	0-0276948	1165	3
GREENWALD EDWARD J	LTC	0-2024456	0167	1
GREENWALD IRVING	CPT	0-0430194	1045	2
GREENWALD LOUIS	LTC	0-0306109	0165	3
GREENWALD NATHANIEL	LTC	0-0330272	1167	1
GREENWALT EMMETT A	LTC	0-1314624	0867	3
GREENWALT GILBERT C	COL	0-0102170	1148	2
GREENWAY EDWARD F	CPT	0-0531631	0547	2
GREENWAY JAMES C	COL	0-0253000	1164	3
GREENWAY JOSEPH P	CW2	W-2215986	0668	1
GREENWAY THOMAS D	CW2	W-2149293	0960	1
GREENWELL ROBERT J	MAJ	0-2014500	1167	1
GREENWELL WILLIAM J	LTC	0-1017145	0163	1
GREENWOOD DEAN A	LTC	0-1300960	0266	1
GREENWOOD HENRY	CPT	0-1649191	0764	1
GREENWOOD JAMES R	MAJ	0-0499059	0453	1
GREENWOOD MOORE	LTC	0-0242600	1057	3
GREENWOOD ROBERT L	CW3	W-2151046	1158	1
GREENWOOD ROBERT R	CW2	W-2203470	0361	1
GREEP RUDOLPH T	COL	0-0270965	0665	3
GREER BARRY D	COL	0-0238947	0151	2
GREER CHARLES W	CW3	W-2144116	0559	1
GREER CURTIS D JR	CPT	0-0995828	0761	1
GREER DRURY H	WO1	W-2122706	0445	2
GREER EDWARD A	LTC	0-0295224	0968	3
GREER FREDERICK	LTC	0-1059793	0162	1
GREER GEORGE	2LT	0-2055122	1044	2
GREER GERALD L	1LT	0-0549481	0845	2
GREER HAROLD E	LTC	0-2054014	0661	1
GREER HERBERT K	COL	0-0411624	0463	1
GREER JAMES A	MAJ	0-0293725	0260	3
GREER JAMES F	MAJ	0-2096478	0765	1
GREER JAMES F	CPT	0-0522706	1051	1
GREER JEAN M	1LT	N-0703272	0545	1
GREER JIM	MAJ	0-0972264	0964	1
GREER JOHN C	LTC	0-0377193	0961	1
GREER MAURICE J	CW2	W-2208517	0462	1
GREER MELVIN A	MAJ	0-1692131	0446	2
GREER NEAL C	CPT	0-1179871	0960	1
GREER ODAS A	CW3	W-2205137	1157	1
GREER OLIVER W	COL	0-0200543	0758	3
GREER RAYMOND L	CW2	W-2145439	0564	2
GREER ROBERT W	LTC	0-0059983	0168	1
GREER RUSSELL A	COL	0-0198573	1162	3
GREER STANLEY W	LTC	0-0809127	1165	2
GREER STEPHEN	MAJ	0-1550600	0361	1
GREER WILLIAM E	LTC	0-1825530	0767	1
GREER WILLIAM H	LTC	0-0323944	1060	1
GREER WILLIAM O	MAJ	0-0436554	0364	1
GREESON DAVID P	2LT	0-1302639	0646	2
GREESON ROBERT W	CPT	0-0509795	1153	1
GREESON WILLIAM R	CW2	W-2144573	0161	1
GREETHAM RALPH E	CW2	W-2117902	0668	3
GREEVER WILLIAM R	1LT	0-0371631	1044	2
GREFE ARTHUR A	LTC	0-0494841	1155	1
GREGAN MARY	MAJ	N-0757971	0568	1
GREGER ERWIN M	CW4	W-2105337	0666	1
GREGERSON LELAND S	MAJ	0-1179082	0261	1
GREGG ALVA M	CPT	0-0237660	0365	3
GREGG CLIFFORD C	COL	0-0126732	0755	3
GREGG EARL T	CPT	0-1062194	0148	2
GREGG EVERITTE A	1LT	0-1949113	0762	1
GREGG FRANK P	MAJ	0-1703420	1067	1
GREGG HAROLD P	1LT	0-1321304	0246	2
GREGG JAMES A	1LT	0-1309720	1146	2
GREGG JESSE F	MAJ	0-0189954	0845	2
GREGG JOSEPH J JR	LTC	0-0409980	0960	1
GREGG JOSEPH W	CW4	W-2142843	0356	1
GREGG LASSITER E	MAJ	0-2206176	1268	1
GREGG LEROY B	CPT	0-0171877	0656	3
GREGG WILLIAM N SR	LTC	0-0185698	1055	3
GREGOR CLARA C	MAJ	N-0800032	0765	1
GREGOR JOHN W	1LT	0-1062593	0446	2
GREGORIE JAMES B	COL	0-0172185	0953	3
GREGORY ALLEN L	CPT	0-2103784	1052	3
GREGORY ARTHUR L	MAJ	0-2020723	0860	1
GREGORY BEN M	LTC	0-0230321	0563	3
GREGORY BERNICE B	LTC	0-0498289	0954	1
GREGORY BRYAN T	MAJ	0-0226056	0363	1
GREGORY BUNNIE E	CPT	0-1541557	0664	1
GREGORY CLAUDE W JR	2LT	0-1108696	0145	2
GREGORY CLYDE JR	LTC	0-2021149	0468	1
GREGORY CORBETT H	LTC	0-1635975	0266	1
GREGORY DOUGLAS H	CPT	0-0380179	0644	2
GREGORY ELMER O	CPT	0-0672607	0354	2
GREGORY ENID	2LT	N-0743371	0345	1
GREGORY FRANCIS A	LTC	0-0455069	0364	1
GREGORY FRANK B	COL	0-0331030	0463	1
GREGORY FRANK L	LTC	0-1533073	0461	1
GREGORY FRED T	CW3	W-2208009	0968	1
GREGORY GABRIEL S	MAJ	0-0988310	0365	1
GREGORY GEORGE G	2LT	0-1014250	0245	2
GREGORY HUGH B	MAJ	0-0275459	0653	3
GREGORY IRVING F	CPT	0-0468903	1045	2
GREGORY JAMES B	LTC	0-0379871	0767	1
GREGORY JAMES B	MAJ	0-2014718	1264	1
GREGORY JOHN M	LTC	0-0206153	0956	3
GREGORY JOSEPH F	MAJ	0-2204313	1166	1
GREGORY LEO	MAJ	0-0318853	0446	2
GREGORY LEROY J	CW3	W-2129454	0659	1
GREGORY ROBERT E	LTC	0-1017891	1062	1
GREGORY ROBERT L	COL	0-0195031	1062	3
GREGORY ROBERT O	LTC	0-0430354	0562	1
GREGORY RODGERS L	LTC	0-1112733	0462	1
GREGORY SIRAK K	CPT	0-1705717	0146	2
GREGORY STANLEY A	MAJ	0-1050282	0865	1
GREGORY VIRGIL E	WO1	W-2149014	0351	1
GREGORY WAYNE	CW2	W-2145142	0962	2
GREGORY WILLIAM T	LTC	0-1102269	1060	1
GREGSON WILLIAM H JR	LTC	0-0369952	0546	2
GREIG BEN W	COL	0-0243210	0858	3
GREIG CLARENCE E	MAJ	0-0356344	1066	3
GREIG LEONARD I	CPT	0-1061966	0468	3
GREIG ROBERT E	LTC	0-0286481	0363	3
GREIG WALTER	LTC	0-0358456	1266	3
GREILICH EDMUND G	CPT	0-1180921	0559	1
GREILING ROBERT E	1LT	0-0925411	1144	2
GREIM WILLARD N	COL	0-0129885	0850	3
GREINER JOHN R	LTC	0-0378698	1163	1
GREINER NORBERT L	1LT	0-1593599	0945	2
GREINER WILLIAM F	MAJ	0-2284004	0762	1
GREINER WILLIAM W	COL	0-0231095	0365	3
GREIVES ABRAHAM	COL	0-0308981	1059	1
GREIR HAROLD F	COL	0-0260242	1057	3
GREISON HANS P	LTC	0-0192190	1151	3
GREIST JOHN H	COL	0-0277466	0366	3
GREMILLION GUY E	CW2	W-2121337	0560	1
GREMILLION JACK P F	1LT	0-1309253	0645	2
GREMILLION JAMES D	MAJ	0-1594201	0965	1
GREMMEL FRED	COL	0-0316539	0268	3
GREMMELS ARNOLD C	LTC	0-1645615	0966	3
GREMORE WESLEY J	MAJ	0-1948747	1262	1
GRENIG ROBERT E	LTC	0-0400701	0461	1
GRENNAN CHARLES A	COL	0-0259396	0865	3
GRENTZENBERG FLETCHE	LTC	0-1184503	0667	1
GRESHAM GEORGE R	LTC	0-0288689	0661	3
GRESHAM HENRY C	MAJ	0-1171168	0161	1
GRESHAM LAMAR M	LTC	0-1557291	0765	1
GRESHAM NORMAN C	COL	0-0251063	0267	3
GRESHAW GLOVER C JR	1LT	0-1288732	0445	2
GRESS KENNETH L	COL	0-0281342	0262	1
GRESSANG WILLIAM H	1LT	0-1309363	0646	2
GRESZLER PAUL R	MAJ	0-1540874	0264	1
GRETH EUGENE H	CW2	W-2214764	0967	1
GRETHER JOHN A	MAJ	0-2021253	1068	1
GRETTENBERG JACK D	MAJ	0-1291807	0261	1
GREULICH FRANCIS A	MAJ	0-0382199	0766	3
GREUNE FRANCIS W	2LT	0-1327620	1145	2
GREUNKE WILMA A	MAJ	N-0767279	0667	1
GREUP ERNST W	1LT	0-1301917	1047	2
GREVE JOHN H	LTC	0-1548817	1165	1
GREVENBERG DUDLEY L	1LT	0-1590507	0660	1
GREVILLIUS GUSTAV	CPT	0-0887684	0458	1
GREWE HERBERT G	COL	0-0298574	0766	3
GREY ALLEN J	MAJ	0-0220538	0556	3
GREY CARL M	LTC	0-1584310	0468	3
GREY DONALD E	LTC	0-0554419	0868	1
GREY EDGAR W	CPT	0-1014931	0255	2
GREY FERNE B	MAJ	N-0742611	0465	1
GREY HAROLD T	MAJ	0-0246174	0547	2
GREY JACK R	1LT	0-0543229	0946	2
GREY JOHN D	CPT	0-0496845	0647	1
GREY RICHARD P	LTC	0-2289554	0567	1
GREY THOMAS A	MAJ	0-1299877	0963	1
GREYBILL JAMES R	MAJ	0-2014551	0262	1
GREYER CHARLES T	COL	0-0269157	0460	1
GRIB WALTER R	LTC	0-1037017	0767	1
GRIBBIN ROBERT E	LTC	0-0134293	1049	3
GRIBBLE ANDREW W JR	MAJ	0-1841741	0168	1
GRIBBLE ETHELBERT	CPT	0-1574782	1145	2
GRIBBONS WILLIAM L	LTC	0-1315683	0663	1
GRICE DERALD O	CPT	0-1307403	0846	2
GRICE JOSEPH C	CPT	0-1105476	0464	1
GRICE STEPHEN H	LTC	0-0212601	0654	2
GRIDER LLOYD B	WO1	W-2123198	0749	1
GRIEB OLIVER W	CPT	0-0271020	0662	3
GRIECO JOHN A	CPT	0-1931863	1262	1
GRIER CHARLES V	CPT	0-0488861	0649	2
GRIER JOHN B	COL	0-0217691	0861	1
GRIER WILLIAM H	CPT	0-1933802	1054	2
GRIES ALBIN G	2LT	0-0169381	0855	3
GRIESBAUER CHRISTIAN	1LT	0-2262144	0257	1
GRIESE JAMES R	MAJ	0-2056088	1264	1
GRIESHABER HARRY E	CPT	0-0444969	1147	1
GRIESSER FRANK J	CPT	0-1039366	0347	2
GRIEST JOHN R	1LT	0-0367879	1145	2
GRIFFEN FRANK A JR	1LT	0-0537778	0346	2
GRIFFES JAMES S	LTC	0-0521116	0265	3
GRIFFEY DURWARD P	MAJ	0-1289243	0561	1
GRIFFEY MILTON JR	MAJ	0-2263166	0666	1
GRIFFIN ALICE E	1LT	N-0721671	0446	2
GRIFFIN ANDREW D	CW2	W-2141294	0659	1
GRIFFIN ANGUS H	COL	0-0248902	1165	3
GRIFFIN AUBREY C	MAJ	0-0417824	0646	2
GRIFFIN BARTON B	LTC	0-0454274	0461	1
GRIFFIN BENNIE H	MAJ	0-2025951	0363	1
GRIFFIN BERNARD M	2LT	0-1305242	0745	2
GRIFFIN BERTRAM F	LTC	0-0167615	1055	3
GRIFFIN BURL T	WO1	W-2102959	0855	1
GRIFFIN CARL H	LTC	0-0330961	0260	1
GRIFFIN DANIEL C	MAJ	0-1825911	0762	2
GRIFFIN DARRELL E JR	MAJ	0-0532730	0864	1
GRIFFIN EARL R	LTC	0-1326393	0268	2
GRIFFIN EDWARD F	M G	0-0198652	1260	3
GRIFFIN ELMER E	LTC	0-0350905	0759	1
GRIFFIN EUGENE L	MAJ	0-0218952	0564	3
GRIFFIN FRANCIS E	MAJ	0-0337024	0460	1
GRIFFIN FRANCIS P	LTC	0-0267527	1044	2
GRIFFIN FRANK A	COL	0-0297143	0561	1
GRIFFIN FRED C JR	1LT	0-1060113	0846	2
GRIFFIN GARLIN	CW3	W-2145441	0164	1
GRIFFIN GEORGE H	MAJ	0-1686704	0468	1
GRIFFIN GEORGE V	LTC	0-1639103	0661	1
GRIFFIN GERALD	COL	0-0169797	0459	3
GRIFFIN GERALD E SR	LTC	0-1010283	1060	1
GRIFFIN GUY E	LTC	0-0192430	0559	3
GRIFFIN HARRY D	LTC	0-0292600	0265	3
GRIFFIN HARRY S	1LT	0-2026532	1155	1
GRIFFIN HELEN R	CPT	N-0732278	0846	1
GRIFFIN HENRY J	LTC	0-0270358	0661	1
GRIFFIN HENRY R	LTC	0-0948967	0268	1
GRIFFIN HENRY W	LTC	0-2043051	0761	1
GRIFFIN HOWARD L	MAJ	0-1824305	0963	1
GRIFFIN IVY L	CPT	0-1293244	0448	2
GRIFFIN JAMES A	LTC	0-1554375	0962	1
GRIFFIN JAMES D	1LT	0-1052368	0858	1
GRIFFIN JAMES E	LTC	0-0231350	0556	3
GRIFFIN JAMES E	LTC	0-1288733	0347	2
GRIFFIN JAMES H	CW3	W-2149213	0860	1
GRIFFIN JAMES J	LTC	0-0298581	0660	2
GRIFFIN JAMES M	CW3	W-2152672	1062	1
GRIFFIN JAMES R	CPT	0-0971074	1060	2
GRIFFIN JERRY A	COL	0-0358644	0859	1
GRIFFIN JOE R	CW3	W-2205998	0166	1
GRIFFIN JOHN C	CPT	0-0352280	0246	2
GRIFFIN JOHN F	MAJ	0-1030152	0461	1
GRIFFIN JUSTUS D	CW2	W-2216211	1268	1
GRIFFIN LAWRENCE W	CW3	W-2147335	0662	1
GRIFFIN LILLIAN R	2LT	L-0201502	0844	2
GRIFFIN MARGARET M	CPT	N-0727461	0947	1
GRIFFIN MARTIN J	MAJ	0-0387052	0864	3
GRIFFIN MARVIN E	CPT	0-1698202	0648	2
GRIFFIN MARY M	1LT	N-0758192	1147	1
GRIFFIN MEADE F	COL	0-0155279	0354	3
GRIFFIN MITCHELL	CW3	W-2213370	1067	1
GRIFFIN MOSE P	MAJ	0-0488467	0649	1
GRIFFIN NEWELL C	MAJ	0-0181522	0462	3
GRIFFIN NOEL H	MAJ	0-0443416	0459	1
GRIFFIN OLIN A JR	1LT	0-0438588	0845	2
GRIFFIN OLIVE D	MAJ	N-0722140	0361	1
GRIFFIN OSBOURNE A	LTC	0-1172882	0663	1
GRIFFIN OSCAR R JR	MAJ	0-1104697	0259	1
GRIFFIN PAUL A	LTC	0-2289847	1168	1
GRIFFIN PAUL E	LTC	0-0545264	1067	1
GRIFFIN REBA M	2LT	N-0737067	0945	1
GRIFFIN REYNOLDS M	LTC	0-0167900	0259	2
GRIFFIN ROBERT E	CW2	W-2213944	0568	1
GRIFFIN ROBERT T	2LT	0-1948143	0346	2

NAME	GRADE	SVC NO	DATE RET MO YR	RET CODE
GRIFFIN ROBERT V	MAJ	O-1102271	1060	1
GRIFFIN ROBERT W	CPT	O-1287866	1046	2
GRIFFIN ROY A JR	CW2	W-2214668	0868	1
GRIFFIN ROYAL M	COL	O-0197718	1060	3
GRIFFIN SAMUEL A	1LT	O-2011747	0767	1
GRIFFIN THOMAS E	CPT	O-0942972	0758	1
GRIFFIN THOMAS F	LTC	O-1796611	1262	1
GRIFFIN THOMAS F JR	LTC	O-0367731	0660	1
GRIFFIN THOMAS J	LTC	O-0827134	0363	1
GRIFFIN THOMAS M	WO1	W-2134441	0248	1
GRIFFIN WALTER C	MAJ	O-1913911	0566	1
GRIFFIN WAYNE H	1LT	O-1297025	0445	2
GRIFFIN WILBUR D	LTC	O-1037991	0960	1
GRIFFIN WILLIAM B SR	LTC	O-0262841	0168	3
GRIFFIN WILLIAM F	MAJ	O-0209002	1064	3
GRIFFIN WILLIAM H JR	MAJ	O-1281806	0161	1
GRIFFIN WILLIAM J	CW2	W-3430266	0867	1
GRIFFIN WILLIAM K	CPT	O-0342245	1145	2
GRIFFIN WILLIAM R	MAJ	O-0970261	1165	1
GRIFFIN WILLIAM W	COL	O-0234971	0654	3
GRIFFIN WILLIAM W	MAJ	O-1046462	0766	1
GRIFFIN WILLIE B	CW3	W-2141849	0760	1
GRIFFIN WILLIE D	CPT	O-1314133	0547	2
GRIFFIS DORIS S	1LT	N-0770144	0847	2
GRIFFIS HENRY H	LTC	O-0428163	0263	1
GRIFFIS HUGH C	1LT	O-1641344	1145	2
GRIFFIS WILLBERN D	CPT	O-1591164	0358	1
GRIFFITH ARCHIE L	LTC	O-1574784	1162	1
GRIFFITH ARTHUR E	1LT	O-1307538	0445	2
GRIFFITH ARTHUR G	LTC	O-1341778	0868	1
GRIFFITH BENNIE W JR	MAJ	O-1321032	0962	1
GRIFFITH BERTRAND A	LTC	O-0333555	1067	3
GRIFFITH BRANDON H	1LT	O-1111639	1045	2
GRIFFITH BRYAN	LTC	O-0497657	0457	1
GRIFFITH CHARLES M	COL	O-0437311	0968	3
GRIFFITH CLETUS L	MAJ	O-1555218	0268	3
GRIFFITH DEXTER K	COL	O-0324007	0860	1
GRIFFITH DONALD W	LTC	O-0323000	0965	3
GRIFFITH ERNEST F	MAJ	O-1633905	1060	1
GRIFFITH ESTES B	CPT	O-0363682	0446	2
GRIFFITH FULLER G JR	LTC	O-0175227	1059	3
GRIFFITH GORDON R	LTC	O-1017851	0264	1
GRIFFITH HAROLD H	COL	O-0290245	1056	3
GRIFFITH HAROLD P JR	2LT	O-0546706	0345	2
GRIFFITH HENRY H	MAJ	O-1298534	1060	1
GRIFFITH HUGHEY L	CW3	W-2136698	0763	1
GRIFFITH JAMES	MAJ	O-0503094	1054	1
GRIFFITH JAMES A	MAJ	O-0258500	1165	3
GRIFFITH JAMES A	1LT	O-1633247	0544	2
GRIFFITH JAMES C	CPT	O-0246959	0162	3
GRIFFITH JAMES L	CPT	O-0443754	0864	1
GRIFFITH JAMES R	2LT	O-0424649	1044	2
GRIFFITH JAMES R JR	COL	O-0242878	1165	3
GRIFFITH JOE E	MAJ	O-2204308	0366	1
GRIFFITH JOHN W	CW2	W-2142844	0254	1
GRIFFITH JOSEPH	LTC	O-0447950	0158	1
GRIFFITH JOSEPH L	1LT	O-0521854	0645	2
GRIFFITH KEAN	LTC	O-0114461	0154	3
GRIFFITH LESTER J	CW2	W-2208101	1062	2
GRIFFITH LEWIS S	CPT	O-0231116	0446	2
GRIFFITH LINDSAY J	COL	O-0242801	0754	3
GRIFFITH LOUIS H JR	MAJ	O-1043646	0562	1
GRIFFITH PHILLIP S	CW4	W-2119390	1263	1
GRIFFITH ROBERT D	CPT	O-1105445	0867	3
GRIFFITH ROBERT F	LTC	O-1058015	0565	3
GRIFFITH ROBERT J	CPT	O-2262322	0161	2
GRIFFITH ROBERT J S	1LT	O-1053149	0446	2
GRIFFITH WALTER C	COL	O-0166794	0956	3
GRIFFITH WILLIAM E	COL	O-0207262	1060	3
GRIFFITH WILLIAM H	MAJ	O-0231326	1056	3
GRIFFITH WILLIAM W	LTC	O-1558718	0862	1
GRIFFITHS ARTHUR L	MAJ	O-0347980	0661	1
GRIFFITHS BYRON R	CW3	W-2144104	0562	1
GRIFFITHS C R	1LT	O-1785317	0246	2
GRIFFITHS JAMES A	COL	O-0273191	0568	3

NAME	GRADE	SVC NO	DATE RET MO YR	RET CODE
GRIFFITHS LIONEL L	CW3	W-2148463	1065	1
GRIFFITHS MORGAN D	LTC	O-1794937	0863	1
GRIFFITHS WILLIAM J	CPT	O-0497249	0546	1
GRIFFON CLARA ANN	1LT	L-0801200	1045	2
GRIGALAUSKAS JOSEPH	1LT	O-2006452	1046	2
GRIGG JERRY D	CW3	W-2146508	0565	1
GRIGG KENNETH C	LTC	O-1306581	0267	1
GRIGG MAX R	CW3	W-2143093	0165	1
GRIGGERS WILLIAM J	CW2	W-3100425	0367	1
GRIGGINS ANTHONY J	1LT	O-1294463	0946	2
GRIGGS BENJAMIN F	CPT	O-0502494	0546	1
GRIGGS EMMITTE H	1LT	O-1320318	0446	2
GRIGGS ERNEST L JR	COL	O-0234025	0965	3
GRIGGS GRETCHEN	1LT	N-2295195	0862	2
GRIGGS HENRY H	CW2	W-2208917	0664	1
GRIGGS THOMAS D JR	CW2	W-2212015	0466	1
GRIGSBY FRANCIS M	LTC	O-1579727	0661	1
GRIGSBY KENNETH R	LTC	O-0291298	0364	3
GRILL FREDERICK	CPT	O-0277805	0663	3
GRILL JACK	LTC	O-0452649	0161	1
GRILL JAMES T	2LT	O-1016582	0444	2
GRILLO GEORGE F	1LT	O-0332660	1042	2
GRILZ JULIAN J	MAJ	O-0969286	1161	1
GRIM ORVILLE L	MAJ	O-1329352	0863	1
GRIMES ALTON W	CPT	O-1293403	0647	2
GRIMES CHARLES M	CW3	W-2004011	1265	1
GRIMES CLARENCE P	CPT	O-2262775	0261	1
GRIMES DAVID L	CW3	W-2208280	0967	1
GRIMES ERCELL A	CW4	W-2144182	0867	1
GRIMES GEORGE M	COL	O-0960635	0968	1
GRIMES GEORGE R	COL	O-0293108	1060	1
GRIMES HENRY J	CPT	O-1534272	0860	1
GRIMES JESSE R	MAJ	O-1642132	0157	1
GRIMES JOHN H	CPT	O-0226662	0845	2
GRIMES KENNETH A	COL	O-0265248	1263	1
GRIMES LADDIE J	LTC	O-1109335	0866	1
GRIMES PRIESTLY H	WO1	W-2106351	1047	2
GRIMES ROBERT H	WO1	W-2122030	0350	2
GRIMES VERNON S	CW3	W-2005981	0164	1
GRIMES WALTER B	COL	O-0264872	1067	3
GRIMKE GLEN O	MAJ	O-0218759	1154	3
GRIMM GLENN R	MAJ	O-2036055	1060	1
GRIMM LAURENCE F JR	CPT	O-0406988	1145	2
GRIMM WILLIAM C	MAJ	O-1030980	0760	1
GRIMMER BRUCE H	MAJ	O-2210273	0365	1
GRIMMER DONALD R	COL	O-0414010	0867	3
GRIMMER WILLIAM N	LTC	O-1594877	0463	1
GRIMMETT HALL W	MAJ	O-0965920	0363	1
GRIMMETT ROBERT R	CW2	W-2212162	0268	1
GRIMSLEY JAMES H	CPT	O-1309722	1147	2
GRIMSLEY VERN O	CW3	W-2147181	0464	1
GRINAGER CLINTON F	MAJ	O-0959318	0366	1
GRINCH LAWRENCE P	MAJ	O-1559455	1263	1
GRINDELL JOHN E	MAJ	O-1799633	0164	2
GRINDELL JOHN R	LTC	O-0364570	0163	1
GRINDLAY RONALD B	WO1	W-2004212	0465	3
GRINDLEY JOSEPH F	MAJ	O-1796080	0661	1
GRINE EDWARD E	1LT	O-1100566	0745	2
GRINER EDNA W	MAJ	N-0771912	0563	1
GRINER MARTIN E	CPT	O-0418499	0957	1
GRINESTAFF WILLIAM E	MAJ	O-1319735	1262	1
GRINNELL ERNEST D JR	CPT	O-1174872	0246	2
GRINNELL JOHN H	MAJ	O-1172883	0461	1
GRINSLADE PHILLIP R	1LT	O-1552684	0145	2
GRINSTEAD RICHARD F	LTC	O-0114324	0345	2
GRINVALSKY STEPHEN A	1LT	O-0526561	0744	2
GRISBON ROSE M	MAJ	M-0002310	1166	3
GRISDALE EARLE G	CPT	O-1292689	1046	2
GRISDALE ERNEST E	2LT	O-1327621	0246	2
GRISE LEO J	2LT	O-2053932	0149	1
GRISET TED A	CPT	O-1039657	0856	1
GRISHAM C P T	CW4	W-2146983	0656	1
GRISHAM FRED L	CW3	W-2142845	0559	1
GRISHAM HAROLD M	CW3	W-2141929	0261	1
GRISHAM QUITMAN O	LTC	O-0453650	0556	1

NAME	GRADE	SVC NO	DATE RET MO YR	RET CODE
GRISHAM ROSCOE E	LTC	O-1118583	0664	1
GRISSINGER JOHN P	CPT	O*1324311	1046	2
GRISSOM GEORGE T	CW2	W-2147323	0957	1
GRISSOM HORACE B	2LT	O-1640502	0245	2
GRISSOM JOHN E	CW2	W-2119696	0845	2
GRISSOM LAWRENCE B	MAJ	O-0397774	0660	1
GRISSOM MERICA C	LTC	O-0236147	1059	1
GRIST GEORGE E	1LT	O-2001796	0146	2
GRISTHUS ANTHONY	1LT	O-1302299	1152	1
GRISWOLD CARLTON P	CPT	O-0171502	0149	3
GRISWOLD FREDERICK	LTC	O-0393446	0664	1
GRISWOLD JAMES M	2LT	O-1317521	0744	2
GRISWOLD JAMES W	CW4	W-2142074	0461	1
GRISWOLD WESLEY C	1LT	O-1639107	0952	1
GRISWOLD WILLIAM H	LTC	O-0119283	0148	2
GRITIS PETER	LTC	O-0971281	1168	1
GRITMAN LINTON D	LTC	O-0499668	1061	3
GRITSAVAGE ALICE M	COL	N-0755518	1262	1
GRITTA PAUL B	MAJ	O-0455112	0653	1
GRITTON CLAUDE S	CW2	W-2149237	0358	1
GRITTON HAROLD N	MAJ	O-0888585	0565	1
GRITZ WILLIAM	COL	O-0181762	1147	1
GRIVAS JAMES N	CPT	O-0164628	1155	3
GRIVERS STANLEY J	CPT	O-2271708	0863	2
GRIZZARD JACK H	LTC	O-1997228	0466	1
GRIZZARD JOSEPH E	LTC	O-1001139	0557	1
GRIZZARD PHIL S	LTC	O-1003538	0667	3
GRIZZLE CHARLES R	MAJ	O-0964825	0363	1
GRNYA RICHARD M	CPT	O-5418721	1267	2
GROAH MILTON B	MAJ	O-2006191	0763	1
GROARK THOMAS P	1LT	O-1542441	0444	2
GROAT RICHARD D	CW3	W-2144135	0764	1
GROBMEIER B ARTHUR	LTC	O-0221358	1262	3
GRODBERG BURTON C	CPT	O-0541679	0146	2
GROESBECK BYRON	CPT	O-1319301	0247	2
GROESCHEL AUGUST H	B G	O-0345992	0668	3
GROETZINGER PHILIP W	LTC	O-1080285	1264	1
GROFF GEORGE M	1LT	O-1315579	0546	2
GROFF JESSE	CPT	O-1288536	0346	2
GROFF VICTOR L	COL	O-0239282	1162	3
GROGAN DORIS V	2LT	N-0785071	0146	1
GROGAN EDWARD M	CPT	O-0159982	1152	3
GROGAN JOHN	CW2	W-2210028	1163	1
GROGAN JOHN B	LTC	O-0401389	0161	1
GROGAN ROBERT J	MAJ	O-2014655	0564	1
GROGAN THOMAS W	LTC	O-1313028	0561	1
GROGG MILTON R	LTC	O-1167873	0861	1
GROH EDWIN G	LTC	O-1172884	1164	3
GROHGAN FRED A JR	LTC	O-2014479	0168	1
GROHL JOHN B	MAJ	O-0255777	0867	3
GROHNE WILLIAM G	1LT	O-1176646	0347	2
GROHS WILLIAM H	CPT	O-0242997	0149	3
GROKE LINTON R	COL	O-0274324	0956	3
GROLL DONALD J	MAJ	O-1015622	0657	1
GROLLER HERMAN W	LTC	O-1019994	0768	1
GROLLMAN JAYE J	1LT	O-0345595	0741	2
GROMBACH JOHN V	COL	O-0252642	0852	2
GROMER TERRY J	LTC	O-1701143	0546	2
GROMKO JOSEPH W	CPT	O-1013262	0561	1
GRONAU AXEL R	1LT	O-0535798	1044	2
GRONBERG WILFRED E	LTC	O-0290663	0766	3
GRONEMYER RALPH E	CW2	W-2144894	0756	1
GRONKE OTTO H	MAJ	O-1947497	0465	1
GRONSETH INGVALD H	COL	O-0128546	0250	3
GRONVOLD THEODORE C	LTC	O-1107995	0165	1
GROOM HORACE E JR	1LT	O-0461019	1045	2
GROOM WINSTON F	MAJ	O-0499362	1066	3
GROOME CHERRY A	LTC	O-0291921	0563	1
GROOMS RUSSELL E	CW3	W-2149256	0762	1
GROOTMAN PAUL G	MAJ	O-0949287	0366	1
GROOVER FRED E	LTC	O-1823732	0266	1
GROPP FREDDIE L	MAJ	O-1554376	1061	1
GROPP WILLIAM H	COL	O-0293901	1264	3
GROSBERG SAMUEL	LTC	O-0358109	0246	2
GROSE DAVID L	MAJ	O-0289327	0360	3

NAME	GRADE	SVC NO	DATE RET MO YR	RET CODE
GROSE EUDIE E	MAJ	O-1182124	0757	1
GROSECLOSE FORREST K	2LT	O-1642924	0345	2
GROSECLOSE FRANK F	COL	O-0255107	0659	3
GROSECLOSE JAMES H	MAJ	O-0408413	0466	1
GROSENBECK GRETCHEN	MAJ	N-0758169	1066	3
GROSGUTH JOSEPH JR	MAJ	O-0321063	0165	3
GROSHART OSCAR O	COL	O-0221202	1053	2
GROSHOK CRAIG G	1LT	O-1315300	0545	2
GROSOF WILLIAM S	CPT	O-0502082	0146	2
GROSS ARTHUR L	2LT	O-1300792	0744	2
GROSS CHARLES L	MAJ	O-1114953	1158	1
GROSS CHARLES N	CPT	O-0360376	0346	2
GROSS CHRIS L	MAJ	O-0302688	0267	3
GROSS EARL R	LTC	O-1170397	0865	1
GROSS EDWARD C	2LT	O-0455339	0145	2
GROSS EDWARD L	MAJ	O-1014171	0361	1
GROSS EVERETT W	1LT	O-1102272	0744	2
GROSS FRANK F	1LT	O-0495986	0145	2
GROSS FRANK W	CW4	W-2131294	0659	1
GROSS GEORGE J	LTC	O-0253261	0263	3
GROSS HARRY H	LTC	O-0269864	0868	3
GROSS HARRY W	MAJ	O-0150599	0356	3
GROSS HELEN R	MAJ	N-0798935	1265	1
GROSS HOWARD I	2LT	O-1799949	0446	2
GROSS IRVING	CW3	W-2152212	1264	1
GROSS JACQUES	LTC	O-0921291	1066	3
GROSS JOHN G	CPT	O-0238187	0665	3
GROSS JOSEPH M	CPT	O-0341336	0144	2
GROSS KARL R	CPT	O-1299232	0546	2
GROSS LESTER E	COL	O-0340815	0562	1
GROSS MARGARET E	MAJ	N-0723156	0367	3
GROSS MARTIN L	LTC	O-1311143	0158	1
GROSS MICHAEL A	COL	O-0276023	0867	3
GROSS MURRAY M	2LT	O-1081748	0145	2
GROSS NICK	2LT	O-0108485	1029	1
GROSS NORMAN N	LTC	O-0391529	0660	1
GROSS REYNOLDS C	LTC	O-0425309	1054	1
GROSS SAMUEL W	1LT	O-1327949	0646	2
GROSS THEODORE A	COL	O-0297626	1065	3
GROSS THOMAS C	CW3	W-2149408	0662	1
GROSS WAYMON L	LTC	O-1316407	0765	2
GROSS WILMA M	LTC	N-0702058	0647	1
GROSSCUP BLANCHE R	LTC	N-0728886	1066	3
GROSSE WOODROW O	1LT	O-1316408	0546	2
GROSSER JAMES C	MAJ	O-1646213	0662	1
GROSSI MILTON	LTC	O-2014818	0768	1
GROSSMAN AARON	1LT	O-0518319	0444	2
GROSSMAN ALEXANDER	LTC	O-0301112	0259	3
GROSSMAN HAROLD	LTC	O-1056019	1262	1
GROSSMAN JAMES M	MAJ	O-1854862	1223	1
GROSSMAN LESTER	MAJ	O-1330304	0567	1
GROSSMAN MARTIN M	1LT	O-1311765	0845	2
GROSSMAN MAX B	LTC	O-0292324	0447	2
GROSSMAN MORRIS J	WO1	W-2148293	1154	1
GROSSMAN PAUL W	LTC	O-1323312	1062	1
GROSSMAN ROYAL G	COL	O-0236123	1045	2
GROSSMAN SIDNEY W	MAJ	O-0321068	0845	2
GROSSMAN WILLIAM M	CPT	O-0538199	1046	2
GROSSMANN GORDON E	LTC	O-0962213	0868	1
GROSSTEPHAN ARTHUR R	COL	O-0220543	0564	3
GROSVENOR JACK L	CPT	O-1331282	1053	2
GROTE WILLIAM J JR	CPT	O-1715492	0648	2
GROTEFEND OLIVER G	COL	O-0321203	0964	3
GROTELUESCHEN E W	MAJ	O-0887376	0161	1
GROTENRATH JOSEPH A	COL	O-0253633	0154	2
GROTH ALFONS C	MAJ	O-1686538	0961	1
GROTH HOWARD G	LTC	O-1824857	0767	1
GROTHJAN CLETUS A	MAJ	O-0326483	0546	2
GROTHUSEN HAROLD D	LTC	O-0225751	0463	3
GROTON RICHARD W	LTC	O-2200603	0768	1
GROTTS JOHN J	MAJ	O-1649021	0657	1
GROTY CHARLES M JR	MAJ	O-0500270	1059	1
GROTZ CHARLES G	2LT	O-0109306	0227	1
GROTZ CLIFFORD C JR	MAJ	O-1922725	1066	1
GROUNDS MARIE	2LT	N-0761140	0345	1

NAME	GRADE	SVC NO	DATE RET MO YR	RET CODE
GROUSE WALTER C	LTC	0-0499646	0648	3
GROUT JAMES A	LTC	0-2034699	0962	1
GROVE CECIL V	CW4	W-2142846	0565	1
GROVE JOY L	CW3	W-2147308	0861	1
GROVE EARL A	LTC	0-0303292	1168	3
GROVE ELLSWORTH	MAJ	0-0966417	0766	1
GROVE GEORGE K	LTC	0-0445535	0554	1
GROVE HARRY C	WO1	W-2106438	0453	2
GROVE HOMER T	CPT	0-0970380	1060	1
GROVE JOHN A	LTC	0-1685855	1045	2
GROVE LARENCE H	CPT	0-1303498	0246	2
GROVE MERLE H	1LT	0-1314134	1058	1
GROVE PAUL C	MAJ	0-0272405	0246	2
GROVE PAUL D	MAJ	0-0310132	0246	2
GROVE PERCIVAL K	1LT	0-1995098	0946	2
GROVE ROBERT H	MAJ	0-0368584	0945	2
GROVE SAMUEL A C	MAJ	0-0406911	0366	3
GROVE STARKEY	LTC	0-0210425	0358	3
GROVE WENDELL P	CW2	W-2146860	0555	2
GROVER FRANK N	CPT	0-1324534	0147	2
GROVER FRED B	1LT	0-1320319	0146	2
GROVER FREDERICK	MAJ	0-1635983	0562	1
GROVER GEORGE B	CW4	W-2108326	0559	2
GROVER MORRIS L	COL	0-0296698	0964	3
GROVER PHYLLIS P	1LT	N-0751484	0246	1
GROVER WARREN B	CPT	0-0485396	0145	2
GROVES ALFRED H	1LT	0-1798730	0950	1
GROVES CLAIRE E	LTC	0-0261776	0360	1
GROVES GERALD L	CW3	W-2208259	0366	1
GROVES JAMES F	MAJ	0-1181616	0759	1
GROVES LAURENCE W	CPT	0-1314280	0149	2
GROVES LYMAN W	CW4	W-2122593	1057	3
GROVES MELVIN J	LTC	0-0453895	0958	1
GROVES PAUL A	MAJ	0-1548213	0452	2
GROVES ROBERT D	B G	0-0129915	0452	3
GROVES WILLIAM F	LTC	0-1576064	0462	1
GROVESTEEN LOYAL E	MAJ	0-2043170	0961	1
GROW NEVILLE L	LTC	0-0287535	0850	2
GROW PAUL C	LTC	0-0244082	1163	3
GROW STEWART L	MAJ	0-0368670	1045	2
GROWDON JAMES P	COL	0-0155229	0648	3
GRUBB HOMER J	CPT	0-0510087	1146	2
GRUBB MILO W	CW3	W-2150655	0965	1
GRUBB WILLIAM F JR	MAJ	0-1298386	0364	1
GRUBBS HORACE	MAJ	0-1112738	1160	1
GRUBBS HOWARD I	MAJ	0-1298860	1167	1
GRUBBS IRVIN A	MAJ	0-1017872	0965	1
GRUBBS PAUL L	CW2	RW-2209318	0561	1
GRUBE NELSON E	MAJ	0-1118214	0667	3
GRUBE ROY D	LTC	0-0286417	0763	3
GRUBER CHARLES G	COL	0-0110218	0854	2
GRUBER CHARLES N	LTC	0-1000571	0356	2
GRUBER DAVID P	CPT	0-1166075	0246	2
GRUBER GEORGE W	MAJ	0-1342266	0262	1
GRUBER JOHN F	MAJ	0-0362699	0368	3
GRUBER LOUIS G	CPT	0-0466976	0846	2
GRUBER RALPH A	LTC	0-0451112	0960	1
GRUBER RICHARD	1LT	0-1597802	0247	2
GRUBER ROBERT P	2LT	0-0957856	0550	2
GRUBER THOMAS H	LTC	0-1541909	1059	1
GRUBERT BILL	MAJ	0-2037166	1061	2
GRUBIN HAROLD	MAJ	0-0330059	0946	2
GRUBIN SAMUEL	LTC	0-0287063	0746	2
GRUBOWSKI JOSEPH N	CPT	0-1692011	0944	2
GRUDZIEN JOHN J	MAJ	0-2011254	0764	1
GRUELLE ORIE P	2LT	0-0439623	0860	1
GRUESS EMANUEL M	1LT	0-0502971	0643	2
GRUITS LAWRENCE T	MAJ	0-0484547	0154	1
GRULA JOE J	CW4	W-2111330	1054	1
GRUM MARY R	CPT	N-0783763	0146	1
GRUMAN DOROTHY J	1LT	L-0200182	1045	2
GRUMBEIN FRANKLIN K	CW3	W-2152343	0564	1
GRUMBLES TURMAN N	MAJ	0-1599041	1164	1
GRUMBLES WILLIAM H	CPT	0-1645012	0259	1
GRUMET MARVIN	2LT	0-1320726	0545	2

NAME	GRADE	SVC NO	DATE RET MO YR	RET CODE
GRUMMISH CARROLL H	CW3	W-2126087	0962	1
GRUMMON STUART N	COL	0-0234610	0356	3
GRUNDBORG BERTEL H	COL	0-0305051	1058	1
GRUNDEN BERT C	CW2	W-2206238	1060	1
GRUNDER MAYNARD S	CPT	0-0241561	0662	3
GRUNDER RICHARD R	CPT	0-1877221	0163	1
GRUNDMEIER LOWELL C	2LT	0-1333067	0946	2
GRUNDVIG HUGH B	COL	0-0282993	1160	1
GRUNDY MACK G	2LT	0-1015231	0857	1
GRUNDY THOMAS	CPT	0-0109574	0228	1
GRUNECK SIDNEY	COL	0-0174188	0258	1
GRUNER ERNEST F JR	CW2	W-2209161	0664	1
GRUNER LOUIS J JR	CPT	0-1534983	0853	2
GRUNEWALD ERNEST O	MAJ	0-0486772	0254	2
GRUNEWALD EUGENE F	LTC	0-0180509	0844	2
GRUNING ROLF P	MAJ	0-2263531	0365	1
GRUNKE ERIK B	MAJ	0-1324410	0557	1
GRUSINSKI FRED S	MAJ	0-2017051	0661	1
GRUSSENDORF B F	CPT	0-1798988	0866	3
GRUSTAS EDWARD	1LT	0-2263144	1057	2
GRUTERS BERTRAM E	LTC	0-0329686	0446	2
GRUTZA JEROME S	CPT	0-1286116	0246	2
GRUVER JOHN J	LTC	0-0212127	1061	3
GRYMES HERBERT L	COL	0-0126905	0651	3
GRYSIKIEWICZ STANLEY	COL	0-1047147	0868	1
GRZEGOROWICZ VINCENT	LTC	0-1646750	1264	1
GRZESKOWIAK URBAN J	LTC	0-1639108	0561	1
GRZONKA EDWARD J	2LT	0-1328251	0845	2
GRZYBEK EDWARD F	MAJ	0-1045762	0247	2
GRZYBOWSKI CHARLES F	CPT	0-1300313	0561	1
GRZYMALA STELLA O	1LT	N-0774049	0348	1
GRZYWNOWICZ ZIGGI S	LTC	0-1643619	0867	1
GSCHWINDT GEORGE F	MAJ	0-0333204	0648	3
GSTALTER EDMOND A R	CW3	W-2205719	0468	1
GUALILLO SILVIO P	LTC	0-0273604	0667	3
GUANZON RAFAEL L	LTC	0-2028494	0968	1
GUARDIOLA-PEREZ MIG	MAJ	0-1924151	0565	1
GUARIGLIA HUMBERT J	CW2	W-2117922	1044	2
GUARINO RUSSELL J	CW2	W-2143170	0956	1
GUARNIERI DAVID C	MAJ	0-0454213	0461	1
GUAS RAMON R	COL	0-0194051	0963	3
GUBIN EMIL K	COL	0-0922540	0566	3
GUBIN IRVING P	LTC	0-0229252	0364	3
GUBITOSI CLEO A	1LT	0-1635984	0847	2
GUBITOSI VINCENT H	CPT	0-1039013	1046	2
GUBOW LAWRENCE	CPT	0-1308509	0748	2
GUCKEL HERBERT B	CW3	W-2204766	0868	3
GUDDAL IVAN C	CPT	0-1325389	0246	2
GUDENAS PAULINE M	MAJ	N-0795117	0565	1
GUDENKAUF BERNARD J	MAJ	0-0969814	0765	1
GUDGEON RUSSELL D	LTC	0-0910577	0964	3
GUDGER GORDON B	LTC	0-0260861	0468	3
GUDGER JESSE M	MAJ	0-0248320	0964	3
GUDIE GEORGE G	1LT	0-1797118	0654	1
GUDMUNDSON WAYNE A	COL	0-0237351	1158	3
GUDRIDGE FREDERICK	LTC	0-1994918	0267	1
GUDWIN ABRAHAM	CPT	0-0484408	0345	2
GUEDET JOSEPH J	MAJ	0-0383262	0964	1
GUELDNER WALTER J JR	CPT	0-1287518	1060	1
GUENARD JOHN R	LTC	0-0283852	0759	1
GUENTHER CLIFFORD E	LTC	0-0100752	0756	3
GUENTHER ROBERT H	LTC	0-1109968	1062	1
GUENTHER STANLEY H	LTC	0-0319266	0264	3
GUENTHNER FRED	CW4	W-2122178	0161	1
GUERIN COURTLAND	LTC	0-0312744	0467	1
GUERIN DONALD L	WO1	W-2125722	0246	2
GUERNSEY CHARLES	CPT	0-1327733	1167	1
GUERNSEY JAMES C	CW2	W-2153351	0560	2
GUERNSEY RICHARD G	CW3	W-2205196	0866	1
GUERNSEY RUSSELL L	1LT	0-0514596	0846	2
GUERRA MACK A	CW3	W-2212356	0668	1
GUERRIERO HUMBERT	1LT	0-1182848	0963	3
GUERRISSI JOSEPH V	LTC	0-0860841	0267	1
GUERRO THOMAS M	LTC	0-0453428	0261	1
GUERTIN ALBERT R	MAJ	0-1104802	0666	1

NAME	GRADE	SVC NO	DATE RET MO YR	RET CODE
GUESS JULIAN C	MAJ	0-1320837	0658	1
GUESS LUTHER H	MAJ	0-0399305	0762	1
GUESSAZ LOUIS A JR	COL	0-0259517	1160	1
GUEST FRANK	MAJ	0-0970128	0865	1
GUEST JOHN A	LTC	0-0289458	1059	3
GUEST THOMAS W	CPT	0-1120682	0158	1
GUEST WILLIAM C JR	2LT	0-1291181	0146	2
GUETSCHOW FRANK I	CPT	0-0262853	1145	2
GUEVARA ROBERTO	MAJ	0-0963511	0765	1
GUFFAIN TOMAS H	LTC	0-1287699	0165	1
GUFFEY CLARENCE L	MAJ	0-1320000	0758	1
GUFFEY HAROLD W	MAJ	0-0451293	1146	2
GUFFEY HUGH J	LTC	0-1012377	0261	1
GUFFIN WILLIAM B	1LT	0-1043094	1044	2
GUGELER RUSSELL A	LTC	0-1184834	0867	1
GUGGENHEIM MORRIS	LTC	0-0251314	1065	3
GUGGOLZ MURIEL E	MAJ	N-0742616	0364	3
GUGISBURG ALBERT W	LTC	0-0227925	0263	3
GUHL EDWARD R	MAJ	0-1178817	0265	1
GUICE JASON G	1LT	0-2319781	0451	3
GUIDA CRESCENZO	LTC	0-0387075	0662	1
GUIDA DOMINIC P	CPT	0-1309255	0347	2
GUIDO JOSEPH J	CPT	0-1923613	0462	1
GUIDOTTI FRANK P	LTC	0-0350147	0147	2
GUIER DAVID H	MAJ	0-1540852	0266	1
GUIJARRO ANTONIO	LTC	0-0287653	0657	3
GUILBAULT BRIEN L	CW2	W-2101774	0446	1
GUILD WALTER A	COL	0-0206210	0758	1
GUILE SAMUEL H	MAJ	0-1112740	0257	1
GUILFORD MADGE L	2LT	N-0773288	0447	1
GUILFORD WILLIAM B	MAJ	0-2021141	0565	1
GUILFOYLE FRANCIS L	CPT	0-1001796	0146	2
GUILFOYLE KENNETH H	CW3	W-2149902	1166	1
GUILLIAMS IRA	CW4	W-2143575	0466	1
GUILLORY KIRBY	LTC	0-0488432	1156	1
GUILLOT EARL L	LTC	0-0924812	0165	3
GUINAN EDWARD R	CPT	0-1012646	0161	1
GUINAN MATTHEW P	2LT	0-1012865	0345	2
GUINN FLETCHER	1LT	0-2036546	0754	1
GUINN JOHN W JR	CPT	0-0699884	1057	2
GUINN JOSEPH P	LTC	0-1042586	0367	1
GUINN MARTHA S	1LT	N-0744284	0146	1
GUINN WALTER	COL	0-0359941	0868	1
GUINN WILLIAM H JR	LTC	0-2017052	1163	1
GUINNUP GORDON R	CPT	0-0296520	1145	2
GUINOT LUIS	WO1	W-2115620	0359	1
GUINTO FAUSTINO G	1LT	0-1896387	1160	1
GUION JOHN P	CPT	0-2271658	0364	1
GUIOT FERNANDO M	MAJ	0-0508365	0264	1
GUISINGER CARLOS W	MAJ	0-1919231	0667	1
GUISINGER EARL C	COL	0-0240932	0846	2
GUIVER GOLDEN C	LTC	0-0309940	0146	2
GULA ANDREW JR	LTC	0-1000572	0463	1
GULBRANSON IRVIN V	MAJ	0-2030980	1166	1
GULCZYNSKI EDMUND C	MAJ	0-2039544	0563	1
GULDENZOPF ROBERT L	MAJ	0-1175726	1060	1
GULEKE JOSEPH	CW2	W-2206904	0663	1
GULIAN GEORGE	COL	0-0339700	1060	1
GULLANS OSCAR	COL	0-0231362	1262	3
GULLBORG HARRY E	1LT	0-1061710	0845	2
GULLEDGE GEORGE W	CW3	W-2152294	1159	1
GULLEKSON CARL L	MAJ	0-2009615	0765	1
GULLETT PAUL C	2LT	0-0441772	0943	2
GULLETTE ROBERT E	LTC	0-0202350	0263	3
GULLICKSON CARMEN I	CPT	N-0775938	0546	2
GULLIFER WILLIAM H	MAJ	0-0126138	0853	3
GULLIKSON ARTHUR G	COL	0-0304936	0858	1
GULLINGSRUD M J O	MAJ	0-0327720	0945	2
GULLION ROBERT C	2LT	0-0516589	0944	2
GULLIVER HERBERT J	CPT	0-1167012	0854	2
GULLIVER REGINALD E	MAJ	0-0259173	0166	3
GULLIXON RICHARD L	CPT	0-0452044	1045	2
GULMYER GEORGE J	MAJ	0-0228463	0463	3
GUMASKAS PETER J	LTC	0-0418283	1160	1
GUMBRELL ARTHUR J	2LT	0-1315301	0345	2

NAME	GRADE	SVC NO	DATE RET MO YR	RET CODE
GUMBS ALFRED E	CPT	0-0156055	0648	3
GUMM CLARK L	CPT	0-1055021	0747	2
GUMMEL CHARLES P	LTC	0-0475964	1054	1
GUMMIS GEORGE J	2LT	0-4040907	0456	2
GUMMOE ROBERT G	LTC	0-1695216	0768	3
GUMP ALAN M	COL	0-0274087	0364	3
GUNBY RUSSELL A	MAJ	0-1019193	1060	1
GUND LEON J	LTC	0-0378897	0554	1
GUNDECK WALTER S	MAJ	0-0198077	0557	3
GUNDERSEN GEORGE A	LTC	0-1546243	0366	3
GUNDERSON CARL F	CW2	W-2143743	0262	1
GUNDERSON COLEMAN G	LTC	0-0173062	1152	2
GUNDERSON ERNEST O	COL	0-0332033	0166	3
GUNDERSON FRANK N	COL	0-0283558	0464	3
GUNDERSON GEORGE M	MAJ	0-0171449	0554	3
GUNDERSON HARVEY J	LTC	0-0250254	0966	3
GUNDERSON RICHARD L	1LT	0-1324622	0245	2
GUNDERSON RUSSELL A	CPT	0-1016546	0947	2
GUNDLACH PHILIP J	LTC	0-0342498	1057	1
GUNDRUM JEROME D	1LT	0-1317906	0545	2
GUNDRY KENNETH E	MAJ	0-0322433	0847	2
GUNGL JOHN C	COL	0-0162684	0648	3
GUNHUS HARMS J	LTC	0-0930468	0465	1
GUNKEL WILLIAM F	LTC	0-0448356	0763	1
GUNN CYRUS L	LTC	0-0258631	0267	3
GUNN ELDON L	CPT	0-1996646	0547	2
GUNN GEORGE C	LTC	0-1309256	1166	1
GUNN JAN V	MAJ	0-0355328	0246	2
GUNN JOE C	MAJ	0-2018683	1162	1
GUNN JOHN E JR	WO1	W-2120459	0862	2
GUNN JOHN H	LTC	0-0303585	0762	3
GUNN NELLIE L	CPT	L-0200420	0346	2
GUNN RAYMOND F	COL	0-0192294	0561	1
GUNN ROBERT B	CPT	0-2035097	0662	1
GUNN ROBERT K	LTC	0-1824177	0765	1
GUNN SAMUEL A	MAJ	0-0370251	0446	2
GUNN THOMAS F	COL	0-0112193	0859	3
GUNNARSON WALTER S	LTC	0-0278309	0668	3
GUNNE MICHAEL J	MAJ	0-1291458	0960	1
GUNNELL EMMA B	MAJ	N-0783788	0863	1
GUNNERUD SWEN S	CPT	0-0224749	0561	3
GUNNING GORDON W	1LT	0-2025916	0247	2
GUNNING JOHN T	CPT	0-1321507	0746	2
GUNNING LAURENCE G	CW4	W-2152578	0765	1
GUNNOE WILBUR G	CPT	0-0473474	0546	2
GUNSEL ROBERT C	MAJ	0-2200513	0466	1
GUNSTON GEORGE T	COL	0-0194301	0259	3
GUNTER ALBERT A	LTC	0-0485275	0954	1
GUNTER CLARENCE W	CW2	W-3400076	0868	2
GUNTER EDWARD R	1LT	0-0255333	0239	1
GUNTER ELMER E	CPT	0-0302160	0945	2
GUNTER FURMAN N	MAJ	0-5301861	0568	1
GUNTER ROBERT E	MAJ	0-0292601	0444	2
GUNTER ROBERT L	CW3	W-2144885	1062	1
GUNTER SAM H	LTC	0-1635988	0162	1
GUNTHARP GEORGE O	LTC	0-0337281	0657	1
GUNTHARP PAUL M	LTC	0-1013289	0361	1
GUNTHER HERBERT J	COL	0-0267778	0158	1
GUNTHER RAYMOND C	COL	0-0369044	0365	3
GUNTHER WALTER	LTC	0-0132814	0556	3
GUNTHORP CECIL H	LTC	0-0360561	0863	3
GUNTZVILLER HARVEY L	1LT	0-2051159	1046	2
GUPTON BENNETT L	CPT	0-0496366	0645	2
GUPTON GROVER A	CW3	W-2204976	0663	1
GUPTON SAMUEL A	LTC	0-1103190	0462	1
GURAN SIDNEY J	LTC	0-0332411	0646	2
GURAT PANTALEON	1LT	0-0890491	1050	1
GURBAL DOROTHY V	2LT	N-0795164	1046	1
GURIAN BERNARD	CPT	0-0486669	0245	2
GURLEY JAMES H	LTC	0-1649475	0861	1
GURLEY JOSEPH C	LTC	0-1633914	0860	1
GURNEE WILLIAM N	CW3	W-2146332	0962	1
GURNEY EDWARD J JR	LTC	0-1010115	1046	2
GURNEY FAUNTLEROY	CW3	W-2144653	1264	1
GURNEY MYRON F	CPT	0-0888209	1060	1

NAME	GRADE	SVC NO	DATE RET MO YR	RET CODE
GURS GAY	MAJ	0-0400809	0163	1
GURSCH OTTO F	LTC	0-0358141	0663	3
GURTOV BERNARD H	1LT	0-1283759	0246	2
GURZNY JOSEPH L	MAJ	0-0271835	0257	3
GUSHIN PAUL P	LTC	0-1533330	0865	1
GUSIMAT GAVINO L	2LT	0-1896522	0358	1
GUSLER CYRIL L	LTC	0-0348279	0867	3
GUSMEROLI JOSEPH	1LT	0-1324411	0147	2
GUSSAK JOHN J	COL	0-0275458	0160	3
GUSSETT NORWICH B	LTC	0-0189403	0160	3
GUST GEORGE A	1LT	0-0448273	0344	2
GUSTAFSON ALICE C	1LT	N-0758203	0447	1
GUSTAFSON CARL G	CW3	W-2143194	0962	1
GUSTAFSON ERLAND W	1LT	0-1032711	0146	2
GUSTAFSON GERALD A	MAJ	0-0537593	0564	1
GUSTAFSON HARRY L	COL	0-0125927	0754	3
GUSTAFSON HERMAN C	LTC	0-0542428	0764	3
GUSTAFSON NILS R	LTC	0-0207338	0657	3
GUSTAFSON PAUL S	CW3	W-2152383	0763	1
GUSTAFSON VICTOR E	MAJ	0-0132119	0144	2
GUSTAFSON VICTOR V	CPT	0-0409147	1043	2
GUSTAFSON WALTER R	CW3	W-2005711	0167	1
GUSTAFSON WILLIAM C	WO1	W-2148255	0153	2
GUSTAVSON CARL B	LTC	0-1054763	1066	1
GUSTIN DALE D	CPT	0-1541852	0159	1
GUSTIN GEORGE W	LTC	0-1590511	0865	1
GUSTIN NICHOLAS L	CW4	W-2135684	0563	1
GUSTIN ROBERT V	LTC	0-0119793	0648	3
GUSTINA FRANCIS L	LTC	0-1101854	1160	1
GUSTORF FRED	COL	0-0312010	0758	2
GUTH WILLIAM W	MAJ	0-1307685	1163	1
GUTHART WENDELL L	CPT	0-1179084	0946	2
GUTHRIE CHARLES M	MAJ	0-1289724	0246	2
GUTHRIE CLARENCE L	CPT	0-0533127	1145	2
GUTHRIE EDWARD H	MAJ	0-0229836	0845	2
GUTHRIE FRED G	1LT	0-1287701	0346	2
GUTHRIE GEORGE P	COL	0-0232937	0464	3
GUTHRIE GORDON J	MAJ	0-2011594	1162	1
GUTHRIE HUGH H	LTC	0-2289473	0365	1
GUTHRIE JAMES B	MAJ	0-0254304	0465	1
GUTHRIE JAMES C	LTC	0-2048941	1165	1
GUTHRIE JESSE L	MAJ	0-1996348	1160	1
GUTHRIE OTTO F	CW2	W-2150306	0162	1
GUTHRIE PERCY L	LTC	0-0259932	0568	3
GUTHRIE WARREN W	1LT	0-0252299	0446	2
GUTJAHR ARTHUR H	1LT	0-1030571	0645	2
GUTJAHR LYDIA	MAJ	N-0737847	0364	1
GUTMAKER HYMAN R	CPT	0-1696116	0246	2
GUTMAN ALBERT F	MAJ	0-2028586	1267	1
GUTMANN ADDIS	COL	0-0219073	0261	3
GUTOW BENJAMIN P	LTC	0-0322806	0568	3
GUTOWSKY HERBERT S	CPT	0-0401091	0945	2
GUTSHALL RICHARD B	LTC	0-0399424	0860	1
GUTTERMAN GEORGE K	LTC	0-0382928	1060	1
GUTTING JOSEPH L	MAJ	0-0175591	0161	3
GUTTMAN WILLIAM S	MAJ	0-1686596	1062	1
GUTTNER GEORGE	MAJ	0-1647057	0568	3
GUY ALFRED E	CPT	0-0268270	0346	2
GUY GEORGE F	COL	0-0213068	0664	3
GUY JAMES H	CPT	0-0524597	0246	2
GUY JAMES S	MAJ	0-1120060	0761	1
GUY JOHN A	LTC	0-1100568	0567	3
GUY LEONIDE J	MAJ	0-0185684	0842	1
GUY LEWIS H	LTC	0-0285922	0768	3
GUY ROSS O	LTC	0-0138897	0648	3
GUY WILLIAM F	CW3	W-2148569	0567	1
GUYER NATHAN E	MAJ	0-0215199	1154	3
GUYER PAUL M	COL	0-0231780	1059	3
GUYETT HARVEY E	MAJ	0-0258982	0560	3
GUYTON JAY M	CPT	0-0924223	0447	2
GUYTON JOSEPH D	LTC	0-0272089	0768	3
GUYTON SAM M	MAJ	0-0471628	1046	2
GUZICKI RAYMOND A	LTC	0-0384541	1061	1
GUZMAN DONATO P	CPT	0-1896443	0358	1
GUZMAN HENRY M	CPT	0-1644388	0360	1

NAME	GRADE	SVC NO	DATE RET MO YR	RET CODE
GUZMAN MANUEL JR	LTC	0-0293891	0246	2
GUZY STEPHEN W	LTC	0-0286667	0967	3
GUZZARDO SAM	LTC	0-1312760	0662	1
GWALTNEY PERRY M	LTC	0-0245433	1053	3
GWATHMEY CABELL	COL	0-0443908	0662	3
GWIAZDA EDWARD J	CW3	W-2147974	0761	1
GWILLIAM MARK R M	COL	0-0109575	1150	3
GWIN GARLAND L	CPT	0-1294299	0747	2
GWIN JAMES M	LTC	0-0282982	1166	3
GWINN FRANK W	LTC	0-0331898	1054	2
GWINN FRED M JR	1LT	0-1644389	0745	2
GWINN JOHN F	LTC	0-0420987	0563	2
GWINN MACK W	LTC	0-1181274	0167	1
GWINNER HAROLD H	LTC	0-0323360	1060	1
GWINNER JOHN K	MAJ	0-0960495	0264	1
GWOZOZ JOSEPH B	LTC	0-1283596	1264	1
GWYNN CHARLES B	COL	0-0223492	0262	3
GWYNN HAROLD V	LTC	0-1177816	0663	1
GWYNN THOMAS E	1LT	0-1996622	0552	2
GYAMI WILLIAM H	MAJ	0-1313696	0365	1
GYTE MILTON E	MAJ	0-0486579	0954	1
GYZEN KLESS	LTC	0-1340455	1166	1
HAAB HOWARD H	CPT	0-1293404	1047	2
HAACK ROBERT O	CPT	0-1319944	0347	2
HAAG CHARLES F	LTC	0-1588018	0163	1
HAAG ESTELLA W	2LT	N-0700392	0637	1
HAAG HAROLD H	LTC	0-0114972	0557	3
HAAG MERRALD H	CPT	0-0275058	1043	2
HAAG ROBERT H	LTC	0-0102930	0845	2
HAAG ROBERT V	CPT	0-0276203	0961	2
HAAKE HOWARD G	CPT	0-0381554	0545	2
HAAKER ELSIE C	MAJ	L-0220007	1167	3
HAALAND ADLER	LTC	0-0375261	0261	1
HAALAND OTTO E	LTC	0-0368654	0967	3
HAAN DANIEL A	CW3	W-2142681	0459	1
HAAR WALTER P	MAJ	0-1553831	0263	1
HAAS CHARLES W	1LT	0-1931297	1057	2
HAAS DOROTHY R	MAJ	N-0805287	0768	1
HAAS EDWARD F	1LT	0-2035846	0845	2
HAAS FRANK T	CW2	W-2142365	0858	1
HAAS GEORGE JR	CW4	W-2146602	0468	1
HAAS GEORGE M	LTC	0-0307504	0564	3
HAAS JOHN A JR	MAJ	0-2019875	0562	1
HAAS JOSEPH	COL	0-0196248	1050	3
HAAS KENNETH W	COL	0-0311614	1146	2
HAAS MABEL E	1LT	N-0752037	0845	1
HAAS ORAN C	LTC	0-1796460	0264	1
HAAS ROBERT F	WO1	W-2124707	0444	2
HAAS THEOPHIL W	LTC	0-0297191	0367	3
HAAS WILLIAM L	LTC	0-1642931	0267	3
HAASE ANTHONY C	LTC	0-0183464	0948	2
HAASE ELDON A	LTC	0-0384205	0760	1
HAASE ELTON L	CW4	W-2122272	0466	1
HAASE REX L	1LT	0-0298625	1145	2
HAASE WILLIAM F	MAJ	0-1107453	1059	1
HAASIS LOUIS C	LTC	0-1556433	0667	1
HABAL DULCESIMO	1LT	0-1896474	1065	1
HABAS MILTON L	LTC	0-1283418	0561	2
HABEL HENRY W	CPT	0-0478470	1045	2
HABER GERD	LTC	0-0961829	0968	1
HABER JOSEPH	MAJ	0-1173262	0153	1
HABERCOM ALAN L	LTC	0-1043095	0765	1
HABERLE DAVID L	1LT	0-0389637	1145	2
HABERLE JACOB	CPT	0-0183349	0249	3
HABERLIN CHESTER E	COL	0-0162317	0559	3
HABERMAN EDWARD J	CPT	0-1299736	0746	2
HABERSTROH CHARLES F	LTC	0-0251617	0366	3
HABERSTZER D H	CW2	W-3100537	0267	1
HABURNE JAMES D	CPT	0-0890327	0348	2
HACHADORIAN CHARLES	CW2	W-2116212	0962	3
HACHET HARRY A	LTC	0-0301999	0764	3
HACK DON E	CPT	0-1894177	1065	1
HACK FREDERICK JR	LTC	0-0274862	0968	3
HACK RAY B	1LT	0-0477730	0241	1
HACK WILLIAM M JR	CW3	W-2207963	0968	1

NAME	GRADE	SVC NO	DATE RET MO YR	RET CODE
HACKARD CLIFFORD T	LTC	0-1296023	0262	1
HACKENBERGER R J	LTC	0-0299990	0264	3
HACKENYOS GEORGE D	CW2	W-2215362	0967	1
HACKER ALEX	LTC	0-1108709	1065	1
HACKER DONALD N	LTC	0-0398193	0966	1
HACKER HERMAN J	2LT	0-0437094	0945	2
HACKER HUBERT L	2LT	0-1294830	1144	2
HACKER HUGH A	LTC	0-1292171	0855	1
HACKER LAWRENCE W	LTC	0-0264093	0657	3
HACKER PHILIP C	MAJ	0-0239799	0753	3
HACKER PHILIP C JR	LTC	0-0413331	0561	1
HACKER RAYMOND G	LTC	0-1104186	0266	1
HACKETT JAMES W	CW3	W-2145175	0662	1
HACKETT KENNETH L	1LT	0-0535899	1145	2
HACKETT NEIL B	1LT	0-1894824	0846	2
HACKETT ROBERT A	2LT	0-1030476	0844	2
HACKETT THOMAS A	MAJ	0-0365174	0747	2
HACKETT WILLIAM D	MAJ	0-1327836	0263	1
HACKETT WILLIAM F	LTC	0-1591776	0163	1
HACKETT WILLIAM G	2LT	0-1016708	0645	2
HACKFORD LEIGH C	CPT	0-1691402	0845	2
HACKITT JACK	LTC	0-1312761	0663	1
HACKMAN HARRY C	MAJ	0-0126479	0850	3
HACKNEY CHARLES G	1LT	0-1331834	1046	2
HACKNEY JAMES F	LTC	0-0948876	0468	1
HACKNEY JOE G	1LT	0-1175449	1044	2
HACKNEY THOMAS G	CW3	W-2205718	0968	1
HACUMAN SIXTO	1LT	0-1896789	0948	1
HADAWAY JOHN W	MAJ	0-0887470	1058	1
HADAWAY WILLIAM C	CPT	0-1035276	0762	1
HADDAD EDWARD G	CPT	0-0299746	1050	2
HADDAD FREDERICK	COL	0-0339938	0560	1
HADDEN RALPH W	MAJ	0-0969649	1061	1
HADDEN ROBERT L	MAJ	0-1186413	0463	1
HADDEN THOMAS M	COL	0-0325911	0268	3
HADDICK JOHN K	LTC	0-0332478	0161	1
HADDIX PETER E	CPT	0-0164215	0929	2
HADDOCK ANNA C	MAJ	N-0769656	0568	3
HADDOCK JAMES O	LTC	0-2014787	1068	1
HADDOCK JORGE G	CPT	0-1924075	0865	2
HADDOCK RAY D	MAJ	0-0144790	0152	3
HADDON WILLIAM S	CPT	0-0989466	0858	2
HADDOX EDDIS F	CW2	W-2217147	0768	1
HADEN DONALD J	LTC	0-1120319	1065	1
HADEN ROBERT B	LTC	0-1181275	0865	1
HADEN WALTER R	LTC	0-1041781	0466	1
HADJY HARRY	1LT	0-1541702	1046	2
HADLEY BETTIE L A	MAJ	L-0804191	0966	1
HADLEY CHANNING L	LTC	0-0962516	0767	1
HADLEY CHARLES C	CW3	W-2149320	0659	1
HADLEY HERBERT	CPT	0-0110718	0544	2
HADLEY JAMES M	LTC	0-1291810	0166	1
HADLEY JOHN M	LTC	0-0906578	1062	3
HADLEY VIRLEN H	1LT	0-1693009	0146	2
HADLOCK ALBERT E	LTC	0-0907602	0463	3
HADLOW CHARLES E	LTC	0-1582356	1062	1
HAEBERLIN STANLEY M	1LT	0-1180927	0246	2
HAECKER ROSS R	LTC	0-1546028	0562	1
HAEFELI CHARLES L	MAJ	0-2262600	0368	1
HAEFNER EUGENE A	1LT	0-1893976	0156	2
HAEFS GLENN H	WO1	RW-2148726	0858	1
HAEHL MARY J	2LT	N-0704144	0744	1
HAENDIGES WILLIAM A	MAJ	0-0329421	0756	1
HAENE WALTER H	MAJ	0-0415448	0346	2
HAENEL BOB B A	COL	0-0422190	1061	1
HAENSEL FRANCIS S	MAJ	0-1799734	1162	1
HAERING MILSON C	CW4	W-2001677	1265	3
HAERING ROY W	2LT	0-1054258	0945	2
HAERLE CHARLES R	CW4	W-2101782	0560	1
HAERTEL GEORGE H	LTC	0-1697971	0667	1
HAERTEL VINCENT M	CW2	W-2143479	0456	1
HAFEMAN GEORGE B	LTC	0-1284326	0559	1
HAFER HAROLD	MAJ	0-1320693	0556	1
HAFFEN JOHN W	MAJ	0-0263838	0247	1
HAFFEY GEAN B JR	MAJ	0-1533331	0857	1

NAME	GRADE	SVC NO	DATE RET MO YR	RET CODE
HAFFNER CHARLES C JR	M G	0-0142106	0658	3
HAFLER MELBA	1LT	N-0734297	0146	1
HAFLEY OLEN C	CPT	0-1011288	1145	2
HAFLING ERNEST M	CPT	0-0488179	0145	2
HAFNER LENA A	2LT	N-0784184	0945	1
HAFNER RALPH A	LTC	0-0373451	1165	3
HAGA CECIL K	MAJ	0-1917850	0367	1
HAGA RALPH L	LTC	0-0520016	1164	3
HAGAN ALFRED F	LTC	0-0290216	1161	3
HAGAN CHARLES H	CPT	0-1581156	0845	2
HAGAN FRANK E	CPT	0-1312552	0451	1
HAGAN JAMES H	LTC	0-0207777	1047	2
HAGAN JOHN E	1LT	0-0532672	0646	2
HAGAN LLOYD D	MAJ	0-0322081	0746	2
HAGAN OSCAR P	MAJ	0-1328999	0466	1
HAGAN WILLIAM B	LTC	0-0281666	0357	3
HAGAN 3RD WILLIAM J	LTC	0-0386384	0446	2
HAGANS DONALD F	CPT	0-1596340	1060	1
HAGANS LYNDEN A	1LT	0-0361164	0542	2
HAGAR CLYDE V	1LT	0-1703011	1055	1
HAGARTY ELIZABETH	LTC	N-0736466	0961	1
HAGE SAM M	1LT	0-1545009	1145	2
HAGEDORN ENRIQUE	1LT	0-0890287	1152	1
HAGEDORN KENNETH F	CPT	0-0357375	1045	2
HAGEDORN RAYMOND E	MAJ	0-0265755	0244	2
HAGEDUS STEVEN R	CPT	0-1171570	0845	2
HAGEE GEORGE M	LTC	0-0132060	0749	3
HAGEL VINCENT	1LT	0-1300478	0845	2
HAGEMAN EARL L	MAJ	0-0177797	1049	3
HAGEMAN RICHARD F	CPT	0-0958856	0561	1
HAGEMANN MILTON H	LTC	0-1794938	0363	1
HAGEMEIER PAUL E	LTC	0-0409968	1060	2
HAGEMEYER JESSE F	MAJ	0-0311756	0154	1
HAGEN ARNOLD C	CPT	0-1288538	0246	2
HAGEN CHARLES M	1LT	0-0499736	0444	2
HAGEN CLIFFORD W	MAJ	0-0749232	0860	1
HAGEN DAVID P	LTC	0-0475366	0657	1
HAGEN DEAN C	LTC	0-1540944	0665	1
HAGEN DUANE L	CW3	W-2208010	1267	1
HAGEN ENGWARD H	MAJ	0-0286700	0544	2
HAGEN GUY B	LTC	0-1300961	0263	1
HAGEN JOHN E	CPT	0-0390793	0945	2
HAGEN LESLIE H	1LT	0-1304522	0350	2
HAGEN MILDRED A	1LT	N-0745241	0246	1
HAGEN WALLACE C	CPT	0-1309725	0847	2
HAGEN WAYNE S	COL	0-0257096	0467	3
HAGENBUCH FORREST H	LTC	0-0248152	0162	3
HAGENBUSH FRANK L	CW2	W-2144457	0665	1
HAGENDORFF HAROLD G	CPT	0-1341779	0457	1
HAGENMEYER ERNEST A	MAJ	0-0969598	1162	1
HAGENS DAVID K	LTC	0-1167876	0162	1
HAGER ANNA L	MAJ	N-0728187	1065	1
HAGER CARL J	LTC	0-0177667	0655	3
HAGER HOMER H	LTC	0-0983504	0968	2
HAGER JAMES L	COL	0-0269019	1162	3
HAGER JOHN M	MAJ	0-0104655	0949	3
HAGER REUBEN W	LTC	0-0341439	0346	2
HAGER SAMUEL E JR	LTC	0-0277460	0459	3
HAGER VIRGIL G	CW4	W-2107941	0658	1
HAGER WALTER A	CW3	W-2147357	0565	1
HAGER WILLIAM M	MAJ	0-0242374	1056	3
HAGER WILSON C	CPT	0-0365854	1045	2
HAGERMAN DAVID D	MAJ	0-0528724	0565	1
HAGERMAN EDWIN R	LTC	0-1013689	0461	1
HAGERTY CHARLES G	1LT	0-1012438	0445	2
HAGERTY DOROTHY G	CPT	N-0720754	0346	1
HAGERTY GEORGE L	LTC	0-1011552	0957	1
HAGERTY JAMES S	MAJ	0-0490900	0153	1
HAGERTY JOHN D	MAJ	0-0259339	1058	3
HAGERTY RICHARD C	CPT	0-1890410	1062	2
HAGERTY THOMAS L	MAJ	0-1298219	0248	2
HAGERTY WALTER H	LTC	0-1637585	1066	1
HAGEWOOD EUGENE G	CPT	0-1578562	0758	1
HAGEWOOD SHEPHERD D	CW3	W-2147894	0562	1
HAGG EARL R	WO1	W-2139539	0445	2

NAME	GRADE	SVC NO	DATE RET MO YR	RET CODE
HAGGARD CECIL L	MAJ	0-0318675	0768	3
HAGGARD KENNETH L	MAJ	0-0283169	0945	2
HAGGARD LLOYD G	LTC	0-0234338	1264	1
HAGGARD MARION C	LTC	0-1291629	0265	1
HAGGARD MARVIN I JR	CW3	W-2208268	1267	1
HAGGARD MIKE L	CPT	0-0953642	1061	1
HAGGARD NEAL F	COL	0-0351806	0763	1
HAGGARD PAUL L	MAJ	0-0995684	0160	1
HAGGERTY CECIL J	LTC	0-0245557	1261	3
HAGGERTY CHARLES A	COL	0-0148369	0655	3
HAGGERTY CHARLES A	2LT	0-1825469	0845	2
HAGGERTY CLAUDE M	COL	0-0158648	0255	3
HAGGERTY RICHARD J	CW2	W-3151602	0367	1
HAGGERTY ROY H	LTC	0-0520071	1163	2
HAGGERTY WILLIAM O	LTC	0-1316548	1166	1
HAGLER CURTIS E	MAJ	0-0271524	0865	3
HAGLER WILLIAM	1LT	0-2056129	0645	2
HAGMAIER LOUIS C	CW3	W-2149698	1163	1
HAGMAN WILLIAM L	LTC	0-0247137	0858	3
HAGMANN EDWARD A	MAJ	0-0305950	0445	2
HAGNEY FRANK J	MAJ	0-1061711	0361	1
HAGON JOHN D	COL	0-0277461	1061	3
HAGOOD EUGENE A	CW2	W-2146960	1160	2
HAGOOD MONROE J	COL	0-0267972	0663	1
HAGSTRUM JOHN H	LTC	0-2040740	0562	1
HAGSTROM OSCAR JR	1LT	0-1328485	0746	2
HAGSTROM WILLIAM E	MAJ	0-0464112	0947	2
HAGUE RICHARD H JR	MAJ	0-1166730	1061	1
HAGUE WILLIAM W	LTC	0-0158865	0955	3
HAGWOOD HENRY M	CW3	W-2141298	0459	1
HAGY EDWARD M	LTC	0-0467102	1165	1
HAHN AUGUST C	COL	0-0406912	0967	3
HAHN CHARLES J	LTC	0-1552687	0463	1
HAHN CLYDE R	1LT	0-0509189	1043	2
HAHN EUGENE G	CW3	W-2110932	0866	1
HAHN FREDERICK JR	LTC	0-0425223	0862	1
HAHN HAROLD W	2LT	0-0462272	0545	2
HAHN HARVEY L	MAJ	0-1690807	0767	1
HAHN HENRY W	CW2	W-2114999	0845	2
HAHN HUBERT C	LTC	0-0352926	0463	3
HAHN JOHN H	COL	0-0259458	0359	1
HAHN NORBERT L	LTC	0-0281302	0666	3
HAHN PAUL B	CPT	0-0345804	0246	2
HAHN PAUL G	CPT	0-0155612	0354	3
HAHN RUDOLPH R	LTC	0-0321870	0561	1
HAHN WALTER S	COL	0-0243889	0766	3
HAHN WELDON J	CW4	W-2132550	0461	1
HAHN WILFERD K	CW2	W-2111071	0545	2
HAIG GEORGE	LTC	0-0204657	1061	3
HAIG JOSEPH A	COL	0-0167105	0758	3
HAIGH JAMES H	MAJ	0-0219556	1158	3
HAIGH RALPH H	LTC	0-1045445	1062	1
HAIGHT ARTHUR W	CPT	0-1548823	0762	1
HAIGHT ASHLEY B	LTC	0-0148367	0454	3
HAIGHT EARL P	MAJ	0-0291315	0747	2
HAIGHT JULIUS R	COL	0-0318047	0967	3
HAIGHT LESLIE L	CPT	0-1311006	0747	2
HAIGHT WILLIAM C	2LT	0-1597121	1056	1
HAIGHT WILLIAM R	COL	0-0260588	0764	3
HAIGNEY VINCENT J	1LT	0-1635998	1043	2
HAIL CURTIS D	2LT	0-1691705	1145	2
HAIL DOUGLAS L	1LT	0-1309726	0346	2
HAILE ELMER R JR	CPT	0-0281253	0446	2
HAILE HARRY W	1LT	0-1304207	1045	2
HAILEY CARL C	2LT	0-1825952	0345	2
HAILEY JESSE S	MAJ	0-1688429	1263	1
HAILS GEORGE F	1LT	0-1294831	1144	2
HAILSTORK HOWARD H	2LT	0-1318892	0146	2
HAIMAN BERNARD A	MAJ	0-0919819	0847	2
HAIN HENRY F	LTC	0-0314717	0961	3
HAINE EDGAR A	COL	0-0271608	0868	3
HAINER ALBION E	LTC	0-0245871	0245	2
HAINER LINTON	MAJ	0-0323228	0965	3
HAINES ALFRED W	MAJ	0-0205966	0858	1
HAINES ARTHUR L	1LT	0-1014220	1046	2
HAINES BRUNETTO J	MAJ	0-0469571	0347	2
HAINES BURZELOUS	LTC	0-1797638	1266	1
HAINES CHARLES E	MAJ	0-2035607	0157	1
HAINES FRANCIS G	MAJ	0-1634840	0561	1
HAINES GEORGE H	COL	0-0283653	0468	3
HAINES HAROLD E	CW3	W-2207178	0468	1
HAINES HILTON O	COL	0-0317834	1065	3
HAINES HOWARD F	B G	0-0173170	1161	3
HAINES JOHN W	COL	0-0261114	1167	3
HAINES JOHN W	MAJ	0-2262973	0665	1
HAINES JUAN D	MAJ	0-2025324	0267	1
HAINES MELVIN E	CW3	W-2146820	0563	1
HAINES OBERT L	LTC	0-0472969	0257	1
HAINES PAUL F	COL	0-0202889	0755	1
HAINES PAUL L	LTC	0-0329848	1066	1
HAINES RICHARD E	CW2	W-2104120	0661	1
HAINES ROBERT W	LTC	0-1000956	1160	1
HAINES VICTOR H	2LT	0-1549486	0945	2
HAINES WILLIAM A JR	LTC	0-0381789	1167	1
HAINES WILLIAM L	1LT	0-0890125	0350	2
HAINLINE FORREST A	LTC	0-0117396	0651	3
HAIR HARRISON B JR	1LT	0-0341242	0544	2
HAIR RAFORD	CW4	W-2112013	0958	1
HAIR ROBERT	CW3	W-2152607	1165	1
HAIR ROBERT M	CW3	W-2147334	0264	1
HAIR ROGER H	MAJ	0-1342267	1164	1
HAIRE JESSE L	COL	0-0398188	0960	1
HAIRSTON JOSEPH H	CPT	0-1171572	1060	1
HAIRSTON MCCOY F	CW3	W-2152213	0564	1
HAIRSTON ROBERT T	2LT	0-1039016	0146	2
HAIS HARRY I	1LT	0-0398140	1041	2
HAISLIP WILLIAM M	MAJ	0-0389112	0149	2
HAJDU FRANK M	CW2	W-2150269	1162	1
HAJEK JAMES W	MAJ	0-1314137	0861	1
HAKALA HERBERT E	LTC	0-1922555	1168	1
HAKALA PENTTI J	CW3	W-2141299	1160	1
HAKE LUCILE B	MAJ	N-0757450	0568	1
HAKE NEVIN	LTC	0-1050693	0264	1
HAKEN SIDNEY	LTC	0-1646048	0766	1
HAKES CHARLES C	MAJ	0-0909560	0944	2
HAKES JAMES D	CW2	W-2150874	1059	1
HALA OTTO	CPT	0-0339910	0462	1
HALAICO STEPHEN J	CW2	W-2150786	0258	1
HALAS LLOYD V	CW3	W-2203871	1066	1
HALASKA ANTON H	LTC	0-0313682	0657	1
HALBERG ROBERT L	2LT	0-1329118	0246	2
HALBERSTADT FRANK C	1LT	0-1555395	0745	2
HALBERSTADT HENRY J	LTC	0-0279972	0862	3
HALBERT HOWARD F	LTC	0-0399387	0261	1
HALBERT WILBAR	LTC	0-0202620	0663	3
HALBLEIB EDWARD K	LTC	0-0312144	0665	3
HALBROOK ALFRED F	MAJ	0-2288512	1264	1
HALCOMB WILLIAM F	1LT	0-1292024	1045	2
HALCOMB WILLIAM S	LTC	0-0144826	0353	3
HALDEMAN WELLINGTON	LTC	0-0126482	1043	2
HALE BARTLEY F	CPT	0-1318426	0556	1
HALE BOBBY H	MAJ	0-2037053	0762	1
HALE BUNN D	COL	0-0382579	0761	1
HALE CLARENCE W	MAJ	0-1634841	0160	1
HALE DONALD S	1LT	0-1016199	0646	2
HALE EDWARD T	LTC	0-1342179	1266	1
HALE FRANK S	CPT	0-0236157	0462	3
HALE GAITHER F	CPT	0-0142007	0853	3
HALE HARVEY M	CW3	W-2152384	0963	1
HALE HERMAN G	CPT	0-0132221	1054	3
HALE HERMAN J	MAJ	0-1926981	0168	1
HALE HOMER H	CPT	0-1542688	0653	1
HALE JAMES D	MAJ	0-0963980	0467	1
HALE JAMES E	MAJ	0-2026878	0161	1
HALE JOHN P	MAJ	0-2009688	0757	1
HALE JOSEPH W	MAJ	0-0426053	0146	2
HALE JULIUS	MAJ	0-0188803	0847	1
HALE KENNETH G	2LT	0-2011360	0251	2
HALE LELAND E	LTC	0-0355755	1060	1
HALE MURRILL F	MAJ	0-2012599	1161	1
HALE NORMAN H	MAJ	0-0253932	0766	3
HALE OLIVE M	2LT	N-0724072	1044	1
HALE PRESTON W	LTC	0-0919442	1162	3
HALE RICHARD S	LTC	0-1702876	0867	1
HALE RICHARD V	LTC	0-0550244	0664	1
HALE ROBERT E	LTC	0-1313399	0762	1
HALE ROBERT L	1LT	0-0456003	0147	2
HALE SAM T	LTC	0-0308347	1053	2
HALE SHERMAN A	CW3	W-2129496	1060	1
HALE VASCO D	1LT	0-1101470	0446	2
HALE WALTER T	MAJ	0-2018160	0662	1
HALE WARNER S	CPT	0-0406445	0346	2
HALE WARREN C	2LT	0-1317908	0245	2
HALE WILEY J	CPT	0-0365874	0363	3
HALE WILLIAM F JR	LTC	0-1180196	0457	1
HALE WILLIAM H	CPT	0-1167015	1045	2
HALE WILLIAM L	MAJ	0-1180523	1060	2
HALES GEORGE J	LTC	0-0251655	0167	3
HALES JOHN C	MAJ	0-0969196	0762	1
HALES JOHN D	CPT	0-1556143	0253	2
HALES MARVIN H	LTC	0-0264717	0561	3
HALETSKY ANTHONY D	CW3	W-2147224	0763	1
HALEY DONALD W	COL	0-0920439	0267	3
HALEY HENRY P	LTC	0-0382280	1166	3
HALEY JOHN	MAJ	0-0509221	1047	2
HALEY JOHN F	CPT	0-0461751	0745	2
HALEY JULIUS F	1LT	0-0379688	1044	2
HALEY LAWRENCE C	CW2	W-2118092	0953	1
HALEY PAUL V	CPT	0-1308947	1047	2
HALEY ROBERT E	LTC	0-1011002	0163	1
HALEY ROBERT W	CPT	0-0969282	0161	1
HALEY VINCENT E	MAJ	0-0587209	0660	1
HALEY WILLIAM R JR	LTC	0-1173632	1166	1
HALEY WILLIAM T	LTC	0-1321179	0465	1
HALFERTY ALMA	2LT	N-0700242	0832	1
HALFERTY ANGIE F	CPT	N-0775394	0947	1
HALFF MAYER H	COL	0-0272172	0166	3
HALFORD HARRY E	MAJ	0-2006850	0161	1
HALFORD WILLIAM D	MAJ	0-1573863	0357	1
HALISKY JOHN R	LTC	0-1554384	0264	1
HALKEWICZ MICHAEL JR	1LT	0-1051985	1146	2
HALL ALAN W	LTC	0-0240087	0247	1
HALL ALFONSO O	LTC	0-0379328	0153	2
HALL ALFRED H	COL	0-0290711	1154	1
HALL ALLEN C	MAJ	0-0477572	0745	2
HALL ALTON G	COL	0-0230252	0864	3
HALL ALVIN C	CPT	0-1292451	0847	2
HALL ANDREW A	COL	0-0296023	0460	1
HALL ANTHONY C	MAJ	0-1295203	0460	1
HALL ARTHUR A	MAJ	0-1063066	0258	1
HALL ARTHUR B	MAJ	0-0187624	0549	3
HALL AUSTIN J JR	COL	0-0340914	0268	1
HALL BETTY J	MAJ	N-0792332	0864	2
HALL BILLY C	MAJ	0-0989363	0267	1
HALL BRUCE	MAJ	0-1923574	0766	1
HALL CARL E	MAJ	0-0327282	1045	2
HALL CARLISLE	CPT	0-0181105	1051	3
HALL CARLSON W	CPT	0-1303717	0358	1
HALL CECIL D	CPT	0-0218602	1157	3
HALL CHARLES D	CPT	0-0494445	0653	1
HALL CHARLES D	LTC	0-1323925	0761	1
HALL CHARLES E	LTC	0-0324407	1264	3
HALL CHARLES F	CW2	W-2214826	0567	1
HALL CHARLES K	MAJ	0-1116224	1057	1
HALL CHARLES L	CPT	0-0251782	1150	3
HALL CHARLES L	LTC	0-1579740	0563	1
HALL CHARLES W	COL	0-0329562	0565	3
HALL CLAIR L	MAJ	0-0291610	0160	1
HALL CLARENCE W	COL	0-0378335	0664	3
HALL LLOYD R	LTC	0-0323768	0347	2
HALL DALLAS A	2LT	0-1330421	1145	2
HALL DANIEL E	MAJ	0-0980547	1061	1
HALL DANIEL F	LTC	0-0476313	0867	1
HALL DANIEL M	CW3	W-2152461	0662	1
HALL DAVID B	CPT	0-1700741	0945	2
HALL DIXIE G	COL	0-0331832	0660	1
HALL DON	CW2	W-2149889	0562	1
HALL DON C	CPT	0-2202214	0658	2
HALL DONALD F	COL	0-0107297	0654	2
HALL DONALD S	CPT	0-2035098	1262	1
HALL EARL C	MAJ	0-0274537	0854	3
HALL EDGAR F	1LT	0-1314704	1145	2
HALL EDWARD B	LTC	0-0223988	0463	3
HALL EDWARD C	CW4	W-2106462	1057	1
HALL EDWIN P	LTC	0-0282523	1062	3
HALL ELLIS H	CPT	0-0377748	0744	2
HALL ERNEST B	COL	0-0323410	0966	1
HALL ERNEST J	COL	0-0206743	0648	3
HALL EVERETT C	1LT	0-1594882	0648	1
HALL FAYETTE G	COL	0-0270317	0561	1
HALL FLETCHER H	CW4	W-2108019	1058	1
HALL FLOYD A	LTC	0-1542856	1060	1
HALL FORREST D	MAJ	0-0980724	0363	1
HALL FRANCES W	MAJ	N-0735445	0163	1
HALL FRANK D	CPT	0-1011431	1045	2
HALL FRANK J	LTC	0-0327624	0848	3
HALL FRED A	MAJ	0-0165844	0754	3
HALL FRED C	LTC	0-1797124	1060	1
HALL FRED W	LTC	0-0131062	0355	3
HALL FREDERIC A	LTC	0-0138316	0359	3
HALL FREDERIC H	MAJ	0-1946275	0953	1
HALL FREDERICK	MAJ	0-0264240	0462	3
HALL GARNET E	LTC	0-0238359	0464	3
HALL GEORGE A JR	COL	0-0909524	0966	3
HALL GEORGE F	COL	0-0254703	0767	3
HALL GLENN O	COL	0-0287545	1065	1
HALL GORDON	COL	0-0128255	1055	3
HALL GORDON F	2LT	0-0441469	0344	2
HALL GORDON L	CW2	RW-3350135	0165	1
HALL GORDON S	CW2	W-2215283	1066	2
HALL HAROLD K	CPT	0-2262399	0261	1
HALL HAROLD L	MAJ	0-2262290	0863	2
HALL HARRY A	LTC	0-0115135	0744	2
HALL HARRY J	LTC	0-0355183	0863	3
HALL HARRY O	1LT	0-2030472	1053	2
HALL HARRY W	CW2	W-2209217	0564	1
HALL HARVEY A	MAJ	0-0103884	0155	3
HALL HENRY C	LTC	0-0235258	0153	3
HALL HENRY C	2LT	0-1998121	0149	1
HALL HENRY H	LTC	0-0124559	0648	3
HALL HENRY W	LTC	0-0247318	0564	3
HALL HERBERT H	MAJ	0-0148387	0551	3
HALL HILLARD JR	CW3	W-2149069	0762	1
HALL HIRAM C	COL	0-0292912	0858	1
HALL HIRAM R	CPT	0-1178169	0846	2
HALL HORACE L	LTC	0-0410866	1064	1
HALL HORACE W	CPT	0-0155610	0251	3
HALL HOWARD F	1LT	0-1325890	1045	2
HALL HUBERT P	CPT	0-0450879	0345	2
HALL HULON C	2LT	0-1308425	1144	2
HALL JACK T	LTC	0-1541328	0959	1
HALL JAMES C	LTC	0-0421951	1263	3
HALL JAMES D	LTC	0-1104809	0965	1
HALL JAMES L	LTC	0-0348888	0467	3
HALL JAMES M	MAJ	0-1018408	0457	1
HALL JAMES M JR	LTC	0-0291141	0466	3
HALL JAMES N SR	LTC	0-1010420	0863	1
HALL JAMES P	LTC	0-0265988	0544	2
HALL JAMES T JR	MAJ	0-1288539	0457	1
HALL JAMES W	CPT	0-0900248	0845	2
HALL JAMES W	MAJ	0-1878699	0268	2
HALL JAY L	LTC	0-0349614	0467	3
HALL JESSE E	MAJ	0-2018878	1266	1
HALL JESSE T	CW2	W-2149214	0762	1
HALL JOHN	COL	0-0207585	1163	3
HALL JOHN E	LTC	0-1301405	1065	3
HALL JOHN K	CPT	0-1997973	0656	1
HALL JOHN L	LTC	0-0488777	0254	1
HALL JOHN R W	LTC	0-0144352	1044	2
HALL JOHN W	CW2	W-2210375	0267	1

NAME	GRADE	SVC NO	DATE RET MO YR	RET CODE
HALL JOSEPH	LTC	0-1824859	0666	1
HALL JOSEPH C	CPT	0-1286276	0446	2
HALL JULIAN H	LTC	0-0996894	1268	1
HALL KARL S	LTC	0-0304345	0962	1
HALL LAURENCE W	LTC	0-0245788	0359	3
HALL LAWRENCE M	CW3	W-2152791	1163	1
HALL LAWRENCE P	CW2	W-2144532	0958	1
HALL LAWRENCE W	COL	0-0301381	0962	1
HALL LEON M	COL	0-0189382	0-49	3
HALL LEONA J	MAJ	N-0752466	0267	1
HALL LESTER H	COL	0-0242228	1155	3
HALL LUTHER B	CPT	0-0279700	0858	3
HALL MARTYN L	MAJ	0-0187318	1054	3
HALL MAX K	1LT	0-1293707	0246	2
HALL MEDWIN E	WO1	W-2143793	0960	1
HALL MERLE W	LTC	0-0362725	0964	1
HALL MERRITT W	CW2	W-2143391	0456	1
HALL MILLARD W	COL	0-0245542	0646	2
HALL MUNROE	MAJ	0-1919105	0866	1
HALL MONROE S	MAJ	0-1168700	0267	1
HALL NORMAN B	LTC	0-0249393	0659	3
HALL OLIVER H	CPT	0-0279144	0460	3
HALL OMER N	MAJ	0-1319199	0164	1
HALL PAUL L	LTC	0-0297084	1262	3
HALL PERCY G	COL	0-0246273	0953	3
HALL PERCY L	CW4	W-2149386	1168	1
HALL PHIM SR	2LT	0-1289416	1045	2
HALL RALPH H	LTC	0-0922052	0-51	3
HALL RAYMOND C	MAJ	0-0510491	1060	1
HALL REGINALD S	LTC	0-0230070	1262	3
HALL REUBEN B JR	COL	0-1574249	0767	1
HALL RICHARD C	MAJ	0-1918977	0564	1
HALL ROBERT A	1LT	0-0497516	0953	1
HALL ROBERT E	MAJ	0-0978780	1264	1
HALL ROBERT JR	CW3	W-2206283	0867	1
HALL ROBERT M	MAJ	0-0367927	0645	2
HALL ROBERT M JR	CW2	W-2147817	1061	2
HALL ROBERT P	CPT	0-0254281	0960	3
HALL ROBERT P	1LT	0-0366904	0245	2
HALL ROBERT W	LTC	0-0186337	0155	3
HALL ROSS C	CPT	0-0230502	0662	3
HALL ROSWELL B	WO1	W-2113830	0345	2
HALL ROY C	LTC	0-0924260	0268	3
HALL RUPERT L	MAJ	0-2005494	0461	1
HALL RUTH I	MAJ	N-0742231	0463	1
HALL SAM W	MAJ	0-0380096	0645	2
HALL SAMMIE A	MAJ	0-1336503	0764	1
HALL SAMUEL B	CPT	0-0413920	0653	1
HALL SHERWOOD IV	1LT	0-5342441	1268	2
HALL STANTON A	COL	0-0203487	0761	3
HALL STEPHEN E	LTC	0-0241660	0765	3
HALL STERLING J	MAJ	0-1182128	0164	1
HALL SYDNEY H	LTC	0-0230741	0857	3
HALL THEODORE L	LTC	0-0983751	0568	1
HALL THOMAS B	CW4	W-2125297	0559	1
HALL THOMAS E	LTC	0-1175142	1162	1
HALL THOMAS E	MAJ	0-1798256	0867	3
HALL THOMAS L	COL	0-0911644	0647	2
HALL THOMAS T	CW2	W-2005634	0268	3
HALL TOM	COL	0-0291795	0862	3
HALL VERNON	1LT	0-1049502	0259	1
HALL WALLACE B	LTC	0-0335743	1160	2
HALL WALTER D	LTC	0-1314737	0568	1
HALL WALTER E	MAJ	0-1332699	1155	2
HALL WALTER W	LTC	0-0474341	0657	1
HALL WARNER W	LTC	0-0223672	1164	3
HALL WARREN G	1LT	0-1647064	0150	1
HALL WENDELL L	LTC	0-2037978	0765	2
HALL WILBUR A	CPT	0-1307966	1046	2
HALL WILL E	CPT	0-0235148	0459	3
HALL WILLIAM	COL	0-1535187	1068	2
HALL WILLIAM E	CW3	W-2144072	0964	1
HALL WILLIAM L	LTC	0-0265913	0959	3
HALL WILLIAM M	1LT	0-1325751	1045	2
HALL WILLIAM P	LTC	0-1549959	0966	1

NAME	GRADE	SVC NO	DATE RET MO YR	RET CODE
HALL WILLIAM R	LTC	0-1030667	1161	1
HALL WILLIAM R	WO1	W-2153085	1054	2
HALL WINDELL B	MAJ	0-2032920	1062	1
HALL WINSLOW G JR	MAJ	0-1878893	1168	1
HALL WOODBURY K	LTC	0-0262662	0966	3
HALL WYATT E	MAJ	0-1340886	0765	1
HALLAHAN WILLIAM J	LTC	0-1012115	0563	1
HALLAHAN WILLIAM J	MAJ	0-1577276	1045	2
HALLAM RICHARD E	CW3	W-2141160	0464	1
HALLAM ROBERT M	LTC	0-0300240	0567	3
HALLARMAN EDWIN	2LT	0-0540319	0945	2
HALLBECK CLARENCE E	CPT	0-0508059	0749	1
HALLBERG ROBERT E	CPT	0-0455637	0952	2
HALLDOW HARRY R	MAJ	0-1312006	0960	1
HALLE ARNE F	CPT	0-1645016	0247	2
HALLE EUGENE L	LTC	0-0374408	1163	1
HALLE HERMAN L	LTC	0-1292335	0261	2
HALLEN WALTER E	LTC	0-0225270	0555	3
HALLENBECK ALONZO G	CPT	0-0168022	0453	3
HALLENBECK GEORGE G	MAJ	0-0195736	0246	2
HALLENBECK KENNETH L	COL	0-0223564	1060	3
HALLER FRANKLIN P JR	COL	0-0177364	0944	2
HALLER JEROME B	LTC	0-0193152	1153	3
HALLER ROBERT B	LTC	0-1054607	0465	1
HALLER WILLIAM M	LTC	0-1104813	1265	1
HALLER 3RD F P	1LT	0-0440896	0944	2
HALLETT BEN S	CW4	W-2148093	0368	1
HALLETT CHARLES S	LTC	0-0315968	0462	1
HALLETT EDWARD A	COL	0-1100571	0463	1
HALLETT EMMALINE W	MAJ	N-0778349	0665	1
HALLETT JACK O	MAJ	0-1030668	1060	1
HALLEY HARRY L S	COL	0-0142333	0954	3
HALLEY THOMAS V	CW4	W-2127246	0859	1
HALLEY WILBUR G	2LT	0-0524437	0645	2
HALLFORD DANIEL C	CPT	0-0388737	0346	2
HALLIBURTON KENNETH	LTC	0-1582702	0467	1
HALLIDAY EUGENE F	LTC	0-0494126	0555	1
HALLIDAY GRANT T	CW4	W-2121033	1057	1
HALLIDAY KENNETH G	LTC	0-1583045	1062	1
HALLIDAY MICHAEL	LTC	0-0371459	0657	1
HALLIDAY RALPH H	LTC	0-1010045	1065	1
HALLIDAY ROBERT J	COL	0-0331237	0467	3
HALLIN CYRIL A	LTC	0-1533079	0557	1
HALLINAN JOHN J	CPT	0-0131081	1050	3
HALLINAN JOHN J	MAJ	0-1633922	1057	1
HALLIWELL HARRY A	LTC	0-0568468	0465	1
HALLIWELL WARREN L	1LT	0-1061712	0854	1
HALLMAN PAUL E	LTC	0-0233922	0365	3
HALLMARK DALE E	MAJ	0-2263334	1264	1
HALLMARK KENITH V SR	MAJ	0-1011038	0557	1
HALLOCK DONALD H V	COL	0-0258371	0568	3
HALLOCK HARRY E	LTC	0-0272347	0668	3
HALLOR FREDERICK	COL	0-0246937	1047	2
HALLORAN ALFRED J	1LT	0-1019136	1045	2
HALLORAN HENRY E	COL	0-0220424	0262	3
HALLORAN PAULINE L	CW3	V-0820489	0365	1
HALLOWAY EDWARD A	CPT	0-0164021	0345	1
HALLOWELL NOEL E	LTC	0-0265005	1265	3
HALLOWELL RAYMOND M	MAJ	0-1114151	0954	1
HALLOWES WALTON B	LTC	0-0910149	0263	1
HALLSTROM IRVING T	LTC	0-0214330	1061	3
HALLSTROM NILS F	MAJ	0-1030154	0956	1
HALLSWORTH HERBERT I	MAJ	0-2204101	0965	1
HALLUM FRANK E	LTC	0-0249431	1165	3
HALPERIN BARNET	COL	0-0321356	0867	3
HALPERIN HERMAN J	CPT	0-0447733	0146	2
HALPERN HARRY L	CPT	0-0504929	1044	2
HALPERT WALTER	LTC	0-0320728	0967	3
HALPIN DAVID F	LTC	0-1560023	1263	1
HALPIN GEORGE E JR	MAJ	0-2021072	1267	1
HALPIN JAMES M	LTC	0-1060790	0167	1
HALPIN MICHAEL P	LTC	0-0220838	0954	1
HALPIN ROBERT D	LTC	0-1305243	0562	1
HALPIN THOMAS A	LTC	0-0382262	0967	3
HALPIN THOMAS F JR	1LT	0-2284007	0960	2

NAME	GRADE	SVC NO	DATE RET MO YR	RET CODE
HALPRIN ROBERT S	1LT	0-1303718	0446	2
HALSALL EARL B	LTC	0-0299639	1068	3
HALSALL JOHN S	MAJ	0-1337569	1263	1
HALSEY CLIFFORD W	CPT	0-1171175	1045	2
HALSEY EDWARD L JR	MAJ	0-1596344	0564	1
HALSEY EDWARD N	LTC	0-0322191	0468	3
HALSEY JOHN E	1LT	0-1317294	0546	2
HALSEY RICHARD V	CW2	W-2144497	0261	1
HALSO ALTON K	CW3	W-2142159	1064	1
HALSTEAD ALICE S	CPT	N-0727775	0547	1
HALSTEAD EARL T	COL	0-0109786	0347	2
HALSTEAD FELIX G	COL	0-0161189	0754	3
HALSTEAD FRANK B	CW3	W-2205717	0467	1
HALSTEAD RAYMOND N	MAJ	0-1585553	0164	1
HALSTEAD T S	COL	0-0187623	0150	3
HALSTEAD WOODROW W	CW2	W-2142705	0157	1
HALSTED HAROLD S	COL	0-0275266	0359	3
HALSTED WILLIAM B JR	LTC	0-1103672	0164	1
HALSTROM LLOYD C	MAJ	0-1895431	0762	1
HALTER WILLIAM E SR	MAJ	0-0971206	0663	1
HALTERMAN GEORGE A	MAJ	0-1101473	0764	1
HALVERSON CLARIBEL A	1LT	N-0771365	0345	1
HALVERSON KARL L	MAJ	0-0506700	0954	1
HALVERSON KENNETH L	COL	0-0342280	1165	1
HALVERSON LESTER P	MAJ	0-0975684	1061	1
HALVERSON WALTER L	MAJ	0-0351021	0758	1
HALVERSON WILLIAM I	MAJ	0-1050287	1062	1
HALVIN MILTON S	CPT	0-1821862	0556	2
HALVORSEN CLIFFORD	MAJ	0-0258017	0450	2
HALVORSON EDWIN W	CPT	0-0532242	0845	2
HALVORSON GLADYS M	1LT	N-0741346	1045	1
HALVORSON HARRY A	LTC	0-0450298	1057	1
HALVORSON MELVIN A	1LT	0-0385204	0643	2
HALVORSON NORRIS P	MAJ	0-0346629	0364	3
HALVORSON THEODORE B	CPT	0-0234953	1056	3
HALVORSON VERNON C	MAJ	0-4074815	0567	1
HALWER MURRAY M	LTC	0-0452362	0267	3
HAM ARTHUR C	CPT	0-0522522	0747	2
HAM HARRY C	1LT	0-1323833	0546	2
HAM JOHN K JR	MAJ	0-5405016	0967	1
HAM JULIUS W	CW4	W-2143588	0766	1
HAM LEWIS W	1LT	0-2207762	0353	2
HAM WALTER A	MAJ	0-0183555	0750	3
HAM WILLIAM F	LTC	0-0377991	1166	3
HAM WILLIAM P JR	COL	0-0311404	0562	3
HAMAKER HAROLD F	CW2	W-2148728	0161	1
HAMAKER ROBERT F	COL	0-0330806	0257	1
HAMAN FRANK	CW2	W-2142640	0157	1
HAMASAKI RICHARD N	MAJ	0-1683429	0461	1
HAMBAUGH RAYMOND K	LTC	0-1100572	0364	1
HAMBLETON CECILE S	2LT	N-0745365	0845	1
HAMBLETON HARRY B	COL	0-0234731	0547	2
HAMBLEY HELEN E	2LT	N-0729134	1144	1
HAMBLIN MELVIN M	CPT	0-0370955	1144	2
HAMBLIN O B	1LT	0-1176043	0458	1
HAMBLIN WILLARD M	MAJ	0-0384143	0244	2
HAMBLIN WILLIE L	CPT	0-0968205	1057	1
HAMBURG HENRY JR	1LT	0-1337427	0151	2
HAMBURGER ALBERT C	MAJ	0-0448724	0847	2
HAMBURY ROLAND T	MAJ	0-0557767	0367	3
HAMBY FRANK M	LTC	0-0330465	0560	1
HAMBY LEWIS M	MAJ	0-0222508	1059	1
HAMBY MYRL W	MAJ	N-0779611	0566	2
HAMBY ROBERT D	MAJ	0-1876398	0268	1
HAMEL ALBERT L	CPT	0-0404066	0146	2
HAMEL EDWARD P	1LT	0-0177426	1147	2
HAMEL JOHN J JR	LTC	0-0173582	0662	3
HAMEL LEON A	CW2	W-2126003	0850	1
HAMEL PAUL R	CPT	0-0397076	0645	2
HAMEL RICHARD J	MAJ	0-1885735	0767	1
HAMEL RICHARD L	LTC	0-0723610	0563	1
HAMELL GLENN P	MAJ	0-0257888	1266	3
HAMER GLENN R	LTC	0-1555827	0366	1
HAMER JOSEPH E	CPT	0-1043649	0164	1
HAMER LEONARD	MAJ	0-1103196	0562	1

NAME	GRADE	SVC NO	DATE RET MO YR	RET CODE
HAMER ROBERT P	CPT	0-0282438	0467	3
HAMERLE JAMES W	LTC	0-2021269	0868	1
HAMES LUTHER C JR	CPT	0-0101142	1045	2
HAMIL J O	CW2	W-2153027	1062	1
HAMIL JACK H	CPT	0-1303719	0762	1
HAMIL LEELON L	MAJ	0-1544923	0762	2
HAMILL CHARLES H	CPT	0-0158420	1046	1
HAMILL WALTER L	COL	0-0242088	0965	3
HAMILL WARREN C	COL	0-0208683	1058	1
HAMILTON ALEXANDER	LTC	0-1170401	1164	1
HAMILTON ANTHONY R	LTC	0-1001355	0457	1
HAMILTON ARTHUR D	LTC	0-0262481	1266	3
HAMILTON AUGUSTUS W	MAJ	0-1293945	0450	2
HAMILTON CHARLES C	CPT	0-1001143	0954	1
HAMILTON CHARLES E	CPT	0-1003246	0246	2
HAMILTON CHARLES M	LTC	0-0967323	1168	1
HAMILTON CHESTER D	1LT	0-0503450	1045	2
HAMILTON CHRISTOPHE	WO1	W-2147157	0564	2
HAMILTON CLARENCE W	LTC	0-0229110	1262	3
HAMILTON CLAUD D	MAJ	0-1637598	1056	1
HAMILTON CONRAD F	COL	0-0119463	1058	1
HAMILTON DANA R	COL	0-0233394	0557	3
HAMILTON DELBERT S	CW2	W-2146244	0962	1
HAMILTON DENNIS J	LTC	0-0385904	1164	3
HAMILTON DEWEY C	1LT	0-0232733	1057	3
HAMILTON EARL A	CPT	0-0508898	0246	2
HAMILTON EARL O	CPT	0-0239664	0155	3
HAMILTON EDISON K	CPT	0-1104187	1147	2
HAMILTON EDWARD O	COL	0-0279519	0768	3
HAMILTON EDWARD R	COL	0-0208420	0257	3
HAMILTON EDWARD S JR	MAJ	0-0372480	0147	2
HAMILTON ELINOR L	MAJ	N-0751420	0265	1
HAMILTON ELIZABETH	MAJ	N-0751859	1063	1
HAMILTON EMMETT A	1LT	0-1177427	0447	2
HAMILTON ERNEST L	LTC	0-1290415	0761	1
HAMILTON EUGENE A	MAJ	0-0406276	0546	2
HAMILTON EVERETT T	LTC	0-2083813	0768	1
HAMILTON EZEKIEL A	LTC	0-0336374	0363	1
HAMILTON FRED L	MAJ	0-0206376	0663	3
HAMILTON G T	2LT	0-1686481	0446	2
HAMILTON GEORGE A	CPT	0-1799049	0155	2
HAMILTON GEORGE W	LTC	0-0272252	0268	3
HAMILTON GRADY P	LTC	0-1305244	0561	1
HAMILTON HAROLD F	MAJ	0-0225576	1155	3
HAMILTON HAROLD R	LTC	0-0274853	0960	3
HAMILTON HARRY M	MAJ	0-1877757	0868	1
HAMILTON HENRY A	CW3	W-2142848	0763	1
HAMILTON HENRY C JR	MAJ	0-0977110	0865	1
HAMILTON HERALD H	CW4	W-2142234	0564	1
HAMILTON HERBERT H	MAJ	0-0479502	0746	2
HAMILTON HERSCHEL L	CW2	W-2115118	0650	2
HAMILTON HOBART G	CPT	0-0440542	0946	1
HAMILTON HOWARD G	1LT	0-1295542	1045	2
HAMILTON HUBERT E JR	LTC	0-0293715	0867	3
HAMILTON HUBERT T	LTC	0-0290631	0245	2
HAMILTON HUGH	MAJ	0-0965438	0465	1
HAMILTON HUGH A	MAJ	0-0146676	0945	2
HAMILTON IAN M	CPT	0-1297357	1145	2
HAMILTON JACK E	1LT	0-0414339	0845	2
HAMILTON JAMES C	COL	0-0230242	1061	3
HAMILTON JAMES C	1LT	0-0527814	0346	2
HAMILTON JAMES F	LTC	0-1169552	0663	1
HAMILTON JAMES L	2LT	0-1544940	1044	2
HAMILTON JAMES M	LTC	0-0167491	0648	3
HAMILTON JAY M	LTC	0-0554299	0663	1
HAMILTON JOHN	CW3	W-2146059	0861	1
HAMILTON JOHN D	LTC	0-1296025	1062	1
HAMILTON JOHN L	LTC	0-0165774	0844	2
HAMILTON JOHN R	1LT	0-2055796	1046	2
HAMILTON JOHN W	1LT	0-0382467	0645	2
HAMILTON KENNETH C	LTC	0-1586634	1160	2
HAMILTON KENNETH O	LTC	0-0981147	0868	1
HAMILTON LAURENS A	LTC	0-0177680	0758	3
HAMILTON LAWRENCE F	CPT	0-0278945	0544	2
HAMILTON LENWOOD C	CW2	W-2211387	0766	1

NAME	GRADE	SVC NO	DATE RET MO YR	RET CODE
HAMILTON LEROY W	COL	0-0489649	1167	3
HAMILTON M STEELE	MAJ	0-0275887	0545	2
HAMILTON MARGARET C	2LT	N-0727327	0145	1
HAMILTON MORRIS H	LTC	0-1590519	0967	1
HAMILTON MORRIS R	LTC	0-0451297	0557	1
HAMILTON OATHER L	WO1	W-2127652	0352	2
HAMILTON PAUL J	MAJ	0-1286119	0657	1
HAMILTON PHILIP M	CW3	W-2147254	0365	1
HAMILTON RAY	1LT	0-0363583	0644	2
HAMILTON RAY H	CW2	W-2144264	0457	1
HAMILTON RAY W	MAJ	0-0147173	0355	3
HAMILTON RICHARD	LTC	0-0253076	0262	3
HAMILTON RICHARD D	CPT	0-1049370	1060	1
HAMILTON ROBERT A	LTC	0-1014470	1157	1
HAMILTON ROBERT F	COL	0-0106243	0648	3
HAMILTON ROBERT M	COL	0-0127005	0152	3
HAMILTON ROBERT M	MAJ	0-1003776	0655	1
HAMILTON THEODORE L	CPT	0-0102571	0-52	3
HAMILTON THOMAS J	MAJ	0-4009033	0767	1
HAMILTON W P JR	CPT	0-1041565	0645	2
HAMILTON WALTER F JR	CPT	0-2305037	0766	1
HAMILTON WARD L	COL	0-0243563	0364	3
HAMILTON WASH H JR	CW2	W-2110205	0647	2
HAMILTON WESLEY 3	B G	0-0172732	0658	3
HAMILTON WEST A	COL	0-0114687	0649	3
HAMILTON WILLIAM E	MAJ	0-1300163	1160	1
HAMILTON WILLIAM H	1LT	0-1775152	1046	2
HAMILTON WILLIAM H	MAJ	0-2055147	1154	1
HAMILTON WILLIAM M	B G	0-0262501	0761	3
HAMILTON WILLIAM T	LTC	0-0359263	0259	1
HAMILTON WILLIAM W	LTC	0-0300414	0757	3
HAMILTON WILLIAM W	LTC	0-0341655	1066	1
HAMILTON WILLIAM W	CPT	0-0373744	0545	2
HAMILTON WILLIAM W	LTC	0-1305245	0866	3
HAMITER JOHN C	1LT	0-1541207	1045	2
HAMITER STANLEY M	1LT	0-0212954	0654	3
HAMLETT LAMAR	MAJ	0-1798668	1060	1
HAMLETT OTIS L	MAJ	0-2000607	0257	1
HAMLETT ROBERT L	CW4	W-2208132	1068	2
HAMLIN JAMES F	COL	0-0244284	0544	2
HAMLIN JAMES T JR	LTC	0-0479718	0147	2
HAMLIN JOHN T	MAJ	0-0990305	0366	1
HAMLIN MARGARET M	MAJ	N-0764351	0467	1
HAMLIN PERCY G	LTC	0-0201372	0354	3
HAMLIN ROBERT	CPT	0-1102748	1046	2
HAMLIN RUSSELL E	COL	0-0265974	0347	2
HAMM BRUCE S	MAJ	0-1588619	1160	1
HAMM CLIFTON M	COL	0-0181629	0857	3
HAMM JACK W SR	CPT	0-1540903	0460	1
HAMM RALPH E	CW3	W-2148792	1264	1
HAMM WILBUR V	2LT	0-1304070	0545	2
HAMM WILLIAM D	2LT	0-1114957	1144	2
HAMMACK EARL J	MAJ	0-1171573	0466	2
HAMMACK EMORY R	LTC	0-1115620	0463	1
HAMMACK JAMES W	MAJ	0-0168754	0260	3
HAMMACK LEWIS T	CPT	0-1013018	0357	1
HAMMACK ROBERT D	CPT	0-2033942	1061	1
HAMMACK ROBERT H	CPT	0-1015368	0960	1
HAMMACK WILLIAM J	MAJ	0-1581769	1053	2
HAMMAN FRED I	MAJ	0-0111010	0255	3
HAMMAN MARION A	CW3	W-2152295	0665	1
HAMMARLUND E R	CPT	0-0554317	0347	2
HAMME RICHARD J	CPT	0-1636000	0161	2
HAMMEL RICHARD L	MAJ	0-0949640	0667	1
HAMMELL MARJORIE	1LT	N-0723334	0552	2
HAMMELL ROBERT J	MAJ	0-2010938	1061	1
HAMMER AVERILL J	CPT	0-0278279	0161	3
HAMMER CHARLES R	LTC	0-0493487	0157	1
HAMMER EDWARD A	MAJ	0-0144929	0352	3
HAMMER HARRY C	MAJ	0-2006325	0158	1
HAMMER HELMUT E	2LT	0-0556397	0745	2
HAMMER HENRY	CW2	W-2115475	0846	2
HAMMER JOHN K	LTC	0-0303083	0768	3
HAMMER JOSEPH	CPT	0-0321299	0746	2
HAMMER MARTIN A	MAJ	0-0283047	0166	3

NAME	GRADE	SVC NO	DATE RET MO YR	RET CODE
HAMMER PERRY C	MAJ	0-0148410	0753	3
HAMMER STONEY	CPT	0-2026198	0758	1
HAMMER STEVENS F	1LT	0-0453494	0544	2
HAMMERICK JOHN M	MAJ	0-1576079	1060	1
HAMMERLUND JOHN M	LTC	0-0377482	0966	1
HAMMERNESS CARL E	LTC	0-0132714	0650	3
HAMMERSLEY WARD	COL	0-0194379	0463	3
HAMMERSMITH AMOS F	1LT	0-1324700	0946	2
HAMMERSTONE JESSE	MAJ	0-0887422	0561	1
HAMMERSTROM R B	1LT	0-0550608	0847	2
HAMMETT CECIL E	MAJ	0-0258079	0566	3
HAMMETT FRED M JR	LTC	0-0249369	0566	3
HAMMETT THOMAS D	2LT	0-1300164	0661	2
HAMMETT WALTER M H	MAJ	0-1646222	0861	1
HAMMILL HENRY S	CPT	0-1316290	0947	2
HAMMOCK DELBERT J	MAJ	0-2262935	1164	1
HAMMOCK ROBERT E	2LT	0-1999885	0446	2
HAMMON GEORGE D JR	LTC	0-1796270	0262	1
HAMMOND BENTON I	CPT	0-1285748	0357	2
HAMMOND BERNARD E	COL	0-0302918	1168	3
HAMMOND BERTRAM L	LTC	0-0384224	1060	1
HAMMOND CELIA	2LT	N-0721942	1044	1
HAMMOND CHARLES F	LTC	0-1043355	0665	1
HAMMOND CHESTER L	MAJ	0-0969385	0263	1
HAMMOND DEWITTF	CW4	W-2116961	0755	2
HAMMOND FLORICH N	MAJ	0-1591169	0662	1
HAMMOND FORLINE	LTC	0-0517044	0954	1
HAMMOND FRED L	CPT	0-0376973	0143	2
HAMMOND FREDERICK	WO1	W-2107068	0945	2
HAMMOND GEORGE B	CW3	W-2210376	0766	2
HAMMOND GEORGE M	LTC	0-1054260	0861	1
HAMMOND GERALD E	1LT	0-1182591	0947	2
HAMMOND GILBERT C	WO1	W-2118218	0545	2
HAMMOND GORDON B	COL	0-0119644	0857	3
HAMMOND HAROLD C	LTC	0-0406176	0461	1
HAMMOND HAROLD T	LTC	0-0298122	0667	3
HAMMOND HOMER H	LTC	0-0033507	0158	2
HAMMOND JOHN A	1LT	0-1040236	0245	2
HAMMOND JOHN A SR	CW3	W-2200421	0668	3
HAMMOND JOHN H	1LT	0-1286480	0645	2
HAMMOND JOHN M	WO1	W-2109988	0349	1
HAMMOND JOHN R	COL	0-0277048	1265	3
HAMMOND LYLE R	MAJ	0-1284327	0255	1
HAMMOND MARTIN L	LTC	0-0483596	0761	1
HAMMOND MATTHEW	COL	0-0124562	0648	3
HAMMOND MAURICE W	LTC	0-0297376	0665	3
HAMMOND OZIE G	CW2	W-2208888	0363	1
HAMMOND RALEIGH L	2LT	0-1822796	0445	2
HAMMOND REGINALD W	MAJ	0-0506865	0246	2
HAMMOND RICHARD T	MAJ	0-0276661	0347	2
HAMMOND ROBERT H	LTC	0-1117005	0866	1
HAMMOND RUTH P	2LT	N-0720831	0844	1
HAMMOND STEPHEN P	MAJ	0-2263020	0963	1
HAMMOND THOMAS B	LTC	0-0132713	0758	3
HAMMOND THOMAS T	1LT	0-1590520	1144	2
HAMMOND WILLIAM C JR	COL	0-0270407	0460	1
HAMMOND WILLIAM F	MAJ	0-0231906	0656	3
HAMMOND WILLIAM H	COL	0-0347192	0568	3
HAMMOND WILLIAM J	LTC	0-0419631	0964	2
HAMMOND WOODROW W SR	1LT	0-0373114	1066	2
HAMMONDS JOHN J	MAJ	0-2018510	0865	1
HAMMONDS KENNETH P	CPT	0-1574794	0466	1
HAMMONS TROY B	MAJ	0-1182130	0862	2
HAMNER GEORGE B	MAJ	0-0449460	0857	2
HAMNER LEWIS M	LTC	0-0404238	0556	2
HAMNER LOUIS	CPT	0-1181279	0758	1
HAMNER SHEPHERD L	CPT	0-0947743	0663	1
HAMNER WALTER C	MAJ	0-0583818	016.	1
HAMOR WADE H	1LT	0-1031091	0745	2
HAMPE HOWARD W	COL	0-2042700	1168	3
HAMPSHIRE EARL E	CPT	0-0510542	1144	2
HAMPSON EDMUND R	MAJ	0-0197735	0754	3
HAMPSON RONALD H	1LT	0-1946745	0146	2
HAMPSON RUSSELL J JR	MAJ	0-1304640	0563	1
HAMPTON CLARENCE R	MAJ	0-2021179	0965	1

NAME	GRADE	SVC NO	DATE RET MO YR	RET CODE
HAMPTON CLIFFORD A	CW3	W-2143912	1162	1
HAMPTON CORNEL S	COL	0-0297405	1060	1
HAMPTON EUGENE G	LTC	0-0179401	0944	2
HAMPTON GEORGE S JR	MAJ	0-1554556	0754	2
HAMPTON HAROLD D	LTC	0-0463640	1054	1
HAMPTON JAMES H	MAJ	0-0216865	0847	2
HAMPTON JAMES H	1LT	0-4059058	1057	2
HAMPTON JAMES M	MAJ	0-1688825	0165	1
HAMPTON JAMES W	MAJ	0-0987101	0465	2
HAMPTON JASEPH A	CW2	W-2142437	0360	1
HAMPTON LUTHER A	CW4	W-2146726	0167	1
HAMPTON OSCAR P JR	B G	0-0403301	0465	3
HAMPTON RALPH W	LTC	0-0417501	1066	1
HAMPTON WALTER D JR	LTC	0-1046471	1058	1
HAMRE JOSEPH	LTC	0-0129295	0450	3
HAMRICK GEORGE D	CPT	0-0493171	0846	1
HAMRICK NATHAN G	MAJ	0-2251950	1167	1
HAMRICK TOM A	LTC	0-0968212	0868	1
HAMRICK WALTERN C	MAJ	0-1048001	0661	1
HAMRICK WILLIAM H	COL	0-0219806	0657	3
HAMSHER KENNETH M	LTC	0-1184939	0360	1
HAMSON GEORGE V	LTC	0-1647067	0363	1
HANAGAMI SHUNIGHI	CW2	W-2214751	1168	1
HANASEK FRANK J	LTC	0-0319810	0966	3
HANAVAN LOUIS W	1LT	0-1175145	0447	2
HANAW JUSTIN J	LTC	0-0202468	0363	3
HANAWAY BLANCHE F	CPT	N-0734700	1263	1
HANBERRY HOMER B	MAJ	0-0345005	0659	2
HANBURY REES G	CW4	W-2134346	1262	1
HANCAMMON WILLIAM H	LTC	0-0364187	0665	1
HANCHETT HADDEN L	1LT	0-0469177	1044	2
HANCHEY WILLIAM J	LTC	0-0228180	1162	1
HANCOCK ALBERTA W	1LT	N-0772651	1045	1
HANCOCK CLEO E	MAJ	0-1011054	0461	1
HANCOCK CLIFTON D	MAJ	0-1541033	0961	1
HANCOCK DARRELL B	1LT	0-1047153	1045	2
HANCOCK DOY L	LTC	0-0226057	0660	3
HANCOCK FRED J	LTC	0-0453437	0661	1
HANCOCK HAMPTON S	LTC	0-1640520	0866	1
HANCOCK HELMER W	LTC	0-0437076	0366	3
HANCOCK HENRY H	MAJ	0-1657040	0346	2
HANCOCK HOBART T	MAJ	0-0230981	0856	3
HANCOCK JOHN I	CPT	0-1002790	0556	1
HANCOCK JOHN W	LTC	0-0398383	0157	1
HANCOCK JOSEPH M	LTC	0-1053157	0463	1
HANCOCK KNOX H	LTC	0-0987657	0868	1
HANCOCK LESTER A	COL	0-0253753	0254	3
HANCOCK LINDLE W	2LT	0-2030376	0964	2
HANCOCK LYNN D	COL	0-0336440	0966	3
HANCOCK MARVIN R	CW4	W-2108788	0761	1
HANCOCK MONTIE C	MAJ	0-0214453	1046	1
HANCOCK RALPH R	CW2	W-2147142	0661	1
HANCOCK ROBERT J	CW2	W-2127547	0946	1
HANCOCK ROMERO A	MAJ	0-0223047	1148	1
HANCOCK STANLEY M	CPT	0-1299881	0647	2
HANCOCK WILLIAM A	LTC	0-0259224	0361	1
HANCOCK WILLIAM I	2LT	0-1055312	0664	2
HANCOCK WINFIELD S	1LT	0-1031247	0945	2
HAND BENJAMIN F	COL	0-0357431	0346	2
HAND CHARLES R	1LT	0-0386088	1143	2
HAND CHARLIE T	CW2	W-2145906	1061	1
HAND CLIFFORD A	LTC	0-0333328	0760	3
HAND EDGAR L JR	MAJ	0-2042768	1061	1
HAND ELIZABETH	1LT	N-0742222	0346	1
HAND JOSEPH G	CPT	0-1166277	0548	2
HAND KENNETH W	CPT	0-1112195	0446	2
HAND MARK M	LTC	0-0490331	1045	2
HAND NOAH S	MAJ	0-0238287	0164	3
HAND OLIVER T	CW3	W-2205447	0165	1
HAND WILLIAM A	MAJ	0-1924510	1067	1
HAND WILLIAM D	MAJ	0-1686732	0864	1
HANDBERG ROGER B	MAJ	0-0383010	0859	1
HANDELMAN EUGENE V	CPT	0-1757070	0346	2
HANDELMAN SAMUEL R	MAJ	0-0240655	0364	3
HANDFIELD CHARLES K	MAJ	0-1636002	0860	1

NAME	GRADE	SVC NO	DATE RET MO YR	RET CODE
HANDLER ALLEN A	CPT	0-0520021	1046	2
HANDLER IRVING	CPT	0-1825858	0447	2
HANDLER PHILIP F	CPT	0-0167972	0555	3
HANDLER WILLIAM	1LT	0-1306841	0846	2
HANDLEY ALVIE J	1LT	0-1647482	0852	1
HANDLEY ARTHUR	CW2	W-2153028	1059	1
HANDLEY CAMERON L	LTC	0-0321469	0163	3
HANDLEY JAMES C B	LTC	0-0308304	0268	3
HANDLEY JAMES J	MAJ	0-0152016	0846	2
HANDLEY JAMES P	MAJ	0-0344151	0246	2
HANDLEY KENNETH E	MAJ	0-1552292	0847	2
HANDLEY LEE R	MAJ	0-1824746	0966	1
HANDLEY PATRICK J	MAJ	0-0240056	0663	3
HANDLEY WALTER C	LTC	0-0450406	0657	1
HANDLY RUSSELL E	MAJ	0-1287704	0361	1
HANDSCHUH JAMES R	CW3	W-3430136	0968	1
HANDY DONALD E	CW2	W-2205939	0263	1
HANDY ELSIE M	MAJ	N-0778119	0965	1
HANDY HARRY W	CPT	0-0143761	0648	3
HANDY JOSEPH L	LTC	0-1796463	0762	1
HANDY ROLAND L	WO1	W-2147271	0753	2
HANER RUSSELL D	CPT	0-1592894	0466	3
HANER WILLIAM F	MAJ	0-1685715	0964	1
HANES ARCHIBALD	MAJ	0-4003617	0462	2
HANES ARTHUR E	2LT	0-1175729	1044	2
HANES CLARENCE W	LTC	0-0219940	0553	3
HANES GLEN C	MAJ	0-1045451	0256	1
HANES GUY L	1LT	MN-0805848	0157	2
HANES RAYMOND G	MAJ	0-0496513	1055	1
HANES ROBERT C	COL	0-0216331	0763	3
HANESS MORRIS	CPT	0-1846444	1053	1
HANEWINCKEL WILLIAM	MAJ	0-1643633	0666	1
HANEY ANNE C	MAJ	N-0760684	0663	1
HANEY ARTHUR F	COL	0-0396846	0763	1
HANEY CHARLES T	CW4	W-2114977	0556	1
HANEY HARRY L	MAJ	0-2262834	0961	1
HANEY JILES W	LTC	0-0192403	0445	2
HANEY LELAND F	CPT	0-2309162	1066	2
HANEY OVEL M	LTC	0-0304244	1160	1
HANEY RALPH T	CPT	0-0348208	0768	3
HANEY ROY R	MAJ	0-0114596	0858	3
HANEY THOMAS R	1LT	0-1325797	0446	2
HANGARTNER JOHN A	LTC	0-1016275	0363	2
HANGEN RUSSELL J	CPT	0-1695340	0343	2
HANGER BRUCE B JR	LTC	0-0910254	0747	2
HANGER JAMES F	LTC	0-0314632	0465	3
HANGER WALLACE C	CPT	0-1301296	0251	2
HANGER WALLACE S	2LT	0-0367796	0344	2
HANGERUD ERLING J	LTC	0-0258191	1057	3
HANIFIN ROBERT E JR	MAJ	0-1166079	0446	2
HANISCH CECIL L	CPT	0-1319493	0846	2
HANKINS COLEMAN	CW2	W-2144081	1059	1
HANKINS JOHN B	CPT	0-0372519	0147	2
HANKINS WILLIAM T	LTC	0-1946746	0463	1
HANKS ALGER	LTC	0-0109294	0549	1
HANKS CLIFTON M	MAJ	0-1116497	1059	1
HANKS EVA B C	2LT	N-0787728	0945	1
HANKS JACK A	1LT	0-1313159	0947	2
HANKS JACK L	LTC	0-0318008	0460	3
HANLEN GEORGE S	CW3	W-2146991	0561	1
HANLEY ARTHUR W	CW3	W-2208694	0667	1
HANLEY CHARLES W	LTC	0-1165869	0360	1
HANLEY DAVID J	MAJ	0-1944465	0460	1
HANLEY DONALD B	CPT	0-0502613	1046	2
HANLEY EDWARD S	LTC	0-0304613	0467	3
HANLEY JACK J	LTC	0-1636003	0368	1
HANLEY PAUL C	LTC	0-1578569	0860	1
HANLEY PHILIP W	CPT	0-1307817	1065	2
HANLEY WILLIAM E	LTC	0-1014635	1162	1
HANLEY WILLIAM J	MAJ	0-1043975	0661	1
HANLIN GEORGE B	LTC	0-1105491	0661	1
HANLIN JAMES E	MAJ	0-1951154	0263	1
HANLON CATHERINE	2LT	N-0721378	0345	1
HANLON ELIZABETH	CPT	N-0723533	1266	3
HANLON FRANK E	COL	0-0382105	0767	3

NAME	GRADE	SVC NO	DATE RET MO YR	RET CODE
HANLON GEORGE T	CW4	W-2151818	0468	1
HANLON JOHN J	LTC	0-0229298	0665	3
HANLON JOHN P	2LT	0-1326396	1145	2
HANLON JOHN R	1LT	0-1035799	0845	2
HANLON JOSEPH W	MAJ	0-1293764	1060	1
HANLON PAUL A	LTC	0-1945369	0565	3
HANLON RAYMOND J	LTC	0-1593607	0867	1
HANLON ROBERT E	CW2	W-2213499	0167	1
HANLON THOMAS J	LTC	0-0320060	0668	3
HANLON THOMAS J	CW3	W-2211219	1267	2
HANMER WILLIAM	CPT	0-1176360	0846	2
HANN CHARLES J	CW2	W-2110955	0246	2
HANN DALE E	MAJ	0-0810651	0866	1
HANN GEORGE D JR	LTC	0-0352830	0565	3
HANN HAROLD C	LTC	0-1309730	0463	1
HANN JOHN R	COL	0-0183425	0957	3
HANNA ARTHUR J	LTC	0-0136802	0152	3
HANNA AUSTIN R	LTC	0-0399455	0546	2
HANNA CARL	COL	0-0183285	0950	3
HANNA CHARLES C	1LT	0-2044296	0546	1
HANNA CHARLES T	CW3	W-2152296	1164	1
HANNA CLAIR E	CPT	0-1062200	0347	2
HANNA CLOVIS S	CPT	0-2001003	0357	1
HANNA GALIL	MAJ	0-1283762	0952	1
HANNA GEORGE W	CPT	0-1634849	1045	2
HANNA HUGH E	2LT	0-1895495	0244	2
HANNA LEE A JR	CW3	W-2206540	1067	1
HANNA MARTIN L	MAJ	0-1041566	0860	1
HANNA NELSON H	MAJ	0-1311250	0863	1
HANNA OBA T JR	1LT	0-1060333	0346	2
HANNA RALPH E	LTC	0-0217081	1063	3
HANNA ROBERT A	CPT	0-2253336	1262	1
HANNA ROGER J	LTC	0-0473971	0446	2
HANNA THOMAS E	MAJ	0-0263842	0658	2
HANNA VIRGINIA R	2LT	N-0732204	0645	1
HANNA WALTER J	M G	0-0171549	0164	3
HANNA WILLIAM A	MAJ	0-1285581	0657	1
HANNA WILLIAM C	LTC	0-0392766	1163	1
HANNABASS CARDWELL F	1LT	0-0409307	0644	2
HANNAH CARL W	MAJ	0-1796464	0555	1
HANNAH CLAUDE R	MAJ	0-0305556	0247	2
HANNAH HAROLD W	LTC	0-0295978	1045	2
HANNAH JOEL M	1LT	0-2202488	0453	2
HANNAH LAWRENCE W	LTC	0-0494193	1166	3
HANNAH PAUL D	LTC	0-0213969	0361	3
HANNAH RICHARD E	LTC	0-1297875	1264	3
HANNAN JOSEPH M	CPT	0-0513572	0216	2
HANNAN WILLIAM S	COL	0-0148971	0648	3
HANNAN WILLIAM T	MAJ	0-1685554	0562	1
HANNAWALKER FRANCIS	CPT	0-0335863	0963	3
HANNAY WILLIAM V	LTC	0-0257044	0556	3
HANNEGAN WILLIAM J	LTC	0-0494828	0555	1
HANNEKE IGNATIUS H	MAJ	0-1540904	1160	1
HANNEN HAROLD P	CW3	W-2145442	1063	1
HANNES EDWIN A	CW3	W-2143027	0264	1
HANNETT HENRY D	LTC	0-1042046	0861	1
HANNEY LEONARD O	LTC	0-1316190	1267	1
HANNIGAN EDWARD V	1LT	0-1639126	0745	2
HANNIGAN WALTER J	MAJ	0-0995743	0364	1
HANNINGTON GEORGE A	CW3	W-2206943	1265	1
HANNON HARRY T	LTC	0-1185622	1167	1
HANNON JOSEPH C	MAJ	0-0356740	0347	2
HANNON MILLARD W	MAJ	0-0272088	1165	3
HANNON PAUL E	CPT	0-0287286	1162	2
HANNON WILLIAM M	MAJ	0-1106791	1059	1
HANNULA JACK	MAJ	0-0474995	0747	1
HANNUM JOHN H	2LT	0-1640524	1044	2
HANNUSCH WILLIAM K	LTC	0-0519727	0765	3
HANNY AELLEN H	MAJ	0-0207401	0160	3
HANOLD CHRIS H	CW3	W-2104703	1154	1
HANON HARRY L	LTC	0-1316150	0366	1
HANOVER BILLY D	2LT	0-2000661	0646	2
HANOVER CHARLES A JR	MAJ	0-0409333	0966	3
HANOVER CHESTER E	LTC	0-0282139	0155	1
HANOVER FRANK J	CPT	0-1174881	0246	2

NAME	GRADE	SVC NO	DATE RET MO YR	RET CODE
HANOVER LAURENCE R	LTC	0-0256076	0467	3
HANRAHAN CLEMENT J	CW4	W-2106497	0857	1
HANRAHAN MARGARET F	MAJ	N-0752670	0464	1
HANRETTY JOHN J	LTC	0-1585561	1265	1
HANSBEARRY ERNEST C	CPT	0-0319610	1145	2
HANSBROUGH ELIZABETH	MAJ	N-0700907	1044	1
HANSBROUGH JOHN H	LTC	0-0198230	0262	3
HANSCHEN JOHN A	1LT	0-1050701	0446	2
HANSCOM HOMER W	LTC	0-0232683	1264	3
HANSEL JACK H	MAJ	0-0426837	0557	1
HANSELL ADOPH	CPT	0-0278826	1148	1
HANSELL HOMER P JR	LTC	0-1298002	1060	1
HANSELL ROBERT J	CPT	0-0297213	1144	2
HANSELMAN WAYNE E	LTC	0-1169554	0461	1
HANSELMANN WALTER W	LTC	0-1037525	0561	1
HANSEN AGNES D	1LT	N-0756745	1045	1
HANSEN ALBERT W	2LT	0-0887685	0257	1
HANSEN ALFRED M	CPT	0-0481794	0347	2
HANSEN ALTON S	MAJ	0-1701105	0146	2
HANSEN ANITA M	1LT	N-0795429	0948	2
HANSEN ARNOLD A	MAJ	0-0299321	0464	3
HANSEN ARTHUR B	MAJ	0-0216058	0757	3
HANSEN BOYD S	MAJ	0-0406494	0657	1
HANSEN CARL V	MAJ	0-0115659	1147	2
HANSEN CHARLES G	CW3	W-2145443	0566	1
HANSEN CHARLES H	CW3	W-2142235	1159	1
HANSEN CLARENCE P	MAJ	0-1534750	0761	1
HANSEN CLARENCE W	MAJ	0-1822994	0257	1
HANSEN DONALD A	CPT	0-0962171	1064	1
HANSEN DONALD A	1LT	0-1177824	0945	2
HANSEN DOROTHY	2LT	N-0751781	0345	1
HANSEN EARL H	1LT	0-0321209	0646	2
HANSEN EDWARD N	CPT	0-1644400	0358	1
HANSEN EDWIN	COL	0-0124563	1152	3
HANSEN ELLSWORTH	LTC	0-1289727	1160	1
HANSEN ERIC	CW3	W-2141733	0758	1
HANSEN EUGENE J	CPT	0-0349085	0150	1
HANSEN FRANKLIN C	MAJ	0-1544176	0662	1
HANSEN FRANKLIN S	LTC	0-1030372	0457	1
HANSEN FRED E	LTC	0-0155356	0253	3
HANSEN GEORGE R	LTC	0-0451299	0260	1
HANSEN GEORGE R	CW3	W-2208305	0668	1
HANSEN GLEN A	CW2	W-2145444	0659	1
HANSEN GODFRIED N	LTC	0-1329833	1265	1
HANSEN HAROLD M	1LT	0-1110532	0146	2
HANSEN HARRY	MAJ	0-0162261	0652	3
HANSEN HARRY P R	COL	0-0218906	0655	3
HANSEN JOHN C	CPT	0-0236201	0463	3
HANSEN JOHN C	CW3	W-2150286	1163	1
HANSEN JOHN E	LTC	0-0452621	1062	1
HANSEN JOHN H	LTC	0-0242142	0843	2
HANSEN KENNETH C	MAJ	0-0821160	0762	1
HANSEN LESTER E	MAJ	0-0450240	1046	2
HANSEN LOUIS A	COL	0-0410115	0465	1
HANSEN LOUIS A	MAJ	0-0987744	0963	1
HANSEN MABEL C	MAJ	N-0799337	0265	2
HANSEN MERLIN A	2LT	0-1998690	0845	2
HANSEN NEIL E	1LT	0-1633255	1145	2
HANSEN OSCAR M	COL	0-0266259	0868	3
HANSEN OTTO M	CW2	W-2114419	0949	1
HANSEN PAUL G	COL	0-0303357	0665	3
HANSEN PERCY M	COL	0-0143887	0150	3
HANSEN RALPH E	COL	0-0185147	0346	2
HANSEN RALPH W	MAJ	0-0245809	0447	2
HANSEN RALPH W	COL	0-0300198	1060	1
HANSEN RICHARD H	LTC	0-1582361	1164	1
HANSEN ROBERT H G	MAJ	0-1341538	0664	1
HANSEN ROBERT W	MAJ	0-0971294	0164	1
HANSEN RUSSELL H	CW4	W-2101799	0756	1
HANSEN SVEND C	MAJ	0-1645021	0756	1
HANSEN THEODORE B	COL	0-0238153	0964	3
HANSEN THEONE H	2LT	0-1108721	0944	2
HANSEN VERNON A	LTC	0-0239266	0166	3
HANSEN VICTOR L	LTC	0-0473008	1051	1
HANSEN VICTOR R	LTC	0-0217166	0466	3

NAME	GRADE	SVC NO	DATE RET MO YR	RET CODE
HANSEN WELLS R	WO1	W-2115607	0561	2
HANSEN WILHELM G	CPT	0-1689461	0645	2
HANSEN WILLIAM H	LTC	0-0172752	0853	3
HANSER SAMUEL A	LTC	0-0355900	0146	2
HANSFORD GEORGE M	1LT	0-1288541	0545	2
HANSFORD JACK D	LTC	0-1307231	0262	1
HANSFORD JOHN W	MAJ	0-1291463	1060	1
HANSHAW EBBERT H	MAJ	0-0967345	1263	1
HANSHAW HORACE C	CW4	W-2112559	1159	1
HANSIS MARJORIE R	2LT	N-0742367	0844	1
HANSKETT JOSEPH F	CPT	0-1796785	1059	1
HANSMANN LEONARD J	MAJ	0-1924538	0268	1
HANSMEIER ROBERT H	LTC	0-0308384	0457	2
HANSON ALTON D	CPT	0-1585562	0352	2
HANSON ARCHIE E	CPT	0-1292519	0157	1
HANSON ARTHUR C	CPT	0-0266580	0245	2
HANSON ARTHUR F	COL	0-0335203	0164	1
HANSON CARL R	MAJ	0-1304208	0266	1
HANSON CHARLES K	MAJ	0-2009795	0465	1
HANSON DANIEL	MAJ	0-1280716	0755	1
HANSON EARL A	COL	0-0297547	0168	3
HANSON ERNEST C	1LT	0-1996591	0647	2
HANSON GEORGE W	COL	0-0263629	0158	1
HANSON HARRY A JR	MAJ	0-0976657	0862	1
HANSON JOHN A	LTC	0-0266148	0465	3
HANSON JOHN E	CPT	0-0423200	1144	2
HANSON JOHN E	1LT	0-1113727	0446	2
HANSON JOHN N	LTC	0-0194648	1059	3
HANSON LEO S	MAJ	0-2037130	1160	1
HANSON LINDLEY J	CPT	0-1544970	0762	2
HANSON LLOYD H	MAJ	0-1030572	0558	1
HANSON LYLE G	CW3	W-3430064	0968	1
HANSON MERLE L	CPT	0-0961634	0860	1
HANSON OLIVER B	CPT	0-1113728	1146	2
HANSON ORVILLE G	LTC	0-0270150	0968	3
HANSON PHILIP F	CPT	0-1017890	1046	2
HANSON RICHARD F	CPT	0-0389067	0444	2
HANSON RICHARD G	LTC	0-2262910	0868	1
HANSON RICHARD H	LTC	0-1307686	1254	1
HANSON ROBERT E	CPT	0-0413442	0345	2
HANSON STEPHEN	LTC	0-0247975	1163	3
HANSON THOMAS C	CPT	0-0415620	0544	2
HANSON THOMAS S	LTC	0-2289382	0461	1
HANSON VIRGIL E	MAJ	0-1312007	0657	1
HANSON WARREN W	LTC	0-0548175	0663	1
HANSON WILLARD D	MAJ	0-0451300	0258	1
HANSON WILLIAM L	LTC	0-0117230	0152	3
HANSON ZELMA F	MAJ	L-0900134	0448	2
HANSS ARMAND W	MAJ	0-0328867	1045	2
HANSSEN HANS I	MAJ	0-0185313	0854	3
HANSSEN KEITH E	LTC	0-1542291	0667	1
HANST BENJAMIN F	LTC	0-0234722	0648	3
HANTELMANN HAROLD E	COL	0-0295837	1046	2
HANTKE RUSSELL C	LTC	0-0382985	1163	1
HANZEL CHARLES A	1LT	0-1797642	0567	1
HANZLIK CHARLES J JR	1LT	0-0541599	0845	2
HAO WILLIAM K	MAJ	0-4005803	0568	1
HAPGOOD DAVID W	2LT	0-1996742	0346	2
HAPGOOD MILES M	MAJ	0-0162958	0156	3
HAPHEY ROBERT O	LTC	0-0316825	0960	1
HAPP WALTER J	CW3	W-2141983	0259	2
HAPPEL GEORGE W N	CPT	0-0224801	0747	2
HAPPEL JOHN H	MAJ	0-0276204	1267	3
HAPWORTH KENNETH C	COL	0-0369790	1060	1
HARABOSKY ROMAN H	WO1	W-2105792	0557	1
HARADA RAYMOND K	LTC	0-0979651	1166	1
HARADA SATORU	MAJ	0-1899432	0262	1
HARADEN ELMER E	LTC	0-0278260	1057	3
HARALSON CHESNEY G	1LT	0-1316749	1045	2
HARASIMOWICZ PAUL P	LTC	0-0297475	0146	2
HARBAUGH CHARLES W	LTC	0-1106796	1063	1
HARBAUGH HELEN H	MAJ	L-1020051	0866	1
HARBAUGH ORIL S	COL	0-0252277	0763	3
HARBECK GARNARD E	CPT	0-2005338	0158	1
HARBERGER CHARLES H	COL	0-0271379	0966	3

NAME	GRADE	SVC NO	DATE RET MO YR	RET CODE
HARBERT EDGAR D	MAJ	0-2203301	0462	1
HARBERT EDWARD D	CPT	0-1845899	1155	2
HARBERT JAMES M	CW3	W-2148410	0966	1
HARBERT JASON T	LTC	0-0330582	0446	2
HARBIDGE KENNETH R	MAJ	0-0938977	0264	1
HARBIN THOMAS R	MAJ	0-0462232	0657	1
HARBIN WILLIAM R	MAJ	0-1551218	0860	1
HARBISON DOUGLAS H	MAJ	0-0274847	1157	3
HARBISON HUNTER G	LTC	0-1168705	0361	1
HARBISON JOHN C	1LT	0-1305050	0146	2
HARBISON JOSEPH S	COL	0-0205893	1054	3
HARBOR JOHN C	CW2	W-2149015	1060	1
HARBOUR WAYNE R	MAJ	0-2000919	0161	1
HARBRIDGE FREDERICK	LTC	0-0273060	1065	3
HARBULA MICHAEL G	MAJ	0-0106283	0455	3
HARBY HORACE D	COL	0-1015803	0566	1
HARD HELEN L	CPT	N-0779304	1147	1
HARD ILO B	LTC	0-0397703	0763	2
HARD THORNTON F	LTC	0-1293407	0865	1
HARDAKER JOHN H W	LTC	0-1551021	0164	1
HARDART ROBERT J	CPT	0-1116156	0847	2
HARDCASTLE DALLAS C	LTC	0-1167883	0561	1
HARDCASTLE LOUIS V	LTC	0-1648282	0163	1
HARDEE FRANK S	LTC	0-0308470	0961	3
HARDEGREE HARMON B	CW3	W-2152996	0763	1
HARDEGREE JOHN P	MAJ	0-1930938	1268	1
HARDEGREE WILLIAM P	COL	0-0276900	1061	3
HARDEMAN ALFRED A	WO1	W-2108346	0146	2
HARDEN ACHESON A JR	LTC	0-1650402	0468	1
HARDEN ANN R	CPT	N-2298815	0863	2
HARDEN BENJAMIN F	LTC	0-0550820	0568	1
HARDEN BERNARD A	LTC	0-0308534	0367	3
HARDEN HOLLIS C	CPT	0-1323690	0346	2
HARDEN JAMES A	CPT	0-0361538	0846	2
HARDEN ROBERT E	1LT	0-1059137	0546	2
HARDEN SAMUEL G JR	CPT	0-0248469	1066	3
HARDEN THADDEUS E	CPT	0-0368355	1044	2
HARDENBERG WILBUR J	CW4	W-2104127	0656	1
HARDENBERGH W A	COL	0-0182732	0848	3
HARDENBURG WILLIAM L	LTC	0-0241044	1063	3
HARDER CARL F	LTC	0-0235122	0861	1
HARDER EDMUND A	LTC	0-0420092	1060	1
HARDESTY CHARLES M	LTC	0-1018359	0563	1
HARDESTY CLAUDE A	MAJ	0-2015779	0261	1
HARDESTY JOHN R	LTC	0-1003249	0556	1
HARDESTY RAYMOND L	LTC	0-0975466	0268	1
HARDESTY W H JR	COL	0-0305862	1060	1
HARDEY CHARLES A JR	MAJ	0-2014808	1065	1
HARDGRAVE LAWRENCE W	1LT	0-2012492	0862	1
HARDGROVE EVERETT A	LTC	0-0515776	1164	1
HARDGROVE GEORGE G	LTC	0-0409866	0663	1
HARDGROVE THOMAS J	COL	0-0492467	0265	3
HARDIE EMMETT F	MAJ	0-1039665	0964	1
HARDIE RALPH E	CPT	0-0337449	0468	3
HARDIE WADE E	LTC	0-0248300	1164	3
HARDIE WILBUR C	CW2	W-2149339	0157	1
HARDIMAN JOSEPH F	LTC	0-0450882	0457	1
HARDIMAN SYLVESTER	CW2	W-2119553	0347	1
HARDIN ARLTON W	LTC	0-1110533	1166	1
HARDIN BAKER B	CPT	0-0338529	1044	2
HARDIN CHARLES F	CPT	0-0332259	1044	2
HARDIN DAVID B	COL	0-0260922	0766	3
HARDIN DELL B	COL	0-0171321	1055	3
HARDIN FRED	CW2	W-2114591	0445	2
HARDIN HARRY T	LTC	0-1296365	0565	1
HARDIN HARVEY M	LTC	0-0469311	0662	1
HARDIN JAMES E	LTC	0-0443991	0854	1
HARDIN JAMES N	LTC	0-0530860	0765	3
HARDIN JAMES W	CPT	0-0485398	0145	2
HARDIN JOHN E	CW2	W-2105251	0546	1
HARDIN JOHN J JR	CPT	0-0465770	0846	2
HARDIN LEO J	LTC	0-0198718	0962	3
HARDIN MERLE C	CW2	W-2150127	0661	1
HARDIN PARKER C	MAJ	0-0241295	0245	2
HARDIN VIRGIL L	CW2	W-2150130	0957	1

NAME	GRADE	SVC NO	DATE RET MO YR	RET CODE
HARDIN WAITUS H	LTC	0-1845725	0662	1
HARDIN WILLIAM B	1LT	0-1317606	0365	2
HARDIN WILLIAM H	LTC	0-0317466	0157	1
HARDIN WILLIAM S	1LT	0-0538726	0945	2
HARDING ALARD C	1LT	0-1013424	0646	2
HARDING ARTHUR L	COL	0-0247067	0866	3
HARDING CHARLES D	MAJ	0-0274108	0656	3
HARDING EDGAR C	1LT	0-2045218	0147	2
HARDING EDWIN JR	LTC	0-0403971	0855	1
HARDING ELIZABETH	LTC	N-0700050	0245	1
HARDING EMORY M	2LT	0-1039373	1044	2
HARDING FRANK R	LTC	0-0324334	0658	2
HARDING FREDERICK	CPT	0-1294657	1146	2
HARDING GEORGE	CPT	0-4504410	0958	1
HARDING HAROLD F	M G	0-0263728	0464	3
HARDING HAROLD F	MAJ	0-1555829	0466	2
HARDING HARRISON W	CPT	0-0409864	0461	1
HARDING HARRY J	LTC	0-0392110	0849	2
HARDING HENRY A	COL	0-0224101	0655	3
HARDING LEONARD B	1LT	0-1642943	1045	2
HARDING MABEL V	2LT	L-0902835	0345	2
HARDING NEIL G JR	MAJ	0-1311890	1057	1
HARDING RICHARD D	CPT	0-0275009	0168	3
HARDING ROBERT A	MAJ	0-1824179	0261	1
HARDING ROBERT R SR	LTC	0-1180936	0666	1
HARDING TOM D	LTC	0-0301320	1263	3
HARDING WARREN G	CPT	0-1876970	1164	2
HARDISON MARVIN G	CW2	W-3152279	1168	2
HARDISON ROBERT S	MAJ	0-1172048	0361	1
HARDISTER CHARLES J	LTC	0-0404456	0364	1
HARDISTY DALE A	LTC	0-0351267	0363	1
HARDISTY HERSCHEL C	LTC	0-0362225	1145	2
HARDMAN SHERMAN W	MAJ	0-1326629	1163	1
HARDSOG HARRY N	COL	0-0261461	1263	3
HARDT DAN A	COL	0-0231170	0662	3
HARDT EDWARD J	CW4	W-2114867	0561	3
HARDT JOHN R	2LT	0-1301823	0844	2
HARDWICK EMMET V	COL	0-0262522	0551	3
HARDWICK EUGENE R JR	1LT	0-0524399	0146	2
HARDWICK GEORGE F SR	MAJ	0-2021069	0868	1
HARDWICK ROY	MAJ	0-1011894	0856	1
HARDWICK RUSSELL V	CPT	0-0274907	0447	1
HARDWICK SYDNEY C	LTC	0-0261426	1066	3
HARDY ARTHUR W	LTC	0-0354209	1045	2
HARDY ASHBY W	LTC	0-1585566	0266	1
HARDY BENJAMIN D JR	COL	0-0301886	0457	3
HARDY CHARLES H	LTC	0-1030573	0166	1
HARDY CLYDE	CW2	W-2110753	0446	1
HARDY FRANK	COL	0-0201407	0262	3
HARDY GEORGE C	LTC	0-0440790	1266	3
HARDY GEORGE C	CW3	W-2141574	0159	1
HARDY GEORGE M	CPT	0-0545497	0946	2
HARDY GEORGE R	1LT	0-2262195	0557	1
HARDY HENRY W	COL	0-0163148	0961	3
HARDY HOLMES L	MAJ	0-1305766	0363	1
HARDY JACKSON L	LTC	0-0250977	0162	1
HARDY JOHN E	CW3	W-2142849	0662	1
HARDY JOHN F JR	CPT	0-0361839	0845	2
HARDY JOHN G	COL	0-0212436	0561	3
HARDY JOHN H	LTC	0-1002023	0267	3
HARDY JOHN R	LTC	0-2007768	0167	1
HARDY JULIAN D	MAJ	0-1020533	0465	1
HARDY LEVI J	CPT	0-0518490	0447	1
HARDY OPAL	2LT	N-0726888	0445	1
HARDY OSCAR L	LTC	0-1823152	1061	2
HARDY PAUL	LTC	0-0327295	0867	3
HARDY RALPH L	CPT	0-1174882	0146	2
HARDY ROBERT B	MAJ	0-1584327	0568	3
HARDY ROBERT M	COL	0-0237858	0166	3
HARDY RUPERT T	2LT	0-1544864	0845	2
HARDY RUSSELL L	1LT	0-1328033	0447	2
HARDY SILAS G	COL	0-1634851	0767	1
HARDY THOMAS J	CPT	0-0399699	0846	2
HARDY THOMAS J	CW3	W-2210162	1068	1
HARDY WILBERT C	LTC	0-0125712	0154	3

NAME	GRADE	SVC NO	DATE RET MO YR	RET CODE
HARDY WILLARD J	MAJ	0-0887996	0861	1
HARDY WILLIAM E	CW3	W-2211479	0467	1
HARDZOG JAMES R	1LT	0-0535288	0946	2
HARE CHARLES A	LTC	0-0504368	0763	3
HARE CHARLES R	MAJ	0-0905574	1068	3
HARE HENRY H	LTC	0-0263891	1064	3
HARE JEAN M	MAJ	0-0940163	1167	1
HARE PERCY R	MAJ	0-2204408	0164	1
HARE WILLIAM H	CPT	0-1012986	1154	1
HAREN FERDINAND	MAJ	0-0775342	0164	1
HARENZA JOSEPH M	MAJ	0-1590522	0360	1
HARFORD BERENICE N	1LT	N-0730710	1044	1
HARFORD DON L	COL	0-0207084	0355	3
HARGADON BERNARD A	LTC	0-1334284	0365	1
HARGENS AUGUSTM	1LT	0-1301140	0951	1
HARGER BERNARD A	CPT	0-0397936	1048	2
HARGETT CLAUDE E	LTC	0-1182377	0864	1
HARGETT YUELL S	MAJ	0-0415280	0546	2
HARGIS BERNIE S	LTC	0-0236409	0750	3
HARGIS JAMES	LTC	0-0450018	1154	1
HARGITT KENNETH A	CPT	0-0571941	0368	1
HARGRAVE CLARENCE E	COL	0-0406844	0263	1
HARGRAVE CLIFFORD E	LTC	0-0927511	0764	1
HARGRAVE ELMO H	LTC	0-0388188	0647	2
HARGRAVE GARNETT D	MAJ	0-1299402	1057	1
HARGRAVES ALLEN P	2LT	0-1173270	0843	2
HARGRAVES RAYMOND	LTC	0-0116267	0155	3
HARGREAVES GEORGE M	COL	0-0280736	0666	3
HARGREAVES WILSON	LTC	0-0335346	1165	3
HARGROVE GEORGE JR	MAJ	0-0387525	0346	2
HARGROVE GRADY T	LTC	0-2035045	0168	2
HARGROVE HARRY W	LTC	0-0373261	1265	3
HARGROVE RICHARD L	CPT	0-0974068	0861	1
HARGROVE ROY T	CW3	W-2145124	0757	1
HARGROVE WILLIAM H	MAJ	0-1996493	0855	1
HARIG OSCAR	MAJ	0-2263263	1061	2
HARING STUART F	LTC	0-0352718	1060	1
HARJES HERMAN H	CW3	W-2148529	0864	1
HARKCOM SAMUEL F	2LT	0-1323834	0644	2
HARKER ELROY E	CW3	W-2153319	0863	1
HARKIN VICTOR H	LTC	0-1944467	0368	3
HARKINS CHARLES R	1LT	0-0530665	0146	2
HARKINS FREDERICK	MAJ	0-1686372	0361	1
HARKINS HAROLD E	LTC	0-0236324	1065	3
HARKINS KELLOGG W	COL	0-0213812	0558	3
HARKINS THOMAS P	LTC	0-0215554	0760	3
HARKNESS GEORGE W	MAJ	0-0234543	1065	3
HARKNESS LESLIE Y	CW3	W-2000624	1060	1
HARKNESS ROBERT B	COL	0-0245187	0162	3
HARLAN CLARENCE B	LTC	0-0299441	0467	3
HARLAN HAROLD R	LTC	0-0273201	0765	3
HARLAN JACK J	MAJ	0-1312919	0660	1
HARLAN ORVILLE A JR	CPT	0-1320366	0746	2
HARLAN STEWART M	LTC	0-1103679	0366	2
HARLAN WILLIAM H	LTC	0-0305386	0646	2
HARLAND ALGER G	MAJ	0-2039403	0964	1
HARLAND RUSSELL O	MAJ	0-1886336	1166	1
HARLANDER ALBERT C	COL	0-0277347	0858	3
HARLEM ALFRED E	LTC	0-0310991	1264	3
HARLEM ROBERT L	LTC	0-1171576	0763	1
HARLEY JAMES D	CW2	W-2149150	1058	1
HARLEY JAMES O	LTC	0-0337188	0758	1
HARLEY RICHARD J	MAJ	0-2033526	0761	1
HARLEY THOMAS	CPT	0-1287707	0246	2
HARLIN CLARENCE R	LTC	0-0392205	0760	1
HARLIN EDGAR F	1LT	0-0177129	0660	3
HARLIN HUGH F	CPT	0-0480854	0849	1
HARLING EDWIN A	LTC	0-0349730	1162	1
HARLOW DOROTHY C	1LT	N-0755742	0946	1
HARLOW GERALD H	1LT	0-1313400	0745	2
HARLOW IRVIN L	COL	0-0371607	0660	1
HARLOW JAMES R	1LT	0-0244673	0154	3
HARM CHARLES J	WO1	W-2122644	0546	2
HARM HENRY W	1LT	0-1283765	0945	2
HARM WINFRED B	CPT	0-0126552	1153	3

NAME	GRADE	SVC NO	DATE RET MO YR	RET CODE
HARMAN CAREY C	COL	0-0272776	0867	3
HARMAN CHARLES C	LTC	0-0250010	0667	3
HARMAN CLYDE E	CPT	0-1174883	0655	1
HARMAN LEO D	MAJ	0-0203194	0249	2
HARMAN MAX C	LTC	0-1548828	0568	1
HARMAN ROBERT D	LTC	0-0265901	1043	2
HARMAN ROBERT J	MAJ	0-0974058	0463	1
HARMAN ROBERT L	MAJ	0-1317630	0165	1
HARMAN WILLIAM C	LTC	0-1294302	0965	1
HARMER EARLE J JR	COL	0-1541268	0466	1
HARMISON LIONEL L	MAJ	0-0266673	0257	3
HARMOLING KARL C	LTC	0-0231112	0563	3
HARMON ALTON F	LTC	0-0276074	1265	3
HARMON BENJAMIN C	CPT	0-0215101	0556	3
HARMON BILLY	MAJ	0-1884179	0167	1
HARMON CHARLIE P	CW2	W-2152039	1055	1
HARMON DAVID M JR	MAJ	0-1116515	1160	1
HARMON DELMAR R	MAJ	0-2102874	0168	1
HARMON ELLIS D	LTC	0-0282239	1145	2
HARMON ERNEST S	1LT	0-1307408	0246	2
HARMON FREDERICK	1LT	0-1825121	1046	2
HARMON GEORGE G	CW3	W-2149402	1263	1
HARMON HARLEY B	CW2	W-2141303	0555	1
HARMON HAROLD M	LTC	0-0454692	0265	1
HARMON HERBERT H	LTC	0-0475177	0656	2
HARMON JACK T	LTC	0-1289247	1160	1
HARMON JEROME B JR	LTC	0-0955100	0168	1
HARMON JOHN D	MAJ	0-0205740	1055	3
HARMON LEO C	LTC	0-0405481	0363	1
HARMON LEO E	LTC	0-1177826	0962	1
HARMON LLOYD V	LTC	0-0245506	1051	3
HARMON NEALE K	MAJ	0-1341539	0365	1
HARMON ODIS L	COL	0-0240018	1063	3
HARMON PAUL A	COL	0-1040537	0468	1
HARMON PAUL C	WO1	W-2142850	0153	2
HARMON RICHARD A	CPT	0-1648251	0257	1
HARMON RICHARD W	LTC	0-1014946	0966	1
HARMON ROBERT	CW3	W-2208891	0467	1
HARMON ROBERT C	CW3	W-2106734	0359	1
HARMON RONALD C	CPT	0-0249645	0267	3
HARMON THOMAS D	MAJ	0-1321774	0962	1
HARMON WILMER P	CPT	0-0381762	0944	2
HARMS FRANK C	LTC	0-0293929	0562	1
HARMS GEORGE E	CPT	0-0435559	0546	2
HARMS GEORGE S	1LT	0-1321917	1147	2
HARMS GLENN L	LTC	0-0295782	0362	3
HARMS ROY C	LTC	0-1338229	0967	1
HARMS WILBUR C	LTC	0-1574798	0462	1
HARNED JOHN W	LTC	0-0168264	0461	3
HARNED LELAND D	1LT	0-1794940	0345	2
HARNED MARK L	COL	0-0232250	1151	3
HARNES ALVIN R	LTC	0-0170020	0454	3
HARNESS FOREST A	CPT	0-0119413	0655	3
HARNESS HAROLD D	CW3	W-2102981	0957	1
HARNESS LEROY R	LTC	0-0240278	0166	3
HARNESS MARSHALL D	CPT	0-1292877	0163	1
HARNETT ROBERT W	COL	0-0379206	1262	1
HARNETT SYDNEY G	COL	0-0174583	0554	3
HARNEY GLENN A	1LT	0-0435921	0546	2
HARNEY JAMES D	MAJ	0-1306717	0665	1
HARNEY JAMES M	MAJ	0-0452566	0746	2
HARNEY MARIE A	1LT	N-0751163	1045	2
HARNEY RALPH G	WO1	W-2149111	0157	1
HARNEY ROBERT G	MAJ	0-0957246	0962	1
HARNEY ROBERT G	LTC	0-1032090	1167	1
HARNISH ROBERT L	LTC	0-0371504	1265	3
HARNISH ROBERT O	MAJ	0-1050705	1064	1
HARNLY ROBERT C	COL	0-0325556	0660	1
HARONIAN FRANK J	CPT	0-0202585	1051	3
HAROVER ROBERT W	CPT	0-0974969	0161	1
HARP ALONZO M	CPT	0-0242911	0753	3
HARP PERCY F	MAJ	0-0202743	0446	2
HARP WILLIAM D	CW4	W-2149811	0862	1
HARPER ALLEN J	CPT	0-1290941	0747	2
HARPER ARDIS C JR	MAJ	0-2014348	1262	1

NAME	GRADE	SVC NO	DATE RET MO YR	RET CODE
HARPER BLAND F	MAJ	0-0252166	0553	3
HARPER CARL M	LTC	0-0499709	0155	1
HARPER CECIL K	MAJ	0-0472495	0555	1
HARPER CHARLES B	MAJ	0-1181288	1163	1
HARPER CHARLES I	MAJ	0-1996927	0662	1
HARPER CHARLES O	CPT	0-0331342	1244	2
HARPER CLIO A	COL	0-0232778	0765	3
HARPER DONALD A	1LT	0-0326373	0645	2
HARPER DOROTHY K	LTC	N-0722377	0561	1
HARPER EDWARD N	LTC	0-0278819	0656	3
HARPER EDWIN O	COL	0-0250159	0647	2
HARPER FRANK D	MAJ	0-1635897	0161	1
HARPER FREDERICK	LTC	0-0403328	0846	2
HARPER GEORGE G	CPT	0-1310837	0956	1
HARPER GERALD F	CW2	W-2210610	0866	2
HARPER GRANT E	CPT	0-0551753	1047	2
HARPER HAROLD	COL	0-0169566	0852	3
HARPER HAROLD I	MAJ	0-1113241	0358	1
HARPER HENRY C	LTC	0-0165089	1146	2
HARPER IVAN	1LT	0-0446834	0246	2
HARPER JAMES B	LTC	0-0254834	1156	3
HARPER JAMES K	LTC	0-0323759	1056	3
HARPER JAMES L	MAJ	0-1688452	0565	1
HARPER JAMES W	1LT	0-1114961	0246	2
HARPER JEAN C	MAJ	N-0804489	1162	2
HARPER JESSE P	CPT	0-0244576	1159	3
HARPER JOE T	1LT	0-1287708	0545	2
HARPER JOHN H	COL	0-0213733	1262	3
HARPER JOHN T	MAJ	0-2033096	0963	1
HARPER LAMAR E	1LT	0-1636011	0546	2
HARPER LEWIS H	COL	0-0116195	0648	3
HARPER LOUIS M	CPT	0-1287344	0747	2
HARPER MILTON N	CPT	0-0735578	0866	1
HARPER OWEN E	MAJ	0-2020808	0164	1
HARPER PAUL F	COL	0-0274317	0860	3
HARPER RILEY A	MAJ	0-0335981	0546	2
HARPER RILEY A	MAJ	0-0355981	0559	2
HARPER ROBERT B	LTC	0-1633259	0162	1
HARPER ROBERT C	LTC	0-1015787	0861	2
HARPER ROBERT H	CPT	0-2263718	0163	2
HARPER ROBERT J	COL	0-0215051	0564	3
HARPER ROBERT J	CPT	0-0979355	0260	2
HARPER ROBERT S	MAJ	0-2014553	0663	1
HARPER ROY H	CW4	W-2116249	0161	1
HARPER VICTOR E	COL	0-0472457	1264	2
HARPER WALLACE I	MAJ	0-2007870	0161	1
HARPER WARD R	2LT	0-1301141	0744	2
HARPER WILLIAM E JR	COL	0-0238584	0457	1
HARPER WILLIAM L	LTC	0-0289147	0944	2
HARPER WILLIE F	LTC	0-1299742	0760	1
HARPIN CHARLES H	LTC	0-1589879	0367	2
HARR GERALD J	MAJ	0-0965429	0763	1
HARR HOWARD R JR	CPT	0-1288224	0346	2
HARR WILLIAM H	MAJ	0-1020499	1165	1
HARR WILLIAM L	LTC	0-0306820	1267	3
HARRAH CALVIN S	COL	0-0108134	0-53	3
HARRALSON HUGH T	LTC	0-2018340	0968	2
HARREL THOMAS H	LTC	0-0304359	1045	2
HARRELL ARTHUR E	COL	0-0306807	0760	1
HARRELL BEVERLEY T	LTC	0-0225854	0364	3
HARRELL CHARLES W	COL	0-0282437	0368	3
HARRELL DALLAS W JR	CW3	W-2151056	1163	1
HARRELL DAWSON L	CW3	W-2120963	0657	1
HARRELL EDWARD M	LTC	0-1285582	0862	1
HARRELL EUGENE J	CW4	W-2144918	0263	2
HARRELL FREDERICK	COL	0-0284779	0157	3
HARRELL GEORGE B	CW2	W-2146333	0560	1
HARRELL GEORGE D	LTC	0-0259058	0167	3
HARRELL GUS W	CPT	0-0455135	0645	2
HARRELL LEIGHTON E	COL	0-0338414	1060	3
HARRELL LEROY J	CW2	W-2212023	0866	2
HARRELL ROBERT L	1LT	0-1999875	0646	2
HARRELL TRUMAN W	CW3	W-2142320	0157	1
HARRELL WALTER F	MAJ	0-0280045	1165	3
HARRELL WILLIAM R	CPT	0-1292447	0557	1

NAME	GRADE	SVC NO	DATE RET MO YR	RET CODE
HARRELSON CHARLIE S	MAJ	0-2206221	1065	1
HARRELSON LARREL C	LTC	0-0281064	0865	1
HARRELSON LAWRENCE E	CW2	W-2152673	1060	1
HARRELSON WALTER N	CPT	0-0362888	0545	2
HARRIES BERNICE M	MAJ	N-0734449	0664	1
HARRIG MARION S	LTC	0-0442618	0464	3
HARRIGAN WILLIAM H	LTC	0-1319412	0763	1
HARRILL CHARLIE H	COL	0-0255876	1047	2
HARRILL ROBERT H	CPT	0-0258729	1043	2
HARRIMAN EARL L	CW2	W-2215293	0368	1
HARRIMAN GRANT D	CPT	0-0317591	1144	2
HARRIMAN LOREN E	MAJ	0-1822397	1265	1
HARRIMAN ROGER L	LTC	0-0222082	0262	3
HARRIMAN WALLACE R	LTC	0-0278949	0864	3
HARRINGTON ALBERT T	COL	0-0217716	0454	3
HARRINGTON DAVID B	LTC	0-0284720	1060	3
HARRINGTON EDWARD R	LTC	0-0919821	0365	3
HARRINGTON EUGENE S	CW2	W-2210190	1264	1
HARRINGTON FERDINAND	LTC	0-0251707	1266	3
HARRINGTON HARRY J	CW3	W-2142851	0359	1
HARRINGTON HUGH T	LTC	0-0906151	1167	3
HARRINGTON JACK	MAJ	0-1550399	1158	1
HARRINGTON JACK	MAJ	0-1557014	1161	1
HARRINGTON JACK P	CPT	0-1583064	0950	2
HARRINGTON JAMES A	MAJ	0-2031855	0363	1
HARRINGTON JAMES C	1LT	0-1321630	0746	2
HARRINGTON JAMES L	MAJ	0-1555980	0460	1
HARRINGTON JANET H	MAJ	N-0728117	0361	1
HARRINGTON JOHN J	LTC	0-1170408	1067	1
HARRINGTON JOHN V	CW3	W-2145445	1061	1
HARRINGTON LEO J	CPT	0-1556436	0454	1
HARRINGTON OMAR L	MAJ	0-1112199	0764	1
HARRINGTON PATRICK	1LT	0-1321918	0445	2
HARRINGTON PAUL F	MAJ	0-1586643	0861	2
HARRINGTON RALPH B	LTC	0-0188183	0358	3
HARRINGTON ROBERT C	CPT	0-0114613	0355	3
HARRINGTON SAMUEL H	MAJ	0-1578573	0757	1
HARRINGTON TIM J	1LT	0-1019074	0946	2
HARRINGTON V B	1LT	0-1045453	1044	2
HARRINGTON WILLIAM H	MAJ	0-1313601	0565	1
HARRINGTON WILLIAM J	CPT	0-0374234	0650	1
HARRINGTON WILLIAM J	LTC	0-1039375	0467	1
HARRIS ALBERT R	LTC	0-0263747	0961	3
HARRIS ALVIN V	LTC	0-1543476	0765	2
HARRIS ANTHONY B	LTC	0-0156196	0655	3
HARRIS ARCHIE M	LTC	0-0450966	0258	1
HARRIS ARTHUR C	LTC	0-1106799	1167	1
HARRIS ARTHUR D	LTC	0-0495957	0855	1
HARRIS BARTON L	COL	0-0281638	0963	1
HARRIS BENJAMIN	COL	0-0137703	0852	3
HARRIS BENJAMIN F	CW3	W-2146451	1057	1
HARRIS BRACE W	2LT	0-0493104	0443	2
HARRIS BRUCE W	CW3	W-2206865	0666	1
HARRIS CARL M	LTC	0-1283251	1265	1
HARRIS CARMON C	LTC	0-0345016	1264	3
HARRIS CARROLL T	COL	0-0187527	1051	3
HARRIS CATHERINE	MAJ	N-0735196	0962	1
HARRIS CECIL F	CW3	W-2148595	0564	1
HARRIS CECIL M	LTC	0-0119840	0750	3
HARRIS CECIL O	LTC	0-0419673	0562	1
HARRIS CECIL R	CW2	W-2150569	0361	1
HARRIS CHARLES A	LTC	0-1956744	0966	1
HARRIS CHARLES B	CPT	0-0451302	0647	2
HARRIS CHARLES C	CPT	0-1899396	0157	1
HARRIS CHARLES E	LTC	0-0279038	0958	3
HARRIS CHARLES E	LTC	0-0420465	0860	1
HARRIS CHAUNCY L	MAJ	0-0348773	0746	2
HARRIS CHESTER S	COL	0-0102898	0648	3
HARRIS CLEVELAND	LTC	0-1103680	0962	1
HARRIS CLIFFORD W	LTC	0-0372739	0360	1
HARRIS CLYDE A	MAJ	0-0301078	0766	3
HARRIS CURTIS A	2LT	0-1642154	0245	2
HARRIS DANIEL G	1LT	0-1341424	0649	2
HARRIS DAVID M	LTC	0-1591784	1162	1
HARRIS DON C	CPT	0-0921676	1045	2
HARRIS DUANE W	LTC	0-1558274	0768	1
HARRIS DUPONT G	LTC	0-0275754	1063	3
HARRIS EARL B	LTC	0-1018891	0867	1
HARRIS EARL G	CW3	W-2205683	0668	1
HARRIS EARL M JR	MAJ	0-1796616	0965	1
HARRIS EARL R	MAJ	0-1822797	0262	1
HARRIS EDMUND P	CPT	0-1994925	0261	2
HARRIS EDWARD N JR	COL	0-0205238	0646	2
HARRIS EDWARD S	LTC	0-0290420	0263	2
HARRIS EDWIN M	1LT	0-1283068	0557	1
HARRIS ELMER J	MAJ	0-0417848	0347	2
HARRIS ELWOOD L	CPT	0-0361560	0346	2
HARRIS ELWOOD O	LTC	0-1176654	0763	1
HARRIS EUGENE	MAJ	0-2033146	0661	1
HARRIS EUGENE D	LTC	0-1637615	0264	1
HARRIS FLETCHER W JR	2LT	0-0438987	0445	2
HARRIS FORREST C	MAJ	0-2019736	0758	1
HARRIS FRANCIS J	CPT	0-0194461	0648	3
HARRIS FRANCIS W	MAJ	0-1542648	1165	1
HARRIS FRANK W	MAJ	0-0303000	0666	3
HARRIS FRED G	MAJ	0-1885275	0867	1
HARRIS FRED M	COL	0-0389405	0965	1
HARRIS FRED P	MAJ	0-0322550	0962	3
HARRIS FREDERICK	MAJ	0-0388785	0846	2
HARRIS GEORGE B	MAJ	0-0544855	0267	3
HARRIS GEORGE E	LTC	0-1308212	1266	1
HARRIS GEORGE H	CPT	0-1577289	1043	2
HARRIS GLEN W	LTC	0-1106800	1262	1
HARRIS GLYNN M	CPT	0-2204305	1063	2
HARRIS GOLDN B	LTC	0-0182665	0351	3
HARRIS GUY J	LTC	0-1322221	0963	1
HARRIS HARDIE F JR	2LT	0-1039376	1044	2
HARRIS HAROLD	CPT	0-2262251	0960	1
HARRIS HAROLD A	LTC	0-0168169	1055	3
HARRIS HAROLD B	MAJ	0-0356609	0745	2
HARRIS HAROLD E	MAJ	0-0983561	1262	1
HARRIS HARRY E	MAJ	0-0245160	1054	3
HARRIS HARRY L	WO1	W-2149194	0256	1
HARRIS HAWES C	LTC	0-0224890	0559	3
HARRIS HENRY C	LTC	0-0206404	0753	3
HARRIS HENRY U JR	1LT	0-1339989	1047	2
HARRIS HERBERT H	MAJ	0-0255573	0146	2
HARRIS HERBERT L	1LT	0-2030520	0458	2
HARRIS HERSHEL M	1LT	0-1167889	0744	2
HARRIS HIRAM S	1LT	0-0108744	0529	1
HARRIS HOWARD W	LTC	0-2033258	0965	1
HARRIS HOYETTE E	LTC	0-1285583	0555	1
HARRIS IRVING	CPT	0-0468823	1044	2
HARRIS IRVING C	1LT	0-0960747	0352	2
HARRIS IVAN H	LTC	0-0264500	0152	2
HARRIS J C	CW2	W-2151765	1163	1
HARRIS JACK M	1LT	0-1824311	0253	1
HARRIS JAMES C	LTC	0-0158082	0660	3
HARRIS JAMES C	CW3	W-2141850	0967	1
HARRIS JAMES E	LTC	0-0492972	0854	1
HARRIS JAMES E	CPT	0-1920224	0463	1
HARRIS JAMES F	1LT	0-1049873	1144	2
HARRIS JAMES O	CW2	W-2210406	0562	1
HARRIS JAMES R	MAJ	0-1820965	0668	1
HARRIS JOHN O	1LT	0-0499845	1144	2
HARRIS JOHN E	LTC	0-0370107	0860	1
HARRIS JOHN E	MAJ	0-1174313	1060	1
HARRIS JOHN J	MAJ	0-0998380	0161	1
HARRIS JOHN L	MAJ	0-0243366	0864	3
HARRIS JOHN M	CPT	0-0317096	0446	2
HARRIS JOHN P	MAJ	0-0218312	0648	3
HARRIS JOHN R	COL	0-0154469	0451	3
HARRIS JOHN R	MAJ	0-2033200	0763	1
HARRIS JOSEPH M	MAJ	0-0239716	0146	2
HARRIS KARL S	MAJ	0-1550183	1160	1
HARRIS KARL W	LTC	0-0262086	0964	3
HARRIS LEO E	1LT	0-1313240	0446	2
HARRIS LEONARD R	CW2	W-2144785	0862	1
HARRIS LESLIE H	MAJ	0-2037795	0863	1
HARRIS LESTER A	1LT	0-1048004	0447	2
HARRIS LLOYD F	COL	0-0204390	0346	2
HARRIS LOUIS C	LTC	0-0300046	0866	3
HARRIS LOWRY R	COL	0-0264290	0855	3
HARRIS LOYD E	COL	0-0215001	1060	3
HARRIS MAN E	LTC	0-0422348	0962	1
HARRIS MARTIN H JR	LTC	0-0403176	0562	1
HARRIS MAURICE H	CPT	0-0281100	1043	2
HARRIS MCGREW	LTC	0-0250299	0859	1
HARRIS MEADE C	CPT	0-1108725	0647	2
HARRIS MERLE E	MAJ	0-1579574	0859	1
HARRIS MERLE G	LTC	0-1108005	0768	3
HARRIS MERRILL F	CPT	0-1110538	1046	2
HARRIS MILAM K	1LT	0-0399472	0145	2
HARRIS MILDRED G	2LT	N-0779012	0445	2
HARRIS MILTON	MAJ	0-0273215	0368	3
HARRIS NATHAN	MAJ	0-0129180	1045	2
HARRIS NEMI	CW2	W-2210158	1262	1
HARRIS NORMAN J	CPT	0-0321754	0144	2
HARRIS ONTY L	MAJ	0-0491943	1155	1
HARRIS PAUL	LTC	0-1114530	0762	1
HARRIS PAUL C	MAJ	0-2006625	0656	1
HARRIS PAUL D	CPT	0-1303500	0447	2
HARRIS PAUL D	LTC	0-1311646	0265	1
HARRIS PAUL P	1LT	0-1797820	0446	2
HARRIS PERRY F	CPT	0-1113243	1262	1
HARRIS PRICE F	MAJ	0-1599128	0563	1
HARRIS RAY A	1LT	0-1299743	0546	2
HARRIS RAY C	CPT	0-0416966	0546	2
HARRIS RAY M	COL	0-0900666	1067	3
HARRIS RAYMOND C	COL	0-0455641	0267	3
HARRIS RHETT G	COL	0-0445690	0667	1
HARRIS ROBERT A	1LT	0-1032715	1045	2
HARRIS ROBERT K	CPT	0-1046474	0847	2
HARRIS ROBERT L	COL	0-0255543	1057	3
HARRIS ROBERT L	CW2	W-2150636	1263	2
HARRIS ROBERT M	LTC	0-0239413	0865	1
HARRIS ROBERT R JR	MAJ	0-2266396	0267	1
HARRIS ROBERT W	LTC	0-1579755	0861	1
HARRIS RODGERS F	CW4	W-2142641	0968	1
HARRIS RONALD M	COL	0-0223254	0451	3
HARRIS ROSS	1LT	0-1324332	0845	2
HARRIS ROY J	COL	0-0217844	1062	3
HARRIS RUSSELL B	2LT	0-1334568	0246	2
HARRIS SAMUEL M	LTC	0-1039022	1165	1
HARRIS SHIRLEY W	LTC	0-0473720	0863	1
HARRIS STACY C	CW4	W-2106546	0358	1
HARRIS THEODORE D	CW4	W-2141576	0962	1
HARRIS THOMAS A	CPT	0-1341781	1060	1
HARRIS THOMAS G	CPT	0-1945599	0851	2
HARRIS THOMAS R	LTC	0-0902293	0663	1
HARRIS TOWNES M	LTC	0-0242497	0859	3
HARRIS TRUITT W	MAJ	0-1290942	0865	2
HARRIS VENOIA M	CPT	0-0307454	0944	2
HARRIS VERNER C	MAJ	0-1171578	0361	1
HARRIS VICTOR W	LTC	0-0348241	0560	1
HARRIS WARREN S	CPT	0-0954090	1159	2
HARRIS WEST J	CW3	W-2152067	0363	1
HARRIS WILLIAM C	CPT	0-1301138	1050	2
HARRIS WILLIAM C	MAJ	0-2262487	1061	1
HARRIS WILLIAM C	CPT	0-2262489	0161	1
HARRIS WILLIAM D	LTC	0-1300030	0959	1
HARRIS WILLIAM E	MAJ	0-1303501	0462	2
HARRIS WILLIAM F	MAJ	0-2262669	0266	1
HARRIS WILLIAM G	MAJ	0-2039652	1060	1
HARRIS WILLIAM H	MAJ	0-0405468	0865	1
HARRIS WILLIAM L	LTC	0-0502315	0856	1
HARRIS WILLIAM O	CW2	W-2150359	0662	1
HARRIS WILLIE P	MAJ	N-0700231	1044	1
HARRIS ZEO C	LTC	0-0401427	0560	1
HARRISON ALFRED H	1LT	0-1310438	1044	2
HARRISON ANNA L	2LT	N-0777557	0746	1
HARRISON ARTHUR B	CW2	W-2145257	1058	1
HARRISON ARTHUR G	CPT	0-0513037	0649	1
HARRISON BENNIE J	LTC	0-1017561	0663	1
HARRISON BRUCE F	1LT	0-5517230	1265	2
HARRISON BRUCE W	LTC	0-1013454	0758	1
HARRISON BUFORD M	MAJ	0-1002236	0861	1
HARRISON CECIL W	LTC	0-2000522	0965	1
HARRISON CHARLES L	COL	0-0406909	0168	1
HARRISON CHARLES R	CPT	0-0979224	1060	1
HARRISON CHARLES W	LTC	0-1167890	1262	1
HARRISON CLIFFORD W	CW3	W-2143339	0162	1
HARRISON CLINT H	COL	0-0163204	0255	3
HARRISON DAVID G	CPT	0-1293768	0146	2
HARRISON DAVID S	MAJ	0-1594218	1064	3
HARRISON DESALES JR	1LT	0-1181900	1046	2
HARRISON EDMUND W	MAJ	0-0256879	0464	3
HARRISON EDWARD R	MAJ	0-1305922	1060	1
HARRISON EDWIN S	LTC	0-1019760	0567	1
HARRISON ERNEST L	MAJ	0-0932982	1065	2
HARRISON EUGENE L	LTC	0-1594219	0563	1
HARRISON FESTUS E JR	MAJ	0-1037826	0161	1
HARRISON FRANCIS L	CPT	0-0405990	0547	2
HARRISON FRANCIS M	LTC	0-0260554	0763	3
HARRISON FRANKLIN P	LTC	0-1587062	0463	1
HARRISON FRED L	COL	0-0224163	0355	2
HARRISON GEORGE R	LTC	0-1325390	0155	1
HARRISON GEORGE W	CPT	0-2034969	1145	2
HARRISON GRAYDON N	LTC	0-0279802	0260	1
HARRISON HAROLD J	1LT	0-1925631	0657	2
HARRISON HARRY	LTC	0-1295544	0666	1
HARRISON HARVEY G	CW4	W-2104129	0659	1
HARRISON HASKEL O	MAJ	0-0975499	0763	1
HARRISON HENRY H	COL	0-0195101	0648	3
HARRISON HOWARD W	CPT	0-1295016	0861	1
HARRISON IVAN H	LTC	0-1011440	0661	1
HARRISON JAMES C	MAJ	0-1183308	0961	1
HARRISON JAMES D JR	2LT	0-1336062	0747	2
HARRISON JESSE W	CW2	W-2146152	0856	1
HARRISON JOE T	LTC	0-1333970	0865	1
HARRISON JOHN D JR	CPT	0-0384036	0646	2
HARRISON JOHN E	COL	0-0497068	0163	1
HARRISON LESLIE R JR	MAJ	0-0938013	0163	1
HARRISON LESLIE S	CPT	0-0528798	1145	2
HARRISON LUCIUS A	MAJ	0-0199917	0756	3
HARRISON LUDY C JR	MAJ	0-2210014	0263	1
HARRISON MERRIT F	COL	0-0232498	0260	1
HARRISON MICHAEL	1LT	0-1326630	0546	2
HARRISON OLIN C	LTC	0-1306584	0763	1
HARRISON OLSON A	MAJ	0-0495958	1050	2
HARRISON PAUL	MAJ	0-0482998	1046	1
HARRISON PETER J JR	2LT	0-1824460	0943	2
HARRISON RICHARD B	CPT	0-1698866	0350	1
HARRISON RICHARD H	COL	0-0152984	0146	2
HARRISON RICHARD H	MAJ	0-0298035	0859	1
HARRISON ROBERT B	COL	0-0392375	0568	1
HARRISON ROBERT C	CW3	W-2153161	0763	1
HARRISON ROBERT D	LTC	0-0222663	0765	3
HARRISON ROBERT G	LTC	0-0182944	0749	1
HARRISON ROBERT M	LTC	0-0308305	0545	2
HARRISON ROLLIE M	LTC	0-0338969	1160	3
HARRISON ROYAL A	MAJ	0-0510573	1061	2
HARRISON SAMUEL G	COL	0-0184461	0851	3
HARRISON SAMUEL L	CW4	W-2122915	0456	1
HARRISON SEIDEL W	CW2	W-2151820	1059	2
HARRISON SHELBY A	MAJ	0-1552083	0759	1
HARRISON STANLEY L	COL	0-0272773	0367	3
HARRISON THOMAS O	LTC	0-0540392	0964	1
HARRISON VERCIL	CW2	W-2112224	0845	2
HARRISON W H JR	M G	0-0235649	0361	3
HARRISON WILBERT G	MAJ	0-1049874	0460	1
HARRISON WILLIAM F	MAJ	0-1560279	0363	1
HARRISON WILLIAM H	CW3	W-2149047	0365	1
HARRISON WILLIAM JR	MAJ	0-0469752	0647	2
HARRISON WILLIAM L	LTC	0-0313433	0854	1
HARRISS ANDREW H JR	COL	0-0204938	0458	3
HARRISS LYNN M F	LTC	0-0248644	0567	3
HARRITT GILBERT N	CPT	0-0225818	0762	3
HARRDD CARROLL O	CPT	0-1178179	0951	2
HARRDD DENNETTE A	CPT	0-0423194	1046	2

332-811 O - 69 - 13

NAME	GRADE	SVC NO	DATE RET MO YR	RET CODE
HARROD GEORGE W	CPT	0-1039023	0166	3
HARROD WILLIAM E	LTC	0-1331286	1167	1
HARROFF ROBERT F	COL	0-0271930	1067	3
HARROLD DONALD W	LTC	0-1013019	0364	2
HARROVER WILLIAM W	1LT	0-1291913	0446	2
HARROW JACK H	LTC	0-0316350	1267	3
HARROW NORMAN L	1LT	0-1047475	0845	2
HARROWER PAUL D	LTC	0-0124427	0153	3
HARRSCH SYLVANUS O	CW2	W-2150364	0563	1
HARRY EDWARD B	COL	0-0173200	0455	3
HARRY JAMES F	LTC	0-1328900	1265	1
HARRY JOHN C JR	CPT	0-0503250	0845	2
HARRY JOSEPH H	LTC	0-0275118	0866	3
HARRY ROBERT H	1LT	0-0527817	0446	2
HARRY WAYNE F	CW3	W-2150121	1265	1
HARSFIELD RAPHAEL E	1LT	0-2043077	0547	2
HARSHBARGER GLENN A	COL	0-0278982	0961	3
HARSHMAN CHARLES F	MAJ	0-0233812	0250	3
HARSHMAN CLARENCE C	COL	0-0190062	1153	3
HARSIN ALVA	MAJ	0-0501303	1053	1
HARSKI KAZIMIERZ	CW2	W-2211684	0567	1
HARSON MAYO JR	CW3	W-2146509	0264	1
HARSTER ARNOLD	1LT	0-1306093	1145	2
HARSTON EDWARD B	LTC	0-2014478	0868	1
HART ALAN L	COL	0-0154184	0854	3
HART ALFORD A	COL	0-0379761	1267	3
HART ALLAN S	1LT	0-1315823	0945	2
HART ANDREW D JR	LTC	0-0443559	0245	2
HART ANNA P	CPT	N-0700579	0945	1
HART AUGUST	MAJ	0-4023015	1268	1
HART BAYARD W	COL	0-0421879	0960	1
HART CARROLL P JR	CPT	0-1307012	0246	2
HART CHARLES H JR	COL	0-0262474	0967	3
HART CHARLES W	LTC	0-0262990	0166	3
HART CLARENCE	COL	0-0410164	0767	1
HART CLARENCE P	LTC	0-1051588	0765	1
HART CLIFFORD C	CPT	0-1185405	0759	1
HART DANIEL F	CW3	W-2132546	1159	1
HART DON D	MAJ	0-1165871	1050	2
HART DONALD F	CW2	W-2149439	0560	2
HART EARL E	CW4	W-2142462	1058	1
HART EARL P	CW3	W-2146775	0959	1
HART EDWARD F	LTC	0-0318601	0160	1
HART EUGENE D	COL	0-0306252	0968	3
HART FRANK J JR	1LT	0-1287873	0645	2
HART GEORGE E	COL	0-0286445	0268	3
HART GEORGE H	MAJ	0-0146786	0748	3
HART H B JR	LTC	0-1319277	0165	1
HART HAL I	CPT	0-1319945	0946	2
HART HAROLD L	COL	0-0324325	0865	3
HART HUGH H	LTC	0-0241562	0265	3
HART IRVIN	CPT	0-1018423	0948	2
HART JAMES A	LTC	0-0252037	0765	3
HART JEROME G	1LT	0-1012526	0444	2
HART JOHN A	CPT	0-0267766	0445	2
HART JOHN P	CPT	0-0225299	0750	1
HART JOHN R	MAJ	0-1032091	0867	3
HART JOHN T	LTC	0-1291465	0766	1
HART JOSEPH F	COL	0-0322932	0657	1
HART KENNETH P	LTC	0-1645028	1162	1
HART LEONARD W	LTC	0-1103727	0865	1
HART LUTHER	MAJ	0-0472323	0953	1
HART OLIVER J	CPT	0-0193361	0254	3
HART OLIVER J	COL	0-0230566	1161	3
HART PAUL M	COL	0-0276506	0361	3
HART PHIL C	MAJ	0-0332497	0465	3
HART RALPH L	1LT	0-1011723	0745	2
HART RICHARD L	LTC	0-1550815	0955	1
HART RICHARD M	CPT	0-0426660	0747	2
HART RICHARD W	2LT	0-1310102	0445	2
HART ROBERT F	CW3	W-2152546	0265	1
HART ROBERT H	LTC	0-1944960	1060	1
HART RUSSELL C	LTC	0-2036909	0465	1
HART SCOTT P	COL	0-0132717	1049	3
HART STANLEY F	LTC	0-1643647	1166	3

NAME	GRADE	SVC NO	DATE RET MO YR	RET CODE
HART THOMAS J JR	LTC	0-1347967	0868	2
HART WALTER P	MAJ	0-0167311	0655	3
HART WILLARD L	LTC	0-0499727	0557	3
HART WILLIAM	COL	0-0231439	0864	3
HART WILLIAM S	MAJ	0-1104195	0961	1
HART WILLIAM S	CW2	W-2145007	0463	1
HART WILLIAM T	CPT	0-0293226	0146	2
HARTOEGEN RICHARD P	COL	0-0178112	0255	3
HARTE LAWRENCE A	MAJ	0-0191495	0762	3
HARTEL GUNTHER E	LTC	0-1105496	0261	1
HARTEL JOSEPH N	LTC	0-1683457	0768	3
HARTEN CLARENCE D	CPT	0-0263122	0345	2
HARTENSTINE ELIAS H	WO1	W-2113764	0547	1
HARTER DONALD H	MAJ	0-1288544	0158	1
HARTER JEAN A	CW3	V-0500835	0263	1
HARTER JOHN D	CPT	0-0442269	0447	2
HARTER PAUL D	COL	0-0194154	0758	3
HARTER RAYMOND A	LTC	0-0254778	0166	3
HARTFORD WILLIAM S	2LT	0-2009545	0448	1
HARTH LEO B	CW4	W-2144113	0568	1
HARTHCOCK CLYDE A	MAJ	0-1115919	0358	1
HARTLE HARVEY L	MAJ	0-1031490	0261	1
HARTLERODAD FRANK G	LTC	0-0223923	1047	2
HARTLEY ALBERT I	CPT	0-1879141	0863	2
HARTLEY CARNEY JR	1LT	0-0384104	0758	1
HARTLEY CLYDE P	MAJ	N-0727268	0264	2
HARTLEY HARRY	MAJ	0-0187432	1047	1
HARTLEY JACK H	MAJ	0-1001145	0960	1
HARTLEY JAMES R	CW3	W-2148117	0562	1
HARTLEY RICHARD S	MAJ	0-0497062	1151	2
HARTLEY ROBERT D	COL	0-0274471	1065	3
HARTLEY RUSSELL W	2LT	0-1324727	0545	2
HARTLEY SAMUEL H	LTC	0-0903042	1062	3
HARTLEY WILLIAM A	CPT	0-2017541	0460	2
HARTLINE NOEL V	CPT	0-0498836	1153	2
HARTLMUELLER GEORGE	LTC	0-0964591	0768	1
HARTMAN ALBERT W JR	MAJ	0-0322328	0146	2
HARTMAN AMMON N	COL	0-0317322	1060	1
HARTMAN CARL	MAJ	0-0970419	0762	1
HARTMAN EDWARD W	LTC	0-0319423	0159	1
HARTMAN FRED L	COL	0-0246993	0662	3
HARTMAN GEORGE J	CPT	0-0451116	0345	2
HARTMAN GEORGE L	MAJ	0-0371470	0545	2
HARTMAN GLENN W	LTC	0-0402908	0161	1
HARTMAN HENRY H	WO1	W-2116465	0245	2
HARTMAN HIRAM K	MAJ	0-1341968	0961	1
HARTMAN IRA F	CPT	0-1697044	0745	2
HARTMAN JEAN F	CPT	0-1288225	0347	2
HARTMAN JOSEPH W P	MAJ	0-0987426	0764	1
HARTMAN LEROY F	1LT	0-1297028	0844	2
HARTMAN MATTHEW J	CPT	0-1341969	0866	1
HARTMAN PAULINE A	1LT	N-0755843	0946	2
HARTMAN ROBERT W	LTC	0-0474092	0350	1
HARTMAN RUSSELL M	LTC	0-0478846	0859	2
HARTMAN SIDNEY J	MAJ	0-1542919	0557	1
HARTMAN STANLEY E	COL	0-0256165	0659	3
HARTMAN WILLIAM T	LTC	0-0307566	1067	3
HARTMANN CATHERINE	MAJ	N-0775664	0865	1
HARTMANN ELIZABETH	MAJ	N-0732882	0248	1
HARTMANN FRANKLYN J	LTC	0-0360342	0963	3
HARTMANN WILLIAM F	LTC	0-0309525	0267	3
HARTNER ALVIN H JR	LTC	0-1642162	1263	1
HARTNESS GEORGE Y	LTC	0-0279579	0860	3
HARTNESS ROBERT W	LTC	0-0324162	1060	3
HARTNESS WILLIAM M	LTC	0-0738553	0763	1
HARTNETT RICHARD J	CPT	0-0318809	0244	2
HARTNETT THOMAS T	CPT	0-1287874	0745	2
HARTOM ELBERT M	MAJ	0-0178232	0760	3
HARTON WILLIAM M	COL	0-0335116	0953	3
HARTS CLEMENT B	B G	0-0241711	0864	3
HARTSELL CHARLES F	MAJ	0-1548831	0558	1
HARTSELL JULIUS W	CW2	W-2208344	1063	1
HARTSHORN DUANE F	COL	0-0296731	0859	3
HARTSHORN JACK W	MAJ	0-0975880	0962	1
HARTSIG RALPH G	1LT	0-1016661	1145	2

NAME	GRADE	SVC NO	DATE RET MO YR	RET CODE
HARTUNG ALBERT H	1LT	0-0277313	1045	2
HARTUNG JOHN S	WO1	W-2128670	0845	2
HARTUNG JOSEPH P	MAJ	0-1303502	0356	1
HARTUNG KENNETH B	LTC	0-0555376	0764	1
HARTWELL GEORGE N	MAJ	0-0424333	0948	2
HARTWELL OLIVER W	LTC	0-0323150	0267	3
HARTWELL VINTON J	MAJ	0-1045104	0461	1
HARTWICK FRED W	LTC	0-0270112	0863	3
HARTWICK ROBERT	CPT	0-1113732	0146	2
HARTWIG CARL J	LTC	0-0262245	0761	3
HARTWIG HARVEY H	LTC	0-0431351	0865	1
HARTWIG HOWARD C	LTC	0-1592262	1267	1
HARTY JAMES A	CPT	0-1284866	0755	1
HARTY JAMES R	LTC	0-0320390	0159	1
HARTY NORMAN C	1LT	0-1323692	0446	2
HARTY PATRICK H	MAJ	0-1047561	0161	1
HARTZ FRANCIS M	MAJ	0-0322699	1045	2
HARTZ WALTER F	MAJ	0-2017848	0262	1
HARTZEL NATHAN S	LTC	0-1755896	0562	1
HARTZELL CLYDE S	MAJ	0-0236260	0447	1
HARTZELL HAROLD P	COL	0-0292196	0759	1
HARTZELL HERBERT E	COL	0-1633935	0867	1
HARTZUG GEORGE N	LTC	0-0475273	0954	1
HARUM GEORGE K	MAJ	0-0360880	1267	3
HARUTUN JAMES J	LTC	0-0270579	1066	3
HARVEL BENJAMIN H	CW4	W-2143277	0160	1
HARVELL CATHERINE	1LT	N-0721814	1146	1
HARVELL CLAUDIA M	CPT	N-0764234	1047	1
HARVEY ALBERT W	LTC	0-0397020	0557	2
HARVEY ANDREW F	LTC	0-1318789	1167	1
HARVEY CARL S	CW2	W-2127172	0457	1
HARVEY CHARLES E	MAJ	0-0464523	0154	3
HARVEY CHARLES F	LTC	0-1308577	0468	2
HARVEY CLINTON D	LTC	0-1038003	0564	1
HARVEY CURTIS B	CW2	W-3150903	0566	1
HARVEY EDWIN	CPT	0-1946981	0164	1
HARVEY EDWIN R	LTC	0-1589882	0968	3
HARVEY FRANK E	LTC	0-1116961	0263	1
HARVEY FRANK E	CW2	W-2206367	0163	1
HARVEY FRANK N	CPT	0-0319499	0245	2
HARVEY GEORGE G	LTC	0-0196708	0358	3
HARVEY GEORGE M	MAJ	0-1052382	0747	2
HARVEY HOWARD A L	MAJ	0-0314538	0752	2
HARVEY JAMES D	MAJ	0-4009149	0868	1
HARVEY JAMES H	MAJ	0-1010594	1062	1
HARVEY JAMES L	CPT	0-0155478	0450	3
HARVEY JAMES C	MAJ	0-0377294	0860	1
HARVEY JOHN E	CPT	0-0954250	0661	1
HARVEY JOHN F	COL	0-0214401	0254	3
HARVEY JOHN F	1LT	0-1633936	0644	2
HARVEY JOHN J	LTC	0-1043979	1162	1
HARVEY JOSEPH S JR	CPT	0-1317911	1046	2
HARVEY KENNETH L	CW4	W-2145059	0166	1
HARVEY LEAMAN C	MAJ	0-0963133	0662	1
HARVEY LILA P	CPT	N-0775974	1153	2
HARVEY MARVIN E	CW2	W-2212822	0268	1
HARVEY MURLAN E	LTC	0-2029767	0467	1
HARVEY ORVILLE M	CW3	W-2141577	0659	1
HARVEY OWEN G	MAJ	0-1341542	0765	1
HARVEY QUINTON C	COL	0-0152983	0455	3
HARVEY RALPH N	LTC	0-0284889	1158	1
HARVEY RALPH C	CPT	0-0370690	0856	1
HARVEY RAYMOND	LTC	0-1286281	0562	1
HARVEY RICHARD C	LTC	0-0266952	0968	3
HARVEY STEPHEN A	CPT	0-0477062	0554	1
HARVEY THOMAS J JR	COL	0-0238586	0565	3
HARVEY WALTER W	LTC	0-1297362	1162	2
HARVEY WARREN E	LTC	0-0453471	1157	1
HARVEY WILLIAM A	CPT	0-0214301	1062	3
HARVEY WILLIAM L	MAJ	0-1917979	0765	1
HARVEY WILLIAM V	CPT	0-1314629	1160	1
HARVILL HALBERT	LTC	0-0131580	1153	3
HARVIN CHARLES M	MAJ	0-0183825	1046	2
HARVIN LUCIUS H JR	2LT	0-0336319	1043	2
HARWARD JAMES B	MAJ	0-1951482	0364	1

NAME	GRADE	SVC NO	DATE RET MO YR	RET CODE
HARWELL ALDEN C	1LT	0-1016154	1045	2
HARWELL J LESTER	COL	0-0263244	0368	3
HARWELL JOHN D	LTC	0-1596351	0761	1
HARWELL JOHN T	2LT	0-1799446	0748	1
HARWELL WARNOCK D	LTC	0-0531981	0763	1
HARWELL WILLIAM J	MAJ	0-0296218	1068	3
HARWOOD DEWEY S	LTC	0-0274709	0658	3
HARWOOD FREDRICK C	CPT	0-1650568	0647	2
HARWOOD GILBERT W	CW2	W-2110324	0653	1
HARWOOD HARRY L	1LT	0-0335442	0146	2
HARWOOD HORACE E	COL	0-0224578	0359	1
HARWOOD LANDRY JR	CPT	0-0273654	0868	3
HARWOOD VICTOR K	LTC	0-1291112	0766	1
HASAL DIOGENES B	CPT	0-1896588	0557	1
HASBROOK WILLIAM	CPT	0-0383890	0746	2
HASBROUCK ELEANOR T	MAJ	N-0756145	0663	2
HASCALL FRANK L	CPT	0-0336265	0845	2
HASCALL JOHN L	COL	0-0131772	0648	3
HASCALL ROBERT E	COL	0-0289291	0861	1
HASE RAYMOND C	LTC	0-0239524	1265	3
HASELDEN JOSEPH H	1LT	0-1585587	0545	2
HASELTINE DUDLEY J	LTC	0-0374656	0964	1
HASEN JOHN S	CPT	0-0188086	0648	3
HASENRITTER ELBERT	COL	0-0250537	1166	3
HASFJORD HAROLD	LTC	0-0392279	0860	1
HASH AGNES P	1LT	L-0302632	1147	2
HASH CECIL J	CPT	0-2046609	0455	1
HASH CHARLES W	COL	0-0335608	0265	1
HASH STANLEY G	LTC	0-1101478	0760	1
HASHAGEN ALBERT J	COL	0-0171477	0549	2
HASHAGEN EDWARD H	MAJ	0-0382555	0260	1
HASHAGEN RICHARD D	LTC	0-0317746	0360	1
HASHAM GEORGE J	MAJ	0-1080112	0260	1
HASHAM POLUS K	MAJ	0-0203504	0755	3
HASHIMOTO MASAYUKI	CW4	W-2136381	0865	1
HASIE PAT W	MAJ	0-1645642	0361	1
HASIS HERBERT	LTC	0-1823294	0563	1
HASKELL CHARLES C	1LT	0-1059484	0746	2
HASKELL FRANCIS W	COL	0-0466971	0667	3
HASKELL FRED L	CW3	W-2145678	0261	1
HASKELL GERALD G	CW4	W-2142044	0959	1
HASKELL HAROLD G	LTC	0-0470884	0240	2
HASKELL JOHN H F	COL	0-0222339	0246	2
HASKELL JOHN W	MAJ	0-1342331	0861	1
HASKELL LAURENT	LTC	0-0558049	0665	1
HASKELL LEROY	MAJ	0-0152704	0648	3
HASKELL WARREN B	LTC	0-0450473	0257	1
HASKETT REMEL	LTC	0-1303264	0761	1
HASKIN JOHN H	MAJ	0-0278414	0565	3
HASKIN JOHN J	MAJ	0-1054617	0859	1
HASKIN JOHN M	LTC	0-1010208	0164	1
HASKINS EDWARD T	MAJ	0-0410892	1146	2
HASKINS HAROLD A	MAJ	0-1341265	1065	1
HASKINS HOWARD E	MAJ	0-0412212	0162	1
HASKINS THOMAS C	LTC	0-1120114	0166	1
HASKINS WILLIAM R	CW3	W-2205168	1064	1
HASLAM JOHN H	WO1	W-2102986	0250	1
HASLAM JOHN W	CPT	0-1948118	1061	2
HASLAM LEGRAND	1LT	0-0377091	0451	2
HASLE HARTVICK K	MAJ	0-0461641	0246	2
HASLER GEORGIA I	MAJ	N-0769490	0268	2
HASLETT WILLIAM H	MAJ	0-1999025	0556	1
HASLIP JOHN L	LTC	0-1041568	0361	1
HASPEL JAMES E	2LT	0-2006409	1145	2
HASPETT HARRY A	CPT	0-1342269	0559	1
HASS ERNEST M	MAJ	0-0204405	1056	3
HASSE WILLIAM H	2LT	0-0542210	1045	2
HASSEL CLARENCE A	LTC	0-1062729	0767	1
HASSELBRINK DONALD H	CW3	W-2151756	0266	1
HASSELL ARTHUR S	COL	0-0208230	1063	3
HASSELL CHARLES W	MAJ	0-1286834	0465	1
HASSELL ELVIN	CW4	W-2132346	0763	1
HASSELL GEORGE E	MAJ	0-1876324	0765	1
HASSELL JOHN S	LTC	0-0319369	1160	1
HASSELL VERNON C	CPT	0-1305424	0959	1

NAME	GRADE	SVC NO	DATE RET MO YR	RET CODE
HASSELD IRVING D	CPT	0-1298061	0647	2
HASSELTINE LEE L	COL	0-0334943	1267	3
HASSEMER ERWIN H	MAJ	0-0309375	0265	3
HASSEN ERWIN	CPT	0-0436757	0845	2
HASSETT HAMAN S	COL	0-0178083	0255	3
HASSIG JOHN L	LTC	0-0302409	0164	1
HASSLER MILBURN	LTC	0-0280065	0767	3
HASSMANN RUSSELL P	CPT	0-0949221	0163	1
HASTAIN JAMES F	COL	0-0243772	0960	3
HASTEN JOHN W	LTC	0-1039379	1163	1
HASTIE FRANCIS A	MAJ	0-1100584	0656	1
HASTIE FRANK B	LTC	0-0257500	0355	3
HASTIE ROBERT T	LTC	0-1703944	1061	1
HASTINGS CHARLES D	MAJ	0-0450884	1054	1
HASTINGS CHARLES W	1LT	0-0354647	0445	2
HASTINGS CLIFTON W	CW3	W-2203378	0766	1
HASTINGS DONALD H	MAJ	0-1301139	0167	1
HASTINGS DONALD W	CPT	0-1302096	0657	1
HASTINGS EMORY P	MAJ	0-0292364	1047	1
HASTINGS EUGENE F	MAJ	0-1117006	0263	1
HASTINGS JACK A	CPT	0-0439149	1048	2
HASTINGS JAMES L	MAJ	0-0360086	0549	1
HASTINGS RICHARD M	1LT	0-1055318	1145	2
HASTY FRANK G	LTC	0-0255191	0662	3
HASTY WINFRED L JR	LTC	0-0398480	0763	1
HASWELL JAMES H	1LT	0-1794941	1045	2
HATCH ALDEN C	COL	0-0306092	1060	1
HATCH AMOS C	LTC	0-0277056	0553	3
HATCH AZEL F JR	1LT	0-0476380	0344	2
HATCH BERNARD F	COL	0-0218725	1057	3
HATCH DAVID B	MAJ	0-2025609	0461	1
HATCH DONALD P	1LT	0-5001161	1160	2
HATCH DONALD W	COL	0-1012006	0960	1
HATCH FRANK M JR	LTC	0-0196156	0262	3
HATCH GRACE M	MAJ	N-0722109	0261	1
HATCH HAROLD F	LTC	0-0917085	1267	1
HATCH WILLARD C	LTC	0-0320393	1059	1
HATCH WILLARD C	LTC	0-2293991	0565	1
HATCH WILLIAM L	CPT	0-1317265	0146	2
HATCH WILLIAM M	LTC	0-0274555	0961	3
HATCHER CHARLES L	LTC	0-0157878	1045	2
HATCHER GEORGE A	COL	0-0143454	0149	3
HATCHER HERBERT C	COL	0-0116222	0549	3
HATCHER HOWELL J	COL	0-0327179	0460	3
HATCHER JAMES E	COL	0-0196357	0558	3
HATCHER JAMES J	CPT	0-1651673	0953	2
HATCHER JAMES W	LTC	0-0947281	1067	1
HATCHER JOHN M	CW3	W-2146472	0960	1
HATCHER JOHN W JR	MAJ	0-0450750	0558	1
HATCHER ROBERT J	LTC	0-0888599	1054	1
HATCHER THOMAS A	CPT	0-0180817	0163	3
HATCHER WILLIAM E JR	MAJ	0-1101325	0161	1
HATCHER WILLIAM J	COL	0-0264151	0264	2
HATCHER WILLIAM L	CW2	W-2142360	0960	1
HATCHETT JAMES R	MAJ	0-1324730	0164	1
HATFIELD AMMON L	CPT	0-0438276	0455	1
HATFIELD ARTHUR P	LTC	0-1950177	0663	1
HATFIELD BENJAMIN F	COL	0-0272253	0866	3
HATFIELD CARSON A	MAJ	0-0156106	0650	3
HATFIELD CLYDE E	WO1	W-2146608	0966	3
HATFIELD ELMER L	2LT	0-1184222	0944	2
HATFIELD ELMER W	MAJ	0-2017699	0463	1
HATFIELD HILBERT H	CPT	0-2006375	0847	2
HATFIELD LEONARD J	CW3	W-3430024	0868	1
HATFIELD RAYMOND W	CW2	W-2144276	0661	1
HATFIELD ROBERT A	MAJ	0-2042703	0457	1
HATFIELD THEODORE C	CPT	0-0220567	0263	3
HATFIELD WEBSTER C	LTC	0-0162973	1061	3
HATHAWAY CHARLES F	LTC	0-1290148	0361	1
HATHAWAY CLAYTON T	LTC	0-0398264	0257	1
HATHAWAY EDWARD E	LTC	0-1020064	1068	1
HATHAWAY EUGENE F	LTC	0-0455175	0265	3
HATHAWAY GEORGE C	MAJ	0-1637633	0257	1
HATHAWAY KENNETH E	LTC	0-1313473	0157	1
HATHAWAY PHILIP J	COL	0-0366135	1059	3
HATHAWAY ROY A	CPT	0-1001359	0759	1
HATHAWAY STILLMAN J	MAJ	0-0186576	1154	3
HATHAWAY THOMAS C JR	CPT	0-0966978	1266	1
HATHAWAY VERNON L	CW2	W-2210624	0266	1
HATHCOCK JESSE C	LTC	0-1298866	0867	1
HATHEWAY MAURICE JR	COL	0-0251464	0261	1
HATHORN PAUL A	COL	0-0348015	0162	3
HATKE KENDALL J	LTC	0-0266875	0855	1
HATLEN CHARLES H	MAJ	0-0302281	0259	3
HATLEY CHARLES A	CW2	W-2145094	0659	1
HATLEY JAMES P	LTC	0-1173636	0857	1
HATLEY LLOYD E	MAJ	0-0425587	0247	2
HATSUKANO TOM S	MAJ	0-1699982	1061	1
HATT EARL	MAJ	0-0510517	0953	1
HATT KENDRICK A	MAJ	0-0119556	0358	3
HATT REGINALD L	COL	0-0208930	0161	3
HATTAN EMERSON W	MAJ	0-0711669	1262	1
HATTAWAY JOHN	CW2	W-2147874	0160	1
HATTEN CAS M	MAJ	0-2035189	0255	1
HATTEN GROVER C	LTC	0-0322029	0847	2
HATTEN JOHN H	MAJ	0-1176657	0861	1
HATTEN LEO A	LTC	0-1646235	0865	1
HATTEN WILLIAM H	CPT	0-0229441	0945	2
HATTENDORF ANTON P	MAJ	0-1684639	0346	2
HATTER MENZO E	CPT	0-1702977	0547	2
HATTER RICHARD L	CW3	W-2207567	0668	1
HATTERSLEY ELWOOD V	LTC	0-1048808	1165	1
HATTON BOYCE L	CPT	0-1598754	0557	1
HATTON ELMER	MAJ	0-0300034	0161	1
HATTON ELMO	MAJ	0-1001146	1055	1
HATTON THEODORE J	MAJ	0-0402250	1146	2
HATTORI EUGENE H	MAJ	0-2033622	0163	1
HATTOX JAMES H	2LT	0-1058539	1046	2
HATTY SAMUEL JR	CPT	0-0490295	1049	1
HAUBENNESTEL JOHN W	LTC	0-0207382	0659	3
HAUBERG HAROLD J	CPT	0-1342270	1058	1
HAUBNER WILLIAM P	MAJ	0-0974466	0266	1
HAUBRICK ROBERT T	WO1	W-2144387	0853	1
HAUCHMAN AARON	CW2	W-2148452	0654	2
HAUCK ARTHUR W	CPT	0-0237607	0554	3
HAUCK GEORGE F	COL	0-0213190	0363	3
HAUCK GEORGE K	CPT	0-0900513	0343	2
HAUCK RAYMOND L	LTC	0-0454099	1163	1
HAUCK WILLIAM F	1LT	0-1322334	1045	2
HAUER GEORGE T	1LT	0-0796063	0545	2
HAUER JOE M	LTC	0-1303882	1060	1
HAUER WALTER	CW3	W-2153156	0865	2
HAUFRECHT FRED	CPT	0-0354788	0246	2
HAUG HAROLD J	2LT	0-1304384	0644	2
HAUG WARREN G	2LT	0-1314472	0245	2
HAUGE HARRY K	LTC	0-0435925	0651	2
HAUGE HOWARD L	LTC	0-0429733	0167	3
HAUGEN CARL H	LTC	0-0258908	1267	3
HAUGEN OBERT O	CW4	W-2135573	0964	1
HAUGENS EDWARD E	CPT	0-0543136	0846	2
HAUGH CALVIN J	1LT	0-1172897	1045	2
HAUGH JOSEPH G	MAJ	0-0509873	0747	2
HAUGHEY JOHN T	LTC	0-0227337	0961	3
HAUGHS HOMER	MAJ	0-0488710	0447	1
HAUGHT LLOYD W	1LT	0-1821713	1044	2
HAUGHT WILLIAM D JR	CW3	W-2150021	0265	1
HAUGHTON DOROTHY E	MAJ	M-0002849	0968	1
HAUGHWOUT FREDERICK	LTC	0-0320049	0268	3
HAUGNESS HAAKON A	1LT	0-1633940	0344	2
HAUGUM ELLA A	LTC	N-0732394	0464	3
HAUKENBERRY EVERETT	LTC	0-0225782	1163	3
HAUMAN ADAM J	CPT	0-1726214	0146	2
HAUMAN HAZEN L	MAJ	0-0491770	1045	2
HAUN ALLISON J	COL	0-0290556	0668	3
HAUN BRUCE W	CW3	W-2148968	1064	1
HAUN LEROY W	WO1	W-2147521	0762	2
HAUN MADELINE M	MAJ	N-0795974	0865	1
HAUN PAUL	CPT	0-0473275	0246	2
HAUN ROLLAND C	LTC	0-0319866	0265	3
HAUPL JOHN	LTC	0-1575349	1162	1
HAUPT LOUIS L	LTC	0-0324377	0660	1
HAUPT MELVILLE I	1LT	0-1032447	0745	2
HAUPT WERNER R	LTC	0-1291466	0666	1
HAUPT WILLIAM G	LTC	0-0289312	0467	3
HAUPTMANN DAVID M	1LT	0-0523911	1045	2
HAUSAM HERBERT C	CPT	0-1646236	0765	1
HAUSAUER KARL F	MG	0-0142022	0257	3
HAUSE FRANK	CW2	W-2144119	0755	1
HAUSE HOWARD E	MAJ	0-0374633	0854	1
HAUSE WATSON L	1LT	0-1304526	0450	1
HAUSER FREDERICK	COL	0-0311304	0660	3
HAUSER GEORGE J	LTC	0-1117441	0963	1
HAUSER GUS E	CPT	0-0401499	0246	2
HAUSER HENRY F	COL	0-0409744	0661	1
HAUSER ISADOR J	LTC	0-0300800	0246	2
HAUSER JOHN W	CPT	0-1693510	1145	2
HAUSER ROBERT J	LTC	0-1553651	0368	1
HAUSER WALTER F	MAJ	0-1036186	0764	1
HAUSER WILLIAM F	MAJ	0-1186414	0762	1
HAUSER WILLIAM J	LTC	0-0288610	0263	3
HAUSLE PAUL M	CW2	W-2108498	0459	1
HAUSMAN JAMES H	LTC	0-0372397	0758	1
HAUSMANN ALBERTA	1LT	N-0723098	0845	1
HAUSWIRTH ERVING J	CPT	0-0254758	0463	3
HAUT ALLEN A	LTC	0-1579765	0268	1
HAVELY PAUL L	LTC	0-0350312	0767	3
HAVEN ALBERT P	LTC	0-0239267	0458	3
HAVEN FRANK S	MAJ	0-0257349	0446	2
HAVEN JAMES A	CPT	0-1933987	1265	2
HAVENICK NATHANIEL	COL	0-0348076	0560	2
HAVENS FLOYD	LTC	0-0446032	0862	1
HAVENS HENRY L	LTC	0-0397090	0766	1
HAVENS LEONARD M	MAJ	0-1651532	0465	1
HAVENS MILTON L	MAJ	0-0310812	0845	2
HAVENS ORIN D	CW3	W-2203483	1263	1
HAVENS RICHARD M	CW3	W-2148596	1063	1
HAVER JOHN H	CPT	0-1015260	0565	2
HAVER ROBERT W	1LT	0-1313744	0945	2
HAVERSTICK HARRY L	LTC	0-0185786	0447	2
HAVERSTICK HARRY R	MAJ	0-1030672	0454	2
HAVIS CHRISTIAN	LTC	0-0451781	0158	1
HAVIGHURST RUSSEL K	COL	0-0113127	0352	3
HAVILAND EUGENE	MAJ	0-1290243	0965	1
HAVILAND HAROLD L	COL	0-0288842	1061	3
HAVILAND SCOTT D	CPT	0-1307819	0561	1
HAVILAND WARREN F	1LT	0-1055320	1152	2
HAVILAND WILLIAM A	COL	0-0161169	0855	1
HAVILL REGINALD	MAJ	0-0134874	0552	3
HAVILLAND HARLAN L	1LT	0-0239137	1162	3
HAVLE ROBERT J	CW2	W-2213376	0468	2
HAVLIK JOHN	MAJ	0-1038669	0964	1
HAVLIN WILLIAM G	1LT	0-1105500	0846	2
HAVOLA ANTERO	LTC	0-0985351	0268	1
HAVRANEK JAMES C	1LT	0-0367486	1045	2
HAVRE ANDREW H	MAJ	0-0964994	0765	1
HAVRILLA JOSEPH M	MAJ	0-0958886	0262	2
HAVRON JAMES C	LTC	0-0392494	0968	3
HAW ALBERT S	COL	0-0911965	0868	3
HAW HARRY H	1LT	0-0134872	0154	3
HAW MARVIN T JR	MAJ	0-0330924	0145	2
HAW PHILLIP	WO1	W-2123434	1045	2
HAWERKOTTE JOHN H	1LT	0-1012318	1145	2
HAWES ALBERT L	1LT	0-0162375	0645	2
HAWES HENRY H JR	CW4	W-2143917	0369	2
HAWES HOWARD R	LTC	0-0379193	0758	1
HAWES MILTON D	LTC	0-0239299	0554	2
HAWETHORNE ELLIOTT G	1LT	0-1825123	0862	1
HAWFIELD ROBERT R	MAJ	0-0525321	1161	1
HAWK ALLEN D	CPT	0-0995589	0364	2
HAWK ASHER M JR	2LT	0-0441400	1143	2
HAWK ERNEST F JR	1LT	0-0452601	1044	2
HAWK GEORGE W	MAJ	0-1291634	1160	1
HAWK JACK H	CPT	0-0367124	0960	2
HAWK JOE C JR	CPT	0-1169146	0646	2
HAWK JOHN F	1LT	0-2097197	1054	2
HAWK LEWIS L	LTC	0-0327176	0262	3
HAWK OSMON R	LTC	0-0263123	0262	3
HAWK TOMMY C	MAJ	0-1890484	0766	1
HAWK WALTER D	CPT	0-0439320	0745	2
HAWKE HARRY L	1LT	0-0395312	0644	2
HAWKE LEONARD T	LTC	0-0415561	0163	1
HAWKER CHARLES W	MAJ	0-0476486	0757	1
HAWKES HOWARD G	MAJ	0-0185918	1054	3
HAWKES KENNETH	LTC	0-1552084	0460	1
HAWKES MAX V	CPT	0-2262583	0266	1
HAWKES PHILLIP C	MAJ	0-0381408	1267	3
HAWKES THOMAS A	CPT	0-0181758	0845	2
HAWKES WINSLOW D JR	LTC	0-1697879	0164	1
HAWKING KENNETH T	COL	0-0469908	0764	1
HAWKINS BYRON R	MAJ	0-1919497	1267	1
HAWKINS CHARLES B	MAJ	0-1701526	0961	1
HAWKINS CHARLES E	CW2	W-2146885	1061	1
HAWKINS CLARENCE C	LTC	0-0340746	0561	1
HAWKINS DAMON	MAJ	0-1314286	0856	1
HAWKINS EDWARD S	MAJ	0-2016326	0265	1
HAWKINS EDWIN O	CW3	W-2147270	0865	1
HAWKINS ELGIN G	CW3	W-2142424	0865	1
HAWKINS ELIM L	1LT	0-1291987	0761	1
HAWKINS FORREST D	1LT	0-0425640	0945	2
HAWKINS FRED R	CPT	0-1884165	0964	1
HAWKINS GEORGE A	MAJ	0-0269513	1164	3
HAWKINS GEORGE B	CPT	0-2262114	1060	1
HAWKINS GEORGE F	COL	0-0233005	0765	3
HAWKINS GEORGE W	LTC	0-0353401	1059	1
HAWKINS GEORGIA M	MAJ	N-0734128	1266	3
HAWKINS HAROLD L	MAJ	0-1176658	0859	2
HAWKINS HARRY H	1LT	0-1184064	0749	1
HAWKINS HAZEL E	LTC	N-0730270	0962	1
HAWKINS HEFLIN N	MAJ	0-0407576	0264	3
HAWKINS HIRSCHLE H	LTC	0-1317733	0763	1
HAWKINS JAMES E	LTC	0-1313602	0766	1
HAWKINS JAMES R	CPT	0-0454388	0453	2
HAWKINS JOHN C	2LT	0-1331359	0354	3
HAWKINS JOHN E	MAJ	0-1288546	0361	1
HAWKINS JOHN F	MAJ	0-1648611	0457	1
HAWKINS JOHN T	CPT	0-2262918	0367	2
HAWKINS JULIAN A	MAJ	0-1304074	1060	1
HAWKINS LAWRENCE R	1LT	0-5340201	0768	2
HAWKINS LESLIE L	CW2	W-2117529	0155	1
HAWKINS LOUIS A JR	COL	0-0216201	0564	3
HAWKINS MALCOLM	LTC	0-0413711	0761	1
HAWKINS MARVIL P	LTC	0-0374121	0661	1
HAWKINS MARVIN L	MAJ	0-1107468	0461	1
HAWKINS MELVIN J	CPT	0-1922549	0764	1
HAWKINS MILDRED R	2LT	N-0768315	0347	1
HAWKINS MILTON	LTC	0-0469225	0146	2
HAWKINS OLIN L	MAJ	0-0971804	0264	1
HAWKINS ORINGTON H	LTC	0-1320383	0163	1
HAWKINS RALPH G	1LT	0-0435644	1045	2
HAWKINS REGINALD	MAJ	0-0360009	1060	1
HAWKINS ROBERT D	CW3	W-2206778	0266	1
HAWKINS ROBERT L	LTC	0-1298225	1161	1
HAWKINS ROBERT R JR	MAJ	0-1050717	0562	1
HAWKINS RUFUS K	CW4	W-2118487	0361	1
HAWKINS THOMAS H	MAJ	0-1923547	1163	1
HAWKINS WESLEY E	LTC	0-0225056	1064	3
HAWKINS WIL	MAJ	0-1599042	1262	1
HAWKINS WILLIAM A	MAJ	0-1308426	0461	1
HAWKINS WILLIAM A	CW3	W-2151646	1165	1
HAWKINS WILLIAM A JR	LTC	0-1303883	0760	1
HAWKINS WILLIAM B	COL	0-0310311	1263	1
HAWKINS WILLIAM G JR	2LT	0-2026987	0246	2
HAWKINS WILLIAM J	LTC	0-2018690	0568	1
HAWKINS WILLIAM K	CPT	0-0491515	0357	1
HAWKINS WILLIAM R	LTC	0-0451608	0256	1
HAWKINS WILLIAM S	CPT	0-0255274	0145	2
HAWKINS WILLIAM S	MAJ	0-0416747	0846	2
HAWKO RICHARD J	LTC	0-0402229	0764	3
HAWLEY CHARLES C	LTC	0-0452738	0766	1
HAWLEY CHARLES D	MAJ	0-0201589	1046	1

NAME	GRADE	SVC NO	DATE RET MO YR	RET CODE
HAWLEY CHARLES L	LTC	0-1100515	0565	1
HAWLEY DORIS L	2LT	N-0760018	0545	1
HAWLEY GEORGE E	MAJ	0-0150315	0150	3
HAWLEY GEORGE F	MAJ	0-0375262	0461	1
HAWLEY HAROLD D	MAJ	0-2025332	0859	2
HAWLEY IVAN A	CW2	W-2145774	0365	1
HAWLEY MARGERY C	LTC	L-0707024	0862	1
HAWLEY PHILIP C	LTC	0-0167133	0955	3
HAWLEY RAY T	CW2	W-2145679	0561	1
HAWLEY RICHARD A	CPT	0-1289729	0546	2
HAWLEY ROBERT F	MAJ	0-0909694	1048	2
HAWLEY ROBERT L	LTC	0-0436830	0159	1
HAWLEY SHERMAN R	COL	0-0299333	1162	3
HAWLEY STANLEY S	LTC	0-0216463	0663	3
HAWLEY VERNON C	LTC	0-0193414	0955	3
HAWLEY WILLIAM G	CPT	0-4006451	0365	1
HAWN MATHEW	MAJ	0-1640538	0657	1
HAWORTH JAMES G	LTC	0-0148452	0648	3
HAWORTH JAMES G	MAJ	0-0987107	0962	1
HAWORTH LEONARD S	2LT	0-2055334	0353	2
HAWORTH MONTIE M	CPT	0-0500381	0654	1
HAWORTH TEDDY L	LTC	0-0269543	1066	3
HAWRO VINCENT A	MAJ	0-0250266	0446	2
HAWRYLAK FRANK	MAJ	0-2018513	0863	1
HAWS LAWRENCE E	LTC	0-0271466	0565	3
HAWTHORNE EMIL F	LTC	0-1106805	0663	1
HAWTHORNE JAMES A	LTC	0-1576101	0564	1
HAWTHORNE JAMES E	1LT	0-1061722	0446	2
HAWTHORNE JOHN H	2LT	0-5405281	0460	2
HAWTHORNE RAMONA M	2LT	N-0797872	0646	1
HAWTHORNE ROY O	COL	0-0201442	0648	3
HAWTIN RAYMOND F	LTC	0-1321306	0662	1
HAWTOF E MANUEL	LTC	0-0276609	1059	3
HAY CARL F	MAJ	0-0463473	0456	1
HAY ELMER M	LTC	0-0263849	0660	3
HAY FLOYD H	CPT	0-0375213	0845	2
HAY KENNETH M	LTC	0-0525155	0764	3
HAY MALCOLM	MG	0-0284748	0667	3
HAY REGINALD W	LTC	0-0148426	0648	3
HAY ROBERT H	LTC	0-1080204	0461	1
HAYASHI HAJIME	MAJ	0-2030796	0863	1
HAYASHI RICHARD K	CPT	0-1326049	0263	1
HAYCOCK CHARLES A JR	CPT	0-0947573	1060	1
HAYCOCK ROBERT D	CPT	0-2036058	0646	2
HAYCOCK ROBERT W	CPT	0-1541731	0845	2
HAYDAHL JOHN T	CW4	W-2116007	0555	1
HAYDEN ALVIN C	CPT	0-0279209	1046	1
HAYDEN BERNARD	WO1	W-2104133	0853	1
HAYDEN CLIFFORD W	CPT	0-2011194	0658	1
HAYDEN CURTIS B	LTC	0-0452617	0161	1
HAYDEN DEBORAH E	1LT	N-0736757	0746	1
HAYDEN GEORGE F	MAJ	0-0524501	1146	2
HAYDEN HERMAN C	CW3	W-2152040	0466	1
HAYDEN PHILIP P	CPT	0-5327067	0668	2
HAYDEN RAYMOND W JR	LTC	0-0454270	0766	1
HAYDEN THOMAS C JR	MAJ	0-1584337	0960	1
HAYDEN VERNON L	CPT	0-1289080	0454	1
HAYDEN WILSON A	LTC	0-2017355	1163	1
HAYDON GERTRUDE M	MAJ	N-0773177	0364	2
HAYDON JULIUS H	MAJ	0-0888281	1062	1
HAYEK WILL J	COL	0-0163685	0756	3
HAYES ANDREW W	COL	0-0281103	0859	1
HAYES ARTHUR F	LTC	0-1001147	0964	1
HAYES BEDA M	1LT	N-0703415	1045	1
HAYES CATHERINE	CPT	N-0730102	0261	1
HAYES CLINTON C	CPT	0-1914917	0661	1
HAYES DONALD F	CPT	0-1291816	1045	2
HAYES DONALD R	LTC	0-1060474	1162	1
HAYES DOUGLAS A	1LT	0-1317913	0945	2
HAYES EDMOND M	CW2	W-2141985	1159	1
HAYES EDWARD J	1LT	0-1179884	1045	2
HAYES EDWARD K	LTC	0-0469769	0455	2
HAYES ENOS W JR	MAJ	0-0344135	0566	1
HAYES ERWIN H	LTC	0-1683489	1264	1
HAYES FLOYD M	COL	0-0208873	0655	2
HAYES GEORGE H	CW3	W-2205435	1164	1
HAYES GEORGE P JR	LTC	0-0337953	0962	3
HAYES GORDON B	CPT	0-0224220	1058	3
HAYES HARLEY L	WO1	W-2151039	1163	2
HAYES HAROLD F	LTC	0-1642952	0964	1
HAYES HARROLD H	COL	0-0342877	1167	3
HAYES J BENJAMIN JR	LTC	0-0274031	1167	3
HAYES JAMES A	LTC	0-0912802	0268	3
HAYES JAMES E	MAJ	0-0300547	0954	1
HAYES JAMES F	LTC	0-0518787	0663	1
HAYES JAMES H	MAJ	0-1283424	0957	1
HAYES JAMES J	MAJ	0-1650105	0261	1
HAYES JAMES M	CW4	W-2139549	0261	1
HAYES JAMES P	MAJ	0-0288628	0363	3
HAYES JAMES R	1LT	0-1284136	0845	2
HAYES JAMES T	CPT	0-0491633	1052	2
HAYES JEREMIAH F	LTC	0-1646238	0263	1
HAYES JESSE C	MAJ	0-0372702	0860	1
HAYES JOHN H	CPT	0-0311856	0345	2
HAYES JOHN J	COL	0-0354750	0168	3
HAYES JOHN J	1LT	0-1012477	114N	2
HAYES JOHN J	CPT	0-1797996	0547	2
HAYES JOHN P	LTC	0-0319397	1045	2
HAYES JOHN T	LTC	0-0446443	1264	1
HAYES JOHN T	MAJ	0-2203412	0965	1
HAYES KENNETH M	CPT	0-1010128	1045	2
HAYES LEON C	CPT	0-1010188	0747	2
HAYES LUTHER Z	CPT	0-1878867	1066	1
HAYES MATTHEW R	MAJ	0-1324478	0668	3
HAYES MIKE H	CW3	W-2209643	0868	1
HAYES REX S	1LT	0-2206811	0454	2
HAYES RICHARD G	2LT	0-1018701	0644	2
HAYES RICHARD L	COL	0-0109248	0546	2
HAYES RICHARD L	CPT	0-1293697	0554	2
HAYES ROBERT C	MAJ	0-0558085	1154	2
HAYES ROBERT L	COL	0-0155366	1155	3
HAYES ROBERT W	LTC	0-1035809	1163	1
HAYES RUDOLPH V	CW3	W-2207964	0666	1
HAYES RUTHERFORD	CPT	0-0261080	1267	3
HAYES SAMUEL E	CPT	0-0388295	0746	2
HAYES THEODORE C	COL	0-1825674	0468	1
HAYES THOMAS F	COL	0-0311367	0664	3
HAYES THOMAS F JR	MAJ	0-0282375	1045	2
HAYES THOMAS J	1LT	0-1286121	1043	2
HAYES THOMAS T H	1LT	0-5310888	0763	2
HAYES WALTER J	CW4	W-2111601	1067	1
HAYES WALTER L	CPT	0-0903755	0845	2
HAYES WARREN H	1LT	0-1307233	0845	2
HAYES WILLARD L JR	MAJ	0-0413689	1045	2
HAYES WILLIAM G	MAJ	0-2263423	1266	1
HAYES WILTON B	CPT	0-1648614	0347	2
HAYGOOD EVERETT A	COL	0-0348351	0667	3
HAYHURST JERIMIAH V	MAJ	0-1918966	0663	1
HAYKEL NORMAN A	CW4	W-2143028	0664	1
HAYKIN ROBERT B	LTC	0-0956965	0768	1
HAYMAKER KENNETH G	COL	0-0398389	1055	1
HAYMAKER WEBB E	LTC	0-0291133	0762	3
HAYMAN ALAN P	LTC	0-0355661	0662	3
HAYMAN ARLEY A JR	LTC	0-0331026	0561	1
HAYMAN FIRMAN K	COL	0-0225647	0657	1
HAYMAN HARRY B	CPT	0-0237480	0464	3
HAYMON WILLARD	CW3	W-2149930	1162	1
HAYNE ORLANDO V	LTC	0-0524490	0965	1
HAYNE PAUL T	LTC	0-0215678	0364	3
HAYNE WILLARD W	COL	0-0325710	0566	3
HAYNER ROBERT L	CPT	0-1300031	0945	2
HAYNES ARTHUR L	CW4	W-2116101	0559	1
HAYNES ARTHUR S	2LT	0-1914401	0345	1
HAYNES BILLIE J	CW2	W-2211141	1265	1
HAYNES BLANDY C JR	LTC	0-1282361	0567	1
HAYNES CHARLES J	CPT	0-1636021	0153	1
HAYNES CLIFFORD G	MAJ	0-0325052	0767	3
HAYNES CLIFFORD L	1LT	0-1301637	0348	2
HAYNES DAVID I	CW2	W-2149920	0661	1
HAYNES DEWITT	1LT	0-2034023	1063	2
HAYNES EARL F	LTC	0-1332814	1065	2
HAYNES EASIL C	CW3	W-2145158	0656	1
HAYNES EDWARD C	MAJ	0-1256370	0261	1
HAYNES EMERSON L	LTC	0-0452499	0153	1
HAYNES FRAZIER J	MAJ	0-1845049	0761	1
HAYNES FRED A	MAJ	0-1051591	1062	1
HAYNES GEORGE H	LTC	0-0275408	1043	2
HAYNES GORDON B	LTC	0-1996586	0265	1
HAYNES HARALD J	LTC	0-0291859	0468	3
HAYNES HORACE S	CW2	W-2127644	1151	1
HAYNES LEWIS M	MAJ	0-1548834	0565	1
HAYNES ORREN F	MAJ	0-0450885	1154	1
HAYNES PAUL E	LTC	0-1101483	0866	3
HAYNES PHILIP F	COL	0-0171548	1046	2
HAYNES RAY	COL	0-0172730	1059	1
HAYNES RUSSELL M	CPT	0-1317789	0267	3
HAYNES SCOTT C	CW3	W-2208864	0967	1
HAYNES STANLEY L	CPT	0-0120124	0654	3
HAYNES STUART G	2LT	0-2210396	1150	2
HAYNES THOMAS E	1LT	0-1551417	0445	2
HAYNES WALTER G	LTC	0-0369487	0246	2
HAYNES WHITWORTH	1LT	0-1313529	0146	2
HAYNES WILLIAM A	LTC	0-0454616	0263	1
HAYNES WILLIAM P III	LTC	0-1283951	0766	1
HAYNES WILLIE E	CPT	0-0987607	0853	2
HAYNIE CLYDE M	CPT	0-0321372	0954	1
HAYNIE JACK D	CPT	0-0167724	0456	3
HAYNIE JEWELL G	LTC	0-0257248	0660	1
HAYNIE ROBERT C	COL	0-0921254	1046	2
HAYNOSCH FRED J	MAJ	0-1294836	1263	1
HAYNSWORTH THOMAS B	MAJ	0-0234162	0965	3
HAYS CLOYD A	COL	0-0308957	0846	2
HAYS FRED J	LTC	0-0451461	1156	1
HAYS GEORGE M	LTC	0-0352715	0546	2
HAYS HARRY F	LTC	0-0291471	0262	3
HAYS HUGH G	LTC	0-0323960	1161	3
HAYS JOHN W	CPT	0-0352281	1045	2
HAYS LEOPOLD M	LTC	0-0347342	0566	3
HAYS MARSHALL A	COL	0-0285948	0468	3
HAYS NORMAN M	CW3	W-2151416	0865	1
HAYS ORREN L	LTC	0-0272582	0263	3
HAYS OTIS E JR	COL	0-0363584	1066	1
HAYS RAY W	COL	0-0113566	0749	3
HAYS ROBERT H	MAJ	0-0289322	0664	3
HAYS ROBERT L	CPT	0-2262612	0261	1
HAYS SAMUEL D	COL	0-0170950	0454	3
HAYS STANLEY	COL	0-0374722	0861	1
HAYS VERYL R	1LT	0-1036187	0845	2
HAYS WALTER L	MAJ	0-0413587	0461	1
HAYSON CECIL J	CW3	W-2143916	0262	1
HAYTON RALPH E	MAJ	0-1108008	0264	2
HAYUNGS HENRY A	LTC	0-0275367	0167	3
HAYWARD CHARLES P	COL	0-0129842	0760	3
HAYWARD DONALD R	2LT	0-0554347	0346	2
HAYWARD EDWARD G JR	LTC	0-0191096	0649	3
HAYWARD EVERETT F	LTC	0-0308138	0762	3
HAYWARD GEORGE E	CPT	0-0380449	1158	1
HAYWARD JOHN A	CPT	0-1922925	0867	2
HAYWARD LAURA F	2LT	N-0720023	0442	1
HAYWARD ORVILLE C	WO1	W-2123084	1049	2
HAYWARD PAUL H	COL	0-0107150	0445	2
HAYWARD VINCENT	CW2	W-2142961	0356	1
HAYWARD WILLIAM A	MAJ	0-0487157	0553	2
HAYWARD WINSTON R	COL	0-0281028	0260	1
HAYWOOD BLANCHE	1LT	N-0901630	0155	2
HAYWOOD HERALD F	LTC	0-0488239	0264	3
HAYWOOD TED M	COL	0-0278946	0561	3
HAYWOOD WILLIAM R	LTC	0-0321302	1265	3
HAYWOOD WILLIE	CPT	0-1324811	0753	2
HAZARD DOUGLAS D	CPT	0-0977613	0861	1
HAZARD FRANCIS J	LTC	0-0450412	1060	1
HAZARD FRED	LTC	0-1574057	1057	1
HAZEL ARTHUR T	LTC	0-1552694	0462	1
HAZEL HAROLD E	LTC	0-0262488	1160	1
HAZEL JOHN J	COL	0-0228093	0365	3
HAZEL R H	MAJ	0-0494263	0154	1
HAZELBAKER HARRY D	LTC	0-0230735	1062	3
HAZELBAKER PHILMON F	LTC	0-0505045	1057	2
HAZELET VINCENT W	MAJ	0-1324931	1061	1
HAZELETT CHARLES W	COL	0-0361771	0668	3
HAZELIP WARNER S	LTC	0-0392116	0263	3
HAZELL WILLIAM C	1LT	0-0109813	0633	1
HAZELTON GERALD A	CPT	0-5321940	1068	2
HAZELWOOD EDWARD L	1LT	0-1822877	0945	2
HAZELWOOD JAMES A	COL	0-0900684	1055	1
HAZELWOOD WENDELL H	LTC	0-0262719	1049	1
HAZEN CHARLES L	COL	0-0362173	1168	1
HAZEN JACK P	LTC	0-1293046	1063	1
HAZEN RAYMOND E	MAJ	0-1289081	0954	1
HAZEN RICHARD G	LTC	0-1058830	0663	1
HAZEN THOMAS F	LTC	0-0246529	0753	3
HAZENBUSH THOMAS G	COL	0-0188511	0252	3
HAZER KALEEM	LTC	0-1165398	0962	1
HAZLETT EDWARD A	COL	0-0220848	1055	1
HAZLETT WALTER R	MAJ	0-0991556	1265	2
HAZLETT WILLIAM L	MAJ	0-0354756	0162	3
HAZLEWOOD IVAN O	LTC	0-1533085	0954	1
HAZLEWOOD JERRY W	1LT	0-5337720	0868	2
HAZLEWOOD UPSALA H	1LT	N-0725435	0646	1
HAZUCHA RUDOLPH F	MAJ	0-1553273	1061	1
HAZUDA ALEX W	LTC	0-0450886	0355	1
HAZZARD STEPHEN B	CPT	0-0446660	1044	2
HEACOCK CHESTER S	2LT	0-1172063	0444	2
HEACOCK FREDERICK	LTC	0-1327354	1065	2
HEACOCK HAROLD W	MAJ	0-0321851	0445	2
HEACOCK ROLAND T	CPT	0-0502079	0845	2
HEAD ALAN S	WO1	W-2111725	0845	2
HEAD ALLEN W	LTC	0-0405470	0363	1
HEAD ARTHUR E	COL	0-0262013	0867	3
HEAD BERNARD R	CW4	W-2132863	0561	1
HEAD CHARLES S JR	COL	0-0254573	0466	3
HEAD CLIFFORD M	LTC	0-1310440	0862	1
HEAD FREDERICK	LTC	0-1299744	1266	1
HEAD HUGH G JR	LTC	0-0346630	0166	3
HEAD JOHN H	MAJ	0-2012524	1166	1
HEAD JOSEPH JR	LTC	0-0284976	1267	3
HEAD LAWRENCE W JR	LTC	0-1641376	0862	1
HEAD MORRIS W	CPT	0-1117142	0465	1
HEAD RAYMOND J	CPT	0-0381956	1145	2
HEAD WILLIAM	CPT	0-0204875	0128	1
HEADLAND VIOLET M	2LT	N-0700580	0535	2
HEADLEY CHALON S	LTC	0-1308951	1266	1
HEADLEY HOLLAND C	LTC	0-0122515	0153	3
HEADLOUGH WARREN E	MAJ	0-1925712	1165	1
HEAGY CHARLES F	LTC	0-0289840	0264	1
HEALD GEORGE P	LTC	0-1301482	0466	1
HEALD HARRY C	MAJ	0-0222615	0644	2
HEALEY ANDREW S JR	CPT	0-1304075	0347	2
HEALEY EDWARD F	CPT	0-0331666	0445	2
HEALEY EUGENE T	MAJ	0-1298703	0958	1
HEALEY GRANT	COL	0-2034424	0466	1
HEALEY JOSEPH T	CPT	0-0441572	1047	2
HEALEY JOSEPH W JR	CPT	0-1110549	0564	1
HEALEY OWEN R	CPT	0-1049199	0746	2
HEALEY THEODORE	CPT	0-0885627	0250	1
HEALY ANNE P	1LT	N-0755984	0546	1
HEALY EDWARD A	MAJ	0-1796278	1060	1
HEALY EDWARD J	MAJ	0-0320184	0564	3
HEALY EDWARD J JR	LTC	0-0311355	0562	1
HEALY EDWARD M	LTC	0-0142028	0257	3
HEALY EDWARD W	MAJ	0-0336060	0347	2
HEALY FRANCIS D	LTC	0-0918722	0165	3
HEALY FRANCIS H	CPT	0-1032016	1162	1
HEALY JAMES K	LTC	0-0450019	1056	1
HEALY JEREMIAH F JR	CPT	0-0453036	0846	2
HEALY JOHN F	CPT	0-1036555	0546	2
HEALY LEONARD H	LTC	0-1176364	1267	1
HEALY MARTIN J	1LT	0-1307123	0945	2
HEALY MAURICE J	CPT	0-0356249	0246	2
HEALY MAURICE J	MAJ	0-1335003	0163	1

NAME	GRADE	SVC NO	DATE RET MO YR	RET CODE
HEALY PAUL E	1LT	0-1324514	1145	2
HEALY RADCLIFFE	MAJ	0-0977900	1167	1
HEALY TIMOTHY J	COL	0-0204385	0261	3
HEALY TRACY K	COL	0-0159645	0751	3
HEANEY BERNARD F	CPT	0-1181626	0947	2
HEANEY ELBRIDGE	LTC	0-0318211	1263	3
HEANEY MICHAEL K	1LT	0-5013463	0267	2
HEANEY WILLIAM J	CW2	W-2143620	1055	1
HEAP GEORGE P	LTC	0-0155112	0648	3
HEAPE ARTIE M	LTC	0-0251330	1156	3
HEAPE GRAHAM	CW4	W-2113418	0763	2
HEAPHY JOHN J	MAJ	0-1578586	0361	1
HEARD ALBERT S	CW2	W-2146785	0557	1
HEARD CHARLES	MAJ	0-1303335	0961	1
HEARD CHARLES R	CPT	0-1535337	0746	2
HEARD EARL D	1LT	0-2212085	0966	2
HEARD GUNION M	LTC	0-0483218	0667	3
HEARD ISAAC J	WO1	W-2149658	1055	2
HEARD JAMES L	MAJ	0-0500032	0146	2
HEARD JOHN C JR	LTC	0-1169148	1160	1
HEARD JOHN W	MAJ	0-1685655	0964	1
HEARD SAMUEL R	1LT	0-1303336	0245	2
HEARD WALTER S JR	MAJ	0-1046121	1263	1
HEARFIELD HAROLD H	LTC	0-0112560	0450	3
HEARICK JAMES G	COL	0-1633949	0664	1
HEARLIN BERTRAM S JR	LTC	0-1100535	1060	1
HEARN ANNA E	MAJ	N-0760790	0764	1
HEARN CHARLES A	COL	0-0294025	1159	1
HEARN CHARLES L	MAJ	0-0406367	0146	2
HEARN CHAUNCEY M	COL	0-0257081	1264	3
HEARN FREDERICK	COL	0-0257135	0859	1
HEARN GEORGE J	M G	0-0295111	0667	3
HEARN GEORGE F	2LT	0-1059805	1144	2
HEARN HENRY G	MAJ	0-0499915	0447	2
HEARN JAMES M JR	MAJ	0-1338091	0765	1
HEARN LYNN E	CPT	0-1314364	0446	2
HEARN OSA M	LTC	0-1014718	0160	1
HEARN THOMAS W	CPT	0-1320279	0964	2
HEARN VIRGINIA E	1LT	N-0762413	0650	2
HEARNE CHARLES F JR	CPT	0-1578537	0745	2
HEARNE FRANK T	1LT	0-0422953	1144	2
HEARNE JULIAN G JR	COL	0-0229386	0660	1
HEARNE WILLIAM A	LTC	0-1039398	1068	3
HEARST MORRIS	LTC	0-0294792	0468	3
HEARTFIELD RICHARD C	COL	0-0130367	0662	3
HEARTSILL CHARLES E	MAJ	0-0260405	0158	2
HEASTY JOHN C	CPT	0-0984194	0862	1
HEATH CHARLES C	MAJ	0-1543128	1064	1
HEATH CHARLEY S	LTC	0-1331130	1068	1
HEATH CLARENCE P	COL	0-0253726	0562	3
HEATH CLIFFORD S	CPT	0-0487913	0247	2
HEATH DENVER Y	CPT	0-0497946	0553	1
HEATH DONALD R	CPT	0-1020150	1059	1
HEATH FOY K	CW4	W-2117550	0659	1
HEATH FRANCIS C	LTC	0-1016373	0363	1
HEATH FREDERICK	MAJ	0-0482330	1059	1
HEATH FREDERICK	MAJ	0-1551220	0957	1
HEATH HARRIET	MAJ	N-0726510	0764	1
HEATH HENRY S	LTC	0-0314065	1047	2
HEATH JAMES N SR	MAJ	0-0953932	0462	1
HEATH JAMES W	LTC	0-1284137	1164	1
HEATH JOHN R	COL	0-0216294	0850	3
HEATH MORRIS L	LTC	0-1056114	0667	3
HEATH PAUL W	COL	0-0261717	1165	3
HEATH PHILLIP C	LTC	0-0463924	0962	1
HEATH RAYMOND A	LTC	0-0274354	0160	1
HEATH STANLEY H	MAJ	0-1238740	1158	1
HEATH THOMAS D	LTC	0-0229990	0344	2
HEATH WILLIAM R SR	MAJ	0-1577303	1058	1
HEATH WILLIAM S	2LT	0-1825675	0344	2
HEATHCOTE EDWIN J	CPT	0-0985460	0162	1
HEATHCOTE CARLYLE J	MAJ	0-1186924	0366	1
HEATHER FRED H JR	MAJ	0-0488158	0348	2
HEATHERINGTON FRED P	CPT	0-1166282	0645	2
HEATHERLY EDWARD S	MAJ	0-1031648	0457	1

NAME	GRADE	SVC NO	DATE RET MO YR	RET CODE
HEATHERLY JAMES A	MAJ	0-0501316	0747	1
HEATHMAN ROBERT C	LTC	0-1002442	0465	3
HEATLEY SELDEN E	CPT	0-1592265	0162	1
HEATLY CLYDE B	MAJ	0-1291636	0960	1
HEATLY HERBERT L	CW2	W-2141578	0161	2
HEATLY MAURICE O	MAJ	0-0379014	0246	2
HEATLY ROBERT L	CPT	0-1111660	0345	2
HEATON CHARLES C	LTC	0-0361792	0446	2
HEATON CHARLES E	MAJ	0-0885430	0653	1
HEATON CHARLES E	MAJ	0-1544716	0657	2
HEATON DOROTHY A	2LT	N-0745264	0345	1
HEATON EDWARD C	CPT	0-1648288	0956	1
HEATON GEORGE P	MAJ	0-0497522	1054	1
HEATON HUGH O	1LT	0-1055867	0664	1
HEATON JAMES W JR	CPT	0-0368764	0346	2
HEATON NELSON E	CPT	0-0261652	0956	3
HEATON RALPH S	CPT	0-1584342	0165	1
HEATON WILLIAM E	MAJ	0-0297494	0449	3
HEATON WILLIAM P	LTC	0-0456161	1060	1
HEAVEN PAUL J	LTC	0-1015670	1061	1
HEAVER JOHN P	LTC	0-1179887	1267	1
HEAVEY JOHN O	MAJ	0-0236483	0764	3
HEAVEY THOMAS J JR	LTC	0-0720499	0165	1
HEBARD GEORGE A	1LT	0-1286284	1044	2
HEBBE VERNE W	LTC	0-0403050	1060	1
HEBBLE JOHN C JR	CPT	0-0211099	0563	3
HEBBLETHWAITE L M	MAJ	0-0496866	1050	2
HEBEL AUGUST R	MAJ	0-0970432	0364	1
HEBERT ALFRED J	1LT	0-1637641	0446	2
HEBERT GLENN L	1LT	0-1113736	1045	2
HEBERT JULIEN A	CPT	0-0501378	0745	2
HEBERT ROBERT J	LTC	0-1315825	0564	1
HEBLICH FREDERICK	LTC	0-0263481	0845	2
HECHINGER RUSSELL W	LTC	0-1585600	1163	1
HECHT CHRIS M	LTC	0-0132233	0558	3
HECHT HARRY W	LTC	0-0205134	0247	2
HECHT LOUIS W JR	MAJ	0-1322448	0764	1
HECHT MORTON E JR	MAJ	0-1167896	0962	1
HECHT VERNON C	2LT	0-1322839	0845	2
HECHT WORTHY O	LTC	0-0917142	1166	3
HECK ALEXANDER	2LT	0-0389446	0647	2
HECK CHARLES A	MAJ	0-0980549	0564	1
HECK HAROLD J	COL	0-0236258	0966	3
HECK JESSE E JR	MAJ	0-2049572	0965	1
HECK LEWIS O	COL	0-0230478	0260	3
HECK ROBERT R	MAJ	0-2018515	0663	1
HECKART PAUL R	CW4	W-2148322	0168	1
HECKELBECK EDWARD E	MAJ	0-0968737	1168	1
HECKER GEORGE L	LTC	0-0288071	0546	2
HECKER GEORGE M	1LT	0-1297878	0645	2
HECKERMAN SEELEY E	LTC	0-0445958	0852	1
HECKERT ROBERT J	COL	0-0392652	0868	1
HECKMAN EDWARD A	CPT	0-1557606	0847	2
HECKMAN KENNETH A	CW3	W-2129916	0859	1
HECKMAN RAYMOND M	COL	0-0173540	0257	3
HECQ CHARLES A	LTC	0-1297363	0162	1
HEDBERG OSCAR G	MAJ	0-0332472	1054	3
HEDDAEUS GILBERT T	MAJ	0-0148547	0757	3
HEDDEN DOUGLAS J	2LT	0-1935248	1053	2
HEDDEN JULIUS C	LTC	0-0381256	0346	2
HEDDEN ORVE K	COL	0-0217767	0963	3
HEDDEN RANDALL	1LT	0-1589889	1044	2
HEDDLESTON ROY R	MAJ	0-1113737	0461	1
HEDEBECK GEORGE H	LTC	0-0140907	0856	3
HEDGCOCK CHARLES G	MAJ	0-0134894	0648	3
HEDGE ALBERT A	COL	0-0174974	0550	3
HEDGE LAFAYETTE	LTC	0-0292843	0447	2
HEDGECOCK ARCHIE W	MAJ	0-1647491	0157	1
HEDGECOCK EDWARD E	LTC	0-1062682	0163	1
HEDGECOCK JOHNIE C	CPT	N-0726681	0347	1
HEDGECOCK LAVERNE L	CW2	RW-2149467	1164	1
HEDGER HAROLD E	COL	0-0224544	1058	3
HEDGES BEN W	LTC	0-1795898	0461	1
HEDGES FRANK H	MAJ	0-1821177	0446	2
HEDGES LAWRENCE R	LTC	0-1541724	1257	1

NAME	GRADE	SVC NO	DATE RET MO YR	RET CODE
HEDGES WILLIAM R	MAJ	* 0-0981917	0263	1
HEDGLIN LESLIE H	CW2	W-2110107	0353	2
HEDGPETH LOUIS G	LTC	0-0520785	0465	1
HEDLESTON WINN D III	MAJ	0-1100586	0763	1
HEDLEY GEORGE A	MAJ	0-0370056	0654	1
HEDLEY JOSEPH J	MAJ	0-1338460	0264	1
HEDLUND CLIFFORD R	CW2	W-2153346	1263	1
HEDMAN FRITZ A	LTC	0-0921971	1066	3
HEDMAN HARRIS W	CW2	W-2148969	0456	1
HEDRICK CHARLES B	MAJ	0-4046714	0468	1
HEDRICK CHARLES T	MAJ	0-1996650	1160	1
HEDRICK CLARENCE B	1LT	0-1017915	1045	2
HEDRICK CLYDE C JR	CW2	W-2211501	1264	1
HEDRICK GEORGE E JR	LTC	0-0327051	0962	1
HEDRICK JOHN R	MAJ	0-2029136	1060	1
HEDRICK WILLIAM P	CPT	0-1173280	1151	2
HEDSTROM FREDERICK	CW3	W-2144312	0959	1
HEEGUM LYLE E	MAJ	0-1174436	1163	1
HEEGEL GORDON C	CW3	W-2144184	0559	2
HEEKE ANGUS J	LTC	0-0272242	0262	1
HEELAN ROBERT W	MAJ	0-0162618	0858	3
HEER FRIDOLIN A	CPT	0-0198617	0662	3
HEER RUTH E	1LT	N-0767097	0347	1
HEERLEIN CHARLES E	CPT	0-0163695	0557	3
HEESCH HERMAN F	COL	0-0241932	0560	3
HEESCHEN ROBERT O	COL	0-0212056	1162	3
HEFFELFINGER H B	LTC	0-0405490	0261	2
HEFFELFINGER WARREN	MAJ	0-1014294	0965	2
HEFFERNAN HENRY J	LTC	0-0288092	1166	3
HEFFERNAN WILLIAM J	LTC	0-1173991	0563	1
HEFFNER J C JR	LTC	0-1577304	0866	1
HEFFNER RICHARD W	CPT	0-2032938	1056	1
HEFFNER WILLIAM M	CPT	0-1048401	0958	1
HEFLEY GENERAL P	LTC	0-1030373	0763	1
HEFLEY JESSE L	MAJ	0-0234246	0965	3
HEFLEY RAYMOND C	LTC	0-0370161	0860	1
HEFLIN CARL W	COL	0-0125704	1052	2
HEFLIN EARL J	1LT	0-1289249	0761	2
HEFLIN FRANK D	MAJ	0-0159105	0456	3
HEFLIN HENRY D	CPT	0-2028697	1263	1
HEFT ROBERT G JR	MAJ	0-1307264	0960	1
HEG WINSLOW	CPT	0-1037045	0746	2
HEGAR JOSEPH A	COL	0-0453590	1268	1
HEGARTY JAMES I JR	MAJ	0-1923587	1163	2
HEGARTY MARY M	MAJ	N-0754098	0866	1
HEGE FELIX D	LTC	0-0450617	0557	1
HEGELMAN THEODORE N	1LT	0-0401463	1045	2
HEGEMAN RICHARD C	LTC	0-1548221	0161	1
HEGEMANN OTTO H	LTC	0-0249429	0464	3
HEGGELUND EMIL M	CW4	W-2141307	0561	1
HEGGIE WALTER B	CW4	W-2115545	0861	1
HEHULT ALBERT C	1LT	0-1557607	0246	2
HEIB HARLEY F	LTC	0-0890424	0157	1
HEID JOHN B	1LT	0-0381817	1043	2
HEIDELBERG EDWARD W	CW3	W-2149215	0265	1
HEIDELBERG F H	MAJ	0-0497814	0546	2
HEIDEMANN WILLIAM B	1LT	0-1544138	0345	2
HEIDEN FLOYD A	WO1	W-2124378	0448	1
HEIDEN HARRY H	LTC	0-0327816	0648	3
HEIDENREICH JAMES F	CW3	W-2152964	0863	1
HEIDENREICH JOHN C	LTC	0-0116245	0949	3
HEIDER JULIUS F	CW2	W-2146355	1057	1
HEIDER LEWIS G	LTC	0-0110562	0648	3
HEIDGEN MARTIN F	CPT	0-0386492	1044	2
HEIDGERD DIEDERICH	LTC	0-0333499	0668	3
HEIDINGER EDWIN J	CW3	W-2141308	1058	1
HEIDINGER WILLIAM G	MAJ	0-1299745	1055	1
HEIDMANN HERBERT A	CPT	0-1935648	0464	1
HEIDT PAUL W	COL	0-0450291	0868	1
HEIDT WOODROW W	CW2	W-2152768	0160	2
HEIDTMAN RALPH M	LTC	0-0248522	0254	1
HEIFETZ ARTHUR	LTC	0-0255475	0468	3
HEIFETZ RALPH	LTC	0-0287991	1066	3
HEIKEN BYARD J	1LT	0-1591794	0645	2
HEIKENS GLADYS R	MAJ	N-0741909	0566	3

NAME	GRADE	SVC NO	DATE RET MO YR	RET CODE
HEIKER ANTHONY E	1LT	0-2051468	0853	1
HEIKKINEN SULO H	MAJ	0-0976855	1165	1
HEIL RICHARD D	LTC	0-1312922	0867	1
HEILBRUN ROBERT M	LTC	0-0243329	0166	3
HEILIG JAMES L	MAJ	0-0226281	0864	3
HEILMAN CHARLES	LTC	0-0497438	1167	3
HEILMAN EDWIN F	LTC	0-0174706	0145	2
HEILMAN EMMA H	MAJ	N-0727525	0964	1
HEILMAN GUS M	LTC	0-1289015	0449	2
HEILMAN JAMES M	MAJ	0-0268604	1144	2
HEILMAN MARION F	1LT	N-0728261	0645	1
HEILMAN RAYMOND J	LTC	0-0138161	1051	3
HEILMANN WILLIAM A	CW3	W-2211814	1068	1
HEILPERN ALVIN	LTC	0-0283352	0559	1
HEIM LEWIS W	MAJ	0-0481114	0252	2
HEIMANN HERSCHEL G	CW3	W-2146062	0261	1
HEIMBAUGH HAYS M	LTC	0-0248723	1065	3
HEIMBROOT CARL E	COL	0-0200079	0651	3
HEIN ALVIN H	MAJ	0-2002293	0963	1
HEIN CORWIN E	LTC	0-0313499	1266	3
HEIN GORDON E	LTC	0-0401610	0345	2
HEIN MERRITT E	LTC	0-1320457	0266	1
HEINARD WHILDEN G	CPT	0-0544563	0347	2
HEINBACH CLAIR E	MAJ	0-0934205	1167	1
HEINDL LEOPOLD A	MAJ	0-1165507	0648	2
HEINE EDWIN J	CPT	0-1179438	1047	2
HEINE KARL G	COL	0-0246427	0766	3
HEINECCIUS BERYL R	1LT	N-0728726	0545	1
HEINEMAN ALBERT H	MAJ	0-2014997	0163	1
HEINEMAN PAUL F	MAJ	0-1312677	0261	1
HEINEMANN JOHN C	LTC	0-0322676	0662	2
HEINEMANN LAMBERT C	MAJ	0-1184065	0665	1
HEINEN EMIL JR	CW2	W-2214533	1267	1
HEINEN JULIUS B	MAJ	0-0316460	1047	2
HEINETZ ALBERT	CW2	W-2146849	0157	1
HEINEY JOSEPH H	CPT	0-0198062	0357	3
HEINICHEN HENRY J	LTC	0-0337124	0660	1
HEINKE MARTHA M	1LT	N-0736834	0647	1
HEINKE ROBERT W	LTC	0-1583089	0365	1
HEINLEIN LAWRENCE L	B G	0-0233033	0960	3
HEINLY DALE H	2LT	0-0453452	1143	2
HEINMILLER CARL W	MAJ	0-0381754	1046	2
HEINRICH JOSEPH E	B G	0-0255083	0465	3
HEINRICH ROBERT L	CW3	W-2136714	1265	2
HEINRICHS LOUIS M	CPT	0-0234559	0451	3
HEINS MILTON H	MAJ	0-1886245	0268	1
HEINTZ LAMBERT W	CPT	0-0420423	0246	2
HEINTZELMAN ROBERT N	CPT	0-0343670	1044	2
HEINTZLEMAN ROBERT W	LTC	0-1300032	0962	1
HEINY FREDERICK	2LT	0-2050252	0446	2
HEINZ ALBERT R	CPT	0-1102286	0845	2
HEINZ CHARLES L	MAJ	0-1551866	0764	1
HEINZ ERNEST F	CPT	0-0391135	0252	2
HEINZ RICHARD J	COL	0-0268485	0364	2
HEINZE BERNARD T	LTC	0-0162581	0961	3
HEINZE MARION O	MAJ	0-2035582	0760	2
HEINZMANN FRANK M	MAJ	0-0245758	0957	3
HEIR JOHN H	LTC	0-1333336	1067	1
HEISE JOHN O	LTC	0-0209633	1160	3
HEISER ANN	MAJ	N-0772903	0760	2
HEISEY ELVIN N	LTC	0-1592269	1061	1
HEISEY JOHN W	CW2	W-3100528	0967	2
HEISHMAN CLAUDE R	MAJ	0-1012448	0355	1
HEISHMAN ROBERT L	1LT	0-2053975	0645	2
HEISIG GILBERT W JR	1LT	0-0552629	0946	2
HEISKELL EDWARD V	COL	0-0112714	0952	3
HEISLER JOSEPH C	CW3	W-2150711	0364	1
HEISLER KERMIT J	CW2	W-2143242	0756	1
HEISS EARL H	LTC	0-1321407	0967	1
HEISS SIMON W	LTC	0-0196005	0648	3
HEISS WILLIAM H	CPT	0-0131593	1049	3
HEITT GEORGE C	CPT	0-0146635	0751	3
HEIT PHILIP	CPT	0-0473104	1044	2
HEITHAUS JOHN	MAJ	0-2055214	1055	1
HEITMAN WALLACE H	MAJ	0-1171585	1165	1

NAME	GRADE	SVC NO	DATE RET MO YR	RET CODE
HEITMUELLER RUDOLF	MAJ	O-0450887	0958	1
HEITZ JOSEPH C	CW2	W-2106748	1047	1
HEITZMAN HARRY M	1LT	O-1285239	0545	2
HEIZER EMORY W	LTC	O-0272430	0968	3
HEIZER JAMES H	LTC	O-0324153	1048	2
HELBERG WALFRED J	MAJ	O-0965176	0966	1
HELBERT VICTOR C	CW3	W-2141309	0758	1
HELD ALBERT E	LTC	O-0459719	0646	2
HELD FREDERICK	MAJ	O-1558361	1062	1
HELD GEORGE F JR	CPT	O-1170411	0747	2
HELD ISIDORE	1LT	O-1304212	0140	2
HELD LEONARD J	1LT	O-1315164	1045	2
HELD SHELDON G	CW3	RW-2209545	0667	1
HELDE ERLING A	MAJ	O-0472863	1057	1
HELDENFELS GROVER C	COL	O-0268253	0756	3
HELDFOND ALFRED J	CPT	O-0486870	1045	2
HELDT WALTER H	MAJ	O-0269051	0566	3
HELES PATRICK F	MAJ	O-1319347	0357	1
HELFERD LYNN W	LTC	O-1341783	0168	1
HELFERTY JOHN K	LTC	O-0321065	0966	3
HELFF NORMAN E	1LT	O-0509341	0244	2
HELFRICK MURRAY D	LTC	O-0231339	0248	2
HELGREN DONALD H	CPT	O-0490357	0946	2
HELGREN ELVIRA H	LTC	N-0700099	0346	1
HELINA ANNE M	MAJ	N-0736865	0567	3
HELINSKI JOSEPH A	MAJ	O-1058833	1262	1
HELLAND ARNE A	CPT	O-1288380	0660	1
HELLAND CLARENCE W	LTC	O-1633956	1060	1
HELLAND ELMER D	MAJ	O-0494328	0547	1
HELLE ROBERT L	CW3	W-2145223	1157	1
HELLEBRANDT EDWIN T	LTC	O-0230303	0764	3
HELLEN JOHN H	MAJ	O-1922597	0663	2
HELLENTHAL GEORGE M	CW2	W-2211921	1066	1
HELLER ARNOLD G	CPT	O-1310713	0246	2
HELLER BERNARD R	CPT	O-1284329	0145	2
HELLER EMIL E	LTC	O-1102761	0764	1
HELLER FRED E	CPT	O-0404353	0645	2
HELLER HARRY D	CW3	W-2129195	1065	3
HELLER HOMER K	COL	O-0222207	0864	3
HELLER JOHN S	1LT	O-1324539	0545	2
HELLER JOSEPH	CPT	O-0500412	0843	2
HELLER LAWRENCE R	CPT	O-1552699	1154	2
HELLER LOREN J	LTC	O-0318429	0265	1
HELLER NATHAN	LTC	O-1341097	0768	1
HELLER RAYMOND G	LTC	O-1285753	0960	1
HELLER ROBERT C	CPT	O-0356962	0545	2
HELLER THEODORE M	CPT	O-0526181	0446	2
HELLIESEN HOWARD E	COL	O-0312905	0261	1
HELLINGER KENNETH F	LTC	O-0541090	0464	1
HELLMAN JOHN P	MAJ	O-0467505	0847	1
HELLMAN NATHANIEL	CPT	O-0554103	1046	2
HELLMAN OSCAR W	MAJ	O-0284658	1167	3
HELLMAN ROBERT S	MAJ	O-0523766	0768	3
HELLMAN ROGERS H	MAJ	O-2288096	0567	1
HELLMANN JACOB G	LTC	O-1038179	0263	1
HELLWEGE JOHN K	LTC	O-1108011	1162	1
HELM DONALD L	2LT	O-1999887	0945	2
HELM HERBERT J	MAJ	O-1100588	1060	1
HELM JOHN P	CPT	O-5201545	0566	2
HELM LEONARD S	LTC	O-0324891	0265	3
HELM PRUETT B	CW2	W-3152839	0867	2
HELM THOMAS P	CW2	W-2146172	1160	1
HELM WILLIAM F	WO1	W-2116208	1044	2
HELMAN NATHANIEL	CPT	O-1321512	0146	2
HELMBOLDT HENRY F	COL	O-0310312	0961	1
HELMERS HANS T	1LT	O-1003404	1058	1
HELMERS RAYMOND A	1LT	O-1285240	1044	2
HELMICK CHARLES R	LTC	O-0461785	1165	3
HELMICK FLOYD F	LTC	O-0180534	1056	3
HELMICK ROBERT W	MAJ	O-1586654	1165	1
HELMICK RUDOLPH W	1LT	O-1176664	0246	2
HELMICKI EDWARD F	MAJ	O-1798790	1263	1
HELMKEN GILBERT M	CPT	O-0441401	0446	2
HELMLING RALPH W	CW3	W-2153226	1264	1
HELMOLD NORMAN C	MAJ	O-2014000	0562	1
HELMS AARON J	MAJ	O-2010799	1063	1
HELMS AUGUSTINE	LTC	O-1546481	0562	1
HELMS CHARLES L	LTC	O-0370308	0563	1
HELMS DONALD R	MAJ	O-2028698	0167	1
HELMS GEORGE W	WO1	W-2149216	1061	2
HELMS HAROLD H	CPT	O-0140279	0854	3
HELMS HUBERT D	LTC	O-0455788	0757	1
HELMS JACOB	LTC	O-0232642	0258	3
HELMS JAMES R	LTC	O-0204370	0658	3
HELMS LLOYD C	LTC	O-1063104	0267	1
HELMS MERCER D	MAJ	O-0258578	1043	2
HELMS RAYMOND W	CW2	W-2143517	0157	1
HELMS ROSCOE R	MAJ	O-2012189	1158	1
HELMS WALTER A	CW3	W-2152997	0264	1
HELMS WARREN E	CW3	W-2150908	1065	1
HELPBRINGER RALPH S	1LT	O-1581173	0644	2
HELPHINSTINE CARL B	COL	O-0327162	0758	3
HELPHREY LOUIS H	MAJ	O-0444082	0144	2
HELQUIST GEORGE B	LTC	O-0464855	0365	3
HELRING WILLIAM J	MAJ	O-1295876	0961	1
HELSEL CLAUDE O	LTC	O-2048011	0962	1
HELSEL DONALD B	MAJ	O-0982296	1066	1
HELSEL FRANK H	1LT	O-0452617	0444	2
HELSEL MARIAN E	MAJ	N-0760762	0665	1
HELSER JOHN H	MAJ	O-0221729	0263	3
HELSING RALPH W	LTC	O-0341561	0968	3
HELSLEY GORDON F	LTC	O-0244320	0850	3
HELSLEY OSCAR S	CPT	O-1846296	0262	2
HELTERBRAN ROBERT E	CW3	W-2145806	0361	1
HELTON HERMAN	CW3	W-2149701	1262	1
HELTON JAMES B JR	1LT	O-0439505	0845	2
HELTON PELHAM G	LTC	O-0948733	0868	1
HELTON ROY M	1LT	O-0865249	0263	2
HELTON WILLIAM P	1LT	O-2011507	0747	2
HELWIG CARL	MAJ	O-1172489	0156	1
HELWIG CARL M	LTC	O-0213373	1161	3
HELWIG EDWARD W	LTC	O-1102287	0462	1
HELWIG FERDINAND	LTC	O-0204730	1058	3
HELWIG WALTER A	CPT	O-1037529	0361	1
HELY JOSEPH W	LTC	O-1329944	1264	1
HELZERMAN RALPH F	CPT	O-1687156	0146	2
HEMANN JAMES E	MAJ	O-0523776	0763	1
HEMBREE HUGH R	MAJ	O-0366162	0647	2
HEMBY NORMAN N	CW4	W-2121281	1057	1
HEMENWAY PAUL E	LTC	O-1994777	0862	1
HEMEYER KARL P M	LTC	O-0328120	0365	1
HEMINGER HAROLD R	MAJ	O-0160225	0457	3
HEMINGTON RALPH W	CPT	O-0313334	0246	2
HEMINGWAY WILLIAM W	CPT	O-1295877	0447	2
HEMKER JOSEPH F	COL	O-1000579	0867	1
HEMMER ANDREW P	CPT	O-0920085	1046	2
HEMMINGS ESTHER H	MAJ	N-0721196	0464	2
HEMMRICH FRED W	LTC	O-0453928	0358	1
HEMOVICH MICHAEL A	LTC	O-0388262	0567	1
HEMPERLY ROBERT W	MAJ	O-5210340	1061	2
HEMPHILL EDWARD S	COL	O-0116274	0852	3
HEMPHILL JAMES E	CW2	W-2214414	0568	1
HEMPHILL WILLIAM H	MAJ	O-2024172	0561	1
HEMPHILL WILLIAM T	MAJ	O-0405504	0349	1
HEMPLEY OSCAR L B	LTC	O-0301458	0555	1
HEMPSTEAD COURTNEY W	LTC	O-0335539	1061	3
HEMRY CHARLES S	COL	O-0226355	0565	3
HENAGAN JOHN C	M G	O-0163943	0157	3
HENAGE CADDIE L	MAJ	O-1306718	0561	1
HENAHAN JOHN P	LTC	O-0256884	1267	3
HENBY ELIJAH B	LTC	O-0326375	0546	2
HENCHEY WILLIAM J JR	1LT	O-1017760	0746	2
HENDEE DONN C	CPT	O-1334572	1263	1
HENDEE PAUL C	LTC	O-1895538	0361	1
HENDERSHOT EDGAR A	COL	O-0264329	0267	3
HENDERSHOT JOHN B	MAJ	O-1282334	0361	1
HENDERSHOT STERLING	CW2	W-2109886	0362	3
HENDERSHOTT H B	1LT	O-1043362	1045	2
HENDERSHOTT JACOB E	LTC	O-0376965	0756	1
HENDERSHOTT WALTER E	1LT	O-1165874	1146	2
HENDERSON ALBERT E	M G	O-0264146	0455	3
HENDERSON ALPHEUS L	COL	O-0212286	1156	3
HENDERSON ARLIE O	MAJ	O-0484511	0847	1
HENDERSON ARTHUR A	CW3	W-2005577	0966	1
HENDERSON ARTHUR F	MAJ	O-1553098	0157	1
HENDERSON ARTHUR H	COL	O-0191695	0962	3
HENDERSON AUSTIN M	LTC	O-0288050	0868	3
HENDERSON CARL E	CW3	W-2152386	1264	1
HENDERSON CHARLES D	COL	O-0328148	1060	3
HENDERSON CHARLES R	CW2	W-3150661	0965	1
HENDERSON CHARLES W	LTC	O-0706174	0563	1
HENDERSON CHARLES W	MAJ	O-1299235	0462	1
HENDERSON CLAIR B	MAJ	O-1595552	0462	1
HENDERSON CLARENCE P	LTC	O-1844829	0762	1
HENDERSON CLYDE F	LTC	O-0307831	0265	3
HENDERSON CYRIL O	LTC	O-0507177	0864	3
HENDERSON DALE E	LTC	O-1013232	0463	1
HENDERSON DAVID L	2LT	O-1052811	0345	2
HENDERSON DICK K	MAJ	O-1825750	0360	2
HENDERSON DONALD L	CW2	W-2214973	0968	1
HENDERSON DONALD R	LTC	O-2000844	1264	1
HENDERSON EDDIE C	CW4	W-2141310	0765	1
HENDERSON EDDYTH H	1LT	O-1104203	0745	2
HENDERSON EDGAR G	MAJ	O-0354798	0245	2
HENDERSON EDGAR L	LTC	O-0236319	0166	3
HENDERSON ELIZABETH	CPT	N-0720595	1150	2
HENDERSON ERNEST W	MAJ	O-0354903	1146	2
HENDERSON FLOYD W	CW2	W-3200702	0768	1
HENDERSON GENEVA E	MAJ	N-0727567	0863	3
HENDERSON GEORGE	COL	O-0125665	0648	3
HENDERSON GEORGE G	MAJ	O-1649484	0864	1
HENDERSON GEORGE H	LTC	O-0495430	1064	3
HENDERSON GEORGE H	CW4	W-2106046	0456	1
HENDERSON GEORGE M	LTC	O-2012707	0367	3
HENDERSON GEORGE R	MAJ	O-0310905	0344	2
HENDERSON GEORGE R	MAJ	O-0976135	0565	1
HENDERSON HAROLD	MAJ	O-0372986	0145	2
HENDERSON HUBERT C	CW2	W-2141176	1154	1
HENDERSON IRENE	MAJ	N-0736847	1264	1
HENDERSON J P	MAJ	O-2018882	0164	1
HENDERSON JACK	1LT	O-0499456	0847	1
HENDERSON JACKSON G	LTC	O-0239298	0266	3
HENDERSON JAMES E	LTC	O-1313241	0367	1
HENDERSON JAMES H	1LT	O-0945884	0853	2
HENDERSON JESSIE T	1LT	N-0744263	0346	1
HENDERSON JOE R	MAJ	O-0336661	0261	3
HENDERSON JOHN D	LTC	O-2208633	0268	1
HENDERSON JOHNNIE C	1LT	O-1288741	0945	2
HENDERSON JOSEPH J	LTC	O-1302816	0761	1
HENDERSON LESTER J	LTC	O-1113248	1262	1
HENDERSON LINDSEY P	LTC	O-0963477	0168	1
HENDERSON LLOYD A	2LT	O-1297366	1043	2
HENDERSON LYLE H	MAJ	O-0248936	0763	3
HENDERSON MARVIN J	CW3	W-2114280	1154	1
HENDERSON MATTHEW G	LTC	O-0263853	0159	3
HENDERSON MAURICE E	COL	O-0242833	1154	3
HENDERSON MAXWELL	2LT	O-2323933	0648	3
HENDERSON OTIS W	LTC	O-1104836	0763	1
HENDERSON RALPH O	MAJ	O-0123080	0352	3
HENDERSON RALPH L	CPT	O-1168284	0454	1
HENDERSON RALPH W	MAJ	O-1639161	0765	3
HENDERSON RALPH W	CW2	W-2109328	1148	1
HENDERSON RAYMOND D	COL	O-0335228	0151	3
HENDERSON ROBERT G	MAJ	O-0450889	0459	1
HENDERSON ROBERT L	MAJ	O-1584346	1263	1
HENDERSON ROBERT M	CPT	O-0396589	0845	2
HENDERSON ROBERT P	CW3	W-2207476	0567	1
HENDERSON ROBERT W	LTC	O-0186543	0748	3
HENDERSON RUPERT C	LTC	O-0489727	0954	1
HENDERSON SIDNEY A	MAJ	O-1101864	0561	1
HENDERSON SIDNEY L	MAJ	O-0262709	0861	3
HENDERSON THOMAS E	CW3	W-2207444	0566	1
HENDERSON THOMAS J	MAJ	O-1294306	1147	2
HENDERSON THOMAS W	1LT	O-0506186	0844	2
HENDERSON VIRGIL L	LTC	O-0299365	0954	1
HENDERSON WALTER H	COL	O-0399792	0767	1
HENDERSON WILLIAM A	LTC	O-1103207	1066	1
HENDERSON WILLIAM B	LTC	O-0415969	0663	3
HENDERSON WILLIAM F	MAJ	O-1288050	0353	2
HENDERSON WILLIAM H	CW3	W-2152965	0965	1
HENDERSON WILLIAM R	MAJ	O-0354670	0246	2
HENDERSON WILLIAM R	CPT	O-1913727	0744	1
HENDLER FREDERIC E	COL	O-0494895	0458	2
HENDLEY ARCHIBALD	MAJ	O-1693114	1160	1
HENDON ROBERT R	COL	O-0199678	0354	3
HENDREN IRVIN K	COL	O-0279730	0966	3
HENDREN KENNETH H	MAJ	O-1794942	0760	1
HENDRESCHKE ROBERT H	CW3	W-3430004	0667	1
HENDRICK PAUL H	MAJ	O-1287350	0961	1
HENDRICK ROBERT E	MAJ	O-0280303	0567	3
HENDRICK ROBERT M JR	LTC	O-1579774	0463	1
HENDRICKS AZRO S	LTC	O-0247923	1266	3
HENDRICKS BILLY	MAJ	O-1338820	0363	1
HENDRICKS CHARLES S	COL	O-0176710	1150	3
HENDRICKS CHARLES Y	CPT	O-0402244	0445	2
HENDRICKS CLEO J	MAJ	O-0972519	0363	1
HENDRICKS EARL F	CPT	O-0286901	0245	2
HENDRICKS EDWARD	CPT	O-1306587	1052	2
HENDRICKS FRANK J	CW2	W-2142236	0160	1
HENDRICKS GEORGE H	MAJ	O-0291911	0760	2
HENDRICKS GLENN W	MAJ	O-0395978	0863	1
HENDRICKS HAROLD L	CW3	W-2101825	0761	1
HENDRICKS HARRY H	COL	O-0203293	0557	3
HENDRICKS JAMES H	MAJ	O-1301484	0757	1
HENDRICKS JENNIE K	MAJ	N-0757951	0265	3
HENDRICKS JOSEPH	MAJ	O-0483111	1053	1
HENDRICKS LAMBERT M	COL	O-0132219	0352	3
HENDRICKS LAURETTA L	MAJ	N-0737757	0468	1
HENDRICKS PORTER	MAJ	O-0312987	1045	2
HENDRICKS RAPHAEL R	1LT	O-1012463	0445	2
HENDRICKS SHELBOUR	1LT	O-1293771	0245	2
HENDRICKS SIMON S	CPT	O-0246905	0855	3
HENDRICKS THOMAS A	LTC	O-0503203	1057	1
HENDRICKSON AGNES G	2LT	N-0784884	0345	1
HENDRICKSON ARTHUR	CPT	O-1319740	104N	2
HENDRICKSON BURTON L	LTC	O-1333972	0866	1
HENDRICKSON CHARLES	CW3	W-2206109	1066	1
HENDRICKSON DEAN M	MAJ	O-0392078	1146	2
HENDRICKSON F R	CPT	O-1010046	1147	2
HENDRICKSON FREDOLPH	MAJ	O-0463993	0546	2
HENDRICKSON GEORGE C	COL	O-0311127	0767	3
HENDRICKSON GEORGE G	MAJ	O-2007311	0164	1
HENDRICKSON GEORGE W	LTC	O-0917197	1264	3
HENDRICKSON HARLAN R	CW4	W-2102998	0659	1
HENDRICKSON HARRY R	CPT	O-1013560	0546	2
HENDRICKSON HUGH J	MAJ	O-1283771	0157	1
HENDRICKSON HUGO R	MAJ	O-1555059	0863	1
HENDRICKSON JACK M	CW3	W-2147550	1264	1
HENDRICKSON JAMES C	MAJ	O-0970124	0864	1
HENDRICKSON JOHN L	CPT	O-2035323	0348	2
HENDRICKSON L R	CPT	O-0488161	1155	1
HENDRICKSON LYDON E	WO1	W-2102999	0943	2
HENDRICKSON OLE Q	LTC	O-0379820	0767	3
HENDRICKSON RALPH G	MAJ	O-0318224	0160	1
HENDRICKSON ROY G	MAJ	O-0024093	0157	1
HENDRICKSON W E	MAJ	O-1289423	0257	1
HENDRIE JONATHAN A	LTC	O-0502865	1266	3
HENDRIKS JOHN	MAJ	O-1874276	0566	1
HENDRIKSMA ELLERT	1LT	O-1317011	0646	2
HENDRIX CHARLES H	LTC	O-1924656	0968	1
HENDRIX DUPREE	CW3	W-2005006	0468	3
HENDRIX ERNEST V	MAJ	O-0197138	0360	3
HENDRIX HAROLD B	LTC	O-0281639	0468	3
HENDRIX JACK S	CW2	W-2149295	0861	1
HENDRIX JAMES S	WO1	W-2107771	0646	2
HENDRIX MIKE Y	COL	O-0417829	1167	1
HENDRIX PHILIP C	LTC	O-1824313	0862	1
HENDRIX RALPH L	MAJ	O-1533086	1148	2
HENDRIX RALPH W	CPT	O-1103208	1047	2
HENDRIX REYNARD E	LTC	O-0283956	0868	3

NAME	GRADE	SVC NO	DATE RET MO YR	RET CODE
HENDRIX SAMUEL B JR	LTC	0-1168285	0462	1
HENDRIX TRACY M	MAJ	0-0190845	0453	3
HENDRIX WILLIAM H	MAJ	0-0998502	0764	1
HENDRIXSON LOGAN B	MAJ	0-0279339	0547	1
HENDRY CHARLES	LTC	0-1796791	0864	1
HENDRY DONALD C	CW3	W-2205716	1165	1
HENDRY FRANK	LTC	0-1315932	0562	1
HENDRY GERALDINE	2LT	N-0773108	0345	1
HENDRY HENRY A	COL	0-0298626	0966	3
HENDRY JOHN E JR	LTC	0-0267511	0657	1
HENDRYX ANDREW B	1LT	0-0482403	1145	2
HENEBERY JOHN J JR	LTC	0-1054620	0866	1
HENEGAR ELMER	MAJ	0-1301640	0358	1
HENEGAR HELEN E	1LT	N-0732156	0846	2
HENEGAR WILLIAM H	MAJ	0-4063713	0868	1
HENEY EDWARD J	LTC	0-0346409	0861	3
HENFLING GEORGE W	MAJ	0-0385001	1047	2
HENGTGEN ARNOLD W	MAJ	0-1043104	1059	1
HENIKA ROBERT G	CPT	0-0317949	0545	2
HENIN ROBERT	CPT	0-1294838	0946	2
HENISE CHARLES E	LTC	0-0334222	0861	1
HENIUS HAROLD H H	COL	0-0359863	0864	3
HENKE KENNETH E	MAJ	0-1314141	0461	1
HENKE ROBERT C	LTC	0-2263741	0868	1
HENKEL BLAINE M	2LT	0-1314477	0144	2
HENKEL ROBERT S	1LT	0-0416482	0743	2
HENKLE CLAIRE V	LTC	0-0229299	0463	3
HENLE ELMO A	CW2	W-2144016	1060	2
HENLEY DELLIS L	CW3	RW-2144949	0761	1
HENLEY ESCOE H	CW3	W-2205136	0463	1
HENLEY GLADYS I	MAJ	N-0783452	0466	3
HENLEY JESS W	LTC	0-0452636	0859	1
HENLEY LOWELL D	LTC	0-0336721	0563	3
HENLEY MANFORD G	COL	0-0119204	0648	3
HENLEY MICHAEL F	WO1	W-3151258	0964	2
HENLEY ROBERT H	1LT	0-1298395	0945	2
HENLINE WENDELL 7	MAJ	0-0522533	0446	2
HENN EMMA C	1LT	N-0724084	1046	1
HENN ROBERT H	1LT	0-1039386	0745	2
HENNE CARL	LTC	0-0288687	0753	3
HENNEBERG ROBERT E	CW3	W-2144023	0258	1
HENNELL KENNITH I	MAJ	0-2046699	1161	1
HENNEMAN FREDERICK	COL	0-0273933	0746	2
HENNEMUTH JOHN R	CPT	0-1102763	0646	2
HENNESEY WILLIAM A	CPT	0-0905711	0946	2
HENNESSEE PATRICK H	WO1	W-2105690	0551	1
HENNESSEY DON P	WO1	W-2121051	0844	2
HENNESSEY EDWARD M	COL	0-0269097	0168	3
HENNESSEY JOSEPH J	CW2	W-2145447	0856	1
HENNESSEY JOSEPH M	CPT	0-0491281	0347	2
HENNESSEY THOMAS P	LTC	0-0530788	0167	1
HENNESSEY WILLIAM J	MAJ	0-2001092	0163	1
HENNESSEY WILLIAM L	1LT	0-0393234	0145	2
HENNESSY CARL D	MAJ	0-0311837	0460	1
HENNESSY CHARLES F	LTC	0-1293049	0663	1
HENNESSY EDWARD J	LTC	0-1295210	0461	1
HENNESSY FRANCIS W	CW2	W-2151616	0160	1
HENNESSY HAROLD R	COL	0-0275788	0963	3
HENNESSY HERBERT J	MAJ	0-0163301	0453	3
HENNESSY JOHN R	LTC	0-0278153	0868	3
HENNESSY JOSEPH J	MAJ	0-0980981	0964	1
HENNESSY LEON G	MAJ	0-1650903	1065	1
HENNEY RICHARD B	CPT	0-1030674	0147	2
HENNICKE CAROLINE D	1LT	L-0900045	0645	2
HENNICKE RAYMOND O	LTC	0-1180535	0859	1
HENNIE OLIVER J	LTC	0-1552496	0367	1
HENNIGAN FRANCIS A	MAJ	0-0220898	0764	3
HENNIGAN PATRICK C	LTC	0-1295478	0863	2
HENNIGAR WILLIAM C	CPT	0-0302615	0246	2
HENNING BERNARD A	CW2	W-2151389	1061	1
HENNING DORA M	LTC	N-0741655	0562	1
HENNING ERWIN R	LTC	0-1182597	0367	3
HENNING GEORGE E	LTC	0-1313607	1165	1
HENNING HARVEY R	2LT	0-1913724	1040	1
HENNING JOHN	1LT	0-1101865	0245	2
HENNING LUTHER T	CPT	0-1292881	0847	2
HENNING MARION M	2LT	N-0795719	0147	1
HENNING ROBERT W	CW2	W-2214823	0868	1
HENNINGER HALLIE B	MAJ	0-0503937	1054	1
HENNINGS ARNIT F	MAJ	0-0274445	0854	2
HENNINGS FRED W	LTC	0-0365461	0568	3
HENNINGS LAWRENCE R	COL	0-0299985	0160	3
HENNINGS WALTER O	COL	0-0278751	1160	3
HENNINGSEN MELVIN G	CPT	0-0535564	0346	2
HENNINGSGAARD B J	CPT	0-0515563	0846	2
HENNINGTON HAROLD M	MAJ	0-0750389	1060	2
HENNIS HARRY W	LTC	0-0179774	1053	3
HENNRIKUS ARTHUR W	1LT	0-1170004	1144	2
HENNRIKUS GEORGE F	LTC	0-0464194	0755	3
HENRECHON JOSEPH L	CPT	0-0275658	0951	3
HENRI ARTHUR V	LTC	0-2046337	0762	1
HENRI AXEL W	COL	0-1549733	1068	1
HENRICH CARL A	MAJ	0-0396942	0561	1
HENRICHSEN ARTHUR L	CPT	0-0349338	1043	2
HENRICKS ALBERT M	LTC	0-1636029	0263	1
HENRICKSON JACOB	CPT	0-0128227	0648	3
HENRIETTA JOHN P SR	MAJ	0-1639164	0462	1
HENRIKSEN FRANCIS R	CPT	0-0321733	1048	1
HENRIKSEN VENITA B	2LT	N-0726925	0945	1
HENRY ANDREW J	CPT	0-4010845	1266	1
HENRY CHARLES E	COL	0-0353730	0557	1
HENRY CHARLES H	MAJ	0-0510889	0757	1
HENRY CHRISTOPHE	2LT	0-1994928	0644	2
HENRY CLARENCE R	CPT	0-0269516	1266	3
HENRY DALE E	MAJ	0-1536181	0765	1
HENRY DALE F	LTC	0-1544984	0962	1
HENRY DEAN T	MAJ	0-0400744	1145	2
HENRY DEWITT C JR	MAJ	0-1175460	0762	2
HENRY EDWARD F	COL	0-0301584	0265	3
HENRY EDWARD R	MAJ	0-1685006	1264	1
HENRY ELLSWORTH	MAJ	0-0967033	1262	1
HENRY ELMER T	COL	0-0271679	0656	1
HENRY ERDEAN L	COL	0-0402798	1164	1
HENRY EUGENE O	MAJ	0-0302890	0245	2
HENRY EVART R	1LT	0-2023735	0847	2
HENRY FRANCIS J	LTC	0-1646142	0263	1
HENRY FRANK D	CPT	0-1885938	0365	1
HENRY FREDERICK	LTC	0-0515166	1065	3
HENRY G B	MAJ	0-1108733	0157	1
HENRY GEORGE	LTC	0-1040938	0363	1
HENRY GEORGE W	WO1	W-2150090	0556	1
HENRY HERBERT H	CW2	W-2105284	0449	1
HENRY HERMAN K	LTC	0-0216776	0263	3
HENRY JAMES A	CW3	W-2116055	0457	1
HENRY JAMES E	1LT	0-1112760	1044	2
HENRY JAY E	LTC	0-0331462	0568	3
HENRY JOHN	MAJ	0-0492424	0456	1
HENRY JOHN D	1LT	0-1289250	0744	2
HENRY JOHN W	CW3	W-2142237	0955	1
HENRY JOSEPH M SR	LTC	0-0183740	0862	3
HENRY JOSEPH P JR	LTC	0-1315063	1162	1
HENRY JUSTUS R JR	2LT	0-1303886	1044	2
HENRY LELAND D	CW3	W-2144878	0862	1
HENRY LOWELL G	LTC	0-0402453	0361	1
HENRY MARY B	MAJ	N-0726747	0356	2
HENRY MERRITT H	COL	0-0186401	0949	3
HENRY MERTON F	2LT	0-1576111	0245	2
HENRY MORDICA M	1LT	0-0274822	0756	3
HENRY NORMAN E	CPT	0-1104840	0962	3
HENRY PATRICK J	CW2	W-3430368	0866	1
HENRY PAUL D	CW2	W-2152387	0361	1
HENRY RALPH J	MAJ	0-0358757	0647	2
HENRY REX T	LTC	0-2042869	0463	1
HENRY ROBERT G	LTC	0-1686701	0868	1
HENRY ROBERT L	CW2	W-3430203	1166	1
HENRY ROBERT M	LTC	0-0399030	0757	2
HENRY RUSK G	LTC	0-2204074	0967	1
HENRY RUSSELL B	WO1	W-2111351	1053	1
HENRY SAMUEL C	LTC	0-1574822	0966	1
HENRY THOMAS L	CPT	0-0450890	0853	2
HENRY TRUMAN K	CPT	0-1823871	0761	1
HENRY WALTER L	1LT	0-1288549	1045	2
HENRY WILLIAM B	MAJ	0-1588633	0355	1
HENRY WILLIAM G	MAJ	0-0721074	1060	2
HENRY WILLIAM J	MAJ	0-0181048	0946	2
HENRY WILLIAM J	1LT	0-0461526	1045	2
HENRY WILLIAM J	CW4	W-2119838	0157	1
HENRY WILLIAM R	MAJ	0-0291809	0467	3
HENRY WILLIAM R	1LT	0-2043035	0246	2
HENSARLING THERON A	MAJ	0-0169188	0360	3
HENSCHEL DENSMORE F	LTC	0-2263258	1068	1
HENSCHEN HAROLD G	CW3	W-2145776	1262	1
HENSEL JOSEPH W	COL	0-0266185	0160	2
HENSEL WILLIAM A	CW3	W-2150914	0863	1
HENSEL WILLIAM B	CPT	0-1309182	0664	1
HENSEN ROBERT A	2LT	0-0968436	0151	2
HENSHAW FRED M	COL	0-0255509	0755	3
HENSHAW WILLIAM R	MAJ	0-1641384	0361	1
HENSKE WILLIAM C	LTC	0-0218686	0756	3
HENSLER DOROTHA E	1LT	N-0726910	0146	1
HENSLER HAROLD A	COL	0-0301076	0663	3
HENSLEY ARTHUR D	CW4	W-2108025	0660	1
HENSLEY BILLY G	MAJ	0-1879043	1264	1
HENSLEY CHARLES E	CW3	W-2210157	0868	1
HENSLEY HENRY	1LT	0-0496804	0846	1
HENSLEY JAMES E	CW2	W-2144682	0461	1
HENSLEY JOHN M	MAJ	0-1299746	0557	1
HENSLEY KENNETH R	LTC	0-0291335	0868	3
HENSLEY LESTER J	COL	0-0174226	0162	3
HENSLEY ROBERT B	COL	0-0303867	0560	1
HENSLEY ROBERT J JR	CPT	0-1642178	0155	1
HENSLEY ROBERT W	CPT	0-1685259	0846	2
HENSON BERNIE C	MAJ	0-2055957	0557	1
HENSON EDGAR L	CPT	0-0210717	0446	2
HENSON HAROLD E	LTC	0-0190960	1055	3
HENSON HOWARD W	LTC	0-0337911	0358	1
HENSON JAMES A	2LT	0-1298537	0945	2
HENSON JAMES T SR	CW2	W-2121063	0955	1
HENSON JOHN W L	WO1	W-2143767	0152	2
HENSON NAPOLEON B	MAJ	0-0125664	0453	3
HENSON OLEN D	LTC	0-0707691	0463	1
HENSON ROBERT G	WO1	W-2107217	0953	1
HENSON ROBERT J	MAJ	0-1919133	0964	1
HENSON ROBERT R	MAJ	0-0815698	0663	1
HENSON WALTER A	CPT	0-1171186	0346	2
HENSTELL HENRY H	CPT	0-0360869	1044	2
HENTERLY JAMES K	2LT	0-1325702	0245	2
HENTGES KENNETH B	CW4	W-2142406	0464	1
HENTGES LESTER J	MAJ	0-2262643	1164	1
HENTGES ROBERT E	CW3	W-2144967	0862	1
HENTIG ROBERT G	CW3	W-2210735	0368	1
HENTON RUFUS JR	CW3	W-2146019	0964	1
HENTSCHEL GEORGE W	CW2	W-2151669	0560	1
HEPBURN EARLE	COL	0-0164564	0652	3
HEPBURN JAMES W	LTC	0-1035012	0556	1
HEPBURN JOHN W	LTC	0-0973231	1067	1
HEPNER GEORGE A	LTC	0-0924625	0468	3
HEPNER SERENE J	CW3	W-2152846	0562	1
HEPP DANIEL H	CPT	0-1030578	1046	2
HEPP WILLIAM	CPT	0-1693450	1145	2
HEPPARD GLENN R	2LT	0-0385297	0843	2
HEPPARD JOHN K	MAJ	0-1178502	1062	1
HEPPERLEN THOMAS A	CPT	0-0195700	0349	3
HEPPTING CHARLES E	CPT	0-0471514	0745	2
HERALD BANKS E	CW2	W-2107966	0753	1
HERALD FRANK B	LTC	0-0292842	1068	3
HERALD VIRGIL H	LTC	0-0234251	0557	1
HERB CHARLES F	MAJ	0-1165876	0261	1
HERB FRANK H	LTC	0-0266622	1065	1
HERB ROBERT E	MAJ	0-0415418	1047	2
HERBERT CHARLES E JR	CPT	0-2262183	1060	1
HERBERT CHARLES T	MAJ	0-0319406	1045	2
HERBERT DONALD L	LTC	0-0286253	0368	3
HERBERT EDWIN C	2LT	0-1183536	0645	2
HERBERT FRANK L JR	CW2	W-2116287	1053	2
HERBERT GERARD W	MAJ	0-1181630	0859	1
HERBERT GILBERT T	CPT	0-1284139	0758	1
HERBERT MARDEN A	MAJ	0-0220298	1162	3
HERBERT PHILIP S	LTC	0-0102123	0655	3
HERBERT ROBERT L	LTC	0-1686665	0767	2
HERBERT WILLIAM S	CPT	0-0419244	1045	2
HERBERTS HERBERT L	COL	0-0142018	1155	3
HERBIN JOHN L	MAJ	0-1686709	0268	1
HERBORN KENNETH D	MAJ	0-1015271	0261	1
HERBSLEB CARL F	LTC	0-0142026	0356	3
HERBST CARL S	COL	0-0216887	0463	3
HERBST EDWARD JR	LTC	0-1108013	0760	1
HERBST KENNETH J	LTC	0-1004781	0363	1
HERBST PAUL W	LTC	0-0502764	0357	1
HERBST WALTER R	CPT	0-0513978	0148	2
HERBSTER ALBERT H	CW4	W-2005717	0868	3
HERBUY DAN	MAJ	0-2007203	0157	1
HERD FRANK E	CPT	0-1308818	0546	2
HERD WILFRED R	LTC	0-0245434	0565	3
HERDENER WILLIAM R	COL	0-0330688	1061	1
HERDMAN HAROLD	CPT	0-0483469	0747	1
HERDMAN ROBERT F	COL	0-0132640	0954	3
HEREDIA MANUEL JR	MAJ	0-2265135	0868	1
HEREDIA TRINIDAD M	MAJ	0-1281463	0757	1
HEREFORD LESLIE R JR	1LT	0-0519386	0346	2
HERES SERAFIN D	1LT	0-1896621	1049	1
HERETH RAYMOND J	MAJ	0-1052387	0261	1
HERGENRATHER CHARL	1LT	0-1171187	0246	2
HERGENROEDER CHARL	2LT	0-0521211	0246	2
HERGERT FRED N	1LT	0-0491029	0258	1
HERGET GEORGE H	LTC	0-1642964	0663	1
HERGET RICHARD P	COL	0-0324038	0868	1
HERIDER HARRY V	MAJ	0-0194318	0146	2
HERINA JOHN	LTC	0-1103689	1060	1
HERING ROBERT H JR	CPT	0-1552698	0553	2
HERIOT JAMES D	COL	0-0409040	0268	1
HERIOT JULIAN C	LTC	0-0376207	1263	1
HERIS GEORGE C	COL	0-0290976	0567	3
HERIT JOHN E	WO1	W-2148794	1064	1
HERITAGE CHRISTIAN	LTC	0-0918480	0867	3
HERITAGE WADE F	COL	0-1821202	0765	1
HERL MARGARET E	1LT	N-0729145	0746	1
HERLIHY FREDERICK	LTC	0-0473553	1066	3
HERLIN STANLEY	LTC	0-1547007	0368	3
HERLONG ROBERT P	CPT	0-0964065	0159	2
HERLT ARTHUR J	1LT	0-0497873	0860	1
HERMAN ALPHONSE G	LTC	0-0195295	0259	3
HERMAN EARL E	CW3	W-2150174	0665	1
HERMAN ELMER B	1LT	0-1316414	0546	2
HERMAN MURRAY	LTC	0-0312338	0567	3
HERMAN RALPH	1LT	0-0444816	1145	2
HERMAN RAY E	MAJ	0-0255149	0361	3
HERMAN SANFORD	1LT	0-1286287	1045	2
HERMAN VINCENT J	LTC	0-1555022	0967	1
HERMAN WELDON P	1LT	0-1301301	0246	2
HERMAN WILLIAM J	LTC	0-1283427	0864	1
HERMANN CHARLES S	CPT	0-1015289	0846	2
HERMANN EDWIN C JR	CW3	W-2208203	0868	1
HERMANSON HUGO E	CW3	W-2148537	0765	1
HERMANSON JACK	LTC	0-1545156	0462	1
HERMANSON JOHN H	MAJ	0-1636031	1060	1
HERMENING GLEN L	MAJ	0-1337707	0962	1
HERMES ROBERT B	1LT	0-1168286	114N	2
HERMEY WALTER E	MAJ	0-1104841	0762	1
HERMITAGE WILLIAM H	LTC	0-0216266	0648	3
HERNANDEZ ARMANDO	MAJ	0-2041427	0965	1
HERNANDEZ ELIGIO B A	1LT	0-1897060	0350	2
HERNANDEZ JOAQUIN	1LT	0-1310340	0945	2
HERNANDEZ JOSEPH C	2LT	0-1016436	0445	2
HERNANDEZ LAZARO M	MAJ	0-1592820	0660	1
HERNANDEZ LUIS F	MAJ	0-0993850	0266	1
HERNANDEZ MICHAEL B	MAJ	0-2005985	0263	1
HERNANDEZ RAFAEL	MAJ	0-0464520	0345	2
HERNANDEZ RAPHAEL S	COL	0-0177554	0961	3
HERNANDEZ RICHARD P	MAJ	0-1597476	0862	1

NAME	GRADE	SVC NO	DATE RET MO YR	RET CODE
HERNANDEZ WALTER R	LTC	0-18[illegible]183	1264	3
HERNANDEZ-NATIVIDAD JOSE	COL	0-0580739	0460	3
HERNANDEZ VALENTINE	WO1	W-2152292	1055	2
HERNDON CLARENCE V	CPT	0-04[illegible]	0746	2
HERNDON DONALD V	COL	0-0173345	1060	3
HERNDON J [illegible]	COL	0-0183543	0757	3
HERNDON JAMES W N	LTC	0-0293334	0860	1
HERNDON JAMES W	COL	0-1294512	0759	1
HERNDON JOHN S	CW2	W-2120109	0445	2
HERNDON MARY E	MAJ	N-0799105	0565	1
HERNDON QUINTUS T	2LT	0-2055136	0944	2
HERNDON WILLIAM [illegible]	WO1	W-2149257	1060	1
HERNDON WILLIAM [illegible]	CW2	W-2214574	1166	1
HEROLD AMBROSE L	LTC	0-1102765	0464	1
HEROLD GERALD M	MAJ	0-1047567	0364	1
HEROLD MARY S	MAJ	N-0721615	1062	1
HERON CHARLES R	CPT	0-1914404	1135	1
HERON DAVID F	COL	0-0490234	0666	2
HERON WILLIAM F JR	LTC	0-0358260	0860	1
HERP CLARENCE F	LTC	0-0334283	0668	3
HERPERS FERDINAND	CPT	0-0324220	104N	2
HERR BAYARD S JR	COL	0-0305111	1068	3
HERR JOSEPH F	MAJ	0-0940016	0462	1
HERR LAURISTON	LTC	0-0103870	1051	3
HERR NORMAN P	COL	0-0406323	0362	2
HERR PAUL S	MAJ	0-0323024	0445	2
HERREN JAMES M JR	LTC	0-0237459	0466	3
HERREN JOHN C	LTC	0-0264485	0661	1
HERREN WESLEY M	LTC	0-0257709	0366	3
HERRERA FERNANDO A	MAJ	0-1641386	0464	1
HERRERA JOHN C	COL	0-0258813	0467	3
HERRERA RAYMOND M	LTC	0-0455254	1158	1
HERRERA WILLIAM	MAJ	0-1284330	0562	1
HERRICK BOBBY L	CW2	W-3200162	1065	1
HERRICK CHARLES C	COL	0-0172228	0251	3
HERRICK HAROLD A	LTC	0-0109320	0648	3
HERRICK JAMES A	MAJ	0-1004783	0457	1
HERRICK ROBERT D	MAJ	0-0157102	0657	3
HERRICK ROBERT E	CW3	W-2123215	0661	1
HERRICK WILLIAM H	MAJ	0-2262601	0165	1
HERRICKS ROBERT N	LTC	0-1010159	0160	1
HERRIN BURK Y	CPT	0-0356157	1146	2
HERRIN NORMAN A	1LT	0-1324933	0854	1
HERRIN WILLIAM M JR	COL	0-0269307	0362	3
HERRING CATHRYN C	1LT	N-0787015	0246	1
HERRING CHARLES P	LTC	0-0142337	1149	3
HERRING CLARENCE B	1LT	0-1112762	1047	2
HERRING GEORGE F	CPT	0-0363388	0646	2
HERRING HERBERT J	MAJ	0-1014238	0759	1
HERRING HERMAN H	CPT	0-0898598	1054	1
HERRING LESTER W	CPT	0-0291798	0564	3
HERRING PETER K	MAJ	0-2204033	1168	1
HERRING THOMAS A	MAJ	0-1640547	0461	1
HERRING THOMAS F	LTC	0-0650530	1062	1
HERRINGTON ARTHUR T	1LT	0-0502109	0744	2
HERRINGTON CECIL P	COL	0-0306826	0367	3
HERRINGTON CHARLES F	CW2	W-2216244	0868	1
HERRINGTON ELMO	CW3	W-2206086	0766	1
HERRINGTON JOHN C	CW3	W-2145077	0365	1
HERRINGTON JOHN T	LTC	0-0422187	0957	1
HERRINGTON LINWOOD	CPT	0-0358123	1143	2
HERRIOTT RUSSELL K	LTC	0-1298704	0561	1
HERRIS WILLIAM R	MAJ	0-1337186	0465	1
HERRLICH WILLIAM E	MAJ	0-0179044	1061	3
HERRMAN RUSSELL T	CW2	W-2209901	0165	1
HERRMANN ALBERT	LTC	0-0246853	0264	3
HERRMANN ERNEST F	LTC	0-0281741	1066	3
HERRMANN FREDERICK	MAJ	0-0216646	0962	3
HERRMANN HARRY C	CPT	0-1184315	0347	2
HERRMANN HENRY J	MAJ	0-0247506	0550	3
HERRMANN HOWARD W	MAJ	0-0299348	1054	1
HERRMANN WESLEY P	LTC	0-0279929	0463	3
HERRMANN WILLIAM H	1LT	0-1032354	1145	2
HERRMANN WILLIAM J	CPT	0-0343540	0145	2
HERRON CARROLL F	CPT	0-5301688	1268	1

NAME	GRADE	SVC NO	DATE RET MO YR	RET CODE
HERRON CLAIR E	CPT	0-0488160	0752	1
HERRON DORWARD P	MAJ	0-1826275	0557	1
HERRON EARL	COL	0-1821274	0764	3
HERRON FREDERICK	LTC	0-0171819	0649	3
HERRON HENRI L	WO1	W-2149941	1262	1
HERRON JAMES R	LTC	0-0309073	0863	3
HERRON NAPOLEON	WO1	W-2108077	0861	1
HERRON RAYMOND K	LTC	0-0906820	0662	1
HERRON RICHARD A	COL	0-0259948	0365	3
HERRON WILLIAM D	CW3	W-3150583	0268	1
HERRSTROM CHARLES E	COL	0-0195914	0263	3
HERSCHBACH SIGMUND R	MAJ	0-1018167	0961	1
HERSCHEL PAUL F JR	MAJ	0-0254358	0252	3
HERSCHLEDER FRED J	LTC	0-0451583	1060	1
HERSEY IRVING W	LTC	0-0919855	1262	3
HERSEY JAMES R	1LT	0-1331395	0846	2
HERSEY WALTER E	LTC	0-1183881	0464	1
HERSEY WINTHROP P	LTC	0-0247535	0466	3
HERSH ELMER R	LTC	0-1584351	0362	1
HERSH HAROLD	MAJ	0-1534755	0666	1
HERSH HARRY	CW2	W-2142316	1054	1
HERSHBERGER HAROLD R	MAJ	0-0954538	0366	1
HERSHBERGER RALPH E	CPT	0-1693789	1045	2
HERSHCUCK MICHAEL	1LT	0-1302900	104N	2
HERSHEY CHARLES E	CPT	0-0158873	1060	3
HERSHKOWITZ LEON	LTC	0-0225525	1263	3
HERSHON IRVING J	LTC	0-0293878	0966	3
HERSKER HERBERT S	2LT	0-0444116	0945	2
HERSMAN WILLIAM M	CW2	W-2200859	0168	3
HERSMER GENE S	CW2	W-2146462	1060	1
HERSTEIN DAVID	CPT	0-1821444	1045	2
HERSTON HOYT R	CW4	W-2002873	0568	1
HERSUM HAROLD D	LTC	0-0183713	0856	3
HERSUM LEROY M	COL	0-0102375	0658	3
HERTEL LORAINE A JR	LTC	0-2262893	0368	1
HERTEL OLIVER R	COL	0-0381328	1163	1
HERTGEN PAUL F	LTC	0-0915344	1165	3
HERTGES NICK F	LTC	0-0494051	0455	1
HERTHEL STEPHEN W	MAJ	0-1576116	0852	2
HERTSCHE JOEL C JR	COL	0-0236133	1065	3
HERTWECK EDWARD C	MAJ	0-0509442	0951	1
HERTZ ALBERT L	LTC	0-0918848	1047	2
HERTZ CLYDE E	COL	0-0165972	0757	3
HERTZ EVELINE R	MAJ	L-0201040	0163	1
HERTZ PAUL B	LTC	0-0464466	1067	3
HERTZ RAY F	1LT	0-1113252	0545	2
HERTZBERG LOUIS	CPT	0-0450022	1048	1
HERTZBERG ROBERT E	COL	0-0257139	0365	3
HERTZKE JOHN J	CW2	W-2215251	0468	1
HERTZOG BERNARD E	CW2	W-2144223	0259	1
HERTZSCH C T JR	1LT	0-0350596	0145	2
HERTZSCH OTTO L	CW2	W-2000503	0253	3
HERVEY DAMON JR	CW2	W-2151790	0957	1
HERVEY HARCOURT	B G	0-0108621	0846	2
HERVOL EMIL C	1LT	0-2203642	1152	2
HERWICK JOHN T	CPT	0-1687100	1144	2
HERWITT HAROLD H	COL	0-0208922	0165	3
HERWITZ ROBERT I	2LT	0-1179094	0645	2
HERYFORD GLEN L	MAJ	0-1540914	0962	1
HERZBERGER ARTHUR C	MAJ	0-0381845	0446	2
HERZFELD JOHN G	LTC	0-0537021	1266	3
HERZKE WILLIAM J	LTC	0-1301824	0165	1
HERZOG LOUIS F	CPT	0-2046296	0949	1
HERZOG MANUEL	1LT	0-1321775	1045	2
HERZOG OTTO LA VE	1LT	0-1314478	0251	2
HERZOG PAUL E	CPT	0-0484294	0345	2
HERZOG VIRGINIA G	2LT	N-0785072	1045	1
HERZOG WILLIAM	LTC	0-0178534	0648	3
HERZOG WILLIAM	CPT	0-1298396	104N	2
HERZSTEIN BERNARD	1LT	0-1637660	0246	2
HESBY ERNEST K	MAJ	0-0273777	1167	3
HESCH MARTIN J	LTC	0-0474902	0268	3
HESELTON CHARLES R	LTC	0-1017828	0561	1
HESFORD HUGH A	LTC	0-0491605	0954	1
HESKETH JAMES P	1LT	0-1335923	0453	2

NAME	GRADE	SVC NO	DATE RET MO YR	RET CODE
HESKETT HARRISON A	CPT	0-0208051	0445	2
HESLEP EDWARD A	2LT	0-1043658	0243	2
HESLER GALEN J	LTC	0-0370604	1165	1
HESLEIN WILLIAM G	MAJ	0-1038399	0262	2
HESS CHARLES J	CW2	W-2149113	0762	1
HESS CHARLES M	LTC	0-0917237	0467	3
HESS CHARLES W	2LT	0-1825124	0144	2
HESS CYRIL G	MAJ	0-0985949	0866	1
HESS EMIL F	MAJ	0-1554563	0464	1
HESS F W	LTC	0-1175157	0561	1
HESS FRANK J	LTC	0-1044550	1167	1
HESS GEORGE J	LTC	0-0888261	0263	1
HESS HAROLD E	MAJ	0-0223645	1154	3
HESS HAROLD S	MAJ	0-1253549	1160	1
HESS HOWARD J	1LT	0-1578598	0845	2
HESS IRWIN H	1LT	0-0978015	0353	2
HESS JAMES M	MAJ	0-0977243	1167	1
HESS JAY R SR	MAJ	0-0908166	1157	3
HESS JOHN J	CPT	0-0918696	0945	2
HESS KENNETH H	COL	0-0290342	0467	3
HESS LAURIE F	LTC	0-0272847	0961	3
HESS LAWRENCE E	LTC	0-0380039	0667	1
HESS MYRON T	CPT	0-0347703	0457	1
HESS ORVAN W	COL	0-0284820	0766	3
HESS WALTER F	LTC	0-0371618	0467	3
HESS WILLIAM F	CW2	W-2210668	1266	1
HESS WILLIAM J	MAJ	0-1846004	0255	1
HESSE CLYDE E	LTC	0-0312542	1159	1
HESSE DAVID F	LTC	0-1542828	1165	1
HESSE GEORGE A	LTC	0-0306012	0863	3
HESSELBARTH PAUL K	CPT	0-1300326	1046	2
HESSELBERG ABRAHAM L	MAJ	0-0168091	0460	3
HESSER LOWELL W	LTC	0-1289424	0863	2
HESSER ROBERT N	CPT	0-0399404	1045	2
HESSEVICK GEORGE I	LTC	0-0502795	0658	1
HESSLER EDWARD A	CPT	0-0514151	0745	2
HESSON DONALD K	LTC	0-0524750	0268	2
HESSON JAMES J	LTC	0-0348153	0767	3
HESTER BURDETTE L	LTC	0-1108737	0462	1
HESTER DAVID C	COL	0-0287113	0858	2
HESTER GEORGE C	CPT	0-0201948	0649	3
HESTER JOE A	MAJ	0-0964236	0164	1
HESTER JOSEPH A JR	MAJ	0-0256132	1067	3
HESTER JOSEPH L	CW3	W-2114487	0356	1
HESTER LEONARD C	LTC	0-1634881	0858	1
HESTER MARION W	CPT	0-0332088	0845	2
HESTER ROBERT J	MAJ	0-1589262	1055	1
HESTER WARREN E	CW3	W-2150158	0764	2
HESTER WILLIAM A	CPT	0-2000425	0368	2
HESTON ROBERT B	CPT	0-0367799	0346	2
HETEJI PAUL S	1LT	0-0414854	0745	2
HETH MABEL S	MAJ	N-0732829	1263	3
HETHCOAT CHARLES L	MAJ	0-2015761	0262	1
HETHCOAT REUBEN	CW2	W-2141313	0753	1
HETHCOTE WILLIAM E	MAJ	0-1821584	0363	1
HETHERINGTON FERRALL	CW3	W-2141164	0561	1
HETHERINGTON JACK S	LTC	0-0449215	1066	1
HETHERINGTON RICHARD	MAJ	0-1846006	0359	1
HETHERINGTON VINCENT	LTC	0-0547580	1157	2
HETHERLY WILLIAM A	CW3	W-2147481	1065	1
HETLAND VICTOR A	LTC	0-0191485	0554	3
HETRICK DONALD R	MAJ	0-2018348	0865	1
HETRICK EDGAR C	MAJ	0-0499998	0753	1
HETRICK ROBERT J	LTC	0-2018349	1267	1
HETTEL CHARLES L	MAJ	0-0990449	1165	1
HETTEL EARL F	LTC	0-0230373	0663	3
HETTLE DONALD B	CPT	0-0410799	1047	2
HETTLER WILLIAM F	LTC	0-0296157	0563	3
HETTRICH ALBERT L	COL	0-0356455	0657	1
HETZEL JOHN B JR	LTC	0-1104843	0966	1
HETZEL KATHARINE	MAJ	N-0786514	0665	1
HETZEL RUDOLPH F	MAJ	0-4009071	0268	1
HETZLER VAUGHN G	2LT	0-0107048	0353	3
HEUCK ROBERT A	CPT	0-1634882	0251	1
HEUER ERNEST E	LTC	0-0324731	0368	3

NAME	GRADE	SVC NO	DATE RET MO YR	RET CODE
HEUBLEIN LOYAL J	1LT	0-1297373	0546	2
HEUSER CHARLES K	MAJ	0-2044573	0853	1
HEUVEL VIRGINIA C	1LT	N-0783644	0446	1
HEWERLIN JOSEPH W	CW2	W-2118114	1066	1
HEWERLY PAUL M	COL	0-0152154	0756	3
HEWES WILLIAM F	CPT	0-1055146	0557	1
HEWETT ARTHUR A	LTC	0-0268037	0167	3
HEWETT ERNEST W	LTC	0-0907915	0167	3
HEWETT GEORGE M	LTC	0-0182399	0160	3
HEWETT JAMES D	B G	0-0910307	1265	3
HEWITT JAMES E	CW2	W-2205266	0861	1
HEWITT ABEL N JR	MAJ	0-1042053	0262	1
HEWITT CARTER E	LTC	0-0904564	1167	3
HEWITT CHARLES F JR	LTC	0-1634883	1065	1
HEWITT CHARLES H	CW3	W-2152515	0664	1
HEWITT CHARLES K JR	CPT	0-4026504	0860	2
HEWITT CHARLES K SR	MAJ	0-1636034	0156	1
HEWITT CHESTER J	LTC	0-0405876	0860	2
HEWITT DANIEL A JR	LTC	0-1293773	0961	1
HEWITT FRANCIS M	LTC	0-0404316	0261	1
HEWITT HARRY H JR	LTC	0-0274759	0668	3
HEWITT LAWRENCE P	LTC	0-0289892	0665	3
HEWITT NORMAN D	LTC	0-1115922	0868	3
HEWITT RALPH E	LTC	0-0289150	1167	3
HEWITT STEPHEN A SR	LTC	0-0233909	1160	1
HEWITT WALTER J D	LTC	0-0341418	0759	1
HEWITT WILLIAM C	LTC	0-1573275	0661	1
HEWLETT ARTHUR F	MAJ	0-0238324	0565	3
HEWSON HAROLD F	MAJ	0-0953846	0365	1
HEXT CHARLES M	LTC	0-0404369	0860	1
HEXTELL CLARE O	MAJ	0-1287880	0764	2
HEY RUSSELL	MAJ	0-0479453	0654	1
HEYDE ALBERT E	CW3	W-2150561	0762	1
HEYDT WILLIAM H	CPT	0-0989999	0661	1
HEYENGA LAWRENCE E	LTC	0-0367045	0859	1
HEYER GLENN A	LTC	0-0326771	0763	1
HEYING CLAIRMONT	MAJ	0-1822998	0966	1
HEYL HENRY L	CPT	0-0436847	0744	2
HEYL THEODORE C	1LT	0-0585017	0254	2
HEYL THOMAS D JR	LTC	0-0109444	0847	1
HEYLIGER FREDERICK	CPT	0-1010235	0147	2
HEYMAN LEO	COL	0-0266340	1053	3
HEYMANNS PETER P	CPT	0-1106200	0355	2
HEYRMAN JOHN H	MAJ	0-1594899	0758	1
HIATT CHESTER L	LTC	0-1080031	0665	1
HIATT CLIFFORD R	LTC	0-0170701	1061	1
HIATT ENAH C JR	LTC	0-0947424	1167	1
HIATT FRED	LTC	0-0534759	0163	1
HIATT JOSEPH S JR	CPT	0-0464893	0145	2
HIATT LOUIS E	1LT	0-0146191	0357	3
HIATT MAURICE F	CPT	0-0973831	1162	2
HIATT NORMAN R	CPT	0-1293252	0447	2
HIATT PAUL F	MAJ	0-2018351	0563	1
HIBALA PAUL S	CPT	0-0503258	0152	1
HIBARGER DON W	2LT	0-1547964	0345	2
HIBBARD CARL H	1LT	0-1115629	1045	2
HIBBARD CHARLES	COL	0-1101493	0263	1
HIBBARD CURT W	CPT	0-0178146	1045	2
HIBBARD LEE M	1LT	0-1287351	0544	2
HIBBARD WALTER C	COL	0-0270662	0560	1
HIBBARD WILLIAM J	MAJ	0-0245630	0258	3
HIBBERT CHESTER A	LTC	0-0166054	1160	3
HIBBETTS EDGAR M	1LT	0-1825272	0247	2
HIBBS CARL W	CW2	W-2148379	0161	1
HIBBS JERAL F	1LT	0-2023876	1047	2
HIBLER BERNARD C	COL	0-0261839	0566	3
HIBNER LOWELL J	LTC	0-2037058	0961	1
HICE GILBERT D	LTC	0-1844615	0967	2
HICHAK MICHAEL	LTC	0-1578601	0862	1
HICK FORD K	LTC	0-0291843	0146	2
HICKAMBOTTOM ELRIE J	MAJ	0-0988674	0567	1
HICKCOX PERCY M	COL	0-0256872	0854	3
HICKEL NED R	MAJ	0-1283257	0947	2
HICKERSON JOE R JR	CPT	0-1184070	0346	2
HICKERSON LEONARD A	CPT	0-1107476	0146	2

NAME	GRADE	SVC NO	DATE RET MO YR	RET CODE
HICKEY CLARENCE A	COL	0-0450891	0655	1
HICKEY DENNIS A	1LT	0-0501148	1045	2
HICKEY EDWARD B	LTC	0-0351366	0667	2
HICKEY EDWARD J	MAJ	0-0103711	0648	3
HICKEY EDWARD J JR	CPT	0-1081475	0858	1
HICKEY EUGENE P JR	LTC	0-1535196	0262	1
HICKEY FREDERICK	LTC	0-0372700	0959	1
HICKEY GRANVILLE	MAJ	0-1894180	0367	1
HICKEY HARRY B	CPT	0-2262361	0161	1
HICKEY JAMES F	COL	0-0332047	0559	1
HICKEY JAMES H	MAJ	0-0344676	0346	2
HICKEY JOHN	CPT	0-1300485	0555	1
HICKEY JOHN F	COL	0-0373364	0867	3
HICKEY LEO K	2LT	0-1295019	1043	2
HICKEY MILDRED N	CPT	N-0786313	0857	2
HICKEY MORRIS J	MAJ	0-0364192	0346	2
HICKEY PATRICK V	CPT	0-1302971	0945	2
HICKEY PETER J	MAJ	0-0338512	1046	2
HICKEY RAYMOND P	CW4	W-2142160	0159	1
HICKEY RUBY P	MAJ	N-0765236	1066	1
HICKEY THOMAS J	COL	0-1043983	1168	1
HICKIE PAUL F	LTC	0-0262866	0165	3
HICKLE WALTER L	LTC	0-0993683	0968	1
HICKLIN HARRY M	CW2	W-2150808	0357	1
HICKLIN WENDELL C	MAJ	0-0920453	0567	3
HICKMAN ARTHUR J	LTC	0-0384495	0166	3
HICKMAN CARLOS S	CPT	0-0234664	0845	2
HICKMAN EDWARD T	MAJ	0-0269432	1068	3
HICKMAN GEORGE F	MAJ	0-1340284-	1165	1
HICKMAN GERALD H	1LT	0-1598756	0747	2
HICKMAN GLENN H	LTC	0-1326240	0367	1
HICKMAN HAROLD D	MAJ	0-1797133	1057	1
HICKMAN HOWARD D	COL	0-0104100	0558	3
HICKMAN JAMES R	LTC	0-1181299	1062	1
HICKMAN JEWETT C	CW2	W-2118255	0356	1
HICKMAN JOE C	MAJ	0-0272272	0359	1
HICKMAN JOHN W	LTC	0-0230327	0164	3
HICKMAN LYLE W	CW3	W-2152731	0463	1
HICKMAN PAUL W	CW3	W-2141584	1056	1
HICKMAN RAYMOND B	MAJ	0-2025403	0863	1
HICKMAN SPURGEON	CW3	W-2145664	1061	1
HICKMAN THOMAS E	LTC	0-0406011	1160	1
HICKMAN WILLIAM H	LTC	0-1059491	0968	3
HICKMAN WILLIAM H	CW2	W-2142963	1053	2
HICKMAN WILLIAM R	1LT	0-1544022	0448	1
HICKOK ARNO J	CW2	W-2208233	0862	1
HICKOX CHARLES	1LT	0-1103212	1145	2
HICKOK DONALD L SR	LTC	0-1104209	0759	1
HICKS ACLE V JR	MAJ	0-1106816	0661	2
HICKS AMP F JR	1LT	0-0533904	1045	2
HICKS ARTHUR	1LT	0-2023800	1146	1
HICKS AUBREY	MAJ	0-1287007	0158	1
HICKS CARL F	LTC	0-1844381	0257	1
HICKS CHARLES E	LTC	0-0343549	0363	1
HICKS CHARLES W	CPT	0-1299883	0560	1
HICKS CLARENCE C	LTC	0-0346738	0764	1
HICKS CLARISSA	MAJ	M-0002734	1163	1
HICKS CLIFTON H	CW3	W-2209103	0367	1
HICKS DAVID N	MAJ	0-1331837	0664	1
HICKS EARL A JR	LTC	0-1057100	0364	1
HICKS EARL D	LTC	0-1646146	0765	1
HICKS ELMER B	COL	0-0209279	1059	3
HICKS FLOYD S	LTC	0-0492413	0855	1
HICKS FRANCIS O	1LT	0-1178188	0146	2
HICKS FRED C JR	LTC	0-0463925	0762	1
HICKS FREDERICK	MAJ	0-1823156	0859	1
HICKS HAROLD D	CW2	W-2148970	0261	1
HICKS HAROLD N	MAJ	0-0948651	0663	1
HICKS HAROLD W	CPT	0-0510745	0455	1
HICKS HENRY K	COL	0-1745564	1267	3
HICKS JAMES	1LT	0-0885624	0945	2
HICKS JAMES C	1LT	0-1319741	0652	1
HICKS JAMES E	1LT	0-1168719	0346	2
HICKS JAMES L	2LT	0-0466481	0144	2
HICKS JAMES M	CPT	0-1183702	0457	2

NAME	GRADE	SVC NO	DATE RET MO YR	RET CODE
HICKS JOHN J	LTC	0-0381966	0655	1
HICKS JOHN P	2LT	0-1303727	1143	2
HICKS KENNETH C JR	LTC	0-1052390	0762	1
HICKS LARUE C	1LT	0-1030880	0856	1
HICKS LOUIS E	LTC	0-1548435	0266	1
HICKS MATTIE D	MAJ	N-0765793	0466	1
HICKS MELVIN A	1LT	0-2010622	0153	2
HICKS MILFORD H	LTC	0-0290257	0456	3
HICKS ORA P	MAJ	N-0726589	0961	1
HICKS RAYMOND E	LTC	0-1296031	0258	1
HICKS ROBERT N	COL	0-0285411	[illegible]	2
HICKS ROBERT O	CPT	0-1879143	0364	1
HICKS SAM E	LTC	0-0402700	0361	2
HICKS SHELDON	LTC	0-1299884	1267	1
HICKS STANFORD R	COL	0-1550620	0868	1
HICKS THOMAS J	CW3	W-2146247	0760	1
HICKS THOMAS M B III	LTC	0-0379455	0760	1
HICKS WESLEY	CPT	0-1823598	1044	2
HICKS WILLARD E	CW2	W-2212281	1265	1
HICKS WILLIAM L	LTC	0-0425289	0961	1
HICKS WILLIAM L	WO1	W-2151674	0956	1
HICKS YALE JR	CPT	0-0412919	0745	2
HICKSON JOHN C	1LT	0-0421722	1044	2
HICKSON ROBERT W	CW3	W-2146972	0363	1
HICOCK RUSSELL	LTC	0-0244058	0965	3
HIDA MIRIAM I	1LT	N-0767126	1145	1
HIDALGO BENITO T	MAJ	0-0341151	1148	2
HIDALGO JACINTO	LTC	0-0255693	0764	3
HIDALGO JOHN P	CPT	0-1284140	0660	1
HIDALGO VINCENT M	COL	0-0245520	1262	3
HIDDEN MORTON E	LTC	0-1642969	0568	1
HIDEN CHARLES S	LTC	0-0237201	0957	3
HIEFIELD ALFRED T	MAJ	0-1057466	0167	3
HIEGERT LEONARD P	MAJ	0-2038840	1058	1
HIEMSTRA CLIFFORD H	LTC	0-1339166	0466	1
HIEN CLARENCE R	LTC	0-0297303	0165	3
HIENTON TRUMAN E	COL	0-0253922	0558	3
HIEPLER JACOB F	MAJ	0-0946831	1062	1
HIERONYMUS CHARLES D	2LT	0-2044522	0445	2
HIERS ROBERT E	CPT	0-0981430	0960	1
HIETT DARRELL D	CPT	0-0884916	0147	2
HIETT EDWARD A	1LT	0-1336064	1051	2
HIGASHI YOSHIKAZU	LTC	0-2037059	0263	1
HIGBEE CLARENCE E	COL	0-0212694	0462	3
HIGBEE ELLSWORTH	2LT	0-1288742	0644	2
HIGBEE WALTER V JR	LTC	0-1041170	0767	1
HIGBY LEONARD G	CPT	0-0360478	0956	3
HIGDON EBB	CW3	W-2152344	0765	1
HIGDON EDGAR H	MAJ	0-2210454	0564	1
HIGDON GLENNIAL	CPT	0-1183462	0161	1
HIGDON KENNETH T	MAJ	0-1335005	0664	1
HIGDON RALPH T	CW3	W-2143205	0563	1
HIGGINBOTHAM EARL A	MAJ	0-0416232	0547	2
HIGGINBOTHAM GEORG	MAJ	0-0476253	1047	1
HIGGINBOTHAM ILIFF S	COL	0-0254440	0463	3
HIGGINBOTHAM IRA	1LT	0-1168720	1145	2
HIGGINBOTHAM MEADE	CPT	0-1924754	0961	1
HIGGINBOTHAM ORGETT	CW3	W-2131712	0368	2
HIGGINBOTHAM V M	1LT	N-0735453	0446	1
HIGGINBOTHAM WILLIAM	LTC	0-1300033	0361	1
HIGGINS ALBERT F	LTC	0-0487452	0265	3
HIGGINS BERT A	CW3	W-2209842	0268	1
HIGGINS CATHERINE	1LT	N-0720621	114N	1
HIGGINS CLIFTON L	LTC	0-1104848	1062	2
HIGGINS EDWARD F	LTC	0-0408897	0963	1
HIGGINS EDWARD J	LTC	0-0276583	0846	2
HIGGINS EDWIN L	MAJ	0-1693590	0646	2
HIGGINS EMERSON H	CPT	0-1042054	0160	3
HIGGINS EVERETT K	LTC	0-0162120	1046	2
HIGGINS FORREST W	CPT	0-2263641	1162	1
HIGGINS FRANCIS V	LTC	0-0399120	0867	3
HIGGINS HARVEY N	1LT	0-0497529	0453	1
HIGGINS HERBERT G	CW2	W-3150398	0767	1
HIGGINS HERMAN N	1LT	0-1285758	0745	2
HIGGINS HUBERT M	MAJ	0-0368164	0844	2

NAME	GRADE	SVC NO	DATE RET MO YR	RET CODE
HIGGINS JAMES J	MAJ	0-0288902	0467	3
HIGGINS JAMES M	COL	0-0916271	0665	3
HIGGINS JOHN F JR	LTC	0-1299336	0767	1
HIGGINS JOHN T	CW2	W-2150672	1057	1
HIGGINS JOSEPH A	2LT	0-1581177	0745	2
HIGGINS JOSEPH F	LTC	0-1645659	0960	1
HIGGINS JOSEPH P	LTC	0-0372824	1068	3
HIGGINS LAWRENCE M	LTC	0-0422019	0661	1
HIGGINS LEMUEL W	MAJ	0-0207018	0656	3
HIGGINS LESLIE B	MAJ	0-1051177	0161	1
HIGGINS MARK P	CW4	W-2002246	0767	1
HIGGINS MICHAEL P JR	1LT	0-1302305	1145	2
HIGGINS MILES W	2LT	0-2049277	1144	2
HIGGINS NORMAN E	MAJ	0-2262758	0864	1
HIGGINS OTTIS C	CPT	0-1690965	0248	2
HIGGINS PAUL M	CW2	W-2210572	0465	1
HIGGINS RALPH P	CPT	0-0524938	1045	2
HIGGINS RAYMOND T	COL	0-0254206	1058	3
HIGGINS ROBERT E	MAJ	0-0971731	0364	1
HIGGINS ROY	MAJ	0-0885813	0358	1
HIGGINS STANLEY P	1LT	0-0395139	0145	2
HIGGINS TIMOTHY G	MAJ	0-0465096	0667	1
HIGGINS WALTER D	CPT	0-0488604	0545	2
HIGGINS WALTER K	LTC	0-0959422	0868	1
HIGGINS WILLIAM B	COL	0-0219816	0356	3
HIGGINSON WILLIAM M	MAJ	0-2034534	0661	1
HIGGS ARDEN J	1LT	0-2033677	0554	2
HIGH CALVIN E	MAJ	0-1299885	0858	1
HIGH OLAY B	MAJ	0-2083351	0465	1
HIGH HOYLE O JR	WO1	W-2151090	0456	2
HIGH VINCENT C	LTC	0-0337303	0158	1
HIGHBERG GEORGE M	LTC	0-0266899	0568	3
HIGHBERGER EDITH M K	1LT	N-0784550	1148	2
HIGHBY PAUL R	LTC	0-0374617	0264	3
HIGHERS THOMAS B	WO1	W-2116691	0145	2
HIGHLEY GLEN H	WO1	W-2112893	1043	2
HIGHLEY HAROLD O	LTC	0-0199047	0258	2
HIGHSMITH LLOYD G	MAJ	0-1166740	0157	1
HIGHSMITH ROBERT M	LTC	0-2206036	1267	1
HIGHT ROBERT H	MAJ	0-2007604	0464	1
HIGHT WALTER	2LT	0-1637667	1048	1
HIGHTOWER L L JR	CPT	0-0366305	1045	2
HIGHTOWER GRACE L	CPT	N-0800092	0652	2
HIGHTOWER JOHN H JR	LTC	0-1168721	1167	1
HIGHTOWER NASH R	LTC	0-0450289	0161	1
HIGHTOWER NORRIS E	MAJ	0-1917989	0568	2
HIGHTOWER RUBIN F	MAJ	0-1309062	0958	1
HIGHTOWER WAYNE R	CPT	0-0432155	0756	2
HIGINBOTHAM WILLIAM	LTC	0-1320688	1162	1
HIGLEY ROBERT P	LTC	0-0374222	0263	1
HIGUCHI HIRO	COL	0-0527027	0267	3
HIKEL NOLAN G	COL	0-0292264	0857	1
HILARY HENRY R	LTC	0-0350501	1266	3
HILBERT MARQUIS D	LTC	0-0934721	0568	1
HILBURN NATHANIEL	LTC	0-0453721	0962	1
HILBURN WILLIAM S	1LT	0-1012378	1145	2
HILBUSH WILLIAM E	CW3	W-2143319	0864	1
HILDEBRAND EUGENE JR	CPT	0-1684802	0344	2
HILDEBRAND GEORGE	CPT	0-0557524	1045	2
HILDEBRAND MIKE	CPT	0-0492946	0350	1
HILDEBRAND PAUL R	COL	0-0317545	0766	3
HILDEBRAND RAYMOND	COL	0-0202793	0451	3
HILDEBRAND ROBERT W	LTC	0-0322605	0263	3
HILDEBRANDT FRANK B	LTC	0-2040802	0667	1
HILDEBRANDT H F	CW2	W-2142065	0755	1
HILDEBRANDT SIEGFRIE	CW3	RW-2151671	0364	1
HILDEBRANT LEO H	CPT	0-1765901	1045	2
HILDER PETER F	MAJ	0-0325723	0645	2
HILDERBRAND LEONARD	LTC	0-0258642	0660	3
HILDETON HILBERT O	LTC	0-0488767	1154	1
HILDRETH CLIFFORD W	CPT	0-0497095	0146	2
HILDRETH DONALD P	CW3	W-2207736	0967	1
HILDRETH EUGENE F	CW3	W-2146818	1162	1
HILDRICH FRANCIS	CW2	W-3250445	1167	1
HILDYARD VICTOR H	CPT	0-0469295	0146	2

NAME	GRADE	SVC NO	DATE RET MO YR	RET CODE
HILE WARREN J	CW2	W-2146774	0758	2
HILEMAN THOMAS E	MAJ	0-1931253	1268	1
HILER ELVA L	MAJ	N-0783600	1265	1
HILEY JULIAN	CPT	0-1044848	0961	2
HILFERTY WILLIAM R	CPT	0-0335374	0647	2
HILGERSON FRANK J	MAJ	0-2036548	1162	1
HILKE WILLIAM J	COL	0-0266017	0460	1
HILKERT WILLIAM B	MAJ	0-0194150	0545	2
HILL ALBERT E	MAJ	0-2200003	1165	1
HILL ALFRED D	LTC	0-1286288	0961	1
HILL AMBROSE H	CW3	RW-2207555	1267	1
HILL ARCHIE D	1LT	0-1308336	0946	2
HILL ARTHUR A	CW2	W-2147489	0164	1
HILL ARTHUR B	CPT	0-2005657	1058	2
HILL ARTHUR E	LTC	0-0261862	0864	3
HILL BENJAMIN F	MAJ	0-0161360	0156	3
HILL BOYD B	COL	0-0204151	1044	2
HILL BOYD V	LTC	0-1103213	0961	1
HILL BURNIS E	1LT	0-1305925	1145	2
HILL BURTON S	COL	0-0198908	1049	3
HILL CATHERINE	1LT	N-0743503	0546	1
HILL CECIL R	COL	0-0243924	1158	1
HILL CHARLES F	CW2	RW-2147450	0463	1
HILL CHARLES F	1LT	0-0885793	0845	2
HILL CHARLES L JR	2LT	0-1650882	1145	2
HILL CHARLEY R	1LT	0-0495993	1144	2
HILL CHAUNCEY V	CPT	0-0887433	0263	1
HILL CLIFTON C	LTC	0-0196207	0660	3
HILL CLYDE W	LTC	0-0983161	0568	1
HILL CYRUS N	LTC	0-0323911	0354	2
HILL DANA E	CPT	0-0152228	0455	3
HILL DARRELL F	LTC	0-0450054	0455	1
HILL DARRELL M	CPT	0-1311513	0847	2
HILL DARWIN M	LTC	0-1542718	0557	1
HILL DAVID D	MAJ	0-0446320	0663	1
HILL DAVID F	CPT	0-1287713	1159	1
HILL DOUGLAS D	CW2	W-2143325	1057	1
HILL EDGAR M	LTC	0-1172494	0663	1
HILL EDWARD B	LTC	0-1307013	0463	2
HILL EDWARD S	1LT	0-1644422	0553	2
HILL EDWARD W	2LT	0-1317793	0545	2
HILL EDWIN V	COL	0-0381660	0868	3
HILL ELLIOTT B	CPT	0-1045112	0859	1
HILL ELLIS D	LTC	0-0532769	0468	1
HILL ELMER A	CW2	W-2149931	1162	1
HILL ELMER C	1LT	0-1291990	0146	2
HILL ERNEST I JR	LTC	0-1167029	0460	1
HILL EUGENE L	MAJ	0-0263814	0949	3
HILL EUGENE R	CW4	W-2002774	1264	3
HILL EVAN	CPT	0-0417992	0848	2
HILL FLOYD G	LTC	0-1559343	0168	1
HILL FORREST S	CPT	0-1178832	0661	1
HILL FRANCIS T	MAJ	0-1798260	0860	1
HILL FRED C	MAJ	0-0178612	0457	3
HILL FRED J	1LT	0-0405423	0145	2
HILL FREDERICK	COL	0-0298862	1066	3
HILL FREDRIC S	LTC	0-0417312	1262	1
HILL GEORGE	MAJ	0-0499638	0747	1
HILL GEORGE A	LTC	0-0390680	0146	2
HILL GEORGE H	MAJ	0-1030155	0258	2
HILL GEORGE JP	LTC	0-0284412	0967	3
HILL GEORGE M	COL	0-0224702	1054	3
HILL GEORGE W	CW4	W-2142382	0757	1
HILL GERALD W	MAJ	0-1185055	1060	1
HILL GLENN H	LTC	0-1291638	0468	2
HILL GRAHAM	CPT	0-0962951	1060	1
HILL GROVER L	CW2	W-2143484	0357	1
HILL HAROLD N	LTC	0-0195325	0562	3
HILL HAROLD R	MAJ	0-1043660	0962	1
HILL HARVEY G JR	CW3	W-2148856	0166	1
HILL HARVEY W	CW2	W-2150691	0264	1
HILL HECTOR W SR	CW2	W-2139428	0962	1
HILL HENRY E	1LT	0-1101868	0345	2
HILL HOMER E	CPT	0-2262112	0958	1
HILL HORACE H	LTC	0-1286124	0662	1

NAME	GRADE	SVC NO	DATE RET MO YR	RET CODE
HILL HOWARD H	LTC	0-1184227	1167	1
HILL HOWARD G	COL	0-0174003	0455	3
HILL HOYT H JR	2LT	0-0425231	1143	2
HILL IRVING [illegible]	MAJ	0-1551969	0461	1
HILL JACK [illegible]	WO1	W-2125436	0945	2
HILL JAMES [illegible]	CW2	W-2205560	0363	1
HILL JAMES E	LTC	0-1342375	0268	1
HILL JAMES B	COL	0-0351368	0666	1
HILL JAMES [illegible]	CW3	W-2149956	1064	1
HILL JAMES R	MAJ	0-0547268	0962	2
HILL JAMES R JR	MAJ	0-1685703	1265	1
HILL JAMES R P	MAJ	0-0298668	0546	1
HILL JAMES W	COL	0-0261395	0654	1
HILL JAMES W	LTC	0-0381654	0960	1
HILL JIM D	MG	0-0176433	0257	3
HILL JOE M	COL	0-0152186	0948	3
HILL JOHN A	CW3	W-2209878	0666	1
HILL JOHN B	COL	0-0191132	0857	3
HILL JOHN D	COL	0-0106115	0950	3
HILL JOHN E	CPT	0-0288457	0861	3
HILL JOHN F	1LT	0-1315167	0545	2
HILL JOHN J	LTC	0-1174285	0560	1
HILL JOHN L	COL	0-0359886	0162	1
HILL JOHN P	CPT	0-0473748	1044	2
HILL JOHN S	CPT	0-0376403	0244	2
HILL JOHN W	CPT	0-0173816	0852	3
HILL KENNETH F	CPT	0-1290245	0947	2
HILL LEE U	LTC	0-1573278	0157	1
HILL LINFORD E	LTC	0-0451481	0457	1
HILL LLOYD M	1LT	0-1309930	0845	2
HILL LONNIE M	CPT	0-1897741	0462	1
HILL LOUIS A	LTC	0-0253101	1058	3
HILL MARION E	MAJ	0-1341786	0463	1
HILL NUGENT	CPT	0-0178149	0654	3
HILL OGDEN H	CPT	0-0377524	0446	2
HILL OLAN F	2LT	0-2012518	0746	2
HILL ORVILLE C	MAJ	0-0503576	0955	1
HILL OTHO R	COL	0-0318401	0768	3
HILL RALPH L JR	LTC	0-0273602	0268	3
HILL RALPH O	CPT	0-0354465	0850	2
HILL RAY E JR	CPT	0-1693643	0668	1
HILL RAYMOND H	MAJ	0-0299932	1044	2
HILL RAYMOND JR	MAJ	0-1305926	0758	1
HILL RICHARD V	CPT	0-1314618	0747	2
HILL ROBERT A	COL	0-0232567	1056	3
HILL ROBERT A	LTC	0-1100147	0662	1
HILL ROBERT L	COL	0-0319333	1059	3
HILL ROBERT L	MAJ	0-1118590	0664	1
HILL ROBERT N	COL	0-0243571	0763	3
HILL ROBERT W	1LT	0-1058024	1145	2
HILL ROY A	MAJ	0-0387054	0460	1
HILL ROYAL H	1LT	0-1958099	0346	2
HILL RUBY E	MAJ	N-0763533	1266	1
HILL SAMUEL D	LTC	0-0295473	1263	3
HILL SAMUEL P JR	MAJ	0-1303504	0263	1
HILL THOMAS G	MAJ	0-1640551	0163	1
HILL THOMAS P	LTC	0-0263038	0962	3
HILL URAD G	1LT	0-1325789	1046	2
HILL VANCE	CW2	W-2205689	0762	1
HILL VANCE V JR	LTC	0-0422518	1262	1
HILL VERNON	CPT	0-1012719	0148	2
HILL WALTER B	CPT	0-0416593	1145	2
HILL WALTER S	LTC	0-0186079	0554	3
HILL WARREN A	MAJ	0-0259303	0767	3
HILL WARREN W	MAJ	0-0335777	0845	2
HILL WAYNE	CPT	0-0182154	0731	1
HILL WETZEL	1LT	0-0451118	0949	1
HILL WILLIAM A	COL	0-0264435	1164	3
HILL WILLIAM A	CW4	W-2003646	0668	3
HILL WILLIAM A JR	CPT	0-0968435	0660	1
HILL WILLIAM F	CPT	0-0174341	1056	3
HILL WILLIAM G	CPT	0-1012291	0246	2
HILL WILLIAM H	LTC	0-0319653	0454	1
HILL WILLIAM L	1LT	0-0490975	1047	1
HILL WILLIAM L	MAJ	0-0887896	1060	1

NAME	GRADE	SVC NO	DATE RET MO YR	RET CODE
HILL WILLIAM M	LTC	0-0333298	0959	3
HILL WILLIAM R	1LT	0-0497379	0151	1
HILL WILLIAM T	LTC	0-0884917	0954	1
HILLABRANT WALTER J	LTC	0-0444649	0768	1
HILLARD THOMAS R	COL	0-0371060	0763	1
HILLARD WILLIAM J	LTC	0-1583109	0561	1
HILLARY MARK	LTC	0-0182696	1047	2
HILLEARY EARL W	CW2	W-2145860	0962	1
HILLEBERT LAWRENCE	CPT	0-1636043	0653	2
HILLEGAS LARRY G	1LT	0-5258742	0968	2
HILLEN JEANNE B	MAJ	N-0737980	0767	1
HILLER ELMER C	CW2	W-2153255	0958	1
HILLER JOHN A	MAJ	0-0125935	0656	3
HILLER JOHN W	2LT	0-1291992	0455	1
HILLER LA MOINE E	1LT	0-0360183	1143	2
HILLER MAURICE L	LTC	0-0270079	0468	3
HILLER ROBERT I	MAJ	0-0483337	1143	2
HILLER WILLIAM L	CPT	0-0299091	0945	2
HILLERY ARTHUR M JR	COL	0-0410116	1167	1
HILLEY LARRY T	CW3	W-2147758	0157	1
HILLEY PAUL E	1LT	0-2005707	1047	2
HILLHOUSE DOUGLAS P	LTC	0-1038401	0862	1
HILLIARD ALBERT L	COL	0-0336824	0267	3
HILLIARD CHARLES N	WO1	W-2103008	1046	2
HILLIARD CLARK	LTC	0-1314781	0762	1
HILLIARD CLAUDE R	CW2	W-2148623	0262	1
HILLIARD EMERSON E	MAJ	0-1010578	0261	1
HILLIARD EVELYN B	1LT	N-0741948	0346	1
HILLIARD JOHN H	CW3	W-2153256	1262	1
HILLIARD JOHN T	MAJ	0-1553470	0462	1
HILLIARD LEON W	COL	0-0212170	1052	3
HILLIARD MILORED A	CPT	N-0733780	0847	1
HILLIARD OLEN	MAJ	0-0451579	0657	1
HILLIARD PAUL	2LT	0-1324839	1144	2
HILLIARD RUSSELL E	MAJ	0-0185819	0945	2
HILLIARD SHERMAN E	1LT	0-0491484	1046	1
HILLIARD SPENCER G	LTC	0-0212354	1061	3
HILLIARD TEMPLE W JR	MAJ	0-0440741	0350	2
HILLIARD WILLIAM F	CW2	W-2206941	0466	1
HILLIER ERNEST H	CPT	0-0279344	0267	3
HILLIKER HERBERT G	1LT	0-1303728	0346	2
HILLIN ROY P JR	CW3	W-2205131	0268	1
HILLIS GEORGE W	LTC	0-0257108	1264	3
HILLIS HUGH W	LTC	0-0271137	0368	3
HILLIS LLOYD E JR	CW2	W-2210998	0367	1
HILLIS ROBERT O	COL	0-0922216	0664	2
HILLIS ROBERT W	MAJ	0-0303692	1167	3
HILLIS WILLIAM C	MAJ	0-0450288	0556	1
HILLMAN ARTHUR F	CW3	W-2135686	0860	1
HILLMAN ENDOCEN H	LTC	0-0177701	0660	3
HILLMAN HAROLD	CW3	W-2116659	1262	1
HILLMAN JIMMYE S	1LT	0-0446745	0545	2
HILLMAN JOHN A JR	CW4	W-2144520	0258	1
HILLMAN LEROY R	1LT	0-1549736	1056	2
HILLMAN LEWIS C	LTC	0-1292522	0966	1
HILLMAN WILLIAM O	COL	0-0258906	0466	3
HILLMON KENNETH K	WO1	W-2104144	0951	1
HILLMON WILLIAM R	MAJ	0-1637675	0656	1
HILLS LYMAN W	1LT	0-0129854	0354	3
HILLS RALPH W	1LT	0-1307015	0645	2
HILLSDALE CHARLES J	LTC	0-1013367	0866	2
HILLSMAN MARVIN C	COL	0-0269399	0957	2
HILLY ARTHUR J	CPT	0-1320320	1052	2
HILLYER JUSTIN D	LTC	0-0243510	0761	3
HILMES EDWARD R JR	LTC	0-0294391	0268	3
HILPERT JOSEPH	LTC	0-2020914	0868	1
HILSHER JOHN M	COL	0-0241435	0463	3
HILT PAUL S	CPT	0-0503073	1049	1
HILTGEN WILLIAM F	CW4	W-2143392	0867	2
HILTNER JEROME M	1LT	0-1299564	1044	2
HILTON ARTHUR W	CW4	W-2142395	0456	1
HILTON EARL L	CPT	0-0240440	0646	2
HILTON ELMER R	MAJ	0-0450251	0154	1
HILTON EUGENE W	LTC	0-0200623	0659	2
HILTON GEORGE W JR	CW4	W-2114297	0359	1

NAME	GRADE	SVC NO	DATE RET MO YR	RET CODE
HILTON HAROLD B	LTC	0-0235847	0847	1
HILTON HENRY F	CPT	0-1287176	1045	2
HILTON JAMES W	COL	0-0266360	0860	3
HILTON JOHN F	CPT	0-0451610	0245	2
HILTON RAY	COL	0-0328146	1266	1
HILTON WILLIAM W	LTC	0-0397792	0946	2
HILTY CHARLES F	LTC	0-0372447	0763	1
HILTY DONALD F	CPT	0-1693759	1044	2
HILTY ROBERT L	LTC	0-0367881	0861	1
HILTZ ROBERT G	1LT	0-1177470	0145	2
HIME LESLIE J	MAJ	0-0996796	0265	1
HIMELSTEIN LOUIS	LTC	0-0251770	0848	2
HIMEON HAROLD T	LTC	0-0263980	0152	3
HIMES CHESTER D JR	LTC	0-1541070	1066	1
HIMES DELBERT R	MAJ	0-1642973	0361	1
HIMES JACK E	MAJ	0-2210180	0665	1
HIMES JOHN R	LTC	0-0516265	0663	1
HIMES ROBERT A	MAJ	0-1299886	0164	1
HIMMELE IRVIN H	COL	0-0217860	1163	3
HIMMELMAN GEORGE R	LTC	0-0259977	0555	3
HIMMELREICH HOWARD W	CW4	W-2134664	1163	1
HIMMELRIGHT JOHN R	LTC	0-1100148	1060	1
HINAMON HUBERT B	MAJ	0-0274539	0950	1
HINAJ JOSEPH	1LT	0-0244389	1153	3
HINCH RICHARD L JR	LTC	0-0195009	0962	3
HINCHBERGER C C	MAJ	0-0247280	0346	2
HINCHBERGER PAUL A	CPT	0-0356587	0145	2
HINCHEY JAMES J	CW2	W-2205628	0262	1
HINCHLIFFE ARTHUR J	CPT	0-0303742	0545	2
HINCKLEY BENJAMIN H	1LT	0-1289864	0145	2
HINCKLEY CHARLES R	LTC	0-0274600	1055	3
HINCKLEY JAMES L	LTC	0-0363240	0666	3
HINCKLEY JOHN B	LTC	0-1636045	0966	3
HINCKLEY MARY J	1LT	N-0756834	0646	1
HINCKLEY ROBERT C	COL	0-0321742	1061	1
HINCKLEY ROBERT W	1LT	0-1303505	0346	2
HINCKLEY WILLIAM G	COL	0-0229918	0662	3
HINDEN EARL L	COL	0-0225783	0465	3
HINDEN ELIZABETH	1LT	N-0725827	0246	1
HINDIN HERMAN	MAJ	0-1035819	0659	2
HINDIN HERMAN	CPT	0-1702466	0945	2
HINDLEY CECIL J	CPT	0-1180541	0646	2
HINDLEY FREDERICK	LTC	0-0511533	1064	2
HINDMAN CURTIS O	MAJ	0-1284141	0761	1
HINDMAN HUBERT	MAJ	0-1577323	0457	1
HINDS BEN M	CW4	W-2148692	0957	1
HINDS GARLAND C	MAJ	0-1104850	0161	1
HINDS HOWARD K	1LT	0-1325089	1162	1
HINDS NORVIL T	LTC	0-0327014	0557	3
HINDS PAUL L	CW3	W-2149258	0267	1
HINDS W D	MAJ	0-5301759	1168	1
HINDS WARREN F	MAJ	0-0425323	0459	1
HINDS WILLIAM T	CW2	W-2145886	0761	1
HINE BUTLER P JR	LTC	0-2205413	1168	1
HINELINE EDWIN C	LTC	0-0377726	1162	1
HINEMAN RICHARD E	LTC	0-1765094	0167	1
HINENBURG LOUIS	CPT	0-1560174	0555	2
HINER GLENN L	LTC	0-1313406	0662	2
HINES CAROL C	COL	0-0336885	1059	1
HINES CHARLES G	CW3	W-2004341	1066	3
HINES EDWARD G	MAJ	0-1589269	0461	1
HINES EDWARD L	1LT	0-1949560	0661	1
HINES EMMETT L III	LTC	0-1172907	1266	1
HINES FLOYD W	COL	0-0260638	0866	3
HINES FRANK M	LTC	0-0373782	0764	1
HINES GAIL W	LTC	0-0516409	0964	3
HINES GEORGE P	CPT	0-0441384	1045	2
HINES HORACE H	1LT	0-0450448	0645	2
HINES HUBERT C	1LT	0-0494072	0148	1
HINES JOSEPH F	LTC	0-0253987	1161	3
HINES LUCY P	CPT	N-0761085	0458	2
HINES MERRILL O	CPT	0-0475643	1144	2
HINES NICHOLAS J	MAJ	0-1172908	0761	1
HINES NORMAN F	COL	0-0183470	0262	1
HINES PERCY A	LTC	0-2034536	0660	1

NAME	GRADE	SVC NO	DATE RET MO YR	RET CODE
HINES RALPH F	MAJ	0-1018863	0664	2
HINES RICHARD D	CW2	W-2142928	0554	1
HINES ROBERT T	COL	0-0180114	1148	3
HINES TED W	CPT	0-1997550	0861	1
HINES THOMAS G	MAJ	0-1637847	0859	1
HINES VANCE V	LTC	0-0442038	0664	1
HINES WALTER W	CW4	W-2144285	0267	1
HINES WILLIS V	LTC	0-0414751	0568	3
HINESLEY DALE F	CPT	0-0488342	0546	2
HINESLEY JOSEPH D	MAJ	0-1556599	0262	2
HINEY MONROE N	MAJ	0-0370855	0949	1
HINGERTY OTIS J JR	CW3	W-2143188	0966	1
HINGLE JULES L	2LT	0-1822273	0344	2
HINISH JOHN F JR	2LT	0-1316553	0445	2
HINKEL JOHN V	COL	0-0270141	1266	3
HINKEL JOSEPH L	LTC	0-1030041	0557	1
HINKLE ELIZABETH	1LT	N-0776231	1045	1
HINKLE GEORGE R	CPT	0-0488431	0847	1
HINKLE HENRY L	COL	0-0312474	0365	3
HINKLE JOHNNIE J	CW3	W-2146990	0762	1
HINKLE KENNETH L	COL	0-0269220	0464	3
HINKLE OSCAR	LTC	0-0496934	0255	1
HINKLE WALTER J	MAJ	0-0375613	0346	2
HINKLE WILBUR E	MAJ	0-0450893	1055	1
HINKLE WILLIAM A	CPT	0-0495922	1151	1
HINKLEY FRANK R	COL	0-0272047	0159	1
HINKLEY HAROLD R	MAJ	0-1821585	0560	1
HINKLEY OLIN T	COL	0-0476454	0854	1
HINKO EDWARD N	1LT	0-0345518	0742	2
HINKSON DEHAVEN	LTC	0-0142156	1051	3
HINKSON EDWARD D	LTC	0-1286650	0463	1
HINKSON HAROLD M JR	2LT	0-0495576	1043	2
HINMAN ALANSON F	MAJ	0-0287271	0166	3
HINMAN CLIFTON F	CPT	0-0216384	1153	3
HINMAN GEORGE W JR	COL	0-0220552	0653	3
HINMAN GERALD H	CPT	0-0504291	0954	1
HINMAN HUBERT H	CW3	W-2205135	0265	1
HINMAN PAUL W JR	LTC	0-1037534	1061	1
HINNANT AUGUSTUS R	CPT	0-1533579	1053	2
HINNER RALPH E	LTC	0-0509496	1054	1
HINO KENNETH S	MAJ	0-0242002	0264	1
HINOJOSA JUAN H	LTC	0-0370944	0367	3
HINOTE RUSSELL C	COL	0-0217861	0355	1
HINRICHSEN JOHN C	MAJ	0-0961521	1163	1
HINRICHSEN ROBERT L	CW3	W-2144919	1056	1
HINSEY LOUIS F	LTC	0-0347295	0161	1
HINSHAW ALFRED H	COL	0-0334295	0967	3
HINSHAW JACOB R	MAJ	0-0231977	0145	2
HINSON ARTHUR	LTC	0-0384891	1266	3
HINSON BENJAMIN F	MAJ	0-0108383	0938	1
HINSON CHARLES F	LTC	0-1288667	0462	1
HINSON CLYDE A	CW4	W-2143574	0661	1
HINSON ELVIS R	1LT	0-0366165	1043	2
HINSON ERNEST R	2LT	0-1999121	0845	2
HINSON JESSE J	COL	0-0245719	1060	3
HINSON LUTHER O	COL	0-0260353	0561	1
HINSON MARVIN G	MAJ	0-1179891	0265	1
HINSON MASON W	LTC	0-1045775	1266	1
HINSON ROBERT J	2LT	0-1325569	0545	2
HINSON ROBERT L	MAJ	0-0286809	0868	3
HINSON SEDGIE V	MAJ	0-0395714	0746	2
HINTERMISTER F A	MAJ	0-0183040	0550	2
HINTON ANDREW H	LTC	0-0312681	1264	3
HINTON EARL D	MAJ	0-1546650	0258	2
HINTON EDGAR A	LTC	0-1647951	0863	1
HINTON HENRY W	MAJ	0-0249152	0866	3
HINTON HERMAN C	MAJ	0-0473274	1264	1
HINTON JOHN JR	LTC	0-1641393	0463	1
HINTON JOSEPH F	LTC	0-0332299	0665	3
HINTON PUGH H	MAJ	0-0979935	0961	1
HINTON ROBERT L	CW4	W-2141585	0559	1
HINTON WALLACE R	MAJ	0-1688781	0265	1
HINTZ WARREN L	LTC	0-1052815	0165	1
HINTZ WILLIAM F	LTC	0-1316755	1262	1
HINTZ WILLIS A	MAJ	0-1336912	0763	1

NAME	GRADE	SVC NO	DATE RET MO YR	RET CODE
HINUEHER ROBART C	1LT	0-1286487	0145	2
HINYARD JAMES N	COL	0-0267421	1267	3
HINZ ROBERT H	CPT	0-0370932	0745	2
HINZ WALTER H	LTC	0-0244191	0862	3
HIOTT ROY	LTC	0-0271062	0261	1
HIPKINS OTHO F	MAJ	0-0912356	0847	2
HIPP DAVID W	CW3	W-2146894	0765	1
HIPP EDWARD B	CPT	0-1319742	0147	2
HIPP HAROLD W	LTC	0-1573867	0860	1
HIPP WILLIAM N	MAJ	0-1013181	0364	1
HIPPEY MARGARET	LTC	N-0722948	1066	3
HIPPLE JAMES B	COL	0-0265951	0263	3
HIPPLE JAMES W	LTC	0-0263182	0466	3
HIPPS BUFORD L	CPT	0-1317166	0854	2
HIPPS JUANITA R	LTC	N-0702902	0846	1
HIPSCHMAN IRVING S	1LT	0-1280759	0646	2
HIPSEN JOHN C	MAJ	0-1173644	0261	1
HIRABAYASHI TAKEO	MAJ	0-1899430	0162	1
HIRAI ERNEST	MAJ	0-0964947	0964	1
HIRANO ROY M	LTC	0-0425914	0467	1
HIRD THOMAS B	CPT	0-0925097	0448	2
HIRKO GEORGE J JR	LTC	0-1318432	0361	1
HIRONAKA MASAO F	CW2	W-2215064	0568	2
HIRONS KENNETH W	CPT	0-1041361	0748	2
HIRSCH BERTRAM H	COL	0-0269771	0868	3
HIRSCH CARL P	MAJ	0-0240896	1063	3
HIRSCH CONRAD G	LTC	0-0374591	1161	2
HIRSCH DONALD A	LTC	0-0309553	1264	3
HIRSCH GEORGE O	COL	0-0347286	0164	3
HIRSCH GUS J	LTC	0-1592927	1162	1
HIRSCH HARRY A	LTC	0-0207095	0446	2
HIRSCH LEO	MAJ	0-1314633	0162	1
HIRSCH OSCAR G	MAJ	0-1010709	0265	1
HIRSCH RICHARD C	MAJ	0-1111667	0161	1
HIRSCH SAMUEL	1LT	0-1017201	0346	2
HIRSCH SIDNEY	1LT	0-4000392	0355	2
HIRSCH STANLEY C	MAJ	0-1280809	1157	1
HIRSCH VICTOR H	MAJ	0-0150234	0247	1
HIRSCH WILLIAM L	MAJ	0-0981855	1264	1
HIRSCHBERG MICHAEL M	1LT	0-1934927	0354	2
HIRSCHLER RICHARD J	CW3	W-2152793	0464	1
HIRSCHMAN LOUIS J	LTC	0-0168340	0648	3
HIRSCHMAN RAYMOND S	MAJ	0-1170416	1266	1
HIRSCHOWITZ SIMON J	CW4	W-2109995	1155	1
HIRSCHY IRVIN A	COL	0-0210460	0854	1
HIRSCHY JAMES B	MAJ	0-1637681	1060	1
HIRSCHY LUTHER C	MAJ	0-1499130	0161	1
HIRSH BERNARD S	2LT	0-1588640	1044	2
HIRSH CLARENCE	MAJ	0-0228949	0365	3
HIRSH HARRY A	LTC	0-1316505	1062	1
HIRSHFIELD HOWARD A	1LT	0-1589906	0946	2
HIRT ARTHUR D	COL	0-0274797	0966	3
HIRT JAMES R	LTC	0-0288629	0965	3
HIRT RICHARD C	CPT	0-1287714	0246	2
HIRTH CARL E	LTC	0-1822980	0168	1
HISAW BOBBIE L	CPT	0-2009407	0455	1
HISAW LUTHER G	CW2	W-2151105	0960	1
HISCOCK IRA V	COL	0-0170951	0552	3
HISE KENNETH W	MAJ	0-1913305	0967	1
HISER CLEM C	MAJ	0-0220859	0755	3
HISEY ROBERT G	CPT	0-1011073	0545	2
HISLE WILLIAM J	CW3	W-2144963	0764	2
HISS ALEXANDER	WO1	W-2135555	0246	2
HISSIGER HENRY L	LTC	0-0233736	0946	2
HISSONG JAMES S	CPT	0-0324165	0647	1
HITA VICENTE JR	LTC	0-0291062	0761	3
HITCH RICHARD J	MAJ	0-0248094	0966	3
HITCH ROBERT A	COL	0-0288190	0466	3
HITCH WILLIAM H JR	MAJ	0-0977556	0764	1
HITCHCOCK CLARENCE J	LTC	0-0275581	0763	3
HITCHCOCK DONALD G	MAJ	0-0885659	0261	1
HITCHCOCK EDWARD G	LTC	0-0259440	0466	3
HITCHCOCK FRANK D	LTC	0-0270138	0468	3
HITCHCOCK GEORGE P	COL	0-0181803	0462	3
HITCHCOCK LAWRENCE S	COL	0-0132920	0958	3

NAME	GRADE	SVC NO	DATE RET MO YR	RET CODE
HITCHCOCK LLYOD H	CW2	W-2152625	0161	1
HITCHCOCK LYMAN H	LTC	0-0229226	0563	3
HITCHCOCK ROBINSON	B G	0-0309266	0558	3
HITCHCOCK RUSSELL W	LTC	0-0269313	0359	1
HITCHCOCK WILLIAM L	CPT	0-0513503	0247	2
HITCHCOX GEORGE H	CPT	0-0253612	1046	2
HITCHINGS AULBRY C	MAJ	0-1298230	0461	1
HITCHNER CHARLES E	CW2	W-2101843	0646	1
HITCHNER RICHARD C	1LT	0-1014664	0745	2
HITE DOROTHY E	2LT	N-0783256	1043	1
HITE HENRY A	MAJ	0-1303729	0765	1
HITE JOSEPH N JR	MAJ	0-1648272	0559	1
HITSELBERGER JAMES F	LTC	0-0264444	1057	1
HITT ARNOLD D	COL	0-0129310	1055	3
HITT JAMES H	2LT	0-2009766	1045	2
HITTLE KENNETH I	LTC	0-0289522	0864	3
HITZEL JOSEPH M JR	LTC	0-0922544	0665	3
HITZEL RAYMOND C	2LT	0-0558521	0145	2
HITZGES EMMETT R	CW2	W-2214534	0966	1
HIVELY HARLAN P	CPT	0-0985631	0758	1
HIVELY JAMES R	CPT	0-1725517	1046	2
HIVELY SHERMAN E	LTC	0-0305723	0246	2
HIX CLAY W	MAJ	0-1173288	0462	2
HIX JOHN C	LTC	0-1114552	0768	1
HIX WILLIAM J	LTC	0-1179894	0463	1
HIX WILLIS R	MAJ	0-5304116	0868	1
HIXON JOHN L	CPT	0-1303341	0747	2
HIXON WALLACE C	CPT	0-0161895	1153	3
HIXSON CHARLES H	CPT	0-1823872	0346	2
HIXSON CLAYTON H	LTC	0-0238973	0362	3
HIZAR DONALD A	CPT	0-0545809	0965	1
HJALMARSON DOPI	LTC	0-0331841	0353	2
HJELMSTAD LODIE O	MAJ	0-1181303	1062	1
HJELMSTROM ANDREW F	CPT	0-0283654	0962	1
HJELT GEORGE B	CW3	W-2150550	0464	1
HJELTNESS MELVIN J	MAJ	0-1291641	1046	2
HLAD RUDOLPH E	2LT	0-1031408	0943	2
HLADIK CHARLES A	CW2	W-2000217	0145	2
HLADKY FRANK P	LTC	0-0415733	1165	3
HLAVAC ALBERT	LTC	0-0136792	0648	3
HOADLEY MAX L	1LT	0-1296210	1044	2
HOAG EDITH A	2LT	N-0745157	0545	1
HOAG GEORGE W	MAJ	0-1548840	0762	1
HOAG JAMES F	LTC	0-1582373	0363	2
HOAG JAMES H JR	CW2	RW-2208479	0465	1
HOAG MEREDITH W	2LT	0-1649161	1045	2
HOAG THOMAS R	COL	0-0334350	0561	1
HOAG VICTOR R	COL	0-0125411	0555	3
HOAG WILLIAM	1LT	0-0442106	104N	2
HOAGLAND CARROLL H	LTC	0-0414713	0760	1
HOAGLAND EARNEST P	MAJ	0-0479404	0154	1
HOAGLAND ELIZABETH	MAJ	L-1010068	1063	1
HOAGLAND KENNETH C	CPT	0-0526403	0246	2
HOAGLAND MELVIN J	1LT	0-1306097	0750	2
HOAGLAND ROGER	1LT	0-0335354	0765	3
HOALT MARRIA M	MAJ	M-0002383	0963	1
HOAR JOHN	MAJ	0-0502782	0447	2
HOAR JOHN B JR	COL	0-0276599	0761	1
HOAR JOHN W	LTC	0-0398787	0166	1
HOAR RALPH D	CPT	0-0277537	0854	3
HOAR WALTER G	COL	0-0309682	0146	2
HOARD JAMES L	CPT	0-0299350	0267	1
HOBAN EUGENE F	CPT	0-0491965	1047	1
HOBAN THOMAS L	B G	0-0176644	1053	3
HOBAN VERN J	CPT	0-0517638	0548	1
HOBART JAMES H	1LT	0-1316048	1144	2
HOBBIE RICHARD M	LTC	0-0442738	0368	3
HOBBS CARL A	CPT	0-1291820	1145	2
HOBBS CREIGHTON	CW2	W-3430180	0267	1
HOBBS EARL B	1LT	0-1294473	1153	1
HOBBS EDWIN G	MAJ	0-0224992	0758	3
HOBBS EDWIN P	CW3	W-2152217	0665	1
HOBBS EUGENE S	MAJ	0-1056120	1262	1
HOBBS EVERETT G	CPT	0-0393019	0146	2
HOBBS FRANK C	MAJ	0-0432946	0146	2

NAME	GRADE	SVC NO	DATE RET MO YR	RET CODE
HOBBS FRANK J	COL	0-0200955	0961	3
HOBBS HENRY R	CW3	W-2152190	0762	1
HOBBS HIBBERT	MAJ	0-1017936	0365	1
HOBBS J BRYAN	COL	0-0444332	1146	2
HOBBS JOHN O JR	COL	0-0245440	0167	3
HOBBS MARIAN	1LT	L-0701581	0746	2
HOBBS NORMAN H	CW4	W-2110460	0556	1
HOBBS RICHARD H	COL	0-0156169	1262	3
HOBBS ROBERT E	LTC	0-0466055	0346	2
HOBBS ROSSITER H	COL	0-0202355	1058	3
HOBBS STANLEY C	MAJ	0-2202817	0667	1
HOBBS VICTOR H	1LT	0-2055132	1148	1
HOBBS WILBUR G	MAJ	0-0887555	0662	1
HOBBS WILLIAM C	LTC	0-0286467	0959	1
HOBBS WILLIAM H	MAJ	0-0219107	0352	3
HOBBS WOODROW H	LTC	0-1030676	1264	1
HOBBY RICHARD D	MAJ	0-1640557	0162	1
HOBER ANTHONY R	LTC	0-1050720	0763	1
HOBER ISABELLE V	1LT	N-0751897	0546	1
HOBERG HENRY G	LTC	0-0142283	0154	3
HOBERG INGEMAR E	COL	0-0219055	1263	3
HOBERG INGOMAR A	LTC	0-0201645	1160	3
HOBERG WILBUR	CPT	0-1799141	0557	1
HOBGOOD RICHARD G	CPT	0-1776042	0450	2
HOBIN FRED J	CW3	W-2150319	0363	1
HOBLITZELL ALAN P	COL	0-0150311	0951	3
HOBSON ALLEN R	2LT	0-1797648	0245	2
HOBSON STANLEY L	CW3	RW-2152778	1167	1
HOBSON WALTER	LTC	0-0314006	0261	1
HOBSON WILLIAM S	CPT	0-1798734	1164	1
HOBSON WINFRED P	CPT	0-2011624	1060	1
HOCHBERG CLIFFORD M	MAJ	0-1112219	1164	1
HOCHBERG PAUL P	CPT	0-0504503	0246	2
HOCKE MERVIN P	MAJ	0-1176060	0561	1
HOCKEBORN CHESTER F	MAJ	0-1050303	0762	1
HOCKENBEAMER EMBREE	LTC	0-0224980	1163	3
HOCKENBERRY E D	COL	0-0269635	0947	2
HOCKENBERRY HAROLD L	LTC	0-1114167	1264	1
HOCKER AUGUSTUS S	COL	0-0266180	1158	1
HOCKETT KENNETH J	MAJ	0-0450898	0459	1
HOCKING ALBERT W	MAJ	0-0196378	0563	3
HOCKLANDER CECIL W	CPT	0-1297368	0247	2
HOCKMAN JOHN K	CPT	0-2055528	0756	1
HOCKMAN OLIVER M	MAJ	0-0992716	0662	1
HOCUTT WRENCHER H	CW3	W-2210164	0168	1
HODAPP RAYMOND J	LTC	0-0249215	0446	2
HODEN BENJAMIN R	1LT	0-1113258	0745	2
HODES WILLIAM A	1LT	0-0917520	0744	2
HODGDON GEORGE E	1LT	0-1285941	0745	2
HODGE CHARLES J	B G	0-0332486	0967	3
HODGE CLAUDE W	CPT	0-0116912	0349	3
HODGE FREDERIC W	COL	0-0241338	1059	1
HODGE GEORGE J	LTC	0-0337849	0966	3
HODGE GERALD O	B G	0-0253172	0760	3
HODGE NORMAN L	CW3	W-2145093	0864	1
HODGE PAT E	MAJ	0-0309964	0245	2
HODGE ROY B	MAJ	0-2289396	0263	1
HODGE SAMUEL R	1LT	0-1913750	1146	1
HODGE WALTER	MAJ	0-2006425	1263	1
HODGES ALLEN T JR	LTC	0-0493189	0465	1
HODGES BILLY M	MAJ	0-4034476	1068	1
HODGES BURGESS G	COL	0-1290070	0561	1
HODGES CLARENCE W	LTC	0-0360647	0955	1
HODGES CLAUDE A	MAJ	0-0250609	1266	3
HODGES DALE F	MAJ	0-1052393	0958	1
HODGES DAN A	LTC	0-0293144	0668	3
HODGES DANIEL W	MAJ	0-0382313	1153	1
HODGES DEAN M	2LT	0-0520423	0145	2
HODGES DUNCAN	COL	0-0449647	0956	3
HODGES GEORGE H	CPT	0-0499451	1154	1
HODGES GEORGE H JR	COL	0-0272540	0268	3
HODGES GORDON S	CPT	0-1167032	0953	2
HODGES HAROLD W	CW3	W-2150148	0865	1
HODGES HARRY D	1LT	0-1598757	0752	2
HODGES HARRY W	CPT	0-1535476	0449	2

NAME	GRADE	SVC NO	DATE RET MO YR	RET CODE
HODGES HARRY V	MAJ	0-1299045	0766	1
HODGES JAMES F	2LT	0-1881458	1052	3
HODGES JESSE W	MAJ	0-1289734	0357	1
HODGES JESSIE A	MAJ	0-5405220	0968	1
HODGES JOHN B	CPT	0-4005448	0866	1
HODGES LA VERN L	LTC	0-1293591	0168	3
HODGES LILLIE M F	CPT	N-0760526	0947	1
HODGES MARK L	MAJ	0-0406106	0247	2
HODGES MILLARD B	LTC	0-0389911	0867	3
HODGES RALPH O	LTC	0-0236762	0765	3
HODGES RAYMOND E	WO1	W-2149973	0753	1
HODGES ROBERT M	MAJ	0-0967100	1267	1
HODGES WILLIAM H	LTC	0-0302116	0660	1
HODGIN JOHN L	LTC	0-0116813	0757	3
HODGIN NELSON C	LTC	0-1310444	1068	3
HODGKIN JOHN B JR	1LT	0-1591802	1045	2
HODGKINS EARL H	CW2	W-2150896	0862	1
HODGKINS HOWARD W	COL	0-0118559	0851	3
HODGKINS LAFOREST E	LTC	0-0538869	0565	3
HODGKINS LELAND M	CW4	W-2139849	0363	1
HODGKINS PIERCE N	MAJ	0-0126335	1151	3
HODGKINSON HENRY R	LTC	0-0273738	0557	1
HODGKINSON WILLIAM F	MAJ	0-0249930	0265	3
HODGKISS JOHN T	CPT	0-1633976	0250	1
HODGSON HAROLD B	CPT	0-0101277	1043	2
HODGSON JAMES F	COL	0-0146759	0254	3
HODGSON MELVIN E	LTC	0-0292197	1166	3
HODGSON RAY W	LTC	0-2036594	1262	1
HODGSON REGINALD M	COL	0-1574830	0765	1
HODNETT JOHN H	MAJ	0-2008394	1060	1
HODNETTE PAUL W	LTC	0-1307412	1262	1
HODSDON GEORGE M JR	CPT	0-0364572	0345	2
HODSHON PETER	2LT	0-1032531	0646	2
HODSON NEVILLE F	LTC	0-0313629	1045	2
HODSON RUSSEL L	CW3	W-2147852	0862	1
HODYKE STEPHEN S	MAJ	0-1796622	0561	1
HOECHSTETTER STANTON	LTC	0-0251872	0464	3
HOEFELMEYER HENRY L	CPT	0-0568642	1147	2
HOEFER CARL F	CPT	0-0277629	0854	3
HOEFER HAROLD W	CPT	0-0307617	0444	2
HOEFFEL CARL G	MAJ	0-0326770	0168	3
HOEFFLIGER FRANCIS L	CW3	W-2147044	0260	1
HOEFGEN NELSON G	1LT	0-1018932	1145	2
HOEGH LEO A	COL	0-0258935	0468	3
HOEHLE ARMAND F	COL	0-0225855	0163	3
HOEHN MARTIN C	LTC	0-0438949	0462	1
HOEHN ROBERT G	MAJ	0-1290602	0864	1
HOEHNEN EUGENE O	CPT	0-0428644	0347	2
HOEING HARLEY T	CW3	W-2143495	0963	1
HOELLER FRANCIS R	CPT	0-0311148	0552	2
HOELSCHER FRANK J	1LT	0-0553376	1047	2
HOELSCHER LEO J	CPT	0-0502686	0746	1
HOENER IRWIN R	LTC	0-0343096	0653	2
HOENINGER CARL L	CW3	W-2146567	0763	1
HOENSHELL FRANCIS E	MAJ	0-1946292	1065	3
HOERGER WINFIELD S	LTC	0-0208297	0359	3
HOERNER EMIL	MAJ	0-0481887	0754	1
HOERNSCHEMEYER JOSEP	LTC	0-0248248	0462	3
HOESE WALTER F	CPT	0-5301618	0968	1
HOEY HARRISON	MAJ	0-2006232	0663	1
HOEY WILLIAM F JR	COL	0-0202517	0648	3
HOFACKER CARL F	CW2	W-2111197	1150	1
HOFER JOHN A	2LT	0-2006233	0461	1
HOFF ARTHUR P	MAJ	0-1045776	0966	1
HOFF CLYDE W	MAJ	0-1331947	0560	1
HOFF CORNELL L	CPT	0-1702442	1145	2
HOFF EDWARD A	CPT	0-1106207	0544	2
HOFF HERBERT	LTC	0-0531226	1063	1
HOFF IVAN R	LTC	0-1948758	1067	3
HOFF ROBERT J	LTC	0-1822798	0962	1
HOFF WILLIAM J	2LT	0-1583120	0844	2
HOFFAY MEREDITH F	LTC	0-1555404	0964	1
HOFFENBACHER W E	COL	0-0237540	0259	3
HOFFENBERG JACOB	MAJ	0-0920724	1045	2
HOFFER FREDERIC S JR	LTC	0-0283404	0668	3

NAME	GRADE	SVC NO	DATE RET MO YR	RET CODE
HOFF[illegible]	MAJ	[illegible]	[illegible]	3
HOFFMAN MARY [illegible]	[illegible]	[illegible]	[illegible]	[illegible]
HOFFMAN [illegible]	[illegible]	W-21[illegible]	[illegible]	1
[illegible]	[illegible]	[illegible]	[illegible]	[illegible]
HOFFMAN A[illegible]	MAJ	[illegible]	[illegible]	[illegible]
HOFFMAN [illegible]	[illegible]	[illegible]	[illegible]	[illegible]
HOFFMAN AL[illegible]	MAJ	[illegible]	[illegible]	[illegible]
HOFFMAN AL[illegible]	[illegible]	[illegible]	[illegible]	3
HOFFMAN AL[illegible] W	[illegible]	[illegible]	1061	3
HOFFMAN [illegible]	MAJ	[illegible]	[illegible]	3
HOFFMAN [illegible]	[illegible]	O-11[illegible]	[illegible]	1
HOFFMAN [illegible]	[illegible]	[illegible]	0561	1
HOFFMAN [illegible]	CPT	[illegible]	0758	2
HOFFMAN [illegible] N	LTC	O-1175815	0464	1
HOFFMAN [illegible]	LTC	O-0341[illegible]12	0559	3
HOFFMAN [illegible]	MAJ	O-2217005	0663	1
HOFFMAN [illegible]	1LT	O-1945506	1045	2
HOFFMAN FRANK [illegible]	CPT	O-0364311	0246	2
HOFFMAN FRANK [illegible]	MAJ	O-0188134	0546	2
HOFFMAN [illegible]	CW3	W-2211780	1164	1
HOFFMAN [illegible] N	MAJ	O-0916363	1063	3
HOFFMAN [illegible] W	LTC	O-1557730	0961	1
HOFFMAN GUSTAV	MAJ	O-0233702	0456	1
HOFFMAN HARRY [illegible] JR	1LT	O-0441261	1145	2
HOFFMAN HARRY W	LTC	O-1315446	0163	1
HOFFMAN HOMER [illegible]	MAJ	O-0266593	1057	3
HOFFMAN ISRAEL L	LTC	O-0335181	0666	3
HOFFMAN JACK [illegible]	LTC	O-0352411	0542	1
HOFFMAN JACK T	CW3	W-2143282	1167	1
HOFFMAN JACK W	CPT	O-2007294	0945	2
HOFFMAN JAMES F	MAJ	O-0270251	1058	3
HOFFMAN JAMES F	CPT	O-0373032	0945	2
HOFFMAN JAY H	CW2	W-2213701	1167	1
HOFFMAN JEAN M	CPT	N-0737769	0449	2
HOFFMAN JOHN C	COL	O-0220154	0157	3
HOFFMAN JOHN J	MAJ	O-0990615	0163	1
HOFFMAN JOHN J	MAJ	O-1000132	0453	1
HOFFMAN JOHN J	LTC	O-2288601	1267	1
HOFFMAN JOHN L	LTC	O-0266579	0668	3
HOFFMAN JOHN R	1LT	O-1010993	0646	2
HOFFMAN JOSEPH	LTC	O-0310727	0567	3
HOFFMAN JOSEPH A	CW2	W-2213087	0667	1
HOFFMAN LAWRENCE C	LTC	O-1229530	0457	1
HOFFMAN LEO L	COL	O-0246989	0167	3
HOFFMAN LLOYD H	MAJ	O-1101872	0861	1
HOFFMAN MARGARET R	1LT	L-0600027	0944	2
HOFFMAN MAX	1LT	O-1322027	0545	2
HOFFMAN MEREDITH F	CW3	W-2141782	0361	1
HOFFMAN MILTON S	LTC	O-0344155	0466	3
HOFFMAN MYRON P	MAJ	O-1112220	0559	1
HOFFMAN PHILIP	CPT	O-0513066	0145	2
HOFFMAN RALPH J	MAJ	O-1297036	0957	1
HOFFMAN RAYMOND H	LTC	O-0168935	0661	3
HOFFMAN RICHARD F	CW2	W-3430107	1267	1
HOFFMAN ROBERT F	2LT	O-1316049	0844	2
HOFFMAN ROBERT G	CW2	W-2214632	0467	1
HOFFMAN ROBERT H	MAJ	O-1051600	0459	1
HOFFMAN ROBERT L	LTC	O-0450449	0359	1
HOFFMAN ROBERT R	CPT	O-0221959	0554	3
HOFFMAN RUDOLPH	MAJ	O-0962109	1262	1
HOFFMAN SIDNEY	MAJ	O-1031219	0759	1
HOFFMAN SIDNEY D	LTC	O-0401949	0568	3
HOFFMAN VIOLA E	CPT	N-0759554	0746	1
HOFFMAN WALTER F	WO1	W-2141084	0949	2
HOFFMAN WESLEY G	CPT	O-1534757	0754	2
HOFFMAN WILLIAM A	MAJ	O-2034971	0662	1
HOFFMAN WILLIAM F	LTC	O-1314634	0864	1
HOFFMANN ARTHUR F	CPT	O-0325667	1144	2
HOFFMANN BURTON E F	LTC	O-0492868	0454	2
HOFFMANN CHARLES W	COL	O-0174036	0848	2
HOFFMANN EDWARD D	CPT	O-1039376	1063	1
HOFFMANN GEORGE A	LTC	O-0254804	0766	3
HOFFMANN GREGORY J	MAJ	O-1112221	0361	1
HOFFMANN HERMAN F	MAJ	O-0301224	0555	1
HOFFMANN JACQUES G	1LT	O-0991736	0255	2

NAME	GRADE	SVC NO	DATE RET MO YR	RET CODE
HOFFMANN [illegible] S	LTC	[illegible]	0163	3
HOFFMANN JULIAN P	LTC	O-2047360	1167	1
HOFFMANN [illegible] W	LTC	O-1117402	1062	1
HOFFMANN WILLIAM J	COL	O-0142237	0648	3
HOFF[illegible] ARTHUR P	1LT	O-1296021	114N	2
HOFF[illegible] WILLIAM [illegible]	LTC	O-0361169	0859	1
HOFFNAGLE IRVIN [illegible]	1LT	O-0904347	0345	2
HOFFNER BURTON P	CPT	O-5013078	0467	2
HOFFRATH JESSE S	LTC	O-0202713	0854	3
HOFFSTADT JOHN P	LTC	O-0264431	0742	2
HOFFSTATTER EDWARD W	LTC	O-0288518	0267	3
HOFMANN ADOLPH A	1LT	O-4009702	0962	2
HOFMANN GEORGE C	LTC	O-0328049	0265	3
HOFMANN JOSEPH E	LTC	O-0379857	0964	3
HOFNESS RUSSEL W	COL	O-0269175	1267	3
HOFSTETTER LOUIS G	COL	O-1546697	1068	1
HOGAN ALBERT M	LTC	O-1052002	0565	1
HOGAN ARTHUR J	LTC	O-0281793	1266	3
HOGAN CHARLES D	CW2	W-2152095	1060	1
HOGAN CHARLES E	COL	O-0415266	1061	1
HOGAN DANIEL J	LTC	O-1575364	1057	1
HOGAN DANIEL W	COL	O-0162772	0354	3
HOGAN EDGAR W	MAJ	O-1106823	0462	3
HOGAN EDWARD	CW3	W-2149114	0562	1
HOGAN EDWIN G	COL	O-0326768	0367	3
HOGAN ELTON R	LTC	O-0495606	1062	1
HOGAN GEORGE A	CPT	O-0176086	0355	3
HOGAN GEORGE J	CPT	O-0467336	0852	1
HOGAN GEORGE W SR	CW2	W-2151076	0163	1
HOGAN GERALD F	MAJ	O-2206089	0867	1
HOGAN HENRY J	1LT	O-1559089	0546	2
HOGAN JAMES F	1LT	O-1315689	1045	2
HOGAN JAMES H	LTC	O-0124705	0849	3
HOGAN JAMES L	1LT	O-1013552	0948	2
HOGAN JOHN J	LTC	O-0255669	0867	3
HOGAN JOHN J JR	MAJ	O-0370602	0768	3
HOGAN JOSEPH J JR	CW2	W-2148256	0461	1
HOGAN LULABEL S	1LT	N-0761184	104N	1
HOGAN MARY H	2LT	N-0728454	0644	1
HOGAN MICHAEL P	MAJ	O-1313522	0361	1
HOGAN RALPH W	CW3	W-2146043	1158	2
HOGAN ROBERT C	1LT	O-1825281	1045	2
HOGAN ROBERT D	MAJ	O-1575796	0464	1
HOGAN ROBERT L	MAJ	O-1341545	0561	1
HOGAN ROWE L	LTC	O-0314441	0261	2
HOGAN ROY E	LTC	O-0450287	0157	1
HOGAN THOMAS F JR	MAJ	O-0320741	0145	2
HOGAN THOMAS J	WO1	W-2120173	0958	1
HOGAN THOMAS J	CW3	W-3150436	0867	1
HOGAN WILLIAM R	2LT	O-1031641	1059	2
HOGAN WOODROW W	MAJ	O-1013800	1056	1
HOGBERG DAN A	1LT	O-1637689	0144	2
HOGE CHARLES S	LTC	O-1796280	0762	2
HOGE ELMER E	COL	O-0447872	0954	1
HOGE ROY D JR	LTC	O-0565667	1062	1
HOGEBOOM CORNELIUS	LTC	O-0249721	1065	3
HOGELAND LEONARD H	CPT	O-0508060	0653	1
HOGG ABNER G	CPT	O-1293253	1146	2
HOGG ALEXANDER JR	CPT	O-0563328	0549	2
HOGG BRUCE M	MAJ	O-0497094	0745	2
HOGG EDWARD J	LTC	O-0349524	0967	3
HOGG GEORGE B JR	MAJ	O-1945607	1265	3
HOGG HAROLD K	COL	O-0245634	1060	3
HOGG HIRAM JR	CPT	O-0182043	0654	3
HOGG JAMES B	CPT	O-0406966	0761	1
HOGG JOHN H	CPT	O-1548074	1045	2
HOGG JOHN T	CPT	O-0411799	0246	2
HOGG WILLIAM C	LTC	O-0320189	1061	3
HOGGAN MELVIN J	CPT	O-0278571	1044	2
HOGGAN WILFORD G	CW2	W-2146728	0661	1
HOGGE FRED M	MAJ	O-1925074	0367	1
HOGHAUG MAURICE A	COL	O-0310166	0964	3
HOGHAUG PHILIP A	CPT	O-0452490	0946	2
HOGLE ALBERT F	COL	O-0241918	0455	3
HOGLE JOHN R	CPT	O-1696808	0448	2

NAME	GRADE	SVC NO	DATE RET MO YR	RET CODE
[illegible]	CPT	[illegible]	[illegible]	1
HOGUE [illegible]	MAJ	[illegible]	[illegible]	1
HOGUE JOHN V	CW3	W-21[illegible]	[illegible]	1
HOGUE [illegible]	MAJ	[illegible]	[illegible]	2
HOGUE WILLIAM [illegible]	WO1	W-21[illegible]	[illegible]	1
HOHAM JOHN [illegible]	1LT	[illegible]	0658	2
HOHL JOHN W	MAJ	O-1013[illegible]	0361	1
HOHL ROBERT A	CW2	W-21[illegible]13	0562	1
HOHM FRANK J	CW3	W-2145311	0664	1
HOHMAN JOHN [illegible]	LTC	O-1011[illegible]	1162	1
HOHMANN BENJAMIN W	CPT	O-104[illegible]	0352	2
HOHN EUGENE B	LTC	O-2010864	0264	1
HOHNSTEIN CLAYTON J	1LT	O-0395[illegible]	0143	2
HO[illegible] EDMUND K	CPT	O-0242689	1059	3
HOISINGTON ROGER A	MAJ	O-0974941	1268	1
HOIVIK TONY H	CPT	O-0530539	0445	2
HOJNACKI WILLIAM J	MAJ	O-1297170	0658	1
HOKANSON DEAN T	LTC	O-0248757	0769	3
HOKE GEORGE A	CPT	O-0451853	1044	2
HOKE VERNON T	MAJ	O-1330172	0863	1
HOKENSON EDWARD D	CW2	W-2150765	0758	1
HOKENSON HARRY S	2LT	O-2017695	0746	2
HOLADAY BEN G	1LT	O-1233604	0745	2
HOLADAY MELVIN F	CPT	O-1014104	1163	1
HOLAHAN DANIEL P	1LT	O-1173291	0644	2
HOLAN MARIE E	2LT	N-0701143	0645	1
HOLANDA PEDRO P	WO1	W-2124051	0349	2
HOLANIK GEORGE V	MAJ	O-1284342	1158	1
HOLASEK RAFAEL F	1LT	O-1856804	1062	1
HOLBERT JAMES F	2LT	O-0108941	0425	1
HOLBERT RAY L	MAJ	O-1016078	0761	1
HOLBERT ROY G	MAJ	O-0113693	0352	3
HOLBERTON TERRY H	COL	O-0112652	0160	1
HOLBRITTER MILTON A	CW4	W-2129612	1167	1
HOLBROOK ARTHUR A	LTC	O-0470511	0246	2
HOLBROOK BERTHAL A	MAJ	O-0442369	0855	1
HOLBROOK CHARLES E	LTC	O-1108024	1062	1
HOLBROOK EDWIN C	CPT	O-0126340	1049	3
HOLBROOK FRANK M	MAJ	O-2000719	1060	1
HOLBROOK GEORGE M	CPT	O-1176670	0546	2
HOLBROOK GORDON R	CW2	W-2149206	1262	1
HOLBROOK GUERNIE	MAJ	O-2006453	0863	1
HOLBROOK HAROLD B	LTC	O-0213104	0762	3
HOLBROOK HORACE N	1LT	O-0386393	114N	2
HOLBROOK JOHN L	LTC	O-0225591	1062	3
HOLBROOK JOHN S	LTC	O-1169574	0662	1
HOLBROOK PAUL F	LTC	O-0171681	0246	2
HOLBROOK ROBERT E	MAJ	O-1913335	0968	1
HOLBROOK ROBERT W	LTC	O-1533591	0568	2
HOLBROOK SAMUEL S	CW3	W-2144808	0461	1
HOLBROOK WALTER C	1LT	O-0408698	0944	2
HOLBROOK WILLIAM	MAJ	O-1640562	0656	1
HOLBROOK WINIFRED V	1LT	N-0775312	0146	1
HOLCOMB FLOYD R	CPT	O-0298797	0644	2
HOLCOMB FREEHORN P	MAJ	O-0474574	0557	1
HOLCOMB GORDON V	COL	O-0224425	0964	3
HOLCOMB HARLEY J	LTC	O-0227244	0664	3
HOLCOMB HERBERT K	CPT	O-0889534	0849	1
HOLCOMB HOYT C	CPT	O-1289255	0945	2
HOLCOMB JOE A	1LT	O-0985436	0760	2
HOLCOMB LAMAR	MAJ	O-1335008	0160	1
HOLCOMB MARK E	COL	O-0344800	0767	3
HOLCOMB MERRITT R	LTC	O-1924585	0468	1
HOLCOMB MONROE F	CW2	W-2145450	0459	1
HOLCOMB RUSSELL F	COL	O-0290907	1061	3
HOLCOMB THOMAS H	MAJ	O-0965866	0862	1
HOLCOMBE MILBURNE L	LTC	O-1579798	0565	1
HOLCOMBE RUSS M	MAJ	O-0464157	0846	2
HOLCOMBE THEODORE G	COL	O-0172417	1058	3
HOLCOMBE THOMAS H	MAJ	O-1297037	0658	1
HOLCOMBE WILLIAM T	CW2	W-2152315	1263	1
HOLDE ERLING M	2LT	O-2053827	0245	2
HOLDEMAN BILLY F	CW3	W-2146717	0966	1
HOLDEN ALFRED W	CPT	O-0494105	0946	2
HOLDEN CHARLES A	COL	O-0173924	0648	3

NAME	GRADE	SVC NO	DATE RET MO YR	RET CODE
HOLDEN FRANCIS W JR	LTC	O-1183329	1262	1
HOLDEN FRANK H	COL	O-0112756	0447	2
HOLDEN HARMON	CPT	O-2912838	0258	1
HOLDEN HAR[illegible] F	COL	O-0199049	0956	3
HOLDEN JACKSON W	1LT	O-1631451	0847	2
HOLDEN MILES F	LTC	O-1065337	0859	1
HOLDEN [illegible]BERT R	MAJ	O-0285559	0268	1
HOLDEN TIMOTHY N	CPT	O-0213365	0950	3
HOLDER ALFRED [illegible]	CPT	O-1646039	0754	1
HOLDER ALPHA W	CW3	W-2149975	0164	1
HOLDER DANIEL F	2LT	O-1305266	0844	2
HOLDER EVERETT A	MAJ	O-1598758	0164	1
HOLDER HACE G	COL	O-0292689	0159	3
HOLDER JOHN C	LTC	O-0239600	1052	2
HOLDER LOUIS L	MAJ	O-2205109	0968	1
HOLDERER MADELINE	2LT	N-0700715	0436	1
HOLDERMAN WILLIAM F	LTC	O-1323928	0161	1
HOLDREN EDWARD A	MAJ	O-1534512	0359	1
HOLDRIDGE JOHN F	LTC	O-2021233	0267	1
HOLDSTOCK JAMES	COL	O-0257064	0663	3
HOLDSWORTH EDITH J	1LT	N-0735391	1144	1
HOLDSWORTH EDWARD H	COL	O-0332614	0459	1
HOLFORD LEWIS A	LTC	O-0474997	1048	1
HOLIEN GERALD M	CW3	W-2152237	0762	1
HOLIEN MAURICE J	LTC	O-1542282	1157	1
HOLINGER ERIC V	CPT	O-1649162	1162	2
HOLIWAY THOMAS C	CPT	O-0959410	0557	2
HOLK CHARLES	CPT	O-0498972	1145	1
HOLL CHARLES F	MAJ	O-1935955	0368	1
HOLLADAY CHARLES R	1LT	O-0558706	1045	2
HOLLADAY CHARLES T	1LT	O-1305429	0357	2
HOLLADAY WILLIAM N	LTC	O-0245969	1160	1
HOLLAHAN MARGARET E	CPT	N-0733501	0746	1
HOLLAHAN THOMAS M	1LT	O-1823300	0648	1
HOLLAND ALGIE B	MAJ	O-0264465	1067	3
HOLLAND ARTHUR C	CW2	W-2206797	1162	1
HOLLAND ARTHUR G JR	MAJ	O-1325496	0758	1
HOLLAND BENJAMIN F	MAJ	O-0496986	0853	1
HOLLAND BERNARD W	CPT	O-1899415	1160	1
HOLLAND CHARLES A	CW3	W-2149195	1262	1
HOLLAND CHARLES R	LTC	O-1592281	0763	1
HOLLAND CLYDE L	LTC	O-1173292	0658	1
HOLLAND DELBERT D	1LT	O-0353763	1158	3
HOLLAND EDMUND L	LTC	O-0246866	0966	3
HOLLAND EDWARD F	CPT	O-1540907	0562	1
HOLLAND ELWOOD W	COL	O-0310198	0667	3
HOLLAND FRANK	1LT	O-0290250	0844	2
HOLLAND FRANK W	WO1	W-2120296	0448	2
HOLLAND GEORGE C	MAJ	O-0411429	0545	2
HOLLAND HARRISON H	MAJ	O-1285592	0558	1
HOLLAND HARVEY H JR	1LT	O-0545150	0346	2
HOLLAND HENRY	CPT	O-1914145	1125	1
HOLLAND JACK G	LTC	O-0525406	0963	1
HOLLAND JAMES D	COL	O-0473478	0267	1
HOLLAND JAMES M	COL	O-0213728	0667	1
HOLLAND JESSE R	WO1	W-2131169	1149	1
HOLLAND JOHN D	LTC	O-0291232	0963	3
HOLLAND JOHN H	MAJ	O-1996575	0356	1
HOLLAND JOHN L	CW3	W-2142023	0662	1
HOLLAND JOSEPH A	LTC	O-0171940	0561	3
HOLLAND JOSEPH J	LTC	O-1166287	1161	1
HOLLAND JOSEPH P	CW3	W-3150327	0667	1
HOLLAND LOUNA W	CPT	O-0197161	0252	3
HOLLAND MARIE A D	1LT	N-0721752	0345	1
HOLLAND MARVIN L	MAJ	O-0488878	1154	1
HOLLAND MICHAEL J	CPT	O-0498325	0747	1
HOLLAND REBA L	MAJ	N-0779785	0968	1
HOLLAND ROBERT P	LTC	O-0499132	0247	2
HOLLAND ROSCOE C	LTC	O-0496152	0257	1
HOLLAND SAM R	LTC	O-1283776	0857	1
HOLLAND URBAN D	CPT	O-0387473	0145	2
HOLLAND VON Q	MAJ	O-2014572	0166	1
HOLLAND WILBUR F	LTC	O-0445702	1262	1
HOLLAND WILLIAM O	COL	O-0254165	1046	2
HOLLAND WILLIAM H	COL	O-0215521	0962	3

NAME	GRADE	SVC NO	DATE RET MO YR	RET CODE
HOLLAHDSWORTH ALBERT	LTC	O-0225434	0265	3
HOLLAR FRANK F	MAJ	O-0299272	0559	1
HOLLE HOBART N	1LT	O-1596910	0746	2
HOLLEY MELVYN G	CW2	W-2203461	0760	1
HOLLENBECK CHESTER D	LTC	O-1541227	1160	1
HOLLENBAUGH HOWARD G	CW2	W-2216633	0667	1
HOLLENBECK DALE V	MAJ	O-1591405	0862	1
HOLLENBECK MELVIN M	CPT	O-1951589	0456	2
HOLLENBECK THOMAS A	LTC	O-0925214	0254	2
HOLLERAN EDWARD J	1LT	O-0383422	0743	2
HOLLERBACH JOSEPH T	MAJ	O-1334290	0463	1
HOLLEY EMERSON	1LT	O-0344335	0542	2
HOLLEY FREDERICK	MAJ	O-0543798	0364	1
HOLLEY JOE W	CW4	W-2143378	0667	1
HOLLEY JOSEPH R	MAJ	O-0964520	0965	1
HOLLEY LEMUEL T JR	COL	O-0341140	1160	1
HOLLEY RICHARD T	MAJ	O-0946977	1265	1
HOLLEY RICHMOND E JR	MAJ	O-0452526	1062	1
HOLLEY SAM J	CW4	W-2144933	0367	1
HOLLIDAE MERLE E	MAJ	O-0123131	0254	3
HOLLIDAY CARL H	CPT	O-0371512	0444	2
HOLLIDAY CLARENCE E	MAJ	O-1017444	0158	1
HOLLIDAY DANIEL D	COL	O-0322310	0368	3
HOLLIDAY DENNIS H	LTC	O-0215400	0264	3
HOLLIDAY DONALD V	LTC	O-0216040	0264	3
HOLLIDAY FREDERICK	LTC	O-0420760	0256	1
HOLLIDAY JOHN C	CPT	O-0202519	0555	2
HOLLIDAY JOSEPH A	COL	O-0217476	0563	2
HOLLIDAY OSCAR W	CW2	W-2106705	0665	3
HOLLIDAY ROBERT D	LTC	O-1585629	0964	1
HOLLIDAY TERRELL C	LTC	O-1285241	0854	1
HOLLIDAY VERNA M	MAJ	N-0726017	1160	1
HOLLIDAY WILLIAM L	LTC	O-1646260	0561	1
HOLLIHAN JAMES R	CPT	O-1586670	0947	2
HOLLIHAND JAMES E	LTC	O-1056743	0861	1
HOLLIMAN CHARLES L	MAJ	O-0983968	0466	1
HOLLIMAN WILLIAM J	MAJ	O-0177999	0453	3
HOLLINGSHEAD L JR	CPT	O-1577228	1044	2
HOLLINGSHEAD LYMAN A	LTC	O-0931792	0667	1
HOLLINGSWORTH DAVID	LTC	O-2201444	0759	1
HOLLINGSWORTH GERALD	MAJ	N-0763766	1163	3
HOLLINGSWORTH HARRY	1LT	O-1060130	0646	2
HOLLINGSWORTH J L	1LT	O-2010499	0261	2
HOLLINGSWORTH J S	COL	O-0382335	0860	1
HOLLINGSWORTH J T	CW3	W-2145136	0656	1
HOLLINGSWORTH JAMES	LTC	O-1541178	0166	2
HOLLINGSWORTH JESSE	MAJ	O-1053641	0864	3
HOLLINGSWORTH L Z	WO1	W-2146248	1059	2
HOLLINGSWORTH MARION	LTC	O-0309367	0258	3
HOLLINGSWORTH NED W	MAJ	O-1327740	0859	1
HOLLINS EDWARD P SR	CW2	RW-2206420	0366	1
HOLLINS HELEN B	MAJ	N-0763658	0468	1
HOLLINSWORTH HANSEL	CW3	W-2143355	0966	1
HOLLIS BENJAMIN	LTC	O-0455867	0867	1
HOLLIS DERAL	CPT	O-0969052	0956	1
HOLLIS HAROLD E JR	CW2	W-2209874	0663	1
HOLLIS HELEN I	1LT	N-0733764	0546	2
HOLLIS JAMES S	MAJ	O-1642193	0563	1
HOLLIS KENNETH L	CPT	O-0115079	0855	3
HOLLIS LAWRENCE C	LTC	O-0173489	1060	3
HOLLIS LEVY V	CPT	O-2262168	0763	1
HOLLIS MARSHALL F	LTC	O-0407545	0863	1
HOLLIS PATRICK M	MAJ	O-0357324	0960	2
HOLLIS STEPHEN L JR	CPT	O-1688341	0358	1
HOLLIS WILLIAM C	COL	O-0138446	1158	3
HOLLIS WILLIAM G	MAJ	O-1943592	0368	1
HOLLIS WILLIAM J	CW3	W-2150123	0865	1
HOLLISTER GEORGE E	LTC	O-0315104	1047	2
HOLLISTER HOWARD J	CPT	O-0239611	0445	2
HOLLISTER JOHN W	COL	O-0267570	1159	3
HOLLISTER KATHERINE	2LT	N-0743604	0445	1
HOLLIWAY HAROLD W	COL	O-0244579	0764	3
HOLLMAN THURMAN H	LTC	O-0413140	0266	1
HOLLORAN HOBERT J	CW3	W-2103718	1057	1
HOLLOW LETTON H	LTC	O-0194517	0850	2

NAME	GRADE	SVC NO	DATE RET MO YR	RET CODE
HOLLOWAY AUBREY T	LTC	O-0250979	0267	3
HOLLOWAY C F JR	CPT	O-1305774	0647	2
HOLLOWAY CARL L	MAJ	O-0310077	0646	2
HOLLOWAY CHARLES F	LTC	O-0348278	1061	1
HOLLOWAY CLAUD L JR	2LT	O-1421588	0344	2
HOLLOWAY GEORGE E	COL	O-0264946	0266	3
HOLLOWAY HAROLD K	COL	O-0286720	0361	1
HOLLOWAY HENRY G	MAJ	O-0995763	1065	1
HOLLOWAY HERBERT D	MAJ	O-1283606	0446	2
HOLLOWAY HERBERT K	LTC	O-0192688	1062	3
HOLLOWAY JESSE G	COL	O-0301946	0960	1
HOLLOWAY JOHN A	CW3	W-2009904	0868	3
HOLLOWAY ROY L	LTC	O-1638901	0962	1
HOLLOWAY STEPHEN O	LTC	O-0903050	0766	3
HOLLOWAY WILLIAM	LTC	O-0281313	1162	3
HOLLOWELL CHARLES W	2LT	O-1176671	0644	2
HOLLOWELL EARL O	1LT	O-1824465	0745	2
HOLLOWELL ELMER A	CW3	W-2152316	0765	1
HOLLSTEIN CHARLES C	LTC	O-1280708	0360	1
HOLLSTEIN JOSEPH P	CPT	O-0497124	0147	1
HOLLSTEIN ROBERT H	CPT	O-0512307	0845	2
HOLLYFIELD MERWYN H	WO1	W-2128022	1046	2
HOLLYWOOD JAMES L	CPT	O-0535975	0445	2
HOLM AARON E	CPT	O-2263684	0862	1
HOLM CLIFFORD A	CW4	W-2151496	0268	1
HOLM EMIL G JR	CPT	O-0409668	1046	2
HOLM ERNEST O	WO1	W-2115847	1051	1
HOLM LIONEL C	MAJ	O-0225784	1264	3
HOLM PAUL C	MAJ	O-1296211	0661	1
HOLMAN CLYDE E	2LT	O-1318795	0844	2
HOLMAN EDWARD L	LTC	O-0225307	0854	3
HOLMAN EDWIN A	2LT	O-2043039	1044	2
HOLMAN HAROLD S	MAJ	O-0370891	0745	2
HOLMAN HORACE F	LTC	O-0224612	1264	3
HOLMAN JACK C	CW2	W-2141316	0655	1
HOLMAN LAWRENCE M	LTC	O-0352334	0157	1
HOLMAN NATHAN A	LTC	O-0272241	0168	3
HOLMAN ROSCOE E	2LT	O-1894588	0545	2
HOLMBERG ERNEST F	LTC	O-0272952	1066	3
HOLMBERG HAROLD B	MAJ	O-0251761	0445	2
HOLMBERG JEAN M	1LT	O-1287533	0146	2
HOLMBERG KENNETH N	LTC	O-1116551	0961	1
HOLMES ADOLPH	MAJ	O-1823158	0856	1
HOLMES ALPHEUS F	MAJ	O-2021259	0366	1
HOLMES ANDREW L	2LT	O-1796474	0645	2
HOLMES ARTHUR A	COL	O-0276591	0960	2
HOLMES ARTHUR D	MAJ	O-0385291	0947	2
HOLMES AUBREY N	COL	O-0293415	0968	3
HOLMES CHARLES K	COL	O-0162054	0452	3
HOLMES CHARLES M	2LT	O-1115924	1143	2
HOLMES CHARLES W	LTC	O-0400264	0163	1
HOLMES CLYDE F S	LTC	N-0727200	0466	3
HOLMES DAVID B	CW4	W-2115846	0559	1
HOLMES DELBERT H	MAJ	O-1292176	0458	1
HOLMES DELTON	CW2	W-2149948	0559	1
HOLMES EARL J	WO1	W-2123638	0257	1
HOLMES EDWARD B	MAJ	O-0333687	1145	2
HOLMES ELVIE H	LTC	O-1283608	1166	1
HOLMES FRANK C	1LT	O-0301186	0343	2
HOLMES FRANKLIN J	LTC	O-0402480	0757	1
HOLMES GASTON L	LTC	O-0172759	0648	3
HOLMES HAROLD H	1LT	O-1182860	0946	2
HOLMES HARRY G	MAJ	O-1105302	1060	1
HOLMES HELEN E	MAJ	L-0803000	0548	2
HOLMES JAMES D	LTC	O-0300415	1162	1
HOLMES JAMES E	MAJ	O-0134345	0449	3
HOLMES JAMES M	MAJ	O-1598093	0263	1
HOLMES JAMES R	MAJ	O-2010648	0859	1
HOLMES JAMES S	MAJ	O-2202912	0964	1
HOLMES JAY M	LTC	O-0168112	0850	3
HOLMES JOHN E	CPT	O-1949124	0955	1
HOLMES JOHN F	LTC	O-0474938	0661	1
HOLMES JOHN H	LTC	O-0361767	0355	1
HOLMES JOHN M	CW3	O-0297203	0968	3
HOLMES JOSEPH A	LTC	O-0154966	0555	3

NAME	GRADE	SVC NO	DATE RET MO YR	RET CODE
HOLMES JOSEPH A	MAJ	O-0197071	0258	1
HOLMES JOSEPH B	CPT	O-1166509	0652	1
HOLMES K J	MAJ	O-1631980	1060	1
HOLMES KENNETH L	LTC	O-0182920	0755	3
HOLMES LESLIE	1LT	O-0923563	0145	2
HOLMES LESTER H	LTC	O-0376074	0166	1
HOLMES LESTER L	LTC	O-0245978	0561	1
HOLMES MERLE V	LTC	O-0192795	0648	3
HOLMES NILS R	MAJ	O-2035272	0560	1
HOLMES OLIVER W	MAJ	O-1846448	0961	1
HOLMES PETER N	LTC	O-0514159	0563	1
HOLMES RAYMOND	WO1	W-2143730	0962	1
HOLMES REAFORD C	LTC	O-0357774	0860	3
HOLMES RICHARD R	MAJ	O-1051206	0962	1
HOLMES RICHARD W	CW3	W-2208122	0268	1
HOLMES ROBERT H	1LT	O-4755591	0661	1
HOLMES ROBERT C JR	COL	O-1134455	1167	1
HOLMES RUSSELL A JR	1LT	O-0556883	0445	2
HOLMES RYLAND C	CW3	W-2146363	0262	1
HOLMES STERLING O	CW4	W-2120737	0563	2
HOLMES THOMAS J	LTC	O-0203471	0963	1
HOLMES THOMAS S	1LT	O-1043992	0245	2
HOLMES WENDELL S	COL	O-0354103	1167	3
HOLMES WILLIAM E	CPT	O-0541093	1145	2
HOLMES WILLIAM F	MAJ	O-1309487	1055	1
HOLMES WILLIAM F	CW3	W-2124248	0257	1
HOLMES WILLIAM H	LTC	O-0455632	0157	1
HOLMES WILLIAM O	MAJ	O-1555062	0161	1
HOLMES WILLIAM W	CPT	O-0184134	0353	3
HOLMGREN CLIFTON G	LTC	O-0297515	0558	3
HOLMGREN SAMUEL T	COL	O-0205315	0745	2
HOLMGREN WARNER E	CPT	O-0445191	0445	2
HOLMQUIST GEORGE F	CPT	O-0110517	0850	3
HOLMQUIST HAROLD F	1LT	O-1291277	0746	2
HOLMSTROM HUGO R	CPT	O-1116552	1060	1
HOLMSTROM ROY C	1LT	O-2006969	1046	2
HOLMSTROM VICTOR R	CW3	W-2143390	0564	1
HOLMWOOD HARLAN W	MAJ	O-0193765	0363	1
HOLOCH ELROY C	LTC	O-1183985	0862	1
HOLOD JOSEPHINE	1LT	N-0794172	0547	1
HOLOM VICTOR	1LT	O-1304216	0845	2
HOLOMAN WILLIAM D JR	2LT	O-4063195	1157	2
HOLROYD BENN S	LTC	O-1585532	0268	3
HOLSAPPLE CLIFFORD A	CW2	W-2151054	0358	1
HOLSCHER EDWARD C	COL	O-0281181	1267	3
HOLSCHER GORDON H	MAJ	O-1952044	0164	1
HOLSINGER HARRIS W	LTC	O-0246345	0360	3
HOLSONBACK BERNARD L	MAJ	O-1877748	0868	1
HOLST RALPH V	CW2	W-2152289	1157	1
HOLST WILLIAM W	LTC	O-0389559	0661	1
HOLSTAD JERRY E	LTC	O-2014321	0168	1
HOLSTE MERLIN L	CW3	W-2148021	0659	1
HOLSTEIN CHARLES F	2LT	O-1053542	0845	2
HOLSTEIN JANE E	MAJ	N-0741882	0862	2
HOLSTEIN RICHARD H	CPT	O-0292611	0445	2
HOLSTEN HERBERT N	COL	O-0334346	0450	1
HOLSTER HENRY P	LTC	O-1175467	0267	1
HOLSTLAW CHARLES H	LTC	O-0171195	0953	3
HOLSTON CLARENCE E	CW3	W-2148857	0161	1
HOLSTON SEYMOUR A	CPT	O-1185505	0648	2
HOLSTROM GEORGE	MAJ	O-1017594	0462	1
HOLSTROM JAMES R	CW3	W-2153344	1264	1
HOLSTON BEVERLY R	CPT	O-0196138	1062	3
HOLT ARTHUR W	COL	O-0460185	0763	1
HOLT CHARLES O	CPT	O-5304117	0768	1
HOLT CHARLES T	MAJ	O-5405157	0568	1
HOLT EARL C	CW4	W-2146115	0168	1
HOLT ELMER M	LTC	O-0224947	1054	3
HOLT ESTHER S	CPT	N-0767467	0546	1
HOLT FLOYD W	WO1	W-2127312	0749	1
HOLT FRANK B	MAJ	O-0977667	1062	1
HOLT FRANK L	LTC	O-1291642	0861	1
HOLT GEORGE T	COL	O-0235386	0965	3
HOLT HAROLD N	MAJ	O-0955431	0264	1
HOLT HERBERT	1LT	O-0535421	1044	2

NAME	GRADE	SVC NO	DATE RET MO YR	RET CODE
HOLT HILAND J D	LTC	O-0306396	1167	3
HOLT HOWARD K	CPT	O-0979136	1061	1
HOLT JAMES M	LTC	O-1306098	0161	1
HOLT JOHN C	1LT	O-1913730	0132	1
HOLT JOHN P	MAJ	O-0359130	0865	3
HOLT LAWRENCE E	CPT	O-1031096	0460	1
HOLT LORRAINE C	2LT	N-0774816	1046	1
HOLT MACK C	MAJ	O-1591208	0160	1
HOLT MARVIN W	CW3	W-2153111	0764	1
HOLT MONT	CW3	W-2141587	0860	1
HOLT PARKER M	COL	O-0296927	0968	3
HOLT RALPH J	1LT	O-1308645	0546	2
HOLT RANSOM A	CPT	O-1688262	1061	1
HOLT RICHARD L SR	CW4	W-2005619	1265	1
HOLT ROBERT A	CPT	O-1876277	0466	1
HOLT ROBERT T	COL	O-0312216	1262	3
HOLT SAMUEL E	MAJ	O-0220798	0858	3
HOLT TAYLOR JR	COL	O-0270614	0663	3
HOLT THOMAS A	MAJ	O-2204407	0166	1
HOLT VICTOR R	CPT	O-1032156	1047	2
HOLT VINCENT J	CW2	W-2151662	0855	1
HOLT WAYLAND G	CPT	O-0454386	1045	2
HOLT WILLARD C	CPT	O-1548438	1160	2
HOLT WILLIAM J JR	MAJ	O-1300036	1262	1
HOLT WILTHELMA	1LT	N-0765382	0847	1
HOLTA BJOHN T	MAJ	O-1633982	0868	3
HOLTE ALFRED O	CPT	O-0441292	1045	2
HOLTE OLAV H JR	CW2	W-3410009	0867	1
HOLTEGAARD LEONARD E	CPT	O-1703028	0246	2
HOLTER HOWARD H	MAJ	O-2038857	0962	1
HOLTHAUS FRANCIS J	LTC	O-1198748	0663	1
HOLTMEIER MILTON J	1LT	O-1586672	0157	1
HOLTON ARCHIE D JR	COL	O-0350609	0160	1
HOLTON CHARLES O JR	LTC	O-1104212	1067	1
HOLTON CLARENCE A	MAJ	O-1182385	0562	1
HOLTON DARWIN S	LTC	O-0276183	1166	3
HOLTON FRANK N	CW3	W-2152579	1164	1
HOLTON GEORGE J	CW2	W-2153086	0462	1
HOLTON JAMES E JR	LTC	O-0299899	0166	3
HOLTON JAMES L	LTC	O-0170580	1059	3
HOLTON JOHN C	LTC	O-1913443	1268	2
HOLTON RAYMOND F	LTC	O-0498908	1155	1
HOLTON ROBERT G	LTC	O-1551226	1065	1
HOLTZ JOHN J	CPT	O-0167811	0752	3
HOLTZ PAUL R	COL	O-0280590	0155	3
HOLTZ ROBERT E	CPT	O-1113759	0862	1
HOLTZCLAW HAPPY L	CPT	O-0281107	0665	3
HOLTZCLAW LOUIE H JR	1LT	O-0423208	1043	2
HOLTZMAN ABRAHAM	1LT	O-1061134	0645	2
HOLTZMAN RAYMOND S	COL	O-0212596	1057	1
HOLUB CHARLES R JR	CW2	W-2154668	0564	1
HOLWAY ORLANDO G	CPT	O-0235886	0352	3
HOLY RUTH L	1LT	N-0772561	0848	2
HOLYBEE MARVIN L	CW2	W-3430285	0968	1
HOLZ ARTHUR J	2LT	O-1319744	1044	2
HOLZ LOUIS F	MAJ	O-1321518	0457	2
HOLZ LOUIS T	MAJ	O-1897756	1063	1
HOLZAEPFEL DAVID W	1LT	O-2202321	1053	2
HOLZER KENNETH W	LTC	O-0534760	0468	1
HOLZER ROY W	MAJ	O-0905867	0468	3
HOLZHAUER FRANKLIN L	MAJ	O-2010065	0962	1
HOLZMAN ROBERT A	COL	O-0422395	1062	1
HOLZMAN SIDNEY T	LTC	O-0205094	1146	2
HOLZMUELLER OSCAR W	CPT	O-0452656	1045	2
HOLZWORTH ELMER J	MAJ	O-0524319	0157	1
HOMAN FREDERIC F	CPT	O-1683612	0744	2
HOMAN GEORGE E	LTC	O-1585637	1166	3
HOMAN HARRY	CPT	O-0395563	0345	2
HOMAN HARRY W	CPT	O-0275841	0859	3
HOMAN LAWRENCE H	CPT	O-0371248	0746	2
HOMAN RALPH F JR	MAJ	O-1172499	1061	1
HOMAN WAYNE E	COL	O-0173541	1051	2
HOMAN WILLIAM J	1LT	O-0112653	1058	3
HOMAN WILLIAM L	COL	O-0183865	0852	2
HOMANICH ANDREW	MAJ	O-0424195	0848	2

NAME	GRADE	SVC NO	DATE RET MO YR	RET CODE
HOMAN JOEL	LTC	0-1057110	0263	1
HOMER ARTHUR H	CPT	0-[illegible]696	1062	[illegible]
HOMER DAVID	LTC	[illegible]	0765	3
HOMER LEROY W	CW3	W-2147311	1065	2
HOMER RUSSELL	CPT	0-1636392	0466	2
HOMERICK PAUL A	2LT	0-1325441	1144	2
HOMEWOOD CHARLES E	MAJ	0-1826019	0263	1
HOMFELD JOHN F	MAJ	[illegible]	0864	3
HOMME FRANCIS [illegible]	LTC	0-1551427	0167	3
HOMME [illegible]	LTC	0-1044667	0461	1
HOMMEL EDWARD H	1LT	0-0497174	1043	2
HOMMEYER PAUL [illegible]	COL	0-0355158	0762	3
HOMZA STEVE A	CW2	W-2147776	0561	1
HON REX J	1LT	0-1167035	0659	1
HONAKER FRANK [illegible]	MAJ	0-1946243	0662	1
HONAKER KEITH J	LTC	0-0407834	0563	1
HONAKER ROBERT L	2LT	0-2005565	0346	2
HONAKER SAMUEL A	COL	0-0125401	0749	3
HONAN J JOSEPH	2LT	0-1591809	1144	2
HONAUTON LAWRENCE JR	MAJ	0-2265136	1168	1
HONDERICH FELIX S	CPT	0-1311893	0362	2
HONEA HENRY	2LT	0-2055841	1044	1
HONEA JAMES L JR	MAJ	0-0964195	0966	1
HONEA WILEY S	MAJ	0-1796624	0957	1
HONECK HOWARD D	MAJ	0-1030677	1164	1
HONECK ROBERT H	LTC	0-1556444	0466	1
HONEY MIKE S	MAJ	0-0512352	0755	1
HONEY ARTHUR C	LTC	0-0507462	0263	1
HONEY JOHN S	LTC	0-0322791	1059	1
HONEY WARREN	CPT	0-1285943	0545	2
HONEY WILLIAM V	LTC	0-0254484	0363	3
HONEYCUTT EUGENE J	MAJ	0-0228738	1164	3
HONEYCUTT LEE D	CW4	W-2134324	0957	1
HONEYCUTT TOWNSELL N	CPT	0-1586674	0746	2
HONEYCUTT WILLIS E	MAJ	0-1342378	1066	1
HONEYWELL ROY J	LTC	0-0132034	0648	3
HONEYWELL STANLEY S	MAJ	0-0976519	0263	1
HONIG RICHARD P	MAJ	0-2055103	0161	1
HONN FERRILL F	CW3	W-2141588	1061	1
HONNELL PIERRE M	COL	0-0271216	0268	3
HONODEL FRANCIS A	LTC	0-1695693	1064	1
HONOLD HENRY W	MAJ	0-0355212	0646	2
HONORE ALEXANDER	CPT	0-1796283	0764	2
HONORE MAGRETHE E	CPT	N-0784595	1047	1
HONOUR JOHN H	MAJ	0-1647506	1057	1
HONSA WILLIAM M	MAJ	0-0264969	0566	3
HONSBERGER JOHN H	LTC	0-1573288	0257	1
HONTS CHAYLON F	1LT	0-1119838	0352	2
HONTS EMORY R	COL	0-0200080	1045	2
HONTZ MARIE V	MAJ	N-0742292	1064	3
HOOBLER DANIEL H	LTC	0-1645056	0264	1
HOOD BOB C	MAJ	0-0995683	0865	1
HOOD CARL M	LTC	0-0360504	0646	2
HOOD CHARLES R	CPT	0-0499654	0946	1
HOOD DANIEL L	1LT	0-1913731	0520	1
HOOD DAVID JR	LTC	0-1575367	0861	1
HOOD DWIGHT L	COL	0-0251182	0462	3
HOOD ELMER C	1LT	0-1300037	0845	2
HOOD ERNEST A	1LT	0-1117275	0460	1
HOOD FRANCES	MAJ	N-0764681	0563	1
HOOD FRANCIS C	COL	0-0274286	0853	1
HOOD FRANK	CW4	W-2145861	0567	1
HOOD FRANK U	COL	0-0146678	1048	3
HOOD FREDERICK	LTC	0-0212703	0845	2
HOOD GLEN D	CW3	W-2144186	0559	1
HOOD GUTHRIE H	CW4	W-2121059	0864	3
HOOD HELEN A	MAJ	N-0773137	0868	3
HOOD HOWARD H	LTC	0-1294132	0863	1
HOOD JAMES A	WO1	W-3200870	0967	1
HOOD JAMES V	CPT	0-0985687	0561	1
HOOD JOHN G	LTC	0-0278444	1159	3
HOOD JOHNNY	MAJ	0-2262802	1162	1
HOOD JULIAN R	CW3	W-2149184	0764	1
HOOD MARY E	2LT	N-0790846	0545	1
HOOD JULIE A	LTC	0-0421849	1162	1

NAME	GRADE	SVC NO	DATE RET MO YR	RET CODE
HOOD RANDOLPH P	MAJ	0-1547969	0756	1
HOOD THURMAN	MAJ	0-1647092	0955	1
HOOD WALTER [illegible]	LTC	0-0260977	0568	3
HOOD WILLIAM B	CW2	W-2207479	0961	1
HOOD WILLIAM D	LTC	0-1030780	0465	1
HOOGLAND DIRK	CW3	W-2205507	0767	1
HOOK ARTHUR	CPT	0-0318202	1058	1
HOOK BRUCE F	CPT	0-4002395	0667	1
HOOK ENOS F	LTC	0-0920015	0446	2
HOOK GEORGE M W	1LT	0-1016836	1045	2
HOOK HAROLD J	LTC	0-1823876	1062	2
HOOK HAROLD O	LTC	0-0301150	0357	1
HOOK IRA T	MAJ	0-0115075	0648	3
HOOK LAWRENCE H	MAJ	0-0335738	0862	3
HOOK LILLIAN M	1LT	N-0760030	0946	1
HOOK LOUIS A	MAJ	0-0995685	1166	1
HOOK RALPH E	MAJ	0-0405381	0346	2
HOOK RALPH G	MAJ	0-1583126	0259	1
HOOK ROBERT W	CW3	W-2146335	1063	1
HOOK WALTER F	LTC	0-0406277	0346	2
HOOK WALTER S	CPT	0-1184521	1158	1
HOOKER ALLEN E	MAJ	0-1881767	1066	1
HOOKER DEWITT E	MAJ	0-0146012	1057	3
HOOKER HERBERT T	MAJ	0-1324623	0468	1
HOOKER JOHN C JR	LTC	0-1822007	0164	1
HOOKER KEITH G	LTC	0-0267032	1068	3
HOOKER LANGSFORD	CW2	W-2151633	0259	1
HOOKER WARREN L	CPT	0-1320919	0846	2
HOOKER WILLIAM A	2LT	0-1301489	0144	2
HOOKER WILLIAM F	MAJ	0-2055410	1158	1
HOOKIE LOWELL D	CPT	0-2032939	0457	1
HOOKS CHARLIE D	MAJ	0-1878544	0968	1
HOOKS JOHN A	CW2	W-2145448	0761	1
HOOKS ROBERT G	LTC	0-0258683	0467	3
HOOKS ROBERT J	1LT	0-0694372	0346	2
HOOLE RALPH D	1LT	0-0405527	0453	2
HOOLIHAN WILLIAM J	CW2	W-2210081	0167	1
HOOPER ALVIN E JR	MAJ	0-0973948	0567	1
HOOPER CHARLES H	LTC	0-0227580	0564	3
HOOPER CHARLES R JR	CW3	W-2151008	1162	1
HOOPER FREDERICK	CPT	0-0307901	0345	2
HOOPER HENRY G	MAJ	0-0949722	1262	1
HOOPER JAMES F	LTC	0-0383877	0557	1
HOOPER JAMES R	COL	0-0438225	1154	1
HOOPER JOHN C SR	MAJ	0-0970669	0363	1
HOOPER LAWRENCE H	2LT	0-1576146	0445	2
HOOPER LORETTA A	1LT	N-0722484	0846	1
HOOPER MELVIN H	LTC	0-0254590	0562	1
HOOPER ROBERT W	MAJ	0-0498729	1044	2
HOOPER SIDNEY R	COL	0-0326834	1055	3
HOOPER WALTER S	WO1	W-2110291	1053	1
HOOPER WILLIAM T JR	LTC	0-1317014	1062	1
HOOPERT JOSEPH D	LTC	0-0371431	0260	1
HOOPMAN RICHARD B	LTC	0-1165514	0962	1
HOOPS RAYMOND	MAJ	0-1019301	0757	1
HOOPS THEODORE H	CW4	W-2000228	1159	3
HOOS HAROLD W	1LT	0-1640570	0646	2
HOOSE CLINTON M	MAJ	0-0253220	1057	2
HOOTS WILLIAM C	MAJ	0-0973458	0263	1
HOOVER CARL H	LTC	0-0273826	0246	2
HOOVER CLARENCE F	COL	0-0265957	0362	3
HOOVER DONALD O	COL	0-0264616	0264	3
HOOVER FRANCIS C	MAJ	0-2011121	1162	1
HOOVER FRANK R JR	LTC	0-0256354	0361	1
HOOVER GILES N	CPT	0-0477221	0448	2
HOOVER HOBERT H	LTC	0-0364957	1264	1
HOOVER HOMER L	LTC	0-0169565	0648	3
HOOVER J D	1LT	0-2008405	0448	2
HOOVER JACOB D	MAJ	0-0250316	0862	3
HOOVER JOHN L	1LT	0-1331626	0546	2
HOOVER JOHN P	MAJ	0-0443857	0364	1
HOOVER JOSEPH H	CW3	W-2208503	0266	1
HOOVER LLOYD H	COL	0-0252181	1064	3
HOOVER MARION J	2LT	0-2049585	0252	2
HOOVER MELVIN L	2LT	0-0887886	0845	2

NAME	GRADE	SVC NO	DATE RET MO YR	RET CODE
HOOVER MERLE M	WO1	W-21[illegible]	1145	2
HOOVER RALPH [illegible]	MAJ	0-2261101	0168	1
HOOVER ROBERT E	W3	W-2152733	1164	1
HOOVER ROBERT V	2LT	0-2007156	0447	2
HOOVER ROSE F	MAJ	0-1561231	0763	1
HOOVER SAMUEL [illegible]	1LT	0-1686713	1051	2
HOOVER SAMUEL [illegible] JR	LTC	0-133[illegible]	0661	1
HOOVER WILLIAM M JR	COL	[illegible]	0751	2
HOOVER WILLIAM [illegible]	LTC	0-1646357	0954	1
HOOVLER JAMES A	1LT	0-1318306	0949	1
HOPEHART HARVEY J	CPT	[illegible]	1045	[illegible]
HOPE ALVIN L	COL	0-0163[illegible]	0955	3
HOPE CHARLES A	MAJ	0-0282591	0949	2
HOPE CHARLES W	MAJ	0-1289085	0760	1
HOPE GEORGE K	1LT	0-2055071	0745	2
HOPE JAMES C	CW3	W-2207056	1066	1
HOPE NOEL S	CW3	W-2145909	0561	1
HOPE ROBERT H	LTC	0-0226458	0964	3
HOPE ROBERT L	LTC	0-1112230	0464	1
HOPE ROBERT R	LTC	0-0914387	1159	3
HOPE WILLIAM M JR	LTC	0-1173838	0562	1
HOPELAIN RICHARD	COL	0-0245460	1062	3
HOPEWELL ROLF K	CPT	0-1320532	1064	1
HOPFNER WALTER R L	MAJ	0-1874899	0865	1
HOPKE JACK A	LTC	0-0309341	0163	3
HOPKINS HENRY S	MAJ	0-1995482	0258	1
HOPKINS BILL H	LTC	0-1183703	0765	1
HOPKINS CECIL W	CPT	0-2010995	1160	1
HOPKINS CHARLES K	CW3	W-2144031	0461	1
HOPKINS CHARLES M	LTC	0-0453819	0157	1
HOPKINS CHARLES M	CPT	0-1312770	1149	1
HOPKINS CHRISTOPHE	LTC	0-0311002	0746	2
HOPKINS CLACK O	COL	0-0347340	1045	2
HOPKINS CLARENCE A	LTC	0-0213726	0263	3
HOPKINS CLARENCE L	LTC	0-0522409	1267	1
HOPKINS CLARK	LTC	0-0166673	0955	3
HOPKINS DANIEL B	MAJ	0-1798262	0163	1
HOPKINS EDWARD E	MAJ	0-1314637	0461	1
HOPKINS EDWARD S	COL	0-0205045	1156	3
HOPKINS FLORIAN G	LTC	0-0357059	0264	3
HOPKINS GEORGE H	COL	0-0263835	0354	3
HOPKINS GEORGE J	1LT	0-1286291	1045	2
HOPKINS GEORGE S	COL	0-0332985	0467	3
HOPKINS HARRY K	MAJ	0-1031812	1061	1
HOPKINS HENRY A	CW2	W-2206099	0660	1
HOPKINS HENRY S	CPT	0-1289582	0449	1
HOPKINS HENRY U	LTC	0-0253268	0946	2
HOPKINS HOWARD H	1LT	0-1016113	0346	2
HOPKINS JACK	LTC	0-0344306	0954	1
HOPKINS JOHN F	CW2	W-2211462	0967	1
HOPKINS JOHN S	COL	0-0245574	0566	3
HOPKINS JOHN T	1LT	0-1314484	0347	2
HOPKINS JOHN W	LTC	0-1173293	0557	1
HOPKINS JOSEPH R	CW3	W-2209484	1267	1
HOPKINS JULIAN H	2LT	0-0530673	0645	2
HOPKINS LESLIE B	LTC	0-0446998	0150	1
HOPKINS LYMAN R	MAJ	0-1284876	0258	1
HOPKINS PAUL F	MAJ	0-2019744	0263	1
HOPKINS PAUL L	LTC	0-1304217	0862	1
HOPKINS RALPH L	MAJ	0-1080789	0660	1
HOPKINS RAYMOND A	MAJ	0-2209962	0568	1
HOPKINS RICHARD H	B G	0-0245902	0766	3
HOPKINS ROBERT F	CPT	0-1000382	0555	1
HOPKINS ROBERT W	MAJ	0-2208531	0666	1
HOPKINS ROSCOE B	MAJ	0-0308637	1067	3
HOPKINS ROY O	CW2	W-2209871	1063	1
HOPKINS ROY H	MAJ	0-1648291	0157	1
HOPKINS THOMAS J	LTC	0-0174367	0561	3
HOPKINS WALTER F	CW4	W-2113954	0659	1
HOPKINS WALTER K	MAJ	0-0400916	1163	1
HOPKINS WAYNE D	MAJ	0-1176375	0561	1
HOPKINS WILLIAM C	MAJ	0-0222185	1145	2
HOPMANN URBAN C	CPT	0-0383804	0247	2
HOPP CHARLES I	CW3	W-2205355	0466	1
HOPP HARVEY M	COL	0-0190899	0158	3

NAME	GRADE	SVC NO	DATE RET MO YR	RET CODE
HOPP RICHARD [illegible]	LTC	[illegible]	1162	1
HOPPE ARTHUR C	LTC	0-0428106	0164	1
HOPPE LAWRENCE S	CW2	W-2144367	1156	[illegible]
HOPPE RICHARD [illegible] JR	1LT	[illegible]	1144	2
HOPPE ROBERT [illegible]	LTC	0-0488[illegible]	0159	1
HOPPE WILLIAM G	MAJ	0-0555[illegible]	0466	2
HOPPE WOODROW E	MAJ	0-0402219	0866	1
HOPPER CLEO W	CW[illegible]	W-2145485	0463	1
HOPPER DANIEL A JR	LTC	[illegible]	0663	[illegible]
HOPPER DAVID W	[illegible]	[illegible]	1159	[illegible]
HOPPER ELBERT B	MAJ	[illegible]	0565	[illegible]
HOPPER ELVIN F	MAJ	[illegible]	1161	1
HOPPER FRANCIS L	LTC	0-0337002	0660	1
HOPPER FRED L JR	LTC	0-1921219	1266	1
HOPPER HERBERT W	CW3	W-2152266	1166	1
HOPPER JAMES A	MAJ	0-1588474	1160	1
HOPPER JOSEPH C	LTC	[illegible]	1155	1
HOPPER KATHERINE	2LT	N-0757469	0646	1
HOPPER M FRANCES	CPT	N-0755303	0546	1
HOPPER OBED A	LTC	0-1176068	0442	1
HOPPER RALPH T	MAJ	0-1877160	1266	1
HOPPER REX	LTC	[illegible]	1162	1
HOPPER STUART C	COL	0-0131928	0648	3
HOPPER WILLIAM F	1LT	0-1324165	0957	1
HOPPES JAMES W	1LT	0-0442791	0946	2
HOPPING JOHN S	MAJ	0-1889044	0944	2
HOPPLE HOMER H	CPT	0-0513231	0650	[illegible]
HOPPOCK NOEL F	2LT	0-1174894	0445	2
HOPPS CARL W	MAJ	0-0191979	0740	3
HOPPUS HOWARD C	MAJ	0-1911472	0164	1
HOPSON EDISON	MAJ	0-1798353	0760	1
HOPSON HOWARD E	COL	0-0302751	0965	3
HOPSON TROY D	MAJ	0-1922674	0567	1
HOPSON WILLIAM H	LTC	0-0257575	0444	3
HOPTIAK TED J	CW2	W-2142930	0361	1
HOPWOOD DUANE J	CW3	W-2153347	0465	1
HORAK RUFUS V	2LT	0-1595573	0746	1
HORAMAN CHAUNCEY E	LTC	0-1648403	0461	1
HORAN ALICE M	1LT	N-0751430	0146	1
HORAN CHARLES A JR	LTC	0-1533815	0365	1
HORAN DONALD J	MAJ	0-2262621	0263	1
HORAN JAMES O	MAJ	0-1049894	0464	1
HORAN JOHN C	1LT	0-1041794	1046	2
HORAN JOHN F	MAJ	0-0347543	0261	1
HORAN JOHN J	CPT	0-1302926	0463	2
HORAN JOHN P	LTC	0-0338284	0760	1
HORAN LYNOTT F	2LT	0-1591811	1043	2
HORAN MARY A	1LT	N-0721855	0646	1
HORAN THOMAS J	MAJ	0-0391646	0146	2
HORAN WILLIAM H	LTC	0-1291278	0660	1
HORBALY WILLIAM V	LTC	0-1941536	0256	2
HORD ASA A	LTC	0-0466013	0367	1
HORD J T	CPT	0-0901205	1044	2
HORDAN RICHARD	LTC	0-0278896	0559	3
HORDECHUCK JOHN F	1LT	0-1327440	0152	2
HORDER HERBERT L	LTC	0-0468680	0854	1
HORDT CHARLES F	LTC	0-0921391	0766	3
HORESTA ELIZABETH	MAJ	N-0757587	0767	1
HORGAN FLORENCE E	1LT	N-0741481	0946	1
HORGAN WILLIAM D	CW2	W-2111889	0446	2
HORGEN CLARENCE A	LTC	0-0319879	0167	3
HORIMOTO WILLIAM S	MAJ	0-1923050	0765	1
HORKOTT JOHN	CPT	0-1081477	0747	2
HORLANDER DERYL	LTC	0-0400092	0457	1
HORLOCK REGINALD J	MAJ	0-0185626	0656	3
HORMAN ARLAN W	MAJ	0-1101045	0564	1
HORMAN DOROTHY	2LT	N-0729262	1043	2
HORMAN GLEN W	LTC	0-1169163	0265	1
HORMEL HAROLD M	CPT	0-1040943	1146	2
HORN ALBERT N	LTC	0-0261944	0156	2
HORN ANDREW W	1LT	0-1179449	0160	2
HORN ANTHONY W	CPT	0-1042603	0247	2
HORN ARTHUR A	CW4	W-2136640	0459	1
HORN CHARLES W	COL	0-0374658	0263	1
HORN DONALD L	CPT	0-1307242	0857	2

NAME	GRADE	SVC NO	DATE RET MO YR	RET CODE
HORN EDITH E	MAJ	N-0741844	1063	3
HORN ERLING	MAJ	0-0239069	0965	1
HORN EUGENE A	CW4	W-2143011	0568	1
HORN GERALD R	LTC	0-0489061	0357	1
HORN JOHN M	MAJ	0-1553278	0767	3
HORN JOHN P	LTC	0-0228739	0365	3
HORN JOSEPH A	LTC	0-0221296	1163	3
HORN JULIUS J	MAJ	0-1634900	1060	1
HORN LESLIE D	LTC	0-0565685	0562	1
HORN LESLIE T	LTC	0-0304768	0668	3
HORN LEWIS E	MAJ	0-0256244	0159	3
HORN MEZICK T	MAJ	0-1051148	0854	1
HORN NORMAN G	CW4	W-2002903	1267	3
HORN ORLANDO K	LTC	0-0361085	0864	1
HORN RICHARD W	LTC	0-0221789	0753	3
HORN ROBERT B JR	CW2	W-2213943	0968	1
HORN ROY A	LTC	0-0228635	0264	3
HORN SIDNEY	MAJ	0-1169575	0560	1
HORN WALTER R	MAJ	0-0531270	0847	2
HORN WOODROW W	MAJ	0-0490430	0960	1
HORNADAY DONALD E	MAJ	0-0972268	0464	1
HORNADAY THOMAS F	COL	0-0267334	0550	1
HORNBEAK PAUL M	MAJ	0-0182502	0449	3
HORNBECK HUGH M	CPT	0-2033047	0762	2
HORNBERGER EVANS Z J	MAJ	0-0469007	1146	2
HORNBUCKLE CHARLES R	MAJ	0-0348067	0263	1
HORNBY WILLIAM F	COL	0-0372899	0665	1
HORNE FRANCIS L SR	LTC	0-0954398	1068	1
HORNE GERARD F	1LT	0-1051607	0246	2
HORNE IVAN W	LTC	0-1104860	0361	1
HORNE JAMES W	WO1	W-2153257	0660	2
HORNE JOHN D JR	1LT	0-5300535	0459	2
HORNE KENNETH	MAJ	0-0312371	0144	2
HORNE LEM O	CW2	W-3350246	0467	1
HORNE LLOYD F	CW3	W-2144187	0958	1
HORNE NORMAN P	LTC	0-1003257	0558	1
HORNE ROBERT G	LTC	0-2263669	0868	1
HORNE ROGER R	WO1	W-2107348	0846	2
HORNE STEPHEN F	CPT	0-0430249	0346	2
HORNE THOMAS C JR	COL	0-0200482	0356	1
HORNE WILFORD W	CPT	0-0254517	1044	2
HORNE WILLIAM A	2LT	0-1175745	1143	2
HORNE WILSON R	MAJ	0-1690975	1066	1
HORNER CHARLES E	1LT	0-1167906	1145	2
HORNER CLYDE L	MAJ	0-1030379	0158	1
HORNER DONALD C	WO1	W-2146667	0765	2
HORNER DONALD D	MAJ	0-1329482	0860	2
HORNER ELIJAH W	LTC	0-0265772	0553	3
HORNER FRANKLYN E	CPT	0-0143062	1055	3
HORNER FREEMAN V	MAJ	0-2014546	0962	1
HORNER HAROLD	LTC	0-0418652	0763	1
HORNER HAROLD A	CW2	W-2151066	0560	1
HORNER JACK C	MAJ	0-0356621	1046	2
HORNER JOHN E W	LTC	0-0374789	0264	1
HORNER MARION R	LTC	0-1586360	1163	1
HORNER NORMAN S	COL	0-0412392	0767	1
HORNER PENNINGTON	MAJ	0-1946990	0356	1
HORNER REUBEN	CPT	0-0164135	1139	1
HORNER REUBEN L	LTC	0-1313746	0163	1
HORNER ROBERT	2LT	0-1321087	0544	2
HORNER ROBERT W	LTC	0-0194587	1155	3
HORNESBY ERNEST F	LTC	0-4090113	0254	1
HORNEY DANIEL J	LTC	0-0321558	0965	3
HORNEY PHILIP S	CW4	W-2143051	0866	1
HORNICK HARRY	CPT	0-0274066	0345	2
HORNICK RICHARD L	CW3	W-3100518	0568	1
HORNING CLYDE H	CW3	W-2143796	0667	1
HORNING GEORGE J	MAJ	0-0980395	0962	1
HORNING HAROLD F	COL	0-0320617	0163	3
HORNING JACKSON G	COL	0-0181021	0652	3
HORNING LEE W	MAJ	0-4074395	1068	1
HORNING STEWART D	LTC	0-1551228	1264	3
HORNING THEODORE R	LTC	0-0283913	0364	3
HORNOR WILLIAM L	B G	0-0250277	0555	3
HORNSBY IRVING R	CW3	W-2149070	0760	1

NAME	GRADE	SVC NO	DATE RET MO YR	RET CODE
HORNSBY JOHN A	CW3	W-2151922	0266	1
HORNSBY ROBERT C	COL	0-0245252	1162	3
HORNSEY JOHN W JR	LTC	0-1119798	1166	2
HORNSTEIN ISIDORE	COL	0-0234525	0158	3
HORNUNG WILLIAM W	COL	0-0193775	1054	1
HORONY JAMES L	CW2	W-2214816	0766	1
HOROWITZ ABRAHAM H	MAJ	0-0215821	0555	3
HORR PHILIP F	COL	0-0218608	1059	1
HORR ROBERT J	COL	0-0171189	0757	3
HORRELL NORBERT C	1LT	0-1010355	1145	2
HORSEY ELDRIDGE J	MAJ	0-0451469	0157	1
HORSFALL WILLIAM R	LTC	0-0513051	0268	3
HORSLEY JAMES L	CPT	0-1587328	0259	1
HORSLEY JOHN W	COL	0-0255162	1055	3
HORSMAN GEORGE L	LTC	0-0347605	0758	1
HORSMAN JESSE L JR	LTC	0-1328605	0865	1
HORST URIAS S	MAJ	0-1799955	0263	1
HORST WALTER H	LTC	0-0309943	1162	3
HORSTMANN OTTO C	2LT	0-0916552	0344	2
HORT HENRY J	COL	0-0265593	1059	1
HORTA JUAN E	LTC	0-0253764	0266	3
HORTMAN ALTON M	CPT	0-0386145	1267	3
HORTON ALFRED W	LTC	0-0171598	0748	3
HORTON ALTON E	MAJ	0-0190430	0760	3
HORTON ARNOLD G	CPT	0-1001154	0547	2
HORTON CHARLIE T	MAJ	0-1176377	0860	1
HORTON CLAUDE C	MAJ	0-2014563	1163	1
HORTON DENNIS W	CPT	0-0238247	0666	3
HORTON DONALD F	COL	0-0245393	0966	3
HORTON DONELSON B	2LT	0-1332495	0446	2
HORTON DWIGHT	COL	0-0103651	0648	3
HORTON EDGAR M	CW3	W-2141589	0259	1
HORTON EDWARD V	CPT	0-0362631	1044	2
HORTON FRANK B	COL	0-0269857	1060	3
HORTON FRED C	MAJ	0-2010489	0258	1
HORTON FREDERICK	LTC	0-0497102	0657	1
HORTON GERALD B	LTC	0-0333837	0463	3
HORTON GUY L	LTC	0-0120785	0648	3
HORTON HAL C	COL	0-0150307	0648	3
HORTON HARRY W	LTC	0-1111674	0664	1
HORTON JAMES D	CPT	0-0272141	0243	2
HORTON JOHN I	CPT	0-0414356	0345	2
HORTON JOHN T	MAJ	0-1697920	1057	1
HORTON LEE F	CPT	0-0198932	0944	2
HORTON MURRAY E	MAJ	0-1899453	0363	1
HORTON NORMAN B	LTC	0-0246789	1058	3
HORTON ORA L	CW2	W-2205889	1161	1
HORTON PAUL H	LTC	0-0242420	0864	3
HORTON ROBERT H	MAJ	0-0308559	0867	3
HORTON ROGER L	LTC	0-1307547	0463	1
HORTON RUTH K	2LT	N-0735870	0645	1
HORTON STERLING R	LTC	0-0915420	0563	2
HORTON TENTON N	2LT	0-1339997	0255	2
HORTON THOMAS R	LTC	0-0244926	1052	3
HORTON WALTER	MAJ	0-1185207	0561	1
HORTON WILLIAM F	1LT	0-1016686	1045	2
HORTON WILLIAM F	CPT	0-2048658	0363	1
HORTON WILLIAM S	2LT	0-0929828	0351	2
HORTON ZACH A	CPT	0-0524338	0745	2
HORVATH ROSE V	LTC	N-0757107	0466	3
HORVATH WILLIAM S	2LT	0-1692557	0545	2
HORWATH FRANK S	1LT	0-0938045	0961	2
HORWITZ ALBERT	1LT	0-1181639	0946	2
HORWITZ ALEX	1LT	0-1302630	1145	2
HORWITZ BURNERD	CW4	W-2147043	1267	1
HORWITZ DAVID	CW3	W-2145200	1061	1
HORWITZ EMANUEL	COL	0-0319781	0468	3
HORWITZ MARTIN	1LT	0-1323320	0146	2
HOSCH JAMES E	MAJ	0-0565689	0161	1
HOSCH JOHN A	COL	0-0200305	0563	3
HOSE FRED H	CW2	W-2121157	0746	2
HOSE GEORGE E	MAJ	0-0408730	0868	3
HOSE ORION E	LTC	0-0475240	0655	1
HOSEASON MARRETT P	1LT	0-0172588	0643	2
HOSENFELD FLORENCE A	MAJ	N-0722271	0564	1

NAME	GRADE	SVC NO	DATE RET MO YR	RET CODE
HOSEY CHARLIE M	MAJ	0-0495255	0854	1
HOSEY JAMES H	LTC	0-2204531	0968	1
HOSEY RICHARD L	CPT	0-1295883	0847	2
HOSFORD HARRY E	LTC	0-0973587	0468	1
HOSHALL EDWARD M	COL	0-0255073	0867	3
HOSIER ROBERT D	2LT	0-1172912	0545	2
HOSKIN ANDREW D	LTC	0-0258582	0166	3
HOSKINS ELEANOR	1LT	N-0742179	0846	1
HOSKINS FRANCIS	LTC	0-1310600	1263	1
HOSKINS JOHN H	MAJ	0-0496154	0554	2
HOSKINS MARSHALL D	LTC	0-1796960	0462	2
HOSKINS ORVILLE E	CW3	W-2145641	0364	1
HOSKINS STUART W	LTC	0-1575368	0467	2
HOSLER HAROLD M	COL	0-0370842	0161	1
HOSODA PAUL Y	CW4	W-2005578	1068	1
HOSTAGE FABIAN	2LT	0-0326765	1062	3
HOSTER GEORGE M	LTC	0-0243389	1160	3
HOSTLER ROBERT D	CW2	W-2214547	0668	1
HOTALEN RUDOLPH B	LTC	0-0291364	0166	3
HOTALING EUGENE	COL	0-0452496	0668	3
HOTALING PERRY R	CPT	0-1302133	0968	3
HOTCHKIN HARRY	MAJ	0-0200609	0554	3
HOTCHKISS DALE C	LTC	0-0885806	0358	1
HOTCHKISS HERVEY D	LTC	0-0351288	0267	3
HOTCHKISS JESSIE A	MAJ	L-0125890	1265	1
HOTCHKISS MERLE S	COL	0-0173168	0557	1
HOTCHKISS THOMAS A	LTC	0-0352530	0865	1
HOTELLING LEWIS A	1LT	0-0999546	1056	2
HOTOPP RAYMOND F	LTC	0-0454521	0258	1
HOTOVY GEORGE S	1LT	0-2047367	0246	2
HOTSENPILLER HARRY A	LTC	0-1545639	0763	1
HOTSKO GEORGE	LTC	0-2019037	0267	1
HOTT JAMES J	MAJ	0-0315307	0446	2
HOTT ROBERT J	CPT	0-0530101	1044	2
HOTT WILLIAM A	MAJ	0-0394789	0760	1
HOTTA YOSHIO	MAJ	0-0944659	1062	1
HOTTEN JACK	LTC	0-0484846	0657	1
HOTTENSTEIN CHARLES	MAJ	0-0288952	0756	3
HOTTINGER RAYMOND C	LTC	0-0278229	0265	3
HOTZ EUGENE B	LTC	0-1047169	0865	1
HOUBLER CLAUDE O	MAJ	0-1038011	0161	1
HOUCHIN EDWARD L	LTC	0-0501706	0563	1
HOUCK DAVID C	CPT	0-0522762	0746	2
HOUCK ELGG L	CW3	W-2205613	0966	1
HOUCK FREDERICK	LTC	0-0275930	0965	3
HOUCK RICHARD	CW2	W-2143203	0157	1
HOUFF CHARLES W	LTC	0-0474149	0163	1
HOUGEN JOHN H	COL	0-0260529	1154	2
HOUGH CECIL H	CPT	0-0504586	0949	1
HOUGH FLOYD W	LTC	0-0114626	0658	3
HOUGH GERALD L	LTC	0-1169576	0762	1
HOUGH HUGH P	LTC	0-1040244	0359	1
HOUGH KENNETH J	COL	0-0205551	0657	3
HOUGH ROBERT E	LTC	0-1588057	0563	1
HOUGH SUSANN Z	CPT	L-0502123	0450	2
HOUGHTALING HENRY M	MAJ	0-1799291	0264	1
HOUGHTALING JULES V	COL	0-0155552	0153	3
HOUGHTALING LESTER J	LTC	0-0431595	0566	2
HOUGHTALING ROBERT G	CW3	W-2209659	1068	1
HOUGHTON ALBERT R JR	LTC	0-0291930	0264	1
HOUGHTON CHARLES K	CPT	0-0364479	1044	2
HOUGHTON GEORGE A	CPT	0-0999315	0561	1
HOUGHTON HOLDEN R	LTC	0-0225683	0762	3
HOUGHTON HORACE	MAJ	0-1797999	0757	1
HOUGHTON RALPH H	MAJ	0-0263249	0367	3
HOUGHTON THURSTON T	COL	0-0187639	0556	3
HOUGHTON WENDELL T	CPT	0-1951486	1162	1
HOUGHTON WILLIAM S	COL	0-0234946	0246	2
HOUGLAND ARNOLD L	LTC	0-1000244	0159	1
HOUGLAND GERALD T	LTC	0-0499031	1164	1
HOUGLUM EDGAR J	1LT	0-2006949	0947	2
HOUK ELIJAH P S	CPT	0-1747016	0548	2
HOUK JAMES N	MAJ	0-1946296	0958	1
HOUK MOULTON	LTC	0-1011277	0968	3
HOUK THEODORE W	1LT	0-1702379	1042	2

NAME	GRADE	SVC NO	DATE RET MO YR	RET CODE
HOULDIN JOSEPH F	COL	0-0261838	0367	3
HOULEHAN FORREST G	LTC	0-0201947	0253	3
HOULEY JOSEPH P	COL	0-0115273	0546	2
HOURIHAN MARGARET A	LTC	N-0722062	0261	1
HOUSAND CHARLES	MAJ	0-0916681	0447	2
HOUSE CHARLES O	LTC	0-0570095	0865	1
HOUSE DOYLE F	MAJ	0-2007002	0156	1
HOUSE ELMER S	CW4	W-2127036	1154	1
HOUSE FRANK M	COL	0-0104262	1050	3
HOUSE GORDON H	LTC	0-1183091	1167	1
HOUSE HAROLD	2LT	0-1003550	0945	2
HOUSE HOWARD H	LTC	0-0255303	1148	3
HOUSE JAMES H	LTC	0-1179106	0761	1
HOUSE JERRY D	LTC	0-0257502	0454	1
HOUSE KENNETH	COL	0-0330566	0860	1
HOUSE LEON F	CPT	0-0496106	0550	1
HOUSE LLOYD JR	LTC	0-1030254	0258	1
HOUSE ORVAL D	MAJ	0-0256245	0658	3
HOUSE RAY W	CPT	0-0536489	1047	2
HOUSE ROBERT J	CW2	W-2214822	0866	1
HOUSE RUFUS W	LTC	0-2042893	0656	1
HOUSE WILLIAM J	CPT	0-0265364	0147	1
HOUSE WILLIAM J	LTC	0-0290652	1267	3
HOUSECROFT MAURICE	LTC	0-0230988	0646	2
HOUSEHOLDER EDGAR S	CW3	W-2209101	0167	2
HOUSEHOLDER ERNEST D	COL	0-0113398	0648	3
HOUSEL JAMES R JR	1LT	0-0414801	0546	2
HOUSEMAN DONELSON M	1LT	0-1062941	1046	2
HOUSEMAN EDGAR W	CPT	0-1283609	0461	1
HOUSEMAN EUGENE B	COL	0-0126762	0648	3
HOUSER CARL F	CPT	0-1016011	0557	1
HOUSER CHARLES H	CW4	W-2110981	1055	1
HOUSER DONALD S	LTC	0-0349402	0761	1
HOUSER EDWARD C	LTC	0-0225002	0160	3
HOUSER EDWIN F	LTC	0-0330734	1063	1
HOUSER HARRY W	MAJ	0-1579809	0758	1
HOUSER JOHN A	CW3	W-2145555	0761	1
HOUSER JOHN F	LTC	0-1184670	0364	1
HOUSER JOHN F	CW3	W-2207098	1265	1
HOUSER RAYMOND L	1LT	0-2023884	1045	2
HOUSER RICHARD A	MAJ	0-1036573	0962	1
HOUSER STEWART L	COL	0-0329609	1153	2
HOUSER WILLIAM E	MAJ	0-1799292	0465	1
HOUSER WILLIAM F	CPT	0-1291469	0960	1
HOUSER WILLIAM F	CW4	W-2111887	1155	1
HOUSETON MARVIN	MAJ	0-1686530	1057	1
HOUSH ROSCOE B	MAJ	0-0271833	0650	1
HOUSHOLDER BAYLESS G	COL	0-0307202	1060	1
HOUSHOLDER EARL R	LTC	0-0142434	1053	3
HOUSHOLDER QUENTIN L	1LT	0-0401775	0445	2
HOUSMAN CLIFFORD A	LTC	0-1546433	0966	1
HOUSNER WILLIAM F	2LT	0-0445610	0145	2
HOUSSEAS CONSTANTIN	LTC	0-0962316	1168	1
HOUSTON ALBERT W	CPT	0-0917504	0346	2
HOUSTON CORNELIUS	1LT	0-0524918	0545	2
HOUSTON GEORGE H	CW3	W-2207054	0366	1
HOUSTON GEORGE W	MAJ	0-1633016	1056	1
HOUSTON GLENN N	MAJ	0-0345358	1156	2
HOUSTON HAROLD A	MAJ	0-0147195	0648	3
HOUSTON HARRY A	LTC	0-1648304	0566	1
HOUSTON JAMES A	MAJ	0-1019098	1262	1
HOUSTON JAMES L	MAJ	0-1914039	1021	1
HOUSTON JOSEPH A	LTC	0-0241571	1146	1
HOUSTON KEITH R R	LTC	0-0279850	1164	3
HOUSTON NEWELL F	CPT	0-0527553	0650	1
HOUSTON NORMAN J	MAJ	0-0271364	0867	3
HOUSTON ROBERT W	LTC	0-0264741	0467	3
HOUSTON ROSCOE	CPT	0-0521297	0349	1
HOUSTON STEPHEN	LTC	0-1169577	0661	1
HOUY CHARLES F	CPT	0-1289584	0146	2
HOUY CORNELIUS	CPT	0-0525316	0154	2
HOUZE JESSE N	2LT	0-1534995	0647	2
HOUZVICKA OTTO A	MAJ	0-0274386	0960	3
HOVANEC JAMES F	LTC	0-1305872	0462	1
HOVANETZ CHARLES J	MAJ	0-1080205	0761	1

NAME	GRADE	SVC NO	DATE RET MO YR	RET CODE
HOVANSKI AUGUSTINE	1LT	0-1838077	0155	[illegible]
HOVAS EDWARD S	LTC	0-[illegible]	0151	3
HOVIOUS CARL C SR	CW4	W-0913170	0267	1
HOVE EVERETT	2LT	0-0888221	0343	2
HOVE OLIVER B	CPT	0-0510739	1066	1
HOVER RALPH	COL	0-0266197	0669	3
HOVER GALEN W	LTC	0-0214117	0857	3
HOVER HARRY S	LTC	0-0229840	0664	3
HOVER THEODORE W	LTC	0-0333405	1159	1
HOVEY ALLEN E	CPT	0-1043369	0966	1
HOVEY RICHARD B	LTC	0-0944758	1268	1
HOVIOUS JAMES W	MAJ	0-1332787	0265	1
HOVIS CARL A	LTC	0-0244568	0659	3
HOVIS CARL F	MAJ	0-1019157	1057	1
HOVIS HERBERT C	1LT	0-0291463	0844	2
HOVLAND DENNIS A	LTC	0-1331185	1165	1
HOVLAND HAROLD L	1LT	0-1041407	0845	2
HOVLAND MELVIN L	1LT	0-0314412	0743	2
HOVORKA KEITH J	1LT	0-0453209	0644	2
HOVSEPIAN JOSEPH	2LT	0-1081652	0545	2
HOWARD ALVA B	LTC	0-1548442	0561	1
HOWARD AMPLUS D	CPT	0-0406352	1043	2
HOWARD ANSEL B JR	2LT	0-0538432	0646	2
HOWARD ARNOLD J	LTC	0-0385190	0763	1
HOWARD ARTHUR G	CPT	0-0316923	1144	2
HOWARD BUCKLEY	CPT	0-0254332	0547	1
HOWARD CARROL J	MAJ	0-1018051	0657	1
HOWARD CHARLES A	MAJ	0-2263538	1065	1
HOWARD CHARLES B	LTC	0-0110895	0554	3
HOWARD CHARLES C	MAJ	0-1300489	0457	1
HOWARD CHARLES F	COL	0-0182482	0354	3
HOWARD CHARLES E	CPT	0-0451009	0754	1
HOWARD CHESTER A JR	1LT	0-1059156	0646	2
HOWARD CHESTER B	LTC	0-0324630	0867	3
HOWARD CLAIR L	LTC	0-0302920	0561	2
HOWARD DAN	MAJ	0-0985361	1164	1
HOWARD DAVID B	CPT	0-0365577	0646	2
HOWARD DAVID L	1LT	0-1577334	0858	2
HOWARD DAVID S	MAJ	0-1650913	0962	1
HOWARD DONALD K	COL	0-0277847	0363	3
HOWARD EDGAR M	MAJ	0-2206278	0766	1
HOWARD EDWARD B	CW3	W-2146249	0166	1
HOWARD EDWARD W	CPT	0-1583650	0263	1
HOWARD ELMER H	MAJ	0-0974703	0664	1
HOWARD EZRA E	LTC	0-0212841	0759	3
HOWARD FRANCIS M	MAJ	0-1683435	1154	1
HOWARD FRANK E	MAJ	0-0486217	1047	1
HOWARD FRANK N	LTC	0-0445142	1062	3
HOWARD FRANKLIN V	LTC	0-0365446	0547	2
HOWARD FRED F	1LT	0-2096512	0557	2
HOWARD FREDERICK	CPT	0-0147413	0846	2
HOWARD GASTON S	COL	0-0178234	0758	3
HOWARD GORDON	LTC	0-1175468	0263	1
HOWARD GROVER C	MAJ	0-1642205	0265	1
HOWARD HARRY	LTC	0-0979647	1168	1
HOWARD HARVEY E	CPT	0-0186389	0258	3
HOWARD HORACE G	2LT	0-1308822	0444	2
HOWARD IKE	CW2	W-2148012	0555	1
HOWARD IRA J	CW4	W-2105545	0260	1
HOWARD ISERAL JR	CW2	W-2148926	0560	1
HOWARD JAMES C	LTC	0-1551029	0762	1
HOWARD JAMES D JR	LTC	0-0230451	0265	3
HOWARD JAMES E	LTC	0-0284719	1265	3
HOWARD JAMES T	CW3	W-2152119	0864	1
HOWARD JEAN W	2LT	N-0764492	0546	1
HOWARD JENNINGS	1LT	0-1314486	0946	2
HOWARD JOHN	LTC	0-0271138	0966	3
HOWARD JOHN A	LTC	0-0467323	0267	1
HOWARD JOHN L	MAJ	0-1642994	1160	1
HOWARD JOHN T	CPT	0-0211684	0146	2
HOWARD JOHN W	LTC	0-0227343	0654	3
HOWARD JOSEPH B	MAJ	0-0285356	0349	2
HOWARD JOSEPH H	COL	0-0326698	0864	3
HOWARD JOSEPH J	MAJ	0-2049445	0457	1
HOWARD KENNETH D	CW3	W-2206132	0866	1

NAME	GRADE	SVC NO	DATE RET MO YR	RET CODE
HOWARD LAWRENCE J	LTC	0-1052822	0863	1
HOWARD LEONARD M	MAJ	0-0243662	1165	3
HOWARD LUCILLE F	MAJ	N-0761773	0964	1
HOWARD MARY D	1LT	L-0401064	0446	2
HOWARD MARY G	1LT	N-0720469	1144	1
HOWARD MELVIN W	CPT	0-1925929	0963	2
HOWARD RALPH I	CW3	W-2147685	0964	2
HOWARD RALPH M	LTC	0-1035490	0861	1
HOWARD RALPH S	LTC	0-1554753	0164	1
HOWARD RICHARD C	LTC	0-1546420	0165	1
HOWARD RICHARD F	COL	0-0192522	0862	3
HOWARD RICHARD F	CW3	RW-2141126	1161	1
HOWARD RICHMOND F	CPT	0-2028972	0655	1
HOWARD ROBERT	MAJ	0-1334708	0964	1
HOWARD ROBERT B	LTC	0-1338825	0866	1
HOWARD ROBERT B	MAJ	0-1591432	0667	3
HOWARD ROBERT H	CPT	0-0370311	0146	2
HOWARD ROBERT L	CW4	W-2108637	0555	1
HOWARD ROBERT L SR	CW2	W-2209976	0965	1
HOWARD ROBERT N	MAJ	0-1048025	0561	1
HOWARD ROBERT W	CW4	W-2143241	0562	1
HOWARD SAMUEL P	1LT	0-0497378	0552	1
HOWARD SANFORD S	CPT	0-0500266	0645	2
HOWARD SHELTON	WO1	W-2145811	0557	1
HOWARD SIMON	LTC	0-0300708	0960	1
HOWARD STEPHEN B	CW3	W-2152743	0560	1
HOWARD STERLING B	COL	0-0221575	0157	1
HOWARD SUMNER E	MAJ	0-1581809	0859	2
HOWARD TAYLOR D	LTC	0-0400090	0760	2
HOWARD TELFORD C	MAJ	0-1824024	1263	1
HOWARD THOMAS L	LTC	0-0266780	1060	3
HOWARD VAUGHAN H	CPT	0-0463811	0447	2
HOWARD VIRGIL F	LTC	0-0306293	0462	3
HOWARD WALTER A	MAJ	0-0147048	0648	3
HOWARD WALTER C	MAJ	0-1047583	1163	1
HOWARD WALTER R	MAJ	0-1876251	1065	1
HOWARD WILLIAM	CPT	0-1944709	0858	1
HOWARD WILLIAM R	LTC	0-0252190	0764	3
HOWARTH GEORGE A	COL	0-0254264	0146	2
HOWARTH JACOB M	MAJ	0-0209989	0948	3
HOWARTH JAMES W	LTC	0-0485426	1164	3
HOWARTH ROBERT F	2LT	0-1294477	1143	2
HOWARTH WILLIAM F	LTC	0-0505317	0361	3
HOWATT LESTER C	LTC	0-1647956	0562	1
HOWDEN DAVID C	CW2	W-2212344	0466	1
HOWE ARLAND G	CW3	W-2151517	0663	1
HOWE CHARLES F	LTC	0-0410503	1145	2
HOWE CLARENCE S	COL	0-0221768	0958	2
HOWE CLIFFORD W	CW3	RW-2146752	0166	1
HOWE DONIVAN J	CW3	W-2125915	0756	1
HOWE DOUGLAS K	LTC	0-0326700	0367	3
HOWE EDWARD W	COL	0-0311510	0347	2
HOWE EDWIN S	CW3	W-2117885	0460	1
HOWE EUGENE C	LTC	0-0247319	0866	3
HOWE JACK E	LTC	0-0391052	0261	1
HOWE JOHN H	MAJ	0-0969493	0762	1
HOWE JOSEPH G	COL	0-0273896	1061	3
HOWE NORMAN E	MAJ	0-0981607	1066	1
HOWE PAUL	LTC	0-0108019	1044	2
HOWE PAUL E	COL	0-0133473	0648	3
HOWE ROBERT E	LTC	0-0469178	0768	1
HOWE ROBERT H	CPT	0-0272869	0968	3
HOWE RUSSELL R	CPT	0-0297534	1044	2
HOWE WILLIAM M	CW3	W-2144886	0464	1
HOWE WISTAR C	MAJ	0-0217402	0844	2
HOWELL ALBERT	LTC	0-0436983	1047	2
HOWELL ALBERT O	MAJ	0-1081557	0767	1
HOWELL BEN O	CPT	0-0514304	0747	2
HOWELL BENJAMIN R	COL	0-0334097	1060	3
HOWELL CECILE M	2LT	N-0741109	0545	1
HOWELL CHARLES M	CW4	W-2203295	0766	1
HOWELL DALLAS C	2LT	0-1637710	0345	2
HOWELL DILLON J	LTC	0-0358938	0866	3
HOWELL EDGAR M	MAJ	0-0361620	0149	2
HOWELL EDWARD C JR	2LT	0-1591214	0644	2

NAME	GRADE	SVC NO	DATE RET MO YR	RET CODE
HOWELL ELI H	CPT	0-0472716	0645	2
HOWELL ERNEST W	COL	0-0269965	0159	1
HOWELL EUGENE J	CPT	0-0169919	0161	3
HOWELL EUGENE M	LTC	0-0275441	0768	3
HOWELL GEORGE F	1LT	0-0541130	0446	2
HOWELL GEORGE H JR	LTC	0-1307696	0560	1
HOWELL GORMAN H	CPT	0-0237451	0853	3
HOWELL HELEN K	2LT	N-0790415	0545	1
HOWELL HOWARD L	MAJ	0-1645690	0564	1
HOWELL IRA L	MAJ	0-0374971	0446	2
HOWELL J ALLEN	CPT	0-0434704	0745	2
HOWELL JACK K	2LT	0-1692955	0451	2
HOWELL JAMES C	CW2	W-2211090	1266	1
HOWELL JAMES W	CPT	0-1941678	0161	2
HOWELL JEFF D	2LT	0-1913712	0737	1
HOWELL JOHN S	COL	0-0358830	1067	1
HOWELL JOHN S JR	CW2	W-2205596	0263	1
HOWELL JOHNIE C JR	CW3	W-2147778	0563	1
HOWELL JOSEPH C	2LT	0-2055057	1045	2
HOWELL LEON	LTC	0-2031868	0955	2
HOWELL LESLIE D	LTC	0-0184616	0648	3
HOWELL LESSLIE S	COL	0-0150696	0357	3
HOWELL NED S	CPT	0-0172103	0953	3
HOWELL RALPH D	COL	0-0159900	0557	3
HOWELL ROBERT	CPT	0-1309884	1046	1
HOWELL ROBERT P	MAJ	0-2020994	0468	1
HOWELL ROBERT S	CPT	0-0312261	0546	2
HOWELL ROY K	MAJ	0-4030637	0666	2
HOWELL THOMAS P	CW3	W-2151911	0565	1
HOWELL VERNER L	CPT	0-0454248	0545	2
HOWELL WENDELL B	CW2	W-2202306	0367	3
HOWELL WILLIAM A	LTC	0-1294309	1163	1
HOWELL WILLIAM R	CPT	0-0323447	0345	2
HOWER EDWARD E	WO1	W-2147976	1053	1
HOWERTON MARION J	MAJ	0-0967032	0862	1
HOWERTON WILLIAM A	LTC	0-0249428	0262	3
HOWERY EMBLETON R	LTC	0-0155045	0953	3
HOWES ALFRED L	COL	0-0347348	0566	3
HOWES JOHN E	CPT	0-1933976	0364	1
HOWES WILLIAM R	CPT	0-0271965	0368	3
HOWEY CECIL A	CPT	0-1002945	0748	2
HOWEY ROBERT F	MAJ	0-2035326	0760	1
HOWEY STEPHEN H	1LT	0-0171178	0648	3
HOWEY THOM S L	WO1	W-2114840	1147	2
HOWITZ CLIFTON I	LTC	0-1180962	1163	1
HOWLAND BERNARD F	LTC	0-0512552	0548	2
HOWLAND CHARLES F	COL	0-0909099	0958	2
HOWLAND CHARLES T	CW4	W-2120855	0859	3
HOWLAND FRANCIS C	LTC	0-0396887	1147	2
HOWLAND JOHN A	CPT	0-0285445	0965	3
HOWLAND MERLE B	CPT	0-1061137	1057	1
HOWLAND RALPH G	2LT	0-2001032	1045	2
HOWLAND ROBERT D	LTC	0-1545490	0363	1
HOWLAND STANLEY E	CPT	0-0223062	0461	3
HOWLAND THOMAS R	1LT	0-5336768	0568	2
HOWLE WAYNE H	CPT	0-1919290	0862	1
HOWLETT ALICE M	2LT	N-0726947	0445	1
HOWLETT ARTHUR E	LTC	0-0901058	0847	2
HOWLETT EMMETT T	2LT	0-1304528	1044	2
HOWLETT ERNEST JR	1LT	0-1015746	1144	2
HOWLETT WALTER M	LTC	0-0500772	0145	2
HOWLEY FRANK L	B G	0-0299977	0363	3
HOWLEY HELENA M	MAJ	N-0721442	1264	2
HOWLEY WALTER R	CW3	W-2203330	1265	1
HOWLEY WAYNE F	1LT	0-0949024	0254	2
HOWRY HAMILTON H	LTC	0-0204595	1053	3
HOWSE JOHN B	MAJ	0-1932445	1266	1
HOWSON CHARLES F	MAJ	0-0148769	0549	3
HOWSON LEO B	LTC	0-0361763	1050	2
HOWTON FLOYD D	COL	0-0332443	0368	3
HOWZE GEORGE W	LTC	0-0427924	1264	1
HOWZE JOHN W	LTC	0-0378337	0163	1
HOXIE ALBERT T	MAJ	0-1899417	0863	1
HOXIE HARRIE E	COL	0-0225642	1055	3
HOXIE THEORA G	1LT	N-0755993	0646	1

NAME	GRADE	SVC NO	DATE RET MO YR	RET CODE
HOXSIE CLARENCE F	LTC	0-0272025	1066	3
HOXSIE NELSON C	LTC	0-0292407	0862	1
HOXSIE RUTH E	CPT	N-0722859	1047	1
HOY HENRY S	CPT	0-1290948	1048	1
HOY JAMES M	1LT	0-1045118	1045	2
HOYER HERBERT W	CPT	0-0945307	0360	1
HOYER JACK C	LTC	0-2215171	0169	1
HOYER JAMES R	2LT	0-2262541	1053	2
HOYER RAY F	CW3	W-2149115	0263	1
HOYLE ENOCH M	LTC	0-0558636	0468	3
HOYLE IRBY H	LTC	0-0271026	0643	2
HOYLE IVAN T	MAJ	0-0916440	1064	1
HOYT CHARLES F	1LT	0-1584380	0445	2
HOYT CLIFFORD R	CW2	W-3430469	1266	1
HOYT EMMETT G	COL	0-0192458	0555	3
HOYT FORD E	LTC	0-0414714	0668	3
HOYT FRED L SR	LTC	0-0190142	0648	3
HOYT GENEVIEVE	2LT	N-0727110	0647	1
HOYT HAZEN L	COL	0-0188925	0648	3
HOYT HOWARD A	CW2	W-2211771	0866	1
HOYT JACK M	CW3	W-2150635	1265	1
HOYT KENNETH D	MAJ	0-1081520	0563	1
HOYT OSCAR T	CPT	0-1557024	0557	2
HOYT RALPH F	CW2	W-2148604	0459	1
HOYT RALPH W JR	CW2	W-2152238	0763	1
HOYT RICHARD L	CPT	0-0454926	0260	1
HOYT RICHARD M	LTC	0-0214091	0162	3
HOYT WARREN J	COL	0-0155402	1155	3
HOYT WILLIAM C JR	CW3	W-2208171	0661	1
HOYT WILLIAM G	1LT	0-1302631	0646	2
HRDY EUGENE E	CW3	W-2148412	0965	1
HRICINAK WILLIAM E	CW4	W-2145014	0859	1
HRITZ JOHN G	COL	0-0260220	0747	2
HRNCIR EDITH M	2LT	N-0734715	0746	1
HROMADKA NICOLAS J	CW4	W-2114338	0656	1
HROMADKA THEODORE V	MAJ	0-1825912	0655	1
HRYSENKO PHILIP M	LTC	0-1302632	0167	1
HUANG RAYMOND L	CPT	0-0546494	0647	2
HUARD EDWARD J	LTC	0-1061432	0163	1
HUBACEK WILLIAM G	CW2	W-2213889	0168	1
HUBACH CLIFFORD E	MAJ	0-0243735	1161	3
HUBACH RALPH L	MAJ	0-0235381	0763	3
HUBAN GEORGE H	CPT	0-0370386	1051	2
HUBATA ROBERT	MAJ	0-0335218	1166	3
HUBBARD ALFRED W	CPT	0-0503228	1043	2
HUBBARD ARNOLD B	LTC	0-0323574	0364	3
HUBBARD ARTHUR W	CPT	0-0257325	0649	3
HUBBARD FRANK E	LTC	0-0205790	0346	2
HUBBARD FREDERICK	MAJ	0-1288840	0146	2
HUBBARD GEORGE R	1LT	0-0450263	0445	2
HUBBARD GLENN S	LTC	0-0326714	1063	3
HUBBARD HAROLD J	COL	0-0146581	1050	3
HUBBARD HENRY V S	MAJ	0-0117590	0648	3
HUBBARD JAMES R	CPT	0-1173297	0546	2
HUBBARD JOHN G	LTC	0-0169422	1158	3
HUBBARD JULIUS C JR	1LT	0-0461528	0146	2
HUBBARD KEITH B JR	LTC	0-0445097	0563	1
HUBBARD LEWIS E	LTC	0-0327798	0755	3
HUBBARD LOUIS D	LTC	0-0269400	0247	2
HUBBARD MACK J JR	CW2	W-2149217	0358	1
HUBBARD MAHLON G	LTC	0-0183411	0646	2
HUBBARD MCKINLEY	CW3	W-2145728	0860	1
HUBBARD PAUL W	COL	0-1547337	1067	1
HUBBARD PERCY C	MAJ	0-2265807	0168	1
HUBBARD SHELTON P	COL	0-0136858	0954	3
HUBBARD WILLIAM	COL	0-0228915	1047	2
HUBBARD WILLIAM D	LTC	0-0174562	0750	3
HUBBARD WILLIAM L	CW2	W-2149048	0460	1
HUBBARD WILLIAM M	MAJ	0-1323323	0357	1
HUBBARD WILLIAM R	COL	0-0212428	0954	3
HUBBELL EDWARD L	MAJ	0-0122389	0156	3
HUBBELL MARVIN F	LTC	0-0307207	0368	3
HUBBELL PORTER H	LTC	0-0343230	0467	3
HUBBELL RAYMOND M	MAJ	0-1303891	0457	1
HUBBELL WILBERT I	LTC	0-0309288	0958	3

NAME	GRADE	SVC NO	DATE RET MO YR	RET CODE
HUBBERT CECIL F	COL	0-1845901	0666	3
HUBBERT GEORGE O	MAJ	0-0450052	0568	3
HUBBS DONALD H	1LT	0-1283963	1044	2
HUBBS RONALD M	COL	0-0233350	0569	3
HUBBS ROY S	COL	0-0273122	0156	3
HUBER ALBERT F	LTC	0-0273895	0368	3
HUBER ALBERT W	CW2	W-2208597	0267	1
HUBER ALFRED E	2LT	0-1294478	1043	2
HUBER ARTHUR L	MAJ	0-4010575	1168	1
HUBER CARL J	MAJ	0-0353383	1166	3
HUBER CHARLES B	LTC	0-0492278	0960	3
HUBER CHARLES R	MAJ	0-0196697	0848	2
HUBER ERNEST A	CPT	0-0298116	1064	3
HUBER FRANCIS D	MAJ	0-0466903	0844	2
HUBER FRANCIS J	CW4	W-2145997	0768	1
HUBER JOSEPH P	1LT	0-1173999	1144	2
HUBER NATHAN	2LT	0-2306199	1061	1
HUBER WILLIAM J	LTC	0-0250907	0162	1
HUBER WILLIAM J	LTC	0-2208149	1158	1
HUBERT JAMES H JR	MAJ	0-0273089	0267	3
HUBERT MARION A	COL	0-0246028	0660	3
HUBERT ROLLAND F	LTC	0-0106322	0850	3
HUBIAK WILLIAM	MAJ	0-1177010	0258	1
HUBIN ELDOR F	CPT	0-0450189	0659	1
HUBKA CHARLES H	CW3	RW-2205940	0167	1
HUBKA WOODROW W	CPT	0-1322030	0647	2
HUBLER NORMAN W	COL	0-0334136	0565	1
HUBNER KARL	2LT	0-1777574	0845	1
HUBNER ROBERT R	MAJ	0-0200023	0559	3
HUBSCH ERWIN R	CW3	W-2142326	0361	1
HUC HARRY J	CW3	W-2148525	0264	1
HUCHISON ELDON A	COL	0-0189304	1150	3
HUCKABAY BEN M JR	LTC	0-1168731	0960	1
HUCKABAY JOHN B	MAJ	0-0476157	0346	2
HUCKABAY ZACHARY T	COL	0-1581812	1067	1
HUCKABEE JAMES G JR	1LT	0-1323432	1145	2
HUCKABY EDWARD V	MAJ	0-2000433	0562	2
HUCKABY THOMAS L	LTC	0-0248378	1265	3
HUCKINS JOSEPH	COL	0-0183637	1059	1
HUCKLEBERRY BOWEN C	LTC	0-0338158	0764	3
HUCKS HERBERT M JR	LTC	0-0293754	0647	2
HUDACEK JOSEPH M	MAJ	0-1796090	0262	1
HUDAK CHESTER A	CW3	W-2152023	1164	1
HUDAK CLARK J	1LT	0-0545152	0546	2
HUDAK DONALD M	MAJ	0-1546613	0267	1
HUDAK JOHN J JR	CPT	0-1584383	1144	2
HUDAK JOHN J JR	CW2	W-2148972	1155	1
HUDDART MAURICE	LTC	0-1313697	0161	1
HUDDELSON ALFRED JR	LTC	0-0135323	0653	3
HUDDERS EUGENE R	LTC	0-0927398	0765	1
HUDDLESON JAMES H	COL	0-0136700	0648	3
HUDDLESTON ALLAN E	CPT	0-1544555	1057	1
HUDDLESTON GRADY L	1LT	0-0513504	1145	2
HUDDLESTON JOSEPH B	CPT	0-0512589	0947	2
HUDDLESTON LESLIE E	LTC	0-1579817	1162	1
HUDDLESTON ORA L	LTC	0-0494942	0546	2
HUDDLESTON ROBERT A	LTC	0-0492159	1053	2
HUDDLESTON ROBERT C	CW3	W-2142643	0462	1
HUDDLESTON TERRELL D	LTC	0-1018753	0562	1
HUDDY DONALD C	LTC	0-1946995	0563	1
HUDELSON DANIEL H	M G	0-0247417	0562	3
HUDGINS JAMES W	LTC	0-0371018	0560	1
HUDGINS JETHRO T	LTC	0-0310669	1060	2
HUDGINS ROBERT J	LTC	0-0390289	0861	1
HUDGINS RUTH O	1LT	N-0764718	0547	1
HUDOCK JOSEPH A	MAJ	0-2015665	0263	1
HUDOCK STEVEN A	LTC	0-1585652	1162	1
HUDON JAMES R	MAJ	0-0310847	0560	1
HUDON RONALD E	CW3	W-2142965	1060	1
HUDSON ADDISON M	MAJ	0-1594914	0268	3
HUDSON ALFRED E A	MAJ	0-0443814	0847	2
HUDSON ANDREW C	CW3	W-3150353	1267	1
HUDSON CARL R	1LT	0-0436604	0946	2
HUDSON CARY A	LTC	0-0141134	1050	3
HUDSON CHARLES E	1LT	0-2007192	0747	1

NAME	GRADE	SVC NO	DATE RET MO YR	RET CODE
HUDSON CHARLES H JR	CW3	W-2146725	0860	1
HUDSON CHARLES R	CPT	0-0446447	1146	2
HUDSON CHARLES W	LTC	0-0452274	1265	1
HUDSON CLYDE J	1LT	0-2016467	0748	1
HUDSON COLLIS P	COL	0-0205664	0559	3
HUDSON DOWELL B	MAJ	0-2018519	0665	1
HUDSON EDWARD B	CPT	0-1321928	0447	2
HUDSON EDWIN	CPT	0-0208347	0653	3
HUDSON ERNEST B	MAJ	0-1179453	0756	1
HUDSON EVERETT B	LTC	0-1165630	0656	1
HUDSON GEORGE E	LTC	0-0249023	0667	3
HUDSON GEORGE H	COL	0-0215378	0659	3
HUDSON GEORGE H	MAJ	0-1688206	1262	1
HUDSON GERALD W	LTC	0-1633991	1163	1
HUDSON HEARL E	LTC	0-1574847	0763	1
HUDSON HENRY E	LTC	0-0397586	0365	3
HUDSON HOWARD V	CPT	0-0953569	0960	1
HUDSON JACK E	MAJ	0-0409969	0556	1
HUDSON JOHN L	1LT	0-1018290	0745	2
HUDSON JOHN M	MAJ	0-0521093	0767	3
HUDSON JOHN N	LTC	0-0346575	1058	1
HUDSON KING C	LTC	0-0106892	0354	3
HUDSON LLOYD D	1LT	0-1309150	0547	1
HUDSON LOIS	2LT	N-0726713	0146	1
HUDSON LYMAN I	WO1	W-2113867	1146	2
HUDSON NORMALL O	LTC	0-2000556	0764	1
HUDSON PAUL C	MAJ	0-1686722	0765	1
HUDSON PAUL L	LTC	0-1101050	0461	1
HUDSON PAUL R	CPT	0-0275476	0157	3
HUDSON RAYMOND B	CPT	0-1048027	1162	1
HUDSON RICHARD C	CW4	W-2142966	0663	1
HUDSON ROBERT O	1LT	0-2035945	0545	2
HUDSON ROBERT T	LTC	0-0450551	0960	1
HUDSON ROBERT T	MAJ	0-1018934	0161	1
HUDSON ROGER W	LTC	0-2035946	0960	1
HUDSON ROSS B	1LT	0-0332356	0264	3
HUDSON RUTH M	2LT	N-0722061	1143	1
HUDSON SUMNER JR	LTC	0-1574848	1265	1
HUDSON THEODORE K	LTC	0-1104871	0263	1
HUDSON TRUEMAN A	CPT	0-0345471	0447	2
HUDSON WALESTINE	CW3	W-2144749	0657	1
HUDSON WILBUR G	MAJ	0-2206398	0466	1
HUDSON WILLIAM A	CPT	0-1937185	1065	1
HUDSON WILLIAM F	1LT	0-0504127	0650	1
HUDSON WILLIAM R	WO1	W-2147039	0156	1
HUDSON WILLIAM T	LTC	0-0368369	0662	1
HUDSPETH BENJAMIN T	MAJ	0-0168093	0145	2
HUDSPETH JOHN H	LTC	0-0289090	0968	3
HUEFTLEIN HOWARD B	MAJ	0-0315303	0965	3
HUELSENKAMP ROY C	WO1	W-2116005	0447	1
HUERTA SALVADOR J	MAJ	0-1821154	0346	2
HUESER JOHN L	CW3	W-2207665	0767	1
HUESTON NORMAN R	LTC	0-0270669	0861	1
HUET MARCEL A	LTC	0-1640575	0762	1
HUET MARGARET L	2LT	N-0725692	0245	1
HUETTER BERNARD R JR	LTC	0-1100601	0666	1
HUEY ELLA	MAJ	N-0700356	0246	1
HUEY ELLIS J	COL	0-0326699	0365	3
HUEY HAMILTON G	LTC	0-0293953	0859	3
HUEY JAMES R	MAJ	0-0959241	0664	1
HUEY JAMES T JR	1LT	0-0376772	1042	2
HUEY REX R	LTC	0-0525323	0951	1
HUEY ROBERT L	LTC	0-1293776	0862	1
HUEY VICTOR B	LTC	0-0400216	0457	1
HUEY WILLIAM C	MAJ	0-0406826	0156	1
HUF WILLIAM F	LTC	0-0461543	0868	3
HUFF ALVIN	CW2	W-3151321	0467	1
HUFF CECIL G	CW3	W-2150559	0459	1
HUFF CHESTER A	MAJ	0-2210167	1264	1
HUFF CLARENCE W	COL	0-1646763	0268	1
HUFF CLYDE	WO1	W-2123763	0747	1
HUFF DAVID H	MAJ	0-0307353	0545	2
HUFF EDGAR C	LTC	0-1331047	1067	1
HUFF EDWARD G	1LT	0-1000588	0346	2
HUFF EMMETTE D	LTC	0-0258682	1157	2

NAME	GRADE	SVC NO	DATE RET MO YR	RET CODE
HUFF ERNEST H	LTC	0-0123934	0648	3
HUFF ERNEST R	COL	0-0241320	0350	2
HUFF FRED L JR	MAJ	0-1019542	1163	1
HUFF GARD P	1LT	M-0539309	0146	2
HUFF GEORGE O	CW2	W-2120860	0253	2
HUFF GILMON A	COL	0-0408081	0957	1
HUFF GORDON R	LTC	0-0438791	0864	1
HUFF HORACE A	LTC	0-1649497	1067	1
HUFF HUGHLEN	CW4	W-2105909	0959	1
HUFF JAMES R	MAJ	0-1010281	1062	1
HUFF JOHN P	LTC	0-1113264	0365	1
HUFF JOHN R	MAJ	0-1312160	0259	1
HUFF JOHN W	CPT	0-1649498	0553	1
HUFF LEE JR	LTC	0-0200491	0859	3
HUFF LEO E	LTC	0-0424444	1162	1
HUFF OWEN W	COL	0-0283957	1057	1
HUFF RALPH P	CW4	W-2115497	0661	1
HUFF REID B	LTC	0-0390555	0760	1
HUFF ROBERT E	MAJ	0-2266234	0665	1
HUFF RODERICK	LTC	0-1010967	0464	1
HUFFAKER HOWELL F	MAJ	0-0474027	1044	2
HUFFCUTT GORDON L	LTC	0-1633292	0965	1
HUFFER ELMER D	LTC	0-1017416	0866	1
HUFFER ROBERT W	CPT	0-0321249	1058	1
HUFFERD RALPH W	COL	0-0230956	0952	3
HUFFINE RODNEY C	MAJ	0-0390761	1161	1
HUFFINE ROY W	LTC	0-1584385	0367	3
HUFFMAN ARTIE C	CW3	W-2149703	1065	1
HUFFMAN CARROLL W	1LT	0-0419660	0542	2
HUFFMAN CLEO	CPT	0-0509978	0146	2
HUFFMAN JEAN D	LTC	0-0927177	1166	3
HUFFMAN FRANK L	MAJ	0-0504241	0456	1
HUFFMAN GEORGE H	LTC	0-0494380	1059	1
HUFFMAN HERBERT M	CW2	W-2145324	0459	1
HUFFMAN ISAIAH K	CPT	0-1919431	0462	1
HUFFMAN JAMES E	COL	0-0135322	0247	2
HUFFMAN JAMES V	CW3	W-2143598	0762	1
HUFFMAN ORVILLE L	CW3	W-2143000	0760	1
HUFFMAN ROBERT O	MAJ	0-0449769	0854	1
HUFFMAN RUSSELL L	MAJ	0-4074280	0867	1
HUFFMAN SAM H	MAJ	0-0237372	0566	3
HUFFORD BERLE K	LTC	0-0354872	0865	1
HUFFORD FLETCHER N	LTC	0-0121395	0154	3
HUFFORD FRANCIS G	COL	0-0164355	0758	3
HUFFSTUTLER THOMAS L	MAJ	0-0278000	1147	1
HUFFT RAYMOND F	LTC	0-0345018	1046	2
HUFSTADER ROBERT R	LTC	0-0243136	0659	3
HUGGETT EDWARD S	WO1	W-2148168	0457	1
HUGGINS CLARENCE N	LTC	0-1637713	0668	3
HUGGINS CLEVELAND	LTC	0-1056752	0864	1
HUGGINS EDWARD J	LTC	0-1544222	1060	1
HUGGINS ELMER P	1LT	0-1574849	0447	1
HUGGINS JAMES H	MAJ	0-0489825	0152	1
HUGGINS JAMES R	CPT	0-0337817	0445	2
HUGGINS JESSE M	LTC	0-0255751	0967	3
HUGGINS KENNETH L	MAJ	0-0346805	0663	3
HUGGINS MEREDITH M	LTC	0-0367960	0246	2
HUGGINS NEWMAN A	CW2	W-2152463	0663	1
HUGGINS NOAH L	CW4	W-2145887	1157	1
HUGGINS THOMAS V JR	CW4	W-2142518	0667	1
HUGGINS WILLIAM S	CPT	0-0394447	0245	2
HUGHES ALBERT G	1LT	0-1312418	0347	2
HUGHES ALBERT T	CW4	W-2109962	0959	1
HUGHES ALLEN G JR	MAJ	0-2018520	0563	1
HUGHES ALVAH F JR	MAJ	0-2049590	0765	1
HUGHES ARTHUR J JR	2LT	0-1312377	0745	2
HUGHES ARTHUR T	MAJ	0-0956066	0862	1
HUGHES AUGUST T	1LT	0-1949564	0546	2
HUGHES BEN M SR	CW2	W-2000417	0157	3
HUGHES BENJAMIN P JR	LTC	0-0522390	0768	3
HUGHES BODE	LTC	0-0214243	0662	1
HUGHES BYRON B	LTC	0-0392447	0361	1
HUGHES BYRON Z	LTC	0-0203706	0352	3
HUGHES CARL K	CPT	0-2015592	0860	1
HUGHES CARROLL V	LTC	0-1001369	0763	1

NAME	GRADE	SVC NO	DATE RET MO YR	RET CODE
HUGHES CHARLES E	CPT	0-1534763	104N	2
HUGHES CHRISTOPHE	1LT	0-0553476	1147	2
HUGHES CLIFFORD M	CPT	0-0508033	1045	2
HUGHES DANIEL A	1LT	0-1825958	0146	2
HUGHES DANIEL F	LTC	0-1285055	1061	1
HUGHES DANIEL J	COL	0-0273327	0646	2
HUGHES DAVID W	LTC	0-1055334	0466	1
HUGHES DAVIS G	LTC	0-0385747	1047	2
HUGHES DELBERT D	CW3	W-2210165	1168	2
HUGHES DONALD C	MAJ	0-1920239	0464	2
HUGHES DONALD M	LTC	0-0253153	0165	3
HUGHES EDWARD A	LTC	0-0277545	0756	3
HUGHES EDWARD J	1LT	0-1112770	1145	2
HUGHES EDWARD P JR	1LT	0-1321186	0448	2
HUGHES EDWIN A	CW2	W-2145159	0859	1
HUGHES ERNEST V	COL	0-0146725	0855	3
HUGHES ETHELYN	MAJ	N-0737493	0264	1
HUGHES FLOYD F JR	LTC	0-2210452	0768	1
HUGHES FRANK W JR	1LT	0-1114558	0945	2
HUGHES GEORGE B JR	LTC	0-1541518	0961	2
HUGHES GORDON R	MAJ	0-1056753	0465	3
HUGHES GUSS C	CW3	W-2106918	0960	1
HUGHES HAROLD C	MAJ	0-1685558	0666	1
HUGHES HARRY J	LTC	0-0451120	0857	1
HUGHES HARRY W	COL	0-0261543	0766	3
HUGHES HAWTHORNE	CPT	0-0450188	0146	2
HUGHES HOLLIS M	CPT	0-0398175	0466	2
HUGHES HONOR L	1LT	N-0723313	0846	1
HUGHES HORACE D	COL	0-0270638	0546	2
HUGHES HOWARD L	2LT	0-1058555	0345	2
HUGHES HOWELL P	CPT	0-1597520	1148	2
HUGHES HUGH A	MAJ	0-1168732	0662	1
HUGHES HUGH I	LTC	0-1107496	0367	3
HUGHES JAMES S	COL	0-0291135	0467	3
HUGHES JAMES T	MAJ	0-1651824	0461	1
HUGHES JESSE G	1LT	0-0237585	0642	2
HUGHES JOHN A JR	COL	0-0275063	0555	3
HUGHES JOHN G	MAJ	0-0236764	0965	3
HUGHES JOHN G	MAJ	0-0370159	1045	2
HUGHES JOHN J	COL	0-0271022	0848	1
HUGHES JOHN W	LTC	0-0349509	0664	3
HUGHES JOSEPH E	MAJ	0-0919342	0644	2
HUGHES JOSEPH H	COL	0-0257084	0757	3
HUGHES JOSEPH O JR	CW2	W-3430330	0567	1
HUGHES JOSEPH W	CW3	W-2152805	1062	1
HUGHES KEVIN G	LTC	0-1645684	1163	1
HUGHES LAVERNE F	2LT	0-1175503	0445	2
HUGHES LOTUS P	LTC	0-1578632	0261	1
HUGHES MARCELLUS	LTC	0-0453529	0861	1
HUGHES MARK P	COL	0-1577345	1064	1
HUGHES MARY R	2LT	N-0734061	1142	1
HUGHES MELVERN C	MAJ	0-1013215	0866	1
HUGHES OWAIN J	COL	0-0167288	1055	3
HUGHES PAUL	MAJ	0-0480645	1154	2
HUGHES PAUL W	LTC	0-1173656	0763	1
HUGHES RAYMOND L	CW2	W-2105152	0946	2
HUGHES RICHARD M	1LT	0-1104874	0248	2
HUGHES RICHARD M	1LT	0-1283434	0346	2
HUGHES RICHARD W	1LT	0-1312162	0246	2
HUGHES ROBERT C	LTC	0-0144667	0461	1
HUGHES ROBERT E	LTC	0-2007075	0768	1
HUGHES ROBERT G	MAJ	0-1327355	0562	1
HUGHES ROBERT S	LTC	0-1633992	1155	1
HUGHES ROBERT T	LTC	0-0251491	0766	3
HUGHES ROBERT W	COL	0-0232267	0156	3
HUGHES ROBERT W	1LT	0-1167037	0446	2
HUGHES ROY E	COL	0-0110519	0154	3
HUGHES ROY J	MAJ	0-1951623	0361	1
HUGHES SAM E	MAJ	0-0420242	0747	2
HUGHES SIDNEY	1LT	0-0510921	0553	1
HUGHES SIDNEY W	MAJ	0-0327246	0246	2
HUGHES THEODORE JR	LTC	0-1291280	1068	2
HUGHES THOMAS A	CW2	W-3151027	0868	1
HUGHES THOMAS H	2LT	0-1581185	0246	2
HUGHES THOMAS M	MAJ	0-0271467	0568	3

332-811 O - 69 - 14

NAME	GRADE	SVC NO	DATE RET MO YR	RET CODE
HUGHES THOMAS M	MAJ	0-1284777	0154	1
HUGHES THOMAS P	COL	0-0251576	0964	3
HUGHES WALTER B	LTC	0-0220372	0648	3
HUGHES WALTER J	MAJ	0-0216485	1057	3
HUGHES WARREN B	WO1	W-2126080	0245	2
HUGHES WILLIAM F	LTC	0-0280511	0868	3
HUGHES WILLIAM J	CW3	W-2152130	1162	2
HUGHES WILLIAM J JR	COL	0-0162756	0256	3
HUGHES WILLIS B	1LT	0-1285056	0146	2
HUGHES WINIFRED A	MAJ	N-0723604	0163	1
HUGHEY ALBERT K	MAJ	0-0509487	0248	1
HUGHEY ALVIN H	CPT	0-0305443	0444	2
HUGHEY DANIEL W	CPT	0-1578634	0745	2
HUGHEY EUGENE V	LTC	0-0506241	0456	1
HUGHEY WILLIAM O	CPT	0-0971338	0860	1
HUGHLETT RICHARD E	MAJ	0-0886397	0266	1
HUGHLING WALLACE C	LTC	0-0742423	1163	1
HUGHS MARVIN P	MAJ	0-0282592	0245	2
HUGHSON DAVID N	CPT	0-1823302	1264	1
HUGILL WILLIAM W	MAJ	0-0394848	0960	1
HUGINS HOLLIS N	LTC	0-0242642	1063	3
HUGO ALAN N	LTC	0-2034972	1067	1
HUGO HOWARD W	LTC	0-1574850	1060	1
HUGO MERRILL S	LTC	0-0251785	0858	3
HUGUELET ADALBERT F	MAJ	0-0506605	1145	2
HUGULEY THOMAS C	COL	0-0228181	0365	3
HUHN RICHARD C	1LT	0-1106836	1045	2
HUIE NELSON F	MAJ	0-0357972	0745	2
HUIET BEN T	COL	0-0188451	0355	3
HUINKER FLORIAN F	CW3	RW-2149828	1167	1
HUITT EVERT L	MAJ	0-2046393	1054	1
HUITT GEORGE J	LTC	0-1101881	0861	1
HULBERT DAVID P	CPT	0-0465144	0446	2
HULBERT MILDRED Y	1LT	N-0727715	1045	1
HULBERT NORMAN B	CPT	0-2034794	1152	2
HULETT ALBERT G	COL	0-0180036	0550	3
HULETT HENRY J	CPT	0-2262415	0161	1
HULGUS HELENE	MAJ	N-0788206	1267	1
HULIN DONALD F	MAJ	0-2035108	1062	1
HULIT CHARLES E	MAJ	0-1644955	1059	1
HULL ALBERT O	COL	0-0189752	0358	3
HULL CHARLES A	LTC	0-1000590	0657	1
HULL CHARLES L	LTC	0-0266121	0265	3
HULL CLARENCE G JR	COL	0-0268840	0668	3
HULL HARMON H	MAJ	0-0195032	0663	3
HULL HARRY G	LTC	0-0259746	0367	3
HULL HARRY J	2LT	0-1301491	0744	2
HULL HOWARD O JR	1LT	0-0535300	1046	2
HULL JAMES O	CW4	W-2005816	0867	1
HULL JOHN N	LTC	0-1592749	0357	1
HULL JOHN W	CPT	0-0252315	1266	3
HULL JOSEPH H	MAJ	0-1167478	0561	1
HULL MARION L	CPT	0-1933705	0165	1
HULL MAURICE E	CW4	W-2110550	0863	3
HULL MILTON E	LTC	0-0242659	0559	3
HULL ROBERT A	MAJ	0-1591218	0163	1
HULL ROBERT J	2LT	0-1058030	0145	2
HULL T G	2LT	0-2000016	0946	2
HULL TRAVIS A	LTC	0-1039690	0764	1
HULL WALKER F	COL	0-0211923	0648	3
HULL WILLIAM E	MAJ	0-1118910	1163	1
HULL WILLIAM M	MAJ	0-1799297	0359	1
HULL WILLIS O	LTC	0-0276217	0264	3
HULLER VERNON W	COL	0-0909273	0862	1
HULLEY OLIVER S	COL	0-0195268	0862	3
HULLINGER CLARENCE W	COL	0-0272403	0766	3
HULMER ERIC C	MAJ	0-1169170	0350	2
HULSE CHARLES M	MAJ	0-0889573	0762	1
HULSE CHESTER T	MAJ	0-2055365	1055	1
HULSE JOHN V SR	CW3	W-2141593	0163	1
HULSE KENNETH P	MAJ	0-0949784	1262	1
HULSER JULIAN V	LTC	0-0919646	0763	3
HULSEY CHARLES E	LTC	0-1845602	1164	1
HULSEY HOB	LTC	0-2011198	1068	1
HULSEY JOHN M JR	COL	0-0321630	0967	3

NAME	GRADE	SVC NO	DATE RET MO YR	RET CODE
HULSEY LLOYD W	CW3	W-2207666	0867	1
HULSLANDER DONALD J	MAJ	0-1576158	0564	1
HULSLANDER ROBERT E	MAJ	0-1288841	0847	2
HULTGREN HAROLD H	CPT	0-0170380	1051	3
HULTIN ALICE J	MAJ	N-0731487	0368	1
HULTZ ROY E	LTC	0-0183355	0753	3
HULTZEN GILBERT N	MAJ	0-1104875	0762	1
HULVERSON FREDERIC	CPT	0-0484621	1047	1
HUMASON DAN W	MAJ	0-0283240	0545	2
HUMBERT LOCKE R	COL	0-0237633	1165	3
HUMBERT REUBEN L	LTC	0-0292368	0960	3
HUMBERTSON CHARLES E	1LT	0-1324264	0147	2
HUMBLE DRURY L	1LT	0-1307244	0947	2
HUMBLE JUNIOR R	1LT	0-0919126	0945	2
HUME FRANCES M	2LT	N-0735008	0545	1
HUME FRANCIS	MAJ	0-0964064	0762	1
HUME JAMES N	LTC	0-0197747	1062	3
HUME JAMES T	2LT	0-2012472	1045	2
HUME JOSEPH F	CW2	W-2104165	0748	1
HUME MANSON E	1LT	0-1642210	1046	2
HUME ROBERT	MAJ	0-0218083	0664	3
HUME ROBERT C	COL	0-0352881	0568	3
HUMENANSKY HELEN C	MAJ	N-0725861	0962	1
HUMENCZUK WILLIAM M	1LT	0-1106218	0745	2
HUMENICK DANIEL F	MAJ	0-1881287	1066	1
HUMISTON FLOYD E	MAJ	0-1926880	0867	1
HUMKE LEWIS H	CW3	W-2203384	0567	1
HUMM EDWARD L	CPT	0-1549298	0961	1
HUMMEL CHESTER R	CW3	W-2147570	1165	1
HUMMEL DONALD J	MAJ	0-2266040	0268	1
HUMMEL FREDERICK	COL	0-0117319	0648	3
HUMMEL GLEN O	1LT	0-1010378	0144	2
HUMMEL JOHN D	LTC	0-1638957	1161	1
HUMMEL LYNN F	LTC	0-0271644	0668	3
HUMMEL MARSHALL L	LTC	0-1576855	0657	1
HUMMEL MARVIN J	LTC	0-0165936	0456	3
HUMMEL MATHIAS	LTC	0-0397092	0760	1
HUMMEL OSWALD R	COL	0-0318691	0660	1
HUMMEL VICTOR W	LTC	0-0451122	0656	1
HUMMEL WALTER A	LTC	0-1334150	0864	1
HUMMER EARL E	1LT	0-1182864	0346	2
HUMMER JOHN F	MAJ	0-1922705	1266	1
HUMMER ROBERT B F	1LT	0-2009786	0348	2
HUMMER ROBERT T	COL	0-1030781	1167	1
HUMMERT LLOYD C	LTC	0-1288555	1060	1
HUMMON DALE L	CPT	0-1633294	0760	3
HUMPHREY CHARLES D	MAJ	0-1330926	1163	1
HUMPHREY CLEMENT E	COL	0-0271741	1068	3
HUMPHREY ELMER W	LTC	0-0323528	1162	3
HUMPHREY EUGENE I	LTC	0-1036204	0662	1
HUMPHREY FRANK L	LTC	0-0452376	0361	1
HUMPHREY GEORGE L	2LT	0-1052006	1144	2
HUMPHREY GLENN	CPT	0-1186978	0357	1
HUMPHREY GORDON K	LTC	0-1319951	0162	1
HUMPHREY HERMAN G	CPT	0-0503229	1046	1
HUMPHREY JAMES E	LTC	0-0239832	0164	3
HUMPHREY JOHN A	CW3	W-2147577	0867	1
HUMPHREY JOHNNIE W	1LT	0-0885774	1148	1
HUMPHREY JOSEPH F	MAJ	0-1545264	0349	2
HUMPHREY JOSEPH R	COL	0-0234079	0356	3
HUMPHREY NEAL D	MAJ	0-0510904	0949	1
HUMPHREY OMAR J JR	LTC	0-0367274	0767	3
HUMPHREY PAUL J	CW3	W-2143922	1164	1
HUMPHREY ROBERT A	LTC	0-0505286	0966	1
HUMPHREY ROBERT L	1LT	0-1042841	1145	2
HUMPHREY STEADMAN F	LTC	0-1175173	0165	1
HUMPHREY THOMAS	CW3	W-2142101	1157	1
HUMPHREY WALTER T	CW2	W-3250606	0668	1
HUMPHREYS BURTON W	LTC	0-0288907	0961	1
HUMPHREYS JOHN B	MAJ	0-0416085	1060	1
HUMPHREYS ROBERT E	LTC	0-0266581	0858	1
HUMPHREYS ROBERT L	LTC	0-0235384	0165	3
HUMPHREYS TALMADGE W	LTC	0-1559708	1068	1
HUMPHREYS TREVOR R	1LT	0-1285058	0543	2
HUMPHREYS WILLIAM H	LTC	0-1553100	0662	2

NAME	GRADE	SVC NO	DATE RET MO YR	RET CODE
HUMPHRIES CECIL L	CPT	0-0410530	0246	2
HUMPHRIES EDWARD G	CW4	W-2143052	1263	1
HUMPHRIES JAMES M	1LT	0-0432691	0847	2
HUMPHRIES JEAN B	CW2	W-2149071	1162	1
HUMPHRIES RUFUS R	CW3	W-2146066	1058	1
HUMPHRIES WILLIAM C	MAJ	0-0442545	0946	2
HUMPHRY ROBERT E	MAJ	0-1036575	0661	1
HUMRIGHOUSE EUGENE B	LTC	0-1180550	0765	2
HUMSTON JOHN L	LTC	0-1553101	1265	1
HUNCILMAN HARRY A	COL	0-0225325	0357	1
HUNCILMAN ROBERT M	LTC	0-0258840	1267	3
HUNDERTMARK HENRY	MAJ	0-2019745	1063	1
HUNDLEY DALLAS B	MAJ	0-0319522	0749	1
HUNDLEY EMMETT G	LTC	0-0260636	1166	3
HUNDLEY PRESTON J	COL	0-0359751	0164	1
HUNDLEY ROY W	CPT	0-1173657	0147	2
HUNDLEY SEYMOUR	CPT	0-0517597	0863	1
HUNESS HARRY	LTC	0-0375767	0360	1
HUNEKE JOSEPH H	1LT	0-1046139	0568	2
HUNEKEN FREDERICK	LTC	0-0919635	0464	3
HUNEYCUTT ANDREW J	LTC	0-0265837	0463	3
HUNEYCUTT WILLIAM H	MAJ	0-1165182	1148	2
HUNGATE WILLIAM C JR	COL	0-0466386	0562	2
HUNGER ROLF	CW3	W-2152051	0864	1
HUNGERFORD CHARLES F	CW2	W-2205351	0361	1
HUNGERFORD HARLEY	LTC	0-1655644	0363	1
HUNGERFORD VICTOR JR	MAJ	0-1300567	0460	2
HUNICHEN GEORGE A	CW3	W-2152041	1062	1
HUNKE HARRY M JR	CPT	0-0965939	1061	1
HUNKE HOWARD R	1LT	0-1292885	0745	2
HUNKIN ALFRED J	1LT	0-1048029	0246	2
HUNN CLIFTON E	CW4	W-2144827	0857	1
HUNNELL CHARLES H	LTC	0-0345867	0561	3
HUNNICUTT GEORGE S	MAJ	0-0965592	1262	1
HUNNICUTT J R	MAJ	0-0232973	0754	3
HUNNICUTT JACK D	COL	0-0182344	0862	3
HUNNICUTT LAURENCE F	MAJ	0-0508982	0947	1
HUNSAKER GRAHAM	1LT	0-0483408	0348	1
HUNSAKER HARRIE E	MAJ	0-0332510	0246	2
HUNSAKER LYNN M	MAJ	0-1299891	0261	1
HUNSAKER WALTER S JR	LTC	0-1557945	1166	3
HUNSICKER JOHN F	2LT	0-1062732	0145	2
HUNSINGER CARL J	LTC	0-0346556	1060	1
HUNSINGER PAUL O	CPT	0-0469912	1053	2
HUNSTON THOMAS J	MAJ	0-0488986	0546	2
HUNSUCKER MARTIN R	MAJ	0-1648271	0365	1
HUNT ARTIS	CPT	0-1289429	0261	1
HUNT DOUGLAS N	MAJ	0-2013838	0661	1
HUNT EDGAR C	WO1	W-2147933	0255	1
HUNT EDWIN T	MAJ	0-1180218	1162	2
HUNT EUGENE A	CPT	0-1109785	0467	1
HUNT FRANK M	CPT	0-1641422	0763	1
HUNT FREDERICK	LTC	0-0193211	0561	3
HUNT FREDERICK	1LT	0-1556448	0446	2
HUNT GEORGE C	LTC	0-0466119	0657	1
HUNT GEORGE W	COL	0-0287236	1061	3
HUNT GRANT J JR	1LT	0-0514599	1145	2
HUNT HAROLD I	LTC	0-0285409	0356	3
HUNT HARRY A	MAJ	0-0478818	0955	1
HUNT HENRY	LTC	0-0241077	1265	3
HUNT HENRY A	MAJ	0-0990889	0468	1
HUNT HENRY C	CW3	W-2211546	0968	1
HUNT HERBERT F	MAJ	0-1180551	0561	1
HUNT HERBERT P	MAJ	0-2008389	0263	1
HUNT HERBERT T	LTC	0-0114051	1144	2
HUNT HORACE S	CW4	W-2002864	0666	3
HUNT JACK R	LTC	0-1590554	1262	1
HUNT JAMES A	MAJ	0-1684955	0165	2
HUNT JOE W	MAJ	0-0966811	0365	1
HUNT JOHN H	LTC	0-0288621	0860	1
HUNT JOHN P	MAJ	0-0510460	0954	1
HUNT JOSEPH B	CW4	W-2115886	0659	1
HUNT JOSEPH F	LTC	0-0281521	1055	2
HUNT KATHLEEN H	1LT	N-0733709	0346	1
HUNT KENNETH A	LTC	0-0324415	0258	1

NAME	GRADE	SVC NO	DATE RET MO YR	RET CODE
HUNT LESLIE R	LTC	0-1285763	0262	1
HUNT LINCOLN B	LTC	0-1557025	0167	1
HUNT MCCOWN E	LTC	0-0306091	1046	2
HUNT MELVIN B	MAJ	0-0312988	1145	2
HUNT MERWIN G	LTC	0-0450960	0257	1
HUNT NICHOLAS P	2LT	0-0109425	0447	1
HUNT PAUL D	MAJ	0-0298328	0367	3
HUNT PAUL R	LTC	0-0287938	0253	2
HUNT RALPH S JR	LTC	0-0265502	0947	2
HUNT RALPH W	LTC	0-0422585	1163	1
HUNT ROBERT M	CPT	0-2096574	1161	1
HUNT RUTH B	1LT	L-0200257	1145	2
HUNT SINGLETON	CW2	W-2101870	0753	1
HUNT STANLEY B	COL	0-0324525	0865	3
HUNT THOMAS C	LTC	0-0292612	0368	3
HUNT THOMAS L	WO1	W-2106964	1157	1
HUNT WALTER E	LTC	0-0382141	0960	1
HUNT WARREN T	LTC	0-0888460	0765	1
HUNT WENDELL K	1LT	0-1301999	0145	2
HUNT WILLARD C	MAJ	0-1300491	0761	1
HUNT WILLIAM A	CW3	W-2151929	0864	1
HUNT WILLIAM H	MAJ	0-0143742	0658	3
HUNT WILLIAM H	LTC	0-0350477	0259	1
HUNT WILLIAM T	MAJ	0-1316232	1058	1
HUNT WILLIAM W	MAJ	0-1536482	0562	1
HUNT WILLIAM W	LTC	0-1576163	0319	1
HUNTER ALFRED E	MAJ	0-2032956	0868	1
HUNTER ALLEN M	LTC	0-1297895	0167	1
HUNTER ARNOLD A	1LT	0-2025140	0352	1
HUNTER BARTON H	LTC	0-1289430	0466	3
HUNTER BERNARD A	1LT	0-1553280	0445	2
HUNTER CARL M	CW3	W-3150329	1068	1
HUNTER CETH T	CW3	W-2147761	0763	1
HUNTER CHARLES F	CW3	W-2144454	0459	1
HUNTER CHARLES S	LTC	0-0405172	0561	1
HUNTER CHARLES S JR	LTC	0-1001593	0368	3
HUNTER CLYDE E	CW2	W-3430005	0866	1
HUNTER DAMIE R	LTC	0-0915052	1064	3
HUNTER DARALD E	CPT	0-1581819	0353	2
HUNTER EARL H	MAJ	0-1583148	1164	3
HUNTER EDGAR L	LTC	0-0215154	0462	3
HUNTER EDWARD H	MAJ	0-0407672	1060	1
HUNTER EDWARD J	CPT	0-0397143	1157	2
HUNTER ELMO J	1LT	0-1050318	0245	2
HUNTER ELVIE	2LT	N-0733539	0144	1
HUNTER EVERETT D	CW3	W-2142852	0961	1
HUNTER F DONIVAN	MAJ	0-1581820	1046	2
HUNTER FRANK A	COL	0-0143666	1148	3
HUNTER FREDERICK	LTC	0-0949375	1068	1
HUNTER GEORGE C	LTC	0-1112774	0763	1
HUNTER GEORGE W	MAJ	0-0366052	0447	2
HUNTER GEORGE W	MAJ	0-1315832	0963	1
HUNTER HAROLD H	LTC	0-1645685	0365	1
HUNTER HARRY M	CPT	0-0918568	0544	2
HUNTER HELEN B	MAJ	N-0786402	0665	1
HUNTER HENRY F	MAJ	0-0451298	1057	1
HUNTER HOWARD J	LTC	0-0194742	1062	3
HUNTER HOWARD V	LTC	0-0111978	0953	3
HUNTER IRENE M	2LT	N-0724952	0545	1
HUNTER JAMES E	LTC	0-1289261	0762	1
HUNTER JAMES W	MAJ	0-0301643	0263	3
HUNTER JOHN	CPT	0-1824321	1163	1
HUNTER JOHN C	MAJ	0-1177012	1161	1
HUNTER JOHN E	LTC	0-1578637	0360	1
HUNTER JOHN G	MAJ	0-1688343	0963	1
HUNTER JOHN H	CPT	0-0262573	1265	3
HUNTER JOHN M	CPT	0-0399999	1044	2
HUNTER JOHN W	CW3	W-2144791	1061	2
HUNTER JOSEPH L	COL	0-0296064	0758	1
HUNTER KELVIN H	COL	0-0236203	0660	1
HUNTER KENNETH E	LTC	0-1633996	1163	1
HUNTER LEO E	MAJ	0-1591814	0862	1
HUNTER LESLIE C	LTC	0-0467517	0557	1
HUNTER LILLARD C JR	MAJ	0-2008198	0663	1
HUNTER NATHAN H	LTC	0-0118236	0955	3

NAME	GRADE	SVC NO	DATE RET MO YR	RET CODE	NAME	GRADE	SVC NO	DATE RET MO YR	RET CODE	NAME	GRADE	SVC NO	DATE RET MO YR	RET CODE	NAME	GRADE	SVC NO	DATE RET MO YR	RET CODE
HUNTER POLLY L	MAJ	N-0727520	1263	3	HURLEY PAUL F	MAJ	0-0322309	0665	3	HUSSEY JOHN C JR	2LT	0-2265996	0553	2	HUTCHISON ALEXANDER	CW3	W-2150771	0166	1
HUNTER RALPH L	LTC	0-0359088	0862	3	HURLEY PIERCE P	LTC	0-0336627	0163	3	HUSSEY JOHN J	CPT	0-1322554	1047	2	HUTCHISON AMOS M	CPT	0-0135020	0253	1
HUNTER RICHARD U	LTC	0-1576167	1162	1	HURLEY RANDALL V	LTC	0-0334447	0361	1	HUSSEY PIERCE L	LTC	0-0384432	0247	2	HUTCHISON BILLY J	MAJ	0-2012459	0365	1
HUNTER ROBERT R	CW2	W-2215294	0968	1	HURLEY ROBERT J	2LT	0-0946649	1051	2	HUSSMAN CARL A	CPT	0-0157472	0355	3	HUTCHISON DAVID W	MAJ	0-0281540	1267	3
HUNTER ROY V JR	LTC	0-2069781	0866	1	HURLEY SYDNEY J III	LTC	0-2033919	0168	1	HUSSMAN ROBERT R	2LT	0-1054275	0145	2	HUTCHISON EMMA B	1LT	N-0722471	1044	2
HUNTER SYDNEY B	CW2	W-2209411	0663	1	HURLEY THOMAS F	CPT	0-1012679	0647	2	HUSSONG CYRUS C	MAJ	0-1884150	1166	1	HUTCHISON GUY T	MAJ	0-1822574	0662	1
HUNTER SYLVESTER	MAJ	0-1302469	0761	1	HURLEY THOMAS F	CPT	0-2043251	0368	3	HUSSONG ROLAND W	COL	0-0476191	0968	3	HUTCHISON HERBERT A	CW3	W-2146924	0667	1
HUNTER THOMAS O	1LT	0-1325008	0146	2	HURLEY THOMAS J	MAJ	0-2018005	0563	1	HUSTACE CHARLES H JR	MAJ	0-1859375	0661	1	HUTCHISON JOSEPH C	M G	0-0209436	0354	3
HUNTER WALLACE L	MAJ	0-1698609	1262	1	HURLEY WILLIAM L	CW3	W-2153369	1265	1	HUSTED ARTHUR L	1LT	0-0302022	1160	3	HUTCHISON MACK J JR	LTC	0-1043115	0960	1
HUNTER WALTER C	CPT	0-0456464	0446	2	HURLEY WILLIAM T	LTC	0-2006084	0263	1	HUSTED ARTHUR L JR	CPT	0-1589282	0163	1	HUTCHISON MELVIN L	MAJ	0-1177013	0159	2
HUNTER WILLARD N	MAJ	0-1342379	1060	1	HURON BENJAMIN S	MAJ	0-0978571	0167	3	HUSTED DARWIN E	CW3	W-2144544	0262	1	HUTCHISON R R JR	1LT	0-1011258	0745	2
HUNTER WILLIAM D	LTC	0-2042677	0655	1	HURON HERBERT S	COL	0-0309683	0249	3	HUSTED KENNETH W	LTC	0-1105839	1267	3	HUTCHISON ROBERT L	MAJ	0-0307989	1144	2
HUNTER WILLIAM H	MAJ	0-1824026	1062	1	HURR HERMAN L	MAJ	0-2096795	1065	1	HUSTED ROBERT C	CPT	0-1299412	0947	2	HUTCHISON ROBERT S	CPT	0-0413712	1146	2
HUNTER WILLIAM R	LTC	0-1312934	0966	1	HURSEY FRANK H	CPT	0-0973477	0862	1	HUSTON CLYDE R	CPT	0-1995279	0446	2	HUTCHISON ROBERT W	CPT	0-0286296	1061	3
HUNTER WILMA A	1LT	N-0804147	0651	2	HURSEY WILBURN W	MAJ	0-1116603	1062	1	HUSTON DWIGHT H	2LT	0-2006268	1145	2	HUTCHISON SHELTON M	MAJ	0-0316449	1062	3
HUNTER WINFIELD K	LTC	0-0310724	0666	3	HURSH GUY C	MAJ	0-0510751	1047	2	HUSTON HARRY C	MAJ	0-1050731	0457	1	HUTCHISON THOMAS O	CPT	0-0949426	0161	1
HUNTINGTON BEN	COL	0-0130828	1151	3	HURST CHARLES E	MAJ	0-0498011	0346	2	HUSTON JOHN L	LTC	0-0311401	0457	3	HUTCHISON WILLIAM R	LTC	0-1799741	0768	1
HUNTINGTON HARRY W	LTC	0-2000222	0668	3	HURST CHILTON N	CW2	W-3150872	0666	1	HUSTON PHILIP S	LTC	0-0372177	0556	1	HUTEHKLES ALLEN G	LTC	0-0225754	0862	3
HUNTINGTON PARK W	COL	0-0180021	0755	3	HURST COY F	LTC	0-1102310	1162	1	HUSTRULID CLARENCE A	CPT	0-0525011	0546	2	HUTESON JOHN P	1LT	0-1645168	0949	2
HUNTINGTON RICHARD S	MAJ	0-0969468	0963	1	HURST DANIEL R	CW3	W-3150208	1068	1	HUSZCZA ANTHONY	CPT	0-1116086	0657	1	HUTH ELMORE P	1LT	0-0528172	1044	2
HUNTINGTON ROBERT A	LTC	0-0263253	1266	3	HURST ELMER F	LTC	0-1003947	0962	1	HUTCHENSON ESTELLA	MAJ	0-0491516	0851	1	HUTH GILBERT H	1LT	0-1291123	0545	2
HUNTINGTON ROBERT W	MAJ	0-1114976	0757	1	HURST FRANCIS M	CPT	0-0390560	0246	2	HUTCHEON FRANK G	2LT	0-1645687	1144	2	HUTH JOHN J	CW3	W-2146756	1160	1
HUNTINGTON ROY T	LTC	0-0373573	0963	1	HURST HENRY L	MAJ	0-1283073	0555	1	HUTCHERSON ABNER C	COL	0-0351785	0155	1	HUTH MARGARET M	2LT	N-0725707	0745	1
HUNTLEY DUANE L	LTC	0-1316903	1066	1	HURST HOWARD P	LTC	0-1287883	0657	1	HUTCHERSON GEORGE B	CPT	0-1120761	0457	1	HUTH MELVIN F	COL	0-0377452	0568	3
HUNTLEY FRANK B	LTC	0-1577353	0760	1	HURST ROBERT P	LTC	0-1059817	0466	1	HUTCHERSON KENNETH R	LTC	0-1319841	0962	1	HUTHOEFER GERALD E	1LT	0-5023828	0767	2
HUNTLEY FRANK P	2LT	0-2034679	0744	2	HURST ROBERT R	LTC	0-0301517	0868	3	HUTCHERSON PAUL M	LTC	0-0732706	0162	3	HUTMAKER MATTHEW A	LTC	0-0297672	0547	2
HUNTLEY HARVEY J	1LT	0-1288747	0145	2	HURST SAMUEL N	MAJ	0-2036605	0556	1	HUTCHERSON SAMUEL J	MAJ	0-0315241	0846	2	HUTNER SYDNEY	MAJ	0-0492328	0545	2
HUNTLEY OREN O	CW2	W-2143265	0563	1	HURST SIDNEY J	CPT	0-0386176	0146	2	HUTCHESON CHARLES B	LTC	0-1555704	0263	1	HUTSCHLER HELEN D	2LT	N-0723979	1043	1
HUNTLEY ROBERT M	CPT	0-0982263	0261	1	HURST THOMAS N	LTC	0-1182148	0768	1	HUTCHESON CHARLES F	MAJ	0-1002256	1158	1	HUTSON ARNOLD	LTC	0-0305003	0968	3
HUNTON 4TH ERPA	MAJ	0-0448389	0146	2	HURST THOMAS T	MAJ	0-0298484	0646	2	HUTCHESON GUILFORD J	LTC	0-0296625	0766	3	HUTSON ARTHUR E	COL	0-0247867	0167	3
HUNTOON DAVID H	COL	0-0345772	1060	1	HURST WARREN L	MAJ	0-2014462	1167	1	HUTCHESON JACK R	LTC	0-0315618	0745	2	HUTSON CLARENCE	LTC	0-1280431	0962	1
HUNTOON DONALD F	MAJ	0-0163592	0450	3	HURST WILLIAM E	LTC	0-0185771	0655	3	HUTCHESON PHILIP T	LTC	0-0946122	0667	1	HUTSON CLYDE	1LT	0-0887643	1147	2
HUNTOON JOHN E	CPT	0-0981978	0957	1	HURST WILLIAM P	1LT	0-2055193	0845	2	HUTCHESON ROBERT W	CPT	0-1894760	0958	1	HUTSON JAMES W	LTC	0-1101508	0647	2
HUNTSMAN GEORGE R	COL	0-0348057	0361	3	HURT ANDREW	CPT	0-2262286	1160	1	HUTCHESON WILLIAM M	CPT	0-0959320	0261	1	HUTSON RAYMOND C	LTC	0-2001806	0268	1
HUNTTER RAY F	CW2	W-2146836	0658	1	HURT CECIL A	COL	0-0322051	0267	3	HUTCHINGS ARTHUR	CW2	W-2105004	0160	1	HUTSON ROY O	CPT	0-0252977	0356	3
HUNZIKER LUTHER A	MAJ	0-1633998	0555	1	HURT CHARLES S	CPT	0-1319748	1047	2	HUTCHINGS CHARLES JR	COL	0-0439146	1153	1	HUTSON STANTON C	COL	0-2273266	1065	1
HUNZIKER ROBERT J	LTC	0-0371611	0258	1	HURT FREDERICK	LTC	0-1640581	0666	1	HUTCHINGS FRANK F	MAJ	0-0124967	0648	3	HUTT IRVIN C	CPT	0-1041580	0546	2
HUPFER CLARENCE G	COL	0-0274322	0855	1	HURT HOLCOMBE H	COL	0-0326697	0461	3	HUTCHINGS GEORGE E	LTC	0-1118224	0266	1	HUTT WILLIAM W	LTC	0-1014355	0667	1
HUPFER JOHN H	CW2	W-2203476	1062	1	HURT IRA H	COL	0-0204539	1150	3	HUTCHINGS HAROLD E	COL	0-0259395	0567	3	HUTTAR RICHARD V JR	MAJ	0-1341883	0766	1
HUPP WILLIAM O	CPT	0-1704229	0758	1	HURT JAMES E	CW2	W-2141594	0955	1	HUTCHINGS WILLIAM P	LTC	0-0487984	0855	1	HUTTENHAUER EDWARD A	CW4	W-2002978	0866	3
HUPPE ARTHUR C	LTC	0-0222272	0454	3	HURT JOSEPH G SR	CW2	W-2145920	0355	1	HUTCHINS ANDREW F	LTC	0-1013030	0462	1	HUTTER JAMES W	MAJ	0-1041799	1162	1
HUPPERICH CHARLES M	1LT	0-1551874	1058	3	HURT PETE E	CPT	0-0976882	1161	1	HUTCHINS BENTLEY S	LTC	0-0202197	0959	3	HUTTER ROBERT J	MAJ	0-1080291	1263	1
HURD ARCHIE G	CW4	W-2111695	0260	1	HURT ROBERT Z	LTC	0-0201931	0545	2	HUTCHINS CECIL C	LTC	0-0277028	0167	3	HUTTER STANLEY E	MAJ	0-0299343	1057	1
HURD ARNOLD H JR	MAJ	0-0535895	0763	1	HURT WILLIAM C JR	LTC	0-0255099	0168	3	HUTCHINS CHARLES F	COL	0-0113299	0648	3	HUTTINGER WILLIAM D	1LT	0-0460566	0352	2
HURD ELINOR K	CW3	V-0712068	1164	2	HURTEAU EVERETT F	MAJ	0-0356250	0446	2	HUTCHINS DAVID W JR	CW2	W-3430023	0963	1	HUTTLIN FRANK L	1LT	0-0926834	0647	2
HURD HERBERT N JR	CW2	W-2150541	1061	1	HURTES MILTON	2LT	0-1306274	1044	2	HUTCHINS ERNEST L	MAJ	0-0992429	1163	1	HUTTLINGER WILLIAM O	1LT	0-0943337	0653	2
HURD JARVIS C	1LT	0-0349943	0942	2	HURTGEN DONALD C	LTC	0-0296086	0968	3	HUTCHINS JAMES G JR	1LT	0-1116852	0646	2	HUTTNER RAYMOND D	LTC	0-0528748	0668	3
HURD JOHN A	MAJ	0-0297052	0868	3	HURTT CHARLES A	CW2	W-0906805	0157	1	HUTCHINS JAMES R	CW2	W-2150977	1055	2	HUTTO ALEXANDER	CW2	W-2123096	0452	2
HURD LESTER J	MAJ	0-0298324	0568	3	HURTT JESSE H	CW3	W-2143421	0265	1	HUTCHINS JOE L	MAJ	0-1922544	0866	1	HUTTO ARTHUR P	CW4	W-2142162	0860	1
HURD WILLIAM	2LT	0-1042059	0345	2	HURTT JOSEPH B	MAJ	0-2262458	0565	1	HUTCHINS JOHN P	1LT	0-0524382	1146	2	HUTTO JAMES B JR	CW2	W-2146153	0158	1
HUREAU WILFRED J JR	CW3	W-2207291	0765	1	HURTT JOSEPH T	MAJ	0-0259550	0167	3	HUTCHINS LEONARD B	MAJ	0-1030382	0257	1	HUTTO LIGE	1LT	0-1998404	0847	1
HUREWITZ SAMUEL	LTC	0-0488352	0466	1	HURWITH ALBERT E	CPT	0-0478885	0445	2	HUTCHINS LEROY W	LTC	0-1046498	0565	3	HUTTO TROY N	LTC	0-0252017	1265	3
HURIANEK JEROME W	CPT	0-1845446	0566	1	HURWITT FRANK	LTC	0-0131090	0648	3	HUTCHINS PAUL A	CPT	0-1550556	0960	3	HUTTON BRUCE M	LTC	0-1059818	0367	1
HURLBERT CHARLES E	CPT	0-4006455	0464	1	HURWITZ MORRIS H	LTC	0-0288428	0867	3	HUTCHINS ROBERT E	LTC	0-1019175	0457	1	HUTTON DONALD J	COL	0-0276370	1064	3
HURLBERT DWIGHT E	LTC	0-0973230	0367	1	HUSBAND FRANK J JR	MAJ	0-0374249	0447	2	HUTCHINS RUSSELL J	1LT	0-0386882	104N	2	HUTTON ELGIN T	CPT	0-1298402	0747	2
HURLBERT MARION R	CW4	W-2119543	0753	1	HUSBANDS SAMUEL	CPT	0-0973586	0562	1	HUTCHINSON BRYAN W	CW3	W-2153383	0663	1	HUTTON FRANK V	MAJ	0-2006928	1060	1
HURLBERT WILLIAM F	LTC	0-0219604	0456	3	HUSCH CHARLES J	CPT	0-1062210	0960	1	HUTCHINSON DORIS H	1LT	N-0756320	1145	2	HUTTON LORA E	1LT	N-0779071	0746	1
HURLBUT HAROLD L	LTC	0-1286491	0555	1	HUSCH LEWIS L	CW3	W-2111485	0456	1	HUTCHINSON GEORGE A	COL	0-0101910	1055	3	HUTTON LOUIS C	LTC	0-0195453	0653	3
HURLBUTT RALPH C	CPT	0-1646766	0846	2	HUSCHER EDWARD A	2LT	0-0558785	1145	2	HUTCHINSON GEORGE W	CPT	0-0358556	0168	3	HUTTON MAX P	MAJ	0-1019106	0163	1
HURLEN SEVERIN JR	CW4	W-2144156	1067	1	HUSEBYE WILLIAM V	2LT	0-1291643	0144	2	HUTCHINSON HENRY P	1LT	0-1166511	0545	2	HUTTON PHILIP W	LTC	0-0239370	1060	1
HURLEY ALICE K	LTC	N-0742358	0865	1	HUSEMAN CHARLES P	MAJ	0-1889827	1267	1	HUTCHINSON JAMES H	LTC	0-0246148	1149	3	HUTTON ROBERT L	MAJ	0-0497660	0652	1
HURLEY EDGAR J	2LT	0-0357991	0867	3	HUSEMAN GEORGE F	CW3	W-2142592	0356	1	HUTCHINSON LEWIS J	MAJ	0-0444775	1266	1	HUTTON ROBERT S	LTC	0-1170783	0966	2
HURLEY EDWARD J	LTC	0-1634913	1262	1	HUSEMANO ALTON	MAJ	0-0967757	0960	1	HUTCHINSON MANLY E	LTC	0-0236622	0355	3	HUTTON ROBERT W	MAJ	0-0355768	0446	2
HURLEY EDWIN P	COL	0-0901378	1263	3	HUSING RUDOLPH C	1LT	0-0522418	0845	2	HUTCHINSON MANNING E	LTC	0-1042842	0860	2	HUTTY HENRY F	1LT	0-0138134	0751	1
HURLEY FLEMING K	MAJ	0-1584389	1162	1	HUSKEA VICTOR G	CPT	0-0006099	0938	1	HUTCHINSON MILFORD B	LTC	0-1186107	1266	1	HUXFORD WILLIAM E	MAJ	0-0436471	0146	2
HURLEY GLADYS E	1LT	N-0755161	0747	1	HUSKEY EUGENE C	1LT	0-0353483	0244	2	HUTCHINSON OLIVER H	LTC	0-0422392	1066	3	HUXLEY WALTER F	MAJ	0-2033150	0563	1
HURLEY HOWARD W	CW3	W-2141089	0364	1	HUSKEY HOYLE H	MAJ	0-1588654	0157	1	HUTCHINSON P C	COL	0-0152716	1060	3	HUXTABLE JAMES T	MAJ	0-0964242	0061	1
HURLEY JAMES E JR	LTC	0-1048832	0261	1	HUSON CHARLES R	1LT	0-2262164	0558	1	HUTCHINSON ROBERT	MAJ	0-2035330	0562	1	HUYLER FRANK K	1LT	0-0450630	0345	2
HURLEY JOHN C	LTC	0-0299330	0257	1	HUSOS ALEXANDER	LTC	0-0448906	1060	1	HUTCHINSON SAM C	LTC	0-0257973	0762	1	HYATT ALLEN T	LTC	0-0325271	1064	1
HURLEY JOHN G	MAJ	0-2043263	1162	1	HUSS LAWRENCE B	2LT	0-0299960	0843	2	HUTCHINSON T G	LTC	0-1101883	1160	1	HYATT ARTHUR G	LTC	0-1541725	0161	1
HURLEY JOHN S	1LT	0-1298710	0945	2	HUSS WILLIAM J	CW2	W-2113620	0866	1	HUTCHINSON WILLIAM E	CW3	W-2205103	0864	1	HYATT FARRELL P	COL	0-0326695	1059	1
HURLEY JOHN S	CPT	0-2041434	0962	1	HUSSEY ALLIS F	MAJ	L-0706100	0763	1	HUTCHINSON WILLIAM H	COL	0-0254229	0659	3	HYATT FRANKLIN G	1LT	0-1031948	0146	2
HURLEY JOSEPH W	2LT	0-1648311	0545	2	HUSSEY ALPHONSE T	LTC	0-0110493	0848	3	HUTCHINSON WILLIAM L	MAJ	0-2042835	0559	1	HYATT HAROLD R B	MAJ	0-1998411	0661	1
HURLEY LAWRENCE E	MAJ	0-1931204	1168	1	HUSSEY BERNARD J	LTC	0-0450279	0651	2	HUTCHINSON WILLIAM T	CW3	W-2149072	0664	1	HYATT HOWARD C	MAJ	0-0979956	0864	1
HURLEY MARSHALL R	MAJ	0-2014784	1262	1	HUSSEY JOE W	MAJ	0-0470132	0862	1	HUTCHINSON 3RE E S	1LT	0-0425672	0144	2	HYATT JAMES F	MAJ	0-1924725	0868	1

NAME	GRADE	SVC NO	DATE RET MO YR	RET CODE
HYATT PAUL L	MAJ	0-1913290	0766	1
HYATT VIRLUS F	1LT	0-1295549	1044	2
HYDAKER VERNON F	COL	0-0221745	0459	3
HYDE ALBERT J	LTC	0-1551647	1162	2
HYDE ALLEN R	1LT	0-1102780	0443	2
HYDE ALVAN L	LTC	0-0194743	1162	3
HYDE BEATRICE N	MAJ	L-0221070	0168	3
HYDE BYRON G	LTC	0-0449553	0263	3
HYDE CLIFFORD L	1LT	0-1031326	1145	2
HYDE DAVID A	1LT	0-1645688	0148	2
HYDE DAVID T	1LT	0-1173101	1045	2
HYDE GARY	CPT	0-1178194	1056	1
HYDE GILBERT F	LTC	0-0336564	0163	3
HYDE HAROLD A	LTC	0-0301128	0868	3
HYDE HAROLD G	LTC	0-0241965	0452	3
HYDE HERBERT E	CW3	W-2146408	0463	1
HYDE JOHN B	MAJ	0-0230989	0856	3
HYDE MARTINA	MAJ	N-0767263	0765	3
HYDE ROBERT G	LTC	0-1167911	0760	1
HYDE ROBERT N	MAJ	0-1106222	1058	2
HYDE SYDNEY F	COL	0-0499610	1063	3
HYDE THEODORE L	MAJ	0-0241297	0744	2
HYDE THOMAS E	CW2	W-2210407	0865	1
HYDE VIRGIL F	CPT	0-0392001	0 45	2
HYDE WALTER H	LTC	0-0100531	1053	3
HYDE WILLARD N	CW4	W-2122908	0261	1
HYDE WILLIAM H	MAJ	0-0199396	0245	2
HYDEN CLYDE E	CPT	0-2016037	0358	1
HYDER BRYAN H	1LT	0-0255554	0967	3
HYDER WARREN L	CPT	0-0889746	0358	1
HYDRICK JOHN F	CPT	0-0249156	0465	3
HYDRICK LUTHER G JR	CW3	W-2210850	0768	1
HYDRICK ONAN A	COL	0-0102159	1048	3
HYDUK JAMES R	CPT	0-0907655	1147	2
HYDUSIK HARRY J	1LT	0-1636076	0945	2
HYER JOHN J	CW2	W-2145160	1055	1
HYER JULIEN C	COL	0-0199392	0454	3
HYER LAWRENCE E	1LT	0-4049704	1159	2
HYGYSCIAN PARASKA M	2LT	N-0704062	0244	1
HYKKONEN HERBERT W	1LT	0-1297727	1045	2
HYLAND CHARLES J	CPT	0-0425936	0445	2
HYLAND FREDERICK	COL	0-0921420	0567	3
HYLAND FREDERICK	LTC	0-1943998	0866	1
HYLAND GEORGE N	LTC	0-0144693	1054	3
HYLAND JOHN E	LTC	0-0470041	0668	3
HYLAND JOHN H	LTC	0-0302673	0948	1
HYLAND MARTIN J	LTC	0-0461549	1265	3
HYLER DONALD W	LTC	0-0971025	1164	1
HYLL FREDERICK	LTC	0-0451558	0452	2
HYLTON DOUGLAS M	LTC	0-1309370	0367	1
HYMAN HARRY H	LTC	0-0208135	0944	2
HYMAN HARRY J	LTC	0-0386394	0368	1
HYMAN JOSEPH A	1LT	0-1583150	0245	2
HYMAN MORRIS	MAJ	0-0335504	0246	2
HYMAN MORRIS	1LT	0-1296861	0446	2
HYMER WILLIAM L	CW3	W-2210342	1068	1
HYMES SYLVAN	CW3	W-2145107	0464	1
HYND ROBERT B	MAJ	0-0258391	0266	3
HYNDMAN THOMAS L JR	1LT	0-1877764	0755	2
HYNDS ANNE E	LTC	N-0701401	0746	1
HYNE HOWARD W	MAJ	0-0138045	0749	3
HYNES EDWARD P	WO1	W-2115151	0348	1
HYNES JAMES J	1LT	0-1014914	0147	2
HYNES JOHN J	LTC	0-0913035	0957	2
HYNES WALTER T	CW2	RW-3200114	0366	1
HYNES WILLIAM P	LTC	0-0183642	0346	2
HYRDOP GILBERT L	LTC	0-0337973	0849	2
HYROWSKI STANLEY	MAJ	0-2028504	0765	1
HYSICK ANDREW W	CPT	0-1012563	0140	2
HYSLOP GLEN	CW2	W-2205378	0157	1
HYTER ELMER L	CW4	W-2117905	0664	1
HYUN JOHN K H	LTC	0-1003116	0868	2
HYZER LELAND	MAJ	0-0155628	0157	3
HYZINSKI WALTER V	LTC	0-1101054	0357	1
IACOVELLA RICHARD G	MAJ	0-1175174	0862	1

NAME	GRADE	SVC NO	DATE RET MO YR	RET CODE
IADANZA IGINO J	MAJ	0-1927650	0666	1
IAFRATI JOHN G	MAJ	0-2017701	0463	1
IANNELLA DANIEL R	MAJ	0-0367085	0646	2
IANNIELLO RALPH J	2LT	0-2055283	0745	2
IANNONE ROBERT C	CPT	0-1886357	0463	1
IBANEZ SABINIANO	MAJ	0-0369949	0257	1
IBBOTSON HARRY F	LTC	0-1293594	0263	1
IBSEN CHRISTIAN	CPT	0-1108759	0157	1
IBSEN MAXWELL	CPT	0-1038016	0446	2
ICENHOWER GEORGE A	MAJ	0-1633299	0760	1
ICENOGLE DALE F	CW2	W-2208297	0164	1
ICHIYASU BENJAMIN M	1LT	0-2030601	0751	2
ICKES CHARLES V	LTC	0-1310115	0465	1
ICKES SARAH M	1LT	N-0771720	0146	1
ICKS ROBERT J	COL	0-0236090	1060	3
IDE HARVEY W	CPT	0-0245582	0361	3
IDE HERVEY V	LTC	0-0309066	0662	1
IDEKER HENRY J	CPT	0-2019595	1162	1
IELMINI JOHN C	2LT	0-1824028	0944	2
IFFT DANIEL G	LTC	0-1308341	0962	1
IFFT MURRY M	MAJ	0-0290908	1165	3
IFLAND WILLIAM J	CW3	W-2146845	0663	2
IGLESIA FRED	CPT	0-0325033	0651	1
IGLOE MAX C	LTC	0-0274490	0961	3
IGNACIO MARCELINO	CW2	W-2151069	0361	1
IGNACIO RICARDO	CPT	0-0890550	0758	1
IGNELZI MICHAEL A	LTC	0-0425122	1264	3
IGOE JAMES P	MAJ	0-1342380	0664	2
IHARA ELEANOR C	MAJ	M-0002742	0967	3
IHLENFELD HANEY E	COL	0-0101889	0156	3
IHLENFELDT BRUCE O	LTC	0-0528244	0364	1
IHLING CHARLES F	CW3	W-2153181	1164	1
IIDA HARRY S	MAJ	0-2030797	0163	1
IJAMES FRED L	MAJ	0-1292886	0662	1
IKARD ANNIE L	MAJ	L-0402681	0264	1
IKE JOSEPH C	1LT	0-0887641	0146	2
IKE WILLIAM P	CPT	0-0884923	0668	3
IKEGUCHI JOSEPH	LTC	0-2024413	0966	1
IKELER EARL R	CPT	0-0174782	0546	2
IKERMAN CHARLES R	LTC	0-1103233	0765	1
ILARDI JOSEPH P	LTC	0-1035121	0962	1
ILGENFRITZ JOSEPH J	LTC	0-0250698	0467	3
ILLES JOSEPH W	CPT	0-4009160	0966	1
ILLINGSWORTH ONEIDA	CPT	0-1172923	0558	1
ILLINGSWORTH R E	1LT	0-0501512	0946	1
ILLSCHE EDWARD A	1LT	0-0364520	1044	2
ILSLEY WILLIAM E	MAJ	0-4006342	[illegible]	1
ILSON JACOB L	1LT	0-0229424	0643	2
ILYAS SHAKIR T	MAJ	0-0357613	0145	2
ILYUS EDMUND B	MAJ	0-0146258	0558	3
IMBER ROBERT J	1LT	0-1315425	0846	2
IMBLEAU LOUIS C	WO1	W-2107006	1049	1
IMBODEN WILEY P	MAJ	0-2008030	0565	1
IMBODY GERALD R	LTC	0-0250756	0664	3
IMBRIACO NICHOLAS	MAJ	0-0970867	1063	1
IMBURGIA FRANK J	COL	0-0303360	0267	3
IMER OSCAR A	MAJ	0-2289516	0962	1
IMERMAN CARLYLE P	CPT	0-0504832	0446	2
IMES JAMES K	MAJ	0-2011314	0666	1
IMHOF WILLIAM L	CPT	0-1113268	0761	1
IMMEL DONALD C	MAJ	0-1318437	0762	1
IMMELL RALPH M	M G	0-0155458	1054	3
IMMER WILLIAM L	COL	0-0225801	0864	3
IMMING MILDRED M	MAJ	L-0703099	0167	1
IMMLER CHARLES W JR	1LT	0-1341429	0949	2
IMMROTH FRANK H	MAJ	0-0857421	0767	1
IMORI HENRY T	MAJ	0-2033003	1161	1
IMRE RAYMOND P	LTC	0-0323155	0868	3
IMSANDE LEMOINE E	LTC	0-0308634	1060	1
INABINET SHELTON E	1LT	0-1577360	0147	1
INABINETTE WILEY G	CW4	W-2201031	0867	3
INANO TOM	CW2	W-2209503	0365	1
INBODY ROY M	LTC	0-0114435	0353	3
INCE MARION M	CW3	W-2153228	1057	1
INO ALLISON W	COL	0-0304920	1160	1

NAME	GRADE	SVC NO	DATE RET MO YR	RET CODE
INO WALTER W	LTC	0-0309182	0758	3
INOACI ROBERT W	LTC	0-1301829	0265	1
INDERMILL ROY C	1LT	0-0370073	0845	2
INDERMILL WILLIAM G	LTC	0-2200203	1067	1
INDINGARD GEORGE T	1LT	0-0395646	1044	2
INDYK WALTER A	LTC	0-1647518	0958	1
INERFIELD ABRAHAM M	1LT	0-0531255	0245	2
INFANTI WALTER C	LTC	0-1057116	0767	1
ING EDMUND T K	LTC	0-0214636	0362	3
ING KENNETH	CW2	W-2148288	0761	1
INGALLS FRANCIS G	CPT	0-0519823	1044	2
INGALLS KEITH I	LTC	0-0258392	0866	3
INGALLS ROBERT H	COL	0-0226934	0565	3
INGARGIOLA HENRY B	MAJ	0-2039583	0661	1
INGE GEORGE H	COL	0-0243053	0560	3
INGEBRITSEN MELVIN B	CW3	W-2143167	0659	1
INGERSOLL CHARLES F	LTC	0-0460271	0846	2
INGERSOLL HAROLD H	LTC	0-1054007	0766	1
INGHAM RAY L	MAJ	0-2007977	1065	1
INGLE CLEO G	COL	0-0192407	0762	3
INGLE DAWN V	CW2	W-2141320	0960	1
INGLE JOHN D	1LT	0-1775825	0645	2
INGLE WADE H	LTC	0-0470487	0947	1
INGLEHART IRENE T	MAJ	N-0723336	0565	1
INGLIS CHARLES R	CPT	0-0287915	0368	3
INGLIS LESTER B	LTC	0-0177290	0860	3
INGLIS PETE	1LT	0-0909836	0445	2
INGLIS WALTER	CW2	W-2114274	0653	2
INGLIS WEBSTER P	CPT	0-1329009	0163	1
INGLIS WILLIAM G	MAJ	0-0254441	0866	3
INGOJO JOSE B	MAJ	0-1595649	1061	1
INGOLD E DEE	COL	0-0345701	1065	1
INGOLD WINFRED L	LTC	0-0204648	0146	2
INGOLDSBY BERTRAM T	MAJ	0-0455571	0546	2
INGRAHAM ARTHUR K	LTC	0-0158671	0654	3
INGRAHAM ERIC E	LTC	0-1587340	0862	1
INGRAHAM FRANCES A	MAJ	N-0727419	0268	2
INGRAHAM HERBERT S	LTC	0-0123532	0460	1
INGRAHAM PAUL S	CPT	0-1323572	0946	2
INGRAHM MERTON	2LT	0-0109513	0329	1
INGRAM CLAUDE R	COL	0-0286662	1059	1
INGRAM FRANK W	CPT	0-0239297	0964	3
INGRAM HAMILTON	CW2	W-2150003	0561	1
INGRAM HENRY L JR	1LT	0-1334295	0453	2
INGRAM JACK D	CW3	W-2149296	0561	1
INGRAM JAMES R	CPT	0-1951692	1159	1
INGRAM JAMES E	LTC	0-1179905	1163	1
INGRAM KENNETH	CW3	W-2206736	0866	1
INGRAM NEAL H	LTC	0-0250219	0965	3
INGRAM ROBERT C	COL	0-0315489	0962	3
INGRAM ROBERT W	CW4	W-2111353	1058	1
INGRAM RUBY K	2LT	N-0763415	0445	1
INGRAM TIMOTHY A	LTC	0-1595007	1265	1
INGRAM VERNON R	MAJ	0-0971815	0364	1
INGRAM VIRGINIA	MAJ	L-0402682	1267	1
INGRAM WILLIAM I	LTC	0-1323434	0260	1
INGRAM WILLIAM W	CPT	0-0376315	1143	2
INGRASCI JOE	1LT	0-1306942	0945	2
INGRUM ROBERT P	COL	0-0311741	0367	3
INGUI THOMAS	CPT	0-1294842	1058	1
INLOW EDGAR B	2LT	0-1322996	0245	2
INLOW GEORGE E	MAJ	0-1643706	1060	1
INMAN BUIS T	LTC	0-0265705	0868	3
INMAN DANIEL W	LTC	0-0446838	0263	1
INMAN ERNEST R	CW3	W-2153109	0563	1
INMAN HARRY H	WO1	W-2106907	0946	1
INMAN HOLLIS C	1LT	0-1549970	0245	2
INMAN JACK H	CW2	W-3420017	0967	1
INMAN JAMES E	COL	0-0217843	0862	3
INMAN MARJORIE C	2LT	N-0720868	1144	1
INMAN WILLIAM R	MAJ	0-0319923	0962	3
INNES CALDER	COL	0-0114045	0953	3
INNES RUCKER G	LTC	0-1288748	1266	1
INNES WILLIAM H	LTC	0-0102182	0648	3
INOMOTO SATORU T	MAJ	0-1999529	0564	1

NAME	GRADE	SVC NO	DATE RET MO YR	RET CODE
INOUYE DANIEL K	CPT	0-1998638	0547	2
INOUYE KIYOSHI	CW4	W-2132700	1064	1
INOUYE MASATO	LTC	0-0983466	0867	1
INSCOE THOMAS W	CW3	W-2203365	1166	1
INSKEEP CURTIS B	WO1	W-2166087	0744	2
INSKEEP HAZEL M	1LT	N-0771605	0146	1
INSLEY ALAN W	1LT	0-1948765	0946	2
INTAS EDWARD D	MAJ	0-0249365	0665	3
INUZUKA MINEO	LTC	0-2262986	0468	1
INZER EUGENE G	1LT	0-2007106	0347	2
INZER RAY L	COL	0-1288560	0860	1
IOERGER GEORGE A	LTC	0-0451143	0755	1
IORIO FRANK P	CPT	0-0509550	0746	2
IORIO HERMAN	MAJ	0-1341975	0761	1
IORIO JOSEPH P	MAJ	0-1081348	0865	1
IOSBAKER ERGO	COL	0-0275596	0767	3
IOVANELLA FRED	LTC	0-1844879	0763	1
IPPOLITO JOSEPH	CPT	0-1299571	0246	2
IPPOLITO LUCIANO	LTC	0-1576173	1156	1
IPSEN JAMES E	MAJ	0-4009161	0767	1
IPSON DONALD K	CPT	0-0368722	0146	2
IRBY B G	LTC	0-1301492	0664	1
IRBY WILLIAM I	CPT	0-0208185	0253	3
IRELAN WILLIAM E	LTC	0-0372411	0761	1
IRELAND EARL C	MAJ	0-1691951	0259	1
IRELAND EDWIN H	MAJ	0-1167913	0559	2
IRELAND EMMETT E	LTC	0-1316156	1264	1
IRELAND HARRY B	CPT	0-0410727	1044	2
IRELAND JOHN A	CPT	0-1922669	0564	1
IRELAND JOHN T	MAJ	0-2009289	0264	1
IRELAND LLOYD L	CPT	0-1165633	0355	1
IRELAND PAUL M	COL	0-0287277	0756	3
IRELAND THOMAS S	CPT	0-0278307	1043	2
IRELAND WILLIAM H	1LT	0-1546686	0146	2
IRESON ALFRED T	CPT	0-0548950	0347	2
IRGENS EDWIN R	LTC	0-0226759	0664	3
IRICK HAROLD L	CPT	0-1176073	0446	2
IRIE ROBERT K	1LT	0-1318638	1145	2
IRION VALENTINE	COL	0-0193283	1059	3
IRISH BLAINE S	MAJ	0-1015571	0364	1
IRISH EDWARD B	CPT	0-0179285	0648	3
IRISH EVERETT A	MAJ	0-0241119	0446	2
IRISH ROBERT J	COL	0-0180542	0450	2
IRISH WILLARD E	LTC	0-0368897	1066	1
IRIZARRY RAMIR-	CPT	0-0268111	0345	2
IRIZARRY RUDDIE E	MAJ	0-1326709	0165	1
IRIZARRY-ALVARE LUIS	MAJ	0-1685837	0769	1
IRLENBORN HENRY N	MAJ	0-0499575	1054	1
IRMEN CLAYTON R	CW3	W-2152847	1164	1
IRMISCH GEORGE W	CPT	0-0326838	0445	2
IRMSCHER ALDEN L	1LT	0-1116466	0346	2
IRONS GEORGE V	LTC	0-0195606	0962	3
IRONS MAURICE C	CW4	W-2109789	1061	3
IRONS TIMOTHY H	LTC	0-0555239	0768	1
IRONS WILLIAM	LTC	0-1581187	0861	1
IRSFELD HUBERT L	CPT	0-0338011	0447	2
IRTZ FREDEICK G	MAJ	0-0352819	0846	2
IRVIN DAVID F	CPT	0-1295721	0346	2
IRVIN FRANK P	CPT	0-1319418	0959	1
IRVIN JAMES M	1LT	0-1288901	1145	2
IRVIN RALPH D	MAJ	0-1935782	0167	1
IRVIN RAWLEIGH N	CW4	W-2149779	1164	1
IRVIN RICHARD K	CPT	0-0354527	1068	1
IRVINE ATHILL W	CPT	0-0242946	0156	3
IRVINE GEORGE W	COL	0-0310440	1266	1
IRVINE JAMES A	LTC	0-0158672	0150	3
IRVINE JAMES P	COL	0-0290867	0660	1
IRVINE JAMES W C	LTC	0-0490774	1165	3
IRVINE PERCY S JR	LTC	0-0258960	0866	3
IRVINE RAYMOND G JR	1LT	0-5006799	0463	2
IRVINE RICHARD R	MAJ	0-2014653	1262	1
IRVINE ROBERT F	LTC	0-0240959	1263	3
IRVINE ROBERT M	CPT	0-0413669	0945	2
IRVINE STANLEY R	1LT	0-0342533	1043	2
IRVINE WILLIAM L JR	1LT	0-0381985	0546	2

NAME	GRADE	SVC NO	DATE RET MO YR	RET CODE
IRVING CHARLES G	1LT	0-0992913	0253	2
IRVING EUGENE J	COL	0-0193054	1055	3
IRVING FRANK R	MAJ	0-0247858	0850	2
IRVING JAMES G	MAJ	0-0492541	1045	2
IRVING KENNETH J	LTC	0-1322748	1063	1
IRVING LOUIS C	LTC	0-0395485	0562	1
IRVING RICHARD H	CPT	0-0279782	0645	2
IRVING ROBERT L	COL	0-0224063	1160	3
IRVING WILLIAM	CPT	0-1284707	0146	2
IRWIN CARL H	COL	0-0307919	0457	1
IRWIN CHARLES W	1LT	0-0468943	0645	2
IRWIN DOUGLAS H	MAJ	0-2047693	0366	1
IRWIN EDWARD R	CPT	0-0506235	0356	1
IRWIN EMORY	CW3	W-2141110	1059	1
IRWIN FRANCIS L	COL	0-0233883	0865	3
IRWIN GEORGE A	LTC	0-0184886	1053	3
IRWIN GERALD B	CW3	W-2206595	0766	1
IRWIN HAL F	COL	0-0197769	0749	2
IRWIN HAROLD S	CPT	0-0155457	0353	3
IRWIN JAMES H	1LT	0-1932461	0467	2
IRWIN KNOX H JR	1LT	0-1698024	1144	2
IRWIN LAWRENCE J	LTC	0-0411471	0667	3
IRWIN LAWRENCE M	LTC	0-1755088	1268	1
IRWIN LILBURN C	CPT	0-0971315	1161	1
IRWIN LUTHER W	COL	0-0281661	0662	3
IRWIN MARGUERITE	MAJ	N-0735155	1267	1
IRWIN RICHARD C	MAJ	0-1002257	1156	1
IRWIN ROBERT B	LTC	0-1627734	0962	2
IRWIN RUEL C	MAJ	0-1543125	0954	1
IRWIN SAMUEL R	COL	0-0255291	0753	3
IRWIN THOMAS J	1LT	0-1102782	1045	2
IRWIN THOMAS N	MAJ	0-0529949	0545	2
IRWIN WILLIAM C	MAJ	0-0347966	1266	3
ISAAC AARON A	CPT	0-1951533	0763	1
ISAAC EVARD E	LTC	0-0265586	0868	3
ISAAC JAMES E	MAJ	0-4009639	0568	1
ISAAC THOMAS J	1LT	0-0467404	0546	2
ISAACS COLEMAN L	CPT	0-0474882	0244	2
ISAACS FREDERICK	2LT	0-1043000	0245	2
ISAACS LEONARD S	1LT	0-1581825	0145	2
ISAACS RAY C	COL	0-0284090	0462	1
ISAACS ROY R	LTC	0-1167914	0457	1
ISAACS SAM	1LT	0-1306721	1045	2
ISAACSON SAMUEL	2LT	0-1301830	0445	2
ISABELL JAMES C	CPT	0-1181494	0258	1
ISACCO ANDREW J	CPT	0-0921805	0146	2
ISACKSEN FRED R	COL	0-0432654	1063	3
ISBELL EARL B	2LT	0-1316422	0451	2
ISBELL FLETCHER F	LTC	0-0384699	0466	3
ISBELL JOSEPH B	MAJ	0-1583156	0457	1
ISBERG EDWIN S	MAJ	0-0166509	1053	3
ISCH ALFRED E	LTC	0-1285764	0560	1
ISCH IRA L	MAJ	0-1933753	0467	1
ISEKE HAROLD J	MAJ	0-2043182	0860	1
ISEL JOHN W	1LT	0-1117883	0646	2
ISELEY WILLARD L	CW3	W-2152806	1262	1
ISELY CHARLES C JR	LTC	0-0268258	0565	3
ISEMINGER BERTRAND L	CW4	W-2128185	0659	1
ISEMINGER BOYD A	LTC	0-0192302	0660	3
ISENBARGER JOHN P	1LT	0-2019882	0452	2
ISENBERG BEATRICE T	1LT	N-0723808	0846	1
ISENBERG CARL L	COL	0-0236930	0163	1
ISENBERG FRANCIS R	MAJ	0-1106847	0264	1
ISENBERG GEORGE W	LTC	0-0445101	0166	1
ISENBERG WILBUR M	CW3	W-2153288	0867	1
ISENBERG WILLIAM G	LTC	0-0915606	1062	1
ISENHART JACK V	CW2	W-2211213	0165	1
ISERMAN FLOYD C	1LT	0-1551034	0146	2
ISERMANN CHRISTIAN	MAJ	0-0265965	0662	3
ISETT ROBERT L	LTC	0-1015281	0165	1
ISGRIGG JOHN G	LTC	0-0415076	0662	1
ISHAM HELEN J	1LT	N-0757859	0847	1
ISHAM ORVILLE A	LTC	0-0396860	0960	1
ISHEE VAUGHN E	LTC	0-0332028	0646	2
ISHER JOHN J	WO1	W-2151647	1058	1
ISHLER ANSCEL I	LTC	0-1684505	0466	3
ISHMAEL JOHN R	CW3	W-2145301	1162	1
ISHMAEL WILLIAM K	MAJ	0-1701707	0246	2
ISHMAEL WILLIAM P	MAJ	0-1176075	0758	1
ISIKOFF MORRIS F	1LT	0-1316423	0346	2
ISLAN ALFRED F JR	1LT	0-1043371	104N	2
ISLER NATHANIEL	LTC	0-0244541	0663	3
ISLER SIMMONS H III	LTC	0-1041582	0162	1
ISLEY CARL J	LTC	0-0348085	1045	2
ISLEY LAMONT O	1LT	0-1289913	1045	2
ISOARO MAX C	LTC	0-0267266	0960	3
ISOLA CHARLES J	1LT	0-1303893	0246	2
ISOM CLEBURNE R	CW3	W-2123148	0256	1
ISOM OLIN G JR	CPT	0-0363081	0645	2
ISON FRANCIS Z	2LT	0-0355116	0342	2
ISON JASPER G JR	CW2	W-2208700	0864	1
ISON VENON H	MAJ	0-2014663	1262	1
ISRAEL ERNEST A	LTC	0-0345014	0868	3
ISRAEL HARRY P	LTC	0-1114175	0163	1
ISRAEL LEONARD	CPT	0-1306426	0946	2
ISRAEL MURRAY	CPT	0-0317984	1144	2
ISRAEL THEODORE J	MAJ	0-0183286	1053	3
ISRAELSON CARL I	MAJ	0-0252972	0949	3
ISTA MYRON H	1LT	0-1318800	1045	2
ITERMAN GEORGE E	LTC	0-0205619	1048	3
ITO KANEMITSU	MAJ	0-1336220	0363	1
ITO PAUL H	CW3	W-2133589	0365	1
ITZEN HERBERT W	MAJ	0-1296216	1159	1
IVANHOE HERMAN	CPT	0-0520997	0147	2
IVANUSHKA MICHAEL	MAJ	0-1322155	0462	1
IVERS JERE J	LTC	0-0283583	0758	1
IVERS JERE J	MAJ	0-1825537	0263	1
IVERSEN CHESTER A JR	COL	0-0912598	1068	3
IVERSEN ERNEST C	MAJ	0-1574265	0561	1
IVERSEN LYLE L	COL	0-0297912	0867	3
IVERSEN MERLE G	MAJ	0-0254495	0167	3
IVERSON JAMES R	2LT	0-1290424	0544	2
IVES ARTHUR D	COL	0-1306844	1067	1
IVES HOWARD S	COL	0-0204678	0860	3
IVES JOHN B	LTC	0-0496991	0356	1
IVES JOHN P	WO1	W-2148393	0752	2
IVES LAVERN V	1LT	0-1996716	1049	1
IVES ROBERT M	B G	0-0140472	0459	3
IVES ROBERT P JR	CW2	W-2212541	1166	1
IVES WILLIAM	CPT	0-1588657	0551	2
IVEY ALBERT J	LTC	0-0294028	1165	3
IVEY CURTIS	MAJ	0-1300493	0656	1
IVEY CURTIS J	LTC	0-0450034	1160	1
IVEY DANIEL W	MAJ	0-1002950	0356	1
IVEY EVAN W	CW2	W-2205134	0662	1
IVEY FRANCIS D	MAJ	0-0450962	0858	1
IVEY JACK B	MAJ	0-0561349	0361	1
IVEY JAMES E	2LT	0-2018171	0559	1
IVEY JOHN C	LTC	0-0369179	0955	1
IVEY JOHN O	MAJ	0-1113763	0949	2
IVEY KENNETH R	CW4	W-2003927	0768	1
IVEY MARJORIE T	MAJ	N-0774927	0568	1
IVEY OLIVER T	LTC	0-0246237	1167	3
IVEY PAUL B	1LT	0-1283439	0745	2
IVEY ROBERT U	MAJ	0-1280770	0256	1
IVINS RICHARD	1LT	0-1053190	0946	2
IVINS WILLIAM O	LTC	0-1643708	0365	1
IVORY MAURICE L	CPT	0-1999768	0860	1
IVY ELDRIDGE L SR	MAJ	0-1931833	1066	1
IVY JAMES M	MAJ	0-2033261	0758	1
IVY ROBERT H	COL	0-0150639	0648	3
IVY WILLIAM J	CW3	W-2141910	0559	1
IVY WILLIAM R	MAJ	0-0374129	0760	1
IWAI GERO	LTC	0-0282546	0657	1
IWAKIRI GEORGE K	CW4	W-2135973	0767	1
IWANAGA SAM S	MAJ	0-2030799	1263	1
IWASA WALTER M	1LT	0-2046479	0347	2
IWICKI GEORGE T	LTC	0-0350705	0768	3
IZER STEWART G JR	LTC	0-1541656	1063	1
IZON GEORGE W JR	MAJ	0-1102783	1061	2
IZQUIERDO OSVALDO M	LTC	0-0349023	0260	1
IZZO WALLACE J	LTC	0-1634004	0661	1
JABBO JOHN J	CPT	0-0504839	0745	2
JACK ARCH M	MAJ	0-1299750	0564	3
JACK CARL R	LTC	0-0240287	1160	3
JACK CHARLES W	CPT	0-0464730	0146	2
JACK RALPH E	CW3	W-2144094	1057	1
JACK WHITFIELD	M G	0-0267915	0866	3
JACKETT ROBERT W	CW3	W-2147272	1162	1
JACKLEY LESTER J	MAJ	0-1016242	0262	1
JACKLIN BARBARA A	1LT	N-0741190	1045	1
JACKMAN GLEN R	LTC	0-0415813	0767	1
JACKMAN REESE H	COL	0-0441876	0854	1
JACKS CARL L	1LT	0-1318439	1046	2
JACKS GEORGE R	COL	0-0250352	0747	1
JACKS HERMAN R	LTC	0-1641429	0160	1
JACKS HOLON E	MAJ	0-0453483	0655	1
JACKSON ALBERT H	CW3	W-2141321	0564	1
JACKSON ALFRED C	CPT	0-0103491	0648	3
JACKSON ARCILCUS E	1LT	0-0411484	0946	2
JACKSON ARTHUR A JR	LTC	0-1167915	1064	1
JACKSON ARTHUR E	MAJ	0-2011598	0163	1
JACKSON AUBRA G	CW4	W-2150725	0558	1
JACKSON AUSTIN F	MAJ	0-1179461	0364	1
JACKSON BAYARD	CPT	0-1170433	0551	1
JACKSON BERNARD F	CPT	0-1288384	0747	2
JACKSON BESSIE M	2LT	N-0700246	0835	1
JACKSON BILLY G	CPT	0-4010896	0768	1
JACKSON BIRKHEAD	MAJ	0-1172924	0461	1
JACKSON BRYAN H	CW2	W-3153425	0968	1
JACKSON BYRON B	1LT	0-0441753	1045	2
JACKSON CALVIN A	1LT	0-1302002	0446	2
JACKSON CALVIN G	COL	0-0282071	1053	2
JACKSON CECIL M	LTC	0-1290607	1161	1
JACKSON CHARLES A	MAJ	0-1541797	0362	2
JACKSON CHARLES A JR	LTC	0-0260355	0767	3
JACKSON CHARLES F	LTC	0-1043672	0161	1
JACKSON CHARLES H	CPT	0-1574266	1061	1
JACKSON CHARLES K	CPT	0-0386346	1057	1
JACKSON CHARLES L	CW2	W-2147149	1166	1
JACKSON CHARLES S	1LT	0-1325992	1045	2
JACKSON CHESLEY C	MAJ	0-0414358	0647	2
JACKSON CHESTER T	MAJ	0-1999177	1157	1
JACKSON CHRISTENE	MAJ	N-0768550	0266	1
JACKSON CLAUDE L	MAJ	0-0251738	0346	2
JACKSON CLIFFORD C	1LT	0-0499777	0250	1
JACKSON CLIFFORD T	LTC	0-1634922	0261	1
JACKSON COLUMBUS S	LTC	0-0283241	0168	3
JACKSON DALE	MAJ	0-1313350	0157	2
JACKSON DAVID G	LTC	0-0164014	1145	1
JACKSON DAVID W	CW2	W-2148859	1157	1
JACKSON DONALD F	MAJ	0-1323066	0865	1
JACKSON DONALD W	MAJ	0-1336068	0164	1
JACKSON DUANE P	LTC	0-1177850	1062	1
JACKSON DUGALD C JR	COL	0-0125948	0855	3
JACKSON DWIGHT M	CPT	0-0258583	0867	3
JACKSON EARL L	LTC	0-0248839	0557	3
JACKSON EDGAR A	CW4	W-2103047	0156	1
JACKSON EDWARD J	CW2	W-2109217	0450	1
JACKSON EDWARD R	CW2	W-2213145	0866	1
JACKSON EDWARD W	MAJ	0-1299751	0163	1
JACKSON EMERY D K	COL	0-0361657	1160	1
JACKSON EMERY L	LTC	0-0903529	0565	1
JACKSON EUGENE K	LTC	0-0909554	1265	3
JACKSON EUGENE W	1LT	0-2025390	1157	1
JACKSON EVERETTE H	LTC	0-0103633	0648	3
JACKSON FLOYD L	LTC	0-0238738	0562	3
JACKSON FORREST A	CW3	W-2150768	0266	1
JACKSON FOSTER G	LTC	0-0216019	0945	2
JACKSON FRANK	1LT	0-2055816	1145	2
JACKSON FRED A	2LT	0-1013843	0844	2
JACKSON GAYLON C	LTC	0-1318801	0764	1
JACKSON GEORGE	MAJ	0-2053916	0157	1
JACKSON GEORGE A	MAJ	0-0258855	1266	3
JACKSON GEORGE O	MAJ	0-0949983	0762	1
JACKSON GEORGE S	CW2	W-2217243	0868	2
JACKSON GEORGE W	LTC	0-0272495	0967	3
JACKSON GEORGE W	CW3	W-3430026	1068	1
JACKSON GERALD G	CW2	W-3410003	0666	1
JACKSON GERTRUDE Q	MAJ	N-0758319	0161	2
JACKSON HAROLD	MAJ	0-1647522	1163	1
JACKSON HAROLD D	CPT	0-0280717	0545	2
JACKSON HARVEY C	LTC	0-1331052	0467	1
JACKSON HERBERT H	COL	0-0321939	0468	3
JACKSON HORACE R	LTC	0-1174004	0366	1
JACKSON HORACE W	COL	0-0261815	0361	3
JACKSON HOWARD	MAJ	0-1059507	0557	1
JACKSON HOWARD A	CW3	W-2145934	0268	1
JACKSON HOWARD G	MAJ	0-1637740	0558	1
JACKSON HOWARD H	MAJ	0-0158534	0453	3
JACKSON HUGH O	1LT	0-0447796	0646	2
JACKSON IGAL C	LTC	0-1556736	1067	3
JACKSON JAMES	WO1	W-2150986	0957	1
JACKSON JAMES A	MAJ	0-0995669	0463	1
JACKSON JAMES C	COL	0-0146123	0856	3
JACKSON JAMES D	MAJ	0-0971329	0265	1
JACKSON JAMES L	MAJ	0-2263352	0563	1
JACKSON JAMES M	2LT	0-0556908	1045	2
JACKSON JAMES M JR	COL	0-0311245	1262	1
JACKSON JAMES P	MAJ	0-1311896	0862	1
JACKSON JAMES T	1LT	0-1317308	0746	2
JACKSON JAMES T	CW3	W-2119651	0454	1
JACKSON JERRY	MAJ	0-1283779	0749	1
JACKSON JESSE A	LTC	0-0161782	0648	3
JACKSON JESSE R	LTC	0-0904506	1046	2
JACKSON JOE	1LT	0-1317242	0644	2
JACKSON JOE N	MAJ	0-1919436	0967	1
JACKSON JOHN	LTC	0-0975865	0868	1
JACKSON JOHN E	LTC	0-0296148	0140	2
JACKSON JOHN F	1LT	0-0936121	0848	2
JACKSON JOHN M	CW4	W-2114227	1052	1
JACKSON JOHN W	LTC	0-1295551	0962	2
JACKSON JOHN W	CW3	W-2113841	1057	1
JACKSON JOSEPH	LTC	0-0461773	1053	1
JACKSON KENNETH	LTC	0-0321905	0662	1
JACKSON KENNETH L	LTC	0-1647964	0566	1
JACKSON KERMITT H	CPT	0-1299752	0957	2
JACKSON KIRBY E	LTC	0-0150462	1053	3
JACKSON KYLE R	LTC	0-0888596	0560	1
JACKSON LELAND A	MAJ	0-0281065	0945	2
JACKSON LEO M	COL	0-0241757	1049	3
JACKSON LEWIS A	CPT	0-0289372	0662	3
JACKSON LEWIS R JR	1LT	0-1002794	0545	2
JACKSON LLOYD S	MAJ	0-0671551	0764	1
JACKSON LONNIE H	CPT	0-0439999	0752	1
JACKSON LYNN S	MAJ	0-0249027	1059	2
JACKSON MARION G	MAJ	N-0720999	0965	3
JACKSON MAURICE W	1LT	0-1287886	0646	2
JACKSON MERVIN E	CW2	W-2110155	1046	1
JACKSON MILFORD G	LTC	0-1577366	0266	1
JACKSON NEIL	LTC	0-0393372	1160	1
JACKSON NEIL C	CPT	0-0385816	1045	2
JACKSON PAUL V JR	MAJ	0-1169585	0561	2
JACKSON PAUL W	MAJ	0-1015385	0157	1
JACKSON PETER F	CW3	W-2150543	0763	1
JACKSON RALPH L	CW2	W-2147492	0563	1
JACKSON REUBEN A	CPT	0-0487993	0948	1
JACKSON REX H	CW3	W-2143923	0160	1
JACKSON RILEY V	COL	0-0368342	0167	1
JACKSON ROBERT C	CW3	W-2144476	0561	1
JACKSON ROBERT F	MAJ	0-0949185	0465	2
JACKSON ROBERT F	MAJ	0-1690937	1061	1
JACKSON ROBERT G	CPT	0-0690574	1063	1
JACKSON ROBERT H	MAJ	0-1646273	0562	1
JACKSON ROBERT I	1LT	0-0439602	0346	2
JACKSON ROBERT L	CPT	0-0485087	0450	1
JACKSON ROBERT T	CW3	W-2147977	0263	1
JACKSON ROY D	CW3	W-2207643	0668	1
JACKSON ROY T	COL	0-1030044	1167	1
JACKSON S LESTER	CPT	0-1765098	0648	2

NAME	GRADE	SVC NO	DATE RET MO YR	RET CODE
JACKSON SAM L	MAJ	0-0213491	1060	3
JACKSON SAMUEL O	CW4	W-2109338	0452	1
JACKSON SAMUEL S	WO1	W-2129767	0745	2
JACKSON SAMUEL T JR	MAJ	0-1304223	1162	2
JACKSON STANFORD L	MAJ	0-0345545	0647	2
JACKSON TEDDY	CPT	0-0973442	1160	1
JACKSON THOMAS F	LTC	0-0517859	0866	3
JACKSON THOMAS H	1LT	0-1109380	1046	2
JACKSON THOMAS J	CW3	W-2205938	1065	1
JACKSON THOMAS K	MAJ	0-1293417	0857	1
JACKSON THOMAS R	COL	0-0121010	0556	3
JACKSON THOMAS S	CPT	0-0419595	1145	2
JACKSON VERNE D	LTC	0-0188125	0752	2
JACKSON VESTER A	LTC	0-0257685	0463	3
JACKSON WALLACE B	MAJ	0-1945173	0164	1
JACKSON WAYNE C	CPT	0-0396281	0845	2
JACKSON WELDON L	MAJ	0-0949905	0168	1
JACKSON WILBUR P	CPT	0-0888906	0447	1
JACKSON WILBURN E	LTC	0-1062211	0766	1
JACKSON WILLIAM A	1LT	0-0989508	0153	2
JACKSON WILLIAM A JR	CPT	0-1294843	0755	1
JACKSON WILLIAM B	MAJ	0-1283967	0662	2
JACKSON WILLIAM B	1LT	0-2048028	1045	2
JACKSON WILLIAM C	COL	0-0271925	0268	3
JACKSON WILLIAM C	COL	0-1633303	1163	1
JACKSON WILLIAM D	B G	0-0169668	0751	3
JACKSON WILLIAM F	CW3	RW-2208811	0766	1
JACKSON WILLIAM G	MAJ	0-0274365	0855	3
JACKSON WILLIAM H	COL	0-0115612	0351	3
JACKSON WILLIAM H	1LT	0-1316757	0146	2
JACKSON WILLIAM J	MAJ	0-0411432	1161	2
JACKSON WILLIAM L	CPT	0-1292530	0646	2
JACKSON WILLIAM M	COL	0-0202774	0556	3
JACKSON WILLIAM N	LTC	0-1324540	0767	1
JACKSON WILLIAM S	MAJ	0-0376831	1060	1
JACKSON WILLIE	CW2	W-2114588	0348	1
JACKSON WILLIS	1LT	0-1335009	0252	2
JACKY ALFRED W	MAJ	0-1935039	0167	1
JACO PAUL M	MAJ	0-0982552	0465	1
JACOB CARROLL D	2LT	0-1177851	0544	2
JACOB GLADYS L	CPT	N-0736423	0247	1
JACOB HAROLD D	MAJ	0-1885251	1165	1
JACOB PABLO	CW2	W-3440010	0866	1
JACOBBERGER BERNARD	MAJ	0-0224257	0164	3
JACOBELLI AMADEO J	LTC	0-0452898	0156	1
JACOBERGER PHILIP F	1LT	0-1945387	0957	1
JACOBI FRED W	COL	0-0349477	0865	1
JACOBI LEE	LTC	0-0117720	0953	3
JACOBS ARTHUR H	CW3	W-2148323	0162	1
JACOBS BURL	CW4	W-2148380	1266	1
JACOBS CHARLES E	LTC	0-1325395	0163	1
JACOBS CHARLES R	CPT	0-1300971	0346	2
JACOBS EDWARD J	CW4	W-2136700	0966	1
JACOBS FRANK H	LTC	0-0224803	1154	3
JACOBS GEORGE C	MAJ	0-0477360	0253	1
JACOBS GERALD JR	LTC	0-0443753	1064	1
JACOBS HAROLD H	LTC	0-1554402	1266	3
JACOBS HELEN	MAJ	M-0002574	0366	1
JACOBS HERBERT	LTC	0-0502664	0964	3
JACOBS HERBERT S	MAJ	0-0312114	0145	2
JACOBS HUBERT L	COL	0-0114761	0160	3
JACOBS JOHN R	COL	0-0237210	0458	3
JACOBS JOSEPH W	LTC	0-1541922	1161	1
JACOBS JULIUS C	CPT	0-1304736	0546	2
JACOBS LESTER A	LTC	0-0182316	0845	2
JACOBS LEWIS	CPT	0-0484653	0945	2
JACOBS LOUIS L JR	MAJ	0-1335010	0465	1
JACOBS MARTIN H	CPT	0-0436240	0348	2
JACOBS MAURICE R	2LT	0-0108933	1040	1
JACOBS MELVIN W	CPT	0-0477934	0945	2
JACOBS MURRAY J	1LT	0-1639211	0646	2
JACOBS NELSON E	MAJ	0-2033974	1162	1
JACOBS NEWTON N	COL	0-0255001	0954	1
JACOBS PAUL E	COL	0-0251138	0267	3
JACOBS PAUL H	COL	0-0238903	0760	1

NAME	GRADE	SVC NO	DATE RET MO YR	RET CODE
JACOBS RALPH E	CW3	W-2147257	0764	1
JACOBS REGINALD F	COL	0-0241186	0763	3
JACOBS RENE L	MAJ	0-0964850	0666	1
JACOBS ROBERT E	LTC	0-1895665	0966	1
JACOBS ROYAL A	COL	0-0296454	0360	1
JACOBS SAMUEL S	1LT	0-1310116	0945	2
JACOBS SHIRLEY C	MAJ	0-2033082	0461	1
JACOBS SIMSON	WO1	W-2124023	0745	2
JACOBS STANLEY J	CPT	0-1306276	1047	2
JACOBS STEPHEN T	LTC	0-0503353	0756	1
JACOBS UEDE L	CW4	W-2104720	0559	1
JACOBS VINCENT H	B G	0-0237721	0749	3
JACOBS WILLIAM A SR	CPT	0-1919345	0562	1
JACOBSEN CARL E	LTC	0-0363522	0959	1
JACOBSEN CHARLES W	COL	0-0176712	0154	3
JACOBSEN EDWARD H	LTC	0-0137779	0648	3
JACOBSEN ERIC M	1LT	0-0469849	0546	2
JACOBSEN ERIC S	MAJ	0-1326305	0759	1
JACOBSEN FRANK E	LTC	0-0194856	0461	3
JACOBSEN GEORGE C	LTC	0-2035332	0667	1
JACOBSEN GORDON F	CPT	0-1053653	0755	1
JACOBSEN SOPHUS C	COL	0-0121535	0352	3
JACOBSEN WALTER C	1LT	0-1060820	1045	2
JACOBSMEYER ROBERT R	COL	0-0272121	0868	3
JACOBSON AL	CW3	W-2152298	0862	1
JACOBSON ALFRED H	LTC	0-0295767	1147	2
JACOBSON ANDREW K	2LT	0-1297201	0644	2
JACOBSON ARVID O	LTC	0-1644446	0968	3
JACOBSON CARL A	COL	0-0263399	0565	3
JACOBSON CLARENCE M	CW3	W-2144290	0661	1
JACOBSON EINO M	LTC	0-0308344	0666	3
JACOBSON GEORGE H	CW2	W-2118644	0162	2
JACOBSON GRANT H	CPT	0-0453870	0145	2
JACOBSON HJALMER A	LTC	0-0256997	0447	2
JACOBSON JAMES W	LTC	0-0242620	1065	3
JACOBSON JOHN JR	M G	0-0102326	0457	3
JACOBSON JOHN P	MAJ	0-1105538	0357	1
JACOBSON JOSEPH S	LTC	0-0323289	0559	1
JACOBSON JULIUS	LTC	0-0255046	0745	2
JACOBSON LEONARD F	2LT	0-1059508	0145	2
JACOBSON RAYMOND L	LTC	0-1042344	0566	1
JACOBSON ROLLAND E	CW3	W-2143117	1160	1
JACOBSON SAMUEL S	MAJ	0-0278140	1263	3
JACOBSON WILLIAM J	LTC	0-2047371	0865	1
JACOBUS FREDERIC A	2LT	0-0538798	0445	2
JACOBY BERNARD R	2LT	0-0531890	0246	2
JACOBY GLENN J	COL	0-0290884	1067	3
JACOBY HARRY J	LTC	0-0303340	1046	2
JACOBY HENRY G	COL	0-1294314	0168	3
JACOMB WILLIAM M	1LT	0-1106849	0446	2
JACOT EARL C	CW2	W-2119479	0853	2
JACQUART DAVID R	CW2	W-2214545	0167	1
JACQUES BRYAN H	MAJ	0-0255881	0967	3
JACQUES ERNEST A	MAJ	0-0974445	1062	1
JACQUES FRED W	CW3	W-2147682	0464	1
JACQUES GABRIEL	CPT	0-0262922	0946	2
JACQUES GEORGE W	LTC	0-0206341	1059	3
JACQUES LEWIS H	MAJ	0-0438587	1146	2
JACQUES MYRON E	CW2	W-2143344	0858	1
JACQUES SOLOMON J	CW4	W-2145275	0268	1
JACQUOT HOWARD E	CPT	0-0326575	1144	2
JACQUOT ROBERT H	MAJ	0-0985790	0866	1
JAEGER ELCAINOR	CW3	W-2145340	0462	1
JAEGER EVELYN W	2LT	N-0772700	0744	1
JAEGER MARVIN F	LTC	0-1308148	0364	1
JAEGER RAYMOND B	MAJ	0-0416791	0945	2
JAEGER WALTER H E	COL	0-0186367	1062	3
JAEGY HUBERT J	LTC	0-0275540	1056	3
JAEKELS DALLAS C	COL	0-0370520	0964	1
JAFFA ROBERT B	LTC	0-0384833	0560	1
JAFFE AARON A	LTC	0-0184669	0450	3
JAFFE SEYMOUR A	1LT	0-1322831	0746	2
JAFFEE MORRIS	LTC	0-1030160	0656	1
JAGER ROLAND V	LTC	0-1048032	0964	1
JAGERS SAMUEL	CPT	0-0965009	0364	2

NAME	GRADE	SVC NO	DATE RET MO YR	RET CODE
JAGGEARS MARVIN E JR	1LT	0-1294137	0646	2
JAGGERS HERMAN L	MAJ	0-1289434	0456	1
JAGGERS THEODORE	MAJ	0-2036382	0764	1
JAGGIE EDWARD A	LTC	0-0903332	0662	1
JAGO EARL F	LTC	0-0190048	0657	3
JAGODA STANLEY A	LTC	0-1177017	1057	2
JAGOE CHARLES W	LTC	0-1306427	0262	1
JAGOW EMIL B	MAJ	0-0916524	0948	2
JAHN WILLIAM M	LTC	0-0235159	0452	3
JAHNIGEN HERMAN W	2LT	0-1997800	1045	2
JAHNS LEWIS E	LTC	0-0121609	0648	3
JAHNSEN OSCAR J	B G	0-0943408	0959	3
JAHR LOWELL G	2LT	0-1180560	0344	2
JAILLET AQUILA	1LT	0-0497508	0647	1
JAILLET ENGLE L JR	1LT	0-1298068	0347	2
JAIME ALFRED C JR	MAJ	0-2055972	0954	1
JAIMES PHILIP M	MAJ	0-2206397	0867	1
JAKAITIS BRUNO L	COL	0-0320071	0865	1
JAKATIS ARTHUR D	2LT	0-1639009	0745	2
JAKCSY JOSEPH	CW3	W-2147148	0962	1
JAKES WILLIAM E JR	CPT	0-0405915	1045	2
JAKOP JOHN W	1LT	0-1292181	0246	2
JAKOPICH WILLIAM F	CPT	0-0504178	1043	2
JAKOVICH DANIEL JR	LTC	0-1101510	1262	1
JAKSHA BERNARD G	MAJ	0-1030991	0364	1
JAKUBIEC JOSEPH B	LTC	0-0486160	0667	1
JAKUBOWSKI JOHN J	MAJ	0-1634926	0457	1
JALBERT MAGLOIRE	1LT	0-0108443	1022	1
JAMERSON OSMOND T	COL	0-0245618	0866	3
JAMERSON SOLOMON J	LTC	0-1686814	0168	1
JAMES ARCHIBALD	CPT	0-0258507	0444	2
JAMES BYRD L	MAJ	0-2000943	1059	1
JAMES DAVID L	LTC	0-1080456	0268	1
JAMES EDGAR A	CPT	0-0360185	0656	2
JAMES EDWARD	MAJ	0-1685698	0263	2
JAMES EDWARD D	MAJ	0-2018007	1062	1
JAMES ELIZABETH	CPT	N-0737430	0548	1
JAMES ELLIS L	WO1	W-2149179	0956	1
JAMES EMMETTE A	LTC	0-1576179	0662	1
JAMES EVAN E	CPT	0-1030992	1047	2
JAMES FELTHAM S	MAJ	0-0249793	0846	2
JAMES FRANK	MAJ	0-2262449	0163	1
JAMES GEORGE B JR	MAJ	0-2204014	0767	1
JAMES GEORGE L	LTC	0-0212808	0363	3
JAMES GEORGE M	1LT	0-0512104	1044	2
JAMES GEORGE R	MAJ	0-1796481	0761	1
JAMES GOMER	LTC	0-1110361	1262	1
JAMES HAROLD D	CPT	0-0381515	0346	2
JAMES HAROLD R	MAJ	0-1557617	0360	2
JAMES HARRY B JR	1LT	0-1322036	1045	2
JAMES HARRY JR	MAJ	0-1342381	0366	1
JAMES HARRY M	MAJ	0-1697868	0456	1
JAMES HATCHER M JR	MAJ	0-1327957	1163	1
JAMES HOWARD E	MAJ	0-1042850	0864	1
JAMES HUBERT I	MAJ	0-1559576	1163	1
JAMES JAMES W	CW2	W-2206038	0659	1
JAMES JESSE R	CPT	0-1557858	0847	2
JAMES JOHN R C	CPT	0-0419173	1047	2
JAMES JOSEPH A	COL	0-0148520	0451	3
JAMES KENNETH L	LTC	0-1172926	0865	2
JAMES LAWRENCE D	MAJ	0-1166515	0761	1
JAMES LEE E	COL	0-0342172	0766	1
JAMES LEO E	MAJ	0-0390463	0446	2
JAMES LEONARD N	LTC	0-0349340	0760	1
JAMES LOUIE W	LTC	0-0269946	1067	3
JAMES LOUIS D	CW3	W-2144357	0766	1
JAMES MAURICE D	LTC	0-0244057	0366	3
JAMES MAXWELL	COL	0-0222145	0849	1
JAMES MELVIN E	MAJ	0-0254805	C166	3
JAMES MOWBRAY R	LTC	0-0359368	0646	2
JAMES NOYELLES L	MAJ	0-2023333	0762	1
JAMES PRESTON E	COL	0-0172462	0259	3
JAMES RALPH V	COL	0-0289138	0668	3
JAMES RICHARD E	MAJ	0-0309179	0754	3
JAMES RICHARD L	LTC	0-0450629	0161	1

NAME	GRADE	SVC NO	DATE RET MO YR	RET CODE
JAMES ROBERT F	MAJ	0-1109381	1164	1
JAMES ROBERT G	CW3	W-3150399	0968	1
JAMES ROBERT S	MAJ	0-0497714	0955	1
JAMES SARA B	1LT	N-0768128	0946	1
JAMES THERESA V	MAJ	N-0732530	0667	1
JAMES THOMAS G	LTC	0-1178843	1167	1
JAMES THOMAS L	LTC	0-0172755	0245	2
JAMES ULRIC N	COL	0-0171127	0151	3
JAMES WALTER G	LTC	0-1636087	0766	1
JAMES WILARD	CW4	W-2144188	0764	1
JAMES WILLIAM D	COL	0-0349879	1166	3
JAMES WILLIAM F JR	LTC	0-0236095	0662	1
JAMES WILLIAM H	CPT	0-0953640	0159	1
JAMES WILLIAM L	COL	0-0313426	0856	1
JAMES WILLIAM L JR	MAJ	0-0998774	1065	1
JAMES WILLIAM M JR	MAJ	0-2262769	0762	1
JAMES WILLIE R	CW3	W-2143283	0561	1
JAMESON EUGENE J	MAJ	0-1185711	0660	1
JAMESON KLIDE A	MAJ	0-2018357	0165	1
JAMESON LLOYD H	COL	0-0225664	1060	3
JAMESON MERRILL E	LTC	0-1177854	0167	1
JAMESON WALTER G	LTC	0-1557469	0263	1
JAMESON WILLIAM S	CPT	0-2040949	0764	1
JAMGOCHIAN VAUGHN M	COL	0-0224475	0158	3
JAMIESON GEORGE T	LTC	0-0542702	0367	3
JAMIESON ROBERT	LTC	0-0265555	0662	3
JAMISON CHARLES E	MAJ	0-1294672	0363	1
JAMISON FENTON W	CPT	0-0114499	1151	3
JAMISON HOMER C	CPT	0-0442275	1045	2
JAMISON MADISON L	CW3	W-2142766	1060	1
JAMISON THURSTON E	LTC	0-0324126	0462	1
JAMISON WILBUR G	MAJ	0-2006273	0465	1
JAMISON WILLIAM E	CPT	0-0391307	0745	2
JAMISON WILLIAM Q	CPT	0-0359407	0645	2
JAMKOCHIAN KEHAN	LTC	0-2002457	0366	2
JAMMES JOSEPH M	MAJ	0-0973457	0862	1
JAMNICKI AUGUST	MAJ	0-2009532	0966	1
JAMPEL SYDNEY	CPT	0-1689081	0746	2
JAMROS JOSEPH J JR	1LT	0-1313248	1045	2
JANACEK FELIX V	MAJ	0-1167044	0757	1
JANAK MATILDA A	MAJ	N-0734402	0464	1
JANASIEWICZ JOHN E	WO1	W-2113766	1050	2
JANCO PETER P	WO1	W-2104721	0750	1
JANCURA CLARENCE J	MAJ	0-1639215	0957	1
JANDA CHARLES A	LTC	0-0470483	0768	3
JANDA WALTER M	1LT	0-2047372	0446	2
JANDRO DONALD H	MAJ	0-1688438	0663	1
JANEBA HUGO B	LTC	0-0961827	0465	3
JANER ENRIQUE A	MAJ	0-0957872	0868	1
JANER JOSE R	LTC	0-0269841	0468	3
JANERETTE VERSEAL A	CPT	0-0535827	0845	2
JANES BEN C	LTC	0-0268323	1065	3
JANES CHARLES F	LTC	0-0493881	0357	1
JANES CHARLES R	COL	0-0911793	0966	3
JANES EUGENE C	1LT	0-0236407	0648	3
JANES FRANK T	COL	0-0421282	0347	2
JANES RAYMOND L	1LT	0-1644449	0250	1
JANES WILLIAM O	CPT	0-1325899	0348	2
JANETIS MICHAEL JR	CW2	W-3430057	0566	1
JANEWAY AUGUSTINE	COL	0-0157793	0845	2
JANEWAY CHARLES H	MAJ	0-0148246	0257	3
JANICKI JOSEPH W	CPT	0-0138319	0852	3
JANIFER EDWARD F O	1LT	0-0245136	1151	3
JANIFER JAMES V	MAJ	0-1291995	0164	1
JANIGER NATHANIEL	CPT	0-0448354	1045	2
JANIN RICHARD A	LTC	0-1634929	0664	1
JANIS RAYMOND A	LTC	0-1574454	0461	1
JANISS HENRY W	CPT	0-2017549	0757	1
JANKOVICH JOSEPH S	LTC	0-1110584	1162	1
JANKOWIAK HENRY	LTC	0-1001814	1262	1
JANKOWICZ BRUNO J	LTC	0-1536061	1068	1
JANKOWSKI CHARLES J	CPT	0-1321373	0654	2
JANKUSKAS FRANK J	LTC	0-0358645	0966	1
JANNACE ATTILIO F	CPT	0-0527947	0645	2
JANNASCH JAMES R JR	2LT	0-2011900	0346	2

NAME	GRADE	SVC NO	DATE RET MO YR	RET CODE
JANNELLE ARMAND E	MAJ	0-0217969	0455	3
JANNETT ANTHONY V	LTC	0-0339327	0268	3
JANNETTE LAWRENCE J	1LT	0-0383494	0146	2
JANNEY ELWOOD A	LTC	0-1291646	0760	1
JANNUSCH GLENWOOD L	CW3	W-2145454	1263	1
JANNUSCH HARRIS T	LTC	0-1640589	0562	1
JANNUZI WILLIAM R	MAJ	0-1548857	1046	2
JANOSIK GABRIEL E	MAJ	0-1284145	1146	2
JANOTA ERWIN J	LTC	0-1585668	1060	1
JANQUART MERVIN	1LT	0-0885710	0446	2
JANSAK ANDREW	CW4	W-2127882	0368	1
JANSEN CLARENCE T	MAJ	0-0410891	0746	2
JANSEN EDWARD T	CPT	0-1295723	0446	2
JANSEN ELMER	CPT	0-0172666	0858	3
JANSEN LAWRENCE C	LTC	0-1038194	0367	1
JANSEN MARIE T	MAJ	N-0756527	0963	1
JANSEN WILLARD S	MAJ	0-1917880	1066	1
JANSEY FELIX	LTC	0-0494598	0247	2
JANSKY ERNEST F	LTC	0-1795915	0657	1
JANSKY STEPHEN J JR	1LT	0-1309741	0845	2
JANSMA CLAYTON B	1LT	0-0410073	1044	2
JANSMA ROBERT K	MAJ	0-0966279	0863	1
JANSSEN HERMAN G	COL	0-0319236	1060	3
JANSSEN THEODORE A	COL	0-0274753	0967	3
JANSSEN WILLIAM A	1LT	0-1001156	0444	2
JANTZ RUDOLPH A	MAJ	0-2263207	0568	1
JANUARY LEWIS E	MAJ	0-0356981	0446	2
JAPINGA MARTIN	LTC	0-0272823	0859	3
JAPPE FRANK K	CPT	0-2028926	0958	1
JAQUES CHARLES	LTC	0-1308149	1162	1
JAQUES ROBERT	MAJ	0-0199386	0648	3
JARAMILLO ELOY	CW3	W-2143603	1162	1
JARANILLA TIBURCIO	1LT	0-0890544	0750	1
JARDEE HERSCHEL H	CW3	W-2142855	0761	1
JARDINE BARBARA M	1LT	N-0721629	0745	1
JARDINE JOHN E JR	LTC	0-0112963	0859	3
JARECKI JOHN T	LTC	0-0266930	0768	3
JARED GEORGE B	LTC	0-0452682	0266	1
JARED MYRON S	LTC	0-0231039	1045	2
JARED RUSSELL W	LTC	0-1590564	1262	1
JARIS LOUIS C	MAJ	0-1183550	0260	2
JARK MARVIN A	LTC	0-1300173	0161	1
JARLETT OSCAR J JR	MAJ	0-1649832	1263	1
JARMAN CECIL C	COL	0-0102205	0156	3
JARMAN GORDON N	LTC	0-0243180	1264	3
JARMAN JOHN W S JR	LTC	0-1592950	0667	1
JARMON JOSEPH K	COL	0-0277047	1265	3
JARMON WILLIAM R	LTC	0-0260464	0766	3
JARNAGIN JAMES B	LTC	0-0105022	0655	3
JAROCH CHESTER J	LTC	0-1549506	0562	1
JAROMAY DELFIN	CPT	0-1896887	1266	1
JAROSKY WALTER	CW2	W-2213120	0767	1
JARRARD CLEMUEL L	2LT	0-1299513	1043	2
JARRARD FRANK C	MAJ	0-1165437	0461	1
JARRARD GEORGE V	LTC	0-2204062	0767	1
JARRATT HENRY M	LTC	0-1701427	1166	3
JARRELL HOWARD R	COL	0-0144639	0157	3
JARRELL RAYMOND E	MAJ	0-1951571	1165	1
JARRELL REMBERT L	1LT	0-0441964	1045	2
JARRETT EARL H	2LT	0-1296217	0944	2
JARRETT EDWIN S	LTC	0-1166296	0867	3
JARRETT ELMER J	MAJ	0-1331400	1059	1
JARRETT GEORGE B	COL	0-0241836	1161	3
JARRETT HARRIS H	CPT	0-1825914	1047	2
JARRETT IOELLA N	2LT	N-0702619	1036	1
JARRETT LOWEY E	2LT	0-1308241	0705	2
JARRETT PAUL J	COL	0-0346140	0661	1
JARRETT WALTER L	CW3	W-2148860	0966	1
JARRETT WILLIAM H	LTC	0-0416086	0861	2
JARRETT WILLIAM T JR	CW3	W-2206357	1167	1
JARRIEL ELLIS B	1LT	0-1306723	1045	2
JARVIS CHARLES W	MAJ	0-0403991	1044	2
JARVIS EDWARD J	2LT	0-1307160	0145	2
JARVIS GEORGE	COL	0-0229934	1064	3
JARVIS HAROLD D	LTC	0-1549972	0563	1

NAME	GRADE	SVC NO	DATE RET MO YR	RET CODE
JARVIS JACK J	MAJ	0-0314115	0646	2
JARVIS JOHN E	LTC	0-0360982	0567	3
JARVIS JOHN S	CPT	0-1823604	0846	2
JARVIS NORMAN F	LTC	0-0374509	0863	1
JARVIS ROGER B	CW3	W-2205409	0968	1
JASEPH ROLAND H	LTC	0-0339926	0361	1
JASINSKI BERNARD M	LTC	0-1291282	1061	1
JASIO JOHN J SR	CW4	W-2117395	1060	1
JASPER CAROLINE E	1LT	N-0775513	1145	1
JASPER ROBERT B	CPT	0-0417763	0146	2
JASS DONALD U	MAJ	0-2021275	1068	1
JASTROW PAUL W	1LT	0-0940747	0149	2
JASTRZEMBSKI JOHN R	MAJ	0-1042608	0158	1
JASUTA EDWARD B	LTC	0-1102315	0757	1
JAUBERT G WILFRED	LTC	0-0412052	0761	1
JAUCH ROLAND S	COL	0-0202231	0160	3
JAUCK WALTER M	1LT	0-1060144	0845	2
JAUDON ELBERT W	MAJ	0-0939665	1062	1
JAUVTIS ELIHU B	LTC	0-1995111	0466	3
JAVIER-BOSCIO BEN	CPT	0-0413007	0960	1
JAVINS REXFORD R	LTC	0-2055327	0963	1
JAVOIS ALEXANDER	LTC	0-0241879	0859	3
JAWOREK JOHN C	1LT	0-0415419	0666	3
JAWORSKI FRANK A	LTC	0-0370666	0760	1
JAWORSKI HENRY	CPT	0-0485652	0946	1
JAY ANDREW L	LTC	0-1583163	0563	1
JAY BYRON	WO1	W-2145729	1153	1
JAY JOSEPH E	LTC	0-0270233	0961	3
JAY THOMAS J JR	CW4	W-2143558	0767	1
JAYCOX CLAUDE E	CW2	W-2101883	0762	2
JAYJOCK LEO J	MAJ	0-1311154	1160	1
JEALOUS WILLIAM K	COL	0-0109136	0354	3
JEAN GUY B	CW3	W-2208401	0567	1
JEAN HOMER W JR	CPT	0-1701169	1265	1
JEAN WILLIAM W	LTC	0-1030680	0958	1
JEAN WILMER F	LTC	0-1286847	0847	2
JEANE HAROLD T	1LT	0-1554759	0950	2
JEANNETTE ROBERT F	CPT	0-1319885	1147	2
JEANSONNE FLOYD E	1LT	0-1106229	0452	2
JEBO ELMER H	1LT	0-1284708	0745	2
JECKEL FREDERICK	MAJ	0-1283266	0264	1
JEDAMUS MARIE	2LT	N-0700725	0734	1
JEDEIKIN LAZARUS	2LT	0-1945618	0545	2
JEDLICKA ANTON G	LTC	0-0106797	1051	3
JEDLICKA FRANK C	MAJ	0-1321414	1057	1
JEEP CLEMENT S	CPT	0-0236454	0762	3
JEFFCOAT CLYDE E	CW3	W-2147880	0763	1
JEFFCOAT OTIS A JR	LTC	0-0261045	0766	3
JEFFE EPHRAIM F	B G	0-0138243	0256	3
JEFFERIES JOHN W	COL	0-0148427	1156	3
JEFFERS BERT M	MAJ	0-1111143	1162	1
JEFFERSON BILLY R	MAJ	0-1330821	1062	1
JEFFERSON EDWIN R	MAJ	0-0348758	0565	3
JEFFERSON JAMES R	CW2	W-2145645	1163	1
JEFFERSON JOSEPH F	CW2	W-2141325	1159	1
JEFFERSON PAUL L	1LT	0-1287887	0545	2
JEFFERSON WILLIAM M	LTC	0-0341625	0556	1
JEFFERY WILLIAM A	COL	0-0172360	0648	3
JEFFORDS ALEXANDER	MAJ	0-1296379	0260	2
JEFFREY ALLAN S	CPT	0-1313895	1145	2
JEFFREY ALVIS	MAJ	0-1998722	0264	1
JEFFREY BERNARD	LTC	0-0464213	0151	1
JEFFREY DORIS R	2LT	L-0602566	0345	2
JEFFREY JOHN G	1LT	0-5403215	0762	2
JEFFREY WALTER R	COL	0-0117104	0752	3
JEFFREYS DAVID E	CPT	0-2033541	0859	1
JEFFRIES ALBERT G	CPT	0-1167483	1147	2
JEFFRIES GURLEY T	MAJ	0-1922601	0866	1
JEFFRIES JAMES F	LTC	0-0172566	0959	3
JEFFRIES JOHN M	LTC	0-0236766	1064	3
JEFFRIES LYMAN B	CPT	0-1293961	1046	2
JEFFRIES LYNN	CPT	0-0281109	0344	2
JEFFRIES ONDE H	CPT	0-2262448	0963	1
JEFFRIES ROBERT F	1LT	0-1060146	0446	2
JEFFRY KENNETH W	CW4	W-2105241	0864	1

NAME	GRADE	SVC NO	DATE RET MO YR	RET CODE
JEFFS DEAN R	LTC	0-0376473	0666	1
JEHL JOSEPH R	COL	0-0295444	0967	3
JEHLE EDWARD J	LTC	0-1554018	0566	1
JEHN ERNST J C	LTC	0-0485813	0967	3
JEKEL ALEX S JR	CW2	W-2215182	0667	1
JELINEK ENGELBERT	MAJ	0-0238430	0865	3
JELINEK JERRY R	LTC	0-1060497	1062	1
JELINEK JOSEPH J	CW2	W-2152388	0857	1
JELKS THOMAS O	MAJ	0-1897772	0666	1
JELLINGS HAZEL T	2LT	N-0789363	0645	1
JELLINGS RAYMOND R	MAJ	0-1311395	1060	1
JELLISON DONALD H	1LT	0-2034539	0561	2
JELLISON EDWARD C	LTC	0-0926830	1164	1
JELSMA MEREDITH H	LTC	0-0295854	0456	1
JELSO SAMUEL J	MAJ	0-0336666	0246	2
JELY OTTO	CW2	W-2147947	0555	1
JEMERIN EDWARD E	MAJ	0-0429233	1045	2
JEMISON JOHN H	MAJ	0-1045650	0561	1
JENCKS FREDERICK	LTC	0-0263540	0864	3
JENDRZEJCAK JOHN G	2LT	0-1688442	0450	2
JENEFSKY JOHN J	CW2	W-2143127	0554	1
JENISON DANIELL A	MAJ	0-1170435	1265	1
JENISON EDWIN	COL	0-0288326	1267	3
JENISTA ERNEST F	LTC	0-0270970	0968	3
JENISTA JOHN E	LTC	0-0418915	0860	1
JENKE HERBERT R	MAJ	0-0981987	1061	1
JENKINS ALLISON W	CPT	0-0506931	1053	2
JENKINS ALTON A	COL	0-0311956	0964	3
JENKINS ALVIN R	MAJ	0-1304225	0963	1
JENKINS ARCHIE M	MAJ	0-0184490	0648	3
JENKINS BILL M	1LT	0-2066454	1058	1
JENKINS CHARLES H	LTC	0-0495633	0767	1
JENKINS CLAUDE JR	2LT	0-1292183	0544	2
JENKINS DANIEL P	LTC	0-0508955	1263	1
JENKINS DELBERT R JR	CW2	W-2210186	0964	1
JENKINS DON A	LTC	0-0167537	0253	3
JENKINS EDWARD L	CW3	RW-2141596	0162	1
JENKINS ELLSWORTH	CW2	W-2152141	0261	1
JENKINS ELMER L	CPT	0-1177019	1158	2
JENKINS ELZIE H	1LT	0-1293595	0945	2
JENKINS EUGENE	CW2	W-2145939	1057	1
JENKINS EVERETT H	MAJ	0-0257141	0457	3
JENKINS FRANK R	LTC	0-0470964	0565	3
JENKINS FRANK W	CW2	W-2152317	0960	1
JENKINS FREDERICK	LTC	0-2016899	0168	1
JENKINS GENEVA	1LT	N-0736283	0547	1
JENKINS GEORGE L JR	MAJ	0-1685731	0565	1
JENKINS GEORGE S	LTC	0-0481129	0155	1
JENKINS HADLEY E	COL	0-1548085	0661	1
JENKINS HAROLD A	LTC	0-0441117	0863	1
JENKINS HARRY S JR	LTC	0-1545218	0762	1
JENKINS HAZEL O	CPT	N-0783542	0646	1
JENKINS HERBERT G	CPT	0-0253110	0948	1
JENKINS HERBERT H	CPT	0-1318803	0546	2
JENKINS HORACE R	WO1	W-2149381	0557	2
JENKINS HUBERT A	2LT	0-2000482	0460	1
JENKINS HUGHES B	COL	0-0275384	0661	3
JENKINS JAMES M	CPT	0-0228744	0362	3
JENKINS JOHN P	MAJ	0-1101891	0164	1
JENKINS JOHNS K	CPT	0-1046145	0645	2
JENKINS JOSEPH D	CW3	W-2149770	1162	1
JENKINS JOSEPH H	CPT	0-0495049	0946	2
JENKINS JOSEPH J	MAJ	0-4010722	0168	1
JENKINS JOSEPH W	LTC	0-1100165	0263	1
JENKINS JOSEPH W	LTC	0-1323138	0863	1
JENKINS LEWIS B	1LT	0-0918844	0145	2
JENKINS LLOYD P	CW2	W-2120922	1049	1
JENKINS LYNN EARLE	MAJ	0-0361189	0762	1
JENKINS MARTIN H	MAJ	0-0438222	0154	1
JENKINS MELVIN	2LT	0-1053191	0644	2
JENKINS MITCHELL	LTC	0-0233967	0156	3
JENKINS MORRISON D	1LT	0-1061742	0763	1
JENKINS NELSON B	MAJ	0-0921266	1146	2
JENKINS NYE P	CPT	0-1302825	0947	2
JENKINS PLINY W	LTC	0-0410693	0761	1

NAME	GRADE	SVC NO	DATE RET MO YR	RET CODE
JENKINS RICHARD V	MAJ	0-1645077	0756	1
JENKINS RICHARD W	LTC	0-1284340	0862	1
JENKINS ROBERT O JR	LTC	0-1103237	0662	1
JENKINS SIDNEY C	LTC	0-0234720	0657	1
JENKINS STANLEY G	CPT	0-1557470	0248	2
JENKINS THOMAS	LTC	0-0146157	0544	2
JENKINS VERL P	LTC	0-0309006	0165	3
JENKINS VERNE W	CPT	0-0269852	0857	3
JENKINS WILBERT L	1LT	0-0385460	0545	2
JENKINS WILFORD M	MAJ	0-2034092	0166	1
JENKINS WILLIAM E	MAJ	0-1924117	0365	1
JENKINS WILLIAM F	MAJ	0-1555998	0557	1
JENKINS WILLIAM H	MAJ	0-1948323	1060	1
JENKINS WILLIAM J	LTC	0-1061984	0463	1
JENKINS WILLIAM N	COL	0-0210890	0955	3
JENKINS WILLIAM R	1LT	0-1058561	0846	2
JENKINS WILLIAM W	LTC	0-0263039	1262	3
JENKINS WILLIE E JR	LTC	0-0987743	0968	1
JENKINS WOODROW R	1LT	0-1288060	0145	2
JENKINSON DONALD R	MAJ	0-2096481	0863	1
JENKS ALLEN R	MAJ	0-4030664	0868	1
JENKS DONALD M	1LT	0-1945843	0146	2
JENKS RICHARD L	LTC	0-1030257	1061	1
JENKS WILLIAM L	MAJ	0-0759939	1064	2
JENKS WILLIAM S JR	1LT	0-0401651	0445	2
JENNE EDWARD S	LTC	0-0484291	0753	1
JENNE JOSEPH H	CW4	W-2143252	0668	1
JENNER WILLIAM B	CW2	W-2000902	1262	3
JENNES SIDNEY W	1LT	0-0502131	1143	2
JENNESS KENNETH L	MAJ	0-0970629	0666	1
JENNEY ALEXANDER	MAJ	0-0420852	0766	3
JENNI CLARENCE M	COL	0-0277433	1156	3
JENNINGS ALBERT W	WO1	W-2106756	0646	1
JENNINGS ARTHUR J	COL	0-0224361	0963	3
JENNINGS CATLIN R	1LT	0-1167485	0448	2
JENNINGS CHARLES H	CPT	0-0515842	0846	2
JENNINGS CLAUDE C	2LT	0-1845055	0544	2
JENNINGS CLINTON S	CW3	W-2146895	0565	1
JENNINGS CURTIS E	CPT	0-1949806	0157	1
JENNINGS DOROTHY V	1LT	N-0901342	0155	2
JENNINGS EARL J	MAJ	0-1646285	0957	1
JENNINGS EDWARD O	CPT	0-1915452	1060	2
JENNINGS FLOYD C JR	1LT	0-1011282	0346	2
JENNINGS HAMLET G	1LT	0-0327924	0445	2
JENNINGS HARRY G	LTC	0-0438963	1163	1
JENNINGS HARRY T	CW3	W-2145455	1064	2
JENNINGS HOWARD M	LTC	0-1052406	1262	1
JENNINGS HOWARD W	CPT	0-1305930	0452	1
JENNINGS JAMES H	CW4	W-2001521	0358	3
JENNINGS JAMES R	LTC	0-0268460	0657	1
JENNINGS JASON E	COL	0-0238451	0265	3
JENNINGS JOHN C JR	CPT	0-0324726	0146	2
JENNINGS JOHN F JR	LTC	0-1101512	0764	1
JENNINGS JOHN L	MAJ	0-0478387	0646	2
JENNINGS JOHN L	LTC	0-0948577	0368	1
JENNINGS JOHN M JR	MAJ	0-1540860	0764	1
JENNINGS LESTER E	MAJ	0-0173950	0945	2
JENNINGS LOUIS A	MAJ	0-1107506	0761	1
JENNINGS LOUIS V	CPT	0-1926518	0464	1
JENNINGS MARY R	1LT	N-0792622	1150	2
JENNINGS MAURICE R	LTC	0-0234482	0962	3
JENNINGS OWEN R	CPT	0-0334842	1054	3
JENNINGS ROBERT S	CW3	W-2148796	0963	1
JENNINGS ROY A	CPT	0-1845448	1047	2
JENNINGS ROY L	2LT	0-1293418	1143	2
JENNINGS RUFUS E	CW3	W-2205918	1065	1
JENNINGS SAMUEL K	CPT	0-0977720	0760	2
JENNINGS T J	CW3	W-2205286	0666	1
JENNINGS THOMAS C	MAJ	0-1300650	0958	1
JENNINGS VERNE H	CPT	0-0148522	0757	3
JENNINGS WALTER F	MAJ	0-0463355	0446	2
JENNINGS WALTER G	COL	0-0174217	0157	3
JENNINGS WILLIAM I	MAJ	0-1321119	1058	1
JENNINGS ZACK O	CPT	0-0348093	1045	2
JENNY JOHN M JR	CPT	0-0412009	0745	2

NAME	GRADE	SVC NO	DATE RET MO YR	RET CODE
JENNY LOUIS A	COL	0-0245627	0648	1
JENS CHARLES A	COL	0-0477494	1068	1
JENSEN AVON P	1LT	0-1295029	0246	2
JENSEN ARNOLD L	COL	0-0174743	0446	2
JENSEN AXEL	COL	0-0209635	0756	3
JENSEN CARL P N	LTC	0-0979407	0158	2
JENSEN CHESTER H	CW2	W-2147312	0261	1
JENSEN CHRISTIAN	LTC	0-0297348	0263	1
JENSEN CLAUDE I	MAJ	0-0981366	0768	2
JENSEN ELERY N	MAJ	0-0327273	0365	3
JENSEN EVALYN D	2LT	N-0775107	1046	1
JENSEN GEORGE F	MAJ	0-1315468	0259	1
JENSEN HANS W	MAJ	0-0437001	0950	1
JENSEN HAROLD A	LTC	0-1558863	0168	1
JENSEN HAROLD W	MAJ	0-0152304	0955	3
JENSEN HARRY P	LTC	0-1103027	0861	1
JENSEN HOMER F	COL	0-0304122	0568	3
JENSEN JAMES H	CPT	0-0229438	0844	2
JENSEN JAMES W	LTC	0-1050325	0766	1
JENSEN JOHN T	LTC	0-0276191	0866	3
JENSEN JORGEN P	MAJ	0-0246073	1166	3
JENSEN LANDRY	1LT	0-0888958	0448	1
JENSEN LARS K	WO1	W-2141324	1053	1
JENSEN LEO R	COL	0-0905961	0662	1
JENSEN LEOTA M	CPT	N-0736752	0546	1
JENSEN LESLIE M	COL	0-0200134	0246	2
JENSEN LLOYD O	LTC	0-1330732	0766	1
JENSEN LYLE H	WO1	W-2141735	0654	2
JENSEN LYMAN	MAJ	0-2210925	0868	1
JENSEN NIELS R	MAJ	0-0503330	0346	2
JENSEN NORMAN C	LTC	0-0375770	0760	1
JENSEN NORMAN P	1LT	0-2010357	0147	2
JENSEN ORVIE A	MAJ	0-0301863	0468	3
JENSEN ROBERT J	CPT	0-1015098	1046	2
JENSEN ROBERT J	CPT	0-1306510	0146	2
JENSEN ROBERT L	LTC	0-1647970	0666	1
JENSEN ROSS F	LTC	0-0225598	0663	3
JENSEN UFFE T	CPT	0-0422669	0443	2
JENSEN VERNE M	LTC	0-1555574	0663	1
JENSEN WILLARD W	LTC	0-0454648	1158	1
JENSON GEORGE W	CW3	W-2152318	0263	1
JENTES CLARENCE L	CW3	W-2142035	1160	1
JENTZ GILBERT L	LTC	0-0261018	1266	3
JEPSON AUSTIN W	1LT	0-1010218	0346	2
JEPSON HERBERT A JR	CPT	0-0947429	0361	2
JERABECK JOSEPH R	LTC	0-0406012	0267	3
JERABEK MARGARET F	1LT	N-0751242	0146	1
JERAM FREDERICK JR	CPT	0-1327746	0947	2
JEREMIAS JOSEPH H	MAJ	0-1554566	0460	1
JEREMIAS RICHARD A	CW3	W-2146510	1162	1
JERGE SUTTON	LTC	0-0498909	0550	2
JERKINS DANIEL M JR	CPT	0-0450725	1145	2
JERLES ROBERT F	MAJ	0-0252762	0246	2
JERMAIN LEONARD L	1LT	0-0388132	1044	2
JERMAN RICHARD G	MAJ	0-2263677	0868	1
JERNBERG CARL E JR	CPT	0-0360061	0545	2
JERNIGAN JACK	MAJ	0-1012369	1059	1
JERNIGAN JOHN H	MAJ	0-0889075	0954	1
JERNIGAN LAWRENCE C	CPT	0-1172929	0858	2
JERNIGAN OTIS M	LTC	0-0253442	0467	3
JERNIGIN RUSSELL C	LTC	0-0108044	0956	3
JEROME EDWARD	1LT	0-0466978	0345	2
JERRETT FRANCIS A	1LT	0-2035948	1046	2
JERRETT FRANKIE L	2LT	N-0703470	1046	2
JERRISON DOROTHY L	MAJ	L-1010359	1067	1
JERRY GEORGE JR	LTC	0-1798354	0766	1
JERSIN HAROLD E S	MAJ	0-0261199	0167	3
JERSIN PEARL D G	MAJ	N-0742262	0562	1
JERVEY CHARLES H	MAJ	0-0261557	0661	1
JERVEY JESSIE M	2LT	N-0763724	0145	1
JERVIS FREDERICK	1LT	0-0547320	0147	2
JESS JAMES P	LTC	0-1061143	0763	2
JESSE FRANCIS R	MAJ	0-1336652	0962	1
JESSE HAROLD L	CW3	W-2148002	1164	1
JESSE MARIE	2LT	N-0721984	0345	1

NAME	GRADE	SVC NO	DATE RET MO YR	RET CODE
JESSEE GEORGE W	CPT	0-0405010	0645	2
JESSEE ROBERT D	2LT	0-0105388	0855	3
JESSEE WILLIAM D JR	MAJ	0-1893739	0766	1
JESSEE YANTIS R	MAJ	0-1299054	0468	3
JESSEN HOWARD W	CPT	0-2262522	1062	1
JESSUP DALE C JR	MAJ	0-1314071	0761	1
JESSUP DANIEL A	CPT	0-0375234	0144	2
JESSUP ERNEST D	COL	0-0354716	0348	2
JESSUP WALTER E	LTC	0-0105378	0648	3
JESTER JOHN C JR	MAJ	0-0257346	1167	3
JETER ANDREW H	CW3	W-2206284	1065	1
JETER LEWIS X	LTC	0-0348682	0660	1
JETER OMER L	COL	0-0335303	0968	3
JETER ROYAL D	CPT	0-0953637	0161	1
JETT BONNIE	CW2	W-2149844	0356	1
JETT CHARLES E	LTC	0-1292889	0966	1
JETT JACKSON B	1LT	0-0454308	0944	2
JETT JOHN D	MAJ	0-2033048	0662	1
JETT OSCAR H R	LTC	0-1046837	1161	1
JETT PRESTON R JR	CPT	0-0971298	0762	1
JETT SHELBY	2LT	0-0410978	0943	2
JETTON CLYDE T	MAJ	0-0454140	0547	2
JETTON MARION W	CPT	0-0309693	0461	3
JETTON MARTIN A	CW3	W-3150330	0468	1
JEWASINSKI STANLEY A	LTC	0-0190982	0456	3
JEWEL CHARLES A	LTC	0-0917076	0866	3
JEWELL DEAN M	LTC	0-0049924	0766	1
JEWELL EDWARD S	CPT	0-0248904	1163	3
JEWELL FRANK JR	MAJ	0-1283968	0862	1
JEWELL FRED J	LTC	0-0520673	0764	1
JEWELL HORACE J	CPT	0-2009972	0556	1
JEWELL JOSEPH L	CPT	0-2001014	0860	1
JEWELL LOIS R	LTC	N-0729397	0163	1
JEWELL WALTER H	MAJ	0-0954540	1262	1
JEWETT ALLEN C	MAJ	0-0989286	0467	2
JEWETT ARNO J	COL	0-0297516	0867	3
JEWETT DAVID G	1LT	0-0888281	0645	2
JEWETT HARVEY E	MAJ	0-1300335	0663	1
JEWETT KELSEY H	LTC	0-0177286	1059	3
JEWETT LOUIS F	LTC	0-0346604	0561	1
JEWETT MAURICE G	COL	0-0166442	0556	3
JILES JAMES W	MAJ	0-1579836	0756	2
JILES JULIAN C	MAJ	0-1307700	0859	1
JILES NEIL L	CPT	0-1286849	1045	2
JILES VIRGIL L SR	CW2	W-2205295	0261	1
JILL HERBERT G	MAJ	0-0369820	0154	2
JIMENEZ ERNEST J	CW2	W-2147052	1059	1
JIMENEZ JORGE J	COL	0-0306443	1068	3
JIMENEZ JOSEPH W	CPT	0-1923149	0667	1
JIMENEZ RUFINO	1LT	0-1896815	0150	1
JIMERSON NORMAN C	1LT	0-0539296	0147	2
JIMERSON WILLIE J	CPT	0-1936972	0366	1
JIMMERSON ALLEN M	1LT	0-1647105	0445	2
JINDRA GEORGE V	MAJ	0-2039482	0361	1
JINES ARTIE	LTC	0-1945174	1055	1
JINKENS GEORGE M JR	LTC	0-0508560	0357	1
JINKS ALVIS H	CPT	0-1286653	1265	1
JINKS CLARENCE A	MAJ	0-1167920	0857	1
JIPSON FLOYD L JR	LTC	0-0380837	0565	1
JIRIKOWIC EDWARD L	MAJ	0-2023634	0862	2
JOBE OWEN J	CW4	W-2144438	0968	1
JOBE WERNER H	CW2	W-2205381	0361	1
JOBERT ARTHUR H	MAJ	0-0277521	1058	3
JOBES CHARLES A JR	2LT	0-1316810	1044	2
JOBES JAMES E	COL	0-0269368	0263	3
JOBSON ROBERT C	LTC	0-1824753	0967	1
JOCA JOHN G	2LT	0-0462582	1045	2
JOCHEM ROBERT N	WO1	W-2121217	1044	2
JOE PHILLIP Y	MAJ	0-2266337	1164	1
JOE WILLIAM G	COL	0-0366342	0168	1
JOERG THOMAS F	MAJ	0-1296530	1061	1
JOERIN WILLIAM A	MAJ	0-1687034	0547	2
JOERN ALBERT E	2LT	0-2025303	0761	1
JOERS WILLIAM H	CW3	W-2150211	1163	1
JOFFE SAMUEL M	CPT	0-1695882	0145	2

NAME	GRADE	SVC NO	DATE RET MO YR	RET CODE
JOHANNES URBAN J	CPT	0-1296862	0258	1
JOHANNESSON BLANCHE	MAJ	N-0777280	0765	1
JOHANNESSON JOHN F	2LT	0-1309742	1044	2
JOHANSEN EIVER W	CPT	0-0240881	0965	1
JOHANSEN WILLARD W	MAJ	0-0954590	1263	1
JOHANSON ELLIS C	LTC	0-0310942	0667	3
JOHANSON HANS C	CW4	W-2142056	1055	1
JOHENNING ALVY G	LTC	0-0280397	0660	1
JOHN CLINTON E	COL	0-0131631	0656	3
JOHN HENRY J	LTC	0-0219873	0750	3
JOHN THEODORE J	1LT	0-1308825	0546	2
JOHNDROW HAROLD F	CW2	W-3150650	0166	1
JOHNER PAUL	LTC	0-0357355	1063	3
JOHNS ALEXANDER	CPT	0-1693408	0143	2
JOHNS ARTHUR	MAJ	0-2012264	0461	1
JOHNS CECIL	LTC	0-1053192	1161	1
JOHNS DAVID E	CPT	0-1577375	0852	1
JOHNS DAVID M	MAJ	0-2020424	1062	1
JOHNS EDWARD J	CPT	0-1174010	0347	2
JOHNS FORREST R	2LT	0-1081015	0960	1
JOHNS GEORGE E	2LT	0-1598427	0247	1
JOHNS GEORGE J	MAJ	0-0169929	0559	3
JOHNS GEORGE W	LTC	0-0202979	0856	3
JOHNS GRANVILLE	MAJ	0-1296381	0461	1
JOHNS HYLAND R	LTC	0-0170857	0350	3
JOHNS JAMES B	CPT	0-1314495	0764	1
JOHNS JAMES T	2LT	0-2008406	1058	1
JOHNS JESSE R	CPT	0-1103718	0253	2
JOHNS JOHN L	LTC	0-0505047	0263	1
JOHNS JOHN N	MAJ	0-1636095	1154	2
JOHNS SAMUEL L	MAJ	0-1576191	0655	1
JOHNS SAMUEL N	MAJ	0-0332512	0866	3
JOHNSEN JOHN L	2LT	0-1286133	1044	2
JOHNSEN MELVIN M	MAJ	0-1550199	1060	1
JOHNSEN NORMAN M	MAJ	0-0319364	0846	2
JOHNSEN RAYMOND K	CPT	0-1698177	0454	2
JOHNSON AARON J	1LT	0-0961468	0851	2
JOHNSON ABRAHAM L	WO1	W-2108067	0944	2
JOHNSON ADAM B	2LT	0-1310249	0245	2
JOHNSON ADOLPH F	LTC	0-0212433	0861	3
JOHNSON AINAR F	1LT	0-1314022	0246	2
JOHNSON ALAN M JR	MAJ	0-0324490	0451	2
JOHNSON ALBERT E	MAJ	0-0146886	0550	3
JOHNSON ALBERT S	LTC	0-0214532	1060	1
JOHNSON ALBERT S	M G	0-0269201	1058	3
JOHNSON ALBIN I	CW4	W-2105220	0766	1
JOHNSON ALEX	CW2	W-2118121	0361	1
JOHNSON ALFRED L JR	CW2	W-2152193	0660	2
JOHNSON ALFRED W	LTC	0-1031328	1060	2
JOHNSON ALGON B	COL	0-0118356	0855	3
JOHNSON ALLAN W	MAJ	0-0349774	0158	2
JOHNSON ALLEN M	1LT	0-1166745	0361	1
JOHNSON ALTEN R	1LT	0-0493386	1153	1
JOHNSON ALVIN B	MAJ	0-0258526	0966	3
JOHNSON ALVIN W	MAJ	0-1577378	0759	1
JOHNSON ANDREW	MAJ	0-0320635	0653	1
JOHNSON ANDREW J JR	MAJ	0-2262761	1064	1
JOHNSON ANNIE B	2LT	N-0725920	1044	1
JOHNSON ARNIE A	2LT	N-0728605	0545	1
JOHNSON ARTHUR	CPT	0-1178202	0247	2
JOHNSON ARTHUR C	MAJ	0-1285948	0361	1
JOHNSON ARTHUR D	LTC	0-1574868	0561	1
JOHNSON ARTHUR D	CW4	W-2115869	0156	2
JOHNSON ARTHUR L	MAJ	0-1314023	1059	1
JOHNSON ARTHUR O	CPT	0-0231878	0448	2
JOHNSON ARTHUR W JR	CW3	W-2203497	1165	1
JOHNSON ARVID T	MAJ	0-0546640	1047	2
JOHNSON ARVIL E	CW4	W-2141911	0765	1
JOHNSON ASBURY H L	CW2	W-2148088	0958	2
JOHNSON ATWOOD N	MAJ	0-2039443	0363	1
JOHNSON AUGUSTUS R	CPT	0-1113279	1263	1
JOHNSON AYRES W	COL	0-0154169	1052	3
JOHNSON BASCOM JR	LTC	0-0333077	0266	3
JOHNSON BAZLEY W	COL	0-0284580	0968	3
JOHNSON BERENOT E	COL	0-0106073	0255	3

NAME	GRADE	SVC NO	DATE RET MO YR	RET CODE
JOHNSON BERNARD C	CPT	0-0516944	0654	1
JOHNSON BERNARD F	CPT	0-0351914	0450	2
JOHNSON BERTEL H	1LT	0-0384821	0845	2
JOHNSON BETTY J	MAJ	L-1010130	0964	1
JOHNSON BILLY J	CW3	W-2210843	1068	1
JOHNSON BOTHWELL R	COL	0-0327315	1265	3
JOHNSON BURKE	MAJ	0-0337630	0448	2
JOHNSON CAIFSON	COL	0-0337085	0865	1
JOHNSON CAMPBELL C	COL	0-0114668	1055	2
JOHNSON CARL F	MAJ	0-1554019	1163	1
JOHNSON CARL H	LTC	0-2049594	1166	1
JOHNSON CARL L	CPT	0-1914032	0641	1
JOHNSON CARL P	CW2	W-2214544	0967	1
JOHNSON CARLTON A JR	LTC	0-1849167	1168	1
JOHNSON CARTER H	LTC	0-0486797	0655	1
JOHNSON CARTER S	LTC	0-0258818	1264	3
JOHNSON CHARLES C	1LT	0-1945175	0446	2
JOHNSON CHARLES E	CPT	0-0888035	1048	1
JOHNSON CHARLES E	CW3	W-2152889	1263	1
JOHNSON CHARLES E	LTC	0-0485295	1165	3
JOHNSON CHARLES E	WO1	W-2115168	0157	1
JOHNSON CHARLES G	2LT	0-1334156	0446	2
JOHNSON CHARLES H	LTC	0-0338848	0760	1
JOHNSON CHARLES L	CPT	0-0538615	1050	2
JOHNSON CHARLES O	CW3	W-2150212	0866	1
JOHNSON CHARLES R	1LT	0-1044565	1145	2
JOHNSON CHARLES R	1LT	0-1549744	0345	2
JOHNSON CHARLES R	MAJ	0-4030816	0167	1
JOHNSON CHARLES R	CW2	W-3430453	1266	1
JOHNSON CHARLES S	MAJ	0-0213493	0344	2
JOHNSON CHARLES V	COL	0-0188542	0648	3
JOHNSON CHARLES W	LTC	0-0543869	0364	1
JOHNSON CHARLES W	MAJ	0-1107508	0160	1
JOHNSON CHARLES W	1LT	0-1289435	0245	2
JOHNSON CHARLES W	CW2	W-2152551	0365	1
JOHNSON CHARLIE W JR	LTC	0-0406703	0560	1
JOHNSON CLAIRE E	MAJ	0-2096522	1166	1
JOHNSON CLARENCE A	LTC	0-0225815	1164	3
JOHNSON CLARENCE B	M G	0-0268791	1168	3
JOHNSON CLARENCE B	LTC	0-0475903	0352	2
JOHNSON CLARENCE E	COL	0-0125764	0855	3
JOHNSON CLARENCE E	LTC	0-0346290	0967	3
JOHNSON CLARENCE R	CPT	0-1168299	1057	1
JOHNSON CLARK E	LTC	0-1302005	0764	1
JOHNSON CLARKE E JR	1LT	0-0553497	0546	2
JOHNSON CLAUDE	CPT	0-0208711	0648	3
JOHNSON CLAUDE E	LTC	0-0169399	0958	3
JOHNSON CLIFFORD J	MAJ	0-0993291	0165	1
JOHNSON CLIFFORD J	CPT	0-1581838	1057	1
JOHNSON CLIFFORD M	CW2	W-2110602	104N	2
JOHNSON CLIFFORD R	CW2	RW-2144369	0664	1
JOHNSON CLIFTON E	LTC	0-0311333	0267	3
JOHNSON CLIFTON R	MAJ	0-1304226	0862	1
JOHNSON CLYDE O	MAJ	0-1685672	0664	1
JOHNSON CLYDE P	MAJ	0-1685588	0562	1
JOHNSON CURTISS S	1LT	0-1062895	1045	2
JOHNSON DALE N	LTC	0-1680453	0266	1
JOHNSON DARWIN L	LTC	0-0310111	0859	1
JOHNSON DAVID A JR	CW2	W-2147631	0562	1
JOHNSON DAVID F	2LT	0-5505448	0860	2
JOHNSON DAVID R	1LT	0-1061743	0352	2
JOHNSON DAVID S	MAJ	0-0974259	0268	1
JOHNSON DAVID T JR	MAJ	0-1013764	0163	1
JOHNSON DECATUR	CPT	0-0293950	0648	1
JOHNSON DELOS L	1LT	0-0362398	0945	2
JOHNSON DENTON A	MAJ	0-2206161	0167	1
JOHNSON DONALD A	1LT	0-1599171	0950	2
JOHNSON DONALD B	COL	0-0329471	0364	3
JOHNSON DONALD C	MAJ	0-1341435	0267	1
JOHNSON DONALD C	CW3	W-2207966	1265	1
JOHNSON DONALD F	MAJ	0-0977390	0365	1
JOHNSON DONALD F	CW3	W-2126086	0559	1
JOHNSON DONALD M	1LT	0-1031252	0845	2
JOHNSON EARL C	MAJ	0-1595598	1055	1
JOHNSON EARLE K	MAJ	0-0230340	1263	3

NAME	GRADE	SVC NO	DATE RET MO YR	RET CODE
JOHNSON EARLING H	LTC	0-0451127	1059	1
JOHNSON EBEN C	1LT	0-1016147	0146	2
JOHNSON EDDIE L	CW3	W-2149117	0564	1
JOHNSON EDGAR A J	LTC	0-0165488	0260	3
JOHNSON EDGAR F	CPT	0-0465014	1046	1
JOHNSON EDGAR W	MAJ	0-2036662	0561	1
JOHNSON EDSEL I	CPT	0-0441958	0152	2
JOHNSON EDWARD	CPT	0-0156230	1046	1
JOHNSON EDWARD A	COL	0-0920578	0267	3
JOHNSON EDWARD H	CW2	W-2150966	0563	1
JOHNSON EDWARD H JR	CPT	0-1111692	1163	1
JOHNSON EDWARD J	LTC	0-0481602	1154	1
JOHNSON EDWARD L	CW2	RW-2209414	0461	1
JOHNSON EDWARD S	MAJ	0-0323815	0861	3
JOHNSON EDWARD W	LTC	0-0285505	0968	3
JOHNSON EDWIN H	MAJ	0-0174299	1060	3
JOHNSON EDWIN N	MAJ	0-1797469	0859	1
JOHNSON ELLSWORTH	2LT	0-1312938	0645	2
JOHNSON ELMER O	LTC	0-0174165	0658	3
JOHNSON ELMER G	LTC	0-1533356	1162	1
JOHNSON ELMER H	LTC	0-0283914	0166	3
JOHNSON ELMER R	MAJ	0-1109387	0665	1
JOHNSON ELVA K	COL	0-0192444	0858	1
JOHNSON ELWYN O	COL	0-0131878	1055	3
JOHNSON EMIL W	MAJ	0-0269677	0262	1
JOHNSON EMMETT N	1LT	0-1303897	0246	2
JOHNSON ERNEST A	MAJ	0-0487520	0354	1
JOHNSON ERNEST B	MAJ	0-0517777	0149	2
JOHNSON ERNEST C	CW4	W-2104176	0761	1
JOHNSON ERNEST S	LTC	0-0288273	0764	3
JOHNSON EUGENE C	CW4	W-2006440	0566	3
JOHNSON EUGENE E	LTC	0-1174604	0961	1
JOHNSON EVERETT H	MAJ	0-1335928	0565	1
JOHNSON FLORENCE L	1LT	N-0741479	0346	1
JOHNSON FLOYD M	1LT	0-1301313	0545	2
JOHNSON FLOYD W	MAJ	0-0183243	0853	3
JOHNSON FOBIAN E	MAJ	0-0237539	0655	3
JOHNSON FRANCIS M	CPT	0-1115303	0847	2
JOHNSON FRANCIS M	LTC	0-1577382	0463	1
JOHNSON FRANK A	MAJ	0-0902857	1044	2
JOHNSON FRANK C	CPT	0-0189536	1149	3
JOHNSON FRANK E JR	MAJ	0-2020425	0563	1
JOHNSON FRANK P	COL	0-0221977	0555	3
JOHNSON FRANK S	MAJ	0-0309235	0767	3
JOHNSON FRANK W	MAJ	0-1049228	0660	1
JOHNSON FRANK W JR	CW3	W-2146982	1164	1
JOHNSON FRANKLIN C	COL	0-0261960	0158	1
JOHNSON FRANKLIN Q	CPT	0-0449153	0247	2
JOHNSON FRANKLYN A	1LT	0-0444613	0845	2
JOHNSON FRED	LTC	0-0503770	0954	1
JOHNSON FRED H JR	1LT	0-1633312	0246	2
JOHNSON FREDERICK	COL	0-0232180	0860	1
JOHNSON FREDERICK	LTC	0-0353717	0162	1
JOHNSON GABRIEL	CW4	W-2142163	0466	1
JOHNSON GEORGE C	LTC	0-0268286	0254	2
JOHNSON GEORGE C	MAJ	0-1283782	1063	1
JOHNSON GEORGE E	MAJ	0-0468899	1262	1
JOHNSON GEORGE E	CW3	W-2208633	0367	1
JOHNSON GEORGE H	COL	0-0259644	1060	3
JOHNSON GEORGE L	CPT	0-0264655	0645	2
JOHNSON GEORGE M	LTC	0-0289353	1166	3
JOHNSON GEORGE R	1LT	0-0482029	0845	1
JOHNSON GEORGE T	LTC	0-0422634	0361	1
JOHNSON GEORGE T	CW3	W-3150269	1267	1
JOHNSON GEORGE W J	LTC	0-0916620	0858	2
JOHNSON GEORGE Y	MAJ	0-2025116	0862	1
JOHNSON GERALD L	CW2	W-2212098	0368	1
JOHNSON GERALDINE	MAJ	N-0755060	0665	1
JOHNSON GEROEN F	COL	0-0303751	0747	2
JOHNSON GILBERT E	LTC	0-0284734	0265	3
JOHNSON GILMOR L	CPT	0-1317018	0457	1
JOHNSON GLEN H	MAJ	0-0976221	0162	1
JOHNSON GLENN A	CW2	W-2110018	0461	1
JOHNSON GORDON H	LTC	0-1181314	0663	1
JOHNSON GORDON R	MAJ	0-1319125	1063	1
JOHNSON GORDON W	LTC	0-0356765	1160	1
JOHNSON GOVE	LTC	0-1011303	1062	1
JOHNSON GRACE L	MAJ	N-0778361	0665	1
JOHNSON GRANVILLE	MAJ	0-0336578	0862	1
JOHNSON GRANVILLE	CPT	0-1332707	0157	1
JOHNSON GRAYDON W JR	LTC	0-1578663	0662	1
JOHNSON GREETA M E	CPT	L-0912231	0151	2
JOHNSON GROVER G	CW2	W-3400020	0267	1
JOHNSON GUSTAV E	COL	0-0309611	1166	3
JOHNSON GUSTAVE E	LTC	0-1314496	0964	1
JOHNSON GUY S	MAJ	0-1686622	0665	1
JOHNSON GWAIN L	CW3	W-3150560	1268	1
JOHNSON HAL C	LTC	0-0333651	0450	3
JOHNSON HARLEY E	COL	0-0107934	0648	3
JOHNSON HAROLD A	LTC	0-1285247	0661	1
JOHNSON HAROLD C	LTC	0-0324461	0446	2
JOHNSON HAROLD E	CPT	0-0249030	1051	2
JOHNSON HAROLD E	LTC	0-0324127	1060	1
JOHNSON HAROLD E	MAJ	0-2021635	0767	1
JOHNSON HAROLD E	CW4	W-2104178	0660	1
JOHNSON HAROLD E JR	MAJ	0-2032958	0263	1
JOHNSON HAROLD H JR	MAJ	0-2289514	0962	1
JOHNSON HAROLD J	LTC	0-0503623	0546	2
JOHNSON HAROLD L	1LT	0-1548865	1146	2
JOHNSON HAROLD R	2LT	0-1317534	0344	2
JOHNSON HAROLD S	LTC	0-1284882	0761	1
JOHNSON HAROLD T	CW3	W-2206110	1266	1
JOHNSON HARRIS E	COL	0-0320609	1067	3
JOHNSON HARRY A	COL	0-0247662	0965	3
JOHNSON HARRY B	LTC	0-0359908	1161	1
JOHNSON HARRY H	M G	0-0172820	0655	3
JOHNSON HARRY JR	LTC	0-0172268	1050	3
JOHNSON HARRY Q	CW3	W-2120884	0154	1
JOHNSON HARVEY B	CPT	0-1175182	0646	2
JOHNSON HAYDEN C	CPT	0-0268509	0568	3
JOHNSON HENRY A JR	COL	0-0206579	0754	1
JOHNSON HENRY S	MAJ	0-0204471	0250	3
JOHNSON HENRY T	LTC	0-1042846	0561	1
JOHNSON HENRY W	MAJ	0-2056263	0967	3
JOHNSON HERBERT B	CPT	0-1690112	0745	2
JOHNSON HERBERT W	MAJ	0-1585676	0765	3
JOHNSON HERBY L	LTC	0-0361231	0568	3
JOHNSON HERMAN F	CW3	W-2007994	0566	3
JOHNSON HERMAN J JR	CPT	0-0311177	1043	2
JOHNSON HERMAN T	COL	0-0249157	0461	3
JOHNSON HILMER O E	COL	0-1581198	1066	1
JOHNSON HORACE L	COL	0-0181114	0959	3
JOHNSON HOWARD	MAJ	0-0969453	0562	1
JOHNSON HOWARD A JR	CPT	0-0965264	1160	1
JOHNSON HOWARD W	MAJ	0-1298070	0456	1
JOHNSON HUBERT V	COL	0-0330842	0565	1
JOHNSON IRA J	WO1	W-2146470	0253	2
JOHNSON IRA T	CPT	N-0763334	0652	2
JOHNSON IRVING J	LTC	0-0916580	0668	3
JOHNSON IVAN S C	CPT	0-0197952	0145	2
JOHNSON JACK H	LTC	0-1183898	0167	1
JOHNSON JACK H	LTC	0-1332070	0463	1
JOHNSON JACK W	CPT	0-1183097	0257	1
JOHNSON JAMES A	CPT	0-1109388	0252	2
JOHNSON JAMES B	CPT	0-0487948	0250	1
JOHNSON JAMES B	MAJ	0-2019598	1162	1
JOHNSON JAMES B JR	LTC	0-1331738	1068	2
JOHNSON JAMES O	1LT	0-1113773	1045	2
JOHNSON JAMES O	2LT	0-1302656	0446	2
JOHNSON JAMES D	CW4	W-2143925	1055	1
JOHNSON JAMES E	MAJ	0-0452066	0655	1
JOHNSON JAMES E	MAJ	0-0909986	0846	2
JOHNSON JAMES E	CPT	0-1317019	0457	1
JOHNSON JAMES E JR	CW3	W-2141724	0360	1
JOHNSON JAMES H	LTC	0-0314237	0962	2
JOHNSON JAMES H	2LT	0-0446746	1044	2
JOHNSON JAMES H	LTC	0-0902420	1167	3
JOHNSON JAMES O	MAJ	0-1636096	1058	1
JOHNSON JAMES P	CPT	0-2004965	0764	2
JOHNSON JAMES R	LTC	0-1117637	1263	1
JOHNSON JAMES R	CW3	W-2209158	0568	1
JOHNSON JAMES T JR	COL	0-0195328	0561	1
JOHNSON JAMES V	CPT	0-1951624	0259	1
JOHNSON JAMES W	CPT	0-0266598	1263	3
JOHNSON JAY F	CPT	0-1017495	0147	2
JOHNSON JAY R	LTC	0-0390228	0766	1
JOHNSON JENNINGS B	CPT	0-0246335	1044	2
JOHNSON JENS C	LTC	0-1108766	1166	1
JOHNSON JERRELL G	LTC	0-1015224	0163	1
JOHNSON JESS K	MAJ	0-1293598	1060	1
JOHNSON JESSE J	LTC	0-1589930	1162	1
JOHNSON JESSE J	MAJ	0-2025368	0266	1
JOHNSON JESSE L	LTC	0-1595599	0967	1
JOHNSON JOE P	LTC	0-1594922	0859	1
JOHNSON JOEL E	LTC	0-1303898	0762	1
JOHNSON JOHN	CPT	0-0495207	0847	1
JOHNSON JOHN C	MAJ	0-0173657	1148	3
JOHNSON JOHN C	CPT	0-1312170	1047	2
JOHNSON JOHN E	MAJ	0-0471291	0244	2
JOHNSON JOHN F	LTC	0-0490169	0357	2
JOHNSON JOHN H	CPT	0-2262898	0861	1
JOHNSON JOHN H	CW3	W-2149900	1262	1
JOHNSON JOHN I SR	LTC	0-0359702	1067	3
JOHNSON JOHN J JR	1LT	0-1283616	1047	2
JOHNSON JOHN L JR	1LT	0-1061153	1045	2
JOHNSON JOHN R	COL	0-0290015	0765	1
JOHNSON JOHN R	CPT	0-1293765	0763	1
JOHNSON JOHN R	CW4	W-2104179	1054	1
JOHNSON JOHN T	CPT	0-0352134	1145	2
JOHNSON JOHN W	2LT	0-1183553	0444	2
JOHNSON JOHNNIE	2LT	0-2055386	1044	2
JOHNSON JOHNNIE G	MAJ	0-1885428	1165	1
JOHNSON JONATHAN L	LTC	0-0115364	0160	3
JOHNSON JOSEPH	CPT	0-1575380	0155	1
JOHNSON JOSEPH A JR	LTC	0-0336504	0856	1
JOHNSON JOSEPH C	LTC	0-0327797	0155	3
JOHNSON JOSEPH K	LTC	0-0182792	0157	3
JOHNSON JOSEPH M	COL	0-0287586	0159	1
JOHNSON JOSEPH M	LTC	0-0342994	0859	1
JOHNSON JOSEPH S	LTC	0-0687946	0964	1
JOHNSON JOSEPH T	LTC	0-0346960	1164	3
JOHNSON JUANITA G	MAJ	N-0798882	0665	1
JOHNSON JULIAN B	MAJ	0-1874876	0565	1
JOHNSON JULIE R	CPT	N-0776209	1046	1
JOHNSON KATHARINE	LTC	N-0720816	0162	1
JOHNSON KEITH E	CPT	0-0985688	0561	1
JOHNSON KELSEY R	LTC	0-0494846	0265	3
JOHNSON KENNETH A	LTC	0-0295950	0157	1
JOHNSON KENNETH A	1LT	0-1091521	0746	2
JOHNSON KENNETH C	LTC	0-0945591	0368	1
JOHNSON KENNETH S	MAJ	0-0234895	0765	3
JOHNSON KERMIT M	COL	0-0287486	0646	2
JOHNSON KIRBY W	CW2	W-2211847	1066	1
JOHNSON KNUTH L	MAJ	0-0447988	0148	1
JOHNSON L R JR	LTC	0-0410072	0161	1
JOHNSON LACY L	1LT	0-2055797	0960	1
JOHNSON LANCELOT N	CW2	W-2151672	1060	1
JOHNSON LAURIE L	LTC	0-0321267	0568	3
JOHNSON LAVERNE F	WO1	W-2149073	0965	1
JOHNSON LAWRENCE C	MAJ	0-0409967	0844	2
JOHNSON LAWRENCE E	COL	0-0107071	0356	3
JOHNSON LAWRENCE JR	LTC	0-1176681	0667	1
JOHNSON LAWRENCE K	MAJ	0-1594923	1067	1
JOHNSON LAYMON A	CW2	W-2147129	0565	1
JOHNSON LEE F	CW2	W-3100508	1266	1
JOHNSON LEE R	1LT	0-1592956	0568	2
JOHNSON LEGRAND K	CPT	0-0415454	0346	2
JOHNSON LEIGH W	LTC	0-0298201	0255	2
JOHNSON LEMUEL R	LTC	0-1295030	0361	1
JOHNSON LEMUEL S	MAJ	0-1294062	0661	1
JOHNSON LEO L	MAJ	0-0976992	0961	1
JOHNSON LEON C	LTC	0-0427932	0266	1
JOHNSON LEONARD A	LTC	0-0927228	0765	1
JOHNSON LEONARD E	CW3	W-2144600	0160	2
JOHNSON LEROY G	1LT	0-0440615	0647	2
JOHNSON LESLIE H	1LT	0-0405334	1044	2
JOHNSON LEWIS M	LTC	0-0500757	0446	2
JOHNSON LEWIS N	2LT	0-1320046	0245	2
JOHNSON LEWIS S	LTC	0-1633314	0667	1
JOHNSON LLOYD F	WO1	W-2143029	1151	2
JOHNSON LORAINE O	MAJ	N-0787740	0668	1
JOHNSON LORIN K	COL	0-0338745	0859	1
JOHNSON LOUIS E	MAJ	0-2262137	0364	1
JOHNSON LOYD R	MAJ	0-1030585	0759	1
JOHNSON LUTHER B	CPT	0-0370095	0462	2
JOHNSON LUTHER B	MAJ	0-2289190	0566	1
JOHNSON LUTHER D	CPT	0-0507789	1045	2
JOHNSON LYLE E	1LT	0-1039700	1047	2
JOHNSON LYMAN E	LTC	0-0228316	0761	3
JOHNSON MAJOR M	CW3	W-2151831	0562	2
JOHNSON MANNON A	MAJ	0-0410140	0656	2
JOHNSON MARCUS M	CW2	W-2113589	0247	2
JOHNSON MARGARET B	2LT	N-0743129	0944	1
JOHNSON MARION I	LTC	0-1181647	1262	1
JOHNSON MARION T	LTC	0-0229116	1158	1
JOHNSON MARK	CW2	W-2149219	0861	1
JOHNSON MARK H	COL	0-0319765	0257	1
JOHNSON MARTIN L	CW2	W-2150975	0159	1
JOHNSON MARTIN W	MAJ	0-1644459	0260	1
JOHNSON MARVIN D	LTC	0-1280338	0868	3
JOHNSON MARVIN E	1LT	0-0470846	1045	2
JOHNSON MAURICE E	LTC	0-0212566	0364	3
JOHNSON MAX E	MAJ	0-0232256	0246	2
JOHNSON MAX K	LTC	0-0389043	0361	1
JOHNSON MAXWELL	CPT	0-0508107	0647	1
JOHNSON MELVERN E	CPT	0-0373099	0244	2
JOHNSON MELVIN A	MAJ	0-1639058	0654	1
JOHNSON MELVIN A	CW2	W-2150919	0562	1
JOHNSON MELVIN I	1LT	0-1552527	0744	2
JOHNSON MELVIN P	MAJ	0-1796964	0868	3
JOHNSON MELVIN W	LTC	0-0426848	0860	1
JOHNSON MERLIN S	MAJ	0-1553669	0762	1
JOHNSON MILORED L	2LT	N-0700124	0531	1
JOHNSON MILO H	MAJ	0-0212826	1262	3
JOHNSON MIZE	CPT	0-0977099	1262	1
JOHNSON MOSES O	COL	0-0228747	0756	1
JOHNSON MOZELLE	CPT	L-0802041	0247	2
JOHNSON MUMPFORD R	LTC	0-0990825	0968	1
JOHNSON MURRY S	MAJ	0-1686387	0562	2
JOHNSON MYRON L	CPT	0-2055930		1
JOHNSON NELLIS I	LTC	0-0385731	1167	1
JOHNSON NILS B	CPT	0-0168363	0853	3
JOHNSON NORMAN F	1LT	0-0466723	0546	2
JOHNSON NORRIS L	MAJ	0-0964196	0261	1
JOHNSON O B	2LT	0-1291373	0544	2
JOHNSON OGDEN	LTC	0-1047270	0668	1
JOHNSON OLIVER	COL	0-0240388	0165	3
JOHNSON ORESTES B JR	2LT	0-1059851	1044	2
JOHNSON OSCAR H JR	CW3	W-2151018	0463	1
JOHNSON OSCAR HUGH	CW2	W-2146546	1058	1
JOHNSON OSCAR JR	CW3	W-3150465	0968	1
JOHNSON PAUL	MAJ	0-1168302	0656	1
JOHNSON PAUL C	LTC	0-1105552	0965	1
JOHNSON PAUL H	2LT	0-0415027	0542	2
JOHNSON PAUL I	2LT	0-2023352	1046	2
JOHNSON PAUL L	CW3	W-2149321	1061	1
JOHNSON PAUL N	CPT	0-0347816	0753	1
JOHNSON PAUL W	CW3	W-2149443	0267	2
JOHNSON PEARL V	CPT	N-0732350	0848	2
JOHNSON PERCY S JR	CPT	0-0502461	0546	2
JOHNSON PETER B	MAJ	0-2208566	0267	1
JOHNSON PETER L	LTC	0-0178991	0648	3
JOHNSON PHILIP	LTC	0-0407957	0747	2
JOHNSON PHILIP M	COL	0-0123801	0955	2
JOHNSON PRESTON E	2LT	0-1003555	0144	2
JOHNSON QUENTIN L	CPT	0-1303512	0859	2
JOHNSON RALPH	LTC	0-0274407	0848	1
JOHNSON RALPH	MAJ	0-2025569	0760	1
JOHNSON RALPH C	LTC	0-1307250	0662	1
JOHNSON RALPH E	MAJ	0-0295864	1263	3

NAME	GRADE	SVC NO	DATE RET MO YR	RET CODE
JOHNSON RALPH E	MAJ	0-1895420	0363	1
JOHNSON RALPH E	1LT	0-2031412	0553	1
JOHNSON RALPH J	MAJ	0-1559819	0159	1
JOHNSON RALPH V	1LT	0-1317516	0845	2
JOHNSON RANDOLPH E	2LT	0-0102815	1133	1
JOHNSON RAY F	LTC	0-1058778	0967	1
JOHNSON RAY M	LTC	0-1591200	1062	1
JOHNSON RAYBURN W	COL	0-0152034	0454	3
JOHNSON RAYMOND	MAJ	0-0450306	1047	1
JOHNSON RAYMOND	LTC	0-0551952	1062	1
JOHNSON RAYMOND F	LTC	0-0358205	0567	3
JOHNSON RAYMOND H	2LT	0-1104399	0145	2
JOHNSON RAYMOND I	LTC	0-0998439	1168	2
JOHNSON RAYMOND JR	MAJ	0-4006059	0567	1
JOHNSON RAYMOND M	MAJ	0-1893538	0567	1
JOHNSON RAYMOND W	MAJ	0-1169588	1058	1
JOHNSON REUBEN H	CPT	0-2010330	0457	1
JOHNSON RICHARD A	2LT	0-2007358	1145	2
JOHNSON RICHARD C	LTC	0-0230095	1053	1
JOHNSON RICHARD D	LTC	0-0355811	0261	1
JOHNSON RICHARD E	1LT	0-0970990	0552	2
JOHNSON RICHARD K	MAJ	0-0300313	1060	1
JOHNSON RICHARD L	LTC	0-0280576	1066	3
JOHNSON RICHARD L	1LT	0-1745202	0647	2
JOHNSON RICHARD S	MAJ	0-2052591	1068	3
JOHNSON RILEY R	MAJ	0-0963700	0664	1
JOHNSON ROBERT B	LTC	0-0265638	0560	3
JOHNSON ROBERT B	1LT	0-1062230	1045	2
JOHNSON ROBERT C JR	MAJ	0-5301624	0968	1
JOHNSON ROBERT D	MAJ	0-0976339	0765	1
JOHNSON ROBERT E	1LT	0-0548259	0346	2
JOHNSON ROBERT E	MAJ	0-1255386	1265	2
JOHNSON ROBERT E	MAJ	0-1305590	0358	1
JOHNSON ROBERT E	1LT	0-1312311	0845	2
JOHNSON ROBERT E	CW4	W-2153359	0264	1
JOHNSON ROBERT E L	MAJ	0-1554762	0357	2
JOHNSON ROBERT F	CW2	W-2149765	0857	1
JOHNSON ROBERT G	CPT	0-0422236	0146	2
JOHNSON ROBERT G	LTC	0-0444953	1054	1
JOHNSON ROBERT H	LTC	0-0377725	0759	1
JOHNSON ROBERT H	MAJ	0-0391137	0146	2
JOHNSON ROBERT H	CPT	0-0971208	0261	1
JOHNSON ROBERT J	LTC	0-0243110	0151	3
JOHNSON ROBERT L	COL	0-1001375	1161	1
JOHNSON ROBERT L	CPT	0-1917955	1061	1
JOHNSON ROBERT M	MAJ	0-0503137	0645	2
JOHNSON ROBERT M	CPT	0-1324338	0558	1
JOHNSON ROBERT W	COL	0-0252454	1163	3
JOHNSON RODNEY	1LT	0-0490374	0653	1
JOHNSON ROGNAR P JR	CPT	0-4007069	0764	2
JOHNSON ROLAND	MAJ	0-1170022	0561	1
JOHNSON ROLAND	MAJ	0-2023286	0762	1
JOHNSON RONALD A	MAJ	0-1797828	0361	1
JOHNSON RONALD G	CPT	0-0104513	0849	3
JOHNSON ROY B	CPT	0-0121711	1052	3
JOHNSON ROY F	CPT	0-0296683	0246	2
JOHNSON ROY M	CPT	0-0490416	1052	1
JOHNSON ROY W	MAJ	0-0182262	0952	3
JOHNSON ROY W	LTC	0-0467556	1160	3
JOHNSON RUFUS R	MAJ	0-1948937	1263	2
JOHNSON RUSSEL D	LTC	0-1585681	0960	1
JOHNSON RUSSELL W JR	LTC	0-1905457	0566	1
JOHNSON RUTH E	1LT	N-0758543	0546	1
JOHNSON SAMUEL M	2LT	0-1316758	1044	2
JOHNSON SAMUEL N JR	1LT	0-0407361	0846	2
JOHNSON SIDNEY E	CPT	0-1300496	1058	1
JOHNSON SIDNEY W	MAJ	0-0162501	1059	3
JOHNSON STANFORD R	LTC	0-0342285	0161	1
JOHNSON STANLEY	LTC	0-0254708	0664	3
JOHNSON STANLEY R	1LT	0-1016398	0849	2
JOHNSON STEN JR	LTC	0-1317537	0968	1
JOHNSON STEPHEN V	1LT	0-1322450	0851	2
JOHNSON STEWART C	LTC	0-0274551	0867	3
JOHNSON STONE	CPT	0-1913744	0634	1
JOHNSON STUART L V	MAJ	0-0243338	1264	3

NAME	GRADE	SVC NO	DATE RET MO YR	RET CODE
JOHNSON SVEN E	MAJ	0-2014156	0563	1
JOHNSON SWAN A	LTC	0-0913767	1262	3
JOHNSON SYLVESTER	CPT	0-1420329	1046	2
JOHNSON TED	COL	0-0309651	1067	3
JOHNSON THEODORE L	MAJ	0-0967030	0763	1
JOHNSON THOMAS E	LTC	0-1322342	1162	1
JOHNSON THOMAS F	LTC	0-1924795	0668	1
JOHNSON THOMAS L	LTC	0-1310119	0166	1
JOHNSON THOMAS S	LTC	0-2008051	0967	1
JOHNSON THOMAS T	CW3	W-2149247	0166	1
JOHNSON THOMAS W	LTC	0-0240181	0762	3
JOHNSON THOMAS W	LTC	0-0311059	0167	3
JOHNSON VANNER J	CW4	W-2001732	0762	3
JOHNSON VAND J	LTC	0-0280660	0665	3
JOHNSON VANSEL S	COL	0-0122541	0858	3
JOHNSON VERNON W	CW2	W-2119262	0647	2
JOHNSON VICTOR C	2LT	0-1574871	1044	2
JOHNSON VIRGINIA A	1LT	N-0727740	0946	1
JOHNSON WALDO E	LTC	0-0955020	1168	1
JOHNSON WALLACE L	CPT	0-1556004	0346	2
JOHNSON WALTER A	MAJ	0-0114680	0352	3
JOHNSON WALTER A JR	MAJ	0-1050776	0661	1
JOHNSON WALTER B JR	LTC	0-1640599	1265	1
JOHNSON WALTER C	CPT	0-0453531	0246	2
JOHNSON WALTER E	COL	0-0300290	0666	3
JOHNSON WALTER E	CW4	W-2144920	0966	1
JOHNSON WALTER G	CW2	W-215[illegible]21	0159	1
JOHNSON WALTER K	MAJ	0-0241187	0765	3
JOHNSON WALTER R	MAJ	0-1876320	0267	1
JOHNSON WALTER S	MAJ	0-0270157	0367	3
JOHNSON WALTER T	1LT	0-1170437	0345	2
JOHNSON WALTER T	CW2	W-2205356	0958	1
JOHNSON WARREN L	WO1	W-2115555	1156	1
JOHNSON WARREN W JR	1LT	0-1283078	0346	2
JOHNSON WAYNE C	LTC	0-0245689	0760	3
JOHNSON WAYNE E	MAJ	0-1105554	0657	1
JOHNSON WAYNE H	LTC	0-0367294	0365	1
JOHNSON WAYNE L	COL	0-0333366	0348	2
JOHNSON WELBY K	CPT	0-0236204	1147	2
JOHNSON WELDON H	CPT	0-1169589	0551	2
JOHNSON WELDON S	CPT	0-1651538	0258	1
JOHNSON WENDALL S	MAJ	0-1639222	1062	1
JOHNSON WILDER A	MAJ	0-1895169	0858	1
JOHNSON WILLARD C	CPT	0-1303071	0646	2
JOHNSON WILLIAM	CPT	0-0505629	0246	2
JOHNSON WILLIAM A	LTC	0-0563433	1062	1
JOHNSON WILLIAM B JR	LTC	0-0241434	0364	3
JOHNSON WILLIAM E	LTC	0-0219948	0948	1
JOHNSON WILLIAM E	LTC	0-1037845	1162	1
JOHNSON WILLIAM G	COL	0-0319804	0657	1
JOHNSON WILLIAM G	MAJ	0-1284710	0759	1
JOHNSON WILLIAM J	CPT	0-0402701	1144	2
JOHNSON WILLIAM M	CPT	0-0266676	0265	3
JOHNSON WILLIAM M	LTC	0-0515697	0468	3
JOHNSON WILLIAM M	LTC	0-0922698	0147	2
JOHNSON WILLIAM M	1LT	0-1182393	0453	1
JOHNSON WILLIAM P	CPT	0-1303606	1046	2
JOHNSON WILLIAM R	LTC	0-0395844	0760	1
JOHNSON WILLIAM R	WO1	W-2120024	0353	1
JOHNSON WILLIAM R	CW3	W-2144018	0157	1
JOHNSON WILLIAM R	CW2	W-2211903	0567	1
JOHNSON WILLIAM S JR	CW4	W-2109662	1060	1
JOHNSON WILLIAM T	LTC	0-0110238	0648	3
JOHNSON WILLIAM T	MAJ	0-1166301	1054	1
JOHNSON WILLIAM T	MAJ	0-2007241	1060	1
JOHNSON WILLIAM T	CW3	W-2205166	1160	1
JOHNSON WILLIAM V	MAJ	0-1010063	0458	2
JOHNSON WILLIAM W	COL	0-0114429	0749	3
JOHNSON WILLIAM W	COL	0-0266698	0160	3
JOHNSON WILLIE H	CPT	0-4072235	0262	2
JOHNSON WILLIE L	WO1	W-2109940	0648	1
JOHNSON WINCE A J	CPT	0-0106055	1145	2
JOHNSON WINIFRED P	1LT	N-0744996	1045	1
JOHNSON WOODROW A	LTC	0-1114983	0667	1
JOHNSON WOODROW W	LTC	0-0451613	0858	1

NAME	GRADE	SVC NO	DATE RET MO YR	RET CODE
JOHNSON YOUBERT T	LTC	0-0252217	0762	3
JOHNSON ZAC M	1LT	0-1896995	0949	1
JOHNSTON ADDY F	1LT	N-0714382	0147	1
JOHNSTON ALAN E	MAJ	0-0170146	0661	1
JOHNSTON ALBERT E JR	1LT	0-0495608	1064	2
JOHNSTON ALBERT M	LTC	0-0369374	0146	2
JOHNSTON AMBROSE F	COL	0-0335687	0761	3
JOHNSTON ARCHIE B	LTC	0-0431990	1160	1
JOHNSTON BYNUM G	MAJ	0-1685656	0564	1
JOHNSTON CARL R	MAJ	0-0208684	0651	1
JOHNSTON CECIL F	MAJ	0-2055135	0361	1
JOHNSTON CLOVIS H	CPT	N-0763975	0546	2
JOHNSTON CLYDE H	LTC	0-0271545	0168	3
JOHNSTON CLYDE J	CPT	0-0423683	0546	2
JOHNSTON DEWEY S	MAJ	0-1598199	0763	1
JOHNSTON DONALD H	CW3	W-2143030	0559	1
JOHNSTON DONALD W	CW3	W-2205934	1255	1
JOHNSTON EDWARD G	COL	0-0265991	0655	3
JOHNSTON ELMER S	CW3	W-2143013	0161	1
JOHNSTON ELMO J	1LT	0-1032359	0346	2
JOHNSTON ETHEL L	CPT	N-0732165	0647	1
JOHNSTON EUGENE F	LTC	0-1293262	1163	1
JOHNSTON FLOYD R	LTC	0-1030681	0162	1
JOHNSTON FRANCIS I	MAJ	0-1051616	0261	1
JOHNSTON FRANK	LTC	0-0444449	0260	1
JOHNSTON FRANK H JR	LTC	0-0472371	0167	1
JOHNSTON FRANKLIN V	LTC	0-2205315	0758	1
JOHNSTON FREDERICK	LTC	0-0148199	0648	3
JOHNSTON FREDERICK	LTC	0-1639225	0666	1
JOHNSTON GEORGE A	COL	0-0218162	0850	3
JOHNSTON GEORGE B	LTC	0-0259121	1067	3
JOHNSTON GEORGE F	LTC	0-0138892	0444	2
JOHNSTON GEORGE H JR	CPT	0-2287823	1162	2
JOHNSTON GEORGE M	MAJ	0-1297544	0961	1
JOHNSTON GEORGE R	1LT	0-1104890	0444	2
JOHNSTON GEORGE W JR	CPT	0-0408520	0246	2
JOHNSTON GORDON A	1LT	0-0405293	0745	2
JOHNSTON GORDON D	LTC	0-0254307	1263	3
JOHNSTON HANNAH A	1LT	N-0700192	0641	2
JOHNSTON HAROLD A	LTC	0-0496956	0266	1
JOHNSTON HAROLD H	MAJ	0-1015548	0860	1
JOHNSTON HAROLD W	LTC	0-0188607	1057	3
JOHNSTON HARRY A	COL	0-0172860	0955	3
JOHNSTON HARVEY G	LTC	0-0361999	0261	1
JOHNSTON HOMER W	LTC	0-1184241	0263	1
JOHNSTON HOWARD R	LTC	0-0308714	0566	3
JOHNSTON HOWARD R	LTC	0-0995042	0968	1
JOHNSTON J C JR	CW3	W-2106054	1057	1
JOHNSTON JACOB A	COL	0-0148641	0754	3
JOHNSTON JAMES H	MAJ	0-0269592	1057	3
JOHNSTON JAMES R	COL	0-0344996	0167	3
JOHNSTON JAMES R	LTC	0-1165518	0866	1
JOHNSTON JAMES V	COL	0-0208060	0950	3
JOHNSTON JAMES W	MAJ	0-1178520	1066	3
JOHNSTON JAMES W	WO1	W-2111118	1147	1
JOHNSTON JESSE E	COL	0-0354998	0566	1
JOHNSTON JOHN E	CPT	0-0487074	0446	1
JOHNSTON JOHN F	CPT	0-0235733	0151	3
JOHNSTON JOHN G JR	CW2	W-2152267	0263	1
JOHNSTON JOHN K	COL	0-0354227	1160	3
JOHNSTON JOHN L	COL	0-0235490	0858	3
JOHNSTON JOHN M	LTC	0-0264726	0166	3
JOHNSTON JOHN M	1LT	0-0548456	0346	2
JOHNSTON JOHN M	LTC	0-1575382	0763	1
JOHNSTON JOSEPH O	MAJ	0-1057794	0464	1
JOHNSTON JULIUS P JR	MAJ	0-0955456	0565	1
JOHNSTON LEE R	CW2	W-2146848	1059	2
JOHNSTON LEROY F	LTC	0-0254776	0265	3
JOHNSTON MARGARET M	CPT	N-0783796	0847	1
JOHNSTON MARION R	CW2	W-2145121	1059	1
JOHNSTON MELVIN T	MAJ	0-0322424	1045	2
JOHNSTON MILTON E	CPT	0-1689622	0152	2
JOHNSTON NATHAN J	LTC	0-0215490	0446	2
JOHNSTON OWEN A	MAJ	0-1284148	1057	1
JOHNSTON PAUL E	LTC	0-1114569	0664	1

NAME	GRADE	SVC NO	DATE RET MO YR	RET CODE
JOHNSTON RALPH S	LTC	0-1195555	0762	1
JOHNSTON RICHARD B	2LT	0-1173665	1044	2
JOHNSTON RICHARD Y	CPT	0-0965640	0367	1
JOHNSTON ROBERT A	COL	0-0428273	0866	1
JOHNSTON ROBERT D	1LT	0-1323575	1145	2
JOHNSTON ROBERT I	MAJ	0-0277084	0252	3
JOHNSTON ROY P	CW3	W-2205121	0965	1
JOHNSTON ROY C	LTC	0-0485409	0656	1
JOHNSTON ROY F	MAJ	0-0184735	0456	1
JOHNSTON ROY T	MAJ	0-1322156	0265	1
JOHNSTON RUFUS Z JR	LTC	0-1646601	0766	1
JOHNSTON RUTH A	1LT	N-0735005	0445	1
JOHNSTON STANLEY J	CW3	W-2205199	1067	1
JOHNSTON TEDDY L	MAJ	0-0243709	0763	3
JOHNSTON THOMAS A	LTC	0-0288715	0562	3
JOHNSTON THOMAS B	MAJ	0-0258211	0749	2
JOHNSTON THOMAS N	LTC	0-0291259	1264	3
JOHNSTON TRUMAN J	1LT	0-1754993	0544	2
JOHNSTON WESLEY W	2LT	0-1951222	1046	2
JOHNSTON WILLARD A	COL	0-0172869	0360	3
JOHNSTON WILLARD T	CPT	0-0242790	0444	2
JOHNSTON WILLIAM A	LTC	0-0260538	0265	3
JOHNSTON WILLIAM A	CPT	0-1541251	1065	1
JOHNSTON WILLIAM C	1LT	0-0310215	1045	2
JOHNSTON WILLIAM D	COL	0-0266507	0857	1
JOHNSTON WILLIAM G	COL	0-0119145	0349	3
JOHNSTON WILLIAM H	LTC	0-0217080	0764	3
JOHNSTON WILLIAM J	LTC	0-0466724	0863	1
JOHNSTON WILLIAM J	MAJ	0-1327624	0361	1
JOHNSTON WILLIAM L	CPT	0-0462496	1145	2
JOHNSTON WILLIAM L	LTC	0-1289589	1159	1
JOHNSTON WILLIAM R	MAJ	0-1577389	0963	1
JOHNSTON WILLIAM R	MAJ	0-1882330	0966	1
JOHNSTON WILLIAM T	CPT	0-0974559	1060	1
JOHNSTON WOODROW K	1LT	0-1544508	0657	1
JOHNSTONE CHARLES W	CW3	W-2148693	1265	1
JOHNSTONE EDWARD L	LTC	0-0359540	0861	1
JOHNSTONE JOHN D	MAJ	0-1103241	0261	1
JOHNSTONE MYRON H	MAJ	0-1031889	0462	1
JOHNSTONE PARKER L	CPT	0-0311776	0645	2
JOHNSTONE RICHARD S	MAJ	0-2204172	0865	1
JOHNSTONE ROBERT H	MAJ	0-1049913	1062	1
JOHNSTONE RUTH B	CPT	N-0724636	0147	1
JOHNSTONE WILLIAM	COL	0-0450628	0963	1
JOHS ALBERT G	LTC	0-1003406	1262	1
JOINER GUS	1LT	0-1105556	0545	2
JOINER HARTWELL	LTC	0-0264424	1162	3
JOINER JOHN R	CPT	0-1584421	0754	2
JOINER KATHRYN L	2LT	N-0785246	0847	1
JOINER NANCY E	1LT	N-0702960	1045	1
JOINER ROWELL A	1LT	0-2025664	0847	2
JOINES ARMWELL J	1LT	0-1824193	1051	1
JOKI WILLIAM M	1LT	0-0384905	0244	2
JOLICOEUR LOUIS A	CPT	0-1114570	0162	2
JOLIE ROBERT P	MAJ	0-2028595	1265	1
JOLIN LEO E	MAJ	0-0327187	0764	3
JOLIN PHILIP W	1LT	0-1285432	0545	2
JOLLEY CHARLES A JR	MAJ	0-0415282	0246	2
JOLLEY JAMES B	MAJ	0-1575384	0162	1
JOLLEY ORAN B	MAJ	0-1044853	0258	1
JOLLIFFE KENNETH R	1LT	0-2262200	0460	1
JOLLIMORE ELIZABET	1LT	N-0758160	0945	1
JOLLY AB	MAJ	0-0242831	0859	3
JOLLY BENJAMIN R	CPT	0-0304067	0245	2
JOLLY BYRON F	LTC	0-0266670	0758	1
JOLLY ROBERT V	CW3	W-2149409	0363	1
JOLLY ROY H	WO1	W-2146045	0858	1
JOLLY THOMAS 3 JR	COL	0-0243727	1151	3
JOMOK MARCELO G	1LT	0-1896670	0261	1
JONAS CHARLES R	COL	0-0224860	0165	3
JONAS CHARLES S	CPT	0-1688069	0845	2
JONAS HENRY M	LTC	0-0396888	0168	3
JONAS HERMAN W	CPT	0-0293064	0945	2
JONAS JOHN F	LTC	0-0302035	0167	3
JONAS WILLIAM	MAJ	0-0177678	0846	2

NAME	GRADE	SVC NO	DATE RET MO YR	RET CODE
JONELIS FRANK G	LTC	O-0362228	1158	1
JONES AARON L SR	WO1	W-2152675	0560	2
JONES ADEN A	COL	O-0298786	0560	3
JONES ADRIAN H	LTC	O-1646294	1162	1
JONES ALBERT	LTC	O-0426300	0457	1
JONES ALBERT F	LTC	O-0452919	0361	2
JONES ALBERT S JR	CPT	O-2047697	0446	2
JONES ALBERT W	MAJ	O-0942365	0963	1
JONES ALEXANDER	MAJ	O-0281365	0858	1
JONES ALFRED	CPT	O-0455233	0467	1
JONES ALFRED H	CPT	O-0286764	1063	3
JONES ALFRED O	LTC	O-0250697	1065	3
JONES ALFRED P	CPT	O-1695360	0945	2
JONES ALFRED S	2LT	O-1004150	0245	2
JONES ALICE N	CPT	M-0000587	0147	1
JONES ALLEN	CW4	W-2004186	0268	1
JONES ANN	CPT	N-0721562	1059	2
JONES ARCHIBOLD R	COL	O-0114497	1056	3
JONES ARCHIE A	2LT	O-1305156	0544	2
JONES ARNOLD C	MAJ	O-0360794	0466	1
JONES AUGUST E	MAJ	O-0975281	0861	1
JONES BARNETT L JR	MAJ	O-1899421	0961	1
JONES BARRY W	CW3	W-2152968	1162	1
JONES BENJAMIN C	COL	O-0148197	0656	3
JONES BERNICE F	LTC	O-0903263	1264	1
JONES BERRY F	LTC	O-0238471	1264	3
JONES BERTRAND H	MAJ	O-1046504	0261	1
JONES BETTY L	MAJ	N-0787151	0768	1
JONES BEUFORD D	1LT	O-1297046	0146	2
JONES BILL JR	MAJ	O-4031375	1266	1
JONES BILL T JR	MAJ	O-1577390	0960	1
JONES BILLY F	1LT	O-5317187	0565	2
JONES BOB K	1LT	O-1944980	0545	2
JONES BRUCE H	CW3	W-2142477	1064	1
JONES BUD L	MAJ	O-1340080	0764	1
JONES CALVIN	CW2	W-2211363	1166	1
JONES CARL D	LTC	O-1020561	0768	1
JONES CARL S	LTC	O-0295127	0562	1
JONES CARL W	LTC	O-0348108	0355	1
JONES CAROL R	CPT	O-0494741	0946	1
JONES CARROLL F	1LT	O-1295559	0445	2
JONES CARROLL J SR	MAJ	O-1115934	0564	1
JONES CECIL R	MAJ	O-2043010	0962	1
JONES CHARLES A JR	CPT	O-1322451	0947	2
JONES CHARLES B	CPT	O-0320560	0246	2
JONES CHARLES C	CPT	O-0170117	0161	3
JONES CHARLES C	LTC	O-0221592	0757	3
JONES CHARLES D	CW3	W-2146941	0664	1
JONES CHARLES E	LTC	O-1282048	0868	1
JONES CHARLES E	1LT	O-1577391	1061	3
JONES CHARLES F	MAJ	O-1305592	1057	1
JONES CHARLES F	1LT	O-1329597	1045	2
JONES CHARLES G JR	2LT	O-1032805	0351	2
JONES CHARLES H	COL	O-0224956	0165	3
JONES CHARLES H	COL	O-0307644	1047	2
JONES CHARLES H JR	COL	O-0216752	0160	1
JONES CHARLES H JR	CPT	O-0537859	0247	2
JONES CHARLES L	LTC	O-0363543	0766	1
JONES CHARLES L	LTC	O-1053657	0661	1
JONES CHARLES P	LTC	O-0372926	1266	3
JONES CHARLES R	1LT	O-1999265	0547	2
JONES CHARLES P	CW3	W-3150633	0168	1
JONES CHARLES S	LTC	O-0187192	0648	3
JONES CHARLES T	LTC	O-0267549	0645	2
JONES CHARLES T	MAJ	O-0527307	1054	1
JONES CHARLES W	LTC	O-0247925	0466	3
JONES CHARLES W	LTC	O-0981957	0868	1
JONES CHARLIE P	LTC	O-0480797	0354	1
JONES CLARENCE F JR	LTC	O-0257719	0964	3
JONES CLARENCE L	COL	O-0248036	0361	3
JONES CLARENCE Q	LTC	O-0298243	0257	1
JONES CLAUDE A	MAJ	O-0887887	0656	1
JONES CLAUDE P	1LT	O-1016457	0746	2
JONES CLEO W	CW2	W-2150585	0357	1
JONES CLEVELAND	CW3	W-2143592	1059	1

NAME	GRADE	SVC NO	DATE RET MO YR	RET CODE
JONES CLIFFORD R	CPT	O-0154480	0955	3
JONES CLYDE A	LTC	O-0323037	0547	2
JONES CLYDE W	MAJ	O-2007862	0662	1
JONES CONWAY R	LTC	O-1285597	0961	2
JONES DAN C	2LT	O-4063315	1058	2
JONES DANIEL H	CW2	W-2122377	0847	2
JONES DANIEL W	COL	O-0163455	1054	3
JONES DARWIN M	CW3	W-2150091	1066	1
JONES DAVID A	CPT	O-0381768	1057	1
JONES DAVID A	CPT	O-0447034	0447	2
JONES DEFOREST	MAJ	O-0456208	1160	1
JONES DEOLINDA C	MAJ	N-0736538	0966	1
JONES DEWITT	LTC	O-0259611	0364	3
JONES DILLARD F	LTC	O-0353009	0766	1
JONES DIXON H	LTC	O-1301753	0457	1
JONES DONALD B	LTC	O-1040742	0866	1
JONES DONALD B JR	LTC	O-0399857	0661	1
JONES DONALD C	1LT	O-1306280	0745	2
JONES DONALD F	1LT	O-1310252	1045	2
JONES DONALD F	CPT	O-0178223	1156	3
JONES DONALD S	1LT	O-1037846	1145	2
JONES DOUGLAS R	CPT	O-5023829	1168	2
JONES DOVA L	MAJ	O-1115305	1262	1
JONES DOYLE	1LT	O-1058279	0847	2
JONES DOYLE W	CW2	W-2131053	0862	1
JONES DUDLEY B	LTC	O-0154389	0354	3
JONES DUKE F	COL	O-0219968	0654	1
JONES EBEN	1LT	O-1172938	0445	2
JONES EDGAR A	MAJ	O-2053871	1155	1
JONES EDGAR B	MAJ	O-0249158	1266	3
JONES EDGAR C JR	1LT	O-1173666	0646	2
JONES EDMUND C	CPT	O-1644464	0560	1
JONES EDWARD	MAJ	O-0978207	0264	1
JONES EDWARD B	CPT	O-1598013	1162	1
JONES EDWARD C	MAJ	O-0236190	1064	3
JONES EDWARD C	1LT	O-1321313	0847	2
JONES EDWARD E	LTC	O-2018174	1167	1
JONES EDWARD L	LTC	O-0144901	0954	3
JONES EDWARD M	CW3	W-2147007	0667	1
JONES EDWARD P	1LT	O-1821876	0445	2
JONES EDWARD T JR	CPT	O-0304253	0944	2
JONES EDWARD W	MAJ	O-1003266	1154	1
JONES EDWARD W JR	LTC	O-0524912	0763	1
JONES EDWIN G	CW2	W-3430062	1264	1
JONES EDWIN L	MAJ	O-0227047	0163	3
JONES EDWIN N	CW2	W-2143031	0957	1
JONES EDWIN T JR	MAJ	O-0404300	0662	1
JONES ELBERT T	LTC	O-0265464	0956	3
JONES ELLIE B	LTC	O-0238304	0262	3
JONES ELLIE C	MAJ	O-0187069	0852	3
JONES ELMER L	1LT	O-0404299	0142	2
JONES ELMER W	COL	O-0274353	0568	3
JONES ELWOOD T	MAJ	O-0567183	0761	1
JONES EMERSON R	LTC	O-1293063	0766	1
JONES EMMETT B	CPT	O-0468631	0745	2
JONES EMMETT L JR	LTC	O-0227080	0746	2
JONES ERNEST F	MAJ	O-1693794	1060	1
JONES ERNEST S	LTC	O-0179324	0648	3
JONES ERNEST T	MAJ	O-1168740	1160	1
JONES EUGENE JR	MAJ	O-2014610	0967	1
JONES EUGENE L	COL	O-0232552	0864	3
JONES EVERETT L	MAJ	O-1548868	0860	1
JONES EVERETT L	CPT	O-5326918	0968	2
JONES EVERTON	MAJ	O-0239558	1162	3
JONES FOREST A	MAJ	O-1944483	0260	1
JONES FORREST E	LTC	O-0190349	1152	3
JONES FRANK O	COL	O-0397755	0859	1
JONES FRANK O JR	LTC	O-0253911	0767	3
JONES FRANK E	CPT	O-0517632	0646	2
JONES FRANK M	MAJ	O-1333829	0262	1
JONES FRED K JR	LTC	O-0358816	0767	3
JONES FRED L	LTC	O-0183358	1056	3
JONES FREDERICK	LTC	O-1035843	0761	1
JONES FREDERICK	MAJ	O-1291648	0157	1
JONES FREDERICK	LTC	O-1873455	1166	3

NAME	GRADE	SVC NO	DATE RET MO YR	RET CODE
JONES FREEMAN	LTC	O-1798005	0861	1
JONES GEORGE A	MAJ	O-0978238	0964	1
JONES GEORGE A	MAJ	O-1876603	0765	1
JONES GEORGE D	LTC	O-0259783	0964	3
JONES GEORGE D	LTC	O-0320069	0460	3
JONES GEORGE W	CPT	O-0430264	0752	2
JONES GEORGE W	LTC	O-0580867	0963	3
JONES GEORGE W	2LT	O-1692513	0845	2
JONES GERALD A	CW3	W-2144546	0365	1
JONES GLEN W	1LT	O-0911354	1044	2
JONES GLEN W	LTC	O-2050842	1167	1
JONES GLENN L	CW4	W-2145731	1167	1
JONES GLENN W	LTC	O-0307691	0358	3
JONES GLENN W	CW3	W-2143926	0962	1
JONES GORDON L	1LT	O-0476017	0245	2
JONES GRANT P	LTC	O-0377156	0567	3
JONES GRANT S	CPT	O-1176682	0662	1
JONES GRIFFITH G	LTC	O-1951091	0166	1
JONES GUY O	MAJ	O-0418096	0760	1
JONES GUY H	CPT	O-0997911	0564	1
JONES HARLOW G	LTC	O-0254135	1064	3
JONES HAROLD	MAJ	O-0402296	0949	1
JONES HAROLD B	LTC	O-0319811	0159	1
JONES HAROLD C JR	2LT	O-0390566	1242	2
JONES HAROLD J	CPT	O-1574456	0658	1
JONES HAROLD R	LTC	O-0354836	0161	1
JONES HARRY L	CW4	W-2104184	0255	1
JONES HARRY P	COL	O-0260778	1160	3
JONES HARRY R	CW4	W-2145471	0768	1
JONES HELEN J	MAJ	N-0744855	1062	1
JONES HENRIETTA	1LT	N-0783903	0446	1
JONES HENRY A	1LT	O-1320737	0645	2
JONES HENRY H	LTC	O-1686549	0767	1
JONES HENRY L II	COL	O-0171546	1060	3
JONES HENRY W	CPT	O-0514007	0646	2
JONES HENRY W	CPT	O-1011642	0146	2
JONES HERBERT D	LTC	O-1794949	1065	1
JONES HERSCHEL C	MAJ	O-1923631	1067	1
JONES HILBERT G	LTC	O-1015981	0468	1
JONES HILLERY D	CPT	O-0973178	0463	1
JONES HIRAM F	MAJ	O-0286268	1053	1
JONES HOLMES A	COL	O-0240794	0363	1
JONES HOWARD B	LTC	O-0418206	0152	2
JONES HOWARD C	COL	O-0241041	0862	3
JONES HOWARD P	COL	O-0208883	0159	3
JONES HOWARD R	1LT	O-1184078	0845	2
JONES HOWARD R	2LT	O-1551651	0645	2
JONES HOWARD S JR	MAJ	O-2035479	1160	1
JONES HUGH D	MAJ	O-0964076	1062	1
JONES HUGH JR	LTC	O-0527809	1264	1
JONES HUGH M	LTC	O-0154641	1153	3
JONES HUMPHREY B	CW2	W-2148653	0461	1
JONES J K	CW3	W-2208938	0168	1
JONES JACK	MAJ	O-0975603	0964	1
JONES JACK A .	CW3	W-2153352	1163	1
JONES JACK C	LTC	O-1554568	1262	1
JONES JACK I	LTC	O-1312010	0865	1
JONES JACK L	MAJ	O-1055878	0866	1
JONES JACK W	MAJ	O-1258240	0364	1
JONES JACKSON S	LTC	O-1577393	1064	1
JONES JAMES A	COL	O-0168857	0647	2
JONES JAMES A	CPT	O-0461070	0345	2
JONES JAMES C	1LT	O-0519685	0146	2
JONES JAMES C JR	MAJ	O-2262695	1065	1
JONES JAMES E	1LT	O-0219894	1053	3
JONES JAMES F	1LT	O-0286392	0442	2
JONES JAMES H	MAJ	O-1172939	0561	1
JONES JAMES H	WO1	W-2115435	1053	1
JONES JAMES L	CPT	O-0504807	0245	2
JONES JAMES L JR	CPT	O-1824867	0861	1
JONES JAMES M	COL	O-0277141	0760	3
JONES JAMES M	MAJ	O-0960814	0863	1
JONES JAMES M	2LT	O-1913506	0747	1
JONES JAMES M	WO1	W-2146992	1157	1
JONES JAMES M JR	COL	O-0330151	1061	3

NAME	GRADE	SVC NO	DATE RET MO YR	RET CODE
JONES JAMES N	LTC	O-0422325	0262	1
JONES JAMES P	MAJ	O-0395437	0457	1
JONES JAMES R	MAJ	O-1325755	0863	1
JONES JAMES S JR	COL	O-0192812	1059	3
JONES JAMES T	LTC	O-1116674	0264	1
JONES JAMES W	CW2	W-2206366	0861	1
JONES JAMES W	CW2	W-3411009	0965	1
JONES JANE C	2LT	N-0729899	0244	1
JONES JAY L	CPT	O-1030484	0147	2
JONES JAY M	CW3	W-2147440	0964	1
JONES JEFFERSON	1LT	O-1331841	0959	1
JONES JERALD R	1LT	O-1284149	0645	2
JONES JEROME B	LTC	O-0152773	0844	2
JONES JESSE J	COL	O-0888537	0854	1
JONES JESSIE M	CW4	W-2125674	1162	1
JONES JEWELL F	LTC	O-0299880	1165	3
JONES JOHN B	MAJ	O-0487427	0547	2
JONES JOHN B	WO1	W-2122811	0745	2
JONES JOHN D	LTC	O-0340817	1160	1
JONES JOHN D	CW2	W-2101901	0344	1
JONES JOHN D	CW2	W-3000404	1267	1
JONES JOHN F	MAJ	O-0972482	0265	1
JONES JOHN F	CW2	W-2205596	0561	1
JONES JOHN H	CPT	O-0363965	1044	2
JONES JOHN J	COL	O-0223454	1164	3
JONES JOHN L	CPT	O-0193156	0456	3
JONES JOHN P	MAJ	O-0148196	0648	3
JONES JOHN P	LTC	O-0275523	0662	3
JONES JOHN P	MAJ	O-0916953	1062	1
JONES JOHN P	1LT	O-1323576	0845	2
JONES JOHN R	LTC	O-0411430	0765	1
JONES JOHN R	WO1	W-2118306	0550	1
JONES JOHN W	COL	O-0197705	0263	3
JONES JOHN W	MAJ	O-1597146	0358	1
JONES JOSEPH A	LTC	O-0291045	1066	3
JONES JOSEPH A	LTC	O-1171209	0966	1
JONES JOSEPH A JR	LTC	O-0249033	0664	3
JONES JOSEPH J	MAJ	O-1044572	1263	1
JONES JOSEPH L	LTC	O-0225833	0365	3
JONES JOSEPH R	MAJ	O-0392726	0667	3
JONES JOSEPH R	MAJ	O-0491051	0146	2
JONES JOSEPH W	MAJ	O-0973828	1165	1
JONES JULIET M	2LT	N-0726166	0644	1
JONES KATHERINE	2LT	N-0700179	1139	1
JONES KENNETH	1LT	O-0419530	0655	2
JONES LARREN L	CPT	O-1103244	0957	1
JONES LARRY C	CPT	O-5417865	1268	2
JONES LAWRENCE A	CW2	W-2214743	1067	1
JONES LAWRENCE H	MAJ	O-0982723	1062	1
JONES LAWRENCE T	MAJ	MN-2299375	1168	2
JONES LELAND N	COL	O-0167383	1055	3
JONES LEO L	2LT	O-0504201	0743	2
JONES LEONARD M	LTC	O-1300336	0364	1
JONES LESLIE F	LTC	O-0446274	0966	3
JONES LEWIS H	COL	O-0204162	0360	3
JONES LINCOLN S	LTC	O-0212204	0264	3
JONES LINDBERGH	MAJ	O-4010795	0767	1
JONES LINZEY D	1LT	O-1321680	0745	2
JONES LLEWELLYN	LTC	O-0407531	0764	1
JONES LLOYD A	LTC	O-1314497	1165	1
JONES LLOYD D	LTC	O-0284624	0768	3
JONES LLOYD D	MAJ	O-1339872	0464	1
JONES LOREN W	CPT	O-2103050	0962	2
JONES LOUIS K	CW4	W-2141329	0766	1
JONES LUTHER C	LTC	O-1540695	0965	1
JONES LYLE	CPT	O-1300807	0654	1
JONES LYLE V	LTC	O-0347709	0365	3
JONES LYLE W	LTC	O-0204722	0961	3
JONES LYNN P	1LT	O-0446747	1145	2
JONES LYTLE R	MAJ	O-0278419	0666	3
JONES MAJLE H	CW4	W-2146155	0767	1
JONES MALCOLM A	COL	O-0288056	0856	3
JONES MALCOLM S	COL	O-0182149	1155	3
JONES MANION F	CPT	O-0180266	0648	3
JONES MARCUS L	MAJ	O-1546401	0261	1

NAME	GRADE	SVC NO	DATE RET MO YR	RET CODE
JONES MARGARET E	MAJ	L-0500986	0165	1
JONES MARGARET F	2LT	N-0751172	1044	1
JONES MARION A	LTC	0-1310120	0764	1
JONES MARION C	1LT	0-1313647	0146	2
JONES MARSHALL W JR	CPT	0-1530378	0446	2
JONES MARTHA R	MAJ	N-0761318	0165	1
JONES MARVIN	MAJ	0-0505398	0255	1
JONES MARVIN J	MAJ	0-0273113	0968	3
JONES MARVIN L	MAJ	0-1170023	0747	2
JONES MARVIN L	1LT	0-1175475	0346	2
JONES MARVIN L JR	MAJ	0-0988155	0964	1
JONES MARY F	2LT	N-0743409	0445	1
JONES MELVIN H	COL	0-0192266	0455	1
JONES MELVIN R	LTC	0-1542233	1062	1
JONES MELVIN T	LTC	0-0297012	0568	3
JONES MILES D	MAJ	0-4011135	0568	1
JONES MILDRED W	CW3	W-2147074	0763	1
JONES MILTON C JR	1LT	0-5323979	1066	2
JONES MILTON H	LTC	0-0297711	0162	1
JONES MINNIS M	1LT	0-1302473	1044	2
JONES MORRIS F	LTC	0-1677774	0964	1
JONES MORRIS A	MAJ	0-1115935	0964	1
JONES MORRIS W	1LT	0-1318181	0145	2
JONES MYRON S	CW3	W-2144472	1165	1
JONES NELSON R	MAJ	0-0418330	0663	1
JONES OLIVER G	CW3	W-2210095	0664	1
JONES OLLIE F	LTC	0-0287488	0366	3
JONES ORION C	MAJ	0-0122177	0252	1
JONES ORVILLE H	MAJ	0-1051626	1054	1
JONES PAUL	MAJ	0-0359070	0854	1
JONES PAUL	CPT	0-0489774	0347	1
JONES PAUL	CW3	W-2150276	0659	1
JONES PAUL A	CW2	W-2115113	0351	1
JONES PAUL J	LTC	0-1111699	1062	1
JONES PAUL J	LTC	0-1296863	0562	1
JONES PAUL L	COL	0-0305788	0366	3
JONES PAUL L	LTC	0-0327132	0760	3
JONES PAUL S	MAJ	0-0111946	0648	3
JONES PAUL W	LTC	0-0194725	0746	2
JONES PAUL W	MAJ	0-1038021	0767	3
JONES PAULINE	MAJ	N-0729075	1062	1
JONES PHILIP I II	LTC	0-1042851	0451	1
JONES PRESTON F	LTC	0-1115306	0167	1
JONES RALPH C	MAJ	0-0258545	1162	1
JONES RALPH K	LTC	0-0361305	0459	1
JONES RALPH O	CW2	W-2214376	1266	1
JONES RALPH V	1LT	0-1333346	0549	2
JONES RAY	CW3	W-2144153	0660	1
JONES RAY G	COL	0-0247770	0556	2
JONES RAY L	MAJ	0-1301156	1059	1
JONES RAY J	2LT	0-1015950	0345	2
JONES RAY V	LTC	0-0136596	0454	3
JONES RAYMOND C	MAJ	0-0452125	1054	1
JONES RAYMOND F	LTC	0-0322331	0868	3
JONES RAYMOND F	CPT	0-0335313	0346	2
JONES RAYMOND F	1LT	0-1014532	0261	2
JONES REBEL J	CPT	0-0444354	1148	1
JONES RICHARD C	MAJ	0-1544872	0457	1
JONES RICHARD H	COL	0-0233409	1064	3
JONES RICHARD H	LTC	0-0503703	0157	1
JONES RICHARD H	MAJ	0-1296038	1146	2
JONES RICHARD L	LTC	0-0421426	0664	1
JONES RICHARD M	LTC	0-0273029	0257	3
JONES RICHARD P	MAJ	0-1552528	1164	3
JONES RICHARD S	1LT	0-1056776	0553	2
JONES RICHARD W	CPT	0-1684357	1060	1
JONES RILEY G	MAJ	0-0468285	0754	1
JONES ROBERT A	COL	0-0345653	0261	1
JONES ROBERT A	MAJ	0-4004290	0168	1
JONES ROBERT B	COL	0-0231269	0561	1
JONES ROBERT B	COL	0-0296455	0864	3
JONES ROBERT B	MAJ	0-1315904	0264	1
JONES ROBERT C	CPT	0-1533595	0962	1
JONES ROBERT E	CW2	W-2144540	1163	1
JONES ROBERT F SR	LTC	0-1574271	0267	1

NAME	GRADE	SVC NO	DATE RET MO YR	RET CODE
JONES ROBERT F	MAJ	0-0472303	0854	1
JONES ROBERT G	MAJ	0-0260476	0164	3
JONES ROBERT G	CW2	W-2216826	0769	1
JONES ROBERT H JR	CW2	W-2205630	0361	1
JONES ROBERT J	MAJ	0-1032218	0157	2
JONES ROBERT J F	CW3	W-2145456	1060	1
JONES ROBERT K	LTC	0-1664466	1156	1
JONES ROBERT L	LTC	0-1325295	1162	1
JONES ROBERT L JR	COL	0-1946302	1068	1
JONES ROBERT M	M G	0-0270821	1164	3
JONES ROBERT M	1LT	0-1589626	0662	2
JONES ROBERT O	MAJ	0-0408580	1045	2
JONES ROBERT P	1LT	0-0440638	1143	2
JONES ROBERT P	MAJ	0-0973544	0861	1
JONES ROBERT R	LTC	0-2052210	0667	3
JONES ROBERT R	CW4	W-2113654	0155	1
JONES ROBERT S	LTC	0-0250614	0467	3
JONES ROBERT S	LTC	0-0273436	0963	3
JONES ROBERT T	CPT	0-1177475	0647	2
JONES ROBERT W	MAJ	0-0353930	0856	2
JONES ROBERT W	LTC	0-0373794	0257	2
JONES RODNEY H	COL	0-0401840	0961	3
JONES ROGER W	COL	0-0262202	0363	3
JONES ROSAMOND R	LTC	0-0407835	0657	1
JONES ROY	COL	0-0304857	0847	2
JONES ROY D	MAJ	0-1176087	0853	1
JONES ROY L	COL	0-0336206	0859	3
JONES RUDOLPH M	LTC	0-0370312	0763	1
JONES RUFUS	CW2	W-2141330	0657	1
JONES RUSSELL T	COL	0-0265281	0367	3
JONES RUTH F	MAJ	N-0771209	0867	1
JONES SALLIE T	MAJ	N-0722413	0765	3
JONES SAM H	MAJ	0-0207538	0757	3
JONES SAMUEL A JR	MAJ	0-0995134	0465	1
JONES SCOTT S	LTC	0-0227812	0257	3
JONES SHERMAN A	CPT	0-1183101	0464	1
JONES SHERMAN F	CPT	0-0496266	0454	1
JONES STANFORD F	MAJ	0-0237785	0763	3
JONES STANLEY F	1LT	0-0447220	0446	2
JONES STARR W	LTC	0-1285249	0266	3
JONES STENSON R	CPT	0-2103030	0662	1
JONES STUART M	MAJ	0-0262022	0664	3
JONES THOMAS B	MAJ	0-0201436	1155	3
JONES THOMAS B	CPT	0-1996351	0551	2
JONES THOMAS D	CPT	0-1286135	1045	2
JONES THOMAS G	CW4	W-2002787	0464	3
JONES THOMAS H	CW4	W-2141600	1060	1
JONES THOMAS JR	CW2	W-2207354	1263	1
JONES THOMAS K	MAJ	0-0273781	0945	2
JONES THOMAS N	COL	0-0249161	0764	3
JONES THOMAS R	MAJ	0-0358910	0546	2
JONES THOMAS W JR	MAJ	0-1922571	1163	1
JONES TORRENCE V	LTC	0-2006092	1163	1
JONES VERNA D	CW3	W-2145969	0166	1
JONES VERNON F	LTC	0-1103720	0861	1
JONES VERNON F	MAJ	0-1300337	0161	1
JONES VERNON O	MAJ	0-0572197	0562	1
JONES VERYL L	2LT	0-1032593	0445	2
JONES VIRGINIA O	1LT	N-0770051	0244	1
JONES WALTER	CW3	W-2141147	0863	1
JONES WALTER B	COL	0-0102768	0255	3
JONES WALTER F	2LT	0-1577396	0245	2
JONES WALTER H	CPT	0-1012293	0847	2
JONES WALTER P	LTC	0-0423283	0660	1
JONES WALTER S	LTC	0-0155500	0648	3
JONES WALTER T	LTC	0-0265856	0154	1
JONES WALTER W	LTC	0-0284685	0854	1
JONES WARD A	LTC	0-0246065	0862	3
JONES WAYNE T	MAJ	0-0572298	1061	1
JONES WENDELL H	1LT	0-1179114	0146	2
JONES WESLEY H	LTC	0-0301497	0967	3
JONES WESLEY S	CW4	W-2113286	1055	1
JONES WILBERT L	MAJ	0-0383676	0460	1
JONES WILBUR A	MAJ	0-0997488	1266	1
JONES WILBUR M	1LT	0-1036582	1051	1

NAME	GRADE	SVC NO	DATE RET MO YR	RET CODE
JONES WILFRED H	MAJ	0-1559928	1066	1
JONES WILLARD A	CPT	0-1951625	1057	1
JONES WILLARD E	LTC	0-1244372	1258	2
JONES WILLIAM	CW2	W-2104660	0853	1
JONES WILLIAM B	COL	0-0311529	1062	3
JONES WILLIAM B	CPT	0-0975435	0265	2
JONES WILLIAM C	MAJ	0-2017245	0764	1
JONES WILLIAM C	COL	0-0225031	0451	3
JONES WILLIAM C	CW3	W-2144572	0460	1
JONES WILLIAM F	LTC	0-0281909	0262	3
JONES WILLIAM G JR	LTC	0-1634345	1264	1
JONES WILLIAM H	MAJ	0-0966176	0563	1
JONES WILLIAM H	MAJ	0-1934423	0760	1
JONES WILLIAM J	LTC	0-0438619	0462	1
JONES WILLIAM J	1LT	0-1317607	0346	2
JONES WILLIAM J	CW3	W-2136580	1262	1
JONES WILLIAM L	CPT	0-0970211	0361	1
JONES WILLIAM L	LTC	0-1010154	0866	1
JONES WILLIAM M	MAJ	0-0177617	0861	3
JONES WILLIAM M	MAJ	0-1798159	1060	3
JONES WILLIAM P JR	LTC	0-0257588	0168	3
JONES WILLIAM R	1LT	0-1297735	0145	2
JONES WILLIAM S	2LT	0-1165097	1144	2
JONES WILLIAM T	MAJ	0-1176583	0464	2
JONES WILLIAM W	CPT	0-0117209	1155	3
JONES WILLIE A	CPT	0-1585685	0557	1
JONES WILLIE F	CW2	W-2145222	0358	1
JONES WILLIE L	MAJ	0-0946620	1263	1
JONES WINIFRED F	MAJ	L-1010723	0866	1
JONES WOODROW A	LTC	0-0345551	0358	1
JONES YOUNG G	WO1	W-2145721	0257	1
JONES ZETTA W H	LTC	L-0607722	0968	2
JONES 3RD JOHN C	MAJ	0-0508477	1047	2
JONESCHILD WILLIAM R	LTC	0-0342552	1061	1
JONGEWAARD LAWRENCE	LTC	0-0403430	0661	3
JONSON LESLIE M	MAJ	0-0955530	0660	1
JOPLIN JOHNNIE P	CW3	W-2153010	0764	1
JOPLIN TROY M	LTC	0-1688514	0567	1
JOPLING DANIEL W	LTC	0-0417923	0561	2
JOPLING HARVEY M	LTC	0-0903835	1166	3
JORAY PHILIP A	LTC	0-0904117	0468	3
JORDAHL MARTIN	CPT	0-0307620	1144	2
JORDAN ALBERT B	CW4	W-2101006	0255	2
JORDAN ARLINGTON	CW2	W-2151478	0363	1
JORDAN ARTHUR L	CW3	W-2149759	0551	1
JORDAN ARTHUR W	LTC	0-0171634	1061	3
JORDAN ASHFORD T	COL	0-0397148	0760	1
JORDAN BENJAMIN R	CPT	0-0349926	0446	2
JORDAN BERTRAND	LTC	0-0321675	0766	3
JORDAN BOREN H	CW3	W-2142425	0965	1
JORDAN CECIL F	CW3	W-2141602	1059	1
JORDAN CHARLES A	LTC	0-0411577	0660	1
JORDAN CHARLES E	CW2	W-2151007	0853	1
JORDAN CURTIS L	CW3	W-2210364	0969	1
JORDAN DONALD F	CPT	0-1299414	0847	2
JORDAN DONALD R	1LT	0-0374110	1145	2
JORDAN DOSIE	CPT	0-0486795	1145	2
JORDAN EARLAND R	LTC	0-0337166	0963	1
JORDAN EARLE H JR	LTC	0-1256600	0561	1
JORDAN EDMUND A	1LT	0-1313748	0545	2
JORDAN EDWARD B	MAJ	0-1302138	0355	1
JORDAN EDWARD E	LTC	0-0444835	0458	3
JORDAN EDWARD M	LTC	0-0379266	0767	1
JORDAN ELAINE M	2LT	N-0735503	1044	1
JORDAN ELMO C	CPT	0-1010090	0446	2
JORDAN ERLAND F	CPT	0-1311794	0647	2
JORDAN EVERETT C	CPT	0-0260621	1147	2
JORDAN FRANCIS N	COL	0-0114248	1055	3
JORDAN FRANKLIN E	LTC	0-0271033	0464	4
JORDAN FRED A JR	CPT	0-0412956	0149	2
JORDAN FRED W	MAJ	0-0444391	0357	3
JORDAN GEORGE F	LTC	0-1826151	0263	1
JORDAN GERARD A	CW3	W-2153125	1062	1
JORDAN GORDAN A	LTC	0-0336818	0860	1
JORDAN H T JR	CPT	0-1571229	0347	2

NAME	GRADE	SVC NO	DATE RET MO YR	RET CODE
JORDAN HARRY A JR	1LT	0-0980669	0547	2
JORDAN HARVIE B	CW2	W-2152932	1057	1
JORDAN HENRY H JR	MAJ	0-0565786	0163	1
JORDAN HENRY M	LTC	0-0386141	0867	1
JORDAN HENRY S	CPT	0-2055162	0356	2
JORDAN HERBERT P	[illegible]	0-0181117	1054	3
JORDAN HOWARD B	COL	0-0282053	0567	3
JORDAN HOWARD P	LTC	0-0271066	0168	3
JORDAN IVA M	CPT	N-0764519	0463	2
JORDAN JAMES A	CW3	W-2145558	1067	1
JORDAN JAMES F	1LT	0-0534368	0246	2
JORDAN JAMES L	CW3	W-2135536	0163	1
JORDAN JAMES M	1LT	0-2034529	0356	1
JORDAN JESSE A	MAJ	0-0290047	0866	3
JORDAN JOHN	LTC	0-1574879	0163	1
JORDAN JOHN A	CPT	0-0449052	0247	2
JORDAN JOHN P	COL	0-0235938	0460	3
JORDAN JOSEPH C	MAJ	0-0327315	0860	3
JORDAN LAURENCE O	MAJ	0-1030047	0665	1
JORDAN LAWRENCE H	LTC	0-0319628	0852	2
JORDAN LEON H	MAJ	0-0962415	0861	1
JORDAN LESTER F	COL	0-0264907	0167	3
JORDAN LEVI	COL	0-0334196	0263	1
JORDAN LOUIS L	LTC	0-0384153	1263	3
JORDAN OCTAVIO L	MAJ	0-0339600	1160	1
JORDAN PATRICK	LTC	0-0451458	1160	1
JORDAN PAUL H	M G	0-0241877	0964	3
JORDAN PAUL H	COL	0-0258985	0164	3
JORDAN RICHARD L	MAJ	0-0274529	0864	3
JORDAN ROBERT B	CW3	W-2141819	0957	1
JORDAN ROBERT H	MAJ	0-0377040	0561	1
JORDAN RUFUS P	CW2	W-2151337	0663	1
JORDAN RUSSELL C	LTC	0-0224951	0844	2
JORDAN STEVE JR	MAJ	0-0986049	1063	1
JORDAN THEODORE W	CPT	0-1166523	0645	2
JORDAN WALTER H	CPT	0-1120154	0564	1
JORDAN WILLIAM B	COL	0-0123854	0857	3
JORDAN WILLIAM I	LTC	0-2267179	0864	1
JORDAN WILLIAM M	CPT	0-1175759	0764	1
JORDAN WILLIAM P	CPT	0-0344528	0545	2
JORDAN WILLIAM P	COL	0-0121579	0552	3
JORGENS JOSEPH	1LT	0-1765043	1044	2
JORGENSEN CHARLES J	LTC	0-0284501	1058	1
JORGENSEN CHRIST	CW2	W-2141332	1157	1
JORGENSEN CLEMENT A	CPT	0-0331443	0445	2
JORGENSEN GALE W	CW2	W-3200182	0165	1
JORGENSEN JAMES M JR	LTC	0-0465588	1066	1
JORGENSEN MABEL G	1LT	N-0732623	0145	1
JORGENSEN WILHELM	COL	0-0308731	0368	3
JORGENSEN WILLIAM F	LTC	0-0183409	0754	3
JORGENSON ANDREW F	MAJ	0-1938017	0869	1
JORGENSON DONALD K	1LT	0-1017406	0946	2
JORGENSON EARL A	1LT	0-1171619	0248	1
JORGENSON ROY E	CW4	W-2116004	1055	1
JORGENSON WALTER R	LTC	0-1285434	0658	1
JORNS HOMER P	1LT	0-1945848	0145	2
JORTE CHARLES H	CPT	0-0166855	0130	1
JORTH AARON M	CPT	0-0509535	0545	2
JOSEPH ALFRED A	LTC	0-0366133	0665	1
JOSEPH ALVIN A	CPT	0-1112789	0164	1
JOSEPH CHARLES N	MAJ	0-2049970	0461	1
JOSEPH EDWARD G	COL	0-0138440	0254	3
JOSEPH JOHN A	COL	0-0251523	1066	3
JOSEPH LESTER G	CPT	0-0378356	0145	2
JOSEPH MARGARET M	MAJ	N-0773598	0667	1
JOSEPH ROBERT D	MAJ	0-2263167	1162	1
JOSEPHS WILLIAM W	COL	0-0317977	0566	3
JOSEY ALLEN I	COL	0-0302692	0346	2
JOSIFEK LUCILLE H	2LT	N-0702292	0832	1
JOSLIN GEORGE B	CPT	0-0193928	1262	3
JOSSERAND NEWTON	CPT	0-1923548	0162	1
JOST GEORGE R	LTC	0-1287189	0965	1
JOST HERMAN H JR	LTC	0-0268282	0567	3
JOST LEWIS M	MAJ	0-1186647	0763	2
JOST LOYD G	LTC	0-0301542	0766	3

NAME	GRADE	SVC NO	DATE RET MO YR	RET CODE
JOST WILLIAM R	LTC	0-0258393	1067	3
JOUBERT MARY L	MAJ	N-0729294	0965	3
JOUETT JOHN K	LTC	0-0439375	1064	1
JOUJON-ROCHE JEAN E	LTC	0-0254508	0666	3
JOURDAN CARMER L	MAJ	0-1683459	0762	1
JOURDEN FOREST J	CPT	0-0472012	1058	1
JOURGLMON NEIL	LTC	0-0261311	0667	1
JOUVE PAUL A	CPT	0-1329755	0461	1
JOVES EUSEBIO R	1LT	0-1396836	1149	1
JOWELL LEWIS L	CW4	W-2116842	0559	1
JOWELL MAITLAND A	CW2	W-3150999	0467	1
JOY FREDERICK	MAJ	0-0235954	0346	2
JOY HAROLD W	CPT	0-0123853	0751	3
JOY ROBERT A	LTC	0-0456299	0264	1
JOY ROBERT D	CPT	0-0408898	0945	2
JOYAL JEANNE G	CW4	V-0123144	1263	1
JOYCE EDWARD H	LTC	0-0917077	0263	3
JOYCE EDWARD P	MAJ	0-0963842	0166	1
JOYCE EUGENE V	LTC	0-0451320	0658	1
JOYCE HAROLD D	LTC	0-0324964	0762	3
JOYCE JOHN A	LTC	0-0308290	0650	1
JOYCE JOHN J	CW4	W-2105647	0557	1
JOYCE JOSEPH R J	CPT	0-0438811	0146	2
JOYCE MARY I	2LT	N-0731054	1044	1
JOYCE MERLE L	COL	0-0244898	0362	3
JOYCE MICHAEL	CW3	W-2148733	0662	1
JOYCE RAY T	LTC	0-0235279	0359	2
JOYCE RAYMOND N	CPT	0-1178852	0347	2
JOYCE ROBERT J	MAJ	0-1824871	0461	2
JOYCE THOMAS B J	LTC	0-0924036	0165	3
JOYCE THOMAS F	LTC	0-0903231	0655	2
JOYCE WALDO V	COL	0-0224704	0164	3
JOYCE WILLIAM A	CW2	W-2123431	1046	2
JOYCE WILLIAM G	CW3	W-2149989	1064	1
JOYCE WILLIAM J	LTC	0-0534672	0848	1
JOYCE WILLIAM L	CW3	W-2142791	0760	1
JOYE JAMES L	CW2	W-2208403	0463	1
JOYER BOYD J	LTC	0-0286728	0667	3
JOYNER HENRY C	MAJ	0-1554494	0659	1
JOYNER HOUSTON L	COL	0-0212284	0958	1
JOYNER JAMES JR	MAJ	0-2205423	0268	2
JOYNER JOHN R	MAJ	0-0199090	0949	1
JOYNER JOHNY F	CPT	0-0505539	0457	1
JOYNER JONES S	LTC	0-0308099	0166	3
JOYNER LESLETTE E	WO1	W-2127714	1062	1
JOZWIAK CASS J	LTC	0-1307059	0367	1
JUBA JOHN	LTC	0-2021130	0668	1
JUBECK JOHN A	LTC	0-0246122	0560	1
JUCKETT RUSSELL A	CPT	0-1315526	0147	2
JUDAH CARTER M	LTC	0-0229258	0464	1
JUDD HARLAN A	LTC	0-0377140	1267	3
JUDD LEROY A JR	CPT	0-0498630	1061	1
JUDD ROLAND B JR	CPT	0-1176905	0263	1
JUDD VERNON C	2LT	0-0503827	1144	2
JUDD WARREN C JR	CW3	W-2148257	0163	1
JUDD WENDELL O	WO1	W-2148473	0969	1
JUDD WILLABEL E	MAJ	L-0501294	0855	2
JUDGE THOMAS J	1LT	0-1593180	0451	2
JUDKINS DONALD S	MAJ	0-1061745	1265	1
JUDKINS PAUL A	LTC	0-0373933	1161	1
JUDKINS ROBERT O	CW2	W-2146464	1050	1
JUDKINS ROGER H	1LT	0-0443759	0945	2
JUDKINS ROY	CW3	W-2207014	0366	1
JUDKINS VERNON T	LTC	0-0714429	0368	1
JUDKINS WELDON R	1LT	0-2267184	1161	2
JUDSON CARL J	LTC	0-0155505	0455	3
JUDSON FREDERICK	COL	0-0301120	0459	1
JUDSON HOWARD F SR	CW4	W-2118145	1054	2
JUDSON LYMAN C	COL	0-0114250	0755	3
JUDSON WILLIAM L	MAJ	0-0302171	0266	3
JUDY FERRIS M	COL	0-0144895	0957	3
JUDY JOHN H	LTC	0-1639105	0864	1
JUDY KENNETH N	COL	0-0319594	0368	3
JUDY WILLIAM R	CPT	0-4022380	1265	1
JUELL ADOLPH B	COL	0-0230684	0262	3

NAME	GRADE	SVC NO	DATE RET MO YR	RET CODE
JUENGER GREGORY M	MAJ	0-1552711	0760	1
JUGE JAMES J	WO1	W-2128054	0257	1
JUGO JOSE	2LT	0-1896606	1148	1
JUHL LEE K	LTC	0-0283491	0967	3
JUHL MILFORD L	LTC	0-0746360	0765	2
JUHRING JOHN C	LTC	0-0202999	0962	3
JUILFS ROBERT W	CPT	0-0980420	1060	1
JULA JOHN	CW2	W-2101910	1152	1
JULIAN ALLEN P	COL	0-0184492	0356	2
JULIAN DAVID P	2LT	0-0540377	0244	2
JULIAN ERLE H	COL	0-0138896	0155	3
JULIAN LAWRENCE C	CPT	0-1179115	1053	2
JULIAN ORMAND C	MAJ	0-0490238	0146	2
JULIANA HORACE F	CPT	0-0422151	0258	1
JULIANO ANDRE V	LTC	0-1185368	0264	1
JULICH ARNOLD C	LTC	0-1184858	0763	2
JULIEN RICHARD	CPT	0-0275528	0457	1
JULIEN THEODORE F	CW3	W-2004803	1267	3
JUMP CLARENCE E	LTC	0-0243052	0863	3
JUMP GEORGE V	LTC	0-1170790	0860	1
JUN EDWARD J	LTC	0-0386215	0846	2
JUNE RALPH A	CW4	W-2106813	1154	1
JUNEAU CHARLES G	LTC	0-0382763	0760	1
JUNEAU LINUS M	LTC	0-1302979	1167	1
JUNEK LAVONNE K	MAJ	N-0775557	0664	2
JUNG ASHTON W	1LT	0-1276535	0545	2
JUNG GEORGE P	MAJ	0-0170795	0550	3
JUNG PHILIP E S	1LT	0-0348370	0446	2
JUNG WERNER F	MAJ	0-0213790	0460	3
JUNGE CARL L	COL	0-0166169	1059	3
JUNGE GORDON H	CPT	0-1646298	0650	2
JUNGE ROBERT O	CPT	0-0282342	0244	2
JUNGERS KENNETH G	MAJ	0-2263328	0765	1
JUNI ARTHUR H	CPT	0-0110411	0251	3
JUNIEWICZ ALEX J	CPT	0-0490565	0547	1
JUNKER CARL F	LTC	0-0922169	0765	3
JUNKERMANN CARL S	B G	0-0278976	0563	3
JUNKERMANN EDGAR B	LTC	0-0199465	0252	3
JUNKINS ROBERT A	MAJ	0-1037082	0359	1
JUNKINS WALTER F	MAJ	0-0979955	0463	1
JUPIN JOHN	1LT	0-1306850	0745	2
JURADO GUADALUPE	CW3	W-2209514	1068	1
JURANTY EDWARD	MAJ	0-0560838	1154	1
JURHALA JOHN	LTC	0-1057480	1161	1
JURBERG EDWARD R	CW2	W-2152848	0655	1
JURCAK FLORIAN F	LTC	0-1050328	0862	1
JURGENS CHARLES J	CW2	W-2149473	1263	1
JURGENS HAROLD L	LTC	0-1557173	1066	1
JURGENSEN MERTON P	CW4	W-2109801	1065	3
JURKOWSKI A D	MAJ	0-1290077	0248	2
JUROSZ ALFRED S	CPT	0-0540814	0146	2
JURY EARL W	CW3	W-2149911	0565	1
JUST BIENVENIDO	2LT	0-1096816	1047	2
JUSTESEN WAYNE O	CPT	0-1172943	1046	2
JUSTICE BIRCHETTE	CW2	W-2210198	1164	1
JUSTICE CARROLL J	CW2	W-2147221	0662	1
JUSTICE EUGENE P	CW3	W-2149871	0359	2
JUSTICE FRANK K	LTC	0-0245945	1066	3
JUSTICE HAROLD G	MAJ	0-2262678	0462	1
JUSTICE HENRY G	2LT	0-1820010	0245	2
JUSTICE HOWARD	MAJ	0-0301949	0652	1
JUSTICE JAMES E	CPT	0-1341436	0860	1
JUSTICE MARVIN L	CPT	0-0260121	0865	1
JUSTICE PERRY T	CW4	W-2126329	0156	1
JUSTICE THELMA E	CPT	N-0745212	0445	1
JUSTICE VERNELL O	1LT	0-1913016	0153	2
JUSTICE WILLIAM C	LTC	0-1697950	0457	1
JUSTICE WILLIAM F	1LT	0-0303276	0844	2
JUSTIN JOSEPH A	MAJ	0-2026362	0865	1
JUSTINIANO RUBEN	CPT	0-1924108	1163	1
JUSTISS WILLIS	CW2	W-2149221	1057	1
JUSTUS HAL C	LTC	0-0243396	0345	2
JUSTUS JOHN H	CPT	0-0281066	1146	2
JUTH ROBERT J	2LT	0-0468533	1144	2
JUTRAS PHILIP L	CW2	W-2111607	0461	1

NAME	GRADE	SVC NO	DATE RET MO YR	RET CODE
JUTZ DONALD G	MAJ	0-4005904	0768	1
JUWIG GUENTHER P	MAJ	0-2006104	1159	1
JUZA KENNETH J	MAJ	0-4108777	1168	1
JUZWIAK MICHAEL N	MAJ	0-1557311	1162	1
KAATZ ERVIN A	2LT	0-2010501	0248	2
KAB BENJAMIN J	LTC	0-0275192	0868	3
KABACK EDNA M	1LT	N-0725314	0345	1
KABAKJIAN ARMON E	COL	0-0263148	0962	3
KABERLE OTTO H	LTC	0-0174712	0156	3
KABUT MEYER	1LT	0-5008941	1262	2
KACANDA JOHN A	1LT	0-1037562	1045	2
KACHELRIES WALNETTA	MAJ	N-0755955	0268	1
KACHMARIK MIKE	LTC	0-0500945	0657	1
KACKAJUKAS JOSEPH P	CW3	W-2145457	0167	1
KACZKA EDWARD F	CPT	0-1038706	0646	2
KACZORJNSKI FELIX F	CPT	0-1289715	0656	1
KACZYNSKI EDWARD J	LTC	0-1000007	0457	1
KADEL RICHARD C	LTC	0-0239917	1146	2
KADEL ROBERT B	LTC	0-1548453	0951	1
KADELA JOHN L	CPT	0-1167057	1045	2
KADET CHARLES L	COL	0-0254358	0466	3
KADIN MAURICE	CPT	0-0361283	0345	2
KADING LEE F	CPT	0-0491324	1147	2
KADUK ROBERT J	CPT	0-0919379	1044	2
KADUMAKI ROBERT N	1LT	0-2046477	1146	2
KADZUK WILLIAM W	LTC	0-1323436	0563	1
KADYSIEWSKI EDMUND	CW3	W-2145143	0661	1
KAEISER WILLIAM H	LTC	0-0345300	1266	3
KAELIN HARRY J JR	MAJ	0-1304255	0963	2
KAELLNER JOHN W	1LT	0-1549304	0545	[illegible]
KAEMPFE ELMER H W	LTC	0-1012573	0763	1
KAEPPEL ARTHUR F	LTC	0-0159960	0648	3
KAEPPLINGER R P	2LT	0-1552713	0944	2
KAETZER THOMAS H	LTC	0-1844871	1163	1
KAFTER THEODORE	LTC	0-1573765	0562	1
KAH JAKE C	LTC	0-0103904	1159	1
KAHAN BORIS S	1LT	0-0526186	0644	2
KAHANIAK JOHN	MAJ	0-1103722	0258	1
KAHAPEA ALEXANDER	LTC	0-1300477	0465	1
KAHL GEORGE G	LTC	0-1640617	1163	1
KAHL KENNETH W	MAJ	0-2016685	0762	1
KAHL ROLAND E	MAJ	0-2006014	1264	1
KAHL-WINTER RANDOLF	MAJ	0-4006051	0167	1
KAHLENBERG JAMES F	LTC	0-0319279	1267	1
KAHLER HARRY E	CW3	W-2203552	1061	1
KAHLER WALTER E	CPT	0-0536420	0848	1
KAHLSTROM CARL F	CPT	0-0336347	0546	2
KAHN EARL A	MAJ	0-2025583	1061	1
KAHN EDWARD	1LT	0-0469502	1043	2
KAHN FRANK D	LTC	0-0370112	0165	1
KAHN HARRY	LTC	0-1574460	0357	1
KAHN HARRY	MAJ	0-1586702	0161	1
KAHN HOWARD C	MAJ	0-0540989	0147	2
KAHN MARCIA L	1LT	N-0772616	0650	2
KAHN RALPH H	MAJ	0-0963677	0764	1
KAHN RAYMOND A	MAJ	0-2051660	0862	1
KAHOE JOSEPH C JR	MAJ	0-1017761	0762	1
KAHRER LOUIS J	WO1	W-2111916	0746	1
KAI HERBERT J	CPT	0-0243466	0461	3
KAIBLER CHARLES G	LTC	0-1874474	0265	1
KAILEY JACK G	MAJ	0-0970639	1062	1
KAIN DONALD M	MAJ	0-1038023	0964	1
KAIN MARY P	MAJ	N-0745250	1168	1
KAINER MARIAN H	MAJ	N-0730530	1051	1
KAISER CHARLES G	COL	0-0271943	0862	2
KAISER DAVID W	1LT	0-1583183	0846	2
KAISER EMANUEL	CW3	W-2150648	1263	1
KAISER FRANK	MAJ	0-1315005	1054	1
KAISER GEORGE F	MAJ	0-0238754	1064	3
KAISER JEROME	MAJ	0-0372711	0446	2
KAISER JOHN O	2LT	0-0502446	0445	2
KAISER ROBERT A	MAJ	0-0358960	0453	1
KAISER RUDOLPH	MAJ	0-1297016	0963	1
KAISER RUSSELL F	COL	0-0320009	1068	3
KAISER STANLEY C	CPT	0-0445806	1144	2

NAME	GRADE	SVC NO	DATE RET MO YR	RET CODE
KAISER WALTER J	COL	0-0348478	0367	3
KAISER WILLIAM J JR	MAJ	0-2019174	0564	1
KAITIS CHESTER S	2LT	0-1016084	0645	2
KAITIS EILEEN M	MAJ	L-0504815	0363	1
KAITZ SIDNEY L	LTC	0-1534524	0261	1
KAJFAS JOHN	CPT	0-1013021	0550	2
KAJIHARA HIROSHI R	WO1	W-3440204	0868	1
KAKIMOTO TOMMY T	CPT	0-0969596	1161	1
KAKLIKIAN HARRY Z	MAJ	0-0990916	0265	1
KAKNAVICH WILLIAM A	CPT	0-1644471	1055	1
KALAHER CHARLES T	MAJ	0-2025424	0260	1
KALAMARIDES JOHN J	CPT	0-0378534	0545	2
KALB EVERETT L	CPT	0-0449710	0846	2
KALBERG TED	CPT	0-1305521	0357	1
KALBFELL ROBERT F	1LT	0-0384822	0544	2
KALBFLEISCH M C	CPT	N-0760633	0654	2
KALBUS CLARA W	CPT	N-0783238	0946	1
KALCOW MICHAEL	CW3	W-2145862	0663	1
KALDENBAUGH HENRY JR	1LT	0-1309373	0644	2
KALDIZAR LEWIS	MAJ	0-0438983	0848	1
KALE HERBERT W	LTC	0-0360514	0240	2
KALE SAMUEL S S	LTC	0-0326650	0860	2
KALEN SYLVESTER	CW4	W-2142483	0764	1
KALER OSCAR A	COL	0-0224735	0661	3
KALINOWSKI JOSEPH W	MAJ	0-2033204	0662	1
KALISCH BERTRAM	COL	0-0415761	0762	3
KALISH ARTHUR L	MAJ	0-1103724	1160	1
KALISH CHARLES	2LT	0-1636112	1044	2
KALISH DANIEL E	MAJ	0-1036218	0161	1
KALK RUSSELL E	CPT	0-1796292	0646	2
KALKUT LEON J	1LT	0-1310257	0146	2
KALLAM JOHN F	MAJ	0-0937945	0862	1
KALLBERG HARRY A	LTC	0-0373110	0256	2
KALLBRIER WILLIAM P	CW2	W-2208274	1061	1
KALLINA FREDERICK	CPT	0-0465830	0948	2
KALLIO HUGO A	CW3	W-2211045	0868	1
KALLMINZER MALCOLM A	1LT	0-1018208	0746	2
KALLMYER LEWIS K	LTC	0-0264791	0665	3
KALLUNKI WAYNE J	LTC	0-0522163	0155	1
KALMAN JOHN N	MAJ	0-1643029	0760	1
KALMAN MANUEL	LTC	0-0361819	0963	3
KALMAN ROSALIE C	1LT	N-0744281	1045	1
KALMBACH JACK R	CW3	RW-2210096	1166	1
KALMON MORRIS	LTC	0-0311334	0465	3
KALP JOHN R	CW3	W-2148861	0364	1
KALSOW ERNEST E	LTC	0-0220699	0646	2
KALTENBACH ERWIN J	LTC	0-0223653	0363	1
KALTSUKIS SPIROS G	CW3	W-2208596	1164	2
KALUSH PAUL J	CW3	W-2136757	0261	1
KALVAR EDWARD S	LTC	0-1113283	0662	1
KALVIN GEORGE B	MAJ	0-0298058	1058	1
KAMAR CHARLES M	CPT	0-1895420	0660	1
KAMBERG SAMUEL	COL	0-0474495	1167	3
KAMBOS GUS	CW3	W-2152066	0463	1
KAMIL CHARLES	1LT	0-1302139	0645	2
KAMIN ERVIN O	1LT	0-2024312	1151	2
KAMINESTER HERBERT M	MAJ	0-0498532	0446	2
KAMINSKE ROY	MAJ	0-0992313	0365	1
KAMINSKI MICHAEL B	MAJ	0-2055525	1057	1
KAMINSKY JOSEPH	COL	0-0471172	0554	1
KAMINSKY MORRIS	CPT	0-0371801	0245	2
KAMM ERNEST R	1LT	0-1881376	0857	2
KAMM WILBUR F	LTC	0-0205823	0651	3
KAMMAN COURTENAY	MAJ	0-0196845	0849	3
KAMMEL HARRY J	LTC	0-1055881	0366	1
KAMP CHARLES F	LTC	0-0198061	0262	3
KAMP GORDON K	CW3	W-2141603	1057	1
KAMPE KLEMENS A	LTC	0-0283895	0864	3
KAMPS JOHN H	CPT	0-0451705	1145	2
KAMRIN BENJAMIN B	LTC	0-0290785	0245	2
KANA FRED J	CPT	0-0307457	0446	2
KANAK FRANK	LTC	0-0485000	0557	1
KANANEN EDWARD M	MAJ	0-0258046	0663	3
KANCIUS STANLEY C	2LT	0-0974833	1051	2
KANDEL ALFRED	CPT	0-0528048	1045	2

NAME	GRADE	SVC NO	DATE RET MO YR	RET CODE
KANDELIN WALTER W	MAJ	0-1329327	0365	1
KANDIGAN CHARLES A	LTC	0-1061740	0464	1
KANDLEY MARGARET A	1LT	N-0724757	0843	2
KANDLER JACOB P	LTC	0-1114590	1067	1
KANE AGNES E	CPT	N-0759142	0349	2
KANE ALLEN E	LTC	0-1546428	0962	1
KANE ANGELA M	2LT	N-0720174	1144	1
KANE ANTHONY S	CPT	0-1040459	0346	2
KANE ARNOLD	LTC	0-1042614	0261	1
KANE BERTRAM J	LTC	0-0495302	0968	3
KANE CARL L	LTC	0-0133412	1048	3
KANE CHARLES R	CW3	W-2151388	1068	1
KANE DANIEL F	CPT	0-0451130	0552	1
KANE EDWIN A	COL	0-0100587	0852	3
KANE GENE L	CPT	0-1599172	1060	1
KANE GEORGE C	CPT	0-1646309	1047	1
KANE GEORGE R	LTC	0-1236473	0366	1
KANE HAROLD M	MAJ	0-1316298	0461	1
KANE HENRY S	MAJ	0-0163498	0648	3
KANE HERBERT W JR	WO1	W-2109740	1045	2
KANE HOWARD H	MAJ	0-0267461	0968	3
KANE JOHN K JR	CPT	0-1030164	0862	3
KANE JOHN T	LTC	0-0328937	0859	1
KANE JOHN W	CW3	W-2152160	1059	1
KANE JOSEPH P	1LT	0-0491385	0745	2
KANE JOSEPHINE	MAJ	N-0783143	0566	3
KANE LAURENCE B	1LT	0-1795799	1059	1
KANE LEO F	LTC	0-0451551	0457	1
KANE MAX	LTC	0-2014795	1068	1
KANE PAUL R	MAJ	0-1299830	1146	2
KANE RAYMOND E	COL	0-1165519	1167	1
KANE ROBERT J	CPT	0-1297546	0346	2
KANE THEODORE F	LTC	0-0346880	0360	1
KANE THOMAS C	MAJ	0-0164281	0545	1
KANE WALTER J	LTC	0-0276454	0265	3
KANEALII FRANCES C	MAJ	N-0730420	0665	3
KANEALY JOHN F	CPT	0-0531253	0146	2
KANEGAI YOSHIO G	MAJ	0-2037067	0662	1
KANGAS TYKO R	LTC	0-1548879	0662	1
KANIA FRANK W	MAJ	0-1111156	0658	2
KANIA JOSEPH F	LTC	0-1167490	0166	2
KANICH JOSEPH J	COL	0-0315962	0768	3
KANNER SIDNEY	CPT	0-1313055	0163	1
KANOUSE CHESTER F	CPT	0-0924266	0747	2
KANSKY ELI	LTC	0-1038024	1067	3
KANSKY WALTER A	LTC	0-0234773	0557	2
KANSTRUP ALFRED H	LTC	0-1319286	0468	3
KANSTRUP ARTHUR A	CPT	0-0327511	0866	3
KANTARIAN HAIG A	1LT	0-1560028	0348	2
KANTER MARVIN W	CPT	0-1172944	104N	2
KANTOLA HELEN F	2LT	N-0723999	0645	1
KANTOR GEORGE J	COL	0-0286419	0866	1
KANTOR JACK	CPT	0-1689762	0445	2
KANTORIK JOHN L	1LT	0-1641107	1155	1
KANTRIMAITIS JOHN	WO1	W-2148734	0154	1
KANZENBACH MELVIN A	CW3	W-2214188	1167	1
KAPAUN WALLACE A	1LT	0-0411174	0745	2
KAPELOWITZ MAX	MAJ	0-0450969	1054	1
KAPICA FRANCIS A	LTC	0-0546784	0464	1
KAPINOS JOHN R	CW2	RW-2211052	1264	1
KAPLAN ABRAHAM H	CPT	0-0336283	1153	3
KAPLAN ALBERT	1LT	0-1002458	0646	2
KAPLAN ARTHUR	1LT	0-1289741	1045	2
KAPLAN ARTHUR T	LTC	0-0174929	1161	3
KAPLAN BEN B	1LT	0-0529308	0544	2
KAPLAN CHARLES	MAJ	0-0375136	0755	2
KAPLAN DAVID	CW2	W-2152177	0261	1
KAPLAN FRANK	WO1	W-2147898	0457	1
KAPLAN FRANK D	1LT	0-1302476	1146	2
KAPLAN GEORGE	LTC	0-0475357	0945	2
KAPLAN GEORGE G	LTC	0-0363344	0864	1
KAPLAN HAROLD L	MAJ	0-1015805	0955	1
KAPLAN HYMAN J	LTC	0-0309528	1045	2
KAPLAN ISADORE	MAJ	0-0371542	0445	2
KAPLAN ISADORE	MAJ	0-0485750	0249	2

NAME	GRADE	SVC NO	DATE RET MO YR	RET CODE
KAPLAN JOSEPH	CPT	0-0333873	1145	2
KAPLAN JOSEPH A	LTC	0-0207597	0756	3
KAPLAN LEO	MAJ	0-1047603	0661	1
KAPLAN LOUIS	CPT	0-0507982	1145	2
KAPLAN MORRIS L	2LT	0-1578684	1044	2
KAPLAN MURRAY J	MAJ	0-0972904	0462	1
KAPLAN NATHAN	CW3	W-2146336	0264	2
KAPLAN RONALD R	COL	0-0374105	0964	3
KAPLAN SAMUEL D	MAJ	0-0413446	1046	2
KAPLAN SEYMOUR T	CPT	0-1534053	1145	2
KAPLAN SOL	2LT	0-2015782	1160	1
KAPLAN THEODORE H	1LT	0-0533958	1145	2
KAPLAN WILLIAM	2LT	0-1591841	0645	2
KAPLANOFF CARL G	LTC	0-1053665	1168	1
KAPLOW LEONARD S	1LT	0-1039715	0746	2
KAPNER WALTER H	LTC	0-0308403	0162	3
KAPOPOULOS GARY J	COL	0-0264450	1061	3
KAPP AUGUST F	LTC	0-1822147	0868	3
KAPP CHARLES L	1LT	0-1543253	0144	2
KAPP ERVIN J	CPT	0-0949095	1059	1
KAPP JOHN M	MAJ	0-1037087	0361	1
KAPP RICHARD C	2LT	0-2006391	0346	2
KAPP ROLLIN W	MAJ	0-1037088	0961	1
KAPP SERGIUS N	CPT	0-0451892	0952	2
KAPPANADZE ROMAN	MAJ	0-0525285	1045	2
KAPPEL VERNON E	1LT	0-1314645	0345	2
KAPPELMAN LESTER B	CPT	0-1313098	1146	2
KAPPEN CHARLES V	MAJ	0-0305259	0653	2
KAPPIE ANTHONY	2LT	0-1592319	0145	2
KAPRAL JOSEPH J	LTC	0-0450185	1154	1
KAPS FRED A	LTC	0-1698187	0748	2
KAPSA RICHARD L	COL	0-0309092	0750	2
KAPUA JOSEPH K	1LT	0-0286934	0858	3
KAPUTA JOSEPH M	LTC	0-0378179	1059	1
KARABA MARTIN F	CW3	W-2142767	0165	2
KARAHALIS GREGORY G	CW4	W-2142858	0361	1
KARALIUS ALBERT L	CW3	W-2144809	1060	1
KARAM EMILE	MAJ	0-1059511	0467	3
KARAM ROBERT	MAJ	0-1634954	0861	1
KARAPATSKIE JOHN E	CW2	W-2153192	1057	1
KARAS STANLEY A	LTC	0-0885734	0557	1
KARAS WILLIAM J	LTC	0-0334805	0945	2
KARASEK JAMES J	1LT	0-1059512	0247	2
KARAU WILLIAM A	2LT	0-4068352	0658	2
KARBEL HOWARD W	LTC	0-0452720	1047	2
KARBER JON F	CPT	0-1039418	0346	2
KARBLEY HAROLD L	LTC	0-1577400	0860	1
KARCH HARRY A	MAJ	0-1823306	1060	1
KARCH HERBERT S	LTC	0-0203543	1058	3
KARCHER CHARLES E	CPT	0-1016891	0346	2
KARCHER FREDERICK	CPT	0-1282391	1059	1
KARDEGG WALTER M	MAJ	0-2049601	0661	1
KAREIVA CHARLES T	MAJ	0-0578126	0164	1
KAREN JOSEPH W	2LT	0-1997421	0646	2
KARESH HARRY A	LTC	0-0246791	1063	3
KARESKY SIDNEY I	1LT	0-1294318	0550	2
KARGE THERON F	1LT	0-0379222	0445	2
KARGEL FREDDIE F	CPT	0-0495403	0358	1
KARICHER NELSON R	LTC	0-1646787	0462	1
KARIG HOWARD L	COL	0-0505267	0863	3
KARIKA CHARLES	CW2	W-2151694	0761	1
KARIUS FRED	2LT	0-1913783	0844	1
KARKALAS ARTHUR A	LTC	0-0177415	0960	3
KARL BENJAMIN F	CW4	W-2151617	0963	1
KARL NORBERT E	2LT	0-1996680	0346	2
KARLAK JOHN M	CPT	0-1289094	1045	2
KARLEEN CONRAD I	LTC	0-0263420	0747	2
KARLEN HARVEY M	1LT	0-1010885	1044	2
KARLSON JOHN R	MAJ	0-0408700	0761	1
KARMATH JOHN I	CW4	W-2002357	1059	3
KARNES KENNETH C	MAJ	0-1543291	1063	1
KARNILOWICZ ANN C	2LT	N-0767925	0645	1
KARNS FREDERICK	MAJ	0-0165795	0750	3
KAROL JOHN E	LTC	0-0287603	0168	3
KAROLCHUCK PHOEBE N	2LT	N-0701474	1131	1

NAME	GRADE	SVC NO	DATE RET MO YR	RET CODE
KAROW JOSEPH J	COL	0-0263041	0464	3
KARP LEWIS S	1LT	0-0509431	0445	2
KARP ROSE	MAJ	N-0723997	0964	3
KARP STANLEY F	LTC	0-0250376	0666	3
KARP WILLIAM A	COL	0-0168226	0555	3
KARPELCHIK JOHN	2LT	0-1874755	0145	2
KARPEL SAUL	MAJ	0-0378439	0646	2
KARR ALBERT W	MAJ	0-0289782	0167	3
KARR CARL R	MAJ	0-0534199	0856	1
KARR FRANK W	CW2	W-2118531	0447	1
KARR RUSSELL H	MAJ	0-1633321	0561	1
KARSNITZ CHARLES R	LTC	0-1548878	0962	1
KARST JOSEPH P	CW4	W-2144608	0967	1
KARSTEN ERNST W	LTC	0-0349496	0863	1
KARWASKI LEOPOLD J	LTC	0-1109397	0960	1
KARWOSKI JOSEPH A	1LT	0-2042974	1055	1
KARYTA STANISLAW	MAJ	0-1549237	0753	1
KASARDA RALPH W	MAJ	0-1011129	1157	1
KASBEER MAX E	CW3	W-2152466	1262	1
KASCHKO HAROLD L	LTC	0-1167491	0862	1
KASCKOW ALEXANDER	MAJ	0-1894563	0860	1
KASCMER JOSEPH	2LT	0-1308517	1044	2
KASE CECIL B	LTC	0-0888242	1062	1
KASEFF BERNARD H	1LT	0-1302094	0845	2
KASEN JACOB	1LT	0-0537052	0245	2
KASHNER HAZEL A	LTC	N-0728633	1266	3
KASHPUREFF NIKOLAI	CW2	W-2101282	0945	2
KASICH ANTHONY M	LTC	0-0228196	0146	2
KASIK OTTO	CPT	0-0499156	1046	2
KASKIN ALVIN	MAJ	0-0279584	0253	1
KASL GLEN M	MAJ	0-0258297	0267	3
KASMALA FRANK G	CW3	W-2208278	0968	1
KASMER JULIUS J	LTC	0-1579853	0661	1
KASOLD EDWARD F	LTC	0-1174018	0860	1
KASPAR ALBERT F L	CW3	W-2145061	0663	1
KASPAR ED A	CW3	W-2207455	0968	1
KASPAR JOE L	CPT	0-0531858	0847	2
KASPER EDWARD C	CPT	0-0460843	0845	2
KASPER HERBERT E	LTC	0-0885822	0557	1
KASPER RAYMOND L	LTC	0-0522302	0864	1
KASPER STANLEY F	LTC	0-0451493	0960	1
KASPER WALTER F	MAJ	0-2032871	0960	1
KASPRAK LEON	COL	0-0343478	1062	1
KASPROWSKI EDWARD	MAJ	0-2008634	0263	1
KASS ALBERT	MAJ	0-0424482	0547	2
KASS DAVID R	CPT	0-0471636	1145	2
KASS HAROLD M	MAJ	0-0509145	0146	2
KASSAB JOSEPH	MAJ	0-0271346	0868	3
KASSAN DAVID	1LT	0-1796484	0444	2
KASSEL HARRY T	CPT	0-0288515	1146	2
KASSEL MAXWELL S	CPT	0-0509894	0446	2
KASSELS MAURICE E	CPT	0-0490239	0845	2
KASSEN WILLIAM C	COL	0-0184493	0562	3
KASSLER FRED R	1LT	0-1825297	1045	2
KASSNER ERNEST	MAJ	0-0963948	0663	1
KASTANOWSKI JOHN A	MAJ	0-2039379	0164	1
KASTEN EMIL W	MAJ	0-1306727	0364	2
KASTEN PETER H	CW3	W-2142353	0758	1
KASTENBAUM HARRY	CPT	0-0201287	0453	3
KASTLE JOHN	CW3	W-2206416	0665	1
KASTLER GEORGE J	CPT	0-1797144	0458	2
KASTLER PATRICK H	LTC	0-0202839	0857	3
KASTNER AUGUST A	LTC	0-0276649	0760	1
KASUN JOSEPH F	LTC	0-1296040	0264	1
KATALENICH THOMAS S	1LT	0-0371231	0145	2
KATALINAS JOSEPH A	LTC	0-0328994	0560	1
KATES DON B	COL	0-0267215	1067	3
KATES HOWARD A W	LTC	0-0266543	0154	3
KATH CHESTER	LTC	0-0276630	0647	1
KATIN JACQUES H	CW3	W-2136713	0664	2
KATO MATT J	LTC	0-1035086	0261	1
KATSCHKE WILLIAM	1LT	0-0976476	0657	1
KATSIAFICAS NICHOLAS	LTC	0-0448789	0165	1
KATSONES PALMER G	CPT	0-2263696	0265	1
KATTNER FRANCIS R	CPT	0-0503235	0947	2

NAME	GRADE	SVC NO	DATE RET MO YR	RET CODE
KATZ ARTHUR	1LT	0-1302411	1045	2
KATZ CHARLES	CW3	W-2145201	0259	1
KATZ CHARLES I	COL	0-0297818	0767	3
KATZ GEORGE	LTC	0-1035039	0865	1
KATZ HAROLD	CW2	W-3430293	1265	1
KATZ HERMAN E	1LT	0-1114986	0146	2
KATZ IRVIN J	COL	0-0476775	0954	1
KATZ JACOB	LTC	0-0224960	0864	3
KATZ JULIAN H	1LT	0-0308356	1044	2
KATZ LESTER F	CW2	W-2208676	1166	1
KATZ LEWIS M	CPT	0-1716476	0645	2
KATZ MAX L	LTC	0-0509437	0156	1
KATZ MORRIS J	LTC	0-1577403	0364	1
KATZ RACHEL	2LT	N-0771383	0545	1
KATZ RAYMOND	1LT	0-1311018	0146	2
KATZ SEYMOUR M	MAJ	0-0404638	0645	2
KATZ SOL	MAJ	0-0332387	0246	2
KATZ STANLEY M	1LT	0-1002460	1045	2
KATZ STANLEY R	1LT	0-1305785	0246	2
KATZ WILLIAM J	1LT	0-1336511	1152	2
KATZBECK JOHN W	LTC	0-1101520	0161	1
KAUFER LAURENCE E	LTC	0-1037565	0463	1
KAUFFMAN CARL H	MAJ	0-0345122	0762	1
KAUFFMAN HARVEY E	COL	0-0111285	0851	3
KAUFFMAN HERBERT V	MAJ	0-2262282	0464	1
KAUFFMAN JAMES W	CPT	0-2014539	1162	1
KAUFFMAN JEROME A	CPT	0-1725521	0347	2
KAUFFMAN JOHN F	LTC	0-1341273	0665	1
KAUFFMAN JOHNNY G	MAJ	0-2085518	0163	1
KAUFFMAN STACY M	CW4	W-2129286	1058	1
KAUFFMAN WILLIAM A	2LT	0-2028708	0452	2
KAUFMAN ABRAHAM A	COL	0-0248738	0167	3
KAUFMAN ALKIE C	LTC	0-0336603	0460	1
KAUFMAN ALVIN J	CPT	0-1556157	0459	1
KAUFMAN CARL K	LTC	0-0322366	0367	3
KAUFMAN DON R	CPT	0-1685023	0855	2
KAUFMAN EDWARD	MAJ	0-0109108	0234	1
KAUFMAN ERNEST	MAJ	0-1318310	0151	2
KAUFMAN ERWIN R	1LT	0-1062215	0246	2
KAUFMAN HARRY	CPT	0-0498253	1263	1
KAUFMAN HERMAN P	LTC	0-0334706	0263	3
KAUFMAN JACK	CPT	0-1703582	0645	2
KAUFMAN JAMES K	MAJ	0-0381466	0443	2
KAUFMAN LOUIS A	LTC	0-0422101	0566	1
KAUFMAN LOUIS L	1LT	0-1112795	0858	1
KAUFMAN MARTHA M	MAJ	N-0790197	0364	1
KAUFMAN MORTON E	1LT	0-0944669	0848	2
KAUFMAN MORTON L	1LT	0-1287720	1045	2
KAUFMAN RALPH J	CPT	0-2262748	0857	1
KAUFMAN RUSSELL H	COL	0-0227321	0159	3
KAUFMAN SAUL D	1LT	0-0502866	0545	2
KAUFMAN WILLIAM	MAJ	0-2033938	0963	1
KAUFMANN BERTRAM	MAJ	0-0197727	0648	3
KAUFMANN MAURICE	CPT	0-0333954	0945	2
KAUFMANN ROBERT J	COL	0-1170792	0868	3
KAUFMANN ULRICH G	MAJ	0-0945757	0165	1
KAUFMANN WILLIAM R	MAJ	0-0958845	0463	1
KAUKA KAIPO F	LTC	0-0387314	1060	1
KAUL LLOYD K	CW3	W-3150331	1167	1
KAULAKIS EDWARD S	LTC	0-0452114	1155	1
KAUPPILA HANS N	CPT	0-0239150	0648	1
KAUSEK BERT G	MAJ	0-1595614	0461	1
KAUTH JOHN W	1LT	0-1824195	104N	2
KAUTZ GEORGE W	LTC	0-0419139	0763	3
KAUTZ HARRY G	LTC	0-0260294	0751	3
KAUTZ RICHARD W	MAJ	0-0977319	0962	1
KAUTZ WILLIAM K	LTC	0-0543609	0464	1
KAVADAS DANIEL S	LTC	0-1765358	1060	2
KAVANAGH WILLIAM P	MAJ	0-0402444	0546	2
KAVANAGH WILLIAM T	1LT	0-1296536	0945	2
KAVANAUGH FRANCIS E	COL	0-0265627	0566	3
KAVANAUGH MYLES T	CPT	0-1695207	0445	2
KAVANAUGH THOMAS E	LTC	0-1046511	0957	1
KAVANAUGH WINIFRED C	MAJ	N-0762521	0864	1
KAVENEY JOHN J	1LT	0-1590582	1045	2

NAME	GRADE	SVC NO	DATE RET MO YR	RET CODE
KAVENEY WALTER J	CW2	W-2106319	0947	2
KAVENY CHARLES V	LTC	0-0534160	0468	3
KAVITT HENRY HYMA	CPT	0-0370250	0246	2
KAVKA ANTHONY J	MAJ	0-1651101	0960	1
KAVLI HOWARD E	MAJ	0-1949487	0560	1
KAVNER IRVING	2LT	0-1046512	0146	2
KAVOVIT CHARLES	CPT	0-0475475	0446	2
KAWA CASMERE J	2LT	0-2000683	1145	2
KAWA WALTER	1LT	0-1295224	0445	2
KAWAGUCHI KATSUMI T	MAJ	0-1899378	0864	1
KAWALEK WALTER P	LTC	0-2021263	0968	2
KAWALESKI FRANK	WO1	W-2108607	0255	1
KAWAMOTO NOBUO	MAJ	0-1925341	0166	1
KAWASAKI ISAAC A	MAJ	0-0420945	1046	2
KAWASAKI TOSHIO	CW4	W-2136005	1168	1
KAWASHIMA ISAMU S	CW4	W-2144108	0468	1
KAWECKI EDWIN	CPT	0-1103252	0146	2
KAY CARNIG	LTC	0-0355140	1162	3
KAY FLOYD F	LTC	0-0216236	0763	3
KAY FRANK J JR	CW3	W-2148862	0766	1
KAY ISRAEL H	MAJ	0-1080870	0866	3
KAY JAMES G	MAJ	0-0971001	0564	1
KAY ROBERT B	CPT	0-1290613	0646	2
KAY ROBERT L	LTC	0-0543489	1063	1
KAY TED	MAJ	0-0451453	0854	1
KAY WILFRED S	COL	0-0186240	0848	3
KAYE BERNARD F	CPT	0-1533364	0545	2
KAYE JOHN P	COL	0-0165185	0751	3
KAYE PAUL M	CPT	0-0402339	0944	2
KAYES STEPHEN J	1LT	0-1103774	1048	1
KAYHS ERNEST W	CPT	0-1016249	0148	2
KAYLOR JOHN D	MAJ	0-2283917	0363	1
KAYLOR JOHN P	LTC	0-1845294	1162	1
KAYNER HOWARD L	LTC	0-0310956	0558	3
KAYRUKSTIS ALBIN K	LTC	0-1115939	0868	3
KAYRUKTIS ALFONSE E	2LT	0-1592964	1044	2
KAYS HAROLD V	LTC	0-1331192	0867	1
KAYSER F P	LTC	0-2041029	1167	1
KAZANJIAN BEARJ G	COL	0-0255616	0862	2
KAZARNOWICZ EDWARD J	LTC	0-1303735	0660	1
KAZERMAN JOSEPH	LTC	0-0349088	0860	1
KAZMAREK HELEN F	2LT	N-0728235	1143	1
KAZMIERCZAK STELLA	CPT	N-0727394	1162	2
KEACH WILLIAM P	MAJ	0-2044316	0958	1
KEADLE HOMER H	1LT	0-0383449	0745	2
KEAG HELEN G	CPT	N-0760031	1047	1
KEAGLE LEONADUS R	MAJ	0-1646304	1056	1
KEALA SAMUEL L	LTC	0-0242006	1059	1
KEALEY GEORGE I	MAJ	0-0273039	0455	1
KEALEY HORACE M	CW4	W-2111470	0658	1
KEAN JOHN R	1LT	0-1039719	1145	2
KEAN RUSSELL E	COL	0-0131673	1059	3
KEAN THOMAS V	LTC	0-0187542	0648	3
KEAN WILLIAM M	1LT	0-1688794	1051	2
KEANE CHARLES F	CW3	W-2150668	0366	1
KEANE JOHN M	LTC	0-1113290	1060	1
KEANE JOSEPH P	LTC	0-1948167	1162	1
KEANON FRANCIS P SR	MAJ	0-1114190	0461	1
KEARIN LAWRENCE E	LTC	0-1292001	0866	1
KEARINS BARTLEY E JR	MAJ	0-1320705	0261	1
KEARLEY ALICE G	2LT	N-0726870	1043	1
KEARNEY BERNARD W	B G	0-0161703	0649	3
KEARNEY BRYANT	COL	0-0274398	0664	3
KEARNEY CHARLES R	COL	0-0309819	0559	2
KEARNEY ERICK W	MAJ	0-0250862	0366	3
KEARNEY JOHN A JR	CW3	W-2143274	0263	1
KEARNEY JOHN J	CW3	W-2151661	1263	1
KEARNEY JOHN O	1LT	0-1046514	0146	2
KEARNEY KENNETH J	LTC	0-1293786	0166	1
KEARNEY MARY F	MAJ	L-0125005	1066	3
KEARNEY RAYMOND C	LTC	0-1010619	0761	1
KEARNEY ROBERT M	1LT	0-1341792	0553	2
KEARNEY WILLIAM F	MAJ	0-2007719	1056	1
KEARNS CECIL	MAJ	0-0963473	1059	2
KEARNS CHARLES E	CPT	0-0462339	0746	2
KEARNS CHARLES M JR	COL	0-0228706	0365	3
KEARNS GILBERT P SR	LTC	0-0152991	0346	1
KEARNS JOHN A	MAJ	0-1031183	0461	1
KEARNS JOHN F	LTC	0-1039425	1163	2
KEARNS RALPH E	LTC	0-2047379	0566	1
KEARNS ROBERT J	CW2	W-2150686	0857	1
KEARNS SYLVESTER	CPT	0-0108624	1049	1
KEARNS WILLIAM S	LTC	0-1044575	0566	1
KEARNY CRESSON H	MAJ	0-0324605	1045	2
KEARTON JOHN G JR	1LT	0-0496742	0845	2
KEAS ARTHUR H	CW3	W-2146069	0964	1
KEASEY GEORGE	1LT	0-1174019	1045	2
KEAST WILLIAM J	1LT	0-1304395	0146	2
KEATHLEY CLAUDE C	CPT	0-0421497	1145	2
KEATING JAMES M	LTC	0-0289817	0960	3
KEATING JOHN A	LTC	0-1018691	0862	1
KEATING LINDALE	CW4	W-2146126	0359	1
KEATING PAUL G	LTC	0-0359743	0256	1
KEATING RAYMOND G	LTC	0-1011237	0862	1
KEATING REGINALD B	LTC	0-0253411	0663	1
KEATING ROBERT G	LTC	0-1305260	0568	1
KEATING THOMAS JR	1LT	0-1823167	0246	2
KEATON EARL R	MAJ	0-0410054	1160	1
KEATON MORGAN	COL	0-0113685	0-51	3
KEATS SIDNEY	MAJ	0-0391404	0845	2
KEAY LUTHER B	1LT	0-1015092	1145	2
KECKLER FRELYN L	CPT	0-0482134	0753	1
KECKLER RALPH J	LTC	0-0364690	0560	1
KEDZIOR CASIMIR J	CPT	0-1184083	0547	2
KEE GEORGE H	CW3	W-2209510	1166	2
KEE PAT M	MAJ	0-1061751	1162	1
KEE SAM R	MAJ	0-1646305	0361	1
KEE WILLIAM V	CPT	0-0507588	0245	2
KEEBLER JOSEPH F	LTC	0-1280920	0764	1
KEEFE ANSELM M	COL	0-0190892	0355	3
KEEFE CHARLES B	LTC	0-0166618	1154	3
KEEFE DONALD J	CPT	0-2032940	0357	1
KEEFE ETHEL A	CPT	L-0105072	0358	2
KEEFE EUGENE K	LTC	0-2200719	0668	1
KEEFE JAMES W	CW3	RW-3000287	0868	1
KEEFE JOHN D	LTC	0-0291407	1160	1
KEEFE JOHN E JR	LTC	0-0252558	1165	3
KEEFE RINO	LTC	0-0453114	0763	1
KEEFER HAROLD A	1LT	0-2024104	0747	2
KEEFER RUSSELL L	MAJ	0-1171216	1160	1
KEEGAN MICHAEL J	CPT	0-1307705	0847	2
KEEHN HARRY D	1LT	0-1320004	1045	2
KEEHNEN KENNETH K	LTC	0-1289270	0860	1
KEEL JAMES R	CPT	0-1327551	0760	2
KEEL PATRICK G	CPT	0-1288754	0947	2
KEELE JOHN C JR	LTC	0-1533106	0761	1
KEELEAN DELOS E	LTC	0-2040808	0168	1
KEELER EARL R	LTC	0-2016902	0768	1
KEELER EDMUND L	LTC	0-0195033	0146	2
KEELER ELIZABETH	2LT	N-0720401	0144	1
KEELER ROBERT	CPT	0-2046400	0147	1
KEELER ROBERT C	1LT	0-0887431	0147	2
KEELER ROBERT D	CPT	0-1295893	1051	2
KEELER ROBERT J	LTC	0-0475976	0164	3
KEELER ROBERT L	LTC	0-2033270	0966	1
KEELER THADDEUS B	CW3	W-2146761	0764	1
KEELER WILLIAM	CPT	0-2016292	0257	1
KEELING FORREST E	COL	0-0119822	0657	3
KEELING REX G	LTC	0-0404550	0246	2
KEELING ROY E	COL	0-0149671	1054	3
KEELING WILLIAM B	2LT	0-0533452	0945	2
KEELY JAMES E	MAJ	0-0273340	0147	2
KEELY ROBERT W JR	2LT	0-1822885	0745	2
KEEN CLARENCE N	LTC	0-0365873	0255	1
KEEN DONALD E	MAJ	0-1885978	1166	2
KEEN FRANKLIN A	LTC	0-2040885	0766	1
KEEN MARLIN O	CW3	W-2205930	0465	1
KEENA CHARLIE F	LTC	0-0384059	0266	3
KEENA CLAIR S	LTC	0-1295895	0859	1
KEENAN DANIEL R	LTC	0-1876262	0968	1
KEENAN FRANCIS	MAJ	0-0298302	0453	1
KEENAN JAMES B	CW3	W-2148227	1058	1
KEENAN JAMES P	1LT	0-1011194	0444	2
KEENAN JAMES P	CW3	W-2142970	0659	1
KEENAN JASPER E	CW3	W-2142164	0559	1
KEENAN JOHN T	CPT	0-0505455	1044	2
KEENAN JOHN V	MAJ	0-1010928	0550	2
KEENAN THOMAS G	LTC	0-1554918	1262	3
KEENE CECIL B	2LT	0-0544508	0847	2
KEENE ERNEST H	MAJ	0-0199953	0648	3
KEENE JOSEPH P	CW3	W-2149705	0962	1
KEENE LAWRENCE E	MAJ	0-1185369	0456	1
KEENE LYNDELL F	LTC	0-0426724	1062	1
KEENE PURLEY L	CPT	0-0188445	0151	3
KEENE RAYMOND E	MAJ	0-2200122	1266	1
KEENE RUDOLPH C	CW2	W-2149196	0161	1
KEENER CARL T	CW2	W-2149993	0958	1
KEENER GRACE E	CPT	N-0700415	0946	1
KEENEY DONALD P	MAJ	0-2020303	0168	1
KEENEY FRANCIS R	LTC	0-1104902	1160	1
KEENEY HARRY C	COL	0-0455689	1059	1
KEENEY HERMAN F	CPT	0-0217794	0262	3
KEENON JOHN F	LTC	0-0228707	0959	1
KEENUM JOHN C	LTC	0-1637793	1062	1
KEENY LESLIE B	LTC	0-0256684	0857	3
KEEP ELINOR R	MAJ	N-0736940	1166	1
KEEPERS HUGH V	LTC	0-2712561	0168	3
KEESE CHARLES J	CPT	0-0409561	1045	2
KEESE HENRY G	CW4	W-2136535	0559	1
KEESE OLIVER C	COL	0-0215091	0752	3
KEESEE RALPH V	LTC	0-1312312	0461	1
KEESHEN WILLIAM J JR	MAJ	0-2051194	0960	1
KEESLAR RALPH L	CPT	0-1266499	0246	2
KEESLING FRANCIS V	COL	0-0333710	0468	3
KEESLING WILEY E	WO1	W-2107954	0650	1
KEESTER DONOVAN E	LTC	0-2020032	0868	1
KEESTER JOHN F	LTC	0-1169593	0760	1
KEESY EUGENE R	1LT	0-1168311	0746	2
KEETER CLINTON W	MAJ	0-2011528	0361	1
KEETER WALTER C	CPT	0-0502518	0948	2
KEETON HILLES G	CPT	0-1557622	0746	2
KEETON OZRO	CPT	0-0509850	0547	1
KEEVIL SIDNEY G	CW3	W-2200521	0966	3
KEGLEY GUY B	LTC	0-1573324	1060	1
KEGLOVITS WILLIAM F	CW3	W-2145915	0958	1
KEHM RONALD C	COL	0-0235399	0454	3
KEHOE BERNARD	MAJ	0-0108987	0344	1
KEHOE JAMES A	B G	0-0330837	1056	3
KEHOE ROBERT T	WO1	W-2121405	0344	2
KEHRER RICHARD F	CW2	W-2141607	0755	1
KEIDER JOHN O	LTC	0-0397548	1060	1
KEIDSER JOHN A	MAJ	0-0486124	0355	1
KEIFER GEORGE W	CW3	W-2143498	0562	1
KEIL LOYD E	1LT	0-0391220	0445	2
KEIL MARCUS A	CPT	0-0430092	0645	2
KEIL WALTER F	CW2	W-2206288	0963	1
KEIL WILLIAM A	LTC	0-1949918	0467	1
KEILCH RALPH F	MAJ	0-2002088	0660	1
KEILEN DANIEL H	1LT	0-0969402	1061	1
KEILLOR GEORGE D	MAJ	0-1110593	0557	1
KEILMAN CHARLES H	MAJ	0-0497455	0657	1
KEIM HOWARD H	MAJ	0-0257176	0557	3
KEIM JOHN H	LTC	0-0454503	0760	1
KEINSLEY WALTER O	LTC	0-2047392	1162	1
KEIPE HENRY A	LTC	0-0221163	0862	3
KEIPER THEODORE W	LTC	0-0299353	1159	3
KEIR WILFRED G	2LT	0-0400381	0143	2
KEIRN IRA J	MAJ	0-0183053	0546	2
KEIRN JAMES D	LTC	0-0718662	0367	1
KEISER DONALD J	CPT	0-1166303	0946	2
KEISER ELLSWORTH	MAJ	0-0262392	0766	3
KEISER FRANK G	LTC	0-0964329	1067	1
KEISER GEORGE	CPT	0-1826281	0260	1
KEISER JOHN T	COL	0-0146292	0752	3
KEISER MARTIN F	MAJ	0-1166753	1157	1
KEISER ROBERT P	CPT	0-0511561	0845	2
KEISER WILLIAM H SR	CW3	W-2209156	0968	1
KEISERMAN JOSEPH	CPT	0-1695981	1045	2
KEISLER BRODIE E	LTC	0-0270823	0368	3
KEISTER GUY A	LTC	0-0121623	1045	1
KEISTER STEVE E	CPT	0-1746087	0549	2
KEITH BERTHA B	MAJ	N-0761348	1263	1
KEITH CLARENCE M	1LT	0-1179118	0646	2
KEITH CLYDE D	COL	0-0131504	1057	3
KEITH DONALD M	COL	0-0333858	1054	3
KEITH EDWARD J	CPT	0-0328843	1044	2
KEITH ELSWICK C	LTC	0-0270716	0668	3
KEITH EUEL M	CPT	0-1556005	1068	3
KEITH FRANCIS C	LTC	0-0162319	0260	3
KEITH GLEN B	LTC	0-0374689	0760	1
KEITH JACK B	MAJ	0-1637796	0558	1
KEITH JAMES W	LTC	0-0204072	0557	1
KEITH JOHN D	LTC	0-0354022	0665	1
KEITH JOHN J	MAJ	0-0401514	0246	2
KEITH LEWIS W	LTC	0-1105567	1062	1
KEITH PAUL R	CW4	W-2110637	0261	1
KEITH RICHARD W	1LT	0-0242384	0342	2
KEITH ROBERT G	1LT	0-1109404	0445	2
KEITH ROY L	2LT	0-1060838	1145	2
KEITH WARREN S	COL	0-0124708	0652	3
KEITH WILLIAM E JR	LTC	0-0335739	0860	1
KEITH WILLIAM H	CW3	W-2141334	0858	1
KEITHAHN CHARLES H	MAJ	0-1845741	0847	2
KEITHLY OSCAR W	CPT	0-0359454	0846	2
KEITHLY PAUL E	MAJ	0-1822280	0261	1
KEIZUR WARREN S	MAJ	0-1885439	0866	1
KEKAHUNA JAMES I P	2LT	0-0276622	0455	3
KELCH PAUL	LTC	0-1895794	0863	1
KELCHAK PAUL J	LTC	0-1102326	0767	1
KELCHNER CLYDE H	MAJ	0-0501523	1046	2
KELCHNER WILLIAM R	1LT	0-1319214	0947	2
KELDER WILLIAM L	MAJ	0-1947206	0464	2
KELEMEN CHARLES	LTC	0-0375487	0562	1
KELEMEN PETE S	CPT	0-0355854	0346	2
KELKER JAMES J A	COL	0-0262378	0666	3
KELL CHARLES F	LTC	0-0367049	0567	1
KELL JAMES D	1LT	0-0890318	1162	1
KELL WILLIAM L	MAJ	0-1584447	0561	1
KELLAN DAYTON J	1LT	0-1039724	0346	2
KELLAR CLAYTON L	MAJ	0-1557314	0158	1
KELLAR KENDALL H	LTC	0-0228097	0954	1
KELLAS DONALD	2LT	0-0508865	0245	2
KELLEHER JAMES F	MAJ	0-0246252	0945	2
KELLEHER JAMES J	CPT	0-0486626	1147	1
KELLEHER JEROME M	CW3	W-2117184	1154	1
KELLEHER JOHN J	MAJ	0-1797474	0464	3
KELLEHER THOMAS C	CPT	0-0492919	0546	2
KELLER ALVIN M	1LT	0-1320950	0947	2
KELLER ARTHUR E	LTC	0-0472967	0657	1
KELLER CARL J	CW4	W-2106232	0359	1
KELLER CHARLES	CW4	W-2144953	0365	1
KELLER CHARLES C	1LT	0-1114584	0445	2
KELLER DALLAS C	LTC	0-0287374	1055	3
KELLER DAVID M	MAJ	0-0946912	1167	1
KELLER DAVID W	1LT	0-1057125	0446	2
KELLER DOWNING D	COL	0-0229164	1164	3
KELLER DWIGHT L	CW3	RW-2148120	0262	1
KELLER EDWARD J	1LT	0-0517889	0944	2
KELLER ELLIS O	LTC	0-0230952	1057	3
KELLER ELVIN F	MAJ	0-1779150	0361	1
KELLER EUGENE JR	COL	0-0103324	0554	2
KELLER FRANK C	LTC	0-1578694	0364	1
KELLER FRANK G	CW3	W-2142860	0561	1
KELLER FRANK M	COL	0-0180763	0762	3
KELLER GEORGE W	MAJ	0-1010524	0155	1
KELLER GORDON H	MAJ	0-0115192	1150	3
KELLER HAROLD A	MAJ	0-1016837	0761	1
KELLER HAROLD E	LTC	0-0250123	0866	3
KELLER HAROLD W	COL	0-0223037	0455	3
KELLER HAROLD W	LTC	0-0409482	0261	1

NAME	GRADE	SVC NO	DATE RET MO YR	RET CODE
KELLER FRANK	[illegible]	[illegible]	[illegible]	1
KELLER HENRY W	COL	[illegible]	1262	1
KELLER HERMAN W	MAJ	[illegible]	0663	3
KELLER HERSCHEL W	COL	0-0296734	0155	1
KELLER JAMES	COL	0-0290622	0257	1
KELLER JOHN	LTC	0-0473924	0357	1
KELLER JOHN	LTC	0-0474775	0960	1
KELLER JOHN S	COL	0-0177757	0761	3
KELLER JOHN W	CPT	0-0404669	0345	2
KELLER JOSEPH F	CW2	W-2151962	1161	1
KELLER JOSEPH L	MAJ	0-1593013	0868	3
KELLER KARL J	CW2	W-2143436	1156	1
KELLER KENNETH F	LTC	0-0359448	0954	1
KELLER LEONARD F	CPT	0-0236786	0445	2
KELLER LUTHER II	COL	0-1241129	0867	1
KELLER MARVIN F	1LT	0-1055639	1044	2
KELLER MARVIN E	LTC	0-1639166	0663	1
KELLER NEIL	LTC	0-1305262	0962	1
KELLER NICHOLAS F	CW4	W-2143572	0659	1
KELLER OLIN T	1LT	0-1754356	0745	2
KELLER OSCAR S	MAJ	0-0147567	1151	3
KELLER OWEN V	LTC	0-0214609	0957	2
KELLER RAYMOND JR	CPT	0-0384070	0944	2
KELLER REX E	LTC	0-0113451	1155	3
KELLER ROGER F JR	1LT	0-0547322	0946	2
KELLER WILFRED J	MAJ	0-0223122	0357	3
KELLER WILLIAM H	COL	0-0276579	1058	1
KELLER WILLIAM H	CW2	W-2151105	0361	1
KELLER WILLIAM J	CPT	0-0176729	0956	3
KELLETT HARRY P	CPT	0-0516226	1045	2
KELLETT NORMAN M	1LT	0-1180985	1045	2
KELLETT RALPH F	CPT	0-1922629	0662	1
KELLEY BARNEY L	MAJ	0-1179918	0761	1
KELLEY BYRON E	LTC	0-0460272	0866	3
KELLEY CARL C	CPT	0-4043198	0562	2
KELLEY CHARLES C	LTC	0-0171373	0560	3
KELLEY CHARLES F	MAJ	0-0262309	0967	1
KELLEY CHARLES W	CPT	0-0473476	0955	1
KELLEY EDGAR C	COL	0-0318972	1263	3
KELLEY EDWARD W	LTC	0-1035847	0262	1
KELLEY ELLEN E	1LT	N-0793182	0849	2
KELLEY ELLERY F	LTC	0-0299877	0966	3
KELLEY ERNEST L JR	CW3	W-2147233	0953	1
KELLEY EVERETT L	CPT	0-1175186	1160	1
KELLEY FRANCIS J	LTC	0-0178444	0760	3
KELLEY FRED	MAJ	0-0208435	0953	3
KELLEY FRED H	COL	0-0174046	0855	3
KELLEY FREDERICK	1LT	0-0490721	0953	1
KELLEY GEORGE P	CPT	0-0414258	0945	2
KELLEY GEORGE W	CPT	0-0492044	1155	1
KELLEY GEORGE W	LTC	0-1576226	0363	1
KELLEY GERARD W	B G	0-0235809	0263	3
KELLEY HARMON JR	1LT	0-1317918	0845	2
KELLEY HAROLD L	MAJ	0-0270341	1266	3
KELLEY HAYWARD K	LTC	0-0143651	0857	3
KELLEY HENRY D	LTC	0-0270359	0467	3
KELLEY JAMES L	MAJ	0-0531428	0146	2
KELLEY JOHN R	CPT	0-0496168	0949	1
KELLEY JOHN T JR	CPT	0-0367549	0545	2
KELLEY JOSEPH C	LTC	0-0499800	0753	2
KELLEY JOSEPH J	MAJ	0-0502112	1152	1
KELLEY KENDRICK K	LTC	0-0378974	1167	3
KELLEY KENT A SR	CPT	0-1924769	0963	1
KELLEY LAWRENCE W	CW3	W-2146429	1162	1
KELLEY LEROY G	CW3	W-2142861	0961	1
KELLEY LOUIS R	CW3	W-2150315	1062	1
KELLEY MARY F	1LT	N-0752446	0646	1
KELLEY MORRIS S	LTC	0-1171219	0960	1
KELLEY NELLE A	MAJ	N-0767572	0365	1
KELLEY NICHOLAS L	LTC	0-0960581	0767	1
KELLEY PATRICK H	WO1	W-2151698	0458	2
KELLEY PAUL L	LTC	0-1102327	0157	1
KELLEY RALPH L	CPT	0-1052420	0261	1
KELLEY RAYMOND W	COL	0-1826331	0968	1
KELLEY ROBERT J	MAJ	0-1951697	0366	1

NAME	GRADE	SVC NO	DATE RET MO YR	RET CODE
KELLEY ROBERT E JR	CW3	W-2150111	0365	1
KELLEY ROSALIND H	1LT	N-0756526	0646	1
KELLEY RUTH A	CPT	0-0282963	0444	2
KELLEY STANLEY R	COL	0-0255222	0360	1
KELLEY STANLEY R	COL	0-0957175	0363	1
KELLEY THOMAS F	MAJ	0-1280940	0556	1
KELLEY THOMAS R	COL	0-0392669	0761	1
KELLEY TOM M	MAJ	0-1044860	1057	1
KELLEY TONY H	MAJ	0-1292188	1058	1
KELLEY VINCENT P	LTC	0-1290434	0861	1
KELLEY WARREN T	COL	0-0178222	1161	3
KELLEY WILLIAM A	MAJ	0-1337440	0264	1
KELLEY WILLIAM F	1LT	0-1304229	1145	2
KELLEY WILLIAM J	MAJ	0-0979215	1262	1
KELLEY WILLIAM J	MAJ	0-1048850	0461	1
KELLEY WILLIAM P	MAJ	0-1018692	0263	1
KELLEY WILLIAM R	LTC	0-0274443	0466	3
KELLEY WILLIS F	LTC	0-1824757	1062	1
KELLEY WINFORD R	MAJ	0-1311159	0361	1
KELLICK FRANK E	2LT	0-1110039	0444	2
KELLIHAN LOUIS L	CPT	0-1595704	0166	1
KELLIHER HENRY J	COL	0-0280247	0767	3
KELLNER HERMAN A	MAJ	0-0335315	0660	1
KELLNER JOHN JR	MAJ	0-0103880	0150	3
KELLNER LOUIS F	CPT	0-0397843	0263	1
KELLNOF ARTHUR	CPT	0-0343827	0544	2
KELLOGG ALBERT R	COL	0-0131505	0648	3
KELLOGG BESSIE I	2LT	N-0700226	0439	1
KELLOGG DOROTHY D	MAJ	J-0101288	1065	1
KELLOGG FREDERICK	COL	0-0284789	0766	3
KELLOGG GAYLE R	1LT	0-1318311	0352	2
KELLOGG GEORGE T	LTC	0-1596920	0668	3
KELLOGG HAMILTON H	COL	0-0257163	1057	3
KELLOGG HARRY W	1LT	0-1012902	0246	2
KELLOGG HENRY K	M G	0-0286132	1161	3
KELLOGG JESSE I	LTC	0-0166477	1056	3
KELLOGG JOHN G	LTC	0-0443619	0948	1
KELLOGG JOHN H	MAJ	0-0217764	0364	3
KELLOGG KENNETH O	1LT	0-0994290	0756	2
KELLOGG RAY E	2LT	0-1825862	0145	2
KELLOGG ROBERT P	LTC	0-0288791	1262	3
KELLOND JAMES K	MAJ	0-0361139	0745	2
KELLS RAYMOND G	LTC	0-0298046	1166	3
KELLSTROM CARL W	MAJ	0-0400219	0861	1
KELLUM FELIX	CPT	0-1596382	0852	1
KELLUM THOMAS B	COL	0-0206755	0956	3
KELLY AIDAN C	COL	0-0109178	0350	1
KELLY ALLAN B	1LT	0-1686427	1059	1
KELLY ALTON L	LTC	0-1037851	0761	1
KELLY ANTHONY D	LTC	0-1031099	1265	1
KELLY ARNOLD A	CW2	W-2205713	0161	1
KELLY ARTHUR F	1LT	0-1284523	104N	2
KELLY AUBREY R	LTC	0-0251410	0266	3
KELLY AUSTIN F	1LT	0-1311087	1146	2
KELLY BAYARD L	CPT	0-1292189	0955	1
KELLY BENNIE W	CW3	W-2152024	0164	1
KELLY BRUCE L	LTC	0-1105568	1263	2
KELLY CARROLL R	CW2	W-2144061	1059	1
KELLY CECIL R	CPT	0-2044301	1148	1
KELLY CHARLES C	CW4	W-2146070	0567	2
KELLY CHARLES G	COL	0-0268586	0467	3
KELLY CHESTER B	MAJ	0-2204086	0166	1
KELLY CLYDE W	1LT	0-0233517	0747	2
KELLY CYRIL A	LTC	0-0450971	1160	1
KELLY DAN JR	2LT	0-0351189	0945	2
KELLY DANIEL D	CPT	0-0418624	1043	2
KELLY DAVID E	CW2	W-2151175	1158	1
KELLY DENNIS H	LTC	0-0486252	0545	2
KELLY DONALD F	CPT	0-5322417	0868	2
KELLY DOROTHY N	1LT	N-0755804	0746	1
KELLY EARL B	LTC	0-1175188	1163	1
KELLY EDWARD	CPT	0-1690967	0557	2
KELLY EDWARD C	CW4	W-2114233	0858	1
KELLY EDWARD C C	CPT	0-0186384	0851	3
KELLY EDWARD F	MAJ	0-0488867	0757	2

NAME	GRADE	SVC NO	DATE RET MO YR	RET CODE
KELLY EDWARD [illegible]	MAJ	[illegible]	[illegible]	1
KELLY EDWARD [illegible]	CW3	[illegible]	[illegible]	1
KELLY EDWARD J	LTC	[illegible]	1063	1
KELLY EDWARD J JR	LTC	[illegible]	1157	1
KELLY EDWARD L	CW4	W-2137158	0659	1
KELLY EDWARD L	CW3	W-2144446	0764	1
KELLY EDWARD S	CPT	[illegible]	1354	1
KELLY EDWARD T	1LT	[illegible]	0744	2
KELLY ELMER F	CPT	0-1014442	0547	2
KELLY ERIC T	LTC	0-0139637	0953	3
KELLY ERNEST A	MAJ	0-0972063	0463	1
KELLY EUGENE C	MAJ	0-1645103	0364	1
KELLY EUGENE L	CPT	0-0246297	1058	3
KELLY FRANCIS J	1LT	0-1999752	0648	2
KELLY FRANCIS P	1LT	0-1302778	0445	2
KELLY FRANK A	CPT	0-0918705	0647	2
KELLY FRED A	LTC	0-0205671	0656	3
KELLY GEORGE A	CPT	0-0243424	0152	3
KELLY GEORGE W	1LT	0-1324420	1145	2
KELLY GEORGE W	MAJ	0-1543373	1058	1
KELLY GLENN M	LTC	0-1547308	0462	1
KELLY HARRY P	LTC	0-1104245	1055	1
KELLY HOWARD F	LTC	0-0223365	1159	3
KELLY HOWARD M	CPT	0-0487061	0549	1
KELLY HUGH J	MAJ	0-0248037	0555	3
KELLY IRA O S	COL	0-0173948	0560	3
KELLY IRVIN V	CPT	0-1013553	0658	1
KELLY JACK S	LTC	0-1179479	1063	1
KELLY JAMES A	CW3	W-2147471	0865	1
KELLY JAMES E	LTC	0-1917745	0868	1
KELLY JAMES M	MAJ	0-2035711	0960	1
KELLY JAMES P	CPT	0-0277626	1057	3
KELLY JAMES P	LTC	0-0300090	0546	2
KELLY JAMES T	CPT	0-0404383	0240	2
KELLY JAMES W	1LT	0-0383131	0146	2
KELLY JEROME K	LTC	0-1334298	0368	1
KELLY JESSE J	LTC	0-0400558	0963	2
KELLY JOHN A	COL	0-0480095	0762	3
KELLY JOHN B	WO1	W-2148173	0455	1
KELLY JOHN E	CPT	0-1304230	0947	2
KELLY JOHN F	LTC	0-1574491	0157	1
KELLY JOHN J	1LT	0-0509352	0245	2
KELLY JOHN J	MAJ	0-1646155	0861	1
KELLY JOHN J JR	CW4	W-2125246	0266	1
KELLY JOHN M	LTC	0-0374988	0254	1
KELLY JOHN N	LTC	0-1308152	0257	3
KELLY JOHN P	COL	0-1252898	1066	1
KELLY JOHN T	CPT	0-0488200	0948	1
KELLY JOHN W	COL	0-0253421	1064	3
KELLY JOHN W	MAJ	0-0888320	0762	2
KELLY JOSEPH F	COL	0-0261366	0261	3
KELLY JOSEPH G	MAJ	0-1999818	0163	1
KELLY JOSEPH J	LTC	0-0324804	0156	2
KELLY JOSEPH J	WO1	W-2124674	0745	2
KELLY JOSEPH P	MAJ	0-0267442	0463	3
KELLY JOSEPH F	COL	0-0336430	0868	3
KELLY JOSPEH X	MAJ	0-0394820	0859	1
KELLY KATHRYN J	2LT	N-0733428	0845	1
KELLY KEITH O	1LT	0-1181925	1159	1
KELLY LAWRENCE B	COL	0-0415911	0568	1
KELLY LAWRENCE R	LTC	0-1589305	0160	1
KELLY LEE C	LTC	0-1031655	0761	1
KELLY LEE W	LTC	0-1291832	0662	1
KELLY LESTER H	WO1	W-2153259	0560	1
KELLY LLOYD E	COL	0-0114560	0757	3
KELLY LOUIS G	COL	0-0186474	0257	3
KELLY MAJOR L	LTC	0-0292163	0668	3
KELLY MARTIN J	CPT	0-0959268	0261	1
KELLY MARTIN J	1LT	0-1310605	0345	2
KELLY MAURICE F	MAJ	0-0919675	0355	2
KELLY MAURICE W	LTC	0-0461485	1166	3
KELLY MICHAEL J	COL	0-0125609	0648	3
KELLY MICHAEL W	LTC	0-0313665	0945	2
KELLY MILES F	1LT	0-0323901	0944	2
KELLY OLIVER H	COL	0-0445808	0662	1

NAME	GRADE	SVC NO	DATE RET MO YR	RET CODE
KELLY [illegible] J	[illegible]	[illegible]	[illegible]	3
KELLY PAUL J	CPT	[illegible]	[illegible]	2
KELLY PAUL T	MAJ	0-1335428	0863	1
KELLY PERRY A	LTC	[illegible]	0967	3
KELLY PHILLIP A	CPT	[illegible]	1056	3
KELLY RALPH A	LTC	0-1558166	1062	1
KELLY RALPH S	MAJ	[illegible]	0957	3
KELLY RAYMOND F	MAJ	[illegible]	0266	1
KELLY RAYMOND J	COL	0-0146223	1156	3
KELLY RAYMOND J	LTC	0-0325619	0367	2
KELLY RICHARD B JR	CPT	0-1128934	0752	2
KELLY ROBERT A	LTC	0-1966086	1062	1
KELLY ROBERT D	MAJ	0-1039788	0264	1
KELLY ROBERT E	MAJ	0-0976541	0764	1
KELLY ROBERT F	MAJ	0-1294317	1060	1
KELLY ROBERT G	CPT	0-0221751	[illegible]	2
KELLY ROBERT J	MAJ	0-0564081	0864	1
KELLY ROBERT M	CW3	W-2143930	0163	1
KELLY ROBERT O	MAJ	0-1599433	1264	1
KELLY RODERICK J	2LT	0-1798580	1157	2
KELLY RUSSELL M	LTC	0-1104246	0657	1
KELLY SAM	CW3	W-2145276	0363	1
KELLY SAMUEL F	LTC	0-1337716	0166	1
KELLY SYLVESTER	COL	0-0342923	0560	3
KELLY THOMAS A	1LT	0-0514713	1045	2
KELLY THOMAS A	LTC	0-2035813	1165	1
KELLY THOMAS J	MAJ	0-0251874	1059	3
KELLY THOMAS J	COL	0-0269351	1059	3
KELLY THOMAS J	COL	0-0452242	1068	1
KELLY THOMAS J	1LT	0-1304231	0646	2
KELLY THOMAS J	LTC	0-1822582	0961	1
KELLY THOMAS R	MAJ	0-0496780	0657	3
KELLY TOM S	LTC	0-1103727	0763	1
KELLY VICTOR O	CPT	0-0532674	0147	2
KELLY WALTER H	MAJ	0-0188453	0748	3
KELLY WALTER L	LTC	0-0331042	0259	1
KELLY WALTER N	MAJ	0-0344504	1060	1
KELLY WALTER R	1LT	0-1019309	0747	2
KELLY WALTER T JR	MAJ	0-1308815	0865	1
KELLY WILLIAM A	LTC	0-0297037	1060	1
KELLY WILLIAM C	CW2	W-2110112	1047	2
KELLY WILLIAM D	LTC	0-0485654	0954	3
KELLY WILLIAM G	MAJ	0-0234484	0468	3
KELLY WILLIAM L JR	CW2	W-2211855	0268	1
KELLY WILLIAM M	COL	0-0189293	0656	3
KELLY WILLIAM P	LTC	0-0957402	0767	1
KELLY WOODROW W	CPT	0-2041030	0161	1
KELM CAROL V	MAJ	M-0002572	0266	1
KELM JACK R	LTC	0-1637799	0663	1
KELM PAUL H	LTC	0-0242752	1165	3
KELM ROBERT F	MAJ	0-1291650	0160	1
KELSAY JESSE O	COL	0-0885824	1160	1
KELSEY ALBERT J	MAJ	0-0231225	0960	3
KELSEY CLARENCE W	MAJ	0-0128603	1056	3
KELSEY LEE C JR	LTC	0-0296066	1267	3
KELSEY LOUIS F	MAJ	0-0337556	0966	3
KELSEY OREN L JR	1LT	0-1288066	0245	2
KELSEY ROBERT G	CW4	W-2146252	0168	1
KELSEY ROSS F	1LT	0-1293068	0345	2
KELSO BILLY P	2LT	0-1287362	0144	2
KELSO CHARITY T	2LT	N-0703007	0644	1
KELSO EARL H	COL	0-0279109	1159	1
KELSO ELMER G	LTC	0-0244296	0563	3
KELSO FRED D	COL	0-0170740	0352	3
KELSO HOMER C	MAJ	0-0473010	0852	1
KELSO MARIE L	2LT	N-0732074	0145	1
KELSO RUPERT F	MAJ	0-0300217	1064	3
KELSO VICTOR C	LTC	0-1798582	0563	1
KELSO WALTER F	COL	0-0447606	0862	1
KELSTON ROBERT H	CW2	W-2123327	0246	2
KELTNER EDGAR H JR	CPT	0-1302477	0246	2
KELTNER JACOB G	CPT	0-0445742	1045	2
KELTNER MARVIN B	CPT	0-1284154	0944	2
KELTON JOHN E	LTC	0-0388681	0660	1
KELTY HENRY J	CPT	0-0982488	0458	1

NAME	GRADE	SVC NO	DATE RET MO YR	RET CODE
KELTY JAMES F	MAJ	0-1113780	0863	1
KELTZ CHARLES E	LTC	0-0321108	0560	1
KELTZ JOHN F JR	MAJ	0-0173329	1160	3
KEMBLE LEWIS G	LTC	0-1591849	0263	1
KEMELHOR MICHAEL C	MAJ	0-1690514	1045	2
KEMICK IRVIN B	CPT	0-0371436	1047	2
KEMMERER FRANK	LTC	0-0486914	0356	1
KEMNITZ LESTER E	CW2	W-2142971	0862	1
KEMNITZ WILLIAM H JR	LTC	0-1573980	0367	2
KEMP ARTHUR D	LTC	0-0363716	0867	3
KEMP ARTHUR H	COL	0-0258136	0967	3
KEMP CHARLES E	1LT	0-0452472	0145	2
KEMP FRED J	LTC	0-0954900	0665	1
KEMP GIBSON D	MAJ	0-1272349	0361	1
KEMP HARDY A	COL	0-0226089	0862	3
KEMP HENRY J III	MAJ	0-1951097	0661	1
KEMP IRA J	LTC	0-1950891	0766	2
KEMP JAMES M	CW3	RW-2145733	1163	1
KEMP KARL	MAJ	0-1576228	0758	1
KEMP LAVERNE R	LTC	0-1314297	0163	1
KEMP LILBURN R	LTC	0-0252018	0964	3
KEMP MARVIN E	CPT	0-0954306	0468	1
KEMP MURRAY G	1LT	0-2001060	0147	2
KEMP NEAL R	LTC	0-1031733	1066	1
KEMP PAUL H JR	LTC	0-1826153	1062	1
KEMP ROBERT M	LTC	0-1314808	0757	1
KEMP ROBERT W	1LT	0-1283788	0943	2
KEMP SILAS M	CPT	0-4009044	0563	1
KEMP VICTOR H	LTC	0-0406359	0663	1
KEMP WILBUR D JR	2LT	0-0253536	1266	3
KEMP WRIGHT C	LTC	0-0224493	0955	3
KEMP WYMAN W	LTC	0-0271359	0967	3
KEMPA WALTER	CW2	W-2144576	0664	1
KEMPER CECIL E	LTC	0-0188952	0758	3
KEMPER GEORGE E	LTC	0-1043381	0762	1
KEMPER RICHARD V	2LT	0-1647539	0745	2
KEMPER WAYNE C	MAJ	0-2030523	0967	1
KEMPER WILLIAM P	1LT	0-0903506	0444	2
KEMPF FRANCIS E	COL	0-0263780	1161	3
KEMPF FRANK J	LTC	0-0482059	0654	1
KEMPLE JOHN L	LTC	0-0906911	0566	3
KEMPSTER GEORGE A	MAJ	0-0370513	0746	2
KEMPTON JOHN	CW3	W-2149933	0862	2
KENDALL ANTOINETTE	2LT	N-0730443	0844	1
KENDALL ARTHUR W	LTC	0-0280434	0261	3
KENDALL BRUCE P	CPT	0-1041813	0245	2
KENDALL BURTON L	MAJ	0-2102528	1262	1
KENDALL CHARLES L	CPT	0-0450554	1053	1
KENDALL DONALD A	MAJ	0-1700179	0246	2
KENDALL DONALD L	MAJ	0-0392144	0363	1
KENDALL FREDERICK	COL	0-0176670	0853	2
KENDALL GEORGE P	1LT	0-0276932	1145	2
KENDALL GEORGE R SR	1LT	0-1301911	0546	2
KENDALL JACKSON W	LTC	0-0105380	0156	3
KENDALL MILTON	COL	0-0177923	0262	3
KENDALL OTHEL	MAJ	0-0235060	0954	3
KENDALL RALPH M	2LT	0-0127187	1056	3
KENDALL ROBERT M	LTC	0-0262740	1166	3
KENDALL ROBIN S	MAJ	0-2296604	1163	1
KENDALL WALLACE C	CPT	0-0412542	0945	2
KENDERDINE JOHN D	COL	0-0146176	0249	3
KENDLE ERNEST F	LTC	0-0426178	1161	1
KENDLE WALTER E	MAJ	0-0206877	0858	3
KENDRICK CHARLES W	MAJ	0-0295003	1068	3
KENDRICK FRANK J	COL	0-0263876	0162	3
KENDRICK FREDERICK	CPT	0-1577413	0845	2
KENDRICK GEORGE M JR	COL	0-0256424	1067	3
KENDRICK HAROLD C	CW3	W-2141988	0657	1
KENDRICK HAROLD P	CPT	0-1534527	0346	2
KENDRICK HARRISON F	MAJ	0-0287089	0558	3
KENDRICK JAMES O JR	MAJ	0-2025152	0765	1
KENDRICK JOSEPH F	MAJ	0-0103329	1154	3
KENDRICK WILLIAM T	2LT	0-1306855	0444	2
KENDRIGAN MARTIN F	CPT	0-0490020	0948	1
KENEALY EDWARD R	LTC	0-0403404	0746	2

NAME	GRADE	SVC NO	DATE RET MO YR	RET CODE
KENES KATHERINE	1LT	N-0723245	0746	1
KENESEY GEORGE F	CW3	W-2152419	0463	1
KENION ALONZO W JR	CPT	0-1310723	0646	2
KENISON AMELIA	MAJ	N-0703502	0666	1
KENISON RAY S	MAJ	0-0262535	0766	3
KENISTON CLIFFORD W	CW4	W-2126963	1068	3
KENLER MYRON L	CPT	0-1690644	0945	2
KENLEY MELVIN L	2LT	0-0538279	0545	2
KENLY GLENN H	MAJ	N-0762491	0864	1
KENNA ALPHA H	LTC	0-0170815	0648	3
KENNALEY JOHN J	COL	0-0384162	0361	2
KENNAMAN JACK R	CPT	0-0890141	0555	2
KENNARD ELEANOR F	MAJ	L-0200880	0263	2
KENNARD ERNEST W	CW2	W-2144359	0561	1
KENNARD FRANKLAND	LTC	0-0205808	1163	3
KENNAUGH MILTON C	CPT	0-1542691	0846	2
KENNEDY ALLEN B	CW4	W-2104918	0662	1
KENNEDY ALLEN K	CW2	W-2143310	0157	1
KENNEDY ALTA S	MAJ	N-0763721	0561	2
KENNEDY ARCHIBALD	MAJ	0-0908957	0747	2
KENNEDY ARCHIE J	LTC	0-1585709	1062	1
KENNEDY ARTHUR L	CW2	W-2144245	0255	1
KENNEDY CECIL J	M G	0-0243189	0360	3
KENNEDY CHARLES C	CPT	0-1320952	1047	2
KENNEDY CHARLES H	MAJ	0-0960221	0165	1
KENNEDY CHARLES H	MAJ	0-1177026	0657	1
KENNEDY CHARLES H	2LT	0-1549751	0145	2
KENNEDY CHARLES R	MAJ	0-2028464	0864	1
KENNEDY CLEMENT E	COL	0-0210104	0853	3
KENNEDY DALE E	LTC	0-0204750	1058	3
KENNEDY DAVID C JR	LTC	0-0304256	0866	3
KENNEDY DAVID I	LTC	0-1002041	0367	1
KENNEDY DONALD D	CW2	W-2146688	0557	1
KENNEDY DONALD J	LTC	0-0386875	0147	2
KENNEDY DONALD J	LTC	0-2076198	0768	1
KENNEDY EARL G	LTC	0-0495551	0952	1
KENNEDY EDMUND F	LTC	0-0287143	0562	3
KENNEDY EDWARD J	CW3	W-2205392	0264	1
KENNEDY EDWARD R	CPT	0-1325577	0346	2
KENNEDY EDWIN R JR	COL	0-0345113	1262	3
KENNEDY ESTUS	MAJ	0-0108636	1047	1
KENNEDY EUGENE C	CW4	W-2003738	0865	1
KENNEDY FRANCIS I	COL	0-0140204	0553	3
KENNEDY FRANCIS J	CPT	0-0335267	0545	2
KENNEDY FRANCIS J	LTC	0-0907819	0455	1
KENNEDY FRANCIS J	CPT	0-2011324	0654	1
KENNEDY GARNETT L	CW2	W-2142996	1163	1
KENNEDY GEORGE E	MAJ	0-2262311	0664	1
KENNEDY GEORGE H	CPT	0-1341673	0458	2
KENNEDY GEORGE M	MAJ	0-1334586	0661	1
KENNEDY GEORGE W	CPT	0-1184681	1165	1
KENNEDY GLADYS	MAJ	M-0002577	0864	1
KENNEDY GRODON A	MAJ	0-1646793	0959	1
KENNEDY HAROLD M	LTC	0-0390571	0860	1
KENNEDY HARRY V	COL	0-0108871	1047	2
KENNEDY HELEN E	MAJ	N-0743168	0465	1
KENNEDY HELEN G	1LT	N-0752793	0747	1
KENNEDY HENRY	CPT	0-0422539	0446	2
KENNEDY HUGH H	COL	0-0255148	0864	3
KENNEDY IRA W	WO1	W-2121268	0452	2
KENNEDY JAMES A	LTC	0-0357960	0668	3
KENNEDY JAMES O	CW2	W-3430342	1067	1
KENNEDY JAMES F JR	CPT	0-2030193	0455	1
KENNEDY JOHN A	MAJ	0-2020736	0767	1
KENNEDY JOHN C	LTC	0-0324080	1163	1
KENNEDY JOHN D	COL	0-0185280	0751	3
KENNEDY JOHN D	1LT	0-1551882	0346	2
KENNEDY JOHN E	MAJ	0-1168314	0960	1
KENNEDY JOHN J	1LT	0-1002959	0553	2
KENNEDY JOHN J JR	MAJ	0-0124601	0253	3
KENNEDY JOHN L	LTC	0-0308521	1057	1
KENNEDY JOHN M III	COL	0-0232684	0361	3
KENNEDY JOHN N	MAJ	0-1320635	1062	1
KENNEDY JOHN T	LTC	0-1120198	0463	2
KENNEDY JOHN T JR	2LT	0-1319076	0146	2

NAME	GRADE	SVC NO	DATE RET MO YR	RET CODE
KENNEDY JOHN W	COL	0-0492205	1168	3
KENNEDY JOSEPH R	1LT	0-1316429	0346	2
KENNEDY JOSEPHINE	1LT	N-0700146	1141	1
KENNEDY KENNETH E	WO1	W-2119592	0656	2
KENNEDY KLEIN W	LTC	0-0239415	1165	3
KENNEDY LAWRENCE H	MAJ	0-1298878	0662	1
KENNEDY LEO W	1LT	0-0522612	0746	2
KENNEDY LOWELL H	2LT	0-2000119	0447	2
KENNEDY LUTHER M	2LT	0-1824327	0744	2
KENNEDY LYLE J	LTC	0-0272854	0566	3
KENNEDY MARGARET M	LTC	N-0700629	0546	1
KENNEDY MAY D	2LT	N-0783463	1044	1
KENNEDY MILDRED D	MAJ	N-0724502	0661	1
KENNEDY OWEN R	CW4	W-2105919	0858	1
KENNEDY PAUL	2LT	0-2010538	0351	2
KENNEDY PAUL C	CW4	W-2149845	0467	1
KENNEDY PAUL J	1LT	0-2207531	0152	2
KENNEDY PAUL R	LTC	0-1280316	0367	3
KENNEDY PAUL T	1LT	0-1333434	0347	2
KENNEDY RALPH P	LTC	0-0984484	1165	1
KENNEDY RAYMOND J	MAJ	0-1114586	0762	2
KENNEDY ROBERT A	LTC	0-1292190	1061	1
KENNEDY ROBERT C	LTC	0-0211174	0154	3
KENNEDY ROBERT C	CW2	W-3100657	1068	1
KENNEDY ROBERT E	MAJ	0-0113079	0368	3
KENNEDY ROBERT E	1LT	0-1573492	0260	2
KENNEDY ROBERT E	MAJ	0-1885533	0966	1
KENNEDY ROBERT H	2LT	0-0442406	0745	2
KENNEDY ROBERT H	LTC	0-0482132	0851	1
KENNEDY ROBERT M	COL	0-0231654	0565	3
KENNEDY ROBERT M	MAJ	0-0406448	0462	1
KENNEDY ROBERT N	CW3	0-2262788	0358	1
KENNEDY ROY L	CW4	W-2142304	1059	1
KENNEDY RUTH P	MAJ	N-0775335	0563	1
KENNEDY SHERROD O	CPT	0-1596922	1057	1
KENNEDY TAYLOR L	1LT	0-1168315	104N	2
KENNEDY TERRENCE S	LTC	0-0548538	1064	1
KENNEDY THOMAS J	CPT	0-0410849	0746	2
KENNEDY THOMAS J	LTC	0-1013257	0762	1
KENNEDY THOMAS J	MAJ	0-1302314	1060	1
KENNEDY THOMAS M	2LT	0-1001159	0344	2
KENNEDY WALTER J	MAJ	0-0126092	1055	3
KENNEDY WALTER J JR	CW2	W-2148552	0363	1
KENNEDY WALTER U	COL	0-0120081	0648	3
KENNEDY WARREN J	COL	0-0270670	0868	3
KENNEDY WILLIAM	MAJ	0-1312680	0657	1
KENNEDY WILLIAM C	MAJ	0-0410342	0164	1
KENNEDY WILLIAM C	MAJ	0-2204189	1066	1
KENNEDY WILLIAM F	CPT	0-0213189	0446	2
KENNEDY WILLIAM M	COL	0-0249839	0362	3
KENNEDY WILLIE B	LTC	0-1543296	0157	1
KENNEDY WILLIS H	1LT	0-0209531	0858	3
KENNELLY EDWARD M	MAJ	0-0227122	0460	3
KENNERLY JOHN D	CW2	W-2214820	1068	1
KENNERSON COLLIE C	MAJ	0-0498001	0946	2
KENNETH DONALD W	MAJ	0-0191336	0357	3
KENNEY AMASA R JR	LTC	0-0318376	0564	3
KENNEY ANDREW A	1LT	0-0269477	0949	1
KENNEY CHARLES W	MAJ	0-2018368	0557	1
KENNEY EARL D	CPT	0-1589945	0846	2
KENNEY EDWARD L	LTC	0-0498825	0268	3
KENNEY GARDNER B	MAJ	0-0971341	1061	1
KENNEY HARVEY A	LTC	0-0386528	0367	3
KENNEY HESTER S	2LT	N-0751428	0944	1
KENNEY JACK P	LTC	0-1106250	0467	3
KENNEY JOHN M	CPT	0-0211445	0120	1
KENNEY MATTHEW R	MAJ	0-1825298	0455	1
KENNEY MILTON M	COL	0-0367304	0264	3
KENNEY OLNEY E	CW4	W-2117853	0967	3
KENNEY PATRICK J	LTC	0-1698005	0463	1
KENNEY PAUL J	LTC	0-0182667	0855	3
KENNEY ROBERT N	CPT	0-1296707	0346	2
KENNEY THOMAS J	MAJ	0-0489009	0155	2
KENNEY WILLIAM F	CPT	0-1101523	0145	2
KENNEY WILLIAM N JR	LTC	0-1304396	0261	1

NAME	GRADE	SVC NO	DATE RET MO YR	RET CODE
KENNIGER CHARLES F	COL	0-0326828	0666	3
KENNING FRANK W	1LT	0-1053670	0245	2
KENNINGTON CLYDE B	LTC	0-0240061	0660	2
KENNISON SAMUEL M	LTC	0-2026815	1163	1
KENNON ROBERT F	COL	0-0185885	0962	3
KENNOY JOHN S	MAJ	0-0227537	0664	3
KENNY ELIZABETH	2LT	N-0700843	0641	2
KENNY JACK O	MAJ	0-0445507	0348	2
KENNY JOHN P	1LT	0-0377921	0344	2
KENNY MARY A	CPT	N-0700663	1044	1
KENNY RAYMOND J	1LT	0-1295384	0545	2
KENNY ROBERT W	B G	0-0205944	0362	3
KENNY ROY W	M G	0-0176730	0255	3
KENNY SIMON E	LTC	0-0524846	0867	1
KENUST ROBERT	CPT	0-1011812	0246	2
KENSOK EDMUND F	MAJ	0-1553486	1059	2
KENT ALBERT E	1LT	0-1798358	0945	2
KENT ALPHONSE J	1LT	0-1302829	0350	2
KENT ARTHUR	LTC	0-0287644	0966	3
KENT EARL W	COL	0-0190852	0260	3
KENT FRANCIS E	MAJ	0-0485656	1147	1
KENT FRED S	COL	0-0216103	0252	3
KENT FREDERICK JR	COL	0-0030172	1060	1
KENT GEORGE R	COL	0-0246364	1154	3
KENT GLEN W	MAJ	0-0418205	0646	2
KENT HAROLD W	COL	0-0118876	0460	3
KENT JAMES W	MAJ	0-1294848	1263	1
KENT JESSE M	CW3	W-2149821	0765	1
KENT JOHN H JR	MAJ	0-0415865	1046	2
KENT JOHN R	CPT	0-1323935	1047	2
KENT JOSEPH J	COL	0-0470757	0353	1
KENT JOSEPH J	LTC	0-1579905	0363	1
KENT MALCOLM F	COL	0-0232939	0663	1
KENT MARK O	LTC	0-0460872	0657	1
KENT ROBERT C	MAJ	0-2263418	1061	1
KENT ROBERT E	1LT	0-1060153	1045	2
KENT ROBERT S	2LT	0-0540336	1045	2
KENT ROY L	2LT	0-1323145	0945	2
KENT ROYAL P	MAJ	0-1692508	0762	1
KENT THADDEUS F	CPT	0-1014268	0561	1
KENTY WILLIAM S	MAJ	0-1018202	1266	1
KENTZEL JOHN J	MAJ	0-1291651	0161	2
KENVIN CLARA P	1LT	N-0759912	0346	2
KENWORTHY HARRY S	MAJ	0-2009361	0360	1
KENWORTHY RAY W	MAJ	0-0247444	1158	3
KENWORTHY WILLIAM B	1LT	0-0491097	114	2
KENYON CHARLES W	COL	0-0289601	1058	1
KENYON ESTHER L	LTC	N-0751427	0865	3
KENYON FRANK C	LTC	0-0184092	1056	3
KENYON JAMES J	CPT	0-2009390	0657	1
KENYON LEE W	MAJ	0-1320134	0359	1
KENYON LEONARD G	1LT	0-1316831	0447	2
KENYON ORLAN E	MAJ	0-1922593	0665	1
KENYON PINCKNEY M	CPT	0-0266110	1054	1
KEOUGH JACK L	CPT	0-1924978	0864	1
KEOUGH JOHN	MAJ	0-0249644	0267	3
KEOUGH JOSEPH M	CW2	W-2211446	1265	1
KEOWN GORDON	CW3	W-2142103	0559	1
KEOWN LAURISTON	COL	0-0336274	0767	3
KEPHART CALVIN I	COL	0-0175037	0648	3
KEPHART FLOYD	LTC	0-2262368	0268	2
KEPHART SAMUEL W	CPT	0-0112211	0648	3
KEPLEY RODNEY S	LTC	0-1295227	0163	1
KEPPARD GORDON C	LTC	0-1577417	0261	1
KEPPERLING GEORGE K	CW2	W-2145195	1163	1
KERAVUORI AITO	COL	0-0985350	0268	1
KERBAUGH LESTER W	MAJ	0-0983741	0962	2
KERBOW HERBERT L	CW2	W-2142711	0755	1
KERCE WOODROW	MAJ	0-1165247	1060	2
KERFOOT DONALD W	CW2	W-2209612	0267	2
KERG JAMES F	1LT	0-2265218	0254	2
KERKER HERBERT V	MAJ	0-1170449	1061	1
KERKSIS SYDNEY C	CW3	W-2136635	0957	1
KERL JULES J	CPT	0-0507127	1044	2
KERLEY THOMAS L	COL	0-1287363	0966	1

NAME	GRADE	SVC NO	DATE RET MO YR	RET CODE
KERLEY WILLIAM G	CW3	W-2206993	0366	1
KERLIN HOMER F	CPT	0-1297364	1046	2
KERLIN ROBERT F	CPT	0-2262342	1062	1
KERLIN WILLIAM S	1LT	0-1321216	0746	2
KERMEN WILLIAM R	COL	0-0323685	0868	1
KERMISCH ALBERT	LTC	0-1577419	0863	1
KERMOTT PHILIP W P	LTC	0-0944109	0868	1
KERN ANNE C	1LT	N-0743446	0746	1
KERN DANIEL J	LTC	0-0269195	0468	3
KERN DONALD B	MAJ	0-1297050	1158	1
KERN GEORGE F	COL	0-0320864	1067	3
KERN HARRY J	LTC	0-1167066	0165	1
KERN HERBERT	1LT	0-1171221	0153	2
KERN JOSEPH W	LTC	0-0214154	0257	3
KERN LEON W	LTC	0-0524469	1266	3
KERN RAY W	2LT	0-0489241	0445	2
KERN RICHARD W	LTC	0-0262222	0368	3
KERN ROBERT J	CPT	0-1636135	0244	2
KERN THEOPHILUS	LTC	0-0230616	0165	3
KERN WALTER	MAJ	0-1047610	0757	1
KERN WILLIAM R	LTC	0-1000142	0262	1
KERNAN REDMOND F JR	B G	0-0173014	0147	2
KERNANDER WILLIAM H	CPT	0-1641464	1055	1
KERNELL LOUIS D	LTC	0-1554761	1166	1
KERNEN DELMAR L	CPT	0-0885445	0447	2
KERNEN WALTER R	2LT	0-0549851	1045	2
KERNER OTTO JR	B G	0-0358530	0868	3
KERNER ROBERT H	MAJ	0-1553677	0259	1
KERNICK CHARLES E	CPT	0-0513679	0847	1
KERNODLE JOHN R	CPT	0-0539741	1046	2
KERNODLE MARION	2LT	0-0183347	0833	1
KERNODLE ROBERT E	COL	0-0129518	0248	2
KERNS BERTHA L	MAJ	N-0756890	0663	1
KERNS MALCOLM B	CW3	W-2152072	0564	1
KERNS MINNIE R	1LT	N-0743323	0546	2
KERNSTOCK ELWYN N	MAJ	0-1185075	1062	1
KERR ALLEN D	LTC	0-0297680	0958	1
KERR CHARLES A II	MAJ	0-1798740	0160	1
KERR CHARLES P	COL	0-0185899	1049	3
KERR CLAYTON D	MAJ	0-0259674	0563	3
KERR CLAYTON P	M G	0-0164979	0962	3
KERR CLYDE E	LTC	0-0349089	0568	3
KERR DONNELL F	CW2	W-2113429	0945	2
KERR EDWARD F	1LT	0-0485418	0346	2
KERR EDWARD J	MAJ	0-1341551	0463	1
KERR FRANCIS R	B G	0-0232181	1050	3
KERR FRED M	CPT	0-1297381	0246	2
KERR GERALD J	1LT	0-1295897	1052	1
KERR GERALDINE	1LT	N-0767219	0745	1
KERR GLADYS	1LT	L-0602094	0445	2
KERR GLENN E	LTC	0-1597507	0364	1
KERR HARRY R	MAJ	0-0964237	0263	1
KERR HERBERT H	MAJ	0-1634965	0-53	1
KERR JACK H	MAJ	0-2019179	0860	1
KERR JAMES E	CW2	W-2148553	0659	1
KERR JAMES F	COL	0-0175290	0760	3
KERR JAMES T JR	CPT	0-0996797	1061	1
KERR JOHN C	LTC	0-0272833	1160	3
KERR JULIA B	LTC	N-0723571	0768	1
KERR KEITH I	MAJ	0-1341674	0862	1
KERR RAYMOND F	MAJ	0-0966618	0964	1
KERR RICHARD H	LTC	0-1310455	1066	1
KERR ROBERT M	COL	0-0229302	0764	3
KERR SAMUEL R JR	LTC	0-1172514	0462	1
KERR WENDELL H	LTC	0-0262090	0563	3
KERR WILLIAM A	LTC	0-0260065	1167	3
KERR WILLIAM C	CPT	0-0197751	0562	3
KERR WILLIAM E JR	MAJ	0-1824759	0864	1
KERRIGAN JOHN T	CPT	0-1010847	0146	2
KERRIGAN WILLIAM C	MAJ	0-0309601	0967	3
KERRIN WILLIAM A	CW3	W-2126646	1162	1
KERRON SETH M	COL	0-0224044	0648	3
KERRY MARSHALL	LTC	0-0261725	1165	3
KERSBERGEN G P W	LTC	0-0374334	0461	1
KERSBERGEN JAY	LTC	0-0299123	0564	3

NAME	GRADE	SVC NO	DATE RET MO YR	RET CODE
KERSBERGEN ROBERT M	MAJ	0-2288265	1166	1
KERSEY JOHN M	MAJ	0-1286299	0360	2
KERSH RUTH J	MAJ	N-0778243	0765	1
KERSHAW JAMES R	COL	0-0402712	1166	3
KERSHAW PETER G D	LTC	0-0261556	0368	3
KERSHAW ROBERT C	CPT	0-1599130	0959	1
KERSHAW SELWYN	CPT	0-0298307	0561	3
KERSHINAR LOUIS P	MAJ	0-1062219	1161	1
KERSHNER GEORGE	MAJ	0-0481558	0346	1
KERSHNER JESS K	COL	0-0123199	0651	3
KERSHNER WARREN E	LTC	0-0167874	0648	3
KERSKI JOHN R	MAJ	0-1118921	0363	1
KERST FRANK	MAJ	0-0913295	0750	2
KERSTEIN CHESTER C	CW3	W-2122932	0160	1
KERSTEIN KARL W	CW3	W-2150778	0864	1
KERSTEN FREDERICK	COL	0-0370560	0964	1
KERSTNER WILLIAM F	WO1	W-2143086	1058	1
KERT MILTON D	LTC	0-0327507	0668	3
KERT MORTON	LTC	0-2035713	0265	1
KERTING WERNER H	MAJ	0-0925876	0560	1
KERTTULA WALTER T	LTC	0-0390744	0567	2
KERWIN EDWARD M	MAJ	0-0117776	0648	3
KERWIN EDWARD W	MAJ	0-1328374	0662	1
KERWIN JAMES J J	MAJ	0-0480985	1144	2
KERWIN WILLIAM	CPT	0-1014715	0346	2
KESECKER HARVEY B	1LT	0-0495379	?946	1
KESHEIMER JULIAN F	LTC	0-1685173	0168	3
KESLER D CLAUDE	CPT	0-1309570	0648	2
KESLER JOHN H	CPT	0-0968384	0258	2
KESLER OLLA A	CPT	0-2043179	0-48	2
KESLER PAT	MAJ	0-4006827	0867	1
KESLER WINFRED A	MAJ	0-1301160	1060	1
KESLIK JOHN	MAJ	0-0889326	0163	1
KESLING CLIFFORD Y	CW2	W-2145916	0657	1
KESNER SAM	MAJ	0-0465480	0646	2
KESSELRING HERBERT M	MAJ	0-1116089	0566	1
KESSELS ANN C	MAJ	N-0737098	1063	3
KESSIE MARSHALL K	1LT	0-0479119	0445	2
KESSINGER RICHARD S	MAJ	0-0438274	1046	1
KESSLER ALBERT E	CW2	W-2122827	0255	2
KESSLER EDWIN	LTC	0-0219819	1063	3
KESSLER FRED J	MAJ	0-2007283	0765	1
KESSLER GEORGE D	COL	0-0427849	0463	1
KESSLER HARRY	LTC	0-0490782	1166	3
KESSLER HERBERT E	MAJ	0-0292142	1166	3
KESSLER JAMES E	MAJ	0-0454362	1059	1
KESSLER JAMES H	CW3	W-2143493	0861	1
KESSLER JOHN	CPT	0-0385142	0546	2
KESSLER LAVIE F	CW2	W-2147432	0361	1
KESSLER MARY M	1LT	N-0790521	0147	2
KESSLER RAYMOND L	LTC	0-0285990	0564	3
KESSLER SAM C	CPT	0-0493795	0547	1
KESSLER WILLIAM H	MAJ	0-0889360	0868	3
KESSLING JOHN F	MAJ	0-0887336	0661	1
KESTER ALFRED J	CPT	0-1299250	0747	2
KESTER WILLIAM R	LTC	0-0223608	0152	3
KESTERSON JAMES C	MAJ	0-1317544	0359	1
KESTLE ROBERT C	MAJ	0-0262379	0146	2
KESTLINGER ROBERT S	CPT	0-1310359	1057	1
KESTNER ROBERT N	CW3	W-2004229	0668	1
KETCH HERBERT L	LTC	0-0279638	1147	2
KETCHAM EARL F	COL	0-0159766	0755	3
KETCHAM FRANK G	COL	0-0224023	0558	1
KETCHAM GEORGE H	LTC	0-0192491	0860	3
KETCHAM HARRY T	COL	0-0218780	0546	2
KETCHAM RAYMOND R	MAJ	0-1935867	0868	1
KETCHER FREDERIC A	LTC	0-0339306	1046	2
KETCHERSID FOY R	CW3	W-2209251	0866	1
KETCHERSIDE HILLARY	LTC	0-0200236	1045	2
KETCHUM ADDISON R	LTC	0-0358157	1166	3
KETCHUM DOUGLAS H	CPT	0-0405209	0859	1
KETCHUM WILLIAM B	MAJ	0-0280719	0568	3
KETKER EDWIN W	CW2	W-2147725	1262	1
KETNER ROBERT R	1LT	0-1587364	1045	2
KETRON HUBERT W	MAJ	0-0310033	0359	3

NAME	GRADE	SVC NO	DATE RET MO YR	RET CODE
KETRON WILLIAM G	LTC	0-1010665	0868	1
KETT CHARLES N	MAJ	0-0450307	0557	1
KETTELL HOLLISTER	MAJ	0-0457626	0155	1
KETTERER PAUL E	LTC	0-0240461	0965	3
KETTERING WILLARD S	CPT	0-0106646	1142	2
KETTERMAN CHARLES W	LTC	0-1576233	1045	2
KETTINGER JOHN P	LTC	0-1324422	0657	1
KETTLE STANLEY C	LTC	0-1015466	0965	1
KETTLE WILLIAM H	1LT	0-1591855	1149	1
KETTLER CHARLES J	LTC	0-0308656	0362	3
KETTNER EUGENE C	MAJ	0-0180809	1055	3
KETTRING LEON C W	LTC	0-0244877	0460	3
KETZ MAX T	COL	0-0227123	1061	3
KETZENBARGER CLIFFOR	LTC	0-0471743	0467	1
KETZLER KENNETH N	LTC	0-0275046	0262	1
KEULING RUSSELL J	MAJ	0-1596079	0560	1
KEUPP PETER	LTC	0-0266760	0868	3
KEVELIGHAN HOWARD J	1LT	0-1536188	0852	2
KEVELL WALTER M	LTC	0-0940761	0867	1
KEVER LUTHER D	MAJ	0-0971828	1062	1
KEVEREN KENNETH A	COL	0-0210514	0559	3
KEVIN RICHARD C	LTC	0-1294853	0266	1
KEY CARL E	CPT	0-0452687	0146	2
KEY CLAYTON N	CPT	0-0485733	1047	1
KEY GILBERT P	LTC	0-0258047	0466	3
KEY JAMES A	LTC	0-0194938	0562	3
KEY JOHNNIE J	WO1	W-2143595	0953	1
KEY WALTER W	LTC	0-0265893	1063	3
KEY WARREN E JR	MAJ	0-1290381	0461	1
KEYES BALDWIN L	COL	0-0140977	0556	3
KEYES CARLETON C	LTC	0-0290330	0460	1
KEYES EARL R	CPT	0-0270659	0264	3
KEYES FREDERICK	MAJ	0-0340676	0944	2
KEYES HARMON E	LTC	0-0230283	0-52	3
KEYES ROBERT C	1LT	0-1541125	1045	2
KEYES ROBERT M	1LT	0-1295230	1144	2
KEYES ROY B	1LT	0-1288907	1045	2
KEYES WILLIAM E	COL	0-0323361	0560	3
KEYFETZ BENJAMIN	CPT	0-0532329	0145	2
KEYMAS PETER G	MAJ	0-2020737	0765	1
KEYS CHARLES B	CPT	0-1294321	0764	1
KEYS DANA L	CW4	W-2122627	0656	1
KEYS EDWARD F	MAJ	0-0117105	0853	3
KEYS EDWARD M	MAJ	0-0346487	1157	2
KEYS JAMES W	MAJ	0-0947689	0465	1
KEYS JOHN J	LTC	0-0248647	0663	1
KEYS JOHN J	1LT	0-1798584	1148	1
KEYS LEE F	MAJ	0-0525251	0961	2
KEYS THEODORE F	CW3	W-2146071	0661	1
KEYS THOMAS B	CPT	0-1286504	0746	2
KEYS WILLIAM C	CPT	0-2262866	0361	1
KEYS WILLIAM J	CW4	W-2114228	0756	1
KEYSER DAVID D	2LT	0-2005392	0845	2
KEYSER GAIL S	LTC	0-0359075	0561	1
KEYSER HAROLD W	MAJ	0-1015444	0762	1
KEYSER MERRIEL D	MAJ	0-0214615	0649	1
KEYSER RICHARC C	1LT	0-1291479	0545	2
KEYSON JOHN A	MAJ	0-0987177	1263	1
KEYSON WESLEY A	COL	0-0388063	0760	1
KHAIL EMIL	MAJ	0-0274293	0966	3
KHALIEL DAVID	MAJ	0-0264080	1050	1
KHALIL SAAD	LTC	0-1314149	0666	1
KHARITONOFF ALEXAND	LTC	0-0367468	1159	1
KIAUNIS PAUL N	CW2	W-2145183	0456	1
KIBBLE HARRY L	MAJ	0-0523289	0656	1
KIBBLE HOWARD P	CW3	W-2143932	0760	1
KIBBY SYDNEY V	LTC	0-0164687	0648	3
KIBELE ELBERT E	LTC	0-2040810	0862	1
KIBER DANIEL H	COL	0-0189393	0554	3
KIBLER HAROLD R	COL	0-0221711	0456	3
KIBLER JOHN W	LTC	0-0246410	0365	3
KIBLER NELSON F	LTC	0-0373200	0561	2
KIBLER THOMAS E	1LT	0-1016452	0448	2
KIBLINGER PAUL L	MAJ	0-1582405	1167	1
KICKLIGHTER JESSE W	LTC	0-1541074	1163	2

NAME	GRADE	SVC NO	DATE RET MO YR	RET CODE
KICTARIK FLORIAN	CW2	W-2205559	0460	1
KIDD CHARLES H	COL	0-0396656	0866	1
KIDD JOHN R	MAJ	0-0269438	0657	3
KIDD ELVIN J	MAJ	0-2003835	0867	1
KIDD HOLLICE F	CPT	0-1920244	1061	1
KIDD JEFFERSON	COL	0-0395415	1161	3
KIDD WADE I	MAJ	0-1101904	0964	1
KIDD WESLEY S	LTC	0-0481121	0857	1
KIDD WILLIAM M	MAJ	0-1019278	0258	1
KIDDER GUY S	LTC	0-0174610	1060	3
KIDDER JAMES H	B G	0-0248043	0262	3
KIDDER JAY H	MAJ	0-5301877	0568	1
KIDDER SHELDON E	MAJ	0-1552531	0562	1
KIDDER WILLIAM	MAJ	0-1555233	0861	1
KIDDEY ANDREW N	CW3	W-2153260	0264	1
KIDDIE ERLAND G	MAJ	0-1544644	1059	1
KIDDOO ROBERT W	LTC	0-1106251	1162	1
KIDNEY JOHN H	CPT	0-0164315	0638	2
KIDWELL HUBERT H	MAJ	0-0499694	0948	1
KIDWELL JOSEPH A	LTC	0-0291466	0145	2
KIDWELL WILLIAM M	LTC	0-0236098	0965	3
KIEF JOSEPH A	MAJ	0-1325996	1162	1
KIEF LEON A	LTC	0-1035040	0161	1
KIEFER EMIL C	2LT	0-1639250	0445	2
KIEFER OSCAR G	LTC	0-0231537	1057	3
KIEFFER CHARLES F	CPT	0-1171224	1160	1
KIEFFER GENE A	MAJ	0-2048671	0161	1
KIEFFER PAUL M	LTC	0-0253308	0961	3
KIEGLER DONALD F	CW3	W-2133202	1057	1
KIEHL MARVIN E	CW4	W-2145078	0167	1
KIEL HAROLD J	MAJ	0-2049815	1163	1
KIELBASA MITCHELL R	LTC	0-1011092	0361	1
KIELICH BRUNO B JR	MAJ	0-1691049	0346	2
KIELKOPF EDWARD C	COL	0-0101934	0249	2
KIELLMAN ALVIN J	MAJ	0-1342386	1262	1
KIELY RALPH J	MAJ	0-0320379	1145	2
KIENHOLZ MARFRED J	CPT	0-1311306	0148	2
KIENLY JOSEPH C JR	MAJ	0-0455688	0655	1
KIENZLE PAUL M	COL	0-0247297	0654	3
KIERAN JAMES J	1LT	0-1038028	0745	2
KIERAN JOHN F JR	1LT	0-0447442	0644	2
KIERNAN JOHN L JR	CPT	0-0890215	0248	2
KIERNAN JOHN M JR	LTC	0-1797307	0562	1
KIERNAN LOYD J	CPT	0-0151934	1055	3
KIERNAN WILLIAM T	1LT	0-0983270	0754	2
KIERULFF DUDLEY E H	1LT	0-1167496	1045	2
KIESELMANN HOWARD T	2LT	0-1825006	0544	2
KIESSLING CHARLES J	CPT	0-0902871	0745	2
KIESZEK STANLEY J	CPT	0-1305595	0747	2
KIETZMAN CARL W	COL	0-0241545	0365	3
KIEVIT DONALD J	COL	0-0391835	0363	2
KIFER JOSEPH H	LTC	0-0223945	1262	3
KIFFIN MONTE R	MAJ	0-0227065	0763	3
KIGER JACK A	CW3	W-2146320	0763	2
KIGER STANLEY W	COL	0-0292882	0160	1
KIGGEN THOMAS E JR	MAJ	0-0974480	0664	1
KIGGINS THOMAS R	LTC	0-1289095	0258	1
KIGHT ROBERT J	MAJ	0-0382997	0157	1
KIGIN LEO S	CPT	0-0204583	0254	3
KIHLGREN AXEL G	LTC	0-0507367	0263	1
KIJEK WALTER A	1LT	0-2200009	1053	2
KIJIMA MASARU	MAJ	0-1922681	1166	1
KIKER JOHN E JR	MAJ	0-0371793	0646	2
KIKER RUSSELL L	LTC	0-0109972	0948	2
KIL HENRY L	1LT	0-1305788	0346	2
KILAND THURLOW N	1LT	0-1323713	1045	2
KILBANKS LESTER H	1LT	0-1997258	0751	2
KILBOURN RUTH H	1LT	L-0900236	0346	2
KILBOURNE JAMES	LTC	0-0279256	0867	3
KILBOURNE LAWRENCE W	LTC	0-0279897	0167	3
KILBOURNE WILLIAM C	CW2	W-2213664	0867	1
KILBRIDE JOHN P	MAJ	0-1287017	0857	1
KILBURN LEW J	CPT	0-1302315	0245	2
KILCAULEY ELMER W	LTC	0-1639253	0467	1
KILCOYNE AUGUSTIN G	COL	0-0916066	1061	3

NAME	GRADE	SVC NO	DATE RET MO YR	RET CODE
KILCREASE DALLAS F	CPT	0-0285899	0145	2
KILDAY JOHN	MAJ	0-0329319	0344	2
KILDUFF FRANCIS X JR	LTC	0-1167934	0561	1
KILE JOHN P	CPT	0-1312565	0551	2
KILE MORTON F	1LT	0-1302013	0347	2
KILE RAYMOND M	1LT	0-1311522	0246	2
KILE ROBERT E	MAJ	0-0456294	0647	2
KILE ROBERT W	MAJ	0-1115558	0557	1
KILESKI FREDERICK	LTC	0-0124409	0156	3
KILEY GERALD G	LTC	0-0265373	1262	3
KILEY RICHARD H	LTC	0-1643751	1065	2
KILEY THOMAS P	MAJ	0-0947352	1163	1
KILGALLEN RAYMOND F	MAJ	0-1170803	0261	1
KILGARIFF ANDREW J	MAJ	0-1186418	0162	1
KILGO STANLEY H	MAJ	0-0578176	1062	1
KILGORE AUSTIN J	LTC	0-0130032	1051	3
KILGORE BENJAMIN M	COL	0-0457420	0846	2
KILGORE LYNDON E	CPT	0-1315947	1046	2
KILGORE MAX G	LTC	0-1579876	0866	1
KILGORE WILEY M JR	CW3	W-2147121	0167	2
KILGORE WILLIAM D	MAJ	0-0947228	0661	1
KILGORE HAROLD C	CW3	W-2142165	0863	1
KILGUS EDWARD J	1LT	0-1184247	1046	2
KILIAN JAMES F	MAJ	0-1342089	1262	1
KILKENNY BERNARD J	CW3	W-2145184	1060	1
KILKER JEROME V	CPT	0-1641467	0855	1
KILLABREW ROSS D	MAJ	0-1290766	0461	1
KILLEBREW JAMES A	CW4	W-2144121	0164	1
KILLEBREW KAZIE T	WO1	W-2150324	0668	2
KILLEBREW ROBERT J	CW2	W-2151772	0157	1
KILLEBREW ROLAND L	LTC	0-2096883	0968	1
KILLEEN FRANCIS M	MAJ	0-0964222	0162	1
KILLEEN JAMES F	1LT	0-1170029	1045	2
KILLEFFER JOHN J	MAJ	0-0329974	0246	2
KILLEN ROSS B	LTC	0-1555234	0665	1
KILLENE ELMER C JR	1LT	0-2055174	1045	2
KILLERLAIN WILLIAM C	2LT	0-1309750	0544	2
KILLETT ERNEST B	LTC	0-1017841	1263	1
KILLEY GLENN C	LTC	0-1956767	0266	2
KILLGORE ALLEN G	MAJ	0-0293223	1168	3
KILLIMETT JOHN J JR	MAJ	0-1639254	1058	1
KILLIN ARTHUR M	COL	0-0271920	0767	3
KILLIN HUGH E	LTC	0-0193996	1044	2
KILLINGER WILMA R	1LT	R-0000417	0846	1
KILLINGSWORTH L J	CW3	W-2146253	1157	1
KILLION JAMES F	CW2	W-2148865	1059	1
KILLION WILLIAM J	MAJ	0-2262191	0965	1
KILLMASTER RICHARD G	1LT	0-0919054	0145	2
KILLMER DONALD F	COL	0-0314177	0764	1
KILLOUGH CLINTON W	MAJ	0-0384943	0862	1
KILLOUGH EDWARD M	LTC	0-0138492	0648	3
KILMAN HOWARD T	LTC	0-1180571	1162	1
KILMER DONALD E	MAJ	0-4006978	0767	1
KILMER GEORGE M	MAJ	0-1182403	0163	1
KILP ALFRED J	LTC	0-0550555	0568	3
KILPATRICK ALMER W	MAJ	0-1686341	0363	1
KILPATRICK BENJAMI	MAJ	0-2051488	1062	1
KILPATRICK CHARLES	CPT	0-1106874	1159	1
KILPATRICK CHARLES J	CPT	0-0128650	0354	3
KILPATRICK CHARLES W	MAJ	0-1291133	1056	1
KILPATRICK GEORGE E	COL	0-0103632	0754	3
KILPATRICK J M	WO1	W-2126920	0546	2
KILPATRICK JAMES E	2LT	0-1825137	C446	2
KILPATRICK R V JR	LTC	0-1325500	0161	1
KILPATRICK RICHARD T	LTC	0-1291288	0656	1
KILPATRICK ROBERT L	LTC	0-1119203	0665	1
KILPATRICK ROBERT W	CW4	W-2141137	0565	1
KILPATRICK WILLIAM B	MAJ	0-1325185	0860	1
KILPATRICK WRIGHT R	CW4	W-2006176	0268	1
KILROE JOHN C	LTC	0-0136798	0945	2
KILROE ROBERT H	COL	0-0193603	0861	3
KILTS CLINTON E	CW2	W-2206409	0364	1
KILTZ CHESTER V	1LT	0-0373931	0244	2
KIM ALBERT K H	CPT	0-1688408	0755	2
KIM ERVIE	CPT	0-1318675	0747	2
KIM PETER	MAJ	0-2024527	1164	1
KIM WALTER Y W	CW2	W-3400077	0167	2
KIM YOUN P	LTC	0-0544054	0661	1
KIM YOUNG D	MAJ	0-0956856	0166	1
KIMBALL BLANCHE	1LT	N-0702255	1046	1
KIMBALL CHANDLEF S	MAJ	0-0281032	0968	3
KIMBALL CHASE	CPT	0-0217317	0262	3
KIMBALL EDGAR R	LTC	0-0902988	0266	3
KIMBALL ELBERT T	COL	0-0151255	0864	2
KIMBALL GEORGE H JR	LTC	0-0388444	1061	1
KIMBALL HUNTER H	MAJ	0-0129547	0347	2
KIMBALL JOHN W	LTC	0-0176334	0361	3
KIMBALL LESLIE G	CW3	W-2146988	0764	1
KIMBALL MILTON S	LTC	0-0211727	0651	3
KIMBALL RALPH L	CPT	0-0227778	0646	2
KIMBALL RAYMOND W	CPT	0-1003565	0555	1
KIMBALL RICHARD V	LTC	0-1012288	0761	1
KIMBALL THOMAS F	1LT	0-1040255	1145	2
KIMBELL JACK G	1LT	0-0355000	0946	2
KIMBLE FRANCIS E	CPT	0-0371728	0661	1
KIMBLE HORTON E	CPT	0-0401617	0747	2
KIMBLE JOHN M	MAJ	0-0244204	0765	3
KIMBLE RALPH A	COL	0-0118168	0953	3
KIMBLE WILLIAM A	LTC	0-0158891	0-51	3
KIMBLE WILLIAM D	LTC	0-0250134	0746	2
KIMBRELL JAMES R	CPT	0-1337442	0358	2
KIMBROUGH JAMES D	CW2	W-2124224	0955	1
KIMBROUGH JOSEPH O	MAJ	0-2036818	0466	1
KIMBROUGH JOSEPH F	MAJ	0-2005278	0760	1
KIMBROUGH ORMAN L	CPT	0-1299754	0450	2
KIME JAMES S	CPT	0-0318050	0246	2
KIME ROBERT C	1LT	0-0393656	1044	2
KIMEL RACHEL T	MAJ	N-0726269	0561	1
KIMELDORF ABRAHAM E	LTC	0-0345686	1068	3
KIMLIN DONALD W	MAJ	0-1584461	0261	1
KIMMEL GEORGE C	LTC	0-0306802	1060	1
KIMMEL JOHN E	MAJ	0-0353821	0367	3
KIMMEL KEED B	MAJ	0-0402023	0860	1
KIMMEL WILLIAM J	MAJ	0-0275550	0758	3
KIMMERLE FOREST E	LTC	0-0360746	0267	3
KIMMONS NEIL C	2LT	0-1054284	0645	2
KIMPEL EDWARD W	1LT	0-1317401	1046	2
KIMPTON EDWARD K	MAJ	0-0118167	0654	3
KIMSEY CHARLES L	COL	0-0373117	0866	1
KIMURA JIROS	MAJ	0-0426755	0446	2
KINARD CHARLES M	LTC	0-0226778	0546	2
KINARD ETHEL S	LTC	0-1293423	0263	1
KINARD LYMAN V	CPT	0-1845910	0546	2
KINARD ULYSSES G	CW3	W-2144217	0361	1
KINARD WILLIAM C	CW4	W-2113636	0266	1
KINBACK GEORGE E JR	MAJ	0-1937112	1168	1
KINCADE GEORGE L	CW2	W-2147476	0860	1
KINCAID CLEMENT J	LTC	0-0241583	1060	3
KINCAID HENRY C	MAJ	0-1640628	0157	1
KINCAID JAMES L	B G	0-0522288	0648	3
KINCAID JOHN I	MAJ	0-0249506	1066	3
KINCAID ORESTUS J	1LT	0-0164033	0936	1
KINCER ALFRED L JR	LTC	0-1101905	0462	1
KINCHELOE JAMES M	CPT	0-0200812	0948	1
KIND WALTER A	LTC	0-0345554	1168	3
KINDALL ROBERT A	1LT	0-1574276	1058	1
KINDELL JOHN W	LTC	0-0187601	1054	3
KINDER CHARLES H	LTC	0-0522097	0847	1
KINDER CHARLES W	CPT	0-2017554	0457	1
KINDER DONALD L	MAJ	0-2014159	1063	2
KINDER HAROLD	MAJ	0-0247546	0567	3
KINDER JACOB F	2LT	0-0939662	0848	2
KINDER SIDNEY R	WO1	W-2121007	0254	1
KINDER THURMAN A	COL	0-0268363	1046	2
KINDICK CHARLES M	MAJ	0-1055884	0164	1
KINDRED FRANK H	MAJ	0-0479907	0147	1
KINDRED WENDELL H	LTC	0-0510909	0347	2
KINEHAN VINCENT W	CW3	W-2147353	1064	1
KINER GEORGE A	CPT	0-2102902	1062	1
KINERK ROBERT L	CPT	0-1296866	0546	2
KING AARON L	MAJ	0-0114565	1052	3
KING ALBERT	CPT	0-1555236	1042	1
KING ALBERT B	LTC	0-0248154	1047	2
KING ALBERT K	COL	0-0415391	C461	1
KING ALBERT T	CPT	0-0235591	1265	3
KING ALFRED F	COL	0-0166704	0750	3
KING ALLYN P	CPT	0-0223333	0153	1
KING ALTON J	MAJ	0-2043185	0765	1
KING ANDRE F	COL	0-0117122	0252	3
KING ARCHIE	LTC	0-0472390	0968	3
KING ARLEN J	LTC	0-0493368	0455	1
KING ARTHUR G	COL	0-0273830	0966	1
KING ARTHUR P	1LT	0-1061441	1046	2
KING BAIRD A	LTC	0-1181326	0762	2
KING BEAUREGARD	CPT	0-0412501	0849	2
KING BENJAMIN F	MAJ	0-2008573	0263	1
KING BENJAMIN J	MAJ	0-0195095	0-51	3
KING BERNARD F	CPT	0-1767474	0348	2
KING BRON T	CW2	W-2208998	0865	1
KING BRUCE R	COL	0-0247245	0758	2
KING BYRON B	LTC	0-1314299	1062	1
KING BYRON F	LTC	0-0270436	0467	3
KING BYRON K	LTC	0-0300469	0359	1
KING CALEB J JR	COL	0-0238587	0666	3
KING CARLIALE P	MAJ	0-0291067	0868	3
KING CARLOS E	CW2	W-2213518	0566	1
KING CARSON H	CPT	0-1010366	0147	2
KING CECIL W	2LT	0-1298716	0744	2
KING CHARLES	LTC	0-1116386	0866	1
KING CHARLES A	1LT	0-1331519	0646	2
KING CHARLES F	MAJ	0-1554573	0361	1
KING CHARLES H	CW3	W-2149075	0165	1
KING CHARLES W	CW2	W-2103088	0750	1
KING CHARLEY L	1LT	0-1826209	0255	1
KING CHESTER L	1LT	0-1013965	0644	2
KING CLAUDE E	CW4	W-2146965	0268	1
KING CLINTON A	LTC	0-0453065	0758	1
KING DALTON L JR	CPT	0-2023777	1057	1
KING DAN W	CPT	0-0327451	1143	2
KING DANIEL P	COL	0-0196319	0761	3
KING DELBERT S	LTC	0-0237486	1263	3
KING DONALD M	MAJ	0-0988555	0668	1
KING DOWELL B	CPT	0-1919207	0363	1
KING E B JR	1LT	0-1306598	0645	2
KING EARL	CPT	0-1922677	0563	1
KING EARL C	MAJ	0-0502357	0555	1
KING EARL E	CPT	0-0220682	1057	3
KING EDMOND H	LTC	0-0369687	0860	1
KING EDWARD F	WO1	W-2111721	0958	1
KING EDWARD V	MAJ	0-0475815	0846	1
KING EDWIN D	COL	0-0254756	1164	3
KING EDWIN H	CPT	0-0111537	1054	3
KING EDWIN H	2LT	0-1548885	0843	2
KING ELIZABETH	1LT	N-0772488	0646	1
KING ELLIS R	COL	0-0107618	1045	2
KING ELMO C	CW3	W-2144849	1262	1
KING ELMO R	CPT	0-2033206	0361	1
KING ELZAH D	MAJ	0-0504180	0761	1
KING ERNEST G	CW3	C-2262345	0557	1
KING ERNEST L	MAJ	0-0360673	0667	3
KING ERNEST Q	COL	0-0299340	1265	3
KING ESTUS R	CW2	W-2211444	0465	1
KING FRANK W	CW3	W-2148738	0561	1
KING FREDDIE L	CW4	W-2141338	1167	1
KING GEORGE B	LTC	0-0408242	1159	3
KING GEORGE B	1LT	0-1106253	0362	3
KING GEORGE J	1LT	0-1822584	0246	2
KING GEORGE W	LTC	0-1294436	0963	1
KING GERALD C	LTC	0-1845195	0365	1
KING GERALD V SR	CW3	W-2210097	0968	1
KING GERALDINE	1LT	N-0770059	0247	1
KING GERARD W	MAJ	0-0179302	1053	3
KING GILBERT W	LTC	0-0269616	1061	1
KING GORDON A	LTC	0-1587369	0962	1
KING GRENVILLE	CPT	0-5531426	C468	2
KING HAROLD C	LTC	0-0371346	1060	1
KING HARRY L	MAJ	0-0245294	0967	3
KING HELEN	MAJ	N-0736083	0361	2
KING HENRY A	COL	0-0240214	0965	3
KING HERBERT G	COL	0-0288120	1160	3
KING HERBERT S	CPT	0-0476332	1047	2
KING HIRAM I	1LT	0-1285603	0448	2
KING HUBERT H	CW4	W-2142104	0666	1
KING HUGH J	CPT	0-2008509	0559	1
KING ILENE C	MAJ	N-0765496	0765	2
KING ISAAC R JR	COL	0-1165888	0865	1
KING JAMES A	CPT	0-1010001	0847	1
KING JAMES D	1LT	0-1015255	0545	2
KING JAMES E JR	MAJ	0-1920267	1264	1
KING JAMES F	LTC	0-1309071	0664	1
KING JAMES F JR	2LT	0-1031253	1044	2
KING JAMES J	CW3	W-2144329	1163	1
KING JAMES T	MAJ	0-0378105	0845	2
KING JENKINS O	2LT	0-2035428	0645	2
KING JOHN C	CPT	0-0246617	0161	3
KING JOHN D	MAJ	0-1013190	0161	1
KING JOHN H	1LT	0-0488536	0745	2
KING JOHN H	LTC	0-1299755	0561	1
KING JOHN H	CW2	W-2150885	0663	1
KING JOHN J	CW4	W-2144269	1061	1
KING JOHN L	1LT	0-1011993	1145	2
KING JOHN L	CPT	0-1052425	0847	2
KING JOHN M	COL	0-0346800	1263	1
KING JOHN O JR	1LT	0-0485932	1045	2
KING JOHN P	CPT	0-0255706	0967	3
KING JOHN P	COL	0-0474073	0859	1
KING JOHN P	MAJ	0-2043172	0668	3
KING JOHN R	LTC	0-1294145	0262	1
KING JOHN S	MAJ	0-0354919	1046	2
KING JOHN T	COL	0-0231533	0250	3
KING JOHN W	LTC	0-1284714	0965	1
KING JOSEPH D B	CPT	0-0474522	0447	2
KING JOSEPH M R	CW3	W-2142863	1160	1
KING KEITH D	1LT	0-1309072	0346	2
KING KENNETH E	1LT	0-1316062	0645	2
KING LAWRENCE A	MAJ	0-1644491	0961	1
KING LAWRENCE G	COL	0-0196305	0449	3
KING LEO L	MAJ	0-0332107	0268	3
KING LEONARD	CW3	W-2150717	0765	2
KING LEONARD B	1LT	0-0488817	0844	2
KING LESLIE R	COL	0-0270986	0367	3
KING LESTER G	MAJ	0-0242975	0849	3
KING LEW	1LT	0-1945182	0945	2
KING LEWIS J	CW4	W-2117178	0261	2
KING LUDLOW	LTC	0-0278463	0945	2
KING LYLE T	LTC	0-0304942	0347	2
KING MARTIN L	1LT	0-1313501	0745	2
KING MARY D	CPT	N-0757320	0249	2
KING MAURICE E	LTC	0-0322622	0361	3
KING MERLE K	MAJ	0-1925524	0866	1
KING MILTON M	MAJ	0-0260005	1267	3
KING MOSES	COL	0-0146245	0648	3
KING MOSES G	MAJ	0-0461358	1146	1
KING NATHANIEL	MAJ	0-0320596	0361	1
KING NICHOLAS	CW3	W-2150882	1262	1
KING NOAH G	MAJ	0-1301650	1160	1
KING NORMAN D	COL	0-0203021	0761	3
KING NORMAN J	LTC	0-1894740	1067	2
KING ORVAL A	CW2	W-2152268	0263	1
KING ORVILLE R	1LT	0-1104915	0745	2
KING OSCAR	COL	0-1289591	0157	1
KING OTIS W	2LT	0-2040952	0252	2
KING PAUL H	CW4	W-2101930	0560	1
KING PAULINE E	1LT	N-0729273	0946	1
KING PHILIP F	COL	0-0262737	0159	3
KING RALPH C	CW4	W-2149342	1068	1
KING RALPH J	COL	0-0255695	1065	3
KING RANDOLPH C	MAJ	0-2042879	0760	1
KING RAYMOND R JR	CW2	W-2147586	1064	1
KING RAYMOND W	MAJ	0-1540868	0164	1

NAME	GRADE	SVC NO	DATE RET MO YR	RET CODE
KING RICHARD M	CPT	0-0299227	1163	3
KING RICHARD M JR	LTC	0-0482349	0262	1
KING ROBERT B	CW2	W-2144070	1265	1
KING ROBERT H	MAJ	0-1317853	0661	1
KING ROBERT J	CPT	0-1321917	0956	2
KING ROBERT V	CW3	W-2145279	0960	1
KING ROBERT W	1LT	0-1167336	0552	2
KING ROBERT W	MAJ	0-1259421	1147	2
KING ROBERT W	CW3	RW-2149303	0264	1
KING ROLLIN W	MAJ	0-0403260	0257	2
KING ROY H	CW4	W-2147599	1268	1
KING RUFUS G	CPT	0-0206721	1163	3
KING RUFUS K	CW2	W-2210523	0264	1
KING RUSSELL W	COL	0-0244102	0647	2
KING S EDWARD	COL	0-0256728	1060	3
KING SAMUEL L	LTC	0-0450038	0560	1
KING SAMUEL R	MAJ	0-0555570	1167	1
KING SEYMOUR D	MAJ	0-0970136	0163	1
KING SHERMONT L	CW3	W-2148004	0862	1
KING SLOAN	CW2	W-2146072	0757	1
KING STANHOPE H JR	LTC	0-0290313	0257	1
KING STARR M	LTC	0-0124788	0355	3
KING STEPHEN H	MAJ	0-0353861	0346	2
KING THEODORE R	LTC	0-0261274	0257	1
KING THOMAS B	MAJ	0-1533109	1047	2
KING THOMAS C	1LT	0-1316559	0845	2
KING THOMAS F	MAJ	0-2046475	0454	2
KING THOMAS J	CPT	0-1291834	0146	2
KING THOMAS R	CW4	W-2002746	1165	1
KING TOMMY E	MAJ	0-0901027	1041	1
KING VERNE D	MAJ	0-2103004	0365	1
KING WALLACE A	LTC	0-1547987	0968	1
KING WALLACE N	MAJ	0-1056433	0264	1
KING WALTER P	MAJ	0-0148505	0648	3
KING WARREN L	2LT	0-5534248	1265	2
KING WILBUR B	LTC	0-0195329	0360	3
KING WILLIAM	MAJ	0-1796807	1060	1
KING WILLIAM A	MAJ	0-0471767	0353	1
KING WILLIAM C	CPT	0-0294839	0955	3
KING WILLIAM D	LTC	0-1944720	0562	1
KING WILLIAM E	COL	0-0268277	1060	3
KING WILLIAM E	MAJ	0-1037577	0164	1
KING WILLIAM F	MAJ	0-1306857	0957	1
KING WILLIAM G	LTC	0-1014973	0463	1
KING WILLIAM H	LTC	0-1323714	0163	2
KING WILLIAM H	CW2	W-2148579	0264	1
KING WILLIAM H JR	COL	0-0404532	0465	1
KING WILLIAM J	COL	0-0443105	1061	3
KING WILLIAM J	LTC	0-1284156	0666	1
KING WILLIAM M	LTC	0-0300825	1047	2
KING WILLIAM M	1LT	0-0447036	0146	2
KING WILLIAM P	LTC	0-1595624	1262	1
KING WILLIAM R	LTC	0-1794755	1263	1
KING WILLIAM S	CPT	0-0387692	1045	2
KING WILLIAM T JR	LTC	0-1035299	1266	1
KING WILLIAM W	CW3	W-2144087	0660	1
KING WILLIE D	CW2	W-2150128	0262	1
KING WILLIS J	MAJ	0-1284200	0847	2
KING WOODROW W	1LT	0-0460570	0244	2
KINGDOM MARK W	LTC	0-1011134	0860	1
KINGERY DANIEL R	LTC	0-0172999	1158	3
KINGHORN ALICE D	MAJ	N-0724887	0168	3
KINGMAN JOHN P	LTC	0-0901793	0666	3
KINGMAN WARREN A	MAJ	0-0344722	0467	3
KINGREY LAWRENCE G	CW2	W-2210313	1063	1
KINGRY WILLIAM F	MAJ	0-1826240	1060	1
KINGSBURY FRANK E	CW2	W-2147819	0760	1
KINGSBURY HOWARD T	LTC	0-0229837	1064	3
KINGSBURY JOHN B	MAJ	0-1634971	1050	2
KINGSBURY KENNETH R	MAJ	0-0509613	0348	2
KINGSBURY LEONARD L	LTC	0-0216898	0763	3
KINGSBURY RALPH N	CPT	0-0266560	1262	3
KINGSFORD CARLETON L	MAJ	0-0252634	0552	3
KINGSLAND FRANK C	LTC	0-0142709	0856	3
KINGSLAND LAWRENCE C	COL	0-0183836	0648	3

NAME	GRADE	SVC NO	DATE RET MO YR	RET CODE
KINGSLEY EDWIN M	CPT	0-0274326	0943	2
KINGSLEY GEORGE R	LTC	0-0490302	0466	3
KINGSLEY JOHN G	LTC	0-1013199	0462	1
KINGSLEY NEIL S	LTC	0-0166219	0549	3
KINGSTEDT CHARLES M	LTC	0-1594212	0462	1
KINGSTON CLARENCE R	MAJ	0-0241311	1165	3
KINGSTON FRANK M	LTC	0-1081074	0662	1
KINGSTON THOMAS J	MAJ	0-2025126	0863	2
KINKEMA ALFRED C	LTC	0-0229222	0159	3
KINKENNON OMAR A	LTC	0-1055055	1162	1
KINKLE FRANKLIN S	LTC	0-1314787	0564	1
KINKOR ROBERT C	COL	0-0355126	0468	1
KINLEY JAMES D	LTC	0-0311780	1064	3
KINLEY JOSEPH F	1LT	0-1318902	0158	1
KINLEY NORMAN J	COL	0-0396938	0767	1
KINLOCH JAMES P	CW2	W-2146338	0762	1
KINMAN RUSSELL B	MAJ	0-0330466	0262	3
KINMONTH CHARLES R	MAJ	0-2033050	0561	1
KINNAMAN JOHN JR	CW2	W-2144468	0461	1
KINNAN JOHN D	LTC	0-2262863	0868	1
KINNE MILTON J	CPT	0-1043383	0465	2
KINNER EDGAR L	LTC	0-0376277	1262	1
KINNER ROBERT K	LTC	0-0266520	0563	3
KINNER STEPHEN G	MAJ	0-1325132	0664	1
KINNETT MAURICE E	CPT	0-1890141	0463	1
KINNEY CLARENCE P	MAJ	0-0292398	1054	3
KINNEY DANIEL J	CW4	W-2107117	0762	1
KINNEY EDWARD J	LTC	0-1641470	1062	2
KINNEY GEORGE F	CPT	0-1304398	1156	2
KINNEY HARRY A	LTC	0-1339450	0666	1
KINNEY JAMES L	CPT	0-0113953	1051	3
KINNEY JAMES W	2LT	0-1315992	0444	2
KINNEY JOHN E	COL	0-0312950	0158	1
KINNEY JOSEPH C	MAJ	0-2026469	1164	1
KINNEY JOSEPH M	LTC	0-2047389	0768	1
KINNEY KENNETH K	1LT	0-0113952	1056	3
KINNEY LAWRENCE E	MAJ	0-0453126	1060	1
KINNEY ROY W	CW2	W-2110459	0450	1
KINNEY WALTER W	COL	0-0366264	0859	1
KINNEY WILLIAM H	LTC	0-1103732	0664	1
KINNEY WILLIAM R	MAJ	0-0979906	0764	1
KINNISON LEWIS A JR	LTC	0-0842126	0968	1
KINNS WILMOT J	LTC	0-1174615	0865	1
KINOSHITA ROBERT S	MAJ	0-0258299	0646	2
KINSAUL WALLACE B	CPT	0-1016265	1060	1
KINSAUL WILLIAM W JR	CPT	0-1589953	1047	2
KINSEL KENNETH G	MAJ	0-1031818	0261	2
KINSELLA JOHN J	LTC	0-1577428	1054	1
KINSER ROBERT L	MAJ	0-4005461	0968	1
KINSEY CHARLES H	LTC	0-0410050	0966	1
KINSEY FREDERICK	2LT	0-1323329	1045	2
KINSEY GEORGE M	LTC	0-0905533	1065	3
KINSEY GEORGE W SR	CW3	W-2144792	0762	1
KINSEY JOSEPH D	CPT	0-0524829	0545	2
KINSEY PAUL S	1LT	0-2055832	0645	2
KINSEY ROBERT S JR	1LT	0-1315948	0845	2
KINSEY ROY E	MAJ	0-0339572	1045	2
KINSINGER JAMES R	MAJ	0-1552532	1060	1
KINSINGER JOSEPH	CPT	0-1303903	1159	1
KINSLEY WILLIAM H	MAJ	0-0984064	0168	1
KINSMAN JOHN M	MAJ	0-2019330	1161	1
KINSOLVING HERBERT L	LTC	0-0909563	0667	3
KINSON ARTHUR E	CW4	W-2144228	0868	1
KINTER MARY A	LTC	N-0763032	0163	1
KINTLER FRANK C	LTC	0-0918942	1067	3
KINTNER FLOYD M	1LT	0-1293972	1145	2
KINTNER ROBERT E	LTC	0-0420703	0944	2
KINTZ JOHN S	LTC	0-0321514	0955	2
KINZER HUGH R	MAJ	0-0249165	0362	3
KINZER OSBORN A	LTC	0-0229928	0863	3
KINZER WALTER L	MAJ	0-0228749	0364	3
KINZIE CHARLES N	1LT	0-1307708	1044	2
KINZIE DONALD H	CW2	W-2130727	1060	1
KINZIE DONALD R	LTC	0-0242921	0861	1
KINZIE JOSEPH R	LTC	0-0455334	1062	1

NAME	GRADE	SVC NO	DATE RET MO YR	RET CODE
KINZIE JULIAN M	1LT	0-1000862	0150	2
KINZIE ROBERT D	MAJ	0-0966925	0867	1
KINZLER RICHARD [illegible]	LTC	0-1171175	0255	1
KIPE OMAR W	CW3	W-2208013	0668	1
KIPLINGER JULES [illegible]	COL	0-1317873	0565	3
KIPP ARTHUR W	CPT	0-1101526	0161	1
KIPP WILLIAM A	LTC	0-0532482	0865	3
KIPPENBROCK MICHAEL	LTC	0-0502234	1063	3
KIPPS HAROLD F	CPT	0-0938178	0156	2
KIPPS HENRY F	LTC	0-1103736	0665	1
KIPPS LEWIS C	1LT	0-1114791	1064	2
KIPPS THOMAS G	1LT	0-1648336	1146	2
KIRBY ALEXANDER	COL	0-0212967	1055	1
KIRBY AUGUSTUS V	MAJ	0-0299601	0468	3
KIRBY CHARLES R	MAJ	0-0223615	0762	3
KIRBY COURTNEY F	CPT	0-0387124	1045	2
KIRBY DARIOUS F	LTC	0-1173333	0165	1
KIRBY EDWARD M	COL	0-0245267	0766	3
KIRBY EDWARD P	1LT	0-1692512	0646	2
KIRBY EUGENE B	LTC	0-1581869	0762	1
KIRBY EUGENE W	LTC	0-1794818	0962	1
KIRBY FERNANDER	LTC	0-0455721	0858	1
KIRBY FRANK L	MAJ	0-0412764	0450	2
KIRBY GEORGE O	CPT	0-1332174	0563	1
KIRBY GORDON I	MAJ	0-0277136	0551	3
KIRBY GRANVILLE JR	MAJ	0-1049928	1265	1
KIRBY HARLEY T	LTC	0-0370111	0657	1
KIRBY HILLIARD F	1LT	0-1014245	0146	2
KIRBY JAMES H	MAJ	0-1685666	0464	1
KIRBY JEFFERSON JR	MAJ	0-1297365	0561	1
KIRBY JOHN L	1LT	0-0397817	0451	2
KIRBY KENNETH C	MAJ	0-0936175	0163	1
KIRBY MARION A	2LT	0-5875010	0161	2
KIRBY NORMAN L	LTC	0-0547547	1068	1
KIRBY RANDALL G	CW2	W-2110516	0145	2
KIRBY RUSSELL	CPT	0-1284157	0152	2
KIRCH ALBERT M	LTC	0-0301424	1068	1
KIRCHER EDWIN JR	1LT	0-2006067	1046	2
KIRCHHOFER MELVIN L	LTC	0-0297304	0463	3
KIRCHHOFF WILLIAM A	LTC	0-1108074	0161	1
KIRCHNER JOHN F	CW3	W-2149445	0665	1
KIRCHNER LOUIS R	CPT	0-0473029	0546	2
KIRCHNER MARVIN M	MAJ	0-1018543	1160	1
KIRCHNER PAUL C	MAJ	0-1174616	0262	1
KIRCHNER PHILLIP N	1LT	0-1030993	0246	2
KIRCHNER WILLIAM R	LTC	0-0287775	0856	1
KIRDAHY GABRIEL T	COL	0-1574901	0268	1
KIRK CLEVELAND JR	MAJ	0-2010502	0161	1
KIRK DONOVAN	LTC	0-0475382	1151	1
KIRK EUGENE P	CPT	0-1319509	0547	2
KIRK FRANK J	COL	0-0327199	0561	2
KIRK FREDERIC D	LTC	0-0413479	0860	1
KIRK FREDERICK	MAJ	0-1004351	0163	1
KIRK GENE	LTC	0-1646319	1262	1
KIRK ISIDOR L	1LT	0-1560215	0648	2
KIRK JESSE K	COL	0-0205990	1160	3
KIRK JOSEPH L	LTC	0-1634973	1166	1
KIRK KAY K	CPT	0-0498018	1044	2
KIRK LEWIS H JR	LTC	0-0396958	0560	2
KIRK NORRIS J	COL	0-0261745	0664	3
KIRK PATRICK J	MAJ	0-0464918	0849	2
KIRK PAUL G	COL	0-0201090	1064	3
KIRK ROBERT J III	LTC	0-0535968	0763	1
KIRK RUFUS H	1LT	0-1645111	0146	2
KIRK THOMAS M	COL	0-0229724	0465	3
KIRK THURSTON S	2LT	0-2047390	0345	2
KIRK WILLIAM F	MAJ	0-0260453	0246	2
KIRK WYATT W	2LT	0-0924500	0844	2
KIRKEL SIDNEY	LTC	0-1550633	0865	1
KIRKENDALL CLARK F	LTC	0-0225984	0962	3
KIRKHAM BEUFORD C	MAJ	0-0490177	0247	1
KIRKHAM CHARLES A JR	MAJ	0-1933583	1168	1
KIRKHAM HENRY P	COL	0-0167010	0648	3
KIRKHAM JACK V	2LT	0-2009585	1158	1
KIRKHAM JOHN S	CW3	W-2143688	0557	1

NAME	GRADE	SVC NO	DATE RET MO YR	RET CODE
KIRKHART ANDREW A	MAJ	0-1288505	0955	2
KIRKLAND [illegible] F	CW3	W-2149656	0761	1
KIRKLAND [illegible]	CW3	W-2145560	0955	1
KIRKLAND ROBERT H	MAJ	0-0475303	0550	1
KIRKLAND GEORGE A	2LT	0-1081298	0943	2
KIRKLAND GEORGE W	MAJ	0-1590109	0165	1
KIRKLAND HENRY F	CPT	0-0470967	0745	1
KIRKLAND JAMES A	LTC	0-0232998	1065	2
KIRKLAND JAMES C	1LT	0-0455313	1051	1
KIRKLAND JAMES G	MAJ	0-0415653	0145	2
KIRKLAND LAURANCE G	COL	0-0260054	0168	1
KIRKLAND LONNIE N JR	LTC	0-1289593	0267	1
KIRKLAND PARKS	CPT	0-1328706	0457	1
KIRKLEY DANIEL C	LTC	0-0235196	1265	3
KIRKLEY JIMMIE J	CW3	W-3150299	0667	1
KIRKMAN CLAUDE R	CPT	0-0477447	0650	1
KIRKMAN PAUL H	MAJ	0-0445581	0960	2
KIRKMAN VAUGHN E	MAJ	0-0570991	0764	1
KIRKPATRICK CHASE P	LTC	0-0252498	0144	2
KIRKPATRICK DAVID V	COL	0-0392561	0661	1
KIRKPATRICK EARL R	LTC	0-1317174	1164	1
KIRKPATRICK FRANCIS	LTC	0-0910990	0968	3
KIRKPATRICK FRANK B	CPT	0-0419481	0646	2
KIRKPATRICK H O	CPT	0-0270628	0354	2
KIRKPATRICK H E	CPT	0-0529844	0746	2
KIRKPATRICK HENRY	COL	0-1576238	0764	2
KIRKPATRICK JAMES E	LTC	0-0489038	1062	1
KIRKPATRICK JOSEPH D	LTC	0-1574277	0461	1
KIRKPATRICK MARK A	MAJ	0-1824761	0365	1
KIRKPATRICK MARTIN D	LTC	0-0262380	0866	3
KIRKPATRICK MAXWELL	MAJ	0-1691470	0759	1
KIRKPATRICK R A JR	MAJ	0-1643759	1160	2
KIRKPATRICK R E	LTC	0-0450184	0655	1
KIRKPATRICK ROBERT H	LTC	0-1285958	0868	1
KIRKPATRICK T L JR	MAJ	0-0336737	1045	2
KIRKPATRICK WILLIAM	LTC	0-0419138	0861	1
KIRKS HENRY G	CPT	0-0439811	1148	1
KIRKSEY FRED	CPT	0-0966617	0259	1
KIRKSEY JAMES W JR	LTC	0-0290140	1067	3
KIRKSEY LOUIS A	CPT	0-0412898	0746	2
KIRKWOOD CLETUS F	MAJ	0-0976570	0166	1
KIRKWOOD GLADYS	CPT	L-0801499	0858	2
KIRKWOOD MAYWOOD	2LT	0-1913793	0942	1
KIRKWOOD ROBERT H	COL	0-0192304	0363	3
KIRLAND ERNEST J	CW4	W-2120835	0858	1
KIRLIN EUGENE D	MAJ	0-1012356	0161	1
KIRLIN LINDEN K	MAJ	0-2096955	1268	1
KIRN HENRY JR	CPT	0-0291946	0847	2
KIRSCH DONALD H	1LT	0-0538616	0845	2
KIRSCH MYRON R	2LT	0-1535011	1144	2
KIRSCH RUSSELL O	LTC	0-0533639	0964	1
KIRSCHBAUM DAVID	MAJ	0-1285604	0961	1
KIRSCHBAUM WILLIAM F	LTC	0-1342190	1167	1
KIRSCHNER JOHN G	LTC	0-0410475	1160	1
KIRSCHNER KENNETH B	LTC	0-0451132	0764	1
KIRSH OLGA D	1LT	N-0761800	0746	1
KIRSHBAUM IRVING J	MAJ	0-0524982	0450	2
KIRSHE HENRY A	1LT	0-4034336	0658	2
KIRSTEIN MELVIN B	CPT	0-0485090	0446	2
KIRSTIEN MARTIN C	CW4	W-2002732	1163	1
KIRT NORMAN F	CPT	0-2035112	1145	2
KIRTHLINK TOWNSEND J	LTC	0-1298075	0262	1
KIRTLEY BUFORD S	LTC	0-0365407	0846	2
KIRTLEY GROVER C JR	LTC	0-1035504	0864	1
KIRTLEY ROBERT D	CW3	RW-2206024	0866	1
KIRTON GRAHAM G	LTC	0-0451324	0559	1
KIRVEN LAMAR L	MAJ	0-1951226	1162	1
KIRWAN FRANCIS M JR	LTC	0-1105575	0962	1
KIRWIN FRANCIS M	MAJ	0-1825477	0661	1
KISCH NICHOLAS M	MAJ	0-1950740	1163	1
KISE CHARLES O	COL	0-0343557	1265	1
KISELYK JOHN	MAJ	0-0384332	0259	1
KISER ADOLPHUS G	1LT	0-1303435	0444	2
KISER CARLTON H	1LT	0-1288398	0645	2
KISER FREDERICK	CPT	0-0347297	1057	1

NAME	GRADE	SVC NO	DATE RET MO YR	RET CODE
KISER GEORGE F	1LT	0-0372178	1144	2
KISER HOWARD M	MAJ	0-1293793	0263	1
KISER ROBERT J	1LT	0-1012421	1051	1
KISER WILLIAM M	2LT	0-1316162	0545	2
KISER WILLIAM N	MAJ	0-0945111	0163	1
KISH FRANK S	CW4	W-2151303	0966	1
KISH GEORGE F	MAJ	0-2030475	0166	1
KISH HELEN L	2LT	N-0767933	0944	1
KISH IVAN J	LTC	0-0290152	0664	3
KISH PETER J	MAJ	0-1299591	0957	1
KISH STEPHEN A	LTC	0-1552309	0564	1
KISH WALTER C	CPT	0-0366134	1143	2
KISHIDA TATSUO	CW3	W-2144191	0764	1
KISHTER HARRY L	WO1	W-2128827	0348	1
KISINGER CHARLES E	CPT	0-1292194	1154	2
KISINGER HOWARD J JR	MAJ	0-1825544	0362	2
KISLIK ROBERT F	CPT	0-1583216	0246	2
KISLOW EDWARD E	CW2	W-0900991	1147	1
KISOR LORENZ	LTC	0-0133026	0158	3
KISPERT HENRY F	MAJ	0-2029753	0864	1
KISSAMETTER MARTHA K	MAJ	N-0742480	0662	1
KISSEL VICTOR T	CPT	0-0521722	0647	2
KISSELL DEWITT C	CPT	0-0345412	1045	2
KISSICK JAMES W	CW3	W-2136601	1165	1
KISSILEFF ALFRED	LTC	0-0319315	0968	3
KISSINGER LESTER G	MAJ	0-2010780	0961	1
KISSINGER MARVIN S	CPT	0-2011203	0757	1
KISSINGER PAUL L	MAJ	0-2262509	0366	1
KISTER CLAUDE V	LTC	0-0284570	1262	3
KISTLER NORMAN L	COL	0-0241336	0766	3
KITAGAWA KIYOSHI	MAJ	0-0336256	1163	1
KITARJGERS GEORGE K	LTC	0-0986376	0768	1
KITCHELL ROBERT	MAJ	0-0202403	1058	3
KITCHEN BETHUEL M	COL	0-0310568	0657	1
KITCHEN CORTEZ A	LTC	0-0358416	0647	2
KITCHEN ELDON L	LTC	0-1533110	0761	1
KITCHEN GEORGE H	COL	0-0406699	1166	1
KITCHEN H DEAN	MAJ	0-0178498	0761	3
KITCHEN JAMES K	LTC	0-1594279	1060	1
KITCHEN JAMES W	LTC	0-1287194	1160	1
KITCHEN ROBERT E	CPT	0-0349480	0268	3
KITCHEN WILLIAM W	COL	0-0291804	1262	1
KITCHENS JOHN G	CPT	0-0352138	0946	2
KITCHENS MILTON G	CPT	0-2262106	1053	2
KITLEY DAYTON V	MAJ	0-0295683	0968	3
KITNER EDWIN F	MAJ	0-0983435	0561	1
KITSELMAN CHARLES H	COL	0-0125121	0855	3
KITSELMAN HENRY A JR	LTC	0-0376003	0859	1
KITSONAS NICHOLAS T	LTC	0-1047612	0866	1
KITT GUSTAV A	CW4	W-2106186	0962	1
KITT WILLIAM	MAJ	0-2000135	0662	1
KITTEL WILLIAM	LTC	0-0235907	0664	3
KITTELL ROY B	CPT	0-0983419	0761	1
KITTELSAA IRVIN	CPT	0-0504451	0750	1
KITTERMAN HOWARD I	CPT	0-1017267	0656	1
KITTERMAN JOHN W	CW2	W-2101935	0648	1
KITTINGER EDWARD R	CPT	0-0165827	1051	3
KITTINGER ROBERT L	LTC	0-0454221	0765	1
KITTLE KENNETH W	CPT	0-1315003	0646	2
KITTLE OTIS A	MAJ	0-0236846	0166	3
KITTLE WALTER F	MAJ	0-0472540	0146	2
KITTLE WILLIAM R	MAJ	0-0917757	0346	2
KITTO LELAND H	CPT	0-1306286	0547	2
KITTRELL THOMAS S	COL	0-0183982	1158	3
KITTS ANDREW F	CW3	W-2150964	0365	1
KITTS HOWARD L	LTC	0-0919495	0364	3
KITZELMAN JAMES W	LTC	0-0488938	0954	1
KIVETT DAVID F	CPT	0-0353485	0146	2
KIVETT NOBLE W JR	CW3	W-2145161	0762	1
KIVG AARON L	CPT	0-1689375	0845	2
KIYFES ANDREW JR	MAJ	0-1648061	0961	1
KIYOTA WILLIE K	1LT	0-1999530	1045	2
KIZER RICHARD M	LTC	0-0422176	0163	1
KIZINSKI IGNATZ M	CPT	0-0499589	0145	2
KIZIS CLIFFORD F	LTC	0-1574905	0463	1

NAME	GRADE	SVC NO	DATE RET MO YR	RET CODE
KJELLAND THOMAS K	CPT	0-1324340	0746	2
KJELLMAN HARRY A	MAJ	0-0149252	0754	3
KJELSTROM WILLIAM C	CPT	0-1286141	0247	1
KJER WINFRED E	1LT	0-1319574	0445	2
KJERNER MAX H	LTC	0-0495234	0663	3
KJONAAS ROBERT A	MAJ	0-0955474	0962	1
KLABANCFF BENJAMIN	MAJ	0-0381247	0548	1
KLACIK GEORGE	MAJ	0-1111713	0964	1
KLAES JAMES G JR	CPT	0-1341981	0860	1
KLAFEHN WILLARD J	LTC	0-1894961	0966	1
KLAHR ELLSWORTH	CPT	0-0417987	0744	2
KLAIBER JOHN J JR	CPT	0-0381710	0346	2
KLAINER MAX J	CPT	0-1686128	1145	2
KLAMBOROWSKI CONSTAN	CW3	W-2208935	1068	1
KLAMER GEORGE F	MAJ	0-1289920	0958	1
KLAMON CHARLES	CPT	0-1062921	0947	2
KLAMPERT MORRIS	CPT	0-1011848	0147	2
KLANCHER LADDIE F	CW2	W-2210589	1162	1
KLANIECKI EDWARD S	LTC	0-1177874	0862	1
KLAPMAN DAVID J	CPT	0-0400187	1045	2
KLAPPSA JOSEPH J	WO1	W-2107904	0945	2
KLARFIELD RICHARD	LTC	0-1846463	0767	3
KLARKOWSKI FRANK G	MAJ	0-2262420	1262	1
KLASE ROBERT F	LTC	0-0885028	1159	1
KLATT HAROLD D	MAJ	0-1292352	0348	2
KLAUBER LOUIS A	LTC	0-0229075	0665	3
KLAUDT MILTON	LTC	0-1581219	0363	1
KLAUS ADOLPH A	CPT	0-0224510	0956	3
KLAUSNER JOHN T	LTC	0-0235542	1165	3
KLAWITTER ARNOLD G	1LT	0-2055401	0145	2
KLEBER VICTOR A	COL	0-0167034	0452	3
KLECH WILLIAM S	MAJ	0-1040041	1052	2
KLECKNER EARL J	COL	0-0182983	0850	3
KLECKNER FRANK C	CW3	W-2145734	0464	1
KLECKNER LEONARD	LTC	0-1292900	0466	1
KLECZKA JOSEPH W	MAJ	0-1185947	1160	1
KLEE WILLIAM W	1LT	0-1183105	1144	2
KLEEB FREDERICK JR	CW4	W-2005737	1067	1
KLEEB WILLIAM H	CW4	W-2119449	1053	1
KLEEFIELD ELMER A	MAJ	0-0501088	0246	2
KLEEFISCH F R	1LT	0-1589955	0545	2
KLEESE JAMES G	LTC	0-0437663	1152	1
KLEIER JOSEPH	LTC	0-1646324	1167	1
KLEIKAMP HERMAN G	LTC	0-1017546	0562	1
KLEIMAN LEO	LTC	0-1012404	0564	1
KLEIMAN MAX	LTC	0-0161586	0157	3
KLEIN BERNARD H	2LT	0-1042336	1144	2
KLEIN CHARLES W	CPT	0-2020559	1058	1
KLEIN CLARENCE W	CW3	W-2150653	0962	1
KLEIN DAVID	CPT	0-0250389	0845	2
KLEIN DONALD C	1LT	0-1036233	0447	2
KLEIN EDITH M	1LT	N-0900062	0956	2
KLEIN ELIZABETH	MAJ	N-0702600	0359	1
KLEIN ELVIN W	LTC	0-1544800	0266	1
KLEIN ERNEST T	LTC	0-0276785	1062	3
KLEIN FRANK N	2LT	0-1913792	0542	1
KLEIN FRED	MAJ	0-1301162	0559	1
KLEIN GEORGE C	COL	0-0253744	0761	3
KLEIN HERMAN	CPT	0-0535218	0445	2
KLEIN HERMAN E	MAJ	0-0297875	1164	3
KLEIN JACK E	1LT	0-1316431	0146	2
KLEIN JACOB W	LTC	0-0426233	0868	3
KLEIN JAMES A	LTC	0-0467405	0962	1
KLEIN JENNINGS B	LTC	0-0261029	0449	2
KLEIN JEROME E	1LT	0-1594946	1145	2
KLEIN JOHN J	LTC	0-0286361	0868	3
KLEIN JOHN J	COL	0-0407195	1265	1
KLEIN JOSEPH	CPT	0-1291134	0446	2
KLEIN JOSEPH N	LTC	0-1535353	1162	1
KLEIN JULIUS	B G	0-0327822	1061	3
KLEIN LAURA M	MAJ	L-0405397	0966	3
KLEIN LOUIS H A	LTC	0-1534305	0262	1
KLEIN MILDRED J	1LT	N-0755043	0745	1
KLEIN MILTON A	LTC	0-0451609	0261	1
KLEIN MILTON D	LTC	0-0296989	0268	3

NAME	GRADE	SVC NO	DATE RET MO YR	RET CODE
KLEIN MILTON F	LTC	0-0002318	0655	2
KLEIN MURRAY M	1LT	0-0522180	0745	2
KLEIN PATRICK L	LTC	0-1044862	0267	1
KLEIN PRESSLEY B	LTC	0-0149284	0853	3
KLEIN ROBERT W	CW3	W-2209008	1268	1
KLEIN ROSE S	2LT	N-0762362	1144	1
KLEIN RUDOLPH	CPT	0-0524324	1145	2
KLEIN SAMUEL	2LT	0-1048047	1044	2
KLEIN THEODORE A	COL	0-0241061	0657	1
KLEIN TOBIAS	LTC	0-0919270	0446	2
KLEIN WILLIAM	MAJ	0-0492705	0957	1
KLEINAU CARL S	LTC	0-0171140	0359	3
KLEINBERG MAURICE S	COL	0-0494322	1167	1
KLEINEGGER CHARLES J	LTC	0-0323115	0960	1
KLEINER ADELBERT F	LTC	0-1585725	1060	1
KLEINER MARY C	1LT	N-0759994	1045	1
KLEINFELD ABRAHAM H	1LT	0-0513968	0644	2
KLEINFIELD HERBERT L	1LT	0-0436968	1043	2
KLEINHANS RUSSELL W	CW2	W-2214540	0966	1
KLEINKNIGHT L R	COL	0-0107218	1056	3
KLEINMAN ABRAHAM M	MAJ	0-1683246	1046	2
KLEINMAN FORREST K	LTC	0-0335972	1060	1
KLEINMAN WILLIAM W	COL	0-0200976	0564	3
KLEINMANN WILLIAM	1LT	0-1037103	1046	2
KLEINSASSER PAUL P	1LT	0-1547989	1145	2
KLEINSCHMIDT B W	CPT	0-0370992	0251	2
KLEISER ROY H	MAJ	0-0122225	0648	3
KLEKNER ARTHUR A	LTC	0-1325997	0366	1
KLEM STEPHEN	2LT	0-1302985	1043	2
KLEMANN JOHN H	CW3	W-2147358	0164	1
KLEMENS FRED W	CW3	W-2121223	0357	1
KLEMENS THADDEUS E	LTC	0-0406736	1059	1
KLEMES ISAUDRE S	CPT	0-0462136	0945	2
KLEMM DEWEY	CPT	0-0496909	0852	1
KLEMM GEORGE J	COL	0-0298403	0266	1
KLEMM WILLIAM H	1LT	0-0200846	1053	3
KLEMP RAYMOND A	CPT	0-0292078	1044	2
KLEMP WALTER A	2LT	0-1949368	0745	2
KLENIK RALPH L	MAJ	0-1048854	0761	1
KLENK FRED	CPT	0-0149784	0857	3
KLENK JOHN M	COL	0-0299982	0760	1
KLEPAC JOHN	1LT	0-0358078	0363	1
KLEPACZ MITCHELL V	LTC	0-1042622	1062	1
KLEPADLO WALTER F	MAJ	0-2097136	0265	1
KLEPEIS WALTER J	MAJ	0-1685011	0465	1
KLEPPEN NORMAN T	CW4	W-2141339	0765	1
KLEREKOPER MAURICE R	LTC	0-1324868	1061	1
KLETT ELEANOR V	MAJ	M-0002034	1164	1
KLETT JOHN R	MAJ	0-0504517	1155	1
KLETT WILLIAM M	1LT	0-1308519	0446	2
KLEUPFER JOHN J	CPT	0-2034007	1268	2
KLEWIN ROBERT E	COL	0-0546959	1267	1
KLIMA PAULINE M	1LT	N-0724236	1144	1
KLIMAS HELEN G	1LT	N-0729189	0646	1
KLIMAS WILLIAM J	WO1	W-2103099	0443	2
KLIMASZEWSKI WILFRED	CW2	W-3200265	0167	1
KLIMES GEORGE V	COL	0-0170713	0446	2
KLINCK JOHN M	LTC	0-0449973	0364	1
KLINDIENST EDWARD F	CPT	0-1040418	0952	1
KLINE ALFRED S	LTC	0-0428982	1063	3
KLINE CHARLES E	LTC	0-0263129	0767	3
KLINE CLAUDE N	1LT	0-0890240	0248	2
KLINE CONRAD W SR	MAJ	0-0162129	0648	3
KLINE DORIS M	1LT	N-0751999	0546	1
KLINE FLOYD F	MAJ	0-1080212	0550	1
KLINE HARLAND R	LTC	0-0265350	0467	3
KLINE HARRY H	CW3	W-2147177	0862	1
KLINE HELEN	MAJ	N-0760036	0764	3
KLINE HELEN T B	1LT	N-0761888	0847	1
KLINE IRVING H	1LT	0-0248920	0446	2
KLINE JAMES A JR	MAJ	0-0974511	1063	1
KLINE JAMES H	1LT	0-0327541	0544	2
KLINE LEE A	CPT	0-0197693	1262	3
KLINE MARTIN L JR	MAJ	0-1041592	0261	1
KLINE MURRAY M	CW2	W-2101213	0346	2

NAME	GRADE	SVC NO	DATE RET MO YR	RET CODE
KLINE NELSON F	CW2	W-2110117	0747	1
KLINE SIDNEY	CPT	0-0238431	0666	3
KLINE STANLEY N	1LT	0-0428144	1043	2
KLINE WILLIAM P	LTC	0-1845676	0862	1
KLINEFELTER PAUL M	CPT	0-0547634	1147	2
KLING HERMAN A	CPT	0-0483382	0945	2
KLING JULIUS W	1LT	0-0549960	0347	2
KLINGBEIL HERMAN F	CPT	0-4006246	0664	1
KLINGE RUDOLF	CW4	W-2145095	1068	1
KLINGENBECK ROBERT F	CW2	RW-2206111	0664	1
KLINGENSMITH M J	2LT	0-0158772	0756	3
KLINGER HARRY F JR	1LT	0-1292003	1045	2
KLINGER KENNETH P	LTC	0-0118192	1056	3
KLINGER WARREN V	1LT	0-1288071	0145	2
KLINGER WILLIAM H	LTC	0-0375170	0756	1
KLINGER WILLIAM L	LTC	0-1557031	1066	1
KLINKACEK FRANCIS	LTC	0-0482129	0962	1
KLINKBEIL CHARLES E	MAJ	0-2262253	0466	1
KLINKEL EDSON	CPT	0-0284915	0159	3
KLINKER DARRELL E	LTC	0-1296867	0163	1
KLINKO AGNES M	1LT	N-0722550	1046	1
KLIPA JOHN JR	CPT	0-1307709	0248	2
KLIPSCH PAUL W	LTC	0-0225960	0464	3
KLIPSTINE CHARLES W	LTC	0-1319960	1262	1
KLISE CARLYLE	COL	0-0329798	1060	1
KLISS VICTOR L	MAJ	0-1174916	0164	1
KLITCH EDWIN M	MAJ	0-1297052	1064	1
KLOBY JOHN J	CPT	0-1692181	0845	2
KLOC CHESTER S	CPT	0-1050338	0258	2
KLOE DONALD R	CPT	0-0547099	0763	1
KLOEB WILLIAM C	LTC	0-1306952	1062	1
KLOECKLER CECILIA L	CPT	N-0735200	0549	2
KLOEFKORN EARL W	1LT	0-1171632	0546	2
KLOETZER ADELBERT O	MAJ	0-0226144	0863	3
KLOMAN CURT C	MAJ	0-2020165	0563	1
KLOO WALTER E	CPT	0-1332710	0265	3
KLOOSTERMAN JOHN	LTC	0-1014660	0567	1
KLOPFER HENRY I	CPT	0-1646327	0557	1
KLOPP CHARLES F	LTC	0-1584469	0364	1
KLOPP HARRY J	MAJ	0-0510770	1051	1
KLOPPEL KEITH M	2LT	0-1324223	0145	2
KLOPSTOCK ARTHUR	COL	0-0198721	0253	1
KLORFINE MILTON	LTC	0-0235662	0764	3
KLOSKI HERMAN A	CPT	0-0346293	0745	2
KLOSTER GEORGE O	CW2	W-2208896	0763	1
KLOSTER IVER J JR	LTC	0-0514489	0261	1
KLOSTER RUSH E	MAJ	0-1200657	0860	1
KLOSTERMAN WARREN W	LTC	0-0426106	0864	1
KLOTCH EDWARD P	LTC	0-1102806	1062	1
KLOTCH FREDERICK	2LT	0-1639261	1045	2
KLOTE EDWARD J	1LT	0-0375865	1145	2
KLOTHE CHARLES A	CW2	W-2118051	1145	2
KLOTZ FRANK A	LTC	0-1016424	0368	1
KLOTZ MAURICE	COL	0-0324235	0766	3
KLOTZ WALTER	MAJ	0-0497030	1154	1
KLUBERTANZ ALBERT J	1LT	0-0221022	1147	1
KLUCHER GEORGE	CW3	W-2152468	0364	1
KLUCZINSKY VINCENT C	LTC	0-1703895	1056	1
KLUEGEL OSWALD E	MAJ	0-0344989	0645	2
KLUG BERNADINE	MAJ	N-0729633	0368	1
KLUGLER JOSEPH	CPT	0-0526830	1046	2
KLUMBACH JOSEPH J	LTC	0-1283977	1165	3
KLUMP EMMETT J	CW3	W-2208283	1266	1
KLUMPP JOSEPH J	COL	0-0153094	1045	2
KLUMPP JOSEPH P	1LT	0-1314150	1145	2
KLUSKY RICHARD V	LTC	0-1314031	0565	1
KLUSMEIER FREDERICK	MAJ	0-0983838	0864	1
KLUSMEIER PAUL C	MAJ	0-0349147	0667	3
KLUTMAN WALTER J	2LT	0-1322832	1044	2
KLUTSCH JOSEPH JR	CPT	0-1289922	1046	2
KLUTTZ WALTER H	LTC	0-0304069	0966	3
KLUTTZ WILLIAM H	CW2	W-2151791	0563	1
KLYVERT EMMETH L	CW3	W-2205201	0867	1
KNAACK WILLIAM H	LTC	0-0337657	1259	1
KNABB JOSEPH H	CW2	W-2205026	0760	2

NAME	GRADE	SVC NO	DATE RET MO YR	RET CODE	NAME	GRADE	SVC NO	DATE RET MO YR	RET CODE	NAME	GRADE	SVC NO	DATE RET MO YR	RET CODE	NAME	GRADE	SVC NO	DATE RET MO YR	RET CODE
KNAPP [illegible]	CPT	[illegible]	[illegible]	1	KNIERIM HENRY E	MAJ	0-0140039	0256	3	KNISS [illegible]	2LT	[illegible]	1067	1	KNOX [illegible] A	CPT	[illegible]	1060	1
KNAPP [illegible]	LTC	[illegible]	[illegible]	3	KNIERIM JOHN H	1LT	0-1649230	0158	1	KNITT [illegible]	CW3	[illegible]	[illegible]	1	KNOX [illegible] W	CPT	[illegible]	1165	2
KNAPP [illegible]	CPT	[illegible]	1069	3	KNI[illegible] WILLIAM E	CW4	W-2144778	1167	1	KNOBEL [illegible]	CW2	[illegible]	1267	1	KNOX JOHN H	[illegible]	[illegible]	0463	1
KNAPP [illegible]	LTC	[illegible]	0764	3	KNIESS GEORGE P SR	MAJ	0-0309717	0259	1	KNOBLAUCH [illegible]	MAJ	[illegible]	[illegible]	1	KNOX [illegible] E	MAJ	[illegible]	0143	1
KNAPP [illegible] A	LTC	[illegible]	1050	1	KNIESTEDT EWALD M	LTC	0-0282566	0862	3	KNOBLAUCH [illegible]	LTC	[illegible]	[illegible]	3	KNOX [illegible] A	CPT	[illegible]	0646	2
KNAPP [illegible]	LTC	0-0297351	0465	1	KNIFFEN CECIL G	CW2	W-2141340	0655	1	KNOBLAUCH [illegible]	LTC	[illegible]	0661	1	KNOX [illegible]	CPT	0-2034062	0745	2
KNAPP MARTHA M	2LT	N-0733417	0944	1	KNIFONG EUGENE	CPT	0-0435409	1049	1	KNOBLETT THOMAS [illegible] JR	CW3	[illegible]	[illegible]	1	KNOX [illegible]	LTC	0-0264736	0261	3
KNAPP [illegible]	LTC	0-0403302	0966	3	KNIFTON FRANCIS H	LTC	0-0226279	0763	3	KNOBLOCH [illegible]	MAJ	[illegible]	0764	2	KNOX [illegible]	1LT	[illegible]	0659	2
KNAPP [illegible]	LTC	0-0147336	0753	3	KNIGHT ALBERT L	MAJ	0-2262937	0866	1	KNOBLOCH HENRY P	1LT	[illegible]	[illegible]	2	KNOX ROBERT W	CPT	[illegible]	1155	3
KNAPP [illegible]	CPT	0-0333170	0662	2	KNIGHT ALEXANDER	COL	0-0128718	0546	2	KNOBLOCK ROBERT J	1LT	[illegible]	1145	2	KNOX WALTER [illegible]	LTC	[illegible]	0264	3
KNAPP [illegible]	LTC	0-0373439	0458	3	KNIGHT CHARLES B	LTC	0-2276376	0563	1	KNODE [illegible]	LTC	0-0252173	0953	3	KNOX WALTER H	LTC	0-0351750	0553	2
KNAPP ANTHONY J	CW3	W-2146588	0959	1	KNIGHT CHARLES E	CPT	0-1312018	1059	1	KNODE LEWIS H	MAJ	0-0102125	1153	3	KNOX WARREN P	CPT	0-0644729	0647	2
KNAPP CHARLES J	CW3	W-2134735	1057	2	KNIGHT CHARLES W	LTC	0-0172624	1146	2	KNODE THOMAS E	CPT	0-0364328	1143	2	KNOX WILLIAM M	LTC	0-0464575	1164	3
KNAPP [illegible]	MAJ	0-0243789	0464	3	KNIGHT CHESTER R	MAJ	0-0976742	0663	1	KNOEALL LAWRENCE W	CPT	0-1573338	0746	2	KNOX NORRIS J	CPT	0-1744729	1152	2
KNAPP EDWARD J	LTC	0-1033334	0267	3	KNIGHT CLARENCE G	MAJ	0-0945723	1066	1	KNOELLER CHARLES R	MAJ	0-0504139	0258	1	KNOX VERGIL G	MAJ	0-2047993	0261	1
KNAPP ETHEL M	2LT	N-0702206	0240	1	KNIGHT DANIEL D	CW2	W-3400053	0968	1	KNOELL ALBERT H	LTC	0-0322279	1162	3	KNUCKLES C W	MAJ	0-1551658	0547	2
KNAPP FREDERICK	LTC	0-0108285	0858	3	KNIGHT EDWIN K	MAJ	0-1109424	1065	3	KNOELL KENNETH H	1LT	0-0554719	0646	2	KNUDSEN EUGENIUS R JR	CPT	0-0259739	0167	3
KNAPP GEORGE S	MAJ	0-0416164	0145	2	KNIGHT ERNEST E	COL	0-0451511	0766	2	KNOELS IRENE M	MAJ	L-1013047	0764	1	KNUDSEN FRED J	CPT	0-0315771	0845	2
KNAPP GEORGE [illegible]	CW3	RW-0908102	0168	1	KNIGHT ERNEST G	CW2	W-2149118	0761	1	KNOOP FREDERICK	CW3	W-2005373	0363	1	KNUDSEN FREDRIK L	LTC	0-1288302	1262	1
KNAPP GORDON A	MAJ	0-0133628	0452	3	KNIGHT FERRIS	MAJ	0-1320540	0859	1	KNOPE FRANCIS N	MAJ	0-0221272	0563	3	KNUDSEN JUNE M	CW3	W-2150606	0656	1
KNAPP [illegible] W	MAJ	0-1103262	0461	1	KNIGHT FRANCIS A	LTC	0-0996131	0868	1	KNOPF SAMUEL N	CPT	0-0524343	0745	2	KNUDSEN MORGAN G JR	LTC	0-1554303	0767	1
KNAPP HOWARD H	CW3	W-2150575	0962	2	KNIGHT GEORGE C	LTC	0-0243128	0861	3	KNOPP FRANCIS X	CPT	0-1015462	0847	[illegible]	KNUDSEN TORE B	CPT	0-2022345	1046	2
KNAPP KELVIN J	LTC	0-0332595	0746	2	KNIGHT GERALD E	1LT	0-1030487	1046	2	KNOPP JAMES A	MAJ	0-1106261	1157	1	KNUDSON [illegible] E	COL	0-0138735	1152	3
KNAPP KENNETH J JR	LTC	0-1045137	1061	1	KNIGHT HAN JR	MAJ	0-1342082	0363	1	KNOPP JAMES H	CW3	W-2141612	0962	1	KNUDSON KENNETH F	COL	0-1576250	0261	1
KNAPP KINGSTON [illegible]	MAJ	0-0673471	0161	1	KNIGHT HENRY J	1LT	0-1045931	0347	2	KNORR ERNEST A JR	LTC	0-0330295	0265	3	KNUPP GILBERT B	CPT	0-1295730	0949	2
KNAPP LLOYD H	LTC	0-1556302	1165	3	KNIGHT HERBERT G	CPT	0-0108628	0438	1	KNORR JAMES S	MAJ	0-0969378	1060	1	KNUTH EARL L	2LT	0-1916222	0253	2
KNAPP RAYMOND S	LTC	0-0118133	0355	3	KNIGHT HOWARD W JR	CPT	0-0885740	0846	2	KNORZER NORVAL P	CPT	0-0510822	1055	1	KNUTSEN CLARA S	2LT	N-0700834	0738	1
KNAPP ROBERT S	MAJ	0-0278249	0256	3	KNIGHT HUGH E	MAJ	0-0215489	1058	3	KNOTT ARTHUR W	CPT	0-0213744	0-50	3	KNUTSEN LLOYD B	COL	0-0285486	0967	3
KNAPP VERNON R	CW2	W-2150776	0661	1	KNIGHT HUGH F	COL	0-0348385	0860	1	KNOTT ARTHUR W JR	LTC	0-1166103	0161	1	KNUTSON HAROLD A	COL	0-0371181	0368	3
KNAPP WILLIAM A	LTC	0-0118270	1158	3	KNIGHT JACK C	MAJ	0-0307184	0866	3	KNOTT ERNEST J	COL	0-0197098	1150	1	KOART VIRGIL P	CPT	0-1340292	1057	1
KNAPPEN CHARLES H JR	1LT	0-0514836	1045	2	KNIGHT JEROME P	LTC	0-0287480	0357	1	KNOTT JAMES P	MAJ	0-0180814	0657	3	KOBBE MAX J	CPT	0-1011905	0946	2
KNAPPIK JACK F	MAJ	0-1599316	1159	1	KNIGHT JOHN W JR	LTC	0-1116165	0661	1	KNOTT NORMAN L	1LT	0-0536373	0645	2	KOBECK HARNEY F	CPT	0-0406523	1060	2
KNAUB JACK JR	MAJ	0-0994560	0463	1	KNIGHT JOSEPH	WO1	W-2147188	0154	2	KNOTTS FRED JR	CPT	0-0405507	0945	2	KOBERNAT ARLEIGH L	LTC	0-0381560	0854	1
KNAUERHASE CARL O	LTC	0-0374654	1060	1	KNIGHT JOSEPH M	CW4	W-2145927	1268	2	KNOTTS HALLECK S	CPT	0-4073684	0459	2	KOBLARCHICK PAUL W	CPT	0-1173334	0467	1
KNAUF CHARLES F	CPT	0-1699779	0945	2	KNIGHT JULIUS A	LTC	0-1573336	1061	1	KNOTTS WILLIAM H	COL	0-0231776	0363	3	KOBLIS PETER S	CW2	W-2210506	1060	1
KNAUF LAWRENCE W	COL	0-0302424	0663	1	KNIGHT KENNETH L	1LT	0-0976569	0953	2	KNOUF JAMES M	MAJ	0-0329799	0146	2	KOBS CHARLES J	LTC	0-0343486	0461	1
KNAUF PAUL W JR	LTC	0-0170994	0760	3	KNIGHT LAWRENCE O	LTC	0-2206259	1067	1	KNOUSE BILLY J	MAJ	0-2262125	0264	2	KOBS ELMER O	CPT	0-0285174	1066	3
KNAUF WILLIAM J	MAJ	0-0175157	0959	3	KNIGHT LEONARD M	1LT	0-0493518	1157	1	KNOUSE BOYD F	CPT	0-1062836	0255	1	KOBS RUDOLPH A	MAJ	0-0371559	0947	2
KNAUFF CHARLES H	MAJ	0-0961378	0862	1	KNIGHT LEROY A	1LT	0-0141963	1153	3	KNOWE BENJAMIN A	MAJ	0-0333277	0557	3	KOBUS ALEXANDIUM	LTC	0-0496714	1055	1
KNAUFF FRANCIS T	1LT	0-0454129	0955	1	KNIGHT LESTER R	MAJ	0-0528113	1154	1	KNOWELS ROBERT J	1LT	0-1319753	0546	2	KOBUS WALTER S	CW4	W-2103103	0957	1
KNAUS FRED	1LT	0-0187154	0753	3	KNIGHT LLEWELLYN	LTC	0-0259722	0368	3	KNOWLDEN RONALD L	CPT	0-2012908	0156	1	KOCER JAMES C	1LT	0-1054655	1045	2
KNAUSS RUTH F	2LT	N-0724996	0345	1	KNIGHT LOUIS J	MAJ	0-0158054	0655	3	KNOWLES ALFRED R JR	MAJ	0-1913364	0365	1	KOCH BERNARD	LTC	0-0334930	0665	3
KNAZOVICH ALEX	MAJ	0-1174918	1062	1	KNIGHT LOYD W	LTC	0-1825007	0667	1	KNOWLES CARL F	LTC	0-1797146	0267	1	KOCH CARL K	LTC	0-0963920	0668	1
KNECHT LAWRENCE F	CW4	W-2118164	0659	1	KNIGHT MARION J	LTC	0-1284159	1161	1	KNOWLES CLARENCE H	MAJ	0-0144593	0349	3	KOCH CASPER F	MAJ	0-2019185	0264	1
KNECHTEL LLOYD W	LTC	0-0903360	0867	3	KNIGHT MAX J	CPT	0-0515281	0844	2	KNOWLES CONRAD A	CPT	0-1588686	1266	3	KOCH CHESTER J	CW3	W-2142166	0767	1
KNEE ROBERT G	LTC	0-0466460	0951	2	KNIGHT PHILIP A	LTC	0-0453610	0662	1	KNOWLES DAVE [illegible]	2LT	0-0547597	1145	2	KOCH CLINT M	MAJ	0-1299758	0959	1
KNEECE BOLDRIDGE	LTC	0-0146409	0254	3	KNIGHT RALPH T	COL	0-0177521	0648	3	KNOWLES GEORGE F JR	MAJ	0-1935262	0866	1	KOCH EDWARD M	LTC	0-0268617	0462	1
KNEECE THURMAN C	CPT	0-0970811	1060	1	KNIGHT RAYMOND	CW2	W-2208404	1263	1	KNOWLES JAMES S	LTC	0-0131813	0549	3	KOCH EDWIN G	LTC	0-0247976	1065	3
KNEELAND BERNARD T	LTC	0-0442478	1262	1	KNIGHT RAYMOND F	MAJ	0-1322558	0363	1	KNOWLES JAMES W	1LT	0-1242201	0845	2	KOCH EDWIN M	CPT	0-1014659	1047	2
KNEELAND THEODORE R	1LT	0-1305269	1048	2	KNIGHT REAMS R	CW4	W-2115520	0559	1	KNOWLES JOHN W	LTC	0-1577436	0461	1	KOCH ELLWOOD L	LTC	0-0377292	1154	1
KNEER BERNARD J	1LT	0-1169603	1045	2	KNIGHT RICHARD F	MAJ	0-1309282	0659	2	KNOWLES LEWIS W	CPT	0-2300147	0160	3	KOCH ERNEST P	LTC	0-1551659	1265	3
KNEESE EDGAR A	LTC	0-1047191	1062	1	KNIGHT ROBERT	MAJ	0-1999062	0460	1	KNOWLES ROBERT F	MAJ	0-1547753	1058	1	KOCH GLENN F	1LT	0-1049933	0962	1
KNEFEL CLEMENT A	MAJ	0-0427993	0261	1	KNIGHT ROBERT F	CW2	W-2143094	1155	1	KNOWLES ROBERT G	CPT	0-1636158	1160	1	KOCH HAROLD C	LTC	0-0475511	0367	3
KNEIB CHARLES F	LTC	0-1641478	0455	1	KNIGHT ROBERT H	1LT	0-2004645	0554	2	KNOWLES ROBERT P	MAJ	0-1557863	0764	1	KOCH JAMES F	1LT	0-1170036	0146	2
KNEISEL WILLIAM G	1LT	0-0524130	0245	2	KNIGHT ROBERT I	LTC	0-1080723	0258	1	KNOWLES ROBERT W	CW3	W-2203494	0666	1	KOCH LLOYD W	LTC	0-0320754	0161	1
KNEISLER JAMES [illegible]	MAJ	0-1191906	1160	1	KNIGHT RUSSELL F	MAJ	0-0589659	0466	3	KNOWLES WILLARD E	LTC	0-0339166	0146	2	KOCH LUTHER F	LTC	0-0272937	0663	3
KNEISLER WALDEMAR	1LT	0-1302317	1045	2	KNIGHT SAMUEL R	COL	0-0243537	0963	1	KNOWLTON CHARLES F	COL	0-0234235	0159	1	KOCH RALPH F	LTC	0-0307866	0668	3
KNEPHER JACK T	CW4	W-2127546	0859	2	KNIGHT THOMAS H	MAJ	0-0972033	0761	1	KNOWLTON CHARLES P	CW2	W-2206282	0962	2	KOCH STANLEY G	1LT	0-1285439	0745	2
KNEPKA EARL H	CW3	W-2145243	0267	1	KNIGHT VIRGLE D	LTC	0-1684952	0968	1	KNOWLTON DONALD F	CPT	0-1165326	0446	2	KOCH THEODORE A	MAJ	0-0272381	0867	3
KNEPLEY JAMES F	LTC	0-1103745	1164	1	KNIGHT WILBURN W	CPT	0-0535442	0846	2	KNOWLTON HORACE A	MAJ	0-0465544	1045	2	KOCH WALTER A	MAJ	0-1798677	0258	2
KNERR LEWIS F	LTC	0-0101960	1149	3	KNIGHT WILEY JR	MAJ	0-0359843	0552	2	KNOWLTON KENNETH H	COL	0-0101850	0557	3	KOCH WILLIAM H	MAJ	0-0411675	1151	2
KNETTLE LEROY J	LTC	0-0295426	0460	3	KNIGHT WILLIAM F	LTC	0-1543614	0163	1	KNOWLTON LE[illegible] F	CPT	0-1556390	0963	1	KOCH WILLIAM R	MAJ	0-2030448	0367	2
KNEUPPER WILFRED A	LTC	0-0341787	0946	2	KNIGHT WILLIAM F	LTC	0-1277741	0965	1	KNOWLTON REX F	1LT	0-1590249	0752	2	KOCHAN PETER S	CPT	0-0186472	1054	3
KNEWITZ RALPH W	MAJ	0-0304065	0645	2	KNIGHT WILLIAM G	COL	0-0130141	0648	3	KNOWLTON RICHARD P	LTC	0-1593221	0261	1	KOCHANSKI CHESTER	CPT	0-1556163	0964	2
KNEZEVICH DONALD M	2LT	0-1574310	0744	2	KNIGHT WILLMER F	CPT	0-0267276	0866	3	KNOX CARMEN B	MAJ	L-0303839	0764	3	KOCHANSKI JOSEPH	LTC	0-0311435	0366	3
KNEZOVICH FRANCIS M	MAJ	0-1108082	0157	1	KNIGHTON CURTISS E	LTC	0-1039732	0868	1	KNOX CAROLINE C	1LT	N-0783473	0446	2	KOCHER BERNARD R	MAJ	0-2014357	0764	1
KNICK RUTH	LTC	L-1010093	0768	1	KNIGHTON HARRY A	LTC	0-1172122	0361	1	KNOX CHARLES V	MAJ	0-1032631	0663	1	KOCHERT JAMES F	MAJ	0-2203026	0363	1
KNICKERBOCKER F	MAJ	0-1548888	1054	1	KNIGOFF MORRIS	CPT	0-0321325	1045	2	KNOX CHESTER N	CW3	W-2147301	1263	1	KOCHNOWER WILLIAM	1LT	0-0523838	1045	2
KNICKERBOCKER G F	2LT	0-1558342	1044	2	KNIPE GEORGE F	MAJ	0-1106260	0862	1	KNOX EDDIE C	CPT	0-0430165	1048	1	KOCHY ERNEST A	MAJ	0-1874872	1065	1
KNICKERBOCKER WILLIA	LTC	0-1102333	1264	1	KNIPHFER DWIGHT O	CPT	0-2006741	0959	1	KNOX ERMA J	MAJ	N-0777509	0365	1	KOCHY STEPHEN B	MAJ	0-1292004	0960	1
KNIE DONALD W	1LT	0-1042623	0446	2	KNIPP OTHAL V	MAJ	0-0357674	0168	1	KNOX FREDERICK JR	MAJ	0-0443360	0147	2	KOCIC DANIEL	MAJ	0-1924747	1264	1
KNIE WALTER M	CW3	W-2152314	0966	1	KNISELY EARL P	LTC	0-0381538	1045	2	KNOX GEORGE W	MAJ	0-0288732	0446	2	KOCIEMBA VICTORIA E	MAJ	N-0786038	0565	1
KNIERIEM CLIFFORD W	LTC	0-1547683	0168	1	KNISHKOWY EMANUEL S	CPT	0-0517242	0545	2	KNOX GLEN H	1LT	0-0958416	1051	2	KOCIUBINSKA MANKA	1LT	N-0759416	0646	1
KNIERIEM JOHN P	LTC	0-0387397	0960	1	KNISLEY ELMER W	CPT	0-1293425	0763	1	KNOX HARRY	COL	0-0256118	1065	3	KOCZAK RICHARD	MAJ	0-1059836	0862	1
KNIERIM GEORGE W J	CPT	0-1314789	0653	2	KNISLEY EVERETT M	CW3	W-2152365	0964	2	KNOX HENRY A	MAJ	0-0278208	0954	3	KOCZON WILLIAM J	MAJ	0-1633338	0762	1

NAME	GRADE	SVC NO	DATE RET MO YR	RET CODE
KOOIS CHARLES	CW2	W-2146847	0161	1
KOEBBE NORVIL G	MAJ	0-1300976	0463	1
KOEBENSKY MICHAEL W	CPT	0-1308065	0654	2
KOEBER ERWIN C	LTC	0-0400703	1263	2
KOEBRICH LOUIS A	MAJ	0-0371619	0568	3
KOECHLIN ROBERT J	1LT	0-1288757	104N	2
KOEGEL CHARLES F	MAJ	0-4010728	1068	1
KOEHLER ARNO P	LTC	0-1004352	0867	3
KOEHLER MILFORD A	LTC	0-0241716	0258	1
KOEHLER MILTON E	LTC	0-0241756	0260	3
KOEHLER WILLIAM H	LTC	0-1797147	0262	1
KOEHNE KENNETH K	CW2	W-2122177	0367	3
KOEHS ROBERT P SR	MAJ	0-1849969	0263	1
KOELLER REUBEN J	MAJ	0-1648341	0258	1
KOELLNER CARL G	COL	0-0319648	0160	1
KOELMEL WILLIAM A	MAJ	0-1798015	1060	1
KOEN JOSEPH T	MAJ	0-1043388	0860	1
KOENEMAN NATHANIEL	COL	0-0029106	0564	3
KOENEMAN THOMAS	LTC	0-1647557	0361	1
KOENIG AUGUST	LTC	0-0451326	0960	1
KOENIG FRED	LTC	0-0154370	1153	1
KOENIG FREDERICK JR	1LT	0-0549293	0346	2
KOENIG JOSEPH A	CW3	W-2146597	0659	1
KOENIG KARL J	1LT	0-0417407	0146	2
KOENIG MERLE C	CPT	0-0974246	1068	1
KOENIG RAYMOND R	MAJ	0-2262172	0163	1
KOENIG THOMAS J	MAJ	C-1640638	0859	1
KOENIG VICTOR L	1LT	0-0409478	0145	2
KOENIG WILBUR C	LTC	0-1000252	0957	2
KOENNE JAMES E	CW3	W-2205863	1167	1
KOEPF FRANCIS J	COL	0-1637846	0868	1
KOEPKE ROBERT A	2LT	0-2006930	0357	1
KOEPP ARTHUR W	MAJ	0-0242869	C855	3
KOEPPE CLARENCE E	COL	0-0199942	0546	2
KOEPPEL ROBERT C	CW4	W-2146374	0668	1
KOERBER HENRY A	CW2	W-2152678	0562	1
KOERNER CHARLES	MAJ	0-0480750	0455	1
KOERNER JULIAN A	CPT	0-0300446	1145	2
KOERNER PAUL C	LTC	0-0403532	0960	1
KOERNER ROBERT L	CPT	0-1292811	0546	2
KOERNER WILLIAM E	MAJ	0-2266237	0468	1
KOERT CORNELIUS	CPT	0-0502746	1144	2
KOERTING VERNON H	CPT	0-0284165	0446	2
KOESTER HERMAN A	CPT	0-0837702	0858	1
KOESTER WILLIAM T	LTC	0-0300274	0262	1
KOETTNER FRANK X	CW4	W-2141117	0162	1
KOFFLER BURTON A	LTC	0-0319882	1065	3
KOFFMAN CECIL W	MAJ	0-0146477	1053	3
KOFLER JOHN M	LTC	0-1822154	1162	1
KOFMAN JAMES W	CPT	0-0244891	0966	3
KOGEL MARCUS C	COL	C-0246239	1063	3
KOGER CARLINE E	MAJ	N-0760578	0167	1
KOGON SAMUEL E	1LT	0-0916337	0546	2
KOGUT FRANK	1LT	0-1012524	0146	2
KOHAN NATHAN H	CW3	W-2144038	0562	1
KOHANIK PAUL J	MAJ	0-1001166	0961	1
KOHL CLEMENT J	LTC	0-0385680	0661	1
KOHL GERALD C	MAJ	0-0250804	0463	3
KOHL JOHN M	CW2	W-2151895	0361	1
KOHL LEONARD L	LTC	0-1100184	0767	1
KOHL WILLIAM A	MAJ	0-1587378	1060	1
KOHLENBERG FRED JR	MAJ	0-0444340	0246	2
KOHLER CLARENCE W	LTC	0-0273548	0468	3
KOHLER DANIEL E	CW2	W-2145079	0656	1
KOHLER FRANK L	2LT	0-1301327	0545	2
KOHLER GORDON E	CPT	0-1045797	0545	2
KOHLER JOHN J	MAJ	0-1106882	0564	1
KOHLER KENT F	MAJ	0-0235719	1164	3
KOHLER OTTO C	LTC	0-0285068	0263	3
KOHLER VINCENT D	MAJ	0-1645123	0361	1
KOHLHAGEN WERNER S	LTC	0-1049541	0361	1
KOHLOSS ROBERT A JR	COL	0-0396691	0844	2
KOHN ARNOLD	MAJ	0-1166758	0762	1
KOHN ARTHUR A	LTC	0-0495047	0867	3
KOHN FRANCIS M	MAJ	0-0235011	1165	3

NAME	GRADE	SVC NO	DATE RET MO YR	RET CODE
KOHN LOUIS A	CPT	0-0254247	0467	3
KOHN ROY E JR	MAJ	0-0365706	0565	1
KOHUT MICHAEL J	1LT	0-0296167	0145	2
KOHUTEK WALTER W	MAJ	0-0987478	1265	1
KOHUTH ROBERT J	CW2	W-3152604	1067	2
KOIVISTO ALFRED K	MAJ	0-0450615	0446	2
KOJASSAR ARAM	COL	0-0464410	0650	1
KOKE RAYMOND D	MAJ	0-0352585	0246	2
KOKENZIE HENRY F	CPT	0-1002964	0646	2
KOKKO CARL W	CW2	W-2150612	0760	1
KOKOL MARY D	LTC	N-0760324	0563	2
KOLAR JOSEPH	MAJ	0-0177805	0347	1
KOLB ELMER R	LTC	0-0290445	0564	3
KOLB EUGENE J	LTC	0-0552569	0963	1
KOLB FRED W JR	CW4	W-2103096	1057	1
KOLB JAMES M	MAJ	0-0297861	1045	2
KOLB JOHN W	CPT	0-1324424	0458	2
KOLB ROBERT W	LTC	0-1287898	0461	1
KOLCUN EDWARD J	MAJ	0-2017077	0867	1
KOLDA CARL E	LTC	0-0303154	0664	3
KOLESAR JOE	LTC	0-0450183	1157	1
KOLESAR NICHOLAS	CW4	RW-2148740	0868	1
KOLGEN ANTHONY J	LTC	0-0290815	0768	3
KOLHONEN BRUNO	LTC	0-1553860	1062	1
KOLKS RICHARD H	LTC	0-0444100	0367	3
KOLL CORNELIUS	LTC	0-1174030	1061	1
KOLLARS THOMAS M	MAJ	0-0959322	1066	1
KOLLIAS NICHOLAOS	CPT	0-0185399	1160	3
KOLM ALWIN S	LTC	0-0291756	0267	3
KOLMAN ALBERT J	LTC	0-0442960	0-53	1
KOLMAN LAWRENCE L	2LT	0-1823460	1144	2
KOLO JOHN F	LTC	0-0377149	1055	1
KOLODY JOHN F	1LT	0-0887496	0757	1
KOLODZIEJ PETER R	MAJ	0-0455195	0756	1
KOLOFER EDWARD A	LTC	0-0320190	1060	1
KOLOSKI JOSEPH L	LTC	0-1548893	0861	1
KOLPACK HERMAN W	LTC	0-0447840	0646	2
KOLSTAD HENRY C	1LT	0-0921696	1043	2
KOLTUN MICHAEL	LTC	0-1647559	0664	2
KOMANCSEK ALEXANDER	MAJ	0-0240242	0864	3
KOMAR JAMES R	1LT	0-1948011	0855	1
KOMAR JOSEPH J	MAJ	0-4022180	0268	1
KOMAROSKI JOHN R	MAJ	0-0450977	0858	1
KOMMERS WILLIAM K	1LT	0-1583224	1143	2
KOMOROSKE ALEXANDER	LTC	0-1649303	1162	2
KOMOSA ADAM A	LTC	0-0378898	1057	1
KONAR ALBERT V	1LT	0-1293605	0945	2
KONAR GEORGE E	2LT	0-1299759	0844	2
KONCEK JOHN	MAJ	0-2262447	1268	2
KONDLER FRANK G	CPT	0-1283447	1154	1
KONECKI LEON W	COL	0-0374164	0161	1
KONEK EDWARD A	MAJ	0-1304913	0163	1
KONESKI CHESTER F	CPT	0-0510150	0446	2
KONIK EDWARD P	MAJ	0-0890185	0758	1
KONING IGNATIUS J JR	CW4	W-2136743	1066	1
KONKEL EDWARD G	1LT	0-1299906	1043	2
KONKEL LEONARD A	MAJ	0-0937483	0268	3
KONKRIGHT MILTON T	LTC	0-0220970	0958	3
KONO YEIJE	1LT	0-1019822	0950	2
KONOP MATT F C	COL	0-0261376	0366	3
KONOPASKE OTTO T	CW3	W-2004143	0865	1
KONOZA JOHN S	MAJ	0-1315696	0961	1
KONRAD ADOLF M	CPT	0-0201403	0762	3
KONRAD ELMER W	MAJ	0-2266260	0466	1
KONRAD GEORGE M	LTC	0-0284132	0668	3
KONTRA GEORGE	LTC	0-1039064	0862	1
KONTZ ERNEST C JR	LTC	0-0253781	0167	3
KONZE ALICE S	MAJ	L-0910059	1163	1
KONZE WILLIAM K	LTC	0-1306217	1163	1
KOOISTRA JACK J	1LT	0-1634043	0246	2
KOOMJAN HELEN	1LT	N-0737376	0146	1
KOON WILLIAM B	CPT	0-0496794	0457	1
KOONCE VANCE T	LTC	0-0443667	0758	1
KOONS CRANDALL I	COL	0-0268527	0763	1
KOONS EVERETT A	LTC	0-0544743	1067	1

NAME	GRADE	SVC NO	DATE RET MO YR	RET CODE
KOONS HERBERT N	MAJ	*0-0481107	0547	2
KOONS VERNON E	MAJ	0-0166716	0749	3
KOONS WILLIAM B	LTC	0-1309575	1162	2
KOONS WILLIAM E	MAJ	0-0978254	1268	1
KOONTZ CLYDE F	LTC	0-0304302	0161	1
KOONTZ ELIAS A JR	CPT	0-1936571	1165	1
KOONTZ EMERY R	COL	0-0310369	0166	3
KOONTZ RUSSELL H	1LT	0-1823171	0245	2
KOONTZ WILLIAM F	LTC	0-1552724	0965	1
KOOP CHARLES F	MAJ	0-2263350	1265	1
KOOP JOHN L	LTC	0-1042338	1263	1
KOOP LOUIS D	MAJ	0-0138412	0648	3
KOOPERSTEIN SAMUEL I	LTC	0-0500798	0446	2
KOOPMAN ROBERT K	MAJ	0-0352769	0858	2
KOOPMANN FREDERICK	LTC	0-1313903	1162	2
KOOPS FRANK F	LTC	0-0244239	1044	2
KOOS RICHARD B	LTC	0-0451638	0663	1
KOOSA FRED L	COL	0-0206959	0457	3
KOOSE HAROLD W	CW4	W-2148797	1068	2
KOPAN LORYN E	LTC	0-0919719	0168	3
KOPANSKI STEPHEN	LTC	0-1293071	0164	1
KOPASZ JOHN C	1LT	0-1582409	0745	2
KOPCHAK JOHN JR	CPT	0-1017790	0347	2
KOPCHELL GILMORE R	MAJ	0-1541066	0647	2
KOPEC EMILY G	1LT	N-0731879	0646	1
KOPEC JOSEPH J	LTC	0-0497116	0756	1
KOPEIKIN ROBERT	2LT	0-1574913	0351	2
KOPELKE KEITH E	LTC	0-1822285	1060	1
KOPER EVA L J	CPT	N-0734376	0946	1
KOPESCHKA EDWARD C	MAJ	0-1930884	0967	1
KOPF FRANK A	COL	0-0202782	1045	2
KOPF JOHN H	LTC	0-1825626	1162	1
KOPICKI ANTHONY J	LTC	0-1640639	0862	1
KOPICKI CHESTER F	LTC	0-1824874	0462	1
KOPKE JOHN N	LTC	0-1012351	0363	1
KOPMAN PHILIP	1LT	0-1039830	0845	2
KOPNICKY ANDREW M	CW3	W-2145349	0162	1
KOPP ARTHUR R	MAJ	0-0982535	1065	1
KOPP FRED H	1LT	0-1045138	1145	2
KOPP RAYMOND J	LTC	0-0297518	0868	3
KOPP WILLIAM L	COL	0-0242065	0554	2
KOPP WILLIAM R	LTC	0-0439392	0566	1
KOPPA KARL K	MAJ	0-1015664	0758	1
KOPPENHAVER FRED B	CPT	0-0503541	1045	2
KOPPENHOEFER ERVIN J	CW3	W-2141930	1058	1
KOPPERL BERTRAM B JR	1LT	0-1047195	0347	2
KOPPES LAWRENCE M	MAJ	0-1650617	0863	1
KOPPLER CARL E	1LT	0-2043023	0145	2
KOPPLIN EDWARD M JR	MAJ	0-1921451	0868	1
KOPS HERMAN	MAJ	0-1289924	0557	1
KOPSTEIN PHILIP E	MAJ	0-1798994	0967	3
KOR OLEG H	LTC	0-0466449	0862	1
KORACH SAMUEL	LTC	0-0493710	1165	1
KORANDOVITCH MIKE	1LT	0-0496167	0447	2
KORANEK JEROME	CW3	W-2205645	0464	1
KORB LELAND C	MAJ	0-0910512	0549	2
KORB WILLIAM C	COL	0-0271597	0868	3
KORBAL FLOYD J	MAJ	0-0200392	0763	1
KORBHOLZ OSCAR	2LT	0-1300978	0744	2
KORDA ALEXANDER	CPT	0-1996512	1264	1
KORDECKI MELVIN A	LTC	0-0492124	0957	2
KORECKI STEVEN	MAJ	0-1051231	0157	1
KOREN MARY J	MAJ	L-0603229	1265	3
KORESJOSKI FRANK	MAJ	0-0502859	0656	1
KORHAN HERMAN H	2LT	0-1288758	1044	2
KORIATH WILLIAM G	MAJ	0-1299255	1060	1
KORN DAVID	MAJ	0-0453500	1053	2
KORN MARTIN P	LTC	0-0144240	0648	3
KORN MATTHEW F	LTC	0-0239155	0865	3
KORN RICHARD R	2LT	0-1582849	0446	2
KORNEGAY SILAS	MAJ	0-2030197	1060	1
KORNFELD MURRAY I	1LT	0-1012429	0446	2
KORNHAUSER LESTER L	LTC	0-0220788	1051	2
KORNS WILLIAM L	2LT	0-0927147	1045	2
KORNSE EUGENE H JR	CW2	W-2214612	0368	1

NAME	GRADE	SVC NO	DATE RET MO YR	RET CODE
KOROL ALEXANDER	1LT	0-1303741	0546	2
KOROTSKY HENRY	MAJ	0-1897775	0661	1
KORP EDWARD M	MAJ	0-1337718	0663	1
KORPONIC ALEX J	MAJ	0-0337029	0853	2
KORRASIK SAMUEL	1LT	0-1634985	0446	2
KORRISON DAVID W	MAJ	0-1013027	0647	2
KORSCHGEN LEON W	LTC	0-0285599	0954	1
KORSE HARRY	CW2	W-2110277	0545	2
KORSGREN DAVID C	CPT	0-0199922	0153	3
KORSTANGE HERBERT J	CPT	0-2288263	0960	1
KORTEN HENRY J	MAJ	0-0923965	0845	2
KORTVESE STEPHEN J	LTC	0-0364457	0166	1
KORVER KENNETH J	LTC	0-1328709	0866	1
KORY JACK I	LTC	0-0581968	1162	1
KOSACK SUSAN E	1LT	N-0757204	1051	2
KOSAK ADAM A	CPT	0-2018121	0459	1
KOSAK JOSEPH C	MAJ	0-1285771	0962	1
KOSAKA FRED I	LTC	0-1544980	0165	1
KOSEBUTZKI VINCENT J	COL	0-1286144	0661	1
KOSEN JOSEPH	1LT	0-1289747	0246	2
KOSHIRE JOSEPH J	CW4	W-2120828	0166	1
KOSHOFFER JOSEPH T	LTC	0-1302988	1262	1
KOSICKI BERNARD A	COL	0-0211365	0660	3
KOSINSKI LEN V	2LT	0-1322189	1044	2
KOSKI AUGUSTUS A	MAJ	0-2026396	0768	3
KOSKI WILLIAM A	LTC	0-0492648	1166	3
KOSKI WILLIAM N	LTC	0-1104257	0465	1
KOSLOW JOSEPH	CW4	W-2003154	1167	3
KOSMALSKI STEPHEN J	2LT	0-1311789	0244	2
KOSMATKA WITOLD C	2LT	0-1174921	0644	2
KOSON ANDRE D	MAJ	0-1950002	0264	1
KOSOREK VALERIE W	LTC	0-2055213	0565	1
KOSSA FRANK R	COL	0-0219748	1157	3
KOST HARRY	2LT	0-1546879	0644	2
KOST MICHAEL	CPT	0-1922658	0765	1
KOST WILLIAM L	LTC	0-0245515	1160	3
KOSTENBAUDER MARION	MAJ	N-0759394	0466	1
KOSTENICK STEVEN L	MAJ	0-1823888	0365	1
KOSTENSKI LESTER M	MAJ	0-1100627	0955	1
KOSTER CLIFFORD C	MAJ	0-0981878	0665	1
KOSTER DOROTHY B	2LT	L-0601416	1144	2
KOSTIN RUDOLPH A	LTC	0-0460661	1062	1
KOSTOCH FREDERICK	CPT	0-1540896	0862	1
KOSTOWICZ STEVEN	1LT	0-1303613	1145	2
KOTARSKY JOSEPH M	LTC	0-1332973	0164	1
KOTCH DONALD J	MAJ	0-1579895	1159	1
KOTCH RICHARD E	LTC	0-1552921	0266	1
KOTELES ALEXANDER JR	1LT	0-1541055	0245	2
KOTH BEN	CW2	W-2146695	0761	1
KOTILAINEN REINO L	CW2	W-2143663	0657	2
KOTINEK JAMES J	MAJ	0-0982982	1062	1
KOTNIK VICTOR J	CW3	W-2106394	0461	1
KOTRE NICHOLAS O	1LT	0-1323006	1045	2
KOTTKE ELMER E	CPT	0-0174684	0944	2
KOTTLER CARL F JR	2LT	0-1536068	0745	2
KOTTMAN CLARENCE A	CPT	0-0471966	1046	1
KOUCKY GEORGE W	1LT	0-1948493	0448	2
KOUDELKA HAROLD A	MAJ	0-1639257	0156	1
KOUKES LEE N	MAJ	0-1597709	0866	1
KOUKOL AUGUST JR	COL	0-0320663	0562	1
KOUMJIAN PETER	MAJ	0-0456647	1061	2
KOUNTZE ELMER B	2LT	0-1284527	1043	2
KOVACH ALEXANDER	MAJ	0-0695354	0765	1
KOVACH JOHNNIE	MAJ	0-1651110	0662	1
KOVACH JOSEPH J	MAJ	0-0354543	0853	2
KOVACIC JOSEPH J	CW4	W-2151666	1265	1
KOVACS STEPHEN L	LTC	0-0268585	0762	3
KOVALCHIK GEORGE JR	CW3	W-2150526	0158	1
KOVE BERNARD S	COL	0-0296281	1065	3
KOWALCHICK MICHAEL	CPT	0-1000984	0546	2
KOWALCIK RUDOLPH V	CW4	W-2122981	0268	1
KOWALESKI JOHN F	CPT	0-0212919	1044	2
KOWALKOWSKI STANLEY	MAJ	0-1030389	0258	1
KOWALOFF MEYER	COL	0-0330274	0968	3
KOWALSKI JEROME J	1LT	0-1314926	0845	2

NAME	GRADE	SVC NO	DATE RET MO YR	RET CODE
[illegible]	[illegible]	[illegible]	1167	1
[illegible]	[illegible]	[illegible]	[illegible]	1
[illegible]	[illegible]	[illegible]	[illegible]	1
[illegible]	[illegible]	[illegible]	[illegible]	1
[illegible]	[illegible]	[illegible]	0866	1
[illegible]	CPT	[illegible]	0766	2
[illegible]	MAJ	[illegible]	0364	2
[illegible]	[illegible]	[illegible]	0567	1
[illegible]	CPT	[illegible]	[illegible]	2
[illegible]	[illegible]	[illegible]	[illegible]	2
[illegible]	LTC	[illegible]	0662	1
[illegible]	LTC	[illegible]	0756	1
[illegible]	CW2	[illegible]	0763	1
[illegible]	LTC	[illegible]	1267	1
[illegible]	CPT	[illegible]	0746	2
[illegible]	MAJ	[illegible]	0262	1
[illegible]	LTC	0-1694426	0563	1
[illegible]	WO1	W-2152052	0155	1
[illegible]	1LT	0-1300814	0945	2
[illegible]	2LT	0-1641447	0344	2
[illegible]	MAJ	0-1587393	0454	1
[illegible] WILLIAM F	LTC	0-0283480	0663	1
[illegible] JOHN	CPT	0-2027035	0562	1
[illegible]	MAJ	0-0174713	0747	2
[illegible] EARL	MAJ	0-0497601	0748	1
KRAEMER EDWIN	LTC	0-0404561	0668	3
KRAEMER FRITZ G A	LTC	0-2012160	0868	3
KRAEMER GEORGE S	MAJ	0-0326080	1045	2
KRAEMER HORST [illegible]	CPT	0-1512473	0446	2
KRAEMER JOE JR	MAJ	0-0298142	0963	3
KRAEMER WENDELL J	MAJ	0-1175177	0866	1
KRAETTLI HAROLD J	MAJ	0-0366630	0248	2
KRAETZER KENNETH G	LTC	0-1170814	0261	1
KRAFFT ROBERT F	2LT	0-2032268	0946	2
KRAFT AL	CPT	0-1554415	1147	2
KRAFT ALLISON F	2LT	0-0544683	1045	2
KRAFT EMMITT F	CW3	W-2147324	0662	1
KRAFT HAROLD C	CPT	0-1165523	0157	2
KRAFT JOHN F	CW3	W-2142864	0161	1
KRAFT NED J	LTC	0-0237147	0166	3
KRAFT PAUL B	1LT	0-0325722	1043	2
KRAFTSCHIK ERNEST W	LTC	0-0333284	0360	1
KRAHN WILLIAM G	2LT	0-1317636	1144	2
KRAISEL MORRIS	LTC	0-0298678	0167	3
KRAJESKI WILLIAM S	LTC	0-0563977	1160	1
KRAJEWSKI STANLEY J	MAJ	0-1795924	1154	1
KRAKAJEK MAX F	CPT	0-1542197	0367	1
KRAKAJSKAS WALTER A	LTC	0-1323938	0862	1
KRAKER JOHN JR	CW2	W-2148673	0964	1
KRAKOWER ARNOLD R	MAJ	0-1636168	0447	2
KRAL JOSEPH F	MAJ	0-1547359	0964	1
KRALL MICHAEL	MAJ	0-1873612	0762	1
KRALOVEC JOHN G	LTC	0-0173060	1060	3
KRAMER ALBERT A	MAJ	0-1293608	0661	1
KRAMER BERTRAM W	LTC	0-1560135	1267	1
KRAMER CHARLES T	LTC	0-0113112	0850	3
KRAMER CLARENCE A	2LT	0-2034546	0545	2
KRAMER CLAUDE J	LTC	0-0300364	0162	1
KRAMER DAVID F	MAJ	0-1540989	1266	1
KRAMER DEWIGHT F SR	MAJ	0-1924894	1066	1
KRAMER DONALD W	LTC	0-2036433	0361	1
KRAMER FRANK J	CPT	0-2262999	0461	1
KRAMER FREDERICK	CPT	0-0350042	1144	2
KRAMER GERTRUDE M	CPT	N-0784609	0747	1
KRAMER HERBERT J	1LT	0-1047196	0545	2
KRAMER IRVIN H	CPT	0-1014110	0647	2
KRAMER JEROME D	CPT	0-0916139	0646	2
KRAMER JOHN	CPT	0-0508489	0646	2
KRAMER JOHN J	CW3	W-2141912	0959	1
KRAMER JOSEPH F	COL	0-0109291	0147	2
KRAMER JOSEPH F	MAJ	0-0808283	0767	1
KRAMER LEO J	LTC	0-2037069	0866	2
KRAMER MARCUS	CPT	0-0534326	0146	2
KRAMER PAUL R	1LT	0-1292405	0545	2
KRAMER RICHARD A JR	MAJ	0-1644500	0662	1

NAME	GRADE	SVC NO	DATE RET MO YR	RET CODE
KRAMER RITA S	2LT	N-0721588	0944	1
KRAMER ROBERT J	LTC	0-0375122	0859	1
KRAMER ROBERT L	MAJ	0-0281280	0844	2
KRAMER SEYMORE	1LT	0-1592494	104N	2
KRAMER STEWART G	MAJ	0-2053836	1055	1
KRAMER WILBUR P	MAJ	0-0188708	0646	2
KRAMER WILLIAM O	LTC	0-1644501	0868	3
KRAMER WILLIAM F	LTC	0-1647132	0969	3
KRAMER WILLIAM J JR	1LT	0-1012779	0246	2
KRAMER WILLIAM R	1LT	0-1323146	1045	2
KRAMKOWSKI BENJAMIN	MAJ	0-1318187	0461	1
KRAMP MERLE W	CW2	W-2144610	0763	1
KRAMP RICHARD O	MAJ	0-0384632	0146	2
KRAN WILLIAM A	LTC	0-0290893	0954	1
KRANICHUCK JOHN M	MAJ	0-0442736	0547	2
KRANTZ HARRY	CPT	0-1689887	0245	2
KRANTZ MARVIN J	MAJ	0-0985938	1163	1
KRANTZ NORBERT J	2LT	0-1110054	1144	2
KRANTZ ROBERT L	CW2	R W-2210947	0664	1
KRANTZ WALTER A	CPT	0-1303162	0258	1
KRANZ DWIGHT O	CW4	W-2005624	1265	1
KRANZ WALTER L	MAJ	0-1325820	1060	1
KRASHOC JOE T	LTC	0-1644502	1062	1
KRASNE LEO R	COL	0-0309808	0860	3
KRASNE PAUL M	1LT	0-0422211	0846	2
KRASNOFF HARRY M	COL	0-0489953	0863	3
KRASSNER WILLIAM V	2LT	0-2048677	1044	2
KRASZEWSKI THADDEUS	LTC	0-1050345	0864	1
KRATCH FRANCIS J	LTC	0-1113308	0664	1
KRATOCHVIL REGIS H	1LT	0-1319512	1045	2
KRATZ DOROTHY M	MAJ	N-0724057	0468	1
KRATZ FRANCIS F	MAJ	0-1648980	0766	1
KRATZ ORA A	2LT	0-1846018	0745	2
KRATZER DONALD A	CPT	0-1017859	1046	2
KRATZER NORWOOD W	CW3	W-2150848	0864	1
KRAU HAROLD N	LTC	0-0395809	0862	1
KRAUCHI CHARLES A	MAJ	0-0973503	0561	1
KRAUS ARTHUR I	LTC	0-0207562	0652	2
KRAUS CHARLES H	COL	0-0931705	0864	3
KRAUS FREDERICK	1LT	0-1705813	0645	2
KRAUS GEORGE H	CW2	W-2145458	0364	1
KRAUS HERBERT H	CW3	W-2153290	0768	1
KRAUS JOHN L	CPT	0-0494479	0249	1
KRAUS JOSEPH A	1LT	0-1174922	1045	2
KRAUS LEO J	COL	0-0307551	1266	3
KRAUS RUSSELL E	2LT	0-2012480	0352	1
KRAUS WILLIAM	CW4	W-2136612	0666	1
KRAUS WILLIAM A	LTC	0-0199901	0544	2
KRAUS WILLIAM E	CPT	0-0367573	0145	2
KRAUSE ALBERT	LTC	0-1825010	0763	1
KRAUSE CHARLES F	MAJ	0-0153832	0648	3
KRAUSE CLARENCE R	CW3	W-2148324	0862	1
KRAUSE CLAUDE G	LTC	0-1292713	0263	1
KRAUSE DONALD A	MAJ	0-1845197	0361	1
KRAUSE EDWARD A	LTC	0-0243697	0845	2
KRAUSE EDWARD C	COL	0-0375296	0859	1
KRAUSE FRANCIS T	CPT	0-1542100	1144	2
KRAUSE GEORGE M	MAJ	0-1039735	0468	3
KRAUSE GUSTAV J	LTC	0-0400034	0647	2
KRAUSE JAMES R	1LT	0-1644503	0646	2
KRAUSE MARTIN W	MAJ	0-0201581	0763	3
KRAUSE NELSON	LTC	0-1576257	1059	1
KRAUSE ROBERT R	MAJ	0-1014388	0161	1
KRAUSE RUDOLPH	CPT	0-2265771	0268	1
KRAUSE VIRGIL E P	CW3	W-2205692	0766	1
KRAUSE WILLIAM A	LTC	0-0319569	1068	3
KRAUSE WILLIAM J	MAJ	0-1824763	0361	1
KRAUSE WILLIAM O	CW2	W-3150682	0166	1
KRAUSHAR CARL	1LT	0-1588998	104N	2
KRAUSS ALBERT	2LT	0-0266491	1156	3
KRAUSS HERBERT M	CPT	0-1292714	0346	2
KRAUSS JOHN J	1LT	0-1047619	0445	2
KRAUSS WALTER E	CPT	0-2041377	0661	1
KRAUT ARTHUR M	LTC	0-0256685	0957	3
KRAUTER JOHN H JR	CW4	W-2124449	1168	1

NAME	GRADE	SVC NO	DATE RET MO YR	RET CODE
KRAVEC EMIL	MAJ	0-1637457	0859	1
KRAVITZ JAMES	LTC	0-0294122	0657	1
[illegible] MICHAEL V	MAJ	[illegible]	0166	1
KRAWCZYK ARTHUR J	LTC	0-1647133	0863	1
[illegible]	COL	[illegible]	0154	3
KRAYNICK MICHAEL	MAJ	0-1302017	1266	1
KREAMER JOHN H	1LT	[illegible]	0244	2
KREBER LEO M	MAJ	0-0171657	0658	3
KREBS CHARLES A	LTC	0-0354421	0161	1
KREBS EDWARD G	LTC	0-1030448	0657	1
KREBS FRED	1LT	0-2046566	0149	1
KREBS LEON A	CPT	0-0327515	0242	2
KREBS NITA	MAJ	N-0785656	0465	1
KREBS RAYMOND F JR	MAJ	0-0966959	1062	1
KREBS RUDOLPH J	COL	0-0302402	1162	3
KREHSBACH VERNON G	CPT	0-0984340	0461	1
KREGER CLARENCE J	MAJ	0-0887585	0161	1
KREGER WILLIAM G	B G	0-0348066	1268	3
KREH LEWIS V B	MAJ	0-0210663	0753	3
KREHER GERHARDT P	CPT	0-0328184	0746	2
KREIBICH ROBERT F	CW3	W-2142299	0860	1
KREIDER ABRAM H	CW3	W-2205511	0567	1
KREIDER GEORGE P	MAJ	0-0100517	0455	3
KREISA FRANCIS J	MAJ	0-0130631	0953	3
KREISER HENRY F	MAJ	0-1055360	0560	1
KREITNER HERMAN G	CPT	0-2034748	0145	2
KREITNER PAUL A	MAJ	0-1293795	1165	1
KREITZ WILLIAM P	LTC	0-1001384	1263	1
KREIZENBECK FRANK W	LTC	0-0172904	0352	3
KREIZENBECK JOHN W	MAJ	0-2050091	0761	1
KREJCI ERVIN C	CPT	0-1113310	1045	2
KRELL BESSIE S	CPT	N-0702418	1045	1
KRELO GEORGE	LTC	0-1055057	0568	1
KREMBS DONALD W	LTC	0-1309941	1061	1
KREMENS VICTOR	1LT	0-1756590	0645	2
KREMER PAUL G	CW3	W-2208131	0768	1
KREMER PAUL P	CW2	W-2146671	0463	1
KREMER WILLIAM H	LTC	0-0263082	0268	3
KREML FRANKLIN M	B G	0-0909816	0267	3
KREMP FRED W	1LT	0-1287018	0447	2
KREMPELKI STANLEY W	1LT	0-1111720	114N	2
KREMPEL JA'S A	LTC	0-0497536	0756	1
KRENCICKI THEODORE	CPT	0-2018373	0662	2
KRENITSKY THOMAS D	LTC	0-2040813	1065	1
KRENKEL HARRY N	COL	0-0125117	1055	3
KRENZ ROBERT W	LTC	0-0254429	1066	3
KREPAK MICHAEL	1LT	0-1644506	0945	2
KREPS ADAM	LTC	0-0414840	0766	1
KREPS JOSEPH L	CW4	W-2151979	0466	1
KRESKOSKY MIKE	1LT	0-1308227	0745	2
KRESS CYRIL G	COL	0-0255190	0564	3
KRESS GEORGE L	COL	0-0302438	0368	3
KRESS JOHN J	1LT	0-1317313	0746	2
KRESS MARVIN	1LT	0-0512958	1145	2
KRESS WALTER J	COL	0-0141621	0653	3
KRESYMAN CLARENCE V	CW3	W-2211856	0768	1
KRESYMAN EDWARD J	CW2	W-2151905	0961	1
KRET FRANCIS J	CPT	0-0410046	0846	2
KRETSCHMER ALFRED A	MAJ	0-0335612	0963	3
KRETZ HAROLD	MAJ	0-0889892	0160	1
KRETZINGER WILLIAM	CW2	W-2103110	0650	1
KRETZMEIER CALVIN L	WO1	W-2146609	0457	1
KREUSLING EMIL W	MAJ	0-1048453	1162	1
KREUTER CHARLES L	CW4	W-2000903	0861	3
KREWITZ WILLIAM D	LTC	0-1108086	1165	3
KREWSON CLAYTON B	LTC	0-1700598	0367	3
KREY NORBERT W	CW3	W-2146694	1263	1
KRICK CHARLES P	LTC	0-0307182	0355	3
KRICKL HOWARD F	1LT	0-1287368	0345	2
KRIDLER GEORGE G	2LT	0-1285772	1144	2
KRIECHBAUM JOSEPH R	COL	0-0200597	0855	3
KRIEG CAMERON E	1LT	0-1300342	1045	2
KRIEG FRED H JR	LTC	0-2047394	0466	1
KRIEG JOHN L	LTC	0-0411090	0161	1
KRIEG WILBERT A JR	MAJ	0-1553492	0966	1

NAME	GRADE	SVC NO	DATE RET MO YR	RET CODE
KRIEGEL WILLIAM W	LTC	0-0262963	0168	1
KRIEGER BURTON E	CW3	W-2141342	1055	1
KRIEGER EDWIN H	1LT	0-1112275	1045	2
KRIEGER IRVING	CPT	0-1285441	0967	2
KRIEGER RICHARD H	CW2	W-2206725	1161	1
KRIENHAGEN LEE F	CW2	W-2148903	0860	1
KRIER HENRY L	LTC	0-0400847	1060	1
KRIESE CLINTON J	LTC	0-0344780	0560	1
KRIGBAUM WILLIAM L	COL	0-0187363	1046	2
KRIGER EUNICE R	MAJ	0-2021160	0164	1
KRIGLINE EDMUND G	CPT	0-0235788	1148	1
KRIGSTEN WILLIAM M	COL	0-0270285	0446	2
KRIKAC STANLEY J	COL	0-0302377	0961	3
KRIM GEORGE A	COL	0-0446273	0854	1
KRIMBILL JACK B	LTC	0-0421206	0461	1
KRIMSLEY MALCOLM	1LT	0-1689588	0944	2
KRING HUGH F	COL	0-0275674	1264	3
KRINGS LOUIS W	MAJ	0-0254199	1064	3
KRISE LEO	CW4	W-2146254	0857	1
KRISH EDWARD P	LTC	0-0294736	1154	1
KRISHNA IKBAI	CPT	0-0483414	0245	2
KRISHNER THEODORE	MAJ	0-0303869	0951	2
KRISKE HERBERT A	MAJ	0-1647562	0657	1
KRIST CHESTER J	LTC	0-2292561	0766	1
KRIST LOUIS M	MAJ	0-1309073	1161	2
KRISTAL JACKSON J	MAJ	0-0371940	0146	2
KRISTIANSEN HARRY E	1LT	0-1317922	104N	2
KRISTIANSEN STANLEY	MAJ	0-0719963	1163	1
KRITKAUSKY ANTHONY R	1LT	0-0373095	0144	2
KRITZMAN CHARLES W	MAJ	0-2023633	0258	1
KRIVI ANDREW H	CPT	0-1306522	0364	1
KRIVISKEY GEORGE	LTC	0-0284502	0568	3
KRIVUNOS ABRAHAM F	MAJ	0-0536374	0945	2
KRIZ JOSEPH R	COL	0-0323535	0963	3
KRIZ ROBERT F	COL	0-1553684	0665	1
KRIZAN EMIL J	WO1	W-2115700	0647	1
KRIZIN STEPHEN E	LTC	0-0481880	1167	3
KROB DEAN M	MAJ	0-0968683	0863	1
KROCHMAL EMIL SR	CW3	W-2144170	0956	1
KROCHMALNY MICHAEL	MAJ	0-1823891	0261	L
KROCK RUPERT T	LTC	0-1281516	0765	3
KROEGER ARTHUR F	MAJ	0-0255246	0858	3
KROEGER CHARLES F	CW4	W-2107166	1057	1
KROEGER FRANK B	CPT	0-0320948	0545	2
KROEGER HOWARD E	MAJ	0-2103071	0764	1
KROEHL GEORGE F	LTC	0-0392387	0164	1
KROELL JOHN T	MAJ	0-0258380	0745	2
KROENCKE EDWARD J	COL	0-0220175	0560	3
KROENCKE FRED J	MAJ	0-0271716	0863	3
KROEPSCH KARL A	COL	0-0243588	1154	2
KROFCHICK JOHNNIE	MAJ	0-2000585	0459	1
KROFCHIK MICHAEL	MAJ	0-1637739	0756	1
KROFCHIK PAUL	LTC	0-0451327	0158	1
KROFT ANDREW P	CPT	0-1339281	1147	2
KROFT DAVID F	LTC	0-1056436	0967	1
KROGEL ROBERT W	LTC	0-1703897	0560	1
KROGH ELMER L	1LT	0-2210819	0854	2
KROGH RICHARD H	CPT	0-0221129	0863	3
KROHE THEODORE D	LTC	0-1533608	0765	1
KROHN NORRIS F	LTC	0-0327314	0566	3
KROKENBERGER JOHN	MAJ	0-0362023	1060	1
KROKUS THEODORE J	COL	0-0179937	0556	3
KROL WALTER J	MAJ	0-2263772	0168	1
KROLAK GEORGE	MAJ	0-1115943	0163	1
KROLL MARGARET W	CPT	N-0728655	0556	2
KROMM FRED	1LT	0-0155239	0952	1
KROMREY ROBERT P	LTC	0-0216061	0364	3
KRON ARTHUR	MAJ	0-2025240	0462	1
KRONE EARL M	MAJ	0-1115318	0257	1
KRONE MILTON F	CW3	W-2146074	1062	1
KRONENBERGER GEORGE	LTC	0-1312569	0663	1
KRONHEIM ALBERT S	MAJ	0-1288759	1145	2
KRONHEIM PAUL O	LTC	0-1636172	0857	1
KRONICK LLOYD	2LT	0-2036664	0645	2
KRONK ADAM B	CPT	0-1309074	0146	2

NAME	GRADE	SVC NO	DATE RET MO YR	RET CODE
KRONTZ WENDELL K	1LT	0-4007013	0259	2
KROON PHILIP C	CPT	0-1170816	0465	1
KROPOSKY CHARLES P	LTC	0-0373205	0760	1
KROSCHEL FRED M JR	COL	0-0452418	0766	2
KROTTS PAUL G	LTC	0-0334555	0860	1
KROTZ DANIEL F	WO1	W-2119454	0545	2
KROULIK ALFRED R	LTC	0-0260868	0266	3
KROUNGOLO MILTON L	CPT	0-0436082	0146	2
KROUSEY WYMONC C	1LT	0-1541944	0457	1
KROVITSKY ELY Y	1LT	0-0451133	1045	2
KROWCHUN JOHN T	1LT	0-2000066	0248	2
KRSUL JOHN W	CW2	W-2145459	0159	1
KRUCKENBERG CARL W G	CW2	W-2150314	0860	1
KRUCKER HERBERT F	COL	0-0254436	0646	2
KRUCZEK BERNARD C	CW2	W-2205912	0160	1
KRUCZEK JOSEPH F	MAJ	0-1584481	1160	1
KRUCZEK WALLACE B	LTC	0-0387181	0657	1
KRUEGER ALBERT T	LTC	0-0232614	0364	3
KRUEGER CLARENCE J	COL	0-0242192	0364	3
KRUEGER ELMER J	CPT	0-0159413	0951	3
KRUEGER EUGENE F	LTC	0-1294148	0361	1
KRUEGER FRED	CPT	0-0488077	0857	1
KRUEGER FREDERICK	LTC	0-0182033	0659	3
KRUEGER GERARD	MAJ	0-0274456	0664	3
KRUEGER HERBERT A	2LT	0-1290617	0144	2
KRUEGER JESS	LTC	0-0240503	0648	3
KRUEGER LESLIE F	MAJ	0-2262257	0565	1
KRUEGER MARION H	MAJ	0-1120550	0965	1
KRUEGER NORBERT M	LTC	0-1284719	0665	1
KRUEGER PAUL M	CW2	W-3430151	0364	2
KRUEGER RALPH H	CW3	RW-2143173	1061	1
KRUEGER ROBERT A	LTC	0-1924805	1068	1
KRUEGER ROBERT F	CPT	0-1048055	1163	1
KRUEGER WILLIAM L	1LT	0-1297053	0745	2
KRUEGER WILLIS E	LTC	0-0252247	0263	3
KRUG JAMES M	LTC	0-0420992	0667	3
KRUG MARIE A	2LT	N-0755960	0845	1
KRUG RICHARD C	LTC	0-1305438	0767	1
KRUG ROBERT C	1LT	0-0556413	0152	2
KRUG ROBERT H	MAJ	0-1925344	1165	1
KRUGER ELMER L	LTC	0-0351068	1061	1
KRUGER JOHN H	MAJ	0-1589324	0547	2
KRUGER LESTER O	1LT	0-1549526	0146	2
KRUGER LOUIS F	LTC	0-0155872	1145	2
KRUGER WILLIAM F	LTC	0-2020658	0568	3
KRUGH ROBERT C	CPT	0-2288464	1264	1
KRUI FRANK	1LT	0-1108790	0247	2
KRUK JOHN S	LTC	0-1173339	1162	1
KRUKAR JOHN	MAJ	0-1548090	0455	1
KRULL GEORGE W	CW3	W-2143748	0263	1
KRULL HAROLD E	LTC	0-0346200	1059	1
KRULL SAMUEL	MAJ	0-0138606	0646	2
KRUMBHAAR CHARLES C	LTC	0-0311737	1262	1
KRUMDIECK NEWTON	MAJ	0-0427963	0146	2
KRUMENACKER GEORGE A	CPT	0-1308969	0647	2
KRUMHAR THOMAS R	1LT	0-0478242	1047	2
KRUML JOSEPH G	COL	0-0267803	0964	3
KRUMLAUF ERNEST J	2LT	0-1298720	0444	2
KRUMM CARL F	COL	0-0301842	0860	3
KRUMM ROBERT A	WO1	W-2120011	0746	2
KRUMM ROGER V	CPT	0-1035863	0446	2
KRUMMEY LLOYD F	MAJ	0-0453385	0357	1
KRUMPOCH QUIDO T	LTC	0-1182624	0766	1
KRUMSICK CALVIN P	CW2	W-2151619	0662	2
KRUPINSKI FRANCIS T	LTC	0-0353323	1061	1
KRUSE JACK H	LTC	0-1184685	1064	1
KRUSE JESSE E	CPT	0-1031735	0547	2
KRUSE JIM T	CPT	0-1693845	0557	1
KRUSE LEE G	CPT	0-2016229	0656	1
KRUSE LOUIS F JR	LTC	0-0334404	0960	1
KRUSE MARVIN O	LTC	0-0308951	0468	3
KRUSEMARK LEO E	MAJ	0-0949471	0666	1
KRUSZYNSKY CHESTER	CW3	W-2142167	1156	1
KRUTAK FRANK J	CPT	0-1312570	0947	2
KRUTHERS JOHN V	CPT	0-1053678	1065	1

NAME	GRADE	SVC NO	DATE RET MO YR	RET CODE
KRUTSCH DEXTER R	MAJ	0-1100629	0654	1
KRYLOFF EUGENE B	LTC	0-0298273	0560	2
KRYSTON MATTHEW E	LTC	0-1583238	0261	1
KRYTER LAURENCE H	LTC	0-0407581	0765	1
KRYZAN FRANK X	1LT	0-1183340	0446	2
KRZYZANOWSKI W M	CPT	0-1691389	0445	2
KUBA JOHN	WO1	W-2131790	0650	1
KUBACH OSCAR C	COL	0-0267287	0956	3
KUBACKI PETER	LTC	0-0403620	0659	2
KUBE ROBERT B	LTC	0-0456435	0466	1
KUBELCK VERN E	2LT	0-0454519	0944	2
KUBELIUS ANTHONY J	LTC	0-1100186	0665	1
KUBIAK FRANK E	LTC	0-0496974	0657	1
KUBICEK ADOLPH R	CPT	0-0488691	1049	1
KUBICHEK FAYE M	1LT	N-0732619	0845	1
KUBIK GEORGE J	MAJ	0-1185232	1067	3
KUBISIAK NORBERT J	MAJ	0-1799526	0258	1
KUBISTAL LESTER M	CPT	0-1643054	0258	2
KUBISZEWSKI RAYMOND	LTC	0-1647564	0963	1
KUBIT THADDEUS A	MAJ	0-1558872	0464	1
KUBLICK WILLIAM G	1LT	0-1101533	0346	2
KUBOOSH EDWARD	CPT	0-1307033	0347	2
KUC WALTER J	CPT	0-0400415	0750	2
KUCERA FRANK H J	CW2	W-2211499	0768	1
KUCERA WILLIE J	MAJ	0-0920269	1262	1
KUCHAR EMIL H	MAJ	0-1634994	0258	2
KUCHERA EARL A	LTC	0-1053679	0662	2
KUCHEVAR ANNE M	1LT	N-0730143	1146	1
KUCHINSKAS ERNEST V	MAJ	0-1598609	0760	1
KUCHINSKI WILLIAM H	CW3	W-2141344	0258	1
KUCHTA FRANK I	LTC	0-1589671	0567	1
KUCIA JOHN J	LTC	0-0408569	0668	3
KUCKUK ROLLAND A	LTC	0-0261016	0267	3
KUCZMARSKI LEO N	CPT	0-0327019	0746	2
KUDEK BERNARD	LTC	0-0194297	0263	3
KUDER WILLIAM R	LTC	0-0333442	1060	1
KUDO FRANCIS M	2LT	0-2055905	0945	2
KUDRLE CHARLES A	LTC	0-1010123	1060	1
KUDZIA ALBERT G	MAJ	0-1306287	0753	2
KUEBER PAUL C	LTC	0-1171636	1164	1
KUEBLER WILLIAM D	COL	0-0268894	0764	3
KUECHLER JAMES R	MAJ	0-0506854	0868	3
KUECKER EDWIN A	COL	0-0549216	0568	3
KUEHL FREDERICK	LTC	0-0322483	0867	3
KUEHL GREGORY J	MAJ	0-1329956	0364	2
KUEHL RUSSELL C	COL	0-0318545	0465	3
KUEHN CHARLES E	MAJ	0-2263794	0466	1
KUEHN MORTMER H	MAJ	0-1578730	0262	2
KUEHN RILEY	COL	0-0227871	0960	3
KUEKER WILLIAM G	LTC	0-1542776	1161	1
KUEKES JOHN H	2LT	0-0539443	0945	2
KUENY GUSTAVE JR	CW3	W-2200110	0766	3
KUENZ PAUL H	2LT	0-1282396	0859	1
KUES OSCAR G	CPT	0-2007716	0648	2
KUESTER JOHN JR	2LT	0-1996667	1145	2
KUETHE RALPH W	LTC	0-1319289	1163	1
KUGEL CHARLES R	LTC	0-1053680	0167	3
KUGLER OLGA R	MAJ	N-0756911	1065	1
KUGLIN HERMAN E	CPT	0-0242932	1055	3
KUHAR ALBERT G	MAJ	0-1822286	0161	1
KUHFELD FRANK W	MAJ	0-0273531	0167	3
KUHL MARIJN T	MAJ	0-0288075	0567	3
KUHL WALTER A JR	2LT	0-1012659	0444	2
KUHLING WALTER W	MAJ	0-1581885	0265	1
KUHLMAN MILTON F	1LT	0-0908739	0643	2
KUHLMAN ROSS E	MAJ	0-0200108	1054	3
KUHLMANN ROBERT L	CW2	W-2152654	0862	1
KUHN ARDELLA B	1LT	N-0730336	0246	1
KUHN CARL B	LTC	0-0274222	0965	3
KUHN CHARLES E	LTC	0-1293610	0657	1
KUHN CHRISTOPH	LTC	0-0537575	0466	3
KUHN CLIFFORD W	LTC	0-0311652	0866	3
KUHN DAVID R	CW3	W-2208889	1263	1
KUHN EDMUND D	COL	0-2053849	0867	3
KUHN ERNEST G	LTC	0-0221590	0559	3

NAME	GRADE	SVC NO	DATE RET MO YR	RET CODE
KUHN FRANK J JR	MAJ	*0-1109433	1161	1
KUHN GEORGE D	LTC	0-0366668	0763	1
KUHN HAROLD E	LTC	0-0246290	0557	3
KUHN HERMAN	MAJ	0-0499571	1057	1
KUHN HOWARD R	LTC	0-1120026	0867	1
KUHN IRVING	CPT	0-1169205	0346	2
KUHN JAMES P	CW3	W-2144458	1263	2
KUHN JIMMIE G	CW2	W-3151087	0468	1
KUHN JOHN J	CW2	W-2153198	0758	1
KUHN KENNETH	COL	0-0325919	0265	3
KUHN LLOYD R	CW4	W-2109259	1165	3
KUHN NICHOLAS J	LTC	0-0392006	0161	1
KUHN RALPH R	1LT	0-0148004	0655	3
KUHN RICHARD P JR	1LT	0-0531551	0346	2
KUHN WILLARD R	LTC	0-0166039	0650	1
KUHN WILLARD W	WO1	W-2118537	0665	1
KUHN WILLIAM F	LTC	0-0296893	0159	1
KUHN WILLIAM H	LTC	0-0290156	0968	3
KUHNE ROBERT F	LTC	0-0384128	0561	1
KUHNS CLINTON W	LTC	0-0325003	0761	2
KUHNS EDWIN J	MAJ	0-1298881	0664	3
KUHNS GLENN E	2LT	0-0335807	1045	2
KUHNS JAMES F	LTC	0-0423026	1046	2
KUHNS JOSEPH B	LTC	0-0281254	0268	3
KUHNS LLOYD L	LTC	0-0211536	0259	3
KUHNS LOGAN L	LTC	0-0212785	1063	3
KUHNS RUSSELL K	COL	0-0359599	0760	1
KUHNS WALTER A	MAJ	0-0483371	0355	2
KUHR LESTER F	LTC	0-1313257	1262	1
KUHS JACK J	LTC	0-0972500	0868	3
KUITE GEORGE B	MAJ	0-0239868	1062	3
KUJALA EARL W	CPT	0-1543839	0552	2
KUKA JOSEPH E	CW2	W-2211216	0764	1
KUKER EUGENE W	CW3	W-2141852	0959	1
KUKIELKA CASIMIR A	MAJ	0-1548901	1160	1
KUKLA EDWIN A	LTC	0-1640647	0563	1
KUKLA RALPH B	LTC	0-1335938	0367	1
KUKUCKA ANDREW J	LTC	0-1996440	0464	1
KULA HELEN S	2LT	N-0720997	1044	2
KULAS SOPHIA	1LT	N-0758704	0847	1
KULBES PHILIP A	MAJ	0-1109434	1262	1
KULESHA KASMIER J	1LT	0-0488059	0344	2
KULHAN EDWARD F	MAJ	0-0426131	0546	2
KULICK CHARLES G	CW3	W-2153170	1264	1
KULICK LEE R	CPT	0-0404201	0146	2
KULIK JOSEPH A	1LT	0-1312388	1045	2
KULINA PETER T	MAJ	0-1116092	0163	1
KULINA STEPHEN	LTC	0-1945629	0968	3
KULKOSKY FRANK	MAJ	0-1318050	0565	1
KULL BERTHA N	1LT	N-0742416	0146	1
KULL CHARLES W JR	LTC	0-0317913	1065	3
KULL FRANCIS C	MAJ	0-1060161	0557	1
KULL FREDERICK	CPT	0-1308970	0246	2
KULLBACK SOLOMON	COL	0-0300670	0567	3
KULLMAN JOHN T	1LT	0-1637969	1144	2
KULO EDWIN W	LTC	0-0989458	0968	1
KULP DURWARD S SR	CW4	W-2152890	0165	1
KULZER FRANK M	WO1	W-2106220	0644	2
KULZER NORBERT J	CPT	0-0307594	0246	2
KUMER MICHAEL R	2LT	0-1002801	0245	2
KUMM KARL G	LTC	0-0443096	0662	3
KUMPF MARGARET L	MAJ	N-0722514	0867	1
KUNCEK JOECK	1LT	0-0457752	0547	1
KUNCL JOSEPH JR	LTC	0-0255109	0146	2
KUNDERT REUMOND P	LTC	0-1300659	0962	1
KUNDERT RUPERT J	MAJ	0-0293222	0368	3
KUNDRA PAUL P	1LT	0-0455317	0645	2
KUNDRAT ANN M	2LT	N-0741367	1144	1
KUNDRATH JOSEPH J	CW2	W-2007415	0361	3
KUNELLIS CHRIS E	CW2	W-2144491	0758	1
KUNEMAN LEO E	1LT	0-1090876	0654	1
KUNIHIRO SHIZUO	MAJ	0-0967756	0763	1
KUNKEL CLEMENTS F	1LT	0-1013373	1045	2
KUNKEL PAUL A JR	LTC	0-0400174	0446	2
KUNKELMAN RAYMOND E	LTC	0-0222789	0355	3

NAME	GRADE	SVC NO	DATE RET MO YR	RET CODE
KUNKLE GERALD F	LTC	0-0391043	0149	2
KUNKLE MARTIN L	CW4	W-2118360	0762	1
KUNKLE PAUL A	LTC	0-0284585	0562	1
KUNKLE WALTER F	2LT	0-2023857	0146	2
KUNS GEORGE G	COL	0-0271725	0264	1
KUNSEMILLER C F	CPT	0-0323199	0346	2
KUNSMAN GLENN W	1LT	0-2035952	0547	2
KUNTER THOMAS N	2LT	0-2089252	1050	2
KUNTZ JOSEPH T	CW3	W-2148741	0765	1
KUNTZ LOUIS F	MAJ	0-0133840	0648	3
KUNTZ PHILIP L	1LT	0-4036865	0356	2
KUNZ CLAUDE A	LTC	0-0322447	1060	3
KUNZ GEORGE P	MAJ	0-2032959	0360	2
KUNZ JOSEPH F	LTC	0-0436589	0264	1
KUNZ K STUART	MAJ	0-2035118	1160	1
KUNZ OTTO JR	1LT	0-1013575	1045	2
KUNZ RITA D	2LT	N-0702148	1031	1
KUNZE ARTHUR I	MAJ	0-0119143	0154	3
KUNZE JOHN H	CPT	0-1318051	1052	2
KUNZE JOSEPH J	LTC	0-0182196	0157	3
KUNZI STANTON P	MAJ	0-1019315	0663	1
KUNZMAN HENRY W	1LT	0-1175199	0945	2
KUPERSTEIN ABNER D	CPT	0-0385612	1145	2
KUPFRIAN LAURANCE B	1LT	0-1645739	0847	2
KUPP HARLEN P	CW2	W-2211744	1166	1
KUPPER CHARLES J	LTC	0-0903698	1045	2
KUPSINEL HERBERT R	MAJ	0-0972512	0564	1
KURDY THOMAS J	LTC	0-0291337	0366	3
KURIATNYK STEVE	CW3	W-2152705	0862	1
KURIS DAVID B	MAJ	0-0375798	0246	2
KURITZKY WILLIAM	1LT	0-1311526	1044	2
KURKA RALPH J	LTC	0-0974853	1168	1
KURKOWSKI JOSEPH P	CPT	0-1559359	1053	2
KURLAND LEON K	COL	0-0284283	0760	1
KURTENBACH EUGENE A	MAJ	0-1639281	1159	1
KURTH AGATHA R	1LT	N-0760584	0545	1
KURTH ARNO W	1LT	0-1103740	0545	2
KURTH ERVIN F	MAJ	0-0242202	0663	1
KURTH RICHARD A	CW2	W-2000106	0546	2
KURTH WILLARD C	CPT	0-1061162	0550	2
KURTTI JOHN W	1LT	0-0316850	0543	2
KURTZ EDWARD E	1LT	0-0108986	1137	1
KURTZ FLOYD E	MAJ	0-0287093	1165	3
KURTZ IRVING M	CPT	0-0317943	0745	2
KURTZ JAMES M	CW2	W-2150028	0164	1
KURTZ JOHN R	LTC	0-0293956	0168	3
KURTZ JOHN R	1LT	0-1639283	1044	2
KURTZ JOHN W	1LT	0-2024272	0148	2
KURTZ MILLARD E	COL	0-0113385	0450	3
KURTZ WALTER H	MAJ	0-0530166	0146	2
KURTZ WILLIAM J	LTC	0-1823893	0961	1
KURTZWEIL SYLVESTER	CW3	W-2148866	0163	1
KURZ DONALD A	MAJ	0-1797313	0962	1
KURZ PHILIP W	LTC	0-0134034	0254	3
KURZAWSKI WILLIAM C	CW3	W-2143376	0462	1
KURZEJEWSKI LOUIS S	MAJ	0-1650183	1057	1
KURZEKA PAUL J	LTC	0-1547995	0468	1
KUSCHEL VICTOR H	COL	0-0288805	0365	3
KUSEL ROBERT L	CPT	0-1289750	0458	2
KUSENER WALTER C	MAJ	0-0578248	0560	1
KUSHMER FRED W	COL	0-0243339	0156	3
KUSHNER JOSEPH P	MAJ	0-0502512	0159	2
KUSHNER SAMUEL J	LTC	0-1103271	0461	1
KUSKA GEORGE W	CPT	0-0491359	0347	2
KUSKI PETER JR	CW3	W-2151673	1061	1
KUSLER CALVIN	LTC	0-2210299	1267	1
KUSMIERZ JOSEPH T	MAJ	0-1289097	0653	2
KUSNER FRANK	MAJ	0-0569001	0663	1
KUSSEROW OLIVER A	LTC	0-0414989	0961	1
KUSTER ALBERT J	1LT	0-1823310	1045	2
KUSTER KENNETH F	COL	0-0216853	1160	1
KUSTERMAN OSCAR B	LTC	0-0916306	0367	3
KUSZEWSKI BERNARD J	LTC	0-1290089	1063	1
KUTAUSKAS ANTHONY F	LTC	0-1296046	0361	1
KUTCHER NATHANIEL	COL	0-0451543	0967	3

NAME	GRADE	SVC NO	DATE RET MO YR	RET CODE
KOTCHEN? THOMAS [illegible]	CW3	W-21[illegible]	0461	1
KOTIS? [illegible]	CW2	W-[illegible]	0968	2
KOTLICK? FRANK A	CPT	0-13[illegible]	1060	1
KOTLIN? MILTON	LTC	0-1533376?	1166	2
KOTSCHEVAR? JOSEPH?	CPT	0-[illegible]	0752	2
KOTTESCH? [illegible]	LTC	0-1124219?	0663	2
KOTTKE? ARNE? [illegible]	CPT	0-01[illegible]	0755	3
KOTTN? [illegible]	LTC	0-027[illegible]	1068	3
KOTTN? JAMES H	COL	0-0171252?	0554	3
KOTTN? WILLIAM J	LTC	0-0[illegible]45	1266	3
KOTTN? WILLIAM J	2LT	0-1462274?	0345	2
KOTY [illegible]	MAJ	0-0357651	0646	2
KOTYS JOSEPH J	CPT	0-1304540?	1153	2
KOTZ ROBERT	LTC	0-0241564	0468	3
KOTZ VERNON A	CPT	0-0895728	1047	2
KOTZEN? JACK	CPT	0-1292196	0140	2
KOTZER JEAN R?	MAJ	0-1170043	1053	2
KOTZER MELVIN D	MAJ	0-0360755	0944	2
KUWAHARA HENRY H	LTC	0-0937926	0163	1
KUWAYE SATORU	CW2	W-2215090	0167	1
KUYKENDALL JOE R	1LT	0-2019753	0951	2
KUZA ANTHONY J	CW4	W-2006420	0866	3
KUZMA JOHN J	CW4	W-2110305	1054	1
KUZNIK FLORENCE E	1LT	N-0759730	0646	1
KVAAS MARTIN G	LTC	0-1329362	0267	1
KVESETH PER U	CPT	0-1703972	0347	1
KVIDT REUBEN O	MAJ	0-0966092	0961	1
KVITEK RICHARD G	2LT	0-0539548	0945	2
KWAN HENRY A	MAJ	0-1896514	0761	1
KWIATKOWSKI EDWARD A	MAJ	0-1923051	0367	1
KWIECINSKI FRANK F	CPT	0-2033128	0556	1
KWINN FRANK C	CPT	0-0372835	0246	2
KWOCK JOHN F	LTC	0-1798681	0765	1
KYDLAND WALLACE A	LTC	0-1013231	0960	1
KYER CHARLES M	CW2	W-2148929	0959	1
KYLCE DONALD F C	LTC	0-1589315	1167	3
KYLE ANGEL E	CW2	W-2143609	0859	1
KYLE BRIDGE E	COL	0-0178764	1061	3
KYLE ERIE E	1LT	0-0491223	1046	1
KYLE FRANK K	1LT	0-0405094	1044	2
KYLE GEORGE R	MAJ	0-0154523	0447	2
KYLE JAY A	LTC	0-0917732	1266	3
KYLE LESLIE R	LTC	0-1919992	1068	1
KYLE LESTER H	LTC	0-0184939	0654	1
KYLE RICHARD E	COL	0-0233019	0765	3
KYLER MONTELL	MAJ	0-1300816	0961	1
KYLES CLAYTON P	CPT	0-0356327	0145	2
KYLES ROGER B	CW2	RW-2144828	0361	1
KYNARD WARREN P	LTC	0-1688678	1168	1
KYNES CHARLES A	CW3	W-2150633	1163	1
KYNETT LAURENCE E	LTC	0-0321700	0766	3
KYRISS HAROLD A	CW4	W-2143749	1068	1
L HEUREUX HENRY F	LTC	0-0168110	1048	2
LA BARBERA VINCENT A	CW3	W-2149706	1064	1
LA BARRE RENE L	LTC	0-0276047	1266	3
LA BELLA JOHN J	MAJ	0-2019894	0962	1
LA BELLA LOUIS	LTC	0-1994793	0568	3
LA BLANC DONALD E	1LT	0-2204192	1253	2
LA BOLLE RICHARD L	COL	0-0267089	0355	1
LA BONNE LEE	LTC	0-1058471	0367	1
LA BONTE JOVITE SR	CW4	W-2000124	0559	1
LA BOUNTY ALVIN B	MAJ	0-2263212	0968	1
LA BOZETTA WILLIAM C	LTC	0-1323332	0563	1
LA BRECQUE EDWARD J	LTC	0-2014962	0868	1
LA BREE FRED M	LTC	0-0265738	0959	1
LA BRIE JOSEPH D JR	LTC	0-1549756	1065	3
LA BUDA MARTHA F	MAJ	N-0759540	1067	1
LA BUTIS CONSTANTIN	LTC	0-0333192	0766	3
LA CAFF ROBERT F	LTC	0-2033291	0966	1
LA CAZE CECIL G	CPT	0-2262865	0461	1
LA CAZE STEPHEN C	CW3	W-2209918	1267	1
LA CHANCE BERTRAND	1LT	0-1926888	0154	2
LA CHANCE PAUL A	CPT	0-0452419	0859	1
LA CORE IVAN A	MAJ	0-0491241	0246	2
LA COUR HARDIE J	LTC	0-0546687	0464	1

NAME	GRADE	SVC NO	DATE RET MO YR	RET CODE
LA COUR HERBERT A	CPT	0-1920094	0162	1
LA COY ROBERT H	LTC	0-1105590	0163	1
LA CRAFT FLOYD	WO1	W-2120653	0159	1
LA CROIX DONALD P	LTC	0-1584489	0263	1
LA CROIX JAMES L	CPT	0-0511440	0746	2
LA DOUCEUR ALBERT J	CPT	0-0266815	0753	3
LA DUE ROBERT W	1LT	0-0460515	0944	2
LA DUE CHARLES J	1LT	0-1177878	0147	2
LA DUE JACK W	MAJ	0-2097628	0367	1
LA FERNEY ROEL L	CW3	W-2152850	0959	1
LA FERRIERE REED J	MAJ	0-1899380	0461	1
LA FEVERS WARREN A	CPT	0-0329575	0746	2
LA FEVOR JAMES W	MAJ	0-0970511	0266	1
LA FLAMME VINCENT J	CPT	0-1646341	0163	1
LA FLEUR ALEXANDER	COL	0-0348118	0857	3
LA FLEUR WILLIAM N	CW2	W-3430519	0968	1
LA FOND ARTHUR F	MAJ	0-1822589	1264	1
LA FOND MARGARET R	2LT	N-0789837	1044	1
LA FOREST WILSON H	MAJ	0-2033630	0361	1
LA FRAGE SUSAN W	COL	N-0743556	0962	1
LA FRANCE GILBERT	LTC	0-0500238	0157	2
LA FRANCIS CYRIL J	CW4	W-2000103	0255	2
LA FRATTA CARL W	COL	0-0281608	0868	3
LA FRENIERE IDA M	1LT	N-0757238	0547	1
LA GATTUTA JOSEPH W	LTC	0-1298411	0762	1
LA GRANGE RICHARD M	LTC	0-1894612	0566	1
LA GRONE WINFRED C	LTC	0-0370020	0865	3
LA HAIE ROBERT JR	LTC	0-0806701	0666	1
LA HAYE NORBERT E	1LT	0-1030996	0446	2
LA HAYE ROBERT G	LTC	0-1821881	0664	1
LA JEUNESSE WILLIAM	LTC	0-1175776	0664	1
LA JOIE RUSSELL E	LTC	0-0332086	1064	1
LA LOGE DAVID	MAJ	0-1010982	0760	1
LA LONE RALPH E	CW3	W-2147382	0665	1
LA LUZ ENRIQUE	MAJ	0-0426225	1163	1
LA MANNA JOSEPH J	MAJ	0-0278940	0150	1
LA MAR ANDREW W	COL	0-0165154	1055	1
LA MARCA JOSEPH T	CW3	W-2105509	0961	1
LA MARCHE LOUIS J	1LT	0-1307426	0144	2
LA MARCHE PAUL J	MAJ	0-0147093	0648	3
LA MASTRA GERARD G	CW2	W-2214022	0866	1
LA MOE OMAR T JR	MAJ	0-1170817	0662	1
LA MONT KENNETH L	CW3	W-2147539	0566	1
LA MONT WILLIS H	CW4	W-2117104	0567	1
LA MONTHE ARTHUR E	LTC	0-1177879	0461	1
LA MONTIA JOHN A	MAJ	0-2020565	1159	1
LA MOTHE RAYMOND H	LTC	0-1052854	0766	1
LA MOTTE FRANK W	COL	0-0211021	1063	3
LA MOTTE ROBERT S	LTC	0-0182599	0455	3
LA PISTO THOMAS R	MAJ	0-1178870	0862	1
LA PLANTE EDWARD J	CPT	0-1319514	1047	2
LA PLANTE JOHN B	CPT	0-0483756	1049	1
LA PLANTE RENE J	CW3	W-2113729	0657	1
LA POINT LEON	CW2	W-2002823	0566	3
LA POINT ROBERT F	LTC	0-1287726	0960	1
LA POINTE FRANK A	LTC	0-0452847	0958	1
LA POINTE HENRY J	CW2	RW-2209939	1064	1
LA POINTE PAUL A	LTC	0-1544566	0562	2
LA POINTE RAYMOND R	MAJ	0-1582731	1162	1
LA PORTE RAY B	LTC	0-0291910	0165	3
LA RAE EVA S	MAJ	N-0743156	0867	1
LA RAE LEWIS L	MAJ	0-1542075	0459	1
LA REAU HARVEY H	CW2	W-2152470	0361	1
LA REAU JOHN T	LTC	0-1574936	0758	1
LA ROCCA XAVIER M E	LTC	0-1594291	1164	1
LA ROCCO JACK A	1LT	0-1556013	0645	2
LA ROCCO JOSEPH L	1LT	0-1294324	0146	2
LA ROCQUE ERNEST A	CW3	W-2144655	1062	1
LA ROCQUE GEORGE A	MAJ	0-0273770	0968	3
LA ROCQUE ROBERT J	CW2	W-3250528	1268	1
LA ROSA PETER A	CW3	W-2207990	0866	1
LA ROSA WILLARD E	COL	0-0379639	0964	3
LA RUE DENTON L	MAJ	0-0440054	0954	1
LA RUE HUGH B	MAJ	0-0119578	0648	3
LA RUE LEMUEL L	1LT	0-1175204	0845	2

NAME	GRADE	SVC NO	DATE RET MO YR	RET CODE
LA RUE ROBERT [illegible]	LTC	0-0216396?	0554	2
LA RUSSA PIERRE? [illegible]	2LT	N-0724065?	0465	1
LA RUSSO RUDOLPH? [illegible]	CW2	W-2111369?	1267?	2
LA SALLE ROBERT M	LTC	0-1684354	1045	2
LA SALLE WILBUR? M	MAJ	0-0240235?	1064	3
LA SCHELL MURRAY	COL	0-1745859?	1163	1
LA SHELLE? GEORGE K	1LT	0-0477452?	0655	2
LA SHOMB LEON V	CW3	W-2207967	0266	1
LA SORSA FRANCIS P	MAJ	0-0303788	0346	2
LA TOUCHE ROBERT C	CW3	W-2152830	1062	1
LA TOURETTE K? B	MAJ	0-1012905	0258	1
LA VAL VERNON H	MAJ	0-0365906?	0866	3
LA VALLEE JOSEPH E	MAJ	0-1798744	0565	3
LA VALLEY LESLIE F	MAJ	0-0294121	0459	3
LA VELLE EDWARD H	CPT	0-1535790	0955	1
LA VERDE SANTO	MAJ	0-1047148	0561	1
LA VERE LARRY T	2LT	0-1958700	0559	1
LA VERTU BRUNO P	CPT	0-1341985	0862	1
LA VIGNE FRED JR	CW3	W-2141350	0361	1
LA VIOLETTE HOMER P	LTC	0-0327006	0163	3
LA VOICE BRUCE W	CW3	W-2205423	0964	1
LA VRENZ ROLAND H	2LT	0-1996562	1045	2
LAAS MOYLAN E	MAJ	0-0356122	1046	2
LABADZ HENRY A	MAJ	0-1994792	0658	1
LABADIE EMILE L	CPT	0-1284343	1146	2
LABARGE ALPHONSE	CW3	W-2146837	1164	1
LABART DORSEY M	MAJ	0-1322073	0263	2
LABBE FRANK E	CW2	W-2143290	0358	1
LABBE MARTIN	MAJ	0-0494710	0856	1
LABELLE GEORGE A	2LT	0-1304915	1043	2
LABELLE HENRY A	LTC	0-1294149	0868	3
LABEN ROBERT C	CPT	0-0464660	0646	2
LABER ORVILLE J	MAJ	0-0984002	1166	1
LABONGE CARL A	LTC	0-0365023	1057	1
LABRADOR CHARLIE	MAJ	0-1896817	0561	1
LABRIOLA CHARLES S	CPT	0-1690626	0245	2
LABRIOLE JOHN	MAJ	0-2006492	0762	1
LACAGNINA PATSY M	MAJ	0-2011205	0467	1
LACAP TEDY N	CPT	0-1896499	0858	1
LACAPRIA ARTHUR	COL	0-0296764	0560	1
LACASSE ROBERT A	MAJ	0-0444075	1057	1
LACAVA FREDERICK	1LT	0-0512534	0645	2
LACE WILLIAM R	MAJ	0-0234152	0459	3
LACEDONIA JULIO R	LTC	0-0300495	1059	1
LACEFIELD EUGENIA M	1LT	N-0779002	0448	2
LACERTE OSWALD J	COL	0-0238781	0264	3
LACEY CLARENCE	COL	0-0446977	1054	1
LACEY DAVID T	1LT	0-1308348	0544	2
LACEY GEORGE T	MAJ	0-0260066	1067	3
LACEY HARLYN W	MAJ	0-0421876	0662	1
LACEY HOWARD W	2LT	0-1031613	0944	2
LACEY JACK L	LTC	0-0724951	0961	1
LACEY JOHN E	CW4	W-2148339	1168	1
LACEY JOHN F	COL	0-0216605	0862	3
LACEY JOHN H	CPT	0-0970845	0962	2
LACEY ROBERT D	1LT	0-0556755	0147	2
LACEY ROLLAND L	LTC	0-1030054	1054	1
LACEY ROSAMOND F	1LT	N-0721700	0945	1
LACHAT JULIETTE	2LT	N-0743428	1044	1
LACHENMAN ALFRED H	1LT	0-2018533	0459	1
LACHEY FRANCIS J	MAJ	0-1546461	0263	1
LACHICOTTE LOUIS H	MAJ	0-0151033	0858	3
LACHMAN MAX	LTC	0-0309223	0958	3
LACK ERNEST A	COL	0-0233907	1058	3
LACK ROBERT P	2LT	0-0922268	0644	2
LACKERMANN EARL E	2LT	0-1329131	1045	2
LACKEY CARVER M	LTC	0-0334837	0660	1
LACKEY LEE G	2LT	0-1913763	0140	1
LACKEY RAYMOND J	1LT	0-0338017	0142	2
LACKEY VAUEN M	COL	0-0267322	0162	3
LACKEY WOODWARD H	1LT	0-0410391	1044	2
LACKNER CLARENCE	CPT	0-2262892	0460	2
LACKO JOHN R	WO1	W-2112578	1145	2
LACOCK WALTER B	COL	0-0213374	1057	3
LACOMBA MIGUEL A	LTC	0-1327246	C164	1

NAME	GRADE	SVC NO	DATE RET MO YR	RET CODE
[illegible] GILBERT S	CPT	0-0469966?	0765	2
LACY AGNES?	1LT	N-0735525?	0546	1
LACY ALAN S	LTC	0-1171686?	0961	1
LACY CECIL C JR	CW3	W-2142065?	0461	1
LACY DELVIN? W	COL	0-0266206?	0253	3
LACY EUGENE [illegible]	MAJ	0-2262429	0861	1
LACY HAROLD S	COL	0-0234397	0953	3
LACY HENRY C	CPT	0-1284528	0246	2
LACY JACK B	1LT	0-1302018	0845	2
LACY LYNN? C	CW2	W-2119248	0165	1
LACY VILAS F	LTC	0-0389668	0765	1
LACY WILLIAM C	CPT	0-1001612	0346	2
LACY WILLIAM D	CPT	0-0972062	1061	1
LADA CHARLES	CW2	W-2146375	1059	1
LADAS GEORGE	MAJ	0-2262300	0963	1
LADD ALMA D	LTC	N-0737564	1062	1
LADD ANGELE	COL	0-0164481	0952	3
LADD ARNOLD B	2LT	0-1168765	1043	2
LADD EDGAR A	LTC	0-0255646	0167	3
LADD FREDERICK JR	LTC	0-0309547	1168	3
LADD JOHN C JR	MAJ	0-2262915	0165	1
LADD LEON F	LTC	0-0405499	0463	1
LADD WILLIAM F	B G	0-0111693	0256	3
LADD WILLIAM P	CPT	0-0488205	1162	1
LADICO ANDREW	CW2	W-2105468	0347	2
LADIGES RICHARD P	1LT	0-1319290	0546	2
LADNER HILLMON P	CW2	W-2144999	0957	1
LADNEY WILLIAM M	LTC	0-0451134	0157	1
LADSON WILLIAM F	COL	0-0366314	0965	1
LADUE DENNIS	MAJ	0-2000000	1061	1
LADWIG ARNOLD H	1LT	0-1042079	1044	2
LADY JAMES R	CPT	0-0402074	0545	2
LAEDLEIN WILLIAM A	CPT	0-0251817	0665	3
LAEVSKY MARCUS H	CPT	0-0216437	0256	3
LAEZZA ALBERT	CW3	W-2153146	0564	1
LAFACE DONALD A	LTC	0-0884118	0356	1
LAFAILLE PETER J JR	CPT	0-0497659	0754	1
LAFALGIO ANTHONY	2LT	0-1185722	1044	2
LAFAYETTE JOHN F	LTC	0-2203999	0968	1
LAFAYETTE KENNETH	COL	0-0287383	035	2
LAFENE BENJAMIN W	MAJ	0-0288196	0346	2
LAFEVER NANCY M	CPT	N-0727155	0554	2
LAFFAL LEON D	MAJ	0-0966695	0662	1
LAFFERTY CHARLES F	LTC	0-0153536	1052	3
LAFFERTY JEFF O	MAJ	0-0477472	0353	2
LAFFERTY LEROY E	LTC	0-1581889	0364	1
LAFFERTY THOMAS J	LTC	0-0885877	1162	1
LAFFERTY WARREN F	MAJ	0-1284720	0658	1
LAFFIN THOMAS M	CPT	0-0405852	0446	2
LAFFITTE CHARLES O	LTC	0-0348397	1061	1
LAFFLER JOSEPH A	CPT	0-0325065	0345	2
LAFLER CZERNA C	CPT	0-0221911	0845	1
LAFON LELAND F	CPT	0-1281838	0347	2
LAFOON JESSE H	LTC	0-2049618	0368	2
LAFORGE CHARLES V JR	2LT	0-1183562	1044	2
LAFOUNTAIN GEORGE J	LTC	0-1011967	0556	1
LAFRANCE RICHARD P	1LT	0-1017434	0546	2
LAGANA JAMES S	CW4	W-2143128	1163	1
LAGEN JOHN A	B G	0-0235968	0166	3
LAGEN ROBERT C	MAJ	0-1307424	1157	2
LAGER BUTLER H	1LT	0-1299760	1054	1
LAGER HERMAN J	CW3	W-2151082	0964	1
LAGER RALPH	CPT	0-1312022	1046	2
LAGERGREN MILTON A	CPT	0-0304622	0945	2
LAGERGREN OSCAR A	CW3	W-2144810	0761	1
LAGERQUIST EDWARD A	2LT	0-1589328	0644	2
LAGERQUIST HOWARD D	COL	0-0300126	0458	3
LAGERSTROM LEANDER A	CPT	0-0975929	1160	1
LAGISH GEORGE T	MAJ	0-0191514	0248	1
LAGLER LESLIE L	COL	0-1637879	0968	1
LAGNEAUX LEONARD	MAJ	0-0338690	1168	3
LAGOUROS JOHN E	LTC	0-0415660	1061	1
LAGOW WHITE F	CW4	W-2144407	0659	1
LAGRAND CHARLES A	MAJ	0-0162542	0-53	1
LAGREW EMARY O	COL	0-0298494	0346	2

NAME	GRADE	SVC NO	DATE RET MO YR	RET CODE
LAGRONE GEORGE N	CPT	0-0249166	1065	3
LAHAR EDMOND E	CW2	W-2151814	0361	2
LAHAR RAYMOND T	MAJ	0-1293612	0648	2
LAHDENPERA ERKKI	COL	0-0985338	0368	2
LAHENS PIERRE P JR	CPT	0-0907282	0845	2
LAHEY GERALD B	COL	0-0348158	0567	1
LAHNER WILLIAM F JR	CPT	0-0537186	0646	2
LAHNSTEIN JOSEPH J	LTC	0-1878819	1268	1
LAHOURCADE SIDNEY F	MAJ	0-0329409	0944	2
LAIDLAW ELLIOT C	LTC	0-0268249	0646	2
LAIDLAW HARRY H JR	LTC	0-1547690	0567	3
LAIER LEO SR	2LT	0-0176850	0653	1
LAIER OTTO J	MAJ	0-1648351	1060	1
LAIGE RAYMOND J	LTC	0-0239495	0846	2
LAIN JAMES W	1LT	0-1323943	0146	2
LAIN ROYCE L	LTC	0-2010958	1068	1
LAINE ARTHUR J	MAJ	0-2103031	0766	1
LAINE FRANK R	CW2	W-2152641	1060	1
LAING FREDERICK	1LT	0-1293613	0545	2
LAING JOHN B	LTC	0-0287622	0464	3
LAING KENNETH T	CPT	0-1011204	1058	1
LAING WALTER A	MAJ	0-0370991	1166	3
LAIR HERLEY D	LTC	0-1185462	0767	1
LAIRD ARCHIBALD	COL	0-0261916	1062	3
LAIRD CLAIRE B	LTC	0-0201469	1055	3
LAIRD DONALD G	LTC	0-2020168	1268	1
LAIRD DONALD J	MAJ	0-0983439	0161	1
LAIRD EUGENE E	LTC	0-0272496	1167	3
LAIRD GEORGE A	MAJ	0-0480506	0-52	1
LAIRD WILLIAM D	CW2	W-2208097	1061	1
LAIRD WILLIAM J JR	1LT	0-1299584	1064	1
LAKE CLARK B	CPT	0-0264564	0764	3
LAKE DANIEL M	CPT	0-1115321	0256	1
LAKE DANIEL W	MAJ	0-0198501	0453	3
LAKE EARL W	MAJ	0-1040257	0761	1
LAKE JAMES A	B G	0-0234350	1065	3
LAKE JOHN I	MAJ	0-0960407	1263	1
LAKE JOHN R	2LT	0-1556744	0645	2
LAKE JOHN V	CW2	W-2143938	0962	1
LAKE LISLE B	LTC	0-0452416	0461	1
LAKE RICHARD H	LTC	0-0386487	0361	1
LAKE ROBERT A	LTC	0-1574075	0960	1
LAKE ROBERT E	CW3	W-2148454	0463	1
LAKE WILLIAM F	COL	0-1001615	0365	1
LAKE WILLIAM S	CPT	0-1650186	0962	1
LAKEMAN WILLIAM D	LTC	0-0294867	0265	3
LAKEY CLETIS M	CW4	W-2101963	0757	1
LAKICH JOSEPH S	MAJ	0-1303355	0561	1
LAKICH OGNJAN I	LTC	0-0944676	0568	1
LAKIN SEYMOUR	LTC	0-1016031	1267	1
LAKITS GORDON E	1LT	0-1016148	0147	2
LALLANDE JOSEPH P	LTC	0-0422053	1060	1
LALLIS EVERETT	CW2	W-2152345	1058	1
LALLY JAMES W JR	MAJ	0-0126008	0848	3
LALLY JOHN J JR	MAJ	0-0436900	1163	1
LALLY JOHN N	LTC	0-1795927	0463	1
LALLY JOHN S JR	MAJ	0-0956082	0765	1
LALLY RICHARD M	LTC	0-1307425	0361	1
LALLY ROBERT E	1LT	0-0429217	0260	2
LALOS THOMAS K	2LT	0-1308834	0745	2
LAM DALE C	1LT	0-1336079	0750	2
LAMAN JOSEPH G	CPT	0-1285607	0848	1
LAMAR BARNEY D JR	CPT	0-0959297	0861	1
LAMAR CARLOS P	CPT	0-0386672	1144	2
LAMAR FRANK L	CW4	W-2111854	0960	1
LAMAR H G	WO1	W-2144657	0458	1
LAMAR LAW JR	1LT	0-0523228	1045	2
LAMAR LUCIUS Q C	LTC	0-0912320	1266	3
LAMAR RALPH H	LTC	0-1574926	0867	1
LAMAR RAYMOND J	LTC	0-0446264	1147	1
LAMAR WILMER A	2LT	0-1309758	0144	2
LAMATSCH ROBERT J	LTC	0-0371960	0662	1
LAMB ALBERT W	WO1	W-2108962	1057	1
LAMB ALLAN J	COL	0-0359348	0267	1
LAMB ALVIN R	LTC	0-0119902	0450	3
LAMB ELAINE A	MAJ	L-1010030	0366	1
LAMB EMMRICH D JR	LTC	0-0410547	0961	1
LAMB EUGENE B	CW2	W-3100573	0968	1
LAMB FREDERICK JR	COL	0-0337551	0161	3
LAMB GAIL V	MAJ	0-2053868	1060	1
LAMB GEORGE J	CPT	0-2017714	1062	1
LAMB GILBERT B	COL	0-0255269	0564	3
LAMB HORACE W	1LT	0-1824330	1058	1
LAMB HOWARD M	COL	0-0306471	0146	2
LAMB IVAN B	1LT	0-0984834	0353	2
LAMB JOHN A	LTC	0-1948342	0664	1
LAMB JOHN T	CW3	W-2143549	0664	1
LAMB JOHN W JR	CW2	W-2149369	0561	1
LAMB KENNETH D	COL	0-0181022	1154	3
LAMB LEROY E JR	MAJ	0-1822412	1263	1
LAMB MELVELL M	CW2	W-2152178	0656	1
LAMB MURRAY E	LTC	0-2023676	0167	1
LAMB NORMAN E	MAJ	0-1283981	0346	2
LAMB OTIS C	CW3	W-2125294	0257	1
LAMB PAUL A	COL	0-0177213	0455	2
LAMB PAUL J	LTC	0-0274119	0853	3
LAMB RAYMOND	WO1	W-2120901	0657	1
LAMB ROBERT F	MAJ	0-1555713	0867	1
LAMB THOMAS M	COL	0-0446302	0965	3
LAMBARD MASSEY S	COL	0-0396770	0862	1
LAMBDEN BILLIE G	1LT	0-2023659	0662	1
LAMBDIN ALLEN B	COL	0-0186043	0849	3
LAMBERSON CHARLES G	CPT	0-1031333	0648	2
LAMBERSON RAYMOND E	CW3	W-2113907	1154	1
LAMBERSON RUSSELL L	CW3	W-2149076	0763	1
LAMBERT ALBERT J	LTC	0-1104260	0563	1
LAMBERT CLAYED P	CPT	0-1116856	1050	2
LAMBERT CRAIG W	LTC	0-1334174	0266	1
LAMBERT DANA C	MAJ	0-0119622	0356	3
LAMBERT EDGAR J	LTC	0-0306316	0568	3
LAMBERT EDWARD J	COL	0-0482714	0667	1
LAMBERT ELDON W	WO1	W-2142168	0454	1
LAMBERT ELLWOOD R	MAJ	0-1287196	1060	1
LAMBERT ERNEST E	CPT	0-0385307	1043	2
LAMBERT FRANCIS A	LTC	0-0324793	0460	1
LAMBERT FRANK P SR	LTC	0-0158386	0655	2
LAMBERT HORACE W	LTC	0-1062855	1262	1
LAMBERT JACK E	LTC	0-0556412	1267	1
LAMBERT JAMES W	1LT	0-2055180	0849	1
LAMBERT JOSIAH	1LT	0-1825761	0746	2
LAMBERT LESLIE A	MAJ	0-0494907	1045	2
LAMBERT LUTHER R	COL	0-0245422	1056	3
LAMBERT MYLES B	MAJ	0-1288243	0861	1
LAMBERT ROBERT P	1LT	0-1308653	1145	2
LAMBERT TRUMAN P	LTC	0-1306433	1165	1
LAMBERT WARREN R	LTC	0-0332394	0460	1
LAMBERT WILLIAM A	2LT	0-4015323	0654	2
LAMBERT WILLIAM H	LTC	0-0381843	1059	1
LAMBERT WILLIAM H	CW4	W-2004521	1066	3
LAMBERTON FLOYD H	CW3	W-2146547	1264	1
LAMBERTSON WAYNE C	LTC	0-0320815	0259	1
LAMBETH CHARLES J	LTC	0-0464995	0658	1
LAMBKINS FREDERICK	CW3	W-2141347	1058	1
LAMBRECHT CONRAD J	CW4	W-2143150	0159	1
LAMBRUSCATI PAUL	MAJ	0-0969784	0862	1
LAMEY JAMES L	MAJ	0-0386040	0346	2
LAMEY JOHN D	CPT	0-0257386	0346	2
LAMIRAND FRANKLIN W	CPT	0-0353862	0544	2
LAMKIN CHARLES E	LTC	0-1030685	0766	1
LAMKIN CLARENCE M	MAJ	0-0342104	0345	2
LAMM GEORGE D	MAJ	0-1287020	0361	1
LAMM GORDON W	LTC	0-1108794	0965	1
LAMM HERMAN R	COL	0-0257570	1166	3
LAMM IRVING	CW3	W-2115542	1157	1
LAMM VINCENT P	MAJ	0-0310490	0559	3
LAMM WILLIS D	LTC	0-1555242	1165	1
LAMMEL GEORGE A	2LT	0-1179929	0346	2
LAMMERS THEODORE Q	CPT	0-0580898	0760	1
LAMOND JOHN P	MAJ	0-1913360	0865	1
LAMONDA MICHAEL J	1LT	0-2018896	0451	2
LAMONS CHARLES P	MAJ	0-1542707	0658	2
LAMONT CLAUDE W	CPT	0-0506430	1045	2
LAMONT GEORGE E	1LT	0-1287904	1145	2
LAMONT JACK D	MAJ	0-1765099	0147	2
LAMONT NEIL	LTC	0-0399730	1147	2
LAMONT WALTER S	LTC	0-0271326	0651	2
LAMOREAUX FRANCIS	CW2	W-2152679	0957	1
LAMORTE NICHOLAS D	COL	0-0245168	1061	3
LAMOTHE ANDREW H	MAJ	0-1547361	0657	1
LAMOURE PAUL A	LTC	0-0382404	0261	1
LAMOUREAUX ARMAND J	COL	0-0279032	1148	1
LAMOUREUX ARTHUR F	CPT	0-1114997	0446	2
LAMP FRED B JR	MAJ	0-2262423	0263	1
LAMP JOHN	LTC	0-1556166	0964	1
LAMP JOHN V	LTC	0-0962092	0868	1
LAMPARTER CARL R	MAJ	0-1558950	0458	2
LAMPE ALERD S	LTC	0-0362574	0262	1
LAMPE ELVAN W	CW4	W-2003232	0665	1
LAMPERT ALBERT J	CW2	RW-2209681	0368	1
LAMPERT EMIL A	1LT	0-1304744	1147	2
LAMPERT HERBERT H	MAJ	0-1650592	1146	2
LAMPERT JOSEPH	LTC	0-0134848	0654	3
LAMPHEAR LAURENCE H	LTC	0-0444042	0953	2
LAMPHEAR RAY D	LTC	0-0297409	1167	3
LAMPHERE ROY	LTC	0-0381742	0968	3
LAMPKIN PHILIP	LTC	0-0372908	1265	3
LAMPKINS MYLES F	CW3	W-2135371	0858	1
LAMPL HOWARD J	CPT	0-2234079	0462	1
LAMPMAN GEORGE I R	LTC	0-0346532	0960	1
LAMPMAN ROY M	MAJ	0-0162533	0949	2
LAMPNER HAROLD	COL	0-0486637	1068	1
LAMPORT MORTON H	CPT	0-0507472	0346	2
LAMPORT WILLIAM A	CW2	RW-2143769	0461	1
LAMPOS NICHOLAS T	LTC	0-1633349	1059	1
LAMPRECHT ALAN F	LTC	0-1579915	0461	1
LAMPREY GEORGE W	1LT	0-1012158	0745	2
LAMPSON ALBERT W	2LT	0-1825354	0545	2
LAMPSON MERT M	COL	0-0523862	0963	1
LAMPTON WILLIAM R	MAJ	0-2020037	0361	1
LAMSON PERRY B	COL	0-0301841	0460	3
LAMSON ROY JR	COL	0-0910053	0368	3
LAMUTT FREDERICK	LTC	0-0342481	0759	1
LANCASTER AUGUSTUS H	COL	0-0486636	0146	2
LANCASTER CLIFTON H	CW2	W-2151417	0664	2
LANCASTER EARLE W	COL	0-0198166	1143	2
LANCASTER FRED D	1LT	0-1287022	0944	2
LANCASTER GEORGE W	MAJ	0-0487060	0750	2
LANCASTER HARLAND F	MAJ	0-0464323	0146	2
LANCASTER JAMES J	CPT	0-0386469	0146	2
LANCASTER JOHN W	2LT	0-0887548	0653	2
LANCASTER LAMAR L	LTC	0-0310146	0464	3
LANCASTER LELON E	CPT	0-1821599	0157	1
LANCASTER OSCAR W	LTC	0-0217416	0463	3
LANCASTER RALPH A	COL	0-0174557	1155	3
LANCASTER RUSSEL M	LTC	0-0288338	1266	3
LANCASTER VAL	CW2	W-2150816	0760	1
LANCASTER VIRGIL M	LTC	0-0262108	0565	3
LANCE ARVIL M	CPT	0-0504220	0247	1
LANCE LAWRENCE W	CPT	0-0405229	0345	2
LANCE WILLIAM J	CPT	0-0335884	1143	2
LANCER GEORGE	CPT	0-0505199	0846	1
LANCER JOHN J	LTC	0-0186190	1156	3
LANCON RAYMOND R JR	COL	0-0276144	0163	3
LANCTO JOSEPH W	1LT	0-0255992	1053	3
LAND CARROL P	MAJ	0-2033794	1265	1
LAND CECIL D	CPT	0-0382373	0649	1
LAND HARRY D	MAJ	0-0494142	1054	1
LAND HARVEY A	MAJ	0-1686560	0560	1
LAND JACK C	MAJ	0-0366799	1045	2
LAND LOGAN	1LT	0-0229499	1160	3
LAND PAUL E	1LT	0-1294150	0845	2
LAND WALTER C	LTC	0-0279323	1062	3
LAND WILLIAM E	LTC	0-0250981	0764	3
LAND WILLIAM H	MAJ	0-0266989	0348	1
LAND WILLIAM J	LTC	0-1573350	0261	1
LANDAU HAROLD S	CPT	0-1012435	0147	2
LANDAUER JOSEPH P	LTC	0-0279682	0360	1
LANDAUER NORMAN E	LTC	0-0247847	0167	3
LANDAW CLAUDE R	COL	0-0287389	0561	3
LANDBECK ALTON J	2LT	0-1581230	1044	2
LANDE ORIN	1LT	0-1030491	0146	2
LANDEN CORNELIUS	CPT	0-1693399	0945	2
LANDENBERGER J W	LTC	0-0497421	0960	3
LANDER ALICE M	2LT	N-0755212	0245	1
LANDER FRANK T JR	1LT	0-0378986	0844	2
LANDER QUINTIN S	COL	0-0261015	0859	1
LANDER STANTON N	MAJ	0-1636182	0866	1
LANDERS HAROLD P	CPT	0-2262471	1060	1
LANDERS JACK M	CPT	0-0520454	0645	2
LANDERS WARREN D	CW3	W-2141348	1057	1
LANDERS WILLIAM E	LTC	0-1104939	0862	1
LANDERS WILLIAM H	MAJ	0-1634050	0262	1
LANDES LEWIS	COL	0-0138767	0246	2
LANDFRIED ROBERT P	WO1	W-2145037	0653	1
LANDGRAFF JAMES A	CPT	0-1948776	1164	1
LANDINI AMELIA Z	1LT	N-0731712	0746	1
LANDIS ALBERT B	LTC	0-0330714	0561	1
LANDIS FRED S	LTC	0-0424343	0746	2
LANDIS NORMAN E	MAJ	0-1878676	0867	1
LANDIS RAYMOND B	LTC	0-1300051	1061	1
LANDIS ROBERT H	1LT	0-1293976	0745	2
LANDOM LEROY A	COL	0-0354297	0868	1
LANDON FLOYD J	CW2	W-2109470	1046	1
LANDON LAWRENCE B	MAJ	0-2210028	0866	1
LANDRETH CHESTER G	1LT	0-1552729	1060	1
LANDRIGAN HERBERT W	CPT	0-0497552	0347	2
LANDROCK ARTHUR H	1LT	0-1304605	0145	2
LANDRUM ARIE H SR	CW2	W-2101969	1155	1
LANDRUM BERNARD L	1LT	0-1011058	1045	2
LANDRUM WILLIAM K	LTC	0-0113382	0349	3
LANDRY ANTOINE	CW3	W-2149223	0463	1
LANDRY CATHERINE	MAJ	L-0303726	0564	1
LANDRY EMERY A	MAJ	0-1106272	1060	2
LANDRY ERNEST J	LTC	0-1058581	0567	1
LANDRY ERNEST J	MAJ	0-1692113	0345	2
LANDRY HOWARD P	LTC	0-0328285	0760	1
LANDRY JAMES A	CPT	0-1292199	1046	2
LANDRY JAMES P	CPT	0-0990150	0161	1
LANDRY JOHN J	1LT	0-0407564	0146	2
LANDRY MAURICE T	MAJ	0-0984682	1062	1
LANDRY MILTON J	LTC	0-0342179	0146	2
LANDRY PIERRE O	CPT	0-0122731	0654	3
LANDRY WALTER J	CW2	W-2150594	0959	1
LANDRY WALTER J JR	LTC	0-0452053	0361	1
LANDRY WILLIAM B	MAJ	0-1648352	0762	1
LANDSMAN GEORGE D	LTC	0-1688742	0168	1
LANDSMAN HARRY	LTC	0-0309866	1058	3
LANDSMAN HARRY	LTC	0-1040964	0862	1
LANDSMAN SOL	LTC	0-1596093	0361	1
LANDT HENRY L	LTC	0-1185233	0863	1
LANDVOIGT MILTON J	MAJ	0-0161986	0651	3
LANDY JAMES J	1LT	0-1173685	1045	2
LANE ABBOT J	MAJ	0-0988087	1167	2
LANE ANDREW J	CW4	W-2148122	0668	1
LANE ARTHUR J	LTC	0-0510726	0255	1
LANE AUGUSTUS H	1LT	0-0455726	1144	2
LANE BILLIE I	MAJ	N-0786669	0467	1
LANE BOND E	LTC	0-0216945	1062	3
LANE CHARLES K	LTC	0-0469431	0546	2
LANE CHARLES L	LTC	0-0324279	0460	1
LANE CLARENCE L	LTC	0-0389433	0557	1
LANE CLARENCE M	CPT	0-0953844	1060	1
LANE DANIEL P	LTC	0-0104038	0648	3
LANE DARRELL T	LTC	0-0182484	0552	3
LANE DEWEY L	WO1	W-2133205	0357	1
LANE EDMUND T	MAJ	0-0274916	0146	2
LANE EDWARD	LTC	0-0229375	0956	3
LANE EDWARD W	LTC	0-0174191	0161	3
LANE ELTON A	CW2	W-2141349	1054	1
LANE FORREST L	CW2	W-2213032	1166	1

NAME	GRADE	SVC NO	DATE RET MO YR	RET CODE
LANE [illegible]	1LT	[illegible]	[illegible]	[illegible]
LANE GILBERT T	LTC	[illegible]	0462	1
LANE HAROLD A V	CW2	W-21[illegible]745	0964	1
LANE HARRY P	COL	0-04[illegible]	0962	1
LANE HARRY W	LTC	0-02[illegible]	0451	3
LANE HENRY A	MAJ	0-0[illegible]591	0459	1
LANE HENRY J	LTC	0-02[illegible]52	0164	3
LANE HIRAM T	MAJ	0-1646470	0953	1
LANE JAMES [illegible]	LTC	0-04[illegible]36	0764	3
LANE JAMES O	CW3	W-2136787	0461	1
LANE JOHN [illegible]	CPT	0-1698141	0964	2
LANE JOHN E	CW4	W-2118107	0755	1
LANE JOHN F	CPT	0-0242635	0464	3
LANE JOHN M	LTC	0-1172131	0766	1
LANE JOHN R	LTC	0-0358496	0160	1
LANE JOHN S	LTC	0-0905593	0453	2
LANE JULIE E	LTC	N-0743641	0168	3
LANE JULIUS F	LTC	0-1325299	0163	1
LANE KENNARD E	LTC	0-2015531	0768	1
LANE LAWRENCE G	MAJ	0-1297274	0564	1
LANE LAWRENCE W	LTC	0-1595538	0568	3
LANE MARY P	2LT	N-0720113	0244	1
LANE MERRITT JR	1LT	0-1182627	0345	2
LANE RAYMOND J	COL	0-0255610	1157	3
LANE RICHARD J	CPT	0-1895189	1052	2
LANE RICHARD O	CW3	W-2146815	1157	1
LANE RICHARD S	MAJ	0-0330277	0146	2
LANE RICHARD S	CPT	0-1038213	0352	2
LANE ROBERT C	MAJ	0-1699358	0161	1
LANE ROBERT C	CW4	W-2111206	1055	1
LANE ROBERT J JR	CW2	W-3200496	0967	1
LANE ROBERT W	MAJ	0-0172628	0656	3
LANE ROY L	LTC	0-0236598	1064	3
LANE RUSSELL G	1LT	0-1172132	0246	2
LANE STANLEY S	LTC	0-0314958	0855	1
LANE THERON I	COL	0-0254185	0654	2
LANE THOMAS J	CW3	W-2208351	0966	1
LANE VINCENT A	COL	0-0208424	0862	3
LANE WENDELL F	2LT	0-0220407	0360	3
LANE WILLIAM T JR	LTC	0-0115530	0656	3
LANELLI LESTER R	LTC	0-1040562	0266	1
LANEVE JOHN J	CPT	0-0525582	0845	2
LANEY JAMES O O	CW3	W-2206839	0966	1
LANFEAR ALMIRA A	LTC	N-0736827	0667	3
LANFORD JOHN L	LTC	0-0285601	0668	3
LANFORD LEROY C	MAJ	0-0258680	0960	3
LANG ABEL	LTC	0-1002267	0466	3
LANG ANTON A	MAJ	0-0159050	1045	2
LANG ARCHIE F	MAJ	0-0134039	0253	3
LANG ARTHUR P	1LT	0-0365167	0945	2
LANG CECIL H	COL	0-0147739	0351	3
LANG CHARLES M	CPT	0-0253502	0952	3
LANG CLEMENT M	MAJ	0-0162989	0546	2
LANG DAVID	MAJ	0-1325831	1059	1
LANG DONALD J H	COL	0-1080726	0968	1
LANG EMIL	CW2	W-2114181	1149	1
LANG FRANCIS C	LTC	0-0283037	1057	1
LANG GEORGE E	CPT	0-0230877	0846	1
LANG GEORGE H	MAJ	0-1948947	1163	1
LANG GEORGE K	CPT	0-0354640	0445	2
LANG GERALD M	LTC	0-1321530	0965	1
LANG HENRY J JR	1LT	0-1335940	1053	2
LANG JAMES O	MAJ	0-1799454	0361	1
LANG JOHN M	CPT	0-0120547	0554	3
LANG JOSEPH	CPT	0-0492257	0645	2
LANG LAWRENCE P	COL	0-0177708	0262	3
LANG LAWRENCE R	1LT	0-1179495	0346	2
LANG LEROY E	WO1	W-2105664	0744	2
LANG ROBERT W	MAJ	0-2263763	0964	1
LANG ROBERT W	1LT	0-4031770	0157	2
LANG STANLEY B	MAJ	0-0194390	0362	3
LANG SYLVAN	COL	0-0185644	0751	3
LANG WALTER P	LTC	0-0324617	1057	1
LANG WILLIAM	CPT	0-1327015	1158	1
LANG WILLIAM F	LTC	0-0928361	0465	3

NAME	GRADE	SVC NO	DATE RET MO YR	RET CODE
LANG WILLIAM F	CW2	W-2206659	0763	1
LANG WILMER J	MAJ	0-0606960	1263	3
LANGAN DAVID [illegible] JR	COL	0-0331831	0565	1
LANGDON ROY B	MAJ	0-1574889	0151	1
LANGDON THOMAS J	1LT	0-1017266	0247	2
LANGE ALBERT	COL	0-0241676	0759	3
LANGE AUSTIN J	LTC	0-0327685	0566	3
LANGE CHARLES A	WO1	W-3155393	1167	2
LANGE CLARENCE C	MAJ	0-0109793	0855	3
LANGE EDWIN J	2LT	0-1913774	0640	1
LANGE ELMER A	CPT	0-1293074	1146	2
LANGE EUGENE W	LTC	0-1181937	1163	1
LANGE FRANK F E	LTC	0-1019931	0165	1
LANGE FREDERICK	LTC	0-0133151	0949	3
LANGE GEORGE J	LTC	0-1030055	0265	1
LANGE JAMES A	CPT	0-1174345	0859	1
LANGE JOHN A	CW3	W-2146021	0967	1
LANGE LAWRENCE W	LTC	0-1294151	0759	1
LANGE LESLIE F	LTC	0-0888756	0363	1
LANGE WILLIAM A	CPT	0-1686874	1046	2
LANGE WILLIAM F	LTC	0-1588110	0368	1
LANGEBARTEL RALPH W	1LT	0-1174039	1045	2
LANGELUTTIG ALBERT C	LTC	0-0171236	1061	3
LANGENDERFER SYLVEST	CW4	W-2145618	0962	1
LANGER FRANK	MAJ	0-0435951	0254	1
LANGERAK DUDOK B	LTC	0-1178541	0758	1
LANGEVIN EVELYN	1LT	N-0785847	0649	2
LANGEVIN MARIE F L	1LT	N-0753058	1046	1
LANGFITT JOSEPH A	LTC	0-0107894	0350	3
LANGFORD CECIL T	CPT	0-0170043	0956	3
LANGFORD ELLIS C	MAJ	0-1185440	0961	1
LANGFORD JAMES A	CW2	W-2152025	0460	1
LANGFORD THEODORE H	MAJ	0-1292200	0157	1
LANGFORD WILLIAM B	LTC	0-0249508	0366	3
LANGGLE PAUL	CW2	W-2148742	0262	1
LANGGUTH ELMER E	LTC	0-1592363	0564	3
LANGHAM BURKE E	MAJ	0-1796811	1060	1
LANGHAM CARL E	MAJ	0-0985160	0668	1
LANGHAM CECIL D	CPT	0-1062687	0747	2
LANGHAM JAMES W	LTC	0-0147761	0648	3
LANGHAM VERNON R	CW3	W-2150299	0466	1
LANGHER GORDON N	LTC	0-1574933	0766	3
LANGLAIS TEDDY	1LT	0-0100016	1037	2
LANGLEY CLAIRE	LTC	0-0307019	0360	1
LANGLEY FRANCIS H	COL	0-0225676	1159	3
LANGLEY HARRY J	LTC	0-1179128	0467	1
LANGLEY JAMES W JR	2LT	0-1553495	0845	2
LANGLEY LEOTA M	MAJ	N-0720740	1061	1
LANGLEY ORVILLE E	COL	0-0299336	1068	3
LANGLEY ROBERT P	LTC	0-0192713	1060	1
LANGLEY THORPE M	LTC	0-0153675	0352	3
LANGLEY WILLIAM A	CPT	0-1583249	1156	2
LANGLOIS ALFRED E	CPT	0-0982084	0653	2
LANGLOIS FLOYD A	MAJ	0-1637892	0862	1
LANGNER ROY W	LTC	0-1639331	0962	1
LANGO SAMUEL A	CPT	0-1824047	0764	1
LANGRUM GODFREY G	CW2	W-2145736	0357	1
LANGSTAFF CHARLES W	CW3	W-2000506	1253	3
LANGSTAFF JOHN M	1LT	0-1299588	0546	2
LANGSTON AUSTINN F	MAJ	0-1108796	0247	2
LANGSTON CHARLES R	1LT	0-1100634	1044	2
LANGSTON CZAR D JR	2LT	0-2050540	0346	2
LANGSTON JAMES H	CW3	W-2148975	1164	1
LANGSTON JAMES L	MAJ	0-1844382	0855	1
LANGSTON JAMES T	MAJ	0-2289142	1165	1
LANGSTON JEAN C	LTC	0-1109438	0664	1
LANGSTON NORRIS O	MAJ	0-0243390	0544	2
LANGSTON PERRY O	CPT	0-0346693	0444	2
LANGSTON ROSS B	MAJ	0-1686669	0964	1
LANGSTON WILLIAM H	MAJ	0-1590300	0465	1
LANGTON LUTHER L	CW3	W-2118104	0657	1
LANGUARO CHARLES J	WO1	W-2104191	0643	2
LANGUEMI FRANK C	MAJ	0-1013440	0546	2
LANGWASSER FRANK	LTC	0-1845063	0562	1
LANGWICK RALPH B	LTC	0-1633352	0261	1

NAME	GRADE	SVC NO	DATE RET MO YR	RET CODE
LANGWORTHY WILLIAM J	LTC	[illegible]	[illegible]	[illegible]
LANHAM [illegible]	MAJ	[illegible]	[illegible]	[illegible]
LANHAM [illegible]	LTC	[illegible]	[illegible]	1
LANHAM [illegible] A	MAJ	[illegible]	[illegible]	3
LANHAM TRAVIS L	MAJ	[illegible]	[illegible]	2
LANIER [illegible]	CW2	W-2143720	[illegible]	2
LANIER [illegible] V	LTC	[illegible]	[illegible]	1
LANIER CARL H	CW4	W-2215522	1066	1
LANIER FELIX T	CPT	0-1334392	1064	3
LANIER GENE D SR	CW3	W-2137136	0661	1
LANIER HAROLD L	LTC	0-1339453	0966	1
LANIER JOHN F	CW2	W-2211659	0666	1
LANIER TEX H	2LT	0-1130047	1045	2
LANIER WILLIAM O	LTC	0-0102562	0249	3
LANIGAN JAMES M JR	LTC	0-0174352	1062	1
LANKFORD B R	CW3	W-2143319	0959	1
LANKFORD HERMAN H	1LT	0-2262720	0463	1
LANKFORD JOHN L	1LT	0-0457725	0945	2
LANKFORD ROGER F	CW3	W-2145203	0662	1
LANKS VIOLA F	CPT	L-0305323	0756	2
LANMAN EDWARD O	MAJ	0-1172959	0262	1
LANN CLYDE E	CPT	0-0217471	0860	3
LANNAN LEONARD C	LTC	0-1946415	0761	1
LANNEY MARY K	MAJ	L-0604558	0965	1
LANNING EDWARD H	CPT	0-1004165	1050	1
LANNON CHARLES E	CW4	W-2103938	0364	1
LANPHERE CLARK P	CW2	W-2108763	1045	2
LANS WILLIAM J	LTC	0-0163299	0647	2
LANSFORD WILLIAM C	LTC	0-1583251	1065	1
LANSFORD WILLIS R	COL	0-0128645	0150	3
LANSFORD WILSON A	MAJ	0-0311287	0361	1
LANSING DANIEL H	LTC	0-0269348	0564	3
LANSING FRED JR	MAJ	0-0490196	0655	1
LANSING HAROLD J	MAJ	0-4009705	1068	1
LANSING JESSE E JR	LTC	0-1003779	0566	1
LANSING LLOYD S	CPT	0-0288453	1045	2
LANSKI MAXWELL J	MAJ	0-0504497	0655	1
LANSROD LLOYD H	LTC	0-1030167	0368	3
LANSTRUM GEORGE F	LTC	0-1298722	1066	1
LANTAJ MARTIN	COL	0-0163040	0959	3
LANTHIER JOSEPH R	MAJ	0-1686793	0165	1
LANTIS JAMES R	MAJ	0-2020308	0364	1
LANTON JAMES R	CW3	W-2150319	0963	1
LANTZ ALFRED C	MAJ	0-1546341	1159	1
LANTZ CHARLES N	MAJ	0-1013755	0860	1
LANTZ DARRELL M	LTC	0-1552105	1160	1
LANTZ DAYLE R	LTC	0-1042347	1055	1
LANTZ ROBERT M	LTC	0-0289402	0460	1
LANTZ WARREN	MAJ	0-0534610	0946	1
LANZA ARTHUR J	1LT	0-1326286	0846	2
LANZA CHARLES V	CPT	0-2019334	0758	1
LANZILLI FERDINAND	1LT	0-1000607	0645	2
LAPERE CARL L	CW2	W-2212217	0167	1
LAPEYRI FERDINAND	COL	0-0264295	0660	3
LAPHAM DANA M	MAJ	0-0986076	0366	1
LAPHAM HARRY H JR	MAJ	0-1326855	0563	1
LAPHAM HOWARD H	WO1	W-2109340	0245	2
LAPHAM JOHN G JR	MAJ	0-1040966	0563	1
LAPHAM ROBERT H	MAJ	0-1893930	1266	1
LAPHAM SAMUEL JR	COL	0-0188456	0952	3
LAPIDUS REUBEN T	CPT	0-0344289	0745	2
LAPINE DOUGLAS P	MAJ	0-1949581	0155	1
LAPINE GLEN H	LTC	0-1997759	0663	1
LAPINER ARNOLD J	MAJ	0-1331847	1263	1
LAPINSKI ROMOALD J	MAJ	0-1845753	0657	1
LAPKE ROBERT H	MAJ	0-1052040	0860	1
LAPLANT PALMER L	LTC	0-1040753	0461	1
LAPLANTE BERNARD H	CPT	0-0410035	1044	2
LAPNIEWSKI CHESTER	MAJ	0-0473595	0645	2
LAPO CHESTER H	MAJ	0-2014564	0563	1
LAPOINTE ROGER J	LTC	0-0388474	0760	1
LAPOTA PAUL M	2LT	0-1108797	0244	2
LAPOTKA JOHN	LTC	0-0439605	0863	1
LAPPIN WILLIAM E	COL	0-0402927	0760	1
LAPPLEY WALTER F	CPT	0-0350043	0745	2

NAME	GRADE	SVC NO	DATE RET MO YR	RET CODE
LAR[illegible]	CW3	[illegible]	[illegible]	3
LAR[illegible] JR	[illegible]	[illegible]	[illegible]	2
LAR[illegible]	[illegible]	[illegible]	[illegible]	1
LAR[illegible] MICHAEL	CW3	W-2117219	[illegible]	1
LAR[illegible]	MAJ	[illegible]	[illegible]	3
LARA MANUEL P	[illegible]	[illegible]	[illegible]	1
LAR[illegible]	[illegible]	[illegible]	[illegible]	3
LAR[illegible]	LTC	[illegible]	[illegible]	1
LARATA HENRY A	[illegible]	[illegible]	[illegible]	1
LAR[illegible] ALBERT R	COL	[illegible]	[illegible]	3
LARAWAY RUSSELL G	CPT	0-0182142	[illegible]	2
LAR[illegible] WILLIAM H	CW2	W-2216667	[illegible]	1
LAR[illegible] CHARLES [illegible]	CW2	W-2154311	0153	1
LAR[illegible] FRED H JR	LTC	0-0275637	0568	3
LARDINAIS LAURA J	2LT	N-0725137	1044	1
LAR[illegible] JOSEPH A	MAJ	0-1015360	0457	2
LARGE BERNARD [illegible]	LTC	0-1313617	1263	1
LARGE CLOIS F	MAJ	0-0265546	0958	1
LARGE JAMES R	CPT	0-1286146	0147	1
LARIMER SIMON P	1LT	0-0175199	0455	3
LARIMORE DONALD E	MAJ	0-0367054	0946	2
LARIMORE PHILIP B	MAJ	0-0511509	0747	2
LARIOS ERNEST F	MAJ	0-0233985	1158	3
LARIOSA BENJAMIN	2LT	0-0890511	0947	2
LARIVEE BERNARD S	MAJ	0-0526055	0655	1
LARKE THOMAS H JR	CPT	0-0172910	0557	3
LARKIN CHARLES F	COL	0-0267856	0451	3
LARKIN EMMETT P	MAJ	0-0973616	0962	1
LARKIN GEORGE V	MAJ	0-0253960	0767	3
LARKIN HERSCHEL R	CPT	0-0463814	1045	2
LARKIN JOSEPH V	LTC	0-1585978	0562	1
LARKIN RALPH R	CW3	W-2145737	1166	1
LARKIN WALLACE S	MAJ	0-0297072	1166	3
LARKIN WILLIAM J JR	LTC	0-1686677	0767	1
LARKIN WILLIAM S	MAJ	0-1821732	0157	1
LARKINS ARTHUR H JR	COL	0-0905041	0168	3
LARKINS JOHNB JR	WO1	W-2118090	0553	1
LARKINS SIMEON J	MAJ	0-1302147	0962	1
LARKINS WALTER W	MAJ	0-2262891	0766	1
LARKUM NEWTON W	COL	0-0229432	0757	3
LARMORE ROBERT C	CPT	0-0407539	0146	2
LARMOYEUX CYRUS	MAJ	0-0354120	0348	2
LARNER HUGH R	LTC	0-0363746	0866	1
LARNER RAY A	MAJ	0-0140698	0255	3
LARRABEE DWIGHT H	MAJ	0-1797481	0360	1
LARRABEE WILLIAM F	COL	0-0268498	1055	3
LARREMORE GENE F	MAJ	0-0455288	0456	1
LARRERE PHILLIP P	CW4	W-2125100	1268	1
LARRICK MYRON E	LTC	0-1533612	1165	1
LARRICK THOMAS	MAJ	0-0250125	0765	3
LARRIMER JOHN B	CW2	W-2146255	0756	1
LARRIMER WALTER D	CW4	W-2000306	0155	1
LARRINAGA CESAR	CPT	0-1326505	0266	1
LARRISON CHARLES B	CW4	W-2119556	1163	3
LARRIVEE ELPHEGE A	WO1	W-2145261	1053	1
LARROUX ROBERT W	LTC	0-0422332	0662	1
LARRY GEORGE	MAJ	0-1332612	0863	1
LARSEN AAGE	MAJ	0-0242259	0651	1
LARSEN ALBERT L	MAJ	0-0172636	0355	3
LARSEN ALF B	LTC	0-0483030	0241	1
LARSEN ANDERS	COL	0-0203145	0-53	3
LARSEN EMIL	MAJ	0-0393384	0146	2
LARSEN ESTHER L	CW3	VR-0602675	0368	3
LARSEN FRED N JR	COL	0-0268007	0366	1
LARSEN HANS C	COL	0-0197313	0553	3
LARSEN HAROLD W	CPT	0-1895782	0964	2
LARSEN IVY T	1LT	N-0736654	0145	1
LARSEN JOHN P	COL	0-0186867	0152	3
LARSEN LAWRENCE H	COL	0-0314138	0260	3
LARSEN LAWRENCE L	LTC	0-0352065	0360	1
LARSEN MELVIN J	MAJ	0-1917845	0665	1
LARSEN WALTER T	MAJ	0-1185409	0958	1
LARSEN WILLIAM C	CW2	W-2144995	0357	1
LARSEN WILLIAM L	CW3	W-2144966	1165	1
LARSON ARTHUR A	COL	0-0215700	1054	1

NAME	GRADE	SVC NO	DATE RET MO YR	RET CODE
LARSON ARTHUR H	LTC	0-0177795	0750	3
LARSON ARTHUR J	CPT	0-1014955	0746	2
LARSON CALVIN L	MAJ	0-1668449	0664	1
LARSON CHESTER G	LTC	0-1108798	0166	3
LARSON CONRAD L	CW4	W-2106810	0559	1
LARSON DAVID J	CPT	0-0524386	0546	2
LARSON DONALD G	CPT	0-0326207	0246	2
LARSON EDMOND H	LTC	0-0917187	1062	1
LARSON EDWARD L	1LT	0-1544059	0146	2
LARSON EDWIN C	CPT	0-0107886	0154	3
LARSON ELSA F	CPT	N-0736954	1046	1
LARSON FRANK L	LTC	0-1169610	0466	1
LARSON FRED O	1LT	0-1290441	1145	2
LARSON GEORGE R	LTC	0-1011157	0758	1
LARSON HARRY	LTC	0-0196584	0655	3
LARSON HARRY E	CPT	0-0401072	0445	2
LARSON JUANNA M	MAJ	N-0779303	0264	1
LARSON JOHN W	MAJ	0-0311440	1045	2
LARSON KEITH D	MAJ	0-0515773	0947	2
LARSON KERMIT E	MAJ	0-1547362	0556	1
LARSON LEANDER T	CW2	W-2103124	0757	1
LARSON LELAND R	CPT	0-0426590	0246	2
LARSON LINNE C	MAJ	0-0169136	0259	3
LARSON LOUIS A	COL	0-0351269	0663	1
LARSON MARIAN L	1LT	N-0730612	1045	1
LARSON MEDERITH J	MAJ	0-1101539	0257	1
LARSON MERLE E	WO1	W-2108852	0255	1
LARSON MERRILL L	COL	0-0296664	0660	2
LARSON OLAF R	CPT	0-0182721	0954	3
LARSON OSCAR W	MAJ	0-0321647	1159	3
LARSON PETER	MAJ	0-0384739	0561	1
LARSON RAYMOND J	LTC	0-0253427	0757	3
LARSON RICHARD P	MAJ	0-1633356	1160	1
LARSON ROBERT A	LTC	0-1321374	0767	1
LARSON ROBERT A	1LT	0-1551893	0944	2
LARSON ROY E	MAJ	0-0481737	0146	2
LARSON SHERWOOD G	CPT	0-1103275	0746	2
LARSON STANLEY O	LTC	0-1592366	0861	1
LARSON SYDNEY S	1LT	0-1587398	0451	2
LARSON THOMAS A	LTC	0-2053934	0263	1
LARSON TURE L B	MAJ	0-0224606	0457	3
LARSON VERNET H JR	LTC	0-1318907	1167	1
LARSON VERNON R	MAJ	0-1635004	0954	1
LARSON WALTER C	CW3	W-3150354	0767	1
LARSON WILLIAM B	LTC	0-1183112	1064	1
LARSSON BROR H	COL	0-0170691	0648	3
LARY JACK K	MAJ	0-1058295	0459	1
LARY VIRGIL P JR	1LT	0-1181338	0845	2
LASA RAFAEL A	1LT	0-0414590	0745	2
LASATER BUREN F	1LT	0-0957115	1053	2
LASATER JOHSA L	LTC	0-0490373	0757	1
LASATER NORMAN E	WO1	W-2110882	0558	1
LASCOLA ANTHONY G	LTC	0-0395230	0461	1
LASEK EUGENE L	CW3	W-2203270	0862	1
LASELL MILO G	LTC	0-1297391	1165	1
LASH CLEO L	COL	0-0183069	0155	3
LASH JAMES W	COL	0-0649510	1166	1
LASH JOHN A	MAJ	0-0256853	1264	3
LASH RUSSELL J	2LT	0-1032536	0145	2
LASHE PETER	CW3	W-2105392	0861	1
LASHER WILLIS W	COL	0-0136968	0448	2
LASHKOFF GALENA	1LT	N-0756778	0646	1
LASHLEY WISTAR J	CW2	W-2145889	0960	1
LASHMAN RUTH E	2LT	N-0788848	0845	1
LASHUA WILLIAM C	CW3	W-2144700	0460	1
LASK WALTER M	MAJ	0-0305786	0950	2
LASKA LEONARD P	MAJ	0-1549906	0161	1
LASKER EDWIN C	LTC	0-1291656	1068	3
LASKOWSKI CLARENCE	MAJ	0-1997268	0767	1
LASKOWSKI FRANK W	LTC	0-0349657	0661	1
LASKOWSKI HELEN C	1LT	N-0721209	0246	1
LASKY JOHN A	LTC	0-0485193	0953	1
LASKY JOHN F	1LT	0-2005658	0147	2
LASKY JOSEPH	CW4	W-2118196	1154	1
LASKY MORTIMER A	LTC	0-0244904	0364	3
LASLEY DONALD G	LTC	0-1284347	0968	1
LASLEY FRED	MAJ	0-0285388	0863	3
LASLEY HAROLD L	LTC	0-0953685	0567	1
LASLEY OLIVER P	CW4	W-2119373	0862	1
LASPINA GATIN T	MAJ	0-1032223	0160	1
LASSELLE HERBERT W	COL	0-0258394	1066	3
LASSELLE PERCY A	LTC	0-0173097	1060	3
LASSETER PAUL L	CW2	W-3151611	0367	1
LASSETER WILLIAM W	CW2	W-2143053	0462	1
LASSETTER BURL G	LTC	0-0291598	0366	3
LASSILA EINO E	COL	0-0985339	0268	1
LASSITER BASIL	LTC	0-1173686	0962	1
LASSITER JAMES	CPT	0-1290769	0550	2
LASSITER RUBY S	LTC	L-0502525	1167	1
LASSMAN MORRIS L	LTC	0-1691273	0168	3
LASSOFF THEODORE	LTC	0-2001062	0661	1
LASSWELL J R	MAJ	0-0960063	1266	1
LASSWELL RICHARD E	CPT	0-1030794	0847	2
LASTER JOHN S	MAJ	0-1036247	0366	1
LASTON FREDERICK	MAJ	0-0476734	0946	2
LASWELL ROBERT A	LTC	0-1017972	1262	2
LATART LELAND J	1LT	0-1170458	0944	2
LATCHEM CLYDE G	LTC	0-0122825	1052	3
LATENDRESSE DONALD P	1LT	0-1106280	1045	2
LATENDRESSE WALDON G	MAJ	0-0962178	0961	1
LATERRIERE JOHN R	LTC	0-0393324	0261	1
LATEY KEITH P	CW3	W-2000712	0356	3
LATHAM ALMON L	LTC	0-0992120	0568	1
LATHAM ARTHUR A	LTC	0-1322641	0464	2
LATHAM BILL C	MAJ	0-1289595	0457	1
LATHAM BILL M	1LT	0-0389647	1045	2
LATHAM ELWIN E	CPT	0-5417986	1268	2
LATHAM GEORGE W	LTC	0-1183715	0168	1
LATHAM LEON D JR	COL	0-0315169	1065	3
LATHAM LYMAN A	MAJ	0-1635006	0266	1
LATHAM ROBERT F	CPT	0-1645750	0647	2
LATHAM RUDOLPH L	CW3	W-2152221	0161	1
LATHAM WALTER O	1LT	0-1797667	1049	1
LATHERS MARTIN L	CPT	0-0494009	0653	1
LATHOM HAROLD E	CW2	W-2103125	0955	1
LATHROP EARL S JR	CPT	0-0426088	0246	2
LATHROP FRANK P	1LT	0-5422762	1168	2
LATHROP LAURENCE L	LTC	0-0313407	0857	3
LATIMER CLAUDE A	COL	0-0211151	0149	3
LATIMER GEORGE W	COL	0-0174611	1060	3
LATIMER HUGH M	LTC	0-0258022	0857	1
LATIMER ROBERT G JR	CPT	0-0504909	0346	2
LATIMER WILLIAM G	CPT	0-0157423	1143	2
LATIMER WILLIAM H	LTC	0-1184870	0965	1
LATOFF THOMAS J	MAJ	0-1695789	1045	2
LATOUR ADRIAN R	LTC	0-0288340	0267	3
LATOUR LUCILE G	MAJ	N-0737818	0163	1
LATRONICO LOUIS	CPT	0-1574939	0655	1
LATSKO WILLIAM S	2LT	0-0538764	0845	2
LATSON CLAUDE H	LTC	0-0277830	1160	3
LATTA ALEXANDER	CPT	0-0276429	0865	3
LATTA SAMUEL C	MAJ	0-0153038	0745	2
LATTA WILLIAM M	MAJ	0-0334700	0265	3
LATTAL ANTON JR	LTC	0-0365929	0860	1
LATTARI DANIEL	1LT	0-1175484	0845	2
LATTERMAN ALBERT J	LTC	0-0134694	0754	3
LATTIMER GEORGE W	CW2	W-3430439	0867	1
LATUCHA ALBERT	CPT	0-1715974	0347	2
LATZ HELEN C	1LT	N-0761120	0746	1
LATZER PAUL J	COL	0-0201853	1061	3
LATZO JOSEPH	CPT	0-1554923	0556	1
LAU BENEDICT W	2LT	0-1019850	0943	2
LAU CHARLES E	MAJ	0-1284348	0345	2
LAU CHARLES H	2LT	0-1314227	0944	2
LAU FRANCIS X	LTC	0-1825762	1168	1
LAU FRANK O	CPT	0-0201081	1056	3
LAU JOSEPH F C	1LT	0-0405176	0843	2
LAU KENNETH K	LTC	0-0366921	0550	2
LAU ROBERT H	MAJ	0-0292884	0545	2
LAU WILSON B	1LT	0-1300344	0746	2
LAUBENHEIMER WILLIAM	COL	0-0281642	0764	1
LAUBER DANIEL A	CW2	W-2209397	0965	1
LAUBY GLENN D	COL	0-0931417	1268	1
LAUCK MERRILL A	1LT	0-1181339	0745	2
LAUDENSLAYER OSCAR G	MAJ	0-1554030	1156	1
LAUDER EDWARD W	LTC	0-0243157	0563	3
LAUDER JOHN R	1LT	0-1174347	0744	2
LAUDERDALE GEORGE W	CW3	W-2146591	0364	1
LAUDERDALE SAMUEL M	MAJ	0-0913983	0546	2
LAUE ALBERT R	LTC	0-1648530	0767	1
LAUER ALBERT G	MAJ	0-0323143	1058	3
LAUER BYRON E	LTC	0-0259260	0567	3
LAUER CHARLES F	LTC	0-1101541	0166	1
LAUER FRANK C JR	LTC	0-0406842	0445	2
LAUER JOSEPH G	LTC	0-1576278	0765	1
LAUER MARGARET B	MAJ	N-0733980	0463	1
LAUER MARY H	2LT	N-0759807	0245	1
LAUGERMAN HAROLD W	1LT	0-1303166	0246	2
LAUGHLIN ALFRED J	MAJ	0-0335431	0546	2
LAUGHLIN CHARLES V	LTC	0-2051832	0667	3
LAUGHLIN JOHN C	1LT	0-2024324	0147	2
LAUGHLIN LORENZO D	MAJ	0-1949831	0663	2
LAUGHLIN SEDRICK G	CW4	W-2143202	1168	1
LAUGHMAN HARRY E	CW2	W-2211403	1265	1
LAUGHNER JOHN H	COL	0-0316755	1264	3
LAUGHRUN WILLIAM A	MAJ	0-1702203	1044	2
LAUGHTER JOHN E	CPT	0-0428743	0647	2
LAUIGAN ESTANISLAO	2LT	0-0890499	0562	1
LAULETTA CYPRIAN M	LTC	0-0484120	0467	1
LAUNDER JOHN E JR	CPT	0-0390139	1045	2
LAUR CLIFFORD N	MAJ	0-2263162	0262	1
LAUREA GERALD	MAJ	0-1305797	0655	1
LAURENCE LESLIE T	MAJ	0-2036248	0958	1
LAURI WAINO A	COL	0-0265474	0468	3
LAURIA PHILIP C	CW3	W-2146980	0964	1
LAURIE GEORGE C	LTC	0-0553095	1066	1
LAURIE ROBERT R	1LT	0-1301656	0146	2
LAURITANO EUGENE J	MAJ	0-1637899	1146	2
LAUSIER CLAUDE D	CW2	W-2153162	0565	1
LAUSMAN HAROLD J	1LT	0-2047038	0246	2
LAUTH ALBERT W	CPT	0-2018535	1058	2
LAUTHERS CHARLES W	LTC	0-0179968	1153	3
LAUTNER ELMER F	MAJ	0-0919847	0447	2
LAUTZENHEISER C N	CPT	0-1945632	0547	2
LAUZZE ANTHONY R	CPT	0-1314032	1045	2
LAVALLE LAWRENCE L	COL	0-0324811	0364	3
LAVALLEE LEON J	COL	0-0206797	0953	3
LAVAN RAY E	LTC	0-0347905	0761	2
LAVELL JOHN B	MAJ	0-1331296	0762	1
LAVELLE JAMES J	MAJ	0-1325904	0863	1
LAVENDER CHARLES E	MAJ	0-0178646	1054	3
LAVENDER ROBERT P	MAJ	0-1298724	1264	1
LAVERDURE LOUIS A	MAJ	0-1578749	0460	1
LAVERY ARTHUR T	CW4	W-2103753	0757	1
LAVERY EUGENE H	1LT	0-1289928	0545	2
LAVERY EUGENE L	LTC	0-0884210	0465	1
LAVERY HAROLD S	CPT	0-1177045	1045	2
LAVETT JOHN S	1LT	0-1015561	0546	2
LAVEY PATRICK J	CW3	W-2146339	1163	1
LAVICK DONALD H	2LT	0-1642304	0745	2
LAVIGNE DAVID F	MAJ	0-1166538	0961	1
LAVIN JOHN A	COL	0-0165493	0156	3
LAVIN JULIA F	MAJ	N-0758300	0165	1
LAVIN MARGUERITE	LTC	N-0731436	1166	3
LAVIN MARSHALL R	2LT	0-2036822	0345	2
LAVINE BERNARD	CPT	0-1304407	1047	2
LAVIS FRANK J	1LT	0-1299911	0344	2
LAVOIE RICHARD J	MAJ	0-1704216	0957	1
LAVOIE WARREN R	MAJ	0-1113316	0261	1
LAVRAKAS CHARLES	LTC	0-0288968	0865	3
LAW ALLEN L	CW4	W-2132131	0857	1
LAW AUGUST	1LT	0-1288404	0551	1
LAW BUELL S	MAJ	0-0201479	0652	3
LAW CHARLTON E	MAJ	0-0239316	0166	3
LAW DAVID F	CPT	0-0499756	0450	1
LAW DON E	CPT	0-1798366	0566	3
LAW EARL J	MAJ	0-0965312	1061	1
LAW ELLIE D JR	LTC	0-0227690	0265	3
LAW FRANCIS M	CW4	W-2143433	0164	1
LAW FRASER C	LTC	0-0219175	0263	3
LAW JAMES E	1LT	0-1548909	1150	2
LAW JOHN T	CPT	0-0505984	1048	1
LAW KENNETH D	LTC	0-2262339	0168	1
LAW ROBERT S	MAJ	0-1950202	0764	1
LAW ROBERT W JR	1LT	0-1294153	0447	2
LAW RUSSELL E	COL	0-0413124	0767	1
LAW RUSSELL E	MAJ	0-1289086	0857	1
LAW RUTH A	2LT	N-0762560	0746	1
LAW WYATT L	CPT	0-0939700	0457	1
LAWDER DOUGLASS J	CPT	0-0247732	1057	3
LAWER JAMES R	CW3	W-2151208	0264	1
LAWES CHARLES O	COL	0-0135743	0755	2
LAWLER AMY K C	CPT	N-0752430	0547	1
LAWLER EDWARD J	LTC	0-0380799	0557	1
LAWLER ERNEST H	LTC	0-1010471	1267	3
LAWLER GEORGE B	LTC	0-0203301	0454	3
LAWLER GEORGE H	CPT	0-1186513	0957	2
LAWLER JACK P	MAJ	0-0981789	1165	1
LAWLER JOHN D	MAJ	0-1642305	0764	1
LAWLER JOHN M	LTC	0-0153801	1149	3
LAWLER RUSSELL B	MAJ	0-0236528	1265	3
LAWLER THOMAS H	MAJ	0-1017337	0265	1
LAWLER VERNON J	CW3	W-2111061	0960	1
LAWLESS CHARLES E	LTC	0-1035514	0367	1
LAWLESS JOHN J	CW3	W-2203284	0263	1
LAWLESS WILBUR D	2LT	0-1823314	0745	2
LAWLEY DOUGLAS N	COL	0-0149915	0955	3
LAWLEY JAMES M	WO1	W-2146055	0653	1
LAWLIS LAUREN L	CPT	0-2033066	1060	1
LAWLIS TILDEN T	LTC	0-1060527	0666	3
LAWLOR CLARENCE A	CW3	W-2145562	0861	1
LAWLOR FRANK E	MAJ	0-0292228	1056	3
LAWLOR HARRY J	CPT	0-1309577	0450	2
LAWLOR JAMES	COL	0-0245444	0863	3
LAWLOR JAMES P	CPT	0-0522220	1045	2
LAWLOR JOHN T	CPT	0-1574076	0855	1
LAWLOR WILLIAM J	LTC	0-1639341	0463	1
LAWRENCE ALBERT W	LTC	0-1574942	0557	1
LAWRENCE ALFRED W	LTC	0-0918926	0568	3
LAWRENCE ALLAN R	COL	0-0305208	0862	2
LAWRENCE ALVIN P	CPT	0-1688542	1057	2
LAWRENCE ANTHONY A	1LT	0-0454929	1143	2
LAWRENCE ANTONIO J	LTC	0-0454077	0258	1
LAWRENCE ARTHUR J	CPT	0-0499440	1054	1
LAWRENCE BERTRAM I	COL	0-0200311	0648	3
LAWRENCE BESSIE	LTC	N-0742101	0164	3
LAWRENCE CHARLES R	1LT	0-1172141	0245	2
LAWRENCE CHENEY E	LTC	0-0297099	0648	3
LAWRENCE CLARENCE D	LTC	0-0438275	1047	1
LAWRENCE CLAUDE W	CW2	W-2152794	1262	1
LAWRENCE EDWIN T	MAJ	0-0312368	0762	3
LAWRENCE EUGENE A	MAJ	0-1796103	1059	1
LAWRENCE GEORGE E	LTC	0-1179499	1265	1
LAWRENCE GEORGE E	1LT	0-1576280	0344	2
LAWRENCE GEORGE H	MAJ	0-1283798	1064	1
LAWRENCE GUY L	CW2	W-2149078	1064	1
LAWRENCE HANS W	COL	0-0246295	0546	2
LAWRENCE HAROLD	CPT	0-1845200	0747	2
LAWRENCE HAROLD M	COL	0-0404626	0766	3
LAWRENCE HARRY L JR	LTC	0-2056251	0265	1
LAWRENCE HELEN V	CPT	N-0763871	0547	1
LAWRENCE HENRY E	CW2	W-2143545	1158	1
LAWRENCE HENRY F	MAJ	0-1047630	0457	1
LAWRENCE HENRY J	COL	0-0311151	0360	3
LAWRENCE HENRY S	LTC	0-0202689	0159	3
LAWRENCE HOWARD J	CPT	0-0310404	0746	2
LAWRENCE HOWARD J	CW3	W-2146410	0168	1
LAWRENCE JAMES K	COL	0-0417236	0368	3
LAWRENCE JAMES P	LTC	0-1168772	0264	1
LAWRENCE JAMES S	1LT	0-1016774	0645	2

NAME	GRADE	SVC NO	DATE RET MO YR	RET CODE
LAWRENCE [illegible]	COL	0-0143090	0563	3
LAWRENCE [illegible]	CPT	0-0211742	1061	3
LAWRENCE [illegible]	MAJ	0-0227817	0560	3
LAWRENCE [illegible]	MAJ	0-1295348	0761	1
LAWRENCE MILTON M	LTC	0-1309167	0262	1
LAWRENCE MI[illegible] L	1LT	0-0988772	0552	2
LAWRENCE [illegible]	COL	0-0453040	0755	1
LAWRENCE PATRICK A	CPT	0-0499677	0747	1
LAWRENCE PAUL M	MAJ	0-0213992	0157	3
LAWRENCE PAUL M	CPT	0-1329403	0157	2
LAWRENCE PHILLIP E JR	2LT	0-0578793	0545	2
LAWRENCE RAY [illegible]	COL	0-0221184	0263	3
LAWRENCE [illegible]	LTC	0-0372900	0966	1
LAWRENCE [illegible]	MAJ	0-1951132	0267	1
LAWRENCE ROBERT [illegible]	CPT	0-0326389	0945	2
LAWRENCE ROBERT L JR	CPT	0-1179542	0947	2
LAWRENCE ROY [illegible]	MAJ	0-1181670	0562	1
LAWRENCE STEWART S	LTC	0-0274087	1154	2
LAWRENCE VERNON [illegible]	LTC	0-0827047	0768	1
LAWRENCE WILLIAM A	CW3	W-2147477	1064	1
LAWRENCE WILLIAM F	COL	0-0450744	1058	1
LAWRENCE WILLIAM T	CPT	0-0309687	1046	2
LAWRENCE WILLIS R	1LT	0-1294154	0145	2
LAWRENCE WINSTON J	LTC	0-0419312	0665	1
LAWRENZ CHARLES A	LTC	0-1284152	1061	2
LAWRIE CLYDE H	CW2	W-2206364	1263	1
LAWRY ARTHUR T	LTC	0-0914875	1264	1
LAWRY DAVID S	CW2	W-3100665	0268	1
LAWRY [illegible] L	MAJ	0-0345090	0145	2
LAWS GEORGE M	MAJ	0-0145711	0648	3
LAWS HAROLD C	MAJ	0-1540911	0661	1
LAWS JAMES R	MAJ	0-1645353	1047	2
LAWS THOMAS F	CPT	0-1100191	1059	1
LAWS WALTER L	MAJ	0-0483834	0852	2
LAWSON ALBERT H	CW2	W-2150897	1162	1
LAWSON ALLAN L	LTC	0-1288075	1062	1
LAWSON ARTHUR D	LTC	0-0386934	0860	1
LAWSON CHARLES F	LTC	0-1947010	1262	1
LAWSON DAVID S	COL	0-0312079	1058	3
LAWSON EARL L	CPT	0-1702567	0246	2
LAWSON EDWARD J	CPT	0-0459463	0947	1
LAWSON ELMER L	MAJ	0-0525778	0349	1
LAWSON GEORGE M	1LT	0-1297390	0446	2
LAWSON GLASSELLE	MAJ	0-0450612	1155	1
LAWSON HAROLD L	1LT	0-1293616	0862	2
LAWSON HARRY A	LTC	0-1550641	0563	1
LAWSON J E	CPT	0-1018109	0863	1
LAWSON JOHN D	2LT	0-1636196	0144	2
LAWSON JOHN L	LTC	0-0476714	0565	1
LAWSON JOSEPH F	1LT	0-1576281	0547	2
LAWSON JOSEPH R	CPT	0-0271457	0445	2
LAWSON RUTH E	MAJ	M-0000479	0566	2
LAWSON WARREN G	CW3	W-2151333	0567	1
LAWSON WILLIAM	CPT	0-0444561	1144	2
LAWSON WILLIAM E	LTC	0-0171028	0260	3
LAWSON WILLIAM F	MAJ	0-1594969	0460	1
LAWSON WILLIS	CPT	0-0452117	1145	2
LAWTER JAMES R	1LT	0-5339037	0968	2
LAWTON ERNEST L	CW4	W-2144076	1066	1
LAWTON FRANK R	LTC	0-1583260	1168	1
LAWTON JAMES K	COL	0-0117701	0751	3
LAWTON JOHN D	LTC	0-1579751	0963	1
LAWTON MARION R	MAJ	0-0390578	1046	2
LAWTON MORGAN B	CPT	0-0907994	1045	2
LAWTON PHILIP C	LTC	0-0447764	1051	1
LAWTON ROBERT C	LTC	0-1311793	0563	1
LAWTON RODNEY E	LTC	0-1945192	1166	1
LAWTON VERA A	MAJ	N-0700948	1044	1
LAWYER CHARLES	CPT	0-0181151	0546	2
LAWYER HIRAM L	LTC	0-0906413	0766	3
LAWYER KEITH H	LTC	0-1595640	1267	1
LAX MARTIN J	1LT	0-0929249	0154	2
LAXTON AMOS H	LTC	0-0262896	0467	3
LAY FOREST A	MAJ	0-1286511	0446	2
LAY JAMES S	MAJ	0-1685003	1064	1
LAY JOHN W	LTC	0-1311756	0865	1
LAY KERMIT K SR	CPT	0-0890211	0451	2
LAYBOURN EUGENE P	MAJ	0-0344648	0147	1
LAYCOCK CLAUDIA G	2LT	N-0761500	0645	1
LAYCOCK WALTER F	1LT	0-1896049	0845	2
LAYDEN CHARLES K	CPT	0-1557180	0864	1
LAYDEN JAMES F	MAJ	0-4006883	1066	2
LAYDEN RICHARD J	MAJ	0-1336232	1161	1
LAYER BARBARA L	1LT	N-0721825	0946	1
LAYLE HERBERT F	COL	0-0322510	1059	3
LAYLE THEODORE W	LTC	0-0370711	1266	3
LAYMAN FRED H	MAJ	0-1308657	0557	2
LAYMAN JAMES W	LTC	0-0479798	0659	2
LAYMAN PHILLIP J	MAJ	0-1109444	1160	1
LAYMAN ROBERT P	CPT	0-1696549	0345	2
LAYMON HOWARD O	LTC	0-1798587	1264	1
LAYMON RICHARD S	2LT	0-1546624	1044	2
LAYNE LORENE	2LT	N-0702269	0132	1
LAYOS JOSEPH K	CPT	0-1821600	0344	2
LAYSON JUNIUS C	MAJ	0-1825867	0261	1
LAYTHE GATHEL C	MAJ	N-0727390	0862	1
LAYTON ALAN W	CPT	0-0416409	1045	2
LAYTON ARTHUR F	LTC	0-0265010	1265	3
LAYTON BENJAMIN T	LTC	0-1290351	0463	1
LAYTON CHARLES F	LTC	0-0475963	0653	1
LAYTON LEWIS L	CW3	W-2006467	0366	3
LAYTON MYRON M	COL	0-0270907	0859	2
LAYTON ROBERT R JR	COL	0-0404693	0946	2
LAYTON WILLIAM P	COL	0-0264732	0667	3
LAYUS AGUSTIN V	2LT	0-1896457	0762	1
LAYWELL RAYMOND L	MAJ	0-1796815	0360	1
LAZAR ISIDOR	MAJ	0-0490627	1155	1
LAZAR WILLIAM H JR	1LT	0-1179500	0546	2
LAZARUS FRANK L	B G	0-0242867	0861	3
LAZARUS JACOB	1LT	0-1593016	0946	2
LAZARUS LUCIUS T	CW2	W-2151197	0961	2
LAZARUS RICHARD S	1LT	0-1059525	0646	2
LAZICKI DANIEL F	MAJ	0-1542143	0762	1
LAZZARI AMERICO	LTC	0-0288573	0867	3
LE BLANC EDWARD H	COL	0-0297080	1166	3
LE BLANC LEO R	MAJ	0-0508040	0357	1
LE BOEUF HERVEY J JR	LTC	0-1100638	1065	1
LE BOEUF JOSEPH R	LTC	0-1293617	0863	1
LE BRETON EDWIN L	MAJ	0-1104951	0763	1
LE BRUN WILFRED J	COL	0-0381999	1068	3
LE CLAIR ADRIEN O	CW4	W-2104232	0157	1
LE CLAIR ARTHUR A	CPT	0-1080639	0157	1
LE CLAIR EDWARD C	LTC	0-1647573	0164	1
LE CLAIR ERNEST W	CW3	W-2002985	0963	1
LE CLAIR ISIDORE G	LTC	0-1822414	0965	1
LE CLEAR FRANCIS E	CPT	0-0393420	0561	1
LE CLERC LEON A	CPT	0-1044277	0955	1
LE CLERG VERNON C	COL	0-0267772	0463	3
LE COMPTE HOWARD C	CW3	W-2151203	0365	1
LE COMPTE THEODORE L	1LT	0-1321221	0246	2
LE COUNT ETHEL G	1LT	N-0772334	0446	1
LE COUNT LOUIS K	LTC	0-0234811	1065	3
LE CRAW ARTHUR E	LTC	0-0175791	1061	3
LE CRAW JOHN W	LTC	0-0116667	0945	2
LE CRONE NAOMI L	1LT	R-0000106	0247	1
LE CROY KERMIT B	MAJ	0-1296872	0866	3
LE DEAUX ANDERSON T	MAJ	0-2324398	0668	1
LE DOUX EDWARD L	CPT	0-0480613	0848	2
LE DUC VINCENT J	CW3	W-2205178	1266	1
LE FEVRE GEORGE L JR	LTC	0-0223104	0955	3
LE FLEUR WAYNE D	LTC	0-1554926	0762	1
LE GATH EVERETT A	LTC	0-0289278	0167	3
LE GAULT MILTON L	LTC	0-1291138	0461	1
LE GORE LOY C	CW3	W-2148438	1065	1
LE GRAND EDWIN C	MAJ	0-0159534	0456	1
LE HARDY JULIUS C	1LT	0-2204117	1054	2
LE JEUNE JOSEPH H	CW3	W-2146341	1162	1
LE LACHEUR EMBERT A	LTC	0-0256180	1053	3
LE LIEVRE EFFIE	MAJ	N-0757474	1163	1
LE MAR DORIS	1LT	N-0736265	0746	1
LE MASTER FRED P	CW4	W-2121143	0864	1
LE MASTER IRA V	LTC	0-0261820	0666	3
LE MASTER ROBERT L	MAJ	0-4005819	0267	1
LE MASTER ROGER H	LTC	0-1044149	0760	1
LE MAY DAVID M	CW2	W-2140170	0959	1
LE MAY EDWARD F	MAJ	0-1547675	0561	2
LE MAY HAROLD W	CPT	0-1325501	1056	2
LE MAY ROBERT H	CW2	W-3430541	1167	1
LE MON TRUE F	MAJ	0-1951678	0564	1
LE NOIR JOSEPH T	CPT	0-1307784	0163	1
LE PAGE MILTON F	LTC	0-0327756	0262	3
LE QUIRE JOHN B	CW3	W-2145760	1160	1
LE RAY THOMAS	MAJ	0-1081851	1067	3
LE TANG LINUS L	LTC	0-0572401	0562	2
LE TRENT JOHN A	LTC	0-1304246	1067	1
LE VALLEY MILLER W	LTC	0-1049069	0562	1
LE VAN FRANKLIN P	CPT	0-0509727	1045	2
LE VAN RAYMOND F	LTC	0-1996661	0465	1
LE VASSEUR EDWARD F	CPT	0-1322048	0347	2
LE VASSEUR PROSPER J	CPT	0-0966290	0762	1
LE VEY ARTHUR F	LTC	0-0348696	0465	3
LE VIEN BERTRAM M	CPT	0-1030795	0662	1
LE VINE SAUL E	CPT	0-0355083	0845	2
LE VINES CHESTER W	CW4	W-2142242	0460	1
LE VITIN MORRIS L	LTC	0-0480611	0663	3
LEA EDWIN B	CW3	W-2146256	0962	1
LEA ELLIS	LTC	0-0288044	0859	1
LEA LUDWELL L	2LT	0-0415791	1042	2
LEA THOMAS R	LTC	0-0365930	0859	1
LEACH ALBERT A	CPT	0-0388065	0846	2
LEACH ANTHONY D	LTC	0-0452965	0566	3
LEACH CHARLES F	MAJ	0-2048990	0968	3
LEACH EDWARD M	CPT	0-1822289	0361	1
LEACH ELEANORE A	1LT	N-0733227	1145	1
LEACH HAROLD D	LTC	0-1995468	0962	2
LEACH HENRY C	COL	0-0358301	0862	1
LEACH HERMAN E	MAJ	0-1296871	0158	1
LEACH JOHN E	CPT	0-0444915	1045	2
LEACH JOSEPH A	CW3	W-2147055	0161	1
LEACH LOREN F	LTC	0-0949332	0866	1
LEACH RAYMOND E	LTC	0-0369957	0766	3
LEACH RICHARD F	MAJ	0-0338387	0946	2
LEACH TIMOTHY	MAJ	0-1047200	0361	1
LEACH WILLIAM P	LTC	0-0365423	0462	1
LEACHMAN THOMAS E	LTC	0-0358474	0461	1
LEACOCK CHARLES E	LTC	0-1913412	0867	1
LEACY BLANCHARD	1LT	0-2010583	0547	2
LEADBEATER HERBERT B	MAJ	0-0456112	1047	2
LEADER GLENN C JR	MAJ	0-0388761	0845	2
LEADER SAMUEL A	COL	0-0311934	0261	3
LEADY CLAUDE L	CW3	W-2152971	1265	1
LEAF JENNIE E	2LT	N-0724135	0244	1
LEAF JOHN M	MAJ	0-0955899	0765	2
LEAF LOUIS	COL	0-0268895	1166	3
LEAFSTONE JOHN H	1LT	0-1702998	0748	2
LEAGUE EDGAR A	CW3	W-2001718	1059	3
LEAGUE JAMES W	1LT	0-1598917	1047	2
LEAH LOUIS D	MAJ	0-1306109	0461	1
LEAHEY EDWARD W	LTC	0-0192077	1062	3
LEAHEY WALLACE J	LTC	0-1327017	0967	1
LEAHY ARTHUR E	CW3	W-2150714	0863	1
LEAHY ARTHUR L	1LT	0-1170822	1145	2
LEAHY BERNARD P	LTC	0-1585760	0762	1
LEAHY MARY E	MAJ	N-0736246	0166	1
LEAHY ROBERT G	MAJ	0-1308837	0165	1
LEAHY WALTER R	MAJ	0-1798868	1160	1
LEAIRD JOHN B JR	CW3	W-2147151	1062	1
LEAK EDWARD D	LTC	0-0953561	0567	1
LEAKE BAIN	CPT	0-1701359	0545	2
LEAKE HADLEY W	LTC	0-0445218	0247	2
LEAKE HARRY L	LTC	0-0116670	0753	3
LEAKE JOHN L	1LT	0-1321192	1147	2
LEAKEN RICHARD M	MAJ	0-1081659	0365	1
LEAKINS JOHN A	2LT	0-0106499	0720	1
LEAL GEORGE P	MAJ	0-1046169	1160	1
LEAMAN LEONARD S	1LT	0-1057698	0366	2
LEAMING ANDREW W	MAJ	0-0376077	0647	2
LEAMING ARTHUR C	1LT	0-1306605	0565	2
LEAMING EARL F	COL	0-0198602	0759	3
LEAMING JEREMIAH C	CPT	0-0177457	0662	3
LEAMING WILLIAM V	1LT	0-0531583	0545	2
LEAMON NICHOLAS J	MAJ	0-1102814	1059	1
LEAMY FRANK P	COL	0-0900549	1265	3
LEAP ARTHUR G	LTC	0-1108802	0960	1
LEAP FRANCIS G	MAJ	0-1844311	0960	1
LEAPHEART SHELTON P	WO1	W-2145907	0657	1
LEAR IRA H	MAJ	0-0992283	0166	1
LEAR LESLIE A	CPT	0-1823016	0162	1
LEAR MERRILL O	CW2	W-2213463	1167	1
LEARD ROBERT N	LTC	0-0338763	0860	1
LEARN GERALD H	MAJ	0-1546667	1262	1
LEARNED NORMA G	MAJ	J-0100135	1166	1
LEARNIHAN THOMAS JR	2LT	0-1305798	0757	2
LEARY ALEXANDER	MAJ	0-2008673	0365	1
LEARY DANIEL F	LTC	0-1302321	1262	1
LEARY EDGAR T	CPT	0-0506474	1044	2
LEARY EDWARD H	CPT	0-0504370	0343	2
LEARY EDWARD J	COL	0-0329499	0561	3
LEARY FRANCIS P	COL	0-0290627	1066	3
LEARY FRANK R	MAJ	0-0537476	0346	2
LEARY HOWARD P	LTC	0-0349255	1162	3
LEARY JOHN J JR	CPT	0-1016332	0147	2
LEARY LEONARD W	1LT	0-1107546	0345	2
LEARY WARREN F JR	LTC	0-1313422	0866	1
LEARY WILBUR A	LTC	0-1000256	0457	1
LEARY WILLIAM E	LTC	0-0351609	0461	1
LEAS JOHN B	MAJ	0-1325302	0961	1
LEAS LARRY D	LTC	0-1290442	0861	1
LEASK ARTHUR A	MAJ	0-2021264	1165	1
LEASK GEORGE D	MAJ	0-0122826	1144	2
LEASURE CLYDE B	LTC	0-0186047	1148	3
LEASURE DAN S	LTC	0-1101088	0163	1
LEASURE ELMER E	MAJ	0-0106908	0754	3
LEASURE THOMAS J	MAJ	0-0287202	1161	3
LEASURE WILLIAM C	1LT	0-0403832	0244	2
LEATH HAROLD W	LTC	0-0323298	1161	3
LEATH JAMES G	CW3	W-2141879	0962	1
LEATH LUTHER C	LTC	0-2047721	0768	1
LEATHAM LOUIS S	LTC	0-0385131	1264	3
LEATHART WAYNE C	CW2	W-2144509	1068	1
LEATHERMAN HAROLD E	2LT	0-1320469	1051	2
LEATHERMAN HARRY L	MAJ	0-0185907	0648	3
LEATHERMAN JAY C	LTC	0-1177499	0567	1
LEATHERS CECIL C	CPT	0-0502771	1047	1
LEATHERS CHARLES A	CPT	0-2036665	0448	2
LEATHERS ERNEST B	1LT	0-0288835	1264	3
LEATHERWOOD ABRAHAM	LTC	0-0228441	0465	3
LEAVELL FRED W	CPT	0-0288408	0356	3
LEAVELL LEWIS L	COL	0-0141686	0148	2
LEAVENS EDWIN T	CPT	0-1293274	0147	2
LEAVER ELMER R	CPT	0-2025264	0858	1
LEAVER THOMAS D	MAJ	0-0224810	0151	3
LEAVITT ARTHUR S	CPT	0-0297115	0446	2
LEAVITT ERNEST E	LTC	0-0244274	1160	3
LEAVITT GEORGE H	COL	0-0172183	0556	2
LEAVITT HARRY	CW4	W-2104231	0552	2
LEAVITT JAMES W	CW2	W-3200452	0267	1
LEAVITT JOHN M	CW2	W-2105967	0753	1
LEAVITT LEIGHTON T	CW2	W-2147100	0661	1
LEAVITT MERVYN W	COL	0-0430745	0261	1
LEAVITT MILO D	CPT	0-0477196	0345	2
LEAVITT MORRILL W	MAJ	0-0292251	0945	2
LEAVITT STANLEY L	MAJ	0-1331298	1264	1
LEAVITT TOD J JR	COL	0-0262870	1167	3
LEAVITT WENDELL D	2LT	0-0529115	0645	2
LEAX WILLIAM F	CPT	0-1295039	0546	2
LEAZAR MARVIN F	MAJ	0-1186044	0459	1
LEBAR JOSEPH	CW3	W-2110684	0357	1
LEBAY WILLIAM H	MAJ	0-0348306	0358	3
LEBEL LUCIEN E	MAJ	0-2036666	0461	1

NAME	GRADE	SVC NO	DATE RET MO YR	RET CODE
LEBER EUGENE I	LTC	O-0317478	1059	1
LEBLANC JOSEPH R JR	CPT	O-0982986	0161	1
LEBOEUF WILFRED F	CPT	O-0484848	1158	2
LEBRON EUDUVIGIS	1LT	O-0155976	0648	3
LEBRON LAMAR C	LTC	O-0168208	0959	3
LEBRUM ERNEST	CPT	O-0513412	0847	1
LECHLEITER EDWARD A	MAJ	O-0240348	0646	2
LECHMAN OTTO	MAJ	O-1648354	0854	1
LECHWAR MARTIN J	MAJ	O-0410868	0358	1
LECKAR LEO	MAJ	O-1648691	1263	1
LECKART HARVEY H	CPT	O-0487096	0246	2
LECKLITNER MYRON D	MAJ	O-1693315	0446	2
LECKVARCIK NICHOLAS	WO1	W-2145738	0863	2
LECKY GEORGE C	LTC	O-0270080	1068	3
LECKY JOSEPH L	1LT	O-0281110	0946	2
LECLERC ADRIAN	CW4	W-2113731	0555	1
LECOCQ HENRY J	1LT	O-0237345	0255	3
LEDBETTER ARVOR M	CPT	O-0176536	1055	3
LEDBETTER CARL E	COL	O-0182694	0754	3
LEDBETTER CARL S	COL	O-0410688	1061	1
LEDBETTER CHARLES O	CPT	O-0385234	0943	2
LEDBETTER JOE S	CW4	W-2143735	0868	1
LEDBETTER LAVERN E	LTC	O-1330327	0766	1
LEDBETTER ONIE C	CW2	W-2108961	0454	1
LEDBETTER PAUL L	CW2	W-2115848	0157	1
LEDBETTER VIRGIL K	MAJ	O-1824049	0258	1
LEDBETTER WILLIAM B	COL	O-0105674	0155	3
LEDBETTER WILLIAM M	MAJ	O-1950549	0860	1
LEDDON JAMES A JR	LTC	O-0426288	0263	1
LEDOY CHARLES P	MAJ	O-0372277	1066	3
LEDDY JOHN F	LTC	O-1542689	1063	1
LEDDY ORVILLE J	1LT	O-0351174	0745	2
LEDDY SAM W	LTC	O-1297058	1160	1
LEDERER WOLFGANG	CPT	O-1012737	0446	2
LEDESMAAGUIAZ FRANK R	CPT	O-0482711	0746	2
LEDFORD JAMES J	2LT	O-1328496	1045	2
LEDFORD LARK JR	1LT	O-1306110	0546	2
LEDGERWOOD MARVIN C	1LT	O-0348617	0942	2
LEDIG ROY E	LTC	O-0409322	0961	1
LEDLIE JOHN P	CPT	O-1575409	0347	2
LEDOGAR CLARENCE G	LTC	O-1320697	1267	3
LEDOUX ALFRED C	LTC	O-0485430	1045	2
LEDWITH OLINON N	LTC	O-0351304	0868	3
LEE AARON A	MAJ	O-1285776	0557	1
LEE ALAN S	1LT	O-1310464	0546	2
LEE ANNA V	2LT	N-0723064	0845	1
LEE ARVEL L	CW2	W-2142397	0861	1
LEE AUBRY E	CPT	O-1284579	1150	2
LEE AUGUSTUS S	CPT	O-0212283	0757	3
LEE BENOTE H	LTC	O-0333168	0350	3
LEE BILLY H	MAJ	O-1879615	1267	1
LEE BRUNER S JR	LTC	O-1167510	0963	1
LEE BUNNIE H	2LT	O-0108808	0833	1
LEE BYRON M	1LT	O-1581902	1145	2
LEE CARL R	CPT	O-1307038	1047	2
LEE CARLETON H	CPT	O-0498771	0844	2
LEE CHANG W	LTC	O-0313400	1058	3
LEE CHARLES E	LTC	O-0477061	0246	2
LEE CHARLES W	LTC	O-0401998	0261	1
LEE CHESTER A	LTC	O-0172554	0859	1
LEE CLARENCE J	COL	O-0289619	0747	2
LEE CLARENCE J	MAJ	O-1309077	0762	1
LEE CLARENCE O JR	MAJ	O-1923588	1064	1
LEE CLIFFORD M	CPT	O-1999851	1052	2
LEE CLIFTON H	1LT	O-0971261	0461	2
LEE CURTIS R	1LT	O-1032758	104N	2
LEE DARREL G	CPT	O-1294495	0446	2
LEE DON F JR	1LT	O-1306943	0846	2
LEE DONALD R	LTC	O-0922411	0263	1
LEE DONALD R	MAJ	O-1057500	0567	1
LEE DUDLEY	CW3	W-2148123	0659	1
LEE EDWARD V	CW2	W-2148143	0461	1
LEE EDWIN C M	MAJ	O-1101090	1046	2
LEE ELEANOR D	CPT	N-0703072	0747	1
LEE EMMETT C	LTC	O-0125145	0945	2

NAME	GRADE	SVC NO	DATE RET MO YR	RET CODE
LEE ERIC	COL	O-0193691	0142	1
LEE ERNA E	MAJ	N-0783864	0165	3
LEE ERNEST W	MAJ	O-1306606	0256	1
LEE EUGENE	MAJ	O-0985115	0363	1
LEE FAIRMAN B	LTC	O-0237131	0656	3
LEE FELIX L	CW3	W-2153169	0766	1
LEE FRANK J JR	CPT	O-1324343	1047	2
LEE FRANK Y F JR	MAJ	O-0976053	0766	1
LEE FREDERICK	1LT	O-1578755	1052	1
LEE GEORGE YUN	CW3	W-2147383	0166	1
LEE GERALD V	LTC	O-0331038	1066	3
LEE GLENN A	LTC	O-1112816	0864	1
LEE GORDON S	COL	O-0204538	0363	3
LEE GROVER C	CPT	O-0499363	0853	1
LEE HAN K	LTC	O-1645756	0763	1
LEE HAPLBERT R	MAJ	O-0424525	1060	1
LEE HAROLD D	LTC	O-1100193	0657	1
LEE HAROLD R	LTC	O-0274425	0355	3
LEE HARRELL E	LTC	O-0245781	0267	3
LEE HARRY S	COL	O-1642311	0567	1
LEE HENRY B	1LT	O-1105606	0344	2
LEE HENRY H	CW2	W-2147117	0961	1
LEE HENRY L	MAJ	O-0247105	0660	1
LEE HERMAN A JR	1LT	O-0462589	0544	2
LEE IRA L	CPT	O-1578756	0346	2
LEE IRWIN	LTC	O-0888575	0964	1
LEE JACK A	LTC	O-0888837	1267	1
LEE JACK G	COL	O-0288223	0967	3
LEE JACK W	1LT	O-1315954	1045	2
LEE JAMES A	CW2	W-2144584	0761	1
LEE JAMES K F	LTC	O-0282547	1168	3
LEE JAMES S	MAJ	O-0445137	0264	2
LEE JESSE V	CPT	O-1637908	0854	1
LEE JESTWIN E JR	CPT	O-1646356	0946	2
LEE JOHN	CW3	W-2149261	0862	1
LEE JOHN F JR	COL	O-0234448	0457	3
LEE JOHN G	LTC	O-1102750	0457	1
LEE JOHN GRIDL	MAJ	O-0908106	1045	2
LEE JOHN L	COL	O-0164294	0946	2
LEE JOHN W	COL	O-0126000	1055	3
LEE JOHNSON C	LTC	O-0472618	0964	3
LEE JONAS R	LTC	O-0154682	1149	3
LEE JOSEPH B	CW4	W-2113908	0659	1
LEE JULIAN R	CPT	O-1341887	0158	1
LEE JULIUS	LTC	O-0232041	0248	1
LEE KENNETH D	MAJ	O-1945861	0168	3
LEE KIRWAN O	LTC	O-1325134	0465	1
LEE LAIN L	WO1	W-2108771	0744	2
LEE LAWRENCE J	MAJ	O-0967826	0465	1
LEE LEOPOLD L	MAJ	O-0501604	0547	2
LEE LESLIE F	2LT	O-0108261	1038	1
LEE LLOYD L	CPT	O-4026388	0965	1
LEE LOUIS W	1LT	O-1319077	0446	2
LEE MAJOR JR	CW3	W-2151726	0666	2
LEE MALVEN F	CW3	W-2147078	0265	1
LEE MARION M	CPT	O-0164459	1128	1
LEE MARY E	2LT	N-0726957	1144	1
LEE MARY V	1LT	N-0778332	0448	2
LEE MATTHEW J	CW2	W-2144028	1154	1
LEE MAXWELL E	1LT	O-1825479	1145	2
LEE MAYNARD E	CW4	W-2101263	1158	1
LEE NEWELL B	LTC	O-0156297	1055	3
LEE ORVILLE E	CPT	O-1307430	0661	1
LEE OSCAR B	1LT	O-0475875	0746	1
LEE PAUL	MAJ	O-0889890	0257	1
LEE PAUL D	MAJ	O-0228325	1046	1
LEE PHILIP A	LTC	O-0197031	1059	3
LEE POWELL A	CPT	O-2037732	0360	2
LEE RANDAL E	LTC	O-0256242	1056	3
LEE RAYMOND A	LTC	O-0154428	1049	3
LEE RAYMOND C	CPT	O-0953544	0356	2
LEE RAYMOND J	1LT	O-1312023	0246	2
LEE RAYMOND N	COL	O-0269596	0360	3
LEE RICHARD B	LTC	O-1287024	0756	1
LEE RICHARD H	COL	O-0182052	0162	3

NAME	GRADE	SVC NO	DATE RET MO YR	RET CODE
LEE RICHARD M	MAJ	O-1014198	0965	1
LEE ROBERT A	MAJ	O-2033685	0465	1
LEE ROBERT B	LTC	O-1579928	0761	1
LEE ROBERT E	CPT	O-0279330	0143	2
LEE ROBERT E	CPT	O-0424537	1045	2
LEE ROBERT E	MAJ	O-1310609	1063	1
LEE ROBERT E	LTC	O-1635012	1063	1
LEE ROBERT E	CPT	O-2263347	0366	1
LEE ROBERT E	CW3	W-2151337	0965	1
LEE ROBERT E JR	LTC	O-1309151	0261	1
LEE ROBERT H	CW3	W-2205050	0765	1
LEE ROBERT H C	MAJ	O-0461762	0856	2
LEE ROBERT J	CPT	O-1534789	1048	2
LEE ROBERT N	MAJ	O-1316065	1162	1
LEE ROLAND P	LTC	O-0921761	0167	3
LEE ROY E	WO1	W-2147145	1154	1
LEE ROY M	MAJ	O-0305339	0446	2
LEE RUSSELL K	LTC	O-0503974	0965	2
LEE SMITH	LTC	O-0110741	0946	2
LEE THEODORE C	CPT	O-0311815	0145	2
LEE THOMAS E	MAJ	O-2033637	1061	1
LEE THOMAS F	LTC	O-1591885	0562	1
LEE THOMAS S	LTC	O-1824481	1066	3
LEE THURSTON L	MAJ	O-1166112	0359	1
LEE WILFRED C	2LT	O-1340784	0647	2
LEE WILLARD D	MAJ	O-1341800	1060	1
LEE WILLARD H	CW3	W-2210065	0168	1
LEE WILLIAM	LTC	O-1651785	0966	1
LEE WILLIAM A	MAJ	O-1589986	0457	1
LEE WILLIAM B	COL	O-0258590	0764	1
LEE WILLIAM D	MAJ	O-1184092	1162	1
LEE WILLIAM D	CW3	W-2147729	0463	1
LEE WILLIAM E	CPT	O-1305799	0546	2
LEE WILLIAM E	CPT	O-2012060	1058	2
LEE WILLIAM EL	2LT	O-1307836	1144	2
LEE WILLIAM F	CPT	O-0203484	0863	3
LEE WILLIAM J	COL	O-0348258	1268	1
LEE WILLIAM J	LTC	O-0383424	0461	1
LEE WILLIAM M	CPT	O-1109447	1046	2
LEE WILLIAM P	LTC	O-0153910	0448	2
LEE WILLIAM P	LTC	O-1291294	0763	1
LEE WILLIAM T	MAJ	O-0310099	0346	2
LEE WILSON A	CW2	W-2209845	0763	1
LEE WILTON A	LTC	O-0349581	0464	1
LEE 3RD ASBURY W	COL	O-0336510	0247	2
LEEB HENRY L	MAJ	O-0205028	0163	3
LEECH HARRY O	LTC	O-1558397	0765	1
LEECH HENRY E	MAJ	O-0473534	0360	3
LEEDHAM DONALD W	LTC	O-2061729	0868	1
LEEDLE ROBERT B	2LT	O-1324630	0644	2
LEEDOM JOE W	COL	O-0131231	0749	3
LEEDS CHARLES F	LTC	O-2028717	1268	1
LEEDS CHARLES T JR	COL	O-0267703	0166	3
LEEDS DANIEL J	CPT	O-0320780	0645	2
LEEDS HARVEY S	LTC	O-1646364	0862	1
LEEGATE CARNEY B	CW2	W-2145564	0959	1
LEEK CALVIN B	LTC	O-0346816	0560	1
LEEK JAMES W	LTC	O-0319740	0567	3
LEEK NORMAN M	MAJ	O-1018141	1062	1
LEEK WALLACE R	MAJ	O-0285982	1067	3
LEEL CHARLES W	LTC	O-0311695	0567	3
LEEN MARVIN J	CW4	W-2109843	0659	2
LEENERTS THEODORE H	CPT	O-0335498	0144	2
LEEP CHARLES M	CPT	O-1857720	1057	1
LEER EDWIN H	COL	O-0341910	1158	1
LEER RALPH H	LTC	O-0298927	1047	2
LEEROY ARTHUR	MAJ	O-0475405	0246	2
LEES GORDON S	LTC	O-1110068	0262	1
LEES HARRY G	CPT	O-1556016	0647	2
LEES HOWARD S	CPT	O-1290621	0146	2
LEES RICHARD S	1LT	O-1173689	0545	2
LEESE MERLE E	MAJ	O-0235223	1265	3
LEET WILLIAM L	COL	O-0183058	0962	3
LEETCH MARION L	CPT	O-1644946	0864	1
LEETY ROSS E	LTC	O-1287198	0166	1

NAME	GRADE	SVC NO	DATE RET MO YR	RET CODE
LEFEBVRE HENRY C	1LT	O-0244451	1058	3
LEFF ABRAHAM	COL	O-0414231	0267	3
LEFF WILLIAM A	LTC	O-0374490	0445	2
LEFFEL DELBERT F	LTC	O-2028378	1068	1
LEFFEL VERNE M	LTC	O-1309078	0963	1
LEFFERTS JAMES C	MAJ	O-2203048	0763	1
LEFFERTS WILLIAM G	LTC	O-0252129	0466	3
LEFFINGWELL W M	LTC	O-0134805	0656	3
LEFKOVICH HAROLD H	2LT	O-1057504	0845	2
LEFKOVITS AARON M	LTC	O-0319905	0761	3
LEFKOWITZ MICHAEL P	CPT	O-0404777	1045	2
LEFLER DANIEL S	MAJ	O-0335514	0157	1
LEFLER JAMES H	LTC	O-0534807	1062	1
LEFLER JEWELL C	CPT	O-1320905	0846	2
LEFLER ROBERT C	MAJ	O-1165188	0446	2
LEFORS ARCHIE O	LTC	O-0247265	0563	3
LEFTON IRVIN M	CPT	O-1533120	0747	2
LEFTWICH JOE	LTC	O-0328045	0446	2
LEFTWICH JOHN V	MAJ	O-1010263	0456	1
LEGAKO IRENE F	MAJ	N-0734536	0868	2
LEGAN WANDLE	MAJ	O-1798018	1060	1
LEGARE EUGENE V JR	MAJ	O-0445978	0762	1
LEGAS FRANK	CPT	O-0981278	0960	1
LEGATE CARL H	CW3	W-2207474	1068	1
LEGAULT LEO A	CPT	O-0478681	0655	1
LEGER HERBERT J	COL	O-0503272	0664	1
LEGER LEROY A	LTC	O-0451262	0857	1
LEGEP LOUIS P	CW3	W-2150842	0659	1
LEGG JACKIE D	MAJ	O-2262713	0463	1
LEGG LLOYD E	COL	O-0163785	0861	3
LEGG PHILLIP N	CW2	W-2142867	1056	1
LEGG ROBERT O	LTC	O-2033157	0367	1
LEGGE TOLLEY B	CW2	W-2147313	0364	2
LEGGETT JAMES H JR	LTC	O-1281265	1067	1
LEGGETT JAMES L JR	CPT	O-0371518	1046	2
LEGGETT JOHN W	COL	O-0166591	0948	3
LEGGETT KENNETH E	MAJ	O-0989450	1167	1
LEGION ELBERT C	MAJ	O-1051249	0259	1
LEGNER HAROLD J	LTC	O-1637912	0764	1
LEGNER LUCIUS S	COL	O-0280594	0658	3
LEGRO ARCHIE W	MAJ	O-0171358	0351	3
LEGRO WILBUR H	CW3	W-2205509	0365	1
LEHAN ANDREW F	LTC	O-1056776	0965	1
LEHANE DECLAN B	MAJ	O-1039467	0661	1
LEHANE LAWRENCE L	MAJ	O-0325977	1045	2
LEHDE JOHN R	LTC	O-0327763	0459	2
LEHDE RAYMOND C	CPT	O-0227454	1262	3
LEHMAN ALFRED C	1LT	O-0242796	0860	3
LEHMAN CHARLES M	CW4	W-2144835	0268	1
LEHMAN ERNEST E	LTC	O-1637913	0466	1
LEHMAN GEORGE W	LTC	O-0979577	0768	1
LEHMAN HENRY E	LTC	O-0323954	0346	2
LEHMAN LEON N	CW2	W-2209491	0361	1
LEHMAN LESTER	CPT	O-1689061	0246	2
LEHMAN ORIN A	CPT	O-0440430	0947	2
LEHMAN RAY	CW4	W-2106911	1054	1
LEHMAN ROBERT H	MAJ	O-1320955	0358	1
LEHMAN ROBERT H	LTC	O-2049312	0563	1
LEHMANN CORNELIUS	LTC	O-0157864	0555	3
LEHMANN RICHARD C	LTC	O-1044589	1163	1
LEHMANN ROBERT A	MAJ	O-2024300	0560	1
LEHMBERG FRITZ G	1LT	O-0490049	0145	2
LEHN DALLAS G	2LT	O-1296225	0445	2
LEHNE CHRISTIAN	LTC	O-0403234	0661	1
LEHNERT DIEDRICH	LTC	O-0205803	0858	3
LEHNERT FRANK H	LTC	O-0397308	0966	3
LEHNING JOHN W	WO1	W-2113091	0944	2
LEHNUS ELWOOD G	MAJ	O-0978662	0765	1
LEHR FREDERIC B	MAJ	O-0225632	0764	3
LEHR MILTON A	LTC	O-0182881	0956	3
LEHR WILLIAM	COL	O-0228253	0362	3
LEHRBASS MARY J	2LT	N-0784279	1045	1
LEHRER JOHN J	CW2	W-2147656	0456	1
LEIB CHARLES A	COL	O-0297328	1266	3
LEIBBRAND PHILO H	COL	O-0251525	1154	2

NAME	GRADE	SVC NO	DATE RET MO YR	RET CODE
LEIBFUKE ROBERT C	MAJ	[illegible]	[illegible]	1
LEIBEL ROBERT M	1LT	[illegible]	[illegible]	1
LEIBLY FRANK J	LTC	[illegible]	[illegible]	3
LEIBOLD JOHN P	CPT	[illegible]	0667	
LEI[illegible] MARK S	MAJ	[illegible]	0662	1
LEICH ROBERT M	LTC	[illegible]	0268	3
LEICHTLING JULIUS J	CPT	[illegible]	0666	2
LEICHTMAN DAVID L	MAJ	[illegible]	[illegible]	1
LEICK RUSSELL W	LTC	[illegible]	0967	1
LEIDAL FLOYD L	MAJ	[illegible]	0664	3
LEIDEL FREDERICK	LTC	[illegible]	0854	1
LEIDENHEIMER LARRY H	COL	[illegible]	1060	1
LEIDLER FRANZ	1LT	[illegible]	0545	2
LEIGH ALFRED H	LTC	[illegible]	0464	3
LEIGH GEORGE H	1LT	0-2007498	1051	1
LEIGH KEITH R	MAJ	0-1845304	1059	1
LEIGH RALPH G	LTC	0-0460311	0960	1
LEIGH ROBERT A	CW2	W-2214649	0158	1
LEIGH THOMAS F	LTC	0-0521923	0763	1
LEIGH THOMAS L	LTC	0-0130704	0855	3
LEIGHT WILLIAM J	COL	0-0317326	0261	1
LEIGHTENHEIMER W E	1LT	0-1184253	1047	2
LEIGHTON ALBERT C	CPT	0-0940777	0957	1
LEIGHTON GEORGE E	CW3	W-2007509	0866	3
LEIGHTON HENRY B	MAJ	0-0244329	1144	2
LEIGHTON HENRY P	MAJ	0-0515345	0549	1
LEIGHTON JEFFRED W	COL	0-0246649	0254	1
LEIGHTON RICHARD A	MAJ	0-2096992	0665	1
LEIGHTTY RALPH S	MAJ	0-1535931	0564	1
LEIGHTY LESTER S SR	MAJ	0-1303519	1160	1
LEIGHTY MAX	LTC	0-0420938	0357	1
LEIHY CHARLES W	COL	0-0236216	0245	2
LEIKER SEVERIN F	1LT	0-0486675	0356	1
LEIKER VICTOR C	CPT	0-0372027	0146	2
LEIKIND ELIAS R	CPT	0-0335099	0944	2
LEIMKUEHLER PAUL E	2LT	0-1328159	0446	2
LEIN MARTIN R	CPT	0-0360789	1144	2
LEINBACH CHARLES L	WO1	W-2103134	0356	1
LEINEN CLETUS N	MAJ	0-0436080	0454	1
LEININGER OLIVER O	MAJ	0-0949480	0866	1
LEINSTER ESTEN B	LTC	0-0331830	0360	1
LEINWEBER ARTHUR R	COL	0-0302549	1265	3
LEINWEBER CHARLEY A	CPT	0-0490051	0251	1
LEINWEBER RAYMOND	WO1	W-2154869	1053	1
LEIPOLD CARL M	LTC	0-1574470	1152	1
LEISER GEORGE E	MAJ	0-1587404	0856	1
LEISER WILLIAM W	1LT	0-1018935	0547	2
LEISINGER LEWIS M	LTC	0-0273620	0768	3
LEISK JAMES H	MAJ	0-1315179	1266	3
LEISTER MICHAEL A	LTC	0-0404222	0761	1
LEISTER ORVILLE T	CW4	W-2122145	0563	1
LEITCH KENNETH H	COL	0-0338022	0167	1
LEITCH WILLIAM H	MAJ	0-0541958	0-48	2
LEITEM EDWARD E	CW3	W-2147707	0263	1
LEITER CLEMENT L	CW2	W-2150707	1060	1
LEITH ALEXANDER	LTC	0-0336121	0760	1
LEITH MILTON B	COL	0-0237723	0562	3
LEITNAKER JOHN M	LTC	0-2035011	1262	1
LEITNER CHARLES J	MAJ	0-1175489	0466	1
LEITNER GEORGE R	CPT	0-1296049	0658	1
LEITZ FRED	1LT	0-1945403	0653	1
LEITZEL HARRY M	LTC	0-1637915	1165	1
LEITZELL ROBERT A	LTC	0-1821883	0861	1
LEITZINGER W A E	COL	0-0190066	0958	3
LEJA EDWARD	1LT	0-0546334	0448	2
LEKNISKAS BENEDICT C	WO1	W-2115383	1043	2
LEKOM BEATRICE T	MAJ	N-0751468	0766	1
LELAND FRANK E	MAJ	0-0472663	0947	1
LELAND HERBERT A	CW2	W-2208608	0765	1
LELAND ROBERT O	1LT	0-0454372	0745	2
LELAND WALTER I	LTC	0-0327748	1060	3
LELAND WALTER J	1LT	0-0375924	0845	2
LELEKIS PETER J	LTC	0-1300182	0763	1
LELEVICH JOSEPH J	CPT	0-1112818	0349	2
LELONG ROBERT L	LTC	0-1341447	0966	1
LEMAIRE PAUL G	CPT	0-0508039	0765	2
LEMAN BROOKE W	LTC	0-0298598	1052	3
LEMAN LLOYD D	LTC	0-0193317	1157	3
LEMAN LOUIS	MAJ	0-1108809	0761	1
LEMANN ARTHUR A	MAJ	0-0373961	0246	2
LEMANN PAUL B	COL	0-0284980	0968	3
LEMAY CHARLES M	CPT	0-1100197	0845	2
LEMBACH CARL L	CW2	W-2115977	0547	1
LEMBURG B HOMER	1LT	0-1292354	0746	2
LEMCHAK JOHN	CW2	W-2145302	0562	1
LEMCKE MARY F	2LT	N-0775723	0245	1
LEMELLE GILBERT	CW4	W-2146117	0768	1
LEMENS WILLIAM V	LTC	0-0263493	1060	3
LEMERIS PAUL F	CW4	W-2126088	0262	1
LEMERISE DAVID B	MAJ	0-1285608	0461	1
LEMERT AMOS C	MAJ	0-0302440	1167	4
LEMIEUX JOSEPH W	MAJ	0-0953659	0563	1
LEMING HOWELL E	LTC	0-0269703	0260	3
LEMIRE HENRY J	LTC	0-0371376	1160	1
LEMKE GORDON H	MAJ	0-1049950	1062	1
LEMKE WALTER B	COL	0-0321373	1159	3
LEMLEY FRED A	LTC	0-0279776	0463	1
LEMM RALPH H	MAJ	0-0241617	0-52	3
LEMM ROBERT J	MAJ	0-2009228	0764	1
LEMME RAYMOND W	MAJ	0-1649010	0164	1
LEMMON GLENN P	COL	0-0110742	0752	3
LEMMON JOHN M JR	LTC	0-0217400	1047	2
LEMMON MARY J K	MAJ	N-0778255	1265	1
LEMMOND PARS H	LTC	0-0212125	0659	3
LEMMOND WALTER H JR	LTC	0-0225644	0664	3
LEMOINE CLAIRE	1LT	N-0745107	0646	1
LEMOINE HERBERT G	1LT	0-1861996	1053	2
LEMON BURTON J	COL	0-0107889	0648	3
LEMON CARL R	CPT	0-0284044	0244	2
LEMON CECIL W	MAJ	0-0436664	0446	2
LEMON CHARLES C	1LT	0-1285256	1145	2
LEMON FRED C	CW2	W-2115965	0545	2
LEMON GEORGE E	1LT	0-1100199	1043	2
LEMON JOSEPH F	LTC	0-0399815	0663	1
LEMON LEONARD D	LTC	0-0978910	0468	1
LEMONS CARL A	1LT	0-2262869	0267	1
LEMOS CARLOS B	CW3	W-2146971	1163	1
LEMP HARRY J	MAJ	0-0126189	0243	2
LEMP JOHN	COL	0-0273986	0367	3
LEMP WILLIAM A	LTC	0-0360815	1262	1
LENAHAN DANIEL W	COL	0-0223503	0464	3
LENAHAN GEORGE T	MAJ	0-1702812	1045	2
LENAHAN WALTER	1LT	0-0398696	0945	2
LENART CLARENCE P	COL	0-0185550	0953	3
LENCHNER GEORGE	1LT	0-1290093	0945	2
LENDVAY EUGENE E	MAJ	0-1057505	0560	1
LENETTI DOMINICK	WO1	W-2124122	0146	2
LENGYEL ALEXANDER	WO1	W-2125870	1046	1
LENGYEL JOSEPH W	MAJ	0-1015420	0160	1
LENHARDT BENJAMIN F	COL	0-0237999	1058	1
LENHARDT BERTRAM	LTC	0-1002269	1065	1
LENHART ALGERS N	CPT	0-0450981	0747	1
LENHART FRANK H	LTC	0-0372463	1263	3
LENHART HAROLD W	CPT	0-1302676	1057	1
LENHART HARRY A	LTC	0-0298296	0963	3
LENHART KENNETH G	LTC	0-0205015	0648	3
LENIC SIGMOND C	LTC	0-1551050	0564	1
LENIHAN JAMES W	1LT	0-1180242	0247	2
LENINGTON EARL E	1LT	0-1286147	0246	2
LENIUS JOHN E	CPT	0-0953683	0261	1
LENK DAVID A	COL	0-0223493	0656	3
LENN LOYD L	CPT	0-1546321	1166	2
LENNA GEORGE	CPT	0-0501236	0550	1
LENNON FRANCIS A	COL	0-0238361	1164	3
LENNON JOHN M	LTC	0-0330661	0147	2
LENNON JOHN T	MAJ	0-1796648	1160	1
LENNON JOSEPH T	CPT	0-1307714	0246	2
LENNON MERWYN C	LTC	0-0250074	1265	3
LENNON ROBERT H	LTC	0-1284892	0463	1
LENNON WILLIAM T	MAJ	0-0506144	1146	2
LENNOX GEORGE	COL	[illegible]	0759	1
LENNOX RICHARD L	LTC	[illegible]	0363	3
LENNY MARY P	MAJ	[illegible]	0765	1
LENT [illegible] J	LTC	[illegible]	0961	1
LEN[illegible] KIRK	CPT	0-1637716	0766	2
LEN[illegible] JAMES F JR	LTC	0-1605714	1067	1
LEN[illegible] GEORGE M	COL	[illegible]	0961	3
LENT DAVID J	COL	0-0506507	[illegible]	3
LENTINE JOSEPH	MAJ	0-0348315	0346	2
LENTINI VINCENT	COL	0-0321481	0763	3
LENTINI-BOITEY PASCU	CW3	[illegible]	0667	1
LENTINO JOSEPH W	CPT	0-0354829	0750	2
LENTZ ELMER L	COL	0-0184531	0555	2
LENTZ JOHN J	LTC	0-0506569	0955	1
LENTZ LAWRENCE E	CW2	W-2146118	1157	2
LENTZ RALPH F JR	LTC	0-1117288	0267	1
LENTZ ROBERT E	LTC	0-0352652	0860	1
LENTZ THOMAS C	CPT	0-1330741	0657	1
LENTZ VALENTINE	LTC	0-0124024	0857	3
LENTZER FRANK M	2LT	0-1300564	0145	2
LENZ GEORGE W JR	CW3	W-2123119	0661	1
LENZ JOHN H	LTC	0-1015724	0462	1
LENZ LEONARD J	1LT	0-1305942	0546	2
LENZ OSCAR L	CW4	W-2002776	0862	3
LENZ ROBERT K	CPT	0-1691243	0845	2
LENZEN KENNETH R	MAJ	0-0491917	0849	1
LEO ARTHUR J	WO1	W-2122776	1058	1
LEO ROBERT T	MAJ	0-1686229	0364	1
LEO SAMUEL	CPT	0-0457113	1044	2
LEON LEO R	LTC	0-0369099	0764	3
LEON THOMAS W C	LTC	0-1584513	0561	1
LEON VICTORIA A	2LT	N-0753738	1046	1
LEON WILFREDO	MAJ	0-0970127	0762	1
LEONARD ALFRED M	LTC	0-1294534	1162	1
LEONARD ARIEL J	LTC	0-1081755	0766	1
LEONARD ARTHUR L	WO1	W-2141353	1055	1
LEONARD BILL	CW2	W-2146900	0261	1
LEONARD BYRL D	WO1	W-2139607	0646	2
LEONARD CHARLES F	CW3	W-2145221	0161	2
LEONARD CLARENCE E	COL	0-0274285	0160	3
LEONARD DAVID E JR	LTC	0-1120458	1068	1
LEONARD DON E	MAJ	0-2011976	0256	1
LEONARD EMMETT T	CW3	W-2146160	0959	2
LEONARD GEORGE	CPT	0-0485194	0347	1
LEONARD GEORGE A	COL	0-0111174	0648	3
LEONARD GEORGE A	COL	0-0380820	0165	1
LEONARD HUBERT C	COL	0-0327753	0565	3
LEONARD JACK D	LTC	0-1544062	0866	1
LEONARD JAMES H JR	LTC	0-1949833	0467	1
LEONARD JAMES J	MAJ	0-1323713	1060	2
LEONARD JAMES M	LTC	0-0320429	0862	1
LEONARD JAMES M	CPT	0-2263561	1062	1
LEONARD JOHN H	CW3	W-2147213	0762	1
LEONARD JOHN M	LTC	0-1338103	0268	1
LEONARD KLEIN J	MAJ	0-1924537	0564	1
LEONARD LAURENCE E	CW3	W-2141913	0762	1
LEONARD LEO B	LTC	0-1651780	1155	1
LEONARD LLOYD	2LT	0-0496950	0944	2
LEONARD LOUISE K	MAJ	N-0765826	0567	1
LEONARD MATTHEW B	CPT	0-1285609	0845	2
LEONARD MAX S	CPT	0-1081350	0757	1
LEONARD QUIRINUS W	WO1	W-2002232	0467	3
LEONARD RALPH B	1LT	0-1294496	0844	2
LEONARD RALPH J	LTC	0-2042831	0158	1
LEONARD RAYMOND F	CW2	W-2213392	0867	1
LEONARD RAYMOND H	1LT	0-1285610	0845	2
LEONARD RICHARD K	LTC	0-0273722	1060	1
LEONARD ROBERT J	MAJ	0-0969202	0564	1
LEONARD ROBERT L	MAJ	0-1535218	0862	1
LEONARD ROGER L	LTC	0-0362840	0463	1
LEONARD RUPERT A	CPT	0-0420120	0461	1
LEONARD SANFORD A	CW2	W-2209107	0661	1
LEONARD THOMAS B	MAJ	0-1646813	1264	1
LEONARD THOMAS J	CW2	W-2141783	0456	1
LEONARD WALLACE M	LTC	0-0275423	0657	3
LEONARD WILLIAM A	[illegible]	[illegible]	1166	1
LEONARDI MARK [illegible]	LTC	[illegible]	0657	1
LEONARDO ALBERT	LTC	[illegible]	[illegible]	1
LEONE JOHN A	CPT	[illegible]	0667	2
LEONE JOSEPH C	CPT	[illegible]	0162	1
LEONE SAM J	1LT	[illegible]	0665	2
LEONETTI CHARLES	MAJ	[illegible]	[illegible]	3
LEONG [illegible]	MAJ	[illegible]	[illegible]	1
LEONHARDT HANS A	LTC	[illegible]	0863	3
LEONHARDT HARRY H	LTC	[illegible]	[illegible]	3
LEONHARDT JOHN W	COL	[illegible]	0155	3
LEONZANIDA QUIRINO	2LT	[illegible]	0654	1
LEOPOLD JESSE T	CW2	[illegible]	1047	1
LERAK ALFRED J	CPT	[illegible]	0665	2
LERAK LOUIS T	CPT	0-0348508	0145	2
LEPERA DOMINICK F	LTC	0-0888577	1154	1
LEPERA ERNEST O	MAJ	0-0453124	1056	1
LEPICIER LEONARD R	LTC	0-1290094	1161	1
LEPINE ADELAND	2LT	0-0153907	0443	1
LEPINE MARSHALL J	MAJ	0-1822023	0264	1
LEPISTO VICTOR F	CPT	0-0416129	0346	2
LEPKE RICHARD P	LTC	0-1113808	0565	1
LEPO PAUL P	MAJ	0-2020568	0563	1
LEPORS CHARLES	MAJ	0-1177050	0757	1
LEPOW HENRY N	CPT	0-1018895	0147	2
LEPP LOUIS B	COL	0-0268093	0763	3
LEPPER NORMAN	LTC	0-0502159	0364	3
LEPPER WILLIAM P	COL	0-0153021	0651	2
LEPPERT ROBERT O	CW2	W-2147424	0660	1
LEPPERT THEODORE J	2LT	0-1045811	0744	2
LERCH PAUL F	1LT	0-1014034	0245	2
LERCH ROBERT W	COL	0-0399094	1060	3
LERDRUP JENS P	CPT	0-0450456	0552	1
LERNER DAVID G	CPT	0-0322054	1243	2
LERNER JAY S	LTC	0-0187690	0355	3
LERNER MARTIN H	LTC	0-0485169	1054	1
LERNER WILLIAM	1LT	0-1319148	0545	2
LERUE EDWARD P	CW4	W-2115859	1163	1
LEROY JOSEPH F	CPT	0-0451545	0758	1
LEROY LEO B	CPT	0-1101091	0246	2
LEROY WARREN S	COL	0-0347628	0259	2
LESAGE ARTHUR F	WO1	W-2125143	0746	2
LESAR WILLIAM J	LTC	0-1048873	0766	1
LESCARBEAU WILFRED J	CPT	0-1046864	0958	1
LESCH ALBERT S	MAJ	0-1581235	0657	1
LESCH DONALD M	CW4	W-2004573	0468	1
LESCH JOSEPH A	CPT	0-1824769	0148	2
LESCHINSKY FRANK A	LTC	0-0261525	0165	3
LESEMANN EDWARD A	CPT	0-0256564	1039	2
LESEMANN F J JR	LTC	0-0406302	1047	2
LESENEY JOE M	LTC	0-0507327	1264	3
LESH EDNA M	2LT	N-0762295	0645	1
LESH WILLIAM T	MAJ	0-0252019	0966	3
LESHER JOHN H	COL	0-0341486	1066	3
LESHIN NORMAN	LTC	0-0511355	1045	2
LESHNE SAMUEL	CPT	0-1690430	0345	2
LESIKAR ADOLPH A	LTC	0-0269577	0166	3
LESIKAR GEORGE	LTC	0-0256650	0867	3
LESINSKI WALTER	MAJ	0-0452099	0660	1
LESKE HELMUTH F	MAJ	0-1293276	1162	3
LESKOVEC RAYMOND F	MAJ	0-1010439	0158	1
LESKOWITZ DAVID	LTC	0-0230269	1162	3
LESLEY CLETUS M	LTC	0-0305682	1060	1
LESLEY JAMES H	CW2	W-2149411	1060	1
LESLIE BENJAMIN L	CW4	W-2116106	1265	1
LESLIE BERTRAM L	MAJ	0-2014555	1262	1
LESLIE CHARLES A	CPT	0-0248221	0346	2
LESLIE CHARLES J	CPT	0-2103005	0962	1
LESLIE CLAUDE E JR	MAJ	0-1643794	0261	1
LESLIE ELWYN E JR	COL	0-1051646	1268	1
LESLIE GAIL C	CPT	0-0452628	0945	2
LESLIE GEORGE W	LTC	0-0264397	1267	3
LESLIE GRAHAM M	COL	0-0140614	0650	3
LESLIE HAROLD C	1LT	0-2035269	0845	2
LESLIE JAMES B JR	COL	0-0246738	0566	3

NAME	GRADE	SVC NO	DATE RET MO YR	RET CODE
LESLIE JESSE H JR	1LT	0-0521707	0646	2
LESLIE RICHARD C	MAJ	0-0939027	0762	1
LESLIE ROLAND R	LTC	0-0190956	0753	3
LESLIE ROMAN C	LTC	0-0243418	0766	3
LESLIE SHIRLEY	LTC	0-0253091	0158	3
LESLIE WESTRAY B	COL	L-0303512	0547	2
LESMERISES CONRAD R	WO1	W-2124172	0346	2
LESNESKI KATHERINE	2LT	N-0721191	0744	1
LESNICKI FRANK T	MAJ	0-1236748	1163	1
LESOWITZ EDWARD	LTC	0-1544475	0761	1
LESPERANCE L J	LTC	0-0344163	0557	1
LESPERANCE STANLEY G	LTC	0-0285070	1057	1
LESPIER MANFREDO E	MAJ	0-0970175	1065	1
LESSARD ROBERT J	MAJ	0-2018901	0363	1
LESSARD WILLIAM G	2LT	0-1310466	1043	2
LESSEL JAMES L	CW2	RW-2145319	0963	1
LESSER KINTELS	CW3	W-2144153	0357	1
LESSIG LESTER L	LTC	0-0150122	0653	3
LESSMAN DALE A	CPT	0-0969203	0561	1
LESSOR PETER J	MAJ	0-1579938	1052	2
LESTCHER STANLEY A	1LT	0-0509299	0345	2
LESTER BERTRAND M	CPT	0-0410907	0545	2
LESTER CALVIN D	WO1	W-2141061	0552	1
LESTER GRAHAM W JR	CPT	0-0520863	1047	2
LESTER GUY D	LTC	0-0351468	0460	1
LESTER JAMES A	CW3	W-2153068	0664	1
LESTER JAMES V	LTC	0-1169617	0960	1
LESTER JOHN C JR	MAJ	0-0970106	1165	1
LESTER LEE J	1LT	0-1327635	0347	2
LESTER LEROY F	COL	0-0334415	0662	2
LESTER MELVIN J	1LT	0-1170461	0845	2
LESTER MICHAEL	CPT	0-1017076	0546	2
LESTER ROBERT M SR	CW3	W-2151792	0564	2
LESTER SPURGEON	CW3	W-2144635	0863	1
LESTER VAN E JR	MAJ	0-1686389	0467	3
LESTER VANCE B	CW3	W-2149396	0864	1
LESTER VESTAL R	CPT	0-1304245	0546	2
LESTER WILBURN L	LTC	0-1010144	1067	1
LESTER WILLIAM E	MAJ	0-0380628	0446	2
LESURE FLOYD A	MAJ	0-1543409	0661	1
LETALIEN ARTHUR	CPT	0-1300664	0546	2
LETCHER HARRISON G	2LT	0-1894797	0646	1
LETHOD EARL R	MAJ	0-1635020	0255	1
LETHERBY JOHN L	MAJ	0-5405090	1168	1
LETHERMON ROBERT H	MAJ	0-0109702	0945	2
LETHOD PERRY TURN	CPT	0-0450983	1051	2
LETKEMANN ADELLE F	2LT	N-0702801	1037	1
LETOURNEAU LESTER C	CW2	W-2203273	0357	1
LETOURNEAU ROGER N	LTC	0-1173351	0161	1
LETOURNEAU SYLVA J	MAJ	0-1017410	0961	1
LETSCHER PAUL J	CW3	W-2149120	0868	1
LETSEN CARL W SR	CPT	0-1579939	0562	1
LETSON WILLIAM A	1LT	0-0313581	1144	2
LETT ELOISE	MAJ	N-0776492	1167	3
LETT JOSEPH R	CPT	0-0424827	0345	2
LETT MAX A	MAJ	0-0230523	0144	2
LETT MAX E	MAJ	0-1299433	0860	1
LETTENMAIER NORBERT	MAJ	0-0980096	0364	1
LETTERMAN OSCAR	CPT	0-0113898	0251	3
LETTIRE WILLIAM J	MAJ	0-1637925	0960	1
LETTRICK LESLIE G	MAJ	N-0701259	0446	1
LEU HENRY G	LTC	0-1057147	0163	1
LEUBNER CHRIS H	CW2	W-2215060	1068	1
LEUCINGER JACOB	1LT	0-1844851	0349	2
LEUPP FRANCIS L	CPT	0-0350242	1047	2
LEUSMAN PATRICIA A	1LT	N-0776703	1145	1
LEUTHARD WALTER H	CW3	W-2152239	1163	1
LEUTHEN BUEL F	MAJ	0-0972294	0563	1
LEUTHYLER EDWARD T	CPT	0-0278500	1055	3
LEVADI SOLOMON S	MAJ	0-0275352	0258	3
LEVAKE CLIFFORD S	LTC	0-0252847	0166	3
LEVANTHAL HARRY	CW4	W-2126127	0653	1
LEVASSEUR GERARD L	CW3	W-2150214	0263	1
LEVECK HENRY H	COL	0-0215548	0164	3
LEVEILLE LOUIS A	LTC	0-0300817	1059	1
LEVEL JOSEPH P	WO1	W-2152496	1153	1
LEVELY HARRY P JR	MAJ	0-1010282	1160	1
LEVEN JOSEPH J	LTC	0-0297217	1167	3
LEVENDORF ABRAHAM	LTC	0-0153490	0156	3
LEVENDOSKY CHARLES L	CW4	W-2111897	0862	1
LEVENDUSKY HARRY G	LTC	0-0451333	0658	1
LEVENS FRANKLIN J	LTC	0-1947297	1265	1
LEVENSALER JAMES L	LTC	0-0262201	0967	3
LEVENSON DANIEL J	MAJ	0-1296051	0646	2
LEVENSON JOSEPH M	CPT	0-0366687	0745	2
LEVENSTEIN JOEL A	LTC	0-1636216	0961	1
LEVENTHAL ISIDOR	LTC	0-0915919	0768	3
LEVENTIS PETER P JR	MAJ	0-0422356	0347	2
LEVENTRITT DAVID	CPT	0-1310467	0546	2
LEVER SAMUEL B	CPT	0-1577474	0848	2
LEVER SHELBY N	LTC	0-0315900	0246	2
LEVERENZ EDWIN W	LTC	0-0434206	0462	1
LEVERET ROBERT L JR	1LT	0-1050353	0252	2
LEVERETTE BLAND K JR	LTC	0-1103283	1166	1
LEVERETTE JAMES W	COL	0-1101916	0861	2
LEVERING GEORGE H	CW2	W-2142241	1057	1
LEVERING WILLIAM C	2LT	0-1014869	0146	2
LEVERS RICHARD C	MAJ	0-1314503	0259	1
LEVESQUE ALBERT G	MAJ	0-1080043	0857	1
LEVESQUE ARTHUR J	MAJ	0-1899406	1162	1
LEVESQUE BARNEY J	1LT	0-1551666	0645	2
LEVESQUE RAYMOND W	CW2	W-2213626	1168	1
LEVETT JOSEPH C	LTC	0-1013908	0960	1
LEVEY MEYER L	LTC	0-0349666	0159	1
LEVI ELIEZER A	CPT	0-0888068	1045	2
LEVI EUGENE G	CPT	0-1299763	0846	2
LEVI ROBERT O	MAJ	0-1545666	0858	1
LEVIA HARRY E	LTC	0-1575418	0157	1
LEVIA LUCILLE A	MAJ	N-0722428	0763	1
LEVICKEY JAMES M	MAJ	0-2262160	0664	1
LEVIE JAMES K JR	LTC	0-0382883	0859	1
LEVIN AARON J	MAJ	0-0230829	0863	3
LEVIN ALLEN R	MAJ	0-1003784	1068	3
LEVIN CYRIL M	1LT	0-0368594	1041	2
LEVIN HARRY	MAJ	0-0912839	1047	2
LEVIN HERBERT S	1LT	0-1288914	0245	2
LEVIN JEAN Z W	CPT	N-0760097	1046	1
LEVIN JOE G	MAJ	0-0271093	0168	3
LEVIN LEO M	MAJ	0-0318995	0646	2
LEVIN MOSES J	MAJ	0-0481314	0445	2
LEVIN ROBERT	1LT	0-1170058	0744	2
LEVIN SAMUEL	MAJ	0-0296100	1145	2
LEVIN SAMUEL A	CW3	W-2005938	0768	3
LEVIN WILLIAM	COL	0-0264259	1150	3
LEVINE ALEXANDER	LTC	0-1049554	0361	1
LEVINE DAVID	MAJ	0-0242364	0864	3
LEVINE DAVID B	LTC	0-0238976	0162	3
LEVINE DAVID L	CW3	W-2152999	0765	1
LEVINE EDWARD P	MAJ	0-0499873	0447	2
LEVINE EMANUEL	1LT	0-1061771	0646	2
LEVINE HARRY	LTC	0-1552735	0566	3
LEVINE IRVING	CPT	0-0487250	0845	2
LEVINE JOEL C	2LT	0-2006365	0846	2
LEVINE MAX A	CPT	0-0546777	0845	2
LEVINE MILTON A	1LT	0-1596100	0246	2
LEVINE RALPH	COL	0-0266189	1164	1
LEVINE RALPH H	MAJ	0-1045150	0464	1
LEVINE ROSE L	2LT	N-0762352	0646	1
LEVINE SAMUEL K	CPT	0-0506571	0745	2
LEVINE SOPHIE A	MAJ	N-0720749	0167	3
LEVINS EDWARD A	MAJ	0-0464234	1145	2
LEVINS EMANUEL	CW4	W-2101994	0557	1
LEVINS JAMES E	MAJ	0-0970585	0266	1
LEVINSOHN NATHAN	CPT	0-0307623	1044	2
LEVINSON CHARLES B	CPT	0-1533125	1047	2
LEVINSON JOSEPH	LTC	0-0984868	0867	1
LEVINSON JULIAN C	1LT	0-0402937	1045	2
LEVINSON MILTON A	MAJ	0-0322561	1146	2
LEVINSON NEWTON S	MAJ	0-0227335	0365	3
LEVINSON PAUL	LTC	0-1535220	0761	1
LEVINSON ROBERT M	MAJ	0-0538118	0346	2
LEVINSON SOL	CPT	0-0472410	0745	2
LEVIS THOMAS C	CW3	W-2120423	0959	1
LEVISON RALPH P	COL	0-0242096	1064	3
LEVITAN SELIG J	B G	0-0276524	0468	3
LEVITIN JOSEPH	COL	0-0227559	1061	3
LEVITT ARTHUR	COL	0-0373480	0760	3
LEVITT EARL N	1LT	0-1822024	1043	2
LEVITT HARRY	MAJ	0-1308155	0361	1
LEVITT ROBERT	COL	0-0343518	0465	1
LEVITT THOMAS J	CW3	W-2109710	0959	1
LEVNO ANTHONY F	COL	0-0276836	0557	2
LEVOEF PHILIP	LTC	0-0466667	0754	1
LEVSTONE KENNETH J	MAJ	0-1112820	0758	1
LEVULIS ALBERT E	LTC	0-1341679	1167	1
LEVY AARON	LTC	0-0349442	0168	3
LEVY ALFRED C	LTC	0-1311314	0663	1
LEVY BENJAMIN H	LTC	0-0242141	0466	3
LEVY BERNARD M	LTC	0-0193622	0561	3
LEVY DAVID	1LT	0-1692039	0545	2
LEVY EDWARD	CPT	0-0465600	0146	2
LEVY EDWARD R	LTC	0-1550645	0561	1
LEVY EZEKIEL	LTC	0-0588822	0468	3
LEVY GEORGE V	2LT	0-1306436	0345	2
LEVY IRVING N	COL	0-2034437	0868	2
LEVY JACK H	MAJ	0-0460670	1146	2
LEVY JEROME S	LTC	0-0214894	1062	3
LEVY LILLIAN	2LT	N-0760863	0245	1
LEVY MILTON	1LT	0-0451599	0346	2
LEVY MILTON A	CPT	0-0253258	0564	3
LEVY MILTON C	MAJ	0-0297071	0968	3
LEVY MILTON G	MAJ	0-0357912	1043	2
LEVY RALPH	MAJ	0-0113721	1148	3
LEVY ROBERT E	1LT	0-1313103	1045	2
LEVY SAMUEL A	CPT	0-0466351	0646	2
LEVY SAMUEL B	MAJ	0-1689873	0346	2
LEVY SIDNEY W	CPT	0-0496983	0146	2
LEW HONOR W	2LT	N-0790059	0945	1
LEW SAM G	LTC	0-0361000	0964	1
LEWANDOWSKI C E	MAJ	0-1595590	0158	1
LEWANDOWSKI DANIEL R	MAJ	0-1301843	0960	1
LEWANDOWSKI EDMUND	CPT	0-1692237	0745	2
LEWANDOWSKI EDMUND W	LTC	0-1039751	0862	2
LEWANDOWSKI VICTOR J	LTC	0-0422225	0761	1
LEWELLEN JOE T	2LT	0-1322049	0645	2
LEWELLYN KEITH	CW2	W-2213495	0268	1
LEWICKA VICTORIA C	2LT	N-0731201	1145	1
LEWIN CHARLES Y	CPT	0-0300738	0961	3
LEWIN JOHN E	CW3	W-2147049	0164	1
LEWIN ROSCOE B	COL	0-0277335	0465	3
LEWIN THEODORE E	COL	0-0355513	1064	1
LEWIS ADLAI R	LTC	0-0191525	0446	2
LEWIS ALBERT B JR	MAJ	0-1648337	0162	1
LEWIS ALBERT E	MAJ	0-1796651	0154	2
LEWIS ALBERT M JR	CPT	0-0353660	0544	2
LEWIS ALEXANDER	MAJ	0-0926983	1164	1
LEWIS ARAMINTA E	MAJ	N-0752554	0966	3
LEWIS ARNOLD M	COL	0-0399798	1164	3
LEWIS ARTHUR N	COL	0-0225183	1264	3
LEWIS BARNEY V	MAJ	0-2033993	0963	1
LEWIS BERNARD M	LTC	0-0211814	0159	3
LEWIS BRUNER A	MAJ	0-1290770	0657	2
LEWIS BURTON W	LTC	0-0341169	0865	1
LEWIS CARLETON H	LTC	0-1110613	0866	3
LEWIS CAROL	2LT	0-1825230	0644	2
LEWIS CARROLL L	MAJ	0-1639307	0157	1
LEWIS CHARLES	CPT	0-1634068	0760	1
LEWIS CHARLES A	LTC	0-0371313	0867	3
LEWIS CHARLES A	CW2	W-2153158	0160	1
LEWIS CHARLES E	LTC	0-1015768	0963	1
LEWIS CHARLES E	MAJ	0-1575421	0451	1
LEWIS CHARLES F	LTC	0-0254507	1265	3
LEWIS CHARLES F	1LT	0-0532198	0350	1
LEWIS CHARLES R SR	LTC	0-1541964	0856	1
LEWIS CHARLES W	MAJ	0-2033937	0365	1
LEWIS CHESTER R	MAJ	0-0496376	1144	2
LEWIS CLARENCE D	CPT	0-1583282	0446	2
LEWIS CLAUDE E	CPT	0-0109177	1024	1
LEWIS CONDIE I	2LT	0-2000842	0960	1
LEWIS CRESLIE W	MAJ	0-2001745	1062	1
LEWIS DALE R	1LT	0-1319982	1045	2
LEWIS DARRELL E	2LT	0-1324550	0244	2
LEWIS DAVID	CW2	W-2101995	1146	2
LEWIS DELMAR J	LTC	0-0308645	0647	2
LEWIS DESSIE R	CPT	0-0486216	0947	2
LEWIS DONALD E	CW2	W-2215177	0468	1
LEWIS DONALD M	LTC	0-1055070	0568	1
LEWIS EARL B	CPT	0-1108106	0558	1
LEWIS EDGAR M JR	COL	0-0171322	0254	2
LEWIS EDWARD C	CPT	0-1306437	0447	2
LEWIS EDWARD J	COL	0-0170841	0752	2
LEWIS EDWARD L	LTC	0-0450984	1265	1
LEWIS EDWARD S	CW3	W-2207714	0667	1
LEWIS EDWIN M	LTC	0-0248028	0152	3
LEWIS ELDRIDGE D	CW2	W-2115496	0645	2
LEWIS ELIZABETH	1LT	N-0761058	0246	1
LEWIS ERIC L	LTC	0-1337592	1065	1
LEWIS EUGENE C	CPT	0-1182172	0647	2
LEWIS EUGENE E	1LT	0-0187038	0657	3
LEWIS FERRELL J	LTC	0-0394935	1160	3
LEWIS FLOYD V	CPT	0-0981777	0761	1
LEWIS FRED G	CW4	W-2101996	1158	1
LEWIS FREDERICK	LTC	0-0251628	0666	3
LEWIS GARLIN H	CW2	W-2211100	1166	1
LEWIS GILBERT H	LTC	0-0262386	0468	3
LEWIS GORDON W	MAJ	0-2037387	0661	1
LEWIS GROVER C	COL	0-0259438	1266	3
LEWIS HAL R	CW3	W-2209469	1068	1
LEWIS HAROLD C	1LT	0-1302150	0945	2
LEWIS HAROLD C	CW4	W-2144968	0367	1
LEWIS HAROLD E	LTC	0-1292206	1163	1
LEWIS HAROLD F JR	MAJ	0-1056147	0265	1
LEWIS HAROLD S	LTC	0-1325758	0863	1
LEWIS HARRY E	MAJ	0-1326254	1164	1
LEWIS HARRY I	LTC	0-0116788	0852	3
LEWIS HARRY J JR	COL	0-0254025	0361	3
LEWIS HARRY L	MAJ	0-0937880	0762	1
LEWIS HARVEY C JR	LTC	0-1107551	0964	1
LEWIS HARVEY D	COL	0-0196815	0662	3
LEWIS HARVEY H	LTC	0-0220615	1145	2
LEWIS HELEN A	1LT	N-0728423	0746	1
LEWIS HENRY E	LTC	0-0269904	0968	3
LEWIS HENRY H W	LTC	0-0215605	0364	3
LEWIS HENRY S	1LT	0-0112354	1157	3
LEWIS HENRY V	MAJ	0-0259105	0167	3
LEWIS HERALD F	LTC	0-0200732	0654	2
LEWIS HOWARD T JR	CPT	0-0475527	0747	2
LEWIS HOWELL C JR	LTC	0-0903536	1162	3
LEWIS HUGH S	CPT	0-1304085	0548	2
LEWIS ISAAC R	CPT	0-1174932	0853	1
LEWIS IVAN L	LTC	0-1001394	1162	1
LEWIS JACOB	1LT	0-0466562	1044	2
LEWIS JAMES C	MAJ	0-0119260	0648	3
LEWIS JAMES C	MAJ	0-0167661	1048	2
LEWIS JAMES H	CPT	0-1311657	0747	2
LEWIS JAMES M	LTC	0-0539813	0663	1
LEWIS JAMES M JR	MAJ	0-1333230	0359	1
LEWIS JAMES N	COL	0-0326716	0263	1
LEWIS JAMES O	LTC	0-0496202	0556	1
LEWIS JAMES R	LTC	0-1017230	0966	1
LEWIS JAMES W	LTC	0-1103752	1160	1
LEWIS JET O	MAJ	0-1647578	0259	1
LEWIS JOHN	WO1	W-2122717	1053	1
LEWIS JOHN D	MAJ	0-1015235	0962	2
LEWIS JOHN D JR	MAJ	0-1688526	0966	1
LEWIS JOHN F JR	LTC	0-1047263	0866	1
LEWIS JOHN G	MAJ	0-0193343	0760	3
LEWIS JOHN P	CPT	0-0370243	1045	2
LEWIS JOHN R	1LT	0-1821884	0345	2
LEWIS JOHN W	CPT	0-1174627	0155	1

NAME	GRADE	SVC NO	DATE RET MO YR	RET CODE	NAME	GRADE	SVC NO	DATE RET MO YR	RET CODE	NAME	GRADE	SVC NO	DATE RET MO YR	RET CODE	NAME	GRADE	SVC NO	DATE RET MO YR	RET CODE
LEWIS JOHN W JR	LTC	0-0286918	0665	3	LEWIS SAUL	CPT	0-0435389	0245	2	LIBY ROBERT A	LTC	0-0358285	1160	1	LIGHT JOHN M	CPT	0-2032941	0557	1
LEWIS JOSEPH H	LTC	0-1112281	1162	1	LEWIS SPENCER R	MAJ	0-1115004	1060	1	LICCIONE WILLIAM J	CPT	0-0380958	1144	2	LIGHTBODY RAYMOND M	COL	0-0184473	1056	3
LEWIS JOSEPH S	CW4	W-2115986	0457	1	LEWIS STANLEY	MAJ	0-1011860	0761	1	LICHEVE STEVE	COL	0-0384161	0954	1	LIGHTBURN WILLIS C	1LT	0-1575425	0445	2
LEWIS JOSEPH V	CW4	W-2145196	0765	2	LEWIS STANLEY D	LTC	0-0293749	0751	2	LICHENSTEIN SIDNEY	MAJ	0-1291842	0252	2	LIGHTBURNE WILLIAM J	LTC	0-0324024	1059	3
LEWIS JULIAN F	LTC	0-0312055	1162	3	LEWIS STELLA C	2LT	N-0771890	1045	1	LICHTENBERGER JOHN W	LTC	0-1581239	0463	1	LIGHTCAP WILLIAM C	LTC	0-2017085	0965	1
LEWIS KARL R	1LT	0-1017053	0347	2	LEWIS STEPHEN A	MAJ	0-0220884	0750	1	LICHTENBERGER L L	1LT	0-1318682	0546	2	LIGHTFOOT BENJAMIN H	1LT	0-0927964	1051	2
LEWIS KELLY H	COL	0-0172315	0654	1	LEWIS STUART	COL	0-0177190	0450	3	LICHTENBERGER M M	1LT	N-0796316	0848	2	LIGHTFOOT ELLISON R	1LT	0-1284536	0744	2
LEWIS KENDRICK D	CW2	W-2141355	0961	2	LEWIS THEODORE K	2LT	0-1296399	0143	2	LICHTENBERGER WILLIA	LTC	0-0322895	0266	3	LIGHTFOOT ROBERT H	CPT	0-4047966	0163	2
LEWIS KENNETH R	MAJ	0-0450800	0544	2	LEWIS THOMAS A	LTC	0-0281111	1167	3	LICHTENEGGER SEIBO	MAJ	0-1048464	0858	1	LIGHTFOOT WHITING R	MAJ	0-0947101	1163	1
LEWIS LAMONT	CW3	W-2146076	0367	1	LEWIS THOMAS A	CPT	0-1309159	0946	2	LICHTENFELS ISAAC	LTC	0-0242265	C566	3	LIGHTMAN PERCY	CPT	0-0200128	1056	3
LEWIS LAWRENCE E	LTC	0-0911912	1162	1	LEWIS THOMAS D JR	1LT	0-1185284	0146	2	LICHTENSTEIN MEYER R	CPT	0-0498776	0446	2	LIGHTSEY G W	CW3	W-2108645	1057	1
LEWIS LAWRENCE H	LTC	0-0150245	0156	3	LEWIS THOMAS F	COL	0-0923745	1068	3	LICHTMAN MELVIN I	1LT	0-1316169	1045	2	LIGHTSEY VIRGIL P	LTC	0-0294973	1068	3
LEWIS LEO R	LTC	0-1303357	0562	1	LEWIS THOMAS E JR	MAJ	0-1823020	0364	1	LICHTMAN WILLIAM T	1LT	0-1080123	1044	2	LIGON EDWARD C JR	CPT	0-0318863	1144	2
LEWIS LEONARD D	CW2	W-3400071	0868	1	LEWIS THOMAS J	MAJ	0-0493465	1152	1	LICKEL WILLIAM C	CPT	0-1100648	1060	1	LIGON RICHARD G	LTC	0-1634071	0864	1
LEWIS LEROY A	LTC	0-0360560	0164	1	LEWIS THOMAS P	LTC	0-1174045	0162	1	LICKLEY REX M	MAJ	0-0298037	1161	3	LIGON ROY W	CW2	W-2101999	0749	1
LEWIS LESTER H JR	MAJ	0-2204125	0167	1	LEWIS THURL D	1LT	0-1306608	0246	2	LICKLIDER BEECHER L	LTC	0-1171648	0963	1	LIGON SEBASTIAN	COL	0-0248474	1166	3
LEWIS LEWIS F	LTC	0-0364931	0547	2	LEWIS TOM	LTC	0-0221566	0354	3	LICKLITER WILLIAM F	CPT	0-0911400	0846	2	LIGON STANHOPE A	COL	0-0245230	1062	3
LEWIS LINDSEY C	1LT	0-0376090	1145	2	LEWIS WALDON K	CPT	0-1168335	0445	2	LIDDELL DONALD M JR	LTC	0-0255278	0467	3	LIKAR FRANK	CPT	0-0504809	0453	1
LEWIS MARION S	CPT	0-0154514	0356	3	LEWIS WALTER J	COL	0-0542613	0468	1	LIDEEN WALTER T	CW2	W-2147406	0962	1	LIKAS DONALD	LTC	0-1289759	0860	1
LEWIS MARTIN E	LTC	0-1110615	1062	1	LEWIS WALTER K JR	CPT	0-0352147	1144	2	LIDKE FRANK J	LTC	0-0262052	1144	2	LIKAS JOSEPH F	LTC	0-0885844	1266	1
LEWIS MARTIN G	LTC	0-1583283	0857	1	LEWIS WARREN R	2LT	0-0526307	0146	2	LIEB FREDERICK	CW4	W-2132752	1162	1	LIKES CREIGHTON	COL	0-0282171	0862	3
LEWIS MEREDITH T	COL	0-0238452	0665	3	LEWIS WAYNE H	CPT	0-0494029	0250	1	LIEBENGUTH MARTIN F	CPT	0-0504538	1046	1	LIKES JOHN L	LTC	0-0417410	0748	2
LEWIS MICHAEL J	LTC	0-1647226	0364	1	LEWIS WILBERT A	LTC	0-0237939	0946	2	LIEBENROOD WILLIAM L	CW3	RW-3100249	0168	1	LIKINS ROBERT A	MAJ	0-1167951	0347	2
LEWIS MILTON C	MAJ	0-1307716	0761	1	LEWIS WILLIAM A	LTC	0-0224258	0762	1	LIEBER GEORGE M	LTC	0-0140611	0358	3	LILES CLAUDE M	COL	0-0246135	0960	3
LEWIS MILTON P	LTC	0-0337224	1057	1	LEWIS WILLIAM A	MAJ	0-1555852	0768	3	LIEBER HARRY S JR	CPT	0-1320057	0547	2	LILES LISTON D JR	MAJ	0-0918208	0746	2
LEWIS MILTON T	MAJ	0-1877696	0764	1	LEWIS WILLIAM C	CW2	W-2149755	0963	1	LIEBER MARSHALL M	LTC	0-0271788	0546	2	LILES RAY L	CPT	0-0497851	1158	1
LEWIS MIRIAM L	2LT	N-0788161	0445	1	LEWIS WILLIAM D	LTC	0-1557953	0268	2	LIEBER SIDNEY	1LT	0-1573366	1045	2	LILES WALLACE G	1LT	0-0436606	0546	2
LEWIS NELLIE C	1LT	N-0765512	0749	2	LEWIS WILLIAM G	CW4	W-2001960	0866	3	LIEBERMAN HARRY A	LTC	0-1315847	0862	1	LILEY WILLIAM L	MAJ	0-2203826	1167	1
LEWIS OLIVER A	CPT	0-1017433	0261	1	LEWIS WILLIAM J	COL	0-0332277	0860	1	LIEBERMAN HEIMAN G	MAJ	0-0488379	0246	2	LILIENTHAL WILBERT H	CPT	0-1295236	0845	2
LEWIS OLIVER D	LTC	0-1574283	0163	1	LEWIS WILLIAM J	LTC	0-1691941	0368	1	LIEBERMAN HERMAN	MAJ	0-2010821	0566	1	LILJEGREEN LEROY R	CW4	W-2101198	0564	1
LEWIS OLIVER P	MAJ	0-0245920	0857	3	LEWIS WILLIAM M	LTC	0-1101920	0561	1	LIEBERMAN JOHN I	MAJ	0-0495429	0350	1	LILJEGREN HARRY E	MAJ	0-0233503	0147	1
LEWIS OSBORNE F	COL	0-0276620	1164	3	LEWIS WILLIAM P	1LT	0-1305801	0354	1	LIEBERMAN LEO	LTC	0-1001175	0468	3	LILL ARCHIE V	LTC	0-0197913	0748	3
LEWIS OSCAR M	LTC	0-0210053	0454	3	LEWIS WILLIF L	CW3	W-2149939	0164	1	LIEBERMAN LEO A	COL	0-0295447	0867	3	LILLARD WALTER H	LTC	0-0101503	0648	3
LEWIS PATRICIA A	1LT	N-0723993	0146	1	LEWIS WODEA	1LT	N-0762765	0850	2	LIEBERMAN LEON R	COL	0-0371941	1167	3	LILLEY CLIFFORD A	LTC	0-1307432	0661	1
LEWIS PAUL B	LTC	0-1577476	1061	1	LEWISON JOEL M	CPT	0-0291051	0468	3	LIEBERSTEIN J H	CPT	0-0495905	0246	2	LILLEY FRANK S	COL	0-0320213	0865	1
LEWIS PAUL W	LTC	0-0241282	1262	3	LEWISON MELVIN A	WO1	W-2132116	1145	2	LIEBERT HERBERT M	MAJ	0-1112824	0461	1	LILLEY GEORGE F	MAJ	0-1598133	1058	1
LEWIS PERLEY M	LTC	0-0329611	0646	2	LEWITZ ERWIN E	MAJ	0-0925453	0446	2	LIEBHARDT ROBERT G	LTC	0-0349662	1060	1	LILLEY GEORGE P	CW2	W-2207133	0962	1
LEWIS PHAON E	WO1	W-2122253	0153	2	LEWMAN CHARLES D	MAJ	0-0341566	1056	3	LIEBIG CHARLES J	CW4	W-2142868	1164	1	LILLEY HALDANE	CPT	0-1311658	1047	2
LEWIS RALPH	LTC	0-1320638	0267	3	LEWMAN R J	CPT	0-1317410	0446	2	LIEBMAN HENRY	LTC	0-0195933	1162	3	LILLEY RICHARD J	COL	0-0418807	0168	1
LEWIS RALPH A	COL	0-0333393	0456	3	LEWSEN RUDOLPH F	LTC	0-0916378	0464	3	LIEBNER BYRON E	1LT	0-1321381	0946	2	LILLEY ROY	LTC	0-0271550	0667	3
LEWIS RAY N	COL	0-0231232	1160	3	LEWY EVERETT	COL	0-0234254	1065	3	LIEBOWITZ HIRSCH R	MAJ	0-0497125	0246	2	LILLGE KARL W	MAJ	0-1289760	0761	1
LEWIS RAYMOND E	MAJ	0-1312176	1061	1	LEX HENRY J	MAJ	0-1031416	0261	1	LIEBRECHT CHARLES F	COL	0-0346155	0864	1	LILLI DOMINIC A	2LT	0-1546085	0944	2
LEWIS RAYMOND J	COL	0-0271706	0260	1	LEX IRWIN A	COL	0-0183427	0455	3	LIECHENSTEIN JOSEPH	LTC	0-0332127	1159	1	LILLIBRIDGE HAROLD D	LTC	0-0244855	0857	3
LEWIS RAYMOND M	1LT	0-1311904	1045	2	LEX ROLAND E	2LT	0-1288761	1044	2	LIECHTY SHERMAN E	CPT	0-1055369	0446	2	LILLICRAP PAUL J	1LT	0-0231331	0943	2
LEWIS REBECCA	2LT	N-0799644	1046	1	LEY MAX O	1LT	0-1574080	0743	2	LIEDER WILLIAM J	MAJ	0-1688607	0264	1	LILLIE BERNARD J	MAJ	0-0349010	0164	2
LEWIS REECE H	COL	0-0288344	0166	3	LEYBOURNE MALCOLM G	MAJ	0-0964581	0163	1	LIEDIGK WERNER M	MAJ	0-1917724	1265	1	LILLIE JOHN N	CW3	W-2146377	1060	1
LEWIS REUBEN G	COL	0-0183217	1150	3	LEYDEN THEODORE J	LTC	0-0337841	0864	3	LIEDMAN LYLE F	LTC	0-2049624	0766	1	LILLIE KENNETH H	LTC	0-0888444	1262	1
LEWIS REX E	1LT	0-0461256	1045	2	LEYDEN WILLIAM G JR	LTC	0-0462172	0765	1	LIEDTKE ALFRED W	LTC	0-0366426	0854	1	LILLIE LEROY D	COL	0-0236654	0261	3
LEWIS RICHARD A	LTC	0-1185718	1263	1	LEYENDECKER C R	1LT	0-1185079	0856	1	LIEN ALTON W	CW3	W-2151146	1062	1	LILLIS ROBERT E	CPT	0-0277294	1045	2
LEWIS RICHARD E	1LT	0-0467309	0145	2	LEYSER GEORGE E	LTC	0-1103286	0765	3	LIEN FLOYD L	LTC	0-1323443	0267	1	LILLY ALEXANDER	MAJ	0-0156444	0451	3
LEWIS RICHARD E	1LT	0-2211846	0653	2	LEYSON JOE O	1LT	0-0890500	0362	1	LIEN VICTOR C	LTC	0-1287027	0263	1	LILLY ALFRED	2LT	0-0109301	0530	1
LEWIS ROBERT A	COL	0-0210051	0-51	3	LEYSON VICTORIO L	2LT	0-1896855	0554	1	LIESE RALPH F	1LT	0-0531865	0447	2	LILLY BASIL G	LTC	0-0208710	0158	3
LEWIS ROBERT A	1LT	0-1170829	0246	2	LEZETTE GEORGE I	1LT	0-1302993	0945	2	LIESINGER RUDOLPH D	1LT	0-0350288	1044	2	LILLY CYRIL R	CPT	0-1048874	0264	2
LEWIS ROBERT A	MAJ	0-1920336	C966	1	LHANON JAMES R	2LT	0-1644530	0345	2	LIESKE HAROLD W	LTC	0-0273532	0766	3	LILLY DONALD E	CW3	W-2205263	0563	1
LEWIS ROBERT B	COL	0-0176533	1153	3	LHEUREUX PHILIP L	LTC	0-1177887	0862	1	LIESKE LOREN F	LTC	0-0998740	0466	1	LILLY FRANCIS W	2LT	0-1299592	0245	2
LEWIS ROBERT B	CPT	0-0179074	1159	3	LHOMME JACQUES M	LTC	0-0267148	1061	1	LIETZ JAMES B	1LT	0-1325224	1045	2	LILLY MAYFIELD JR	CW3	W-2143164	1266	1
LEWIS ROBERT C	CW4	W-2105238	0559	1	LI VECCHI SALVATORE	LTC	0-1591267	1163	1	LIEURANCE CHARLES H	CPT	0-0963188	0459	1	LILLY ROBERT A	CPT	0-1309580	0947	2
LEWIS ROBERT E	1LT	0-0353144	0245	2	LIAKOS STEPHEN	CPT	0-1295041	0546	2	LIEURANCE LLOYD C	MAJ	0-0263822	1060	3	LILLY SHELBY T	1LT	0-1169218	1045	2
LEWIS ROBERT E	MAJ	0-1633366	0746	2	LIASSE EDSON A	CW4	W-2144595	0568	1	LIEVENS JACOB J	CW3	W-2144798	0761	1	LILLY THEODORE E	MAJ	0-0218599	0556	3
LEWIS ROBERT J	MAJ	0-1554422	0661	1	LIBBON FRANK	CW2	W-2214338	1068	1	LIFCHULTZ LEO B	CPT	0-0486903	0745	2	LILYGREN LLOYD E	COL	0-0244934	0848	3
LEWIS ROBERT L	COL	0-0156226	0847	2	LIBBY DONALD M	COL	0-0125236	0956	3	LIFE ARTHUR R	LTC	0-0170046	0859	3	LIM VINCENTE H JR	2LT	0-0549526	0745	2
LEWIS ROBERT L	LTC	0-1286671	0761	1	LIBBY FRED C	CW4	W-2141356	0660	1	LIFSCHUTZ MARY	2LT	N-0722245	1043	1	LIMBACH GERALD H	CW2	W-2213533	0868	1
LEWIS ROBERT M	CPT	0-0319982	0145	2	LIBBY JAMES W	1LT	0-1950009	0247	2	LIFSEY JULIAN H JR	1LT	0-1637936	0145	2	LIMBACH WILTON G	MAJ	0-0276245	0943	2
LEWIS ROBERT P	CPT	0-0238568	0955	3	LIBBY RALPH G JR	CPT	0-0425608	1143	2	LIGDA ANDREW V	LTC	0-2018687	0166	1	LIMBECK JOHN A	LTC	0-1039078	1162	1
LEWIS ROBERT R	CW3	W-2148931	0465	1	LIBBY ROLAND D	LTC	0-0381575	0664	1	LIGEIKIS JOSEPH	1LT	0-1288250	0544	2	LIMBERG EARL W	COL	0-0355304	1060	1
LEWIS ROGER E	MAJ	0-1030170	0254	1	LIBBY THOMAS H	LTC	0-1329365	0265	1	LIGGETT ALBERT L	LTC	0-0905418	0563	3	LIMBOCKER THOMAS B	LTC	0-0113282	0558	3
LEWIS ROSWELL E	WO1	W-2209326	0359	1	LIBBY WILLIAM C	2LT	0-1102355	1043	2	LIGGETT CLARENCE P	CW2	W-2146257	0858	1	LIMERICK JOE B	MAJ	0-0479800	0849	2
LEWIS ROY	LTC	0-0276472	0356	3	LIBCKE JOHN W	M G	0-0233642	1061	3	LIGGETT ROBERT S	MAJ	0-0403327	0146	2	LIMERICK THOMAS J	MAJ	0-0981132	0363	1
LEWIS ROYAL C	LTC	0-1548918	0766	1	LIBERATOR ERCOLE A	LTC	0-0922806	1265	3	LIGHSTON RENOLD B JR	LTC	0-4002377	1066	3	LIMES JOSEPH K	LTC	0-0257895	1163	3
LEWIS ROYER K	COL	0-0472310	0653	1	LIBERATORI FRANCIS J	CPT	0-1100647	1146	2	LIGHT ALEXANDER	MAJ	0-0384241	0964	3	LIMOGES REGIS R	1LT	0-1290772	0547	1
LEWIS RUSSELL C	MAJ	0-0481916	1052	1	LIBERTINI ROBERT M	MAJ	0-0254595	0-51	3	LIGHT CHARLES P JR	COL	0-0190273	0163	3	LIMPERT DANIEL C	1LT	0-0890155	1046	2
LEWIS RUSSELL M	MAJ	0-0991231	1266	1	LIBERTY ALLEN P	MAJ	0-1112823	0360	1	LIGHT ERNEST H	2LT	0-1032368	1063	2	LIMPIC JOHN	1LT	0-1290268	0945	2
LEWIS SAMUEL A	COL	0-0483415	0856	1	LIBERTY JOHN F	MAJ	0-1018095	0662	1	LIGHT GEORGE G	LTC	0-0245872	0966	3	LIMPUS LEROY D	MAJ	0-0416682	0761	1
LEWIS SAMUEL F	1LT	0-1297745	0745	2	LIBERTZ EDWARD F	CW2	W-2149079	1057	2	LIGHT HARLEY E	MAJ	0-0339183	0862	1	LINAGEN EDWARD H	CW2	W-2141614	0257	1
LEWIS SAMUEL L	LTC	0-0205107	1147	2	LIBOUREL HERBERT H	MAJ	0-0312442	0346	2	LIGHT HARRY J	1LT	0-1946101	0347	2	LINARD CHAUNCEY C	LTC	0-0252815	0564	3

NAME	GRADE	SVC NO	DATE RET MO YR	RET CODE
LINCAVAGE PAUL G	1LT	0-1798795	1058	1
LINCK OSWALD H	LTC	0-0326651	1068	3
LINCOLN ELMER D	CPT	0-0276157	0366	3
LINCOLN ELMER F	MAJ	0-1635033	0857	2
LINCOLN ELMER H	MAJ	0-1642324	0456	1
LINCOLN JOHN J	LTC	0-0372657	1166	3
LINCOLN LUCIUS F	LTC	0-0502514	0954	1
LINCOLN LYDIA R	MAJ	N-0737584	0663	1
LINCOLN MILAN A	2LT	0-1016535	0245	2
LINCOLN NELSON H	MAJ	0-0404361	0166	1
LINCOLN ROBERT A	LTC	0-0255372	0967	3
LINCOLN WILBERT J	LTC	0-0243750	0558	3
LIND ARTHUR M	LTC	0-1559661	1266	1
LIND CHARLES W	COL	0-0349961	0646	2
LIND EDMUND L	LTC	0-0320239	0260	3
LIND FREDERICK	LTC	0-0166672	1045	2
LIND HJALMAR A	MAJ	0-0452003	1157	1
LIND JAMES F	LTC	0-0278648	1160	3
LIND LAURIE P	COL	0-0215789	0860	3
LIND LESTER C	2LT	0-1167089	0145	2
LIND NORMAN	2LT	0-1649024	1045	2
LIND WILLIS T	LTC	0-0300086	0265	3
LINDAHL FRANK C	LTC	0-1584528	0662	1
LINDAHL FRANK D	COL	0-0261335	0166	3
LINDAHL JOHN O	MAJ	0-0123225	1053	3
LINDAMOOD ROBERT E	MAJ	0-1295737	0660	1
LINDAU FRED I	LTC	0-0225962	0762	3
LINDBERG ARTHUR J JR	CPT	0-0495777	0848	2
LINDBERG ARTHUR M	CW3	W-2144567	0859	1
LINDBERG HARRY E	CPT	0-0182931	0553	3
LINDBERG STANLEY J	LTC	0-1170463	1162	1
LINDBLOOM EDWIN O	CW4	W-2103755	0659	1
LINDBORG ARTHUR F	COL	0-0245059	0648	3
LINDE KNUD W	MAJ	0-0924713	0547	2
LINDEBERG RUTH R	2LT	N-0762567	0945	1
LINDEGREN GEORGE L	COL	0-0247697	0463	3
LINDELL KERMIT F	MAJ	0-0452857	0456	1
LINDEMAN ELMER H	MAJ	0-1184100	0663	1
LINDEMAN JACK B	COL	0-0311671	0368	3
LINDEMAN LEONARD K	CW4	W-2117128	0659	1
LINDEMAN MARK A	1LT	0-1637938	1046	2
LINDEMAN PHILIP F	M G	0-0272444	0367	1
LINDEMAN WILLIAM N	MAJ	0-0977845	0962	1
LINDEMANN THEODORE T	MAJ	0-0211092	0360	3
LINDEN EUGENE J	CPT	0-1297747	1147	2
LINDEN JAMES E SR	LTC	0-1100202	0157	1
LINDEN JOHN A	MAJ	0-1590609	0263	1
LINDEN JOHN R	LTC	0-0327126	0759	1
LINDEN JOHN W	CPT	0-0289216	1061	3
LINDENMAN SHEPARD	CPT	0-0486796	0445	2
LINDENMUTH LEROY A	CW3	W-2142244	1160	1
LINDENSTRUTH HENRY J	LTC	0-0344106	0263	1
LINDENSTRUTH R W	1LT	0-0384283	0545	2
LINDEQUIST DAVID C	CW3	W-2150094	1162	1
LINDER CLAUDE W	MAJ	0-0113283	0648	3
LINDER JAMES H	MAJ	0-0463051	0147	2
LINDER JESSE L	CW3	W-2146907	0463	1
LINDER ROY L	LTC	0-1579947	0863	1
LINDER VIRGIL R	MAJ	0-1302152	0263	1
LINDERER LAWRENCE W	COL	0-0336425	0865	2
LINDERMAN ALVIN A	CW3	W-2147318	0862	1
LINDERMAN GEORGE W	2LT	0-1291374	1044	2
LINDERMAN LONNIE F	CW4	W-2103145	0360	1
LINDEROSE WILLIAM C	MAJ	0-1020455	0763	1
LINDERSON HAROLD E	COL	0-0188264	0853	3
LINDGREN ALLAN G	MAJ	0-1165306	0662	1
LINDGREN ELMER A	MAJ	0-1318683	0457	1
LINDGREN FRANK M	CPT	0-0986449	1060	1
LINDGREN JOSEPH B	MAJ	0-1796307	0866	1
LINDGREN LLOYD A	CPT	0-1178226	1147	2
LINDH LAWRENCE J	LTC	0-0963808	1167	1
LINDHOLM GEORGE S	1LT	0-1308250	1045	2
LINDHOLM VIRGINIA I	MAJ	N-0774856	0168	1
LINDIMORE CHARLES F	MAJ	0-1286672	0663	1
LINDLE HERBERT A	COL	0-0183620	1047	1
LINDLEY CHARLES L	1LT	0-1798592	1046	1
LINDLEY ELBERT O	CW2	W-2148124	0159	1
LINDLEY ERNEST E	CPT	0-1698890	0854	1
LINDLEY GEORGE F	1LT	0-0215194	0-49	3
LINDLEY ROBERT P	LTC	0-0479730	0457	1
LINDLEY THOMAS A	COL	0-0327212	0658	1
LINDLY HAROLD G	MAJ	0-1932205	1167	1
LINDMAN FRANCIS E	CPT	0-0382160	0347	2
LINDNER CLEMENT P	COL	0-0468974	1061	3
LINDNER EMIL O	COL	0-0299552	0668	3
LINDNER JOHN A	LTC	0-0124058	0952	3
LINDNER KENNETH M	LTC	0-0547089	0666	3
LINDON JAMES T	2LT	0-0446041	1044	2
LINDQUIST GERALD F	MAJ	0-2036608	1057	1
LINDQUIST MABEL P	MAJ	N-0758219	1066	3
LINDQUIST MARSHALL C	MAJ	0-0487593	1054	1
LINDSAY ADAM S	MAJ	0-1037599	0764	1
LINDSAY CHARLES O	LTC	0-1180585	0668	1
LINDSAY GEORGE H	MAJ	0-0505240	1045	2
LINDSAY GEORGE M	LTC	0-1283095	0765	1
LINDSAY GEORGE T	1LT	0-1041826	1044	2
LINDSAY HAROLD J	CPT	0-0105671	0352	3
LINDSAY JAMES B	MAJ	C-0414366	1146	2
LINDSAY JESSE S	B G	0-0237198	0961	3
LINDSAY JOHN E	1LT	0-1299913	0546	2
LINDSAY ROBERT M	MAJ	0-2017086	0665	1
LINDSAY RUSSELL K	1LT	0-0505991	0147	1
LINDSAY WALTER A	MAJ	0-1897788	0765	1
LINDSAY WALTER I	CPT	0-1290269	0446	2
LINDSEY ADRIAN H	COL	0-0200836	0855	3
LINDSEY ALVA E	LTC	0-0279770	1055	3
LINDSEY ARLEN G	CW3	W-2203317	0467	1
LINDSEY CHARLES R	MAJ	0-1688435	0464	1
LINDSEY CLIFTON S	COL	0-0377868	0761	1
LINDSEY EDWARD L	LTC	0-0384546	0662	1
LINDSEY GEORGE W SR	MAJ	0-2033601	1061	1
LINDSEY GILBERT F	1LT	0-1061173	0446	2
LINDSEY HOWARD S	CW2	W-2145917	0558	1
LINDSEY IRVIN B	MAJ	0-1546653	0257	1
LINDSEY JOHN P	CW2	W-2148208	0863	1
LINDSEY JULIA S	1LT	N-0763464	1145	1
LINDSEY LOUIS G	CPT	0-0485989	1146	2
LINDSEY MARTIN L JR	LTC	0-1795032	0766	1
LINDSEY OREL B	LTC	0-0281844	0161	1
LINDSEY ROBERT E	LTC	0-0171946	0757	3
LINDSEY RUBLE	CPT	0-0499774	1052	1
LINDSEY THEARON K	WO1	W-2124443	0353	1
LINDSEY TRAVIS	MAJ	0-1946550	0859	1
LINDSEY WILLIAM R	LTC	0-1553303	0465	1
LINDSKOG MAURICE B	CW2	W-2148352	1159	1
LINDSLEY CHARLES F	MAJ	0-1635036	1060	1
LINDSLEY LOUIS H	LTC	0-0317565	0858	3
LINDSTROM ALTON J	1LT	0-1105614	0345	2
LINDSTROM EDGAR V	MAJ	0-1172967	0364	1
LINDSTROM GUSTAV G	CPT	0-0370455	0346	2
LINDSTROM JOHN W JR	CW3	W-2141615	0462	1
LINDSTROM LEWIS I	MAJ	0-2210337	0866	1
LINDSTROM OLOF R	CPT	0-0267920	1165	3
LINDVALL BERT C	COL	0-0336039	0454	3
LINDY JOHN R	CPT	0-2033158	0855	1
LINE GERALD C	COL	0-0223414	0860	3
LINEAWEVER JOHN K	LTC	0-1052451	0362	1
LINEBARGER EDWARD C	CPT	0-0244450	0-53	3
LINEBARGER RAYMOND C	LTC	0-1845754	1265	1
LINEBAUGH GEORGE E	LTC	0-0450753	0560	1
LINEBERRY CHARLES T	LTC	0-1286859	0361	1
LINEHAN DANIEL J JR	LTC	0-0287700	0467	3
LINEHAN FRANCIS B	COL	0-0249642	0566	3
LINEHAN GILROY F JR	COL	0-0277575	0968	3
LINEHAN RAYMOND J	CW3	W-2146305	0662	1
LINEHAN ROBERT J	MAJ	0-0360913	0146	2
LINEK VICTOR	CW3	W-2103146	0755	1
LINER CARL A	LTC	0-0958914	1267	1
LINER IRVIN S	LTC	0-0265786	0968	3
LINES CLARENCE P	LTC	0-1044875	0666	1
LINES RAYMOND E	COL	0-2046320	0366	1
LINFORD TED P	LTC	0-1167952	0461	1
LING DAVID E	CPT	0-0969189	0261	2
LING THEODORE C	CPT	0-1018295	0547	2
LING WALTER J	CPT	0-1287028	0947	2
LINGENFELTER JOHN F	CPT	0-0931958	0450	2
LINGG JAMES T	CW2	W-2150591	0164	1
LINGK GERHARD F	CW2	W-2105671	1053	1
LINGLE ARNOLD H	LTC	0-1173692	0465	1
LINGNER GEORGE A	CW4	W-2120273	0757	1
LINGO HENRY	CPT	0-1311659	0646	2
LINIK JOSEPH	1LT	0-1316564	0745	2
LINK ANDREW J	LTC	0-0264442	0667	3
LINK ELMER R	1LT	0-0973601	0460	2
LINK EUGENE F	CPT	0-0522209	0448	1
LINK GORDON S	LTC	0-0506221	0567	3
LINK HAROLD S	MAJ	0-1168337	0959	1
LINK HAZEL E	COL	0-0452420	0866	1
LINK HOWARD P	CPT	0-0382416	0446	2
LINK JESSE W	MAJ	0-1583291	0662	1
LINK MAX W SR	CPT	0-0498611	0852	2
LINK ROBERT V	LTC	0-0385069	0368	3
LINK RUSSELL L	1LT	0-1109454	0246	2
LINK THEODORE W	WO1	W-2132128	0646	2
LINKA CLAIRE M	1LT	N-0703632	0548	1
LINKER AURAND E	LTC	0-0328454	1060	3
LINKER JOE B	LTC	0-0140078	0657	3
LINKER ROLAND O	COL	0-0451138	0860	1
LINKHART ROBERT C	CPT	0-0377491	0246	2
LINN ARTHUR C	COL	0-0268912	0852	3
LINN CHARLES A	COL	0-0334160	0465	3
LINN HOWARD M	LTC	0-0385050	0161	1
LINN IRVING	CPT	0-0471642	0648	1
LINN LESLIE A	MAJ	0-0286519	1060	3
LINN STANLEY T	MAJ	0-2203971	0365	1
LINN VIDA R	MAJ	N-0732196	0868	3
LINN WALTER R	COL	0-0179186	0351	3
LINNELL JOHN M	LTC	0-0378305	0557	1
LINNERT CLEMENT W	CPT	0-0215414	0144	2
LINNEWEH WALTER L	CW4	W-2132193	0959	1
LINNVILLE RAYMOND A	CW3	W-2122842	0757	1
LINSCHEID HAROLD E	CPT	0-1700287	0145	2
LINSLEY BRUCE A	LTC	0-1320748	1063	1
LINSTAD HOWARD D	LTC	0-0410037	0161	1
LINT ROBERT S	2LT	0-1947014	1044	2
LINTER LEONARD M	CPT	0-0418991	0845	2
LINTHICUM CECIL I	LTC	0-0253094	0658	3
LINTHICUM EUBERT W	CPT	0-0486065	0347	1
LINTHICUM EVERETTE	CPT	0-0495795	0756	1
LINTNER JULIUS H	COL	0-0213341	0963	3
LINTON GEORGE	LTC	0-0911941	0746	2
LINTON HOWARD L	LTC	0-0328950	0563	1
LINTON JAMES P	CW2	W-2214072	0168	1
LINTON JAMES W	MAJ	0-1551448	0258	1
LINTON JOHN D	COL	0-0164151	0950	1
LINTON WALTER L	LTC	0-0302416	0261	1
LINTON WILLIAM E	CW3	W-2112041	0756	1
LINTZ HARRY E	CPT	0-1822026	1146	2
LINVILLE UNICE K	CPT	0-1179504	0650	1
LINVILLE VERN G	CW2	W-2214720	0267	1
LIOI ALBERT J	MAJ	0-1059858	0261	1
LION FRANCIS L	LTC	0-2017558	0968	1
LIOTTA SALVATORE	CPT	0-1689824	0745	2
LIPARI JOSEPH	MAJ	0-2037627	0363	1
LIPE WILLIAM G	CW2	W-2106291	0960	1
LIPICH JOSEPH	MAJ	0-1597604	0160	1
LIPINSKI JOHN J	CPT	0-1766916	0755	2
LIPMAN ABRAHAM I	LTC	0-0291607	0954	1
LIPMAN BARNEY	CPT	0-0159662	0146	2
LIPMAN JACK M	1LT	0-1012155	0146	2
LIPP JOHN W	LTC	0-0290262	0557	1
LIPP LEONARD C	LTC	0-1287029	0559	2
LIPPAI STEPHEN A	CPT	0-4006738	0266	1
LIPPARD ARTHUR R	LTC	0-0304071	1167	3
LIPPINCOTT HOWARD E	MAJ	0-1306113	1162	1
LIPPINCOTT LOUIS D	MAJ	0-0316057	0153	1
LIPPINCOTT ROBERT	MAJ	0-1796493	0461	1
LIPPITT CHARLES W	COL	0-0272830	0554	3
LIPPITT LOUIS D	CPT	0-1696239	0346	2
LIPPITT SAMUEL B	COL	0-0189632	0756	3
LIPPMAN IRVIN W	MAJ	0-0439147	0649	1
LIPPMAN PAUL	CPT	0-1017813	1146	2
LIPPY HARRY G	MAJ	0-0239192	0563	3
LIPS FRANCIS W	WO1	W-2131946	0557	1
LIPSCH SIDNEY H	1LT	0-1595656	0745	2
LIPSCOMB CHARLES J	CPT	0-0901917	0345	2
LIPSCOMB CHARLES L	LTC	0-0296225	0467	3
LIPSCOMB DAVID H	1LT	0-0409319	0647	2
LIPSCOMB HAROLD J	COL	0-0284152	0363	3
LIPSCOMB HUDSON P JR	LTC	0-0311406	0752	3
LIPSCOMB JOHN S JR	COL	0-0269405	1164	1
LIPSCOMB JOHN W	COL	0-0178966	0-51	3
LIPSCOMB PATRICK C	LTC	0-0237288	1162	3
LIPSCOMB ROBERT L	MAJ	0-2263148	0566	1
LIPSCOMB THOMAS C	MAJ	0-0269437	0767	3
LIPSCOMB WILLIAM N	LTC	0-0122037	0249	3
LIPSCOMB WILLIAM W	CW3	W-2208933	0467	1
LIPSCOMBE ROBERT B	MAJ	0-2283835	0465	1
LIPSETT ZELNER M	COL	0-0179763	0855	3
LIPSEY ARCHIE L	MAJ	0-0499976	0353	1
LIPSEY RAYMOND E	LTC	0-0275761	0757	1
LIPSEY RICHARD C	LTC	0-0403413	0362	2
LIPSIUS ALBERT J	1LT	0-0889951	0759	1
LIPSIUS KURT P	MAJ	0-0193292	0857	3
LIPSKI PETER	MAJ	0-1797485	0257	1
LIPSKY ARTHUR A	LTC	0-0239945	0361	3
LIPSKY HARRY T	MAJ	0-0312195	0862	1
LIPSKY JOSEPH A	LTC	0-0324139	0767	1
LIPSON EDWARD	MAJ	0-0471730	0444	2
LIPSON ROY E	CW3	W-2151080	1163	1
LIPTON ALEXANDER	LTC	0-0253179	0262	3
LIPUT JOSEPH A	CPT	0-2006720	0657	1
LIPUT STANLEY	CPT	0-1321367	0958	1
LIQUE FRANCIS P	CW2	W-2109025	0547	2
LIQUORI VINCENT J	1LT	0-1302678	0945	2
LIS FLORIAN	CPT	0-1331524	0459	1
LIS JOHN J	1LT	0-1060172	0847	2
LIS PAUL M	1LT	0-2005931	1147	2
LISANTI DOMINIC C	CW3	W-2125244	1059	1
LISCINSKY ANDREW G	CPT	0-0411264	1145	2
LISCOMB JESSE R	LTC	0-1314707	0363	1
LISENBE JAMES C	CPT	0-1294160	1157	1
LISENBEE MILLARD K	1LT	0-0492935	0651	1
LISENBY ALBERT S	COL	0-0103566	0757	3
LISENBY RALPH W	MAJ	0-0976853	0762	1
LISH JAMES B	MAJ	0-1185236	1064	1
LISHNESS ARTHUR R	LTC	0-1106286	1158	2
LISK CLIFFORD L	CPT	0-1031959	0647	2
LISKA JOHN J	CW3	W-2152706	1066	1
LISMAN ANDREW J JR	CPT	0-1316651	0248	2
LISOVICZ LEONARD P	1LT	0-1316762	0345	2
LISS LEWIS L	1LT	0-1594307	0146	2
LISS VICTOR T	1LT	0-1309285	1045	2
LISSNER JOHN J J	COL	0-1579949	0866	1
LISSY LEE W	CPT	0-1593031	0564	1
LIST EDWIN O	COL	0-0158541	1046	2
LISTON HOWARD F	LTC	0-0421220	0760	1
LISTON PAUL	MAJ	0-1051656	0665	1
LISZCZ STANLEY A	MAJ	0-0305499	1044	2
LISZT LAWRENCE S	1LT	0-1596405	0646	2
LITCH MILTON B JR	LTC	0-1103759	0561	1
LITCHER VINCENT G	LTC	0-1591897	0568	3
LITCHFIELD VERNON A	LTC	0-0477118	1166	3
LITEHISER ROBERT R	COL	0-0141755	0453	3
LITHERLAND JOHN S	CPT	0-0298080	1263	1
LITHGOW MARION B	CPT	0-0244621	0362	3
LITMAN LEONARD R	LTC	0-0306950	1060	1
LITMAN MILTON D	LTC	0-0312392	0568	3
LITT EDWARD T	CPT	0-1696013	0545	2
LITTELL HOWARD W	LTC	0-0359162	0160	1

NAME	GRADE	SVC NO	DATE RET MO YR	RET CODE
LITTELL LEROY O	CPT	0-0370005	0750	2
LITTERAL KELLEY	CPT	0-1299260	1046	2
LITTERST FRANK C	1LT	0-0519592	1145	2
LITTLE CHARLES C	LTC	0-0424106	0468	2
LITTLE ALBERT M	MAJ	0-0990103	0968	1
LITTLE ALFRED T	CPT	0-1799322	0961	3
LITTLE ANDREW T	1LT	0-0321393	0545	2
LITTLE CARL C JR	CPT	0-1239446	0147	2
LITTLE CLAYTON N	MAJ	0-0456152	0346	2
LITTLE CLIFFORD F	MAJ	0-0286861	0966	3
LITTLE CLYDE L	CW3	W-2145111	1162	1
LITTLE DON D	1LT	0-0519238	0945	2
LITTLE EDWARD R	MAJ	0-0180290	0754	3
LITTLE EPHRAMS S	1LT	0-1796819	0562	1
LITTLE EUGENE T	LTC	0-1324427	0462	1
LITTLE FRED K	CW4	W-2102005	1054	1
LITTLE GEORGE C	LTC	0-2028914	0168	2
LITTLE GEORGE T	WO1	W-2113130	0946	2
LITTLE GEORGE W W	CPT	0-0502915	0545	2
LITTLE GUILBERT R	LTC	0-0232909	0960	3
LITTLE HAROLD C	LTC	0-0335046	0863	3
LITTLE JAMES L	CW3	W-2143102	0360	1
LITTLE JOE M	LTC	0-2016590	0565	1
LITTLE JONATHAN F JR	CPT	0-0219858	1055	3
LITTLE KEITH A	LTC	0-1101553	0663	1
LITTLE LAMAR W	LTC	0-0248135	1045	2
LITTLE LAWRENCE E	CW3	W-2003388	1165	1
LITTLE LEWIS D	MAJ	0-2019479	0962	1
LITTLE LITTLETON	LTC	0-0296187	0546	2
LITTLE LONGINO	CPT	0-0349401	1045	2
LITTLE MARTIN B	LTC	0-0259089	0962	3
LITTLE MILTON R	MAJ	0-0113705	1053	3
LITTLE PERCY R	COL	0-0243887	0161	3
LITTLE RALPH V	MAJ	0-1300666	0761	1
LITTLE ROBERT E	CPT	0-0411350	1263	1
LITTLE ROBERT H	CW2	W-2148868	0761	1
LITTLE ROBERT L	MAJ	0-0225805	0463	3
LITTLE RUSSELL M	CPT	0-0247296	0557	3
LITTLE THOMAS F JR	MAJ	0-1281371	0768	3
LITTLE VERNA B	MAJ	N-0765652	0665	1
LITTLE WILLIAM J	MAJ	0-2016146	1058	1
LITTLE WILLIAM S	LTC	0-0254297	0266	3
LITTLEFIELD CHESTER	MAJ	0-2263230	0462	1
LITTLEFIELD ERNEST A	COL	0-0268573	0646	2
LITTLEFIELD HOWARD C	MAJ	0-2206093	0864	1
LITTLEFIELD JAMES C	COL	0-0174612	0562	3
LITTLEHALES WILLIAM	MAJ	0-0957394	0662	1
LITTLEJOHN ARON M	MAJ	0-2034976	0658	1
LITTLEJOHN CHARLES E	LTC	0-0147840	1155	3
LITTLEJOHN CLYDE	MAJ	0-1322243	0860	1
LITTLEJOHN THOMAS F	MAJ	0-0292631	1068	3
LITTLEPAGE NORRIS	2LT	0-1172148	0845	2
LITTLETON DARCY A	LTC	0-0337844	1059	3
LITTLETON HARRY M	CPT	0-0141768	0553	3
LITTLETON MARVIN V	MAJ	0-1846025	0866	1
LITTLETON REX B JR	1LT	0-4043736	0361	2
LITTMAN ABRAHAM	LTC	0-0247892	0567	3
LITTMAN HERMAN	LTC	0-0379058	1167	3
LITTMAN JEROME R	1LT	0-1053228	0346	2
LITTMAN MAXWELL	1LT	0-1048466	0444	2
LITTON BIRCHELL E	CW2	W-2211478	0766	1
LITTON ROY E	MAJ	0-1876968	0768	2
LITTON STEPHEN M	CPT	0-0450179	0146	2
LITTRELL HOWARD F	MAJ	0-1116926	1063	1
LITTRELL LURA L	1LT	N-0733338	0245	1
LITTRELL WOODROW	WO1	W-2109854	0757	1
LITWIN DONALD J	CW2	W-2116119	0847	2
LITZELMAN JOHN H	MAJ	0-0141758	0857	3
LITZI JERRY	1LT	0-0561525	0653	1
LIUNI FRANK	COL	0-0138218	0558	3
LIUZZI ROCCO V	MAJ	0-0339067	104N	2
LIVAZER HERSH	LTC	0-0527131	0465	2
LIVE ISAAC C	MAJ	0-0325613	0766	3
LIVEAKOS GEORGE H	LTC	0-1186113	0766	1
LIVELY CHESTER A	LTC	0-0346055	0960	1
LIVELY JACK W	CW4	W-2142245	0556	1
LIVELY LABAN G	COL	0-0306318	0865	1
LIVELY RICHARD E	MAJ	0-2000448	0859	1
LIVELY RICHARD P	COL	0-0283172	0547	2
LIVELY ROBERT L	CW2	W-2141359	0858	1
LIVELY WILLIAM P	CPT	0-0182091	0357	3
LIVENGOOD NORMAN D	MAJ	0-0921554	0446	2
LIVENGOOD ROBERT B	1LT	0-1294329	0145	2
LIVENSPARGAR DAVENPO	LTC	0-0370841	0361	1
LIVERMORE EDWIN D	CW3	W-2141360	1057	1
LIVERNOIS EDWARD D	CPT	0-1014788	0464	1
LIVESAY TOLLAND O	CW4	W-2103149	0161	1
LIVESEY HERBERT B JR	LTC	0-0229502	0562	3
LIVINGSTON C E	CPT	0-0125232	1044	2
LIVINGSTON C E	LTC	0-0298814	0857	1
LIVINGSTON CHARLES H	LTC	0-0580929	0563	1
LIVINGSTON CHESTER	CW3	W-2148353	0760	1
LIVINGSTON DANIEL	MAJ	0-0265598	0664	1
LIVINGSTON DONALD B	LTC	0-0220255	0764	3
LIVINGSTON GUS	LTC	0-1999165	0962	2
LIVINGSTON JEROME M	MAJ	0-2046299	1154	1
LIVINGSTON JOE L	CW2	W-2152222	0961	1
LIVINGSTON JOSEPH D	CW2	W-2148744	1162	1
LIVINGSTON KNOX W	1LT	0-1042353	1047	2
LIVINGSTON LAWRENCE	LTC	0-1339641	0268	1
LIVINGSTON LUNSFORD	LTC	0-0315305	0646	2
LIVINGSTON MORGAN L	LTC	0-0375153	0762	2
LIVINGSTON OLIVER E	CW3	W-2152227	0762	1
LIVINGSTON OLLIE B	1LT	0-0518145	1046	2
LIVINGSTON STANLEY R	MAJ	0-1639314	1062	1
LIVINGSTON STANTON K	COL	0-0224935	0458	3
LIVINGSTON THOMAS A	LTC	0-0328422	0662	1
LIVINGSTON WELLINGTO	LTC	0-1595319	0265	1
LIVINGSTON WILLIAM S	1LT	0-0524133	0846	2
LIVINGSTON WILLIS A	1LT	0-1014216	1145	2
LIVINGSTON WOODROW W	MAJ	0-1543881	0261	1
LIVINGSTONE CECIL G	LTC	0-0311179	1063	3
LIWSKI PETER P	COL	0-0312952	0758	1
LIZARDI JOSE C	CPT	0-0217529	1145	2
LIZON JAMES J	CW2	W-2148609	0163	1
LIZZI ARTHUR J	MAJ	0-0422860	0346	2
LJUNGDAHL WILLIAM A	1LT	0-0103190	0746	2
LLATO ANTONIO	1LT	0-1556465	0246	2
LLAVINA RAFAEL	CW2	W-2147664	0360	1
LLEWELLYN BERNARD J	CPT	0-1914384	1044	1
LLEWELLYN ENSLEY M	LTC	0-0246386	1165	3
LLEWELLYN JOHN G	COL	0-0232095	1050	3
LLEWELLYN KENDALL O	CPT	0-0379912	0246	2
LLEWELLYN RUSSELL W	MAJ	0-0199408	0155	1
LLEWELLYN WILLIAM N	LTC	0-1545942	1064	1
LLOMPART JOSEPH A	LTC	0-0208691	1050	3
LLOY HAROLD A	LTC	0-1558734	0463	1
LLOYD ADDINELL W	LTC	0-0286187	1062	3
LLOYD ARTHUR H	CW2	W-2150132	0564	1
LLOYD ARTHUR Y	M G	0-0253763	0268	3
LLOYD BENJAMIN J	1LT	0-1000993	0246	2
LLOYD CARLTON D	MAJ	0-1559720	1164	1
LLOYD CECIL C	CPT	0-1283099	0762	1
LLOYD CHARLES N	MAJ	0-0343693	1167	3
LLOYD CHESTER U	CW3	W-2142647	0561	2
LLOYD DAVID G	LTC	0-0292406	0367	3
LLOYD DOUGLAS P	MAJ	0-0245273	1162	3
LLOYD EARL K	MAJ	0-0996988	0464	1
LLOYD ERIC F	CW4	W-2114431	0857	1
LLOYD FRANK W	LTC	0-0327189	0659	2
LLOYD HENRY W	LTC	0-0330985	1166	1
LLOYD JAMES	CW3	W-2152161	0264	1
LLOYD JANE	MAJ	N-0745186	0867	1
LLOYD JOEL	CW3	W-2148833	0162	1
LLOYD JOHN B	LTC	0-0398441	0368	3
LLOYD JOHN W JR	MAJ	0-0252629	0167	3
LLOYD KATHERINE	1LT	N-0703320	0445	1
LLOYD KENNETH W	CW2	W-2212971	0268	1
LLOYD LEON A	LTC	0-0158034	1057	3
LLOYD MARGARET C	CPT	L-1010317	0554	2
LLOYD MINTA	MAJ	N-0728554	0266	1
LLOYD ROBERT B	CPT	0-0336522	0749	2
LLOYD ROBERT D	MAJ	0-1577485	0568	3
LLOYD ROBERT J	MAJ	0-0244505	1262	3
LLOYD ROBERT W	1LT	0-0452465	1043	2
LLOYD THOMAS D	LTC	0-1285781	0461	1
LLOYD THOMAS R	WO1	W-2005350	1165	3
LLOYD WALTER R	MAJ	0-1338482	0363	1
LLOYD WILLIAM G III	MAJ	0-1919849	1165	1
LLOCH JOSE C	MAJ	0-0170540	0456	3
LO PRESTI JOSEPH M	CW3	W-2143055	1062	1
LO VECCHIO GUY F	LTC	0-0527343	0864	1
LOADER BYRON O	CW4	W-2141616	0767	1
LOADER CLIFFORD F	MAJ	0-0525930	0347	2
LOAR ROBERT R	2LT	0-1032636	1044	2
LOBBY MAURICE E	CW3	W-2150798	0962	1
LOBDELL ARTHUR T	COL	0-0130490	1154	3
LOBDELL HUGH L	LTC	0-0259592	0668	3
LOBEL JACOB	MAJ	0-1104959	0765	1
LOBEL MURRAY R	MAJ	0-0972584	0265	1
LOBERG LAURICE L	LTC	0-1305077	0562	1
LOBIANCO FRANK E	LTC	0-0346946	0351	2
LOBIT JAMES C	LTC	0-0496315	1162	1
LOBO ISMAEL Y	1LT	0-1896526	1157	1
LOBSINGER ALVIN P	LTC	0-1053700	0962	1
LOBUE NICHOLAS J	CPT	0-0359316	1044	2
LOCASCIO JOSEPH R	CW3	W-2206411	0166	1
LOCASCIO NICHOLAS R	MAJ	0-0284406	0246	2
LOCER HARVEY W	MAJ	0-1285448	0661	1
LOCH ELMER V	LTC	0-1303747	0159	1
LOCHEN EVERETTE L	LTC	0-0250441	0466	3
LOCHLIN CLIFFORD A	COL	0-0381008	0157	1
LOCHWOOD FRANK S	CW2	W-2216355	1068	1
LOCK FRANK A JR	MAJ	0-2208581	0867	1
LOCK JAMES W	MAJ	0-2019480	0463	1
LOCKARD CLAIR R	MAJ	0-1319428	1060	1
LOCKARD CLARENCE H	CW2	W-2144642	1060	1
LOCKARD RICHARD J	MAJ	0-1846476	0160	2
LOCKARD WALTER S	CW2	W-3430275	0867	1
LOCKE BRUCE M	MAJ	0-1593035	0863	1
LOCKE CHARLES O	CPT	0-0107876	0752	3
LOCKE HERBERT H	MAJ	0-2020741	0962	1
LOCKE JOHN P	LTC	0-0169467	0360	3
LOCKE JOHN R	COL	0-0301126	0466	3
LOCKE ROBERT	MAJ	0-1011713	0759	1
LOCKE ROBERT L	LTC	0-1577486	0667	1
LOCKE ROBERT M	CPT	0-1057806	1060	1
LOCKE ROLLIN K	MAJ	0-1591899	1160	1
LOCKE RUPERT A	LTC	0-0373342	0758	1
LOCKEN CARL M	MAJ	0-0280533	0566	3
LOCKER LUTHER M	LTC	0-0259133	0746	2
LOCKERMAN JULIAN F	LTC	0-1039443	0863	1
LOCKETT WENDELL W	LTC	0-0391249	1161	2
LOCKETT WILLIAM R	LTC	0-0360122	0766	3
LOCKHART CHARLES G	CPT	0-1103762	1064	1
LOCKHART HAROLD E	MAJ	0-1179506	0763	1
LOCKHART HOWARD C	LTC	0-0317298	0947	2
LOCKHART JACK N	MAJ	0-1177889	0461	1
LOCKHART JAMES J	CW3	W-3150653	0668	1
LOCKHART JOSEPH	LTC	0-0170565	0945	2
LOCKHART RALPH M	COL	0-0241259	1262	3
LOCKHART ROBERT JR	MAJ	0-1168341	0762	1
LOCKLEAR ROBERT W	MAJ	0-1999096	0759	1
LOCKLEAR WILLIAM C	MAJ	0-0509489	1053	1
LOCKLER FRANK T	CW2	W-2207543	0462	1
LOCKLIN HORACE M	LTC	0-0474127	0555	1
LOCKLIN ORVIL L	1LT	0-1796308	0152	2
LOCKMAN EDGAR O	LTC	0-0307681	0458	3
LOCKMAN EDGAR P JR	CW2	W-2209928	1264	1
LOCKNANE BUSH W	MAJ	0-0232826	0460	3
LOCKSLEY HOWARD R	1LT	0-0341673	0246	2
LOCKWOOD ARTHUR W	CPT	0-1295395	0546	2
LOCKWOOD CHERRY L	1LT	J-0100151	0756	2
LOCKWOOD FREDERICK	LTC	0-1648361	0658	1
LOCKWOOD GEORGE W	LTC	0-2277417	0568	1
LOCKWOOD JOHN J	CW3	W-2112271	0256	1
LOCKWOOD JOHN S	CPT	0-0446772	1046	2
LOCKWOOD KENNETH V	CPT	0-1285257	0645	2
LOCKWOOD ROBERT J	MAJ	0-1113324	0165	1
LOCKWOOD RUSSELL A	LTC	0-0491382	0654	2
LOCKWOOD SAMUEL M	MAJ	0-1284723	1061	1
LOCKWOOD WILLIAM F	LTC	0-0112424	0754	3
LOCKWOOD WILLIAM W	LTC	0-0301415	0761	1
LOCKYER ROBERT H	LTC	0-1046182	0961	1
LOCKYER WILLIAM T	LTC	0-0341470	0647	2
LODATO JOHN F	LTC	0-0277761	0662	1
LODATO VICTOR JR	CPT	0-0499835	0145	2
LODDE RALPH H	LTC	0-0386409	0468	1
LODEK CHARLES C	MAJ	0-0289155	0655	1
LODEN EARL	LTC	0-0221482	1056	3
LODER CHARLES	CPT	0-1642329	0654	2
LODER WILLIAM C	COL	0-0451336	0467	1
LODGE HENRY C	M G	0-0188725	0862	3
LODGE SHENTON B	MAJ	0-1115677	0761	1
LODISE FRANCES R	1LT	N-0729064	0545	1
LODL JAMES JR	CW2	W-2110830	0556	1
LOOS LOUIS E	LTC	0-1020029	1067	1
LOEB ROBERT M	LTC	0-0296808	0964	3
LOEBEL GEORGE A	LTC	0-0510496	0762	1
LOEBS CARL H	LTC	0-0166328	1152	3
LOEFFLER ERWIN P	LTC	0-0555185	0565	1
LOEFFLER WILLIAM E	CPT	0-0515414	0249	1
LOEHNERTZ ELFRIEDA E	2LT	N-0774905	0845	1
LOEHR RODNEY C	MAJ	0-1995296	1267	3
LOEHR WILLIAM M	LTC	0-0332668	0753	2
LOER GEORGE W	MAJ	0-0349105	0764	3
LOES EDWIN B	MAJ	0-1297751	0264	1
LOES MURLAND F	COL	0-0350715	0557	1
LOES PAUL F	1LT	0-1325908	0446	2
LOESCH ROBERT J	LTC	0-0421204	0363	1
LOESER JOHN M	WO1	W-2131274	0747	2
LOEWE WILL R	COL	0-0277576	1161	3
LOEWEN FRANK W	CW2	W-2144385	1058	1
LOFFREDO ANTHONY P	MAJ	0-2047409	0261	1
LOFGREEN EARSTON A	CPT	0-0446845	0546	2
LOFGREN CARL R	LTC	0-1317552	1262	2
LOFGREN JAMES T	LTC	0-0383624	1060	1
LOFGREN PAUL F	1LT	0-1305611	0945	2
LOFLAND EDWARD O	CW3	W-2150801	1263	1
LOFLAND WILMER D	LTC	0-2029075	1263	1
LOFLEN LESTER A	MAJ	0-2016488	0660	1
LOFT WILLIAM P	LTC	0-2049316	0168	1
LOFTESNESS CURTIS H	MAJ	0-1685659	0565	1
LOFTFIELD BERNER F	MAJ	0-0280640	0746	2
LOFTFIELD GORM	CPT	0-0199728	0551	3
LOFTHEIM HAAKON L	LTC	0-1032637	0861	1
LOFTIN JAMES C	MAJ	0-0251709	1046	2
LOFTIN ROBERT E	CPT	0-0386043	1043	2
LOFTON HARRY F	COL	0-0265634	1061	3
LOFTUS FRANCIS S	MAJ	0-0971198	0264	1
LOFTUS JOHN J	CW4	W-2148629	0656	1
LOFTUS MARGARET P	2LT	N-0797605	1147	1
LOGAN ALBERT N	2LT	0-1822159	0645	2
LOGAN BENNIE L	CW2	W-2124547	0650	1
LOGAN CHARLES F	MAJ	0-1935052	0966	1
LOGAN CHARLES O	LTC	0-0313173	0258	1
LOGAN CHARLES W	MAJ	0-1825232	1060	1
LOGAN CLYDE B	CW3	W-2152707	1263	2
LOGAN COOLIDGE A	MAJ	0-0963527	0861	1
LOGAN DULANEY C	CPT	0-0514410	0646	2
LOGAN EOSEL G	CPT	0-1533130	0851	2
LOGAN EMMETT H	LTC	0-0411080	0861	1
LOGAN ERNEST J	MAJ	0-0572439	1056	1
LOGAN GEORGE A	LTC	0-0403341	1066	3
LOGAN GORDON W SR	CPT	0-1937201	0864	1
LOGAN HAROLD N	MAJ	0-0388286	0468	3
LOGAN HENRY T	MAJ	0-0455588	0246	2
LOGAN HERBERT A	MAJ	0-2002482	0561	1
LOGAN JAMES W	COL	0-0288875	0860	1
LOGAN JOHN R	CW2	W-3150757	0367	1

NAME	GRADE	SVC NO	DATE RET MO YR	RET CODE
LOGAN JOHN W	LTC	O-1641520	0668	3
LOGAN JOSEPH A	LTC	O-0111700	0453	3
LOGAN JOSEPH A	LTC	O-1845307	0765	3
LOGAN JOSEPH R	LTC	O-0397159	0261	1
LOGAN RAYMOND M	2LT	O-0378088	1044	2
LOGAN ROBERT A	LTC	O-1699152	1144	2
LOGAN ROBERT G	COL	O-0411587	0161	1
LOGAN ROBERT L	COL	O-0101325	1154	3
LOGAN ROBERT M	LTC	O-0389737	1262	1
LOGAN RUSSELL S	MAJ	O-0358073	0945	2
LOGAN SHERMAN D JR	MAJ	O-0969783	0161	1
LOGAN THEOPHILUS	MAJ	O-1311527	0762	1
LOGAN THOMAS H	CPT	O-0962710	1060	1
LOGAN WILLIAM B JR	1LT	O-1057151	0446	2
LOGAN WILLIAM G JR	CW3	W-2151648	1262	1
LOGAN WILLIAM N	2LT	O-1182635	1144	2
LOGAN WYATT Y	CPT	O-2212081	0860	1
LOGEL JOHN	WO1	W-2130729	0956	1
LOGIE MARC J	COL	O-0187529	0853	3
LOGSDON CALE W	LTC	O-0224131	1157	3
LOGUE CHARLES D	MAJ	O-2025630	1063	1
LOGUE CHARLES W	2LT	O-1016663	0545	2
LOHAN ARTHUR E	MAJ	O-1315181	0868	3
LOHMAN KENNETH W	CPT	O-1289600	0257	1
LOHMILLER MATTHEW D	LTC	O-0133472	1056	3
LOHN OVID L	CPT	O-0497877	0547	1
LOHNES HALLET E	CPT	O-0187688	1053	2
LOHNES JAMES E	MAJ	O-1639319	0662	1
LOHR CURTIS H	COL	O-0275251	0157	3
LOHR JOHN M	LTC	O-0240182	0164	3
LOHR LAWRENCE J	CPT	O-0492151	0146	2
LOHRE JAMES F	CW3	W-2209929	1267	1
LOHSE MELVIN D	CW4	W-2124484	0964	1
LOIERO ALPHONSE J	CW2	W-2143196	1161	1
LOIZEAUX PAUL F	COL	O-0225670	0364	3
LOKEN HARRIS	1LT	O-1013648	0346	2
LOKEN LESLIE B	COL	O-0386341	1055	1
LOKEY BENJAMIN F	1LT	O-0424048	0346	2
LOKEY EDWARD L	MAJ	O-2004005	0268	1
LOKEY WILLIAM H	MAJ	O-0232243	0565	3
LOKKER HOMER C	MAJ	O-2035122	0261	1
LOLL LEON E	COL	O-1534546	0868	1
LOLLAR LEON B	CPT	O-2016396	0561	1
LOLLAR RICHARD L	LTC	O-0208237	0654	3
LOLLAR VICTOR G	1LT	O-2204173	1053	2
LOLLIS GEORGE A	LTC	O-0518005	1264	1
LOMAN FREDERICK	CPT	O-0515091	0546	2
LOMAS ATHALEE A	MAJ	N-0703344	1165	1
LOMAS GEORGE A	CW3	W-2141618	0662	1
LOMASNEY JOHN W	LTC	O-0504349	1054	1
LOMAX VIRGIL C	CPT	O-0291437	0968	3
LOMBAES LEO	2LT	O-1174046	0445	2
LOMBARD ARTHUR G	COL	O-0910116	0966	1
LOMBARD EMMONS S	MAJ	O-0253614	0662	3
LOMBARD JAMES O	CW3	W-3150271	1168	1
LOMBARD REGINALD T	COL	O-0196244	0856	3
LOMBARDI LUCIAN	LTC	O-0335036	0746	2
LOMBARDI PHILIP J	LTC	O-0547386	0967	1
LOMBARDO ETHEL M	1LT	N-0794572	1146	1
LOMBARDO LAWRENCE	CW2	W-3150404	0466	2
LOMBARDO ROBERT T	WO1	W-2150355	1153	2
LOMBARDO SAMUEL	LTC	O-1287551	0162	1
LOMET PIERRE JR	LTC	O-0211742	1061	3
LOMITOLA JOHN L	CPT	O-1298256	0863	1
LOMMLER BRYCE W	CPT	O-1321644	0547	2
LOMMORI JOSEPH P	MAJ	O-0358666	0646	2
LOMONACO JOSEPH	2LT	O-1308429	1143	2
LONABAUGH MARTHA M	MAJ	N-0725995	1167	1
LONBERGER FRANK R	1LT	O-0414072	0146	2
LONDON BENJAMIN C	LTC	O-1594628	0762	1
LONDON CLYDE F	MAJ	O-0970213	1061	1
LONDON DANIEL	CPT	O-0497950	0251	2
LONDON ELLIOTT E	CPT	O-0252899	0862	3
LONDON JOHN D	CW3	W-2152580	0664	1
LONERGAN FRANK E	LTC	O-1103764	0763	1

NAME	GRADE	SVC NO	DATE RET MO YR	RET CODE
LONERGAN JOHN D	MAJ	O-0305621	0766	3
LONEY RALPH H	MAJ	O-0968679	0466	1
LONEY ROBERT S	LTC	O-0908137	0367	3
LONG AARON A	CW3	W-2150133	0456	1
LONG ADOLPHUS P	CW3	W-2144811	0862	1
LONG ALBERT W	MAJ	O-0448902	1055	1
LONG ANTHONY	B G	O-0274572	0968	3
LONG ARTHUR	MAJ	O-1994467	0863	1
LONG AVERY P JR	MAJ	O-0239105	0465	3
LONG BILLY J	CW3	W-3150499	0668	1
LONG BROOKS R	2LT	O-2024322	0646	2
LONG BYFORD F	LTC	O-1287553	0665	1
LONG CALVIN	WO1	W-2115901	1044	2
LONG CARL P	MAJ	O-0355154	1166	1
LONG CHARLES D	MAJ	O-4074516	0568	1
LONG CHARLES E	1LT	O-1168782	0846	2
LONG CHARLES J	CPT	O-1010003	1051	1
LONG DON E	MAJ	O-1315849	1060	1
LONG DONALD E	LTC	O-0141656	0953	3
LONG EARL S JR	MAJ	O-1926294	0566	1
LONG EDWARD	LTC	O-1945864	0368	1
LONG EDWARD H	LTC	O-0283656	0467	3
LONG ELMER I	LTC	O-0331646	1067	3
LONG ERNEST W	LTC	O-0402446	0258	1
LONG EUGENE L	LTC	O-0327818	0366	3
LONG EVANS	CPT	O-0282465	0868	3
LONG FAYE L	LTC	O-0373344	0161	1
LONG FLOYD M	2LT	O-1822890	0244	2
LONG FRANK C	CW3	W-2144711	0466	1
LONG FRANK E	MAJ	O-0118407	0648	3
LONG FRANK H	2LT	O-2005637	0356	2
LONG FRANK S	LTC	O-0111105	0648	3
LONG FRED P	LTC	O-0311126	0464	3
LONG GEORGE C	COL	O-0256349	0564	3
LONG GEORGE P	LTC	O-0336542	1154	2
LONG GLEN H	CW2	W-2109853	0857	1
LONG GLENDON R	COL	O-0359901	0563	1
LONG HAMILTON A	MAJ	O-0140380	0359	3
LONG HENRY A	CPT	O-0482079	0845	2
LONG HOWELL G	COL	O-0269953	0266	3
LONG HUBERT F	LTC	O-0299640	0359	1
LONG JAMES B	LTC	O-0235628	1044	2
LONG JAMES E	COL	O-0188220	0460	3
LONG JAMES F R	CPT	O-0171021	0648	3
LONG JAMES J	LTC	O-1541259	0364	1
LONG JAMES M	MAJ	O-2042880	0161	2
LONG JAMES R	MAJ	O-1108119	0663	1
LONG JAMES R	1LT	O-1287554	1145	2
LONG JOHN A	CPT	O-0302427	0546	2
LONG JOHN A	CPT	O-0376777	1045	2
LONG JOHN D	MAJ	O-1012647	1147	2
LONG JOHN L	CW2	W-2149226	0361	2
LONG JOHN W	COL	O-0190011	0355	3
LONG JOHN W	MAJ	O-0333779	1154	2
LONG JOSEPH S	MAJ	O-1637951	1046	2
LONG LAWRENCE M	LTC	O-0372701	0656	1
LONG LAWRENCE V	MAJ	O-1924940	0568	1
LONG LAWRENCE W	COL	O-0239899	0462	3
LONG LEONARD H	1LT	O-1588129	1049	1
LONG LOUIS C JR	CW2	W-2109370	0156	2
LONG MAURICE E	1LT	O-1304249	0245	2
LONG MAX H	CPT	O-0491131	1053	2
LONG NORMAN G	LTC	O-0290255	1164	3
LONG ODUS E	1LT	O-1293430	0752	2
LONG ORAN M	CPT	O-1030687	1048	2
LONG PAUL M	LTC	O-0278156	0758	3
LONG PAUL T	LTC	O-1825423	1166	1
LONG PAUL W	LTC	O-0308417	0466	1
LONG RAYMOND B	CPT	O-0219396	0457	3
LONG REGINALD	CPT	O-1924783	1262	2
LONG RICHARD J	1LT	O-1297060	0146	2
LONG RICHARD J	MAJ	O-2203067	0764	1
LONG ROBERT F	1LT	O-0449410	0344	2
LONG ROBERT F	CW2	W-2142170	0855	2
LONG ROBERT G	LTC	O-0254779	0954	1

NAME	GRADE	SVC NO	DATE RET MO YR	RET CODE
LONG ROBERT W	LTC	O-0201586	0663	1
LONG ROBERT W	LTC	O-1688616	0168	1
LONG RUDOLPH A	CW3	W-2144750	0860	2
LONG RUSSELL A	CPT	O-0304803	0348	2
LONG SAM H	COL	O-0323054	0154	3
LONG SAMUEL M	2LT	O-1322640	0844	2
LONG THEODORE S	MAJ	O-1001398	0861	1
LONG THOMAS J	2LT	O-1304250	0345	2
LONG THOMAS J	1LT	O-1332836	0652	2
LONG THOMAS M	CPT	O-1598137	0165	1
LONG THOMAS TEL	COL	O-0242212	0951	2
LONG THOMAS W	CW3	W-2147505	0268	2
LONG TOMMY L	LTC	O-0423851	0663	1
LONG VERNON A	1LT	O-5230768	0668	2
LONG VINCENT P	1LT	O-1319846	0546	2
LONG WARREN R	WO1	W-2120078	0654	1
LONG WAYNE E	MAJ	O-0238434	0864	3
LONG WENDELL B	LTC	O-0217854	0462	3
LONG WENDELL W	MAJ	O-1175784	0763	1
LONG WILLIAM	MAJ	O-0250163	0947	1
LONG WILLIAM B JR	MAJ	O-1010220	0646	2
LONG WILLIAM C	CW3	W-2142246	1060	1
LONG WILLIAM F	MAJ	O-0151834	0455	3
LONG WILLIAM G	MAJ	O-2262903	0264	1
LONG WILLIAM H	CPT	O-0256924	0866	3
LONG WILLIAM J	MAJ	O-0218889	0254	3
LONG WILLIAM L	CW3	RW-2207647	0866	1
LONG WILLIAM M	MAJ	O-0260018	1267	3
LONG WILLIAM M	CPT	O-0488819	0847	1
LONGACRE M ANNABEL	MAJ	N-0725120	0462	1
LONGENECKER ERNST A	MAJ	O-0156689	0456	3
LONGENECKER HARRY W	MAJ	O-0975473	0165	1
LONGEY LLOYD L	MAJ	O-0490115	0954	1
LONGFELLOW HENRY W	LTC	O-1100205	0863	1
LONGFELLOW LAWRENCE	LTC	O-1172152	0967	1
LONGFELLOW LYMAN E	CW3	W-2146606	0762	1
LONGFELLOW REASEN H	MAJ	O-0298310	1166	3
LONGFELLOW ROY C	LTC	O-0373273	1060	2
LONGLEY ANDREW J	COL	O-0231803	0365	3
LONGLOY FRANCIS E	MAJ	O-2262491	1265	1
LONGMIRE BYRON H	CW2	W-2112107	0450	1
LONGMIRE MARION A	CPT	O-0327821	0745	2
LONGNECKER THOMAS H	1LT	O-1999089	1046	2
LONGO AUGUSTINE	CW3	W-2141361	0461	1
LONGO DANIEL J	CW4	W-2115171	0959	1
LONGOBARDI MARY S	2LT	N-0729149	0745	1
LONGORIA VICTOR M	CPT	O-0284684	0945	2
LONGPRE J H FERNAN	LTC	O-0483795	0346	2
LONGSDON MALCOLM J	MAJ	O-0481434	0546	2
LONGSDORF FORD H	COL	O-0298772	1060	3
LONGSDORF JAMES E	CPT	O-0954994	0467	1
LONGSHORE JOHN R	COL	O-0340189	0957	1
LONGSHORE PAUL J	LTC	O-0236701	0361	3
LONGSTRETH ALVIN E	COL	O-0262824	1267	3
LONGSWORTH HAROLD J	LTC	O-0348582	0261	1
LONGTIN LUDGER P	CW2	W-2206335	0665	1
LONGWELL FREEMAN H	MAJ	O-0332962	0246	2
LONGWILL BENNY F	MAJ	O-2037073	0561	1
LONGWORTH EVERETT	CPT	O-0394898	0562	1
LONNQUIST T OSCARENA	MAJ	N-0741900	0864	3
LONON WILLIAM A	1LT	O-1168342	0747	2
LONSDALE WILLIAM L	MAJ	O-2050550	0567	2
LONSETH CLAYTON D	LTC	O-1550854	0563	1
LONSFORD CHARLES A	MAJ	O-0948809	1060	1
LONSINGER WALLACE F	2LT	O-1179508	0245	2
LONTOS CLARENCE J	MAJ	O-1932459	0667	1
LOOFBOURROW WADE H	LTC	O-0253511	0358	3
LOOMIS DONALD O	CPT	O-0890223	0147	2
LOOMIS GUY A JR	COL	O-0261293	0667	3
LOOMIS JOSEPH M	CPT	O-2262289	0758	2
LOOMIS LEE S	CW3	W-2150037	1060	1
LOOMIS MARVIN A	CPT	O-1297909	1147	2
LOOMIS PAUL A	COL	O-0350599	0366	2
LOOMIS PHILIP L	LTC	O-0351642	0759	1
LOOMIS WILLARD T	CPT	O-0343605	0744	2

NAME	GRADE	SVC NO	DATE RET MO YR	RET CODE
LOOMIS WILLIAM B	LTC	O-0294773	0964	3
LOOMIS WILLIAM E	CW3	W-2109265	1060	1
LOONEY ELIJAH H	COL	O-0310798	0968	3
LOONEY ENNIS M	CW3	W-2146758	0963	1
LOONEY HOUSTON G	LTC	O-1703759	1058	1
LOONEY JACK M	LTC	O-0941991	0767	1
LOONEY JAMES H JR	1LT	O-0461463	1144	2
LOONEY JAMES K	LTC	O-0198078	1056	3
LOONEY MICHAEL L	COL	O-0319890	0764	3
LOONEY MORRIS G	MAJ	O-2012772	0367	1
LOONEY QUENTEN S	MAJ	O-2262797	1062	1
LOOP ALFRED B	WO1	W-2114734	1049	2
LOOP ELVIN J	MAJ	O-0963858	0363	2
LOOP VINCENT C	LTC	O-0401826	0862	1
LOOPER RANSCME T	COL	O-0423260	0666	1
LOORAM JOHN J	CPT	O-1012175	1047	2
LOOS ALDO H	COL	O-0363503	1059	3
LOOS ALFRED R	COL	O-0269197	0568	3
LOOS CARL D	LTC	O-1049250	1057	1
LOOS KARL D	CPT	O-0100047	0351	3
LOOSBROCK JOHN F	CPT	O-1286151	0345	2
LOOSER IRENE A	CPT	N-0730985	1047	1
LOPARDO ANTONIO A	CW3	W-2145216	0460	1
LOPER JAMES F	1LT	O-1319429	0749	2
LOPER WILLIAM H JR	LTC	O-0578362	0262	1
LOPES ALBERT V	CPT	O-2263307	0861	1
LOPEZ ALBERT C	LTC	O-1100653	0358	1
LOPEZ CARLOS	2LT	O-1017649	0945	2
LOPEZ DE VICTORI	1LT	O-1180589	0547	2
LOPEZ FRITOSO R	MAJ	O-1917614	1062	1
LOPEZ JUAN E	MAJ	O-2263330	1268	1
LOPEZ JULIAN JR	MAJ	O-1684994	0365	1
LOPEZ LAURENCE C	CW3	W-2153094	0163	1
LOPEZ LOUIS V	LTC	O-0186282	0154	3
LOPEZ LOUIS V	MAJ	O-0954056	1162	1
LOPICCOLO ERNEST K	LTC	O-1110627	0866	1
LOPSHIRE ARTHUR P	COL	O-0327147	0360	3
LOPUS LESTER R	COL	O-0197030	0454	3
LOPUSNIAK MACK S	1LT	O-0419864	1144	2
LOR ALFRED R	CPT	O-1306292	0857	1
LORAH BRUCE	CW3	W-2005876	0967	1
LORANCE JEROME	MAJ	O-1553502	1060	1
LORANGE HARRY	LTC	O-0278569	1264	3
LORANGER JOHN W	MAJ	O-1844817	0367	1
LORCH ROBERT B	LTC	O-0200850	0850	3
LORD AUSTIN R	MAJ	O-1319093	0565	1
LORD CHARLES E	MAJ	O-0263622	1058	3
LORD CHARLES G	LTC	O-0339355	0765	3
LORD E R	COL	O-0197753	0563	3
LORD EVERETT J	LTC	O-1596710	0768	2
LORD FRANK H	WO1	W-2120361	0347	2
LORD FREDERICK JR	CPT	O-0398404	0544	2
LORD GORDON C	MAJ	O-0251859	1057	3
LORD HANSEL L	CPT	O-1296723	0446	2
LORD HAROLD F	LTC	O-1000405	0261	1
LORD JAMES F	CW4	W-2141141	1168	1
LORD LAURENCE F	LTC	O-0473947	0162	3
LORD M O	MAJ	O-0935963	1163	1
LORD MEDERIC J	CW3	W-2148484	0163	1
LORD RALPH C	CPT	O-0494305	0548	1
LORD ROBERT E	CPT	O-1309766	0546	2
LORD RUSSELL R	COL	O-0253043	0566	3
LORD WILLFRED V	CPT	O-0415334	1044	2
LORD WILLIAM A JR	COL	O-0231053	0364	3
LORD WILLIAM J	1LT	O-0555806	0247	2
LORDEN DANIEL F	1LT	O-0525324	0349	1
LORE GEORGE T W	MAJ	O-2262774	0762	1
LOREE JAMES T	COL	O-0299127	0648	3
LOREN WILLIAM H	LTC	O-1168785	0267	1
LORENTZ CARL B	WO1	W-2150169	1054	1
LORENTZEN JULIUS C	MAJ	O-0202991	0648	3
LORENZ FRANK	CW3	W-2207349	0966	1
LORENZ HERMAN A	MAJ	O-0166566	0545	2
LORENZ THEODORE E	LTC	O-0198949	1053	1
LORENZEN JOHN R	LTC	O-1558593	1167	1

NAME	GRADE	SVC NO	DATE RET MO YR	RET CODE
LORENZO MICHAEL J	LTC	0-1634085	1164	1
LORENZO PEDRO	1LT	0-1896926	0859	1
LORENZO SEBASTIAN	MAJ	0-1401171	0762	2
LORETT ROBERT M	CW3	W-2206133	0868	1
LORETTE EDMOND O	CW4	W-2102014	0955	1
LORETTE FRANCIS B	CW4	W-2148258	0864	1
LORETTE SANFORD D	LTC	0-0449228	0263	1
LOREY PAUL R JR	2LT	0-0545475	1045	2
LORIA JOSEPH A JR	MAJ	0-1054680	0265	1
LORIE JAMES N	LTC	0-0475876	0454	1
LORIMER FRANK M	CPT	0-0476076	0446	2
LORIMER GEORGE H	LTC	0-0245573	0459	3
LORIMER WILLIAM III	COL	0-0297340	0560	1
LORING ALBERT W	CPT	0-1106913	0346	2
LORING ARTHUR P	LTC	0-0301101	1263	3
LORING GLADDON L	LTC	0-1549923	0267	1
LORING WARREN E	LTC	0-0760199	0668	1
LORSUNG LLOYD W	MAJ	0-1549535	0665	1
LORY EARL C	LTC	0-0249340	0766	3
LORY JOSEPH W	CW3	W-2203331	0465	1
LORZ NORBERT W	MAJ	0-0296057	0763	3
LOS BANOS BERN	MAJ	0-1331303	1162	1
LOSEE JOSEPH I	LTC	0-1287377	0667	3
LOSEE LOUIS C	MAJ	0-1556018	1060	1
LOSEE WILFRED J	MAJ	0-1699951	0962	1
LOSEL WILLIAM J	COL	0-0260070	0467	3
LOSER EARL G	LTC	0-0234997	0753	3
LOSER HENRY L	CPT	0-0822033	1166	2
LOSHBAUGH ALBERT O	MAJ	0-0405206	1146	2
LOSHNOWSKY HARRY W	1LT	0-1551051	1044	2
LOSPENNATO AMERICO W	2LT	0-1578786	0543	2
LOSS CHARLES R	LTC	0-0405233	0364	3
LOSSBOM KNUT E	CW4	W-2104249	1058	1
LOSSEF SAMUEL	1LT	0-0490264	0345	2
LOSSING FAY A	LTC	0-0234167	0965	3
LOSTUMBO DOMINICK J	LTC	0-1307923	0162	2
LOTH MORITZ A R	CPT	0-0183213	0254	3
LOTHNER ROY	LTC	0-1324428	1062	1
LOTHROP JACK W	2LT	0-0466486	0344	2
LOTHROP MELFORD M	MAJ	0-0234084	0645	2
LOTSPEICH THERESE M	MAJ	N-0743669	1068	3
LOTT COLON J	LTC	0-1289282	1057	1
LOTT DANIEL P	WO1	W-2119936	0244	2
LOTT ELLIS T	CW3	W-2146430	0361	1
LOTT FREDERICK	CPT	0-0444203	0846	2
LOTT HENRY E	LTC	0-0237461	0664	3
LOTT JOHN H	LTC	0-0294762	0257	3
LOTT JOSEPH W	CW2	W-2106758	0259	2
LOTT WILLIAM B	COL	0-0912404	0567	3
LOTTER CHARLES A	LTC	0-0267564	0157	1
LOTTI DOMINICO T	MAJ	0-0969460	0163	1
LOTTIE RAYMOND C	LTC	0-1117074	0862	1
LOTTIER RAYMOND L	MAJ	0-2033286	0465	1
LOTZ ARNOLD H	CPT	0-1293279	1262	1
LOTZ CHARLES J	1LT	0-1324429	0546	2
LOTZ ERIC A	COL	0-0262537	0668	3
LOTZ HARRY B	1LT	0-0451038	0644	2
LOUCKS JOHN H	CW4	W-2133248	0158	1
LOUCKS JOSEPH A	CPT	0-1700739	0646	2
LOUD EMERY S	LTC	0-0229774	0563	3
LOUDEN MERRILL C	LTC	0-0372206	0860	1
LOUDEN RUSSELL	MAJ	0-0156895	0253	3
LOUDERMILK ALVIN E	CW2	W-2210185	1164	1
LOUDON EUGENE J	MAJ	0-1825145	0661	1
LOUDON JAMES O	MAJ	0-0380936	0746	2
LOUGEE BERNARD R	LTC	0-0557918	0167	1
LOUGH CHARLES M JR	MAJ	0-0932077	0763	1
LOUGH FRANK A	LTC	0-0255611	0360	1
LOUGH GEORGE E	LTC	0-0420864	1160	1
LOUGH LISLE S	CPT	0-1310612	0447	2
LOUGH SAMUEL R	LTC	0-0266082	0353	3
LOUGHEED CHARLES D	MAJ	0-1923522	1065	1
LOUGHRAN EUGENE P	1LT	0-5321972	1066	2
LOUGHRAN JOHN F	CW3	W-2107872	1061	1
LOUGHRAN JOHN J	COL	0-1040046	0466	1
LOUGHRY JOE M	LTC	0-0332504	0868	3
LOUGHRY RICHARD F	MAJ	0-1325304	0161	1
LOUIS FRED W	COL	0-0434726	0462	1
LOUIS JOHN J	MAJ	0-4010509	0567	1
LOUN ELVA M	CW3	V-0322541	0765	1
LOUNSBERRY GEORGE H	MAJ	0-0285837	0862	3
LOUNSBERRY RALPH F	MAJ	0-1037135	0559	2
LOUPE SYLVAIN R	COL	0-0271551	0567	3
LOURDEAUX STANLEY J	CPT	0-0422851	1144	2
LOUSBERY ARTHUR E	LTC	0-0464227	0763	2
LOUSTEAU DANIEL T	LTC	0-1177968	0866	1
LOUT ELSA K	2LT	N-0723841	0645	1
LOUWENAAR DAVID W	MAJ	0-0506953	0268	3
LOVANYAK ERNEST J	LTC	0-1648550	1160	1
LOVAS WILLIAM S	MAJ	0-1687354	0546	2
LOVE AMANDA I	2LT	N-0743131	0846	2
LOVE ARTHUR	1LT	0-1896735	0350	1
LOVE CLAIR L	1LT	0-1646373	0846	2
LOVE DANA W	LTC	0-0212013	1156	3
LOVE DONALD E	1LT	0-4074517	0668	2
LOVE DOYNE M	CW3	W-2150323	0963	1
LOVE ELBERT H	MAJ	0-0396630	0846	2
LOVE FRANK A	CPT	0-0154663	1148	3
LOVE HARRY W	1LT	0-1081353	1045	2
LOVE HOWARD L	CW4	W-2136402	0865	2
LOVE JERRY I	LTC	0-1175216	0161	1
LOVE JOHN	1LT	0-2027443	0254	1
LOVE JOHN E	1LT	0-1108818	0246	2
LOVE LAWRENCE E	MAJ	0-0446500	0954	1
LOVE LOWELL S	COL	0-0222612	0460	1
LOVE MELVIN V	CPT	0-0521351	1147	2
LOVE RAY	COL	0-0170287	1055	3
LOVE ROBERT B	LTC	0-0273386	1061	3
LOVE RUTH A	1LT	N-0728415	0646	1
LOVE WESLEY G	1LT	0-0188757	0535	1
LOVE WILBUR B	MAJ	0-1535022	0161	2
LOVE WILLIAM A JR	CW3	W-2112841	1060	1
LOVE WILLIAM O	MAJ	0-1104964	0463	1
LOVE WILLIAM S JR	COL	0-0246751	0246	2
LOVEJOY CHARLES R	LTC	0-0287282	0968	3
LOVEJOY CLARENCE E	COL	0-0219503	0654	3
LOVEJOY CLIFFORD O	COL	0-0308415	0362	3
LOVEJOY FRANK	MAJ	0-0450626	0660	1
LOVEJOY GRORGE F	LTC	0-0306383	0160	1
LOVEJOY LILLIAN L	1LT	N-0786070	0147	1
LOVEJOY RHEBA O	MAJ	N-0775389	0567	3
LOVEJOY THOMAS C	LTC	0-0257807	0567	3
LOVEJOY WALTER E	2LT	0-1308157	0445	2
LOVELACE HAROLD M	COL	0-0232931	0863	3
LOVELADY WILLIAM B	COL	0-0262588	0766	3
LOVELAND CARL H	MAJ	0-0931280	0966	1
LOVELAND ERWIN H	CW3	W-2146884	1264	1
LOVELAND WILLIS H	CW2	W-2205433	1062	1
LOVELESS HOWARD A	CPT	0-1291661	1044	2
LOVELESS WALTER E	MAJ	0-1823546	0658	1
LOVELL DOW H	CPT	0-0268041	1046	2
LOVELL JAMES L	MAJ	0-1037605	0464	1
LOVELL JAMES W	MAJ	0-0334033	0246	2
LOVELL JOHN W	LTC	0-0384300	0346	2
LOVELL SAMUEL W	CPT	0-1018099	1160	3
LOVELL WILLIAM H	CW4	W-2110664	0860	1
LOVELY GUY R	CW2	W-2148125	1159	1
LOVELY JOHN E	2LT	0-0197116	1029	1
LOVELY JOSEPH D	CW3	W-2005973	1064	3
LOVEMAN ADOLPH B	MAJ	0-0476654	1045	2
LOVENTHAL MARTIN S J	2LT	0-1017714	0744	2
LOVERDE ALBERT A	CPT	0-0308066	0146	2
LOVERIDGE WILLIAM I	MAJ	0-1011822	0760	1
LOVERING FRANK R	LTC	0-0265296	0962	3
LOVERING HARRY D	LTC	0-0126632	0152	3
LOVESTEDT LOYD W	CPT	0-1170064	0446	2
LOVETERE ANGELO A	MAJ	0-0330401	0545	2
LOVETT CLARENCE J	MAJ	0-0181344	1056	3
LOVETT CLAUDE E JR	CPT	0-0521431	1047	2
LOVETT JOE T	COL	0-0210936	0245	2
LOVETTE JASON P	LTC	0-1313503	0961	1
LOVETTE JOE E	1LT	0-0497179	0946	1
LOVINGOOD ESTON A	LTC	0-0303942	0460	1
LOVITT ERNEST C	MAJ	0-2016163	1163	1
LOVKO JOHN F	COL	0-0327761	0263	3
LOVORN RICHARD T	CPT	0-1645772	0557	1
LOVRE STANTON C	MAJ	0-0343899	1045	2
LOVREIN LELAND C	MAJ	0-1894935	1060	1
LOVSETH PERCIVAL C	LTC	0-0935881	0568	1
LOVVORN WILLIAM H JR	LTC	0-1172969	0764	1
LOW CLARENCE A	MAJ	0-0365630	0456	1
LOW FREDERICK	MAJ	0-2208222	0367	1
LOW RICHARD C	COL	0-0316831	0960	1
LOW ROBERT J	COL	0-1166547	0164	1
LOWANDE WILLIAM B	1LT	0-1177062	104N	2
LOWDER JOHN W	CW3	W-2145683	0965	1
LOWDER PAUL J	LTC	0-1996774	0262	1
LOWDERMILK LEE D	COL	0-0279353	0950	2
LOWDERMILK ZEB B	CW3	W-2205542	0165	1
LOWE ACIE	1LT	0-0497647	0346	2
LOWE BENO P	CW2	W-2121116	0845	2
LOWE BESS G	1LT	N-0730285	0146	1
LOWE BILLY D	MAJ	0-2206422	0764	1
LOWE CARL W JR	LTC	0-1030171	0357	1
LOWE CARLTON M	MAJ	0-1329020	0865	1
LOWE CATHERINE	CPT	N-0736516	0951	2
LOWE CHARLES B	CW2	W-2004445	0164	1
LOWE CHARLES W JR	CW4	W-2142870	1064	1
LOWE CLARK	LTC	0-1180248	1060	1
LOWE DENZIL R	COL	0-0278598	0560	3
LOWE DONALD H	LTC	0-1285450	0759	1
LOWE EDCAR P	CW2	W-2144239	0656	1
LOWE EDWARD H	CPT	0-0450384	0356	1
LOWE EDWIN P	MAJ	0-0914214	0665	3
LOWE FARRELL D	LTC	0-0349000	0754	1
LOWE FRANK E	M G	0-0170395	0648	3
LOWE GERALD H	LTC	0-2048060	0264	1
LOWE GIDEON H	LTC	0-0265516	1153	3
LOWE HAROLD T	COL	0-0211491	0751	3
LOWE HENRY W	LTC	0-1954470	1264	1
LOWE HOWARD D	COL	0-0342310	1064	1
LOWE JAMES E	WO1	W-2128075	0447	1
LOWE JAMES L	LTC	0-0374696	0966	3
LOWE JERROL P	MAJ	0-0405931	0960	1
LOWE JOHN A	LTC	0-0160726	0848	3
LOWE JOHN L JR	CPT	0-1302025	0146	2
LOWE KATHRYN F	CPT	N-0751221	0363	1
LOWE MARY E	CPT	N-0763765	0649	2
LOWE MILLS T	2LT	0-2024287	1145	2
LOWE MILTON C	LTC	0-1012026	0655	1
LOWE MITCHELL	CW3	W-2152300	0662	2
LOWE OTTO B	2LT	0-1637958	1043	2
LOWE RALPH W	MAJ	0-0359906	0160	1
LOWE RAYMOND P	MAJ	0-1950204	0564	1
LOWE ROBERT C	COL	0-0350544	0859	1
LOWE ROBERT W	LTC	0-1115681	0766	3
LOWE ROBERT W	MAJ	0-2283838	0859	1
LOWE SAM D	LTC	0-0237898	0863	3
LOWE THEODORE	COL	0-1105625	0266	3
LOWE THOMAS J	LTC	0-0241753	0460	2
LOWE WILLIAM A	MAJ	0-0969791	1263	2
LOWE WILLIAM A	LTC	0-1165898	0159	1
LOWELL EDDIE R	LTC	0-1182900	1262	1
LOWELL JAMES R	LTC	0-0343950	0646	2
LOWELL JOHN C	MAJ	0-1048878	0862	1
LOWELL PARKER	MAJ	0-0297544	0267	3
LOWELL ROBERT L	MAJ	0-1173360	0161	1
LOWENSTEIN BERNARD	COL	0-0308448	0368	3
LOWENSTINE JAMES R	2LT	0-0439208	0645	2
LOWER EDGAR R	COL	0-0194232	0354	3
LOWER ERNEST H	MAJ	0-0290030	0654	3
LOWER GRANT K	MAJ	0-1165252	0860	1
LOWER ROBERT W	LTC	0-1701568	1167	1
LOWERY AGNES R	MAJ	L-0305306	1165	1
LOWERY FRED T	MAJ	0-1918943	1265	1
LOWERY GEORGE W	CPT	0-0283059	1266	3
LOWERY H A	CPT	0-0969773	0261	2
LOWERY JAMES C SR	LTC	0-0290756	1055	3
LOWERY JOHN J	MAJ	0-2262790	0562	1
LOWERY LAWRENCE C	CW2	W-2148456	0559	1
LOWERY ONAS F	LTC	0-0109174	0146	2
LOWERY PAUL J	CPT	0-1038047	1047	2
LOWERY PERCY E	LTC	0-0182648	0846	1
LOWERY RALPH T	LTC	0-1292549	1262	1
LOWERY RAYMOND M	MAJ	0-0106023	0158	3
LOWERY WILLIAM W	CW2	W-3100548	0468	1
LOWES WILLIAM J	MAJ	0-1288252	1161	1
LOWI ALVIN P	MAJ	0-0103452	0246	2
LOWMAN ARDEN W	LTC	0-1299262	0562	1
LOWMAN CECIL B	1LT	0-0537424	1045	2
LOWMAN JENNINGS D	MAJ	0-0490259	0648	1
LOWN CHARLES R	1LT	0-1031192	0544	2
LOWN GROVER E	CW2	W-2118269	0946	2
LOWN JAMES M	MAJ	0-0408118	0157	1
LOWNES EDWARD D	COL	0-0195681	0762	3
LOWRANCE CARLOS U	MAJ	0-0187587	0557	1
LOWRANCE WAYNE H	LTC	0-0502186	0468	3
LOWRANCE WILLIAM R	LTC	0-1635043	0461	1
LOWREY JAMES O	MAJ	0-1581918	0467	3
LOWREY JOHN C	CW2	W-2126737	0651	1
LOWREY NORTON R	LTC	0-0236818	1159	1
LOWREY ROBERT E JR	LTC	0-0300834		2
LOWREY ROBERT W	COL	0-0344894	1045	2
LOWREY WILLIS F	LTC	0-0397690	0561	1
LOWRY ALBERT H	CPT	0-0492936	0847	1
LOWRY BURRIS H	LTC	0-0271263	0166	3
LOWRY DOROTHY K	CPT	L-0800042	1162	1
LOWRY EARL D	MAJ	0-0146542	0653	3
LOWRY GEORGE B	MAJ	0-1112289	0959	1
LOWRY HARRY P	COL	0-0274217	0551	3
LOWRY J C	1LT	0-1920057	0753	2
LOWRY JAMES M	CW4	W-2142172	1162	1
LOWRY JEFFERSON	MAJ	0-1683978	1161	1
LOWRY JOHN A	2LT	0-0541577	0845	2
LOWRY JOHN C	COL	0-0107180	1057	1
LOWRY JOSEPH V	CW4	W-2118534	0155	1
LOWRY MAYMIE I	1LT	N-0771018	0646	1
LOWRY RICHARD E	LTC	0-1048470	0667	1
LOWRY SAMUEL N	COL	0-0262742	0456	2
LOWRY SUMTER L	M G	0-0170909	0853	3
LOWRY TAYLOR T JR	MAJ	0-1333090	0365	1
LOWRY THOMAS M JR	MAJ	0-0170948	1161	3
LOWRY WILLIAM C	LTC	0-0270601	0862	3
LOWRY WILLIAM V SR	CPT	0-1181021	1060	2
LOWTHER BEN W	LTC	0-1646375	0767	1
LOWTHER CHARLES W	CW3	W-2211098	0968	1
LOY FRANKLIN L	LTC	0-0193820	0262	3
LOY JOHN H	CW3	W-2203318	1163	1
LOY JOHN W	CPT	0-2011327	0257	1
LOY LELAND L	LTC	0-0471520	0365	1
LOY WILLIAM A	CPT	0-0360071	1145	2
LOYA MARY	2LT	N-0734863	0744	1
LOYD ALBERT S	CW2	W-2210818	0766	1
LOYD GARRITT W	CW2	W-2145288	0360	1
LOYD GILBERT M	MAJ	0-1297219	0762	1
LOYD KATHERINE	MAJ	N-0735329	0865	1
LOYD LENSEY A JR	CW3	W-2210902	0868	1
LOYD SAMUEL J	MAJ	0-0268047	0459	1
LOYD W C	CW4	W-2152838	0468	1
LOYD WILLIAM E	CW3	W-2205376	1166	1
LOYE HARLAN M	LTC	0-0397927	0760	1
LOZANO CONSUELO R	1LT	N-0728936	0945	1
LOZANO RAUL G	MAJ	0-0988043	0265	1
LOZEAU ROLLAND A	MAJ	0-1105629	0963	1
LOZIER LUE C	LTC	0-0130652	0246	2
LOZITO FRANK	CW2	W-2215075	0968	1
LUBAN FRANCIS	MAJ	0-1899376	0561	1
LUBBEN JOHN F JR	LTC	0-0245673	0658	3
LUBCHANSKY HAROLD W	LTC	0-1101560	0462	1
LUBEN CONRAD J	MAJ	0-0942957	0466	1

NAME	GRADE	SVC NO	DATE RET MO YR	RET CODE
LUBENS HERMAN	CPT	0-0444202	0545	2
LUBERT LOUIS	LTC	0-0346806	1161	3
LUBIN DAVID	1LT	0-1635044	0646	2
LUBIN FRANCES C	1LT	N-0759143	0845	1
LUBITZ BENJAMIN	COL	0-0261651	0160	3
LUBOTSKY IRVING J	MAJ	0-1307226	0964	1
LUBOVSKY BENJAMIN	LTC	0-0443671	0854	1
LUBRAND DOMINICK	CW2	W-2110436	0846	1
LUBY JOSEPH P	CPT	0-1014343	0854	1
LUCA SALVATORE	MAJ	0-0503985	0546	2
LUCANDER VICTOR	2LT	0-1310270	0557	1
LUCAS ALBERT	MAJ	0-0174022	0555	3
LUCAS CLARENCE R	MAJ	0-0451337	0660	1
LUCAS CLIFFORD R	MAJ	0-0475910	1053	1
LUCAS ERNEST	LTC	0-0335347	0760	1
LUCAS ERNEST L	COL	0-0203635	0752	3
LUCAS FRANCES B	1LT	N-0742031	0646	1
LUCAS FRANK C	MAJ	0-0257778	0966	3
LUCAS GEORGE	CW4	W-2111827	0659	1
LUCAS GEORGE	CW3	W-2206964	0267	1
LUCAS GEORGE A	1LT	0-1309675	0751	1
LUCAS GROVER E	MAJ	0-1877158	0165	1
LUCAS GUY P	1LT	0-0168748	0160	3
LUCAS HARLAN S	MAJ	0-0933933	0462	1
LUCAS HERBERT	CPT	0-1293621	1147	2
LUCAS HOWARD C	1LT	0-0365140	1142	2
LUCAS HOYT D	MAJ	0-0193813	1152	3
LUCAS JAMES F	MAJ	0-0491519	0453	2
LUCAS JAMES O JR	1LT	0-0537802	1045	2
LUCAS JOHN	LTC	0-0460117	1053	1
LUCAS JOHN A	MAJ	0-0526929	0155	1
LUCAS JOHN D	COL	0-0412396	0166	1
LUCAS JOHN J	MAJ	0-1695224	0246	2
LUCAS JOHN L	MAJ	0-1177063	0865	1
LUCAS JOHN P	MAJ	0-1548926	0761	1
LUCAS JOHN R	LTC	0-0355044	0660	1
LUCAS JOSEPH N	CPT	0-1011834	0847	2
LUCAS LOUIS F	COL	0-0407117	0546	2
LUCAS MARVIN H	LTC	0-0385794	0760	1
LUCAS MICHAEL	CW2	W-2109531	1152	2
LUCAS PAULINE B	MAJ	N-0724904	1061	1
LUCAS RAY D	CW2	W-2211279	C766	1
LUCAS RICHARD L	MAJ	0-1017939	0263	1
LUCAS ROBERT L	LTC	0-1185846	1062	2
LUCAS ROBERT L	WO1	W-2131792	1044	2
LUCAS ROSEMARY V	MAJ	N-0735591	1064	2
LUCAS RUSSELL S	CPT	0-0423535	1043	2
LUCAS STANLEY M	LTC	0-1050787	0263	1
LUCAS THOMAS C	2LT	0-2006069	0845	2
LUCAS WENDELL S	LTC	0-0444317	0853	2
LUCAS WILLARD J	CPT	0-1796113	1058	1
LUCAS WILMER F	COL	0-0242247	0757	3
LUCE CHARLES M	CPT	0-0580363	0646	2
LUCE EDWIN A	CW4	W-2110534	0957	1
LUCE FRANCIS N	MAJ	0-0251203	0155	3
LUCE GEORGE H	LTC	0-0383362	0660	1
LUCE GILBERT L	LTC	0-0278811	0763	3
LUCE HOWARD J SR	CW4	W-2144812	0968	1
LUCE WALTER A	CW3	W-2113626	0859	1
LUCERI VINCENT F	LTC	0-1168787	0563	1
LUCERO LEO L	MAJ	0-1104970	0960	1
LUCEY ALEXANDER	MAJ	0-0125975	0648	3
LUCHT HAROLD C	CPT	0-0912048	0244	2
LUCHT HERSHEL F	LTC	0-0445362	0463	1
LUCIAN JOHN A	CPT	0-0339802	0346	2
LUCIANO FRANK A	MAJ	0-0955589	0463	1
LUCIANO MICHAEL N	1LT	0-1295912	1044	2
LUCINSKI WILLIAM	LTC	0-0329439	1057	1
LUCIS EDWARD	CW3	W-2144360	0659	1
LUCK DONALD D	2LT	0-0515229	1043	2
LUCK EMORY H	CW2	W-2145890	0961	1
LUCK JULIAN W	LTC	0-0426047	0263	2
LUCK WILLIAM V	MAJ	0-0296540	0865	3
LUCKE CARL E	CPT	0-0117856	0650	3
LUCKES CLINTON E	MAJ	0-1686171	1060	1
LUCKETT GUSTUS	COL	0-0403573	0860	1
LUCKETT LUTHER J	LTC	0-0253347	0155	3
LUCKEY JULIUS J JR	CPT	0-0309404	1148	2
LUCKFIELD HERBERT M	LTC	0-1555721	0763	2
LUCKHURST CHARLES A	LTC	0-0176873	0648	3
LUCKIE CHARLES A	COL	0-0335074	1266	3
LUCKY VIRGIL M	MAJ	0-1924119	0663	1
LUCKY VIRGLE E SR	CW3	W-2151144	0865	1
LUCORE JAMES C	LTC	0-1635047	0862	1
LUCY CLAUD R	MAJ	0-0483623	0747	1
LUCZAK ARTHUR F	MAJ	0-2019341	0463	1
LUDDEN CHARLES F	LTC	0-0212360	0661	2
LUDDEN PAUL W	LTC	0-0510920	0363	1
LUDDEN WALTER E	MAJ	0-1103290	0165	1
LUDES GEORGE M	LTC	0-0318614	0566	3
LUDFORD AARON L	1LT	0-1298257	1145	2
LUDINGTON RALPH E	LTC	0-1016809	0465	1
LUDLOW GEORGE L	CW3	W-2142519	0667	1
LUDLOW PAUL L	CW3	W-2144193	0663	1
LUDOVICI PETER P	1LT	0-1546215	0446	2
LUDWIG DONALD W	LTC	0-0344045	1167	3
LUDWIG EDWARD P	CW4	W-2104254	0664	1
LUDWIG ERWIN P	COL	0-0313148	0767	3
LUDWIG GERALD E	LTC	0-0269519	0566	3
LUDWIG HENRY R	1LT	0-1182636	0946	2
LUDWIG HOWARD G JR	CW3	W-2144691	0660	1
LUDWIG JOHN J	CW2	W-2206848	0962	1
LUDWIG LEROY M	LTC	0-1040762	0861	1
LUDWIG LLEWOLLYN	COL	0-0246406	0762	3
LUDWIG LLOYD A	LTC	0-0370126	0863	3
LUDWIG ROBERT B SR	CW2	W-2213720	0768	1
LUDWIG RODMAN W	LTC	0-1645774	0961	1
LUDWIG ROSS	LTC	0-0364873	0668	3
LUDWIG WILLIAM J	MAJ	0-0411349	0261	1
LUEBBE CLETUS L	CPT	0-1055371	0155	2
LUEBBERS RALPH H	LTC	0-0342611	0466	3
LUEBKERT BERNARD C	LTC	0-0285191	1058	1
LUEBSEN JOHN H	CPT	0-0317031	1044	2
LUEDDE FULLERTON	CPT	0-0345718	0743	2
LUEDEKE OTTO H	MAJ	0-1798021	0358	1
LUEDERS WILLIAM T	MAJ	0-1874397	0666	1
LUEDKE EDWARD A	LTC	0-0193394	0760	3
LUEDKE FREDERICK	CPT	0-0283792	0144	2
LUEDKE GEORGE E	1LT	0-1048474	1045	2
LUEDTKE LEO M	LTC	0-1041603	0367	1
LUEKER ANDREW H	LTC	0-1948501	1167	1
LUELLMAN GEORGE V	CW2	W-2145923	1159	1
LUERNITZ ALBERT W	CW2	W-3200440	0868	1
LUETH HAROLD C	B G	0-0285937	0864	3
LUFBURROW WILLIAM G	LTC	0-1994801	0668	1
LUFKIN BENJAMIN N	CPT	0-0280040	0254	3
LUFTMAN HARRY I	LTC	0-0487763	0946	2
LUFTY ANTHONY	1LT	0-1177510	114N	2
LUGO LUIS A	COL	0-0108281	1049	1
LUGO RAMON L	CPT	0-0198849	0562	3
LUGOWE BOLESLAUS	LTC	0-1331528	1162	1
LUGTU EMILIO L	MAJ	0-0373046	0157	1
LUHN EDGAR R JR	MAJ	0-1922651	1166	1
LUHORN VICTOR E	LTC	0-0444375	0755	2
LUHRING ELWIN E	MAJ	0-0217571	1161	3
LUIDOR CHARLES	CPT	0-0507962	1047	1
LUIKART GORDON A	1LT	0-2103226	1054	2
LUJAN JOE C	LTC	0-1291663	0860	1
LUJAN MANUEL S	MAJ	0-1329959	1061	1
LUKAS CHARLES J	MAJ	0-1171252	0261	1
LUKAS CHESTER T	MAJ	0-1181022	0860	1
LUKE CHARLES D	LTC	0-0299216	1167	3
LUKE FRANCIS F	MAJ	0-0311545	0757	3
LUKE GERALD M	MAJ	0-1644541	1060	3
LUKE JOHN L	2LT	0-0513508	1045	2
LUKE JULIAN S	WO1	W-2129317	1162	1
LUKE LEONARD V	LTC	0-1635049	0368	3
LUKE MARTIN	CPT	0-1292359	0445	2
LUKE WALDENE F	LTC	0-0232777	0765	3
LUKENS CHARLES E	CW2	W-2152973	0464	1
LUKENS REAVES C	COL	0-0167195	0148	2
LUKER WILBUR H	MAJ	0-1554424	0660	1
LUKEY PHILIP E	MAJ	0-1895434	1061	1
LUKITSCH JOSEPH F	LTC	0-1013420	0964	1
LUKOWSKI ANTHONY E	COL	0-0226856	1150	2
LUKOWSKI RAYMOND L	MAJ	0-1550432	0757	1
LULL EVERETT P	LTC	0-1312958	0962	1
LULL WILLIAM C	MAJ	0-2266144	0767	1
LUM CHARLES W	LTC	0-0348836	1266	1
LUM TOM K	LTC	0-0285431	0860	1
LUMAN HARRY J	MAJ	0-1329495	0465	1
LUMAN RALPH M	COL	0-0350086	0661	1
LUMBARDO JOSEPH E	CPT	0-0521133	0559	2
LUMBARDO JOSEPHINE	MAJ	R-0000584	0568	1
LUMLEY JAMES P	CPT	0-1639326	0962	1
LUMMEL JOSEPH J	LTC	0-0383193	0162	2
LUMMUS HELENE V	LTC	N-0722054	0566	3
LUMMUS J W	MAJ	0-1328913	0266	1
LUMPKIN FRANK G JR	LTC	0-0284400	1067	3
LUMPKINS ROY G	MAJ	0-1325502	0860	1
LUMSDEN HOWARD R	CPT	0-2262742	0361	1
LUMSDEN VIRGIL M JR	1LT	0-1587423	0352	2
LUNA HAYES D	COL	0-0312746	0367	3
LUNA JOHN	CW2	W-2142976	0261	1
LUNA W C	CW2	W-2146578	0262	1
LUND ARNOLD	2LT	0-1170468	1144	2
LUND ARTHUR R	LTC	0-0504984	0556	1
LUND CARROLL R JR	CW4	W-2139469	1265	1
LUND GLEN S	1LT	0-1285453	1045	2
LUND MELVIN C	CW3	W-2205500	0367	1
LUND MELVIN E	CW2	W-2209722	0363	1
LUND OSCAR J JR	CW2	W-2147889	0861	1
LUND PAUL O	2LT	0-2043275	0346	2
LUNDAHL CHARLES A	MAJ	0-1317237	1166	3
LUNDAHL GEORGE E	1LT	0-1012822	1144	2
LUNDAHL HELEN M	MAJ	N-0745095	0668	1
LUNDAHL JOHN H SR	CW2	W-2206975	0263	2
LUNDAY ARTHUR R	CW2	W-2149950	0161	2
LUNDBERG ANDREW M	COL	0-0373755	1162	1
LUNDBERG REUBEN O	MAJ	0-0254759	1263	3
LUNDBLAD CLARENCE J	COL	0-0258164	1067	3
LUNDBLAD FRANK W JR	LTC	0-1321793	0766	1
LUNDBLAD ROY A	CPT	0-1700762	0944	2
LUNDEBERG THURSTON R	LTC	0-0234848	0165	3
LUNDEEN WALTER S	CPT	0-0481576	1042	2
LUNDELL LESLIE J	LTC	0-0352208	0264	1
LUNDEN EUGENE B	MAJ	0-0242749	0465	3
LUNDGREN FRED H JR	MAJ	0-0369513	0146	2
LUNDGREN ROY H	LTC	0-0403963	0960	1
LUNDGREN SIDNEY C	MAJ	0-2017876	0463	1
LUNDH JOHN	1LT	0-1017357	0246	2
LUNDHEIM ERLING J	CPT	0-0319208	0845	2
LUNDIN LEONARD W	LTC	0-0272689	0868	3
LUNDQUEST EARL A	1LT	0-0350107	0968	3
LUNDQUIST CARL K	MAJ	0-0452854	0152	2
LUNDQUIST CHARLES G	2LT	0-1688833	0351	2
LUNDQUIST DONALD N	MAJ	0-4074518	1166	1
LUNDQUIST HARRY T	LTC	0-0429568	1158	1
LUNDQUIST RAYNARD V	LTC	0-0227638	0862	3
LUNDSTROM JAMES E	CPT	0-1049961	0147	2
LUNDVALL MERLE E	1LT	0-1286861	1144	2
LUNDY CLAYTON J	MAJ	0-0118382	0556	3
LUNDY CONSTANCE	CPT	N-0752202	1047	1
LUNDY RICHARD P	MAJ	0-1551052	0747	2
LUNDY ROBERT A	LTC	0-0426277	0162	3
LUNDY ROBERT J	CPT	0-1598921	0157	1
LUNDY ROGER J	MAJ	0-1599088	0364	1
LUNDY THOMAS F JR	COL	0-0252065	1263	3
LUNDY THOMAS G	1LT	0-1061777	0146	2
LUNDY WALTER A SR	MAJ	0-1316652	0462	3
LUNG ADOLPHUS V	CPT	0-1289107	1059	1
LUNGARD PETER A	MAJ	0-0306505	1067	3
LUNGER CHARLES	LTC	0-1280069	0354	1
LUNN JESSIE C	CPT	0-1823025	0146	2
LUNN MEREDITH A	1LT	0-1291846	0245	2
LUNN WALTER K JR	CPT	0-0553499	1047	2
LUNN WILBURN V	COL	0-0190586	0260	3
LUNNEY EDWARD J JR	MAJ	0-1302153	0661	1
LUNSFORD DOROTHY L	MAJ	L-0909416	1058	2
LUNSFORD JOHN A	LTC	0-0224386	0145	2
LUNSFORD PRESTON E	LTC	0-1120125	0467	1
LUNSFORD WILLIAM E	2LT	0-0108237	0238	1
LUNSKIS CHARLES P	LTC	0-2040702	0257	1
LUNT ARTHUR W	CPT	0-1586753	0763	1
LUNT CLINTON E	LTC	0-0320801	0960	3
LUNT HOMER K	MAJ	0-0279798	0166	3
LUNTZ BENJAMIN	MAJ	0-0111279	0251	3
LUPARELLO THOMAS G	COL	0-0347625	0665	3
LUPINACCI JOSEPH J	2LT	0-1315508	0145	2
LUPINACCI VINCENT P	COL	0-0225858	0265	3
LUPINDS JOSEPH	MAJ	0-0965876	0164	1
LUPO CARL W	COL	0-0114522	1153	3
LUPO JASPER	MAJ	0-1634089	0764	1
LUPO JOHN M	CW3	W-2207420	1167	1
LUPO RUTH A	MAJ	N-0727855	0867	1
LUPSA GEORGE J	CW2	W-2153030	0663	1
LUPTON GORDON L	MAJ	0-0166616	1158	3
LUPTON HELEN M	MAJ	N-0758784	0964	3
LUPTON WILLIAM R JR	LTC	0-1688550	0768	1
LUQUES DONALD L	LTC	0-0354377	0164	1
LUREY SAM	LTC	0-1111745	0663	1
LURIA SYDNEY	CPT	0-0386060	0140	2
LURIE BENNY	MAJ	0-0484275	0346	1
LURIE GUNTHER J	CW3	W-2149351	0964	1
LURIE JACK	CPT	0-1715087	0545	2
LURQUIN HENRY J	LTC	0-0219003	0253	3
LURVEY RALPH A	CW2	W-2144921	0859	1
LUSBY JAMES W H	LTC	0-0247451	0157	1
LUSCHER HENRY R JR	CPT	0-0399889	0645	2
LUSCHER WILLIAM G	CPT	0-1309770	1047	2
LUSCOMBE HERBERT A	CPT	0-0468875	0846	2
LUSCOMBE NICH A	LTC	0-0390771	1061	1
LUSE WALLACE K	LTC	0-0364124	1047	2
LUSH LEWIS C	MAJ	0-0231355	0260	3
LUSH RICHARD F	LTC	0-0278068	0157	3
LUSIGNAN GERARD A	CW3	W-2153175	0767	1
LUSK AUD E	MAJ	0-0187788	0753	3
LUSK DAVID E	MAJ	0-0431602	0646	2
LUSK DAVIS	LTC	0-0348800	0663	1
LUSK DONALD F	MAJ	0-0983538	0565	1
LUSK EARL M	CPT	0-0357420	0348	2
LUSK FRANK B	COL	0-0116856	0246	2
LUSK GEORGE V	LTC	0-1174051	0261	1
LUSK HAYWOOD W	CPT	0-1636245	0760	1
LUSK JAMES R	CPT	0-1341680	0254	2
LUSK ROBERT A	LTC	0-0223144	0964	3
LUSK ROBERT K	LTC	0-0360894	1165	1
LUSK RUTH L	1LT	N-0764171	0146	1
LUSK VERNON N	MAJ	0-1931401	0167	1
LUSKOSKI JOHN JR	CPT	0-2263576	0163	1
LUSSIER JOSEPH E	MAJ	0-1286316	1158	1
LUSSIER ROSARIO H	LTC	0-0394614	0457	1
LUST HERBERT L	LTC	0-0371232	0468	3
LUSTBADER PHILIP F	CPT	0-0345586	0446	2
LUSTER HARRISON	1LT	0-0495302	1051	1
LUSTGARTEN EARL M	MAJ	0-1821319	0446	2
LUSTIG J MERWIN	LTC	0-0424026	1060	1
LUSTMAN JACK	CW2	W-2106037	1049	2
LUTCAVAGE ZIGMUND C	MAJ	0-1284538	0557	1
LUTE HARRY J	CW2	W-2103161	1268	2
LUTEN CLARENCE R	LTC	0-1286517	0657	1
LUTER ASA B SR	MAJ	0-0313982	1059	1
LUTES JACK L	LTC	0-1182177	0567	1
LUTES JOHN T JR	1LT	0-5204569	0361	2
LUTES ROBERT A	MAJ	0-4009570	0566	1
LUTFRING ANTHONY E	MAJ	0-0276566	0259	3
LUTGEN CONRAD J	MAJ	0-0229241	0363	3
LUTH BEN C	COL	0-0253719	1057	3
LUTH HERMAN W	MAJ	0-0506365	0846	2
LUTH LOUIS H	COL	0-0100721	1051	3

NAME	GRADE	SVC NO	DATE RET MO YR	RET CODE
LUTHER M MARGARET	1LT	N-0773509	1145	1
LUTHER ARTHUR F	CPT	0-0487742	0259	1
LUTHER CHARLES C	MAJ	0-0256646	0867	1
LUTHER FRANCIS C	CPT	0-2262047	0361	1
LUTHER HAROLD S	1LT	0-1756977	1163	2
LUTHER LYLE I	LTC	0-0583926	1164	1
LUTHER MARSHALL K	1LT	0-0433018	0154	1
LUTHER RALPH P	MAJ	0-0550277	0349	2
LUTHER STANLEY W	MAJ	0-0196736	0357	3
LUTHER STANLEY W	COL	0-0256891	1167	3
LUTHER PHILLIP A	CW3	W-2206539	0368	1
LUTIGER LOUIS P	CPT	0-0830132	0846	2
LUTINSKI ALFRED M	LTC	0-1119087	0966	1
LUTMAN CHARLES W	MAJ	0-0437837	0861	1
LUTNER THOMAS R JR	1LT	0-0550355	0347	2
LUTON JAMES N	COL	0-0223344	0864	3
LUTTENBEIN RICHARD W	MAJ	0-0944139	0564	1
LUTTIG NORMAN W	LTC	0-1946556	0463	1
LUTTINGER WILLIAM W	MAJ	0-0969326	1061	1
LUTTON GLENN T	MAJ	0-1636246	0555	1
LUTTRELL EARNEST	LTC	0-0209823	0846	1
LUTTRELL LEWIS	CW4	W-2103162	1064	1
LUTTRELL THORNTON E	LTC	0-2047413	0962	1
LUTTRINGER WILLIAM B	LTC	0-0338000	0760	1
LUTWACK MAURICE	COL	0-0275727	0466	3
LUTYE WILLIAM B	CPT	0-1030798	0161	1
LUTZ ALVIN H	COL	0-0235866	0860	3
LUTZ CHRISTIAN	LTC	0-1105633	1262	1
LUTZ EARL E	LTC	0-0355383	0547	2
LUTZ GEORGE J	1LT	0-1032369	1044	2
LUTZ GEORGE L	MAJ	0-0531305	0956	2
LUTZ GEORGE W	CPT	0-1891104	1164	1
LUTZ HAROLD W	MAJ	0-1546400	0859	1
LUTZ HARRY J	LTC	0-0491313	0859	1
LUTZ HERMAN M	LTC	0-0242784	0567	3
LUTZ HOBART F	1LT	0-1825019	0945	2
LUTZ JOHN W	CPT	0-0458058	0250	1
LUTZ JOSEPH	MAJ	0-0973444	1063	1
LUTZ JOSEPH C	LTC	0-0272105	0767	3
LUTZ KARL C	MAJ	0-1309286	0358	1
LUTZ PAUL F	LTC	0-0266242	0161	2
LUTZ RICHARD W	LTC	0-1311175	0764	1
LUTZ THOMAS F	WO1	W-2146344	1167	2
LUTZ WALTER C	MAJ	0-1285076	0647	2
LUTZ WILLIAM O	LTC	0-0250927	0560	1
LUTZ 2ND JOHN E	MAJ	0-0396832	0446	2
LUTZE FRANK M	CPT	0-1794965	0949	2
LUX GEORGE L	2LT	0-1104275	1044	2
LUX SAMUEL P	1LT	0-2023680	0548	2
LUX TURNER S JR	2LT	0-0557728	0146	2
LUXBACHER JOHN W	MAJ	0-1011819	1263	1
LUXEM JOHN G	2LT	0-2024389	0646	2
LUXFORD RICHARD G	2LT	0-1798593	0445	2
LUXMORE BETTY M F	CW3	V-2205865	1265	1
LUXTON WILLIAM L	LTC	0-0171388	0747	2
LUZADER WILLIAM K	CW3	W-2148259	1067	1
LUZZIE EDWARD E	MAJ	0-0297014	0347	2
LYBARGER EARNEST W	CPT	0-2008220	0557	1
LYBECK CARL W	LTC	0-1646819	1062	1
LYBRAND WENDEL C	CW2	W-2151842	0562	1
LYBROOK ROBERT C	COL	0-0269407	0467	3
LYDAY RANDAL J	LTC	0-0292303	0168	3
LYDDON RICHARD E	CPT	0-2103101	0761	2
LYDECKER LEIGH K	COL	0-0133287	0648	3
LYDEN JOSEPH J	LTC	0-1592392	0648	1
LYDIARD CHARLES W	CPT	0-1165900	0745	2
LYDICK JESSE B	CW2	W-2131818	0246	2
LYDMAN ALVIN C	CPT	0-0374595	0445	2
LYDON ANTHONY M	MAJ	0-1299438	0760	2
LYDON BERNARD J	CPT	0-0979306	0262	1
LYDON JAMES J	1LT	0-1299595	0365	2
LYDON JOHN E	MAJ	0-2037567	1062	1
LYELL JAMES M	CW2	W-2153087	1061	1
LYELL ROSSLYN A	1LT	0-1113815	104N	2
LYERLY JOSEPH E	CPT	0-0909217	0263	1

NAME	GRADE	SVC NO	DATE RET MO YR	RET CODE
LYGA THOMAS E	1LT	0-1996331	0347	2
LYKINS JOSEPH B	1LT	0-0450989	1154	2
LYLE ADRIAN B	CPT	0-1578316	1158	1
LYLE ARCY W	CW2	W-2215127	0667	1
LYLE CHARLES M	LTC	0-1581246	0762	1
LYLE CLARENCE L	LTC	0-0446262	0347	1
LYLE CLAUDE V	LTC	0-0287897	0862	1
LYLE DONALD F	CPT	0-0473182	0146	2
LYLE EMMET B	COL	0-1304753	1268	1
LYLE JAMES F	CW2	W-2148209	0461	1
LYLE JAMES M JR	MAJ	0-0260997	1264	3
LYLE JOHN T	1LT	0-0501238	0746	1
LYLE ORLANDO W	COL	0-0293004	0263	1
LYLE ROGER B	MAJ	0-0116731	1149	3
LYLES EDWARD H	MAJ	0-1186421	0264	1
LYLES FINIS J	CW3	W-2144669	0561	1
LYLES JOSEPH E	LTC	0-0163281	0246	2
LYMAN ANN S	1LT	N-0789213	1045	1
LYMAN EDWARD F	LTC	0-0212983	0362	3
LYMAN FRANK G	LTC	0-0370712	0159	2
LYMAN JOHN	LTC	0-0489048	0363	1
LYMAN JOHN F	CW2	W-2116325	0145	2
LYMAN LAUREN A	MAJ	0-1114629	0263	1
LYMAN LEW G	COL	0-0102915	1050	3
LYMAN RALPH G	MAJ	0-1186010	0464	1
LYMAN RICHARD F	LTC	0-0104159	0352	3
LYMAN WILLIAM S	LTC	0-1103768	0863	1
LYNAS JOHN W	CW3	W-2142648	0966	1
LYNCH ALBERT J	CPT	0-1107960	1046	2
LYNCH ARTHUR E	MAJ	0-1823026	0358	1
LYNCH ARTHUR W	COL	0-0262895	0967	3
LYNCH BERNARD P	LTC	0-1001179	0766	3
LYNCH CHARLES A	LTC	0-1054041	0465	1
LYNCH CHARLES E	LTC	0-0214643	0961	3
LYNCH CLARENCE R	LTC	0-0286197	0967	3
LYNCH DALLAS P	LTC	0-1101561	0761	1
LYNCH DAVID J	LTC	0-1876472	1268	1
LYNCH DAVID R	LTC	0-0205791	0757	3
LYNCH EARL	MAJ	0-0450386	0757	1
LYNCH EDGAR M JR	LTC	0-1334306	0867	1
LYNCH EDMUND B	MAJ	0-4031407	0568	1
LYNCH EDMUND T	LTC	0-1105634	0765	3
LYNCH EDWARD J	LTC	0-0917002	0547	2
LYNCH EDWARD J	COL	0-2015599	1266	3
LYNCH EMZY H	LTC	0-0200759	1155	3
LYNCH FRANCIS A	2LT	0-0502547	0344	2
LYNCH FRANCIS J	1LT	0-1016793	1044	2
LYNCH GEORGE C	1LT	0-1294685	0344	2
LYNCH GIRARD F J	2LT	0-1307044	0545	2
LYNCH GOFFREY J	LTC	0-0486986	1053	1
LYNCH GORDON C	LTC	0-0229024	0365	3
LYNCH GRAYSON L	CPT	0-0966311	1060	1
LYNCH HERBERT J	CPT	0-0900379	0347	2
LYNCH HILTON M	MAJ	0-0341748	0746	2
LYNCH JAMES A	COL	0-0361414	0266	3
LYNCH JAMES H	CPT	0-0133336	0552	3
LYNCH JAMES H	COL	0-1285258	0368	1
LYNCH JAMES M	2LT	0-1016479	0245	2
LYNCH JAMES W	MAJ	0-0977447	0962	1
LYNCH JOHN B	MAJ	0-0262109	0965	3
LYNCH JOHN C	CPT	0-0128445	0445	2
LYNCH JOHN C	CPT	0-0518894	0545	2
LYNCH JOHN E	LTC	0-0343676	0158	1
LYNCH JOHN J	MAJ	0-2208017	0466	1
LYNCH JOHN L	COL	0-0255672	1063	3
LYNCH JOHN M	CPT	0-1325226	0946	2
LYNCH JOHN M	CW4	W-2002030	1165	1
LYNCH JOHN W	MAJ	0-0348197	0846	2
LYNCH JOHN W	LTC	0-1555858	0967	3
LYNCH JOSEPH F JR	LTC	0-1576317	1061	1
LYNCH JOSEPH K	MAJ	0-0284389	1043	2
LYNCH JOSEPH P	1LT	0-1577498	0746	2
LYNCH JOSOPH E	LTC	0-0330823	0650	2
LYNCH KENNY E	LTC	0-0437852	0167	1
LYNCH LEO J	LTC	0-1546803	1265	1

NAME	GRADE	SVC NO	DATE RET MO YR	RET CODE
LYNCH LEONARD P	LTC	0-1744152	1167	1
LYNCH LEONARD F	MAJ	0-0338119	0265	3
LYNCH MAX A SR	CW3	W-2142124	0860	1
LYNCH MICHAEL J	LTC	0-0297813	0552	2
LYNCH MYRL J	LTC	0-1011402	0767	1
LYNCH PATRICK F	MAJ	0-1044597	0861	1
LYNCH PATRICK J	MAJ	0-0127403	0648	3
LYNCH PHILIP M	1LT	0-0375033	1045	2
LYNCH RAYMOND J	LTC	0-0330112	1046	2
LYNCH RICHARD P	MAJ	0-0263840	0351	1
LYNCH RUFF F	MAJ	0-1333988	0461	1
LYNCH SILAS W	MAJ	0-0494981	0854	1
LYNCH THOMAS C	MAJ	0-0959361	0863	1
LYNCH THOMAS F JR	COL	0-0240576	0264	3
LYNCH WALTER J	LTC	0-0252495	0964	3
LYNCH WAYNE F	MAJ	0-1030799	0361	1
LYNCH WILFRED T	MAJ	0-0341567	0256	3
LYNCH WILLIAM D	COL	0-0264603	0963	3
LYNCH WILLIAM J	CPT	0-0337095	1145	2
LYNCH WILLIAM J	LTC	0-2025961	0568	1
LYNCH WILLIAM J	MAJ	0-2262143	0563	1
LYNCH WILLIAM P	MAJ	0-2262564	1266	1
LYNCH WILLIAM RY	MAJ	0-0128414	0247	2
LYNCH WILLIAM S	MAJ	0-0204069	1062	3
LYNCH WOODROW	MAJ	0-1004497	0854	1
LYNCH 3RD THOMAS	CPT	0-0415063	0646	2
LYNDE FRANK T	LTC	0-0208494	0156	3
LYNES GUY B	LTC	0-0229120	0663	3
LYNES WESLEY J	MAJ	0-0366346	0746	2
LYNG LESLIE V	COL	0-0180116	0846	2
LYNN CECIL S	MAJ	0-1117482	1059	1
LYNN CUSTER L	MAJ	0-0373459	0165	3
LYNN DANIEL R JR	LTC	0-0456384	0759	1
LYNN EDWIN A	2LT	0-1170469	0345	2
LYNN ELLIS H JR	LTC	0-1297062	0161	1
LYNN HAROLD B	LTC	0-1634092	0760	1
LYNN HUGH B	CPT	0-0411649	0346	2
LYNN JACK J	LTC	0-1578775	1067	1
LYNN JAMES	LTC	0-0451039	0358	1
LYNN JAMES E	MAJ	0-0456792	0157	1
LYNN JAMES J	MAJ	0-1576318	0952	1
LYNN JOHN S	LTC	0-0300011	1168	3
LYNN JOSEPH R JR	LTC	0-1548928	0862	1
LYNN NOAH F	CPT	0-1305949	0246	2
LYNN REGINALD K	CW3	W-2149671	0568	1
LYNN ROBERT M	MAJ	0-0989759	1165	1
LYNN THOMAS U	WO1	W-2109242	0944	2
LYNN WILLIAM R	MAJ	0-0926828	0466	1
LYNN WILLIAM P	MAJ	0-0980169	0366	1
LYNNE ROBERT N	MAJ	0-0411168	0647	2
LYNSKEY JOSEPH P	COL	0-0230590	0463	3
LYNTON DALE W	MAJ	0-1875551	0966	1
LYNXWILER THOMAS L D	MAJ	0-0285628	0246	2
LYON ALBERT G	CW2	W-2214874	0766	1
LYON ARTHUR J JR	2LT	0-1012837	0145	2
LYON CHARLES A	MAJ	0-0479473	1155	1
LYON CLYDE	MAJ	0-0276069	0959	1
LYON DONALD S	LTC	0-2042739	0661	1
LYON ERNST F	CPT	0-0378704	1145	2
LYON GEORGE B	MAJ	0-0233134	1057	3
LYON GLOYD M	CPT	0-0387293	0246	2
LYON HARRY L	LTC	0-0253782	0163	3
LYON JAMES A	2LT	0-1080728	0744	2
LYON JENNINGS	1LT	0-1036609	0146	2
LYON JOHN F	CPT	0-0477716	0745	2
LYON MAX E	2LT	0-1011920	0545	2
LYON NEVEN R	MAJ	0-1951173	0663	1
LYON OLEN	LTC	0-1059538	0265	3
LYON ORVILLE Y	MAJ	0-1178233	0864	1
LYON PAUL E	LTC	0-1588134	1060	1
LYON RALPH M	MAJ	0-0221968	1262	3
LYON RICHARD J	LTC	0-0408985	1060	1
LYON ROBERT L	LTC	0-0295478	0758	3
LYON ROBERT R	CPT	0-1043411	1050	1
LYON ROSS M	LTC	0-0344849	0865	1

NAME	GRADE	SVC NO	DATE RET MO YR	RET CODE
LYON VELMA S	2LT	N-0721079	0145	1
LYON WOODY K	MAJ	0-1014959	0658	2
LYONS BERNARD A	COL	0-0252679	0446	2
LYONS CATHERINE	MAJ	N-0741679	1166	1
LYONS CECIL R	CPT	0-0380741	0350	2
LYONS CLINTON G	LTC	0-0208776	1045	3
LYONS DANIEL T	CW3	W-2148470	1162	1
LYONS DEWEY B	LTC	0-0231370	1058	3
LYONS EDWARD A	MAJ	0-2017723	0764	1
LYONS EUGENE T	LTC	0-1317247	0866	1
LYONS HAROLD A	1LT	0-1175939	0361	2
LYONS HARRY A	LTC	0-0174767	1060	3
LYONS HARRY W	LTC	0-0319392	0864	3
LYONS JAMES F JR	2LT	0-2034992	1050	2
LYONS JAMES P	CW3	W-2118103	1155	1
LYONS JAMES T	LTC	0-0219700	1146	1
LYONS JAMES V	CPT	0-0438618	1045	2
LYONS JIM R JR	2LT	0-1305279	0744	2
LYONS JOHN A	MAJ	0-1540906	0161	1
LYONS JOSEPH L	CW3	W-2150605	1262	1
LYONS KATHLEEN J	MAJ	N-0730057	0261	1
LYONS LAWRENCE B	LTC	0-1315955	0168	3
LYONS LEONARD H	LTC	0-0194480	0862	3
LYONS MICHAEL J	LTC	0-0465101	0246	2
LYONS MILTON H	LTC	0-0191453	0752	3
LYONS NELSON K	LTC	0-0158442	0257	3
LYONS OLIN F	CPT	0-2018192	0859	1
LYONS OSCAR JR	CPT	0-0976233	0261	1
LYONS PAUL R	1LT	0-1109470	0245	2
LYONS RAYMOND J	LTC	0-0216095	1058	3
LYONS ROBERT L	LTC	0-2262119	0168	1
LYONS STANLEY	LTC	0-1291144	0461	1
LYONS THOMAS G	1LT	0-0145945	0755	3
LYONS THOMAS W	1LT	0-1016110	0445	2
LYONS ULRICH S	MAJ	0-0270955	1154	3
LYONS WILLIAM J	MAJ	0-1950557	0263	1
LYSAGHT CHARLES S	CPT	0-1166550	1145	2
LYSAKOWSKI EDWARD W	MAJ	0-0980258	0263	1
LYSINGER FREDERICK	MAJ	0-0970123	1163	1
LYSNE GERALDINE	1LT	N-0788798	0346	1
LYSNE PAYNEE O	LTC	0-0439108	0563	1
LYSTAD ANDY	LTC	0-0161963	0944	2
LYTAL WILLIAM L	MAJ	0-0973843	0364	1
LYTER RICHARD K	LTC	0-1171264	0562	2
LYTLE CARL S	LTC	0-0294363	0966	3
LYTLE CHARLES B	CPT	0-1299263	0547	2
LYTLE CLEVELAND	LTC	0-0326170	0152	2
LYTLE HUGH W	LTC	0-0267219	0362	3
LYTLE JAMES K	1LT	0-1012491	0845	2
LYTLE ROBERT P	LTC	0-0262279	0865	3
LYTLE THEODORE J	LTC	0-0497664	0155	1
LYTLE WILBUR C	CPT	0-0450610	0753	2
LYTLE WILLIAM T II	1LT	0-5230150	0268	2
LYTLE WILLIAM W	MAJ	0-0324813	0945	2
LYTTLE JOSEPH F JR	CPT	0-5223378	0768	2
LYTTON JACK W	MAJ	0-0386336	0747	2
LYUBLANOVITS ERNEST	LTC	0-1559591	1163	1
MA GEE WILLIAM M	MAJ	0-1312181	0862	1
MA HANNA WILLIAM R	CPT	0-0232192	0157	3
MAAHS RALPH F	CW3	W-2145081	0963	1
MAANUM JOHN O	1LT	0-1307720	1145	2
MAAS HYMAN T	CPT	0-1894659	0545	2
MAAS PAUL O	1LT	0-1292209	0147	2
MAASS VICTOR E	CW3	W-2146912	0960	1
MABBETTE EDWIN A	MAJ	0-0321235	0462	3
MABE RODERICK D	CW4	W-2104257	0557	1
MABE WAYNE L	CW2	W-2214745	0868	1
MABEY JOSEPH G	CPT	0-0223020	0965	3
MABEY JOSEPH L JR	LTC	0-0341473	0546	2
MABILE ERNEST J	CW3	W-2145036	0461	1
MABRA FRED J	LTC	0-1284898	0868	1
MABRY AARON W	CW3	W-2141621	1157	1
MABRY BUFORD S	1LT	0-1306612	0346	2
MABRY JAMES R	CW3	W-2211670	0368	1
MABRY JOHN F	CPT	0-0373438	0545	2

NAME	GRADE	SVC NO	DATE RET MO YR	RET CODE
MABRY OLLIE B	MAJ	0-0269350	1050	3
MABJARY KENNEY C	1LT	0-2005449	1048	1
MAC ADAM DAVID A	LTC	0-0258673	0545	2
MAC ADAM FRANCIS A	LTC	0-0451452	0155	1
MAC ADAMS CHARLES W	MAJ	0-1314510	1163	1
MAC ADOFF JOHN	CPT	0-0982277	1061	1
MAC ALISTER ALEXAN	LTC	0-0113033	0855	3
MAC ALUSO ALFRED C	1LT	0-0470465	1043	2
MAC AREVEY JAMES J	LTC	0-1298766	0966	1
MAC ARTHUR ALBERT D	MAJ	0-0360062	1045	2
MAC ARTHUR FLETCHE	CPT	0-0532553	0647	2
MAC ARTHUR JAMES	CW4	W-2101195	0255	2
MAC ARTHUR JOHN J	LTC	0-1825813	0263	1
MAC ARTHUR KENNETH R	LTC	0-0274762	0367	3
MAC AULAY THOMAS M	CPT	0-4011140	0566	2
MAC BETH NORBERT A	CW3	W-2146708	0264	1
MAC BRIDE MILTON F	2LT	0-1110079	0845	2
MAC CALLUM DANIEL B	COL	0-0120094	0158	3
MAC CARONE SEBASTIAN	CW3	W-2205276	0265	1
MAC CARTHY HOWARD JR	1LT	0-0915325	0744	2
MAC CARTNEY DONALD K	CW2	W-2206194	0360	1
MAC CHLERIE GEORGE W	MAJ	0-1798025	0754	1
MAC CLAIN ALBERT L	CPT	0-0151110	1154	3
MAC CLOSKEY ROBERT W	LTC	0-0293931	0768	3
MAC COMBIE HERBERT F	COL	0-0205739	1059	3
MAC CONNELL HERBERT	1LT	0-0525297	0358	3
MAC CORD HOWARD A	COL	0-1101098	1062	1
MAC COY PAUL W	LTC	0-0206929	0850	2
MAC CREADY DAVID B	LTC	0-0145684	0749	3
MAC DERMAID ALFRED R	LTC	0-1053235	0966	1
MAC DERMID JAMES H	CPT	0-1015442	0759	1
MAC DERMOTT W V	CPT	0-0288027	0944	2
MAC DERMUT EMANUEL G	MAJ	0-1844881	0758	3
MAC DEWITT EAMON D	1LT	0-0437818	0746	2
MAC DONALD ALAN F	MAJ	0-0785700	1064	1
MAC DONALD ALBERT B	LTC	0-0973781	1068	1
MAC DONALD BERNARD H	MAJ	0-1920221	0767	1
MAC DONALD BRUCE W	MAJ	0-1329021	0365	1
MAC DONALD CATHERINE	MAJ	N-0720744	1162	3
MAC DONALD CHARLES	LTC	0-0165259	0349	3
MAC DONALD CHARLES F	1LT	0-2046521	0145	2
MAC DONALD CLARA B	MAJ	N-0759062	0165	2
MAC DONALD DANIEL A	COL	0-0422912	0262	1
MAC DONALD DANIEL P	LTC	0-1558304	0965	1
MAC DONALD DAVID J	CPT	0-1639488	0546	2
MAC DONALD DONALD E	COL	0-0120003	1158	3
MAC DONALD DONALD J	LTC	0-0262741	0767	3
MAC DONALD EDGAR C	LTC	0-0111185	0945	2
MAC DONALD ERIC D	LTC	0-0482392	0954	1
MAC DONALD FLOYD P	LTC	0-0228379	1162	3
MAC DONALD GEORGE A	CPT	0-4007149	1064	1
MAC DONALD GEORGE E	MAJ	0-0428149	0662	1
MAC DONALD GORDON A	M G	0-0193923	0359	3
MAC DONALD GORDON J	2LT	0-4052510	0157	2
MAC DONALD HAROLD	COL	0-0302344	1053	1
MAC DONALD HENRY J	MAJ	0-0520978	0554	1
MAC DONALD IRA A	CPT	0-0411177	0845	2
MAC DONALD JAMES A	MAJ	0-1104340	0756	1
MAC DONALD JAMES L	CPT	0-1702873	0146	2
MAC DONALD JAMES W	MAJ	0-1541000	0754	1
MAC DONALD JEAN E	1LT	L-0200074	0745	2
MAC DONALD JOHN A	CPT	0-2208908	0756	2
MAC DONALD JOHN D	CW2	W-2207530	0761	1
MAC DONALD JOHN N	LTC	0-0418256	0861	1
MAC DONALD JOHN W	LTC	0-0202109	1060	1
MAC DONALD MAUDE C L	1LT	N-0752153	1047	1
MAC DONALD PAUL K	M G	0-0296004	1168	3
MAC DONALD PHILIP J	MAJ	0-2018541	1168	2
MAC DONALD RALPH	COL	0-0216370	0357	3
MAC DONALD RALPH A	LTC	0-0175420	1059	3
MAC DONALD ROBERT B	1LT	0-1286317	0945	2
MAC DONALD THEODORE	LTC	0-1053706	1061	1
MAC DONALD THOMAS JR	MAJ	0-0363804	1045	2
MAC DONALD TOMMYE S	2LT	N-0765295	0947	1
MAC DONALD VINCENT A	COL	0-0314351	0759	1

NAME	GRADE	SVC NO	DATE RET MO YR	RET CODE
MAC DONALD WALLACE	COL	0-0183474	0554	3
MAC DONALD WILLIAM	MAJ	0-0294180	0344	2
MAC DONALD WILLIAM J	CW2	W-2142714	0760	1
MAC DONALD WINSTON A	CPT	0-1291490	0248	2
MAC DONELL ALAN M	LTC	0-0100867	0453	3
MAC DONELL JOHN R	CPT	0-0232807	0464	3
MAC DONNELL JAMES M	LTC	0-1559219	0767	1
MAC DONNELL RAYMOND	CPT	0-1555591	0146	2
MAC DONNELL REGINALD	COL	0-0126174	0856	3
MAC DOUGALD JOSEPH J	CW2	W-3350190	0565	1
MAC DOUGALL ANGUS W	LTC	0-0527602	0557	3
MAC DOWALL MARTHA E	CPT	N-0764082	1148	2
MAC DOWELL MATTHEW	CPT	0-0404975	0960	1
MAC DUFF DOUGLAS	COL	0-0261657	0265	3
MAC EACHERN ROBERT T	LTC	0-1796500	0361	1
MAC EWAN DONALD D	LTC	0-1575437	0168	3
MAC FADDIN JOHN W	MAJ	0-0172582	0165	3
MAC FADYEN ISABEL	CPT	N-0735720	0747	1
MAC FARLAN CHARLES W	LTC	0-0910031	1262	3
MAC FARLAN JOHN G	LTC	0-0263626	0162	3
MAC FARLAND GEORGE W	LTC	0-1327639	0263	1
MAC FARLANE EDWARD L	CPT	0-0153815	0453	3
MAC FARLANE JOHN R	MAJ	0-1688422	0361	1
MAC FARLANE RICHARD	LTC	0-0920655	0467	3
MAC FARLANE WINFIELD	LTC	0-0404596	0164	1
MAC FARLINE PAUL L	CW2	RW-2153031	1063	1
MAC FEDRIES GLADSTON	MAJ	0-0466990	0947	1
MAC GAFFICK CLYDE O	LTC	0-1574288	0954	1
MAC GEER DURWARD	1LT	0-0364696	0650	2
MAC GILL ALLEN J III	LTC	0-0371979	0463	1
MAC GILL ROBERT R	CPT	0-2040956	1146	2
MAC GILLIVRAY RAYNOR	MAJ	0-1946792	1165	1
MAC GRATH DONALD A	COL	0-0260431	0965	1
MAC GREGER DONALD L	COL	0-0174838	0162	3
MAC GREGOR ALAN A	LTC	0-0375064	0267	1
MAC GREGOR CHARLES W	CW2	W-2152852	1060	2
MAC GREGOR ROBERT T	CPT	0-1308980	0948	2
MAC GREGOR WALLACE D	LTC	0-0566117	0661	1
MAC GUIRE EUGENE B	CPT	0-1115947	0962	1
MAC HOTT HYMAN E	MAJ	0-1054316	0264	2
MAC HUGH ROBERT E	LTC	0-1324346	0867	1
MAC INNES MARION K	1LT	N-0720124	0646	1
MAC INNES ROY F	CW3	W-2205302	0965	1
MAC INNIS KENNETH D	1LT	0-1323589	0447	2
MAC INTIRE SAMUEL C	COL	0-0218549	0850	3
MAC INTOSH JOHN M JR	CPT	0-5230198	0468	2
MAC INTOSH RICHARD N	LTC	0-0548221	0663	1
MAC INTYRE JOHN K	LTC	0-0330663	0860	1
MAC INTYRE NORMAN J	CW2	W-2146036	1158	1
MAC INTYRE ROBERT S	1LT	0-1286155	0544	2
MAC ISAAC CHARLES F	LTC	0-0430446	0561	1
MAC IVOR ALEXANDER	1LT	0-1324034	0945	2
MAC IVOR DONALD I	MAJ	0-1685667	0564	1
MAC KAIG KENNETH R	MAJ	0-0300822	0168	3
MAC KAY ALBERT A	MAJ	0-0267112	0164	3
MAC KAY DONALD K	LTC	0-0338741	0965	3
MAC KAY FRANCIS E	CW3	W-2147498	0259	1
MAC KAY JOSEPH J JR	COL	0-0229074	0464	3
MAC KAY STCLAIR C	MAJ	0-0903491	0245	2
MAC KAY WILLIAM C	LTC	0-0235786	0362	3
MAC KELLAR ROBERT S	LTC	0-0250948	0864	3
MAC KENDREE MOFFATT	CW3	W-2144717	0565	1
MAC KENZIE FREDERICK	CPT	0-0155991	0859	3
MAC KENZIE HOWARD A	LTC	0-0236565	0463	3
MAC KENZIE JOHN H	MAJ	0-0444630	0548	1
MAC KENZIE KEITH M	COL	0-0397911	1263	1
MAC KENZIE RODERICK	LTC	0-1281204	0268	3
MAC KENZIE THOMAS T	LTC	0-0226278	0662	3
MAC KIEWICZ W S	CPT	0-0490466	0445	2
MAC KINNON RALPH H	MAJ	0-0273723	0668	3
MAC KINNON WILLIAM G	COL	0-0235018	1165	3
MAC LACHLAN WILLIAM	1LT	0-1558050	1265	2
MAC LAFFERTY JAMES W	LTC	0-0234288	0965	3
MAC LAIN FRANK H	LTC	0-0372272	0368	3
MAC LAIRD KENNETH A	CW2	W-2104259	0147	1

NAME	GRADE	SVC NO	DATE RET MO YR	RET CODE
MAC LAREN HORACE E	LTC	0-0305081	0965	1
MAC LAREN WILLIAM R	LTC	0-0100262	0157	1
MAC LAUGHLIN M C	LTC	0-0330995	0760	2
MAC LAUGHLIN MILLA	LTC	0-0125094	0556	3
MAC LEAN KENNETH J	1LT	0-1913350	1052	2
MAC LEAN WALLACE K	MAJ	0-1582737	0465	1
MAC LEAY FRANCIS R	2LT	0-1166318	0545	2
MAC LEAY RICHARD J	LTC	0-0920265	1262	3
MAC LELLAN ROBERT W	LTC	0-1287730	1161	1
MAC LENNAN JAMES F	LTC	0-0344875	0767	3
MAC LENNAN NINA M	2LT	N-0754286	0646	1
MAC LEOD COLIN G	LTC	0-0275354	1052	3
MAC LEOD DAVID G	LTC	0-0548139	0967	3
MAC LEOD GREGOR A	LTC	0-0305452	1063	1
MAC LEOD RALPH E	COL	0-0128748	0549	3
MAC LEOD ROBERT H	LTC	0-1822031	0462	1
MAC LEOD ROSS	CPT	0-0218054	0948	2
MAC LEOD WALLACE W	LTC	0-1104977	0961	1
MAC LEOD WILFRID A	COL	0-0238681	1163	3
MAC MANNIS HENRY B	CPT	0-0181818	0760	3
MAC MASTER ARTHUR W	MAJ	0-1101935	0263	1
MAC MASTER DONALD H	MAJ	0-0278575	0344	2
MAC MASTER LYLE S	MAJ	0-0242855	0755	3
MAC MILLAN ANDREW R	LTC	0-0234499	1060	3
MAC MILLAN CATHERINE	MAJ	N-0759088	0665	1
MAC MILLAN EDWARD A	COL	0-0133426	0253	3
MAC MILLAN JOHN M	1LT	0-1001842	1045	2
MAC MILLAN MILDRED	1LT	N-0736078	0546	1
MAC MILLEN HESPER N	MAJ	0-0290923	0446	2
MAC MINN DAVID E JR	CW2	W-2148573	0959	1
MAC MURRAUGH ARTHUR	LTC	0-0250508	0664	3
MAC NAB DONALD H	LTC	0-0282944	0765	3
MAC NAB MARION L	1LT	N-0759022	0346	1
MAC NABB BARBARA A	2LT	N-0700200	0236	1
MAC NAMARA JAMES	CPT	0-0356943	0645	2
MAC NAMARA MAURICE E	MAJ	0-1010322	0261	1
MAC NAUGHTON HENRY D	MAJ	0-0322479	0849	3
MAC NEAL ROBERT C	CPT	0-0496060	1045	2
MAC NEIL EDMUND L	CW2	W-2126792	1060	1
MAC NEIL MARK K	MAJ	0-1043711	0960	1
MAC NEIL ROBERT E	CPT	0-4030986	1165	1
MAC NEILL JOHN P	COL	0-0172680	0255	2
MAC NEILL NEIL M	LTC	0-0103911	1149	3
MAC NEILL RALPH M JR	CW3	W-2146559	0365	1
MAC NICOL ALLAN E	COL	0-0117668	0855	3
MAC NICOL HELEN V	MAJ	N-0742650	1268	2
MAC NICOL JAMES J	LTC	0-1592397	1164	1
MAC PHEE KATHERINE	MAJ	N-0783054	0363	1
MAC PHERSON ROBERT H	COL	0-1280231	0165	1
MAC PHERSON WILLIAM	1LT	0-0298406	0156	3
MAC PHETRIDGE EDWARD	1LT	0-1309288	0845	2
MAC QUEEN GEORGE E	COL	0-0365477	1165	1
MAC QUEENEY PATRIC	COL	0-0176532	0552	3
MAC QUIDDY HARROLD H	CPT	0-0451067	0545	2
MAC RAE COLIN D	COL	0-0205981	0658	3
MAC RAE GORDON C	COL	0-0289117	0658	3
MAC RAE JOHN C	MAJ	0-0192198	0959	3
MAC SLARROW JACK A	LTC	0-1823029	0264	1
MAC VANE GLENN F	CW2	W-2210232	1062	1
MAC VEAN JAMES M	LTC	0-0205185	0363	3
MAC VICAR NORMAN	MAJ	0-1287033	0954	1
MAC WILLIAMS JOHN D	CPT	0-1116239	0960	1
MACALI CHARLES M	MAJ	0-1639334	0358	1
MACARTNEY CLEMENT D	CPT	0-1185339	0164	1
MACATANGAY JUAN T	1LT	0-1896725	0854	1
MACATEE WALTER F	LTC	0-1104975	0463	1
MACAULAY EDWARD L	COL	0-0114166	0352	3
MACAULEY IRVING P JR	1LT	0-0517383	0247	2
MACCARONE LIDRE	CPT	0-1799326	0858	1
MACCHIA JOHN J	1LT	0-1167523	0844	2
MACCOUL MELVIN	LTC	0-0520645	0554	1
MACDONALD PETER F	CPT	0-0461187	1046	2
MACDONALD ROBIN W	CPT	0-0461258	0849	2
MACE EUGENE E	CW3	W-2145567	0263	1
MACE GEORGE L	CPT	0-1895016	0457	1

NAME	GRADE	SVC NO	DATE RET MO YR	RET CODE
MACE HERMAN A	LTC	0-0888952	1163	1
MACE JOHN W	MAJ	0-0976219	0562	1
MACE ROBERT H	CPT	0-1286518	0348	2
MACE WILLIAM E	LTC	0-1062238	0866	1
MACE WILLIAM M	CPT	0-2262319	1160	1
MACELLARO GOLDIE L	MAJ	N-0795837	0266	3
MACERA RAYMOND A	MAJ	0-1925202	0264	1
MACEWICZ JOHN G	MAJ	0-0452207	0959	1
MACEY ALLEN C	CW2	W-3150811	0363	1
MACEYAK MICHAEL A	CW3	W-2145646	1263	1
MACGREGOR ARTHUR S	CPT	0-0131802	1051	3
MACHAMER WALDON K	2LT	0-2024273	0346	2
MACHAN HERBERT P	MAJ	0-0194654	0462	3
MACHANN JOSEPH A	MAJ	0-0280995	0760	1
MACHATE JOSEPH V	MAJ	0-1105637	0761	1
MACHEN HENRY B	LTC	0-0271197	1068	3
MACHIK JOHN H	MAJ	0-1552737	0463	1
MACHLE EDWARD P	LTC	0-0163362	0761	3
MACIEL FRANK H	2LT	0-1172154	0545	2
MACK ALONZO E	CPT	0-0460900	1265	2
MACK EDWARD B	MAJ	0-1166551	0663	1
MACK FRANCIS M	COL	0-0100623	0648	3
MACK FREDERICK	1LT	0-0514310	0246	2
MACK FREDERICK	CPT	0-0515323	0249	1
MACK GEORGE L JR	MAJ	0-0984131	0266	1
MACK GERALD C	LTC	0-0543633	0966	1
MACK HENRY D	MAJ	0-0112087	0648	3
MACK JAMES E	MAJ	0-1112831	0763	1
MACK JAMES M	1LT	0-5426526	0868	2
MACK JOHN D	CPT	0-0502035	0849	1
MACK JOSEPH J	COL	0-0297562	0362	3
MACK KENNETH R	MAJ	0-0285644	0944	2
MACK LAWRENCE G	CPT	0-0353270	0945	2
MACK LOUIS J	LTC	0-1289291	0164	1
MACK THOMAS E	LTC	0-0256825	0254	3
MACK THOMAS F JR	MAJ	0-0450747	0557	1
MACK VINCENT H	LTC	0-0990121	0764	1
MACK WALTER R JR	1LT	0-1301333	0645	2
MACK WARREN J	MAJ	0-2033159	1262	1
MACKAY BENTLEY B JR	MAJ	0-1290624	1060	1
MACKAY HOWARD D	MAJ	0-1648016	0560	1
MACKEL JOHN J	MAJ	0-0453839	1158	1
MACKENZIE GORDON S	LTC	0-1116930	0163	1
MACKENZIE IAN J	CPT	0-0750148	0445	2
MACKENZIE WILLIAM	MAJ	0-0126096	0356	3
MACKENZIE WILLIAM	CW3	W-2152680	0663	1
MACKERT JOHN H	LTC	0-0233158	0954	3
MACKEY BENJAMIN E	CPT	0-2263149	0761	1
MACKEY CATHLEEN M	2LT	N-0757624	0345	1
MACKEY CHARLES	CPT	0-1184884	0256	1
MACKEY CLARENCE H SR	COL	0-0298050	0264	1
MACKEY CLARENCE JR	CPT	0-0461555	1146	2
MACKEY CURTIS T	LTC	0-1876612	1268	1
MACKEY EDWARD J	COL	0-0385900	1167	3
MACKEY FRANCIS L	CW4	W-2106433	0366	1
MACKEY HAROLD M	CW4	W-2145998	1168	1
MACKEY JACK B	2LT	0-1300993	1044	2
MACKEY JAMES G	COL	0-0282291	0159	3
MACKEY JOHN J	MAJ	0-0328443	1262	3
MACKEY MARY J	1LT	N-0729734	0947	1
MACKEY PARKER JR	LTC	0-1324106	0768	1
MACKEY PATRICK D	CW3	W-2151822	0463	1
MACKEY PATRICK J	MAJ	0-0982151	0564	1
MACKEY PAUL N	1LT	0-0499939	0853	1
MACKEY WALLACE B	WO1	W-2105784	0645	2
MACKEY WILLIAM B	LTC	0-0374521	0167	3
MACKIE ARTHUR	MAJ	0-1996545	0157	1
MACKIE FRED W	LTC	0-0248610	1166	3
MACKIE JAMES	WO1	W-2109627	1046	1
MACKIE WALTER H	LTC	0-1546675	0963	1
MACKIN HUGH F	LTC	0-0252985	0166	3
MACKIN JOHN P	MAJ	0-2037262	1062	1
MACKINNON GEORGE L	MAJ	0-1492443	0345	2
MACKINTOSH CHARLES D	LTC	0-0110143	0958	3
MACKINTOSH DONALD	CPT	0-0375265	0247	2

NAME	GRADE	SVC NO	DATE RET MO YR	RET CODE
MACKINTOSH HOWARD D	MAJ	0-0504937	0654	1
MACKLEY EVERETT J	MAJ	0-2262846	0463	1
MACKLIN JOHN C	2LT	0-1914205	1047	1
MACKLIN THOMAS P	LTC	0-0506108	1057	1
MACKLIN WILLIAM	CPT	0-0524208	0849	1
MACKLINO PETRA	2LT	N-0731595	0746	1
MACKMILL GOLDEN	MAJ	0-1696086	1045	2
MACKO JOSEPH J	MAJ	0-1048083	0860	1
MACKOFF ABE	1LT	0-0230656	0263	3
MACKOFF CHARLES H	COL	0-0309985	0868	3
MACKSON CHESTER J	CPT	0-0540872	0947	2
MACLACHLAN CLIFTON E	MAJ	0-2000435	0656	1
MACNAK JOSEPH A	MAJ	0-1041607	0447	2
MACNAMARA HOMER P	COL	0-0278625	1249	3
MACNEILL ARTHUR E	MAJ	0-0419624	1044	2
MACOMBER DOROTHY M	2LT	N-0743849	0445	1
MACOMBER FREEMAN G	COL	0-0362090	0261	3
MACON DAVID	LTC	0-0225169	0363	1
MACON WILLIE B	MAJ	0-1592398	0261	1
MACRI JAMES F	LTC	0-1058882	1163	1
MACSPADDEN ARNOLD	LTC	0-0900583	1044	2
MACWETHY RAYMOND E	2LT	0-1289602	1143	2
MACY GERALD A	CPT	0-1289451	0746	2
MACY HAROLD	COL	0-0165308	0155	3
MACY JOSIAH N	COL	0-0275505	0161	3
MACY MELVIN C	COL	0-0405816	0463	1
MACY ROBERT S	MAJ	0-0978063	1268	1
MACY RUSSELL E	MAJ	0-1794824	0568	3
MACY SAMUEL C	CPT	0-0350854	0347	2
MADARA GUY H	LTC	0-0207410	0648	3
MADARY CHARLES R	LTC	0-0389947	1146	2
MADDEN CHARLIE A	MAJ	0-0371370	0447	2
MADDEN DAVID G	CW2	W-2146517	0566	1
MADDEN EDWARD A	COL	0-0179529	0147	2
MADDEN FRANCIS P	LTC	0-0903912	1063	1
MADDEN FRED	CPT	0-1168791	0346	2
MADDEN GRAHAM R	LTC	0-1015290	0463	1
MADDEN JAMES A	MAJ	0-0887329	1057	1
MADDEN JEROME P	1LT	0-1169224	0145	2
MADDEN JOHN B	COL	0-0145779	1052	3
MADDEN JOHN C	MAJ	0-1039501	0865	1
MADDEN JOHN J	LTC	0-0334417	0660	1
MADDEN JOHN W	CW2	W-2151503	1060	1
MADDEN JOSEPH P	LTC	0-0124091	0355	3
MADDEN LOUIS R	CW3	W-2148296	0559	1
MADDEN MARIETTA H	LTC	N-0759962	0767	3
MADDEN MARY J	MAJ	N-0759068	0263	1
MADDEN PAUL H	MAJ	0-2021232	0865	1
MADDEN PETER A	LTC	0-1306868	0968	2
MADDEN THOMAS C SR	2LT	0-1825630	0145	2
MADDEN THOMAS E	MAJ	0-0505940	0147	2
MADDEN THOMAS H	LTC	0-0266326	0246	2
MADDEN THOMAS J	2LT	0-1316700	0544	2
MADDEN THOMAS J	CW4	W-2000611	0765	3
MADDEN WALTER E	1LT	0-1311025	0146	2
MADDEN WILLSON R	MAJ	0-0503279	0854	1
MADDOCK RUTH M	MAJ	N-0795477	0665	1
MADDOCK THEODORE R	LTC	0-1103774	0163	1
MADDOCKS EARLE F	LTC	0-0424809	0563	1
MADDOX ALFRED E	MAJ	0-4010856	0967	1
MADDOX ANDREW A	CW2	W-2148605	0462	1
MADDOX CHARLES W	CPT	0-0475016	0550	1
MADDOX EDWARD W	MAJ	0-0440773	0947	1
MADDOX ELVIS V	MAJ	0-1543735	1163	1
MADDOX JAMES R	1LT	0-0507236	0949	1
MADDOX JOHN B	LTC	0-0213395	1061	3
MADDOX JOHN C	LTC	0-0484286	0554	1
MADDOX JOHN W	MAJ	0-0211106	0849	3
MADDOX JOHN W	2LT	0-1311097	0645	2
MADDOX LINDSEY A	MAJ	0-0401932	0446	2
MADDOX LUTHER R	COL	0-0111176	0648	3
MADDOX RANDOLPH R	CW3	W-2208636	0568	1
MADDOX WARNER V	COL	0-0271267	1166	3
MADDOX WILLIAM A	LTC	0-0239416	0864	3
MADDREY WILLIAM G	CW4	W-2141784	0761	1

NAME	GRADE	SVC NO	DATE RET MO YR	RET CODE
MADORY JOHN A	CPT	0-1941346	0466	1
MADDOX GERARD F	LTC	0-1576324	0454	1
MADDUX MILTON R	COL	0-0242020	0761	3
MADDY IRVIN S	LTC	0-0370138	0467	3
MADEAU JOSEPH I	CW3	W-2149355	0957	1
MADEIRA WARD A JR	1LT	0-1318199	0645	2
MADEN WILLIAM B	CW4	W-2102031	0354	1
MADER EDWARD B	LTC	0-0534747	0267	3
MADIAS DAVID	CW4	W-2102032	0664	1
MADIGAN DONALD L	COL	0-0335480	0646	2
MADIGAN JOHN J	COL	0-0117351	1252	3
MADIGAN JOHN J	CW2	W-2122902	0546	2
MADIGAN SID G	CPT	0-1044883	0552	2
MADIGAN THOMAS J JR	LTC	0-1574988	0661	1
MADISON ALFRED P	CPT	0-0263596	0647	1
MADISON CLAUDE O	MAJ	0-1582442	0858	2
MADISON CLEMENT C	CW3	W-2141968	1060	1
MADISON DALLAS E	MAJ	0-1118936	0166	2
MADISON DOROTHY E	MAJ	N-0734359	1161	1
MADISON EUGENE H	CPT	0-2263651	0263	1
MADISON FRANCES M	MAJ	N-0736802	1161	1
MADISON GILBERT C	LTC	0-0343941	1154	1
MADISON GUY	CW3	W-2148745	0764	1
MADISON HERBERT L	WO1	W-2200006	0767	1
MADISON JAMES R	MAJ	0-1824645	0160	1
MADISON LEO H	MAJ	0-1286319	0155	1
MADISON MARION L	LTC	0-0283452	0368	3
MADISON MAURICE N	CPT	0-1112833	0960	1
MADISON MELVIN L	1LT	0-0491531	0654	1
MADISON ROBERT E	MAJ	0-2081516	1065	1
MADISON STANLEY	CPT	0-1104301	0660	1
MADISON TAYLOR G	CW4	W-2152420	0168	2
MADISON TROY E	LTC	0-1172155	0263	1
MADISON WILLIAM H	CW3	W-2153119	1061	1
MADISON WILLIAM W	LTC	0-1173364	0261	1
MADOKORO SHIGESHI	LTC	0-1331965	0861	1
MADONIA PETER P	MAJ	0-1553505	0459	1
MADRUGA ROBERT	LTC	0-1703071	0368	1
MADSEN EARL A	COL	0-0271688	0466	3
MADSEN EMIL	LTC	0-0288440	0767	3
MADSEN GEORGE R	1LT	0-1553305	0746	2
MADSEN HAROLD M	LTC	0-0219897	0164	3
MADSEN JAMES F	MAJ	0-1688759	1065	1
MADSEN LEO H	MAJ	0-2048062	0661	1
MADSEN OWEN M SR	LTC	0-2053986	1055	1
MADSON NORRIS C	LTC	0-1644549	0361	1
MADZELAN VASIL JR	MAJ	0-1824053	0661	1
MAEGERLEIN MARY J	MAJ	N-0728416	0568	1
MAEKAWA GEORGE	CW2	W-2210899	0566	1
MAERZ FREDERICK	CPT	0-2262757	0361	1
MAES ANDREW J	LTC	0-0488459	1060	3
MAES ROBERT W	MAJ	0-0969255	0263	1
MAESER ARTHUR F	LTC	0-1543419	0367	2
MAFFEO PASQUALE E	1LT	0-1319759	1046	2
MAFFETT CHARLES R	LTC	0-0446325	1065	1
MAFFETT WALLACE G	2LT	0-1299439	0445	2
MAGADIEU WALTER J	COL	0-0237277	0157	3
MAGALOTTI MARION F	CPT	0-0464470	0846	2
MAGARIAN ARAM	MAJ	0-1595669	0665	1
MAGARIAN HAROLD J	MAJ	0-1824208	0860	1
MAGARIAN OSCAR K	LTC	0-0504309	1165	3
MAGAURN ELTON L	LTC	0-1999877	0166	1
MAGAZIN GEORGE A	CW3	W-2143443	0365	1
MAGOITS EDWARD A	CPT	0-1058884	0747	2
MAGOLEN ROBERT J	COL	0-0499478	0568	3
MAGE SIGMUND	LTC	0-0486525	0446	2
MAGEE DUDLEY E	MAJ	0-0272085	0344	2
MAGEE GEORGE R	CPT	0-0910277	0245	2
MAGEE HAROLD J	LTC	0-1585801	0661	1
MAGEE JEWEL L	CW4	W-2151507	0665	1
MAGEE JOHN A	LTC	0-0222776	0859	3
MAGEE LILLIAN E	1LT	N-0721558	0846	1
MAGEE LUTHER D	2LT	0-1172157	0145	2
MAGEE ROBERT D	MAJ	0-2048063	0161	1
MAGEE ROBERT E	LTC	0-1339551	0766	1

NAME	GRADE	SVC NO	DATE RET MO YR	RET CODE
MAGEE ROBERT F	CPT	0-0487954	0246	2
MAGEE ROBERT W	MAJ	0-1799876	0163	1
MAGEE THEODORE F	COL	0-1292550	1162	1
MAGEE VERNON L R	LTC	0-1555426	0867	1
MAGEE VICTOR F	MAJ	0-1016041	0966	1
MAGEE WILLIAM G	CPT	0-0346091	0944	2
MAGEE WILLIAM L	MAJ	0-1646384	0161	2
MAGENOT FRED K	LTC	0-0323619	0153	2
MAGENS HANS J	LTC	0-0197728	0553	3
MAGERS FRANK J	COL	0-0503870	0847	1
MAGERS FREDERICK	LTC	0-0297411	0560	1
MAGERS JESSE E	MAJ	0-1290274	1060	1
MAGGIORE MICHAEL J	LTC	0-0345616	0364	3
MAGID ALLAN	LTC	0-0229372	1044	2
MAGIDOVITCH AVSHALOM	MAJ	0-0980320	0468	2
MAGILL GEORGE W	LTC	0-1292727	0167	1
MAGILL HUGH B JR	COL	0-0339466	0868	3
MAGILL SAMUEL W	LTC	0-1297913	0168	1
MAGILL THOMAS C	MAJ	0-1047645	1162	1
MAGILL WALTER B	LTC	0-0359272	0666	1
MAGIN RALPH G	CPT	0-1945419	1045	2
MAGINNIS PATRICK C	LTC	0-0313745	0367	3
MAGLIO DENNIS C	1LT	0-0245905	0157	3
MAGLIO FRANK R JR	LTC	0-1012063	0767	3
MAGLIONE FRANK D	CPT	0-0970819	0758	2
MAGNAN JOSEPH P	CPT	0-0961626	1058	1
MAGNER GEORGE J	LTC	0-1256874	0765	1
MAGNES MAX	COL	0-0285213	1162	3
MAGNESS GUY N	COL	0-0251187	1059	3
MAGNUS CLARENCE A	CPT	0-0268110	0847	2
MAGNUSEN LEWIS C	COL	0-0305535	1067	3
MAGNUSON GOSTA R	1LT	0-0525989	0944	2
MAGNUSON OSCAR W	MAJ	0-0236948	0264	3
MAGNUSON RICHARD	CW3	W-2144997	0858	1
MAGRI MICHAEL	LTC	0-1182905	0562	2
MAGRUDER ALFRED L	MAJ	0-2027534	0261	1
MAGRUDER HERBERT E	LTC	0-0450609	1058	1
MAGRUDER JERREL E	CPT	0-1290781	0153	1
MAGRUDER ROGER G	COL	0-0349145	0866	3
MAGRUDER VIRGIL E	MAJ	0-1043719	0761	1
MAGUE ALICE I	CW4	V-1001672	1264	1
MAGUFFEE BOBBY L	CW2	W-2211899	0167	1
MAGUIRE ANNA R	1LT	N-0725551	0947	1
MAGUIRE FRANK J	LTC	0-0252360	1266	3
MAGUIRE FRANK J	CPT	0-2263046	0861	1
MAGUIRE GEORGE T	LTC	0-0526336	0949	2
MAGUIRE JAMES C	LTC	0-0363686	1059	1
MAGUIRE JAMES F	CPT	0-1299597	0266	2
MAGUIRE JOHN A	1LT	0-1295046	0454	1
MAGUIRE JOSEPH T	LTC	0-1054047	0168	1
MAGUIRE ROBERT R	MAJ	0-0976884	0664	1
MAGUIRE THOMAS	LTC	0-0284541	0858	2
MAGUIRE WILLIAM E	CPT	0-0297017	1044	2
MAGYAR CHARLES C	CPT	0-1307266	0463	1
MAGYAR STEPHEN J	WO1	W-2123610	1045	2
MAHADY FRANCIS L	LTC	0-0221527	0462	3
MAHADY STEPHEN C	CPT	0-0510401	0645	2
MAHALEY WALTER C	LTC	0-1100210	0760	1
MAHAN BERTHA M P	1LT	N-0783135	0845	1
MAHAN CHARLES F	MAJ	0-0451477	0856	1
MAHAN DAVID V	1LT	0-0438674	0346	2
MAHAN FRANCIS E	CW3	W-2143943	0862	2
MAHAN FRANCIS L	LTC	0-1287378	0666	1
MAHAN GUY S	LTC	0-0251321	0165	3
MAHAN JOHN J	MAJ	0-1947147	0960	1
MAHAN LORENZO B	MAJ	0-1114220	1064	1
MAHAN MILLARD	LTC	0-0453846	0959	1
MAHAN SARAH R	MAJ	N-0802141	0768	1
MAHAN TALLMAN J	LTC	0-1108824	0462	1
MAHAN THOMAS L	CPT	0-1032726	0647	2
MAHANEY CHARLES E	LTC	0-0255940	1059	1
MAHAR EDNA L	LTC	N-0700175	0346	1
MAHAR EDWARD F	1LT	0-1302097	0346	2
MAHAR HAROLD W	CPT	0-1332616	1053	2
MAHAR THOMAS B	CW3	W-2141969	1161	2

NAME	GRADE	SVC NO	DATE RET MO YR	RET CODE
MAHER EDMUND A	LTC	0-0173027	0860	3
MAHER EDWARD A	LTC	0-0299589	0763	3
MAHER EDWARD B	1LT	0-0499826	0754	1
MAHER EDWARD J	CPT	0-1285455	0745	2
MAHER JOHN F	MAJ	0-1693125	1263	1
MAHER JOHN L	1LT	0-1288767	0745	2
MAHER JOHN M	MAJ	0-0541637	1047	2
MAHER RAYMOND W	LTC	0-0451148	1159	1
MAHER THOMAS D	LTC	0-0147553	0854	3
MAHER WALTER G	LTC	0-0396862	0660	1
MAHER WILLIAM J	2LT	0-0507467	1144	2
MAHIKOA AINSLEY K	LTC	0-0315400	0561	1
MAHL HUGH B	LTC	0-1688700	1268	1
MAHLE GERALD E SR	1LT	0-1799465	0559	1
MAHLER ARTHUR I	LTC	0-1547764	0765	1
MAHLER ERIC	MAJ	0-0466085	0648	1
MAHN FREDERICK	MAJ	0-1339075	0263	1
MAHOLTZ JOSEPH A	CW3	W-2132664	0956	1
MAHON BOYD B JR	1LT	0-1179940	1045	2
MAHON GEORGE S	MAJ	0-0468133	0346	2
MAHON JAMES B	CPT	0-1015964	1146	2
MAHON RUSSELL P	MAJ	0-1046545	0955	1
MAHONEY ARTHUR V	CW2	W-2148626	0357	1
MAHONEY BEULAH L	MAJ	N-0734167	0165	3
MAHONEY CATHERINE	LTC	N-0724674	0466	2
MAHONEY DANIEL J	LTC	0-0497990	1053	2
MAHONEY ELBERT W	CPT	0-0279042	1046	2
MAHONEY FRANCIS M	MAJ	0-1051270	0361	1
MAHONEY HAROLD J	LTC	0-0404372	0765	3
MAHONEY HARRY J	MAJ	0-0963254	0563	1
MAHONEY JAMES O	2LT	0-2012596	0746	2
MAHONEY JAMES P	LTC	0-0297477	0666	3
MAHONEY JOHN J	1LT	0-0507705	0663	1
MAHONEY JOHN P	MAJ	0-0415906	0146	2
MAHONEY JOSEPH P	COL	0-0412269	0468	3
MAHONEY MICHAEL E	CPT	0-1304755	1146	2
MAHONEY MURIEL D	1LT	N-0752117	0546	1
MAHONEY ROBERT B	WO1	W-2113943	0145	2
MAHONEY ROSEMARY M	1LT	N-0703702	0645	1
MAHONEY WILLIAM J	LTC	0-0455389	0764	1
MAHONY EDWARD F	1LT	0-1325585	0646	2
MAHONY JOHN W	COL	0-1639521	1267	1
MAHOOD FRANK C	COL	0-0250618	0567	3
MAHORIC FRANK	CW3	W-2207065	0465	1
MAHURIN KENNETH R	1LT	0-1651547	1048	2
MAIDEN BENJAMIN O JR	LTC	0-0348092	0662	1
MAIER FREDERICK	COL	0-0128549	0256	3
MAIER FREDERICK	LTC	0-0210833	0358	3
MAIER HEMO F	1LT	0-1324035	104N	2
MAIER JOHN G	CW2	W-2120127	1055	1
MAIER JOHN L	CPT	0-0419908	0946	2
MAIERS CLARENCE H	CPT	0-1590627	0864	2
MAILE BONIFACE	1LT	0-0911268	1144	2
MAILLARD CHARLES A	1LT	0-0420780	1145	2
MAIN CHARLES E	COL	0-0149442	1057	3
MAIN DONALD G	1LT	0-1327640	0346	2
MAIN GEORGE F	COL	0-0273533	0968	3
MAIN LESLIE J	1LT	0-1287556	0845	2
MAINAR BRUNO	1LT	0-1897031	0565	1
MAINAR JOSEPH O	2LT	0-1896468	0862	1
MAINES ALVIN R	CW2	W-2143645	0656	1
MAINES ARTHUR L	CW4	W-2003463	0768	3
MAINORD HUGH I	COL	0-0109066	0955	3
MAINS CHARLES H	CPT	0-1312183	0147	2
MAINS JESSIE R	1LT	N-0736525	1146	1
MAINS JOHN R	MAJ	0-1310283	0264	1
MAINS PAUL G	LTC	0-0222584	0863	3
MAINS PAUL H	MAJ	0-1556756	0960	1
MAINS WILLIAM O	CPT	0-0406951	1044	2
MAINZ FRANCIS	LTC	0-0253762	1053	1
MAINZER FRANCIS S	LTC	0-0228135	1058	3
MAIORANA JOHN A	LTC	0-1826212	1264	1
MAIRE ROMAN W	MAJ	0-1168795	0258	1
MAISCH WILLIAM	LTC	0-0241426	0652	3
MAISEL FREDERICK	MAJ	0-0418335	1047	2

NAME	GRADE	SVC NO	DATE RET MO YR	RET CODE
MAISENBACHER LEROY A	LTC	0-1824209	1266	1
MAISER CARL J	LTC	0-1322799	0262	1
MAISON HAROLD G	M G	0-0141515	0757	3
MAITEN SAMUEL J	1LT	0-1557323	0346	2
MAITLAND DAVID S	MAJ	0-0244148	0564	3
MAITLAND STEPHEN A	MAJ	0-2262328	0861	1
MAITLAND THOMAS F	LTC	0-0996384	0861	1
MAITLAND WILLIAM F	CPT	0-1081661	0247	2
MAIZE CLYDE H	COL	0-0225987	0565	3
MAIZE LLOYD H	CW2	W-2150996	0959	1
MAIZE WILLIAM	LTC	0-1289453	0461	1
MAJANE WILFRED C	1LT	0-1301508	1044	2
MAJERIC CHARLES	MAJ	0-0507540	0455	2
MAJEWSKI ALEXANDER	1LT	0-1010727	0744	2
MAJOR CLARENCE E	CPT	0-1292026	0146	2
MAJOR ELWOOD P	MAJ	0-0234910	0755	3
MAJOR FERDINAND	COL	0-0194491	1262	3
MAJOR RALPH B	LTC	0-0236300	0460	1
MAJOR RALPH H	LTC	0-0264238	1055	3
MAJOR TERRANCE A	MAJ	0-2006488	0957	1
MAJOR THOMAS H	LTC	0-1299442	0162	1
MAJOR THOMAS W	MAJ	0-1633386	0555	1
MAJORAS MICHAEL J	MAJ	0-2010386	1162	1
MAJORS ALLEN B	MAJ	0-1894436	0657	1
MAJORS GRADY C	LTC	0-1184988	0766	1
MAJORS N A	MAJ	0-1322753	0260	1
MAJORS WEBSTER B	LTC	0-0290523	0556	3
MAJURE ERNEST D	COL	0-0321066	0264	3
MAKAR WALTER V	LTC	0-1163796	0462	1
MAKAREVICH ANDREW J	1LT	0-1049968	0945	2
MAKELA POMONA K	MAJ	N-0744234	1267	3
MAKEPEACE RALPH C	MAJ	0-1052463	0368	1
MAKER NAJMI N	2LT	N-0734011	1044	1
MAKHOLM ARTHUR F	LTC	0-1109479	0767	1
MAKI AUGIE	MAJ	0-1639524	1157	1
MAKI ELMER R	LTC	0-1048983	1062	1
MAKIN GRAHAM	MAJ	0-1595877	1262	1
MAKOWSKI LEONARD D	MAJ	0-1016020	0262	1
MAKOWSKI RICHARD J	CW2	W-2214906	1166	1
MAKRIS JAMES C	CPT	0-0973820	0958	2
MAKUCH WALTER S	LTC	0-1174944	0367	1
MALABED MAURICIO E	1LT	0-2032116	0851	1
MALACH MONTE	1LT	0-1917320	0754	2
MALACHOWSKI STANLEY	MAJ	0-0230348	0748	1
MALAMBRI WILLIAM F	CW3	W-2203356	0164	1
MALAN KENNETT H	MAJ	0-0311297	0844	2
MALANCA FRANCIS X	1LT	0-0501611	1043	2
MALANGA ANGELO P	CW4	W-2143304	0259	1
MALARKEY LEO L	1LT	0-0526058	0744	2
MALATESTA STEPHEN	MAJ	0-0104607	0648	3
MALAY WILLIAM J	MAJ	0-1584552	0862	1
MALCOLM BERNARD L	COL	0-0269145	0858	1
MALCOLM FRANK J	MAJ	0-0773412	0363	1
MALCOLM WALTER F	CPT	0-1945882	1262	1
MALDONADO JESUS M	CW4	W-2103168	0455	1
MALDONADO PEDRO J	MAJ	0-1924096	1063	1
MALDONADO PEDRO M	CPT	0-0298286	0446	2
MALEADY EUGENE L	LTC	0-0543785	0364	1
MALEK EDWARD R	LTC	0-2014468	0566	1
MALEK LEO E	1LT	0-1294501	1045	2
MALENFANT LAURENCE	MAJ	0-0234502	0345	2
MALENSKI ALBERT S	1LT	0-1306737	0767	2
MALET OLGA M	CPT	L-1005152	0847	2
MALEY EDMOND P	COL	0-0350943	0266	1
MALEY JOHN L	MAJ	0-0958403	1168	1
MALICK KENNETH R	1LT	0-1012085	1045	2
MALICK MARVIN P	WO1	W-2125242	0147	1
MALIKO JOSEPH	MAJ	0-1341987	0863	1
MALIKOWSKI STANLEY P	CW3	W-2206641	0166	1
MALIN EDGAR	1LT	0-0452664	0344	2
MALINAUSKI JOSEPH G	MAJ	0-1012932	1060	1
MALINIAK JOHN A	MAJ	0-1648370	0860	1
MALINICK GEORGE	CPT	0-1111751	0855	2
MALINOWSKI ROY E	CPT	0-0959292	0755	2
MALINSKI FLORIAN L	CPT	0-2015745	0760	1

NAME	GRADE	SVC NO	DATE RET MO YR	RET CODE
MALISKEY DONALD C	LTC	0-0380676	1061	1
MALIZOLA JAMES	MAJ	0-1598924	0964	1
MALKEMUS GEORGE R	CW2	W-2109451	0647	1
MALKIN SIDNEY W	1LT	0-1308666	0245	2
MALKOWSKI EDWARD J	CW2	RW-2207062	0565	1
MALL JACOB O	COL	0-0287138	0962	3
MALL LEONARD W	MAJ	0-1845927	0763	1
MALL ROBERT B	MAJ	0-1302999	0965	1
MALLARD INMAN E	LTC	0-1305951	0463	1
MALLARI ELISEO V	CPT	0-0369267	0157	1
MALLAY JULES L	COL	0-0184780	0757	3
MALLEK JAMES R	CW2	W-2212303	0964	1
MALLEN ABRAHAM	LTC	0-0250286	0557	1
MALLENDER CHARLES W	LTC	0-1582445	0163	3
MALLETT CECILE A	MAJ	N-0753369	0965	1
MALLETT DIRRELL E	CW3	W-2136044	0662	1
MALLETT WINIFRED M	2LT	N-0703078	0643	1
MALLEY GEORGE F	1LT	0-1059869	0546	2
MALLEY LEO H	LTC	0-0401414	0966	2
MALLEY WALTER F	LTC	0-0305480	0358	1
MALLIA ANN T	MAJ	N-0729034	0962	1
MALLICOAT JAMES D	CPT	0-0188922	0648	3
MALLIN JOSEPH D	CPT	0-1299338	0246	2
MALLISON EARL D	COL	0-0178812	0458	3
MALLON ARTHUR	LTC	0-0220802	0664	3
MALLON EDWARD P	CPT	0-0887652	0747	2
MALLON ETHAN L	LTC	0-0290312	0467	3
MALLON FRANCIS R	CW2	W-2106104	0545	2
MALLON MAX K	CPT	0-0479353	0444	2
MALLONEE DAVID W	2LT	0-1913804	0642	1
MALLORY BURWELL S	CW4	W-2111461	0161	1
MALLORY CHARLES D	CPT	0-1321431	1167	1
MALLORY EDWARD C	2LT	0-1313107	1045	2
MALLORY FREDERIC	CW2	W-2144524	1266	1
MALLORY GEORGE	CPT	0-0509663	0246	2
MALLORY HALSEY L	LTC	0-0239440	0666	3
MALLORY KIRK R	COL	0-0345786	0858	3
MALLORY MARGARET M	1LT	N-0722820	1146	1
MALLORY ROBERT C	MAJ	0-0889271	1061	1
MALLORY WILLIAM T	LTC	0-0226812	1062	3
MALLOW ALFRED B	LTC	0-1323450	1167	1
MALLOW DONALD JR	CW3	W-2205181	1066	1
MALLOY AGNES A	1LT	N-0901143	0455	2
MALLOY EDWARD J	1LT	0-1576328	1053	1
MALLOY HOWARD F	1LT	0-0499795	1160	1
MALLOY JAMES T E	LTC	0-1577516	1060	1
MALLOY JOSEPH D	MAJ	0-0279271	1044	2
MALLOY JOSEPH J	COL	0-0306391	0657	3
MALLOY LUKE T	MAJ	0-1642345	0361	1
MALLOY ROBERT L	CPT	0-0446224	0744	2
MALLOY WESLEY J	LTC	0-1303362	0162	1
MALLOY WILLIAM F	LTC	0-0296150	0546	2
MALLOZZI PASQUALE J	CPT	0-0317306	0161	1
MALM PIERRE	LTC	0-1557488	0167	3
MALMBERG ARTHUR W	CPT	0-0193994	0662	3
MALMQUIST TORD V	LTC	0-1304416	0364	1
MALMSTROM CARL T	CPT	0-0485478	0761	2
MALMSTROM IVAR T	LTC	0-0261436	0367	3
MALMSTROM VINCENT F	LTC	0-0236107	0266	3
MALONE ALBERT R JR	MAJ	0-1919386	1066	1
MALONE ALVIN R	LTC	0-0357477	0646	2
MALONE ANDREW	MAJ	0-0177090	0360	3
MALONE ARCHIE D	1LT	0-1319627	0445	2
MALONE BEN F	2LT	0-0274635	0543	1
MALONE BERT H	MAJ	0-1683850	0546	2
MALONE CLIFFORD A	MAJ	0-1556470	1162	1
MALONE DONALD J	LTC	0-1588140	0565	1
MALONE EDWARD W	COL	0-0275069	0860	3
MALONE FLOYD D	CW2	W-2209006	0565	1
MALONE FRANCIS H	1LT	0-0997645	0855	2
MALONE FRANK G	COL	0-0912788	0667	3
MALONE HENRY O	LTC	0-0421983	0765	3
MALONE ITHER D	CPT	0-1303913	0547	2
MALONE JAMES F	MAJ	0-0451344	0862	1
MALONE JAMES H	COL	0-0294214	0863	1

NAME	GRADE	SVC NO	DATE RET MO YR	RET CODE
MALONE JOSEPH H	CW2	W-2143033	0160	1
MALONE MORRIS L	CPT	0-0169165	1059	3
MALONE OTIS L	MAJ	0-1999791	0461	1
MALONE PAUL B JR	COL	0-0312074	1053	2
MALONE ROBERT R	COL	0-0436925	0662	2
MALONE STEPHEN N	COL	0-0239339	1265	3
MALONE THOMAS C	LTC	0-0272212	1060	1
MALONE TOM W	CW3	W-2147762	0162	1
MALONE VICTOR A	CW3	W-2127496	1154	1
MALONE VICTOR E	CPT	0-0488380	0547	1
MALONE WILLIAM F	LTC	0-0471033	0851	2
MALONE WILLIAM J	CPT	0-0967827	0661	1
MALONE WILLIAM P	CPT	0-2047415	0868	3
MALONE WILLIS JR	CW3	W-2203483	0766	1
MALONEY ANDREW B	MAJ	0-0402295	0161	1
MALONEY DENIS J JR	CPT	0-1018432	0747	2
MALONEY EDWARD J	MAJ	0-0501140	0346	2
MALONEY EDWARD S	MAJ	0-0176330	0165	3
MALONEY ELDON T	MAJ	0-1634102	0860	1
MALONEY FRANCIS J JR	1LT	0-1686717	0551	2
MALONEY FRANK L	CW2	W-2147528	0760	2
MALONEY GORDON F	MAJ	0-0208707	0347	2
MALONEY HAROLD J	2LT	0-1584554	0344	2
MALONEY JAMES C	CW2	W-2209178	1062	1
MALONEY JAMES G	LTC	0-0299471	0465	3
MALONEY JAMES I	LTC	0-0307010	0460	1
MALONEY JAMES J	CPT	0-2025638	0655	1
MALONEY JOHN B	CPT	0-0315173	0949	1
MALONEY JOHN F	1LT	0-1295913	0246	2
MALONEY JOHN F	MAJ	0-2020445	1167	1
MALONEY JOHN F	CW3	W-2151886	1164	1
MALONEY JOHN P	MAJ	0-0587324	1061	2
MALONEY JOHN R	MAJ	0-0224048	0562	3
MALONEY JOHN T	COL	0-0490451	0267	1
MALONEY JOHN W	2LT	0-1056156	1044	2
MALONEY ORMAND	MAJ	0-0483877	0655	1
MALONEY ROBERT A	LTC	0-2006640	1163	1
MALOOF FREDERIC F	MAJ	0-0483154	0246	2
MALOS LLOYD G	CPT	0-0425878	1047	2
MALOY EWELL W	MAJ	0-1030803	1057	1
MALPASS FRANCIS J	CW3	W-2206404	1264	2
MALSAM WENDELIN R	MAJ	0-0451345	0756	1
MALSBURY FRANK H	LTC	0-1288919	0867	1
MALSBURY JAMES S	LTC	0-0240304	0765	3
MALSBURY LIONEL A	LTC	0-0406410	0660	1
MALTAIS RENAUD J	COL	0-0496988	0859	1
MALTBY LEON M	MAJ	0-0537153	0466	3
MALTRY JOHN M JR	MAJ	0-1797847	0859	1
MALTZ FREDERICK	1LT	0-1284171	1045	2
MALTZ HERBERT L	CW4	W-2148326	1068	1
MALVAL HENRY J	1LT	0-1048483	1044	2
MALZER ARNOLD	CPT	0-0555183	0946	2
MAMA MORA	CPT	0-0890532	0348	2
MAMUKARI JAMES	2LT	0-1305082	0444	2
MAMULA JEANNE D	1LT	N-0901151	0853	2
MANAHAN WILLIAM T	LTC	0-0230536	0347	2
MANARO HELEN L	2LT	N-0764533	0545	1
MANBECK FRANK E	COL	0-0282118	0166	3
MANCE JAMES E	LTC	0-1534800	1262	1
MANCHESTER WILFRED F	WO1	W-2130034	0459	1
MANCIL COLEMAN M	CPT	0-0976983	0861	1
MANCIOCHI LOUIS J	CW2	W-2147890	0660	1
MANCK IRA	MAJ	0-1309582	0864	3
MANCUSO FRANK	MAJ	0-2055228	0660	1
MANCUSO MARCO S	CW3	W-2136620	0761	1
MAND IRWIN	CPT	0-0357890	0651	2
MANDEL GERALD S	CW3	W-2150721	0163	2
MANDEL J D	CW2	W-2144496	0760	1
MANDEL JACOB	1LT	0-2020316	0868	1
MANDEL JEROME	LTC	0-0446288	0447	2
MANDEL NATHAN G	MAJ	0-0313612	0645	2
MANDELL HERMAN	LTC	0-0394593	0866	3
MANDELL HERMAN S	LTC	0-1105644	0266	1
MANDELL LESTER	LTC	0-1043715	0664	1
MANDELL LOUIS D JR	LTC	0-0229504	0564	3

NAME	GRADE	SVC NO	DATE RET MO YR	RET CODE
MANDER DESMOND W	CPT	0-1183570	0347	2
MANDERS WILLIAM G	CPT	0-1010085	1046	2
MANDERSON WILLIAM T	MAJ	0-1913339	0763	1
MANDEVILLE JOHN E	LTC	0-0362693	0568	3
MANDICH BENEDICT R	MAJ	0-0978801	0364	1
MANDL JOSEPH P	LTC	0-0313654	0660	3
MANDLE ALBERT	MAJ	0-1691459	0152	1
MANDOLADO CESARIO	2LT	0-1896660	0761	1
MANEE LEROY A	MAJ	0-0498284	0247	1
MANEGOLD JOHN E	LTC	0-0154005	1050	3
MANER ROY C	MAJ	0-0989685	1267	1
MANES CHARLES D	LTC	0-1579971	0961	1
MANES JOHN H	CW2	W-2101059	0248	2
MANEVAL ROBERT C	COL	0-0307005	0366	3
MANEY HOWARD S	MAJ	0-0964547	0565	1
MANEY MARTIN F	1LT	0-1307438	0946	2
MANEY WILLIAM F JR	LTC	0-1057155	0365	1
MANFRE JOHN G	LTC	0-1001843	0761	1
MANFREDI AUGUSTINE	CW2	W-2211861	0666	1
MANFREDO DOMINIC	CW3	RW-2146814	0264	1
MANGALINDAN PRIMITIV	2LT	0-1896377	0450	2
MANGAN BRUCE J	MAJ	0-1650218	0361	1
MANGAN EDWARD J	CPT	0-1012743	0645	2
MANGANARO PHILIP L	1LT	0-1045823	0745	2
MANGANELLO ARTHUR	CPT	0-0969655	0860	1
MANGELLY THOMAS	CPT	0-1640697	0660	1
MANGELS CONRAD JR	LTC	0-0257153	1267	3
MANGEN ALBERT J	MAJ	0-0288418	0568	3
MANGER LEO	LTC	0-0464915	0257	1
MANGES BINNIE L	1LT	N-0742694	1046	1
MANGHI GENE	CPT	0-1641540	0764	1
MANGIERI CHARLES E	2LT	0-1060544	1045	2
MANGIN CHARLES E	1LT	0-1826241	0745	2
MANGINE WILLIAM J	COL	0-0176734	0260	3
MANGINELLI VITUS W	COL	0-0448101	0665	3
MANGINI JOHN J	1LT	0-1030593	0944	2
MANGINI ROLAND A	COL	0-0239790	0852	3
MANGOLD CLYDE H	LTC	0-0380470	0368	1
MANGRUM ALTON J	LTC	0-1178883	1162	1
MANGUBAT DIOSCORO L	1LT	0-0890528	1048	1
MANGUM HENRY R JR	LTC	0-0958696	0568	1
MANGUM HOWEL C	WO1	W-2131583	0147	1
MANGUM INGLIS P JR	CPT	0-1295574	1047	2
MANGUM JAMES E	COL	0-0157497	0753	3
MANGUM ROBERT G JR	CPT	0-2262963	1266	1
MANGUM WILSON P	1LT	0-1307724	0345	2
MANGUNO JOSEPH D	LTC	0-1292916	1061	1
MANGUSO ANTONINO H	LTC	0-0310672	0161	1
MANHART WALTER	CPT	0-0195808	0641	1
MANIFOLD GEORGE T	CW2	W-2152642	0660	1
MANIFOLD KENNETH M	LTC	0-1291849	0363	1
MANIFOLD ROY J	LTC	0-0919585	1167	3
MANINGO FELIPE N	1LT	0-0890232	0447	2
MANION ESTHER L	2LT	N-0787969	0445	1
MANION JOSEPH P	1LT	0-0531210	0945	2
MANION THOMAS J	1LT	0-1325657	0348	2
MANION WAYNE H	MAJ	0-1291666	0662	1
MANIS CARL JR	LTC	0-0545432	0365	1
MANIX JOHN W	1LT	0-2035124	1045	2
MANKE ELDRED B	1LT	0-1111753	0845	2
MANKE ROBERT L	CPT	0-1582447	0853	2
MANKER RAYMOND D	LTC	0-1035523	1062	1
MANKOWICH ABRAHAM	MAJ	0-0253591	0667	3
MANLEY CARL B	1LT	0-1635090	0661	3
MANLEY EUGENE H	COL	0-0378191	0765	1
MANLEY FRANCIS J	LTC	0-1040432	0366	1
MANLEY HENRY G	MAJ	0-0959381	0767	1
MANLEY JERRY R	2LT	0-1017543	0944	2
MANLEY JOHN G	1LT	0-1322054	1058	1
MANLEY JOSEPH P JR	1LT	0-0359520	0345	2
MANLEY JOSEPH W	CPT	0-0462723	0345	2
MANLEY ROBERT D	1LT	0-1298266	1145	2
MANLEY ROBERT F	MAJ	0-0969378	0267	1
MANLOVE CHARLES H JR	LTC	0-0176656	0648	3
MANLY CLARENCE H	CPT	0-0149577	1152	3

NAME	GRADE	SVC NO	DATE RET MO YR	RET CODE
MANN ANTHONY A	CW2	W-2152553	0161	1
MANN ANTHONY M	CW3	W-2209127	0368	1
MANN BLAIR A	MAJ	O-17[illegible]	1262	3
MANN CARL E	COL	O-0458178	1158	1
MANN CLAUD [illegible]	CPT	O-1914445	1263	1
MANN CURTIS W	LTC	O-040[illegible]	0758	1
MANN DOROTHY A	1LT	N-0742159	1145	1
MANN DURWARD W	WO1	W-2102817	0157	3
MANN EDWARD M	CW3	W-2210320	1064	2
MANN ELTON O	CW2	W-2062214	0866	3
MANN FRANK E	LTC	O-0405372	0660	1
MANN FREDERICK A	COL	O-0274106	0858	2
MANN GEORGE F	MAJ	O-0147813	0554	3
MANN GEORGE L	LTC	O-0143922	0656	3
MANN GRAHAM L	1LT	O-1101565	0845	2
MANN HORACE	LTC	O-1574409	0361	1
MANN HOWARD G	MAJ	O-1311530	0864	1
MANN HUGO S	CW2	W-2151118	0264	1
MANN JACK	MAJ	O-2289274	1166	1
MANN JAMES G	LTC	O-0425285	0961	1
MANN JESS H	LTC	O-0486108	1058	1
MANN JOHN A	LTC	O-0492419	1048	1
MANN JOHN L JR	MAJ	O-0469925	1066	1
MANN JULIUS W	COL	O-0453180	1162	1
MANN LEROY S	COL	O-0245725	0860	3
MANN MAX W	CPT	O-0436344	0246	2
MANN NATHAN J	2LT	O-1643094	1052	2
MANN PAUL H	LTC	O-0350618	0357	1
MANN PAUL W	CW2	W-2142768	1154	1
MANN RALPH H	MAJ	O-0186625	1054	3
MANN ROBERT W	LTC	O-1045824	0964	1
MANN RUSSELL F	MAJ	O-0402257	1045	2
MANN THOMAS J	MAJ	O-1169628	1158	1
MANN THOMAS M	LTC	O-0578500	0358	1
MANN WALTER F	CW2	W-2109980	1049	2
MANN WAYNE G	LTC	O-0405505	1058	1
MANNE EDWARD	COL	O-0240648	0163	3
MANNERSTEDT GERDON D	LTC	O-0446986	0546	2
MANNESCHMIDT GEORG	LTC	O-0257129	0453	2
MANNHEIMER ROBERT E	LTC	O-0322385	0765	1
MANNING BENJAMIN C	CW3	W-2150322	0959	1
MANNING BRECKAN J	CPT	O-0450534	0653	1
MANNING CARL E	CW4	W-2142977	0868	1
MANNING DANIEL F	COL	O-0219354	0559	3
MANNING DONALD V	WO1	W-2108967	0645	2
MANNING DREW A	1LT	O-1312577	0445	2
MANNING FORDYCE G	LTC	O-1010077	0258	1
MANNING FRANK P	LTC	O-1165904	0162	1
MANNING FRED J	LTC	O-1598715	0162	1
MANNING FREDERICK	CPT	O-1577518	1058	1
MANNING GRACE H	MAJ	L-0220085	1163	1
MANNING GRANT W	LTC	O-0506017	1054	1
MANNING HAROLD L	CW3	W-2143616	0760	1
MANNING JACK R	CPT	O-1579973	0646	2
MANNING JAMES D	LTC	O-0398317	1062	1
MANNING JAMES F	1LT	O-11F1026	0450	2
MANNING JEFFREY H	2LT	O-1310929	1044	2
MANNING JERALD F	CW3	W-2203276	0767	1
MANNING JOHN C	MAJ	O-0941958	0463	1
MANNING JOHN F	LTC	O-0414970	0762	1
MANNING JOHN M	LTC	O-0259178	0960	1
MANNING JOHN W	COL	O-0219691	0459	3
MANNING MANFORD J	CPT	O-1041836	0446	2
MANNING RICHARD D	CPT	O-1298563	1047	2
MANNING ROBERT E JR	CPT	O-0461033	1047	2
MANNING VAUGHN E	CW4	W-2141363	0463	1
MANNING VIVIAN F	2LT	N-0702298	0235	1
MANNING WENDELL A	MAJ	O-2096467	1165	1
MANNING WILLIAM E	CW3	W-2141707	0657	1
MANNING WILLIAM J	CPT	O-1304418	1061	1
MANNING WILLIAM S	LTC	O-0189480	1158	3
MANNION JOSEPH W	MAJ	O-1545770	0965	1
MANNLE ROBERT A	LTC	O-1056457	0766	2
MANNON EUGENE L	MAJ	O-0250137	1145	2
MANNS EDDIE F	MAJ	O-0942802	0761	1

NAME	GRADE	SVC NO	DATE RET MO YR	RET CODE
MANNY JAMES W	1LT	O-1933768	0355	2
MANO JOSEPH M	LTC	O-0419532	0261	1
MANOR ROBERT J	MAJ	O-0266915	0862	3
MANOS ANTHONY J	MAJ	O-2008537	0962	1
MANOWN VOYLE F JR	CPT	O-1062899	0346	2
MANRESA MIGUEL JR	CPT	O-0522941	1048	2
MANRIQUE BIENVENIDO	1LT	O-0890441	0858	1
MANROSS FREDERICK	COL	O-0191550	0161	3
MANRY JOHN C	MAJ	O-1305952	0757	1
MANS BILLIE	MAJ	N-0726549	0861	1
MANSEN THEODORE A	LTC	O-0513112	0166	3
MANSER HARRY M	COL	O-0178694	0758	3
MANSER JOHN A	LTC	O-0343381	0863	3
MANSER JULIEN G	CPT	O-0268529	0545	2
MANSFIELD EVE D	CPT	L-0500101	0648	2
MANSFIELD FRANK S	MAJ	O-0121174	0658	3
MANSFIELD GORDON H	CPT	O-5325599	0968	2
MANSFIELD JOSEPH P	CW3	W-2008294	0266	3
MANSFIELD RICHARD D	MAJ	O-0342999	0645	2
MANSFIELD ROBERT C	COL	O-0254985	0153	2
MANSFIELD VIRGIL C	LTC	O-1588716	0862	1
MANSFIELD WILBUR L	LTC	O-0410360	0965	3
MANSFIELD WILLIAM A	LTC	O-0100183	0253	3
MANSHIP LAWRENCE L	LTC	O-0916148	0667	3
MANSKA JACK H	MAJ	O-0964031	1061	1
MANSON GORDON	1LT	O-0436993	0446	2
MANTELL FRANCIS J	LTC	O-0310158	0463	3
MANTER NELSON L	MAJ	O-0251300	1166	3
MANTER RALPH M	COL	O-0131514	0355	3
MANTEUFFEL ERWIN P	MAJ	O-0240005	1048	3
MANTHE CORNELIUS	LTC	O-1111214	1062	1
MANTHEI JOHN E	MAJ	O-1337727	0467	1
MANTIPLY SAMUEL T	1LT	O-0888450	0749	2
MANTO JOSEPH V	MAJ	O-2001784	0562	1
MANTONE PLINIO	MAJ	O-1014003	0966	1
MANTZ HARRY E	MAJ	O-0368520	1144	2
MANTZ JUANITA S	2LT	N-0736936	0445	1
MANUEL ANNIE J	1LT	N-0726756	0446	1
MANUEL FRANK J	MAJ	O-1286157	0547	2
MANUEL JERRY L	CW3	W-3150532	0268	1
MANUEL MILTON L	CPT	O-0414076	1045	2
MANUEL RALPH E	LTC	O-1294689	0860	2
MANUEL THOMAS B	COL	O-0249469	0146	2
MANUEL WEBSTER G	CW3	W-3150355	0667	1
MANULIK JOHN C	LTC	O-1542890	0861	1
MANWELL KARL R	MAJ	O-0889792	0555	1
MANWILLER JOHN A D	LTC	O-0356034	0463	1
MANY EDWARD C	MAJ	O-0292767	0368	3
MANZ HANS J	LTC	O-2200200	1066	1
MANZANO FLORENCIO	1LT	O-0268179	0447	2
MANZIONE JOSEPH A	MAJ	O-0279066	0154	3
MAPEL FRANK B	COL	O-0336161	0963	3
MAPES AMELIA C B	2LT	N-0753286	0546	1
MAPES LESTER R	MAJ	O-0123642	0750	3
MAPES LLOYD A	MAJ	O-0384985	0868	3
MAPES LLOYD T	LTC	O-1331532	0164	1
MAPES MILTON C	COL	O-0193153	0648	3
MAPES WILLIAM M	CPT	O-0231062	0357	3
MAPLE ALPHEUS F	LTC	O-0346504	0662	3
MAPLE CHARLES W	CW3	W-2144308	0861	1
MAPLE HAROLD S	CW4	W-2113439	0461	1
MAPLE TELFORD G	1LT	O-0419398	0944	2
MAPLES CHARLES E	CW2	W-3200417	1168	1
MAPLES FREDERICK	LTC	O-0341482	0647	2
MAPLES GEORGE V	LTC	O-0397330	0868	1
MAPLESDEN GEORGE T	WO1	W-2131089	0546	2
MAR THOMAS A	CW3	W-2145025	1164	1
MAR THOMAS M	CPT	O-0421223	0246	2
MAR WILLIAM F	LTC	O-1949387	0662	1
MARA SAMUEL G	LTC	O-0234825	1154	3
MARABLE BEN F	LTC	O-0264510	0760	1
MARALDI CARL F	LTC	O-0246454	0755	3
MARANA ANDRO S	1LT	O-2031896	0649	1
MARANCHAK STEPHEN M	CW4	W-2151804	1060	1
MARANGONI BRUNO A	MAJ	O-0338956	0345	2

NAME	GRADE	SVC NO	DATE RET MO YR	RET CODE
MARANGONI LOUIS	CW2	W-2214700	0468	1
MARANVILLE HEATHER F	LTC	O-0450173	1158	1
MARATTA JOHN W	CPT	O-0410251	0146	2
MARAZZINI BERNARD J	LTC	O-0551253	0959	1
MARBERRY JOE D	MAJ	O-0451003	0657	2
MARBLE ALEXANDER	B G	O-0241298	0362	3
MARBLE CUSTER T	CW3	W-2141365	0659	1
MARBLE JOHN H	MAJ	O-1049970	1055	1
MARBLE ROBERT D	MAJ	O-1917770	0463	1
MARBLE ROBERT L	LTC	O-0938795	1268	1
MARBLE ROLAND C	CPT	O-2006093	0347	2
MARBRY GEORGE W	CPT	O-0494185	0346	2
MARBUT WILLIAM M	COL	O-0246304	0858	2
MARCACCIO VINCENT	CW4	W-2152151	1168	1
MARCAIS ARSENE F	CPT	O-0172452	0549	3
MARCANTONIO HENRY S	LTC	O-2014465	1267	1
MARCANTONIO R C	1LT	O-2028391	0953	2
MARCEAU PAUL F	LTC	O-0504796	0164	3
MARCELL LEO J	MAJ	O-2055190	0756	1
MARCELLE DAVID A	COL	O-0081005	1167	1
MARCELYNAS ANTHONY F	LTC	O-0368747	0258	1
MARCENKUS ALBERT A	1LT	O-1322566	1045	2
MARCEREAU ARCHIBALD	LTC	O-1288604	1168	1
MARCH HARRY S	LTC	O-0225172	0652	3
MARCH LEONARD W	LTC	O-0217688	1055	3
MARCH WILLIAM E	2LT	O-0451512	0544	2
MARCHAN RAFAEL	LTC	O-0263347	0368	3
MARCHAND CLAYTON P	LTC	O-0510804	0954	1
MARCHAND HANS L	CPT	O-1059542	0649	2
MARCHANT EDWARD J	WO1	W-2111690	0264	3
MARCHANT GORDON L	LTC	O-1550438	1161	1
MARCHANT JAMES O	LTC	O-0251659	0366	3
MARCHBANK ANDREW C	1LT	O-5022862	1067	2
MARCHBANKS JAMES L	MAJ	O-1287731	0954	1
MARCHBANKS VANCE H	CPT	O-0109537	1039	1
MARCHBANKS WILLIAM O	1LT	O-2212022	0656	1
MARCHE DON C	CPT	O-2033160	0662	1
MARCHESE FRANK J	CW3	W-2143584	1263	1
MARCHESELLI V F JR	MAJ	O-1042096	0459	1
MARCHETTI FRANK F	LTC	O-0187983	0847	2
MARCHI BRUNO G	LTC	O-0233093	1163	3
MARCHILLO FRANK N	LTC	O-0977392	0768	1
MARCHIONDA JOSEPH	CW4	W-2141737	0668	1
MARCHIONDO EDDIE	1LT	O-1826353	0346	2
MARCHITELLI HENRY A	LTC	O-1314037	1060	1
MARCHMAN MARY I	2LT	N-0773080	1045	1
MARCHMAN WILLIAM H	CW2	W-2215128	0567	1
MARCHUT WALTER J	2LT	O-2008276	0258	1
MARCIN HILARY J	CPT	O-0535220	0545	2
MARCINAK CASPER F	WO1	W-2119927	1145	2
MARCINKO STEPHEN A	COL	O-0479005	1057	1
MARCINKOWSKI JULIAN	MAJ	O-0450607	0457	1
MARCINKOWSKI THADDEU	LTC	O-0383546	0263	1
MARCK WILLIAM J	MAJ	O-0312795	1044	2
MARCKS RAYMOND H	MAJ	O-0980124	0264	1
MARCO JOSEPH O	CPT	O-0305381	0845	2
MARCO SIDNEY V	LTC	O-1644556	1267	1
MARCOM JAMES W	LTC	O-2294696	1267	1
MARCOTT HELEN M C	2LT	N-0758014	0146	1
MARCOTTE GERALD J	MAJ	O-1702281	0267	1
MARCOTTE PAUL E L	LTC	O-1102369	0968	1
MARCOTTE ROMEO A	COL	O-1822295	0468	1
MARCOUS MARION H	1LT	N-0730350	0445	1
MARCOUX ELI A	LTC	O-0131516	1054	3
MARCROFT JOHN C	LTC	O-0238160	0764	3
MARCUCCI ALDO M	1LT	O-1593301	0746	2
MARCUM ALFRED L	LTC	O-0125162	0546	2
MARCUM HENRY F	2LT	O-1324634	0245	2
MARCUM HERSHEL	1LT	O-1643831	1045	2
MARCUM SAMUEL G	MAJ	O-0336903	0646	2
MARCUM WARREN F	1LT	O-1285967	0945	2
MARCUM WILLIAM C	CPT	O-0263433	0953	3
MARCUM WILLIAM H	LTC	O-1295916	1060	1
MARCUS IRWIN M	CPT	O-1756775	0946	2
MARCUS LAWRENCE F	CPT	O-0370714	0145	2

NAME	GRADE	SVC NO	DATE RET MO YR	RET CODE
MARCUS LEO	1LT	O-1717555	0945	2
MARCUS LOUIS L	LTC	O-0297051	0260	3
MARCUS MAURICE	CPT	O-1312693	0847	2
MARCUS MORRIS D	CPT	O-0314202	0346	2
MARCUS PHILLIP W	CPT	O-0331516	0844	2
MARCUS RUSSELL O	CW3	W-2215027	0868	1
MARCUS SAMUEL	CW3	W-2142251	0665	1
MARCUS SIDNEY R	MAJ	O-0284994	0157	2
MARCUS STANLEY	CPT	O-0511801	0146	2
MARCUS STANLEY S	1LT	O-1048887	0347	2
MARCUSSEN WILLIAM B	LTC	O-0464075	0246	2
MARCY GUY E JR	CPT	O-0419008	0645	2
MARCYES PAUL F	MAJ	O-1043415	0661	1
MARDEN HAROLD C	COL	O-0242841	0860	3
MARDEN HARRY S	1LT	O-0279299	0538	1
MARDER SIDNEY S	CPT	O-0508861	0545	2
MARDIROS ARMEN N	COL	O-0279171	1066	3
MARDIS JOHN R	1LT	O-0408571	0345	2
MARDIS RALEIGH L	CW3	W-2141366	1161	1
MARDOS OTTO	MAJ	O-0969050	0163	1
MAREK CHARLES S	COL	O-0234053	0851	3
MAREK CHESTER J	2LT	O-1302683	0245	2
MAREK FRANK A	MAJ	O-1556175	0557	1
MAREK HATTIE L	MAJ	N-0701687	1163	3
MAREK NORBERT C	MAJ	O-1289934	0147	2
MAREK RICHARD G	CPT	O-0445638	0446	2
MAREKA EDWARD J	MAJ	O-0972667	1066	1
MAREN ADOLPH	CW2	W-2141367	1057	1
MARESCA ROBERT J JR	CW3	W-2152007	0765	1
MARESH EDWARD	MAJ	O-0165496	0447	2
MARFORI EDMUNDO J	LTC	O-1301660	0962	1
MARGESON EDWARD M JR	CW3	W-2152144	0964	1
MARGIN BERNARD J	CW4	W-2147855	1168	1
MARGNER LOUIS J	MAJ	O-1038051	0461	1
MARGOLIASH JACOB S	CPT	O-0399026	0346	2
MARGOLIN BARACH	LTC	O-0321683	0161	1
MARGOLIN SAMUEL	MAJ	O-0250391	0165	3
MARGOLIS ARTHUR	MAJ	O-1001845	1155	2
MARGOLIS SAMUEL L	1LT	O-1543642	0245	2
MARGRAF RAYMOND	LTC	O-1106925	0664	1
MARGULIES CHARLES	MAJ	O-1689285	0346	2
MARIAN JOHN B	COL	O-0192114	0551	3
MARIANI JOSEPH A	LTC	O-1548098	1062	1
MARICLE LECLAIRE R	MAJ	O-0314651	1045	2
MARIGMEN PEDRO B	1LT	O-0280157	0157	1
MARIHUGH CLARENCE H	CW2	W-2205908	0762	1
MARIN ALBERT G	COL	O-1285078	1157	1
MARINACCI ALBERTO A	MAJ	O-0370756	0846	2
MARINAN JOSEPH T	LTC	O-0170828	0349	3
MARINE MICHAEL	CW2	W-2148611	1061	1
MARINER FREEMAN B	MAJ	O-2010387	0864	1
MARING WILBUR F JR	COL	O-0160016	0757	1
MARINO ANTHONY L	CW3	W-2205704	0467	1
MARINO JOSEPH A	MAJ	O-0971308	0665	1
MARINO RAYMOND E	CW4	W-2118200	1065	1
MARINOS HARRY G	MAJ	O-0368262	0445	2
MARINZACK JOHN P	CPT	O-1691725	0457	1
MARION JOE E	MAJ	O-0441403	0445	2
MARION JOHN P	CPT	O-1322643	1047	2
MARION MARIAN M	CPT	L-0400000	1144	2
MARION ROBERT D	LTC	O-1341279	1167	1
MARION THOMAS F JR	CW4	W-2143770	0262	1
MARIS ANNE E	1LT	N-0726866	1046	1
MARIS ARTHUR M	MAJ	O-0270313	0168	3
MARIS LEE M	CPT	O-0491585	0346	2
MARIS THOMAS G JR	LTC	O-0363868	0347	2
MARK CECIL H	CPT	O-0324141	0944	2
MARK COLEMAN B	LTC	O-0189955	0648	3
MARK HILBERT	COL	O-0263440	0266	3
MARK JACK S	2LT	O-1703851	0645	2
MARKARIAN VARSING	2LT	N-0742969	0445	1
MARKEE JOSEPH E	LTC	O-1049972	1266	1
MARKEL BERNICE P	MAJ	N-0800273	0965	1
MARKEN DELOSS I	COL	O-0275539	1155	3
MARKER GEORGE L	LTC	O-1035311	0361	1

NAME	GRADE	SVC NO	DATE RET MO YR	RET CODE
MARKER JOHN I	COL	0-0121088	0445	2
MARKER MARION R	CPT	0-2033162	0459	2
MARKETTE JOHN P JR	CPT	0-0487123	1043	2
MARKHAM CARL W	COL	0-0111181	1048	3
MARKHAM FAY E	CW2	W-2210181	0366	1
MARKHAM HARLEY B	MAJ	0-0261704	0165	3
MARKHAM JOHN H	LTC	0-0153914	0754	3
MARKHAM JOSEPH W	MAJ	0-1288920	0361	1
MARKHAM LAURIE W	MAJ	0-2034088	0468	1
MARKHAM RAYMOND G	COL	0-0217485	0463	3
MARKHEIM HERBERT R	MAJ	0-0367677	1145	2
MARKIEWICZ JAMES	LTC	0-0729776	0264	1
MARKILLIE RICHARD C	LTC	0-1797323	0561	2
MARKIN UREL E JR	CW4	W-2119495	0462	1
MARKKOLA RUSSELL F	1LT	0-0466733	0446	2
MARKLAND CURTIS W	COL	0-0308374	0960	1
MARKLAND GEORGE E	MAJ	0-1919217	0168	1
MARKLAND OLIVER W JR	CW3	W-2206410	0966	1
MARKLAND WALTER H	MAJ	0-1185803	1159	1
MARKLE BYRON M	MAJ	0-0324348	1066	3
MARKLE EARL	1LT	0-1292211	0745	2
MARKLE EUGENE C	MAJ	0-1919420	0464	1
MARKLEY RAYMOND L	LTC	0-0231342	1150	3
MARKLEY ROBERT L	MAJ	0-1636267	0563	1
MARKOFF ABRAHAM	CPT	0-0504723	0346	2
MARKOLA HAROLD J	WO1	W-2118509	0144	2
MARKOVIC ERNEST J	LTC	0-0460186	0866	1
MARKJWICH EDWARD P	1LT	0-1180253	1147	2
MARKOWITZ MAX	MAJ	0-0438292	0246	2
MARKS ARTHUR	MAJ	0-0245674	0653	3
MARKS BERTRAM E	MAJ	0-0382675	0246	2
MARKS DUDLEY B	WO1	W-2149171	0156	1
MARKS FRANCIS W	COL	0-0180245	0863	3
MARKS FRANK H	LTC	0-0168559	0158	3
MARKS GEORGE E	CPT	0-0479214	0148	1
MARKS HARRY S	MAJ	0-0961725	0962	1
MARKS HERMAN	MAJ	0-1080126	1059	1
MARKS HILDA M	MAJ	N-0730887	0267	1
MARKS HOWARD E	WO1	W-2114877	0755	1
MARKS IRA G	1LT	0-1322698	C146	2
MARKS JAMES E	MAJ	0-0572511	1060	1
MARKS JULIAN I	COL	0-0138343	0648	3
MARKS KARL W	LTC	0-0218833	0752	3
MARKS LESLIE M	LTC	0-0347371	1067	3
MARKS MATTHEW D	1LT	0-0539718	1045	2
MARKS MAX	CPT	0-0496557	0646	2
MARKS PAUL H JR	LTC	0-0948307	0768	1
MARKS PERRY D	MAJ	0-2028721	1066	1
MARKS SAMUEL F	MAJ	0-0287805	0360	3
MARKS THEODORE D	MAJ	0-1643833	1163	1
MARKS WILBUR C	MAJ	0-1824058	1162	1
MARKUNAS ELNOR M	1LT	N-0751279	0246	1
MARKUS MURELL F	MAJ	0-0223886	0245	2
MARKUSON REGINA W	MAJ	N-0757268	1163	1
MARLAY RAYMOND V	LTC	0-0210517	0852	3
MARLAND CLIFFORD R	MAJ	0-1649080	0756	1
MARLE WILLIAM D	LTC	0-1341452	0967	1
MARLER ALLEN D	MAJ	0-0976612	0865	1
MARLER JAMES D	LTC	0-0514627	0663	1
MARLEY GEORGE E	LTC	0-1821743	0763	1
MARLEY JOHN F	CPT	0-1106927	0947	2
MARLEY RALPH M	COL	0-0304142	0657	1
MARLEY WALLACE C	LTC	0-0814508	0467	1
MARLIER GASTON P	CW4	W-2142305	0256	1
MARLIN CLIFTON B	CPT	0-0514009	0847	2
MARLIN PERRY S	MAJ	0-0988297	0865	1
MARLIN WILLIAM E	MAJ	0-0982266	1264	1
MARLOW GEORGE R SR	CW3	W-2146753	0559	1
MARLOWE ORVILLE E	MAJ	0-0267069	0760	3
MARMEY ROLAND A	MAJ	0-2018696	0363	1
MARMORSTEIN ROBERT	LTC	0-1035897	1268	1
MARNER PAUL B	COL	0-0188140	0962	3
MARNFELD ROBERT	MAJ	0-0451939	0457	1
MAROHN HAROLD	MAJ	0-1168802	0455	1
MAROHN RALPH L	CPT	0-1181947	0962	1

NAME	GRADE	SVC NO	DATE RET MO YR	RET CODE
MAROLF JOHN F	MAJ	0-1636270	0959	1
MARONEY BERRY D	1LT	0-0508966	0959	1
MARONEY JOHN J	CPT	0-1295746	0857	1
MARONEY PAUL E	MAJ	0-2000831	0861	1
MAROON HABEEB Z	CPT	0-0500027	0246	2
MAROUKIAN MARTIN L	LTC	0-1575444	0266	1
MARQUARDT FREDERICK	CW3	W-2209277	0867	1
MARQUARDT GEORGE W	LTC	0-0166718	1154	3
MARQUARDT OSWALD K	MAJ	0-0374090	0746	2
MARQUARDT VIOLA R	1LT	N-0732468	0246	1
MARQUES LEMUEL JR	MAJ	0-0251478	0164	3
MARQUESS ARTHUR C	1LT	0-1317182	0146	2
MARQUESS STANLEY F	CW3	RW-2147374	0763	1
MARQUEZ JOSE	MAJ	0-0466621	0147	1
MARQUEZ VICTOR	CPT	0-1340673	1160	1
MARQUIS GEORGE W JR	MAJ	0-0264302	0454	3
MARQUIS JAMES F	LTC	0-0310615	0762	1
MARQUIS VANCE B	COL	0-0295830	0559	1
MARQUIS WILLIAM C	1LT	0-1032466	1045	2
MARR CLIFFORD	LTC	0-0453816	0658	1
MARR IRVINE M	MAJ	0-0253937	0267	3
MARR PATRICK J SR	LTC	0-1337978	0868	1
MARRA JOSEPH	MAJ	0-1336406	0264	1
MARRA PELLEGRINO	2LT	0-1104285	0445	2
MARRACCINI EUGENE M	2LT	0-1051669	0845	2
MARRAH GEORGE L	LTC	0-0339069	0846	2
MARRERO JUAN	CPT	0-0255465	0148	1
MARRIN JAMES G JR	LTC	0-0327555	1061	1
MARRIOTT FRANK	LTC	0-0264406	1165	3
MARRON JAMES M	1LT	0-1171661	0745	2
MARRON REGINA M	1LT	N-0758482	0646	1
MARROW WILLIAM M	CPT	0-0347931	1053	1
MARRS ALVERNA I	1LT	N-0784765	0846	1
MARRS BILLY J	CPT	0-0890468	1047	2
MARRS CARL D	MAJ	0-2016437	0258	1
MARRS GEORGE R	WO1	W-2111452	0647	2
MARRS HAROLD F	LTC	0-1047655	0463	1
MARS CHARLES	MAJ	0-0234355	1057	3
MARS EDWARD	CW2	W-2148869	0753	1
MARS EVERETT D	CPT	0-0395780	0961	1
MARSALA ANTHONY J	COL	0-1541293	0761	1
MARSDEN ROSS L	CPT	0-1697748	0145	2
MARSDEN THOMAS A JR	LTC	0-0329458	0960	1
MARSDEN WALLACE T	CW3	W-2211167	0968	1
MARSELLA CLARENCE B	MAJ	0-0230620	1057	3
MARSEY JOHN L	2LT	0-1649081	0445	2
MARSH ANDREW T	LTC	0-0261276	0560	1
MARSH AUBREY L	LTC	0-1288923	1266	1
MARSH CHARLES D	COL	0-0324478	0564	3
MARSH CHARLES E	1LT	0-0973561	0354	2
MARSH CHARLES W	1LT	0-1284900	0244	2
MARSH DANIEL J	MAJ	0-0384049	0267	3
MARSH DONALD L	COL	0-0233924	1054	1
MARSH EDGERLY B	MAJ	0-0374916	0147	2
MARSH ELLIS E JR	LTC	0-0269162	0760	1
MARSH EMER L JR	CW4	W-2118527	0361	1
MARSH EVELYN B	1LT	N-0760297	1145	1
MARSH EVIN H	CW2	W-2150189	0366	1
MARSH FRED	LTC	0-0443521	0851	2
MARSH GARVIS C	1LT	0-0527642	1145	2
MARSH GEORGE M	MAJ	0-2012803	0862	1
MARSH GLENN M	LTC	0-1297562	0757	1
MARSH HARVEY D	CW3	W-2206567	0266	1
MARSH JAMES V	LTC	0-1305953	0862	1
MARSH JAMES W	CW3	W-2206452	0868	1
MARSH JOHN W	LTC	0-0252419	0453	3
MARSH KOSCIE H	1LT	0-1995128	0745	2
MARSH LOREN R	CW2	W-3430166	0467	1
MARSH LOUIS S	CW4	W-2124168	1160	1
MARSH MARION F	1LT	0-1031825	0960	1
MARSH RICHARD	LTC	0-1001010	0667	1
MARSH ROBERT E	LTC	0-0349903	0367	3
MARSH RUTH M	1LT	N-0745237	0446	1
MARSH SAMUEL E	CPT	0-0493791	1059	2
MARSH VICTOR T	MAJ	0-2043221	0960	1

NAME	GRADE	SVC NO	DATE RET MO YR	RET CODE
MARSH WILLIAM C	MAJ	0-1312780	1266	1
MARSH WILLIAM D	MAJ	0-1182644	0859	1
MARSHA EARL M	COL	0-0359891	0660	1
MARSHACK ROBERT C	LTC	0-1177897	0261	1
MARSHALL ALBERT L JR	MAJ	0-0335943	1045	2
MARSHALL ARTHUR A JR	1LT	0-1926899	C454	2
MARSHALL ARTHUR W	LTC	0-0363499	0859	1
MARSHALL BEAUFORD C	CPT	0-1032226	0559	2
MARSHALL BENJAMIN E	CPT	0-1296150	1146	2
MARSHALL CARL A	MAJ	0-0253106	1263	3
MARSHALL CARL M	MAJ	0-0296665	0460	1
MARSHALL CHARLES C	MAJ	0-1015129	0466	3
MARSHALL CHARLES G	CW2	W-2119303	0960	1
MARSHALL CHARLES H	LTC	0-0389033	0455	1
MARSHALL CHESTER R	CPT	0-0318189	0645	2
MARSHALL CLARENCE C	CPT	0-1013503	1154	1
MARSHALL CLARK	LTC	0-0506617	0453	2
MARSHALL CLEMON L	LTC	0-1177516	0760	1
MARSHALL CLIFF B	LTC	0-0260912	0468	3
MARSHALL DALLAS E	MAJ	0-0371493	0466	3
MARSHALL DAVID E	LTC	0-0134221	0656	3
MARSHALL DAVID L	2LT	0-0413205	0845	2
MARSHALL DONALD	CW2	W-3430233	1266	1
MARSHALL DONALD P	2LT	0-1638001	0145	2
MARSHALL DOUGLAS G	MAJ	0-1040435	1165	1
MARSHALL EARL B	WO1	W-2142520	0757	1
MARSHALL EDWARD I	MAJ	0-0268109	0163	1
MARSHALL EDWARD V	WO1	W-2207165	0758	2
MARSHALL EDWARD W	MAJ	0-0217398	0464	3
MARSHALL EDWIN A	LTC	0-0349747	1161	3
MARSHALL ELIZABETH	1LT	R-0002157	0454	2
MARSHALL ELLWOOD J	CW4	W-2149462	0866	2
MARSHALL ELMER P	COL	0-0484151	0962	3
MARSHALL ERNEST D	LTC	0-1038053	0867	3
MARSHALL FRANK A	COL	0-0274032	0166	3
MARSHALL FRANK G	LTC	0-0239374	0666	3
MARSHALL FREDERICK	COL	0-0188790	0456	3
MARSHALL GEOFFREY JR	LTC	0-1535673	1164	1
MARSHALL HARRY W	COL	0-0170342	0361	3
MARSHALL HERBERT D	MAJ	0-0275879	0261	3
MARSHALL HOWARD I	CPT	0-0204112	0648	3
MARSHALL JACK A	CPT	0-0451717	0546	2
MARSHALL JAMES C JR	CW3	W-2142872	0960	1
MARSHALL JAMES E	2LT	0-1300347	0244	2
MARSHALL JAMES F	MAJ	0-1692988	0662	1
MARSHALL JESSE E	COL	0-0177361	0648	3
MARSHALL JOE S	CPT	0-0408666	0850	2
MARSHALL JOHN A	MAJ	0-0477555	0447	1
MARSHALL JOHN A	2LT	0-2026942	1048	1
MARSHALL JOHN H	MAJ	0-0358180	0544	2
MARSHALL JOHN H	CPT	0-0441138	0346	2
MARSHALL JOHN O	LTC	0-1002988	1266	3
MARSHALL JOHN S	LTC	0-0105727	1055	3
MARSHALL JOHN S	CPT	0-0474080	0645	2
MARSHALL JOHN W	LTC	0-0383634	0760	1
MARSHALL JOHN W	MAJ	0-1645791	0358	1
MARSHALL JOSEPH	LTC	0-0454689	0857	1
MARSHALL JULIA P	2LT	N-0761137	0445	1
MARSHALL LEHNHOLF S	COL	0-0228858	0562	3
MARSHALL LORENE M	MAJ	N-0792093	0268	1
MARSHALL LOUIS	MAJ	0-0369940	0268	3
MARSHALL LOUIS E	COL	0-0406404	1163	3
MARSHALL LYLE P	MAJ	0-1653129	0664	1
MARSHALL MITCHELL A	COL	0-0347637	0564	1
MARSHALL NEAL F	MAJ	0-0330740	1157	1
MARSHALL OSCAR E	WO1	W-2114970	0754	1
MARSHALL RALPH J	CW2	W-3151223	0968	1
MARSHALL ROBERT A	CW3	W-2144630	0163	1
MARSHALL ROBERT I	CPT	0-1298267	0957	2
MARSHALL ROBERT P	CW4	W-2004577	0767	2
MARSHALL ROSCOE	CW4	W-2150743	0368	1
MARSHALL RUSSELL C	MAJ	0-0191502	1052	3
MARSHALL SAM L	B G	0-0102920	0860	3
MARSHALL SAMUEL	COL	0-0297504	0451	1
MARSHALL SAMUEL A	LTC	0-0116571	0360	3

NAME	GRADE	SVC NO	DATE RET MO YR	RET CODE
MARSHALL SAMUEL G	MAJ	0-0954863	1162	1
MARSHALL THEODORE H	B G	0-0235213	0762	3
MARSHALL THOMAS L	CW3	W-2144242	0863	1
MARSHALL THOMAS T	MAJ	0-1695710	0163	1
MARSHALL VERN B	CPT	0-0165799	0648	3
MARSHALL VERNON T	LTC	0-1046549	1067	1
MARSHALL WILLIAM	1LT	0-1176719	0847	2
MARSHALL WILLIAM B	2LT	0-1914126	0342	1
MARSHALL WILLIAM J	LTC	0-0455286	0864	1
MARSHALL WILLIAM M	LTC	0-0124734	0950	2
MARSHALL WILLIAM R	CW3	W-2150652	0263	1
MARSHBURN CLARENCE E	1LT	0-1290101	0862	2
MARSHMAN GEORGE F	LTC	0-0216933	0862	3
MARSICO CLEMENT W	LTC	0-1303365	0165	1
MARSTON BURTON W	MAJ	0-0208653	0156	3
MARSTON CHARLES A	LTC	0-0311056	0464	3
MARSTON WALTER E	LTC	0-0321723	0366	3
MART ROY M	1LT	0-0390747	1044	2
MARTAUS JOSEPH A	LTC	0-1284357	0561	1
MARTEL CHARLES A	LTC	0-0919858	0865	3
MARTELL DAVID	MAJ	0-1302840	0960	1
MARTELL DAYLE L	LTC	0-1050365	0666	1
MARTELL JAMES	CPT	0-0499574	0547	1
MARTELL LOUIS E	LTC	0-1000621	0754	1
MARTELL WILLIAM C	MAJ	0-1046550	0959	1
MARTELLO RUDOLF	CPT	0-0373762	1047	1
MARTELLO WALLACE	LTC	0-1548100	1060	1
MARTENS IRVIN J	CPT	0-0556253	0746	2
MARTENS JOSEPH H	MAJ	0-0969026	0761	1
MARTENS LOUIS C	LTC	0-1824647	0764	1
MARTENS ROBERT P	1LT	0-2047421	1045	2
MARTENS ROY E	CW3	W-2203323	1267	1
MARTH ALBERT F	LTC	0-0218616	0764	3
MARTHENS PHILIP M	CPT	0-5023833	0668	2
MARTHINSEN JOHN	2LT	0-0389164	1044	2
MARTHINSEN WILLIAM H	LTC	0-0360134	0960	1
MARTI ALFRED J	CPT	0-1697889	0346	2
MARTIG HOWARD J	2LT	0-1108140	0844	2
MARTIN ALBERT	CW3	W-2144443	1161	1
MARTIN ALBERT E	LTC	0-0266539	0968	3
MARTIN ALBERT H	1LT	0-1317647	0345	2
MARTIN ALFRED J	COL	0-0267981	0359	3
MARTIN ALTON F	CW4	W-2205224	1064	3
MARTIN BENJAMIN G	CPT	0-0945897	0159	2
MARTIN BENJAMIN H	CW4	W-2152433	0867	1
MARTIN BILL M	1LT	0-1556177	1055	1
MARTIN BRUCE	COL	0-0481310	0661	1
MARTIN BUFORD L	CPT	0-0258593	0765	3
MARTIN BURL B	MAJ	0-1540767	1060	1
MARTIN BYRD C	CPT	0-0304543	0744	2
MARTIN CAMILO R	1LT	0-1896370	1148	2
MARTIN CARL H	CPT	0-0334001	0947	2
MARTIN CARL T	LTC	0-0103362	0648	3
MARTIN CARTER E	LTC	0-1043430	0468	3
MARTIN CHARLES D	MAJ	0-0986674	0967	1
MARTIN CHARLES E	WO1	W-2148598	1056	1
MARTIN CHARLES H	MAJ	0-0273056	0648	3
MARTIN CHARLES H	MAJ	0-2017093	1060	1
MARTIN CHARLES J	LTC	0-0268980	0968	3
MARTIN CHARLES M	LTC	0-0134251	0648	3
MARTIN CHARLES M JR	CW2	W-2114824	1044	2
MARTIN CHARLES S JR	CPT	0-0465782	0547	2
MARTIN CHARLES W	MAJ	0-2032927	0765	1
MARTIN CHESTER C	1LT	0-0335359	0547	1
MARTIN CHESTER L	LTC	0-0404844	0760	1
MARTIN CHRISTINE	2LT	N-0743588	0844	1
MARTIN CLARENCE E	CW2	W-2210156	1066	1
MARTIN CLARENCE F	COL	0-0212364	0563	1
MARTIN CLARENCE V	MAJ	0-0230438	0558	3
MARTIN CLARENCE V JR	LTC	0-0308237	0462	1
MARTIN CLAUD M	1LT	0-2020572	0364	2
MARTIN CLIFFORD R	MAJ	0-1013432	0160	2
MARTIN CLYDE L	LTC	0-0382709	0456	2
MARTIN DANIEL	MAJ	0-1176419	0556	1
MARTIN DANIEL D	LTC	0-0450749	0752	1

NAME	GRADE	SVC NO	DATE RET MO YR	RET CODE
MARTIN DOMINIC H	WO1	W-2152708	0656	1
MARTIN DONALD N	CPT	0-1170478	0862	2
MARTIN DONALD R	CPT	0-0342863	1065	1
MARTIN DOUGLAS B	LTC	0-1015087	0762	1
MARTIN DREW W JR	MAJ	0-1881937	0467	1
MARTIN DREW A	COL	0-0363590	1265	1
MARTIN DWIGHT E	CW2	W-2144533	1060	1
MARTIN EARL H	LTC	0-0324046	0968	3
MARTIN EARL J	MAJ	0-1799528	0361	1
MARTIN EDWARD A	1LT	0-2020176	0659	1
MARTIN EDWARD D	CPT	0-1030267	0161	1
MARTIN EDWARD L	1LT	0-1319298	0847	2
MARTIN ELBERT C	CPT	0-0121577	0947	2
MARTIN ELBERT H	COL	0-0103356	0858	3
MARTIN EMMETT J	CW4	W-2124032	1054	1
MARTIN EMMONS A	MAJ	0-0202306	0257	3
MARTIN EMORY H	1LT	0-1303752	1045	2
MARTIN ENOCH G	LTC	0-0373439	0167	1
MARTIN ENOLA M	1LT	N-0797709	0549	2
MARTIN ERNEST H	MAJ	0-1297561	1060	1
MARTIN ERNEST L JR	CPT	0-1303366	0848	2
MARTIN EUGENE C	LTC	0-0293194	0562	2
MARTIN EVERETT E	LTC	0-0251348	0564	3
MARTIN FAY H	MAJ	0-0311951	0458	3
MARTIN FLOYD R	COL	0-0299916	0264	1
MARTIN FORD E	CPT	0-0391188	0346	2
MARTIN FRANK A JR	CW2	W-2113618	0746	2
MARTIN FRANK B	COL	0-0174652	0356	3
MARTIN FRANK R	LTC	0-0918775	1264	3
MARTIN FRANK R	1LT	0-0386931	0145	2
MARTIN FRED B	CPT	0-1703692	0745	2
MARTIN FRED M	CW4	W-2001598	0466	3
MARTIN FRED O	CW4	W-2005904	0964	3
MARTIN FREDERICK	1LT	0-1844797	0854	1
MARTIN FREDERICK	CW2	W-2152274	0661	1
MARTIN FREEMAN G	MAJ	0-0174101	0461	3
MARTIN GARNETT W	LTC	0-0256463	1161	3
MARTIN GENE J	CW2	W-2210696	0566	1
MARTIN GEORGE	LTC	0-0125154	0945	2
MARTIN GEORGE A	MAJ	0-1000815	0747	2
MARTIN GEORGE A	MAJ	0-1775720	1045	2
MARTIN GEORGE E	CPT	0-0490000	1043	2
MARTIN GEORGE E	LTC	0-1945206	0168	2
MARTIN GEORGE G	LTC	0-1310360	0562	1
MARTIN GEORGE H	MAJ	0-0455277	0165	1
MARTIN GEORGE H	MAJ	0-0965091	0665	2
MARTIN GEORGE L	COL	0-0302137	0368	3
MARTIN GERALD J	CW3	W-2148676	0563	1
MARTIN GERTRUDE E	1LT	N-0721991	0646	1
MARTIN GLEN B	CW2	W-2209654	1265	1
MARTIN GLEN W	LTC	0-0284263	0947	2
MARTIN GORDON G	MAJ	0-2103028	1063	1
MARTIN GRACE T	MAJ	N-0756308	1268	1
MARTIN GRANVILLE	1LT	0-0486971	0645	2
MARTIN GUY V	CPT	0-0328763	0754	2
MARTIN HAROLD J	LTC	0-0265037	0862	3
MARTIN HAROLD W	CPT	0-1876591	0967	1
MARTIN HAROLD W	MAJ	0-1886189	0468	1
MARTIN HARRY L	CPT	0-0519434	0949	1
MARTIN HARRY W	MAJ	0-1045165	0157	1
MARTIN HENRY F	CPT	0-0979575	0262	1
MARTIN HENRY H JR	LTC	0-0354250	0563	3
MARTIN HENRY J	MAJ	0-1080570	0162	1
MARTIN HERBERT D	CPT	0-0387633	1144	2
MARTIN HERBERT H	LTC	0-2262776	0468	1
MARTIN HERSCHEL E	CW2	W-2147514	1060	1
MARTIN HERSHEL J	COL	0-0354423	0857	1
MARTIN HOWARD G	LTC	0-0270422	0368	3
MARTIN HOWARD W	MAJ	0-0493637	0252	2
MARTIN HUBERT S	CW2	W-2147464	0157	1
MARTIN HUGH K	MAJ	0-0138490	0449	3
MARTIN IRL R	CPT	0-0980548	0359	2
MARTIN JACK	LTC	0-1691871	0368	2
MARTIN JACK E	LTC	0-0267076	1068	3
MARTIN JAMES	MAJ	0-0202681	0858	3

NAME	GRADE	SVC NO	DATE RET MO YR	RET CODE
MARTIN JAMES	CPT	0-2012526	0757	1
MARTIN JAMES A	CW3	W-2146306	0964	1
MARTIN JAMES C	MAJ	0-0943009	0765	1
MARTIN JAMES C	CW3	W-2141623	0559	1
MARTIN JAMES H	LTC	0-0550222	0265	1
MARTIN JAMES I	COL	0-0177161	0257	1
MARTIN JAMES M	CPT	0-0959460	0161	1
MARTIN JAMES M	CW2	W-2115851	0549	2
MARTIN JAMES T	CPT	0-1292366	1046	2
MARTIN JAMES W	LTC	0-1182645	0667	1
MARTIN JAMES W	MAJ	0-1923504	0665	1
MARTIN JESSE S	LTC	0-0302735	1065	3
MARTIN JEWEL F	MAJ	N-0801342	0468	1
MARTIN JOHN C JR	MAJ	0-2003246	0268	2
MARTIN JOHN D JR	LTC	0-0277077	0863	3
MARTIN JOHN E	1LT	0-0512866	0547	2
MARTIN JOHN G	1LT	0-1318621	0745	2
MARTIN JOHN H	2LT	0-1289293	1044	2
MARTIN JOHN J	LTC	0-0223193	1046	2
MARTIN JOHN J	LTC	0-1181361	0361	1
MARTIN JOHN J	MAJ	0-1593701	0661	1
MARTIN JOHN J JR	MAJ	0-0441461	0662	1
MARTIN JOHN R	MAJ	0-1328825	0163	1
MARTIN JOHN S	COL	0-0181015	1060	3
MARTIN JOHN S	CPT	0-0510805	0649	1
MARTIN JOHN S	LTC	0-0982566	0268	1
MARTIN JOHN T	COL	0-0389056	0268	1
MARTIN JOHN T	MAJ	0-2005675	0756	3
MARTIN JOHN W	MAJ	0-1182184	1060	1
MARTIN JOHN W	MAJ	0-2042866	0257	2
MARTIN JOSEPH V	1LT	0-0540507	0346	2
MARTIN JUSTIN E	MAJ	0-1045196	0765	1
MARTIN KEMP	MAJ	0-0245138	1063	3
MARTIN KENNETH H	CPT	0-0241355	1163	3
MARTIN KURT G	CW3	W-2136694	1061	1
MARTIN LANDRUM E	LTC	0-2000845	0563	1
MARTIN LAWRENCE W	1LT	0-1061392	1045	2
MARTIN LEE M	LTC	0-0408641	0561	1
MARTIN LEON	CPT	0-1302495	0165	1
MARTIN LEONARD D	COL	0-0451140	0459	1
MARTIN LEROY E	MAJ	0-1922599	1163	1
MARTIN LEWE B	1LT	0-1119337	0846	2
MARTIN LEWIS W	CW2	W-2143001	1160	1
MARTIN LINUS B	LTC	0-0304732	0560	1
MARTIN LIONEL E	CW4	W-2103757	1057	1
MARTIN LOCKETT B	CPT	0-0409513	0245	2
MARTIN LUTHER E	MAJ	0-1688532	0666	1
MARTIN LYLE B	1LT	0-1174637	1045	2
MARTIN MARGARET M	2LT	N-0796028	0446	1
MARTIN MARION R	LTC	0-0268962	0546	2
MARTIN MARION S	COL	0-0222449	0256	3
MARTIN MARVIN L	1LT	0-1306738	0545	2
MARTIN MAX A	1LT	0-1313266	0145	2
MARTIN MELROWE O	LTC	0-1185190	0163	1
MARTIN MELVIN L	LTC	0-0175026	0956	2
MARTIN MELVIN L	MAJ	0-1173367	0363	1
MARTIN MERLIN A	LTC	0-0321331	0959	3
MARTIN MILFORD E	LTC	0-0285665	1168	3
MARTIN NORMAN	WO1	W-2144257	0459	2
MARTIN NORMAN H	2LT	0-1584565	0844	2
MARTIN OGLE J	LTC	0-0512544	0157	1
MARTIN ORLANDO A	LTC	0-0491920	1160	1
MARTIN OWEN C	LTC	0-0930670	0465	1
MARTIN PAUL	LTC	0-1590635	1067	1
MARTIN PAUL M	LTC	0-1015882	0461	1
MARTIN PAUL T	MAJ	0-0101971	1036	1
MARTIN PAUL W	1LT	0-1290784	0845	1
MARTIN RALPH A	2LT	0-1544687	1044	2
MARTIN RALPH J	LTC	0-0350004	0368	3
MARTIN RALPH L	LTC	0-1286321	0261	1
MARTIN RAYMOND C	CPT	0-1331200	1057	1
MARTIN RAYMOND D	CPT	0-1549777	0158	2
MARTIN RAYMOND H	CPT	0-0329460	0844	2
MARTIN RAYMOND L	LTC	0-1797682	1167	1
MARTIN REGINALO L	LTC	0-2030131	0266	1

NAME	GRADE	SVC NO	DATE RET MO YR	RET CODE
MARTIN RESBERT P	CPT	0-1320356	1147	2
MARTIN RICHARD D	MAJ	0-1881792	0964	1
MARTIN RICHARD F	CPT	0-1014380	0945	2
MARTIN RICHARD R	LTC	0-0482069	0246	2
MARTIN RICHARD W	CW2	W-2145911	1165	1
MARTIN ROBERT E	COL	0-0279864	0368	3
MARTIN ROBERT E	LTC	0-1039455	0145	1
MARTIN ROBERT M	CW4	W-2104268	0659	1
MARTIN ROBERT O	LTC	0-0210273	0455	3
MARTIN ROBERT P	LTC	0-1322248	0566	1
MARTIN ROBERT S	LTC	0-0365635	0859	1
MARTIN ROBERT W	MAJ	0-1061434	1060	1
MARTIN ROGER C	LTC	0-0318536	0266	3
MARTIN ROLAND L	CW3	W-2205917	0567	1
MARTIN ROY B	LTC	0-0423875	0847	2
MARTIN ROY L	CW3	W-2149775	0865	1
MARTIN ROY S	MAJ	0-0275442	1264	3
MARTIN SAM B	LTC	0-1306739	0566	3
MARTIN SIMPSON G	CW2	W-2149387	0756	1
MARTIN SOPHIA L	1LT	N-0732371	1045	1
MARTIN SPENCER D	MAJ	0-0956866	0563	1
MARTIN STEVE	CW4	W-2117893	0167	1
MARTIN STEVEN J	CPT	0-5323319	0867	2
MARTIN STEVENS J	COL	0-0348433	0866	3
MARTIN THEODORE R	LTC	0-1284540	0757	1
MARTIN THEODORE S	CPT	0-0252249	0865	3
MARTIN THOMAS	CPT	0-0184058	0644	2
MARTIN THOMAS A	CW2	W-2146551	1061	1
MARTIN THOMAS D	CPT	0-0231374	0859	3
MARTIN THOMAS E	1LT	0-0980257	0259	1
MARTIN THOMAS J	LTC	0-0324347	0760	1
MARTIN THOMAS J	1LT	0-1881668	0853	2
MARTIN TOM B	COL	0-0125453	1049	3
MARTIN VAIDEN C	MAJ	0-0510611	0355	3
MARTIN VENVERT W	CPT	0-2033875	0562	2
MARTIN VERNON E	MAJ	0-1535228	0264	1
MARTIN VIRGIL G	LTC	0-0143852	0457	3
MARTIN WALLACE B	MAJ	0-1288089	0859	1
MARTIN WALLACE R	LTC	0-1635097	0761	1
MARTIN WELLINGTON	CW4	W-2118523	1062	3
MARTIN WILFRED J JR	MAJ	0-1115341	0161	1
MARTIN WILLIAM B	2LT	0-1320397	0345	2
MARTIN WILLIAM C	MAJ	0-1174059	0961	1
MARTIN WILLIAM C JR	LTC	0-1284541	0954	1
MARTIN WILLIAM E	MAJ	0-0249052	1064	3
MARTIN WILLIAM F	MAJ	0-0374598	0146	2
MARTIN WILLIAM F JR	CW3	W-2211071	0868	1
MARTIN WILLIAM H	COL	0-0335128	0346	2
MARTIN WILLIAM H	MAJ	0-0585668	1057	1
MARTIN WILLIAM H	CW4	W-2142978	0963	2
MARTIN WILLIAM J	CPT	0-1110640	0846	2
MARTIN WILLIAM J	MAJ	0-1302841	0861	1
MARTIN WILLIAM L	CPT	0-0262095	0458	3
MARTIN WILLIAM M	CW2	W-2109012	1147	2
MARTIN WILLIAM O JR	CW4	W-2144397	1068	1
MARTIN WILLIAM R	LTC	0-0389035	0760	1
MARTIN WILLIAM R	MAJ	0-1634109	1162	1
MARTIN WILLIAM R	CW2	W-2208940	1065	1
MARTIN WILLIAM S	2LT	0-0920694	1044	2
MARTIN WILLIAM T JR	LTC	0-0237226	0962	1
MARTIN WOODIE B	MAJ	0-0970665	0565	1
MARTIN WYATT	1LT	0-0476451	0547	1
MARTINA ALFEO J	1LT	0-1103300	0346	2
MARTINA GENO A	CW2	W-2143570	0358	2
MARTINA SAMUEL A JR	CPT	0-0392464	1145	2
MARTINDALE DICK	1LT	0-1105652	0845	2
MARTINDALE GEORGE H	MAJ	0-0199459	0859	3
MARTINDALE JOHN C	CPT	0-1055910	0163	2
MARTINDALE THOMAS	MAJ	0-0402739	0457	1
MARTINDALE WINFRED L	MAJ	0-0143889	0559	3
MARTINE RALPH L JR	CPT	0-2041221	0562	1
MARTINEAU JOHN A	LTC	0-1306298	1163	1
MARTINEE ROBERT F	MAJ	0-1541244	0847	2
MARTINEK RUDOLPH F	MAJ	0-1939094	0756	2
MARTINELLI JOHN	COL	0-0220297	0355	1

NAME	GRADE	SVC NO	DATE RET MO YR	RET CODE
MARTINEZ DAMIAN	MAJ	0-2262645	0961	1
MARTINEZ DAVID S	MAJ	0-1048890	0966	1
MARTINEZ JAMES O	CPT	0-1305281	1062	1
MARTINEZ JOE	MAJ	0-1824337	0561	1
MARTINEZ JOSE M	LTC	0-0452009	1069	1
MARTINEZ JOSE R	CPT	0-1339897	0462	1
MARTINEZ JUAN D	MAJ	0-1934336	0968	1
MARTINEZ MANUEL A	MAJ	0-1556020	0960	1
MARTINEZ MANUEL H	LTC	0-0386407	0560	1
MARTINEZ NICK M	1LT	0-1315523	0350	2
MARTINEZ RAFAEL G	CPT	0-0396768	0761	1
MARTINEZ RAMON P	MAJ	0-0406948	0960	1
MARTINEZ ROBERT J	MAJ	0-1703935	0361	1
MARTINEZ THOMAS H	LTC	0-1594631	0962	2
MARTINEZ-DAVILA AORI	CW3	W-2151637	0366	1
MARTINEZ-DAVILA RAFA	LTC	0-1288414	0364	1
MARTINEZ-DE ANDINO F	CW2	W-2211962	0266	1
MARTINEZ-RIVERA VIRG	CPT	0-0219699	0165	3
MARTINI ALFRED	CW3	W-2214761	0868	1
MARTINI PAULINA M	1LT	N-0752396	0353	2
MARTINIAK LEONARD J	1LT	0-1100666	0745	2
MARTINO CATHERINE	2LT	N-0751399	0645	1
MARTINO JOSEPH	CPT	0-0984556	0562	1
MARTINO PHILIP T	LTC	0-0451882	0261	1
MARTINO ROBERT A	COL	0-0272815	0859	3
MARTINOT PIERRE M	CPT	0-1313267	1045	2
MARTINSON BERNARD A	MAJ	0-1798874	0461	1
MARTINSON BRADY	CPT	0-2050884	0861	1
MARTINSON VERN H	CPT	0-1285260	0146	2
MARTINUS JOHN L	LTC	0-0302125	0860	1
MARTLEY WILLIAM R	LTC	0-1045531	0665	1
MARTO JOHN P	CPT	0-2015930	0758	1
MARTON GEORGE L	MAJ	0-1080946	0859	1
MARTONE WILLIAM M	2LT	0-1301510	0664	1
MARTORANI WILLIAM	LTC	0-0386859	0560	1
MARTTILA REINO J	1LT	0-1018094	0847	2
MARTTINEN ALPO K	COL	0-0985337	0268	1
MARTYNIAK STANLEY L	LTC	0-1584566	0762	1
MARTYNIAK WILLIAM	MAJ	0-1316306	0657	1
MARTZ ARTHUR A	CPT	0-1030690	1046	1
MARTZ FORREST L	COL	0-0218617	0658	1
MARTZ JOSEPH R	COL	0-0340569	0960	1
MARTZ KARL B	LTC	0-2046561	0257	1
MARULLO LOUIS J	MAJ	0-1998506	0161	1
MARUS GEORGE	LTC	0-0410643	1162	1
MARUSAK PETER	MAJ	0-1012994	0547	2
MARUTANI WILLIAM M	2LT	0-0936289	1047	2
MARVICH MARTIN D JR	CPT	0-1698173	0345	2
MARVILL HOWARD A	LTC	0-0286219	0450	1
MARVIN CHESTER J	CPT	0-1324175	0847	2
MARVIN EDWARD A	LTC	0-1048891	0564	1
MARVIN EDWIN J	MAJ	0-0974430	0264	1
MARVIN NEIL E	LTC	0-0286399	0163	3
MARVIN PAUL H	CW4	W-2136513	0966	2
MARVIN WILLIAM H JR	CPT	0-0422203	0447	2
MARVIN WILMER C	MAJ	0-0957749	0868	1
MARWITZ JULIUS A	LTC	0-0916968	0266	3
MARX EMIL F	COL	0-0178916	1052	3
MARX GEORGE J	LTC	0-1297398	1061	1
MARX GERALD J	CW3	W-2148648	0267	1
MARX JOSEPH N	COL	0-0171350	0953	3
MARX MONROE F	2LT	0-1585829	0644	2
MARXEN EDWARD H	LTC	0-0164883	0550	3
MARXSON FRED R	LTC	0-0282754	0767	3
MARY JACOB	LTC	0-0157487	0948	2
MARY MILTON B	CPT	0-0487140	0844	2
MARYE MADISON E	MAJ	0-1925429	1165	1
MARYMEE JOHN D	CW4	W-2115934	0254	1
MARYNICK TEOFIL	MAJ	0-1825027	0355	1
MARZANO FRANK	LTC	0-0382341	0657	1
MARZANO GALLIO J	CW4	W-2002111	0762	3
MARZANO ROCCO G	MAJ	0-0406109	0546	2
MARZARI GUY J JR	LTC	0-0441965	0964	1
MASAR JOHN J	1LT	0-1317320	0546	2
MASARIK STEPHEN F JR	1LT	0-1823032	0644	2

NAME	GRADE	SVC NO	DATE RET MO YR	RET CODE
MASARSKY HARRY	CW2	W-2149018	0761	1
MASBACH FLORES	LTC	N-0701400	1046	1
MASCARI PAUL F	1LT	O-1685013	0853	2
MASCETTE VINCENT J	2LT	O-1119764	0652	2
MASCHMANN JAMES W	LTC	O-1691914	0966	1
MASCHMEIER EMMETT C	LTC	O-0334976	0947	2
MASCHMEYER WILLIAM L	COL	O-0247928	1066	3
MASCIA FRANKLIN J	CPT	O-0374764	0746	2
MASCOLO ARNOLD D	MAJ	O-1638009	1060	1
MASEM MATTHEW C	MAJ	O-1316909	0761	1
MASEN JOHN M	MAJ	O-0502379	0250	1
MASENGILL HOWARD R	LTC	O-0251099	0260	1
MASHBIR SIDNEY F	COL	O-0151029	0951	3
MASHBURN FRANKLIN B	MAJ	O-1684982	0363	1
MASHBURN SNYDER F	LTC	O-1534553	0865	1
MASHEWSKE CHARLES E	1LT	O-1307440	0446	2
MASI ANTHONY	LTC	O-1549780	0164	1
MASI ROMEO J	MAJ	O-1635098	0766	1
MASICK RUTH V	2LT	N-0796344	0946	1
MASICLAT CIPRIANO	CPT	O-2027043	1149	1
MASIN FRANCIS A	CPT	O-0421796	0345	2
MASK WALTER S	COL	O-0258534	0468	3
MASKEL JOSEPH A	LTC	O-1038753	0563	1
MASKELL JOHN W	LTC	O-1183358	0764	1
MASKIELL JAMES JR	CPT	O-0348196	0745	2
MASKIELL JOSEPH	LTC	O-0302983	1068	3
MASKOWITZ CHARLES W	CPT	O-1296466	0145	2
MASLANSKY MANUEL M	LTC	O-0263476	1263	3
MASLIN MARY M	MAJ	N-0736867	0966	3
MASLOFF RAYMOND E	CW3	W-2143578	0762	1
MASLON VICTOR D	LTC	O-2049638	0766	1
MASLOSKI JOHN J	2LT	O-1644565	0144	2
MASLOWSKI STEPHEN A	MAJ	O-1293287	0661	1
MASLYK JULIAN A	LTC	O-1053714	1264	1
MASON ARTHUR R	CPT	O-1650948	0657	1
MASON BENTON A	LTC	O-2033648	0367	1
MASON BRUCE G	LTC	O-0428721	1066	1
MASON CHARLES E	COL	O-0319903	0565	3
MASON CHARLES J	CPT	O-0349993	1145	2
MASON CHARLES J	MAJ	O-1045828	1059	1
MASON CHARLES R	COL	O-1581267	0767	1
MASON CHARLES W	MAJ	O-0887988	0755	2
MASON EDWARD W	LTC	O-0257531	0961	3
MASON EDWIN D	LTC	O-1044291	0467	1
MASON EUGENE D	COL	O-0454796	0868	1
MASON FRANCIS G	LTC	O-1174060	0665	3
MASON FRANCIS W	COL	O-0162871	0859	1
MASON FRED C	MAJ	O-2102930	0465	1
MASON GEORGE B	LTC	O-0282801	0460	1
MASON GEORGE E	LTC	O-0220495	0562	3
MASON GEORGE E	CW2	W-2142252	1054	1
MASON GEORGE J	COL	O-0251322	0366	3
MASON GEORGE W	MAJ	O-0320951	0664	3
MASON HARRY E	1LT	O-1590021	0957	2
MASON HARRY F	MAJ	O-0412707	1144	2
MASON HAYDEN E	CW4	W-2141625	0559	1
MASON HORATIO C	COL	O-0252798	0965	3
MASON IRWIN	MAJ	O-0480637	0546	2
MASON JACOB W	CPT	O-0477981	0446	2
MASON JAMES B	B G	O-0219601	0458	3
MASON JAMES E	WO1	W-2147730	0654	2
MASON JAMES H	MAJ	O-4006765	0867	1
MASON JAMES J	CPT	O-0980034	0961	1
MASON JAMES L	1LT	O-1320544	0546	2
MASON JANET C	CW4	V-0311097	0466	1
MASON JOHN	CPT	O-2263626	0658	2
MASON JOHN C	CW4	W-2142046	0562	1
MASON JOHN E	LTC	O-1597185	0964	1
MASON JOHN H	LTC	O-1336409	1167	1
MASON JOHN M	WO1	W-2110491	0444	2
MASON JOY J	CW2	W-2113647	0961	2
MASON LEN J	CW3	W-2146680	0560	1
MASON LEONA M	CPT	N-0902533	1061	2
MASON LEROY W	LTC	O-1000053	0964	1
MASON MAURICE M	MAJ	O-0269289	0667	3

NAME	GRADE	SVC NO	DATE RET MO YR	RET CODE
MASON MELVIN I	CPT	O-1287557	0946	2
MASON OMER E	MAJ	O-1585830	0163	1
MASON RALPH	MAJ	O-1285082	0752	1
MASON RAYMOND V	LTC	O-0905956	0264	3
MASON REGINALD P	CW2	W-2215381	0967	1
MASON RICHARD O	CW2	W-2152769	0565	1
MASON ROBERT D	MAJ	O-1020445	0562	1
MASON ROBERT F	CW4	W-2148104	0867	1
MASON ROBERT J	CPT	O-1060548	1046	2
MASON ROBERT P	MAJ	O-0215949	0264	3
MASON ROBERT S	MAJ	O-2049824	0557	1
MASON RUSSELL E	1LT	O-0343180	0141	2
MASON SAM	CPT	O-0331949	0146	2
MASON SAMUEL C	MAJ	O-0501772	1052	2
MASON THOMAS A	LTC	O-0214767	0960	1
MASON THOMAS J	CW3	W-2147856	0357	1
MASON THOMAS W	CW3	W-2112165	0454	1
MASON THOMAS Y	CPT	O-0455269	0446	2
MASON WALTER F	LTC	O-1010865	0366	1
MASON WATSY H	CW3	W-2143074	0258	1
MASON WILLIAM N	CPT	O-1541504	1145	2
MASON WILLIAM S	MAJ	O-0237100	0355	3
MASON WILLIAM W	1LT	O-0373340	0148	1
MASON WILLIAM W	1LT	O-1178556	0646	2
MASON ZELNA V	MAJ	O-0505787	1046	2
MASONCUP SEWELL E	1LT	O-1313505	0945	2
MASOTTI GEORGE M	CPT	O-0347527	0146	2
MASS LEON J	1LT	O-1553871	1045	2
MASSA JOSEPH M	1LT	O-0405912	1143	2
MASSA PAUL L	CPT	O-1167966	0246	2
MASSA RAPHAEL	CPT	O-0450459	0146	2
MASSAD ERNEST L	M G	O-0302186	1268	3
MASSARI SILVIO C	LTC	O-0206248	0562	3
MASSARD JOSEPH O	CW2	W-2214337	0168	1
MASSENGALE RAY	MAJ	O-0464913	0148	1
MASSEY ANDREW J	CW2	W-2206552	0264	1
MASSEY CALVIN L JR	CW3	W-2203643	1166	1
MASSEY EARL D	LTC	O-0298905	0948	2
MASSEY HAROLD L	COL	O-0300147	0364	2
MASSEY JAMES W	MAJ	O-1106932	0860	2
MASSEY OLIVER T	MAJ	O-0112329	1049	3
MASSEY SAM J	WO1	W-2144093	0358	1
MASSEY THOMAS J	MAJ	O-1294167	1052	1
MASSEY VIRGIL H	CPT	O-0484855	0848	1
MASSEY WALTER	MAJ	O-0329419	0260	3
MASSEY WILLIAM O	MAJ	O-1120769	0663	1
MASSEY WILLIAM M	LTC	O-1056163	1165	2
MASSIE HOMER B	MAJ	O-0500976	0347	2
MASSIE IRVIN L	CW2	W-2154867	1057	1
MASSIE WILLIAM K JR	MAJ	O-0357845	0846	2
MASSINGILL AARON W	MAJ	O-1937395	0566	1
MASSINGILL WILLIAM L	MAJ	O-1308529	0255	2
MASSO JOSE C	MAJ	O-2029534	0261	1
MASSON STANLEY F	CPT	O-0438799	1045	2
MASSOTH ALYSE C	1LT	N-0723676	1046	1
MASSOUD ALFRED P	MAJ	O-1295399	1160	1
MAST FRED R	COL	O-0154631	1056	3
MAST OSCAR P	LTC	O-0206112	0960	3
MAST PHIL H	MAJ	O-0258733	0168	3
MAST RAYMOND E	CPT	O-0982684	0363	2
MASTELLAR BRUCE G	LTC	O-1044890	1162	1
MASTENBROOK FRED A	MAJ	O-0299870	1044	2
MASTER GUSTAVE W	LTC	O-0428032	1154	1
MASTERS CHARLES H	LTC	O-0359812	0559	1
MASTERS DONALD B	MAJ	O-1593703	1062	1
MASTERS DONALD F	CPT	O-1018740	0863	1
MASTERS DONALD P	CW4	W-2146707	1268	1
MASTERS DWIGHT S	LTC	O-0916388	0664	3
MASTERS GERALD R	CPT	O-1297914	0951	2
MASTERS JOHN	CPT	O-0100898	1038	1
MASTERS KENNETH JR	CW3	W-2206633	0566	1
MASTERS MILTON B	CW2	W-2149707	0361	1
MASTERS MYRL W	MAJ	O-1318205	0263	1
MASTERS REUBEN H	MAJ	O-1017936	0862	1
MASTERS ROBERT	MAJ	O-1311800	0562	2

NAME	GRADE	SVC NO	DATE RET MO YR	RET CODE
MASTERS ROBERT E L	COL	O-0178254	1159	1
MASTERS STANLEY W	CPT	O-1014008	0248	2
MASTERSON ALVIN M	MAJ	O-0485892	1148	1
MASTERSON RUE B	LTC	O-1543260	1060	1
MASTERSON SAMUEL O	MAJ	O-0961624	0962	1
MASTERSON THOMAS R	CPT	O-0393784	1045	2
MASTERVICH JOHN	MAJ	O-0949829	1062	1
MASTICK GEORGE E	LTC	O-1335552	0768	1
MASTICK MAX B	MAJ	O-0386548	0166	3
MASTIN CHARLES S SR	CPT	O-0984242	0464	1
MASTIN WILLIAM L	WO1	W-2108751	0345	2
MASTON AL	2LT	O-1641548	1044	2
MASTRO HENRY	COL	O-0349748	0460	1
MASTROIANNI ORIZZONT	COL	O-0428072	0966	1
MASTRONARDI FRANK J	CW3	W-2148610	0665	1
MASTROPOLO JOHN J	CPT	O-1690256	0446	2
MASUDA HIROSHI F	CW3	W-2136398	0265	1
MASUDA JOE Y	MAJ	O-0930027	0261	1
MASUR IRVING	CW2	W-2108683	0449	1
MASUYAMA HISAO L	MAJ	O-2030814	1263	1
MATAL HAROLD O	CW2	W-3100598	0568	1
MATCHAN JAMES A	CPT	O-0391584	0159	2
MATCHETTE GORDON T	CW4	W-2131815	0167	1
MATCHICK ANDREW	LTC	O-1169633	1163	1
MATCHIN TOM O	LTC	O-0513922	0865	2
MATECKO ANDY	LTC	O-1287379	0957	1
MATEER ROBERT E	LTC	O-0220430	0246	2
MATEJCZYK JOHN F	LTC	O-0363254	0566	3
MATEO LUCIANO E	1LT	O-1896746	0263	2
MATERA ALBERT A	LTC	O-1595676	1162	1
MATEREWICZ GEORGE L	LTC	O-2054015	0457	1
MATERNIAK ALVIN A	MAJ	O-1179950	0863	1
MATEYKA FRANK F JR	CPT	O-0578540	0961	2
MATHEKE CLARENCE C	MAJ	O-1933610	0466	1
MATHENEY WILLIAM L	MAJ	O-1037868	0560	1
MATHENY ALEXANDER	1LT	O-1303753	0646	2
MATHENY AUSTIN C	COL	O-0275241	0864	3
MATHENY ESTON G	LTC	O-0462652	0862	1
MATHENY REX	MAJ	O-0219757	0648	3
MATHENY WALTER R	CW3	W-2205703	0367	1
MATHER CLAYTON B	LTC	O-0324392	1145	2
MATHER HENRY S	COL	O-0267783	0857	3
MATHER JAMES R JR	1LT	O-4006274	1057	2
MATHER MARGARET B	1LT	N-0783760	1045	1
MATHER MILLARD L	MAJ	O-0496716	0161	3
MATHER THOMAS W	1LT	O-0538341	0945	2
MATHER WILLIAM J	COL	O-0121695	0451	2
MATHERS ROBERT L	MAJ	O-1036294	0960	1
MATHERS WILLIAM C	MAJ	O-1316178	0865	1
MATHES DONALD E	COL	O-0165280	1160	3
MATHES ROBERT C	LTC	O-0272239	0859	1
MATHESON HUGH SR	MAJ	O-0366508	1045	1
MATHESON MARVIN M	1LT	O-1167098	0159	1
MATHESON WENDELL H	MAJ	O-1062411	0261	2
MATHEW CHARLES R	WO1	W-2142594	0856	1
MATHEW THOMAS R	CPT	O-0357919	0545	2
MATHEWS ARTHUR E	MAJ	O-1030395	0854	2
MATHEWS CASEY P	CW3	W-2205483	1263	1
MATHEWS DAVIS L	CPT	O-1593704	1054	2
MATHEWS EARL B	MAJ	O-2007057	0562	1
MATHEWS EDWIN C	CPT	O-0532602	1046	2
MATHEWS EUGENE F	COL	O-0294835	0460	3
MATHEWS FRANK M	CW3	RW-2142296	0461	1
MATHEWS GLEN W	CW2	W-2148781	0855	1
MATHEWS HARVEY W	COL	O-0237769	1263	3
MATHEWS LAFAYETTE	COL	O-0114368	0455	3
MATHEWS LEON L	M G	O-0255628	0267	3
MATHEWS LUCIUS D	COL	O-0274730	0453	3
MATHEWS LUKE G	LTC	O-0333401	0648	3
MATHEWS MILLARD F	MAJ	O-0488864	0153	1
MATHEWS MORRIS M	LTC	O-0547121	1064	3
MATHEWS PAUL L	1LT	O-1176123	0447	2
MATHEWS PERRY C	LTC	O-0167067	1053	3
MATHEWS RAYMOND A	LTC	O-1300348	0662	1
MATHEWS REX D	MAJ	O-0545526	0364	1

NAME	GRADE	SVC NO	DATE RET MO YR	RET CODE
MATHEWS RICHARD T	LTC	O-0408198	1060	1
MATHEWS ROBERT J	MAJ	O-0111909	1150	3
MATHEWS ROBERT S	COL	O-0147733	0453	3
MATHEWS THOMAS D	COL	O-1533853	0463	1
MATHEWS THOMAS R	CW3	W-2141368	0760	1
MATHEWS TROUP H	2LT	O-1012588	1143	2
MATHEWS WENDELL E JR	1LT	O-1872435	1053	2
MATHEWS WILLIAM G	MAJ	O-0502090	0655	1
MATHEWSON DALLAS S	LTC	O-1035526	0167	2
MATHEWSON THEODORE P	LTC	O-0299905	0165	3
MATHEY CHARLES W	CPT	O-1110647	0646	2
MATHEY NORRIS A	MAJ	O-0276490	1165	3
MATHIAS JAMES F	2LT	O-0887522	0745	2
MATHIAS JOHN	1LT	O-1896538	0550	1
MATHIAS LEIGH H	LTC	O-0349659	0647	2
MATHIAS ROBERT D	MAJ	O-1685549	0464	1
MATHIES ARTHUR B	CPT	O-0441997	0768	1
MATHIESEN ROY A SR	CPT	O-0482579	0646	1
MATHIEU GEORGE E	LTC	O-0107777	0752	3
MATHIS ALTON P	LTC	O-0288157	1164	3
MATHIS BENJAMIN H	CW3	W-2149278	0864	1
MATHIS CHARLES B	CW3	W-2007231	0167	3
MATHIS CHARLES C JR	LTC	O-0269524	1066	3
MATHIS JAMES E	CPT	O-5326745	0268	2
MATHIS JOHN E JR	LTC	O-1688406	1067	1
MATHIS JOHN H	MAJ	O-0329890	1145	2
MATHIS MILLARD H	CW2	W-2144241	1163	1
MATHIS ROBERT B	LTC	O-0425906	0762	1
MATHIS ZACK C	LTC	O-0450076	0457	1
MATHISEN CHARLES A	LTC	O-1111222	0964	1
MATHLESS NORMAN	CPT	O-0451154	0345	2
MATHON GEORGE W	LTC	O-1543364	0661	1
MATHUS FRANCIS T	LTC	O-1718638	0368	3
MATHWIG WILLIAM H	MAJ	O-1293622	1146	2
MATIER FRANCIS A	MAJ	O-1329728	0862	1
MATIKIEWICZ CHARLE	1LT	O-1544480	0845	2
MATISH EDWARD J	MAJ	O-1101103	0963	1
MATISI ANTHONY F	MAJ	O-1938991	0454	2
MATISIN JOSEPH J	LTC	O-1297226	0857	1
MATISOFF MAURICE	COL	O-0312605	0657	1
MATLACK EDWARD A	CW2	W-2151742	0659	1
MATLACK JACOB D	MAJ	O-0366118	0368	3
MATLOCK GEORGE J	2LT	O-1117670	0345	2
MATLOCK HOMER B	LTC	O-0403914	0562	1
MATLOCK LLOYD W	LTC	O-0321931	1055	1
MATLOCK RALPH S	1LT	O-0557135	1146	2
MATLOCK WESLEY J	WO1	W-2120094	0945	2
MATLOSZ ANNE K	1LT	N-0722823	0246	1
MATNEY CARL P	CPT	O-0407621	0147	2
MATNEY EUGENE D	CPT	O-0450461	0266	1
MATNEY JAMES B	MAJ	O-1168803	1060	1
MATNEY JAMES F	CW2	W-2205151	0461	1
MATNEY RICHARD L	MAJ	O-0974988	0164	1
MATNEY THOMAS H	MAJ	O-0974893	0863	1
MATOS FRANCISCO	CW2	W-2145001	0562	1
MATOS JORGE A	LTC	O-0927417	0666	1
MATOY GEORGE C JR	MAJ	O-1548101	0960	1
MATSCHE JOHN F	MAJ	O-1053715	0564	1
MATSCHKE ARNOLD W	LTC	O-0263214	0255	2
MATSCHULLAT W F	LTC	O-0250187	0646	2
MATSEN BRADFORD C	LTC	O-1168804	1058	1
MATSON CHARLES W	MAJ	O-1104997	0765	1
MATSON CLAUDE D	CW3	W-2150326	0765	1
MATSON ENOR K JR	LTC	O-0333598	0761	1
MATSON FRANK L	LTC	O-0299514	0168	3
MATSON GUSTAVE A	COL	O-0309147	0659	3
MATSON JOHN W	LTC	O-0374760	0746	2
MATSON JOSEPH JR	COL	O-0233472	0865	3
MATSON RALPH A	LTC	O-0279045	0964	3
MATSON RANDALL E	1LT	O-1170071	0145	2
MATSON VICTOR I	LTC	O-0320317	0660	1
MATSUK AGNES A	2LT	N-0773138	1044	1
MATSUMOTO WALTER T	CPT	O-0315402	0946	2
MATSUNAGA ROY T	CW3	W-2152107	0665	1
MATSUURA GEORGE Y	LTC	O-1899442	0268	1

NAME	GRADE	SVC NO	DATE RET MO YR	RET CODE
MATT ROBERT H	1LT	O-1118425	0766	2
MATT WAYLAND P	CPT	O-0420949	0645	2
MATTAS JOHN A	CPT	O-2014534	0565	2
MATTE RUTH E	MAJ	N-0720510	0562	1
MATTEI JAMES J	LTC	O-0291792	0463	1
MATTEI GUS A	1LT	O-1534805	0745	2
MATTER ANTHONY J	CPT	O-0165878	0552	3
MATTERI ELY S	LTC	O-0877167	0766	1
MATTERN ROSYE B	MAJ	O-1293808	0858	1
MATTES EDWIN E	MAJ	O-1685650	0264	1
MATTES EWARENCE H	1LT	O-1056693	1045	2
MATTES MAX W	CPT	O-0423562	0146	2
MATTESON FLOYD A	CPT	O-0450504	0245	2
MATTESON FRED C	CW3	W-2205474	0466	1
MATTESON FREDERICK	MAJ	O-0214574	1162	3
MATTESON GRACE I	1LT	N-0731967	0546	1
MATTESON MARSHALL E	LTC	O-1312579	0966	1
MATTESON RICHARD L	LTC	O-0273446	1060	1
MATTHEW JOHN R	CPT	O-0297803	0146	2
MATTHEWS ANSEL H	LTC	O-0305472	0463	3
MATTHEWS AUDREY L	MAJ	O-0371617	0148	2
MATTHEWS AUBREY L	MAJ	O-1944742	0367	1
MATTHEWS BRUCE B	LTC	O-0524066	1265	3
MATTHEWS CHARLES D	MAJ	O-0967192	1167	1
MATTHEWS CHARLES M	LTC	O-1013456	0462	1
MATTHEWS CHARLES N	LTC	O-1168359	0258	1
MATTHEWS CHARLES W	LTC	O-0242203	1064	3
MATTHEWS CHARLES W	LTC	O-0374142	0860	1
MATTHEWS CLAUDE F	MAJ	O-2001790	0561	2
MATTHEWS CLAUDE I	CPT	O-0302721	0263	3
MATTHEWS CLIFFORD R	MAJ	O-0989655	0968	1
MATTHEWS COKE S JR	COL	O-0258535	1267	3
MATTHEWS DAISY R	CPT	N-0736073	1048	2
MATTHEWS DEE	CPT	O-0297848	1159	3
MATTHEWS DONALD G	LTC	O-1108142	0868	1
MATTHEWS EARL	LTC	O-0499282	1068	3
MATTHEWS EDITH A	MAJ	N-0722994	0165	1
MATTHEWS EDWARD D JR	CW2	W-2145741	0861	1
MATTHEWS EDWARD H	1LT	O-1325603	0347	2
MATTHEWS ELMER L	LTC	O-0386358	0267	3
MATTHEWS ERIC F	LTC	O-1291952	0461	1
MATTHEWS GEORGE JR	LTC	O-0901516	0948	3
MATTHEWS GILBERT B	COL	O-0300365	0646	2
MATTHEWS HAZEN L	1LT	O-1010226	0446	2
MATTHEWS HENRY S III	MAJ	O-2049012	1266	1
MATTHEWS HENRY S JR	COL	O-0234767	0956	3
MATTHEWS JAMES M JR	CPT	O-0419492	0544	2
MATTHEWS JOHN A	CPT	O-0499645	0551	1
MATTHEWS JOHN D	MAJ	O-1331306	1266	1
MATTHEWS JOHN H	1LT	O-0273031	1044	2
MATTHEWS JOHN H JR	LTC	O-1048911	0463	1
MATTHEWS JOHN P	MAJ	O-1182186	0763	1
MATTHEWS JOHN T	LTC	O-1535229	0862	1
MATTHEWS JOHN W	1LT	O-1795808	0258	3
MATTHEWS JOSEPH A	1LT	O-1102842	0847	2
MATTHEWS JOSEPH C JR	COL	O-0255969	0457	1
MATTHEWS JOSEPH J JR	LTC	O-0531778	0868	2
MATTHEWS JOSEPH S	1LT	O-1002068	0154	1
MATTHEWS KENNETH H	2LT	O-2034615	0344	2
MATTHEWS LLOYD P	LTC	O-0250188	0465	3
MATTHEWS MANASSES J	CW2	W-2210415	0864	1
MATTHEWS MAX A	LTC	O-0255846	0163	3
MATTHEWS MOORE	2LT	O-1038431	0544	2
MATTHEWS MYREL O	MAJ	O-0360319	0360	1
MATTHEWS OLLIE G	LTC	O-0171990	1048	3
MATTHEWS PALMER A	COL	O-0230182	0958	1
MATTHEWS PAUL J JR	CPT	O-1176124	0561	1
MATTHEWS PERCY B	MAJ	O-0348181	0947	2
MATTHEWS PHILIP A	CPT	O-2012858	1160	2
MATTHEWS ROBERT C JR	COL	O-0374230	0862	1
MATTHEWS ROBERT M	CW3	W-2148663	0965	1
MATTHEWS RUDOLPH S	COL	O-0336239	1063	3
MATTHEWS RUSSELL L	CPT	O-0543653	0351	2
MATTHEWS SAMUEL R	LTC	O-0221365	0863	3
MATTHEWS SEALE H	MAJ	O-1284542	0553	1

NAME	GRADE	SVC NO	DATE RET MO YR	RET CODE
MATTHEWS THELMA L	MAJ	N-0742990	0665	1
MATTHEWS THOMAS	WO1	W-2130659	0446	2
MATTHEWS THOMAS J	CPT	O-0289721	0546	2
MATTHEWS THOMAS R	CPT	O-0925225	0246	2
MATTHEWS ORA A	CPT	O-0263782	0845	2
MATTHEWS VIRGIL E	CPT	O-0990440	0662	1
MATTHEWS WALTER L S	CPT	O-0331911	0446	2
MATTHEWS WILLIAM E	MAJ	O-0973174	0264	1
MATTHIAS FRANKLIN T	COL	O-0272612	0468	3
MATTHIAS HOWARD C	LTC	O-0352633	0764	2
MATTHIAS RUSSELL H	LTC	O-0274276	0966	3
MATTHIAS WILLIAM T	MAJ	O-1949852	1160	1
MATTHIES HAROLD F	CPT	O-1292809	0447	2
MATTHYS HAROLD F	COL	O-0131848	0651	3
MATTICE CRAIG S	LTC	O-0309321	1160	3
MATTICE MICHAEL M	LTC	O-0167305	1055	3
MATTICK EDWIN C	LTC	O-0254217	0767	3
MATTICK ROY W	CPT	O-1548490	0261	1
MATTINGLY FRED J	CPT	O-0189860	0452	3
MATTINGLY GUY L JR	MAJ	O-0960321	0668	1
MATTINGLY MARK F	WO1	W-2127498	0944	2
MATTINGLY ORVILLE B	CPT	O-0507056	0747	1
MATTIOLI JOSEPH	MAJ	O-0890174	0256	1
MATTIS MICHAEL C	COL	O-0277644	0164	3
MATTIS WILLIAM	LTC	O-0418730	1160	1
MATTISON ARTHUR C	COL	O-0174193	1059	3
MATTOCKS HAROLD P	MAJ	O-1171666	1158	1
MATTOCKS JESSE P	LTC	O-0314744	1167	3
MATTOCKS KENNETH G	CW3	W-2209278	1267	1
MATTOX ERNEST E	LTC	O-1283807	0757	2
MATTOX HORACE	CPT	O-0490894	0750	1
MATTOX WILLIAM R	1LT	O-0910613	0743	2
MATTSON BERNARD H	LTC	O-0805950	0867	1
MATTSON BRUCE D	1LT	O-1824061	0446	2
MATTSON EDWARD J	LTC	O-0308137	0656	3
MATTSON EILLEEN J	2LT	N-0721469	0744	1
MATTSON HAROLD A	MAJ	O-1316179	1062	1
MATTSON HARRY W	MAJ	O-1996965	0163	1
MATTSON HERMAN G	LTC	O-0303269	1057	3
MATTSON PAUL J	CPT	O-0502302	0653	1
MATTSON RAYMOND J	CW2	W-2143600	1158	1
MATTSON ROBERT A	CW3	W-2148515	0864	1
MATTSON ROY A	MAJ	O-1291493	0661	1
MATTSON SELIM A	MAJ	O-0490615	1053	1
MATUCK GEORGE	CW4	W-2103185	1057	2
MATUKONIS ANTHONY M	MAJ	O-0885797	1056	1
MATUKONIS JOSEPH A	MAJ	O-4074618	0468	1
MATULA THOMAS P	1LT	O-0511256	0745	2
MATULIS FRANK G	1LT	O-1895250	0357	1
MATULIS RAYMOND G	LTC	O-1592414	0363	1
MATUSZAK FRANK A	CPT	O-0492448	0254	2
MATUSZKO EDWARD J	CPT	O-1183360	0946	2
MATYSTIK EDMUND A	LTC	O-0499563	0762	2
MATZ ARTHUR	CPT	O-0157518	0840	2
MATZ FRANK P	LTC	O-1640706	0765	1
MATZ FRED W	1LT	O-0888231	1044	2
MATZ JOHN H	MAJ	O-0924540	0546	2
MATZ ROY W	LTC	O-1101943	0361	1
MATZEN HAROLD P	MAJ	O-0267046	0765	3
MATZKE NORMAN A	CW2	W-2148043	0368	1
MATZKO MICHAEL A	LTC	O-0417830	0164	1
MAU LOWELL H	CW3	W-2147635	0161	1
MAUBORGNE BENJAMIN P	COL	O-0343930	0565	1
MAUCERI CHARLES	MAJ	O-1306790	1063	1
MAUCH ERNEST C	MAJ	O-0956053	0562	1
MAUER RONALD W	MAJ	O-1559945	0862	1
MAUER 3RD JOHN L	2LT	O-0444086	0344	2
MAUGANS JAMES W E	1LT	O-0398790	1144	2
MAUGEL JOHN P	1LT	O-0332765	0545	2
MAUGHAM CECIL L	CW3	W-2151137	1164	1
MAUK DESSIE A	COL	O-0441126	0860	1
MAUK JOHN D	CPT	O-0397237	1044	2
MAULDIN DENNIS E	CPT	O-0495505	1052	1
MAULDIN THOMAS R JR	MAJ	O-0554612	0364	1
MAULE JACK	2LT	O-1331643	0246	2

NAME	GRADE	SVC NO	DATE RET MO YR	RET CODE
MAULE MAX D	LTC	O-1312695	0862	1
MAULE CHARLES C JR	LTC	O-0279260	0268	3
MAUM EUGENE	CW2	W-2147763	0560	1
MAUNEY STONEY F JR	LTC	O-0168315	0461	3
MAUPIN JAMES K	CPT	O-1013296	0446	2
MAUPIN WARREN L	CPT	O-0557136	0347	2
MAUPIN WILLIAM A	1LT	O-1316492	0845	2
MAURELLO BERNARD J	CPT	O-1047760	1045	2
MAURER ARNOLD I	LTC	O-0334282	0465	3
MAURER BUD F	CPT	O-1305452	0947	2
MAURER CHARLES J JR	CW3	W-2148746	1066	1
MAURER FREDERICK	MAJ	O-0784744	0860	1
MAURER JOHN G	1LT	O-1054695	0447	2
MAURER LESLIE D	COL	O-0235417	0663	3
MAURER PAUL H	COL	O-0235474	0457	1
MAURER PHILIP E	CPT	O-0544139	1146	2
MAURER REGINALD A	B G	O-0180740	1159	3
MAURER RICHARD H	CW3	W-2146958	1263	1
MAURER ROBERT P	LTC	O-0388765	1060	1
MAURER ROY B	LTC	O-2053898	1154	1
MAURIER DAVID A	COL	O-0145748	0648	3
MAURITZ FRANK F	CPT	O-0312065	0143	2
MAURO CARL	CPT	O-1321795	0147	2
MAURO LUCIA G	1LT	N-0744538	0646	1
MAURY LEWIS A	COL	O-0172167	0352	3
MAURY MELVIN M	COL	O-1579999	0865	1
MAUS JOHN E	CPT	O-1166778	0647	2
MAUS ROGER G	COL	O-0102228	0155	3
MAUSERT CLAYTON L	COL	O-0183544	0957	1
MAUTE WILLIAM C	CPT	O-0125807	0156	3
MAUTNER RALPH A	2LT	O-1588724	0945	2
MAUZY BYRON E	CW2	W-2203636	1057	2
MAUZY CLAUDE R	COL	O-0350097	0846	2
MAVIS STEPHEN F	COL	O-0252797	0464	3
MAWBY ROBERT H	MAJ	O-1634115	0160	1
MAWHAR LAWRENCE F	CW2	W-2150142	0659	1
MAWHINNEY JAMES D	COL	O-0201060	1058	3
MAWN JOHN J	MAJ	O-2010475	0262	1
MAWN PETER R	MAJ	O-1596111	0760	3
MAX MOSES	MAJ	O-1578820	0361	1
MAX PAUL F	COL	O-0294805	0365	3
MAXAM HARRY A	CW3	W-2129706	0459	1
MAXEDON JAMES P	MAJ	O-1109491	0862	1
MAXEY BERNARD E	LTC	O-0238911	1162	3
MAXEY GEORGE E	MAJ	O-0228884	0357	3
MAXFIELD CHARLES E	LTC	O-0451347	0563	1
MAXFIELD CHARLES L	LTC	O-0165857	0358	3
MAXFIELD DONALD V	CPT	O-0343002	1045	2
MAXFIELD GEORGE G	LTC	O-0242496	0461	1
MAXFIELD HAROLD A	COL	O-0187434	0953	3
MAXFIELD WILLIAM B	MAJ	O-1797328	0360	1
MAXIMINI BURT E	MAJ	O-1799591	0861	1
MAXON MILDRED E	2LT	N-0721146	0843	1
MAXSON KENNETH R	CPT	O-1181365	1063	1
MAXSON MELVIN L	LTC	O-0358736	0260	1
MAXSON PAUL A	LTC	O-1546421	1163	2
MAXSON RHEA F	MAJ	L-0201175	0763	3
MAXTED LAURENCE T	CW2	W-2141627	0159	1
MAXWELL ALEXANDER	MAJ	O-0211299	0549	1
MAXWELL ARTHUR A	CPT	O-0481595	0449	1
MAXWELL ARTHUR J	COL	O-0183032	0555	3
MAXWELL AUGUSTUS B	LTC	O-0401704	0364	1
MAXWELL CARL F	CW2	W-2144371	0157	1
MAXWELL CARLTON F	LTC	O-0473109	0962	1
MAXWELL CLARENCE M	CPT	O-0987401	0762	1
MAXWELL CYRUS H JR	COL	O-0153700	0659	3
MAXWELL DAVID	1LT	O-1913818	0124	1
MAXWELL DAVID D	MAJ	O-1536420	0463	1
MAXWELL DONALD R	MAJ	O-0472858	0345	2
MAXWELL EDWARD H	MAJ	O-1037611	1262	1
MAXWELL EUGENE T	CW3	W-2205871	0962	1
MAXWELL FRANK W	1LT	O-1292028	0346	2
MAXWELL FREDERICK	COL	O-0198200	1153	1
MAXWELL GAINES E	LTC	O-0302272	1068	3
MAXWELL GEORGE F	CW4	W-2143351	1060	1

NAME	GRADE	SVC NO	DATE RET MO YR	RET CODE
MAXWELL GERALD C	COL	O-0358761	0160	1
MAXWELL HAROLD P	CW2	W-2143516	0760	2
MAXWELL HARVEY C	COL	O-0224771	0146	2
MAXWELL HUBERT J	CPT	O-0532861	1145	2
MAXWELL JAMES R	CW3	W-2152681	1065	1
MAXWELL JIM J	CW4	W-2110865	1058	1
MAXWELL JOHN C	COL	O-0925359	0567	3
MAXWELL JOHN F	LTC	O-1545541	0160	1
MAXWELL JOHN R	CW3	W-2102054	1154	1
MAXWELL JOHN W	COL	O-0922176	0663	3
MAXWELL JOSEPH L	LTC	O-0303395	0667	3
MAXWELL JOSEPH M	LTC	O-0255697	0166	3
MAXWELL KENNETH L	MAJ	O-0813544	0661	1
MAXWELL LLOYD F	CW3	W-2151620	0361	1
MAXWELL LOREN C	COL	O-0235535	0146	2
MAXWELL NORRIS K	LTC	O-0450396	0561	1
MAXWELL OLIVER K	LTC	O-1638021	0161	1
MAXWELL PAUL R	CPT	O-0209245	0655	3
MAXWELL QUENTIN R	1LT	O-0702223	0245	2
MAXWELL RAYMOND	LTC	O-0460632	1046	1
MAXWELL ROBERT R	MAJ	O-4005319	1167	1
MAXWELL SAMUEL L	MAJ	O-1313506	0260	1
MAXWELL WALTER P	LTC	O-0268223	0968	3
MAY ANTHONY A	LTC	O-0421984	1147	2
MAY BILLY R	MAJ	O-1919177	1163	1
MAY CHARLES W	LTC	O-0375305	1068	3
MAY CLYDE V	LTC	O-0247225	1166	3
MAY CONDA E	1LT	O-0971548	0357	1
MAY DAVID E	CW3	W-2206332	1165	1
MAY DONAL R	1LT	O-1939784	0955	2
MAY DONALD R	1LT	O-1020311	0647	2
MAY EARL C	MAJ	O-0247929	0446	2
MAY EDISON L	MAJ	O-0981860	0865	1
MAY EDWARD L	CW2	W-2215249	0768	1
MAY EMIL P	1LT	O-0377268	0245	2
MAY ERNEST V	LTC	O-0101324	0150	3
MAY ERNEST W	LTC	O-2206179	0768	1
MAY FRANCIS P	MAJ	O-0907876	0750	2
MAY FREDERICK	LTC	O-0218030	0761	2
MAY GEORGE L	1LT	O-2055328	0147	1
MAY HAROLD F	MAJ	O-0358869	0661	1
MAY HARRY JR	COL	O-0253867	0767	3
MAY HERMAN J	LTC	O-1316517	0161	1
MAY HUGH R	MAJ	O-1540650	0563	1
MAY JAMES A	1LT	O-1030807	0957	1
MAY JAMES B	CW2	W-2143656	0661	1
MAY JAMES W	1LT	O-0983408	1062	2
MAY JOHN S	CPT	O-0456143	0644	2
MAY JOHN T	WO1	W-2109667	0145	2
MAY JOSEPH B	LTC	O-0348929	0856	1
MAY MABEL G	2LT	N-0700445	1038	1
MAY MARJORIE D	MAJ	N-0760887	1166	1
MAY PERCY C	LTC	O-0247472	0466	3
MAY PETER G	LTC	O-0290973	1062	3
MAY ROBERT L	LTC	O-0451150	0257	1
MAY ROBERT T	MAJ	O-2263705	1166	1
MAY RUFUS H	CPT	O-1289605	0544	2
MAY SAMUEL	COL	O-0295650	1060	1
MAY STANLEY E	LTC	O-1577536	0761	1
MAY THEODORE S	LTC	O-1172982	0465	1
MAY WALTER R	MAJ	O-0984351	0563	1
MAY WALTER W	MAJ	O-1290968	1060	1
MAY WILLIAM M	CPT	O-1108143	0363	1
MAY WOODWARD J	MAJ	O-0165581	0157	3
MAYALL JAMES H	LTC	O-1285459	1067	3
MAYAUSKY BERNARD E	CPT	O-0963082	0361	1
MAYBACH LELAND F	COL	O-0280804	0468	3
MAYBEE ORRIN S	MAJ	O-1326247	0860	1
MAYBEE REGINALD W	1LT	O-2000463	1146	2
MAYBERRY ARCHER O	CW3	W-2151153	0764	1
MAYBERRY HENRY E	LTC	O-0365642	0460	1
MAYBERRY LESTER H	MAJ	O-1031259	0162	1
MAYBIN ARTHUR H JR	1LT	O-0460041	0245	2
MAYBIN JOHN A	1LT	O-2033009	0551	2
MAYBURY DANIEL C	COL	O-0246438	0664	1

NAME	GRADE	SVC NO	DATE RET MO YR	RET CODE
MAYCUMBER GUY	MAJ	0-0231886	0445	2
MAYDEN WALTER S	COL	0-0248175	1062	3
MAYE HENRY R	CW4	W-2111862	0356	1
MAYE JOHN E	1LT	0-1055080	0346	2
MAYE VIRGIL F	CW3	W-2142769	0459	1
MAYE WARREN H	MAJ	0-1037612	1060	1
MAYEA ELIZABETH	1LT	N-0722167	0246	1
MAYER ALFRED F	1LT	0-1320249	0945	2
MAYER AUBREY E	CW3	W-2146751	0864	1
MAYER BENJAMIN J	LTC	0-1686184	0761	1
MAYER CARL P	COL	0-0216843	1154	3
MAYER DAVID E	B G	0-0178166	0961	3
MAYER FRANCIS L	LTC	0-0263397	0267	3
MAYER FRANK I	LTC	0-0214382	0652	3
MAYER GEORGE E	LTC	0-1165908	0162	1
MAYER GEORGE F	COL	0-0513049	0568	2
MAYER GEORGE W	COL	0-0176069	1055	3
MAYER HAROLD F	1LT	0-1325587	0847	2
MAYER HARRY R	CW3	W-2144304	0363	1
MAYER HUGO E	LTC	0-0195422	1060	3
MAYER JAMES L	MAJ	0-1170073	0561	1
MAYER JOHN S	COL	0-0217175	1058	3
MAYER JOHN W	1LT	0-1301661	0646	2
MAYER MANETTE L	CPT	N-0733825	1046	1
MAYER MILVOY	MAJ	0-1800109	0161	1
MAYER ORLANDO B JR	COL	0-0207136	0857	3
MAYER ROBERT L	COL	0-0289676	0560	1
MAYER ROBERT R	1LT	0-1756666	0955	1
MAYER ROBERT W	LTC	0-1167967	1060	1
MAYER WERNER A	CW3	RW-2136690	1161	1
MAYER WILLIAM F	CW4	W-2141894	1163	1
MAYER WILLIAM O	LTC	0-0497211	0468	3
MAYERHOFER ALFRED F	1LT	0-1062776	1046	2
MAYERS BENEDICT	MAJ	0-0256243	1166	3
MAYERS HENRY L	CPT	0-0486640	0846	2
MAYERS ISADORE	1LT	0-1294693	0845	2
MAYERS LEO V	CW4	W-2149807	1067	2
MAYES CULLUS M	LTC	0-0266435	0859	1
MAYES DON C	LTC	0-0266726	0667	3
MAYES FRANCIS B	MAJ	0-0193987	0861	3
MAYES HAROLD	MAJ	0-0238553	0865	3
MAYES JAMES L	LTC	0-0405734	0960	1
MAYES JESSE J	LTC	0-1059546	1264	1
MAYES LAWRENCE S	CPT	0-1054696	0564	2
MAYES LOUIS T	MAJ	0-1030808	0363	1
MAYES WALTER A	1LT	0-0403131	1144	2
MAYETTA FRANK R	COL	0-0320736	1161	1
MAYEUX LEVY L	2LT	0-0961737	0652	2
MAYFIELD ALFRED G	CW3	W-2127371	0958	1
MAYFIELD BEATRICE J	1LT	N-0727414	0846	1
MAYFIELD DON W	1LT	0-1322058	1045	2
MAYFIELD EDWARD T	1LT	0-1296555	0346	2
MAYFIELD FRANK G	LTC	0-0365328	0660	1
MAYFIELD GEORGE C	COL	0-0272147	0166	3
MAYFIELD HARRY L	COL	0-0285429	0859	1
MAYFIELD HOWARD F	CW2	W-2149019	0159	1
MAYFIELD LAWRENCE A	CW4	W-2145466	0767	1
MAYFIELD LOUIE A	LTC	0-0256538	1167	3
MAYFIELD ROBERT H	LTC	0-0414749	0964	3
MAYFIELD SAMUEL E	1LT	0-1012464	0751	2
MAYFIELD THOMAS M	M G	0-0168362	0161	3
MAYHALL EMMETT A	COL	0-0265121	0363	3
MAYHERCY ROBERT L	LTC	0-1167510	0361	1
MAYHEW JOHN R	MAJ	0-1312476	0658	1
MAYHEW WALTER P JR	MAJ	0-1298413	0361	2
MAYHEW WILLIAM M	MAJ	0-1297663	0261	1
MAYKOVICH ALBERT A	LTC	0-0451349	0657	1
MAYKOVICH JOHN J	MAJ	0-1050468	1153	1
MAYLAND JACK B	LTC	0-0888603	1160	1
MAYLE LESLIE	LTC	0-0493616	0947	1
MAYLUNAS JOHN A	CW3	W-2141725	0459	1
MAYNARD ALFRED A	LTC	0-0914245	1263	1
MAYNARD ALFRED C	CPT	0-0378988	0346	2
MAYNARD CECIL D	CPT	0-0527836	0147	2
MAYNARD CHARLES A	LTC	0-1550654	1060	1

NAME	GRADE	SVC NO	DATE RET MO YR	RET CODE
MAYNARD HAROLD G	COL	0-0355276	0754	1
MAYNARD HIRAM H	COL	0-0185202	0746	2
MAYNARD HOY P	CW2	W-2112574	0846	1
MAYNARD PERRY C	COL	0-0195920	0662	3
MAYNE CARLTON A	MAJ	0-1588149	1065	2
MAYNE WARREN R	1LT	0-0485500	0145	2
MAYNHART JOHN	CPT	0-1576344	0749	2
MAYNOR CHARLES H	CW2	W-2149366	0660	1
MAYO ANDREW J	1LT	0-1062244	0146	2
MAYO ARTHUR	CPT	0-1913838	1133	1
MAYO CARL N	COL	0-0359546	1059	1
MAYO EDWIN A	CPT	0-1004373	1156	1
MAYO FRANK M	1LT	0-0461218	0845	2
MAYO GLENN M	LTC	0-1698194	0261	1
MAYO JOHN W	COL	0-0171773	1061	3
MAYO LACIE L	2LT	0-1108144	1143	2
MAYO LEON G	MAJ	0-1998044	0360	1
MAYO PAUL E	CPT	0-1286159	0156	1
MAYO STEVEN B	LTC	0-1057163	1162	1
MAYO WILLIE A	LTC	0-1169233	0356	1
MAYOR JOSEPH J	WO1	W-2123101	0249	1
MAYORGA GEORGE W	LTC	0-0275948	0756	3
MAYOROS STEVE J	MAJ	0-0432586	0861	1
MAYOROS WILLIAM F	CPT	0-0550250	0764	1
MAYS ABRAHAM W SR	MAJ	0-0509482	1053	1
MAYS DARYL F	1LT	0-1550861	0167	1
MAYS EARL R	CW2	W-2208218	0263	2
MAYS FRANK A	MAJ	0-1639364	0760	1
MAYS HELENA F	1LT	N-0720893	0147	1
MAYS JOHN P	MAJ	0-0468839	0862	1
MAYS JOHN W JR	MAJ	0-0974460	0964	1
MAYS JOSEPH R	MAJ	0-1172983	0762	1
MAYS NEO G	LTC	0-1035527	0755	1
MAYS RAYMOND R	LTC	0-0334909	1267	3
MAYS REAVUS C	COL	0-0347030	0557	1
MAYS RICHARD J	COL	0-0330072	0960	1
MAYS RICHARD J	LTC	0-0352895	0158	1
MAYS SAMUEL C	LTC	0-0335058	0265	3
MAYSHARK JAMES P	CPT	0-0347088	1044	2
MAYSTER RONALD A	1LT	0-1037173	1045	2
MAZA HERBERT	CPT	0-0378859	0546	2
MAZAITIS EDGAR O	COL	0-0386310	0862	1
MAZE THOMAS A	MAJ	0-0442664	0552	1
MAZEAU JOHN Y	LTC	0-0256740	0960	3
MAZEKE WILSON	CW2	W-2147764	0261	1
MAZETIS WALTER R	LTC	0-1100221	1062	1
MAZIKE WALTER J	LTC	0-0493792	0656	1
MAZNEK NICHOLAS	1LT	0-1326104	1145	2
MAZOL JOSEPH J	LTC	0-0328446	0960	1
MAZUR EDWARD W	LTC	0-1283640	0258	1
MAZUR SEYMOUR	CPT	0-0119185	1153	3
MAZURKIEWICZ HENRY J	CW2	W-2115437	0155	1
MAZZA JOHN V	MAJ	0-1311802	0846	2
MAZZANTI VINCENT F	CPT	0-0471192	1045	2
MAZZARELLA ROBERT A	MAJ	0-0449454	1047	2
MAZZARISI ERNEST S	1LT	0-1168807	1144	2
MAZZEI JOHN C	COL	0-0228045	1165	3
MAZZEI OTTO	CPT	0-1919874	0761	1
MAZZEO WILLIAM	LTC	0-1296232	0265	1
MAZZI EARL J	MAJ	0-1644570	0756	1
MAZZIE GASPERO P	LTC	0-0346388	0261	1
MAZZIE ROLAND R	CW2	W-2141629	0656	1
MAZZIOTTA ROBERT P	1LT	0-0537049	0345	2
MAZZOLA NICHOLAS C	LTC	0-1289936	0357	1
MAZZUCCO PETER R	CPT	0-2010704	1158	1
MAZZUCCO ROBERT R	MAJ	0-2291891	1168	1
MC AHEE GARLAND J	MAJ	0-2263116	0763	1
MC AHEE ORMOND A JR	MAJ	0-1555862	0862	1
MC ADAM WILLIAM A	MAJ	0-0235310	1048	3
MC ADAMS CARL JR	COL	0-1576346	0867	1
MC ADAMS DALE A	MAJ	0-0414371	0163	1
MC ADAMS ROBERT L	CPT	0-0509554	1148	1
MC ADOO HOWARD F	1LT	0-1309170	1165	2
MC ADOO WILLIAM A	MAJ	0-0413995	1165	3
MC ADOO WINFRED E	2LT	0-1690744	0647	2

NAME	GRADE	SVC NO	DATE RET MO YR	RET CODE
MC ADOW VIVIAN N	1LT	N-0732763	0746	1
MC AFEE DEVEAUX J	LTC	0-0299229	0861	3
MC AFEE FOREST S	MAJ	0-2020448	0264	1
MC AFEE JAMES P	CPT	0-1653368	0745	2
MC AFEE MILLS B	MAJ	0-1317034	0460	1
MC AHON JACK F	LTC	0-1315707	0767	1
MC ALEAR DORIS F	MAJ	L-1010358	1165	1
MC ALEVEY ALICE Z	CPT	N-0720222	0847	1
MC ALEXANDER HUGH R	CPT	0-0996747	0564	1
MC ALHANY CARL T	1LT	0-0972003	1168	1
MC ALISTER CLINTON L	MAJ	0-0397124	0646	2
MC ALISTER GUY C	MAJ	0-1179953	0761	1
MC ALISTER JAMES E	CPT	0-0386376	0868	3
MC ALISTER JOHN M JR	LTC	0-0355879	1060	1
MC ALISTER JOHN R	LTC	0-0261405	1051	2
MC ALISTER REID W	MAJ	0-0327074	0946	2
MC ALISTER RENEAU S	LTC	0-0288832	0358	1
MC ALISTER ROBERT T	CW3	W-2146381	0662	1
MC ALLEN WILLIAM T	LTC	0-0458469	1162	1
MC ALLISTER CECIL M	LTC	0-0369824	1066	3
MC ALLISTER CHARLES	MAJ	0-1999027	0462	1
MC ALLISTER GEORGE	MAJ	0-1058893	0461	1
MC ALLISTER JACK	LTC	0-0254164	0468	3
MC ALLISTER JAMES R	LTC	0-0242067	1044	2
MC ALLISTER MAX F	COL	0-0226061	0664	3
MC ALLISTER PHILMORE	LTC	0-0312760	1265	3
MC ALLISTER RICHARD	LTC	0-1592415	0365	1
MC ALLISTER ROBERT B	CPT	0-2034555	1145	2
MC ALLISTER THORNTON	LTC	0-0252438	0946	2
MC ALLISTER WILBUR B	LTC	0-0301037	1061	3
MC ALLISTER WILLIAM	CPT	0-1181033	1162	1
MC ALOON JOSEPH O	MAJ	0-1011325	1263	1
MC ALPIN ESTEL C	LTC	0-0510506	0854	1
MC ALPINE DONALD E	1LT	0-1322567	0945	2
MC ALPINE ELLAYNE E	COL	N-0744720	0767	2
MC ALPINE FRED F	MAJ	0-1297227	0358	1
MC ALPINE RODERICK K	MAJ	0-0213735	1263	3
MC ALPINE WAYNE D	LTC	0-0221489	0760	1
MC AMIS LEWIS A	MAJ	0-1543042	0961	1
MC ANALLY CHARLES W	LTC	0-0286076	1263	3
MC ANALLY HEARL P	CW2	W-2150727	0961	1
MC ANALLY OSCAR N	LTC	0-0328048	0668	3
MC ANALLY WILLIAM F	COL	0-0197607	0947	2
MC ANDREW JOSEPH	CPT	0-2029454	0457	1
MC ANDREW MILES F	LTC	0-0516184	0567	1
MC ANINCH HARRY R	COL	0-0410580	0168	1
MC ANULTY DALE	LTC	0-1589002	0761	1
MC ANULTY HARLEY D	WO1	W-2123416	0148	1
MC ANULTY JAMES S	LTC	0-0233125	0165	3
MC ANULTY WALLACE M	LTC	0-1794827	1061	1
MC ARDLE EDWARD J	CPT	0-1175507	0246	2
MC ARDLE JOSEPH J	CW4	W-2141990	0161	1
MC ARTHUR FRANCIS S	LTC	0-1308355	1167	1
MC ARTHUR STUART C	LTC	0-1115465	0767	1
MC ASKILL WILLIAM D	CPT	0-0259037	0945	2
MC ATAMNEY RICHARD W	2LT	0-1258740	0545	2
MC ATEE EUGENE M	2LT	0-2000738	0645	2
MC ATEE FRANK J	CPT	0-0509927	0745	2
MC ATEE LESLIE B	LTC	0-0135241	0960	3
MC AULEY WILLIAM C	CW3	W-2147102	0463	1
MC AULIFFE ALBERT	MAJ	0-1106339	0660	1
MC AULIFFE FRANK H	LTC	0-0333169	0855	3
MC AUSLAN HAROLD L	LTC	0-0231332	1262	2
MC AVEY THOMAS J JR	MAJ	0-0140172	0958	3
MC AYEAL RUF C	MAJ	0-0924690	0547	2
MC BARRON JOSEPH P	LTC	0-0437743	1164	1
MC BEE JAMES W	CW3	RW-2143129	0761	1
MC BEE JOHN	MAJ	0-0941961	1262	1
MC BEE LEROY S	1LT	0-2012546	0447	2
MC BEE LLOYD W	CPT	0-0974431	0257	1
MC BEE WELDON H	LTC	0-0255299	0859	1
MC BETH NEU	LTC	0-0237842	0468	3
MC BRATNIE ELLEN J	MAJ	N-0726711	0863	1
MC BRAYER ELDON E	LTC	0-1549993	1159	2
MC BRAYER THOMAS E	LTC	0-0220101	1062	3

NAME	GRADE	SVC NO	DATE RET MO YR	RET CODE
MC BREARTY CHARLES F	CPT	0-1552116	0163	1
MC BREEN WILLIAM T	MAJ	0-0954225	0166	1
MC BRIDE ANDREW C	1LT	0-1044293	0646	2
MC BRIDE CECIL M	CW2	W-3430990	1268	1
MC BRIDE ELZIE G	2LT	0-2009595	0146	2
MC BRIDE EMMA B	CPT	N-0755651	1046	1
MC BRIDE GEORGE	LTC	0-1043161	1060	1
MC BRIDE GEORGE A	MAJ	0-0244016	0865	3
MC BRIDE GEORGE W	WO1	W-2126717	1156	1
MC BRIDE JOHN S	1LT	0-1324038	0945	2
MC BRIDE JOHN T	CW3	W-2146693	0661	2
MC BRIDE JOSEPH L	MAJ	0-0450457	0855	1
MC BRIDE JOSEPHINE	MAJ	N-0760621	0566	1
MC BRIDE LAUREN E	LTC	0-0363427	0361	1
MC BRIDE LESTER H	LTC	0-0370288	1154	1
MC BRIDE MALCOLM R	CPT	0-1284732	0952	2
MC BRIDE OTTO L	COL	0-0316013	0168	3
MC BRIDE PAUL T	CPT	0-0968388	0361	1
MC BRIDE RALPH F	CPT	0-0220371	0245	2
MC BRIDE RALPH H	LTC	0-1933713	1168	2
MC BRIDE ROBERT J	2LT	0-1012198	0144	2
MC BRIDE ROGER P	LTC	0-0964800	0768	1
MC BRIDE THOMAS W	CW3	W-2145685	0563	1
MC BRIDE WELDON C	LTC	0-1289286	0161	1
MC BRIDE WILLIAM F	MAJ	0-0480472	0557	1
MC BRIDE WILLIS T	CPT	0-1923615	0764	1
MC BRIEN RUTH E	MAJ	N-0720617	1163	1
MC BRIEN WALDO R	LTC	0-0366008	1165	3
MC BRIER CLYATT	CPT	0-0454452	0846	1
MC BRINN ROBERT J	LTC	0-0970304	1067	1
MC BROOM JAMES F	LTC	0-0384207	1160	1
MC BROOM JOHN C	MAJ	0-1997279	0164	1
MC BROOM ROBERT J	LTC	0-1592416	1263	2
MC BROOM WILLIAM H	MAJ	0-2046601	1155	1
MC BRYDE CHARLES M	2LT	0-1300508	1044	2
MC BURNEY HAROLD H	COL	0-0225884	0959	3
MC CABE ARTHUR E JR	COL	0-0315142	1166	1
MC CABE ARTHUR T	MAJ	0-1290277	0157	1
MC CABE CHARLES J	CPT	0-1338834	0464	1
MC CABE DONNA S	MAJ	N-0723237	0265	1
MC CABE EDWARD J	1LT	0-0514511	0547	2
MC CABE FRANK J	LTC	0-1044609	0761	1
MC CABE GEORGE E	COL	0-0348434	1265	3
MC CABE GEORGE W	1LT	0-1314932	1047	2
MC CABE HENRY V	MAJ	0-1287208	1060	1
MC CABE JAMES F	MAJ	0-1650952	0263	1
MC CABE JAMES M	CW2	W-2107854	0847	2
MC CABE LOUIS C	COL	0-0240760	0364	3
MC CABE LUKE V JR	CPT	0-1116795	1158	2
MC CABE MERRILL J	MAJ	0-0969511	0762	1
MC CABE THOMAS R	LTC	0-1057817	0163	1
MC CABE THOMAS W	MAJ	0-0538117	0646	2
MC CABE WILLIAM B	MAJ	0-2008752	0767	1
MC CABE WILLIAM F	1LT	0-0503584	0445	2
MC CABE WILLIAM S JR	CPT	0-1534558	0647	2
MC CAFFERTY EDWARD E	LTC	0-0994620	0968	1
MC CAFFERTY ROBERT H	LTC	0-0925265	0964	3
MC CAFFERY HAROLD W	CW2	W-2144522	1060	1
MC CAFFERY PATRICK G	MAJ	0-1317322	1161	1
MC CAFFERY WALTER M	CW2	W-2141370	0360	1
MC CAFFREY HOWARD T	LTC	0-1302157	1062	1
MC CAFFREY JAMES A	LTC	0-1180604	0267	1
MC CAFFREY JAMES G	LTC	0-0238377	0961	3
MC CAFFREY JOSEPH E	COL	0-0190366	0856	3
MC CAFFREY JOSEPH F	1LT	0-1284360	0644	2
MC CAFFREY LEE E	CW3	W-2148126	1163	1
MC CAFFREY MICHAEL A	1LT	0-1294168	0246	2
MC CAFFREY RICHARD	LTC	0-1695670	0762	1
MC CAFFREY ROBERT T	LTC	0-1179143	0468	1
MC CAFFREY THOMAS E	LTC	0-1697949	0962	1
MC CAGUE MICHAEL J	LTC	0-1037142	0867	1
MC CAHILL WILLIAM F	COL	0-0387227	0263	1
MC CAIG RAYMOND J	MAJ	0-1797851	0663	1
MC CAIN CLARENCE E	MAJ	0-0971753	1262	1
MC CAIN CLAWSON W	MAJ	0-1651345	0560	1

332-811 O - 69 - 17

NAME	GRADE	SVC NO	DATE RET MO YR	RET CODE
MC CAIN [illegible]	MAJ	[illegible]	[illegible]	1
MC CAIN [illegible] H	LTC	[illegible]	0567	3
MC CAIN HOWARD [illegible]	LTC	[illegible]	0867	3
MC CAIN WILLIAM [illegible]	[illegible]	[illegible]	0467	3
MC CALE ALFRED [illegible]	[illegible]	[illegible]	1058	3
MC CALEB ROBERT [illegible]	LTC	[illegible]	0361	1
MC CALL ANNA [illegible]	MAJ	N-0756824	1264	3
MC CALL BESSIE M	1LT	[illegible]	0548	1
MC CALL BILL [illegible]	[illegible]	W-2146161	0667	1
MC CALL CHARLES S JR	LTC	[illegible]	1046	2
MC CALL FRANCIS L	1LT	[illegible]	1145	2
MC CALL GEORGE A	LTC	0-1543251	1160	1
MC CALL GERALD C	LTC	0-1044491	1066	1
MC CALL HOBART [illegible]	CPT	0-0432737	1045	2
MC CALL IVER F	MAJ	0-1695649	0163	1
MC CALL JOHN [illegible]	COL	0-0911534	0668	3
MC CALL JOHN S	LTC	0-0491081	0668	3
MC CALL JOSEPH H	LTC	0-0266909	0165	3
MC CALL RUSSELL C SR	LTC	0-1295054	0463	1
MC CALL VIRGIL W	MAJ	0-0561566	0761	1
MC CALL WILFRED J	COL	0-0416680	0561	1
MC CALLA LOUIS S	CW3	W-2147069	0766	1
MC CALLEY WALTER S	CPT	0-0235462	1266	3
MC CALLION CHARLES L	CW2	W-2141171	0957	1
MC CALLISTER CURTI	MAJ	0-0159835	0955	3
MC CALLISTER RUSSELL	LTC	0-1183723	0463	1
MC CALLUM ARCHIBALD	MAJ	0-0253497	1065	3
MC CALLUM EDWARD J	CW2	W-2207136	0662	1
MC CALLUM GEORGE C	CPT	0-0419006	0645	2
MC CALLUM GEORGE L	LTC	0-1298259	0367	3
MC CALLUM GORDON A	CPT	0-0509906	0149	1
MC CALLUM HAROLD O	MAJ	0-0451339	1167	1
MC CALLUM HAYES S	MAJ	0-0177592	1045	2
MC CALLUM HERMAN O	LTC	0-1042361	0261	1
MC CALLUM LEROY	CW4	W-2103191	0955	1
MC CALLUM M ANNA	MAJ	N-0783034	0263	1
MC CALLUM ROBERT H	LTC	0-1552327	0161	1
MC CALLUM ROBERT S	LTC	0-0395450	0557	1
MC CAMEY JAMES E JR	1LT	0-1321796	1045	2
MC CAMMON JOSEPH R	COL	0-0279083	0859	1
MC CAMMON PAUL O	CW2	W-2149959	1062	1
MC CANCE CLYDE W	MAJ	0-0406455	0562	1
MC CANDLESS CHARLE	MAJ	0-0507053	0153	1
MC CANDLESS ELMER H	2LT	0-0753382	0750	2
MC CANDLESS GEORGE T	CPT	0-1597535	1065	3
MC CANDLESS JAMES B	CW3	W-2149081	0364	1
MC CANDLESS WILBERT	CW2	W-2147508	0963	1
MC CANDLISS CHARLE	CPT	0-1763319	1045	2
MC CANE GEORGE F	CW2	W-2152892	0161	1
MC CANLESS CHARLES L	LTC	0-0471556	1155	2
MC CANN DONN M	LTC	0-1044610	0261	1
MC CANN EDMUND T	CPT	0-0198190	0747	1
MC CANN EDWARD T JR	2LT	0-1053245	1044	2
MC CANN EUGENE J	CPT	0-0890021	1147	2
MC CANN EUGENE J	2LT	0-2318371	0464	3
MC CANN HAROLD J	LTC	0-0124466	0350	3
MC CANN HOWARD	MAJ	0-2011240	0860	1
MC CANN JAMES R	1LT	0-1336524	0748	2
MC CANN JOHN F	1LT	0-0322244	0446	2
MC CANN JOHN R	COL	0-0156892	0455	3
MC CANN JOHN P	CPT	0-0386282	0245	2
MC CANN JOSEPH F	LTC	0-0456339	0766	1
MC CANN LEONARD J	COL	0-0239167	0156	3
MC CANN PERCY J	CW2	W-2002790	0256	3
MC CANN RICHARD D	CPT	0-1305621	0546	2
MC CANN ROBERT J	1LT	0-0393660	0744	2
MC CANN THOMAS A	MAJ	0-1328164	0563	1
MC CANN WILLIS H	MAJ	0-0265456	0467	3
MC CANNA JOSEPH P JR	LTC	0-0427800	0763	1
MC CANNE JOE P	1LT	0-1182648	0946	2
MC CANSE PHILIP	MAJ	0-1928321	1166	1
MC CANTS LESTER	LTC	0-0422066	0463	1
MC CARDELL FRANCIS J	CW3	W-2205860	0466	1
MC CARDIE CLARENCE E	CW2	W-2207522	0360	1
MC CARDLE JOHN JR	MAJ	0-2097806	1065	1

NAME	GRADE	SVC NO	DATE RET MO YR	RET CODE
MC CARRICK MARJORIE	CPT	N-0712872	0647	1
MC CARRON EDMUND S	CPT	0-1301337	0546	2
MC CARRON ROBERT F	MAJ	0-0282116	1145	2
MC CART JOHN G	CW3	W-2151184	0965	1
MC CART KENNETH A	1LT	0-2042911	1054	1
MC CARTER LEE P	CPT	0-0476402	0147	1
MC CARTHEY RAYMOND M	LTC	0-1103787	0662	1
MC CARTHY ALLEN J	CPT	0-0172141	0951	3
MC CARTHY ALPHONSU	COL	0-0254260	0359	3
MC CARTHY ARNOLD B	MAJ	0-1183575	0261	1
MC CARTHY BARTHOLE	LTC	0-1287036	0657	1
MC CARTHY CORNELIUS	CPT	0-1048488	0859	1
MC CARTHY DAVID J	1LT	0-1174370	0745	2
MC CARTHY DONALD E	MAJ	0-1315708	0261	1
MC CARTHY EDMUND P	MAJ	0-1332840	1166	1
MC CARTHY EDWARD A	MAJ	0-0239029	0266	3
MC CARTHY EDWARD J	LTC	0-1338625	1066	1
MC CARTHY EDWARD R	CPT	0-1288588	0958	1
MC CARTHY EUGENE P	WO1	W-2003839	1067	3
MC CARTHY FLORENCE J	CPT	0-1105339	1046	2
MC CARTHY FRANCIS J	MAJ	0-1050370	0461	1
MC CARTHY FRANK W	LTC	0-0112370	0852	3
MC CARTHY GEORGE V	CW3	W-2146485	0958	1
MC CARTHY HAROLD H	LTC	0-1108146	0462	1
MC CARTHY HENRY A	WO1	W-2118384	0846	2
MC CARTHY HERBERT J	1LT	0-1045171	0945	2
MC CARTHY JAMES A	CPT	0-0471024	0844	2
MC CARTHY JAMES B	CPT	0-0935639	0959	1
MC CARTHY JAMES F	MAJ	0-1947023	0662	1
MC CARTHY JAMES G	CW2	W-2208493	0360	1
MC CARTHY JAMES J	CPT	0-2018381	0456	1
MC CARTHY JAMES M	LTC	0-0359364	0760	1
MC CARTHY JOHN B	1LT	0-5704866	0365	2
MC CARTHY JOHN E	CPT	0-0885733	0155	1
MC CARTHY JOHN F	COL	0-0210475	0956	3
MC CARTHY JOHN J	MAJ	0-0182271	0862	3
MC CARTHY JOHN J	COL	0-0256199	0267	3
MC CARTHY JOHN J	LTC	0-0323278	0560	1
MC CARTHY JOHN J	MAJ	0-0443696	0954	1
MC CARTHY JOHN J	CPT	0-1181367	0846	2
MC CARTHY JOHN J	MAJ	0-1321384	1160	1
MC CARTHY JOHN R	CPT	0-2019624	0656	1
MC CARTHY JOHN W	1LT	0-0495324	0750	2
MC CARTHY JOSEPH E	LTC	0-0957383	0868	1
MC CARTHY JOSEPH H	MAJ	0-1587445	0346	2
MC CARTHY JOSEPH J	LTC	0-1576349	0862	1
MC CARTHY JOSEPHINE	1LT	N-0742068	1045	1
MC CARTHY LESTER	CW2	W-2150168	0860	1
MC CARTHY MARGARET	2LT	N-0700106	1038	1
MC CARTHY MARTIN J	MAJ	0-0463553	0246	2
MC CARTHY MICHAEL J	LTC	0-1112845	0467	1
MC CARTHY PATRICK O	LTC	0-0445099	1166	1
MC CARTHY PAUL E	2LT	0-1646400	0645	2
MC CARTHY PAUL V	COL	0-0220323	0859	3
MC CARTHY PHILIP J	MAJ	0-1574969	0747	2
MC CARTHY PHILIP O	LTC	0-0439628	0666	1
MC CARTHY QUENTIN R	CW2	W-2205505	0563	1
MC CARTHY RAYMOND P	1LT	0-1534088	1043	2
MC CARTHY ROBERT C	MAJ	0-2289515	1060	1
MC CARTHY STEPHEN R	LTC	0-0173623	0853	3
MC CARTHY THOMAS F	CPT	0-0169290	0755	3
MC CARTHY THOMAS J	CPT	0-1285462	0746	2
MC CARTHY THOMAS L	2LT	0-1293809	1044	2
MC CARTHY WILLIAM B	MAJ	0-0255458	0246	2
MC CARTHY WILLIAM F	LTC	0-0406954	0960	1
MC CARTHY WILLIAM J	CW4	W-2106936	0155	1
MC CARTHY WILLIS B	LTC	0-0454462	0161	1
MC CARTNEY CARL P	LTC	0-1945653	0266	1
MC CARTNEY CLINTON E	LTC	0-1585849	0962	1
MC CARTNEY HENRY A	LTC	0-0109901	1048	2
MC CARTNEY HERBERT M	CPT	0-0367464	0450	1
MC CARTNEY JAMES J	MAJ	0-1048489	1056	1
MC CARTNEY JAMES K	MAJ	0-1557045	0663	1
MC CARTNEY JAMES R	LTC	0-1556182	1162	1
MC CARTNEY LOREN	LTC	0-2034796	1062	1

NAME	GRADE	SVC NO	DATE RET MO YR	RET CODE
MC CARTNEY [illegible] J	LTC	[illegible]	[illegible]	1
MC CARTNEY [illegible]	MAJ	0-0484195	0145	2
MC CARTNEY WILLIAM A	LTC	0-0225500	1263	1
MC CARTT JAMES V	CW3	[illegible]	1267	1
MC CARTY CECIL L	CPT	0-1307563	0347	2
MC CARTY CHESTER J	CW2	W-2147410	0761	1
MC CARTY KENNETH T	LTC	0-1312189	1060	1
MC CARTY MARION C	LTC	0-0302793	0661	1
MC CARTY MATTHEW F	1LT	0-1649084	1146	2
MC CARTY OLIN C	MAJ	0-0398399	0946	2
MC CARTY RICHARD E	CPT	0-1080468	1049	2
MC CARTY THOMAS A	CPT	0-1946109	0265	2
MC CARTY THOMAS O	MAJ	0-1001180	0654	1
MC CARTY WILLIAM H	COL	0-0147115	1051	3
MC CARTY WILLIAM J	COL	0-0288864	0758	3
MC CARTY WILLIAM L	LTC	0-0322501	0446	2
MC CARVER EVERETT E	LTC	0-1177901	0763	1
MC CARVILLE ANDREW J	LTC	0-0261693	0168	3
MC CARY MASON B	MAJ	0-1557751	0759	1
MC CASKEY AMBROSE E	LTC	0-0290912	1146	2
MC CASKEY RAYMOND	CPT	0-2033067	1160	1
MC CASKILL JUNIUS M	LTC	0-0444483	0867	3
MC CASKILL MARVIN J	1LT	0-1986716	1054	2
MC CASKILL WILLIAM C	MAJ	0-0170658	0648	3
MC CASLAND STANFORD	LTC	0-0233194	0765	3
MC CASLIN GUY T	MAJ	0-1310959	0246	2
MC CASLIN JAMES F	COL	0-0336629	0553	3
MC CASLIN JOHN W	COL	0-0141603	0755	3
MC CASLIN JOSEPH L	MAJ	0-1135191	0257	1
MC CASLIN MARVIN K	MAJ	0-0239452	0768	3
MC CASTOR JOSEPH T	MAJ	0-0242686	0846	2
MC CAUGHEY PATRICK F	CPT	0-0258157	0267	3
MC CAUL THOMAS F	LTC	0-0405939	1164	3
MC CAULEY ALICE M	2LT	N-0700543	0838	1
MC CAULEY ANTHONY G	CW3	W-2148281	0664	1
MC CAULEY CHARLES	LTC	0-0216483	1161	3
MC CAULEY CHARLES	CPT	0-0545413	0847	2
MC CAULEY CHARLES D	CPT	0-0130947	1145	2
MC CAULEY DONNIE W	2LT	0-2000492	0558	2
MC CAULEY HARRY J	MAJ	0-0331432	0346	2
MC CAULEY JAMES D	LTC	0-0162712	1060	3
MC CAULEY JAMES R	LTC	0-0298083	0867	3
MC CAULEY JOHN B	1LT	0-1043419	1144	2
MC CAULEY JOHN J	LTC	0-1591250	0865	1
MC CAULEY ROBERT D	LTC	0-0450388	0161	1
MC CAULEY ROBERT M	MAJ	0-1323453	0461	1
MC CAULEY VINCENT P	1LT	0-1576350	0345	2
MC CAUSLAND CHARLES	LTC	0-0372606	0364	3
MC CAUSLAND PAUL W	1LT	0-0518719	0547	2
MC CAW THOMAS W	COL	0-0186192	0352	3
MC CAY ALFRED T	LTC	0-1308669	1262	1
MC CHESNEY ARTHUR	CPT	0-1765761	0847	2
MC CHESNEY CLAUDE M	LTC	0-1294170	0961	1
MC CHESNEY DON R	COL	0-0389538	0966	1
MC CHESNEY EDWARD R	CPT	0-0219267	0663	3
MC CHESNEY FRANK A	COL	0-0916342	0555	2
MC CHESNEY VERNETT	1LT	N-0732784	0645	1
MC CLAFLIN FRANK L	MAJ	0-2310448	0768	1
MC CLAIN ARTHUR H	LTC	0-2039437	0167	2
MC CLAIN BRUCE M	CPT	0-1850139	1160	1
MC CLAIN CHARLES J	CPT	0-1795937	1045	2
MC CLAIN COLBERT C	COL	0-0147531	0649	3
MC CLAIN DELPHINA	2LT	N-0762531	0545	1
MC CLAIN EDGAR R	MAJ	0-0505829	1052	1
MC CLAIN ELIZABETH	MAJ	N-0727341	1262	1
MC CLAIN EUGENE F	LTC	0-1308531	0763	1
MC CLAIN GORDON H	CPT	0-0907885	0764	1
MC CLAIN JAMES R	MAJ	0-1946564	1060	1
MC CLAIN THEODORE E	MAJ	0-1010452	0268	1
MC CLAIN THOMAS M	MAJ	0-1951496	0963	1
MC CLAIN VERNAL B	CPT	0-0518570	1047	1
MC CLAIN WILLIAM A	MAJ	0-2001746	0764	1
MC CLAIN WILDFORD A	CPT	0-0452441	1145	2
MC CLAMMA LOYAL	CPT	0-2018547	1054	2
MC CLANAHAN C J	MAJ	0-1643109	1060	1

NAME	GRADE	SVC NO	DATE RET MO YR	RET CODE
MC CLANAHAN JAMES L	LTC	0-1551279	0162	1
MC CLANAHAN PAUL A	1LT	0-1585855	0945	2
MC CLANAHAN ROBERT O	LTC	0-1580006	0662	1
MC CLANATHAN ROBER	LTC	0-0288998	0960	3
MC CLANNAHAN K F	CW4	W-2109841	0755	1
MC CLARNON JOHN F	MAJ	0-0961772	1060	1
MC CLARREN FREDERI	MAJ	0-1101946	1053	1
MC CLARREN RICHARD H	MAJ	0-1745905	0161	3
MC CLARY CLAUDE P	MAJ	0-1291667	0960	1
MC CLASKEY JAMES W	MAJ	0-1301849	0662	1
MC CLATCHEY DAVID H	MAJ	0-2033969	0163	1
MC CLAY ROBERT H	LTC	0-1308670	0166	1
MC CLEAR ROBERT D	COL	0-0251307	0866	3
MC CLELLAN DONALD	LTC	0-0383359	1060	1
MC CLELLAN ERNEST V	LTC	0-0257897	1054	1
MC CLELLAN FRANCIS R	CPT	0-0176397	0462	3
MC CLELLAN IRVIN P	COL	0-0320478	0565	3
MC CLELLAN JAMES T	CPT	0-0358541	0347	2
MC CLELLAN JOHN A	MAJ	0-1576351	0960	[illegible]
MC CLELLAN LLOYD G	LTC	0-1548943	0864	1
MC CLELLAN MAX D	CPT	0-1890037	1165	1
MC CLELLAN THOMAS F	CPT	0-1174945	1045	2
MC CLELLAN WEBSTER J	CPT	0-1641554	0667	3
MC CLELLAN WILLIAM A	MAJ	0-0957259	0364	1
MC CLELLAN WILLIAM D	LTC	0-0404968	0561	1
MC CLELLAND DAN R	LTC	0-0380017	0361	1
MC CLELLAND DONALD J	LTC	0-1042362	0164	1
MC CLELLAND FRANCES	MAJ	N-0728433	0364	2
MC CLELLAND FRANCIS	MAJ	0-0961194	0762	1
MC CLELLAND JAMES H	MAJ	0-0965431	0765	1
MC CLELLAND JAMES J	2LT	0-0551454	1045	2
MC CLELLAND PERRY G	2LT	0-1306872	0945	2
MC CLELLAND ROYCE S	COL	0-0140304	0948	3
MC CLELLAND SAMUEL	MAJ	0-1703832	1156	1
MC CLELLAND STANLEY	CPT	0-0317187	0845	2
MC CLELLAND WALTER B	MAJ	0-0263649	0861	3
MC CLELLAND WILLIAM	MAJ	0-0987787	1066	1
MC CLEMENT VERE E	CPT	0-1293441	0446	2
MC CLENAHAN JOHN L	1LT	0-0413732	0544	2
MC CLENATHEN VERNE W	LTC	0-1542737	1164	1
MC CLENDON BERNARD	1LT	0-0366237	1045	2
MC CLENDON JESSE F	LTC	0-0128527	0648	3
MC CLENNY ERNEST B	MAJ	0-1333681	0761	1
MC CLESKEY CHARLES S	LTC	0-0176569	0357	3
MC CLESKEY DEE T	MAJ	0-0485191	0647	2
MC CLESKEY FELIX E	CW2	W-2146810	0461	1
MC CLEVEY ARTHUR M	LTC	0-0915364	0862	1
MC CLIMANS REUBEN L	MAJ	0-0450529	0357	1
MC CLINTIC GEORGE M	COL	0-0441924	0562	3
MC CLINTIC VIRGIL M	1LT	0-0463445	0845	2
MC CLINTOCK AUSTIN R	LTC	0-0259370	1264	3
MC CLINTOCK CHARLES	CW3	W-2149082	0962	1
MC CLINTOCK JOSEPH G	LTC	0-0408194	0860	2
MC CLINTOCK R D JR	CW4	W-2141630	0859	1
MC CLINTOCK RAYBURN	WO1	W-2124697	0445	2
MC CLINTOCK ROBERT A	CPT	0-1996498	1161	1
MC CLINTOCK VIRGIL H	LTC	0-0159211	0957	3
MC CLINTOCK WALTER L	CPT	0-0499858	0544	2
MC CLINTOCK WILLIA	LTC	0-0398311	0247	2
MC CLINTON JAMES W	MAJ	0-0497651	1162	1
MC CLISH JAMES D	LTC	0-1301236	0657	1
MC CLISTER CECIL M	CPT	0-1302030	0546	2
MC CLOONEY JAMES E	LTC	0-0541793	0763	1
MC CLOSKEY ANTHONY	LTC	0-1574972	0367	1
MC CLOSKEY BERNARD	1LT	0-1175794	0559	1
MC CLOSKEY CHARLES A	WO1	W-2142427	0256	1
MC CLOSKEY EDWARD B	MAJ	0-0992339	0166	1
MC CLOSKEY GERTRUD	1LT	N-0725263	1045	1
MC CLOSKEY JAMES	MAJ	0-1703762	0755	1
MC CLOSKEY JAMES W	LTC	0-1047669	0863	1
MC CLOSKEY JOHN	MAJ	0-0124468	0755	3
MC CLOSKEY JOHN B	MAJ	0-0334424	0960	3
MC CLOSKEY JOHN E	MAJ	0-1327558	0662	1
MC CLOSKEY JOHN T	MAJ	0-0435793	0450	1
MC CLOSKEY JOHN W	LTC	0-1534559	1061	1

NAME	GRADE	SVC NO	DATE RET MO YR	RET CODE
MC CLOSKEY THOMAS	CPT	0-1325658	0947	2
MC CLOUD WALTER D	LTC	0-0244502	0164	3
MC CLOY JAMES S	2LT	0-0416412	0343	2
MC CLUNEY SAMUEL R	COL	0-0295684	0368	3
MC CLUNG ARTHUR J	CPT	0-0402859	0847	2
MC CLUNG BOYD E	LTC	0-1058895	0662	1
MC CLUNG FRED	CPT	0-0496718	0954	1
MC CLUNG HUGH JR	LTC	0-0512728	0268	1
MC CLUNG J C	CPT	0-1690917	1266	1
MC CLUNG JAMES A	LTC	0-0265447	0261	1
MC CLUNG JOHN D	MAJ	0-0480473	0746	2
MC CLUNG WILLIAM A	LTC	0-1283642	0147	2
MC CLURE ALBERT J	MAJ	0-2208479	0867	1
MC CLURE ALMA G	MAJ	N-0786447	0665	1
MC CLURE BOYD E	CW2	W-3440062	0867	1
MC CLURE CHARLES C	COL	0-1041843	1168	2
MC CLURE CHARLES F	2LT	0-1958377	0858	1
MC CLURE COVER G	WO1	W-2107527	0445	2
MC CLURE DEL R	LTC	0-0299282	0867	3
MC CLURE EDWIN S	LTC	0-2073975	0268	1
MC CLURE ERNEST W	LTC	0-0303320	1066	1
MC CLURE FRANK	1LT	0-0487979	0247	1
MC CLURE HAROLD L	2LT	0-1174063	0544	2
MC CLURE HORACE E	MAJ	0-1119084	0763	1
MC CLURE JAMES E	LTC	0-1120690	0266	1
MC CLURE JOHN H JR	LTC	0-0390585	0661	1
MC CLURE LINWOOD D	COL	0-0201182	0346	2
MC CLURE NATHAN F	LTC	0-0233406	0455	3
MC CLURE ROBERT W	LTC	0-1290787	0863	2
MC CLURE ROSS	CPT	0-0959295	0560	1
MC CLURE WALTER C	1LT	0-2008218	1046	1
MC CLURE WALTER M	CW3	W-2144122	0559	1
MC CLURE WILLIAM K	COL	0-0178072	1054	3
MC CLURE WILLIAM M	LTC	0-1287559	0767	1
MC CLURG DONALD C	LTC	0-1949398	0966	2
MC CLUSKEY DONALD W	LTC	0-1894525	0263	1
MC CLUSKEY EAMONN	MAJ	0-0463524	1262	1
MC CLUSKEY RAYMOND V	CPT	0-1885837	0464	1
MC CLUSKY BETTY A	2LT	N-0725170	0145	1
MC CLYMONT JAMES R	MAJ	0-1059196	0361	1
MC COACH JAMES P	COL	0-0357800	0363	2
MC COID CHESTER B	COL	0-0491380	0855	2
MC COIN JOHN F	MAJ	0-0334907	0662	2
MC COLEAY CHARLES D	CW4	W-2151050	0665	1
MC COLGAN AUGUST T	LTC	0-1298262	0463	1
MC COLL BETTY A	1LT	N-0777538	1047	1
MC COLL CHARLES D	COL	0-0199576	0854	1
MC COLLISTER LANDON	MAJ	0-0220458	0764	3
MC COLLISTER WILEY C	LTC	0-0454461	0761	1
MC COLLOM LAWRENCE S	LTC	0-1182649	0466	3
MC COLLOM WALTER W	LTC	0-0143734	1053	3
MC COLLOUGH SOLOMON	CW3	W-2146260	0765	1
MC COLLOUGH VINCEN	LTC	0-0342131	0546	2
MC COLLOUGH WALTER W	MAJ	0-1002276	0860	1
MC COLLUM BERT H	2LT	0-1053718	0744	2
MC COLLUM CHARLES T	CPT	0-2033317	0961	1
MC COLLUM CLARENCE E	LTC	0-1257400	0167	1
MC COLLUM EDWARD E	LTC	0-0404477	0464	1
MC COLLUM FRED JR	COL	0-0284525	1066	3
MC COLLUM JOHNNIE G	CW2	W-3440064	0968	1
MC COLLUM JOSEPH E	CPT	0-1252029	0656	1
MC COLLUM MARVIN F	LTC	0-1294362	1060	1
MC COLLUM REGINALD E	LTC	0-1118611	1067	1
MC COLLUM VESTAL P	LTC	0-1999189	0966	1
MC COLLUM VINCENT F	CPT	0-0481730	0246	2
MC COLLUM VIRGIL O	LTC	0-0253307	0947	2
MC COLLUM WENDELL D	MAJ	0-0289493	0247	2
MC COLLUM WILLIAM A	CPT	0-0116966	0153	3
MC COLLUM WILLIAM R	LTC	0-1552329	0167	3
MC COLLY HARRY A	COL	0-0200788	0255	1
MC COLPIN JOHN J	LTC	0-2009519	1167	1
MC COMAS BEN CURTIS	LTC	0-1823182	1165	1
MC COMAS EARL W	LTC	0-0189237	1154	3
MC COMB ALLAN W	CPT	0-0121951	1057	3
MC COMBS BILLY O	WO1	W-3410032	0967	1

NAME	GRADE	SVC NO	DATE RET MO YR	RET CODE
MC COMBS GEORGE R	MAJ	0-1798032	0660	1
MC COMBS NELSON C	CPT	0-0226696	0561	3
MC COMBS NORA	CPT	N-0725526	0448	1
MC COMMAS DONALD R	CW3	W-2150998	0463	1
MC COMMONS JOHN L	LTC	0-0217543	0549	3
MC CONAGHY LOUIS R	MAJ	0-0270067	0268	3
MC CONAHAY JAMES A	LTC	0-0396886	0463	1
MC CONAHAY JAMES F	CPT	0-0237254	1056	3
MC CONAHAY WILLIAM C	LTC	0-0192663	1160	3
MC CONATHY EDWARD W	1LT	0-1576352	0146	2
MC CONAUGHEY DONALD	CW3	W-2147766	0966	2
MC CONCHIE JAMES K	COL	0-0538843	1165	1
MC CONIGLY RALPH D	COL	0-0310314	0767	3
MC CONKIE EDWIN B	LTC	0-0303450	0768	3
MC CONN EARLE M	LTC	0-1593372	0862	1
MC CONNAUGHEY W E	LTC	0-0226315	1048	3
MC CONNAUGHHAY CLY	MAJ	0-1017346	0657	1
MC CONNEL JOHN P	MAJ	0-1103305	0967	3
MC CONNELL CLIFFORD	1LT	0-2056244	0546	2
MC CONNELL DELMER M	MAJ	0-2263581	0967	1
MC CONNELL ELBRIDGE	MAJ	0-4031024	0667	1
MC CONNELL FREDERICK	LTC	0-0371580	0167	1
MC CONNELL GEORGE E	LTC	0-0366014	1160	1
MC CONNELL HAROLD	MAJ	0-0145954	0554	3
MC CONNELL KENDRED C	LTC	0-0452014	0564	1
MC CONNELL LESTER O	LTC	0-1047670	1061	1
MC CONNELL LOUIS F	MAJ	0-0228751	0161	3
MC CONNELL OSCAR L	CW4	W-2109167	0553	2
MC CONNELL PAUL H	LTC	0-1037146	0666	1
MC CONNELL RICHARD M	LTC	0-1053719	0363	1
MC CONNELL ROY W	LTC	0-0427404	0368	3
MC CONNELL ULYSSES S	COL	0-0333553	0561	1
MC CONNELL WILFORD O	MAJ	0-0264042	0354	3
MC CONNELL WILLIAM H	1LT	0-1107579	0448	2
MC CONNICO JAMES B	LTC	0-1338260	0166	1
MC CONNICO JARRETT C	MAJ	0-1017643	0465	1
MC CONVILLE ROBERT W	LTC	0-1633395	0559	1
MC CODEY VINCENT R	LTC	0-1581928	0260	1
MC COOK FRANK W	COL	0-0182516	1154	3
MC COOL DAVID V	CPT	0-5322566	1068	2
MC COOL DOROTHY N	MAJ	N-0724182	0162	1
MC COOL JAMES D	1LT	0-1549544	1045	2
MC COOL JOHN C	CPT	0-0885080	0555	1
MC COPPIN MARGARET	1LT	N-0737759	0646	1
MC CORD ANDREW	CPT	0-1168811	0759	1
MC CORD CAREY P	COL	0-0198783	0648	3
MC CORD EDGAR B	LTC	0-1534332	1264	1
MC CORD ELMER C JR	LTC	0-1181688	1066	1
MC CORD JAMES A JR	LTC	0-0381252	0860	1
MC CORD JOSEPH F	LTC	0-0224378	0945	2
MC CORD NED J JR	MAJ	0-0927643	0664	1
MC CORD RICHARD F	CW3	W-2147235	0464	1
MC CORD WALTER B	LTC	0-0346197	0660	1
MC CORKELL GORDON W	1LT	0-0525037	0647	2
MC CORKLE BEN W	CPT	0-0285413	0845	2
MC CORKLE ROBERT L	1LT	0-1000820	0752	2
MC CORKLE ROBERT W	MAJ	0-0967561	0463	1
MC CORKLE STANLEY A	MAJ	0-0300541	1062	1
MC CORLEW THOMAS J	MAJ	0-1298415	1060	1
MC CORMAC PAUL C	MAJ	0-0344680	0744	2
MC CORMACK CHARLES R	MAJ	0-0266743	1066	3
MC CORMACK DELOS W	LTC	0-0217570	0962	3
MC CORMACK ELDRIDGE	1LT	0-0491635	1148	1
MC CORMACK FREDERICK	CPT	0-1644575	0950	2
MC CORMACK GEORGE W	COL	0-0372247	0964	1
MC CORMACK HARRIS A	LTC	0-1047226	0164	1
MC CORMACK HARRY E	MAJ	0-1590051	0563	1
MC CORMACK JAMES M	LTC	0-0328933	1264	3
MC CORMACK JOHN C	COL	0-0416702	0365	1
MC CORMACK JOHN F	CPT	0-0397790	1045	2
MC CORMACK JOHN J	CPT	0-1591919	0754	2
MC CORMACK JOSEPH L	LTC	0-1168362	0162	1
MC CORMACK RICHARD	MAJ	0-0546557	0765	1
MC CORMACK ROBERT C	MAJ	0-0738993	0761	1
MC CORMACK ROBERT H	LTC	0-0265678	0549	2

NAME	GRADE	SVC NO	DATE RET MO YR	RET CODE
MC CORMACK WILBUR	LTC	0-1301339	0364	1
MC CORMACK WILLIAM E	LTC	0-0963087	0768	1
MC CORMICK ALFRED A	MAJ	0-1304089	1060	3
MC CORMICK ALVIN G	CPT	0-1319150	1056	2
MC CORMICK CHARLES	B G	0-0332054	0760	3
MC CORMICK CHARLES	MAJ	0-0479972	0646	2
MC CORMICK CHARLES E	CPT	0-0255874	0247	2
MC CORMICK CHRISTI	COL	0-0187429	1052	3
MC CORMICK CYRUS	MAJ	0-0483798	0943	2
MC CORMICK DONALD W	MAJ	0-0374530	1145	2
MC CORMICK EDWARD C	LTC	0-0176896	0846	2
MC CORMICK EVERETT L	MAJ	0-0972263	0766	1
MC CORMICK FRANCIS W	LTC	0-0358779	0262	1
MC CORMICK GEORGE	COL	0-0261650	0457	1
MC CORMICK HARRY	CPT	0-0225025	0758	3
MC CORMICK HARRY W	COL	0-0373126	0255	1
MC CORMICK HOWARD W	LTC	0-1554234	1062	1
MC CORMICK JAMES E	LTC	0-1693201	0246	2
MC CORMICK JAMES J	MAJ	0-2277782	1167	3
MC CORMICK JOHN C	1LT	0-1002277	0858	1
MC CORMICK JOHN F	MAJ	0-1329374	1262	1
MC CORMICK JOHN R	LTC	0-1186212	0768	1
MC CORMICK LARRY M	CW2	W-2108473	0360	1
MC CORMICK LEONARD E	LTC	0-0302663	0755	2
MC CORMICK MORRISON	MAJ	0-0278342	0166	3
MC CORMICK RAYMOND C	CW2	W-2102067	0650	1
MC CORMICK RICHARD F	1LT	0-1322460	0546	2
MC CORMICK ROGER S	1LT	0-1041612	0644	2
MC CORMICK STANLEY	CPT	0-0925000	0345	2
MC CORMICK STEPHEN C	COL	0-1102849	0868	1
MC CORMICK TERRENCE	LTC	0-1288589	0366	1
MC CORMICK THOMAS A	CW2	W-3411034	1266	1
MC CORMICK THOMAS M	LTC	0-1331850	0767	1
MC CORMICK VANE E JR	CPT	0-5331477	1268	2
MC CORMICK WILFRED	LTC	0-0242464	0363	3
MC CORMICK WILLARD P	1LT	0-0538968	0945	2
MC CORMICK WILLIAM B	COL	0-0253191	0958	3
MC CORMICK WILLIAM H	MAJ	0-1583349	0263	1
MC CORMICK WILLIAM J	LTC	0-0495281	1055	1
MC CORMICK WILLIAM J	CPT	0-2292797	1266	2
MC CORMICK WILLIAM L	LTC	0-0231435	0565	3
MC CORMICK WILLIAM N	MAJ	0-4002102	0856	2
MC CORQUODALE ERNEST	CPT	0-1010651	0346	2
MC CORT MERCEDES A	MAJ	N-0759212	0464	1
MC CORVEY JAMES G	CW3	W-2205936	0368	1
MC COUCH NELSON	LTC	0-1105006	0162	1
MC COUN WILEY F	LTC	0-0328057	1060	1
MC COURT KEITH D	LTC	0-0465261	1162	1
MC COWAN EDSEL R	CW2	W-2119613	0657	1
MC COWEN RICHARD H	1LT	0-0431737	0646	2
MC COWN ALBERT S	LTC	0-0280351	0468	3
MC COWN JOHN R	1LT	0-0318818	0944	2
MC COWN LLOYD L	CW2	W-2208082	1060	1
MC COWN LORIN S	CPT	0-0419817	0345	2
MC COWN MARJORIE P	LTC	L-0903592	0766	1
MC COWN ROBERT E	LTC	0-0213659	0556	3
MC COY ANDREW R	MAJ	0-1643494	1160	1
MC COY ARTHUR M	COL	0-0263250	1066	3
MC COY AVERIL O JR	MAJ	0-0271113	0168	3
MC COY BURRILL F	1LT	0-1108840	0544	2
MC COY CARL M	LTC	0-1170850	0264	1
MC COY CAROLYN L	CPT	N-0773604	0648	1
MC COY CLYDE H	LTC	0-0302972	0263	3
MC COY DON L	1LT	0-1949399	1046	2
MC COY DONALD B	2LT	0-4045463	0857	2
MC COY DOUGLAS D	LTC	0-0344588	1047	2
MC COY EDWIN O JR	LTC	0-0533707	0463	1
MC COY ELMER R	CW3	W-2147767	0157	1
MC COY FRED W	CW4	W-2141372	0164	1
MC COY FREDERICK	LTC	0-0569201	0464	1
MC COY GEORGE W	CW2	W-2145004	1165	2
MC COY GERARD J	CW3	W-2147040	0864	1
MC COY HUBERT V	COL	0-0229600	1264	3
MC COY JAMES E	CW3	W-2152084	0361	1
MC COY JAMES H	MAJ	0-1310475	0762	1

NAME	GRADE	SVC NO	DATE RET MO YR	RET CODE
MC COY JAMES M JR	MAJ	0-1002675	0566	3
MC COY JOHN F	MAJ	0-0909446	1046	1
MC COY JOHN J	1LT	0-1284545	0445	2
MC COY JOSEPH B JR	1LT	0-0535875	0346	2
MC COY JOSEPH G	1LT	0-1030801	1045	2
MC COY KEITH L	CPT	0-0370775	0345	2
MC COY MICHELLE B	1LT	N-0720072	0545	1
MC COY PASCHAL G	CPT	0-0887358	0247	2
MC COY PAUL	CPT	0-2007115	1147	2
MC COY PAUL J	CPT	0-1318319	0868	3
MC COY ROBERT C	COL	0-0277712	0858	3
MC COY ROBERT C	LTC	0-0976320	0368	1
MC COY ROBERT W	MAJ	0-0349913	0568	3
MC COY ROGER W	LTC	0-1003579	1062	1
MC COY STATES D	COL	0-0240963	0963	3
MC COY THOMAS A	1LT	0-0449229	0645	2
MC COY TIMOTHY J	COL	0-0153439	0451	3
MC COY WAYNE M	LTC	0-2048700	0166	1
MC COY WILLIAM H JR	MAJ	0-1039778	0661	2
MC COY WILLIAM M	LTC	0-0253340	1046	2
MC COY WILLIE F	MAJ	0-0969608	0167	1
MC CRACKEN BLAKE D	CPT	0-1551268	1047	2
MC CRACKEN CAROL A	CW3	W-2207466	0865	1
MC CRACKEN DAVID H	CW4	W-2133587	1065	1
MC CRACKEN HENRY E	LTC	0-0246633	1066	3
MC CRACKEN IVAN L	LTC	0-0432930	0756	1
MC CRACKEN JOHN T	MAJ	0-1119094	0964	1
MC CRACKEN REED J	LTC	0-0315097	0161	1
MC CRACKEN RICHARD S	CPT	0-1302496	1046	2
MC CRACKEN ROBERT E	2LT	0-1061475	0645	2
MC CRACKEN ROY G	LTC	0-1293988	0461	1
MC CRACKEN SAM J	CW3	W-2210788	0368	1
MC CRACKEN SARA	MAJ	N-0722896	0262	1
MC CRACKEN THOMAS E	LTC	0-0253847	0560	1
MC CRACKEN WALTER M	LTC	0-0365788	1160	1
MC CRACKIN EDWARD D	COL	0-0341543	0163	1
MC CRAE JAMES L	COL	0-0243621	0766	3
MC CRANEY DONALD	MAJ	0-0496265	1046	2
MC CRANEY THOMAS R	LTC	0-1557639	1065	1
MC CRARY GEORGE J	CPT	0-1035531	0260	1
MC CRARY HARVEY P	CW4	W-2134372	0957	1
MC CRARY JOHN M	CPT	0-1297758	0546	2
MC CRARY LAMAR	MAJ	0-0961197	0962	1
MC CRARY LEON F	LTC	0-0336970	0358	1
MC CRARY MARTHA E	LTC	N-0744985	1064	3
MC CRARY MARY S	CPT	N-0703969	0147	1
MC CRARY PAUL E	MAJ	0-0375868	0847	2
MC CRARY ROY P JR	LTC	0-2018384	0965	1
MC CRARY WALTER R	CW2	W-2144737	0656	1
MC CRARY WILLIAM B	MAJ	0-1577546	0258	1
MC CRAVY HOWARD W	MAJ	0-0147620	0855	3
MC CRAW HENRY G	COL	0-0277836	1060	3
MC CRAW ROY	LTC	0-0949973	0966	1
MC CRAY WILLIAM L	MAJ	0-1545717	0464	2
MC CREA DONALD M	LTC	0-0279597	1159	3
MC CREA JOHN A	1LT	0-1018598	1045	2
MC CREA JOHN H	CPT	0-0369066	0346	2
MC CREA ROBERT L	LTC	0-1822596	0665	1
MC CREA WILLIAM C	MAJ	0-0505124	0546	2
MC CREA WILLIAM W	COL	0-0249454	0566	3
MC CREADY CHARLES L	MAJ	0-0174049	0862	3
MC CREADY CLOYD E	MAJ	0-0122131	1052	3
MC CREADY DONALD D	1LT	0-0558097	0946	2
MC CREADY NORMAN J	CW3	W-2142247	0459	1
MC CREADY RICHARD J	1LT	0-1170486	0545	2
MC CREARY GERALD F	CPT	0-1111772	0248	2
MC CREARY JAMES M	MAJ	0-1876653	0367	1
MC CREARY LEROY	CW3	W-2006677	0863	3
MC CREARY ROBERT N	LTC	0-0203633	0853	3
MC CREARY WALTER W	LTC	0-1297070	0963	1
MC CREEDY JOHN J	MAJ	0-0469512	0346	2
MC CREERY SAMUEL JR	1LT	0-1634123	1144	2
MC CREIGHT IAN H	CPT	0-0218159	0758	3
MC CREIGHT REX	CPT	0-2010756	0260	1
MC CRELLEN RICHARD W	CPT	0-2012722	0858	1

NAME	GRADE	SVC NO	DATE RET MO YR	RET CODE
MC CRIGHT HOWARD L	CW2	W-2211778	0667	1
MC CRORIE JACK E	MAJ	0-1290279	0962	1
MC CRORY JOHN R	LTC	0-0291858	1266	3
MC CRORY MARTIN A	CPT	W-0001133	0668	3
MC CRORY ROBERT L	LTC	0-0374470	0859	1
MC CRORY ROY L	MAJ	0-1338835	0165	1
MC CRORY WALTER F	LTC	0-0377910	0266	1
MC CROSKEY NEWELL M	1LT	0-1081431	0246	2
MC CRUM JOHN L	1LT	0-0212405	0363	3
MC CRUM PHILIP H	COL	0-0246129	0959	3
MC CRYSTAL WILLIAM	LTC	0-0124181	0754	2
MC CUBBIN JODIE L	WO1	W-2104904	0760	1
MC CUBBINS ELIZABETH	MAJ	N-0755913	1063	3
MC CUDDEN EDWARD W	CW3	W-2149043	0462	1
MC CUE EARL H	CW3	W-2152974	0760	1
MC CUE ELMER S	MAJ	0-0507980	1148	1
MC CUE FRANK P	COL	0-0327193	0260	3
MC CUE HAROLD E	LTC	0-1039097	1163	1
MC CUE JOHN P	1LT	0-0447040	0746	2
MC CUE LEO M	CW3	W-2152275	0165	1
MC CUE LESLIE L	LTC	0-0535162	1064	3
MC CUE MICHAEL W	1LT	0-5243206	1068	2
MC CUEN JOHN W	MAJ	0-0170554	0855	3
MC CUGH LONNIE E	MAJ	0-1326414	0465	1
MC CUGH SIMON R	MAJ	0-2262136	0663	1
MC CUISTION ARTHUR W	WO1	W-2150588	0158	1
MC CUISTON TREMON W	LTC	0-0363609	0262	1
MC CULLA JAMES A	1LT	0-1645192	0245	2
MC CULLACH GEORGE H	COL	0-0290873	0167	3
MC CULLAGH THOMAS J	2LT	0-0409930	0244	2
MC CULLAH HENRY R	MAJ	0-1799761	0968	1
MC CULLEN MATTHEW L	1LT	0-1314164	0146	2
MC CULLERS CECIL M	MAJ	0-0984550	0963	1
MC CULLERS EDGAR W	CPT	0-0166284	0254	3
MC CULLEY GEORGE H	LTC	0-0151051	1049	3
MC CULLEY JAMES A	MAJ	0-0387210	0746	2
MC CULLEY WAYNE L	LTC	0-0266907	1165	3
MC CULLION FRANCIS E	MAJ	0-1644260	1154	1
MC CULLOCH C P	WO1	W-2129308	0945	2
MC CULLOCH FRANK A	COL	0-0279008	0360	1
MC CULLOCH HORACE W	MAJ	0-1014142	0261	1
MC CULLOCH JAMES E	MAJ	0-0443016	0649	1
MC CULLOCH JAMES H	1LT	0-0455526	1144	2
MC CULLOCH MARGARET	1LT	N-0789917	0747	1
MC CULLOCH MAXWELL A	MAJ	0-0885723	0657	1
MC CULLOGH WILLIAM R	CW3	W-2004988	1262	2
MC CULLOH KENNETH E	1LT	0-0549653	1045	2
MC CULLOUGH CAMPRE	COL	0-0154168	0648	3
MC CULLOUGH EARL	CW3	W-2209644	0568	1
MC CULLOUGH FRANCIS	CW4	W-2001663	1061	3
MC CULLOUGH GEORGE E	LTC	0-0380018	0546	2
MC CULLOUGH HAROLD E	MAJ	0-1302031	0266	1
MC CULLOUGH HAROLD T	COL	0-0107182	1155	3
MC CULLOUGH HAROLD W	LTC	0-0237770	0764	1
MC CULLOUGH HELEN A	CPT	N-0742568	0351	2
MC CULLOUGH HIRAM JR	LTC	0-0225917	0265	3
MC CULLOUGH JACK D	MAJ	0-0450390	0853	1
MC CULLOUGH JAMES	MAJ	0-1298893	0760	1
MC CULLOUGH JAMES D	LTC	0-0227185	1064	3
MC CULLOUGH JESSE F	2LT	0-1055666	0145	2
MC CULLOUGH JOHN R	COL	0-0313702	0467	1
MC CULLOUGH JOSEPH F	MAJ	0-1320387	0565	1
MC CULLOUGH LORY L	MAJ	0-1289780	0958	1
MC CULLOUGH LOYD	CW4	W-2107071	1163	2
MC CULLOUGH MAURICE	LTC	0-0255774	0963	3
MC CULLOUGH ROBERT	LTC	0-0175073	0953	3
MC CULLOUGH THOMAS L	COL	0-0147345	0648	3
MC CULLOUGH WILBUR E	CW2	W-3100541	0668	1
MC CULLOUGH WILLIA	MAJ	0-1636882	0855	1
MC CULLOUGH WILLIAM	2LT	0-1315595	0944	2
MC CUMBER JAMES B	COL	0-0183405	1060	3
MC CUNE GERALD F	2LT	0-1031007	0745	2
MC CUNE JAMES P	CW3	W-3150405	0767	1
MC CUNE MARVIN H	LTC	0-0301714	0359	3
MC CUNE WILLIAM W	CPT	0-0278276	1045	2
MC CURDY CHARLES F	MAJ	0-1101108	1164	1
MC CURDY DAVID S	LTC	0-0346463	0660	1
MC CURDY FORMAN O	LTC	0-0190598	1161	3
MC CURDY FRANKLIN W	LTC	0-0299660	0868	3
MC CURDY HARLEY E	CW3	W-2143034	1263	2
MC CURDY JOHN A	LTC	0-1038237	0764	1
MC CURDY JOHN F	CPT	0-1825151	0156	1
MC CURDY JOHN G	LTC	0-0328047	0560	1
MC CURDY LLOYD L	CPT	0-2018196	0358	1
MC CURDY RICHARD F	1LT	0-1323454	1045	2
MC CURDY ROBERT S	LTC	0-1168366	0666	1
MC CURDY WILLIAM G	LTC	0-0147713	0255	3
MC CURRY CLARENCE D	COL	0-0359032	0852	2
MC CURRY EDWARD P	LTC	0-1534561	0561	1
MC CUSKER ALOYSIUS X	CPT	0-0451145	0849	1
MC CUSKER GEORGE A	1LT	0-0275648	0158	3
MC CUSKER JOHN T	2LT	0-1325163	0844	2
MC CUSKER JOSEPH A	COL	0-0126170	0653	3
MC CUSKER JOSEPH X	1LT	0-1306443	0350	2
MC CUSKER SYLVESTER	1LT	0-2049017	0756	1
MC CUSKEY CHARLES F	LTC	0-0236487	1053	3
MC CUTCHAN EDWARD D	1LT	0-1052469	0868	2
MC CUTCHAN HOWARD E	LTC	0-0344358	0647	2
MC CUTCHEN CHARLES C	CPT	0-0192285	1159	3
MC CUTCHEN DONALD P	LTC	0-0401632	0964	1
MC CUTCHEON GEORGE L	CPT	0-0155968	0452	3
MC CUTCHEON WILLIAM	LTC	0-1314372	0166	1
MC DADE WILLIAM P	CW2	W-2151426	0361	1
MC DANIEL ALVA E	1LT	N-0735986	0745	1
MC DANIEL CECIL A	LTC	0-1048899	1162	1
MC DANIEL CHARLES D	COL	0-0039696	1060	1
MC DANIEL DONOVAN	CPT	0-0405890	1150	2
MC DANIEL EARL	MAJ	0-2212074	0565	1
MC DANIEL EDWARD M	1LT	0-1648596	1045	2
MC DANIEL EDWARD P	CPT	0-0436256	0845	2
MC DANIEL EUGENE	1LT	0-1554589	0450	2
MC DANIEL FAY A	CW3	W-2145472	0760	1
MC DANIEL GEORGE W	LTC	0-0251650	0663	1
MC DANIEL HAROLD C	LTC	0-0922439	0857	2
MC DANIEL HAROLD L	CPT	0-1182419	1164	2
MC DANIEL HARRY W	MAJ	0-1167533	0261	1
MC DANIEL J ZEB	LTC	0-0248095	0267	3
MC DANIEL JAMES C	CPT	0-1293442	0346	2
MC DANIEL JAMES H	LTC	0-1290788	0561	1
MC DANIEL JAMES W	CW4	W-2149197	0367	1
MC DANIEL JOHN F	CPT	0-1594324	1045	2
MC DANIEL JOHN W JR	LTC	0-0534854	0768	1
MC DANIEL LESTER G	CW2	W-2148747	0760	1
MC DANIEL MILTON R	CW3	W-2151500	0266	1
MC DANIEL MONTE	2LT	0-0485670	1161	1
MC DANIEL OLIVER H	LTC	0-0292637	1060	2
MC DANIEL PAUL H	CPT	0-0545107	0445	2
MC DANIEL PAUL L	CPT	0-0329160	0757	3
MC DANIEL PRESTON	CW2	W-3430038	1163	1
MC DANIEL RAYMOND E	CPT	0-0293473	0746	2
MC DANIEL ROBERT B	LTC	0-1182420	0960	1
MC DANIEL ROBERT C	CW4	W-2116976	0562	1
MC DANIEL ROBERT T	LTC	0-0269137	0560	1
MC DANIEL ROBERT W	MAJ	0-0255147	0262	3
MC DANIEL TALBOT A	1LT	0-1645804	0746	1
MC DANIEL VICTOR L	CPT	0-0975623	0665	2
MC DANIEL VIRGINIA	MAJ	N-0751103	0560	2
MC DANIEL WILMER K	COL	0-0224058	0760	1
MC DANIELS ARTHUR W	COL	0-0188426	0454	3
MC DANIELS ELMER L	CW2	W-2141993	0452	1
MC DANIELS FRANK L	MAJ	0-0179945	0155	3
MC DANIELS LYNN L	1LT	0-1822163	1045	2
MC DANIELS ORRIN O	LTC	0-0403714	0860	1
MC DAVITT JEROME A	LTC	0-0307358	0254	2
MC DAVITT JOHN F	2LT	0-1822814	1144	2
MC DEARMON GLADYS	CPT	N-0703278	0946	1
MC DEARMON LACY H	MAJ	0-0226841	0764	3
MC DERMOTT BERNICE M	1LT	N-0723881	0546	1
MC DERMOTT CLARENCE	1LT	0-1685506	1162	2
MC DERMOTT EDWARD E	LTC	0-1302032	0263	1
MC DERMOTT EDWARD T	1LT	0-1047228	1045	2
MC DERMOTT EMERSON M	COL	0-0356361	1058	1
MC DERMOTT FRANCIS L	CPT	0-1015749	0966	2
MC DERMOTT JACK C	MAJ	0-0990037	0868	1
MC DERMOTT JAMES P	CPT	0-1055383	0358	1
MC DERMOTT JAMES P	1LT	0-1060555	0766	2
MC DERMOTT JOHN F	LTC	0-1053249	0565	1
MC DERMOTT JOHN R	CPT	0-1924102	0763	1
MC DERMOTT MARY C	MAJ	N-0727504	0465	3
MC DERMOTT RAYMOND M	LTC	0-1101948	0863	2
MC DERMOTT RICHARD L	MAJ	0-1796117	0259	1
MC DERMOTT ROBERT F	LTC	0-2032856	0867	1
MC DERMOTT THOMAS A	COL	0-0549713	0868	1
MC DERMOTT THOMAS C	COL	0-0200834	1155	3
MC DERMOTT VINCENT T	LTC	0-0439550	0146	2
MC DERMOTT WALTER J	CPT	0-1311413	0947	2
MC DEVITT DONALD J	LTC	0-1057523	0867	1
MC DEVITT JAMES C	LTC	0-0408325	0965	1
MC DEVITT JOSEPH F	MAJ	0-1043421	0463	1
MC DEVITT RICHARD J	LTC	0-1894697	0861	1
MC DEVITT WILLIAM A	CW2	W-2206883	0162	1
MC DEWELL DONALD S	1LT	0-0971748	0967	1
MC DIARMID JAMES C J	CPT	0-0524999	1143	2
MC DILL BRUCE M	MAJ	0-0175725	0851	3
MC DIVITT ARCHIE L	COL	0-0411347	0465	1
MC DONALD ADAM M	LTC	0-0498558	1162	1
MC DONALD ALMA E	2LT	N-0721223	1045	1
MC DONALD ARCH JR	MAJ	0-2001049	0263	1
MC DONALD ARTHUR W	CPT	0-0244764	0462	3
MC DONALD CARL D	CW3	W-2149823	0664	1
MC DONALD CARSON D	CW4	W-2109052	0659	1
MC DONALD CLARENCE M	LTC	0-1011380	0464	1
MC DONALD CRAIG W JR	LTC	0-0376899	1262	1
MC DONALD CRAWFORD J	MAJ	0-2208555	0664	1
MC DONALD DAVID A	CPT	0-0519552	0146	2
MC DONALD DONALD L	CW3	W-2151849	0664	1
MC DONALD EARL B	MAJ	0-0355869	0563	1
MC DONALD EARL F	MAJ	0-0965426	0762	1
MC DONALD EARL L	MAJ	0-0356461	0653	2
MC DONALD EDWARD D J	MAJ	0-0381170	0646	2
MC DONALD EDWARD O	MAJ	0-0283206	0968	3
MC DONALD EDWIN G	MAJ	0-0379514	1267	3
MC DONALD ERNEST D	LTC	0-0409118	0761	1
MC DONALD EUGENE P	LTC	0-1057165	0262	1
MC DONALD FREDERICK	LTC	0-0494302	0968	3
MC DONALD FREEMAN W	CPT	0-1320855	0847	2
MC DONALD GEORGE	CW3	W-2103196	0260	1
MC DONALD GEORGE D	1LT	0-1947774	0247	2
MC DONALD HAROLD J	CPT	0-1299567	0461	2
MC DONALD HAROLD R	MAJ	0-1826423	0860	1
MC DONALD HARRY A	CPT	0-0117938	1053	3
MC DONALD HELEN C	MAJ	N-0759287	1061	2
MC DONALD HENRY S JR	COL	0-0946426	0558	1
MC DONALD HENRY T	MAJ	0-1110014	1264	1
MC DONALD HERBERT E	CW3	W-2147580	0564	1
MC DONALD HOWARD D	LTC	0-0329418	1168	3
MC DONALD HURLEY M	LTC	0-0450995	0562	1
MC DONALD JACK A	MAJ	0-1105664	0662	1
MC DONALD JACK W	LTC	0-0450996	0559	1
MC DONALD JAMES A	CPT	0-0499494	0347	1
MC DONALD JAMES A	LTC	0-1284001	0652	2
MC DONALD JAMES B	LTC	0-1329609	1262	1
MC DONALD JAMES D	2LT	0-1311033	0445	2
MC DONALD JAMES E	2LT	0-1038758	1044	2
MC DONALD JAMES J	CW2	W-2150354	0265	1
MC DONALD JOE M	1LT	0-0493519	0951	2
MC DONALD JOHN A	LTC	0-0164909	0855	3
MC DONALD JOHN A	LTC	0-0445823	0954	1
MC DONALD JOHN A	CW2	W-2214520	0868	2
MC DONALD JOHN E	LTC	0-0236717	0365	3
MC DONALD JOHN E	CW3	W-2152145	0367	1
MC DONALD JOHN H	LTC	0-0162206	1060	3
MC DONALD JOHN R	LTC	0-1301002	0566	1
MC DONALD JOHN R	CW3	W-2141632	0659	1
MC DONALD JOHN T	CW3	W-2145357	1165	1
MC DONALD JOHN W	CW3	W-2112250	0757	1
MC DONALD JOSEPH A	CW3	W-2210934	0968	1
MC DONALD JOSEPH F	LTC	0-1172987	1055	2
MC DONALD KENNETH O	LTC	0-2014896	0966	1
MC DONALD MALCOLM W	CPT	0-1547267	1046	2
MC DONALD MARTIN H	CPT	0-1307126	0947	2
MC DONALD MAURICE H	MAJ	0-1062859	0767	1
MC DONALD MICHAEL	CW2	W-2144976	0157	1
MC DONALD NORTON L	LTC	0-0255929	0759	1
MC DONALD PAULINUS F	CPT	0-0236950	0166	3
MC DONALD QUINTON	CW4	W-2114216	0859	2
MC DONALD RAYMOND J	CW4	W-2003849	0661	3
MC DONALD RICHARD E	LTC	0-0330379	1064	2
MC DONALD ROBERT A	LTC	0-1305781	0865	1
MC DONALD ROBERT F	COL	0-0371299	0261	1
MC DONALD ROBERT H	LTC	0-0163537	0347	3
MC DONALD ROBERT H	LTC	0-2051511	0166	1
MC DONALD ROBERT R	LTC	0-0294047	0660	1
MC DONALD ROGER W	CPT	0-2002072	0860	1
MC DONALD ROLLAND M	CW3	W-2146195	0560	1
MC DONALD RONALD B	LTC	0-0504455	1064	3
MC DONALD RONALD J	LTC	0-0172029	1046	2
MC DONALD ROSE M	1LT	N-0760246	1045	1
MC DONALD ROYCE C	MAJ	0-1300194	0161	1
MC DONALD THOMAS E	1LT	0-0380019	0144	2
MC DONALD THOMAS H	2LT	0-1913546	0447	1
MC DONALD WALTER F	LTC	0-0352921	0258	1
MC DONALD WARD H	LTC	0-0407980	1166	1
MC DONALD WARREN R	MAJ	0-2001792	1061	1
MC DONALD WILLARD A	COL	0-0245131	0560	1
MC DONALD WILLIAM A	LTC	0-0158403	0150	3
MC DONALD WILLIAM A	LTC	0-1174951	1162	1
MC DONALD WILLIAM B	MAJ	0-0237919	0865	3
MC DONALD WILLIS F	LTC	0-1011226	1163	1
MC DONELL GEORGE F	LTC	0-1296726	0860	1
MC DONELL JOHN P	MAJ	0-1058602	0261	1
MC DONIE CARL E	CPT	0-1294341	0346	2
MC DONNELL ALAN J	LTC	0-0489303	0766	3
MC DONNELL FRANCIS J	CW2	W-2146202	0966	1
MC DONNELL GEORGE D	2LT	0-2026996	0448	2
MC DONNELL H E JR	1LT	0-1289607	0246	2
MC DONNELL J F JR	CPT	0-1104294	1045	2
MC DONNELL JAMES F	CW3	W-3410000	1268	1
MC DONNELL JAMES G	LTC	0-1290789	0867	3
MC DONNELL JOHN P	LTC	0-1110111	1262	1
MC DONNELL JOHN P	CPT	0-1297759	0348	2
MC DONNELL JOSEPH W	2LT	0-0964878	1158	2
MC DONNELL ROBERT E	LTC	0-1018666	0962	1
MC DONNELL ROBERT F	CPT	0-1320065	0946	2
MC DONNELL THOMAS J	1LT	0-0346333	0842	2
MC DONNELL WILLIAM D	LTC	0-1299169	0754	1
MC DONOUGH BERNARD A	CPT	0-0324352	0668	3
MC DONOUGH CHARLES E	COL	0-0284143	1065	3
MC DONOUGH DANIEL J	LTC	0-1174066	0766	1
MC DONOUGH EDWARD M	1LT	0-1306618	1045	2
MC DONOUGH EDWARD W	MAJ	0-2017567	0965	1
MC DONOUGH FRANCIS T	1LT	0-1294885	0846	2
MC DONOUGH JOHN E	LTC	0-0102249	0256	3
MC DONOUGH JOHN H	CPT	0-1320151	0347	2
MC DONOUGH MARK D	LTC	0-0507398	0658	2
MC DONOUGH MILES V	LTC	0-0405071	0263	1
MC DONOUGH MONA	2LT	N-0727261	1144	1
MC DONOUGH RAYMOND E	LTC	0-1290102	0661	1
MC DONOUGH REDMOND A	LTC	0-1548496	1062	1
MC DONOUGH ROGERS M	LTC	0-0178544	0853	3
MC DONOUGH THOMAS J	CW3	W-2145973	0962	1
MC DONOUGH WILLIAM	1LT	0-1305956	0246	2
MC DOUGAL HUBERT H	CPT	0-0468096	0246	2
MC DOUGAL LEO E	CPT	0-1587450	0860	2
MC DOUGALD CHARLIE	CW2	W-2152901	0161	1
MC DOUGALL BILLY E	1LT	0-1174953	0844	2
MC DOUGALL CHAUNCY L	CW3	W-2146078	0162	1
MC DOUGALL FRANCIS J	CPT	0-0471831	0945	2
MC DOUGALL HARRY G	COL	0-0287998	0359	1
MC DOUGALL LINDSAY M	CPT	0-0376236	0344	2

NAME	GRADE	SVC NO	DATE RET MO YR	RET CODE
MC DOUGLE RAMON F	CW4	W-2115564	0367	1
MC DOULETT RAYMOND P	CW2	W-2208646	1064	1
MC DOW ALLEN C	CW2	W-2150955	0358	1
MC DOWALL GRAVES H	MAJ	O-0308995	1161	2
MC DOWALL RAYMOND G	CW3	W-2151887	0461	1
MC DOWELL ALVIN L	MAJ	O-2033705	0868	1
MC DOWELL CARL A	CPT	O-0227238	1061	3
MC DOWELL CHARLES K	CW3	W-2141786	0863	1
MC DOWELL CLIFFORD	MAJ	O-0291046	0945	2
MC DOWELL DOUGLAS B	CPT	O-1687007	1045	2
MC DOWELL EDWARD H	CPT	O-1699979	0161	1
MC DOWELL ELISE	2LT	N-0738030	0745	1
MC DOWELL EUGENE A	LTC	O-0385323	0657	1
MC DOWELL EVALYN S	MAJ	N-0742447	0263	1
MC DOWELL HARVEY E	MAJ	O-0309571	0863	3
MC DOWELL JAMES G JR	1LT	O-1845762	0647	2
MC DOWELL JOHN O	1LT	O-1038064	0947	2
MC DOWELL JOUETT S	LTC	O-0231115	1067	3
MC DOWELL MALCOLM H	LTC	O-0454756	0261	1
MC DOWELL NEWTON D	LTC	O-1296065	0363	1
MC DOWELL PETER C	LTC	O-1315086	0762	1
MC DOWELL ROBERT L	CW3	W-2146414	1167	1
MC DOWELL ROMA J	LTC	O-1917612	0568	1
MC DOWELL VERN A	CPT	O-1020037	0965	2
MC DOWELL WALTER J	LTC	O-1035939	0767	1
MC DOWELL WILLIAM F	MAJ	O-1796978	0658	1
MC DOWELL WILLIAM J	1LT	O-1042647	0744	2
MC DUFF ALVIE L	COL	O-0357360	0960	1
MC DUFF GRADY A	MAJ	O-1101573	0861	1
MC DUFF MELVIN A	COL	O-0389808	0265	1
MC DUFFEE DONALD V	LTC	O-0405689	0665	1
MC DUFFEE JAMES M	LTC	O-0214855	0562	3
MC DUFFEY JOHN C	CW3	W-2153657	0167	1
MC DUFFIE JAMES H JR	1LT	O-0407302	0645	2
MC DUFFIE LEON C JR	LTC	O-0904980	0566	3
MC EACHERAN DONALD	CPT	O-0154159	0854	3
MC EACHERN CHARLES	CPT	O-0525795	0252	2
MC EACHIN IVAN B JR	CW2	W-3200656	1168	2
MC EACHIN RAYMOND P	MAJ	O-1685541	0461	1
MC EADDY JAMES D	MAJ	O-0510366	1052	3
MC ELDOWNEY JOSEPH H	LTC	O-1638037	0663	1
MC ELDOWNEY ROBERT R	CPT	O-0241390	0648	3
MC ELFISH CHARLES J	MAJ	O-2037283	1065	1
MC ELHANEY EMERSON	CPT	O-0389032	0544	2
MC ELHENY CLAIR C	COL	O-0260113	1263	3
MC ELHERNE FRANK P	CW4	W-2112334	0559	1
MC ELHOE ALBERT B	COL	O-0299565	0646	2
MC ELLIGOTT THOMAS J	CPT	O-0460436	1146	2
MC ELMURRAY GEORGE L	LTC	O-0357849	1059	1
MC ELREE JOHN W	CW3	W-2146406	0463	1
MC ELROY ALLEN A	LTC	O-1293443	0865	1
MC ELROY CECIL B J	LTC	O-1170356	1060	1
MC ELROY DANIEL R	CPT	O-1595691	0846	2
MC ELROY GEORGE E	LTC	O-0382834	0763	1
MC ELROY JAMES P	CPT	O-0423733	1048	2
MC ELROY JOHN H	LTC	O-0279254	0758	1
MC ELROY JUSTIN	LTC	O-0231562	0955	3
MC ELROY ORVAL J	CW2	W-2150574	1062	1
MC ELROY RAYMOND	CPT	O-0421460	1046	2
MC ELROY RUTH K	MAJ	N-0738032	0162	1
MC ELROY THEODORE J	CW4	W-2136574	0559	1
MC ELVANY GRAYSON E	MAJ	O-1999928	0656	1
MC ELWAINE EDWARD W	MAJ	O-1587451	0466	1
MC ELWEE DAWSON	CW4	W-2100919	0661	1
MC ELWEE PINCKNEY G	COL	O-0311642	0958	3
MC ELYEA ATWOOD M	2LT	O-2046692	0345	2
MC ELYEA BENNIE A	MAJ	O-0243947	0463	3
MC ENANY FRANCIS R	LTC	O-0400133	0860	1
MC ENDARFER MYRON E	MAJ	O-0256953	0264	3
MC ENEANY WILLIAM J	MAJ	O-0395349	0164	1
MC ENIRY CHARLES T	COL	O-0122041	0454	3
MC ENIRY DANIEL N	LTC	O-0122040	0648	3
MC ENROE ROBERT A	CW3	W-2143141	0262	1
MC ENTEE EDWARD J	LTC	O-0889069	0857	1
MC ENTEE JAMES J	LTC	O-1554235	1061	1

NAME	GRADE	SVC NO	DATE RET MO YR	RET CODE
MC ENTYRE CLINTON E	LTC	O-0412865	0457	1
MC EOWEN ALMOND B	CPT	O-7002177	0357	1
MC EVER WILLIAM H	1LT	O-0359219	0542	2
MC EVILLA JAMES A	CW2	W-2213452	0767	1
MC EVOY DUDLEY J	LTC	O-0414602	0254	1
MC EVOY FRANK	MAJ	O-0456287	0646	2
MC EVOY FRED L	CW3	W-2005337	1066	1
MC EVOY HAROLD T	CW4	W-2006275	1065	3
MC EVOY JOHN A	COL	O-0336830	1065	3
MC EVOY RICHARD T	LTC	O-0349773	0860	1
MC EWAN DONALD H	LTC	O-1545623	0467	1
MC EWAN GERALD J	LTC	O-1535236	0964	1
MC EWAN JOHN J	LTC	O-0478042	1144	2
MC EWAN JOHN W	2LT	O-1113354	0844	2
MC EWEN CARL C	CPT	O-1298895	1060	1
MC EWEN LAURENCE B	LTC	O-0174538	0860	3
MC EWEN WILLIAM C	LTC	O-1639625	0563	1
MC EWEN WILLIAM D	LTC	O-1583352	1267	3
MC FADDEN ALICE W	MAJ	R-0001330	0167	3
MC FADDEN DAVID J	COL	O-0224689	0457	1
MC FADDEN EMORY L	1LT	O-1549328	0466	3
MC FADDEN FRANK J	LTC	O-1284002	0864	1
MC FADDEN JOHN P	1LT	O-1315087	0146	2
MC FADDEN PHILLIP D	CW3	W-2152853	0164	1
MC FADDEN ROBERT E	MAJ	O-1174374	0446	2
MC FADDEN ROGER B	1LT	O-1109503	0947	2
MC FADDEN VINCENT B	LTC	O-0325707	0948	2
MC FADDEN VINCENT G	COL	O-0299871	0965	3
MC FADDEN WILLIAM G	CW3	W-2144408	0365	1
MC FADDIN EDWARD F	CPT	O-0101996	1054	3
MC FADDIN NORMAN J	CPT	O-0383141	0260	2
MC FADIN OSCAR L	LTC	O-2027777	0962	1
MC FADYEN WILLIAM B	COL	O-0305737	1065	1
MC FAIL STANLEY H	2LT	O-1798170	0146	2
MC FALL ELMER P	CPT	O-1180255	0559	1
MC FALL LOUISE A	MAJ	N-0800079	0765	1
MC FALL RUSSELL K	CW3	W-2114843	0154	1
MC FARLAND A J	MAJ	O-0970667	0859	1
MC FARLAND COWAN A	MAJ	O-0194249	1046	1
MC FARLAND ERWIN V	CW3	W-2153069	1164	1
MC FARLAND FRED C	COL	O-0133539	0758	3
MC FARLAND GEORGE H	LTC	O-1165651	0459	1
MC FARLAND HARRY L	MAJ	O-0973920	0863	1
MC FARLAND HENRY T	CW3	W-2120181	0962	1
MC FARLAND J B	CW2	W-2210216	1061	1
MC FARLAND JAMES E	MAJ	O-0463931	0165	1
MC FARLAND JAMES F	CPT	O-0243125	0854	3
MC FARLAND JOHN M	LTC	O-0565585	0868	1
MC FARLAND JOHN R JR	MAJ	O-0452232	0346	2
MC FARLAND JOHN W	MAJ	O-2055144	0155	1
MC FARLAND NELSON	1LT	O-1320757	0746	2
MC FARLAND OTTIS H	MAJ	O-0284262	0167	3
MC FARLAND PAUL T	LTC	O-0294516	1056	3
MC FARLAND ROBERT D	CPT	O-1298896	0346	2
MC FARLAND ROBERT M	COL	O-0290787	0561	3
MC FARLAND WILBUR G	MAJ	O-1582743	0562	1
MC FARLAND WILLIAM	1LT	O-0391923	0751	2
MC FARLANE BURR C	MAJ	O-1885766	0668	1
MC FARLANE PAUL S	LTC	O-1557193	1163	1
MC FARLANE SAMUEL J	1LT	O-1914062	1043	2
MC FARLIN GEORGE C	LTC	O-0265945	0958	3
MC FATE THOMAS J JR	1LT	O-1726015	0945	2
MC FAUL MARY E	MAJ	N-0756367	0463	1
MC FEE ALBERT A	CPT	O-0497458	0147	1
MC FEE WALTER E	LTC	O-0186770	0648	3
MC FEELY KENNETH O	MAJ	O-1317985	0563	2
MC FERREN ROBERT H	CPT	O-0552332	1163	2
MC FETRIDGE CAROL F	CPT	O-0982909	0162	1
MC GAFFIGAN JAMES A	CPT	O-0337537	0646	2
MC GAHA CHARLES L	MAJ	O-2027823	1061	1
MC GAHAN PAUL J	COL	O-0147271	1048	3
MC GAHEE NELSON M	CW3	W-2111947	1160	1
MC GALLIARD ALEXAN	LTC	O-0450997	1154	1
MC GALLIARD ANDREW H	CPT	O-0546043	0147	2
MC GANN WILLIAM G	MAJ	O-2007207	0561	1

NAME	GRADE	SVC NO	DATE RET MO YR	RET CODE
MC GARITY ROBERT S	MAJ	O-0282577	1068	3
MC GARR ARTHUR F	LTC	O-0311203	0368	3
MC GARRETT ADDISON M	CW3	W-2144922	0462	1
MC GARRIGLE JOHN T	CW3	W-2139937	0860	1
MC GARRIGLE ROBERT J	CW2	W-2146725	1061	1
MC GARRY EDWARD P	1LT	O-2006919	1067	3
MC GARRY GERALD J	MAJ	O-1573408	0549	2
MC GARRY GERARD B	LTC	O-1584582	0666	1
MC GARRY JOSEPH J	LTC	O-1796979	0465	1
MC GARRY ROBERT L	1LT	O-1110653	0545	2
MC GARRY WILLIAM F	LTC	O-1045519	0762	1
MC GARRY WILLIAM L	LTC	O-1794971	0764	1
MC GARVEY EDMUND F	CW3	W-2152242	1063	1
MC GARVEY HERSCHEL G	MAJ	O-0889254	1264	1
MC GARVEY JOSEPH A	CW2	W-2146715	1263	1
MC GARVEY RICHARD C	COL	O-0454747	0464	1
MC GARVEY SAMUEL E	CW4	W-2141821	0861	1
MC GARVEY WILLIAM G	LTC	O-1104296	0563	1
MC GARY JOHN O	LTC	O-1594326	0366	1
MC GAUGHEY KENNETH E	MAJ	O-1688598	0865	1
MC GAUGHEY MUNSEY	CPT	O-0112074	0655	3
MC GAUHEY MILTON G	MAJ	O-0974702	0666	1
MC GAVOCK ALFRED M	MAJ	O-0260771	0567	3
MC GAVOCK FRANCIS J	2LT	O-0979239	0352	2
MC GAW CHARLES F	2LT	O-1845067	1144	2
MC GEE CARL D	COL	O-0372381	0462	3
MC GEE CHARLES F	LTC	O-1535373	1162	1
MC GEE CHARLES F	2LT	O-1658164	0245	2
MC GEE CHARLES L	LTC	O-0254009	0862	3
MC GEE EDWARD F	2LT	O-1031899	0146	2
MC GEE ERNEST T	CW4	W-2142595	1265	1
MC GEE HENRY J JR	MAJ	O-1047673	1158	1
MC GEE HOKE S	LTC	O-1546645	1262	1
MC GEE JAMES E JR	LTC	O-1182191	1062	1
MC GEE JOSEPH B JR	COL	O-0294448	1160	1
MC GEE LAWRENCE E	MAJ	O-1302846	0261	1
MC GEE MILDRED K	MAJ	N-0772393	0754	2
MC GEE MORGAN B	MAJ	O-1294695	0760	1
MC GEE MORRIS L	CPT	O-0984063	1060	1
MC GEE RALPH W	1LT	O-0518870	1045	2
MC GEE RAYMOND	WO1	W-2005939	1058	3
MC GEE REECE J	COL	O-0171858	1149	3
MC GEE ROBERT J	WO1	W-2129965	0846	2
MC GEE WILLIAM	1LT	O-0341168	0154	1
MC GEE WILLIAM B	LTC	O-0142948	1056	3
MC GEE WILLIAM N JR	1LT	O-0392655	0146	2
MC GEE ZETTIE A	1LT	N-0735187	0546	1
MC GEEGHAN JAMES F	1LT	O-1315596	0146	2
MC GEHEE HARRY C	1LT	O-0546134	0846	2
MC GEHEE JAMES I	CW3	W-2206528	1068	1
MC GEHEE MARIA T	2LT	N-0702257	0635	1
MC GEHEE ROBERT J	1LT	O-0531122	1145	2
MC GEHEE TURNER A JR	1LT	O-1010200	0146	2
MC GERROW SAMUEL V	LTC	O-0327506	0661	2
MC GHEE ADDISON F JR	COL	O-0258592	0867	3
MC GHEE DEWARD A	MAJ	O-1164641	1060	1
MC GHEE DONALD F	CW3	W-2145047	0164	1
MC GHEE EARL R	CPT	O-0109996	0755	3
MC GHEE LEWIS M	MAJ	O-0270041	0447	2
MC GHEE ROBERT B	LTC	O-1824779	0466	1
MC GIBONEY DAVID R	1LT	O-1288773	0945	2
MC GIFFERT ANDREW C	MAJ	O-0285996	0768	3
MC GILL ALFRED A	CPT	O-1895941	0567	3
MC GILL ALLAN C	LTC	O-1300350	0466	1
MC GILL ARTHUR A	LTC	O-0206031	0547	1
MC GILL DONALD K	COL	O-0436956	0462	1
MC GILL DONALD R	MAJ	O-0270440	0468	3
MC GILL GRANT J	LTC	O-0276984	0855	3
MC GILL KENNETH H	LTC	O-1581253	1167	1
MC GILL LLOYD D	CPT	O-0885645	1147	2
MC GILL RICHARD H	CW4	W-2105469	0259	1
MC GILLICUDDY L O	LTC	O-1167548	1166	3
MC GILVERY LAWRENCE	CPT	O-0346408	0667	3
MC GILVRAY HAROLD R	CW3	W-2141633	1057	1
MC GILVRAY JOHN W	COL	O-0221838	0247	1

NAME	GRADE	SVC NO	DATE RET MO YR	RET CODE
MC GIMPSEY WILLIAM T	CW4	W-2107942	0155	1
MC GIMSEY CECIL F	LTC	O-0252748	0649	1
MC GINITY JOSEPH T	CPT	O-1166132	0745	2
MC GINLEY ALICE C	MAJ	N-0720230	0461	1
MC GINLEY VINCENT J	MAJ	O-2014910	0167	1
MC GINN HAROLD J	MAJ	O-0125100	1051	3
MC GINN JOHN P	MAJ	O-0481291	0546	2
MC GINN JOSEPH G	LTC	O-1794829	0561	1
MC GINN JOSEPH L	MAJ	O-1167539	0364	1
MC GINN KATHLEEN	MAJ	N-0758486	0864	1
MC GINN MICHAEL J	MAJ	O-1635071	0648	2
MC GINNESS GEORGE L	LTC	O-0239807	0765	3
MC GINNESS JOHN S	MAJ	O-1047229	1059	2
MC GINNIS EARL L	CW2	W-2124653	1045	2
MC GINNIS EDWARD J	CPT	O-0510084	1147	1
MC GINNIS EVERETT D	CW3	W-2146453	0760	1
MC GINNIS FRANCIS D	WO1	W-2139513	0745	2
MC GINNIS FREDERIC D	LTC	O-0261253	1262	1
MC GINNIS JOHN F	LTC	O-0295501	0768	3
MC GINNIS JOHN L	LTC	O-0422060	0547	2
MC GINNIS MARION L	CW3	W-2148211	0962	1
MC GINNIS PATRICK F	COL	O-1286326	0764	1
MC GINNIS PAUL W	1LT	O-1302847	0945	2
MC GINNIS ROBERT C	WO1	W-2139949	1145	2
MC GINNIS VINCENT F	MAJ	O-1165419	0461	1
MC GINNIS WILLIAM A	MAJ	O-1557328	0959	3
MC GINNIS WILLIAM H	MAJ	O-0491661	0546	1
MC GINNIS WILLIAM T	MAJ	O-0260454	0865	3
MC GINTY GEORGE E	CPT	O-0524853	1146	2
MC GINTY HOWARD C	MAJ	O-0341155	0246	2
MC GINTY RICHARD R	LTC	O-1549330	0864	1
MC GINTY THOMAS F	MAJ	O-1822033	0164	1
MC GINTY WILLIAM R	MAJ	O-1584057	0146	2
MC GIRL JOHN J	MAJ	O-0138383	0853	3
MC GIRR JOHN P	1LT	O-1169243	0853	2
MC GIVEN PAUL L	LTC	O-0377100	1059	1
MC GIVERN PETER M JR	MAJ	O-1299459	1162	1
MC GIVNEY ROBERT B	LTC	O-0354125	1065	1
MC GLAMERY JOHN W	CPT	O-0155808	1044	2
MC GLAUGHLIN W J	CW2	W-2119678	0348	2
MC GLAUN WILLIAM C	MAJ	O-0986436	0963	1
MC GLINN MARY E	CPT	L-0909021	1144	2
MC GLONE ANTHONY J	CW4	W-2200735	1266	3
MC GLONE CLARENCE	MAJ	O-0338246	0656	1
MC GLONE HAROLD W	LTC	O-1168812	0667	3
MC GLOTHLAN JOHN A	MAJ	O-0395007	0547	2
MC GLYNN EDWARD J	CPT	O-0359606	0545	2
MC GLYNN JAMES C	MAJ	O-0383192	0347	2
MC GLYNN JAMES O	LTC	O-0221107	1160	3
MC GLYNN THOMAS F	LTC	O-0343663	0262	1
MC GLYNN THOMAS J	CW3	W-2203312	0864	1
MC GOEY RALPH A	CPT	O-0236600	0266	3
MC GOLDRICK JOHN P	MAJ	O-1549546	0950	2
MC GOLDRICK LESTER C	LTC	O-1578835	0259	1
MC GONAGLE HOWARD F	MAJ	O-0966859	0661	1
MC GOUGAN ERNEST D	MAJ	O-0138551	1054	3
MC GOUGH JOSEPH M	LTC	O-0336075	0464	3
MC GOUGH JOSEPH P	CPT	O-0399137	0346	2
MC GOUGH THOMAS L	CW3	W-2205160	1163	1
MC GOUGHRAN EDWARD H	LTC	O-1550657	1158	2
MC GOVERN ANN	MAJ	N-0720920	0364	3
MC GOVERN ARTHUR J	MAJ	O-0237233	0346	2
MC GOVERN CHARLES	LTC	O-0266276	0860	1
MC GOVERN FLORENCE K	MAJ	N-0759078	1162	1
MC GOVERN FRANK A	LTC	O-0330586	0357	1
MC GOVERN JAMES F	MAJ	O-1041846	0354	2
MC GOVERN JAMES W JR	CW2	W-2145341	0461	1
MC GOVERN JOHN E	LTC	O-1167106	1061	1
MC GOVERN MILTON J	1LT	O-0884172	0644	2
MC GOVERN SYLVESTER	1LT	O-1895310	0944	2
MC GOVERN THOMAS F	CPT	O-1536422	0363	1
MC GOVERN THOMAS J	MAJ	O-0118041	0954	3
MC GOVERN WILLIAM R	2LT	O-1321805	1150	2
MC GOWAN ARTHUR O	CPT	O-1700279	0944	2
MC GOWAN B I JR	CPT	O-0359281	0645	2

NAME	GRADE	SVC NO	DATE RET MO YR	RET CODE	NAME	GRADE	SVC NO	DATE RET MO YR	RET CODE	NAME	GRADE	SVC NO	DATE RET MO YR	RET CODE	NAME	GRADE	SVC NO	DATE RET MO YR	RET CODE
MC GOWAN CHARLES [illegible]	CPT	[illegible]	0365	2	MC GUIGAN GEORGE F	MAJ	0-2052224	1057	2	MC ILROY FRED W	LTC	0-0476815	1153	1	MC KAMY THOMAS W	2LT	0-0685236	0666	2
MC GOWAN CHARLES S	LTC	0-1576159	0961	1	MC GUIGAN JOHN G	CW4	W-2004353	0964	3	MC ILROY JAMES R	COL	0-0311807	0246	2	MC KANNA NEAL B	CPT	0-1165309	0957	1
MC GOWAN CLARENCE M	CPT	0-2036695	0557	1	MC GUIGAN LEONARD M	CPT	0-0489686	0246	2	MC ILVAINE CHARLES W	LTC	0-0312971	0668	3	MC KAY ANDREW J	WO1	W-2146261	0352	2
MC GOWAN EDWARD	1LT	0-1285506	0444	2	MC GUINES ETHEL G	CPT	N-0721701	0746	1	MC ILVAINE HOWARD F	WO1	W-2126496	1065	2	MC KAY GEORGE C	LTC	0-1016201	0263	1
MC GOWAN EDWARD A	MAJ	0-0314409	0363	1	MC GUINESS RICHARD M	CPT	0-1030065	0345	2	MC ILWAIN WALTER N	LTC	0-2015641	0767	1	MC KAY HAROLD W	LTC	0-0365797	0667	3
MC GOWAN FRANCIS	1LT	0-0895778	1153	1	MC GUINESS WILLIAM J	1LT	0-1295407	0444	2	MC ILWAIN WILLIAM T	LTC	0-0214107	0763	3	MC KAY HUNTER B	CPT	0-0206054	0158	3
MC GOWAN FRANCIS J	COL	0-0193258	1147	2	MC GUINNESS JAMES F	LTC	0-1173707	0560	1	MC ILWAINE THEODORE	LTC	0-0322065	0868	3	MC KAY IVOR W SR	LTC	0-1311911	0168	1
MC GOWAN FRANK R	MAJ	0-0957294	0563	1	MC GUINNESS JOHN P	COL	0-0183782	0753	3	MC INANEY WILLIAM F	MAJ	0-2262388	0563	2	MC KAY JAMES H	LTC	0-0455496	0758	1
MC GOWAN GRAEME	LTC	0-1119027	1264	3	MC GUIRE CHARLES F	CPT	0-1545492	0154	2	MC INDOE ELIZABETH	CPT	L-0906009	1055	2	MC KAY JAMES V	CPT	0-1913823	0828	1
MC GOWAN JACK A	MAJ	0-1173177	0468	3	MC GUIRE CLEMENT J	CPT	0-1297566	0446	2	MC INDOE JAMES F	LTC	0-0191162	0860	3	MC KAY JAMES W JR	CPT	0-1292382	1046	2
MC GOWAN JAMES J	LTC	0-0477813	0355	1	MC GUIRE CLYDE W	1LT	0-1181953	1145	2	MC INDOE WILLIAM C	LTC	0-0154517	1054	3	MC KAY JOHN W	CPT	0-0246405	1055	3
MC GOWAN JOHN C JR	CW3	W-2144272	0268	1	MC GUIRE DAVID T	CW2	W-2210617	1064	1	MC INERNEY HENRY B	LTC	0-0376835	0667	1	MC KAY LOYD J	1LT	0-2304298	1060	2
MC GOWAN JOHN R	LTC	0-1324782	0563	1	MC GUIRE ELMER L	LTC	0-1015793	0967	1	MC INERNEY JOHN J	LTC	0-0397940	0346	2	MC KAY NEIL A	1LT	0-1533138	0743	2
MC GOWAN MARGARET	LTC	N-0744396	0465	3	MC GUIRE ERNEST J	CW3	W-2151650	1262	1	MC INERNEY JOSEPH T	1LT	0-1101110	1145	2	MC KAY NEIL H	COL	0-0104944	0151	3
MC GOWAN MARTHA M	CPT	N-0732791	1046	1	MC GUIRE EVERETT A	MAJ	0-1284180	0758	1	MC INERNEY MARY M	1LT	N-0724365	1045	1	MC KAY NEIL P	B G	0-0173091	1055	3
MC GOWAN OREN H	CW3	W-2142878	0656	1	MC GUIRE FRANCIS P	CPT	0-1551910	0859	1	MC INERNEY MARY T	1LT	R-0002148	1045	2	MC KAY ROBERT D	CW4	W-2143286	0867	1
MC GOWAN PAUL H	MAJ	0-1103794	0858	2	MC GUIRE FRANK A	MAJ	0-0497708	1045	2	MC INERNEY MICHAEL J	MAJ	0-2262855	1161	1	MC KAY TERRELL	LTC	0-0245158	0446	2
MC GOWAN ROBERT F	1LT	0-1331646	1147	2	MC GUIRE FRANK X JR	2LT	0-1596726	0245	2	MC INNES GILBERT JR	1LT	0-1046562	0545	2	MC KAY WILLIAM	LTC	0-1297567	0962	1
MC GOWAN SAMUEL F	LTC	0-0285511	0364	3	MC GUIRE GEORGE F	MAJ	0-0217946	0162	3	MC INNES JOHN P	CPT	0-1300831	1164	1	MC KAY WILLIAM A	MAJ	0-1322462	0261	1
MC GOWAN SANFORD	CW3	W-2149472	0662	1	MC GUIRE GERALD A	LTC	0-0232582	0359	3	MC INNES MARGARET M	LTC	N-0751283	1167	1	MC KEAGE THOMAS E	MAJ	0-1310280	0562	1
MC GOWAN THOMAS G	LTC	0-0288741	1064	3	MC GUIRE HERBERT	CPT	0-1914161	0427	1	MC INNES WILLIAM G	LTC	0-0526232	0366	3	MC KEAN ALAN M	MAJ	0-1013759	0965	1
MC GOWAN THOMAS P	LTC	0-1590016	0168	3	MC GUIRE HERMAN M	MAJ	0-1042366	0148	2	MC INNIS GEORGE N	1LT	0-0866027	0146	2	MC KEAN ALEXANDER	LTC	0-0260584	0864	3
MC GOWAN WILLIAM	LTC	0-1541064	0764	1	MC GUIRE HUGH C	MAJ	0-1318370	0760	1	MC INNIS HERRIN E	LTC	0-1548255	0563	1	MC KEAN ALVIN S	MAJ	0-1182193	1159	1
MC GOWAN WILLIAM J	MAJ	0-1548951	0561	2	MC GUIRE JACK J	CPT	0-1323156	1152	2	MC INNIS JANE K	1LT	N-0784480	1146	1	MC KEAN ELROY H	LTC	0-1288774	0955	1
MC GOWAN WILLIAM J	WO1	W-2125104	1043	2	MC GUIRE JAMES B	LTC	0-1000264	0757	1	MC INNIS JOHN W	CW3	W-2143657	1158	1	MC KEAN GORDON W	COL	0-0275888	0468	3
MC GOWAN WILLIAM P	LTC	0-0259750	1065	3	MC GUIRE JOHN A	LTC	0-0234652	1164	3	MC INNIS MERVILLE W	COL	0-0154545	0746	2	MC KEAND JAMES M	LTC	0-0328052	1064	3
MC GRADE GEORGE F	CW3	W-2104760	1154	1	MC GUIRE JOHN C	MAJ	0-0482445	0446	2	MC INNIS RICHARD J	LTC	0-0219004	1059	3	MC KEARNEY J B JR	1LT	0-1997810	1047	2
MC GRADY CATHERINE	MAJ	L-0115788	0367	1	MC GUIRE JOHN M	MAJ	0-1922575	1064	1	MC INROY DAVID J	CW3	W-2153656	0665	2	MC KECHNIE WILLIAM E	MAJ	0-0208599	0959	3
MC GRADY J R	LTC	0-1106350	1064	1	MC GUIRE JOHN P	LTC	0-0294521	0358	3	MC INTIRE DONALD B	1LT	0-0454020	1044	2	MC KEE ALBERT O	MAJ	0-0201416	0359	3
MC GRADY MARION M	LTC	0-1182911	0161	1	MC GUIRE JOSEPH	LTC	0-1598130	0165	1	MC INTIRE JOHN E	LTC	0-0258654	1165	3	MC KEE ARTHUR R	1LT	0-0145578	0648	3
MC GRADY WILLIAM M	2LT	0-1016669	0944	2	MC GUIRE JOSEPH F	COL	0-0439004	0453	1	MC INTIRE LEWIS W	COL	0-0183575	0861	1	MC KEE CHARLES G	LTC	0-1109506	0265	1
MC GRAIN ROBERT A	CW4	W-2002068	0563	1	MC GUIRE LAWRENCE E	MAJ	0-1822597	0861	2	MC INTIRE RILEY B	1LT	0-1323722	0646	2	MC KEE CLARENCE W	LTC	0-1550447	0261	1
MC GRANE GERALD J	1LT	0-1314811	0451	2	MC GUIRE M J JR	1LT	0-1288592	0245	2	MC INTIRE ROBERT B	LTC	0-0463815	0762	1	MC KEE EDWIN	LTC	0-0910432	1046	2
MC GRANE JOHN A	MAJ	0-1043423	0561	1	MC GUIRE MARTIN E	MAJ	0-1326004	1157	1	MC INTIRE ROLAND H	LTC	0-0450375	0258	1	MC KEE EUGENE C	CW3	W-2147768	0562	1
MC GRATH ALBERT J	MAJ	0-2019764	1160	1	MC GUIRE MATTHEW J	LTC	0-0278041	0868	3	MC INTIRE SCOTT L	LTC	0-0256248	0157	3	MC KEE FRANK	LTC	0-0189751	0362	3
MC GRATH ALBERT W	COL	0-0389029	0461	1	MC GUIRE ORLA E	COL	0-0519500	1163	3	MC INTOSH CLAUDE	MAJ	0-0347617	0562	3	MC KEE FRANK J	CPT	0-0493642	0246	2
MC GRATH ANDREW T	LTC	0-1589369	0464	1	MC GUIRE RALPH T	CW3	W-2146741	0866	1	MC INTOSH EDWIN W	MAJ	0-0293747	1162	1	MC KEE GEORGE R	CPT	0-0948641	0361	1
MC GRATH GEORGE F	MAJ	0-0996582	0463	1	MC GUIRE RAYMOND C	MAJ	0-0294291	0544	2	MC INTOSH ERNEST G	CW2	W-2121205	0564	1	MC KEE GEORGE S	LTC	0-0195362	0462	3
MC GRATH GERALD A	MAJ	0-2016918	1162	1	MC GUIRE RICHARD W	1LT	0-1290632	1145	2	MC INTOSH JESSE E	M G	0-0187985	0857	3	MC KEE GERALD F	MAJ	0-1913494	0568	1
MC GRATH HAROLD W	MAJ	0-1341893	0365	1	MC GUIRE SEYMOUR J	CPT	0-0232965	1059	3	MC INTOSH JOSEPH R	LTC	0-0247550	0166	3	MC KEE HERBERT A	MAJ	0-0181140	0245	2
MC GRATH HARRY J	LTC	0-0369432	0267	3	MC GUIRE THOMAS	2LT	0-2263722	0856	1	MC INTOSH KENNETH	LTC	0-0204150	0153	3	MC KEE JAMES E JR	2LT	0-1578840	0843	2
MC GRATH HOWARD L	LTC	0-0346958	0861	1	MC GUIRE THOMAS C	CPT	0-0283247	0966	3	MC INTOSH REGINALD S	2LT	0-1312580	0145	2	MC KEE JAMES R	CPT	0-2036625	0359	2
MC GRATH JAMES A	LTC	0-1177523	0161	1	MC GUIRE VIRGIL P	LTC	0-1913325	0968	1	MC INTOSH RICHARD I	COL	0-0235756	0266	3	MC KEE JAMES W JR	MAJ	0-1821747	1160	1
MC GRATH JOHN C	COL	0-0210522	1064	3	MC GUIRE WALTER T JR	1LT	0-1108157	0146	2	MC INTOSH ROBERT M	1LT	0-0985331	0154	2	MC KEE JOHN A	MAJ	0-0450999	0258	1
MC GRATH JOHN R	CPT	0-4005832	0964	1	MC GUIRE WILLIAM T	CW4	W-2142521	1062	1	MC INTOSH WILLIAM E	CPT	0-1298418	0446	2	MC KEE JOHN C	LTC	0-0121704	0252	3
MC GRATH JOSEPH B	1LT	0-0536975	0946	2	MC GUIRL DANIEL P	CPT	0-2000098	0861	2	MC INTOSH WILLIAM L	MAJ	0-1170489	1263	1	MC KEE MORRIS R	CW3	W-2150328	0666	1
MC GRATH JOSEPH J	CW2	W-3000381	1267	1	MC GUYER GLENN C	MAJ	0-1821609	0958	1	MC INTURFF HARLAND R	CW2	W-2146950	0161	1	MC KEE RALPH H	M G	0-0234931	1165	3
MC GRATH JOSEPH S	CPT	0-0386415	0861	1	MC HALE DONALD J	LTC	0-1796118	0367	3	MC INTURFF J H	CW4	W-2129364	0159	1	MC KEE RAYMOND	COL	0-0313649	1060	1
MC GRATH RAY G	LTC	0-0218378	1059	3	MC HALE DONALD R	1LT	0-1643858	1058	2	MC INTYRE ALEX JR	CPT	0-1304765	1045	2	MC KEE ROBERT A	CW2	W-2115530	0946	2
MC GRATH ROY A	CW2	W-2110679	0653	1	MC HALE LAWRENCE	CW3	W-2141994	0762	1	MC INTYRE ANDREW F	B G	0-0271317	0652	3	MC KEE ROBERT L	MAJ	0-1583358	1156	2
MC GRATH THOMAS J	LTC	0-1559491	0863	1	MC HAN WALTER S	LTC	0-0302452	0347	1	MC INTYRE ANTHONY	CPT	0-0360330	0960	1	MC KEE THOMAS C	COL	0-0420767	0861	3
MC GRATH VINCENT T	CPT	0-0118091	0858	3	MC HARG WILLIAM F	MAJ	0-1946569	0661	1	MC INTYRE CARL M	LTC	0-0420127	0760	1	MC KEE WALDO C	MAJ	0-0348269	0444	2
MC GRATH WILLIAM H	LTC	0-0203053	0758	3	MC HENRY GUY T	MAJ	0-0290022	0163	3	MC INTYRE CHARLES J	COL	0-0175207	0846	2	MC KEEFE ANDREW	COL	0-0266928	1067	3
MC GRATH WILLIAM J	MAJ	0-1945427	1060	1	MC HENRY HARVEY W	CPT	0-0245899	0550	3	MC INTYRE EARL E	CPT	0-0153702	0955	3	MC KEEN CHESTER V	MAJ	0-1293623	0446	2
MC GRAW CARROLL R	LTC	0-1018555	0468	1	MC HENRY HENRY I	LTC	0-0515424	0854	1	MC INTYRE EDWARD J	1LT	0-1012056	0446	2	MC KEEN RAYMOND L	CPT	0-1315597	0346	2
MC GRAW CARRUTTH M	LTC	0-0281119	0866	3	MC HENRY IRVIN	LTC	0-1012617	0357	1	MC INTYRE EUGENE J	MAJ	0-0976064	0167	1	MC KEEVER EDWARD L	MAJ	0-1876990	0265	1
MC GRAW FRANK W	MAJ	0-1311183	0457	1	MC HENRY JAMES L	LTC	0-1031461	0864	1	MC INTYRE GORDON R	LTC	0-0268394	1164	3	MC KEEVER JACK W	CW3	W-2206019	0168	1
MC GRAW GEORGE	MAJ	0-1639381	0354	2	MC HENRY MELVIN C	LTC	0-0888344	1265	1	MC INTYRE JAMES B	LTC	0-0170901	0655	3	MC KEEVER JAMES L	CPT	0-0554875	0948	2
MC GREE NICHOLAS C	LTC	0-1043425	0761	1	MC HENRY ROBERT M	LTC	0-0267315	0767	3	MC INTYRE JAMES O	1LT	0-1301514	0546	2	MC KEEVER THOMAS E	LTC	0-1038761	0761	1
MC GREEVY JOHN M	M G	0-0278060	0262	1	MC HENRY WILLIAM O	MAJ	0-1640725	1160	1	MC INTYRE LORENZO C	MAJ	0-0252736	1268	3	MC KEICH ROBERT W	CW4	W-2142509	1163	1
MC GREGOR ARDEN D	MAJ	0-2023893	0161	1	MC HONE JAMES R	1LT	0-1542511	0845	2	MC INTYRE NATHANIEL	1LT	0-0300257	0665	3	MC KEITH EARL J	CPT	0-0272484	0460	3
MC GREGOR CLIFFORD	WO1	W-2152122	1154	1	MC HUGH CATHERINE	2LT	N-0720723	1043	1	MC INTYRE NILES J	MAJ	0-1011371	0859	1	MC KEITHAN ERNEST H	CPT	0-0423039	0346	2
MC GREGOR ERNEST M	MAJ	0-2032290	0662	1	MC HUGH CHARLES X	LTC	0-1647602	0463	1	MC INTYRE R J JR	LTC	0-0301530	1059	1	MC KEITHEN LONZIE	MAJ	0-0527993	1161	2
MC GREGOR JOEL I	1LT	0-1823754	C153	2	MC HUGH ELIZABETH	LTC	L-0220012	0468	3	MC INTYRE WADE H JR	CPT	0-0396115	1046	2	MC KEITHEN VANN E	CPT	0-0451716	1045	2
MC GREW DANIEL R	MAJ	0-0978982	0764	1	MC HUGH GEORGE M	CW2	W-2102075	1055	1	MC INTYRE WILLIAM O	LTC	0-0424523	1060	1	MC KELL WILLIAM H	LTC	0-1057531	1067	3
MC GREW EDWARD J JR	M G	0-0265015	1162	3	MC HUGH HAROLD J	LTC	0-0359365	0463	3	MC INTYRE WILLIAM L	MAJ	0-1798870	1062	1	MC KELLEGET RICHARD	MAJ	0-0942994	0864	1
MC GREW JAMES W	LTC	0-1646408	0767	1	MC HUGH JOHN T	CPT	0-0509140	0655	1	MC INVALE CECIL W	2LT	0-2010599	0559	1	MC KELLOP BARNEY H	MAJ	0-1062984	0363	1
MC GREW THOMAS J	1LT	0-2033554	0559	1	MC HUGH JOSEPH C	COL	0-1578837	1164	3	MC ISAAC MAURICE J	CW4	W-2122883	0562	2	MC KELLY JOHN S	LTC	0-0350092	0760	1
MC GROGAN WILLIAM J	CPT	0-0307160	1145	2	MC HUGH KATHLEEN J	MAJ	N-0795454	1066	1	MC IVER GEORGE D	CW2	W-2207473	0364	1	MC KELVEY CLYDE C	CPT	0-0224035	0656	3
MC GRUDER ANDERSON	CPT	0-2039430	0657	1	MC HUGH ROBERT F	LTC	0-0917025	0365	3	MC IVERS GRACE J	2LT	N-0790659	0545	1	MC KELVEY PAUL G	MAJ	0-0145720	0246	2
MC GRUDER CLEMENT W	1LT	RW-2149933	0657	1	MC HUGH WILLIAM C	MAJ	0-0417259	0945	2	MC IVERS PAUL T H	CPT	0-1283287	1045	2	MC KELVEY RUSSELL	CW3	W-2141376	0157	1
MC GRUDER ROLAND W	MAJ	0-1799762	1165	1	MC HUGH WILLIAM O	LTC	0-0497997	1048	1	MC KAGUE BERNARD F	MAJ	0-1578839	0762	1	MC KELVEY STUART C	COL	0-1555250	0868	1
MC GUANE FRANK L	COL	0-0251622	0367	3	MC HUGH WILLIAM P	CPT	0-0507696	0746	2	MC KAIN CHARLES L JR	1LT	0-1289781	0646	2	MC KELVEY WILLIAM T	CPT	0-0176845	0737	1
MC GUFFEY BILL E	CPT	0-1643113	0762	*1	MC ILRAITH WILLIAM J	1LT	0-1287918	1146	2	MC KAIN JAMES H	LTC	0-1106944	0667	1	MC KELVIE CLYDE R	CPT	0-1166556	0866	1
MC GUFFIN JOHN W	LTC	0-0285754	1163	3	MC ILREE JOHN L	WO1	W-2132217	0345	2	MC KALIP MARVIN S	MAJ	0-1294697	0963	1	MC KELVY GEORGE M	LTC	0-0401691	1160	1

NAME	GRADE	SVC NO	DATE RET MO YR	RET CODE	NAME	GRADE	SVC NO	DATE RET MO YR	RET CODE	NAME	GRADE	SVC NO	DATE RET MO YR	RET CODE	NAME	GRADE	SVC NO	DATE RET MO YR	RET CODE
MC KENIE JAMES B	LTC	0-1312581	1264	3	MC KEW JOSEPH E JR	CPT	0-1322568	0747	2	MC KINNON JOHN L	MAJ	0-0460364	0232	1	MC LAUGHLIN CLAREN	MAJ	0-0141530	0648	3
MC KENY WILLIAM L JR	CW3	W-2151140	1066	1	MC KEWEN WILLIAM R	CW4	W-2119616	0859	1	MC KINNON RAY	MAJ	0-0183856	0346	2	MC LAUGHLIN CLAYTON	CW3	W-2207740	0767	1
MC KENDREE JAMES L J	1LT	0-0536189	0946	2	MC KIBBEN BEN B JR	LTC	0-1319304	0565	2	MC KINNON WADE L	MAJ	0-1300195	1160	1	MC LAUGHLIN DEROY J	MAJ	0-0419337	0446	2
MC KENDRICK JAMES	COL	0-0470913	1152	3	MC KIBBEN DONALD H	MAJ	0-2010633	1164	1	MC KINNON WILLIAM L	MAJ	0-0382552	0855	1	MC LAUGHLIN DONALD G	CPT	0-0418024	0744	2
MC KENNA ALVIN	LTC	0-1548953	0665	1	MC KIBBEN HERBERT D	LTC	0-1167541	0366	1	MC KINSEY HAROLD I	LTC	0-1323950	0366	3	MC LAUGHLIN EDGAR A	COL	0-0275862	1267	3
MC KENNA CHARLES F	2LT	0-2000439	1145	2	MC KIBBIN MARTIN H	1LT	0-0106440	0244	2	MC KINSEY MILLARD F	LTC	0-0467734	0164	1	MC LAUGHLIN EDWARD D	CPT	0-0218224	0763	3
MC KENNA DANIEL J	LTC	0-0330094	0645	2	MC KIBBON JAMES J	CW2	W-2211443	0166	1	MC KINSEY ROY R	LTC	0-0266594	0565	3	MC LAUGHLIN ELIZAB	1LT	L-0602378	0947	2
MC KENNA ELEANOR C	2LT	N-0783090	1144	1	MC KIE ARTHUR B JR	LTC	0-1318322	1062	1	MC KINSTRY EDWARD N	CPT	0-0280807	0664	3	MC LAUGHLIN ERNEST	1LT	0-0437724	0346	2
MC KENNA GERALD J	LTC	0-0924035	1066	3	MC KIE FORREST W	COL	0-0452676	0361	1	MC KINSTRY ELWYN R	MAJ	0-1012520	0261	1	MC LAUGHLIN FRANCIS	MAJ	0-0252890	0167	3
MC KENNA HAROLD P	LTC	0-0348102	0346	2	MC KIE JAMES K JR	1LT	0-1288267	1045	2	MC KINSTRY GEORGE C	LTC	0-0129283	0547	2	MC LAUGHLIN FRANK	COL	0-0286130	0362	3
MC KENNA JAMES E	LTC	0-0416959	1165	1	MC KIE ROBERT B	LTC	0-0239030	1045	2	MC KINSTRY JEROME D	1LT	0-5217153	0864	2	MC LAUGHLIN GEORGE J	CPT	0-0397294	0248	2
MC KENNA JAMES E	1LT	0-1648035	0146	2	MC KIERNAN JOHN L	CW3	W-2146382	0966	1	MC KINSTRY JOHN O	CW3	W-2145197	0662	1	MC LAUGHLIN GERALD W	LTC	0-0386852	0668	3
MC KENNA JAMES F	LTC	0-0391958	0968	1	MC KIERNON THOMAS B	CPT	0-1590649	1060	1	MC KINZIE LON	MAJ	0-1179533	1160	1	MC LAUGHLIN HAROLD A	LTC	0-0288742	0859	3
MC KENNA JAMES F	2LT	0-1183927	0745	2	MC KILLOP DOUGLAS A	LTC	0-0884909	0660	1	MC KISSICK DOUGLAS R	LTC	0-2047063	1162	1	MC LAUGHLIN HARRY F	MAJ	0-0197603	1055	3
MC KENNA JAMES F JR	COL	0-0264434	0768	3	MC KILLOP KENNETH	COL	0-0197645	0846	2	MC KISSICK FRANK A	LTC	0-1552121	0563	1	MC LAUGHLIN HARRY R	LTC	0-0297336	0546	2
MC KENNA JAMES J	LTC	0-0402245	1262	1	MC KIM HENRY D	LTC	0-1013584	0561	1	MC KISSICK ROY	CW3	W-2143217	1160	1	MC LAUGHLIN HENRY F	CPT	0-0986866	0562	1
MC KENNA JOHN F	CW2	W-2209657	0765	1	MC KIM JOHN V	LTC	0-2014255	0767	1	MC KISSICK VERNON H	LTC	0-0259039	0965	3	MC LAUGHLIN HOMER L	LTC	0-0238664	0164	3
MC KENNA JOHN F JR	2LT	0-0528920	0544	2	MC KIM WILLIAM J	LTC	0-1639646	0862	1	MC KITTRICK KENNETH	MAJ	0-0338634	1144	2	MC LAUGHLIN JACK L	1LT	0-2040960	0246	2
MC KENNA JOHN J	1LT	0-1010060	0346	2	MC KIMM HARRY G	CW3	W-2145823	0665	1	MC KITTRICK PETER	MAJ	0-0510270	0554	3	MC LAUGHLIN JAMES J	CPT	0-2268763	1055	3
MC KENNA JOHN V	LTC	0-1555867	1266	1	MC KIMMEY LEROY L	CW2	W-2210654	0763	1	MC KIVETT JAMES C A	1LT	0-0288489	0258	3	MC LAUGHLIN JOHN E	LTC	0-1014972	1263	1
MC KENNA JUNE M	1LT	N-0798858	0153	2	MC KIMMINS MARK	MAJ	0-0278347	1059	3	MC KNIGHT ALEXANDE	2LT	0-0102935	1155	3	MC LAUGHLIN JOHN E	LTC	0-1287919	1059	2
MC KENNA MICHAEL D	LTC	0-0524293	0963	1	MC KINLAY DUNCAN E	MAJ	0-0104542	0648	3	MC KNIGHT CHARLES	COL	0-0100223	0951	3	MC LAUGHLIN JOHN E	CW2	W-3150564	1266	1
MC KENNA MILAN M	MAJ	0-1314167	0568	3	MC KINLEY ALAN F	1LT	0-0378497	0144	2	MC KNIGHT EUEL E	MAJ	0-0159760	1044	2	MC LAUGHLIN JOHN W	1LT	0-1182912	1045	2
MC KENNA ROBERT L	1LT	0-0494931	0245	2	MC KINLEY ARTHUR D	CPT	0-1684658	1145	2	MC KNIGHT FRANCIS H	CPT	0-0169438	0960	3	MC LAUGHLIN JOSEPH H	LTC	0-0498369	0147	2
MC KENNAN BRADLEY	1LT	0-1032102	0246	2	MC KINLEY CARL E	CW3	W-2151332	0962	1	MC KNIGHT JAMES O	MAJ	0-1703806	0758	1	MC LAUGHLIN KENNETH	LTC	0-0373184	1067	3
MC KENNEY BEN	CW2	W-2148212	1154	1	MC KINLEY HAROLD A	MAJ	0-0205686	0553	3	MC KNIGHT JAMES P	MAJ	0-1876991	1068	1	MC LAUGHLIN LEONARD	MAJ	0-1884167	1067	1
MC KENNEY BERTRAM A	MAJ	0-1174069	0261	1	MC KINLEY HUGH F	MAJ	0-0964162	0863	1	MC KNIGHT JOHN J	MAJ	0-1925433	0968	1	MC LAUGHLIN LESTER L	CW3	W-2146809	0164	2
MC KENNEY CHARLES A	CPT	0-0298753	1064	3	MC KINLEY JAMES R	COL	0-0248534	1163	3	MC KNIGHT JOHN P	B G	0-0258303	0566	3	MC LAUGHLIN M M JR	MAJ	0-1949405	0960	1
MC KENNEY CHARLES L	MAJ	0-1294240	0557	1	MC KINLEY LAMAR M	COL	0-0104600	0648	3	MC KNIGHT JOSEPH W	CPT	0-1176726	0360	1	MC LAUGHLIN MARY J	1LT	N-0742420	0945	1
MC KENNEY DOUGLAS C	1LT	0-1314168	0146	2	MC KINLEY MERLE H	LTC	0-1054710	0766	1	MC KNIGHT RAY A	LTC	0-0202776	0863	3	MC LAUGHLIN MAX D	LTC	0-1011312	1262	1
MC KENNEY HENRY J	MAJ	0-0143189	0151	3	MC KINLEY PAUL	LTC	0-0299489	0167	3	MC KNIGHT ROBERT W	COL	0-0145761	0855	3	MC LAUGHLIN MICHAEL	COL	0-0204673	1051	3
MC KENNEY MARIE M	2LT	N-0700176	0837	1	MC KINLEY RICHARD M	CW3	W-2208961	0967	1	MC KNIGHT ROBERT W	MAJ	0-0233190	1263	3	MC LAUGHLIN MICHAEL	CPT	0-0286903	0446	2
MC KENZIE CHARLES R	CW4	W-2102076	0559	1	MC KINLEY ROBERT B	COL	0-0902417	0364	3	MC KNIGHT STEWART D	LTC	0-0249172	0266	3	MC LAUGHLIN ORRIN L	MAJ	0-1308674	0355	2
MC KENZIE DANIEL B	LTC	0-0268799	0668	3	MC KINLEY RUSSELL C	CW3	W-2145891	0562	1	MC KNIGHT THOMAS J	MAJ	0-0264762	0445	2	MC LAUGHLIN ORVILLE	MAJ	0-0385597	0762	1
MC KENZIE DON M	MAJ	0-0968643	0667	1	MC KINLEY WILLIAM	CPT	0-1116102	0745	2	MC KNIGHT WILLIAM H	LTC	0-0450042	0658	1	MC LAUGHLIN R B	CPT	0-0341317	1145	2
MC KENZIE DONALD W	MAJ	0-2010433	1263	1	MC KINLEY WILLIAM J	LTC	0-1543220	0361	1	MC KNIGHT WILLIAM R	MAJ	0-0224662	0252	3	MC LAUGHLIN RALPH M	LTC	0-0279188	1164	3
MC KENZIE DOUGLAS J	COL	0-0219187	0154	3	MC KINNEY ARTHUR J	MAJ	0-2204178	0664	1	MC KOAN JOHN E	1LT	0-0928344	1051	2	MC LAUGHLIN RAYMOND	LTC	0-0936243	1168	1
MC KENZIE GEORGE O	CPT	0-1582436	1145	2	MC KINNEY CHARLES B	MAJ	0-1288418	0459	2	MC KOAN JOHN W JR	COL	0-0255742	0445	2	MC LAUGHLIN ROLAND C	CW4	W-2002616	0968	3
MC KENZIE GERALD K	LTC	0-1040773	0666	1	MC KINNEY CHARLES H	MAJ	0-1303921	0861	1	MC KOAN THOMAS P	LTC	0-0292266	0366	3	MC LAUGHLIN THEODORE	LTC	0-0250370	0660	1
MC KENZIE HUGH H	LTC	0-1057168	0865	1	MC KINNEY CLARENCE L	1LT	0-0946198	0862	2	MC KONE DON T	MAJ	0-0438363	1045	2	MC LAUGHLIN THOMAS A	LTC	0-1894714	0666	3
MC KENZIE ISABEL C	MAJ	N-0751599	0866	1	MC KINNEY CLYDE T	MAJ	0-2056121	0157	1	MC KONE SAMUEL A	MAJ	0-0107710	1143	2	MC LAUGHLIN THOMAS J	MAJ	0-1177083	1066	1
MC KENZIE JAMES K	1LT	0-0888368	0345	2	MC KINNEY DONALD	CPT	0-2034797	1148	1	MC KOWN CLARENCE O	LTC	0-0348813	0263	1	MC LAUGHLIN W J	1LT	0-1290974	0945	2
MC KENZIE JOHN B	LTC	0-0215996	0249	3	MC KINNEY DONALD E	CPT	0-2262323	0562	1	MC KOWN OMER M	MAJ	0-2206018	1268	1	MC LAUGHLIN WILLIAM	COL	0-0237810	1162	3
MC KENZIE JOHN W	1LT	0-1293084	0944	2	MC KINNEY DONALD L	LTC	0-1585869	0668	1	MC KOWN RUSSELL L	LTC	0-0305197	0155	3	MC LAUGHLIN WILLIAM	LTC	0-0890331	0657	1
MC KENZIE KENNETH O	COL	0-0356276	0248	2	MC KINNEY GEORGE W	CPT	0-0509399	0944	2	MC KOWN WILLIAM N	CW4	W-2149085	1068	1	MC LAURIN JOHN W	LTC	0-0969670	0868	1
MC KENZIE LEONARD C	LTC	0-0509403	0954	1	MC KINNEY GLENN H	LTC	0-1546030	0357	1	MC KOY OTIS L	CW2	W-2105445	1045	2	MC LEAN ANDREW J	LTC	0-0141696	1050	3
MC KENZIE LOUIS H	LTC	0-0528659	0865	1	MC KINNEY HAROLD P	LTC	0-0984375	1067	1	MC KRILL EDWARD M	CPT	0-0335527	1144	2	MC LEAN ARTHUR D	LTC	0-0354616	0460	1
MC KENZIE NORMAN J	LTC	0-0966370	0168	1	MC KINNEY ISAAC P	1LT	0-0186961	0336	1	MC KUIN JOHN W	CPT	0-2262456	1060	1	MC LEAN CECIL M	MAJ	L-0904566	0659	2
MC KENZIE OLA E	COL	0-0207064	1051	3	MC KINNEY JAMES C	MAJ	0-1047234	1059	1	MC KULLA MARIE B	2LT	N-0734187	1043	1	MC LEAN CLAUDE E	MAJ	0-0140805	0648	3
MC KENZIE ROBERT L	MAJ	0-1821893	1047	2	MC KINNEY JERALD F	MAJ	0-1019590	0464	2	MC LACHLAN EDWARD J	CPT	0-0424985	0568	3	MC LEAN DANIEL R	CPT	0-0499198	0645	2
MC KENZIE VIRGIL E	LTC	0-1796980	0864	1	MC KINNEY JOSEPH A	CPT	0-0212118	0648	3	MC LAIN GEORGE F	MAJ	0-0215545	0944	2	MC LEAN DONALD A	LTC	0-1798941	1266	3
MC KENZIE WALTER L	1LT	0-0453319	0744	2	MC KINNEY JOSEPH K	CW3	W-3200252	1067	1	MC LAIN JOHN F	CPT	0-1171673	0946	2	MC LEAN DONALD M	CPT	0-0551704	0647	2
MC KENZIE WILLIAM E	CW3	W-3150759	1068	1	MC KINNEY JOSEPH M	LTC	0-1167109	0461	1	MC LAIN LLOYD S	LTC	0-1291305	0361	1	MC LEAN DUNCAN N JR	CPT	0-0982792	1157	1
MC KENZIE WILLIAM G	1LT	0-1284181	0744	1	MC KINNEY KENNETH G	CPT	0-0981839	0960	1	MC LAIN LOWELL E	MAJ	0-1342198	0962	1	MC LEAN FRANKLIN A	COL	0-0251353	1263	1
MC KENZIE WILLIAM W	CPT	0-0491185	1144	2	MC KINNEY MARVIN E	1LT	0-0970324	1053	2	MC LAIN RALPH E	MAJ	0-0532091	0763	1	MC LEAN HAROLD A	COL	0-0281825	0660	2
MC KEON ANDREW J	LTC	0-0134865	0454	3	MC KINNEY RALPH J	CPT	0-0514942	0247	2	MC LAIN RONALD A	CPT	0-0468165	0753	1	MC LEAN JAMES C D	LTC	0-2048705	1164	1
MC KEON CLIFFORD G	LTC	0-1319630	0665	1	MC KINNEY RALPH L	1LT	0-0389055	0245	2	MC LAIN RUSSELL K	CPT	0-0971801	1160	1	MC LEAN JAMES F	LTC	0-1039108	0465	1
MC KEON HARRY	CW4	W-2152276	0264	1	MC KINNEY RALPH V	COL	0-0217183	0857	3	MC LAIN STUART	LTC	0-0261384	0465	3	MC LEAN JOHN J	1LT	0-0517975	0944	2
MC KEON JOHN P	1LT	0-0222271	0557	3	MC KINNEY REX	LTC	0-2044375	0855	1	MC LAIN THERON N	LTC	0-0323936	0954	1	MC LEAN JOSEPH I	MAJ	0-1039463	0665	1
MC KEON JOHN P JR	MAJ	0-0967059	0662	1	MC KINNEY ROBERT L	COL	0-0453238	0965	1	MC LAINE WILLIAM H	MAJ	0-0238651	0762	3	MC LEAN KEITH E	LTC	0-1017111	0762	1
MC KEON RICHARD T	LTC	0-0212873	0562	3	MC KINNEY ROBERT L	2LT	0-1703043	0145	2	MC LAIRD PAUL L	CPT	0-1695187	1265	1	MC LEAN LUCIEN M	CPT	0-0978674	0960	1
MC KEON THEODORE	1LT	0-1643115	0958	1	MC KINNEY ROLLO J	MAJ	0-0268891	0356	3	MC LANE CAREY	1LT	0-1913824	1128	1	MC LEAN LYLE W	CPT	0-0288462	0457	3
MC KEON THOMAS V	COL	0-1328169	0768	1	MC KINNEY STAN A	LTC	0-2035253	0761	1	MC LANE DORIS M	MAJ	N-0741981	1067	1	MC LEAN MACS B	MAJ	0-1650647	0168	3
MC KEOUGH DONALD J	MAJ	0-1047675	1060	1	MC KINNEY TROYCE R	MAJ	0-0977374	0264	2	MC LANE NEIL G	1LT	0-0313545	0348	2	MC LEAN PAUL F	MAJ	0-0966043	1166	1
MC KEOUGH JOSEPH F	MAJ	0-1543738	0762	1	MC KINNEY VOLTAIRE	CW3	W-3200128	0668	1	MC LANE WOODROW	CW2	W-2149185	1159	1	MC LEAN ROBERT E	CPT	0-1573904	0547	1
MC KEOWN CAROLINE S	MAJ	L-0608150	1163	3	MC KINNEY WALTER H	MAJ	0-1167973	1054	1	MC LAREN DONALD W	MAJ	0-0104509	0646	2	MC LEAN ROBERT N	LTC	0-0130533	0153	3
MC KEOWN DEWEY M	COL	0-0336380	0460	1	MC KINNEY WARREN L	MAJ	0-0288934	0765	3	MC LAREN MILTON W JR	LTC	0-1032225	0664	1	MC LEAN SYDNEY S	CW2	W-2144074	0957	1
MC KEOWN FORREST G	LTC	0-0469557	0563	1	MC KINNEY WESLEY B	CW2	W-2148297	0365	2	MC LARNAN RITA K	MAJ	N-0763016	0868	1	MC LEAN THOMAS N	CPT	0-0290165	0668	3
MC KEOWN LLOYD D	CPT	0-1181038	0946	2	MC KINNEY WILLIAM	MAJ	0-1040050	0558	1	MC LAUCHLIN ALBERT C	CW2	W-2211286	0765	1	MC LEAN WILLIAM J	MAJ	0-1314169	0557	1
MC KERALL SAMUEL G	LTC	0-0287553	0368	3	MC KINNEY WILLIAM B	COL	0-0257555	0760	3	MC LAUCHLIN THOMAS N	1LT	0-1332619	0448	2	MC LEISH MURRAY M JR	1LT	0-0495623	0146	2
MC KERCHAR ROY M	COL	0-0166594	0648	3	MC KINNEY WILLIAM C	LTC	0-0465721	1266	1	MC LAUGHLIN AUBREY A	1LT	0-0547526	0246	2	MC LELLAN ALLAN	LTC	0-0198479	1054	3
MC KERNAN DONALD	MAJ	0-1117491	1061	1	MC KINNEY WILLIAM J	CW2	W-3430346	1267	1	MC LAUGHLIN BERYNE	COL	0-0346413	0960	1	MC LELLAN CURTISS	CPT	0-2055157	1055	1
MC KERNAN EDWARD V	1LT	0-2036020	0745	2	MC KINNON ANGUS G	1LT	0-1309483	0345	2	MC LAUGHLIN CHARLES	LTC	0-0197856	0346	2	MC LELLAN EARL O	WO1	W-2107922	1046	1
MC KERNAN JOSEPH A	MAJ	0-1591301	0163	3	MC KINNON DONALD A	COL	0-0179322	1055	3	MC LAUGHLIN CHARLES	LTC	0-1013371	0866	1	MC LELLAN JAMES H	CPT	0-1317986	0747	2
MC KEVITT JOHN G	1LT	0-1176428	0745	2	MC KINNON EDWARD F	LTC	0-1043168	0957	2	MC LAUGHLIN CHARLES	MAJ	0-1651687	0867	1	MC LELLAN JESSE M	COL	0-0253445	0454	3

NAME	GRADE	SVC NO	DATE RET MO YR	RET CODE
MC [illegible]	CPT	[illegible]	[illegible]	[illegible]
MC [illegible]	CW4	W-2146775	0466	1
MC [illegible]	MAJ	[illegible]	[illegible]	1
MC [illegible]	MAJ	[illegible]	0664	1
MC [illegible] ROBERT F	1LT	[illegible]	1046	2
MC [illegible] JAMES A	LTC	[illegible]	0665	1
MC [illegible] JAMES H	1LT	[illegible]	0965	2
MC [illegible] JAMES A	CPT	[illegible]	0757	1
MC [illegible]	CPT	[illegible]	1044	2
MC [illegible]	MAJ	[illegible]	0657	1
MC [illegible] ARCHIE H	LTC	[illegible]	1056	1
MC [illegible] CHARLES H	LTC	[illegible]	0961	3
MC [illegible] FRANCIS J	LTC	[illegible]	0461	1
MC [illegible] HUGH	MAJ	[illegible]	1156	3
MC LEOD JAMES [illegible]	CPT	0-0342110	0250	2
MC LEOD MURRAY	LTC	[illegible]	0560	1
MC LEOD RICHARD F	MAJ	0-0984087	0464	1
MC LEOD WAYNE L	CW2	W-2214326	0467	1
MC LEOD WILLIAM F	CPT	0-1593364	1058	2
MC LEOD [illegible] DAN	CPT	0-1821610	0945	2
MC LEOD JACK	CPT	0-0458927	0650	1
MC LEROY JOHN T JR	1LT	0-0365254	0144	2
MC LESTER JAMES H	COL	0-0392345	0866	3
MC LIN ARTHUR N	CW2	W-2209721	0762	1
MC LINDEN HELEN E	1LT	N-0768818	0851	2
MC LINTOCK ADDISON W	MAJ	0-0492530	0647	2
MC LOUGHLIN ANTHONY	LTC	0-0409078	0766	3
MC LOUGHLIN JAMES M	MAJ	0-0274406	1162	3
MC LOUGHLIN JOHN A	MAJ	0-0439815	0348	2
MC LOUGHLIN JOHN H	CW3	W-2206018	1065	1
MC LOUGHLIN MICHAEL	LTC	0-0938028	0866	1
MC LOVICH ANDREW	1LT	0-1047235	0146	2
MC LURE JOHN J	COL	0-0154589	0648	3
MC LURE RICHARD A	1LT	0-1348962	0951	3
MC LURKIN CHARLES P	LTC	0-1554236	0763	1
MC MAHAN THEODORE W	COL	0-0342815	0157	1
MC MAHAN WILLIAM T	LTC	0-2046751	0667	1
MC MAHON CHARLENE H	MAJ	L-0502117	1164	1
MC MAHON EDMUND T	2LT	0-1051685	1044	2
MC MAHON EDWARD A	COL	0-0233141	0648	3
MC MAHON EDWARD J	CPT	0-0463271	0746	2
MC MAHON EDWARD M JR	LTC	0-0473229	0656	1
MC MAHON GEORGE J JR	CW2	W-2215286	1068	1
MC MAHON HENRY J	MAJ	0-0264205	0154	3
MC MAHON HUGH J	MAJ	0-1535799	0760	1
MC MAHON JAMES J	1LT	0-1895192	0756	1
MC MAHON JAMES P	MAJ	0-0168882	1056	3
MC MAHON JOHN E	LTC	0-1946332	1165	3
MC MAHON JOHN F	LTC	0-1080730	0464	1
MC MAHON JOHN F	CW2	W-2007564	0667	3
MC MAHON JOHN T	MAJ	0-1823037	0361	2
MC MAHON JOHN W	MAJ	0-0474886	0452	2
MC MAHON JOSEPH E	CW3	W-2119919	0655	1
MC MAHON JOSEPH I	MAJ	0-1288268	1263	1
MC MAHON LESLIE W	LTC	0-0381650	0763	1
MC MAHON RAYMOND G	LTC	0-0264408	0862	3
MC MAHON RICHARD A	MAJ	0-1947348	0568	3
MC MAHON THOMAS G JR	LTC	0-0295308	0666	3
MC MAHON WALTER J	MAJ	0-1106947	0261	1
MC MAHON WILLIAM J	MAJ	0-0548342	0564	1
MC MANAMNA ALAN A	MAJ	0-0428435	0263	1
MC MANIS HAROLD	CPT	0-0505360	1047	1
MC MANUELS ARTHUR J	CW3	W-2151164	1263	1
MC MANUS ADRIAN C JR	1LT	0-0461061	0846	2
MC MANUS CHARLES F	COL	0-0172814	0259	3
MC MANUS CHARLES V	LTC	0-0357476	0446	2
MC MANUS FRANCIS G	2LT	0-1297467	0645	2
MC MANUS HENRY B	LTC	0-0249348	1264	3
MC MANUS HUGH F JR	MAJ	0-0368213	0946	2
MC MANUS JAMES J	MAJ	0-0173661	0753	3
MC MANUS JAMES L	MAJ	0-1318064	1160	1
MC MANUS JOHN J JR	1LT	0-1110122	0546	2
MC MANUS JOSEPH W	COL	0-0202142	0954	1
MC MANUS MARGARET E	CPT	N-0759006	0947	1
MC MANUS ORVILLE O	LTC	0-1291307	1160	1

NAME	GRADE	SVC NO	DATE RET MO YR	RET CODE
MC MANOS PHILIP J JR	LTC	0-0437481	0764	1
MC MANOS RAY J	LTC	0-0419073	1162	1
MC MANOS THOMAS L	LTC	0-0174274	0559	1
MC MANOS WOODROW H	CPT	0-1030904	1251	2
MC MARTIN FINLAY	1LT	0-1590934	0745	2
MC MASTER ARCHIE L	MAJ	0-0317527	0246	2
MC MASTER WILLIAM E	MAJ	0-1285782	0361	1
MC MASTERS JOHN R	LTC	0-0328054	1158	1
MC MAUGHAN GEORGE W	LTC	0-1100682	0662	1
MC MEANS HEATH L	MAJ	0-0187825	0849	3
MC MEANS THOMAS W	LTC	0-0344868	1067	3
MC MEEKIN ANDREW F	COL	0-0342249	0848	2
MC MELLEN ROBERT W	MAJ	0-1924556	0466	1
MC MENAMIN JOSEPH C	CPT	0-0337498	1045	2
MC MICAN STELLA M	2LT	N-0730402	0844	1
MC MICHAEL JOHN H	MAJ	0-0428107	0246	2
MC MICHAEL JOHN W	LTC	0-2007904	0363	1
MC MICHAEL MORRIS H	MAJ	0-0304015	0747	2
MC MILLAN ALBROSE C	LTC	0-0300699	0166	3
MC MILLAN CARLTON F	MAJ	0-1184549	0257	1
MC MILLAN CLARENCE T	CW3	W-2146570	0464	1
MC MILLAN DAVID G	LTC	0-0237378	0362	3
MC MILLAN DONALD J	MAJ	0-1115697	1162	1
MC MILLAN EUGENE A	CPT	0-1919250	1262	1
MC MILLAN EVERETT E	COL	0-0276146	0763	3
MC MILLAN GARLAND D	1LT	0-2016919	0852	2
MC MILLAN GEORGE	LTC	0-0319346	0859	3
MC MILLAN GORDON B	COL	0-0275824	0363	3
MC MILLAN HAROLD F	CW4	W-2148440	1068	2
MC MILLAN HYDE	1LT	0-0461522	0146	2
MC MILLAN JACK W JR	MAJ	0-1171279	0661	1
MC MILLAN JAMES J	CPT	0-1558665	0263	1
MC MILLAN JAMES M	MAJ	0-1646840	0861	1
MC MILLAN JESSE M	MAJ	0-0305295	0767	3
MC MILLAN JOHN A	LTC	0-0270203	0365	3
MC MILLAN JOHN M	MAJ	0-0258532	0667	3
MC MILLAN JOHN W	LTC	0-0302173	1063	1
MC MILLAN LENORE B	CPT	L-0304146	1150	2
MC MILLAN MARSHALL J	WO1	W-2122661	0846	2
MC MILLAN RICHARD J	LTC	0-1580023	0765	1
MC MILLAN ROBERT A	COL	0-0166804	0850	3
MC MILLAN ROGER J	1LT	0-1327753	1145	2
MC MILLAN ROLLAND H	MAJ	0-2033866	0463	1
MC MILLAN ROY A	LTC	0-0166890	0550	3
MC MILLEN EDWARD J	2LT	0-1331072	0864	2
MC MILLEN GERALD O	LTC	0-0266908	1059	3
MC MILLEN NORMAN W	LTC	0-0212451	0948	3
MC MILLIAN PORTER	MAJ	0-1307275	0257	1
MC MILLION OVID M	COL	0-0920572	0465	3
MC MINIMEE WALTER C	LTC	0-0917295	0765	3
MC MINN JACQUES S	MAJ	0-0153181	0-49	3
MC MINN JAMES	LTC	0-0405955	0951	2
MC MINN WALTER P	LTC	0-0497731	0954	1
MC MONAGLE DANIEL S	LTC	0-1824893	0567	1
MC MONIGLE GLENN R	MAJ	0-1688831	0565	1
MC MONIGLE THOS J	1LT	0-1288269	0944	2
MC MORRIS ALFRED W	COL	0-0172466	1050	3
MC MORROW DAN K	1LT	0-1634128	0150	1
MC MORROW JOHN J	MAJ	0-0290781	1147	2
MC MORROW JOHN W	1LT	0-0973188	0353	2
MC MORROW LESLIE P	LTC	0-0323910	0762	1
MC MORROW RALPH J	1LT	0-1311320	0746	2
MC MULLAN JOHN J	1LT	0-1583365	0245	2
MC MULLAN THEODORE N	LTC	0-0271553	0768	3
MC MULLEN CECIL J W	1LT	0-0270997	0667	3
MC MULLEN HERSCHEL H	LTC	0-0285902	0966	3
MC MULLEN JACK W	MAJ	0-1798688	0960	1
MC MULLEN JAMES B	CW3	W-2149796	1167	1
MC MULLEN JOHN A	CW3	W-2147068	1062	2
MC MULLEN JOSEPH E	COL	0-0250140	0766	3
MC MULLEN LEROY A JR	LTC	0-1287212	0163	1
MC MULLEN PHILLIPS R	CPT	0-0117260	0257	3
MC MULLEN RAY W JR	LTC	0-1105018	0864	1
MC MULLEN WILLIAM R	LTC	0-1845313	0158	2
MC MULLIN MICHAEL A	CPT	0-1340568	0358	2

NAME	GRADE	SVC NO	DATE RET MO YR	RET CODE
MC MURPHY ERNEST L	2LT	0-0533494	0645	2
MC MURRAY CRAWFORD A	COL	0-0244613	0464	1
MC MURRAY FLOYD T	CPT	0-0117262	0151	1
MC MURRAY PAUL H	COL	0-0267663	0658	1
MC MURRAY ROBERT J	MAJ	0-2035485	0361	1
MC MURRAY WILLIAM T	CPT	0-0451146	1055	1
MC MURREN IRVIN G	CPT	0-0499517	0449	1
MC MURRER JAMES F	CPT	0-0108836	0753	1
MC MURRY PEARL W	COL	0-0319437	0566	1
MC MURTRAY ROY S	LTC	0-0333367	0963	1
MC MURTRY LESLIE B	LTC	0-0168222	1054	1
MC NABB ALVA C	MAJ	0-1894119	1267	1
MC NABB CHARLES J	MAJ	0-1919472	1265	1
MC NABB HUGH E	LTC	0-0179874	1045	1
MC NABB JAMES H	1LT	0-1313536	0260	1
MC NABB OSCAR J	MAJ	0-0235309	0563	1
MC NAGNY WILLIAM F	1LT	0-0493032	0145	2
MC NAIR ALBERT	CPT	0-4005704	0765	1
MC NAIR ELISHA B	LTC	0-0515951	0963	1
MC NAIR JAMES E P	COL	0-0244674	0846	2
MC NAIR JAMES R	1LT	0-0494993	0453	1
MC NAIR WILLIAM H JR	1LT	0-1319631	1045	2
MC NALLAN JACK D	CW3	W-2152074	0966	1
MC NALLY CARL R JR	1LT	0-0528677	0146	2
MC NALLY GEORGE J	COL	0-0913024	1065	2
MC NALLY HENRY C	MAJ	0-0311243	0358	1
MC NALLY HUGH T	CPT	0-1169244	0546	2
MC NALLY IRA E JR	MAJ	0-1836042	0165	1
MC NALLY JAMES W	CW3	W-2205607	0368	1
MC NALLY JEANETTE M	1LT	N-0752563	1045	2
MC NALLY JOHN G	LTC	0-0307577	0668	3
MC NALLY JOHN H	LTC	0-1536455	0766	1
MC NALLY JOHN M	LTC	0-0279680	0960	3
MC NALLY JOSEPH P	CPT	0-0478519	1045	2
MC NALLY LEE O	1LT	0-0252224	0166	3
MC NALLY RICHARD S	LTC	0-1950220	0663	1
MC NALLY WILLIAM J	CW3	W-2147953	0962	1
MC NAMARA EDWARD O	LTC	0-1550448	0265	1
MC NAMARA JAMES E	MAJ	0-0990630	0463	1
MC NAMARA JAMES O	CPT	0-0497001	0553	1
MC NAMARA JOHN P	MAJ	0-0216093	1051	1
MC NAMARA JOSEPH P	COL	0-0917084	0566	3
MC NAMARA MARVIN F	1LT	0-1823911	0244	2
MC NAMARA MICHAEL F	MAJ	0-0449565	0345	2
MC NAMARA ROBERT C	1LT	0-1012694	0745	2
MC NAMARA THOMAS	CPT	0-0496768	1048	1
MC NAMARA THOMAS F	LTC	0-1342199	1166	1
MC NAMARA WILLIAM F	CPT	0-0445922	0246	2
MC NAMARA WILLIAM J	CPT	0-1285263	0549	2
MC NAMEE EDMUND J	1LT	0-0717722	0745	2
MC NAMEE FRANK A JR	COL	0-0140490	1052	3
MC NAMEE JOHN B	LTC	0-1534564	0765	1
MC NAMEE ROBERT	CPT	0-5329540	0568	2
MC NARY ROBERT P	LTC	0-0232794	1163	3
MC NATT ORVILLE F	CPT	0-1103317	0346	2
MC NAUGHT PERCY C	CPT	0-0382518	1059	3
MC NAUGHTON JOHN N	CPT	0-1914127	0645	1
MC NAUGHTON LAWRENCE	LTC	0-0319779	0467	3
MC NAUGHTON RAY L O	CW3	W-2147574	1262	1
MC NAUGHTON RODGER W	CPT	0-0379071	0245	2
MC NAUL WINFIELD H	COL	0-0410151	0461	2
MC NAY GEORGE H	LTC	0-0244947	0664	3
MC NEAL DAN H	LTC	0-0188541	0159	3
MC NEAL DAVID C	LTC	0-0509141	0547	2
MC NEAL FRED J	LTC	0-1552748	0962	1
MC NEAL THOMAS F	COL	0-0240050	1065	3
MC NEAL WILLIAM A	CW2	W-2206245	0459	1
MC NEARNY THOMAS L	MAJ	0-1015897	0165	2
MC NEE WILLIAM E	LTC	0-2042734	0466	1
MC NEELY JAMES H	LTC	0-0371890	1265	3
MC NEELY MARVIN	CW2	W-2153001	1060	1
MC NEER JAMES W	COL	0-0223703	1154	1
MC NEES HAROLD C	CPT	0-1683019	1144	2
MC NEES PHILIP M	CW4	W-2102083	0256	1
MC NEESE TURNER C	LTC	0-0510607	1060	1

NAME	GRADE	SVC NO	DATE RET MO YR	RET CODE
MC NE[illegible] HARRY D	CW3	W-2203395	0165	1
MC NEIL BURTON [illegible]	LTC	0-1171676	0966	1
MC NEIL CHARLES J	MAJ	0-1530026	1061	1
MC NEIL DANIEL D	CW3	W-2202607	0567	1
MC NEIL DANIEL P	LTC	0-1581961	0456	1
MC NEIL DELBERT S	LTC	0-1304093	0865	1
MC NEIL FRANK J	MAJ	0-0331778	1044	2
MC NEIL HARRY F	CW2	W-2149305	0359	1
MC NEIL JACK G	LTC	0-1295754	1057	1
MC NEIL JOHN O	CPT	0-0507639	1047	1
MC NEIL MABEL B	1LT	N-0772008	0546	1
MC NEIL NEIL A	MAJ	0-1040443	0361	1
MC NEIL PERRY M	LTC	0-0301677	0267	3
MC NEIL RALPH G	MAJ	0-0194888	0152	3
MC NEIL ROBERT B	CPT	0-2024605	1053	2
MC NEIL ROY M	LTC	0-1287939	0961	1
MC NEIL STANLEY R	COL	0-0216015	0847	2
MC NEIL WILLIAM B	MAJ	0-0945545	0163	1
MC NEILL ALLISON	MAJ	0-1645813	0566	3
MC NEILL ALVIN J	WO1	W-2117108	1044	2
MC NEILL CHARLES L	COL	0-0366111	0264	1
MC NEILL FORD N JR	COL	0-0255587	0164	3
MC NEILL JAMES C	MAJ	0-1304094	1060	1
MC NEILL JAMES M	CPT	0-0407746	0144	2
MC NEILL JOSEPH F	LTC	0-1314040	1162	1
MC NEILL LOREN C	CPT	0-0358365	0944	2
MC NEILL THOMAS H	LTC	0-0316289	0252	2
MC NEISH PAUL M	LTC	0-0339474	0762	1
MC NELLY BERTRAM J	MAJ	0-1593080	0163	1
MC NELLY RICHARD L	B G	0-0256304	0662	3
MC NEMAR HAROLD B	LTC	0-0507074	1054	1
MC NERNEY DANIEL P	LTC	0-2036021	0962	1
MC NERNEY EDWARD W	1LT	0-1052076	1145	2
MC NERNEY GORDON	MAJ	0-1574985	1059	2
MC NERNEY NEVILLE O	LTC	0-2202331	0168	2
MC NERNEY THOMAS L	MAJ	0-0360201	0452	2
MC NERNY HERBERT G	COL	0-0134641	0946	2
MC NEVIN ALFRED C B	COL	0-0164797	0648	3
MC NEW HARRY C JR	CPT	0-0266897	1266	3
MC NEW LIFSTER O	2LT	0-1326866	0146	2
MC NICHOL JOHN C JR	LTC	0-1313769	0562	1
MC NICHOL THEODORE	CW2	W-2149086	1058	2
MC NICHOLAS THOMAS G	LTC	0-0128457	0648	3
MC NICHOLL PATRICK J	LTC	0-0139095	0745	2
MC NICHOLL PATRICK J	MAJ	0-0980809	0964	1
MC NICHOLS ROBERT H	LTC	0-0419942	0161	1
MC NICKLE ARTHUR J	LTC	0-1040775	0461	1
MC NIFF MILES S	LTC	0-1106949	0563	1
MC NITT HENRY J R	LTC	0-0212260	1161	3
MC NULTY JAMES F	MAJ	0-1295579	0957	1
MC NULTY JAMES K	MAJ	0-1320760	0262	2
MC NULTY JOHN A	LTC	0-0449828	1266	1
MC NULTY JOHN F JR	LTC	0-1316773	1164	1
MC NULTY JOHN N	LTC	0-2035353	0367	1
MC NULTY JOHN P	CW3	W-2146914	0266	1
MC NULTY JOSEPH O	2LT	0-2005424	0351	2
MC NULTY SARSFIELD	LTC	0-1575462	0260	1
MC NULTY WARREN E	LTC	0-1320690	0763	1
MC NURLEN KEITH A	1LT	0-0513539	0945	2
MC NUTT DALTON W	2LT	0-1307276	0744	2
MC NUTT EUGENE C	2LT	0-2006429	0646	2
MC NUTT LAWRENCE E	MAJ	0-1305622	0159	1
MC NUTT LEONARD M	COL	0-0405892	0660	1
MC NUTT LEROY C	CPT	0-1288091	0556	1
MC NUTT LILLIE B	MAJ	N-0773269	0364	1
MC NUTT WALTER R	CW2	W-2112557	0459	1
MC NUTT WILLIAM P	LTC	0-0272058	1166	3
MC PARTLAND HELEN J	MAJ	N-0720010	0146	1
MC PARTLAND MARION B	MAJ	N-0752236	0965	3
MC PEAK EDGAR M	LTC	0-0247744	0545	2
MC PECK EDWIN K	CPT	0-1649085	0648	2
MC PEEK FRANK D	CPT	0-2300984	1263	1
MC PEEK RICHARD W	LTC	0-1316701	0861	2
MC PHAIL ARTHUR M	LTC	0-0494536	0854	1
MC PHAIL BILLY B	MAJ	0-1174646	0860	1

NAME	GRADE	SVC NO	DATE RET MO YR	RET CODE
MC PHAIL JAMES T	CW3	W-2146538	0165	1
MC PHAILL EARL	CPT	O-1703396	1145	2
MC PHAUL ANDERSON G	LTC	O-1686832	0268	1
MC PHEE EUGENE R	COL	O-0220462	0662	3
MC PHEE JOHN G	2LT	O-1015156	0244	2
MC PHEE MONICA K	1LT	N-0752909	0946	1
MC PHEETERS JAMES H	LTC	O-0471328	0762	1
MC PHERRAN PAUL L	LTC	O-0317706	0861	1
MC PHERSON CHARLES M	CW4	W-2104293	0659	1
MC PHERSON CHARLES W	1LT	O-0450174	0344	2
MC PHERSON DONALD M	1LT	O-1298264	1045	2
MC PHERSON DONALD W	CW4	W-2145566	0168	1
MC PHERSON GEORGE R	LTC	O-0247698	0259	3
MC PHERSON HENRY A	CPT	O-0524983	1044	2
MC PHERSON HUE O	CW2	W-2123368	1058	1
MC PHERSON JACK K	CW3	W-2153322	0865	1
MC PHERSON JAMES R	MAJ	O-1332285	0963	1
MC PHERSON JESSE R	LTC	O-0278546	0954	3
MC PHERSON KENNETH M	COL	O-0345415	1066	3
MC PHERSON MARION V	MAJ	O-1313278	1162	1
MC PHERSON SADIE E	1LT	N-0743336	1145	1
MC POLAND JAMES J	LTC	O-1298265	0768	1
MC PROUD CARL E	LTC	O-1822598	1061	1
MC QUADE EDWARD B	CW4	W-2147820	1155	1
MC QUADE JAMES F	1LT	O-2055251	0849	1
MC QUADE JOSEPH W	LTC	O-0286596	0462	3
MC QUAID KENNETH B	CPT	O-1576375	1145	2
MC QUAIG JAMES A	CW3	W-2205393	1063	1
MC QUAIL MARGARET B	2LT	N-0784833	0845	1
MC QUAIN GUY A	CPT	O-2034449	0258	1
MC QUARRIE HILTON B	CPT	O-0363605	0551	1
MC QUEEN ALBERT H	MAJ	O-0286393	0768	3
MC QUEEN JOHN W	LTC	O-0268979	0967	3
MC QUEEN WILLIAM R	CPT	O-0304866	0247	2
MC QUEENEY WILLIAM A	LTC	O-0242608	0962	1
MC QUIDDY EUGENE R	CW3	W-2205070	0864	1
MC QUILKIN MARTIN F	MAJ	O-0100523	1055	3
MC QUILLAN FRANCIS C	1LT	O-1035946	0845	2
MC QUILLAN JOHN G	LTC	O-1542668	0966	3
MC QUILLAN JOHN J	CPT	O-2027809	0357	1
MC QUILLEN ALVIN K	MAJ	O-1541479	0754	1
MC QUILLEN PETER L	CPT	O-0108980	1038	1
MC QUISTON DANIEL H	COL	O-0147031	0546	2
MC QUISTON WILLIAM H	1LT	O-0259217	1045	2
MC QUISTON WILLIAM J	LTC	O-1573413	0468	3
MC QUOWN LEONARD A	COL	O-0147107	0853	3
MC RAE CHARLES G	CW3	W-2208619	0868	1
MC RAE DAVID E	MAJ	O-0285790	1056	3
MC RAE JOHN S	1LT	O-1330840	1047	2
MC RAE MARGARET C	2LT	N-0723713	0145	1
MC RAE ROBERT W	LTC	O-1874619	1168	1
MC RAINEY MALCOLM A	LTC	O-1284550	0861	1
MC REE CHARLES J	CW3	W-2210109	0168	1
MC REYNOLDS CHARLES	LTC	O-0203466	0563	3
MC REYNOLDS DWIGHT L	B G	O-0278061	0468	3
MC REYNOLDS EDGAR	1LT	O-2024357	0466	2
MC REYNOLDS EDGAR L	MAJ	O-2263501	1262	1
MC REYNOLDS FRANK R	LTC	O-0114199	0648	3
MC RHOADS JAMES P	CPT	O-4006673	0167	1
MC ROBBIE EDITH	MAJ	L-0203219	0563	1
MC ROBERTS PAUL L	CW3	W-2209067	0966	1
MC ROBERTS WILLIAM N	LTC	O-0395083	0263	1
MC SHANE ADRIAN J	CW3	W-2146177	0662	2
MC SHANE FRANK P	CPT	O-1307730	0448	2
MC SHANE KENNETH J	MAJ	O-0487263	0660	1
MC SHERRY LEROY F	LTC	O-0455007	0566	1
MC SORLEY FRANK N	MAJ	O-1559492	1263	1
MC SPADDEN ROBERT S	MAJ	O-1641571	0465	1
MC SPADDEN WILLIAM B	2LT	O-0390291	0542	2
MC SPARREN GEORGE R	CW2	W-2212500	0867	1
MC SWAIN HAROLD V	1LT	O-1298898	1045	2
MC SWAIN OLA M	MAJ	N-0726041	0166	1
MC SWANE RAYMOND	CPT	O-0361191	1152	1
MC SWEEN F D	CW3	W-2143554	0859	1
MC SWEEN HARRY Y	LTC	O-0410271	0845	2
MC SWEEN JOHN M JR	MAJ	O-1635083	0258	1
MC SWEENEY JAMES J	LTC	O-2036022	0562	1
MC SWEENEY JAMES P	1LT	O-0538979	0646	2
MC SWEENEY JOHN	LTC	O-0164741	0753	3
MC SWEENY JOHN	CPT	O-0133227	0944	2
MC TAGGART ALASTAIR	MAJ	O-2021178	0167	1
MC TAGGART HARRY H	2LT	O-1913817	0237	1
MC TAMNEY JOSEPH J	MAJ	O-2200416	0666	1
MC TERNAM WILLIAM R	LTC	O-0204478	0157	1
MC TIER LINDY D	CW3	W-3150468	11?7	1
MC TIERNEY AGNES I	MAJ	N-0723541	0867	3
MC TIGHE JOHN J	CPT	O-1551067	1146	2
MC VAY CLARENCE H	CW3	RW-2207614	0266	1
MC VAY LLOYD R	CW4	W-2141379	0764	1
MC VAY MELVIN J	CPT	O-0201673	0648	3
MC VEA JOHN B	MAJ	O-1018282	0263	1
MC VEIGH GEORGE M SR	MAJ	O-1576378	0361	1
MC VEIGH JAMES H	COL	O-0116330	1049	3
MC VEY ALBERT V	COL	O-0175141	0560	3
MC VEY DELBERT P	1LT	O-0177711	1261	3
MC VEY OTTO T	CPT	O-1634130	0647	1
MC VICKER FOREST R	1LT	O-0519105	0146	2
MC VICKER GEORGE C	CW4	W-2115131	0857	2
MC VICKER PAUL M	CPT	O-0236492	1054	3
MC VOY JOHN A	LTC	O-0221457	1063	3
MC WADE JAMES	MAJ	O-1342288	0361	1
MC WATERS WILLIAM L	LTC	O-1301077	1062	1
MC WAYNE FRANK E JR	MAJ	O-0285725	1046	2
MC WEE NATHANIEL	MAJ	O-0378613	0555	1
MC WHIRTER BONNIE	MAJ	O-0241797	1144	2
MC WHIRTER EDWARD L	CPT	O-0413163	0946	2
MC WHIRTER OSCAR M	MAJ	O-0250012	0567	3
MC WHORTER FRANK R	CPT	O-1556023	0358	1
MC WHORTER JOHN C JR	1LT	O-0449506	0945	2
MC WHORTER JULIAN H	COL	O-0923554	1267	3
MC WHORTER ROBERT E	CW2	W-2120995	0348	2
MC WILLIAM JAMES T	LTC	O-1102858	1066	3
MC WILLIAMS ALVA L	MAJ	O-1878312	0767	1
MC WILLIAMS JOHN	CW2	W-2142250	0953	1
MC WILLIAMS JUDSON H	CPT	O-1593719	0647	2
MC WILLIAMS ROBERTA	LTC	L-0600652	0268	1
MC WILLIAMS WILLIAM	COL	O-0321847	1159	3
MCCAWLEY HARRISON B	1LT	O-0548460	0946	2
MCDONALD LAWRENCE H	1LT	O-0488866	0654	1
MCGOVERN JAMES P	MAJ	O-1057527	0154	1
MCILWAIN JOSEPH E	COL	O-0208728	0456	3
MCMENAMIN EDWARD G	1LT	O-0551924	0846	2
MCNULTY THOMAS J	LTC	O-0492138	1053	1
MEACHAM CARL J	COL	O-0106926	1055	3
MEACHAM GORDON F	CW3	RW-2209559	0467	1
MEACHAM MERLE A	LTC	O-0303610	0962	3
MEACHUM HUBERT J	1LT	O-1324351	0446	2
MEAD ALBERT H	MAJ	O-0206973	0147	2
MEAD ALFRED J	LTC	O-0192105	1157	3
MEAD AMOS R	LTC	O-0262543	0865	3
MEAD DAVID	CPT	O-1924826	0264	2
MEAD DOUGLAS O	MAJ	O-0219943	0154	3
MEAD EMORY A	LTC	O-0309406	0863	3
MEAD EUGENE W	MAJ	O-0230565	0644	2
MEAD HARVEY L JR	LTC	O-0179115	1061	2
MEAD JOHN G	LTC	O-1299774	0663	1
MEAD ROBERT F	CPT	O-0453855	0646	2
MEADE CHARLES H	CW4	W-2103764	0866	1
MEADE EUGENE L	MAJ	O-1945891	0564	1
MEADE JAMES P JR	CW2	W-3155087	0768	2
MEADE JOHN E	LTC	O-0143054	1053	3
MEADE MARVIN W	1LT	O-1000822	0458	2
MEADE WILLIAM H	LTC	O-0503578	1045	2
MEADER EDWARD H	CPT	O-1017348	1060	2
MEADERS GEORGE E	COL	O-0395884	0968	1
MEADERS KIRK A	LTC	O-0397126	0447	2
MEADOR ARLINE R	2LT	N-0761589	0646	1
MEADOR BARCLAY F	COL	O-0140407	0958	3
MEADOR ELTON	WO1	W-2117247	0252	1
MEADOR JOHN D	CPT	O-0416030	0244	2
MEADOR JOHN G	MAJ	O-1577557	0455	1
MEADOR MARVIN E	LTC	O-0272967	1267	3
MEADOR RILEY W	LTC	O-1309328	0358	1
MEADOR WILLIAM	WO1	W-2142997	0756	1
MEADORS JOHN H JR	CW2	W-2147834	1060	1
MEADORS RICHARD M	CW3	W-2144107	0756	1
MEADOW NATHAN	1LT	O-1284737	1143	2
MEADOWS ANDERSON O	LTC	O-0153790	1058	3
MEADOWS CHARLIE E	LTC	O-0386676	0357	1
MEADOWS CLARENCE C	MAJ	O-0266546	0244	2
MEADOWS CLYDE L	CW4	W-2109679	0857	1
MEADOWS ERNEST C	CW2	W-2152435	0461	1
MEADOWS FRED W	MAJ	O-1590655	1264	1
MEADOWS JAMES A	1LT	O-1287920	0245	2
MEADOWS JOHN P O	1LT	O-0251772	1055	3
MEADOWS JOHN W	CPT	O-1744795	0-48	2
MEADOWS OLIVER E	CPT	O-0465376	0447	2
MEADOWS WADE O	MAJ	O-1302501	0457	1
MEADOWS WILLIAM R	CW3	W-2141804	0360	1
MEADS OLIVER F	CPT	O-2008205	0557	1
MEAGHER MARY C	MAJ	N-0771638	0864	1
MEAGHER STELLA M	MAJ	N-0737510	0166	3
MEAGHER THOMAS F JR	MAJ	O-1341561	0666	1
MEALEY JOHN A	MAJ	O-2000494	0264	1
MEALING JOHN P JR	LTC	O-0249055	0462	3
MEANEY MARTIN H	COL	O-0182202	0848	3
MEANEY ROD F	MAJ	O-1645816	0163	2
MEANEY VINCENT J	LTC	O-0933037	0868	3
MEANEY WILLIAM J JR	LTC	O-0323319	0265	3
MEANLEY WILLIAM C JR	COL	O-0326057	0464	1
MEANS DONALD L	LTC	O-0555416	0268	1
MEANS JOHN S	LTC	O-0110055	0453	3
MEANS LEWIS M	B G	O-0133499	0246	2
MEANS RALPH E	LTC	O-0293185	0765	1
MEANS RUSSELL P	MAJ	O-1176131	0765	1
MEANS WILLIAM J	CW4	W-2109848	0157	1
MEANY JOHN H	CPT	O-1685994	0845	2
MEARES JIMMY G	LTC	O-2093379	0268	1
MEARES WALTER A	LTC	O-0220071	0352	3
MEARS CLYDE C JR	CW3	W-2206292	0468	1
MEARS DOUGLAS C	2LT	O-1054714	0445	2
MEARS GLEN G	LTC	O-1047678	1061	1
MEARS JAMES F	LTC	O-1010034	0954	1
MEARS JOHN A	LTC	O-0255473	0967	3
MEARS KENNETH M JR	LTC	O-1823912	0264	1
MEARS RALPH E	MAJ	O-2006144	1163	1
MEASE RUSSELL S	CPT	O-1185291	0962	1
MEASLEY WILBUR T JR	MAJ	O-1326867	C163	1
MEAUT BERMOND J	LTC	O-1168816	0967	1
MEAUT WILLIAM M	2LT	O-0519697	C745	2
MEAUX ELTON J	CW2	W-2146454	0656	1
MEBUS GEORGE B	LTC	O-0197103	0563	3
MECARTEA LOUIS J	MAJ	O-1057823	0763	1
MECCA ANDREW L JR	LTC	O-0378326	0663	1
MECCA THEODORE F	MAJ	O-0969325	0463	1
MECHAM ARNOLD	CW2	W-2215207	0868	1
MECHAM ROSS L	CPT	O-1174957	0251	2
MECHLER FLOYD A	CPT	O-1103799	0246	2
MECHLER WILLIAM J	MAJ	O-0286762	1059	3
MECHLING GEORGE S	LTC	O-0329587	0249	3
MECHTEL NORMAN F	MAJ	O-2262777	0162	1
MECORD PHILIP H	CPT	O-0980044	1060	1
MEDAGLIANI JOSEPH B	LTC	O-1691898	0561	1
MEDALIA LEON S	COL	O-0211525	0546	2
MEDARIS CHESTER T	LTC	O-0300677	1166	3
MEDBERY EDWARD W	LTC	O-0257754	0967	3
MEDCALF RICHARD A	CW2	W-2141995	0661	1
MEDCALF VAN C	LTC	O-0211448	0252	2
MEDD CHARLES B	MAJ	O-2326748	0466	3
MEDDAUGH RALPH T	CPT	O-0204134	0963	3
MEDEIROS WALTER L	CW3	W-2150902	0763	1
MEDENBACH MILTON H	COL	O-0261188	0168	3
MEDER ALFRED O	CPT	O-1285083	1145	2
MEDESY WILLIAM A	CPT	O-0317969	0444	2
MEDFORD EDWARD E	CPT	O-1177087	0865	1
MEDFORD ERNEST D	MAJ	O-0986502	0864	1
MEDFORD WILLIAM T	COL	O-0128641	1055	2
MEDICK ROBERT L	CW2	W-2149934	0960	1
MEDICO SIMON P	CPT	O-2019060	0959	1
MEDINA ANGEL	2LT	O-1896441	0559	1
MEDINA ANTONIO	LTC	O-0267935	0760	1
MEDINA VICTOR	CW3	W-2144988	0861	1
MEDINGER ROBERT E	LTC	O-1110099	0967	1
MEDLEY ARTHUR W	MAJ	O-0487661	0463	1
MEDLEY CHARLES A	CPT	O-1922613	1161	1
MEDLEY MAX W	MAJ	O-1293292	0557	2
MEDLEY OSCAR W	CW3	W-2105019	0656	1
MEDLIN GEORGE C	CW2	W-2211601	0466	1
MEDLIN MAE	MAJ	N-0735821	0165	1
MEDLIN MDEE	LTC	O-0286741	0366	3
MEDLIN NED D	CW3	W-2145899	1160	1
MEDLIN RAYMOND	LTC	O-1305288	0867	3
MEDLIN THOMAS F	CPT	O-2262972	1160	2
MEDLOCK AL S	MAJ	O-1877870	1266	1
MEDLOCK CLARENCE E	LTC	O-0211815	0164	3
MEDLOCK THOMAS L	MAJ	O-1923551	0866	1
MEDSKER ROY R	CW3	W-2153666	0264	1
MEDVED RAYMOND L	MAJ	O-0992736	0365	1
MEDZ GOHAR	1LT	N-0758379	0952	2
MEE JAMES H	CPT	O-0451744	0844	2
MEE JOSEPH W	CW3	W-2151005	0265	1
MEECE FRANK H	LTC	O-0271472	1164	3
MEECH ROBERT A	LTC	O-1104299	0862	1
MEEDS ROBERT E	COL	O-0252580	0959	3
MEEHAN ANNE E	MAJ	N-0755351	0668	3
MEEHAN DAVID R	MAJ	O-0499023	0147	2
MEEHAN FRANK J JR	CW3	W-2151667	0665	1
MEEHAN PAUL F	LTC	O-1319965	1062	1
MEEK EDWIN M	MAJ	O-0506264	0546	2
MEEK HIBBS S	MAJ	O-0510241	0557	1
MEEK JOSEPH C	CPT	O-0275849	1063	3
MEEK LEONARD L	CPT	O-0342059	0146	2
MEEK LESTER I	COL	O-0320351	0256	3
MEEK WILBUR J	LTC	O-0434226	0667	1
MEEK WILLIAM M	CPT	O-0521825	0347	2
MEEKER BRUNS	LTC	O-0395591	0860	1
MEEKER FRANK R JR	LTC	O-1646421	0563	1
MEEKER GEORGE E	COL	O-0201978	0161	3
MEEKER ROBERT M	CPT	O-1312032	0146	2
MEEKINS EDMUND L	LTC	O-0278490	0159	1
MEEKINS GEORGE E	MAJ	O-1172994	0561	1
MEEKINS JOSEPH A	CW2	W-2118459	0146	2
MEEKINS RAYMOND M	COL	O-0179465	0861	3
MEEKS CHARLIE C	MAJ	O-0358194	0347	1
MEEKS LAWRENCE E	COL	O-0299917	0360	1
MEEKS ROBERT B	LTC	O-0122861	0952	3
MEEKS SYDNEY M	CW4	W-2119453	0457	1
MEELER MARION E	CW2	W-2142306	1057	1
MEENAN IGNATIUS J	CPT	O-0182812	0751	3
MEERMAN WILLIAM A	MAJ	O-1296236	0862	1
MEERMANS LEONARD H	COL	O-0257003	1267	3
MEES THOMAS L	1LT	O-1292215	0146	2
MEESE CHARLES M	LTC	O-0922558	0565	3
MEESKE JOHN M	CPT	O-1702352	0346	2
MEFFORD ANDY J	CW4	W-2110431	0361	1
MEFFORD ERNEST A	MAJ	O-0289306	0146	2
MEGAN LEE C	LTC	O-2040939	0566	3
MEGARGEE HENRY P JR	2LT	O-1555102	0445	2
MEGARITY JACK	CPT	O-0968217	0461	1
MEGERLE NEIL O	2LT	O-1913822	1039	1
MEGOWAN FRANK M	1LT	O-0519763	0846	2
MEGOWAN NORBERT F	LTC	O-0292836	0861	1
MEHAFFEY JACK E	MAJ	O-1588166	1160	1
MEHAFFEY JAY H	CPT	O-1321464	0247	2
MEHAFFEY ROBERT E JR	MAJ	O-0384193	0745	2
MEHAFFEY WILSON J	2LT	O-1320286	0944	2
MEHAFFIE HAROLD B	CPT	O-1044615	0154	1
MEHAFFIE KENNETH N	CPT	O-0204820	0362	1
MEHAFFIE TERRENCE C	2LT	O-1046196	0645	2
MEHAL ANDREW A	CPT	O-2262667	0861	2

NAME	GRADE	SVC NO	DATE RET MO YR	RET CODE
MEHARG M I	2LT	0-1311913	1044	2
MEHLIZ RALPH C	CPT	0-4005126	0965	1
MEHLENO JOHN J	CPT	0-1171468	0949	1
MEHLMAN JAMES D	MAJ	0-0533040	1047	2
MEHPOLA DANIEL K	1LT	0-2012516	1058	2
MEHL FRED C	LTC	0-0100786	0657	3
MEHL LOUIS S	LTC	0-1031576	1264	1
MEHLE JAMES T	CPT	0-1943970	1051	2
MEHLER LOUIS A	MAJ	0-1946335	0968	3
MEHLICK CECELIA G	CPT	N-0773630	0764	1
MEHLIN ELIZABETH	MAJ	N-0731412	1162	1
MEHNER HANS H	CW3	W-2136650	0363	1
MEHRHOF FLOYD F	LTC	0-0134256	1055	3
MEHRING WILLIAM C	CW4	W-2109062	0168	1
MEHRTEN JERYLE M	MAJ	0-1693115	1163	1
MEIER ALFRED A	CW3	W-2004721	0765	1
MEIER BERNHARDT	MAJ	0-0378498	0860	1
MEIER CARL J JR	CPT	0-2007718	0457	1
MEIER GEORGE A	CPT	0-1298092	0147	2
MEIER GEORGE R JR	CW2	W-2214395	0868	1
MEIER MERVIN H	MAJ	0-1180615	0458	2
MEIER ROBERT A	LTC	0-0223045	0559	3
MEIER ROBERT J	CW4	W-2102049	0255	2
MEIER RUSSELL F	COL	0-0253923	1059	1
MEIERDIERCKS EDWARD	MAJ	0-1254972	0264	1
MEIGHAN SYLVESTER	LTC	0-0246329	0661	1
MEIGHEN CARL H	CW4	W-2132731	0361	1
MEIGHEN CHARLES P	MAJ	0-0151274	1155	3
MEIGHEN MILES P	CPT	0-0185195	0960	3
MEIGHEN PATRICK H	MAJ	0-1341352	1060	1
MEIGS CHARLES P	1LT	0-0108149	0839	1
MEIGS GEORGE A	LTC	0-0305387	0966	3
MEIHOFF AMIEL D	CPT	0-0921072	0248	2
MEIK FRANCIS J	LTC	0-0287668	1157	3
MEIKLEJOHN WILLIAM R	MAJ	0-1301854	0761	1
MEILSTRUP DREW B	MAJ	0-0347900	0346	2
MEINCKE WALDEMAR	MAJ	0-1799339	1262	1
MEINDERTSMA PETER	MAJ	0-2006946	0461	1
MEINDL JAMES A	LTC	0-0455921	1167	3
MEINERDING ROBERT B	MAJ	0-1320761	0562	1
MEINKE ARTHUR C	CPT	0-0888224	1045	2
MEINSCHEIN BERNARD J	1LT	0-1328381	0146	2
MEINSTEIN SIEGFRIED	1LT	0-0961622	0151	2
MEIS JOSEPH A	LTC	0-0478778	1048	1
MEISEL HAROLD L	LTC	0-1845071	0564	1
MEISENHEIMER JEROME	LTC	0-0244193	1061	3
MEISENHELDER LLOYD E	CPT	0-0904037	1044	2
MEISER EDWARD H	LTC	0-0461148	0862	1
MEISNER ROBERT E	1LT	0-1299925	1045	2
MEISS GUY C	LTC	0-1017397	0463	1
MEISSNER FRED	CPT	0-0182496	0431	1
MEISTER CARL J	MAJ	0-1283648	1046	2
MEISTER ELSIE M	MAJ	N-0742942	0965	1
MEISTER VICTOR M	MAJ	0-0242521	0257	3
MEIXELL GLENN E SR	MAJ	0-0994420	0365	1
MEIXNER ZANE R M	MAJ	0-0983107	0168	1
MEIZLER FRANK	CPT	0-2006049	0160	1
MEJO WALTER L	MAJ	0-0250903	1166	3
MEKLAS JOHN F	2LT	0-0511831	0944	2
MELAD RAFAEL	2LT	0-1896491	0553	1
MELANCON JAMES L	CPT	0-0421159	1144	2
MELANSON EDWARD J	CW2	W-2000108	1159	1
MELANSON JOSEPH W P	LTC	0-0395775	1160	1
MELANSON RICHARD C	MAJ	0-2289007	0763	1
MELBOURNE CLARENCE J	MAJ	0-1559049	0163	1
MELBOURNE RALPH V	CW3	W-2148502	0166	1
MELCHER GEORGE H	MAJ	0-0328155	0145	2
MELCHER PHILIP R	LTC	0-1041848	0862	1
MELCHERS CORA E	CPT	N-0762103	0854	2
MELCHERT HAROLD B	LTC	0-0499798	1263	3
MELCHIOR ARCHIBALD	COL	0-0134768	0454	3
MELDRUM CHARLES B	MAJ	0-0244323	0356	3
MELDRUM GORDON C	LTC	0-0333230	0863	3
MELEGARI WILLIAM	CW2	W-2200462	0562	2
MELENDEZ JUAN R	LTC	0-0406152	1164	1

NAME	GRADE	SVC NO	DATE RET MO YR	RET CODE
MELGARD CHARLES G	2LT	0-0520258	0245	2
MELI CHARLES P	LTC	0-1685671	1267	1
MELIM JOHN V	LTC	0-0363332	0563	3
MELINA SAMUEL R	LTC	0-1097081	0165	1
MELINE WILLIAM C	LTC	0-0378099	0665	3
MELISE SAMUEL	1LT	0-0380708	1144	2
MELISH JOHN R	LTC	0-0191763	0262	3
MELIUS ROVERT C	CW2	W-2204975	0160	1
MELKO JOHN T	MAJ	0-1284363	0457	1
MELKONIAN SAM	MAJ	0-1925535	0467	1
MELL CHARLES M	MAJ	0-1000824	0663	1
MELL CHARLES N	MAJ	0-0522705	1145	2
MELLA HUGO	COL	0-0485466	0846	2
MELLA RALPH J	MAJ	0-0996658	1268	2
MELLARD ROBERT B	CW2	W-2144704	1059	1
MELLARS THOMAS A JR	LTC	0-1058077	1166	1
MELLEN WILLIAM E	LTC	0-0295510	0166	3
MELLEN WILLIAM H	MAJ	0-0266942	0950	3
MELLER JOSEPH	MAJ	0-0274460	0165	3
MELLICK ALDEN B	LTC	0-1175237	1166	3
MELLINGER OLIVER L	LTC	0-0497775	0767	3
MELLION JACOB	COL	0-0276682	1057	3
MELLIS DONALD B	MAJ	0-0172966	1159	3
MELLISH FREDERICK	MAJ	0-0403265	1045	2
MELLMAN SANFORD S	CPT	0-0475019	0649	1
MELLO HELENA R	MAJ	N-0728191	1068	3
MELLOM JULIUS O	MAJ	0-1552334	1055	1
MELLON JAMES E	1LT	0-1934948	0854	2
MELLON JOHN	CPT	0-0496717	0750	1
MELLON JOSEPH R	LTC	0-1312491	0863	1
MELLOR DONALD M	LTC	0-0916805	1167	3
MELLOR MARY E K	CPT	N-0700141	0846	1
MELLOW THOMAS H JR	CPT	0-1305959	0548	2
MELNICK CARL J	COL	0-0443785	0954	1
MELNIKOFF VIADIMIR N	MAJ	0-0981211	1160	1
MELOCHICK GEORGE	LTC	0-1312697	1057	1
MELODY MILNER D	CPT	0-0381555	0148	2
MELOGRANO VINCENT J	MAJ	0-1598639	0164	1
MELONE ORURY	LTC	0-0451005	0568	3
MELOTTE JOHN H	CW4	W-2146553	0968	1
MELPIGNANO JOSEPH P	1LT	0-1298568	0353	2
MELRAGON HENRY A	CPT	0-0425931	1046	2
MELTON ADRUS C	MAJ	0-0364692	0667	3
MELTON ALFRED E	MAJ	0-1947153	1060	1
MELTON CHARLES E	COL	0-0330103	0954	2
MELTON CLARENCE W	WO1	W-2145467	0862	1
MELTON DOYLE E	CW3	W-2208444	1166	1
MELTON EDWARD I	LTC	0-1641575	0263	1
MELTON EDWARD R	COL	0-0222238	1060	3
MELTON ELDRIDGE	COL	0-0223067	0254	3
MELTON ERNEST B	2LT	0-1032291	1044	2
MELTON EUGENE R	LTC	0-1280016	0854	1
MELTON FRANK	LTC	0-1542606	1058	2
MELTON GEORGE D	CW3	W-2142499	0859	1
MELTON JOSEPH	CPT	0-1689515	0146	2
MELTON LUTHER L	LTC	0-0403613	1263	1
MELTON NOEL M	LTC	0-0347347	0768	3
MELTON NORMAN A	CPT	0-1171676	0156	1
MELTON OLIVER Q	2LT	0-0514312	1045	2
MELTON ORVAL W	2LT	0-1897734	0452	2
MELTON ROBERT B JR	LTC	0-0549541	0564	1
MELTON ROBERT L	WO1	W-2118112	0758	1
MELTON ROMIE L	COL	0-0220624	0764	3
MELTON ROSCOE	CPT	0-1341895	0860	1
MELTON TALVIN R	CPT	0-1288932	0558	1
MELTON TILLMAN K	MAJ	0-0288839	0266	3
MELTON WILLIAM R	MAJ	0-0471031	0851	2
MELTZ ROBERT W	MAJ	0-1306302	0462	1
MELTZER DANIEL	LTC	0-2049333	0368	1
MELTZER JACK	MAJ	0-0336050	0246	2
MELTZER JAMES L	CPT	0-1304635	1147	2
MELVILLE ALBERT F	CW3	W-2144772	1055	1
MELVILLE JOHN W	MAJ	0-0299516	0246	2
MELVIN ALLISON O	LTC	0-1636318	0859	1
MELVIN DANIEL L	MAJ	0-1038066	0661	1

NAME	GRADE	SVC NO	DATE RET MO YR	RET CODE
MELVIN GEORGE H	COL	0-0451006	0862	1
MELVIN HERSCHEL I	LTC	0-0288576	0954	1
MELVIN JOHN W	CW3	W-2205163	0766	1
MELVIN ROBERT E	LTC	0-1311897	1062	1
MELVIN THOMAS F	1LT	0-2034564	1044	2
MELVIN WALTER H	CPT	0-1686522	0556	1
MELVIN WILLIAM L	CPT	0-0948715	0361	1
MELZER CLIVE R	LTC	0-0474576	1153	2
MELZER PHILLIPS	LTC	0-1046567	0565	1
MELZER WILLIAM N	CPT	0-0466864	0245	2
MEMNINGER CHARLES B	MAJ	0-0140507	1152	3
MEMORY ROBERT A	CPT	0-0354093	0945	2
MENA ESTEBAN	LTC	0-0357958	0657	1
MENA JOSE A	MAJ	0-0376556	0157	1
MENAPACE LOUIS A	MAJ	0-1338733	1064	1
MENARD JOHN B	MAJ	0-0404866	0248	1
MENARD LEO A	CW3	W-2151889	1065	1
MENARICK GEORGE E	MAJ	0-1637673	0267	1
MENCACCY ALBERT C	LTC	0-0283869	1060	3
MENCACCY FERNANDO C	M G	0-0278275	0762	3
MENCH EDWARD F	1LT	0-0912378	0745	2
MENCH LLOYD G	1LT	0-1101116	0446	2
MENCHER EDWARD W	CPT	0-0330539	0844	2
MENDE RALPH A	MAJ	0-0965177	0563	1
MENDELSOHN ISADOR W	MAJ	0-0234424	0554	3
MENDELSOHN LESTER	WO1	W-2105532	0954	1
MENDELSOHN MATTHEW	COL	0-0296993	0368	3
MENDELSON MARVIN	1LT	0-1306447	0745	2
MENDEN JULIAN	LTC	0-0250392	1165	3
MENDENHALL HERBERT D	COL	0-0116377	0648	3
MENDENHALL JOHN B	COL	0-0321568	1164	3
MENDENHALL RALPH F	LTC	0-1018680	0968	1
MENDENHALL VIRGIL C	WO1	W-2123978	0844	2
MENDEZ EDRIS	LTC	0-0417742	0860	1
MENDEZ JOSE F	LTC	0-0453159	1060	1
MENDEZ PEDRO T JR	CPT	0-1313169	1060	1
MENDEZ-RIOS FRANCISC	CW2	W-2147655	0264	1
MENDLOW SAMUEL	1LT	0-1823039	0246	2
MENDOLA VINCENT S	1LT	0-1050812	0945	2
MENDOZA JOSE T	CPT	0-1313662	0863	1
MENDOZA JULIO E	MAJ	0-1037623	0260	1
MENDOZA VICK	2LT	0-1896671	1148	1
MENDOZA SOFIO P	LTC	0-0888136	0749	2
MENDRES THEODORE J	MAJ	0-0309966	0368	4
MENEGUS GRACE N	MAJ	L-0901371	0566	1
MENEGUZZI ENRICO	MAJ	0-1081085	0866	1
MENGEL GEORGE F	MAJ	0-0962937	0865	1
MENGES ALBERT C	LTC	0-0397125	1060	1
MENGES JOSEPH W	LTC	0-0255642	1163	3
MENGES WILBUR S	CPT	0-0361593	0145	2
MENGHINI ERMA P	1LT	N-0772100	0845	1
MENGHINI RENALDO R	MAJ	0-0318616	1045	2
MENIATIS ARTHUR	MAJ	0-0496373	0451	1
MENICON MENICOS N	LTC	0-0321699	0962	3
MENIFEE RUSSELL R	WO1	W-2126018	0154	1
MENKEMEYER HENRY	CPT	0-1165766	0245	2
MENKEN JOHN J	CW3	W-2136723	0163	1
MENKING ROBERT C	LTC	0-1634135	1067	1
MENMUIR JAMES B	LTC	0-0257169	1061	3
MENNEG PAUL F	CPT	0-1290637	0346	2
MENNELL LORVE F	CPT	0-1301183	0545	2
MENNING EUGENE W	LTC	0-1040270	1266	1
MENNINGER HENRY E	2LT	0-1794932	1145	2
MENSCHING ELMER F	CW2	W-2104236	0458	1
MENSH JENNIE	CPT	N-0723639	0546	1
MENTEMEYER ALFRED O	1LT	0-1055917	1060	1
MENTKOWSKI JOSEPH T	MAJ	0-2262307	0364	1
MENTON LATHERINE	MAJ	N-0797771	0765	1
MENTZER BLISS R	1LT	0-1181957	0745	2
MENTZOS LEWIS G	MAJ	0-2007034	0859	1
MENUSTIK JOHN JR	CPT	0-0542521	0546	2
MENVILLE EUGENE F	LTC	0-0495402	0657	1
MENZIE MARY H	CPT	N-0733999	0947	1
MENZIES GORDON E	COL	0-0346100	0465	3
MENZIES GRALE	MAJ	L-0609389	0963	1

NAME	GRADE	SVC NO	DATE RET MO YR	RET CODE
MERANSKI ARTHUR M	LTC	0-1061790	0968	1
MERBACH EDWARD	MAJ	0-1055207	0459	1
MERBACK ARTHUR A	CPT	0-0535414	0549	2
MERCADO FELIX V	COL	0-0303993	0862	1
MERCADO PAUL	COL	0-0232438	0966	1
MERCAP ANDREW R	MAJ	0-2200128	0866	1
MERCER ARTHUR G	MAJ	0-0988494	0866	1
MERCER BEATRICE E	CW2	V-0135389	0165	1
MERCER CHARLTON W	2LT	0-1821896	0545	2
MERCER EDWIN W	LTC	0-0287369	1264	3
MERCER GARNET E	LTC	0-1413770	0966	1
MERCER GERALD L	1LT	0-1285768	0246	2
MERCER HORACE R	MAJ	0-1339380	0865	1
MERCER HOWELL P	COL	0-0906799	1262	1
MERCER JAMES A	COL	0-0283734	0647	2
MERCER JAMES A	COL	0-0479611	0455	1
MERCER JOE B	CW4	W-2143771	1060	1
MERCER JOHN W	LTC	0-0240935	1163	3
MERCER LEWIS P	CPT	0-1300677	0646	2
MERCER LOIS B	2LT	N-0741940	1043	1
MERCER NELSON	LTC	0-0151140	1251	3
MERCER RAY	COL	0-0117439	0648	3
MERCER RICHARD H	LTC	0-0240470	0763	3
MERCER ROBERT C	CPT	0-1295058	0146	2
MERCER ROY W	MAJ	0-0235051	0454	3
MERCER TIM	LTC	0-1103801	0862	1
MERCER WILLIAM E	MAJ	0-1941699	0368	1
MERCHANT AUSTIN W	COL	0-0262892	1066	3
MERCHANT CHARLES L	MAJ	0-1594333	0363	1
MERCHANT HAROLD E	MAJ	0-1168818	0159	1
MERCHANT HENRY R JR	COL	0-0263739	0568	3
MERCHANT JESSE C JR	CW2	W-2104297	0347	2
MERCHANT MARCIUS H	MAJ	0-0247845	0648	3
MERCHANT MARTIN L V	LTC	0-1313113	0762	1
MERCHANT ROBERT P	LTC	0-0467814	0164	1
MERCHANT THOMAS O	CPT	0-0410858	0946	2
MERCHANT WILLARD R	COL	0-0296377	0265	2
MERCHANT WILLIAM A	CPT	0-0494850	0345	2
MERCHANT WILLIAM B	MAJ	0-0397121	0863	1
MERCIER ALBIN S JR	MAJ	0-2202018	0267	1
MERCIER FRANCIS B	MAJ	0-0454209	0261	1
MERCIER HAROLD A	LTC	0-0551807	1064	3
MERCIER HOWARD S	MAJ	0-1293445	0861	2
MERCIER ROMA R	1LT	N-0752833	1154	2
MERCIL SIMONE Y	MAJ	N-0755584	0965	1
MERCKER ALBERT O	COL	0-0237278	C460	3
MERCURIO ALBERT A	MAJ	0-1118615	0760	2
MERDELL MELVIN E	CPT	0-1101121	1055	2
MEREDITH ARVIN O	LTC	0-1042652	0762	1
MEREDITH CHARLES L	COL	0-0371790	1262	1
MEREDITH DOYLE C	LTC	0-1031666	0957	1
MEREDITH EARL F	LTC	0-1327366	0765	1
MEREDITH ERNEST L	CW4	W-2106048	0562	3
MEREDITH HERBERT J	MAJ	0-0962264	1165	1
MEREDITH JAMES C	MAJ	0-0228543	1156	3
MEREDITH JOSEPH W	1LT	0-0263430	0648	3
MEREDITH KENNETH M	LTC	0-0318004	0455	1
MEREDITH PAUL F	LTC	0-0237978	0864	3
MEREDITH ROBERT L	CW4	W-2005750	0168	1
MEREDITH ROBERT M JR	MAJ	0-1685678	0364	2
MEREDITH WILMER H	LTC	0-0328436	0468	3
MEREHENT DALE O	MAJ	0-0195254	0462	3
MERENBACH WALTER	COL	0-0340814	0663	1
MERGARD VICTOR	MAJ	0-1796506	0759	1
MERGELE MARVIN E	CPT	0-0482577	0145	2
MERGENTHAL RAYMOND O	MAJ	0-2014467	0566	1
MERGET JOHN R	LTC	0-0313897	0661	3
MERICAL CLOYD A	MAJ	0-1648985	0857	1
MERIDETH CLAUDE T	CW3	W-2145892	0464	1
MERIGLIANO JOSEPH J	CW2	W-2147407	0363	1
MERIN HERBERT L	CPT	0-1030908	104N	2
MERIWETHER DON R	1LT	0-0434705	1044	2
MERIWETHER JOHN B	MAJ	0-0162729	0356	3
MERIWETHER WILLIAM M	MAJ	0-1003989	0460	1
MERKEL ARTHUR V	LTC	0-027C120	1166	3

NAME	GRADE	SVC NO	DATE RET MO YR	RET CODE
MERKEL EDWARD J	LTC	O-1577562	0266	1
MERKEL ELLEN H	MAJ	N-0800044	1165	2
MERKEL GORDON D	CPT	O-1325066	1047	2
MERKL FRANK M	LTC	O-0167914	1058	3
MERKLE CHARLES A	COL	O-0275100	0357	1
MERKLE VOLA J	2LT	N-0736420	0345	1
MERKLER FRANK C	CPT	O-1293293	0847	2
MERLE HENRI J	LTC	O-1328280	0563	1
MERLI PETER A	CW4	W-2149414	0967	1
MERLIN SAMUEL A	COL	O-0223970	1161	3
MERLINO LOUIS	CPT	O-1049579	0747	2
MERLO NICHOLAS A	1LT	O-2037860	1047	2
MEROLA ANTHONY A	LTC	O-1332397	0666	1
MERONEY RICHARD H	LTC	O-1042653	1060	1
MEROWIT CLEMENT E	CPT	O-0919438	1045	2
MERRELL HERMAN E	CPT	O-1946573	1060	2
MERRELL STANLEY S	COL	O-0287447	0566	3
MERRIAM BERNARD A	MAJ	O-0167860	0648	3
MERRIAM CHARLES	MAJ	O-0989882	0467	1
MERRIAM CHARLES S	LTC	O-0301344	0859	1
MERRIAM GEORGE C JR	LTC	O-0918333	1067	3
MERRIAM HOWARD K	LTC	O-1639398	0262	1
MERRIAM KENNETH G	COL	O-0171071	1061	3
MERRIAM LUCIUS B	LTC	O-0308608	0358	3
MERRIAM WALTER F	LTC	O-0243939	0943	2
MERRICK BERNARD V	COL	O-0184691	0853	1
MERRICK CHARLES M	MAJ	O-1553702	1067	3
MERRICK JANE A	1LT	N-0742353	0346	1
MERRICK JOSEPH W	LTC	O-1596731	0463	1
MERRICK RICHARD H	COL	O-0273724	0665	1
MERRIFIELD CHARLES C	LTC	O-0252599	0-52	1
MERRIHEW JAMES L	1LT	O-1320155	1045	2
MERRILL ADELBERT H	MAJ	O-0254048	1057	3
MERRILL ALVIE L	COL	O-0207985	0346	2
MERRILL CHAUNCEY D	M G	O-0112486	0758	3
MERRILL EDWARD A	COL	O-0170186	0560	3
MERRILL EDWARD O	MAJ	O-1313771	0666	1
MERRILL ELWIN	MAJ	O-1116964	0463	1
MERRILL FRANKLIN R	LTC	O-1297916	0459	2
MERRILL HAROLD D	LTC	O-0254250	0960	3
MERRILL HARRY E	MAJ	O-1643123	0759	1
MERRILL HENRY B	COL	O-0216111	0754	3
MERRILL HERVEY C	LTC	O-0961851	1068	1
MERRILL HOWARD C	LTC	O-1290282	0465	1
MERRILL JOHN P	COL	O-0181405	0559	1
MERRILL KENNETH J	MAJ	O-1105026	0450	2
MERRILL LEW E	MAJ	O-0350093	1157	3
MERRILL LOUIS M	LTC	O-0296151	1160	3
MERRILL MARRINER W	CPT	O-0497199	0845	2
MERRILL MELVILLE L	LTC	O-0110553	0648	3
MERRILL MELVIN C	2LT	O-0772067	0146	2
MERRILL MICHAEL S	CPT	O-1166784	1047	1
MERRILL RALPH H	CW3	W-2150096	1157	1
MERRILL ROBERT A	MAJ	O-0230255	0345	2
MERRILL ROBERT S	CW4	W-2146080	1067	1
MERRILL ROY A JR	MAJ	O-4018677	0466	1
MERRILL SAM D	MAJ	O-1313699	0661	1
MERRILL WENDELL W	LTC	O-0466490	1162	1
MERRILL WILLIAM B SR	CW2	W-2208587	0662	1
MERRILL WILLIAM H JR	COL	O-0217017	0163	3
MERRIMAN TAYLOR	LTC	O-0909676	0766	3
MERRIMAN WILSON C	MAJ	O-0506577	0846	2
MERRIOTT OTHELL O	LTC	O-1542951	0562	1
MERRIS GILBERT E	LTC	O-1167117	0266	1
MERRITT BENJAMIN F	M G	O-0244836	1267	3
MERRITT BUFORD A	COL	O-0233751	0963	3
MERRITT DELBERT L	CPT	O-1288595	0345	2
MERRITT EARL W	2LT	O-1322645	0645	2
MERRITT ELMER V	MAJ	O-1179967	0260	1
MERRITT EMMETT H	MAJ	O-0497489	0151	1
MERRITT GEORGE W	CPT	O-1016514	0546	2
MERRITT HARRY W	1LT	O-0131861	0554	3
MERRITT I T	CW3	W-2205761	0865	1
MERRITT JOHN M	LTC	O-1309382	0163	1
MERRITT JOHN W	MAJ	O-5301893	1068	1

NAME	GRADE	SVC NO	DATE RET MO YR	RET CODE
MERRITT JOSEPH W	CPT	O-0277282	1266	3
MERRITT MAURICE A	1LT	O-1016613	1145	2
MERRITT NORMAN F JR	CPT	O-1899386	1155	1
MERRITT PAUL D	MAJ	O-1329860	0263	1
MERRITT RICHARD B	CW3	W-2210016	1267	1
MERRITT ROBERT L	LTC	O-1341811	0868	1
MERRITT ROLAND J	MAJ	O-0301705	0261	1
MERRITT SYLVESTER	LTC	O-0475085	0454	1
MERRITT WILLIAM R	MAJ	O-1533862	0759	1
MERROW ELMER J	LTC	O-0411626	1060	1
MERRYMAN JAMES H	CPT	O-0141521	0648	3
MERRYWELL HARRY H	CW2	W-2209515	0165	1
MERRYWELL LOREN W	CW2	W-2119286	0567	1
MERSCHOFF BAYLY E	LTC	O-0395895	1262	1
MERSENSKE J E	1LT	N-0742268	1044	1
MERSHON FREDERICK	MAJ	O-0287073	1158	3
MERSHON WILLIAM B JR	LTC	O-0141550	1149	3
MERTEN FRED W	CW4	W-2103214	0659	1
MERTENS HELMUTH E	LTC	O-0302879	1068	3
MERTENS HERMAN C	MAJ	O-0476861	0149	1
MERTZ LOWELL C	LTC	O-1585889	0164	1
MERTZ PAUL F	LTC	O-2037681	0866	1
MERULLO ROLAND A	MAJ	O-2007468	0864	1
MERVES LOUIS	MAJ	O-0461400	1145	2
MERVINE SAMUEL S	COL	O-0299831	1059	3
MERVINE WILLIAM H	CW3	W-2115366	0255	2
MERVIS WALTER J	LTC	O-1583372	0361	1
MERWIN DONALD W	CW3	W-2149410	0463	1
MERWIN WILLIAM H	CPT	O-0525931	0146	2
MERWINE NETTIE K	1LT	N-0741002	1047	1
MERWORTH ROY C	MAJ	O-1950704	0760	1
MERZ JON P	1LT	O-5248966	1268	2
MERZ ROBERT E	2LT	O-1081086	0545	2
MESA CELSO C	LTC	O-0888117	1063	1
MESARCH VICTOR M	LTC	O-1293810	0762	1
MESAROS ANTHONY C	CPT	O-0454505	0745	2
MESCH FRED P	CW3	W-2147532	1062	1
MESCH JOSEPH A	2LT	O-1298094	0643	2
MESCHAN VINCENT R	1LT	O-1015631	1045	2
MESECK WALTER T	LTC	O-0223941	0954	3
MESEKE VICTOR H	COL	O-0248177	0564	1
MESEKE WILLIAM C	LTC	O-0236069	0163	3
MESHEY WILLIAM P	MAJ	O-2009736	0662	1
MESHKOFF PETER P	MAJ	O-0253659	0267	3
MESICK JACOB R	1LT	O-2035958	0245	2
MESKER THERMON D	1LT	O-1017253	1046	2
MESKIMEN JOSEPH E	MAJ	O-0204436	0755	3
MESSALL CHARLES M	COL	O-1644589	0168	2
MESSEC WENDEL C	LTC	O-0450046	0363	1
MESSENGER KENNETH W	1LT	O-1115700	0545	2
MESSER BERNARD A	CW3	W-2151020	1165	1
MESSER CHARLES F	MAJ	O-0369464	0161	1
MESSER DALLAS C	2LT	O-1032440	1044	2
MESSER DANIEL	MAJ	O-1047238	0657	2
MESSER DOROTHY B	MAJ	N-0752956	0864	1
MESSER DOROTHY S	LTC	L-0200747	1167	1
MESSER FRED W	2LT	O-2012427	0246	2
MESSER MARVIN A	CPT	O-1044304	0663	1
MESSER THOMAS A	CPT	O-2008269	0855	1
MESSER THOMAS V	MAJ	O-1645821	0963	1
MESSER ZORA	LTC	O-0450606	1157	1
MESSERLY NOEL JR	MAJ	O-1333851	0262	1
MESSERSMITH CHARLES	LTC	O-0240306	0862	3
MESSERSMITH LEO H	CW4	W-2108228	0157	1
MESSEY JACK	CPT	O-0233523	1159	3
MESSICK WALTER L	LTC	O-1298971	0461	1
MESSIER BERTRAND G	1LT	O-1013103	0961	1
MESSIER EDMUND G	CPT	O-0501773	0351	1
MESSINA JACK A	2LT	O-1321230	0345	2
MESSINA JOSEPH	LTC	O-1290453	0158	1
MESSINA JOSEPH C	CPT	O-0386835	0146	2
MESSINA PHILIP V	CPT	O-0504318	0645	2
MESSINER FRED	1LT	O-0537041	0145	2
MESSING FREDERICK	LTC	O-1103803	0960	1
MESSINGER CARL	LTC	O-1559948	0168	1

NAME	GRADE	SVC NO	DATE RET MO YR	RET CODE
MESSMER ROBERT L	LTC	O-1548501	0960	1
MESSMORE RALPH E	CPT	O-2262798	0461	1
MESSNER GRANT J	CPT	O-1110662	0963	1
MESSNER LUCILE A	MAJ	N-0777784	0667	3
MESSNER MARK A	LTC	O-0189628	1055	3
MESSNER ROY G	LTC	O-0207692	0451	3
MESSURI JOHN R	LTC	O-1311514	0967	1
MESTAN ALBERT A	MAJ	O-1688488	0962	1
MESTAYER JOHN L	1LT	O-1296729	0546	2
METCALF ALLEN M	2LT	O-0532110	0544	2
METCALF ANNE C	1LT	N-0725926	0746	1
METCALF CHARLES E	1LT	O-1294514	0345	2
METCALF FREDERICK	LTC	O-1322859	0964	1
METCALF GAYLE R	MAJ	O-4018678	0268	1
METCALF HAROLD B	LTC	O-0235663	0862	3
METCALF MAURICE	LTC	O-0508610	0965	1
METCALF ROBERT W	LTC	O-1551068	0361	1
METCALF STANLEY W	COL	O-0264611	0-53	3
METCALF THOMAS F	LTC	O-1285268	0263	1
METCALFE ARTHUR S	LTC	O-1177089	0967	1
METCALFE GEORGE S	LTC	O-0277611	0962	3
METCALFE HERBERT A	MAJ	O-0307677	0163	3
METCALFE REX	1LT	O-1305626	1045	2
METELSKI JOHN J	MAJ	O-0307500	0866	3
METENY ALBERT J	COL	O-0266150	1164	3
METEVELIS DON G	1LT	O-1301856	0147	2
METHENY ARLIE	CPT	O-0966654	0859	1
METHENY ELLSWORTH	LTC	O-0341159	0163	1
METHENY MARVIN O	1LT	O-1556763	0558	1
METHENY RALPH S	COL	O-0277220	0665	3
METHENY WILLIAM E	MAJ	O-1922524	0565	1
METOYER ALFRED L SR	CW2	W-2148976	1165	1
METTENHEIMER JOHN M	LTC	O-0253137	0559	3
METTERNICH JOHN H	MAJ	O-0282277	0968	3
METTLEN LEE R	MAJ	O-1174383	1265	1
METZ HERBERT H	MAJ	O-0203898	0860	3
METZ HERMAN A	CPT	O-1690382	1045	2
METZ HOWARD D	LTC	O-0284813	0568	3
METZ JAMES L	MAJ	O-0333244	0562	1
METZ KARL H	COL	O-0138403	0252	3
METZ PAUL E	CW2	W-2214763	1266	1
METZ THEODORE H	COL	O-0312669	0157	1
METZDOWER SAMUEL O	2LT	O-1338491	0546	2
METZEROTH ERIC C	COL	O-0225837	0862	3
METZEROTT KIRK A	COL	O-0113851	0754	3
METZGAR JOHN M	LTC	O-1176434	1061	1
METZGAR RICHARD A	COL	O-1755543	1268	1
METZGAR THOMAS I	LTC	O-0196870	1061	3
METZGER ALLEN C	MAJ	O-1341283	0461	1
METZGER ERNEST L	LTC	O-1169250	0363	2
METZGER FRITZ R	MAJ	O-0241409	0666	3
METZGER HARRISON A	LTC	O-2068713	0667	1
METZGER HENRY G	LTC	O-0325958	C760	1
METZGER JOHN M	CPT	O-1167981	0765	2
METZGER MICHAEL F	MAJ	O-1309949	0361	1
METZGER RALPH A	LTC	O-0340158	1060	1
METZGER RICHARD J	LTC	O-1557741	0763	1
METZGER RUDOLPH V	COL	O-0321564	0866	3
METZLER WILLIAM F	LTC	O-0276196	0764	3
MEULENERS RUBEN H	LTC	O-1299273	0761	1
MEUNIER HECTOR A	2LT	O-2023907	0553	1
MEUNIER MARCEL P	2LT	O-1080648	0445	2
MEUNIER PAUL A	LTC	O-1110104	1066	3
MEURER FREDERICK	CPT	O-0214096	0762	3
MEURLOTT BYRON M	LTC	O-0264094	0149	1
MEWALDT LEONARD R	CPT	O-1595706	1046	2
MEWHIRTER SYDNEY A	COL	O-0103909	0854	3
MEYER ADOLPHA M	CPT	N-0732164	1048	2
MEYER ALEX	CW3	W-2142881	0257	1
MEYER ANDREW	CW3	W-2149489	0165	1
MEYER ARLEIGH G	MAJ	O-1323596	1060	2
MEYER CAMILLE A	CPT	O-0120902	0648	3
MEYER CARROLL O	LTC	O-1296884	0962	1
MEYER CHARLES C JR	2LT	O-1012637	0544	2
MEYER CHARLES Z	LTC	O-0203309	0755	3

NAME	GRADE	SVC NO	DATE RET MO YR	RET CODE
MEYER CLEBURNE H	CPT	O-1032229	1146	2
MEYER DAN C	1LT	O-1648605	1045	2
MEYER EARL L	CPT	O-0131341	0351	3
MEYER EDWARD J	LTC	O-1545463	1160	1
MEYER EDWIN H	LTC	O-0236265	0645	2
MEYER ELVIN L	MAJ	O-1300354	0665	2
MEYER FRANCIS P	CPT	O-0498132	1044	2
MEYER FRANK J	CW4	W-2144558	0767	1
MEYER FRED J	MAJ	O-0463996	0664	1
MEYER FREDERICK	LTC	O-0386508	0466	3
MEYER GEORGE C JR	LTC	O-1050387	0862	1
MEYER GEORGE E	COL	O-0190136	0651	3
MEYER HAROLD W	LTC	O-1017537	1262	1
MEYER HART E	2LT	O-1176731	0945	2
MEYER HENRY	1LT	O-1178563	114N	2
MEYER HENRY A	MAJ	O-0470583	0746	2
MEYER HENRY H	LTC	O-0254892	0167	3
MEYER HENRY I	CPT	O-1116799	0947	2
MEYER HERSHEL	CPT	O-1821390	0844	2
MEYER IVAN W	LTC	O-0196462	1045	2
MEYER JACK J	CPT	O-4011144	0661	2
MEYER JAKE K	CW4	W-2134476	0557	1
MEYER JOHN D	LTC	O-0989937	0568	1
MEYER JOHN J	LTC	O-1549332	0164	1
MEYER JOSEPH F	CW3	W-2141932	0661	1
MEYER KENNETH L	MAJ	O-0451155	0656	1
MEYER LAWRENCE H	LTC	O-0272498	1068	3
MEYER LEO J	COL	O-0166303	0955	3
MEYER LEONARD O	COL	O-0432911	0266	2
MEYER LEROY A	LTC	O-1327030	1065	1
MEYER LOUIS A	CPT	O-2048710	0156	1
MEYER LUTHER	LTC	O-0112777	0844	2
MEYER MANIE H	LTC	O-0238811	0961	3
MEYER MARVIN C	LTC	O-0512316	0168	3
MEYER MAURICE O	LTC	O-0270121	0258	1
MEYER OSCAR G	CPT	O-1286682	0346	2
MEYER OSCAR W	CPT	O-0251296	0463	3
MEYER PAUL R	LTC	O-0311094	0145	2
MEYER PHILIP L	1LT	O-0575594	0857	1
MEYER RALPH E	CPT	O-1303371	0261	1
MEYER RALPH E	1LT	O-1305960	1044	2
MEYER RAYMOND F	MAJ	O-2048711	0664	1
MEYER ROBERT J	MAJ	O-1165134	0664	1
MEYER RUSSELL A	MAJ	O-0350286	1163	1
MEYER STANTON H	MAJ	O-0230936	0762	3
MEYER STEPEHN J	CW2	W-2119777	1044	2
MEYER THEODORE D	LTC	O-1825966	0862	1
MEYER WALLACE A	LTC	O-2020324	0965	1
MEYER WILLIAM C	CPT	O-0162058	0560	3
MEYER WILLIAM C	MAJ	O-1999856	0361	1
MEYER WILLIAM C JR	LTC	O-1019060	0967	1
MEYER WILLIAM L	CW3	W-2148801	0267	1
MEYER WILLIAM R	LTC	O-0113865	0855	3
MEYERS ALEXANDER JR	LTC	O-1593089	0863	1
MEYERS ANDREW J	CPT	O-0499788	0852	1
MEYERS BEN	1LT	O-1312858	0659	2
MEYERS CHESTER W	LTC	O-0387729	0364	3
MEYERS DAVID G	LTC	O-1175803	0864	1
MEYERS EARL L	COL	O-0271687	1267	3
MEYERS FRANK L	LTC	O-0389104	1060	1
MEYERS FRANK X	COL	O-0305284	0668	3
MEYERS GARTH H	COL	O-0370859	1053	1
MEYERS GEORGE G	2LT	O-1292369	0445	2
MEYERS HAROLD A	MAJ	O-1999415	1262	1
MEYERS HENRY L	MAJ	O-1115960	1059	1
MEYERS J STUART	MAJ	O-0239634	0566	3
MEYERS JAMES L	WO1	W-2114367	0544	2
MEYERS JOHN P	CPT	O-0372849	0567	3
MEYERS JOSEPH H	COL	O-0522688	0864	3
MEYERS LESTER A	MAJ	O-1948512	0157	1
MEYERS LUTHER D	MAJ	O-0194957	0344	2
MEYERS MARGUERITE	1LT	N-0775417	0146	1
MEYERS MARTIN O	COL	O-0244398	1064	3
MEYERS MAX F	MAJ	O-0451008	0253	2
MEYERS ROBERT C	CPT	O-1919040	0262	1

NAME	GRADE	SVC NO	DATE RET MO YR	RET CODE
MEYERS [illegible]	CPT	[illegible]	1160	1
MEYERS [illegible]	LTC	[illegible]	0164	3
MEYERS RUDY [illegible]	CW[illegible]	W-2213463	0664	1
MEYERS [illegible]	1LT	[illegible]	0964	2
MEYERS [illegible]	COL	[illegible]	1155	1
MEYERS WALTER [illegible]	CPT	[illegible]	1168	1
[illegible]	1LT	[illegible]	0166	[illegible]
[illegible]	COL	[illegible]	0664	3
[illegible]	1LT	[illegible]	0767	2
[illegible]	CPT	0-1725141	0645	2
[illegible]	LTC	0-1000324	0763	1
[illegible]	LTC	[illegible]	0755	2
[illegible]	LTC	0-1543661	0666	1
[illegible]	LTC	0-0406819	0556	1
[illegible] CHARLES	CW2	W-2145975	0456	1
MICELI AUGUST [illegible]	COL	0-0347675	0862	3
MICELI JOHN N	CPT	0-0347114	1163	2
MICELI JOSEPH F	MAJ	0-1799693	1160	1
MICHAEL BARBARA S	2LT	N-0742277	0245	1
MICHAEL DONALD T	LTC	0-0288656	0968	3
MICHAEL HORACE D	LTC	0-1176742	0267	3
MICHAEL HOWARD F	2LT	0-1012491	0944	2
MICHAEL JOHN M	LTC	0-0957640	1166	3
MICHAEL JOSEPH H	1LT	0-1845419	0545	2
MICHAEL ROBERT M	1LT	0-0970540	1060	1
MICHAEL RONALD A	CW3	W-2210109	0168	1
MICHAEL SIDNEY J	LTC	0-0313470	0865	3
MICHAEL THOMAS O	MAJ	0-1311346	1162	1
MICHAEL WILLIAM E	CW2	W-2149447	0166	1
MICHAELS ABRAHAM	LTC	0-0523620	0567	3
MICHAELS ABRAHAM J	MAJ	0-1690352	0447	2
MICHAELS ANTON S	CPT	0-2016205	0656	1
MICHAELS ARTHUR C	COL	0-0251964	1066	3
MICHAELS CHARLES F	CW3	W-2205444	0767	1
MICHAELS DAVID J	COL	0-0250223	0765	3
MICHAELS GEORGE M	MAJ	0-1826052	0356	2
MICHAELS HERMAN J	LTC	0-0887423	1167	1
MICHAELS JACOB A	CW2	W-2125055	1154	1
MICHAELS LOUIS A	CW3	W-2152454	0862	1
MICHAELS MICHAEL K	1LT	0-1292561	0644	2
MICHAELS MORRIS	1LT	0-0140180	0549	3
MICHAELS ROBERT M	CW3	W-2144850	0460	1
MICHAELS THOMAS W	2LT	0-2043302	0945	1
MICHAELSKI JOSEPH	LTC	0-1302853	0261	1
MICHAELY JACK	MAJ	0-1030505	1059	1
MICHAL SYLVIA A	LTC	N-0732725	0768	3
MICHAL WILLIAM R	MAJ	0-0976435	0562	1
MICHALAK RAYMOND F	COL	0-0278461	1165	3
MICHALOWSKI HELIODOR	CPT	0-0451471	0160	2
MICHALOWSKI ROMAN	LTC	0-0920687	0646	2
MICHALOWSKI V S	MAJ	0-0279572	0847	2
MICHAJ WERNER T	LTC	0-1017492	0263	1
MICHAJJ OSCAR J	CW2	W-2152630	0460	1
MICHEK FRANK J	MAJ	0-0339131	0645	2
MICHEL ALFRED JR	CPT	0-0966182	0760	1
MICHEL GEORGE L	CW2	W-2139633	0858	1
MICHEL GUSTAVO	2LT	0-2007135	0346	2
MICHEL JULIUS F	CPT	0-0390243	0843	2
MICHELL ALLEN R	COL	0-0223102	0563	3
MICHELLON ROBERT L	MAJ	0-0990439	0365	1
MICHELS OLIVER A	MAJ	0-1308406	0561	1
MICHELSEN RICHARD C	1LT	0-0919344	0445	2
MICHELSON ROBERT A	LTC	0-1182425	1068	1
MICHENER ELIZABETH	MAJ	N-0700865	0646	1
MICHENER GEORGE G	MAJ	0-1316183	0364	1
MICHENER MILTON L	CPT	0-1555038	0147	2
MICHENER PERCY Z	COL	0-0285750	0264	3
MICHIE JOHN JR	LTC	0-1293913	0761	1
MICHIELS SYLVESTER	CW2	W-2211659	0367	1
MICHL JOSEPH P	LTC	0-0242463	1160	1
MICHNY FRANK J	MAJ	0-1597205	0859	1
MICHON STANLEY	CPT	0-2262719	0361	1
MICINOWSKI ANTHONY	MAJ	0-1131694	0264	1
MICIOTTO BRO JOSEPH	1LT	0-1319307	0945	2
MICK WALLACE R	MAJ	0-1917548	0563	1
MICKA BENEDICT W	MAJ	0-1660737	1161	1
MICKELSON EDGAR D	CPT	0-1011755	1047	2
MICKELSON WALLACE V	1LT	0-1103807	1165	2
MICKEY HOWARD H	LTC	0-1928157	0368	1
MICKEY JOHN J JR	LTC	0-1324547	0969	1
MICKLEBERRY STEPHEN	CPT	0-2262358	0261	1
MI[illegible] ROSE A	MAJ	N-0724076	0361	1
MIDDLEBROOK ARTHUR L	CW4	W-2148371	0868	1
MIDDLEBROOK CHARLES	LTC	0-0294096	0465	3
MIDDLEMAN ISADORE G	MAJ	0-0303371	1144	2
MIDDLEMAS JOHN N	MAJ	0-2262644	0167	1
MIDDLESWORTH JOHN P	MAJ	0-0332471	0768	3
MIDDLETON ALDINE M	CW4	W-2110626	0861	1
MIDDLETON CASILEAR	LTC	0-2021294	0967	1
MIDDLETON CHARLES	LTC	0-0487560	0758	1
MIDDLETON CHARLES	CPT	0-1101579	1054	2
MIDDLETON CHARLES H	COL	0-0224905	1057	3
MIDDLETON CHARLES L	MAJ	0-1057174	0259	1
MIDDLETON FRANK V	MAJ	0-1580034	0361	3
MIDDLETON JAMES L	WO1	W-2135263	0146	2
MIDDLETON JOSEPH T	LTC	0-0383605	0647	2
MIDDLETON PAUL F	MAJ	0-0120963	0556	3
MIDDLETON PHILIP H	LTC	0-0279192	1163	3
MIDDLETON ROBERT O	MAJ	0-1922535	0763	1
MIDDLETON ROBERT S	1LT	0-1285269	0745	2
MIDDLETON WILLIAM D	COL	0-0176200	0648	3
MIDDLETON WILLIAM H	CPT	0-1316774	1146	2
MIDDLETON WILLIAM J	2LT	0-1112863	1044	2
MIDGETT DAVID P	LTC	0-0515580	0263	1
MIDGETT JOSEPH W	CPT	0-0243373	0347	1
MIDGLEY CHARLES E	1LT	0-0499787	0346	2
MIDGLEY ROBERT F	MAJ	0-1314525	1364	1
MIDKIFF HAROLD C	CW2	W-2005202	0667	1
MIDKIFF WILLIAM R	CW3	W-2211021	1268	1
MIDUSKI THEODORE A	MAJ	0-2036275	0161	1
MIDYETTE ELOISE H	1LT	N-0764353	0946	1
MIEHE PAUL H	LTC	0-0247966	0267	3
MIELE ADOLPH	LTC	0-0383643	0965	1
MIELE ANTHONY C	MAJ	0-2046297	0356	1
MIELKE JOHN W	LTC	0-1042887	0557	1
MIELLY PAUL F	LTC	0-0223578	0651	2
MIELNIK FRANK C	CW3	W-2203268	0763	1
MIESEGAES JULIUS T	COL	0-0221735	0754	3
MIETLOWSKI JOHN F	CW2	W-2150097	0959	1
MIETUS CONRAD A	CPT	0-1691011	0145	2
MIETZEL EWALD E	LTC	0-0256016	0160	2
MIFCOVIC FRANCIS S	LTC	0-0514338	0663	1
MIGDAIL CARL J	CPT	0-0432924	0750	2
MIGHT THOMAS E	MAJ	0-1294342	0461	1
MIGLIACCIO RICHARD P	CPT	0-1342099	1167	1
MIGLIORINO PAUL P	CW4	W-2005805	1268	1
MIGUEL ANTONIO	1LT	0-0890501	1163	1
MIGUES GEORGE F	1LT	0-1293295	0845	2
MIHACHIK ALFRED D	LTC	0-0482573	1263	3
MIHAL GEORGE	CPT	0-1309790	0146	2
MIHALIK MICHAEL	MAJ	0-1290639	0546	2
MIHALKA JOHN G	CW3	W-2145342	0163	1
MIHARA LAWRENCE L	MAJ	0-0937928	0764	1
MIHOC GEORGE A	MAJ	0-1551069	0461	1
MIJAL KAROL P JR	LTC	0-2200111	0767	1
MIKAL JOSEPH	CW3	W-2143385	0963	1
MIKELONIS FLORIAN F	CPT	0-1112321	0662	1
MIKESELL CARL L	LTC	0-0447755	0759	1
MIKESELL FREDERICK	1LT	0-1575003	1044	2
MIKESELL KEITH L	CPT	0-0402768	1046	2
MIKESELL RAY E	MAJ	0-0173821	0751	3
MIKESELL WILLIAM H	CPT	0-0506812	0246	2
MIKKELSEN JOHN F	LTC	0-0525017	0763	1
MIKLAUTSCH JOSEPH	MAJ	0-1054719	0166	1
MIKLES LOWELL	LTC	0-0779935	0767	1
MIKLES MARVIN E	MAJ	0-1824493	1160	1
MIKO RUDOLPH S	1LT	0-1060887	0452	2
MIKOS JOSEPH W	MAJ	0-0975975	0962	1
MIKU NICHOLAS	MAJ	0-2263562	0764	1
MIKULA HELEN M	1LT	N-0800196	0248	1
MIK[illegible] JOHN F	CPT	[illegible]	[illegible]	1
MIKULAS JOHN JR	MAJ	[illegible]	1156	1
MIKULSKY BEN	MAJ	[illegible]	[illegible]	1
MIK[illegible] WILLIAM J	CW3	W-214[illegible]	0261	2
MIK[illegible] NICHOLAS M	LTC	0-1114658	0363	1
MILAM [illegible] H	CPT	[illegible]	0762	2
MILAM DEWITT T	MAJ	[illegible]	1061	2
MILAM GROVER [illegible]	MAJ	[illegible]	[illegible]	1
MILAM HAROLD [illegible]	CPT	[illegible]	1145	2
MILAM JACK M	2LT	[illegible]	0645	2
MILAM ROBERT M	LTC	[illegible]	1160	1
MILAN EDWARD A	LTC	[illegible]	0555	1
MILAN FRED M	MAJ	0-1648045	0461	1
MILANESE HUGH	CW4	W-2136517	1164	1
MILANI FRANK	COL	[illegible]	1051	1
MILANI ALFRED	MAJ	0-0757400	0261	1
MILANI LOUIS	CW2	W-2234645	1262	1
MILAVETZ SIDNEY D	LTC	0-0345617	0168	3
MILAVITZ LLOYD	1LT	0-1692582	0446	2
MILAZZO CHARLES J	LTC	0-1296730	1060	1
MILAZZO FRANK	MAJ	0-0992115	1161	1
MILBERGER JAMES S	CW3	W-2148977	0567	1
MILBERT ATHUR H	MAJ	0-0457749	1145	2
MILBURN ELIZABETH	MAJ	L-0406211	0468	3
MILBURN GEORGE H	CPT	0-1946574	1162	1
MILBURN ROBERT W	COL	0-0117479	0648	3
MILBUT CHARLES W	MAJ	0-2064177	0660	1
MILCH ELMER	CPT	0-0403026	0145	2
MILDE GEORGE K	MAJ	0-1045135	0664	1
MILDNER RUSSELL E	MAJ	0-1311675	0664	1
MILDONIAN GEORGE A	COL	0-0328453	0954	1
MILEHAM RICHARD L	MAJ	0-2262631	1162	1
MILES ANDREW M	MAJ	0-1342486	0561	1
MILES AURELIUS H	MAJ	0-1322065	0647	2
MILES DEWITT M	MAJ	0-1003990	0855	2
MILES DONALD C	1LT	0-1016210	0945	2
MILES EARL H	CPT	0-1171679	0646	2
MILES EDGAR J	LTC	0-1583380	1161	1
MILES FRANK T	MAJ	0-0302737	0367	3
MILES GEORGE W	CW4	W-2111566	0761	1
MILES HARVEY W	CPT	0-0471965	0147	1
MILES HENRY P	CPT	0-1642389	0464	1
MILES JAMES C	MAJ	0-0307536	0654	1
MILES JOHN B	COL	0-0314226	0463	3
MILES JOHN H	MAJ	0-0195488	0762	3
MILES JOHN H	CW3	W-2141380	0661	1
MILES JOHN J	CPT	0-1303756	0455	1
MILES JOHN L	COL	0-0224888	0861	3
MILES LAURENCE A	MAJ	0-1541467	0848	1
MILES LEE G	LTC	0-0326014	0660	1
MILES LEONARD E JR	LTC	0-2014477	0666	2
MILES LEROY M	COL	0-0256942	1267	3
MILES LOUIS A	CPT	0-1590350	0658	2
MILES MABEL M	1LT	N-0724878	0945	1
MILES MARION L	LTC	0-0216181	0263	3
MILES PAUL N	MAJ	0-1294241	0954	1
MILES RALPH F	COL	0-0247740	0959	1
MILES ROBERT C	CW3	W-2152166	1163	1
MILES STUART C	CPT	0-0463571	0748	1
MILES WARD R	CPT	0-0122892	0551	3
MILES WILBUR O	WO1	W-2131636	1145	2
MILES WILLIAM R	MAJ	0-0371094	0352	2
MILES WOODROW B	CW3	W-2145688	0561	1
MILEWSKI ALEXANDER	WO1	W-2123190	1057	1
MILEWSKI JOHN A	CPT	0-0475679	0655	1
MILEWSKI JOSEPH S	CW2	W-2102095	0948	1
MILEY DAVID W	CPT	0-1825033	0346	2
MILEY DONALD H	CW2	W-2123070	1162	1
MILEY HARRY C	MAJ	0-0386293	0161	1
MILEY JOSEPH P	LTC	0-0257770	0268	3
MILEY PERCY	COL	0-0245679	0966	3
MILEY WILLIAM F	CPT	0-0377401	0146	2
MILFORD HOMER C	COL	0-0370270	0447	2
MILFORD JESS F	LTC	0-0461568	0962	3
MILFORD PHILIP L	WO1	W-2133320	0945	2
MIL[illegible] TOM S	COL	[illegible]	0868	3
MIL[illegible] AMBROSE J	MAJ	[illegible]	1163	1
MIL[illegible] MADELINE F	LTC	N-[illegible]	0447	1
MIL[illegible] JOSEPH J	LTC	[illegible]	0361	1
MIL[illegible] JAY G JR	CW2	W-[illegible]	0456	2
MIL[illegible] ALLAN M	[illegible]	[illegible]	1062	1
MIL[illegible] MAX P	LTC	[illegible]	0667	3
MIL[illegible]VICH NICHOLAS	MAJ	[illegible]	0862	1
MIL[illegible] NATHANIEL	LTC	[illegible]	0960	1
MIL[illegible] CHESTER S	LTC	[illegible]	0764	1
MIL[illegible] GEORGE	LTC	[illegible]	0965	1
MILKOVITCH JOHN J	MAJ	0-0495284	0651	1
MILKOWSKI STANLEY J	LTC	[illegible]	0360	1
MILL FREDERICK L	MAJ	[illegible]	0866	1
MILL GEORGE E	LTC	0-1322506	1263	1
MILLA[illegible] ISIDORE B	CPT	[illegible]	0659	1
MILLAM KENNETH F	CW4	W-2135719	0266	1
MILLAN LEWIS C	LTC	0-1049993	1266	1
MILLAR JAMES G	LTC	0-0384371	1266	3
MILLAR JULIAN Z	COL	0-0177854	0861	3
MILLAR LUCIAN R SR	MAJ	0-0974680	1265	1
MILLAR SAMUEL R JR	COL	0-0152908	0249	3
MILLARD ALLAN L	CW4	W-2112115	0256	1
MILLARD FRANK G	COL	0-0182140	0352	3
MILLARD JACK A	LTC	0-0301383	0667	3
MILLARD MOYER R	LTC	0-0918963	0766	3
MILLARD WILLIAM F	MAJ	0-1054720	0261	1
MILLARD WILLIAM J	MAJ	0-0146071	0648	3
MILLARE ULPIANO D	MAJ	0-0267768	0754	2
MILLAS JOHN G	1LT	0-0538150	1045	2
MILLBERRY HAROLD K E	LTC	0-0277885	0154	3
MILLEA EDWARD D	LTC	0-0166772	0656	3
MILLEN PHILIP H	1LT	0-0391251	0146	2
MILLENTHAL BENJAMI	COL	0-0131390	1052	3
MILLER A L	CW2	W-2150098	0556	1
MILLER ABBOTT R	CPT	0-2284130	1061	2
MILLER ABRAHAM L	CPT	0-2049028	0657	1
MILLER ABRAHAM W	LTC	0-0210728	0761	3
MILLER ADRIAN C	CW2	W-2209291	1159	2
MILLER ALBERT H	MAJ	0-0294761	0346	2
MILLER ALBERT K	CW3	W-2141381	0459	1
MILLER ALBERT L	LTC	0-0224298	0363	3
MILLER ALDEE G	CPT	0-1342100	0861	1
MILLER ALEXANDER	COL	0-0227622	0362	3
MILLER ALEXANDER	LTC	0-0264054	1154	3
MILLER ALFRED R	CPT	0-2042789	0251	2
MILLER ALLISON	COL	0-0227448	0155	3
MILLER ALTON L	CW4	W-2124677	1055	1
MILLER AMZIE F	LTC	0-0288745	0963	1
MILLER ANDREW A	MAJ	0-1046896	0359	1
MILLER ANDREW J	MAJ	0-0491192	0251	1
MILLER ANDREW J	LTC	0-1797685	0261	1
MILLER ANN K	2LT	N-0728740	0145	1
MILLER ANNA J	1LT	N-0703596	0746	1
MILLER ANNA L	MAJ	N-0722389	0562	1
MILLER ANNA T	MAJ	N-0755988	0152	2
MILLER ANSON S	LTC	0-0247898	1059	3
MILLER ARCHIBALD	LTC	0-1289771	0663	1
MILLER ARCHIBALD	CW3	W-2150797	0864	1
MILLER ARLYN C	CPT	0-0363436	0868	3
MILLER ARNOLD	LTC	0-1170088	0763	1
MILLER ARNOLD C	CW3	RW-2142980	0862	1
MILLER ART B	COL	0-0297487	0450	2
MILLER ARTHUR E	MAJ	0-2037471	0361	2
MILLER ARTHUR E	CW2	W-2151515	0461	2
MILLER ARTHUR H	LTC	0-0203684	0647	1
MILLER ARTHUR J	CW3	W-2145940	0660	1
MILLER ARTHUR W	LTC	0-0259768	0867	3
MILLER ARTHUR W JR	1LT	0-1302687	0146	2
MILLER AUGUST W	CW2	W-2151752	0862	1
MILLER BARNEY	MAJ	0-1583381	0860	1
MILLER BAYARD A	LTC	0-0308604	0954	1
MILLER BEN W	COL	0-0403582	1060	1
MILLER BENJAMIN H	CPT	0-2262348	1060	1
MILLER BERNARD	MAJ	0-0983380	0763	1

NAME	GRADE	SVC NO	DATE RET MO YR	RET CODE
MILLER BERNARD A SR	CW4	RW-2143035	0164	1
MILLER BERNARD I	WO1	W-2126310	0845	2
MILLER BERNARD N	CPT	O-1324783	0446	2
MILLER BERTHA A	MAJ	N-0730973	0465	3
MILLER BESSIE I	2LT	N-0700586	0337	1
MILLER BEVERLEY E	MAJ	O-1821897	1146	2
MILLER BILLY H	CW3	W-2205346	0367	1
MILLER BRUCE A	CW2	W-2152601	0561	1
MILLER BURNIE L	CW3	W-2147164	1163	1
MILLER CARL	2LT	O-0189342	0442	1
MILLER CARL F	MAJ	O-1332186	0462	1
MILLER CARL P	LTC	O-0255114	0663	3
MILLER CARL S	CPT	O-1300200	1045	2
MILLER CARLETON	CPT	O-1647608	0468	3
MILLER CARMAN D	LTC	O-0230526	0364	3
MILLER CARSON E	MAJ	O-1174959	1061	1
MILLER CATHERINE	MAJ	L-0702037	1162	1
MILLER CECIL D	LTC	O-0320402	0161	1
MILLER CECIL G	LTC	O-1017842	0167	3
MILLER CHARLES A	LTC	O-0143533	0952	3
MILLER CHARLES A	LTC	O-0344915	0967	3
MILLER CHARLES A SR	MAJ	O-1576390	1161	1
MILLER CHARLES E	LTC	O-0212775	1058	3
MILLER CHARLES E	MAJ	O-0451352	1046	2
MILLER CHARLES E	CPT	O-0958859	0361	1
MILLER CHARLES E	CW2	W-2163767	0759	1
MILLER CHARLES G	LTC	O-0397175	1061	2
MILLER CHARLES H	CW2	W-2144892	0857	1
MILLER CHARLES J	COL	O-0268304	0967	3
MILLER CHARLES J	CW3	W-2145326	0959	1
MILLER CHARLES R	LTC	O-1036634	0867	1
MILLER CHARLES R	LTC	O-1312033	0263	1
MILLER CHARLES W	CW3	W-2142883	0862	1
MILLER CHARLEY W	LTC	O-0507313	0164	1
MILLER CHARLIE A	CPT	O-1290105	0666	1
MILLER CHRISTIAN	MAJ	O-0469211	1143	1
MILLER CHRISTOPHE	CW3	W-2144553	0456	1
MILLER CLARENCE G	2LT	O-1177530	1044	2
MILLER CLARENCE H	CW4	W-2120618	1057	2
MILLER CLARENCE M JR	LTC	O-1002075	0363	2
MILLER CLARENCE T	LTC	O-1294174	0665	1
MILLER CLARENCE W	CPT	O-1552340	0958	1
MILLER CLARKE R	WO1	W-2110948	1056	1
MILLER CLAUDE R	CPT	O-1013940	1164	1
MILLER CLYDE C	COL	O-0137540	0850	3
MILLER CONRAD U	LTC	O-1048498	0763	1
MILLER CURTIS	COL	O-0141891	0660	1
MILLER DALE H	LTC	O-2021101	1168	1
MILLER DAN L	COL	O-0189278	1057	1
MILLER DANIEL H	COL	O-0309917	1159	3
MILLER DAVE	LTC	O-1290978	0861	1
MILLER DAVID	MAJ	O-0300695	0646	2
MILLER DAVID	1LT	O-0544916	0345	2
MILLER DAVID A II	CW2	W-2214886	0767	1
MILLER DAVID C	CPT	O-0474470	0847	2
MILLER DAVID C	CW3	W-2144670	0461	1
MILLER DAVID E	CPT	O-0382079	0445	2
MILLER DAVID E	LTC	O-1335336	0767	1
MILLER DAVID G	CPT	O-0486968	0446	2
MILLER DAVID H	WO1	W-2145778	0855	1
MILLER DAVID M	MAJ	O-0408201	1045	2
MILLER DAVID T	LTC	O-1338980	0766	1
MILLER DEARREL A	LTC	O-1299277	1061	1
MILLER DELBERT G	CW3	W-2152243	0964	1
MILLER DEWEY P	CPT	O-0488388	0546	1
MILLER DONALD C	2LT	O-1307989	1044	2
MILLER DONALD J	LTC	O-1016634	0762	1
MILLER DONALD L	LTC	O-1169654	0961	1
MILLER DONALD L	MAJ	O-2002497	1065	1
MILLER DONALD O	LTC	O-2017734	1166	2
MILLER DONALD T	LTC	O-0349953	0666	1
MILLER DUDLEY D	LTC	O-0451502	0957	1
MILLER E C	CW2	W-2143772	1060	1
MILLER EARL B	COL	O-0117497	0445	2
MILLER EDGAR A	MAJ	O-0145978	0648	3

NAME	GRADE	SVC NO	DATE RET MO YR	RET CODE
MILLER EDWARD A	CW2	W-2212797	0268	1
MILLER EDWARD C	LTC	O-1030910	0562	1
MILLER EDWARD J	LTC	O-0184485	0960	3
MILLER EDWARD L	MAJ	O-2014439	0165	1
MILLER EDWARD O	LTC	O-1594634	0861	1
MILLER EDWARD T	MAJ	O-0171516	1050	3
MILLER EDWARD T JR	LTC	O-0241444	1165	3
MILLER EDWARD W	MAJ	O-0518877	0547	2
MILLER EDWARD Z	CW4	W-2150789	0360	2
MILLER EDWIN	COL	O-0256869	0964	3
MILLER EDWIN A	MAJ	O-0482224	0848	2
MILLER EDWIN E	MAJ	O-0330770	0965	3
MILLER EDWIN J	CW3	W-2136661	0762	1
MILLER ELDEN V	CPT	O-0471855	0348	2
MILLER ELLSWORTH	LTC	O-0282831	1254	1
MILLER ELMER C	CW3	W-2210964	0868	1
MILLER ELMER L	COL	O-0247215	0860	3
MILLER ELMER L	CPT	O-1011171	1163	1
MILLER EMANUEL M	LTC	O-0920930	0964	3
MILLER EMILY U	LTC	L-0801003	0765	1
MILLER ERCIL D	LTC	O-1641584	0662	1
MILLER ERNEST E JR	MAJ	O-2046459	1057	1
MILLER ERNEST R JR	LTC	O-1111788	0263	1
MILLER ERWIN E	MAJ	O-0254768	0546	2
MILLER ESKEL N JR	COL	O-0282880	0868	3
MILLER ESTHER A	CPT	L-0304426	0950	2
MILLER EUGENE M	LTC	O-0397838	1262	1
MILLER EUGENE N	CW3	W-2126131	0659	1
MILLER FLOYD R	LTC	O-0190815	0555	3
MILLER FLOYD R	LTC	O-0452665	0161	1
MILLER FRANCES B	2LT	N-0730775	1043	1
MILLER FRANCIS G	MAJ	O-0229839	0562	3
MILLER FRANCIS L	CW3	W-2146407	0361	1
MILLER FRANCIS M	CW2	W-2212662	1266	1
MILLER FRANCIS X	WO1	W-2109647	0747	1
MILLER FRANK J	LTC	O-2046298	0955	2
MILLER, FRANK W	COL	O-0254710	1165	3
MILLER FRED R	LTC	O-0165357	0359	3
MILLER FRED W	1LT	O-0921181	1045	2
MILLER FREDERICK	CPT	O-0131389	1149	3
MILLER FREDERICK	LTC	O-0257401	0262	3
MILLER FREDERICK	CPT	O-0501574	0245	2
MILLER FREDERICK	CW4	W-2002841	0957	3
MILLER FREDERICK	CW3	W-2142479	0863	1
MILLER GEORGE A	LTC	O-0492335	0867	3
MILLER GEORGE C	LTC	O-0251528	0566	3
MILLER GEORGE D	MAJ	O-0223902	0762	3
MILLER GEORGE E JR	CPT	O-1718614	0547	2
MILLER GEORGE F	CPT	O-0292582	0546	2
MILLER GEORGE F	1LT	O-0922872	0945	2
MILLER GEORGE F	CW3	W-2149344	0666	1
MILLER GEORGE F	CW3	W-2153323	1162	1
MILLER GEORGE H	LTC	O-0527353	0664	3
MILLER GEORGE J	CPT	O-1168825	0745	2
MILLER GEORGE K	CPT	O-0258734	1045	2
MILLER GEORGE L	COL	O-0122550	0648	3
MILLER GEORGE M	CPT	O-1032641	0247	2
MILLER GEORGE N	1LT	O-1010694	0344	2
MILLER GEORGE W	MAJ	O-0242075	0563	3
MILLER GEORGE W	2LT	O-1111789	0943	2
MILLER GERALD E	COL	O-0370129	0168	3
MILLER GERALD G	COL	O-0450398	0557	1
MILLER GERALD H	MAJ	O-1795810	0466	1
MILLER GLEN E	1LT	O-0208851	0645	2
MILLER GLEN I	LTC	O-0112278	1155	3
MILLER GLENN R	MAJ	O-0290563	0368	3
MILLER GRANT W	CW2	W-2148006	0359	1
MILLER GRAY O	LTC	O-1180621	0762	1
MILLER GRETCHEN M	CPT	L-0104147	0847	2
MILLER GROVER C	MAJ	O-0164202	1144	2
MILLER GUSTAV A	MAJ	O-0254872	0964	3
MILLER GUY T	CPT	O-2282698	0666	3
MILLER HADLEY B	1LT	O-1044898	0745	2
MILLER HAROLD	WO1	W-2132183	1154	1
MILLER HAROLD A	MAJ	O-1554237	0261	1

NAME	GRADE	SVC NO	DATE RET MO YR	RET CODE
MILLER HAROLD C	COL	O-0297193	1066	3
MILLER HAROLD D	1LT	O-1107593	1150	2
MILLER HAROLD E	MAJ	O-1289120	0266	1
MILLER HAROLD E	2LT	O-1998402	1046	2
MILLER HAROLD F	LTC	O-0385067	0158	1
MILLER HAROLD G	2LT	O-0423184	0145	2
MILLER HAROLD M	CW2	W-2151832	0656	1
MILLER HAROLD N	MAJ	O-1693644	0146	2
MILLER HAROLD P	LTC	O-0316852	0361	1
MILLER HAROLD R	LTC	O-0217806	0162	3
MILLER HAROLD S	1LT	O-0505149	1058	1
MILLER HAROLD T	COL	O-0256098	0464	3
MILLER HARPER B	LTC	O-0258844	0966	3
MILLER HARRY	CPT	O-4005707	0167	1
MILLER HARRY S	CW2	W-2113657	0848	2
MILLER HARVEY	CPT	O-1596938	0654	1
MILLER HENLEY E	COL	O-0401958	0347	2
MILLER HENRY	CPT	O-0404575	1045	2
MILLER HENRY C	LTC	O-0112414	0357	3
MILLER HENRY H	MAJ	O-0105284	1051	2
MILLER HENRY L	LTC	O-0308670	0562	3
MILLER HENRY W	COL	O-0128148	0648	3
MILLER HERBERT D	MAJ	O-0404474	0347	2
MILLER HERBERT F	MAJ	O-0509074	0748	2
MILLER HERBERT P	COL	O-0168239	1054	3
MILLER HERBERT R	MAJ	O-0304870	0467	3
MILLER HERMAN C	CPT	O-0274985	0249	3
MILLER HERMAN S	MAJ	O-1184739	0660	1
MILLER HILLIARD M	MAJ	O-1951321	0868	3
MILLER HIRAM A	COL	O-0125981	0156	3
MILLER HORATIO	COL	O-0101697	0952	3
MILLER HOWARD A	CPT	O-0234488	1065	3
MILLER HOWARD B	LTC	O-0407664	0461	1
MILLER HOWARD E	MAJ	O-1686661	0264	1
MILLER HOWARD F	1LT	O-1647184	0845	2
MILLER HOWARD F	MAJ	O-1951592	1064	1
MILLER HOWARD P	MAJ	O-1290106	1060	1
MILLER HUGH	CW2	W-2212203	0668	1
MILLER IRV I	1LT	O-1030067	1045	2
MILLER J ALLEE	CPT	O-0334874	1060	1
MILLER JACK	2LT	O-0494662	0445	2
MILLER JACK	1LT	O-1304098	0446	2
MILLER JACK	CPT	O-1306448	0955	1
MILLER JACK E	MAJ	O-1311417	0261	1
MILLER JACK R	1LT	O-1288422	1145	2
MILLER JACKSON H	CW2	W-2150554	1062	1
MILLER JACKSON P	LTC	O-1796833	0464	1
MILLER JACOB	CPT	O-0201260	0147	1
MILLER JAMES A	LTC	O-0131420	0648	3
MILLER JAMES A	CPT	O-1636337	0360	1
MILLER JAMES C	MAJ	O-0360833	1055	2
MILLER JAMES C	CW3	W-2142596	0460	1
MILLER JAMES D	LTC	O-0910016	0564	3
MILLER JAMES E	LTC	O-0569408	0461	1
MILLER JAMES F	COL	O-0190774	0162	3
MILLER JAMES F JR	MAJ	O-0964941	0261	1
MILLER JAMES H	MAJ	O-1168379	0364	1
MILLER JAMES I	MAJ	O-2319721	1267	1
MILLER JAMES K	COL	O-0404244	1060	1
MILLER JAMES L JR	MAJ	O-0414114	1061	1
MILLER JAMES M	COL	O-0456235	0861	1
MILLER JAMES R	LTC	O-1032374	0964	1
MILLER JAMES R	CW2	W-2152710	0562	1
MILLER JAMES S	CW3	RW-2147989	0861	1
MILLER JAMES T	MAJ	O-1308845	0461	1
MILLER JAMES W	LTC	O-0295518	0352	2
MILLER JAMES W	LTC	O-0453632	0661	1
MILLER JOE H	CPT	O-0514146	1145	2
MILLER JOE J	COL	O-0182171	0748	3
MILLER JOHN A	COL	O-0355517	0447	2
MILLER JOHN A	CW3	W-2150752	0358	1
MILLER JOHN B	MAJ	O-1824086	1163	1
MILLER JOHN D	MAJ	O-0282474	1167	3
MILLER JOHN D	2LT	O-1292217	0843	2
MILLER JOHN D	CW4	W-2001993	0365	1

NAME	GRADE	SVC NO	DATE RET MO YR	RET CODE
MILLER JOHN E	LTC	O-0255225	0166	3
MILLER JOHN E	CPT	O-1109518	0467	2
MILLER JOHN E	LTC	O-1294515	1060	1
MILLER JOHN E	CPT	O-2200607	0664	2
MILLER JOHN G	CPT	O-0295829	1045	2
MILLER JOHN H	LTC	O-0238556	0365	3
MILLER JOHN H	1LT	O-0526270	0145	2
MILLER JOHN H	CPT	O-1297405	0147	1
MILLER JOHN M	MAJ	O-0450463	0658	1
MILLER JOHN R	MAJ	O-1551072	0861	1
MILLER JOHN W	LTC	O-0215514	0245	2
MILLER JOHN W	LTC	O-0547130	0367	1
MILLER JOHN W	MAJ	O-0885652	0261	1
MILLER JOHNNIE C	CPT	O-1685616	0261	1
MILLER JOSEPH	COL	O-0368625	1264	1
MILLER JOSEPH	CPT	O-1100693	0446	2
MILLER JOSEPH B	LTC	O-0298989	0562	1
MILLER JOSEPH D	2LT	O-2049657	0545	2
MILLER JOSEPH H	LTC	O-1285472	0258	1
MILLER JOSEPH J	CPT	O-0447936	0744	2
MILLER JOSEPH J	CPT	O-4006595	1264	1
MILLER JOSEPH L	CW3	W-2150538	0167	1
MILLER JOSEPH R	MAJ	O-1826243	0261	1
MILLER JOSEPH T JR	MAJ	O-1283087	0955	1
MILLER JOSEPH W	2LT	O-0202524	1263	3
MILLER JUANITA H	MAJ	N-0804046	0868	2
MILLER JULIUS A	CW4	W-2109161	1059	1
MILLER JUNIOR F	M G	O-0385454	0667	3
MILLER K C	CW3	W-2149301	0463	1
MILLER KELSIE E	COL	O-0201443	0858	3
MILLER KENNETH F	LTC	O-0237807	1263	3
MILLER KENNETH W	MAJ	O-1574294	0757	1
MILLER LA CLAIR P	LTC	O-1691855	0765	3
MILLER LARGENT M	MAJ	O-1649879	0965	1
MILLER LARRY C	1LT	O-1321800	0945	2
MILLER LAURANCE O	LTC	O-1110129	0361	3
MILLER LAWRENCE T	LTC	O-0471964	0855	1
MILLER LEO W	LTC	O-1635118	0462	1
MILLER LEON	CPT	O-1581278	0446	2
MILLER LEONARD L JR	LTC	O-1578867	0761	1
MILLER LEROY K	MAJ	O-0995515	0666	2
MILLER LEROY L	CW3	W-2205250	0863	1
MILLER LESLIE B	LTC	O-2010594	0368	1
MILLER LEWIS C	LTC	O-0451353	1163	1
MILLER LEWIS C	MAJ	O-1917586	0265	1
MILLER LILA G	MAJ	N-0767450	0868	3
MILLER LLOYD E	LTC	O-0445885	0854	1
MILLER LLOYD E	WO1	W-2125447	0747	2
MILLER LOUELLA	MAJ	N-0784584	0364	1
MILLER LOUIS A	1LT	O-2008452	1046	2
MILLER MARCEL V	CPT	O-0302345	0845	2
MILLER MARCUS C	CW4	W-2003563	0464	1
MILLER MARCUS E	LTC	O-0235346	1063	3
MILLER MARGARET J	1LT	N-0767675	0845	1
MILLER MARIE B	MAJ	N-0737540	1162	1
MILLER MARION M	CW2	W-2149352	0659	1
MILLER MARK G	LTC	O-0483957	0163	3
MILLER MARLYN W	LTC	O-0317191	0746	2
MILLER MARTIN J	CW3	W-2142651	0265	1
MILLER MARTIN K	LTC	O-0268160	0568	3
MILLER MARTIN P	1LT	O-1328173	0147	2
MILLER MARVIN C	WO1	W-2146307	0153	2
MILLER MARY A	MAJ	N-0762377	0764	1
MILLER MARY S	1LT	N-0763335	1144	1
MILLER MARY W	MAJ	N-0737027	1063	1
MILLER MAURICE B	LTC	O-1639724	0761	1
MILLER MAXWELL	LTC	O-0492686	0161	1
MILLER MAXWELL E	1LT	O-1308677	0544	2
MILLER MAYNARD B	MAJ	O-0983407	0264	1
MILLER MELVILLE H	LTC	O-0147637	1146	2
MILLER MEYER G	COL	O-0330532	0568	3
MILLER MICHAEL M	MAJ	O-0462720	0945	2
MILLER MICHAEL S	LTC	O-0685766	0361	1
MILLER MILES C	CW3	W-2153331	0467	1
MILLER MILLARD C	MAJ	O-1031740	0158	1

NAME	GRADE	SVC NO	DATE RET MO YR	RET CODE	NAME	GRADE	SVC NO	DATE RET MO YR	RET CODE	NAME	GRADE	SVC NO	DATE RET MO YR	RET CODE	NAME	GRADE	SVC NO	DATE RET MO YR	RET CODE
MILLER MINNIE G	MAJ	N-0741134	0965	1	MILLER ROY L	MAJ	0-1295580	1046	2	MILLER WILLIAM T	CW4	W-2132990	1167	1	MILLS JOHN F	1LT	0-1018939	0348	2
MILLER MOORE H	MAJ	0-0372072	0264	1	MILLER ROY V	MAJ	0-0246716	1165	1	MILLER WILLIAM V	CPT	0-0171228	0753	1	MILLS JOHN F	LTC	0-1117687	0466	2
MILLER MORRIS	COL	0-0291069	0765	1	MILLER RUBIN B	LTC	0-0295766	0566	3	MILLER WILLIE	CW3	W-2153002	0962	1	MILLS JOHN J	MAJ	0-1307551	0862	1
MILLER MORRIS A	LTC	0-0257444	0965	1	MILLER RUDOLPH A	CW4	W-2145468	0767	1	MILLER WILLIE F	LTC	0-0531127	0763	1	MILLS JOSEPH A	MAJ	0-1552753	0166	1
MILLER MORRIS F	2LT	0-0516324	0145	1	MILLER RUSSEL W	LTC	0-0453035	0555	1	MILLER WILLIS C	MAJ	0-1633018	0847	1	MILLS LAWRENCE E	1LT	0-1303177	0546	2
MILLER MYRA F	1LT	N-0796837	0255	2	MILLER RUSSELL B	1LT	0-0310782	0746	2	MILLER WILLIS T	MAJ	0-1176653	0557	1	MILLS LEO W	COL	0-0292356	1059	3
MILLER MYRTLE M	2LT	N-0726405	0145	1	MILLER RUSSELL S	CW2	W-2208073	1060	2	MILLER WOODROW H	CPT	0-1043269	1146	2	MILLS LEONARD J	MAJ	0-1651866	1265	2
MILLER NATHAN	CPT	0-1692028	0546	2	MILLER SAMUEL A	MAJ	0-1185098	0759	1	MILLER WYTHE R	1LT	0-1112868	0845	2	MILLS LLOYD F	LTC	0-0382807	0569	1
MILLER NOEL	LTC	0-0244264	0167	3	MILLER SAMUEL D	1LT	0-0544988	1045	2	MILLERE EDMOND S	2LT	0-0117268	1052	3	MILLS MAMIE E	2LT	N-0702363	0837	1
MILLER NORMAN D	CPT	0-1114660	0348	2	MILLER SAMUEL E	COL	0-0325116	0166	3	MILLERLICE WILLIAM A	CPT	0-1825242	1262	2	MILLS MELBOURNE	LTC	0-0225692	0163	3
MILLER NORMAN J	CW3	W-2152593	0662	1	MILLER SAMUEL F	2LT	0-0368931	0440	2	MILLET GORDON Y	LTC	0-0265012	0367	3	MILLS MILTON E	CW2	W-2139833	0763	1
MILLER NORMAN W	MAJ	0-0493341	0752	1	MILLER SAMUEL H	LTC	0-1014451	0861	1	MILLETT EDWARD B	LTC	0-0450085	1056	1	MILLS ORBIN W	CW3	W-2148127	0460	1
MILLER OLEN F	LTC	0-0519652	0267	1	MILLER SAMUEL L	MAJ	0-0289391	0245	2	MILLETT JOHN C JR	1LT	0-0452118	0-47	2	MILLS OTIS M	MAJ	0-1969615	0356	1
MILLER ORAL D	LTC	0-1684315	0467	1	MILLER SAMUEL R	CPT	0-1688143	0146	2	MILLHAM MERLE P	CPT	0-1553875	0646	2	MILLS PAUL T	CW2	W-2150016	1058	1
MILLER ORAN J	CW4	W-2140687	0963	1	MILLER SANFORD L	1LT	0-1302162	0445	2	MILLHISER CHARLES II	COL	0-0246017	0966	3	MILLS PERCY H	1LT	0-1289297	0761	1
MILLER ORLA G	COL	0-0165260	1150	3	MILLER SAUL	CPT	0-0471863	0246	2	MILLHOLLAND RANDOLPH	COL	0-0259648	1066	3	MILLS RAYMOND C JR	CW3	W-2149172	0866	1
MILLER ORVAL J	COL	0-0257219	0567	3	MILLER SEWELL A	CPT	0-2009709	0960	1	MILLICAN ARNIE L	LTC	0-0455326	0256	1	MILLS REVIS L	MAJ	0-0965267	1060	1
MILLER OTHMAR J	MAJ	0-0275064	0859	1	MILLER SEYMOUR M	1LT	0-0374245	0246	2	MILLICAN CHARLES B	COL	0-0168470	0659	3	MILLS RICHARD F	1LT	0-1281105	1145	2
MILLER PAGE L	LTC	0-0339386	0562	1	MILLER SHELDON F	CW2	W-3440037	0868	1	MILLICAN FRED J JR	LTC	0-1055096	0866	1	MILLS ROBERT E	LTC	0-1647156	1163	1
MILLER PAUL	LTC	0-1311418	0457	1	MILLER SIDNEY C	CPT	0-1286331	0746	2	MILLICAN LEWIS M JR	LTC	0-1324043	1061	2	MILLS ROBERT L	LTC	0-1347781	0663	1
MILLER PAUL C	LTC	0-1291308	1060	1	MILLER STANLEY	1LT	0-1824897	1045	2	MILLICAN MAURICE E	CW3	W-2148750	0760	1	MILLS ROY	MAJ	0-1039802	1054	1
MILLER PAUL C	CW2	W-2152436	0758	1	MILLER STANLEY H	MAJ	0-1577570	1055	1	MILLICAN WOODROW M	WO1	W-2132841	0654	1	MILLS ROY R	CPT	0-0491825	0148	1
MILLER PAUL J	LTC	0-1585905	0763	1	MILLER TAFT	MAJ	0-1648609	0160	1	MILLIGAN ALEXANDER	LTC	0-0143867	0542	2	MILLS WALTER R	LTC	0-0178123	0153	3
MILLER PAUL J	CW4	W-2003418	0163	2	MILLER TED A	CW2	W-3440061	1168	1	MILLIGAN ANDREW J	CPT	0-0272817	1049	1	MILLS WILLIAM H	COL	0-0243756	1163	3
MILLER PAUL M JR	2LT	0-1055674	0545	2	MILLER THERMAN D	CW2	W-2146384	1158	1	MILLIGAN CLARE B	LTC	0-0508805	0557	1	MILLS WILLIAM L JR	MAJ	0-1309591	0946	2
MILLER PAUL R	LTC	0-0333840	1059	3	MILLER THOMAS A	COL	0-0231720	0363	3	MILLIGAN JAMES J	COL	0-0123695	0352	3	MILLSAPS ROBERT M	CW3	W-2149353	1163	1
MILLER PAUL W	LTC	0-0342290	0663	1	MILLER THOMAS A	CPT	0-1011289	0949	1	MILLIGAN JAMES M	CW2	W-3150406	1168	1	MILLSAPS WOODROW W	LTC	0-1303923	0457	1
MILLER PHILIP J	1LT	0-0450399	0246	2	MILLER THOMAS B	LTC	0-0381770	0764	3	MILLIGAN LIONEL C	LTC	0-0218038	0763	3	MILLSPAUGH ROY O	MAJ	0-4063720	1068	1
MILLER PHILIP L	LTC	0-0384270	0161	1	MILLER THOMAS G	COL	0-0248057	0965	3	MILLIGAN LOWELL A	COL	0-0289190	0763	3	MILLSTINE WALTER A	1LT	0-1102868	0745	2
MILLER PHILLIP C	MAJ	0-1877762	0666	1	MILLER THOMAS H	CW2	W-2105345	1048	1	MILLIGAN RICHARD L	CW3	W-2145689	1266	1	MILLWARD JAMES M	MAJ	0-0245164	1047	2
MILLER PHILLIP H	LTC	0-1106314	1263	1	MILLER THOMAS T	LTC	0-0260176	0368	3	MILLIGAN ROBERT L	CPT	0-0329441	1043	2	MILLWOOD WILLIAM H	MAJ	0-0975604	0863	1
MILLER QUENTON C	CW4	W-2145072	1067	1	MILLER VERN W	LTC	0-0273767	1265	3	MILLIKEN BASIL C JR	MAJ	0-0970992	0264	2	MILMORE JOHN F JR	1LT	0-1295926	0145	2
MILLER RALPH D	MAJ	0-4005328	0765	1	MILLER VICTOR	1LT	0-1591318	104N	2	MILLIKEN JOHN O	1LT	0-1327562	0446	2	MILMORE OSWALD H	COL	0-0262617	0258	3
MILLER RALPH E	LTC	0-1548505	0162	1	MILLER VICTOR N	MAJ	0-0169670	0356	3	MILLIKEN LYMAN F	COL	0-0302278	0565	3	MILNE DOUGLAS B	MAJ	0-0362269	0446	2
MILLER RALPH K	2LT	0-2001046	0555	1	MILLER VINCENT A	COL	0-0311937	0963	3	MILLIKEN RAYMOND W	1LT	0-1314175	0551	2	MILNE WALTER L	MAJ	0-1012497	0765	1
MILLER RALPH L	COL	0-1048112	0767	1	MILLER VINCENT F	1LT	0-0528922	0746	2	MILLIKEN ROBERT M	COL	0-1031198	0667	1	MILNER ALFRED S	1LT	0-1326006	0845	2
MILLER RAYMOND	CPT	0-0478194	0556	1	MILLER VIRGIL J	CPT	0-0510577	1049	1	MILLIKEN TOM T	CPT	0-0531128	0248	2	MILNER DONALD S	CW3	W-2146704	0965	1
MILLER RAYMOND A	LTC	0-0343482	0855	1	MILLER VIRGIL L	CW2	W-3430169	0566	1	MILLIKIN WILLIAM E	LTC	0-0157112	0950	3	MILNER EVERETT W	CPT	0-0215048	0346	2
MILLER RAYMOND A	MAJ	0-0451010	1157	1	MILLER WALLACE C	LTC	0-1176134	0267	1	MILLING JAMES W	CPT	0-1062825	1058	1	MILNER GEORGE L	LTC	0-0283149	1168	3
MILLER RAYMOND C	1LT	0-0367479	0645	2	MILLER WALTER C	CW2	W-2114477	0345	2	MILLINGTON CARL A	MAJ	0-0910322	1047	2	MILNER GIFF C	CPT	0-0331485	0850	2
MILLER RAYMOND D	CPT	0-0489753	0847	1	MILLER WALTER J	MAJ	0-0503935	1054	1	MILLINGTON GILBERT E	COL	0-1173387	1268	1	MILNER JAMES E	LTC	0-0397773	0160	1
MILLER RAYMOND E	MAJ	0-1877080	1165	1	MILLER WALTER L	MAJ	0-0415970	1263	2	MILLIREN JAMES L	MAJ	0-1186121	0764	1	MILNER JOE W	1LT	0-0216134	0844	2
MILLER RAYMOND M	CW3	W-2153063	0266	1	MILLER WALTER L	COL	0-0530956	1163	1	MILLIS EDWARD L	COL	0-0203228	0754	3	MILNER JOSEPH A	LTC	0-0333203	0346	2
MILLER REUBEN S	CW3	W-2147906	0861	1	MILLER WALTER M	1LT	0-1113363	1144	2	MILLMAN HYMAN	CPT	0-0499187	0643	2	MILO CHARLES A	1LT	0-1692403	0346	2
MILLER REX K	COL	0-0240936	1045	2	MILLER WALTER R	MAJ	0-1314309	0359	2	MILLNER ROSE	MAJ	N-0720760	0662	2	MILOGLAV OLGA H	2LT	N-0769216	1045	1
MILLER RICHARD A	2LT	0-1306127	0744	2	MILLER WALTER W	2LT	0-0300802	0467	3	MILLNER WILLIAM D	MAJ	0-0502762	0854	1	MILOSOVIC ROBERT T	CPT	0-1119884	0258	1
MILLER RICHARD C	CPT	0-0540381	1046	2	MILLER WARREN S JR	COL	0-0208432	1056	3	MILLON JOHN R	2LT	0-0379676	0541	2	MILROY LOIS M	MAJ	L-0909273	0867	1
MILLER RICHARD S	MAJ	0-1923552	0465	1	MILLER WAYLAND L	COL	0-0190144	0457	2	MILLOT ALFRED E	COL	0-0294601	0768	3	MILSTEAD CLAUDE W	1LT	0-1013564	0845	2
MILLER ROBERT	LTC	0-1315089	0666	1	MILLER WAYNE	LTC	0-0263109	0662	3	MILLS ABRAHAM A	1LT	0-0507310	1144	2	MILSTEAD FINLEY E	LTC	0-0370885	0962	2
MILLER ROBERT A	MAJ	0-1080128	0166	1	MILLER WAYNE J	MAJ	0-0808702	0566	1	MILLS ALBERT R	LTC	0-0307825	0364	3	MILSTEAD JACK F	MAJ	0-1535379	0863	1
MILLER ROBERT A	LTC	0-1581968	0866	1	MILLER WAYNE K	MAJ	0-2020325	0462	1	MILLS ANDREW J	MAJ	0-0103363	0245	2	MILSTEAD OSCAR V JR	CPT	0-1920133	0563	1
MILLER ROBERT B	CW3	W-2208195	1066	1	MILLER WELDON M	MAJ	0-0291139	0968	3	MILLS ARCHIBALD	COL	0-0195197	0457	3	MILSTEIN PHILIP	COL	0-0507374	0967	3
MILLER ROBERT D	CPT	0-0247897	0564	3	MILLER WESLEY A	CPT	0-0312258	0345	2	MILLS ARTHUR E	LTC	0-0540017	0766	1	MILSTER ARTHUR N	MAJ	0-0214915	0462	3
MILLER ROBERT E	1LT	0-1108174	0945	2	MILLER WILBUR K	LTC	0-0298984	0645	2	MILLS AVERY G	MAJ	0-1031010	1058	1	MILTON JAMES A	MAJ	0-0166869	0456	3
MILLER ROBERT E	CW3	W-2208508	0968	1	MILLER WILBUR L	LTC	0-1118952	1063	1	MILLS CHARLES F	MAJ	0-1057539	0562	1	MILTON JOHN O	COL	0-0281807	0346	2
MILLER ROBERT F	CPT	0-0536751	0847	2	MILLER WILBURN M	MAJ	0-1044920	0958	1	MILLS CHARLES H	COL	0-0214538	1061	3	MILTON MAURICE O	MAJ	0-1312197	0758	1
MILLER ROBERT F	MAJ	0-0972891	1267	1	MILLER WILLARD W	MAJ	0-0494698	0759	2	MILLS CLARENCE L	LTC	0-1546070	0167	1	MILTON PAUL H	COL	0-0302684	0657	1
MILLER ROBERT F	LTC	0-1058328	0766	1	MILLER WILLIAM	1LT	0-1534815	0346	2	MILLS CLYDE R	LTC	0-0415788	1160	1	MILTON 2ND HUGH M	M G	0-0154541	0357	3
MILLER ROBERT G	2LT	0-1591317	1044	2	MILLER WILLIAM A	COL	0-0264108	1062	3	MILLS DAVID B	LTC	0-0979574	0368	1	MILTONBERGER B B	M G	0-0197801	0947	2
MILLER ROBERT H	COL	0-0362051	0661	1	MILLER WILLIAM A	CPT	0-0326303	0746	2	MILLS DONALD C	LTC	0-0465011	1154	1	MILTZ CHARLES R	LTC	0-1174385	0763	1
MILLER ROBERT J	LTC	0-0109354	0147	1	MILLER WILLIAM A	CW2	W-2313518	1068	1	MILLS DONALD D	MAJ	0-0443924	0446	1	MILWARD STANLEY	MAJ	0-0265678	0867	3
MILLER ROBERT L	MAJ	0-4006403	0368	1	MILLER WILLIAM D	1LT	0-1796834	0945	2	MILLS DOYLE W	MAJ	0-1014830	0862	1	MILYO RAYMOND L	LTC	0-1341689	1167	1
MILLER ROBERT M	LTC	0-0388301	1160	1	MILLER WILLIAM E	WO1	T-0067512	0962	2	MILLS DREXEL G	MAJ	0-1881215	0266	1	MIMNA CURTIS T	LTC	0-0452477	0957	1
MILLER ROBERT N	1LT	0-1288275	1145	2	MILLER WILLIAM H	MAJ	0-0335423	0465	3	MILLS EARL F	CW3	W-2118539	0262	1	MIMONI LEONARD J	1LT	0-1017717	0945	2
MILLER ROBERT P	M G	0-0256068	1063	3	MILLER WILLIAM H	CPT	0-1308359	1145	2	MILLS ELBERT B	CPT	0-1822600	0259	1	MIMS FLOYD C	MAJ	0-0149919	0849	1
MILLER ROBERT P	1LT	0-1324641	0145	2	MILLER WILLIAM J	LTC	0-0396269	0466	1	MILLS EMMA L	MAJ	N-0752851	1264	2	MIMS RICHARD B	LTC	0-0330997	1060	1
MILLER ROBERT W	LTC	0-0555413	0865	2	MILLER WILLIAM J	MAJ	0-0588548	1060	1	MILLS FRANK R	1LT	0-0108458	0124	1	MIMS ROBERT H	MAJ	0-1046204	0665	3
MILLER RODMAN D	COL	0-0341721	0867	3	MILLER WILLIAM J JR	CW2	W-2148283	0667	1	MILLS GUY G	COL	0-0163227	0648	3	MINARD ALDACE W	LTC	0-0244650	0866	3
MILLER ROGER L	LTC	0-1823759	1167	1	MILLER WILLIAM K	COL	0-0330280	0866	1	MILLS HAROLD N	LTC	0-0226731	1055	3	MINARD CHARLES H	CPT	0-1011242	0359	1
MILLER ROGER R	CW2	W-2142057	0553	1	MILLER WILLIAM L	CPT	0-1322646	1050	2	MILLS HARRISON T	CW3	W-2208568	1267	1	MINARIK GEORGE	LTC	0-0305177	0561	1
MILLER ROGER W	LTC	0-1041618	0267	2	MILLER WILLIAM L	CW2	W-2148329	1262	1	MILLS HENRY L	1LT	0-1016873	0246	2	MINCER CHARLES T	LTC	0-1283996	1064	1
MILLER ROLLAND S	1LT	0-0176897	1044	2	MILLER WILLIAM M JR	MAJ	0-1595710	1262	1	MILLS HENRY P	MAJ	0-0125022	1054	3	MINCEY TALMADGE W	CW2	W-2145825	0359	1
MILLER RONALD D	LTC	0-0273175	1067	3	MILLER WILLIAM P	MAJ	0-0997170	0961	1	MILLS HERMAN W	MAJ	0-1951111	1058	1	MINCHEW JAMES C	LTC	0-1319308	0967	1
MILLER ROY A	CPT	0-1996567	0660	1	MILLER WILLIAM R	1LT	0-1047766	0745	2	MILLS HOWARD M	CPT	0-0223464	0537	1	MINCKE JULIUS H	MAJ	0-0195713	0860	3
MILLER ROY J	LTC	0-0104979	0439	1	MILLER WILLIAM R	LTC	0-1178257	1162	1	MILLS JAMES R	1LT	0-0318819	0146	2	MINEHAN EDWARD H	CW3	W-2144283	0866	1

NAME	GRADE	SVC NO	DATE RET MO YR	RET CODE
MINEHAN ROBERT A	CPT	0-1333996	1060	1
MINER CHESTER C	CPT	0-0183507	0-50	3
MINER GEORGE F	LTC	0-1168832	0161	1
MINER HARRY C	1LT	0-1053261	1144	2
MINER HARRY F	LTC	0-0248501	1055	1
MINER JAMES G	CW3	W-2207995	0667	1
MINER JOE F	COL	0-0281796	0460	1
MINER KENNETH L	CPT	0-0216314	0848	3
MINER MARY C	MAJ	N-0703417	0666	1
MINER RILEY P	CW3	0-0246278	1160	1
MINER WILLIAM R	CPT	0-1299449	0846	2
MINER WILLIS C	LTC	0-0214612	0652	2
MINERVA LOUIS L	CW2	W-2142109	0556	1
MINFORD 3RD LEVIS W	1LT	0-0403159	0245	2
MINGHI LAWRENCE J	LTC	0-1112870	0761	1
MINGLEDORFF MARVIN S	LTC	0-0260266	0864	3
MINGS JAMES W	CW3	W-2004832	0167	1
MINICHIELLO LEWIS A	COL	0-0228378	0463	1
MINICI JOE P	CPT	0-0904614	0545	2
MINICK FLETCHER E	CW3	W-2149672	1165	1
MINICK ROBERT O	CPT	0-0137236	0251	3
MINICUS JOHN F	CPT	0-0513196	1046	2
MINIE ALBERT G	CW2	W-2210521	0763	1
MINIER EARL F	LTC	0-0147687	1156	3
MINIETTA CHARLES	LTC	0-1179545	0763	1
MINIKES SOLETTE E	COL	0-0112356	0154	1
MINIUM DON	CPT	0-0210100	0247	1
MINKE KARL A	CPT	0-0319305	1148	2
MINKIN LJBA F	MAJ	N-0755130	0264	3
MINKIN SARAH R	MAJ	N-0796473	0465	3
MINKS FLOYD A	LTC	0-0287950	0866	3
MINNER MAURICE H	CW3	W-2147179	0662	1
MINNER MORRIS G	COL	0-0190552	0648	3
MINNERATH JOHN M	CW4	W-2146754	0868	1
MINNEY HAROLD F	MAJ	0-1550662	0760	1
MINNICH SAMUEL T	LTC	0-1289942	0457	1
MINNICH THEODORE O	MAJ	0-1334194	0865	2
MINNICK JAMES H	1LT	0-1539004	114N	2
MINNICK KENNETH E	2LT	0-0411476	0245	2
MINNIS JESSE H	CPT	0-0507106	0647	1
MINNIS RAYMOND L	CPT	0-0507105	0448	1
MINNIK ELMER	CW3	W-2141383	0859	1
MINNS ALBERT E JR	COL	0-0389183	0661	1
MINNS JOHN S	MAJ	0-0482313	0951	1
MINOR BRUCE J	2LT	0-1056813	0944	2
MINOR EUGENE M	LTC	0-1575009	0259	1
MINOR JAMES A	CPT	0-0499580	0-53	1
MINOR JOE	COL	0-0211969	0146	2
MINOR MILLER G	1LT	0-2020832	0847	2
MINOR PAYSON S	CPT	0-0211689	0960	3
MINOR WALTER H	LTC	0-0233557	0165	3
MINOR WILLARD H	CPT	0-0491922	0953	1
MINOS ALEXIS P	LTC	0-0191672	1050	3
MINOTT ERNEST L	CPT	0-0282798	0024	1
MINSHAW WILLIAM C	LTC	0-0313437	0948	1
MINSON KENNETH M	MAJ	0-1595713	0961	1
MINSTER RICHARD F	1LT	0-0470930	0545	2
MINTER JOHN E JR	CPT	0-0367122	0345	2
MINTER JOHN L	LTC	0-0259954	0268	3
MINTER LEE R	MAJ	0-1290981	0960	1
MINTER WILLIAM R	LTC	0-0215776	0663	3
MINTHORN BLAIR C	MAJ	0-0497371	0954	1
MINTO THOMAS M	MAJ	0-2014559	0164	1
MINTON RHEUBEN O	MAJ	0-1548260	1056	2
MINTON WILFRED M	LTC	0-1172553	1263	1
MINTZ ABRAHAM	1LT	0-1292040	0845	2
MINYARD ROBERT L	LTC	0-1309793	0167	1
MINYO ANDREW	MAJ	0-1643138	0261	1
MIRAGLIA FRANCIS	LTC	0-1284913	0468	3
MIRAKIAN PETER	COL	0-1286165	0868	1
MIRANDA ANTONIO	MAJ	0-0888977	0760	1
MIRANDA EDUARDO	LTC	0-1320388	C968	1
MIRANDA RAFAEL J	COL	0-0152050	1157	3
MIRE EVARICE C	LTC	0-0125019	0649	2
MIREE JAMES W C	LTC	0-0288908	1266	3

NAME	GRADE	SVC NO	DATE RET MO YR	RET CODE
MIRSKY LOUIS H	1LT	0-0384706	0745	2
MISCHAK WILLIAM	LTC	0-1056814	0268	1
MISCHKE CHARLES G	CW2	W-2214839	0767	1
MISCHKER ERWIN J	MAJ	0-1181375	0163	2
MISCHLER PAUL B	MAJ	0-0988301	0166	1
MISCHO ISADORE W	CW2	W-2103768	0952	1
MISENER EARLE C	LTC	0-1314042	0764	1
MISENHEIMER HARVEY N	COL	0-0222236	0660	3
MISERENDINO ANTHONY	MAJ	0-1882362	0965	1
MISHLER IVAN N	1LT	0-1331539	0961	1
MISHOU THOMAS F JR	LTC	0-0113298	0653	3
MISIEWICZ CHESTER C	MAJ	0-1101580	0758	1
MISIEWICZ VICTOR J	MAJ	0-1535501	0161	1
MISKILL HOWARD P	CPT	0-1117919	0954	2
MISKIMON ROBERT M	CPT	0-0419830	0146	2
MISKOWICH DONALD T	MAJ	0-1053262	1164	1
MISKOWSKI MICHAEL	CW3	W-2150943	1061	1
MISLOCK RAYMOND A	LTC	0-0482480	0-52	1
MISS DAVID C	LTC	0-0404817	1060	1
MISSAL MORRIS E	LTC	0-0465627	0845	2
MISSALL MAYNARD M	LTC	0-0182960	0453	3
MISSALL MAYNARD M JR	LTC	0-0375302	1060	1
MISSILDINE CHARLES E	MAJ	0-4010904	0967	1
MISSILDINE JACK A	2LT	0-2009753	0356	1
MISSIMER CARROLL	LTC	0-0188901	1053	3
MISTLER HERMAN C	LTC	0-1186267	1163	1
MISTRETTA JOSEPH F	MAJ	0-0912061	1067	3
MITCHAM CAMERON L	1LT	0-1284188	1145	2
MITCHAM EDWARD H	LTC	0-0195672	0446	2
MITCHELL ARCHIE B	1LT	0-1286871	1045	2
MITCHELL ARTHUR C	MAJ	0-1340010	0362	2
MITCHELL ARTHUR L	MAJ	0-0258942	1058	1
MITCHELL ARTHUR S	MAJ	0-0108043	0652	3
MITCHELL AUGUSTUS H	LTC	0-0303409	1061	1
MITCHELL BEN F	COL	0-0210697	0362	3
MITCHELL BERNARD A	MAJ	0-1703815	1053	1
MITCHELL BERTHA O	2LT	N-0728048	0343	1
MITCHELL BILL L	LTC	0-1639746	1161	1
MITCHELL BYRON G	MAJ	0-2024125	0466	1
MITCHELL CHARLES A	CW2	W-2152770	0762	1
MITCHELL CHARLES B	LTC	0-0203136	1043	2
MITCHELL CHARLES F	1LT	0-1043173	0145	2
MITCHELL CHESTER E	LTC	0-0276467	0445	2
MITCHELL CLAUDE Q JR	CPT	0-1591943	1265	3
MITCHELL CLIFFORD	MAJ	0-2010959	0457	1
MITCHELL CLYDE F	LTC	0-1331206	0568	1
MITCHELL CLYDE W	MAJ	0-2017102	0363	1
MITCHELL DONALD E	LTC	0-0900769	0364	3
MITCHELL DONALD M	LTC	0-0267390	1068	3
MITCHELL DOUGLAS C	LTC	0-0231068	0263	3
MITCHELL EARL W	LTC	0-1542875	1163	1
MITCHELL EARLE W	LTC	0-0389354	0162	1
MITCHELL ED L	CW3	W-2147126	0164	1
MITCHELL EDWARD E	LTC	0-1283651	0961	1
MITCHELL EDWARD V	CW2	W-2142175	1053	1
MITCHELL EDWIN O	MAJ	0-0374020	0761	1
MITCHELL ELLIOTT C	CPT	0-1648395	0962	1
MITCHELL ELMER E	LTC	0-0256078	0460	1
MITCHELL EUGENE M	MAJ	0-1928160	0167	1
MITCHELL EVAN H	CPT	0-0326110	0644	2
MITCHELL FLOYD	CPT	0-1286532	0147	2
MITCHELL FRANKLIN A	LTC	0-0502254	1164	3
MITCHELL FRED	LTC	0-1319310	1165	1
MITCHELL FRED	CW3	W-2146934	0156	1
MITCHELL FRED G	LTC	0-0371572	1060	1
MITCHELL GABRIEL G	WO1	W-2118109	1044	2
MITCHELL GARLAND H	CPT	0-2006762	0757	1
MITCHELL GEORGE E	MAJ	0-2014794	0266	1
MITCHELL GEORGE F	COL	0-0277610	0260	3
MITCHELL GEORGE J JR	LTC	0-0461738	1262	1
MITCHELL GLADYCE V	CPT	N-0729023	0355	2
MITCHELL GOUVERNEUR	MAJ	0-1535944	1262	1
MITCHELL GUY	CW2	W-2148835	0457	1
MITCHELL HAROLD C	MAJ	0-0480761	0345	2
MITCHELL HAROLD E	CPT	0-0180309	0555	3

NAME	GRADE	SVC NO	DATE RET MO YR	RET CODE
MITCHELL HAROLD W	LTC	0-0276438	0268	3
MITCHELL HARRY H	1LT	0-0432371	0445	2
MITCHELL HERBERT H	COL	0-0218635	1055	3
MITCHELL HOLLAND C	COL	0-0312767	1166	3
MITCHELL HUGH A	LTC	0-0334055	0846	2
MITCHELL IVERSON O	MAJ	0-1690911	1062	1
MITCHELL JAMES A	MAJ	0-0217237	0548	1
MITCHELL JAMES A JR	LTC	0-0174841	0760	3
MITCHELL JAMES F	CPT	0-0369992	0944	2
MITCHELL JAMES F	1LT	0-1307282	0945	2
MITCHELL JAMES F JR	COL	0-0294760	1163	3
MITCHELL JAMES M	CPT	0-1319311	0767	2
MITCHELL JAMES W	LTC	0-0338672	0868	3
MITCHELL JAMES W	CPT	0-2262526	0163	1
MITCHELL JESS	CW4	W-2104311	0259	1
MITCHELL JOHN A	COL	0-0101966	0655	3
MITCHELL JOHN B	CPT	0-0443958	0946	2
MITCHELL JOHN L	LTC	0-0351003	0761	1
MITCHELL JOHN P	1LT	0-2030503	0853	2
MITCHELL JOHN S	LTC	0-0481194	0657	1
MITCHELL JOSEPH A	CW4	W-2120015	0565	1
MITCHELL JOSEPH G	2LT	0-0408839	0844	2
MITCHELL JOSEPH H	LTC	0-0268888	0665	3
MITCHELL JOSEPH H	CW2	W-2152975	1062	1
MITCHELL JOSEPH L	MAJ	0-0275559	0961	3
MITCHELL LAURENCE C	1LT	0-2033208	0264	2
MITCHELL LAWRANCE J	LTC	0-0416477	0466	3
MITCHELL LEONARD T	1LT	0-1305628	0146	2
MITCHELL LEROY S	MAJ	0-1561977	0561	2
MITCHELL LEWIS A	CW4	W-2122604	0466	1
MITCHELL LEWIS B	LTC	0-0511847	0564	2
MITCHELL LIONEL C	CPT	0-1923553	0363	1
MITCHELL LOUIS A	CPT	0-0124251	1049	3
MITCHELL LUTHER M SR	MAJ	0-1185917	0263	1
MITCHELL MACK C	MAJ	0-0964371	1266	1
MITCHELL MALCOLM L	LTC	0-1181041	0862	1
MITCHELL MARION R	MAJ	N-0764579	0768	1
MITCHELL MARVIN E	LTC	0-0342455	0657	1
MITCHELL MAURICE M	COL	0-0122871	0653	3
MITCHELL MAX H	MAJ	0-4031243	0368	1
MITCHELL MERLE S	COL	0-0180305	0251	2
MITCHELL MIZPAH R	MAJ	N-0762465	0468	1
MITCHELL NEAL SR	MAJ	0-1998339	0657	1
MITCHELL NORMAN L	MAJ	0-1825160	1060	1
MITCHELL OLIVER C	MAJ	0-0269117	0965	3
MITCHELL ORREN R	LTC	0-0465218	0967	1
MITCHELL PAUL E	CPT	0-1319433	1163	1
MITCHELL PAUL M	LTC	0-0169397	0758	3
MITCHELL PAUL O	COL	0-0238161	1054	1
MITCHELL PAUL W	MAJ	0-2047073	0665	1
MITCHELL PHILIP H	MAJ	0-0318552	0546	2
MITCHELL RALPH R	MAJ	0-0963857	0862	1
MITCHELL RALPH J	COL	0-0140483	1050	2
MITCHELL RAYMOND L	LTC	0-1312967	0568	1
MITCHELL RICHARD L	COL	0-0308507	1065	3
MITCHELL RICHARD L	CW2	W-3250579	1168	1
MITCHELL ROBERT C	LTC	0-1047690	0761	1
MITCHELL ROBERT F	LTC	0-0237122	1265	3
MITCHELL ROBERT E	LTC	0-0304765	0968	3
MITCHELL ROBERT F	LTC	0-0365295	0859	1
MITCHELL ROBERT L	MAJ	0-0237438	0366	3
MITCHELL ROBERT L	CPT	0-0978766	0960	1
MITCHELL ROBERT W	MAJ	0-0281149	0468	3
MITCHELL ROBERT W	LTC	0-2057983	0168	1
MITCHELL ROGER S	MAJ	0-0506263	0545	2
MITCHELL RUSSELL A	LTC	0-0301357	0967	3
MITCHELL SAMUEL C	1LT	0-1313035	0845	2
MITCHELL SAMUEL T	1LT	0-1031423	0246	2
MITCHELL SANDEFER	LTC	0-0959323	0965	1
MITCHELL SHELTON O	LTC	0-0962243	0766	1
MITCHELL THOMAS A	LTC	0-1039120	0962	1
MITCHELL THOMAS O	COL	0-0316016	0158	3
MITCHELL THOMAS O	MAJ	0-1170095	0264	1
MITCHELL THOMAS R	MAJ	0-1875123	0764	1
MITCHELL VICTOR G	MAJ	0-2097585	1167	1

NAME	GRADE	SVC NO	DATE RET MO YR	RET CODE
MITCHELL WALLACE A	LTC	0-0217850	0163	3
MITCHELL WALTER E	CW2	W-2145826	0457	2
MITCHELL WALTER L	MAJ	0-2032961	1064	1
MITCHELL WALTER M	CPT	0-0301386	0755	3
MITCHELL WAYNE G	CW2	W-2212930	0268	1
MITCHELL WILLIAM	CW2	W-2110106	1044	2
MITCHELL WILLIAM A	CPT	0-0370884	1144	2
MITCHELL WILLIAM A	LTC	0-2009327	1064	1
MITCHELL WILLIAM D	MAJ	0-1111247	0858	1
MITCHELL WILLIAM G	MAJ	0-1032033	0161	1
MITCHELL WILLIAM P	LTC	0-0451075	1146	2
MITCHELL WILLIAM S	LTC	0-0261157	0767	3
MITCHELL WILLIS F	LTC	0-1185590	0264	1
MITCHELL WINIFRED A	CPT	N-0784091	0657	2
MITCHEM WILLIAM E	2LT	0-1324465	0952	2
MITCHUM ARTHUR F	CPT	0-0371640	0247	2
MITMAN THOMAS R	MAJ	0-1287564	0661	1
MITNIK PAUL	CW3	W-2142177	0660	1
MITREGA JOHN P	MAJ	0-2047753	0859	1
MITRICK JOSEPH M	CPT	0-0423573	1045	2
MITRO GEORGE JR	MAJ	0-2000754	0763	1
MITROS ROBERT J	CW3	W-2148089	0563	1
MITTAG HERBERT C	MAJ	0-1115041	0367	3
MITTANCK ERHARD H	COL	0-0238457	0366	3
MITTELSTAEDT R E	B G	0-0102218	0648	3
MITTENTHAL HARRY H	MAJ	0-0890239	0154	1
MITTON WALTER G	MAJ	0-0269470	0866	3
MITTY WILLIAM F	LTC	0-1597872	0667	3
MITZEL PAUL C	CW2	W-2214521	0866	1
MITZEN LAWRENCE	LTC	0-0448383	0954	1
MITZEN STANLEY	COL	0-0885655	1154	1
MIX GALE L	MAJ	0-0212403	1262	3
MIX STANLEY M	LTC	0-0399259	0161	1
MIX WILBUR M	CPT	0-0421918	0146	2
MIXON CHARLIE F	CW3	W-2146262	0764	1
MIXON CLAUDE R	LTC	0-0355028	0566	3
MIXON EARL R	CPT	0-0269583	0151	1
MIXON JACK C	CW2	W-2149053	0660	1
MIXON JOE J	LTC	0-0341003	0668	3
MIXON JOSEPH F	WO1	W-2145827	1155	2
MIXON QUINTON J	2LT	0-2212004	1052	2
MIXON THOMAS F	CW3	W-2149448	1267	1
MIXON WILLIAM M	1LT	0-2016277	1058	1
MIXON WINBOURN M	MAJ	0-1043437	0557	1
MIYAGISHIMA TERUO	MAJ	0-0996127	0865	1
MIYAKE HOWARD Y	CPT	0-2055907	1147	2
MIYAMOTO HARRY H	2LT	0-2055889	0645	2
MIYAMOTO THEODORE T	CW2	W-2214507	1167	1
MIZDAIL EUGENE B	MAJ	0-1172555	0561	1
MIZE ERVIN W	CW3	W-2141385	0761	1
MIZE WALLACE L	LTC	0-0313392	0954	1
MIZELL GEORGE C	LTC	0-2210004	0867	1
MIZELL JOE T JR	COL	0-0310853	0763	3
MIZELL WINTON R	LTC	0-0410532	0966	1
MIZER FLOYD R	CPT	0-1701090	0246	2
MIZER GEORGE L	LTC	0-1580045	0662	1
MIZER WARREN H	CW3	W-2205442	0764	1
MIZUHA JACK H	CPT	0-0331006	0944	2
MIZUTA RICHARD K	MAJ	0-0331007	1046	2
MIZZI DOMENICO	LTC	0-1895743	0567	3
MIZZLES MARVIN R	CW2	W-2212798	1068	1
MLAZGAR JOHN D	1LT	0-2035889	0545	2
MLINAR JOHN F	CW3	RW-2146460	0262	1
MLODZIANOWSKI FRANK	CW2	W-2207055	0766	1
MOA JOHN A	MAJ	0-1541368	0159	1
MOAK GIFFORD E	CW4	W-2112228	0965	1
MOAK HARRY G	1LT	0-1301009	0746	2
MOAK JOHN C JR	MAJ	0-1688359	0266	1
MOAK STERLING L	LTC	0-0262076	0468	3
MOAK VERNON J	CW3	W-2117996	0653	1
MOALE JOHN F	MAJ	0-0462467	0662	1
MOATS GEORGE E	CW2	W-2151622	0463	1
MOATS WENDELL A	CPT	0-1311567	0147	2
MOBERG PHYLLIS H	MAJ	N-0754157	0665	1
MOBILIO JOSEPH A	LTC	0-0237701	0464	3

NAME	GRADE	SVC NO	DATE RET MO YR	RET CODE
[illegible]	LTC	[illegible]	[illegible]	3
[illegible]	1LT	[illegible]	[illegible]	1
[illegible]	LTC	[illegible]	[illegible]	[illegible]
[illegible]	LTC	[illegible]	[illegible]	[illegible]
[illegible]	MAJ	[illegible]	[illegible]	3
[illegible]	LTC	[illegible]	[illegible]	3
[illegible]	1LT	[illegible]	[illegible]	1
[illegible]	LTC	[illegible]	[illegible]	[illegible]
[illegible]	COL	[illegible]	[illegible]	1
[illegible]	MAJ	[illegible]	[illegible]	[illegible]
[illegible]	LTC	[illegible]	[illegible]	3
[illegible]	CW4	W-[illegible]	[illegible]	1
MOCK [illegible]	2LT	[illegible]	1159	1
MOCK [illegible] L	1LT	[illegible]	0465	2
MOCK [illegible]	CPT	[illegible]	0651	2
MOCK HARVEY [illegible]	1LT	0-1540046	[illegible]	1
MOCK JOHN H	LTC	0-1313569	1161	1
MOCK JOSEPH J	CPT	0-0103550	0351	3
MOCK LEWIS V	CPT	0-1011239	0448	2
MOCK [illegible] R	CPT	0-1101123	0448	1
MOCK WALTER H	CPT	0-1307376	0664	1
MOCKBEE JACK	LTC	0-0494370	0854	1
MOCKUS JOHN	LTC	0-0402510	0946	2
MOCNIS JOHN JR	LTC	0-0399992	0457	2
MOCZYGEMBA NORBERT W	CW3	W-2153372	0267	1
MODDER LAWRENCE	CPT	0-0267345	0858	3
MODERN LOUISE	CPT	N-0737751	0646	2
MODICA MARTIN M	MAJ	0-2050304	0463	1
MODINE CARL F	LTC	0-1046569	0261	1
MODISETT SHIRLEY A	CPT	0-0412767	1045	2
MODISETT TOM F	MAJ	0-1339200	0265	1
MODJESKE EUGENE J	LTC	0-0354547	1168	3
MODLIN ELBRIDGE L	COL	0-0142756	1153	1
MODRAK JOHN J JR	1LT	0-1019141	0546	2
MODZIKOWSKI THADDEUS	CPT	0-0508471	1144	2
MOE CHARLES B	MAJ	0-0548345	1166	1
MOE FORREST L	1LT	0-0147261	0456	3
MOE GEORGE F	1LT	0-1181964	0846	2
MOE JAMES	LTC	0-1547722	0763	1
MOE JOHN J	MAJ	0-1540924	0564	1
MOE LEWIS H	COL	0-0240883	0261	3
MOE LLOYD D	2LT	0-1110664	0245	2
MOE MAX E	LTC	0-0399172	0367	1
MOE THEODORE F	MAJ	0-0245284	1065	3
MOEBIUS MARY F	2LT	N-0777458	1046	1
MOEBIUS WILLIAM H	LTC	0-1648768	0267	3
MOECK HOWARD F	MAJ	0-1549555	0557	1
MOECKEL VIOLA L	MAJ	L-1010100	0368	1
MOEGLE EDGAR L	COL	0-0221809	0756	3
MOEHLE EDWIN L	CPT	0-0404785	0645	2
MOEHLMAN ARTHUR H	COL	0-0357462	0367	3
MOELLER ALICE G	MAJ	L-0701347	0463	1
MOELLER GEORGE W	LTC	0-0414178	1065	1
MOELLER LOWELL J	LTC	0-0321229	0461	3
MOELLER SIGURD F	1LT	0-1167548	0745	2
MOELLER WALTER J	LTC	0-1290642	1060	1
MOELLERING CARL W	MAJ	0-0168818	0959	3
MOELLERS LAWRENCE T	LTC	0-0454680	0457	1
MOELLINGER MAX JR	LTC	0-0420562	0761	1
MOEN CHARLES B	1LT	0-1331540	1152	2
MOEN JAMES L	MAJ	0-1583395	0261	1
MOEN MARCUS M	LTC	0-0258702	0945	2
MOERLS JOHN H	MAJ	0-1173717	1060	1
MOESE OTTO H	MAJ	0-0304463	0664	3
MOESSNER KARL F	COL	0-0256125	0467	3
MOFFAT FRASER M JR	COL	0-0140551	0857	3
MOFFATT JOSEPH F	LTC	0-1108177	0462	1
MOFFET ROBERT F	B G	0-0220503	1058	3
MOFFETT ALBERT L	CPT	0-0475296	0947	1
MOFFETT COLEMAN J	LTC	0-1725606	0766	1
MOFFETT DONALD F	MAJ	0-2263097	0164	1
MOFFETT WILLIAM R	1LT	0-1302503	0544	2
MOFFIE ELEANOR E	MAJ	L-0300053	1062	1
MOFFIT FRANCIS G	LTC	0-1016954	1057	1
MOFFITT ALBERT H JR	COL	0-0262184	0268	3

NAME	GRADE	SVC NO	DATE RET MO YR	RET CODE
MOFFITT CARL E	MAJ	0-1812921	0657	1
MOFFITT EDWARD P	MAJ	0-1037732	0962	1
MOFFITT EDWARD V	CW3	W-2152893	0763	1
MOFFITT FREDERICK	MAJ	0-0237376	0646	2
MOFFITT GEORGE N	LTC	0-0256779	0457	3
MOFFITT JOSEPH A	CW3	W-2143222	1262	1
MOFFITT LAWRENCE C	COL	0-0308263	1065	3
MOFFITT LESTER W	CW3	W-2142566	0358	1
MOFFITT MARSHALL T	MAJ	0-2000500	0962	1
MOFFITT RUSSELL F	MAJ	0-0327734	1063	3
MOFFITT THOMAS D	CPT	0-0476234	0434	1
MOGAN EARLEY E	COL	0-0274836	1068	3
MOGAN FRANCIS M JR	MAJ	0-4006494	0867	1
MOGAN THOMAS E JR	MAJ	0-2006843	0262	1
MOGEL VICTOR L	CW3	W-2152497	0764	1
MOGIEL CHARLES J	CW3	W-2089285	0267	3
MOGLIA JOHN J	CPT	0-2262260	0161	1
MOGUL ROBERT	MAJ	0-1535243	0264	1
MOHAN FRANK P	MAJ	0-0328086	1059	3
MOHAN JOHN J	2LT	0-1115042	0145	2
MOHAN RAYMOND P	1LT	0-1168382	0244	2
MOHAN STANLEY P	1LT	0-0372370	1266	3
MOHART HAROLD A	CW3	W-2104315	1054	1
MOHEN EUGENE J	LTC	0-0303602	1059	1
MOHER JEREMIAH W	LTC	0-1298900	0364	1
MOHLER ARTHUR E	MAJ	0-2011796	0465	1
MOHLER CHARLES E	MAJ	0-0122266	0648	3
MOHLER CHARLES R	MAJ	0-2051257	0963	1
MOHLER DON B	MAJ	0-0317963	1159	1
MOHLER DONALD P	1LT	0-1102871	0946	2
MOHLER FRANKLIN C	LTC	0-0361054	0168	3
MOHLER FRANKLIN R	CW3	W-2109142	1060	1
MOHLER GALEN P	WO1	W-2126308	1058	1
MOHLER HARRY A	LTC	0-0278906	0863	3
MOHLER JOHN A	COL	0-0386389	0761	1
MOHLER LEWIS H	CW3	W-2147442	0464	1
MOHLER RALPH H	LTC	0-1550005	1162	1
MOHLER ROBERT L	MAJ	0-0304305	0568	3
MOHLER SAMUEL C JR	MAJ	0-0355683	0660	1
MOHLER SIDNEY G	CPT	0-0492057	1045	2
MOHLER WILLIAM A	MAJ	0-1042115	1148	2
MOHN SAMUEL P	LTC	0-1080049	1061	1
MOHNEY EARL JR	2LT	0-1184264	0446	2
MOHNEY ROBERT R	CPT	0-1165657	0955	1
MOHOLY JOSEPH O	LTC	0-1047246	0764	1
MOHR DONALD M	1LT	0-0382142	0245	2
MOHR FREDERICK	COL	0-0262137	0366	3
MOHR GEORGE W	CPT	0-0515270	1047	2
MOHR GORDON D	LTC	0-1018564	0964	1
MOHR GUSTAV C	LTC	0-0255928	1161	3
MOHR HAROLD D	CW3	W-2147881	0263	1
MOHR HARRY C	LTC	0-1299609	0562	1
MOHR HENRY A	MAJ	0-1045533	0359	1
MOHR JAMES	CPT	0-1295758	0346	2
MOHR NORMAN F	MAJ	0-1184415	0164	1
MOHR RAY M	MAJ	0-0173731	0861	3
MOHR WALTER C	LTC	0-0274257	0347	2
MOHR WILLIAM H	COL	0-0250342	0866	3
MOHRHAUSER ROBERT W	MAJ	0-0265522	1157	3
MOHRMANN JOHN M	COL	0-0347389	0967	3
MOILAN DONALD W	LTC	0-2017737	0866	2
MOIR EDWIN G	CPT	0-0488640	0244	2
MOIR JACK R	LTC	0-0494984	0154	2
MOISAN PHILIP K	COL	0-0208175	0748	2
MOISELLE WILLIAM	LTC	0-0140650	0152	3
MOITOZO JOHN G	CW2	W-2213905	1168	1
MOKLER JOHN F	CW3	W-2152933	0666	1
MOKRI FRANCIS J	CW3	W-2148555	0662	1
MOLO NEIL W	MAJ	0-2208440	0461	1
MOLDENHAUER OSCAR A	COL	0-0232749	1160	3
MOLE ALBERT L	LTC	0-1300065	0461	1
MOLENDA EDWIN A	CW2	W-2149935	0860	1
MOLENGRAFT CORNELIUS	COL	0-0309630	1262	3
MOLETTE ROBERT C	LTC	0-0251787	0465	3
MOLINARI PETER L	LTC	0-0291732	0967	3

NAME	GRADE	SVC NO	DATE RET MO YR	RET CODE
[illegible]	2LT	[illegible]	[illegible]	[illegible]
[illegible]	CPT	[illegible]	[illegible]	[illegible]
[illegible]	LTC	[illegible]	1066	[illegible]
[illegible]	WO1	W-[illegible]	[illegible]	1
[illegible]	CPT	[illegible]	[illegible]	[illegible]
MOLL [illegible]	COL	[illegible]	[illegible]	1
MOLL [illegible]	LTC	[illegible]	[illegible]	[illegible]
MOLLART ARTHUR [illegible]	LTC	[illegible]	1165	3
[illegible] JOSEPH W	MAJ	[illegible]	[illegible]	1
MOLLEMA JOHN	MAJ	[illegible]	[illegible]	1
MOLLENKOPF HERBERT L	MAJ	[illegible]	[illegible]	3
MOLLER JOHN H	MAJ	0-1800134	0163	1
MOLLICA ALFONSO A	CW2	W-2149412	0762	1
MOLLISH FRANK E	MAJ	0-0967825	0263	1
[illegible] JOSEPH M	LTC	0-0550992	0367	3
MOLLOY EDWARD A	MAJ	0-1031175	0561	1
MOLLOY EDWARD T	MAJ	0-1696663	0363	1
MOLLOY JAMES A	1LT	0-0148497	0648	3
MOLLOY LOGAN H	1LT	0-0443034	0645	2
MOLLOY WILLIAM M	LTC	0-0171112	1159	3
MOLMEN ARMAN P	LTC	0-1290286	0364	1
MOLNAR MIKE	CPT	0-0488708	0454	1
MOLNAR PAUL M	1LT	0-1106967	0545	2
MOLNAR STEPHEN G	LTC	0-0272152	0366	3
MOLNAR THEODORE T	COL	0-0257383	0359	3
MOLNER ALBERT Y	1LT	0-0321173	0564	3
MOLOHON ALBIN D	MAJ	0-0250147	0460	3
MOLOHON CHARLES W	MAJ	0-1821499	0861	1
MOLOHON MARTIN J	CW2	W-3440021	0765	1
MOLONEY ROBERT C	CPT	0-0454510	0346	2
MOLONY FRANK E	LTC	0-0125246	0648	3
MOLOVINSKY DAVID E	CW4	W-2146396	0566	1
MOLSEE DAVID C	CW2	W-2147265	0657	1
MOLTER ALBERT C	COL	0-0249936	0160	1
MOLTER HENRY T	LTC	0-1166423	1060	1
MOLTHAN ALBERT L	1LT	0-1341567	0259	1
MOLTRUP CHARLES H	CW3	W-2145044	0162	1
MOLTZ JOHN H JR	CPT	0-1584622	0746	2
MOLTZ LESTER H	LTC	0-1312318	1266	3
MOLUMBY JOHN R	MAJ	0-1555734	0259	1
MOMAN GEORGE H	MAJ	0-1292219	0361	1
MOMCILOVICH MICHAEL	LTC	0-1001196	0758	1
MOMEYER GERALD R	COL	0-0255257	0660	1
MOMEYER KENNETH W	COL	0-0179260	0356	3
MOMII TOM T	LTC	0-1330457	0965	1
MONA JOSEPH D	MAJ	0-0279612	1166	3
MONACO HUGO I	CW2	W-2210697	0865	1
MONACO RAYMOND T	1LT	0-1822431	0344	2
MONACO RAYMOND W	2LT	0-1297080	0344	2
MONAGAN JOHN S III	1LT	0-1575475	0344	2
MONAGHAN JACK H	CW2	W-2005755	0468	3
MONAGHAN LORETTA H	1LT	N-0796175	0147	1
MONAGHAN ORLOFF	LTC	0-0452923	0465	3
MONAGHAN ROBERT W	MAJ	0-1824347	0464	1
MONAGHAN THOMAS J	LTC	0-1287565	0861	1
MONAHAN CHARLES E	CPT	0-0489602	0351	1
MONAHAN FRED V	1LT	0-1666568	0147	2
MONAHAN JAMES J JR	MAJ	0-1314043	0761	2
MONAHAN JOHN P	CPT	0-1170873	0348	2
MONAHAN JOSEPH W	CW2	W-2211148	0365	1
MONAHAN MARTIN C JR	CW3	W-2153126	1062	2
MONAHAN PATRICK	1LT	0-1324562	0550	1
MONAHAN PHILIP D	1LT	0-0408701	0744	2
MONAHAN STEPHEN D	LTC	0-0224102	0149	3
MONAHAN THOMAS F	MAJ	0-2021224	0466	2
MONASMITH MAURICE L	MAJ	0-0305969	0863	1
MONCK QUENTIN U	1LT	0-1167993	1145	2
MONCRIEF HAYWARD A	LTC	0-0302369	0565	3
MONCRIEF JOHN F	MAJ	0-2016632	0962	1
MONCRIEF LEWIS F	LTC	0-0394750	0162	1
MONCRIEF WALLACE B	CW4	W-2142178	1262	1
MONCUR JAMES W	1LT	0-1284914	0945	2
MONCURE WILLIAM A	LTC	0-2052234	1167	3
MONDA ANTHONY	CW2	W-2141386	1154	1
MONDELLI HUGO J	1LT	0-1297081	0546	2

NAME	GRADE	SVC NO	DATE RET MO YR	RET CODE
[illegible]	CW3	[illegible]	[illegible]	1
[illegible]	CPT	[illegible]	1067	1
[illegible]	LTC	[illegible]	[illegible]	3
[illegible]	[illegible]	[illegible]	[illegible]	1
[illegible]	MAJ	[illegible]	[illegible]	1
[illegible]	[illegible]	W-[illegible]	[illegible]	2
[illegible]	MAJ	[illegible]	[illegible]	1
[illegible]	CPT	0-0481288	0267	1
[illegible] CHARLES J	MAJ	[illegible]	0663	1
[illegible]	1LT	0-1018568	0450	2
[illegible] WILLIAM [illegible]	LTC	[illegible]	0363	1
MONGAN HOWARD J	1LT	[illegible]	1146	2
[illegible] NICHOLAS J	CW3	W-2152476	0245	1
MONK ARCHIE [illegible]	1LT	0-2023803	0858	1
MONK GALLOWAY	LTC	0-1551147	0469	1
MONK GEORGE F	LTC	0-0256717	0667	3
MONK JAMES F JR	MAJ	0-0217481	0564	3
MONK LEWIS J	MAJ	0-0323045	1164	3
MONK MARION M	LTC	0-1035417	0263	1
MONK ROBERT S	2LT	0-1302566	0943	2
MONKHOUSE GEORGE R	CPT	0-1524669	0663	1
MONKS CHARLES J JR	LTC	0-1797506	0262	1
MONLEON PETER D	MAJ	0-0523111	0453	2
MONLEZUN CLYDE J	LTC	0-1552341	0757	1
MONNERAT JOSEPH E JR	LTC	0-0419990	0161	1
MONNESS IRA H	LTC	0-1945647	1264	3
MONNIER CHARLES S	COL	0-0353106	0468	3
MONRO WILLIAM J	CW4	W-2144751	1057	1
MONRO 3RD WILLIAM L	1LT	0-0496731	0745	2
MONROE CHARLES H	MAJ	0-1688599	0566	1
MONROE CLYDE W	CPT	0-0283657	1044	2
MONROE DOUGLAS A	CW4	W-2001749	0669	3
MONROE ERNEST M	LTC	0-0267273	0147	1
MONROE HARLAN B	COL	0-0267055	0358	3
MONROE HARMON L	CPT	0-0463655	1045	2
MONROE HOWARD J	COL	0-0302846	0162	3
MONROE JAMES F	CW4	W-2115897	0359	1
MONROE JAMES LEWI	2LT	0-1999889	1051	2
MONROE JOHN JR	MAJ	0-1920319	0766	1
MONROE LEWIS A	1LT	0-2035962	0945	2
MONROE MARION H	1LT	0-1400684	0145	2
MONROE ROBERT W	LTC	0-1054068	1063	1
MONROE STEPHEN C	COL	0-0906558	0466	1
MONROE TONY F	CPT	0-0108514	0829	1
MONROE ULYSSES G	MAJ	0-1298098	0561	1
MONROE WILLIAM J	CPT	0-1174387	1146	2
MONROE WILLYS M	LTC	0-0202966	0850	3
MONSEES ALBERT J	CPT	0-1765987	0247	2
MONSEN MANLEY B	MAJ	0-0264014	0163	3
MONSERRATE LUIS A	CPT	0-1327368	0862	1
MONSON WENDELL L	LTC	0-2046428	0763	1
MONSOUR THOMAS B	LTC	0-1175808	0962	1
MONSSON C DOUGLAS	LTC	0-0242569	0164	3
MONT CHARLES P	CW4	W-2112034	0157	1
MONTAGUE DOROTHY S	2LT	N-0727236	0345	1
MONTAGUE EDGAR S	COL	0-0155971	0355	3
MONTAGUE EDWARD T	CPT	0-0415544	0445	2
MONTAGUE GLEN H	1LT	0-1639417	0648	2
MONTAGUE JAMES L	LTC	0-0175732	0755	3
MONTAGUE LUDWELL L	COL	0-0255454	0967	3
MONTANA FRANK R	CPT	0-0470610	0244	2
MONTANO ANTONIO	CW2	W-2126143	0648	1
MONTASSER AHMAD S	MAJ	0-1647192	0456	1
MONTAVON LORETTA V	1LT	N-0755304	0446	1
MONTBRIAND FRANCIS H	MAJ	0-1648051	0757	1
MONTE ANGELO J	LTC	0-1545833	0366	2
MONTE RUPERTO	1LT	0-1896597	1149	1
MONTEALEGRE FRANCISC	LTC	0-0235390	0564	3
MONTECALVO JOSEPH	CPT	0-0944661	0365	1
MONTEDONICO JAMES H	2LT	0-1587473	1044	2
MONTEE MATTHEW P	CPT	0-0742594	0859	1
MONTEFUSCO EDWARD	COL	0-0266239	0964	3
MONTEGUT JAMES J JR	MAJ	0-1582756	0263	1
MONTEITH CHARLES D	MAJ	0-0187060	0648	3
MONTEITH COLIN S JR	COL	0-0193925	1262	3

ARMY OF THE UNITED STATES RETIRED LIST

NAME	GRADE	SVC NO	DATE RET MO YR	RET CODE
MONTEITH JAMES G	LTC	O-1305459	1266	1
MONTEITH ROBERT E	CPT	O-1291152	0759	1
MONTELEONE MAURICE D	LTC	O-0455268	1163	1
MONTEMARANO VINCEN	CPT	O-0331553	0246	2
MONTER GERALD	1LT	O-1018392	1045	2
MONTERO JOSE A	MAJ	O-0988302	0163	1
MONTES ABRAM	CPT	O-2007393	0566	1
MONTES ISIDRO	1LT	O-1896818	0258	1
MONTFORT GEORGE R	CW2	W-2212981	0467	1
MONTFORT WILLIAM H	CPT	O-0363238	0346	2
MONTGOMERY ALBERTIS	LTC	O-0172919	0450	3
MONTGOMERY ALF R	MAJ	O-1577585	0461	1
MONTGOMERY AVERY L	1LT	O-1050389	0345	2
MONTGOMERY CAL	WO1	W-2120031	0557	1
MONTGOMERY CARMEN	CPT	N-0774446	0847	1
MONTGOMERY CHARLES B	MAJ	O-0989214	0666	1
MONTGOMERY CHARLES C	MAJ	O-0332710	1045	2
MONTGOMERY CHARLES W	LTC	O-1176736	0366	2
MONTGOMERY CLIFFORD	MAJ	O-0237640	1265	3
MONTGOMERY DONALD E	1LT	O-0427901	1044	2
MONTGOMERY DOROTHEA	MAJ	L-0400814	0664	3
MONTGOMERY EARL B	LTC	O-1183370	1266	1
MONTGOMERY EARL W	1LT	O-1308346	0545	2
MONTGOMERY EARLE S	LTC	O-0141589	0553	3
MONTGOMERY EDWARD F	CPT	O-1325230	0248	2
MONTGOMERY EDWARD H	MAJ	O-2020195	0462	2
MONTGOMERY ELIJAH P	LTC	O-0259953	0467	3
MONTGOMERY FRANCIS C	LTC	O-0255015	0752	3
MONTGOMERY GEORGE W	1LT	O-0927578	1046	2
MONTGOMERY HARRY H	CW3	W-2144035	0661	1
MONTGOMERY HENRY K	CPT	O-0345147	0845	2
MONTGOMERY HERMAN E	MAJ	O-0956187	0761	1
MONTGOMERY HOMER T	LTC	O-1110137	0964	1
MONTGOMERY HUGH B	MAJ	O-0358114	0266	1
MONTGOMERY HUGH R	LTC	O-0188089	0648	3
MONTGOMERY JACK	LTC	O-1035545	1164	1
MONTGOMERY JAMES E	MAJ	O-0677104	0766	1
MONTGOMERY JEWEL D	1LT	O-0788380	0752	2
MONTGOMERY JOHN A JR	LTC	O-1112873	0668	3
MONTGOMERY JOHN W	COL	O-0334082	0551	2
MONTGOMERY JONATHAN	CW2	W-2152163	1063	1
MONTGOMERY JOSEPH B	LTC	O-0285862	0646	2
MONTGOMERY JOSEPH M	LTC	O-0339444	0168	3
MONTGOMERY JOSEPH R	LTC	O-1326163	0765	1
MONTGOMERY KENNETH A	CPT	O-0211858	1162	3
MONTGOMERY KENNETH L	CW4	W-2113294	0862	1
MONTGOMERY LLOYD P	CPT	O-1287741	0448	2
MONTGOMERY MAYS E	1LT	O-0462876	0945	2
MONTGOMERY ORIN R	MAJ	O-0226151	0545	2
MONTGOMERY PAUL R	MAJ	O-2035433	1060	1
MONTGOMERY PHILIP V	MAJ	O-1330338	0766	1
MONTGOMERY QUINN F	CPT	O-0232391	0245	2
MONTGOMERY RAY	MAJ	O-1110138	0760	1
MONTGOMERY RAYMOND A	LTC	O-1296561	0361	1
MONTGOMERY ROBERT E	LTC	O-0452913	0357	1
MONTGOMERY ROBERT E	LTC	O-1533403	0462	1
MONTGOMERY ROBERT E	CPT	O-1577587	0656	1
MONTGOMERY ROBERT N	1LT	O-1329271	0147	2
MONTGOMERY THOMAS D	MAJ	O-0500137	0849	1
MONTGOMERY WILLIAM D	MAJ	O-0371780	0246	2
MONTGOMERY WILLIAM H	CPT	O-0890270	1147	2
MONTI DANIEL J	CPT	O-1317186	0155	1
MONTICH EMIL	MAJ	O-1172348	0963	1
MONTIETH LESTER E	CW4	W-2119362	0357	2
MONTJOY ROBERT H JR	LTC	O-1106322	0467	1
MONTO SAUL B	MAJ	O-0470885	0946	2
MONTOOTH CHARLES	CPT	O-0108977	1031	1
MONTOYA ALBERT	1LT	O-1683439	0262	1
MONTROSS HENRY E	MAJ	O-0230786	1047	2
MONTROY ROBERT E	CW3	W-2152554	0762	1
MONTS MILLES M	CW4	W-2103235	0659	1
MONTSTREAM WILLIAM L	MAJ	O-0261337	0666	3
MONYAK CHARLES	MAJ	O-2054023	0255	1
MONYEK MILTON S	1LT	O-0494252	0943	2
MOJO RENE L	CW3	W-2149793	0661	1
MOODY ALVAH E	LTC	O-0223787	0954	3
MOODY DAVID	CW3	W-2151902	0663	1
MOODY DONALD	MAJ	O-1949413	0961	1
MOODY DOUGLASS N	LTC	O-0293598	1163	3
MOODY EDWIN F	COL	O-0341984	1066	1
MOODY ELMER	CPT	O-1060895	0450	2
MOODY FRANK B	MAJ	O-0241027	0445	2
MOODY HARDY O	CW4	W-2143106	0366	1
MOODY JAMES E	1LT	O-0228676	1044	2
MOODY JAMES R	1LT	O-0887531	0667	1
MOODY JERALD J	LTC	O-1173390	0860	1
MOODY JOHN M	CW3	W-2145976	0861	1
MOODY LAFAYETTE	CPT	O-0206718	1142	2
MOODY NARVA L	1LT	O-1047248	0645	2
MOODY OTIS N	MAJ	O-1639776	0961	1
MOODY PHILIP H	CW3	W-2141915	1060	1
MOODY REGINALD H	LTC	O-0174928	0648	3
MOODY RICHARD L	LTC	O-1044308	0868	1
MOODY THOMAS E	MAJ	O-0973995	0568	1
MOODY WALTER L	CW4	W-2114978	0251	1
MOODY WILLIAM	MAJ	O-0949164	0962	1
MOODY WILLIAM T	MAJ	O-0285124	1168	3
MOOERS SAMUEL R JR	MAJ	O-1174656	1060	1
MOOK ANDREW W	LTC	O-0280549	0564	3
MOOK MILO M	1LT	O-0484949	1044	2
MOOK WALTER L	1LT	O-0924412	0648	2
MOOMAW BENJAMIN F JR	MAJ	O-0254827	0466	3
MOON EARNEST P	2LT	O-1299779	0644	2
MOON EDWIN E	MAJ	O-1824662	0465	1
MOON FREDERICK	CW4	W-2111019	0762	3
MOON JAMES B	CPT	O-0205225	1053	3
MOON JAMES W	1LT	O-0352161	0244	2
MOON JAY W	LTC	O-0322954	0166	1
MOON JOSEPH F	CW2	RW-2146685	1164	1
MOON LOYDE P	1LT	O-1592454	0652	2
MOON MAURICE J	COL	O-0145877	0256	3
MOON OSCAR O	LTC	O-0405702	1060	1
MOON SAMUEL	MAJ	O-1923059	1063	1
MOON WILLIAM A	MAJ	O-1303925	0761	1
MOON WILLIAM O	LTC	O-0474057	0457	1
MOONEY CHARLES E	LTC	O-1110139	0265	1
MOONEY DANIEL C	CPT	O-1822603	0566	1
MOONEY EARL R	CPT	O-0174454	1055	3
MOONEY EDWIN J	COL	O-0100062	0952	3
MOONEY GEORGE G	LTC	O-0284072	0668	3
MOONEY GEORGE W	CW4	W-2113848	0257	1
MOONEY GLEN	CPT	O-1307057	0447	2
MOONEY HARRY F	COL	O-1043736	1067	1
MOONEY JAMES W	CW2	W-2111456	0753	1
MOONEY JOHN P	LTC	O-0432759	0765	1
MOONEY LAUREN M	MAJ	O-1634155	1160	1
MOONEY LEON D	MAJ	O-1103328	0666	1
MOONEY LESLIE L	MAJ	O-0227780	0463	3
MOONEY RAUL C JR	1LT	O-0281274	114N	2
MOONEY ROBERT	LTC	O-0372676	0762	1
MOONEY THOMAS L	MAJ	O-1167127	1055	2
MOONEY WILLIAM R	CW2	W-2142736	1061	1
MOONEYHAM BILL M	MAJ	O-2263072	0163	1
MOONEYHAM BOB R	CPT	O-2097061	0363	1
MOOR VINCENT C	MAJ	O-1318246	1165	1
MOORE ABNER B	MAJ	O-2019913	0662	1
MOORE ALBERT F	COL	O-0284740	0564	1
MOORE ALFRED D	MAJ	O-0983214	1262	1
MOORE ALFRED E	CW2	W-2211215	1164	1
MOORE ALLAN B	MAJ	O-1081155	0461	1
MOORE ALLEN L	MAJ	O-2018392	0463	1
MOORE ALLEN R	LTC	O-0177182	0655	3
MOORE ALTON M	LTC	O-0299182	1266	3
MOORE ALTON W	CPT	O-2032896	0257	1
MOORE ALVIN	LTC	O-0145878	0950	3
MOORE ALVIN H	LTC	O-0108682	0147	1
MOORE ALVIN L	CW3	W-2149415	0660	1
MOORE ALVIN R	COL	O-0300054	0454	2
MOORE ANDREW J	CW3	W-2144194	0662	1
MOORE ANGELA C	1LT	N-0775961	0446	1
MOORE ARCHIE	LTC	O-0278078	0263	3
MOORE ARTHUR H	1LT	O-1318624	0546	2
MOORE ARTHUR J	MAJ	O-0231722	0963	3
MOORE AUBREY A	LTC	O-0325752	0168	3
MOORE BARNETT J	1LT	O-1333998	0647	2
MOORE BENJAMIN F	CPT	O-1170097	1057	2
MOORE BERT E	LTC	O-0344419	0362	3
MOORE BESSIE L	MAJ	N-0780061	0767	1
MOORE BUNYAN B	MAJ	O-0229658	1137	1
MOORE BURTON L	LTC	O-0283933	0764	3
MOORE CALVIN L	CPT	O-0211775	1057	3
MOORE CARL C	CW3	W-2149261	1062	1
MOORE CARL R	CW2	W-2210326	0266	1
MOORE CARROTHERS	2LT	O-1584629	0646	2
MOORE CHARLES E JR	LTC	O-0305638	0260	1
MOORE CHARLES F	COL	O-0229895	0960	1
MOORE CHARLES H	COL	O-0199959	1162	3
MOORE CHARLES H	LTC	O-0242512	1055	3
MOORE CHARLES H	LTC	O-0425614	1166	1
MOORE CHARLES I	CW3	W-2209547	1068	1
MOORE CHARLES R	LTC	O-0297732	0764	3
MOORE CHASTAIN	LTC	O-0499922	1155	1
MOORE CLARENCE L JR	MAJ	O-1331973	1065	1
MOORE CLARENCE R	1LT	O-0922794	0745	2
MOORE CLARENCE W	MAJ	O-1315347	0765	1
MOORE CLAUDE I	CPT	O-0480330	1045	2
MOORE CLAUDE JR	CW3	W-2203324	0566	1
MOORE CLIFFORD C	MAJ	O-1951180	1162	1
MOORE CLINTON M	CW2	W-3151354	0667	1
MOORE CLYDE B	MAJ	O-0966109	0262	1
MOORE CORBITT R	LTC	O-1014227	0766	1
MOORE DAVID J	LTC	O-0451357	1058	1
MOORE DELMA G	CPT	N-0768289	0847	1
MOORE DEVERT	CW4	W-2115480	0866	1
MOORE DEWEY C	1LT	O-0291972	1065	2
MOORE DON W	MAJ	O-0505520	1144	2
MOORE DONALD E	COL	O-0155882	0861	3
MOORE DOUGLAS D	LTC	O-0364202	0468	3
MOORE DOWELL L	MAJ	O-1549793	0961	1
MOORE DOYLE L	2LT	O-0379555	0742	2
MOORE EDWARD C JR	COL	O-0231868	0660	1
MOORE EDWARD N	LTC	O-0348074	0954	1
MOORE EDWARD W	1LT	O-1302035	0246	2
MOORE EDWIN C	CPT	O-0885937	0656	1
MOORE EDWIN O	LTC	O-1283652	0164	1
MOORE EDWIN J	CW4	W-2102108	0964	1
MOORE ELIASE L	MAJ	O-0484379	0954	1
MOORE ELLIS	LTC	O-0173774	0345	2
MOORE ELZIE K	COL	O-0223985	0564	3
MOORE ERNEST L	CPT	O-0311980	0365	3
MOORE ERNEST W	LTC	O-0143154	1154	3
MOORE ESCOM L	MAJ	O-0370260	0546	2
MOORE EUGENE M	CPT	O-1291929	1146	2
MOORE EVA E	MAJ	N-0727824	1264	1
MOORE FRANCES W	2LT	N-0783688	0545	1
MOORE FRANCIS C	LTC	O-1645840	1165	1
MOORE FRANCIS P	MAJ	O-0447560	0446	2
MOORE FRANCIS X	MAJ	O-0335257	0662	1
MOORE FRANK A	LTC	O-1636355	0259	1
MOORE FRANK C	CPT	O-4006066	0964	1
MOORE FRANK J JR	LTC	O-1329273	0867	1
MOORE FRANK L	COL	O-0508743	1264	3
MOORE FRANK M	MAJ	O-0439833	1262	1
MOORE FRANK T	COL	O-0307015	0961	3
MOORE FRANKLIN D	LTC	O-0265603	0755	2
MOORE FRED A	1LT	O-1594343	0347	2
MOORE FRED W	MAJ	O-0179108	0959	3
MOORE FREDERICK	LTC	O-0309591	0660	1
MOORE GALE S	CPT	O-1301669	0364	2
MOORE GALLIE	2LT	O-0646247	0750	1
MOORE GARLAND J	MAJ	O-2262356	1164	1
MOORE GEORGE	COL	O-0248303	0367	3
MOORE GEORGE A	CPT	O-0383680	0367	3
MOORE GEORGE P	LTC	O-0360213	0260	1
MOORE GEORGE D	MAJ	O-2288319	1263	1
MOORE GEORGE F	LTC	O-1001857	1162	1
MOORE GEORGE M	MAJ	O-0354624	0255	2
MOORE GEORGE S	CPT	O-0495245	0948	1
MOORE GEORGE T	2LT	O-2011387	1046	1
MOORE GERALD K	LTC	O-0347906	0258	1
MOORE GERALD P	1LT	O-1299929	0846	2
MOORE GLENN A	MAJ	O-0257975	0267	3
MOORE GORDON E	1LT	O-0449063	0745	2
MOORE GRADY W	CW3	W-2149858	1262	1
MOORE GRANT W	1LT	O-0406808	0844	2
MOORE GUS R	CW3	W-2147486	0965	1
MOORE HARLAND B	CPT	O-0161473	0452	3
MOORE HARLIN A	LTC	O-0245504	0860	3
MOORE HAROLD C	CW3	W-2005171	0968	3
MOORE HAROLD E	MAJ	O-0373082	0568	3
MOORE HAROLD E	MAJ	O-1688451	0364	1
MOORE HAROLD G	CPT	O-1035126	0661	1
MOORE HAROLD H	COL	O-0335728	0661	1
MOORE HAROLD Z	MAJ	O-1295582	0752	2
MOORE HARRY H	LTC	O-1170099	0562	1
MOORE HARRY L	MAJ	O-0263851	0864	3
MOORE HENRY D	CPT	O-0304029	0563	3
MOORE HENRY F	CPT	O-0187986	0349	1
MOORE HENRY W	MAJ	O-0252133	0665	3
MOORE HERBERT A	CPT	O-0407681	0562	1
MOORE HERBERT S	CPT	O-1306128	0447	2
MOORE HERMAN R	CPT	O-0174211	0353	3
MOORE HOLMES R	CPT	O-0379922	0562	1
MOORE HOMER L	MAJ	O-0978139	0664	1
MOORE HOOVER C	CW3	W-3150501	0466	1
MOORE HORACE	LTC	O-0925263	0265	3
MOORE HOWARD I	LTC	O-0191834	0762	3
MOORE HOWARD W	LTC	O-0276575	1161	3
MOORE HOWARD W	MAJ	O-1295062	0364	1
MOORE IOUS B	MAJ	O-0504280	0155	1
MOORE ILEAN	CPT	N-0729077	0946	1
MOORE IVEY J JR	CPT	O-2033986	1061	1
MOORE JACK	1LT	O-0443968	0344	2
MOORE JACK B	CW2	W-3350347	0667	1
MOORE JACK M	LTC	O-1293629	0962	1
MOORE JACOB F J	LTC	O-1101124	1055	1
MOORE JAMES A	COL	O-0346936	0264	1
MOORE JAMES A	CW2	W-3420002	0266	1
MOORE JAMES B III	COL	O-0269409	1168	3
MOORE JAMES B JR	MAJ	O-1328918	1060	1
MOORE JAMES C	LTC	O-0412607	0761	1
MOORE JAMES C	CPT	O-1046571	0762	1
MOORE JAMES D	CPT	O-0408329	0245	2
MOORE JAMES D	LTC	O-1596121	0363	1
MOORE JAMES E	LTC	O-0243068	0466	3
MOORE JAMES E	1LT	O-1589388	0346	2
MOORE JAMES E	1LT	O-1947039	0646	2
MOORE JAMES J	CW2	W-2152748	0363	1
MOORE JAMES L	MAJ	O-2019491	0363	1
MOORE JAMES M	COL	O-0237610	0845	2
MOORE JAMES O	MAJ	O-1548262	0754	2
MOORE JAMES O	CW3	W-2152098	0762	1
MOORE JAMES P	MAJ	O-0225521	0562	3
MOORE JAMES P	MAJ	O-1534099	0463	1
MOORE JAMES S	CPT	O-1686143	1050	2
MOORE JAMES W	LTC	O-0378081	1161	1
MOORE JAMES W	LTC	O-1638106	0564	2
MOORE JAMES W	CW3	W-2144673	0860	2
MOORE JARVIS B	2LT	O-1298424	0145	2
MOORE JAY K	MAJ	O-1050836	1263	1
MOORE JEROME W	MAJ	O-1557337	0256	1
MOORE JESSE W	CPT	O-2096817	0564	1
MOORE JOE L	CW3	W-2152796	0264	1
MOORE JOE P	MAJ	O-0290646	1059	3
MOORE JOE R	MAJ	O-1951701	0562	1
MOORE JOHN B	B G	O-0244989	0762	3
MOORE JOHN B	MAJ	O-1826425	0561	1
MOORE JOHN B	CW3	W-2142884	0161	1
MOORE JOHN D	COL	O-0209176	0846	2
MOORE JOHN E	LTC	O-0114183	0850	3

332-811 O - 69 - 18

NAME	GRADE	SVC NO	DATE RET MO YR	RET CODE
MOORE JOHN F	MAJ	0-1540917	0563	1
MOORE JOHN H	2LT	0-0466584	0743	2
MOORE JOHN H	2LT	0-2014910	0254	1
MOORE JOHN H	MAJ	0-2206124	1165	1
MOORE JOHN K	LTC	0-1287218	0465	3
MOORE JOHN K	MAJ	0-1287567	0461	1
MOORE JOHN M	MAJ	0-0258218	0467	3
MOORE JOHN T	CPT	0-0969436	0462	1
MOORE JOHN T	LTC	0-1308678	0667	2
MOORE JOSEPH A	COL	0-0285220	0864	3
MOORE JOSEPH D	LTC	0-1287219	0966	1
MOORE JOSEPH E	LTC	0-0431474	0162	1
MOORE JOSEPH E	MAJ	0-1945025	0565	3
MOORE JOSEPH M	CW3	W-2150980	1163	1
MOORE JOSEPH N	1LT	0-1299452	0246	2
MOORE JOSEPH N SR	CPT	0-0240057	0762	2
MOORE JOSEPH O	COL	0-0319845	0-51	1
MOORE JULIUS B	LTC	0-0549347	1066	1
MOORE KAY D	CPT	0-1031578	0147	2
MOORE KENNETH M JR	CPT	0-2301019	0965	1
MOORE LAWRENCE F	WO1	W-2132299	0854	1
MOORE LAWRENCE F SR	MAJ	0-0364879	1263	1
MOORE LAWRENCE M	CW2	W-2147584	0857	1
MOORE LEE	LTC	0-1253450	0168	1
MOORE LEO	MAJ	0-1698036	0655	1
MOORE LEO B	LTC	0-0354004	0346	2
MOORE LEONARD H	CPT	0-2002178	0659	2
MOORE LOUIS E	MAJ	0-2055434	1054	1
MOORE LUCIUS L	COL	0-0197562	0456	3
MOORE LUKE R	MAJ	0-0938975	0662	1
MOORE LUKE W	LTC	0-0245079	0253	3
MOORE LUM H	CPT	0-1593732	1047	2
MOORE MARION L	LTC	0-0266724	0968	3
MOORE MARION N	CPT	N-0722790	0147	1
MOORE MARTHA D	2LT	N-0736236	1044	1
MOORE MARY M	2LT	N-0759907	1144	1
MOORE MATTHEW C	MAJ	0-0984999	0661	1
MOORE MATTHEW S	1LT	0-0454586	0545	2
MOORE MERLE E	MAJ	0-1822818	1061	1
MOORE MILLARD F	CW3	W-2153658	0665	1
MOORE MILTON M	CPT	0-1035546	0766	1
MOORE MORRIS P	COL	0-0113954	0151	3
MOORE NELSON J	COL	0-0172651	0646	2
MOORE NEWELL V	1LT	0-1305460	0346	2
MOORE NORMAN M	MAJ	0-0914959	0945	2
MOORE ODIS E	CW2	W-2128044	0662	1
MOORE OLAF R	CPT	0-1312968	0546	2
MOORE ORVILLE A	CW4	W-2107902	1160	1
MOORE OSCAR H	WO1	W-2149302	0858	1
MOORE OSCAR S	CW2	W-3200250	0268	1
MOORE OSWALD D	CPT	0-0145817	0854	3
MOORE PAUL B JR	LTC	0-1288780	0261	1
MOORE PAUL J	CPT	0-0347337	0964	3
MOORE PERCY E	MAJ	0-0269216	1064	3
MOORE RALPH B	1LT	0-1014050	1046	2
MOORE RALPH E	MAJ	0-2005660	1262	1
MOORE RALPH H	2LT	0-1050390	0744	1
MOORE RALPH L	LTC	0-1002997	0564	1
MOORE RANDALL S	2LT	0-1330458	0146	2
MOORE RAY A JR	CPT	0-0460927	0448	2
MOORE RAYMOND L	LTC	0-0260958	1045	2
MOORE REX	2LT	0-1554941	1044	2
MOORE REYNOLDS C JR	1LT	0-1115043	0846	2
MOORE RICHARD B	MAJ	0-2266109	0968	1
MOORE ROBERT A	LTC	0-0263684	1059	1
MOORE ROBERT B	LTC	0-0453276	0758	1
MOORE ROBERT B	1LT	0-1287742	0452	2
MOORE ROBERT C	CPT	0-1549560	0346	2
MOORE ROBERT E	2LT	0-1049999	0644	2
MOORE ROBERT E	CW4	W-2129443	0966	1
MOORE ROBERT E JR	LTC	0-0254021	0246	2
MOORE ROBERT H	MAJ	0-0209194	0260	3
MOORE ROBERT H	MAJ	0-1114663	0862	1
MOORE ROBERT H JR	MAJ	0-1548970	1263	1
MOORE ROBERT J	2LT	0-1822432	1045	2
MOORE ROBERT L	LTC	0-0238604	0544	2
MOORE ROBERT L	LTC	0-0348825	0560	1
MOORE ROBERT M	1LT	0-1297573	1044	2
MOORE ROBERT M	CW3	W-2153373	1066	1
MOORE ROBERT N	CW2	W-2150678	1161	1
MOORE ROBERT R	COL	0-0256307	0365	3
MOORE ROBERT R	LTC	0-1107603	0763	1
MOORE ROBERT S	CW3	W-2141387	0960	1
MOORE ROBERT W	2LT	0-1823916	1044	2
MOORE ROBERT W	LTC	0-2048086	0665	1
MOORE RODERICK G	1LT	0-0372356	0745	2
MOORE ROLAND	MAJ	0-1112875	0463	1
MOORE ROY A	CW4	W-2117926	1054	1
MOORE ROY E	MAJ	0-1015667	1266	1
MOORE ROY W	MAJ	0-2204104	1165	1
MOORE ROYCE L	CW2	W-2146879	0657	1
MOORE RUSSELL R	LTC	0-1010955	0661	1
MOORE SAM L JR	LTC	0-1328282	0268	1
MOORE SAM Y	MAJ	0-1300685	0161	1
MOORE SAMUEL A	LTC	0-0346046	1062	3
MOORE SAMUEL W	MAJ	0-0171469	0358	3
MOORE SARAH W	MAJ	N-0742056	0165	1
MOORE SCOTT	MAJ	0-1113847	0162	1
MOORE SHERIDAN B	MAJ	0-1051694	0462	1
MOORE SIDNEY S	2LT	0-0520753	0445	2
MOORE STANLEY B	1LT	0-1317810	1045	2
MOORE STANLEY J	CPT	0-0973595	1060	1
MOORE THADDEUS S	CPT	0-1297408	0448	2
MOORE THED L	MAJ	0-1999609	1060	1
MOORE THEOPHILUS	LTC	0-0319941	0461	1
MOORE THOMAS A	LTC	0-0299986	0361	3
MOORE THOMAS J	LTC	0-1314940	1163	1
MOORE THOMAS V JR	CPT	0-0495702	0546	2
MOORE TOLLY K	COL	0-1557879	0468	1
MOORE TREVOR F	LTC	0-1042102	0462	2
MOORE TROY T	1LT	0-1645225	0855	1
MOORE TROY V	M[illegible]	0-0494992	0849	1
MOORE VERNON O	LTC	0-0393766	0264	1
MOORE VICTOR A	LTC	0-1010457	0767	1
MOORE VICTOR P	CPT	0-1822302	1058	1
MOORE VINCENT H	CPT	0-0924933	0745	2
MOORE VIRGIL S	MAJ	0-0317753	0553	2
MOORE VORDA B	1LT	0-2006320	1046	2
MOORE WALDO W	LTC	0-0129184	0455	3
MOORE WALLACE H	COL	0-0197922	0846	2
MOORE WALTER L	COL	0-0165067	0953	3
MOORE WALTER L	1LT	0-0454603	1045	2
MOORE WALTER T	CPT	0-0282164	1266	3
MOORE WALTER W	MAJ	0-0966639	0662	2
MOORE WALTER W SR	CPT	0-0116797	1159	3
MOORE WARREN H	MAJ	0-2014661	0763	1
MOORE WAYMON L	MAJ	0-1311419	0956	1
MOORE WENDELL T	MAJ	0-0542610	1063	1
MOORE WESLEY G	CPT	0-1576408	0756	1
MOORE WILBUR M	LTC	0-0267722	0265	3
MOORE WILBUR M	MAJ	0-0316544	1144	2
MOORE WILLARD D	MAJ	0-0196277	0961	3
MOORE WILLIAM A	1LT	0-0443540	0745	2
MOORE WILLIAM A	LTC	0-1580056	1161	1
MOORE WILLIAM C	1LT	0-0547661	0546	2
MOORE WILLIAM C	WO1	W-2143692	0555	1
MOORE WILLIAM D	1LT	0-1339462	0448	2
MOORE WILLIAM E	CW2	W-3100522	0268	1
MOORE WILLIAM F	MAJ	0-1823470	0661	1
MOORE WILLIAM H	MAJ	0-0193098	0163	3
MOORE WILLIAM H	1LT	0-0545985	0446	2
MOORE WILLIAM H	MAJ	0-0956659	0967	2
MOORE WILLIAM H	LTC	0-1584631	0261	1
MOORE WILLIAM H	CW2	W-2109372	0256	1
MOORE WILLIAM I	COL	0-0219688	0845	2
MOORE WILLIAM J	MAJ	0-0308919	0163	1
MOORE WILLIAM JR	LTC	0-0143116	1155	2
MOORE WILLIAM L	CPT	0-0372650	0750	1
MOORE WILLIAM R	LTC	0-1289775	0165	1
MOORE WILLIAM R	CW4	W-2143593	0162	1
MOORE WILLIAM P JR	2LT	0-0549781	1145	2
MOORE WILLIAM T JR	1LT	0-0412219	0945	2
MOORE WILLIAM T JR	LTC	0-1573441	1159	1
MOORE WILLIE JR	MAJ	0-2024616	0165	1
MOORE WILSON P	CPT	0-1548504	0745	2
MOORE WOODFORD D	CPT	0-1293451	1047	2
MOORE WRIGHT C	MAJ	0-1554239	0361	1
MOORE WRIGHT T	COL	0-0129066	0853	3
MOORE YOUNG III	LTC	0-1560228	1267	1
MOOREHEAD CHARLES	LTC	0-0453111	0860	1
MOOREHEAD JOE N	1LT	0-1319528	0646	2
MOORER EDWARD A	MAJ	0-1286873	0760	1
MOORES JESSE T	LTC	0-1305291	0665	1
MOORHEAD JOHN T	COL	0-0278223	0559	3
MOORHEAD JOSEPH H	CPT	0-1878179	0355	2
MOORHEAD PAUL A	CPT	0-0336592	0744	2
MOORHEAD ROBERT D	CW3	W-2206939	0666	1
MOORHEAD STEELE L JR	CPT	0-0473500	1044	2
MOORHEAD WAYNE L	CW3	RW-2208764	0467	1
MOORHEAD WENDELL P	CW3	W-2143007	0456	1
MOORMAN ALAN W	LTC	0-0277806	0560	3
MOORMAN CHARLES H	CW2	W-2149708	0261	1
MOORMAN CLINTON R	MAJ	0-2202336	0966	1
MOORMAN FRANK M	LTC	0-0184443	0754	3
MOORMAN JOHN H JR	CPT	0-0424466	0246	2
MOORMAN RALPH	CPT	0-1324887	0946	2
MOORS ARTHUR G	LTC	0-1550230	0264	1
MOORTEL JACK G	CW3	RW-2209724	0467	1
MOOSE ARCHIE E	LTC	0-2034826	0266	1
MOOSEN JOSEPH G	MAJ	0-2017572	0760	1
MORABITO JOHN	LTC	0-0252541	1166	3
MORACE JOHN J	CW3	W-2136672	0661	1
MORAGHAN ANNA G	2LT	N-0728974	0944	1
MORAGON PABLO R	MAJ	0-0336937	0868	3
MORAINE JACK L	CPT	0-2036277	0954	2
MORALES BENITO	COL	0-0301225	0655	1
MORALES EDWARD B	1LT	0-1031347	0346	2
MORALES MARIANO	CW3	W-2145470	1061	1
MORALES RICHARD H	LTC	0-1548109	0257	1
MORAN ALLEN R	LTC	0-1049587	1166	1
MORAN BRIAN P	MAJ	0-1011119	0147	2
MORAN CARL H	CPT	0-1172558	0446	2
MORAN CLEMENT J	MAJ	0-0257616	0461	3
MORAN DAVID J	LTC	0-1014350	0462	1
MORAN EARL E	MAJ	0-0233816	1146	2
MORAN EDWARD B	1LT	0-2053954	0446	2
MORAN EDWARD F	MAJ	0-0215139	1063	3
MORAN EDWARD J	LTC	0-1574101	0858	1
MORAN ERNEST L	MAJ	0-0969051	1066	1
MORAN ETHEL S	LTC	L-0220003	0652	2
MORAN EVAN A	1LT	0-1320159	0745	2
MORAN FRANK P	LTC	0-0240058	0447	1
MORAN FRANK R	CPT	0-1019213	0361	1
MORAN GEORGE C	M G	0-0184043	0657	3
MORAN HALBERT S	LTC	0-0239081	0764	3
MORAN HAROLD A	CW2	W-2209334	0563	1
MORAN JACK T JR	MAJ	0-1580057	0557	1
MORAN JAMES D	LTC	0-1300513	1161	1
MORAN JAMES E	CW2	W-3200476	0868	1
MORAN JOHN F	LTC	0-0180301	0660	1
MORAN JOHN J	MAJ	0-0268932	0146	2
MORAN JOHN J	LTC	0-0487154	0557	1
MORAN JOHN S	COL	0-0166000	1051	3
MORAN JOSEPH F JR	CPT	0-1303634	0844	2
MORAN JOSEPH R	CPT	0-1696608	0745	2
MORAN LUCILLE E	2LT	M-0002218	0446	1
MORAN OWEN W	MAJ	0-0278274	0754	3
MORAN RAYMOND P JR	MAJ	0-1925655	0267	1
MORAN RICHARD T	CW2	W-2211898	0867	1
MORAN ROBERT B	CW3	W-2150866	0865	1
MORAN ROBERT W	1LT	0-0420324	1144	2
MORAN THOMAS E	CPT	0-1288936	0447	2
MORAN THOMAS P	LTC	0-0361356	1061	1
MORAN TIMOTHY F	LTC	0-1695370	0445	2
MORAN VIRGINIA M	1LT	N-0762170	1046	1
MORAN WILLIAM	1LT	0-0959481	0457	2
MORAN WILLIAM D	CPT	0-0483965	0852	2
MORAN WILLIAM H	CPT	0-1703235	1044	2
MORAN WILLIAM J	CW3	W-2206597	0466	1
MORAN WILLIS Y	LTC	0-0286584	0267	3
MORANCIE EDMOND J	MAJ	0-1309875	0656	1
MORANDA LAWRENCE E	LTC	0-1826166	0868	3
MORANO RALPH	LTC	0-0446213	0667	3
MORAVEC RALPH A	2LT	0-2047089	0445	2
MORAVEK STEPHEN	COL	0-0236222	0963	3
MORAVETZ ROBERT L	COL	0-0287686	0868	3
MORAZ ALBERT P	CPT	0-1584635	0546	2
MORCE EARL M	CW3	W-2146919	0258	1
MORCOCK JOHN C JR	LTC	0-0244741	0363	3
MORDEN CARROLL V	MAJ	0-1052087	0258	1
MORDEN HOWARD C	CPT	0-0470248	0145	2
MORE CARLETON	LTC	0-0164435	0353	3
MORE GLENDALE	MAJ	0-1328623	0264	1
MORE JOSEPH F	LTC	0-0177765	0148	2
MORE WILLARD E	CW3	W-2148561	0464	1
MOREAU ALFRED	MAJ	0-1044904	0257	1
MOREAU CECIL J	LTC	0-2043173	0264	2
MOREAU DANIEL	CPT	0-1922630	1162	1
MOREAU GILBERT W	1LT	0-1283295	1045	2
MOREAU LAMAR J	CPT	0-0479350	0962	1
MOREAU LOUIS S	2LT	0-1299454	0345	2
MOREAU RAY A	MAJ	0-4009667	0166	1
MORECRAFT ELWOOD M	1LT	0-1015269	0845	2
MOREDA ARMAND E	MAJ	0-2008067	1060	1
MOREE JAMES A	LTC	0-1639424	0163	1
MOREHEAD GLENN E	LTC	0-0251350	1165	3
MOREHEAD LEMUEL Y	MAJ	0-0283873	1064	3
MOREHEAD LOUIS M JR	COL	0-0312506	1065	3
MOREHEAD WILLIAM F	LTC	0-1593734	0867	3
MOREHEAD WILLIAM H	CW3	W-2205362	0366	1
MOREHISER JOHN E JR	CPT	0-0428136	0344	2
MOREHOUSE COURTLAND	MAJ	0-0919319	1163	1
MOREHOUSE JOSEPH H	MAJ	0-0205361	1159	3
MOREHOUSE VIRGIL A	CW3	W-2150517	0663	1
MOREHOUSE WILLIAM W	LTC	0-0505134	0568	3
MOREL VICTOR J	1LT	0-1638111	0947	2
MORELAND EARL E	CW4	W-2108718	0560	1
MORELAND EUGENE E	MAJ	0-0489729	0754	1
MORELAND HUGH E	CW3	W-2150647	0662	1
MORELAND J L	MAJ	0-1542097	0160	1
MORELAND JOHN W JR	1LT	0-0517677	1145	2
MORELAND KENNETH D	1LT	0-1319434	0450	2
MORELAND RANDALL B	COL	0-0359082	0547	2
MORELAND ROBERT G	LTC	0-1994662	0965	1
MORELAND SAMUEL J	CW3	W-2150815	0564	1
MORELAND WALTER I	LTC	0-1691929	0563	1
MORELL GUSTAVE A	CPT	0-0273554	1064	3
MORELLE GUY J	MAJ	0-0173047	1144	2
MORELLI TONY	2LT	0-1032467	0445	2
MOREN ALBERT A	LTC	0-0235126	0659	3
MOREN WILLIAM R	MAJ	0-1173393	1058	1
MORENCY ANTHONY J	CW2	W-2119961	0949	1
MORENCY JOHN E	MAJ	0-1280480	0860	2
MORENCY JOSEPH N JR	1LT	0-1314310	1045	2
MORENO VICENTE	1LT	0-0346144	0250	1
MORENO YOLANDA M	2LT	N-0798888	0646	1
MORERE RODERIC G	MAJ	0-0433294	0647	2
MOREST FREDERICK	MAJ	0-1699841	0146	2
MORET SIMON	1LT	0-0403267	0745	2
MOREY LEIGHTON G	COL	0-1300835	0567	1
MORFORD ALEXANDER	LTC	0-0280686	1062	3
MORFORD THEODORE	MAJ	0-0200007	0746	2
MORGAN ALOIS A	COL	0-1107014	1167	1
MORGAN ANGELA J	1LT	N-0763826	0747	1
MORGAN ARTHUR C	1LT	0-1186268	0347	2
MORGAN BEAVER C	CW3	W-2206001	1168	1
MORGAN BENJAMIN T	1LT	0-0197356	0161	3
MORGAN BILLY L	CW2	W-2150641	0657	1
MORGAN BOYCE M	CW4	W-2118370	0964	1
MORGAN CAMILLE G	CPT	0-1323160	1262	1

NAME	GRADE	SVC NO	DATE RET MO YR	RET CODE	NAME	GRADE	SVC NO	DATE RET MO YR	RET CODE	NAME	GRADE	SVC NO	DATE RET MO YR	RET CODE	NAME	GRADE	SVC NO	DATE RET MO YR	RET CODE
MORGAN CARL L	LTC	O-0452088	0255	1	MORGAN LEROY JR	2LT	O-1311568	0645	2	MORIN ANDREW E	MAJ	O-0948833	1065	1	MORRIS EVERETTE W JR	CW2	W-2211615	1066	1
MORGAN CARTHEL N	LTC	O-0342878	1058	1	MORGAN LONNIE	CW2	W-2205098	1060	1	MORIN CHARLES E	CW2	W-2149709	1060	1	MORRIS FLOYD D	CPT	O-0254769	0567	3
MORGAN CHARLES A	MAJ	O-1289117	0358	1	MORGAN MARION N	LTC	O-1284744	0261	1	MORIN LEON	CW2	W-2108609	1055	1	MORRIS FRANCIS S	LTC	O-1010155	1055	1
MORGAN CHARLES E	CPT	O-1294703	0348	2	MORGAN MARVIN M	LTC	O-2028617	1268	1	MORIN MARGARET B	2LT	N-0720417	0444	1	MORRIS FRANK E	MAJ	O-0286623	0944	2
MORGAN CHARLES H	LTC	O-0334733	0257	1	MORGAN MAURICE M	CPT	O-1796836	0246	2	MORIN MARGUERITE	MAJ	L-1010131	0164	1	MORRIS FRANK J	COL	O-0521454	0466	3
MORGAN CLIFFORD D JR	1LT	O-3207949	0165	2	MORGAN MILLARD	LTC	O-1285626	0165	1	MORIN ROGER J	LTC	O-1533868	0764	1	MORRIS FRANK S JR	CW3	W-2208445	0167	1
MORGAN CLINTON D	MAJ	O-1294177	1157	1	MORGAN MYRON	LTC	O-1286333	0847	2	MORIN ROY E	CW3	W-2143228	1060	1	MORRIS FRED H	LTC	O-0337059	0555	3
MORGAN DAVID F	COL	O-0145644	0-53	3	MORGAN NEIL B	LTC	O-0204073	0359	3	MORINE MYRON L	2LT	O-1301519	0843	2	MORRIS FRED M JR	MAJ	O-0397891	0364	1
MORGAN DEXTER P	MAJ	O-4074526	0668	1	MORGAN NEWTON B	LTC	O-0149818	0852	3	MORINS DAVIS C	CPT	O-1172559	0148	2	MORRIS GEORGE A	B G	O-0266651	0867	3
MORGAN DON P	MAJ	O-0985328	0365	2	MORGAN NOAH R	CW2	W-2145924	0562	2	MORISON GARLAND M	MAJ	O-1587479	0457	1	MORRIS GEORGE E	1LT	O-0516870	0658	2
MORGAN DONALD A	MAJ	O-0292763	0968	3	MORGAN NORMAN	CPT	O-1915259	0462	1	MORISON JACK P	COL	O-0302028	0647	2	MORRIS GEORGE F	LTC	O-1169662	0561	1
MORGAN DONALD H	LTC	O-2210327	1167	1	MORGAN OLIN F	CW3	W-2147251	0965	1	MORISON WILLIAM C	CW2	W-2213865	0468	1	MORRIS GEORGE P	CW4	W-2142683	0866	1
MORGAN DORSEY	CPT	O-0947729	0861	1	MORGAN OLIN R	CW3	W-2147073	0161	1	MORISSETTE BERTELL P	CW4	W-2143613	0767	1	MORRIS GEORGE R	LTC	O-0900408	0362	3
MORGAN EDNA L	2LT	N-0735926	0546	1	MORGAN PATRICK H	LTC	O-0462401	1266	1	MORITZ ROWLAND T	CPT	O-1845935	0162	1	MORRIS GEORGE W	LTC	O-0397668	0461	1
MORGAN EDWIN R	LTC	O-0300022	0166	3	MORGAN PAUL F JR	MAJ	O-0390602	0347	2	MORITZ WILLIAM R	CPT	O-1032231	0847	2	MORRIS GLENN S	LTC	O-0209437	0755	3
MORGAN ELDON V	CW3	W-2142256	0659	1	MORGAN PRENTICE G	LTC	O-0311202	0660	1	MORIUCHI GONJI	LTC	O-1330459	0464	1	MORRIS GRANT F	1LT	O-0293960	0641	2
MORGAN ELMER H	1LT	O-1286332	0946	2	MORGAN PRESTON W	LTC	O-1308275	0767	1	MORK LEE D	COL	O-0259087	1264	3	MORRIS HARPER K	LTC	O-2066482	1267	1
MORGAN FLETCHER B	CPT	O-0333331	1053	2	MORGAN RALPH B	MAJ	O-0301335	0247	1	MORLA RAFAEL	COL	O-0287456	1047	2	MORRIS HARRY	LTC	O-0257903	0745	2
MORGAN FRANCIS J	LTC	O-0470247	0651	2	MORGAN RALPH E JR	MAJ	O-0966086	0765	1	MORLAN ERNEST F	WO1	W-2148752	0158	2	MORRIS HARRY O	COL	O-0247495	0167	3
MORGAN FRANK C	COL	O-0255235	0156	1	MORGAN RALPH L	LTC	O-0888375	0556	1	MORLAN HAROLD F	WO1	W-2113197	0945	2	MORRIS HARRY W	CPT	O-0175405	0658	3
MORGAN FRANK C	CPT	O-1555109	0352	2	MORGAN RALPH S	LTC	O-0355386	0165	1	MORLEY ABNER S	COL	O-0188516	0949	3	MORRIS HENRY C	MAJ	O-1335818	0864	1
MORGAN FRED	CW3	W-2149466	0166	1	MORGAN RALPH W	LTC	O-0363477	0467	3	MORLEY CHARLES P	CPT	O-2033287	1059	1	MORRIS HENRY L	LTC	O-0401673	0960	1
MORGAN FREDERICK	MAJ	O-0117425	0950	3	MORGAN RAYMOND B	CPT	O-2289500	0562	1	MORLEY JOHN H	MAJ	O-0284937	0946	1	MORRIS HOBART A	1LT	O-2049662	0446	2
MORGAN GENE	1LT	O-1309299	0146	2	MORGAN RAYMOND E	LTC	O-1582468	0565	1	MORLEY JOHN R	1LT	O-0527842	0946	2	MORRIS HORACE M	LTC	O-0241257	0159	3
MORGAN GEORGE A	COL	O-0900096	0954	1	MORGAN RAYMOND J	1LT	O-0419149	0946	2	MORLEY JOHN W	LTC	O-0441704	0662	1	MORRIS HOWARD A	MAJ	O-0196871	0162	3
MORGAN GEORGE E	CW4	RW-2122105	0866	1	MORGAN RICHARD F	MAJ	O-1305963	0157	1	MORNEAU JAMES P	1LT	O-5331646	0368	2	MORRIS HOWARD G	CPT	O-1110143	0646	2
MORGAN GEORGE H	CPT	O-0887573	0646	2	MORGAN RICHARD G	MAJ	O-4074728	1168	1	MORNINGSTAR CLINTON	CW3	W-2205165	1064	1	MORRIS HUGH B	CPT	O-0373291	0445	2
MORGAN GEORGE H	2LT	O-1799945	0545	2	MORGAN RICHARD H	MAJ	O-1016964	1060	1	MORUZ RAYMOND G	LTC	O-2048536	0960	1	MORRIS HUGH E	1LT	O-1312037	0747	2
MORGAN GEORGE N	LTC	O-0342291	1160	1	MORGAN RICHARD J	CPT	O-0910477	0747	2	MORPHEW WALTER L SR	LTC	O-1043739	0565	1	MORRIS J D	CW3	W-2149087	1060	1
MORGAN GEORGE W	CPT	O-2011656	0160	1	MORGAN RICHARD L	COL	O-0297685	0660	1	MORR DARRELL M	1LT	O-1100255	0843	2	MORRIS JACK H	CPT	O-1300514	0459	1
MORGAN GERALD C	COL	O-0451128	1160	1	MORGAN ROBERT G	MAJ	O-2043069	0657	1	MORRA DORIS M	1LT	N-0722424	0346	1	MORRIS JAMES B	WO1	W-2109144	0962	1
MORGAN HAROLD A	COL	O-0215195	1054	3	MORGAN ROBERT H	2LT	O-1638117	0643	2	MORRELL IRA D	CPT	O-0505732	0854	1	MORRIS JAMES C	LTC	O-2204929	0868	1
MORGAN HARRIET P	CPT	N-0720973	1047	1	MORGAN ROBERT M	1LT	O-0425435	0643	2	MORRELL LEO A	1LT	O-1648616	0345	2	MORRIS JAMES E	LTC	O-0453195	0461	1
MORGAN HARRY T	LTC	O-0252987	0949	2	MORGAN ROY L	CPT	O-0504084	1048	1	MORRELL PAUL A	LTC	O-1294555	0266	1	MORRIS JAMES E	LTC	O-0928940	0166	1
MORGAN HELEN M	2LT	N-0755236	0345	1	MORGAN ROY S	CPT	O-0307195	0244	2	MORRELL RONALD F	CW2	RW-2149493	1066	1	MORRIS JAMES H	MAJ	O-1951556	0863	1
MORGAN HELEN S	1LT	N-0721573	0946	1	MORGAN ROY W	CW2	W-2118329	0260	1	MORRIA JAMES I	CW2	W-2150124	0760	1	MORRIS JAMES K	LTC	O-0103358	0156	3
MORGAN HENRY G	1LT	O-1030579	0949	1	MORGAN RUFUS	CPT	O-0499502	1049	1	MORRILL HARVEY J	LTC	O-1645848	0165	1	MORRIS JAMES L	CPT	O-0357608	0345	2
MORGAN HENRY P II	MAJ	O-2200220	0767	1	MORGAN SIDNEY	COL	O-0114527	0550	3	MORRILL HORACE A	LTC	O-0204908	0750	3	MORRIS JAMES S	COL	O-0309173	0460	2
MORGAN HENRY T	LTC	O-1010172	0162	2	MORGAN STANLEY P	MAJ	O-0528115	0155	1	MORRILL JUSTIN S	COL	O-0316696	0967	3	MORRIS JAMES W	CPT	O-0423179	0163	1
MORGAN HORACE R	MAJ	O-0994456	0165	1	MORGAN STANTON A	MAJ	O-0465219	1062	1	MORRILL KEITH S	LTC	O-1102395	0962	1	MORRIS JIMMIE A	WO1	W-2150044	0956	1
MORGAN HOWELL F	CPT	O-0373465	0745	2	MORGAN THEODORE J	CW2	W-2208610	0462	1	MORRILL LESLIE S	COL	O-0118197	0754	3	MORRIS JOHN A JR	CW3	W-2141827	0858	1
MORGAN IRVING H	LTC	O-0232976	0957	3	MORGAN THOMAS J	2LT	O-1292042	0945	2	MORRILL MARIAN A	1LT	N-0751954	0246	1	MORRIS JOHN D	WO1	W-2151823	0357	1
MORGAN JAMES A JR	WO1	W-2005635	1051	2	MORGAN WALTER R JR	MAJ	O-1285088	1046	2	MORRIS AL K	LTC	O-1696548	0147	2	MORRIS JOHN E	LTC	O-1101591	0961	1
MORGAN JAMES D	MAJ	O-1012523	0662	1	MORGAN WARREN E	CW3	W-2147769	0964	1	MORRIS ALBERT C	MAJ	O-0419369	0346	2	MORRIS JOHN E	MAJ	O-2263095	0466	1
MORGAN JAMES F	2LT	O-1059092	0945	2	MORGAN WENDELL H	MAJ	O-1541939	0466	3	MORRIS ALBERT C JR	CPT	O-1553148	0246	2	MORRIS JOHN H	CPT	O-0921478	0846	2
MORGAN JAMES C	LTC	O-0349654	0166	2	MORGAN WILBER L	CW3	W-2151794	0264	1	MORRIS ALFRED M JR	COL	O-0244821	0465	3	MORRIS JOHN R	MAJ	O-0502493	1146	2
MORGAN JAMES R	MAJ	O-1829973	0166	1	MORGAN WILFRED A	COL	O-0170630	0153	3	MORRIS ANSON P	LTC	O-0237316	0768	3	MORRIS JOHN S	MAJ	O-0160895	0648	3
MORGAN JESSE P	LTC	O-0259491	0746	2	MORGAN WILLIAM C JR	COL	O-0174464	0263	3	MORRIS ARCHIE	CPT	O-0173169	0254	1	MORRIS JOHN S	CPT	O-1176740	0753	2
MORGAN JESSIE M	MAJ	N-0755320	0163	1	MORGAN WILLIAM O	LTC	O-0344436	1159	1	MORRIS ARDEN S	LTC	O-0394642	0967	3	MORRIS JOHN T	MAJ	O-0253377	1262	3
MORGAN JOHN A	LTC	O-1550007	1263	1	MORGAN WILLIAM H	LTC	O-0103307	0549	3	MORRIS ARTHUR C	CPT	O-1303929	0953	1	MORRIS JOHN W	MAJ	O-2029521	0363	1
MORGAN JOHN B	MAJ	O-0183812	0250	3	MORGAN WILLIAM H	CW2	W-2211022	0666	1	MORRIS ARVING F	LTC	O-0220200	0250	3	MORRIS JOHNIE L	CW2	W-2148678	0758	1
MORGAN JOHN B	MAJ	O-1587478	0858	1	MORGAN WILLIAM R	LTC	O-1340571	0767	1	MORRIS ASTOR A	LTC	O-1287744	0263	1	MORRIS JOSEPH A	1LT	O-2040895	0847	2
MORGAN JOHN C	COL	O-0260818	0566	3	MORGAN WILLIE E	CW3	W-2147527	0565	1	MORRIS BEE	2LT	N-0737485	0345	1	MORRIS JOSEPH E	COL	O-0278843	0446	2
MORGAN JOHN D	COL	O-0133085	0648	3	MORGAN WILMER G	LTC	O-0326226	0562	1	MORRIS CAROL	CPT	O-0486690	0656	1	MORRIS JOSEPH F	CW2	W-2148753	0561	1
MORGAN JOHN D JR	COL	O-0238334	0-49	3	MORGAN WINSTON J	MAJ	O-1322802	0464	1	MORRIS CECIL E	LTC	O-1169661	1060	1	MORRIS JOSEPH S	MAJ	O-1052489	0857	[illegible]
MORGAN JOHN E	LTC	O-0236368	0165	3	MORGAN WYNNE H	LTC	O-0237382	0664	3	MORRIS CLAUDE B	LTC	O-0365425	0946	2	MORRIS JOSEPH W	CPT	O-0309474	0763	[illegible]
MORGAN JOHN F	2LT	O-1297409	0944	2	MORGANSTERN ALFRED B	MAJ	O-0207643	0355	3	MORRIS CLAUDE H	CW3	W-2141862	0358	1	MORRIS JULIUS	CW4	W-2005756	0867	3
MORGAN JOHN G	LTC	O-1643149	0665	2	MORGANTI JOSEPH M	MAJ	O-1648615	0261	1	MORRIS DANIEL R	LTC	O-0338337	0965	3	MORRIS LAVAL S	LTC	O-0173936	0160	3
MORGAN JOHN R	MAJ	O-1686721	0465	1	MORGENSTERN FLOYD V	1LT	O-1645846	0945	2	MORRIS DON L	MAJ	O-0969898	1160	1	MORRIS LEE	LTC	O-1294178	0754	1
MORGAN JOHN R JR	1LT	O-0551743	1046	2	MORGENSTERN GEORGE E	MAJ	O-0297719	0145	2	MORRIS DONALD	CPT	O-0221897	0958	3	MORRIS LEONARD S	LTC	O-0116820	0652	3
MORGAN JOHN T	COL	O-0105742	0152	3	MORGNER ARTHUR F	MAJ	O-1035548	0461	2	MORRIS DONALD K	COL	O-0365296	0363	1	MORRIS LEW E	COL	O-0189360	0559	3
MORGAN JOHN W	COL	O-1165918	0867	1	MORHAIME LEO S	MAJ	O-1175810	0968	3	MORRIS DONALD V	LTC	O-0394979	0846	2	MORRIS LEWIS B	CW3	W-2148213	0762	1
MORGAN JOHN W	MAJ	O-1924645	1263	1	MORIAN HAROLD L	LTC	O-0282698	0156	2	MORRIS DONALD W	CW2	W-2213915	0768	1	MORRIS LEWIS E	MAJ	O-0472960	1048	2
MORGAN JOSEPH H JR	CW3	W-2145498	0763	1	MORIARITY WILLIAM J	CPT	O-1645847	1263	3	MORRIS DOUGLAS	CW3	W-2142982	0758	1	MORRIS LLOYD M	COL	O-0149745	1055	3
MORGAN JOSEPH L	CW2	W-2206646	1063	1	MORIARTY FRANCIS E	MAJ	O-1305292	0960	1	MORRIS DOUGLAS B	MAJ	O-0983976	0764	1	MORRIS LOUIS W	1LT	O-0112270	0648	3
MORGAN JOSEPH W	COL	O-0285940	0166	3	MORIARTY GEORGE K	LTC	O-0370533	0968	3	MORRIS DREW W	LTC	O-1118955	1166	1	MORRIS LOVELL J JR	LTC	O-1589392	0564	1
MORGAN KATHRYN M	LTC	N-0700058	0346	1	MORIARTY JAMES T	MAJ	O-0255241	0162	3	MORRIS EARL D	CW3	W-2151986	1064	1	MORRIS LUTHER P	LTC	O-0964697	0768	1
MORGAN KENNETH L	MAJ	O-0962162	0263	1	MORIARTY JOHN P	CPT	O-1174390	0246	2	MORRIS EDWARD F	LTC	O-2000982	0768	1	MORRIS MALCOLM E	MAJ	O-1634162	0364	2
MORGAN LAURENCE C	1LT	O-1581984	0545	2	MORIARTY LAUREN R	CPT	O-0367946	0145	2	MORRIS EDWARD H	CPT	O-0172499	0648	3	MORRIS MANUEL R	CPT	O-1846324	0947	2
MORGAN LAURENCE S	1LT	O-1041201	0445	2	MORIARTY RUSSELL S	MAJ	O-1328833	0263	1	MORRIS EDWARD J	LTC	O-1184265	0566	1	MORRIS MARK W	LTC	O-0287926	0666	3
MORGAN LAWRENCE J	COL	O-0347478	0468	3	MORIARTY VEALE F	LTC	O-0393729	0860	1	MORRIS EDWARD J	1LT	O-1283465	0145	2	MORRIS MARTIN M	1LT	O-1172433	1047	1
MORGAN LEANDER J	CW3	W-2119150	0557	1	MORIARTY WILLIAM M	1LT	O-1934950	0654	2	MORRIS EDWARD P JR	CPT	O-1292043	1159	1	MORRIS MARVIN E	MAJ	O-4063811	1168	1
MORGAN LEONARD C JR	MAJ	O-2021129	0965	1	MORIATY JOHN O	LTC	O-0273284	0468	3	MORRIS EDWARD R	COL	O-0183525	0855	3	MORRIS MARVIN J	CW3	W-2142384	1164	1
MORGAN LEONARD F	CPT	O-2032392	1058	1	MORICONI FRANK E	WO1	W-2151300	1066	1	MORRIS ELISHA	CPT	O-2262460	0461	2	MORRIS MELVIN EUG	2LT	O-1292567	0451	2
MORGAN LEROY E	MAJ	O-2000903	0760	1	MORIE GRACE D	1LT	N-0783122	0846	1	MORRIS EVA M	1LT	N-0772715	1045	1	MORRIS MELVIN J	CW3	W-2209289	0868	1

NAME	GRADE	SVC NO	DATE RET MO YR	RET CODE
MORRIS MELVIN L	CW2	W-2150177	0964	1
MORRIS NORMAN	LTC	O-1114668	1061	1
MORRIS NORMAN W	LTC	O-1110675	0962	1
MORRIS ORVAL	CPT	O-1298574	0457	1
MORRIS OSCAR	CW3	W-2116354	0660	1
MORRIS PAUL E	COL	O-0319558	1065	1
MORRIS PERRY L V	MAJ	O-1313116	1160	1
MORRIS QUENTIN P	LTC	O-1551319	0563	3
MORRIS R W	WO1	W-2146348	0459	1
MORRIS RAWLINS M	MAJ	O-1164836	0258	1
MORRIS RAYMOND E	1LT	O-1894763	0958	1
MORRIS ROBERT	CW3	W-2145145	0962	1
MORRIS ROBERT E	MAJ	O-5301544	1268	1
MORRIS ROBERT E	CPT	O-0160946	0651	3
MORRIS ROBERT H	COL	O-0162361	0159	1
MORRIS ROBERT K	WO1	W-2126659	1061	2
MORRIS ROBERT L	LTC	O-1048505	0964	1
MORRIS ROBERT L	1LT	O-1551949	1264	2
MORRIS ROBERT M	MAJ	O-1115713	0757	1
MORRIS ROY C JR	1LT	O-2211233	0553	2
MORRIS ROY H	LTC	O-0270469	0268	3
MORRIS ROY L	CPT	O-1333105	0256	1
MORRIS SAMUEL P	COL	O-0246032	0462	1
MORRIS SIDNEY C	CW3	W-2144344	0664	1
MORRIS STANLEY M	MAJ	O-0359355	0868	3
MORRIS STEPHEN	LTC	O-1573450	1054	1
MORRIS STEPHEN F	COL	O-1633422	0560	1
MORRIS THEODORE F	CPT	O-0498816	0455	1
MORRIS THEODORE L	LTC	O-0507319	1065	3
MORRIS THEODORE N	1LT	O-0536117	0845	2
MORRIS THERON K	CW3	W-2142885	0158	1
MORRIS WALLACE E	CW4	W-2141390	0166	1
MORRIS WALLACE H	LTC	O-0321199	0157	1
MORRIS WALLACE M	MAJ	O-1945897	0966	3
MORRIS WALTER	MAJ	O-1308996	0760	1
MORRIS WALTER C	CW3	W-2209401	0468	1
MORRIS WALTER J JR	2LT	O-1108182	0145	2
MORRIS WALTER T	CW2	W-2102117	0949	1
MORRIS WILLIAM A	LTC	O-0384299	0767	3
MORRIS WILLIAM B JR	MAJ	O-1822173	1160	1
MORRIS WILLIAM C	COL	O-0521542	1147	2
MORRIS WILLIAM C	CW2	W-2210689	1066	1
MORRIS WILLIAM D	CPT	O-0546873	0747	2
MORRIS WILLIAM H	LTC	O-0182784	1047	1
MORRIS WILLIAM H	MAJ	O-0389942	0445	2
MORRIS WILLIAM H JR	MAJ	O-1177915	0162	1
MORRIS WILLIAM R	CW4	W-2141639	0867	1
MORRIS WILLIAM S	CPT	O-0415592	0953	2
MORRIS WILLIAM W JR	LTC	O-1310749	0663	1
MORRIS WILMA B	1LT	O-1108973	0766	1
MORRIS WILSON	MAJ	O-1323955	1160	1
MORRISON ALAN C	CW2	W-2108309	1059	1
MORRISON ALFRED F	CPT	O-1996653	0856	1
MORRISON ALVIN A	LTC	O-0273435	0664	3
MORRISON BENJAMIN A	CW2	W-2144647	1159	1
MORRISON CHARLES H	MAJ	O-0112344	0455	3
MORRISON CHARLES J	1LT	O-0537435	0847	2
MORRISON CHARLES W	1LT	O-1307565	0745	2
MORRISON CLARENCE F	LTC	O-2279330	1167	1
MORRISON CLAUDE B	2LT	O-1686527	0146	2
MORRISON CLIFFORD O	1LT	O-1177105	0562	1
MORRISON CLIFFORD P	COL	O-0300251	0367	3
MORRISON DANIEL W	CPT	O-0450460	0750	1
MORRISON DONALD A	1LT	O-1304770	0146	2
MORRISON DONALD J	MAJ	O-1951702	0266	1
MORRISON DONALD K	LTC	O-0103359	1152	3
MORRISON EDWIN V JR	MAJ	O-0286784	1267	3
MORRISON ELEANOR M	LTC	L-0600001	0163	2
MORRISON EVERT F	CW2	W-2146083	0365	1
MORRISON FRANCIS G	LTC	O-0910754	0765	3
MORRISON FRANK G	1LT	O-0116821	0652	3
MORRISON FRANK H	1LT	O-1321369	0246	2
MORRISON FRED C SR	MAJ	O-0975181	0264	1
MORRISON GARLAND V	CPT	O-0499496	0347	1
MORRISON GEORGE G	CPT	O-1684780	0246	2

NAME	GRADE	SVC NO	DATE RET MO YR	RET CODE
MORRISON GEORGE R	LTC	O-1331078	0964	1
MORRISON HARRY F	MAJ	O-0582160	0955	1
MORRISON HENRY C	CPT	O-1547410	0952	2
MORRISON HENRY G	WO1	W-2148415	0455	1
MORRISON HERMAN H	LTC	O-1031580	0160	1
MORRISON HOMER W	LTC	O-1318999	1066	1
MORRISON ISAAC F	LTC	O-0187219	0951	3
MORRISON IVAN L	2LT	O-1169261	1145	2
MORRISON J ATWOOD	COL	O-0302938	0160	1
MORRISON JAMES O JR	1LT	O-1285274	0845	2
MORRISON JEANNE E	1LT	N-0730551	1045	1
MORRISON JOHN A	LTC	O-1599393	1163	1
MORRISON JOHN L	LTC	O-0360859	0763	3
MORRISON JOHN W	MAJ	O-1318070	0561	1
MORRISON JOSEPH W	LTC	O-0351143	0159	1
MORRISON JOSEPH W	LTC	O-1328730	0563	1
MORRISON LORRAINE G	MAJ	O-0441782	0147	2
MORRISON LOUIS C	CW4	W-2121968	0760	1
MORRISON LOUIS E	LTC	O-1290288	0461	1
MORRISON LOUIS JR	CW3	W-2211602	1168	1
MORRISON LUTHER S	2LT	O-1303375	0645	2
MORRISON MARCUS E	MAJ	O-0369301	0446	2
MORRISON NORMAN B	MAJ	O-0291470	0344	2
MORRISON NORMAN T	MAJ	O-1044906	1164	1
MORRISON PAUL L	COL	O-0121799	1059	3
MORRISON PHILLIPS L	CPT	O-0490097	0343	2
MORRISON PRUDENZA S	MAJ	L-1010055	0163	1
MORRISON RAYMOND C	CPT	O-0498726	0550	1
MORRISON REGINALD G	1LT	O-0401679	0344	2
MORRISON RICHARD A	WO1	W-2139480	0646	2
MORRISON RICHARD L	CW4	W-2009215	0868	3
MORRISON RICHARD R	COL	O-0334421	0648	3
MORRISON RICHARD R	LTC	O-0342190	0746	2
MORRISON ROBERT N	LTC	O-1294345	0563	1
MORRISON ROBERT T	CPT	O-0506149	0146	2
MORRISON THOMAS O	LTC	O-0277609	1266	3
MORRISON THOMAS E	LTC	O-0444359	0257	1
MORRISON VERNE B	MAJ	O-1645850	1166	3
MORRISON WHEELER J	LTC	O-1175252	0863	1
MORRISON WILLIAM D	LTC	O-0161285	0157	2
MORRISON WILLIAM E	MAJ	O-1044912	0666	1
MORRISON WILLIAM E	MAJ	O-1063071	1064	1
MORRISON WILLIAM G	MAJ	O-0258784	1066	3
MORRISON WILLIAM J	MAJ	O-1922590	1265	1
MORRISROE ROBERT	CW2	W-2150626	0157	1
MORRISS ABNER B	1LT	O-0915361	0744	2
MORRISSEY ARTHUR T	CW2	W-3000421	1168	1
MORRISSEY EDWARD L	LTC	O-0507614	0265	3
MORRISSEY FRANCIS C	MAJ	O-1322804	0263	1
MORRISSEY JAMES T	LTC	O-1104309	0562	1
MORRISSEY JOHN	MAJ	O-0286594	0166	3
MORRISSEY JOHN B	LTC	O-0323284	0247	2
MORRISSEY JOHN F	CPT	O-1031011	0459	1
MORRISSEY LAURENCE	LTC	O-1314942	0546	2
MORRISSEY PAUL R	CW3	W-2145779	0666	1
MORRISSEY RAYMOND E	1LT	O-1014408	0460	1
MORRISSEY THOMAS H	CW3	RW-2152164	0166	1
MORROW ALFRED	MAJ	O-1052090	0358	1
MORROW BAILEY M	MAJ	O-2004460	0868	2
MORROW CHARLES H	MAJ	O-0473696	0858	1
MORROW CHARLES M	1LT	O-0513541	0346	2
MORROW DAVID C	LTC	O-1102880	0161	1
MORROW EUGENE F	1LT	O-0141882	0454	3
MORROW FRANK S	LTC	O-0910368	0264	3
MORROW HALE	MAJ	O-0286650	1044	2
MORROW HASKELF E	MAJ	O-0253451	1047	2
MORROW HENRY	1LT	O-0164213	0637	1
MORROW JACK C	1LT	O-2053900	1145	2
MORROW JAMES E	LTC	O-1048910	0866	1
MORROW JAMES E	LTC	O-1641601	0262	1
MORROW JAMES H	1LT	O-0536909	0845	2
MORROW JAMES P	2LT	O-0537436	0345	2
MORROW RAYMOND N	CPT	O-1309385	0754	2
MORROW ROBERT D	LTC	O-0168741	0444	2
MORROW ROBERT P	LTC	O-0315285	1059	1

NAME	GRADE	SVC NO	DATE RET MO YR	RET CODE
MORROW ROBERT P	CPT	O-0158377	0246	2
MORROW ROBERT P	1LT	O-1056177	1051	2
MORROW SIDNEY S	2LT	O-1017572	0146	2
MORROW TALMADGE D	1LT	O-1825235	0767	1
MORROW THADDEUS L	LTC	O-0259854	0666	3
MORROW WALTER R	LTC	O-0334220	0958	1
MORROW WILEY M	MAJ	O-0941525	0667	1
MORROW WILLIAM H	2LT	O-1578892	0566	2
MORROW WILLIAM J	LTC	O-0349971	0246	2
MORROW WILLIAM T	2LT	O-2007671	0346	2
MORROW WINSTON V	LTC	O-0141834	0648	3
MORS GEORGE L	COL	O-0280653	0462	3
MORSE ALBERT W JR	LTC	O-0158330	0760	3
MORSE ANTHONY W	LTC	O-1280220	1060	1
MORSE ARNOLD A	CW4	W-2144224	1265	1
MORSE ARTHUR M	MAJ	O-0240645	1064	3
MORSE CALVIN	MAJ	O-0956057	0962	1
MORSE CLAYTON C	CPT	O-0214026	0264	3
MORSE DONALD S	CW4	W-2004760	0966	1
MORSE EDWARD J	MAJ	O-0976231	0762	1
MORSE FRANK E	MAJ	O-0128460	0350	3
MORSE GEORGE B	COL	O-0121796	0651	3
MORSE HARRISON R JR	CPT	O-1018198	1046	2
MORSE HENRY P	COL	O-0339673	1160	1
MORSE HOWARD C	CPT	O-1044311	0147	2
MORSE HOWARD M	1LT	O-1172561	1044	2
MORSE JACK W	MAJ	O-1059008	0762	1
MORSE JESSE S	MAJ	O-1588187	0260	1
MORSE LEWIS W	COL	O-0909172	0963	3
MORSE LOUIS E	COL	O-0174546	0846	2
MORSE MARIE A	2LT	N-0731605	0445	1
MORSE NORMAN T	MAJ	O-1924648	0368	1
MORSE PERCY	LTC	O-0499561	1054	1
MORSE RAYMOND R	LTC	O-0213600	0955	3
MORSE RICHARD O	CW4	W-2123320	1060	1
MORSE RICHARD L	CW3	W-2144062	0461	1
MORSE ROY F	MAJ	O-0246391	0158	3
MORSE THELMA M	CW4	V-0120159	0967	1
MORSE WILFRED C	CPT	O-0973173	0961	1
MORSE WILLIAM R	LTC	O-0949409	1162	1
MORSON THERON D	1LT	O-0163337	0355	3
MORSS CLYDE L	CW3	W-2144452	0563	1
MORSS VIRGIL R	LTC	O-0242731	0864	3
MORT CHARLES L	MAJ	O-1051696	1066	3
MORT ROBERT T	LTC	O-2030848	0365	1
MORTENSEN DOUGLAS A	MAJ	O-2025138	0163	1
MORTENSEN EDWIN J	1LT	O-1057178	1045	2
MORTENSEN FREDERIC	COL	O-0186181	0253	3
MORTENSEN MARTIN A	2LT	O-1168387	0645	2
MORTENSEN RODNEY F	LTC	O-1171689	0466	1
MORTENSEN WILLIAM J	1LT	O-1057831	0146	2
MORTENSON DONALD R	LTC	O-0975234	0868	1
MORTENSON FRANCINE B	MAJ	L-0201272	0568	2
MORTIMER JOHN C	CW3	W-2209075	0168	1
MORTIMER WINFIELD S	LTC	O-0277665	0867	3
MORTON ALMON W	2LT	O-1308997	0844	2
MORTON CARL	MAJ	O-1289611	0147	2
MORTON EARL D	CPT	O-1298101	1045	2
MORTON EDWIN A	LTC	O-0522529	1163	3
MORTON EDWIN A	CW2	W-2214650	0767	1
MORTON HAROLD S	COL	O-0425611	0646	2
MORTON HENRY A	MAJ	O-0163708	1056	3
MORTON HOWARD W	WO1	W-2152302	1057	2
MORTON IRA H	CPT	O-0353275	1045	2
MORTON JAMES C	CPT	O-1060898	0462	2
MORTON JAMES F	MAJ	O-0228833	0748	1
MORTON JAMES C	CPT	O-0366352	0546	2
MORTON JAMES M	MAJ	O-1183934	0463	1
MORTON JAMES M	MAJ	O-1797859	0264	1
MORTON JIMMIE O	MAJ	O-2262581	0168	1
MORTON JOHN K	MAJ	O-0394613	0660	1
MORTON JOHN K	MAJ	O-0483108	0457	1
MORTON LELAND A	CW2	W-2118146	0553	1
MORTON MANUEL M	CPT	O-1042119	0456	1
MORTON MARY W	2LT	N-0759462	0544	1

NAME	GRADE	SVC NO	DATE RET MO YR	RET CODE
MORTON MATTHEW W	MAJ	O-0933669	0757	1
MORTON NORMAN W	MAJ	O-0994503	0764	1
MORTON OLIVER F	LTC	O-0315222	[illegible]62	1
MORTON PAUL P	MAJ	O-1039481	0262	1
MORTON PAUL S JR	CPT	O-0432950	0646	2
MORTON RALPH E	LTC	O-0490213	0456	1
MORTON RALPH W JR	1LT	O-1014172	1046	2
MORTON RAY W	LTC	O-1947584	1062	1
MORTON ROBERT J	LTC	O-0171235	0460	3
MORTON ROY M	MAJ	O-0191466	1051	3
MORTON THOMAS C	MAJ	O-1323254	1159	2
MORTON ULYSSES	CW3	W-3150273	1068	1
MORTON WILLIAM D	CPT	O-1166788	1145	2
MORTRUDE ELLIS L	MAJ	O-1004380	0168	3
MORUD STANLEY J	MAJ	O-0756659	0667	1
MORYLE FELIX	CW3	W-2148262	1159	1
MOSBY BEATRICE O	2LT	N-0772208	0345	1
MOSBY CLARENCE L	MAJ	O-1297574	0261	1
MOSBY LEON	2LT	O-2027462	0547	1
MOSCICKE LEE F JR	LTC	O-0942977	1066	1
MOSEBACH JAMES A	LTC	O-0301716	0749	2
MOSELEY BRUCE W	MAJ	O-2020328	1065	1
MOSELEY CHAMP G	LTC	O-0219854	0664	3
MOSELEY CRAIG D	MAJ	O-2204041	1065	1
MOSELEY EDWARD F	MAJ	O-1636368	0160	1
MOSELEY FREDERICK	LTC	O-0380670	0462	1
MOSELEY GEORGE C	MAJ	O-1030598	0250	1
MOSELEY GEORGE O JR	CPT	O-1635140	0559	1
MOSELEY HOLSTON G	CW4	W-2147720	0464	1
MOSELEY JAMES R	CW2	W-2153003	1062	1
MOSELEY ROBERT F JR	LTC	O-0228185	0465	3
MOSELEY THOMAS F	CPT	O-1554446	0146	2
MOSELEY WILLIAM L JR	MAJ	O-1318818	0665	1
MOSER CHRIS J	CPT	O-0537895	0847	2
MOSER EUGENE P	MAJ	O-0315912	0162	1
MOSER FLOYD D JR	MAJ	O-1557645	0961	1
MOSER HORACE G	MAJ	O-0966574	0161	2
MOSER JOHN G	LTC	O-1322360	0263	1
MOSER JOSIAH L JR	LTC	O-1577599	0959	1
MOSER MORENO	CPT	O-0497370	0749	1
MOSER MORRIS K	1LT	O-1895874	0557	3
MOSER RICHARD H	1LT	O-0430492	0845	2
MOSER RICHARD J	MAJ	O-2265612	1068	1
MOSER WALTER L	LTC	O-0275289	0854	3
MOSER ZACKUR	LTC	O-0505353	0257	1
MOSES ALAN M	MAJ	O-0116822	1054	3
MOSES BERNARD A	LTC	O-0299961	0462	1
MOSES EDWARD W	MAJ	O-0122955	0654	3
MOSES ELBERT R JR	LTC	O-0903452	0468	3
MOSES FRANK B	COL	O-0451360	0456	1
MOSES GEORGE W	CW3	W-2149124	1063	1
MOSES GEORGE W JR	LTC	O-0236861	0264	3
MOSES HAROLD T	COL	O-0314136	0462	1
MOSES HERMON L	MAJ	O-0335921	0844	2
MOSES JOHN R	1LT	O-1019183	1045	2
MOSES KELLIE H	LTC	O-0354127	0159	2
MOSES MAXMILLIAN	CPT	O-0505040	0744	2
MOSES ROBERT L	CPT	O-0282757	0868	3
MOSES RUTH A	CPT	L-0800006	0347	2
MOSES WALTER E	LTC	O-0279564	0866	3
MOSES WILLIAM G	COL	O-0100078	0360	3
MOSES WILLIAM P	CW4	W-2004977	0267	3
MOSHBERGER MARTIN	COL	O-0249591	0959	1
MOSHER FREDRICK G	WO1	W-2143036	0558	1
MOSHER GRANT O	LTC	O-1310751	0367	1
MOSHER HAROLD S	LTC	O-1332514	0665	2
MOSHER HELEN M	CPT	N-0720317	1046	1
MOSHER JOHN F	COL	O-0240785	0663	1
MOSHER KENNETH A	MAJ	O-1042380	0962	1
MOSHER WILLIAM C	MAJ	O-0140737	0354	3
MOSHIER RALPH M	CW2	W-2213424	1067	1
MOSHOLDER ROBERT M	CW3	W-2141863	0860	1
MOSIER ARTHUR I	CW4	W-2104774	0559	1
MOSIER ULYSSES G JR	CPT	O-0222251	0762	3
MOSIER 2ND LORAL	LTC	O-0429258	*0655	2

NAME	GRADE	SVC NO	DATE RET MO YR	RET CODE
MOSIG JOHN J	CPT	0-0545543	0747	2
MOSKOT EDWARD J	CPT	0-0499596	1053	2
MOSKOWITZ HENRY	CPT	0-0482103	0145	2
MOSKOWITZ IRVING L	LTC	0-0428582	0557	1
MOSLEY ARTHUR P	2LT	0-1998507	0546	2
MOSLEY DONALD C	CW3	W-2147062	0257	1
MOSLEY DOUGLAS	MAJ	0-2018201	0661	1
MOSLEY HENRY D	LTC	0-0281916	0768	3
MOSLEY HENRY G	LTC	0-0269902	1167	3
MOSLEY HUGH G	LTC	0-0296627	0259	3
MOSLEY JAMES W	CW2	W-2144538	0465	1
MOSLEY JOHN E	COL	0-0193883	1157	1
MOSLEY JOHN W	CW2	W-2149673	0168	1
MOSLEY WILLIAM F	CPT	0-2005432	0757	2
MOSMAN HARRY W	1LT	0-0542205	0945	2
MOSMILLER WALTER E	COL	0-0255270	1162	3
MOSS CLARENCE E	CPT	0-0104897	0648	3
MOSS CLAY B	MAJ	0-1182663	0658	1
MOSS CLIFFORD F	CPT	0-0258945	1165	3
MOSS DANIEL R	LTC	0-0502655	0760	3
MOSS DONALD D	CPT	0-1053743	0647	2
MOSS DURWOOD W	CPT	0-0166126	0153	3
MOSS EDWARD W	CPT	0-0978973	0461	1
MOSS JACK E	LTC	0-1290794	0961	1
MOSS JACK G	MAJ	0-1167130	1060	1
MOSS JAMES M	MAJ	0-0416750	0348	2
MOSS JAMES R	CPT	0-2204433	0468	2
MOSS JOHN P	LTC	0-0325614	0660	1
MOSS LEONARD	WO1	W-2121198	0148	1
MOSS MAVOR J	CPT	0-1684790	1045	2
MOSS NOVELLE H	LTC	0-0426912	0365	1
MOSS RAPHAEL S	2LT	0-0462342	0744	2
MOSS RAYMOND W	CW3	RW-2150330	0764	1
MOSS VERDIE S	LTC	0-1307059	0763	1
MOSS WARREN P	LTC	0-1059566	0867	1
MOSS WILBERT	CPT	0-0109581	1121	1
MOSS WILLIAM N	CPT	0-0485883	0245	2
MOSSACK EDWARD L	CPT	0-0134183	1052	3
MOSSAWIR HARVEY H	MAJ	0-0321979	1265	3
MOSSER THOMAS M	2LT	0-1052894	0345	2
MOSTROM ALBERT C JR	LTC	0-1314821	0264	1
MOSTY ROBERT L	CPT	0-0316583	0347	2
MOSURE GAYLORD H	CW3	W-2148129	0461	2
MOTE CARL H JR	2LT	0-0359897	0944	2
MOTE ERSHAL L	CW3	W-2152131	0664	1
MOTE JOHN H	CPT	0-0267755	0446	2
MOTES PETE	WO1	W-2108656	0552	1
MOTHERSHEAD DORIS S	2LT	N-0788490	0644	1
MOTHERSHEAD EARL K	MAJ	0-0921008	0357	2
MOTHERSHEAD ROBERT A	LTC	0-0318360	0446	2
MOTHERWAY WILLIAM	CW4	W-2002570	0858	3
MOTICH MARK	CPT	0-0497201	1049	1
MOTKOWSKI BERNARD S	COL	0-0313164	1054	1
MOTKOWSKI CECELIA J	1LT	N-0796389	0647	2
MOTL ANNA	2LT	N-0700331	0839	2
MOTL JOSEPHINE	MAJ	N-0700344	0246	1
MOTLEY HENRY L	MAJ	0-0967128	0862	1
MOTLEY HULON E	CPT	0-0992063	0162	1
MOTLEY WILLIAM A SR	LTC	0-0961536	0168	1
MOTLONG CHAUNCEY E	CPT	0-0147534	1154	3
MOTOGAWA LAWRENCE N	CW3	W-2136020	0364	1
MOTON RONALD O	LTC	0-1081569	0962	1
MOTSCHALL JAMES N	1LT	0-1047693	0144	2
MOTSCHALL ROBERT E	1LT	0-1796136	0244	2
MOTSON CHARLES E JR	LTC	0-1547086	0568	1
MOTT CHARLES R	1LT	0-1305093	0345	2
MOTT FREDERICK	MAJ	0-0248439	0144	2
MOTT GEORGE F	COL	0-0254500	0767	3
MOTT GEORGE W	CPT	0-1635144	1045	2
MOTT HUBERT A	LTC	0-1686653	0767	1
MOTT JAMES C	M G	0-0176119	1160	3
MOTT JAMES M	LTC	0-0196246	0253	3
MOTT MARSHALL L III	LTC	0-1035549	0563	1
MOTT SELDON R	COL	0-0243462	0158	3
MOTT VERN E	CPT	0-0255281	0162	3

NAME	GRADE	SVC NO	DATE RET MO YR	RET CODE
MOTT WALTER C	MAJ	0-0140735	1057	3
MOTT WILLIARD C	LTC	0-1173394	0561	2
MOTTA ANTHONY F	LTC	0-1280875	0457	1
MOTTERN ALBERT J	LTC	0-0172756	0647	2
MOTTERN LAYTON R	COL	0-0210297	1154	3
MOTTILLA RICHARD A	1LT	0-1017986	0152	2
MOTTLEY ROBERT C	COL	0-0224717	0454	2
MOTTO ROCCO L	CPT	0-0435315	1046	2
MOTTORN JACOB P	COL	0-0248058	0862	3
MOTYLINSKI JOSEPH	CW2	W-2113007	1051	2
MOTZ JOHN R	LTC	0-0316248	0362	3
MOTZ WALTER R	MAJ	0-0492510	0266	3
MOTZNY LEON W JR	LTC	0-1106982	0864	1
MOUDY ALFRED L	LTC	0-0121147	0648	3
MOUDY RALPH W	LTC	0-0415595	0467	1
MOUKAD PAUL R	CW3	W-2153159	1162	1
MOULD GEORGE F	MAJ	0-1574104	0163	1
MOULTHROP HENRY S	MAJ	0-0177808	1051	3
MOULTIS CHARLES A	MAJ	0-1947926	0667	3
MOULTON ALVA H	1LT	0-1185782	0647	1
MOULTON EARL R	LTC	0-0236379	0862	1
MOULTON FREDRICK J	1LT	0-1294346	0945	2
MOULTON GEORGE O	CW3	W-2141640	0156	1
MOULTON JAMES A	LTC	0-0196235	0162	3
MOULTON ROBERT P	CW2	W-2150936	1157	1
MOUNCE KENNETH L	LTC	0-0284526	0866	3
MOUNGER DWYN M	LTC	0-0517998	0866	3
MOUNSEY WILLIAM B	MAJ	0-0450368	0864	1
MOUNT ERMON E	CPT	0-0287000	0655	3
MOUNT GEORGE E	1LT	0-1305631	0146	2
MOUNT HARRY V JR	CPT	0-1107607	0146	2
MOUNT JAMES B	LTC	0-2263342	0968	1
MOUNT JOHN B JR	CPT	0-0254062	0567	3
MOUNT MARK L	LTC	0-0240309	0165	3
MOUNT ROBERT H	1LT	0-0266990	1045	2
MOUNT WILSON H	LTC	0-1796839	1262	3
MOUNTAIN DANIEL J	2LT	0-0495243	0648	1
MOUNTAIN EARLE	LTC	0-0400134	0762	1
MOUNTFORD FRANK A	CW2	W-2145220	0568	2
MOUNTJOY PEARL B	MAJ	0-0361344	0455	1
MOUNTS LEONARD J	CW4	W-2208291	1168	1
MOUNTZ KENNETH B	MAJ	0-0387137	0460	1
MOURAS TED	CW2	W-3430173	1067	1
MOVOLD CLINTON H	2LT	0-1173007	1043	2
MOW KUI P	CW3	W-2154669	0367	1
MOWAT EDITH F	LTC	N-0722629	0263	1
MOWAT WILLIAM J JR	LTC	0-0408677	1060	1
MOWATT GEORGE	CPT	0-0491565	0848	1
MOWBRAY EMMA H	CPT	N-0760627	1052	2
MOWBRAY ORVILLE H	LTC	0-0382566	0364	3
MOWBRAY RICHARD M	MAJ	0-0999552	0965	1
MOWEN JOHN H	CPT	0-0412548	104N	2
MOWER CHARLES J	1LT	0-0507592	0545	2
MOWER FRANK C	LTC	0-0235639	0965	3
MOWER NATHANIEL	COL	0-0319665	0767	3
MOWERS LEONARD F	MAJ	0-0256645	0256	2
MOWERY JAMES F	LTC	0-0448051	0662	1
MOWERY SARAH E	MAJ	N-0797508	0568	1
MOWITZ ARNO P JR	COL	0-0296307	0560	1
MOWLDS WILLIAM L	LTC	0-0168443	0559	3
MOWRAR HAROLD M	MAJ	0-1886487	0864	1
MOWRY DON F	LTC	0-1182429	0762	1
MOWRY FRANK W JR	CW2	W-3100564	0968	1
MOWRY RICHMOND C	MAJ	0-1107608	0353	2
MOWRY ROBERT B	MAJ	0-2096152	0368	1
MOXHAM CYRIL B	MAJ	0-2263438	0665	1
MOXLEY CALVIN I	CPT	0-0495404	0657	1
MOXLEY GEORGE N	CW3	W-2151423	0363	1
MOXON JAMES A	MAJ	0-0324806	0446	2
MOY FRANK	MAJ	0-1580064	0557	1
MOYCO GUALBERTO	1LT	0-0890443	0158	1
MOYE JAMES E	CPT	0-0505111	1045	2
MOYE LEON B	COL	0-0300946	0252	1
MOYE MACON J JR	LTC	0-0742765	0768	1
MOYER BILL A	CW3	W-2205296	0267	1

NAME	GRADE	SVC NO	DATE RET MO YR	RET CODE
MOYER CARL W	2LT	0-1295585	0445	2
MOYER CHARLES D	1LT	0-5201097	0959	2
MOYER CLIFFORD	CPT	0-0174671	0659	1
MOYER DWIGHT L	LTC	0-0423460	0767	3
MOYER EARL H JR	MAJ	0-1999155	0864	1
MOYER EDWARD F	MAJ	0-1296733	0760	1
MOYER ELSIE G	CPT	N-0700560	0644	1
MOYER HARRY	MAJ	0-1302333	0758	1
MOYER IRVIN P	MAJ	0-0151431	0361	2
MOYER JACK A	CPT	0-1289463	0657	1
MOYER JACOB E	MAJ	0-1588763	1058	1
MOYER KENNETH G	CPT	0-0991974	0662	1
MOYER KERMIT W	LTC	0-0401461	0961	1
MOYER LAWRENCE R	LTC	0-1108186	0263	1
MOYER MARY E	2LT	N-0761284	0345	1
MOYER REX L	CW4	W-2122005	0559	1
MOYER REX M	LTC	0-0450678	0863	1
MOYER SHERMAN M	CW3	W-2120038	0159	1
MOYER WILBUR J	CW4	W-2001524	0667	3
MOYERS ALFRED J	WO1	W-2122965	0645	2
MOYERS JAMES P	1LT	0-1797336	0845	2
MOYES WILLIAM S	COL	0-0234721	1262	3
MOYLAN JAMES E	1LT	0-0492231	0246	2
MOYLE JOHN P	CW4	W-2144521	0266	1
MOYLE WALLACE A	COL	0-0171128	1157	3
MOYNIHAN PATRICK J	1LT	0-0494990	0348	1
MOYS NEAL D	MAJ	0-2043112	0761	1
MOYSE HERMANN	LTC	0-0108219	0951	3
MOZES EDWARD	MAJ	0-0326808	0146	2
MOZLEY HUGH A	COL	0-0403781	1060	1
MOZZER ALEXANDER	CPT	0-0465628	1045	2
MRAKAVA MICHAEL J	LTC	0-1633423	0962	1
MRAZ ALEX N	CW4	W-2102122	0656	1
MROCZKOWSKI CHARLES	MAJ	0-2262649	0263	1
MUCHA FRANK R	1LT	0-1634164	1044	2
MUCHEMORE FRANKLIN B	MAJ	0-1593115	0664	1
MUCHKA WALTER A	1LT	0-0420708	1144	2
MUCHMORE PETE M	2LT	0-1822175	0345	2
MUCHMORE WARREN G	1LT	0-1112334	0146	2
MUCK JAMES B	MAJ	0-4005021	1065	1
MUCKELROY ANTHONY	LTC	0-0357555	0762	3
MUCKEY MELVIN J	MAJ	0-0153736	0352	3
MUCKLE CRAIG W	LTC	0-0296339	1065	3
MUCKSTADT JOHN J	1LT	0-1019189	0546	2
MUDD WILLIAM C	CPT	0-1309386	0847	2
MUDGE JOHN W	COL	0-0293576	0861	3
MUDON GEORGE M	LTC	0-1037643	1264	3
MUDRY JOSEPH	CPT	0-0382256	0146	2
MUDSE JOSEPH W	1LT	0-0939701	0158	1
MUEDEN GEORGE F JR	CPT	0-0356187	0746	2
MUEHL FLORY M	1LT	0-1290110	0545	2
MUEHL JOSEPH W	CPT	0-1167995	1060	1
MUEHLBERGER C W	CW3	W-2142179	1157	1
MUELLER ADOLPH R	COL	0-0258180	0965	3
MUELLER CHARLES J	LTC	0-0360067	1057	2
MUELLER CHESTER	COL	0-0208506	0962	3
MUELLER CHESTER R	CPT	0-0554858	0447	2
MUELLER DON J	CPT	0-1999191	0657	1
MUELLER FRANK J	MAJ	0-0370238	0952	2
MUELLER FRANK J	MAJ	0-0988068	0663	1
MUELLER FREDERICK	LTC	0-1583413	0260	2
MUELLER GUSTAV C	MAJ	0-1178905	0256	2
MUELLER HARRIE S	COL	0-0102015	0651	3
MUELLER HENRY J JR	CW4	W-2143420	1067	1
MUELLER HERBERT	MAJ	0-4020995	0168	1
MUELLER HOWARD G	CW3	W-2208640	1167	1
MUELLER JACKSON W	CW3	W-2149825	0464	1
MUELLER JOSEPH E	CPT	0-0406840	1046	2
MUELLER KEITH E	2LT	0-0528029	1045	2
MUELLER LEROY W	LTC	0-0429239	0261	1
MUELLER LESTER W	MAJ	0-2262275	1061	1
MUELLER MILTON O	CW3	W-2150528	1263	1
MUELLER MORRIS A	COL	0-1699868	0166	3
MUELLER OTTE J	MAJ	0-1633424	0262	1
MUELLER REINHOLD	CW3	W-2146811	0559	1

NAME	GRADE	SVC NO	DATE RET MO YR	RET CODE
MUELLER ROY M	LTC	0-0314809	0467	2
MUELLER WALTER E	LTC	0-0196332	0463	3
MUELLER WESLEY H	MAJ	0-0479827	0461	3
MUER JULIUS A JR	CW2	W-3430258	1066	1
MUES DONALD D	MAJ	0-1924799	0666	1
MUFFLEY ROBERT T	1LT	0-1634165	1045	2
MUGAVIN FRANCIS M	CW4	W-2109915	0868	3
MUGERDITCHIAN SHAR	1LT	0-1303009	0745	2
MUGFORD CHARLES	LTC	0-1046577	0162	2
MUHAR ANDREW V JR	LTC	0-1336105	0566	2
MUHL JAMES P	MAJ	0-1052491	0462	1
MUHLBAIER JAMES W	MAJ	0-2020997	0366	1
MUHLENBERG FREDRIC	COL	0-0167177	0648	3
MUHS ELEANOR J	CPT	N-0722208	0953	2
MUHSFELD E W	LTC	0-0442665	0446	2
MUILENBURG TEUNIS H	CPT	0-0309467	1145	2
MUIR CHARLES H JR	LTC	0-0215977	0664	3
MUIR CHARLES W	CPT	0-0523343	1045	2
MUIR HUGH B	1LT	0-0538623	1146	2
MUIR HUGH H	COL	0-0189251	0153	3
MUIR KENNETH L	MAJ	0-0275200	1057	3
MUIR ROBERT L	LTC	0-0221388	0763	3
MUIR SYLVESTER	LTC	0-0298000	1165	3
MUIR WILLIAM W JR	CPT	0-1292926	0846	2
MUIRHEAD GRACIEUSE	MAJ	N-0764249	0364	1
MUIRHEAD RAY J	MAJ	0-0989170	0765	1
MUIRHEAD RICHARD J	LTC	0-1994959	0863	1
MUIZERS JOHN F	CW3	W-2146486	1062	1
MUJICA FRANK E	1LT	0-0398023	0845	2
MUKENSNABLE L K	1LT	N-0731873	0546	1
MULADORE ROBERT W	LTC	0-1050003	0961	1
MULBERRY ALBERT F	LTC	0-1913217	0667	1
MULCAHEY JOHN T JR	LTC	0-1945651	1162	1
MULCAHY HUBERT F	MAJ	0-1552939	0658	1
MULCAHY JOHN J	MAJ	0-1328733	0565	1
MULCAHY ROBERT E	MAJ	0-2053862	0461	1
MULCAHY THOMAS A	LTC	0-1635148	0364	1
MULCAHY TIMOTHY J	MAJ	0-0163855	0846	2
MULDER JOHAN	LTC	0-0467314	0168	3
MULDOON JAMES E	MAJ	0-0410562	1146	2
MULDOON MARY A	MAJ	N-0700528	0546	1
MULDROW HAL L	M G	0-0250319	0665	3
MULDROW JAMES J	LTC	0-0437951	0962	1
MULDROW JOSEPH F	COL	0-0118196	1049	3
MULE WALTER	LTC	0-1047695	0663	2
MULFORD JAMES T	CPT	0-1059216	0246	2
MULFORD JAMES W	LTC	0-0426666	1266	1
MULFORD JOHN A	LTC	0-0293091	0961	2
MULFORD RALPH K	2LT	0-0554456	1145	2
MULFORD TODD M	LTC	0-0371671	1052	2
MULGANNON ROBERT E	CPT	0-1994483	0353	2
MULGREW EDWARD L	MAJ	0-0954202	1263	1
MULHALL LAWRENCE J	COL	0-0178412	0560	1
MULHERN FRANCIS L	LTC	0-1281212	0662	1
MULHERN JOHN J	LTC	0-0243996	0165	3
MULHOLLAN SHERMAN D	MAJ	0-1554942	1160	1
MULHOLLAND EDWARD J	LTC	0-1177112	0665	1
MULHOLLAND JAMES	1LT	0-0476512	0560	1
MULHOLLAND JOHN P	1LT	0-1329621	0746	2
MULHOLLAND JOSEPH E	1LT	0-1018971	0746	2
MULHOLLAND ROBERT T	LTC	0-0278543	1145	2
MULKERN JAMES A	CPT	0-1290795	0657	1
MULKERNE DONALD J D	1LT	0-0546819	0447	2
MULKEY OREN A	CPT	0-1340207	0263	1
MULKY FRANCIS P	LTC	0-0231209	0657	3
MULL CHARLES E	LTC	0-0486973	1065	3
MULL CLELLAND S	2LT	0-1031743	0344	2
MULL LEROY E	CW2	W-2144114	0259	1
MULL ROBERT S	CPT	0-2263748	0163	1
MULLAGHY EUGENE J	LTC	0-1533149	0861	1
MULLAHY WILLIAM J	LTC	0-1115044	0562	1
MULLALLY FRANCIS J	MAJ	0-1913280	1165	1
MULLALY DANIEL L	LTC	0-0448718	0449	1
MULLAN THOMAS L	MAJ	0-0499467	0461	2
MULLANE JAMES P	CPT	0-0450464	0845	3

NAME	GRADE	SVC NO	DATE RET MO YR	RET CODE
MULLANE WILLIAM M	CW3	W-2002110	1155	3
MULLANEY BARTHOLOME	LTC	0-0503740	0157	1
MULLANEY CHARLES P	CW2	W-3200442	0267	1
MULLANEY JOHN T	LTC	0-0529100	1063	1
MULLANEY JOSEPH A	MAJ	0-1112877	1160	1
MULLANEY JOSEPH E	1LT	0-1913954	0543	1
MULLANEY THOMAS F	COL	0-0196495	1062	3
MULLANEY THOMAS J	LTC	0-0472652	0157	1
MULLANEY WILLIAM L	1LT	0-1052092	0845	2
MULLEN BEATRICE M	2LT	N-0744332	0144	1
MULLEN CLIFFORD J	LTC	0-0198423	1058	3
MULLEN DONALD A	CPT	0-1016810	0446	2
MULLEN FORREST H	2LT	0-1845629	0144	2
MULLEN FRANCIS A	CW3	W-2148493	0163	1
MULLEN FRANCIS E	MAJ	0-0256495	0867	3
MULLEN FREDERICK	CPT	0-1299088	0547	2
MULLEN GEORGE F	CPT	0-1266516	0945	2
MULLEN GERALD H	1LT	0-1303930	0457	2
MULLEN JAMES F	LTC	0-1115966	0764	1
MULLEN JAMES P	COL	0-0153734	1051	3
MULLEN JOHN B	CPT	0-0505944	0745	2
MULLEN JOHN F	CPT	0-0454214	1145	2
MULLEN JOHN J	LTC	0-0499996	0657	2
MULLEN JOHN J	CW4	W-2143178	0667	1
MULLEN JOHN P	LTC	0-0236003	0-51	3
MULLEN JOSEPH T	WO1	W-2108959	0350	1
MULLEN KENNETH D	1LT	0-1583415	1045	2
MULLEN LEO F	LTC	0-0244664	1157	3
MULLEN MYRON C	LTC	0-0282813	1265	3
MULLEN OAKMAN E	CPT	0-0300071	0744	2
MULLEN RICHARD D	2LT	0-1641607	0845	2
MULLEN ROBERT V	2LT	0-1290796	0744	2
MULLEN THOMAS V	LTC	0-1325590	0564	1
MULLEN TIMOTHY F	COL	0-0251263	1263	3
MULLEN WALTER J JR	LTC	0-1045191	1064	1
MULLEN WILLIAM J	CW2	W-2150993	0260	1
MULLENAX VEE B H	1LT	0-1692567	0847	2
MULLENDER JOSEPH D	LTC	0-0267238	0662	3
MULLENIOUX WILLIAM H	MAJ	0-0974140	0562	1
MULLENIX JOSEPH P	CPT	0-0485962	0547	2
MULLENMEISTER HUGH F	MAJ	0-0280130	0346	2
MULLER ALBERT B	CPT	0-0216699	0364	3
MULLER ARNOLD	MAJ	0-0260547	1163	3
MULLER FLOYD M	1LT	0-1995306	0145	2
MULLER JAMES	MAJ	0-0973584	1062	1
MULLER JAMES F	LTC	0-0142058	0648	3
MULLER LUIS	CPT	0-0371134	0960	1
MULLER MARCUS J	MAJ	0-0684386	0661	1
MULLER MARK T	COL	0-0375668	0267	1
MULLER MILTON E	COL	0-0305379	0358	1
MULLER PHILIP	CW2	W-2209441	0763	1
MULLER PHILIP H	1LT	0-0402517	0646	2
MULLER RALPH P	1LT	0-5218663	0764	2
MULLER RICHARD F	CPT	0-1312203	0449	2
MULLER WALTER G	LTC	0-1040278	0859	1
MULLER WILLIAM F	MAJ	0-2018397	0663	2
MULLER WILLIAM L JR	CPT	0-2051684	0459	1
MULLERY JAMES V	CPT	0-1183935	0662	1
MULLIGAN JOHN A	COL	0-0254772	1264	3
MULLIGAN ARTHUR M	LTC	0-0267234	1063	3
MULLIGAN CLAIRE A	1LT	N-0745508	0646	1
MULLIGAN JOSEPHINE	MAJ	N-0758370	0864	1
MULLIGAN WELDON L	CW3	W-2151199	0561	1
MULLIN EDWARD P	MAJ	0-1052093	0865	1
MULLIN FRANCIS W	CW3	W-2152132	0265	2
MULLIN HOWARD L	MAJ	0-0258538	1065	3
MULLIN JOHN J	1LT	0-0443992	0945	2
MULLINAX EDWIN H	WO1	W-2143626	0157	1
MULLING EUGENE G	COL	0-0234788	0247	2
MULLINIKS EDWARD C	LTC	0-0367692	1165	3
MULLINIX EARL L	COL	0-0236469	0461	3
MULLINIX RAY	MAJ	0-0264264	0158	3
MULLINS ALVA R	MAJ	0-0509986	0247	2
MULLINS CAROL H	LTC	0-1314312	0765	1
MULLINS HAROLD	LTC	0-1012522	0257	1
MULLINS HAROLD F	MAJ	0-2016158	0963	1
MULLINS JAMES P	LTC	0-0674511	0168	1
MULLINS JASPER C	WO1	W-2142567	1151	2
MULLINS JOHN W JR	CPT	0-1554057	0462	1
MULLINS JOSEPH C	CW3	W-3150408	1268	1
MULLINS LAWRENCE L	MAJ	0-0261624	1167	3
MULLINS LEONARD E	CW2	W-2119611	0852	1
MULLINS MARCUS G	MAJ	0-0407451	0861	2
MULLINS MERVIN F	MAJ	0-1101132	0361	1
MULLINS PAUL F	MAJ	0-1634168	0361	1
MULLINS RICHARD F	LTC	0-0276111	1144	2
MULLINS ROBIN E	MAJ	0-0385848	0761	1
MULLINS SAMUEL L	CW4	W-2003686	0968	1
MULLINS WALTER S	COL	0-0174806	0260	3
MULLINS WILLIAM B	MAJ	0-4030830	0866	1
MULLINS WILLIAM H	2LT	0-1595055	0645	2
MULLINS WILLIAM J	CW4	W-2109946	1164	3
MULLINS WILLICF R	CW4	W-2110528	0959	1
MULLOY PATRICK J	CPT	0-1101133	0546	2
MULQUIN WAYNE D	COL	0-0270344	1067	3
MULRINE GERALD J	LTC	0-1165195	1162	1
MULROONEY WALTER S	LTC	0-1316577	1166	1
MULVANEY BERNARD H	1LT	0-1305815	1044	2
MULVANEY JOHN J	CPT	0-1756343	0747	2
MULVANEY LOUIS C	LTC	0-1703794	0559	1
MULVENNA RICHARD F	MAJ	0-0439922	0551	1
MULVENON JOSEPH T	LTC	0-1110676	1065	1
MULVEY THOMAS P	LTC	0-0383437	0760	1
MULVIHILL JOHN R	CPT	0-1688491	0565	1
MUMBRAUER CHARLES E	LTC	0-0359019	0867	3
MUMFORD BRUTON L	LTC	0-0371209	0968	3
MUMFORD HOWARD F	LTC	0-1059013	1263	1
MUMLER WILLIAM C	MAJ	0-0411537	0346	2
MUMM FRED E	LTC	0-1846041	1162	1
MUMM HARRY G	LTC	0-0252796	1265	3
MUMM KARL B	MAJ	0-0977445	1263	1
MUMMA CECIL J	LTC	0-0420944	0762	1
MUMMA GEORGE J	LTC	0-0385498	0368	3
MUMME FRANK H JR	LTC	0-1312040	0562	2
MUMMEY PAUL F	CPT	0-2011034	0760	1
MUMPOWER WILLIAM B	COL	0-0326088	0160	1
MUNAKER ISRAEL N	MAJ	0-1995307	0564	2
MUNBY WILLIAM A	MAJ	0-0930272	0866	1
MUNCH ARTHUR W	CPT	0-1285093	0746	2
MUNCH FRANCIS J	MAJ	0-1551472	0662	1
MUNCHMEYER LOUIS W	COL	0-0229402	0864	3
MUNCIE CLINTON J	LTC	0-0162231	0349	3
MUNCIE JAMES A	MAJ	0-2034691	1160	1
MUNCK HARRIS R	LTC	0-1685722	0168	1
MUNCY LARKIN K	2LT	0-1913855	0832	1
MUNDALL BERNARD P	CPT	0-0551227	0246	2
MUNDAY AUDWERT L	MAJ	0-1301015	0363	1
MUNDELL GRACE I	LTC	N-0732294	0564	1
MUNDEM GUY O	MAJ	0-0161872	0259	2
MUNDEN CECIL L	COL	0-1055395	0567	3
MUNDEN ERNEST A	CPT	0-1697836	0955	1
MUNDEN KENNETH T	CPT	0-1284190	1055	1
MUNDER MITCHELL F	COL	0-1103825	0468	3
MUNDORFF WILLIAM H	LTC	0-0463584	0854	1
MUNDT CARL P	1LT	0-1590068	1045	2
MUNDT DONALD A	MAJ	0-1331210	0164	1
MUNDT HENRY G	MAJ	0-1111802	1157	1
MUNDTH LYMAN K	2LT	0-1310292	0943	2
MUNDY CHARLES F	MAJ	0-1326652	0465	1
MUNDY HARRY K	2LT	0-0885879	0944	2
MUNDY HENRY L	LTC	0-1594371	0762	1
MUNDY JAMES R	LTC	0-1181383	0766	1
MUNDY JAMES T	CPT	0-0371039	0846	2
MUNDY JOHN T JR	LTC	0-0249058	1266	3
MUNFORD CHARLES W	LTC	0-0293904	1166	3
MUNFORD THOMAS T	1LT	0-1016390	0646	2
MUNGER HARRY A	MAJ	0-1332293	0867	2
MUNGER IRVIA C JR	LTC	0-0252704	0460	3
MUNGER PEARL M	2LT	N-0784255	1044	1
MUNGER RALPH L	LTC	0-0389817	1054	1
MUNGER RAY M	COL	0-0159850	1154	1
MUNGO ALFRED J	1LT	0-0328447	1043	2
MUNGOVAN JOHN F	COL	0-0277608	0565	3
MUNGUIA RAFAEL V	LTC	0-1047255	0263	1
MUNHALL WILLIAM V	LTC	0-0299169	0368	3
MUNIAK JOHN J	CPT	0-0380791	0345	2
MUNIZ BRAULIO	CPT	0-0217528	0249	1
MUNK ROBERT F	CPT	0-1822435	0346	2
MUNKER FREDERICK	LTC	0-1105692	1160	1
MUNKRES GARLYN	LTC	0-0362097	0561	1
MUNN ARTHUR N	2LT	0-1949614	0646	2
MUNN CLEMMON F	LTC	0-0283342	1061	1
MUNN FREDERICK	MAJ	0-0966309	0459	1
MUNN GERALD H	LTC	0-0450168	1060	1
MUNN JAY A	CPT	0-0384753	0546	2
MUNN JOHN F	MAJ	0-1557760	0164	1
MUNN JOHN P	CW3	W-3430120	1168	1
MUNN KELLY C	CPT	0-1951026	0259	1
MUNN LILLIAN M	2LT	N-0701823	1041	1
MUNN MURDOC C JR	CW3	W-2208572	1167	1
MUNN NEIL B	CW2	W-2207592	1162	1
MUNN RALPH B	LTC	0-0217198	C653	3
MUNN RICHARD R	LTC	0-0318489	0266	3
MUNN ROBERT W	CPT	0-0283594	0447	2
MUNN THELMA	LTC	N-0775056	0363	1
MUNNECKE CHARLES M	COL	0-0238096	0859	1
MUNNERLYN LAWRENCE A	CPT	0-1312204	0662	1
MUNOZ CARLOS F	COL	0-0273026	0155	1
MUNOZ CELESTINO	CPT	0-2032079	0263	2
MUNOZ FILBERT	2LT	0-1319152	0245	2
MUNOZ FRANK E	LTC	0-1319532	0563	1
MUNOZ JOHN C	MAJ	0-0198305	0253	2
MUNOZ MIGUEL A	COL	0-0102981	0247	2
MUNOZ WILLIAM P	LTC	0-0335729	C560	1
MUNRO ARTHUR M	CW4	W-2119632	0859	1
MUNRO DONALD M	MAJ	0-1335963	1159	1
MUNROE DUNCAN H	MAJ	0-0268241	0459	1
MUNROE ROBERT F	1LT	0-1019145	0446	2
MUNS GEORGE F JR	2LT	0-0538291	0845	2
MUNSEL HARLEY U	CW4	W-2122255	0259	1
MUNSELL BENJAMIN F	1LT	0-1297923	0248	2
MUNSHOWER ELMER F	COL	0-0210722	0648	3
MUNSKE CHARLES R	COL	0-0243021	0258	1
MUNSON ARTHUR L	MAJ	0-1172566	0361	1
MUNSON CLARENCE S JR	MAJ	0-1317329	1164	1
MUNSON DONALD C	CPT	0-1533870	0145	2
MUNSON EDWARD H	1LT	0-1010089	0445	2
MUNSON GEORGE P JR	M G	0-0257114	1267	3
MUNSON JOHN K	MAJ	0-0954485	0663	1
MUNSON LEO A	CW3	W-2205601	0565	1
MUNSON LEONARD H	LTC	0-0411565	1061	3
MUNSON LEVI CHARL	CPT	0-0265827	0842	2
MUNSON NELSON C	MAJ	0-0511051	0447	2
MUNSON NICHOLAS S	LTC	0-0454670	0961	1
MUNSON WILBUR R	CW2	W-2114087	0858	1
MUNSON WILNER W	1LT	0-0885052	0644	2
MUNSTERMAN ALFRED H	CPT	0-1012893	1145	2
MUNYAN PAUL D C	CW3	RW-2142016	0761	1
MUNYER WILLIAM J	LTC	0-2042864	0466	1
MUNZ RUDOLPH P	LTC	0-0234685	0861	3
MUNZELL PETER C	LTC	0-1012058	0663	1
MURA ROMEO E	LTC	0-0234698	C964	3
MURANAKA REYNOLD T	MAJ	0-2030816	0162	1
MURANE EDWARD E	LTC	0-0245201	0962	3
MURATTI JOSE A	LTC	0-0368534	0660	1
MURAWSKI THEODORE M	MAJ	0-1057184	0162	1
MURAY ALBERT V	LTC	0-0323363	C852	2
MURBACH CLARENCE F	COL	0-0214007	0648	3
MURCH GREENWOOD	MAJ	0-1645233	0158	1
MURCH JAMES E	2LT	0-1287748	0845	2
MURCH ROBERT E	LTC	0-1321326	0363	1
MURCHISON ALBERT R	MAJ	0-0283063	1044	2
MURCHISON BRYAN	CW2	W-2112399	0651	1
MURCHISON CLYDE A JR	1LT	0-0552597	0646	2
MURCHISON JOHN T	COL	0-0238913	0366	3
MURCHISON LEWIS N	LTC	0-0201517	0563	3
MURCHISON ROBERT B	COL	0-0373804	0161	1
MURCHISON WALTER H	MAJ	0-1308363	0163	1
MURCHISON WILLIAM P	CW4	W-2001668	0768	3
MURDOCH ALBERT R	LTC	0-0535265	0167	3
MURDOCK CHARLES E	MAJ	0-2212032	0962	1
MURDOCK EDWARD E	LTC	0-1309594	0264	1
MURDOCK FRED F	LTC	0-0239577	0162	3
MURDOCK JOHN T	CPT	0-2032931	0658	1
MURDOCK PATRICIA M	2LT	N-0785305	0546	1
MURDOCK ROBERT	1LT	0-1325138	0246	2
MURDZA JOHN L	2LT	0-1314944	0345	2
MURDZA JOSEPH L	CW4	W-2146264	0157	1
MURELLO CHARLES E	LTC	0-1041622	0964	1
MUREN GEORGE H	MAJ	0-0387244	0962	1
MURETTA JOE J	1LT	0-1178907	1145	2
MURFIN JACK A	MAJ	0-2265080	1268	1
MURFREE ERVIN E	CW3	W-2151135	0463	1
MURIEL RAFAEL A	CPT	0-0195801	0160	3
MURKBERG MAX A	LTC	0-1824071	1160	1
MURLEY FLORENCE	MAJ	M-0002830	0966	1
MURLIN JAMES S	MAJ	0-1048510	0948	2
MURNAN HERBERT B	COL	0-0300675	1059	1
MURNAN PAUL A	1LT	0-1286688	1044	2
MURNANE RAYMOND C	LTC	0-0508547	0954	1
MUROFF WILLIAM W	CW2	W-2145038	0559	1
MURPHEY ALBERT N	LTC	0-0146213	1054	3
MURPHEY ARLO L	MAJ	0-0318469	0746	2
MURPHEY HORACE F	MAJ	0-0251481	0864	3
MURPHEY MURIEL D	MAJ	0-1177539	0161	2
MURPHEY WALTER H	MAJ	0-1287220	0361	1
MURPHIE DONALD W	MAJ	0-1324354	1160	1
MURPHREE MARY L	MAJ	L-1010033	0864	1
MURPHREE WILLIAM M	LTC	0-0183450	0840	1
MURPHY ALBERT K	LTC	0-0284711	1061	3
MURPHY ALBERT W	CPT	0-1313358	0963	1
MURPHY ALFRED J	LTC	0-0290436	1164	3
MURPHY ALFRED L	1LT	0-1080310	0246	2
MURPHY ALFRED T	1LT	0-0481471	0345	2
MURPHY ALLEN H	LTC	0-0384174	0965	1
MURPHY ALLEN P	LTC	0-0745471	0568	1
MURPHY ALOYSIUS T	LTC	0-0343503	1067	3
MURPHY AUDREY V	COL	0-0919358	0468	3
MURPHY BERNARD J JR	CW2	W-2210789	0568	1
MURPHY CATHERINE	1LT	N-0793256	1047	1
MURPHY CHALMER S	1LT	0-0494238	-0-48	2
MURPHY CHARLES A	LTC	0-0398889	0363	1
MURPHY CHARLES C	CPT	0-0410356	0246	2
MURPHY CHARLES E	LTC	0-0445920	1067	1
MURPHY CHARLES M	1LT	0-0501484	0146	2
MURPHY CLAIR	LTC	0-0386553	0566	3
MURPHY CLARKE JR	1LT	0-0461963	114N	2
MURPHY CLAUD H	MAJ	0-1933579	0468	1
MURPHY CLEMENT B	LTC	0-0494482	0354	1
MURPHY CYRIL R	LTC	0-0304127	0760	1
MURPHY DANIEL J	LTC	0-0450677	1160	1
MURPHY DANIEL J JR	COL	0-0289447	0267	3
MURPHY DANIEL T	LTC	0-0390068	0660	1
MURPHY DAVID D	LTC	0-1559233	0963	1
MURPHY DONALD I	2LT	0-1291314	0943	2
MURPHY DONALD P	MAJ	0-1925540	0668	1
MURPHY DORIS E	1LT	N-0759536	0846	1
MURPHY EARL J	CW2	W-2152711	0561	1
MURPHY EARLE W	LTC	0-1038775	0164	1
MURPHY EDMUND C	LTC	0-0278607	0557	1
MURPHY EDWARD A	LTC	0-0242346	1044	2
MURPHY EDWARD B	LTC	0-0311052	1046	2
MURPHY EDWARD F	CPT	0-1581994	0746	2
MURPHY EDWARD J	CW3	W-2148755	0763	2
MURPHY EDWARD P	LTC	0-0448639	1054	1
MURPHY EMERY W	CW3	W-2205284	0766	1
MURPHY FRANCIS A	LTC	0-1691740	0561	1
MURPHY FRANCIS G	LTC	0-1017237	0763	1
MURPHY FRANCIS J	MAJ	0-2019069	0662	1
MURPHY FRANK W	COL	0-0370163	0853	2

NAME	GRADE	SVC NO	DATE RET MO YR	RET CODE
MURPHY FRANK W	MAJ	0-1185104	0365	2
MURPHY FRED	CW3	W-2144734	0760	1
MURPHY FREDERICK	LTC	0-1585940	1064	1
MURPHY GERARD L	MAJ	0-2005002	1268	1
MURPHY GLENN H	2LT	0-2043011	0445	2
MURPHY GORDON G	CW2	W-2149303	0860	1
MURPHY HAROLD J	LTC	0-0212535	0462	3
MURPHY HARRY G	1LT	0-0136675	0249	3
MURPHY HARRY M	MAJ	0-0403028	0346	2
MURPHY HELENE F	MAJ	N-0796087	1168	3
MURPHY HENRY B	1LT	0-1323725	0845	2
MURPHY HENRY L	LTC	0-1112338	0265	1
MURPHY HERMAN A	1LT	0-0227220	1265	2
MURPHY HOLLIS E	MAJ	0-0962885	0665	1
MURPHY JAMES A JR	MAJ	0-2262692	1065	2
MURPHY JAMES C	MAJ	0-1307568	0864	1
MURPHY JAMES D	LTC	0-2052237	0665	3
MURPHY JAMES E	LTC	0-0969323	1067	1
MURPHY JAMES L JR	CPT	0-0352958	0944	2
MURPHY JAMES M	LTC	0-0413514	1146	2
MURPHY JAMES R	MAJ	0-0969591	1264	1
MURPHY JEREMIAH P	2LT	0-1106328	0445	2
MURPHY JOE	CW3	W-2207691	0966	1
MURPHY JOE H JR	CPT	0-1031581	0446	2
MURPHY JOHN C	LTC	0-0499468	1060	1
MURPHY JOHN C	MAJ	0-1186984	0361	1
MURPHY JOHN E	1LT	0-0441076	0345	2
MURPHY JOHN F	LTC	0-0407843	0163	1
MURPHY JOHN F	CPT	0-1299781	0646	2
MURPHY JOHN J	MAJ	0-1031427	0265	1
MURPHY JOHN J	MAJ	0-1280390	0246	2
MURPHY JOHN J	1LT	0-1585943	0853	1
MURPHY JOHN J	LTC	0-1689055	0754	2
MURPHY JOHN L	COL	0-0905222	1045	2
MURPHY JOHN L	LTC	0-1585944	0860	1
MURPHY JOHN L	CW2	W-2119572	1146	1
MURPHY JOHN L JR	MAJ	0-1060225	1065	1
MURPHY JOHN R	COL	0-0336254	0167	3
MURPHY JOHN T	1LT	0-0382298	0941	2
MURPHY JOHN T	MAJ	0-1175256	0661	1
MURPHY JOSEPH B	MAJ	0-0426226	0546	2
MURPHY JOSEPH C	COL	0-0274358	0659	3
MURPHY JOSEPH P	MAJ	0-0256009	0942	2
MURPHY JOSEPH P	MAJ	0-0673866	1162	1
MURPHY LAWRENCE B	COL	0-0487617	0967	1
MURPHY LAWRENCE D	1LT	0-1823761	0546	2
MURPHY MARGARET L	2LT	N-0744129	0246	1
MURPHY MARVIN H	1LT	0-0468466	0348	2
MURPHY MARY L	MAJ	N-0742217	1064	3
MURPHY MERRITT W	1LT	0-1309801	1046	2
MURPHY MICHAEL J	CPT	0-0329941	0642	2
MURPHY MURRAY P	CW4	W-2003495	0968	1
MURPHY NIGEL C	CW3	W-2144851	1062	1
MURPHY OWEN F	COL	0-0261345	0657	3
MURPHY PATRICK C	1LT	0-1305173	0545	2
MURPHY PAUL J	CW3	W-3150566	0868	1
MURPHY PHILIP G	COL	0-0170848	0-49	3
MURPHY RALEIGH C	CPT	0-0321753	0645	2
MURPHY RAPHAEL A	LTC	0-0343276	1046	2
MURPHY RAYMOND H	LTC	0-1166338	1264	1
MURPHY RAYMOND JR	1LT	0-4036531	0658	2
MURPHY RAYMOND L	CW4	W-2005163	0466	1
MURPHY RICHARD R	MAJ	0-1879071	0467	1
MURPHY ROBERT A	MAJ	0-1044319	0258	1
MURPHY ROBERT A	MAJ	0-2019205	1063	2
MURPHY ROBERT J	MAJ	0-0268324	0664	3
MURPHY ROBERT J	CPT	0-0380776	0645	2
MURPHY ROBERT J SR	COL	0-0255702	0961	1
MURPHY ROBERT M	LTC	0-1046590	0966	1
MURPHY ROLAND E	COL	0-0100686	1053	3
MURPHY ROY F	CPT	0-0281956	1145	2
MURPHY RUSSELL C	2LT	0-1106989	1044	2
MURPHY SAMUEL D	2LT	0-0374022	0142	2
MURPHY SAMUEL S	CW3	W-2143690	0564	1
MURPHY THEODORE E	LTC	0-0329902	0263	3

NAME	GRADE	SVC NO	DATE RET MO YR	RET CODE
MURPHY THOMAS A	LTC	0-1292223	0461	1
MURPHY THOMAS E	CPT	0-1683515	0457	1
MURPHY THOMAS F	MAJ	0-0351779	0347	2
MURPHY THOMAS G	LTC	0-1341692	1066	1
MURPHY THOMAS J	LTC	0-0320267	0258	1
MURPHY THOMAS J	CPT	0-1595058	0553	2
MURPHY THOMAS O	CPT	0-0471558	0949	1
MURPHY THOMAS T	MAJ	0-1013377	1263	1
MURPHY TIMOTHY H	COL	0-0138469	0450	3
MURPHY TIMOTHY J	LTC	0-0450605	0860	1
MURPHY VALERIA K	MAJ	N-0745231	0865	1
MURPHY VIRGIL L	CPT	0-1684325	0546	2
MURPHY WAYMON T	LTC	0-1284920	0461	1
MURPHY WILLIAM A	CW4	W-2004344	0668	1
MURPHY WILLIAM C	LTC	0-1045534	0560	1
MURPHY WILLIAM E	COL	0-0400136	1062	1
MURPHY WILLIAM E	MAJ	0-1922898	0866	1
MURPHY WILLIAM F	LTC	0-0149778	0756	3
MURPHY WILLIAM F	LTC	0-1295067	1061	2
MURPHY WILLIAM H	LTC	0-0261697	0266	3
MURPHY WILLIAM J	CPT	0-1046209	0864	1
MURPHY WILLIAM R	CPT	0-1297768	0646	2
MURR CLYDE E	MAJ	0-1950911	1159	1
MURRAY ACY	MAJ	0-2042845	1059	1
MURRAY ALBERT S	1LT	0-0298144	0648	3
MURRAY ALFRED E	CPT	0-1645237	0961	1
MURRAY ARTHUR L	LTC	0-0395670	0547	2
MURRAY ARTHUR R	WO1	W-2110950	0461	3
MURRAY BENJAMIN M	LTC	0-0483816	0468	2
MURRAY BETHEL R	1LT	0-1308681	0246	2
MURRAY BILLIE J	CPT	0-1922806	0164	1
MURRAY CARL M	CPT	0-0475674	0252	1
MURRAY CARL M	CW3	W-2105263	0662	1
MURRAY CHARLES A	LTC	0-0284140	1061	1
MURRAY CHARLES L	2LT	0-0216315	1042	1
MURRAY CHARLES W	MAJ	0-1048917	0661	1
MURRAY CHRISTOPHE	LTC	0-0475008	0546	2
MURRAY CLARENCE M	LTC	0-0227455	0664	3
MURRAY CLIFFORD E	COL	0-0322528	1059	3
MURRAY CLIVE E	COL	0-0291912	0955	3
MURRAY DAVID J	CPT	0-0461080	0648	1
MURRAY DAVID T	1LT	0-1012685	0945	2
MURRAY DENNIS F	CPT	0-0108249	0944	1
MURRAY EDMUND J	LTC	0-0440013	0567	3
MURRAY EDWARD R	LTC	0-1308168	0568	1
MURRAY EDWIN F	CW4	W-2117246	0862	1
MURRAY EMERY G	MAJ	0-1081157	0461	1
MURRAY FRANCIS D	CW2	RW-2206453	0361	1
MURRAY FREEMAN C	1LT	0-2035134	0645	2
MURRAY GEORGE E	MAJ	0-0415673	1057	1
MURRAY GERALD J	LTC	0-0450088	0762	1
MURRAY GERTRUDE J	MAJ	J-0100043	1266	1
MURRAY HAROLD W	LTC	0-1298576	0861	1
MURRAY HERMAN D	CPT	0-0283252	1067	3
MURRAY HERMAN T	1LT	0-0583991	0755	1
MURRAY HUBERT W	CPT	0-1797862	1060	1
MURRAY JACK S	1LT	0-0299112	0642	2
MURRAY JAMES C	CW2	W-2147438	0360	1
MURRAY JAMES F	1LT	0-1560302	0955	1
MURRAY JAMES R	CPT	0-0451689	0246	2
MURRAY JAMES T	CW3	W-2207593	0668	1
MURRAY JOHN A	LTC	0-0802934	1167	1
MURRAY JOHN D	2LT	0-0113211	0655	3
MURRAY JOHN G	MAJ	0-1559234	0668	3
MURRAY JOHN J	CPT	0-0479714	1143	2
MURRAY JOHN J	MAJ	0-0506115	1054	1
MURRAY JOHN L	LTC	0-1341569	0567	1
MURRAY JOSEPH D	LTC	0-0134004	0850	3
MURRAY KENNETH E	1LT	0-1306454	0546	2
MURRAY LEONARD E JR	LTC	0-1291680	0960	1
MURRAY LEWIS G	LTC	0-0429458	0167	1
MURRAY LIONEL T	2LT	0-0555506	0247	2
MURRAY MELVILLE M	CPT	0-0451629	0757	1
MURRAY MICHAEL D	MAJ	0-0277606	1062	3
MURRAY NATHAN A	LTC	0-1584657	0361	1

NAME	GRADE	SVC NO	DATE RET MO YR	RET CODE
MURRAY NORMAN C	LTC	0-1057548	0667	1
MURRAY OLIVER J	LTC	0-0478207	0255	1
MURRAY PHILIP F	LTC	0-0140942	0151	3
MURRAY RAYMOND A	LTC	0-1103827	0765	1
MURRAY RAYMOND A	CW3	W-2144989	0663	1
MURRAY RICHARD J	MAJ	0-1336679	1064	1
MURRAY RICHARD R	MAJ	0-0320250	0755	1
MURRAY ROBERT M	LTC	0-0453636	0860	1
MURRAY ROBERT M JR	2LT	0-1031260	1044	2
MURRAY ROGER	CPT	0-0213015	0745	2
MURRAY ROSCOE L	COL	0-0171812	0347	2
MURRAY SAMUEL S	LTC	0-0208480	0351	3
MURRAY SARSFIELD	CW2	W-2149354	0561	1
MURRAY THADDEUS H	CW2	W-2151684	0161	1
MURRAY THEODORE C	MAJ	0-1591338	0263	1
MURRAY THOMAS C	COL	0-0405133	0461	2
MURRAY THOMAS F	CW3	W-2104328	0659	1
MURRAY THOMAS J	COL	0-0298105	0968	3
MURRAY THOMAS W	CW3	W-2153004	0567	1
MURRAY VIRGINIA M	1LT	N-0772922	0445	1
MURRAY WALTER G	LTC	0-0190795	0858	3
MURRAY WAVERLY C	MAJ	0-1634172	1047	1
MURRAY WILLIAM	MAJ	0-0460121	0746	1
MURRAY WILLIAM F	MAJ	0-0396595	0247	2
MURRAY WILLIAM J	COL	0-0251773	1159	1
MURRAY WILLIAM J	MAJ	0-0405709	1045	2
MURRAY WILLIAM J	2LT	0-1698108	1043	2
MURRAY WILLIAM J	2LT	0-2049042	0147	2
MURRAY WILLIAM K	LTC	0-1335564	0268	1
MURRAY WINTHROP P	LTC	0-1060567	0267	1
MURRELL BILLIE	CPT	0-0497005	0650	1
MURRELL PAUL M	LTC	0-0452288	0463	1
MURRELL WALTER L	CPT	0-0328076	0843	2
MURREY CHARLES T	COL	0-0264095	1059	3
MURRY MILTON J	CW2	W-2107950	1058	1
MURSELL GEORGE R	COL	0-0337942	1058	3
MURTAGH JAMES R	1LT	0-1045192	0745	2
MURTHA JOSEPH J	COL	0-0260553	0262	3
MUSARD ALBERT E	CW2	W-2145219	0868	2
MUSARRA JOE S	CW3	W-2147248	1164	1
MUSCHANY GEORGE V	MAJ	0-1035928	0662	1
MUSE ALFRED L	CPT	0-1298275	1152	2
MUSE BRADFORD F	MAJ	0-1050394	0657	1
MUSE ERNEST D	MAJ	0-1647199	0954	1
MUSE JAMES A	MAJ	0-1686154	0461	1
MUSE JAMES B JR	1LT	0-1300689	0846	2
MUSE JAMES G	WO1	W-2130496	1146	2
MUSE MOSE J	CW3	W-2205992	0568	1
MUSE RAYMOND W JR	CW2	W-2152146	0858	1
MUSE ROBERT S	CPT	0-1698180	0953	2
MUSE SAMUEL P	MAJ	0-2014460	0463	1
MUSEGADES WALTER F	LTC	0-0277166	1061	3
MUSGRAVE ARTHUR F	COL	0-0146276	1056	3
MUSGRAVE CLARENCE S	COL	0-0204902	1063	3
MUSGRAVE HARRY G	LTC	0-0111355	0648	3
MUSGROVE EARL E	MAJ	0-0970652	1062	1
MUSGROVE JAMES W	MAJ	0-0497037	0353	1
MUSGROVE ORA E	COL	0-0170309	0348	2
MUSHAKE WILLIAM I	COL	0-0184821	0461	3
MUSHET GERALD S	MAJ	0-0229271	0762	3
MUSHKATIN MAX H	COL	0-0336358	0268	3
MUSICH RICHARD	CW2	W-3350502	1168	1
MUSICK EGBERT S	1LT	0-1573461	0861	1
MUSICK PAUL F	LTC	0-2000524	0666	1
MUSICK ROBERT M	MAJ	0-0262302	1047	1
MUSICO SEBASTIAN	2LT	0-1015864	0644	2
MUSIELEWICZ C A	1LT	0-1170107	1046	2
MUSIL FRANCIS J	CW2	W-2208150	0963	1
MUSINSKI SIGMUND W	CW4	W-2105651	1058	1
MUSKE HARRY B	CPT	0-1321370	0846	2
MUSKRAT JEFFIE W	LTC	0-0964066	0767	1
MUSOLF EARL R	CPT	0-0974709	1161	1
MUSOLINO ANTHONY R	CW2	W-3000400	0668	1
MUSSATTO KATHARINE	CPT	N-0783350	0547	1
MUSSELMAN ARTHUR C	COL	0-0250210	1165	3

NAME	GRADE	SVC NO	DATE RET MO YR	RET CODE
MUSSELMAN JOHN M	MAJ	0-0396983	0246	2
MUSSELMAN LOUIS J	CW3	W-2142533	1060	1
MUSSELWHITE EMORY L	LTC	0-1081158	0562	1
MUSSELWHITE JOHN O	CPT	0-1798948	0259	1
MUSSER CARROLL L	LTC	0-1575022	0161	2
MUSSER HARVEY H	LTC	0-0201964	1148	3
MUSSER MILTON S	COL	0-0379505	0259	2
MUSSER ROBERT S	2LT	0-1031744	0945	2
MUSSLER LOUIS H	COL	0-0333559	0947	2
MUSSOMELI MARINO	LTC	0-0455073	0663	1
MUSTAIN RHOADS	MAJ	0-0493652	1147	2
MUSTONE ALBERT A	LTC	0-2042790	0962	1
MUSZKIEWICZ STANLE	MAJ	0-1289947	0860	1
MUTERT LESTER F	MAJ	0-1560047	0264	1
MUTH DANIEL M	COL	0-0234295	1159	1
MUTHIG JAMES V	1LT	0-0547351	1046	2
MUTIK ADAM J	CW3	W-2141998	0659	1
MUTINSKY EDWARD J	LTC	0-0268169	1167	3
MUTKALA WAINO J	1LT	0-1824350	0760	1
MUTTER ALVIE M	CPT	0-0149906	0950	3
MUTTER CLYDE S	CW4	W-2149125	0165	1
MUTTY JOHN E	COL	0-0221727	1056	3
MUXO EDUARDO	MAJ	0-1108882	1060	1
MUZIO JOHN A	COL	0-0299581	0568	3
MUZZY HOWARD L	CPT	0-1290985	0947	2
MYATT ALFRED R JR	LTC	0-0310227	0263	1
MYATT FRED B	MAJ	0-0986859	0964	1
MYCO JAMES W	MAJ	0-0394933	0968	3
MYCOCK EDWIN S	CPT	0-1317656	0647	2
MYGLAND OIDRIK B	LTC	0-0525101	0863	1
MYER ALFRED	WO1	W-2117234	0946	1
MYER AUSTIN H	LTC	0-0369838	1052	2
MYER CARL T	CPT	0-0242894	1150	3
MYER LLOYD W	CW4	W-2004194	0864	3
MYER THOMAS L	1LT	0-1170504	0545	2
MYERS ABEL	CW2	W-2147689	0757	1
MYERS ALBERT I	CW4	W-2134988	0959	1
MYERS ALVIN L	CPT	0-0334062	0145	2
MYERS ARTHUR E	LTC	0-1284921	0547	1
MYERS B F JR	MAJ	0-1185106	0560	1
MYERS CARLTON B	MAJ	0-0104861	1155	3
MYERS CECIL L	1LT	0-0286849	0762	3
MYERS CHARLES A	MAJ	0-1645238	0655	1
MYERS CHARLES A	CW3	W-2206807	0367	1
MYERS CHARLES E	CPT	0-1315603	0148	2
MYERS CHARLES L	MAJ	0-1548979	1163	1
MYERS CHARLES R	CW3	W-2147182	1263	1
MYERS CHARLES W	LTC	0-0340562	0763	1
MYERS CHESTER C	MAJ	0-0426492	1157	1
MYERS CHESTER R	CPT	0-1104313	0465	1
MYERS CHRISTIAN	1LT	0-0152901	0942	2
MYERS CLIFFORD L	LTC	0-1011828	0264	1
MYERS COLLIN S JR	MAJ	0-1332090	0964	1
MYERS DONALD C	LTC	0-0484371	0157	1
MYERS DOREL M	MAJ	0-4011059	0368	1
MYERS EDWIN M	WO1	W-2143519	0953	2
MYERS ELMER F	MAJ	0-0414618	1046	2
MYERS ELMER L	MAJ	0-1293092	0964	1
MYERS ERLAND F	LTC	0-1041854	0264	1
MYERS EUGENE B	CW3	W-2205913	1164	1
MYERS EVELYN L	MAJ	N-0727795	1262	1
MYERS FRED	CPT	0-0177715	0958	3
MYERS FRED J	1LT	0-1285277	0844	2
MYERS G TAYLOR	LTC	0-0472237	0945	2
MYERS GENE	COL	0-0354384	1265	1
MYERS GEORGE A	1LT	0-1298104	0145	2
MYERS GEORGE C	CW3	RW-2136649	0564	1
MYERS GEORGE N	COL	0-0301722	0760	1
MYERS GEORGE W	MAJ	0-0278117	1047	1
MYERS GERALD	CPT	0-0923023	0446	2
MYERS GLENN D	CW2	W-2147900	0763	1
MYERS HAROLD	MAJ	0-1686718	0463	2
MYERS HAROLD E	CW2	W-2147303	0263	1
MYERS HARRY	LTC	0-0103039	0848	2
MYERS HARRY A	MAJ	0-0189757	0250	3

NAME	GRADE	SVC NO	DATE RET MO YR	RET CODE
MYERS HENRY R	LTC	0-1001649	1162	1
MYERS HENRY F	CW3	W-2104778	1152	2
MYERS HORACE W	MAJ	0-0276[illegible]38	1266	3
MYERS IRVIN L	2LT	0-20[illegible]145	0944	2
MYERS IRVING	MAJ	0-03[illegible]33	0855	3
MYERS ISAAC C	LTC	0-01[illegible]308	0351	3
MYERS IVAN J	1LT	0-131[illegible]7	0746	2
MYERS JACK W	LTC	0-04[illegible]156	0555	1
MYERS JAMES K	MAJ	0-045[illegible]0	0151	2
MYERS JAMES L	MAJ	0-168[illegible]14	0765	1
MYERS JAMES M	LTC	0-031[illegible]01	0162	3
MYERS JAMES O	LTC	0-0912[illegible]62	0567	3
MYERS JAMES P	LTC	0-1044908	0263	1
MYERS JAMES W	1LT	0-1312970	1045	2
MYERS JEFFERSON	COL	0-0238095	0666	3
MYERS JENNINGS	MAJ	0-1283467	0853	1
MYERS JESSE D	LTC	0-0491012	0547	2
MYERS JOE	CW4	W-2118499	0156	1
MYERS JOHN B	MAJ	0-0426011	0764	1
MYERS JOHN C	CW2	W-2210225	0865	1
MYERS JOHN P JR	LTC	0-2096487	1268	1
MYERS JOHN T	MAJ	0-0947479	0765	1
MYERS JOHN W	2LT	0-0864753	1145	2
MYERS JOSEPH A	MAJ	0-0980968	0562	1
MYERS KEITH O	MAJ	0-1922874	0466	2
MYERS LAWRENCE	LTC	0-1001650	0568	3
MYERS LEONARD O	LTC	0-0295305	0757	2
MYERS LEWIS E	LTC	0-0459740	0554	1
MYERS LLOYD V	MAJ	0-1016276	1060	1
MYERS LONNIE	2LT	0-1112885	0660	1
MYERS MARCUS A	MAJ	0-0585148	0962	1
MYERS MARVIN R	CW3	W-2146896	0962	2
MYERS MICHAEL J	LTC	0-1062777	0763	1
MYERS MILTON H	1LT	0-2005569	0850	2
MYERS ONNIE P	LTC	0-0337888	0965	3
MYERS ORVIS G	MAJ	0-0968382	0564	1
MYERS OSCAR L	LTC	0-0239540	0560	1
MYERS PAUL A	LTC	0-1296071	1165	1
MYERS PAUL A	2LT	0-2000100	1147	2
MYERS PELHAM L JR	MAJ	0-1595061	0163	1
MYERS PHILIP	CPT	0-0216700	0962	3
MYERS PORTIA H	1LT	N-0729674	0645	1
MYERS RALPH N	LTC	0-0328158	0364	3
MYERS RALPH R	MAJ	0-1947156	0157	1
MYERS RICHARD E	LTC	0-0323204	0945	2
MYERS RICHARD H	1LT	0-1313631	0247	2
MYERS ROBERT B	MAJ	0-1046210	0461	1
MYERS ROBERT D	2LT	0-0508680	1044	2
MYERS ROBERT E	COL	0-0349098	1060	1
MYERS ROBERT E	LTC	0-1032035	1062	1
MYERS ROBERT F	MAJ	0-1650667	0465	1
MYERS ROBERT H	COL	0-0276581	0845	2
MYERS ROBERT J	MAJ	0-1310752	0267	1
MYERS ROBERT J	CPT	0-1634173	0346	2
MYERS ROBERT K JR	LTC	0-0350087	0161	1
MYERS ROBERT N	MAJ	0-0183189	0-53	3
MYERS ROBERT O	1LT	0-0420532	0344	2
MYERS ROBERT O	CPT	0-0958653	0162	2
MYERS ROBERT O	MAJ	0-1645239	0160	1
MYERS ROBERT P	MAJ	0-0273995	0268	3
MYERS ROY P	MAJ	0-1320699	0257	1
MYERS SAM M	COL	0-0260983	0864	3
MYERS SHERRY B	COL	0-0286810	1265	3
MYERS STANTON L	LTC	0-0266450	0860	1
MYERS TEX G	LTC	0-1325919	0263	1
MYERS THEODORE A	LTC	0-0246828	0846	2
MYERS THEODORE E	LTC	0-1110677	0468	3
MYERS THEODORE M	CPT	0-1018342	1163	1
MYERS THOMAS A	CW2	W-2208982	0166	1
MYERS THOMAS A JR	MAJ	0-0993963	0363	1
MYERS THOMAS J	CW4	W-2143693	0766	2
MYERS THOMAS W	LTC	0-0915162	0663	1
MYERS TYVER W	LTC	0-0209435	0648	3
MYERS VIRGIL V	LTC	0-0918706	0965	3
MYERS WALTER P	LTC	0-0382551	0761	1

NAME	GRADE	SVC NO	DATE RET MO YR	RET CODE
MYERS WILBUR J	COL	0-0403508	0166	1
MYERS WILLIAM E	LTC	0-0279876	0762	1
MYERS WILLIAM L	MAJ	0-0971399	1167	1
MYERS WILLIAM L	CPT	0-0973593	1158	1
MYERS WILLIAM N	COL	0-0270043	0460	1
MYERS WILSON J	CPT	0-1169668	0448	2
MYETTE CHARLES L	CPT	0-0364186	1148	2
MYLAN CLYDE	CW3	W-2147133	0361	1
MYLAK JAMES L	LTC	0-0371465	0665	1
MYLAR WILBER K	COL	0-0156229	1050	3
MYLES RAYMOND J	MAJ	0-1549797	0461	1
MYLES WILLIAM S	1LT	0-5708088	0765	2
MYLKE ERNEST R	CPT	0-0489395	0450	1
MYLOD JAMES A	COL	0-0278694	1059	3
MYNCHENBERG GEORGE C	LTC	0-0248485	0543	2
MYNES CLARENCE M JR	MAJ	0-1919994	0466	1
MYNSBERGE MAURICE	LTC	0-2055420	0561	1
MYRA EUGENE L	CW3	W-2149810	1166	1
MYRANT ROBERT R	WO1	W-2144288	1160	1
MYRDEK JOHN F	MAJ	0-2053834	0456	1
MYRE HERMAN T	MAJ	0-1322581	0846	2
MYREN HATTIE L	MAJ	N-0742810	0766	1
MYRICE ALVIN G	MAJ	0-0469425	0747	2
MYRICK CHARLES E	LTC	0-0476384	1153	1
MYSAK FRANK C	CPT	0-1012615	0747	2
NAAB HENRY	COL	0-0106227	0650	3
NABB GLENN R	MAJ	0-1284374	0259	1
NABBE PHILIP M	COL	0-0358059	1057	1
NABER EUGENE J	LTC	0-1178909	0962	1
NABERS WILLIAM F JR	MAJ	0-0276920	0868	3
NABORS JAMES F	COL	0-0397813	1160	1
NABORS JOHN H	CPT	0-0257359	1046	2
NABORS WILLIE R	CPT	0-1998338	0355	1
NACCI VINCENT	LTC	0-2029594	0966	1
NACE DAVID S	CPT	0-1103831	1146	2
NACE LLOYD E	CPT	0-0333191	0964	3
NACHAZEL CATHERINE	MAJ	N-0773977	0567	1
NACHIN JOSEPH J	LTC	0-1583428	1061	1
NACHTIGALL HENRY B	MAJ	0-0368965	0246	2
NACK ARTHUR W	LTC	0-1302336	0260	1
NACKE CLAUS K	LTC	0-0554457	1167	2
NADDEO MIKE	CPT	0-1319221	0148	2
NADEAU CHARLES E	MAJ	0-0343164	0446	2
NADEL HIRSCH	CPT	0-1118778	0148	2
NADELL MILTON J	LTC	0-0971310	0667	1
NADEN DOYT M	LTC	0-0334316	1061	1
NADER CHARLES	CPT	0-1694362	0744	2
NADER ROBERT E	2LT	0-1590409	0345	2
NADER ROBERT L	CPT	0-1037197	0863	1
NADLER MAX	1LT	0-0298566	0546	2
NADOLA SANTO J	LTC	0-1115716	0463	1
NADOLSKI ROBERT W	1LT	0-5340928	1168	2
NADOR GEORGE W	CPT	0-0385083	0346	2
NADWORNIK HANS A	CPT	0-0980235	1061	1
NAEGELI FLOYD C	COL	0-0217566	0163	3
NAEGELI HAROLD L	COL	0-0252251	0864	3
NAESS ERLING W	MAJ	0-0504912	0946	2
NAFE JOHN O	1LT	0-0430033	0647	2
NAFTEL WILLIAM H	LTC	0-1824667	0868	1
NAFTULIN IRVING L	CPT	0-1693551	0146	2
NAGAO HENRY J	LTC	0-2263161	0868	1
NAGEL FRANCES	MAJ	L-1010036	0764	1
NAGEL GEORGE E	LTC	0-0301391	0968	3
NAGEL HENRY	CPT	0-1039814	0862	2
NAGEL LEONARD E	1LT	0-1294889	1045	2
NAGEL RICHARD E	LTC	0-0451562	0859	1
NAGEL WALTER E	LTC	0-1108193	0461	1
NAGELMANN BERNARD R	LTC	0-0413632	0863	1
NAGLE BERNARD J	LTC	0-0301890	0762	1
NAGLE LOIS E	MAJ	N-0805665	1163	1
NAGLE VANCE E	MAJ	0-0515183	0453	1
NAGLE WILLIAM B JR	1LT	0-5316070	0467	2
NAGLEE COOPER M	MAJ	0-1693113	0263	1
NAGY ARNOLD A	CW3	W-2152192	0666	1
NAGY JAMES	1LT	0-1016802	1147	2

NAME	GRADE	SVC NO	DATE RET MO YR	RET CODE
NAGY JOE H	1LT	0-2206436	0953	2
NAGY LEONARD	MAJ	0-0982191	0768	1
NAGY MICHAEL F	CPT	0-1927718	1067	2
NAHAN JOSEPH F	MAJ	0-0731406	0161	1
NAHATZKI CARVEL F	LTC	0-0500012	0668	3
NAIBERT ARTHUR C	MAJ	0-0259008	1265	3
NAIDORF CARROL P	COL	0-0471232	0664	3
NAILL WILLIAM Y	LTC	0-0237342	0463	3
NAIMO ALFRED J	LTC	0-0383246	1059	1
NAIRN HARRY J	CW2	W-2148589	0361	1
NAIRN WILLIAM H JR	COL	0-0207582	0-50	3
NAISBITT FRANK J	MAJ	0-0947436	0564	1
NAJDUCH MICHAEL J	MAJ	0-1548266	0756	1
NAJJAR SAMMY A	CW4	W-2102135	0659	1
NAKAMURA GEORGE T	MAJ	0-0985628	0864	1
NAKANISHI KOICHI	CW4	W-2136060	1066	1
NAKASHIAN SAMUEL J	1LT	0-0488979	1043	2
NAKATA CHARLES T	LTC	0-2027787	0564	1
NAKAYAMA JIMMIE T	MAJ	0-1998049	0963	1
NALBONE CHARLES J	MAJ	0-0347741	0263	1
NALEPA JOHN F	MAJ	0-4031495	0868	1
NALER LAWSON H JR	MAJ	0-1036648	0661	1
NALL CARL B	1LT	0-0469590	0645	2
NALL JACK A	CW2	W-2142181	0157	1
NALL JAMES E	2LT	0-0787408		2
NALL JOHN R	CW4	W-2136015	0766	2
NALL VELMA E	CPT	N-0726649	1146	1
NALLE GEORGE S	LTC	0-0239055	0957	3
NALLEY CHARLES E SR	CW3	W-2152807	0864	1
NALLEY EDWARD F	LTC	0-0414179	0749	1
NALLEY JAMES T	CW2	W-2146038	1161	1
NALLEY JOHN P	CPT	0-0505895	1047	1
NALLI MARY J C	2LT	N-0756947	0945	1
NALLY JOHN F	CPT	0-0992821	1262	1
NALON PAUL E	LTC	0-0486059	1067	3
NALTY FRANK K	CPT	0-0885390	0150	1
NALJAI MOSES K	LTC	0-0375365	0365	3
NAMETH LYALL J	MAJ	0-1293093	0961	2
NANCARROW ROBERT C	CPT	0-1638154	0963	1
NANCE CLARENCE B	MAJ	0-1582000	1057	2
NANCE CLYDE D	LTC	0-1167558	1068	3
NANCE ELMER P	MAJ	0-1167137	0746	2
NANCE HERSCHEL G	LTC	0-1114681	0664	1
NANCE HUBERT M	LTC	0-1290292	0562	1
NANCE JACK A	MAJ	0-2206118	1163	1
NANCE JAMES W	LTC	0-0449163	0547	1
NANCE JOHN H	LTC	0-0482990	0453	2
NANCE RICHARD H	LTC	0-1323163	0263	1
NANCE ROGER J	MAJ	0-1647200	0859	1
NANCE TAYLOR M	CPT	0-0277666	1160	3
NANKERVIS BYRON J	MAJ	0-0184465	0754	3
NANTZ WILSON A	CPT	0-1011180	0161	1
NANZ ALBERT J	CPT	0-0286074	0245	2
NAOMI CHARLES A SR	COL	C-0255300	0862	3
NAPEROLA STANLEY J	CPT	0-1322070	0248	2
NAPIER ALEXANDER	LTC	0-0312612	0168	3
NAPIER CHARLES G	CPT	0-1014310	0747	2
NAPIER DAVID R	MAJ	0-0483780	0847	2
NAPIER FRANK C	MAJ	0-1165315	0448	2
NAPIER GREEN	MAJ	0-1322648	0859	1
NAPIER GUY J	MAJ	0-0221569	1149	1
NAPIER JAMES B	LTC	0-0282759	0766	3
NAPIER JOHN T	CPT	0-1030818	0258	1
NAPIER THOMAS J	CW4	W-2150589	1268	2
NAPIER THURMAN W	LTC	0-1576433	0961	1
NAPIER VICTOR H	CW3	W-2206047	0368	1
NAPIER WILLIAM T	CPT	0-0889081	0953	1
NAPLES ANGELO S	COL	0-0284826	0963	3
NAPLES RALPH V	LTC	0-0451359	0465	1
NAPOLIELLO CEASARE D	MAJ	0-2096511	0365	1
NAPOLITANO ANDREW J	MAJ	0-1894750	0757	1
NAPORA JOHN J	CW4	W-2115452	1065	1
NAPP RALPH R	2LT	0-0977170	1050	2
NAQUIN JOSEPH U	CPT	0-1593743	0165	1
NARA EDWIN A	LTC	0-1825245	1165	1

NAME	GRADE	SVC NO	DATE RET MO YR	RET CODE
NARAMOR GILBERT E	LTC	0-0230938	0547	1
NARAMORE EARL	LTC	0-0199478	0545	2
NARAMORE JOHN E	MAJ	0-2209275	1168	1
NARAMORE STUART	LTC	0-0224590	0651	3
NARAMORE WILLIAM W	COL	0-0345529	0666	3
NARANJO LUCAS	MAJ	0-2030589	0650	2
NARDELLA RALPH A	MAJ	0-1337073	1059	1
NARDI PACIFICO A	2LT	0-1017126	1044	2
NARDI THOMAS JR	1LT	0-1014183	0446	2
NARDIN GENE	CPT	0-0342908	0146	2
NARDIN JOHN G	COL	0-0296888	1265	1
NARDONE ANTHONY A	COL	0-0263156	0965	3
NARDONE GEORGE J	LTC	0-1544518	0167	2
NARDUCCI JOSEPH J	1LT	0-0532683	0645	2
NARIGON DWAIN M	MAJ	0-2046323	0262	1
NARINS SAMUEL R	CPT	0-1691009	0445	2
NARMORE JOSEPH W	MAJ	0-0450089	0846	2
NARSAVAGE PETER P	LTC	0-1799593	0168	2
NARUM ARTHUR J	LTC	0-0236217	0161	3
NARVIS CHARLES S	LTC	0-0194521	0450	3
NARWID RAYMOND J	1LT	0-1550667	1144	2
NARY THOMAS M	1LT	0-1293300	0646	2
NASAW JOSHUA J	2LT	0-1533410	0344	2
NASE DANIEL R JR	MAJ	0-1326511	1063	1
NASER VIRGIL S	LTC	0-0364832	0859	1
NASH ALFRED G	MAJ	0-0978055	1065	1
NASH BENJAMIN E	1LT	0-1059016	1145	2
NASH EDWIN B	1LT	0-1031349	0145	2
NASH ELTON E	MAJ	0-0493164	0556	1
NASH GARVIN W	COL	0-0238309	0462	3
NASH GERALD S	COL	0-0278641	0661	1
NASH HERMAN B	CPT	0-0211369	0655	3
NASH JACK S	MAJ	0-0887320	0261	1
NASH JOHN C	CPT	0-0505019	1147	1
NASH JOHN F	2LT	0-0524353	0944	2
NASH JOHN M	MAJ	0-0295957	1045	2
NASH JOHN W	CPT	0-0986027	1060	1
NASH JOSEPH S	1LT	0-1063043	104N	2
NASH NEWMAN C	1LT	0-0360013	0645	2
NASH PERCY L	LTC	0-0284373	0154	1
NASH RICHARD A	MAJ	0-2209851	0668	1
NASH RICHARD C	LTC	0-1170863	0468	1
NASH ROBERT E	LTC	0-0966772	1064	1
NASH ROBERT O	MAJ	0-1996577	0257	1
NASH SIMEON	COL	0-0143033	0648	3
NASH THOMAS H	LTC	0-0407838	0263	1
NASH THOMAS J	MAJ	0-1080311	0863	1
NASH TOM	CW3	W-2119897	0753	2
NASH VERNA M	LTC	0-0962303	0768	1
NASH WALLACE C	CPT	0-1341816	0960	1
NASH WALLIS G	1LT	0-1325410	0645	2
NASIS ALEJANDRO	CW2	W-2151392	1160	1
NASIS HELEN	1LT	N-0805651	1154	2
NASLUND JULIUS W	CPT	0-0370272	0444	2
NASON BENNETT E	LTC	0-0569542	1060	1
NASON DONALD J	1LT	0-1878823	0559	2
NASON JOHN	1LT	0-1320163	0947	1
NASON LEONARD H	COL	0-0171735	0955	3
NASON RICHARD B	LTC	0-1056479	0267	1
NASR FRED G	LTC	0-0397673	1047	2
NAST CHARLES C	M G	0-0298840	0165	3
NAST HERMAN F	1LT	0-1184555	0646	2
NAST WALTER H	LTC	0-0332820	0257	1
NASVIK ADOLPH C	LTC	0-0230686	0564	3
NATAL ERNEST C	MAJ	0-1047698	0858	1
NATAL STEVE M	MAJ	0-1042659	0158	1
NATALE ANTHONY J	1LT	0-1185842	0246	2
NATALINI CARLO A	LTC	0-1534581	1262	1
NATE CHARLES'R	MAJ	0-0173980	1159	3
NATHAN AARON	LTC	0-1296245	0960	1
NATHAN ALBERT S	MAJ	0-0439697	1059	2
NATHAN BENJAMIN	LTC	0-1634174	0868	3
NATHAN DELORIS E	2LT	N-0786834	0746	1
NATHAN ELROY N	LTC	0-1949617	0962	1
NATHAN HERMAN	LTC	0-0261856	0667	3

NAME	GRADE	SVC NO	DATE RET MO YR	RET CODE
NATHANSON NATHANIEL	LTC	0-0173288	0159	3
NATHANSON YALE S	LTC	0-0182155	0355	3
NATION FRANKLIN E	1LT	0-1920216	0865	2
NATIONS KENNETH L	CPT	0-2212052	0765	1
NATIONS OSCAR T	LTC	0-0312882	0257	2
NATKE STANLEY F	2LT	0-1945231	0445	2
NATTRAS EDWARD D SR	CW2	W-2214797	0168	1
NATTRESS JOHN A	CPT	0-0535379	1047	2
NATTRESS ROY K	CW2	RW-2143008	0163	1
NATZKE RICHARD H	LTC	0-0312272	0861	1
NAU GEORGE I	MAJ	0-1060901	0165	1
NAUCK DONALD A	LTC	0-0306114	0661	1
NAUDAIN GLENN G	COL	0-0213613	1054	3
NAUERT GEORGE V	1LT	0-2262828	0254	2
NAUGHER WILLIAM A	MAJ	0-1195241	0162	1
NAUGHTEN EDWARD T	LTC	0-0435642	1062	1
NAUGHTON FRANCIS L	LTC	0-1043447	0463	1
NAUGHTON JOHN E	LTC	0-0396243	0768	1
NAUGHTON JOHN J	MAJ	0-0411021	0766	3
NAUGHTON THOMAS J	MAJ	0-2009297	0261	1
NAUGLE DONALD E	CW3	W-2150502	1064	1
NAUGLE JEFFERSON	MAJ	0-1100265	1162	1
NAUGLE WILLIAM R	CPT	0-1296407	0347	2
NAULT GERALD H	LTC	0-0451159	0157	1
NAULT ROLLAND F	CPT	0-2006431	0162	2
NAUM ALBERT A	LTC	0-0487837	0555	1
NAUMAN CHARLES F JR	CPT	0-0486184	1048	1
NAUMANN WILLIAM F	COL	0-0441445	0562	3
NAUSE FRANK X	MAJ	0-1578903	0957	1
NAVARRE CHRISTOPHE	CW3	W-2149710	0663	1
NAVARRE ELMER C	LTC	0-0404332	0760	1
NAVARRE GEORGE	LTC	0-1533874	1058	1
NAVARRE VINCENT J	CPT	0-0976679	1151	2
NAVARRETTE GABRIEL L	1LT	0-2055833	0845	2
NAVARRO PATRICK	CPT	0-0890320	0154	1
NAVARRO ROCCO	MAJ	0-4010626	0968	1
NAVARRO ROSENDO	1LT	0-2030387	1049	1
NAVAS STANLEY R	1LT	0-0412838	1045	2
NAVAS VICTOR M	MAJ	0-2262637	0961	1
NAVAZIO ATTILIO	CPT	0-0500566	1045	2
NAVE CLARENCE F	LTC	0-0360053	0157	1
NAVE JOHN A	LTC	0-1165768	0264	1
NAVIDOMSKIS JOHN N	MAJ	0-1016827	1161	1
NAVIN JOHN W	1LT	0-1192433	0746	2
NAVY SOPHIA I	MAJ	N-0763486	0664	1
NAWROCKI GEORGE J JR	MAJ	0-2033109	0764	1
NAY WARREN M	MAJ	0-1338633	0365	1
NAYFIELD CHESTER L	CPT	0-0494030	0446	2
NAYLON GEORGE E JR	CPT	0-1165316	1044	2
NAYLOR ARTHUR S	COL	0-0268904	1160	1
NAYLOR CHARLES R	MAJ	0-1012963	0357	1
NAYLOR EUSTACE I	1LT	0-1548981	0959	3
NAYLOR JOSEPH W	COL	0-0357746	0568	3
NAYLOR JUSTUS B	LTC	0-0246338	1266	3
NAYLOR MYREL E	LTC	0-0289185	1061	1
NAYLOR ROBERT J	1LT	0-1590688	1045	2
NAYLOR WALTER C	1LT	0-0390780	1044	2
NAYLOR WILLIAM H	B G	0-0265997	0965	3
NAYLOR WILLIAM H	1LT	0-1030819	0250	1
NAYLOR WILLIAM R	MAJ	0-0470795	0247	2
NAZAK MICHAEL	2LT	0-1821902	0743	2
NAZARENO VICENTE V	CPT	0-1896537	1159	1
NAZARETE BLAS N	1LT	0-1896878	0751	1
NAZARIO MANUEL A	LTC	0-0245832	0753	3
NAZZARO JOHN J	LTC	0-2211317	1064	1
NEACE LAWRENCE T	CPT	0-0435053	0246	2
NEAGLE CHARLES W	LTC	0-1639866	0662	1
NEAL ALLEN B	WO1	W-2121331	0345	2
NEAL BILLIE J	MAJ	0-4074529	0867	1
NEAL CHARLES M JR	CW3	W-3150685	1268	1
NEAL CHARLEY G	CW2	W-2120789	0450	1
NEAL CHARLIE L JR	LTC	0-1303763	0861	1
NEAL CLARK A	LTC	0-0448099	0962	1
NEAL CORNELIUS	1LT	0-0449239	0646	2
NEAL DAVID L	CW3	W-2147194	0964	1

NAME	GRADE	SVC NO	DATE RET MO YR	RET CODE
NEAL EDWARD B	MAJ	0-0321628	0546	2
NEAL EDWARD J	MAJ	0-1926423	0767	2
NEAL HERESCHELL JR	LTC	0-0972707	0162	2
NEAL HUGH A	LTC	0-0243951	0346	2
NEAL JACK O	1LT	0-1115362	0745	2
NEAL JAMES E	LTC	0-0340150	0446	2
NEAL JAMES P	MAJ	0-0260291	1147	2
NEAL JOSEPH D	1LT	0-0451430	0857	1
NEAL JOSEPH W JR	CPT	0-0398348	0144	2
NEAL KENNETH R	1LT	0-1045858	1045	2
NEAL LENUAL C	CW3	W-2143426	0864	1
NEAL LETTY G	LTC	N-0702522	0960	1
NEAL LILY W	LTC	N-0772841	1263	1
NEAL MARILU	LTC	N-0763498	1068	3
NEAL MILLS F	COL	0-0172100	0852	3
NEAL OLIN F	MAJ	0-1555443	0561	1
NEAL REXFORD B	MAJ	0-0885741	1060	1
NEAL RICHARD K	CPT	0-0246976	0764	3
NEAL ROBERT W	LTC	0-0308715	1160	1
NEAL ROBERT W	COL	0-1283468	0966	1
NEAL THOMAS E JR	CW3	W-2143435	1163	1
NEAL WILLIAM A JR	LTC	0-0370120	0361	1
NEAL WILLIAM W	LTC	0-0374734	0267	1
NEALE ALTON D	COL	0-0505230	0266	3
NEALE JUSTICE R	COL	0-0338492	0366	1
NEALING WILLIAM H	COL	0-0444446	1054	1
NEALON JAMES F	LTC	0-1168004	0261	1
NEALON ROBERT T	CPT	0-1011306	1045	2
NEAMTZ JOHN C	MAJ	0-2265735	0266	1
NEARHOOF RALPH L	LTC	0-1555256	0566	1
NEARY JAMES E	MAJ	0-0451015	0455	1
NEARY JOHN F JR	MAJ	0-0293339	0168	3
NEARY JOHN S	LTC	0-1169670	0964	1
NEARY PHILIP J	LTC	0-0689264	0468	1
NEASE DARIUS H	MAJ	0-1036319	1047	2
NEAT LEYDEN K	CPT	0-0902414	0546	2
NEAVERTH ELMER J	COL	0-0305289	0866	3
NEAVLES JACKSON C	CPT	0-0465740	0945	2
NEBEL DAVID A	CPT	0-1309301	0848	2
NEBEL HAROLD	LTC	0-0245780	0346	2
NEBINGER JOHN F	LTC	0-0333718	0563	1
NEBINGER RANKIN A	MAJ	0-0261757	1063	3
NEBLETT DOUGLAS C	CPT	0-0349917	0145	2
NEBLETT GEORGE L	LTC	0-0228219	1055	1
NECEL ROMUALD H	CW2	W-2144040	0761	1
NEDER ELLIS E	2LT	0-0920507	0145	2
NEDOPAD LOUIS F	MAJ	0-1533645	0457	1
NEDZELNITSKY OLEG V	2LT	0-1017155	0545	2
NEEB MILTON T	CPT	0-1302696	0548	2
NEED OMAR U JR	1LT	0-0335844	0943	2
NEEDHAM ARTHUR C	1LT	0-0397868	0244	2
NEEDHAM ARTIE C	LTC	0-0254317	0562	3
NEEDHAM DANIEL	M G	0-0179136	0551	3
NEEDHAM HARRY C	LTC	0-0953549	0568	1
NEEDHAM HARRY H	COL	0-0203824	0954	3
NEEDHAM JOHN A	LTC	0-0328926	0766	3
NEEDHAM LESLIE E	MAJ	0-0261970	0346	2
NEEDHAM RAYMOND H	2LT	0-1301018	0844	2
NEEDHAM SUMNER H JR	MAJ	0-0242858	0859	1
NEEDHAM WILLIAM A	1LT	0-1590689	0140	2
NEEDHAM WILLIAM A	MAJ	0-2200108	0566	1
NEEDLES FLOYD L	LTC	0-0499383	0962	1
NEEFE WARREN E	CW2	W-2205909	0763	1
NEEL JAMES E	MAJ	0-1283500	0960	1
NEEL TALLY M	LTC	0-0383562	1065	3
NEELEMAN LEONARD J	1LT	0-0465263	0145	2
NEELEY ANDERSON P	LTC	0-0238349	1064	3
NEELEY JOHN A	1LT	0-1030177	0845	2
NEELLY JOHN W	LTC	0-1287391	1166	3
NEELY ARNOL R	CPT	0-0366878	0246	2
NEELY CARL C	B G	0-0270845	0667	3
NEELY CECIL F	MAJ	0-0559771	0561	1
NEELY CHARLES V	CW4	W-2113912	0562	2
NEELY FRED P	CW2	W-2146719	0455	1
NEELY JAMES F	COL	0-0328441	0467	3

NAME	GRADE	SVC NO	DATE RET MO YR	RET CODE
NEELY PAUL F	MAJ	0-1107615	0457	1
NEELY WORLEY R	CPT	0-0493217	1053	1
NEENER ELWOOD H	MAJ	0-0267034	0253	2
NEENER ELWOOD H JR	CPT	0-0990105	0961	1
NEER JAMES R	CPT	0-0182724	0648	3
NEES LEO C	CW4	W-2142182	0858	1
NEESE JOHN D	LTC	0-0361901	0868	3
NEESON JAMES F	MAJ	0-2012108	1163	1
NEETZ HAROLD B	2LT	0-1305463	0644	2
NEFF ANDREW M	LTC	0-0198882	1153	3
NEFF CLYDE A	CPT	0-0120235	0853	3
NEFF CONRAD R JR	2LT	0-0528096	0944	2
NEFF ELSIE	LTC	N-0700021	0344	1
NEFF EMERY B	COL	0-0193482	0245	2
NEFF EUGENE P	MAJ	0-1633425	1065	1
NEFF GARLAND M	2LT	0-1331856	0446	2
NEFF HUGH E	CW3	W-2209467	1068	1
NEFF MARTIN H	CPT	0-1695874	1045	2
NEFF PAT M JR	MAJ	0-0912005	0444	2
NEFF ROBERT D	CW2	W-2150545	0560	1
NEFF THEODORE H	2LT	0-1302173	1043	2
NEFF WILLIAM S JR	MAJ	0-4074531	1268	1
NEGLIA PHILIP P	CPT	0-1116737	1046	2
NEGRI MARY J	1LT	N-0788984	1046	1
NEGRON CARLOS R	CW2	W-2151663	1060	1
NEGRON JESUS M	MAJ	0-0169963	0357	3
NEGRUCCI ROBERT A	CW4	W-2142332	0868	2
NEHF ANDREW J	LTC	0-0254558	0366	3
NEHLS LAURA T	1LT	N-0759601	0845	1
NEHODA FLORENCE K	2LT	N-0794260	0346	1
NEHRLING ROBERT E	LTC	0-1115363	0165	1
NEIBAUR AURILLIS S	WO1	W-2107050	0568	3
NEICHIN SIDNEY N	LTC	0-0385320	0767	3
NEICHTER JOSEPH C	CPT	0-0487575	1058	3
NEIDBALLA EDWARD G	CPT	0-1684598	0146	2
NEIDER DONALD F	MAJ	0-0379118	0260	1
NEIDER NORMAN L	LTC	0-1018130	1062	1
NEIDERMEYER ELMER J	LTC	0-1110680	0368	1
NEIDHAMER THOMAS V	LTC	0-1011268	1263	1
NEIER RICHARD E	CPT	0-1011349	0347	2
NEIGHBARGER R M	CPT	0-1301673	0453	2
NEIGHBORS MELVIN H	MAJ	0-2019071	0862	1
NEIGHBORS WILLIAM R	LTC	0-1824668	0263	1
NEIGUM GOTLIEB G	1LT	0-0944682	0857	1
NEIL AUBREY R	MAJ	0-0500418	0653	1
NEIL TERRANCE	COL	0-0420187	0753	1
NEILL ANDRUS B	COL	0-0359884	0455	1
NEILL CHARLES R	CPT	0-0184878	0845	2
NEILL CHESTER H	CPT	0-1700692	0446	2
NEILL EUGENE P	CW3	W-2108838	0760	1
NEILL GARLAND G	CW4	W-2145571	0968	1
NEILL JEREMIAH F	MAJ	0-0223268	1060	3
NEILL JESSE L	1LT	0-1048119	0545	2
NEILL JOHN B	CW3	W-2203260	0666	1
NEILL JOHN L M	LTC	0-0295202	0665	3
NEILL LEX T	CPT	0-0472531	0146	2
NEILL OWEN C	CPT	0-0263088	0466	3
NEILL ROBERT G	MAJ	0-1289118	0159	1
NEILL ROBERT W	1LT	0-0529430	0945	2
NEILL THOMAS J	1LT	0-1294890	1044	2
NEILLY HAROLD J	CW3	W-2151695	1265	2
NEILON DANIEL F	MAJ	0-0296740	0843	2
NEILSON ROBERT C	CPT	0-1697874	0652	2
NEILSON ROBERT E	2LT	0-0464057	0245	2
NEIPLING LAWRENCE E	LTC	0-1341817	0563	1
NEIS BONNEVILLE	COL	0-0159299	0853	2
NEISS HELEN C	MAJ	N-0759283	1263	1
NEISWANGER HAROLD A	CW3	W-2143950	1262	1
NEISWENDER C P SR	LTC	0-0245290	1058	3
NEISWENDER WILLIAM G	MAJ	0-1284005	0361	2
NEIWIRTH LEO	1LT	0-1647621	0247	2
NEKICH JOSEPH	WO1	W-2112241	0348	1
NELDENGER EDWIN J	LTC	0-1585958	0361	3
NELKA STANLEY E	CPT	0-5218408	0968	2
NELL MARVEL G	LTC	0-0248306	0366	3

NAME	GRADE	SVC NO	DATE RET MO YR	RET CODE
NELLEN ROBERT S	CPT	0-1016207	0864	1
NELLES PHILIP A JR	LTC	0-0288750	1056	3
NELLIGAN HARRY A	WO1	W-2004427	0458	3
NELLIS CHARLES N JR	LTC	0-0262021	0467	3
NELLIS JOSEPH L	CPT	0-0955981	1058	1
NELLOR EDWARD K	1LT	0-0450374	0544	2
NELLOR TUDOR M	1LT	0-1319567	1045	2
NELSEN HANS	2LT	0-1291681	1044	2
NELSEN KENNETH W	MAJ	0-1320767	0563	1
NELSON A JANE R	1LT	N-0724710	0846	1
NELSON AARON W	MAJ	0-0301167	1158	3
NELSON ADOLPH H	MAJ	0-0288743	0844	2
NELSON ALFRED C	LTC	0-2056120	1168	1
NELSON ALFRED H	CPT	0-0385118	0145	2
NELSON ALFRED W JR	1LT	0-1298745	0345	2
NELSON ANTON	CW4	W-2101086	1052	1
NELSON ARTHUR G	MAJ	0-2025119	0465	1
NELSON ARTHUR P	MAJ	0-1893738	0267	1
NELSON AUGUST W	CW3	W-2208677	0366	1
NELSON BERNICE A	MAJ	N-0771704	0448	1
NELSON CARL W	COL	0-0335637	0564	3
NELSON CARL W	LTC	0-1285278	0657	1
NELSON CHARLES G JR	CPT	0-1647623	0361	1
NELSON CHESTER H	CW4	W-2144871	0867	1
NELSON CHESTER L	MAJ	0-0210912	0648	3
NELSON CLARENCE A	LTC	0-0317003	1057	3
NELSON CLAUDE L	MAJ	0-0888275	1054	1
NELSON CLAYTON J JR	MAJ	0-0996656	0966	1
NELSON CLIFFORD R	WO1	W-2114449	0454	2
NELSON CLIFTON B	COL	0-0502250	1054	1
NELSON CLIFTON W	CPT	0-1282055	1054	1
NELSON CURTIS A	COL	0-0279146	0365	3
NELSON DAVID A	LTC	0-0240580	1152	2
NELSON DONALD M	LTC	0-1646448	0567	1
NELSON DONALD T	CPT	0-1165920	0346	2
NELSON EARL J	LTC	0-0243326	0963	3
NELSON EARL W	CPT	0-0270345	1144	2
NELSON EDWARD D JR	LTC	0-1948025	0164	1
NELSON EDWARD G	CW3	W-2151934	0666	1
NELSON EDWARD H	MAJ	0-0256142	1063	3
NELSON EDWARD P	LTC	0-0257402	1265	3
NELSON EDWARD S	LTC	0-0254072	0768	3
NELSON EDWIN A	LTC	0-0487022	0357	1
NELSON EDWIN C	MAJ	0-0451160	0853	1
NELSON EDWIN J	LTC	0-1042660	0766	1
NELSON ELBERT L	COL	0-0245306	1158	3
NELSON ELMER L	LTC	0-1111805	1062	1
NELSON ELMER L	CW2	W-2147045	0663	1
NELSON ELVEN C	LTC	0-0529465	0967	3
NELSON EMERSON M JR	CW3	W-2211015	0868	1
NELSON EMERY E	CW3	RW-2207401	1267	1
NELSON EMIL H	1LT	0-1169268	1044	2
NELSON ERNEST L	1LT	0-1172754	0845	2
NELSON ETHEL M	1LT	N-0703015	0646	1
NELSON FRANCIS H	CPT	0-0252405	0965	3
NELSON FRED C JR	2LT	0-1316579	1044	2
NELSON FREDERICK	LTC	0-1010307	1262	1
NELSON FREDERICK	MAJ	0-1110153	0761	1
NELSON FREDERICK	MAJ	0-1885994	1068	1
NELSON GEORGE E	COL	0-0256043	0159	3
NELSON GEORGE R	LTC	0-1646865	1162	1
NELSON GEORGE W	CW2	W-2113090	1151	1
NELSON GLENN E	LTC	0-1554449	0765	1
NELSON GORDON N	CW3	W-2141643	0959	1
NELSON GORDON W	1LT	0-1297771	1045	2
NELSON GRETCHEN A	2LT	N-0734403	0944	1
NELSON GRIFFIN G	1LT	0-1294891	0446	2
NELSON HAROLD A	COL	0-0353173	0166	1
NELSON HAROLD S	COL	0-0100959	0350	3
NELSON HARRY A	LTC	0-0232989	1060	3
NELSON HEDRICK C	MAJ	0-1030399	1060	3
NELSON HENRY N SR	MAJ	0-0125857	0452	3
NELSON HERBERT R	1LT	0-0921320	0544	2
NELSON HERMAN	CW4	W-2146922	1268	2
NELSON HILDURE	1LT	N-0735659	0946	1

NAME	GRADE	SVC NO	DATE RET MO YR	RET CODE
NELSON HOWARD L	LTC	0-0405241	1157	1
NELSON HOWARD W	MAJ	0-1305097	0363	1
NELSON IRA	LTC	0-1013058	0257	1
NELSON IRA J	1LT	0-1300515	0454	1
NELSON IRENE M	1LT	N-0751765	0246	2
NELSON IRVING E	MAJ	0-0497136	1047	2
NELSON IVAR V JR	2LT	0-1110681	1044	2
NELSON JACK J	MAJ	0-2033803	0865	1
NELSON JACK W	CW3	W-2150899	0862	1
NELSON JAMES A	CPT	0-2056700	0564	2
NELSON JAMES D	LTC	0-0404694	0546	2
NELSON JAMES H	CPT	0-0298722	0346	2
NELSON JAMES H	1LT	0-1285279	1045	2
NELSON JAMES L	CPT	0-4073465	0968	1
NELSON JESSE G	LTC	0-0305161	0768	3
NELSON JOHN A	COL	0-0173086	0753	3
NELSON JOHN A	CPT	0-0450091	1145	2
NELSON JOHN C	MAJ	0-0500691	0756	1
NELSON JOHN J	LTC	0-1577621	0755	1
NELSON JOHN L	CW2	W-2118406	0653	1
NELSON JOHN L JR	MAJ	0-1338840	1060	1
NELSON JOHN M	2LT	0-1633427	1044	2
NELSON JOHN R	CPT	0-0920250	0845	2
NELSON JOHN R	LTC	0-1546367	0363	1
NELSON JOHNNIE L	CW2	RW-2210416	1164	1
NELSON JOSEPH N	MAJ	0-0509879	0661	1
NELSON KENNETH L	CPT	0-0261646	0166	3
NELSON KENNETH S	CPT	0-0456093	0745	2
NELSON KINLOCH	MAJ	0-0400345	0245	2
NELSON KLEMENS M	LTC	0-2034896	1060	1
NELSON LAWRENCE A	COL	0-0267617	0554	1
NELSON LAWRENCE J	LTC	0-0394215	0660	1
NELSON LAWRENCE M	MAJ	0-0290814	0146	2
NELSON LAWRENCE M	LTC	0-0377911	0662	1
NELSON LLOYD C	MAJ	0-1552943	0157	1
NELSON LLOYD L	1LT	0-2042848	0348	1
NELSON LOWELL	LTC	0-0445978	0956	1
NELSON LYMAN A	LTC	0-0200076	0358	3
NELSON MANSFIELD	COL	0-0230627	0955	1
NELSON MARION M	LTC	0-1080890	0161	1
NELSON MARVIN L	CPT	0-0151598	0554	3
NELSON MARY E	MAJ	L-0906370	0166	1
NELSON MARY M	1LT	N-0763157	1045	1
NELSON MELVIN	CPT	0-2032889	1263	1
NELSON MELVIN W	CW2	W-2153043	0957	1
NELSON MERLAND W	LTC	0-2014442	0768	1
NELSON MERLIN N	LTC	0-0417550	0762	2
NELSON MURRAY R	CW3	W-2146455	1264	1
NELSON NEAL D	LTC	0-0226233	0464	3
NELSON NORMAN A	WO1	W-2104945	0946	2
NELSON ORVAL E	CW2	W-2151700	0561	1
NELSON ORVILLE L	CW2	W-2210214	1062	1
NELSON ORVIN E	1LT	0-1325509	0648	2
NELSON OSCAR H	CW4	W-2116143	0359	1
NELSON OTTO A	LTC	0-0364863	0859	1
NELSON OTTO F	MAJ	0-1574734	0365	1
NELSON PAUL L	LTC	0-2001109	0968	1
NELSON QUENTIN V	CW3	W-2144342	0963	1
NELSON RALPH H	1LT	0-1054731	0346	2
NELSON RANDALL H	CPT	0-1036653	0347	2
NELSON RAYMOND A	COL	0-0286649	0655	1
NELSON RAYMOND F	2LT	0-1796139	0845	2
NELSON RAYMOND J	CPT	0-0387542	0144	2
NELSON RAYMOND N	2LT	0-1314398	0744	2
NELSON RICHARD O	MAJ	0-0977394	0264	1
NELSON RICHARD V	1LT	0-0160198	0854	3
NELSON RICHARD V	MAJ	0-0230873	0958	3
NELSON ROBERT A	CPT	0-1799068	0854	2
NELSON ROBERT C	LTC	0-1591341	0960	1
NELSON ROBERT O	MAJ	0-1318819	1063	1
NELSON ROBERT O	CW4	W-2105228	1060	1
NELSON ROY E	MAJ	0-0102250	0658	3
NELSON ROY E	COL	0-0294136	0866	3
NELSON ROY E	LTC	0-0750667	0761	1
NELSON ROY R	CPT	0-1324181	1047	2

NAME	GRADE	SVC NO	DATE RET MO YR	RET CODE
NELSON ROY W	LTC	0-1063013	1062	1
NELSON RUSSELL C	LTC	0-0256045	1159	1
NELSON RUSSELL E	CW2	W-2151659	0361	1
NELSON SIGURD S	MAJ	0-0482712	1148	1
NELSON STANLEY O	MAJ	0-117C111	1161	1
NELSON STEADMAN P	LTC	0-1944766	1265	1
NELSON SUE C	1LT	N-0763435	0346	1
NELSON SUMTER R	LTC	0-0420240	0660	1
NELSON TEDDY B	MAJ	0-1168391	0158	1
NELSON TERRY N	CPT	0-0913072	0445	2
NELSON THOMAS C SR	MAJ	0-0974457	0764	1
NELSON THOMAS H	1LT	0-0250872	1044	2
NELSON THOMAS W	2LT	0-1052525	0245	2
NELSON THOMAS W	1LT	0-1845630	0446	2
NELSON THURSTON D	MAJ	0-0975931	0763	1
NELSON VINCENT H	MAJ	0-0978797	0364	1
NELSON WALDO	COL	0-0351054	0567	3
NELSON WALLACE E	MAJ	0-2262188	1263	1
NELSON WALTER S JR	LTC	0-1284924	0760	1
NELSON WARREN H	CW4	W-2004440	1167	1
NELSON WILLIAM A	MAJ	0-1080651	0863	1
NELSON WILLIAM A	CW2	W-2102144	0846	1
NELSON WILLIAM A JR	LTC	0-0454102	0859	1
NELSON WILLIAM F	MAJ	0-1181970	1062	1
NELSON WILLIAM III	LTC	0-0412771	0167	1
NELSON WILLIAM S JR	COL	0-0174566	0358	3
NELSON WILLIAM V	LTC	0-1319319	0168	1
NELSON WILLOUGHBY	MAJ	0-0965143	0966	2
NELSON WOODROW L	LTC	0-0412285	1060	1
NEMEC FRANK A	CPT	0-0517258	0445	2
NEMETH ALBERT J	1LT	0-0885791	1145	2
NEMETH ERNEST A	CPT	0-2263137	0761	1
NEMETH LELIA L	MAJ	N-0797837	0765	1
NEMETH STEPHEN JR	MAJ	0-0488480	0457	1
NEMETH THEODORE W JR	CPT	0-1055680	0147	2
NEMIC ALBERT L	LTC	0-0350061	0566	3
NEMISH CHARLES	LTC	0-1323021	1162	1
NENN WILLIAM H	CW2	W-2006562	1057	2
NENNINGER HAROLD F	LTC	0-1823336	0562	1
NENNO ARTHUR C	MAJ	0-1548982	0161	1
NENOW NIKOLAI	CW2	W-2210841	1265	1
NERI FRANK D	MAJ	0-0494495	0350	2
NERI HENRY J	LTC	0-0359280	0367	3
NERRIE ROBERT A JR	MAJ	0-0252884	0460	1
NESBETT GEORGE H JR	COL	0-0313384	0961	1
NESBIT ARTHUR P	COL	0-0244574	0357	1
NESBIT VIRGIL C	CW3	W-2148874	0563	1
NESBITT CARL E	COL	0-0192853	0146	2
NESBITT DAVID A	CW3	W-2148574	0862	2
NESBITT GARVEN S	LTC	0-0925250	0666	3
NESBITT GEORGE B	WO1	W-2126752	0145	2
NESBITT LEROY J	LTC	0-0322010	1062	1
NESBITT RUSSELL G	MAJ	0-0201136	0958	3
NESBITT THOMAS M JR	COL	0-0223246	1064	3
NESBITT WILLIAM E	CPT	0-0249595	0762	3
NESBITT WILLIAM J	1LT	0-1309805	0146	2
NESEWICH MARTIN	CW3	W-2148357	1262	1
NESLEN CLARENCE C	COL	0-0368733	0267	3
NESMITH JAMES II	COL	0-0163241	1061	3
NESOM CHARLES N JR	LTC	0-0321381	1267	3
NESS DONALD L	LTC	0-0419311	0263	1
NESS JULIUS B	CPT	0-1285479	0945	2
NESS MARTIN K	MAJ	0-1173728	0656	1
NESS PAUL F	CW2	W-2152976	1057	1
NESS RICHARD C	LTC	0-1322071	1066	1
NESS VERNELLE J	CPT	0-1698201	0646	2
NESSELHOF WILLIAM	CPT	0-0133905	0254	3
NESSLEY EDWARD J	LTC	0-1703892	0163	1
NESSMITH REX D	WO1	W-2117962	0759	1
NESSON JOHN H	LTC	0-0220385	1058	3
NESTER GILBERT C	LTC	0-1634176	0960	1
NESTER LOUIS T	CW3	W-2205593	0268	1
NESTER NORMAN W	LTC	0-0282761	0865	3
NESTOR MARION E	LTC	L-0203227	0667	1
NESTOR MONA E S	1LT	N-0742988	1046	1

NAME	GRADE	SVC NO	DATE RET MO YR	RET CODE
NETHERLAND RAYMOND A	CPT	0-1320769	1146	2
NETHERTON CHARLES J	MAJ	0-1109555	0865	1
NETHERTON GROVER T	CPT	0-0446464	0645	2
NETHERY SAMUEL C	LTC	0-0234867	1159	1
NETHERY WILLIAM M	LTC	0-0322004	0566	3
NETSKY MARGARET P	1LT	N-0743611	0747	1
NETTERS JIMMIE C	1LT	0-0360051	1043	2
NETTLES ALBERT A	CPT	0-0330906	1045	2
NETTLES EARL W	LTC	0-0429341	0162	1
NETTLES FRANK K	WO1	W-2147343	0853	2
NETTLES HOWARD C	MAJ	0-1639451	1160	1
NETTLES ROBERT L	MAJ	0-0249903	1057	3
NETTLES WILLIAM F JR	CPT	0-0257161	1267	3
NETZER ERWIN	MAJ	0-1889862	0766	1
NETZLOFF HAROLD H	MAJ	0-1287045	1060	1
NEU EUGENE G	WO1	W-2119381	1044	2
NEU RICHARD F	LTC	0-0298271	0468	3
NEU WARREN E	COL	0-0369942	0862	1
NEUBAUER ADOLPH	CW3	W-2118064	1060	1
NEUBAUER KENNETH H	MAJ	0-1062031	0762	1
NEUBAUM FREDERICK	CW3	W-2206377	0966	1
NEUDEK ELSIE V	2LT	N-0728999	0145	1
NEUDORFF KARL A	CW2	W-2150347	1066	1
NEUENDORF RAY C	LTC	0-0484316	0655	1
NEUFELD CHARLES M	LTC	0-0981221	1063	1
NEUFELD LEWIS	2LT	0-1597877	104N	2
NEUGEBAUER WILLIAM F	COL	0-1994666	0562	1
NEUHAUSER HARRY M	LTC	0-0235424	0760	1
NEUMANN ARTHUR	LTC	0-1281037	0766	1
NEUMANN ARTHUR T	CPT	0-1290987	0249	1
NEUMANN CARL E	CW3	W-2148397	1062	1
NEUMANN EARNEST O	MAJ	0-1936344	0967	1
NEUMANN EDWARD E	COL	0-0279600	0254	1
NEUMANN OSCAR D	LTC	0-0374430	0860	1
NEUMANN PAUL M	LTC	0-0376918	1060	1
NEUMANN RAYMOND J	LTC	0-1944535	1060	1
NEUMANN SIDNEY S	CPT	0-1308849	0947	2
NEUMANN WALTER E	CPT	0-0425940	0954	1
NEUMARK GEORGE	COL	0-0254403	0765	3
NEUMYER ROBERT J	LTC	0-1582831	0863	1
NEUNEWS ROY T	CPT	0-1303010	0146	2
NEUROCK JOHN	MAJ	0-1336682	1161	1
NEUWIRTH ABRAHAM	MAJ	0-1554947	0756	1
NEUWIRTH ABRAHAM A	LTC	0-0274171	0544	2
NEVELING WALDO	1LT	0-2032300	0646	2
NEVELLS FREDERICK	LTC	0-0241272	0762	3
NEVELS ALICE P	CPT	L-0401524	0445	2
NEVENZEL HARVERD L	LTC	0-1174089	0668	1
NEVERICK ALFRED A	MAJ	0-1795954	1267	3
NEVILL GALE E	COL	0-0286060	0167	3
NEVILLE ANDREW P	COL	0-0510313	0660	3
NEVILLE CATHERINE	MAJ	N-0751945	0666	1
NEVILLE DELMAR S	CW4	W-2147130	0868	1
NEVILLE HOWARD T	2LT	0-1947265	0345	2
NEVILLE JAMES M	LTC	0-4021577	1059	2
NEVILLE JOHN F	1LT	0-1030179	1044	2
NEVILLE JOHN W	1LT	0-0958911	0554	2
NEVILLE JOSEPH H JR	1LT	0-0269525	0445	2
NEVILLE JOSEPH M	COL	0-0114956	0754	3
NEVILLE LEWIS J	MAJ	0-2263114	0465	1
NEVILLE WALTER L	LTC	0-0289686	1060	3
NEVILLE WALTER S	CPT	0-2043070	0968	3
NEVILLE WILLIAM D	CPT	0-0130045	0453	3
NEVILLE WILLIAM G	LTC	0-0452778	0547	2
NEVILLE WILLIAM H JR	2LT	0-1292047	0545	2
NEVIN JOSEPH P JR	MAJ	0-1583438	0357	1
NEVINS EDWARD F	CW2	W-2210882	1068	1
NEVINS GLEN	1LT	0-1316915	1045	2
NEVINS WILLIAM B	MAJ	0-1923599	0665	2
NEVITT JAMES R	COL	0-0321833	0959	3
NEVITT OLNEY L	MAJ	0-1577625	0761	1
NEVITT PEYTON G	COL	0-0178264	1154	3
NEVITT THOMAS R	MAJ	0-0173732	1060	3
NEVIUS CARL W	MAJ	0-0309576	1153	3
NEVLING CLAYTON T	MAJ	0-0969463	1263	1

NAME	GRADE	SVC NO	DATE RET MO YR	RET CODE
NEVUE FRANCIS E	MAJ	0-1634179	0657	1
NEW CHARLES A	COL	0-0226473	1063	3
NEW CHARLES J	LTC	0-1032545	1266	1
NEW JAMES O	CW2	W-2213521	0566	1
NEW JOHN R	CPT	0-0460044	0647	2
NEW MARVIN H	1LT	0-1179553	0945	2
NEW WILLIAM J	COL	0-0237900	0665	3
NEWBEGIN FRANCIS N	MAJ	0-1299284	0564	1
NEWBERG MILDRED	MAJ	L-010C089	0965	1
NEWBERN HOWARD E	LTC	0-0355976	1067	3
NEWBERRY DONALD C	MAJ	0-2203250	1166	1
NEWBERRY GUY F	2LT	0-1549799	1043	2
NEWBERRY JARREL M	CPT	0-2262392	1160	1
NEWBERRY LOUIS M	LTC	0-0954162	0367	1
NEWBERRY MARK	WO1	W-2146977	0659	1
NEWBERRY Y T	CW4	W-2109971	1062	1
NEWBILL MARION L	CW3	W-2144852	0661	1
NEWBILL ROBERT N	LTC	0-0454816	1161	1
NEWBOLD JOHN W	1LT	0-0441319	0544	2
NEWBURGER SIDNEY JR	LTC	0-0243248	0365	3
NEWBURGER STANLEY W	WO1	W-2107176	1045	2
NEWBURN ALVA O	LTC	0-0490479	0159	3
NEWBURY FRED L	CPT	0-0485186	0647	1
NEWBY RALPH D	LTC	0-117C113	0563	1
NEWCOMB ARTHUR M	CW4	W-2131484	0760	1
NEWCOMB CARMEN A JR	MAJ	0-0303003	0245	2
NEWCOMB GEORGE L	CW4	W-2111703	0559	1
NEWCOMB LESTER D	1LT	0-0925226	0445	2
NEWCOMBE HAZEL J	2LT	N-0720556	0545	1
NEWCOMER DONALD R	CW3	W-2205108	1067	1
NEWCOMER ROBERT	CW4	W-2124709	1060	1
NEWELL BEN A	1LT	0-0413864	0343	2
NEWELL CLYDE R	MAJ	0-0135827	0648	3
NEWELL FRANCIS M	LTC	0-0274205	1061	3
NEWELL HAROLD L	CPT	0-0323160	0351	1
NEWELL HARVEY P	2LT	0-1104319	0855	1
NEWELL JACK D	2LT	0-1114686	1044	2
NEWELL JAMES J	CW3	W-2149797	0462	1
NEWELL JOHN L	MAJ	0-0273837	1043	2
NEWELL JOSEPH J JR	CW3	W-2152610	1163	1
NEWELL LELAND R	LTC	0-1844959	0862	3
NEWELL LOU P	1LT	N-0726011	0646	1
NEWELL MELVIN S	CW2	W-2111718	0945	2
NEWELL RICHARD E	MAJ	0-2042909	0258	1
NEWELL ROBERT L JR	CW2	W-3151848	0966	2
NEWELL SHEPARD B	MAJ	0-0977562	0763	1
NEWELL WESLEY S	1LT	0-1550880	1158	1
NEWELL 3RD JOHN	1LT	0-0538805	0246	2
NEWGARD JOSEPH M	MAJ	0-0119972	0648	3
NEWHALL HARRY B	LTC	0-117C114	0864	1
NEWHARD CHARLES H	1LT	0-1298107	1045	2
NEWHARDT CLIFFORD J	2LT	0-0966507	0550	2
NEWHART ARTHUR H	MAJ	0-2024105	0860	1
NEWHOUSE ARVID B	COL	0-0338755	0568	3
NEWHOUSE ELBERT A	LTC	0-0278536	1066	3
NEWHOUSE FRED L	MAJ	0-2211504	0667	1
NEWHOUSE JESSE P	MAJ	0-2262882	0567	1
NEWHOUSE WILLIAM C	CPT	0-1325920	0856	1
NEWINGTON ELMER J	MAJ	0-1298578	1262	1
NEWITT BERENICE E	2LT	N-0700986	0737	1
NEWKIRK ARTHUR C	COL	0-0119081	1150	3
NEWKIRK HAROLD J	1LT	0-1038779	0146	2
NEWKIRK JAMES R	LTC	0-0364415	1266	1
NEWKIRK KENNETH L	CPT	0-0384606	0346	2
NEWKIRK LEWIS R	MAJ	0-1646868	0162	1
NEWKIRK MARION J	LTC	0-0516992	1167	1
NEWKIRK WILLIAM G	LTC	0-1333372	0166	1
NEWLAND FLETCHER F	MAJ	0-2279879	0366	1
NEWLAND HAROLD	COL	0-0123883	0953	3
NEWLAND LEROY T JR	MAJ	0-0889794	0263	1
NEWLANDER JULIAN A	COL	0-0269989	0860	1
NEWLIN ARTHUR E	LTC	0-1116801	1267	1
NEWLIN DALE A	COL	0-0221176	0150	1
NEWLIN DONALD M	MAJ	0-2263451	1168	1
NEWLIN FLOYD W	1LT	0-1542501	1045	2

NAME	GRADE	SVC NO	DATE RET MO YR	RET CODE
NEWLIN LEWIS K	LTC	0-1558186	0467	1
NEWMAN BERNARD J	1LT	0-1172574	0246	2
NEWMAN BERYL R	CPT	0-0346726	1045	2
NEWMAN CARL F	1LT	0-1113374	104N	2
NEWMAN CHARLES C	CPT	0-0508492	0946	1
NEWMAN CHARLES E	COL	0-0193139	0553	3
NEWMAN CHARLES E	CW3	W-2148875	1266	1
NEWMAN CHARLES W	LTC	0-0244778	0964	3
NEWMAN DELMAR J	CPT	0-0361166	1045	2
NEWMAN DONALD R	LTC	0-0518442	0767	1
NEWMAN DWIGHT R	CW2	W-2150153	1160	1
NEWMAN EARL L B	CPT	0-0501427	0145	2
NEWMAN ELMER C	LTC	0-0365773	0760	1
NEWMAN ELMER A	MAJ	0-0185120	0156	3
NEWMAN EZRA H JR	LTC	0-1165754	0263	1
NEWMAN FLOYD W	MAJ	0-0179097	0944	2
NEWMAN FRED [illegible]	MAJ	0-1874692	1061	1
NEWMAN GEORGE J	CW3	RW-2142090	0859	1
NEWMAN HAROLD T	LTC	0-0220847	1061	3
NEWMAN HENRY	2LT	0-0395267	0345	2
NEWMAN HENRY E	MAJ	0-1185506	0255	2
NEWMAN HOWARD E	LTC	0-1312586	1166	1
NEWMAN IRVING J	COL	0-0248739	0357	3
NEWMAN JACK W	1LT	0-1314823	1045	2
NEWMAN JAMES S	MAJ	0-1918978	0863	1
NEWMAN JESSE V	1LT	0-0479016	0447	1
NEWMAN JOE L	1LT	0-0373003	0544	2
NEWMAN JOE W	2LT	0-2101162	1045	2
NEWMAN JOHN F	CPT	0-0361508	0945	2
NEWMAN JOHN H	CW4	W-2103259	0168	1
NEWMAN JOSEPH	WO1	W-2115377	0845	2
NEWMAN KENNETH F	CW2	W-2207074	1062	1
NEWMAN KENNETH F	LTC	0-0387412	0258	1
NEWMAN LESLIE	CPT	0-0167755	0745	2
NEWMAN MANCEL L SR	LTC	0-0494730	0654	2
NEWMAN MARCEL J	CPT	0-1341233	1058	1
NEWMAN MARTIN C	LTC	0-0302716	0167	3
NEWMAN MAURICE A	LTC	0-1541951	0661	1
NEWMAN MILTON B	1LT	0-1594158	0446	2
NEWMAN MOSES C JR	CW2	W-2219642	0466	1
NEWMAN OLFUS L	1LT	0-0487776	0644	1
NEWMAN OLIVER L	LTC	0-1257929	0962	1
NEWMAN PATTI C	MAJ	0-0484276	0451	1
NEWMAN PAUL D	CPT	0-0511397	1045	2
NEWMAN PETER J	CPT	0-1925217	0764	1
NEWMAN PHILIP H	CPT	0-0485514	1045	2
NEWMAN RALPH C	WO1	W-2117940	1046	2
NEWMAN SAMUEL W	CW2	W-2152475	1161	1
NEWMAN STEWART L	MAJ	0-1684988	0564	1
NEWMAN TAYLOR E	CW2	W-2115933	0949	2
NEWMAN THOMAS C	MAJ	0-1100702	0359	1
NEWMAN WALTER C	LTC	0-0327155	1265	3
NEWMANN NORMAN F	LTC	0-1322651	1262	1
NEWMARK PHILIP M	MAJ	0-1001203	0347	2
NEWMARK TED	LTC	0-1001864	0567	3
NEWNAM ALONZO F	LTC	0-1316580	0466	1
NEWNAM JOHN H	CPT	0-0480979	0447	1
NEWPORT EARL M	2LT	0-0391989	0741	2
NEWPORT NORSUDA M	LTC	0-0346850	0367	3
NEWPORT ROBERT A	LTC	0-0961939	0268	1
NEWSHAM ARTHUR J	CPT	0-1315092	0747	2
NEWSOM HAROLD R	MAJ	0-0504917	0457	1
NEWSOM HERMAN L	1LT	0-0171602	0355	3
NEWTON ABRAM M	COL	0-0224539	0548	3
NEWTON ALBERT	CW3	W-2205260	0464	1
NEWTON ARTHUR P	MAJ	0-0322177	1165	1
NEWTON CECIL J	LTC	0-0915388	1067	3
NEWTON GORDON E	CPT	0-1120668	0760	1
NEWTON HAROLD D	MAJ	0-0137271	0355	3
NEWTON HARVEY P	1LT	0-0555150	0446	2
NEWTON HENRY C	B G	0-0104029	0756	3
NEWTON HERBERT P	MAJ	0-0267374	0261	3
NEWTON IOUS W	CW3	W-2145894	0866	1
NEWTON JAMES E	COL	0-0290054	1064	3
NEWTON JOHN G	1LT	0-2002693	0753	2
NEWTON JOHN H	LTC	0-0255882	0967	3
NEWTON JOSEPH B	MAJ	0-1302042	0462	1
NEWTON JOSEPH C	CW4	W-2114199	0655	3
NEWTON JOSEPH L	CPT	0-1289471	0146	2
NEWTON LAWRENCE R	LTC	0-0328437	0763	3
NEWTON LULU J	LTC	N-0700371	1046	1
NEWTON PAUL V	LTC	0-1105061	0862	1
NEWTON PETER J	LTC	0-0359139	0647	2
NEWTON RUFFUS H	MAJ	0-0976054	0962	1
NEWTON RUSSEL M	1LT	0-5331492	0767	2
NEWTON WILLIAM A	MAJ	0-1894193	0167	1
NEWTON WILLIAM H	COL	0-0277999	0159	3
NEWTON WILLIAM T	CW3	W-2149229	1265	1
NEXSEN SAMUEL M	1LT	0-0460045	0845	2
NEY VIRGIL	COL	0-0227473	1057	1
NIBALI VINCENT C	MAJ	0-1598986	0462	1
NIBBELINK HARRY L	MAJ	0-1548985	0164	1
NIBBELINK WAYNE R	1LT	0-0467220	0445	2
NIBERT WILLIAM E	LTC	0-0408942	0765	1
NIBLACK CARLTON D JR	LTC	0-0296230	1161	1
NICCOLLS FRANCIS A	LTC	0-1796142	0361	1
NICCUM JOHN F	CPT	0-0959998	1061	1
NICCUM LEWIS L	CW2	W-2105726	0845	2
NICE HERBERT D	COL	0-0171524	0864	3
NICELY ROY E	CW3	W-2203261	0266	1
NICEWANDER WILLIAM A	MAJ	0-2202225	0866	1
NICHOL DEANE M	CPT	0-1324566	0746	2
NICHOL EFFIE B	MAJ	N-0788572	0963	1
NICHOL ERNEST R	COL	0-0262044	0165	3
NICHOL RAYMOND R	CPT	0-1039823	0862	1
NICHOLAS GEORGE D	LTC	0-1289472	0763	1
NICHOLAS GEORGE W	CW2	W-2141396	0667	2
NICHOLAS HARRY I JR	LTC	0-1030508	0668	3
NICHOLAS JESSE T	COL	0-0261951	1157	3
NICHOLAS JOHN F JR	LTC	0-0392659	0761	1
NICHOLAS JOSEPH	MAJ	0-1580088	0960	1
NICHOLAS LANDON G	CPT	0-1290647	0748	2
NICHOLAS ROBERT W JR	CPT	0-0525069	1057	1
NICHOLLS EARLE R JR	MAJ	0-1639871	0165	1
NICHOLLS EDWARD W	LTC	0-1181705	0868	1
NICHOLLS HAROLD C	COL	0-0317492	0265	3
NICHOLLS MALCOLM A	CW3	W-2146119	0264	1
NICHOLS ARTHUR T	LTC	0-0291561	0167	3
NICHOLS BENNIE B	LTC	0-2017888	0967	1
NICHOLS BRYANT L	LTC	0-1303765	0464	1
NICHOLS BYRON D	MAJ	0-1929037	0167	1
NICHOLS CARNIE F	WO1	W-2115173	0750	1
NICHOLS CHESTER A	COL	0-0255671	0160	1
NICHOLS CHESTER W	LTC	0-0229776	0165	3
NICHOLS CLYDE R	COL	0-0336407	1068	3
NICHOLS DEAN M	1LT	0-1018444	0246	2
NICHOLS EARL T SR	CW2	W-2145331	0758	1
NICHOLS EDWIN O	LTC	0-0309796	1063	1
NICHOLS ELIJAH E JR	2LT	0-1822440	0252	2
NICHOLS ERNEST A	CPT	0-1574108	0664	1
NICHOLS FLOY L	CPT	0-0239663	1065	3
NICHOLS FRANCIS L	CPT	0-0222946	0860	3
NICHOLS FRANK	CPT	0-0497456	0447	1
NICHOLS FRANK S	LTC	0-0977938	0868	1
NICHOLS FRANKLIN L	MAJ	0-1081828	1166	1
NICHOLS FRED Z JR	CPT	0-1040988	0447	2
NICHOLS FREDERIC H	COL	0-0155985	0355	3
NICHOLS FREDERICK	LTC	0-0507789	0363	1
NICHOLS GAYLE H	LTC	0-0321348	0459	3
NICHOLS GROVER T	LTC	0-0258598	1267	3
NICHOLS HENRY C	MAJ	0-0186169	0155	3
NICHOLS HERBERT A	2LT	0-1688282	1054	1
NICHOLS HERBERT B	LTC	0-0298554	1167	3
NICHOLS HERSHEL R	MAJ	0-0576895	0666	1
NICHOLS JAMES A	COL	0-0224989	1058	1
NICHOLS JAMES A	CW3	W-2147255	0361	1
NICHOLS JAMES D	LTC	0-0981437	0468	1
NICHOLS JAMES R JR	MAJ	0-0270044	0667	3
NICHOLS JASPER W	MAJ	0-0151391	1150	3
NICHOLS JOHN A	CPT	0-0353254	0444	2
NICHOLS JOHN H	COL	0-0336909	0465	3
NICHOLS JOHN H	MAJ	0-1554791	0447	2
NICHOLS JOHN L	LTC	0-0496317	0463	1
NICHOLS JOHN M	CW3	W-2208438	0866	1
NICHOLS JOHN W	MAJ	0-1798288	0556	2
NICHOLS LAWRENCE G	LTC	0-0450642	0561	2
NICHOLS LEON H	CW4	W-2142076	1164	1
NICHOLS LEONARD I	MAJ	0-0284865	0566	3
NICHOLS MARON J	CPT	0-0987710	1057	1
NICHOLS MAURICE L	1LT	0-0401659	0544	2
NICHOLS ORVIN N	COL	0-0358054	0354	3
NICHOLS RALPH M	MAJ	0-2026804	0563	2
NICHOLS RICHARD O	1LT	0-1648630	0653	2
NICHOLS RICHARD T	COL	0-0206550	1155	1
NICHOLS ROBERT E	CPT	0-2263516	0764	1
NICHOLS ROBERT F	CW3	W-2203361	0565	1
NICHOLS ROBERT J	COL	0-0210064	1057	3
NICHOLS THEODORE J	1LT	0-1636876	0849	2
NICHOLS THOMAS F	COL	0-0372276	0968	3
NICHOLS WALTER R	COL	0-0301532	1057	2
NICHOLS WALTER S	MAJ	0-1824073	0264	1
NICHOLS WALTER V	LTC	0-0481946	0566	1
NICHOLS WALTER W	MAJ	0-1172575	1265	1
NICHOLS WILLIAM C	LTC	0-1593750	0862	1
NICHOLS WILLIAM F	CPT	0-0379281	0447	2
NICHOLS WILLIAM G	LTC	0-1168393	1163	1
NICHOLS WILLIAM H	CPT	0-1882370	0267	1
NICHOLS WILLIAM V	COL	0-0908968	0862	1
NICHOLS WILLIS F	MAJ	0-0259789	0267	3
NICHOLS WOODROW E	LTC	0-0396953	0961	1
NICHOLSON ALFRED D	COL	0-0238561	0566	3
NICHOLSON ALVIN F	1LT	0-1285098	0944	2
NICHOLSON DAVID S	MAJ	0-1646870	0561	1
NICHOLSON ERNEST R	CPT	0-0394004	0862	1
NICHOLSON EUGENE C	LTC	0-0397766	1060	1
NICHOLSON FLORENCE C	LTC	L-0700205	0363	1
NICHOLSON FRANCIS L	CW3	W-2103261	0356	1
NICHOLSON FRANK A	MAJ	0-1040989	0961	1
NICHOLSON FRANKLIN W	MAJ	0-1285692	0850	2
NICHOLSON FRED E	COL	0-0195424	1158	3
NICHOLSON FREEMAN M	WO1	W-2122636	0951	1
NICHOLSON HARRY L	LTC	0-2055275	0866	1
NICHOLSON HENRY H	MAJ	0-0266814	0257	3
NICHOLSON JAMES G	1LT	0-1320770	0747	2
NICHOLSON JAMES L	LTC	0-0287171	0165	3
NICHOLSON KENNETH B	LTC	0-1043003	1061	1
NICHOLSON MALCOLM E	CW4	W-2122943	0859	1
NICHOLSON MILTON E	COL	0-0301539	0566	3
NICHOLSON NELSON C	1LT	0-1293457	0746	2
NICHOLSON RENAUD	CPT	0-0454309	1145	2
NICHOLSON ROBERT H	COL	0-0182727	1149	3
NICHOLSON ROBERT V	CPT	0-0130040	0950	3
NICHOLSON S J JR	1LT	0-0437793	0646	2
NICHOLSON THOMAS I	CPT	0-0481408	0244	2
NICHOLSON THOMAS W	CW3	W-3150307	0968	1
NICHOLSON W R JR	CPT	0-1100269	0248	2
NICHOLSON WILLIAM S	1LT	0-1300840	0546	2
NICKEL ALBERT W	COL	0-0408559	0561	1
NICKEL LOUIS F	COL	0-0200669	0646	2
NICKEL PAUL H	LTC	0-0499433	1154	1
NICKELL DENNIS C	MAJ	0-0523015	0448	2
NICKELL JOE	M G	0-0246192	0658	3
NICKELL WALLACE H	B G	0-0234267	1161	3
NICKELS ORVIN F	1LT	0-1179556	1045	2
NICKERSON FRANK C	MAJ	0-0259420	1164	3
NICKERSON GEORGE D	CW3	W-2150099	0764	1
NICKERSON GEORGE L	CW2	W-2151914	0561	1
NICKERSON MAXWELL E	COL	0-0249382	0665	3
NICKERSON OSGOOD A	COL	0-0168518	1052	2
NICKERSON PHILIP E	COL	0-0419110	1267	1
NICKERSON WENDELL R	2LT	0-1825969	1044	2
NICKETAKIS GEORGE	1LT	0-1045862	0844	2
NICKEY RALPH SR	MAJ	0-1308850	0161	1
NICKLAS WILLIAM G	COL	0-0223346	0362	3
NICKLE FERN L	LTC	0-0254155	0864	3
NICKLES HERBERT L	MAJ	0-0248361	0762	3
NICKLIN BRYAN G	CW2	W-2211500	0563	1
NICKOLAISEN DARREL L	1LT	0-4006934	0157	2
NICKOLAUS HENRY F	LTC	0-0178532	0146	2
NICKOLI THOMAS R	1LT	0-2288829	0962	2
NICKROSE JOHN J	CW2	W-2104342	0649	1
NICKS BRYAN	MAJ	0-0246994	1056	3
NICKS CLIFFORD W	1LT	0-1298909	0248	2
NICKS FRANK I	MAJ	0-0318241	0346	2
NICKUS VINCENT	CW4	W-2142183	0659	1
NICOL WILLIAM D	CPT	0-1304935	0962	3
NICOLAIT EUGENE B	2LT	0-1593132	0944	2
NICOLETTE ANGELO D	MAJ	0-2012340	0360	1
NICOLL HARRY A JR	LTC	0-1641625	0466	1
NICOLOSI AMEDEO A	MAJ	0-0291733	0258	1
NICOLSON DANIEL M	LTC	0-1063087	0367	1
NICOLSON W P JR	COL	0-0193326	0553	3
NIDA ORR L	MAJ	0-1595737	0363	1
NIDAY MARY D	2LT	N-0783723	0744	1
NIDEVER ELZA E	CW4	W-2002085	0964	3
NIDOSITKO MICHAEL	MAJ	0-1824904	0661	1
NIEBELS ALVA C	LTC	0-0283825	0268	3
NIEBLING LOUIS H	LTC	0-0255605	0366	3
NIEBRUEGGE LYLE H	CPT	0-1933526	0265	1
NIEBUR CLARENCE H	LTC	0-0298333	0265	3
NIEC STANISLAW	LTC	0-0395006	0356	1
NIEDER SAMUEL	CPT	0-0393265	0844	2
NIEDERHAUSER ALBERT	1LT	0-0453684	1044	2
NIEDERMAYER WALTER T	LTC	0-1326209	0465	1
NIEDERNHOFER SADIE M	CPT	N-0728157	1046	1
NIEDEROEST ROBERT J	COL	0-0334282	0568	3
NIEDRACH CHARLES A	1LT	0-1289782	104N	2
NIEDRICH WILLIAM V	LTC	0-1576443	0961	1
NIEHANS ALFRED A	CPT	0-0555610	0946	2
NIEHAUS GOLDIE A	2LT	N-0765083	1146	1
NIEHAUS SMITH S	CW3	W-2148804	0565	1
NIEHOFF ERNEST H	WO1	W-2153033	0165	2
NIELSEN ANDRES F	LTC	0-0233925	0254	3
NIELSEN ANDREW J	2LT	0-0131029	0249	3
NIELSEN BERNHARD M	MAJ	0-0287870	0668	3
NIELSEN BERNICE C	MAJ	N-0774998	1265	1
NIELSEN CARL E	MAJ	0-1334612	0564	1
NIELSEN CARL W	LTC	0-0923079	1167	3
NIELSEN CHARLES W	LTC	0-0254852	0854	1
NIELSEN DONALD L	LTC	0-0969122	0868	1
NIELSEN EARL W	MAJ	0-1913220	0665	1
NIELSEN EDWARD V	CPT	0-1640775	1147	2
NIELSEN EMMA J	2LT	N-0732308	0443	1
NIELSEN GLENN Z	LTC	0-0383591	0759	3
NIELSEN HENRY M	MAJ	0-1321543	0163	1
NIELSEN HOLGER O	CPT	0-0212989	1163	3
NIELSEN HOWARD R	CW3	W-2144530	0263	1
NIELSEN JAMES J	LTC	0-1018858	0666	1
NIELSEN KAJ T G	CPT	0-0497369	0553	1
NIELSEN MAURICE O	MAJ	0-1590697	0561	1
NIELSEN NIEL W	1LT	0-1038078	0745	2
NIELSEN NORMAN L	CPT	0-1541006	0246	2
NIELSEN RALLEN B	CPT	0-2008409	0668	1
NIELSEN RALPH W	WO1	W-2123111	0246	2
NIELSEN RAY	LTC	0-1111271	0858	1
NIELSEN RAYMOND H	MAJ	0-0452119	0658	1
NIELSEN RICHARD W	1LT	0-1295761	0446	2
NIELSON DARREL R	1LT	0-2016525	0746	2
NIELSON DAVID J	COL	0-0135938	0855	3
NIELSON JAMES G	MAJ	0-1258283	0546	2
NIEMAN CHARLES H	CW3	W-2146084	0765	1
NIEMAN HERBERT A	LTC	0-0225026	1152	3
NIEMAN WALTER E	MAJ	0-0340822	1045	2
NIEMAND HENRY D	1LT	0-0141428	0251	3
NIEMCZURA BENNIE S	CW3	W-2152629	0263	1
NIEMCZYK PAUL M	CPT	0-2033069	0257	1
NIEMEN ANN N	1LT	N-0784316	0447	2
NIEMEYER CLARENCE A	1LT	0-0356362	1154	1
NIEMEYER NELSON E	MAJ	0-2263154	0762	2
NIEMI ELVIN F	MAJ	0-1046591	1157	2

NAME	GRADE	SVC NO	DATE RET MO YR	RET CODE
NIEMI WILLIAM J	COL	0-0228905	0464	3
NIEMIRO BERNARD J	CPT	0-0309039	0745	2
NIEMZ ARTHUR M	LTC	0-0103747	1049	3
NIEMZ RICHARD F	COL	0-0274424	1163	3
NIER MARTIN E	MAJ	0-0971908	0963	1
NIERGARTH JOHN F	MAJ	0-1180646	0263	1
NIERMANN FRED W	LTC	0-0404666	0761	2
NIESSE JOHN L	LTC	0-0119109	0155	3
NIETSCH CLARENCE H	CPT	0-0489482	0549	1
NIEVES JOSE M	MAJ	0-0387465	1160	1
NIEVES RAUL	MAJ	0-2262193	0766	1
NIFFENEGGER ORA F	LTC	0-0324817	0166	3
NIFFENEGGER RALPH E	LTC	0-0033084	1060	1
NIFORO CHESTER R	1LT	0-0405329	1046	2
NIFORTH WARREN M	MAJ	0-1822819	0560	1
NIGALAN PEDRO	2LT	0-1896601	0151	2
NIGHTINGALE ARTHUR B	LTC	0-0294366	0468	3
NIGHTINGALE ROBERT L	CW3	W-2152682	0962	1
NIGHTINGALE WILLIAM	CW3	W-2203471	1164	1
NIGRO DOMINIC	CPT	0-0512492	1145	2
NIGRO THEODORE M	CPT	0-1548112	0246	2
NIHART GEORGE W	CPT	0-0983366	0962	1
NIKKEL DONALD A	1LT	0-1302176	1045	2
NIKKEL GEORGE W	LTC	0-0262219	0560	1
NIKRANDT ROGER F	LTC	0-2021157	0568	1
NIKSTAITIS WALTER C	2LT	0-1288942	0244	2
NILAND JACK N	LTC	0-1634185	0161	1
NILAND THOMAS J JR	1LT	0-1309955	0845	2
NILAYAN CARPIO V	MAJ	0-1896253	0662	1
NILES CHARLES E	COL	0-0217922	0958	3
NILES LELAND G	MAJ	0-0123054	1057	3
NILES LYLE E	CPT	0-1290294	0247	2
NILES NORMAN E	LTC	0-0279599	0668	3
NILES ROBERT G	CPT	0-0451020	0960	1
NILL JACK G	CW3	W-2136633	0865	1
NILLES AL C	CPT	0-1173729	1161	2
NILO ALPHONSO	LTC	0-1103839	0263	1
NILSEN NILS	LTC	0-1534829	1061	1
NILSON OSCAR J	MAJ	0-2202315	0268	1
NILSSON CHARLES J	LTC	0-0355419	0763	1
NIMITZ ERNEST H	MAJ	0-0175282	1060	3
NIMMERFROH RAYMOND J	MAJ	0-1341900	0261	1
NIMS HENRY H	MAJ	0-1120484	0864	1
NIN LUIS L	COL	0-0238367	0965	3
NIOLET JAMES W	MAJ	0-2288311	0463	1
NIPPER JAMES L	MAJ	0-1798603	0657	1
NIPPS THOMAS H	MAJ	0-1252450	0555	1
NISBET LEIGH M	COL	0-0162233	0157	3
NISBET ROY D	CPT	0-0386954	0261	1
NISBETT JAMES M	LTC	0-0222476	1156	3
NISBETT STUART L	MAJ	0-0373034	0665	3
NISEVICH STANLEY J	CW2	W-2147654	0858	1
NISEWANER RAYMOND E	LTC	0-0256357	1059	1
NISHIKAWA JAY K	CW2	W-2215180	0167	1
NISHIMURA THOMAS H	CW3	W-2133592	0662	1
NISI FRANK J	CPT	0-1295258	0556	1
NISKA OIVA R	MAJ	0-1105062	1060	1
NISLEY JOHN F	CW2	RW-2214852	0866	1
NISLEY RICHARD E	1LT	0-1316916	0445	2
NISSBLATT EDWARD	CW3	W-2146808	0957	1
NISSEN WALLACE E	LTC	0-0484133	0646	2
NISSENBAUM JAMES	CPT	0-0502503	0946	2
NITCH JAMES F	LTC	0-1040054	0666	1
NITKOSKI KAROL A	MAJ	0-0986228	0664	1
NITSCHE RICHARD E	CPT	0-1081294	0754	2
NITTISKIE JOSEPH N	CW3	W-2142654	1055	1
NITZ WILLIAM C	LTC	0-1542795	0464	1
NIVER LISLE H	LTC	0-0320157	0460	1
NIX ANDREW T	MAJ	0-1882371	0268	1
NIX DILLARD L	CPT	0-1735738	0656	2
NIX HENRY B	CW3	W-2143037	0161	1
NIX HENRY E	CW2	W-3150713	0467	1
NIX JAMES C	MAJ	0-2017577	0462	1
NIX JAMES H JR	LTC	0-1055927	0764	1
NIX ROBERT R	MAJ	0-1558891	0763	1
NIX WILLIAM M	1LT	0-1111811	0146	2
NIX WILLIAM T	CPT	0-0979237	0761	1
NIXDORF JAMES R	LTC	0-1335452	0966	1
NIXDORFF BOYCE G	LTC	0-0278100	0767	3
NIXON ALBERT M	WO1	W-2112358	0854	1
NIXON DRURY M	LTC	0-0163512	0861	3
NIXON EUGENE L	COL	0-0280998	0368	3
NIXON EWING M	MAJ	0-0381094	0446	2
NIXON GWINN H	LTC	0-0301543	0266	3
NIXON HUBERT A	MAJ	0-1924830	0467	1
NIXON JACK H	WO1	W-2143336	0457	1
NIXON RAY A	COL	0-0290461	0462	1
NIXON VINCENT F JR	CW2	RW-2152165	1062	1
NIZENSKI STANLEY F	CPT	0-1013899	1047	2
NOACK HAROLD R	LTC	0-0297033	0565	3
NOACK WILLIAM R	LTC	0-0244077	0463	3
NOAH EDWARD C	CW3	W-2148805	0165	1
NOAH EMERAL O	MAJ	0-1280961	0856	1
NOAH GHOLSTON N	1LT	0-1302043	1045	2
NOAH LEOPOLD S	2LT	0-1845631	0145	2
NOAH ROSS E	LTC	0-0936483	0568	1
NOAKES RAY W	MAJ	0-1688283	1163	1
NOARD JOHN W	MAJ	0-1290114	0757	1
NOBILE JEANETTE M	1LT	N-0755980	0845	1
NOBLE CARTER	1LT	0-0440608	0845	2
NOBLE CHARLES L	CW2	W-2209468	1264	1
NOBLE CURTIS A	COL	0-0178886	0547	2
NOBLE DAVID H	CPT	0-2019072	0161	1
NOBLE EDNA L	CPT	N-0795541	1160	2
NOBLE HAZEL P	MAJ	L-0903105	1162	1
NOBLE HENRY J	LTC	0-0286680	1266	3
NOBLE HENRY P JR	LTC	0-0260725	0267	3
NOBLE HOWARD T	MAJ	0-0225240	0450	3
NOBLE JAMES W	CPT	0-1921743	0252	2
NOBLE KENNETH L	COL	0-0360235	0364	3
NOBLE MARVIN B	CPT	0-0420085	0246	2
NOBLE MYRTLE E	2LT	N-0729562	1144	1
NOBLE NATHAN M	COL	0-0326658	0566	3
NOBLE ROYCE J	COL	0-0220702	0857	3
NOBLE RUFUS B	WO1	W-2146266	1051	2
NOBLE RUSL P	CPT	0-0464298	0145	2
NOBLE SPENCER C	MAJ	0-0242929	0354	3
NOBLE THEODORE R	MAJ	0-0977561	0963	1
NOBLE WILLIAM H	LTC	0-1176146	0767	1
NOBLES BOB T	LTC	0-0959325	0567	1
NOBLES CLARENCE G	CW2	W-2206418	1263	1
NOBLES GERRY	CW4	W-2108957	0756	1
NOBLES GLEN C	CW2	W-2216257	0868	1
NOBLES JAMES L	MAJ	0-0327751	0667	3
NOBLES LAWRENCE E JR	MAJ	0-2020192	0763	1
NOBOA JUAN JR	COL	0-0191260	0462	3
NOBUNAGA TADASHI	CW3	W-2144422	0266	1
NOCELLA ROCCO J	1LT	0-0527871	0445	2
NOCH CLIFFORD J	1LT	0-1544967	0646	2
NODDER WILLIAM R	LTC	0-0254683	0767	3
NODDINGS FREDERICK	MAJ	0-2262179	1161	1
NODEN ROGER H	CPT	0-0521994	0347	2
NOE LAWRENCE J	MAJ	0-2050107	1060	1
NOE ROBERT S JR	MAJ	0-1945441	0460	2
NOECKER LEWIS R	MAJ	0-0373027	0467	3
NOEL ALBERT E	CPT	0-0268428	0544	2
NOEL CHESLEY J	LTC	0-1102889	0465	2
NOEL CLAUDE B JR	WO1	W-2119293	1145	2
NOEL EARL E	LTC	0-0331119	0161	1
NOEL ELIZABETH	2LT	N-0730743	0845	1
NOEL FRED V	LTC	0-0418493	1060	1
NOEL JAMES D B	LTC	0-0170995	1055	3
NOEL JOSEPH W R	CPT	0-1926670	1163	1
NOEL LOUIS A	MAJ	0-1585408	1054	1
NOEL MAE H	1LT	N-0786721	0749	2
NOEL MARSHALL E	MAJ	0-2033665	0264	1
NOEL WRAY H	LTC	0-0319848	1148	2
NOELL CHARLES E	LTC	0-0962507	1160	1
NOESGES THOMAS M	1LT	0-2056715	1147	2
NOETH JOHN A	CW4	W-2136712	0966	1
NOFTE MONTELL S	CPT	0-0528492	0745	2
NOFTZ GEORGE P	1LT	0-1559109	0251	2
NOFZIGER JAMES C	1LT	0-0525039	0847	2
NOGAR EDMUND J	LTC	0-0495818	0460	1
NOGAY EDWARD	1LT	0-1018368	0247	2
NOGGLE MYRL K	LTC	0-1287572	0765	1
NOGUERA IGNACIO	2LT	0-1949422	1045	2
NOGUERA JOSE R	MAJ	0-1947785	1163	1
NOKES ARTHUR J JR	CW2	W-2210483	0962	1
NOKES JAMES C	CW3	W-2141645	1059	1
NOKES LEWIS H	MAJ	0-0505901	1046	1
NOLAN CHARLES H	COL	0-0172210	1056	3
NOLAN CONWAY G	CPT	0-1015766	0155	2
NOLAN DANIEL B	CPT	0-1322861	0747	2
NOLAN DONALD J	CPT	0-0486697	1145	2
NOLAN EDWARD T	CW3	W-2148950	0662	1
NOLAN FRANCIS A	MAJ	0-0339447	0947	2
NOLAN FRANCIS J	CPT	0-1318921	1047	2
NOLAN JOHN E	LTC	0-0335793	0563	1
NOLAN JOHN F JR	MAJ	0-1596753	0861	1
NOLAN JOHN R	LTC	0-1590081	1065	1
NOLAN LAWRENCE F	MAJ	0-0955590	1060	1
NOLAN MAURICE J JR	MAJ	0-1184914	0266	1
NOLAN PAUL H	LTC	0-1553137	0561	1
NOLAN RICHARD J	LTC	0-1166797	0463	1
NOLAN THOMAS F JR	1LT	0-1825434	0545	2
NOLAN THOMAS J	LTC	0-0364508	0465	1
NOLAN WILLIAM A	LTC	0-0910225	0762	3
NOLAN WILLIAM F	CW2	W-2148018	0961	1
NOLAN WILLIAM H	1LT	0-1306311	0746	2
NOLAN WILLIAM J	2LT	0-0373221	0442	2
NOLAN WILLIAM J	MAJ	0-1168845	1059	1
NOLAND ALLEN K	MAJ	0-1685702	1064	1
NOLAND AUGUSTUS T	LTC	0-0419301	1160	1
NOLAND CLIFTON M	LTC	0-1171300	0266	2
NOLAND HARRY C JR	LTC	0-1043182	0968	1
NOLAND HORACE V	LTC	0-0246951	0866	3
NOLAND LOREN O	CW4	W-2143951	0367	1
NOLAND VERNON	MAJ	0-0899176	0560	1
NOLEN BOB [illegible]	CPT	0-0484787	0745	2
NOLEN CALVIN E	LTC	0-0911016	0866	3
NOLEN CHARLES A	MAJ	0-1173730	0958	1
NOLEN CHARLES W	LTC	0-0394001	1162	1
NOLEN GEORGE M	COL	0-0482477	1054	1
NOLEN NEIL D	LTC	0-0281918	0660	1
NOLEN TITUS R	CW2	W-2145474	0761	1
NOLET ROY W	LTC	0-0966389	0568	1
NOLF JAMES H JR	CPT	0-1303933	1146	2
NOLFO LOUIS A	COL	0-0279538	0563	3
NOLIN ALBERT R	MAJ	0-0139722	1057	3
NOLKER WILLIAM F	MAJ	0-1650677	0567	1
NOLL ELOISE A	2LT	N-0769557	1046	1
NOLL JOHN V JR	MAJ	0-0081095	0566	1
NOLL WILLARD J	CPT	0-1312437	0547	2
NOLLEN FREDERICK	MAJ	0-0502277	1154	1
NOLLENBERGER ROBERT	LTC	0-1299093	0965	1
NOLLER WALTER H	LTC	0-0203465	0659	3
NOLLETTE FRANCIS C	MAJ	0-2262457	0663	1
NOLLKAMPER RALPH W	1LT	0-0338917	1045	2
NOLT ROY E	MAJ	0-0966601	0862	1
NOLTE HANS F	CW4	W-2144793	1166	1
NOLTE HENRY A JR	LTC	0-1288602	0167	1
NOLTE JOHN F	LTC	0-0145130	0648	3
NOLTE LAWRENCE W	COL	0-0239064	1065	3
NOLTEN EVERT	MAJ	0-1284560	0353	1
NOLTENSMEYER M H	CPT	0-0418770	0846	2
NOLTING JOHN P	LTC	0-0261255	0366	3
NOLTING PAULA J	MAJ	N-0742958	0646	1
NONEMAKER AUBREY G	1LT	0-0412635	0344	2
NONES BENITO O	CPT	0-0282303	0949	2
NONES ROBERT H JR	COL	0-0145131	0648	3
NONTE GEORGE C JR	MAJ	0-1688654	0764	1
NOON SAMUEL H	1LT	0-1319535	0446	2
NOON THEODORE W JR	CPT	0-1285480	0146	2
NOONAN CHARLES J	CPT	0-1292048	0848	2
NOONAN CHARLES J	MAJ	0-1946822	0865	1
NOONAN EDWARD J	MAJ	0-2032067	0963	1
NOONAN FRANCIS J	CPT	0-0353778	0446	2
NOONAN GEORGE S	1LT	0-1285280	0851	2
NOONAN HENRY R	LTC	0-0448039	1168	3
NOONAN THOMAS F	CPT	0-1309388	0147	2
NOONAN THOMAS J	LTC	0-0251586	1061	3
NOONS EDWARD J	COL	0-0260289	0452	3
NORAT ANGEL R	CPT	0-1924125	0263	1
NORAT DOMINGO	1LT	0-0452010	0956	1
NORBERG ERNEST L	LTC	0-0104225	0-49	3
NORBERG JOHN H	LTC	0-0461338	0263	3
NORBERG SHERWOOD M	1LT	0-1324436	0246	2
NORBUT ALEX J	MAJ	0-0394756	0644	2
NORCROSS ELLSWORTH	CW2	W-2146388	0559	1
NORCROSS FERNANDO T	COL	0-0173258	0352	3
NORCROSS WILLIAM H	MAJ	0-1282073	1162	1
NORD EDGAR B	1LT	0-1300365	0146	2
NORDEAN MAURICE E	1LT	0-2055456	1146	2
NORDELL CHARLES A	MAJ	0-0413796	0447	2
NORDELL ELMER	MAJ	0-1301867	0960	1
NORDGREN EDWIN J	CW2	W-2115781	0552	1
NORDGREN KARL E.	COL	0-0264143	0465	3
NORDGREN WILLIAM J	1LT	0-1897733	0158	1
NORDIN JAMES T	CW3	W-2148046	0865	1
NORDIN WILLIAM J	MAJ	0-0498240	0754	1
NORDLING JOHN H	MAJ	0-1013786	1265	1
NORDLINGER LEROY F	CW3	W-2144498	0862	1
NORDLINGER STEPHEN L	COL	0-0201113	0358	3
NORDLUND HOWARD D	CW3	W-2147916	0861	1
NORDLUND KEITH L	LTC	0-1288783	0662	1
NORDMANN BERNARD J	LTC	0-0367194	0964	1
NORDMANN FRED M	1LT	0-0353672	0142	2
NORDQUIST HARRY O V	CPT	0-0170435	1152	3
NORDSTROM ARTHUR H	COL	0-0228068	0357	3
NORDSTROM CARL T	COL	0-0167942	0450	3
NORDSTROM FRANCIS G	LTC	0-1011070	0668	1
NORDSTROM MAURICE D	LTC	0-0901110	0148	2
NORDWELL ALFRED W	LTC	0-0104324	0648	3
NORDYKE DALTON L	LTC	0-0450377	0557	1
NORDYKE HERBERT F	CW2	W-2214588	0866	1
NOREEN EUGENE L	LTC	0-0453147	0361	1
NORELIUS EMIL F	COL	0-0217964	0648	3
NOREN WILLIAM L	MAJ	0-2028731	0965	1
NORFLEET WILLIAM J	COL	0-0262071	0845	2
NORGARD CARL E	CW3	W-2143952	1159	1
NORLEY EARL M	CPT	0-0359354	0463	3
NORLIN JAMES E	COL	0-0237414	1150	3
NORLING MALCOLM R	MAJ	0-1042127	1060	1
NORLING OSCAR S	CPT	0-0278035	0354	3
NORMAN ABRAHAM	COL	0-0268570	0861	3
NORMAN AUSTIN H	LTC	0-1587499	0461	1
NORMAN BERKIE E	MAJ	0-1885193	0867	1
NORMAN CHARLES J	COL	0-0217653	0154	1
NORMAN EARLE T	COL	0-0249315	0462	3
NORMAN FRED W	2LT	0-1004387	0545	2
NORMAN GENE L	2LT	0-1327973	0439	2
NORMAN GEORGE S JR	LTC	0-1312042	0862	1
NORMAN HENRY A	MAJ	0-1182211	0862	1
NORMAN HENRY R	LTC	0-0507594	0946	2
NORMAN HUGH W	MAJ	0-0970802	0267	1
NORMAN JACK J	MAJ	0-1016804	0463	1
NORMAN JAMES C	CW4	W-2113308	0559	1
NORMAN JAMES D	LTC	0-1585975	0166	2
NORMAN JAMES R	1LT	0-1184558	0758	1
NORMAN JANET H	2LT	N-0703000	0540	1
NORMAN JOHN	MAJ	0-1651491	0261	1
NORMAN JOHN A	LTC	0-0288753	0666	3
NORMAN LEWIS E	LTC	0-1298108	0662	1
NORMAN MEADE B	LTC	0-0234471	1062	1
NORMAN OLIVER V	MAJ	0-1178274	0960	1
NORMAN RAYMOND	CPT	0-0967107	0262	2
NORMAN RICHARD L	CW2	W-2212429	0567	1
NORMAN ROBERT A	COL	0-0404481	0661	1
NORMAN ROBERT T	COL	0-0246528	1266	3

NAME	GRADE	SVC NO	DATE RET MO YR	RET CODE
NORMAN THOMAS G	MAJ	0-0502019	0959	1
NORMAN WILLIAM L	CPT	0-0199023	0563	3
NORMAN WILLIAM S	LTC	0-0511716	1059	1
NORMAN WILLIAM T	LTC	0-0285495	0862	3
NORMAND FELIX A JR	CW2	W-2207529	0960	1
NORMANDIN LOUIS A	CW3	W-2209176	1266	1
NORMINGTON LEONARD R	CW3	W-2152977	0465	1
NORQUIST SAMUEL G	CPT	0-0441267	0947	2
NORQUIST STANLEY E	CW4	W-2112555	0759	2
NORRED LLOYD H	MAJ	0-1100704	0353	1
NORRELL LUCIAN H	1LT	0-1296891	0645	2
NORRELL OLIVER L JR	LTC	0-1997452	0568	1
NORRGARD WARREN J	CW2	W-2149979	0463	1
NORRICK GORDON D	1LT	0-1533158	1264	1
NORRIS ALBERT M	CPT	0-1303012	0447	2
NORRIS ARTHUR H	CPT	0-0174541	0648	3
NORRIS BERGERON J	CW3	W-2152712	0762	1
NORRIS CHARLES A	LTC	0-0498434	0265	3
NORRIS EDWARD J	LTC	0-0285071	0468	3
NORRIS GEORGE W	CPT	0-0973571	1161	1
NORRIS HARRY R	LTC	0-0391842	0965	1
NORRIS HUGH H	LTC	0-0259805	0567	3
NORRIS IDA M	1LT	N-0730306	0345	1
NORRIS JAMES E	CW2	W-3430594	1168	1
NORRIS JOHN C	LTC	0-0483040	0962	1
NORRIS JOHN G	MAJ	0-0978859	1061	1
NORRIS JOHN L	CPT	0-0513369	0946	2
NORRIS JOHN M JR	LTC	0-1825876	0767	1
NORRIS JOHN W	MAJ	0-0267478	1068	3
NORRIS KATHRYN N	2LT	N-0760871	0744	1
NORRIS LOUIS	2LT	0-1913868	0634	1
NORRIS LYNN W	LTC	0-1545772	0161	2
NORRIS MILTON R	CPT	0-0516067	0846	2
NORRIS OSCAR J	CPT	0-0263231	0745	2
NORRIS OTIS L	COL	0-0358917	0264	3
NORRIS PAUL T	COL	0-0292587	0260	1
NORRIS RAYMOND C JR	CW2	W-2210112	0365	1
NORRIS RICHARD M	MAJ	0-0264917	0645	2
NORRIS RIDLEY L	CW3	W-2147075	0560	1
NORRIS SAMUEL D	MAJ	0-1999801	1060	1
NORRIS WALTER C	MAJ	0-1038448	0663	1
NORRIS WALTZ W	CPT	0-0103697	114N	2
NORRIS WILLARD	COL	0-0367195	0165	1
NORRIS WILLIAM L	LTC	0-1172200	0261	1
NORRISH VERNON M	LTC	0-0225760	0664	3
NORSWORTHY BERNARD A	LTC	0-0187230	1054	3
NORTH CARL E JR	MAJ	0-0975621	0963	1
NORTH EDGAR	LTC	0-1324284	1167	1
NORTH JIMMIE	1LT	0-1323164	1045	2
NORTH JOHN E	CW3	W-2151857	1060	1
NORTH JOHN P	COL	0-0230783	0261	3
NORTH JOHN W	1LT	0-1290463	0945	2
NORTH ROBERT E	CPT	0-1642430	0364	1
NORTH THOMAS M	2LT	0-1305972	0445	2
NORTHAM EDWARD A	MAJ	0-0149429	0857	3
NORTHAM FLOYD A	CW3	W-2153659	0464	1
NORTHAM HOWARD L	CPT	0-0242440	1264	3
NORTHCUTT JACK E	LTC	0-1015944	0962	1
NORTHEY WILBERT	WO1	W-2114768		2
NORTHFIELD IVAN H	COL	0-0127979	0551	3
NORTHRIDGE BEN J	COL	0-0275042	1263	3
NORTHROP ALLEN C	LTC	0-1107000	1165	1
NORTHROP CHARLES R	MAJ	0-1051708	0164	2
NORTHROP HENRY H	MAJ	0-0813561	1262	1
NORTHROP LEROY M	LTC	0-0454595	0758	1
NORTHROP MARY E	LTC	N-0701782	0346	1
NORTHROP THOMAS E	LTC	0-0322658	0467	3
NORTHRUP HARRY E	LTC	0-0275026	0159	2
NORTHRUP HOBART E	COL	0-0185047	0454	1
NORTHRUP JOSEPH	MAJ	0-2283946	1160	1
NORTHRUP PAUL E	CW3	W-2210615	0668	1
NORTHRUP ROBERT C	MAJ	0-1920360	0166	1
NORTHUP HARRISON	CPT	0-0127154	0153	3
NORTON ALLYN S	1LT	0-0285801	1044	2
NORTON ARTHUR O	MAJ	0-0161198	1052	3

NAME	GRADE	SVC NO	DATE RET MO YR	RET CODE
NORTON CLARK L	MAJ	0-1797694	1160	1
NORTON CLIFFORD J	MAJ	0-1031430	0261	1
NORTON CURTIS C	MAJ	0-1017001	1057	1
NORTON EDWIN W	LTC	0-0497465	0764	3
NORTON ELLIOTT M JR	LTC	0-0374886	0361	1
NORTON EUGENE E	MAJ	0-2204169	0265	1
NORTON FRED L	CPT	0-0333142	0246	2
NORTON GRADY H	MAJ	0-1016338	1262	1
NORTON JEAN G	LTC	0-0336169	0247	2
NORTON JERRY J	MAJ	0-1951664	0166	1
NORTON JOHN D	1LT	0-0541186	0844	2
NORTON JOHN D	CW2	W-2147431	0661	1
NORTON JOHN E	LTC	0-0903347	0468	3
NORTON JOHN H	LTC	0-1041210	0361	1
NORTON JOHN W	LTC	0-1950025	0767	1
NORTON JOHN W R	COL	0-0287167	0758	3
NORTON LAWRENCE E	COL	0-0905946	0868	3
NORTON LEROY P	CW4	W-2115448	1057	1
NORTON LESTER C	1LT	0-1325923	0346	2
NORTON MALCOLM A	MAJ	0-1876586	1068	1
NORTON MATTHEW V	CPT	0-0463342	0645	2
NORTON MAXFIELD W JR	CPT	0-0394857	0246	2
NORTON MERVIN L	LTC	0-0975753	0768	1
NORTON MICHAEL E	LTC	0-0370657	0161	3
NORTON ROBERT H	1LT	0-1913871	0446	1
NORTON ROBERT S	LTC	0-0217435	0648	3
NORTON WILLARD A	LTC	0-0481316	0968	3
NORTON WILLIAM	2LT	0-1646457	0744	2
NORTON WILLIAM D	LTC	0-0337828	0266	3
NORTON WILLIAM V	LTC	0-0299055	0968	3
NORTON WILLIE B	CW3	W-2151145	0863	1
NORUK HAROLD A	1LT	0-1319[illegible]	1052	2
NORUM ELMER C	MAJ	0-1338121	0363	1
NORUM MILTON G	LTC	0-0397867	0457	1
NORVE LESTER H	1LT	0-1998651	1151	2
NORVELL ROY E	COL	0-0265029	0962	3
NORVIEL JOHN W	LTC	0-0194962	0759	1
NORVILLE ATKINS W	LTC	0-0480574	1054	1
NORWOOD ANTHONY E	CPT	0-1573482	0746	1
NORWOOD ARTHUR H JR	LTC	0-0299763	0660	1
NORWOOD AUBURN	MAJ	0-0992928	0265	1
NORWOOD EARL	CW2	W-2142110	0254	1
NORWOOD JAMES W	COL	0-0854123	1268	1
NORWOOD JAMES W	LTC	0-1300071	0361	1
NORWOOD LUTHER M	CW2	W-2150024	0961	1
NORWOOD MILLER E	CW4	W-2153006	0868	1
NORWOOD RAY A	CW3	W-2149675	0861	1
NOSSAL LEWIS P	MAJ	0-0975624	1163	1
NOSSAMAN CALVIN W	MAJ	0-1879074	1167	1
NOSSOV MORRIS A	CPT	0-0380351	0545	2
NOSUN ALBERT H	B G	0-0264243	1163	3
NOTARD MARIANNE E	1LT	L-0500328	1046	2
NOTGRASS CHARLES D	LTC	0-0435237	0944	2
NOTGRASS JAMES C JR	LTC	0-1290649	0761	1
NOTHOURFT ROBERT H	LTC	0-1636401	0765	1
NOTT CARTER	1LT	0-1052502	1045	2
NOTTINGHAM DOLBY M	CW3	W-2148876	0466	1
NOTTROOT RUDOLPH F	LTC	0-1560557	0866	1
NOTTROTT CARL G	LTC	0-0348034	1263	3
NOURSE KEITH C	LTC	0-1283300	0564	1
NOVACK DAVID	CPT	0-1298647	0447	2
NOVACK FELIX	COL	0-0252669	0851	2
NOVACK FRANCIS L	MAJ	0-1289122	0858	1
NOVACK JOHN A	LTC	0-1004389	0767	1
NOVACK LOUIS	CPT	0-0490355	0645	2
NOVAK ANDREW J	CPT	0-2262622	0361	1
NOVAK FRANK	LTC	0-0403221	0258	1
NOVAK FRANK W	LTC	0-0329558	0454	1
NOVAK GEORGE A	LTC	0-0209030	0556	3
NOVAK LEONARD J	MAJ	0-0989084	0268	1
NOVAK LEONARD J	LTC	0-1018372	0663	1
NOVAK MARION M	1LT	0-1016283	1045	2
NOVAK ROBERT A	1LT	0-1335040	0252	2
NOVAK THEODORE W	MAJ	0-0308196	0546	2
NOVAK WALTER S	CPT	0-0465725	0246	2

NAME	GRADE	SVC NO	DATE RET MO YR	RET CODE
NOVAKY FRANK S	MAJ	0-2011181	0261	1
NOVARO JOSEPH A	LTC	0-0230743	0165	3
NOVASCONE MARJORIE F	1LT	N-0731433	0646	1
NOVELLINO JOSEPH J	MAJ	0-0339890	0140	2
NOVEY ERNEST E	COL	0-0240017	1051	3
NOVGROD IRVING	LTC	0-1643177	0565	1
NOVICK JOHNNY T	LTC	0-1043185	0166	1
NOVINSKI CLEMENT J	2LT	0-2027470	0557	2
NOVIS CARMIN G	LTC	0-0310236	1147	2
NOVITT NORTON T	2LT	0-1574303	0745	2
NOVO AMERICO L	2LT	0-1949877	0745	2
NOVOSAD JERRY J	MAJ	0-0964576	1065	1
NOVOSAD ROMAN B	CPT	0-1300366	0747	2
NOVOSEL NICHOLAS	COL	0-0393387	0760	1
NOVOTNEY JOSEPH W	MAJ	0-1011200	0457	1
NOVOTNY ARCHIE A	CPT	0-0451918	0258	1
NOVOTNY FRANK C	LTC	0-0258898	0266	3
NOVOTNY REGINA A	MAJ	N-0762623	1064	1
NOWACK EUGENE E	1LT	0-4038357	0159	2
NOWAK SYLVESTER	LTC	0-2033129	0866	1
NOWASKI JOE L	1LT	0-0964933	0951	2
NOWELL CLAUDE R	MAJ	0-0232276	1054	3
NOWELL JAMES W	MAJ	0-1018718	0557	1
NOWELL TOM E JR	LTC	0-0347948	0462	1
NOWELL WILLIAM D	CW3	W-2109741	0157	1
NOWERS GEORGE C	LTC	0-1035952	0361	1
NOWICK JOE	LTC	0-0359995	0560	1
NOWICKI ALBERT L	LTC	0-0314330	0367	3
NOWICKI JAMES J	LTC	0-1303014	0462	2
NOWICKI JOHN S JR	CW3	RW-2209596	0167	1
NOWICKI JOSEPH M	MAJ	0-1300516	0756	2
NOWICKI WILLIAM J	CW2	W-2146932	0355	1
NOWILL WILLIAM K	CPT	0-0475118	0647	2
NOWINSKI STANLEY M	LTC	0-1288426	0761	1
NOWLAND LEE J	LTC	0-0472339	0461	1
NOWLIN EDGAR E	CW3	W-2151987	0962	1
NOWLIN GEORGE A	1LT	0-0371646	0845	2
NOWLIN IRVIN J	COL	0-0294302	0563	3
NOWLIN KATHERINE	MAJ	L-0800676	0358	2
NOWLIN OTIS D	CPT	0-2005357	1158	1
NOWLIN STANLEY E	MAJ	0-2005317	0957	1
NOWOSLAWSKY WALTER F	CW2	W-2126921	1144	2
NOXON WILLARD M	1LT	0-0887542	0546	2
NOYES ALBERT L	CPT	0-1589412	0656	1
NOYES FRANK E	COL	0-0186936	0156	3
NOYES HARRISON C JR	1LT	0-0548466	1046	2
NOYES ROBERT H	LTC	0-0910227	0165	3
NOYES SHERMAN F JR	LTC	0-1285986	1060	1
NOYES STEPHEN D	LTC	0-1039492	1263	1
NOYES WILFRED	CW2	W-2117125	0559	1
NUCE HARRY R	CPT	0-0212210	1157	3
NUCKELS CLIFFORD R	CW2	W-2152181	1162	1
NUCKOLLS DRUSILLA N	CPT	N-0792603	0758	2
NUCKOLLS LEONARD A	LTC	0-1110691	0262	1
NUCKOLS GEORGE M	MAJ	0-1176754	0859	1
NUCKOLS MILTON F	MAJ	0-0260775	0347	2
NUERENBERG KARL A	CPT	0-0530981	0346	2
NUGENT AMBROSE H	LTC	0-0387162	0460	1
NUGENT CATHERINE	1LT	N-0724006	1044	1
NUGENT GEORGE L	LTC	0-1650259	1262	1
NUGENT JOHN	MAJ	0-1040992	0856	1
NUGENT JOHN J	LTC	0-0908501	1066	3
NUGENT JOHN P	CW2	W-2142111	1159	1
NUGENT MICHAEL	LTC	0-1292572	0263	1
NUGENT OLAN	MAJ	0-0979307	0965	1
NUGENT PEGEEN	1LT	N-0783325	0146	1
NUGENT ROBERT P III	LTC	0-0282650	0167	1
NUGENT WILLIAM E	1LT	0-1297238	0146	2
NULL CARROLL H	2LT	0-0960105	0751	2
NULTA MAURICE C	LTC	0-1574304	0455	2
NULTON HENRY G	M G	0-0205635	0161	3
NULTY JOHN C	1LT	0-0970234	1157	1
NUNAMAKER EDWARD M	LTC	0-1799354	0468	2
NUNES RICHARD E	COL	0-0360390	0762	1
NUNEZ ROBERT F JR	MAJ	0-0289914	1053	3

NAME	GRADE	SVC NO	DATE RET MO YR	RET CODE
NUNGESSER WILLIAM C	MAJ	0-0263089	0265	3
NUNLEY CHESLEY O	LTC	0-1327650	0965	1
NUNLEY ROY M	MAJ	0-0997867	0267	1
NUNLEY THOMAS J	CW3	W-3150309	0368	2
NUNN CARROLL L	LTC	0-1289787	0658	1
NUNN CHARLES F	LTC	0-1169675	1059	1
NUNN CLIFFORD T	2LT	0-1055689	1044	2
NUNN ERNEST W	MAJ	0-1030275	0857	1
NUNN JOHN T	MAJ	0-2017269	0561	1
NUNN LESLIE L	COL	0-0213016	1058	3
NUNN WALTER A	CW3	W-2203279	0659	1
NUNN WILLIAM A JR	COL	0-0231161	0359	1
NUNN WILLIAM J	CPT	0-1170121	1045	2
NUNNALLY OTIS	CW3	W-2146039	0861	1
NUNNALLY W B JR	CPT	0-1105713	0446	2
NUNNELLEY JAMES R JR	CPT	0-0305351	0459	1
NUNVAR FRANCIS E	LTC	0-0184367	0850	3
NUQUI DANIEL	2LT	0-1896971	0950	1
NUQUI RENE B	1LT	0-1896590	1061	2
NURNEY BERNARD T	CW2	W-2152978	0359	1
NURSS RICHARD E	CPT	0-0888533	0160	1
NUSBAUM CHARLES S	LTC	0-0337056	0261	2
NUSBAUM JACK B	1LT	0-1315095	1045	2
NUSE GEORGE H	MAJ	0-1333252	0663	2
NUSSBAUM PERRY E	COL	0-0526719	0368	3
NUSSBAUM WILLIAM V	MAJ	0-1582015	0662	1
NUSSDORFER ALFRED E	MAJ	0-0262874	0864	3
NUSSDORFER JOHN H	COL	0-0182251	0646	2
NUSSE DANIEL T	CPT	0-1822180	0960	1
NUSSER WILLIAM A	COL	0-0369320	0962	1
NUTLEY VICTOR L	LTC	0-0155848	0952	3
NUTT CECIL E	MAJ	0-1648938	0457	1
NUTT JOHN F	COL	0-0452910	0763	1
NUTTER LLOYD B	CPT	0-0255667	0544	2
NUTTER ROBERT L	MAJ	0-1014834	0760	2
NUTTING DANIEL C	COL	0-0216473	0563	3
NUTTING HARRY D JR	COL	0-0252609	1165	3
NUTTING LOWELL D	LTC	0-2045143	0564	1
NUWER JOHN E	LTC	0-0350002	0561	1
NUZIE SAMUEL B	MAJ	0-0500136	0546	2
NUZUM JOHN B	LTC	0-1114245	0764	1
NUZUM PAUL B	CW2	W-2114959	0848	1
NUZZO JOHN	2LT	0-1038252	0454	1
NUZZO JOSEPHINE	2LT	N-0753186	0546	1
NUZZOLO CHARLES A	CPT	0-0508897	0752	2
NYBURG WILLARD M	LTC	0-0221794	1061	1
NYCE VINCENT W	LTC	0-1307064	0668	3
NYE DOUGLAS B	CW3	W-2143038	0862	1
NYE IRWIN C	LTC	0-1636407	1167	1
NYE MAURICE B	COL	0-0221014	0456	3
NYE STEPHEN G	LTC	0-0165599	0258	3
NYE WILLIAM F	COL	0-0163877	0648	3
NYEMASTER MARC	CW2	W-2150687	1063	1
NYENHUIS EDWARD J	LTC	0-0394053	0960	1
NYERS JAMES J	1LT	0-1307291	0348	1
NYGAARD MABEL D	MAJ	N-0732031	0468	3
NYGARD WILBUR A	MAJ	0-0991829	1262	1
NYGREN BURDETTE J	LTC	0-1184275	0767	1
NYHAN STANLEY L	LTC	0-2274644	0463	1
NYITRAY JOSEPH A	1LT	0-1289305	0544	2
NYLAND LAWRENCE E	CPT	0-1312208	0463	1
NYLANDER EVA	CPT	N-0756610	0647	1
NYMAN ROBERT A	2LT	0-0392892	0647	2
NYMAN WILLIAM M	MAJ	0-0964562	0862	1
NYQUIST ELBERT A	LTC	0-0384133	1150	2
NYSTROM ERNEST G	LTC	0-0213096	0551	3
NYSTROM JOSEPH B	2LT	0-1305298	1061	2
NYSTROM MARIAN A	2LT	N-0732245	0145	1
OAKES MILTON C	LTC	0-0283068	0764	3
OAKES THEODORE C	2LT	0-1288605	1044	2
OAKES WALTER M	LTC	0-0314048	0349	1
OAKES WILLIAM F	LTC	0-1052105	0662	1
OAKEY GEORGE J	LTC	0-1185244	0762	1
OAKLEY ALBERT P	MAJ	0-1797866	0663	1
OAKLEY CARL L	MAJ	0-1294179	0858	1

ARMY OF THE UNITED STATES RETIRED LIST

NAME	GRADE	SVC NO	DATE RET MO YR	RET CODE	NAME	GRADE	SVC NO	DATE RET MO YR	RET CODE	NAME	GRADE	SVC NO	DATE RET MO YR	RET CODE	NAME	GRADE	SVC NO	DATE RET MO YR	RET CODE
OAKLEY DONALD L	1LT	0-1135917	0549	2	OBRIEN EDWARD B	CPT	0-0491528	0855	1	OBRIEN WILLIAM L	CPT	0-0404205	0445	2	OCONNOR FREDERICK	LTC	0-1323388	1262	1
OAKLEY JACK D	CPT	0-1299977	0456	1	OBRIEN EDWARD J	LTC	0-0812124	1262	1	OBRIEN WILLIAM M	COL	0-0303372	0146	2	OCONNOR GEORGE L	MAJ	0-2038016	0865	1
OAKLEY RALPH W	COL	0-0181119	1055	3	OBRIEN EDWARD J	LTC	0-0996026	0768	1	OBRIEN WILLIAM M	CPT	0-0511415	0347	1	OCONNOR GEORGE M	COL	0-0178379	0362	3
OAKLEY WARD S	MAJ	0-1055438	1062	1	OBRIEN EDWARD J	1LT	0-1575496	1043	2	OBRIENE PATRICK F	CW2	W-2142259	1057	1	OCONNOR GEORGE M JR	LTC	0-1066912	0467	1
OAKNER MERVIN G	2LT	0-1943202	0945	2	OBRIEN EDWARD J	CPT	0-2043029	1046	2	OBRION EDWARD H	MAJ	0-0287613	0868	3	OCONNOR GERALD A	CPT	0-1686497	0954	2
OAKS ALFRED W	LTC	0-1844604	0462	1	OBRIEN EDWARD T	LTC	0-0236365	0567	3	OBRIST ROBERT A	MAJ	0-0522367	0266	1	OCONNOR GERALD J	LTC	0-1947355	0164	1
OAKS JAMES W	CW3	W-2211135	0868	1	OBRIEN EVERETT M	LTC	0-1285806	1162	1	OBROCK JOHN C	CPT	0-0515676	0854	1	OCONNOR GERALD T	MAJ	0-0482556	0747	2
OAKS THOMAS R F	MAJ	0-1356409	0166	2	OBRIEN FRANCIS R	1LT	0-0387615	1145	2	OBRYAN HARRY L JR	COL	0-0454879	0266	1	OCONNOR HOWARD	COL	0-0339823	1157	3
OAKSFORD HOMER H JR	LTC	0-1291124	0461	1	OBRIEN FRED F	MAJ	0-0969859	1060	1	OBRYAN LARRY E	CPT	0-1304105	0947	2	OCONNOR JAMES J	1LT	0-1011821	0945	2
OAS CLAYTON S	MAJ	0-1311345	1158	1	OBRIEN FREDERICK	MAJ	0-0967332	0865	1	OBRYAN RAPHAEL L	1LT	0-0493787	1049	1	OCONNOR JAMES W	MAJ	0-1049290	1060	1
OATES AGNES	1LT	N-0764536	1047	1	OBRIEN GEORGE L JR	COL	0-0265746	1064	1	OBRYAN RONALD I	LTC	0-1304336	0766	1	OCONNOR JEROME B	MAJ	0-0260254	0468	3
OATES CALVIN W	MAJ	0-0955543	0765	1	OBRIEN GERALD J	2LT	0-0479268	0445	2	OBRYANT ALBERT H	1LT	0-1825703	0146	2	OCONNOR JOHN A	MAJ	0-1578933	0564	1
OATES CHARLES R	LTC	0-1047277	0263	1	OBRIEN HARRY J	COL	0-1040587	0366	1	OBRYANT CHARLES W	M G	0-0328896	1059	3	OCONNOR JOHN C	1LT	0-1305620	0853	1
OATES EDWARD F JR	CPT	0-1182671	0965	2	OBRIEN HELEN J	CPT	N-0724558	0147	1	OBUCHOWSKI ALPHONSE	LTC	0-2047766	0662	1	OCONNOR JOHN J	CPT	0-0298327	0245	2
OATES OTIE F	MAJ	0-0208991	1054	3	OBRIEN HENRY W	CW2	W-2146086	0956	1	OBURG HAROLD G JR	CPT	0-0348695	1164	1	OCONNOR JOHN M	COL	0-0311187	0861	2
OATES WALTER M	MAJ	0-0230982	0450	1	OBRIEN ISABEL M	MAJ	N-0776728	1166	1	OBYE CHARLES H	LTC	0-0117768	0854	3	OCONNOR JOSEPH R JR	CPT	0-0445039	0463	1
OATES WILLIAM A	MAJ	0-0346606	0450	2	OBRIEN IVAN T	LTC	0-0358206	0263	1	OBYRNE CHARLES T	MAJ	0-2266504	1167	2	OCONNOR JOSEPH F	CPT	0-0191257	0361	3
OATES WILLIAM H	LTC	0-1548991	0661	1	OBRIEN JAMES E	LTC	0-1798505	0765	1	OBYRNE THOMAS W	CW3	W-2145114	0659	1	OCONNOR JOSEPH L	MAJ	0-1302866	0861	1
OATIS ALICE S	1LT	N-0788720	0646	1	OBRIEN JAMES J	LTC	0-1032380	0465	1	OCALLAGHAN EDMOND J	LTC	0-1574305	0963	2	OCONNOR JOSEPH M	1LT	0-0922783	1043	2
OATLEY CHARLES W	MAJ	0-0325489	0264	1	OBRIEN JOHN A	CW4	W-2116079	1158	1	OCALLAGHAN ROBERT J	LTC	0-1101145	1060	1	OCONNOR KEVNEY	MAJ	0-0477440	0-50	3
OATMAN ALFRED S	MAJ	0-1105068	1160	3	OBRIEN JOHN D	MAJ	0-0139740	0257	3	OCAMPO ALFREDO	CPT	0-0984312	1062	1	OCONNOR MORGAN P	COL	0-0381892	0562	1
OATMAN CHESTER G	2LT	T-0003234	1047	2	OBRIEN JOHN J	CPT	0-0515793	1045	2	OCAMPO-EUSTAQUI	2LT	0-1896591	0555	1	OCONNOR NORMAN J	WO1	W-2116221	0544	2
OATMAN JOHN R	COL	0-0286282	0468	3	OBRIEN JOHN J	CPT	0-1105717	0455	2	OCARROLL MARY A	MAJ	N-0756727	0663	1	OCONNOR PATRICK J	CPT	0-1638181	0455	1
OBAN NEMISIO	1LT	0-2030388	1047	2	OBRIEN JOHN J	CPT	0-1305100	0146	2	OCASEK MILES F	CPT	0-0459328	0445	2	OCONNOR PAUL E	LTC	0-1001206	0862	1
OBANNON JAMES B	1LT	0-1293459	0346	2	OBRIEN JOHN L	MAJ	0-1634187	0664	1	OCHOJSKI B CHARLES	1LT	0-0416170	0945	2	OCONNOR PHILIP J	LTC	0-0518206	0467	3
OBANNON LLOYD W	CPT	0-0402425	0453	2	OBRIEN JOHN M JR	MAJ	0-0250413	0365	3	OCHRAN EDWARD P	CPT	0-0500809	1048	1	OCONNOR RICHARD P	1LT	0-0370015	0346	2
OBANNON ROBERT F	LTC	0-1282354	0466	1	OBRIEN JOHN P JR	LTC	0-1641116	1167	1	OCHS ADOLPH S	MAJ	0-0151353	0643	2	OCONNOR ROBERT G	LTC	0-1043450	1262	2
OBARR HUGH A	CW3	W-2144207	0660	1	OBRIEN JOHN W	LTC	0-0209814	0661	3	OCHS ALFRED H JR	MAJ	0-0279481	0268	3	OCONNOR THOMAS	CPT	0-1012539	1265	1
OBATA BENJAMIN T	LTC	0-2030779	1263	1	OBRIEN JOHN W	LTC	0-1321725	0968	1	OCHS ERVIN J JR	MAJ	0-1292049	1060	1	OCONNOR THOMAS J	LTC	0-0888542	0663	1
OBAUGH FREDERICK	CPT	0-1036658	0353	2	OBRIEN JOSEPH C	CW4	W-2148241	0867	2	OCHS ISIDOR	MAJ	0-0311705	0144	2	OCONNOR THOMAS J	1LT	0-1321943	1045	2
OBBINK JACK D	CPT	0-0405344	0646	2	OBRIEN JOSEPH E	LTC	0-0995082	0463	1	OCKER HENRY III	CW3	W-2151795	1165	1	OCONNOR THOMAS W	LTC	0-1596943	0163	1
OBEN JOHN H	LTC	0-0307705	0665	3	OBRIEN JOSEPH F	LTC	0-0202717	0857	3	OCKINGA HAROLD H	MAJ	0-0972815	0466	1	OCONNOR WILLIAM D	CW2	W-2212253	0267	1
OBENAUF HOMER A	MAJ	0-0234985	0251	3	OBRIEN JOSEPH F	LTC	0-1578932	0662	1	OCKULY EUGENE A	MAJ	0-0515877	0545	2	OCONNOR WILLIAM H	LTC	0-0192183	1053	3
OBENOUR MERLE W	COL	0-0287515	0955	3	OBRIEN JOSEPH L	CPT	0-0261393	0545	2	OCONNELL ANNETTE M	CPT	N-0805493	0555	2	OCONNOR WILLIAM J	CPT	0-0193821	0453	3
OBENOUR WILLIAM H	COL	0-0243089	0658	3	OBRIEN JOSEPH L	LTC	0-0293009	0758	1	OCONNELL BARTHOLOME	LTC	0-1176148	0464	1	OCONNOR WILLIAM R	MAJ	0-1291158	0261	1
OBER EDWARD	LTC	0-1081571	0268	1	OBRIEN LAURENCE A	LTC	0-0404760	0660	1	OCONNELL DANIEL F	CPT	0-1533416	0844	2	ODA WILLIAM S	LTC	0-1695694	0967	1
OBER THEODORE M	LTC	0-0908473	0263	3	OBRIEN LEONARD C	LTC	0-1000057	0461	1	OCONNELL EARL J	1LT	0-1548992	1044	2	ODAHL WILLIAM R	CPT	0-1542010	0754	1
OBER WILLIAM L	CW2	W-2117547	0251	2	OBRIEN LYNN H	CPT	0-0297749	0248	1	OCONNELL EARLE R	1LT	0-0133146	0357	3	ODANIEL PAUL A	CW2	W-2211678	0766	1
OBERFELL GEORGE J	1LT	0-1299618	0745	2	OBRIEN MADELINE J	CPT	N-0722315	0848	2	OCONNELL EDMUND W	CPT	0-1299619	0446	2	ODAWE NICHOLAS	CPT	0-0370486	0946	2
OBERG ALICE I	CPT	N-0731530	0646	1	OBRIEN MARRIN J	MAJ	0-1015807	0165	3	OCONNELL FRANK B	COL	0-0190132	0252	3	ODAY MARY M	CPT	N-0725512	1046	1
OBERG HENRY C	MAJ	0-1060231	0967	3	OBRIEN MARY ANN E	MAJ	N-0794306	0365	1	OCONNELL FRANK V	2LT	0-1051310	1043	2	ODAY THOMAS H	CPT	0-1044327	1153	1
OBERG JOHN A	1LT	0-1301868	0845	2	OBRIEN MARY E	MAJ	N-0723981	1162	1	OCONNELL GEORGE E	COL	0-0911789	0864	3	ODDI VICTOR L	LTC	0-0335210	0864	1
OBERHAUSEN FRANK C	LTC	0-0963892	0269	1	OBRIEN MAXWELL A	B G	0-0295693	1150	3	OCONNELL GERALD F	CW3	W-2147280	0862	1	ODEA EDWARD B	LTC	0-0258419	0565	3
OBERLANDER MAURICE I	1LT	0-1588779	0450	2	OBRIEN MAYO M	CPT	0-0496487	1060	1	OCONNELL JOHN	LTC	0-1171704	0-53	1	ODEA JAMES J	CPT	0-1303625	0646	2
OBERLE EDWARD F	1LT	0-0408506	0861	2	OBRIEN MICHAEL	1LT	0-1913900	1019	1	OCONNELL JOHN A	LTC	0-1003003	1065	1	ODEA MILTON L	CW4	W-2104167	0659	1
OBERLE HENRY J	2LT	0-1557963	0345	2	OBRIEN MICHAEL J	LTC	0-0482097	0654	2	OCONNELL JOHN J	CW4	W-2111686	0568	3	ODEA PADRAIG M	LTC	0-1030181	0963	1
OBERLIN BENJAMIN G	MAJ	0-0139739	1054	3	OBRIEN MICHAEL L	LTC	0-0276680	0957	3	OCONNELL JOSEPH A	LTC	0-1323469	0567	1	ODEGAARD ERLING A	2LT	0-1172203	1044	2
OBERLIN WILLIAM W	MAJ	0-0442039	0946	2	OBRIEN MICHAEL R	LTC	0-1593759	0668	3	OCONNELL LAWRENCE O	CPT	0-1166148	0845	2	ODEGARD HENRY O	LTC	0-1177559	0965	1
OBERMEIER CHARLES F	CW3	W-2148905	0363	1	OBRIEN PATRICK C	MAJ	0-1111816	0861	1	OCONNELL MARY C	MAJ	L-0115997	1065	3	ODELL ALBERT M	COL	0-0210109	0249	1
OBERNDORFER ABBOTT	COL	0-0139706	0154	3	OBRIEN PATRICK J	CPT	0-0227501	0463	3	OCONNELL MICHAEL H	MAJ	0-2263297	0168	1	ODELL BILLIE E	CW2	W-2214674	0667	1
OBERRY LEE R	CW3	W-2206549	0968	1	OBRIEN PATRICK J	CPT	0-1041409	0744	2	OCONNELL PAUL R	LTC	0-1176455	0161	1	ODELL BRUCE	MAJ	0-0431606	0757	1
OBERSCHLAKE ALBERT F	CW3	W-2205388	1065	1	OBRIEN RAYMOND F	1LT	0-2021285	0954	2	OCONNELL PHILLIP D	COL	0-0269526	1167	3	ODELL CATHERINE	MAJ	N-0702785	0968	3
OBERSEIDER JOHN R C	CW3	W-2142597	0559	1	OBRIEN RAYMOND J	LTC	0-0411023	0363	1	OCONNELL PHYLLIS A	2LT	N-0721193	1043	1	ODELL CLAUDE W	MAJ	0-0246896	0455	3
OBERST ARTHUR L	LTC	0-0215184	1151	3	OBRIEN RICHARD A	MAJ	0-0247995	0842	2	OCONNELL ROY I	CW2	W-2147417	0259	1	ODELL COURTNEY J	COL	0-0235919	1061	3
OBERST MARY J	CPT	N-0702985	0947	1	OBRIEN RICHARD C	MAJ	0-1922577	0164	1	OCONNELL THOMAS B	MAJ	0-2023688	0161	1	ODELL DONALD E	CW3	W-2143724	0159	1
OBERSTER HOWARD J	1LT	0-1287048	1059	1	OBRIEN RICHARD D	CPT	0-0970525	0363	1	OCONNELL THOMAS M	1LT	0-1176456	1150	2	ODELL DOUGLAS V	CPT	0-1309306	0446	2
OBERWEGNER MARION T	LTC	0-0300337	0562	1	OBRIEN ROBERT A	LTC	0-0565624	0762	2	OCONNELL THOMAS P	MAJ	0-1000273	0366	1	ODELL EDWARD P	1LT	0-1172579	0146	2
OBETZ ROBIN C	MAJ	0-0500586	1044	2	OBRIEN ROBERT E	LTC	0-0330160	1060	1	OCONNELL THOMAS R	CPT	0-0538754	0247	2	ODELL ERNEST E	MAJ	0-1341693	0463	1
OBITZ FREDERICK	LTC	0-1001422	1163	1	OBRIEN ROBERT E	CPT	0-1306133	1147	2	OCONNELL WILLIAM	CPT	0-0468566	1047	1	ODELL GORDON E	CW3	W-2206588	1165	1
OBLACK ELMER F	CW2	W-2212609	0266	1	OBRIEN ROBERT E	CPT	0-1316778	0347	2	OCONNELL WILLIAM H	LTC	0-0475922	0256	1	ODELL HAROLD H	LTC	0-1105070	1266	3
OBLEY WILLIAM M	MAJ	0-1287573	0164	1	OBRIEN ROBERT G	CPT	0-1697973	1046	2	OCONNELL WILLIAM J	CPT	0-0344454	0346	2	ODELL HAROLD S	MAJ	0-1683967	0954	1
OBLINGER FRANK O SR	CW2	W-2119547	0248	1	OBRIEN ROBERT L	1LT	0-1316918	1045	2	OCONNELL WILLIAM J	CPT	0-1584690	0347	2	ODELL JACK D	CPT	0-2009612	0864	1
OBRANOVICH JOHN	MAJ	0-1591960	0957	1	OBRIEN ROGER J	CPT	0-1291157	1045	2	OCONNOR ALBERT R	CPT	0-0887710	1046	2	ODELL JAMES L	1LT	0-0545988	0147	2
OBRANOVICH PETE	WO1	W-2147770	0854	1	OBRIEN THOMAS	LTC	0-0919555	0467	3	OCONNOR ANSON	MAJ	0-1998524	1054	1	ODELL JAMES W	CW3	W-2139701	1062	2
OBRASKY GEORGE H	COL	0-0202658	1046	2	OBRIEN THOMAS A	MAJ	0-1314374	0762	1	OCONNOR BERNARD C	MAJ	0-0373574	0747	2	ODELL JOSEPH E	CW2	W-2210083	1264	1
OBREMSKI EGAN A	MAJ	0-0974715	1063	1	OBRIEN THOMAS J	CPT	0-1324473	0847	2	OCONNOR CHARLES	CW4	W-2143238	1265	1	ODELL LORRENCE JR	LTC	0-2018739	0466	1
OBRIAN GEORGE R JR	CPT	0-1285100	1146	2	OBRIEN THOMAS L	MAJ	0-2021093	0766	1	OCONNOR DANIEL J	MAJ	0-1639467	0656	1	ODELL MARION C	CPT	0-0973480	0561	1
OBRIEN ALVIN F	CW3	W-2146185	0857	1	OBRIEN TYRRELL W	CW3	W-2136038	0862	1	OCONNOR DAVID J	CPT	0-0509431	0148	1	ODELL RALPH E	LTC	0-1822043	0567	2
OBRIEN AMBROSE R	LTC	0-0382969	0559	2	OBRIEN WALTER H	MAJ	0-0450539	0560	1	OCONNOR EMMET L	LTC	0-0270707	1161	1	ODELL ROBERT E	COL	0-0209219	0253	3
OBRIEN CARLTON P	CPT	0-0538292	0447	2	OBRIEN WILLIAM F	COL	0-0299919	0446	2	OCONNOR EVERETT W	CW3	W-2150593	0566	1	ODELL VIRGIL L JR	MAJ	0-1338843	0867	1
OBRIEN CHARLES E	LTC	0-1108896	0962	1	OBRIEN WILLIAM H	COL	0-0307803	1062	1	OCONNOR FRANCIS E	1LT	0-1322945	0246	2	ODELL WALTER	LTC	0-0393506	0468	3
OBRIEN DALE E	LTC	0-1108897	0263	1	OBRIEN WILLIAM J	LTC	0-0301287	0867	3	OCONNOR FRANCIS J	CPT	0-0386309	0961	1	ODELL WILLIAM R	MAJ	0-1108210	0267	1
OBRIEN DALTON C	COL	0-0490225	0962	3	OBRIEN WILLIAM J	LTC	0-0345945	0962	1	OCONNOR FRANCIS J	2LT	0-0424460	0944	2	ODEM NORMAN H	LTC	0-1314537	0867	3
OBRIEN DANIEL A	COL	0-0369366	0766	3	OBRIEN WILLIAM J	CPT	0-0439442	1046	2	OCONNOR FRANK A	CW3	W-2144552	0663	1	ODEN PHILIP W	CPT	0-0322494	0143	2
OBRIEN DAVID B	1LT	0-0481693	0845	2	OBRIEN WILLIAM J	LTC	0-1287223	0466	1	OCONNOR FRANK W	LTC	0-0287487	0645	2	ODEN WILLIAM O	MAJ	0-0423216	0560	1

ARMY OF THE UNITED STATES RETIRED LIST

NAME	GRADE	SVC NO	DATE RET MO YR	RET CODE	NAME	GRADE	SVC NO	DATE RET MO YR	RET CODE	NAME	GRADE	SVC NO	DATE RET MO YR	RET CODE	NAME	GRADE	SVC NO	DATE RET MO YR	RET CODE
ODENBRETT JOSEPH J	MAJ	0-1303381	0159	1	OESTREICH ROY H	LTC	0-1298278	0860	1	OHANLON FRANCIS B	1LT	0-0904505	0845	2	OKIE FREDERICK	COL	0-0259965	0767	3
ODENWALDER CHARLES M	LTC	0-0412129	0960	1	OETINGER GEORGE JR	COL	0-0218245	0859	1	OHANLON JOSEPH D	LTC	0-0282328	0558	1	OKIN HARRY	MAJ	0-0119766	0950	3
ODENWELLER RICHARD F	LTC	0-0181701	0553	2	OETJEN GEORGE F	MAJ	0-0199757	0745	2	OHARA CHARLES R	LTC	0-0415679	0161	1	OKINS JOHN L	CW2	W-2214611	0668	1
ODER JOHN T	MAJ	0-0490167	0356	1	OETKEN BYRON W	CW3	W-2144065	0766	1	OHARA DANIEL	LTC	0-2200216	1168	1	OKOLOWICH THOMAS J	MAJ	0-0413337	0647	2
ODESS SAMUEL L	1LT	0-1292574	0545	2	OETTINGER LEON JR	1LT	0-0539719	0146	2	OHARA FRANCIS D	CW3	W-2150754	0163	1	OKONOGI HUGO S	COL	0-0527069	1065	3
ODETTE MARJORIE F	2LT	N-0772477	0834	1	OFARRELL FRANCES W	1LT	N-0735830	0946	1	OHARA JAMES T	COL	0-1107002	0562	1	OKONSKI LEONARD J	MAJ	0-2097082	0867	1
ODIL EMMETT C	1LT	0-1172906	0646	2	OFFEN ROGER L JR	CPT	0-0361632	0945	2	OHARA JOHN L	CW2	W-2119313	0447	2	OKULICK AMBROSE	CW2	W-2115176	0457	1
ODIOSO RAYMOND C	1LT	0-0549112	0346	2	OFFER PAUL J	CPT	0-1639469	1060	1	OHARA JOHN J	MAJ	0-1296411	0755	2	OKUMURA MAKOTO	MAJ	0-2030780	1061	1
ODLAND CLIFFORD	MAJ	0-0347749	0566	3	OFFER RICHARD F	1LT	0-2037085	0247	2	OHARA RICHARD G	LTC	0-1290990	0561	1	OKUSA MUNEO M	MAJ	0-0935440	0765	1
ODLAND THEODORE E	COL	0-0220399	0652	3	OFFERMAN JACOB	CW2	W-2148696	0859	1	OHARA THOMAS J SR	CW2	W-2148341	0457	1	OLAH THOMAS F	MAJ	0-1580119	0164	1
ODLEY RALPH L	MAJ	0-0319649	0146	2	OFFICER BREAMON A	LTC	0-2020754	0766	1	OHARA THOMAS P	MAJ	0-0968682	0163	1	OLANDER EDWIN J	1LT	0-2055861	0445	2
ODLIN WALTER C	CW2	W-2141788	0758	1	OFFICER VERNON W	LTC	0-0275722	1160	3	OHARAN PAUL F	LTC	0-0541059	0466	1	OLANDER FRANK H	LTC	0-0349133	0860	1
ODOM ALFRED D	CPT	0-0147515	0748	3	OFFIE SAMUEL J	LTC	0-1944772	0660	2	OHARE FRANK J	COL	0-0349595	0466	3	OLANDER RALPH C	CPT	0-0272589	0545	2
ODOM ANN W C	MAJ	N-0737807	0366	3	OFFNER DAVID I	CW2	W-3430216	0863	2	OHARE JACK	LTC	0-1646467	1163	1	OLAUGHLIN PHILIP J	LTC	0-0309043	0259	1
ODOM BERRYMAN H	CPT	0-1316194	0359	1	OFFNER JOSEPH A	MAJ	0-1588782	0361	1	OHARE JAMES P	CW3	W-2144295	0562	1	OLAZABA AURELIO R JR	CW3	W-2146349	0364	1
ODOM BOBBIE M	WO1	W-2110389	1044	2	OFFNER WILBUR H	LTC	0-1180651	1059	1	OHARE JOHN F	MAJ	0-1288785	0564	1	OLBON CLAY	B G	0-0246675	0663	3
ODOM CLIFFORD K	CPT	0-1594365	0849	2	OFFRIL PAUL D	1LT	0-1896966	0551	1	OHARE KENNETH W	LTC	0-0300188	0546	2	OLCOTT BEN L	COL	0-1291159	1267	3
ODOM EDWARD E	MAJ	0-0105734	0552	3	OFFRINGA ROBERT J	1LT	0-1330107	0747	2	OHARE WILLIAM F	1LT	0-2017271	1166	1	OLD ALVY O	MAJ	0-2046374	0447	2
ODOM HAYNES	LTC	0-0164048	0335	1	OFFUTT EDWARD W JR	MAJ	0-1685658	0366	1	OHARRA JAMES J	MAJ	0-1325926	0760	1	OLD DODGE H	CPT	0-0397913	0546	2
ODOM HUBERT L	MAJ	0-0927267	0957	1	OFFUTT REGINALD J	CPT	0-0149696	0150	3	OHARROW JOHN W	CPT	0-0492356	0447	1	OLDENDORFF ERNEST	MAJ	0-1593763	1156	1
ODOM IRA J	CW3	W-2206591	0966	1	OFFUTT ROBERT K	MAJ	0-0119176	0952	3	OHART THEODORE C	MAJ	0-0260115	0767	3	OLDHAM FAITH A	LTC	N-0757406	1268	1
ODOM JAMES J	MAJ	0-0237874	0765	3	OFLAHERTY JOHN C	MAJ	0-0179829	1145	2	OHEARN JAMES P	WO1	W-2132302	0345	2	OLDHAM OWEN L	MAJ	0-1119106	0365	1
ODOM JOHN W	CPT	0-0988987	0461	2	OFLYNN GEOFFREY J	COL	0-0101392	0648	3	OHEARN JOHN J	LTC	0-0210527	1150	3	OLDHAM RODNEY L	LTC	0-1100707	0964	1
ODOM OWEN W JR	LTC	0-1116979	1062	1	OGAN BOYINGTON	MAJ	0-1590708	1063	1	OHEARN RAYMOND L	LTC	0-1946352	0566	1	OLDOM FRED	CPT	0-0508487	0347	1
ODOM ROBERT H	MAJ	0-1541303	0761	1	OGARA JOHN F	2LT	0-1552762	0544	2	OHEREN PAT	MAJ	0-1596560	0959	2	OLDS CORWIN H	COL	0-0265810	0455	3
ODOM ROPERT F	LTC	0-1919390	0268	1	OGAWA HARUJI	MAJ	0-0958733	0563	1	OHL THOMAS H	LTC	0-0375794	1064	1	OLDS OMAR G	COL	0-0191489	0859	3
ODOM WILLIAM F	CW3	W-2142717	0661	1	OGAWA KATSUMI	2LT	N-0784086	0545	1	OHLAND FREDRICK C	CPT	0-1107004	0347	2	OLDZIEWSKI LEO M	MAJ	0-1575041	0557	1
ODONNAL MELVIN C	LTC	0-0398879	0960	1	OGBURN LORANZY D	1LT	0-1289951	0347	2	OHLHEISER HAROLD R	LTC	0-0242139	0163	3	OLEAIR JOHN J	CPT	0-0302403	0156	3
ODONNELL ANTHONY W	1LT	0-1876252	1055	2	OGDAHL HARMON T	CPT	0-1316319	0646	2	OHLINGER NORBERT B	CW2	W-2149090	0157	1	OLEARCZYK STANLEY R	MAJ	0-0939629	0764	1
ODONNELL BERNARD J	LTC	0-1060234	0363	1	OGDEN ALAN	CW3	W-2209084	0868	1	OHLMAN GERALD G	MAJ	0-1257932	0761	1	OLEARY ARTHUR E	LTC	0-0441778	0748	1
ODONNELL CORNELIUS	CPT	0-1320910	0257	1	OGDEN CARL J	CW3	W-2147901	0666	1	OHLRICH VIRGIL C	MAJ	0-1062779	0363	1	OLEARY CORNELIUS	LTC	0-0123614	0361	3
ODONNELL DANIEL P	LTC	0-0127245	0648	3	OGDEN CARLOS C	CPT	0-1299287	0448	2	OHLSEN HENRY L	WO1	W-2151778	0361	2	OLEARY DANIEL R	CPT	0-1014452	1060	1
ODONNELL FRANCIS J	1LT	0-1102410	0145	2	OGDEN CLAIR F	LTC	0-1551922	0657	1	OHLSEN WALTER C	LTC	0-0252317	0163	3	OLEARY FRANCIS A	CPT	0-0977204	0856	1
ODONNELL JAMES D	LTC	0-0344985	0463	1	OGDEN CLAUDE H	LTC	0-0115709	0251	3	OHLSON LEROY J	1LT	0-1184560	0147	2	OLEARY GLENA B	CPT	N-0763636	1046	1
ODONNELL JAMES P	LTC	0-1756338	1161	2	OGDEN FREDERICK	CPT	0-0305640	0246	2	OHLSON RUTH H	2LT	N-0736540	0244	1	OLEARY LAWRENC A	COL	0-0261808	1067	3
ODONNELL JAMES T	CPT	0-1080892	0748	2	OGDEN HAROLD F	COL	0-0204623	0557	3	OHMAN RINOLD L	LTC	0-0280260	0652	3	OLEARY LEO W	LTC	0-0500349	1262	1
ODONNELL JOHN B	MAJ	0-1585979	0466	3	OGDEN HORATIO W	LTC	0-0933029	1067	3	OHMERT WINFIELD L	COL	0-0151245	0548	3	OLEARY TIMOTHY J	COL	0-1577647	0967	3
ODONNELL JOSEPH G	CW3	W-2141964	1060	1	OGDEN JAMES O	1LT	0-1746362	0645	2	OHRBECK JOSEPH F	CPT	0-0129749	1059	3	OLECH RAY A	CPT	0-0535521	0146	2
ODONNELL JOSEPH J	CPT	0-0905323	1145	2	OGDEN JAMES P	1LT	0-0392338	1143	2	OHRSTROM HILDING E	CW4	W-2109191	0368	3	OLECK DAVID	1LT	0-1547093	1045	2
ODONNELL JOSEPH M	MAJ	0-0969254	1063	1	OGDEN LEVI J	MAJ	0-1925115	0468	1	OHRVALL ADOLPH F	LTC	0-0288954	1060	1	OLEFIROWICZ C P	CPT	0-1845223		2
ODONNELL LEO P	MAJ	0-0229201	1056	3	OGDEN VAN L	LTC	0-0261296	0565	3	OHSIEK LEROY E	COL	0-0346546	0468	3	OLEJAR PAUL D	LTC	0-0911598	1066	3
ODONNELL MALCOLM F	COL	0-0350013	0346	2	OGDEN WALTER H	MAJ	0-0162938	1151	3	OJA CARL A	LTC	0-1305821	0266	1	OLEJARZ BOLESLAW	LTC	0-1115725	0368	1
ODONNELL MORGAN J	CW3	W-2141398	0262	1	OGESEN EVER J	CPT	0-0239562	0745	2	OJE LYLE F	MAJ	0-1551349	1162	1	OLEKSIW JEROME J	LTC	0-0273600	0668	3
ODONNELL PAUL T	LTC	0-0549030	0566	1	OGEZ JOHN J	LTC	0-1056185	1267	1	OJEDA FRANK W	CW4	W-2151624	1267	1	OLENBERGER CARL F JR	1LT	0-0405346	0246	2
ODONNELL THOMAS H	COL	0-0210680	0554	3	OGG JACK L	CPT	0-0528680	0846	2	OJI SUKEO	MAJ	0-1339091	0863	1	OLENTINE JULIE E	CPT	0-0528280	1045	2
ODONNELL THOMAS W	CW2	W-2144605	0259	1	OGG RICHARD L	1LT	0-0762486	1067	2	OJIBWAY PHILIP J	CPT	0-0424555	0845	2	OLES FLOYD	LTC	0-0189508	0556	3
ODONNELL VINCENT R	CPT	0-1283823	0846	2	OGG STODDARD L	CPT	0-1013983	0247	2	OKADA ICHIRO	1LT	0-0410147	0246	2	OLES PAUL F	CW2	W-2141647	0556	1
ODONNELL WALDROP L	COL	0-0177056	0560	3	OGILBEE HARRY L	CW2	W-2147637	0259	1	OKANE MORTIMER J	COL	0-0247071	0959	1	OLESHEVTZ MIKE	MAJ	0-2039501	0666	1
ODONNELL WILLIAM J	LTC	0-2033962	0168	1	OGILVIE JOHN O	MAJ	0-0454123	0755	1	OKANE ROY	1LT	0-1914070	0748	1	OLESON EVERETT E	MAJ	0-1014673	0565	1
ODONOGHUE FRANCIS F	1LT	0-0497511	1043	2	OGINSKY THEODORE J	1LT	0-1292929	1044	2	OKEEFE DANIEL M	MAJ	0-1324183	0862	1	OLESON LLOYD F	CPT	0-0366962	0545	2
ODONOGHUE NICHOLAS R	CPT	0-0441093	0743	1	OGLE ELMER E	COL	0-0182425	0559	3	OKEEFE DONALD A	CPT	0-5325617	1168	2	OLESZAK MAX W	MAJ	0-0887342	0261	1
ODONOHUE EDWARD	LTC	0-0498564	0153	1	OGLE ELWOOD L	LTC	0-1327272	0968	1	OKEEFE FRANCIS A	LTC	0-1165139	0159	1	OLESZCZUK JOHN	MAJ	0-0348309	0768	3
ODONOVICH PAUL	LTC	0-1698133	1263	1	OGLE WALTER A	MAJ	0-1556195	0358	1	OKEEFE FRED T	MAJ	0-0465381	0365	1	OLEZ GLENN	2LT	0-1896607	0666	1
ODOR HUGH E	LTC	0-0906164	0866	3	OGLE WILLIAM E	CW4	W-2135378	1055	1	OKEEFE HERBERT A SR	CPT	0-1326109	0347	2	OLFKY ANTHONY E	MAJ	0-1534108	0546	2
ODRAIN MARIE E	MAJ	N-0760190	0868	3	OGLES OTIS R	LTC	0-0373396	0760	1	OKEEFE JOHN A	B G	0-0277514	0551	2	OLIG FRANCIS A	LTC	0-1826217	0164	2
ODUM ODIS R	CW2	W-2149172	0461	1	OGLESBY DAVID H JR	CPT	0-1692643	0663	1	OKEEFE JOHN F	LTC	0-0369837	0862	1	OLIHOVIK JOHN	LTC	0-0799622	0562	1
ODWYER BERNARD L	MAJ	0-1533418	0960	1	OGLESBY ERNEST J JR	CPT	0-0449004	0750	2	OKEEFE JOHN P	CPT	0-1523162	0645	2	OLIJAR MICHAEL	LTC	0-1177926	1163	1
OECHSLE ELMER H	COL	0-0155715	0762	3	OGLESBY OSCAR D	CPT	0-1339386	0858	1	OKEEFE JOHN P	MAJ	0-1645886	0958	2	OLIN FRANK R	COL	0-0203254	0646	2
OECHSLE HERMAN P	1LT	0-1315606	1044	2	OGLESBY PAUL C	CPT	0-1774793	1054	2	OKEEFE JOHN W	CPT	0-1035953	0246	2	OLIN JOHN H	LTC	0-0324955	0358	1
OED PAUL	COL	0-0463583	0950	1	OGLESBY WALTER P	CW4	W-2119769	1263	1	OKEEFE MAURICE P	CPT	0-1301869	0960	1	OLIN MORSE E	LTC	0-0322710	0457	1
OEDER LAMBERT R	MAJ	0-0255243	0151	3	OGLESBY WILLIAM B JR	WO1	W-2148978	0359	1	OKEEFE PAUL T	LTC	0-0248261	0759	3	OLIND JOHN H	CPT	0-0110583	0355	3
OEHLER JAMES C	COL	0-0162708	0155	3	OGLETHORPE RAYMOND J	MAJ	0-1636421	0560	1	OKEEFE ROBERT P	LTC	0-1947788	0965	1	OLIND JOHN H JR	CW2	W-2206629	1063	1
OEHMKE BENJAMIN H	COL	0-0329930	1264	1	OGLETREE CLYDE	MAJ	N-0727702	0365	1	OKEEFE TIMOTHY L JR	MAJ	0-1881685	0468	1	OLINE JOSEPH R	LTC	0-0390795	0366	3
OEHNE FORD A	2LT	0-1031354	1045	2	OGRADY FRANCIS D	CW2	W-2148263	0261	1	OKEEFFE ELBERT R	LTC	0-0416856	1060	1	OLINGER ALLEN M JR	1LT	0-1702791	0645	2
OELKERS ALBERT L	LTC	0-1110694	1164	3	OGRADY GERALD B	COL	0-0164475	1056	3	OKEEFFE ELLEN L	MAJ	N-0745391	0664	1	OLINGER WILLIAM A	CPT	0-0469788	0945	2
OELRICH WILFRED C	LTC	0-0465108	0567	1	OGRADY JOHN J	MAJ	0-0499844	1045	2	OKEEFFE JAMES JR	1LT	0-0449005	0645	2	OLIPHANT CHARLES F	CPT	0-1054742	1047	2
OELSCHLAGER JAMES A	2LT	0-1165770	1044	2	OGRADY MICHAEL P	CPT	0-0925069	0446	2	OKELLEY GOLMER P	MAJ	N-0727632	0962	1	OLIPHANT FLOYD W	COL	0-0235017	0260	3
OELTJEN GUS J	CPT	0-0437024	0350	1	OGREEN RUDOLPH C	LTC	0-0258051	0155	3	OKELLEY HOKE S	CPT	0-0135949	0747	2	OLISZEWSKI CASIMIR	COL	0-0300907	1056	1
OENNING LESTER C SR	LTC	0-1329387	0966	1	OGREN CECIL C	CPT	0-0229811	0261	3	OKELLEY HORACE W	CPT	0-0510480	0647	1	OLIVARI-AMILL WILLIA	LTC	0-1325772	1162	1
OERTEL WILLY M	CW4	W-2115682	0658	1	OGWYNN PAUL D	LTC	0-1044636	0562	1	OKELLY ARTHUR P	1LT	0-1013531	0645	2	OLIVE GEORGE S	MAJ	0-1280304	0446	2
OERTER HERBERT L	MAJ	0-2046395	0956	1	OHACO MICHEL J	CPT	0-0446852	0847	2	OKELLY FIELDING K JR	CPT	0-1578935	0145	2	OLIVE HAROLD P	WO1	W-2150100	0855	1
OERTER KARL C	CW4	W-2122139	1160	1	OHAGAN FRANCIS G	CPT	0-1796515	0163	1	OKEN MORRIS H	CPT	0-0512411	1044	2	OLIVE LEONARD J JR	CW3	W-2203369	0963	1
OESCH WILLIAM H	LTC	0-0133147	0459	3	OHAIR JAMES A	MAJ	0-2266278	0568	1	OKERT FRED H	CPT	0-0495166	0849	1	OLIVE ROBERT H JR	MAJ	0-1331979	0960	1
OESER RICHARD W	MAJ	0-1642443	1264	1	OHAIR JOHN E	COL	0-0237115	0556	1	OKEY ELMER E	MAJ	0-0115713	0556	3	OLIVE WILLIAM M JR	MAJ	0-1590710	0262	1
OESTREICH FORREST C	LTC	0-0391007	0157	1	OHALLORAN MARY A	MAJ	N-0744796	1162	1	OKEY KEITH M	CW2	W-2151173	0966	1	OLIVER ALFRED	LTC	0-0149406	0654	3

NAME	GRADE	SVC NO	DATE RET MO YR	RET CODE
OLIVER ALFRED L	COL	0-0269527	0860	1
OLIVER CALVIN C	CW2	W-2102162	0866	2
OLIVER CHARLES W	MAJ	0-0255592	0451	3
OLIVER CLARENCE E	LTC	0-1591658	0968	2
OLIVER CLARENCE R	MAJ	0-1920264	1163	1
OLIVER DAVID T	COL	0-1331427	1068	1
OLIVER DONALD B JR	LTC	0-1116967	0467	1
OLIVER EVERETT J	CPT	0-0967061	1060	1
OLIVER FRANCIS J	MAJ	0-1291868	0860	1
OLIVER GEORGE F	LTC	0-0985581	0468	1
OLIVER GEORGE L	LTC	0-0288338	0246	2
OLIVER HAROLD L	LTC	0-1921555	0968	1
OLIVER HENRY C	CPT	0-1283122	0546	2
OLIVER JACK L	LTC	0-2070542	0867	1
OLIVER JAMES G	COL	0-0506051	0266	3
OLIVER JESSE	CW4	W-2145869	0765	1
OLIVER JOHN G	MAJ	0-0971200	0365	1
OLIVER JOHN W	COL	0-0205398	0659	3
OLIVER LEO P	MAJ	0-1548115	0559	1
OLIVER LEONARD E	MAJ	0-1579937	1054	1
OLIVER LOUIS O	MAJ	0-1899405	0263	1
OLIVER NORMAN	MAJ	0-0442262	0146	2
OLIVER OVIE	CPT	0-1293103	0668	2
OLIVER RALPH	CW2	W-2151314	1160	2
OLIVER REX G	MAJ	0-1877824	0264	2
OLIVER THOMAS H	LTC	0-1573489	0961	1
OLIVER THURMAN W	LTC	0-1305973	0266	1
OLIVER WALTER E	MAJ	0-1922573	1263	1
OLIVER WILLARD E	CPT	0-0989036	0161	1
OLIVER WILLIAM H	MAJ	0-0342230	0346	2
OLIVER WILLIAM P	MAJ	0-0220733	1158	3
OLIVER WILLIAM R	COL	0-1310139	0466	1
OLIVER WILLIAM W	LTC	0-0910454	0864	3
OLIVERAS RAFAEL	1LT	0-0425592	0446	2
OLLER J C	CW2	W-2152392	0563	1
OLLER JOSE A	COL	0-0523909	0667	1
OLLER JOSEPH W	1LT	0-1319327	0646	2
OLLIFF CHARLES K	LTC	0-2287715	1267	1
OLLIFFE ARTHUR J	CW2	W-2150358	1161	1
OLLS VICTOR	LTC	0-1290295	0663	1
OLMSTEAD ALFRED S	MAJ	0-2263443	0367	1
OLMSTEAD KENNETH A	LTC	0-1549904	0961	1
OLMSTEAD THOMAS	1LT	0-1340797	1152	2
OLMSTED ALFRED M	MAJ	0-0373968	1160	1
OLMSTED GENE S	COL	0-0244935	0447	2
OLMSTED GEORGE H	M G	0-0199581	0461	3
OLMSTED JOSEPH N	LTC	0-1030699	0964	3
OLMSTED RANDOLPH F	COL	0-0290497	0659	3
OLMSTED ROBERT Q	CPT	0-1010718	0346	2
OLMSTED WALTER C	1LT	0-0396890	0245	2
OLNEY FRANCIS X	LTC	0-0341358	1159	1
OLJANS JOHN M	CW3	W-2136361	0163	1
OLOUGHLIN ROSEMARY	MAJ	L-0311291	1163	1
OLSCHEWSKE JOHN A	COL	0-0421916	1061	1
OLSEN AARON B	MAJ	0-0401643	0649	2
OLSEN ALBERT L	LTC	0-0248307	1164	3
OLSEN ALBERT M	LTC	0-0301651	0461	1
OLSEN ALFRED W	CPT	0-0496976	0249	1
OLSEN ARNOLD	LTC	0-0201821	0455	3
OLSEN ARNOLD C	MAJ	0-2018043	0264	1
OLSEN ARTHUR T	WO1	W-2152244	0557	1
OLSEN BEN JR	CPT	0-0365730	0246	2
OLSEN BOB G	LTC	0-0451364	0758	1
OLSEN BODO	CW3	W-2148299	1061	1
OLSEN BORGA R	LTC	0-1105722	1062	1
OLSEN CARL T	CPT	0-0223237	0756	3
OLSEN CLARENCE M	LTC	0-0233467	1050	2
OLSEN DONALD H	MAJ	0-2090150	0966	1
OLSEN EARL	CW2	W-2109539	0949	2
OLSEN EARL M	MAJ	0-0973224	1160	1
OLSEN EDWARD H	LTC	0-0422757	0856	1
OLSEN GORDON N	COL	0-0244795	1055	3
OLSEN HANFORD T	LTC	0-0901865	0666	3
OLSEN IVAN C E	CW2	W-2214539	0667	1
OLSEN JAMES E	LTC	0-0283676	0864	3

NAME	GRADE	SVC NO	DATE RET MO YR	RET CODE
OLSEN JOHN R D	MAJ	0-1115369	0958	1
OLSEN KNUD	CPT	0-0278975	0447	1
OLSEN LEROY J	1LT	0-1595080	0146	2
OLSEN ODIN F	MAJ	0-1330953	0163	1
OLSEN ROBERT N	LTC	0-1594370	0566	1
OLSEN ROGER C	CW2	W-2215799	0968	1
OLSEN ROLF	MAJ	0-0992458	0764	1
OLSEN ROY J	MAJ	0-1308367	0164	1
OLSEN SAM N	CPT	0-0888359	1145	2
OLSEN SAMUEL G JR	MAJ	0-1798388	0764	1
OLSEN VICTOR L	COL	0-0297916	1162	3
OLSEN WILLIAM S	CPT	0-1306882	0447	2
OLSON ALBERT J	MAJ	0-1894700	1053	2
OLSON ALBERT N	MAJ	0-2007117	1265	1
OLSON ALBIN J	CW3	W-2150093	0363	1
OLSON ALLAN M	CPT	0-1765343	1045	2
OLSON ANDREW G	CW4	W-2107818	0562	1
OLSON CARL A	1LT	0-0487084	0744	1
OLSON CARL G	CW4	W-2109834	0959	1
OLSON CARROLL A	CPT	0-1020028	0252	2
OLSON CHARLES H	LTC	0-1167147	0166	1
OLSON CHARLES W	CPT	0-1293821	0258	1
OLSON CLARENCE H	COL	0-0201092	0560	3
OLSON CLINTON W	MAJ	0-2021181	0565	1
OLSON DONALD D	CW2	W-2148216	0962	1
OLSON EARL J	MAJ	0-1684271	0346	2
OLSON EDWARD	1LT	0-1322166	1046	2
OLSON EDWARD	LTC	0-1585985	1262	1
OLSON EDWARD T	CPT	0-1341034	0265	1
OLSON EDWIN O	CPT	0-0232591	0355	3
OLSON EINO O	CPT	0-0329632	0146	2
OLSON ELLEN M	LTC	N-0728322	1161	1
OLSON ELMER A JR	CPT	0-0520545	0146	2
OLSON ELMER J	1LT	0-0549966	0946	2
OLSON ELMER M	MAJ	0-2026946	0467	1
OLSON ELVIN N	MAJ	0-2097007	0864	1
OLSON FRANCIS J	MAJ	0-0487611	0863	3
OLSON FRANKLIN R	LTC	0-1039493	0964	1
OLSON FRANZ L	LTC	0-1036664	0162	1
OLSON FREDERICK	WO1	W-2128101	0456	1
OLSON GEORGE H	LTC	0-1311042	0662	1
OLSON GEORGE W	LTC	0-0475020	0762	1
OLSON GUSTAF R	B G	0-0275721	1062	3
OLSON HAROLD W	LTC	0-1557764	0564	1
OLSON HARRY E	CW2	W-2113563	0947	1
OLSON IHLINE G	2LT	N-0732606	0843	1
OLSON JAMES O	MAJ	0-0376428	0846	2
OLSON JOHN E	MAJ	0-0246155	0463	3
OLSON JOHN E	MAJ	0-1103845	0859	1
OLSON JOHN R	1LT	0-0372399	1143	2
OLSON KENNETH M	LTC	0-1039096	0968	3
OLSON LEONARD A	LTC	0-1797174	1162	1
OLSON LEROY B	CPT	0-1555115	0661	2
OLSON LESTER E	CPT	0-0503271	0746	2
OLSON LUDWIG F	WO1	W-2103274	1056	1
OLSON MARVIN A	CW3	W-2207223	1165	1
OLSON MARVIN V	LTC	0-1182674	0563	1
OLSON MELVIN W	LTC	0-1284927	0665	2
OLSON NORMAN J	CPT	0-2020960	0558	1
OLSON OLIVE	2LT	N-0783041	0944	1
OLSON OLIVER S	COL	0-0180111	0457	1
OLSON OSCAR	2LT	0-1324184	0544	2
OLSON OSCAR A	LTC	0-0182367	0357	3
OLSON PALMER F	CPT	0-1291161	0662	1
OLSON RALPH J	M G	0-0232882	0468	3
OLSON RICHARD	CPT	0-0504962	0745	2
OLSON RICHARD A	CW2	W-2213047	0667	1
OLSON RICHARD J	LTC	0-0946195	1068	1
OLSON RICHARD W	CPT	0-0948898	0161	1
OLSON ROBERT B	LTC	0-1697845	0363	1
OLSON ROBERT M	1LT	0-1322806	0148	2
OLSON ROBERT R	CW3	W-2113658	0658	2
OLSON RUSSELL L	MAJ	0-1114693	0959	1
OLSON RUSSELL L	COL	0-1550473	1168	1
OLSON THEODORE A	LTC	0-0369628	0246	2

NAME	GRADE	SVC NO	DATE RET MO YR	RET CODE
OLSON THEODORE P	MAJ	0-0490438	0466	1
OLSON THOMAS C	2LT	0-1313886	1048	1
OLSON VERNON G	2LT	0-0888239	0744	2
OLSON WALTER L	1LT	0-0452943	0848	2
OLSON WALTER P	LTC	0-0350467	0964	1
OLSON WALTER W	MAJ	0-0270928	0667	3
OLSON WALTON S	MAJ	0-1659184	0861	1
OLSON WILLIAM A	LTC	0-1106378	0664	1
OLSON WILLIAM P	LTC	0-0486694	0156	2
OLSON WILLIS E	1LT	0-1312706	0845	2
OLSOWSKY EDWARD C	WO1	W-2108372	0445	2
OLSSON JOHN F	LTC	0-0264993	1060	3
OLSSON ROY H SR	MAJ	0-1891227	0167	1
OLSTAD MYRTLE A	LTC	N-0731096	1165	3
OLSTYNSKI STANLEY A	CW3	W-2208129	1268	1
OLSZEWSKI JOHN P	MAJ	0-1946125	1154	1
OLSZEWSKI JOSEPH L	LTC	0-1870076	1268	1
OLSZEWSKI WALTER J	2LT	0-1298427	0745	2
OLTARZEWSKI WALTER J	CPT	0-0397870	0867	1
OLTJENBRONS ELIZABET	MAJ	L-0801279	1065	1
OLTJENBRONS WALTER W	MAJ	0-1032106	0460	1
OLTMAN ALBERT O	1LT	0-1301198	0548	2
OLTMANN OSCAR F	MAJ	0-1019277	0361	1
OLTS CHARLES A	LTC	0-0453655	1061	1
OLUFS HAROLD F	MAJ	0-0402543	0368	3
OLVER THOMAS W	LTC	0-1281357	0864	2
OLVERSON JOHN B JR	MAJ	0-0900528	0146	2
OLVIS CHARLES J	COL	0-0290522	1059	3
OLWIN JOHN H	LTC	0-0259418	0667	3
OLYNICK MILTON	CW3	W-2152269	1264	1
OMAHONEY JOHN F	LTC	0-2049349	0263	1
OMALLEY EDWARD A	LTC	0-0291024	0260	1
OMALLEY EDWARD F	1LT	0-1000636	0750	2
OMALLEY EDWARD P	LTC	0-0308495	1065	3
OMALLEY FRANCIS E	1LT	0-1916517	0452	2
OMALLEY FRANK W	CPT	0-0444661	0245	2
OMALLEY GEORGE E	MAJ	0-1016721	0467	1
OMALLEY JAMES E	LTC	0-1636428	0761	1
OMALLEY JAMES F	CW3	W-2149711	0461	1
OMALLEY JOHN E	CPT	0-0143883	0751	3
OMALLEY VIRGINIA L	1LT	0-0539933	0750	2
OMALLEY WILLIAM D	1LT	0-0349937	0957	1
OMALLEY WILLIAM P	COL	0-1321238	0668	1
OMAN ERNEST H	MAJ	0-0319767	0266	3
OMAN RALPH W	MAJ	0-0166871	0657	3
OMARA JAMES J	CPT	0-0408508	1045	2
OMARA THOMAS J	1LT	0-1317736	1145	2
OMEARA ARTHUR A	LTC	0-0905136	0662	1
OMEARA CHARLES E	CW2	W-2142385	1055	1
OMEARA HOWARD F	LTC	0-1556031	1262	1
OMEARA JAMES J	CPT	0-1822607	1162	1
OMEARA MILDRED M	1LT	N-0724094	0146	1
OMEARA WILLIAM F	MAJ	0-0204802	0759	3
OMELANUK MICHAEL	CW3	W-2203862	0965	1
OMELIA JOSEPH J	CW3	W-2152734	0564	1
OMELIA MALCOLM B	CPT	0-1323728	1264	1
OMER DANIEL O	COL	0-0195630	0960	3
OMER JAMES M	MAJ	0-1296074	0546	2
OMHOLT ELMER V	1LT	0-1294351	0145	2
OMHOLT GARTH O	MAJ	0-4010593	1167	1
OMOHUNDRO ROBERT L	LTC	0-1041413	0962	1
OMORI RICHARD T	MAJ	0-2030794	0866	1
OMSTEAD FRED A	CW4	W-2118032	1053	1
ONASCH WILLIS E	CW2	W-2209400	0763	1
ONDECK MICHAEL	LTC	0-1336948	0466	1
ONDECKER ANDREW M	MAJ	0-0406796	0947	2
ONDO JOSEPH	LTC	0-1542849	1161	2
ONEAL ARVIL C	LTC	0-1288106	0755	1
ONEAL AUBREY M	MAJ	0-2011718	1056	1
ONEAL BUFORD L	LTC	0-0295494	0867	3
ONEAL CECIL S	MAJ	0-2263113	0865	1
ONEAL CECIL T	CPT	0-0192590	0151	3
ONEAL DOCK L	CW3	W-2143365	0861	1
ONEAL EDMUND J	CPT	0-0532434	0946	2
ONEAL FRANK W	LTC	0-1056496	0365	1

NAME	GRADE	SVC NO	DATE RET MO YR	RET CODE
ONEAL GEORGE A JR	LTC	0-0439797	1262	1
ONEAL HAROLD F	LTC	0-0238871	0760	3
ONEAL JACK O	MAJ	0-0988881	1065	2
ONEAL JAMES G	CW3	RW-2149741	1163	1
ONEAL JAMES M	LTC	0-0383537	1044	2
ONEAL LEON H	CW3	W-2149798	0667	2
ONEAL LOWELL W	MAJ	0-1108215	0760	1
ONEAL MONCURE C	LTC	0-0248329	0567	3
ONEAL ORVILLE W	COL	0-1544041	1067	3
ONEAL THOMAS F	CW2	W-2145863	0754	1
ONEAL WALTER D	MAJ	0-2042311	0960	1
ONEAL WILLIAM H	CW2	W-2211221	1165	1
ONEAL WILLIAM L JR	MAJ	0-1938025	0367	1
ONEAL WILLIAM T	MAJ	0-2042870	1157	1
ONEAL WILTON K	COL	0-0348056	1063	1
ONEALE MINERVA	LTC	N-0700135	0846	1
ONEIL ALBERT O	CW4	W-2145162	0767	1
ONEIL ARTHUR	CPT	0-0977921	0160	2
ONEIL GERALD W	CW3	W-2119585	1159	1
ONEIL GILBERT M	LTC	0-0292375	0859	1
ONEIL JAMES E	LTC	0-0181248	0953	3
ONEIL JOHN P	LTC	0-1112899	1062	1
ONEIL JOSEPH F	MAJ	0-1947790	1165	1
ONEIL MABELLE M	LTC	N-0751261	0766	3
ONEIL ORLANO J	CPT	0-2097059	0762	1
ONEIL RAYMOND F	LTC	0-1338504	0466	1
ONEIL ROBERT	COL	0-0346053	0667	3
ONEIL THOMAS F	CPT	0-0101817	0648	3
ONEIL THOMAS F	CW4	W-2135976	0766	1
ONEILL CHARLES T	COL	0-0191567	0748	3
ONEILL CLEMENT J	LTC	0-0962977	1267	1
ONEILL CLIFFORD L	1LT	0-1176757	1046	2
ONEILL DONALD F	CW2	W-2147602	0766	1
ONEILL EDWARD M	CPT	0-1646472	0348	2
ONEILL ELEANOR E	CPT	N-0700666	0446	1
ONEILL ELIZABETH	1LT	N-0763568	0746	1
ONEILL FREDERICK	COL	0-0281043	0866	3
ONEILL GERALD M	LTC	0-1305467	0561	1
ONEILL HAROLD L	MAJ	0-1109569	0861	1
ONEILL JAMES D	CW4	W-2006890	1067	1
ONEILL JAMES E	CW3	W-2144678	1060	1
ONEILL JAMES F	LTC	0-1945446	0568	3
ONEILL JAMES J	CPT	0-0381006	0647	2
ONEILL JAMES L JR	MAJ	0-1298114	0864	1
ONEILL JAMES W	MAJ	0-1297578	1157	2
ONEILL JEREMIAH F	LTC	0-0131039	0353	3
ONEILL JOSEPH A	MAJ	0-0266972	1068	3
ONEILL JOSEPH A	LTC	0-0361262	0756	1
ONEILL JOSEPH L	MAJ	0-0887355	0564	1
ONEILL KATHRYN M	MAJ	N-0758770	1264	1
ONEILL LEANDER W	LTC	0-1328392	0765	1
ONEILL PAUL S	MAJ	0-2033945	0664	2
ONEILL PETER M	LTC	0-0189753	0558	1
ONEILL RICHARD F	CW3	W-2144053	0564	1
ONEILL ROBERT B	MAJ	0-0454222	0261	1
ONEILL THOMAS J	MAJ	0-1650682	1062	1
ONEILL THOMAS P	MAJ	0-1294002	1060	1
ONEILL TIMOTHY J	2LT	0-1644637	0146	2
ONEILL WALTER L	CPT	0-1004392	0962	1
ONEILL WILLIAM H	MAJ	0-0369043	0267	3
ONEILL WILLIAM J	CPT	0-0479558	1144	2
ONEILL WILLIAM R	CPT	0-2017579	1057	2
ONELLION WILLARD M	1LT	0-0480139	0248	1
ONEY WALTER	MAJ	0-2007204	1157	1
ONGERT WALTER J	CPT	0-1280235	0760	2
ONGIES JEROME H	LTC	0-1688789	0767	1
ONION 3RD WILLIAM F	1LT	0-1284379	0346	2
ONKES WILLIAM R	CPT	0-0450468	0847	1
ONKST DOROTHY O	1LT	N-0767746	0147	1
ONOSZKO WALDEMAR P	LTC	0-1700994	1068	3
ONSRUD MYRTLE S	CPT	N-0736615	0946	1
ONSTOT CLEMENT C	CW3	W-2123023	0361	1
ONSTOTT EDWIN C	LTC	0-1845326	1062	1
OOLEY WAYMAN R	CPT	0-0197139	0262	3
OOSTERLING WALTER H	LTC	0-0266032	0653	2

NAME	GRADE	SVC NO	DATE RET MO YR	RET CODE	NAME	GRADE	SVC NO	DATE RET MO YR	RET CODE	NAME	GRADE	SVC NO	DATE RET MO YR	RET CODE	NAME	GRADE	SVC NO	DATE RET MO YR	RET CODE
OPAL EDWARD A	CPT	0-1998388	0750	2	ORIORDAN CHARLES P	LTC	0-1583463	0662	1	ORTLER LESLIE A	LTC	0-1683441	1065	1	OSHEA HOWARD F	1LT	0-1177562	0446	2
OPALEK ELLA	MAJ	N-0793429	0365	1	ORITT LOUIS	1LT	0-1592490	0645	2	ORTLIP HENRY T	COL	0-0332093	0760	1	OSHEA JAMES	CW3	W-2142362	0561	1
OPENSHAW FRANK	CPT	0-0407912	0245	2	ORIVIS HARRIET S	MAJ	L-0909571	0463	1	ORTMANN ARNOLD E	MAJ	0-0278221	0365	3	OSHEA JOHN F	LTC	0-0308591	0159	3
OPENSHAW FRED	MAJ	0-0104330	1058	3	ORLANDI MANUEL	CW2	W-2605005	0767	3	ORTNER RICHARD E	CPT	0-1573920	0946	2	OSHEA OBIE M	MAJ	0-0498140	1052	1
OPENSHAW GLEN A	CW2	W-2205156	1163	1	ORLANDO DOMINICK J	LTC	0-1310754	0368	1	ORTON JACK L	LTC	0-1648658	0762	1	OSHEE PATRICK C	COL	0-0216153	1063	3
OPENSHAW JAMES	LTC	0-1634188	0665	1	ORLANDO THOMAS	COL	0-1310630	0567	1	ORTON LEONARD C	CPT	0-1557201	0453	2	OSHEROFF WILLIAM	MAJ	0-0426611	0645	2
OPENSHAW ROBERT G	LTC	0-1339910	0268	1	ORLOFSKY CHARLES F	CPT	0-1555452	1060	1	ORTON RAY	MAJ	0-1285988	0957	1	OSHIRO WILLIAM C	1LT	0-1998050	0147	2
OPENSHAW THOMAS E	1LT	0-2043266	1046	2	ORLUK ALPHONSE J	1LT	0-1325234	1045	2	ORTZMAN PHILIP	LTC	0-1100712	1061	1	OSICKEY BENJAMIN L	LTC	0-1647216	0267	1
OPHAUG ORVILLE H	LTC	0-1300519	0463	1	ORMOND CLYDE R	MAJ	0-0975476	0765	1	ORVINO JOSEPH R	CPT	0-2049675	0346	2	OSIER ROLLAN	1LT	0-1183151	0747	1
OPIE EVARTS W	B G	0-0172561	0953	3	ORMSBY DONALD F	CW2	W-2107923	0257	1	ORY MURPHY A	COL	0-0348261	0860	1	OSMAN JAMES A	CPT	0-1285989	1151	2
OPIE SIDNEY P	LTC	0-0353607	0559	1	ORMSBY EDWARD T	CPT	0-0904121	0847	2	ORYAN JAMES E L	MAJ	0-0137825	0648	3	OSMAN LEO D	CPT	0-0196449	0944	2
OPILLA PAUL C	CW2	W-2209665	0464	1	ORMSBY JUSTIN R	LTC	0-1050846	0961	1	ORZECHOWSKI EDWARD A	MAJ	0-2012774	0962	1	OSMAN LEROY J	MAJ	0-1794843	1060	2
OPITZ WILLIAM A	CW2	W-2123826	1256	2	ORMSBY THOMAS C	CW2	W-2152612	0262	1	ORZECHOWSKI HENRY E	LTC	0-0497708	0657	1	OSMANSKY MORTIMER	MAJ	0-0285380	0460	3
OPLIGER PAUL G	MAJ	0-1948365	0460	1	ORMSBY WADE E	1LT	0-0428539	1045	2	ORZEL JOHN F	COL	0-0557586	0768	1	OSMUN ELMER E	MAJ	0-0242138	0263	3
OPPENBERG IRVING L	1LT	0-1822901	0547	2	ORNDOFF JOSEF M	CPT	0-2263675	0263	1	ORZEPOWSKI WALTER S	CPT	0-1303383	0647	2	OSMUN JAMES W JR	1LT	0-2037581	1047	2
OPPENHEIM ARMAND	1LT	0-1288428	1045	2	ORNDORF WENDELL R	LTC	0-0913385	1165	3	OSAGE ANTHONY J	CPT	0-1179169	0750	2	OSMUN WALTER JR	CW3	W-2148758	1062	1
OPPENHEIM NORMAN W	COL	0-0291873	0847	2	ORNDORFF CLARENCE A	COL	0-0174803	0646	2	OSBORN ARTHUR W	LTC	0-0323211	0962	3	OSMUN WILLIS R	CPT	0-0133189	0648	3
OPPENHEIMER LOUIS R	CPT	0-1010039	0960	1	ORNELAS MANUEL	CPT	0-1287575	1047	2	OSBORN BILL F	MAJ	0-1030279	0447	2	OSMUSSEN JOHN S	1LT	0-1177563	0246	2
OPPER CHARLES G	LTC	0-0331749	0161	1	ORNER RALPH J	MAJ	0-0272759	0668	3	OSBORN DAVID A	LTC	0-0969643	1167	1	OSOLIN ALFRED J	LTC	0-0282120	0868	3
OPPIDI ALBERT A	1LT	0-0915145	1047	2	ORNSTEIN DAVID	LTC	0-0485678	1265	1	OSBORN FRED P	LTC	0-0177896	1155	3	OSOSKY BERNARD H	CW2	W-2143273	1056	2
OPPLEMAN HERMAN F	CPT	0-0428292	0144	2	ORNSTEIN HAROLD A	LTC	0-0300174	0262	3	OSBORN GEORGE C JR	MAJ	0-0340691	0646	2	OSTEEN AL F	MAJ	0-1922871	0968	1
OPUDA JOHN	LTC	0-0485030	0363	1	OROSCO ERNEST D	MAJ	0-1325349	0859	1	OSBORN JAMES F	MAJ	0-1303626	0761	1	OSTEEN BERNARD V	CW3	W-2144332	0961	1
OQUINN JAMES D	MAJ	0-0260380	1266	3	OROURKE ALEXANDER	LTC	0-0208723	0447	1	OSBORN NORTON J	LTC	0-0264000	0666	3	OSTEEN JACK A	CPT	0-0959358	1064	1
OQUINN THOMAS J	CW2	W-2125153	0161	1	OROURKE DAVID J	LTC	0-1698130	0364	2	OSBORN PRESTON H	MAJ	0-1300846	1061	1	OSTENDORF WALTER A	COL	0-0213614	0550	3
OQUINN TRUEMAN E	COL	0-0917160	0665	3	OROURKE JAMES J	LTC	0-0309594	1065	3	OSBORNE ALBERT B	MAJ	0-0369355	0867	3	OSTERBY BARBARA M	2LT	N-0778196	0147	1
OQUINN WILLIAM A	LTC	0-1322167	0766	1	OROURKE JOSEPH V	MAJ	0-0361452	0246	2	OSBORNE ALBERT C	CPT	0-0512255	0755	1	OSTERDAHL ETHEL V	CPT	N-0793684	0956	2
ORAM GEORGE F	WO1	W-2125199	0647	2	OROZCO EMIL M	1LT	0-1315002	0347	2	OSBORNE ALBERT J	MAJ	0-1105077	0556	1	OSTERHOLM ORRIN C	2LT	0-1307292	0144	2
ORAMAS FELIX	CW4	W-2113844	0760	1	ORR AUGUSTUS B	LTC	0-0968934	0868	1	OSBORNE ALICE L	1LT	N-0793327	1046	1	OSTERHOUDT PHILIP J	LTC	0-0192147	0156	3
ORATE BRAULIO D	CW3	W-2135150	1063	1	ORR CLAUDE H	MAJ	0-0456677	0557	1	OSBORNE ARTHUR H	CPT	0-0259711	0363	3	OSTERKAMP FRANCIS R	MAJ	0-0474962	0647	1
ORAVEC ANDREW H	CPT	0-1686564	0946	2	ORR DONALD J	CPT	0-0139863	0156	3	OSBORNE CECIL M	CW3	W-2144556	0565	1	OSTERMAN JAMES K	COL	0-0378433	0461	1
ORAVEZ JAMES J	MAJ	0-0372731	0954	1	ORR DOROTHY L	MAJ	N-0754526	0665	1	OSBORNE CHARLES C	CPT	0-1280954	0460	2	OSTERMAN MARTIN G	MAJ	0-1884092	1066	1
ORAZEN JOHN	MAJ	0-0471096	1154	1	ORR ELI H	COL	0-0286382	0658	3	OSBORNE CHESTER M JR	MAJ	0-1285485	1060	1	OSTERMANN RAYMOND J	MAJ	0-0962883	1266	1
ORBECK MARTIN J	LTC	0-0165416	0450	3	ORR FOSTER W	LTC	0-2262481	0268	1	OSBORNE CLARENCE F	MAJ	0-0311420	1144	2	OSTERMEIER RUSSELL L	LTC	0-0242396	0757	1
ORBISON FRANK H	MAJ	0-0486043	0547	2	ORR FRANK M	LTC	0-0193848	0661	3	OSBORNE EARL E	MAJ	0-0488880	1148	1	OSTERNDORF LOGAN C	1LT	0-0372981	0147	2
ORCHARD WINIFRED M	MAJ	N-0783925	0963	1	ORR FREDERICK	LTC	0-0885525	0861	1	OSBORNE ERNEST T	CPT	0-0491923	0349	1	OSTERSTOCK GEORGE A	LTC	0-1291872	0960	1
ORCUTT HAROLD W	COL	0-0393762	0557	1	ORR FREDERICK	CW3	W-2205946	0764	1	OSBORNE FRANCIS H	CPT	N-0726177	0147	1	OSTERWALD HERBERT P	MAJ	0-0258138	0766	3
ORCUTT ROBERT D	LTC	0-0364494	1065	3	ORR HILOUR D	2LT	N-0742904	0545	1	OSBORNE GEORGE M	CPT	0-1106381	1045	2	OSTEYEE WILLIAM W	CW3	W-2105776	0456	2
ORDAHL STAFFORD N	COL	0-0273570	0165	2	ORR JAMES E	CW3	W-2146587	0361	1	OSBORNE HAROLD L	LTC	0-0555421	0765	1	OSTLUND VICTOR S	1LT	0-1180654	0546	2
ORDOYNE LUCIEN P	MAJ	0-1302868	0761	1	ORR JOHN K JR	MAJ	0-0394151	0547	2	OSBORNE HUGH D	CPT	0-1017887	0466	2	OSTRAND CHARLES J	MAJ	0-4021162	0167	1
ORDWAY FRED D	LTC	0-0130099	1049	3	ORR LEWIS P	MAJ	0-1000438	0155	1	OSBORNE JACK A	COL	0-0392552	0368	1	OSTRANDER GILBERT G	MAJ	0-0423867	1162	1
ORDWAY ROBERT E	2LT	0-1698079	0145	2	ORR MORRIS M	MAJ	0-0123577	0550	3	OSBORNE JOSEPH F	MAJ	0-0994496	1066	1	OSTRANDER WILLIAM G	CW2	W-2148144	0659	1
OREAR JOHN H	MAJ	0-1540636	0757	1	ORR SAMUEL S JR	CW3	W-2203277	1266	2	OSBORNE JULIUS F	MAJ	0-1588213	0262	1	OSTREM VICTOR L	LTC	0-0463472	0954	1
OREARDON DANIEL G	MAJ	0-0207825	0455	3	ORR SAMUEL V	CPT	0-0456166	0646	2	OSBORNE LOUIS	MAJ	0-1845336	0461	1	OSTRO HARRY	1LT	0-0563969	0845	2
OREBAUGH LOUIS F	CW3	W-2208329	0366	2	ORR WILLIAM R	LTC	0-0328931	0360	1	OSBORNE LOUIS G	COL	0-0102317	0158	3	OSTROFF DAVID S	CPT	0-1313786	1044	2
OREFICE WILLIAM R	CPT	0-1288287	0647	2	ORR WILLIAM T	CPT	0-0328105	0446	2	OSBORNE OTIS S	LTC	0-1297784	0261	2	OSTROM ERNEST S	LTC	0-1315356	1062	1
OREGAN SAMUEL G	LTC	0-0350838	0662	1	ORRELL ELISE	2LT	N-0727885	0745	1	OSBORNE RICHARD	CPT	0-0371448	0346	2	OSTROM PAUL G	LTC	0-1646475	0367	3
OREGAN TERENCE P	MAJ	0-1303533	0361	1	ORRICK CHARLES H	MAJ	0-0264006	0561	3	OSBORNE ROBERT E	LTC	0-0229270	1263	3	OSTROM PAUL L	2LT	0-1825877	0845	2
OREILLEY JAMES H	COL	0-0151663	1054	3	ORRICK LUTHER F	M G	0-0357391	0667	3	OSBORNE RUPERT S JR	CW3	W-2203305	0861	1	OSTROM RALPH K	CPT	0-0343776	0854	2
OREILLEY WILLIAM C	WO1	W-2108304	1064	3	ORRICO FRANK A	CW2	W-3200459	0968	2	OSBORNE SYDNEY G	LTC	0-0474918	0647	2	OSTROW JAMES D	LTC	0-0330621	0446	2
OREILLY BERNARD F	MAJ	0-1015379	0861	1	ORRIS HAROLD J	MAJ	0-0317842	0745	2	OSBORNE THOMAS B D	CW2	W-2147070	1154	1	OSTROW LOUIS B	CPT	0-0209897	0661	3
OREILLY DANIEL F	CPT	0-0438940	0246	2	ORRISON HOWARD C	MAJ	0-1031503	0661	1	OSBORNE VINCENT C	CW2	W-2148217	0757	1	OSULLIVAN DELLA F	2LT	N-0752736	0246	1
OREILLY HUGH P	MAJ	0-1339208	1060	1	ORSAY ELMER P	1LT	0-1112351	1145	2	OSBORNE WALTON L H	COL	0-0147059	0648	3	OSULLIVAN EDMOND J	LTC	0-1011329	0860	1
OREILLY JOHN V	MAJ	0-0406998	0961	1	ORSBORN ERNEST V	LTC	0-0319827	0264	3	OSBORNE WILLIAM	CW4	W-2131047	0566	1	OSULLIVAN FRANK D	1LT	0-1310869	104N	2
OREILLY JOSEPH G	1LT	0-1323346	114N	2	ORSBORN GEORGE E JR	1LT	0-0443610	0345	2	OSBOURN GEORGE R	CPT	0-2032942	0859	1	OSULLIVAN GEORGE W	COL	0-0284871	0646	2
OREILLY ROBERT M	MAJ	0-1826293	0666	2	ORSER LYON C	MAJ	0-1582333	0862	2	OSBOURN WARREN F	CPT	0-2263271	0961	1	OSULLIVAN JACK M	CPT	0-0338920	0445	2
OREM CHARLES W	CPT	0-0318723	1044	2	ORSINI PAUL	LTC	0-1002701	0658	1	OSBURN BENJAMIN F	LTC	0-1584703	1054	1	OSULLIVAN JAMES V	1LT	0-0962623	0157	1
OREM WILLIAM W	MAJ	0-0208231	0257	3	ORSON ELLIOTT A	CPT	0-0468163	0745	2	OSBURN EMMITT W	CW4	RW-2133714	0564	1	OSULLIVAN JOHN F	CPT	0-1014318	0448	2
OREN WILLIAM C	LTC	0-0529605	0867	3	ORSON OLIVER W	MAJ	0-0301522	0147	2	OSBURN GABRIEL W	1LT	0-0532149	1047	2	OSULLIVAN ROBERT W	MAJ	0-0990939	0268	1
OREND JACK F	LTC	0-1585988	0766	1	ORSTAD EDWARD L	COL	0-0298776	0857	1	OSBURN JAMES C	MAJ	0-1178923	0161	1	OSWALD CLETUS J	LTC	0-0263866	1057	3
ORENDORF CARROLL A	1LT	0-1176460	0945	2	ORSZULAK MICHAEL J	MAJ	0-1323266	0261	1	OSBURN LEROY	LTC	0-1295262	0954	1	OSWALD RALPH J W	COL	0-0294657	0863	1
ORENDORFF LLOYD E	CPT	0-0117859	0554	3	ORT JOHN P	MAJ	0-0225795	0165	3	OSBURN RICHARD P	MAJ	0-1799979	0658	1	OSWALT JAMES D	2LT	0-1181398	0944	2
ORENDORFF ROBERT D	MAJ	0-2012665	0663	1	ORT VEE L	MAJ	N-0768381	0968	1	OSCHWALD EMIL C	CW2	W-2111341	0650	2	OTENBERGER JOHN L	MAJ	0-2263383	1065	1
ORENSTEIN LEO L	MAJ	0-0346845	0446	2	ORTEGA MANUEL M	CW2	W-2209157	0964	1	OSCHWALD LAWRENCE W	MAJ	0-0340813	0966	3	OTERI JOHN	CW4	W-2110317	0859	1
ORESCHAK ANDREW	1LT	0-2007045	0647	2	ORTEGO CRESENCIO	WO1	W-2129629	1146	2	OSEKOWSKI THOMAS J	LTC	0-1101149	1160	1	OTERO TULIO	CW3	W-2147638	1160	1
ORESS CHARLES E	CW3	W-2149582	0964	1	ORTH FRANKLIN L	COL	0-0307198	0667	3	OSEN BERT U	MAJ	0-1686197	0166	1	OTEY IVO F	COL	0-0246568	1264	3
ORF ROBERT C	MAJ	0-0390145	0847	2	ORTH HAYES J	MAJ	0-1031671	0960	1	OSENKOWSKI KAROL P	WO1	W-2122710	0345	2	OTIS EARL R	LTC	0-0290632	0868	3
ORFANOS CONSTANTIN	LTC	0-0908532	0166	3	ORTH JOHN M	CPT	0-0153923	0751	3	OSGOOD BASIL F	MAJ	0-1046559	1061	1	OTIS FREDERIC S	MAJ	0-1305101	0665	3
ORFF DALE V	MAJ	0-1285484	0163	1	ORTHEY GEORGE F	LTC	0-0185187	0653	3	OSGOOD DEXTER T	LTC	0-0273283	0367	3	OTIS HAROLD	CPT	0-0477958	0247	1
ORGEL SAMUEL Z	LTC	0-0104405	0255	3	ORTHNER WALTER H	MAJ	0-0480583	0657	1	OSGOOD DONALD W	LTC	0-1252744	0262	1	OTIS WILLIAM L	MAJ	0-1042665	0859	1
ORI GEORGE	LTC	0-1309308	0261	1	ORTIZ ALEJANDRO	CPT	0-0108224	0848	2	OSGOOD FRANK G	CPT	0-0220153	1050	3	OTOOLE CHARLES V	CPT	0-0938143	0956	1
ORI STEPHEN J	MAJ	0-1173026	1060	1	ORTIZ CLEMENTE M	1LT	0-1896679	0365	2	OSGOOD FRANKLIN H	COL	0-0305623	1164	3	OTOOLE JOHN H	MAJ	0-0312499	0946	2
ORILEY LESTER E	LTC	0-1011852	0163	1	ORTIZ JOSE A	CPT	0-0401879	0461	1	OSHAUGHNESSY JOHN	1LT	0-1799069	0851	2	OTOOLE JOSEPH F	CPT	0-1593156	0457	1
ORILEY ROBERT M	LTC	0-2010615	0866	1	ORTIZ JOSE R	2LT	0-1318820	0445	2	OSHAUGHNESSY JOHN F	MAJ	0-1824356	0459	2	OTOOLE WILLIAM F	CW4	W-2142307	0758	2
ORIN LAWRENCE E	LTC	0-1108216	0962	1	ORTIZ SILVESTRE	LTC	0-0382119	0960	1	OSHAUGHNESSY PATRI	1LT	0-1017747	0846	2	OTOOLE WILLIAM J	2LT	0-1054744	0645	2
ORINGDERFF LOYD G	CPT	0-2009493	0956	1	ORTIZ-CUENCAS JOSE	CW2	W-2210743	0865	1	OSHEA EDWARD A	LTC	0-0258474	0466	3	OTOOLE WILLIAM L	CPT	0-1172973	0949	2

NAME	GRADE	SVC NO	DATE RET MO YR	RET CODE
OTDUSA JANE C	2LT	N-0762090	0245	1
OTSEA MARSHALL S	MAJ	0-1339305	0365	1
OTSTOT RICHARD G	LTC	0-0295563	0666	3
OTT ARTHUR A	LTC	0-1168402	1060	1
OTT CHARLES H JR	COL	0-0218491	0159	2
OTT CLIFFORD S	LTC	0-0297025	0263	1
OTT DONALD I	LTC	0-2021291	0968	1
OTT DOYLE C	MAJ	0-0508917	0646	2
OTT EDWARD V	1LT	0-1311199	0945	2
OTT GLENN J	1LT	0-0382090	1044	2
OTT JOHN F	LTC	0-0319035	0762	1
OTT JOHN J JR	CPT	0-0464204	0744	2
OTT JOSEPH T	CPT	0-0333097	0450	2
OTT LLOYD V	LTC	0-1337332	0468	2
OTT RALPH J W	CPT	0-1322365	0847	2
OTT RICHARD R	MAJ	0-0151726	0357	3
OTT ROBERT S	CW2	W-2141400	1057	1
OTT ROBERT T	CW2	W-2146890	0661	1
OTT ROBERT W	LTC	0-1036665	0664	2
OTTAVI ROMOLO F	LTC	0-1302871	0767	1
OTTAVIANO ANTONIO F	CW2	W-2145476	0660	1
OTTAWAY LESTER R	WO1	W-2116023	1055	1
OTTE FREDERICK	WO1	W-2114665	0756	1
OTTE JOSEPH S JR	CW3	W-3200166	0668	1
OTTE RALPH E	LTC	0-0242019	0456	3
OTTEN JACK A	MAJ	0-0364545	0667	3
OTTEN JOHN H	MAJ	0-1307065	0459	1
OTTEN WILLIAM C	B G	0-0470649	0761	3
OTTERPOHL HENRY J	2LT	0-1914152	1046	1
OTTERSON GEORGE L	LTC	0-0273535	0868	3
OTTINGER GEORGE W	CW3	W-2142598	0161	1
OTTINGER LOWELL T	LTC	0-0454089	0561	1
OTTMAN EDWARD J JR	LTC	0-2262277	0868	1
OTTMANN EDWARD C	MAJ	0-0455988	0757	1
OTTO CARL E	LTC	0-0235939	1155	3
OTTO EARL F JR	COL	0-0460664	0768	1
OTTO ELIZABETH	MAJ	L-0220094	0168	3
OTTO EMIL H	1LT	0-1032383	0845	2
OTTO GEORGE N	MAJ	0-0337802	0567	3
OTTO JOHN	LTC	0-1030182	0661	1
OTTO RAYMOND H	MAJ	0-0229777	0365	3
OTTO ROBERT G	CW2	W-2146889	0764	1
OTTOFY LADIS H	1LT	0-0131120	0657	3
OTTOVICH LOUIS	MAJ	0-1048521	0268	3
OTTS SHERMAN R	CW2	W-2142121	0662	1
OTTWILLER ROBERT F	CW2	W-2210893	0762	1
OUELLETTE CHARLES E	CW4	W-2106323	1066	1
OUILETTE JAMES J	CPT	0-0410376	1144	2
OUSLEY IVON L	CW2	W-2145900	1057	1
OUTEN DEWEY L	MAJ	0-0220938	1051	2
OUTLAND ORLANDO T	MAJ	0-0948897	0462	1
OUTLAW ARTHUR T	LTC	0-1584705	0963	1
OUTLAW VENIRA E	MAJ	N-0763230	0966	2
OUTMAN HARL F	MAJ	0-1103849	0863	1
OUTSEN ROBERT K	1LT	0-1549001	0145	2
OUTTEN ALMA J	1LT	N-0743610	1145	1
OUTTEN EDGAR C	LTC	0-0153650	0-51	3
OUTTERSON CHARLES W	CPT	0-0256112	1160	3
OVELMEN HERMAN D	COL	0-0289573	0965	3
OVENS MELVON J	MAJ	0-0284053	1166	3
OVER FRANK JR	LTC	0-0103033	0256	3
OVERACKER ALVIN G	CW2	W-3430442	0966	1
OVERALL RALPH E	CW3	W-2212877	1168	1
OVERBAY CLARENCE M	CW3	W-2142014	0764	1
OVERBAY JOSEPH G JR	CW4	W-2004581	1168	1
OVERBAY ROY V	2LT	0-1322587	0745	2
OVERBECK ALVIN H	MAJ	0-0552007	0664	1
OVERBY EDWARD J	MAJ	0-0525219	1045	2
OVERCASH DENNIS B	MAJ	0-0162580	0158	3
OVERFIELD ELIJAH H	LTC	0-0487651	0452	1
OVERGAARD TERANCE E	LTC	0-0264314	0866	3
OVERHOLSER DEWEY L	MAJ	0-0242622	1058	3
OVERHOLTZER HARRY A	LTC	0-0332234	0461	1
OVERLEE DONALD	CPT	0-1553329	0755	1
OVERLEY RAYMOND J	CW2	W-2143518	1156	1

NAME	GRADE	SVC NO	DATE RET MO YR	RET CODE
OVERLOCK WALTER E JR	MAJ	0-1590088	0761	1
OVERMAN GERARD B	MAJ	0-1897800	1162	1
OVERMAN GLEN W	LTC	0-0294852	0668	3
OVERMYER CALVIN J	COL	0-0218884	0257	3
OVERMYER CHARLES E	MAJ	0-0400482	0462	1
OVERSTREET CHARLES O	MAJ	0-1000836	0860	1
OVERSTREET CLAUDE L	MAJ	0-2002513	0762	1
OVERTON AMOS	CW2	W-2205568	0961	1
OVERTON GLEN D	1LT	0-1304781	0646	2
OVERTON IRVING J	CPT	0-0527129	0345	2
OVERTON LEMUEL H	1LT	0-0281225	0345	2
OVERTON MACK W	1LT	0-0483157	0447	1
OVERTON ROBERT H	LTC	0-0271857	0361	3
OVERTURF ARCHIE M	1LT	0-0506237	0351	1
OVERTURF ARNOLD A	LTC	0-2048737	0564	1
OVERTURF VERNON E	MAJ	0-0979458	0762	1
OVIATT WELLS	MAJ	0-0168986	0647	2
OWEN ALBERT E	1LT	0-1325351	0147	2
OWEN ALBERT S	COL	0-0247659	1265	3
OWEN BASCOM S	MAJ	0-0293481	0368	3
OWEN CHARLES J	LTC	0-0313585	1058	1
OWEN CLARENCE I	COL	0-0210363	1156	3
OWEN EDWARD E	MAJ	0-2006071	1160	1
OWEN GARLAND M	MAJ	0-0287408	0264	3
OWEN GEORGE R	LTC	0-0343412	0759	1
OWEN HARRY M	MAJ	0-0153640	0456	3
OWEN HOLLAND M	CW4	W-2145980	1268	1
OWEN HOWARD P	CW2	W-2150773	1061	1
OWEN JACK D	MAJ	0-0358568	0449	1
OWEN JACK S	COL	0-0363845	0761	1
OWEN JAMES B	LTC	0-1824907	0867	1
OWEN JAMES D	1LT	0-0885727	1045	2
OWEN JAMES G	CPT	0-0968077	0461	1
OWEN JAMES R	1LT	0-0108535	0134	1
OWEN JOHN M	LTC	0-0535161	1267	3
OWEN JOSEPH A	MAJ	0-0252138	1166	3
OWEN JOSEPH H	MAJ	0-1996623	0162	1
OWEN PHILIP M	CW3	W-2211116	0868	1
OWEN RICHARD W	COL	0-0211765	0960	1
OWEN ROBERT D	CPT	0-1048522	0647	2
OWEN ROBERT W	COL	0-0358421	0461	1
OWEN ROY W	LTC	0-1174095	0461	1
OWEN RUTH W	MAJ	N-0741649	0164	3
OWEN SAMMIE H	MAJ	0-1048131	1060	1
OWEN SEWARD E	COL	0-0201536	1058	3
OWEN WALTER O	CPT	0-0413993	1062	2
OWEN WESLEY C	LTC	0-0220752	0461	1
OWEN WILLIAM W	MAJ	0-2014057	0567	1
OWEN WILLIE J	CPT	0-0409572	0146	2
OWENS ANDRE H	MAJ	0-1001025	0664	1
OWENS BENJAMIN T	MAJ	0-0328932	1164	3
OWENS BENNETT G	COL	0-0224270	0361	3
OWENS BILLIE G	CW2	W-3430427	0966	1
OWENS CHARLES F	LTC	0-1171303	0962	1
OWENS CHARLES W JR	MAJ	0-2212019	0464	1
OWENS CLARENCE P	CW4	W-2000628	0261	3
OWENS CLEO H	LTC	0-1052113	0166	1
OWENS EARL H	CPT	0-0969228	1061	2
OWENS EDWARD A	CPT	0-1726066	0146	2
OWENS EDWARD H	CW2	W-2142888	0764	1
OWENS EDWARD J	MAJ	0-0137488	0648	3
OWENS EUGENE R	1LT	0-1111820	1046	2
OWENS FRED	CW4	W-2146677	0757	1
OWENS FREDERICK	1LT	0-4030832	0459	2
OWENS GLADYS E	MAJ	N-0759878	0263	1
OWENS HAROLD C	MAJ	0-1636435	0960	1
OWENS HENRY M	LTC	0-1580130	0658	1
OWENS HERBERT T	MAJ	0-1057556	0865	1
OWENS HERMAN	2LT	0-1951630	0750	2
OWENS JAMES C	LTC	0-1180655	0663	1
OWENS JAMES E	MAJ	0-1578945	0261	1
OWENS JAMES M	1LT	0-1015162	0367	1
OWENS JAMES W JR	CPT	0-0309861	0442	2
OWENS JESSE L	CW4	W-2153265	0166	1
OWENS JOHN B	MAJ	0-1108908	0466	1

NAME	GRADE	SVC NO	DATE RET MO YR	RET CODE
OWENS JOHN D JR	CPT	0-1326015	0647	2
OWENS JOSEPH F	LTC	0-1108909	0962	1
OWENS JOSEPH H	LTC	0-0230093	1165	3
OWENS JUDSON E JR	LTC	0-0555567	1265	1
OWENS KENNETH G	1LT	0-1590714	0245	2
OWENS LAWRENCE H	MAJ	0-1323024	0963	1
OWENS LAWTON K	MAJ	0-0462605	0862	1
OWENS MARVIN A	CW2	W-3150536	0365	1
OWENS MARY H	1LT	N-0723333	0146	1
OWENS MATTHEW J	CPT	0-0157787	1059	3
OWENS MAURICE J	LTC	0-0336916	0762	3
OWENS MAURICE T	LTC	0-0259389	1166	3
OWENS MERVIL C	MAJ	0-2262288	0863	1
OWENS ROBERT E	MAJ	0-2047098	0759	1
OWENS ROBERT J	COL	0-0515777	0568	3
OWENS ROBERT V	LTC	0-0524053	0763	1
OWENS ROBERT W	1LT	0-1823924	0546	2
OWENS ROSS	COL	0-0263873	0966	3
OWENS THEODORE R	LTC	0-0558201	1064	1
OWENS THOMAS M	LTC	0-0420739	0566	1
OWENS TRACY C	LTC	0-0490887	0545	2
OWENS WILLIAM C	1LT	0-2026911	1046	2
OWENS WILLIAM F	CPT	0-0918660	0445	2
OWENS WILLIAM H	LTC	0-0444895	0747	1
OWENS WILLIAM H JR	CPT	0-1303384	0147	2
OWENS WILLIAM I	CPT	0-0472007	1047	2
OWENS WILLIAM L	CW2	W-2152831	0557	1
OWINGS DORSEY	COL	0-0286518	0256	3
OWINGS ORVILLE M	LTC	0-1289473	0157	1
OWINGS WALTON A	2LT	0-0507896	0144	2
OWNBY KEITH M	MAJ	0-1304108	1163	1
OWNEY HOLMAN E	MAJ	0-1016070	0561	1
OWSLEY EDWARD A	COL	0-0414501	0466	1
OWSLEY GUY A	COL	0-0254641	0364	3
OWSLEY LINTON L	MAJ	0-0981680	0764	1
OXENDINE MELYAR R	MAJ	0-2014445	0662	1
OXENREIDER GEORGE O	CW3	W-2205183	1068	1
OXFORD WILLIAM D	CPT	0-0238589	0761	3
OXLEY DELBERT F	2LT	0-1999304	0448	2
OXLEY JOSEPH C	LTC	0-0204148	0756	3
OXLEY LAWRENCE A	1LT	0-0127499	0648	3
OXLEY LEWIS P	MAJ	0-4074732	0967	1
OXTON CHARLES A	2LT	0-1946128	1144	2
OXWANG MARGARET	1LT	N-0736483	0247	1
OYLER DONALD C	CW3	W-2147364	0165	1
OYLER FRANK H	CPT	0-1556774	0561	1
OYLER MAURICE W JR	CW4	W-2006319	1168	1
OYLER URAL E	MAJ	0-1013294	0860	1
OZENBERGER PETER F	MAJ	0-1285284	1056	1
OZIER RAYFIELD SR	CW2	W-2141401	0856	2
OZMUN CHARLES G	CPT	0-0279175	0844	2
OZSVATH DANIEL R	CPT	0-0500057	1046	2
PAAR EDWARD G	LTC	0-0298649	0159	1
PAAR ROBERT J	MAJ	0-1608496	0765	1
PABLO AGAPITO R	1LT	0-1896490	0366	1
PABON&RAMIREZ W	WO1	W-2113970	0446	2
PABST EDWIN D	1LT	0-0516715	1047	2
PACE BONNIE L	CW3	W-2150035	0962	1
PACE CARL	MAJ	0-0995805	0668	1
PACE CHARLES M	CPT	0-1535611	0366	1
PACE FRED C	1LT	0-1103358	1045	2
PACE GEORGE A	MAJ	0-1107018	0267	3
PACE GEORGE D	2LT	0-1039499	1044	2
PACE GEORGE E	CW2	W-3100690	0968	1
PACE LORAN A	LTC	0-0545451	0364	1
PACE OTIS	MAJ	0-1634194	0854	1
PACE RENTIS E	LTC	0-1548273	0757	1
PACE SMITH H JR	LTC	0-1578946	0461	1
PACEK LOUIS E	CW2	W-2143393	1157	2
PACELLA RALPH M	1LT	0-1168854	0146	2
PACETTI AMEDEO E	CPT	0-0517459	0545	2
PACHECO EDWARD F	LTC	0-1100714	1160	1
PACHECO EDWARD J	CW2	W-2146737	0561	1
PACHECO ESTHER M	CPT	N-0900805	0263	2
PACHL LADDIE J	CPT	0-0255656	0862	3

NAME	GRADE	SVC NO	DATE RET MO YR	RET CODE
PACIFICO ALEXANDER	MAJ	0-0969838	1064	2
PACK HENRY B JR	MAJ	0-0315065	0646	2
PACK LAMONT A	LTC	0-0232389	0757	3
PACK MYRTLE I	1LT	N-0730647	0946	1
PACK PHILIP C	COL	0-0170735	0554	3
PACKARD BRUCE G	MAJ	0-0285931	1066	3
PACKARD FRANK O JR	LTC	0-2206423	1267	1
PACKARD JOHN K	MAJ	0-0172335	1048	2
PACKARD LYLE O	MAJ	0-0390934	0861	1
PACKARD RUSSEL L	LTC	0-1039277	0962	1
PACKER ALMA S	COL	0-0199890	0-52	3
PACKER DAVID A	LTC	0-2051271	1166	1
PACKER JACOB L	MAJ	0-0400694	0163	1
PACKER NORMAN N	1LT	0-1040997	0445	2
PACKER ROY F	CPT	0-1060579	0447	2
PACOCHA EDMUND S	CPT	0-1684346	0545	2
PACULA STEVEN J	1LT	0-0402302	1044	2
PACULIS GEORGE B	MAJ	0-1062622	0164	1
PADALINO MARTIN L	LTC	0-0070463	1167	1
PADAN FRANK L	2LT	0-1116536	0946	2
PADAONG CONSTANTIN	1LT	0-2031920	0149	1
PADDENBURG JOHN A	LTC	0-0451370	0660	1
PADDOCK CLINTON T	LTC	0-0232005	0465	3
PADDOCK FREDERICK	MAJ	0-0417328	0946	2
PADDOCK HOWARD P	LTC	0-0178103	0648	3
PADDOCK LEROY	CW4	W-2103782	0957	1
PADDOCK RALF C	COL	0-0182590	0446	2
PADDOCK ROBERT H	COL	0-0234415	1065	3
PADDOCK STILES R	LTC	0-0300501	1065	1
PADEN DONALD G	CW4	W-2136333	1160	1
PADEN FREDERICK	LTC	0-1590555	0868	3
PADGET HENRY F JR	1LT	0-0540402	0446	2
PADGETT BENNIE	MAJ	0-1303017	0459	1
PADGETT EDMOND J	LTC	0-0345017	0660	1
PADGETT EUGENE C	COL	0-0314533	0559	1
PADGETT EWART M	1LT	0-2025253	0168	2
PADGETT JOEL J	LTC	0-0209103	1147	2
PADGETT JOHN L	MAJ	0-1876933	1166	1
PADGETT LORENZO D	MAJ	0-0497004	0756	1
PADGETT MEADE M	CW2	W-2207366	0762	1
PADGETT PAUL J	MAJ	0-2033068	1262	1
PADGETT PHILIP G	CPT	0-0482455	0447	2
PADGETT ROBERT G	LTC	0-0177274	1161	3
PADGITT JAMES T	MAJ	0-0244920	1144	2
PADIAL ISABEL R	MAJ	N-0800252	0865	1
PADILLA FRANCISCO	COL	0-0360316	0868	3
PADILLA JAIME L	CPT	0-0450379	1060	1
PADLAR PEGGY A	2LT	L-0210160	0645	2
PADLEY EVERETT J	LTC	0-0297913	0864	3
PADLON JOSEPH F	COL	0-0205557	0760	3
PADMORE WILLIAM G	CW3	W-2149876	0663	1
PADRICK WALTER R	LTC	0-0254414	0162	1
PADRTA NORMAN L	2LT	0-1590093	0344	2
PADUA MARIANO	2LT	0-1896608	0750	1
PADVORAC VICTOR A	1LT	0-1308853	1044	2
PAEPER HENRY	MAJ	0-0256353	0662	3
PAEPKE HAROLD M	MAJ	0-1181069	0963	1
PAFENBERG ROY E	MAJ	0-2027357	0562	1
PAFFORD PARNELL M	COL	0-0272214	0563	1
PAFFORD ROBERT B JR	MAJ	0-0960103	0264	1
PAGAC BENEDICT B	LTC	0-1339559	1066	1
PAGAN FRANCISCO	LTC	0-0298806	0467	3
PAGAN LUIS R	CW2	W-2154862	1060	1
PAGANI FEDERICO JR	CPT	0-2262642	0261	1
PAGANO RICHARD L	CPT	0-1017855	0346	2
PAGE CANNON R	MAJ	0-0241933	0962	3
PAGE CHARLES A	LTC	0-0361734	0859	1
PAGE CHARLES E	LTC	0-0422077	0760	1
PAGE DAVID P	COL	0-0204809	0262	3
PAGE DON E	MAJ	0-1923696	1068	1
PAGE EDSEL F	CPT	0-2014548	0366	1
PAGE EDWIN R	MAJ	0-0199862	0648	3
PAGE GEORGE H	LTC	0-1635187	1266	1
PAGE HENRY L JR	MAJ	0-0990415	1064	2
PAGE HERMAN R	LTC	0-0151845	1054	3

NAME	GRADE	SVC NO	DATE RET MO YR	RET CODE
PAGE IVAN H	MAJ	0-1020515	0768	1
PAGE JAMES A	MAJ	0-0272102	1166	3
PAGE JAMES E	CPT	0-1290991	0348	2
PAGE JESSE B	MAJ	0-0247287	0167	3
PAGE JOHN B	1LT	0-0498039	0846	1
PAGE JOHN J JR	MAJ	0-1012226	0361	1
PAGE JOHN W JR	MAJ	0-0385136	0646	2
PAGE JOSEPH E	LTC	0-2030621	0267	1
PAGE KENNETH J	1LT	0-1645899	0145	2
PAGE LESLIE K	MAJ	0-0972813	0962	1
PAGE NOBLE W	1LT	0-0404282	0745	2
PAGE OTTO C	CPT	0-0448618	0547	2
PAGE PAUL E	MAJ	0-1340924	1163	1
PAGE ROBERT C	MAJ	0-0324117	1145	2
PAGE ROBERT L JR	2LT	0-1289789	0645	2
PAGE ROBERT R JR	CPT	0-5301900	0768	1
PAGE VICTOR S	MAJ	0-0475727	0953	1
PAGE WILLIAM F	CPT	0-1881954	0963	1
PAGE WILLIAM M	MAJ	0-2208586	0766	1
PAGE WILLIS M	MAJ	0-1104328	0961	1
PAGEL HERBERT E	MAJ	0-1045546	1065	1
PAGELS EDWARD A	CPT	0-2262921	0361	1
PAGLIERANI LOUIS J	LTC	0-1101981	0161	1
PAGNOTTA FRANK R	LTC	0-2000817	0965	1
PAHL JOSEPH W	1LT	0-0539209	0446	2
PAHLE JOSEPH F	1LT	0-0524626	1046	2
PAIGE BYRON L	COL	0-0018704	1060	1
PAIGE CLAUDE	CPT	0-1323607	0455	2
PAIGE JOSEPH	1LT	0-1596460	114N	2
PAIGE ROLAND W	MAJ	0-1895512	0466	3
PAINE ALBERT W	COL	0-0151120	0648	3
PAINE ANDREW	LTC	0-0815226	0767	1
PAINE CHARLES B	LTC	0-0359132	1046	2
PAINE CHARLES G JR	2LT	0-2010796	0746	2
PAINE EDWARD V	1LT	0-1547098	0266	1
PAINE EUGENE M	CPT	0-0401873	0645	2
PAINE FRANK L	CPT	0-0256979	1064	3
PAINE HENRY E	MAJ	0-1181400	0760	1
PAINE JOHN R	LTC	0-0284794	1266	3
PAINE MELVIN R	WO1	W-2151635	1053	1
PAINE ROBERT L	CW3	W-2146350	0363	1
PAINTER BENJAMIN F	CPT	0-0149083	0653	3
PAINTER CHARLES O	CPT	0-0238740	0264	3
PAINTER DAVID R	WO1	W-2142773	0756	1
PAINTER FREDERICK	MAJ	0-1585996	0447	2
PAINTER HARRY J	LTC	0-0941993	0366	1
PAINTER JAMES P	1LT	0-0447044	1145	2
PAINTER KENNETH D	1LT	0-1924797	0753	2
PAINTER LOWELL	1LT	0-1107021	1051	2
PAINTER MARY L	1LT	N-0755031	0646	2
PAIRSH JOHN R	CPT	0-1546019	1051	1
PAISLEY HAROLD	CW2	W-2141403	1054	1
PAISLEY OLDHAM	COL	0-0120285	0553	3
PAISTE ALBERT J	MAJ	0-1885650	1166	1
PAJELA FELIPE R	2LT	0-1896837	0858	1
PAJU OLAF E	CPT	0-2033097	0959	1
PAJUNAS ALBERT	LTC	0-0384447	1060	1
PAKELE PETER N JR	LTC	0-0224738	0954	3
PALACIO FRANK J	MAJ	0-0398123	0248	2
PALACKY FRANK A	LTC	0-1536209	0263	1
PALAGI SETH	LTC	0-0372551	0658	1
PALASKY FRANK	CW2	W-2149936	0261	1
PALAU OTTO G	2LT	0-2009644	0646	2
PALUA ROBERT R	LTC	0-0953903	0764	1
PALEDES NICHOLAS P	LTC	0-1294892	0961	1
PALERMO JOSEPH O	MAJ	0-1297414	0757	1
PALETTA VINCENT R	LTC	0-0999301	0568	1
PALETZ EUGENE	LTC	0-0248086	1058	1
PALEY AARON	CPT	0-0428323	0745	2
PALEY JAMES F	LTC	0-0322368	0662	1
PALEY SIDNEY O	LTC	0-0262271	0668	3
PALFREY THOMAS R	COL	0-0178635	1055	3
PALIN AGNES J	MAJ	N-0757411	0164	3
PALKA STANLEY J	CW2	W-2152280	0860	1
PALKOVIC MICHAEL J	CPT	0-0478880	1059	1

NAME	GRADE	SVC NO	DATE RET MO YR	RET CODE
PALL THOMAS O	1LT	0-1796995	1060	1
PALLA RINALDO F	LTC	0-1648640	0166	1
PALLADINO RALPH A	M G	0-0232912	1064	3
PALLMAN GEORGE H	LTC	0-0282985	0760	1
PALLO GEORGE S	1LT	0-0515634	0446	2
PALLOTTI FRANCIS P	MAJ	0-0102293	1055	3
PALM WILLIAM J	1LT	0-1035332	1045	2
PALMA ANTHONY V	MAJ	0-0346304	0764	3
PALMACCIO CHARLES P	LTC	0-1052913	1167	1
PALMATARY ERNEST E	CPT	0-0346190	0245	2
PALMATIER CHARLES M	1LT	0-1035025	0666	1
PALMER ALBERT J	CPT	0-0524533	0845	2
PALMER ALFRED H	COL	0-0284096	1067	3
PALMER ALGER A	MAJ	0-0168549	0551	3
PALMER ALONZO S	MAJ	0-097C812	1161	1
PALMER BEATRICE B	MAJ	L-1010010	0165	1
PALMER BILLIE F	CW2	W-2214628	0668	1
PALMER CARL J	MAJ	0-1311047	0862	1
PALMER CARL L	LTC	0-1030701	0865	1
PALMER CHARLES B	LTC	0-0451024	0258	2
PALMER CHARLES E	LTC	0-1111286	0464	1
PALMER CHARLES K	CW3	W-2205899	0266	1
PALMER CHARLES L	CPT	0-0202124	0362	3
PALMER CLARENCE E	LTC	0-0285819	0665	3
PALMER CLARK F	CPT	0-1323960	1048	2
PALMER CLETUS T	1LT	0-1280379	0945	2
PALMER CUSTIN C	MAJ	0-1184918	0761	1
PALMER DOMINIC M	MAJ	0-0469827	1045	2
PALMER DONALD B	LTC	0-0166974	0648	3
PALMER EARL J JR	LTC	0-0407863	0663	1
PALMER EDWARD J JR	1LT	0-0983007	0458	1
PALMER ERNEST O	MAJ	0-0226475	0763	3
PALMER FRANCIS J	LTC	0-0388839	1060	1
PALMER FRANK	LTC	0-0492154	0157	1
PALMER FRANK C	CPT	0-1577668	1048	2
PALMER FREDERICK	LTC	0-1290992	0959	1
PALMER GAIL A	CW2	W-2104788	1044	2
PALMER HELEN L	LTC	N-0723014	0562	1
PALMER HENRY U	LTC	0-1057557	0166	1
PALMER JACK	CPT	0-1300370	1053	1
PALMER JACK M	CPT	0-2012844	0457	1
PALMER JAMES P	MAJ	0-0257215	1159	3
PALMER JESSE I	CPT	0-0255262	0766	3
PALMER JEWEL W	CW3	W-2151324	0564	1
PALMER JOHN L	1LT	0-1822721	1145	2
PALMER JOHN W	2LT	0-1332190	0746	2
PALMER JOSEPH H	1LT	0-0201939	0753	3
PALMER JOSEPH P	1LT	0-1320170	1045	2
PALMER JOSEPH W	COL	0-0110603	0754	3
PALMER KARL V	COL	0-0123590	0755	3
PALMER LELAND H	LTC	0-1533882	0461	2
PALMER MAC A	LTC	0-0401497	0453	2
PALMER MARVIN E	1LT	0-1185115	0645	2
PALMER MC KEE A	MAJ	0-0300097	0167	3
PALMER MILBURN L	MAJ	0-0295826	0968	3
PALMER NOBLE E	LTC	0-1551286	0462	1
PALMER NOYES S	MAJ	0-1318077	0457	1
PALMER OSBORN	LTC	0-0100314	0648	3
PALMER OSCAR C JR	CW3	W-3150877	0968	1
PALMER OTIS B	COL	0-0390721	1266	1
PALMER R V	LTC	0-0540396	1063	1
PALMER RALPH J	CW3	W-2145218	1160	1
PALMER RANDOLPH M	MAJ	0-1030400	0459	1
PALMER RAY H	MAJ	0-0212280	0453	3
PALMER RAYMOND C	MAJ	0-0127307	0844	2
PALMER RICHARD H	LTC	0-0911640	0665	3
PALMER ROBERT E	1LT	0-1019973	0647	2
PALMER ROBERT R	CPT	0-0182567	1043	2
PALMER STANLEY A	LTC	0-0357957	0667	3
PALMER THERA O JR	MAJ	0-0268801	1046	2
PALMER THURSTON J	MAJ	0-0317139	0367	3
PALMER TRUMAN G	LTC	0-0299873	0960	1
PALMER WALTER E	COL	0-0115125	0648	3
PALMER WILLIAM E	LTC	0-1172208	1066	1
PALMER WILLIAM G	1LT	0-1825249	0346	2

NAME	GRADE	SVC NO	DATE RET MO YR	RET CODE
PALMER WILLIAM H	MAJ	0-0352010	1262	1
PALMERLEE ALBERT S	COL	0-0261800	0268	3
PALMERLEE JOHN D	1LT	0-0481336	0445	2
PALMERTON RUSSELL J	MAJ	0-1313441	0858	2
PALMIERI FRANK F	WO1	W-2124067	0443	2
PALMORE AARON D	LTC	0-0412866	0560	1
PALMQUIST HOWARD D	MAJ	0-0963863	0761	1
PALMQUIST MILFORD H	MAJ	0-0508058	0159	1
PALMQUIST ROY M	CPT	0-1313787	0159	2
PALUMBO ALFRED	COL	0-1172209	1168	1
PALUMBO ANTHONY A	LTC	0-0372960	1164	1
PALUMBO GERALD A	MAJ	0-0397068	0146	2
PALUMBO JOSEPH G	CPT	0-0240964	1161	3
PALUMBO LEONARD J	MAJ	0-0423164	1262	1
PALUMBO RICHARD J	LTC	0-1580137	1066	1
PALYOK JOHN JR	MAJ	0-1171306	0262	1
PALZKILL ANNA M	LTC	N-0730227	0561	1
PAMER JOHN A JR	1LT	0-1326229	1145	2
PAMPLIN JOHN W	COL	0-0266829	0968	3
PAMPLIN LLOYD	CPT	0-1575052	0358	1
PANAGOPOULOS PETER P	CW3	W-2144978	0962	1
PANAGOT GEORGE J	2LT	0-1302872	1044	2
PANAK VINCENT	CPT	0-1101608	0747	2
PANAPOLIS PETER J	CPT	0-0274859	0160	3
PANCOAST KATHERINE	CPT	N-0729053	0646	2
PANCOOK ARTHUR J	COL	0-0299366	0567	3
PANEK JOHN M	1LT	0-1634200	0947	2
PANGBORN RICHARD K	CW3	W-2208127	0566	1
PANIAN DONALD J	MAJ	0-1876994	1264	1
PANICH HAROLD L	1LT	0-1171307	0346	2
PANISH CHARLES K	COL	0-0908231	0567	3
PANIZZI RICHARD J	CPT	0-5301791	0768	1
PANKER JOSEPH F	LTC	0-1535049	1266	1
PANKEY ELDRIDGE T	MAJ	0-1301202	0761	1
PANKEY HENRY G	WO1	W-2127650	0550	1
PANKEY JAMES E	CW2	W-2143341	0162	1
PANKOSKY JOHN J	LTC	0-1283475	0657	1
PANKRATZ ROBERT R	CW2	W-2210842	0765	2
PANNEBAKER CHARLES P	CW2	W-2142568	0761	1
PANNECK THEODORE W	LTC	0-0407704	1060	1
PANNELL EARL R	1LT	0-1318572	1045	2
PANNELL GEORGE E	LTC	0-1050855	0162	1
PANORA ANTHONY	MAJ	0-0125985	0858	3
PANORI ARTHUR	CPT	0-5419813	0868	2
PANOS MICHAEL	CPT	0-0941998	0657	1
PANOTES RICARDO	1LT	0-1896757	0862	1
PANTALEO FRANK A	1LT	0-1003425	0652	2
PANTAZI SPIROS G	1LT	0-0550183	1045	2
PANTERA ALBIN M	CPT	0-1717800	1046	2
PANTON WILLIAM A	LTC	0-0203771	0553	3
PANTSARI ERIC W	MAJ	0-1306137	0563	1
PANUZIO FRANK L	LTC	0-0273647	0867	3
PANZARINO ANGELO	MAJ	0-1298585	0461	1
PAOLI LOUIS S	1LT	0-1317106	0645	2
PAOLINI MARIO	MAJ	0-1039587	0860	1
PAOLUCCI VINCENT P	LTC	0-0540812	0667	2
PAONESSA ROBERT A	MAJ	0-0968640	0764	1
PAPA ANTHONY T	MAJ	0-0420351	0863	1
PAPAE NORMAN	LTC	0-0229696	0262	3
PAPAS ALEXANDER	CPT	0-0510202	114N	2
PAPAZOGLOU GEORGE	CPT	0-1301355	0646	2
PAPE GLENN H	LTC	0-0332584	0561	1
PAPE LEWIS C	2LT	0-1822902	0344	2
PAPE MIRIAM A	CPT	N-0773313	0348	1
PAPEN BERNARD P	COL	0-0236606	0758	1
PAPERNO SAMUEL	CW3	W-2142000	0159	1
PAPIERNIK ADOLPH J	WO1	W-2105891	1146	1
PAPIN JACKIE L	LTC	0-1039148	0868	1
PAPKEE EDWARD E	CPT	0-1535511	0647	2
PAPKEE GUSTAVE A	1LT	0-0127498	0753	3
PAPP EDWARD A	MAJ	0-1636443	0960	1
PAPP EDWIN A	1LT	0-1331326	0946	2
PAPPALARDO CARMELO	CW4	W-2121633	0862	1
PAPPALARDO JOHN	1LT	0-5019627	0566	2
PAPPAS ANGELO	1LT	0-1547738	0146	2

NAME	GRADE	SVC NO	DATE RET MO YR	RET CODE
PAPPAS ANTHONY	CPT	0-1718586	1049	2
PAPPAS ANTHONY J	1LT	0-0438715	0844	2
PAPPAS CONSTANTIN	LTC	0-1041624	0163	1
PAPPAS ERIC W	2LT	0-1996342	0246	2
PAPPAS GEORGE W	1LT	0-2008001	0652	2
PAPPAS NICHOLAS G	LTC	0-1324571	0763	1
PAPPAS NICK G JR	CPT	0-2265239	0765	1
PAPPERITZ ALVIN N	1LT	0-0490114	1050	1
PAPROCI LEONARD C	CPT	0-0544888	0246	2
PAQUETTE HENRY L	LTC	0-1640800	0965	1
PAQUETTE MAURICE G	MAJ	0-2011270	1060	1
PAQUIN JEAN C	CW2	W-2216241	0768	1
PARADIS OMAR M	CW4	W-2001602	1265	3
PARADIS ROGER	2LT	0-1299785	0544	2
PARADISE HAROLD W	2LT	0-0420454	0344	2
PARADY RANSOM O JR	WO1	W-2108634	0844	2
PARAGON LOUIS	LTC	0-0531223	1264	1
PARAISO RUDY V	LTC	0-2210134	1067	1
PARANGAN ANDRES M	2LT	0-1897010	0652	1
PARANO JOSEPH	2LT	0-1176154	0545	2
PARAS BENJAMIN P	2LT	0-1896602	0662	2
PARAYOS STEVE	CW3	W-2142067	0862	1
PARCE CARLTON R	LTC	0-0305834	0168	3
PARCHMAN DAVID S SR	1LT	0-0493992	0650	1
PARDI RICHARD A	1LT	0-4C85201	0260	2
PARDILLA CRISPIN C	2LT	0-2031888	1047	2
PARDO JAMES	CPT	0-0516706	1153	1
PARDON PHILIP V JR	CPT	0-0258599	0568	3
PARDUE ROBERT J	MAJ	0-2285822	0967	1
PARDUE VICTOR E	MAJ	0-1794845	0560	1
PARDUE WOODROW W	1LT	0-0518953	1045	2
PARDUN ERNEST W	1LT	0-1017999	0346	2
PARE JOSEPH A E	1LT	0-0979616	1159	1
PARELLA WILLIAM P	2LT	0-1589424	0444	2
PARENT FRANK R	CPT	0-1289954	1060	1
PARENT JOSEPH A JR	CPT	0-2017745	0762	1
PARENT JOSEPH L C	1LT	0-2046511	0755	1
PARENT LEO J	LTC	0-2208507	0667	1
PARENT ROBERT L	MAJ	0-2035435	1060	1
PARES CESAR	MAJ	0-027C619	0247	1
PARFITT CARL L	LTC	0-1280775	0160	1
PARHAM BILLY S	CPT	0-0527848	0846	2
PARHAM CHARLOTTE	2LT	N-0701925	0642	1
PARHAM CLAUDE	CPT	0-0496380	0647	1
PARHAM FOSTER B	MAJ	0-0491822	1049	1
PARHAM HARRY C	1LT	0-0462660	1045	2
PARHAM JOHN A	1LT	0-0541386	0946	2
PARHAM LLOYD	CPT	0-1301204	0347	2
PARHAM MALVIN J	1LT	0-0833984	1147	2
PARHAM MASTON S	B G	0-0299244	0468	3
PARHAM ROBERT H	CW2	W-2147234	0763	1
PARHAM ROBERT W JR	LTC	0-0227404	0964	3
PARIENT WILLIAM R	LTC	0-0345869	0 47	2
PARILLA JOSEPH	COL	0-0172250	0250	3
PARIS FRANKLYN G	COL	0-0327280	1060	1
PARIS JEWEL M	1LT	0-1294182	0967	1
PARIS JOSEPH	1LT	0-1013540	0945	2
PARIS JOSEPH W	1LT	0-1926184	0454	2
PARIS WILLIAM W	LTC	0-1166804	0266	1
PARISE PETER	1LT	0-2007266	1064	1
PARISEAU WILLIAM E	LTC	0-1289480	0757	1
PARISH ELMO R	COL	0-0397170	1068	3
PARISH JAMES W	CW3	W-2121017	0456	1
PARISH JOHN E	MAJ	0-0310222	0645	2
PARISH JOHN M	LTC	0-1284383	0661	1
PARISH LEAFY M	MAJ	N-0763660	0568	1
PARISH WYATT M	1LT	0-2265154	0354	2
PARISOT LEE J	1LT	0-1686801	0752	2
PARK ALTON E	LTC	0-1332521	1266	1
PARK ANDREW IV	LTC	0-0261338	0462	1
PARK ARTHUR	MAJ	0-0190133	0259	3
PARK BRYCE W	LTC	0-1583473	1161	1
PARK EDWARD L	LTC	0-1795962	1163	1
PARK FRANCIS C	CW4	W-2110422	0258	1
PARK GEORGE A	MAJ	0-4043698	0767	1

NAME	GRADE	SVC NO	DATE RET MO YR	RET CODE
PARK GLENN H	LTC	0-0131319	0854	2
PARK HALL C	COL	0-0261395	0667	1
PARK JAMES H	CPT	0-1283659	0945	2
PARK JAMES K	LTC	0-1016736	0464	1
PARK LUTHER A	CPT	0-0149089	0950	3
PARK MARY B	1LT	N-0728841	0546	1
PARK PRINTES V	CPT	0-0447116	0745	2
PARK RALPH R JR	LTC	0-2033214	0966	1
PARKE FRANCIS W	LTC	0-0182019	0357	3
PARKE JAMES W	LTC	0-0423829	1063	3
PARKE LOUIS L	LTC	0-0223928	0262	3
PARKE ORLAND M JR	CPT	0-1285107	0946	2
PARKER ADAM G	CPT	0-1051324	0651	2
PARKER ADEAN	CPT	N-0735499	0649	2
PARKER ALFRED C	LTC	0-0410125	0565	1
PARKER ALVIN H	COL	0-0341989	0861	1
PARKER ARNOLD G	MAJ	0-2017444	0367	1
PARKER AUSTIN J	MAJ	0-0795621	0866	1
PARKER AUSTIN L	MAJ	0-1825169	0566	1
PARKER BRAXTON C	CPT	0-1303773	1055	1
PARKER BURTON E	LTC	0-0219292	104N	2
PARKER CHALMERS M	LTC	0-0141012	0256	3
PARKER CHARLES A	CW3	W-2210639	0668	1
PARKER CHARLES D	CPT	0-0257755	0467	3
PARKER CHARLIE M	LTC	0-0507677	0154	1
PARKER CLARABEL	CPT	N-0735759	1048	2
PARKER CLARENCE E	COL	0-0102390	1054	3
PARKER CLARENCE E	CPT	0-0127303	0253	3
PARKER CRAYTON A	LTC	0-1182675	0867	1
PARKER DAVID R	LTC	0-1290993	1164	1
PARKER DELBERT	MAJ	0-0454771	0448	2
PARKER DONALD L	CW2	W-3440005	0967	1
PARKER DONALD R	LTC	0-0400271	1060	1
PARKER DONOVAN W	1LT	0-1331764	0347	2
PARKER DUYANE A	LTC	0-0975606	1167	1
PARKER EDGAR A	COL	0-0397877	0860	1
PARKER EDGAR L JR	LTC	0-1168858	0661	1
PARKER EDWARD A	CPT	0-1894938	0354	3
PARKER ELLIS J	CPT	0-2026019	0867	3
PARKER ELMER K	MAJ	0-1300521	0658	1
PARKER EMULON B	1LT	0-0500762	1043	2
PARKER EUAN J	CPT	0-1174098	0661	1
PARKER FORREST R	CW2	W-2145930	0555	1
PARKER FRANCIS W JR	COL	0-0175056	0648	3
PARKER FRANKLIN D	CW3	W-2143773	0764	1
PARKER FRED H	MAJ	0-0413165	1161	1
PARKER FREDERIC T	COL	0-0195994	1157	3
PARKER GARDNER E	CW2	W-2143218	0657	1
PARKER GEORGE C	WO1	W-2114266	0545	2
PARKER GEORGE E	MAJ	0-2263067	1064	1
PARKER GEORGE F	COL	0-0249063	0460	1
PARKER GEORGE J	LTC	0-0305148	1047	2
PARKER GEORGE M	MAJ	0-1639479	1060	1
PARKER GEORGE W	2LT	0-0286882	0368	3
PARKER GUY W	CW2	RW-2149389	0468	1
PARKER HAROLD D	LTC	0-1640802	1165	1
PARKER HARRISON D	MAJ	0-0163028	1048	3
PARKER HARRY	CPT	0-0231121	0949	3
PARKER HARRY S	LTC	0-0229368	1058	3
PARKER HARVEY C	CW3	W-2142125	0662	1
PARKER HOMER V JR	2LT	0-1037666	0745	2
PARKER HOWARD M	MAJ	0-1101610	1053	2
PARKER JACK C	WO1	W-2146839	0755	1
PARKER JAMES A	LTC	0-1310870	0163	1
PARKER JAMES R	LTC	0-0386484	0761	1
PARKER JIMMY W	MAJ	0-1998501	0460	1
PARKER JOEL R	LTC	0-1010182	1047	2
PARKER JOHN A	2LT	0-0538806	0844	2
PARKER JOHN A	CW2	W-3250453	0167	1
PARKER JOHN B	LTC	0-0271347	0666	3
PARKER JOHN R JR	CW2	W-2211054	1167	1
PARKER JOHN L	MAJ	0-0241050	0266	3
PARKER JOHN L	MAJ	0-1577663	0761	1
PARKER JOHN R	LTC	0-0451635	0756	1
PARKER JOHN T	MAJ	0-0168130	0163	3
PARKER JOHNNIE G	CW3	W-2206378	1065	1
PARKER JOSEPH A	LTC	0-1048134	0764	1
PARKER KERMIT R	MAJ	0-1640803	1057	1
PARKER LAURANCE T	MAJ	0-2037087	0866	1
PARKER LEE T F	LTC	0-1946129	1165	3
PARKER LEON	LTC	0-0531649	0746	2
PARKER LEONARD F	MAJ	0-1115731	0559	1
PARKER LESLIE E	LTC	0-0249750	0855	3
PARKER LESLIE T	LTC	0-1641652	0164	1
PARKER LOREN L JR	CPT	0-1595751	0748	2
PARKER LOUIS E	CW2	W-2210640	1065	1
PARKER LOWELL W	MAJ	0-1924052	0963	1
PARKER LUTHER C	CPT	0-1046225	0346	2
PARKER LYLE A	MAJ	0-1643950	0563	1
PARKER MARGARETTE	LTC	L-0701119	1167	1
PARKER MART R	COL	0-1294355	0968	1
PARKER MARY B	LTC	L-0510098	0664	1
PARKER MEYER H	CPT	0-0493868	0345	2
PARKER NELSON H JR	MAJ	0-0276294	0967	3
PARKER OLIVER F	COL	0-0312592	0157	1
PARKER OSCAR D	MAJ	0-0957668	0264	1
PARKER PARKER	COL	0-0220849	1047	2
PARKER PAUL E	MAJ	0-0517937	1045	2
PARKER PAUL R	LTC	0-1331327	0165	1
PARKER PERCY E	LTC	0-0309887	0465	3
PARKER PERCY O	COL	0-0312257	1164	3
PARKER PETER A	MAJ	0-1640804	0760	1
PARKER PHILANDER	CW4	W-2123138	0462	2
PARKER RALPH M	CPT	0-0198644	0954	3
PARKER RAY D	CW2	W-2144079	0959	1
PARKER RAY J	1LT	0-0361382	0445	2
PARKER RICHARD L	CPT	0-1168859	0446	2
PARKER RICHARD M	LTC	0-0350297	0265	1
PARKER RICHARD W	MAJ	0-1639480	0363	1
PARKER RONALD	CW3	W-2117156	0755	1
PARKER SAMUEL I	LTC	0-0180686	1051	3
PARKER SHERROW G	COL	0-0169207	1158	3
PARKER STANTON C	LTC	0-0276236	0157	1
PARKER STEPHEN E	LTC	0-1171710	0261	1
PARKER STEVIE B	MAJ	0-0277992	1046	2
PARKER THOMAS R	LTC	0-0275501	0961	3
PARKER THOMAS S	COL	0-0288816	0665	3
PARKER VIRGIL A	1LT	0-0174948	0362	3
PARKER WALTER J	CPT	0-1292053	0348	2
PARKER WALTER J	CPT	0-2021039	0166	1
PARKER WALTER L	LTC	0-0245980	0155	1
PARKER WALTER L	WO1	W-2117239	1055	1
PARKER WARREN E	LTC	0-0954623	1267	1
PARKER WILBUR E	LTC	0-0194460	1156	3
PARKER WILLARD V	MAJ	0-1690791	0960	1
PARKER WILLIAM	CPT	0-4030933	0765	1
PARKER WILLIAM C	LTC	0-0268316	0868	3
PARKER WILLIAM C	CPT	0-1550675	0661	1
PARKER WILLIAM C	MAJ	0-1686288	1155	1
PARKER WILLIAM D	CPT	0-0417995	0645	2
PARKER WILLIAM E	COL	0-0169349	1060	1
PARKER WILLIAM F	MAJ	0-1885324	1067	1
PARKER WILLIAM M	MAJ	0-0133510	0156	3
PARKER WILLIAM M	LTC	0-2014857	0568	1
PARKER WILLIAM R	CW2	W-2000809	0745	2
PARKER WILLIAM V	LTC	0-0258396	0468	3
PARKER 3RD HERVEY E	1LT	0-0466737	0344	2
PARKERSON HAROLD C	LTC	0-1546848	0662	1
PARKERSON W W SR	WO1	W-2110893	0346	2
PARKES COLIN G	MAJ	0-1100720	0346	2
PARKEY JACK L	CW3	W-2143824	0764	1
PARKHURST CHARLES	1LT	0-1294405	1044	2
PARKHURST DAVID S	MAJ	0-1877812	1266	1
PARKHURST ORVILLE J	MAJ	0-0269653	1057	3
PARKIN CLAIR A	1LT	0-2027426	0646	2
PARKIN HENRY E	CW4	W-2002482	1060	3
PARKINS FREDERICK	MAJ	0-2014470	0865	1
PARKINS GUY W	MAJ	0-0210679	0852	3
PARKINSON DEE R	CPT	0-0478493	0346	2
PARKINSON DON M	1LT	0-1012236	0446	2
PARKINSON GILBERT N	MAJ	0-2055042	0961	1
PARKINSON JOHN F	LTC	0-0139732	1057	3
PARKINSON THOMAS V	MAJ	0-1177130	1163	1
PARKISON RALPH R	CW3	W-2152393	0563	1
PARKMAN EDWARD L	LTC	0-2014619	0968	1
PARKO HENRY J	MAJ	0-2000766	0661	1
PARKS ALVIN J	CW3	W-2144888	1160	1
PARKS BEAUMONT M	MAJ	0-1032300	0768	3
PARKS BERYL F	LTC	0-1284384	0561	1
PARKS CECIL W	MAJ	0-1285487	0856	1
PARKS CECIL W	CPT	0-1822046	0161	2
PARKS CLARENCE C	LTC	0-0445063	1047	2
PARKS CLARENCE F	LTC	0-0273925	1064	3
PARKS DOROTHY R	MAJ	L-1010203	0766	1
PARKS EARL W	LTC	0-0106254	0857	3
PARKS EDWARD D	MAJ	0-1101982	0160	1
PARKS GEORGE M	LTC	0-1895832	0562	1
PARKS GORDON M	LTC	0-2010934	0963	1
PARKS GROVER T	CPT	0-2033291	0554	2
PARKS HARRY E	1LT	0-2055163	0146	2
PARKS HOMER H	CW2	W-2145666	0657	1
PARKS JAMES B	MAJ	0-2017893	0862	1
PARKS JAMES C	COL	0-0153005	0754	3
PARKS JAMES F	MAJ	0-1592498	0859	1
PARKS JAMES L	1LT	0-0492184	0350	1
PARKS JASPER D	1LT	0-1312976	1044	2
PARKS JOHN H	LTC	0-0217807	1262	3
PARKS JOSEPH W	1LT	0-0536437	0145	2
PARKS LAWRENCE	COL	0-0270346	0766	3
PARKS LORENZO L	COL	0-0247996	0466	3
PARKS RALPH G	WO1	W-2116220	0344	2
PARKS RALPH R	COL	0-0221112	0362	3
PARKS RECTOR	CPT	0-0306740	0468	3
PARKS ROWLAND M	LTC	0-0511578	0360	1
PARKS SAMUEL F	MAJ	0-2020459	0161	1
PARKS VELLA E	MAJ	M-0002250	0667	3
PARKS WARREN E	CW2	W-2207506	0663	1
PARKS WILLIAM E	MAJ	0-0386251	0661	1
PARKS WILLIAM E	1LT	0-1950918	0650	2
PARKS WILLIAM T JR	LTC	0-1634202	0761	1
PARLAS JOSEPH L	1LT	0-0483032	0944	2
PARLEE ARTHUR E	LTC	0-0182141	0457	3
PARLIAMENT ALLEN D	MAJ	0-1341186	1265	1
PARLIN GEORGE S	LTC	0-0508804	0246	2
PARLINI CATHERINE	1LT	N-0758750	0847	1
PARMAKIAN JOHN	COL	0-0274135	0968	3
PARMAN KENNETH C	CPT	0-0319712	0768	3
PARMELE LESLIE P	LTC	0-0270085	0467	3
PARMELEE ERNEST H	LTC	0-0295117	0658	3
PARMELEE GLENN C	COL	0-1544021	0661	3
PARMELEE JAMES T	LTC	0-0377895	0646	2
PARMELEE THERON S	LTC	0-0207654	0656	3
PARMENTER ALFRED C	CPT	0-0393242	0646	2
PARMENTER CAROLINE S	1LT	N-0764153	0846	1
PARMENTER EDWARD D	MAJ	0-0387247	0960	1
PARMENTIER HAROLD J	1LT	0-2035664	0945	2
PARMER GLENN G	COL	0-0399914	1262	1
PARMETER BERNARD W	2LT	0-1294525	0645	2
PARMETT ALAN	2LT	0-1638221	0944	2
PARNASS EMANUEL R	LTC	0-0171701	0653	3
PARNELL CHARLES F	CW3	W-2152735	1063	1
PARNELL CHARLIE L	CPT	0-0238058	0745	2
PARNELL GEORGE A	LTC	0-1103852	0162	1
PARNELL HUBERT N	LTC	0-0168648	1060	3
PARNELL RICHARD	LTC	0-0160310	1056	3
PARNELL SAMUEL A	CW3	W-2142048	0863	1
PARNELL WILLIAM C	LTC	0-0199729	1045	2
PARNELLE MILTON H	LTC	0-1171711	0960	1
PARNESS HENRY	LTC	0-1165771	0562	1
PARNIN JOHN R	COL	0-0201334	0957	3
PAROLARI BERT W	LTC	0-1020491	0866	1
PARR CHARLES H	MAJ	0-1327038	1061	1
PARR FRANKLIN A	CW3	W-2149400	0263	1
PARR GEORGE W	LTC	0-1001658	0463	1
PARR HENRY H	MAJ	0-2262688	0168	1
PARR J C	MAJ	0-0472647	0955	1
PARR JOE B	COL	0-0261548	0568	3
PARR JOHN E	MAJ	0-0496952	1047	1
PARR PERRY L	LTC	0-0175561	0756	3
PARR VIRON P	COL	0-0231727	0763	3
PARRA FRANCISCO	COL	0-0253714	0646	2
PARRACK CECIL T	MAJ	0-1181072	0358	1
PARRACK DONALD L	MAJ	0-1703002	1060	1
PARRAMORE BENJAMIN B	LTC	0-1306463	0763	1
PARREN JOSEPH S	LTC	0-1186774	0567	2
PARRES LAWRENCE J	CW3	W-2150101	0564	1
PARRETT JOSEPH W	MAJ	0-1558603	0863	1
PARRILLO ANTHONY C	CPT	0-0502829	0146	2
PARRINO PAUL S	LTC	0-0198992	0561	3
PARRIS RALPH D	LTC	0-1310144	0263	1
PARRIS TOM B	LTC	0-1307776	1063	1
PARRIS WARREN M	1LT	0-0539297	0645	2
PARRISH BRUCE W	LTC	0-0935765	0968	2
PARRISH COLIN D	MAJ	0-1336951	0464	1
PARRISH DUDLEY T	COL	0-0926221	1162	1
PARRISH EDWIN T	LTC	0-1111823	0263	1
PARRISH JAMES M	CPT	0-1592499	1056	1
PARRISH JAMES W SR	LTC	0-1284011	0658	1
PARRISH JOSEPH W	LTC	0-0468044	0347	1
PARRISH LESLIE H	MAJ	0-1643951	0757	2
PARRISH MINTON D	MAJ	0-0322478	0352	2
PARRISH ROBERT B	MAJ	0-0488548	0355	2
PARRISH SIDNEY F	1LT	0-0536545	0759	1
PARRISH SPENCER D	MAJ	0-1638223	0860	1
PARRO WILLIAM J	2LT	0-1119356	0246	2
PARRON WALTER C JR	2LT	0-1296417	0244	2
PARROT DAVID L	CPT	0-0396141	0545	2
PARROTT ARTHUR E	COL	0-0249522	0265	3
PARROTT BEN C	LTC	0-0344461	0563	1
PARROTT ERNEST M	LTC	0-0490352	0164	3
PARROTT JOHN B	COL	0-0282024	0660	1
PARROTT JOHN H	MAJ	0-0331763	0846	2
PARROTT JOHN R	CW4	W-2146389	0962	1
PARROTT WILLIAM R	LTC	0-0887434	0666	1
PARRY EDWARD A JR	MAJ	0-0388854	0861	1
PARRY HOWELL J	LTC	0-1635194	0960	1
PARRY PRISCILLA	MAJ	N-0759338	1262	1
PARRY ROBERT S	1LT	0-1317238	0446	2
PARRY STEPHEN H	MAJ	0-1342345	1163	1
PARSEK CLARENCE R	MAJ	0-1796997	0361	1
PARSHALL CECIL S	MAJ	0-1284201	0352	2
PARSHALL CHARLES J	LTC	0-0279125	0962	3
PARSHALL HARVEY G	MAJ	0-1308857	1160	1
PARSON JOHN	1LT	0-0450381	0345	2
PARSON KENNETH B	MAJ	0-0502673	0347	2
PARSONS CARY C	CPT	0-0289375	1163	3
PARSONS CHARLES A	1LT	0-1184706	0745	2
PARSONS CHARLES L	CW4	W-2143446	1066	1
PARSONS CHESTER N	LTC	0-0307368	1067	3
PARSONS DAVID B	LTC	0-1554604	0967	1
PARSONS DOROTHY	LTC	N-0720025	0161	1
PARSONS GEORGE C	LTC	0-1578953	1061	1
PARSONS HAROLD K	COL	0-0197578	0750	3
PARSONS J D	MAJ	0-1291749	0359	1
PARSONS JACK G	COL	0-0343358	0466	1
PARSONS JAMES M	LTC	0-1105083	1161	1
PARSONS JOHN F	MAJ	0-1107028	1264	1
PARSONS JOHN G	1LT	0-0360870	1043	2
PARSONS KELLY	1LT	0-0462163	0444	2
PARSONS LAWRENCE B	CPT	0-0248104	1043	2
PARSONS LESLIE H	COL	0-0350927	1267	3
PARSONS LYMAN	MAJ	0-0227576	0665	3
PARSONS MARIAN C	1LT	N-0789171	0546	2
PARSONS PRESTON	1LT	0-0109498	0637	1
PARSONS PRESTON P	MAJ	0-1825250	1057	1
PARSONS RALPH A	COL	0-0168874	1055	3
PARSONS RICHARD W	CW3	W-2205787	0566	1
PARSONS ROBERT B	MAJ	0-1174099	0665	1
PARSONS ROBERT L	CPT	0-1846047	1045	2
PARSONS RODNEY T	MAJ	0-0386970	0547	2

NAME	GRADE	SVC NO	DATE RET MO YR	RET CODE
PARSONS THEODORE W	LTC	0-0369810	1057	1
PARSONS VERIL D	MAJ	0-1949185	0759	1
PARSONS WILLIAM B	COL	0-0221205	0264	3
PARSONS WILLIAM G	CW3	RW-2148013	1163	1
PARTANEN GEORGE O	CPT	0-1287053	1046	2
PARTCH ELDON R	MAJ	0-1951504	0465	1
PARTEN JOHN D	MAJ	0-0986835	1264	2
PARTHUM CHARLES F	2LT	0-1004657	0944	2
PARTIN WALTER F	COL	0-0407006	1163	1
PARTLOW GEORGE L	LTC	0-0350357	0459	1
PARTLOW RAY W	CW4	W-2006400	0866	2
PARTON BENJAMIN F	CPT	0-1299625	1051	1
PARTON GEORGE P JR	LTC	0-0491867	0366	1
PARTRIDGE GEORGE F	CPT	0-0412221	0245	2
PARTRIDGE JOHN S	MAJ	0-0266334	0262	1
PARTRIDGE LEON S	CPT	0-0231728	0165	3
PARTRIDGE STANLEY H	COL	0-0378455	0160	2
PARTRIDGE WILLIAM J	MAJ	0-2033298	0662	1
PARTRIDGE WILLIAM T	MAJ	0-2203051	0566	1
PARULIS DANIEL A	2LT	0-2040975	0944	2
PARUN BERNARD	MAJ	0-0276135	0664	3
PARVEY MARCUS A	1LT	0-0384704	0646	2
PARVIS CHARLES F	CW3	W-2145343	0165	1
PARZNIK JOHN T	CW4	W-2106594	0259	1
PASAHOW SAMUEL	CW3	W-2142655	1164	1
PASCAL LOUIS R	1LT	0-1177131	1047	2
PASCALE FRANK L	1LT	0-1321810	0345	2
PASCALE VITO P	CPT	0-1287935	0648	1
PASCH HARRY A	LTC	0-0553607	0765	1
PASCH LOUIS N	CPT	0-0411671	0545	2
PASCH THOMAS C	CW2	W-2212935	0767	1
PASCHAL MERLE B	LTC	0-0182371	0157	1
PASCHAL WALTER R	MAJ	0-1105084	0761	1
PASCHALL CHARLES R	CW3	W-2152902	0263	2
PASCHALL HUNTER H	LTC	0-1590586	1262	1
PASCOE BENJAMIN O	1LT	0-0888197	1045	2
PASCOE JOHN T	MAJ	0-2102980	1165	1
PASCUAL NICOLAS	CPT	0-1297773	0246	2
PASCUCCI LUCIEN M	MAJ	0-0357139	0246	2
PASH BORIS T	COL	0-0275706	1157	2
PASH LEONARD O	CPT	0-0499515	0446	1
PASKELL ARCHIBALD	CW2	W-2129724	0566	3
PASKLER JUNIUS	2LT	0-1541933	0552	1
PASKO JOSEPH W	MAJ	0-1335573	0764	1
PASKOPOULOS GEORGE E	COL	0-0243685	1062	3
PASKUS JOHN G	1LT	0-2008369	0450	2
PASMORE JOHN L	MAJ	0-0323943	0345	2
PASOLA JOSEPH	2LT	0-2008515	0446	2
PASQUALINO FELIX	LTC	0-0524440	0946	2
PASQUARIELLO VINCENT	CPT	0-1874821	1167	1
PASQUINO JOSEPH JR	CW4	W-2143418	0866	1
PASS BERNARD J	CPT	0-1821497	0145	2
PASS PASQUAL F	CW2	W-2110327	0762	1
PASSAGE CLAYTON C	LTC	0-1555877	0668	3
PASSARO RAMON	MAJ	0-4074840	1168	1
PASSER JEROME	1LT	0-0514150	0345	2
PASSEY WILLIAM H	MAJ	0-0979985	1062	1
PASSON WALTER	CPT	0-1917762	0263	1
PASSONS ROBERT J	MAJ	0-1691774	0563	1
PASTELL JOHN S	LTC	0-2018046	0266	1
PASTER EMANUEL	1LT	0-1592197	0853	2
PASTERNAK CHESTER J	MAJ	0-1283661	0746	2
PASTERNAK JOSEPH A	MAJ	0-1292227	0366	1
PASTON DAVID G	COL	0-0189428	0647	2
PASTOR AMELIA	CPT	N-0757027	0247	1
PASTOR JOHN E	1LT	0-1320911	0346	2
PASTOR LOUIS J	CPT	0-1310871	0747	2
PASTORET AL L	LTC	0-0135312	0352	3
PASTUSZYNSKI EDWARD	MAJ	0-1999315	0156	1
PASVOLSKY VALENTINE	MAJ	0-0184269	0759	1
PATACSIL LAUREANA F	2LT	N-0783899	0246	1
PATAKI GEORGE D	COL	0-1643952	0566	1
PATANE JOSEPH S	MAJ	0-1280943	0657	1
PATANIA JOSEPH M	CW3	W-2141805	0661	1
PATCH EDGAR M JR	MAJ	0-2262229	1167	1
PATCH RUSSELL B	CPT	0-0290865	0244	2
PATCH VERNON T	MAJ	0-0183969	0362	3
PATCHETT HOWARD F	CW2	W-2205851	1162	2
PATCHIN WILLIAM F	CPT	0-0108982	1035	1
PATE ARTHUR A	CPT	0-0497788	0553	2
PATE CHARLES G	MAJ	0-1342208	0963	1
PATE DAVID C	CW4	W-2149263	1166	1
PATE DURWOOD L	CW3	W-2142523	0263	1
PATE EUGENE H	CW3	W-2141405	0662	1
PATE GERALD B	CW3	W-2108257	1057	1
PATE JAMES F JR	1LT	0-4024060	0159	2
PATE JEWELL M	1LT	0-1636449	1054	1
PATE JOE N	WO1	W-2151509	0255	1
PATE JOHN L	MAJ	0-1324703	0561	1
PATE JOSEPH B JR	LTC	0-1010298	1061	1
PATE LEO B	1LT	0-1322946	1045	2
PATE OTHO S	1LT	0-0528063	0744	2
PATE RALPH R	LTC	0-0413633	0657	1
PATE TOM D	1LT	0-0505831	0855	1
PATE VERNE E	COL	0-0361205	0567	1
PATEE JAMES C	MAJ	0-0993226	0864	1
PATER EDWIN F	MAJ	0-2032979	0961	2
PATERSON CHARLES	LTC	0-1286175	1060	1
PATERSON GLEN S	MAJ	0-0257757	0865	3
PATEY ELWOOD K	MAJ	0-1303020	0560	1
PATHE TIMOTHY J	CPT	0-0925842	0347	2
PATIN TADDY	CPT	0-1574498	0958	1
PATNESKY EDWARD	CPT	0-1535392	0746	2
PATREM JOHN B	MAJ	0-1337084	0963	1
PATRENOS FRANCIS P	CPT	0-0961232	0463	1
PATRICIO RAYMOND	MAJ	0-1110172	0962	1
PATRICK CARL	CPT	0-0486611	0548	1
PATRICK CLAUDE B	LTC	0-1535512	0165	1
PATRICK FLAY R	CPT	0-1644651	0256	1
PATRICK FOREST	CPT	0-1037217	0959	1
PATRICK FRANK J	MAJ	0-1549807	0363	1
PATRICK GEORGE A	MAJ	0-1105085	0157	1
PATRICK GEORGE M	2LT	0-2011808	0146	2
PATRICK GEORGE P	1LT	0-0444863	0744	2
PATRICK HARTFORD L	2LT	0-0467225	0244	2
PATRICK JAMES R	LTC	0-0113918	0253	3
PATRICK JASPER R	CW2	W-2147534	0860	1
PATRICK JOHN D	CW4	W-2103295	1058	1
PATRICK JOHN F D	COL	0-0290515	0560	1
PATRICK JOHN K	CW3	W-2148578	0965	1
PATRICK JOHN N	MAJ	0-0297721	1044	2
PATRICK KENNETH J	LTC	0-1325165	0663	1
PATRICK MARION L	CPT	0-0104811	0821	1
PATRICK MILTON L	2LT	0-1182934	1044	2
PATRICK NOBLE M	LTC	0-1172588	1265	1
PATRICK OSCAR F	MAJ	0-2081349	1066	1
PATRICK THOMAS E	CPT	0-1047716	0160	1
PATRICK VERNON P	CW2	W-2212250	0168	1
PATRINELIS JOHN E	COL	0-0178905	0753	3
PATRITCH JOHN J	LTC	0-0389827	0561	1
PATRYLO RUDOLPH M	CPT	0-1113386	1262	1
PATSCHKE MILDRED L	1LT	N-0794919	1047	1
PATSY GLORIO J	LTC	0-1534357	0857	1
PATT EMANUEL	CPT	0-0553820	0346	2
PATTEE KARL M	COL	0-0208962	0457	3
PATTEN ALBERT J	CW3	W-2144985	0962	1
PATTEN ALLEN P	1LT	0-1296418	1045	2
PATTEN FRANKLIN W	LTC	0-0168150	0760	3
PATTEN LAWTON M	CPT	0-0239083	0565	3
PATTEN RAYMOND L	LTC	0-0481389	1157	3
PATTEN WILLIAM W	MAJ	0-1586005	0359	1
PATTERSON ADNA R	MAJ	0-2049679	1262	1
PATTERSON ALAN F	CW3	W-2146862	0765	1
PATTERSON ALLEN A	LTC	0-0170070	1057	3
PATTERSON ARTHUR J	MAJ	0-1917574	1064	1
PATTERSON BARTON H	MAJ	0-1926187	1168	1
PATTERSON BEN	CW2	W-2144353	0659	1
PATTERSON BRUCE E	2LT	0-0336287	0666	3
PATTERSON BUEL R	LTC	0-0248158	0664	3
PATTERSON BUNYAN L	MAJ	0-1285488	1154	1
PATTERSON BURTON R	LTC	0-0478161	0858	2
PATTERSON CALVIN W	1LT	0-2042871	0851	2
PATTERSON CARL D JR	LTC	0-1165928	0161	1
PATTERSON CARROLL G	LTC	0-1053766	0865	3
PATTERSON CECIL	MAJ	0-2262285	0761	1
PATTERSON CHARLES C	COL	0-0204232	0547	2
PATTERSON CHARLES H	CPT	0-0488822	0153	1
PATTERSON CHARLES L	MAJ	0-2262615	0764	1
PATTERSON CHARLIE L	LTC	0-0278103	0366	3
PATTERSON CUTHBERT	MAJ	0-0492977	0547	1
PATTERSON DANIEL S	MAJ	0-0499043	0257	1
PATTERSON DONALD W	CW3	W-2150073	0566	1
PATTERSON DOROTHY D	CPT	N-0763685	0747	1
PATTERSON DREXEL P	MAJ	0-0189698	0647	2
PATTERSON EDWARD L	WO1	W-2115183	0844	2
PATTERSON EDWIN M	MAJ	0-0351574	1047	2
PATTERSON EMERY F	LTC	0-1000839	0358	2
PATTERSON EUGENE K	CPT	0-0145029	1055	3
PATTERSON EUGENE R	COL	0-0998481	0863	2
PATTERSON FARREL S	CPT	0-1287397	1047	2
PATTERSON FRANK B	LTC	0-0135012	1056	3
PATTERSON FRANK S	WO1	W-2112285	0859	1
PATTERSON FRED L JR	MAJ	0-0335105	0746	2
PATTERSON GEORGE P	CW4	W-2136699	0666	1
PATTERSON GORDON E	CPT	0-0361769	0345	2
PATTERSON HAROLD J	CW2	W-2153266	0261	1
PATTERSON HAROLD R	LTC	0-1342108	0167	1
PATTERSON HARRY F	CPT	0-0489907	0352	2
PATTERSON HOWARD A	CPT	0-1108920	0359	1
PATTERSON HOWARD L	1LT	0-2055089	0849	2
PATTERSON HOWARD S	COL	0-0125844	0648	3
PATTERSON ISAAC N	CPT	0-0473175	0943	2
PATTERSON JAMES D	2LT	0-2006029	0945	2
PATTERSON JAMES N	COL	0-0255586	0656	3
PATTERSON JAMES P	MAJ	0-1298751	0561	1
PATTERSON JOHN C	COL	0-0366882	0864	1
PATTERSON JOHN C	LTC	0-0392197	0262	1
PATTERSON JOHN H	CPT	0-0256903	0952	1
PATTERSON JOHN J	1LT	0-1698071	0245	2
PATTERSON JOHN K	COL	0-0193473	1160	3
PATTERSON KENNETH L	LTC	0-1017168	0268	1
PATTERSON LAWRENCE P	MAJ	0-0112674	0645	2
PATTERSON LEON C	MAJ	0-0129514	0648	3
PATTERSON LLOYD C	CPT	0-0452690	1043	2
PATTERSON LOWELL H	LTC	0-1002706	1166	1
PATTERSON LUTHER E	COL	0-0269810	1067	3
PATTERSON LYNN T	CW2	W-2102187	0958	1
PATTERSON MATTIE L	2LT	N-0701964	0243	1
PATTERSON MC LEOD	LTC	0-0381437	0347	2
PATTERSON OSCAR A	CPT	0-0995076	1161	1
PATTERSON PAUL H	2LT	0-0581068	0945	2
PATTERSON PAUL J	MAJ	0-0278723	1060	3
PATTERSON RALPH B	MAJ	0-1307571	0657	1
PATTERSON RALPH B	1LT	0-1589430	0762	1
PATTERSON RALPH E	COL	0-0201550	0751	3
PATTERSON RAY C	2LT	0-1597237	0945	2
PATTERSON RAYMOND	COL	0-0279296	0468	3
PATTERSON RAYMOND	CW2	W-2205603	0760	1
PATTERSON ROBERT A	1LT	0-0416417	0444	2
PATTERSON ROBERT A	MAJ	0-0421001	0161	1
PATTERSON ROBERT B	LTC	0-0261383	1265	3
PATTERSON ROBERT B	1LT	0-1290651	0946	2
PATTERSON ROBERT C	COL	0-0262952	0964	3
PATTERSON ROBERT C	LTC	0-0350408	0562	1
PATTERSON ROBERT E	MAJ	0-1922512	0965	1
PATTERSON ROBERT E	CPT	0-5230203	0768	2
PATTERSON ROBERT G	COL	0-0218143	1047	2
PATTERSON ROBERT H	CPT	0-1323168	1047	2
PATTERSON ROBERT M	LTC	0-0153811	0355	3
PATTERSON ROBERT M	MAJ	0-2055079	0857	1
PATTERSON ROY J	MAJ	0-1304109	0266	1
PATTERSON ROY M	1LT	0-1301531	1045	2
PATTERSON STANLEY J	LTC	0-1294183	0261	1
PATTERSON THADDEUS M	LTC	0-1593167	1067	1
PATTERSON THOMAS C	LTC	0-0180439	0746	2
PATTERSON THOMAS D	LTC	0-0287492	0661	1
PATTERSON THOMAS J	1LT	0-1309600	1045	2
PATTERSON THOMAS L	CW3	W-2142410	0361	1
PATTERSON WARREN E	CW3	W-2211117	0868	1
PATTERSON WARREN J	MAJ	0-2097589	0667	1
PATTERSON WARREN W	LTC	0-0283524	0268	3
PATTERSON WILLIAM D	LTC	0-0260126	0264	1
PATTERSON WILLIAM G	LTC	0-1295591	0763	1
PATTERSON WILLIAM M	CW2	W-2214748	1066	1
PATTERSON WILLIAM T	LTC	0-1320556	1262	1
PATTERSON WILLIS D	LTC	0-1019840	1066	1
PATTERSON WINFRED E	MAJ	0-0931190	0260	1
PATTI ARCHIMEDES	LTC	0-0372453	0757	1
PATTI JOSEPH A	MAJ	0-2023922	0559	1
PATTIE CHARLES M	LTC	0-0349650	0657	1
PATTIE MARY T	CPT	N-0742073	1046	1
PATTILLO LEWIS C	B G	0-0244386	1063	3
PATTIS GEORGE J	LTC	0-1332857	0667	1
PATTISON CLARENCE L	MAJ	0-2202211	0665	1
PATTISON GEORGE P	2LT	0-0919386	0545	2
PATTISON HARLAND G	LTC	0-0268746	1063	3
PATTISON PAUL F	LTC	0-0753921	0163	1
PATTISON PHILIP R	COL	0-0188917	0558	3
PATTISON RAYLINN	CPT	0-1170131	0953	2
PATTISON VIRGINIA R	1LT	N-0776312	0147	2
PATTON BERNARD W	COL	0-0335451	1168	3
PATTON BYRON R	COL	0-0103082	1056	3
PATTON CHARLES G	CPT	0-1591974	0954	1
PATTON CHARLES W	CPT	0-1001872	1145	2
PATTON CLIFFORD M	CW2	W-2147639	0357	1
PATTON CLOYD E	CPT	0-1576479	0546	2
PATTON COREY E	COL	0-0244766	0561	3
PATTON EDWARD K	2LT	0-1321660	0344	2
PATTON ELMO L	B G	0-0229128	0463	3
PATTON FREDERICK	2LT	0-2019777	0846	2
PATTON JACK F	LTC	0-1549576	0765	1
PATTON JAMES B	COL	0-0179705	0755	3
PATTON JAMES H JR	MAJ	0-1295932	0163	1
PATTON JAY D	LTC	0-0266996	1067	3
PATTON JOHN A	COL	0-0201965	0753	3
PATTON JOHN B	MAJ	0-1825705	0363	1
PATTON JOHN O	MAJ	0-0450644	1054	1
PATTON JOHN W	COL	0-0149119	0855	3
PATTON KARL S	LTC	0-1184919	0564	1
PATTON KENDALL K	2LT	0-1080655	0844	2
PATTON RAYMON E	1LT	0-1298915	0246	2
PATTON SAMUEL A	CPT	0-0994231	1061	1
PATTON STEWART H JR	CPT	0-0465291	0559	1
PATTON THOMAS E	MAJ	0-0350044	0745	2
PATTON THOMAS R	MAJ	0-0474643	0559	1
PATTON WENDELL B	LTC	0-0220999	1057	2
PATTON WILLIAM E	CPT	0-1685873	0844	2
PATTON WILLIAM M	1LT	0-1824358	0845	2
PATTON WILLIAM T	CPT	0-2033553	0566	1
PATTUGALAN SANTIAGO	1LT	0-2030550	0950	1
PATTY DAVID O	MAJ	0-0234258	0844	2
PATURZO MICHAEL R	1LT	0-1925830	0254	2
PATY BYRD F JR	1LT	0-0538807	0446	2
PATY WILLIAM W	CPT	0-0481696	0846	2
PATZE RICHARD A	LTC	0-1102418	0860	1
PATZIG W J	CW2	W-3150656	0466	1
PAUGH DELMER I	LTC	0-1293466	1062	1
PAUL ARTHUR T	LTC	0-1172214	1067	1
PAUL CALVIN	WO1	W-2145575	0560	2
PAUL CARL J	COL	0-0494043	0268	3
PAUL CARROLL D	LTC	0-0164084	0647	2
PAUL CHARLOTTE	CPT	M-0000472	1047	1
PAUL CHESTER V	MAJ	0-0947156	0765	2
PAUL DELBERT A	CW3	W-3150249	1068	1
PAUL DONALD K	MAJ	0-0959244	1266	1
PAUL GROVER S	MAJ	0-1798392	0361	1
PAUL HARLOW L	LTC	0-1183155	1065	1
PAUL JACK D	MAJ	0-0305265	0846	2
PAUL JAMES H	CW3	W-2152476	1263	1
PAUL JAMES R	MAJ	0-1031115	0658	1

NAME	GRADE	SVC NO	DATE RET MO YR	RET CODE
PAUL JAMES A	CPT	0-2010876	0256	1
PAUL JESSIE A JR	CW3	W-2208415	0765	2
PAUL JOSEPH B JR	WO1	W-2142057	0254	2
PAUL LACY A	CW2	W-2103797	0854	1
PAUL LELAND B	LTC	0-2012490	0765	1
PAUL LEMUEL E	CW3	W-2112817	0159	1
PAUL LEO J SR	1LT	0-1012090	0159	1
PAUL LESLIE J	COL	0-0176650	0959	3
PAUL NICHOLAS T	CW4	W-2111542	1065	1
PAUL RACHEL C	1LT	N-0745475	1146	1
PAUL ROBERT D	MAJ	0-1703407	0946	2
PAUL RODGER R	LTC	0-0229341	1061	3
PAUL ROLAND M	LTC	0-0408088	0263	1
PAUL THEODORE S	COL	0-0176640	0250	3
PAUL THOMAS B	MAJ	0-0996291	0164	1
PAUL WARREN D	LTC	0-0116272	1056	3
PAUL WERNER M	MAJ	0-1800159	0264	1
PAUL WILLIAM E	LTC	0-0233607	0648	3
PAUL WILLIAM C	CPT	0-0378414	0246	2
PAUL WILLIS L JR	LTC	0-1115357	1066	1
PAULDING JOHN	CPT	0-0255665	0364	3
PAULETTE WILLIE N	MAJ	0-1594168	0763	1
PAULEY ARTHUR R	LTC	0-0506999	0163	1
PAULEY DENVER	CPT	0-1182677	1162	1
PAULEY HAROLD C	CW3	W-3150602	0568	1
PAULEY WARREN B	LTC	0-1285545	0261	1
PAULHAMUS KENNETH H	LTC	0-0450544	0656	1
PAULI AUGUST	2LT	0-2005218	0646	2
PAULIN ALBERT A	WO1	W-2115516	1046	1
PAULIN ANDREW C	LTC	0-1546000	0862	1
PAULIN HOWARD P	MAJ	0-0236640	0166	3
PAULINO CAMILO	CW2	W-2152245	0263	1
PAULK BILLIE B	2LT	0-1043968	0345	2
PAULK CLYDE A	CW4	W-2003983	0168	3
PAULL FREDERICK	CW3	W-2143774	1060	1
PAULL JULIUS J	MAJ	0-1242435	0662	1
PAULL ROBERT P	2LT	0-1048969	0744	2
PAULL ROSS	COL	0-0267130	0746	2
PAULLIN PERRY E	1LT	0-1575505	0366	3
PAULOS GEORGE F JR	MAJ	0-0340947	1043	2
PAULS HENRY J	MAJ	0-0493017	1151	1
PAULSEN ARTHUR F	LTC	0-1105090	1163	1
PAULSEN CARL C	COL	0-0321477	0756	1
PAULSEN CLARENCE I	MAJ	0-0900430	0245	2
PAULSEN EDWARD D	2LT	0-0520756	0445	2
PAULSEN OSCAR	CPT	0-1540543	0349	1
PAULSON EUGENE C	MAJ	0-1646489	0461	1
PAULSON JACK C	CPT	0-0321892	0744	2
PAULSON KENNETH D	CW2	W-3250490	1167	1
PAULSON MARGARET M	CPT	N-0745125	1147	1
PAULSON ROBERT L	CPT	0-0401916	0146	2
PAULSON ROY B	CW3	W-2142774	1162	1
PAULSON WILLIAM C	CPT	0-0342870	0945	2
PAUS JOSEPH H	LTC	0-2033545	0965	1
PAUSTIAN MARGRET K	1LT	N-0799510	0747	1
PAUSZEK FELIX H	LTC	0-1550677	0668	3
PAUTENIS EDWARD A	MAJ	0-1051327	0265	1
PAUTSCH LAWRENCE D	COL	0-0907472	0162	2
PAUTZ EDGAR F	LTC	0-1641659	1168	1
PAVELKA MILTON E	CPT	0-1016049	0949	2
PAVEY ROBERT F	MAJ	0-1881809	0967	1
PAVIA ALBERT J	CPT	0-2262730	0361	1
PAVLAK ALEXANDER	MAJ	0-2045102	0455	1
PAVLICK JOHN J	MAJ	0-1895539	0261	1
PAVLICK MARY A	MAJ	N-0728374	0962	1
PAVLIK ALEX G	1LT	0-1291163	0144	2
PAVLIK JOSEPH R	1LT	0-1181724	0246	2
PAVLIK STEPHEN G	CW4	W-2104792	0768	2
PAVLOCK EDWARD S	LTC	0-0496086	1154	1
PAVLOVICH PAUL L	1LT	0-1324948	0246	2
PAVY EDMUND F	CPT	0-0260575	0145	2
PAWLAK NORMAN C	2LT	0-1823053	0245	2
PAWLENKO ALEX	LTC	0-1284931	0959	2
PAWLING GEORGE F	LTC	0-0343006	0163	1
PAXMAN RALPH S	MAJ	0-1185415	0361	1
PAXTON ALEXANDER	M G	0-0129178	1058	3
PAXTON CALVIN N	CPT	0-1554801	0465	1
PAXTON FLOYD M	MAJ	0-0350572	0447	2
PAXTON GEORGE W JR	CW3	W-2150724	0164	1
PAXTON JACK L	LTC	0-1000442	0461	1
PAXTON JEROME M	MAJ	0-1634207	1047	2
PAXTON JOSEPH M	CPT	0-1013665	0547	2
PAXTON WILLIAM J JR	CW3	W-2144459	0868	1
PAYETTE ANDRE H	LTC	0-0504985	0163	1
PAYNE ADAM G	LTC	0-0303071	0154	1
PAYNE ARCHIE L	LTC	0-1041626	1062	1
PAYNE BROWN H	WO1	W-2119405	1143	2
PAYNE CARLOS	CW4	W-2127911	1165	1
PAYNE CARTER H	CW2	W-2206681	0463	1
PAYNE CHARLES B	LTC	0-1535950	0965	1
PAYNE CHARLES E	MAJ	0-1688286	0663	1
PAYNE CHARLES M	CPT	0-0382449	0843	2
PAYNE CLAUD M	MAJ	0-1304562	0160	1
PAYNE CLYDE M	CW2	W-2214019	0568	1
PAYNE CYRIL J	1LT	0-1014300	0845	2
PAYNE ELMER R	LTC	0-0189396	0646	1
PAYNE ELWOOD M	LTC	0-0365998	0566	3
PAYNE GEORGE A	LTC	0-0924022	1264	3
PAYNE GEORGE A	MAJ	0-2014269	0760	1
PAYNE GEORGE R	CPT	0-0123726	1055	3
PAYNE GEORGE S	CW2	W-2102192	0349	1
PAYNE GLENN A JR	LTC	0-1594384	0966	1
PAYNE GRAYFORD C	CW4	W-2142484	1068	1
PAYNE HAROLD J	MAJ	0-1697944	0557	1
PAYNE HARRY N	LTC	0-0310691	0658	1
PAYNE HENRY C	CPT	0-1312215	0550	2
PAYNE HERBERT M	LTC	0-0252819	0863	3
PAYNE HOUSTON	MAJ	0-1013971	0862	1
PAYNE JAMES E JR	MAJ	0-2262117	1263	2
PAYNE JOHN R JR	LTC	0-0151860	0259	3
PAYNE JOHN E	2LT	0-2008478	0157	1
PAYNE JOHN J	LTC	0-0479784	1067	3
PAYNE KENNETH B	2LT	0-1298916	0644	2
PAYNE LEONARD W	LTC	0-1894591	0269	3
PAYNE LUTHER	LTC	0-1101156	0758	1
PAYNE OTHA F	LTC	0-1295078	0964	1
PAYNE RALPH S	LTC	0-0209690	0955	3
PAYNE RICHARD H	MAJ	0-1016753	0954	1
PAYNE RICHARD M	LTC	0-1328838	1067	1
PAYNE ROBERT E	LTC	0-0337998	0565	3
PAYNE ROBERT E	CW2	W-2210813	0865	1
PAYNE THOMAS L	LTC	0-0382032	1165	3
PAYNE VERA F	1LT	N-0756287	0546	1
PAYNE WALTER K	COL	0-0198278	0656	1
PAYNE WILLIAM F JR	LTC	0-0325122	0562	1
PAYNE WILLIAM H	MAJ	0-0179088	0948	3
PAYNE WILLIAM H	CPT	0-2042972	0755	1
PAYNE WILLIAM N	LTC	0-1324704	0165	1
PAYNTER FLOYD L	LTC	0-0212966	0358	3
PAYONK ANDREW L	MAJ	0-1311923	0761	1
PAYSON MICHAEL J	1LT	0-1822451	0747	2
PAYTE SAMUEL G JR	1LT	0-1314322	0945	2
PAYTON LELAND E	LTC	0-0123722	0554	3
PAYTON RALPH H	LTC	0-1104331	0961	1
PAYTON ROBERT C	CPT	0-0116273	1157	3
PAYTON ROY A JR	MAJ	0-1946594	0754	2
PAYTON VEROLD W	CW4	W-2146562	0666	2
PAZICH STEPHEN	2LT	0-1308043	0844	2
PAZZELLI LOUIS P	2LT	0-0430461	0445	2
PEABODY BURTON W	MAJ	0-0901918	1043	2
PEABODY CARY S	CPT	0-0411501		2
PEABODY HUGH D	LTC	0-1638233	1164	1
PEABODY JOHN W	MAJ	0-1951032	0261	1
PEABODY LAURENCE A	LTC	0-0257983	0768	3
PEABODY RODNEY W	CW3	W-2207596	0568	1
PEABODY SELIM D	COL	0-0156281	0355	1
PEACE JAMES M	WO1	W-2108263	0245	2
PEACH ERIC A	COL	0-0328475	1163	3
PEACH ROBERT E JR	LTC	0-1636455	1061	1
PEACH THOMAS R	CPT	0-2019360	1159	1
PEACH WILLIAM C	CPT	0-0477470	0546	1
PEACOCK CURTIS A	MAJ	0-1846593	1060	1
PEACOCK DAVID R	MAJ	0-1020161	0164	2
PEACOCK FREDERICK	MAJ	0-1035464	0760	1
PEACOCK GORDON H	CPT	0-1894013	0763	1
PEACOCK JAMES H	LTC	0-0291276	0863	3
PEACOCK JAMES J	1LT	0-1046921	0447	1
PEACOCK JOSEPH A	LTC	0-1320476	0461	1
PEACOCK RICHARD S	MAJ	0-1050031	1064	1
PEACOCK WILLIAM R	LTC	0-0118032	0249	3
PEAK ELSIE M	2LT	N-0727897	0944	1
PEAK RAYMOND M	LTC	0-0203350	0959	1
PEAK REUBEN T	MAJ	0-0131330	0451	3
PEAKE CHARLES H	CPT	0-0184958	0856	3
PEAKE MARTHA C	MAJ	N-0757341	0967	1
PEAKE RALPH A	LTC	0-0353685	0959	1
PEARCE ALTON A	MAJ	0-2021128	0264	1
PEARCE ARTHUR B JR	LTC	0-0372534	0667	3
PEARCE CHARLES M	LTC	0-0139309	0548	3
PEARCE EDWARD L	LTC	0-0914530	0265	3
PEARCE EDWIN L	LTC	0-1555746	0965	3
PEARCE FRANCIS M JR	2LT	0-0494471	1143	2
PEARCE FRANKLIN E	LTC	0-1118112	0665	3
PEARCE JACK R	LTC	0-0884557	0657	1
PEARCE JAMES M	LTC	0-0221936	0563	3
PEARCE JOHN E	LTC	0-0215444	0862	3
PEARCE JOHNSON L	WO1	W-2134293	0660	1
PEARCE LOVICK B	COL	0-0137718	0554	3
PEARCE MARGARET H	CPT	N-0752899	0952	2
PEARCE NIEL A	CPT	0-1301206	0646	2
PEARCE RUFUS H	LTC	0-0185113	1148	3
PEARCE VERA H	1LT	N-0700759	0245	1
PEARCE WESLEY C	1LT	0-0392833	1145	2
PEARCE WILLIAM H JR	1LT	0-1996430	0847	2
PEARCE WILLIAM J	CW2	W-2151322	0765	1
PEARCE WILLIAM N	COL	0-0235879	0462	3
PEARCY EVANS C	CW4	W-2103306	0656	1
PEARDON ROBERT F	1LT	0-2262805	1158	1
PEARLMAN HUBERT S	CPT	0-0999551	0854	2
PEARMAN EARL O	CPT	0-0507865	0546	2
PEARMAN JAMES N JR	LTC	0-0390615	0860	1
PEARS DONALD R	CPT	0-0180316	1059	3
PEARSALL ARTHUR J	LTC	0-0414772	0763	1
PEARSALL MARTIN L	CPT	0-1294195	0546	2
PEARSON ALEXANDER	LTC	0-1105092	0163	1
PEARSON AUBREY D	1LT	0-1550399	0246	2
PEARSON BENJAMIN F	COL	0-0343145	0147	2
PEARSON CARL A JR	MAJ	0-1925831	0566	1
PEARSON CARL L	CW4	W-2128069	1054	1
PEARSON CHARLES B	COL	0-0352071	0165	1
PEARSON CHARLES L	MAJ	0-2206424	1166	1
PEARSON CHARLES T	LTC	0-0505014	0157	1
PEARSON CLARENCE E	MAJ	0-0973172	0365	2
PEARSON CLEMENS P	LTC	0-1285290	1155	1
PEARSON ELINOR	MAJ	R-0000531	0766	1
PEARSON EMMET F	COL	0-0272149	0466	3
PEARSON GEORGE C	LTC	0-0113146	0648	3
PEARSON HERBERT C	1LT	0-1012535	0145	2
PEARSON HOWARD E	LTC	0-0320143	0544	2
PEARSON HUBERT B	CPT	0-0436960	0846	2
PEARSON JOHN P	LTC	0-0325400	0647	2
PEARSON JOSEPH F	LTC	0-0271503	0547	2
PEARSON JULIUS R	MAJ	0-1683871	0546	2
PEARSON KARL M	LTC	0-0230034	0465	3
PEARSON LENDON P	MAJ	0-0578833	1164	1
PEARSON LEROY	COL	0-0127299	0648	3
PEARSON LEROY F	MAJ	0-1638237	0261	1
PEARSON LOYCE F	1LT	0-2026850	0148	1
PEARSON MORRIS	1LT	0-1309010	1045	2
PEARSON OLEN	CW2	W-2145896	1054	2
PEARSON OVID F	LTC	0-0253096	0240	2
PEARSON RAYMOND C	1LT	0-1644654	0860	1
PEARSON RICHARD H	CPT	0-1643957	0658	1
PEARSON ROBERT L	CW4	W-2145830	1061	1
PEARSON RUSSELL C	1LT	0-1312793	1045	2
PEARSON SHEPARD S JR	MAJ	0-1552144	0568	3
PEARSON THOMAS D	LTC	0-0359288	0965	1
PEARSON THOMAS R	MAJ	0-1951631	0263	1
PEARSON THOMAS V JR	MAJ	0-1440576	0364	1
PEARSON VERN K	1LT	0-1795963	0844	2
PEARSON WELTON D	LTC	0-0345376	1166	3
PEARSON WHITMAN	LTC	0-0357818	0866	3
PEASE ARCHIE G	COL	0-0284505	0769	3
PEASE AUSTIN H	CW3	W-2147710	1061	1
PEASE EDWIN J	COL	0-1172218	1164	1
PEASE EVERETT B	MAJ	0-2096631	0768	1
PEASE JAMES N	COL	0-0214497	0643	3
PEASE LAURENCE T	LTC	0-0366564	0463	3
PEASE LOYAL M	LTC	0-1548123	1060	1
PEASE ROOSEVELT	CPT	0-0224332	0747	1
PEASE WILLIAM H	LTC	0-1020389	0966	1
PEASE WILLIAM K	CPT	0-1172219	0555	1
PEASLEY ELMUS D	LTC	0-0257314	0663	1
PEASNER ALMA W	1LT	0-0516707	0848	1
PEATROSS 3RD SETH C	CPT	0-0520899	1045	2
PEATTIE JOHN J	LTC	0-0450469	0858	1
PEAVEY FRANK H	COL	0-0266490	1163	3
PEAVY HENRY J JR	MAJ	0-0213955	1145	2
PEAVY JERRY L	LTC	0-1289617	0664	1
PEAY JAMES H B JR	COL	0-0259910	1267	3
PEAY ROBERT E	MAJ	0-1581316	0261	1
PEBEROY CHARLES A	LTC	0-0485319	0268	3
PEBLER CAROLINE M	MAJ	N-0795431	0167	1
PECAUT RAYMOND W	MAJ	0-0499017	0655	1
PECAWICZ JOHN W	MAJ	0-1591361	0862	1
PECHIN FREDERIC W	MAJ	0-1287754	0361	1
PECHIN JAMES P	CPT	0-0974795	0666	1
PECHON ERNEST F	CPT	0-1580147	0253	2
PECHULIS FRANK V	LTC	0-1041216	1163	1
PECK ALBERT B	2LT	0-1173417	0444	2
PECK ALLEN S JR	LTC	0-0331955	1060	1
PECK CALVIN R	MAJ	0-1919937	0963	1
PECK EARL W	CW3	W-2141650	0559	1
PECK ELAM A	MAJ	0-0260907	0365	3
PECK ERNEST	LTC	0-0321478	1058	1
PECK GEORGE A JR	LTC	0-1035336	0661	1
PECK HARLAND K	MAJ	0-0810210	0263	2
PECK HARRY M	COL	0-0163234	0948	3
PECK JAMES C	MAJ	0-1924598	0867	1
PECK JAMES E	COL	0-0338204	0467	1
PECK JESSE M	CPT	0-0105336	0527	1
PECK JOHN C	1LT	0-1302703	104N	2
PECK JOHN S SR	CPT	0-1175532	0562	1
PECK KENNETH	LTC	0-0289854	0757	3
PECK LOUIS P	CPT	0-0418983	1047	2
PECK PHILIP B	CPT	0-0254285	1065	3
PECK RALPH W	CW2	W-2209573	1060	1
PECK ROBERT G	CPT	0-1292937	0247	2
PECK RODNEY H	LTC	0-0322305	0868	3
PECK ROLAND B	LTC	0-0229525	0545	2
PECK SAMUEL W	MAJ	0-1305978	0561	1
PECK WYATT N	MAJ	0-0102084	0856	3
PECKENS MARK R	CW2	W-2109610	0456	1
PECKHAM CHARLES L	LTC	0-1287939	0367	2
PECKHAM GEORGE M	MAJ	0-0331670	1046	2
PECKHAM VIVIAN R	COL	0-0201150	0763	3
PECKINPAUGH R L	CPT	0-1575506	0446	2
PECKLERS HERBERT R	2LT	0-1545728	1044	2
PECOR ROBERT F	MAJ	0-1885431	0966	1
PECOR VIRGEL F	CPT	0-0483031	0154	1
PEDDICORD JAMES O	CW3	W-2141806	0158	1
PEDDIE EDGAR C	CW3	W-2145041	0963	1
PEDDIE JAMES	LTC	0-0494136	0657	1
PEDDRICK ELMER M	COL	0-0180194	0752	3
PEDDY ROY L	CW3	W-2141406	0659	1
PEDEN ROSIE L	2LT	N-0703797	1042	1
PEDERSEN ANKER C	LTC	0-1584724	0957	1
PEDERSEN CHRISTIAN	COL	0-0104176	0648	3
PEDERSEN CONRAD H	COL	0-0201855	0860	3
PEDERSEN CORA M	MAJ	M-0002630	1164	1

NAME	GRADE	SVC NO	DATE RET MO YR	RET CODE
PEDERSEN FRANK S	MAJ	O-0276148	0963	3
PEDERSEN HAROLD	MAJ	O-0984537	0862	1
PEDERSEN JOHN W	2LT	O-1592503	0446	2
PEDERSEN NORMAN C	CW3	W-2152394	0866	1
PEDERSEN WARREN F	MAJ	O-1304432	0861	1
PEDERSEN WILLIAM W	MAJ	O-4006745	1067	1
PEDERSON DALE V	MAJ	O-2048104	0763	1
PEDERSON ERNEST O	LTC	O-0275712	0567	3
PEDERSON HANS F	CPT	O-0235338	0752	3
PEDERSON HAROLD W	WO1	W-2108611	1044	2
PEDIGONE HENRY A	LTC	O-1176760	0768	1
PEDIGO PAUL C	CPT	O-0406089	0344	2
PEDIGO ROGER L	MAJ	O-0366539	0961	1
PEDLOW ROBERT W	COL	O-2036695	0968	1
PEDNEAULT GEORGE J	LTC	O-0301487	0152	2
PEDONE GASPAR J	2LT	O-0965078	1151	2
PEDONE JOSEPH J	LTC	O-1595093	0864	1
PEDREIRA LUIS A	LTC	O-0262057	0448	2
PEDRI HENRY G	MAJ	O-0305307	1068	3
PEDRONI PETER J	1LT	O-1111427	0745	2
PEDROTTI PETER W	LTC	O-0361670	0358	1
PEEBLES BARCLAY	LTC	O-1319438	0566	3
PEEBLES FRANCIS E	CPT	O-1304110	1146	2
PEEBLES SNYDER L	B G	O-0238690	0862	3
PEEBLES THOMAS A	MAJ	O-0204341	1052	2
PEEBLES WARD K	MAJ	O-2033675	1065	1
PEED JAMES E	CW3	W-2149264	1265	1
PEEK CLIFFORD L	LTC	O-0917164	0765	3
PEEK DUNCAN G	LTC	O-0307644	0364	3
PEEK GEORGE J	CW3	W-2152856	0764	1
PEEK JAMES E	MAJ	O-2014783	0165	1
PEEK NOHEA J A	COL	O-0245525	0161	3
PEEK ROBERT P	LTC	O-0453710	0656	1
PEEKE RAYMOND G	COL	O-0203608	1055	3
PEEL ROBERT G	LTC	O-1103350	1066	3
PEELER ALLEN L	LTC	O-0305473	0661	2
PEELING ORRAL J	MAJ	O-0247369	0749	3
PEEPLES HAZAEL L	MAJ	O-1342294	0867	1
PEEPLES HEARL A	MAJ	O-0235763	0565	3
PEEPLES WILLIAM H JR	MAJ	O-0204633	1062	3
PEER CHARLES W	LTC	O-2210018	1167	1
PEERSON JAMES H	1LT	O-1048136	0548	2
PEERY KENNETH B	LTC	O-1587527	0868	3
PEET MARLIN D	MAJ	O-0268122	0759	3
PEET WILLIAM H	CPT	O-0312969	0545	2
PEET WILLIAM W	MAJ	O-0119031	0648	3
PEETOON PETER W	LTC	O-0341563	0252	2
PEGELOW EDWIN F	LTC	O-1053032	0767	1
PEGG HAROLD J	LTC	O-0236279	0457	3
PEGG JOHN T	B G	O-0905691	1168	3
PEGG ROBERT W	COL	O-0404164	1060	1
PEGRAM ALBERT A	MAJ	O-0373611	0964	1
PEGRAM HOWARD M	LTC	O-0495400	0955	1
PEGRAM JAMES C	MAJ	O-1102420	0359	1
PEHOVIC JOHN V	LTC	O-0461466	0568	1
PEHRSON ARTHUR J	LTC	O-0299991	0966	1
PEIFER ELSIE S	MAJ	N-0723632	0965	1
PEIFER GEORGE T	CPT	O-0147918	0559	3
PEIFFER DONALD R	CW2	W-2214506	0866	1
PEIFFER JAMES L	LTC	O-0450757	0857	2
PEIFFER RAY D	CW3	W-2111715	1054	1
PEIFFER ROBERT D	LTC	O-1580152	1056	1
PEIKERT ALBERT B	CPT	O-0277743	0850	2
PEIL RODMAN H	1LT	O-2033247	0450	2
PEINE PATRICK E	MAJ	O-1550479	0960	1
PEIRCE BYRON H	LTC	O-0272005	1166	3
PEIRCE EUGENE W	LTC	O-0237139	0664	3
PEIRCE HEMAN W	CW2	W-2104794	0853	1
PEIRCE LEONARD K	LTC	O-1589437	1164	1
PEIRCE MERVIN W	CW3	W-2146025	0960	1
PEIRCE SHELDON J	CPT	O-0254752	0267	3
PEISER HARRY	LTC	O-0499215	0150	1
PEISER MILDRED B	MAJ	N-0795848	0465	1
PEISER WILLIAM S	CPT	O-0421924	0547	2
PEITROWSKI EDWARD E	CPT	O-1545364	0351	2

NAME	GRADE	SVC NO	DATE RET MO YR	RET CODE
PEITZER BERNARD	LTC	O-0499368	0965	3
PEIXOTTO EDGAR P	CPT	O-0234832	0844	2
PELAK WILLIAM T	1LT	O-1030077	0144	2
PELAVA MIKE	CW3	W-2145344	0659	1
PELEBECKY GEORGE W	1LT	O-0436280	0744	2
PELET MARISKA J	MAJ	N-0726646	1162	1
PELFREY WILLIAM C	2LT	O-2010884	0449	1
PELHAM THOMAS W JR	LTC	O-0174461	0147	2
PELHAM WALTER C	MAJ	O-0888437	0860	1
PELINSKI P ELEANOR	1LT	N-0730677	0646	1
PELISH MAX	2LT	O-1297417	0943	2
PELISSIER LOUIS R	CW2	W-2145253	0660	1
PELL CLEMENS A	LTC	O-0271718	0663	1
PELL EARL R	CW3	W-2205948	0965	1
PELL FRANCIS H	MAJ	O-1688368	1262	1
PELL HARRY S	LTC	O-1044921	1066	1
PELL HOWLAND H JR	COL	O-0139975	0957	3
PELL JOE C JR	LTC	O-0966363	0168	1
PELL WENCE P	1LT	O-0289181	1042	2
PELLACANI ROMOLO	LTC	O-1639504	0666	1
PELLE JOHN J	CPT	O-0553870	0461	1
PELLEGREN LEONARD	CW2	W-3000419	1168	1
PELLEGRENE ADA D	MAJ	N-0727807	0165	1
PELLEGRINI MARIO	CW3	W-2152147	0663	1
PELLEGRINO HAROLD L	MAJ	O-0416867	0646	2
PELLEGRINO HENRY R	LTC	O-0373635	0368	3
PELLEGRINO JAMES M	LTC	O-1688640	0268	1
PELLEGRINO PETE A	CPT	O-0234785	0563	3
PELLEGRINO PETER J	1LT	O-0404139	0346	2
PELLENS GERARD G	MAJ	O-2263057	0865	1
PELLER IVAN M	MAJ	O-0486782	0563	1
PELLER JOSEPH R	COL	O-0145929	0456	3
PELLETIER CHARLES E	WO1	W-2104795	0346	2
PELLETIER IRVING	CW4	W-2000113	0165	3
PELLETIER JAMES J	LTC	O-1294186	0761	1
PELLETTIERI JAMES E	COL	O-0282309	0356	3
PELLING PETER	1LT	O-1178285	0646	2
PELLISH ALEX	LTC	O-0390212	0258	1
PELLISH MAXWELL C	LTC	O-0193465	1159	3
PELLOUX ROBERT L	LTC	O-0378525	0261	2
PELLOWSKI JOSEPH A	CW3	W-2104879	0860	1
PELLS HARRISON W	LTC	O-0385101	0161	1
PELOQUIN RUSSELL V	CW3	W-2210213	1068	1
PELOSI LEON	CW3	W-2145290	1063	1
PELOT MELL S	LTC	O-1546188	0867	1
PELOUZE CANNING C	LTC	O-0362142	1059	1
PELOW CHARLES A	1LT	O-1326295	0246	2
PELT AUGUSTUS H	MAJ	O-0980438	1266	1
PELT JOSEPH S	MAJ	O-1104333	0846	2
PELTIER NORMAN A	CPT	O-0947336	0668	3
PELTIER RAYMOND J JR	MAJ	O-1885939	0968	1
PELTIER REGINALD A	LTC	O-2026564	0366	1
PELTOLA HENRY W	LTC	O-1845424	0168	3
PELTON CHARLES E	CW3	W-2148807	0564	1
PELTON WILLIAM C	LTC	O-0371514	0161	1
PELUSO SAMUEL A	CW2	W-2150242	0765	1
PELZER GROSS A	LTC	O-0250371	0367	3
PELZMAN IVY A	LTC	O-0197221	0146	2
PEMBERTON BILLIE J	CPT	O-1999323	0847	2
PEMBERTON CHARLES S	MAJ	O-1320173	0563	1
PEMBERTON FRANK S	LTC	O-1586012	1162	2
PEMBERTON HOWARD L	2LT	O-2000137	1145	2
PEMBERTON JAMES E JR	COL	O-0112677	1058	3
PEMBERTON WILFRED G	LTC	O-0398965	0862	1
PENA JOSEPH A	LTC	O-1301207	0263	1
PENA WILLIAM M	CPT	O-0465382	0647	2
PENAS FRANK D	LTC	O-2033166	0366	1
PENCE ALFRED W	LTC	O-0250044	0565	3
PENCE ARTHUR P	CW3	W-2141652	1058	1
PENCE DAN	1LT	O-0221858	1044	2
PENCE HARRY S	LTC	O-0289287	0661	3
PENCE YARD W JR	MAJ	O-4005253	1067	1
PENCHAN BENJAMIN	CPT	O-1587528	0461	1
PENDARVIS ADRIAN E	1LT	O-0450505	0345	2
PENDER HAROLD E	CPT	O-0309648	0255	2

NAME	GRADE	SVC NO	DATE RET MO YR	RET CODE
PENDER HENRY L	1LT	O-2054039	0747	1
PENDER HERBERT W	CW3	W-2151910	1163	1
PENDER MURRAY T	CPT	O-0390616	0146	2
PENDER RICHARD H	LTC	O-0485672	0159	1
PENDERGAST HERBERT C	LTC	O-0198441	0455	3
PENDERGAST JAMES A	CW2	W-3100960	0368	1
PENDERGRAFT GEORGE W	CPT	O-0445626	0447	1
PENDERGRAFT HENRY C	CPT	O-2331637	1166	3
PENDERGRAPH GARLAND	LTC	O-0511671	0268	3
PENDERVILLE EDGAR R	CPT	O-0467010	0448	2
PENDLETON ARTHUR G	LTC	O-0451462	0960	1
PENDLETON FRANK S	2LT	O-0494666	0345	2
PENDLETON HERMAN E	CW4	W-2146411	1168	1
PENDLETON HUNTER A	CPT	O-0194576	1057	3
PENDLETON ROBERT W	LTC	O-0450342	1054	1
PENDLETON THOMAS H	MAJ	O-1341698	0166	1
PENDLETON WILLIAM E	1LT	O-1115058	0946	2
PENDLETON WILLIAM E	CW2	RW-2211288	0764	1
PENDLETON WILLIAM W	1LT	O-1245079	0646	2
PENDLETON WILLIE G	CPT	O-1101949	0447	2
PENER WILLIAM H	LTC	O-1324092	1262	1
PENFIELD JOEL F	MAJ	O-0207910	1146	2
PENFIELD JOHN R	LTC	O-1002709	0966	1
PENFIELD RICHARD	COL	O-0133618	1051	3
PENFIELD RONALD W	LTC	O-0256505	0563	3
PENGELLY HAROLD	COL	O-0360761	0154	1
PENGILLY JOSEPH H	COL	O-0133755	0648	3
PENHALLOW RICHARD	LTC	O-0242757	0266	3
PENICK EDGAR C JR	MAJ	O-1643214	0963	3
PENINGTON RALPH A	LTC	O-1185300	1061	1
PENKUNAS ISABELL C	MAJ	N-0725488	0767	1
PENMAN JAMES T	CPT	O-1822613	0447	2
PENN CLARK J	LTC	O-1650690	0765	1
PENN JULIUS H	MAJ	O-0168717	0959	3
PENN MARION B	LTC	O-0226773	0962	3
PENN WILLIAM A	MAJ	O-0502893	0850	2
PENNDORF WILLIAM B	CPT	O-0498215	0946	1
PENNEFATHER RICHARD	2LT	O-1104334	0445	2
PENNELL GLENN F	CW2	W-2152134	0361	1
PENNELL HENRY B	2LT	O-0221308	1062	3
PENNELL LOCKWOOD M	LTC	O-0274890	0466	3
PENNELL VIRGINIA H	1LT	N-0731130	1046	1
PENNER ELWOOD G	MAJ	O-1951186	1059	1
PENNER EMANUEL J	CW3	W-2147119	0763	1
PENNETT JOHN A	LTC	O-1013171	0962	1
PENNEWELL NOAH A	LTC	O-0280456	0261	1
PENNEY DAVID F JR	COL	O-0320260	0866	3
PENNEY EDWARD C JR	1LT	O-1556930	0746	2
PENNEY HAROLD C	MAJ	O-0575870	1159	1
PENNEY JAMES S III	1LT	O-5323448	1067	2
PENNEY JEAN M	MAJ	O-2292184	0468	1
PENNEY MAYNARD M	MAJ	O-0109433	0946	2
PENNEY MYERS F	MAJ	O-1941324	0966	1
PENNEY THOMAS F	LTC	O-0451374	0658	1
PENNIMAN EDWARD G	CPT	O-1315205	1047	2
PENNING EDWIN W	CPT	O-1166152	0260	1
PENNINGA WILLIAM J	LTC	O-0361460	0161	1
PENNINGTON ALTON R	1LT	O-1931279	0357	2
PENNINGTON CLARK W	LTC	O-0254551	0954	1
PENNINGTON CLYDE H	CW3	W-2146456	0859	1
PENNINGTON CLYDE L	LTC	O-0305618	0549	1
PENNINGTON DAVID	LTC	O-1168863	1065	1
PENNINGTON FRED P	1LT	O-0564004	0956	1
PENNINGTON JAMES H	LTC	O-1550240	0666	1
PENNINGTON JOHN A	MAJ	O-0301529	0160	3
PENNINGTON LORETTA N	1LT	N-0755245	0546	1
PENNINGTON LUTHER T	1LT	O-1736095	0645	2
PENNINGTON RALPH W	CW3	W-2145694	0166	1
PENNINGTON REDUS M	MAJ	O-0457642	0156	1
PENNINGTON WILLIAM P	MAJ	O-1821763	1056	2
PENNINO WALTER A	LTC	O-0371010	1059	1
PENNOCK JOHN S	MAJ	O-0453107	0356	1
PENNOCK JOSEPH L	CW3	W-2152421	0663	1
PENNOYER GEORGE O	MAJ	O-1686221	1265	1
PENNY ALLEN L	MAJ	O-0984895	0763	1

NAME	GRADE	SVC NO	DATE RET MO YR	RET CODE
PENNY FOREST L	1LT	O-0887680	1145	2
PENNY HAROLD G	COL	O-0191995	0157	1
PENNY LEON J	LTC	O-1045209	1165	1
PENNY NEWTON M	CPT	O-0308539	0545	2
PENNY WILFRED F	CW2	W-2206644	0661	1
PENNYWITT LESLIE H	2LT	O-2050825	0250	3
PENOFF ALEXANDER	CPT	O-2015805	0359	1
PENOYER MARK H	LTC	O-0406260	0464	1
PENROD CHARLES W	CW3	W-2149676	0162	1
PENROD CLAUDE M	LTC	O-0497492	0355	1
PENROD HAROLD L	LTC	O-1582042	0567	1
PENROD HOMER F	CW2	W-2144097	0960	2
PENROD PAUL F	CW3	W-2148979	0962	1
PENROSE CHARLES	LTC	O-1291508	0954	1
PENRY WILLARD W	LTC	O-0194750	1060	3
PENSKE WILLIAM W	LTC	O-0145468	0351	3
PENSTONE GILES H	MAJ	O-0256908	0867	3
PENSYL JOSEPH D	CW3	W-2143506	0862	1
PENSYL WILLIAM H	LTC	O-0546887	0265	1
PENTECOST FATE J	CPT	O-1290118	1163	1
PENTER KENNETH L	1LT	O-1290997	1145	2
PENTON GUY	CPT	O-0493957	0550	1
PENTON JAMES P	CPT	O-1822614	1047	2
PENTZ CARL M	WO1	W-2111763	0851	2
PENTZ WILLIAM R	MAJ	O-0216876	0755	3
PENUEL BENJAMIN H JR	MAJ	O-2014692	0465	1
PENWELL GUY C	LTC	O-0191368	0162	3
PENZENIK JOHN J JR	MAJ	O-0395026	0257	1
PEOPLES AVERY G	MAJ	O-0981134	0961	1
PEOPLES CLAUDE F	CPT	O-0308326	0346	2
PEOPLES HOWARD G	LTC	O-1104335	0860	1
PEOPLES PAUL F	1LT	O-1109584	1045	2
PEOPLES SAMUEL M	CW2	W-2215221	0868	1
PEPAS JOHN J	MAJ	O-1000841	0462	2
PEPIN BERNARD J	MAJ	O-1551486	0161	1
PEPLAU WALTER C	MAJ	O-1165282	0657	1
PEPPARD HAROLD J	MAJ	O-2009351	1162	1
PEPPEL BLAIR W	MAJ	O-1300524	0561	1
PEPPER DICKINSON	COL	O-0296317	0667	3
PEPPER GRADY S	LTC	O-0911830	1062	3
PEPPER JACK A	1LT	O-0484997	1046	1
PEPPER JOE C	MAJ	O-2026891	0260	1
PEPPER ROBERT H	1LT	O-1288610	0750	2
PEPPERDENE JOHN H	MAJ	O-1825170	1262	1
PEPPERS DONALD F	COL	O-0211217	0453	3
PEPPERS TRACY D	LTC	O-0224152	1044	2
PEPPIN HULL C	LTC	O-0298604	0261	3
PEPPLE RAYMOND F	MAJ	O-0270163	0151	2
PEPPLER FRANCIS K	LTC	O-0285669	0668	3
PERAK JOHN S	2LT	O-5325476	0366	2
PERANTONI DAVID T	1LT	O-5706838	0565	2
PERCEFULL PAYNE H	CPT	O-2024211	1058	1
PERCIFIELD JAMES O	LTC	O-1105095	0261	1
PERCIVAL GEORGE M	COL	O-0114533	0254	3
PERCIVAL HAROLD C	COL	O-0117958	0454	3
PERCIVAL RICHARD G	CW3	W-2145653	0663	1
PERCIVAL WILLIAM J	MAJ	O-4074736	0367	1
PERCOCO FRANK A	WO1	W-2120622	0745	2
PERCY RANDOLPH H	LTC	O-0103685	1056	1
PERCY ROBERT J	LTC	O-1549010	0967	1
PERDELWITZ LEE E	MAJ	O-1341288	0766	2
PERDUE EDWARD F	LTC	O-0181385	0455	3
PERDUE GEORGE T JR	MAJ	O-1643215	0159	1
PERDUE LOREE V	1LT	N-0779790	0547	1
PERDUE LOVIC P JR	LTC	O-0260786	1264	3
PERDUE WILLIAM L	1LT	O-0525884	0646	2
PEREDO FRED U	CPT	O-0890288	0150	1
PEREGO FORDYCE L	LTC	O-0107805	0648	3
PEREIRA FRED E	COL	O-0206204	0746	2
PEREL MILTON	CPT	O-0360512	1044	2
PERELL SYDNEY C	COL	O-0242681	0346	2
PERELLA DORWIN H	LTC	O-0315977	0760	1
PERELMAN ROBERT	CPT	O-2212068	1068	2
PERETTI SERAFINO	CPT	O-1846048	1150	1
PERETTIE DANIEL J	COL	O-0109568	0148	2

NAME	GRADE	SVC NO	DATE RET MO YR	RET CODE
PEREW ROBERT W	CW2	W-3350341	0968	1
PEREZ CHARLES F	LTC	0-1296420	1061	2
PEREZ ERNESTO	CPT	0-0156277	0655	3
PEREZ EUGENE F	LTC	0-0372172	0845	2
PEREZ JOSE M	CPT	0-2027328	0557	1
PEREZ MANUEL S	CPT	0-0156276	0653	3
PEREZ OVIDIO JR	CW3	W-2144996	0361	1
PEREZ REYESTER	CPT	N-0804211	0357	2
PEREZ ROBERT	COL	0-0274105	1065	3
PEREZ TEMISTOCLE	1LT	0-1896919	0162	1
PEREZ-GARCIA RAFAEL	LTC	0-0422056	0461	1
PEREZ-VEGA HECTOR	MAJ	0-0988480	1162	1
PERFATER GEORGE M	COL	0-0267540	0454	1
PERFETT FLORENCE A	1LT	N-0722467	0346	1
PERHAM BERTRAM S	CPT	0-1692350	1045	2
PERHAM CLIFFORD A	LTC	0-0280025	0859	1
PERHAM MARSHALL	LTC	0-0488369	0964	1
PERICONE VINCENT J	CW2	W-2146964	0854	1
PERIGNY CHARLES H	LTC	0-0491397	0365	1
PERIH CHARLES	CW3	W-2151210	0865	1
PERILLI CHARLES	LTC	0-1323731	0163	1
PERINA FRANK A JR	1LT	0-2055298	0146	2
PERING CHARLES L	CW2	RW-2211208	0165	1
PERKIN FRANK S	MAJ	0-0470551	1045	2
PERKINS ALBERT H	LTC	0-0375871	0664	1
PERKINS ANTHONY B	LTC	0-1037228	1268	1
PERKINS AUGUST T	LTC	0-0494289	1166	3
PERKINS CALVIN F	LTC	0-0436542	0664	3
PERKINS CHARLES F	CW3	W-2149407	0565	1
PERKINS CHARLES L	MAJ	0-0395829	0947	2
PERKINS CHYDE A	CPT	0-0333907	0166	3
PERKINS CLARENCE A	1LT	0-0263990	1054	3
PERKINS CLAUD F	MAJ	0-1287756	0358	2
PERKINS CLIFFORD A	MAJ	0-0477479	0944	2
PERKINS DAVID M	LTC	0-0448179	0560	3
PERKINS DUNCAN C	LTC	0-1306139	0165	2
PERKINS EARL	CW3	W-2151370	0665	1
PERKINS EARLE F	MAJ	0-1650281	0956	1
PERKINS EDWARD	CW2	W-2104686	0650	2
PERKINS EDWARD M	LTC	0-0281287	0363	3
PERKINS ELDON R	MAJ	0-1933577	0665	1
PERKINS ELGIN A	MAJ	0-1582044	0762	1
PERKINS ERWIN F	COL	0-0255141	1054	3
PERKINS FRANK A	MAJ	0-2056114	0762	1
PERKINS FRED FRED	CPT	0-0494052	0852	1
PERKINS GEORGE H	CW4	W-2131831	0762	1
PERKINS GRADY R	1LT	0-1043752	0545	2
PERKINS HANSON T	MAJ	0-0200661	0959	3
PERKINS HARRISON H	COL	0-0439841	0-53	1
PERKINS HENRY N JR	CW3	W-2149231	0466	1
PERKINS HUGH V	MAJ	0-0204381	0151	3
PERKINS JAMES R	1LT	0-2208142	1152	2
PERKINS JAMES W	COL	0-0279636	0861	3
PERKINS JOHN	COL	0-0103397	0648	3
PERKINS JOHN H	MAJ	0-1797345	0561	1
PERKINS JOHN K	LTC	0-0981901	0668	1
PERKINS JOHN P	CW2	W-2215050	0968	1
PERKINS JOHN T	CW2	W-2210641	0263	1
PERKINS JOHN W	CW3	W-2142349	0659	1
PERKINS JOHN W	CW2	W-2147496	1058	1
PERKINS LEON W	LTC	0-0181935	0150	3
PERKINS LLOYD A	LTC	0-0450470	0855	1
PERKINS MELVILLE F	COL	0-0170762	0554	3
PERKINS NORRIS H	MAJ	0-0325782	0246	2
PERKINS ORVILLE O	1LT	0-1690945	1047	2
PERKINS OSCAR L	LTC	0-0180951	0862	3
PERKINS PERCY H JR	COL	0-0239342	1065	3
PERKINS RAY	COL	0-0143725	0856	3
PERKINS RAYMOND K	COL	0-0908549	0466	3
PERKINS ROBERT	LTC	0-1703784	1060	1
PERKINS ROBERT A	CW2	W-2152659	0960	2
PERKINS RODNEY	CW2	W-2119677	1060	1
PERKINS ROSCOE JR	COL	0-0149123	0651	3
PERKINS RUSSELL V	MAJ	0-1650541	0259	1
PERKINS SAMUEL M	LTC	0-1297244	0361	1.

NAME	GRADE	SVC NO	DATE RET MO YR	RET CODE
PERKINS THOMAS F	LTC	0-2263420	1168	1
PERKINS WHEELER R	COL	0-0250625	0466	3
PERKINS WILLIAM A	LTC	0-0236053	0449	3
PERKOWSKI JOHN	MAJ	0-1688424	0561	1
PERKOWSKI STEPHEN P	CW3	W-2144881	0960	1
PERKOWSKY WILLIAM	MAJ	0-1311814	1058	2
PERL WILLIAM H	LTC	0-0555149	1066	3
PERLEY ALLAN H	CW2	W-2146026	0259	1
PERLEY SYDNEY H	LTC	0-0124279	0345	2
PERLMAN JEROME	CW3	W-2145831	0163	1
PERLMAN SAM S	LTC	0-1549011	1064	1
PERLOFF WILLIAM H	CPT	0-0465633	0945	2
PERLOW DAVID	LTC	0-0221212	0-53	1
PERLSWEIG BERNARD L	CPT	0-1311537	1046	2
PERMAN MAXWELL L	MAJ	0-0434710	0446	2
PERMENTER GAIL M	2LT	0-2048108	0644	2
PERNA ALFONSO A	MAJ	0-0334901	0846	2
PERNETTI ANTHONY M	CPT	0-0310977	1045	2
PERNICK HARRY C	COL	0-0510666	1167	1
PERNISH PAUL J	LTC	0-0348225	0965	3
PERO JAMES P	MAJ	0-1014838	0862	1
PERONE NICHOLAS A	MAJ	0-1796147	0458	2
PEROTTI JAMES D	LTC	0-0379600	0663	1
PERREAULT ALBERT F	MAJ	0-1874288	0664	1
PERRETTA CANIO O	CPT	0-1549013	0447	2
PERREY JOSEPH I	COL	0-0240311	0964	3
PERREY RAPHAEL E	LTC	0-0319875	1160	1
PERRIN AUBREY H	LTC	0-0224675	0662	3
PERRIN FRANK Y	1LT	0-1108229	0562	1
PERRIN HORACE C	2LT	0-1050860	0743	2
PERRIN HUBERT E	CW3	W-2142984	0960	1
PERRIN VIRGIL C	MAJ	0-1312326	0559	1
PERRIN WILLIAM C	LTC	0-1118269	0868	1
PERRINE ALFRED T	CPT	0-0469123	0946	2
PERRINE EARL R	CW3	W-2208545	0866	1
PERRINE FLOYD V	LTC	0-0384766	0666	1
PERRINE GILBERT E	CW2	W-2142186	0266	1
PERRINE NAT S JR	LTC	0-0406897	0461	1
PERRINGTON ALBERT W	MAJ	0-1292747	0558	1
PERRITT ELLIOTT E JR	LTC	0-0272976	0868	3
PERRON HENRY F	LTC	0-1576491	0157	1
PERRON ROBERT C	MAJ	0-1595756	0157	1
PERRONE DOMINIC A	MAJ	0-1795034	1058	1
PERRONE VINCENT R	MAJ	0-2200222	0563	1
PERROTTA DONATO F	CPT	0-1047290	0353	1
PERROW EARNEST A	LTC	0-0162232	0146	2
PERRY ALBERT N	MAJ	0-2023306	0467	1
PERRY ALEXANDER	COL	0-0378492	0365	3
PERRY ANNA A	CPT	N-0731147	0547	1
PERRY ANTHONY G	CW2	W-2123318	0963	3
PERRY ARVEL H	MAJ	0-1322404	0158	1
PERRY BREWSTER	COL	0-0450163	1162	1
PERRY CARL B	CPT	0-1302705	1054	1
PERRY CHARLES E	LTC	0-0127159	1156	3
PERRY CHARLES H	LTC	0-1645908	1266	3
PERRY CLARENCE L	LTC	0-1287232	0661	1
PERRY CLAUDE S	COL	0-0227626	0659	3
PERRY CLYDE L	MAJ	0-1183592	0860	1
PERRY COLLINS R	LTC	0-0270368	0345	2
PERRY DOUGLAS B	CW4	W-2121777	0963	1
PERRY EDWIN R	COL	0-1107033	0463	1
PERRY ELTON L	CW4	W-2142599	0464	1
PERRY EVERETT W	1LT	0-1309816	0845	2
PERRY EZRA B	CPT	0-0466237	0546	2
PERRY FANNY S	2LT	N-0767374	0145	1
PERRY FRANCIS E	1LT	0-0443131	0345	2
PERRY FRANK O	MAJ	0-1578962	1062	1
PERRY GEORGE J	CW2	W-2000115	0354	3
PERRY GERALD F	CPT	0-0191974	0158	3
PERRY GLENN G	MAJ	0-0441331	0346	2
PERRY HAROLD E	CW3	W-2150220	0166	1
PERRY HAROLD W	CW2	W-2212234	0367	1
PERRY HASKELL O	CW4	W-2104367	0659	1
PERRY HERBERT J	CPT	0-1169684	0863	1
PERRY HERMAN A	2LT	0-1914169	0348	1

NAME	GRADE	SVC NO	DATE RET MO YR	RET CODE
PERRY HERMAN M	MAJ	0-0252685	0550	1
PERRY HIRAM S	LTC	0-0205596	0648	3
PERRY HOWARD E	2LT	0-2017502	0354	2
PERRY HOWARD W	MAJ	0-2034839	0462	1
PERRY JAMES A	LTC	0-0311057	0866	3
PERRY JAMES F	LTC	0-1315610	1162	1
PERRY JAMES G	1LT	0-0920481	1045	2
PERRY JAMES I JR	CPT	0-2212099	0960	1
PERRY JAMES M	CPT	0-2293414	0666	1
PERRY JAMES Z	1LT	0-0430551	0845	2
PERRY JASON A	LTC	0-0250255	0654	2
PERRY JOHN B	MAJ	0-0495628	1064	1
PERRY JOHN C	MAJ	0-0331360	0851	2
PERRY JOHN M	MAJ	0-0982790	0468	1
PERRY JOHN P JR	LTC	0-0397171	0561	1
PERRY JOHN W	COL	0-0257066	0854	1
PERRY JOSEPH H	1LT	0-2263425	0461	1
PERRY JOSEPH R	2LT	0-2034454	1044	2
PERRY JOSEPH W	LTC	0-1310489	0562	1
PERRY LAYTON M	MAJ	0-1166351	0546	2
PERRY LEBERT F	CPT	0-0410098	0647	2
PERRY LEE C	CPT	0-1013640	1047	2
PERRY LEE G	CW3	W-2129091	0461	2
PERRY LEE ROY	1LT	0-1583491	0447	2
PERRY LEON J	2LT	0-1288437	0744	2
PERRY LESTER E	MAJ	0-1309310	0661	1
PERRY LONNIE W	MAJ	0-2016018	0860	1
PERRY LYNN	LTC	0-0166912	0648	3
PERRY MARLIN F	1LT	0-1081093	1045	2
PERRY MARSHALL E	MAJ	0-0963206	0863	1
PERRY MARVIN J	CW4	W-2132192	0559	1
PERRY MERLIN H	LTC	0-1181728	0762	1
PERRY MILTON J	LTC	0-0297959	0268	3
PERRY NORBERT V	CPT	0-0333426	0140	2
PERRY REGINA B	2LT	N-0788806	0744	1
PERRY RICHARD T	MAJ	0-0244560	0562	3
PERRY ROBERT E	LTC	0-1287581	0661	2
PERRY ROBERT K	1LT	0-0404805	0245	2
PERRY RONALD H	MAJ	0-2029435	0763	1
PERRY RYLAND B	CPT	0-0309478	0345	2
PERRY SANFORD C	MAJ	0-0305352	1067	3
PERRY THEODORE A	MAJ	0-0545770	0464	1
PERRY THERON H	LTC	0-2017275	0367	1
PERRY THOMAS C	MAJ	0-0203961	0647	2
PERRY THOMAS E	CW4	W-2102208	0656	1
PERRY THOMAS L	2LT	0-1050032	0145	2
PERRY THURSTON R	MAJ	0-1560378	0263	1
PERRY VERNON B	CW2	W-2145345	0255	2
PERRY VIRGIL L	CW3	W-2152713	0564	1
PERRY WADE B	MAJ	0-0320261	0546	2
PERRY WALTER S	CPT	0-1301208	0747	2
PERRY WARREN B	LTC	0-0505206	0264	3
PERRY WELDON W	CPT	0-2020199	0561	1
PERRY WILLIAM	LTC	0-0180556	0444	2
PERRY WILLIAM	MAJ	0-0501603	1046	2
PERRY WILLIAM A	MAJ	0-1589439	0861	1
PERRY WILLIAM H	CW3	W-2142657	0860	1
PERRY WILLIAM O	COL	0-0181268	1055	3
PERRY WILLIAM W	CW2	W-2214845	0667	1
PERRY WINFRED O	MAJ	0-0166270	0353	3
PERRYMAN JULIAN G	WO1	W-2115997	0156	1
PERRYMAN KENNETH C	2LT	0-2018406	0547	2
PERRYMAN LEON T	LTC	0-0267257	0960	3
PERRYMAN MARK F	1LT	0-0888981	0350	1
PERRYMAN TAYLOR O	LTC	0-0267020	0157	1
PERRYMAN VIRGIL O	LTC	0-1597238	0666	1
PERSELL RALPH M	LTC	0-0300553	0968	3
PERSICHINI ARCHIE D	CPT	0-2053991	0756	1
PERSING DAN H	LTC	0-0273174	0468	3
PERSION MATTHEW M	MAJ	0-0209693	0558	3
PERSON DON E	LTC	0-0491798	0959	1
PERSON EPHRAIM E	MAJ	0-0265996	0859	3
PERSON ERNEST A	LTC	0-0934864	1266	1
PERSON LAWRENCE E	MAJ	0-1312379	1163	1
PERSON RUFUS M JR	CPT	0-0250873	1166	3

NAME	GRADE	SVC NO	DATE RET MO YR	RET CODE
PERSON VERNON E	LTC	0-1105097	0863	1
PERSON WILLIAM F	MAJ	0-0123555	1052	3
PERSONETTE CHESTER A	LTC	0-2065107	0866	1
PERSONS DONALD B	LTC	0-1639900	0760	1
PERSONS ELAINE O	2LT	N-0737043	0444	1
PERSONS JOHN C	MG	0-0203751	0648	3
PERSONS JOSEPH H	CPT	0-1102901	0762	1
PERSONS LAWRENCE L	LTC	0-0402050	0464	1
PERUGINI MORRIS F	MAJ	0-0965933	0864	1
PERUSO LOUIS P	1LT	0-1012489	0945	2
PESANO JAMES	CW2	W-2123410	1044	2
PESAVENTO ROBERT F	LTC	0-1314053	0862	1
PESCATORE VINCENT V	LTC	0-1576492	1162	1
PESCHELL ALBERT E	CW4	W-2148761	1168	1
PESCI RICHARD G	CPT	0-1557060	1147	2
PESHAK GEORGE J	1LT	0-1183390	0546	2
PESHMALYAN BARUYR	MAJ	0-0242817	0448	2
PESKIN AARON R	MAJ	0-0236129	1043	2
PESSA JOSEPH J	COL	0-1101991	0867	1
PESSIN JOSEPH	LTC	0-0473463	0546	2
PESSUTTI JOSEPH P	1LT	0-1046608	0546	2
PESTER EARL H	1LT	0-1825314	0346	2
PETER ALBERT G	COL	0-0202671	0450	3
PETER ALEXANDER	LTC	0-0243896	0646	2
PETER DONALD P	2LT	0-1316084	0745	2
PETER JOHN A	1LT	0-0513647	0445	2
PETER MAURICE G	LTC	0-0239090	0758	3
PETERKA CHARLES	MAJ	0-0230652	0260	3
PETERKIN GEORGE W JR	MAJ	0-1945453	0954	1
PETERKIN WILBUR J	COL	0-0270347	0364	3
PETERS ALEXANDER	MAJ	0-0165079	0-49	3
PETERS BENARD	LTC	0-0183104	0157	1
PETERS BURNHAM L	1LT	0-0888267	0145	2
PETERS CARL F	CW3	W-2206652	0766	1
PETERS CECIL A	CW2	W-2150360	0160	1
PETERS CLARENCE C	MAJ	0-1105362	0660	2
PETERS CLAUDE P	CPT	0-0114001	1154	3
PETERS CLIFFORD	1LT	0-1913201	0553	2
PETERS DONALD W	MAJ	0-2034980	1060	1
PETERS DWAIN P	1LT	0-1316200	0645	2
PETERS EARL V	1LT	0-1012277	0744	2
PETERS EDWARD A	CW3	RW-2144398	0365	1
PETERS EDWARD R	CW2	W-2205281	0761	1
PETERS EVA G	1LT	N-0721125	0446	1
PETERS GERALD O	1LT	0-1636464	0544	2
PETERS GORDON K	MAJ	0-1582495	0363	1
PETERS GREGORY H	1LT	0-5336550	0468	2
PETERS HARRY C	MAJ	0-1019601	0461	1
PETERS HARRY E	LTC	0-0399371	0164	1
PETERS HENRY T	MAJ	0-1081669	1060	1
PETERS IONE H	2LT	N-0733334	1044	1
PETERS JAMES G	COL	0-0212784	0362	3
PETERS JOHN A	COL	0-0376228	0261	1
PETERS JOHN D	COL	0-0348995	0767	3
PETERS JOHN L	MAJ	0-1328289	1061	1
PETERS JOSEPH A	CW2	W-2144516	0557	1
PETERS JOSEPH F	LTC	0-0450471	0657	1
PETERS KENNETH C	CPT	0-1822447	0966	2
PETERS KENNETH E	CPT	0-2012376	0457	1
PETERS KENNETH H	COL	0-0299590	0668	3
PETERS LAWRENCE E	1LT	0-1312710	0745	2
PETERS LEO J	MAJ	0-2262396	0862	1
PETERS MARTIN A	LTC	0-1294188	0859	1
PETERS NYREN L	CW3	W-2147134	0760	1
PETERS PAUL E	CW3	W-2148628	0762	1
PETERS PETER H	LTC	0-0377948	0667	3
PETERS RAYMOND	MAJ	0-2035553	0661	2
PETERS RAYMOND S	2LT	0-1691588	1045	2
PETERS ROBERT H	COL	0-0228620	0663	3
PETERS RUPERT E	MAJ	0-0889772	1262	1
PETERS VERNON E	MAJ	0-0969025	1160	1
PETERS WALTER	MAJ	0-1011238	0859	1
PETERS WALTER C	LTC	0-0169074	0660	3
PETERS WALTER H JR	CW3	W-2150312	1064	1
PETERS WALTER J JR	LTC	0-1011551	0961	1

NAME	GRADE	SVC NO	DATE RET MO YR	RET CODE
PETERS WAYNE A	CW4	W-2115898	0359	1
PETERS WILLIAM C	LTC	O-1547108	1262	1
PETERS WILLIAM F	CPT	O-2036738	0759	1
PETERS WILLIAM H	CPT	O-0166125	0648	3
PETERS WILLIAM H JR	COL	O-0161346	0356	3
PETERS WILLIAM I	CPT	O-0471949	0846	1
PETERS WILLIAM R	MAJ	O-0379286	0560	1
PETERSEN ADOLF S	LTC	O-0428455	0168	3
PETERSEN CHRISTIAN	LTC	O-0463470	0748	1
PETERSEN CLARENCE W	1LT	O-1946833	0246	2
PETERSEN DONALD F	MAJ	O-0453561	0161	1
PETERSEN EMIL	MAJ	O-0966964	0964	1
PETERSEN ERNEST	MAJ	O-1575510	0557	1
PETERSEN FRED M	1LT	O-1306641	1062	1
PETERSEN GLEN N	1LT	O-1311925	0646	2
PETERSEN HANS G	COL	O-0153212	0652	3
PETERSEN HAROLD W	CPT	O-0495739	1045	2
PETERSEN HENRY F	MAJ	O-0242380	0158	3
PETERSEN HENRY F	CW3	W-2003877	1064	3
PETERSEN HENRY R	LTC	O-0425006	0662	1
PETERSEN JIMMIE P	1LT	O-1699973	0965	2
PETERSEN JOHN W	LTC	O-1826058	1267	1
PETERSEN JOHN W	CW2	W-2128587	0662	1
PETERSEN JOHNS W	CW2	W-2148301	0757	1
PETERSEN JOSEPH C	CPT	O-1102402	0646	2
PETERSEN KERMIT	MAJ	O-0752017	0651	1
PETERSEN LAVERNE H	LTC	O-1305104	1067	1
PETERSEN MELVIN E	CW3	W-2142308	0558	1
PETERSEN MERLE E	LTC	O-1114709	1266	3
PETERSEN NORMAN F	MAJ	O-1332529	0263	1
PETERSEN PATRICK J	CPT	O-0509882	1045	2
PETERSEN RAYMOND L	CW2	W-2143806	0664	1
PETERSEN SIDNEY O	MAJ	O-0214543	0963	3
PETERSEN SIDNEY M	LTC	O-1115738	0263	1
PETERSEN WILLIAM B	CPT	O-1583498	0557	1
PETERSEN WILLIAM H	CPT	O-2033567	0859	1
PETERSEN WILLIAM W	LTC	O-1292750	0463	1
PETERSILIE HENRY	1LT	O-0483046	0343	2
PETERSON ALDEN E	LTC	O-0261598	0366	3
PETERSON ALFRED	CPT	O-0887562	1053	1
PETERSON ALICE E	CPT	N-0721454	0350	2
PETERSON ANDREW J	CPT	O-1302185	1051	2
PETERSON ARTHUR K	LTC	O-0258746	0667	3
PETERSON BERTHEL W	COL	O-0202729	1160	3
PETERSON BORDEN F	LTC	O-0336889	0662	1
PETERSON BRADY	CPT	O-2262395	0161	1
PETERSON BURTON C	1LT	O-1303774	0545	2
PETERSON CAPERS L	LTC	O-0261555	0167	3
PETERSON CARL A	CPT	O-0333178	1044	2
PETERSON CARL E	CW4	W-2115947	0355	1
PETERSON CARL H	LTC	O-0284479	0266	3
PETERSON CARL L	COL	O-0176731	0646	2
PETERSON CHARLES	COL	O-1315479	0968	1
PETERSON CHARLES A	COL	O-0301533	1054	1
PETERSON CHARLES E	CPT	O-0392003	0346	2
PETERSON CHARLES R	LTC	O-0241007	1144	2
PETERSON CHESTER	COL	O-0226963	0564	3
PETERSON CHESTER A	MAJ	O-0975123	0266	2
PETERSON CHESTER I	MAJ	O-0994780	1064	1
PETERSON CHESTER W	LTC	O-1017496	0865	1
PETERSON CLARENCE	CPT	O-1689506	0845	2
PETERSON CLARENCE W	MAJ	O-0216301	0149	1
PETERSON CLEMENT	1LT	O-0169409	0156	3
PETERSON COLEMAN A	1LT	O-1051727	1062	1
PETERSON DERRELL F	COL	O-0396378	0964	3
PETERSON DON A	LTC	O-0341451	1167	3
PETERSON DONALD H	CPT	O-0412857	1045	2
PETERSON EARL O	LTC	O-0280682	0268	3
PETERSON EARL J R	LTC	O-1549015	0764	1
PETERSON EDWARD J	CW3	W-2147858	0263	1
PETERSON EDWARD W	MAJ	O-1333116	0164	1
PETERSON EDWIN W	LTC	O-0159540	0962	3
PETERSON EMIL H	CW2	W-2143956	0656	1
PETERSON EVELYN S	MAJ	N-0772646	1063	1
PETERSON FRANCIS S	MAJ	O-0343979	0846	2
PETERSON FRANK J JR	MAJ	O-2291540	1167	1
PETERSON GENE	MAJ	O-1299993	0164	1
PETERSON GEORGE E	MAJ	O-1055417	1156	2
PETERSON GEORGE G	CW3	W-2152194	0964	1
PETERSON GEORGE O	1LT	O-1797873	0146	2
PETERSON GILMAN P	CPT	O-1685250	1145	2
PETERSON GLENN D	2LT	O-1797347	1143	2
PETERSON GUSTAVE R	LTC	O-0244307	0164	3
PETERSON HAROLD	CPT	O-0106347	0648	3
PETERSON HAROLD	LTC	O-0364540	0460	1
PETERSON HAROLD W	COL	O-0355052	0667	3
PETERSON HAROLD W	CW3	W-2150782	1165	1
PETERSON HARRY L	MAJ	O-1285639	0162	1
PETERSON HARTWELL E	LTC	O-1593777	0863	1
PETERSON HARVEY L	2LT	O-1336252	0747	2
PETERSON HENRY E	MAJ	O-1018916	1055	1
PETERSON HENRY P	MAJ	O-0444900	0357	1
PETERSON HERBERT D	LTC	O-0408055	0961	1
PETERSON HOWARD G	LTC	O-1113390	0863	1
PETERSON I LILBOURN	COL	O-0210073	0154	3
PETERSON IRA R	CPT	O-0116725	0654	3
PETERSON IVAR E	LTC	O-1559810	0464	2
PETERSON JACK W	LTC	O-1307296	0264	1
PETERSON JAMES C	1LT	O-1325166	0850	2
PETERSON JAMES M	CW3	W-2005926	1266	1
PETERSON JAMES N	2LT	O-0436580	0345	2
PETERSON JAMES W	WO1	W-2119929	0464	1
PETERSON JOHN E	MAJ	O-4023236	0367	2
PETERSON JOHN F	MAJ	O-1179171	0661	1
PETERSON JOHN J	MAJ	O-0959222	1068	1
PETERSON JOHN J	CPT	O-0967893	0960	1
PETERSON JOHN L	LTC	O-0187294	0955	3
PETERSON JOHN R	LTC	O-1012012	0961	1
PETERSON JOSEPH H JR	1LT	O-1016203	1145	2
PETERSON JOSEPH L	COL	O-0235033	0259	3
PETERSON JOSEPH L	CW4	W-2111531	0261	1
PETERSON JULIAN J	MAJ	O-0974128	0264	1
PETERSON KENDALL L	LTC	O-1048137	0463	1
PETERSON KENNETH F	2LT	O-1090753	0746	2
PETERSON LARS W	CPT	O-1921728	0456	2
PETERSON LEONARD D	LTC	O-0421473	0761	1
PETERSON LEROY R	MAJ	O-1695725	0859	1
PETERSON LESLIE W	CW4	W-2150154	0568	1
PETERSON LLOYD E	LTC	O-0301614	1046	2
PETERSON LOUIS A	CPT	O-0527271	0667	1
PETERSON LOUIS G JR	LTC	O-1293308	0263	1
PETERSON LYLE E	CPT	O-1182223	1146	2
PETERSON LYLE M	MAJ	O-0964598	0565	1
PETERSON LYMAN K	MAJ	O-0393309	1047	2
PETERSON MANFRED O	CW3	W-2144756	0564	1
PETERSON MARCEL G	CPT	O-0975945	1060	1
PETERSON MARLIN A	CPT	O-1013796	0756	1
PETERSON MARTIN B	1LT	O-1925832	0254	2
PETERSON MARTIN J	CPT	O-0452391	0944	2
PETERSON MARTIN W	MAJ	O-0452863	0657	1
PETERSON MILTON F	LTC	O-1294359	0859	1
PETERSON NATHANIEL	LTC	O-0151221	0149	3
PETERSON OSCAR G	LTC	O-1588805	0363	1
PETERSON PALMA L	1LT	N-0732403	0646	1
PETERSON PHILIP H	MAJ	O-1913224	0167	1
PETERSON QUENTIN E	CW2	W-2140252	0546	2
PETERSON RALPH M	LTC	O-0450102	0657	1
PETERSON RAY A	1LT	O-0387470	0144	2
PETERSON REBECCA F	2LT	N-0742621	0944	1
PETERSON RICHARD P	CW4	W-2110157	0365	3
PETERSON ROBERT A	LTC	O-1329277	1064	1
PETERSON ROBERT A	MAJ	O-4009104	1066	1
PETERSON ROBERT F	MAJ	O-1298121	0661	1
PETERSON ROBERT H	CPT	O-1314545	0561	2
PETERSON ROBERT N	LTC	O-1182440	0968	1
PETERSON ROBERT W	2LT	O-1302186	0145	2
PETERSON RUSSELL C	CPT	O-1036333	0966	1
PETERSON RUSSELL W	CW2	W-2153048	0261	1
PETERSON SEVERIN O	CW2	W-2150134	0659	1
PETERSON SOREN A JR	MAJ	O-0788080	0762	1
PETERSON STANLEY C	CPT	O-0307598	0145	2
PETERSON STANLEY J	LTC	O-0251340	0764	3
PETERSON THADDEUS E	MAJ	O-0141721	0152	3
PETERSON THEODORE H	MAJ	O-1692901	0963	1
PETERSON THEODORE M	COL	O-0249281	1264	3
PETERSON THOMAS J	MAJ	O-1018635	0461	1
PETERSON THOMAS O	LTC	O-1182441	0264	1
PETERSON TITUS T	WO1	W-2128828	0845	1
PETERSON VAUGHN	LTC	O-0265570	0259	1
PETERSON VERNON	COL	O-0120748	0953	1
PETERSON VERNON A	MAJ	O-1634211	0358	1
PETERSON VERNON W	LTC	O-0544631	0865	1
PETERSON VICTOR R	CW4	W-2128202	1066	1
PETERSON VICTOR W	2LT	O-1999958	0347	2
PETERSON VIRGIL J	LTC	O-1104339	1054	1
PETERSON WILBUR G	1LT	O-0103117	1045	2
PETERSON WILLIAM A	COL	O-0289225	0167	3
PETERSON WILLIAM H	MAJ	O-0250830	1057	3
PETERSON WILLIAM J	CPT	O-0252942	0153	3
PETERSON WILLIAM V	LTC	O-1796856	0464	3
PETERSON WYATT B	LTC	O-1650285	1065	1
PETH JOHN C	LTC	O-0149383	0-52	3
PETHICK FRANK I JR	B G	O-0248060	0467	3
PETICOLAS JOHN D	MAJ	O-0361241	1044	2
PETIGROW NORMAN B	1LT	O-1043460	1045	2
PETINGA SALVATORE	CPT	O-1297418	0655	1
PETIT ALEXANDER	CPT	O-0108349	0134	1
PETIT JOE F	MAJ	O-1558191	0358	1
PETIT WILFRED D	MAJ	O-1010174	0957	2
PETITBON LEO A	CPT	O-2055486	0456	1
PETITE FREDERICK	MAJ	O-0257877	0446	2
PETITO PETER A	COL	O-0369209	0661	1
PETORJCK JOHN J	MAJ	O-0964828	1162	1
PETRA RUDOLPH A	1LT	O-1110184	1044	2
PETRABORG JARROLD A	COL	O-0102227	1153	2
PETRAITIS MARTHA C	MAJ	N-0743319	0967	3
PETRAKIS MANUEL M	LTC	O-0533338	1266	1
PETRAS JOSEPH W	CPT	O-1283827	0345	2
PETRASEK ALBERT C	CPT	O-0487934	0346	2
PETRASH EDWARD B	MAJ	O-0467392	0364	1
PETRE JOSEPH K	CW4	W-2111037	0454	2
PETREE NOEL H	MAJ	O-0164569	0255	2
PETRESKY JOHN J	LTC	O-1044645	0461	1
PETRI JOHN	MAJ	O-0435927	1157	1
PETRICH ARTHUR G	LTC	O-0372655	0860	1
PETRICK JOSEPH L	LTC	O-0290075	0159	3
PETRICK LAWRENCE R	LTC	O-1291512	0960	1
PETRIE ANDREW H	MAJ	O-0186471	0356	3
PETRIE HAROLD J	MAJ	O-1010855	0546	2
PETRIE ROY A	1LT	O-0129614	1252	3
PETRIE WALTER E	LTC	O-0965406	1067	1
PETRILLI FRANK	CW3	W-2205685	0765	1
PETRING RALPH W	LTC	O-0913386	0862	2
PETRINI NEVIO	LTC	O-1101617	0261	1
PETRO ANDREW P JR	CW3	W-2206421	0468	1
PETRO VASIL W	CPT	O-1686049	0844	2
PETROCHKO WASIL F	CW2	W-2208504	0564	1
PETRONE FRANK R	CPT	O-1557061	0747	2
PETRONE JOHN C	MAJ	O-0325014	0146	2
PETRONE JOSEPH A	CPT	O-0508527	0345	2
PETROSKE LOUISE C	1LT	N-0721531	0546	1
PETROSKI STANLEY	1LT	O-1324647	0140	2
PETROVICH ENRIQUE	LTC	O-0373942	1160	1
PETROVICH JOHN J	2LT	O-1636467	0844	2
PETROVICH WALTER C	CW3	W-2150232	0659	1
PETROVSKY PAUL	LTC	O-1030738	0362	3
PETROWSKI JOSEPH P	1LT	O-0157571	0658	3
PETRU FRANK L	COL	O-0259436	0967	3
PETRY FRANCIS J	MAJ	O-0949938	0963	1
PETRY WILLIAM A	LTC	O-0490522	1145	2
PETSCH ALFRED P C	LTC	O-0103398	1153	3
PETSCH DOROTHY L	MAJ	N-0741491	0767	3
PETT MARLIN J	1LT	O-1300849	0246	2
PETTAWAY JOHN T	CPT	O-1559608	1161	1
PETTAY JOSEPH F	CW2	W-2116100	0553	1
PETTENGELL ROBERT E	1LT	O-1182224	0461	1
PETTENGILL HENRY G	1LT	O-1797003	1143	2
PETTERSEN HERBERT C	COL	O-0198588	0463	3
PETTERSEN HERBERT F	LTC	O-0481234	0954	1
PETTERSEN PEDER G	COL	O-0300160	1057	3
PETTERSON MARCUS A	LTC	O-1576497	0660	1
PETTET JOSEPH W	LTC	O-0358201	0261	2
PETTI GEORGE H	CPT	O-0513680	0545	2
PETTIE FLOYD W	CW3	W-2152772	1160	1
PETTIE RICHARD C	CPT	O-4011155	1166	1
PETTIFORD ROBERT L	CW3	W-2144645	0363	2
PETTIFORD SAMUEL E	MAJ	O-1049609	0964	1
PETTIGREW GEORGE W	MAJ	O-1060922	0758	1
PETTIGREW ROBERT JR	MAJ	O-1948650	0165	1
PETTIGREW VERNEL W	2LT	O-1540694	1045	2
PETTIGREW WILLIAM B	MAJ	O-0678449	1062	1
PETTINE ULDRICH H	LTC	O-1168411	0165	1
PETTINGER JOHN L	LTC	O-0367610	0862	1
PETTINGER MARY E	CPT	N-0758038	0947	1
PETTINGER NEIL S	1LT	O-1700613	0443	2
PETTIS GEORGE S	CPT	O-0500064	0246	2
PETTIT ALFRED B	1LT	O-0351120	0145	2
PETTIT BILLY	MAJ	O-2262330	0263	1
PETTIT CHARLES A	LTC	O-0297868	0366	3
PETTIT EDWARD Y	MAJ	O-0468407	0248	2
PETTIT JOHN G	1LT	O-0227697	1263	3
PETTIT LOYDE A	CPT	O-1649909	0954	1
PETTIT ROYCE E	MAJ	O-0210666	0555	3
PETTIT WILMER S	CPT	O-0911910	0545	2
PETTS FRANCES	1LT	N-0788871	1046	1
PETTUS BACON P	LTC	O-0156519	0253	3
PETTUS ELINOR S	2LT	N-0700167	0638	1
PETTUS FITZHUGH	CPT	O-0505224	1149	1
PETTWAY RICHARD W	LTC	O-0162562	0459	3
PETTY ADDISON E	LTC	O-0224594	0162	3
PETTY ALBERT W	CW2	W-2147491	0961	1
PETTY BENNIE	CPT	O-4000208	1262	2
PETTY CARL G	MAJ	O-0299953	0668	3
PETTY CHARLES D	LTC	O-1184130	0366	1
PETTY JEFFERSON	COL	O-0204557	0-53	1
PETTY JESSE M	CPT	O-0496523	0449	1
PETTY JOHN S	CPT	O-1167580	1045	2
PETTY MAUDE L D	2LT	N-0700831	1140	1
PETTY MILDRED L	MAJ	N-0755560	0767	3
PETTY PAUL L	CPT	O-0289983	0944	2
PETTY ROY C	CPT	O-1552356	0561	1
PETTY VERNON H	CW2	W-2212752	0865	1
PETTY VERNON L	CW3	W-2149799	0864	1
PETTY WILLIAM A	WO1	W-2130127	0445	2
PETTY WILLIE E	1LT	O-1648669	0852	2
PETTYJOHN H C	CW2	W-2209897	0664	1
PETTYJOHN WILLIAM J	CW3	W-2141410	1160	1
PETZOLD THEODORE A	CPT	O-0280005	1144	2
PEURA JAMES G	MAJ	O-2263610	0367	1
PEVERELL HAROLD D	CPT	O-1333698	1151	2
PEVERILL WILLIAM L	COL	O-0236437	0165	3
PEW FRANK W	MAJ	O-2009563	0663	1
PEYRONNIN CHESTER A	LTC	O-0286620	1163	3
PEYSER JULIAN I	2LT	O-1170522	1043	2
PEYTON ALLEN T JR	LTC	O-1552956	0264	1
PEYTON CLIFFORD E	LTC	O-1648576	0463	1
PEYTON DONALD	MAJ	O-1897782	0563	1
PEYTON HAMILTON S	LTC	O-0284689	0164	3
PEYTON PHILIP B	1LT	O-0317658	1042	2
PFAFF CHARLES W	MAJ	O-1542335	0548	2
PFAFF JULIAN F	COL	O-0328894	1165	1
PFAFF RICHARD H	1LT	O-1881404	0453	2
PFAFF WALTER	CPT	O-1588808	1168	2
PFAFFMANN VALENTINE	1LT	O-1166811	0140	2
PFANNENSCHMIDT A R	LTC	O-0262855	0958	2
PFAUTZ JOE H	LTC	O-0962260	0768	1
PFEFER ABRAHAM	LTC	O-0488229	0449	1
PFEFFER ALBERT J	LTC	O-0289377	0962	1
PFEFFER FRANCIS A	MAJ	O-0304105	0766	3
PFEIFER CHARLES R	LTC	O-1183392	0465	1

NAME	GRADE	SVC NO	DATE RET MO YR	RET CODE
PFEIFER JOSEPH	1LT	0-1054363	1044	2
PFEIFFER ALEXIS V	LTC	0-0540948	0966	1
PFEIFFER BERNARD C	LTC	0-1945246	0967	1
PFEIFFER CARL F H	LTC	0-0247837	0465	3
PFEIFFER ERIC P	MAJ	0-0255730	0146	2
PFEIFFER FLOYD L	COL	0-0291257	0760	1
PFEIFFER HERBERT G	CPT	0-0259569	0144	2
PFEIFFER JOHN L	MAJ	0-1004660	0661	1
PFEIFFER THEODORE	LTC	0-0359068	0451	2
PFEIL WILLIAM A	LTC	0-1182681	0467	1
PFERSCH FRANK R	MAJ	0-1107040	0961	1
PFIEFER HAROLD E	LTC	0-1115063	1162	1
PFIESTER ALFRED C	CW4	W-2143087	0268	1
PFINGST ADOLPH	1LT	0-1319771	0246	2
PFIRRMANN KARL B	MAJ	0-1293469	0346	2
PFISTER EARL F	LTC	0-1553182	0661	1
PFISTER FRANCIS F	LTC	0-0295222	1067	3
PFISTER PAUL G	WO1	W-2132288	1150	1
PFISTER RALPH L	MAJ	0-1545554	0660	1
PFLEPSEN NICHOLAS M	2LT	0-1334741	0746	2
PFLIEGER JOHN A	LTC	0-0170096	0559	3
PFLUGER CLEMENS A	CPT	0-0241572	1061	3
PFLUGER WALTER L	LTC	0-0207686	1163	3
PFLUGLER JOSEPH E	LTC	0-2283717	0568	2
PFOHL RICHARD A	1LT	0-1166583	0444	2
PFROMM GEORGE L	LTC	0-0277793	1065	3
PFROMMER FRED G	2LT	0-0540501	1045	2
PFUNKE WINSTON F	CPT	0-1318695	0 46	2
PHAGAN JULIUS G	CW2	W-2150609	0957	1
PHALEN THEODORE R	LTC	0-0181753	0855	3
PHANEUF VICTOR S	COL	0-0222296	0758	3
PHARAOH FRANK H	COL	0-0149398	1155	1
PHARR FRANK W	MAJ	0-1176763	0264	1
PHARR GEORGE T	MAJ	0-1105739	0465	1
PHARR JAMES M	LTC	0-0293483	0768	3
PHARR ROBERT W	COL	0-0309783	0768	3
PHARR STANLEY M	MAJ	0-1118104	0462	1
PHEASANT CLYDE D	CW3	W-2208550	0967	1
PHELAN JOHN A JR	CPT	0-0447294	1146	2
PHELAN JOHN J	1LT	0-0889183	0260	1
PHELAN MICHAEL V	MAJ	0-1559112	0962	1
PHELAN PAUL L	LTC	0-0257811	1047	2
PHELPS DOUGLAS L	CW2	W-2213709	0368	1
PHELPS ELBERT S	1LT	0-1108927	0945	2
PHELPS ELLIS H	MAJ	0-0383614	0368	3
PHELPS FOSTER C	LTC	0-0236472	0765	3
PHELPS FREDERICK	LTC	0-2047105	1262	1
PHELPS HAMILTON H	LTC	0-0293024	0860	1
PHELPS HAPPER K	LTC	0-0104959	1151	3
PHELPS HAROLD B	LTC	0-0224525	1164	3
PHELPS HAROLD P	COL	0-0264456	0147	2
PHELPS HARRY E	LTC	0-0264624	0856	3
PHELPS IRVIL D SR	CW3	W-2104373	0257	1
PHELPS JEWELL D	CPT	0-1557657	0947	2
PHELPS MAX W	LTC	0-0321968	0757	2
PHELPS NEIL T	COL	0-0241643	0765	3
PHELPS RAYMOND A	COL	0-0219572	0853	3
PHELPS ROBERT J	MAJ	0-0452352	0848	2
PHELPS ROBERT J	2LT	0-1105103	1144	2
PHELPS ROSSWELL F	LTC	0-1167157	0258	1
PHELPS STANLEY K	CW3	W-2149677	0866	1
PHELPS WILLIAM S	LTC	0-1293107	0766	1
PHERIGO JOHN B	2LT	0-1108237	1044	2
PHERO NORMAN F	LTC	0-1184921	0766	1
PHETTEPLACE RAY F	CW2	W-2152281	0861	1
PHIBBS ANDREW F	MAJ	0-0486072	0965	3
PHIFER OLLIE A	MAJ	0-1103862	0960	1
PHIFER PAUL H	CPT	0-1330218	1055	1
PHIFER WALTER L	1LT	0-1319227	0246	2
PHILBECK ROBERT H	CW3	W-2147291	1166	2
PHILBIN JOHN A	MAJ	0-0187193	0147	2
PHILBIN LEO P	2LT	0-2006468	1145	2
PHILBRICK ARNOLD D	CPT	0-0286888	1059	3
PHILBRICK LEON G JR	MAJ	0-0824713	0465	1
PHILBROOK MORTIMER	CW2	W-2116232	1146	1

NAME	GRADE	SVC NO	DATE RET MO YR	RET CODE
PHILIP HERBERT A	MAJ	0-0447959	0246	2
PHILIP RUSSEL E	LTC	0-0308432	0568	3
PHILIP VAN N	COL	0-0204001	0756	3
PHILIPPS CARL J	2LT	0-1107631	0744	2
PHILIPS BILLY U SR	MAJ	0-2038853	1159	2
PHILIPS HOWARD E	LTC	0-0229094	0764	3
PHILIPS JULIAN H	LTC	0-1298919	0761	1
PHILIPS VINCENT D	LTC	0-0235188	1045	2
PHILIPSEN CLIFFORD A	MAJ	0-2019364	0865	1
PHILIPSEN GEORGE E	LTC	0-0268745	1063	3
PHILLABAUM C O	MAJ	0-1545996	0758	2
PHILLABAUM DONALD E	2LT	0-1309601	0444	2
PHILLABAUM JACK O	MAJ	0-4009456	0966	1
PHILLEBAUM LEONARD P	CW2	W-2205700	0663	1
PHILLEO ROLLAND A	LTC	0-0236164	0266	3
PHILLIPP JOSEPH J JR	CW3	W-2203496	0766	1
PHILLIPP LOUIS S N	COL	0-0100564	1053	3
PHILLIPPE CLAUDE C	1LT	0-1298753	1045	2
PHILLIPS ALBERT H	1LT	0-0376413	1044	2
PHILLIPS ALBERT S	CW3	W-2152832	0263	1
PHILLIPS ALBERT W	MAJ	0-1994554	0367	3
PHILLIPS ALBERT W JR	LTC	0-0271729	0668	3
PHILLIPS ALFRED	LTC	0-0540323	0968	1
PHILLIPS ANTON A	CPT	0-0342944	0545	2
PHILLIPS ARTHUR W	CW3	W-2149371	0463	1
PHILLIPS BARRETT H	1LT	0-0452610	0352	2
PHILLIPS BASHAN B	CW4	W-2129116	0556	1
PHILLIPS BOBBY M	CW2	W-2210811	0767	1
PHILLIPS BUEL R	MAJ	0-0966635	0459	1
PHILLIPS CARL E	CPT	0-0120954	0456	3
PHILLIPS CARL E	MAJ	0-2262459	0662	1
PHILLIPS CARO E	1LT	0-0372678	0844	2
PHILLIPS CECIL F	MAJ	0-1309961	0965	1
PHILLIPS CHARLES B	MAJ	0-1173034	1162	1
PHILLIPS CHARLES E	LTC	0-0305856	0861	1
PHILLIPS CHARLES G	MAJ	0-1941900	0267	1
PHILLIPS CHARLES H	LTC	0-0200998	0545	2
PHILLIPS CHARLES I	LTC	0-1552770	1061	1
PHILLIPS CHARLES W	1LT	0-1170910	0546	2
PHILLIPS CHARLES W	LTC	0-2033741	0768	1
PHILLIPS CLARENCE I	CW3	W-2145115	0561	1
PHILLIPS CLAUDE C JR	COL	0-0427865	0668	1
PHILLIPS CLAUDE R JR	MAJ	0-1307848	0862	1
PHILLIPS CLAURICE M	COL	0-0308484	0964	3
PHILLIPS CLYDE J	CW2	W-2145832	1155	1
PHILLIPS CYRIL J	MAJ	0-2023805	0762	1
PHILLIPS DOUGLAS H	CW4	W-2113946	0563	2
PHILLIPS EARL	1LT	0-0149160	0648	3
PHILLIPS EARL E	LTC	0-0209641	0450	3
PHILLIPS EARL G	1LT	0-1177138	1045	2
PHILLIPS EARL G	CPT	0-1947163	1046	2
PHILLIPS EDWARD C	LTC	0-0165699	0552	3
PHILLIPS EDWARD J	CPT	0-1541036	0964	1
PHILLIPS EDWARD L	MAJ	0-2263111	0264	1
PHILLIPS EDWARD R	MAJ	0-1284758	0561	1
PHILLIPS EDWARD W	LTC	0-0503637	0657	1
PHILLIPS ESKILL A	CW3	W-3150472	0168	1
PHILLIPS FLETCHER	CW4	W-2124184	1153	1
PHILLIPS FRANCIS J	MAJ	0-0238914	1164	3
PHILLIPS FRANCIS J	LTC	0-1553535	0760	1
PHILLIPS FRANKLIN A	2LT	0-1171718	0244	2
PHILLIPS FRED L	LTC	0-1284013	0564	1
PHILLIPS FREDERICK	LTC	0-0217885	0761	3
PHILLIPS FREDERICK	MAJ	0-2055164	0459	1
PHILLIPS GEORGE M	LTC	0-0550120	0565	1
PHILLIPS GILES T	LTC	0-0299638	0264	3
PHILLIPS GLENN J	CPT	0-0282762	0145	2
PHILLIPS HAL B	LTC	0-1051728	0862	1
PHILLIPS HAROLD	LTC	0-1302046	0263	1
PHILLIPS HAROLD W	CW2	W-2142187	1058	1
PHILLIPS HARRISON M	LTC	0-1321547	0764	1
PHILLIPS HARRY	CPT	0-0290609	0257	3
PHILLIPS HARRY	CPT	0-0498350	0549	2
PHILLIPS HARRY L SR	CW4	W-2127847	0659	1
PHILLIPS HARTSELL O	MAJ	0-0949714	1263	1

NAME	GRADE	SVC NO	DATE RET MO YR	RET CODE
PHILLIPS HERBERT R	LTC	0-0473066	0865	3
PHILLIPS HERSCHEL A	1LT	0-0552047	0-48	2
PHILLIPS HORACE B II	MAJ	0-0461737	0347	2
PHILLIPS IVAN J	CW3	W-2147711	0766	1
PHILLIPS JACK R	MAJ	0-1339846	1164	1
PHILLIPS JAMES E	CPT	0-0980340	0662	1
PHILLIPS JAMES O	MAJ	0-1000170	0350	2
PHILLIPS JAMES O	CW3	W-2148880	0962	1
PHILLIPS JAMES R	LTC	0-1945038	0864	1
PHILLIPS JAMES T	COL	0-0245171	0461	3
PHILLIPS JAMES W	CPT	0-0509181	0546	2
PHILLIPS JAMES Y	MAJ	0-0515042	0146	2
PHILLIPS JESSE W	WO1	W-2113711	0558	1
PHILLIPS JOHN B	CPT	0-0420208	1144	2
PHILLIPS JOHN E	2LT	0-2005705	0646	2
PHILLIPS JOHN F	MAJ	0-4031101	0768	1
PHILLIPS JOHN H	LTC	0-0439925	0954	1
PHILLIPS JOHN H	CW2	W-2208507	0463	1
PHILLIPS JOHN M	COL	0-0187445	1160	3
PHILLIPS JOHN M	LTC	0-0298606	0246	2
PHILLIPS JOHN P	MAJ	0-0103893	0850	3
PHILLIPS JOHN R	CPT	0-0558458	0946	2
PHILLIPS JOHN R	LTC	0-1596147	0764	1
PHILLIPS JOHN R	MAJ	0-2007797	1060	1
PHILLIPS JOHN R	MAJ	0-2097077	0565	1
PHILLIPS JOHN T	CW2	W-2206836	1064	1
PHILLIPS JOHNIE F	MAJ	0-1822904	1164	1
PHILLIPS JOHNNIE T	CPT	0-1108238	0245	2
PHILLIPS JOSEPH B JR	COL	0-0330996	0262	1
PHILLIPS JOSEPH J	CPT	0-1060588	0947	2
PHILLIPS JOSEPH J	CW4	W-2003511	0267	3
PHILLIPS JOSEPH R	MAJ	0-0488809	0448	1
PHILLIPS KARL E	LTC	0-1055698	0465	1
PHILLIPS KENNETH L	1LT	0-1312980	1048	2
PHILLIPS KENNETH P	CPT	0-1920269	1162	1
PHILLIPS LAYMAN	CW2	W-2141323	0357	1
PHILLIPS LEE	WO1	W-2109487	1045	2
PHILLIPS LEE J	1LT	0-1845944	1045	2
PHILLIPS LELAND J	1LT	0-1293826	0146	2
PHILLIPS LESTER L	CW2	W-2152395	1055	1
PHILLIPS LOYD B	CPT	0-0499504	0855	1
PHILLIPS MARK H	CPT	0-0480013	0746	2
PHILLIPS MELVILLE	CPT	0-0465385	0747	1
PHILLIPS MERRILL F	MAJ	0-0222820	0656	3
PHILLIPS MORGAN L SR	COL	0-0201552	0762	3
PHILLIPS MORTON E	CW3	W-2152903	0764	1
PHILLIPS NANCY S	CW4	V-0406204	0168	1
PHILLIPS NOEL F	CPT	0-0262075	0866	3
PHILLIPS ORRIE F	CW2	W-2141882	1055	1
PHILLIPS PAUL	MAJ	0-1552957	0958	1
PHILLIPS PAUL E JR	CPT	0-1558520	0863	1
PHILLIPS PURDY	LTC	0-1291690	0361	1
PHILLIPS RALPH E	MAJ	0-1878228	0967	1
PHILLIPS RALPH L	MAJ	0-0382171	0746	2
PHILLIPS RALPH L	MAJ	0-1173038	1162	1
PHILLIPS RANDOLPH E	LTC	0-0528004	1268	1
PHILLIPS RAY O	MAJ	0-0510965	0855	1
PHILLIPS RAYMOND E	COL	0-0219287	0660	3
PHILLIPS RAYMOND L	CPT	0-0342312	0363	1
PHILLIPS RAYMOND M	COL	0-0270641	0868	3
PHILLIPS RAYMOND M	2LT	0-1328840	1145	2
PHILLIPS RENDEP T	2LT	0-2006867	0146	2
PHILLIPS RICHARD F	1LT	0-0409691	0644	2
PHILLIPS ROBERT C	CPT	0-1015494	0462	1
PHILLIPS ROBERT JR	CPT	0-1635206	0945	2
PHILLIPS ROBERT M	MAJ	0-0292892	0244	2
PHILLIPS ROBERT O	LTC	0-0402745	0765	1
PHILLIPS ROLAND J	MAJ	0-0885647	0457	1
PHILLIPS ROYAL G	CPT	0-0178231	0756	3
PHILLIPS RUPERT E	CW2	W-2214946	1066	1
PHILLIPS RUSSELL E	CPT	0-1325595	0246	2
PHILLIPS SAM B	MAJ	0-1179572	1058	1
PHILLIPS SAMUEL	LTC	0-1283501	1054	1
PHILLIPS STONEWALL	LTC	0-0288522	1145	2
PHILLIPS TALMAGE J	MAJ	0-1589441	0662	1

NAME	GRADE	SVC NO	DATE RET MO YR	RET CODE
PHILLIPS THOMAS J	LTC	0-0420538	0152	2
PHILLIPS THOMAS R	CW2	W-2152506	1057	1
PHILLIPS THOMAS W	MAJ	0-1030405	0960	1
PHILLIPS VIRGIL G	LTC	0-1643967	1060	1
PHILLIPS WADE H	LTC	0-0208417	0648	3
PHILLIPS WALLACE G	CPT	0-0309854	1145	2
PHILLIPS WALTER G	1LT	0-1181730	0646	2
PHILLIPS WALTER J	CW3	W-2151729	0964	1
PHILLIPS WALTER JR	MAJ	0-1297419	1061	1
PHILLIPS WAYNE G	MAJ	0-0100621	0928	1
PHILLIPS WENDELL B	CW2	W-2112672	1049	2
PHILLIPS WENDELL P	LTC	0-0452534	0764	1
PHILLIPS WILLIAM C	LTC	0-0321702	1060	3
PHILLIPS WILLIAM E	1LT	0-2262270	0358	1
PHILLIPS WILLIAM H	MAJ	0-0116969	0449	3
PHILLIPS WILLIAM H	MAJ	0-1020243	0161	1
PHILLIPS WILLIAM J	LTC	0-0362687	0766	3
PHILLIPS WILLIAM L	MAJ	0-1035047	0360	1
PHILLIPS WILLIAM T	LTC	0-1291513	0860	1
PHILLIPS WILLIAM T	WO1	W-2152683	0753	1
PHILLIPS WILLIAM W	1LT	0-1295426	1045	2
PHILLIPSEN EDWIN R	LTC	0-1302345	0762	1
PHILLPOTTS RONALD A	MAJ	0-0413497	0656	1
PHILMAN JACK M	1LT	0-0475318	0445	2
PHILMON LEE B	MAJ	0-2263578	0465	1
PHILP GEORGE B	LTC	0-1639495	0164	1
PHILPOT ERNEST W	LTC	0-0030627	1060	1
PHILPOT JAMES S	CW3	W-2149813	0166	1
PHILPOT MARION M	CW4	W-2146146	0966	2
PHILPOTT ROBERT J	COL	0-0256799	1066	3
PHILQUIST HARRIS E	MAJ	0-1578972	0865	1
PHINIZY JOHN A	CPT	0-0288633	1046	2
PHINNEY CARL L	M G	0-0244577	1164	3
PHINNEY EDWARD T	COL	0-0355187	0267	3
PHINNEY MABLE A	CPT	N-0787461	0346	1
PHINNEY WALLACE S	LTC	0-0300731	0667	3
PHIPPS ALTON T	LTC	0-1822051	0662	1
PHIPPS GENE O	CW2	W-3430652	0468	1
PHIPPS GEORGE E	1LT	0-0297705	0844	2
PHIPPS HARRY R	COL	0-0282815	0361	1
PHIPPS JAMES M	1LT	0-1692539	0447	2
PHIPPS WILBUR H	LTC	0-1646887	1067	1
PHLEEGER GUY D	MAJ	0-1172222	0261	1
PHOEBUS JOHN W	1LT	0-0452904	0245	2
PHOENIX MERRILL W	LTC	0-0432315	1054	1
PHYSIOC JOHN U	LTC	0-1101994	1061	1
PIASECKI DONALD E	1LT	0-5706534	0963	2
PIASECKI EDMUND B	1LT	0-1297941	0845	2
PIASECKI STANLEY F	1LT	0-1289959	0945	2
PIASECZNY JOSEPH J	MAJ	0-1331220	0861	1
PIATT MALCOLM K	2LT	0-1108239	0145	2
PIAZZA EUGENE S	MAJ	0-1937583	0566	1
PICARD COLICE P	LTC	0-0397531	0757	1
PICARD HARRY L	1LT	0-1172225	0346	2
PICARD HENRY J	LTC	0-0970453	1268	1
PICARD JOHN J	2LT	0-1316086	0644	2
PICARD POLLY A F	1LT	L-0303818	0145	2
PICCIALLO BENJAMIN	2LT	0-1108929	0645	2
PICCININO JOSEPH	CW2	W-2206347	0863	1
PICCININO LEONARD J	CW3	W-2152396	0863	1
PICCIUOLO CHARLES	LTC	0-2042806	0461	1
PICCOLO SEBASTIAN	1LT	0-1921227	1052	2
PICHICHERO LARRY J	MAJ	0-0966610	0462	1
PICK CHARLES	WO1	W-2105821	1043	2
PICK CHARLES A	CW2	W-2204114	0862	1
PICK JOHN F	LTC	0-0513489	0646	2
PICKAR DANIEL N	COL	0-0307997	0868	3
PICKARD CHARLES M	LTC	0-0260288	0646	2
PICKARD HELEN E	1LT	N-0724432	0146	1
PICKARD JOSEPH A	CPT	0-1283828	0847	2
PICKARD RICHARD H	CW2	W-2214756	0868	1
PICKEL FRNCIS M JR	1LT	0-0953769	0852	2
PICKEL ROBERT H JR	MAJ	0-0327827	0746	2
PICKELL HEYWARD M	LTC	0-0229071	0465	3
PICKENHEIM WALTER H	CW3	W-2147444	0566	1

NAME	GRADE	SVC NO	DATE RET MO YR	RET CODE
PICKENS JAMES J	MAJ	0-4010765	0868	2
PICKENS JAY W	LTC	0-0259568	1145	2
PICKENS JOE B	2LT	0-1823345	0944	2
PICKENS RALPH D	1LT	0-1102906	0546	2
PICKENS WILEY M	COL	0-0235829	0956	3
PICKERING FRANK I	MAJ	0-0165318	1047	1
PICKERING GEORGE E	LTC	0-1553521	0767	1
PICKERING GEORGE J	CPT	0-1167159	0547	1
PICKERING HILDEN D	MAJ	0-1060250	0762	1
PICKERING JAMES A	1LT	0-2037091	0745	2
PICKERING JOHN A	MAJ	0-1110186	0663	1
PICKERING RAMON H	CPT	0-1305639	1060	1
PICKERING S J JR	CW2	W-2149015	1058	1
PICKERING WALTER J G	LTC	0-0223143	0364	3
PICKETT CHARLES M JR	LTC	0-0231917	0265	3
PICKETT CLYDE N	2LT	0-1177937	0245	2
PICKETT ELLIS H	LTC	0-1182226	0966	1
PICKETT EVAN S	LTC	0-1101167	0461	1
PICKETT FRED B	LTC	0-0324301	0265	3
PICKETT GEORGE H	CPT	0-4020972	1264	1
PICKETT HENRY F	CPT	0-0246325	1262	3
PICKETT HOWARD D	LTC	0-1994505	0764	1
PICKETT HOWARD L	CW3	W-2150761	0562	1
PICKETT JOHN L	COL	0-0245342	0658	3
PICKETT JOHN T	1LT	0-0423176	1047	2
PICKETT RICHARD B	2LT	0-1798509	0345	2
PICKETT SAMUEL P	COL	0-0232452	0261	3
PICKETT WALTER F	LTC	0-0206360	0446	2
PICKETT WILLIAM J	COL	0-0206366	0853	3
PICKETT WILLIAM JR	CW3	W-2205283	0766	1
PICKETTE WILLIE B	CW4	W-2141411	0966	1
PICKHARDT ISAAC J	MAJ	0-1311358	0960	2
PICKHARDT OTTO C	LTC	0-0445678	0844	2
PICKING GLENN E	MAJ	0-1300526	0948	2
PICKINPAUGH THOMAS E	CPT	0-2023329	0761	1
PICKLE CHARLES F	MAJ	0-1316325	0859	1
PICKLE OLIVER W	CW3	W-2142889	1160	1
PICKLE OWEN B	MAJ	0-2204160	1263	1
PICKRELL ISAAC R	CW2	W-2147239	0260	1
PICKUP MICHAEL	LTC	0-0455106	0560	2
PICKWICK GEORGE B	COL	0-0241088	1060	1
PICO THOMAS M	LTC	0-1302513	0266	1
PICOTTE CARYL L	LTC	0-0131258	0947	2
PICOU DRA F	1LT	N-0734929	0746	1
PIDCOCK FINLEY S	MAJ	0-0223665	0458	3
PIDGEON DONALD F	CPT	0-1284933	0662	1
PIDGEON LARRY	CPT	0-0325594	0644	2
PIECUKONIS ALEXANDER	CW3	W-2145578	0164	1
PIEDRA CHARLES	LTC	0-1283665	0763	1
PIEKARSKI KASIMIR J	MAJ	0-0940741	0862	1
PIEKARSKI LEONARD J	LTC	0-1111835	0763	1
PIEKLIK WILLIAM	CW4	W-2103315	0267	1
PIEMME WALTER C	LTC	0-1171719	1264	1
PIENKOWSKI OLIVER E	LTC	0-0244145	0864	3
PIEPENBURG ARTHUR K	MAJ	0-0956864	0863	1
PIEPER CARL A	LTC	0-0512616	1065	1
PIEPER GEORGE F	CPT	0-0422267	1045	2
PIEPKORN ARTHUR C	COL	0-0340801	0767	3
PIER WALTER F	LTC	0-1289960	0861	1
PIERCE ALONZO R	LTC	0-0374814	0859	1
PIERCE BOLTON S	LTC	0-0330045	1059	1
PIERCE BURTON	MAJ	0-1317338	1059	1
PIERCE CARL B	CPT	0-0959782	1061	1
PIERCE CHARLES H	CW3	W-2152773	0667	1
PIERCE CHESTER H	CPT	0-0169390	0850	3
PIERCE CLYDE W	MAJ	0-1313511	1057	1
PIERCE DAVID P	1LT	0-1015577	0146	2
PIERCE EARL S	LTC	0-1945675	0463	1
PIERCE EDMUND P	CPT	0-0978064	1058	2
PIERCE EMERSON J	CPT	0-0219184	0459	3
PIERCE ERIE F	LTC	0-0350149	0859	1
PIERCE FRANKLIN M	MAJ	0-1636474	0360	1
PIERCE GEORGE B	LTC	0-0338858	0660	1
PIERCE GEORGE J	1LT	0-1010644	0846	2
PIERCE HAROLD K	CPT	0-1045211	0248	2
PIERCE HARRY G	COL	0-0171807	0449	3
PIERCE HARRY W	MAJ	0-1297584	0462	1
PIERCE HORACE E	LTC	0-0334242	0865	1
PIERCE HORACE LEE	MAJ	0-0496140	0851	2
PIERCE IRA L	LTC	0-1686534	0166	1
PIERCE ISAIAH B	LTC	0-0422443	1067	3
PIERCE JACK B	MAJ	0-0312830	0654	1
PIERCE JACKSON A	MAJ	0-0966898	0263	1
PIERCE JAMES A	COL	0-0276201	1063	3
PIERCE JAMES F	CPT	0-0984364	0762	1
PIERCE JAMES L	CW2	W-3200290	0866	1
PIERCE JAMES T	LTC	0-0108366	0748	1
PIERCE KEITH Z	CW3	W-2208701	0268	2
PIERCE LAWRENCE R	LTC	0-0393278	1267	3
PIERCE LAWRENCE S	MAJ	0-0224514	0862	3
PIERCE LEON G	CPT	0-1180296	1046	2
PIERCE LESLIE W	MAJ	0-1950236	0966	3
PIERCE LESTER W JR	LTC	0-1041275	0665	1
PIERCE LLOYD G	CPT	0-2011962	0562	2
PIERCE LOUIS I	MAJ	0-2289503	0967	1
PIERCE MILLARD H	LTC	0-0287372	1059	2
PIERCE PAUL F	MAJ	0-2262764	0961	1
PIERCE PHILLIPS H	CW4	W-2007731	0968	3
PIERCE RALPH W	COL	0-0163825	0548	2
PIERCE ROBERT E	LTC	0-0376628	0263	1
PIERCE ROBERT F	COL	0-0182125	0462	3
PIERCE ROBERT H	CW2	W-2144448	0559	1
PIERCE ROBERT L	LTC	0-1285116	0861	1
PIERCE ROBERT W	2LT	0-1327763	1045	2
PIERCE RUBY L	2LT	N-0737134	0545	1
PIERCE RUSSEL F	LTC	0-0341148	0463	3
PIERCE SUMNER W	COL	0-0241644	0363	3
PIERCE WILLIAM A	LTC	0-0358582	0663	1
PIERCE WILLIAM A	LTC	0-1300375	0764	1
PIERCE WILLIAM B	LTC	0-1289313	0261	1
PIERCE WILLIAM L	LTC	0-1551084	0462	1
PIERCE WILLIAM W	MAJ	0-0117674	0648	3
PIERCE WILLIAM W	LTC	0-0500250	1146	2
PIERCY EDITH T	MAJ	L-1010042	0466	1
PIERCY GAY V	LTC	0-0379785	0660	1
PIERCY KATHERINE	MAJ	N-0797446	0665	1
PIERCY WALTER W	MAJ	0-2014669	0163	1
PIERDOLLA EUGENIA	1LT	N-0702530	0243	1
PIERLUISI GUILLERMO	MAJ	0-0425132	1145	2
PIERNICK ROMAN T	LTC	0-0383287	0364	1
PIERPOINT OWEN W	CW3	W-2152714	0563	1
PIERPONT ROGER L	MAJ	0-0447904	104N	2
PIERPONT WILSON R	LTC	0-0376669	1262	1
PIERSALL RUSH C	WO1	W-2150357	0555	1
PIERSALL SHIRLEY L	LTC	0-1795965	0461	1
PIERSON BERT	MAJ	0-2014499	0666	1
PIERSON CLIFFORD G	2LT	0-1948808	0945	2
PIERSON DALTON T	MAJ	0-2052403	0866	3
PIERSON DON E	MAJ	0-0889244	1060	1
PIERSON EDWARD C	COL	0-0102199	0457	3
PIERSON FRANK M	LTC	0-0904895	0267	2
PIERSON GEORGE W	LTC	0-1001435	1161	2
PIERSON HAROLD R	CPT	0-0254364	1045	2
PIERSON HARRY T JR	MAJ	0-1333258	0263	1
PIERSON JOSEPH R	LTC	0-0290500	0346	2
PIERSON LEROY C	COL	0-0406996	0866	1
PIERSON RUSSELL H	LTC	0-1030920	0562	1
PIERSON STANLEY D	CPT	0-0948977	0860	1
PIERSON VAL S	LTC	0-0418474	0262	1
PIERSON WARREN R	MAJ	0-0349733	0560	1
PIET JOHN F	MAJ	0-1944552	0763	1
PIETRANTONIO NICHOLA	MAJ	0-1924116	0566	1
PIETRI VICENTE	1LT	0-0180059	0352	3
PIETRO JOSEPH N	CPT	0-0510399	0747	1
PIETROVITO JEREMIAH	MAJ	0-1923601	1163	1
PIETRZYK JOSEPH A	2LT	0-1181408	1144	2
PIETTE HUBERT J	LTC	0-0235036	0662	3
PIETZ MARTAIN	MAJ	0-1015450	0759	1
PIFER FERDINAND JR	MAJ	0-1298125	0861	1
PIFER JAMES R	LTC	0-0335133	1054	3
PIGEAULT RENE J	MAJ	0-2262836	0267	1
PIGEON CARL R	MAJ	0-2020759	0963	1
PIGFORD CHARLES A	COL	0-0301607	0745	2
PIGG HERMAN E	CW2	W-2149315	0161	1
PIGG ROBERT W	MAJ	0-2029564	1263	1
PIGGOTT KENNETH S	LTC	0-0523915	1054	1
PIGHETTI JOHN C	LTC	0-0194021	0546	2
PIGMAN CHARLES F	MAJ	0-1342113	1162	1
PIGOTT THOMAS R	LTC	0-1041631	0866	1
PIKAITIS ANTHONY P	1LT	0-1302188	0456	1
PIKE CHARLES W	CW2	W-2116049	1154	1
PIKE ENIS H	MAJ	0-1165322	0765	1
PIKE JAMES T	CPT	0-1310342	0355	2
PIKE MILES N	LTC	0-0172307	1059	3
PIKE WAYNE S	MAJ	0-0522293	0947	2
PIKE WILLIS H	CPT	0-1294010	0447	2
PIKON STANLEY W	CPT	0-1302515	0646	2
PIKULSKI JOSEPH A	MAJ	0-1308175	0662	1
PIKUS HARRY	COL	0-0212654	0261	1
PILACHOWSKI LEO B	CPT	0-0948050	0361	1
PILAT JOHN L	CW4	W-2107246	1053	1
PILAWSKI JOHN A	CPT	0-1178596	0851	2
PILCH IRVING	CW2	W-2112380	1055	1
PILCHER CHARLES D	CW2	W-2210206	0266	1
PILCHER LEWIS S	LTC	0-0468963	0646	2
PILE WENDELL J	CPT	0-1766608	1048	2
PILERT EDWARD JR	1LT	0-1586028	0647	2
PILEWSKI EDWARD J	LTC	0-1545716	1266	1
PILEWSKI JOSEPH M T	CW3	W-2127182	1054	1
PILGRIM CHARLES W	CW3	W-2141924	0762	1
PILGRIM OLLASTER C	MAJ	0-1951707	0762	1
PILGRIM VINCENT W	WO1	W-2141412	0259	1
PILKENTON WILLIAM H	2LT	0-0540598	1045	2
PILKINGTON GEORGE P	MAJ	0-1114263	1059	2
PILKINGTON JOSEPH	LTC	0-1184923	0966	2
PILLAR WILLIAM T	1LT	0-1305304	0445	2
PILLEPICH JOHN A	CPT	0-0445050	0546	2
PILLIFANT THOMAS H	1LT	0-0439374	1045	2
PILLING EVERETT H	MAJ	0-1897754	0365	1
PILLON JAMES P	MAJ	0-1542248	1060	2
PILLSBURY MARJORIE A	1LT	N-0720169	0346	1
PILON JOHN P SR	CPT	0-2014880	0861	1
PILON OLIVER J	CPT	0-0507434	0253	2
PILSEN LOUIS	COL	0-1170915	1064	1
PILTZ GEORGE F	LTC	0-1692129	0345	2
PILUSO CARLO	COL	0-0248908	0764	3
PIMENTEL MERRILL A	COL	0-0236906	0466	3
PINALI FRANK	MAJ	0-1296421	0361	1
PINAUD GEORGE C	MAJ	0-1642470	0855	1
PINCKNEY FRANK D	M G	0-0246920	0464	3
PINCKNEY MURRAY S	LTC	0-1183595	0461	1
PINCKNEY SAMUEL M JR	MAJ	0-2009680	0263	1
PINCOMBE JOHN D	2LT	0-1822052	0645	2
PINCOSKE ANDREW M	CW3	W-2121280	0155	1
PINDER ROBERT F JR	MAJ	0-2028739	1166	1
PINE HELEN M	1LT	N-0763887	0745	1
PINE IRVING	CPT	0-0322114	1045	2
PINE PAUL H	CPT	0-0232693	0665	3
PINE SEYMOUR	CPT	0-1797522	0146	2
PINEDA MICHAEL V	CPT	0-0978132	0466	2
PINEIRO-RUIZ JOSE	CW4	W-2142260	0465	1
PINER RAYMOND E	MAJ	0-0317316	0666	3
PINET ALFRED J	MAJ	0-1845481	0860	3
PINETTE MATTIE A	LTC	L-0303523	0363	3
PINGREE JOHN	MAJ	0-1588228	0259	1
PINK HAROLD H	CW4	W-2144195	0466	1
PINKEL DONALD P	1LT	0-1874268	0355	2
PINKERTON CLIFFORD C	1LT	0-1055120	1145	2
PINKERTON JACKSON D	MAJ	0-0266821	0157	3
PINKERTON JAMES R	LTC	0-0252141	0465	3
PINKERTON JAY W	LTC	0-1641676	1266	1
PINKERTON JOHN F	MAJ	0-0957807	0964	1
PINKERTON JOHN G	LTC	0-0497000	1154	1
PINKERTON JOHN P	LTC	0-0295799	1145	2
PINKERTON PETER F	COL	0-0276293	1267	3
PINKERTON REX	CW2	W-3000429	0968	1
PINKERTON WILLIAM R	MAJ	0-0274078	0358	3
PINKHAM ARTHUR G	MAJ	0-0492183	0857	1
PINKHAM FREDERICK	1LT	0-1048933	1145	2
PINKHAM VERNON C D	LTC	0-0162135	0460	3
PINKHAM WALTER R	LTC	0-1047730	0962	1
PINKLEY GEORGE R	LTC	0-0233069	0565	3
PINKLEY WILLIAM M	CPT	0-0308580	1045	2
PINKOWSKY FRANCIS T	MAJ	0-0344234	0662	1
PINKSTAFF WILLIAM O	CW2	W-2152303	0561	1
PINKSTON HUGH O	LTC	0-0271476	1263	3
PINKSTON LAMON H	LTC	0-1103359	1065	1
PINKSTON WILLIAM E	COL	0-0123349	0749	3
PINKUS PHIL F	2LT	0-1592515	0944	2
PINNELL WILLIAM H	CW4	W-2145654	0157	1
PINNEO JAMES A	CW4	W-2001597	0567	3
PINNEY THEODORE C	CPT	0-1081670	0547	2
PINNEY WARREN B	LTC	0-0259161	0864	3
PINNICK RALPH E	MAJ	0-0252024	0765	3
PINSKY DANIEL J	MAJ	0-0322713	0246	2
PINSON ANDREW J	CW4	W-2118026	0659	1
PINSON CHARLES N	MAJ	0-1106404	0563	2
PINSONEAULT RAYMOND	MAJ	0-1307745	0461	1
PINTEL JAMES J	COL	0-0167525	0352	3
PINTHER HAROLD D	COL	0-0190978	0656	3
PINZAK STEPHEN	CW3	W-2145199	0862	1
PINZINO DOMINICK J	MAJ	0-0494315	0962	1
PINZOLO JOHN P	MAJ	0-2055482	0460	1
PINZON FILIBERTO	CW3	W-2151625	0862	1
PIO MYRON B	CW2	W-2213475	0964	2
PIOMBINO NICHOLAS	CW3	W-2106470	1055	1
PIOMBO ANDREW T	2LT	0-1323964	0446	2
PIOS ANTHONY L	LTC	0-1322809	0267	1
PIOTROWSKI FRANK E	CPT	0-1015117	1047	2
PIOTROWSKI SIGMUND A	MAJ	0-0365787	0564	3
PIPALA JOSEPH S	MAJ	0-1636478	0861	1
PIPER BURGETT W	CPT	0-1683966	0158	2
PIPER DONALD W	LTC	0-1341235	0866	1
PIPER ELLIS G	COL	0-0228863	1157	1
PIPER FLOYD P	CW3	W-2153324	1263	1
PIPER HOMER S	COL	0-0288433	0860	1
PIPER KENNETH R	CW2	W-3154235	0868	2
PIPER LLOYD L	COL	0-0332585	0557	1
PIPER MARGARET B	CPT	N-0760117	0147	1
PIPER RALPH A	LTC	0-0188915	0246	2
PIPER SAM M	MAJ	0-1797004	0262	1
PIPER WILLIAM C	COL	0-0244113	0462	3
PIPKIN COMPERE	1LT	0-0378976	1065	3
PIPKINS TROY C	MAJ	0-1937420	0868	1
PIPOLO SANDY E	CW4	W-2152108	0860	1
PIPPEN AUBREY J	MAJ	0-0486607	0760	1
PIPPERT RAY E	1LT	0-1111309	0545	2
PIPPIN MILLARD F	COL	0-0195444	1046	2
PIPPINS CALEB E	CW2	W-2150972	1262	1
PIPPITT LESLIE S	CW2	RW-2150512	1064	1
PIRC JOHN R	LTC	0-1913232	0468	1
PIRIBEK JERRY	LTC	0-1049612	1167	1
PIRKLE JACK D	MAJ	0-1919988	0665	1
PIRKLE RUSSELL L JR	COL	0-0341790	0559	1
PIRKLE TYRUS J	CW2	W-2150989	1161	1
PIRNACK RICHARD O	LTC	0-0276515	0953	2
PIRNIE ALEXANDER	COL	0-0196965	0563	3
PIRONE ADELINA E	MAJ	M-0000513	1263	1
PIRSCH JOSEPH H	LTC	0-0159243	0648	3
PIRTLE LLOYD A	CW4	W-2113304	0659	1
PISANELLO ALFRED J	CW2	W-2110343	1060	1
PISANI GEORGE	CW4	W-2145292	0664	1
PISCOP JORDAN	LTC	0-0322705	1064	3
PISEGNA ANOSTA	LTC	0-1107046	1059	1
PISINSKI LUCY I	MAJ	N-0751424	0863	2
PISKORSKI VAL B	LTC	0-0331768	0868	3
PITA FRANK L	COL	0-0305150	0668	3
PITCHER GLEE J	CPT	0-1947440	1047	2
PITCHER HORACE E	1LT	0-0560229	0645	2
PITCHERALE JOSEPH	CW3	W-2122638	1055	1

NAME	GRADE	SVC NO	DATE RET MO YR	RET CODE
PITCHFORD CARL R	CW4	W-2129520	0962	1
PITCHLYNN PETER P	CPT	0-0274790	0464	3
PITKETHLY DAVID A	LTC	0-0314472	0263	2
PITKIN HERBERT D	CW2	W-2211791	0766	1
PITLIK CLARENCE C	LTC	0-0250831	1263	3
PITMAN CLYDE F	CW2	W-2147098	0561	1
PITMAN IVY C	CPT	0-0379288	1145	2
PITMAN ROBERT B	2LT	0-1584742	0545	2
PITMAN ROBERT M	2LT	0-1314413	104N	2
PITMAN WILFORD G	1LT	0-1998452	0767	1
PITNEY GUY B	LTC	0-0188540	0-52	3
PITNEY MARVIN J	MAJ	0-0406632	0746	2
PITONIAK GREGORY M	CPT	0-2263698	1162	1
PITOSCIA GUSSIE D	MAJ	0-1304941	0263	1
PITPITAN GABINO	1LT	0-1896839	1049	1
PITRE CHARLES D	MAJ	0-2042897	0960	2
PITRE GEORGE L SR	COL	0-0194486	1262	3
PITT FRANK R	MAJ	0-0916217	0347	2
PITT HAMILTON	2LT	0-0411878	0442	2
PITT GRACE G	CW3	W-2008040	1066	3
PITT PERRY	CPT	0-1319541	0247	2
PITT STANTON	LTC	0-0473397	0862	1
PITTARO JOHN S	MAJ	0-0268470	0563	3
PITTENGER AUBREY O	COL	0-0298215	0955	1
PITTENGER JAMES S	LTC	0-0405349	0247	2
PITTENGER PAUL N	LTC	0-0103050	0648	3
PITTENGER RAY L	LTC	0-0328971	0559	3
PITTENGER THAD H JR	1LT	0-1032038	1045	2
PITTMAN CECIL	CW2	W-2146269	0659	1
PITTMAN CLAY M	CW3	W-2149346	0959	1
PITTMAN DUDLEY E	LTC	0-2047780	1262	1
PITTMAN FLOYD H	LTC	0-0447547	0247	1
PITTMAN HARRY R	LTC	0-0263190	0166	3
PITTMAN JIMMIE L	LTC	0-1047295	0563	1
PITTMAN JOHN C JR	LTC	0-0419075	0860	1
PITTMAN LEON E	LTC	0-1111836	1161	1
PITTMAN PAUL C	1LT	0-0417524	0745	2
PITTMAN ROBERT T JR	LTC	0-1293110	0163	1
PITTMAN ROY P	MAJ	0-2008161	0861	1
PITTMAN SAMUEL H	CW2	W-2120888	0946	1
PITTMAN WALTER D	MAJ	0-0283344	0968	3
PITTMAN WILLIAM A	CPT	0-1693001	0146	2
PITTS ALFRED H	CW3	W-2146778	1064	1
PITTS BAYNARD Y	CPT	0-1180002	0547	2
PITTS CHARLES A	CPT	0-1341819	0563	1
PITTS CHARLES L	MAJ	0-2262383	0966	1
PITTS FRANK P	LTC	0-0400527	0255	3
PITTS HARVEY C	LTC	0-0269965	1265	3
PITTS JOHN E	COL	0-0103336	1153	3
PITTS LEMUEL T	CPT	0-1303941	1045	2
PITTS NELSON A	CPT	0-1301032	0548	2
PITTS RALPH J	MAJ	0-1885927	0167	1
PITTS RICHARD G	1LT	0-1639501	0246	1
PITTS ROBERT L	COL	0-1301033	0965	1
PITTS ROY B	LTC	0-1634227	0865	1
PITTS RUFUS K	1LT	0-1582052	0745	2
PITTS THEODORE R	COL	0-0341150	0363	1
PITTS THOMAS V	CW3	W-2152304	0762	1
PITTS WALTER E	CPT	0-0499776	1046	1
PITTS WILLIAM	LTC	0-1330960	0866	1
PITZER GEORGE T	CW2	W-2209337	0864	1
PIURKOWSKY JOHN P	CPT	0-2033542	0257	1
PIVOVARNICK JOHN J	LTC	0-0268455	0657	3
PIXTON ROBERT C	COL	0-0236404	0746	2
PIZER VERNON	LTC	0-0406007	0763	1
PIZZILLO JOHN T	MAJ	0-1012339	0267	1
PLACE JOHN P JR	CPT	0-1590729	0945	2
PLACE KENNETH M	COL	0-0217699	1059	3
PLACE RICHARD C	CPT	0-0370893	0344	2
PLACE ROBERT H	CPT	0-0203646	1053	3
PLACHINSKI FLORIAN C	CPT	0-0385188	0147	2
PLACKO FRANK	LTC	0-0372230	0460	1
PLACKSIN SAMUEL Z	LTC	0-1108242	0868	3
PLAENERT ALFRED B	LTC	0-0286615	1064	3
PLAGMANN REGINALD F	CW2	W-2144763	1155	1

NAME	GRADE	SVC NO	DATE RET MO YR	RET CODE
PLAIN FERDINAND	LTC	0-0255295	0462	3
PLAIN IRVING H	1LT	0-0482554	0144	2
PLAINE ROBERT C	LTC	0-1285640	0954	1
PLAISANCE EDWARD B	COL	0-0366821	0766	1
PLAISANCE HARRY A	CW3	W-2146777	0664	1
PLAISTED MARK S	COL	0-0214424	1262	3
PLAKORUS MIKE G	MAJ	0-1643971	0263	1
PLAMBECK ERNEST	MAJ	0-0254031	0163	3
PLAMONDON WARREN A	MAJ	0-1686461	0363	1
PLANCE ROBERT E	CW2	W-2209077	0667	1
PLANDOR FRANCISCO	2LT	0-1896801	1047	1
PLANDOWSKI HENRY S	CPT	0-1176161	0862	1
PLANER JAMES E	LTC	0-1102426	0661	1
PLANITZ ARTHUR E	LTC	0-0456676	0261	1
PLANK ALLAN K	MAJ	0-0237423	1142	2
PLANK WILBUR L	COL	0-0227022	0963	3
PLANKENHORN CHARLES	LTC	0-0253299	0267	3
PLANKERS DEWEY A	MAJ	0-1296254	0259	1
PLANT EDWARD D	LTC	0-1542347	0461	1
PLANT PHILIP	LTC	0-1308540	0467	3
PLANT ROSS H	MAJ	0-0326118	1045	2
PLANT THOMAS G	COL	0-0900295	0150	3
PLANT WILLIS L	LTC	0-0314220	1060	1
PLANTAMURA JOSEPH A	LTC	0-0397767	0960	1
PLANTE MARGARET J	CW4	V-0204894	0266	1
PLANTS JAMES L	CPT	0-1944553	0846	2
PLANUTIS ALEX J	MAJ	0-1175539	0666	1
PLAPP ELMER B	MAJ	0-0167412	0554	3
PLAPUS JOHN S	CW2	W-2210401	0361	1
PLARR ROBERT J	MAJ	0-1649580	1161	1
PLASKOW ELI P	COL	0-0409855	0765	1
PLASKY JOHN	CPT	0-1111839	0450	2
PLASS JOHN B	CPT	0-0473152	0745	2
PLASTER ROY W	MAJ	0-1823769	1163	1
PLASTRIDGE ROBERT A	MAJ	0-0162974	0557	3
PLATANACK JOHN	MAJ	0-0502579	0852	2
PLATEK DANIEL A	CW3	W-2144689	0157	1
PLATH RICHARD I	1LT	0-1321812	1145	2
PLATKO MICHAEL A	MAJ	0-1575517	1164	1
PLATNER PAUL G	CW4	W-2101210	0257	1
PLATO ELKEN J	COL	0-0222560	0747	2
PLATSON KENNETH F	LTC	0-1994678	0461	1
PLATT ARTHUR F	MAJ	0-0298897	0368	3
PLATT CHESTER L	MAJ	0-0443692	1053	2
PLATT DONALD L	MAJ	0-1173744	0162	1
PLATT DONALD M	MAJ	0-0255839	0967	3
PLATT DWIGHT H	CW2	W-2124074	1050	2
PLATT FREDERICK	CPT	0-0393283	0842	2
PLATT MATTHEW	CPT	0-0461610	1045	2
PLATT PHILLIP B	LTC	0-1041002	1065	3
PLATT ROBERT J	MAJ	0-1580170	0963	1
PLATT VINCENT J	WO1	W-2106728	0854	1
PLATT WILLIAM C	COL	0-0185924	0251	3
PLATUS LOUIS	CW2	W-2119879	0952	1
PLATZ JAMES L	LTC	0-1573511	0860	2
PLATZ JULIUS E	LTC	0-0270648	0467	3
PLAUTZ ARTHUR V	CW3	W-2205422	0266	1
PLAUTZ FREDERICK	MAJ	0-0968380	1065	2
PLAVNICKY CHARLES J	CW4	RW-2136733	0166	1
PLAXICO WILLIAM L	MAJ	0-0280769	0568	3
PLAZAK JAMES J	LTC	0-1648647	0363	1
PLEASANT MONROE	CPT	0-0479779	0347	1
PLEDGER LYLE J	LTC	0-0408804	0864	1
PLEFKA GEORGE	MAJ	0-2263009	0664	1
PLEMMONS ALTON W	MAJ	0-0491530	1047	2
PLEMMONS CLARENCE W	MAJ	0-1178292	0660	1
PLEMONS ELMORE S	MAJ	0-0347283	0965	3
PLEMP FRANK M	1LT	0-0346503	0942	2
PLESS NICK G	CW3	W-2113911	0659	1
PLETSCHER HARVEY W	WO1	W-2120909	104N	2
PLETTA DAN H	MAJ	0-0229509	0164	3
PLETZER GOTTFRIED	MAJ	0-2020760	0563	1
PLEVINSKY RAYMOND	1LT	0-1296422	0245	2
PLEXICO CLAUDE H	MAJ	0-0966764	0263	1
PLIER MILTON F	CW4	W-2126654	0961	1

NAME	GRADE	SVC NO	DATE RET MO YR	RET CODE
PLINSKE VERNON H	MAJ	0-0975459	0966	1
PLISH STEVE	LTC	0-1552578	0464	1
PLISKIN REUBEN R	LTC	0-0319000	0746	2
PLITT EDWARD T	LTC	0-0512121	0368	3
PLOLICA JOSEPH E	MAJ	0-1796523	0263	1
PLOCK EDGAR F	CPT	0-0251969	0160	3
PLOGER VERNE R	MAJ	0-0575915	0957	1
PLONNINGS HERMAN JR	MAJ	0-1017233	0459	1
PLONSKE MARION E	CPT	N-0755473	1047	1
PLOSS ROY C	MAJ	0-0229246	0345	2
PLOTT PORTER I	LTC	0-1575518	0658	1
PLOUGH HAROLD H	MAJ	0-0127422	0452	3
PLOURDE THOMAS	LTC	0-1304942	1264	1
PLOUTZ DENNIS A	CW2	W-2145482	1055	2
PLOWDEN ALFRED J JR	COL	0-0340629	0547	2
PLOWMAN BLAIR E	CPT	0-0226271	1061	3
PLOWMAN STEPHEN W	MAJ	0-1297422	1161	1
PLUCINSKI FRANCIS A	CW2	W-3200301	1168	1
PLUE RUSSELL J	LTC	0-0257693	1264	1
PLUIM WILLIS A	CW3	W-2144853	1060	1
PLUM HARRY E	MAJ	0-0481690	0348	1
PLUM RAYMOND J	CPT	0-1745091	1146	2
PLUMB HARRY A	CPT	0-0192232	0847	2
PLUMB RALPH E	LTC	0-0428174	0960	1
PLUMER PAUL R	MAJ	0-0262764	0567	3
PLUMLEE BILLIE L	1LT	0-1913361	0754	2
PLUMLEY FRANCIS H	1LT	0-1294717	1146	2
PLUMLEY GUILFORD A	2LT	0-1288946	0445	2
PLUMLEY ROY R	LTC	0-1294718	0161	1
PLUMLEY WALTER P	LTC	0-0261530	1066	3
PLUMMER CHARLES E	MAJ	0-0126810	0356	3
PLUMMER EDWARD W SR	CPT	0-1319542	1062	1
PLUMMER HAROLD L	MAJ	0-0151444	0754	3
PLUMMER KENNETH C	LTC	0-0413498	0856	1
PLUMMER LEONARD B	LTC	0-0222397	0951	1
PLUMMER LOUIS F	MAJ	0-0382618	0646	2
PLUMMER MICHAEL J	LTC	0-1587541	0167	2
PLUMMER NATHAN S	CPT	0-2289282	0563	1
PLUMMER ROBERT J	CW3	W-2123367	1053	1
PLUMMER THOMAS H	COL	0-0211395	0654	1
PLUMMER WILLIAM	CPT	0-1299104	1047	2
PLUMMER WILLIAM E	COL	0-0261205	0166	3
PLUNKETT ELMER G	CPT	0-0399237	1144	2
PLUNKETT ELMER L	1LT	N-0734990	1046	1
PLUNKETT FREDERICK	LTC	0-0976224	1167	1
PLUNKETT HENRY P	COL	0-0180254	0161	3
PLUNKETT ROBERT	CW3	W-2142261	0757	1
PLUNKETT ROBERT T	1LT	0-1102131	0345	2
PLUNKETT WOODROW C	CPT	0-1290999	0246	2
PLUTZ ANDREW	1LT	0-1112374	0345	2
PLYBON PAUL C	CPT	0-0419682	0145	2
PLYLER ORELL F	MAJ	0-0443424	1052	1
PLYLEY RAYMOND C	COL	0-0173944	0159	3
PLYMALE RAYMOND D	CW2	W-2215178	0767	1
PLYMATE ELEANOR A	MAJ	N-0732269	0262	1
PLYMEL ERNEST L	CPT	0-1590110	0761	1
PLYMIRE HAROLD N	1LT	0-1301034	0945	2
POAGE JAMES D	2LT	0-0384180	0142	2
POBLOCKI ROBERT J	MAJ	0-0453735	0446	2
POCHODOWICZ S J	CPT	0-0331064	0345	2
POCILUYKO NICHOLAS D	MAJ	0-2027772	0260	1
POCOCK CLIFFORD H	LTC	0-1338849	0766	1
POCZIK LESLIE J	MAJ	0-1105113	0164	1
PODBIELSKI ANTHONY K	LTC	0-1294719	0868	3
PODCASY BERNARD J	CPT	0-1316326	1047	2
PODEYN EMIL M	LTC	0-0279934	0753	3
PODGORSKI ELIZABET	2LT	N-0744433	0944	1
PODLEWSKI NICK S	MAJ	0-0585185	0557	1
PODSCHUN WILLIAM A	CW3	W-2150253	0662	1
PODSIAULY EDWARD	LTC	0-1541111	0959	1
PODSOBINSKI MAURICE	CPT	0-1555460	0663	1
PODWORNY EDWARD C	LTC	0-0408485	0863	1
POE BRYCE	LTC	0-0274050	0447	2
POE CHARLES F	COL	0-0114486	1146	2
POE CHARLES T	1LT	0-0345121	0646	2

NAME	GRADE	SVC NO	DATE RET MO YR	RET CODE
POE JAMES E	LTC	0-1533423	0757	1
POE LEWIS M JR	MAJ	0-0912574	1043	2
POE RALPH A	COL	0-0234977	0262	1
POE VICTOR F	CPT	0-1823347	1158	1
POE WILLIAM A	COL	0-0185905	0358	1
POEHLMAN FRANK F	COL	0-0178980	0650	3
POEHLMANN GEORGE	CPT	0-0365733	0546	2
POEHLMANN JOHN L	1LT	0-1177583	0446	2
POEHLMANN THEODORE H	CW3	W-2148507	0566	1
POER MELVYN R	LTC	0-1109594	0762	1
POFF JOSEPH E	CW4	W-2112257	0659	1
POFFENBERG SCOTT B	LTC	0-0202068	1061	3
POFFENROTH JOHN E	1LT	0-1289794	1045	2
POGAR JOHN	MAJ	0-1181412	0358	1
POGGI JOHN J	1LT	0-2007039	0847	2
POGGIONE JOSEPH J	LTC	0-0361405	0963	3
POGUE EARL W	CPT	0-0331375	0562	3
POGUE FRANK L	MAJ	0-1291515	1159	1
POGUE HERBERT L	CPT	0-0977671	0161	1
POGUE JACK	CPT	0-0885620	0947	2
POGUE JAMES C	LTC	0-1166586	0164	1
POGUE JOSEPH G	MAJ	0-1591373	0959	1
POGUE ROGER R	CW2	W-2215049	0567	1
POH LAWRENCE C	MAJ	0-1177940	0560	1
POHL CHARLES M	MAJ	0-0336637	0346	2
POHL GLYN W	LTC	0-0365065	0161	1
POHL HARRY W	LTC	0-1580172	0761	1
POHLSON CARL I	LTC	0-0336289	0356	3
POHOWSKY ALEX JR	CPT	0-0441415	0146	2
POHZEHL LOUIS C	CPT	0-1319645	0246	2
POINDEXTER JAMES A	LTC	0-1171722	0457	1
POINSETT EDGAR H	LTC	0-1297247	0261	1
POINT ROBERT C	LTC	0-2206394	0867	1
POINTON HERBERT A	CW3	W-2151390	0866	1
POIRIER JOHN	CW4	W-2108001	0951	1
POIS JOHN	CPT	0-0213635	1045	2
POISSON PAUL H JR	CW3	W-2145294	0463	1
POITRAS MAURICE WX	WO1	W-2217379	1168	1
POKORNEY FRED M	LTC	0-0233070	1162	3
POKORNY ALBERT E	LTC	0-1102429	0262	1
POKORNY JERRY	MAJ	0-0417735	0848	1
POKORNY JOHN E	LTC	0-0189460	1046	2
POKORSKI MAX F	LTC	0-1823056	0866	1
POKRAS JACOB	LTC	0-2050330	0368	1
POKUSA STANLEY M	1LT	0-1052127	1045	2
POLACEK JAMES V	MAJ	0-0133793	0948	3
POLAK BENJAMIN E	MAJ	0-2032276	0860	1
POLAND ARTHUR E	MAJ	0-2026038	0861	1
POLAND EUSTIS L JR	MAJ	0-0453085	0161	1
POLAND RAYMOND A	CW4	W-2104924	1059	1
POLAND ROBERT R	CPT	0-0217514	0656	3
POLASKO JOHN	2LT	0-0108262	1030	1
POLASKY LOIS I	CPT	N-0733648	0450	2
POLATIN ALVIN H	CPT	0-1938852	0654	2
POLCYN EDWARD W	MAJ	0-1926914	1264	1
POLERETCKI JOSEPH	MAJ	0-1115745	0256	1
POLHAMUS ALBERT A	1LT	0-4010815	1158	2
POLICANI GASPER V	MAJ	0-1542420	0857	1
POLICASTRO ARMONDO	1LT	0-1998350	0845	2
POLICH FRANK J	COL	0-0391844	0760	1
POLICHNIA ERNEST	CPT	0-1542425	0160	1
POLICOFF LOUIS	2LT	0-0967829	0453	2
POLING ANDREW W	1LT	0-2262948	0957	1
POLING CARL M	CPT	0-0298811	1045	2
POLING RICHARD R	2LT	0-1590732	1044	2
POLITZER FRANK	1LT	0-1285296	0546	2
POLK ARDITH T	CW3	W-2153034	1164	1
POLK ARTHUR B	MAJ	0-1638278	0356	1
POLK CHARLES K	MAJ	0-2033787	1265	1
POLK HARVEY E SR	CW3	W-2143675	0965	1
POLK J L	CW2	W-2143166	0456	1
POLK JAMES K	COL	0-0448177	0166	3
POLK JAMES K	LTC	0-1103364	0161	1
POLK JOHN H	1LT	0-1315210	1052	2
POLK ROBERT L	CW2	W-2146156	0560	1

NAME	GRADE	SVC NO	DATE RET MO YR	RET CODE
POLK SAMUEL T JR	CPT	0-1307073	0646	2
POLK WILLIAM F	MAJ	0-0348195	0857	2
POLKA JAMES B	COL	0-0287125	0262	3
POLL DAVID J	1LT	0-2210426	1053	2
POLLACK IRVING S	CPT	0-0534155	1045	2
POLLACK JOSEPH A	LTC	0-1549024	1061	1
POLLACK JOSEPH J	CPT	0-1635211	0860	1
POLLAK LEO C	MAJ	0-2018215	0365	1
POLLARD ALBERT H	LTC	0-0347669	0161	3
POLLARD ANDREW M III	LTC	0-0254368	0867	3
POLLARD DONALD G	CPT	0-1642475	0457	1
POLLARD JACK	LTC	0-1103865	1161	1
POLLARD KENNETH B	CW3	W-2148219	0262	1
POLLARD RICHARD H	CPT	0-0171486	0854	3
POLLARD RICHARD R	CW3	W-2152566	0661	1
POLLARD ROBERT L	LTC	0-0162291	0348	2
POLLARD THOMAS D	LTC	0-0964554	0463	1
POLLARD VAN B	LTC	0-1576508	0760	1
POLLARD WILLIAM F	LTC	0-1055123	0164	1
POLLARO MARY T	CPT	N-0725439	1147	1
POLLET IRVING L	MAJ	0-0210134	0146	2
POLLEY GEORGE D	MAJ	0-1284572	0861	1
POLLICK ALBERT P	MAJ	0-1302876	0847	2
POLLINQUE EUGENE F	2LT	0-0519702	0845	2
POLLITT JAMES J	1LT	0-1822723	0551	2
POLLITZER HENRY H	CW3	W-2144247	0257	1
POLLOCK ALFRED L	LTC	0-0357460	1056	3
POLLOCK CARL A	LTC	0-0425238	0862	1
POLLOCK CLINTON A	CPT	0-1800114	0656	2
POLLOCK GEORGE M	MAJ	0-0275253	0457	1
POLLOCK GORDON R	COL	0-1313058	1067	1
POLLOCK KATHERINE	MAJ	N-0724089	0561	1
POLLOCK KEITH A	CW3	W-2141865	1160	1
POLLOCK OTTO G JR	1LT	0-0397338	0345	2
POLLOCK ROBERT W	LTC	0-0328962	0466	3
POLLOCK WILLIAM M	COL	0-0264656	0466	3
POLONSKI JOSEPH	CW3	W-2152336	0364	1
POLSE MAX L	MAJ	0-0492829	0146	2
POLSON EARL H	CPT	0-2212093	0556	1
POLSON JAMES L	LTC	0-0238310	0863	3
POLSTER ALVIN F	CW4	RW-0906955	0860	1
POLVOROSA CARLOS	CPT	0-1896710	1268	2
POLY ERNEST W	CPT	0-2014385	0357	1
POMEROY FRANKLIN I	COL	0-0101351	0154	3
POMEROY MARGUERITE	MAJ	L-0603914	0463	1
POMEROY PHILIP S JR	COL	0-0451035	1266	1
POMEROY PLAYFORD R	LTC	0-0290886	0144	2
POMEROY ROLAND E	LTC	0-0389953	0846	2
POMEROY ROSCOE E	COL	0-0308718	1063	1
POMMETT FRANCIS A SR	MAJ	0-1821908	0761	1
POMO RALPH J	1LT	0-1011944	1045	2
POMPER WALTER C	CPT	0-1113397	0766	1
PONADER CARMAN W	1LT	0-1041223	1045	2
POND CLIFTON R	LTC	0-0196487	0256	3
POND HARRY S	LTC	0-0104334	0648	3
POND LESLIE L JR	CW4	W-2115846	1054	2
POND MACK A	LTC	0-0272586	0967	3
POND ROBERT C	CPT	0-0289929	0146	2
POND THOMAS B	CPT	0-1310760	0247	2
POND WOODY	1LT	0-1824504	0545	2
PONDELICEK MILES J	CPT	0-0965801	0959	1
PONDER CHARLES F	2LT	0-0504543	1048	1
PONDER HOYETT A	CPT	0-0328783	0645	2
PONDER MARY E	1LT	N-0737351	1152	2
PONDS WILLIAM J	1LT	0-1301679	0745	2
PONEBSHEK CARL M	MAJ	0-4005255	0568	1
PONS FRANK J	MAJ	0-0944653	1061	1
PONT WALTER F	MAJ	0-1041880	0358	1
PONTIUS HERMAN W	LTC	0-0195011	0452	2
PONZAR WALTER F	LTC	0-0345128	0860	1
PONZIO HAROLD J	1LT	0-1308045	0945	2
POOL BERNARD E	CW3	W-2134685	0861	1
POOL FLOYD R	COL	0-0225269	0154	3
POOL FRANK M	MAJ	0-0394513	0146	2
POOL GEORGE F	MAJ	0-0911829	0246	2

NAME	GRADE	SVC NO	DATE RET MO YR	RET CODE
POOL HANDFORD E	MAJ	0-0224674	0-52	3
POOL JOHN	LTC	0-0243580	1045	1
POOL LAFAYETTE	CW2	W-2149816	0960	2
POOL SANFORD M JR	COL	0-0202292	0959	1
POOL WALTER C	CW3	W-2121156	0857	1
POOLE ALBERT	CW3	W-2150160	0566	1
POOLE ARTHUR J	MAJ	0-2282586	1166	1
POOLE CHARLES E	CW3	W-2145483	1058	1
POOLE GEORGE D	COL	0-0255265	0655	3
POOLE JESSE O	CW2	W-2145484	0462	1
POOLE JOHN M JR	WO1	W-2148499	0855	1
POOLE KENNETH W	1LT	0-1012290	1045	2
POOLE LAVERNE S	LTC	0-0520972	1064	3
POOLE LLOYD G	LTC	0-0258647	0947	2
POOLE LYNWOOD H	LTC	0-0320173	0464	1
POOLE MAURICE L	LTC	0-1284573	0666	3
POOLE REGINALD M	CW3	W-2144597	0264	1
POOLE RICHARD W	CPT	0-1545726	0157	1
POOLE ROBERT E	MAJ	0-0249803	0865	3
POOLE ROBERT H	LTC	0-0423576	0462	3
POOLE ROLAND J	MAJ	0-0171263	0648	3
POOLE WILLIAM	MAJ	0-0266161	1060	1
POOLE WILLIAM B	MAJ	0-1111311	0266	1
POOLE WILLIAM C	LTC	0-0292403	1160	1
POOLER JAMES T	CPT	0-1924748	0763	1
POOLER PAUL L	LTC	0-0299087	0863	3
POOLEY RICHARD L	COL	0-0269386	1159	1
POORE ARCHIE P	COL	0-0247028	0747	2
POORE FREDERIC L	LTC	0-1583517	0267	1
POORE RAYMOND H	LTC	0-0379123	1062	1
POORE STUART H	LTC	0-0518007	1262	3
POORMAN DOROTHY E	1LT	N-0704040	0546	1
POORMAN FRED S	COL	0-0173458	1061	3
POORMAN JOHN A	LTC	0-0741622	0767	1
POPA RALPH	CW3	W-2152282	0963	1
POPE ALBERT H	CPT	0-0336437	1144	2
POPE BENJAMIN W	CPT	0-0469231	0650	1
POPE CARL W	2LT	0-2040753	0568	2
POPE CHARLES A	MAJ	0-0354070	0367	3
POPE CHARLES F	LTC	0-0335733	0345	2
POPE CHARLES F JR	1LT	0-0445745	1146	2
POPE CHARLES R	LTC	0-1054367	1166	3
POPE CHARLES S	LTC	0-0241190	0664	3
POPE CLAUDE F	MAJ	0-1550481	0157	1
POPE CLYDE F	MAJ	0-1695634	1153	1
POPE EDGAR A	CPT	0-0522415	1060	1
POPE EMIL S	MAJ	0-0980398	0264	1
POPE EZRA T JR	COL	0-0151557	0457	3
POPE HARRIS M	LTC	0-1306466	0960	1
POPE HOWARD E	CW2	W-2150191	0760	1
POPE JAMES T	CW2	W-2208806	0668	1
POPE JOHN B	LTC	0-1113399	1263	1
POPE JOHN G	CPT	0-1110726	1047	2
POPE LAWRENCE F	1LT	0-2035018	1145	2
POPE MARY H	CW4	V-0609411	1263	1
POPE NORMAN L	1LT	0-1292585	1046	2
POPE RALPH P	LTC	0-0172693	0950	3
POPE RALPH W	CW4	W-2145087	1058	1
POPE RICHARD F	CW4	W-2146351	0868	1
POPE RUFUS A	LTC	0-1300706	0161	1
POPE SIDNEY K	LTC	0-0268166	1065	3
POPE SOWELL G	LTC	0-1168036	0759	1
POPE WALTER C	LTC	0-0286400	0866	3
POPE WILLIAM E JR	CW3	W-2149158	0465	1
POPE WILLIAM J	CW2	W-2145695	0257	1
POPERNIK MAX M	LTC	0-0307287	1168	3
POPHAM JOHN S R	LTC	0-0484149	0763	3
POPLINE VIOLET M	MAJ	N-0759677	0268	1
POPOVICH ELLIOT G	CW3	W-2142263	0659	1
POPOVICH JAMES M	LTC	0-1797875	0961	1
POPOVICH MARCUS J	LTC	0-1945678	0861	2
POPOVICS JOHN	MAJ	0-2011617	0665	1
POPOVSKY NICHOLAS T	LTC	0-0275566	1065	3
POPP LEWIS	CW4	W-2114860	0559	1
POPPAS GEORGE JR	LTC	0-1173747	0466	1

NAME	GRADE	SVC NO	DATE RET MO YR	RET CODE
POPPELL MASON L	MAJ	0-2262334	0763	1
POPPLE RICHARD W	CW3	W-2144714	0164	1
POPPLEWELL ARCHIE L	CW3	W-2144492	0659	1
POPPLEWELL ARVINE G	CPT	0-0936111	1148	2
POPWELL JOHNNIE C	CW3	W-2148935	0364	1
PORADA EDMUND S	LTC	0-2210138	0767	1
PORAT ALBERT	MAJ	0-0484074	0551	2
PORCARI STEPHEN	CPT	0-0332906	0962	1
PORCH JOSEPH W	MAJ	0-1329514	0764	1
PORCHE STANLEY E	LTC	0-1030406	0557	1
PORCHER PHILIP G	CPT	0-0258715	1045	2
PORGES ARTHUR	1LT	0-1166356	0744	2
PORISCH ADOLPHE H	1LT	0-1312219	0446	2
PORR GEORGE L	LTC	0-0338428	1062	3
PORT AUGUST G	LTC	0-0151827	0648	3
PORT CHARLES S	CPT	0-0509356	0246	2
PORT HORACE W	MAJ	0-0342462	0645	2
PORT JOHN Y	MAJ	0-1047297	0465	1
PORT MURRAY	LTC	0-0314930	0266	3
PORT THOMAS D	1LT	0-1309823	1145	2
PORTE DAVID S	1LT	0-0331717	0664	1
PORTELROY JOHN C	COL	0-0278916	1065	3
PORTEOUS WILLIAM L	MAJ	0-0418833	0647	2
PORTER ALEXANDER	CPT	0-1168037	0153	2
PORTER ALLEN T	LTC	0-1170923	1163	1
PORTER BERNARD R	LTC	0-0268008	0666	3
PORTER BERNARD U	LTC	0-1291164	0465	1
PORTER CHARLES B	LTC	0-0382176	0854	1
PORTER CHARLES P	1LT	0-0885654	0744	2
PORTER CHARLES W	LTC	0-0244951	1048	2
PORTER DALLAS E	CPT	0-0248634	0865	3
PORTER DANIEL B JR	COL	0-0295018	0966	1
PORTER DONALD E	CW2	W-2207141	0568	1
PORTER EARNEST E	1LT	0-0457156	0452	1
PORTER FRANK H	2LT	0-1324648	0944	2
PORTER FRANK P	CW2	W-2144365	1157	1
PORTER GEORGE I	CPT	0-2262995	0461	1
PORTER GEORGE L	LTC	0-0170035	0755	3
PORTER HARLAN E	MAJ	0-0526800	0755	1
PORTER HAROLD A	LTC	0-1289361	0961	1
PORTER HAROLD E	LTC	0-0254419	0164	3
PORTER HARRY JR	MAJ	0-2033070	0962	1
PORTER HOBART O	CW2	W-2210038	0664	1
PORTER HOMER A	CPT	0-1321580	1145	2
PORTER HOWARD O	LTC	0-0183055	0962	3
PORTER JAMES F	MAJ	0-2034803	0657	1
PORTER JAMES H	LTC	0-1305827	0461	1
PORTER JAMES M	1LT	0-1644675	1045	2
PORTER JAMES M	CW2	W-2146391	1059	1
PORTER JAMES W	MAJ	0-1174684	0563	1
PORTER JAMES W	LTC	0-1558249	0166	1
PORTER JOHN D	LTC	0-0404281	1060	1
PORTER JOHN D	LTC	0-0415053	0161	1
PORTER JOHN E	LTC	0-0372119	0246	2
PORTER JOHN F	CW4	W-2111975	0559	1
PORTER JOHN V	CPT	0-1309824	0346	2
PORTER JOHN W JR	MAJ	0-1332412	0760	1
PORTER JOSEPH H	1LT	0-1043464	1045	2
PORTER KENNETH A	WO1	W-2129446	0751	1
PORTER LANDON C	CPT	0-1058630	0567	3
PORTER LEON E	1LT	0-1172603	0846	2
PORTER LEONARD R	CPT	0-1599183	1058	1
PORTER MORRIS C	LTC	0-0462471	0368	1
PORTER PAUL B	COL	0-0241305	0849	3
PORTER PAUL E	MAJ	0-2017114	1265	1
PORTER PHILIP D	MAJ	0-1560379	0564	1
PORTER PHILIP H JR	LTC	0-0184342	0744	2
PORTER RICHARD L	1LT	0-1297943	0246	2
PORTER RITA A	MAJ	N-0756108	1267	3
PORTER ROBERT E	MAJ	0-1015056	0361	1
PORTER ROBERT J	CPT	0-1533674	1062	1
PORTER ROBERT P	LTC	0-0277601	1057	3
PORTER ROBERT W	LTC	0-1646510	1163	1
PORTER ROBERT W	CPT	0-2202303	0466	1
PORTER THOMAS H	1LT	0-2207939	0553	2

NAME	GRADE	SVC NO	DATE RET MO YR	RET CODE
PORTER THOMAS R	CW3	W-2000620	0159	1
PORTER THOMAS W	CPT	0-1289318	1146	2
PORTER WENDELL A	2LT	0-1309825	0545	2
PORTER WILBUR E	CW3	RW-2152613	0363	1
PORTER WILLIAM C	LTC	0-1286887	0561	1
PORTER WILLIAM E	MAJ	0-1291325	0558	1
PORTER WILLIAM L	LTC	0-1010008	1066	3
PORTERA JOHN J	LTC	0-0939691	0765	1
PORTERA JOHN O	MAJ	0-2263754	0565	1
PORTERFIELD ARTHUR R	1LT	0-1310876	1045	2
PORTERFIELD FRANK H	LTC	0-0971115	0868	1
PORTERFIELD HARRY B	MAJ	0-0991254	0563	1
PORTERFIELD JAMES W	CPT	0-0866520	1062	1
PORTERFIELD RICHARD	CW3	W-2152750	0867	1
PORTEUS JAMES H	LTC	0-2086997	0768	1
PORTFOLIO DONALD N	MAJ	0-1635214	1064	1
PORTH RICHARD J	CPT	0-0331733	0664	3
PORTMAN ABRAHAM	1LT	0-0507805	1043	2
PORTMANN FREDERICK	CW2	W-2145485	0660	1
PORTNOFF BERT	1LT	0-0455585	0645	2
PORTNOY BRADFORD M	MAJ	0-1696212	0646	2
PORTO PEDRO	1LT	0-1311849	0356	1
PORTOR LAWRENCE W	WO1	W-2144401	0853	1
PORTWOOD VERA W	CPT	N-0784670	1047	1
PORTWOOD WESLEY C	1LT	0-0507384	1052	1
POSCHNER GEORGE W	CPT	0-0523320	1148	2
POSES ABRAHAM L	MAJ	0-0246134	0847	2
POSES MEYER	LTC	0-1948032	0767	3
POSEY ARBRADE J	CPT	0-0949126	0365	2
POSEY BARRON B	MAJ	0-1823057	0457	1
POSEY CARROLL L	CPT	0-1877815	1065	1
POSEY EVERETT D	LTC	0-0257650	0863	1
POSEY FARRIS J	LTC	0-1548287	0361	1
POSEY GENE K	LTC	0-0482358	0668	2
POSEY HERMAN C	CW3	W-2151989	0766	1
POSEY HORACE E	LTC	0-1323029	1262	1
POSEY JAMES O	1LT	0-1307746	0656	1
POSEY PAUL W	CW3	W-2144306	0261	1
POSEY ROBERT K	MAJ	0-0228681	0564	3
POSEY WALTER J	LTC	0-0508105	0865	3
POSHARD HERBERT M	CPT	0-0187864	0145	2
POSIK JOSEPH W	1LT	0-4010133	0757	2
POSLIK JOSEPH	MAJ	0-1313040	1048	1
POSNER CHARLES	CPT	0-1703244	0744	2
POSNER GEORGE E	MAJ	0-1185416	0258	1
POSNER SAUL	1LT	0-1043465	0447	2
POSPICHAL ARNOLD B	LTC	0-1577703	0258	1
POSS DAVID H	LTC	0-0378961	1066	1
POSS RUBY	1LT	N-0701935	0742	1
POST ARTHUR E JR	LTC	0-1280195	1163	1
POST BURNAP	1LT	0-1015067	0745	2
POST CHALMER F	LTC	0-1638290	0466	1
POST CHARLES G	CPT	0-0371104	0344	2
POST CHARLES W JR	CPT	0-0518139	1147	2
POST FRANK S	COL	0-0237338	0345	2
POST GEORGE R	LTC	0-1170142	0860	1
POST GEORGE W	CW3	W-2202248	0368	3
POST GERALD V	CPT	0-0315992	0844	2
POST HARRY W	LTC	0-0395845	0960	1
POST JOHN A	MAJ	0-0401848	1050	2
POST MAURICE F	MAJ	0-1032385	0265	3
POST PAUL L	1LT	0-1018539	0846	2
POST RUTH E	MAJ	L-0125590	0563	1
POST SAMUEL S	COL	0-0352866	1266	1
POST WALTER H	1LT	0-1110727	1144	2
POST WESLEY V B	COL	0-0221425	1057	1
POST WILLIAM	CPT	0-1081715	0451	2
POSTEL MILO J	LTC	0-1640824	0861	2
POSTER RUSSELL E	CPT	0-1285493	1044	2
POSTICK FRED G	CPT	0-1342346	0159	1
POSTLETHWAIT VIRGIL	MAJ	0-1824909	0862	1
POSTLEWATE JAMES F	CPT	0-1997997	0863	1
POSTON CHARLES B JR	MAJ	0-0954838	0463	1
POSTON JOHN W	LTC	0-1054091	0467	1
POSVAR VLADIMIR L	LTC	0-0163100	0362	3

NAME	GRADE	SVC NO	DATE RET MO YR	RET CODE
POSZ CHARLES H	MAJ	0-1285494	0859	3
POSZ JOSEPH A	LTC	0-0260253	0467	3
POTASZ THOMAS M	COL	0-0325967	0246	2
POTEET HOMER F	CPT	0-0427991	0552	1
POTEET HORACE E	LTC	0-1590190	1060	1
POTEET JOHN W JR	LTC	0-0225684	0264	3
POTEET ROBERT W	MAJ	0-1645294	0859	1
POTEETE LEON	CW2	W-2144349	1164	1
POTENZA LOUIS F	CW3	W-2152397	1162	1
POTESKY ANTHONY	CPT	0-0164125	1026	1
POTHIER DOROTHY M	MAJ	N-0752421	0464	2
POTIER JOE E	CW2	W-2150732	0658	1
POTKONSKI LEOPOLD A	CPT	0-0357140	0446	2
POTOCKI JOHNNIE A	LTC	0-0312075	0758	1
POTOLICCHIO GORDON G	MAJ	0-4002910	0466	1
POTRECZ JULIAN K	CW4	W-2119310	0157	1
POTSAID MAJIC S	CPT	0-1533653	0246	2
POTTEIGER ALFRED A	LTC	0-0410724	0658	1
POTTEIGER ROBERT W	CPT	0-1287056	0155	1
POTTER ALICE	2LT	N-0763538	1144	1
POTTER ALICE W	CPT	N-0787707	1047	1
POTTER ARTEMAS C	CW3	W-2152979	1063	1
POTTER BENJAMIN P	MAJ	0-1692078	0745	2
POTTER BRYAN W	LTC	0-0450344	0256	1
POTTER CECIL E	LTC	0-1004213	0966	3
POTTER CECIL V	MAJ	0-1881412	0266	1
POTTER CHARLES E	MAJ	0-1306316	1046	2
POTTER ELEANOR V	CPT	N-0744101	0549	2
POTTER EUGENE W	COL	0-0139969	0857	3
POTTER FRANK M	COL	0-0212683	0763	3
POTTER FRANKLIN J	MAJ	0-0220720	1058	3
POTTER GABE W	CPT	0-1920280	0262	1
POTTER GEORGE H	CPT	0-0285478	0747	2
POTTER HAROLD C	LTC	0-0453884	1260	1
POTTER HAROLD W	LTC	0-0212257	0245	2
POTTER HENRY J SR	CPT	0-0308663	1154	3
POTTER HERBERT S	LTC	0-0125792	1150	3
POTTER IRA	LTC	0-0256040	0359	3
POTTER JAMES D	LTC	0-0972924	1166	1
POTTER JAMES W	WO1	W-2110027	1145	2
POTTER JOHN C	MAJ	0-1649334	0357	1
POTTER JOHN F JR	MAJ	0-0948978	0861	1
POTTER JOHN W	LTC	0-0255800	0668	3
POTTER LELAND L	CW3	W-2141789	0864	1
POTTER LESLIE S	LTC	0-1319647	0665	1
POTTER MARSHALL D	COL	0-0219891	0161	3
POTTER MORELAND N	WO1	W-2105374	0364	1
POTTER NELSON A	CPT	0-0374394	0468	2
POTTER RALPH A	CW2	W-2118731	1049	1
POTTER ROBERT B	LTC	0-1289484	0466	1
POTTER ROBERT C	LTC	0-1101399	0464	1
POTTER ROBERT H	CPT	0-1821765	0647	2
POTTER RUPERT W	CW2	W-2147726	0863	1
POTTER SIDNEY D	CW4	W-2149232	0968	1
POTTER STANLEY R	LTC	0-0493443	0566	3
POTTER THERESA C	2LT	N-0761736	1045	1
POTTER THOMAS F	1LT	0-1304944	0745	2
POTTER VERNON N	LTC	0-1044391	0166	1
POTTER WILLARD	MAJ	0-0147891	0557	3
POTTHOFF BERNARD B	LTC	0-1547748	0566	1
POTTLE CLARENCE E	CW2	W-2213574	0867	1
POTTORF HAROLD R	MAJ	0-1177579	1162	1
POTTRATZ WAYNE B	CW3	W-2146792	0562	1
POTTS ABEL	LTC	0-2035144	0760	1
POTTS BENNIE B	CW4	W-2146519	0968	1
POTTS BENNIE R	LTC	0-0493144	0159	3
POTTS C HARRIS	COL	0-0181094	1154	3
POTTS CHARLES T JR	MAJ	0-1635528	0459	1
POTTS DAVID F	CPT	0-0500046	0647	1
POTTS EDITH W	CPT	N-0765400	0757	2
POTTS EDWARD J	CW4	W-2112025	0662	1
POTTS EDWIN L	CPT	0-1921727	0753	2
POTTS FRANCIS M	CW2	W-2150813	0961	1
POTTS GEORGE W	MAJ	0-0147757	1052	3
POTTS HORACE F	LTC	0-1167589	1160	1
POTTS JIMMIE N	CW2	W-2152148	0761	1
POTTS JOHN R	1LT	0-1284048	1045	2
POTTS JOHN W	2LT	0-1304440	0145	2
POTTS MABEL	1LT	N-0726345	0348	1
POTTS RICHARD H	MAJ	0-1171724	0466	1
POTTS WILLIAM G JR	MAJ	0-1001661	0855	1
POTTS WILLIAM H	CW3	W-2148980	0163	1
POTTS 2ND ALFRED M	MAJ	0-0265075	0145	2
POTVIN ROLAND L	LTC	0-1554609	1063	1
POTWIN EARLE A	1LT	0-0453023	0757	1
POTWIN MAURICE L	CW3	W-2142775	0258	1
POTZ DAVID F	CPT	0-0973905	1265	2
POU CAYETANO R	LTC	0-0329569	0849	3
POU FRANK E S	LTC	0-0234496	1045	2
POU-LINES MANUEL R	LTC	0-0962654	0268	1
POUDRE LOUIS J	LTC	0-0405897	0954	1
POUJOL HARLEY K	MAJ	0-1559246	1263	2
POULIN HOWARD C	COL	0-0396517	0967	1
POULIOT GERARD N	CW2	W-2111614	1046	2
POULIS BYRON	CPT	0-0213184	1262	3
POULNOT ROBERT J	1LT	0-2018051	0551	2
POULOS RICHARD L	MAJ	0-1177588	1060	1
POULSEN NIELS I	COL	0-0115069	0256	2
POULSEN OTTO L	2LT	0-0532152	0944	2
POULSON DAHL F	MAJ	0-2263308	0968	1
POULSON WILLIAM R	CPT	0-0212705	1060	3
POUND JOHN H	MAJ	0-0177221	0861	3
POUND JOHN M	COL	0-0358338	1062	3
POUND MARVIN F	LTC	0-0348999	0756	1
POUND MARVIN G	1LT	0-0115068	0352	3
POUND ROBERT L	MAJ	0-1999738	0561	1
POUNDERS PORTER C	LTC	0-2263192	1168	1
POUNDS RUSSELL G	CW3	W-2142891	0163	1
POUNDS VEON O	CW2	W-2146901	0460	1
POUNDS WILLIAM M	MAJ	0-0481203	1049	1
POUNDSTONE ANSEL F	LTC	0-0151416	0153	2
POUSARD ALFRED W	LTC	0-0419374	0661	1
POUSKA ALEXANDER JR	LTC	0-0411881	0966	1
POUSSON NICHOLAS	CPT	0-0510679	0847	1
POUST CASSIUS	COL	0-0178869	0-51	3
POUTTU THOMAS C	CPT	0-1300379	0847	2
POUTTU THOMAS E	MAJ	0-1688835	0264	1
POVEROMO PAUL	LTC	0-1010858	0963	1
POVEROMO WILLIAM F	LTC	0-1115382	0464	1
POVEY PHILIP F	2LT	0-0511602	1244	2
POVSHA ROBERT J	CPT	0-2096962	0163	1
POW FREDERICK	LTC	0-0163052	0350	2
POWDERLY PATRICK J	CPT	0-4030937	0464	2
POWE HAROLD D	CPT	0-1293310	0347	2
POWELL ALFRED B	MAJ	0-0208362	0648	3
POWELL ARMOND V	CW2	W-2148681	0158	1
POWELL ARTHUR E	COL	0-1586844	0661	1
POWELL ARTHUR P	LTC	0-1102000	0166	3
POWELL BERRY F	MAJ	0-0364584	0262	1
POWELL BRADFORD G	LTC	0-2274882	0762	1
POWELL CECIL P JR	1LT	0-0989206	0967	2
POWELL CHARLES A	LTC	0-1634519	0966	3
POWELL CHARLES E	MAJ	0-0107925	0648	3
POWELL CHARLES F	LTC	0-1305474	0762	1
POWELL CHARLES S	CPT	0-0310352	1145	2
POWELL CHARLES W	CPT	0-1333001	1060	1
POWELL CLARENCE J	LTC	0-0278749	0764	3
POWELL CLAUDE	LTC	0-1573517	0954	1
POWELL CLAUDE M	LTC	0-0139159	0249	3
POWELL CLEMENT J	LTC	0-0201485	0459	3
POWELL CLIFFORD R	M G	0-0102214	0753	3
POWELL CLIFFORD S	MAJ	0-1593785	0764	1
POWELL CLIFFORD W	CW2	W-2148096	0859	1
POWELL DAVID M	CPT	0-0328485	0249	2
POWELL DUPERT	CPT	0-0485477	0448	1
POWELL EDWARD	CW2	W-2147452	0462	1
POWELL EDWARD T	CW2	W-2149088	0761	2
POWELL ELDRED L	MAJ	0-1636495	1060	1
POWELL EVERETT A	MAJ	0-0491038	1046	2
POWELL FLOYD G	LTC	0-0237945	0645	2
POWELL FLOYD M	CW2	W-2103328	1046	2
POWELL FRANK M	CPT	0-0182507	0154	3
POWELL FRANK T JR	MAJ	0-2011964	0461	1
POWELL FRED A	MAJ	0-0742946	0865	1
POWELL FREDERICK	COL	0-0197777	0359	3
POWELL GEORGE M	LTC	0-0297045	1059	3
POWELL GEORGE W	MAJ	0-0183711	1045	2
POWELL GLENN A	LTC	0-0325933	0859	1
POWELL HAROLD A	CPT	0-0375507	1145	2
POWELL HAROLD N	LTC	0-0265365	0667	3
POWELL HAROLD R	CPT	0-0232583	1156	3
POWELL HERBERT G	CPT	0-0166129	0648	3
POWELL JOHN D JR	MAJ	0-2033937	0466	1
POWELL JOHN G JR	MAJ	0-1061821	0962	1
POWELL JOHN M	MAJ	0-0245151	0352	3
POWELL JOHN F	MAJ	0-0309776	0358	1
POWELL JOHN P	LTC	0-1554786	0461	1
POWELL JOHN R	MAJ	0-1684424	0645	2
POWELL JOHN R JR	CPT	0-0984395	0162	2
POWELL JOHN W	1LT	0-1113394	0246	2
POWELL JOSEE R	1LT	0-1645920	0246	2
POWELL JOSEPH C	CPT	0-0197642	0644	2
POWELL JOSEPH C	CW4	W-2109425	0659	1
POWELL JOSEPH W	LTC	0-0332121	0359	1
POWELL LAMAR W	CW3	W-2150929	1062	1
POWELL LELAND T	MAJ	0-1172604	0258	1
POWELL LEO T	CPT	0-0394775	1047	2
POWELL LESTER	CW3	W-2150338	0657	1
POWELL LLOYD F	MAJ	0-1924573	0565	1
POWELL MARTIN E	LTC	0-0272626	0667	3
POWELL MCCLELLAN	CPT	0-1313125	0462	1
POWELL MILTON F	LTC	0-0217838	0662	3
POWELL NEVILLE A	LTC	0-0120707	0648	3
POWELL NORMAN F	LTC	0-1313012	0461	1
POWELL OWEN I	MAJ	0-1047737	1158	1
POWELL PAUL L	MAJ	0-1999954	0861	1
POWELL PHILLIP B	LTC	0-1582505	0163	1
POWELL RICHARD L	CW3	W-2152182	0764	1
POWELL RICHARD T	CW2	W-2215006	1166	1
POWELL ROBERT F	LTC	0-0318170	1267	3
POWELL ROBERT W	LTC	0-1291001	0263	1
POWELL ROBERT W	CPT	0-1549816	0746	2
POWELL STEPHEN B	1LT	0-1043466	0245	2
POWELL THEO L JR	CW4	W-2111473	1158	1
POWELL THOMAS D	LTC	0-0485098	1155	2
POWELL VIRGIL O	CPT	0-0239343	0464	3
POWELL WALTER G	CPT	0-2003797	0667	1
POWELL WALTER H	MAJ	0-1686295	0765	1
POWELL WARREN C	MAJ	0-0270348	0363	3
POWELL WILLIAM	MAJ	0-1035978	0968	1
POWELL WILLIAM A	LTC	0-0330435	0268	3
POWELL WILLIAM B	LTC	0-0257287	0547	2
POWELL WILLIAM P	COL	0-0319490	0868	3
POWELL WILLIAM R	CPT	0-0963865	0761	1
POWELL WILLIAM S	MAJ	0-0389319	0861	1
POWELL WILLIAM T	LTC	0-0320749	0360	1
POWELL WILLIAM T	LTC	0-0534156	0868	3
POWELL WILLIAM W	1LT	0-0444865	0844	2
POWELL WILLIE H	CW3	W-2145487	0659	1
POWELL WILLIS F	1LT	0-1174108	0647	2
POWELL WILLIS G	CPT	0-4006348	1065	1
POWELL WILSON B	COL	0-0288169	0161	1
POWELL WILSON F	MAJ	0-1290126	0557	1
POWER ALICE F	2LT	N-0789718	0645	1
POWER ERNEST F	LTC	0-1643237	1262	1
POWER ERNEST J	MAJ	0-0476639	0446	1
POWER FRANK K	MAJ	0-0242793	1061	3
POWER GEORGE C	CPT	0-1534601	0746	2
POWER HENRY F	CW2	W-2110768	0556	1
POWER JACK	MAJ	0-1112920	0464	1
POWER JOHN E	2LT	0-1183162	0844	2
POWER JOHN F	LTC	0-0248791	0461	1
POWER LAURENCE R	LTC	0-1894716	0662	2
POWER SAMUEL H JR	MAJ	0-0270850	0868	3
POWER THOMAS F	LTC	0-0261700	0265	3
POWERS ALEXANDER	LTC	0-1573519	0251	2
POWERS ARTHUR B	COL	0-0384256	0460	1
POWERS CARLTON J	LTC	0-0234416	0245	2
POWERS CATHERINE	2LT	N-0703756	0942	1
POWERS CHARLES A	MAJ	0-1103867	1163	1
POWERS CHARLES L	2LT	0-1593787	0645	2
POWERS DAVID H	COL	0-0229803	0863	3
POWERS DONALD M	MAJ	0-0286933	1063	3
POWERS EDDIE J	CW2	W-2141415	0954	1
POWERS EDGAR N	LTC	0-1041420	0361	1
POWERS EDWARD L	CPT	0-2018567	0758	1
POWERS EUGENE A	1LT	0-1107636	0146	2
POWERS EUGENE E	LTC	0-0452342	0666	1
POWERS FRANCIS I	LTC	0-0322594	0447	2
POWERS FRANK F	MAJ	0-0232036	0954	3
POWERS FREDERICK JR	MAJ	0-1947519	0468	1
POWERS GEORGE H	LTC	0-0302376	0167	3
POWERS GEORGE H	CPT	0-1055125	0963	2
POWERS HARLOW C	LTC	0-1280355	0761	1
POWERS JAMES G	MAJ	0-0301480	0959	3
POWERS JAMES J	LTC	0-0129924	0145	2
POWERS JAMES P	COL	0-0167517	0355	3
POWERS JAMES W	LTC	0-0415349	1161	1
POWERS JOHN A JR	LTC	0-1544239	0166	2
POWERS JOHN F	COL	0-0261340	1064	3
POWERS JOHN J	LTC	0-0453281	1163	1
POWERS JOHN R	COL	0-0245243	0866	3
POWERS JOHN T H	MAJ	0-0110260	1050	3
POWERS JOSEPH A	CPT	0-1686058	0745	2
POWERS JOSEPH M	1LT	0-1057221	0546	2
POWERS JOSEPH W	LTC	0-0483024	0546	1
POWERS MAX H	LTC	0-1330963	0768	1
POWERS RALPH M	LTC	0-0331964	0563	1
POWERS RAYMOND F JR	CW3	W-2206116	0466	1
POWERS RICHARD C	LTC	0-1305306	0765	1
POWERS RICHARD E	CPT	0-1558195	0347	2
POWERS ROBERT H	2LT	0-1182684	1045	2
POWERS ROBERT W	CPT	0-0466510	0245	2
POWERS ROGER F	1LT	0-0414764	0447	2
POWERS RONALD V	MAJ	0-0127451	1155	3
POWERS THOMAS R	1LT	0-0582261	0546	2
POWERS WILLIAM J	LTC	0-1112921	1062	1
POWERS WILLIAM J	LTC	0-1287057	0461	1
POWERS WILLIAM J	CW3	W-2146027	0860	1
POWERS WILLIAM J JR	1LT	0-1012137	0547	2
POWERS WILLIE G	1LT	0-0169270	1146	1
POWERSGHEALD F	MAJ	0-1703237	0146	2
POWIS EARL W	MAJ	0-0975068	1068	1
POWNALL ROGER F	COL	0-0261341	0867	3
POWNALL VIRGIL P	COL	0-0147842	0154	3
POYER CHARLES E JR	MAJ	0-1648991	0361	1
POYNER THOMAS E	1LT	0-1300527	1043	2
POYNER VERNON C	WO1	W-2109636	0245	2
POYNTER HAROLD E	MAJ	0-2035436	1062	1
POYNTER VERNON L	LTC	0-1030606	0260	1
POYNTER WILLIAM M	CPT	0-1301682	0145	2
POYTHRESS CLYDE L	CW2	W-2150510	0258	1
POZARNSKY CHARLES H	COL	0-0441294	0868	1
POZARO WILLIAM M	LTC	0-1000447	1055	1
PRABLEK FAITH C	MAJ	N-0771111	0168	1
PRACHER ALTHA M	MAJ	N-0795658	0565	1
PRACHT WILMER A	2LT	0-1059245	0745	2
PRACHYL LEWIS F	MAJ	0-1885813	1266	1
PRADO MIGUEL A	LTC	0-0963010	0864	1
PRAEGER HOWARD A	MAJ	0-0331861	0668	3
PRAEL ROBERT F	LTC	0-1634236	1266	1
PRAETZ EDWARD F	LTC	0-0158657	0260	3
PRAGER ALEXANDER	COL	0-0308792	0166	3
PRAGER JOSEPH L	1LT	0-1173043	0449	2
PRAIL CHARLES F	CPT	0-1639915	0847	2
PRAISNAR ADAM	CW2	W-2116050	0155	1
PRANGE ERNEST S	MAJ	0-1683464	0960	1
PRANT CHARLES E	CW4	W-2145206	0267	1
PRATER CHARLES L	MAJ	0-1889763	1267	1
PRATER GUY T	LTC	0-1287403	1060	1

NAME	GRADE	SVC NO	DATE RET MO YR	RET CODE
PRATER JOHN P	LTC	0-1004216	0163	1
PRATER VEALEY	1LT	0-0176549	0648	3
PRATHER ARDEN	CW2	W-2148912	0763	1
PRATHER CARROLL W	LTC	0-0222704	0950	3
PRATHER JAMES W	2LT	0-1113966	1145	2
PRATHER JOHN E	WO1	W-2105931	1150	2
PRATHER JOHN W	MAJ	0-0988680	0564	1
PRATHER RICHARD C	MAJ	0-1110731	0258	1
PRATHER THOMAS J	CPT	0-0544744	0647	2
PRATSCHER EDWARD J	CW3	W-2147860	0965	1
PRATT ALFRED S JR	MAJ	0-0466997	0245	2
PRATT ARTHUR F	MAJ	0-0325574	0965	3
PRATT ARTHUR F	WO1	W-2126744	0545	2
PRATT CHARLES H	COL	0-0439160	1064	1
PRATT CHARLES L	MAJ	0-1923614	0865	1
PRATT CLARENCE O	CPT	0-0342954	1046	2
PRATT EDWARD B	COL	0-0171230	1052	3
PRATT ERNEST A	2LT	0-1286354	0944	2
PRATT EUGENE E	LTC	0-0213560	0552	3
PRATT FRANCIS W	COL	0-0100827	0454	3
PRATT GILBERT S	MAJ	0-0184460	0145	2
PRATT GORDON L	LTC	0-0505938	1062	3
PRATT JAMES M	CW3	W-2144362	0263	2
PRATT LAWRENCE A	LTC	0-0348940	0246	2
PRATT LAWRENCE H	MAJ	0-2288312	1060	1
PRATT LEMUEL F JR	COL	0-0352562	0665	1
PRATT LYMAN M	LTC	0-0249728	0365	3
PRATT MARY E	1LT	N-0788298	0945	1
PRATT MERRITT C	LTC	0-0223693	0857	3
PRATT MILTON R	CW3	W-2205271	0364	1
PRATT REMUS S	LTC	0-1589637	0862	1
PRATT ROBERT H	COL	0-0261012	0368	3
PRATT ROGER F	CPT	0-1013568	0447	2
PRATT RUPERT J	WO1	W-2007668	0565	3
PRATT SHERMAN W	LTC	0-2006846	1059	1
PRATT STUART S	MAJ	0-0260720	0167	3
PRATT STUART W	CPT	0-1303944	0649	2
PRATT THELMA A	MAJ	N-0752104	1063	1
PRATT WALTER M	LTC	0-0100321	1150	3
PRATT WESLEY F	MAJ	0-1949896	0758	1
PRATT WILLARD M	CPT	0-0129963	1055	3
PRATT WILLIAM B SR	CW4	W-2144504	0462	1
PRAUGHT CLARENCE H	COL	0-0334323	0967	3
PRAUGHT JOHN P	1LT	0-0507210	0850	1
PRAY EUGENE W	1LT	0-2007499	1046	2
PRAY KENT R	MAJ	0-0996344	0168	1
PRAZENKA STEPHEN	CPT	0-0998775	0264	1
PREAS HUGH L	LTC	0-0319109	0467	3
PREBLE CLARENCE E	MAJ	0-1177590	0758	1
PREBLE EUGENE W	COL	0-0237315	0665	3
PREBLE FRANK H	MAJ	0-1181735	1262	1
PREBLE ROBERT J	LTC	0-0347316	0864	1
PREBLE WELDON P	CPT	0-0502350	0251	1
PRECHEL EVERETT A	LTC	0-0254182	0767	3
PRECHTEL EARL D	MAJ	0-2008173	1160	1
PREDGO CHARLES J	CW3	W-2104385	1060	1
PREDMORE ARTHUR L	LTC	0-0347001	0861	3
PREDMORE CLAYTON L	MAJ	0-1039514	0267	1
PREDMORE LESTER C	LTC	0-0202695	0458	3
PREDOVICH MILAN F	CPT	0-0367660	0145	2
PREECE HARRY W	MAJ	0-1174110	0966	3
PREGER DANIEL A	1LT	0-0524356	0346	2
PREGGE CLIFFORD C	CPT	0-1258922	0-48	2
PREHEIM DICK H	WO1	W-2150749	0853	1
PREHLE JOHN	MAJ	0-0977607	0162	1
PREININGER LOUIS J	CPT	0-0496030	1045	2
PREISCH WILLIAM W	COL	0-0149529	0352	3
PREISCHE HENRY F	MAJ	0-1689551	0246	2
PREISS JOSEPH L	MAJ	0-1183947	0664	1
PREISS ROBERT C	MAJ	0-0958147	0768	1
PREJEAN PAUL G	CW2	W-2149492	0461	1
PREM DONALD J	LTC	0-1182495	0467	1
PREMISLER HARRY	CPT	0-1690531	0545	2
PREMO HOWARD L	MAJ	0-2102983	0765	1
PREMPAS THOMAS G	COL	0-0277734	0558	3

NAME	GRADE	SVC NO	DATE RET MO YR	RET CODE
PRENDERGAST JOHN F	1LT	0-1535613	1045	2
PRENDERGAST THOMAS A	2LT	0-4051896	0257	2
PRENN JAMES L	LTC	0-0352807	1147	2
PRENTICE ALLEN F	LTC	0-1046926	0365	1
PRENTICE CURTIS C	CPT	0-0976915	0264	2
PRENTICE JAMES M	LTC	0-0328973	0456	3
PRENTICE JOHN C	MAJ	0-1285672	0760	1
PRENTICE MAX G O	MAJ	0-0277758	1160	1
PRENTICE WILLIAM A	MAJ	0-1822054	1062	1
PRENTISS CHARLES H	MAJ	0-0325463	0546	2
PRENTISS HARRY A	MAJ	0-0172061	0653	3
PRENTISS HENRY M	MAJ	0-0209422	0853	3
PRENTISS JAMES A	MAJ	0-0303467	1060	3
PRENTISS NORVAL O	CW3	W-2143423	1160	1
PRENTISS ROBERT F	LTC	0-1302050	0967	1
PRENTISS ROBERT J	CPT	0-0346443	1041	2
PRENTISS STANTON H	LTC	0-0245212	0966	3
PRES WALTER P	CPT	0-1181415	0753	1
PRESBERG MOWEY	LTC	0-0320244	1164	3
PRESCOTT DONALD P	LTC	0-0350576	0466	3
PRESCOTT ELMO	LTC	0-1031912	1054	1
PRESCOTT FRANK L	CPT	0-0331276	0559	3
PRESCOTT GEORGE D	MAJ	0-0953862	1266	1
PRESCOTT HARRY W	LTC	0-0202194	0145	2
PRESCOTT JACK W	1LT	0-1296083	1043	2
PRESCOTT JOSEPH C	CPT	0-1919000	1263	1
PRESCOTT JULIAN P	LTC	0-0289116	1265	3
PRESCOTT KENNETH E	MAJ	0-0488422	0346	2
PRESCOTT LEONA B	MAJ	M-0000438	1262	1
PRESCOTT LUCAS M	LTC	0-0314011	0163	1
PRESCOTT MANFRED U	B G	0-0224176	1059	3
PRESCOTT REX K	2LT	0-1177941	1044	2
PRESCOTT RICHARD D	COL	0-0155888	0649	3
PRESCOTT THOMAS M	CPT	0-0409418	1045	2
PRESENT JULIAN D	CPT	0-0321289	0446	2
PRESLEY JAMES H	1LT	0-0401705	0444	2
PRESLEY JONES B	CW2	W-2205541	0262	1
PRESLEY ROBERT K	CPT	0-1167166	0561	1
PRESLEY THEODORE F	LTC	0-0346296	0354	1
PRESLEY VERDIE B	MAJ	0-1052920	0958	1
PRESNELL FRED P	CPT	0-0989015	0763	1
PRESNELL ROBERT R	COL	0-0107557	0454	3
PRESNELL TOM	COL	0-0345783	0668	3
PRESS GEORGE L	MAJ	0-0971184	1060	1
PRESS JOHN J	CW2	W-2149453	1057	1
PRESSER MEYER I	LTC	0-4003826	0856	2
PRESSEY HERBERT E	LTC	0-0328972	1156	3
PRESSLER JOHN I	MAJ	0-1109599	0447	2
PRESSLY CHARLES R JR	1LT	0-1542683	0246	2
PRESSMAN CLARENCE S	MAJ	0-0487853	0557	1
PRESSMAN ROBERT S	MAJ	0-0411540	0646	2
PRESSON JAMES H	CW4	W-2005158	0167	3
PRESSON WILLIAM	1LT	0-1165200	0544	2
PRESTEL STANLEY V	CPT	0-0477450	0645	2
PRESTHOLT BENJAMIN M	LTC	0-0253917	0267	3
PRESTIDGE T J	CW2	W-2146138	1155	1
PRESTIN FRED J	1LT	0-1634238	0345	2
PRESTON ALBERT G JR	MAJ	0-0333846	1047	2
PRESTON ARTHUR M	CPT	0-0100189	0152	3
PRESTON CHARLES M	1LT	0-1289135	0561	2
PRESTON CLAUDE P	CPT	0-0921081	1152	1
PRESTON CLAY	MAJ	0-0279966	0653	3
PRESTON EDWIN R	COL	0-0468939	1062	3
PRESTON FRANK R JR	CW4	W-2148358	0568	1
PRESTON HAROLD G	CPT	0-0302601	1143	1
PRESTON HARRY H	MAJ	0-1054368	1060	1
PRESTON HENRY C	WO1	W-2147772	0755	1
PRESTON JACK I	MAJ	0-2017752	0765	1
PRESTON JAMES L	CW2	W-2148981	0757	1
PRESTON JAMES W	CW4	W-2146089	0767	1
PRESTON JESSE D	MAJ	0-0291973	0761	1
PRESTON JOHN	1LT	0-1298434	1160	1
PRESTON JOHN D	LTC	0-1592520	0262	1
PRESTON JOHN W	CW2	W-2147990	0654	1
PRESTON JON P	CW2	W-2148549	0160	2

NAME	GRADE	SVC NO	DATE RET MO YR	RET CODE
PRESTON LEONARD T	LTC	0-0251694	0963	3
PRESTON LILLIAN T	1LT	N-0702958	0644	1
PRESTON LLOYD R	MAJ	0-0196195	0562	3
PRESTON MALCOLM H	2LT	0-1173748	1043	2
PRESTON ROBERT B JR	1LT	0-1113896	0251	2
PRESTON SAMUEL P JR	CPT	0-1165144	0945	2
PRESTON THOMAS R	LTC	0-0492109	0847	2
PRESTON WALTER M	MAJ	0-0403270	0763	1
PRESTON WILLIAM C	2LT	0-0286783	0564	3
PRESTON WILLIAM G	CPT	0-1948034	0751	2
PRESTRIDGE ARTHUR	1LT	0-1633460	0545	2
PRESTRIDGE GEORGE N	LTC	0-1253471	1163	1
PRESTRUD CARL G	CPT	0-0173033	0648	3
PRESTWOOD GLADYS E	MAJ	N-0726184	0765	1
PRESTWOOD JAMES G JR	CPT	0-0352166	0446	2
PREUETT FRED D	MAJ	0-1293472	0461	1
PREUSKER WERNER C	LTC	0-1107642	0564	1
PREVATT ERNEST G	MAJ	0-2029761	0961	1
PREVATTE CHARLES C	CW3	W-2204995	1164	1
PREVICS MARTIN	LTC	0-0370946	0761	1
PREVOST ALBERT F	MAJ	0-0953666	0263	1
PREVOST JOHN R	CW3	W-2144395	0653	1
PREVOST MABEL C	LTC	N-0759860	0568	1
PREVOST THURMAN E	1LT	0-1551931	1160	2
PREWETT JOHNNIE J	1LT	0-0415295	0843	2
PREWITT AUBREY R	MAJ	0-1317940	0159	1
PREWITT CLIFFORD W	MAJ	0-4010382	0868	1
PREWITT LOUIS L	MAJ	0-0502016	0461	1
PREWITT MALCOLM L	LTC	0-0272832	0367	3
PRIBYL JEROME W	2LT	0-1112382	0545	2
PRICE ALBERT A	LTC	0-0452797	1162	1
PRICE ALBERT F	1LT	0-0547691	1045	2
PRICE AMIT J	MAJ	0-2014675	1164	1
PRICE ANDREW F	LTC	0-0219892	1144	2
PRICE ARCHIE N	CPT	0-0367454	0946	2
PRICE BLAIR W	MAJ	0-2262325	0765	1
PRICE BLISS A	LTC	0-1305640	0765	1
PRICE BRUCE C	COL	0-0290603	0668	3
PRICE CALVIN W	MAJ	0-2016108	0660	1
PRICE CARLTON B	LTC	0-1319773	1061	1
PRICE CHARLES E	MAJ	0-0981040	0167	1
PRICE CHARLES L JR	1LT	0-0423070	0646	2
PRICE CHARLES W	LTC	0-0194453	0457	3
PRICE DANA H	CW2	W-2142985	0753	1
PRICE DONALD A	LTC	0-1635220	1162	2
PRICE DONALD L	MAJ	0-1648096	0557	1
PRICE EARL R	LTC	0-0297768	1046	2
PRICE EDWARD F JR	COL	0-1588236	1264	1
PRICE EDWARD W	CPT	0-0109808	0244	1
PRICE ELBERT C	LTC	0-0176539	0656	3
PRICE ELLIS R	2LT	0-0947361	0251	2
PRICE ELMER C	MAJ	0-0510902	0153	1
PRICE ENOCH R JR	MAJ	0-0966340	1165	2
PRICE ERNEST T	MAJ	0-1107055	1263	1
PRICE EVA M	MAJ	N-0754475	0665	1
PRICE FRANCIS F JR	MAJ	0-0461039	0264	1
PRICE FRANK C JR	MAJ	0-2266283	0866	1
PRICE FREDERICK	MAJ	0-1822323	0261	1
PRICE GENE F	CW2	W-2211956	0768	1
PRICE GEORGE P	LTC	0-0380798	0562	1
PRICE GLENN A	COL	0-0267396	1068	3
PRICE HAROLD G	COL	0-0314972	1166	1
PRICE HARRY	LTC	0-0182062	0862	3
PRICE HARRY E	CPT	0-1324573	0968	3
PRICE HOLLIS A	MAJ	0-2026292	1165	1
PRICE HOMER I	MAJ	0-1285300	0759	1
PRICE HOWARD E	COL	0-0329365	0363	1
PRICE HOWARD P	CPT	0-0885722	0764	1
PRICE HOWARD T	1LT	0-0885642	1047	1
PRICE HUBERT O	MAJ	0-0245186	1149	3
PRICE IRVEY M	WO1	W-2123801	0547	2
PRICE JACK J	LTC	0-1176469	0466	1
PRICE JAMES I	CW3	W-2208491	0267	1
PRICE JAMES R	1LT	0-1314188	0547	2
PRICE JAMES T	MAJ	0-1053306	0364	1

NAME	GRADE	SVC NO	DATE RET MO YR	RET CODE
PRICE JIMMIE R	CW2	W-2207717	0365	1
PRICE JOE P	COL	0-0236100	0965	3
PRICE JOHN C	CW2	W-2148907	1060	1
PRICE JOHN E JR	MAJ	0-0537444	0765	1
PRICE JOHN H	MAJ	0-0521640	1154	1
PRICE JOHN L JR	2LT	0-1951119	0947	2
PRICE JOHN M	2LT	0-1644681	0944	2
PRICE JOHNNY C	LTC	0-2029844	0567	2
PRICE JULIAN R	COL	0-1573522	0261	1
PRICE KERMIT D	1LT	0-0889273	1057	1
PRICE KERMIT F	CW3	W-2143669	0961	1
PRICE LEE F	CW3	W-2205297	0767	1
PRICE LESLIE F	CPT	0-0401019	0346	2
PRICE LLOYD G	CPT	0-1013727	0748	2
PRICE LOTT W	CPT	0-1577709	0549	1
PRICE LOUIS	MAJ	0-0298551	0145	2
PRICE LOYD A	1LT	0-1167167	0145	2
PRICE MILTON L	1LT	0-1046231	0545	2
PRICE MITCHELL R	1LT	0-1310151	1046	2
PRICE MOSES C	MAJ	0-0976152	0861	1
PRICE OSCAR O	LTC	0-0294911	1065	3
PRICE PAUL T SR	2LT	0-2006230	1045	2
PRICE RALPH A	LTC	0-0297876	1163	3
PRICE RALPH C	COL	0-0270719	1266	3
PRICE RAYMOND J	MAJ	0-0322825	0862	3
PRICE REYNOLD E	MAJ	0-1686755	0564	1
PRICE RICHARD M	LTC	0-0244219	0665	3
PRICE ROBERT J	LTC	0-0213544	0245	2
PRICE ROBERT K	MAJ	0-1554612	0163	1
PRICE ROBERT L	CW3	W-2104390	1059	1
PRICE ROBERT M	LTC	0-0185118	0958	3
PRICE ROBERT Y	MAJ	0-1648097	0160	1
PRICE RUPERT A	CPT	0-0976525	0960	1
PRICE RUSSELL S	LTC	0-0246978	0857	2
PRICE SAMUEL H	MAJ	0-1686632	0762	1
PRICE SAMUEL J	COL	0-0145202	0353	3
PRICE THEODORE P	1LT	0-0538382	0446	2
PRICE THOMAS	MAJ	0-1874878	0365	1
PRICE THOMAS A	LTC	0-0224586	1055	3
PRICE THOMAS A JR	LTC	0-1042140	1262	1
PRICE THOMAS M	MAJ	0-0320102	0153	2
PRICE VAL	LTC	0-0195648	0162	3
PRICE VAUGHN A	LTC	0-0176912	0260	3
PRICE VERNON C	CPT	0-0186034	0446	1
PRICE WALTER	COL	0-0306078	0368	3
PRICE WALTER O	CW4	W-2128803	0856	1
PRICE WILBUR M	1LT	0-1325669	0646	2
PRICE WILLIAM A	CPT	0-2039152	0657	1
PRICE WILLIAM E	CW3	W-2143342	0665	1
PRICE WILLIAM G	CW4	W-2147422	0364	1
PRICE WILLIAM H	MAJ	0-1288118	1266	1
PRICE WILLIAM R	CPT	0-1284394	0359	1
PRICE WILLIAM S JR	CPT	0-1030510	0655	2
PRICE WILLIAM T	MAJ	0-0137474	1151	2
PRICER JOHN D	MAJ	0-1822454	0758	1
PRICHARD ELBERT M	COL	0-0183990	0258	3
PRICHARD ELMER C	LTC	0-0388265	0768	3
PRICHARD GEORGE W	LTC	0-0166914	0354	3
PRICHARD LESLIE A	COL	0-0246085	1161	3
PRICHARD MASON C	COL	0-0246804	0559	3
PRICHARD STANLEY N	LTC	0-1015320	1066	1
PRICHARD VERNON R	CPT	0-2212031	0960	1
PRICHARD WALDEMAR L	MAJ	0-0413167	0546	2
PRICKETT HENRY G	LTC	0-0196016	0650	3
PRIDDY CECIL T	LTC	0-0343680	0761	1
PRIDDY NEWTON O	LTC	0-0353921	0465	3
PRIDE ARCHIE C	CW3	W-2006728	0767	3
PRIDE HAROLD E	COL	0-0121493	0554	3
PRIDE RICHARD	MAJ	0-1061823	0561	1
PRIDE ROBERT S	LTC	0-0261451	0567	3
PRIDEAUX GEORGE E	1LT	0-2035371	0745	2
PRIDEMORE WILLIAM H	1LT	0-1573932	1051	2
PRIDGEN ROBERT H	2LT	0-1913881	0930	1
PRIDMORE GEORGE M	LTC	0-0354031	0561	1
PRIEBE ARTHUR H	CPT	0-0241810	1062	3

NAME	GRADE	SVC NO	DATE RET MO YR	RET CODE
PRIEBE AUDREY W	LTC	O-1596190	0863	1
PRIEBE EGON A	1LT	O-1312591	1145	2
PRIEBE RUBY M	MAJ	N-0741810	0247	1
PRIEM CARROLL G	LTC	O-1798701	0358	1
PRIEM RICHARD S	LTC	O-2019216	0868	1
PRIESS CONRAD E JR	CPT	O-0394182	0544	2
PRIESS HAROLD F	LTC	O-0250427	1064	3
PRIEST ARCHIE W	COL	O-0102803	0648	3
PRIEST CLARENCE L	LTC	O-0285917	1058	3
PRIEST CLIFTON H	1LT	O-1050427	0845	2
PRIEST NORMAN F	LTC	O-1031834	0164	1
PRIEST ROY R	MAJ	O-0181718	0455	3
PRIEST WILLIAM L	LTC	O-1309395	1163	1
PRIESTER PETER J	CW4	W-2001864	0354	3
PRIGAL ROBERT	WO1	W-2134238	1045	2
PRIGG LEIGH P	1LT	O-1302517	0945	2
PRIGGE HENRY T	MAJ	O-1641701	0158	2
PRILLER JAMES H	LTC	O-0925554	0765	3
PRIMAKOW MAX J	COL	O-0307493	1166	3
PRIME JESSE M	MAJ	O-0109948	1137	1
PRIME LOUIS J	LTC	O-0256030	0760	3
PRIME NICHOLAS P	COL	O-0313877	0657	1
PRIMEAUX ALEXANDER	MAJ	O-0968073	0561	1
PRIMEAUX OLIVER J JR	CW2	W-2213048	1168	1
PRIMER BENJAMIN M	COL	O-0368715	0460	3
PRIMER MABEL C	CPT	N-0700788	1146	2
PRIMM BENY J	1LT	O-2202681	0953	2
PRIMM CHARLES T	LTC	O-1644683	0762	1
PRIMM HUGH R	LTC	O-1031969	0564	1
PRIMM JOHN L	MAJ	O-0308581	1045	2
PRIMPAS CONSTANTIN	MAJ	O-0297463	1043	2
PRIMROSE FRANK	2LT	O-1872981	0453	2
PRIMROSE JAMES W	CPT	O-0219864	0955	3
PRIMROSE JOHN W	LTC	O-0246524	0346	2
PRINCE FRED A JR	CW2	W-2213704	1268	1
PRINCE CHARLES C	LTC	O-0552228	0766	3
PRINCE DWIGHT E	LTC	O-1293312	0567	1
PRINCE EDWARD E	LTC	O-1323476	0661	2
PRINCE EUGENE	COL	O-0135384	0253	3
PRINCE FORREST	CW2	W-2103330	0960	1
PRINCE FRANK C	LTC	O-0131364	0352	2
PRINCE HAROLD R	LTC	O-1703067	0962	1
PRINCE JAMES C	MAJ	O-1635518	0260	1
PRINCE JULIUS E	CW4	W-2109972	0863	1
PRINCE RAYMOND D	LTC	O-0366267	1060	1
PRINCE ROBERT C	LTC	O-0400547	0762	1
PRINCE WILLIAM	CW2	W-2152398	0862	1
PRINCE WILLIAM G	LTC	O-0281124	0867	3
PRINCIGALLI PASQUALE	COL	O-1638307	1268	1
PRINDEVILLE CHARLES	LTC	O-0168059	0157	3
PRINDLE ROBERT C	LTC	O-0339162	1166	1
PRINE GLYNN L	LTC	O-0358794	0562	1
PRINE WEBSTER C	1LT	O-0507989	1148	1
PRING NORVAL L	LTC	O-1173749	1060	1
PRINGLE JAMES L	MAJ	O-1049619	1059	2
PRINS JOHN M	MAJ	O-0163690	1061	3
PRINTUP ROY S	MAJ	O-0291617	0653	2
PRIOR IRVIE L	CW3	W-2136725	1162	1
PRIOR RAYMOND W	LTC	O-0346531	0655	1
PRIOR WILLIAM E	CW4	W-2146297	0265	2
PRISET GEORGE F	CW3	W-2148982	0566	1
PRISMON DONALD R	2LT	O-1295429	1143	2
PRITCHARD ARCHIE A	MAJ	O-1821909	0161	1
PRITCHARD CHARLES K	LTC	O-1582773	1066	1
PRITCHARD CHARLES N	1LT	O-1104348	0344	2
PRITCHARD EZRA L	CW3	W-2143636	1060	1
PRITCHARD FRANK R	LTC	O-0282598	0459	1
PRITCHARD FRANK S	COL	O-0139855	0659	3
PRITCHARD GEORGE B	LTC	O-0254314	0865	3
PRITCHARD GEORGE R	COL	O-0296032	0647	2
PRITCHARD GROVER E	2LT	O-1115987	0345	2
PRITCHARD HOWARD C	CW3	W-2003908	0667	1
PRITCHARD JACOB L	COL	O-0104146	0547	2
PRITCHARD JOHN M	2LT	O-0456203	0145	2
PRITCHARD ROWLAND	MAJ	O-0282600	0946	2

NAME	GRADE	SVC NO	DATE RET MO YR	RET CODE
PRITCHARD THOMAS F	MAJ	O-1799659	0861	1
PRITCHER OWEN E	MAJ	O-0292644	0468	3
PRITCHETT BRUMLEY O	COL	O-0272215	0867	3
PRITCHETT CHARLES M	CPT	O-1596555	1052	2
PRITCHETT CLARK P	MAJ	O-0319001	0945	2
PRITCHETT DEAN	1LT	O-1048935	0856	1
PRITCHETT IRENE M	1LT	N-0728295	0945	1
PRITCHETT JAMES W	CW3	W-2152049	0563	1
PRITCHETT T H	LTC	O-2049687	1162	1
PRITCHETT THOMAS W	LTC	O-2209854	0868	1
PRITIKIN ROLAND I	COL	O-0278803	0266	3
PRIVETT JOE H	1LT	O-0527853	0845	2
PRIVETTE WILLIAM P	COL	O-0264574	0367	3
PRIZZIA KATHARINE	2LT	N-0757241	0245	1
PROBASCO CYRIL E	MAJ	O-0990953	0366	1
PROBASCO MORGAN C JR	MAJ	O-1645297	0660	1
PROBECK ROBERT V	1LT	O-0486939	1045	2
PROBERT ALICE O	MAJ	N-0771374	0366	3
PROBES DONALD J	LTC	O-0294745	0658	1
PROBST ARNOLD M	COL	O-0131365	0648	3
PROBST RUDOLPH O	COL	O-0163266	1149	3
PROBST WILLIAM JR	MAJ	O-0982947	0364	1
PROCH RICHARD S	2LT	O-1294192	1144	2
PROCHASKA RALPH E	LTC	O-0328201	0563	1
PROCHAZKA JOSEPH	1LT	O-1303184	1144	2
PROCHKA JOHN S	1LT	O-1103369	0845	2
PROCISSI FREDERIC P	MAJ	O-1307998	0364	1
PROCK HARRY F	MAJ	O-2025826	0859	2
PROCTER CLAUDE M	LTC	O-0300705	0446	2
PROCTER HARRY L JR	CPT	O-0401500	0145	2
PROCTOR CARL E	CPT	O-1169694	0146	2
PROCTOR CARLTON S	COL	O-0173630	1043	2
PROCTOR EMMETT F	MAJ	O-1117711	1165	1
PROCTOR HARRY W	LTC	O-0379640	1166	3
PROCTOR JAMES H	LTC	O-0539945	0564	1
PROCTOR JOE K	LTC	O-1309605	0261	1
PROCTOR JOHN G	1LT	O-0499522	0661	1
PROCTOR ROBERT L	CW4	W-2003992	0765	1
PROCTOR ROBERT M	CPT	O-0278244	0846	1
PROCTOR ROLAND G	1LT	O-0291737	0645	2
PROCTOR SAMUEL E	LTC	O-0202435	0863	3
PROCTOR STEPHEN M	LTC	O-0481233	0555	2
PROCTOR WALTER J	CW2	W-2150221	0263	1
PROCTOR WARREN S	CPT	O-1102914	0755	2
PROCTOR WILLIAM A	1LT	O-2008544	0648	2
PROEHL WILLIAM H	LTC	O-1102915	0559	2
PROESCHEL ROBERT L	CW2	W-2129295	0949	2
PROETTO JOHN	WO1	W-2123426	1044	2
PROFFER CLEVEL C	CW3	W-2147362	0465	1
PROFFER ESTES E	LTC	O-0360087	0761	1
PROFFITT JOHN M	CW3	W-2146873	1263	1
PROFFITT JOSIAH C	COL	O-0295725	0861	3
PROFFITT SAMUEL L	MAJ	O-0885425	0347	1
PROFFITT SCOTT	MAJ	O-1306642	1156	1
PROFFITT WOODROW W	CW2	W-2148584	0859	1
PROHASKA RAYMOND J	LTC	O-0268743	0568	3
PROHASKA ROBERT A	LTC	O-1105121	0561	1
PROKOP ALEXANDER	MAJ	O-0535955	0467	1
PROKOP GEORGE S	MAJ	O-0258358	0268	3
PROKOP VENNA V	MAJ	O-1303945	0158	1
PROMIN JOHN	CPT	O-0234964	0447	1
PRONCAVAGE WILLIAM F	MAJ	O-1181087	0863	1
PROPER FRANCIS J	CPT	O-1294237	0658	2
PROPER THEODORE R	LTC	O-0491841	0646	2
PROPES WELDON O	LTC	O-0456102	0961	1
PROPHITT RAYMOND E	CW3	W-3150871	1168	1
PROPST CLIFFORD H	MAJ	O-1310637	0561	1
PROPSTER HOWARD A	LTC	O-1291878	0961	1
PROSCENO HARRY A	CPT	O-0326665	0446	2
PROSE BOBBY B	CW3	W-2144423	1065	1
PROSERPI RAYMOND H	MAJ	O-1061221	0364	1
PROSKE DOROTHY L	2LT	N-0700690	0141	1
PROSNAK JOHN P	MAJ	O-1845090	0461	1
PROSNIT DANIEL R	1LT	O-1544548	0445	2
PROSS DALE F	CW2	W-2110775	1159	2

NAME	GRADE	SVC NO	DATE RET MO YR	RET CODE
PROSSER BIRNEY E	MAJ	O-0408934	1060	1
PROSSER CORTLAND R	CPT	O-1650701	0959	1
PROSSER EVAN W	MAJ	O-1817869	0665	1
PROSSER HOLLIS P	CW2	W-2211132	0865	1
PROSSER LEWIS R	2LT	O-1587551	1045	2
PROTAS STANLEY J	1LT	O-1002504	0945	2
PROTEAU ROSE M	1LT	N-0720835	0946	1
PROTENIC JOSEPH A	CW4	W-2109090	0657	1
PROTHERO WALTER K	MAJ	O-1320859	1061	1
PROTHEROE LORANA R	2LT	L-0100333	0247	2
PROTHEROE MAURICE R	LTC	O-0224930	0165	3
PROTHRO RUFUS C	LTC	O-0451042	0156	1
PROUDE JAMES J A	COL	O-0264337	0655	2
PROULX ENNIS A	LTC	O-1102435	0162	1
PROULX THOMAS E	MAJ	O-1685514	0561	1
PROVAN RICHARD D	CPT	O-1294013	1146	2
PROVOST LOUIE	LTC	O-0946462	0667	1
PROVOST MURREL G	MAJ	O-0322538	1061	3
PROVOST RAYMOND J	LTC	O-1584761	1160	1
PROVOST RAYMOND L	CW3	W-2211124	0868	1
PROVOST ROLAND E	2LT	O-1334345	0146	2
PROVOW CHARLES O	MAJ	O-1291327	0862	1
PRUCE I JAMES	LTC	O-1636505	0865	1
PRUCNAL PETER G	MAJ	O-1011658	0954	1
PRUDDEN HORTON R	2LT	O-1557660	1144	2
PRUDEN JOSEPH O	MAJ	O-0527442	0665	1
PRUDEN KNOX P	COL	O-0273918	0950	2
PRUDHOMME LENANCE J	LTC	O-0289293	1060	1
PRUEGERT JOSEPH	CPT	O-0139856	0648	3
PRUEITT FELIX N	MAJ	O-0509636	1157	1
PRUEITT RAYMOND V	MAJ	O-0296433	0157	1
PRUET HENRY M	CW2	W-2205193	0262	1
PRUETT ALLEN K	MAJ	O-0575962	0660	1
PRUETT CARL A	CPT	O-2262984	0764	1
PRUETT FLOYD H	MAJ	O-1166357	1046	2
PRUETTE JAMES	2LT	O-2026334	1059	2
PRUITT GORDON A	CW4	W-2113623	0456	1
PRUITT JAMES C	MAJ	O-0231997	0665	3
PRUITT OSBIE T	CPT	O-1342115	1060	1
PRUITT ROBERT E	2LT	O-1290127	0644	2
PRUITT THOMAS W	1LT	O-0447926	0846	2
PRUITT VAN F	CPT	O-0135542	0949	3
PRUITT VESTER L	CW2	W-2148330	1055	1
PRUITT WILLIAM R	LTC	O-0249068	0367	3
PRUNER CLINTON E	CPT	O-0279534	1044	2
PRUNER HAROLD M	1LT	O-1633463	0345	2
PRUNTY PAUL P	LTC	O-1822186	1161	1
PRUSIK CHARLES C	MAJ	O-0973153	1160	1
PRUSINOWSKI S J	2LT	O-1301875	0545	2
PRYCE LESLIE P	MAJ	O-1308375	0464	1
PRYDE THOMAS	LTC	O-0272499	1263	3
PRYOR BERNARD B	MAJ	O-1342347	0563	1
PRYOR FRANCIS J III	MAJ	O-0513055	0564	3
PRYOR HAROLD R	MAJ	O-1298756	1060	1
PRYOR JOHN R	LTC	O-0167494	0152	2
PRYOR MARY S	CPT	L-0502413	0455	2
PRYOR WILLIAM I JR	1LT	O-0212577	0363	3
PRYOR WILLIAM L	MAJ	O-1293474	0261	1
PRYPLESH STEPHEN	MAJ	O-1950241	0764	1
PRZYBYSZ BOGUMIL	CW3	W-2210110	0568	1
PSAKI CONSTANTIN	MAJ	O-0265888	0550	3
PSCHORR WILLIAM J	LTC	O-0276288	1057	3
PSILEKAS VASSIL L	MAJ	O-1117713	0765	1
PSURNY EDWARD S	LTC	O-1183949	1061	1
PSZEKAZA JOHN J	MAJ	O-2014700	0864	1
PTASZEK JOHN F	MAJ	O-1328930	1059	1
PUCHBAUER JOHN H	LTC	O-0335041	0351	1
PUCHER MIKE A	CPT	O-0484491	0256	1
PUCK EMERSON E	CW3	W-2147537	0564	1
PUCKETT ALVIN L	COL	O-0454883	1267	1
PUCKETT ANDERSON H	MAJ	O-2096816	0165	2
PUCKETT JAMES A	LTC	O-0241895	1065	3
PUCKETT JAMES D	CPT	O-1576525	0255	2
PUCKETT JOHN P	LTC	O-0482845	0368	3
PUCKETT JUDSON	MAJ	O-0959289	1061	1

NAME	GRADE	SVC NO	DATE RET MO YR	RET CODE
PUCKETT LAWRENCE C	CW2	W-2116348	0146	2
PUCKETT LAWRENCE K	MAJ	O-1924654	0464	1
PUCKETT MERTON T	CW3	W-2203482	0765	1
PUCKETT ORVILLE	2LT	O-1288121	0657	1
PUCKETT SAMUEL R	WO1	W-2120046	0251	1
PUCKETT THOMAS T JR	CW3	W-2148049	0963	1
PUCKETT WILFRED R	MAJ	O-1650294	1063	2
PUDDY MARY M	2LT	N-0701662	1044	1
PUDIL HOWARD M	CW2	W-2142986	1054	1
PUDLINER WILLIAM G	1LT	O-1298757	1154	1
PUERNER LEO W	CPT	O-0279580	0958	3
PUETT JOSEPH F	COL	O-0288767	0559	1
PUFFER FRANCES B	1LT	N-0751441	104N	1
PUFFER NORMAN M	CW3	W-2147980	1264	1
PUGATCH MAX M	1LT	O-1578992	0346	2
PUGENS ERWIN R	CPT	O-1559841	0565	1
PUGH ALFRED E	CPT	O-0254316	0663	3
PUGH DELBERT J	MAJ	O-0258795	1267	3
PUGH EDWARD E	2LT	O-1302192	0944	2
PUGH GRAYDON J	LTC	O-0282489	1167	3
PUGH IRVING E	MAJ	O-0166598	0446	2
PUGH LAURENCE J	LTC	O-0329195	0547	2
PUGH LUSTER T	CW2	W-2147773	1060	1
PUGH MARY M	LTC	L-0909017	1162	1
PUGH PETER J JR	CW3	W-2153335	0864	1
PUGH THOMAS	LTC	O-1533655	0661	1
PUGH THOMAS F	MAJ	O-1696199	0646	2
PUGH WALTER S	COL	O-0209559	0556	3
PUGH WILLIAM C	COL	O-0911595	0564	1
PUGH WILLIAM V	CW3	W-2151128	1262	1
PUGIL WALTER F	CW3	W-2146392	0161	1
PUGLIA FRANK A	MAJ	O-0310859	0159	1
PUGLIESE JOHN	LTC	O-1643985	0862	1
PUGLIESE MARY J	CPT	N-0724169	1146	2
PUGZLES ANTHONY O	2LT	O-1287758	0844	2
PUIG BALDEMERO JR	CPT	O-0215501	1060	3
PUJOLS JAIME	1LT	O-0155889	1053	3
PUKL STEPHEN A	MAJ	O-0969642	0361	1
PULAKIS STRATO J	1LT	O-1300851	0746	2
PULASKI RAY C	LTC	O-1041004	1061	1
PULCIPHER KFELER O	COL	O-0121596	1056	3
PULHAM CHARLES T	COL	O-0102224	1054	3
PULLEN LARRY B	MAJ	O-1946135	1265	3
PULLEN MACK J	CW2	W-2149937	1160	2
PULLEN MARVIN C	CW3	W-2141420	1065	1
PULLEN ROYAL R	MAJ	O-0147551	0648	3
PULLEY BENJAMIN J	LTC	O-1299470	0261	1
PULLEY BOYD H	CPT	O-0305162	0945	2
PULLEY EDWIN E	CPT	O-4005843	0766	1
PULLEY LUBY C JR	MAJ	O-1170928	1059	1
PULLIAM HARVEY L V	1LT	O-1045293	0844	2
PULLIAM THOMAS P	LTC	O-1586051	0562	1
PULLIN WILLIAM M	LTC	O-1686761	1067	1
PULLINEN DIVA E	MAJ	O-1293644	1060	1
PULLIUM RAY C	CW4	W-2143607	0864	1
PULLIUM VENISON G	LTC	O-0287198	0861	1
PULLMAN GEORGE J	CPT	O-1575085	0954	1
PULLUM WILLIAM C	LTC	O-2055052	0566	1
PULLY ASHTON H	COL	O-0327943	0461	1
PULLYBLANK WILLARD R	LTC	O-1576527	1066	3
PULMAN PETER B	LTC	O-0227290	0359	3
PULSIFER WALTER T	LTC	O-0241089	0166	3
PULTZ ROBERT J	LTC	O-0494667	0963	1
PULVER MILTON B	LTC	O-0244405	0962	1
PUMP FREDDIE E	1LT	O-1013349	0345	2
PUMPHREY EDWARD A JR	CPT	O-0377052	0144	2
PUMPHREY FRED H	LTC	O-0141492	0758	3
PUMPHREY GORDON H	COL	O-0447761	0967	3
PUMPHREY LEON P	CW3	W-2144301	0261	1
PUMPHREY LOIRA C	LTC	O-0253914	0162	3
PUMPHREY OTHO S	LTC	O-0297182	0262	1
PUNCH FRANK G	CW4	W-2006939	0667	3
PUNCOCHAR LEE B	2LT	O-1320558	0944	2
PUNLA BONIFACIO	1LT	O-1896448	1154	1
PUNLA MACARIO	1LT	O-1896776	1154	1

NAME	GRADE	SVC NO	DATE RET MO YR	RET CODE
PUNTENNEY IRVING	CPT	0-0400081	1043	2
PURCELL ARTHUR L JR	LTC	0-0364867	0760	1
PURCELL BURGO	LTC	0-0114491	0648	3
PURCELL EDWARD A	LTC	0-0956554	1168	1
PURCELL FRANCIS J	MAJ	0-0243992	1263	3
PURCELL FRANCIS R	COL	0-1324115	1265	1
PURCELL GEORGE W	MAJ	0-1923029	0964	1
PURCELL ISMAEL A	CPT	0-0209892	0859	3
PURCELL JAMES B	1LT	0-1288947	0145	2
PURCELL JOHN J	COL	0-0308693	1067	3
PURCELL PHILIP J	MAJ	0-0239656	0361	3
PURCELL WILLIAM E	CW4	W-2152583	0161	1
PURCHASE RALPH K	1LT	0-0408987	1144	2
PURDIE KENNETH S	COL	0-0234586	0152	3
PURDON JOHN	LTC	0-1797704	0268	3
PURDUN ROBERT L	CW3	W-2207598	0666	1
PURDUE ORREN L	COL	0-0255242	0663	3
PURDY EDWARD	COL	0-0221572	0859	1
PURDY ERNEST V	CPT	0-0412266	0845	2
PURDY JULIAN M	CW4	W-2104398	0261	1
PURDY RALPH A	LTC	0-0530590	1063	1
PURDY TILDEN J JR	MAJ	0-1312795	0258	1
PURFIELD EMMETT J	COL	0-0203083	0358	3
PURINGTON GEORGE I	LTC	0-1300081	0457	1
PURINGTON WILLIAM H	CW2	W-2110519	0853	1
PURINTON JOHN A JR	MAJ	0-0443093	0346	2
PURINTON RUSS E	LTC	0-0410895	0163	1
PURKHISER CHARLES W	1LT	0-1286181	1153	2
PURKHISER WILLIAM H	LTC	0-1647351	1067	1
PURLEE MENLO M	COL	0-0372205	0660	1
PURMAN RONALD R	CW3	W-2144073	0763	1
PURNELL FRANK J	CW2	W-2100026	0161	1
PURNELL LILLIE G	2LT	N-0745292	0945	2
PURNELL WILLIAM C	M G	0-0183312	1063	3
PURNHAGEN JOHN F JR	2LT	0-1301037	0444	2
PURPURA ANTHONY J	LTC	0-0237703	0663	1
PURRINGTON ALFRED L	COL	0-0253310	0562	3
PURSGLOVE PHILIP E	CPT	0-1294362	0860	1
PURSLEY JOHN D	MAJ	0-1576528	0462	1
PURSLEY JOSEPH R	MAJ	0-0322824	0745	2
PURSLEY LUTHER M	MAJ	0-1553198	0954	1
PURTELL WILLIAM E	1LT	0-0553650	0746	2
PURVES JAMES H	CPT	0-1293475	0257	1
PURVIANCE ROBERT E	CW3	W-2136744	0963	1
PURVIN LLOYD Z	LTC	0-1548289	0961	2
PURVINE HAROLD O	1LT	0-2000163	0453	1
PURVINE PAUL L	LTC	0-0291228	0958	1
PURVIS BURNETT A	CW3	W-2143429	0962	1
PURVIS DARVIN D	CPT	0-1998482	1155	1
PURVIS GEORGE B	CPT	0-0971825	0161	1
PURVIS JAMES C	MAJ	0-1549030	0257	1
PURVIS JOHN E	1LT	0-1315861	0645	2
PURVIS MILTON D	LTC	0-0338504	0964	3
PURVIS OTIS	COL	0-0211397	0251	1
PURVIS RUTH D	MAJ	N-0760663	0268	1
PURVIS SIMON M	MAJ	0-0950340	0163	1
PURVIS TARANTULA	MAJ	0-0956451	0661	1
PURVIS WALTER M	LTC	0-0425341	0245	2
PUSATERI ANTHONY J	CW4	W-2129858	1060	1
PUSEL HENRY G	1LT	0-0508168	0653	1
PUSEY OSCAR L	1LT	0-2033854	0154	2
PUSEY RUSSELL A	CW4	W-2122141	0853	1
PUSITZ MANUEL E	MAJ	0-0487521	0146	2
PUSKAR JOHN	MAJ	0-2055829	1057	1
PUSKARICH JOHN	CPT	0-1549031	1044	2
PUSKARICH JOSEPH M	CW2	W-2214350	0566	1
PUTEGNAT GEORGE W	MAJ	0-0343380	0467	3
PUTIGNANO SAM	MAJ	0-1015452	0164	1
PUTMAN FREDERICK	LTC	0-0365395	0261	1
PUTMAN JAMES H	MAJ	0-0312005	0246	2
PUTMAN MILTON F	COL	0-0269321	0168	3
PUTMAN RICHARD G	MAJ	0-0451168	0257	1
PUTMAN ROBERT L	COL	0-0284945	0758	3
PUTMAN ROSS D	1LT	0-1017634	0346	2
PUTNAM BILLY	CW2	W-2214276	0468	1

NAME	GRADE	SVC NO	DATE RET MO YR	RET CODE
PUTNAM DARRELL J	MAJ	0-2016432	0563	1
PUTNAM EDWIN A	1LT	0-1045894	0845	2
PUTNAM FRANK L	COL	0-0178330	0755	3
PUTNAM GEORGE F	CW3	W-2143973	0563	1
PUTNAM HAROLD O	LTC	0-1328843	1068	1
PUTNAM MILES A	LTC	0-0253688	0557	3
PUTNAM PAUL M	LTC	0-0260456	1266	3
PUTNAM THOMAS R	COL	0-0228257	1063	3
PUTNEY CHARLES A	MAJ	0-0949231	0262	1
PUTRYAE EDWARD J	LTC	0-0487624	0266	3
PUTT ALLEN A	COL	0-0139845	1157	3
PUTTERMAN SAMUEL	2LT	0-1014868	0844	2
PUTZ ARTHUR E	LTC	0-0257849	0261	1
PUTZIER RAYMOND E	MAJ	0-2036881	0962	1
PUYLARA JOHN A	CPT	0-0963856	0262	1
PYDESKI LEONARD B	LTC	0-0454096	0966	1
PYFRIN SHERMAN A	LTC	0-0210750	0658	3
PYKE THOMAS N	LTC	0-0294055	0668	3
PYLAND JOE W	CW3	W-2144196	0659	1
PYLAND VAN H	COL	0-0236089	0957	3
PYLE BELTON	CW2	W-2141421	0359	1
PYLE BEN E	CW2	W-2208775	0860	1
PYLE CLYDE B	LTC	0-0217136	0648	3
PYLE DONALD F	WO1	W-2209474	1058	1
PYLE EDWIN R	1LT	0-2049361	0246	2
PYLE GEORGE S	MAJ	0-0263092	1143	2
PYLE NORMAN J	LTC	0-0143418	0145	2
PYLE REA M JR	LTC	0-1325515	0765	1
PYLE ROBERT L	MAJ	0-1549032	1060	1
PYLE THEODORE H	LTC	0-0173397	0861	3
PYLE WILLIAM A	COL	0-0247500	0659	3
PYLE WILLIAM K	MAJ	0-2002520	0363	1
PYLES RAY S	CPT	0-0358168	0646	2
PYLYPETZ CATHERINE	MAJ	N-0721455	0864	1
PYNDUS MILTON H	CW2	W-2118904	0545	2
PYNE FREDERICK	LTC	0-0257045	1062	3
PYNE JAMES F	CW3	W-2145147	0162	2
PYNE WILLIAM E	CPT	0-1287237	0845	2
PYNN THOMAS E	LTC	0-0347530	0966	3
PYSIENSKI JOHN W	LTC	0-0450652	1163	1
PYTEL ALEK G	MAJ	0-1692975	0562	1
PYTLAK EDWARD E	LTC	0-0204650	0755	3
PYZIK STANLEY W	COL	0-0346382	0867	3
QUAAS MARION J	LTC	0-1166587	1055	1
QUACKENBOSS JOHN W	LTC	0-1542183	0267	3
QUACKENBUSH FRANK A	COL	0-0305180	1056	3
QUACKENBUSH ROGER W	LTC	0-2034573	0562	1
QUACKENBUSH RUSSELL	LTC	0-0269106	0461	1
QUAID WILLIAM H	LTC	0-0436872	0264	3
QUAINTANCE RICHARD E	LTC	0-0139055	0157	3
QUALLINS GEORGE A	MAJ	0-0276758	0161	3
QUALLS EVERETTE H	B G	0-0216229	0963	3
QUALLS GUY L	1LT	0-0415871	0646	2
QUALLS OPAL B	CW3	W-2151022	0666	1
QUALLS ROY J	CPT	0-0270334	0947	1
QUAMMEN CLARENCE	2LT	0-1686291	1166	3
QUAN THOMAS J	COL	0-0322885	1160	3
QUANTZ HERMAN C	MAJ	0-0368651	0643	2
QUANTZ WILLIAM	CPT	0-0191963	1039	1
QUARLES GEORGE P	LTC	0-0240984	0844	2
QUARLES HUGH L JR	LTC	0-0918770	1066	3
QUARLES JAMES T	MAJ	0-0153190	0648	3
QUARLES ROBERT W	MAJ	0-0382813	0856	1
QUARRY JOHN H	MAJ	0-0977324	1266	1
QUARTERMAN C H JR	CPT	0-0316268	1044	2
QUARTERMAN LEE S	MAJ	0-0340631	0661	1
QUATSOE ROSS J	LTC	0-0219106	0758	3
QUATTLEBAUM M G	LTC	0-1283836	1160	1
QUATTLEBAUM MANNING	MAJ	0-1047744	1161	1
QUEBBEMAN FORREST K	MAJ	0-1645300	0361	1
QUEBEDEAU ELIE P	MAJ	0-1544079	0559	1
QUEEN CLARON	CW4	W-2123193	0956	1
QUEEN DANIEL	CPT	0-0971793	0860	1
QUEEN DONALD R	MAJ	0-1047745	0158	1
QUEEN HOWARD D	COL	0-0166002	1153	3

NAME	GRADE	SVC NO	DATE RET MO YR	RET CODE
QUEEN JAMES C	MAJ	0-1340929	0561	2
QUEEN RICHARD K	2LT	0-1017733	0644	2
QUEEN RICHARD R	1LT	0-0177817	0952	3
QUEISSER 3RD R L	1LT	0-0526958	1046	2
QUEL OTTO J	CPT	0-1648100	0657	1
QUENELLE OWEN G	CPT	0-0249181	0361	3
QUENTIN WILLIAM J	MAJ	0-0172611	0649	3
QUERRY CHARLES D	LTC	0-0318192	0767	3
QUERY ALDRICH	LTC	0-0213183	0862	3
QUESADA ANTONIO	MAJ	0-0443967	1160	1
QUESADA EUGENE	2LT	0-2264472	1147	1
QUESENBERRY GUY E	CPT	0-1937725	0165	1
QUESINBERRY POSEY B	LTC	0-0498125	0263	3
QUIAMBAO GORDULO P	1LT	0-1896747	0163	1
QUIAT GERALD M	1LT	0-0553278	1045	2
QUICK CLYDE N	CW2	W-2142189	1057	1
QUICK GERALD	1LT	0-0445525	0254	2
QUICK GUY H	LTC	0-1557770	0763	1
QUICK HOWARD D	CPT	0-0244318	0358	3
QUICK KARL E	MAJ	0-1334019	0864	1
QUICK LEROY	1LT	0-0501065	1146	1
QUICK MADELEINE	MAJ	L-1000103	0363	1
QUICK RILEY R	2LT	0-2054004	0645	2
QUICK ROY T	COL	0-0121165	0648	3
QUICK WALTER J	CW3	RW-2148081	0961	1
QUICK WAYNE E	MAJ	0-0421399	0464	1
QUIGEL EDWARD M	CW3	W-2143042	0462	1
QUIGG NORMAN L	CW4	W-2102239	0355	1
QUIGGIN RAYMOND H	CPT	0-1577716	0446	2
QUIGLEY BENJAMIN F	LTC	0-0276388	1267	3
QUIGLEY DAVID W	2LT	0-1175548	0344	2
QUIGLEY FRANCIS C	LTC	0-1046615	0267	1
QUIGLEY HARVEY E	1LT	0-1297093	0645	2
QUIGLEY HARVEY P	CW4	W-2115358	1055	1
QUIGLEY JAMES F	MAJ	0-0976602	1164	1
QUIGLEY JAMES L	COL	0-0926042	0666	3
QUIGLEY JOHN A	LTC	0-1010985	0563	1
QUIGLEY J A	COL	0-0181510	1052	3
QUIGLEY THOMAS A	MAJ	0-1577717	0262	1
QUIJANCE URBANO	CPT	0-1896485	1058	1
QUILICI LEO J	CW2	W-2205100	0562	1
QUILLEN CLYDE H	COL	0-0311913	0957	1
QUILLEN EUGENE K	MAJ	0-1293645	0164	1
QUILLEN JOSEPH E	CPT	0-0376414	0248	2
QUILLEN LOUIE L JR	MAJ	0-2028742	0768	1
QUILLEN MARVIN L	2LT	0-1031358	0445	2
QUILLIN EUGENE F	1LT	0-0161481	0155	3
QUILLIN FRANK V	LTC	0-0396882	0557	2
QUILLIN WALTER F	CPT	0-1165324	0548	2
QUILLINAN MAURICE W	CW3	W-2143112	0661	1
QUILTY LAWRENCE A	2LT	0-2006571	0246	2
QUILTY RALPH G	LTC	0-0286315	0661	3
QUIMBY CALVIN A	CPT	0-0269044	0756	3
QUIMBY RALPH W	LTC	0-0320613	0162	3
QUIMBY ROBERT C	LTC	0-0451169	0954	1
QUIMBY WILLIAM R	CW2	W-2142563	0761	1
QUIMBY WILLIAM W	LTC	0-0407150	0862	1
QUINBY UPSHUR B	MAJ	0-1333872	0463	1
QUINET RAMON I	LTC	0-0299623	0960	3
QUINLAN JAMES P	CW4	W-2151796	1160	1
QUINLAN JOHN F	MAJ	0-0487368	0445	2
QUINLIVAN ROBERT J	1LT	0-1010038	1044	2
QUINLIVAN WILLIAM O	CPT	0-1014306	0657	1
QUINN ARVIL B	LTC	0-1016561	0963	1
QUINN AUGUSTINE JR	1LT	0-0439235	1043	2
QUINN CHARLES A	CPT	0-2042829	1162	2
QUINN CHARLES E	MAJ	0-1919205	0365	1
QUINN CLEMENT P	LTC	0-0139882	0954	3
QUINN DAVID E	COL	0-0272464	0561	3
QUINN DONALD T	1LT	0-1057570	0346	2
QUINN EDWARD	CW2	W-2145293	0960	1
QUINN EDWARD E JR	1LT	0-1546486	0545	2
QUINN EDWARD J	CW3	W-2205808	0365	1
QUINN FRANCIS J	CPT	0-1598990	0763	1
QUINN FRANCIS P	CPT	0-2014914	1263	1

NAME	GRADE	SVC NO	DATE RET MO YR	RET CODE
QUINN FRANCIS S	MAJ	0-0377856	0961	1
QUINN FRANCIS W	LTC	0-1012317	0263	1
QUINN FRANK J	LTC	0-1290305	1062	1
QUINN FRANKLIN C	MAJ	0-0257303	0146	2
QUINN GUS G	CPT	0-0240202	1043	2
QUINN HAROLD P	CW3	W-2205398	0265	1
QUINN HERBERT B	COL	0-0499272	0168	3
QUINN JAMES E	CW4	W-2145834	0865	1
QUINN JAMES K	MAJ	0-0963256	0865	1
QUINN JAMES M	COL	0-0114820	0745	2
QUINN JAY W	1LT	0-0460050	0247	2
QUINN JOHN E	COL	0-0235067	0765	3
QUINN JOHN F	CPT	0-1541505	0446	2
QUINN JOHN F	LTC	0-1949440	1167	1
QUINN JOHN P	CPT	0-1294014	0851	2
QUINN JOHN R	MAJ	0-0127369	0149	3
QUINN JOHN T	COL	0-0272170	0847	2
QUINN JOHN W	2LT	0-2023926	1045	2
QUINN LEONARD T JR	1LT	0-0985767	0757	2
QUINN MAURICE F	CPT	0-1797524	0446	2
QUINN RICHARD F JR	CW2	W-2214749	0767	1
QUINN ROBERT J	2LT	0-0440489	0445	2
QUINN ROBERT L.	LTC	0-1324848	1267	1
QUINN THOMAS J	COL	0-0163890	1056	3
QUINN TIMOTHY P	CPT	0-1321949	0146	2
QUINN WILLIAM E	LTC	0-0108639	1147	1
QUINNETT JAMES G	MAJ	0-2263326	0967	1
QUINNEY AUSTIN F	MAJ	0-1325140	0264	1
QUINONES PEDRO J	CW3	W-2144980	0960	1
QUINSEY CARL L	MAJ	0-1919014	0865	1
QUINT HERBERT S	LTC	0-1035576	0361	1
QUINT ROY T JR	LTC	0-0340504	0762	1
QUINTANA PEDRO	LTC	0-0108225	0947	2
QUINTANA ROBERT	CW4	W-2004154	0767	1
QUINTAS JOSEPH C	MAJ	0-1948655	0464	1
QUINTON CARROLL D	MAJ	0-0421472	0957	1
QUINTON HOWARD E	CW2	W-2210489	0164	1
QUINTON MILTON T JR	LTC	0-1326662	0264	1
QUIRK EMMETT G	LTC	0-0394611	0760	1
QUIRK FRANCIS W	LTC	0-1310761	0662	1
QUIRK JOHN E	LTC	0-1695704	0761	1
QUIRK THOMAS C	2LT	0-0460451	0245	2
QUIRK WILLIAM J	LTC	0-1545262	0364	1
QUIROS EVAN B	LTC	0-0421393	0747	2
QUISENBERRY CURTIS D	MAJ	0-1542931	0363	1
QUIST ARVID F	CW3	W-2120897	0461	1
QUIST JASON N	MAJ	0-0368437	0547	2
QUIST LLOYD E	CW3	W-2109916	0856	1
QUIST NORMAN M	COL	0-0321226	0262	1
QUITTNER JOSEPH	LTC	0-0135386	0648	3
RA ZOR JAY F SR	LTC	0-1295317	0461	1
RAAH CARL H JR	MAJ	0-1685560	1264	1
RAAB MELVIN H	MAJ	0-1597896	0661	1
RAAB RUSSEL R	LTC	0-0259861	0867	3
RAABE DONALD F	LTC	0-1000173	0756	1
RAABE DONALD H	2LT	0-2000813	0945	2
RAABE ERNEST W	LTC	0-0318172	0561	3
RAABE ORVAL J	MAJ	0-0280540	0347	2
RAABE WALLACE M	CW2	W-2210683	0965	1
RAABERG LEO C	CPT	0-0219230	0256	3
RAACK PAUL A	CPT	0-1104350	0253	2
RAASCH FRANK D	COL	0-0212985	0459	3
RABB EVERETT E	CW2	W-2115948	0466	1
RABB WILLIAM E	COL	0-0172393	0253	3
RABBITT FRANCES C	MAJ	N-0737263	1164	1
RABBITT ROBERT S	CW4	W-2141657	0862	1
RABBITT VERNON W	CW3	W-2146120	1263	1
RABBOTT DONALD F	LTC	0-1639522	0667	1
RABE LUCID R	MAJ	0-1306752	0662	1
RABE ROBERT F	MAJ	0-2210060	0864	1
RABEDEAU MELBOURNE	LTC	0-0243354	0760	3
RABELL FORREST J	LTC	0-1329746	0165	1
RABER EDWARD B	CW4	W-2145490	0559	1
RABER HOWARD C	LTC	0-1552152	1166	1
RABIDEAU RAYMOND J	2LT	0-2048452	0345	2

332-811 O - 69 - 20

NAME	GRADE	SVC NO	DATE RET MO YR	RET CODE
RABINAK PETER P	1LT	0-1049621	1150	2
RABINER NATHAN M	1LT	0-0511998	1145	2
RABINOWITZ DAVID L	CPT	0-0470476	1046	2
RABINOWITZ HERMAN	COL	0-0253312	0262	3
RABOGLIATTI ALFREDO J	MAJ	0-1110751	1063	2
RABOLD LEONARD J	MAJ	0-0419799	0646	2
RABON WILLIAM D	LTC	0-1548533	0960	1
RABUANO JOSEPH W	CW3	W-2144958	1065	1
RABUCHA WILLIAM M	CPT	0-2046791	0647	2
RABUN JOSEPH R	CPT	0-2262276	0456	1
RABUN THOMAS E	CW3	W-2209473	0568	1
RABURN MARY T	MAJ	N-0735615	0664	1
RACE GEORGE W	COL	0-0229168	0565	3
RACEK JOHN E	LTC	0-0366274	1060	1
RACEK WILLIAM D	MAJ	0-1334020	0766	1
RACH AUGUST J JR	LTC	0-1759368	0165	1
RACHAL WILLIE JR	CPT	0-1576533	0950	1
RACHEFF THEODORE N	LTC	0-0322323	0562	3
RACHEK JOHN W	LTC	0-1589452	1160	1
RACHEK WILLIAM D	LTC	0-0547742	0720	1
RACHELS JOCK K	MAJ	0-1301878	1060	1
RACHELS THOMAS R JR	MAJ	0-0959656	0966	1
RACHKO JOHN JR	CW4	W-2101043	0357	1
RACHLIN IRVING	CPT	0-0344392	1145	2
RACHMEL LEO	LTC	0-1580193	1061	1
RACHUI WILLIAM T	MAJ	0-0974141	0866	1
RACICOT NAPOLEON A	COL	0-0169276	0559	3
RACICOT PHILEAS A	MAJ	0-0129417	0648	3
RACICOT ROBERT P	CW4	W-2110512	0958	1
RACINE NORMAN D	MAJ	0-2019785	0565	2
RACKLEY ANNETTE S	2LT	N-0764543	0547	1
RACKLEY PEYTON L	LTC	0-0414705	0562	1
RACKOW ELBERT J	CW3	W-2148660	0966	1
RACY FLOYD D	MAJ	0-1640838	1157	1
RACZKIEWICZ JOHN W	CPT	0-1050432	0847	2
RACZYNSKI JOHN F	CPT	0-1895894	0757	1
RACZYNSKI JOSEPH L	LTC	0-1313548	1265	1
RADAKOVICH NICHOLA	1LT	0-1329048	1047	2
RADCLIFFE CLIFFORD B	LTC	0-1292586	0561	1
RADCLIFFE DONALD E	1LT	0-0490511	1045	2
RADCLIFFE HAROLD L	2LT	0-0333829	0366	3
RADCLIFFE HARRY	LTC	0-0979257	0968	1
RADCLIFFE HERBERT E	COL	0-0230345	0663	3
RADCLIFFE HERBERT W	COL	0-0272478	1165	2
RADCLIFFE WILLIAM D	LTC	0-0257398	0767	3
RADDATZ NORMAN G	CW3	W-2126867	1060	1
RADDIN JESSE T	WO1	W-2144705	0860	1
RADDIN REGINALD F	COL	0-0276790	1058	3
RADDING IRVING M	CW3	W-2150715	0764	1
RADE JOSEPH J JR	1LT	0-1171320	0546	2
RADECKI JOSEPH A	CPT	0-0345721	0246	2
RADEK JOE F	LTC	0-0308719	1060	1
RADEMAKER CHARLES C	MAJ	0-1340493	0562	1
RADER COLUMBUS M	CPT	0-1640839	0656	1
RADER JOSEPH A	1LT	0-0468838	1045	2
RADER LAURENCE G JR	LTC	0-1757877	1060	1
RADER MARK E	CW2	W-2210149	0663	1
RADEZ ERNEST	1LT	0-1591382	1145	2
RADFORD DUANE E	MAJ	0-1059041	0260	1
RADFORD EDGAR D	CPT	0-0510715	1050	1
RADFORD HAROLD G	LTC	0-1648654	0563	1
RADICK WILLIAM J	CPT	0-2042954	0746	2
RADIGAN JOHN T	LTC	0-0299798	0562	1
RADIKE MELVIN N	LTC	0-1109253	1262	1
RADKE WALTER L	LTC	0-0901115	0861	3
RADL ROBERT B	COL	0-0197958	0761	3
RADLAUER EDWARD	2LT	0-1946137	1144	2
RADLEY J M JR	1LT	0-1897798	1051	2
RADLOFF LAWRENCE J	LTC	0-0250910	1055	3
RADNEY WALTER S	MAJ	0-1329879	1063	1
RADNOR JESS C	COL	0-0303215	0264	3
RADO IRVING M	CPT	0-1060259	0561	2
RADOSEVICH JOSEPH J	LTC	0-1924815	0768	1
RADOSZEWSKI B H	MAJ	0-1289622	0261	1
RADOW SAMMY F	LTC	0-0888438	1163	1
RADSCH REX W	COL	0-0251592	0761	1
RADTKE ALBERT H	MAJ	0-1877071	0666	1
RADTKE LAURENCE H	LTC	0-0559331	0759	1
RADTKE MERTON P	2LT	0-0543946	1144	2
RADTKE ROBERT F	CW3	W-2150959	1062	1
RADTKE WILLIAM D	MAJ	0-1699953	0163	1
RADULESCU GEORGE	1LT	0-0536087	0747	2
RADZYMINSKI S F	LTC	0-0308768	0161	3
RAE DUDLEY D	LTC	0-0366573	0364	1
RAE JOHN T	MAJ	0-1284935	0947	2
RAEL SOL	1LT	0-1016926	114N	2
RAEZER LESTER N	MAJ	0-2046336	0364	1
RAFF JOSEPH S	COL	0-0310359	0462	3
RAFFA DOMENICK R	MAJ	0-1100291	0355	2
RAFFA LEO L	CPT	0-1284936	0547	2
RAFFENBEUL OTTO H	2LT	0-2006547	1045	2
RAFFENSBERGER E E	LTC	N-0700030	0246	1
RAFFENSPERGER HAROLD	LTC	0-0337917	0160	2
RAFFERTY DAVID M	MAJ	0-1017752	1262	1
RAFFERTY GEORGE W	COL	0-0542652	0364	1
RAFFERTY GLENN A	COL	0-0271906	0360	2
RAFFERTY JOHN C	1LT	0-0407841	0547	2
RAFFERTY JOHN J	MAJ	0-2023983	0161	1
RAFFERTY LOUIS L	LTC	0-0443006	0348	1
RAFFERTY LYLE T JR	CW3	W-3430019	1268	1
RAFFETY CHARLES A	LTC	0-0309111	0868	3
RAFFIELD ZENUS W	MAJ	0-1105127	0956	1
RAFTER EDWIN J	COL	0-0238993	0357	3
RAFTER PHILIP C	CPT	0-0298117	0966	3
RAFTER WILLIAM E	MAJ	0-0474842	0563	1
RAFTERY BERNARD G	LTC	0-1185783	1265	1
RAFTERY WILLIAM C	COL	0-0924046	1059	3
RAFY JAMES	MAJ	0-1798295	0560	1
RAGAN REX	LTC	0-0207223	0955	3
RAGAN ROBERT E	LTC	0-0332666	1054	1
RAGAN TILLMAN A	LTC	0-0300811	1063	3
RAGER RALPH E	MAJ	0-2020762	1063	1
RAGLAND ELBERT M	CW3	W-2142554	0164	1
RAGLAND JAMES C	MAJ	0-0345566	0557	1
RAGLAND JOHN J	MAJ	0-2000748	0463	1
RAGLAND MAURICE A	LTC	0-0964569	1067	1
RAGON FRANKLIN L	MAJ	0-1324870	0660	1
RAGONNET OLIVER E	LTC	0-0341867	0468	3
RAGSDALE BILLY E	MAJ	0-1042922	0263	1
RAGSDALE CHARLTON L	LTC	0-0232347	0347	2
RAGSDALE JAMES W JR	CW4	W-2150661	1058	1
RAGSDALE JOHN W	MAJ	0-0475319	1046	2
RAGSDALE ROBERT E	LTC	0-1580195	0960	1
RAGSDALE ROBERT G	LTC	0-0414192	1058	2
RAGUCKAS JOSEPH JR	1LT	0-1307166	1045	2
RAGULA JULYAN	CW3	W-2152980	1163	1
RAGUSA VINCENT J	MAJ	0-1556340	1059	1
RAGUSIN GEORGE A	LTC	0-0890116	0363	1
RAGUSKY FRANK	CW2	W-2118222	0257	1
RAHAIM MAZICK	LTC	0-1297094	0165	1
RAHAL DERDUN E	LTC	0-1288441	0165	1
RAHE JOSEPH Y	MAJ	0-0377446	0648	1
RAHILLY FRANCIS H	LTC	0-1825055	1064	1
RAHLMANN DONALD F	2LT	0-0556948	0546	2
RAHM LAMBERT P	CPT	0-0504152	0445	2
RAHN CHARLES W JR	CW2	W-2210231	0465	1
RAHN LAWRENCE J	1LT	0-1881384	0556	2
RAHN LEON F	1LT	0-0438316	0744	2
RAHTE WALTER E	CPT	0-0372015	0959	2
RAIDER JACK H	MAJ	0-0313181	1045	2
RAIDER JOSEPH	LTC	0-0348105	0446	2
RAIGOZA JUAN	LTC	0-1059599	0761	1
RAILEY HILTON H	COL	0-0127454	0855	3
RAIN CHARLES R	COL	0-0255263	0859	1
RAINBOLT HENRY E JR	MAJ	0-1175836	0662	1
RAINBOLT NAPOLEON	COL	0-0153224	0950	2
RAINE JOHNNIE S	CW3	W-2210880	0768	1
RAINER LELAND L	1LT	0-1325321	0745	2
RAINES FRANK	CPT	0-0282294	0447	1
RAINES JAMES M	1LT	0-1103872	0146	2
RAINES RAY T	LTC	0-0274679	1044	2
RAINES RAYMOND W	LTC	0-1011276	0866	1
RAINES ROBERT M	LTC	0-2038084	0865	1
RAINES WILLIAM P JR	LTC	0-1043759	1061	1
RAINEY DAVID E	MAJ	0-0238271	0763	3
RAINEY DONALD	LTC	0-1289139	0165	1
RAINEY FRANCIS E	MAJ	0-1283837	0358	1
RAINEY HARRY J	MAJ	0-0260211	0368	3
RAINEY HARRY T	1LT	0-1288791	0945	2
RAINEY HERBERT W	LTC	0-0535876	0764	1
RAINEY JAMES JR	1LT	0-1103873	0544	2
RAINEY LLOYD J	MAJ	0-0454116	0256	1
RAINEY MARION W	LTC	0-1545225	0967	1
RAINEY RAYMOND E	1LT	0-1298924	1045	2
RAINEY RICHARD N	MAJ	0-0329492	1267	3
RAINEY SAMUEL L	MAJ	0-2015594	0764	1
RAINEY WALTER P	MAJ	0-0320181	0168	1
RAINEY WILLIAM	CW3	W-2151353	0263	1
RAINFORD CLIFFORD J	LTC	0-1311050	0162	1
RAINS ARTHUR C	LTC	0-0211114	0350	1
RAINS FLOYD A	COL	0-0440157	0446	2
RAINS FLOYD D	MAJ	0-0276890	0655	3
RAINS MYRTLE L	2LT	N-0700253	0836	1
RAINWATER CHARLES C	MAJ	0-1824364	0765	1
RAINWATER HAROLD G	CPT	0-0415896	1044	2
RAINWATER HOWARD L	MAJ	0-2206223	0866	1
RAINWATER LESTER F	CPT	0-1307572	0446	2
RAINWATER PAUL	MAJ	0-2023213	0362	2
RAINY CURTIS W	MAJ	0-0975817	0253	2
RAITCH THEODORE R SR	2LT	0-1996720	1052	1
RAITHEL ERNEST J	LTC	0-2006129	0263	1
RAJALA OLIVER M	LTC	0-0889598	1265	1
RAJCHEL THADDEUS P	MAJ	0-1330591	0565	1
RAJOTTE EDWIN J	MAJ	0-1998116	0261	1
RAJSKI ROMAN L	MAJ	0-1686311	0363	2
RAKOWSKI ANTHONY W	CPT	0-0962186	1160	2
RALEIGH JOHN M	COL	0-0383797	0764	1
RALEIGH WALTER O	CPT	0-0425946	104N	2
RALEY ROBERT L	LTC	0-1327282	C166	1
RALLS EUGENE D	1LT	0-1574507	0849	1
RALPH CARL C	CPT	0-0979362	1160	1
RALPH CLIFFORD W	MAJ	0-0358859	0464	1
RALPH GEORGE F JR	CW2	W-2152057	0761	1
RALPH JOHN S	LTC	0-1321061	C462	1
RALSTON EUGENE J	MAJ	0-0483201	0461	1
RALSTON FRANK G JR	CPT	0-0540876	0647	2
RALSTON JAMES G	LTC	0-0261748	0963	3
RALSTON JOHN N	LTC	0-0259766	0568	3
RALSTON LLEWELLYN	LTC	0-0250099	0167	3
RALSTON RAY R	MAJ	0-0101223	1056	3
RALSTON ROBERT C	CPT	0-0445131	0247	2
RALSTON THOMAS A JR	CW3	W-2151529	0766	1
RALSTON WAYNE M	COL	0-0131445	0254	3
RALSTON WILLIAM A	CW2	W-2149152	1058	1
RALSTON WILLIAM A	CW3	W-2206474	0168	1
RALSTON WILLIAM C	LTC	0-0145253	0346	2
RAMAGE DANIEL O	CW3	W-2153267	0666	1
RAMAGE THOMAS W H JR	CW3	W-2149279	0162	1
RAMAGLIA ALFRED A	2LT	0-0885794	0444	2
RAMAGLIA JOSEPH	LTC	0-0482637	0163	2
RAMAY JAMES H	MAJ	0-1549037	0562	1
RAMBICUR ROBERT	MAJ	0-2016049	1264	1
RAMBIN AGNES I	CPT	N-0737785	0855	2
RAMBO CARLTON W	CW2	W-2209986	0862	1
RAMBO CHARLES R	LTC	0-1295769	0265	1
RAMBO DAVID A	LTC	0-0197507	0961	3
RAMBO EDWIN	COL	0-1012296	1068	1
RAMBO LOUIS B	CPT	0-1061520	0747	2
RAMEL ROBERT E	CPT	0-1311329	1046	2
RAMEY JACK A	CPT	0-0972834	0561	1
RAMEY MEDFORD G	COL	0-0162466	0961	3
RAMEY SAMUEL M	CPT	0-1327462	1064	1
RAMEY VERNON E	CW4	W-2144363	1262	1
RAMICK GEORGE A	CW3	W-2150045	0163	2
RAMIL AMBROSIO	1LT	0-1896805	0657	1
RAMIRES CARLOS L	LTC	0-0337668	1066	3
RAMIREZ AGUSTIN A	LTC	0-0373943	1160	1
RAMIREZ ALBERTO	LTC	0-0362566	0248	2
RAMIREZ JOSE A	2LT	0-1319126	0545	2
RAMIREZ JOSEPH	LTC	0-0440035	1062	1
RAMIREZ LUIS R	LTC	0-1542607	0365	1
RAMIREZ PEDRO C	2LT	0-1896920	0348	1
RAMIREZ RAFAEL	LTC	0-0330564	1168	3
RAMIREZ RAFAEL G	MAJ	0-1289365	0363	1
RAMIREZ RAMIRO R	LTC	0-1280753	0257	1
RAMIREZ VICTOR M	LTC	0-0365724	1160	1
RAMIREZ-ACEVEDO R H	MAJ	0-1339916	0965	1
RAMIREZ-VINAS VIDAL	1LT	0-0271307	0568	3
RAMME PETER F	MAJ	0-0392694	0361	1
RAMNES OSCAR A	COL	0-0355065	0760	1
RAMO ARTHUR	1LT	0-1000846	0444	2
RAMONT GUSTAVE O	MAJ	0-0289125	0559	2
RAMOS EDILBERTO	CPT	0-1896288	0948	2
RAMOS EMILIO	CPT	0-1896436	0259	1
RAMOS FLORO B	MAJ	0-0888107	0962	1
RAMOS JOHN A	1LT	0-0890502	0750	1
RAMOS JOSE J	CW2	W-2214798	1167	1
RAMOS MAXIMIANO	1LT	0-1896764	0450	2
RAMOS PEDRO R	MAJ	0-1170150	0353	2
RAMOS ROBERT B	MAJ	0-0981423	1167	1
RAMOS SEGUNDO	1LT	0-0217526	0637	1
RAMOS-RODRIGUEZ CARL	MAJ	0-1329158	0763	1
RAMP JACK G	LTC	0-1286182	0262	1
RAMPTON WALTER E	MAJ	0-0778557	0565	1
RAMPULLA BENNIE	CPT	0-0410138	1143	2
RAMSAY ELLIOT	LTC	0-0192531	1159	3
RAMSAY GEORGE E SR	MAJ	0-1593793	0559	1
RAMSAY JAMES M	CPT	0-0498457	0655	1
RAMSAY JAMES M	MAJ	0-1599061	0163	1
RAMSAY JOHN A	2LT	0-1048150	1043	2
RAMSAY MALCOLM JR	LTC	0-0452405	0363	1
RAMSAY ROBERT M	1LT	0-0472990	0246	2
RAMSAY WALTER D	LTC	0-0506189	1060	1
RAMSAY WALTER G	COL	0-0319378	1262	3
RAMSAY WILLIAM F	CW3	W-2207293	0868	1
RAMSDELL EUGENE E	LTC	0-1578997	1058	1
RAMSDELL JACK A	2LT	0-0444735	0344	2
RAMSDEN JOHN C	COL	0-0299766	0167	3
RAMSDEN JOHN T	LTC	0-0396665	0157	1
RAMSDEN ROBERT H	CW2	W-2146393	0666	3
RAMSEL CURTIS D	LTC	0-0465528	0962	1
RAMSEUR ARTHUR R	1LT	0-0270854	0345	2
RAMSEY CARL D	LTC	0-0885750	0556	1
RAMSEY CHARLES E	MAJ	0-1031208	0761	1
RAMSEY CHARLIE	CW4	RW-2119839	0762	1
RAMSEY CLYDE R	MAJ	0-0197008	1056	3
RAMSEY EARLE G	1LT	0-1103874	0446	2
RAMSEY EDWARD A	MAJ	0-0139440	1052	3
RAMSEY EDWARD W	MAJ	0-0349608	0246	2
RAMSEY FELIX	MAJ	0-0285016	0361	3
RAMSEY FRANK B	COL	0-0278183	0862	3
RAMSEY HAROLD L	MAJ	0-1304442	1158	1
RAMSEY HARVEY E	CPT	0-1176771	1055	2
RAMSEY HENRY H	CPT	0-0153125	0754	3
RAMSEY IRA C	CPT	0-0495405	0550	1
RAMSEY JACKIE B	CPT	0-1939372	0360	2
RAMSEY JAMES D	CPT	0-0301047	0746	2
RAMSEY JAMES G JR	CW2	W-2151816	0760	1
RAMSEY JAMES O	CPT	0-1105128	0446	2
RAMSEY JOHN W	MAJ	0-1688456	1265	1
RAMSEY JOSEPH L	CPT	0-0450158	0545	2
RAMSEY KIRWIN R W	CPT	0-0199215	0351	3
RAMSEY LAWRENCE F	CW4	W-2120714	1165	1
RAMSEY MARLIN W	LTC	0-0704979	0868	1
RAMSEY RALPH J	MAJ	0-0331834	0646	2
RAMSEY RICHARD E	MAJ	0-0234582	1160	3
RAMSEY ROBERT A	CPT	0-0281805	1162	1
RAMSEY ROBERT E	LTC	0-0377304	0858	1
RAMSEY ROSS G	MAJ	0-0323400	0161	1
RAMSEY RUSSELL A	M G	0-0215598	0664	3

ARMY OF THE UNITED STATES RETIRED LIST

NAME	GRADE	SVC NO	DATE RET MO YR	RET CODE
RAMSEY THEODORE V	LTC	O-0322833	0560	1
RAMSEY WILLIAM	MAJ	O-1950839	0564	1
RAMSEY WILLIAM H	CW3	W-2115783	0159	1
RAMSEY WILLIAM L	LTC	O-1586057	1162	1
RAMSEY WILLIAM T	CW2	W-2104404	1057	1
RAMSEY 3RD FRANCIS W	1LT	O-1647663	1145	2
RAMSLAND MAXWELL O	CPT	O-1107646	0248	2
RANAGER GAINES A	LTC	O-0360100	1262	3
RANCE RICHARD H	LTC	O-2096887	1068	2
RANCK JAMES B	LTC	O-0954800	1168	1
RANCK WILLIAM A	COL	O-0179924	0452	3
RAND DEWEY	MAJ	O-0258648	0758	3
RAND GEORGE L	COL	O-0311927	1266	3
RAND HENRY D JR	1LT	O-1316087	1045	2
RAND JOHN H JR	1LT	O-5334610	0968	2
RAND PAUL	CPT	O-1726077	0247	2
RAND WARREN R	1LT	O-1331661	0452	2
RAND WILLIAM T JR	1LT	O-2210059	0651	2
RANDA SHERMAN D	LTC	O-1037247	0467	1
RANDACK MARGUERITE	MAJ	L-0705070	0667	1
RANDAL ZACK	MAJ	O-1922582	0865	1
RANDALL BEURELL V	CW2	W-2147193	0457	1
RANDALL CALVIN R	MAJ	O-2035971	0358	1
RANDALL CARL D JR	LTC	O-0388478	1146	2
RANDALL CLARENCE K	CPT	O-0301518	0357	1
RANDALL CLYDE L	LTC	O-0220299	0358	3
RANDALL EDWIN H	CPT	O-1080742	0147	2
RANDALL FLETCHER S	CPT	O-0488714	0250	1
RANDALL GERALD C	LTC	O-1551498	1161	1
RANDALL GLEN L	LTC	O-1821910	0461	1
RANDALL GUY N	WO1	W-2104405	1055	1
RANDALL JOHN F	LTC	O-0323135	1262	3
RANDALL JOHN J	LTC	O-0285887	0964	3
RANDALL LAWRENCE F	LTC	O-1257589	1161	1
RANDALL MORTON H	MAJ	O-0481052	0346	2
RANDALL OSCAR	COL	O-0273022	1156	3
RANDALL RICHARD F	LTC	O-0422062	0960	1
RANDALL RUSSELL B	CPT	O-1100292	0354	1
RANDALL WILLIAM E	CPT	O-0204520	1044	2
RANDAZZISE ANTHONY	CPT	O-1312044	0446	2
RANDAZZO JOSEPH S	MAJ	O-1081303	0958	1
RANDEL CHARLES A	MAJ	O-0229641	0264	3
RANDELL LAURI A	CW4	W-2143564	0968	1
RANDELL ROLLAND P	LTC	O-1534119	0665	1
RANDELL RUSSELL R	LTC	O-0321940	0755	2
RANDER JOSEPH G	CW4	W-2117257	1154	1
RANDLE TOM	2LT	O-0179690	1150	3
RANDLES JOHN M	MAJ	O-0400400	0657	2
RANDOLPH BENJAMIN	WO1	W-2129817	0344	2
RANDOLPH DURWARD W	LTC	O-1305310	0364	1
RANDOLPH FREDERICK	MAJ	O-0271167	0667	3
RANDOLPH JAMES M	CW2	W-2114361	0659	1
RANDOLPH JAMES P	2LT	O-1306753	0544	2
RANDOLPH PHILIP S P	1LT	O-1030706	0645	2
RANDOLPH ROBERT A	MAJ	O-0236306	1162	3
RANDOLPH ROBERT E	LTC	O-1012924	0862	1
RANDOLPH SAMUEL D	LTC	O-1104352	1060	1
RANDOLPH WILLIAM J	CPT	O-0373882	1045	2
RANDOW THOMAS E JR	LTC	O-1004666	0763	1
RANER NORMAN G	2LT	O-2055880	0346	2
RANEY AIDAN A	MAJ	O-0331615	0646	2
RANEY ARTHUR	LTC	O-0315705	0754	1
RANEY BATES O	LTC	O-0195429	0559	3
RANEY BEN B	CPT	O-1684722	1045	2
RANEY JAMES G	MAJ	O-2005525	1160	1
RANEY JOHN K	MAJ	O-0139403	0550	3
RANEY MARGARET M	MAJ	N-0744458	1065	1
RANEY OLIVER C	2LT	O-1329159	0545	2
RANFT ROBERT L	CW3	W-2103343	0356	1
RANG JOHN T	MAJ	O-1548535	0759	1
RANGE ARTHUR R	LTC	O-0709894	0763	1
RANGER ROBERT A	1LT	O-1309398	0446	2
RANGOLO WILLIAM M	CW4	W-2143294	0468	2
RANGOON ELLEN M	1LT	N-0721693	0448	1
RANIERI BENJAMIN J	MAJ	O-2262628	0266	1
RANK EDWARD J	1LT	O-2035894	1045	2
RANK ROBERT D	LTC	O-1048542	1264	1
RANKE RUDOLPH F	CPT	O-0444122	0447	2
RANKIN CARL H	LTC	O-0969855	1167	1
RANKIN EDGAR R	MAJ	O-0139422	1151	3
RANKIN ELMO C	CPT	O-0238715	1165	3
RANKIN FRANK B	CPT	O-0450672	0346	2
RANKIN GEORGE G	MAJ	O-1030926	0968	3
RANKIN HARVEY R	CPT	O-0182769	1050	3
RANKIN HARVEY W	MAJ	O-0162406	104N	2
RANKIN HENRY H	LTC	O-1001031	0657	1
RANKIN HUGH F	1LT	O-1116969	0346	2
RANKIN JAMES L JR	LTC	O-0244986	0760	1
RANKIN JOHN H JR	LTC	O-2047121	1162	1
RANKIN LLOYD F	1LT	O-1012591	0646	2
RANKIN LLOYD F JR	2LT	O-2263472	0453	2
RANKIN OTIS W	2LT	O-2007723	0960	1
RANKIN RALPH K	MAJ	O-0344604	0546	2
RANKIN ROBERT D JR	1LT	O-1823058	0847	2
RANKIN RUSSELL L	LTC	O-0311405	0754	3
RANKIN VERNON H	MAJ	O-1294721	0547	2
RANKIN WALTER R	COL	O-0379860	0165	3
RANLET ROBERT JR	LTC	O-0400166	0964	3
RANNELLS WILLIAM B	LTC	O-0280915	0846	2
RANNEY LAWRENCE L	1LT	O-1895525	0446	2
RANNEY RALPH R	COL	O-0177460	0662	3
RANNEY RAYMOND F	1LT	O-1289140	0245	2
RANNEY WILLIS E	LTC	O-0237049	0364	3
RANSBOTTOM RICHARD N	1LT	O-1283672	0446	2
RANSDELL GEORGE W	MAJ	O-0399756	0245	2
RANSIER RONALD	COL	O-0414186	0466	1
RANSLER NICHOLAS	MAJ	O-0139430	0648	3
RANSOM HENRY C	COL	O-0166512	0648	3
RANSOM PAUL W	LTC	O-0302420	0464	3
RANSOM RAYMOND A	LTC	O-0248584	0665	3
RANSOM SETH J JR	1LT	O-2010541	0947	2
RANSOME JOSEPH T	CW2	W-2122512	0862	1
RANSON ODYLE M	LTC	O-0365361	0666	1
RANTA GILBERT D	CW3	W-2213489	0868	2
RANUS DON H	MAJ	O-0915454	0962	1
RANVIER GENE M	COL	O-0313834	0465	1
RAPACH ANNA B	MAJ	N-0756008	0663	1
RAPACH JOHN D	1LT	O-2053910	1052	1
RAPAPORT REUBEN	CPT	O-1689011	0646	2
RAPEE RUBY O A S	1LT	N-0733599	1046	1
RAPERTO RALPH B	LTC	O-1058103	0162	1
RAPHAEL THEODORE	LTC	O-0302523	0468	3
RAPHUN CHARLES M	LTC	O-1633470	0764	1
RAPKIN HAROLD	1LT	O-1718580	1048	2
RAPLEY LUCIA A	CPT	N-0725699	0348	2
RAPP ELIZABETH	MAJ	N-0760181	0264	1
RAPP ERNEST E	1LT	O-0281555	1045	2
RAPP JAMES H	1LT	O-1322368	1145	2
RAPP OLIVER L	LTC	O-0277053	0161	3
RAPP RUPERT B	CW4	W-2103787	0955	1
RAPP VIVIAN	COL	O-0235306	0354	3
RAPPAPORT BERNARD	LTC	O-1542780	0765	1
RAPPE LOGAN R	COL	O-0385255	0260	1
RAPPLEYEA JOHN C	COL	O-0230492	0461	3
RAPPOLT WILLIAM H	1LT	O-1042141	1144	2
RAPPORT HERMAN	CW4	W-2105045	0457	1
RAPPORT MILTON H	CPT	O-1794986	1045	2
RAPPORT VICTOR A	COL	O-0290340	0164	3
RAREY DONALD R	MAJ	O-0265721	0159	3
RARICK WILMER E	CW3	W-2142058	0160	1
RASAY JOYCE W	MAJ	N-0758835	1264	1
RASBERRY HOWARD A	CW2	W-2208476	1159	1
RASBERRY JAMES A	CW3	W-2210340	1168	1
RASBURY MANNING S	LTC	O-0410420	0661	1
RASBURY MURRAY P	CPT	O-1586061	0155	1
RASCH RICHARD F JR	MAJ	O-1331662	1266	1
RASCHKE RUPERT T	LTC	O-0313435	0367	3
RASH CLARENCE E	MAJ	O-1300853	0158	1
RASH DILLMAN A	M G	O-0274004	0867	3
RASHLEIGH HELEN M	2LT	N-0772894	0345	1
RASIK FRANK A	CW4	W-2126156	1265	1
RASINEN EDWIN M	CPT	O-0364514	0144	2
RASMUS REX B	MAJ	O-0301770	0262	1
RASMUSSEN CLAIR H	LTC	O-0403634	0664	1
RASMUSSEN CLARENCE H	MAJ	O-0444443	0646	2
RASMUSSEN GARTH R	LTC	O-1104354	0963	1
RASMUSSEN HAROLD P	LTC	O-0347643	1066	3
RASMUSSEN HOWARD B	LTC	O-0242437	1164	3
RASMUSSEN JACK G	LTC	O-0373478	0461	1
RASMUSSEN JOHN O	COL	O-0176904	0957	3
RASMUSSEN JOHN P	MAJ	O-0502930	0645	2
RASMUSSEN RALPH W	LTC	O-1297779	0561	1
RASMUSSEN RAYMOND C	1LT	O-0408095	0544	2
RASMUSSEN ROGER J	MAJ	O-1105129	0163	1
RASMUSSEN TRACY A	MAJ	O-0417526	0358	1
RASMUSSEN VERNON F	2LT	O-1823931	1143	2
RASMUSSEN WILLIAM	MAJ	O-0525292	0354	2
RASOR LEO E	2LT	O-1316209	1145	2
RASPBURRY ALMA J	2LT	N-0763702	0645	1
RAST JAMES E	1LT	O-1881961	0953	2
RAST ROBERT L	CW3	W-2148519	1267	1
RASZKOWSKI RAYMOND J	CW3	W-2141916	0159	1
RATACZAK ROBERT L	MAJ	O-0427345	0658	1
RATCLIFF ERMEL R	WO1	W-2150878	0356	1
RATCLIFF JAMES R	MAJ	O-1108255	0461	1
RATCLIFF KENNETH P	LTC	O-1549038	0468	1
RATCLIFF WILLARD A	LTC	O-0971149	0968	1
RATCLIFFE ELLIS C	MAJ	O-1326131	1159	1
RATCLIFFE FRED H	CPT	O-0496663	0356	1
RATCLIFFE GERALD R	CW2	W-2112264	0747	1
RATCLIFFE JAMES J	CPT	O-1170152	0761	1
RATCLIFFE ROBEY S	MAJ	O-0201172	0257	3
RATCLIFFE THOMAS E	MAJ	O-1168874	0646	2
RATH HAROLD G	CPT	O-0247112	1055	3
RATH HOWARD G	CPT	O-0104435	0648	3
RATH HOWARD W	MAJ	O-2006342	1159	1
RATH JAMES J JR	1LT	O-1323969	0346	2
RATHBUN DONALD	MAJ	O-1120082	1062	1
RATHBUN FRANK F	LTC	O-1303027	0463	1
RATHBUN GLENN E	LTC	O-0423333	0946	2
RATHBUN HAROLD V	LTC	O-0231255	0465	3
RATHBUN HOWARD JAM	MAJ	O-1320182	1265	1
RATHBUN WILLIAM A	LTC	O-0545449	1064	1
RATHERT RICHARD W	CW3	W-2147395	0663	1
RATHERT WILFRED E	1LT	O-1018974	0845	2
RATHIEWICZ WACISLAW	1LT	O-0510852	0447	1
RATHJEN GERALD A	LTC	O-1172238	0865	3
RATHKE FRED A	COL	O-0273410	0164	3
RATHKE HERBERT W	LTC	O-0153291	0851	3
RATHKE THEODORE O	CPT	O-0183348	0449	1
RATHMAN EDWARD	LTC	O-0507624	0154	1
RATHMANN ERNEST A	COL	O-0454530	0663	1
RATHMANN THOMAS M	1LT	O-1287406	0845	2
RATIGAN JOHN F	LTC	O-0170527	1058	3
RATLIFF ALVIN W	CW3	W-2153155	1065	1
RATLIFF JOHN H JR	MAJ	O-0450503	0657	1
RATLIFF LON	CPT	O-1555126	0446	2
RATLIFF MANFRED D	LTC	O-0311328	1155	1
RATLIFF THOMAS W	1LT	O-1181419	0346	2
RATNER CHARLES H	MAJ	O-0473844	0949	2
RATNER JULIUS B	1LT	O-0494927	0646	2
RATNER MILTON H	CPT	O-0508663	0444	2
RATTENBURY GEORGE S	LTC	O-0310738	0868	3
RATTERMANN MARION F	LTC	O-0265600	0959	1
RATTRAY ALEXANDER	LTC	O-1301364	0664	1
RATTRAY CHARLES T	CPT	O-0168214	1155	3
RATY RAYMOND	LTC	O-0451046	0961	1
RAU JACOB F	LTC	O-0325766	0665	3
RAU JOHN F	LTC	O-0151573	0648	3
RAU WILLIAM C JR	CPT	O-1059250	0547	2
RAUCH ALFRED P	COL	O-0255694	1160	1
RAUCH GORDON L	CPT	O-0495204	0246	2
RAUCH HAROLD D	2LT	O-1309879	0944	2
RAUCH KENNETH A	CW3	W-2203280	0165	1
RAUCH LAWRENCE J	CW2	W-3250216	0164	1
RAUCH ROBERT L	2LT	O-0495667	0545	2
RAUCH THOMAS R	MAJ	O-1107061	0647	2
RAUCHWERGER SOLOMON	COL	O-0485456	0768	3
RAUCK LINNAFUR B	CPT	O-0185238	0944	2
RAUGHLEY ALAN H	LTC	O-0402146	0468	3
RAUGUST ARNOLD W	LTC	O-0475222	0662	2
RAUH JOSEPH C	LTC	O-0235092	0360	1
RAUHAUSER DONALD M	MAJ	O-0998106	1268	1
RAUKOHL VERNER E	MAJ	O-0282188	0868	3
RAULERSON MAURICE J	CPT	O-1996484	1046	2
RAUSCH EMIL H JR	LTC	O-0270241	1168	3
RAUSCH KENNETH E	2LT	O-0120391	0545	2
RAUSCHENBERG CHARLES	MAJ	O-2011591	0862	1
RAUSCHER JOHN E	LTC	O-0967102	0268	1
RAUSCHKOLB FREDERI	2LT	O-1047307	0743	2
RAUTENSTRAUCH CHESTE	MAJ	O-4006667	1168	1
RAUTENSTRAUCH WALTER	LTC	O-0335779	1165	3
RAUTERBERG CARL B	LTC	O-0437685	0351	2
RAUZI FRANCIS A	LTC	O-1298288	0461	1
RAVELY MARVIN D	MAJ	O-1824683	0761	1
RAVEN CLARA	COL	K-0528130	0565	3
RAVEN WILBUR R	LTC	O-0494582	0557	1
RAVENSCRAFT DAIL F	CW3	W-2144086	1060	1
RAVENSCROFT ESTILL P	LTC	O-1100738	0661	1
RAVERTY MARY J	1LT	N-0728648	0946	1
RAVITZ BENJAMIN B	1LT	O-1554619	1145	2
RAVITZ SAMUEL F	MAJ	O-0213636	0660	3
RAWCLIFFE WILLIAM F	LTC	O-0451751	0162	1
RAWDON ROBERT M	1LT	O-0420262	1043	2
RAWHOUSER DONALD W	MAJ	O-1686806	0166	1
RAWLEY PALMER B	COL	O-0145217	0152	3
RAWLEY STUART D	CPT	O-1315727	0946	2
RAWLINGS AUBREY J	MAJ	O-0167881	1054	3
RAWLINGS FREMONT G	LTC	O-1647665	1165	3
RAWLINGS HERBERT R	CW3	W-2150987	0862	1
RAWLINGS HERBERT L	LTC	O-1299472	0262	1
RAWLINGS JOHN A JR	LTC	O-0115990	1062	1
RAWLINGS MORRIS G	LTC	O-1165938	0564	1
RAWLINGS WILLIAM L	MAJ	O-0314995	0361	1
RAWLINS DANIEL H	MAJ	O-1923056	0664	1
RAWLINS VICTOR F JR	MAJ	O-1555745	0963	1
RAWLINS WALTER A	1LT	O-0490924	0653	1
RAWLINS WILLIS H	LTC	O-0388353	1060	1
RAWLINSON HAVARD T	COL	O-0404980	0948	1
RAWLINSON HUBERT N	MAJ	O-1291006	1161	2
RAWLS BEN H	MAJ	O-0325959	0147	2
RAWLS CHARLES B	LTC	O-1001033	1167	3
RAWLS ELIZABETH	1LT	N-0728514	0845	1
RAWLS JOE P	MAJ	O-2263279	0962	1
RAWLS JOHN M	LTC	O-1646893	1162	1
RAWLS MARCELLUS	CPT	O-0510032	0549	1
RAWLS WALLACE G	MAJ	O-2102644	1165	1
RAWN ARNOLD E	CPT	O-0432156	0847	1
RAWSON GORDON H	LTC	O-1280975	0361	1
RAWSON JAMES S	CPT	O-1590937	1164	1
RAWSON JUSTIN L	CPT	O-0137347	1043	2
RAWSON VINTON R	LTC	O-0237420	0962	3
RAY ALBERT	CW2	W-2151028	0463	1
RAY ALFRED	CPT	O-1595114	0961	1
RAY ANDREW	CPT	O-2044403	0350	1
RAY CHARLIE C	MAJ	O-1177946	1060	1
RAY CLARK	CPT	O-2007518	0357	1
RAY DAVID W	MAJ	O-1018286	0855	1
RAY DUARD L	LTC	O-0219926	0258	3
RAY ERNEST A	LTC	O-0163503	0257	3
RAY FRANK D JR	CPT	O-1638330	0946	2
RAY FRANK S	LTC	O-0452862	1060	1
RAY FRANK W	COL	O-0322539	0166	3
RAY GARD W	CPT	O-0922774	1044	2
RAY GEORGE C JR	LTC	O-1010908	0763	1
RAY GILBERT M	MAJ	O-1115390	0359	2
RAY GRANT L	1LT	O-0502105	1047	1
RAY HENRY G SR	1LT	O-0288512	0752	1
RAY HOWARD K	CPT	O-0404140	0862	1
RAY HOWARD L	CW4	W-2127791	1060	1

NAME	GRADE	SVC NO	DATE RET MO YR	RET CODE
RAY ROBERT L	CW3	W-2143548	0161	2
RAY JACK L	MAJ	O-1688752	0765	1
RAY JACK O	LTC	O-0974775	0268	1
RAY JAMES A	LTC	O-1055705	1162	1
RAY JAMES E	CPT	O-1298591	0962	1
RAY JAMES M	MAJ	O-1311928	0960	1
RAY JAMES P	CW3	W-2205516	0666	1
RAY JASPER L	MAJ	O-1555127	0361	1
RAY JOE A	MAJ	O-0967751	1061	1
RAY JOHN G JR	LTC	O-0127368	0957	3
RAY JONNIE B L	CW2	W-2144146	0258	1
RAY KEITH C	MAJ	O-0279840	0247	2
RAY KINLEY L	1LT	O-1323778	0546	2
RAY LOWELL R	1LT	O-0414086	0944	2
RAY LORA JJ	MAJ	N-0726654	0764	1
RAY LUTHER G JR	MAJ	O-1168044	0657	1
RAY MARCUS H	COL	O-0267261	0158	2
RAY MARY E	1LT	N-0700229	0644	1
RAY MICHAEL K	MAJ	O-0981027	0767	1
RAY PAUL J	LTC	O-0555974	0360	3
RAY RALPH K	LTC	O-0280490	0663	3
RAY REUBIN W	CPT	O-2263172	0857	1
RAY ROBERT L	CW3	W-2126318	0654	1
RAY WARNER C	CW4	W-2131586	1166	1
RAY WILBURN A JR	CPT	O-5314099	1268	2
RAY WILLARD R	MAJ	O-1334623	0165	1
RAY WILLIAM	CW3	W-2109434	0558	1
RAY WILLIAM E JR	CW4	W-2144392	0468	1
RAY WILLIAM H	CPT	O-0386064	0644	2
RAYBOULD LOUIS C	MAJ	O-2210221	0761	1
RAYBOURN JESSE S	LTC	O-0949590	0967	1
RAYBUCK CLYDE W	LTC	O-1587561	0962	1
RAYBUCK VERNON J	LTC	O-1593208	0965	1
RAYBURN ELLIS T	LTC	O-1545962	0568	2
RAYBURN FREDERICK	MAJ	O-0920489	0847	2
RAYBURN KENNETH W	LTC	O-0946973	0967	1
RAYCEVICH MIKE N JR	2LT	O-0442886	1144	2
RAYCRAFT MARJORIE E	1LT	N-0773581	0647	1
RAYFIELD BENTON A SR	LTC	O-1551089	1061	2
RAYFIELD BEVERLY E	1LT	O-1325777	0645	2
RAYFIELD GEORGE E	LTC	O-1051464	0166	1
RAYFIELD PAUL W	MAJ	O-1876352	0468	1
RAYKOWSKI HARLEY A	CPT	O-1700736	1143	2
RAYL JOHN E	MAJ	O-1575090	0162	1
RAYMAN MARTIN	2LT	O-1183954	0346	2
RAYMER JACK L	CPT	O-0368095	0846	2
RAYMOND ANAN	COL	O-0121596	1150	3
RAYMOND ARTHUR L	LTC	O-0282765	0167	3
RAYMOND BASIL J	1LT	O-1012606	1145	2
RAYMOND CHARLES F	CPT	O-1295268	1046	2
RAYMOND EDWARD A	COL	O-0339955	0766	1
RAYMOND EDWARD A	MAJ	O-1634246	0656	1
RAYMOND FRANK	COL	O-0268672	0460	1
RAYMOND FREDERIC E	MAJ	O-1342001	0266	1
RAYMOND GEORGE E	MAJ	O-1311428	0960	1
RAYMOND JOHN M	COL	O-0124453	0854	3
RAYMOND LAUREN A	CPT	O-0386652	1045	2
RAYMOND NORMAN K	LTC	O-0260504	0667	3
RAYMOND RICHARD T	LTC	O-0248731	0865	3
RAYMOND ROBERT	COL	O-0250473	0866	3
RAYMOND ROY L	WO1	W-2115865	0261	1
RAYMOND VICTOR G	CPT	O-0424224	1066	3
RAYMOND VIRGINIA G	1LT	N-0771091	1045	1
RAYMOND WALTER A	CW2	W-2208142	1163	1
RAYMOND WILLIAM	MAJ	O-1924535	1265	1
RAYNER CHARLES E	CPT	O-1170932	0159	2
RAYNER JAY C	LTC	O-0376265	0661	1
RAYNOR GLEN H	CW2	W-2217228	0968	1
RAYNOR J E JR	CPT	O-0358586	1064	2
RAZLER FRANK J	1LT	O-1944788	0446	2
RE VEAL IVAN	MAJ	O-0101891	0655	3
REA GEORGE S JR	LTC	O-1284763	1060	1
REA HOWARD W	MAJ	O-1334624	0666	1
REA JAMES E	CPT	O-1299628	1045	2
REA JOHN P	LTC	O-1113901	0365	1
REA ROBERT G	MAJ	O-1688590	0567	1
REA WILLIAM N	CPT	O-0474750	0447	1
READ ALAN W	LTC	O-1341704	0567	1
READ CLARK R	LTC	O-1314328	0566	1
READ FRANK L	LTC	O-0253648	0560	1
READ HENRY C	LTC	O-0341399	0457	2
READ JOHN P	COL	O-0255741	1060	3
READ JOSEPH C	CPT	O-0471005	0963	3
READ LATHROP B JR	LTC	O-0243340	0346	2
READ LESLIE A	LTC	O-1101630	0458	2
READ NORWOOD G	LTC	O-1011393	0161	1
READ WILLIAM H	MAJ	O-1915588	0367	1
READ WILLIE H	COL	O-0272271	0568	3
READE ARTHUR C	LTC	O-0211398	0957	3
READE BRUCE M	MAJ	O-0311843	0546	2
READE VINCENT J JR	CPT	O-0370757	0445	2
READER CHARLES H	MAJ	O-0224754	1054	3
READMAN GEORGE B	MAJ	O-1301213	0762	1
READY DANIEL	LTC	O-0357794	0765	3
READY WILLIAM C	COL	O-0172282	0562	3
REAFSNYDER VICTOR J	COL	O-0333729	1162	1
REAGAN ARVIL R	CPT	O-1185808	0762	1
REAGAN CHARLES H	COL	O-0175178	0360	3
REAGAN EUGENE M	CPT	O-1292398	0448	2
REAGAN FRANK A	COL	O-0211502	0460	3
REAGAN GEORGE M	CW3	W-2211841	1268	1
REAGAN HOMER L	1LT	O-1298926	104N	2
REAGAN JOHN F	COL	O-0400167	0760	1
REAGAN JOHN W	LTC	O-0533717	0864	1
REAGAN REGINALD	MAJ	O-0329891	0546	2
REAGIN CHARLES E	LTC	O-0239034	0658	3
REAGLES JOHN G	MAJ	O-1885435	1267	1
REAKSECKER JOHN H	CPT	O-1052535	0157	1
REAL STEWART G	LTC	O-1698087	0765	1
REALS BERNARD B	CW4	W-2110538	0560	1
REALY FRED O JR	WO1	W-2122820	0147	2
REAM BERTRAND A	LTC	O-0410704	0964	3
REAM EDWARD F JR	LTC	O-0272716	1067	3
REAM ELWOOD P	CPT	O-1182690	0254	2
REAM GEORGE G	COL	O-0292060	0365	2
REAM GRANVILLE	MAJ	O-1917912	0763	1
REAMER GEORGE W	1LT	O-0407647	1044	2
REAMES CARL J	CW3	W-2144315	0860	1
REAMES EDWARD E	CPT	O-2010342	0157	1
REAMES JOHN P	LTC	O-0452094	1059	1
REAMES JULIAN T	MAJ	O-0352167	1145	2
REAMEY SANFORD	MAJ	O-1313447	1164	1
REAMS BERNARD D	MAJ	O-0302333	0662	1
REAMS CHARLES E	CPT	O-0498466	1047	2
REAMS EDWARD L	LTC	O-0381918	1165	2
REAMS JACK W	MAJ	O-1334208	0464	1
REAMS LUTHER	CPT	O-1041424		2
REAMS PATRICK P	MAJ	O-0750842	0562	1
REAMS WILLIAM D	CPT	O-0441978	0-48	2
REARDON BERNARD A	LTC	O-1319249	1059	1
REARDON CURTIS R	CW2	W-2149714	0557	1
REARDON EUGENE E	MAJ	O-2200445	0366	1
REARDON EVELYN D	2LT	N-0753044	0846	1
REARDON JAMES H	COL	O-0338723	0857	1
REARDON JOHN W	MAJ	O-1913496	0166	1
REARDON MARTIN L JR	LTC	O-1319545	1168	2
REARDON MICHAEL A	LTC	O-0198945	0557	3
REARDON WILLIAM B	LTC	O-0277800	0-48	2
REARICK IRA P	MAJ	O-1559746	0760	1
REARICK PHILIP D	CPT	O-0307913	0943	2
REASENBERG MAX	1LT	O-1946839	0945	2
REASONOVER GEORGE D	MAJ	O-2206251	0264	1
REASONOVER JOHN R	LTC	O-0256718	1265	3
REASOR LEO C	CW2	W-2211840	0268	1
REAVELEY ROBERT Q	LTC	O-0382821	1160	1
REAVES GEORGE W	CW2	W-2145857	0858	2
REAVES JOHN R	LTC	O-1284575	0461	1
REAVES ROBERT J	1LT	O-0491529	1146	2
REAVES THOMAS P	MAJ	O-0334279	0648	1
REAVES WALKER G	LTC	O-2047793	0261	1
REAVEY GEORGE J	2LT	O-1306782	0545	2
REAVIS EDNA M	2LT	N-0742253	0545	1
REAVIS ELIZABETHH	1LT	N-0757243	0646	1
REAVLEY JACK W	LTC	O-0309913	1165	3
REAVLEY JOE M	CPT	O-0494458	0245	2
REAZIN VERNON D	CW2	W-2143725	1268	2
REBER ROBERT J	CPT	O-1289805	0-48	2
REBHUN LESTER	2LT	O-0734602	0445	2
REBISZ CASIMIR	LTC	O-1050878	0962	2
REBMANN EDWARD D	MAJ	O-0224206	1264	3
REBO JOHN H	CW2	W-2145655	0659	1
RECH HAMEN	2LT	O-0192577	0527	1
RECHER FRED S	LTC	O-0463646	0854	1
RECHTINE GLENN R	LTC	O-0400742	0360	2
RECK ALBERT P	CW3	W-2205662	0364	1
RECK FRANKIE E	1LT	N-0735223	0546	1
RECK WILLIAM R	MAJ	O-1800022	1160	1
RECKARD OSCAR J	LTC	O-0157766	0648	3
RECKLINGHAUSEN WILLI	MAJ	O-1304790	1264	1
RECKORD LELAND T	COL	O-0358311	0555	3
RECKORD MILTON A	M G	O-0102176	0546	2
RECKSIEK DANIEL M	LTC	O-1060601	0862	1
RECORDS THOMAS H	LTC	O-0250545	1265	3
RECTOR CARROLL R	MAJ	O-0191326	0656	3
RECTOR CHARLES G	MAJ	O-1645305	0457	1
RECTOR CHARLES W	CPT	O-0546686	0846	2
RECTOR CHESTER H	CPT	O-1002101	0646	2
RECTOR GARRETT I	CW2	W-2115784	0647	1
RECTOR HENRY V	COL	O-0208908	0346	2
RECZEK WALTER A	1LT	O-0444324	0544	2
RED CARL L	WO1	W-2152058	1059	1
REDD BENJAMIN D	MAJ	O-0399883	0257	1
REDD CHARLES F	MAJ	O-0197279	0662	3
REDD LOCK W	LTC	O-0164208	0147	2
REDD SAMUEL C	CPT	O-2025279	0956	1
REDDEN GEORGE D JR	CPT	O-1321128	0258	3
REDDEN LARRY D	CW3	W-2146270	0363	1
REDDEN LLOYD H	LTC	O-0548280	0664	1
REDDEN WALTER M	LTC	O-0373146	0260	1
REDDICK CLEVELAND	LTC	O-1824366	1263	1
REDDICK RICHARD D	LTC	O-1166359	0446	2
REDDICK WILLIS C	COL	O-0229527	0164	3
REDDIN CLARENCE W	LTC	O-0289566	1267	3
REDDIN GEORGE B	COL	O-0198329	1060	3
REDDIN RUBY C	MAJ	N-0759450	0967	1
REDDING CHARLES H JR	CW2	W-2112987	1043	2
REDDING EDWIN T	CW3	RW-2145835	0163	1
REDDING HERBERT J	CPT	O-0453282	0744	2
REDDING HOWARD R	CW3	W-2142190	0960	1
REDDING JOHN B	CW2	W-2150048	0860	1
REDDING JOHN D	LTC	O-1596948	1262	1
REDDING JOHN H	LTC	O-0215512	1157	3
REDDING JOSEPH A	M G	O-0126852	0754	3
REDDINGTON JOHN F	COL	O-1290130	0767	3
REDDY ALBERT J	LTC	O-0124659	0157	3
REDDY ANITA S	MAJ	N-0736969	0562	1
REDDY BERNARD E JR	LTC	O-0498052	1057	1
REDDY JOHN G	CW4	W-2008811	0867	3
REDDY JOHN H	LTC	O-0300043	1065	3
REDELL ARCHIBALD	1LT	O-0335660	0559	1
REDELLA FRANCIS R	CPT	O-2049366	0746	2
REDELLA JOHN A	WO1	W-2109428	0845	2
REDENBAUGH CLETUS R	CW2	W-2205370	0562	1
REDENBO ROSS M	CPT	O-0160768	1155	3
REDFEARN PERCY R	LTC	O-0273756	1266	3
REDFEARN RUTH	MAJ	N-0765664	0565	1
REDFERN EDGAR F	LTC	O-0499711	0665	3
REDFIELD CHANDLER S	LTC	O-1291518	0662	1
REDFIELD ETHEL M	MAJ	N-0788499	0165	3
REDFIELD JOHN F	CPT	O-0341993	0558	1
REDFIELD RONALD L	MAJ	O-1694351	0146	2
REDHAIR GEORGE I	LTC	O-0236335	0863	3
REDICAN THOMAS F	CW3	W-2145240	0167	1
REDICK FLOYD C	LTC	O-0332140	0765	3
REDIFER RAYMOND D	MAJ	O-2212082	0465	1
REDIHAN BERNARD F	COL	O-0276670	0359	1
REDINGER JOSEPH C	MAJ	O-1051740	0260	1
REDINGTON DICK P	1LT	O-0527855	0947	2
REDISKE HAROLD J	CW2	W-2214772	0868	1
REDKEY EARL G	CW3	W-2145656	0564	1
REDLINGSHAFER I A	LTC	O-0349973	0559	1
REDMAN CHARLES H	COL	O-0908443	0365	3
REDMAN ELMA W	LTC	O-0263545	1062	3
REDMAN HERBERT E	LTC	O-0123103	0644	2
REDMAN JAMES N	CW3	W-2211451	1068	2
REDMAN WILLIAM F	1LT	O-1581331	1045	2
REDMON JASON A	LTC	O-0104053	0849	3
REDMON JOHN C	LTC	O-1554620	0163	2
REDMON L GORDON	LTC	O-0509692	0456	2
REDMON WILLIAM F	MAJ	O-1945464	0762	1
REDMON WILLIAM V JR	MAJ	O-1180679	0464	1
REDMOND ODYTT D	MAJ	O-1685525	0462	1
REDMOND EDWARD M	MAJ	O-0256227	1266	3
REDMOND ERNEST R JR	CW3	W-2008191	0868	3
REDMOND GLINNIS	CPT	O-0499495	0854	1
REDMOND JOHN P	LTC	O-1636524	0967	1
REDMOND MARGARET Z	2LT	N-0760137	0445	1
REDMOND ROBERT F	MAJ	O-1876915	0365	1
REDMOND ROBERT J	LTC	O-1080066	0263	1
REDMOND ROBERT L	1LT	O-1994514	0951	2
REDMOND SPENCER W	MAJ	O-1885672	0466	1
REDMOND WILLIAM F	LTC	O-0399956	1161	2
REDMOND WILLIAM H	1LT	O-5252093	1068	2
REDNER FRANCIS B	COL	O-0139449	0554	3
REDUS ED P JR	LTC	O-1551296	1161	1
REDUS JAMES L	MAJ	O-0290963	0364	3
REDUS THELMA A	CPT	N-0734603	0445	1
REDWINE RUFFIN E	MAJ	O-0948893	0560	1
REDZICH JOHN	1LT	O-0497190	0860	1
REECE CLARENCE W	LTC	O-0320428	0754	1
REECE DAVID P	MAJ	O-1643490	0560	1
REECE FREDERICA	MAJ	N-0723132	0662	1
REECE GEORGE J	MAJ	O-0104570	0848	3
REECE HOWARD P	MAJ	O-0583489	0758	1
REECE JOHN W	MAJ	O-0322646	0262	2
REECE MILLARD F	LTC	O-0956990	1168	1
REECE WALTER F	LTC	O-0289126	0247	2
REED ADOLPHUS O	CW4	W-2121393	0365	1
REED ALBERT J	CPT	O-1640850	0447	2
REED ALFRED G	CW3	W-2209340	0767	1
REED ARCHIE F	LTC	O-0145222	0452	3
REED ARTHUR N	CW2	W-2149800	0156	1
REED BENJAMIN M	COL	O-0194773	0663	3
REED BERNARD E	MAJ	O-1935718	1066	1
REEC CARL D	LTC	O-1590938	0261	1
REED CARL E	LTC	O-1635242	1154	1
REED CHARLES A JR	MAJ	O-0999268	0562	1
REED CHARLES E JR	MAJ	O-1119241	0863	1
REED CHARLES E JR	WO1	W-2116259	0346	2
REED CHARLES H	MAJ	O-0207517	1150	3
REED CHARLES H	COL	O-0245471	0660	2
REED CHARLES L	LTC	O-0398196	0665	3
REED CHARLES L JR	COL	O-0220498	0262	3
REED CHARLES O	LTC	O-0326709	0260	1
REED CHARLES S	CPT	O-0192982	0258	3
REED CHESTER A	CW2	RW-2153007	0363	1
REED CLAUDE H	LTC	O-1293317	0966	1
REED CLAYTON W	2LT	O-1641714	1068	2
REED CLYDE S JR	LTC	O-0489404	0767	1
REED DAVID E	2LT	O-1015605	0844	2
REED DAVID R SR	MAJ	O-2262673	0962	1
REED DENTON H	COL	O-0478830	0261	3
REED DENZEL V	MAJ	O-1699988	0561	1
REED DICK R	LTC	O-0133696	0449	3
REED DONALD F	CW2	W-2151928	0762	1
REED EARCLE R	LTC	O-1288122	0261	1
REED EARNEST L	MAJ	O-1320964	0557	1
REED EDWARD M	MAJ	O-1922667	1265	1
REED EMILY J	2LT	N-0735661	0745	1
REED ERNEST J	CPT	O-0108205	0836	1

NAME	GRADE	SVC NO	DATE RET MO YR	RET CODE
REED ERNEST V	COL	0-0114826	0648	3
REED FENWICK T	LTC	0-0263850	0757	3
REED FRANCIS B	CPT	0-2262613	1057	2
REED FRANK H JR	COL	0-0261883	0161	1
REED FRED R	LTC	0-1299109	0562	1
REED GAROLD E	LTC	0-1633476	0364	1
REED GEORGE A	LTC	0-2035493	0867	1
REED GEORGE C	CPT	0-1298927	0146	2
REED GEORGE H	MAJ	0-0264338	0166	3
REED GEORGE JR	CPT	0-0540499	1046	2
REED GEORGE M	2LT	0-1059601	0545	2
REED GEORGE N	LTC	0-0171300	1061	3
REED GEORGE NOR	LTC	0-0149567	1050	2
REED GEORGE W F	CW4	W-2145836	0868	1
REED GLEN G	CPT	0-0523871	0945	2
REED GUY A	LTC	0-0187539	1053	3
REED HEBER L	2LT	0-1306933	0244	2
REED HENLY E	LTC	0-1549361	1262	1
REED HENRY C	MAJ	0-0474819	0947	1
REED HENRY D	LTC	0-0304040	0346	2
REED HOWARD B	CPT	0-0513222	0847	1
REED HOWARD E	COL	0-0200133	0655	3
REED HUBERT N	MAJ	0-2055894	0863	1
REED IRVIN T	COL	0-0311254	1164	1
REED JACK	2LT	0-1322712	0345	2
REED JACK C	1LT	0-1031017	0445	2
REED JAMES A	2LT	0-1576545	1044	2
REED JAMES D	CW2	W-2214652	0966	1
REED JAMES E	CW2	W-2150758	0360	1
REED JAMES F	MAJ	0-1114721	0557	1
REED JAMES L	LTC	0-0209107	1153	3
REED JAMES R	LTC	0-0269968	0259	1
REED JAMES R JR	LTC	0-1251696	0361	1
REED JAMES W SR	MAJ	0-2206657	0968	1
REED JEAN R	LTC	0-0379366	0146	2
REED JOHN C	MAJ	0-0278890	0760	1
REED JOHN E	MAJ	0-0242458	0764	3
REED JOSEPH	CPT	0-1550748	1153	1
REED JOSEPH R	LTC	0-0477778	0651	2
REED JOSEPH V	CW2	W-2203315	1164	1
REED LAUREN R	CPT	0-1321553	0146	2
REED LAURENCE F	CPT	0-0169935	0860	3
REED LELAND M	CW3	W-2206117	1066	1
REED LEO B	COL	0-0121483	0455	3
REED LEON J	COL	0-0260961	0468	3
REED LOUIS B	COL	0-0153457	1151	3
REED LOUIS J	MAJ	0-0139678	0858	3
REED MARY L	2LT	N-0772602	0245	1
REED MAX E	LTC	0-0550107	0364	1
REED MYRON W	1LT	0-1294901	0645	2
REED OSCAR R	MAJ	0-0184417	0648	3
REED PAUL F	LTC	0-0275645	0665	3
REED PAUL W	MAJ	0-0218932	0357	3
REED PHILIP W	LTC	0-0468026	0851	2
REED RAYMOND J	CW4	W-2141424	1264	1
REED REXTON M	LTC	0-1311203	0861	1
REED ROBERT C	1LT	0-1115391	0646	2
REED ROBERT E	CW3	W-2147375	0761	2
REED ROBERT J	LTC	0-1167170	0161	1
REED ROBERT L	CW2	W-2214483	0968	1
REED ROBERT P	MAJ	0-2019932	0863	1
REED ROBERT R	COL	0-0355021	0859	1
REED ROY E JR	LTC	0-1342116	0767	1
REED RUFUS R	CPT	0-0261631	0952	3
REED RUSSELL H	LTC	0-0231402	0165	3
REED SHELTON	CPT	0-0355074	0548	1
REED TED E	MAJ	0-1015381	0149	2
REED THOMAS J	CW2	W-2150748	0258	1
REED THOMAS W	MAJ	0-0949452	1263	1
REED VIRGIL O	MAJ	0-0118886	1056	3
REED WALTER J	LTC	0-0313434	1059	3
REED WARREN G	LTC	0-0443155	0967	1
REED WILLARD W	CPT	0-1295269	0758	1
REED WILLIAM A	COL	0-0274513	0648	3
REED WILLIAM A	CPT	0-1253477	0750	2

NAME	GRADE	SVC NO	DATE RET MO YR	RET CODE
REED WILLIAM C	COL	0-0203100	1154	3
REED WILLIAM C	CPT	0-0533901	0848	2
REED WILLIAM D	LTC	0-1037252	0957	3
REED WILLIAM D	CW3	W-2149372	0762	1
REED WILLIAM N	CW3	W-2209618	0868	1
REED WILLIAM P JR	CW3	W-2141425	0760	1
REED WILLIAM R	COL	0-0224667	0857	3
REED WILLIAM R	MAJ	0-1651169	1062	1
REED WILLIAM R	CW3	W-2148082	1062	1
REED WILLIAM W JR	LTC	0-0417334	0767	1
REED WILLIE J	CPT	0-2012591	0765	2
REEDER CHARLES G	1LT	0-0319582	0945	2
REEDER FRANK	CW2	W-2116046	1151	1
REEDER GERALD W	CPT	0-0275985	0447	1
REEDER HENRY H	LTC	0-0265453	0850	3
REEDER HERMAN W	LTC	0-0228621	1264	3
REEDER JACK M	CPT	0-0423337	1146	2
REEDER JULIAN T	LTC	0-0323392	0860	1
REEDER JULIUS C	LTC	0-1300743	0662	1
REEDER TORRENCE W	CW3	W-2006655	0666	1
REEDER WILLIAM S	LTC	0-0248181	0166	3
REEDIE ARTHUR C	LTC	0-0502563	0964	3
REEDY CHARLES F	LTC	0-2262493	0868	1
REEDY JAMES J	LTC	0-1646526	0768	1
REEDY MORRIS	MAJ	0-0201266	0763	3
REEDY PAUL W	1LT	0-1108260	1044	2
REEDY RAYMOND D	LTC	0-0445056	0155	1
REEDY ROBERT J	LTC	0-0444423	0468	3
REEDY WILLIAM H	MAJ	0-1176473	0565	1
REEGD JAMES H	LTC	0-1635243	0963	1
REEKS LLOYD O JR	CPT	0-1000455	0147	2
REEL LEIDY R JR	LTC	0-1167171	0361	1
REEMS ALBERT B	WO1	W-2151079	1154	1
REENSTJERNA ROBERT L	LTC	0-0331918	0862	1
REENTS JOHN H	LTC	0-0415532	1161	3
REEP MURLEY A	LTC	0-0946869	0258	3
REES FREDERICK	MAJ	0-0420237	0246	2
REES GOMER S	LTC	0-0400670	0960	1
REES HENRY E	CPT	0-0110920	0749	3
REES JACK JR	1LT	0-0408335	0945	2
REES JOHN E JR	LTC	0-1544279	0267	1
REES JOHN L	LTC	0-1017048	0757	1
REES JOHN W	LTC	0-0172263	0951	3
REES MAGDALENE	1LT	N-0733987	0546	1
REES MAHONE JR	COL	0-0255296	1165	3
REES MALCOLM C	COL	0-0124553	0455	3
REES MAX I	1LT	0-1113407	1045	2
REES THOMAS A JR	MAJ	0-0974616	0665	1
REES WILLIAM D	2LT	0-1058362	1144	2
REESE ALICE L	CPT	N-0771655	0547	1
REESE ARVAN D	LTC	0-0281168	0761	1
REESE CHARLES D	MAJ	0-2033818	0465	1
REESE CHARLES T	LTC	0-1333535	0967	1
REESE CLYDE F	MAJ	0-0370567	0547	2
REESE EDGAR P	COL	0-0258772	1165	3
REESE EDWARD J JR	MAJ	0-2029596	1264	1
REESE FRANKLIN W	COL	0-0204229	0156	1
REESE GARLAND S	1LT	0-4025691	0162	2
REESE HAROLD B	CW2	W-2206551	0665	1
REESE HAROLD K	1LT	0-1172239	0546	2
REESE HARRY S	CW4	W-2101026	0855	1
REESE HATTIE P	MAJ	L-0807862	0868	3
REESE HOMER S	COL	0-0143110	1055	3
REESE JACK N	1LT	0-1313129	0745	2
REESE JAMES C	LTC	0-2037240	0866	1
REESE JEP H	1LT	0-0411620	1044	2
REESE JOHN A JR	MAJ	0-1016986	0765	1
REESE JOHN D	MAJ	0-1822189	0861	1
REESE JOHN L	LTC	0-0357268	1151	2
REESE LAWRENCE W	LTC	0-0271042	1167	3
REESE OSCAR N	MAJ	0-0197227	1151	3
REESE ROBERT	LTC	0-1295937	1162	1
REESE ROBERT M	COL	0-0380691	0861	1
REESE ROBERT P	CPT	0-1305644	0866	1
REESE TOMMY L	CW2	W-2118458	0945	2

NAME	GRADE	SVC NO	DATE RET MO YR	RET CODE
REESE VICTOR C	MAJ	0-0162258	0648	3
REESE WILLIAM E	COL	0-0507949	0655	2
REESE WILLIAM F	CW2	W-2144147	0160	1
REESE WILLIAM G	MAJ	0-0413211	0255	2
REESE WILLIAM N	LTC	0-0371143	0849	1
REESER JOHN A	1LT	0-0504159	0744	2
REESER ROBERT L	LTC	0-1043204	1265	1
REEVE CHESTER L	LTC	0-0507732	0556	1
REEVE EZEKIEL B	LTC	0-1542759	0557	1
REEVE HAROLD I	CW2	W-2146955	0466	1
REEVE THOMAS B	2LT	0-0446319	0645	2
REEVES ALLAN E	CW2	W-2150352	1164	1
REEVES ALLEN	LTC	0-0924305	1047	2
REEVES BERTIE L	CW3	W-3430110	0568	1
REEVES CHARLES	CW2	W-2142937	1155	1
REEVES CLARENCE E	CW4	W-2144898	0567	2
REEVES CURTIS C	1LT	0-0507352	0146	2
REEVES DANIEL F C	LTC	0-0273786	0868	3
REEVES FOLK O	COL	0-0228242	1263	3
REEVES FRED D JR	COL	0-1080660	1267	1
REEVES GEORGE R	MAJ	0-1294534	0447	2
REEVES JAMES E	LTC	0-1169046	1163	1
REEVES JOHN A	MAJ	0-0444674	0762	1
REEVES JOSEPH C	LTC	0-1169702	0361	1
REEVES JOSEPH S	LTC	0-1846513	1060	2
REEVES JULIUS B JR	2LT	0-1292588	0545	2
REEVES LEROY W	COL	0-0347583	0166	3
REEVES LOUIS P	COL	0-0150418	0462	3
REEVES LUNSFORD T	COL	0-0287966	1067	3
REEVES OSCAR E	MAJ	0-1878400	0667	1
REEVES PAUL W	LTC	0-0378981	0165	1
REEVES RALPH P SR	MAJ	0-1173046	1160	1
REEVES RAOUL B	LTC	0-0420077	0361	1
REEVES RAY C	COL	0-0208218	0842	2
REEVES ROBERT L	CPT	0-2036693	0547	2
REEVES ROBERT N	MAJ	0-0378625	0246	2
REEVES TED R	1LT	0-0312281	1061	3
REEVES THOMAS W	LTC	0-1342297	1266	1
REEVES WALTER P JR	CPT	0-0926805	0646	2
REEVES WALTER T JR	1LT	0-0966991	0952	2
REEVES WILLIAM A	MAJ	0-1110207	1062	1
REEVES WILLIAM C	CPT	0-0496193	1051	1
REFAKES ARISTIDES	MAJ	0-0236914	0265	3
REFFEL EDWARD W	CW2	W-2209859	0464	1
REFFETT LEROY R	LTC	0-1293649	0864	1
REFFNER HOWARD S	LTC	0-1332099	0967	1
REGA JOHN A	COL	0-0264334	1151	1
REGA JOHN J	CW4	W-2121195	0459	1
REGA MICHAEL	CW4	W-2145262	1059	1
REGALA ALFONSO M	2LT	0-1896503	0849	2
REGAN DAVID M	CPT	0-1697656	0845	2
REGAN EDWARD J	COL	0-0388223	0851	2
REGAN FRANK C	LTC	0-1588245	0966	3
REGAN JAMES M	LTC	0-0493711	1062	1
REGAN JOHN J	1LT	0-1038093	0446	2
REGAN JOHN M JR	1LT	0-0509451	0246	2
REGAN LELAND S	CPT	0-0224098	1160	3
REGAN TIMOTHY J JR	B G	0-0266143	0368	3
REGAUER OTTO	WO1	W-2150340	0255	1
REGEHR CORNELIA	MAJ	N-0785271	0165	1
REGENS LOU	CPT	0-1294902	0147	2
REGENWETHER MARY E	1LT	N-0733890	0745	1
REGER CHRIS G	COL	0-0219877	0652	2
REGER HERMAN T	MAJ	0-1293117	0366	3
REGER 2ND WILLIAM H	CPT	0-0389167	0346	2
REGILIO FRANK JR	MAJ	0-0970685	0864	2
REGISTER BARNEY W	2LT	0-1104357	0644	2
REGLI WERNER F	LTC	0-0905579	0846	2
REGNIER JOSEPH C	CW3	W-2145492	0359	1
REGNIER WALTER D	MAJ	0-0239504	0560	3
REGUERA CESAREO	COL	0-0268662	1054	1
REH CHRISTIAN	LTC	0-0485393	0965	1
REHAGEN CLARENCE T	CPT	0-0292350	0268	3
REHAK DONALD E	2LT	0-1289487	1043	2
REHANEK JAMES J	COL	0-0118061	0948	3

NAME	GRADE	SVC NO	DATE RET MO YR	RET CODE
REHBACH WILLIAM E	CW3	W-2152305	0765	1
REHE AUGUST J	LTC	0-0438425	1152	1
REHFUSS JAMES M	MAJ	0-1169703	0968	3
REHKOP RUSSELL G	COL	0-0223467	0660	1
REHM CHARLES H	1LT	0-0378591	0745	2
REHM EVERETT R	LTC	0-0932867	0765	3
REHPOHL WILFRED L	CPT	0-1944790	0246	2
REIBER WILLIAM O	LTC	0-0294872	0155	1
REIBER WILLIAM E JR	MAJ	0-1542488	0361	1
REIBERG RUFUS	CPT	0-1038463	0246	2
REICH DANIEL J	LTC	0-1647667	0161	1
REICH EMIL J	2LT	0-1796526	0444	2
REICH MERRILL O	1LT	0-0443533	1144	2
REICH PAUL F	CPT	0-1691047	0545	2
REICH RALPH J	MAJ	0-1923578	1066	1
REICH ROBERT L	1LT	0-1796692	0146	2
REICH RUDOLPH M	LTC	0-1019324	0966	1
REICH RUDOLPH S	LTC	0-0193290	0254	3
REICH SAMUEL	CW2	W-2153139	0266	1
REICH WILLIAM	MAJ	0-2034695	0960	1
REICH WILLIAM F	LTC	0-0454137	0761	1
REICHARD JAMES C	LTC	0-0518310	0668	3
REICHARD JOHN S	LTC	0-0532467	0268	1
REICHE LAWRENCE E	CPT	0-1283839	1058	1
REICHEL ALBERT J	WO1	W-2002260	0267	3
REICHEL CHARLES P	MAJ	0-0295149	1043	2
REICHEL PAUL A	LTC	0-0222814	1049	3
REICHENAUER IRWIN E	MAJ	0-0265708	0358	3
REICHENBACH GLEN H	MAJ	0-0258311	0867	3
REICHENBACHER DAVI	MAJ	0-1799006	0757	1
REICHERS WILLIAM N	MAJ	0-0443400	0662	1
REICHERT DAVID L	LTC	0-1691474	0663	1
REICHERT FRED H	CPT	0-0298210	1044	2
REICHERT JOSEPH E	MAJ	0-1685710	0164	1
REICHERT MARION E	1LT	N-0777874	1046	1
REICHLE HENRY C JR	CPT	0-0977501	0762	1
REICHLE SAMMY L	MAJ	0-1920046	0365	1
REICHLING FRANKLIN A	CW3	W-2153178	1163	1
REICHMAN DOROTHY S	1LT	N-0704026	0745	1
REICHMAN JULIAN F	1LT	0-1551938	0545	2
REICHMANN FRANCIS J	B G	0-0219282	0458	3
REICHMANN RICHARD S	MAJ	0-1101177	1146	2
REID ALEXANDER	LTC	0-0919378	0764	3
REID AUBREY O	COL	0-0255099	0867	3
REID BEN C	CW2	W-2203348	0462	1
REID BOYD M	1LT	0-1593212	0145	2
REID CARN R	LTC	0-1107775	1062	1
REID CHARLES A	MAJ	0-1112932	1155	1
REID DAVID F	CPT	0-0961962	1161	1
REID DAVID T JR	CPT	0-2263093	0661	1
REID DONALD R SR	MAJ	0-2263081	0165	1
REID EDWARD E	COL	0-0215648	0664	3
REID EDWIN M	LTC	0-1166163	0464	1
REID EDWIN P	CW3	W-2144142	1155	1
REID FRANCES E	MAJ	N-0732566	0165	3
REID FREDERICK	CW2	W-2215778	0668	1
REID GEORGE E	LTC	0-1553539	0766	3
REID GILMORE W	1LT	0-1102926	0345	2
REID GLENN R	MAJ	0-1327177	0566	2
REID HARRY L	MAJ	0-4009721	0768	1
REID HERBERT D	2LT	0-1047309	0344	2
REID HOWARD A	MAJ	0-0230443	0648	3
REID HUGH M	CPT	0-0268063	0868	3
REID HYTHE A	1LT	0-0540042	0745	2
REID JACKSON B	CPT	0-0461729	0547	2
REID JAMES F	CPT	0-1314060	1154	2
REID JAMES J	MAJ	0-0334724	0862	1
REID JESSE P	MAJ	0-0297727	1267	3
REID JOHN C	CPT	0-0403229	1045	2
REID JOHN M	1LT	0-1166591	0148	2
REID JOHN M	LTC	0-1646898	0367	1
REID JOHN W	LTC	0-0281795	0261	1
REID KENNETH R	MAJ	0-0948802	0165	1
REID KINNEY E JR	1LT	0-1294723	0846	2
REID LANDON J	LTC	0-2014725	0168	1

NAME	GRADE	SVC NO	DATE RET MO YR	RET CODE
REID LESLIE W	MAJ	0-1597804	0457	1
REID MARTIN T	CPT	0-0522351	1045	2
REID PATRICK M	MAJ	0-0505264	1052	1
REID ROBERT E	CPT	0-1013272	0760	2
REID ROBERT H	LTC	0-0180743	0952	3
REID ROBERT L	LTC	0-1554465	0863	1
REID ROBERT M	LTC	0-1551297	0457	1
REID ROBERT N	LTC	0-0271939	0468	3
REID ROBERT V	LTC	0-0241472	0366	3
REID ROBERT V	CW4	W-2144926	1068	1
REID ROGER D	COL	0-0287344	0865	3
REID STUART W	MAJ	0-1324890	0361	1
REID THOMAS G	CW3	W-2148588	0564	1
REID THOMAS J E JR	2LT	0-1311540	0744	2
REID TRUMAN J	CPT	0-1168048	0746	2
REID VERNON	1LT	0-0216042	0260	3
REID WESLEY G	COL	0-0282855	0663	3
REID WILLIAM J	LTC	0-0434990	0464	3
REID WILLIAM S JR	LTC	0-0311239	0448	2
REID WILLIAM T	LTC	0-0503233	0258	1
REIDELBACH FRANK	LTC	0-0382713	0761	1
REIDELBACH JAMES V	LTC	0-1638342	1265	1
REIDENBACH RICHARD C	1LT	0-0468425	0546	2
REIDPATH CHARLES D	COL	0-0178760	0949	3
REIDY DANIEL J	COL	0-0236915	0265	3
REIDY JOHN P	CPT	0-0505028	1046	1
REIDY PATRICK F	CPT	0-1107065	0855	1
REIDY RUDOLPH W	LTC	0-1951337	0967	1
REIDY WILLIAM F	1LT	0-1295270	0745	2
REIF FRED W	COL	0-1825184	1068	1
REIF LEONARD	1LT	0-1546126	0346	2
REIFEL BENJAMIN	LTC	0-0281241	1066	3
REIFENRATH HAROLD C	LTC	0-1003313	1160	1
REIGEL FRANK B	MAJ	0-0186417	0648	3
REIGHARD ROBERT H	MAJ	0-0316969	1048	2
REIHER ARNOLD F	LTC	0-0248833	0348	2
REIL HERMAN N	COL	0-1579003	0862	1
REILERT HAROLD	CPT	0-0481266	0246	2
REILEY RICHARD H	1LT	0-0497319	0845	2
REILING DANIEL L	MAJ	0-0955709	0262	1
REILLEY JOHN H	LTC	0-0131614	1146	2
REILLY CHRISTOPHE	LTC	0-1319441	0868	1
REILLY DONALD E	LTC	0-1324952	0367	1
REILLY EDWARD M	COL	0-0274391	0666	3
REILLY FRANCIS B	LTC	0-0513042	0463	2
REILLY FRANCIS J	LTC	0-0396871	0664	1
REILLY FRANK F	LTC	0-2005962	0766	1
REILLY GERTRUDE F	2LT	N-0723439	0944	1
REILLY GORDON G	LTC	0-0240586	0559	1
REILLY HOWARD E	MAJ	0-0452165	0346	2
REILLY JACK P	CW2	W-2110204	1053	1
REILLY JAMES F	COL	0-0339918	0660	1
REILLY JOHN A	LTC	0-0373790	0167	1
REILLY JOHN A JR	LTC	0-1825437	0167	1
REILLY JOHN B	CPT	0-0410567	1046	2
REILLY JOHN F	MAJ	0-1596776	1061	1
REILLY JOHN M	COL	0-1635245	0767	2
REILLY JOHN R	COL	0-0187096	1046	2
REILLY JOHN R	COL	0-0198558	0758	3
REILLY JOSEPH A	LTC	0-0199108	0563	3
REILLY JOSEPH A	2LT	0-1799894	0949	1
REILLY JOSEPH F	COL	0-0453075	0963	1
REILLY MICHAEL J	LTC	0-0205050	0961	3
REILLY PHILIP J	COL	0-0264597	0864	3
REILLY ROBERT J	MAJ	0-0520606	0447	2
REILLY STEPHEN J	CW2	W-2113454	0959	3
REILLY THOMAS F	CPT	0-1325141	0846	2
REILLY THOMAS J	CPT	0-1176474	0161	1
REILLY VINCENT E	1LT	0-1324788	0646	2
REILY PAUL A	CPT	0-1017870	0246	2
REIMAN LAWRENCE N	LTC	0-0319493	0461	1
REIMANN CURT A	LTC	0-1795819	0861	1
REIMER GEORGE L	LTC	0-1289624	1060	1
REIMERS O KENNETH	COL	0-0271586	0864	1
REIMLER GEORGE C	CW3	W-2150949	0464	1

NAME	GRADE	SVC NO	DATE RET MO YR	RET CODE
REIN JOSEPH J JR	MAJ	0-1635247	0359	1
REINA DAVID J	COL	0-0319583	0661	1
REINA WILLIAM F	1LT	0-0477713	0144	2
REINBERG EINAR	LTC	0-0302686	0967	3
REINBERG MARTIN H	CPT	0-0542397	0346	2
REINBOTHE ALFRED H	LTC	0-0275497	1059	1
REINCKE FREDERICK	M G	0-0322850	1059	3
REINDERS HENRY A	LTC	0-1176475	0664	1
REINDL EDWARD W	CPT	0-2037092	1145	2
REINECK JOHN F	LTC	0-0288585	0559	1
REINECKE CALVIN C	CPT	0-0718020	0560	1
REINECKE CARL W	LTC	0-0225967	0364	3
REINECKE ERWIN P	LTC	0-0343794	0363	1
REINEKE ROY R	CW3	W-2143197	0762	1
REINEMEYER JOHN T	MAJ	0-1549584	0364	1
REINER ROBERT H	LTC	0-0258623	1160	1
REINER WALTER M	CPT	0-0442264	0144	2
REINERS CHARLES	1LT	0-2048459	1045	2
REINERS LILLIAN J	1LT	N-0703790	0146	1
REINERT GERVASE T	MAJ	0-0258271	0266	3
REINERT HOWARD D JR	MAJ	0-1291519	0859	1
REINERT PRICE D	MAJ	0-0428066	0462	1
REINES JOSE A	LTC	0-1284397	0266	1
REINFELD MARTIN H	MAJ	0-0549038	0564	1
REINFURT JOSEPH A	MAJ	0-0984327	0763	1
REINHARD WALTER F	CW3	W-2208929	0167	1
REINHARD WILLIAM S	MAJ	0-1017278	0264	1
REINHARDT BERT L	CPT	0-1302197	0662	1
REINHARDT CLARENCE W	LTC	0-0508448	0657	1
REINHARDT EDITH A	MAJ	N-0756360	0265	3
REINHARDT FRANK F	2LT	0-0440900	1144	2
REINHARDT GEORGE N	MAJ	0-1651875	0763	1
REINHART BERNARD J	CPT	0-1556341	0267	2
REINHART GEORGE P	CW3	W-2143445	1061	1
REINHART JAMES W	CPT	0-0510898	0141	1
REINHOLZ LEONARD J	LTC	0-0505429	1065	3
REININGER WILLIAM G	CW2	W-2205579	0760	2
REINISCH MAX	CPT	0-0927480	1146	2
REINKE HARRY A	COL	0-0275853	0166	3
REINKE RICHARD F	LTC	0-0341397	0467	3
REINKING HAROLD C	LTC	0-0360070	0761	1
REINOLD ARTHUR J	MAJ	0-1558609	1161	1
REINSMITH MARTIN C	CPT	0-1182232	0846	2
REIS FRANKLIN A	MAJ	0-1284576	0961	1
REIS ROBERT	1LT	0-0347091	0945	2
REIS ROBERT	MAJ	0-0969183	0468	1
REISCH HERMAN P	LTC	0-1580209	0461	1
REISEN WILLIAM E	CW4	W-2115263	0658	1
REISER CARLETON C	MAJ	0-0277060	1057	3
REISER FRANK J	COL	0-0909934	0568	3
REISER JOSEPH	CPT	0-1308870	0446	2
REISIG CONRAD	1LT	0-0493959	0946	1
REISINE PHILIP	CW2	W-2210429	0662	1
REISING ANDREAS F	2LT	0-1575095	0743	2
REISING HENRY	MAJ	0-1173753	1057	1
REISING JOSEPH A	LTC	0-0219501	0664	3
REISINGER EDWARD A	CW2	W-2215284	0566	2
REISINGER EDWARD L	CW4	W-2148020	1067	1
REISINGER JOHN P VI	LTC	0-1796693	0461	1
REISLER BENNO J	CW3	W-2136728	0663	1
REISNER EDWARD H JR	CPT	0-0495055	1045	2
REISS FREDERICK	LTC	0-1181094	0467	1
REISS JACK	LTC	0-0322390	0866	3
REISS ROBERT S	CPT	0-0926070	0246	2
REISS SIDNEY A	COL	0-0321368	0766	3
REISSE GEORGE B JR	LTC	0-0907900	0268	3
REISTROFFER ROBERT J	LTC	0-1117195	0163	1
REISZ FRED C JR	MAJ	0-0450476	0557	1
REISZ LOUIS L	CPT	0-1576550	0948	1
REITEMEYER JOHN R	COL	0-0308796	0458	3
REITENBACH RUTH E	1LT	N-0728282	0346	1
REITER EDWARD	CPT	0-1306320	0347	2
REITH RICHARD T	MAJ	0-1924666	1264	1
REITHEL ROBERT J	LTC	0-0373115	0647	2
REITZ CHARLES B	LTC	0-0145088	0150	3

NAME	GRADE	SVC NO	DATE RET MO YR	RET CODE
REITZ DELMAR A	2LT	0-2000752	0945	2
REITZ HENRY M	CPT	0-0466332	0745	2
REJMER STANLEY J	2LT	0-1323612	0145	2
RELAC PETER	LTC	0-1326169	0967	1
REMALEY CLARENCE A	COL	0-0295333	1052	2
REMALEY JOHN W C	COL	0-0237781	0566	3
REMALIA NEAL Z	1LT	0-0552584	0446	2
REMBIJAS MICHAEL F	MAJ	0-1041425	0660	1
REMEIN QUENTIN P	2LT	0-1288950	1044	2
REMER OSWALD M	LTC	0-1583553	0962	1
REMILY CONSTANCE	MAJ	N-0783231	0963	1
REMINGTON CECIL G	COL	0-0329403	1161	3
REMINGTON CHARLES F	COL	0-0329833	0365	3
REMINGTON KENNETH K	CW2	W-2149715	0565	1
REMINGTON LUCIUS D	1LT	0-0488722	1049	1
REMINGTON VYAN K	LTC	0-0510643	0563	3
REMLEY NORMAN W	LTC	0-0218024	0464	3
REMLEY ROBERT G	LTC	0-1797879	0658	1
REMMEL JOHN E	LTC	0-0354232	0767	3
REMMERS BERNHARD J	CPT	0-1586077	0154	1
REMMERS HERMAN R SR	CPT	0-0440589	0653	1
REMMIE JOHN A	LTC	0-1081717	0263	1
REMPE JAMES R	WO1	W-2147305	0866	2
REMPFER PAUL	CW3	W-2147561	1168	1
REMSTER WALTER A	2LT	0-1341705	0349	2
REMUND DONALD E	LTC	0-0232275	0152	1
REMUS MERLE R	CW3	W-2210961	0868	1
REMY JAMES G J	LTC	0-1576551	1163	1
REMY JOHN P	COL	0-0360539	1065	1
RENAK EDWARD T	CW4	W-2111903	1154	1
RENAKER CLINE R	CW2	W-2119135	1055	1
RENALD JOSEPH P	LTC	0-0250309	0857	3
RENARD LOUIS J	CW4	W-2003453	0765	3
RENAUD FRED F	CPT	0-2033868	0260	1
RENAUD ROGER J	MAJ	0-1258593	1060	1
RENBUDR CARL L	CW3	W-2152584	0765	1
RENCH CLIFFORD H	MAJ	0-2263466	1162	2
RENDEIRO CHRISTIAN	MAJ	0-1003151	0447	2
RENDEL ALLEN D	LTC	0-0225292	1159	3
RENDER ANDREW J	CW4	W-2142192	1265	1
RENDER HAROLD L	MAJ	0-1285642	0546	2
RENDINA RICHARD J	MAJ	0-1822626	0261	1
RENE JOSEPH L	CW2	W-2119603	0457	1
RENE VICTOR E	CW2	W-2211096	1263	1
RENEAU BILLY R	CW3	W-3150212	0768	1
RENEAU LONNIE M	CPT	0-0480752	1048	1
RENEAU THOMAS A	MAJ	0-0305285	1165	3
RENEGAR GERALD E	LTC	0-1045569	1058	1
RENFER RUDOLF A	CPT	0-0435028	0246	2
RENFRO DONALD M	CPT	0-0162811	0160	3
RENFRO HENRY M	COL	0-0349066	1166	2
RENFRO IVOR B	CW2	W-2103355	0654	1
RENFROE DANIEL J	COL	0-0249999	0167	3
RENFROE EARL W	COL	0-0300463	0267	3
RENFROE GEORGE J	MAJ	0-1289806	1160	1
RENFROW ARTHUR C JR	MAJ	0-1305991	0661	1
RENFROW DOUGLAS O	2LT	0-1318225	0445	2
RENFROW LOUIS H	B G	0-0160948	0157	3
RENGER JULIUS J	MAJ	0-1703289	0446	2
RENICK FRED T	MAJ	0-0281613	0446	2
RENICK MAURICE O	CPT	0-0434159	0845	2
RENICK SAMUEL T	CPT	0-0444967	0349	1
RENIER REMI O	COL	0-1107068	1068	1
RENIKER EVERETT T	COL	0-0418653	0662	1
RENK ROMAN J	CPT	0-1294903	1147	2
RENKEL FREDERICK	CW3	W-2209253	0568	1
RENKEN GUSTAV W	CPT	0-1699903	0445	2
RENKEN HENRY E	COL	0-0223855	0857	3
RENN HAROLD J	CPT	0-0345916	1045	2
RENNA CARMEN J	1LT	0-1994981	0151	2
RENNARD ROBERT E	COL	0-0286163	0667	3
RENNEBAUM W C	1LT	0-1014279	0346	2
RENNER AUGUST N	CPT	0-0536913	1046	2
RENNER DONALD A	LTC	0-0395548	0960	1
RENNER GEORGE M JR	1LT	0-1299790	1045	2

NAME	GRADE	SVC NO	DATE RET MO YR	RET CODE
RENNER HANS H	2LT	0-1644003	0944	2
RENNER JOSEPH	1LT	0-1102927	0744	2
RENNIE EDWARD F	CW2	W-2150600	1157	1
RENNIE JAMES F	LTC	0-0440901	0962	1
RENNIE SYLVESTER	MAJ	0-1683605	1044	2
RENNINGER GORDON K	LTC	0-1183599	0568	1
RENO BILL E	CW3	W-2141661	1159	1
RENO FLOYD M	MAJ	0-5304148	0868	1
RENO RUSSELL P	LTC	0-0230250	1164	3
RENOFF GEORGE J	CPT	0-0359309	0146	2
RENSEMA ROBERT H	MAJ	0-1289965	0361	1
RENTMEESTERS WHILOME	MAJ	N-0773493	0661	2
RENTON BENJAMIN E	1LT	0-0447310	0646	2
RENTON JAMES M	1LT	0-0445189	0746	2
RENTON MAURICE F	CPT	0-0919604	0846	2
RENTZ ERIN E	LTC	0-0331427	1061	3
RENTZ NORMAN H	CW3	W-2114312	0860	1
RENZ ADEN D	LTC	0-0397814	0161	1
RENZI VERGINIO	LTC	0-1102586	0764	1
REODICA HERMOGINES	2LT	0-2032081	1047	1
REOH LYLE H	1LT	0-2040706	1144	2
REORDAN ROBERT E	LTC	0-1178303	1162	1
REPINE CLARENCE E	CW2	W-2207430	0263	1
REPKA ERIC J	CPT	0-2036929	0156	1
REPKE ALEXANDER	MAJ	0-0454401	0761	1
REPLOGLE NELSON R	MAJ	0-1576552	0961	1
REPLOGLE WILLIAM K	1LT	0-1018442	0446	2
REPPLINGER ELMER R	MAJ	0-2263063	0865	1
REPPOND CLYDE M	CW2	W-2149727	0467	1
REPSHER JEROME J	LTC	0-2014474	0268	1
REQUA EUGENE M	MAJ	0-0188371	0255	3
REQUEJO MARIANO P	1LT	0-1896712	0655	1
RESCHKE EDWARD F	1LT	0-1110758	0345	2
RESEK EPHRAIM F JR	COL	0-0198589	0762	3
RESEL FRANK L	CPT	0-1597259	0957	1
RESER JOHN W	LTC	0-1010715	0965	1
RESKEY BENJAMIN F	LTC	0-1533429	1057	1
RESNICOFF MURRA	LTC	0-0172906	0454	3
RESNICK WILLIAM V JR	MAJ	0-2008507	0161	1
RESNIKOFF ABRAHAM	1LT	0-1012581	1151	2
RESPESS BENJAMIN R	1LT	0-1305992	0445	2
RESSEGER JAMES L	1LT	0-1183600	0445	2
RESSL WILLIAM L	CW3	W-2003742	0666	1
RESSLER EDWIN A	MAJ	0-1013269	0561	1
RESSLER MARLIN A	CW2	W-2144969	1056	1
RESTEMAYER CLINTON E	CPT	0-1170159	0845	2
RESTERER ROBERT T	LTC	0-1012366	0161	1
RESTITUTO NICOLAS	1LT	0-1896791	0950	1
RESTO-VAZQUEZ JOSE A	CW3	W-2154864	0163	1
RESZCZYNSKI EUGENE	MAJ	0-1645942	0260	1
RETALLACK SHIRLEY W	CW2	W-2141896	1052	2
RETHEMEYER LLOYD D	MAJ	0-1105779	0262	1
RETTAGLIATA JOHN B	LTC	0-0402553	0661	1
RETTER EUGENE R	MAJ	0-1015947	0759	1
RETTERER ALFRED C	LTC	0-1584784	0861	1
RETTIE WILLIAM	LTC	0-0371623	0757	1
RETZER RUTH M	MAJ	N-2292539	1167	1
RETZKY CLARENCE	COL	0-0454052	0564	1
RETZLAFF ERNEST W	2LT	0-0397932	1041	2
REUBEN ARTHUR W	CPT	0-0451171	0149	1
REUBLIN KENNETH C	MAJ	0-1899407	1264	1
REUKEMA RUSSELL R	LTC	0-0193978	0860	3
REULET JEAN P	CW3	W-2149867	0865	1
REUM HARVEY E	MAJ	0-1648109	1056	1
REUPKE GORDON E	LTC	0-1170158	0462	1
REUS JOHN F JR	CW2	W-2208077	0559	1
REUSS GEORGE J	MAJ	0-1331868	0261	1
REUTER ALBERT J	LTC	0-1110760	0961	1
REUTER EUGENE A	LTC	0-1535266	0965	1
REUTER GEORGE J	CPT	0-0115754	0146	2
REUTER LESLIE S	CW4	W-2129190	0557	1
REUTER LOUIS JR	MAJ	0-1288706	1046	2
REUTER ORVILLE E	CW2	W-2116664	1143	2
REUTER ROBERT W	COL	0-0297767	1155	1
REUTERSHAN ALFRED D	COL	0-0167700	0558	3

ARMY OF THE UNITED STATES RETIRED LIST

NAME	GRADE	SVC NO	DATE RET MO YR	RET CODE
REUTHER CHARLES R	CPT	0-0477955	0148	1
REUTTER DALLAS C	2LT	0-0524778	1044	2
REVELEY ROBERT W	LTC	0-0109429	0945	2
REVELL JAMES V	MAJ	0-1012979	0761	1
REVELL JOHN H	MAJ	0-0272872	0167	3
REVELLE RICHARD T	CW4	W-2144675	0360	1
REVERE DONALD J	LTC	0-1579009	0361	1
REVES NORMAN	CW3	W-2142265	0861	1
REVIER DONALD E	MAJ	0-0342229	0647	2
REVIS JOSEPH E	CPT	0-1290134	0446	2
REVIS JOSEPH H	CW2	W-2120833	0247	1
REVOIR RAY	2LT	0-1316091	1144	2
REW CLIFFORD P	CPT	0-1103262	0661	1
REW EDWARD A	COL	0-0245439	0759	1
REW HOWARD B	COL	0-0223420	0749	3
REWEY ORMOND F	COL	0-0179837	0756	3
REX SCOTT T	COL	0-0226748	0464	3
REXFORD CLARENCE E	COL	0-0129971	0648	3
REXFORD SIDNEY S	MAJ	0-1643268	0662	1
REXRODE HARRY M	LTC	0-0443979	0452	1
REY ANGEL	CPT	0-0203233	0563	3
REY BRUCE E	LTC	0-0353765	0868	3
REYBURN JOHN F	LTC	0-1055709	0366	2
REYER KARL D	COL	0-0167376	0959	3
REYES JESUS	CPT	0-0260437	0744	2
REYES JOSE V	CW2	W-3150889	0168	1
REYES LOUIS F	LTC	0-1549045	0765	1
REYES OSMUNDO R	1LT	0-1856840	1162	1
REYES ROBERT L	MAJ	0-1913357	0564	1
REYES VIVIANO	CPT	0-1692559	0764	1
REYKALIN MARIE G	1LT	N-0784658	0546	1
REYNALDS GERALD H	LTC	0-0241521	0245	2
REYNARD LAWRENCE R	2LT	0-1020573	0348	2
REYNIERS ELMER E	MAJ	0-0504991	1056	1
REYNOLDS ALBERT G	CPT	0-0976814	1051	2
REYNOLDS BERNARD D	LTC	0-0312757	1065	3
REYNOLDS BERNARD E	LTC	0-2031828	0766	1
REYNOLDS BURNS	CPT	0-2262497	1264	2
REYNOLDS CHARLES L	LTC	0-0178451	0554	3
REYNOLDS CHARLES R	CPT	0-0942792	0357	1
REYNOLDS CHARLES W	LTC	0-0364123	0362	3
REYNOLDS CHARLES W	LTC	0-1030294	0961	1
REYNOLDS CYRIL H	LTC	0-1105758	0157	1
REYNOLDS DALE L	CPT	0-0539319	0747	2
REYNOLDS DONALD E	CW3	W-2150290	0265	1
REYNOLDS DONALD K	2LT	0-1303387	0344	2
REYNOLDS EARL E	LTC	0-1545021	1064	1
REYNOLDS EARL R	LTC	0-0376951	1060	1
REYNOLDS ERNEST W	1LT	0-1300219	0250	1
REYNOLDS EUGENE G	2LT	0-1047310	1051	1
REYNOLDS EUGENE J	MAJ	0-2020836	0660	1
REYNOLDS EUGENE P	MAJ	0-1015961	0760	1
REYNOLDS FLOYD H	WO1	W-2109024	0448	2
REYNOLDS FRANK J	CPT	0-1042147	0547	2
REYNOLDS FREDERICK	1LT	0-1283308	0745	2
REYNOLDS GEAN H	MAJ	0-1288621	0161	1
REYNOLDS GEORGE W	1LT	0-0405903	0345	2
REYNOLDS GILBERT B	2LT	0-1112389	0144	2
REYNOLDS GRANT	CPT	0-0408560	0444	2
REYNOLDS GUY D	MAJ	0-2038879	0361	1
REYNOLDS HAROLD C	2LT	0-2055183	1044	2
REYNOLDS HELENE W	2LT	L-0402260	1044	2
REYNOLDS HENRY L	MAJ	0-0309458	0259	3
REYNOLDS HERSCHEL E	LTC	0-2038027	0966	1
REYNOLDS HORACE L	COL	0-0243518	0864	3
REYNOLDS HORATIO N	LTC	0-0498911	0864	1
REYNOLDS HOWARD W	LTC	0-0299989	0667	3
REYNOLDS HUBER H	LTC	0-1577737	0760	1
REYNOLDS HUGH	LTC	0-1646902	0259	1
REYNOLDS JACK	LTC	0-2029763	0466	1
REYNOLDS JAMES A	LTC	0-0374485	0167	3
REYNOLDS JAMES E	LTC	0-0455553	0261	1
REYNOLDS JAMES E	CW3	W-2142658	0862	1
REYNOLDS JAMES H	LTC	0-0456568	0664	1
REYNOLDS JAMES H	2LT	0-1303546	0543	2
REYNOLDS JAMES M	LTC	0-0521016	0255	1
REYNOLDS JAY F	LTC	0-0230083	0756	3
REYNOLDS JESSE F	MAJ	0-0962188	0767	1
REYNOLDS JOHN	COL	0-0168122	0443	2
REYNOLDS JOHN F	CPT	0-1292760	1046	2
REYNOLDS JOHN L JR	LTC	0-1044932	0161	1
REYNOLDS KENNETH P	MAJ	0-0334454	0847	2
REYNOLDS LEON K	MAJ	0-0151356	1055	3
REYNOLDS LEONARD E	MAJ	0-1291332	1062	1
REYNOLDS LEROY C JR	MAJ	0-0967622	0268	1
REYNOLDS LLOYD A	LTC	0-0242551	0764	3
REYNOLDS MEFLIN E	LTC	0-1004222	0962	1
REYNOLDS MICHAEL E	LTC	0-0535972	0264	1
REYNOLDS MILES H	CPT	0-0364947	0148	1
REYNOLDS OLIVER W	2LT	0-0108254	0936	1
REYNOLDS OSCAR H	CW2	W-2151502	1060	1
REYNOLDS OSCAR L	CW4	W-2104412	0556	1
REYNOLDS PAUL L	CPT	0-0250404	0246	2
REYNOLDS PHILIP S	LTC	0-1320073	0367	1
REYNOLDS RAYMOND L	MAJ	0-2014571	0863	1
REYNOLDS RICHARD	LTC	0-1100299	1160	1
REYNOLDS RICHARD C	1LT	0-1103878	0246	2
REYNOLDS ROBERT C	MAJ	0-0982938	1262	1
REYNOLDS ROBERT H	LTC	0-0662826	0762	1
REYNOLDS ROBERT I	CPT	0-1685635	0857	2
REYNOLDS ROBERT J	MAJ	0-0958805	0163	1
REYNOLDS ROBERT V	MAJ	0-0977500	0164	1
REYNOLDS ROLAND W	CPT	0-0236165	1065	3
REYNOLDS ROY J	CPT	0-0969216	0860	1
REYNOLDS THOMAS J	CW4	W-2110682	1064	1
REYNOLDS ULRIC H	1LT	0-0372933	0846	2
REYNOLDS VIRGIL H	MAJ	0-1102010	0861	1
REYNOLDS WALTER A JR	MAJ	0-0959514	0166	1
REYNOLDS WARREN C	CPT	0-2011127	0557	1
REYNOLDS WATSON J	CW3	W-2148222	0860	2
REYNOLDS WAYNE C	MAJ	0-1287411	1167	1
REYNOLDS WILLIAM D	LTC	0-1328402	1062	1
REYNOLDS WILLIAM G	CW3	W-2145496	0263	1
REYNOLDS WILLIAM J	1LT	0-1775506	0246	2
REYNOLDS WILLIAM M	COL	0-0274219	0453	3
REYNOLDS WILLIAM R	LTC	0-0175689	0157	3
REYNOLDS WILLIAM R	CW2	W-2146841	1060	1
REYNOLDS WILLIAM W	COL	0-0180526	0657	3
REZA BEULAH B	1LT	N-0801008	1047	1
REZABEK RICHARD A	2LT	0-1794989	0444	2
REZAC MARVIN J	MAJ	0-1341189	0166	1
REZARCH FRANK A	MAJ	0-1947936	1264	1
REZNICK IRWIN	CPT	0-1689543	1044	2
RHATIGAN BERNARD J	CPT	0-1286550	0265	1
RHEA GEORGE M	CW2	W-2209581	1164	1
RHEAUME FRANK D	CW2	W-2122494	1059	1
RHEAUME WALTER A	CW2	W-2151127	1163	1
RHEDMON DONALD T	MAJ	0-1304444	0157	1
RHEIN LEO A	LTC	0-2036336	0468	1
RHEINGANS WILLIAM J	LTC	0-0151435	0858	3
RHEUBY ELIZABETH	1LT	N-0763986	0846	1
RHEUPORT RICHARD W	MAJ	0-2028439	0866	1
RHINE DONALD C	MAJ	0-1636532	0847	2
RHINE RAYMOND D	LTC	0-0443100	0662	1
RHINEHART CLARENCE G	CW3	W-2207618	1066	1
RHINEHART FORREST H	MAJ	0-0280999	1161	3
RHOAD DANIEL L JR	LTC	0-0227699	0365	3
RHOADES CARL A	2LT	0-1305832	0545	2
RHOADES DONALD A	LTC	0-1101631	1061	1
RHOADES DONALD H	1LT	0-1542364	0868	1
RHOADES EARL A	LTC	0-1584785	1161	1
RHOADES FLETCHER D	MAJ	0-4006514	0267	1
RHOADS ALBERT W	LTC	0-0900284	0562	1
RHOADS D I	CW3	W-2210073	0168	1
RHOADS EUGENE J	MAJ	0-1884210	0467	1
RHOADS GLENN W	LTC	0-0182961	0160	3
RHOADS HARLEY R	MAJ	0-0277841	0744	2
RHOADS RAYMOND D	1LT	0-1048547	0462	2
RHOADS WAYLAND	LTC	0-0199504	1152	3
RHOADS WILLIAM H JR	LTC	0-1552585	1062	1
RHODA WILLIAM D	MAJ	0-0889805	0863	1
RHODE RAYMOND H	MAJ	0-0400100	0760	1
RHODE RICHARD F	LTC	0-1112391	1062	1
RHODES CARL E	MAJ	0-0941040	0167	1
RHODES CHARLES C	LTC	0-2263348	0468	1
RHODES CHARLES D JR	1LT	0-0557736	1045	2
RHODES CHARLES M	CW2	W-2001744	0867	1
RHODES CHARLIE E JR	CPT	0-0488308	0255	1
RHODES COOPER B	M G	0-0258656	1164	3
RHODES EARL D	CPT	0-0139818	1058	3
RHODES EDMOND A	MAJ	0-0972474	0865	1
RHODES EDNA F	2LT	N-0770019	0646	2
RHODES EDWARD A	LTC	0-2210462	0668	2
RHODES EDWARD J	CPT	0-0273344	0167	3
RHODES EDWARD R	MAJ	0-0442891	1044	2
RHODES FRED H	CPT	0-1057218	0747	2
RHODES FRED H JR	LTC	0-0224793	1061	3
RHODES GEORGE M	COL	0-0274359	1055	3
RHODES HENRY C	LTC	0-1002930	0961	1
RHODES HERMAN L	CPT	0-1683491	0647	2
RHODES JACK L	1LT	0-0543693	114N	2
RHODES JAMES A	CPT	0-0302295	0760	1
RHODES JOHN L	LTC	0-1302709	1263	1
RHODES JOHN M	CPT	0-0440586	0244	2
RHODES JOHN M	CPT	0-1308545	0847	2
RHODES PRENTICE B	MAJ	0-0494562	0347	1
RHODES RAY F	CPT	0-0345227	1045	2
RHODES RAYMOND E	MAJ	0-0958799	0965	1
RHODES RAYMOND K	2LT	0-2009579	1046	2
RHODES RAYMOND R	WO1	W-2123284	0754	1
RHODES THOMAS D	CW3	W-2150844	0161	1
RHODES WILLIAM H	CW3	W-2148184	1059	1
RHODES WILLIAM J	LTC	0-1590753	1164	1
RHONE THOMAS B	LTC	0-0293624	0763	3
RHOTEN LOREN J	LTC	0-1172243	1262	1
RHU HERMAN S JR	MAJ	0-0518808	0646	2
RHUDY JAMES T	COL	0-0156199	1059	3
RHULE WALTER A	MAJ	0-1282392	1060	1
RHYNE DONNY A	CPT	0-5424243	0968	2
RHYNE LEE	CW2	W-2209342	1064	2
RHYNE PLATO S	LTC	0-0288255	0267	3
RIALES JAMES B	CW3	W-2207242	0568	1
RIALS THOMAS E	CW3	W-2154670	1164	1
RIANT IDNEY A	CW3	W-2103359	0151	1
RIBA LEANDER W	LTC	0-0135397	0757	3
RIBAL RAYMOND R	COL	0-0243815	0761	3
RIBERDY BERNARD	MAJ	0-0959611	0865	1
RIBINSKY JOSEPH A	CW3	W-2142470	0261	1
RIBYAT MORRIS	2LT	0-0377897	0944	2
RICCARDI JOSEPH J	MAJ	0-2014543	0165	1
RICCARDI LOUIS S	CPT	0-0504590	0140	2
RICCI ALFRED P	LTC	0-1301368	0958	1
RICCI ANTHONY J	MAJ	0-0260234	0364	3
RICCI FRANK G	CW2	W-3200715	1067	2
RICCI GABRIEL R JR	MAJ	0-1103880	0965	1
RICE ALFRED G	COL	0-0910429	0962	1
RICE ALLEN F	COL	0-0230223	0260	1
RICE CHARLES G	MAJ	0-1114274	0165	1
RICE CHARLES H	LTC	0-0277754	0966	3
RICE CHARLES H	LTC	0-0391963	0860	1
RICE CHESTER	CPT	0-0989920	0561	1
RICE CLARENCE C	MAJ	0-1016327	0564	1
RICE CLARK C	COL	0-0106255	0450	2
RICE DELANO G	LTC	0-0360308	0167	3
RICE DONALD G	LTC	0-1580220	0963	1
RICE DONOVAN J	COL	0-0257599	0665	1
RICE EARL J	LTC	0-0252434	0765	3
RICE EARL L	MAJ	0-0221546	0848	3
RICE ELDRIDGE N	1LT	0-1308706	0845	2
RICE ELLA M	MAJ	N-0743138	0165	1
RICE ELLSWORTH	MAJ	0-0118064	0256	3
RICE ERWIN M	LTC	0-1280542	0962	3
RICE EZEKIEL H	CPT	0-0476501	0348	1
RICE FREDERICK	MAJ	0-1107656	0363	1
RICE FREDERICK	CW2	W-2210211	0865	1
RICE FREEMAN D	CPT	0-0451733	0950	2
RICE G W	LTC	0-2018417	0766	1
RICE GEORGE	CPT	0-1290815	0357	1
RICE GLENN T	LTC	0-0371147	0861	1
RICE GUY V	LTC	0-0249317	0964	3
RICE HANS G	LTC	0-0355703	0346	2
RICE HARRISON S	CPT	0-0488967	1148	1
RICE HARVEY I	1LT	0-1167175	1045	2
RICE HELEN E	CPT	N-0742602	0647	2
RICE HENRY C	LTC	0-0189144	0846	1
RICE HORACE	CW2	W-2148985	0862	1
RICE HORACE G	LTC	0-0253152	1055	3
RICE HOWARD P	LTC	0-0304448	0864	3
RICE IRWIN G	MAJ	0-0546768	1264	1
RICE J MERRITT	CPT	0-0189958	0249	3
RICE JACK	CW3	RW-2150254	1265	1
RICE JAMES E JR	COL	0-0237316	0964	3
RICE JOHN B	COL	0-0276173	1168	3
RICE JOHN D	LTC	0-0435639	0863	1
RICE JOHN F	CPT	0-1577739	1265	3
RICE JOHN L JR	1LT	0-1291883	0346	2
RICE JOHN M	LTC	0-0414649	0564	1
RICE JOHN M	MAJ	0-1555610	0667	3
RICE JOSEPH	1LT	0-1913909	0235	1
RICE JOSEPH A	LTC	0-0407537	0762	1
RICE JOSEPH C JR	LTC	0-1285499	0962	1
RICE JOSEPH E	LTC	0-0102977	1044	2
RICE JOSEPH E	LTC	0-1014327	0167	3
RICE JOSEPH L	LTC	0-0260000	0762	1
RICE JULEANNE J	MAJ	N-0756747	0165	1
RICE KEITH M	LTC	0-0329868	0858	1
RICE LEE JR	CPT	0-0465790	0546	2
RICE LELAND E	MAJ	0-0415919	1164	1
RICE LEONARD R	LTC	0-1294368	0657	1
RICE LEONARD W	CPT	0-1116970	0461	1
RICE LEROY	2LT	0-1045570	0844	2
RICE LESTER M	LTC	0-1011669	1064	1
RICE LOWELL D	LTC	0-0406827	1060	1
RICE LUIS F	MAJ	0-1288622	1160	1
RICE MARIAN K	CPT	L-0225400	0863	1
RICE MARWIN F	CW4	W-2110489	0659	1
RICE MELVIN W	MAJ	0-0324618	0961	1
RICE MERIDA	CPT	0-1286551	1052	1
RICE MILLARD F	MAJ	0-1882500	0365	1
RICE NEAL W	CPT	0-1184289	0962	2
RICE NOBLE R T	MAJ	0-0961199	0663	1
RICE NOLAND W	WO1	W-2128223	0756	1
RICE ORVILLE W	COL	0-0243847	1060	3
RICE PAUL W	MAJ	0-1557207	0455	1
RICE PETE L	MAJ	0-0493662	0557	1
RICE RALPH E	2LT	0-0258622	0266	3
RICE RALPH R	CW2	W-2211766	0468	1
RICE RAYMOND R	2LT	0-0378676	0442	2
RICE REGINALD M	CPT	0-0321216	1046	1
RICE RICHARD D	MAJ	0-2033632	0259	1
RICE RICHARD F	LTC	0-1109618	0962	1
RICE ROBERT C	COL	0-0247824	0255	3
RICE ROBERT J	LTC	0-1544768	0367	1
RICE ROBERT L	MAJ	0-1170937	0562	1
RICE SHEPHERD	MAJ	0-0270366	1167	3
RICE SIDNEY C	LTC	0-0174105	1263	3
RICE SUSAN K	2LT	N-0755339	0545	1
RICE THOMAS A	COL	0-0342841	1060	1
RICE THOMAS H	CW4	W-2147076	0468	1
RICE THOMAS R	LTC	0-1550690	0864	1
RICE TRUMAN A	LTC	0-0451384	0758	1
RICE WALTER A	MAJ	0-1318329	0861	1
RICE WALTER M	CPT	0-1297591	0247	2
RICE WALTER W	LTC	0-0274867	0963	3
RICE WILLIAM C	MAJ	0-1101632	0860	1
RICE WILLIAM G	CW4	W-2108850	1262	1
RICETTI JOHN	CW3	W-2205329	0264	1
RICH ARCHIE G	CPT	0-2007444	0857	1
RICH AUGUSTUS C	LTC	0-0195291	0454	3
RICH BRUCE A	MAJ	0-1844384	0757	1

NAME	GRADE	SVC NO	DATE RET MO YR	RET CODE
RICH CHARLES	MAJ	0-1010472	0859	1
RICH CHARLES J	COL	0-0309612	0168	3
RICH EMORY J	1LT	0-1293118	0246	2
RICH GORDON	LTC	0-0918416	0864	3
RICH HAN H	MAJ	0-1055952	0261	1
RICH HENRY A	COL	0-0245146	0648	3
RICH LAWRENCE M	LTC	0-0313953	0863	3
RICH MAHLON S	LTC	0-1556475	0864	1
RICH MARGARET P	MAJ	N-0763304	0353	2
RICH ROBERT R	MAJ	0-1877102	1264	1
RICH SHERMAN G	2LT	0-1057219	0245	2
RICH THOMAS L	COL	0-0291118	0167	3
RICH THOMAS L	CPT	0-0965596	1057	1
RICH WALKER J	CPT	0-1281749	0846	2
RICH WILLIAM	COL	0-0188364	0455	2
RICH WILLIAM	CPT	0-0476383	1048	1
RICH WILLIAM L	LTC	0-0137038	0450	3
RICHARD ALLAN C	CPT	0-0411988	0844	2
RICHARD CHARLES A	1LT	0-2009737	0562	2
RICHARD ELI O	LTC	0-0310887	0559	3
RICHARD ERNEST C	LTC	0-0179963	0861	3
RICHARD GILBERT	2LT	0-2035973	0445	2
RICHARD HAROLD V	LTC	0-1289808	0960	1
RICHARD HENRY T	CPT	0-0248339	0444	2
RICHARD JOHN R	LTC	0-0276493	0862	3
RICHARD ROBERT E	MAJ	0-1285500	0446	2
RICHARD STANLEY G	LTC	0-1319338	0263	1
RICHARD W WAYNE	CW3	RW-2136741	1264	1
RICHARD WILTON J	LTC	0-0415804	0761	1
RICHARDE HENRY P	LTC	0-1185784	0163	1
RICHARDS ADDIE R	MAJ	N-0700464	0146	1
RICHARDS ANCIL D	CPT	0-0992539	0461	1
RICHARDS ARTHUR E JR	CPT	0-1180313	0947	2
RICHARDS ARTHUR F	COL	0-0317506	0255	1
RICHARDS ARTHUR J	LTC	0-1039173	0961	1
RICHARDS BARBARA	CPT	L-0115605	0746	2
RICHARDS BURKE F	CPT	0-1058635	0855	2
RICHARDS BURT L JR	CW4	W-2102269	0565	1
RICHARDS CHARLES R	LTC	0-1556044	0366	1
RICHARDS CHARLES S	LTC	0-0170645	0254	3
RICHARDS CHARLES T	LTC	0-1102931	0562	1
RICHARDS CHARLES W	LTC	0-0471318	1167	3
RICHARDS CHARLES W	LTC	0-1053316	0763	3
RICHARDS CLAUDE	2LT	0-0157437	0940	1
RICHARDS DOROTHY M	MAJ	N-0799096	0765	1
RICHARDS EDWARD J	COL	0-0241036	0655	3
RICHARDS EDWARD R	1LT	0-1302350	1046	2
RICHARDS FRANK	8 G	0-0329568	1159	3
RICHARDS FRANK B	MAJ	0-0184676	1038	1
RICHARDS FRED J	1LT	0-1823750	1045	2
RICHARDS GEORGE E	LTC	0-0469768	0157	1
RICHARDS GEORGE H	1LT	0-0527535	1048	1
RICHARDS GEORGE H	CW2	W-2212985	1166	1
RICHARDS GEORGE S	1LT	0-0274065	0459	1
RICHARDS HAROLD	CW3	W-2210133	0168	1
RICHARDS HAROLD T	LTC	0-1031753	0862	1
RICHARDS HARRY A	LTC	0-0231598	0264	3
RICHARDS HARTZEL E	LTC	0-0309310	0760	1
RICHARDS HERMAN	LTC	0-1534846	0561	1
RICHARDS HERMAN O	CPT	0-0303903	0544	2
RICHARDS HILTON	CPT	0-0491204	1147	1
RICHARDS HORACE S E	LTC	0-0313489	0863	1
RICHARDS HORACE W S	LTC	0-0336745	0968	3
RICHARDS JACK	LTC	0-0409694	1167	1
RICHARDS JAMES B	CW4	W-2001920	0467	3
RICHARDS JAMES H	CW3	W-2146739	0863	1
RICHARDS JAMES V	MAJ	0-1318930	1065	1
RICHARDS JESSE H	MAJ	0-1688376	0462	1
RICHARDS JOE G	COL	0-0405199	0946	2
RICHARDS JOHN P	LTC	0-1000458	0860	1
RICHARDS JOSEPH A	CW2	W-2144699	0663	1
RICHARDS KENNETH E	CPT	0-0353894	1046	2
RICHARDS LEE C	CW2	W-2147120	0760	1
RICHARDS LEROY E	CW2	W-2205801	0863	2
RICHARDS MARCUS S	CPT	0-0482428	0145	2
RICHARDS MARY H K	2LT	N-0773740	1045	1
RICHARDS MAURICE E	MAJ	0-0888403	1056	2
RICHARDS NORMAN E	CW4	W-2143377	1166	1
RICHARDS PAUL H	MAJ	0-1172244	0264	1
RICHARDS REED H	COL	0-0272932	0464	3
RICHARDS ROBERT B	COL	0-0180646	0550	3
RICHARDS ROBERT E	MAJ	0-1171327	0862	1
RICHARDS ROBERT R	CPT	0-1693576	0345	2
RICHARDS ROBERT W	LTC	0-1547433	0263	1
RICHARDS STEPHEN L	CW4	W-2106144	0361	1
RICHARDS THOMAS D	MAJ	0-0961892	0263	1
RICHARDS THOMAS E JR	COL	0-0343445	1066	3
RICHARDS THOMAS K	CPT	0-1634258	0748	2
RICHARDS WALTER L JR	1LT	0-0412840	0845	2
RICHARDS WALTER W	LTC	0-1896005	0566	3
RICHARDS WILLIAM A	CPT	0-1113410	0846	2
RICHARDS WILLIAM JR	CW2	W-2148265	0857	1
RICHARDS WILLIAM S	COL	0-0290735	1261	1
RICHARDS WILLIAM S	CPT	0-0507899	0955	1
RICHARDS WILLIAM S	MAJ	0-1044654	0862	1
RICHARDSON ALAN	COL	0-0231005	0565	3
RICHARDSON ALBIN E	2LT	0-2033000	0448	2
RICHARDSON ALLEN	MAJ	0-0494046	0-53	1
RICHARDSON AMOS M	COL	0-0205661	0648	3
RICHARDSON ARTHUR K	2LT	0-1290660	1044	2
RICHARDSON ATLEE S	LTC	0-0884165	1264	3
RICHARDSON AUSTIN P	COL	0-0310165	0966	3
RICHARDSON BAXTER K	1LT	0-0180127	0450	3
RICHARDSON BRYANT E	LTC	0-1640866	0363	1
RICHARDSON CHARLES	LTC	0-0382112	1045	2
RICHARDSON CHARLES J	LTC	0-0113591	0747	2
RICHARDSON CHARLIE R	CPT	0-1998384	0455	1
RICHARDSON CHESLEY C	MAJ	0-0209648	0849	3
RICHARDSON CLAUDE	CPT	0-0245647	0648	3
RICHARDSON DALE N	CW3	W-2209409	0466	1
RICHARDSON DAVIS P	LTC	0-0253530	1162	3
RICHARDSON DEWEY E	CW2	W-2210343	1265	2
RICHARDSON DONALD V	LTC	0-0501015	1263	1
RICHARDSON DONALD W	1LT	0-1174690	1144	2
RICHARDSON EARL M	MAJ	0-1295273	0566	1
RICHARDSON EDWARD B	MAJ	0-0372778	0960	1
RICHARDSON EDWARD C	LTC	0-0209549	1059	3
RICHARDSON EDWARD R	LTC	0-0442234	0865	1
RICHARDSON EMMETT V	COL	0-0269032	1066	3
RICHARDSON FRANCIS C	MAJ	0-1950617	0563	1
RICHARDSON FRANKLIN	LTC	0-1584789	0866	1
RICHARDSON GEORGE	CPT	0-0404921	0363	1
RICHARDSON GEORGE E	LTC	0-0374671	0962	1
RICHARDSON GEORGE H	LTC	0-0115944	0255	3
RICHARDSON GERALD A	CW2	W-2210450	0864	1
RICHARDSON GERALD E	LTC	0-1111330	1064	1
RICHARDSON GERALD I	CW3	W-2211452	1168	1
RICHARDSON HAMILTON	MAJ	0-1634259	0859	1
RICHARDSON HANCL C	CW2	W-3151914	0668	1
RICHARDSON HARLAN G	CW2	W-2116194	0347	2
RICHARDSON HAROLD W	CPT	0-1651990	0557	1
RICHARDSON HENRY B	CPT	0-1534367	1045	2
RICHARDSON HOLLIS M	MAJ	0-0287595	0768	3
RICHARDSON HUGH F	LTC	0-1170164	0758	1
RICHARDSON IVAN D	MAJ	0-1644700	0157	1
RICHARDSON JAMES C	LTC	0-0329488	0365	1
RICHARDSON JAMES H	LTC	0-0384569	0564	3
RICHARDSON JESSE T	1LT	0-1914055	0247	1
RICHARDSON JOHN P	CW2	W-2214466	0768	1
RICHARDSON JOHN Q	MAJ	0-0206761	0749	3
RICHARDSON JOHN T JR	MAJ	0-0336419	0665	3
RICHARDSON JOHN W	CPT	0-1574128	0868	3
RICHARDSON LAWRENC	1LT	0-1286002	0145	2
RICHARDSON LOUIS K	CW3	W-2152981	1062	1
RICHARDSON LYMAN K	COL	0-0308070	0567	3
RICHARDSON MARION B	COL	0-0109403	0352	3
RICHARDSON MARVIN R	CPT	0-1165041	1150	2
RICHARDSON MARY S	MAJ	R-0002010	0266	1
RICHARDSON MELVIN D	CW2	W-2150951	0563	1
RICHARDSON NELSON R	LTC	0-0312503	0663	3
RICHARDSON NORWOOD G	LTC	0-1595782	0866	1
RICHARDSON ORRIE H	LTC	0-0372227	0862	1
RICHARDSON OVA K	MAJ	0-0534732	0950	1
RICHARDSON PAUL B	MAJ	0-2007278	1262	2
RICHARDSON PHILIP	CPT	0-1302351	0546	2
RICHARDSON RALPH W	LTC	0-0361978	0162	1
RICHARDSON ROBERT	MAJ	0-1644701	1159	1
RICHARDSON ROBERT A	MAJ	0-1115396	0259	1
RICHARDSON ROBERT B	2LT	0-1013488	1044	2
RICHARDSON ROBERT M	MAJ	0-1032041	0161	1
RICHARDSON RODNEY K	CW3	W-2205554	1266	1
RICHARDSON ROY L	2LT	0-1638359	0644	2
RICHARDSON WALTER F	LTC	0-0183087	1148	1
RICHARDSON WILLIAM	1LT	0-2036739	0556	1
RICHARDSON WILLIAM A	MAJ	0-2033619	0261	1
RICHARDSON WILLIAM B	COL	0-0285799	0568	3
RICHARDSON WILLIAM K	MAJ	0-1041008	1059	2
RICHARDSON WILLIAM L	LTC	0-0553312	0166	1
RICHARDSON WILLIAM N	LTC	0-1108266	0564	1
RICHARDSON WILLIAM W	LTC	0-0175793	0961	3
RICHARDSON WILLDUG	LTC	0-0472669	1045	2
RICHARDSON WILSON D	CW2	W-2121062	0649	1
RICHARDSON WINNICK K	MAJ	0-1036353	0459	1
RICHBOURG ROBERT K	CPT	0-0271087	0146	2
RICHDORF MICHAEL L	CPT	0-0253942	0958	3
RICHE CHARLES H	CPT	0-0499814	0951	1
RICHERD ERNEST E	LTC	0-1577746	0267	1
RICHERSON JOHN L	LTC	0-0267039	0961	3
RICHERT ROBERT E A	COL	0-1583556	1166	2
RICHES HARRY L	LTC	0-0175155	0755	3
RICHESON EUGENE	CW2	W-2150050	0860	1
RICHESON LIONEL L	LTC	0-0229975	0963	3
RICHESON MARVIN G	COL	0-0185942	0348	2
RICHESON VOORHEIS	MAJ	0-0164834	1149	1
RICHEY CLAUDE G	MAJ	0-0282168	1058	3
RICHEY DWAIN W	2LT	0-1582075	0445	2
RICHEY ELBA L	MAJ	0-2097199	0767	1
RICHEY ELDEN H	CW4	W-2149234	1068	1
RICHEY FRANK H	LTC	0-0277603	1162	3
RICHEY GEORGE H	2LT	0-1340808	1147	2
RICHEY GERALD L	MAJ	0-1641727	0463	1
RICHEY TIM V	CPT	0-0368524	1045	2
RICHIE CHARLES W	CPT	0-0992463	0863	1
RICHIE ELLIS B	COL	0-0329574	0465	1
RICHIE JESSE T	LTC	0-1036695	0967	1
RICHIE JOHN L	LTC	0-1550904	0167	1
RICHIE OLLIE B	MAJ	0-1310372	0160	1
RICHISTER WOODROW L	1LT	0-1301688	0958	1
RICHMAN ELMER	MAJ	0-0498207	0345	2
RICHMAN JOHN H	MAJ	0-1580222	0157	1
RICHMAN KENNETH	CPT	0-1014963	0854	1
RICHMAN MILTON H	COL	0-0361120	0758	3
RICHMAN MURRAY L	MAJ	0-1080141	0261	1
RICHMOND ALLEN P JR	COL	0-0131011	0452	3
RICHMOND CHARLES B	COL	0-0266010	0166	3
RICHMOND CLARENCE	COL	0-0287025	0656	3
RICHMOND EDWARD A	MAJ	0-0127510	0648	3
RICHMOND FREDERICK	MAJ	0-1922648	0164	1
RICHMOND HARRY R	MAJ	0-0139164	0950	3
RICHMOND JOHN F	CPT	0-0461659	0347	1
RICHMOND JOSEPH F JR	LTC	0-0454132	0267	1
RICHMOND LEROY M	MAJ	0-0959288	0163	1
RICHMOND LILLYN L	1LT	L-0700390	1045	2
RICHMOND MALCOLM F	CPT	0-1057573	0859	1
RICHMOND PAUL A	CW4	W-2002032	0468	3
RICHMOND PAUL C	LTC	0-0329823	0267	3
RICHMOND RAYMOND E	CW4	W-2002900	0865	3
RICHMOND SIDNEY T	2LT	N-0726371	1145	1
RICHMOND WILLIAM E	MAJ	0-1894196	0564	2
RICHSTATTER ROBERT L	CPT	0-0949614	1060	1
RICHTER ALBERT E JR	LTC	0-1114725	1163	1
RICHTER ARLINE E	CPT	N-0788035	0961	2
RICHTER EMANUEL J	MAJ	0-0272901	0246	2
RICHTER EUGENE A	LTC	0-0319441	0460	2
RICHTER EUGENE F	LTC	0-0342296	0346	2
RICHTER FORREST E	CPT	0-0456149	0645	2
RICHTER HIBBARD	COL	0-0127509	0546	2
RICHTER JOSEPH F	LTC	0-0264098	1145	2
RICHTER JULIUS J	CPT	0-0206975	0756	3
RICHTER ROBERT J	1LT	0-1304950	1145	2
RICHTER STANLEY M JR	CW2	W-3430316	0967	1
RICHTER VIRGINIA D	2LT	N-0768100	0845	1
RICHWINE MARTIN W JR	COL	0-0291235	0463	3
RICK CHARLES J	LTC	0-1691377	0368	3
RICK FRANK E	MAJ	0-0286487	0359	1
RICK LEO E	CPT	0-1319778	0446	2
RICKARD ERIC M	MAJ	0-0160718	0858	3
RICKARD HARRY C	LTC	0-0509682	0263	1
RICKARD WALLACE D	MAJ	0-1100741	0348	2
RICKARDS JOHN A	CPT	0-1583558	0362	2
RICKELL WILLIAM F	MAJ	0-1185379	0361	1
RICKER BERLE C	1LT	0-1016413	0446	2
RICKER CHESTER M	LTC	0-0124381	0846	2
RICKER ELMER J	LTC	0-0298518	0161	1
RICKER EUGENE K	MAJ	0-0133694	0945	2
RICKER RENARD	MAJ	0-1799185	0666	1
RICKER SHERWIN M	LTC	0-0244592	1064	3
RICKERT ALBERT A	LTC	0-2200539	1067	1
RICKES JOHN A	MAJ	0-1635255	0258	1
RICKETSON LEONARD W	COL	0-0233404	0355	2
RICKETSON MARION S	MAJ	0-0968508	0264	1
RICKETT JOHN F	CPT	0-5329833	0768	2
RICKETT NEO	CPT	0-0410426	0245	2
RICKETT WILLIAM F	LTC	0-2055429	1262	2
RICKETTS WARREN E	CPT	0-0349514	0653	2
RICKEY HARRY W	COL	0-0125073	0459	3
RICKEY VICTOR	MAJ	0-1597787	1060	1
RICKLE FRED M	CPT	0-0477704	1044	2
RICKLY FRANCIS A	COL	0-0133173	0156	3
RICKMAN JOSEPH B	LTC	0-0949232	0268	1
RICKMOND CHARLES A	MAJ	0-0956274	0767	1
RICKS CECIL C	2LT	0-1286004	0157	1
RICKS GLENN W	CW3	W-2152109	0761	1
RICKSON RECY L	LTC	0-0451508	0255	1
RICOTTA SAMUEL J	2LT	0-1796153	0745	2
RIDDEL ALEXANDER JR	LTC	0-1535408	0968	1
RIDDEL JAMES L	LTC	0-0526062	0446	2
RIDDELL HARRY M	1LT	0-1104365	0246	2
RIDDELL ROGER A	CPT	0-1110213	1059	1
RIDDER ALBERT T	LTC	0-0283573	0568	3
RIDDER DON W	MAJ	0-1885369	0767	1
RIDDER PAUL A	1LT	0-1013223	0345	2
RIDDICK JOHN A	LTC	0-0242277	0164	3
RIDDICK JOHN F	MAJ	0-1031439	0360	1
RIDDICK WILBUR E	CW3	W-2145581	1060	2
RIDDINGER PHILIP H	COL	0-0288285	0961	1
RIDDLE AMOS J	CPT	0-0189691	0456	3
RIDDLE ARTHUR E	CPT	0-1579015	0762	2
RIDDLE BURGESS P	LTC	0-0460882	0763	3
RIDDLE GLENN N	MAJ	0-0145177	0648	3
RIDDLE LLOYD E	LTC	0-0322637	1164	3
RIDDLE PASKEL T	1LT	0-1016780	1154	1
RIDDLE RAYMOND L	MAJ	0-1641728	1160	1
RIDDLE ROBERT H	LTC	0-1684876	1266	3
RIDDLE ROY A	COL	0-1555612	1268	1
RIDDLEBARGER G E	CPT	0-0958853	1060	1
RIDDLESWORTH A A	1LT	0-1582518	0347	2
RIDENOR WALTER C	CW4	W-2142938	1068	1
RIDENOUR EMWOOD J	CW3	W-2152512	0964	1
RIDENOUR RUSSEL R	LTC	0-0107207	0450	3
RIDENOUR SAMUEL J	2LT	0-1845240	0245	2
RIDEOUT ERNEST W	1LT	0-1043208	0844	2
RIDEOUT EUGENE W	COL	0-0113245	0256	3
RIDER EUGENE E	MAJ	0-0205521	0642	2
RIDER IRVIN S	1LT	0-2012056	0358	1
RIDER JOHN F	LTC	0-0901783	0645	2
RIDER RALPH R	WO1	W-2126253	1047	1
RIDGAWAY BERT E	CW2	W-2147341	0264	1
RIDGE ALVIN	1LT	0-1302884	104N	2
RIDGE BURRELL B	CPT	0-1176780	1150	2

NAME	GRADE	SVC NO	DATE RET MO YR	RET CODE
RIDGEWAY CLEM E	LTC	0-1176174	0967	1
RIDGEWAY DONALD F	LTC	0-0491196	0465	1
RIDGEWAY MARION E	CW2	W-2112999	0145	2
RIDGEWAY PAUL E	CPT	0-2263666	0663	1
RIDGLEY ALDAS S JR	CW3	W-2005772	0768	1
RIDGWAY DONALD D	MAJ	0-1016297	1061	1
RIDGWAY ROBERT J	CPT	0-0533718	1046	2
RIDING CECIL K	2LT	0-1048166	0244	2
RIDLEY JOHN H	CW3	W-2149302	1062	1
RIDLEY MARY JO	2LT	N-0703037	1041	1
RIDLEY WILLIAM V	CW4	W-2152661	1068	1
RIDLON ERNEST S	CPT	0-0233903	1164	3
RIEBE JOHN	LTC	0-0495495	0758	1
RIEBE NORMAN J	COL	0-0299997	0463	3
RIEBER CHARLES W	CPT	0-0324232	1045	2
RIECK WILLIAM F	CW3	RW-2135664	0862	1
RIECK WILLIAM J JR	LTC	0-1171736	0864	1
RIECKEN JIMMIE F	LTC	0-1285305	0563	1
RIEDEBURG HERMAN W	LTC	0-0420529	0363	1
RIEDEL CHARLES A	MAJ	0-0177926	0462	3
RIEDEL ROBERT H	LTC	0-0251191	1045	2
RIEDL CHARLES A	LTC	0-2051862	1167	3
RIEDL DONALD F	COL	0-0288504	1267	3
RIEDLEY EARLE C	LTC	0-0453647	0357	2
RIEDY OWEN L	CPT	0-1947812	0149	2
RIEF ROLAND W	1LT	0-0502919	0449	1
RIEFLING RICHARD G	LTC	0-0204397	0363	3
RIEGEL FRANK E	CPT	0-1039527	0364	1
RIEGEL LEO A	LTC	0-0322208	1059	3
RIEGELMAN HAROLD	COL	0-0211708	0852	3
RIEGER MORRIS J	CPT	0-1307077	0746	2
RIEGER WRAY M	COL	0-0223926	0662	3
RIEGERT LOUIS C JR	CPT	0-0480266	1045	2
RIEGLE ROY W	COL	0-0177389	0456	3
RIEGLER RICHARD D	MAJ	0-0375530	0560	1
RIEHM RICHARD W	LTC	0-1553160	0766	1
RIEKE BENNY A	CW3	W-2145497	1263	1
RIEKSE ROBERT J	MAJ	0-1165040	1047	2
RIEL DAVID H	MAJ	0-0304451	0954	1
RIEL JOSEPH L	CW2	W-2147411	0659	1
RIELAND GEORGE D	CPT	0-0397591	0944	2
RIELLY JAMES B	LTC	0-1544098	0465	1
RIELLY ROBERT W	CPT	0-0872093	1146	2
RIENDEAU NELSON N	CPT	0-0496689	0547	1
RIERSON GLENN D	LTC	0-0451050	0258	1
RIESBOL HERBERT S	LTC	0-0260992	0668	3
RIESENBERG MARGARET	1LT	N-0726496	0145	2
RIESINGER SIMON	MAJ	0-1300220	1166	1
RIESMEYER JOHN F	CPT	0-1107658	1050	1
RIESS ANDREW J	1LT	0-1593932	1147	2
RIESS WALTER G	CPT	0-1930335	0463	2
RIESSBECK JOHN	CPT	0-2103026	0462	1
RIEWERTS ERROLL S	MAJ	0-0974524	0563	1
RIFE BYRON	COL	0-0120862	0852	3
RIFE JOHN W	LTC	0-0337820	0660	1
RIFE STANLEY S	1LT	0-1312719	1045	2
RIFFEL EMERY J	CW3	W-2142892	0561	1
RIFFEL JOSEPH D	1LT	0-1648450	0159	2
RIFFENBURG WALTER V	CPT	0-0200328	0253	3
RIFFERT REYNOLDS H	1LT	0-1590135	1044	2
RIFKIN JULIAN S	CPT	0-0343983	1045	2
RIFLEMAN JAMES D	MAJ	0-1844700	1162	1
RIGAL WALDO A	MAJ	0-0268380	0755	3
RIGBY DONALD M	COL	0-0179611	1160	3
RIGBY HENRY S	CPT	0-0438993	0446	2
RIGBY JACK B	LTC	0-1580225	1062	1
RIGBY JOURDAN	CPT	0-0443564	1045	2
RIGBY LINDEN G	LTC	0-0410769	1045	2
RIGBY LOEHR M JR	LTC	0-1821913	0265	1
RIGBY LUCY	MAJ	L-0807500	0663	1
RIGBY PAUL T	COL	0-0331137	0360	1
RIGBY ROBERT L	LTC	0-1579018	0261	2
RIGDON HAROLD E	LTC	0-1000656	1061	1
RIGDON RALPH E	LTC	0-1287062	0164	1
RIGG CLIFTON F	CW4	W-2147774	0866	1

NAME	GRADE	SVC NO	DATE RET MO YR	RET CODE
RIGG JOHN P	LTC	0-0464205	1154	1
RIGGAN JOHN W	CPT	0-2263500	0162	1
RIGGIN BENJAMIN F	CPT	0-0278089	0855	3
RIGGIN BENJAMIN F JR	1LT	0-0420041	0146	2
RIGGIN GEORGE B	LTC	0-1000462	0657	1
RIGGINS CHARLES F	LTC	0-0580183	0268	3
RIGGINS EMMETT	MAJ	0-0487839	0946	1
RIGGINS JAMES L	LTC	0-2289189	0462	2
RIGGLE CLORAN D	LTC	0-0219947	0446	2
RIGGLE PAUL	MAJ	0-0271798	0442	2
RIGGLEMAN ESKER H	MAJ	0-1635548	0954	1
RIGGS CHARLES E	MAJ	0-0908662	0845	2
RIGGS CHARLES R	CPT	0-1644008	0746	2
RIGGS CLARENCE B	LTC	0-0267439	0240	2
RIGGS EDWARD C	MAJ	0-0971981	0163	2
RIGGS FRANK P	1LT	0-1327042	0746	2
RIGGS GLENN E	CPT	0-1289626	1045	2
RIGGS GROVER C	LTC	0-0921986	1067	3
RIGGS LEO J	MAJ	0-1306471	1060	1
RIGGS ROBERT C	LTC	0-0239891	0559	3
RIGGS RUTH J	2LT	N-0701710	1040	1
RIGGS WILLIAM H	CW3	W-2110331	0158	1
RIGHTER HALL T	CW3	W-2143959	0163	1
RIGLER RALPH L	LTC	0-0383942	0764	1
RIGLER RAYMOND H	LTC	0-0382755	0766	1
RIGLEY ALBERT J	2LT	0-1318228	0344	2
RIGNEY HUBERT M	1LT	0-0185327	0151	3
RIGO CHARLES P	LTC	0-0339923	0862	2
RIGO WILLIAM F	MAJ	0-1934859	0968	1
RIGSBY CHARLES H	MAJ	0-0286367	1044	2
RIGSBY VERL W	MAJ	0-0407279	0646	2
RIHA JOHN D	MAJ	0-1060609	0760	1
RIHELDAFFER WILLIAM	COL	0-0234376	1065	3
RIKARD WILLIAM F	MAJ	0-0336493	0467	3
RIKER CHARLES E	LTC	0-0920312	1165	3
RIKER DAVID C	LTC	0-0405986	0155	1
RILEY ANDREW P	LTC	0-1294371	0658	1
RILEY CHARLES H	LTC	0-0373448	0567	3
RILEY DOMNICK G	LTC	0-1590136	0464	1
RILEY FLOYD A	MAJ	0-1031835	0361	1
RILEY FRANCIS E JR	1LT	0-1594422	104N	2
RILEY FRANK	MAJ	0-1686289	0155	1
RILEY FRANK E	CPT	0-0422826	0561	1
RILEY FRED A	CPT	0-1698848	0156	1
RILEY FRED T	CW4	W-2004524	0865	3
RILEY GALYE	1LT	0-0444112	0145	2
RILEY GEORGIA S	2LT	N-0742741	1044	1
RILEY HAROLD B	LTC	0-0173966	1057	1
RILEY HARRY A JR	CPT	0-1284399	0246	2
RILEY HARRY T	LTC	0-1177610	0864	1
RILEY HERBERT E	2LT	0-1558076	0245	2
RILEY JAMES A	2LT	0-1321332	1045	2
RILEY JAMES F	CW3	W-2142266	1058	1
RILEY JAMES L	CPT	0-1049630	0460	2
RILEY JAMES L	CW3	W-2147918	0762	2
RILEY JAMES R	MAJ	0-0466568	0646	2
RILEY JOHN C	MAJ	0-0396950	0847	2
RILEY JOHN E	CW2	W-2151730	1062	1
RILEY JOHN P JR	MAJ	0-0493899	0354	1
RILEY JOHN W	MAJ	0-1030708	1060	1
RILEY JOHN W	LTC	0-1534610	0362	2
RILEY MARTIN G	COL	0-0888371	0862	1
RILEY MARVIN M	LTC	0-1166816	1059	1
RILEY MARY B	1LT	N-0735643	0447	1
RILEY MASON H	CPT	0-0129344	0354	3
RILEY MAX W	CPT	0-0260546	0949	1
RILEY MEDFRED S	COL	0-0397904	0768	3
RILEY PAGE M	CPT	0-1305112	0346	2
RILEY PERRY N	CPT	0-0450667	0757	1
RILEY PLEASANT O	CW2	W-2211906	0566	1
RILEY RENWICK N	LTC	0-1037904	0361	1
RILEY RICHARD C	1LT	0-2047799	0945	2
RILEY ROBERT R	MAJ	0-1015566	1162	1
RILEY ROY	1LT	0-0450508	1043	2
RILEY SAMUEL W	LTC	0-1288446	0764	1

NAME	GRADE	SVC NO	DATE RET MO YR	RET CODE
RILEY THOMAS F	1LT	0-1113913	0246	2
RILEY THOMAS M	2LT	0-0539800	1045	2
RILEY VIVIAN F	CPT	0-0261011	1045	2
RILEY WALTER F	CPT	0-1683473	1059	1
RILEY WARREN S	LTC	0-0226038	0964	3
RILEY WILLIAM C	1LT	0-1283841	0644	2
RILEY WILLIAM H	CW4	W-2145498	0968	1
RILEY WILLIAM J	CPT	0-0401637	0461	1
RILEY WILLIAM J	2LT	0-1797530	1043	2
RILEY WILLIAM L	CW3	W-2147027	0165	1
RILEY WILLIAM P	COL	0-1796859	0266	3
RILEY WILSON M	COL	0-0245769	0467	3
RILLONA CESAR C	1LT	0-1896932	0849	1
RIMBACK JOSEPH A	LTC	0-1574130	0561	1
RIMER HOWARD W	MAJ	0-0278092	0466	3
RIMES WILLIAM G	CPT	0-1285501	0846	1
RIMMER BENNIE H JR	CPT	0-0579005	0746	2
RINALDUCCI RALPH J	LTC	0-0573117	1163	1
RINAMAN JAMES C	COL	0-0317293	0663	3
RINCK ROBERT E	LTC	0-0831804	0466	1
RINEBOLD WILLIAM C	CPT	0-1577750	0954	1
RINEHART BERNARD F	LTC	0-0280916	0467	3
RINEHART CLEO A	LTC	0-0175751	0162	3
RINEHART DEVOE A	1LT	0-0301575	0450	1
RINEHART ELWELL D	CPT	0-0295641	0645	2
RINEHART JOHN C	CW3	W-2208152	1067	1
RINEHART JOHN W	LTC	0-1013609	0261	1
RINEHART JOSEPH F	CW3	W-2150802	1068	2
RINEHART MIKE	LTC	0-0371635	0164	3
RINEHART OMRO W	CW3	W-2148599	0963	1
RINEHART ROBERT L	MAJ	0-1046624	1163	1
RINEHART STANLEY L	CW2	W-2103366	0447	1
RINER ROBERT D	CW2	W-2149083	0357	1
RING ADOLPHUS L	COL	0-0346915	0554	3
RING CARLYLE D	MAJ	0-2010344	1160	1
RING GUSTAVE A	COL	0-0282568	0263	3
RINGE CHARLES L JR	CPT	0-0332698	0146	2
RINGEL HAROLD L	1LT	0-1581338	0843	2
RINGEL WILLIAM F	LTC	0-0181161	0162	3
RINGENBACH RAYMOND F	2LT	0-1322125	1044	2
RINGER EDWARD L	CPT	0-0440799	1145	2
RINGER JOHN F	LTC	0-1041535	1165	1
RINGER MATTHEW J	LTC	0-1174121	1262	1
RINGER SMITH	1LT	0-0165777	0151	3
RINGEY LAWRENCE E	MAJ	0-1924536	1064	1
RINGGOLD GORDON B	COL	0-0205501	1163	3
RINGKVIST ROBERT C	LTC	0-0524656	0667	1
RINGLAND AUGUSTUS G	2LT	0-1012187	0944	2
RINGLAND EDWARD D	MAJ	0-1635258	0555	1
RINGLE LEO W	CW2	W-2143488	1054	1
RINGLER LEWIS J	1LT	0-0524161	1045	2
RINGLER MILTON E	CPT	0-0473320	0846	2
RINGLER WILLIAM F	MAJ	0-0909388	1044	2
RINGSRUD RONALD H	LTC	0-0355009	0467	1
RINGSTROM BERTIL L	CW3	W-2149737	0558	1
RINGWALD ROBERT K	1LT	0-1822056	0546	2
RINGWALT CHARLES C	LTC	0-0139999	0655	3
RINK EMMETT A	COL	0-0309444	0268	3
RINK TED O	MAJ	0-1298958	0656	1
RINKAVAGE JOSEPH P	CW2	W-2440015	0566	1
RINKE JOSEPH G	CPT	0-0372822	0464	1
RINKER ALBERT E	MAJ	0-1021754	0360	1
RINKER CHARLES J	LTC	0-0912021	1164	3
RINKES EARL W	CW3	W-2144291	1062	2
RINKLE BILL	MAJ	0-1824370	0258	1
RINKS ZACK H	CPT	0-0483745	0248	1
RINN RALPH E	COL	0-0310109	0846	2
RINSLAND HENRY D	MAJ	0-0214922	0346	2
RINTLEMAN GLEN C	2LT	0-2023626	1045	2
RINTOUL WILLIAM	LTC	0-2051296	0266	1
RIOLLANO CARLOS	LTC	0-0354321	0960	1
RION GEORGE P	CW2	W-2119514	0553	1
RION HOWARD G	LTC	0-0349233	0447	2
RIORDAN DON F	LTC	0-1548133	1060	1
RIORDAN RALPH E	LTC	0-0247427	0457	2

NAME	GRADE	SVC NO	DATE RET MO YR	RET CODE
RIORDAN THOMAS M	MAJ	0-1301881	1064	2
RIOS DAN J	2LT	0-1306789	0145	2
RIPALDA ANTONIO	1LT	0-1896889	1164	1
RIPICH JOHN W	CPT	0-0344742	1045	2
RIPLEY FREDERICK	1LT	0-1824371	0246	2
RIPLEY GORDON M	COL	0-0443763	1168	2
RIPLEY JOSEPH M JR	2LT	0-1699970	0848	2
RIPLEY PAUL H	CPT	0-1180687	0748	2
RIPP JACOB	MAJ	0-0356597	0446	2
RIPP JOHN P	LTC	0-1583563	0462	1
RIPPE HENRY A	LTC	0-0522179	0863	3
RIPPEE ROBERT L	MAJ	0-1542633	0661	1
RIPPER LLOYD E	CW2	W-2146978	0361	1
RIPPERTON NADINE	2LT	N-0771458	0246	1
RIPPETOE DAVID L	MAJ	0-2263424	0167	1
RIPPLINGER ORLEY K	LTC	0-0279855	0267	3
RIPPY BAYARD W	2LT	0-1309834	0451	2
RIPPY EDWIN L	LTC	0-0280981	0268	3
RIPPY ELKIN L	LTC	0-0239890	0845	2
RIPPY PAUL	MAJ	0-1573541	1157	1
RIPSTRA EARL F	COL	0-0242610	1163	3
RIPSTRA HENRI I	LTC	0-1183172	0965	3
RIQUELME ALEXANDER	LTC	0-0476176	0-52	1
RISBURG RUBIN C	COL	0-0193640	0756	3
RISDEN EDWARD J	LTC	0-1168052	0468	1
RISDEN MILFORD	CPT	0-0989046	1060	1
RISELEY JERRY B JR	1LT	0-0414699	0545	2
RISEN ROLLIN F	COL	0-0334411	1057	3
RISER GEORGE M	LTC	0-0228767	0664	3
RISH EARL B	CPT	0-2289641	0762	1
RISHE MARK N	LTC	0-1107076	0962	2
RISHEBARGER EDWARD S	LTC	0-1119536	0164	1
RISHEILL CLARENCE E	MAJ	0-1170939	0561	1
RISHELL CHESTER A	MAJ	0-0341497	0364	3
RISING CAROLL A	LTC	0-0273557	0765	3
RISING FREDERIC D	LTC	0-0168232	1157	3
RISING STANLEY A	LTC	0-1038805	1263	1
RISINGER ERMA E	2LT	N-0729401	1144	1
RISK EDWARD	CW2	W-2208337	0364	2
RISKE CHARLES W	LTC	0-1100304	0960	1
RISKIN SAMUEL	1LT	0-0157943	0355	3
RISKO EDWARD F	CW3	W-2141135	0959	1
RISKO MICHAEL A	CW4	W-2145837	0468	1
RISLEY DANIEL L	LTC	0-0909704	0463	1
RISPOLI FRANK V	1LT	0-1229347	1045	2
RISSE EUGENE J	CPT	0-0255887	0141	1
RISSER ANDREW A	LTC	0-0242165	1163	3
RISSLER JOHN C	LTC	0-1534369	0661	1
RIST AUSTIN S	COL	0-1040061	0866	1
RIST CHARLES M	COL	0-0320384	0859	3
RISTAINO JOHN P	CW3	W-2141738	0860	1
RISTEDT ERNEST J	COL	0-0104062	0648	3
RISTINE LEONARD P	LTC	0-0354208	1146	2
RISTROPH PAUL L	COL	0-0271557	0968	3
RITCH ALLEN	LTC	0-0233845	1061	3
RITCHARDSON WALTER L	CPT	0-1341708	1160	1
RITCHEY HAROLD E	1LT	0-1176781	1046	2
RITCHEY JOHN A	MAJ	0-0318573	0243	2
RITCHEY ROY V	CW2	W-2209613	0363	1
RITCHIE CECIL C	LTC	0-1286362	0866	2
RITCHIE DAVID K	CW3	W-2145233	0963	1
RITCHIE DAVID O	CW3	W-2148148	1163	1
RITCHIE GUY G	MAJ	0-0970225	1264	1
RITCHIE JOHN G	MAJ	0-0567381	0965	1
RITCHIE JOHN III	COL	0-0911465	0464	3
RITCHIE KENNETH W	CPT	0-1824085	1056	2
RITCHIE LLOYD C	COL	0-0145369	0350	3
RITCHIE RALPH D	CPT	0-1878174	1265	1
RITCHIE RAY M	MAJ	0-0156782	0653	3
RITCHIE ROBERT B	LTC	0-0243946	0564	3
RITCHIE ROBERT E	LTC	0-1643279	0768	1
RITCHIE THOMAS N	COL	0-0280542	0460	1
RITCHIE VERL C	2LT	0-1589463	0743	2
RITCHIE WILLIAM B	CW2	W-2153188	0460	1
RITENOUR HAROLD R	CW3	W-2205537	0267	1

NAME	GRADE	SVC NO	DATE RET MO YR	RET CODE
RITENOUR PAUL A	CW2	W-2150163	0659	1
RITHMAN CHARLES	1LT	0-2046705	0158	1
RITKO JOSEPH J	LTC	0-1645948	1063	1
RITNER JOHN A	MAJ	0-1634515	0260	1
RITTENBERG EDITH F	1LT	L-0116025	0446	2
RITTENER LOUIS G J	MAJ	0-0504311	0460	1
RITTENHOUSE WILLIAM	CPT	0-1285821	1265	1
RITTER ARTHUR E	CW4	W-2109013	0659	2
RITTER CHARLES S JR	1LT	0-1795973	1144	2
RITTER CLOVIS O	LTC	0-0316589	0266	1
RITTER DONALD L	LTC	0-0398471	0561	2
RITTER EUGENE S	CW4	W-2141664	0762	1
RITTER FRED J	LTC	0-0282898	0456	3
RITTER GEORGE T	LTC	0-0347649	0558	3
RITTER HAROLD F	MAJ	0-1944571	0546	2
RITTER HAROLD K	CW3	W-2149965	0461	1
RITTER JOHN J	LTC	0-0267716	0140	2
RITTER LEONARD C	1LT	0-0885711	1055	1
RITTER LEROY A	LTC	0-0213535	0164	3
RITTER LESTER W	CPT	0-1596396	0566	1
RITTER RAYMOND N	CPT	0-1691736	1154	1
RITTER ROBERT J	CPT	0-1795974	0345	2
RITTER WARREN W	CPT	0-0976778	0657	1
RITTERHOLZ BERNARD J	CPT	0-0445821	1048	1
RITTERMAN HENRY	CPT	0-0485591	1045	2
RITTERSPACHER PHILLI	LTC	0-0297704	0867	3
RITZ ANTHONY A	LTC	0-1111331	0261	1
RITZ RALPH K	LTC	0-1335979	0766	1
RITZ ROBERT S JR	LTC	0-1166818	1060	1
RITZ SHERWOOD F	LTC	0-0909530	0657	2
RITZO EUGENE	LTC	0-1332420	0663	1
RIVARD REGINALD J	LTC	0-0451172	0658	1
RIVCHUN FREDERICK	MAJ	0-1010341	0446	2
RIVELLESE JULIUS C	CPT	0-0495949	0346	2
RIVELY JOSEPH C	LTC	0-0317309	1159	1
RIVENBARK GEORGE M	CW4	W-2125292	0758	1
RIVER HENRY L	CPT	0-1577756	0457	1
RIVERA ALFREDO	1LT	0-2263290	0460	1
RIVERA ANIBAL R	CPT	0-0417257	0261	1
RIVERA CESAR L	1LT	0-0504779	0847	2
RIVERA EDELMIRO	MAJ	0-1288447	0358	1
RIVERA EUGENIO M	LTC	0-0173227	0460	3
RIVERA GIL A	1LT	0-2027038	0951	1
RIVERA JACINTO	LTC	0-0405131	1060	1
RIVERA JOSE	2LT	0-1583564	0247	1
RIVERA JOSE A	COL	0-0513618	0365	3
RIVERA JOSE A	MAJ	0-1288450	1060	1
RIVERA JOSE R	CW3	RW-2147670	0965	1
RIVERA JUAN J	MAJ	0-0200739	0352	3
RIVERA LUIS A	MAJ	0-1328748	1063	1
RIVERA MARIA G	MAJ	N-0779152	1065	3
RIVERA MIGUEL	1LT	0-0468066	0867	1
RIVERA PATRICIA M	1LT	N-0732092	0745	1
RIVERA RAFAEL M	CPT	0-0528185	1145	2
RIVERA RAMON	2LT	0-0275562	1051	1
RIVERA ROSLINA	1LT	N-0901539	1153	2
RIVERA VICTOR M	CPT	0-0420511	0645	2
RIVERA&NEGRON JORGE	2LT	0-0445091	0144	2
RIVERA-PEREZ SANTOS	CW3	W-2151665	0962	1
RIVERO HARRY	MAJ	0-4005259	0566	2
RIVERS FORREST E	1LT	0-0494271	0946	1
RIVERS HENRY F	2LT	0-1999789	0858	1
RIVERS JAMES D	MAJ	0-0977095	1262	1
RIVERS JOHN L SR	CW2	W-3430449	1167	1
RIVERS LA VERNE L	LTC	0-0274547	0958	1
RIVERS LANGDON U	2LT	0-1311206	0944	2
RIVERS LEO A	CPT	0-1651656	0458	2
RIVERS THOMAS N	MAJ	0-0410870	0563	1
RIVERS THOMAS N III	CPT	0-1686684	0465	1
RIVES JOHN C	CPT	0-2262868	0461	1
RIVES POWELL F	1LT	0-0545693	0146	2
RIVES ROBERT C	LTC	0-0156785	1052	3
RIVIERE WILLIAM T	LTC	0-0151226	0347	2
RIVKIN NORMAN	2LT	0-0887699	0945	2
RIVKIN RAYMOND	CPT	0-0371893	0144	2
RIVOIRE EMMA C	LTC	N-0722502	0761	1
RIX THEODORE A	CW3	RW-2209602	0264	1
RIXEY GEORGE Y	COL	0-1583565	1266	1
RIZER ARTHUR L	1LT	0-1303547	0845	2
RIZNER ANDREW	MAJ	0-0262242	1058	3
RIZZARDI ALBERT J	2LT	0-2023754	0446	2
RIZZIO ANTHONY P	1LT	0-5013917	0865	2
RIZZO DOMINICK A	MAJ	0-1648114	0965	1
RIZZO FRANK A	CPT	0-2055149	0647	2
RIZZO FRANK P	COL	0-0252646	0963	3
RIZZO TOAY	MAJ	0-2055165	0958	1
RIZZO VICTOR P	CPT	0-1175846	1060	1
ROACH AUSTIN S	MAJ	0-0977670	0961	1
ROACH CHARLES A	2LT	0-1914343	1036	1
ROACH CURTIS O	MAJ	0-0220581	0861	3
ROACH HENRY B	COL	0-0276004	1266	3
ROACH IRA L	CW4	W-2115961	0957	1
ROACH JAMES E	CPT	0-1041887	0245	2
ROACH JOHN P	WO1	W-2123436	0744	2
ROACH JOHN W	LTC	0-0922381	0862	3
ROACH MARVIN E	MAJ	0-1053319	0760	1
ROACH PATRICK W	CPT	0-0509483	0945	2
ROACH REX D	B G	0-0337895	1165	3
ROACH RICHARD J	CPT	0-0521090	0145	2
ROACH SAMUEL P	COL	0-0910412	0263	1
ROACH WALTER J	MAJ	0-1053897	0158	1
ROACH WILLIAM C JR	MAJ	0-1542134	1059	1
ROACH WILLIAM L	COL	0-0141476	1057	3
ROACHE RUSSELL F	CPT	0-1011855	0945	2
ROADCAP ROBERT S	CPT	0-0302654	0753	3
ROADIFER HAROLD M	MAJ	0-1821770	0862	3
ROADMAN BERNICE M	MAJ	N-0732491	0264	3
ROAM WILLIAM E JR	CPT	0-1882390	0662	1
ROAN EARL H	2LT	0-1914052	0238	1
ROAN ROY R	CW3	W-2152246	0164	1
ROANE LAWRENCE H	MAJ	0-0214692	0345	2
ROANE WAYNE R	LTC	0-0257057	0967	3
ROARK BILL	LTC	0-1542036	0261	1
ROARK CHARLES V	MAJ	0-1588837	0462	1
ROARK FRANK E	CPT	0-0356993	0146	2
ROARK HAROLD E	CW2	W-2149089	1160	2
ROARK ROGER	CPT	0-2026991	0647	2
ROARK WILLIAM C	CW3	W-2206252	0966	2
ROARKE OWEN A	MAJ	0-0163186	0454	3
ROAT CHARLES E	CW3	W-2146271	0760	1
ROATEN SHELLEY P	1LT	0-1182693	0946	2
ROATH STEPHEN J	CW3	W-2153325	1066	1
ROBACK GEORGE S	CPT	0-1785728	0 47	2
ROBARDS WOODFORD L	CPT	0-0407376	0146	2
ROBAS FREDERICK	CW4	W-2103372	0153	2
ROBB DARYL G	LTC	0-0543212	0166	1
ROBB EDWIN P	1LT	0-0305196	1144	2
ROBB HARRY J	MAJ	0-0467142	0346	2
ROBB JAMES F	COL	0-0263191	1262	3
ROBB JOHN A	LTC	0-1633495	0163	1
ROBB JOHN R	LTC	0-0355393	1058	1
ROBB KENNETH P	LTC	0-1287762	1060	1
ROBB ROBERT H	MAJ	0-1889870	1067	1
ROBB WILLIAM A JR	MAJ	0-1889767	0966	1
ROBBEN GEORGE M JR	MAJ	0-1634263	0757	1
ROBBEN GERHARD G	MAJ	0-0305807	0962	3
ROBBERS JOSEPH C	LTC	0-0129637	0353	3
ROBBERSON ROY L	MAJ	0-1635260	0657	1
ROBBERT ALBERT A JR	MAJ	0-1013861	0747	2
ROBBIN HARRY N	CPT	0-0243220	0756	3
ROBBINS BERL	LTC	0-0330841	1059	1
ROBBINS BRAMBLE	CPT	0-1179592	0161	1
ROBBINS CHARLES E	LTC	0-1644705	1063	1
ROBBINS CHARLES H	LTC	0-0455913	0559	1
ROBBINS ELSIE	2LT	N-0700160	0733	1
ROBBINS ERNEST P	MAJ	0-0981600	0164	1
ROBBINS FLADGE	CPT	0-0499042	0250	1
ROBBINS FLOYD O	LTC	0-0288188	1045	2
ROBBINS FRED E	COL	0-0262702	0757	1
ROBBINS GERALD	LTC	0-0378694	0859	1
ROBBINS GERALD O	CPT	0-1313705	0646	2
ROBBINS HERBERT JR	MAJ	0-1003154	1267	3
ROBBINS HERBERT S	1LT	0-0334246	0444	2
ROBBINS HOMER O	MAJ	0-1172245	1065	1
ROBBINS HORACE M	COL	0-0235672	1052	3
ROBBINS JAMES A	LTC	0-1165552	0264	1
ROBBINS JAMES N	COL	0-0104939	0346	2
ROBBINS KENNETH R	CW3	W-2147103	1060	1
ROBBINS LEE O	LTC	0-0377750	0861	1
ROBBINS LEO G	CW3	W-2148625	1065	1
ROBBINS MAC	CPT	0-1636510	0845	2
ROBBINS MCINTYRE	CPT	0-0509635	0346	2
ROBBINS MORRISON B	COL	0-0326621	0367	1
ROBBINS RENNIE	MAJ	0-0266057	0250	3
ROBBINS RICHARD C	1LT	0-1292944	0245	2
ROBBINS RICHARD C	LTC	0-1557018	0667	1
ROBBINS ROBERT C	CPT	0-0411138	0747	2
ROBBINS ROBERT L	CW4	W-2109442	0960	1
ROBBINS ROY L	MAJ	0-0956991	0468	1
ROBBINS SIDNEY	1LT	0-0438798	0844	2
ROBBINS STANLEY E	CW4	W-2117102	1157	1
ROBBINS STANTON O	CPT	0-0487023	0247	1
ROBBINS STEPHEN M	1LT	0-1317229	0147	2
ROBBINS TENNIS L	CW4	W-2149781	1067	1
ROBBINS THEODORE	MAJ	0-1297782	0161	1
ROBBINS WALTER C	MAJ	0-0303344	0266	3
ROBBINS WARREN E	WO1	W-2153052	1162	2
ROBBINS WELDON L	LTC	0-0920203	0568	3
ROBBINS WILLIAM L	CW3	W-2209689	1067	1
ROBBINS WINSTON C	LTC	0-0925427	0568	3
ROBBLEE DONALD E	CPT	0-1288952	0849	1
ROBEL CHARLES A	1LT	0-2042867	0146	2
ROBERG ALFRED A	LTC	0-0139076	0853	3
ROBERSON BRUCE W	LTC	0-0865389	0860	1
ROBERSON CLARENCE W	LTC	0-0249529	1043	2
ROBERSON HOSMER M	LTC	0-0343385	0760	3
ROBERSON MARION J	CW4	W-2115458	1163	1
ROBERSON THEO F JR	CPT	0-2287555	0467	1
ROBERSON WILLIAM C	COL	0-0261812	1158	3
ROBERSON WILLIAM H	CW4	W-2142317	0463	1
ROBERSON WORSHAM B	MAJ	0-2050124	0663	1
ROBERTO FREDERICO	LTC	0-2016401	0663	1
ROBERTO PATRICK M	LTC	0-1036355	0962	1
ROBERTS ALBERT O	LTC	0-0255072	1155	3
ROBERTS ALEXANDER	LTC	0-0100022	0658	3
ROBERTS ALFRED R	CW2	W-2149868	0961	1
ROBERTS AMSTER	CPT	0-0450458	0944	2
ROBERTS ARCHIBALD	LTC	0-1542803	1065	1
ROBERTS ARTHUR H	LTC	0-0291644	1061	1
ROBERTS ARTHUR J	2LT	0-1307855	0145	2
ROBERTS ARTHUR W	MAJ	0-0979617	1162	1
ROBERTS BRAXTON L	MAJ	0-0135036	1145	2
ROBERTS BURCH J	COL	0-0347242	0346	2
ROBERTS CARL P	CW3	W-2207600	0666	1
ROBERTS CHARLES C	COL	0-0451387	1067	1
ROBERTS CHARLES D	MAJ	0-1116465	1058	1
ROBERTS CHARLES H	MAJ	0-0187477	0555	3
ROBERTS CHARLES H	CPT	0-2262268	1060	1
ROBERTS CHARLES R	MAJ	0-0260901	0367	3
ROBERTS CHARLES W	MAJ	0-0237748	0651	3
ROBERTS CHARLEY	CW2	W-2002964	0268	3
ROBERTS CLARENCE B	LTC	0-1824900	0968	1
ROBERTS CLARENCE W	1LT	0-1338641	1047	2
ROBERTS CLAUDE	CW3	W-2147002	0961	1
ROBERTS CLAUDIUS H	COL	0-0173117	0954	3
ROBERTS CLIFFORD A	CW2	W-2146806	0758	1
ROBERTS CLINTON F	CPT	0-0496999	0845	2
ROBERTS CLYDE J	LTC	0-0554323	0968	1
ROBERTS DANIEL J	1LT	0-0395081	1045	2
ROBERTS DARRELL S	MAJ	0-0402785	0761	1
ROBERTS DEE F	MAJ	0-2019795	1262	1
ROBERTS DONALD A	CW2	W-2118453	0553	1
ROBERTS DONALD B	MAJ	0-0251973	0966	3
ROBERTS DONALD L	COL	0-0284112	0247	2
ROBERTS EARL D JR	LTC	0-2020345	1066	1
ROBERTS EDGAR W	1LT	0-2262627	0759	1
ROBERTS EDWARD A	CW3	W-2208544	0268	1
ROBERTS EDWARD P	CW4	W-2145582	0668	2
ROBERTS EDWIN T	1LT	0-1014909	1044	2
ROBERTS ELBERT M	LTC	0-0309204	0365	3
ROBERTS ELLIS M	2LT	0-1301690	0144	2
ROBERTS ELTON W	CPT	0-1576563	0454	1
ROBERTS EMITT	1LT	0-0496791	0953	1
ROBERTS ERASTUS W	LTC	0-2288982	0868	1
ROBERTS ERNEST J	MAJ	0-1999915	1060	1
ROBERTS ERVIN L	CW2	W-2143864	0158	1
ROBERTS ESKELL F	1LT	0-1108273	0645	2
ROBERTS EUGENE	CPT	0-2263234	0957	1
ROBERTS EUGENE M	LTC	0-1109624	0965	3
ROBERTS EUGENE V	MAJ	0-0226000	0864	3
ROBERTS EVAN R	MAJ	0-0244486	0664	3
ROBERTS FLOYD P	CPT	0-0105166	0454	3
ROBERTS FRED B	CW2	W-2206118	0266	1
ROBERTS FRED E	LTC	0-0224340	0260	3
ROBERTS GEORGE	CPT	0-0556998	0268	3
ROBERTS GEORGE A	COL	0-0359310	0268	3
ROBERTS GEORGE A	LTC	0-1583566	0261	1
ROBERTS GEORGE A	CPT	0-1718017	0651	2
ROBERTS GEORGE J	1LT	0-1320920	114N	2
ROBERTS GEORGE W	LTC	0-2045221	0766	1
ROBERTS GORDON D	MAJ	0-0327297	0958	3
ROBERTS GORDON E	COL	0-0235801	0857	3
ROBERTS GRADY A	WO1	W-2107093	0155	1
ROBERTS GUY R	MAJ	0-2263774	0368	2
ROBERTS HAROLD F	LTC	0-1118792	1065	1
ROBERTS HAROLD L	MAJ	0-0977203	0464	1
ROBERTS HARRY W	LTC	0-1894663	0760	1
ROBERTS HENRY F JR	CW3	W-2152717	0563	1
ROBERTS HERBERT C	COL	0-0256363	1056	3
ROBERTS HERBERT J	LTC	0-0199886	0560	3
ROBERTS HERMAN H	CPT	0-1032596	0255	1
ROBERTS HERMAN M	MAJ	0-1947221	0961	2
ROBERTS HOLLIS V	CW3	RW-2147686	1064	1
ROBERTS HOWARD	MAJ	0-1913386	0966	1
ROBERTS HOWARD H	LTC	0-0201308	0555	3
ROBERTS HOYT K	MAJ	0-1590759	0561	1
ROBERTS IRVING E	LTC	0-0295246	1267	3
ROBERTS JACK F	LTC	0-1544847	1055	1
ROBERTS JACK K	CPT	0-1002719	0257	1
ROBERTS JACK R	CW3	W-2209059	0968	1
ROBERTS JACK W	MAJ	0-1062930	1065	1
ROBERTS JACKSON R	CPT	0-1330755	0763	1
ROBERTS JAMES B	CW2	W-2141665	0865	1
ROBERTS JAMES C	CPT	0-1998063	0347	2
ROBERTS JAMES F	CPT	0-1928407	0264	2
ROBERTS JAMES O	MAJ	0-0435058	0446	2
ROBERTS JAMES R	CW3	W-2122047	0258	2
ROBERTS JAMES T	B G	0-0220864	1060	3
ROBERTS JESSE L	CW2	W-2142659	1054	1
ROBERTS JOHN C	CW4	W-2003256	1066	3
ROBERTS JOHN D SR	MAJ	0-2033872	0265	1
ROBERTS JOHN E	1LT	0-1856821	0154	2
ROBERTS JOHN G	1LT	0-1321249	0846	2
ROBERTS JOHN J	MAJ	0-0151821	0649	3
ROBERTS JOHN L	1LT	0-1004071	0952	1
ROBERTS JOHN O	MAJ	0-0514923	1054	1
ROBERTS JOHN W	1LT	0-0558237	114T	2
ROBERTS KEITH O	CW3	W-2148066	0161	1
ROBERTS KEITH M	COL	0-0340350	1066	1
ROBERTS KENNETH B	LTC	0-0264730	0965	3
ROBERTS KIT C JR	CW3	W-2211435	0968	1
ROBERTS LEONARD F	CW2	W-2115595	0654	2
ROBERTS LEWIS S	MAJ	0-0962545	0764	1
ROBERTS LOUIS	1LT	0-1281473	1048	2
ROBERTS MALCOLM	LTC	0-1031441	0562	1
ROBERTS MARSHALL O	MAJ	0-1053326	0759	1
ROBERTS MARTIN W	CPT	0-0919248	0145	2
ROBERTS MARVIN F	2LT	0-1303777	0845	2
ROBERTS MARVIN L	CW3	W-2149901	0760	1
ROBERTS MILO A	CPT	0-0910596	0447	2

NAME	GRADE	SVC NO	DATE RET MO YR	RET CODE
ROBERTS MOULTRIE Q	LTC	0-0265210	0762	3
ROBERTS OLIVER M	CW3	W-2208678	0367	1
ROBERTS ORA F	COL	0-0167377	1045	2
ROBERTS PAUL E	1LT	0-1328186	0546	2
ROBERTS PAUL J	COL	0-0172671	0958	1
ROBERTS PAUL J	MAJ	0-0205083	0459	3
ROBERTS PAUL M	MAJ	0-5301556	0968	1
ROBERTS PAUL P	2LT	0-1319442	0945	2
ROBERTS PAUL P	LTC	0-1639555	0363	1
ROBERTS PEBBLE V	1LT	0-1315728	0168	1
ROBERTS PERCY S	CPT	0-1002107	1157	1
ROBERTS QUENTIN R	CPT	0-1018495	1045	2
ROBERTS RAYMOND E	CW3	W-2141429	1057	1
ROBERTS REX F	MAJ	0-1014097	0959	1
ROBERTS RICHARD L	CPT	0-0174436	0654	3
ROBERTS RICHARD L	1LT	0-2035373	0146	2
ROBERTS RICHARD T	LTC	0-0889685	0868	1
ROBERTS ROBERT D	LTC	0-0941978	0266	1
ROBERTS ROBERT H	LTC	0-1826059	1268	1
ROBERTS ROLAND H	2LT	0-0538925	0845	2
ROBERTS RONALD J	COL	0-1115084	0768	1
ROBERTS ROSCOE L	LTC	0-0276073	1164	3
ROBERTS RUPERT J	MAJ	0-1995041	0855	2
ROBERTS SAMUEL L	MAJ	0-0451383	0860	1
ROBERTS SAMUEL N	CW2	W-2144927	0157	1
ROBERTS SIDNEY E JR	LTC	0-1101636	0363	1
ROBERTS SIDNEY J	1LT	0-1994837	0745	2
ROBERTS STANLEY J	MAJ	0-0105757	0150	3
ROBERTS THEODORE J	LTC	0-0343363	1160	1
ROBERTS THOMAS C	CPT	0-0452475	1144	2
ROBERTS THOMAS H	LTC	0-1560059	0761	1
ROBERTS THOMAS J	MAJ	0-2028629	0265	1
ROBERTS THOMAS L	CPT	0-0331880	0346	2
ROBERTS THOMAS N	MAJ	0-0121846	0-53	3
ROBERTS THOMAS O	LTC	0-0909497	0762	1
ROBERTS WALTER C	COL	0-0156786	0959	1
ROBERTS WALTER J	WO1	W-2102287	0344	2
ROBERTS WALTER W	CW2	W-3150793	0965	1
ROBERTS WILEY L	CPT	0-2025254	0857	1
ROBERTS WILLIAM	MAJ	0-0325747	0153	1
ROBERTS WILLIAM A	1LT	0-1535268	1044	2
ROBERTS WILLIAM C	LTC	0-0274007	0467	3
ROBERTS WILLIAM E	B G	0-0233906	0258	3
ROBERTS WILLIAM G	MAJ	0-1924534	0563	1
ROBERTS WILLIAM J	CPT	0-0502706	1147	1
ROBERTS WILLIAM P	LTC	0-0222460	0358	3
ROBERTS WILLIAM R	LTC	0-0302926	0767	3
ROBERTS WILLIAM T	1LT	0-0531135	1045	2
ROBERTS WILLIAM W	CW3	RW-2206135	1065	1
ROBERTS WOODROW A	CW3	W-2148882	0363	1
ROBERTSON ALAN G	LTC	0-1998454	1162	1
ROBERTSON ALBERT W	LTC	0-0370706	0960	1
ROBERTSON ALFRED P	LTC	0-0247936	1058	1
ROBERTSON ANDREW C	CPT	0-1283491	1154	1
ROBERTSON ANDREW G	CPT	0-1256259	1146	2
ROBERTSON CHARLES A	LTC	0-0275816	0564	3
ROBERTSON CHARLES C	LTC	0-1316588	0166	1
ROBERTSON CHARLES M	MAJ	0-1312798	0447	2
ROBERTSON CHARLES W	CW3	W-2147482	1162	1
ROBERTSON CHESTER B	COL	0-0350788	0760	1
ROBERTSON CLARE E	WO1	W-2134507	1045	2
ROBERTSON DELLA M	2LT	N-0701723	0731	1
ROBERTSON DICKSON	1LT	0-0167734	0660	3
ROBERTSON DON	1LT	0-0402029	0344	2
ROBERTSON DON O C C	LTC	0-0239529	0446	2
ROBERTSON DONALD R	LTC	0-0217053	0958	3
ROBERTSON DOUGLAS A	COL	0-0169705	0161	3
ROBERTSON DURWOOD W	1LT	0-0405258	0746	2
ROBERTSON EARL A	MAJ	0-0299848	1064	1
ROBERTSON ELGAN C	B G	0-0100407	1149	3
ROBERTSON ELGIN G	MAJ	0-0471391	0356	1
ROBERTSON ERNEST O	MAJ	0-0949168	1262	1
ROBERTSON ERVIN E	MAJ	0-0887390	0561	1
ROBERTSON EVERETT L	LTC	0-1287065	0959	1
ROBERTSON F G	CPT	0-0377758	1147	2

NAME	GRADE	SVC NO	DATE RET MO YR	RET CODE
ROBERTSON FRANCIS E	LTC	0-1051344	0264	1
ROBERTSON FRANCIS M	MAJ	0-1038273	0963	1
ROBERTSON FRANK D	MAJ	0-0355656	0345	2
ROBERTSON GARLAND R	1LT	0-2207643	0253	2
ROBERTSON GENE	MAJ	0-2283834	0463	1
ROBERTSON GEORGE C	MAJ	0-0450604	0658	1
ROBERTSON GEORGE H	COL	0-0450475	0560	1
ROBERTSON GORDON L	LTC	0-0215580	1046	2
ROBERTSON HAROLD D	CPT	0-1685623	0165	1
ROBERTSON HARRY B	MAJ	0-0491159	0944	2
ROBERTSON HARRY H	LTC	0-0425484	0960	1
ROBERTSON HARRY L	WO1	W-2119561	0848	2
ROBERTSON HAYWOOD	CPT	0-0948327	0859	1
ROBERTSON IRWIN J	LTC	0-0175154	0462	3
ROBERTSON IVIE M	CW3	W-2146272	0366	1
ROBERTSON JAMES A	LTC	0-1640869	0866	1
ROBERTSON JAMES B JR	COL	0-0196886	0163	3
ROBERTSON JAMES C	CPT	0-1700842	0446	2
ROBERTSON JAMES C	WO1	W-2119463	1146	1
ROBERTSON JAMES G JR	CPT	0-0482186	0546	2
ROBERTSON JAMES J	MAJ	0-0283672	0168	3
ROBERTSON JAMES M	MAJ	0-2038875	0759	1
ROBERTSON JAMES R	CPT	0-1170538	0947	2
ROBERTSON JEROME R	CPT	0-0987291	1061	1
ROBERTSON JOE V	MAJ	0-1018583	0157	1
ROBERTSON JOEL C	LTC	0-0280643	0968	3
ROBERTSON JOEL P	CW2	W-2152124	0158	2
ROBERTSON JOHN C	CPT	0-0466931	0744	2
ROBERTSON JOHN D	MAJ	0-1897721	0265	1
ROBERTSON JOHN G	LTC	0-0331849	0466	3
ROBERTSON JOHN O JR	LTC	0-1180317	0163	1
ROBERTSON JOHN R	LTC	0-0371533	0561	1
ROBERTSON JOHN R	MAJ	0-1172623	0662	1
ROBERTSON JOSEPH L	CW3	W-2151776	1061	1
ROBERTSON LAWRENCE D	CW2	W-2145696	0960	1
ROBERTSON LORRAINE G	MAJ	N-0761198	0967	1
ROBERTSON LYLE J	COL	0-0341360	0161	1
ROBERTSON MARSHALL J	CPT	0-0450509	0246	2
ROBERTSON OLIVER W	MAJ	0-0956836	1062	1
ROBERTSON PHILLIP J	CPT	0-1552589	0562	1
ROBERTSON PORT G	CPT	0-0353886	1045	2
ROBERTSON RALPH H	MAJ	0-2263401	0865	1
ROBERTSON RAYMOND	MAJ	0-1596783	1058	1
ROBERTSON RICHARD T	MAJ	0-1102015	1061	1
ROBERTSON ROBERT C	COL	0-0121896	0859	3
ROBERTSON ROBERT L	COL	0-0452864	0457	1
ROBERTSON RUTH O	MAJ	N-0785118	1064	2
ROBERTSON SAMUEL V	2LT	0-1290816	0344	2
ROBERTSON STANLEY	CPT	0-1794858	0247	2
ROBERTSON SYDENHAM B	CPT	0-1648115	1046	2
ROBERTSON THOMAS	CW3	W-2141430	0659	1
ROBERTSON THOMAS V	MAJ	0-1794859	0361	1
ROBERTSON TUCK M	CW3	W-2145838	0656	1
ROBERTSON VICTOR M	LTC	0-0220939	0356	1
ROBERTSON VIVIAN D	LTC	0-0286114	0661	3
ROBERTSON WILLIAM	CW3	W-2148360	0567	1
ROBERTSON WILLIAM B	1LT	0-0512869	0145	2
ROBERTSON WILLIAM B	1LT	0-2003618	0753	2
ROBERTSON WILLIAM J	LTC	0-0913087	0966	3
ROBERTSON WILLIAM J	LTC	0-1325239	1061	1
ROBERTSON WILLIAM JR	MAJ	0-0135716	0959	3
ROBERTSON WILLIAM M	CPT	0-0131132	0157	3
ROBERTUS HENRY JR	MAJ	0-0362463	0261	1
ROBEY BENJAMIN F JR	CW3	W-2113941	0562	1
ROBEY JOHN M	CW2	W-2135177	0 55	2
ROBEYSEK JAMES W	LTC	0-1101188	1160	1
ROBICHAUD ALBERT	LTC	0-2045268	1165	1
ROBICHAUD PHILIP A	CW3	W-2208842	0966	1
ROBICHAUD ROGER E	CPT	0-4010768	0266	1
ROBICHEAUX LAWRENC	MAJ	0-1180689	0562	1
ROBICHEAUX MABLE M	1LT	N-0745299	0949	2
ROBIDOUX EUGENE J	CPT	0-1107079	1047	2
ROBIE EVERTT M	LTC	0-0378308	1060	1
ROBIE THEDOORE R	MAJ	0-0466530	1143	2
ROBIESON FRANK W	MAJ	0-0194342	1054	3

NAME	GRADE	SVC NO	DATE RET MO YR	RET CODE
ROBIN HARRY J	MAJ	0-1937449	0768	1
ROBINETT CLIFTON H	MAJ	0-0149292	1150	3
ROBINETTE CHARLES	1LT	0-[illegible]648116	0948	1
ROBINETTE CHARLES K	CW2	W-2146140	0855	1
ROBINETTE DELMAS D	LTC	0-0354301	0358	1
ROBINETTE ELMER R	MAJ	0-1181431	0868	3
ROBINETTE GLENDON H	CW4	W-2145066	0665	2
ROBINETTE HAROLD L	CW3	W-2149023	1262	1
ROBINETTE HERBAL E	LTC	0-0477097	1051	1
ROBINETTE JAMES W	MAJ	0-1342300	0863	1
ROBINETTE JOE H	CPT	0-0511189	0346	1
ROBINS FOYE C	MAJ	0-1336825	1164	1
ROBINS LEON D	CW2	W-2210812	0363	1
ROBINS ROBERT F	1LT	0-2017590	0763	2
ROBINS WILLIAM E	LTC	0-0471314	1164	3
ROBINSON ADRAIN M	LTC	0-0309386	0247	2
ROBINSON ALBERT E	CPT	0-0109250	1131	1
ROBINSON ALBERT F	MAJ	0-1881566	0167	1
ROBINSON ALBERT L	CPT	0-1059607	0447	2
ROBINSON ALBERT P	CW3	W-2143360	0959	1
ROBINSON ALBERT S	2LT	0-1594430	0944	2
ROBINSON ALFRED A	COL	0-0298499	0852	1
ROBINSON ALFRED V	MAJ	0-0443702	0750	1
ROBINSON ANNIE L	2LT	N-0727726	0246	1
ROBINSON ANSON F	COL	0-0161708	0648	3
ROBINSON ARTHUR C	MAJ	0-1549365	0161	1
ROBINSON B C	LTC	0-0282871	0956	3
ROBINSON BEN B	COL	0-0210681	0155	3
ROBINSON BESTOR	COL	0-0900111	0258	3
ROBINSON BEULAH R	1LT	N-0702707	1146	1
ROBINSON BILL A	MAJ	0-2265434	0767	1
ROBINSON BOGGS A	LTC	0-0313922	1065	1
ROBINSON CECIL W	LTC	0-0443156	0562	1
ROBINSON CHARLES M	LTC	0-0524330	0466	3
ROBINSON CHARLES O	LTC	0-0153526	0951	3
ROBINSON CHARLES S	LTC	0-0147047	0152	3
ROBINSON CHARLES W	CPT	0-1894817	0351	2
ROBINSON CHARLEY B	LTC	0-0360068	0259	3
ROBINSON CLIFFORD E	CPT	0-1104371	0852	1
ROBINSON DAVIS	LTC	0-1583570	1160	1
ROBINSON DAVID S	CW2	W-2144625	0263	1
ROBINSON DOROTHY E	MAJ	N-0741289	1264	3
ROBINSON EDGAR L	LTC	0-2023594	0163	1
ROBINSON EDNA L	2LT	N-0777362	0846	1
ROBINSON EDWARD E	COL	0-0275267	0458	3
ROBINSON ELMER	LTC	0-1634266	0760	1
ROBINSON ELMER C	1LT	0-1171332	0645	2
ROBINSON ERNEST B	CPT	0-0383810	0346	2
ROBINSON ERNEST B	CPT	0-1173054	0447	1
ROBINSON EUGENE L	1LT	0-1185124	0845	2
ROBINSON EVERT A	CPT	0-1053321	0446	2
ROBINSON FRANK E	MAJ	0-0167006	0156	3
ROBINSON FRED	LTC	0-0359321	0764	3
ROBINSON FRED E	CW3	W-2141939	1159	1
ROBINSON FRED P JR	LTC	0-0271901	0968	3
ROBINSON FREDERICK	LTC	0-0282934	0467	3
ROBINSON GENE L	2LT	0-1999309	0945	2
ROBINSON GEORGE D	1LT	0-0425442	1043	2
ROBINSON GEORGE H	LTC	0-0913474	0266	3
ROBINSON GEROLD D	1LT	0-1031512	0346	2
ROBINSON HAMILTON	COL	0-0274008	0868	3
ROBINSON HAROLD E	LTC	0-1102940	0658	1
ROBINSON HAROLD P	LTC	0-0364339	0854	1
ROBINSON HARRY H	MAJ	0-0133442	1159	3
ROBINSON HARRY W	MAJ	0-2203038	0766	1
ROBINSON HENRY A	COL	0-0186377	0547	2
ROBINSON HENSON L	COL	0-0178720	1056	3
ROBINSON HERBERT E	LTC	0-1554262	1055	1
ROBINSON HERBERT O	COL	0-0184201	0555	3
ROBINSON HOWARD A	CW2	W-2146532	0967	1
ROBINSON HUBERT F	CW2	W-2152567	1160	1
ROBINSON HUBERT R	CW2	W-2117939	0753	1
ROBINSON HUGHES A	MAJ	0-0402437	0847	2
ROBINSON IVAN E	LTC	0-1894718	0863	1
ROBINSON IVAN E	MAJ	0-2020208	1060	1

NAME	GRADE	SVC NO	DATE RET MO YR	RET CODE
ROBINSON JACK S	CPT	0-0486604	0653	1
ROBINSON JAMES H	LTC	0-1062627	1166	2
ROBINSON JAMES H JR	1LT	0-1017006	0646	2
ROBINSON JAMES W	MAJ	0-0323890	0546	2
ROBINSON JOEL W	CPT	0-1315547	0647	2
ROBINSON JOHN A	1LT	0-1015389	1144	2
ROBINSON JOHN C	LTC	0-0449468	0663	1
ROBINSON JOHN H	CPT	0-1011205	1047	1
ROBINSON JOHN J	MAJ	0-0888208	0647	2
ROBINSON JOHN M	CW4	W-2110416	0554	1
ROBINSON JOHN T	LTC	0-1695675	0761	1
ROBINSON JOHNSTON	MAJ	0-0988327	0258	1
ROBINSON JOSEPH D JR	CW3	W-2203662	1068	1
ROBINSON JOSEPH G	1LT	0-0499445	0553	1
ROBINSON JOSEPH M	LTC	0-0101402	1053	3
ROBINSON KENNETH A	COL	0-0231490	0963	3
ROBINSON KERNEY L	CW2	W-2148808	0358	1
ROBINSON LASTER E	CW2	W-2146573	1057	1
ROBINSON LAURENCE E	2LT	0-1045223	1045	2
ROBINSON LEON E	COL	0-0279414	1057	3
ROBINSON LEONARD R	LTC	0-0361770	0657	1
ROBINSON LESTER T	1LT	0-1308002	0745	2
ROBINSON LEWIS H	MAJ	0-2263286	0264	1
ROBINSON LLOYD L	MAJ	0-0278861	1158	3
ROBINSON LUTHER E	CW3	W-2205778	1165	1
ROBINSON MACK L	CW2	W-2210515	0666	1
ROBINSON MARY B	CPT	N-0700291	1045	1
ROBINSON MELVIN C	MAJ	0-1180692	1054	1
ROBINSON MICHAEL T	CPT	0-1826174	0862	2
ROBINSON MORDECAI L	LTC	0-0249279	0262	3
ROBINSON NANCY	CPT	L-0115761	0263	1
ROBINSON NORMAN A	LTC	0-0777023	0867	1
ROBINSON NORMAN F	LTC	0-0253597	0259	3
ROBINSON OLIVER K	CPT	0-0297975	1144	2
ROBINSON OLIVER T	LTC	0-0514480	0164	1
ROBINSON PAUL V	LTC	0-0425556	0462	3
ROBINSON PHILIP E	LTC	0-1315619	0763	1
ROBINSON RALPH E	CPT	0-0505477	0553	1
ROBINSON RALPH R	MAJ	0-1307120	0857	2
ROBINSON RALPH R	CW3	W-2144411	1264	1
ROBINSON RANDOLPH	MAJ	0-0270325	1263	3
ROBINSON RICHARD A	LTC	0-1103891	0861	1
ROBINSON RICHARD C	MAJ	0-0119587	1057	3
ROBINSON RICHARD W	COL	0-0214075	0163	3
ROBINSON ROBERT A JR	COL	0-0465391	0868	1
ROBINSON ROBERT H	CPT	0-0390210	0845	2
ROBINSON ROBERT H	CPT	0-2262980	0561	1
ROBINSON ROBERT L JR	MAJ	0-0843007	0568	1
ROBINSON ROBERT M	MAJ	0-0995145	0568	1
ROBINSON ROLAND W	LTC	0-0363215	0957	2
ROBINSON RONALD W	1LT	0-1167184	0645	2
ROBINSON SAMMIE L JR	LTC	0-0558600	1264	1
ROBINSON SAMUEL J	LTC	0-0264346	0966	3
ROBINSON SAMUEL J	LTC	0-1109625	1162	1
ROBINSON SETH B JR	COL	0-0221530	0163	3
ROBINSON SHERRILL E	MAJ	0-0185407	0953	3
ROBINSON SPENCER J	LTC	0-0151225	0857	3
ROBINSON THOMAS T	CPT	0-0268517	0566	3
ROBINSON TIMOTHY E	COL	0-0299849	0661	1
ROBINSON VINCENT H	1LT	0-1047746	0845	2
ROBINSON VIRGIL B	MAJ	0-1060614	0561	1
ROBINSON VIRGIL E	MAJ	0-1051345	0366	1
ROBINSON VIVIAN F	MAJ	N-0736416	0168	1
ROBINSON WALTER	WO1	W-2151063	1060	1
ROBINSON WALTER B	2LT	0-1581344	0643	2
ROBINSON WALTER J	MAJ	0-1577765	1160	1
ROBINSON WELD S	CPT	0-0498727	0262	2
ROBINSON WILFRED F	LTC	0-0260479	1166	3
ROBINSON WILL G	COL	0-0276227	0553	3
ROBINSON WILLIAM A	MAJ	0-0279997	1054	1
ROBINSON WILLIAM E	COL	0-0114873	0654	3
ROBINSON WILLIAM F	CPT	0-0256929	1052	3
ROBINSON WILLIAM F	CW3	W-2147238	1056	1
ROBINSON WILLIAM J	COL	0-0182744	0955	3
ROBINSON WILLIAM J	MAJ	0-0983953	0867	1

NAME	GRADE	SVC NO	DATE RET MO YR	RET CODE
ROBINSON WILLIAM R	MAJ	0-1169711	0261	1
ROBINSON WILLIAM T	CW4	W-2149266	1264	1
ROBINSON WILLIS J	1LT	0-0532285	0845	2
ROBINSON WINFORD W	CW3	W-2143490	0157	1
ROBISON FRANK P	LTC	0-0125082	1050	3
ROBISON FRED J	CPT	0-0948994	0661	1
ROBISON HERBERT V	CPT	0-4010677	0368	1
ROBISON HOSTON E	MAJ	0-1756698	0159	1
ROBISON JAMES K	LTC	0-0264549	0555	3
ROBISON JESSE H	2LT	0-1305835	0544	2
ROBISON JOHN H	CW4	W-2142944	0561	1
ROBISON JOSEPH F JR	LTC	0-0303933	0559	1
ROBISON RAY G	MAJ	0-1335358	0165	1
ROBISON THOMAS J	LTC	0-0240610	0444	2
ROBLES JOSE JR	MAJ	0-0970430	1061	1
ROBLYER OLLOS A	CPT	0-1288953	104N	2
ROBOHM JOHN F	COL	0-0127602	0154	3
ROBOHM JOHN F	LTC	0-1165443	0561	1
ROBOLD VIRGIL G	CW3	W-2146394	0959	1
ROBOTTI JOHN J	MAJ	0-1825643	0361	1
ROBSON FRANK W	LTC	0-0915169	0766	1
ROBSON GEORGE L JR	CPT	0-2300363	0765	1
ROBSON GORDON E	CPT	0-0260235	0566	3
ROBSON JAMES E	LTC	0-0399087	0758	1
ROBSON WALLACE W	MAJ	0-0402595	0647	2
ROBSON WARREN H	LTC	0-1636552	0763	1
ROBSON WILLIAM A	1LT	0-1309406	0246	2
ROBY DALE W	CPT	0-2023957	0458	2
ROBY JAMES F	LTC	0-1059256	0666	1
ROBY OLIVER C	MAJ	0-0980741	0464	1
ROCAP CHARLES F JR	LTC	0-1116741	0663	1
ROCCANOVA BERNARD	2LT	0-1645953	0445	2
ROCCHIO LOIS C	CPT	N-0702237	0546	1
ROCHE ANDREW M	CPT	0-0475131	0546	2
ROCHE FRANCIS T	CW3	W-2142194	0662	1
ROCHE JOHN J	CW2	W-2152808	0960	1
ROCHE JOSEPH F	MAJ	0-1296261	0865	1
ROCHE RICHARD B	MAJ	0-0393813	0966	1
ROCHE SIDNEY J	LTC	0-0569970	0966	1
ROCHEL EDWARD M	CW2	W-2207049	0461	1
ROCHEL HENRY J	MAJ	0-0274123	0744	2
ROCHELEAU WILFRED E	LTC	0-0287245	0456	2
ROCHESTER WILLIAM R	MAJ	0-2274852	1168	2
ROCHFORD STEPHEN H	MAJ	0-2033033	0364	1
ROCHFORD THEODORE J	MAJ	0-1903372	0162	1
ROCHMAN GEORGE H	COL	0-0299825	0962	1
ROCHNOWSKI ARTHUR R	MAJ	0-1185953	1162	1
ROCHON HAROLD R	1LT	0-1180027	0245	2
ROCHOW HAROLD E	LTC	0-0318236	0963	3
ROCK ADA F	MAJ	N-0730233	1165	1
ROCK ALBERT H	LTC	0-1035585	0263	1
ROCK FONDA F	LTC	0-0353146	0868	3
ROCK JOHN J	LTC	0-0453569	0961	1
ROCK JOHN W	LTC	0-0515707	0649	3
ROCK JOSEPH G	MAJ	0-1035995	1062	1
ROCK ROBERT F	LTC	0-1534372	0261	1
ROCK THOMAS F	1LT	0-1182949	0646	2
ROCKAFELLOW EDNA M	LTC	N-0700043	0245	1
ROCKAWAY JOHN D	COL	0-0268146	0468	3
ROCKE HERSCHEL M	1LT	0-0342452	0346	2
ROCKEFELLER CHESTER	1LT	0-1300085	0346	2
ROCKEFELLER EARL S	LTC	0-0100796	1053	3
ROCKER ROY H	CW2	W-2145501	0962	1
ROCKETT CARLTON A	CPT	0-1825257	0660	1
ROCKETT GRADY L	CW2	W-2113205	0144	2
ROCKETT RICHARD W	CW2	W-2147478	0261	1
ROCKETT THOMAS A	LTC	0-0245614	0648	3
ROCKEY CARLTON G	LTC	0-0263613	1052	2
ROCKEY FRANCIS C	LTC	0-0331239	0460	1
ROCKHILL ROBERT A	MAJ	0-0246118	1154	3
ROCKIS JOSEPH	COL	0-0331792	1159	1
ROCKNE LLOYD M	1LT	0-1183750	1045	2
ROCKOFF RICHARD M	LTC	0-0338588	0968	3
ROCKWELL ALICE A	2LT	N-0722260	0845	1
ROCKWELL CHARLES F	2LT	0-0246314	0648	3

NAME	GRADE	SVC NO	DATE RET MO YR	RET CODE
ROCKWELL DONALD L	MAJ	0-0885663	1160	1
ROCKWELL EDGAR A	CW3	W-2119223	0659	1
ROCKWELL LLOYD H	COL	0-0324566	0660	1
ROCKWELL MILTON B	LTC	0-1577766	0261	1
ROCKWELL NORMAN H	CW2	W-2148987	0859	1
ROCKWELL WILLARD F	LTC	0-0176711	0855	3
ROCKWELL WILLIAM O	MAJ	0-1951710	0466	1
ROCKWELL WILLIAM S	COL	0-0194679	0256	1
ROCKWERK LOUIS	MAJ	0-1308378	0863	1
ROCKWOOD BERT JR	CW3	W-2147218	1262	2
ROCUS JAMES T	LTC	0-1053322	0468	3
ROD HERBERT L	1LT	0-1015272	0947	2
RODAK STANLEY R	1LT	0-1308003	0446	2
RODAT WARREN K	CPT	0-1011738	1045	2
RODAWALT LEE R	MAJ	0-0959802	0466	1
RODD LAVERN E	LTC	0-1551505	0768	1
RODDA BILL T	MAJ	0-0384617	1060	1
RODDEN LEO	CW3	W-2206626	1264	1
RODDEY OTHA C	LTC	0-0104408	0854	3
RODDICK WILLIAM C	1LT	0-1291887	0852	2
RODDY FRANCIS G	COL	0-0211947	0648	3
RODDY FRANCIS J	LTC	0-0310345	0560	1
RODDY GUINDEL J	LTC	0-1634270	0460	1
RODDY THOMAS J	MAJ	0-1576560	0361	1
RODE JOHN A	MAJ	0-1313646	0957	1
RODECKER HAROLD H	COL	0-0311403	0365	3
RODEN CALVIN T	2LT	0-1287066	0744	2
RODEN CHARLES J	LTC	0-1103387	0164	1
RODEN HUGH F	MAJ	0-0135470	0-52	3
RODEN JOHN B	CW3	W-2114372	0461	2
RODENBAUGH ETHEL W	MAJ	L-0200412	0968	3
RODENBERG ELMER J	COL	0-0309707	1063	3
RODENMAYER HAROLD W	LTC	0-0362989	1160	1
RODERICK ARTHUR R	LTC	0-1550490	0565	1
RODERICK EDWARD M	MAJ	0-0225994	0863	3
RODERICK EDWARD T	MAJ	0-1686654	0764	1
RODERICK JAMES W	MAJ	0-1010279	0658	1
RODERICK JOHN L	MAJ	0-0552588	1061	1
RODES ROBERT D	LTC	0-0277788	0760	3
RODES THOMAS L	LTC	0-0197141	0547	2
RODES WILLIAM R	LTC	0-1042151	0767	1
RODEWALD ERIC E	MAJ	0-1312048	0366	1
RODGERS ALBERT I	LTC	0-1167185	0261	3
RODGERS ALLAN	MAJ	0-1555274	1159	1
RODGERS ANNIE M	1LT	N-0726234	0748	2
RODGERS ARTHUR P	MAJ	0-1540875	0767	1
RODGERS CALVIN M	COL	0-0256873	0567	3
RODGERS DAVID E	MAJ	0-0243575	0957	3
RODGERS DENNIS D	CW3	W-2142004	0156	1
RODGERS EDWARD A	LTC	0-1289143	0657	1
RODGERS FORREST G	CPT	0-0522904	1047	2
RODGERS GEORGE H	MAJ	0-1030827	0161	1
RODGERS GEORGE T	MAJ	0-1552976	1147	2
RODGERS GROVER	LTC	0-0186663	0844	2
RODGERS HARRY B	CW3	W-2145583	1165	1
RODGERS HONZIE L	LTC	0-0407750	1160	1
RODGERS JAMES	CPT	0-2035231	0250	1
RODGERS JESSE A	CW4	W-2145322	0159	1
RODGERS JOHN	CW2	W-2148334	0956	1
RODGERS JOHN E	LTC	0-1013897	0863	1
RODGERS JOHN F	LTC	0-0395315	0268	3
RODGERS JOSEPH W	CPT	0-1290481	0753	2
RODGERS KENNETH W	MAJ	0-1110769	0661	2
RODGERS LOWELL D	CW3	W-2146354	1056	1
RODGERS MARTIN H	LTC	0-1590761	0662	1
RODGERS PATRICK G	LTC	0-2029640	1263	1
RODGERS PAUL C	MAJ	0-0957432	1065	1
RODGERS PAUL L	LTC	0-0175042	0654	1
RODGERS RAYMOND A	MAJ	0-1579030	0954	1
RODGERS RICHARD M	LTC	0-5322171	1166	2
RODGERS ROBERT D	CW2	W-2210302	0765	1
RODGERS THOMAS E	LTC	0-0247278	0263	3
RODGERS TOM JR	LTC	0-1635268	0760	1
RODGERS VINCENT W	COL	0-0244372	0766	3
RODGERS WALTER F	LTC	0-1107664	0762	1

NAME	GRADE	SVC NO	DATE RET MO YR	RET CODE
RODGERS WALTER H H	CW2	W-2152645	0460	1
RODGERS WALTER I	LTC	0-0982344	0768	2
RODGERS WAYNE	CW3	W-2152479	1262	1
RODGERS WILLIAM W	LTC	0-0957254	0267	1
RODIACK ROBERT F	2LT	0-0948275	0452	2
RODIER LOUIE B	COL	0-0440767	0659	2
RODISH ANDREW	CW2	W-2115785	0448	1
RODMAN GAGE R JR	CPT	0-1323482	1047	2
RODMAN HARRY A	1LT	0-1590140	0850	2
RODMAN OLIVER W	LTC	0-1172626	1066	1
RODMAN WILEY C JR	LTC	0-0299970	1067	3
RODNEY HARRY J	MAJ	0-0109188	0539	1
RODNEY JOSEPH A	MAJ	0-0361184	1044	2
RODOSEVICH KATHERINE	1LT	N-0775055	0946	1
RODRICK EUGENE L	LTC	0-0249370	0167	3
RODRIGO AUSTIN V JR	CW3	W-2210909	0968	1
RODRIGO JOSEPH	COL	0-0247085	1065	3
RODRIGUES GEORGE	MAJ	0-1012818	1059	1
RODRIGUES VICTOR M	CW3	W-2146395	0562	1
RODRIGUEZ ALPHONSE	CW4	W-2144298	0966	1
RODRIGUEZ CARLOS E	1LT	0-0471844	0645	2
RODRIGUEZ CHARLES C	LTC	0-0275165	0158	3
RODRIGUEZ DAVID O	MAJ	0-1948817	0760	1
RODRIGUEZ EMILIO	CW3	W-2151644	0265	1
RODRIGUEZ FERNANDO E	1LT	0-0448044	1143	2
RODRIGUEZ FRANCISCO	CW3	W-2151660	1063	1
RODRIGUEZ HUMBERTO G	CPT	0-5405075	0368	1
RODRIGUEZ JOSE	MAJ	0-0243628	0951	1
RODRIGUEZ JOSE JR	MAJ	0-0985363	0464	1
RODRIGUEZ JOSE M	LTC	0-0462235	0461	3
RODRIGUEZ JOSEFINA M	MAJ	N-0726861	0363	1
RODRIGUEZ LUIS C	CW3	W-2147667	0265	1
RODRIGUEZ LUIS R	MAJ	0-1338514	0960	1
RODRIGUEZ MANUEL	CW3	W-2147469	0965	1
RODRIGUEZ OVIDIO JR	1LT	0-2028630	1053	2
RODRIGUEZ RAYMOND T	CW2	W-2107098	0851	2
RODRIGUEZ RENATO A	MAJ	0-0272165	0867	3
RODRIGUEZ SAMUEL L	COL	0-0259902	1162	3
RODRIGUEZ-GARCI MAN	CW3	W-2147499	1061	1
RODRIGUEZ-LLABR ANTO	CPT	0-0257612	0666	3
RODRIGUEZ-MOLIN RAF	LTC	0-0231483	1061	3
RODRIGUEZ-SERRA TULI	CPT	0-0166891	0554	3
RODWELL JOSEPH J	CW4	W-2114861	0265	1
ROE CHARLES H	COL	0-0137380	0649	3
ROE DENER A	CPT	0-1175292	0450	2
ROE EDWIN L	MAJ	0-0168850	0359	3
ROE JAMES B	LTC	0-0275517	1066	3
ROE JAMES V	LTC	0-1300222	0358	1
ROE JIMMIE	CW3	W-2205818	0367	1
ROE THEODORE J	CPT	0-0382415	0345	2
ROEBKE HARRISON L	LTC	0-1628384	0563	1
ROECKER RAYMOND H	MAJ	0-0971487	0962	1
ROEDE CHARLES B	LTC	0-0265175	0168	3
ROEDEL ESTELLA	1LT	N-0728480	1046	1
ROEDEL LLOYD A	MAJ	0-1315367	0861	1
ROEDER CHESTER C JR	MAJ	0-0465392	0365	1
ROEDER GEORGE W JR	CW3	W-2150279	0760	1
ROEDER HENRY J	CPT	0-5229866	1068	2
ROEDER HENRY W	CPT	0-0496583	0848	1
ROEDER WALTER L	CW2	W-3200488	1167	1
ROEDER WILLIAM E	CW3	W-2151797	1262	1
ROEDLER GEORGE R	1LT	0-1294016	0345	2
ROEDTS GEORGE H	CW2	W-2143468	1057	1
ROEGNER FLOYD O	MAJ	0-1754992	0862	1
ROEGNER KENNETH A	MAJ	0-0156933	1055	3
ROEHLEN BURCHARD G	CW3	W-2150814	0662	1
ROEHM DONALD F	2LT	0-1114279	1044	2
ROEHRIG FREDERICK	LTC	0-0112812	1046	2
ROELING LOYOLA G	LTC	0-0257789	0865	3
ROEMER BERNARD F	LTC	0-0415430	0168	3
ROEMER CHARLES T	LTC	0-0922456	0346	2
ROEMER HERBERT S	COL	0-0302756	0767	3
ROEMER JOHN R	LTC	0-0139769	0962	3
ROEMER MARGARET M	MAJ	L-0221000	0564	2
ROEMER ORLAND A	LTC	0-0259072	0261	1

NAME	GRADE	SVC NO	DATE RET MO YR	RET CODE
ROENIGK JOHN A	CPT	0-0949167	0160	2
ROEPER EDWARD J	LTC	0-0353394	0766	3
ROES TONY	CPT	0-0276690	0248	1
ROESCH JULIUS A	LTC	0-0245563	0366	3
ROESCH ROBERT E	COL	0-0163191	0861	3
ROESCH WILBER H	CPT	0-1175560	0447	2
ROESSER MILLARD H	COL	0-0414188	0166	1
ROETTGER DON F	1LT	0-0885029	0744	2
ROETTGER WALTER H	CPT	0-0962492	1060	1
ROEWERT OTTO H	1LT	0-0536794	0250	1
ROFF EARL H	CPT	0-0968509	0261	1
ROFF STANLEY R	MAJ	0-0266636	0166	3
ROGACKI ALFRED G	MAJ	0-0497526	0457	1
ROGALA MARION A	MAJ	0-2011925	0963	1
ROGALESKIE JOHN H	MAJ	0-0481643	0747	1
ROGAN FRANCIS E	COL	0-0332098	1055	1
ROGAN JAMES L	MAJ	0-1923532	0565	1
ROGAN OWEN D	1LT	0-1305650	0745	2
ROGAN WILLIAM J	MAJ	0-1638385	0858	1
ROGASKI CHESTER A	LTC	0-1286553	0664	1
ROGELL HAROLD I	LTC	0-0226383	1061	3
ROGERS ALAN J	2LT	0-0556272	0646	2
ROGERS ALBERT J	LTC	0-2010879	1165	1
ROGERS ALBERT T	CW2	W-2149267	0758	1
ROGERS ALFRED W	CW2	W-2152558	1061	1
ROGERS ALVIN L JR	1LT	0-1322267	0545	2
ROGERS ARTHUR G	COL	0-0286758	1263	3
ROGERS BEN C	MAJ	0-0122193	0756	3
ROGERS BETTY D	LTC	L-0500836	0865	2
ROGERS CARL L	CW2	W-2103377	0359	1
ROGERS CECIL B	LTC	0-0220619	1052	3
ROGERS CHARLES E	LTC	0-1648815	0662	1
ROGERS CLARENCE B	CPT	0-0135030	0857	3
ROGERS CLARENCE M	COL	0-0246371	1166	3
ROGERS CLIFFORD A	CW2	W-2150524	0859	1
ROGERS DON G	CW3	W-2203897	0467	1
ROGERS DONALD F	COL	0-0456346	0563	1
ROGERS DRAKE E	LTC	0-0386235	0962	1
ROGERS EDGAR A JR	CPT	0-1533903	0147	2
ROGERS EDWARD C	LTC	0-1280002	0958	1
ROGERS EDWARD H	CW2	W-2114446	0154	1
ROGERS EDWIN R	LTC	0-0282494	0268	3
ROGERS ELLERY R	LTC	0-1173932	0461	1
ROGERS ELMER L	LTC	0-0281309	0168	3
ROGERS EMORY S	LTC	0-0183051	0455	3
ROGERS ERLO L	1LT	0-1112398	0246	2
ROGERS EUGENE C	LTC	0-1166822	0258	1
ROGERS FAY R	CW2	W-2209343	1264	1
ROGERS FLORENTINE	2LT	N-0702521	0440	1
ROGERS FRANK A JR	1LT	0-1307078	0345	2
ROGERS GALEN A	COL	0-0316131	0966	3
ROGERS GEORGE A	MAJ	0-1330861	1163	1
ROGERS GEORGE N	1LT	0-0495581	0552	1
ROGERS GLENN W	LTC	0-1581345	1262	2
ROGERS GRACE B	CPT	N-0725318	0247	1
ROGERS GRANVILLE	MAJ	0-2053904	1159	1
ROGERS HAROLD B	CPT	0-1824916	0667	1
ROGERS HASKEL R	1LT	0-0492380	1044	2
ROGERS HENRY	LTC	0-0112662	0648	3
ROGERS HENRY H	CPT	0-0525704	1046	1
ROGERS HENRY H	LTC	0-1642519	0763	1
ROGERS HERMAN M	CW3	W-2135992	0662	1
ROGERS HOMER R	1LT	0-1015469	0446	2
ROGERS HORACE I	COL	0-0182487	0355	3
ROGERS HOWARD	MAJ	0-0516308	0448	2
ROGERS HOWARD A	WO1	W-2150074	0961	2
ROGERS HUGH R	LTC	0-0194075	0853	2
ROGERS HUNTER B	LTC	0-0246546	0264	3
ROGERS IRVIN W	CPT	0-1947069	1167	1
ROGERS JAMES A	MAJ	0-0508594	0947	2
ROGERS JAMES B	MAJ	0-1113417	0165	1
ROGERS JAMES C	MAJ	0-1321596	1060	1
ROGERS JAMES C	CW3	W-2152183	0665	1
ROGERS JAMES E	COL	0-0280049	0461	3
ROGERS JAMES F	CPT	0-0498995	1146	1

NAME	GRADE	SVC NO	DATE RET MO YR	RET CODE
ROGERS JAMES H	MAJ	0-1285503	0450	1
ROGERS JAMES L	MAJ	0-0967662	1163	1
ROGERS JAMES V JR	1LT	0-1735906	0647	2
ROGERS JANSEN H	LTC	0-1636555	1066	1
ROGERS JOE D	CPT	0-1823064	0357	1
ROGERS JOHN	CPT	0-1030296	0650	1
ROGERS JOHN E	COL	0-0168967	0960	3
ROGERS JOHN F	LTC	0-1586104	0768	3
ROGERS JOHN L	LTC	0-0450099	0163	1
ROGERS JOHN M	MAJ	0-2034829	0167	1
ROGERS JOHN T JR	CPT	0-0532114	0447	2
ROGERS JONATHAN C JR	1LT	0-0519530	1145	2
ROGERS JOSEPH E	1LT	0-0416238	0245	2
ROGERS JOSEPH V	LTC	0-0467946	0254	1
ROGERS KENT C	CPT	0-1825492	0346	2
ROGERS LANNES F	1LT	0-1042929	1044	2
ROGERS LAURENCE A	LTC	0-2044401	0761	1
ROGERS LEO K	LTC	0-1289627	0954	1
ROGERS LEON L	CW3	W-2203328	0167	1
ROGERS MARVIN C	LTC	0-0230617	0664	3
ROGERS MIKE	CW4	W-2114208	1052	1
ROGERS MILFORD J	COL	0-1786483	0368	3
ROGERS ORIN L	CPT	0-0364933	0668	3
ROGERS OTTO F JR	CPT	0-0309121	0145	2
ROGERS PAUL D	CPT	0-1639566	0146	2
ROGERS PAUL E	CPT	0-1919500	0662	1
ROGERS RALPH H	1LT	0-0206772	0251	3
ROGERS RAY J	LTC	0-0977728	0968	1
ROGERS RAYMOND L	LTC	0-0350019	0664	3
ROGERS RICHARD A	MAJ	0-0351653	0947	2
ROGERS RICHARD M	LTC	0-0949623	1067	1
ROGERS ROBERT A	MAJ	0-2021088	1264	1
ROGERS ROBERT E	MAJ	0-0972473	0661	1
ROGERS ROBERT E	MAJ	0-1881968	0367	1
ROGERS ROBERT E	MAJ	0-1941418	0267	1
ROGERS ROBERT E JR	LTC	0-0267360	1166	3
ROGERS ROBERT L	LTC	0-0165346	0261	3
ROGERS ROBERT R	CPT	0-0414087	0761	1
ROGERS ROBERT W	LTC	0-0202893	0957	3
ROGERS ROBERT W	LTC	0-0225406	0564	3
ROGERS ROBERT W	WO1	W-2107494	0745	2
ROGERS ROLAND H	MAJ	0-1041388	1266	1
ROGERS ROSCOE D	MAJ	0-1876993	1163	1
ROGERS ROY E	LTC	0-0271998	0560	1
ROGERS ROY L JR	CW2	W-2154866	0263	1
ROGERS ROYCE J	LTC	0-1586105	0762	1
ROGERS RUDOLF J	MAJ	0-1545538	0261	1
ROGERS SAMUEL	1LT	0-1696810	0144	2
ROGERS SAMUEL L	MAJ	0-0238984	0957	3
ROGERS SHIRLEY N	CPT	0-0173964	0161	3
ROGERS THOMAS E JR	LTC	0-1177164	1162	1
ROGERS THOMAS J	COL	0-0323474	0655	1
ROGERS THOMAS J	CPT	0-0914064	0146	2
ROGERS THOMAS O	LTC	0-1050442	0864	1
ROGERS THOMAS P	COL	0-0173616	1057	3
ROGERS THOMAS P	LTC	0-1322954	0267	3
ROGERS VELVIN D	MAJ	0-1049653	0357	1
ROGERS WALTER C	CPT	0-1167189	0857	1
ROGERS WALTER P	CPT	0-0492387	1049	1
ROGERS WALTER R	LTC	0-0336851	1055	1
ROGERS WAYNE S	2LT	0-0554879	0445	2
ROGERS WELDON A	CW2	W-2210030	1159	1
ROGERS WILLIAM C	COL	0-0256838	1162	1
ROGERS WILLIAM E	MAJ	0-1185774	1157	1
ROGERS WILLIAM F JR	LTC	0-1640873	0762	1
ROGERS WILLIAM J	MAJ	0-0205555	0352	3
ROGERS WILLIAM J	COL	0-0242898	0-53	1
ROGERS WILLIAM R	COL	0-0347861	0167	3
ROGERS WILLIAM S JR	CW3	W-2152306	0665	1
ROGERS WINTHROP H	COL	0-0266339	0957	2
ROGERSON DONALD J	MAJ	0-1101639	1262	1
ROGERSON GEORGE E	LTC	0-1292762	1263	1
ROGERSON WESLEY L	LTC	0-0322831	0266	3
ROGGE MYRON R	1LT	0-1170539	0445	2
ROGGE WILBUR E	CW3	W-2150795	0167	1

NAME	GRADE	SVC NO	DATE RET MO YR	RET CODE
ROGGENKAMP JOSEPH M	LTC	0-0456232	0161	1
ROGGENSTEIN CHARLES	LTC	0-1297096	0765	1
ROGINSON DAVID S	CW2	W-2150617	0361	1
ROGNEY ROGER W	CW3	W-2146697	0962	1
ROGNLIEN OYVART G	MAJ	0-0254461	0664	3
ROGNSTAD RALPH J	LTC	0-1688729	0168	1
ROGOISH DANIEL D	CPT	0-4030617	0667	1
ROGOWSKI ARTHUR A JR	LTC	0-0366502	0666	1
ROGOWSKI JULIAN J	WO1	W-2102297	0744	2
ROGOWSKI STANISLAUS	CW3	W-2118656	0760	1
ROHALY MICHAEL	CW4	W-2003008	1262	3
ROHAN WILLIAM R	LTC	0-0377269	0767	1
ROHDE GEORGE M	LTC	0-1579035	0960	1
ROHDE PAUL F	WO1	W-2124031	0661	2
ROHDE RAYMOND H	LTC	0-1115403	1064	1
ROHDE RUSSELL H	MAJ	0-2043228	0860	1
ROHLEDER GILBERT V	1LT	0-0441452	1145	2
ROHLER ALFRED I	MAJ	0-0969651	1267	1
ROHLF EDWARD L	MAJ	0-1700326	0246	2
ROHLFING ROBERT F	LTC	0-0299591	0854	1
ROHLING ARTHUR H	MAJ	0-0442669	0245	2
ROHLING EUGENE M	CW2	W-2213896	0268	1
ROHNER EUGENE A	MAJ	0-1685561	1064	1
ROHNER PRESTON E	COL	0-0260506	0367	3
ROHNER ROBERT W	MAJ	0-1043216	0160	1
ROHR FRANK	COL	0-0145925	1152	3
ROHR IGNATIUS R	CPT	0-0442732	0749	2
ROHR JOHN M	1LT	0-1311254	0745	2
ROHR NEVA I	MAJ	N-0728964	0168	1
ROHR THEODORE E	MAJ	0-1583577	0860	1
ROHRBACH RICHARD R	MAJ	0-0184642	0848	1
ROHRBACHER CLARENCE	CPT	0-0887891	0548	2
ROHRBACHER HARRY W	MAJ	0-0331962	1046	2
ROHRE STUART M	LTC	0-0234806	1057	3
ROHRER JAMES R	LTC	0-0294883	1266	3
ROHRER JAY E	CPT	0-0195332	0362	3
ROHRER KENWOOD B	COL	0-0250526	0865	3
ROHRMAN FREDERICK	LTC	0-0226292	0264	3
ROHRMOSER ROBERT	MAJ	0-2208002	1265	1
ROHRS FLORENCE S	MAJ	N-0786520	0466	1
ROHRS FRANK A	COL	0-0133449	0351	3
ROHYANS KENNETH A	MAJ	0-1305836	1064	1
ROICKI STANLEY A	CPT	0-1040462	0767	1
ROIG FRANK N	LTC	0-1012223	1060	1
ROININEN EINO K	1LT	0-1051347	0546	2
ROISTACHER ALBERT S	LTC	0-0289029	0646	2
ROISUM JEROME O	LTC	0-1845618	1162	1
ROJAS PABLO	MAJ	0-1890176	0868	1
ROJAS WILLIAM O	CW2	W-2211753	1266	1
ROJO FERNANDO S	LTC	0-1543795	0556	1
ROLAN GEORGE T	LTC	0-0225158	0459	1
ROLAND CHARLES	1LT	0-1307468	1146	1
ROLAND EUGENE S	CW4	W-2121371	0459	1
ROLAND JEAN L	1LT	M-0000753	0946	1
ROLAND VICTOR E	MAJ	0-1825062	0961	1
ROLANDER ARTHUR E	MAJ	0-0287755	0857	1
ROLF EDWARD O	CPT	0-1300386	0746	2
ROLF RAY H	MAJ	0-1291170	0954	1
ROLFE ARVIL E	LTC	0-1702987	0166	1
ROLFE RALPH E	CW2	W-2113701	0665	3
ROLFF HELEN M	CPT	N-0722124	1053	2
ROLFING HENRY W	MAJ	0-1314840	0164	1
ROLL BENJAMIN F	LTC	0-1115088	1167	1
ROLL CHARLES V	MAJ	0-0561936	1262	1
ROLL FRITA F	CPT	0-0377244	1145	2
ROLLASON RICHARD N	LTC	0-0452074	0358	2
ROLLASON SAMUEL H	CW2	W-3154252	0968	2
ROLLE JEROME O	MAJ	0-1574133	0560	1
ROLLER ARNOLD E	CPT	0-0466894	0550	1
ROLLER JOHN B	MAJ	0-0216389	1044	2
ROLLER ROBERT C	1LT	0-1316589	0646	2
ROLLINS CHARLES C JR	COL	0-0307324	0462	1
ROLLINS EDWARD W	LTC	0-0918697	1065	3
ROLLINS FISKE	LTC	0-0262466	0766	3
ROLLINS FRED G	LTC	0-0173354	0955	3

NAME	GRADE	SVC NO	DATE RET MO YR	RET CODE
ROLLINS GEORGE C J	MAJ	0-1107083	0856	1
ROLLINS HARRY W	LTC	0-1312334	0467	1
ROLLINS HELEN S	MAJ	N-0741083	0167	1
ROLLINS HERBERT R	1LT	0-0147939	0353	3
ROLLINS JACK P	1LT	0-1639568	0845	2
ROLLINS JOHN W	2LT	0-1048169	0944	2
ROLLINS JOSEPH	LTC	0-0482913	0954	1
ROLLINS LOUIS B	CPT	0-1314192	0954	1
ROLLINS MAYNARD A	MAJ	0-0504630	0854	1
ROLLINS MELVIN L	2LT	0-1011820	0344	2
ROLLINS OLIVER E	LTC	0-0342373	1060	1
ROLLINS ORVAL W	MAJ	0-1174694	0562	1
ROLLINS PAUL C	LTC	0-1324363	0866	1
ROLLINS ROBERTA F	MAJ	N-0763059	1066	3
ROLLINS WILLIAM R	LTC	0-1111336	0163	1
ROLLMAN FREDERICK	CW3	W-2147101	1263	1
ROLLSTIN GILBERT C	LTC	0-0318068	0664	3
ROLLY DOROTHY L	1LT	L-0915323	0945	2
ROLLY JOHN W	CPT	0-0488483	0647	1
ROLPH ARTHUR B	LTC	0-0361584	0960	1
ROLPH CARL J	MAJ	0-0110790	0955	3
ROLSON CARL L	1LT	0-1944795	1044	2
ROLWES BERNARD A	CPT	0-0244388	0855	3
ROM GEMINIANO	1LT	0-0890482	1047	1
ROMAINE ALLIE H	LTC	0-0310108	0646	2
ROMAINE FRANK E	CPT	0-0509705	0745	2
ROMAN ALFRED J	LTC	0-0422778	0161	1
ROMAN CHARLES E	MAJ	0-0885747	0657	1
ROMAN FORTUNATO	COL	0-0167712	1053	3
ROMAN STEPHEN J	WO1	W-2008164	0668	3
ROMANCHEK JOSEPH J	MAJ	0-2047804	0258	1
ROMANCHEK LOUISE J	LTC	N-0702892	1060	1
ROMANI LOUIS A	1LT	0-0885726	0246	2
ROMANO FRANK E	1LT	0-1000280	1044	2
ROMANO FRANK J	LTC	0-1057231	0166	1
ROMANO GEORGE	CPT	0-1543723	0246	2
ROMANO PASQUALE A	LTC	0-1045904	0964	1
ROMANO PLACIDO	1LT	0-1579037	0844	2
ROMANOFF ALEXANDER	1LT	0-2030998	1056	1
ROMANOV PAUL A	CPT	0-0507203	0845	2
ROMANOVICH SELMA R	MAJ	N-0734374	0961	2
ROMANOWSKI WILLIAM J	CPT	0-0888225	1047	2
ROMANSKI RAYMOND N	CPT	0-0976947	0851	2
ROMBACH PETER	MAJ	0-0888600	0753	1
ROME HOWARD J	CPT	0-0330383	1145	2
ROME MANUEL	1LT	0-0573161	0644	2
ROMER MAXIMILIAN	1LT	0-2046520	1044	2
ROMERO EDMUND J	MAJ	0-1021514	1157	1
ROMERO VICTOR M	CW3	W-2144440	0160	1
ROMERSBERGER RICHARD	1LT	0-0543332	0746	2
ROMEU LUIS A	LTC	0-1644713	1164	1
ROMICH NEIL G	MAJ	0-0228428	0544	2
ROMIG EVERETT A	LTC	0-0336103	1166	3
ROMINIECKI ANDREW J	LTC	0-0257071	1267	3
ROMITI ALDO S	CPT	0-0304179	1046	2
ROMM BARNET I	CPT	0-0543542	1045	2
ROMM MILTON	1LT	0-1325672	0146	2
ROMMEL SENTILE A	CPT	0-1000659	0252	2
ROMP THOMAS H	2LT	0-1542138	0466	2
ROMPOT EDWARD	LTC	0-1257593	0263	1
RONALD SIDNEY C JR	LTC	0-0302810	0467	3
RONAS JOHN S	MAJ	0-1540922	1262	1
RONCI FRANK A	1LT	0-0540242	0646	2
RONCONE EDWARD A	CW2	W-2000328	0147	2
RONDEAU EDMUND	MAJ	0-2008057	0563	1
RONDEAU JAMES C	CW4	W-2002831	0965	3
RONEY DONALD R	MAJ	0-1861667	0967	1
RONEY WALTER D	LTC	0-0288416	0463	3
RONEY WARD W	COL	0-0235727	0663	3
RONGAUS LEON F	2LT	0-1824917	1044	2
RONGEN JOHN A	1LT	0-0505265	1154	1
RONICKER FREDERICK	1LT	0-0396730	0646	2
RONING HARRY C	CW4	W-2001664	0364	3
RONINGER LOUIS E	LTC	0-0392113	0361	1
RONK RAPHAEL R	1LT	0-0445446	0245	2

NAME	GRADE	SVC NO	DATE RET MO YR	RET CODE
RONKA ENSIO K F	COL	0-0303930	0158	3
RONN SIGFRED A	MAJ	0-2007279	0965	1
RONNE ROBERT P	LTC	0-0372893	0752	2
RONNEBERG CONRAD E	LTC	0-0135325	1153	3
RONNEL ELIOT A	LTC	0-0377456	0268	3
RONNING LILY V	1LT	N-0727556	0446	1
RONNINGEN OTTO I	COL	0-0336200	0648	3
RONNOW DERRILL C	CPT	0-0453697	0245	2
RONQUILLO JOSE	CW2	W-2205697	0863	1
RONQUILLO MAXIMO C	1LT	0-1896646	0350	2
RONQUILLO TEODORO M	CPT	0-1896440	0357	2
RONSHAUSEN WILBER A	MAJ	0-0969843	0964	1
ROOD HAROLD	MAJ	0-1557779	0961	3
ROOD REGINALD S	LTC	0-0311198	0365	3
ROOF DONALD B	LTC	0-2034900	0962	1
ROOF EDWARD F	LTC	0-1109629	0862	1
ROOF ORA W JR	LTC	0-1577770	0961	1
ROOF WILLIAM J JR	MAJ	0-2007571	0960	1
ROOK ELMER D	CPT	0-0200991	1154	3
ROOKS ROBERT D	CPT	0-0348302	1165	3
ROOKS WILLIAM A	COL	0-0216137	1263	3
ROONAN JOHN J	LTC	0-0372207	0568	3
ROONEY ARTHUR E	LTC	0-0394471	0866	1
ROONEY CHARLES D	LTC	0-0419113	0460	1
ROONEY CHARLES H	CW3	W-2205231	0963	1
ROONEY DENNIS A	CPT	0-0961900	0163	1
ROONEY IRVING J JR	2LT	0-1298294	0345	2
ROONEY JOHN F	1LT	0-2047805	0745	2
ROONEY JOHN H	LTC	0-0397204	0563	2
ROONEY MARGARET A	2LT	N-0756533	0845	1
ROONEY RALPH F	MAJ	0-0404034	0163	1
ROONEY ROBERT F	LTC	0-1821916	0264	1
ROONEY ROBERT T	2LT	0-1635570	0445	2
ROONEY THOMAS C	LTC	0-2049701	1066	1
ROONEY VINCENT J	CW3	W-2102299	0557	1
ROOP DONALD R	LTC	0-0360318	0865	3
ROOP GERALD D	CW2	W-3430477	0267	1
ROOPE WILLIAM A	CW3	RW-2148070	1061	1
ROORDA HENRY M	CPT	0-0490212	0946	1
ROOS HAMPUS E	MAJ	0-0294914	0445	2
ROOS MAURICE I	2LT	0-1822907	0744	2
ROOSE CLARENCE N	MAJ	0-1054776	0265	3
ROOSEVELT ARICHIBA	LTC	0-0143128	0143	2
ROOT AMOS P	CW2	W-2110663	1149	1
ROOT CHARLES L	MAJ	0-0151045	0852	3
ROOT CHESTER L	MAJ	0-0465712	0452	2
ROOT DONALD S	MAJ	0-0137661	0252	3
ROOT ERNEST E	COL	0-0266181	0463	3
ROOT HOWARD S	CPT	0-0163728	0449	3
ROOT JAMES A	CPT	0-0417274	0744	2
ROOT JAMES H	MAJ	0-0404759	0464	1
ROOT JAMES W	CPT	0-0959546	0160	1
ROOT KARL E	MAJ	0-1639572	1058	1
ROOT LEWIS A	1LT	0-1949642	0846	2
ROOT MURPHY A	LTC	0-0257511	0867	3
ROOT NICHOLAS V	MAJ	0-4005500	0265	1
ROOT PAUL F	CW2	W-2146192	0958	1
ROOT RICHARD M	CW3	W-2152559	0863	1
ROOT ROBERT L	LTC	0-0902819	0146	2
ROOT ROBERT R	LTC	0-0400844	0466	1
ROOT RODERICK M	MAJ	0-0261342	0367	3
ROOT ROY B	LTC	0-1302527	0867	1
ROOTE JESSE T	CPT	0-0365641	0447	2
ROOTS CLYDE C	1LT	0-1111875	0447	2
ROPER ARTHUR E	CPT	0-2018574	0156	1
ROPER BENJAMIN S	LTC	0-0310091	0347	2
ROPER EDWIN	MAJ	0-1331437	0768	3
ROPER ROBERT G	CPT	0-1311931	0547	2
ROPER WILLIS W	MAJ	0-1922536	0465	2
ROQUEMORE RICHARD D	COL	0-0282162	0954	3
ROQUETTE HENRY L	LTC	0-0174804	0454	3
RORBY EBBA C A	1LT	N-0700410	0443	1
RORICK ROLAND M	1LT	0-0515575	1148	1
RORICK SHIRLEY M	LTC	0-1177619	1067	1
RORK CATHERINE	MAJ	N-0800137	0865	2

NAME	GRADE	SVC NO	DATE RET MO YR	RET CODE	NAME	GRADE	SVC NO	DATE RET MO YR	RET CODE	NAME	GRADE	SVC NO	DATE RET MO YR	RET CODE	NAME	GRADE	SVC NO	DATE RET MO YR	RET CODE
RORK PHILIP J	LTC	0-1580244	0463	1	ROSE ROBERT B	COL	0-0103668	1150	3	ROSENBLUM MEYER	MAJ	0-0352587	0466	2	ROSS ELLWOOD H	LTC	0-0250346	0566	3
RORRER WOODROW W II	1LT	0-5331225	1068	2	ROSE ROBERT J	CPT	0-0539345	0747	2	ROSENCRANZ ARTHUR	1LT	0-1592552	0845	2	ROSS ELTON [illegible]	COL	0-0313594	0147	2
ROSA ANGEL	1LT	0-0371126	0945	2	ROSE ROBERT O	CW2	W-2148137	0856	1	ROSENDAHL EDWARD E	COL	0-0458037	0766	3	ROSS ERNEST	LTC	0-0291740	0868	3
ROSA CHARLES W	CW3	W-2110009	0760	1	ROSE ROGER J	LTC	0-1821632	0162	1	ROSENECK FREDERICK	CW3	W-2146671	0763	1	ROSS EUGENE A	CPT	0-1826394	0547	2
ROSADO FRANCISCO	1LT	0-2162965	0456	3	ROSE SIDNEY	LTC	0-0279044	1056	3	ROSENFELD ABRAM H	COL	0-0213685	1163	3	ROSS EUGENE P	CW3	W-2146943	0563	1
ROSAL PAUL M	LTC	0-1101191	0365	1	ROSE STANLEY W	CW2	W-2147446	1059	1	ROSENFELD IRVING	MAJ	0-0545448	1068	2	ROSS FRANK A	CW4	W-2112139	1159	1
ROSALES BENNY	COL	0-0179150	1040	1	ROSE SYDNEY A	1LT	0-1716582	1045	2	ROSENFELD LOUIS	2LT	0-1640881	0445	2	ROSS FRANK A	CW3	W-2152283	0765	1
ROSALES JOSEPH A JR	CW3	W-2152984	1065	1	ROSE THOMAS O	LTC	0-1284402	0762	1	ROSENFELD ROBERT T	MAJ	0-0366847	0246	2	ROSS FRANK E	COL	0-0300004	0165	3
ROSAMINO PAUL H	1LT	0-3533468	0946	2	ROSE VIRGIL L	CPT	0-1300388	1047	2	ROSENFIELD ABRAHAM B	MAJ	0-0157984	0246	2	ROSS FRANK P	LTC	0-1796157	1055	1
ROSARIO ABRAHAM	MAJ	0-0475822	0154	1	ROSE WERNER J	COL	0-0225884	0962	3	ROSENGREN ROSWELL P	COL	0-0420484	0262	3	ROSS FRED F	LTC	0-0203820	0648	3
ROSARIO LUIS	MAJ	0-0423215	1057	1	ROSE WESLEY E	CW3	W-2203876	1064	1	ROSENHEIM HARRY T JR	LTC	0-0324508	0865	3	ROSS FRED J	1LT	0-1306152	1045	2
ROSBACH JACK N	2LT	0-1592549	1043	2	ROSE WILLIAM B	COL	0-0353261	0267	1	ROSENKRANS DONALD R	LTC	0-0324567	0968	3	ROSS GEORGE H	COL	0-0212356	0262	3
ROSBOROUGH JAMES C	COL	0-0179173	0155	3	ROSE WILLIAM R	CPT	0-1755913	0447	2	ROSENSTEIN JACOB J	LTC	0-0904981	0268	3	ROSS GILBERT I	COL	0-0177289	0462	3
ROSCOE ELI JR	2LT	0-1284954	0644	2	ROSE WILLIAM Y	MAJ	0-1165084	0862	1	ROSENSTOCK FRANCIS C	CW2	W-2145594	0452	1	ROSS GORDON M	MAJ	0-1285120	0447	2
ROSCOE JOSEPH P	CW3	W-2203368	0965	1	ROSE WINSLOW A	CPT	0-0287496	0457	1	ROSENTHAL ABNER H	CPT	0-1689371	0545	2	ROSS GORDON W	LTC	0-0900477	0563	1
ROSCOE VROOM W	CW4	W-2003794	1061	3	ROSEBERRY FLOYD M	1LT	0-1647675	0845	2	ROSENTHAL CARL J	CW2	W-2150680	0259	1	ROSS HAROLD B	MAJ	0-2041372	0765	1
ROSDAHL CONRAD E	CPT	0-0461519	0146	2	ROSEBOROUGH JOSEPH	CW3	W-2209339	0866	1	ROSENTHAL HARRY W JR	CPT	0-0969320	0859	2	ROSS HARRY W	MAJ	0-1796357	0660	1
ROSE ALFRED J	CW3	W-2210711	1168	1	ROSEBRAUGH REBECCA C	MAJ	N-0763121	1067	1	ROSENTHAL IRVING A	CPT	0-1683851	0544	2	ROSS HENRY F	COL	0-0307704	0661	1
ROSE BENJAMIN F	COL	0-0264769	0968	3	ROSEBRAUGH STANLEY M	MAJ	0-0218891	0559	3	ROSENTHAL JEROME B	2LT	0-1181437	0445	2	ROSS HERBERT F	CPT	0-0500154	0848	1
ROSE BOBBIE L	MAJ	0-2211468	0965	1	ROSEFIELD IRVING	LTC	0-0490436	1062	1	ROSENTHAL JOHN	LTC	0-0456304	0264	1	ROSS HERMAN	1LT	0-1289013	0545	2
ROSE BURNICE E	CW4	W-2148683	0468	1	ROSEKRANS FREDERICK	CW4	W-2110544	0267	3	ROSENTHAL LIONEL H	LTC	0-0263908	0756	3	ROSS HOWARD A	CPT	0-0461715	0646	2
ROSE CHARLES F	MAJ	0-1938070	0466	1	ROSELER HERBERT W	LTC	0-1543401	1163	1	ROSENTHAL MAURICE	CW4	W-2101078	0953	1	ROSS HUBERT W	MAJ	0-1020185	0461	1
ROSE CHARLES F	LTC	0-0338522	1066	3	ROSELL CHARLES T	LTC	0-1586112	0962	1	ROSENTRATER ROBERT E	2LT	0-1293836	0845	2	ROSS JACK	CW4	W-2145277	1167	1
ROSE CHARLES L	LTC	0-1798298	1166	1	ROSELL HENRY	1LT	0-1039623	0346	2	ROSENWALD ARTHUR W	CW2	W-2112152	0361	2	ROSS JACK J	MAJ	0-0558616	0766	1
ROSE CHARLES N JR	COL	0-0402206	0868	1	ROSELL MARTIN R	LTC	0-0283922	1265	3	ROSER ROBERT H	1LT	0-1292061	0646	2	ROSS JAMES A	MAJ	0-1167195	0561	1
ROSE CLIFFORD E	MAJ	0-1643294	0260	1	ROSELLE CLIFFORD H	CW3	W-2153133	0164	1	ROSESCO ALFRED W	LTC	0-1014847	1161	1	ROSS JAMES A JR	CPT	0-1101192	1164	3
ROSE DAVID L	1LT	0-1285311	0944	2	ROSEMAN LEO L	CPT	0-1821292	0646	2	ROSETO BENJAMIN J	LTC	0-1295943	0463	1	ROSS JAMES H	COL	0-0901972	0266	3
ROSE DEWEY W	2LT	0-2011481	1145	2	ROSEMAN REUBEN	COL	0-0449652	1168	3	ROSEVEAR WILLIAM B	COL	0-0101987	0250	3	ROSS JAMES J	LTC	0-0403379	0163	1
ROSE DONALD C	CW3	W-2147665	0664	1	ROSEMARK RICHARD I	MAJ	0-0358549	0567	3	ROSFELD EMANUEL	CW3	W-2204478	0756	1	ROSS JAMES W	COL	0-0100079	1149	1
ROSE EARL A	LTC	0-0266619	0757	3	ROSEMOND JAMES	1LT	0-2262765	1053	2	ROSHON CHARLES O JR	MAJ	0-0475935	0366	3	ROSS JAMES W	CPT	0-4031259	0666	1
ROSE EDWARD C	MG	0-0102685	0954	3	ROSEMONT BERNARD N	LTC	0-0254221	0763	3	ROSIE LOUIS O	CW2	W-2152125	0559	1	ROSS JAY H	LTC	0-0360840	0264	3
ROSE EMYLE	LTC	0-0502021	0257	1	ROSEN CHARLES	CPT	0-0514941	0545	2	ROSINETTE THURMAN W	CW2	W-2144762	0957	1	ROSS JESS	MAJ	0-0297819	0868	3
ROSE FRANCIS J	COL	0-0272741	1067	3	ROSEN CLOYCE B	LTC	0-1295605	0462	1	ROSKAM CHARLES A	CW3	W-2144434	0263	1	ROSS JOHN P	CPT	0-1573735	0958	1
ROSE FRED L	CW2	W-2209536	0961	1	ROSEN DAVID	LTC	0-0289340	0957	1	ROSKAMP HUBERT A	MAJ	0-2033658	1262	1	ROSS JOSEPH L	LTC	0-0301827	1161	3
ROSE FREDERICK	MAJ	0-0410886	1047	2	ROSEN HARRY E	LTC	0-1593812	1162	2	ROSKOPP JOHN G	2LT	0-1323175	0344	2	ROSS JOSEPH V M	CPT	0-1695284	1045	2
ROSE GEORGE E	COL	0-0175750	0360	3	ROSEN HERMAN L	CPT	0-0318408	0945	2	ROSKOSKI JOHN	1LT	0-1825259	0157	2	ROSS KENNETH P	CPT	0-0143186	0858	3
ROSE GLEN	CPT	0-0248387	0344	2	ROSEN JACK	LTC	0-1651174	0667	1	ROSKOSZKA ROMAN S	CW2	W-2151062	0658	2	ROSS LARRY M	CPT	0-5320629	0868	2
ROSE HANNIBAL C	CPT	0-0508064	0157	2	ROSEN JEROME	CPT	0-0121913	0648	3	ROSLER ROLAND R	CW3	W-2151520	0668	1	ROSS LELAND G	CW3	W-2146488	0862	1
ROSE HAROLD F	LTC	0-0323516	0646	2	ROSEN JOSEPH	MAJ	0-0321736	1267	3	ROSLUND OLIVER S	CPT	0-0330423	0262	3	ROSS LEO	LTC	0-0384867	0967	3
ROSE HARRY A	COL	0-1169057	1168	1	ROSEN JULIUS B	MAJ	0-1030929	0761	1	ROSNER ADOLPH G	MAJ	0-1288302	0152	2	ROSS LILLIAN R	2LT	N-0737610	0745	1
ROSE HORACE S	LTC	0-0423035	0765	1	ROSEN MICHAEL M	MAJ	0-0253241	0945	2	ROSNER HAROLD	2LT	0-1056214	0944	2	ROSS LIONEL E	CPT	0-0393559	0748	2
ROSE HOWARD E	1LT	0-1059045	0846	2	ROSEN MURRAY	CW3	W-2152149	0357	1	ROSNER WILLIAM P	CPT	0-1799898	0858	1	ROSS LUTHER J	COL	0-0288815	0760	1
ROSE IRVIN H	MAJ	0-0448582	0148	1	ROSEN SAMUEL C	LTC	0-0337711	1063	3	ROSNICK MANNING J	CPT	0-1683922	0145	2	ROSS MARTIN C	CW2	W-2153150	0459	1
ROSE IVAN G	CW2	W-2212424	0568	1	ROSEN SYDNEY S	LTC	0-1183405	0467	3	ROSOFF LEONARD	CPT	0-0400515	1045	2	ROSS MARVIN A	LTC	0-1170541	0258	1
ROSE JACK W	LTC	0-1825493	0663	1	ROSENBALM CARL	CW4	W-2126852	1054	1	ROSPOND ROBERT T	2LT	0-0557644	0347	2	ROSS MONETTE C	LTC	0-0310755	0558	1
ROSE JAMES P	CW3	W-3200133	1268	1	ROSENBALM JAMES L	LTC	0-2035148	0866	1	ROSQUIST ARNE E	MAJ	0-1535957	0266	1	ROSS PETER W	MAJ	0-0305886	0546	2
ROSE JO E	MAJ	0-1535819	0663	1	ROSENBAUM ALEXANDER	LTC	0-0294102	1062	3	ROSS ALEX J	1LT	0-2017243	0852	2	ROSS PHILIP R	COL	0-0245130	0967	3
ROSE JOE W	LTC	0-1552978	1060	1	ROSENBAUM CHARLES R	COL	0-0303326	1160	1	ROSS BASIL E	MAJ	0-1935078	0868	1	ROSS RALEIGH R	LTC	0-0332186	1046	2
ROSE JOHN L	LTC	0-0500463	0-53	1	ROSENBAUM FRANK W	CW2	W-2210432	0163	1	ROSS CARLOS A	LTC	0-0168746	0358	3	ROSS RICHARD A	WO1	W-2133161	1045	2
ROSE JOHN F	MAJ	0-1108278	0359	1	ROSENBAUM HAROLD D	CPT	0-0476074	0547	2	ROSS CHARLES A	MAJ	0-0523752	0347	2	ROSS RICHARD S	2LT	0-1534850	0146	2
ROSE JOHN H	MAJ	0-0109500	1145	2	ROSENBAUM JOHN A	MAJ	0-0213760	0962	3	ROSS CHARLES E	LTC	0-0176127	0961	3	ROSS ROBERT	CPT	0-1166365	0446	2
ROSE JOHN J	CPT	0-1635276	0156	1	ROSENBAUM LEONARD	CPT	0-1284026	0645	2	ROSS CHARLES F	MAJ	0-0968332	0967	1	ROSS ROBERT B	2LT	0-1111877	0645	2
ROSE JOHN M	MAJ	0-0167313	0653	3	ROSENBERG ERNEST R	COL	0-0184256	1152	3	ROSS CLARENCE E	LTC	0-0257676	0958	3	ROSS ROBERT H P	LTC	0-0277927	1055	3
ROSE JOHN O JR	LTC	0-0406024	0364	1	ROSENBERG JOSEPH W	LTC	0-1592019	0167	3	ROSS CLIFTON M	MAJ	0-0287859	1058	3	ROSS ROBERT R	CPT	0-1543796	0547	2
ROSE JOSEPH	MAJ	0-0310144	0845	2	ROSENBERG LEWIS B	LTC	0-0268872	1267	3	ROSS CONSTANCE	2LT	N-0778439	0348	1	ROSS RODERICK D	CW2	W-2152736	0161	1
ROSE JOSEPH P	LTC	0-0403516	0761	1	ROSENBERG LOUIS	MAJ	0-0109441	1135	1	ROSS COSBY F	CW2	W-2149090	0662	1	ROSS ROLLIN G	COL	0-0211735	1048	2
ROSE KEITH L	LTC	0-1845096	0761	1	ROSENBERG LOUIS I	MAJ	0-0255413	0967	3	ROSS CYRIL C	CPT	0-0287214	1057	1	ROSS ROY W	COL	0-0331231	1066	3
ROSE KYLE L	LTC	0-0250229	0263	3	ROSENBERG NATHAN	LTC	0-0336315	0654	3	ROSS CYRIL M	CW3	W-2004449	1164	1	ROSS RUDOLPH R JR	MAJ	0-1579056	0455	1
ROSE LANGTON F	WO1	W-2107649	0746	2	ROSENBERG ROBERT E	MAJ	0-1105147	0266	1	ROSS DANIEL F SR	CPT	0-1686173	1053	2	ROSS SAMUEL	LTC	0-0310437	0246	2
ROSE LENA M	CPT	N-0734736	0248	1	ROSENBERG SEYMOUR J	COL	0-0284615	1066	3	ROSS DANIEL JR	1LT	0-1878392	0355	2	ROSS THOMAS W	MAJ	0-0334206	1266	3
ROSE LEONARD J	LTC	0-0114604	0951	3	ROSENBERG VERNON L	CPT	0-1716129	0645	2	ROSS DAVID	COL	0-0355468	0960	1	ROSS VICTOR G	2LT	0-1003156	0145	2
ROSE LLEWELLYN	LTC	0-0276840	0457	1	ROSENBERGER BRUCE N	2LT	0-0517610	0944	2	ROSS DAVID C	1LT	0-2200332	0458	2	ROSS VIRGIL	CW2	W-2208930	0265	1
ROSE LUTHER I	MAJ	0-1914061	0725	1	ROSENBERGER FIETTA K	LTC	N-0722523	0462	1	ROSS DAVID W	LTC	0-1570041	0266	3	ROSS WADE H	CPT	0-2054003	1045	2
ROSE LUTHER S	WO1	W-2102301	0243	2	ROSENBERGER FINLEY O	1LT	0-1308709	1144	2	ROSS DOMINIC R	CPT	0-1018205	0947	2	ROSS WALTER E	MAJ	0-1745229	0647	2
ROSE MILTON F	MAJ	0-0228559	0465	3	ROSENBERGER HARRY A	MAJ	0-1282089	0860	1	ROSS DONALD A	MAJ	0-0349161	0967	3	ROSS WEBSTER K	MAJ	0-0227329	0162	3
ROSE MURRELL S	CW4	W-2121006	0355	1	ROSENBERGER JOSEPH O	COL	0-0228187	0565	3	ROSS DONALD J	1LT	0-0393370	114N	2	ROSS WILLARD C	LTC	0-0137299	0654	3
ROSE MYRON F	MAJ	0-1541941	0667	3	ROSENBERGER ROBERT E	MAJ	0-0955274	0563	1	ROSS DONALD R	CPT	0-0920518	0645	2	ROSS WILLIAM	1LT	0-1320185	1046	2
ROSE NORVAL R	MAJ	0-2262440	0267	1	ROSENBERGER ROBERT L	CPT	0-0290288	1068	3	ROSS DONALD R	CW3	W-2145621	0363	1	ROSS WILLIAM B	LTC	0-1324792	0761	3
ROSE OTIS B	MAJ	0-0494375	0954	1	ROSENBLATT JOSEPH K	CPT	0-1111876	0664	1	ROSS DWIGHT H	CPT	0-0238067	0446	2	ROSS WILLIAM E	LTC	0-0351952	0660	1
ROSE PAUL A	COL	0-0922248	0967	3	ROSENBLATT WILLIAM H	CPT	0-1685108	0346	2	ROSS EARL B	COL	0-0205844	0754	3	ROSS WILLIAM I	CW2	W-2122884	0762	1
ROSE PETER	LTC	0-1167193	0766	1	ROSENBLOOM PHILIP J	MAJ	0-0481677	0746	2	ROSS EDITH M	2LT	N-0772394	0445	1	ROSS WOODROW	CW4	W-2122576	0859	2
ROSE PHILIP	COL	0-0253309	0662	1	ROSENBLOOM SELIG	MAJ	0-1551301	0355	1	ROSS EDWARD H	MAJ	0-1330596	0666	3	ROSSBERG RAYMOND A	COL	0-0209818	1153	3
ROSE RALPH F	LTC	0-0923112	0865	3	ROSENBLUM CHARLES	CPT	0-0256635	1065	3	ROSS EDWARD J	1LT	0-1055432	1045	2	ROSSEAU BILLY P	CW4	W-2005890	0868	1
ROSE RICHARD A	MAJ	0-0501428	1145	2	ROSENBLUM HOWARD M	CPT	0-0447230	1045	2	ROSS EDWIN B	MAJ	0-0248880	0667	3	ROSSEN JOSEPH M	CPT	0-0498678	0545	2
ROSE RICHARD I	CPT	0-0925467	1151	2	ROSENBLUM HYMAN	LTC	0-0176959	0347	2	ROSS EDWIN F	CPT	0-1544647	0647	2	ROSSER BERNADINE	1LT	N-0784646	0747	1

NAME	GRADE	SVC NO	DATE RET MO YR	RET CODE
ROSSER BERNARD H	CPT	0-0372587	1145	2
ROSSER GLEN H	MAJ	0-1181745	1057	1
ROSSER LANDON C	COL	0-0236911	1054	3
ROSSETTE HENRY J	CPT	0-0201873	1145	1
ROSSETTER JAMES W	LTC	0-0259535	0865	3
ROSSETTI CHRISTOPHE	LTC	0-1638391	0164	1
ROSSETTI STEPHEN D	LTC	0-1295088	1066	1
ROSSI ALDO R	LTC	0-0443636	0755	1
ROSSI HAROLD F	CPT	0-1306321	0746	2
ROSSI MARY M	CPT	N-0720093	0546	1
ROSSI NEIL J	CW3	W-2147519	0862	1
ROSSI RALPH A	CPT	0-0497726	0446	2
ROSSIO FRANK	CPT	0-0498102	0352	1
ROSSITER RUSSELL F	CPT	0-1312049	0848	2
ROSSITTO ANTHONY F	CPT	0-0369627	0343	2
ROSSKOPF JOHN K	LTC	0-1046251	1161	1
ROSSKOPF JOHN W	COL	0-0174206	0657	1
ROSSLOW ALWIN F	LTC	0-0206264	0263	3
ROSSLOW FRED S	1LT	0-1313134	0845	2
ROSSMAN BERNARD	CPT	0-0441419	0945	2
ROSSMAN FRANK E	LTC	0-0220685	0161	3
ROSSMAN HENRY C JR	MAJ	0-0370943	0945	2
ROSSNAGEL FREDERICK	LTC	0-1648463	0663	1
ROSSNAGEL JOHN M	COL	0-0364936	0765	1
ROSSON JULION C JR	CPT	0-1648464	1159	1
ROSSON SAMUEL I	LTC	0-0248388	0745	2
ROSSOW BENJAMIN O	COL	0-0239101	0166	3
ROSSOW DOMINIC	CPT	0-0971746	0961	2
ROST CECIL I	LTC	0-1326171	0366	1
ROST CLYDE J	CW4	W-2146416	1069	1
ROSTEN HERBERT	LTC	0-1945930	0662	1
ROSTET WILHO W	LTC	0-0479053	1166	3
ROSTON MARK A	1LT	0-0536690	0246	2
ROSWELL KENNETH E	LTC	0-0302522	1167	3
ROSWOLD ROBERT E	CW2	W-2152775	0961	1
ROSZKOWSKI JOSEPH W	CW2	W-2141434	1054	1
ROTCHFORD FREDERICK	CW2	W-2149348	0561	1
ROTCHFORD HENRY M	LTC	0-1894983	0165	3
ROTELL RELLA T	1LT	N-0797575	0648	1
ROTH ADOLPH J	WO1	W-2128423	0347	1
ROTH ADOLPH R	LTC	0-0513908	0865	3
ROTH ALFRED J	LTC	0-1169714	1163	1
ROTH ARTHUR I	LTC	0-0234893	0162	3
ROTH CARROLL W	LTC	0-0246347	1166	3
ROTH CHARLES H	MAJ	0-0127593	0649	3
ROTH CLEMENT E JR	MAJ	0-0982216	0568	1
ROTH DALE E	MAJ	0-0263014	0446	2
ROTH DANIEL B	MAJ	0-0356291	0745	2
ROTH DAVID A	1LT	0-1744894	1045	2
ROTH EDWARD	LTC	0-1310880	1062	1
ROTH ERGAN V	MAJ	0-1061842	0562	1
ROTH EUGENE	COL	0-0299374	1066	3
ROTH GEORGE H	1LT	0-1794862	0145	2
ROTH GEORGE R	LTC	0-0359909	0461	1
ROTH HAROLD R	LTC	0-1316513	1063	1
ROTH HAROLD W	CPT	0-1745543	0646	2
ROTH HENRY J	1LT	0-1546403	0346	2
ROTH HERMAN M	COL	0-0331991	0168	3
ROTH HOWARD E	2LT	0-1293838	0145	2
ROTH JAMES F	1LT	0-0426033	0744	2
ROTH JOSEPH P	2LT	0-1015859	0445	2
ROTH KENNETH L	MAJ	0-4006984	0466	1
ROTH LAWRENCE A	CW3	RW-2152423	0566	1
ROTH MAX	LTC	0-0315410	0449	1
ROTH MERALL	CPT	0-0422622	0648	2
ROTH MICHAEL M	LTC	0-0380690	0564	3
ROTH MILTON	LTC	0-1001453	0168	3
ROTH MORTON A	LTC	0-2026404	0168	3
ROTH ROBERT E	LTC	0-1165668	0161	1
ROTH RUBEN	WO1	W-2123800	0850	2
ROTH SIGMUND	LTC	0-1999267	0562	2
ROTH VERNAL G L	LTC	0-0389443	0865	2
ROTH WAYNE W	CW2	W-2210074	0963	1
ROTH WILLIAM A	WO1	W-2130925	1045	2
ROTH WILLIAM E	CPT	0-0201823	0650	3

NAME	GRADE	SVC NO	DATE RET MO YR	RET CODE
ROTHE CHARLES R	MAJ	0-1055960	0766	3
ROTHE MARSCHAL D	LTC	0-0147645	0456	3
ROTHE VINCENT L	MAJ	0-1182695	1058	1
ROTHERT PAUL P	LTC	0-0298774	1064	1
ROTHFEDER JOSEPH L	CPT	0-0471213	0546	2
ROTHGEB EDWIN E	CPT	0-0236938	0964	3
ROTHMAN ARTHUR F	CPT	0-1584826	0655	1
ROTHMAN BERNARD M	MAJ	0-0453024	0746	2
ROTHMAN DAVID	COL	0-0398936	0666	3
ROTHMAN HERMAN	CPT	0-1690473	0146	2
ROTHMAN HYMAN	1LT	0-0499226	0543	2
ROTHMAN MILTON M	LTC	0-2019509	1266	1
ROTHMAN SANFORD	CPT	0-0244180	1045	2
ROTHNER JACOBY T	MAJ	0-0232354	0962	3
ROTHNIE JAMES B	COL	0-0181896	1057	3
ROTHROCK HUBERT D	LTC	0-0252602	0960	3
ROTHROCK JESSE	CW4	W-2148810	1268	1
ROTHROCK KENNETH M	MAJ	0-0277701	0864	3
ROTHROCK PHILIP W	CPT	0-0411231	0645	2
ROTHROCK ROBERT W	COL	0-0494576	0550	2
ROTHROCK WILLIAM G	LTC	0-1011891	0464	1
ROTHSCHILD BERNARD W	1LT	0-1535071	0146	2
ROTHSCHILD RICHARD	MAJ	0-0925749	1162	1
ROTHSEID MAURICE	CPT	0-1298600	0845	2
ROTHSTEIN ISADORE	MAJ	0-0336067	1045	2
ROTHWELL CLIFTON J	MAJ	0-0484395	0-53	1
ROTHWELL RALPH K	MAJ	0-1014155	0963	1
ROTHWELL STUART C	1LT	0-1173059	0444	2
ROTHWELL WALTER H	LTC	0-0957118	0667	1
ROTKOW MAURICE J	CPT	0-1700368	0446	2
ROTONI ROGER J	CPT	0-1290482	1047	2
ROTTENBERG MARVIN	LTC	0-1305319	0762	1
ROTTNER JOHN S G	COL	0-0345534	0467	3
ROTWEIN ABE A	1LT	0-1166824	1044	2
ROTZ SOLOMON G	CPT	0-0475847	0154	1
ROUDABUSH LESTER S	LTC	0-1304272	0363	1
ROUDAKOFF PAUL P	LTC	0-0918559	0168	3
ROUDEBUSH GEORGE JR	MAJ	0-1183608	0461	1
ROUFFY FERNAND E	MAJ	0-0184106	0445	2
ROUGAS JON N	1LT	0-1011118	0645	2
ROUGH JOSEPH M	MAJ	0-1649929	0664	1
ROUGHAN MARTIN P	CW2	W-2144761	0559	1
ROUGHSEDGE WALTER L	COL	0-2044395	0764	2
ROUILLE CHARLES V	CW4	W-2145503	0160	1
ROULEAU JOHN K	LTC	0-0251608	0167	3
ROUND JAMES H	1LT	0-0444121	1046	2
ROUNDS ARVIN O	CPT	0-0102226	0752	3
ROUNDS DALE G	WO1	W-2126120	0444	2
ROUNDS DAVID E	LTC	0-1644026	0667	3
ROUNDS FRANCIS E	CPT	0-1308549	0762	1
ROUNDS GAIL S	1LT	0-1825260	0245	2
ROUNDS JACK S	MAJ	0-017 -88	0861	3
ROUNDS PAUL H	CW3	W-2152[illegible]14	0165	1
ROUNDY PAUL H	LTC	0-1185464	0966	1
ROUNDY WILLIAM D	CW3	RW-2207601	0966	1
ROUNER THOMAS J	COL	0-0240077	1158	3
ROUNSAVALL CLYDE M	MAJ	0-1176180	0561	1
ROUNSEVILLE HOWARD W	1LT	0-1165314	0446	2
ROUNTREE JAMES R	CPT	0-0373676	0645	2
ROUNTREE LEWIS G	LTC	0-1309838	0562	1
ROUNTREE MCIVER	LTC	0-0305057	0263	1
ROUNTREE RALPH R	2LT	0-1299116	0145	2
ROUNTREE WALTER S	LTC	0-0234661	0161	3
ROURKE JAMES L	MAJ	0-0371630	0163	1
ROUS LOUIS	LTC	0-1641747	0767	3
ROUSE CHARLES A	LTC	0-1306473	0263	1
ROUSE EDWARD B JR	LTC	0-0311342	0861	2
ROUSE ELWOOD T	COL	0-0328791	0360	1
ROUSE GLENNIE L	MAJ	N-0765644	1068	1
ROUSE HAROLD A	MAJ	0-1638395	0457	1
ROUSE HENRY F	LTC	0-0405512	0261	1
ROUSE HERMAN L	MAJ	0-1056215	0256	1
ROUSE HOWARD J	COL	0-0235030	0648	3
ROUSE JAMES W H	COL	0-0291502	0467	3
ROUSE JERRY E	COL	0-0339275	1061	1

NAME	GRADE	SVC NO	DATE RET MO YR	RET CODE
ROUSE JOHN A	LTC	0-0200870	1056	3
ROUSE JOHN J	CPT	0-0270295	0445	2
ROUSE MILFORD E	CPT	0-0443411	0658	1
ROUSE RALPH E	CW2	W-2214875	0267	1
ROUSE WALTER J	CPT	0-0503047	1046	1
ROUSE WAYNE W	MAJ	0-0455266	1060	1
ROUSE WILLIAM V	MAJ	0-1576586	0254	1
ROUSER RICHARD F	CW4	W-2150581	0764	1
ROUSER VELMA M C	1LT	N-0701920	0542	1
ROUSH CALVIN T	LTC	0-1291013	0761	1
ROUSH DEFOREST R	COL	0-0264430	0760	3
ROUSH DONALD E	MAJ	0-1111880	1264	1
ROUSH GARY W	LTC	0-0444420	0662	1
ROUSH GEORGE W	1LT	0-1292235	0845	2
ROUSH HOWARD W	LTC	0-1258762	1060	1
ROUSH JEAROLD S	CPT	0-0886927	1045	2
ROUSH JOHN V JR	LTC	0-1822462	1163	1
ROUSH JOHN W	MAJ	0-1320196	0262	1
ROUSH KENNETH W	MAJ	0-1549063	0161	1
ROUSH ROBERT W	CW4	W-2131797	0862	2
ROUSH SAMUEL F	CPT	0-0415711	0444	2
ROUSSEAU CECIL	LTC	0-1949644	0765	1
ROUSSEAU GENARO W	MAJ	0-0365018	0847	2
ROUSSEAU JACQUES M	CW3	W-2112558	0855	1
ROUSSEAU SAMUEL D JR	LTC	0-0337533	0760	1
ROUSSEAU WALTER S	LTC	0-0382412	1160	1
ROUTE HOWARD S	MAJ	0-1184580	0165	1
ROUTEN EUGENE V	LTC	0-1325706	1262	1
ROUTH ROSS H	B G	0-0287602	1065	1
ROUTSON CLARENCE E	CPT	0-1310765	0564	1
ROUTT RAYMOND J	CPT	0-2011219	0457	1
ROUTZAHN CHARLES O	LTC	0-1645535	0562	1
ROUTZOHN NORMAN E	COL	0-0299129	0862	3
ROUX ERNEST V	1LT	0-1896831	0861	1
ROUZIE THOMAS J	COL	0-0254145	0158	3
ROVANSEK JOSEPH S	LTC	0-0451390	0258	1
ROVIN MAURICE E	COL	0-0129244	0648	3
ROVNER EDWARD	2LT	0-1177620	0646	2
ROVNER MIAH H	1LT	0-0471301	1043	2
ROVZAR ROBERT R	CPT	0-0409861	1045	2
ROW ANDREW W JR	CPT	0-0408453	0846	2
ROWAN CLAUDE P	COL	0-0151087	0359	3
ROWAN DONALD W	CPT	0-0117936	0857	3
ROWAN FRANK E	CW3	W-2213910	0967	1
ROWAN JOHN E	LTC	0-0277789	1063	3
ROWAN JOHN L	LTC	0-0292740	0563	1
ROWAN JOHN P	CW4	W-2119574	0657	1
ROWAN JOSEPH E	CPT	0-0374349	0149	2
ROWAN LAWRENCE H	CPT	0-1325933	0261	1
ROWAN MELVIN R	LTC	0-0269767	0466	3
ROWAN RICHARD S	CPT	0-0181378	0557	3
ROWAN ROBERT W	CPT	0-2204401	1060	1
ROWAN WILLIAM K	CPT	0-1062743	0647	2
ROWAND JAMES C	1LT	0-0500062	0647	1
ROWE ELMER B	MAJ	0-1335985	0964	1
ROWE GRANVILLE	LTC	0-0317902	0768	3
ROWE HERBERT O	1LT	0-1014254	0245	2
ROWE JOHN J	CPT	0-1324657	1047	2
ROWE LLOYD F	LTC	0-0294280	0168	3
ROWE MARION W	1LT	0-1306153	0846	2
ROWE PHILIP A	MAJ	0-0228151	0465	3
ROWE PRESTON B	MAJ	0-0201740	0854	3
ROWE RALPH L	CPT	0-1994987	1065	3
ROWE RAPHAEL R	1LT	0-0147641	0956	3
ROWE RICHARD J	CPT	0-1755519	0846	2
ROWE ROBERT R	LTC	0-0206511	0554	3
ROWE SAMUEL	LTC	0-0382543	0166	3
ROWE WILLIAM H	1LT	0-0372025	1147	2
ROWE WILLIAM J	MAJ	0-1176181	0661	1
ROWE WILLIAM P	CPT	0-1884185	0965	1
ROWE WILLIAM T	1LT	0-1107092	0855	1
ROWELL IRVING H	LTC	0-0262960	0964	1
ROWEN BRYCE C	LTC	0-0446095	0563	1
ROWIN WILLARD C	CW2	W-2151060	0962	1
ROWLAND BILLY L	LTC	0-2010996	0566	1

NAME	GRADE	SVC NO	DATE RET MO YR	RET CODE
ROWLAND CHARLES C	MAJ	0-2262654	1063	1
ROWLAND DWIGHT R	MAJ	0-1823350	0966	1
ROWLAND FYNES J	MAJ	0-2262462	0563	1
ROWLAND GEORGE G	LTC	0-0372158	0460	1
ROWLAND HARRY W JR	2LT	0-1177170	0344	2
ROWLAND LAWRENCE O	LTC	0-0324661	0266	3
ROWLAND NANCY T	1LT	N-0741773	0845	1
ROWLAND PRESTON B	1LT	0-0420964	0544	2
ROWLAND QUENTIN R	MAJ	0-1289146	0557	1
ROWLAND RALPH E	1LT	0-2006623	0147	2
ROWLAND ROGER W	1LT	0-0526388	1047	2
ROWLAND RUFUS S	2LT	0-1823777	0844	2
ROWLAND SIDNEY A	COL	0-0165030	0648	3
ROWLAND THOMAS N	LTC	0-0197033	1155	3
ROWLAND WILL C	COL	0-0342971	0566	1
ROWLAND WILLIAM C JR	LTC	0-0225179	0657	1
ROWLAND WILLIE W	CPT	0-2007445	0656	1
ROWLANDS ROBERT W	WO1	W-2132436	0246	2
ROWLETT CAIUS A	COL	0-0229668	0251	3
ROWLETT JOSEPH G	COL	0-0226715	0362	3
ROWLETTE AVERY P	COL	0-0258182	0166	3
ROWLEY ALBERT E G	MAJ	0-0332488	0446	2
ROWLEY JAMES S	1LT	0-1018284	1147	2
ROWLEY JAMES T	CPT	0-0962621	1065	2
ROWLEY MARIE	LTC	N-0722819	0262	1
ROWLEY NORMAN O	MAJ	0-1577777	0557	1
ROWLEY TONY W	CW4	W-2118119	0464	1
ROWORTH JOHN M	LTC	0-0347714	0560	1
ROWSE ROBERT J	COL	0-0127755	0147	2
ROWSELL LELAND R	LTC	0-0298028	0466	3
ROWSTON JOHN	CPT	0-0207665	0728	1
ROY ERMIL L	LTC	0-1165943	0461	1
ROY HAROLD	MAJ	0-1166597	1059	1
ROY HAROLD C	LTC	0-1823213	0462	1
ROY JOSEPH FOL	1LT	0-0443157	0147	2
ROY JOSEPH H R	LTC	0-0961770	0163	1
ROY LAWRENCE B	LTC	0-1636570	0557	1
ROY LUTHER W	LTC	0-1307470	0361	1
ROY MICHAEL D	1LT	0-1311819	0846	2
ROY ROBERT G	CPT	0-0983498	0557	2
ROY THOMAS L	MAJ	0-1289628	0258	1
ROY WALLACE R	CPT	0-0243634	0845	2
ROY WENDELL P	MAJ	0-0255959	0867	3
ROYAL EDWARD E	MAJ	0-1798812	0165	1
ROYAL L J	CW4	W-2002839	0166	3
ROYAL RHEUTILIOU	MAJ	0-0216690	0363	3
ROYAL THAYER L	LTC	0-0221300	1061	3
ROYAL THOMAS E	LTC	0-1102022	0561	1
ROYALL LUBY F	MAJ	0-0296058	0255	3
ROYALL WALTER H	MAJ	0-1935684	0465	1
ROYALL WILLIAM A	LTC	0-0139085	0158	3
ROYALTY DAVID B	CW3	W-2209672	0468	1
ROYCE FRANK F	CW2	W-2114624	0466	3
ROYCE JAMES D	LTC	0-0211089	0159	3
ROYCE JOHN F	LTC	0-0277445	0866	3
ROYCROFT FRANK F	CW3	W-2142507	0259	1
ROYE ROBERT L	MAJ	0-0423022	0960	1
ROYE WYATT F	CPT	0-0281614	0846	2
ROYER CLARENCE E	CPT	0-0966431	0161	1
ROYER CLARK W	CPT	0-0317845	1045	2
ROYER HERMAN L	MAJ	0-0248780	1165	3
ROYER MANSEL G	CPT	0-1305838	0160	1
ROYER WALTER J	COL	0-0500009	0463	3
ROYLE DONALD H	CW2	W-3400070	0967	1
ROYONG SIMPLICIO	1LT	0-2027447	0349	1
ROYSE FRANCIS J	CPT	0-1018689	0263	1
ROYSTER JACK A	CPT	0-0375814	0946	2
ROYSTON CHARLIE A	COL	0-0221632	1061	3
ROYSTON WILLIAM R	MAJ	0-1031360	0557	1
ROZAK FRANK J	CW3	W-2142457	0761	1
ROZALSKY HERMAN	CPT	0-0392473	0346	2
ROZAR ROBERT L	CW2	W-2150731	0262	1
ROZEA CYRIL E	COL	0-0286006	0162	3
ROZECKI EDMUND D	LTC	0-2019227	0967	1
ROZER WILLIAM H	CW2	W-2205046	0960	1

NAME	GRADE	SVC NO	DATE RET MO YR	RET CODE
ROZETT OSCAR	MAJ	0-0510509	0546	2
ROZGA ANTHONY A	COL	0-0421553	0365	1
ROZICH FRANCIS R	MAJ	0-1644724	0761	1
ROZIER HAROLD F	MAJ	0-0222352	0945	2
ROZMAN JOHN J	CW2	W-2146846	1066	1
ROZMAN MARIE R	1LT	N-0724874	0945	1
ROZMAN ROBERT W	LTC	0-2023703	1265	1
RUANO WILLIAM J	LTC	0-0259741	0568	3
RUARK PARKE R	CPT	0-0209237	0943	2
RUBARD JAMES J	MAJ	0-0947482	0862	1
RUBASH REUBEN S	CPT	0-0443354	0146	2
RUBBELKE LLOYD F	LTC	0-1251889	0962	1
RUBEL ERNEST N JR	LTC	0-0284510	1059	1
RUBEL GEORGE R	COL	0-0193524	1061	3
RUBELMAN LOUIS F	COL	0-0299417	0646	2
RUBEN JOSEPH E	CPT	0-0357105	0140	2
RUBEN LEAH M	2LT	N-0736892	0445	1
RUBENSON BERNARD	LTC	0-0368774	0460	1
RUBENSTEIN BARRY L	CPT	0-5012683	0963	2
RUBENSTEIN EDWIN V	LTC	0-0456622	1160	1
RUBENSTEIN JACOB F	LTC	0-1575123	0466	1
RUBENSTEIN ROBERT	1LT	0-0470809	0744	2
RUBERTON LOUIS A	LTC	0-2032280	0768	1
RUBIN DEAN L	LTC	0-0497161	0667	3
RUBIN HAROLD S	CPT	0-1705950	0248	2
RUBIN IRVING	1LT	0-1697849	1144	2
RUBIN MANDEL	CPT	0-1012309	0247	2
RUBIN MARVIN H	1LT	0-1644726	0146	2
RUBIN NATHAN N	MAJ	0-1946151	0562	1
RUBIN RALPH R	1LT	0-0551326	0547	2
RUBIN ROGER W	CW2	W-3430446	1168	1
RUBIN SAMUEL	MAJ	0-0491389	0546	2
RUBIN WALTER E	LTC	0-0481013	0263	1
RUBINOFF JACOB	MAJ	0-0135765	1052	3
RUBINOWITZ STANLEY H	COL	0-1577778	1064	1
RUBINTON SAMUEL	LTC	0-0453982	1157	1
RUBIO BERNARDO	CPT	0-1896625	0359	1
RUBLE CLYDE R	CPT	0-0493962	0755	1
RUBLE ROY T	WO1	W-2107975	0757	1
RUBLE VIRGIL E	MAJ	0-0991264	1167	1
RUBLE WILLIS V	LTC	0-0441786	1154	1
RUBLEE EDMUND O	LTC	0-0231471	0364	3
RUBOTTUM ERNEST L	CPT	0-1031125	0257	1
RUBY JOHN L	LTC	0-0318744	0358	1
RUCH LAWRENCE W	CW3	W-2151682	0364	1
RUCINSKI JOHN	1LT	0-1549593	0646	2
RUCKER AARON E	LTC	0-0275001	0156	3
RUCKER CLYDE F	CW2	W-2144928	0459	1
RUCKER FRANK H	2LT	0-0538296	0145	2
RUCKER JAMES J	LTC	0-0451058	0357	1
RUCKER JOHN P	MAJ	0-1283143	0 48	2
RUCKER ROBERT H	CPT	0-0365364	0144	2
RUCKER ROY J	MAJ	0-2293194	0662	1
RUCKLE JAMES G	LTC	0-0239964	0665	3
RUCKMAN CHARLES W	MAJ	0-0226063	1262	3
RUCKMAN WILLIAM C	LTC	0-0252168	0755	2
RUDAT ROBERT L	LTC	0-1552782	0664	1
RUDBERG JEROME	LTC	0-1845098	1165	1
RUDD CHARLES	COL	0-0181205	0452	2
RUDD JOEL W	CPT	0-2048766	0448	2
RUDD JOHN H	CPT	0-2009672	1155	1
RUDD RAY V S	CPT	0-0241976	0648	3
RUDDELL DORIS N	1LT	N-0767888	0546	1
RUDDER SARAH E	MAJ	L-1010038	0665	1
RUDDER FRED F	COL	0-0248000	0462	3
RUDDER PAUL L	LTC	0-1341583	1066	1
RUDDOCK WILLIAM M	LTC	0-0284926	0260	3
RUDDY JOHN G	2LT	0-1047321	1143	2
RUDDY JOSEPH C	MAJ	0-1688492	0765	2
RUDE HARRY E	1LT	0-1822194	0745	2
RUDE JAMES L	1LT	0-0544462	0646	2
RUDEEN PAUL F SR	CW3	W-2152776	0165	1
RUDELL ROBERT C	LTC	0-1307082	0862	1
RUDER JESSE H	LTC	0-0179094	0649	2
RUDERMAN JOSEPH D	1LT	0-0369381	0342	2
RUDERMAN MAURICE	CW3	W-2145586	0463	1
RUDICEL CHANDLER C	LTC	0-0253575	1160	2
RUDIN PHILIP G	LTC	0-0301204	0762	3
RUDIN STUART	2LT	0-4037586	0256	2
RUDINE CLIFFORD	LTC	0-0153310	0-53	3
RUDINE FRANCIS B	1LT	0-1787142	1147	2
RUDIS ALGIRDAS M	LTC	0-1057588	1064	1
RUDISEL CARL V	2LT	0-1586121	0943	2
RUDISILL HENRY D	COL	0-0279096	0465	3
RUDISILL RICHARD E	COL	0-0174598	0254	3
RUDLEY EDWARD J	LTC	0-0255374	0458	3
RUDMAN NATHAN A	WO1	W-2122715	0645	2
RUDMAN PAUL	1LT	0-1048555	0345	2
RUDNICK EMILY M	CPT	N-0900066	1060	2
RUDNICKI EDWARD M	LTC	0-0673961	0268	2
RUDNICKI FRANCIS	LTC	0-1287067	0258	1
RUDNICKY JAMES M	1LT	0-1317426	0350	2
RUDOLPH CHARLES W	CPT	0-0485455	0944	2
RUDOLPH DIXON	CPT	0-0300451	1144	2
RUDOLPH ELMER M	COL	0-0237596	0557	3
RUDOLPH FRANCIS F	CPT	0-0444871	114N	2
RUDOLPH JACK A	MAJ	0-0249857	0547	2
RUDOLPH JULES E	CPT	0-4022165	0957	2
RUDOLPH KORRA F	MAJ	L-0704163	0467	1
RUDOLPH MARSHALL K	COL	0-0236354	1056	3
RUDOLPH PHILIP S	CPT	0-0305503	1044	2
RUDOLPH SAMUEL F JR	MAJ	0-1885210	1067	1
RUDSER ORLANDO J	LTC	0-0291901	0967	3
RUDULPH ROBERT M	MAJ	0-0414482	0354	2
RUDY CHARLES A	LTC	0-0412098	1057	1
RUDY HAROLD A	MAJ	0-1686091	0546	2
RUDY THOMAS M	CPT	0-0490203	0646	1
RUDY WILBUR D	LTC	0-1697953	0557	1
RUE CHARLES H	COL	0-0394223	0958	1
RUE CLARENCE A	MAJ	0-0165206	1059	3
RUEF WERNER H	CPT	0-0192483	1160	3
RUEFF WILLIAM F	LTC	0-1113421	0464	1
RUEGSEGGER BOYD A	LTC	0-1001671	0859	1
RUEHE RICHARD W	MAJ	0-0973632	0867	1
RUEHLE CLARENCE C	CW3	W-2103386	0455	1
RUELAS BYRON H	MAJ	0-2018421	1162	1
RUESCH HAROLD R	LTC	0-1584833	0661	1
RUESLER NORMAN A	CW4	W-2150571	0868	1
RUEST GILBERT J	LTC	0-0347050	1164	2
RUETH ANTON	CW2	W-2105963	0750	1
RUFF CARL N	MAJ	0-1294018	0347	2
RUFF DAVID J	CW2	W-2107847	0361	1
RUFF DONALD C	1LT	0-0446961	1044	2
RUFF HERMAN A	LTC	0-0393838	1060	1
RUFF RICHARD R	CPT	0-1557073	1062	1
RUFF WILLIE A	MAJ	0-0504006	0650	1
RUFF 3RD WILLIAM H	CPT	0-0362665	1045	2
RUFFEL EDWARD W	MAJ	0-1018364	1266	1
RUFFNER FREDERICK	LTC	0-0147654	0154	3
RUFFNER ROBERT B	LTC	0-1293123	1262	1
RUFFNER WILLIAM A	CW4	W-2146642	0468	1
RUFKAHR CLOYDE B	CW2	W-2146804	0859	1
RUFLETH ELMER H	MAJ	0-0411635	1146	2
RUFO SANDY R	LTC	0-1598217	0367	1
RUFSVOLD OLAV M	LTC	0-0207516	0952	3
RUGG BENJAMIN	1LT	0-1294907	0645	2
RUGG JACK	CW2	W-2151393	0264	1
RUGGERI AUGUSTUS A	CPT	0-1690390	0745	2
RUGGIERI JOSEPH M	COL	0-0276267	0568	3
RUGGIERI JOSEPH P	LTC	0-0524857	0366	1
RUGGIERO MICHAEL B	LTC	0-1012784	0467	1
RUGGIERO ORLANDO	MAJ	0-1015710	0661	1
RUGGLES GEORGE C	LTC	0-0312859	0967	3
RUGGLES WILLIAM B	COL	0-0151250	0351	3
RUGHEIMER EDGAR W	COL	0-0245727	0459	3
RUHL HARRY C	COL	0-0214353	0650	3
RUHL HOMER L	CW2	W-2117931	0649	1
RUHL JOSEPH R	LTC	0-1115095	0767	1
RUHL LEVI W	MAJ	0-0179851	1053	3
RUHL MAX N	LTC	0-1116973	0568	1
RUHL PAUL V	CPT	0-1016806	1053	1
RUHOFF JOHN R	COL	0-0264923	1046	2
RUIS RONALD H	2LT	0-1307083	1044	2
RUISH DUDLEY C	CW2	W-2149980	0764	1
RUIZ FRANCIS V	2LT	0-1896577	1159	1
RUIZ HERBERTO	CPT	0-0406949	0860	1
RUIZ JOSEPH T	1LT	0-1896661	1060	1
RUIZ LOUIS	COL	0-1036704	1268	2
RUIZ LUIS	CPT	0-0940758	1158	1
RUIZ RAFAEL T	1LT	0-1182241	0450	1
RULAND HAROLD C	CPT	0-1996561	1057	1
RULAND LEWIS O JR	1LT	0-1540884	1050	2
RULE MERTON R	2LT	0-1551101	0145	2
RULE MILTON L	LTC	0-0288202	1047	2
RULE PERCY R	MAJ	0-0979123	0965	1
RULFS CARL H JR	LTC	0-0307326	1168	3
RULISON VERNON	COL	0-0450694	0766	1
RULLMAN EDWARDS F	1LT	0-1651318	1146	2
RULLMAN WILLIAM M	MAJ	0-1045233	0761	1
RULON BLANCHE S	CPT	N-0700004	1039	1
RUMANS EARL C	MAJ	0-1547769	0159	1
RUMANS WALTER D	MAJ	0-1019554	0564	1
RUMAZZA CARLO R	MAJ	0-0308842	0947	2
RUMBAUGH EARL E	COL	0-0184349	1058	3
RUMBAUGH ROBERT M	LTC	0-1113422	0967	1
RUMBAUGH ROY M	CPT	0-0151271	1044	2
RUMBLE WILLIAM A	LTC	0-0293112	0761	1
RUMFLIED CHARLES L	CPT	0-2025295	1060	1
RUMM RAYMOND F	CW4	W-2150706	0168	1
RUMMAGE ROBERT E	1LT	0-1018671	0845	2
RUMMEL DAVID J	CPT	0-0266316	0760	3
RUMMEL JOSEPH L	CPT	0-1583598	0959	1
RUMMEL WILMER E	CPT	0-1686198	1147	2
RUMMIG JAMES A	CW3	RW-2209664	1166	1
RUMOLD WILLIAM F	LTC	0-1645962	1163	1
RUMP ROBERT L	MAJ	0-0995162	0265	1
RUMPF CARL W	COL	0-0275564	0157	3
RUMPF FRANK H	1LT	0-1327768	1046	2
RUMPF MILDRED C	LTC	N-0775305	1166	3
RUMPFF ROY R	COL	0-0139787	0655	3
RUMPH ALBERT R	CW2	W-2109776	0354	2
RUMPLE PAUL V	1LT	0-0479643	1044	2
RUMPLER JAMES J	MAJ	0-0347116	1060	1
RUMSE WILLIAM F	LTC	0-0176695	0-52	3
RUMSEY CLEO E	LTC	0-0217751	0363	3
RUMSEY HARRIS	CW3	W-2120707	0356	1
RUMSEY LEMUEL G	MAJ	0-1116353	0662	1
RUMSEY ORACE J	LTC	0-1312594	0567	3
RUNDALL JOHN R	MAJ	0-2019510	0361	1
RUNDE PAUL S	MAJ	0-1577781	0954	1
RUNDELL HUGH A	1LT	0-1319121	0446	2
RUNDLE JOSEPH T	MAJ	0-0362821	0356	1
RUNDLE PERCIVAL J	LTC	0-0206304	1157	3
RUNDLE THOMAS L	1LT	0-1044940	0945	2
RUNDQUIST CHARLES F	LTC	0-0354319	0546	2
RUNDQUIST WILLIAM A	MAJ	0-0286444	0266	3
RUNEWITSCH HERMAN A	CW3	W-2147895	0866	1
RUNG ADAM A	2LT	0-1305167	0744	2
RUNG PETER R JR	1LT	0-0502261	0344	2
RUNGE WILLIAM F	LTC	0-0306294	0259	3
RUNION ALLEN R	2LT	0-0363292	1166	3
RUNK JAMES E	LTC	0-1046253	0768	1
RUNKLE ALBERT L	CPT	0-1174103	0761	1
RUNKLE DONALD R	CPT	0-1296430	1046	2
RUNKLE GEORGE A	MAJ	0-1016548	1061	1
RUNKLE SAMUEL C	CW2	W-2104436	1055	1
RUNNELS W L	LTC	0-0979535	0268	1
RUNNER WILLIAM R	CW3	W-2146157	0461	1
RUNNING FRED	MAJ	0-1030710	0256	1
RUNNION BILLY L	CW2	W-3411029	0568	1
RUNYAN FRANK	MAJ	0-0404665	0846	2
RUNYAN HUGH M	CPT	0-1321828	0346	2
RUNYAN PAUL H	COL	0-0191588	0657	3
RUNYON AGNES M	MAJ	N-0778091	0565	1
RUNYON GEORGE L	MAJ	0-1534851	1160	1
RUNYON HAROLD M	MAJ	0-0266349	1161	3
RUNYON JOHN K	LTC	0-0173446	0562	3
RUNYON ROLLIN A	CW3	W-2152004	0860	1
RUP CHESTER S	MAJ	0-1003028	0657	1
RUPE FRED O	COL	0-0498256	1050	2
RUPERT HOWARD L	LTC	0-0141202	1149	3
RUPERT JAMES K	MAJ	0-1293839	0862	1
RUPERT MARIE L	MAJ	0-0442994	1062	2
RUPERT ORAN H	LTC	0-0331356	0962	2
RUPERT PASCAL W	LTC	0-0205706	0845	2
RUPERT ROBERT L	COL	0-1335347	0868	1
RUPERT ROBERT P	MAJ	0-1919017	0464	1
RUPERT WILLIAM D	LTC	0-0800052	0366	1
RUPERT WILLIAM P	CPT	0-2011879	0557	1
RUPP FREDERICK	MAJ	0-1120513	0663	1
RUPP HERMAN B	LTC	0-0307810	0962	1
RUPP KARL K	MAJ	0-0268651	1060	3
RUPP KENNETH J	LTC	0-0255975	0966	3
RUPPART HOWARD H	COL	0-0296102	0655	1
RUPPEL HENRY M	MAJ	0-0139784	0857	3
RUPPEL RAYMOND P	MAJ	0-1081672	0761	1
RUPPERSBERG ANTHONY	COL	0-0306198	0767	3
RUPPERT HENRY	LTC	0-1331228	0764	1
RUPPLE HARRY F	LTC	0-0238721	0962	3
RUPRECHT CYRIL M	CW2	W-2211965	0368	1
RUPY STANLEY B	1LT	0-1287068	1044	2
RUS ALBERT F	MAJ	0-0272765	0568	3
RUSBARSKY FRANK R	LTC	0-1948215	0164	1
RUSCH RODERIC F	CW3	W-2144663	0760	2
RUSCITTO PETER G	CPT	0-1281131	0646	2
RUSEK STEPHEN C	MAJ	0-0476732	1154	1
RUSH ELLIS F	LTC	0-0395348	1157	1
RUSH ERNEST J	COL	0-0165604	0647	2
RUSH GEORGE F	1LT	0-0553039	0847	2
RUSH HOWARD C JR	LTC	0-0213244	1262	3
RUSH JACK L	2LT	0-0887349	0645	2
RUSH MERLE K	MAJ	0-0306754	0146	2
RUSH ORA W	LTC	0-0287242	1060	3
RUSH RALPH R	CW4	W-2106913	0955	1
RUSH RAYMOND J JR	LTC	0-1286897	1167	1
RUSH ROBERT	LTC	0-0318541	0559	1
RUSH ROY C	1LT	0-1018316	0147	2
RUSH SAMUEL E	LTC	0-0402991	0163	1
RUSH THOMAS H	CPT	0-1825063	1047	2
RUSH WARD D	MAJ	0-1303195	1060	1
RUSHAKOFF OSCAR	CPT	0-1821508	1045	2
RUSHE BERNARD J	1LT	0-0885775	1145	2
RUSHER WILLIAM A	MAJ	0-1014592	0367	1
RUSHING CALVIN L	LTC	0-1924916	1168	2
RUSHING EDGAR	COL	0-0130080	0956	3
RUSHING EDWARD C	CW2	W-2205118	0462	1
RUSHING REGINALD	LTC	0-0911140	0666	3
RUSHTON ALLEN	LTC	0-0234926	0264	3
RUSHTON BENJAMIN W	COL	0-0264404	0965	1
RUSHTON ELSMORE	LTC	0-0220022	0549	1
RUSHTON MARION	COL	0-0208099	1053	3
RUSHTON PIERCE A	COL	0-0246481	1166	3
RUSHTON WILLIAM J	COL	0-0211867	0860	3
RUSINKO GEORGE	LTC	0-0475961	0255	1
RUSK RICHARD A	LTC	0-2021029	0868	1
RUSNOCK ANN R	MAJ	N-0725333	0166	1
RUSOKOVITCH MICHAEL	COL	0-1821633	0868	2
RUSS ALFRED L	CW2	W-2212301	1068	1
RUSS ANTHONY	1LT	0-1081500	0745	2
RUSS JAMES R	1LT	0-1293484	0944	2
RUSS JOHN D	CPT	0-0280652	1054	1
RUSS JOHN T	CW3	W-2209435	0668	1
RUSS KENNETH L	MAJ	0-2011708	0261	1
RUSS RICHARD W	CPT	0-1874863	0962	1
RUSSELL ALAN G	CW2	W-2105014	0145	2
RUSSELL ALLEN B	MAJ	0-1540935	0763	1
RUSSELL ANDREW G	COL	0-0278235	0957	2
RUSSELL BLANTON E	COL	0-0329864	0268	3
RUSSELL BRUCE W	COL	0-0217631	0256	3
RUSSELL CARLOS L	LTC	0-0907094	0662	1

NAME	GRADE	SVC NO	DATE RET MO YR	RET CODE
RUSSELL CHARLES L	MAJ	0-1549065	0461	2
RUSSELL CHARLES S	LTC	0-1591416	0162	2
RUSSELL CHESLEY B	LTC	0-0383357	0662	1
RUSSELL CHESTER A	CPT	0-0492980	0354	1
RUSSELL CLIFFORD A	CPT	0-1551728	0855	1
RUSSELL DEAN	CW3	W-2144609	0260	2
RUSSELL DONALD L	MAJ	0-5201540	0468	1
RUSSELL DONALD W	WO1	W-2118415	1052	2
RUSSELL DOUGLAS C	MAJ	0-1646915	0264	1
RUSSELL EDMOND E	COL	0-0195885	1162	3
RUSSELL EDWARD J	MAJ	0-0364011	0346	2
RUSSELL EDWARD J	LTC	0-1297257	0962	1
RUSSELL EUGENE	MAJ	0-0975886	0164	1
RUSSELL EZEKIEL B	LTC	0-1167607	0463	1
RUSSELL FRANCIS T	LTC	0-0884912	1160	1
RUSSELL FRANK	LTC	0-0889327	0765	1
RUSSELL GEORGE D	CW2	W-2118191	1047	2
RUSSELL GEORGE G	LTC	0-0294684	0367	3
RUSSELL GEORGE G JR	LTC	0-1047761	1163	1
RUSSELL GILBERT A	CW2	W-2104439	0444	2
RUSSELL GORDON B	CPT	0-0270266	0668	3
RUSSELL HENRY	COL	0-0286872	0363	1
RUSSELL HENRY	CPT	0-0966085	1060	1
RUSSELL HENRY D	M G	0-0212769	0251	3
RUSSELL HERBERT S	MAJ	0-1634279	1055	1
RUSSELL HOMER A	MAJ	0-0382704	0846	2
RUSSELL HOWARD C	MAJ	0-0163129	0648	3
RUSSELL HOWARD M	LTC	0-0309093	0660	1
RUSSELL JACK L	CPT	0-1031126	0847	2
RUSSELL JAMES A	LTC	0-0371280	0866	3
RUSSELL JAMES H	MAJ	0-1324953	0963	1
RUSSELL JAMES J	CW4	W-2002750	0768	3
RUSSELL JAMES M	1LT	0-1105774	1147	2
RUSSELL JAMES M	MAJ	0-2103044	0467	1
RUSSELL JAMES R	MAJ	0-1298766	0861	1
RUSSELL JAMES S	CPT	0-0123965	0752	3
RUSSELL JEROME E	MAJ	0-0996685	0664	1
RUSSELL JIM	LTC	0-1641751	0464	1
RUSSELL JOHN A	LTC	0-2046458	0157	1
RUSSELL JOHN E	CW4	W-2147861	0861	1
RUSSELL JOHN F	MAJ	0-0395011	1045	2
RUSSELL JOHN F	CW4	W-2108393	0962	1
RUSSELL JOHN H	COL	0-0900185	0268	3
RUSSELL JOHN W	LTC	0-1032246	0261	1
RUSSELL JOSEPH J	LTC	0-1544731	0865	1
RUSSELL JOY A	MAJ	0-0229303	0263	3
RUSSELL KENNETH W	CW2	W-2149759	0662	1
RUSSELL KENT R	MAJ	0-0994365	0466	1
RUSSELL L B	CPT	0-1297595	0546	2
RUSSELL LAWRENCE JR	LTC	0-0264382	0159	1
RUSSELL LEWIS H	CW3	W-2210421	1268	1
RUSSELL LOUIS C	MAJ	0-1684013	0862	1
RUSSELL MARK W	MAJ	0-1173761	0661	1
RUSSELL MELVIN B	MAJ	0-1326172	0363	2
RUSSELL ORVILLE L	MAJ	0-1176497	0161	1
RUSSELL PAUL S	MAJ	0-1598373	0463	1
RUSSELL RALPH W	1LT	0-0212832	0757	3
RUSSELL RICHARD T	MAJ	0-0966895	0164	1
RUSSELL RILEY J	CW2	W-2143369	0554	1
RUSSELL ROBERT	CPT	0-1292236	0246	2
RUSSELL ROBERT S	LTC	0-0274796	0965	3
RUSSELL ROY H	LTC	0-1102027	0463	1
RUSSELL RUBY H H	MAJ	N-0764034	0964	3
RUSSELL RUFUS R	LTC	0-0473394	0557	1
RUSSELL RUHL J	COL	0-1010348	0968	2
RUSSELL SAMUEL	COL	0-0137945	0560	3
RUSSELL SOLON F	COL	0-0163960	0655	3
RUSSELL STEPHEN B	CPT	0-0503040	0650	1
RUSSELL TED S	CPT	0-0457248	1053	1
RUSSELL THEODORE S	MAJ	0-0456617	0164	1
RUSSELL THOMAS R	CPT	0-1289631	0550	2
RUSSELL WALTER A	CPT	0-1179600	0163	2
RUSSELL WALTER B	LTC	0-0901598	0763	3
RUSSELL WALTER E JR	MAJ	0-2096492	0763	1
RUSSELL WILLIAM A	MAJ	0-0383844	0366	1

NAME	GRADE	SVC NO	DATE RET MO YR	RET CODE
RUSSELL WILLIAM A	1LT	0-1540897	1058	1
RUSSELL WILLIAM B	CPT	0-1297097	0146	2
RUSSELL WILLIAM E	MAJ	0-1335473	0363	1
RUSSELL WILLIAM E	MAJ	0-1797012	0161	1
RUSSELL WILLIAM G	LTC	0-0383319	0961	1
RUSSELL WILLIAM H	CW4	W-2110500	1056	1
RUSSELL WILLIAM K	CPT	0-2055151	0847	1
RUSSELL WILLIAM L	LTC	0-0423169	0765	1
RUSSERT LAWRENCE J	CPT	0-4005503	1264	1
RUSSIAN JOHN L	MAJ	0-1924824	0266	1
RUSSIE LESTER W	CW4	W-2114822	0565	1
RUSSO FRANK J	1LT	0-0389435	0645	2
RUSSO HAROLD J	COL	0-0903286	0763	3
RUSSO JAMES A JR	1LT	0-0556562	0947	2
RUSSO JOSEPH J	1LT	0-0445605	0844	2
RUSSO JOSEPH J	MAJ	0-1103900	0664	1
RUSSO OLGO A	1LT	0-1295277	0845	2
RUSSO PATRICK R	CW2	W-2147677	0262	1
RUSSO THOMAS J	LTC	0-1337492	1167	1
RUSSO VICTOR JR	CW2	W-3350355	0867	1
RUSSON RAYMOND S	CW3	W-2149902	0964	1
RUSSUM CARROLL B	CW2	W-2212493	1267	1
RUST CHARLES L	MAJ	0-0346332	0557	1
RUST JOSEPH H	CW2	W-2000517	0562	3
RUST MALCOLM B	LTC	0-0445651	0164	3
RUST VICTOR H	MAJ	0-0335838	0962	1
RUSTAD JOHN H	2LT	0-1316333	0944	2
RUSTARI EINO A	1LT	0-0507773	1157	1
RUSTICK JOSEPH S	CW3	W-2150621	1160	1
RUSTIN ARTHUR L	MAJ	0-1543557	0960	1
RUSTIN NATHAN E SR	WO1	W-2145999	1163	2
RUSTON GEORGE M	CPT	0-0452978	0551	2
RUSZALA HENRY J	1LT	0-1640896	0445	2
RUT ADAM G	MAJ	0-0885147	0753	1
RUTA EDWARD J	MAJ	0-1821920	0457	1
RUTAN JAMES H	MAJ	0-0504198	0163	1
RUTAN WILTON L	COL	0-0105479	0155	3
RUTCAVAGE CHARLES J	CPT	0-1695226	1046	2
RUTH ALEX F	CPT	0-0299833	0749	1
RUTH BEVERLY P	MAJ	0-0205042	0352	2
RUTH FRANCIS D	LTC	0-1894773	0862	1
RUTH FRANCIS J	CW3	W-2003735	1266	1
RUTH WALTER H	COL	0-0298794	0963	3
RUTHE ALICE	MAJ	M-0002210	0963	2
RUTHERFORD ARTHUR B	MAJ	0-1108288	0961	1
RUTHERFORD ARTHUR L	CW3	W-2151187	0864	1
RUTHERFORD CARL R	1LT	0-1305652	1045	2
RUTHERFORD CHESTER A	1LT	0-1015639	1045	2
RUTHERFORD FLOYD A	COL	0-0102388	0554	1
RUTHERFORD FRANCIS H	LTC	0-0261506	1164	3
RUTHERFORD JAMES S	CW2	W-2203120	0962	1
RUTHERFORD JOE H	MAJ	0-1165329	0157	1
RUTHERFORD KENNETH M	MAJ	0-1544063	0259	2
RUTHERFORD RAYMOND E	LTC	0-0127799	0455	3
RUTHERFORD RICHARD E	CW2	W-2115786	0346	2
RUTHERFORD ROBERT B	COL	0-0317606	0346	2
RUTHERFORD SAMUEL A	LTC	0-1320288	0762	1
RUTHERFORD WILLIAM	CPT	0-2046542	0157	1
RUTHERFORD WILLIAM A	CPT	0-0487891	0446	2
RUTHERFORD WILLIAM C	COL	0-0247324	0962	3
RUTHERFORD WILLIAM G	LTC	0-2094932	0467	1
RUTHERFORD WILLIAM M	CPT	0-0505704	1047	2
RUTHERFORD WILSON R	MAJ	0-1112412	1163	1
RUTKA JOHN	1LT	0-0452100	0848	1
RUTKIN JOSEPH	LTC	0-1292592	0462	1
RUTKOSKI STANLEY	1LT	0-1825494	0862	1
RUTKOVSKY PAUL	MAJ	0-1080959	0259	1
RUTKOWSKI HENRY B	CPT	0-0940770	0557	1
RUTKOWSKI STEPHEN J	CPT	0-1307169	0646	2
RUTLAND ALSIE L	CPT	0-1333543	0158	1
RUTLAND LEROY E	LTC	0-0390627	0266	1
RUTLAND ROGER M	CW3	W-2149236	0662	1
RUTLEDGE ALBERT F	LTC	0-1284584	0764	1
RUTLEDGE ANGUS V	COL	0-0386987	0866	1
RUTLEDGE GEORGE A	CW4	W-2152284	1068	2

NAME	GRADE	SVC NO	DATE RET MO YR	RET CODE
RUTLEDGE GLENN C	COL	0-0245264	0966	3
RUTLEDGE JAMES A	CW3	W-2150051	0665	1
RUTLEDGE JAMES H	COL	0-0243288	0757	3
RUTLEDGE JAMES R	MAJ	0-0673731	1058	1
RUTLEDGE JOHN M	LTC	0-0401827	0163	1
RUTLEDGE LLOYD A	CPT	0-1908748	0463	2
RUTLEDGE MELVIN M	MAJ	0-0169602	1048	3
RUTLEDGE ROBERT A	MAJ	0-1877846	1166	1
RUTLEDGE WAYNE M	MAJ	0-2025247	0359	1
RUTLEDGE WILLIAM M	LTC	0-1946154	0962	2
RUTLEDGE WILLIAM W	CPT	0-0502784	0358	1
RUTLEDGE WYATT A	MAJ	0-1296265	1157	1
RUTMAN HARRY	LTC	0-0496877	1166	3
RUTSTEIN RALPH	2LT	0-1321953	0445	2
RUTTAN FRANCIS M	MAJ	0-0267149	0562	3
RUTTAN MELVIN	CPT	0-1181108	0647	2
RUTTER ROBERT M	CW3	W-2150880	0765	1
RUTTER ROBERT R	CW3	W-2206056	0167	1
RUTTER THOMAS T	LTC	0-1045235	1162	1
RUTTLE JOSEPH F	CW4	W-2005358	1063	3
RUTZ CLARENCE A	CPT	0-0890302	1046	2
RUUD LOUIS A	LTC	0-0257785	0665	3
RUUD PHILLIP D	1LT	0-1824513	0947	2
RUX JAMES P	2LT	0-2040759	1044	2
RUYLE EDWIN W	MAJ	0-1112951	1162	1
RUZIC EMIL R	LTC	0-1186957	0768	1
RYALL VERN B	MAJ	0-0237171	0162	3
RYALS JULIUS W	1LT	0-0984155	0753	2
RYAN ALICE L	1LT	N-0751118	1045	1
RYAN AMBROSE A	LTC	0-0232404	0558	3
RYAN ARCHIBALD JR	2LT	0-2204858	0852	2
RYAN ARLAND D	CPT	0-0496287	0346	2
RYAN AUSTIN J	CPT	0-1112413	0253	2
RYAN BARRY A	COL	0-0453198	0862	1
RYAN BERNARD C	1LT	0-0390756	0245	2
RYAN BERNARD P	CW2	W-2146122	0861	1
RYAN CHARLES F	COL	0-0254037	0261	3
RYAN CHARLES J	LTC	0-1323487	0761	1
RYAN CHRISTOPHE	LTC	0-0215032	0160	3
RYAN CYRIL B	LTC	0-0400086	0960	1
RYAN DANIEL J	MAJ	0-0218285	0556	3
RYAN DANIEL P	CPT	0-1055962	1062	1
RYAN DON C	MAJ	0-0224497	1158	3
RYAN DONALD E	LTC	0-0209466	0164	3
RYAN DONALD E	LTC	0-1301546	0164	1
RYAN DONALD H	LTC	0-1057869	0867	1
RYAN DONALD H	CW3	W-2146882	0164	1
RYAN EDWARD F	2LT	0-1328525	0945	2
RYAN EVERETT W	COL	0-0335054	1164	3
RYAN FRANCIS A	MAJ	0-0250032	1060	3
RYAN FRANK S	MAJ	0-0361484	1060	1
RYAN FRANKLYN J	CPT	0-2017593	0756	1
RYAN FREDERICK	LTC	0-0191577	0646	2
RYAN GEORGE F	WO1	W-2145215	0853	1
RYAN GLENROY	LTC	0-1108289	1262	1
RYAN GOLDEN D	MAJ	0-0254467	0159	3
RYAN HAROLD F	CPT	0-1297597	0261	1
RYAN HAWARD V	CPT	0-0973288	1061	1
RYAN HELEN G	1LT	N-0754505	1047	1
RYAN HERBERT V	COL	0-0209801	0264	3
RYAN HERSCHEL D JR	CPT	0-5417830	0968	2
RYAN HUGH E	LTC	0-0420488	0947	2
RYAN JAMES F	LTC	0-0278410	0551	1
RYAN JAMES F	MAJ	0-0410346	0846	2
RYAN JAMES H	LTC	0-0365004	0463	3
RYAN JAMES J	CW2	W-3000411	0767	1
RYAN JAMES L	LTC	0-0403376	0761	1
RYAN JAMES L	CW2	W-2152646	0659	1
RYAN JAMES M	CW2	W-2004375	0568	3
RYAN JOHN A JR	CPT	0-1115098	0753	2
RYAN JOHN J	LTC	0-1797189	0163	1
RYAN JOHN L	MAJ	0-0981900	0765	1
RYAN JOHN M	LTC	0-0273389	0960	3
RYAN JOHN V	MAJ	0-0337831	0262	1
RYAN JOSEPH A	MAJ	0-1003321	1068	3

NAME	GRADE	SVC NO	DATE RET MO YR	RET CODE
RYAN JOSEPH G	LTC	0-1107673	1161	2
RYAN JOSEPH G	MAJ	0-1551304	0763	1
RYAN JOSEPH H	LTC	0-1106442	0366	1
RYAN JOSEPHINE	1LT	N-0751896	0645	1
RYAN KENNETH N	LTC	0-0267610	0468	3
RYAN LAWRENCE E	LTC	0-0407276	0561	1
RYAN LAWRENCE F	LTC	0-0277835	0158	3
RYAN LEO F	LTC	0-0471793	0548	1
RYAN MARGARET A	MAJ	N-0798929	0865	1
RYAN MARGARET M	2LT	N-0732575	0145	1
RYAN MARK F JR	LTC	0-1000852	0757	1
RYAN MARTIN S	LTC	0-0247742	0456	1
RYAN MATTHIAS J	MAJ	0-0190640	0850	3
RYAN NEAL C	MAJ	0-2014077	1063	1
RYAN PETER J	LTC	0-0168942	0758	3
RYAN RAY E	LTC	0-0290532	0862	1
RYAN ROBERT W	CPT	0-1643305	0762	1
RYAN RUSSELL	LTC	0-0113483	0648	3
RYAN RUSSELL C	MAJ	0-0162219	0749	3
RYAN THOMAS A	CPT	0-0235617	0750	3
RYAN THOMAS D	MAJ	0-0962290	0368	1
RYAN THOMAS E	2LT	0-1060907	0345	2
RYAN THOMAS J	MAJ	0-1582535	1060	1
RYAN THOMAS J	MAJ	0-1999959	0162	1
RYAN VERONICA L	MAJ	N-0786149	0665	1
RYAN VINCENT L	CW3	W-2150516	0163	1
RYAN WILLIAM	LTC	0-0335357	0464	3
RYAN WILLIAM A	MAJ	0-2034577	0460	1
RYAN WILLIAM C	COL	0-0167604	0755	3
RYAN WILLIAM E	COL	0-0162000	1056	3
RYAN WILLIAM F	1LT	0-1110225	0445	2
RYAN WILLIAM H	LTC	0-1048970	0662	1
RYAN WILLIAM J	2LT	0-1323617	0545	2
RYAN WILLIAM V	MAJ	0-0270901	0865	3
RYBA HENRY H	LTC	0-0344041	0465	3
RYBA SYLVESTER	1LT	0-1041638	1044	2
RYBECK WILLIAM H	LTC	0-0111676	0354	3
RYBERG ROBERT W	CPT	0-2263147	0863	1
RYBKA WILLIAM J	LTC	0-1166825	0459	1
RYBOLT HENRY C	MAJ	0-1305840	1161	1
RYCRAFT CLARENCE A	COL	0-0200192	1047	2
RYDER EDWARD A	COL	0-0208454	1059	3
RYDER EDWIN W	MAJ	0-0366074	0765	1
RYDER EUGENE H	CPT	0-0281762	0458	2
RYDER FRANK A	MAJ	0-0323104	1044	2
RYDER HARRY L	LTC	0-1168449	0167	1
RYDER HOWARD G	LTC	0-0561965	1060	1
RYDER MYRON W	LTC	0-0261505	1265	3
RYDER OLIVER A	MAJ	0-1588268	1157	1
RYDZINSKI LAURENCE E	CW3	W-2209726	0866	1
RYE BURNIE W JR	MAJ	0-1296909	0960	1
RYKEN WILLIAM P	CPT	0-1325327	0946	2
RYKER TRUMAN C	MAJ	0-0259598	0668	3
RYKERT GEORGE L	LTC	0-0204168	0155	3
RYKKEN VICTOR T	LTC	0-1650724	0868	1
RYLAND HARRY H	MAJ	0-0247435	0466	3
RYLAND JACK	CW4	W-2004586	0268	1
RYLE JESSE T JR	MAJ	0-0198836	0658	3
RYMAN DEAN E	COL	0-0101073	1048	3
RYMER GRADY	CW3	W-2142309	0958	1
RYMILL ROBERT J	LTC	0-1894879	0767	1
RYMUS JAMES D	MAJ	0-2266399	0368	1
RYNDERS GEORGE M	1LT	0-1317822	0845	2
RYNDERS THOMAS J	CW3	W-2209562	0967	1
RYNIEWICZ HILARY L	MAJ	0-0955708	0863	1
RYNN ROBERT A	MAJ	0-1599115	0963	1
RYON ALTON H	LTC	0-0264835	1164	3
RYON JOHN C	LTC	0-0415772	0866	1
RYSE ROY L	CPT	0-2009761	0258	1
RYSHKUS EUGENE J	MAJ	0-1636580	0160	1
RYUN FRANCIS H	CW2	W-2104441	0758	1
SAAL WILBERT G	CPT	0-1823649	0662	1
SAALMAN FRANK E	CPT	0-0155957	0954	3
SAALMAN OTIS E	MAJ	0-0348986	0751	2
SAAR WERNER R	LTC	0-0432772	0960	1

332-811 O - 69 - 21

NAME	GRADE	SVC NO	DATE RET MO YR	RET CODE
SAARI LEONARD V	COL	0-0250456	0266	3
SAATHOFF ROBERT L	CPT	0-5301795	0868	1
SABATELLI JOHN D	2LT	0-0529130	1044	2
SABATINI JOHN A	CW3	W-2203374	1161	1
SABATINO GERALD V	LTC	0-0438186	1264	1
SABATINO LAWRENCE J	MAJ	0-1949913	1067	3
SABATINO NATALE A	MAJ	0-0339457	0746	2
SABEL JAMES T	MAJ	0-0269536	0666	2
SABEL NORMAN A	MAJ	0-1345533	0567	1
SABERHAGEN HAROLD A	LTC	0-1040465	0355	1
SABEY WALTER O	CW3	W-2105864	0166	1
SABIA AGNES S	MAJ	N-0757538	0765	1
SABIA ANGELO J	1LT	0-1826104	0447	2
SABIA BERNARD J	1LT	0-1644742	0245	2
SABIK JOHN	CW2	W-2114807	1051	1
SABIN ANTHONY G	LTC	0-1249752	0961	3
SABIN CLAYTON C	CW2	W-2104443	0746	2
SABIN CORNELIUS	CPT	0-1302529	1147	2
SABIN HAROLD	MAJ	0-1108941	0254	1
SABIN WILLIAM A	MAJ	0-1594441	0556	1
SABIN WINFRED A	LTC	0-0144064	0354	3
SABINE FRANK A	LTC	0-0297077	1061	3
SABIO LIBERATO E	2LT	0-1897033	0358	1
SABISTON THOMAS J	LTC	0-1101646	1160	1
SABLE PHILIP R	2LT	0-1031515	0145	2
SABO JACK	MAJ	0-0109257	0647	1
SABOL JOSEPH S	CPT	0-1014760	0657	2
SABOM WILLIAM O	CPT	0-0325635	0147	2
SABOTNIK REX E	LTC	0-0273419	0861	1
SABRINSKY MICHAEL J	LTC	0-1797014	0863	1
SABRSULA WILLIE L	CW2	W-2149981	0761	2
SACCO GREGORY E	CPT	0-1688124	1143	2
SACCONE ERO	CW4	W-2152720	1060	1
SACHEROWITZ ALVIN	COL	0-0199907	0854	3
SACHAJ DONALD F	1LT	0-1555759	0846	2
SACHLEBEN RAYMOND	CW3	W-2128011	1155	1
SACHS CARL W	LTC	0-1535414	0363	1
SACHS ELIHU M	LTC	0-0401299	0346	2
SACHS HENRY N	COL	0-0223120	0464	3
SACHS MANUEL J	MAJ	0-0348491	1046	2
SACHSE MARGARET E	MAJ	N-0799171	0665	1
SACHSE WILLIAM O	LTC	0-1997765	1064	1
SACHT ALBERT R	MAJ	0-1798201	0159	1
SACK ERNEST A	MAJ	0-0187935	1259	3
SACK FRANK R	COL	0-0232218	0665	3
SACKETT CALVIN B	LTC	0-0233534	0459	1
SACKETT ROGER W	LTC	0-1541294	1262	1
SACKIN STANLEY	CPT	0-1688145	1145	2
SACKMAN HAROLD A	MAJ	0-0959287	0561	1
SACKMANN KARL C	LTC	0-0131578	1051	3
SACKRIDER GORDON	CW3	W-2146398	0463	1
SACKRIDER HAROLD A	MAJ	0-1876980	0965	1
SACKS EARL	CPT	0-1055438	0946	2
SACKS HAROLD J	CPT	0-0475259	0546	2
SACKS JEROME J	LTC	0-1824374	0368	2
SACKSTEDER MARY E	MAJ	M-0002178	0165	1
SACRAMO NICHOLAS	CW2	W-2110255	0247	1
SADDLER GLENN W	LTC	0-0425618	0261	1
SADILEK JULIUS B	LTC	0-0396948	0960	1
SADJA ELLIOT D	1LT	0-1580261	0145	2
SADLER ALBERT A	LTC	0-0489401	0463	1
SADLER AUBREY E	COL	0-0250635	0964	3
SADLER BYRON P	MAJ	0-0371338	0248	2
SADLER CHARLES F	CW3	W-2145839	1262	1
SADLER CHARLES G	MAJ	0-1599136	0361	1
SADLER HARRY V	2LT	0-1118280	1045	2
SADLER PAUL W	LTC	0-0294851	1264	3
SADLER S ELOISE	1LT	N-0742900	1046	1
SADLER WARREN H	MAJ	0-0953592	1264	1
SADLER WOODSON A	MAJ	0-1168060	0960	1
SADOWSKI FRANCIS A	LTC	0-0456682	0261	1
SADOWSKI HENRY P	CPT	0-2262780	0358	1
SADOS MARY E	MAJ	N-0743492	1262	3
SAEFKE JOHN F	LTC	0-1167608	0162	1
SAEMENES PETER J	CW4	W-2003289	0967	3

NAME	GRADE	SVC NO	DATE RET MO YR	RET CODE
SAENZ ALBERT Z	CW2	W-3150993	0963	1
SAEZ JOSE B	CW2	W-2147207	1060	1
SAFARIK EDWIN W	LTC	0-0257482	0168	3
SAFIR JACOB V	CPT	0-0491787	0365	2
SAFRA LEONARD T	1LT	0-1175301	0750	2
SAFFER SIDNEY H	CPT	0-0496071	0745	2
SAFFOLD JESSE O	LTC	0-0179617	0154	3
SAFFORD EDWARD L	COL	0-0160722	0647	2
SAFFORD EMORY P	COL	0-0306053	0665	1
SAFFORD HARVEY D	CPT	0-0380120	0645	2
SAFFORD WINFIELD F	LTC	0-0438600	0355	1
SAFFRON MORRIS F	LTC	0-0288415	0246	2
SAFKO LEE C	MAJ	0-2046319	0761	1
SAFOUREK NORBERT J	LTC	0-0108307	0650	1
SAFSTROM ALLEN I	LTC	0-1304449	1163	2
SAGE ALFRED E	CPT	0-1081172	0859	1
SAGE ARTHUR L	MAJ	0-0476476	0962	1
SAGE CHARLES L	LTC	0-0463024	0954	1
SAGE GILBERT B JR	LTC	0-1043219	1262	1
SAGE ORA G JR	MAJ	0-1552161	0346	2
SAGE WINFIELD W	LTC	0-0141844	1058	3
SAGENDORF DOUGLAS	CW3	W-2210718	0764	1
SAGENDORF VINCENT W	CW2	W-2205298	0159	1
SAGER BERNARD	MAJ	0-0483363	0346	2
SAGER EMIL W	MAJ	0-0509523	0155	1
SAGER JAMES T	1LT	0-1292403	0644	2
SAGER WESLEY C	LTC	0-0355664	1060	1
SAGERT JAMES B	MAJ	0-1106443	0363	1
SAGIN GEORGE N	COL	0-0274399	0160	3
SAGMOEN CLARENCE M	COL	0-0196451	0663	3
SAGNERI JOSEPH	1LT	0-1551950	0647	2
SAGONA ROBERT G	MAJ	0-2265088	0667	1
SAHADI RAY	1LT	0-1591420	0347	2
SAHLI EDWARD A	COL	0-0372990	0564	3
SAHLIN BRUCE A	LTC	0-1551510	1061	1
SAHLIN ERNEST H	CPT	0-0527880	0549	2
SAHLIN WERNER G	2LT	0-2035732	1044	2
SAHM CLARENCE E	MAJ	0-1933726	0967	1
SAHM FRANCIS P	MAJ	0-1170959	0464	1
SAHM JOSEPH P	LTC	0-1635589	0258	1
SAHS ROBERT E	LTC	0-0545597	0968	1
SAIBER JACOB	MAJ	0-0313904	1146	2
SAIKI BARRY	LTC	0-1338279	1266	1
SAIKI GEORGE	2LT	0-1331992	1045	2
SAIKLEY MITCHELL F	COL	0-0286019	0367	2
SAILER ADELINE J	CPT	N-0722477	0248	2
SAILER JAMES A	1LT	0-1055439	0651	2
SAILOR VANCE L	COL	0-0205088	1054	3
SAILORS JOHN J	COL	0-0265379	0246	2
SAILORS WILLIAM M	LTC	0-0442668	0265	3
SAIN JOSEPH R	LTC	0-1030828	0667	1
SAIN ROBERT L	CPT	0-0503651	0652	2
SAINIO PAUL H	MAJ	0-1947225	0962	1
SAITES LOUIS N	MAJ	0-0976223	0762	1
SAKAI KINICHI	CPT	0-0153837	0853	3
SAKAI TOSHIYUKI	MAJ	0-0961663	1263	1
SAKAMATO SAMUEL M	LTC	0-0349640	0666	1
SAKAMOTO KIYOSHI K	MAJ	0-1686540	0661	1
SAKANARI GEORGE R	LTC	0-1328405	1165	1
SAKELLARIOU EVANS N	LTC	0-0512713	1163	3
SAKER ANTHONY O	LTC	0-1286007	0364	1
SALADOW EDWARD C	1LT	0-1716674	1044	2
SALAMATA METRO	CPT	0-0494039	0550	1
SALAMEDA JOSEPH	1LT	0-1105853	0146	2
SALAMONE FRANK L	MAJ	0-0958899	0565	1
SALANCE CHARLES	CPT	0-1634284	0766	2
SALAS CHARLES F JR	WO1	W-2149177	0753	2
SALAS MERLA F	1LT	N-0731591	0246	1
SALAZAR ALBINO	1LT	0-2027442	0753	1
SALAZAR DAVID C	LTC	0-1045585	0161	1
SALAZAR JOSEPH L	2LT	0-0492768	0345	2
SALBERG ARTHUR K	1LT	0-0311215	1143	2
SALCEDO MARIANO	1LT	0-1896947	1150	2
SALCIDO AUGUSTINE	MAJ	0-1544761	0161	1
SALDANA-BIASCOE	LTC	0-1328850	0367	1

NAME	GRADE	SVC NO	DATE RET MO YR	RET CODE
SALDIN ROBERT S	CPT	0-2007550	0148	2
SALDIVAR JULIAN T	LTC	0-0327257	1167	3
SALE POWELL J	MAJ	0-2262740	0663	1
SALEE HARTFORD F	COL	0-0339336	0960	1
SALEEBY CLAIRE	MAJ	0-1031913	0963	1
SALEN [illegible]	LTC	0-0176788	0267	3
SALENSKY SELMA	CPT	N-0720877	0946	2
SALERNO SAM A	LTC	0-1287536	0461	1
SALES LAWRENCE N	CPT	0-1322311	0147	2
SALFEI AMBROSE G	CPT	0-0496682	0147	2
SALFINGERE FRANK W	LTC	0-0155535	0652	3
SALGET GEORGE R	CPT	0-1296890	0746	2
SALGUERO ARTHUR R JR	MAJ	0-0224609	1150	1
SALHANY EDWARD T	LTC	0-0410384	0860	1
SALHANY THEODORE T	CPT	0-1321665	0446	2
SALI VICTOR	CPT	0-0951496	0156	1
SALIC NICHOLAS F	2LT	0-2006290	0246	2
SALIN WARREN E	LTC	0-0243311	0266	3
SALINAS BASILEIO G	CPT	0-1688416	0760	1
SALISBURY ARTHUR J	COL	0-0331720	0256	1
SALISBURY CHARLES J	1LT	0-1327289	0346	2
SALISBURY CLAUDE W	LTC	0-2019373	1167	1
SALISBURY EDWARD A	MAJ	0-0964442	0461	3
SALISBURY F W	MAJ	0-0328323	0647	2
SALISBURY GEORGE H	LTC	0-0247756	0164	3
SALISBURY JAMES E	MAJ	0-0354411	0348	2
SALISBURY LAURON F	LTC	0-0267859	0359	3
SALISBURY LUCIUS A	COL	0-0101747	0648	3
SALISBURY RALPH D	COL	0-0100643	0453	3
SALISBURY SAMUEL T	LTC	0-0116234	1145	2
SALISBURY THOMAS M	CW2	W-2153107	0764	1
SALITERMAN H I	MAJ	0-0238130	0347	2
SALIVAR THEODORE J	1LT	0-1287069	1064	1
SALLADA HOMER R	CW3	W-2145506	0157	1
SALLADAY ISAIAH R	MAJ	0-0120071	0947	2
SALLE JEWEL B	MAJ	N-0737516	0168	2
SALLEY CLARENCE L	1LT	0-1043777	1045	2
SALLEY EDWARD M JR	COL	0-0231831	0665	3
SALLEY HARRY G	1LT	0-0377413	1144	2
SALLEY ROBERT L	MAJ	0-1924629	1068	1
SALLEY WILLIAM B JR	LTC	0-0390628	1160	1
SALLEY WILLIAM H	LTC	0-2033751	0967	1
SALLICK GEORGE	MAJ	0-1300533	0655	1
SALLINGER ELMER E	MAJ	0-1576600	0358	1
SALLIS HELEN N	MAJ	L-0130178	1163	1
SALLIS JESSIE I	CW4	W-2111078	0161	1
SALLMAN EDWIN L	COL	0-0264071	0555	1
SALLS KENNETH T	MAJ	0-0186834	0958	3
SALLY JOSEPH F	LTC	0-0324875	0646	2
SALMAN HARRY A	CPT	0-0393271	1052	1
SALMELA OLGA O P	CPT	N-0752613	0248	1
SALMON ARMAND J	COL	0-0230475	1061	3
SALMON EUGENE H	LTC	0-0305037	0860	1
SALMON I CHENERY	COL	0-0231944	0763	3
SALMON PHILIP A	LTC	0-0230561	0165	3
SALMON RICHARD	1LT	0-1294320	1045	2
SALMONS CLYDE R JR	MAJ	0-0961244	0263	1
SALMONS ELLIOTT D	MAJ	0-0256174	0967	3
SALMONS OREN R	MAJ	0-1037274	1160	1
SALO TOIVO E	CPT	0-1111345	1065	2
SALOME BEVERLEE M	MAJ	N-0728656	0462	1
SALON DAYTON D	MAJ	0-0468638	0846	2
SALOPEK THOMAS	CPT	0-0982514	0263	1
SALSBERY DANIEL F	MAJ	0-1105791	1168	3
SALTER ABRAHAM	WO1	W-2140410	1146	2
SALTER ALYS L	LTC	N-0727063	1146	1
SALTER BILLY B	LTC	0-0378079	0857	1
SALTER BYRON M	MAJ	0-0299947	0356	3
SALTER CHARLES F	LTC	0-0456619	0861	1
SALTER GEORGE B	COL	0-0284797	0663	3
SALTER HIRAM P	CPT	0-0295496	0146	2
SALTER JAMES W	CPT	0-1309611	0446	2
SALTESS ALEX	1LT	0-2000816	1047	2
SALTSMAN MARVIN L	CW3	W-2214701	1168	1
SALTUS SEYMOUR	LTC	0-0906454	1267	3

NAME	GRADE	SVC NO	DATE RET MO YR	RET CODE
SALTZ NATHAN J	CPT	0-0381418	0745	2
SALTZMAN CHARLES E	MG	0-0275984	1063	3
SALUGA STEPHEN J	CW2	W-2003883	1167	1
SALVA CALVIN V	CPT	0-2027445	1058	2
SALVATOR ROBERT A	LTC	0-1324178	0163	2
SALVAS PAUL G	1LT	0-5320377	0666	2
SALVATO EDWARD T	LTC	0-0246813	0966	3
SALVICE LEWIS W	2LT	0-1081309	0944	2
SALVO CHARLES	CW2	W-2207330	1162	1
SALVO WALTER W	2LT	0-1291528	0243	2
SALYER GEORGE R	LTC	0-0347996	0658	1
SALYER HARRY T	MAJ	0-1573564	1158	1
SALYERS JAMES G C	CPT	0-0108947	1044	2
SALZ LEO	1LT	0-1012630	0745	2
SALZ LOUIS C	COL	0-0139369	0155	3
SALZBERG LAWRENCE L	LTC	0-1105160	0961	1
SALZBERG THEODORE H	CPT	0-1112953	0446	2
SALZILLO WILLIAM H	LTC	0-1108291	0663	1
SALZMAN ALLE L	2LT	N-0700492	1034	1
SALZMAN BERNARD	LTC	0-1845101	0961	1
SALZMAN JAY M	CPT	0-0258183	0566	3
SALZMAN ROBERT R	MAJ	0-5405038	0968	1
SAMANIEGO GEORGE	CPT	0-1318090	1053	2
SAMARAS GEORGE D	CPT	0-1303202	0346	2
SAMDAHL LEO B	LTC	0-0453676	0760	1
SAMMIS HERBERT F	MAJ	0-1001224	0860	1
SAMMON EDWARD F	CW4	W-2006638	1068	3
SAMMON MARLAN C SR	MAJ	0-0970637	1163	1
SAMMOND WILLIAM A	1LT	0-0915282	0944	2
SAMMONS EUGENE	CPT	0-0450474	0762	1
SAMMONS FRED S	COL	0-0273787	0866	3
SAMMONS ROBERT L	CPT	0-1313177	0847	2
SAMMONS WILLIAM	1LT	0-0508705	0350	1
SAMONDS JOHN M JR	MAJ	0-1116183	0962	1
SAMOTIN MAXWELL E	LTC	0-0920762	0665	3
SAMOUCE GEORGE A	MAJ	0-0200876	0259	3
SAMOURIAN HARRY A	CPT	0-0503102	0545	2
SAMPAGA CLEMENTE	1LT	0-0890545	0649	2
SAMPAGA DOMINADOR	1LT	0-1896915	0751	1
SAMPAYAN RUPERTO O	MAJ	0-1110783	0263	1
SAMPERE JEROME S	MAJ	0-1826223	0267	3
SAMPIER FRANK D	LTC	0-0338446	0768	3
SAMPIER JOHN W	LTC	0-0250045	1065	3
SAMPIERI HORACE M	CW3	W-2207046	0967	1
SAMPLE ADIS D	MAJ	0-1115769	0966	2
SAMPLE CHARLES	CW3	W-2145657	0662	1
SAMPLE JOHN W	LTC	0-0282498	0747	2
SAMPLE KATHRYN E	1LT	N-0787760	0646	1
SAMPLE THOMAS E	MAJ	0-2285585	0568	1
SAMPLES CECIL L	WO1	W-2148812	0160	2
SAMPLES GILBERT	2LT	0-1178962	1145	2
SAMPLES JACK L	LTC	0-2023864	0664	1
SAMPLES ORVAL E	CW3	W-3430048	0868	1
SAMPSELLE JACK S	CPT	0-0347165	0254	1
SAMPSON ARNOLD I	MAJ	0-2262363	0266	1
SAMPSON BERNARD L	MAJ	0-0346914	1045	2
SAMPSON CATHERINE	2LT	N-0721191	0844	1
SAMPSON CHARLES W	COL	0-0411864	1266	1
SAMPSON DAVID C	CW3	W-2141809	0757	1
SAMPSON FRANCIS A	LTC	0-1047326	1060	1
SAMPSON GEORGE L	LTC	0-0440000	0357	1
SAMPSON GEORGE V	COL	0-0344465	1165	3
SAMPSON JAMES B	LTC	0-0171684	0455	3
SAMPSON JOSEPH R	MAJ	0-1894496	0254	1
SAMPSON PAUL L	LTC	0-0887576	0466	1
SAMPSON PAULINE R	1LT	N-0751125	0746	1
SAMPSON PHILIP	LTC	0-0167113	0147	2
SAMPSON RAYMOND H	CPT	0-1633515	0246	2
SAMPSON RICHARD F	CPT	0-0980890	0163	1
SAMPSON RICHARD L	CW4	W-2136683	0668	1
SAMPSON ROBERT W	1LT	0-1557524	1044	2
SAMPSON SELVIN E	1LT	0-1309840	0945	2
SAMS FARRIS V	CW2	W-2129943	0159	1
SAMS UPSHAW H	MAJ	0-0541442	1163	1
SAMSON JOHN A	MAJ	0-1013888	0462	1

NAME	GRADE	SVC NO	DATE RET MO YR	RET CODE
SAMTER MAXIMILLIA	CPT	0-0534486	0146	2
SAMUEL JAMES B	CPT	0-0490351	0962	1
SAMUELL JOHN H	LTC	0-0508771	0761	3
SAMUELS ANTHONY	LTC	0-1554082	0965	1
SAMUELS GEORGE	2LT	0-0556931	0146	2
SAMUELS GEORGE J	CPT	0-2133125	0266	1
SAMUELS JACK H	CW3	W-2205273	1068	1
SAMUELS JOHN P	MAJ	0-0357063	0762	1
SAMUELS JULIUS A	LTC	0-1041639	0162	1
SAMUELS NATHAN	COL	0-0499937	0866	3
SAMUELS WILLIAM S	COL	0-0220530	0452	3
SAMUELS WINFIELD H	CPT	0-1294320	1046	2
SAMUELSEN HERMAN W	CW2	W-2141773	0859	1
SAMUELSON ELWYN F	MAJ	0-0981992	0864	1
SAMUELSON MYRON I	COL	0-0267282	1068	3
SAMUELSON ROLAND	CPT	0-1336551	0465	1
SAMUELSON ROMAIN N	WO1	W-2210820	0461	2
SAMULEVICH PETER J	MAJ	0-1923604	0567	1
SAN BORN ARTHUR C	CPT	0-0307999	0845	2
SAN MILLAN RAFAEL JR	MAJ	0-0203440	0963	3
SAN PABLO FELICIANO	1LT	0-1896535	0351	1
SAN VITO JAMES A	2LT	0-1309018	0744	2
SANABRIA RAFAEL	CPT	0-0163621	0159	3
SANANO ANDRES S	CPT	0-0395419	0157	1
SANANO JUSTINO	1LT	0-1896704	1163	1
SANAVITIS ANTHONY	1LT	0-0495501	0449	1
SANBORN EDWARD J	1LT	0-1303031	1150	2
SANBORN GERDA C	CPT	N-0778368	0655	2
SANBORN HARRY F	LTC	0-1181748	0266	1
SANBORN MERLE M	MAJ	0-0309600	0766	3
SANBORG FRANK E	MAJ	0-0263982	0762	2
SANCHES DANIEL F	LTC	0-0442356	0756	1
SANCHEZ ARNOLD R	MAJ	0-2047481	1162	1
SANCHEZ ELIAS S	CW3	W-2141669	0659	1
SANCHEZ EUGENE M JR	MAJ	0-1946157	0466	1
SANCHEZ GERARDO	CW2	W-2142792	0357	1
SANCHEZ JOHN J	CPT	0-1014058	0664	1
SANCHEZ PHILIP P P	CPT	0-0477532	0844	2
SANCHEZ RAFAEL	CW4	W-2001052	1060	1
SANCHEZ RAYMOND	CPT	0-1333382	0960	1
SANCHEZ SALVADOR F	CW3	W-2143292	0263	1
SANCHEZ6CAMACHO A	1LT	0-1685783	1056	2
SANCHEZ-RIVERA GUILL	MAJ	0-1322744	0663	1
SANCHIS JOSEPH M	LTC	0-0524520	0961	3
SAND ALEXANDER	MAJ	0-0207397	1143	2
SAND DONNA M	1LT	N-0769753	1147	1
SAND JOHN D	MAJ	0-0930382	0168	1
SAND RUSSELL A	COL	0-0263415	0967	3
SAND WILLIS R	LTC	0-0387954	0368	3
SANDBERG CARL R	LTC	0-0240427	1165	3
SANDBERG DAVID W	CPT	0-0205999	1163	3
SANDBERG ELMER T	MAJ	0-0278055	0365	3
SANDBERG ERLAND L	COL	0-0213877	0163	3
SANDBERG FLOYD A	LTC	0-0217563	0862	3
SANDBERG RALPH L	MAJ	0-1548545	0361	1
SANDBERG TOIVO A	LTC	0-1645337	0367	1
SANDELIN ROBERT W	LTC	0-0261965	0265	3
SANDEN MILTON V	LTC	0-0232067	0361	3
SANDERCOCK WILLIAM J	LTC	0-1320364	1064	1
SANDERLIN JOE H	LTC	0-0192819	0253	3
SANDERS ADMIRAL O	LTC	0-0176414	0560	3
SANDERS ALERIE	MAJ	0-1644736	0156	1
SANDERS ARNOLD L	LTC	0-0362668	0647	2
SANDERS ARTHUR R	MAJ	0-0216252	0460	3
SANDERS BERLINE J	2LT	N-0702641	0235	1
SANDERS BERNARD	MAJ	0-0450662	1060	1
SANDERS BERNARD	MAJ	0-1923621	1165	1
SANDERS BERNARD A	CW2	W-2113175	0746	1
SANDERS BERNARD C	MAJ	0-1046255	0161	1
SANDERS BUCK	LTC	0-2054305	0754	1
SANDERS CARL W	2LT	0-0298253	0643	2
SANDERS CHARLES	1LT	0-1913916	0946	1
SANDERS CHARLES A	LTC	0-0346343	0856	1
SANDERS CHARLES C	CW2	W-2210590	0565	1
SANDERS CHARLES L	1LT	0-1018305	1047	2

NAME	GRADE	SVC NO	DATE RET MO YR	RET CODE
SANDERS CHARLES R	CPT	0-1336966	0552	2
SANDERS CHRIS	MAJ	0-2030175	0363	2
SANDERS DALE	LTC	0-1310767	0866	1
SANDERS EARL C	MAJ	0-0441380	1057	1
SANDERS EARL E	LTC	0-1290665	0267	1
SANDERS EDWARD	MAJ	0-0213431	1163	3
SANDERS ELBERT	CW2	W-2152324	1060	1
SANDERS ELIZABETH	1LT	L-0116993	1045	2
SANDERS ERIC A	MAJ	0-0979279	0365	1
SANDERS ERNEST C	COL	0-0267867	0964	3
SANDERS ERNEST L	CPT	0-1030829	0759	1
SANDERS ERVIN J	LTC	0-0888202	0266	1
SANDERS ERVIN L	LTC	0-1543305	0267	1
SANDERS EWING B	CW2	W-2149809	0961	1
SANDERS FATE	CW2	W-2142196	0662	2
SANDERS FRANK W	MAJ	0-1877929	0267	1
SANDERS FRED R JR	CW3	W-2205856	0567	1
SANDERS GEORGE F	MAJ	0-1304164	0365	1
SANDERS GRADY A SR	2LT	0-1897736	0758	1
SANDERS GUY N	CW2	W-2149457	0357	1
SANDERS HERMAN	CW2	W-2121738	0845	2
SANDERS JACK D	CPT	0-1638864	0857	2
SANDERS JAMES F	MAJ	0-2020068	1160	1
SANDERS JOHN D	COL	0-0327130	0761	1
SANDERS JOHN T	LTC	0-1170548	1263	1
SANDERS KEITH F	CPT	0-0250500	0266	3
SANDERS LESTER	1LT	0-1298136	1045	2
SANDERS LOUIS	CPT	0-1541160	0761	1
SANDERS LUCIEN S	LTC	0-0184380	0848	3
SANDERS MURRAY	LTC	0-0512356	0546	2
SANDERS NEIL H	CPT	0-0284169	0964	3
SANDERS PALMER W	LTC	0-0223484	0562	3
SANDERS PAUL L	LTC	0-0470828	0263	3
SANDERS QUINCY A	LTC	0-0202289	0864	3
SANDERS RICHARD D	LTC	0-0474117	1046	2
SANDERS RICHARD L	MAJ	0-0271086	0468	3
SANDERS ROBERT C	LTC	0-1055965	1066	1
SANDERS ROBERT E	2LT	0-2011726	0347	2
SANDERS ROBERT H	CW3	W-2206886	0566	1
SANDERS ROBERT J	CPT	0-1322087	0646	2
SANDERS ROBERT L	LTC	0-1120779	0868	1
SANDERS ROBERT W	COL	0-0270860	1067	3
SANDERS ROBERT Y	LTC	0-0487905	0157	1
SANDERS ROSCOE C	CW2	W-2147510	1263	1
SANDERS SAMUEL M	COL	0-0100233	0360	3
SANDERS SIDNEY	LTC	0-2200506	0968	1
SANDERS TROY H	LTC	0-1037702	0262	1
SANDERS WALTER C	LTC	0-1590963	0766	1
SANDERS WALTER F	CPT	0-0450487	0560	1
SANDERS WALTER W	MAJ	0-2030148	0160	1
SANDERS WILLIAM B	CW2	W-2151328	0563	2
SANDERS WOODROW W	1LT	0-1303032	0857	1
SANDERSON BURDETTE E	CPT	0-0259073	0765	3
SANDERSON CLINTON E	COL	0-0246484	1061	3
SANDERSON DUDLEY B	MAJ	0-5800440	0368	1
SANDERSON LLOYD B	LTC	0-0143030	0858	3
SANDERSON ROBERT B	1LT	0-0406798	0644	2
SANDERSON ROLAND O	MAJ	0-0782025	0267	1
SANDERSON VIRGIL	MAJ	0-1001225	0557	1
SANDERSON WILLIAM H	MAJ	0-1013104	0261	1
SANDFORD CHARLES B	1LT	0-0547263	0446	2
SANDICO MELAND	CPT	0-0324507	1053	1
SANDIDGE CHARLES R	COL	0-0294767	0565	1
SANDIFER FRED M JR	MAJ	0-0480302	1045	2
SANDLER WILLIAM	MAJ	0-1645338	1061	1
SANDLIN JACK L	MAJ	0-2048770	0560	1
SANDLIN JAMES L	LTC	0-0299856	0562	3
SANDLIN KENNETH E	CW4	W-2153387	0868	1
SANDMAN OTTO E	M G	0-0184611	0550	3
SANDO FREDRICK D	MAJ	0-4010272	0268	1
SANDOE CLAYTON JR	CPT	0-1176499	0567	1
SANDOVAL FILIBERTO	CW3	W-2147862	0959	1
SANDOZ THOMAS R	COL	0-0293213	0762	1
SANDRIDGE HENRY R	LTC	0-0287801	0659	3
SANDS CHARLES E	COL	0-0255387	0767	3

NAME	GRADE	SVC NO	DATE RET MO YR	RET CODE
SANDS CLOYD D	MAJ	0-0277816	1060	3
SANDS FRANK N JR	COL	0-0244062	0666	3
SANDS JOSEPH E	LTC	0-0483735	0960	1
SANDS MAX	2LT	0-1011495	0545	2
SANDS OLIVER J JR	COL	0-0243184	1165	3
SANDS ROBERT L	MAJ	0-0985926	0965	1
SANDS SPENCER C	LTC	0-0311835	0867	3
SANDS THOMAS F JR	COL	0-0324311	0363	3
SANDS WILLIAM B	MAJ	0-1822463	0461	1
SANDS WILLIAM H	M G	0-0174202	0652	3
SANDSTROM CARL R	COL	0-0363207	0261	1
SANDSTROM CUTHBERT F	CPT	0-0249593	0157	3
SANDSTROM DONALD G	MAJ	0-0954247	1163	1
SANDSTROM RICHARD A	CW2	W-2214739	0368	1
SANDUSKY PAUL	CW2	W-2151892	0461	1
SANDUSKY WILLIAM R	LTC	0-0295497	1166	3
SANDYGREN ELBERT W	MAJ	0-0492096	0347	2
SANFACON GEORGE A	2LT	0-1554631	1144	2
SANFILIPPO A A	2LT	0-1548865	1044	2
SANFILIPPO PAUL J	CPT	0-0466189	0246	2
SANFORD EMMONS M	LTC	0-0507570	0447	2
SANFORD GEORGE A	1LT	0-1108293	0645	2
SANFORD JOHN G	LTC	0-0201281	0957	3
SANFORD JOHN P	CPT	0-0306634	1146	2
SANFORD JOHN T	COL	0-0182976	0560	3
SANFORD LEONARD C	MAJ	0-1994518	0661	1
SANFORD MARVIN D	CW2	W-2150120	0959	1
SANFORD ROBERT H	MAJ	0-1316675	0864	1
SANFORD SLOAN M	MAJ	0-0213655	0544	2
SANFORD WALTER A	MAJ	0-1120165	1059	1
SANFORD WILBER E	CW4	RW-2141670	0867	1
SANGER GORDON L	LTC	0-0494878	1062	1
SANGER ISADORE J	CW3	W-2145840	1162	1
SANGER JOHN L	MAJ	0-0269529	1168	3
SANGER NED	LTC	0-0884114	1057	1
SANGER STEPHEN S	LTC	0-0232607	0263	3
SANGO GEORGE J	MAJ	0-1173444	1158	1
SANGSTON LAURENCE P	COL	0-0328942	1162	3
SANGUINET EDGAR Y	LTC	0-0298524	0161	1
SANGUINETTI JOHN H	LTC	0-0361561	1160	1
SANIGA ERWIN	LTC	0-1311688	0264	1
SANKEY GEORGE K	LTC	0-1686472	1067	1
SANKEY WILLIAM C	LTC	0-0314945	0461	3
SANLAND CLARK	MAJ	0-0203399	0453	3
SANNEBECK FRANK A	WO1	W-2114126	0345	2
SANNEMAN LAWRENCE F	WO1	W-2109786	0545	2
SANNER CHARLES G	COL	0-0182591	0554	3
SANNER ROBERT J	CW3	W-2153268	0959	1
SANNING FRANCIS G	COL	0-0310863	0368	3
SANSARONA SANY M	2LT	0-0890533	0358	1
SANSBURY SHELLEY S	CPT	0-0211957	1063	3
SANSKY MICHAEL J	MAJ	0-2018928	0165	2
SANSOM JAMES F	CPT	0-1058643	0763	1
SANSONE DOMINICK J	CW4	W-2143044	0264	1
SANSONE JAMES W	1LT	0-1112419	0546	2
SANT GEORGE R	LTC	0-1111348	0168	3
SANTA ANA ERIBERTO	MAJ	0-1896787	0864	1
SANTAGNIVI ERNEST	MAJ	0-0171392	1145	2
SANTAGO ANTHONY C	MAJ	0-1333883	1059	1
SANTARSIERO C J	CPT	0-1304275	1147	2
SANTELISES MARIANO O	1LT	0-2030389	0648	2
SANTERRE FRANK	MAJ	0-0108959	0945	2
SANTIAGO JOSE I	LTC	0-0489706	0954	1
SANTIAGO JUAN G	CW4	W-2113948	1163	1
SANTIAGO TOMAS	1LT	0-0274261	1040	1
SANTIAGO WILLIAM	CW4	W-2147642	1268	1
SANTIAGO-VAZQUE FRA	CW2	W-2208966	0861	1
SANTILLI ALCIDE	LTC	0-0500498	0965	1
SANTILLI JOSEPH F	COL	0-0252768	0559	3
SANTINI LUIS H	MAJ	0-0370993	0560	1
SANTINI RAMON	2LT	0-1318847	1044	2
SANTINO MATHEW	LTC	0-0293048	0656	1
SANTNER JOHN C	1LT	0-1320010	1145	2
SANTO CARL A	MAJ	0-0493763	0464	3
SANTO JOSEPH	LTC	0-0309425	0560	1

NAME	GRADE	SVC NO	DATE RET MO YR	RET CODE
SANTONI GENEVIEVE	MAJ	N-0755665	0664	3
SANTOR WALTER	MAJ	0-0492195	0348	1
SANTORO ANGELO M	LTC	0-1822196	0862	1
SANTORO JOHN A	LTC	0-0358751	0364	1
SANTORO JOSEPH M	LTC	0-0261701	0967	3
SANTORO MARTIN P	MAJ	0-1895237	1160	2
SANTORO SAMUEL L	2LT	0-1292595	0144	2
SANTORO VINCENT H	LTC	0-0453477	0157	1
SANTOS AUGUSTIN L	MAJ	0-1305322	0264	1
SANTOS ROBERT A	1LT	0-4006830	0359	2
SANTOYAN RUTH	CPT	L-0201146	0263	1
SANTURBANE ERNEST F	LTC	0-1553548	0762	1
SANTY FRANK G	LTC	0-0421162	1156	1
SANVITO J VINCENT	CPT	0-0510277	1045	2
SANWALD FRED J	MAJ	0-0163753	1146	1
SANZONE JOSEPH	CW4	W-2122144	1059	1
SAPER NORMAN	CPT	0-0904212	0346	2
SAPHIR EDWARD	MAJ	0-0143082	0255	3
SAPIO ANGELO J	MAJ	0-2034578	0557	1
SAPORA GEORGE E	LTC	0-0302203	0858	1
SAPP DEWITT T	COL	0-0438344	1146	2
SAPP GEORGE E	LTC	0-1059623	1066	1
SAPP JOSEPH E	CW3	W-2121162	0552	1
SAPP PAUL P	CW3	W-2144591	0765	1
SAPP WHITNEY P JR	1LT	0-1174194	1045	2
SAPP WILLIAM B	CW3	W-2205837	0268	1
SAPP WILLIE	CW2	W-2145984	0855	1
SAPPER CARL H	COL	0-0171132	1159	3
SAPPER FRED E	LTC	0-0171148	0858	3
SAPPER WILLIAM L	LTC	0-0250563	1166	3
SAPPINGTON HOMER A	COL	0-0209912	0357	3
SAPPINGTON JOHN W JR	LTC	0-1994690	0757	1
SAPRIO JEROME JR	CPT	0-5709466	1168	2
SAPUDAR JOSEPH J	CW3	W-2144774	1161	1
SARADARIAN ALBERT V	CPT	0-0421228	0546	2
SARAS VICENTE	MAJ	0-0430507	0755	1
SARASIN GEORGE F	CPT	0-0384306	0547	2
SARAZEN JAMES F	CW4	W-2110546	1266	3
SARCANDER WILLIAM A	COL	0-0112306	0356	3
SARCONE JOSEPH A	MAJ	0-2011035	0864	1
SARDY INA	1LT	N-0730975	1045	1
SARELAKOS T C	1LT	0-1055624	0452	2
SARGENT CHARLES H JR	COL	0-0127021	0658	3
SARGENT FRANCIS A	LTC	0-0249898	1263	3
SARGENT FRED M	CPT	0-0504430	0249	1
SARGENT GEOFFREY W	COL	0-0245784	0852	1
SARGENT GEORGE W	LTC	0-0153050	0745	2
SARGENT HAROLD A	LTC	0-1291706	0357	1
SARGENT HERBERT D	MAJ	0-0997862	1162	1
SARGENT HUGH H	COL	0-0272171	0557	1
SARGENT JAMES H JR	MAJ	0-0961243	0167	1
SARGENT JOHN F	MAJ	0-1120609	0965	1
SARGENT LLOYD G	LTC	0-0227775	1064	3
SARGENT MAURICE V	LTC	0-0323189	0665	3
SARGENT RONALD W	1LT	0-5320227	0767	2
SARGENT WARREN B	CPT	0-0374644	0345	2
SARGENT WARREN N	CPT	0-1290666	0346	2
SARGENT WILLIAM H	LTC	0-1176790	1167	1
SARGIS GEORGE R JR	COL	0-1165559	0865	1
SARGOOD LEROY T SR	CW3	W-2208480	1268	1
SARIA RICARDO C	MAJ	0-1934864	1268	1
SARIK MICHAEL J	CPT	0-1640913	0661	1
SARINE WALTER G	CPT	0-0322144	1262	2
SARKA RUDOLPH A	MAJ	0-1534853	1060	1
SARKA STEPHEN	CPT	0-1319446	0446	2
SARKISIAN SARKIS G	MAJ	0-0251623	0367	3
SARKOVITZ LAWRENCE P	CW3	W-2149024	0266	1
SARLES DUANE Y	COL	0-0184900	0555	3
SARLES EARLE R	COL	0-0149534	1055	3
SARLES ROBERT S	CW2	W-2150716	0561	1
SARLES THEODORE	LTC	0-0455100	0966	1
SARMAN ADOLPH F	CPT	0-0496949	0549	1
SARMIENTO IGNACIO M	CPT	0-1822465	1063	1
SARMIENTO PEDRO	CPT	0-0324272	0957	1
SARNER DAVID S	CPT	0-1323618	0947	2

NAME	GRADE	SVC NO	DATE RET MO YR	RET CODE
SARNES OLIVER A	CPT	0-0255322	0148	1
SARNOFF DAVID	B G	0-0208338	0651	3
SAROCH THOMAS M	CPT	0-1586886	0268	1
SARRA ERNEST L	LTC	0-0237337	1064	3
SARROW ALFRED F	CW4	W-2105864	1061	1
SARTELL ERVIN J	CW4	W-2000604	1054	2
SARTHOU PETER F	MAJ	0-0394896	0846	2
SARTOR JOLLY C	MAJ	0-1115773	0860	1
SARTOR RALPH H	COL	0-0137411	0648	3
SARTOR WARREN W	CPT	0-0428123	0643	2
SARTOR WILLIAM M	MAJ	0-1543370	0958	1
SARTORE ARTHUR J	1LT	0-1822827	0346	2
SARTWELL ROBERT F	CPT	0-1298767	0445	2
SARVER HOMER B	LTC	0-1283319	0164	1
SARWARK HENRY F	LTC	0-1549074	1167	1
SAS WALTER J	MAJ	0-1339664	0466	1
SASAKI JOSEPH Y	CW3	W-2144402	1064	1
SASAKI KAY K	CW3	W-2133596	0365	1
SASEEN CHARLES A	CPT	0-0399161	0944	2
SASICH LOUIS	1LT	0-1037276	1045	2
SASKI WALTER H	CW3	W-2149886	0164	1
SASS ISIDORE	COL	0-0256882	0262	3
SASS RAYMOND W	MAJ	0-0210189	0264	3
SASSER JEFFERSON	CW2	W-2210405	1163	1
SASSER LUTHER S	COL	0-0378215	0358	1
SASSER RALPH L	CW3	W-2205101	0866	1
SASSER THADDEUS L JR	WO1	W-2109166	0854	1
SASSEVILLE EZRA M	LTC	0-0237064	0460	3
SASSO CHARLES A	LTC	0-0275872	1051	3
SASSO LOUIS A	1LT	0-4047417	0658	2
SATERWHITE R C	CW3	W-2205395	0667	1
SATHER DONALD E	1LT	0-1552785	0446	2
SATHER RICHARD N	CPT	0-0464814	0446	2
SATKOFF FRANK	MAJ	0-1587598	0163	1
SATO JAMES K	MAJ	0-1922579	1165	1
SATT CARL V	LTC	0-0275758	0347	2
SATTENSTEIN SIDNEY L	MAJ	0-0267400	0448	2
SATTERFIELD BARNEY C	CW4	W-2143337	0667	1
SATTERFIELD JAMES M	1LT	0-0449010	1044	2
SATTERFIELD MILMAN I	LTC	0-0366110	0267	3
SATTERFIELD SHELBY A	LTC	0-2055130	0960	1
SATTERLEE IRL G	MAJ	0-1544830	0160	2
SATTERLEE RUFUS B JR	MAJ	0-0967816	1162	1
SATTERLEY EARL O	MAJ	0-1820983	0868	1
SATTERLY ROBERT I	MAJ	0-0974960	0463	1
SATTERTHWAITE PHILIP	COL	0-0251974	1164	3
SATTERWHITE ALONZO V	LTC	0-0365545	0765	3
SATTERWHITE THURMAN	CW2	W-2209991	1265	1
SATURNINE JOHN F	CPT	0-1639592	1146	2
SAUCER ALVIN B	1LT	0-1321597	1149	1
SAUER ALVIN	COL	0-0244542	0363	3
SAUER BUDDY B	CPT	0-1326199	0846	2
SAUER JOHN	CW2	W-2000314	1156	3
SAUER JOHN A	MAJ	0-0220903	0664	3
SAUER RALPH H	CW2	W-2216448	1268	1
SAUER WILLIAM A	CPT	0-0488545	0655	1
SAUERBIER JOHN O SR	CW3	W-2148988	1164	1
SAUERWEIN JAMES T	CW2	W-2147836	0859	1
SAUGSTAD RANDOLF C	MAJ	0-0235892	0956	3
SAUL BARTON A	LTC	0-1315972	0465	1
SAUL FREDRIC H	MAJ	0-1651495	0561	1
SAUL HAROLD L	MAJ	0-1281097	0862	2
SAULS MARCUS F JR	LTC	0-0329199	0257	1
SAULS NIRAM L	COL	0-1287415	0663	1
SAUM COURTNEY W	LTC	0-1113927	0163	1
SAUM OTIS O	LTC	0-1295609	0862	1
SAUMER JAMES M	LTC	0-2006934	0568	1
SAUNAR JOAQUIN	1LT	0-1896464	0564	1
SAUNDERS ALFRED M	LTC	0-1291018	0964	1
SAUNDERS BENJAMIN B	MAJ	0-1635298	0366	1
SAUNDERS CHANDLER W	MAJ	0-0513161	0452	1
SAUNDERS CHARLES H	CPT	0-0495054	0248	1
SAUNDERS DOUGLAS I	MAJ	0-1822197	0561	1
SAUNDERS EARL E	CPT	0-1556347	0346	2
SAUNDERS EARL G	LTC	0-1292405	0563	1
SAUNDERS EDWARD H	MAJ	0-1302203	0763	1
SAUNDERS EVERETT L	CPT	0-0357253	0445	2
SAUNDERS FREDERICK	LTC	0-0254599	0267	3
SAUNDERS HARRY W JR	2LT	0-0466709	0144	2
SAUNDERS HORACE G	LTC	0-1556496	1267	1
SAUNDERS HOWARD C	MAJ	0-2042984	0857	1
SAUNDERS IRVING F JR	LTC	0-0440578	0263	2
SAUNDERS JAMES H	2LT	0-1822909	0545	2
SAUNDERS JAMES K	COL	0-0149850	0648	3
SAUNDERS JAMES P	CPT	0-1031589	0949	2
SAUNDERS JOSEPH W	LTC	0-0323422	0961	3
SAUNDERS LADDIE	CW4	W-2111363	0757	1
SAUNDERS LESLIE M	LTC	0-0291615	0947	2
SAUNDERS MILTON S	MAJ	0-2035559	0660	1
SAUNDERS MYRLE J	CW2	W-2119622	0654	1
SAUNDERS NORMAN H	COL	0-0171661	0659	3
SAUNDERS RAYMOND W	LTC	0-0297827	1058	1
SAUNDERS RAYMOND W	LTC	0-0382765	0761	2
SAUNDERS RICHARD C	MAJ	0-0225539	0964	3
SAUNDERS ROBERT S	MAJ	0-1586137	0959	2
SAUNDERS RODNEY V JR	MAJ	0-1108987	0563	1
SAUNDERS WALTER W	CW2	W-2147497	0860	1
SAUNDERS WILLIAM H	LTC	0-0295625	0858	2
SAUNDERS WILLIAM H	MAJ	0-0312078	0646	2
SAUNDERS WILLIAM H	CPT	0-0450548	0759	1
SAUNDERS WILLIAM L	LTC	0-0264694	0559	3
SAUNDERS WILLIAM R	CPT	0-0351062	0146	2
SAUNDERS WOODROW W	CPT	0-0686280	0561	1
SAUNDERSON DONALD H	MAJ	0-2020839	0862	1
SAURENMAN DONALD G	LTC	0-0250127	0366	3
SAURER HOWARD D	LTC	0-1316676	1065	3
SAURWEIN GEORGE K	MAJ	0-0163657	0649	3
SAUSSER EDWIN J	CPT	0-1795980	0148	2
SAUSSER WARREN E	LTC	0-1289817	0361	1
SAUSVILLE WILLIAM C	1LT	0-1301691	1045	2
SAUTER HENRY	1LT	0-1319789	0146	2
SAUTER JOSEPH L	1LT	0-1324660	0246	2
SAUTER JULIAN C	1LT	0-1994520	1045	2
SAUTER OTTO J	LTC	0-1845102	0662	1
SAUVE NATHANIEL	COL	0-0205029	1063	3
SAVACOOL KENNETH L	MAJ	0-0888309	0166	1
SAVAGE ARNO A	MAJ	0-1897718	0961	1
SAVAGE ARTHUR R	CPT	0-0211962	0744	2
SAVAGE FRANK L	LTC	0-1107105	1163	1
SAVAGE FRANKLIN W	CW2	W-2208298	0658	2
SAVAGE GEORGE S	MAJ	0-0104148	0648	3
SAVAGE GRADY H	CW4	W-2106072	0558	1
SAVAGE JAMES M	1LT	0-1579065	1146	2
SAVAGE JEREMIAH J	MAJ	0-0204476	0746	1
SAVAGE JOHN H JR	COL	0-0266668	0465	3
SAVAGE JOSEPH W	CPT	0-1017966	1047	2
SAVAGE JUDSON W	LTC	0-0183283	0752	3
SAVAGE LAWRENCE L JR	CPT	0-0959720	0967	1
SAVAGE LEORU H	COL	0-0295534	1066	3
SAVAGE PAUL J	LTC	0-1559848	1062	1
SAVAGE ROBERT B	COL	0-1547443	1067	3
SAVAGE ROBERT O	MAJ	0-0256547	0557	1
SAVAGE THOMAS A	1LT	0-1320653	0545	2
SAVAGE WALTER O	1LT	0-0451392	0361	2
SAVARD ARTHUR M	LTC	0-0346292	0655	1
SAVARD CHARLES E	CPT	0-1923627	1065	1
SAVASTANO F	1LT	0-1295610	114N	2
SAVEDGE LEWIS B	CW3	W-2152355	0964	1
SAVEL AALE A	CPT	0-1319790	0846	2
SAVELL WILLIAM H	CPT	0-1311932	0646	2
SAVERANCE GLENN E	LTC	0-2033873	0268	1
SAVERY CHARLES R	MAJ	0-1331996	1059	1
SAVICH JOHN	WO1	W-2123637	1051	1
SAVICKAS BRUNO F	MAJ	0-1693112	0461	1
SAVICKAS MECISLAWAS	MAJ	0-1284404	1062	1
SAVIGNY HARRY A	COL	0-0249376	0466	3
SAVILLE RICHARD F	COL	0-0220917	0966	1
SAVILLO RALPH F	2LT	0-1013439	1043	2
SAVINAR NORMAN O	LTC	0-0377012	0246	2
SAVINE HENRY J	1LT	0-1309680	0246	2
SAVINGTON HOWARD J	CW2	W-2207015	0762	1
SAVINI JOHN	CPT	0-0394474	0346	2
SAVIO WAYNE E	LTC	0-1107677	0465	1
SAVITSKE GEORGE	COL	0-1549371	0868	1
SAVITSKY DAVID V	2LT	0-1056874	0644	2
SAVOIA BRUNO J	CPT	0-0446473	0845	2
SAVOIE JOSEPH A	CPT	0-1011077	0949	2
SAVOIE XAVIER	CW2	W-2145272	0355	1
SAVORY CHESTER J JR	CW4	W-2145365	0268	1
SAVOY AUGUST T	MAJ	0-0373359	0963	1
SAVOY JOSEPH E	CW4	W-2109440	0158	1
SAVOY MICHAEL F	1LT	0-1165948	0645	2
SAWAJA YUKIO K	MAJ	0-2030783	0165	1
SAWALLESH ERNEST F	COL	0-0298911	0859	1
SAWARYNSKI WILLIAM C	1LT	0-1018448	1045	2
SAWDON ROBERT J	CPT	0-1300862	0346	2
SAWEY HAROLD G	CPT	0-2055245	0859	1
SAWICKI HENRY N	CPT	0-0488096	1047	1
SAWIN ALTON JR	1LT	0-0521965	1145	2
SAWIN DWIGHT H JR	LTC	0-2288257	0668	1
SAWIN HARRY C	LTC	0-0270992	0467	3
SAWTELLE CHARLES W	MAJ	0-0924716	0667	3
SAWYER BENJAMIN F	MAJ	0-1303205	0662	1
SAWYER BERTRAM H	MAJ	0-0127350	0854	3
SAWYER BROOKE E	COL	0-0104580	0157	3
SAWYER CARROLL H	LTC	0-0184221	1062	3
SAWYER CHARLES F	LTC	0-0282300	0565	3
SAWYER FERDINAND	LTC	0-0395280	0163	1
SAWYER FRANK N	MAJ	0-0209012	0344	2
SAWYER GILBERT C	LTC	0-0888212	0862	1
SAWYER GRENVILLE	1LT	0-0331516	0743	2
SAWYER HUGH	COL	0-0958602	0765	2
SAWYER JAMES C	MAJ	0-0450113	0566	2
SAWYER JAMES H	CPT	0-0480689	0847	1
SAWYER JOHN H	LTC	0-1334754	0665	1
SAWYER JOHN J	MAJ	0-1055720	1160	1
SAWYER JOSEPH C E	LTC	0-1293321	0666	1
SAWYER JOSEPH O	LTC	0-0276484	0257	1
SAWYER LESLIE F	CPT	0-1171746	0145	2
SAWYER LESTER L	LTC	0-0178209	0853	3
SAWYER LYMAN E	MAJ	0-1636592	0761	1
SAWYER MABEL E	2LT	N-0757661	1044	1
SAWYER PRESTON W	1LT	0-0358086	1041	2
SAWYER SIMEAR F	MAJ	0-0916594	0246	2
SAWYER SPENCE F	CW3	W-2144495	0664	1
SAWYER THOMAS J	CW2	W-2142197	0765	1
SAWYER TOM J	LTC	0-0385499	0461	1
SAWYER WAYNE	CPT	0-0382725	0856	1
SAWYER WILLARD C	MAJ	0-1874570	0568	1
SAWYER WILLIAM E	MAJ	0-0278977	0257	3
SAWYER WILLIAM H	CPT	0-0419699	0346	2
SAX HAROLD W	COL	0-0218989	0761	1
SAXBY LEWIS W	MAJ	0-1309844	1062	1
SAXE EARLE B	CPT	0-3059498	1162	2
SAXER ELWOOD F	COL	0-0304926	0661	2
SAXON CLIFFORD T	LTC	0-0496715	0557	1
SAXON HERSCHEL A	LTC	0-0301181	0561	3
SAXON KEENE	LTC	0-0206497	0363	1
SAXON ROBERT O	LTC	0-0304755	0160	1
SAXTON ALTON J	LTC	0-0298709	1264	3
SAXTON ELMER O SR	CW3	W-2147691	0165	1
SAXTON ROBERT O	LTC	0-1326926	0866	1
SAXTON VINCENT L	CPT	0-2102944	1062	1
SAY GEORGE K JR	2LT	0-1340695	1265	2
SAYE HENRY W	MAJ	0-1638426	0757	1
SAYE MAYNARD	CW3	W-2142412	0161	1
SAYEN HARRISON K	COL	0-0147906	1058	3
SAYER EDWIN J	1LT	0-1183613	0646	2
SAYER JOHN M	WO1	W-2110702	0562	3
SAYERS ANDREW J	MAJ	0-0940780	0862	2
SAYERS FREDERICK	LTC	0-0910481	1068	3
SAYERS JOHN K	LTC	0-0403614	1165	2
SAYERS MILTON F	COL	0-0301652	0857	1
SAYFORD ALAN N	CPT	0-0371413	0445	2
SAYLE JACK	1LT	0-2262138	0856	1
SAYLES ARTHUR L	LTC	0-0245124	0867	3
SAYLES GRACE	2LT	N-0759114	0345	1
SAYLES JOHN J A	LTC	0-0277791	0866	3
SAYLIN RALPH R	COL	0-0401933	0166	1
SAYLOR DAVID R	CW3	W-2205172	0768	1
SAYLOR HAROLD O	COL	0-0147905	0752	3
SAYLOR LOUIS F	COL	0-0021733	1060	1
SAYLOR ROBERT L JR	LTC	0-0506777	0967	3
SAYLOR WILBERT O	CPT	0-0432416	0152	2
SAYNER WILLIAM V	COL	0-0238890	0963	3
SAYNISCH VICTOR L	MAJ	0-1559849	0563	1
SAYPOL GEORGE M	LTC	0-0332954	0947	2
SAYRE ALBERT L	LTC	0-0221323	0959	3
SAYRE CLIFFORD L	B G	0-0201040	1059	3
SAYRE GEORGE M	LTC	0-0903694	0264	3
SAYSON CONRADO S	CPT	0-1896649	0966	1
SAZAKI HARUO	MAJ	0-2262474	0364	1
SAZZMAN THEODORE	LTC	0-1116693	0662	1
SBARAGLIA GREGORY	2LT	0-2262749	1151	2
SBERTOLI LAWRENCE	LTC	0-0294823	0560	1
SBROLLA PHILIP A	CPT	0-1551106	0246	2
SCACE WILLIAM B	LTC	0-0251465	0665	3
SCAGLIONE GERALD A	1LT	0-1031268	0146	2
SCAGNELLI JOHN C	MAJ	0-1556656	1059	1
SCALA NICK A	2LT	0-0887509	0146	2
SCALBERG JAMES W	2LT	0-1998518	0146	2
SCALES JAMES M	LTC	0-0246798	1165	3
SCALES JAMES W	LTC	0-0260650	0767	3
SCALES LUCILLE L	1LT	N-0779199	0446	2
SCALES MARCELLUS	LTC	0-1556942	1161	2
SCALF HERBERT R	MAJ	0-1647434	0662	1
SCALION CHARLES	CPT	0-0494848	0953	1
SCALLIN CARLOS	LTC	0-0331280	1058	3
SCALLON HUBERT J	MAJ	0-0309331	0660	3
SCALLY PATRICK J	1LT	0-1011659	0545	2
SCANDELL ROY H JR	2LT	0-1318832	0846	2
SCANDIFFIO N J	2LT	0-1309020	1044	2
SCANLAN EDWARD F JR	LTC	0-1639967	1164	1
SCANLAN GEORGE C	CPT	0-0542642	0845	2
SCANLAN JAMES J	LTC	0-0313389	0359	1
SCANLAN JOSEPH A	LTC	0-1593242	1164	1
SCANLAN WILLIAM V	LTC	0-0513878	0365	3
SCANLON CECIL M	MAJ	0-0348374	0946	2
SCANLON FRANK C	CPT	0-1324740	0357	1
SCANLON JEROME A	2LT	0-1305998	0245	2
SCANLON MARY A	1LT	N-0700809	0943	1
SCANLON ROBERT J	MAJ	0-1638428	0264	1
SCANNELL JOHN W	CPT	0-0386942	0146	2
SCANNELL THOMAS P	CPT	0-0542176	0846	2
SCAPLEN FRANK W	LTC	0-1633656	0966	1
SCARANGELLA N A	MAJ	0-1651086	0957	1
SCARANI LOUIS P	1LT	0-1170179	0251	2
SCARBERRY GLEN N	CPT	0-0358399	0153	1
SCARBOROUGH CHAFFEE	MAJ	0-0215480	1262	3
SCARBOROUGH EARL W	MAJ	0-1797016	1059	1
SCARBOROUGH JAMES W	LTC	0-0363937	0661	2
SCARBOROUGH JOHN H	MAJ	0-0531224	0846	2
SCARBOROUGH JOSEPH C	MAJ	0-0989147	0964	1
SCARBOROUGH LELAND D	COL	0-1309845	0365	2
SCARBOROUGH OSCAR L	LTC	0-0259791	0967	3
SCARBOROUGH SIDNEY	LTC	0-0353033	0945	2
SCARBOROUGH ZACK T	CPT	0-0283931	0946	1
SCARBROUGH CROWELL W	CPT	0-0482447	1046	1
SCARBROUGH LEON T	LTC	0-1165949	0258	1
SCARBROUGH LOUIS R	LTC	0-1177965	0765	1
SCARBROUGH RAYMOND C	CW3	W-2147777	0364	1
SCARDINA ANTONIO	LTC	0-0322727	1164	3
SCARFF INA M	1LT	N-0776116	0745	1
SCARLE CHARLES F	CPT	0-0452975	0663	1
SCARNECCHIA JOHN L	CPT	0-1693543	0145	2
SCARPA JOSEPH	CPT	0-1590155	0648	1
SCARPONE PASQUALE W	LTC	0-1102588	0861	1
SCARRY MICHAEL M	2LT	0-1296095	0744	2
SCATES GEORGE L	MAJ	0-0488328	0249	1
SCATES SHELBY T	1LT	0-4027962	0357	2

NAME	GRADE	SVC NO	DATE RET MO YR	RET CODE
SCATTERDAY JOHN R	LTC	0-0439404	0344	2
SCEARCE TROY W	MAJ	0-1917507	1266	1
SCEFONAS STANLEY A	1LT	0-1823067	0545	2
SCELLATO FRANCIS O	LTC	0-1638430	1162	1
SCHAAD EDWIN M	LTC	0-1638431	0962	1
SCHAAF JAMES C	LTC	0-0304384	1158	1
SCHAAF JAMES C	MAJ	0-0985750	1064	1
SCHAAFSMA FRANK	CPT	0-1081173	0846	2
SCHAAL FRANK J	COL	0-0181800	1054	1
SCHAAR FREDERICK	CPT	0-1794994	0958	2
SCHABA GEORGE E	1LT	0-2027370	0749	1
SCHACHT WALTER G	1LT	0-1053342	0747	2
SCHACHTEL MAURICE	2LT	0-1048568	0145	2
SCHADE CALVIN W	CPT	0-4006911	0266	1
SCHADE CHARLES E JR	MAJ	0-0300389	0762	1
SCHADE FRANK F	COL	0-0269645	1166	3
SCHADE MELVIN A	1LT	0-1309946	1045	2
SCHADLE ALVA C	MAJ	0-1826104	1060	1
SCHADLER FREDERICK	MAJ	0-1534137	0958	1
SCHADOJ MICHAEL V	LTC	0-2011345	0263	1
SCHAEFER AMOS E	LTC	0-0313051	0361	3
SCHAEFER ARTHUR F	COL	0-0275495	0154	2
SCHAEFER DUFRED L	MAJ	0-1945479	0161	2
SCHAEFER FRANCIS H	LTC	0-0260077	0166	3
SCHAEFER HENRY J	CPT	0-1689838	0159	2
SCHAEFER HENRY W	MAJ	0-0958731	1064	1
SCHAEFER IRVING D	M G	0-0110672	0856	3
SCHAEFER JOHN H	COL	0-0104135	09 0	3
SCHAEFER JOHN L	1LT	0-0461377	0944	2
SCHAEFER KENNETH E	WO1	W-2153231	1267	2
SCHAEFER LEO J	LTC	0-0135425	1055	3
SCHAEFER LEROY L	MAJ	0-1825888	0764	1
SCHAEFER LOUIS W	COL	0-0114939	1057	3
SCHAEFER ROBERT R	1LT	0-1645972	0147	2
SCHAEFER ROBERT G	LTC	0-0396361	0660	1
SCHAEFER ROBERT J	2LT	0-1012570	0144	2
SCHAEFER STEPHEN H	CW3	W-2208473	0766	1
SCHAEFER VINCENT W	CPT	0-0238122	0561	3
SCHAEFER WILLIAM H	CPT	0-1930838	1164	1
SCHAEFFER BERTRAM	CPT	0-1533439	1145	2
SCHAEFFER CHARLES D	MAJ	0-1039195	0462	1
SCHAEFFER CHARLES T	LTC	0-1062698	1165	1
SCHAEFLE JAMES M	CW4	W-2142268	0960	1
SCHAERTEL ELMER G	LTC	0-0346901	0167	3
SCHAETZEL NORMAN F	CW3	W-2150166	1165	1
SCHAEUFELE JOHN G	CPT	0-0283643	0647	1
SCHAF LEONARD C	1LT	0-0253596	0244	2
SCHAFER ALBERT M	CPT	0-1945936	0246	2
SCHAFER AUGUST	MAJ	0-0974521	0961	1
SCHAFER HOWARD M	CW3	W-2209186	0868	1
SCHAFER PAUL J	CPT	0-1638433	0446	2
SCHAFER PHILIP R	LTC	0-0518292	0766	3
SCHAFER RAYMOND A	LTC	0-1289633	0358	1
SCHAFER ROBERT J	LTC	0-1293842	0765	1
SCHAFER ROBERT P	LTC	0-1640920	0367	1
SCHAFER VERNON L	LTC	0-1644048	0862	1
SCHAFER WILLIAM F	MAJ	0-2049923	0961	1
SCHAFER WILLIAM H	MAJ	0-2265090	0768	1
SCHAFERSMAN JOE H	CW2	W-3440227	1068	2
SCHAFFER ERWIN A	1LT	0-0360097	0245	2
SCHAFFER JACOB V	MAJ	0-1015215	1068	3
SCHAFFER JOHN G	LTC	0-0299757	0368	3
SCHAFFER MARY C	2LT	N-0734002	1144	1
SCHAFFER ROBERT H	MAJ	0-2263157	0364	1
SCHAFFER WARREN F	CPT	0-0888855	0148	2
SCHAFFER WILLIAM	COL	0-0477533	1266	1
SCHAFFLER ALBERT J	LTC	0-1100319	0857	1
SCHAFHAUSEN MARY C	MAJ	N-0729166	0568	1
SCHAFISH CHARLES H	MAJ	0-1543436	0164	1
SCHAIBLE HERBERT F	COL	0-0296571	0763	3
SCHAIBLY ROBERT L	1LT	0-1296912	0745	2
SCHAIN JAMES T	1LT	0-1845497	0844	2
SCHAIRER KARL G JR	MAJ	0-1041896	0666	1
SCHAKEL CORNELIUS	2LT	0-1300089	0844	2
SCHALK KURT W	LTC	0-0350364	0861	3

NAME	GRADE	SVC NO	DATE RET MO YR	RET CODE
SCHALL ALBERT JR	2LT	0-1015581	0644	2
SCHALL BASTIDA B	MAJ	N-0758097	0267	3
SCHALL MARTIN H	CPT	0-1634296	0647	1
SCHALL SAMUEL M	MAJ	0-0463739	1047	2
SCHALLER HARRY F	CPT	0-0334238	0545	2
SCHALLER KATHRYN C	CPT	N-0737243	0447	1
SCHALLER RALPH J	MAJ	0-1319021	0962	1
SCHALLIOL RICHARD J	MAJ	0-0271898	0668	3
SCHALTEGGER OSCAR B	CW2	W-2148813	1160	1
SCHAM MANUEL J	COL	0-0322590	0267	3
SCHANCK GEORGE P JR	CPT	0-0428094	0346	2
SCHANEN MILTON W	1LT	0-1589484	0845	2
SCHANER LEONARD G	LTC	0-1796705	0266	1
SCHANHOFF SIR GEORGE	CW3	W-2145256	0762	1
SCHANK ROBERT E	LTC	0-0441490	0767	1
SCHANNEN JOSEPH F	CW2	W-2141918	1166	2
SCHANNEN THEODORE R	LTC	0-0240326	1065	3
SCHANTZ EDWARD J	LTC	0-0318167	0868	3
SCHANTZ RICHARD	CPT	0-1684581	0147	2
SCHANZENBACH EMIL E	CW4	W-2128092	0157	1
SCHAPER JACK F	1LT	0-1326173	1045	2
SCHAPIRO ISADORE S	CPT	0-0441327	0346	2
SCHAPIRO MORRIS	MAJ	0-0423064	0346	2
SCHAPLOW WILFRED H	MAJ	0-0381996	0257	2
SCHARDT HENRY P	MAJ	0-1595149	0157	1
SCHARF LEWIS E	CPT	0-0273278	0545	2
SCHARF STANLEY L	LTC	0-0982505	0168	1
SCHARFENSTEIN LOUIS	CPT	0-4006406	0565	1
SCHARFF EDUARD L	LTC	0-0538233	1268	1
SCHARFF EDWARD G	1LT	0-1057592	1045	2
SCHARFF LYNTON L	MAJ	0-0182717	0457	3
SCHARFF RICHARD B	MAJ	0-0224964	0355	3
SCHARPF WILLIAM F	2LT	0-0539496	0745	2
SCHARR ALICE D	MAJ	N-0732333	0563	1
SCHARSCHMIDT LEWIS W	CPT	0-1012410	0546	2
SCHARTAU MELVIN I	CW3	W-2207651	0167	1
SCHARTLE RONALD N	LTC	0-0243468	0766	3
SCHATTE FREDERICK	1LT	0-1309848	0345	2
SCHATTENBERG GUS A	COL	0-0248285	0456	1
SCHATZ GEORGE	COL	0-0310805	0562	3
SCHATZ JOSEPH D	MAJ	0-0985591	0968	1
SCHATZMAN DONALD C	WO1	W-2152481	1053	2
SCHATZMAN EDWARD J	CPT	0-2035440	1063	1
SCHATZMAN THOMAS F	LTC	0-0275517	0264	1
SCHAU NILE C	MAJ	0-0493126	0-52	1
SCHAUB HAROLD W	COL	0-0114333	0251	3
SCHAUB LEWIS W	1LT	0-1058646	0346	2
SCHAUBEL CARL A	LTC	0-0269380	0768	3
SCHAUDT MAURICE H	1LT	0-0506178	0944	2
SCHAUER ERNEST J	LTC	0-1315103	0466	1
SCHAUER GORDON H	CPT	0-1577804	0955	1
SCHAUER ROBERT J	1LT	0-0158861	0650	3
SCHAUERMAN WILLIAM	2LT	0-1306892	0444	2
SCHAUFFELE WALTER H	1LT	0-2014892	0947	2
SCHAUFFLER ALLEN M	LTC	0-0143355	0951	3
SCHAUMBERG HENRY	MAJ	0-0176257	0945	2
SCHAUTZ ARTHUR G	MAJ	0-0183376	0356	3
SCHAYER ISADORE	LTC	0-0336205	0144	2
SCHEAFFER MILTON W	1LT	0-1331667	0546	2
SCHEAFNOCKER RICHARD	LTC	0-1184138	1267	1
SCHEARER JOSEPH L	LTC	0-1288128	0861	1
SCHECHER FRANCIS J	LTC	0-1638437	0965	1
SCHECHTER SIDNEY	CPT	0-0451802	0660	1
SCHECHTMAN EMANUEL	1LT	0-1647256	0145	2
SCHECTER AARON F	CPT	0-0485764	1044	2
SCHECTER BEN	1LT	0-1299121	0545	2
SCHEEL EDWARD A	CPT	0-2036934	0547	2
SCHEEL IRMA C	1LT	N-0737960	0946	1
SCHEER ARTHUR A	LTC	0-0234528	0162	3
SCHEER CHARLES H	COL	0-0103051	0653	2
SCHEERER JOHN B	CPT	0-0277425	0660	3
SCHEERER RICHARD W	1LT	0-1297958	0145	2
SCHEETZ HARRY L	COL	0-0200727	1047	2
SCHEFFEL CHARLES	CPT	0-0446059	0145	2
SCHEFFLER EDMUND B	CW3	W-2206823	1066	1

NAME	GRADE	SVC NO	DATE RET MO YR	RET CODE
SCHEFFLER HAROLD G	CPT	0-0515156	0846	2
SCHEFFLER LEWIS F	LTC	0-0524196	0965	3
SCHEFFNER WARREN H	LTC	0-0418787	0767	1
SCHEGOLIN JOHN E	MAJ	0-0451177	0260	1
SCHEIB JOHN E	CW2	W-2211890	0367	1
SCHEIBE CLARENCE E	CPT	0-0503501	0746	2
SCHEIBE EDMUND	LTC	0-0339013	0361	1
SCHEIBER EDWARD L	LTC	0-1644746	0257	1
SCHEIBLER HERBERT A	LTC	0-0971114	0468	1
SCHEIBNER CARL F	LTC	0-0236401	1053	3
SCHEIBNER CARL F JR	CPT	0-1876602	0868	1
SCHEID GEORGE T JR	CPT	0-1551306	1145	2
SCHEID LLOYD J	2LT	0-1324227	0545	2
SCHEINBERG HOWARD M	CPT	0-0298198	0968	3
SCHEIRER ELEANOR C	1LT	N-0734916	0346	1
SCHEIRER PAUL D	MAJ	0-1552164	1161	1
SCHEITERLE CHARLES	1LT	0-0241936	0554	3
SCHELIN CARL A	CPT	0-1014320	0846	2
SCHELL BERNARD J	LTC	0-1576613	1163	1
SCHELL CHARLES C	CPT	0-1320655	1146	2
SCHELL CHRISTIAN	MAJ	0-0237502	0851	3
SCHELL EMORY T	CPT	0-1317568	0760	1
SCHELL HENRY H	LTC	0-1633519	0561	1
SCHELL LOUIS C	CW2	W-2147617	0659	1
SCHELL VALENTINE	MAJ	0-2200333	0466	1
SCHELL WILLIAM	MAJ	0-0455760	0757	1
SCHELL WILLIAM H	LTC	0-1102031	1262	1
SCHELLHAAS RICHARD B	MAJ	0-1113428	0263	1
SCHELLINGS WILLIAM	2LT	0-1331101	0140	2
SCHELPER LAWRENCE J	2LT	0-1324364	1145	2
SCHEMBER RAYMOND W	1LT	0-1325674	1046	2
SCHEMMEL HENRY E	2LT	0-0130074	1152	3
SCHEMMEL HERMAN H	1LT	0-1311211	0146	2
SCHEMMEL RUTH L	1LT	R-0000971	0346	2
SCHENA CHARLES J	MAJ	0-2032904	0364	1
SCHENCK HERSCHEL W	MAJ	0-0320391	0760	3
SCHEND JAMES E	CW3	W-2150518	1064	1
SCHENECK EDWIN B	1LT	0-0912613	0746	2
SCHENK CLINTON O	CPT	0-0164191	1126	1
SCHENKER BENJAMIN N	CPT	0-1692311	0145	2
SCHEPPACH MAXIMILIAN	MAJ	0-0151664	0-50	1
SCHEPPACH RAYMOND C	LTC	0-0302223	0265	3
SCHEPPLER FRED F	CPT	0-0117449	0550	3
SCHER LOUIS I	CW3	W-2145295	0656	1
SCHERBA JOHN M	WO1	W-2152325	0855	1
SCHERBA STEPHEN	MAJ	0-0345795	0446	2
SCHERCK JAMES P	MAJ	0-1922801	0868	1
SCHERECK WILLIAM J	2LT	0-1306955	0245	2
SCHERER ALFRED C	COL	0-0329340	0661	1
SCHERER EARL A	CPT	0-0182020	1154	3
SCHERER EDWARD A	CW2	W-2209997	1162	1
SCHERER LELAND H	1LT	0-0426658	0946	2
SCHERER WILLIAM R	LTC	0-1169320	0867	1
SCHERFF HARRY J	MAJ	0-0123246	0246	2
SCHERGER JOHN P	MAJ	0-0938025	0661	1
SCHERLEN EMIL D	LTC	0-0143977	0947	2
SCHERMER ALBERT B	CPT	0-0301154	1043	2
SCHERMER TED	LTC	0-0275094	0168	3
SCHERMERHORN A E	MAJ	0-1644748	0960	1
SCHERMERHORN H A	CPT	0-1015978	0846	2
SCHERMERHORN JOHN W	COL	0-0193213	0461	3
SCHEROTTER HOWARD	2LT	0-2207975	1151	2
SCHERTZ JEAN E	2LT	N-0795245	0846	1
SCHERWAT WILLIAM C	CPT	0-0120089	0453	3
SCHERWERTS DANIEL	CPT	0-0226392	1040	1
SCHETTLER HAYDN A	LTC	0-0236212	0665	3
SCHEUER GEORGE B	MAJ	0-1573571	0854	1
SCHEUERMANN DANIEL G	MAJ	0-2010670	1068	1
SCHEUFLER ROBERT C	MAJ	0-0870670	0163	1
SCHEUMACK JOHN T	COL	0-0253907	0351	3
SCHEUPLEIN JOHN W	CW3	W-2147366	0757	1
SCHEVIS JOHN JR	MAJ	0-0966636	1262	1
SCHEWE CLIFFORD H	CPT	0-1540646	1046	2
SCHEYD WILLIAM F JR	COL	0-0300787	0767	1
SCHIAVELLI GEORGE F	LTC	0-0249625	0367	3

NAME	GRADE	SVC NO	DATE RET MO YR	RET CODE
SCHIBLER JOHN M	LTC	0-1636605	1060	1
SCHICK CHARLES F	LTC	0-1169722	0860	1
SCHICK GEORGE A	LTC	0-0451549	0258	1
SCHICK HERBERT M	CPT	0-0105183	0455	3
SCHICK LOUIS T	1LT	0-1316219	0146	2
SCHICK WALTER R	CPT	0-0554058	0947	2
SCHICKEL JOSEPH	CPT	0-1685237	0347	2
SCHICKER ROBERT D	MAJ	0-0955800	0566	1
SCHIDZIG ANDREW J	MAJ	0-1293322	1047	1
SCHIEBER HERMAN A	CW2	W-2143340	0461	1
SCHIEFER GEORGE R	CPT	0-0977262	0462	1
SCHIEFERSTEIN CARL J	COL	0-0290258	0962	1
SCHIEK IRVING E JR	CPT	0-0532406	0246	2
SCHIELD EMMETT L	LTC	0-0129410	0459	3
SCHIELDGE W C JR	1LT	0-1306476	0945	2
SCHIELE GEORGE C	COL	0-0281767	0866	3
SCHIENDELMAN LEON M	MAJ	0-2000776	1060	1
SCHIERHORST EDWIN C	CPT	0-1100321	0944	2
SCHIERS ROBERT A	2LT	0-2055120	0645	2
SCHIERZ PEARLE I	1LT	N-0784460	0348	1
SCHIFF ABE L	MAJ	0-0499353	0247	2
SCHIFF ISADORE J	CPT	0-0382052	1142	2
SCHIFFBAUER JOHN E	2LT	0-1698159	0944	2
SCHIFFMAN WILLIAM L	MAJ	0-0498571	0646	2
SCHILDKNECHT OTTO C	CW3	W-2146614	0561	1
SCHILDT JAMES F	MAJ	0-1183409	0860	1
SCHILHABEL LAUREL H	LTC	0-1848567	0268	1
SCHILL JOHN S	1LT	0-1110790	0146	2
SCHILLER DANIEL	CW3	RW-2145362	0663	1
SCHILLER HERBERT A	CPT	0-0420203	1044	2
SCHILLER HORACE G	LTC	0-0238459	0666	3
SCHILLER MAX	CPT	0-0885811	0646	2
SCHILLER MELVIN O	2LT	0-1173769	0444	2
SCHILLETTER W A	COL	0-0149003	0354	2
SCHILLING CHARLES A	CW3	W-2151207	1164	1
SCHILLING GEORGE W	COL	0-0350170	0265	1
SCHILLING GEORGE W	LTC	0-0408205	0768	3
SCHILLING JOSEPH F	MAJ	0-1330969	0962	1
SCHILLING RUSSELL R	1LT	0-1105795	0847	2
SCHILLINGER EDWARD N	COL	0-0234012	0550	3
SCHIMENTI MATTHEW L	CPT	0-0406232	0445	2
SCHIMMACK AUGUST F	MAJ	0-0192969	0-51	3
SCHIMMEL CARL L	MAJ	0-0266948	0163	3
SCHIMMEL JOHN III	LTC	0-0196173	0363	3
SCHIMSA JOSEPH J	CW4	W-2006084	1068	1
SCHINAZI LEON R	COL	0-0214429	0954	3
SCHINDEL JOHN B	LTC	0-0312495	1067	3
SCHINDELHEIM SAMUE	MAJ	0-0497224	0246	2
SCHINDLER EDWARD C	MAJ	0-1560071	1062	1
SCHINDLER WARREN H	CW3	W-2144760	0464	1
SCHIPPERS RICHARD J	1LT	0-1823495	0550	2
SCHIPPDREIT GEORGE P	LTC	0-0300132	0658	1
SCHIRA PEDRO G	CPT	0-0263957	0259	3
SCHIRMACHER THEODORE	COL	0-0918017	0366	1
SCHIRMER FREDERICK	LTC	0-1118281	0866	1
SCHIRMER ROY E	CPT	0-0337290	1045	2
SCHIRRU SPARTACO R	CW4	RW-2144930	0767	1
SCHISGALL LEO	LTC	0-0205262	0460	3
SCHISKA MARTIN T	MAJ	0-0129356	0958	3
SCHLABAUGH DONALD	CPT	0-1015836	1146	2
SCHLACHTA FRANK J	CPT	0-1882393	0463	2
SCHLAFLI ALFRED JR	COL	0-0380570	0861	1
SCHLAFLY JOHN P	CW3	W-2142607	1057	1
SCHLAGER EDWARD D	CPT	0-0548193	0846	2
SCHLAGER ROLAND G	LTC	0-0453214	1066	3
SCHLAIRET CHARLES V	CPT	0-0486448	0546	2
SCHLAPPER LLOYD H	1LT	0-0132457	0547	2
SCHLAUERSBACH ADAM	CW4	W-2136534	1263	1
SCHLECHTE ARNOLD W	CW2	W-2115352	1048	1
SCHLECHTWEG CHARLES	WO1	W-2215168	0764	2
SCHLEDER GEORGE JR	CW2	W-2209996	0264	1
SCHLEGEL CHARLES E	CW4	W-2102327	0657	1
SCHLEGEL FRANCIS J	CW2	W-2119653	0852	2
SCHLEGEL LESLIE H	1LT	0-1305485	1045	2
SCHLEGELMILCH EARL G	CPT	0-1182700	0562	3

NAME	GRADE	SVC NO	DATE RET MO YR	RET CODE
SCHLEEI ELMER W	LTC	0-0308483	0256	3
SCHLEIDER EMIL J	MAJ	N-0734288	0154	2
SCHLEIFFER THEODORE	MAJ	0-4006620	1167	1
SCHLEIGH RUSS D	MAJ	0-0153249	0744	2
SCHLEMMER MILTON C	CPT	0-2265331	1267	1
SCHLEMMER NORMAN C	1LT	0-0545334	0745	2
SCHLEINER C F	1LT	0-1056877	0146	2
SCHLENKER IRVIN	MAJ	0-4011514	0265	1
SCHLENKER JAMES A	CW3	W-2143113	1059	1
SCHLENKER ROBERT D	1LT	0-1013172	0446	2
SCHLESINGER LEE H	COL	0-0284361	0665	3
SCHLESINGER MELVIN H	COL	0-0129714	1155	3
SCHLESINGER MEYER	LTC	0-1544136	1166	3
SCHLESINGER MORTON	2LT	0-1101303	0844	2
SCHLESINGER NOLAN R	1LT	0-1324955	0146	2
SCHLESINGER SAM	COL	0-1822910	1267	1
SCHLESINGER THOMAS O	MAJ	0-0947274	1064	1
SCHLEUDER ERNEST A	LTC	0-0205571	0857	2
SCHLEY ERVIN L	MAJ	0-1169901	0561	2
SCHLEICHER ROYCE E	CPT	0-1015530	0561	1
SCHLEICHTMAN JOHN D	CW2	W-2152660	0463	1
SCHLICKER EDWARD H	CPT	0-1554473	0164	2
SCHLIEPER ARTHUR W	CPT	0-1058647	0547	2
SCHLIETER WILLARD R	CW3	W-2141439	0561	1
SCHLIEVE RUTH T	2LT	N-0777256	0548	1
SCHLITZKUS GUS W	LTC	0-0337620	0958	1
SCHLOBOHM WILLIAM A	MAJ	0-1633522	1160	1
SCHLOEGEL LOUIS J	LTC	0-2212098	0568	1
SCHLOESSER DOROTHY M	2LT	R-0001151	0945	1
SCHLOSSBERG MAX	MAJ	0-1182701	1263	1
SCHLOSSER JOSEPH D	LTC	0-1635305	0768	3
SCHLOSSER RICHARD W	1LT	0-1796707	0448	2
SCHLOTH WILLIAM J	MAJ	0-0330137	0246	2
SCHLUEDER THOMAS D	1LT	0-1824234	0763	1
SCHLUETER DEAN A	MAJ	0-1342302	0860	1
SCHLUETER JOHN F	WO1	W-2150363	0756	2
SCHLUETER KENNETH W	COL	0-0453324	1061	1
SCHLUETER THEODORE L	MAJ	0-0264641	1059	1
SCHLUNTZ JOACHIM M	LTC	0-0262416	0166	3
SCHLUSSEL MAURICE J	LTC	0-0313090	0867	3
SCHMADER WILBUR P	LTC	0-0372984	0160	1
SCHMAHLENBERGER CARL	MAJ	0-2208020	0564	1
SCHMAL ROBERT E	LTC	0-0306795	0162	1
SCHMALHOFER GEORGE F	MAJ	0-2005693	0263	1
SCHMALL ALEXANDER	WO1	W-2123740	0253	2
SCHMALZIGAN JACK B	CPT	0-0969260	0167	1
SCHMANSKA KATHERIN	1LT	N-0751021	1145	1
SCHMECKERT RAYMOND H	WO1	W-2109812	0864	3
SCHMEDEMAN ALBERT G	LTC	0-0279442	1161	3
SCHMEDEMANN ALBERT J	MAJ	0-0170840	0153	3
SCHMEICHEL JULIUS	LTC	0-0166550	0156	3
SCHMELA WOODROW W	MAJ	0-0356237	0346	2
SCHMELING ALFRED	CPT	0-0491080	0348	1
SCHMELTZER C H	MAJ	0-0166461	0956	3
SCHMELTZER ROBERT M	LTC	0-1030930	0962	1
SCHMELZER JOHN H	LTC	0-0223971	0157	3
SCHMENK CATHERINE	MAJ	N-0769562	0467	1
SCHMERBAUCH HUBERT B	CPT	0-1295091	1049	2
SCHMICKLE ROBERT D	LTC	0-0250785	0966	3
SCHMICKLEY PAULINE	MAJ	N-0784400	0164	1
SCHMID EARL W	MAJ	0-1289819	0856	1
SCHMID ELLS P	MAJ	0-1341908	1060	2
SCHMID HAROLD W	LTC	0-0216959	0164	3
SCHMID HELMUT K	COL	0-0372521	0260	1
SCHMID JAMES J	CW4	W-2150291	0868	1
SCHMID KARL A	LTC	0-0405239	0547	2
SCHMIDGALL FRANK W	CPT	0-1881262	0863	1
SCHMIDHAMER KATHRYN	MAJ	N-0759952	0368	1
SCHMIDT CHARLES A	CPT	0-1316677	0657	1
SCHMIDT DANIEL H	LTC	0-0279862	0868	3
SCHMIDT DAVID G	COL	0-0311206	1166	3
SCHMIDT DELMER A	MAJ	0-1169725	1161	1
SCHMIDT EDWARD J	COL	0-0159420	0753	3
SCHMIDT EDWARD L JR	LTC	0-0251825	0660	1
SCHMIDT EDWIN A	CPT	0-1580281	0546	2

NAME	GRADE	SVC NO	DATE RET MO YR	RET CODE
SCHMIDT ELDON M	CW4	W-2114259	0359	1
SCHMIDT ELVIRA C	2LT	N-0737038	0943	1
SCHMIDT ERNEST A	CW3	W-2151686	0864	1
SCHMIDT EUGENE A	LTC	0-0403751	1163	1
SCHMIDT FRED J	LTC	0-1101206	0761	1
SCHMIDT FREDERICK	COL	0-0256280	1058	3
SCHMIDT FREDERICK	LTC	0-0323579	0963	3
SCHMIDT FREDERICK	LTC	0-1300396	0657	1
SCHMIDT GEORGE F	CW2	W-2210356	1063	1
SCHMIDT GEORGE P	CPT	0-0253298	0142	2
SCHMIDT GEORGE W	CW2	W-2148266	0163	1
SCHMIDT HANS W	COL	0-0312696	0765	3
SCHMIDT HARRY	CPT	0-0244523	0445	1
SCHMIDT HARRY E	MAJ	0-0502554	1045	2
SCHMIDT HILTON A JR	1LT	0-0396183	0443	2
SCHMIDT HUGO A	CPT	0-0415069	0345	2
SCHMIDT JAMES R	MAJ	0-0356908	0846	2
SCHMIDT JOHN B	LTC	0-0329186	0864	1
SCHMIDT JOHN H	CPT	0-0427910	0644	2
SCHMIDT JOSEPH I JR	CPT	0-1171749	0862	1
SCHMIDT KENNETH G	MAJ	0-0273447	0366	3
SCHMIDT LEONARD B	1LT	0-1297259	104N	2
SCHMIDT LEROY A	MAJ	0-1185347	0361	1
SCHMIDT LINDLEY G	COL	0-0177834	0547	2
SCHMIDT LORRIMER M	MAJ	0-0505658	1146	2
SCHMIDT LOUVERA B	LTC	0-0230718	0460	3
SCHMIDT MARVIN T	MAJ	0-0964471	0662	1
SCHMIDT MAURICE S	LTC	0-1534138	0863	1
SCHMIDT OTTO H	LTC	0-0332063	0152	3
SCHMIDT PAUL W	COL	0-0123534	0556	3
SCHMIDT PHILIPP E	MAJ	0-0257330	0157	3
SCHMIDT RICHARD P	2LT	0-0552401	0845	2
SCHMIDT ROBERT A	COL	0-0332201	0665	3
SCHMIDT ROBERT D	COL	0-0332392	1145	2
SCHMIDT ROBERT F	CW2	W-2144429	1060	1
SCHMIDT WALTER	CW3	W-2129412	1154	1
SCHMIDT WALTER G	LTC	0-1639606	0162	1
SCHMIDT WALTER J	MAJ	0-0481638	0845	2
SCHMIDT WARREN R	CPT	0-1340405	1064	1
SCHMIDT WILLIAM C	LTC	0-0220704	0553	3
SCHMIDT WILLIAM G	CPT	0-1295438	0747	2
SCHMIDT WOODROW C	MAJ	0-2007691	1058	1
SCHMIED WILLIAM C	MAJ	0-0378730	0747	2
SCHMIEDEKE JOHN A	LTC	0-1319023	0466	1
SCHMIER ADOLPH A	MAJ	0-0508973	0646	2
SCHMILSKI RHINEHARD	MAJ	0-1541681	1159	1
SCHMINK ELWOOD P	LTC	0-0262995	0168	3
SCHMINKE GEORGE C	LTC	0-0240733	1264	3
SCHMITCKE RALPH B	CW4	W-2127514	0659	1
SCHMITS LOUIS H	CW3	W-2143961	0363	1
SCHMITT BENEDICT C	CW2	W-2205809	0164	1
SCHMITT CHARLES J	MAJ	0-0239995	1164	3
SCHMITT CHRIST G	LTC	0-0302168	0167	3
SCHMITT EDWARD	COL	0-0127926	0956	3
SCHMITT MARTIN J	CPT	0-0996075	0158	2
SCHMITZ ARTHUR H	LTC	0-0290618	0860	2
SCHMITZ ENGELBERT	MAJ	0-0330449	0657	3
SCHMITZ FLORA D	MAJ	N-0767013	0563	1
SCHMITZ GEORGE A	CW4	W-2004899	0368	1
SCHMITZ JOHN T	COL	0-0319265	0861	1
SCHMOLDT EDGAR R	LTC	0-1282255	1268	1
SCHMOLL EDWARD A JR	LTC	0-1533910	0461	1
SCHMOLZE FREDERICK	CPT	0-1031991	0468	2
SCHMOOCK WALDEMAR C	LTC	0-0910100	0866	3
SCHMOTZER STEVE	CW4	W-2003968	0568	1
SCHMOYER ARTHUR R	1LT	0-0508304	0845	2
SCHMUCK EDWARD J	LTC	0-0349795	0546	2
SCHMUHL LORENZ C	LTC	0-0121598	0358	3
SCHMUS JACK C	MAJ	0-0524502	0954	1
SCHNABEL HERMAN J	MAJ	0-0445787	0962	1
SCHNABEL IRVING D	2LT	0-1110792	0145	2
SCHNABEL JAMES F	LTC	0-1176795	0964	1
SCHNABEL LOUIS F	COL	0-0374673	0764	1
SCHNACKENBERG FREDER	LTC	0-1326587	0763	;
SCHNAKENBERG WILLIAM	CW2	W-3410013	0468	1

NAME	GRADE	SVC NO	DATE RET MO YR	RET CODE
SCHNAP ISIDORE	COL	0-0467348	0866	3
SCHNATHORST WILLIA	MAJ	0-0504491	1044	2
SCHNAUTZ WILLIAM J	CPT	0-0223519	0653	3
SCHNECK JACOB O	LTC	0-0451432	0957	1
SCHNECK ROSE H	1LT	N-0730517	0546	1
SCHNEDLER WILFRED J	LTC	0-0316443	0664	3
SCHNEE CHARLES W	LTC	0-0371229	1167	3
SCHNEIDER ALBERT C	MAJ	0-0468090	0247	1
SCHNEIDER ALBERT L	MAJ	0-1054111	1064	1
SCHNEIDER ARLON B	1LT	0-0370992	1044	2
SCHNEIDER CATHEREN M	LTC	N-0733277	1162	1
SCHNEIDER CHARLES L	MAJ	0-1545259	1067	3
SCHNEIDER CHARLES P	CPT	0-0446271	0845	2
SCHNEIDER CHRISTIAN	CW2	W-2209730	0863	1
SCHNEIDER CLAUDE R	MAJ	0-0217496	1054	3
SCHNEIDER CLEMMENS	LTC	0-0333525	1159	3
SCHNEIDER EARL A	CPT	0-1011763	0557	1
SCHNEIDER EDWARD H	LTC	0-0312191	1264	3
SCHNEIDER ELMER V	COL	0-0311507	0868	3
SCHNEIDER EMMA F	1LT	N-0772790	0746	1
SCHNEIDER EUGENIE H	1LT	N-0743964	0645	1
SCHNEIDER FREDDIE J	WO1	W-2148937	0656	1
SCHNEIDER FREDERICK	MAJ	0-0286816	0260	3
SCHNEIDER GEORGE M	MAJ	0-2026412	1162	1
SCHNEIDER GLENN W	LTC	0-1317685	0664	1
SCHNEIDER HAROLD B	1LT	0-1581359	0756	1
SCHNEIDER HARRY	LTC	0-1299315	1055	1
SCHNEIDER HENRY J	COL	0-0451570	1166	2
SCHNEIDER HERBERT A	1LT	0-1302206	114N	2
SCHNEIDER JOHN	2LT	0-1051773	1043	2
SCHNEIDER JOHN M	CPT	0-0452061	0156	1
SCHNEIDER JOHN T	COL	0-0290102	0655	3
SCHNEIDER JOSEPH A	LTC	0-0325570	1068	3
SCHNEIDER JOSEPH H	LTC	0-1307942	1162	1
SCHNEIDER KENNETH E	LTC	0-1255780	0765	1
SCHNEIDER LOUIS	LTC	0-0250394	0164	3
SCHNEIDER MAURICE H	MAJ	0-2262364	0462	1
SCHNEIDER MORRIS D	LTC	0-0344521	0262	1
SCHNEIDER ORVILLE N	CPT	0-0348493	0767	3
SCHNEIDER OTTO H	LTC	0-0397929	0860	1
SCHNEIDER PHILIP	CW3	RW-2147923	1163	1
SCHNEIDER RALPH W	LTC	0-0903531	0865	3
SCHNEIDER ROBERT	2LT	0-0420310	0545	2
SCHNEIDER ROLLAND E	LTC	0-1059272	0867	1
SCHNEIDER WILLIAM N	MAJ	0-1597917	1063	1
SCHNEIDER WILLIAM R	MAJ	0-0989014	1165	1
SCHNEIDEWIND A R	COL	0-0184070	1058	3
SCHNELL HERMAN F	CPT	0-0322691	1153	2
SCHNELL JACK C	MAJ	0-1583632	0565	2
SCHNELL JOHN H	LTC	0-0301325	1054	2
SCHNELL MICHAEL W	MAJ	0-1549599	1158	2
SCHNELLENBACH KURT	COL	0-0475887	0255	1
SCHNELLER RAYMOND J	MAJ	0-0370406	0746	2
SCHNETZLER ROBERT H	CW4	W-2141440	1167	1
SCHNIERING JOHN	LTC	0-1303780	0966	1
SCHNIRCH LESTER R	LTC	0-1950785	0768	1
SCHNITTMAN JOSEPH L	CW2	W-2153153	0364	1
SCHNOOK HENRY L	COL	0-0229240	0465	3
SCHNUR JAMES F	LTC	0-1041645	0352	2
SCHNURR FREDERICK	MAJ	0-1826248	1165	1
SCHOCH FRANCIS J	CW3	W-2149951	0764	1
SCHOCH JAMES B	MAJ	0-0167344	0455	3
SCHOCH LEO M	CPT	0-0479593	0955	1
SCHOEBEN BERNARD W	WO1	W-2129906	0144	2
SCHOEBERL GEORGE M	LTC	0-1574136	0556	1
SCHOEBERL ROBERT H	MAJ	0-0971964	1063	1
SCHOECH OSCAR W	LTC	0-0376641	0860	1
SCHOEL LOUIS H	LTC	0-0283902	0168	3
SCHOELLER JULIUS E	LTC	0-1042425	1062	1
SCHOEN JOSEPH F	COL	0-0916551	0763	3
SCHOEN LEON W	LTC	0-0272021	0964	3
SCHOENBAECHLER GILBE	MAJ	0-2033995	0566	1
SCHOENBAUM GEORGE H	MAJ	0-0290871	0745	2
SCHOENBECK EDWIN H	CPT	0-1030714	1046	2
SCHOENBERG HARRY I	CPT	0-1305469	0567	2

NAME	GRADE	SVC NO	DATE RET MO YR	RET CODE
SCHOENBERG T F	1LT	0-1823219	0346	2
SCHOENBERGER LAURENC	MAJ	0-0302901	0962	1
SCHOENBORN FREDERICK	LTC	0-0239840	0864	3
SCHOENENBERGER A R	CPT	0-1697773	0645	2
SCHOENKOPFF EDWARD E	LTC	0-0200387	0552	3
SCHOENMAN HARRY P JR	LTC	0-1052152	0764	1
SCHOENTAG DAVID C	CPT	0-1312232	0848	2
SCHOENWETHER KENNETH	LTC	0-0295753	1165	1
SCHOENY RICHARD L	LTC	0-1011963	0763	1
SCHOETTLE JACOB F JR	2LT	0-1335700	0446	2
SCHOFFSTALL WAYNE	CPT	0-0219692	0347	1
SCHOFFSTOLL LOUIS E	LTC	0-1824924	1162	1
SCHOFIELD EVERETT H	CW4	W-2116195	0359	2
SCHOFIELD FLOYD O	CPT	0-0114942	0156	3
SCHOFIELD HERBERT M	COL	0-0210660	0643	3
SCHOFIELD JOHNC	MAJ	0-0293375	1048	1
SCHOFIELD LAWRENCE E	MAJ	0-0300439	1145	2
SCHOFIELD MORGAN G	LTC	0-1587605	0156	1
SCHOFIELD OSCAR	CPT	0-0331367	0745	2
SCHOFIELD THEODORE H	MAJ	0-0978170	0062	1
SCHOLEY THEODORE R	LTC	0-0238692	0462	3
SCHOLL CLYDE L	LTC	0-1944587	0562	1
SCHOLL DONALD E	CPT	0-1919170	1264	1
SCHOLL EARL S	2LT	0-1014860	1045	2
SCHOLL GEORGE A	LTC	0-1294540	1060	1
SCHOLL GEORGE W JR	MAJ	0-1930900	1068	1
SCHOLL HAROLD I	WO1	W-2146274	0558	1
SCHOLL HENRY	2LT	0-0217219	1024	1
SCHOLL JAMES N	1LT	0-1014395	0846	2
SCHOLL JOHN A	CPT	0-0358382	0145	2
SCHOLL STANLEY F	LTC	0-0347738	0354	2
SCHOLLARD JOHN	1LT	0-0404981	0745	2
SCHOLLE JESS L	LTC	0-0315820	0564	1
SCHOLLER JOSEPH P	CPT	0-0322308	0645	2
SCHOLLIAN HAROLD F	MAJ	0-1316678	0864	3
SCHOLLMEYER KURT	1LT	0-1289149	1045	2
SCHOLLY WILLIAM C	MAJ	0-1336429	1164	1
SCHOLOM JACOB	CPT	0-1171750	0646	2
SCHOLTZ ERWIN V	LTC	0-1575694	1055	1
SCHOLTZ FRANK C	MAJ	0-0297317	0545	2
SCHOLTZ JULIUS R	LTC	0-0463600	1145	2
SCHOLZ HARVEY A	LTC	0-1994848	1060	1
SCHOLZ JOSEPH W	2LT	0-1312803	0346	2
SCHOLZ RUDOLPH J	COL	0-0167879	0656	3
SCHOLZE JACK J	CPT	0-1305486	0248	2
SCHOMBURG CARL F	MAJ	0-1582889	0760	1
SCHOMISCH ROBERT C	MAJ	0-0464000	0347	2
SCHON HUBERT A	COL	0-0276627	0367	3
SCHON RUTH	1LT	N-0775197	0945	1
SCHONE CARL G	COL	0-1573573	0963	1
SCHONFELD PAUL O	2LT	0-1003160	0445	2
SCHONFELD SEYMOUR A	CW2	RW-2108332	0560	1
SCHONFELD WILLIAM A	MAJ	0-1690600	0946	2
SCHONGAR GEORGE P	1LT	0-0423021	0545	2
SCHOOK ROBERT N	CW2	W-3250218	0466	1
SCHOOLER ERNEST JR	MAJ	0-2019655	0263	1
SCHOOLEY JESSE B	LTC	0-0422581	0261	1
SCHOOLFIELD HUGH M	LTC	0-1107106	0862	1
SCHOOLING JAMES F	LTC	0-0220325	1053	3
SCHOONDYKE ROBERT E	2LT	0-1328937	0845	2
SCHOONMAKER FRED T	1LT	0-0345538	0347	2
SCHOONOVER FRED E	CPT	0-1300864	0147	2
SCHOONOVER KENNETH E	MAJ	0-1112425	0361	1
SCHOPP ALVIN C	MAJ	0-0356511	0746	2
SCHOPPER WALTER P	COL	0-0508664	0863	2
SCHOR HOWARD P	LTC	0-0310416	1061	3
SCHORK CHRISTIAN	MAJ	0-0482545	0849	1
SCHORR HYMAN J	CPT	0-0517041	1145	2
SCHORSTEN EDWARD S	MAJ	0-2016036	0363	1
SCHOTT FRANK L	1LT	0-1040063	1144	2
SCHOTT NAOMI R	2LT	N-0723945	1044	1
SCHOTT ROYAL M	CW4	W-2202629	0867	3
SCHOTT STUART	CPT	0-0490716	0146	2
SCHOTTLAND STANLEY A	1LT	0-1315624	0745	2
SCHOUVALOFF PETER	LTC	0-0922661	1065	3

NAME	GRADE	SVC NO	DATE RET MO YR	RET CODE
SCHOWALTER HERBERT P	COL	O-0210991	0953	3
SCHOWENGERDT WILLIAM	COL	O-0314849	0864	3
SCHRADE RALPH E	CW3	W-2150122	0463	1
SCHRADER CHARLES H	COL	O-0348211	0863	1
SCHRADER JOHN P	MAJ	O-0248635	1044	2
SCHRADER JULIUS J	MAJ	O-2208417	0466	1
SCHRADER LOWELL G	MAJ	O-0239567	1146	2
SCHRAEDER EDNA	CPT	N-0726899	1045	1
SCHRAGER ARTHUR J	LTC	O-0368623	0166	3
SCHRAM CHARLES JR	1LT	O-1321034	0745	2
SCHRAM CHARLES R	COL	O-0349908	0558	3
SCHRAMAR JOHN	1LT	O-1913978	0336	1
SCHRAMM ERIC	MAJ	O-1850063	1061	1
SCHRAMM MARVIN L	MAJ	O-1108992	0959	1
SCHRANDT CHARLES C	MAJ	O-0345437	0855	3
SCHRANK JOHN W	LTC	O-0354186	0867	3
SCHRANTZ GEORGE N	COL	O-0287238	0961	2
SCHRANTZ MYRON A	COL	O-0409076	1068	3
SCHRANZ FRANCIS M	1LT	O-1298604	0745	2
SCHRAVESANDE JOHN B	COL	O-0916433	0364	3
SCHRECK FRANCIS C	1LT	O-1308551	104N	2
SCHRECK ROBERT W	MAJ	O-1554085	0366	1
SCHREIBER RICHARD C	CW3	W-2141867	0861	1
SCHREIBER ROBERT E	2LT	O-0513948	0145	2
SCHREIBER WALTER R	CPT	O-0515152	1144	2
SCHREIBER WILLIAM A	COL	O-0358623	0864	1
SCHREIBSTEIN ROBERT	LTC	O-1644754	0964	1
SCHREINER CARL E	MAJ	O-1045591	1160	1
SCHREINER FRANK	MAJ	O-2016118	0467	1
SCHREINER GEORGE W	MAJ	O-2014716	0167	1
SCHREINER ORA C	LTC	O-0294281	1066	3
SCHREINER ROGER W	LTC	O-1598394	0667	1
SCHREINER WILLIAM J	LTC	O-0202351	0163	3
SCHREMP WILLIAM R	CPT	O-1173067	1264	1
SCHREPEL DONALD W	MAJ	O-0297553	0667	3
SCHREY JACK W	CPT	O-0351805	1045	2
SCHREYER MILTON M	MAJ	O-1297789	0361	1
SCHRICKER ROBERT L	1LT	O-1928319	1156	2
SCHRIMPF KENNETH A	MAJ	O-1050069	1162	1
SCHRODER EDWARD G	LTC	O-0397816	1068	3
SCHRODER CARLTON J	MAJ	O-0548194	0966	2
SCHRODER CHARLES	2LT	O-0328981	1041	2
SCHROEDER ALFRED J	LTC	O-0504313	0457	1
SCHROEDER CARL J	LTC	O-0225311	0360	3
SCHROEDER CLARENCE H	MAJ	O-1892458	0967	1
SCHROEDER CLEMONS C	2LT	O-1642556	0944	2
SCHROEDER CLOYDE P	LTC	O-0182898	0850	2
SCHROEDER DIETRICH	LTC	O-1591433	1063	3
SCHROEDER EARLE W	LTC	O-0303914	0562	1
SCHROEDER EDGAR A	CPT	O-1172645	0149	2
SCHROEDER EDGAR E	COL	O-0183128	1160	3
SCHROEDER EDWARD P	1LT	O-1326666	0346	2
SCHROEDER EDWIN E	MAJ	O-0102023	0156	3
SCHROEDER ERNEST J	MAJ	O-0423272	0246	2
SCHROEDER FREDERIC W	COL	O-0219333	0159	3
SCHROEDER GEORGE R	LTC	O-1046259	1064	1
SCHROEDER JAMES M	LTC	O-1338863	0766	1
SCHROEDER JULIUS T	MAJ	O-1930961	1066	1
SCHROEDER LESLIE L G	CPT	O-0221812	0764	3
SCHROEDER NORMAN C	LTC	O-0494871	0645	2
SCHROEDER RAYMOND H	COL	O-0231897	0356	3
SCHROEDER RICHARD J	2LT	O-0783635	0361	2
SCHROEDER ROBERT F	CW2	W-2142721	0157	1
SCHROEDER RUTH E	CPT	N-0773620	0448	1
SCHROEDER WALTER	LTC	O-0253680	1055	3
SCHROEDER WILFRED G	CPT	O-1319664	0647	2
SCHROEDER WILLIAM K	MAJ	O-0242674	1051	2
SCHROEER LORRAINE	1LT	N-0703097	0143	1
SCHROETER HERBERT F	CPT	O-1305487	0762	1
SCHROETER THOMAS I	LTC	O-0496194	0456	1
SCHROLL GERALD C	MAJ	O-1640929	0567	1
SCHRON JOHN E	CW2	W-2215819	0868	1
SCHROTH EDWARD W	MAJ	O-1922723	1167	1
SCHROYER GEORGE W	CW2	W-2131443	0348	1
SCHRYER LAWRENCE M	LTC	O-1580289	1162	1

NAME	GRADE	SVC NO	DATE RET MO YR	RET CODE
SCHRYVER LEWIS A	CPT	O-0165526	0350	2
SCHUBERT CHARLES A	LTC	O-0270991	0858	1
SCHUBERT GEORGE E	LTC	O-0364531	0459	1
SCHUBERT HAROLD J	COL	O-0375822	0658	1
SCHUBERT JAMES A	LTC	O-0907498	0463	1
SCHUBERT JOSEPH R	2LT	O-1588871	0944	2
SCHUBERT PAUL W	COL	O-0314331	1062	2
SCHUBERT URIEL	CPT	O-1048573	1045	2
SCHUBERT WARREN F	COL	O-0387733	0963	1
SCHUBERT WOODROW H	LTC	O-1101209	0461	1
SCHUBKEGEL PAULINE	1LT	N-0783817	1046	2
SCHUBMEHL WILLIAM J	LTC	O-0299762	0960	2
SCHUCH ADAM F	LTC	O-0265293	0667	3
SCHUCHAT VICTOR E	2LT	O-1588273	0744	2
SCHUCK GEORGE E	LTC	O-0494987	0854	1
SCHUCK LAWRENCE A	1LT	O-1289326	1045	2
SCHUCK RALPH T	MAJ	O-2042840	1054	1
SCHUCKER HARRY P	MAJ	O-0109183	0744	1
SCHUE CHARLES S	CW3	W-2113744	0659	1
SCHUE EDWARD B	MAJ	O-1335065	0762	1
SCHUE LLOYD	CPT	O-0264316	0846	1
SCHUELLER JOHN P	2LT	O-1310507	0645	2
SCHUENEMAN HELEN L	1LT	N-0703852	0646	1
SCHUERMEYER CARLYLE	LTC	O-0281127	0365	3
SCHUESSLER GEORGE D	LTC	O-0307268	0268	3
SCHUETTE EARL R	LTC	O-1556943	0863	1
SCHUETTE ROBERT F	LTC	O-0178323	0660	3
SCHUETTNER RICHARD C	LTC	O-0290776	0467	3
SCHUETZ GORDON R	CW3	W-2147597	0863	1
SCHUETZ LILLIAN H	MAJ	N-0737416	0665	3
SCHUFF EUGENE J JR	COL	O-0276659	0466	3
SCHUG ANTHONY JR	MAJ	O-1950786	1067	3
SCHUGAR EMANUEL	LTC	O-0320854	0746	2
SCHUGG CARL V	1LT	O-0264120	0256	3
SCHUH MARION G	MAJ	N-0703828	1263	1
SCHUH WILLIAM P	MAJ	O-1321338	0957	2
SCHUHERT WILLIAM A	CPT	O-0977604	0261	1
SCHUL JOSEPH	MAJ	O-2012085	0263	1
SCHULD WALTER O	2LT	O-1177627	0744	2
SCHULENBERG DONALD F	LTC	O-0479286	0965	1
SCHULER LESTER W	MAJ	O-0235834	0861	3
SCHULER PAUL H	LTC	O-0378828	0660	1
SCHULER REFO H	CPT	O-0291078	1267	3
SCHULHOFF JOSEPH	1LT	O-1175857	1145	2
SCHULKIN LESLIE M	2LT	O-1300433	0245	2
SCHULLER JOHN C	LTC	O-0291856	0467	3
SCHULMAN DANIEL B	1LT	O-1584865	0345	2
SCHULSTAD LAWRENCE M	LTC	O-0309339	0866	3
SCHULTE ARDEN C	CPT	O-0991592	0961	1
SCHULTE JESSE J	CW4	W-2142777	1264	1
SCHULTE JOHN H	CPT	O-1644756	0357	1
SCHULTE LOUIS C	COL	O-0100913	1053	3
SCHULTZ ALBERT V	CW3	W-2151860	0960	1
SCHULTZ ARCHIE D	1LT	O-1322088	0945	2
SCHULTZ CHRISTIAN	LTC	O-2042770	0757	1
SCHULTZ DALE L	MAJ	O-1798068	1060	1
SCHULTZ DELBERT E	B G	O-0309296	0666	3
SCHULTZ EDWARD G	LTC	O-0221581	0755	3
SCHULTZ EDWARD J	LTC	O-0327619	1045	2
SCHULTZ FRANK B	LTC	O-0333503	0958	3
SCHULTZ FRANK R	MAJ	O-1055725	0460	1
SCHULTZ HARRY H	COL	O-0343384	0962	3
SCHULTZ HERMAN C	LTC	O-2262779	0867	2
SCHULTZ JAMES F	1LT	O-1288454	0445	2
SCHULTZ JAMES H	CPT	O-1924979	1063	1
SCHULTZ JOHN H	MAJ	O-1052558	0764	1
SCHULTZ JOHN H JR	MAJ	O-0997293	0667	1
SCHULTZ JOHN M	LTC	O-0333189	0547	2
SCHULTZ JOHN M	CPT	O-1104390	0947	1
SCHULTZ JOSEPH F	LTC	O-2037018	0762	1
SCHULTZ LEONHARDT	CPT	O-1010057	0646	2
SCHULTZ LORRAINE A	MAJ	L-0704059	0765	2
SCHULTZ NATHAN	CW2	W-2152535	1063	1
SCHULTZ ORVILLE W	1LT	O-1113430	0645	2
SCHULTZ OSCAR E	MAJ	O-0238072	1155	3

NAME	GRADE	SVC NO	DATE RET MO YR	RET CODE
SCHULTZ PAUL E	2LT	O-1315376	1043	2
SCHULTZ PAUL H	LTC	O-1794996	1162	1
SCHULTZ ROBERT R	CPT	O-1293323	0147	2
SCHULTZ SAMUEL K	COL	O-0316804	0668	3
SCHULTZ THOMAS P	CW3	W-2146275	1063	1
SCHULTZ WALTER A	COL	O-0216955	0563	3
SCHULTZ WILLIAM C	CW2	W-2148684	1055	2
SCHULTZ WILLIAM F	CW3	W-2153361	0760	1
SCHULTZE BENJAMIN R	MAJ	O-1059631	0361	1
SCHULTZE MAX O	COL	O-0437754	0666	3
SCHULZ ARTHUR W	LTC	O-0153609	0452	3
SCHULZ CHARLES T	MAJ	O-0247015	1056	3
SCHULZ ELDOR J	LTC	O-0438416	0767	1
SCHULZ JAMES G	1LT	O-1598226	0147	2
SCHULZ LYNN W	2LT	O-1290485	1144	2
SCHULZ MILTON J	LTC	O-0219527	0361	3
SCHULZ ROBERT P	M G	O-0330078	1065	3
SCHULZ VERNIE A	MAJ	O-2037768	0567	3
SCHULZ WILLIAM J JR	CPT	O-1320658	1146	2
SCHULZE KENNETH C	WO1	W-3100719	0667	1
SCHULZE LUTHER M	LTC	O-0329613	0866	3
SCHULZE THEODORE L	CW2	W-2144557	1163	1
SCHUMACHER ADOLPH G	LTC	O-1590789	0366	3
SCHUMACHER ARTHUR B	LTC	O-0292510	1165	3
SCHUMACHER ARTHUR F	COL	O-0247786	0852	3
SCHUMACHER ARTHUR L	LTC	O-1289493	0762	1
SCHUMACHER B F	CPT	O-0169812	0159	3
SCHUMACHER CHARLES A	LTC	O-0256143	0363	3
SCHUMACHER ERNST F	LTC	O-1317946	0962	1
SCHUMACHER FRED W	CW3	W-2146168	1160	1
SCHUMACHER HENRY A	MAJ	O-0170945	0757	3
SCHUMACHER IRWIN C	COL	O-0184311	1153	3
SCHUMACHER JOHN H	LTC	O-1105798	0166	1
SCHUMACHER LELAND L	LTC	O-1550048	0561	2
SCHUMACHER MELVIN M	MAJ	O-2024239	1160	1
SCHUMACHER WALTER L	LTC	O-0919998	0867	3
SCHUMACHER WILLIAM F	MAJ	O-1315455	0463	1
SCHUMACHER WILLIAM G	CW4	W-2002197	1163	3
SCHUMAKER FREDERICK	CPT	O-1917927	1264	2
SCHUMAKER JAMES K JR	MAJ	O-0928483	0168	1
SCHUMAN IRVING	COL	O-0329342	0567	3
SCHUMAN STANLEY	2LT	O-1294913	0344	2
SCHUMANN HARVEY H	LTC	O-0924273	0367	3
SCHUMANN ROLF A P	MAJ	O-1885626	1166	1
SCHUMANN WILLIAM F	1LT	O-1017625	0945	2
SCHUMMERS WILLIAM M	LTC	O-1001674	0566	1
SCHUNIOR GEORGE F	COL	O-0294918	0463	1
SCHUPACK ISADOR B	LTC	O-0314043	0968	3
SCHUPP DONALD L	MAJ	O-1168070	1061	1
SCHUPPER NATHAN	COL	O-0373510	0768	3
SCHUPPNER HARRY R	COL	O-0125468	1047	2
SCHURIG OTTO R	COL	O-0246936	0550	3
SCHURMAN ERICH R	1LT	O-0499493	0557	1
SCHURR EMILE H	CW4	W-2000434	0961	3
SCHURTZ JACK C	CPT	O-1044946	0662	1
SCHUSSLER EDWARD	2LT	O-1595814	1044	2
SCHUSSLER EDWARD W	LTC	O-0419627	0760	2
SCHUSTER ARTHUR A	1LT	O-1325837	1045	2
SCHUSTER EDWARD J	LTC	O-0262005	0468	3
SCHUSTER HAROLD F	CW4	W-2148187	1068	1
SCHUSTER HERMAN F	B G	O-0366569	1168	3
SCHUSTER JAMES D	LTC	O-0131128	1048	3
SCHUSTER JOHN C	MAJ	O-0107997	1054	3
SCHUSTER JOSEPH A	1LT	O-0918794	0551	2
SCHUSTER MAYNARD B	1LT	O-1825191	1145	2
SCHUTT ERNEST C JR	MAJ	O-1052156	0361	1
SCHUTT LESTER F	LTC	O-1895255	0562	1
SCHUTTLER WALTER H	CPT	O-0973582	1060	1
SCHUTZ CHARLES D	MAJ	O-0389669	0446	2
SCHUTZE WALTER	LTC	O-0260899	0367	3
SCHUYLER GEORGE B	LTC	O-0193012	0458	3
SCHUYLER JOHN J	COL	O-0377465	0265	1
SCHUYLER PHILIP	CPT	O-0290768	1044	2
SCHUYLER PHILIP G	CPT	O-1308768	0146	2
SCHWAB ARTHUR J	1LT	O-1307857	0945	2

NAME	GRADE	SVC NO	DATE RET MO YR	RET CODE
SCHWAB DONALD K	1LT	O-1290315	1045	2
SCHWAB ERWIN N	MAJ	O-1052559	0962	1
SCHWAB FLORENCE C	CPT	N-0725836	0947	1
SCHWAB GEORGE P	CPT	O-0400720	0450	2
SCHWAB JOHN S JR	MAJ	O-1319344	0264	1
SCHWAB JOSEPH F	CW4	W-2001832	0767	3
SCHWAB LOUIS	CPT	O-1745651	0947	2
SCHWABE ADOLPH R	1LT	O-0890411	0252	2
SCHWABE OTTO	2LT	O-1174136	0351	2
SCHWAEBLE ELSIE	MAJ	N-0700220	0946	1
SCHWAGER VINCENT V	1LT	O-1032600	0945	2
SCHWAGER WILLIAM P	CPT	O-1638462	0157	1
SCHWAIGER LUDWIG A	CW4	W-2108306	1154	1
SCHWALBACH PARK J	CPT	O-0534949	0848	1
SCHWALL ALFRED J	2LT	O-1060964	1044	2
SCHWALL REFOE L	MAJ	O-0453927	0758	1
SCHWALM ARTHUR W	1LT	O-0451178	0246	2
SCHWAMBERGER RALPH F	CPT	O-1295946	0546	2
SCHWANECK JOHN T	LTC	O-0325066	0246	2
SCHWANKE JAMES W	LTC	O-0258066	0465	3
SCHWARCZ GILBERT G	LTC	O-0284884	0162	3
SCHWARM ERNEST P	MAJ	O-0272766	0367	3
SCHWARTZ AARON	1LT	O-1574524	0944	2
SCHWARTZ ABNER B	CPT	O-1011661	1044	2
SCHWARTZ ALBERT F	2LT	O-1594458	1045	2
SCHWARTZ ANDREW J	LTC	O-0189682	0956	3
SCHWARTZ BENJAMIN	LTC	O-0906870	0765	3
SCHWARTZ BYRON W	COL	O-0183844	1055	1
SCHWARTZ DAVID	2LT	O-1177628	0244	2
SCHWARTZ EDWARD	CPT	O-0316805	0845	2
SCHWARTZ EDWARD A	CW3	W-2148188	0262	1
SCHWARTZ ELMER L	CW3	W-2152519	0862	1
SCHWARTZ ELWOOD G	LTC	O-1042163	0157	1
SCHWARTZ EMANUEL	CPT	O-0540606	0446	2
SCHWARTZ FLOYD K	MAJ	O-1011473	1167	1
SCHWARTZ FRANCIS R	CW4	W-2136043	0661	1
SCHWARTZ GEORGE E	CW3	W-2150719	0267	1
SCHWARTZ GEORGE T	LTC	O-1303209	1262	1
SCHWARTZ GERALD D	1LT	O-1715610	0545	2
SCHWARTZ HARRY L	MAJ	O-1697685	0646	2
SCHWARTZ HERMAN J	LTC	O-1555132	0463	1
SCHWARTZ ISADORE R	LTC	O-0274499	0164	3
SCHWARTZ JEROME	1LT	O-1062287	0747	2
SCHWARTZ JOHN F	COL	O-0296471	1064	1
SCHWARTZ JOSEPH SR	MAJ	O-1113431	0959	1
SCHWARTZ KENNETH C	COL	O-0239778	0465	3
SCHWARTZ LEO R	MAJ	O-0503778	1045	2
SCHWARTZ LOUIS	LTC	O-0344456	0363	3
SCHWARTZ MARCUS	COL	O-0240038	0663	3
SCHWARTZ MELVIN B	CPT	O-0390674	0246	2
SCHWARTZ MORRIS L	COL	O-0167009	1156	3
SCHWARTZ MORRIS S	COL	O-0185522	0358	3
SCHWARTZ NATHAN F	CPT	O-0503972	1145	2
SCHWARTZ ROBERT J	2LT	O-1294731	1044	2
SCHWARTZ ROBERT L	LTC	O-1308233	0666	1
SCHWARTZ ROBERT M	LTC	O-0401669	1160	1
SCHWARTZ SAMUEL Z	CPT	O-0381978	0663	1
SCHWARTZ SEYMOUR H	1LT	O-1303036	0745	2
SCHWARTZ STANLEY L	CPT	O-0484258	1147	2
SCHWARTZ THEODORE	CPT	O-0503443	0845	2
SCHWARTZ THOMAS A JR	MAJ	O-1877113	1168	1
SCHWARTZ WILLAIM A	CPT	O-0474489	1045	2
SCHWARTZ WILLIAM A	CW3	W-2149459	1162	2
SCHWARTZ WILLIAM F	CW4	W-2115268	0359	1
SCHWARTZ WILLIAM W	MAJ	O-0988416	0965	1
SCHWARZ CHARLES E	CW3	W-2145508	0959	1
SCHWARZ HENRY F	LTC	O-1040810	1060	1
SCHWARZ HOWARD C	LTC	O-0255632	0767	3
SCHWARZ JOHN H	COL	O-0319969	1059	3
SCHWARZE FREDERICK	LTC	O-0832254	0666	1
SCHWARZKOPF DONALD F	MAJ	O-0364181	1163	1
SCHWARZKOPF LEROY C	LTC	O-1337096	0966	1
SCHWARZMILLER R E	1LT	O-1312385	0246	2
SCHWECKE HUGH R	COL	O-0274636	1153	1
SCHWEDE WALTER A	CPT	O-0342966	0444	2

NAME	GRADE	SVC NO	DATE RET MO YR	RET CODE
SCHWEDERSKY GEORGE H	COL	O-0295051	0457	3
SCHWEERS ROBERT J	CPT	O-1699634	0267	2
SCHWEICKIST LOWELL G	COL	O-0264979	0267	3
SCHWEINERT ALBERT C	MAJ	O-0404609	1163	1
SCHWEINHARD FRED H	MAJ	O-0450796	0858	1
SCHWEINHART HARRY C	CPT	O-1230143	0746	2
SCHWEINLER FRANCIS F	B G	O-0277772	0966	3
SCHWEITER OTIS	COL	O-0260486	0268	3
SCHWEITZER CHARLES N	2LT	O-1032391	0345	2
SCHWEITZER ELMER	MAJ	O-1174703	0358	2
SCHWEITZER GEORGE C	CPT	O-1053348	0764	1
SCHWEITZER GEORGE M	CPT	O-1110799	0656	2
SCHWEITZER JEROME W	LTC	O-0270635	1268	3
SCHWEITZER RICHARD H	CW3	W-2207580	1168	1
SCHWEITZER WILLIAM H	CW4	W-2111335	0255	1
SCHWEIZER HERMAN W	LTC	O-0311683	0765	3
SCHWEND GEORGE F	1LT	O-1174704	0246	2
SCHWENDEMANN EDWARD	COL	O-0272767	0968	3
SCHWENDINGER ROYAL C	MAJ	O-0386377	1046	2
SCHWENGEL FRANK R	B G	O-0175046	0653	3
SCHWENK HERMAN R D	MAJ	O-0172283	0650	3
SCHWENKA MEDRIC C	CW2	W-2150614	0660	1
SCHWENN GAYHART M	MAJ	O-1015862	0261	1
SCHWEPPE HENRY I	COL	O-0202666	0359	3
SCHWERIN WILLIAM E	LTC	O-0994929	0360	1
SCHWERIN WILLIAM F	MAJ	O-0233509	0454	3
SCHWIDDE JESSE T	CPT	O-0407253	0546	2
SCHWIEBERT EDWARD H	CPT	O-0332675	0446	2
SCHWIED WILLIAM E	CPT	O-0471158	0548	2
SCHWIEGER DEKOVEN L	LTC	O-0307657	0665	3
SCHWIEKER PAUL B	COL	O-0324147	0861	1
SCHWIMER JOSEPH	LTC	O-1039903	0668	3
SCHWINHART THOMAS J	LTC	O-0259946	0965	3
SCHWOERKE ORVILLE L	COL	O-0242205	0964	3
SCHWOLSKY HARRY	COL	O-0322770	0954	3
SCHWOYER ARTHUR J	1LT	O-1996442	0646	2
SCHWULST ROLAND C	MAJ	O-0509417	0260	2
SCIALLA DOMINIC A	1LT	O-1018894	0346	2
SCIALLY JOHN	LTC	O-0137887	0854	3
SCILLIAN OSCAR T	1LT	O-1590791	0162	2
SCIOTTI FRED	LTC	O-0257452	0246	2
SCIRE JAMES	CPT	O-2262996	0561	1
SCIULLO VINCENT F	CPT	O-0490810	0646	2
SCOBEY JOSEPH W	COL	O-0203095	0255	2
SCOBIE FRANK G JR	CW3	W-2150327	1062	1
SCOBY DONALD L	LTC	O-1293128	0561	1
SCOBY MARION L	WO1	W-2144590	0858	1
SCOFIELD JOSEPHINE	2LT	N-0785530	0546	1
SCOFIELD KENDALL C	CPT	O-1697983	0246	2
SCOFIELD MARGARET M	1LT	N-0730580	1045	1
SCOFIELD RALPH G	MAJ	O-0923127	0946	2
SCOFIELD TIMOTHY C	CPT	O-0253638	0853	2
SCOFIELD VERNON	1LT	O-1557084	1045	2
SCOGGIN BERT L	MAJ	O-1590164	1263	1
SCOGGIN JAMES F	COL	O-0161315	0954	3
SCOGGIN WILLIAM C	COL	O-0241938	1159	1
SCOGGIN WILLIAM G JR	CPT	O-1297961	0547	2
SCOGGINS JAMES E JR	LTC	O-0426651	0557	1
SCOGGINS WALTER P	COL	O-0277640	0557	1
SCOGGINS WILLIS L JR	MAJ	O-2295413	1066	1
SCOLA ROY J	MAJ	O-0274897	0968	3
SCOLES EARL E	MAJ	O-0957154	1165	1
SCOLES PAUL B JR	2LT	O-1304125	0853	1
SCOLLARD LLOYD T	CW4	W-2145658	1161	1
SCOLLARD PAUL T	LTC	O-0246873	0962	3
SCOLLON ROBERT B	CW2	W-2209183	0667	1
SCOLNIK AVERN B	LTC	O-0189658	1155	3
SCONYERS JOSEPH M	LTC	O-1290669	0863	1
SCOPEL FRANCIS E	LTC	O-0960035	1067	1
SCOPELLETI FRANK R	CW2	W-2145296	0557	1
SCOPELLITI PATSY J	CW3	W-2152809	1163	1
SCOPOLI MARIANO	CPT	O-2212007	0860	1
SCORDO LEO	MAJ	O-0404679	1046	2
SCOTHORNE WILFRED F	CPT	O-0255430	0854	3
SCOTT ALBA L	LTC	O-1313804	0562	3
SCOTT ALBERT E	1LT	O-1043490	0145	2
SCOTT ALBERT L	CPT	O-4058584	1063	2
SCOTT ALFRED F	1LT	O-1575087	0546	2
SCOTT ALLISON F	COL	O-0167998	0955	3
SCOTT ALVESTER	LTC	O-1301221	0166	1
SCOTT ARNOLD D	CW2	W-2212628	1268	1
SCOTT ARNOLD W	CW4	W-2000419	0260	1
SCOTT ARTHUR B	LTC	O-0226970	0360	3
SCOTT ARTHUR G	LTC	O-1597266	0763	1
SCOTT BEVERLY R	MAJ	O-1001229	1059	1
SCOTT BILLIE L	LTC	O-1059941	0266	1
SCOTT BIRDIE	CPT	O-0966758	0761	1
SCOTT BLANCHE L	MAJ	L-0303576	1265	1
SCOTT BRUCE F	CPT	O-2008083	0556	1
SCOTT BURT A	LTC	O-0346193	0866	3
SCOTT CARROLL F	LTC	O-0244661	0454	3
SCOTT CARSON R	CPT	O-1286715	1059	1
SCOTT CECIL H	LTC	O-1030715	0858	1
SCOTT CHARLES H	COL	O-0268200	0747	2
SCOTT CHARLES H	CW3	RW-2152985	0663	1
SCOTT CHARLES W	LTC	O-1798070	0667	1
SCOTT CHARLEY B	LTC	O-1287764	1054	1
SCOTT CHESTER F	CPT	O-1288630	0766	3
SCOTT CHRIS S	LTC	O-0265473	1061	1
SCOTT CLAIR	CPT	O-0246856	0745	1
SCOTT CLAIR J	CW2	W-3430492	0668	1
SCOTT CLARENCE E	CPT	O-0492665	0847	1
SCOTT CLYDE O	LTC	O-0200921	0959	3
SCOTT CORNELIUS	CPT	O-1296100	0945	2
SCOTT DANIEL J	CW3	W-2117027	0261	1
SCOTT DANIEL J JR	CPT	O-1304957	1146	2
SCOTT DANIEL W JR	CPT	O-0472673	0145	2
SCOTT DAVID A	MAJ	O-0286175	0553	3
SCOTT DELMONT H	CW3	W-2152520	1065	1
SCOTT DONALD A	MAJ	O-1324120	0365	1
SCOTT EDWARD F	CPT	O-0929909	0868	3
SCOTT EDWARD J	1LT	O-1043515	0545	2
SCOTT EDWARD M	CPT	O-0481243	0345	2
SCOTT ENOS P	COL	O-0188435	0353	3
SCOTT EUGENE W	CW2	W-2210153	0464	1
SCOTT EWING B	2LT	O-0501434	0144	2
SCOTT FRANCIS E	LTC	O-0988738	0868	1
SCOTT FRANK E	COL	O-0295626	0967	3
SCOTT FRANK J	CW2	W-3440041	0968	1
SCOTT FRANK W	LTC	O-0512311	0463	1
SCOTT GARY L	CW3	W-2209983	0968	1
SCOTT GENEVIEVE	1LT	N-0744479	0446	1
SCOTT GEORGE C	2LT	O-0251326	0354	3
SCOTT GEORGE D	LTC	O-0306010	0663	3
SCOTT GEORGE J	COL	O-0320024	1062	3
SCOTT GEORGE J	CW2	W-2110174	0347	2
SCOTT GEORGE R	LTC	O-1286371	1062	1
SCOTT GEORGE W	MAJ	O-0226022	0564	3
SCOTT GEORGE W	LTC	O-0323424	0864	3
SCOTT GEORGE W	COL	O-1821922	0667	1
SCOTT GLENN A	CW3	W-3150539	1068	1
SCOTT GLENN W	MAJ	O-2000810	0263	1
SCOTT GORDON W	COL	O-0303546	0961	1
SCOTT HAL L	CW2	W-3430208	1265	2
SCOTT HARRY E	WO1	W-2127663	0450	1
SCOTT HARRY L	CW2	W-2151196	0859	2
SCOTT HARRY R	1LT	O-0491407	0651	1
SCOTT HARVEY J JR	CPT	O-0970512	1060	1
SCOTT HELEN	1LT	N-0722972	0646	2
SCOTT HENRY B	LTC	O-0213984	0646	2
SCOTT HOWARD D	CPT	O-0887345	0147	2
SCOTT INMAN O	MAJ	O-1286372	0857	1
SCOTT IRA G	MAJ	O-1897716	0563	1
SCOTT IRVING J	MAJ	O-0508734	1153	2
SCOTT JAMES	CW3	W-2147903	0659	1
SCOTT JAMES A	COL	O-0301794	0460	1
SCOTT JAMES P JR	CPT	O-0981441	1262	1
SCOTT JAMES R	MAJ	O-1686825	0566	1
SCOTT JESSE C	CW2	W-2150931	0161	1
SCOTT JESSE D	1LT	O-1288796	0545	2
SCOTT JOE H	CPT	O-0990610	1161	1
SCOTT JOE JR	CW3	W-2142413	0862	1
SCOTT JOHN B	1LT	O-0500400	0545	2
SCOTT JOHN E	COL	O-0247175	0854	3
SCOTT JOHN H	COL	O-0242287	1059	2
SCOTT JOHN T JR	MAJ	O-0251791	0146	2
SCOTT JOHN T JR	LTC	O-0384678	0164	1
SCOTT JOHN W	LTC	O-0451416	1054	2
SCOTT JOHN W	LTC	O-1040085	1264	1
SCOTT JOHN W	MAJ	O-1844748	1164	1
SCOTT JUDSON R	COL	O-0301173	1160	1
SCOTT KELTON M	LTC	O-2037512	0964	1
SCOTT LANE T	MAJ	O-2041297	0863	1
SCOTT LAWRENCE R	MAJ	O-0956931	1166	2
SCOTT LEON	1LT	O-1019121	1045	2
SCOTT LESLIE R	MAJ	O-2262691	0961	1
SCOTT LEVERNE W	MAJ	O-1588278	0856	2
SCOTT LEWIS C	MAJ	O-0182184	0644	2
SCOTT LORIN A	MAJ	O-1340939	0468	1
SCOTT MALCOLM F	CPT	O-1301041	0845	2
SCOTT MARION H	LTC	O-0522200	0464	1
SCOTT MILTON R	LTC	O-0222164	1062	3
SCOTT MINOT E	COL	O-0287087	0267	3
SCOTT MONROE A	MAJ	O-1854790	1157	1
SCOTT NORMAN	LTC	O-1105904	0862	1
SCOTT OKEY H	MAJ	O-1328938	0565	2
SCOTT OLIVER E	LTC	O-0230378	0751	3
SCOTT OLIVER J	1LT	O-1534139	0351	2
SCOTT OTIS	CW2	W-2150255	0662	2
SCOTT OTIS T	COL	O-0179687	0346	2
SCOTT PATRICIA C	MAJ	N-0757856	0464	1
SCOTT PAUL A	MAJ	O-0953910	1262	1
SCOTT PAUL M	MAJ	O-1182248	0666	1
SCOTT PETER W	COL	O-0291958	0260	1
SCOTT PHALAS W	CW2	W-2110296	0348	1
SCOTT RALPH	2LT	O-1038837	0844	2
SCOTT RAY J	1LT	O-0929715	0844	2
SCOTT RAYMOND	MAJ	O-0977200	0363	1
SCOTT RAYMOND M	CPT	O-0218274	1057	3
SCOTT RAYMOND O	LTC	O-0284362	0364	3
SCOTT RAYMOND P	MAJ	O-2035980	0665	1
SCOTT RAYMOND R	MAJ	O-0981136	0563	1
SCOTT REID K	MAJ	O-0962241	0265	1
SCOTT REYNOLDS G	CPT	O-0903872	0545	2
SCOTT RICHARD L	1LT	O-0453891	0144	2
SCOTT RICHARD P	LTC	O-0408650	0761	1
SCOTT RICHARD P JR	CW3	W-2146048	0861	1
SCOTT ROBBIE L	MAJ	N-0734993	1066	1
SCOTT ROBERT C	MAJ	O-0295923	0467	3
SCOTT ROBERT D	LTC	O-0296127	0759	1
SCOTT ROBERT D	CW3	W-2151685	0464	1
SCOTT ROBERT F	LTC	O-1292633	0766	1
SCOTT ROBERT L	2LT	O-1326667	0545	2
SCOTT ROBERT P	CPT	O-0420442	0745	2
SCOTT ROBERT R	WO1	W-2116300	0657	1
SCOTT ROBERT S	LTC	O-0432792	1167	1
SCOTT ROBERT W	COL	O-0313706	0263	1
SCOTT ROLLAND G	LTC	O-0228937	1057	1
SCOTT ROSS W	MAJ	O-0442711	1165	1
SCOTT ROY J	LTC	O-0440772	1049	1
SCOTT RUPERT W	MAJ	O-1300092	1057	1
SCOTT STANLEY L	CW4	W-2118525	0953	2
SCOTT STONEWALL	CW3	W-2148285	0163	1
SCOTT STUART W	CW2	W-2141675	0961	1
SCOTT THOMAS J	LTC	O-0241239	0964	3
SCOTT THOMAS P JR	CPT	O-1036721	0147	2
SCOTT VELDON M	CPT	O-0451179	0657	1
SCOTT VERNON M	LTC	O-0407156	0760	1
SCOTT VICTOR	LTC	O-1643316	0365	1
SCOTT VIVIAN N	COL	O-0178724	0958	3
SCOTT WALTER J	MAJ	O-1534858	0257	1
SCOTT WALTER L	CW3	W-2148764	0963	1
SCOTT WALTER M	COL	O-0170870	1152	3
SCOTT WALTER M	1LT	O-0222781	0256	3
SCOTT WESLEY H	LTC	O-1557085	0163	1
SCOTT WILBUR W	CW4	W-2143425	1065	1
SCOTT WILLIAM H	2LT	O-1597267	0445	2
SCOTT WILLIAM H SR	2LT	O-1557979	0645	2
SCOTT WILLIAM L	1LT	O-1297791	0945	2
SCOTT WILLIAM L	LTC	O-1338520	0267	1
SCOTT WILLIAM M	MAJ	O-0972311	0667	1
SCOTT WILLIAM P	CPT	O-2008366	0657	2
SCOTT WINFORD T	CW2	W-2206622	0763	1
SCOTT WOODSON D	COL	O-0227543	0859	3
SCOTT-SMITH QUENTIN	MAJ	O-1330230	0464	1
SCOTTI ELIO	LTC	O-1295282	0564	2
SCOTTI STEPHEN G	MAJ	O-1938655	0267	1
SCOVEL CHARLES E	MAJ	O-1324058	0355	1
SCOVILLE CHAUNCEY W	LTC	O-0196603	0262	3
SCOVILLE CLARENCE E	1LT	O-0408117	0345	2
SCOVILLE CURTISS W	LTC	O-0175940	0662	3
SCOVILLE DUANE J	MAJ	O-0966649	1061	1
SCRACHTEL MAURICE W	CPT	O-0537631	0246	2
SCRANAGE ROBERT B	CPT	O-0361070	0744	2
SCRANTON JOHN A	LTC	O-1317200	0467	1
SCRANTON WALTER A	CPT	O-1291178	0846	2
SCREWS CARROLL S SR	CW2	W-2211986	0968	1
SCRIBNER ROBERT W	MAJ	O-0977682	1062	1
SCRINOPSKIE ROBERT M	2LT	O-1822637	0944	2
SCRIPTER DONALD L	CW2	W-2206375	1262	1
SCRIVNER JAMES	LTC	O-0141328	1055	3
SCROGHAM JOSEPH P	CPT	O-2019938	1059	1
SCROGHEM ALPHEUS M	LTC	O-0224449	0956	3
SCRUBY DELBERT K	COL	O-0164939	0249	3
SCRUGGS BAXTER S	LTC	O-0204182	0354	3
SCRUGGS CLINTON W	LTC	O-0390057	0660	1
SCRUGGS EDWARD P	LTC	O-0180169	0553	3
SCRUGGS ERNEST N	1LT	O-1045592	1045	2
SCRUGGS JAKE C	CW3	W-2148702	0261	1
SCRUGGS JOHN H	1LT	O-0219453	0164	3
SCRUGGS KATHRYN	MAJ	N-0732928	1062	1
SCRUGGS MALCOLM F	MAJ	O-1935891	1165	1
SCRUGGS WILLIAM R JR	LTC	O-0376335	0765	1
SCRUGHAM ETHELBERT	MAJ	O-0302644	0162	3
SCRUTON ROBERT A	LTC	O-1319142	0455	1
SCUDDER CHARLES P	MAJ	O-0253743	1045	2
SCUDDER ELMER E	COL	O-0330191	0264	3
SCUDDER HUGH G	CPT	O-0369781	0746	2
SCUDDER JAMES	MAJ	O-0984157	0568	1
SCULL JOHN L JR	LTC	O-1165564	0266	1
SCULL ORVILLE E	LTC	O-0493543	1049	1
SCULL THOMAS R	CPT	O-1576626	1044	2
SCULLEY HAROLD F	MAJ	O-1302365	0361	1
SCULLY EDWARD F JR	CW2	W-2148814	0567	1
SCULLY ERNEST W S	CPT	O-0496404	0246	2
SCULLY GRANT H	MAJ	O-0349696	1051	1
SCULLY HAROLD R	CW3	W-2144267	0960	1
SCULLY JAMES W III	LTC	O-0919320	1063	3
SCULLY JOHN J	2LT	O-2029320	1147	2
SCULLY LEO L	1LT	O-1181119	0945	2
SCULLY RAYMOND E	LTC	O-1595820	0464	1
SCULLY RICHARD F	LTC	O-0418297	0361	1
SCULLY THOMAS G	1LT	O-1013819	0846	2
SCULLY WILLIAM A	LTC	O-0309909	0765	3
SCURR KENNETH R	COL	O-0179563	0156	3
SEABORN WALTER J	1LT	O-1314963	1046	2
SEABOURNE JOSIAH G	COL	O-0137662	0846	2
SEABRIDGE FREDERICK	LTC	O-0288406	0362	3
SEABRIGHT GLENN W	MAJ	O-0407532	1147	2
SEABROOK STERLING W	1LT	O-0533895	0346	2
SEABURG GENE H	MAJ	O-0957271	1065	1
SEABURY GORDON H	MAJ	O-0277882	0345	2
SEABURY JOHN C	LTC	O-1285648	0762	1
SEABURY ROLAND T	MAJ	O-0218216	0963	3
SEACORD CHARLES L	CPT	O-0445073	0645	2
SEAGER CHARLES W	MAJ	O-0218391	0564	3
SEAGER NORMAN	1LT	O-1107111	0646	2
SEAGLE GLADYS I	2LT	L-0302151	0644	2
SEAGO ERNEST W	CPT	O-0341010	0944	2
SEAGO WILNA J	LTC	O-0320268	0262	1

ARMY OF THE UNITED STATES RETIRED LIST

NAME	GRADE	SVC NO	DATE RET MO YR	RET CODE
SEAGRAVE DANIEL W	LTC	O-1555285	0962	1
SEAGRAVE DAVID C	COL	O-0105046	0351	3
SEAGRAVE GERALD K	LTC	O-0453584	0860	1
SEAGRAVE RODMAN G	LTC	O-1554476	0662	1
SEAGRAVES EDWARD L	LTC	O-1173970	1267	1
SEAGRAVES WALTER B	MAJ	O-2035545	0261	1
SEAGROVES MAE	MAJ	N-0724554	0365	3
SEAHA BRUNO J	1LT	O-1292598	1045	2
SEAL J L	CW3	W-2146093	0864	1
SEALANDER MELVIN W	MAJ	O-1056544	0661	1
SEALE BRYAN P	MAJ	O-0576222	1058	1
SEALE EDWIN L SR	CW3	RW-2148051	0762	1
SEALE ERNEST F	1LT	O-2017907	0651	2
SEALE JOHN C	LTC	O-1108999	0962	1
SEALE MAXWELL L	MAJ	O-2055523	0358	1
SEALE THOMAS F SR	2LT	O-2052558	0246	2
SEALE WILLIAM A	1LT	O-1322593	0646	2
SEALES LOYT C	WO1	W-2149268	0953	1
SEALS JAMES D	2LT	O-1323358	0745	2
SEALS JAMES F	MAJ	O-0451393	0657	1
SEALS RAY D	MAJ	O-0927996	0965	1
SEALS RAY E	CPT	O-4074425	0965	2
SEALS VERNELL V	CW2	W-3430376	1268	1
SEAMAN CHARLES H	MAJ	O-1308715	1161	1
SEAMAN CLIFTON E	MAJ	O-2010507	0164	2
SEAMAN EDWARD W	1LT	O-0320915	1157	1
SEAMAN GEORGE A	LTC	O-1945485	0361	1
SEAMAN HENRY	LTC	O-0205962	0546	2
SEAMAN JOHN T	LTC	O-0194025	0662	3
SEAMAN PAUL M	CW2	W-2209220	1263	1
SEAMAN VICTOR B SR	WO1	W-2150135	0556	2
SEAMAN WAYNE R	1LT	O-0522632	0146	2
SEAMANDS GEORGE A	LTC	O-2044314	0557	1
SEAMANS JOHN E	MAJ	O-0354164	1045	2
SEARNO RAMON Y	1LT	O-2032115	0853	1
SEARCH WILLIAM C	CPT	O-1321957	0346	2
SEARCY DONALD M	1LT	O-1102590	0944	2
SEARCY JOSEPH W	LTC	O-1535524	0766	1
SEARCY KENNETH F	LTC	O-0385633	1160	1
SEARCY LEE R	MAJ	O-2050634	0263	1
SEARCY RALPH C JR	COL	O-0359141	0163	1
SEARCY WILLIAM C	LTC	O-1335482	0168	1
SEARIGHT GEORGE T	MAJ	O-2047818	1057	1
SEARIGHT WILLIAM H	2LT	O-1045913	1044	2
SEARL SHERBURN C	1LT	O-0447472	0746	2
SEARLE GERALD F	MAJ	O-2055175	0761	1
SEARLE HOWARD S	B G	O-0123165	0-51	3
SEARLE JOHN G	MAJ	O-1012390	0261	1
SEARLES DONALD E	LTC	O-1307471	0866	1
SEARLES JOHN W	LTC	O-0231609	0764	3
SEARLES PAUL W	COL	O-0307601	0468	3
SEARLES STANLEY N SR	MAJ	O-2033324	0865	1
SEARLS CHESTER B	LTC	O-1300856	0866	1
SEARLS WELLINGTON	COL	O-0234322	0753	3
SEARS ARTHUR M	MAJ	O-1287074	0358	1
SEARS CECIL W	LTC	O-1174967	0263	1
SEARS DAVID M	2LT	O-1540769	0246	2
SEARS DEMAS L	COL	O-0160472	0254	3
SEARS DONALD R	LTC	O-1554355	0164	1
SEARS EDWARD W	COL	O-0171330	0551	3
SEARS EUGENE E	CW3	W-2150112	0165	2
SEARS GEORGE W	LTC	O-0278300	1160	2
SEARS JAMES E	CW3	W-2208374	0867	1
SEARS JOSEPH H JR	LTC	O-1181122	0762	1
SEARS JULIAN A	MAJ	O-1332320	0463	1
SEARS MILLICENT	MAJ	L-1010498	0866	1
SEARS RICHARD E	MAJ	O-0951239	0364	1
SEARS RICHARD L	1LT	W-0903787	0359	1
SEARS RICHARD M	CPT	O-1554633	0261	1
SEARS ROY C	1LT	O-0257759	1166	3
SEARS SAMUEL	LTC	O-0264330	1055	3
SEARS THOMAS E	LTC	O-1341909	0768	1
SEARS THOMAS P JR	MAJ	O-1172646	0561	1
SEARS THURMAN E	CPT	O-0399854	1045	2
SEARS WILLIAM B	LTC	O-0423173	0763	1
SEARS WILLIAM G	MAJ	O-0331227	1046	2
SEARS WILLIAM H	1LT	O-1320782	0447	2
SEARSON REX L	MAJ	O-1341588	0666	1
SEASE ELBERTA W	MAJ	N-0726895	0864	1
SEASE GEORGE A	LTC	O-0312289	0361	1
SEASHOLES HENRY C	LTC	O-0203462	1060	3
SEASTRAND CONRAD M	1LT	O-1015554	0161	2
SEATON JOHN A	1LT	O-0918762	0844	2
SEATON THOMAS W	CW2	W-2154671	0657	2
SEATON VICTOR T	LTC	O-1796163	0461	1
SEATVET JOHN	LTC	O-0437665	0554	1
SEAVER ROBERT S	COL	O-0330966	0765	1
SEAVEY CALVIN C	COL	O-0129701	0458	3
SEAVEY EDGAR S	MAJ	O-1030612	0559	1
SEAVEY HAROLD V	CPT	O-1314066	0859	1
SEAVEY POWELL J	CW2	W-2148335	1059	1
SEAVEY REX W	LTC	O-1289152	0454	1
SEAVY LOUIS M	LTC	O-0903944	1167	3
SEAWELL COLUMBUS J	MAJ	O-1055454	0747	2
SEAWELL VERGIL L	LTC	O-1549088	0663	1
SEAWELL WALTER	LTC	O-0471714	0366	3
SEAWELL WILLIAM A	MAJ	O-0259331	0345	2
SEAWELL WILLIAM A	2LT	O-1324442	0145	2
SEAWRIGHT PATRICK E	M G	O-0277902	0957	3
SEAY ALBERT E	1LT	O-1303392	0346	2
SEAY DANIEL E	1LT	O-1169329	0444	2
SEAY EMBREY W	LTC	O-1166176	0761	1
SEAY FURMAN R	CW3	W-2151349	1063	1
SEAY RICHARD R	1LT	O-0765108	0945	2
SEAY ROGER	CW3	W-2152839	0966	1
SEBASTIAN HARRY M	LTC	O-0481709	0854	1
SEBENY GEORGE J JR	CW2	W-2214095	0868	1
SEBEY GEORGE G	CW4	W-2113619	0368	3
SEBOLD GEORGE	CW4	W-2136623	1064	1
SEBJORN ALBERT C	MAJ	O-1181123	0555	1
SEBJORN JAMES	CPT	O-0492204	0945	2
SEBRING HARRY D	2LT	O-2000139	1050	1
SEBRING HARVEY D	1LT	O-2018226	0647	2
SECHREST PAUL T	CW2	W-3150989	1168	1
SECHREST THOMAS P	CPT	O-2037513	0956	2
SECHRIST DAVID C	CPT	O-2001686	1051	2
SECHRIST WILLIAM R	MAJ	O-2021416	1161	1
SECK HARRY F	LTC	O-1636627	0956	1
SECKINGER GEORGE M	LTC	O-0308541	1060	1
SECOR ALLEN F	LTC	O-1112079	0668	3
SECOR ERNEST P	CPT	O-4031110	0167	1
SECOR RICHARD W	LTC	O-0408926	0361	1
SECOR WILLIAM H	LTC	O-1795982	0557	1
SECREST HORACE G JR	MAJ	O-0974679	0464	1
SECRIST ESTHER D	1LT	N-0704000	0745	2
SEDA DELYLE L	LTC	O-1031678	0966	1
SEDDON ARTHUR J JR	CPT	O-1597074	0159	1
SEDDON FRANK	MAJ	O-0370432	0246	2
SEDDON WILLIAM A	LTC	O-0230623	0663	3
SEDGWICK ALEXANDER	COL	O-0188448	0259	1
SEDGWICK HARRY K	CPT	O-0406106	1046	2
SEDGWICK WALTER E	LTC	O-0476037	0457	1
SEDILLO JUAN A A	COL	O-0224107	0362	3
SEDILLO RUFINO R	COL	O-0334777	1053	2
SEDLACEK LEO B	COL	O-0257063	0756	3
SEDLAK ANTHONY T	LTC	O-0348342	0157	1
SEDLAK MARY R	MAJ	L-0506791	1163	1
SEDMAK MICHAEL P	CPT	O-1306156	0947	2
SEDOLA PHYLLIS W	2LT	N-0723117	0444	1
SEDWICK JACK D	MAJ	O-0356304	0346	2
SEE DANIEL M	2LT	O-1182249	0345	2
SEE HENRY S	LTC	O-0244311	0245	2
SEE LEROY	CW3	W-2142778	0859	1
SEE MACK	CW2	W-2148443	0757	1
SEE MAXWELL W	LTC	O-1645354	1163	1
SEE WILLIAM T	LTC	O-0323531	0260	1
SEEBER JOHN A	MAJ	O-1043491	0258	1
SEEDORF HERBERT G	1LT	O-1314400	1045	2
SEEDS ERNEST E	CW3	W-2153269	0762	1
SEFFELD WILLIAM F	1LT	O-1307579	0146	2
SEEGAR EARLIE B	MAJ	O-0981483	0663	1
SEEGER GEORGE H	LTC	O-1542236	0167	1
SEEGERT NEAL	CPT	O-0423517	1045	2
SEEKER MAX D	MAJ	O-1165788	0860	1
SEEKINS WINFIELD T	LTC	O-1018059	0867	1
SEELAND ELIAS	LTC	O-0285842	0566	3
SEELER ALFRED J JR	CW2	RW-2147276	0762	1
SEELEY ALLAN H JR	1LT	O-1641779	0149	2
SEELEY DOUGLAS C	MAJ	O-0311488	1067	3
SEELEY ELWOOD W	MAJ	O-0350327	0246	2
SEELEY GEORGE E	MAJ	O-0379356	0444	2
SEELEY HARLAN A	2LT	O-2010594	0957	1
SEELEY THOMAS C	MAJ	O-0239965	1263	3
SEELIG LAWRENCE A	CW3	W-2211681	1168	1
SEELY CHESTER E	COL	O-0472781	0468	1
SEELY DAVID F	MAJ	O-2033861	0562	1
SEELY GEORGE M	CW3	W-2152865	0862	1
SEELY LAWRENCE P	COL	O-0385051	0561	1
SEELY MITT	MAJ	O-0502154	1048	1
SEELY ROGER G	LTC	O-0281842	0867	3
SEELYE RICHARD M	MAJ	O-4009979	0667	1
SEELYE WALTER B	CPT	O-1702431	0645	2
SEEM DONALD L	LTC	O-1342304	0966	1
SEEMAN MARVIN P	CW2	RW-2150397	0464	1
SEEMANN JULIUS A	MAJ	O-0486819	0347	2
SEEMEYER ROGER F	MAJ	O-2038032	0264	1
SEENEY DALTON E	CW3	W-2203660	0165	1
SEERY JAMES L	LTC	O-1315734	0261	1
SEES JOHN C	LTC	O-1579090	1263	1
SEESHOLTZ RAMON C	MAJ	O-1590168	0461	1
SEETON LELAND W	MAJ	O-0258248	1267	3
SEEWER RAY H	CPT	O-1118285	0957	1
SEEWER TRUMAN A	CW2	W-2144129	0559	1
SEFCAK EDWARD J	MAJ	O-1555895	0760	1
SEFCIK DEL F	1LT	N-0737854	0346	1
SEFCIK EDWARD F	CPT	O-0386763	1045	2
SEFCIK STEPHEN P	1LT	O-1284586	0744	2
SEFF BERNARD	CPT	O-0488876	1044	2
SEFRIT GEORGE W	LTC	O-1056227	1068	3
SEFTEN EUGENE H	LTC	O-0283826	0468	3
SEFTON BINGER H	MAJ	O-0268121	0656	3
SEFTON HARRY B	LTC	O-0282149	0264	3
SEGAL BERNARD	LTC	O-0348904	1267	3
SEGAL JEROME M	1LT	O-1259799	0146	2
SEGAL MOREY M	MAJ	O-0509525	0746	2
SEGALL LOUIS	LTC	O-0120101	0747	1
SEGARS JAMES J	1LT	O-0294464	0146	2
SEGEL PAUL	LTC	O-0319668	0167	3
SEGERSTROM HAROLD A	MAJ	O-0378325	0245	2
SEGERSTROM HENRY T	CPT	O-0547000	0647	2
SEGESKY MIKE	CPT	O-1181819	0660	1
SEGNA FRANCIS R	CPT	O-0519779	0450	2
SEGUIN MARCEL G	CW3	W-2205232	0666	1
SEGUIRANT REGINALD M	MAJ	O-0965454	0762	1
SEHRING GEORGE H	CPT	O-0510156	0346	2
SEHRT VERNON R	MAJ	O-1289974	0446	2
SEIB VINCENT J	COL	O-0277038	0963	3
SEIBEL JOHN J	LTC	O-0439477	1150	1
SEIBEL ROBERT H	MAJ	O-1877046	1065	1
SEIBERT EUGENE R	LTC	O-0400621	0367	1
SEIBERT WALTER E JR	1LT	O-1318252	1045	2
SEIBOLD CHARLES A	LTC	O-1002122	1162	1
SEIBT ALVIN W	LTC	O-0444628	0256	1
SEICSHNAYDRE DAVID T	CW2	W-2108821	0867	3
SEIDEL CARL L	LTC	O-1045248	0962	1
SEIDEL OTTO K	COL	O-0133756	0353	3
SEIDEL ROBERT D	CW3	W-2150147	0461	1
SEIDEL RUSSELL Z	LTC	O-1534621	1167	1
SEIDELMANN HERBERT W	CPT	O-1111359	0347	2
SEIDENER ROBERT S	COL	O-0303407	0467	3
SEIDENFELD BERNICE O	1LT	N-0772155	1045	1
SEIDENFELD MORTON A	COL	O-0246681	1066	3
SEIDENGLANZ CHARLES	LTC	O-0238416	1265	3
SEIDENGLANZ LEONARD	COL	O-0919082	1065	3
SEIDENZAHL AUGUST T	COL	O-0330561	1262	3
SEIDL AUGUSTINE	CW4	W-2002716	0567	1
SEIDL CLARENCE F	CW4	W-2142897	0468	1
SEIDL PETER J	1LT	O-1053804	1045	2
SEIDLER FRANK B	MAJ	O-0971802	0563	1
SEIDMAN JACOB S	WO1	W-2149802	1154	1
SEIDMAN JOSHUA I	CPT	O-0503977	1045	2
SEIDNER NORBERT W	LTC	O-0463020	0954	1
SEIFARTH CHARLES K	LTC	O-1692622	0861	2
SEIFARTH VIRGINIA M	1LT	N-0767128	1045	1
SEIFERLEIN A L	CPT	O-0301352	0845	2
SEIFERT ANN P	1LT	N-0722844	0546	2
SEIFERTH SOLIS	MAJ	O-0123254	0255	3
SEIFFERLEIN HILMER F	CPT	O-1554478	0446	2
SEIFFERT FRANK H	MAJ	O-1683432	0255	1
SEIFRIED JOHN O	CPT	O-1015097	0346	2
SEIFRIED WALTER G	CPT	O-1284032	1146	2
SEIGEL BURTON H	WO1	W-2120030	1047	1
SEIGNEUR WILLIAM B	MAJ	O-0976998	0264	2
SEIL NOLAND B	CPT	O-0117362	1054	3
SEILER DONALD J	LTC	O-1323359	1163	1
SEILER FRANK B	LTC	O-0321972	0667	1
SEILER GEORGE B	COL	O-0276853	0358	3
SEILING JOHN M	1LT	O-1301695	0545	2
SEILLER EDWARD F	LTC	O-0183886	0857	3
SEIND JAMES W	MAJ	O-1922652	0465	1
SEIP WILLIAM H	CPT	O-0981817	0960	1
SEIPEL ALOYSIUS	LTC	O-0465577	1049	1
SEIPT DEWEY F	MAJ	O-0480852	1148	1
SEITELBACH LEO	CW3	W-2150865	1165	1
SEITNER ROBERT L	COL	O-0127486	0255	3
SEITZ ALFRED G	COL	O-0324662	0665	3
SEITZ CHARLES R	MAJ	O-0253745	0153	3
SEITZ EDWARD H	CW4	W-2151527	0868	1
SEITZ FRANK C	COL	O-0214945	0957	1
SEITZ GEORGE H JR	COL	O-0236275	0266	3
SEITZ JOE	1LT	O-1644068	0556	1
SEITZ LEONARD F	LTC	O-1175307	0462	1
SEITZ WILLIAM H JR	LTC	O-0358442	0160	1
SEITZER PAUL W	MAJ	O-1549091	0861	1
SEITZINGER EDWARD F	2LT	O-0507660	0944	2
SEITZINGER JOHN R	MAJ	O-1686714	0767	1
SEIX ERNEST J	CW3	W-2143553	0161	1
SEKAN EDWARD J	LTC	O-0423876	1057	1
SEKULIC PHIL M	CPT	O-1553358	0358	1
SEKULOVICH MILO	1LT	O-1327187	0546	2
SELANDER GEORGE W	CW2	W-2143963	0361	2
SELBY CHARLES A	COL	O-0332894	1067	3
SELBY EDWARD H SR	CPT	O-2007242	0168	3
SELBY EDWIN O	COL	O-0430193	0163	1
SELBY ORVAL C	LTC	O-0127887	0848	3
SELDEN JOSEPH H	LTC	O-0420230	0763	1
SELDEN METELLUS D	LTC	O-0341647	0765	3
SELDEN WILLARD W	MAJ	O-0280161	1065	3
SELDNER MAC E	LTC	O-1181124	0866	1
SELENSKI LEONARD S	2LT	O-1640934	1144	2
SELF CHARLES B	LTC	O-0378987	0853	1
SELF CHARLES M	MAJ	O-2021183	0764	1
SELF CHARLIE E	CW2	W-2108565	0758	1
SELF COYE R	LTC	O-2005480	0766	1
SELF DAN J	CW3	W-2144855	0460	1
SELF ELBERT E	LTC	O-1305846	0361	1
SELF JAY D	CW3	W-2144502	1162	1
SELF JOSIE	1LT	N-0702546	0444	1
SELF RICHARD B	LTC	O-1012363	0760	1
SELF ROY M	CW2	W-2143403	0755	1
SELFE HILBERT A	CPT	O-0218838	1058	3
SELIG SETH J	CW2	W-2214940	0766	1
SELISKAR CARL E	1LT	O-1055634	1145	2
SELK HAROLD F	MAJ	O-1542851	1157	1
SELKIRK WYATT O	COL	O-0149168	0648	3
SELL ALLEN M	CPT	O-0288460	0454	3
SELL EMERSON F	CPT	O-1186295	0268	1
SELL ESTHER G	1LT	N-0775833	0746	1
SELL FREDERICK	1LT	O-0476886	1144	2
SELL GUY S	CPT	O-0261647	0667	3

NAME	GRADE	SVC NO	DATE RET MO YR	RET CODE
SELL HOWARD E	CPT	0-1551105	1146	[illegible]
SELL RAY R	1LT	[illegible]	[illegible]	[illegible]
SELL ROBERT A	LTC	0-2039147	1168	1
SELLARS DENNIS P	MAJ	0-1326031	0366	1
SELLARDS DAVID L JR	COL	0-0171206	1061	3
SELLARS MURRAY	MAJ	0-0217355	0257	3
SELLARS RALPH N	MAJ	0-1937927	0267	1
SELLARS RICHARD D JR	1LT	0-1060658	0643	2
SELLE FRED A	LTC	0-0760563	0763	1
SELLECK LLOYD [illegible]	LTC	0-1015896	0367	3
SELLECK WALTER B	1LT	0-1309419	0745	2
SELLEN LEROY W	LTC	0-1041742	0662	1
SELLERS PAUL J	MAJ	0-0105290	0650	3
SELLERS ALBERT R	LTC	0-1190326	0266	3
SELLERS CLYDE G	LTC	0-0378419	0757	1
SELLERS EMMETT L	MAJ	0-1917735	1163	1
SELLERS FREDERICK	MAJ	0-0211716	1163	3
SELLERS GEORGE J	CPT	0-1917893	0254	2
SELLERS GEORGE W JR	CW4	W-2150274	0968	1
SELLERS HERBERT P	LTC	0-0239230	0363	3
SELLERS JOHN M	MAJ	0-0207368	0453	2
SELLERS NORMAN G	MAJ	0-0866102	1265	1
SELLERS PHILIP A	CW2	W-2190210	0259	1
SELLERS ROBERT L	MAJ	0-1304176	1160	1
SELLERS ROSCOE A	MAJ	0-0390316	0757	1
SELLERS THOMAS E	MAJ	0-1559065	1063	1
SELLERS WILBUR R	MAJ	0-2212017	0564	1
SELLERS WILFRED J	LTC	0-0404285	0464	1
SELLERS WILLIAM L JR	CPT	0-1683024	1144	2
SELLERS WILLIAM Z	MAJ	0-0321878	0661	1
SELLETT LEONARD V	CPT	0-0496290	1145	2
SELLEW ROLAND W	COL	0-0186566	1055	3
SELLIN JACK D	MAJ	0-1825778	0464	1
SELLING HOLGER C	MAJ	0-0184084	0557	3
SELLINGER CECIL T	COL	0-0447596	1262	3
SELLMAN EUGENE E	LTC	0-2204418	1168	1
SELLS JACK D	CPT	0-1013747	0361	1
SELMAN JOHN E	MAJ	0-1535824	0768	3
SELMAN JOSEPH R	LTC	0-1642570	0565	1
SELNAU FREDERICK	CW2	W-2153187	1162	1
SELOGIE LOUIS A	CPT	0-1935336	0347	2
SELSEMEYER JOHN	LTC	0-0200089	0849	3
SELTZ ROLAND L	1LT	0-1105809	0345	2
SELTZER EUGENE P	COL	0-0143727	1056	3
SELTZER MAURICE	MAJ	0-0231307	0661	3
SELTZER RAYMOND F	MAJ	0-0394546	0247	2
SELVIDGE KENNETH W	CPT	0-0360190	0145	2
SELVIG KERMIT H	MAJ	0-1296270	0361	1
SELWYN GEORGE V	COL	0-0359926	1263	3
SEMANCIK MICHAEL A	MAJ	0-1016389	0963	1
SEMANS WILLIAM D	LTC	0-0169277	0652	3
SEMBRA NICK	CW3	W-2141791	1157	1
SEMEL MAX	1LT	0-1307087	0645	2
SEMELMAKER MORTON	LTC	0-1019109	0163	1
SEMENJEF PETER	LTC	0-1295321	0957	1
SEMENJEF WALTER	LTC	0-1295831	1057	1
SEMKEN SEVERT	1LT	0-0277855	0960	3
SEMKEN HOMER L	MAJ	0-2029424	0662	1
SEMLEK ROBERT	MAJ	0-0452971	0163	1
SEMLER ADOLPH	CPT	0-0178633	0239	2
SEMLER ALBERT E	LTC	0-0302245	0261	1
SEMLER ROBERT K	2LT	0-0982559	1051	2
SEMMENS RICHARD T	LTC	0-1581363	0762	1
SEMMES BUFORD B A	LTC	0-1038283	1167	1
SEMMES GEORGE W	COL	0-0210229	0249	3
SEMMES HARRY H JR	1LT	0-1013698	0945	2
SEMOFF MILTON C F	1LT	0-0357648	1142	2
SEMON JOHN A	CPT	0-1036019	0662	1
SEMON NORMAN N	MAJ	0-2208463	0167	1
SEMPLE WILLIAM R	COL	0-0266649	0461	3
SEMRAW RUSSELL R	WO1	W-2128135	0950	1
SEMSKER ALBERT	LTC	0-0906573	0862	3
SEMSTEAD ALLAN R	MAJ	0-1181125	0855	1
SEN JOHN J	LTC	0-1331948	1266	1
SENCY LOUIS F	CPT	0-1284947	0862	1

NAME	GRADE	SVC NO	DATE RET MO YR	RET CODE
SENDERS JOHN A	MAJ	0-0447131	0657	1
SENDROFF DAVID	1LT	0-0547138	1146	2
SENECAL FRANCIS G	1LT	0-1945274	1048	2
SENFRITE LEONARD A	CPT	0-1306157	1158	1
SENEY RODGER E	2LT	0-1315868	1144	2
SENFT HENRY M	MAJ	0-0308477	0145	2
SENFT CRAIG T	CPT	0-1326114	1146	2
SENG LEA M	2LT	N-0729120	0944	1
SENGER JOSEPH W	LTC	0-1312054	1060	1
SENGPIEHL ARTHUR P	LTC	0-0311825	1160	3
SENIL GEORGE	1LT	0-1288310	0744	2
SENIK JOSEPH	2LT	0-1550497	0145	2
SENIOR LEO V	CW3	W-2147934	1061	1
SENIOR SOLOMON F	COL	0-0260079	1063	3
SENKER RICHARD F	CW4	W-2152616	0866	1
SENKEWICH WILLIAM	CW2	W-2147309	0457	1
SENKO JOSEPH M	LTC	0-1306481	0461	1
SENN EDWARD L JR	1LT	0-0194754	1056	3
SENN HANS	1LT	0-1174706	0549	2
SENN JACQUES L	2LT	0-1303393	1144	2
SENN NORMAN H	CPT	0-0478510	0360	1
SENNE ARTHUR M	LTC	0-0312823	1046	2
SENNE WALTER W	MAJ	0-1593259	1160	1
SENOWSKI JOHN R	1LT	0-0922357	1143	2
SENSE GEORGE A	LTC	0-0423095	0661	1
SENSENBACH ELMER F	LTC	0-0682398	0966	1
SENSOR EARL C	CPT	0-0251591	0257	3
SENTELL JOHN E	LTC	0-0151026	0145	2
SENTGERATH GEORGE J	CW3	W-2147981	0464	1
SENTI GENE C	MAJ	0-2055187	0161	1
SENZ FRANCIS J	MAJ	0-0934557	0361	1
SEPULVEDA EUGENIO E	CW3	W-2147649	0963	1
SEPULVEDA JOSE JR	CW2	W-2209226	1060	1
SEQUIRA DANIEL	CW3	W-2208299	0168	2
SERAFIN EDWARD J	CW3	W-2208428	0863	1
SERAFIN THADDEUS R	2LT	0-1307758	0762	1
SERAFINI FRANCIS H	LTC	0-1825192	0661	1
SERAFINI LOUIS	CPT	0-1060290	0448	2
SERAFINI LOUIS J	2LT	0-1061857	1145	2
SERBENSKI JOSEPH J	CPT	0-4009200	0366	1
SERHOUSEK EMIL E	LTC	0-0495624	0554	1
SERBY JESSE L	CPT	0-0497298	0345	2
SERDA JOSEPH F	1LT	0-1321958	1045	2
SERENA JOSEPH R	LTC	0-0314540	0761	1
SERETAN MORRIS A	1LT	0-1302714	0446	2
SERFAS LELAND E	CW3	W-2141741	1057	1
SERFASS HARRY A	LTC	0-0246755	1046	2
SERFIN ADOLPH T	LTC	0-0435618	0164	1
SERGIO JAMES J	LTC	0-0407562	1060	1
SERGIO LOUIS S	CPT	0-1302208	1046	2
SERLES ROBERT T	LTC	0-1648487	0263	1
SEROKA GEORGE	MAJ	0-1919498	1265	1
SEROLA MICHAEL M	CW2	W-2141960	0161	1
SERPA JAMES D	WO1	W-2144531	0353	2
SERPE ANTHONY D	LTC	0-1081720	0768	2
SERTICH JOHN	1LT	0-2044297	0553	1
SERVICE ALBERT	1LT	0-1822063	1044	2
SERVIN DONALD K	CPT	0-1321555	0646	2
SERVIS CLYDE E	MAJ	0-0337954	0954	1
SERYAK FRANK W	LTC	0-0382830	0665	3
SESE GERVASIO G	MAJ	0-1324812	1162	1
SESINGER ESTHER A	MAJ	N-0752517	0164	1
SESINGER HAROLD B	MAJ	0-1014716	0761	1
SESIT MYRON F	LTC	0-0348352	0965	3
SESLOWE HYMAN	LTC	0-0329938	0766	3
SESNA GERALD T	2LT	0-1080149	0643	2
SESSA CARL L	CPT	0-0429547	0245	2
SESSION ALBERT S	1LT	0-4034363	0259	2
SESSIONS ALVIN	COL	0-0165560	0250	3
SESSIONS EDGAR H	MAJ	0-1321341	1157	1
SESSIONS JAMES L	CPT	0-0239311	1265	3
SESSIONS JAMES R	LTC	0-1309852	0366	1
SESSIONS LEWIS B	CPT	0-2043992	0263	1
SESSIONS THADDEUS J	CPT	0-0419104	0945	2
SESSIONS THOMAS M	COL	0-0291592	1059	2

NAME	GRADE	SVC NO	DATE RET MO YR	RET CODE
SESSIONS WILL A JR	LTC	[illegible]	[illegible]	[illegible]
SESSUMS JAMES C	CPT	[illegible]	[illegible]	1
SESTERO MICHAEL	LTC	[illegible]	[illegible]	1
SETARO JOHN G	LTC	[illegible]	[illegible]	1
SETH GEORGE E	COL	[illegible]	[illegible]	[illegible]
SETH RICHARD C	CPT	[illegible]	[illegible]	2
SETHER HOWARD B	CPT	[illegible]	[illegible]	2
SETLAK VINCENT S	CW3	W-2211315	1168	1
SETSER HORACE L	CW2	W-2149718	1057	1
SETTANNI MICHAEL D	1LT	0-1305158	1044	2
SETTERSTEN WARD F	LTC	0-0249777	[illegible]	1
SETTLE HERBERT R	LTC	0-2031038	1266	3
SETTLE LYLE L	MAJ	0-0302812	0762	1
SETTLE WALTER R	MAJ	0-1605528	0862	1
SETTLES HENRY D	LTC	0-0382640	0757	1
SETTLES RALPH H	CPT	0-0910148	0945	2
SETZE TOM B	LTC	0-1577826	1161	1
SETZER JAMES L	1LT	0-2204475	0453	2
SETZER SHELTON H	2LT	0-1735324	0544	2
SETZER WORTH A	LTC	0-0289846	1153	3
SETZKE MAX A	MAJ	0-0407310	0959	1
SEUFERT JAMES F	MAJ	0-1114744	0566	1
SEVALL JOSEPH R JR	LTC	0-1016469	0962	1
SEVAREID JOHN W	COL	0-1556558	0868	1
SEVCHIK WILLIAM	1LT	0-1299975	0254	1
SEVENER BERNARD C	LTC	0-1107113	0366	3
SEVENER CLINTON J	CPT	0-0300764	0943	2
SEVER JOSEPHINE	LTC	N-0759518	0463	1
SEVERANCE GUY C	MAJ	0-1630627	0657	1
SEVERANCE MYRTLE	MAJ	L-0117418	0963	1
SEVERE LILLIAN M	MAJ	N-0724077	0361	1
SEVERIN OLVAR	LTC	0-1330014	0768	1
SEVERINI CAMILLO G	CW3	W-2148618	0763	1
SEVERSON GERTRUDE A	2LT	N-0761364	1044	1
SEVERSON HARVEY H	LTC	0-0306054	0163	1
SEVERSON RONALD A	LTC	0-2210465	0768	1
SEVERSON STANLEY H	2LT	0-1114745	0844	2
SEVERSON THOMAS B	MAJ	0-1019499	0960	1
SEVEY WILLIAM B	LTC	0-0941613	1267	1
SEVIER GEORGE B	CW2	W-2209744	0263	1
SEVIER JAMES H	LTC	0-0287516	0260	3
SEVIER JOHN C	WO1	W-2125150	1046	2
SEVY VERNON K	COL	0-0155983	0954	1
SEWALL THOMAS K	CPT	0-0350742	0545	2
SEWARD GILBERT M	CW2	W-2006794	1266	3
SEWARD ROYAL H JR	LTC	0-1173073	1265	1
SEWART GEORGE F	WO1	W-2122639	0151	1
SEWELL BENNIE R JR	LTC	0-2036446	0962	1
SEWELL GILBERT H	2LT	0-1320187	1044	2
SEWELL HOMER S	CW2	W-2145008	0358	1
SEWELL JACK H	CPT	0-1302715	1051	2
SEWELL JONATHAN F	CW4	W-2103435	0756	1
SEWELL MILTON A	LTC	0-0510769	0353	1
SEWELL ORAL C	MAJ	0-0972042	0461	1
SEWELL PRESTON D	MAJ	0-1584005	0656	1
SEWELL RALPH F	MAJ	0-1112432	0264	1
SEWELL ROBERT F	MAJ	0-1563244	0163	1
SEWELL ROBERT M	MAJ	0-1031839	1066	2
SEWELL VIRGIL T	CPT	0-1166602	0645	2
SEXSMITH WILFRED H	LTC	0-1646575	0766	1
SEXSON JACK	MAJ	0-1004839	0957	1
SEXSON JOSEPH H	CW3	W-2150934	0953	1
SEXTON BARBARA H	2LT	N-0721074	0944	1
SEXTON CHARLES R	LTC	0-0209720	1057	3
SEXTON CHARLES V	CPT	0-0335064	0644	3
SEXTON JAMES N	COL	0-0252712	1047	2
SEXTON LAURENCE H	COL	0-0201307	0-48	3
SEXTON LOUIS A	MAJ	0-1045723	0261	1
SEXTON MARGARET C	1LT	N-0760264	1048	1
SEXTON WILLIAM N	LTC	0-1948394	0463	1
SEYB DILLON W	LTC	0-1845645	0967	3
SEYBERT GEORGE I	LTC	0-0274492	0454	3
SEYFRIED CARL L	MAJ	0-0250289	0965	3
SEYFRIED RUDOLPH J	COL	0-0163771	0749	3
SEYKOSKI MICHAEL	1LT	0-1303555	0266	2

NAME	GRADE	SVC NO	DATE RET MO YR	RET CODE
SEYLE [illegible]	CPT	0-0317536	0863	3
SEYMOUR CLARENCE W	LTC	0-0115468	0668	3
SEYMOUR EDWARD C	LTC	0-1877419	1168	1
SEYMOUR ERNEST H	MAJ	0-0196438	0661	3
SEYMOUR FREDERICK	MAJ	0-0917290	0953	2
SEYMOUR FREDERICK	LTC	0-1107114	0264	1
SEYMOUR HOBERT E JR	1LT	0-0538562	0865	2
SEYMOUR JOHN H	MAJ	0-0427489	0954	1
SEYMOUR KENNETH W	LTC	0-0392173	0957	2
SEYMOUR MARMADUKE	MAJ	0-0110531	0648	3
SEYMOUR PERSHING K	MAJ	0-1646931	1062	1
SEYMOUR ROBERT A	2LT	0-1311216	0344	2
SEYMOUR STUART L	LTC	0-0297758	0964	3
SEYSTER MICHAEL E	LTC	0-0243752	0162	1
SGARRO MICHAEL J	LTC	0-1796165	0567	3
SHAAD ROBERT R	1LT	0-0554934	0747	2
SHACHTMAN JOSEPH M	MAJ	0-0403096	0745	2
SHACKEL EDWARD G	LTC	0-1636633	0158	1
SHACKELFORD B W	CPT	0-0905337	0-49	2
SHACKELFORD GORDON E	CPT	0-0407966	0646	2
SHACKELFORD HOWARD F	CW2	W-2145871	1058	2
SHACKELFORD JAMES A	LTC	0-2054033	0862	1
SHACKELFORD JAMES E	CW2	W-2107537	1045	2
SHACKELFORD JAMES F	MAJ	0-0258542	1066	3
SHACKELFORD JAMES M	LTC	0-0293880	1068	3
SHACKELFORD RICHARD	COL	0-0215595	0662	3
SHACKELFORD ROBERT O	MAJ	0-1535076	1061	1
SHACKELFORD TOM G	LTC	0-0304890	1059	1
SHACKELFORD TRAVIS P	CW4	W-2146029	0368	1
SHACKLEFORD EARL E	LTC	0-1016172	0962	1
SHACKLEFORD PAUL A	CPT	0-0390762	0546	2
SHACKLEFORD R H	CW2	W-2147672	1155	1
SHACKLETTE ELMER C	CPT	0-2009973	0255	1
SHACKLETTE JOSEPH W	CW2	W-2144220	1059	2
SHACKMAN ALEXANDER	WO1	W-2128397	0146	2
SHACKTON ROBERT W	1LT	0-1309971	0845	2
SHADDEAU WILLIAM A	LTC	0-1015181	1060	1
SHADDIX HERMAN L	CW4	W-2148189	0568	1
SHADDOCK HENRY	CPT	0-2055116	0647	2
SHADE ADELAIDE E	CPT	N-0724721	0649	2
SHADE ERVIN H	LTC	0-0232165	1047	2
SHADE KENNETH N	1LT	0-0311768	0144	2
SHADE RAYMOND A	CPT	0-0246241	1145	2
SHADE RICHARD E	LTC	0-1341590	0666	1
SHADE VERONICA R	MAJ	N-0799206	0665	1
SHADFORD EUGENE S	CPT	0-0184591	0851	3
SHADIS ARTHUR	MAJ	0-1794998	0157	1
SHADLE FREDERICK	LTC	0-1297793	0166	1
SHADRICK JAMES B	CPT	0-1296919	1063	1
SHAEFER HENRY C	MAJ	0-1641786	0564	1
SHAEFFER CLAYTON C	CW3	W-2144961	0159	1
SHAEFFER FRANCES Z	2LT	N-0785488	0946	1
SHAFE LOWELL F	CPT	0-1110247	1163	1
SHAFER ALBERT H	LTC	0-0213022	0446	2
SHAFER DELPHA F	MAJ	N-0732023	1165	1
SHAFER DONALD M	MAJ	0-0345171	0346	2
SHAFER ERNEST A	MAJ	0-0133784	0349	3
SHAFER HENRY A	CPT	0-0967815	1060	1
SHAFER HERBERT J	2LT	0-1102954	0545	2
SHAFER QUINTON R	CW3	W-2144345	1164	1
SHAFFER ALBERT JR	1LT	0-0357677	0145	2
SHAFFER BENJAMIN F	LTC	0-0190185	1151	3
SHAFFER CARLETON B	COL	0-0145143	0648	3
SHAFFER CHARLES N	MAJ	0-0414948	1145	2
SHAFFER CLYDE G	CW4	W-2122622	0266	1
SHAFFER DONALD Y	COL	0-0296906	0566	3
SHAFFER FRED W	LTC	0-0285731	0163	3
SHAFFER FREDERICK	LTC	0-0212550	0249	3
SHAFFER GEORGE D	LTC	0-1636635	0463	1
SHAFFER HARRY T	CW2	W-2145622	0957	1
SHAFFER HOWARD P	COL	0-0256375	0958	3
SHAFFER J D	MAJ	0-2017767	0560	1
SHAFFER JACK G	MAJ	0-0885757	0261	1
SHAFFER JAY O	CW4	W-2142898	0367	2
SHAFFER JOHN W	LTC	0-2026806	0668	1

ARMY OF THE UNITED STATES RETIRED LIST

NAME	GRADE	SVC NO	DATE RET MO YR	RET CODE
SHAFFER JOHN W	WO1	W-2141826	0854	1
SHAFFER LEE J	COL	0-0237094	1064	3
SHAFFER LYLE B JR	1LT	0-1182959	1048	2
SHAFFER MORRIS	CW3	W-2104451	1054	1
SHAFFER ORRIN G	LTC	0-1165952	0765	1
SHAFFER PAUL R	LTC	0-0213300	0462	3
SHAFFER SUSAN	1LT	N-0761078	0847	1
SHAFFER WALTER G	LTC	0-0916527	1062	1
SHAFFER WAYNE C	MAJ	0-0513034	0265	1
SHAFFER WILLIAM D	COL	0-0186287	0848	3
SHAFFER WILLIE L	MAJ	0-0205610	1059	1
SHAFFER XENOPHON B	LTC	0-0156913	0857	3
SHAFFRAN JOHN	CW2	W-2104463	0753	2
SHAHAN WILLIAM H	LTC	0-0900536	1062	3
SHAHON HENRY I	MAJ	0-0492592	0346	2
SHAIA FONAD T	CW2	W-2110438	1052	1
SHAKARIAN CHARLES G	MAJ	0-0998771	1165	1
SHAKE JULIAN P	MAJ	0-0962436	0363	1
SHAKULA JOHN H	MAJ	0-2000792	0562	1
SHALALA JOHN S	LTC	0-1100762	0966	1
SHALE JOHN H	1LT	0-1283330	0245	2
SHALL MORRIS J	CPT	0-0263054	1065	3
SHALLCROSS DONALD C	CPT	0-0444623	0646	2
SHALLCROSS FRANK A	LTC	0-0179946	0253	3
SHALLCROSS LAWRENCE	COL	0-0298593	1267	3
SHALLER DOROTHY E	2LT	N-0761526	1044	1
SHALLER SIDNEY B	CPT	0-1309421	0246	2
SHALLINGTON THOMAS W	COL	0-0394475	0263	1
SHALVEY JOSEPH P	MAJ	0-1184296	0962	1
SHAMBAUGH GORDON I	LTC	0-0368062	1265	3
SHAMBAUGH HOWARD T	LTC	0-1549094	0662	2
SHAMBAUGH WILSON R	MAJ	0-1286017	0760	2
SHAMBLIN HOWARD C	MAJ	0-1013256	0760	1
SHAMBURG DUANE L	CW2	W-3000439	0969	1
SHAMBURGER SAMUEL L	CPT	0-2263647	0864	1
SHAMEL WILLIAM L	LTC	0-0203675	1154	3
SHAMLIN ED M	LTC	0-1324583	0865	1
SHAMP WALTER R	LTC	0-0292808	1168	3
SHAMPER OLIVIA K	2LT	N-0730209	0943	1
SHANABARGER ROBERT G	CPT	0-0970660	1060	1
SHANAFELT JOHN L	1LT	0-1010864	0446	2
SHANAHAN CHARLES M	MAJ	0-1998440	1163	1
SHANAHAN CORNELIUS	MAJ	0-1297794	0661	1
SHANAHAN JOHN R	MAJ	0-1300536	0147	2
SHANAHAN ROBERT E	LTC	0-1577830	0660	1
SHANDS JSCE H	CPT	0-0473719	0460	3
SHANE HENRY K	LTC	0-0175740	0562	3
SHANE SEYMOUR L	MAJ	0-1182960	0165	1
SHANER ELMER E	LTC	0-1112433	0765	1
SHANGRAW CLAYTON C	MAJ	0-0172697	0556	3
SHANK OLIVER D JR	LTC	0-1052958	1165	1
SHANK WILLIAM W	LTC	0-0332215	0968	3
SHANKEY ANASTATIA	CPT	R-0001309	1246	1
SHANKMAN ROBERT A	MAJ	0-1031444	1160	1
SHANKS JOHN N	LTC	0-0219050	0947	1
SHANLEY JOHN M	MAJ	0-0229850	0665	3
SHANLEY PATRICK J	LTC	0-0451548	0962	1
SHANLEY WILLIAM T	CPT	0-1113438	0846	2
SHANNON ALBERT L	COL	0-0415427	0264	1
SHANNON BURDETTE A	LTC	0-1102956	0856	1
SHANNON CHARLES H	CW3	W-2107943	1060	1
SHANNON DALLAS L	MAJ	0-1334362	0662	1
SHANNON DONALD C	LTC	0-0361301	0363	1
SHANNON EDMUND W	LTC	0-1327387	1067	1
SHANNON FRANK W	CW3	W-2147899	1161	1
SHANNON GEORGE I	LTC	0-0141147	0946	2
SHANNON HARRY J	CPT	0-0885883	0848	1
SHANNON HARRY L	LTC	0-1108314	1060	1
SHANNON JACK T	COL	0-0361736	1160	1
SHANNON JACKSON G	1LT	0-1286906	0943	2
SHANNON JAMES JR	CW3	W-2153326	0766	1
SHANNON JOE A	CPT	0-1638490	0456	1
SHANNON JOHN A	CPT	0-0486570	0843	2
SHANNON JOSEPH J	CW2	W-2114759	0962	1
SHANNON JOSEPH K	LTC	0-1649939	0366	1

NAME	GRADE	SVC NO	DATE RET MO YR	RET CODE
SHANNON MILDRED C	MAJ	N-0744644	0163	1
SHANNON RALPH T	LTC	0-0312190	0846	1
SHANNON ROGER R	MAJ	0-0321597	0345	2
SHANNON ROY A	LTC	0-1823073	0561	1
SHANNON STANLEY E	MAJ	0-0289745	0861	1
SHANNON THOMAS J	MAJ	0-1639632	0863	1
SHANNON WILLIAM H	COL	0-0158250	0648	3
SHANNON WILLIAM V	MAJ	0-0172750	0162	3
SHANOR GEORGE B	COL	0-0172546	0564	2
SHAPBELL EDITH M	CPT	N-0760779	0153	2
SHAPIRA JAKE	MAJ	0-0430282	0246	2
SHAPIRO ALBERT	CPT	0-0449521	0745	2
SHAPIRO GEORGE W	CPT	0-1690020	0246	2
SHAPIRO HERMAN H	COL	0-0409140	1264	3
SHAPIRO HERMAN L	COL	0-0530972	1064	3
SHAPIRO HYMAN O	LTC	0-0482271	0446	2
SHAPIRO JACOB	LTC	0-0341427	0146	2
SHAPIRO JOHN L	CPT	0-0419805	0945	2
SHAPIRO JOSEPH	MAJ	0-1689607	0646	2
SHAPIRO MAX	1LT	0-0399281	0444	2
SHAPIRO MORRIS	CW3	W-2109212	0159	1
SHAPIRO SOLOMON S	LTC	0-0233755	0546	2
SHAPIRO SYDNEY H	1LT	0-1544484	1045	2
SHAPIRO THEODORE	CPT	0-1173455	0446	2
SHAPLAND LESTER B	COL	0-0133811	1151	3
SHAPLEY BENJAMIN S	LTC	0-0317612	0561	3
SHAPPELL EARL R	LTC	0-1039913	0364	1
SHAPPY FOSTER F	1LT	0-1299802	0348	1
SHAPRO FRANK	COL	0-0222190	1047	2
SHAPTER PETER L	MAJ	0-1289976	0657	1
SHARBONDA VIVIAN P	1LT	N-0783852	1045	1
SHARIN BERNARD	2LT	0-1997339	0945	2
SHARKEY EDWARD M	1LT	0-1310158	0845	2
SHARKEY JOSEPH J	MAJ	0-1324195	0359	1
SHARKEY MARY E	2LT	N-0768346	0845	1
SHARO SAMUEL M	COL	0-0220678	1161	3
SHARON JOSEPH L	2LT	0-1895655	0944	2
SHARON MAY	MAJ	N-0727866	0762	2
SHARP ALVA C	CPT	0-1649610	0657	1
SHARP BENJAMIN C	CPT	0-0400953	0345	2
SHARP BOYD F	LTC	0-0253131	0960	1
SHARP CHARLTON D	CW2	W-2103796	0652	2
SHARP CLARENCE L	CPT	0-0102933	0250	3
SHARP DALLAS A	LTC	0-0412071	0463	1
SHARP DAVID M	CPT	0-1876047	0966	2
SHARP DON E	LTC	0-2263469	0766	1
SHARP EVERETT W	LTC	0-0249907	0165	3
SHARP FRANK L	1LT	0-0221432	0353	3
SHARP FRED E	MAJ	0-0307940	0168	3
SHARP HAROLD K	COL	0-1586170	1268	2
SHARP HAROLD K	LTC	0-1593264	1062	1
SHARP HIRAM F	LTC	0-0269531	0467	3
SHARP JOE A	LTC	0-1797365	0668	3
SHARP JOHN H	COL	0-0194054	0-48	2
SHARP JOHN H	COL	0-0219789	0557	1
SHARP JOHN H	CPT	0-1287420	1045	2
SHARP JOSEPH C	MAJ	0-0276252	0458	3
SHARP PAUL W	COL	0-0218792	0758	3
SHARP RALPH T	1LT	0-2055198	0951	2
SHARP RALPH V	MAJ	0-0544630	0264	1
SHARP ROBERT E	LTC	0-0470969	0750	2
SHARP ROLLINS H	MAJ	0-0966759	1062	1
SHARP THEODORE L	LTC	0-0306298	1166	3
SHARP WILLARD H	LTC	0-0908255	1068	3
SHARP WILLIAM R	CW2	W-2215380	0867	1
SHARP WILLIAM R SR	MAJ	0-1185497	0858	1
SHARPE CLIFFORD M	LTC	0-0396845	1045	2
SHARPE GEORGE A	CW2	W-2145587	1056	1
SHARPE JOHN H	LTC	0-0300514	0860	1
SHARPE JOHN R	CPT	0-1080149	0347	2
SHARPE LUTHER E JR	COL	0-0450765	0166	1
SHARPE PATRICK C	MAJ	0-4005510	0968	1
SHARPE PHILIP J	LTC	0-1322479	0164	1
SHARPE THEODORE G	MAJ	0-0966771	0164	1
SHARPES KENNETH	1LT	0-1544105	0551	2

NAME	GRADE	SVC NO	DATE RET MO YR	RET CODE
SHARPNACK GEORGE L	CPT	0-1180043	0648	2
SHARPS FRANK	1LT	0-0381805	0145	2
SHARRETT VICTOR A	MAJ	0-0235488	1265	3
SHARTEL PAUL W	MAJ	0-1015167	0357	1
SHARY 2ND JOHN H	CPT	0-0533475	1047	2
SHASTEEN JOHN L	CW4	W-2118339	0560	1
SHATTAN BOAZ	1LT	0-1716661	0245	2
SHATTUCK LEE C	CPT	0-4005511	1063	1
SHATTUCK WILLIAM R	LTC	0-0225808	0762	3
SHAUB BENJAMIN M	MAJ	0-0215960	0153	3
SHAUB DAVID P	1LT	0-0490769	0146	2
SHAUB ROBERT C	1LT	0-0512913	1043	2
SHAUCK CHARLES W	LTC	0-0360912	0760	1
SHAUGHNESSEY PETER G	CPT	0-1595827	0953	1
SHAUGHNESSY MICHAEL	LTC	0-2011055	1163	1
SHAUGHNESSY ROBERT C	MAJ	0-2017768	0763	1
SHAUKLAS VICTOR F	MAJ	0-0940786	0162	2
SHAUL REX K	COL	0-0313126	0464	1
SHAULIS CALVIN F	LTC	0-0151323	0955	3
SHAULIS MILDRED A	2LT	N-0789066	0844	1
SHAULIS MITCHELL	CW2	W-2142899	0453	2
SHAVE HENRY A	MAJ	0-2262454	0267	2
SHAVER CHARLES D	CPT	0-1180044	0747	2
SHAVER DANIEL M	CPT	0-0177187	1058	3
SHAVER GARNETT M	WO1	W-2151323	1054	1
SHAVER GEORGE E	MAJ	0-1165954	0960	1
SHAVER GLENN A	WO1	W-2118483	0750	1
SHAVER RALPH B	CW4	W-2152833	0368	1
SHAVER WILLIAM E	LTC	0-1924930	1068	1
SHAVERS IVERSON E	LTC	0-1593266	1062	1
SHAW ALEXANDER JR	CPT	0-1291753	0844	2
SHAW ALLAN G	2LT	0-1311823	0545	2
SHAW ALTON D	COL	0-0453215	0261	1
SHAW ARTHUR F	COL	0-0143824	1044	2
SHAW ARTHUR R	COL	0-1165334	0662	1
SHAW ARTHUR W	MAJ	0-0492417	0758	1
SHAW BERNARD G	MAJ	0-0454162	0850	2
SHAW BILL	LTC	0-1016658	0468	1
SHAW CHARELS E JR	MAJ	0-1186367	1265	1
SHAW CHARLES R	COL	0-0444074	1054	2
SHAW CLARKE M	COL	0-0202190	0758	1
SHAW DAVID S	LTC	0-0291059	0761	1
SHAW DELOYD C	MAJ	0-0220053	1059	3
SHAW DENNIS J	LTC	0-1032602	0961	2
SHAW DONALD B	MAJ	0-0200574	0258	3
SHAW DONALD F	LTC	0-1019546	0463	2
SHAW DOROTHY J	1LT	N-0789136	0546	1
SHAW DWIGHT B	COL	0-0284882	0658	3
SHAW EARL A	LTC	0-0258199	0746	2
SHAW EARL W	MAJ	0-1584885	0655	1
SHAW EDWIN D	COL	0-0124037	0756	1
SHAW EMMON R	COL	0-0360495	0960	1
SHAW EUGENE D	MAJ	0-1304451	0962	1
SHAW FRANK H	LTC	0-1633538	1262	1
SHAW FRANK L	COL	0-1184145	0368	2
SHAW FRANK W	LTC	0-0966600	1068	1
SHAW FRANK W JR	CPT	0-0339456	0645	2
SHAW GLEN E	COL	0-0296573	0766	1
SHAW HALBERT C	MAJ	0-0266976	1145	2
SHAW HAROLD R	COL	0-0243589	0364	3
SHAW HARRY D	MAJ	0-2017289	0463	1
SHAW HELEN L	1LT	N-0728145	0744	1
SHAW HESTER C	MAJ	N-0759615	0368	1
SHAW HOBART D JR	LTC	0-1100331	0868	3
SHAW HOWARD W	CPT	0-1549095	0854	1
SHAW HUGH P	MAJ	0-1289154	0660	1
SHAW JAMES A	MAJ	0-0291515	0365	1
SHAW JAMES E	COL	0-0281282	0761	2
SHAW JAMES G	COL	0-0331544	1267	3
SHAW JAMES H	LTC	0-1299803	1057	1
SHAW JANDON	CPT	0-0341343	0144	2
SHAW JEWEL M	1LT	N-0783682	0447	1
SHAW JOHN B	MAJ	0-0145123	0457	3
SHAW JOHN C	COL	0-1654200	0267	1
SHAW JOHN C JR	LTC	0-0379739	0160	2

NAME	GRADE	SVC NO	DATE RET MO YR	RET CODE
SHAW JOHN D M	MAJ	0-0282000	0862	1
SHAW JOHN E	CPT	0-1111907	0559	1
SHAW JOHN E	CPT	0-1318713	0646	2
SHAW JOHN T	CPT	0-1925128	0959	2
SHAW JOHNNIE J	LTC	0-1924544	0968	1
SHAW JOSEPH	LTC	0-1594472	0766	3
SHAW JOSEPH C	CPT	0-0503679	0246	2
SHAW JOSEPH E	COL	0-0147367	0256	3
SHAW JUNE M	1LT	N-0784377	0546	1
SHAW KENNETH E	MAJ	0-1108316	0167	1
SHAW LAUREN L	LTC	0-0278587	0756	3
SHAW LELAND H JR	1LT	0-1032652	104N	2
SHAW LESLIE A	MAJ	0-0236784	0266	3
SHAW LLEWELLYN	LTC	0-0224322	0559	1
SHAW LOUISE A	MAJ	N-0754266	0565	3
SHAW LUTHER D	COL	0-0464434	1064	3
SHAW LYMAN A	COL	0-0141123	0250	3
SHAW MARJORIE A	1LT	N-0751178	0146	1
SHAW MARVIN H	MAJ	0-1645529	0461	1
SHAW MARVIN W	LTC	0-2009039	0767	1
SHAW MAURICE A	CPT	0-1173456	0557	1
SHAW MELVIN	1LT	0-1178332	0744	2
SHAW MILTON	LTC	0-0182370	0749	3
SHAW MILTON S	MAJ	0-1103399	0662	1
SHAW MINARD P	LTC	0-1583661	0558	1
SHAW MURRAY L	MAJ	0-1546771	0857	1
SHAW OREN V	COL	0-0221230	0858	3
SHAW ORVILLE T	MAJ	0-1326521	0559	1
SHAW PAUL A	MAJ	0-1306324	0861	1
SHAW QUINCY A JR	COL	0-0127600	0457	3
SHAW RALPH W	CPT	0-1540778	0659	1
SHAW RAYMOND C	MAJ	0-0449990	1061	3
SHAW RICHARD A	CW2	W-2217655	1268	1
SHAW RICHARD J	LTC	0-1340940	0968	1
SHAW ROBERT E	CW2	W-2129945	0261	1
SHAW ROBERT H	LTC	0-0360547	0757	2
SHAW ROBERT H	LTC	0-0915768	0867	3
SHAW ROBERT R	2LT	0-1031445	0643	2
SHAW ROLIN W	LTC	0-0198002	0648	3
SHAW ROY L	MAJ	0-0222187	0249	1
SHAW SIDNEY E	CPT	0-1117077	0854	1
SHAW THOMAS M	1LT	0-1295443	0645	2
SHAW VAUGHAN A	MAJ	0-0357108	0146	2
SHAW WALTER F	MAJ	0-1946378	1060	1
SHAW WARD M JR	1LT	0-1315528	0547	2
SHAW WARREN C	2LT	0-0540043	0945	2
SHAW WILLIAM A	MAJ	0-0300720	0344	2
SHAW WILLIAM F	MAJ	0-1286019	1060	1
SHAW WILLIAM J	COL	0-0235610	1052	3
SHAW WILLIAM J	LTC	0-1042428	0365	1
SHAW WILLIAM R	LTC	0-0342833	1160	2
SHAW WILLIS F	2LT	0-1309973	0644	2
SHAW WILLOUGHBY	1LT	0-1292071	1043	2
SHAWHAN OLEN B	COL	0-0180370	1057	3
SHAWVER DORIS A	1LT	N-0737205	0846	1
SHAWVER WILLIAM C	LTC	0-1111361	0257	1
SHAY CLARENCE R	MAJ	0-1690918	0960	1
SHAY DAN B	LTC	0-1016762	0766	1
SHAY HARRY	LTC	0-0484089	1054	1
SHAY NEIL E	CPT	0-0903212	0344	2
SHAYDAK JOHN C	MAJ	0-0838226	0960	1
SHEA CHARLES A JR	2LT	0-0917666	0445	2
SHEA CHARLES R	CW4	W-2111636	0660	1
SHEA CLARENCE J	CW4	W-2141677	1062	2
SHEA CLIFFORD H	LTC	0-1324705	1062	1
SHEA DAVID S	CPT	0-0383832	0146	2
SHEA DONALD W	CPT	0-1047345	0965	2
SHEA ELEANOR F	1LT	N-0720358	0946	1
SHEA ELISABETH	1LT	N-0752519	0146	1
SHEA FRANCIS B	CPT	0-1593840	0346	2
SHEA FRANK H	1LT	0-2034700	1045	2
SHEA FRANK S	MAJ	0-0220865	1158	3
SHEA GEORGE H	LTC	0-1697994	0268	3
SHEA GEORGE S	LTC	0-2035896	0767	1
SHEA HENRY B	LTC	0-0288693	0164	3

NAME	GRADE	SVC NO	DATE RET MO YR	RET CODE
SHEA IRVING [illegible]	LTC	0-0913370	0962	1
SHEA JAMES [illegible]	LTC	0-0147454	0455	1
SHEA JAMES M	LTC	0-1581466	0868	1
SHEA JAMES M JR	LTC	[illegible]	0264	1
SHEA JOHN	LTC	0-0981776	0368	1
SHEA JOSEPH [illegible]	LTC	0-0475725	0753	1
SHEA [illegible]	CW4	W-2132455	0958	1
SHEA LAWRENCE	MAJ	0-0475012	0946	1
SHEA RALPH [illegible]	COL	0-0264078	1267	1
SHEA RAYMOND [illegible]	MAJ	0-1167214	0356	1
SHEA ROBERT S	CW3	W-2144190	0963	1
SHEA STANLEY C	COL	0-1280374	1060	1
SHEA THOMAS [illegible]	MAJ	0-0445255	0346	2
SHEA WILLIAM J JR	1LT	0-1017652	0446	2
SHEAD WALTER J	CW4	W-2144414	1059	1
SHEAFE EARLE V	COL	0-0103743	0648	3
SHEAFFER CHARLES G	CW2	W-2151689	0760	1
SHEAFFER DANIEL H	CW4	W-2005411	0568	1
SHEAFFER WALTER A	1LT	0-0476676	1145	2
SHEAHAN FRANCIS R	CW4	W-2151040	0967	1
SHEAHAN JOHN J	CPT	0-0283368	1145	2
SHEAHAN WILLIAM M	LTC	0-1643938	0661	1
SHEAKS ELBERT F	CPT	0-1169458	0153	2
SHEALY JESSE A	LTC	0-0475261	0446	1
SHEALY JOHN R	LTC	0-2014737	0666	1
SHEAR ALEX E	1LT	0-1030711	0945	2
SHEAR SIDNEY P	CPT	0-0336241	0246	2
SHEARD WILDER H	COL	0-0301496	0560	1
SHEARER HARRY F	MAJ	0-2033599	0965	1
SHEARER CYRUS M	MAJ	0-0201419	1046	2
SHEARER FRANCIS B	COL	0-0211630	0658	1
SHEARER FRED C JR	1LT	0-0537485	1147	2
SHEARER GEORGE M	LTC	0-0218770	1058	3
SHEARER JAMES G	CW4	W-2148052	0968	1
SHEARER JAMES L	COL	0-0248843	0852	3
SHEARER LEE	WO1	W-2110133	0350	2
SHEARER MARK D	LTC	0-1103403	0764	1
SHEARER MARY E	MAJ	N-0760395	0165	1
SHEARER OSCO	MAJ	0-0449671	0550	2
SHEARER ROBERT L	CPT	0-0361206	1145	2
SHEARIN GEORGE E	CW4	W-2143667	0164	1
SHEARIN WILLIAM F	MAJ	0-0332338	0660	1
SHEARROW CHARLES W	CW2	W-2150017	1262	1
SHEARS CLARA B	2LT	N-0763804	0245	1
SHECKELS JOHN E	CW3	W-2105031	1151	1
SHECKLER CHARLES L	LTC	0-1183969	0565	1
SHEDD GEORGE C	WO1	W-2130241	0653	1
SHEDER LAWRENCE S	1LT	MN-2321219	0268	2
SHEEDY JOHN	LTC	0-0463643	1054	1
SHEEHAN BERNARD J	LTC	0-1591558	0967	1
SHEEHAN CHARLES J	2LT	0-0979236	0152	2
SHEEHAN DANIEL F	LTC	0-0220216	1046	1
SHEEHAN EARL J	MAJ	0-1036373	0665	3
SHEEHAN EDWARD L	LTC	0-0166809	0246	2
SHEEHAN EVELYN M	2LT	L-0601837	0245	2
SHEEHAN GEORGE T	MAJ	0-0123212	0648	3
SHEEHAN JAMES G	LTC	0-0407192	0351	2
SHEEHAN JOHN G	COL	0-0224570	1156	3
SHEEHAN JOHN P	LTC	0-0232039	0666	3
SHEEHAN JOHN G	1LT	0-0432962	1045	2
SHEEHAN KATHERINE	2LT	N-0759755	0944	1
SHEEHAN RICHARD D	CPT	0-0370930	1046	2
SHEEHAN THOMAS F	LTC	0-2018586	1164	1
SHEEHE NORMAN L	LTC	0-0195769	0853	3
SHEEHY JOSEPH S	CPT	0-1825929	0454	2
SHEEHY JULIAN R	MAJ	0-1996412	1158	1
SHEEHY OLIVER J	CPT	0-0109095	0953	3
SHEEHY ROBERT J	1LT	0-1325067	0265	1
SHEEHY THORNTON F	MAJ	0-1635323	1060	1
SHEELEY WALTER L	CW3	W-2209784	1167	1
SHEELY ARTHUR C	COL	0-0207217	1058	3
SHEELY CHARLES W	LTC	0-0179203	1060	3
SHEELY EARL D	1LT	0-0498851	0547	1
SHEELY GILBERT H	CPT	0-1030932	0747	2
SHEEN CHARLES F	LTC	0-0123270	0157	3
SHEER HERBERT	LTC	0-1013579	1061	1
SHEERAN JAMES H	CPT	0-0199310	0546	2
SHEERAN LAWRENCE W	LTC	0-1291182	0565	1
SHEERIN JOHN J	CW2	W-2215390	0368	1
SHEETINGER ERNEST J	MAJ	0-0220075	0760	3
SHEETS ALBERT E	LTC	0-0191271	0-53	3
SHEETS HARRY D	COL	0-0260649	0857	1
SHEETS JACK O	COL	0-0242069	0566	3
SHEETS ROBERT V	CPT	0-0444947	0744	1
SHEETZ CHESTER R	CW2	W-2213972	1168	1
SHEETZ GEORGE E	LTC	0-0265023	0158	3
SHEFF NATHAN W	CW2	W-3430225	0268	1
SHEFFER WILLIAM B	LTC	0-0335786	1057	1
SHEFFIELD AZOR D	1LT	0-0383428	1045	2
SHEFFIELD CLYDE T	MAJ	0-4074551	0768	1
SHEFFIELD DOUGLAS A	CPT	0-0285908	1067	3
SHEFFIELD HAROLD C	LTC	0-0370204	0361	1
SHEFFIELD JOHN W	LTC	0-0242722	0566	3
SHEFFIELD LOUIS MC C	WO1	W-2123551	1044	2
SHEFFIELD RICHARD F	LTC	0-1165736	0761	2
SHEFFLER ABBOTT M JR	1LT	0-0514656	0945	2
SHEFFY CARY L	CPT	0-1322090	1162	1
SHEFRIN NORMAN	CPT	0-0543884	1145	2
SHEFT THADDEUS J	CPT	0-0410919	1047	2
SHEHAB ALFRED H M	LTC	0-1012319	0363	1
SHEHAN CHARLES F	MAJ	0-1923593	1063	1
SHEHAN MILLARD P	CW2	W-2148815	1166	1
SHEHANE BARNEY A	COL	0-0263758	0863	3
SHEIL JOHN J	CPT	0-0510291	1047	1
SHEIL NICHOLAS F	LTC	0-1306325	0762	1
SHEIMAN SAMUEL C	CPT	0-1690196	0346	2
SHELBAER ROSS	CW4	W-2102359	0557	1
SHELBERT MICHAEL R	CW2	W-2152617	0858	1
SHELBY CECIL P	MAJ	0-1881825	0166	1
SHELBY CHARLES T	1LT	0-1558977	0346	2
SHELBY CHARLES T	MAJ	0-1592047	0667	1
SHELBY HERMAN J	MAJ	0-1821777	1060	1
SHELBY HOWARD J	MAJ	0-0248682	0164	3
SHELBY JOHN D	MAJ	0-0885777	0259	2
SHELBY ROBERT W	MAJ	0-0450153	0952	2
SHELBY TROY H	COL	0-0314663	0764	1
SHELDEN HOWARD W	LTC	0-0193770	0951	3
SHELDON ARVID K	MAJ	0-2292024	0866	1
SHELDON EDGAR E	1LT	0-0213973	0347	2
SHELDON HARRY B	CPT	0-1715057	1047	2
SHELDON HOLLIS F	MAJ	0-1580314	0264	1
SHELDON HOYNE S	COL	0-0300039	1065	2
SHELDON JOSEPH V	COL	0-0401466	0157	1
SHELDON NINUS W	MAJ	0-0497428	0762	3
SHELDON RAYMOND W	CW4	W-2000126	1051	2
SHELDON ROBERT B	LTC	0-0371964	0657	1
SHELDON ROSS A	CPT	0-2017909	0662	1
SHELDON WILLIAM H	MAJ	0-0133605	0944	2
SHELEY MAURICE C	LTC	0-1344705	0362	2
SHELHORN ROBERT H JR	LTC	0-0523405	0963	1
SHELINE WILLIAM H	CPT	0-0234655	0544	1
SHELL HERBERT	1LT	0-1283856	0246	2
SHELLER EUGENE W	1LT	0-1309102	0146	2
SHELLER SAMUEL M	MAJ	0-2015502	0562	1
SHELLEY AUBREY F	LTC	0-0408491	1263	1
SHELLEY FRANCIS R	2LT	0-1080816	0744	2
SHELLEY HARRY S	COL	0-0291116	0761	3
SHELLEY HOLLIOUS R	1LT	0-1995168	0347	2
SHELLEY JOHN E	MAJ	0-1699971	1061	1
SHELLEY MACK C	LTC	0-1286195	0157	1
SHELLEY OTTO S	MAJ	0-1308191	0357	1
SHELLEY ROBERT G SR	CW3	W-2146881	0760	1
SHELLEY THOMAS L	LTC	0-0271957	0960	3
SHELLEY WILSON E	MAJ	0-1306326	0257	1
SHELLMAN ERNEST J	MAJ	0-0196575	0356	3
SHELLOW HAROLD	MAJ	0-0496516	0946	2
SHELMAN PHILLIP T	CW3	W-2144719	1264	1
SHELNUTT HENRY F	MAJ	0-1639637	0563	2
SHELNUTT HOMER H	CW3	W-2144628	0966	2
SHELTON A L	CW3	W-2152866	0962	2
SHELTON ALBERT E	1LT	0-1304211	0346	2
SHELTON ALDEAN L	MAJ	0-0417956	0361	1
SHELTON AUBREY J	LTC	0-1328531	0363	1
SHELTON BAKER D JR	LTC	0-1584899	0666	3
SHELTON CHARLES L	LTC	0-0364075	0267	3
SHELTON CLARENCE B	LTC	0-1044176	0366	3
SHELTON GUY F	CW2	W-2148191	0756	1
SHELTON DAVID S	MAJ	0-1238449	1047	2
SHELTON EDWARD F	LTC	0-1996368	0665	1
SHELTON ELDRED V	CW3	W-2148738	0168	1
SHELTON FAY S	2LT	0-1174710	0445	2
SHELTON FRED T	LTC	0-1168912	1060	1
SHELTON GEORGE L	LTC	0-2053835	0764	1
SHELTON GERALDINE	CW2	W-2119863	0545	2
SHELTON IRWIN D	MAJ	0-1113245	0962	1
SHELTON JAMES F	MAJ	0-1319587	0357	1
SHELTON JAMES H JR	LTC	0-1337630	1268	1
SHELTON JAMES R	MAJ	0-1823949	0760	1
SHELTON JOHN B	CPT	0-0497878	0548	1
SHELTON JOHN W	CPT	0-0988095	0162	1
SHELTON LEONARD A	2LT	0-2003775	0552	2
SHELTON LLOYD W	2LT	0-2006236	0864	2
SHELTON LOUIS F	CPT	0-1540786	0557	1
SHELTON LYNN C	MAJ	0-1335189	0864	1
SHELTON MARVIN C JR	MAJ	0-2023521	1267	1
SHELTON MILLER F	CPT	0-0402300	0144	2
SHELTON MILTON	MAJ	0-0211315	0450	3
SHELTON ORVILLE F	1LT	0-1031446	0945	2
SHELTON PRESTON K	CW2	W-2007227	0767	1
SHELTON RALPH W	MAJ	0-5304065	0968	1
SHELTON RAYMOND P	LTC	0-1322273	0166	1
SHELTON ROLAND H	MAJ	0-0959181	0865	1
SHELTON RUFUS B	MAJ	0-0968430	0961	1
SHELTON WILLIAM A	LTC	0-1291712	0760	1
SHELTON WILLIAM A	CW2	W-2211049	1165	1
SHELTON WILLIAM B	1LT	0-0323744	1146	2
SHELY REX	CW2	W-2120937	0853	1
SHEMELYNEC STEPHEN	CW3	W-2152439	0564	1
SHEMIDT ANTHONY R	CPT	0-0444103	0944	2
SHENBERGER JACK W	MAJ	0-1930905	0967	1
SHENK DAVID H	1LT	0-1032177	0447	2
SHENK EDGAR L	LTC	0-1636641	0461	2
SHENK HAROLD H	1LT	0-1303784	0347	2
SHENK MERRITT M	CW2	W-2119548	0147	1
SHENKEL JOHN H	LTC	0-0145280	1153	3
SHENKYR JUNITA H	1LT	N-0776445	0446	1
SHENOSKY PETER S	1LT	0-1174436	0545	2
SHEON JESSE P	LTC	0-0338842	0468	3
SHEPARD ALAN B	LTC	0-0131392	0951	3
SHEPARD ARTHUR C	CPT	0-2206106	0265	1
SHEPARD BURLEIGH W	1LT	0-1113940	0446	2
SHEPARD CHAUNCEY B	MAJ	0-1996501	1159	1
SHEPARD COREY R	1LT	0-1284225	0246	2
SHEPARD EARL W	CW3	W-2144213	0161	1
SHEPARD EDMOND C	WO1	W-2115843	1048	1
SHEPARD FRED E	MAJ	0-0173319	0460	3
SHEPARD FREDERICK	COL	0-0252889	1155	3
SHEPARD GEORGE M	LTC	0-0127840	0748	3
SHEPARD GEORGE W	MAJ	0-1168915	0258	1
SHEPARD HAROLD P	CPT	0-0297089	1043	2
SHEPARD HARRY D	CPT	0-0211189	0354	3
SHEPARD IRVIN G	LTC	0-0386076	1056	2
SHEPARD JOHN B	COL	0-0169298	0860	3
SHEPARD JOSEPH E	LTC	0-1822467	0168	1
SHEPARD JULIUS T	COL	0-0380688	0867	1
SHEPARD KENNETH T	1LT	0-1701703	1044	2
SHEPARD MERRILL L	LTC	0-1184147	0767	1
SHEPARD RICHARD A	MAJ	0-0474187	1047	2
SHEPARD ROBERT A	MAJ	0-0360931	0846	2
SHEPARD ROY C	CPT	0-0505580	0356	1
SHEPARD VINCENT N	MAJ	0-1291183	0261	1
SHEPARD WILLIAM A	MAJ	0-0271973	0668	3
SHEPARDSON FRANK A	COL	0-0271203	0568	3
SHEPARDSON PEARL H	MAJ	N-0744517	0962	1
SHEPEK JOE H	CPT	0-0279904	0744	2
SHEPHARD PHILIP G	CW2	W-3350238	0868	1
SHEPHARD WILLIAM G	1LT	0-0556676	1154	2
SHEPHERD ALTA R	CPT	L-0115797	0847	2
SHEPHERD AVERY D	LTC	0-0265883	0668	3
SHEPHERD CARLETON H	LTC	0-1446582	0664	1
SHEPHERD CHARLES H	COL	0-0239197	0556	3
SHEPHERD CLARENCE F	MAJ	0-0223131	0351	3
SHEPHERD EARL L	COL	0-0355057	0566	3
SHEPHERD EDWIN M	MAJ	0-0989671	0746	2
SHEPHERD GEORGE S	1LT	0-1313652	0845	2
SHEPHERD GLENN L	COL	0-0232608	0365	3
SHEPHERD HAROLD K	LTC	0-1291055	0161	1
SHEPHERD HENRY B	CPT	0-0482203	0845	1
SHEPHERD JOHN T	MAJ	0-0948901	0162	1
SHEPHERD REGINALD	CW2	W-2102364	1047	1
SHEPHERD ROY D	1LT	0-1113441	1145	2
SHEPHERD RUFUS W	COL	0-0265899	1067	3
SHEPHERD WALTON S JR	MAJ	0-0261261	1065	3
SHEPHERD WILLIAM E	COL	0-0108833	0151	3
SHEPLER MYRON E	COL	0-0340566	1264	1
SHEPPARD ALBERT D	LTC	0-0190904	0845	2
SHEPPARD BAZEL B	MAJ	0-0203951	1063	3
SHEPPARD DON A	COL	0-0225568	1163	3
SHEPPARD ELAINE C	MAJ	N-0723199	0168	1
SHEPPARD FORREST N	LTC	0-0225567	1262	3
SHEPPARD HARLO J JR	LTC	0-1013013	1060	1
SHEPPARD HILLIARD G	CW2	W-2144358	0361	1
SHEPPARD JAMES D	LTC	0-1167216	0961	1
SHEPPARD JAMES Y	LTC	0-0805993	0268	1
SHEPPARD JESSE J	MAJ	0-1797024	1266	3
SHEPPARD LAWRENCE C	LTC	0-0974515	0968	1
SHEPPARD LOUIS B	MAJ	0-0494595	0645	2
SHEPPARD LOVIC P	1LT	0-0496582	0446	1
SHEPPARD REGINALD R	MAJ	0-0452027	0457	1
SHEPPARD ROBERT B	MAJ	0-1004685	0857	1
SHEPPARD ROBERT W	2LT	0-1326115	0745	2
SHEPPARD STANLEY R	MAJ	0-0261813	0959	1
SHEPPARD SYLVESTER	LTC	0-0451180	0663	1
SHEPPARD W J III	MAJ	0-2055166	1152	2
SHEPPE ARTHUR T	COL	0-0256119	1164	3
SHEPPERD ALSTON L	COL	0-0267602	0362	3
SHER ABO S	COL	0-0285247	0666	3
SHER JOSEPH	CPT	0-1543639	1045	2
SHERARD ROY L	MAJ	0-0955272	0166	1
SHERBERT HENRY G JR	MAJ	0-2204411	0367	1
SHERBURN MERL L	COL	0-0246356	0959	1
SHERER ELLIS H	MAJ	0-2001700	0161	1
SHERER JOHN D	LTC	0-0199769	0159	3
SHERET VIRGINIA	LTC	R-0002399	0568	3
SHERFESEE CHARLES M	LTC	0-0282030	0768	3
SHERFY KAY L	CW4	W-2113305	0764	1
SHERIDAN EDWIN H	MAJ	0-0263734	0461	1
SHERIDAN FRANCIS E	MAJ	0-0570218	0755	1
SHERIDAN HARRY H	LTC	0-1797190	0562	2
SHERIDAN HENRY R SR	CW2	W-2206572	0562	2
SHERIDAN JAMES D	LTC	0-0358084	0948	1
SHERIDAN JOHN J	1LT	0-1312345	1045	2
SHERIDAN LAWRENCE V	COL	0-0186728	0648	3
SHERIDAN MARTIN J	CW2	W-2117089	0957	1
SHERIDAN PHILIP J	WO1	W-2127795	0646	2
SHERIDAN ROBERT E	LTC	0-2009574	0268	1
SHERIDAN ROBERT J	MAJ	0-1551115	1054	1
SHERIDAN VICTOR A	MAJ	0-0908060	0347	2
SHERIDAN WILLIAM C	CPT	0-0495311	1048	1
SHERIDAN WILLIAM E	LTC	0-1584890	0562	1
SHERIDAN WILLIAM J	LTC	0-1645363	0565	1
SHERIDAN 2ND HARRY C	2LT	0-2017600	0546	2
SHERIFF ELMER E	CPT	0-1004394	0261	1
SHERK JOHN T	MAJ	0-0248358	0462	3
SHERLING JAMES E	CPT	0-0274765	1266	3
SHERLOCK FRANCIS J	CW4	W-2102366	0165	1
SHERLOCK JOHN E JR	CPT	0-1107122	0750	2
SHERLOCK THOMAS J JR	LTC	0-0443405	0663	1
SHERMAN ARTHUR	LTC	0-0359661	0864	3
SHERMAN ARTHUR W	CW4	W-2115156	0559	1

NAME	GRADE	SVC NO	DATE RET MO YR	RET CODE
SHERMAN CARLETON W	COL	O-0297094	0464	3
SHERMAN CHARLES F	MAJ	O-1049343	1163	1
SHERMAN CORNELIUS	MAJ	O-1335071	0763	1
SHERMAN DANA	1LT	O-1170192	1046	2
SHERMAN DORA J	2LT	N-0743644	0845	1
SHERMAN EARL F	CPT	O-0290360	0247	1
SHERMAN EARNEST G	CW3	W-2205419	0966	1
SHERMAN ELLIOTT W	LTC	O-0231036	0349	1
SHERMAN ELMER R	COL	O-0255745	0658	3
SHERMAN FRANK J JR	COL	O-0142150	0662	3
SHERMAN FRANK S	COL	O-0495219	0756	1
SHERMAN GEORGE C	COL	O-0251377	0954	3
SHERMAN HAROLD F	LTC	O-1118491	1167	1
SHERMAN HENRY T	CPT	O-0314968	0546	2
SHERMAN JAMES A SR	MAJ	O-0546145	0265	1
SHERMAN JAMES B	CPT	O-1115106	0862	1
SHERMAN JESS M	CPT	O-1297601	0759	1
SHERMAN JOHN H	COL	O-0100828	0149	3
SHERMAN JOHN T	2LT	O-0449999	0945	2
SHERMAN KATHLEEN E	1LT	N-0754709	0947	1
SHERMAN LEO E	MAJ	O-0235268	0861	3
SHERMAN LESLIE K	LTC	O-0490387	0567	3
SHERMAN MAURICE	COL	O-0266870	1055	3
SHERMAN RALPH E	CPT	O-0389410	0445	2
SHERMAN ROGER N	CPT	O-1638502	0868	3
SHERMAN SAMUEL P	CPT	O-0444942	0746	2
SHERMAN THOMAS M JR	LTC	O-0258939	0760	1
SHERMAN WILLIAM A	LTC	O-0215090	0963	3
SHERMAN WILLIAM H	LTC	O-1106464	0767	1
SHERMAN WILLIAM M	CPT	O-0422279	0961	1
SHERMAN WINCHESTER	1LT	O-0447452	1044	2
SHERNER ROBERT E	WO1	W-2148514	0254	2
SHERMETTA MICHAEL	CW3	W-2147959	0960	2
SHERON RAYMOND H	WO1	W-2121066	0145	2
SHERR EARLE J	LTC	O-1584894	0565	1
SHERRARD HERMAN H	MAJ	O-0113511	0251	3
SHERRARD JACK G	MAJ	O-0391028	0646	2
SHERRATT LLOYD C	MAJ	O-2262967	1263	1
SHERREN JOSEPH E	MAJ	O-0406848	1060	1
SHERRER JOHN O	LTC	O-0272314	0765	3
SHERRICK PAUL H	COL	O-0217535	0259	3
SHERRILL ELWOOD E	CPT	O-1294546	1047	2
SHERRILL FRANKLIN C	MAJ	O-0454420	0958	1
SHERRILL FRED G	COL	O-0236194	1054	3
SHERRILL PARKS R	CW2	W-2151926	0460	1
SHERRILL RALPH E	CPT	O-0889800	1058	1
SHERRIS SAMUEL	LTC	O-1555901	0567	1
SHERROD JULIAN A	CPT	O-0498231	0150	1
SHERROD VINCENT A	1LT	O-0475652	0744	2
SHERRON ALBERT E	LTC	O-0493531	0657	1
SHERRY DEAN	COL	O-0151719	0550	3
SHERRY FRANCIS J	MAJ	O-1573579	0461	1
SHERRY JOSEPH E	LTC	O-0370118	0357	1
SHERRY PAUL J	MAJ	O-1922583	0164	1
SHERRY ROY J	COL	O-0357432	0165	1
SHERTZER ROBERT S	LTC	O-0167183	0953	3
SHERVA CHESTER O	1LT	O-0345555	1143	2
SHERVANICK THOMAS S	MAJ	O-0509639	0857	1
SHERVEN EDWARD P	CPT	O-0340723	1059	3
SHERWIN EDWARD P	LTC	O-0392879	0361	1
SHERWIN GRAMMAR C	2LT	N-0724557	0844	1
SHERWIN HERBERT	LTC	O-0263292	0863	3
SHERWIN JOHN L	CW2	W-3200340	0468	1
SHERWIN MITCHELL J	1LT	O-1589498	0140	2
SHERWOOD CALVIN L	WO1	W-2107401	1052	1
SHERWOOD DAVID J	CPT	O-1038940	0648	2
SHERWOOD DORA M	CPT	L-0500013	0945	2
SHERWOOD ELMER W	MAJ	O-0257335	0356	3
SHERWOOD GEORGE M	MAJ	O-0342976	0168	3
SHERWOOD GRANT M	CW4	W-2111676	0756	1
SHERWOOD HERBERT A	CPT	O-0199743	0352	3
SHERWOOD JACK C	MAJ	O-1337389	1162	1
SHERWOOD JOHN A	MAJ	O-1040812	0661	1
SHERWOOD REX E	LTC	O-1101212	0260	1
SHERWOOD ROBERT	COL	O-1638503	0968	1
SHERWOOD ROGER B	MAJ	O-0488644	0752	1
SHERWOOD WARREN E	LTC	O-0982616	1163	3
SHERWOOD WILLIAM E	COL	O-0237052	0865	3
SHEVALIER WATSON R	MAJ	O-1579105	0263	1
SHEVCHIK WALTER V	MAJ	O-0450117	0256	1
SHEVICK JOSEPH	CPT	O-1311334	0958	1
SHEVIN SELIG A	1LT	O-0498208	0843	2
SHEW OPAL E	WO1	W-2132154	0960	2
SHEWAN WILLIAM H JR	2LT	O-0516875	0445	2
SHIBER JOHN S	MAJ	O-0371804	1045	2
SHICK DANIEL E	MAJ	O-1165448	0646	2
SHICK JOHN R	LTC	O-1293134	0261	1
SHICK WAYNE L	1LT	O-0396736	1043	2
SHIDEL FREDERIC C JR	LTC	O-0297555	0466	3
SHIELD ELGEAN	MAJ	O-0262924	0945	2
SHIELDS BILLY F	CW3	W-2149460	0864	1
SHIELDS CECIL C	MAJ	O-2038117	0564	1
SHIELDS CHARLES J	CPT	O-1306002	1047	2
SHIELDS DORIS I P	1LT	N-0774637	0547	1
SHIELDS F W JR	2LT	O-2049099	0146	2
SHIELDS GAYLE	CPT	O-1178338	0361	1
SHIELDS GEORGE C JR	LTC	O-0451181	0854	2
SHIELDS GEORGE H	CW2	W-2211519	0765	1
SHIELDS HAROLD A	CPT	O-1822065	0163	1
SHIELDS HOMER E	COL	O-0393280	0165	1
SHIELDS JAMES F	CW2	W-3430552	0868	1
SHIELDS JAMES H JR	CPT	O-1822322	0246	2
SHIELDS JAMES R	MAJ	O-1017091	0747	2
SHIELDS JOHN E	CW3	W-2150811	0563	1
SHIELDS JOHN M	MAJ	O-1109006	0663	1
SHIELDS JOHN R	COL	O-0137582	0753	3
SHIELDS LEE G	CPT	O-0437756	0346	2
SHIELDS LEM W	COL	O-0330839	0462	1
SHIELDS LIN	LTC	O-0224242	0154	1
SHIELDS LUKE S	LTC	O-0379818	0764	3
SHIELDS PAUL P	MAJ	O-0426230	0764	1
SHIELDS R T JR	MAJ	O-0441859	0945	2
SHIELDS ROBERT R	2LT	O-2017136	0851	2
SHIELDS WILLIAM I	CPT	O-1172653	0161	1
SHIELDS WILLIAM M	2LT	O-0553677	0246	2
SHIELDS ZOLLIE H	LTC	O-1591441	0761	2
SHIELS THOMAS O	COL	O-0174845	0361	3
SHIER SIGMUND	LTC	O-1583668	0361	1
SHIERMAN HAROLD D	LTC	O-0239148	1061	3
SHIFFER LAVERNE K	LTC	O-0282651		3
SHIFFMAN ROBERT	CPT	O-1715169	0846	2
SHIFLETT ELBERT O	MAJ	O-2262265	0764	1
SHIGLEY FRED M	MAJ	O-0282462	0656	3
SHIKANY SAMUEL E	CPT	O-1702370	1145	2
SHIKOSKI LEO F	MAJ	O-1334763	0864	1
SHILDT HARRY P	CW2	W-2104468	1049	1
SHILLCOCK JOHN G	CW4	W-2114643	0860	1
SHILLER EDWIN S	CPT	O-1635513	0262	2
SHILLING MARVIN F	LTC	O-0141648	0354	3
SHILLING RUSSELL T	MAJ	O-0207134	1263	3
SHILLING WILLIAM K	LTC	O-0364070	1265	3
SHIMAMOTO FRANK M	CW3	W-2136039	0465	1
SHIMBERG HARRY W	CPT	O-2033119	0658	1
SHIMEL ROY E	LTC	O-1649944	1163	1
SHIMER RALPH W	1LT	O-1826349	0747	2
SHIMMEL FRANK W	MAJ	O-0479058	0254	1
SHIMMEL JOHN B	CPT	O-1649220	0957	1
SHIMODA SATORU C	CW4	W-2136383	1266	2
SHIMUNEK FRANK J	2LT	O-1540603	0645	2
SHINABERGER HOWARD L	LTC	O-0199136	0962	3
SHINDELAR EDWARD	LTC	O-1168462	1263	1
SHINE BERNICE C	CPT	L-0312381	0158	2
SHINE DUDLEY S III	MAJ	O-0370665	1160	1
SHINE JOHN C	CPT	O-1325600	1047	2
SHINE ROBERT H	1LT	O-0557360	0446	2
SHINER WILLIAM F JR	1LT	O-1824517	0146	2
SHINKLE JOHN E	2LT	O-0988138	0152	2
SHINN FLOYD C	LTC	O-0258965	0567	3
SHINN FRANK R JR	COL	O-0244619	0960	2
SHINN KENNETH E	1LT	O-0537887	1045	2
SHINN ROBERT V	COL	O-0323157	1060	1
SHINN WILLIAM E	MAJ	O-0192941	0760	3
SHIPE CHARLES E	LTC	O-0225966	0265	3
SHIPE WESLEY Z	MAJ	O-1116697	0657	1
SHIPE WILBERT G JR	CW3	W-3250251	0868	1
SHIPEK ALICE V	LTC	L-0909306	0268	1
SHIPES WILLIE O	CW2	W-2149153	0757	1
SHIPFERLING GEORGE E	COL	O-0397006	0267	3
SHIPLETT DAVID A	LTC	O-0904185	0947	2
SHIPLEY ALEX B	COL	O-0332350	0965	3
SHIPLEY ALVIN J	MAJ	O-0965793	0965	1
SHIPLEY B H JR	2LT	O-0532117	0945	2
SHIPLEY DOUGLAS B	CW3	W-2147960	1063	2
SHIPLEY ERVIN W	CW3	W-2150659	0566	1
SHIPLEY JOHN S	CPT	O-0257697	1265	3
SHIPLEY MICHAEL	MAJ	O-0188491	1045	2
SHIPLEY NORMAN M	COL	O-0351412	0846	2
SHIPMAN GERALD A	CW3	W-2150292	1163	1
SHIPMAN WALTER H	CW2	W-2118369	1047	1
SHIPMAN WILLIAM F	MAJ	O-0159543	1043	2
SHIPPEE GARELD A	2LT	O-1320189	1143	2
SHIPPEY KELLEY F	COL	O-0267157	1068	3
SHIPPEY PAUL M	CPT	O-1844429	0446	2
SHIPPEY THOMAS L	LTC	O-0292653	0546	2
SHIPPEY WEBSTER B	MAJ	O-0120185	1156	3
SHIPPEY WILLIAM L	CPT	O-0292336	0744	2
SHIPTON FRANCIS F	LTC	O-0358371	0555	1
SHIPTON WAYNE F	CW3	W-2146802	0760	1
SHIPWAY JOHN N	MAJ	O-2037175	0658	1
SHIRE HERBERT	2LT	O-0544387	0345	2
SHIRES HARRY F	MAJ	O-1175310	0366	1
SHIRES HENRY G	MAJ	O-0149980	0855	3
SHIRES SARA D	1LT	N-0722232	0146	1
SHIREY ERVIN L	COL	O-0932580	1168	1
SHIREY MERLE M	MAJ	O-0179844	0347	1
SHIREY ROBERT E	CPT	O-1922553	0768	1
SHIREY WILLIAM B	LTC	O-0153723	0159	3
SHIRK AMOS D	CW2	W-2114474	0846	2
SHIRK DAVILLA C	COL	O-0239768	1065	3
SHIRK HAROLD G	MAJ	O-0275392	1155	3
SHIRK JOSEPH O	CW2	RW-2152737	0661	1
SHIRLAW HELEN A	LTC	L-0903697	0867	1
SHIRLEY BARKER L	1LT	O-0336986	0263	1
SHIRLEY CARL R	MAJ	O-2017466	0158	1
SHIRLEY CHARLES L JR	MAJ	O-0959330	0162	1
SHIRLEY CYRUS	CW3	W-2102370	0953	1
SHIRLEY HARVEY G	LTC	O-0169686	0949	3
SHIRLEY HARVEY J	LTC	O-0509361	1046	2
SHIRLEY HERMAN M	1LT	O-2046554	0846	2
SHIRLEY JAMES C	LTC	O-0166146	0852	3
SHIRLEY JOE H	CW2	W-2208379	0461	1
SHIRLEY JOSEPH W	LTC	O-1289156	0762	1
SHIRLEY LEWIS H	WO1	W-2149390	1052	2
SHIRLEY NOYES D	CPT	O-0262112	0168	3
SHIRLEY OTHO A	MAJ	O-1319350	0557	1
SHIRLEY RILEY P JR	1LT	O-1306761	0946	2
SHIRLEY ROBERT H	MAJ	O-0256754	0966	3
SHIRLEY WARREN B	CW3	W-2203370	0965	1
SHIRLEY WILLIAM K	CPT	O-0460001	0647	2
SHIRLEY WILLIAM M	MAJ	O-0151725	0555	3
SHIRLING MILO R SR	CW3	W-2145909	0562	1
SHIROMA HARRY I	1LT	O-1998658	0251	2
SHIRREFF JOHN A	CW2	W-2215010	0167	1
SHIRVANIAN LEVON H	CPT	O-0139389	0944	2
SHIVEL HUBERT L	CW2	W-2111331	1153	1
SHIVELEY HARRY T	LTC	O-0452569	1060	1
SHIVELY DONALD L	MAJ	O-1338365	0367	1
SHIVELY HARMON G	LTC	O-0284771	0768	3
SHIVELY JOWARREN B	MAJ	O-1340589	0965	1
SHIVELY ROBERT J	MAJ	O-0968674	0768	1
SHIVELY VERNON H	LTC	O-1173457	1160	1
SHIVELY WILLARD R	LTC	O-0230736	0153	3
SHIVER NOBLE C	CPT	O-0168635	0560	3
SHIVERS GERALD W	LTC	O-0401127	0761	1
SHIVES JAMES O	1LT	O-0383015	0845	2
SHIVLEY VIRGIL W	1LT	O-0505753	0846	1
SHLEVIN IDA M	2LT	N-0700402	0839	1
SHOAF CHARLES JR	CPT	O-1294205	0245	2
SHOAF RICHARD R	CPT	O-0291001	1044	2
SHOAFF ROSS L	CPT	O-1593272	0162	1
SHOAFF WALTER R	COL	O-0143930	1056	3
SHOBE DABNEY W JR	CW3	W-2209347	0768	2
SHOBERT CHARLES O	CPT	O-0510320	0750	1
SHOCHET HARRY	CW3	W-2147805	0765	1
SHOCKEY FLOYD E	CPT	O-0269551	0645	2
SHOCKEY JOHN E	LTC	O-0507368	0567	3
SHOCKEY JOHN W	COL	O-0366998	0266	1
SHOCKEY WILLIAM M JR	MAJ	O-0997239	1164	1
SHOCKLEY LEVERT E	CPT	O-0460826	0547	1
SHOCKLEY ORIEN C	CPT	O-1291582	1045	2
SHOCKLEY ROBERT E	1LT	O-0436306	0545	2
SHOCKRO HARRY W	LTC	O-1319450	0962	1
SHOEMAKER ALBERT M	LTC	O-0481876	0962	1
SHOEMAKER CHARLES M	CW3	W-2200672	0165	1
SHOEMAKER ELMER E	LTC	O-0227376	0952	3
SHOEMAKER FORREST M	MAJ	O-1298481	0561	1
SHOEMAKER GEORGE O	LTC	O-0284214	1061	1
SHOEMAKER HARVEY J	COL	O-0183091	0745	2
SHOEMAKER J L JR	MAJ	O-0242055	0645	2
SHOEMAKER JOHN E	CPT	O-5419404	0768	2
SHOEMAKER JOSEPH J	COL	O-0186879	0649	3
SHOEMAKER LEO V	MAJ	O-1996511	0266	1
SHOEMAKER M F	MAJ	N-0727115	0348	1
SHOEMAKER ORVILLE E	COL	O-0329860	0866	3
SHOEMAKER PHILIP C	COL	O-0309114	0964	3
SHOEMAKER ROBERT E	MAJ	O-2051712	0461	1
SHOEMAKER VERNON K	MAJ	O-1326590	0961	1
SHOEMAN GORDON C	CW4	W-2130702	0854	1
SHOENBERGER F P	MAJ	O-1037300	0557	1
SHOGREN PHILIP E	LTC	O-1171353	0361	1
SHOLAR CLARENCE W	MAJ	O-0965899	0662	2
SHOLAR JAMES B	MAJ	O-4002294	0463	2
SHOLARS BRUNSWIG	CPT	O-1170978	0654	2
SHOLL HERBERT A	1LT	O-1292243	0345	2
SHOLL PAUL F	CPT	O-0184533	0557	3
SHOLLENBERGER JOSEPH	LTC	O-1304803	1262	1
SHOLLENBURG RAYMOND	2LT	O-2020766	1051	2
SHOLTIS JOSEPH H	MAJ	O-0482201	1052	1
SHOMER VERN F	CPT	O-1290826	0649	2
SHONERD GEORGE D	CPT	O-1691892	0258	1
SHONKWILER VIRGIL G	MAJ	O-0400626	0246	2
SHONS CHARLES H	LTC	O-0164547	1049	3
SHOOK DALE C	2LT	O-1540687	0754	1
SHOOK EDWIN H	MAJ	O-2262739	1264	1
SHOOK EUGENE F	COL	O-1557669	0165	1
SHOOK GARNETT W	CPT	O-0323859	0367	3
SHOOK MARGARET M	MAJ	N-0700157	0444	1
SHOOK THEODORE	LTC	O-1043790	0361	1
SHOOP CLYDE D	CPT	O-1174971	0967	3
SHOOSHAN MARTIN D	LTC	O-0298417	0663	3
SHOOSTER MARGARET L	MAJ	N-0767932	1164	1
SHOPE CHARLES D	CPT	O-0345071	0446	2
SHOPE WILLARD M	LTC	O-0236925	1060	1
SHOPNITZ JOSEPH W	2LT	O-2012462	0346	2
SHOR ELAINE E	1LT	N-0799056	0847	1
SHOR ROBERT L	CPT	O-5218684	0866	2
SHORE AARON	1LT	O-1297264	0246	2
SHORE JOHN M	CW4	W-2144484	0866	1
SHORE LEON F	MAJ	O-2008766	0763	1
SHORE PAUL D	CPT	O-0483285	0446	2
SHORE SCHILLER F	LTC	O-0330854	0560	1
SHORE VENETA L	MAJ	N-0788718	1063	1
SHORES CHARLES V JR	MAJ	O-2028750	0167	1
SHORES JAMES A	CW2	W-2208551	0264	1
SHOREY HENRY A	1LT	O-1170979	0945	2
SHOREY MILES C JR	LTC	O-0335625	0546	2
SHORT ALBERT W	CPT	O-1300405	0951	2
SHORT CLAIR A JR	MAJ	O-0320513	1143	2
SHORT CLAUD	MAJ	O-1175575	0557	1
SHORT EDWARD L JR	CW2	W-2211513	0266	1

NAME	GRADE	SVC NO	DATE RET MO YR	RET CODE
SHORT [illegible]	MAJ	[illegible]	[illegible]	[illegible]
SHORT [illegible]	MAJ	[illegible]	[illegible]	[illegible]
SHORT [illegible]	[illegible]	[illegible]	[illegible]	[illegible]
SHORT [illegible]	[illegible]	W-2116171	[illegible]	[illegible]
SHORT [illegible]	[illegible]	[illegible]	[illegible]	1
SHORT [illegible]	MAJ	[illegible]	[illegible]	1
SHORT [illegible]	COL	[illegible]	0847	[illegible]
SHORT [illegible]	CPT	[illegible]	[illegible]	[illegible]
SHORT [illegible]	[illegible]	[illegible]	[illegible]	1
SHORT JOHN [illegible]	CW4	[illegible]	[illegible]	[illegible]
SHORT JOHN [illegible]	LTC	0-2010127	[illegible]	1
SHORT KENNETH L	CPT	0-1317[illegible]	0552	1
SHORT [illegible]	MAJ	[illegible]	0646	2
SHORT MELVIN M	MAJ	0-1002340	1052	2
SHORT NORMAN V	CPT	0-1047645	1059	1
SHORT [illegible] T	CPT	0-1541240	0450	1
SHORT RAYMOND W	COL	0-0125028	0848	2
SHORT ROBERT [illegible]	LTC	0-0274277	0268	3
SHORT ROLAND JR	LTC	0-0439611	0665	1
SHORT WELDON M	MAJ	0-0535574	0556	2
SHORT WILLIAM E	CW3	W-2141884	1060	1
SHORTER CHARLES R	LTC	0-1170194	0764	1
SHORTER HASKELL [illegible]	CW3	W-2201744	0268	3
SHORTER WADE H JR	MAJ	0-0261449	1167	3
SHORTER WALTER C	COL	0-0183049	0962	3
SHORTER WILLIE C JR	CW2	W-2106752	0445	2
SHORTER WOODSON S	1LT	0-1325029	1045	2
SHORTESS JULIAN F	CW4	W-2104471	0859	2
SHORTLIDGE JAMES L	CW2	W-2105484	0857	1
SHORTRIDGE JACK M	LTC	0-1556797	0768	1
SHORTRIDGE NORMAN H	LTC	0-0244908	0654	1
SHORTSLEEVES W L	1LT	0-0497275	0646	1
SHORTT BILLY H	MAJ	0-1102591	1060	1
SHORTT PETER J	LTC	0-0917059	0847	2
SHOSTAK MAX R	LTC	0-0225353	0165	3
SHOSTROM EVERETT L	1LT	0-0551206	0746	2
SHOTSMAN HARRY	LTC	0-0912558	0545	2
SHOTT DONALD C	CW2	W-2152400	0961	2
SHOTT JOSEPH W	MAJ	0-1116976	0760	1
SHOTTS JAMES F	COL	0-0216976	1052	3
SHOTWELL JACK B	MAJ	0-1634322	1054	1
SHOUCAIR EDWARD T	CPT	0-0349890	0855	3
SHOUDY CHARLES F	CPT	0-0989406	0366	2
SHOUP MARION L	MAJ	0-0248781	1266	3
SHOUSE JOHN F	MAJ	0-1333722	0661	1
SHOVAR MARK	LTC	0-0230372	0551	2
SHOVER FRANK E	CPT	0-1101657	0861	1
SHOWALTER DANIEL E	LTC	0-1016446	1266	1
SHOWALTER JACKSON H	MAJ	0-2014451	1165	1
SHOWALTER JAMES A	MAJ	0-0526917	0756	1
SHOWALTER JAMES F	COL	0-0442030	0466	1
SHOWALTER JOHN F	LTC	0-0109404	0844	1
SHOWALTER KARL W	COL	0-0261260	1267	3
SHOWALTER MARIE J	MAJ	N-0761329	1164	3
SHOWELL CARTER S	LTC	0-0271572	0865	3
SHOWERS JAMES E	LTC	0-1285320	0760	1
SHOWS JOHN H	CW2	W-2206909	0867	1
SHOWS NORMAN R	CW2	W-2145345	0156	2
SHOWS ROSCOE J	CPT	0-1817352	0562	1
SHRADER BRYANT F W	MAJ	0-2243123	1162	1
SHRADER EARL A	COL	0-0182215	0854	3
SHRAKE ROBERT F	CPT	0-1103406	0964	1
SHRECK GEORGE W	CPT	0-0910055	0146	2
SHRECK HORACE W	COL	0-0332055	0867	3
SHREDER RAYMOND J	LTC	0-1105418	0861	1
SHREEVE CALEB A	COL	0-0279366	1151	3
SHREEVE ORVILLE W	CW2	W-2141427	0656	1
SHREFFLER ROBERT F	LTC	0-0499231	0968	3
SHREVE CHARLES H	COL	0-0158193	0358	3
SHREVE JOHN C	LTC	0-1044676	0966	1
SHREVE PAUL F	2LT	0-1554088	0246	2
SHREVE ROY J	CPT	0-0495779	1157	1
SHREVES JOHN P JR	2LT	0-0354253	1142	2
SHREVES MELVILLE N	MAJ	0-0218399	0648	3
SHREWSBURY ARCHIE K	1LT	0-0956521	0867	2

NAME	GRADE	SVC NO	DATE RET MO YR	RET CODE
SHREWSBURY GEORGE W	CW3	W-2150223	0959	1
SHRIGLEY [illegible]	CPT	0-0108434	0960	1
SHRINER EDWARD C	MAJ	0-0209081	0948	3
SHRINER MARCILES A	LTC	0-0963447	1162	1
SHRIVER ANN	MAJ	N-0767249	0766	3
SHRIVER GLENN G	MAJ	0-0965894	0163	1
SHRIVER JAY M	CPT	0-1700477	0745	2
SHRIVER JOSEPH G	CW3	W-2144261	0461	1
SHRIVER KARL H	COL	0-0108278	0648	3
SHROCK WAYNE T	MAJ	0-0274339	0159	3
SHROPSHIRE JAMES S	LTC	0-0257698	0966	3
SHROUT AMAROS	CPT	0-0479407	0846	1
SHROUT CARL C	CW3	W-2148765	0561	1
SHROY RICHARD F	COL	0-0357372	1162	1
SHROYER FRED N	MAJ	0-1685735	1065	1
SHRUM PAUL L	COL	0-0176857	0759	3
SHUBART STANLEY C	COL	0-0232692	0766	3
SHUDER RUSSELL M	COL	0-0348543	0861	1
SHUE HAROLD I	LTC	0-1018489	0263	1
SHUER JAY J	1LT	0-1283506	0845	2
SHUEY EDWARD W	CW3	W-2146443	0463	1
SHUFELT GEORGE H	COL	0-0266028	0359	3
SHUFF KING W	CW2	W-2149154	0760	1
SHUFFER JACOB M	1LT	0-1040813	1053	1
SHUFFIELD JAMES W JR	1LT	0-1048972	0144	2
SHUFFLEBARGER JOHN H	MAJ	0-1116256	0561	1
SHUFLATA GEORGE J JR	LTC	0-1081097	0861	1
SHUFORD NORMAN C	MAJ	0-0139427	1048	3
SHUGART CLARENCE M	LTC	0-0887425	0463	1
SHUGART GLENN W	MAJ	0-2016145	0359	1
SHUGART MARION L	LTC	0-0244698	0766	3
SHUGART R T	LTC	0-0287005	1060	1
SHUGERT JAMES M H	LTC	0-1050086	0863	1
SHUH JUDSON	1LT	0-0409149	0543	2
SHUKERS CARROLL F	COL	0-0319981	1065	3
SHUKIS EUMANOS	CW4	W-2136652	1167	1
SHULAR WILLIAM A JR	MAJ	0-1295283	0265	1
SHULENBERG LEROY E	MAJ	0-0970230	0365	1
SHULER JOHN H	LTC	0-0252818	1066	3
SHULKCUM EDWARD	MAJ	0-0260648	0864	3
SHULL EDWIN L	B G	0-0335061	0764	3
SHULL HOMER	2LT	0-1913936	1031	1
SHULL LESTER A	LTC	0-0260033	0264	3
SHULL RALPH G	MAJ	0-0947426	1157	1
SHULMAN HERBERT	CPT	0-0368272	1045	2
SHULMAN MAURICE	MAJ	0-0141240	1052	3
SHULMAN MAX L	MAJ	0-0281833	0346	2
SHULT BRUCE E	LTC	0-0399248	0657	1
SHULTIE JAMES E SR	CW3	W-3430090	1268	1
SHULTS CAMERON	LTC	0-0401656	0860	1
SHULTS GEORGE W	LTC	0-0284109	0868	3
SHULTS THOMAS N	1LT	0-0358722	0345	2
SHULTZ EARL H	LTC	0-0947052	0767	1
SHULTZ EDWARD K	LTC	0-0505512	0968	3
SHULTZ HAROLD M	CPT	0-1283858	0448	2
SHULTZ HERMAN N	CW2	W-2145358	0160	1
SHULTZ JAMES D	CPT	0-1589502	0347	2
SHULTZ NANCY S	2LT	N-0760276	1144	1
SHULTZ RALPH	COL	0-0149231	1046	2
SHUMAKER CLARENCE A	LTC	0-0104468	0159	3
SHUMAKER GEORGE L	COL	0-0379230	1067	1
SHUMAKER HENRY	COL	0-0373045	1058	1
SHUMAKER MEREDITH L	COL	0-0377823	0765	1
SHUMAKER WARREN B JR	LTC	0-0674807	0266	1
SHUMAN HAROLD	LTC	0-0306961	0560	1
SHUMAN JAMES R	LTC	0-0404764	0762	1
SHUMAN ROBERT L	CPT	0-0367139	0645	2
SHUMAN RONALD B	COL	0-0343486	0468	3
SHUMATE BAYARD S	COL	0-0234770	1156	3
SHUMATE BRUCE E	COL	0-0316506	0866	3
SHUMATE CARL T	1LT	0-1683492	0346	2
SHUMATE EDWARD M	CW3	W-2152401	0764	1
SHUMOCK EARL F	CW3	W-2152326	0263	1
SHUMPERT FLOYD A	MAJ	0-1303398	0247	2
SHUMWAY HYROM S	1LT	0-0524584	1046	2

NAME	GRADE	SVC NO	DATE RET MO YR	RET CODE
SHUPE ARTHUR [illegible]	LTC	0-1295756	[illegible]	1
SHUPERT [illegible]	2LT	[illegible]	0644	[illegible]
SHUPIS ALEXANDER	CPT	[illegible]	[illegible]	1
SHUPP [illegible]	LTC	[illegible]	[illegible]	1
SHURBUT MICHAEL [illegible]	CW4	W-2142722	1262	2
SHURE [illegible]	MAJ	[illegible]	0647	2
SHURBET WILLIAM [illegible]	CPT	0-0342786	0144	2
SHURE ABRAHAM L	MAJ	[illegible]	[illegible]	2
SHURLEY HOMER [illegible]	2LT	[illegible]	0653	1
SHURLEY WILLIAM R JR	LTC	0-0411527	0261	2
SHURTLEFF CLINTON [illegible]	MAJ	0-0277127	0745	2
SHURTLEFF HORACE W	COL	0-0287321	0658	3
SHURTLEFF L J	COL	0-0133666	[illegible]	1
SHURTLEFF W H JR	COL	0-0135689	1054	1
SHURTLIFF WESLEY O	LTC	0-0327433	1063	1
SHURTS NORMAN	LTC	0-1113443	0267	1
SHURTZ EUGENE F	LTC	0-1576644	0764	1
SHURTZ JOHN F	1LT	0-1822202	0546	2
SHUSTER GERALD L	CW2	W-2215009	1058	1
SHUSTER PHILIP L	CW3	W-2116030	0155	2
SHUTE DONALD M	COL	0-0275817	0161	3
SHUTE EMIL	LTC	0-0397040	1057	1
SHUTE JEAN P	LTC	0-0311170	0859	1
SHUTES HOWARD A	LTC	0-1596496	0166	1
SHUTT GEORGE B	LTC	0-1010056	0360	1
SHYTLE CARL O	COL	0-0267536	0958	1
SIAS HAROLD F	LTC	0-1650828	0962	1
SIAS RUSSELL E	CPT	0-0295547	0644	2
SIBAL CEZAR	MAJ	0-1896748	0151	1
SIBALA HILARIO	CPT	0-1895676	1060	1
SIBBETT WILLIAM A	1LT	0-1055975	1147	2
SIBERT DENNIS W	MAJ	0-1798522	1058	1
SIBERT HAROLD W	LTC	0-0443528	1054	1
SIBERT JOHN W JR	COL	0-0190900	0962	3
SIBERT LUTHER R	COL	0-0352905	0964	1
SIBERT RALPH F	CPT	0-1018589	1156	1
SIBERT RAY S	LTC	0-0399886	0161	1
SIBERT ROBERT L	WO1	W-2129124	1046	1
SIBERZ LLOYD W	LTC	0-1545011	1062	1
SIBLEY KENNETH L	MAJ	0-0488398	0555	1
SIBLEY KENNETH R	MAJ	0-1541593	0457	1
SIBLEY LINWOOD T	LTC	0-1551517	1164	1
SIBRAY DONALD L	LTC	0-0174237	0258	3
SIBRAY WILLIS S JR	1LT	0-1542539	0345	2
SICA ALPHONSO J	CPT	0-0257111	0347	1
SICA FRANK A	CPT	0-0486517	0646	2
SICAY TEOFILO G	MAJ	0-1896752	0461	1
SICHER MAX H	MAJ	0-4013551	0567	1
SICILIA FRANK	LTC	0-2007891	0365	3
SICILIANO JOSEPH M	CPT	0-0337263	0946	2
SICILIANO PHYLLIS V	1LT	N-0740162	0546	2
SICKELS GLENN	2LT	0-1550918	1043	2
SICKENGA JACK W	LTC	0-0388906	1060	1
SICKEROTT CARL O	CPT	0-0462360	1146	2
SICKING ROBERT C	1LT	0-1054411	0946	2
SICKLER JESSE P	COL	0-0317551	1055	3
SICKMAN JONATHAN V	MAJ	0-1105819	1067	3
SICURANZA JACK I	LTC	0-1576857	0557	1
SIDARIS NICKOLAS J	1LT	0-0769764	1147	2
SIDDALL MARY T	1LT	N-0775583	1046	1
SIDDALL WILLIAM S	LTC	0-1102347	0266	1
SIDDONS ARTHUR W	CPT	0-1102466	0954	1
SIDEBOTHAM THOMAS E	LTC	0-0949370	1168	1
SIDEBOTTOM RUSSELL L	CW2	W-2207499	0565	1
SIDEBOTTOM WILFORD L	LTC	0-2008535	0868	1
SIDERIS CHRIS Z	1LT	0-2050133	0847	2
SIDERS WALTER F	LTC	0-0497167	0767	3
SIDLE CHARLES L	COL	0-0266681	0546	2
SIDLER EARL R II	LTC	0-0402191	0566	3
SIDLEY WILLIAM F	MAJ	0-1897423	0165	1
SIDMORE PHILIP R	LTC	0-0327848	0163	1
SIDOTI JOSEPH T	CW3	W-2150973	0763	1
SIDWELL JOSEPH H	CPT	0-0293866	0246	2
SIEBE CHARLES C JR	1LT	0-1050465	1047	2
SIEBEN GERALD M	CPT	0-0481787	0445	2

NAME	GRADE	SVC NO	DATE RET MO YR	RET CODE
SIE[illegible] M	MAJ	[illegible]	[illegible]	1
SIE[illegible] WALTER A	[illegible]	[illegible]	[illegible]	1
SIEBRECHT JAMES [illegible]	CPT	[illegible]	[illegible]	2
SIE[illegible] EVERETT [illegible]	LTC	[illegible]	[illegible]	[illegible]
SIE[illegible] VALENTINE	LTC	[illegible]	[illegible]	[illegible]
SIEDSCHLAG EVERETT W	1LT	[illegible]	[illegible]	[illegible]
SIE[illegible] CLARENCE E	LTC	0-1544313	[illegible]	1
SIEGAL EDWARD I	COL	[illegible]	[illegible]	3
SIEGEL ALVIN	LTC	0-1361714	0467	1
SIEGEL ANNIE N	MAJ	[illegible]	1167	3
SIEGEL ERWIN A	CPT	[illegible]	0262	1
SIEGEL KENNETH I	MAJ	[illegible]	[illegible]	1
SIEGEL LEO	MAJ	[illegible]	0146	2
SIEGEL MARTIN	MAJ	0-1182255	1062	1
SIEGEL MICHAEL	MAJ	[illegible]	0656	1
SIEGEL NATHAN	LTC	[illegible]	0655	1
SIEGEL OSCAR A	2LT	[illegible]	0944	2
SIEGEL PETER	COL	[illegible]	0463	3
SIEGEL SHEPPARD M	CPT	[illegible]	1155	2
SIEGENTHALER S K	1LT	0-1061859	1145	2
SIEGER GILBERT G	CW2	W-2205727	1061	1
SIEGERT SHELDON R	CPT	0-1549839	0947	2
SIEGFRIED CHARLES W	MAJ	0-1294377	0861	1
SIEGFRIED JOHN JR	CPT	0-1786193	0146	2
SIEGLER MARETTA O	1LT	N-0775936	0146	1
SIEGLING CHARLES C	LTC	0-0271085	0368	3
SIEGLING EDMOND M	MAJ	0-1105566	0663	3
SIEGMOND CLEO F	1LT	N-0731739	1146	1
SIEGMOND RUDOLPH A	CPT	0-1100765	0947	2
SIEGRIST ADOLPH W	1LT	0-0342241	1144	2
SIEGRIST C J JR	CPT	0-0348463	0744	2
SIEGRIST KENNETH J	1LT	0-0493712	1045	2
SIEKER JOHN H	CPT	0-0176172	0263	3
SIEKIERSKI ALOISIUS	CW3	W-2143513	0561	1
SIEMASKO ALPHONSE W	1LT	[illegible]	[illegible]	2
SIEMINSKI LEON	MAJ	0-0450358	0854	1
SIEMON ADOLPH V	1LT	0-1288[illegible]	0844	2
SIEMON ROSA L	1LT	N-070[illegible]	0646	1
SIEMONSMA CLARENCE E	LTC	0-0921466	0564	3
SIENES DEMETRIO	2LT	0-0890503	0654	1
SIENKIEWICZ SOPHIE T	2LT	N-0742256	0749	2
SIEPELT HEINZ W	CW4	W-2133663	0468	1
SIER ROBERT M	CW3	W-2146947	0559	1
SIERACKI CHESTER R	CPT	0-1335102	0364	2
SIERRA GEORGE	CW2	W-2214785	1066	1
SIERZEGA EMIL M	1LT	0-1183192	0249	2
SIEVERS BERNARD M	MAJ	0-2021191	0166	1
SIEVERS EDWARD L	LTC	0-1795009	0766	1
SIEVERS EDWIN R	MAJ	0-0338852	0461	3
SIEVERT EDGAR W	CPT	0-0289384	0649	2
SIEVWRIGHT ELMER B	CPT	0-1042709	0863	1
SIEVWRIGHT RICHARD H	MAJ	0-1338967	0567	1
SIEWERS GEORGE M	LTC	0-1823224	0864	1
SIEWERT ORVILLE R	MAJ	0-2014776	0264	1
SIFOOL RAYMOND S	MAJ	0-0175443	0344	2
SIGAUD LOUIS A	LTC	0-0143719	0953	3
SIGEL DAVE	COL	0-0151781	0446	2
SIGELO PATRICK J	LTC	0-1295094	1264	1
SIGETY DAVID P	CW3	W-2152647	0966	1
SIGLER LYNN E	1LT	0-1327671	0646	2
SIGLER MAHLON O	MAJ	0-0268261	1049	1
SIGLER PHARES O	COL	0-0319652	0659	3
SIGLER RUSSELL K	1LT	0-1324584	1045	2
SIGLER THOMAS V	COL	0-0406899	1062	1
SIGLEY ALLEN L	CPT	0-1582129	0347	2
SIGMANN WILLIAM J	MAJ	0-1018431	0963	1
SIGMON ERNEST F	MAJ	0-0585800	0856	1
SIGMOND HENRY I	LTC	0-0253767	0962	3
SIGNORELLI PATRICK L	CW2	W-2143237	0960	1
SIGSBEE HAROLD J	LTC	0-1167221	0967	3
SIGSWORTH ALLYN B	MAJ	0-2017912	0664	1
SIGWALD JOHN J	LTC	0-0231793	0360	1
SIGWELL RUSSELL E	LTC	0-2036080	0860	1
SIHTO THOMAS JR	CPT	0-0285176	1050	1
SIKES DANIEL O	MAJ	0-0249233	0164	3

NAME	GRADE	SVC NO	DATE RET MO YR	RET CODE
SIKES DERRILL F	MAJ	0-1947084	0764	1
SIKES FRANK B	CW4	W-2147611	1067	2
SIKES JAMES I	LTC	0-0441990	0365	1
SIKES JAMES S	CPT	0-1289157	1057	1
SIKES ROBERT L	CPT	0-0499876	0463	1
SIKORA ALFONS	CPT	0-2010659	0359	1
SIKORSKI JOSEPH C	MAJ	0-1050089	0561	1
SIKORSKI WILLIAM	LTC	0-1177183	0658	1
SIKORSKY ANDREW J JR	LTC	0-1294207	0663	1
SILAN STEVE	MAJ	0-1118809	0959	1
SILATA FRANK	1LT	0-1996347	0546	2
SILBAUGH JACK	MAJ	0-2032324	0665	1
SILBER PAUL G JR	1LT	0-1327891	0247	2
SILBER WILLIAM H	LTC	0-1320783	0866	1
SILBERBERG JULES W	MAJ	0-2208409	0666	1
SILBERT ARVID E	CPT	0-1041913	0146	2
SILBERT DAVID	LTC	0-1002128	0766	3
SILCOX ISAAC	CPT	0-2018229	0358	1
SILCOX RAY W	LTC	0-0376231	1146	2
SILENCE JOSEPH F	1LT	0-1822640	1067	2
SILER ARNOLD	MAJ	0-0421254	1060	1
SILER ELMER W	MAJ	0-0307777	0944	2
SILER JAMES G	MAJ	0-0267383	0363	3
SILFEN CHARLES	CPT	0-1325936	0556	1
SILL MORTON H	LTC	0-1011315	0358	1
SILL ROBERT F	LTC	0-1556219	0166	1
SILLER RALPH E	CPT	0-1584906	0246	2
SILLIMAN BENJAMIN D	LTC	0-0122803	0955	3
SILLIMAN CHARLES A	1LT	0-0407478	0346	2
SILLIMAN CHESTER W	MAJ	0-0278582	0667	3
SILLIMAN 3RD FRANK	COL	0-0179174	0157	3
SILLMAN CHESTER W	1LT	0-1311694	0545	2
SILLONA GAUDENCIO	MAJ	0-0267129	0554	1
SILLS JOHN F	LTC	0-0349630	1160	1
SILNER ROBERT C	LTC	0-1037713	1168	1
SILO BENJAMIN	1LT	0-1897023	0164	1
SILSBEE 2ND HENRY O	COL	0-0124188	0749	3
SILSBY DON J	LTC	0-0294813	0865	3
SILSBY HARRY D	COL	0-0332969	1168	3
SILVA ALVIN K	COL	0-0175152	0660	3
SILVA ANTONIO R	LTC	0-0182910	0657	3
SILVA ERNEST P	LTC	0-1012493	0764	1
SILVA EURIPIDES	COL	0-0245105	0555	3
SILVA JOHN B	2LT	0-1112973	1044	2
SILVA JOHN J	MAJ	0-1110804	0562	1
SILVA JULIO N	CPT	0-4010748	1165	1
SILVA SATURNINO	LTC	0-1300095	0848	2
SILVA TORIVIO	MAJ	0-1533675	1060	1
SILVA WALTER G	LTC	0-0453882	1060	1
SILVER CHARLES H	1LT	0-0438331	0646	2
SILVER DAVID	LTC	0-1332749	0766	1
SILVER FRANCIS F	MAJ	0-0369549	0247	2
SILVER GEORGE A	MAJ	0-0475110	0546	2
SILVER HORACE S	CW3	W-2208057	0566	1
SILVER IRVING	CPT	0-1283682	0546	2
SILVER JONAS	CPT	0-1690052	0344	2
SILVER MICHAEL W	1LT	0-0368967	0146	2
SILVER RAYMOND R	CW3	W-2147060	0465	1
SILVER RICHARC F	LTC	0-0285340	1264	3
SILVERA TOM B	CPT	0-0491302	0845	2
SILVERBERG EDWARD M	COL	0-0113728	0754	3
SILVERBERG ISRAEL	LTC	0-1796715	0965	3
SILVERIO BONIFACIO	2LT	0-1896891	1251	2
SILVERMAN ABRAHAM G	COL	0-0170178	0657	1
SILVERMAN ISADOPE	MAJ	0-0251560	0667	3
SILVERMAN MARTIN H	CW3	W-2145297	0464	2
SILVERMAN MAX H	COL	0-0539332	1167	1
SILVERMAN MEYER	1LT	0-0107995	1037	1
SILVERMAN PHILIP	CPT	0-0265770	0855	3
SILVERNAIL EDMOND M	LTC	0-1016169	0864	1
SILVERSTEIN BERNARD	LTC	0-0262629	1163	3
SILVERSTEIN STUART H	1LT	0-1185312	0146	2
SILVERSTRAND CLARENC	COL	0-0900981	0868	3
SILVERTHORN CHARLES	MAJ	0-1951635	0665	1
SILVESTRO THOMAS	CW3	W-2147288	1165	1
SILVEY CHARLES D SR	CW3	W-2152168	0465	1
SILVEY FREDERICK	LTC	0-0356134	0349	2
SILVEY WILLIAM R	COL	0-0208512	0258	3
SILVIA WILLIAM J	WO1	W-2105382	1049	1
SIM ALEX T	1LT	0-0112455	1054	3
SIMANK ARTHUR	CPT	0-1796716	1258	2
SIMARD JOSEPH G E	1LT	0-1577850	0245	2
SIMARD STANLEY B	1LT	0-0339958	1044	2
SIMCHICK JOSEPH L	1LT	0-1317599	0944	2
SIMCOX CLARENCE H	MAJ	0-1301044	0557	1
SIMENSON RAYMOND S	CPT	0-0356719	1045	2
SIMES GARDNER M	LTC	0-0251821	0467	3
SIMI LAWRENCE	1LT	0-1301224	0661	1
SIMICH ALEXANDER	CW4	W-2116025	0157	1
SIMIELE FRANK	COL	0-0456666	0665	1
SIMIONE NICHOLAS A	MAJ	0-1595832	0668	3
SIMKIN THEODOPE T	CPT	0-1015946	0846	2
SIMKINS HOMER A	MAJ	0-0246992	0349	3
SIMKINS LESLIE C	COL	0-0236954	0464	3
SIMKINS MURPAY K	1LT	0-1179709	1144	2
SIMKINS ROY G	MAJ	0-0217147	0145	1
SIMKINS WILLIAM B JR	MAJ	0-1844394	0762	2
SIMMERMAN WALTER H	CW2	W-2210922	0166	1
SIMMERS RICHARD C	CPT	0-1289977	1045	2
SIMMERT ROBERT H	B G	0-0271897	0467	3
SIMMIE ALBERT F	CPT	0-0890373	0847	2
SIMMINGTON T JR	MAJ	0-0417591	0553	2
SIMMONDS GEORGE H	MAJ	0-1306897	0462	1
SIMMONDS HAROLD W	LTC	0-0329913	0158	3
SIMMONDS JOE G	CPT	0-1291024	0847	2
SIMMONDS MAURICE R	LTC	0-0275306	0457	1
SIMMONITE HENRY G	COL	0-0257292	0465	3
SIMMONS A J LOWE	MAJ	0-1172657	0155	1
SIMMONS ABRAM F JR	CW3	W-2152153	1063	1
SIMMONS ALFRED J	CW3	W-2209917	1060	1
SIMMONS AMOS F	MAJ	0-0966292	0163	1
SIMMONS ARTHUF B JR	1LT	0-0341869	1043	2
SIMMONS BESSIE O	1LT	N-0797678	0647	1
SIMMONS CARL A	LTC	0-1685020	0166	1
SIMMONS CARL G	MAJ	0-0341477	0146	2
SIMMONS CHARLES E	CPT	0-0509076	0147	1
SIMMONS CLARENCE C	LTC	0-0466241	0560	3
SIMMONS CLIFFORD H	1LT	0-0382607	0245	2
SIMMONS DANIEL H	LTC	0-1049647	0164	1
SIMMONS EDWARD E	CPT	0-1038289	1154	2
SIMMONS EDWIN R	LTC	0-1175577	0764	1
SIMMONS ELMER M	LTC	0-0164221	0753	2
SIMMONS ELMER N	MAJ	0-0501192	0854	1
SIMMONS ELMORE B	MAJ	0-0514544	0457	1
SIMMONS ELVIS A	1LT	0-0519423	0447	2
SIMMONS EMIL	LTC	0-0493416	0257	1
SIMMONS FARPIS C	MAJ	0-1305328	0761	1
SIMMONS FLAVIUS K	MAJ	0-0936090	0762	1
SIMMONS FLOYD L	COL	0-0100037	0748	3
SIMMONS FRANK G	CPT	0-0353351	0346	2
SIMMONS FRED H	LTC	0-0254748	1163	3
SIMMONS FREMONT	CPT	0-0157514	0238	1
SIMMONS GEORGE E	COL	0-0276427	1164	3
SIMMONS GEORGE E	CPT	0-1306159	0745	2
SIMMONS GEORGF F	MAJ	0-1324795	0163	1
SIMMONS GEORGE H JR	2LT	0-0540601	1144	2
SIMMONS GEORGE L	CW2	W-2000725	0644	2
SIMMONS GERALD W	CW4	W-2103437	0759	2
SIMMONS GORDON H	LTC	0-0522634	0967	1
SIMMONS GRANT A	MAJ	0-0976461	1263	1
SIMMONS HARRIMAN N	LTC	0-0272277	0464	3
SIMMONS HARRY E	MAJ	0-0101999	0258	3
SIMMONS HERBERT W	CW2	W-2109057	0453	1
SIMMONS J W	CPT	0-1184725	1060	1
SIMMONS JAMES L	1LT	0-0393073	0445	2
SIMMONS JAMES W	MAJ	0-1292074	0747	2
SIMMONS JAMES W	LTC	0-1594481	1262	2
SIMMONS JOHN D	LTC	0-1315487	1164	1
SIMMONS JOHN W	LTC	0-0386896	0961	1
SIMMONS JOSEPH F	MAJ	0-2015749	1165	1
SIMMONS LEON G	LTC	0-2055896	0765	1
SIMMONS LLOYD B	MAJ	0-0452179	0762	1
SIMMONS MARVIN H	MAJ	0-1591445	0964	3
SIMMONS MELVIN C	MAJ	0-1639648	1063	1
SIMMONS MELVIN L	CPT	0-0984721	1161	1
SIMMONS NOLA	1LT	N-0744732	0548	1
SIMMONS PHILIP F	MAJ	0-0402298	0649	2
SIMMONS R B	MAJ	0-0967139	0462	1
SIMMONS ROBERT W	1LT	0-1296272	1145	2
SIMMONS ROSS Y	CPT	0-1291025	0657	1
SIMMONS ROY P SR	MAJ	0-1015102	0559	1
SIMMONS SAMUEL D	CW4	W-2002083	1164	3
SIMMONS SIDNEY L	MAJ	0-1112974	0963	2
SIMMONS THOMAS C	MAJ	0-0335235	1044	2
SIMMONS THOMAS S	MAJ	0-1634326	1057	1
SIMMONS TOM R	MAJ	0-0176221	0462	1
SIMMONS VICTOR C	LTC	0-0305785	1047	2
SIMMONS VICTOR H	MAJ	0-1580325	0762	1
SIMMONS WALTER L	MAJ	0-1323622	0257	1
SIMMONS WILLARD C	LTC	0-1000473	0862	1
SIMMONS WILLIAM	MAJ	0-0498544	0953	2
SIMMONS WILLIAM E	LTC	0-0169008	0360	3
SIMMONS WILLIAM H	1LT	0-1824927	0449	2
SIMMONS WILLIAM H	CW2	W-2142051	1061	1
SIMMONS WILLIAM J	MAJ	0-2032866	0463	1
SIMMONS WILLIAM K	MAJ	0-0444345	0150	1
SIMMONS WILTON L	COL	0-0372208	0361	1
SIMMS BERNARD G	LTC	0-0414862	0763	1
SIMMS CHARLES H	LTC	0-0321522	0258	1
SIMMS CLARENCE J	LTC	0-0294922	0866	3
SIMMS EDWARD A	CW3	W-2145510	0264	1
SIMMS EDWARD W JR	LTC	0-1582132	0962	1
SIMMS GEORGE C	LTC	0-0202217	0757	1
SIMMS HAROLD A	CPT	0-0131561	0648	3
SIMMS HARWELL	MAJ	0-1296923	0761	1
SIMMS JAMES E	COL	0-0420774	1068	2
SIMMS RAYMOND F	LTC	0-0413504	1267	3
SIMMS RICHARD B	COL	0-1058380	0268	1
SIMMS WILLIAM H	LTC	0-1320258	1167	1
SIMMS WILLIAM P	1LT	0-1324957	0246	2
SIMON ANNE MARIE	CPT	N-0759050	1147	1
SIMON CHARLES	CPT	0-0372136	0745	2
SIMON CLARENCE G JR	COL	0-1287422	0168	1
SIMON FELIX M JR	CPT	0-0987099	1062	1
SIMON FRANCIS E	CPT	0-1319129	0746	2
SIMON FRANCIS M	CW2	W-3200319	1266	1
SIMON HARRY F	1LT	0-5504381	0860	2
SIMON HENRY	MAJ	0-0501534	1045	2
SIMON JOHN F	COL	0-0337959	0868	3
SIMON JOHN M JR	MAJ	0-2025898	0363	1
SIMON JOHN O	MAJ	0-0270465	0246	2
SIMON KONA	MAJ	0-0371956	0346	2
SIMON LESTER E	MAJ	0-0252535	0647	2
SIMON MAX R	LTC	0-0139439	0648	3
SIMON MICHAEL R	MAJ	0-0558854	1145	2
SIMON MORTON L	1LT	0-1574527	0444	2
SIMON NORMAN	CPT	0-0379670	1045	2
SIMON SAMUEL S	CW2	W-2151870	0361	1
SIMON SIDNEY	2LT	0-1298771	0245	2
SIMON STANLEY J	LTC	0-0291027	0151	2
SIMONDS EDWARD P	LTC	0-1322722	0764	1
SIMONDS ISAAC E	LTC	0-0576286	0757	3
SIMONDS JACK L	MAJ	0-1913374	0265	1
SIMONELLI MARIO	CPT	0-0501735	0245	2
SIMONEN LAURA L	1LT	N-0703604	0546	1
SIMONETTI JOSEPH F	COL	0-1326523	0968	2
SIMONETTI LOUIS J	LTC	0-0520018	0466	3
SIMONIDES HOWARD A	LTC	0-1047781	0264	1
SIMONS BERNARD C	CPT	0-0947033	0557	2
SIMONS CHARLES H	CPT	0-2029673	1059	1
SIMONS EDWARD H	CPT	0-1291187	0560	2
SIMONS KENNETH L	LTC	0-0225909	0265	3
SIMONS LYLE F	LTC	0-1319030	0757	2
SIMONS MILTON N	LTC	0-0294873	0863	1
SIMONS WEBSTER L	COL	0-0221680	0557	1
SIMONSEN EDWARD G JR	1LT	0-1337767	0751	2
SIMONSON ARNOLD L	MAJ	0-0535175	0759	2
SIMONSON CHARLES H	1LT	0-0115084	0555	3
SIMONSON DONALD B	CPT	0-1700686	0246	2
SIMONSON RAE L	1LT	0-1293845	0346	2
SIMONTON RAY M	1LT	0-1322961	1045	2
SIMOWITZ BERNARD	MAJ	0-0241588	0466	3
SIMPKINS SILAS C	MAJ	0-0192813	0655	3
SIMPSON ANDREW JR	CW3	W-2206371	1265	1
SIMPSON ARTHUR L	COL	0-0901337	1068	3
SIMPSON ARTHUR T	MAJ	0-0166463	0648	3
SIMPSON BAILEY L	LTC	0-0206514	1054	1
SIMPSON BEN F JR	CPT	0-0392474	0546	2
SIMPSON CARL C	LTC	0-1178625	0164	1
SIMPSON CHARLES H	WO1	W-2122577	1045	2
SIMPSON CHARLES J	LTC	0-2024342	0461	1
SIMPSON CHARLES W	LTC	0-1686296	0765	2
SIMPSON CHARLIE E	1LT	0-0495768	0951	1
SIMPSON CLAUDE F	CW3	W-2145753	0262	1
SIMPSON CLAUDE S	LTC	0-0401080	0260	1
SIMPSON CLAYTON R	MAJ	0-2263017	0663	1
SIMPSON CLINTON F	LTC	0-0135594	0653	3
SIMPSON DAN C	LTC	0-0214576	0164	3
SIMPSON DAVID R	LTC	0-0172623	0648	3
SIMPSON DAVID V	MAJ	0-0347971	1163	3
SIMPSON DONALD M	1LT	0-0200164	0762	3
SIMPSON EARLE A	CPT	0-2006366	0458	2
SIMPSON EDGAR F	LTC	0-0265622	0759	3
SIMPSON EDWIN H	1LT	0-1592058	0761	1
SIMPSON EUGENE L	MAJ	0-1552384	0760	1
SIMPSON EUGENE R	1LT	0-0971325	0857	1
SIMPSON FELIX T	LTC	0-0184516	0-52	3
SIMPSON GEORGE E	LTC	0-1002528	0166	3
SIMPSON GEORGE T JR	CPT	0-1584917	0568	2
SIMPSON GERALD M	CW3	W-2206305	0867	1
SIMPSON GLENN C	LTC	0-1686537	1166	1
SIMPSON GLYNN W	MAJ	0-1635333	0358	1
SIMPSON GRAYSON	CPT	0-0386271	0254	2
SIMPSON HARRY B	LTC	0-0280646	0260	3
SIMPSON HARVEY A	1LT	0-1302367	0745	2
SIMPSON HOMER O	CPT	0-2262185	0257	2
SIMPSON IRA C	CW3	W-2116011	1154	1
SIMPSON JACK B	MAJ	0-0976050	0466	1
SIMPSON JACK L	1LT	0-1301379	0853	2
SIMPSON JAMES	LTC	0-0275607	0754	3
SIMPSON JAMES B	1LT	0-2042773	1045	2
SIMPSON JOHN A	1LT	0-1038843	0945	2
SIMPSON JOHN E	LTC	0-0373268	1164	1
SIMPSON JOHN M	CW3	W-2147546	0764	1
SIMPSON JOHN P JR	COL	0-0251664	0966	3
SIMPSON JOSEPH M	COL	0-0222086	0560	3
SIMPSON JOSEPH T	MAJ	0-0450904	0459	1
SIMPSON JUBE A	MAJ	0-1550919	0662	2
SIMPSON LAVAUGHAN	CPT	0-1582894	0856	1
SIMPSON MARK H	2LT	0-1633550	0343	2
SIMPSON MARTHA I	MAJ	N-0724090	0361	1
SIMPSON MAURICE M	MAJ	0-1549840	0962	1
SIMPSON NELL A	2LT	N-0786747	1046	1
SIMPSON R B JR	CW2	W-3100520	1167	1
SIMPSON RAY M	LTC	0-0395771	0960	1
SIMPSON RAYMOND	LTC	0-0525864	0463	1
SIMPSON REUBEN J	CW2	W-2209044	0565	1
SIMPSON RICHARD S	1LT	0-0403167	1045	2
SIMPSON ROBERT A	CW4	W-2148989	0958	1
SIMPSON ROBERT B	COL	0-0291975	1061	1
SIMPSON ROBERT S	MAJ	0-0475601	0446	2
SIMPSON SYDNEY E	CPT	0-1307862	0246	2
SIMPSON THOMAS C	LTC	0-0255211	1262	2
SIMPSON THOMAS D	2LT	0-1183414	0245	2
SIMPSON VERNON R	MAJ	0-0959187	0267	1
SIMPSON VERNON W	CPT	0-0515867	0159	1
SIMPSON VICTOR C	LTC	0-1180337	0467	1
SIMPSON WADE H	LTC	0-0984924	0668	1
SIMPSON WALTER L	LTC	0-0127921	0648	3
SIMPSON WILBERT A	LTC	0-0430553	1068	1

NAME	GRADE	SVC NO	DATE RET MO YR	RET CODE
SIMPSON WILLIAM A	1LT	0-1048191	0845	2
SIMPSON WILLIAM A	MAJ	0-1306486	0764	1
SIMPSON WILLIAM E	CPT	0-0153900	0749	3
SIMPSON WILLIAM R	1LT	0-0462475	0246	2
SIMRO JOSEPH R	MAJ	0-2263599	126	1
SIMS ALLEN H	MAJ	0-1535691	1061	1
SIMS CARL C	MAJ	0-1796718	0560	1
SIMS CHARLES F	MAJ	0-0275480	0356	3
SIMS CLAIR W	LTC	0-0253716	0567	3
SIMS CLAUDE F	CPT	0-2026456	0859	2
SIMS CLAYTON C	COL	0-1302537	1263	1
SIMS DEWARD W	MAJ	0-1169739	0361	1
SIMS DURWARD M	MAJ	0-0947791	0865	1
SIMS EDWARD J	COL	0-1286071	1168	2
SIMS ELBURN T	COL	0-0184133	0246	2
SIMS FRED A	CW3	W-2141829	1262	1
SIMS FRED E	LTC	0-0249732	0457	1
SIMS HAROLD S	CPT	0-2011137	0853	1
SIMS HOWARD C	2LT	0-4076205	1158	2
SIMS HUBERT M	CW3	W-2149192	0761	1
SIMS JAMES S	CW4	W-2143236	0466	1
SIMS KENNETH P	LTC	0-1559258	0263	1
SIMS LEONARD F	CPT	0-0477368	0148	1
SIMS MATT B H JR	MAJ	0-1340702	0765	1
SIMS MURPHY M	LTC	0-0388153	0955	2
SIMS ORLEY J	LTC	0-1318717	0964	1
SIMS RALEIGH N	LTC	0-1300724	1060	1
SIMS ROBERT J	MAJ	0-1692935	0559	1
SIMS SAMUEL	CPT	0-1699866	0745	2
SIMS SAMUEL E	CPT	0-1111362	0446	2
SIMS STANLEY P	1LT	0-0404358	0167	3
SIMS THOMAS J	CW3	W-2142199	0756	1
SIMS VIRGIL	WO1	W-2126108	0145	2
SIMS VIVIAN H	MAJ	L-1010027	1164	1
SIMS WALTER K	LTC	0-0338996	0760	1
SIMS WILLIAM F	LTC	0-0294061	0967	3
SIMS WILLIAM H JR	CPT	0-1290672	0146	2
SIMS WILLIAM L	CW2	W-2146957	0358	1
SIMUKA BERNARD F	1LT	0-1318230	1045	2
SINAIKO RUSSELL P	CPT	0-0361553	0346	2
SINCAVAGE JOSEPH J	MAJ	0-0456596	0658	1
SINCIC EDWARD H	1LT	0-1291715	0546	2
SINCLAIR DONALD	CW2	W-2152152	0860	1
SINCLAIR DONALD R	1LT	0-1100766	1044	2
SINCLAIR HARRY	CW3	W-2119411	0157	1
SINCLAIR HARRY B JR	LTC	0-0273640	1046	2
SINCLAIR JOHN M	CPT	0-1598237	0364	1
SINCLAIR LILLIAN H	CPT	N-0760707	1148	2
SINCLAIR RICHARD B	MAJ	0-0280370	0968	3
SINCLAIR THEODORE R	LTC	0-0155556	0556	3
SINDELL BERNARD I	2LT	0-1053811	0644	2
SINDERMAN MARVIN L	MAJ	0-1312598	1059	1
SINE HIRAM K	COL	0-0174486	0955	1
SINEATH LEROY F	CPT	0-0127959	0544	2
SINEATH WALTON A	LTC	0-1053812	0767	1
SINEX JAMES M	CPT	0-0519424	1046	2
SINEX WILLIAM F	LTC	0-0384616	0562	1
SINGE DONALD C	COL	0-0324762	0868	3
SINGER ALFRED L	LTC	0-1041917	1061	2
SINGER BENJAMIN L	CPT	0-0298542	1166	3
SINGER ELEANOR R	2LT	N-0783366	0646	1
SINGER FRANK C	LTC	0-0415652	0647	1
SINGER FRED J	MAJ	0-0151785	0559	3
SINGER HENRY	CW3	W-2207621	0168	1
SINGER IRVING G	CPT	0-0145200	0953	1
SINGER JACK L	CPT	0-0455371	0445	2
SINGER MAX	CPT	0-0529572	0246	2
SINGER THEODORE B	CW2	W-2152630	1262	1
SINGER WILLIAM I	MAJ	0-0249726	1045	2
SINGEWALD GEORGE L	MAJ	0-0275419	0947	2
SINGLE HERMAN J	MAJ	0-1175314	1060	1
SINGLER JOHN W	CPT	0-1684863	0146	2
SINGLETARY ALFRED P	LTC	0-0229543	0964	3
SINGLETARY CONRAD F	CPT	0-1918388	0463	1
SINGLETARY DAVE H	2LT	0-1913709	0547	1
SINGLETARY NED	MAJ	0-0352885	1154	1
SINGLETON BURT N	LTC	0-0243927	0961	3
SINGLETON CLIFTON E	COL	0-0192580	0360	1
SINGLETON ELHANON	1LT	0-0497374	0147	1
SINGLETON FRANK P	MAJ	0-0443625	0657	2
SINGLETON HERBERT J	CW2	W-3430372	0668	1
SINGLETON HOWARD W	2LT	0-1922815	1156	2
SINGLETON NELSON M	MAJ	0-0337092	0261	1
SINGLETON ROBERT R	1LT	0-0482526	1145	2
SINGLETON WALTER T	CPT	0-0402846	0146	2
SINGLETON WILBERT F	LTC	0-1316496	0862	1
SINGLETON WILLIAM D	LTC	0-0263682	0246	2
SINGLETON WILLIAM D	CPT	0-1690844	0258	1
SINGMASTER LAWRENCE	CPT	0-0461445	0745	2
SINGSON AMBROSIO P	1LT	0-0255496	1048	1
SINKLER CECIL I	MAJ	0-0398235	0759	1
SINKOV ABRAHAM	COL	0-0300669	0967	3
SINKOVIC WILLIAM V	MAJ	0-1055978	0160	1
SINNARD HERBERT R	LTC	0-0217278	1263	3
SINNOCK ALBERT J	1LT	0-0243599	0-50	3
SINNOTT JOSEPH J	LTC	0-1823950	0962	1
SINNOTT PHILIP J	LTC	0-0282849	0453	3
SINNOTT WILLIAM W JR	LTC	0-1321669	0368	1
SINOR CLAUDE F	CW2	W-2152251	0765	1
SIPES ROBERT H	LTC	0-0252008	0566	3
SIPILA ARVO W	MAJ	0-0281046	0768	3
SIPLE JOHN J	MAJ	0-1552176	0961	1
SIPOLE ALBERT G	MAJ	0-2042841	0356	1
SIPOLSKI JAMES	LTC	0-0108991	1040	1
SIPOS ANDREW J	MAJ	0-0182519	0851	3
SIPOS ANDREW J	MAJ	0-1997476	0863	1
SIPPEL WALTER A	LTC	0-1044954	0762	1
SIPPLE ERVIN E	CW2	W-2147380	0461	1
SIPPY MALCOLM B	LTC	0-1003843	0461	1
SIRACUSS FRANCES R	2LT	N-0796678	0346	1
SIRAN MATTHEW F	LTC	0-1826062	0865	1
SIRAN WALTER J	1LT	0-1581374	0959	1
SIRDEVAN JAMES F	CPT	0-0920172	0147	2
SIREN SYLVESTER	MAJ	0-0156855	0955	3
SIRES JOSEPH T JR	CPT	0-1036029	0652	2
SIRI EUGENE W	MAJ	0-1035601	0951	2
SIRIANNE RAYMOND A	LTC	0-1556800	1163	1
SIRK WILLIAM S	CPT	0-0451185	0250	1
SIRKIN LOUIS J	MAJ	0-1299130	0463	1
SIRLES CLYDE P	COL	0-0408214	0962	1
SIROIS SAMUEL F	CPT	0-1323781	0547	2
SIROTA JONAS H	CPT	0-0478457	0545	2
SISCO BOBBY J	CW3	W-2205329	0767	1
SISCO ROBERT F L	CPT	0-1795984	0352	1
SISCOE FRED F	MAJ	0-1593280	0865	1
SISEMORE ROBERT L	MAJ	0-0949060	0563	1
SISK HORACE L	MAJ	0-0997097	0866	1
SISK JOHN L	MAJ	0-0346577	0745	2
SISLER BRUCE H	COL	0-0277717	0761	3
SISON JOSE S	CPT	0-1914200	1140	1
SISSON DORIS J	MAJ	L-1010596	0163	1
SISSON GEORGE E	CPT	0-0352662	1044	2
SISSON JAMES A	MAJ	0-0132108	1047	1
SISTAC ARDEN W	LTC	0-1043794	0655	1
SISTEK CHARLES M	MAJ	0-1036741	0755	1
SISTEK EDITH W	2LT	N-0720583	1043	1
SISTI FRANCIS F	MAJ	0-1174440	0361	1
SISTRUNK JOEL H	MAJ	0-2018778	0657	1
SISTRUNK LOHIE W	2LT	0-1053814	0744	2
SITAR STEPHEN B	MAJ	0-1324706	0157	1
SITARIK JOHN P	MAJ	0-2016026	0161	1
SITES CLAUDE W	MAJ	0-1919107	0665	1
SITES HARRY	MAJ	0-1001243	0557	1
SITES LAWRENCE D	LTC	0-2011004	0762	1
SITES MARY E	MAJ	N-0752315	0667	1
SITLER HERBERT G	COL	0-0289444	1164	1
SITNEY JULIAN J	CPT	0-1821410	0446	2
SITNIK BRONISLAW	MAJ	0-1047784	0757	1
SITTON FRANKLIN G	LTC	0-1542137	0960	1
SITTS RALPH J	MAJ	0-0197838	0553	2
SITWELL GEORGE F	LTC	0-0438418	1167	2
SITZMAN PHILIP F SR	LTC	0-1797730	1160	1
SIVAK ANDREW	CW3	W-2147875	0365	1
SIVATON ALBERT R	MAJ	0-0249763	0962	3
SIVERSON ADOLPH G	COL	0-0121526	1155	3
SIVERTSON GAYLORD D	LTC	0-1335072	0663	1
SIVETS JOHN W	MAJ	0-1308047	0162	1
SIVIL CLIFFORD L	LTC	0-1300539	0662	1
SIWINSKI ARTHUR G	COL	0-0240351	0166	3
SIWY WALTER J	1LT	0-0419079	0245	2
SIZEMORE DENVER	MAJ	0-0955782	0262	1
SIZEMORE LAMAR T	LTC	0-2019664	1266	1
SIZER EDMUND A	LTC	0-1573589	1154	1
SJODING HAROLD N E	LTC	0-1644092	0556	1
SJORUP CHRISTOPHE	MAJ	0-0959331	0165	1
SKABLA JAMES C	CW3	W-2151780	0363	1
SKABO TORGER	MAJ	0-0258888	0764	3
SKADDEN JAMES D	LTC	0-1103929	0664	1
SKAER ARTHUR W JR	1LT	0-1846067	0746	2
SKAFF DAVID J	MAJ	0-0287688	1144	2
SKAGGS CLINT H	CPT	0-0124472	1054	3
SKAGGS ELMER M	LTC	0-0265660	0459	2
SKAGGS HORACE G	CPT	0-0402395	1045	2
SKAGGS JAMES S	MAJ	0-0156872	0749	3
SKAGGS LOREN D	COL	0-0479095	1152	1
SKAILES THOMAS J	CPT	0-0924174	0244	2
SKAITH LEROY J	LTC	0-1314558	0763	1
SKALICKY EMIL	LTC	0-0375312	0563	1
SKANSE GEORGE W	MAJ	0-1109013	0463	1
SKARI LUTHER C	CW4	W-2141681	0757	1
SKARRY ARTHUR	COL	0-0234780	0460	3
SKEAHAN THOMAS J	COL	0-0237777	0556	1
SKEEN HENRY C	CPT	0-0164239	0438	1
SKEEN ROBERT P	MAJ	0-1598238	0863	1
SKEEN VICTOR L	1LT	0-1999175	1045	2
SKELLEY LILLIAN L	MAJ	N-0742368	1264	2
SKELLY EDWARD K	LTC	0-0475026	1158	2
SKELLY EDWARD W	COL	0-0299202	0362	3
SKELLY JOSEPH T	MAJ	0-1081031	1160	1
SKELLY MILTON	COL	0-0266873	0665	3
SKELLY WALTER J	COL	0-0199519	0160	1
SKELTON BERYL D	MAJ	N-0756922	0663	3
SKELTON BUSTER L	MAJ	0-0969418	0565	1
SKELTON CLARENCE C	COL	0-0277839	0959	3
SKELTON DOYLE C	COL	0-0277852	1066	3
SKELTON EUGENE	MAJ	0-0984300	1263	1
SKELTON HERBERT J	MAJ	0-0249534	1265	3
SKELTON JAMES H JR	COL	0-0115975	0157	3
SKELTON LAWRENCE R	LTC	0-1302539	0460	1
SKELTON SEWELL G	LTC	0-0327801	1045	2
SKELTON WINIFRED	1LT	N-0721385	0645	1
SKEMP CHARLES P	MAJ	0-0104067	0254	3
SKEMP HAL P	COL	0-0263285	0166	3
SKENDER MILDRED M	2LT	N-0790055	0845	1
SKENDROVIC NORMAN A	LTC	0-1049648	1067	1
SKEOCH RALPH M	CW2	W-2203269	1060	1
SKERKOWSKI FREDERICK	MAJ	0-1686798	1266	1
SKERSTON ISABELLE D	CPT	N-0783768	1146	1
SKERYANC ANTHONY P	MAJ	0-2047831	0359	1
SKEWES CRAIG L	CPT	0-4009084	1162	2
SKIDMORE COOPER	2LT	0-2016963	0161	1
SKIDMORE LYDIA G	MAJ	L-1010108	0964	1
SKIDMORE WILLIAM F	LTC	0-0936767	0866	1
SKIELVIG WALTER H	COL	0-0364891	0460	1
SKIFF HARRY A JR	LTC	0-1946383	0468	3
SKIFF KENNETH H	LTC	0-1549603	0163	1
SKILLEN JAMES R	COL	0-0236520	1262	3
SKILLEN ROBERT W	LTC	0-0311738	0267	3
SKILLING HAROLD C	MAJ	0-0205233	0550	3
SKILLINGER ROBERT C	LTC	0-1551116	0661	1
SKILLMAN F C JR	COL	0-0319783	1058	1
SKILLMAN HAROLD R	COL	0-0203796	0457	3
SKIMIN ROBERT F	MAJ	0-1689536	0867	1
SKINNER ARTHUR L	MAJ	0-1651325	0863	1
SKINNER BAILEY	MAJ	0-0457846	0449	1
SKINNER CHARLES A	CPT	0-0966942	0560	1
SKINNER CHARLES F JR	CPT	0-0137920	0159	3
SKINNER EARL D	MAJ	0-0135501	0955	3
SKINNER EARL M	CPT	0-1183971	1146	2
SKINNER EUGENE O	1LT	0-0473512	0744	2
SKINNER EUGENE L	COL	0-0219850	0763	3
SKINNER HARRY J	MAJ	0-0890440	1160	1
SKINNER JAMES C	MAJ	0-2015515	0863	1
SKINNER JAMES G	MAJ	0-2289184	1060	1
SKINNER JAMES M	MAJ	0-1587631	1062	1
SKINNER KENYON R	LTC	0-0384628	1064	2
SKINNER LEO	CW3	W-2148399	0767	1
SKINNER LOUIS C	CW3	W-2205240	0268	1
SKINNER LOUIS C JR	CPT	0-0472036	0445	2
SKINNER MILLARD E	CPT	0-0343812	1044	2
SKINNER OTIS R JR	CPT	0-1339575	0259	2
SKINNER RAPHAEL S	MAJ	0-0205757	0460	3
SKINNER RICHMOND H	LTC	0-0123155	0651	2
SKINNER ROBERT M	CW2	W-2131519	0747	1
SKINNER ROGER C	MAJ	0-1306676	0364	1
SKINNER THOMAS V S	LTC	0-0275510	0367	3
SKINNER WILLIAM F	MAJ	0-0250677	1165	3
SKINNER WILLIAM J	MAJ	0-2042723	0749	2
SKIPPER JOHN T JR	CW3	W-2145910	0263	1
SKIPTON GERLAD F	1LT	0-1593282	0761	1
SKIPTON ROY K	CPT	0-0463943	1046	2
SKIRVING CHARLES D	LTC	0-1582137	0167	1
SKITSKO GEORGE	MAJ	0-1051783	0259	1
SKLAR MURRAY A	WO1	W-2130597	0647	2
SKLAR SOL H	MAJ	0-0507767	0446	2
SKOBBA JOSEPH S	COL	0-0313015	1164	3
SKOGLUND LAWRENCE L	CPT	0-5423820	1268	2
SKOLD BERNARD H	LTC	0-0052013	1060	1
SKOLNICK MAX H	CPT	0-0486015	0645	2
SKOLNICK SOLOMON H	LTC	0-0442166	0747	2
SKOLUDA ERIC R	COL	0-0359453	0665	3
SKOMSKI ANTHONY J	2LT	0-0974934	0352	2
SKONORD RUDOLPH H SR	COL	0-0309184	0468	3
SKOOG ALMA T	LTC	N-0700207	1045	1
SKOOG CLINTON L	CW3	W-2147555	0767	1
SKOPANSKI MARTIN	CW2	W-2121177	0949	1
SKORHEIM FRANCIS	1LT	0-1055730	0246	2
SKOVIRA ANNA V	MAJ	N-0720863	0263	1
SKOVRON JOSEPH W	MAJ	0-2015684	1057	1
SKOW HAROLD C	CPT	0-1036742	0446	2
SKOWRON JOHN J	CPT	0-0469460	0246	2
SKOWRONEK ANTON J	CPT	0-1697958	0346	2
SKOWRONSKI CASMIR A	CPT	0-0477027	0446	2
SKRAMSTAD DAYLE L	1LT	0-1311696	0347	2
SKRIPSKY STANLEY J	CPT	0-1796169	0261	2
SKULBORSTAD MARK J	CW2	W-3157190	0868	2
SKUTAS BERNICE C	LTC	L-0610745	1167	1
SKUTEVIK RICHARD A	CW3	W-2211709	1268	1
SKUTTLE IRVING M	MAJ	0-0224896	0145	2
SKVARNA JOHN J JR	MAJ	0-1336704	1263	1
SKVORAK MICHAEL J	LTC	0-0886865	0366	1
SLACK EARL V	LTC	0-1549099	0964	1
SLACK HERBERT L	CW3	W-2151893	0764	1
SLACK JOHN K	CPT	0-1646593	0462	1
SLACK ROBERT C	CPT	0-0403314	0549	2
SLADE DONALD S	LTC	0-0220273	0558	3
SLADE EDWARD J	LTC	0-1108328	0761	1
SLADE MELBOURNE JR	LTC	0-1183972	0265	1
SLADE RAY O	LTC	0-0270599	1156	1
SLADE RICHARD S	CPT	0-0403552	0346	2
SLADE WORDIE B	MAJ	0-1551962	0657	1
SLADECK MARIE J	1LT	N-0730532	0946	1
SLADER DANIEL A	CPT	0-1824954	0548	2
SLAGER JACOB J	LTC	0-1115418	1266	1
SLAGLE MARION A	CPT	0-0489783	0450	2
SLAHTOVSKY ANNA C	MAJ	N-0755471	0763	1
SLAKER RAYMOND H	1LT	0-1306900	0146	2
SLAMAN ALBERT	CPT	0-1821641	0747	2
SLAMIN ARTHUR	1LT	0-1313808	0548	2
SLANK CONSTANCE	MAJ	N-0793662	0365	1

NAME	GRADE	SVC NO	DATE RET MO YR	RET CODE
SLANKARD RICHARD G	CW3	W-2143967	0567	1
SLATE CLYDE R	CW3	W-2205315	0867	1
SLATE ROBERT C	1LT	O-1321343	0646	2
SLATER ALFRED T	CPT	O-1307863	1065	1
SLATER EDWIN F	LTC	O-1295953	1066	1
SLATER ELMER S	1LT	O-1304717	0146	2
SLATER FRANK J	1LT	O-1016360	0747	2
SLATER GEORGE F	MAJ	O-0349732	0156	3
SLATER GERALD A	2LT	O-1320568	0744	2
SLATER HAROLD K	LTC	O-0412904	0363	1
SLATER IRVING	LTC	O-1297640	0468	3
SLATER JAMES M	LTC	O-1342400	0966	1
SLATER JAMES R	MAJ	O-0151395	0256	3
SLATER JOEL H	COL	O-0245843	0957	3
SLATER JOHN E	LTC	O-0129379	0551	2
SLATER JOHN E	CW3	W-2146095	0360	1
SLATER JOHN W	MAJ	O-1397764	0561	1
SLATER MABEL B F	1LT	N-0737764	1045	1
SLATER MARION F	MAJ	O-2010627	0763	1
SLATER NORMAN S	LTC	O-0320124	0561	1
SLATER ROLAND A	COL	O-0214845	0660	3
SLATER THOMAS V	LTC	O-1172296	0764	1
SLATER WALTER J	MAJ	O-1638527	0661	1
SLATER WILLIAM K	MAJ	O-1934511	0367	1
SLATES BURL V	MAJ	O-0248355	1065	3
SLATON WILLIAM J	LTC	O-0187866	0-53	3
SLATORE LEE R	MAJ	O-0112723	1155	3
SLATTERY ARTHUR R	LTC	O-0232918	0260	1
SLATTERY BYRON R	CPT	O-1039568	1052	2
SLATTERY EUGENE V	COL	O-0311536	0665	3
SLATTERY JOHN J	1LT	O-1297357	0346	2
SLATTERY ROBERT F	LTC	O-1293329	0964	1
SLATTERY RUTLEDGE	LTC	O-0245210	0766	3
SLATTUM HAWKINS L	LTC	O-1100339	0456	1
SLAUGHTER CHARLES T	LTC	O-1290673	0557	1
SLAUGHTER CLARE E	LTC	O-0196271	0962	3
SLAUGHTER GEORGE R	1LT	O-0304391	1043	2
SLAUGHTER GLEN A	LTC	O-0403928	0467	3
SLAUGHTER HARRY	LTC	O-0185693	1149	3
SLAUGHTER HERBERT C	CPT	O-0342803	1045	2
SLAUGHTER JAMES D	1LT	O-0387266	0845	2
SLAUGHTER JAMES H	LTC	O-0263683	0964	3
SLAUGHTER JOHN C	MAJ	O-0306407	1147	1
SLAUGHTER MARION H	1LT	O-0532740	1146	2
SLAUGHTER ROBERT J	CPT	O-0507733	0849	1
SLAUGHTER ROBERT N	CPT	O-0230159	0948	3
SLAUGHTER SOLOMON W	LTC	O-1081376	0764	2
SLAUGHTER STEPHEN F	LTC	O-0529409	0763	1
SLAUGHTER TALMADGE C	CW2	W-2214865	0966	1
SLAUSON IRVIN D	MAJ	O-2208229	0965	1
SLAVEN ROBERT K	MAJ	O-1633553	0758	1
SLAVENS DWIGHT F	CPT	O-0286136	0348	1
SLAVIN GEORGE F	LTC	O-0346220	1067	3
SLAVINS ARNOLD W	COL	O-0289077	0959	3
SLAVIS ANTHONY	1LT	O-2024167	0347	2
SLAWSON FRED H	CPT	O-1684946	1061	1
SLAWSON JOHN E	LTC	O-0423263	0660	1
SLAY MAURICE S	MAJ	O-1823787	0564	1
SLAY NOEL G	CW2	W-2142430	0655	1
SLAYDEN WALTER S	CPT	O-1285510	0253	1
SLAYMAKER WILLIAM H	CPT	O-1290674	0346	2
SLAYMAN WILLIAM J	LTC	O-1167633	1164	2
SLAYSMAN CLARENCE L	LTC	O-0361381	0163	1
SLAYTER VERNIE	LTC	O-0372343	0858	1
SLAYTON BARNEY W	MAJ	O-1031025	0359	1
SLEATOR RALPH W	LTC	O-0240335	1060	3
SLEE HAROLD M	CW2	W-2151360	0563	1
SLEETER LEROY H	CPT	O-1635342	1047	2
SLEETH ROBERT S JR	1LT	O-1012354	1145	2
SLEIGHT ROBERT G	1LT	O-0888234	0945	2
SLEMMER WILLIAM W	MAJ	O-1317048	0264	1
SLEPIAN ROBERT	LTC	O-1309617	0862	2
SLEPIN MATTHEW M	LTC	O-0309085	0668	3
SLESINGER BENJAMIN	MAJ	O-1638447	1156	1
SLETTEN NORMAN O	MAJ	O-1054818	1162	1

NAME	GRADE	SVC NO	DATE RET MO YR	RET CODE
SLEVIN JOHN G	COL	O-0257857	0263	3
SLEVIN RICHARD A	CW4	W-2126261	1059	1
SLEZAK CLYDE L	MAJ	O-0264830	1164	3
SLEZAK JOHN	COL	O-0203778	0556	3
SLEZAK WILLIAM E	LTC	O-1285511	1060	1
SLICK JOSEPH D	1LT	O-2284025	0455	3
SLIGER AUSTIN K	MAJ	O-1533447	0662	1
SLIGER GLEN T JR	MAJ	O-1031130	1160	1
SLIGER THOMAS F	CPT	O-1311936	0748	2
SLIGH MARION W	CW3	W-2207635	0668	1
SLIGH WILLIAM D	LTC	O-0193109	1060	3
SLIGH WILLIAM L	CW2	W-2145165	0257	1
SLIKER ROBERT R	MAJ	O-1102052	0564	1
SLINGLUFF ROBERT L	LTC	O-0246551	1067	3
SLINGO HERBERT J	COL	O-0183965	1055	2
SLINZAK JOHN E	MAJ	O-0423380	0358	1
SLITER ELMER H JR	COL	O-0180858	0462	3
SLOAN ARTHUR H JR	CW4	W-2152252	0867	1
SLOAN BERNARD W	CW4	W-2206792	1168	2
SLOAN DWIGHT H	LTC	O-0363599	0261	1
SLOAN EDWIN	CW4	W-2147779	1163	1
SLOAN FRANK S	LTC	O-0184163	0656	3
SLOAN GEORGE H	LTC	O-0242549	0564	3
SLOAN HAROLD P JR	MAJ	O-1305658	0764	1
SLOAN JAMES J	CPT	O-0508806	0159	2
SLOAN LAVERN D	1LT	O-1052969	0564	1
SLOAN OWEN K	LTC	O-1542138	1167	3
SLOAN PAUL G	LTC	O-0436615	1147	2
SLOAN RICHARD G	MAJ	O-1994531	0758	1
SLOAN RICHARD V	LTC	O-0258026	1064	3
SLOAN SAMUEL J	1LT	O-1298610	0247	2
SLOAN SHELTON S	MAJ	O-2032833	0863	1
SLOAN WILLIAM S	COL	O-0307271	0968	3
SLOANE GEORGE A	MAJ	O-2017294	0260	1
SLOANE JOSEPH	MAJ	O-1545369	0361	1
SLOANE MEDWYN D JR	COL	O-0302433	0966	1
SLOANE THELMA L	MAJ	N-0724804	0961	1
SLOAT CHARLES A	MAJ	O-0176491	1058	3
SLOAT ERNEST H	1LT	O-1179619	0546	2
SLOBODIAN DANIEL	1LT	O-1295096	1145	2
SLOBODKIN BURTON R	LTC	O-1533918	0768	3
SLOBODKIN MORRIS	COL	O-0313133	0766	3
SLOCOMB DON B	1LT	O-0283271	0645	2
SLOCUM CHARLES R	LTC	O-0277851	0646	2
SLOCUM EUGENE E	CPT	O-1309315	1046	2
SLOCUM HARRIET M	2LT	N-0744939	0545	1
SLOCUM RAYMOND A	MAJ	O-2263615	0662	2
SLOCUM WINFIELD S	COL	O-0179151	0151	3
SLOCUM YUDELL K	LTC	O-0320385	0764	3
SLOCUMB PARKER V	CW4	W-2104823	0559	1
SLOMA FRANCIS M	1LT	O-1038465	0845	2
SLONAKER EDWARD G L	CPT	O-1318837	0547	2
SLONE CHARLES R	1LT	O-1939908	1055	2
SLONE CULLEN R	CW3	W-2145513	0161	1
SLONE WILLIAM R	LTC	O-0360494	0760	1
SLOTE ARTHUR D	CPT	O-1015815	0446	2
SLOTERBECK JOHN B	CW4	W-2106816	0464	2
SLOTKOWSKI EUGENE L	1LT	O-0475257	1045	2
SLOTT NORMAN	MAJ	O-0245465	0966	3
SLOUGH ROY	LTC	O-0121523	0851	3
SLOVER GORDON F	LTC	O-0301936	0866	3
SLOVISCZEK RICHARD P	CPT	O-2034702	0247	2
SLOWIK JOSEPH	CPT	O-1305660	0646	2
SLUSARCHUK ALBERT D	CPT	O-5321711	0268	2
SLUSARCZYK JULIAN W	1LT	O-2042996	0764	1
SLUSS DAVID H	COL	O-0181893	1057	3
SLUSSER ELWOOD K	LTC	O-0359889	1266	3
SLUSSER WILBUR F	CW2	W-2142376	0255	1
SLUTTER JEROME S	MAJ	O-0277850	0544	2
SLUTTS EDWARD J	LTC	O-1591452	0361	1
SLUYTER HARLAN L	LTC	O-1031679	0261	1
SLY ROBERT E	MAJ	O-0386820	0146	2
SLYE DEAN J	MAJ	O-1105826	1060	1
SLYE ERNEST R JR	MAJ	O-0509922	0258	1
SMACHLO WALTER	1LT	O-0542939	0547	2

NAME	GRADE	SVC NO	DATE RET MO YR	RET CODE
SMALL ALLEN L	1LT	O-0924478	1144	2
SMALL ALVIN L	LTC	O-1301225	0363	1
SMALL ARNOLD F	LTC	O-1101218	0361	1
SMALL ARTHUR L	CW4	W-2103443	0955	1
SMALL CALVERT R	COL	O-0329498	1163	3
SMALL CARLTON F	COL	O-0111595	0154	3
SMALL CHARLES H	COL	O-0273299	0168	3
SMALL CHARLES W	1LT	O-0185436	0446	1
SMALL DEE	CPT	O-0121522	1055	3
SMALL EDWARD	LTC	O-0301608	0458	3
SMALL ERNEST L	LTC	O-0123686	1051	3
SMALL FREDERICK	LTC	O-0208769	0959	3
SMALL GEORGE	COL	O-0210049	0958	3
SMALL GEORGE	MAJ	O-0380788	0368	3
SMALL GEORGE W	COL	O-0125531	0650	3
SMALL HIRAM F	CPT	O-0325566	0146	2
SMALL IRVING C	LTC	O-0290706	0466	3
SMALL JAMES G	CPT	O-0384921	0944	2
SMALL LEONARD F	MAJ	O-5301801	1168	1
SMALL MARTIN A JR	LTC	O-1635346	1061	1
SMALL RALPH R	LTC	O-0346419	0265	3
SMALL STEPHEN W	MAJ	O-1312235	0856	1
SMALLEY ARZA G	2LT	O-2012432	0546	2
SMALLEY FREDERICK	MAJ	O-1174441	0356	1
SMALLEY JACK R	LTC	O-1822832	0466	1
SMALLEY JAMES F	MAJ	O-0445272	0854	1
SMALLEY RICHARD M	1LT	O-1017194	1045	2
SMALLEY ROBERT R	CPT	O-0487231	0346	2
SMALLFELT CECIL L	MAJ	O-0211857	0961	3
SMALLING JOHN F JR	CW3	W-2147732	0463	1
SMALLWOOD GLENN R	CW3	W-2210511	1168	1
SMALLWOOD HENRY W	2LT	O-1010699	1144	2
SMALLWOOD HERBERT C	LTC	O-1293491	0466	1
SMALLWOOD THOMAS W	1LT	O-0547395	0446	2
SMALLWOOD WILLIAM	LTC	O-0451290	0258	1
SMARDAK FRANK R	MAJ	O-2037177	1263	1
SMARR KENNETH M	1LT	O-1549100	0345	2
SMARR WYATT C	MAJ	O-2011235	0560	1
SMARSH LEO F	MAJ	O-1573947	0247	2
SMART ALBERT C	CW3	W-2142029	0556	1
SMART DANIEL J	LTC	O-0232212	1057	1
SMART FRED E	MAJ	O-0983707	0259	2
SMART HARRY V	MAJ	O-0181647	0960	3
SMART HELEN G	1LT	N-0760156	104N	1
SMART HENRY C	MAJ	O-1922632	0965	1
SMART HENRY G	LTC	O-1651190	0868	1
SMART OSCAR J	1LT	O-0185466	1048	1
SMART SOLON D	LTC	O-0327122	1068	3
SMART THEODORE T	MAJ	O-0215990	1060	3
SMART WILLARD F	1LT	O-1309432	1045	2
SMATHERS BARBARA S	MAJ	N-0720677	0564	1
SMATHERS CARROLL L	CW3	W-2206330	1265	1
SMATHERS DON L	LTC	O-1311574	0364	1
SMATHERS JAMES L	COL	O-0237648	0459	3
SMATHERS RAY K	COL	O-0106163	0857	2
SMATHERS VAN C	MAJ	O-0507491	0852	2
SMATLICK NADA M	MAJ	L-1010109	0568	1
SMAWLEY JACK G	MAJ	O-1060978	0866	1
SMAY JOSEPH E	CPT	O-0221223	0658	3
SMEAL GLENN W	CW3	W-2206067	0465	1
SMEDES EARLE R	1LT	O-1313656	0651	2
SMEDLEY FRANK H	LTC	O-0253359	1055	3
SMEDS ERLING T	LTC	O-0441298	0467	1
SMEE FREDERICK	LTC	O-1103934	1163	1
SMEED DALLAS B	CW3	W-2148317	1062	1
SMEJKAL JAMES	MAJ	O-1111916	1160	1
SMELLEY EVAN J	CPT	O-1303402	0947	2
SMELLEY HOWARD M	LTC	O-1283154	0163	1
SMELLIE HERBERT H	LTC	O-0354076	0560	1
SMELTER JOSEPH J	CPT	O-2055534	0851	1
SMELTZER GERALD M	CPT	O-0576309	0546	2
SMELTZER PAUL T	COL	O-0420710	0262	1
SMELTZER SAMUEL W	LTC	O-0221368	0562	3
SMERAK EUGENE F	MAJ	O-1020204	0265	1
SMETANA JOHN	MAJ	O-1703937	0657	1

NAME	GRADE	SVC NO	DATE RET MO YR	RET CODE
SMETANA JOSEPH J	MAJ	O-1633558	0158	1
SMETANA LOUIS V	LTC	O-0250198	0763	3
SMETANA PAUL E	2LT	O-1643343	0745	2
SMETHERS SADIE M	1LT	N-0794074	1047	1
SMICK DONALD C	MAJ	O-1287424	1060	1
SMIDT JOHN	MAJ	O-0494989	0145	1
SMIETANOWSKI JOSEPH	CPT	O-1324667	1145	2
SMIGA JOSEPH	MAJ	O-1650748	0663	1
SMIGEN GEORGE A	MAJ	O-1020259	0463	1
SMIGIELSKI LEONARD S	CPT	O-1923580	0664	1
SMILEY ALBERT B	CW2	W-2214840	0767	1
SMILEY FRANK H	LTC	O-0168601	0660	3
SMILEY HOWARD C	LTC	O-0272974	1156	3
SMILEY JAMES A	LTC	O-1107691	0963	1
SMILEY JAMES J JR	MAJ	O-0261885	0765	3
SMILEY JAMES V	LTC	O-1107133	0463	1
SMILEY JOHN H	LTC	O-0242826	0364	3
SMILEY JOHN W	COL	O-0240989	0766	3
SMILEY LLOYD F	MAJ	O-1176512	1160	1
SMILEY ROBERT M	MAJ	O-0507631	0361	1
SMILIE CHARLES R	MAJ	O-1172287	0361	1
SMINK CHARLES E	MAJ	O-2263650	0463	1
SMIRES CLIFFORD L	COL	O-0405792	0760	2
SMIRES MARY L	MAJ	L-1010090	0965	1
SMIRES RALPH C	MAJ	O-0405178	0760	1
SMIT MORTON J	CPT	O-1291716	1046	2
SMITH AARON	CPT	O-0496803	0853	1
SMITH ADAIR M	1LT	O-1301699	1061	1
SMITH ADELBERT P	1LT	O-1544167	0147	2
SMITH ADLEY O	MAJ	O-1302368	0859	1
SMITH ALAN P JR	COL	O-0261399	0855	3
SMITH ALBERT A	MAJ	O-0319766	0658	1
SMITH ALBERT C	LTC	O-0347984	1057	1
SMITH ALBERT E	1LT	O-1638866	0145	2
SMITH ALBERT L	LTC	O-0420976	0861	1
SMITH ALBERT W	MAJ	O-1320193	0662	1
SMITH ALDEN H	LTC	O-0383324	0962	1
SMITH ALEX C	LTC	O-1588297	0860	1
SMITH ALEXANDER	LTC	O-0197897	0358	3
SMITH ALEXANDER JR	LTC	O-1845832	0762	1
SMITH ALFRED F	WO1	W-2210809	1060	2
SMITH ALFRED H	WO1	W-2115253	0950	1
SMITH ALFRED W	MAJ	O-0137611	0648	3
SMITH ALICE E	1LT	N-0721211	0646	1
SMITH ALLEN	CPT	O-1308718	0547	2
SMITH ALLEN A J	CW3	W-2209835	0568	1
SMITH ALTON JR	CPT	O-1293137	0646	2
SMITH ALTON K	LTC	O-1036033	0160	1
SMITH ALVA B JR	CPT	O-1101219	1043	2
SMITH ALVA R	LTC	O-0324739	0460	1
SMITH ALVIN L	MAJ	O-1648832	0563	1
SMITH ALVIN P	MAJ	O-1015520	1263	1
SMITH AMIEL	CW2	W-2143639	0257	1
SMITH ANNA E	MAJ	N-0793551	1263	2
SMITH ANTHONY A	LTC	O-0149525	0552	3
SMITH ARDEN D	LTC	O-1172288	0262	1
SMITH ARGUS F	MAJ	O-1319232	0862	1
SMITH ARTHUR A	LTC	O-0238691	0463	3
SMITH ARTHUR B	LTC	O-0285826	0360	1
SMITH ARTHUR C	LTC	O-0237720	1159	1
SMITH ARTHUR D	CW2	W-2102388	1146	1
SMITH ARTHUR H	MAJ	O-0151794	0649	3
SMITH ARTHUR H	1LT	O-0324593	0261	3
SMITH ARTHUR M	MAJ	O-0238767	0466	3
SMITH ARTHUR M	MAJ	O-2014090	0164	1
SMITH ARTHUR W	COL	O-0174241	0-53	3
SMITH AUSTIN B	LTC	O-0296248	0865	3
SMITH AUSTIN D	COL	O-0205772	0854	3
SMITH AUSTIN W	CPT	O-0280087	1165	3
SMITH AUSTIN W	MAJ	O-1289329	1159	1
SMITH BAILEY B	LTC	O-0196272	0361	1
SMITH BARBARA J	LTC	L-0906078	1167	1
SMITH BASIL	MAJ	O-0497955	1046	1
SMITH BEECHER L	COL	O-0292482	0862	3
SMITH BEN H JR	CPT	O-1328760	1160	2

332-811 O - 69 - 22

NAME	GRADE	SVC NO	DATE RET MO YR	RET CODE
SMITH BEN W	CW2	W-2147090	0159	1
SMITH BENJAMIN F	MAJ	0-2206425	0162	1
SMITH BENJAMIN H	CPT	0-0445496	0247	2
SMITH BENJAMIN N	MAJ	0-0962546	0663	1
SMITH BERNARD H	CPT	0-0113989	0-50	3
SMITH BERNARD J	2LT	0-1181462	0844	2
SMITH BERNARD L	CPT	0-0370606	0847	2
SMITH BERNARD L	MAJ	0-1020301	0165	1
SMITH BERT I	LTC	0-0766738	0167	1
SMITH BERTRAM B	LTC	0-1001244	0860	1
SMITH BERTRAM L	COL	0-0300204	1051	3
SMITH BISHOP B	MAJ	0-0451417	1053	1
SMITH BONNIE	MAJ	0-0469570	1048	1
SMITH BOYD L	2LT	0-0409703	1142	2
SMITH CARL A	LTC	0-1289640	0764	1
SMITH CARL B	COL	0-0175502	0258	3
SMITH CARL W	LTC	0-1165572	0661	1
SMITH CARLESS R	LTC	0-0488515	0-53	1
SMITH CARLETON R	MAJ	0-0229546	0264	3
SMITH CARLOS C	COL	0-0277917	1065	3
SMITH CARLTON H	2LT	0-2035155	0345	2
SMITH CARLTON J	MAJ	0-2267613	0964	2
SMITH CARLTON K	B G	0-0231996	1061	3
SMITH CARLTON P	COL	0-0186359	0847	1
SMITH CARROL B	CPT	0-1649620	0555	2
SMITH CARSON E	CW2	W-2149717	0955	1
SMITH CECELIA	2LT	N-0737684	0644	1
SMITH CECIL C	MAJ	0-0113869	0253	3
SMITH CECIL F	LTC	0-0272957	0368	3
SMITH CHANDLER C	1LT	0-1640961	0645	2
SMITH CHARLES A	LTC	0-0285130	0966	3
SMITH CHARLES A	2LT	0-0302726	0363	3
SMITH CHARLES A	2LT	0-1650334	1045	2
SMITH CHARLES A	CW4	W-2001665	0363	3
SMITH CHARLES C	COL	0-0225519	0564	3
SMITH CHARLES C	COL	0-0288176	0664	3
SMITH CHARLES C	MAJ	0-0972055	0364	1
SMITH CHARLES D	MAJ	0-0343683	0945	2
SMITH CHARLES D	LTC	0-1175316	0267	1
SMITH CHARLES D	1LT	0-1295287	0345	2
SMITH CHARLES E	MAJ	0-0442900	0649	1
SMITH CHARLES E	LTC	0-0495007	0448	2
SMITH CHARLES E	CPT	0-1294378	0257	2
SMITH CHARLES F	MAJ	0-1884175	0866	1
SMITH CHARLES F	LTC	0-0248182	0766	3
SMITH CHARLES F	LTC	0-1536125	1068	1
SMITH CHARLES H	CPT	0-0137766	0857	3
SMITH CHARLES H	MAJ	0-1032047	0759	1
SMITH CHARLES JR	COL	0-0112724	0953	3
SMITH CHARLES L	1LT	0-0379482	0446	2
SMITH CHARLES P	COL	0-0252843	0665	3
SMITH CHARLES P	COL	0-0171852	1060	3
SMITH CHARLES R	LTC	0-0247301	0165	3
SMITH CHARLES R	MAJ	0-0320218	1047	2
SMITH CHARLES R	LTC	0-1550055	0157	1
SMITH CHARLES S	MAJ	0-0245953	0858	3
SMITH CHARLES S	LTC	0-0295905	0867	3
SMITH CHARLES T	CW2	W-3000219	1163	1
SMITH CHARLES W	LTC	0-0177953	1159	3
SMITH CHARLES W	CPT	0-1307475	0847	2
SMITH CHAUNCEY JR	MAJ	0-1011297	0861	1
SMITH CHESTER A	CPT	0-0145609	1055	3
SMITH CHESTER A	LTC	0-0354059	0862	1
SMITH CHESTER A	MAJ	0-1284953	0759	1
SMITH CHESTER A	2LT	0-1299807	0944	2
SMITH CHESTER D	CPT	0-1700935	0646	2
SMITH CLAIR B	MAJ	0-1881274	1065	1
SMITH CLAIRE D	MAJ	0-1644097	0264	1
SMITH CLARENCE A	MAJ	0-1535532	0268	3
SMITH CLARENCE C	1LT	0-0542331	0445	2
SMITH CLARENCE D	MAJ	0-0349334	0968	3
SMITH CLARENCE E	1LT	0-1303554	0753	1
SMITH CLARENCE E	WO1	W-2103448	0659	1
SMITH CLARENCE E	CW3	W-2147394	0958	1
SMITH CLARENCE F	COL	0-0300205	1060	3

NAME	GRADE	SVC NO	DATE RET MO YR	RET CODE
SMITH CLARENCE J	LTC	0-0298155	0356	1
SMITH CLARENCE M JR	LTC	0-1555903	1064	1
SMITH CLARENCE W	MAJ	0-0479933	0859	1
SMITH CLARENCE W	LTC	0-1886429	0968	1
SMITH CLARK B	CPT	0-0255733	0667	3
SMITH CLAUD	LTC	0-1011956	0954	1
SMITH CLAUDE A	CW2	W-2213557	0167	1
SMITH CLAUDE J	MAJ	0-0889095	0864	1
SMITH CLAUDE J	LTC	0-1018750	0168	1
SMITH CLIFF	MAJ	0-0505241	0348	1
SMITH CLIFFORD H	CPT	0-1010248	0860	1
SMITH CLIFFORD W	LTC	0-1647278	0259	1
SMITH CLINE C	1LT	0-1574146	1044	2
SMITH CLINT G	CPT	0-0255541	1064	3
SMITH CLYDE D	COL	0-0242435	0462	3
SMITH CLYDE K	MAJ	0-1283091	0962	1
SMITH CLYDE M	COL	0-0335588	0867	3
SMITH CLYDE W	LTC	0-0279071	1162	1
SMITH CONOVER C	MAJ	0-0234735	1163	3
SMITH CONRAD A	CPT	0-1102470	0453	2
SMITH COURTLAND	LTC	0-0256065	0358	3
SMITH COURTNEY	MAJ	0-0357808	0554	1
SMITH CRAWFORD J	COL	0-0496878	0857	2
SMITH CURTIS H	LTC	0-0313417	1054	1
SMITH CURTIS N	CW3	W-2151006	0563	1
SMITH CURTIS O	MAJ	0-1325791	0561	1
SMITH DALE E	LTC	0-1335485	0766	1
SMITH DAN L	CW3	W-2206942	0167	1
SMITH DANIEL L JR	MAJ	0-0239310	1065	3
SMITH DARREL	LTC	0-1634333	0457	1
SMITH DAVID H	COL	0-0394229	0268	1
SMITH DAVID H	LTC	0-1294030	0862	1
SMITH DAVID L	MAJ	0-0271391	1264	3
SMITH DAVID P	LTC	0-0396827	0262	1
SMITH DAVID R	MAJ	0-0177051	0162	3
SMITH DAVID W	MAJ	0-1799797	1162	1
SMITH DAVIS M	LTC	0-1292951	0663	1
SMITH DEAN E	MAJ	0-0960345	0363	1
SMITH DENNIS F	1LT	0-0557141	1046	2
SMITH DEWAYNE J	COL	0-0330756	0967	3
SMITH DICK D	MAJ	0-1114752	1059	1
SMITH DONALD	LTC	0-1996836	0468	1
SMITH DONALD A	LTC	0-0669521	1168	1
SMITH DONALD B	LTC	0-1041027	0762	1
SMITH DONALD D	LTC	0-0297355	1061	1
SMITH DONALD E	CW4	W-2008913	0868	3
SMITH DONALD F	CW3	W-2148268	0863	1
SMITH DONALD H	MAJ	0-1048193	1263	1
SMITH DONALD H	LTC	0-1321256	0464	1
SMITH DONALD L	CW2	W-2211430	0164	1
SMITH DONALD M	MAJ	0-1686731	0363	1
SMITH DONALD R	LTC	0-0185018	0958	3
SMITH DONALD V	2LT	0-1014074	0744	2
SMITH DONALD W	LTC	0-0234815	0659	3
SMITH DONALD W	CPT	0-1331884	0360	1
SMITH DONET C	CPT	0-0490178	0747	1
SMITH DOTT F	COL	0-0171077	0648	2
SMITH DOUGLAS E	MAJ	0-0967219	0663	1
SMITH DOUGLAS R	MAJ	0-0868411	1163	1
SMITH DUDLEY L	CPT	0-0369849	0943	2
SMITH DURWOOD J	CPT	0-0413358	0646	2
SMITH E RAY	CW3	W-2114347	0856	1
SMITH EARL C	2LT	0-1325055	0645	2
SMITH EARL D	1LT	0-1946859	0546	2
SMITH EARL E	MAJ	0-0326286	0358	1
SMITH EARL E	CW3	W-2149142	1262	1
SMITH EARL F	LTC	0-0364238	1064	3
SMITH EARL W	MAJ	0-0477974	0150	1
SMITH EDGAR E	LTC	0-0885434	1055	1
SMITH EDGAR H	CW3	W-2210078	1068	1
SMITH EDGAR K JR	1LT	0-1042958	0246	2
SMITH EDGAR W	LTC	0-0486186	0157	1
SMITH EDMOND J	CW4	W-2117929	0457	1
SMITH EDWARD	1LT	0-1017735	0845	2
SMITH EDWARD	CPT	0-2042002	1262	1

NAME	GRADE	SVC NO	DATE RET MO YR	RET CODE
SMITH EDWARD B	LTC	0-1946171	0964	2
SMITH EDWARD C	MAJ	0-0264371	0668	3
SMITH EDWARD F	1LT	0-1168083	1046	2
SMITH EDWARD F	LTC	0-1178630	0864	1
SMITH EDWARD J	LTC	0-0272673	0268	3
SMITH EDWARD J	MAJ	0-1693111	1061	1
SMITH EDWARD L	COL	0-0137621	1049	3
SMITH EDWARD L	CW3	W-2213410	0968	1
SMITH EDWARD S	MAJ	0-0190167	0648	3
SMITH EDWARD T	LTC	0-0206142	0860	3
SMITH EDWARD V	MAJ	0-1110262	0964	1
SMITH EDWIN E	LTC	0-0125495	0652	3
SMITH EDWIN H	CW4	W-2109279	0966	1
SMITH EDWIN M	LTC	0-0335127	0560	1
SMITH EDWIN S	CW2	W-2141446	1158	1
SMITH EDWIN T	CPT	0-0391163	0244	2
SMITH EDWIN W	CPT	0-0364298	1045	2
SMITH EDWIN W	CW2	W-2209431	0764	1
SMITH ELDON E	CPT	0-0419639	1145	2
SMITH ELGIN	MAJ	0-0163486	0648	3
SMITH ELIJAH M	LTC	0-0338863	0461	3
SMITH ELIZABETH	MAJ	N-0729893	0563	2
SMITH ELIZABETH	2LT	N-0735109	1044	1
SMITH ELLA J	2LT	N-0700140	0336	1
SMITH ELLIOTT V	LTC	0-0220960	0563	3
SMITH ELLIS I	LTC	0-0281425	1166	3
SMITH ELMER D	1LT	0-0441082	0944	2
SMITH ELTON R	MAJ	0-0313751	0465	3
SMITH ELWYN W	MAJ	0-1103936	0547	2
SMITH EMBUR V	LTC	0-0313492	1158	3
SMITH EMERSON W	LTC	0-0361176	0367	3
SMITH EMERY V	CPT	0-0497933	0845	2
SMITH EMMETT A	MAJ	0-1056237	1162	1
SMITH EMURY C	LTC	0-0278039	1067	3
SMITH ERNEST A	LTC	0-0375114	0666	3
SMITH ERNEST A	1LT	0-1285324	0146	2
SMITH ERNEST C	CPT	0-0967238	1159	1
SMITH ERNEST C	CPT	0-0920218	0245	2
SMITH ERNEST G JR	1LT	0-1706236	0346	2
SMITH ERNEST L	CPT	0-0966619	0862	2
SMITH ERNEST M	COL	0-0251007	0161	3
SMITH ERNEST W	LTC	0-1011144	0165	1
SMITH ERSKINE O	CW3	W-2141898	1054	1
SMITH EUGENE A JR	LTC	0-0342354	0163	1
SMITH EUGENE B	MAJ	0-1913349	1265	2
SMITH EUGENE H	1LT	0-1284411	0245	2
SMITH EUGENE P	CW2	W-2143438	0261	1
SMITH EVERETT C	LTC	0-0469754	0552	1
SMITH EVERT E	MAJ	0-1184726	0364	1
SMITH EZEKIEL C	MAJ	0-1298611	0347	2
SMITH EZRA L	CPT	0-4003709	1166	2
SMITH FANNIE E	MAJ	N-0744643	1068	1
SMITH FATIMA D	2LT	N-0727474	0744	1
SMITH FELIX J	MAJ	0-0339268	0545	2
SMITH FELIX R	MAJ	0-0953879	1161	1
SMITH FENELON O	LTC	0-0284858	0566	3
SMITH FINIS M	CPT	0-1012315	0446	2
SMITH FISHER J	LTC	0-0320360	0667	3
SMITH FLORIE B	LTC	0-1590190	1062	1
SMITH FLOYD D	MAJ	0-0332883	0161	3
SMITH FLOYD H	CW3	W-2210079	1068	1
SMITH FLOYD R	LTC	0-2021182	0868	1
SMITH FOREST R	MAJ	0-1300873	0263	1
SMITH FORREST G	COL	0-0288366	1155	3
SMITH FORREST H	CW2	W-2141941	0655	1
SMITH FORREST W	COL	0-0268636	0661	3
SMITH FRANCIS B	LTC	0-1293875	1060	1
SMITH FRANCIS J	MAJ	0-2018829	1265	2
SMITH FRANCIS T	MAJ	0-1013513	1062	2
SMITH FRANCIS V	LTC	0-0283550	0860	1
SMITH FRANK	LTC	0-1080581	0461	1
SMITH FRANK	CW3	W-2207999	0368	1
SMITH FRANK A	LTC	0-0450360	0355	1
SMITH FRANK A	1LT	0-1286723	0745	2
SMITH FRANK B	LTC	0-1324796	1061	1

NAME	GRADE	SVC NO	DATE RET MO YR	RET CODE
SMITH FRANK B	CW4	W-2127161	1155	1
SMITH FRANK C	COL	0-0103254	1058	1
SMITH FRANK C	COL	0-0272930	1061	1
SMITH FRANK E	LTC	0-0471606	0762	1
SMITH FRANK H	CPT	0-0500677	0554	1
SMITH FRANK H	MAJ	0-1641807	0161	1
SMITH FRANK J	CPT	0-0491955	0847	1
SMITH FRANK M	CW2	W-2149718	1058	1
SMITH FRANK P	CPT	0-1691077	0146	2
SMITH FRANK W	MAJ	0-2032829	1059	1
SMITH FRANKLIN A	MAJ	0-0174702	1049	3
SMITH FRANKLIN H	CPT	0-0411279	1045	2
SMITH FRANKLIN W	LTC	0-0310606	0168	3
SMITH FRED A	LTC	0-0504120	0156	1
SMITH FRED A	LTC	0-1639662	0658	1
SMITH FRED A	CPT	0-2262400	0160	1
SMITH FRED C	1LT	0-1031520	1045	2
SMITH FRED D	MAJ	0-2000434	1262	1
SMITH FRED D	CW2	W-2105252	0649	2
SMITH FRED L	COL	0-0403597	1060	1
SMITH FRED L	MAJ	0-2102973	0565	1
SMITH FREDERICK	MAJ	0-0237926	0262	3
SMITH FREDERICK	LTC	0-0314283	1058	1
SMITH FREDERICK	MAJ	0-0412246	1045	2
SMITH FREDERICK JR	1LT	0-0181464	1051	2
SMITH GENE W	MAJ	0-1338753	1164	1
SMITH GEORGE A	MAJ	0-1052971	0961	2
SMITH GEORGE A	LTC	0-1332649	1166	1
SMITH GEORGE A	1LT	0-2043269	0151	2
SMITH GEORGE A	2LT	0-4032436	1055	2
SMITH GEORGE A JR	CPT	0-1284037	0845	2
SMITH GEORGE B	COL	0-0263356	0267	3
SMITH GEORGE B	MAJ	0-2263600	1163	1
SMITH GEORGE C	LTC	0-0304747	0968	3
SMITH GEORGE C	1LT	0-0582425	0645	2
SMITH GEORGE C III	LTC	0-0955163	0368	1
SMITH GEORGE D	LTC	0-1581376	0861	1
SMITH GEORGE E	MAJ	0-1120410	0962	1
SMITH GEORGE E	CPT	0-1173783	0258	1
SMITH GEORGE E	LTC	0-1280219	0768	3
SMITH GEORGE F	MAJ	0-0476884	1046	2
SMITH GEORGE F JR	1LT	0-1317951	0867	1
SMITH GEORGE G	LTC	0-0506665	1265	3
SMITH GEORGE H	LTC	0-0464988	0854	1
SMITH GEORGE H	2LT	0-1018450	0844	2
SMITH GEORGE J	MAJ	0-1045256	1163	1
SMITH GEORGE L	MAJ	0-0119511	0855	3
SMITH GEORGE P	MAJ	0-1037722	0557	1
SMITH GEORGE R	CPT	0-0280078	0459	1
SMITH GEORGE R	CW2	W-2148990	0760	2
SMITH GEORGE W	CPT	0-0227268	0165	3
SMITH GEORGE Y	CPT	0-0400985	0346	2
SMITH GEORGIA H	MAJ	L-0603303	0363	1
SMITH GERALD L	LTC	0-1167227	0961	1
SMITH GERALD W	LTC	0-0470151	1262	2
SMITH GILBERT	WO1	W-2123132	0445	2
SMITH GLEN E	CPT	0-2006263	0261	1
SMITH GLEN L	MAJ	0-0396960	0168	3
SMITH GLENN A	LTC	0-0386948	0361	1
SMITH GLENN A	LTC	0-0902721	1157	2
SMITH GLENN E	MAJ	0-0222875	0754	3
SMITH GLENN H	COL	0-0293587	1065	3
SMITH GLENN M	LTC	0-0256057	0558	3
SMITH GORDON	COL	0-0187398	0947	2
SMITH GORDON E	CPT	0-5536750	0768	2
SMITH GORDON L	MAJ	0-1102058	0158	1
SMITH GORDON W	LTC	0-0378126	0765	3
SMITH GRANT H JR	LTC	0-0370697	0949	2
SMITH GRANVILLE	LTC	0-0206840	0154	2
SMITH GROVER C	MAJ	0-1032654	1060	1
SMITH GROVER C	2LT	0-1290322	1044	2
SMITH GROVER C JR	MAJ	0-2208627	0768	1
SMITH GUY R	CW3	W-2150552	1265	2
SMITH HAMMOND B	LTC	0-0501013	1068	3
SMITH HARDY	MAJ	0-0218985	0244	2

NAME	GRADE	SVC NO	DATE RET MO YR	RET CODE
SMITH HAROLD A	2LT	0-0468433	0344	2
SMITH HAROLD A	2LT	0-1176806	0545	2
SMITH HAROLD B SR	MAJ	0-2262180	0761	1
SMITH HAROLD C	LTC	0-0327848	0954	1
SMITH HAROLD C	LTC	0-0917336	0164	3
SMITH HAROLD C	2LT	0-1308281	0345	2
SMITH HAROLD F	MAJ	0-1117744	0966	3
SMITH HAROLD F	1LT	0-1328086	1046	2
SMITH HAROLD J	MAJ	0-1544544	0561	2
SMITH HAROLD L	1LT	0-2003139	0954	2
SMITH HAROLD T	MAJ	0-1173080	1163	1
SMITH HAROLD V	1LT	0-0498604	0752	1
SMITH HAROLD V	CW2	W-2209892	0763	1
SMITH HAROLD W	MAJ	0-0127402	1055	3
SMITH HAROLD W	LTC	0-0361814	0467	1
SMITH HAROLD W	MAJ	0-1105193	0968	3
SMITH HARRIS C	LTC	0-1638538	0762	1
SMITH HARRIS L	LTC	0-1044404	1165	1
SMITH HARRY	CPT	0-2046704	1046	2
SMITH HARRY B	CPT	0-0231469	0164	3
SMITH HARRY C	MAJ	0-0948737	0263	1
SMITH HARRY E	COL	0-0171203	1047	2
SMITH HARRY E	CPT	0-0488559	0248	1
SMITH HARRY E	CW2	W-2143015	1059	1
SMITH HARRY F	LTC	0-1056556	1166	1
SMITH HARRY F	CW2	W-2119029	0454	1
SMITH HARRY F	CW3	W-2205185	0267	1
SMITH HARRY G	MAJ	0-1309168	1060	1
SMITH HARRY K	MAJ	0-0248782	0665	3
SMITH HARRY O	COL	0-0330759	0468	3
SMITH HARRY P	COL	0-0345224	0555	1
SMITH HARRY R	COL	0-0423294	1054	1
SMITH HARRY W	COL	0-0172357	0353	3
SMITH HARRY W	LTC	0-0552312	0764	1
SMITH HARVEY A	LTC	0-0230533	0163	3
SMITH HARVEY A	LTC	0-0294924	0168	3
SMITH HARVEY J	CW2	W-2111322	0154	1
SMITH HARVEY L	CW3	W-2121079	0755	1
SMITH HARVEY W	LTC	0-1639664	0967	3
SMITH HAZELETT	LTC	0-1797373	1168	1
SMITH HEBARD P	MAJ	0-0272517	0967	3
SMITH HELEN O	MAJ	N-0737763	1262	1
SMITH HELEN S	CPT	N-0787429	1148	2
SMITH HENRY B	1LT	0-1171772	0245	2
SMITH HENRY C	MAJ	0-0306637	0567	3
SMITH HENRY C	LTC	0-0329357	1162	1
SMITH HENRY E	CPT	0-0234609	0757	3
SMITH HENRY G	LTC	0-0343373	0960	1
SMITH HENRY L	MAJ	0-1112984	0964	1
SMITH HENRY M	COL	0-0233408	1156	3
SMITH HENRY M	MAJ	0-1316965	0457	2
SMITH HENRY T	COL	0-0196001	0951	3
SMITH HENRY V	MAJ	0-1298972	1162	1
SMITH HERBERT A	M G	0-0189961	0761	3
SMITH HERBERT A JR	2LT	0-1798210	0844	2
SMITH HERBERT B	LTC	0-1280034	0148	2
SMITH HERBERT E	CPT	0-1299131	0347	2
SMITH HERBERT E JR	LTC	0-0399732	0646	2
SMITH HERBERT H	COL	0-0280596	0353	1
SMITH HERBERT J	MAJ	0-1646602	1066	1
SMITH HERBERT K	1LT	0-0371716	0146	2
SMITH HERBERT M	LTC	0-0241957	0444	2
SMITH HERBERT W	MAJ	0-0213999	1153	3
SMITH HERMAN	CPT	0-0975643	0154	2
SMITH HERMAN E	LTC	0-0141907	0652	3
SMITH HERMAN T	MAJ	0-1688524	0965	1
SMITH HEYBURN O	LTC	0-0228867	0863	3
SMITH HIRAM N	COL	0-0360645	0154	1
SMITH HOBART V	COL	0-1548145	1165	1
SMITH HOKE	CW3	W-2143532	1059	1
SMITH HOMER	CW2	W-2148193	1061	2
SMITH HOMER A	WO1	W-2107639	0648	1
SMITH HOMER L	LTC	0-0169120	0758	3
SMITH HOMER L	LTC	0-0500331	0157	1
SMITH HOMER W	CW3	W-2147919	1060	1

NAME	GRADE	SVC NO	DATE RET MO YR	RET CODE
SMITH HORACE R	LTC	0-1651191	1263	1
SMITH HOWARD A	LTC	0-0410504	1160	1
SMITH HOWARD A	LTC	0-1333555	0965	1
SMITH HOWARD B	MAJ	0-0407561	0960	1
SMITH HOWARD C	CPT	0-1326116	0448	2
SMITH HOWARD C	LTC	0-2033884	0868	1
SMITH HOWARD D	MAJ	0-1295954	0747	2
SMITH HOWARD D	MAJ	0-1878144	0166	1
SMITH HOWARD H	LTC	0-0198580	0562	3
SMITH HOWARD K	2LT	0-1299809	0445	2
SMITH HOWARD R JR	CPT	0-1318585	0859	1
SMITH HOWLAND C	LTC	0-0242098	1164	3
SMITH HOYT P	MAJ	0-0349510	0952	2
SMITH HUBERT F	CPT	0-0207413	0547	1
SMITH HUBERT M	LTC	0-2053970	0657	1
SMITH HUGH J	CW3	W-2139899	0967	1
SMITH HUGH P	LTC	0-0473796	0745	2
SMITH IRA W	MAJ	0-0478548	0642	1
SMITH ISAAC R	CPT	0-1695101	1043	2
SMITH ISAAC V	MAJ	0-1875476	1166	1
SMITH IVAN C	LTC	0-0234333	0346	2
SMITH IVAN J	MAJ	0-0344638	0750	2
SMITH J B	2LT	0-0557374	0750	2
SMITH J W	LTC	0-0451769	0160	1
SMITH J WINTER	CPT	0-0133525	0648	3
SMITH JACK	CPT	0-0970058	1060	1
SMITH JACK C	CW4	W-2146163	0666	1
SMITH JACK E	LTC	0-2040912	0960	1
SMITH JACK R	1LT	0-0441156	0750	2
SMITH JACKSON A	COL	0-0173781	0557	3
SMITH JAMES A JR	2LT	0-1825985	0750	2
SMITH JAMES B	LTC	0-0399187	0367	1
SMITH JAMES B	CPT	0-2202342	0866	1
SMITH JAMES C	LTC	0-0195976	0161	3
SMITH JAMES C	COL	0-0248289	0655	3
SMITH JAMES E	LTC	0-0198969	0955	3
SMITH JAMES E	CW4	W-2002242	0768	3
SMITH JAMES E	CW2	W-2209813	1060	1
SMITH JAMES F	COL	0-0295183	0961	1
SMITH JAMES F	CPT	0-0501587	0450	1
SMITH JAMES F	LTC	0-1010687	0464	1
SMITH JAMES F	2LT	0-1115795	0244	2
SMITH JAMES G	LTC	0-1106480	0766	1
SMITH JAMES G	LTC	0-1577861	0462	1
SMITH JAMES H	2LT	0-0445211	0545	2
SMITH JAMES H	CPT	0-1015218	0556	1
SMITH JAMES H	CPT	0-1299488	0446	2
SMITH JAMES H	MAJ	0-1554617	0161	1
SMITH JAMES H	LTC	0-1822472	0658	1
SMITH JAMES H JR	1LT	0-0450840	1044	2
SMITH JAMES J	MAJ	0-2295218	0866	1
SMITH JAMES L	LTC	0-0282233	0868	3
SMITH JAMES L	CPT	0-1320346	0547	2
SMITH JAMES L	CW3	W-2103453	1157	1
SMITH JAMES L	CW3	W-2146489	0765	1
SMITH JAMES L	CW3	W-2149129	0464	1
SMITH JAMES M	LTC	0-0973949	0768	1
SMITH JAMES N	LTC	0-0248546	0566	3
SMITH JAMES P	COL	0-0176961	0956	3
SMITH JAMES Q	MAJ	0-0504419	0850	2
SMITH JAMES R JR	LTC	0-0570300	0867	1
SMITH JAMES S	CW3	W-2152127	0262	1
SMITH JAMES S SR	CW2	W-2212406	1066	1
SMITH JAMES T	1LT	0-0417896	1046	2
SMITH JAMES T JR	MAJ	0-2263084	0665	1
SMITH JAMES W	1LT	0-1177983	0646	2
SMITH JAMES W	LTC	0-1592612	0968	1
SMITH JAMES W	CW4	W-2143536	0868	1
SMITH JASPER K	CPT	0-0337098	0263	3
SMITH JASPER K	LTC	0-1169744	0161	1
SMITH JAY C	LTC	0-1112449	0765	1
SMITH JAY D	LTC	0-0484980	1145	2
SMITH JENNINGS B	MAJ	0-1004523	0255	1
SMITH JERRY M JR	LTC	0-1314337	1062	1
SMITH JESSE	CW2	W-2109630	0347	1

NAME	GRADE	SVC NO	DATE RET MO YR	RET CODE
SMITH JESSE H	MAJ	0-1558905	0364	1
SMITH JESSE J	MAJ	0-1293330	0562	1
SMITH JESSE R	MAJ	0-1796538	0657	1
SMITH JOE W	LTC	0-1080241	0366	1
SMITH JOHN A	LTC	0-0284672	0366	3
SMITH JOHN A	1LT	0-1014076	0149	2
SMITH JOHN A	MAJ	0-1796171	0961	1
SMITH JOHN B	COL	0-0253622	0154	3
SMITH JOHN C	MAJ	0-0377213	0446	2
SMITH JOHN C	CPT	0-2017771	1161	1
SMITH JOHN D	CPT	0-0525460	0846	2
SMITH JOHN J	LTC	0-1306330	0163	1
SMITH JOHN D	CW3	W-2151709	0664	1
SMITH JOHN E	CPT	0-1323493	0547	2
SMITH JOHN F	COL	0-0289443	0660	1
SMITH JOHN F	2LT	0-5501512	0862	2
SMITH JOHN F	WO1	W-2148666	1162	1
SMITH JOHN H	COL	0-0298701	0264	1
SMITH JOHN H	CPT	0-1294737	0747	2
SMITH JOHN J	LTC	0-0501439	0954	1
SMITH JOHN J	MAJ	0-1923561	0865	1
SMITH JOHN JR	MAJ	0-1552389	0357	1
SMITH JOHN L	LTC	0-0451514	0457	1
SMITH JOHN L	LTC	0-1325032	0462	1
SMITH JOHN L JR	LTC	0-1172289	0167	1
SMITH JOHN M	COL	0-0225480	0550	3
SMITH JOHN P	MAJ	0-1297441	0562	1
SMITH JOHN P	CW3	W-2149308	0665	1
SMITH JOHN P JR	LTC	0-0235292	1162	3
SMITH JOHN R	MAJ	0-0971689	0565	1
SMITH JOHN R	LTC	0-1824522	0765	1
SMITH JOHN R	MAJ	0-1882115	0764	1
SMITH JOHN S	CPT	0-1798622	1162	1
SMITH JOHN S	CW2	W-2153010	0962	1
SMITH JOHN T	LTC	0-0343987	0247	2
SMITH JOHN T	CPT	0-1995530	0359	1
SMITH JOHN V	CW2	W-2129859	0447	1
SMITH JOHN W	CPT	0-1001464	0764	1
SMITH JOHN W	MAJ	0-1030518	0166	1
SMITH JOHN W	1LT	0-2000947	0554	1
SMITH JOHN W	CW3	W-2142900	0659	1
SMITH JOHN W JR	CW3	W-2210492	0768	1
SMITH JOHNNIE T	MAJ	0-0963717	0764	2
SMITH JOSEPH	COL	0-0320251	0256	3
SMITH JOSEPH A	LTC	0-0233196	0255	3
SMITH JOSEPH C	MAJ	0-1555138	0457	1
SMITH JOSEPH C	MAJ	0-2010917	1060	1
SMITH JOSEPH D JR	1LT	0-0281860	0543	2
SMITH JOSEPH D JR	MAJ	0-1299132	0462	1
SMITH JOSEPH H	LTC	0-0172519	0648	3
SMITH JOSEPH M JR	CPT	0-1116257	1148	2
SMITH JOSEPH R	WO1	W-2106051	0256	1
SMITH JOSEPH S	LTC	0-1329998	0863	1
SMITH JOSEPH W	1LT	0-0164574	0157	3
SMITH JOSEPH W	MAJ	0-0483748	0946	2
SMITH JOSEPH W	MAJ	0-1030093	1046	2
SMITH JOSEPH W	1LT	0-1050492	0845	2
SMITH JOSEPH W JR	CPT	0-0301436	0547	2
SMITH JOSHUA C II	LTC	0-1946172	1166	1
SMITH JOSHUA W	CPT	0-1548555	0351	1
SMITH JULE R	COL	0-0159158	1054	3
SMITH JULIAN B	LTC	0-0352469	0662	1
SMITH JUNIUS R	MAJ	0-0226485	1044	2
SMITH KARL J	WO1	W-2113448	0745	2
SMITH KATE M	MAJ	N-0734339	0354	2
SMITH KEMP H	COL	0-0221531	1061	3
SMITH KENNETH C	MAJ	0-4031368	1068	1
SMITH KENNETH E	MAJ	0-0295851	1167	3
SMITH KENNETH E	MAJ	0-1799669	0662	1
SMITH KENNETH H	CPT	0-2262107	1060	1
SMITH KENNETH M	CPT	0-0495919	1052	1
SMITH KENNETH M	CW3	W-2143582	1158	1
SMITH KENNETH T	LTC	0-0358132	0266	1
SMITH KENNETH T	COL	0-1583688	0968	1
SMITH KENNETH W	CPT	0-0310476	0147	2

NAME	GRADE	SVC NO	DATE RET MO YR	RET CODE
SMITH KIRK B	CW2	W-2150875	0461	1
SMITH LAROY A	MAJ	0-2102945	0464	1
SMITH LARUE W	LTC	0-1010851	0761	1
SMITH LAURENCE A	LTC	0-1062432	0962	1
SMITH LAURENCE A	WO1	W-2105975	0153	2
SMITH LAURENCE H	COL	0-0112011	0850	3
SMITH LAVELLE	CPT	0-1634340	0162	2
SMITH LAVERNE E	CW3	W-2147124	0663	1
SMITH LAVON E	MAJ	0-1166376	0960	1
SMITH LAWRENCE D	MAJ	0-4006800	0268	1
SMITH LAWRENCE E	MAJ	0-1294738	0662	1
SMITH LAWRENCE E	MAJ	0-1877147	1165	1
SMITH LAWRENCE S	LTC	0-0269304	0668	3
SMITH LAWRENCE T	MAJ	0-0179019	0644	2
SMITH LEE A	LTC	0-0168587	0958	3
SMITH LEE O	MAJ	0-1185253	0562	1
SMITH LEE R	CW3	W-2149760	0163	1
SMITH LEE R JR	MAJ	0-1688745	0666	1
SMITH LELAND	LTC	0-1307093	0456	2
SMITH LENDALL A	1LT	0-1049354	0845	2
SMITH LENWOOD	CPT	0-0965046	0660	1
SMITH LEO J	MAJ	0-0475772	0846	1
SMITH LEO M	1LT	0-0579279	0362	2
SMITH LEON C	LTC	0-0244011	0560	1
SMITH LEON E	CW2	W-2149160	0661	1
SMITH LEON F	MAJ	0-0239570	0163	3
SMITH LEONARD	CPT	0-0246726	1063	3
SMITH LEONARD A	MAJ	0-0256484	1053	3
SMITH LEONARD C	MAJ	0-0249535	0364	3
SMITH LEONARD H JR	COL	0-0253683	0556	1
SMITH LEONARD J	2LT	0-2263068	1151	2
SMITH LEONIDAS H	LTC	0-1554484	1165	3
SMITH LEROY C	WO1	W-2147535	0957	1
SMITH LEROY J	1LT	0-0967068	0861	2
SMITH LEROY N	CW3	W-2152327	0665	1
SMITH LEROY W	MAJ	0-1592071	0765	1
SMITH LEROY W	MAJ	0-2200013	0268	1
SMITH LESLIE A	MAJ	0-0120275	0350	3
SMITH LESLIE A	CPT	0-0485676	0861	1
SMITH LESLIE F	MAJ	0-0577260	0665	1
SMITH LESSLIE W	LTC	0-0226546	0463	3
SMITH LESTER O	MAJ	0-1334365	0962	1
SMITH LESTER H	LTC	0-0273639	0169	3
SMITH LEVI G	MAJ	0-2036030	1165	1
SMITH LEWIS A	CPT	0-0143432	1155	1
SMITH LEWIS A JR	MAJ	0-0254866	1054	3
SMITH LEWIS C	LTC	0-1039221	0865	3
SMITH LEWIS F	LTC	0-1316497	1062	1
SMITH LEWIS H	CW4	W-2004005	1268	3
SMITH LEWIS V	LTC	0-0260521	0159	1
SMITH LINTON B	MAJ	0-1184586	0462	1
SMITH LLOYD A	LTC	0-1584933	0662	1
SMITH LLOYD N	LTC	0-1102060	0265	1
SMITH LOUIS A	CPT	0-0116538	0349	3
SMITH LOUIS D	LTC	0-0250170	0364	3
SMITH LOUIS M JR	CPT	0-0385222	0745	2
SMITH LUCIEN L JR	CPT	0-1012487	1045	2
SMITH LUKE D	LTC	0-0236955	0960	3
SMITH LUTHER B	LTC	0-1646604	0467	1
SMITH LYLE E	2LT	0-1030802	0645	2
SMITH LYNN C	1LT	0-0499955	0847	1
SMITH M JANE	1LT	N-0756215	0546	1
SMITH MACK	CW3	RW-2210898	0968	1
SMITH MALCOLM J	MAJ	0-0247024	1060	1
SMITH MARCUS G	MAJ	0-0989591	0968	1
SMITH MARINER T	COL	0-0408907	1165	3
SMITH MARION P	LTC	0-0394601	0262	1
SMITH MARION R	MAJ	0-0253229	0464	3
SMITH MARK A	MAJ	0-2008797	0762	1
SMITH MARLO F	1LT	0-1299954	0846	2
SMITH MARVIN C	MAJ	0-0299250	0667	3
SMITH MARVIN C	MAJ	0-0445320	0146	2
SMITH MARVIN C	MAJ	0-1796369	0157	1
SMITH MARVIN D	LTC	0-1173463	0960	1
SMITH MARY E	MAJ	N-0726301	1267	3

NAME	GRADE	SVC NO	DATE RET MO YR	RET CODE
SMITH MARY T	1LT	N-0723379	0246	1
SMITH MAURICE	CW3	W-2154122	0463	1
SMITH MAURICE L	LTC	0-1574594	1064	1
SMITH MAX C	CW2	W-2111178	0368	1
SMITH MAXINE V	LTC	L-0302338	0663	1
SMITH MELVIN I	1LT	0-2026953	0867	3
SMITH MELVIN O	CW2	W-2208116	1266	1
SMITH MERLIN F	MAJ	0-0974120	0966	1
SMITH MERVYN H	LTC	0-0403734	0665	1
SMITH MILTON O	1LT	0-0525722	1045	2
SMITH MILTON R	CW2	W-2136317	0762	3
SMITH MORSE F	LTC	0-0230886	0964	3
SMITH MORTON	COL	0-0242411	1165	1
SMITH MURRY D	LTC	0-2028524	1068	1
SMITH MYRIAM M	LTC	L-0401685	0465	3
SMITH MYRON P	LTC	0-0364042	0859	1
SMITH NEAL D	MAJ	0-0242675	1059	3
SMITH NEDRA L	1LT	N-0729848	0348	1
SMITH NEELAND E	LTC	0-1341481	0967	1
SMITH NEWMANN B	MAJ	0-0214347	0763	3
SMITH NEWTON C	CPT	0-0225280	0950	3
SMITH NICHOLAS R	LTC	0-1554486	1068	1
SMITH NORMAN	MAJ	0-2021782	1168	1
SMITH NORMAN L	CPT	0-0969731	0764	1
SMITH NORMAN W	COL	0-0213878	0147	2
SMITH OCTAVE M	COL	0-0214414	0356	3
SMITH OLIVER M	LTC	0-1295786	0766	1
SMITH ORVILLE A	1LT	0-1016592	1145	2
SMITH OSCAR E	1LT	0-0157778	1048	1
SMITH OSCAR L JR	MAJ	0-1825069	0662	1
SMITH OSCAR T	MAJ	0-0113654	1054	3
SMITH OSCAR W	WO1	W-2102399	0744	2
SMITH OTIS	CW2	W-2144526	0658	1
SMITH OTIS L	LTC	0-1293492	1160	1
SMITH OTIS M	LTC	0-0451473	1065	1
SMITH OTTO E	CPT	0-1030418	0447	1
SMITH PATRICK M	CW3	W-2145588	1264	1
SMITH PAUL	CW3	W-2143105	0960	1
SMITH PAUL H	CW2	W-2120461	0550	1
SMITH PAUL I	MAJ	0-1937060	0267	1
SMITH PAUL M	LTC	0-0885426	1166	1
SMITH PAUL R	LTC	0-0374801	0461	1
SMITH PAUL R	MAJ	0-1108330	0846	2
SMITH PAUL W	MAJ	0-0404876	0546	2
SMITH PAUL W	MAJ	0-1103943	0460	1
SMITH PAULINE E	1LT	N-0767052	0246	1
SMITH PEARL M	CW2	W-2104825	0553	1
SMITH PERCIVAL W	MAJ	0-0231120	0964	3
SMITH PERRY L	CW4	W-2200200	0268	3
SMITH PETER	COL	0-0267426	0150	3
SMITH PHILIP	CPT	0-0453749	0945	2
SMITH PHILIP C	2LT	0-2010629	1045	2
SMITH PHILIP E	COL	0-0278533	0160	1
SMITH PHILIP F	LTC	0-1102061	1060	1
SMITH PHILIP G	CPT	0-1286561	1044	2
SMITH PHILLIP B	CPT	0-0970904	0268	1
SMITH PROSPER D	COL	0-0183939	1146	2
SMITH R ESTON	LTC	0-1288639	0961	1
SMITH RAE M	LTC	0-0888419	1160	1
SMITH RALPH F	LTC	0-0205489	0967	3
SMITH RALPH O	MAJ	0-0301648	0668	3
SMITH RALPH O	1LT	0-1825378	0246	2
SMITH RALPH T	MAJ	0-0181642	0561	3
SMITH RALPH V	CW2	W-2144542	0163	1
SMITH RALPH W	MAJ	0-2012694	1060	1
SMITH RALPH W	1LT	0-5228705	1268	2
SMITH RANDOLPH M	COL	0-0236246	0546	2
SMITH RAYMOND D	CW3	W-2211465	0968	1
SMITH RAYMOND E	LTC	0-1638541	0361	1
SMITH RAYMOND F	CW3	W-2207448	0967	1
SMITH RAYMOND G	MAJ	0-1341128	0167	1
SMITH RAYMOND H	LTC	0-0369037	0763	3
SMITH RAYMOND M	1LT	0-1018641	0846	2
SMITH RAYMOND O	COL	0-0212926	0554	2
SMITH RAYMOND T	LTC	0-0450361	0759	1

NAME	GRADE	SVC NO	DATE RET MO YR	RET CODE
SMITH REID K	LTC	0-0358362	0564	3
SMITH REUBEN W JR	COL	0-0144838	0545	2
SMITH REX A	LTC	0-1797549	0862	1
SMITH REX L	COL	0-0275070	1264	3
SMITH RHEA M	COL	0-0908608	0567	3
SMITH RICHARD A	LTC	0-0556801	0464	1
SMITH RICHARD C	LTC	0-0285333	0868	3
SMITH RICHARD C	1LT	0-0388454	0945	2
SMITH RICHARD E	CPT	0-1287960	0446	2
SMITH RICHARD E	MAJ	0-1596810	1159	1
SMITH RICHARD F JR	1LT	0-1299810	0845	2
SMITH RICHARD H	LTC	0-1100341	1162	1
SMITH RICHARD H	LTC	0-1640966	0266	1
SMITH RICHARD J	LTC	0-1039222	1167	1
SMITH RICHARD M	2LT	0-1177189	0444	2
SMITH RICHARD M	CW3	W-2209344	1068	1
SMITH RICHARD P	CW4	W-2127142	0656	1
SMITH RICHARD R	MAJ	0-1913265	1263	1
SMITH RICHARD W	LTC	0-0264084	0468	3
SMITH RICHARD W	2LT	0-1926933	0358	2
SMITH RICHARD W	LTC	0-2021053	0368	1
SMITH ROBERT	CPT	0-1290830	0647	2
SMITH ROBERT A	LTC	0-0405509	0667	1
SMITH ROBERT A	2LT	0-1180341	0144	2
SMITH ROBERT A	MAJ	0-1644107	0759	1
SMITH ROBERT B	CPT	0-0493922	1044	2
SMITH ROBERT B	2LT	0-1014741	0443	2
SMITH ROBERT C	LTC	0-0113066	0755	3
SMITH ROBERT C	LTC	0-1057289	0166	1
SMITH ROBERT C	MAJ	0-1168924	1057	2
SMITH ROBERT C	CPT	0-1591123	0552	2
SMITH ROBERT C JR	1LT	0-0521838	1145	2
SMITH ROBERT D	MAJ	0-0757095	0863	1
SMITH ROBERT D JR	CPT	0-0401658	0245	2
SMITH ROBERT E	CW3	W-2143456	0564	1
SMITH ROBERT G	CPT	0-1055692	0162	1
SMITH ROBERT H	CPT	0-0463944	0747	2
SMITH ROBERT H	MAJ	0-1062438	0365	1
SMITH ROBERT H	CPT	0-2015385	1159	1
SMITH ROBERT I	LTC	0-1040331	0762	1
SMITH ROBERT I	LTC	0-1287961	0264	1
SMITH ROBERT I	CW3	W-2151124	0563	1
SMITH ROBERT L	LTC	0-0320625	0866	3
SMITH ROBERT L	LTC	0-0421852	0266	1
SMITH ROBERT L	CPT	0-0448148	1147	1
SMITH ROBERT L	MAJ	0-0985653	1163	1
SMITH ROBERT L	LTC	0-1322278	1166	1
SMITH ROBERT L	2LT	0-4017333	0355	2
SMITH ROBERT M	MAJ	0-0418980	0247	2
SMITH ROBERT M	MAJ	0-0477542	0453	2
SMITH ROBERT P	CPT	0-1061265	0546	2
SMITH ROBERT R	MAJ	0-1876401	0164	1
SMITH ROBERT S	MAJ	0-1310946	1046	2
SMITH ROBERT S	MAJ	0-2018782	0964	1
SMITH ROBERT V	CPT	0-1319144	0346	2
SMITH ROBERT W	COL	0-0202616	0262	3
SMITH ROBERT W	MAJ	0-1018151	0461	1
SMITH ROBERT W	CPT	0-1285651	0546	2
SMITH ROBERT W	LTC	0-1638543	1061	1
SMITH ROBERT W JR	COL	0-0287036	1066	3
SMITH RODERICK K	CPT	0-0451418	0648	2
SMITH RODMAN JR	1LT	0-1316706	0345	2
SMITH ROGER F	LTC	0-0492519	0455	1
SMITH ROGER N	MAJ	0-1313737	0861	1
SMITH ROGER W	CPT	0-1311697	0559	1
SMITH ROLAND L	LTC	0-0177966	1160	3
SMITH ROLLIN H	LTC	0-0462700	1262	3
SMITH RONALD D	MAJ	0-2210467	0665	1
SMITH RONALD E	LTC	0-0257177	0244	2
SMITH RONALD F	MAJ	0-0477209	0857	1
SMITH RONALD F	MAJ	0-1290677	0168	1
SMITH RONALD O	LTC	0-0223217	0656	3
SMITH RONALD V	CW2	W-2147961	0457	1
SMITH ROSWALD F	MAJ	0-0103661	1144	2
SMITH ROY A	COL	0-0321441	0766	3

NAME	GRADE	SVC NO	DATE RET MO YR	RET CODE
SMITH ROY B	LTC	0-0257093	0265	1
SMITH ROY B	CPT	0-1543441	0758	1
SMITH ROY H JR	CPT	0-1878062	0165	1
SMITH ROY J	LTC	0-1248405	0859	1
SMITH ROY L	LTC	0-0120339	0345	2
SMITH ROY W	LTC	0-0551554	1067	2
SMITH RUFUS S	WO1	W-2147143	0453	2
SMITH RULON F	COL	0-0322429	0860	3
SMITH RUSSELL	MAJ	0-0450362	1045	2
SMITH RUSSELL C	LTC	0-0360577	0346	2
SMITH RUTH F	1LT	N-0737010	0246	1
SMITH SAM D	MAJ	0-1179713	0760	1
SMITH SAMUEL A	COL	0-0145789	0450	2
SMITH SAMUEL F	1LT	0-0422736	0246	2
SMITH SAMUEL G	LTC	0-0475846	0555	1
SMITH SAMUEL H	MAJ	0-1300099	0955	1
SMITH SAMUEL H	LTC	0-1536249	0464	1
SMITH SAMUEL L	CPT	0-0197758	0960	3
SMITH SAMUEL L	MAJ	0-0249077	0965	3
SMITH SAMUEL L	COL	0-0328065	0247	1
SMITH SAMUEL P	LTC	0-1550703	0957	1
SMITH SCHUYLER P	1LT	0-1913927	0539	1
SMITH SCOTT C	MAJ	0-0209685	0355	3
SMITH SHERMAN W	MAJ	0-1174035	1060	1
SMITH SHERROD S	1LT	0-1545575	0146	2
SMITH SHERWOOD R	COL	0-0439997	0560	3
SMITH SIDNEY C JR	MAJ	0-0959547	0663	1
SMITH SIDNEY F	CW4	W-2122968	0359	1
SMITH SIDNEY F	LTC	0-1555297	1164	1
SMITH SILAS	MAJ	0-1032783	0261	1
SMITH SILAS R	LTC	0-0169156	0957	3
SMITH SOMERS S	LTC	0-0348594	0463	3
SMITH SPENCER D	MAJ	0-1101221	0255	1
SMITH STANFORD	1LT	0-1924609	0155	2
SMITH STANHOPE C	COL	0-0211351	0155	3
SMITH STANLEY	LTC	0-0145681	0851	1
SMITH STEVE S	WO1	W-2109109	0744	2
SMITH STEWARD H	CPT	0-1686013	0645	2
SMITH STUART E	LTC	0-0266397	0263	3
SMITH STUART J	CW3	W-2106983	1165	3
SMITH STUART W	LTC	0-0207122	0457	1
SMITH SUMNER F	COL	0-0206735	0161	3
SMITH SYDNEY	MAJ	0-1108331	1163	1
SMITH T J	MAJ	0-4006258	0168	1
SMITH TAVIS	MAJ	0-1634344	0263	2
SMITH TAYLOR	LTC	0-0163734	0753	2
SMITH TED J	LTC	0-1826304	0565	1
SMITH TEMPLE C	LTC	0-1584939	0961	1
SMITH THEODORE T	LTC	0-1945713	0565	3
SMITH THEODORE W	MAJ	0-0499573	1051	2
SMITH THOMAS A	LTC	0-0477684	0255	1
SMITH THOMAS B	CPT	0-1321758	0347	2
SMITH THOMAS C	MAJ	0-0524318	0565	3
SMITH THOMAS C	MAJ	0-4007079	0267	1
SMITH THOMAS D JR	MAJ	0-0329533	0561	1
SMITH THOMAS F	MAJ	0-1550057	1055	1
SMITH THOMAS F	MAJ	0-2033053	0461	1
SMITH THOMAS J	MAJ	0-0964439	1060	1
SMITH THOMAS J	CW3	W-2149027	0365	1
SMITH THOMAS P	CPT	0-0453030	0845	2
SMITH THOMAS T	COL	0-0277897	0955	1
SMITH THOMAS W E	MAJ	0-2262204	0263	1
SMITH THURMOND S	MAJ	0-0174112	0960	3
SMITH TREMAINE F	LTC	0-1145000	1262	1
SMITH TRUEITT B	LTC	0-1062299	1167	1
SMITH TUTTLE F	COL	0-0238707	0360	1
SMITH U S	2LT	0-1015446	1043	2
SMITH UEL	CW2	W-2143826	0559	1
SMITH ULYSSES G	MAJ	0-1176515	1162	1
SMITH VANNAS C	MAJ	0-1997782	0561	1
SMITH VAUGHN T	CPT	0-1109674	0453	2
SMITH VERNON C	CW2	W-2149655	1261	1
SMITH VICTOR H	LTC	0-0129711	0353	3
SMITH VINSON S	LTC	0-2035982	0461	1
SMITH VIRGIL F	CPT	0-1300100	1145	2

NAME	GRADE	SVC NO	DATE RET MO YR	RET CODE
SMITH VIRGINIA M	CPT	0-0751185	[illegible]	1
SMITH VIVIAN G	COL	0-0254646	0867	3
SMITH W EUGENE	COL	0-0328433	[illegible]	2
SMITH WARDELL F	COL	0-0397209	1155	2
SMITH WALLACE J	CW4	W-2111461	0564	1
SMITH WALLACE P	LTC	0-0234799	0265	3
SMITH WALTER A	LTC	0-1644942	0264	3
SMITH WALTER B	COL	0-0907732	0762	3
SMITH WALTER E	MAJ	0-0210636	0457	3
SMITH WALTER F	MAJ	0-1996349	0261	1
SMITH WALTER G	MAJ	0-0364360	1045	2
SMITH WALTER H	MAJ	0-0281926	1066	3
SMITH WALTER H	LTC	0-0911402	0864	3
SMITH WALTER H	MAJ	0-1315981	0764	1
SMITH WALTER H	LTC	0-1825575	0764	1
SMITH WALTER K	MAJ	0-0178008	0362	1
SMITH WALTER S	CW3	W-2208703	0568	1
SMITH WALTER W	MAJ	0-0493960	0447	1
SMITH WALTER W	LTC	0-0498493	0455	1
SMITH WALTER W	MAJ	0-1646605	0161	1
SMITH WALTON	COL	0-0210101	0646	2
SMITH WARREN D	CW3	W-2152358	0666	1
SMITH WARREN E	1LT	0-1014954	1047	2
SMITH WARREN F	CW3	W-2145012	1059	1
SMITH WARREN M	CW2	W-2148008	1060	1
SMITH WARREN O	LTC	0-1170200	0162	1
SMITH WARREN W	1LT	0-1795670	1161	2
SMITH WAYNE B	LTC	0-1167639	0967	2
SMITH WAYNE D	LTC	0-0395711	0761	1
SMITH WAYNE H	CPT	0-1108332	0847	2
SMITH WAYNE W	LTC	0-0191999	0462	3
SMITH WELDON A	CPT	0-0971967	0361	1
SMITH WELDON D	MAJ	0-0133662	0648	3
SMITH WENFRED W	CPT	0-1683438	0858	1
SMITH WESLEY C	1LT	0-0240432	0545	2
SMITH WILBERT E	MAJ	0-2036703	0764	1
SMITH WILBUR L	CW2	W-2152867	0360	1
SMITH WILLARD A	1LT	0-1112454	0346	2
SMITH WILLARD F	COL	0-0338465	0854	1
SMITH WILLIAM	2LT	0-1583883	1044	2
SMITH WILLIAM A	CPT	0-0450912	1145	2
SMITH WILLIAM A	1LT	0-0476478	0445	2
SMITH WILLIAM B	CPT	0-0193085	0463	3
SMITH WILLIAM B	LTC	0-0287188	0755	2
SMITH WILLIAM C	COL	0-0244543	1160	3
SMITH WILLIAM C	LTC	0-1012121	0466	1
SMITH WILLIAM C	CW2	W-3100551	1068	1
SMITH WILLIAM D	1LT	0-1287426	1044	2
SMITH WILLIAM D	CW3	W-2146279	1059	1
SMITH WILLIAM E	CPT	0-0245508	0150	3
SMITH WILLIAM E	MAJ	0-1112989	0462	1
SMITH WILLIAM E	LTC	0-1303963	1060	1
SMITH WILLIAM E JR	MAJ	0-0965187	0961	1
SMITH WILLIAM F	LTC	0-0107303	0648	3
SMITH WILLIAM F	LTC	0-0240965	0266	3
SMITH WILLIAM F	CPT	0-0954749	0859	1
SMITH WILLIAM F JR	CPT	0-1110263	0350	2
SMITH WILLIAM G	CPT	0-0331585	0849	3
SMITH WILLIAM H	1LT	0-0113350	0455	3
SMITH WILLIAM H	COL	0-0250274	1264	3
SMITH WILLIAM H	CPT	0-0404292	0346	2
SMITH WILLIAM H	MAJ	0-0490862	0155	1
SMITH WILLIAM H	1LT	0-1043228	0744	2
SMITH WILLIAM H	CPT	0-2055870	0453	2
SMITH WILLIAM H JR	LTC	0-0300725	0665	3
SMITH WILLIAM H JR	LTC	0-0378776	0860	1
SMITH WILLIAM H JR	LTC	0-1579144	1162	1
SMITH WILLIAM J	COL	0-0264377	1163	1
SMITH WILLIAM J	1LT	0-0423766	0944	2
SMITH WILLIAM J	1LT	0-1286198	0345	2
SMITH WILLIAM J	1LT	0-1308877	0545	2
SMITH WILLIAM J	LTC	0-1544249	0466	1
SMITH WILLIAM J	CW2	W-2144776	0555	1
SMITH WILLIAM J SR	MAJ	0-0179344	0648	3
SMITH WILLIAM L	1LT	0-1297443	0265	1

NAME	GRADE	SVC NO	DATE RET MO YR	RET CODE
SMITH WILLIAM L	1LT	0-1342214	0749	2
SMITH WILLIAM M	LTC	0-0105400	0745	2
SMITH WILLIAM M	CPT	0-0336553	1045	2
SMITH WILLIAM M	1LT	0-0528929	0146	2
SMITH WILLIAM M	MAJ	0-2283918	0863	1
SMITH WILLIAM O	CW4	W-2144519	0868	1
SMITH WILLIAM O	CW2	W-2147408	0261	1
SMITH WILLIAM P	LTC	0-0474813	1167	3
SMITH WILLIAM Q	LTC	0-1044107	0961	1
SMITH WILLIAM R	MAJ	0-0402334	1044	2
SMITH WILLIAM R	MAJ	0-1296312	0661	1
SMITH WILLIAM T	1LT	0-1292773	0645	2
SMITH WILLIAM T	MAJ	0-1576671	1264	1
SMITH WILLIAM V	MAJ	0-0175663	1161	1
SMITH WILLIAM W	MAJ	0-0222850	1052	3
SMITH WILLIAM W	COL	0-0235789	1065	3
SMITH WILLIE E	MAJ	0-2040992	0363	1
SMITH WILLIE JR	LTC	0-1872512	0968	1
SMITH WILMOT O	LTC	0-0264496	0364	3
SMITH WILSON G	MAJ	0-1032603	0559	1
SMITH WINFIELD W	COL	0-0113527	0744	2
SMITH WINT	B G	0-0123028	1152	3
SMITH WINTHROP G	MAJ	0-0273370	1267	3
SMITH WOODROW H	CW2	W-2142201	0459	1
SMITH WORTHINGTO	COL	0-0231135	0356	3
SMITH WORTHINGTO	LTC	0-1292411	0567	3
SMITH YEVE L	CW3	W-2152402	1264	1
SMITHER GERALD S	MAJ	0-1107139	0961	1
SMITHERMAN BOB	MAJ	0-1182964	0161	1
SMITHERMAN JOHN L	MAJ	0-1823226	0962	1
SMITHERS CHARLES O	CPT	0-0201486	1153	3
SMITHERS LOUIS F	MAJ	0-0165034	0551	3
SMITHERS WILLIAM B	COL	0-0266462	0657	3
SMITHEY CECIL C	1LT	0-1298775	0245	2
SMITHEY THADDEUS R	LTC	0-1104400	0258	1
SMITHGALL HARRY M	LTC	0-0236019	1160	3
SMITHLING JOHN F	CW4	W-2133218	1160	1
SMITHSON ALBERT L JR	LTC	0-0403367	0960	1
SMITHSON ERNEST	CW3	W-2209627	1067	1
SMITHWICK VINCENT J	MAJ	0-1549846	0257	1
SMITHYMAN WILLIAM E	LTC	0-1322845	1067	1
SMITZES GEORGE S	CPT	0-0189322	0852	3
SMOAK ALVA G	MAJ	0-0969415	C966	1
SMOAK LAURIE C JR	CPT	0-0534223	0947	2
SMOAK LILLIAN	MAJ	N-0764476	0567	1
SMOAK TILLMAN T	COL	0-0282504	0368	3
SMOCK LYMAN	MAJ	0-0166649	0647	1
SMOCK WALTER W	CPT	0-0538582	0946	2
SMOKLER JACK	CPT	0-0521522	0845	2
SMOLARK JOHN A	LTC	0-0333360	0167	3
SMOLEN GEORGE	1LT	0-1557673	0146	2
SMOLEN JOHN	CPT	0-0490668	0146	1
SMOLEN JOSEPH	MAJ	0-1300546	0464	1
SMOLEN SEYMOUR S	1LT	0-1012407	0645	2
SMOLENS NATHAN M	COL	0-0314274	0265	3
SMOLIK VINCENT W	CPT	0-1685692	1058	2
SMOLIN EDWIN M	2LT	0-0554880	0346	2
SMOLKA CLARENCE	MAJ	0-0315467	0943	2
SMOLLAN DAVID	CPT	0-0263192	1265	3
SMOLLEN JOHN P	LTC	0-1176198	0667	2
SMOLLON JOHN E	1LT	0-1052972	0848	2
SMOOT ARTHUR F	LTC	0-1306010	0665	1
SMOOT CHARLES H	LTC	0-1636665	0766	1
SMOOT GEORGE W	COL	0-0292123	0667	1
SMOOT JAMES C	COL	0-0102166	0960	3
SMOOT MARVIN L	LTC	0-0346462	1060	1
SMOOT RICHARD H	LTC	0-0294268	1062	1
SMOOT WENDELL M JR	CPT	0-0465272	1145	2
SMOOT WESLEY A	CW2	W-2112561	0461	2
SMOTHERS JOHN W	LTC	0-0371583	0760	1
SMOTHERS ODELL W	LTC	0-0407418	0363	1
SMOUSE JOHN P	LTC	0-0279153	0966	3
SMOUT ETHAN P	1LT	0-1296925	104N	2
SMRCEK MARY	CPT	N-0775905	0959	2
SMRSTIK GEORGE E	CPT	0-1319145	0547	2

NAME	GRADE	SVC NO	DATE RET MO YR	RET CODE
SMUCK JOHN C	COL	0-0141251	0257	3
SMUIN FRANK O	LTC	0-0283923	0468	3
SMULLEN WILLARD C	MAJ	0-0461536	0246	2
SMULLIN THOMAS E	LTC	0-0133611	0760	3
SMULLIN THOMAS E JR	MAJ	0-2021113	0964	1
SMYERS BERTRAND H JR	LTC	0-0172008	0759	3
SMYLE RUSSELL C	LTC	0-1796410	0667	1
SMYRE CARTER JR	CW3	W-2205576	0366	1
SMYRE MELFORD A	CPT	0-0453226	1045	2
SMYTH HARRY	COL	0-0205091	0154	3
SMYTH JOSEPH J	2LT	0-2015705	0655	1
SMYTH LEON L	1LT	0-0180414	0158	3
SMYTHE DANNY H	LTC	0-1825831	1063	1
SMYTHE FRANCIS	LTC	0-1117532	1167	1
SMYTHE MARCUS H JR	CPT	0-0454166	0645	2
SMYTHE SAMUEL S	CW3	W-2116328	0159	1
SNAER BERNARD A	LTC	0-0287600	1168	3
SNAJCZUK STEPHEN R	1LT	0-1283509	1043	2
SNAPP HERBERT L	LTC	0-0265684	0162	3
SNAPP LLOYD E	LTC	0-0450478	1157	1
SNAPP REGINALD E	2LT	0-0552595	0346	2
SNAVELY EARL S R	CPT	0-0510878	0147	1
SNAVELY GUY E JR	LTC	0-0246267	0766	3
SNAVELY HARRY L	LTC	0-0341099	0663	1
SNEAD GORDON P	CW3	W-2148382	0359	1
SNEAD ROSWELL P	LTC	0-0265377	0868	3
SNEAD SAM JR	CPT	0-0441083	0947	2
SNEAD YOUNGER F	LTC	0-0274680	1266	3
SNEAR WILLIAM B	COL	0-0416107	1068	1
SNEATH VERYL L	MAJ	0-1540870	0865	1
SNECINSKI JOSEPH F	1LT	0-0369178	0345	2
SNEDDEN HARRY O	CW3	0-0964191	0458	1
SNEDDON JAMES W	CPT	0-1582153	0657	1
SNEDEKER GEORGE	LTC	0-1031760	0663	1
SNEDEKER RUSSELL S	MAJ	0-1641813	0261	1
SNEE THOMAS J	LTC	0-0253297	0567	3
SNEE THOMAS R	COL	0-0316172	1164	1
SNEED ARTHUR F	CPT	0-1284778	0657	1
SNEED CALVIN JR	CPT	0-5405230	1168	1
SNEED HENRY P	MAJ	0-0108253	0545	1
SNEED REPSIE J	CW3	W-2148361	0961	1
SNEED RICHARD H	MAJ	0-0364076	0558	1
SNEED THEO W	LTC	0-0235197	1265	3
SNEIDER MILTON J	CPT	0-0521717	0845	2
SNELL ARTHUR T	LTC	0-1100343	0656	1
SNELL FRANK L	COL	0-0208972	1059	1
SNELL GILBERT P	LTC	0-0293940	0959	3
SNELL IVAN B	LTC	0-0439212	0853	1
SNELL JAY R	2LT	0-2007428	0156	2
SNELL JOHN R	CPT	0-0222229	0363	3
SNELL LLOYD L	CW2	W-2141449	0760	1
SNELL MAYNARD J	LTC	0-1535297	0462	1
SNELL WALTER M	MAJ	0-1544711	1058	1
SNELLING DAVID B	MAJ	0-0263294	0246	2
SNELLING SIDNEY B	CPT	0-2033980	0262	1
SNELLINGS WILLIAM R	MAJ	0-0415355	0247	2
SNELLMAN WILLIAM F	LTC	0-0299968	1066	3
SNELSON SYDNEY E	MAJ	0-1641814	0857	1
SNEPENGER JOE	CPT	0-1307867	1045	2
SNETHEN ROLLIN K	LTC	0-0272720	1068	3
SNIDER BYRON R	1LT	0-1047335	0745	2
SNIDER EDWIN T	1LT	0-2046516	0350	1
SNIDER ELLWOOD H	COL	0-0207225	0358	3
SNIDER EMORY A SR	MAJ	0-2017138	0462	1
SNIDER JOHN F	COL	0-0188468	0454	1
SNIDER JOHN W	1LT	0-1168086	1145	2
SNIDER JOSEPH O	CW3	W-2150224	0963	1
SNIDER RAYMOND L	MAJ	0-0888923	0157	1
SNIDER RICHARD	CPT	0-1305332	0746	2
SNIDER ROBERT E	LTC	0-1109020	0367	1
SNIDER ROBERT E	MAJ	0-2017606	0164	1
SNIDER ROSS F	MAJ	0-0475300	0853	1
SNIDER WILLIAM A	LTC	0-0544447	1266	1
SNIDER WILLIAM A	CPT	0-1015500	0148	2
SNIDOW LEE C	MAJ	0-2263385	1262	1

NAME	GRADE	SVC NO	DATE RET MO YR	RET CODE
SNIFFIN EDWARD H	1LT	0-1298146	0546	2
SNIPES CHARLIE L	CW3	W-2147109	1163	1
SNITJEN WAYNE J	1LT	0-1053817	0745	2
SNIZER RICHARD G	1LT	0-1648698	0847	2
SNODDY WILLIAM H	MAJ	0-0157000	1054	3
SNODGRASS ANSEL N	MAJ	0-0911800	0246	2
SNODGRASS EDWARD E	LTC	0-0277950	0853	2
SNODGRASS FRANCIS E	MAJ	0-1308195	C966	3
SNODGRASS GEORGE F	COL	0-0273537	0266	3
SNODGRASS HARVEY A	CW3	W-2149904	0165	1
SNODGRASS JOHN M	CW3	W-2151345	1165	1
SNODGRASS LEROY A	CW4	W-2114471	0559	1
SNODGRASS NORMAN K	LTC	0-0405088	0868	3
SNODGRASS ORIS R	LTC	0-0545771	0364	1
SNODGRASS REA L	LTC	0-1577868	0167	3
SNODGRASS RICHARD G	LTC	0-1297975	1060	1
SNODGRASS ROBERT B	LTC	0-1111367	1163	1
SNODGRASS ROGER G	MAJ	0-1584945	1162	1
SNODGRASS WALTER H	MAJ	0-0239789	0760	3
SNODGRASS WALTER M	WO1	W-2121187	0944	2
SNODGRASS WARREN M	LTC	0-1016328	0264	1
SNOOK GLENN D	LTC	0-1316344	0266	1
SNOOK HOWARD P	LTC	0-1546596	0867	1
SNOOK ORRIE V	LTC	0-0278193	0357	2
SNOOK RUSSELL A	COL	0-0267119	0960	3
SNORKOWSKI STEPHEN M	MAJ	0-1048194	0854	1
SNOVER JAMES A	CW3	W-2145213	0963	1
SNOW ABNER L	1LT	0-1290679	0559	1
SNOW AETHRA C	MAJ	0-1038850	1059	1
SNOW ARTHUR W	COL	0-0173907	0751	3
SNOW ASBURY D	COL	0-0291008	0163	1
SNOW BERNARD D	CPT	0-0291156	0147	2
SNOW CHESTER R	CW2	W-2146030	0859	1
SNOW EDITH E	LTC	N-0798927	0765	1
SNOW EDWARD C	COL	0-0214151	0260	3
SNOW ERNEST C	COL	0-1575567	0868	1
SNOW FRANCIS H	CW4	RW-2115964	0861	1
SNOW FRANK	CPT	0-2046339	0355	1
SNOW FRED E	1LT	0-1322814	0745	2
SNOW GALEN	LTC	0-0127070	0755	3
SNOW GEORGE N	CPT	0-0481268	0346	1
SNOW GEORGE W	MAJ	0-0173297	0-51	3
SNOW JACK R	LTC	0-0217896	0246	2
SNOW JAMES W	CPT	0-2020768	1160	2
SNOW JOHN R	LTC	0-0452722	0956	1
SNOW MICHAEL	MAJ	0-1295955	1159	1
SNOW PARKER O	LTC	0-0376194	0363	1
SNOW R E	CPT	0-1691775	0558	1
SNOW RAYMOND	CW2	W-2147921	1157	1
SNOW ROBERT A	LTC	0-0265237	0364	3
SNOW ROGER W JR	LTC	0-0380703	0859	1
SNOW THOMAS R JR	LTC	0-1175321	0962	1
SNOWDEN CHARLES R	MAJ	0-0113351	0952	3
SNOWDEN FRANK M	COL	0-0210148	0648	3
SNOWDEN GLADYS B	MAJ	N-0724295	0763	1
SNOWDEN JAMES C	CW3	W-2113264	0760	1
SNOWDEN JOSEPHINE	MAJ	N-2298647	0467	1
SNOWDEN OBED L	LTC	0-0304758	1168	3
SNOWDER HAROLD W	MAJ	0-1318099	0163	1
SNOZEK JOHN E	MAJ	0-1117026	0557	1
SNURKOWSKI CHARLES V	LTC	0-0268055	0256	3
SNYDER A J	CW2	W-2142113	1056	1
SNYDER ALBERT F	MAJ	0-0345942	1150	2
SNYDER ALLEN L JR	LTC	0-2012535	0266	1
SNYDER ARTHUR B	1LT	0-0149595	1049	3
SNYDER ARTHUR G	LTC	0-0445953	1047	2
SNYDER ARTHUR J	CW3	W-2148991	0664	1
SNYDER BERNARD A	CW3	W-2151205	0863	1
SNYDER BURR M	LTC	0-0435723	1048	1
SNYDER CATHERINE	1LT	N-0737851	1151	2
SNYDER CEDRICK V	1LT	0-1295099	0145	2
SNYDER CHARLES H	CPT	0-0278122	1256	3
SNYDER CHARLES T	MAJ	0-0256584	1044	2
SNYDER CHESTER A JR	CPT	0-1584946	0645	2
SNYDER CHESTER O	CW2	W-2144994	0660	1

NAME	GRADE	SVC NO	DATE RET MO YR	RET CODE
SNYDER CLAUDE F	LTC	0-0490839	0356	1
SNYDER DONALD J	CW3	RW-2209974	0966	1
SNYDER DONALD L	1LT	0-0371097	1044	2
SNYDER DRENNEN	1LT	0-2048784	0945	2
SNYDER EARLE D	COL	0-0174503	0349	3
SNYDER EDGAR M	MAJ	0-2049401	0157	1
SNYDER EDWARD E	CW4	W-2001843	1065	1
SNYDER EDWARD N	LTC	0-1294380	0657	1
SNYDER EDWIN H	MAJ	0-1113453	0855	2
SNYDER ERNEST C	MAJ	0-0574596	1163	2
SNYDER ERNEST C	MAJ	0-1001245	0759	1
SNYDER EUGENE B	CW3	W-2145659	0566	1
SNYDER EUGENE H	MAJ	0-1825278	0161	1
SNYDER FLOYD T	MAJ	0-0912419	0346	2
SNYDER FRANK J	LTC	0-1168925	0664	1
SNYDER FRED D	CW2	W-3440088	1068	1
SNYDER FREDERICK	MAJ	0-1542026	0658	1
SNYDER GARREL O	LTC	0-0282825	0662	3
SNYDER GEORGE G	CPT	0-1575568	0246	2
SNYDER GERALD D	LTC	0-2263475	0568	1
SNYDER GLEN E	MAJ	0-0229723	0458	3
SNYDER HAROLD H	COL	0-0508449	0865	3
SNYDER HAROLD R	LTC	0-1171777	1262	1
SNYDER HERBERT	COL	0-0127580	1055	3
SNYDER HERBERT C	LTC	0-0282779	0868	3
SNYDER HERBERT L	MAJ	0-0982858	1060	1
SNYDER HOLLIS F	MAJ	0-1340706	1161	2
SNYDER HUBERT E	COL	0-0193810	0648	3
SNYDER INEZ V	LTC	L-0115629	0147	2
SNYDER JACK A	LTC	0-1303789	0761	1
SNYDER JACQUES F	LTC	0-1691903	1067	1
SNYDER JAMES B	LTC	0-0240966	0265	3
SNYDER JAMES C SR	1LT	0-1951547	0549	2
SNYDER JAMES F	COL	0-0196604	0463	3
SNYDER JAMES L	CPT	0-1894986	0745	2
SNYDER JAMES M	MAJ	0-0258237	1267	3
SNYDER JAMES W JR	CW3	W-2205508	0468	1
SNYDER JESS W	MAJ	0-0167936	0446	2
SNYDER JOHN B	CW3	W-2150192	0263	1
SNYDER JOHN J	COL	0-1165958	0768	1
SNYDER JOHN T JR	CW3	W-2148886	0663	1
SNYDER JOHN W	COL	0-0103058	0655	3
SNYDER JOHN W	MAJ	0-0974109	1263	1
SNYDER JOSEPH L	1LT	0-0482252	0157	1
SNYDER JOSEPH V	MAJ	0-1296107	0657	1
SNYDER JOSEPH W	1LT	0-0451930	0945	2
SNYDER KATHRYNE R	MAJ	N-0774655	0567	1
SNYDER KENNETH R	MAJ	0-1580345	0268	3
SNYDER LAWRENCE	MAJ	0-1797551	0258	1
SNYDER LAWRENCE M	CW3	W-3150542	1266	1
SNYDER LEROY T	LTC	0-0477828	0865	1
SNYDER LYLE O	LTC	0-0493998	0166	3
SNYDER MAXWELL C	M G	0-0242582	0860	3
SNYDER MELVIN C	COL	0-0253968	1058	3
SNYDER MELVIN L	1LT	0-1167642	0347	1
SNYDER MERLE B	LTC	0-0239597	1263	3
SNYDER MERVIN E	CW2	W-2147733	1056	2
SNYDER MILDRED L	CPT	N-0733816	0946	1
SNYDER MILO O	LTC	0-0100041	0648	3
SNYDER MILTON A	COL	0-0147436	0647	2
SNYDER MORRIS L	LTC	0-0321436	0768	3
SNYDER NATHAN C	COL	0-0229534	1063	3
SNYDER NEIL N	LTC	0-0171204	1049	3
SNYDER NELSON T III	CPT	0-2028636	0366	1
SNYDER OLEY O JP	LTC	0-2006293	0968	1
SNYDER PAUL C	LTC	0-0472597	0259	1
SNYDER PHILIP E	COL	0-0374216	0667	1
SNYDER RAYMOND K	LTC	0-0210368	0360	3
SNYDER RICHARD F	LTC	0-0184241	0656	3
SNYDER ROBERT E	CW3	W-2209933	0568	1
SNYDER ROBERT F	CW2	W-3151923	0668	2
SNYDER ROBERT G	MAJ	0-0257558	1165	3
SNYDER ROBERT G	CW4	W-2146970	1268	1
SNYDER ROBERT L	LTC	0-0303549	0647	2
SNYDER ROBERT V	COL	0-0409985	1265	1

NAME	GRADE	SVC NO	DATE RET MO YR	RET CODE	NAME	GRADE	SVC NO	DATE RET MO YR	RET CODE	NAME	GRADE	SVC NO	DATE RET MO YR	RET CODE	NAME	GRADE	SVC NO	DATE RET MO YR	RET CODE
SNYDER ROBERT W	LTC	0-1553909	0662	1	SOKOL ANTHONY J	LTC	0-0545244	0564	1	SOMMERVOLD WILLIAM A	MAJ	0-2015500	1060	1	SORRICK DAVID C	CW3	RW-3150572	0767	1
SNYDER ROSS M	MAJ	0-1640971	0862	1	SOKOL ARNOLD	LTC	0-0451245	1162	1	SONDEREGGER R P	2LT	0-1181465	0145	2	SORROUGH JAMES E	CPT	0-1688300	0457	1
SNYDER RUFUS A	LTC	0-0402949	0146	2	SOKOLOWSKA ANNA	2LT	N-0722695	0744	1	SONENFELD HOWARD	CPT	0-0508661	0946	2	SORSDAHL DOUGLAS	1LT	0-1324669	0246	2
SNYDER SAMUEL F	MAJ	0-0449522	0749	1	SOKOLOWSKI JOSEPH J	MAJ	0-1184726	1161	1	SONEY RALPH C	LTC	0-0469183	0447	2	SORTOR ROBERT C	LTC	0-1593300	0268	3
SNYDER SHERRILL G	LTC	0-0483996	0568	3	SOKOLSKY SAMUEL	1LT	0-1315226	0146	2	SONGY STANLEY R	1LT	0-0421413	0546	2	SOS JOSEPH P	LTC	0-1060648	0664	1
SNYDER SIDNEY A	CPT	0-0358561	0346	2	SOLA GERALD C SR	LTC	0-0133755	0253	3	SONIAT SIDNEY L	LTC	0-0282242	1060	3	SOSEBEE HERMAN H	CW2	W-2152027	0961	1
SNYDER SIDNEY W	MAJ	0-0110987	0656	3	SOLA MARCELO	CW2	W-2147641	1060	[illegible]	SONIVILLE FRED T	LTC	0-1322097	0765	1	SOSKIN HERSHEL A	LTC	0-0259546	0657	1
SNYDER SIEGFRIED	CPT	0-1798082	0661	1	SOLANDER JOHN O	CW3	W-2146555	0161	1	SONKIN JESSE	LTC	0-0302132	1166	3	SOSKY JOSEPH W	CW2	W-2141451	0557	1
SNYDER STANLEY	CPT	0-1112457	1162	2	SOLANICK WILLIAM C	MAJ	0-1309105	0965	1	SONLEY JOSEPH L	MAJ	0-0969853	0263	1	SOSNA MAX E	MAJ	0-0500160	0658	1
SNYDER THURMAN F	LTC	0-0922018	0867	3	SOLAR LESLIE S	LTC	0-0126211	0855	3	SONNE IRVIN H	LTC	0-0119609	0147	2	SOSNAY THEODORE	LTC	0-1316791	0765	1
SNYDER VICTORY A	CPT	0-0498508	0347	2	SOLARI LOUIS S	LTC	0-0266062	0362	3	SONNEBORN JAMES E	MAJ	0-0949659	0365	1	SOSNOVE WILLIAM	LTC	0-1057606	0667	1
SNYDER WALTER C	COL	0-0270866	0668	3	SOLHAKKEN IVAR A	CPT	0-0453158	0945	2	SONNELAND SIDNEY G	MAJ	0-0206933	0245	2	SOSNOWSKI PETER P	CPT	0-1109676	0163	1
SNYDER WARREN	MAJ	0-2055167	1161	1	SOLBERG CHRIS	LTC	0-0287639	0754	1	SONNEMANN EUGENE H	LTC	0-0552097	0968	1	SOTO CHARLES T III	LTC	0-1577874	0262	1
SNYDER WESLEY E	LTC	0-0900029	0746	2	SOLBERG JOHN C	COL	0-0243102	0251	3	SONNENBURG BILLY J	CW3	W-3200127	1068	1	SOTO LOUIS H	LTC	0-0337463	0459	1
SNYDER WILLIAM J	MAJ	0-0329161	0546	2	SOLBERG NELS G	MAJ	0-0129253	0255	3	SONNET HARRY M	MAJ	0-1579154	0951	2	SOTO-REMOS JULIO	CPT	0-0222444	0563	3
SNYDER WILLIAM D JR	LTC	0-1113454	0664	1	SOLCANY WILLIAM J	MAJ	0-0500004	0950	2	SONNHEIM EDWARD B	LTC	0-0230816	0664	3	SOTOMAYOR BONIFACIO	MAJ	0-0108069	0144	1
SNYDER WILLIAM P	MAJ	0-2067899	0763	1	SOLDATO JOSEPH A	1LT	0-1824242	1059	1	SONNIE JAMES E	MAJ	0-2006873	0165	1	SOTTONG GEORGE V	COL	0-0288253	0857	1
SNYDER WILTON R	LTC	0-0214477	0655	3	SOLOZ LESTER C	CPT	0-1291344	0347	2	SONNIER AMBROSE	CW4	W-2147135	0868	1	SOUCHON CLIFFORD P	LTC	0-1031273	0162	1
SOBCZAK JOHN J	CPT	0-1877853	0963	1	SOLEN ALBERT M	CPT	0-0381872	0444	2	SONNIER JOHN J	MAJ	0-0264216	0966	3	SOUCIER LOUIS R	CPT	0-0289962	0458	3
SOBCZYK NICHOLAS V	2LT	0-1336275	0646	2	SOLINSKY NORMAN T	LTC	0-1635359	0660	1	SONNIER WILLIAM	MAJ	0-0216373	0748	2	SOUCY RAYMOND L	CPT	0-0988380	1061	2
SOBCZYNSKI STANLEY F	MAJ	0-0441140	0868	1	SOLIS JOSEPH	MAJ	0-1642598	0661	1	SONNTAG EUGENE W	MAJ	0-1284780	0161	1	SOUDER ROBERT H	LTC	0-0358306	0161	1
SOBECK CYRIL C	LTC	0-0352191	0646	2	SOLIS LOUIS B	CW2	W-2208300	0565	2	SONNTAG JOSEPH H	LTC	0-0903544	0467	3	SOUHRADA ALBERT H	MAJ	0-0311415	0944	2
SOBEK ADAM J	1LT	0-1844933	0547	1	SOLIS PAUL J	LTC	0-0271560	1066	3	SONNTAG RICHARD W	1LT	0-1702708	1044	2	SOUKARAS KOMNENUS M	MAJ	0-0251575	1165	3
SOBEL LOUIS	LTC	0-0905797	0467	3	SOLKOT ROY	MAJ	0-0518169	0965	1	SONOWSKI JOSEPH F	CW3	W-2142054	0959	1	SOUKUP WILLIAM L	MAJ	0-0971812	0266	1
SOBEL MANUEL	LTC	0-1280334	0168	3	SOLL ANDREW M	1LT	0-1001686	0346	2	SONSTEIN JACK	MAJ	0-1586933	0965	1	SOULOS EDWARD H	LTC	0-1308196	0363	1
SOBEL MIN	LTC	L-0220162	0363	1	SOLLENBERGER WILLIAM	CPT	0-0523257	0746	2	SOOBY JOHN T	CW4	W-2146842	1265	1	SOULE FRANK A	MAJ	0-0218292	1160	3
SOBELL HARRY	COL	0-0411655	0867	3	SOLLEY LOUIE W	MAJ	0-1298613	1057	1	SOOLPOVAR DAVID	LTC	0-1172667	0461	2	SOULES WEBSTER F	COL	0-0285472	0468	3
SOBELL JACK	CPT	0-0310103	0445	2	SOLO ALEXANDER	2LT	0-0158788	0456	3	SOOTOO LINCOLN	CW2	W-3350179	1168	1	SOUPLY RAY A	LTC	0-1179623	0165	1
SOBELMAN JACK S	MAJ	0-0966740	1160	1	SOLOMKIN MARK	CPT	0-0467940	1045	2	SOPER ANN W	MAJ	N-0797057	0767	1	SOUSA JAMES J	MAJ	0-2018594	0664	1
SOBER CLARENCE W	COL	0-1695288	1068	1	SOLOMON ADOLPH F	COL	0-0281510	0561	1	SOPER ARTHUR C	LTC	0-0133535	1054	3	SOUSA LEO	MAJ	0-0939669	1262	1
SOBEY ARTHUR W	LTC	0-1575179	0965	1	SOLOMON BRUCE L	LTC	0-0774338	1167	1	SOPER CLARENCE E	MAJ	0-0282532	0245	2	SOUSA MANUEL B	CW2	W-2144837	0155	1
SOBEY WILFRED M	MAJ	0-2032849	1262	1	SOLOMON BURTON	1LT	0-0514651	0446	2	SOPER DONALD	CPT	0-1649911	0949	2	SOUSA ROBERT J	MAJ	0-1308014	1162	1
SOBIN JULIUS	COL	0-0135456	1053	3	SOLOMON ELKAN F	LTC	0-0247855	0361	1	SOPHER PHILIP	MAJ	0-1556662	0361	2	SOUTH CHESTER E	LTC	0-0997819	0968	1
SOBLEN WALTER J	1LT	0-1636667	1144	2	SOLOMON HUBERT L	MAJ	0-2204331	0863	1	SOPKA JOHN	MAJ	0-0494701	1053	1	SOUTH KEITH H	COL	0-0127880	0657	3
SOBOLESKI STEVEN A	2LT	0-1300726	0244	2	SOLOMON IRA T	CW3	W-2152403	1263	1	SOPPE ANTHONY J	CW2	W-2146400	0155	2	SOUTH ROBERT L	MAJ	0-1930844	0266	1
SOBOLESKY HELEN T	1LT	N-0725923	1045	1	SOLOMON JACOB M	LTC	0-0235402	1165	3	SORADY FRED E	LTC	0-1100791	0760	1	SOUTH SAMUEL D	WO1	W-2121953	1062	1
SOBOLEWSKI WILLIAM C	MAJ	0-1327896	0261	1	SOLOMON JAMES E JR	LTC	0-1102963	1160	1	SORAHAN FRANK R	LTC	0-1298777	0155	2	SOUTH SAMUEL L	COL	0-0240611	0-52	3
SOBOTTA CORNELIUS	MAJ	0-2009409	0860	1	SOLOMON JEROME J	COL	0-0244876	0866	3	SORBELLO MICHAEL	MAJ	0-1044108	0861	1	SOUTHALL COPELAND S	MAJ	0-0151988	0255	3
SOBUT VINCENT T	MAJ	0-1059645	0562	1	SOLOMON JOSEPH C	LTC	0-0536197	0164	1	SORBER MILDRED R	1LT	N-0722768	0745	1	SOUTHALL SAM R	CW3	W-2145842	0163	1
SOCHA EDMUND J	MAJ	0-1102474	0261	1	SOLOMON LOUIS E JR	1LT	0-0495931	1044	2	SORDEN EDWARD H JR	CW2	W-2211477	0167	1	SOUTHALL THOMAS W	CW3	W-2207203	0568	1
SOCHA JOSEPH V	CW3	W-2148223	0362	2	SOLOMON MEYER	CPT	0-0484610	0845	2	SORENSEN AARON L	CW3	W-2206340	0468	1	SOUTHARD FRANK L	LTC	0-0921941	0465	3
SOCHON STANLEY J	CW2	W-2111367	0864	1	SOLOMON NELSON	CPT	0-1895300	1155	1	SORENSEN ARVIC H	LTC	0-1598247	0668	1	SOUTHARD JAMES W F	COL	0-0287441	0559	3
SOCIA MARVIN W	CW2	W-2104491	1045	2	SOLOMON PAUL A	1LT	0-0497189	0848	1	SORENSEN BETTE M	2LT	N-0785579	0546	1	SOUTHARD WESLEY	LTC	0-0397202	0868	3
SODA WILLIAM E	CPT	0-0343913	1143	2	SOLOMON PAUL E	CPT	0-0890311	0556	1	SORENSEN CARLYLE A	CPT	0-0313599	0245	2	SOUTHER CLIFFORD J	LTC	0-1326138	0765	1
SODDY THOMAS B	1LT	0-0403636	0444	2	SOLOMON SAUL	COL	0-0348806	1165	3	SORENSEN CLARENCE N	MAJ	0-0462073	0546	2	SOUTHER JAMES R	MAJ	0-0341944	0145	2
SODEN JAMES B	LTC	0-0906587	1265	3	SOLOMON TOUFIC J	CW3	W-2203488	1266	1	SORENSEN EUGENE E	MAJ	0-1170564	0158	1	SOUTHER JOHN K	LTC	0-0290132	0260	1
SODERBERG EDWARD R	CW3	W-2001523	0762	3	SOLOMONOW EDWARD J	LTC	0-0312332	0646	2	SORENSEN FRED E	CPT	0-1336559	0662	1	SOUTHERLAND C C	CW2	W-2147697	1059	1
SODERBERG JOHN W	2LT	0-1004038	0845	2	SOLON THOMAS F	CPT	0-0470270	0246	2	SORENSEN HARRY L	LTC	0-1302375	0759	1	SOUTHERLAND JOHN A	CPT	0-1031211	1156	1
SODERBERG KERMIT J	MAJ	0-0312878	0146	2	SOLOT MORTON A	CPT	0-1290832	0447	2	SORENSEN HARRY S	CW3	W-2147365	0664	1	SOUTHERLAND LEE V	MAJ	0-0404291	0962	1
SODERBERG ROBERT E	MAJ	0-0446265	0550	1	SOLOVE SAMUEL	CPT	0-1544869	0546	2	SORENSEN JOHN JR	MAJ	0-0982656	0865	1	SOUTHERLAND WILLIAM	CW3	W-2210627	0768	1
SODERGREN CARL I	COL	0-1175865	0861	1	SOLOVEN BOLIESLAU	CW2	W-2143249	0162	1	SORENSEN KEITH A	CW3	W-2140938	1262	1	SOUTHERN BOB N	CPT	0-1337497	0664	1
SODERLIND STEPHEN D	1LT	0-5336398	0368	2	SOLOVSKOY GEORGE P	LTC	0-1297801	0261	1	SORENSEN ORRIL E	CW4	W-2142798	1068	1	SOUTHERN DONALD E	MAJ	0-1885262	0866	1
SODERLUND KENNETH G	MAJ	0-2211319	1262	1	SOLTOW EDWARD A	LTC	0-1059287	0262	1	SORENSEN ORVEL H	LTC	0-1592079	0962	2	SOUTHERN DONALD L	1LT	0-0417056	0345	2
SODERQUIST RICHARD W	MAJ	0-0381626	0745	2	SOLTYS ANDREW T	LTC	0-1045259	0461	1	SORENSEN PETER	MAJ	0-0109994	1044	2	SOUTHERN FREDERICK	MAJ	0-0452611	0162	1
SODERSTROM GLEN A	LTC	0-0350574	0462	1	SOLTYS STANLEY	LTC	0-0860577	0962	1	SORENSEN REUBEN S	CPT	0-0943926	0960	1	SOUTHERN HAROLD K	MAJ	0-0361465	0263	3
SODINI MARIO G	CW4	W-2148345	1268	1	SOLYOM RICHARD L	MAJ	0-0310763	0146	2	SORENSEN VALDEMAR M	CW3	W-2203393	0765	1	SOUTHERN HUBERT A	MAJ	0-1577876	0653	1
SODORFF RICHARD L	1LT	0-0550595	0146	2	SOMBAR MICHAEL J	MAJ	0-2035388	0564	1	SORENSEN VERNAL T	LTC	0-0293944	1051	2	SOUTHERN JOHN A	LTC	0-0360774	0165	3
SOEDER ROBERT G	MAJ	0-2047503	0962	1	SOMERALL JAMES B	1LT	0-1323753	1145	2	SORENSEN WESTON C	MAJ	0-1825832	0264	1	SOUTHERN JOHN W	1LT	0-1169749	1051	2
SOELLNER FRED W	CPT	0-1304135	0659	2	SOMERS DANIEL A	MAJ	0-0335990	0464	3	SORENSON DUWARD J	CW2	W-3155706	1168	2	SOUTHERN ROY	MAJ	0-1555904	0960	1
SOERHOFF ROBERT A	CPT	0-1322096	0347	2	SOMERS GAYLE H	CPT	0-0189064	0453	3	SORENSON ELMER C	LTC	0-0448734	0662	1	SOUTHWARD CHARLES L	B G	0-0329922	1267	1
SOETERS EUGENE L	MAJ	0-0973877	1162	1	SOMERS GORDON	LTC	0-1580352	0668	3	SORENSON HAROLD J	1LT	0-1543625	0646	2	SOUTHWARD WILBUR R	COL	0-0267137	0863	3
SOEURT WILLIAM J	COL	0-0255836	0964	3	SOMERS JAMES F	1LT	0-1586932	0446	2	SORENSON JEROME W JR	MAJ	0-0328672	0346	2	SOUTHWELL EDWIN T	1LT	0-1177990	0945	2
SOFER HERMAN	CPT	0-1690616	1044	2	SOMERS LEE W	CPT	0-2008640	0157	1	SORG ROBERT F	LTC	0-1580353	1061	1	SOUTHWELL JOSEPH A	CW2	W-2210150	0964	1
SOFFE CLYDE C	MAJ	0-0358912	0566	3	SOMERS LOWELL M	CPT	0-1040154	0245	2	SORGI CHARLES F JR	2LT	0-1294212	0745	2	SOUTHWICK THOMAS S	LTC	0-0236169	0765	3
SOFFEL QUINTIN I	MAJ	0-0244776	0146	2	SOMERS PETER	MAJ	0-1101669	0860	1	SORIANO FRED D	MAJ	0-1896563	0561	2	SOUTHWICK WILLIAM B	CPT	0-0447821	0556	2
SOGARD THEODORE L	COL	0-0127573	1053	3	SOMERS VERNON H	MAJ	0-0228809	1163	3	SORIERO WILLIAM A	CPT	0-0386024	0944	2	SOUTHWORTH CHARLES G	MAJ	0-1634349	0557	1
SOHN HYMAN	1LT	0-1317695	1145	2	SOMERVILLE GEORGE W	MAJ	0-2210441	0566	1	SORILLA ROSEN S	MAJ	0-1896781	0861	1	SOUTHWORTH GILBERT E	MAJ	0-1636674	0457	1
SOHN LOUIS S JR	MAJ	0-0394282	0146	2	SOMERVILLE JAMES	CPT	0-1319673	1146	2	SORLEY MILFORD S	MAJ	0-0118143	1044	2	SOUTHWORTH HAVEN F	LTC	0-0242547	0366	3
SOHNGEN WILLIAM F	CPT	0-1693604	0146	2	SOMERVILLE ROBERT L	LTC	0-0480070	1067	3	SOROKA ALEXANDER	LTC	0-1041445	0264	1	SOUTHWORTH JAMES JR	CPT	0-0388847	0446	2
SOIFER IRVIN T	CPT	0-0490808	0646	2	SOMERVILLE ROBERT L	CW3	W-2143180	0660	1	SORRELL HERBERT E	MAJ	0-1926202	0266	1	SOUTHWORTH JOHN A	MAJ	0-0244596	0863	3
SOINE ARTHUR W	LTC	0-0925597	0564	3	SOMES ALFRED H	CPT	0-0468150	0344	1	SORRELL HERBERT S	1LT	0-0482394	0742	2	SOUTHWORTH JOSEPH E	CPT	0-0334996	0545	2
SOISSON JOHN L	2LT	0-0360360	0966	3	SOMMER GEORGE N J JR	COL	0-0296319	0967	3	SORRELL JAMES O	LTC	0-0311936	1057	2	SOUTHWORTH ROBERT B	COL	0-0253035	1166	3
SOISSON WILLIAM H	LTC	0-0294492	0945	2	SOMMER JAMES E	LTC	0-0395721	0464	1	SORRELLS RUSSELL B	MAJ	0-0262579	0468	3	SOUTHWORTH WILLIAM E	2LT	0-2012600	0646	2
SOJKA PATRICK J	MAJ	0-1081033	0860	1	SOMMERMEYER W C	LTC	0-0395329	1060	1	SORRELS AARON I JR	CPT	0-1058658	0556	1	SOUWEINE LEON E	CW3	W-2104493	0862	1
SOKEN EDWARD B	LTC	0-0247205	0966	3	SOMMERS ALBERT P JR	CPT	0-1291719	1046	2	SORRENTINO FELIX G	CW4	W-2105741	0258	1	SOUZA LAWRENCE P	MAJ	0-1301896	1160	1

NAME	GRADE	SVC NO	DATE RET MO YR	RET CODE
SOVA EDWIN H	1LT	O-1292413	0453	1
SOVA STANLEY J	CPT	O-0978203	0164	1
SOVERNS JAMES W	LTC	O-1550056	0462	1
SOVINSKY WILLIAM P	CPT	O-1551522	0348	2
SOVITSKI CHARLES	MAJ	O-1054371	0863	1
SOWA JOSEPH F	LTC	O-1307582	0663	1
SOWA WALTER D	LTC	O-1309106	0762	1
SOWASH CARL O	CPT	O-1081861	0247	2
SOWASH CLARE R	LTC	O-0183951	0159	3
SOWDER SAMUEL P	CW4	W-2113662	0263	1
SOWELL KAVY V	CW3	W-2150036	1055	1
SOWELL LEWIS C	LTC	O-0272267	0767	3
SOWELL ROBERT A	LTC	O-1549604	0962	1
SOWER DONALD L	LTC	O-1107701	0863	1
SOWER WARREN C	MAJ	O-0425487	0361	1
SOWERS HAROLD E	1LT	O-1822326	0746	2
SOWERS JESSE E	CPT	O-1289134	0345	2
SOWERS LOYD G	1LT	O-1291027	104[illegible]	2
SOWKA SAMUEL H	LTC	O-1107024	0862	1
SOWL WILLIAM F	CPT	O-1586936	1058	1
SOWLE CHARLES H	CPT	O-1580356	0263	1
SOXMAN R C	COL	O-0231753	0264	3
SOYKE JOHN R	1LT	O-1307583	0745	2
SOZIO MARIO S	CW3	W-2212611	1068	1
SPAANS HAROLD R	COL	O-0273913	0968	3
SPACKEEN PAUL J	CW3	W-2233355	0963	1
SPACKMAN VERNON S	WO1	W-2124213	0564	1
SPADAFORO JOSEPH F	1LT	O-1314686	1145	2
SPADE JOHN S	LTC	O-1573599	0860	1
SPADEY FRANCIS X	CPT	O-1581381	0446	2
SPADOLA RENATO F	MAJ	O-0389390	0246	2
SPAE WILLIAM M	LTC	O-1317742	0366	1
SPAHN OTTO J	LTC	O-0184303	0959	3
SPAHR ERNEST X	LTC	O-0277741	0159	3
SPAHR KIMBALL	MAJ	O-0413110	0747	2
SPAHR WILLIAM H	LTC	O-0295102	0163	3
SPAHT CARLOS G	COL	O-0284652	0966	1
SPAIN JOSEPH C	LTC	O-0450767	0858	1
SPAIN VERNIE H	1LT	N-0742078	1045	1
SPAINHOWER EARL E	LTC	O-0167245	0954	3
SPAINHOWER JOHN W	LTC	O-0276384	0341	1
SPAKE WILLIAM T	LTC	O-1640976	0261	1
SPALDING MALCOLM C	LTC	O-1287429	0255	1
SPALDING PHILIP C	1LT	O-1304626	1045	2
SPALDING THOMAS J	MAJ	O-0317560	0945	2
SPALDING WESLEY E	CPT	O-1693816	0656	1
SPALDING WILLIAM W	MAJ	O-1924312	0264	1
SPALONE ALFRED L	MAJ	O-0474239	0446	2
SPANGE HUGH W	LTC	O-0276655	0254	3
SPANGENBERG WARREN E	CPT	O-1796723	0446	2
SPANGLER GEORGE R	CPT	O-0272216	1143	2
SPANGLER HENRY A	MAJ	O-0222955	1064	3
SPANGLER MATTHEW J	1LT	O-1310891	1047	2
SPANGLER THOMAS M	LTC	O-0227484	1046	1
SPANIER HAROLD B	LTC	O-0135295	0451	3
SPANIER SEYMOUR E	LTC	O-0504296	1061	1
SPANN ALBERT C	LTC	O-0256221	0967	3
SPANN CHARLES A	MAJ	O-0483747	1043	2
SPANN GARLAND C	LTC	O-0305270	1268	3
SPANNAKE KARL L	LTC	O-1634351	0364	1
SPANNKAFT FRANK O	CW4	W-2111336	0561	1
SPANSKI EDWARD J	LTC	O-0525209	0266	3
SPANUTIUS EDWARD R	MAJ	O-0959286	1064	1
SPARER PHINEAS J	MAJ	O-0525991	0946	2
SPARGER WILBUR L	CW2	W-2147373	0559	2
SPARKMAN GUY A	2LT	O-0940737	0656	1
SPARKMAN LEWIS A	MAJ	O-1798893	1165	1
SPARKMAN MATTISON E	MAJ	O-2021127	0168	1
SPARKMAN MAURICE K	MAJ	O-0921326	1062	1
SPARKMAN THOMAS B	COL	O-0207231	0643	3
SPARKS BENJAMIN F JR	CPT	O-1109677	0446	2
SPARKS CARL A	LTC	O-0187246	0255	3
SPARKS CLIFFORD C JR	MAJ	O-2021138	0364	1
SPARKS COURTLEIGH	LTC	O-1640978	0162	1
SPARKS DELILAH M	LTC	N-0700341	0347	1

NAME	GRADE	SVC NO	DATE RET MO YR	RET CODE
SPARKS DONALD L	CPT	O-1599092	0365	1
SPARKS ENOCH P	LTC	O-1549105	0658	1
SPARKS GEORGE T	MAJ	O-0975202	0365	1
SPARKS JAMES L E	LTC	O-1924867	1068	1
SPARKS JAMES M	CPT	O-1004039	1046	2
SPARKS JAMES V	MAJ	O-0118239	0743	2
SPARKS KING JR	COL	O-0290780	0868	3
SPARKS LARRY E	CW3	W-2143114	1067	1
SPARKS LAWRENCE E	LTC	O-1080584	0766	1
SPARKS LLOYD	CPT	O-1574532	0550	1
SPARKS MERLE A	COL	O-0246627	0966	3
SPARKS RAYMOND W	MAJ	O-0287451	0358	3
SPARKS WALTER D	MAJ	O-0968218	0566	1
SPARKS WAYNE J	1LT	O-1303965	0446	2
SPARKS 4TH ROBERT W	CPT	O-0412234	0346	2
SPARLING HAROLD I	LTC	O-0285132	0756	3
SPARROW HOWARD M	2LT	O-0246066	0356	3
SPARROW RICHARD S	1LT	O-0528410	0246	2
SPARROW WILBUR O	1LT	O-2030199	0747	2
SPARTI JOSEPH F	WO1	W-2144164	0459	2
SPASARO FRANK	MAJ	O-1591011	0563	1
SPASEFF MARY M	1LT	N-0760537	0746	1
SPATCHER FRANCIS	MAJ	O-1341829	1162	1
SPATZ AGNES L	MAJ	L-0702252	0363	1
SPATZ CHARLES G	CPT	O-1011870	0147	2
SPAUGH WILLIAM W	CW3	W-2132070	0254	2
SPAULDING GLENN E	MAJ	O-1922864	0767	1
SPAULDING HORACE M	MAJ	O-0326238	0846	2
SPAULDING JAMES A	1LT	O-1319451	0246	2
SPAULDING JAMES B	COL	O-0160788	0151	3
SPAULDING JAMES F	MAJ	O-0751475	0465	1
SPAULDING MERTON D	MAJ	O-1312004	0853	1
SPAULDING NORBERT V	MAJ	O-1100776	0364	2
SPAULDING THOMAS E	LTC	O-0225514	0557	3
SPAUR GEORGE	COL	O-0214067	0463	3
SPAW CARL S	MAJ	O-0370367	0446	2
SPAYD GEORGE F	MAJ	O-1285652	1060	1
SPEAGLE MICHAEL E	MAJ	O-1974906	0468	1
SPEAK WILLIAM B	CPT	O-2000864	0358	1
SPEAKER HARRY A	LTC	O-0349364	1047	2
SPEAKER HARRY H	LTC	O-0371969	0765	3
SPEAKES EUGENE M	LTC	O-1331895	0168	1
SPEAKS DONALD W	1LT	O-0526962	0845	2
SPEAKS STANFORD S	COL	O-0176665	1046	2
SPEAR CARTER W	MAJ	O-0495741	0654	1
SPEAR CHARLES D JR	LTC	O-0242629	0844	2
SPEAR FRANK A	LTC	O-0286811	0361	3
SPEAR HUNTER J	MAJ	O-1339403	0162	1
SPEAR RAYMOND L JR	MAJ	O-0323362	0462	1
SPEAR RHEA C	MAJ	N-0756177	0364	3
SPEARMAN FRANCIS W	LTC	O-0360366	0564	2
SPEARMAN JAMES P JR	CW3	W-2205487	0263	1
SPEARS AUGUSTUS C	LTC	O-0476882	0464	3
SPEARS CHARLIE P	1LT	O-1547461	0145	2
SPEARS DORMAN A	MAJ	O-0246692	0165	3
SPEARS ELSWORTH W	MAJ	O-1597819	0761	2
SPEARS FRED M	CPT	O-1285386	0264	1
SPEARS HOMER R	2LT	O-2001824	0657	1
SPEARS JOHN E	CW3	W-2143579	0259	1
SPEARS JOHN R	MAJ	O-0410752	0561	1
SPEARS LEROY C	LTC	O-0790730	0964	1
SPEARS RALPH W	MAJ	O-1010361	0357	1
SPEARS WILLIAM K	CPT	O-0979105	0161	1
SPEARY JOHN A	LTC	O-1107144	0461	1
SPEAS KENNETH R	LTC	O-1166615	0761	1
SPECHT CHARLES H	LTC	O-1579158	0469	1
SPECHT FRANCIS X	CW3	W-2150351	1065	1
SPECHT LEE C	1LT	O-5337469	0268	2
SPECHT MALCOLM A	COL	O-0250898	1266	3
SPECHT ORVILLE A	LTC	O-1595839	0964	1
SPECHT VELMA M	CPT	N-0771340	0649	1
SPECK DONALD W	LTC	O-1327189	0464	1
SPECK DUNBAR V	CW4	W-2105933	1154	1
SPECK JEFFERSON	MAJ	O-0377670	0347	2
SPECK MARVIN C	LTC	O-1311338	0368	1

NAME	GRADE	SVC NO	DATE RET MO YR	RET CODE
SPECK WILLIAM R	MAJ	O-1544028	1165	3
SPECKER JOHN C	COL	O-0273225	0367	3
SPECKERT MARIE	1LT	N-0700112	0742	1
SPECKMAN JAMES H	LTC	O-0272355	1068	3
SPECTOR DANIEL H	COL	O-0425494	0963	1
SPECTOR HENRY	LTC	O-0447351	0852	2
SPECTOR MELVIN M	CPT	O-1551119	0857	1
SPECTOR WILLIAM S	1LT	O-1533451	0745	2
SPEDDLE HAROLD F	LTC	O-0395140	1060	1
SPEED ALONZO C	CPT	O-0259546	0265	3
SPEED CARL	MAJ	O-2035528	0656	1
SPEED KARL H	CW3	W-2206918	1068	2
SPEEDMAN RICHARD L	LTC	O-1713256	0968	1
SPEEGLE GLEN H	1LT	O-0104945	1028	2
SPEELMAN RODNEY A	MAJ	O-0545773	0464	1
SPEENBURGH GLEASON B	CPT	O-2062075	1045	2
SPEER FRED C	LTC	O-1122291	0263	1
SPEER JAMES R	COL	O-0143699	0648	3
SPEER JOHN R H	LTC	O-0302525	0459	3
SPEER JOSEPH R	MAJ	O-2262924	1062	1
SPEER RENWICK W	CPT	O-2263409	0162	1
SPEER RICHARD C	LTC	O-1634352	0264	1
SPEER THOMAS J	LTC	O-1634353	0755	1
SPEER WILLIAM C	1LT	O-1575183	0644	2
SPEERS CHESTER C	MAJ	O-0451247	0561	1
SPEERS ROBERT W	CPT	O-2021133	1162	1
SPEES HAROLD L	1LT	O-1548441	0161	1
SPEES MILTON H	1LT	O-1884163	0754	2
SPEEVACK MAHER	CPT	O-1685231	0646	2
SPEHR PETER F	LTC	O-0230689	0964	3
SPEIGHT BILLY R	CPT	O-2029847	0366	1
SPEIGHTS PAUL F	1LT	O-1110818	1045	2
SPEIR ROSS C	COL	O-0102458	0648	3
SPELCE CARL C	MAJ	O-0356181	0547	2
SPELICH MATTHEW P	MAJ	O-1017045	0760	1
SPELL JOSEPH D	CW2	W-2146993	0857	1
SPELLMAN CLARENCE F	CW2	W-2151720	1060	1
SPELLMAN JAMES L	COL	O-0326821	0161	1
SPELLMAN JAMES W	LTC	O-0904329	0263	1
SPELLMAN JOSEPH L	LTC	O-0276794	0766	3
SPELLMAN VERNON C	1LT	O-1017500	0546	2
SPELLMEYER EDWARD L	MAJ	O-3357880	1147	1
SPELMAN HAYES S	CPT	O-1301322	0254	1
SPELTA VICTOR F	LTC	O-1845796	0167	1
SPELTZ REINHARD L	COL	O-0406278	0158	1
SPENCE ADELINE	MAJ	N-0756134	0463	1
SPENCE CURTIS T	LTC	O-0407824	0665	2
SPENCE DAVID A	LTC	O-0171313	0756	3
SPENCE HOMER W	MAJ	O-0363726	0945	2
SPENCE JAMES T	MAJ	O-0109974	1054	3
SPENCE JOHN F	LTC	O-0489854	1057	1
SPENCE JOSEPH W	CPT	O-2025333	0760	1
SPENCE NAVEN D	MAJ	O-5301713	1067	1
SPENCE RALPH K	CPT	O-0172487	0452	3
SPENCE ROBERT J	1LT	O-1316227	0645	2
SPENCE THOMAS E	CPT	O-2262698	0261	1
SPENCE THOMAS P JR	CW3	W-2143778	0161	1
SPENCE WILLIAM L	CPT	O-1441593	0160	1
SPENCER ADAM C	CPT	O-0164258	0340	1
SPENCER ALFRED J JR	LTC	O-0958256	0767	1
SPENCER ALLEN W	LTC	O-0295389	0160	1
SPENCER BURFORD A	CPT	O-0167929	1158	3
SPENCER CLAUDE W	MAJ	O-2262217	0766	1
SPENCER CURTIS JR	MAJ	O-1234412	0757	2
SPENCER DEANE E	2LT	O-1303218	1144	2
SPENCER EDWARD A	CPT	O-2247136	0967	1
SPENCER ELWIN A	COL	O-0315352	0369	3
SPENCER EUGENE A	CPT	O-1543876	1154	2
SPENCER EUGENE M	MAJ	O-0311443	0363	1
SPENCER FLOYD R	COL	O-0359373	0961	1
SPENCER FOREST H	COL	O-0246593	1054	3
SPENCER FRANK W	CPT	O-1013933	0960	1
SPENCER FRANKLIN H	LTC	O-0179191	0557	3
SPENCER GAYLE H	1LT	O-1016843	0945	2
SPENCER GEORGE H	MAJ	O-1320893	1047	2

NAME	GRADE	SVC NO	DATE RET MO YR	RET CODE
SPENCER GEORGE W	LTC	O-1109027	0764	1
SPENCER GERALD W	LTC	O-0284566	0868	3
SPENCER HAL P	MAJ	O-0275350	0258	3
SPENCER HARVEY H	LTC	O-0967240	0363	3
SPENCER HENRY A	CW3	W-2146629	0966	1
SPENCER HENRY R	MAJ	O-1923581	1065	1
SPENCER HERBERT	COL	O-0176785	1054	3
SPENCER HERBERT M	1LT	O-1111926	0246	2
SPENCER JAMES B	LTC	O-0309464	0462	1
SPENCER JAMES O	MAJ	O-0312946	1047	2
SPENCER JIM L	MAJ	O-2024306	0764	1
SPENCER JIMMIE D	MAJ	O-2103079	0265	1
SPENCER JOHN A	COL	O-0314668	0164	1
SPENCER JOHN B JR	MAJ	O-1913227	0767	1
SPENCER JOHN L JR	LTC	O-0943239	0168	1
SPENCER JOHN P	LTC	O-0268224	0462	1
SPENCER JOHNNY H	MAJ	O-0888884	0860	1
SPENCER JOSEPH L	COL	O-0219500	0664	3
SPENCER JOSEPH O	LTC	O-0337530	0658	1
SPENCER JULIUS F	MAJ	O-0385236	0546	2
SPENCER KENNETH A	CPT	O-1882121	1065	1
SPENCER LAILA	CPT	N-0722471	0846	1
SPENCER LAWRENCE D	LTC	O-1297108	0363	1
SPENCER LEWIS R	CW3	W-2144998	1160	2
SPENCER LINCOLN R	1LT	O-1107145	0461	1
SPENCER LOUIS C	MAJ	O-0162304	0160	3
SPENCER MARSHALL E	1LT	O-0539828	0546	2
SPENCER MELVIN	LTC	O-0499642	0446	2
SPENCER MYRON O	WO1	W-2126782	0949	1
SPENCER NEIL	CPT	O-2011168	1066	3
SPENCER OLLIE	CPT	O-0495894	0549	1
SPENCER OTTO F	MAJ	O-0372792	1061	1
SPENCER PAUL A	CPT	O-0977053	0961	1
SPENCER PAUL R	CW3	W-2210155	0668	1
SPENCER RALPH P	CPT	O-2002366	0757	1
SPENCER RALPH V	CW3	W-2142415	0562	1
SPENCER RICHARD R	LTC	O-0420015	0547	2
SPENCER ROBERT B	LTC	O-1012314	0456	1
SPENCER ROBERT C	LTC	O-0327426	1061	1
SPENCER ROBERT P	LTC	O-0321771	0661	3
SPENCER SAMUEL M	MAJ	O-1553366	0765	1
SPENCER SEAVER R JR	LTC	O-1289333	1065	1
SPENCER THOMAS B	CPT	O-1685103	1045	2
SPENCER THOMAS H	LTC	O-0332447	0161	2
SPENCER THOMAS N	LTC	O-0301828	1064	3
SPENCER VERNON H	MAJ	O-0490326	0254	2
SPENCER WALTER E	1LT	O-2[illegible]834	1049	2
SPENCER WILLIAM L	MAJ	O-0450602	1146	2
SPENCER WILLIAM M	LTC	O-0145395	0856	3
SPENCER WILLIAM O	LTC	O-0168715	0860	3
SPENDLOVE KATHERINE	MAJ	N-0752113	0965	1
SPENGEMAN CARL G	CPT	O-1307868	1146	2
SPENIK JOHN	1LT	O-1897765	0555	1
SPER MARTIN T	MAJ	O-0983269	1263	1
SPEREAU HARRY R	1LT	O-1324121	0846	2
SPERL WENZEL F	CW2	W-3430425	1068	1
SPERLING GEORGE R	LTC	O-1553911	0363	1
SPERLING JOSEPH	CPT	O-0492816	0146	2
SPERLING RUTH E	MAJ	N-0735482	1265	3
SPERLING SIDNEY S	LTC	O-1042950	1065	1
SPERRY CLARENCE E	COL	O-0243269	0661	1
SPERRY GEORGE B	MAJ	O-0885120	0666	1
SPERRY JOHN W	CW3	W-2144965	0559	1
SPERRY LEONARD	2LT	O-1643471	1044	2
SPERRY LEONARD E	MAJ	O-5301805	1268	1
SPERRY WILLIAM D	LTC	O-0287014	0557	1
SPERSEN HENRY G	CW4	W-2002257	0864	3
SPESHOCK EDWARD J	COL	O-0357785	1268	1
SPEZZACATENA DANIEL	MAJ	O-2033130	0561	1
SPICE CHARLES E	WO1	W-2142779	0264	1
SPICER CLAUDE H	MAJ	O-0241964	1055	3
SPICER GEORGE H	MAJ	O-0239571	1063	3
SPICER HENRY D	LTC	O-1000869	0359	1
SPICER HOWARD E	LTC	O-0169790	0460	3
SPICER MALCOLM F	LTC	O-1331567	0467	2

NAME	GRADE	SVC NO	DATE RET MO YR	RET CODE
SPICER ROBERT J	COL	0-0284434	0767	3
SPICER WILLIAM L	CW2	W-2141453	0557	1
SPICKARD HAROLD E	COL	0-0271421	0655	3
SPICKELMIER JOHN P	LTC	0-0344327	0457	1
SPICKELMIRE VERNON L	CPT	0-0100839	0648	3
SPICUZZA JOHN H	CW3	W-2142270	0661	1
SPIDLE HARRY W	WO1	W-2152459	1061	2
SPIEGEL DAVID	COL	0-1797034	1065	2
SPIEGEL GEORGE F	COL	0-0359055	0461	1
SPIEGEL LEWIS H	CPT	0-0345215	0144	2
SPIEGEL SIDNEY S	WO1	W-2111528	0145	2
SPIEGELBERG GEORGE R	COL	0-0900951	1045	2
SPIELMAN SOL	1LT	0-1717366	0545	2
SPIER JAMES E	COL	0-0190832	0357	3
SPIERING DONALD P	1LT	0-1299955	1045	2
SPIERS REED A	MAJ	0-2033171	0562	1
SPIERS ROBERT H	CPT	0-0143690	0155	3
SPIES GEORGE R JR	1LT	0-0486038	1043	2
SPIESS FRANK G	COL	0-0266094	0467	3
SPIESS GEORGE G	LTC	0-0243495	1052	2
SPIESS JEROME J	CW3	W-2147419	0962	1
SPIKES RICHARD W JR	LTC	0-1595840	1162	1
SPILLANE JOHN J	LTC	0-0450150	0157	1
SPILLANE ROBERT F	CPT	0-1059649	0746	2
SPILLE FREDERICK	CW3	W-2208538	0367	1
SPILLER DAVID H	1LT	0-1642602	0447	2
SPILLER GEORGE M	LTC	0-1168927	1160	1
SPILLER ROLAND L	CW3	W-2146125	0863	1
SPILLER THOMAS B JR	COL	0-0315078	0466	1
SPILLER WILLIAM F	LTC	0-0149675	0948	3
SPILLERS ARTHUR R	COL	0-0902022	0967	3
SPILLERS CURTIS W	LTC	0-1541242	0661	1
SPILLMAN AMIEL E	CPT	0-1297272	1046	2
SPILLMAN HARVEY M	CW2	W-2145514	0162	1
SPILLMAN KENNETH R	COL	0-0330158	0962	3
SPILLMAN RUSSELL L	CPT	0-1556357	0561	1
SPILLUM WESLEY I	1LT	0-1697841	0145	2
SPILMAN CHARLES M	COL	0-0194719	1058	3
SPILMAN JAMES A	1LT	0-1861989	1153	2
SPINDLER ALFRED C	MAJ	0-0225323	0444	2
SPINDLER CLARENCE F	LTC	0-0313658	0965	3
SPINDLER ELWIN J	1LT	0-1925682	0454	2
SPINELLI GEORGE L	1LT	0-1547159	0147	2
SPINK JOHN E	MAJ	0-1326779	0962	1
SPINKS ALBERT G	MAJ	0-0283432	0968	3
SPIOTTO ANTHONY	LTC	0-1290325	0954	1
SPIRA JACOB I	LTC	0-4055482	0857	2
SPIRES EZRA T	CPT	0-1044110	1162	2
SPIRES L E	CPT	0-0390643	0245	2
SPISHAKOFF NATHAN N	CPT	0-0344257	0145	2
SPITAL JACK	MAJ	0-0544694	0663	1
SPITLER WILLIAM H JR	2LT	0-0504300	1144	2
SPITZ ALLAN G	COL	0-0109603	0652	2
SPITZ JOHN R	1LT	0-1053374	1265	1
SPITZ RUTH L	MAJ	N-0762618	1164	1
SPITZBERG JULIUS	LTC	0-1168477	0268	1
SPITZER ALBERT	LTC	0-0264134	0668	3
SPITZER HAROLD S	LTC	0-0335426	0960	1
SPITZER JACK R	CW2	W-2153168	0464	1
SPITZER LAWRENCE L	CPT	0-0400978	0145	2
SPITZER LOUIS	MAJ	0-1310919	0765	1
SPIVACK ISAAC D	COL	0-0268562	0962	3
SPIVAK JACK	CPT	0-0487682	0546	2
SPIVEK SOLLY A	LTC	0-1013838	0366	3
SPIVEY ALLEN T	CW2	W-2208751	0860	1
SPIVEY ARTHUR W	MAJ	0-0345279	0246	2
SPIVEY DAVID W	LTC	0-1770994	0860	1
SPIVEY EDWARD P	1LT	0-1011045	0545	2
SPIVEY JOSEPH H JR	1LT	0-1317726	0845	2
SPIVEY MARY L	2LT	N-0760087	0545	1
SPIVEY OSCAR M	MAJ	0-1178631	1160	1
SPIVEY THOMAS H	CW3	W-2143699	0560	1
SPIVEY WILLIAM D	MAJ	0-1284594	0346	2
SPLEEN STEPHEN F	LTC	0-0183205	0351	3
SPODE HERMAN H	COL	0-0151951	0952	2
SPOFFORD BOSWORTH F	MAJ	0-0223133	1145	2
SPOHR CHARLES D	CPT	0-0363424	0947	2
SPONAMORE BENJAMIN F	LTC	0-0507003	0466	3
SPONENBURGH ELSTON S	LTC	0-0352827	0960	1
SPONENBURGH JOHN	LTC	0-0383198	0265	1
SPONTAK CHARLES	CW4	W-2120823	0659	1
SPOO CHARLES E	1LT	0-1648706	0652	1
SPOO GEORGE L	1LT	0-2055406	1045	2
SPOON DONALD D	B G	0-0401940	0667	3
SPOONE JAMES N	CW4	W-2141454	1068	1
SPOONER TRUMAN R	COL	0-0206107	0346	2
SPOOR FERRIS G	MAJ	0-0347171	0147	2
SPOOR JOHN A	CW3	W-2152751	0165	1
SPOOR MARIE A	CPT	N-0758367	0447	1
SPOOR WILLIAM J JR	CW2	W-2206813	0963	2
SPORBERT WILLIAM O	1LT	0-1292414	0944	2
SPORCIC STEPHEN	MAJ	0-1037919	0166	3
SPORE HELEN L	CPT	L-0601353	0964	1
SPORER HENRY JR	2LT	0-1861607	1053	2
SPORING GEORGE C	CW3	W-2141455	0163	1
SPORL JONAS C	COL	0-0309171	0966	3
SPORT FRANK S	MAJ	0-2033231	0561	2
SPOTWOOD W R SR	CW2	W-2149719	0758	2
SPRADLIN RANDALL T	CW3	W-2152798	1165	1
SPRADLING QUENTIN M	COL	0-0335126	1062	3
SPRAGGINS GEORGE V	MAJ	0-1923589	0667	1
SPRAGGINS HENRY G	CPT	0-0508765	1147	2
SPRAGUE CARL T	MAJ	0-0169463	0555	3
SPRAGUE DONALD A	CPT	0-0331944	0767	3
SPRAGUE EDWARD H	LTC	0-0318980	0868	3
SPRAGUE ERNEST L	LTC	0-1013714	0765	1
SPRAGUE FLOYD L	CPT	0-1319058	0247	2
SPRAGUE FRANK W	LTC	0-0406263	0667	3
SPRAGUE HERMAN W JR	LTC	0-1917914	1268	1
SPRAGUE RAYMOND S	CPT	0-0264669	0545	2
SPRAGUE ROBERT C	MAJ	0-1797377	0754	2
SPRAGUE ROBERT M	LTC	0-0306295	1164	1
SPRAGUE THOMAS G	LTC	0-1000870	1267	1
SPRAGUE WILBUR E	CW3	W-2209328	0767	1
SPRAGUE WINFIELD A	MAJ	0-1650753	0164	1
SPRANDEL MARTIN E	1LT	0-1290326	0645	2
SPRATLEY DOLORES R	MAJ	L-1010041	0163	1
SPRAUER EDWARD J	MAJ	0-0334503	0446	2
SPRAWLS RICHARD D	CPT	0-0545833	0450	2
SPRAYBERRY WILLIE R	MAJ	0-1923502	1064	1
SPRECHER WILLIAM J	CW2	W-2107573	0246	2
SPREEMANN FREDERIC	CPT	0-1307869	0847	2
SPREEN ELGIN W	1LT	0-0430189	0346	2
SPREITZER ERNEST R	CPT	0-1293668	0649	2
SPRENG FRED C	LTC	0-0250046	0464	3
SPRENG GEORGE W	CW2	RW-2210435	0863	1
SPRENKEL SAMUEL L	MAJ	0-0237594	0158	3
SPRIGGS JOHN A	MAJ	0-1559985	0164	1
SPRIGGS WALTER E JR	MAJ	0-0977498	0662	1
SPRINDIS STEPHEN W	LTC	0-1289671	0948	2
SPRING ARLINGTON	MAJ	0-0168016	0453	3
SPRING CARL C	MAJ	0-0244702	0659	3
SPRING ELBERT B JR	MAJ	0-1114303	0862	1
SPRING JOHN B	1LT	0-1924727	0254	2
SPRING ROBERT B	MAJ	0-0456133	0647	2
SPRINGALL ARTHUR N	COL	0-0332079	0368	3
SPRINGER ALBERT G	LTC	0-0199263	0754	3
SPRINGER ARTHUR G	2LT	0-1328763	1045	2
SPRINGER AVIS J H	2LT	N-0755340	0546	1
SPRINGER EDWARD F	CPT	0-0181442	0643	1
SPRINGER GEORGE W JR	MAJ	0-0123047	1052	3
SPRINGER HARRY B	LTC	0-0302455	0665	3
SPRINGER HENRY C	COL	0-0207770	0257	3
SPRINGER JAMES H	CPT	0-0481692	0448	1
SPRINGER KEITH	MAJ	0-1180348	0163	1
SPRINGER PERCY A	WO1	W-2143471	0853	1
SPRINGER ROBERT C	MAJ	0-1301702	0663	2
SPRINGER ROBERT G	COL	0-0206399	1162	3
SPRINGER SAMUEL S	COL	0-0377449	0968	3
SPRINGFIELD EDWARD L	CW3	W-2142399	1157	1
SPRINGFIELD THOMAS	CPT	0-1824227	0446	2
SPRINGFORD ELBRIDGE	COL	0-0241646	0864	3
SPRINGLE HORACE G	CW2	W-2214225	0564	1
SPRINGMEYER CHARLES	2LT	0-0392542	0643	2
SPRINKEL HAROLD H	CW4	W-2114246	0755	1
SPRINKLE DAVID G	LTC	0-0502398	0962	1
SPRINKLE ERNEST H	MAJ	0-0258496	1059	3
SPRINKLE HARMON G	CW3	W-2144321	0962	1
SPROAT CLARENCE D	WO1	W-2127389	0364	3
SPROAT JOHN R	CPT	0-0177168	0957	3
SPROUL CHARLES B	LTC	0-0251237	0966	3
SPROULL TOM	CW3	W-2152060	0860	1
SPROUSE GEORGE C	CPT	0-0321155	0463	3
SPROUSE ROBERT E	MAJ	0-1302897	0160	2
SPROUT DEANE O	CPT	0-0386197	1045	2
SPROW GUY	CPT	0-0296410	0545	2
SPROWLS DONALD L	COL	0-1594498	1068	2
SPROWLS GEORGE M	MAJ	0-0139282	1048	3
SPRUCK DONALD C	MAJ	0-0969885	0562	1
SPRUILL MARION C	1LT	N-0725929	0745	1
SPRUILL WILLIAM R	LTC	0-1558205	0563	1
SPRUNG CLIFFORD C	LTC	0-0231495	0762	3
SPRY BYRON P	LTC	0-0208880	0850	3
SPRY CLIFFORD	CW2	W-2147806	0661	1
SPRY FRANCIS N	LTC	0-0257578	0162	3
SPUNT EDWARD T	COL	0-0291152	0351	2
SPURGEON GLEN H	CPT	0-0337329	0854	3
SPURGIN EARNEST H	LTC	0-1107147	0565	1
SPURGIN HAROLD S	LTC	0-0324659	0665	3
SPURLIN RUSSELL M	CPT	0-1242415	0845	2
SPURLIN WILLIAM H	MAJ	0-1599189	1161	1
SPURLOCK BEN E	LTC	0-0931497	0465	1
SPURLOCK CARLOS	CW3	W-2205953	0468	1
SPURLOCK FRANCIS M	CPT	0-1640033	0346	2
SPURLOCK PAUL E	LTC	0-1030422	1068	3
SPURLOCK RALPH O	LTC	0-0220786	0558	1
SPURLOCK WILLIAM W	LTC	0-0211076	0747	2
SPURR GENEVA M	2LT	N-0742804	1144	1
SPURRIER JAMES D	MAJ	0-1101226	0847	2
SPURRIER MERRILL D	MAJ	0-0137978	1157	3
SPURRIER RICHARD R	CPT	0-0455131	0146	2
SPURRIER ROBERT F	LTC	0-1290682	0162	1
SPYKER WILLIAM O	LTC	0-1060650	0662	1
SQUALLS CORNELIUS	CPT	0-1876912	0262	1
SQUIER EDWARD M	LTC	0-0143701	0857	3
SQUIER ROGER W	LTC	0-0242956	0863	3
SQUIER WILLARD A	CPT	0-0500307	0158	1
SQUIRE DONALD A	MAJ	0-2048494	1162	1
SQUIRE GEORGE P	CPT	0-1899367	0261	1
SQUIRE JAMES L	CPT	0-0228053	0344	2
SQUIRE MAX E	MAJ	0-1081251	0361	1
SQUIRES BLANNIE	CPT	N-0751028	0955	2
SQUIRES DALE C	CPT	0-1056559	1059	1
SQUIRES LAURICE F	LTC	0-1321673	0167	1
SQUIRES LYNDON H	MAJ	0-0411892	0162	1
SQUIRES WALTER A	CPT	0-5227472	0468	2
SQUITIERI GILBERT D	1LT	0-1114304	0445	2
SQUYERS HORACE M	MAJ	0-1950286	1160	1
SROICH LOUIS P	MAJ	0-0555837	0763	1
SRUKA JOHN C	MAJ	0-0451188	0154	1
SROMOVSKY JOHN A	CW3	W-2145254	0367	1
SRUBAR JOE H	CW3	W-2145149	0859	1
ST AMAND ALBERT P	CW2	W-2110178	0361	1
ST AMANT PHILEMON A	LTC	0-0378772	0859	1
ST ANGELO NICHOLAS	LTC	0-2048159	0762	1
ST AUBIN ROBERT J	LTC	0-0961163	0768	1
ST CLAIR CROMWELL D	MAJ	0-0426910	0266	1
ST CLAIR FORREST W	LTC	0-1292238	0762	1
ST CLAIR MARVIN W	CW3	W-2150777	1057	1
ST CLAIR MATTHEW	MAJ	0-1168479	0358	1
ST CLAIR NORMAN E	COL	0-0269109	0366	3
ST CLAIR WALLACE C	CW3	W-2148373	0565	1
ST CLAIRE FELIX L	LTC	0-0280406	0260	2
ST GEORGE EARL W	LTC	0-0253808	0167	3
ST GEORGE WILFRED C	LTC	0-1651044	0465	1
ST JAMES ROBERT H	CPT	0-0358827	1045	2
ST JEAN WILLIAM J	MAJ	0-1178637	1063	1
ST JOHN ALFRED JR	MAJ	0-1118478	0865	1
ST JOHN CLARENCE C	CW3	W-2141461	0556	1
ST JOHN ELMER G	MAJ	0-0302475	0745	2
ST JOHN HELEN M	MAJ	N-0799295	0665	1
ST JOHN ILA N	MAJ	L-1010054	0263	1
ST JOHN JOHN	MAJ	0-0403557	0546	2
ST JOHN JOSEPH A	1LT	0-1286205	0945	2
ST JOHN JOSEPH W	CPT	0-1018128	0757	1
ST LOUIS DONALD W	MAJ	0-2019388	0363	1
ST LOUIS HAROLD	CPT	0-1634373	0147	1
ST MARTIN WILFRED A	COL	0-0265790	1161	3
ST MARY ERNEST F JR	1LT	0-0548596	0347	2
ST ONGE ARTHUR P	LTC	0-0451480	1263	1
ST ONGE HUBERT L	LTC	0-1285134	1166	1
ST ONGE NORMAN E	CW4	W-2103395	0658	1
ST ONGE VICTOR A	COL	0-0212245	0945	2
STAAB CARLYLE H	LTC	0-0303110	0267	3
STAAB RUDOLPH L	CPT	0-0481091	1045	2
STAAB WILLIAM F	COL	0-0387319	0760	1
STAAK WILLIAM R	MAJ	0-1648838	0364	1
STAAKE HUGH F	1LT	0-1015552	0346	2
STAATS BURTON L	CW2	W-2214977	1168	1
STABINGAS ELEANOR C	MAJ	N-0724962	0467	1
STABLES LINTON D JR	MAJ	0-0926261	0268	1
STACEY HOWARD A	MAJ	0-1543281	0859	1
STACEY THOMAS B	LTC	0-0474210	0954	2
STACEY WILLIAM T	MAJ	0-2046830	0261	1
STACH JAMES A	LTC	0-0268869	0165	3
STACHELSKI ALEXANDER	LTC	0-1051393	0364	2
STACHWICK ROY A	LTC	0-1055162	0163	1
STACK BERNARD D	MAJ	0-0367667	0445	2
STACK JOHN M	CPT	0-0398410	1045	2
STACK LOUIS T	LTC	0-0186301	1057	3
STACK RICHARD J	LTC	0-1062706	1266	1
STACK WILLIAM	LTC	0-1330001	0365	1
STACKHOUSE EARL A	CPT	0-1822477	0646	2
STACKHOUSE GEORGE L	CW2	W-2122574	0754	2
STACKHOUSE HOWARD J	CW4	W-2142271	0360	1
STACKHOUSE WILLIAM M	MAJ	0-0980954	0962	1
STACKLIN ROBERT J	CW2	W-2211655	0766	1
STACKPOLE ALBERT H	M G	0-0103158	0657	3
STACKPOLE LESLIE B	CPT	0-0426771	0546	2
STACKS ROLAND P	LTC	0-1336445	1166	1
STACY ADAM JR	MAJ	0-0494295	0346	2
STACY ALBERT J	1LT	0-1287777	1045	2
STACY HAROLD M	CW3	W-2144479	0559	1
STACY HENRY D	MAJ	0-2055952	0160	1
STACY JOHN F	LTC	0-1049355	0562	1
STACY JOHN T	CPT	0-0406435	1049	1
STACY ROBERT E	2LT	0-0424544	0343	2
STACY SHERWOOD J	COL	0-0372154	1063	3
STACY THEODORE E	CPT	0-0534437	1045	2
STACY WALTER S	LTC	0-0543975	0964	3
STACY WINTON T	COL	0-0214883	0456	3
STADECK ALOIS J	CPT	0-0473612	0946	2
STADIE HERMAN E	CPT	0-0166106	0330	1
STADLER RUTH R	2LT	N-0700193	0838	1
STADNICK THEODORE	MAJ	0-1895426	0457	1
STADTLER GEORGE J JR	COL	0-0242961	1060	3
STADTLER JULIAN P	LTC	0-1315502	0464	1
STADTMILLER JAMES P	MAJ	0-1692732	0668	1
STADTMILLER LEO M	LTC	0-0300317	0668	3
STAEFFLER RICHARD P	COL	0-0285249	0146	2
STAEHLE WILLIAM C	1LT	0-1695702	0346	2
STAELENS IRMA M	MAJ	N-0726442	0761	1
STAELENS JOSEPH C	MAJ	0-1595841	0762	1
STAFF EDGAR J	LTC	0-0185452	0352	3
STAFF HENRY	LTC	0-0345524	0561	3
STAFFIER ANTHONY R	CPT	0-0497050	0845	2
STAFFIERI LEONARD	MAJ	0-0290053	0459	1
STAFFORD ARVEL C	LTC	0-0357949	0758	1
STAFFORD CHARLES E	CW3	W-2150567	0465	2
STAFFORD CLINE	1LT	0-1312351	1051	1

NAME	GRADE	SVC NO	DATE RET MO YR	RET CODE
STAFFORD DAVID F	1LT	0-0446062	1045	2
STAFFORD EMMA M	CPT	N-0726212	0857	2
STAFFORD EUGENE	1LT	0-2046831	0850	2
STAFFORD FREDERICK	CPT	0-0208501	0546	2
STAFFORD GEORGE T JR	CPT	0-0438709	0846	2
STAFFORD GEORGE W	MAJ	0-1693124	0164	2
STAFFORD GEORGE W	1LT	0-2015938	0647	2
STAFFORD GEROME H	1LT	0-1293669	1045	2
STAFFORD HALBERT H	LTC	0-0217216	1160	3
STAFFORD JOHN C	CW3	W-2145515	0661	1
STAFFORD JOHN H	LTC	0-1109683	1163	1
STAFFORD JOSEPH	WO1	W-2115088	1051	2
STAFFORD JOSEPH W	CW3	W-2145873	0357	1
STAFFORD LEE C	LTC	0-0292210	0368	3
STAFFORD MASON L	1LT	0-1920271	1057	2
STAFFORD MIAL D	LTC	0-1317435	0467	1
STAFFORD NICHOLAS T	LTC	0-1167647	0866	1
STAFFORD PHILIP H	COL	0-0127018	0652	3
STAFFORD RAYMOND R	MAJ	0-2212011	1264	1
STAFFORD RUTH V	1LT	N-0721200	1145	1
STAFFORD THOMAS	CPT	0-0192333	0350	1
STAFFORD THOMAS L	MAJ	0-2025479	0663	1
STAGE KENNETH M	CW3	W-2148766	0162	1
STAGE WILLIAM F	CPT	0-0940759	1058	1
STAGER LORANZA C	CW4	W-2142202	0264	1
STAGG GRANVILLE	LTC	0-2029556	0766	1
STAGG GROSJEAN M	MAJ	0-1579165	0161	1
STAGG WILLIAM F	LTC	0-2017944	0266	1
STAGG 3RD HOWARD J	MAJ	0-0351754	1045	2
STAGGS DOUGLAS E	LTC	0-1294382	0359	1
STAGGS JOSEPH B	CW3	W-2114910	0856	1
STAGGS LOWELL C	1LT	0-1109684	0553	1
STAGGS MILLIE L	2LT	N-0734234	0345	1
STAGGS ORVILLE L	MAJ	0-1283511	0155	2
STAHL ADOLPH F	LTC	0-0453754	0763	1
STAHL BENJAMIN F JR	COL	0-0256539	0660	1
STAHL CHOUTEAU P	LTC	0-0203337	0963	3
STAHL HAROLD J	LTC	0-0283456	0467	3
STAHL HERBERT G	1LT	0-0513906	0246	2
STAHL JUDSON H	CW3	W-2144026	0763	1
STAHL LEWIS F	CPT	0-1315973	1047	2
STAHLE BILLY G	LTC	0-2014639	0168	1
STAHLER CHRISTOPHE	MAJ	0-0285969	1045	2
STAHLMAN HAROLD E	MAJ	0-2033936	1165	1
STAHLY LEONARD L	CW3	W-2145317	0467	1
STAIGER FRANKLIN W	COL	0-0147983	0152	3
STAIGER LEA R	COL	0-0319931	0963	3
STAINES WILLIAM L	LTC	0-0166537	0945	2
STAINS WATSON A JR	LTC	0-0364155	0960	1
STAINTON WILLIAM F	LTC	0-0226772	0660	3
STAIR WALTER E	CW2	W-2211968	1068	1
STAIRS CARROLL A	LTC	0-1558096	0367	1
STAKER GORDON L	LTC	0-0334985	0767	3
STALBAUM MAX P	MAJ	0-1686809	0765	1
STALBIRD MERRITT E	CW4	W-2201737	1068	2
STALCUP GENE S	MAJ	0-1317207	0361	1
STALCUP JOHN W	CPT	0-1018252	1146	1
STALEY BAILEY B	LTC	N-0734170	1264	1
STALEY CHARLES N	LTC	0-0210726	0245	2
STALEY DONALD V	LTC	0-0325007	0358	3
STALEY EDGAR E	LTC	0-1553367	0768	3
STALEY FRANCIS S	CPT	0-0385622	0762	1
STALEY GEORGE E	MAJ	0-2006401	0157	1
STALEY HARRY H	MAJ	0-1106501	0962	1
STALEY JACK A	CPT	0-0372679	1045	2
STALEY JAMES F	LTC	0-2036081	1067	1
STALEY JOHN H JR	1LT	0-0535336	0945	2
STALEY KENNETH V	MAJ	0-1330002	0959	1
STALEY LEO C	MAJ	0-2029357	1066	1
STALEY MARCUS P	LTC	0-0225644	0959	3
STALEY MARTIN E	MAJ	0-0167338	1157	3
STALEY RAYMON M JR	MAJ	0-1947949	0761	1
STALGAITIS JOSEPH G	CW3	W-2151298	1167	1
STALIN GUSTAF S	MAJ	0-1050473	0562	1
STALKER RICHARD W	1LT	0-1559207	1047	2
STALL JOSEPH W	MAJ	0-1581384	0558	1
STALLARD ALTON V	COL	0-0195039	1161	3
STALLINGS GEORGE W	COL	0-0253637	1156	1
STALLINGS HARTWELL F	MAJ	0-0238315	0264	3
STALLINGS JESSE D	CPT	0-0371389	1047	2
STALLINGS RICHARD E	CPT	0-1583710	0863	1
STALLINGS TOLBERT L	LTC	0-0175354	0561	1
STALLINGS WILLIAM H	CPT	0-0263058	0245	2
STALLINGS WILLIAM T	LTC	0-0407696	0959	1
STALLWITZ GEORGE	COL	0-0275078	0764	3
STALLWORTH EDWARD	CW3	W-2151731	0764	1
STALLWORTH WILLIAM E	CPT	0-0406255	0447	2
STALTER ROBERT A	MAJ	0-0445498	0562	1
STALZER MILDERD A	1LT	N-0786049	1046	1
STAMAN LILBURN P	LTC	0-0252320	0167	3
STAMAS STANLEY	LTC	0-1301226	1167	1
STAMATE EVA H	2LT	N-0730678	1044	1
STAMBACH ALBERT B	MAJ	0-0135920	0355	3
STAMBACH GERALD M	1LT	0-0885701	0346	2
STAMBACH MAX F	CPT	0-2006548	0461	1
STAMBAUGH CLYDE	CPT	0-1330871	0354	2
STAMBAUGH JACOB L	MAJ	0-0159294	0749	3
STAMBERG STANLEY A	MAJ	0-0230098	0658	3
STAMEY HENRY C	MAJ	0-0488619	1151	2
STAMM JOHN J	LTC	0-1309859	0862	1
STAMM LUTHER A	1LT	0-1995032	0753	2
STAMMER HELEN	2LT	N-0736877	1045	1
STAMMREICH IRVING H	MAJ	0-1640036	0157	1
STAMP EMILY C F	CPT	N-0787375	0946	1
STAMP FRANK T	CPT	0-0375554	0244	2
STAMP WILLIAM M	CPT	0-1312601	0365	1
STAMPA ALLAN J	COL	0-0171139	0762	3
STAMPER CHARLES E	MAJ	0-1284782	0546	2
STAMPER LUCIAN A	CPT	0-1684564	1045	2
STAMPER ROBERT M	MAJ	0-1285653	0461	1
STAMPS MARGARET H	1LT	N-0771821	0945	1
STAMPS MARTIN E	CW2	W-2145247	0563	1
STAMS NICK R	LTC	0-1551753	1162	1
STAN LEONARD J	MAJ	0-2033570	0763	1
STANBACK JEFFREY F	LTC	0-0137644	0154	3
STANBERRY ALLAN W	MAJ	0-1048600	0161	1
STANCARI LOUIS F	LTC	0-1542258	0862	1
STANCATO ANTHONY L	1LT	0-1306332	0451	2
STANCHOS ALVIN A E	MAJ	0-0295686	0662	1
STANCIL WILLIAM C	2LT	0-1303790	0544	2
STANCKIEWITZ WALTER	LTC	0-1555300	0961	1
STANDAFER EZRA E	CW2	W-2147866	1061	2
STANDAL HJALMAR L	MAJ	0-1041655	0862	1
STANDER THOMAS R	COL	0-0287251	0857	3
STANDISH ALBERT	MAJ	0-1297976	0662	1
STANDISH HENRY H	MAJ	0-0984396	0766	1
STANDISH THEODORE C	CPT	0-1113460	1045	2
STANDISH WALTER P	MAJ	0-1317827	0757	1
STANDLEY IRVIN L	MAJ	0-0358547	1045	2
STANDOCK STEPHEN O	CPT	0-1166620	0657	1
STANDRIDGE HAROLD S	CW3	W-2142450	0859	1
STANEK MILLARD A	CW3	W-2150670	0263	1
STANEK ROBERT T	MAJ	0-1182010	0260	1
STANFIELD ELMO L	LTC	0-0110885	0955	3
STANFIELD MERLYN L	CPT	0-5305724	1065	2
STANFIELD ROBERT R	MAJ	0-1174151	0361	1
STANFIELD RUFUS A	MAJ	0-0439634	0946	1
STANFIELD THOMAS J	LTC	0-0573462	0455	1
STANFILL JOHN L	MAJ	0-2262981	0266	1
STANFILL KERMIT J	MAJ	0-1999167	0859	1
STANFORD HENRY J	MAJ	0-0273845	1045	2
STANFORD MARY R P	1LT	N-0772474	1046	1
STANFORD ROBERT F	CW3	W-2110521	0859	1
STANFORD WILLIAM	CPT	0-0496245	0844	2
STANG HENRY J	LTC	0-0170936	0757	3
STANGE RICHARD H	LTC	0-0294637	0968	3
STANGEL VICTOR	CPT	0-0493356	0646	2
STANGER THOMAS A	MAJ	0-1545637	1164	1
STANGL FREDERICK	LTC	0-2031902	0765	1
STANGL TONY F	LTC	0-1283688	0461	1
STANICH MICHAEL A	2LT	0-1288641	1045	2
STANICK BERNARD L	LTC	W-1289988	1055	1
STANIEC STEPHEN	CPT	0-0971744	1060	1
STANIFER ROM D	LTC	0-0245088	0364	3
STANION WARREN F	LTC	0-0285181	0665	3
STANIS JOHN E	LTC	0-0534136	0864	1
STANISH EDWARD A	MAJ	0-2262610	1267	1
STANISH THEODORE J	LTC	0-1286563	1266	1
STANISLO NICK K	LTC	0-0352904	0366	1
STANK ALBERT F	CW2	W-2146280	0657	1
STANKO GEORGE	CPT	0-1998373	0254	2
STANKO WILLIAM M	1LT	0-1185315	0647	1
STANKUS ANTHONY A SR	LTC	0-0495660	0455	1
STANLEY ARTHUR J JR	LTC	0-0234148	0463	3
STANLEY ARTHUR L	CPT	0-0369260	0644	2
STANLEY BEN W	1LT	0-1596511	1045	2
STANLEY CALVIN E	CW3	W-2149270	1162	1
STANLEY CHARLES A	LTC	0-0186381	0648	3
STANLEY CHARLES M	CW4	W-2113272	0555	1
STANLEY CHESTER H	MAJ	0-0983754	0865	1
STANLEY CLEON F	LTC	0-0163285	0761	3
STANLEY CLIFFORD	MAJ	0-1338409	1264	1
STANLEY EDWARD T	MAJ	0-1638626	1061	1
STANLEY EMERY R	LTC	0-0323651	0160	3
STANLEY ERNEST K	CPT	0-2055303	0561	1
STANLEY ERNEST P JR	MAJ	0-0949083	0366	1
STANLEY FELIX W JR	MAJ	0-0036428	1060	1
STANLEY FOSTER L	COL	0-0118912	1055	3
STANLEY FRANK A	LTC	0-1100349	0161	1
STANLEY FRANK C JR	1LT	0-1320349	1045	2
STANLEY FREMONT B	LTC	0-1167649	1160	1
STANLEY GEORGE B	CPT	0-1593309	0350	1
STANLEY GLEN R	1LT	0-1288642	0744	2
STANLEY HARRY D	2LT	0-1293877	0959	1
STANLEY HAYWOOD	LTC	0-1170996	1267	1
STANLEY JOHN G	COL	0-2042895	1160	1
STANLEY JOSEPH	CW3	W-2148651	0963	1
STANLEY LISBETH M	CPT	N-0720348	1054	2
STANLEY MILFORD W	MAJ	0-0410674	0662	1
STANLEY NORMAN O	MAJ	0-0976911	1263	2
STANLEY RAYMOND L	MAJ	0-0360879	0563	1
STANLEY ROBERT	CPT	0-0525215	0347	1
STANLEY ROME	CPT	0-0493534	0447	1
STANLEY RUDOLPH S	LTC	0-0287432	0966	3
STANLEY SAMUEL F	MAJ	0-1182969	1060	1
STANLEY WILFRED B	LTC	0-0268240	0560	1
STANLEY WILLIAM C	LTC	0-0348149	0361	1
STANLY GEORGE B	CPT	0-0173776	1061	3
STANN STANLEY J	MAJ	0-0394649	0861	1
STANN STANLEY S	LTC	0-0387560	0561	1
STANN WALTER A	MAJ	0-1110270	0958	1
STANNACK GUY	LTC	0-1559126	0564	1
STANO FERDINAND	LTC	0-0372168	0358	1
STANPHILL DELMAR R	MAJ	0-0969257	0764	1
STANPHILL ODELL	CPT	0-0804245	0461	1
STANSBURY ALFRED B	MAJ	0-0349899	0156	1
STANSBURY HARRY R	LTC	0-1115805	0966	1
STANSBURY JAMES E JR	LTC	0-0300368	1161	1
STANSBURY MARCELLU	CPT	0-0551878	0846	2
STANSBURY PAUL	COL	0-0384570	1262	1
STANSELL JOHN W	CPT	0-1297110	0747	2
STANSELL ROBERT R JR	1LT	0-1312727	0746	2
STANSIFER JOHN D	2LT	0-1930037	1054	2
STANTON CHARLES W	LTC	0-1041921	0564	1
STANTON CHARLOTTE	1LT	N-0722667	0945	1
STANTON CLARENCE H	MAJ	0-0323800	0164	3
STANTON DOUGLAS W JR	LTC	0-1822072	0865	1
STANTON EDWARD V	MAJ	0-1695920	0246	2
STANTON FARRIS C	1LT	0-0420770	1045	2
STANTON FORD B	LTC	0-0282509	0267	3
STANTON GEORGE M	LTC	0-1594645	0466	3
STANTON HOMER F	CW4	W-2104498	0664	1
STANTON JAMES C	LTC	0-0147997	0250	3
STANTON JOSEPH A	MAJ	0-1306333	1164	1
STANTON KENNETH A	MAJ	0-1101672	1159	1
STANTON KENNETH J	LTC	0-0234914	0965	3
STANTON LEE B	LTC	0-0245303	0966	3
STANTON LEGETTE	CW2	W-2206562	0164	1
STANTON LOUIS E	LTC	0-0217309	0346	2
STANTON LUCIE	2LT	N-0744274	0744	1
STANTON MARK A	MAJ	0-0692520	0759	1
STANTON PAUL M	2LT	0-1322963	0345	2
STANTON ROSS H JR	1LT	0-1316102	0645	2
STANTON THOMAS F	CPT	0-1181467	0354	2
STANTON WILLIAM F	LTC	0-0450914	0658	1
STANTON WYLLYS G	LTC	0-0232800	0346	2
STANULIS EDWARD A	MAJ	0-1303567	0850	2
STANULONIS STANLEY F	MAJ	0-0962235	1161	2
STAPLES ELTON E	LTC	0-0226865	1163	3
STAPLES ERNEST A JR	MAJ	0-1186759	1164	1
STAPLES FRANK	CPT	0-0108439	0326	1
STAPLES JAMES L	2LT	0-1165959	1044	2
STAPLES JEREMIAH G	LTC	0-0297889	0965	3
STAPLES MARGARET F	1LT	N-0700861	0143	1
STAPLES RALPH JR	MAJ	0-1556663	1160	1
STAPLES ROBERT R	LTC	0-0283662	0365	3
STAPLES WILLIAM D	1LT	0-0283185	0842	2
STAPLETON C A JR	MAJ	0-1949222	1060	1
STAPLETON CLAUDE E	CW2	W-2208126	1061	1
STAPLETON CYRIL O	COL	0-0329737	1068	2
STAPLETON EUGENE C	CW2	W-2210862	0766	1
STAPLETON HERBERT N	LTC	0-0270990	0867	3
STAPLETON JAMES A	CPT	0-0369905	0445	2
STAPLETON JOHN L	LTC	0-0288564	1164	3
STAPLETON JOSEPH I	MAJ	0-1032395	0263	1
STAPLETON ROBERT G	CPT	0-1044959	0966	1
STAPLETON SAMUEL J	MAJ	0-0976357	0963	1
STAPOWICH JOSEPH P	LTC	0-0366479	1060	1
STAPP J D	CW4	W-2106984	1058	1
STAPP JAMES B	LTC	0-0262231	0667	3
STAPP JOHN W	MAJ	0-1931343	0866	1
STAPP ROBERT R	LTC	0-0395418	1164	1
STAPP ROY D	CPT	0-0481520	1050	1
STAPP WILLIAM B	LTC	0-1171375	0768	1
STAPP WILLIAM J	LTC	0-0917085	0966	3
STAPPLER FRIEDRICH	LTC	0-1080327	1266	1
STAPULA JAMES E	LTC	0-1114760	1062	1
STARBIRD CHESTER B	CPT	0-0165054	0648	3
STARBIRD JAMES C	MAJ	0-0360905	1051	2
STARBOARD EARL O	CPT	0-0159784	0755	3
STARBUCK CHARLES O	LTC	0-0377271	0862	1
STARBUCK JACK C	1LT	0-1534869	0444	2
STARBUCK JAMES L	WO1	W-2211565	0367	1
STARCEVICH PAUL J	CPT	0-0500585	0643	2
STARCHER EVERETT H	LTC	0-0244772	0857	3
STARCHER LEROY	LTC	0-0468719	1163	1
STARCK CARL O	CPT	0-0496841	1046	2
STARE ANDREW	MAJ	0-1050099	0866	1
STARE EDWARD W	LTC	0-0283740	0168	3
STARICHA LOUIS	CW4	W-2108628	0351	1
STARK ABRAM L	WO1	W-2133269	1047	1
STARK ALFRED R	CPT	0-0232421	0646	2
STARK ALONZO F	LTC	0-0278402	0463	3
STARK BETTY	1LT	N-0736328	1046	1
STARK CHRISTOPHE JR	LTC	0-0269595	1168	3
STARK CLARENCE A	LTC	0-0238110	1062	3
STARK ELDEE R	LTC	0-0274375	1264	3
STARK GEORGE D	CPT	0-0493125	0447	1
STARK HOWARD H	LTC	0-0913289	0264	2
STARK HUGH G	LTC	0-0403790	0954	1
STARK HUGO J	COL	0-0228521	0465	3
STARK JESSE D	COL	0-0291207	0160	3
STARK JOSEPH V	CW3	W-2144206	0562	1
STARK JULIAN H	LTC	0-0177851	1061	3
STARK JULIUS A	B G	0-0143760	1054	3
STARK LOUIS B	LTC	0-0911331	0868	3
STARK MARY E	MAJ	L-1010213	0565	1
STARK MELVILLE I	LTC	0-0334783	1145	2
STARK MERRILL L	2LT	0-1177646	0344	2
STARK MORRIS	CPT	0-0501052	1045	2

NAME	GRADE	SVC NO	DATE RET MO YR	RET CODE
STARK ROBERT R	2LT	0-2006126	0446	2
STARK ROBERT E	LTC	0-0437815	0166	3
STARK ROY W	2LT	0-1109688	0644	2
STARK THOMAS H	MAJ	0-0498072	0947	2
STARKE HORACE M JR	LTC	0-0241481	0259	3
STARKE MILTON B	CW3	W-2152135	0864	2
STARKE ROBERT J	CPT	0-0259186	0666	3
STARKEY BERNARD L JR	CPT	0-1012113	0646	2
STARKEY BILLIE D	MAJ	0-1876273	0668	1
STARKEY CHARLES G	COL	0-0166837	0656	3
STARKEY ELLIS D	CW3	W-2209992	1267	1
STARKEY JOHN A K	1LT	0-0337772	0542	2
STARKEY JOHN E	MAJ	0-1535970	0463	1
STARKEY JOHN H	LTC	0-1289929	1060	1
STARKEY JOHNNY W	MAJ	0-2027369	C961	1
STARKEY RALPH W	MAJ	0-0262821	1265	3
STARKEY RAYMOND F	2LT	0-2005581	1146	1
STARKMAN MICHAEL C	1LT	0-1576688	0844	2
STARKOWICZ STANLEY P	LTC	0-1317828	1062	1
STARKS CHARLES W	LTC	0-0444668	0346	2
STARKS FREDERICK	CW3	W-2152184	0865	1
STARKS WALTER	CW2	W-3430475	0167	1
STARKWEATHER WILLIAM	MAJ	0-0283508	0346	2
STARLING HERMAN W	MAJ	0-1171376	0756	1
STARLING HUIE D	CPT	0-2007881	0454	2
STARLING JOHN C	CPT	0-0438817	1148	2
STARLING RALPH E	CPT	0-1328088	0661	1
STARLING RICHARD G	MAJ	0-0409974	0261	1
STARMAN RAPHAEL F	CPT	0-1318233	0747	2
STARMER JOHN W	1LT	0-0495220	0761	1
STARNES CAMERON S JR	MAJ	0-0291283	0648	2
STARNES GILBERT D	LTC	0-0420278	0957	1
STARNES HAROLD F	CW2	W-2149367	0261	1
STARNES JAMES M	MAJ	0-0199042	0347	1
STARNES JAMES V	COL	0-0341524	1060	1
STARNES JOE JR	1LT	0-0520866	0945	2
STARNES WILLIAM G	COL	0-0901246	0946	2
STARNS CLYDE	CPT	0-0966531	0960	1
STARNS JOE E	LTC	0-1288643	0259	1
STAROW FRANK J	1LT	0-1647292	0445	2
STAROW JOHN M	MAJ	0-0497960	0446	2
STARR AMBROSE M	1LT	0-1643364	0146	2
STARR DAVID J	MAJ	0-1030304	0563	1
STARR DONALD F	COL	0-0455912	1264	1
STARR ERASMUS F	LTC	0-1322381	1262	1
STARR FRANK C	COL	0-0143057	0648	3
STARR FRANK H	MAJ	0-0248356	0848	3
STARR GEORGE	MAJ	0-1059295	0965	1
STARR GEORGE J	LTC	0-0200327	0650	3
STARR HAROLD L	MAJ	0-1919209	1168	1
STARR HERBERT L	CPT	0-0308920	0345	2
STARR JAMES W	LTC	0-0382822	0361	1
STARR JOHN F	LTC	0-0179342	0555	3
STARR JOSEPH L	LTC	0-0401616	0954	1
STARR LORIS B	LTC	0-0358490	0761	1
STARR PETER J	MAJ	0-2016458	1061	2
STARR ROBERT A	LTC	0-0451532	0864	2
STARR ROGERS F	LTC	0-0362308	0460	1
STARR ROSE K	MAJ	N-0724943	0766	3
STARR WALTER W	CW2	W-3430320	1268	1
STARR WILLIAM T	COL	0-0251467	0365	3
STARRET HOWARD A	MAJ	0-0158384	0842	2
STARRETT HENRY A	COL	0-0127579	0156	3
STARRETT JOSEPH C	MAJ	0-1685580	1264	1
STARRETT SAMUEL P	MAJ	0-1167234	0859	1
STARRY DON A	COL	0-0330433	0157	3
STARTT JOHN W	CPT	0-0385183	0550	1
STARTUP ALBERT A	CW3	W-2150303	1263	1
STARZYK WILLIAM J	MAJ	0-1947455	0555	1
STASI EMILIO	MAJ	0-2262653	0264	1
STASKIEWICZ LEO J	LTC	0-0288580	0762	3
STASSI VICTOR B	MAJ	0-0263865	1144	2
STATEN VIRGINIA C	1LT	N-0741459	0846	1
STATESIR VERNON A	CPT	0-0191498	0860	3
STATHIS H ROBERT	LTC	0-2044377	0267	3

NAME	GRADE	SVC NO	DATE RET MO YR	RET CODE
STATHOS VRASIDA D	CW4	W-2003455	1165	1
STATON LORY G	MAJ	0-0495301	1053	1
STATON OLIN G	CW3	W-2207748	1267	1
STATON SAMUEL D	CPT	0-0454786	0847	2
STATON WOODS W	1LT	0-0554509	0546	2
STAUB ROBERT E	LTC	0-1685673	0667	1
STAUBACH WILLIAM S	CW2	W-2215336	0467	1
STAUDENMAIER W G	CPT	0-0185631	1154	3
STAUDIGL HENRY J	CPT	0-0464796	0545	2
STAUDINGER JOSEPH F	LTC	0-0885382	0255	1
STAUDT CHARLES P	CW2	W-2150928	0657	1
STAUDT GEORGE L	LTC	0-0334807	1045	2
STAUDT RAYMOND E	CW3	W-2210748	1068	1
STAUDT WILLIAM S	COL	0-0524259	0568	2
STAUFF JOHN H	CPT	0-1183628	0247	2
STAUFFACHER CHARLES	CPT	0-1699937	0646	2
STAUFFER CARRYL E	MAJ	0-0218373	0564	3
STAUFFER IVERY D	LTC	0-1053377	0464	1
STAUFFER LILA L	1LT	N-0804848	0453	2
STAUFFER MARLIN J	CPT	0-4041244	1268	2
STAUFFER PAUL W	WO1	W-2122633	0852	1
STAUFFER ROYCE A	MAJ	0-1920032	0865	1
STAUFFER WILLARD F	CPT	0-1306164	0949	2
STAUNCH STEPHEN	WO1	W-2104829	0345	2
STAUSS ELMER A	MAJ	0-0257557	0945	2
STAUSS SELMA I	CPT	L-0912496	0348	2
STAVINOHA HENRY F	MAJ	0-0257947	0765	3
STAVISH JEROME W	CPT	0-0920752	1044	2
STAWINSKY JOANN	MAJ	0-1181149	1060	1
STAYNER FLOYD L	COL	0-0258153	0861	1
STAYTON FLOYD E	COL	0-0225339	1264	3
STAYTON SAMUEL A	CPT	0-1599191	0258	1
STEACY HUBERT M	CW3	W-2122113	0655	1
STEAD EARLE C	COL	0-0147004	1055	3
STEAD OLIN W	MAJ	0-0242415	0665	3
STEADLER CLARENCE M	COL	0-0172016	0356	3
STEARN JOSEPH L	LTC	0-0339328	0368	3
STEARNES HARDIN	MAJ	0-0234519	0959	3
STEARNES WILLIE B	CW2	W-2119878	0651	1
STEARNS ALBERT C	MAJ	0-0156210	0555	3
STEARNS CLYDE C	CPT	0-0139245	0955	3
STEARNS FRED S	MAJ	0-0479633	0555	2
STEARNS HARRY A	LTC	0-0193738	0648	3
STEARNS MARGARET E	1LT	N-0765454	0647	1
STEARNS MORRIS L	1LT	0-1062641	0450	2
STEARNS PARLEY M	1LT	0-1554826	1045	2
STEARNS ROBERT J	MAJ	0-0963846	0366	2
STEARNS ROLAND F	LTC	0-0949037	0868	1
STEARNS RUSSEL M	COL	0-0347356	1161	3
STEARNS STEVEN H	1LT	0-0939683	1150	2
STEARNS THOMAS H	CW4	W-2145843	0968	1
STEATES EDWARD C	1LT	0-1292444	0446	2
STEBBING PHILIP A	COL	0-0270230	0363	3
STEBBINS CHESTER F	MAJ	0-0304703	0165	3
STEBBINS GEORGE B	COL	0-0127146	0648	3
STEBBINS JUNE H	LTC	0-0936305	0866	1
STEBBINS LAWRENCE C	CW2	W-2150243	1060	1
STEBBINS ROY W	2LT	0-1638578	0666	3
STECH RICHARD J	CW2	RW-2207678	1163	1
STECHER ADOLPH	CW4	W-2141457	0266	1
STECHER ANTHONY F	COL	0-0117768	0855	3
STECHER HAROLD I	LTC	0-0203116	1061	3
STECHER PETER J	LTC	0-1996566	0761	1
STECK CHARLES F III	LTC	0-1645401	0763	1
STECK HAROLD P	1LT	0-1323496	1145	2
STECK JOHN E	CW2	W-2150759	0864	1
STECKBAUER WILLIAM J	CW4	W-2002676	0761	3
STECKBECK HENRY J	MAJ	0-1575573	0249	1
STECKEL EVERETT J	MAJ	0-0404849	1160	1
STECKLER EDMUND J	MAJ	0-0977594	1265	1
STECKLER PHILIP P	MAJ	0-0504785	0851	2
STEDGE ERNEST J	2LT	0-0464712	0843	2
STEDMAN HARRY E	COL	0-0170516	0654	3
STEDMAN W THACHER	COL	0-0177941	1050	2
STEDRONSKY VICTOR L	MAJ	0-0271750	0968	3

NAME	GRADE	SVC NO	DATE RET MO YR	RET CODE
STEEBER WILLIAM L	CPT	0-2039639	0256	1
STEED ALBERT M JR	2LT	0-1326064	1045	2
STEED BASIL G	2LT	0-1587650	0157	1
STEED HAROLD F	1LT	0-1302064	0546	2
STEED ROBERT	CPT	0-0302971	1047	1
STEED WILLIAM C	LTC	0-1635368	0561	1
STEEL ERNEST W	COL	0-0190874	0853	3
STEEL JOHN A	CPT	0-0403609	0146	2
STEELE ALFRED M	MAJ	0-0340535	1158	1
STEELE ARTHUR F S	1LT	0-1315231	0146	2
STEELE ASA G	WO1	W-2110964	0766	3
STEELE CARL W	CW3	W-2151998	0364	2
STEELE CELIA G	2LT	N-0721172	1144	1
STEELE CHARLES W	COL	0-0469173	0166	3
STEELE CHESTER D	LTC	0-1030095	0664	1
STEELE CLARENCE R	LTC	0-0209669	0648	3
STEELE CLAYTON S	COL	0-0299549	0668	3
STEELE CLIFTON R	1LT	0-1314846	0747	2
STEELE CLYDE F JR	MAJ	0-1307320	0664	1
STEELE CORNELIUS	CPT	0-1634364	0346	2
STEELE DONALD P	1LT	0-1169349	0145	2
STEELE FRANK P	MAJ	0-0965172	0765	1
STEELE GARLAND F	LTC	0-0902116	0947	2
STEELE GEORGE T	CPT	0-2033293	0863	1
STEELE GERALD H	LTC	0-0239732	0765	3
STEELE GORDON K	MAJ	0-0354705	0359	1
STEELE HENRY M	LTC	0-0186177	0750	3
STEELE HOWARD C	CPT	0-1326472	0248	2
STEELE HOWARD J	MAJ	0-1549848	0457	1
STEELE JAMES C	LTC	0-2005287	0666	1
STEELE JAMES H	MAJ	0-0239254	0345	2
STEELE JESSE I	COL	0-0264786	0265	3
STEELE JOHN G	MAJ	0-0338795	0755	1
STEELE JOHN H	MAJ	0-1554095	0364	1
STEELE JOHN N	CPT	0-0369113	1044	2
STEELE JOHN P	MAJ	0-2262181	0163	1
STEELE JOHN W	CPT	0-0528499	0352	1
STEELE JOSEPH C	CPT	0-0331566	0862	1
STEELE MARVIN J	LTC	0-0761338	0467	1
STEELE MARY E	2LT	N-0796012	0346	1
STEELE MERRILL L	COL	0-0199717	0353	3
STEELE MILAN G	MAJ	0-0165347	1159	3
STEELE MYRON T	MAJ	0-1582568	0962	1
STEELE PAUL L	LTC	0-0451421	1055	1
STEELE PAUL O	MAJ	0-0426656	0857	1
STEELE RALPH L	COL	0-0210592	0856	3
STEELE ROBERT P	CW4	W-2142903	1267	1
STEELE ROBERT V	MAJ	0-1101673	0859	1
STEELE ROBERT W	MAJ	0-1282347	0962	1
STEELE ROY R	MAJ	0-1999049	0460	1
STEELE VIRGIL S	MAJ	0-0250001	1045	2
STEELE WARREN B	COL	0-0169296	0960	1
STEELE WILLIAM	MAJ	0-0419676	0746	2
STEELE WILLIS G	1LT	0-2262832	0357	1
STEELMAN JAMES F	MAJ	0-1102970	0361	1
STEELMAN JOSEPH E	CPT	0-0969271	0258	1
STEELMAN ROBERT C	LTC	0-2262861	1068	1
STEELSMITH ERNEST M	MAJ	0-0400846	0146	2
STEELY STEWART L	2LT	0-1556664	1043	2
STEEN DOROTHY M	MAJ	N-0792361	1068	1
STEEN JAMES P	1LT	0-1295957	1044	2
STEEN JOHN M	MAJ	0-1640490	0562	1
STEEN JULIAN P	LTC	0-0237904	0265	3
STEEN MARVIN O	COL	0-0159284	0847	2
STEEN PHILIP M	MAJ	0-1170208	0361	1
STEENBARGER CHARLES	LTC	0-0416914	0364	1
STEENSGAARD RAYMON	CPT	0-1032247	0856	1
STEENSLAND THOMAS T	1LT	0-0540930	1145	2
STEERE MANSON F	MAJ	0-1046961	1060	1
STEERS WALTER A	MAJ	0-0423620	1060	1
STEES ERNEST W	LTC	0-1636690	0766	1
STEFANCIN JOSEPH F	2LT	0-1999880	0546	2
STEFANIAK LEO	MAJ	0-0151952	0648	3
STEFANICH FRANK A	1LT	0-1168930	0646	2
STEFANOWICZ VICTOR A	LTC	0-0382664	0462	1

NAME	GRADE	SVC NO	DATE RET MO YR	RET CODE
STEFFEN WILLIAM	LTC	0-1328194	0566	1
STEFFEN BERTRAM L	CW4	W-2142468	0158	1
STEFFEN GERALD B	MAJ	0-1295451	1061	1
STEFFEN MARTIN H	COL	0-0309853	1159	1
STEFFENHAGEN DEWEY H	MAJ	0-0490010	1045	2
STEFFENS LINCOLN F	COL	0-0297571	0266	3
STEFFENSEN WALLACE H	MAJ	0-0483055	0945	2
STEFFENSON ALBERT P	MAJ	0-1177196	0563	1
STEFFER ORVILLE R	MAJ	0-1011195	0157	1
STEFFER SOPHIE S	MAJ	N-0758698	1064	1
STEFFEY HOWARD L	LTC	0-0311381	0659	2
STEGALL DELBERT L	CPT	0-1550509	0654	1
STEGALL DORSEY F	LTC	0-1118504	1163	1
STEGALL HARRY E	MAJ	0-1688388	1160	1
STEGALL JAMES R	MAJ	0-0926603	1061	1
STEGALL OLIVER N	MAJ	0-0355665	0346	2
STEGALL WHITNEY	MAJ	0-1644813	0747	2
STEGEMAN LEROY C	LTC	0-0253010	0459	3
STEGEMILLER EARL G	LTC	0-0310764	0368	3
STEGENGA MINER	MAJ	0-0171953	0251	3
STEGER LAWRENCE P	CW3	W-2145205	0564	1
STEGER PAUL J	MAJ	0-0285786	0347	2
STEGMAN HAZEL M	2LT	N-0742647	0847	1
STEGMANN DONALD F	LTC	0-1309621	0962	1
STEGMANN HENRY R	CPT	0-1309109	0246	2
STEGMEIER HERBERT D	MAJ	0-1340824	0365	1
STEGNER ALBERT L	COL	0-0240196	0765	3
STEGNER DEWAYNE O	MAJ	0-0131174	0648	3
STEGNER LLOYD E	COL	0-0122093	0556	3
STEHLIN EARL K	MAJ	0-4074753	1167	1
STEIBEL LOUIS R	COL	0-0199618	0149	3
STEIG LESTER P	MAJ	0-0311256	1046	2
STEIG MILAN B	COL	0-0239279	0864	3
STEIGERWALT WILLIAM	LTC	0-1550700	0862	1
STEIMER RALPH N	COL	0-0147006	0955	3
STEIMLE MARTHA L	MAJ	N-0773831	1167	1
STEIN ALFRED E	CPT	0-0283274	0645	2
STEIN ARTHUR D	MAJ	0-0961566	0464	2
STEIN FRANK P	MAJ	0-0265376	0860	3
STEIN FREDRICK A	1LT	0-0400421	0344	2
STEIN HARRY C	LTC	0-0185570	0648	3
STEIN HENRY G	COL	0-0333626	0254	3
STEIN HENRY J	MAJ	0-1951562	0764	1
STEIN JEROME D JR	CPT	0-1298948	1047	2
STEIN JOSEPH P	LTC	0-1586233	0468	3
STEIN KARL E	LTC	0-1037733	0666	1
STEIN LEONARD J	LTC	0-1165756	1160	1
STEIN LOUIS	MAJ	0-0230404	1263	3
STEIN LOUIS H	1LT	0-0167153	0959	3
STEIN MORRIS B	CPT	0-1715558	0346	2
STEIN MORTON P	1LT	0-1586234	1045	2
STEIN RAYMOND S	MAJ	0-1548315	0361	1
STEIN STANLEY S	CPT	0-1039578	0946	2
STEIN THEODORE G	LTC	0-0429877	0268	3
STEINBACH GEORGE C	LTC	0-1633025	0457	1
STEINBAUGH HUBERT D	MAJ	0-0221118	0358	1
STEINBECK PAUL W	COL	0-0017670	0859	2
STEINBERG CHARLES	1LT	0-0885792	1045	2
STEINBERG HARRY	LTC	0-0497593	1065	3
STEINBERG JOE	1LT	0-0417448	0845	2
STEINBERG MARTIN R	LTC	0-0484973	0745	2
STEINBERG SAM	1LT	0-1576694	0246	2
STEINBERG SAMUEL J	LTC	0-0246827	1266	3
STEINBERG SAUL	MAJ	0-0483911	0846	2
STEINBRUEGGE GERTRUD	CPT	N-0787736	0946	1
STEINEBACH WILLIAM J	LTC	0-0969580	0968	1
STEINECK SHIRLEY S	2LT	N-0731351	0345	1
STEINEGEWEG CHARLE	2LT	0-2000823	1045	2
STEINEKER ALFRED W	1LT	0-1018465	0446	2
STEINER ELLIS A	MAJ	0-1894630	0154	1
STEINER HELEN E	CPT	N-0787466	0846	1
STEINER HOWARD A	CPT	0-0493557	1145	2
STEINER JOHN H	MAJ	0-1596195	1264	1
STEINER JOHN J F	COL	0-0206815	0553	3
STEINER LEO E	LTC	0-0179914	0851	3

NAME	GRADE	SVC NO	DATE RET MO YR	RET CODE
STEINER NICHOLAS M	CPT	0-0492676	1043	2
STEINER RANALD F	MAJ	0-1100783	1059	1
STEINER RAYMOND P	LTC	0-0325865	0161	1
STEINER SAMUEL	CPT	0-1551122	0858	2
STEINERT BEVERLY A	1LT	N-0743326	0446	1
STEINES LEO J	CW2	W-2149579	1163	1
STEINFELD HOWARD F	MAJ	0-1294742	0258	1
STEINFIELD THOMAS G	LTC	0-0320760	1059	3
STEINHARDT ALBERT J	LTC	0-0108164	0940	1
STEINHART ARDEN C	LTC	0-0262967	1266	3
STEINHAUER ROBERT A	CPT	0-1317831	0862	1
STEINHAUSEN RICHARD	LTC	0-1292777	0864	1
STEINHILPER JACK H	LTC	0-0450661	0657	1
STEINHOFF CARL F	B G	0-0245045	1054	3
STEINHOUR RUSSELL B	LTC	0-0502106	0657	1
STEINKE RAYMOND L	LTC	0-0480494	0168	3
STEINKRUGER ANTHON	LTC	0-0276952	0359	1
STEINMAN DONALD F	CW2	W-2144389	0463	1
STEINMAN ROBERT E	LTC	0-0279975	0466	3
STEINMAN RUDOLPH	1LT	0-2000795	0756	1
STEINMANN WILLIAM E	MAJ	0-1016042	0761	1
STEINMETZ GEORGE P	LTC	0-0210057	0456	3
STEINMETZ JOHN P	MAJ	0-2002545	0461	2
STEINMETZ THOMAS J	MAJ	0-1118814	0160	1
STEINMEYER HARRY A	MAJ	0-0967145	0861	1
STEINMEYER WILMER H	1LT	0-0233854	0965	3
STEINREICH OTTO S	CPT	0-0369169	0746	2
STEINSIEK CLYDE W	LTC	0-1040311	0561	1
STEINWACHS JON P	LTC	0-0347483	1153	1
STEINWAND DONALD A	CPT	0-0998886	0462	1
STEIRWAGLE WENDELL F	CPT	0-1043235	1058	2
STEIS WILLIAM B	MAJ	0-1291192	0447	2
STEJBACK WILLIAM J	CW3	W-2203874	0967	1
STEJSKAL JULIUS	MAJ	0-0300410	0663	3
STEKERT FRANKLIN	MAJ	0-0233367	0448	2
STELFOX LEONARD F	1LT	0-1109696	0146	2
STELL DAVID J	LTC	0-0279342	0568	3
STELL JAMES L SR	COL	0-0255362	1062	3
STELL OTIS A JR	CPT	0-1594976	0147	2
STELLA ABEL	CPT	0-1283990	1054	1
STELLA MANUEL	MAJ	0-1284595	0763	3
STELLA MICHAEL J	2LT	0-1302409	0144	2
STELLER HOWARD M	CPT	0-0325096	0167	3
STELLINGER CALVIN W	LTC	0-0452983	1163	1
STELLMANN EDWARD B	COL	0-0169358	0960	3
STELLRECHT TROY P	CPT	0-2035391	0547	2
STELMAN HENRY H	LTC	0-0302597	0767	3
STELTZNER LEWIS H	LTC	0-0356035	0868	3
STELTZNER ROGER L	LTC	0-0423268	0863	1
STEM RICHARD C	MAJ	0-0690268	0661	2
STEMBER ABRAHAM	MAJ	0-1634365	1067	3
STEMEN RICHARD J	MAJ	0-1031843	1263	1
STEMLER DAVID R	2LT	0-0495394	0145	2
STEMNOCK LEONARD V	CW3	W-2139657	0559	1
STEMPEL FRANKLIN H	LTC	0-0303482	0647	2
STEMPLE CLYDE F	CPT	0-1324201	1064	1
STEMPLE EARL C	LTC	0-0520970	0464	1
STENBERG FRANCIS R	2LT	0-1303569	0344	2
STENDER LEON S	2LT	0-1590828	0545	2
STENDER WILBUR P	MAJ	0-1545079	0962	1
STENE GORDON S	LTC	0-1312062	0766	1
STENERSON RAYMOND H	LTC	0-1286201	0157	1
STENGEL HENRY J	CPT	0-1821144	0443	2
STENGEL JAMES D	CW2	W-2150514	0656	1
STENGEL WILLIAM M	1LT	0-1178351	0745	2
STENGER FRED C	LTC	0-0227724	0559	3
STENGER ROBERT	LTC	0-1314687	0966	1
STENGLE WILLIAM T	2LT	0-0348314	0555	3
STENHOUSE JOE L	LTC	0-1288136	0959	1
STENINGER HOWARD W	MAJ	0-1542423	0157	1
STENINGER MILO C	1LT	0-0356420	1144	2
STENJEM ELDON M	COL	0-0159397	1054	3
STENMOE CLARENCE S	MAJ	0-1318248	0862	1
STENN ARTHUR	CPT	0-1821195	0843	2
STENNER JOHN	2LT	0-2027513	0549	1

NAME	GRADE	SVC NO	DATE RET MO YR	RET CODE
STENQUIST GEORGE W	COL	0-0268219	0162	3
STENSBY JOHN L	CW3	W-2143139	0560	1
STENSLAND ARTHUR O	CPT	0-0266981	0853	3
STENSLAND ROY F	CPT	0-0386242	0550	2
STENSON RUSSELL C	LTC	0-0406140	0960	1
STENSON VIRGINIA M	1LT	N-0756714	0246	1
STENSTROM ETHEL C	CPT	L-0400546	0549	2
STEPAHIN ALEXANDRIA	MAJ	N-0725794	0862	1
STEPANOVICH NICK	COL	0-0259434	0967	3
STEPHAN CARL	LTC	0-0519006	0954	1
STEPHAN EDWARD W	1LT	0-1052587	0846	2
STEPHAN EMMA E	CW3	V-0217521	0564	1
STEPHAN PAUL J	CW2	W-2205330	0463	2
STEPHAN ROBERT S	CPT	0-2288975	0565	1
STEPHANI PAUL W	LTC	0-1165960	0965	1
STEPHANS FRED L	LTC	0-0254606	0364	3
STEPHANY CARL R	MAJ	0-0137675	0744	2
STEPHEN JAMES E	CW3	W-2148269	0863	1
STEPHEN JOHN M	CW4	W-2002569	0264	3
STEPHENS ALBERT K	CW2	W-2115888	1054	1
STEPHENS ALEXANDER	LTC	0-0263992	0664	3
STEPHENS ALZIE L	CPT	0-1944602	0958	1
STEPHENS BEN T	LTC	0-1010742	0763	1
STERHENS CARL C JR	MAJ	0-1186619	0663	1
STEPHENS CHARLES E	CPT	0-0504404	0157	1
STEPHENS CHARLES H	COL	0-1576695	0665	1
STEPHENS CLARENCE E	CW4	W-2126125	1058	1
STEPHENS EDWARD W	CW4	W-2143449	0466	1
STEPHENS ELMER	LTC	0-0453016	1057	1
STEPHENS FOSTER L	LTC	0-0254822	0764	3
STEPHENS FRANKLIN L	MAJ	0-1575196	0166	1
STEPHENS FRANKLIN T	CW3	W-2150164	0465	2
STEPHENS GEORGE H	LTC	0-1018550	0967	1
STEPHENS GEORGE J	LTC	0-0149068	0449	3
STEPHENS GILES D	LTC	0-0348879	0954	1
STEPHENS HARRY H	CW2	W-3200119	0265	1
STEPHENS HENRY M	LTC	0-1558906	0763	1
STEPHENS HOMER E	CPT	0-0235411	0753	3
STEPHENS HOWARD A	LTC	0-1288969	1159	1
STEPHENS IRA A	LTC	0-0296854	0866	3
STEPHENS JAMES E	LTC	0-1166845	0261	1
STEPHENS JAMES F	CPT	0-0463049	1047	1
STEPHENS JAMES H	LTC	0-0282509	0168	3
STEPHENS JAMES H	MAJ	0-0485270	0747	1
STEPHENS JAMES H	CW3	W-2152688	1265	1
STEPHENS JAMES P	MAJ	0-1638585	0561	1
STEPHENS JAMES P	MAJ	0-0964860	0765	1
STEPHENS JAMES R	WO1	W-2109366	1044	2
STEPHENS JOE B	1LT	0-2263769	0657	2
STEPHENS JOHN R	MAJ	0-0452936	0856	1
STEPHENS JOHN G	LTC	0-0323763	0451	2
STEPHENS JOHN P JR	1LT	0-1101676	0546	2
STEPHENS JOSEPH	CW2	W-2111324	0251	2
STEPHENS JOSEPH P	CPT	0-1640041	0657	1
STEPHENS LAWRENCE W	LTC	0-0332191	1160	1
STEPHENS LLOYD E	MAJ	0-1295958	0161	1
STEPHENS LOUIS B	COL	0-0325866	0864	1
STEPHENS LOUIS P	MAJ	0-1036393	0657	1
STEPHENS LYNN C	1LT	0-1011991	1045	2
STEPHENS MANUEL W	CW4	W-2147650	1161	2
STEPHENS MARION A	MAJ	0-0228442	1150	3
STEPHENS OLEN	CW3	W-2142610	0256	1
STEPHENS OLIN B	CW2	W-3411035	1168	1
STEPHENS OLIVER J	MAJ	0-1110273	0263	1
STEPHENS PAUL W	MAJ	0-0360152	0448	2
STEPHENS RANDALL P	MAJ	0-1303406	0164	1
STEPHENS RAY E	MAJ	0-2055168	0261	1
STEPHENS RICHARD A	CW2	W-2205510	0663	1
STEPHENS RICHARD F	LTC	0-0238590	1060	3
STEPHENS RICHARD T	LTC	0-0247115	0457	3
STEPHENS RUSSELL R	CPT	0-0503351	0447	1
STEPHENS THELMA M	CPT	N-0787467	0448	1
STEPHENS THOMAS W	LTC	0-1913499	0768	1
STEPHENS VINCENT R	1LT	0-0366656	0145	2
STEPHENS WALTER M	1LT	0-0238512	0865	3

NAME	GRADE	SVC NO	DATE RET MO YR	RET CODE
STEPHENS WILFRED R	CPT	0-0375038	1044	2
STEPHENS WILLIAM A	LTC	0-0325796	0761	1
STEPHENS WILLIAM A	MAJ	0-2019813	0263	1
STEPHENS WILLIAM D	CW2	W-2209811	0364	1
STEPHENS WILLIAM H	1LT	0-2042975	0854	1
STEPHENS WILLIAM L	LTC	0-0329164	0559	3
STEPHENS WILLIS E	LTC	0-1634367	0967	1
STEPHENSON ALVIN B	CW3	W-2147963	0863	1
STEPHENSON CHARLES H	MAJ	0-0425821	0746	2
STEPHENSON CHARLES L	COL	0-0194111	1046	2
STEPHENSON CLARK B	COL	0-0354728	1162	1
STEPHENSON DALE J	LTC	0-0399392	0554	2
STEPHENSON DONALD B	2LT	0-1302378	0445	2
STEPHENSON EDGAR H	CPT	0-0501029	0253	1
STEPHENSON EDWARD F	COL	0-0333736	0755	3
STEPHENSON EDWARD R	LTC	0-1642610	1058	1
STEPHENSON EDWIN A	COL	0-0170012	0261	3
STEPHENSON ELLIOTT O	CPT	0-0412434	1144	2
STEPHENSON FRANCIS R	MAJ	0-1177397	0664	1
STEPHENSON GENE R	MAJ	0-0453070	0856	1
STEPHENSON GEORGE W	2LT	0-2049731	0645	2
STEPHENSON HARRY H	CPT	0-2008447	0253	2
STEPHENSON JAMES G	1LT	0-2048160	0746	2
STEPHENSON JOE	LTC	0-1286916	1055	1
STEPHENSON JOSEPH L	CPT	0-1258311	0662	1
STEPHENSON L F JR	LTC	0-1824243	1060	1
STEPHENSON LOUIS B	LTC	0-0311387	0664	3
STEPHENSON MACK C	CPT	0-1184955	0357	1
STEPHENSON OWEN T JR	MAJ	0-1917934	0164	1
STEPHENSON PAUL H	LTC	0-1013999	0963	1
STEPHENSON RAYMOND P	MAJ	0-1030522	0861	1
STEPHENSON ROY E	1LT	0-1059072	1046	2
STEPHENSON STANLEY W	LTC	0-0374755	0666	1
STEPHENSON WALLACE L	CPT	0-1825321	0755	1
STEPHENSON WARD C	LTC	0-1596514	0263	1
STEPHENSON WILBUR F	COL	0-0270178	0257	1
STEPHENSON WILLIAM A	COL	0-0506836	1064	3
STEPHENSON WINNIE M	MAJ	N-0744142	1062	1
STEPHSEN ANN L	MAJ	N-0799717	0865	1
STEPP JOSEPH J JR	LTC	0-2204022	0767	1
STEPPING HENRY	1LT	0-1823666	0246	2
STEPT RAYMOND	CPT	0-0348565	0744	2
STEPTOE ROBERT P	MAJ	0-1165576	0349	2
STERBENZ DONALD L	CPT	0-4074857	0568	1
STERETT JACK L	CW3	W-2147547	0564	1
STERGAR FRANK E	MAJ	0-0956470	0164	1
STERGIADES THEODORE	LTC	0-1544680	1165	1
STERKEN EDWARD J JR	LTC	0-1044399	0561	1
STERLE JOHN H	MAJ	0-1307477	0557	1
STERLING BOBBY G	CW2	W-2212278	1266	1
STERLING CECIL L	1LT	0-0539870	0646	2
STERLING EDWARD A	COL	0-0153579	1154	3
STERLING GERALD B	LTC	0-1634368	0557	1
STERLING HERMAN S	LTC	0-0317482	0762	2
STERLING JACK V	MAJ	0-0967496	0464	1
STERLING JAMES	MAJ	0-5301656	1168	1
STERLING JAMES K	LTC	0-1173795	0962	1
STERLING JOSEPH R	LTC	0-0425503	0167	3
STERLING JULIUS H	CPT	0-0917039	1145	2
STERLING MICHAEL J	CPT	0-1303407	0647	2
STERLING MILDRED A	2LT	N-0731502	0445	1
STERLING RAYMOND C	CW2	W-2117988	0650	1
STERLING THOMAS A	CPT	0-0506841	0350	1
STERMER JOSEPH E	LTC	0-0274190	1060	1
STERMER LEE R	CW3	W-2152880	1263	1
STERN ALBERT P	LTC	0-0277716	1066	3
STERN ARTHUR L	1LT	0-1312813	1145	2
STERN ELMER V	1LT	0-0512365	1043	2
STERN EUGENE C	1LT	0-0489739	0446	2
STERN FRED	CPT	0-1884170	0363	1
STERN GEORGE J	WO1	W-2003850	0567	3
STERN HENRY W	1LT	0-1294745	1044	2
STERN I HENRY	COL	0-0219407	0364	3
STERN JEROME	1LT	0-1541325	1044	2
STERN JOSEPH	2LT	0-1824244	1044	2

NAME	GRADE	SVC NO	DATE RET MO YR	RET CODE
STERN JOSEPH F	COL	0-0323607	0966	3
STERN JOSEPH J	COL	0-0298027	0865	3
STERN OTTO	CPT	0-1586237	1146	2
STERN SAMUEL Z	LTC	0-0294854	0346	2
STERN SIDNEY	COL	0-0288036	0861	1
STERN WALTER F	MAJ	0-1551123	0161	1
STERN WILLIAM A	MAJ	0-2018597	0364	1
STERNBECK LAWTON L	LTC	0-0693572	0962	1
STERNBERG CHARLES	CPT	0-0450494	0865	1
STERNBERG RANDOLPH W	2LT	0-0281133	0343	2
STERNE MORTIMER C JR	LTC	0-0455699	0962	1
STERNE THEODORE E	COL	0-0290549	1267	3
STERNER JOHN H	CW3	W-2145591	0964	1
STERNER THOMAS R	CW2	W-2152721	1163	1
STERNFELD ABRAHAM N	LTC	0-0420251	1068	1
STERNHAGEN JOSEPH P	LTC	0-0137167	0648	3
STERNIG MARTIN	CPT	0-1690002	1145	2
STERNS FRANK W	CPT	0-0242626	0752	3
STERRETT ANDREW G JR	LTC	0-1821646	0761	1
STERRETT PARIS V	1LT	0-0480121	1143	2
STESS IRA Z	CPT	0-1636696	1047	2
STETLER DONALD A	LTC	0-0403574	0164	1
STETLER ELMER	CPT	0-0185129	0648	3
STETSON CHARLES G	CPT	0-0282384	0 43	2
STETTER RAY N	LTC	0-0470763	0750	1
STETTLER LILLIAN C	MAJ	N-0760461	1264	3
STETZ ALBERT W	LTC	0-1796541	1065	1
STETZER JOHN W	LTC	0-0492624	0954	1
STEUART DELL K	COL	0-0336855	1053	2
STEUART GERARD J	CPT	0-0210306	0862	1
STEUDING ERNEST A	LTC	0-0252711	0167	3
STEUERWALD ROBERT C	LTC	0-0291590	0857	3
STEVEN ROBERT A	LTC	0-0226966	0642	2
STEVENS ALBERT A	MAJ	0-1949667	0960	1
STEVENS ALBERT B	LTC	0-0236530	1264	3
STEVENS ALBIN C	COL	0-0336010	0865	1
STEVENS ALLEN	1LT	0-1042955	0945	2
STEVENS ALLEN J	COL	0-0174054	0757	3
STEVENS ALTUS A	CW3	W-2235464	0366	1
STEVENS ARMENIOUS	CW4	W-2143530	0667	1
STEVENS ARTHUR B	CW3	W-2143056	1264	1
STEVENS ARTHUR E	MAJ	0-0496765	0148	1
STEVENS ARTHUR G	COL	0-0111474	0153	3
STEVENS ARTHUR G	MAJ	0-0347066	0766	2
STEVENS ARTHUR H	LTC	0-1030614	0763	1
STEVENS ARTHUR H	CW2	W-2000121	0560	3
STEVENS ARTHUR L	MAJ	0-1824816	0762	1
STEVENS AUBREY D	CW4	W-2145911	1268	1
STEVENS BOYD	MAJ	0-0233800	0664	3
STEVENS BYRON L	MAJ	0-0966308	0762	1
STEVENS CALVIN E	1LT	0-1318249	0553	2
STEVENS CARLETON H	1LT	0-1303966	0246	2
STEVENS CARROLL H	MAJ	0-0268001	0448	1
STEVENS CHARLES D	LTC	0-1322964	0763	1
STEVENS CHARLES E	LTC	0-0309884	0162	1
STEVENS CHARLES F	MAJ	0-2036449	0557	1
STEVENS CHARLES L	LTC	0-1640992	0268	3
STEVENS CHARLES R	LTC	0-0361648	0446	2
STEVENS CLAUDE M	LTC	0-1102592	0265	3
STEVENS CLINTON V	MAJ	0-0184715	0459	3
STEVENS DANIEL	1LT	0-1030721	0346	2
STEVENS DANIEL W	COL	0-0291288	1055	3
STEVENS DAVID A	COL	0-0184023	1153	3
STEVENS DONALD L	MAJ	0-0297065	0367	3
STEVENS DONALD O	CW3	W-2146801	0763	1
STEVENS EDGAR C	WO1	W-2146457	1056	2
STEVENS EDWARD A	LTC	0-0334387	0862	1
STEVENS EDWARD H	LTC	0-0515083	0657	1
STEVENS EDWARD R	LTC	0-1683449	0864	1
STEVENS EDWARD S	LTC	0-1796877	1062	2
STEVENS ELSON H	MAJ	0-1885584	1065	1
STEVENS EMMETT	LTC	0-0261397	0854	1
STEVENS FLORENCE R	MAJ	N-0721017	0362	2
STEVENS FRANCIS J	MAJ	0-1168481	0461	1
STEVENS FRANK O	LTC	0-0248476	0557	1

NAME	GRADE	SVC NO	DATE RET MO YR	RET CODE
STEVENS GEORGE A	MAJ	0-0956840	1158	1
STEVENS GEORGE E	WO1	W-2153144	1058	1
STEVENS GEORGE H	1LT	0-1116541	0146	2
STEVENS GORDON L	CW2	W-3430332	0167	1
STEVENS GRANT JR	LTC	0-2264274	0868	1
STEVENS HAROLD F	MAJ	0-0104032	0949	3
STEVENS HAROLD P	1LT	0-0920261	0944	2
STEVENS HARRY A	LTC	0-1180352	0867	1
STEVENS HARRY F	MAJ	0-0966014	0361	1
STEVENS HENRY L JR	LTC	0-0237057	0156	3
STEVENS HENRY S	LTC	0-0254655	0367	3
STEVENS HERBERT C	1LT	0-0209913	0944	2
STEVENS HERBERT K	1LT	0-1822329	0845	2
STEVENS HERMAN W	LTC	0-1171377	1054	1
STEVENS HOYT C	LTC	0-0131328	0455	3
STEVENS IOWD W	MAJ	0-0486569	0649	2
STEVENS JAMES C	MAJ	0-0984266	0365	1
STEVENS JAMES L JR	CW3	W-3350225	1268	1
STEVENS JOHN A	LTC	0-0349515	1146	2
STEVENS JOHN H	LTC	0-0451466	0657	1
STEVENS JOHN J	CPT	0-0519475	0961	2
STEVENS JOSEPH L	2LT	0-2000930	0246	2
STEVENS JULIAN B	LTC	0-0323578	0361	3
STEVENS LEWIS	MAJ	0-1555911	0158	1
STEVENS LILBURN H	M G	0-0275376	1062	3
STEVENS LOWELL G	CPT	0-1044114	0662	1
STEVENS LOYD	CPT	0-0279588	0144	2
STEVENS LUTHER R	COL	0-0232434	0848	2
STEVENS LYLE V	CW2	W-2151732	1060	1
STEVENS MELDEN L	MAJ	0-0888913	0954	2
STEVENS MERL B	1LT	0-1014845	0948	2
STEVENS MICHAEL S	2LT	0-1580438	0644	2
STEVENS MILES G	COL	0-0271858	0158	3
STEVENS MORRIS W	LTC	0-0172574	0754	3
STEVENS PAUL	MAJ	0-1062449	0861	1
STEVENS PHILIP L	2LT	0-0286241	0659	3
STEVENS RALPH A JR	COL	0-0124322	0755	1
STEVENS ROBERT C	CW3	W-2144794	0763	1
STEVENS ROBERT G	LTC	0-1284229	0766	2
STEVENS ROBERT J	1LT	0-0526769	0146	2
STEVENS ROBERT L	CPT	0-0977052	0361	1
STEVENS ROBERT R	2LT	0-2014969	0446	2
STEVENS ROBERTIE	MAJ	N-0742853	0665	1
STEVENS ROY	CPT	0-2016969	0556	1
STEVENS SAMUEL C JR	CW2	W-2147451	0965	1
STEVENS THOMAS F	MAJ	0-0300571	0667	3
STEVENS WALTER D JR	LTC	0-1291720	0462	1
STEVENS WARREN B	MAJ	0-0547522	0563	1
STEVENS WAYNE R	LTC	0-1105841	1265	1
STEVENS WILLIAM V	CW3	W-2148768	0762	2
STEVENS WINFRED G	MAJ	0-2006202	0960	1
STEVENSON ALFRED S	MAJ	0-0317199	1145	2
STEVENSON BETTY L	2LT	N-0700607	1140	1
STEVENSON CARL A	2LT	0-2009337	0846	2
STEVENSON CHARLES G	B G	0-0233309	0663	3
STEVENSON DEWITT A	CPT	0-0395391	0446	2
STEVENSON EDDIE	1LT	0-2025845	0447	1
STEVENSON EDWARD H	MAJ	0-0277128	1047	1
STEVENSON FRANK M	MAJ	0-0129309	0657	3
STEVENSON GEORGE S	COL	0-0252470	0264	3
STEVENSON GILBERT M	LTC	0-0246838	0861	3
STEVENSON HAROLD F	MAJ	0-0453757	0848	2
STEVENSON HOWARD G	LTC	0-0539378	0963	1
STEVENSON JAMES N	LTC	0-1845248	0364	1
STEVENSON JOHN	CW4	W-2122617	0461	1
STEVENSON JOSEPH W	LTC	0-1302901	0361	1
STEVENSON KARL	CPT	0-1579176	1045	2
STEVENSON MARION W	LTC	0-1290837	0563	1
STEVENSON MARJORIE G	1LT	N-0757616	0745	1
STEVENSON OLEN J JR	MAJ	0-1555190	1162	1
STEVENSON PAUL J	WO1	W-2149417	0753	2
STEVENSON PETER J	COL	0-0143185	0758	3
STEVENSON RICHARD H	LTC	0-0113311	0648	3
STEVENSON RICHARD H	CPT	0-0123939	0648	3
STEVENSON ROBERT H	MAJ	0-0147010	0954	3

NAME	GRADE	SVC NO	DATE RET MO YR	RET CODE
STEVENSON ROBERT L	COL	0-0120958	1154	1
STEVENSON ROBERT L	MAJ	0-1291031	1061	1
STEVENSON ROGER H	MAJ	0-0438060	0146	2
STEVENSON RUSH W	CPT	0-0391628	0861	1
STEVENSON SARA I	LTC	N-0700608	0445	1
STEVENSON THOMAS T	COL	0-0197539	0659	3
STEVENSON WILBUR O	CPT	0-0498497	0853	1
STEVENSON WILLIAM R	LTC	0-1165453	0457	1
STEVER ORVAL R	MAJ	0-1913377	0365	1
STEVESKEY JOSEPH M	1LT	0-0380728	0157	1
STEVICK DONALD J	COL	0-0281724	0368	3
STEWARD HAROLD D	LTC	0-0452025	0261	1
STEWARD JOHN J	LTC	0-0341496	1164	3
STEWARD WILLIAM E	CW2	W-2209539	0765	1
STEWARDSON DON J	LTC	0-1290152	1061	1
STEWART ALBERT R JR	MAJ	0-1175872	0167	2
STEWART ALEXANDER	COL	0-0203758	1062	3
STEWART ALFRED E	CW2	W-2126551	0365	1
STEWART ARCHIE M	LTC	0-0291991	1167	3
STEWART ARCHIE W JR	CPT	0-1296442	1045	2
STEWART ARTEMAS J	LTC	0-0262465	0667	3
STEWART CHANDIS L	CW3	W-2203351	0564	1
STEWART CHARLES	1LT	0-1015392	0745	2
STEWART CHARLES L	MAJ	0-0953702	0667	1
STEWART CHARLES M	MAJ	0-0404732	0146	2
STEWART CHARLES R	CW4	W-2110717	0559	1
STEWART CLARENCE D	LTC	0-1586949	0561	1
STEWART CLARENCE J	COL	0-0260552	1264	3
STEWART CLIFFORD R	LTC	0-1177198	0768	2
STEWART DON L	MAJ	0-1305496	1163	1
STEWART DONALD L	LTC	0-0272779	0862	3
STEWART DOROTHY L	MAJ	N-0732361	0964	3
STEWART EARL C	COL	0-0175687	1061	3
STEWART EDNA M	1LT	N-0778418	0749	2
STEWART EDWARD J	LTC	0-0422612	0965	1
STEWART EDWARD M	CW2	W-2151102	0264	1
STEWART ELDON C	MAJ	0-1110829	0657	1
STEWART EMRY V	COL	0-0262120	1046	2
STEWART ERNEST D	LTC	0-0450593	0758	1
STEWART EVERETT S	LTC	0-0374152	0657	1
STEWART FAYE H	COL	0-0358024	0346	2
STEWART FERGUSON C	LTC	0-0366287	0361	1
STEWART FLOYD W	B G	0-0113310	0553	3
STEWART FRANCIS X	MAJ	0-1325068	1060	1
STEWART FRANK B	LTC	0-0491221	0651	2
STEWART GARNET G	LTC	0-1549118	1066	1
STEWART GENE V	MAJ	0-1799907	1263	1
STEWART GEORGE B	CPT	0-0885059	0662	1
STEWART GEORGE F	MAJ	0-4010390	0767	1
STEWART GEORGE G	LTC	0-1645404	0265	1
STEWART GEORGE L	MAJ	0-2008461	0960	1
STEWART GEORGE T	MAJ	0-0310617	0747	2
STEWART GLENN D	CPT	0-0269487	1158	1
STEWART GLENN S	LTC	0-0972024	1068	1
STEWART GRANVILLE	1LT	0-2262170	0759	1
STEWART HAROLD A	COL	0-0201897	0457	3
STEWART HAROLD L	LTC	0-0227077	1046	2
STEWART HAROLD O	CPT	0-0528508	1145	2
STEWART HARRY G	MAJ	0-0450366	0657	1
STEWART HARRY L JR	LTC	0-1695939	0346	2
STEWART HERMAN E	CPT	0-1308558	0549	2
STEWART HOLLIS P	MAJ	0-1032657	0863	1
STEWART HOMER T	MAJ	0-1596516	0857	1
STEWART HORACE H	COL	0-0350299	0946	2
STEWART HUGH J	LTC	0-0304186	0861	1
STEWART IRWIN M	LTC	0-0239842	1047	2
STEWART JACK K	CW2	W-2149406	1163	1
STEWART JACK L	LTC	0-1291350	1061	1
STEWART JACKSON W	LTC	0-1639694	1262	1
STEWART JACOB M	MAJ	0-0448901	0745	1
STEWART JAMES	WO1	W-2106784	1051	2
STEWART JAMES A	COL	0-0258234	1162	1
STEWART JAMES A	MAJ	0-0977081	0463	1
STEWART JAMES C	1LT	0-1296762	0968	3
STEWART JAMES D	LTC	0-0237881	0265	3

NAME	GRADE	SVC NO	DATE RET MO YR	RET CODE
STEWART JAMES E	COL	0-0357549	1154	1
STEWART JAMES E	CPT	0-0940296	0562	1
STEWART JAMES E W	LTC	0-0536157	0868	1
STEWART JAMES F	CPT	0-1797036	1048	2
STEWART JAMES M	1LT	0-0411895	0245	2
STEWART JAMES N	MAJ	0-2265662	0968	1
STEWART JAMES O	LTC	0-1104346	0161	1
STEWART JAMES O	MAJ	0-2023559	0762	1
STEWART JAMES P	MAJ	0-1104347	0961	1
STEWART JAMES R	2LT	0-1309320	0945	2
STEWART JAMES T	COL	0-0353319	0963	1
STEWART JASPER O	CPT	0-1058388	1146	2
STEWART JOHN A	LTC	0-0357553	0161	1
STEWART JOHN A	CPT	0-0528895	0448	2
STEWART JOHN B	2LT	0-1329174	0560	2
STEWART JOHN C	LTC	0-1635375	0751	1
STEWART JOHN C	1LT	0-0516741	0946	2
STEWART JOHN L	1LT	0-2035739	0745	2
STEWART JOHN R	MAJ	0-0340382	1143	2
STEWART JOHN R	2LT	0-1310166	1045	2
STEWART JOHN W	COL	0-0325908	1161	1
STEWART KATHRYN R	1LT	N-0789231	0946	1
STEWART KENNETH E	LTC	0-0270104	0967	3
STEWART KENNETH M	LTC	0-1058399	0167	1
STEWART KERMIT D	COL	0-0239239	0165	3
STEWART KERMIT G	LTC	0-1319452	1062	1
STEWART LLOYD R	LTC	0-0335458	1058	1
STEWART LOUIS G	MAJ	0-0252817	0666	3
STEWART MARLIN M	LTC	0-0375794	0467	1
STEWART MARVIN R	CPT	0-1106510	1046	2
STEWART MARY V	2LT	N-0742847	0345	1
STEWART MERVILLE E	CPT	0-2016970	1048	1
STEWART MILLER J	MAJ	0-0306005	0766	3
STEWART MURRAY C	LTC	0-0412996	0263	2
STEWART NORMAN R	MAJ	0-0494609	0157	1
STEWART OLIVER W	MAJ	0-0256969	0866	3
STEWART OMER C	LTC	0-0320137	0868	3
STEWART OSWALD B	LTC	0-0223684	0557	1
STEWART OTHEL W	COL	0-0257653	0859	1
STEWART PAUL B	MAJ	0-0201832	0645	2
STEWART PERCY M	1LT	0-0521897	0856	3
STEWART PHILOMENA	1LT	N-0795335	1147	1
STEWART PRICE C	MAJ	0-1535035	0159	1
STEWART RALPH R SR	CW3	W-2211852	1268	1
STEWART RAY E JR	LTC	0-1319037	1162	1
STEWART RAY S	CW3	W-2145592	0361	1
STEWART RAYMOND H	CPT	0-1286565	1045	2
STEWART RICHARD G	COL	0-0231975	0463	3
STEWART RICHARD W	1LT	0-1016711	0247	2
STEWART ROBERT	2LT	0-1305129	0745	2
STEWART ROBERT	2LT	0-1823083	1044	2
STEWART ROBERT A	MAJ	0-1295102	0254	1
STEWART ROBERT B	CPT	0-0303906	1045	2
STEWART ROBERT C JR	LTC	0-1281053	0862	1
STEWART ROBERT G	LTC	0-0244628	0765	3
STEWART ROBERT L	COL	0-0286530	0856	3
STEWART ROBERT L	CW4	W-2121374	0368	1
STEWART ROBERT S	LTC	0-3251067	0267	3
STEWART ROBERT W	1LT	0-0295419	1043	2
STEWART ROBERT W	2LT	0-0407584	0442	2
STEWART ROBY F	MAJ	0-2073424	0765	2
STEWART ROGER S	MAJ	0-0269486	0168	3
STEWART ROY C	CPT	0-0490143	0646	2
STEWART ROY P	LTC	0-0905350	1165	3
STEWART SADIE E	1LT	N-0764773	0247	1
STEWART SAMLEN S	LTC	0-0532118	1164	1
STEWART SELDON C	MAJ	0-0456798	1152	1
STEWART STANLEY O	MAJ	0-1544386	0766	1
STEWART SYDNEY O	LTC	0-0265850	0247	2
STEWART ULYSSES G JR	MAJ	0-1550930	0862	1
STEWART W S	COL	0-0292623	0168	3
STEWART WALLACE	MAJ	0-0315665	0568	3
STEWART WILLIAM H	1LT	0-0305467	0242	2
STEWART WILLIAM H	CPT	0-0890237	1057	2
STEWART WISDOM H	LTC	0-0405378	1158	1

NAME	GRADE	SVC NO	DATE RET MO YR	RET CODE
STEYAART CHARLES L	COL	0-0252446	0762	3
STIBR JOSEPH M	CPT	0-0326188	0253	3
STICE MARC A	MAJ	0-0237403	0648	3
STICE MILTON A	LTC	0-0564408	0555	1
STICE SILAS P	CW3	W-2142990	1057	1
STICKEL VINCENT J	MAJ	0-1947604	1059	1
STICKELS M JEANNE	1LT	N-0774028	0148	1
STICKLE JOHN R	LTC	0-0305961	1060	1
STICKLER LEE R	MAJ	0-0383209	0461	1
STICKLER MERTON H	CPT	0-0165121	0957	3
STICKLES JOSEPH M	MAJ	0-1648810	0961	1
STICKLEY JOSEPH W	1LT	0-1584983	0745	2
STICKNEY EDWIN F	CPT	0-0300095	0757	3
STICKNEY GERALD R	LTC	0-1308016	0465	1
STICKNEY JOSEPH E JR	1LT	0-0514613	0846	2
STICKNEY RICHARD W	CPT	0-1181473	0447	2
STIDHAM JAMES C	CPT	0-1165048	0146	2
STIDHAM TAYLOR	LTC	0-2029462	0667	1
STIEBER GEORGE L	CPT	0-0488907	0649	2
STIEFF RAY A	MAJ	0-1012367	0858	1
STIEGLER ERNEST G	1LT	0-1335709	1047	2
STIEGMAN FRED M	MAJ	0-0186105	0759	3
STIEHL GUSTAV H JR	CPT	0-0295938	1068	3
STIELOW EMIL F	CPT	0-0204672	0455	3
STIENECKER H M	CPT	0-0447765	0647	2
STIER HERBERT E	LTC	0-0321175	0466	3
STIERS WALTER E	CW2	W-2104507	0854	1
STIFF ELBERT H	COL	0-0272722	0566	1
STIFF FREDERICK	LTC	0-0411110	0368	3
STIFFLER PRESTON F	WO1	W-2121825	0645	2
STIGGINS LILLIAN D	MAJ	N-0726333	1264	2
STIGLIANO JAYNE J	2LT	N-0755403	0945	1
STILE LOUIS	CPT	0-0516487	0247	2
STILES AARON K	COL	0-0174798	0760	3
STILES AUSTIN C	LTC	0-0190565	0554	3
STILES EDWARD G	CPT	0-0994765	1061	1
STILES FREDERIC C	CPT	0-0184807	0555	3
STILES GEORGE F	CW4	W-2143115	0964	1
STILES GEORGE M	MAJ	0-1644127	1062	1
STILES HERMAN R	CPT	0-1301556	1146	2
STILES LEO T	MAJ	0-1845798	0757	1
STILES LOOISE L	MAJ	R-0002330	0765	1
STILES MARY K	2LT	R-0000883	1144	1
STILES MELVIN C	CPT	0-1107158	0549	2
STILES ROBERT V	CPT	0-5405079	1068	1
STILES WENDEL A	LTC	0-0175276	1059	3
STILES WILLIAM L JR	MAJ	0-0235052	0345	2
STILEY JOSEPH F JR	CPT	0-0513476	0563	1
STILL EDWARD H	MAJ	0-1553181	0466	2
STILL GEORGE P	LTC	0-0109906	0436	1
STILL JOHN	MAJ	0-0370268	0154	1
STILL NORMAN J	CW2	W-2147675	1059	1
STILL WRIGHT P	CPT	0-1165961	0547	2
STILLE WALTER H	CW3	W-2141458	0659	1
STILLGER RAYMOND C	LTC	0-1304580	0664	2
STILLINGS WILLIAM A	CW4	W-2111966	0760	1
STILLMAN FREEMAN L	MAJ	0-0330529	1043	2
STILLMAN ISADORE W	MAJ	0-0507905	1046	2
STILLMAN ROBERT C	MAJ	0-2019247	0465	1
STILLMAN RUFUS C	1LT	0-1014233	0845	2
STILLMUNKS HARMON L	CW2	W-2211634	0566	1
STILLSON CLAUDE E	MAJ	0-1536226	0463	1
STILLWAGON ARTHUR N	CW2	W-2119688	1163	2
STILLWAGON THOMAS	MAJ	0-1326267	1262	2
STILLWELL CLYDE	CPT	0-0172432	1051	3
STILLWELL HAROLD V	CPT	0-1920292	0663	2
STILSON ALDEN E	B G	0-0320041	0261	3
STILWELL CHARLES A	CW2	W-2213705	1167	1
STILWELL JAMES L	MAJ	0-1111934	1061	1
STILWELL LELAND E	COL	0-0256707	0454	3
STILWELL MELVYN S	LTC	0-0326986	1160	1
STILWELL ROBERT L	COL	0-0119180	0-53	3
STILWELL RONALD L	CPT	0-1796179	0248	2
STIMMELL LEE	LTC	0-1558907	1165	1
STIMPSON DONALD JR	LTC	0-1284961	0361	1

NAME	GRADE	SVC NO	DATE RET MO YR	RET CODE
STIMPSON NABOTH G	CPT	O-1557914	0351	2
STIMSON GORDON	LTC	O-0236613	0665	3
STIMSON ROLLAND H	LTC	O-0285288	1060	1
STINCHCOMB JUDD T	LTC	O-0169529	0852	3
STINCHCOMB PAUL A	MAJ	O-1341331	0765	1
STINE GORDON T	1LT	O-1291351	0446	2
STINE JOSEPH	LTC	O-0455297	1063	1
STINEBAUGH DANIEL L	CPT	O-2035393	0850	2
STINNETT EARL W	CPT	O-0373582	0244	2
STINNETT JAMES H	CW4	W-2149169	0768	1
STINNETT WILLIAM C	MAJ	O-0384287	0763	1
STINSON FORREST A	CPT	O-0294855	0645	2
STINSON HOWARD E	MAJ	O-2211416	1066	2
STINSON JOHN	1LT	O-1109038	0546	2
STINSON LEONARD E	CPT	O-1926566	0366	1
STINSON MARION J	1LT	O-1011167	0945	2
STINSON MAURICE J	CW3	W-2152812	1059	1
STINSON ROBERT V	MAJ	O-5304073	0668	1
STINSON WADE P	1LT	O-1338148	0947	2
STINSON WILLIAM B	COL	O-0265143	0460	1
STIO ROLCO L	CPT	O-0322702	0145	2
STIPE JOHN W M SR	MAJ	O-0526344	0664	3
STIPECH EDWARD F	LTC	O-1876470	1268	1
STIPP GEORGE M	COL	O-0251977	0165	3
STIRES FREDERICK	LTC	O-0432341	1059	1
STIRLING JAMES R	MAJ	O-1298616	1160	1
STIRLING SHELDON L	LTC	O-0205349	1163	3
STITELER CHESTER G	LTC	O-0330991	0866	3
STITELER ROWLAND H	COL	O-0400634	1267	3
STITH BENJAMIN F JR	MAJ	O-1304631	0961	1
STITH CHARLES R	LTC	O-1300229	1162	1
STITH DON J	LTC	O-0464561	0145	2
STITH STEPHEN W	CPT	O-0488095	0251	1
STITHEM DALE D	LTC	O-1031031	0260	1
STITT ALBERT A	CPT	O-0400006	1146	2
STITT GEORGE S	LTC	O-0288379	0958	1
STITT JOHN B	MAJ	O-1821648	0463	1
STITT LYNN B	CPT	O-0361185	0745	2
STITZENBERGER WILBER	LTC	O-0912583	0764	3
STIVERS ROBERT T	2LT	O-1636703	0245	2
STIVERSON WILLIAM K	LTC	O-0292898	0866	3
STIVES JOHN H	MAJ	O-0412554	0546	2
STOAK PHILIP	COL	O-2026416	1168	2
STOBAUGH WILLARD L	LTC	O-0357196	0747	2
STOCK BERNARD A	MAJ	O-0570407	0464	1
STOCK HARRY J	WO1	W-2119336	0747	1
STOCK HOWARD P	1LT	O-0409833	0145	2
STOCK JAMES E	2LT	O-1312456	1144	2
STOCK JOSEPH J	LTC	O-1314235	0361	1
STOCKARD HENRY J JR	1LT	O-0541495	1045	2
STOCKARD THOMAS J JR	1LT	O-1298949	0345	2
STOCKDALE GEORGE R	LTC	O-0407775	0766	2
STOCKDALE PAUL H	1LT	O-2003710	1052	1
STOCKDER HANS J	COL	O-0199905	0951	3
STOCKELL ALBERT W	MAJ	O-0416474	0661	1
STOCKER STEWART J	1LT	O-1299491	1047	2
STOCKETT JOHN H	MAJ	O-0306540	0360	1
STOCKHAMMER S F	LTC	O-0255913	0560	3
STOCKLAND CLARENCE D	LTC	O-0288324	0764	3
STOCKMAN GILBERT	MAJ	O-1186298	0967	1
STOCKMAN PERRY J	1LT	O-1288460	0465	1
STOCKMAN WILLIAM A	CPT	O-0220239	0945	2
STOCKNER LESTER W	CPT	O-0282780	0843	2
STOCKS ERNEST J	LTC	O-0281515	0867	3
STOCKS JESSE T	MAJ	O-0270380	0767	3
STOCKSON MATHEW	LTC	O-0487978	0357	1
STOCKTON ALBERT E	LTC	O-0524649	1168	3
STOCKTON ARTHUR E	MAJ	O-0491303	1044	2
STOCKTON CHRISTOPHE	MAJ	O-0349535	0943	2
STOCKTON DURWARD B	CW3	W-2150491	0748	1
STOCKTON JACK P	LTC	O-1291352	1060	1
STOCKTON JOHN L	1LT	O-1177199	0466	1
STOCKTON PURL A JR	MAJ	O-0537243	0563	1
STOCKTON RICHARD F	COL	O-0253157	0968	3
STOCKTON ROBERT A	MAJ	O-1294926	0865	2

NAME	GRADE	SVC NO	DATE RET MO YR	RET CODE
STOCKTON SHERMAN E	WO1	W-2111128	0456	2
STOCKTON WILLIAM W	LTC	O-1168095	0860	1
STOCKTON WILLIE R	MAJ	O-1309863	0765	1
STOCKUNAS JOSEPH W	CW2	W-2210713	1262	1
STOCKWELL HARVEY L	LTC	O-1113002	0566	1
STOCKWELL RICHARD V	LTC	O-1177998	0266	1
STODART WILLIAM E	MAJ	O-1922644	0567	1
STODDARD ARTHUR E	M G	O-0371507	0558	3
STODDARD CARROLL S	COL	O-0230693	0148	2
STODDARD ELLIOTTE A	LTC	O-0241821	0159	3
STODDARD GLENN G	MAJ	O-0245513	0855	3
STODDARD HENRY R	COL	O-0240838	0363	3
STODDARD JACK C	MAJ	O-1823513	0462	1
STODDARD JAMES K	MAJ	O-0494835	0645	2
STODDARD LEONARD JR	2LT	O-1286391	0945	2
STODDART MARJORIE	1LT	N-0793554	1046	1
STOEBE ROLLAND W	COL	O-0285492	0268	3
STOECKEL JOSEPH F JR	MAJ	O-0175064	0352	3
STOECKLEY CLARENCE F	LTC	O-1304139	1262	1
STOEFEN HARLAN J	LTC	O-1542001	1262	1
STOEHR ERWIN A	CW3	W-2143971	0161	1
STOEHR HENRY G	CPT	O-2263021	0661	2
STOELTZING ERNST R	MAJ	O-2049113	0365	1
STOETZER CHARLES E	LTC	O-0376201	0960	1
STOFFEL JOSEPH F	MAJ	O-1554830	0761	1
STOFFT FREDERICK	B G	O-0273771	0665	3
STOFT JOSEF D	MAJ	O-0346102	0747	2
STOGSDILL JAMES E	COL	O-0212615	1060	3
STOHLER MAURICE H	CPT	O-0545998	0647	2
STOHLMAN ROBERT F	MAJ	O-1577905	0666	1
STOK DANIEL D	LTC	O-0327641	0263	1
STOKAN DONALD A	MAJ	O-2021189	1264	1
STOKE HERSCHEL R	LTC	O-0119778	0754	3
STOKELY CLAYTON E	MAJ	O-0281692	0746	2
STOKER EMORY D	COL	O-0163926	0863	1
STOKER HENRY C	WO1	W-2147084	0457	1
STOKES ARTHUR	1LT	O-0250104	0164	3
STOKES CECIL L	CW4	W-2109818	0468	3
STOKES FRED D	MAJ	O-1306203	0861	1
STOKES JAMES O	1LT	O-1321675	1045	2
STOKES JAMES G	CPT	O-0163509	1155	3
STOKES KENNETH E	COL	O-0213443	0564	3
STOKES MELMOTH Y JR	COL	O-0179148	0454	3
STOKES PAUL L JR	MAJ	O-2033233	0161	1
STOKES REDMOND F	1LT	O-1300727	0846	2
STOKES ROBERT N	MAJ	O-1295620	0561	1
STOKES RUSSELL C	LTC	O-1296601	0168	1
STOKES WILLIAM J	COL	O-0332517	0960	1
STOKES WILLIAM M JR	M G	O-0166391	0658	2
STOKES WILLIAM R	CPT	O-1301705	1057	2
STOKINGER WILLIAM A	LTC	O-0468231	0865	1
STOKKE HENRY C	CPT	O-0410840	0147	2
STOKLEY LAWTON W	LTC	O-0245007	0966	3
STOKLOSA OTTO J	MAJ	O-1648840	1057	1
STOKOE JAMES S	1LT	O-0285544	1044	2
STOKWITZ STANLEY S	CW4	W-2130043	0268	1
STOLAR ROBERT	COL	O-0334213	0867	3
STOLARSKI MACK G	MAJ	O-1172682	0858	1
STOLBERG JOHN C	MAJ	O-0212590	0948	3
STOLEN ERNEST G	CPT	O-0521599	0346	2
STOLL CHARLES G	MAJ	O-1684252	0246	2
STOLL FRANK J	CW2	W-2118251	0548	1
STOLL FRED H	COL	O-0171275	1157	1
STOLL FREDERICK	LTC	O-0492939	0455	1
STOLL HERBERT M	MAJ	O-0177471	0361	3
STOLL JOHN E	LTC	O-0235661	0560	3
STOLL JOSEPH W	CPT	O-1323042	0248	2
STOLLAK JULES S	CPT	O-0949181	0861	1
STOLLE CARL M	LTC	O-0156168	1045	2
STOLLE EDWARD J	MAJ	O-0237129	1144	2
STOLLER LOUIS W	MAJ	O-0488325	1045	2
STOLOFF ALFRED H	1LT	O-1113003	0845	2
STOLPE THEODORE P	LTC	O-0276607	0968	3
STOLPESTAD C T	CPT	O-0501030	1044	2
STOLTZ FLEETWOOD	LTC	O-0255744	0767	3

NAME	GRADE	SVC NO	DATE RET MO YR	RET CODE
STOLTZ JOSEPH H	LTC	O-1168091	1265	1
STOLTZ OTTO W	LTC	O-0287136	1167	3
STOLZ FRED C	LTC	O-0290202	0867	3
STOLZ FREDERICK	LTC	O-1548563	1265	1
STONAKER MARGARET R	MAJ	N-0760800	0964	1
STONBRAKER KENNETH D	CPT	O-2262302	0261	1
STONE ALFRED W	MAJ	O-0979499	0963	1
STONE AMOS E	1LT	O-1179744	0146	2
STONE BARTOL F	MAJ	O-1641831	1163	1
STONE BERNARD W	CPT	O-0317140	0244	2
STONE BOYD W	MAJ	O-0518895	0345	2
STONE CALEB S JR	LTC	O-0473273	0746	2
STONE CARRINGTON	COL	O-0114353	0246	2
STONE CHARLES A	LTC	O-0300081	0464	3
STONE CHARLES R	LTC	O-1310343	0465	3
STONE CURTIS A	LTC	O-0296632	0668	3
STONE DAVID B	COL	O-0019976	1060	1
STONE DEE W	COL	O-0165561	0252	3
STONE DONALD D	LTC	O-0257065	0659	3
STONE DUDLEY J	LTC	O-0320039	0565	3
STONE EARL F	WO1	W-2120927	0447	2
STONE ELRY	COL	O-0207696	0454	3
STONE ERIC P	LTC	O-0173655	0352	3
STONE FRANK L	MAJ	O-1313140	0757	1
STONE FRANKLIN W	1LT	O-0347223	0443	2
STONE GEORGE F	MAJ	O-0903897	0746	2
STONE GEORGE R	2LT	O-2010988	1152	1
STONE GLENN A	MAJ	O-1643371	0764	1
STONE HARVEY L	2LT	O-1595193	1044	2
STONE HENRY C	LTC	O-0411897	0264	1
STONE HUBERT L	CW3	W-2128214	1056	1
STONE IVAN B	MAJ	O-0267919	0367	3
STONE IVAN J	MAJ	O-1320665	0347	2
STONE JAMES H	1LT	O-0520369	0947	2
STONE JAMES M	LTC	O-0323989	0867	3
STONE JEFF D	CW3	W-2142432	0559	1
STONE JEFFREY A	COL	O-0410143	0446	2
STONE JOHN E	LTC	O-0292257	0760	2
STONE JOHN E	LTC	O-1059130	1263	1
STONE JOHN J	MAJ	O-1039234	0562	1
STONE JOSEPH H	CPT	O-1031032	0157	1
STONE JOSEPH P	MAJ	O-1559626	0864	1
STONE JUNIUS F	CPT	O-0502108	0260	1
STONE LEVERETT C	LTC	O-0232405	1051	3
STONE LEWIS E	CW3	W-2206834	1068	1
STONE LOUIS	CPT	O-0109861	0339	1
STONE MALCOLM C	1LT	O-0980300	0854	2
STONE MATTYE L	MAJ	N-0765173	0565	1
STONE MEAD W JR	1LT	O-0527281	0346	2
STONE OTIS L	CW2	W-2207501	0359	1
STONE PAUL M	LTC	O-0451566	0557	1
STONE PHILIP V	MAJ	O-0296094	0868	3
STONE RAYMOND D	MAJ	O-0218339	1054	3
STONE RAYMOND W	LTC	O-1035605	0164	1
STONE RICHARD H	1LT	O-1042962	0443	2
STONE ROBERT H	CPT	O-1169355	1045	2
STONE ROBERT D	LTC	O-1533455	0563	1
STONE ROY	LTC	O-0172249	0553	3
STONE ROY E	LTC	O-0274364	1062	3
STONE RUFUS B	CPT	O-0254829	0763	3
STONE SANFORD J	MAJ	O-1334924	0863	1
STONE THEODORE J	MAJ	O-1692573	0666	1
STONE WALTER C	MAJ	O-0959235	1062	1
STONE WALTER F	CPT	O-0890076	1046	2
STONE WILBUR H	MAJ	O-0919191	0845	2
STONE WILLIAM C	MAJ	O-0251036	0345	2
STONE WILLIAM H	LTC	O-1573706	1157	2
STONE WILLIAM P	COL	O-0482739	0962	3
STONEBACK DONALD F	1LT	O-1293144	1044	2
STONEBERG NORMAN E	MAJ	O-1540869	0364	1
STONEBERGER WARREN H	CW3	W-2141460	0661	1
STONEBRAKER ERNEST M	CPT	O-0222268	0460	3
STONEBRAKER FRANK J	MAJ	O-1285842	0860	1
STONEBRAKER JOHN H D	MAJ	O-1333898	0362	2
STONEBRIDGE W E	MAJ	O-0244804	1054	3

NAME	GRADE	SVC NO	DATE RET MO YR	RET CODE
STONEBRUNER JOHN G	CW2	W-2122735	0645	2
STONEBURG CHARLES K	LTC	O-1599001	0168	1
STONECIPHER BARBARA	1LT	L-0502047	1044	2
STONEHOCKER CLARENCE	LTC	O-0265215	0358	1
STONEKING LEO T	CPT	O-0975981	0162	1
STONEMAN HARRY	MAJ	O-0175871	1058	3
STONER DORWIN E	1LT	O-1320873	1145	2
STONER EDGAR B JR	MAJ	O-1579184	1060	1
STONER FRANK G	COL	O-0110962	0955	3
STONER JOHN W	LTC	O-1318483	0163	1
STONER JOSEPH H	LTC	O-0919053	1267	3
STONER MAURICE F	CPT	O-0436673	1045	2
STONESTREET EUGENE V	CW3	W-2211647	1168	1
STONESTREET GUY W	LTC	O-0382318	0668	3
STONIER LYNN C	MAJ	O-0347807	0660	1
STONIK ANDREW R	LTC	O-1107160	1158	1
STOODLEY GERALD F	CPT	O-0104253	0853	3
STOOL WILLIAM M	CPT	O-0331586	1043	2
STOPFEL MARLIN E	1LT	O-1184954	0647	2
STOPPELLI DANIEL O	COL	O-0308983	0654	1
STORBRAATEN SIDNEY N	COL	O-0253820	0954	1
STORCH ALFRED W	COL	O-0914106	1165	3
STORER JOHN A	LTC	O-1641832	1162	1
STOREY AUGUSTUS A JR	CPT	O-0260893	0567	3
STOREY CARL L	1LT	O-2053873	0546	1
STOREY J S	CPT	O-1584964	0754	1
STOREY JACK A	LTC	O-2263367	0767	1
STOREY JAMES E	LTC	O-1185317	0262	1
STOREY LEONARD W	LTC	O-0418735	0762	1
STOREY LUTHER R	COL	O-0178454	1154	1
STOREY MELVIN H	MAJ	O-0987078	0466	1
STOREY PRINT E	LTC	O-1825719	1262	1
STOREY ROBERT L	CPT	O-1338149	0757	1
STOREY STAR J	WO1	W-2004126	0768	3
STORIE JAMES C	LTC	O-1639700	0860	1
STORLIE CLIFFORD J	CPT	O-1001251	0951	1
STORM CECIL V	COL	O-1101681	0660	1
STORM EDGAR N	CW2	W-2104509	1044	2
STORM ERIC F	COL	O-0188432	0256	3
STORM HARVEY W	COL	O-0245808	0955	2
STORM HOWARD T	MAJ	O-2208412	0266	1
STORM JOSEPH L	CW2	W-2146283	0358	2
STORM JOSEPH P	LTC	O-2012011	0564	1
STORM RUSSELL F	CW2	W-2150296	1058	1
STORM SYLVESTER	1LT	O-0323963	0147	2
STORMES ROBERT G	1LT	O-0342762	0146	2
STORMINGER GEORGE M	LTC	O-0506875	1059	1
STORMS ARNOLD J	2LT	O-1591466	0445	2
STORMS ISAAC D	LTC	O-0485890	1054	1
STORRS BARRIE E	MAJ	O-1017896	0862	1
STORRS JOHN N	MAJ	O-0221663	1061	3
STORTZ FRANK J	LTC	O-0110912	0756	3
STORUP ELTON T	1LT	O-1185467	1051	2
STORY CHARLES G	CW3	W-2152689	0265	1
STORY CHESTER L	CW3	W-2147409	0167	1
STORY DONALD H	CPT	O-1320197	0847	2
STORY DOUGLAS E	CW2	W-2205049	1161	1
STORY EMIL R	CPT	O-0358707	1045	2
STORY FRIEDA P	1LT	N-0731063	0445	2
STORY HARRY R	CPT	O-1298313	0862	1
STORY JOSEPH H	CPT	O-0220629	1046	1
STORY MELVIN E	1LT	O-0473828	0744	2
STORY WILLIAM J	MAJ	O-1685559	0963	1
STOSE JOHN	MAJ	O-4055933	0367	1
STOSHITCH IVAN	MAJ	O-0446937	0263	1
STOSS HELMUT G W	CW3	W-2142991	1163	1
STOTLER CHARLES E	LTC	O-0255390	0566	3
STOTLER HARRY E	WO1	W-2117976	0853	1
STOTSENBURG CHARLES	LTC	O-0548731	0368	3
STOTT GEORGE S JR	2LT	O-1340509	1054	2
STOTT GERTRUDE A	1LT	N-0757298	0946	1
STOTT KENHELM W	COL	O-0191716	0552	3
STOTT LAWRENCE J	MAJ	O-0333087	1058	3
STOTTS EARL E	LTC	O-1106512	0562	1
STOTTS WILCHER C	MAJ	O-1169760	1160	1

NAME	GRADE	SVC NO	DATE RET MO YR	RET CODE
STOTZ JOHN K	COL	0-0145965	0-53	3
STOUCH JOHN R	CW3	W-2148887	0462	1
STOUDT KENNETH M	LTC	0-0934278	0767	1
STOUDT LOGAN H	2LT	0-2000213	0346	2
STOUFFER JAY E	MAJ	0-1542159	0962	1
STOUFFER NELSON W	MAJ	0-0980114	0266	1
STOUFFER THOMAS M	LTC	0-0204386	1157	1
STOUGH WILLIAM P	LTC	0-1080153	0761	1
STOUGHTON CECIL W	MAJ	0-2283315	0567	1
STOUGHTON JOSEPH B	1LT	0-1797553	0452	2
STOUGHTON WILLIAM L	MAJ	0-0285611	1061	3
STOUT ALLEN V	MAJ	0-1941344	1067	1
STOUT BERNARD N	MAJ	0-1181474	0662	1
STOUT CHARLES J	CPT	0-4013585	0655	2
STOUT DAVID G	CW2	W-3410007	0968	1
STOUT DONALD G	CPT	0-0523412	1053	2
STOUT DONALD I	MAJ	0-0405309	0164	1
STOUT GEORGE S	1LT	0-1030525	0645	2
STOUT GROVER C	1LT	0-0176933	0740	1
STOUT HARRY R	2LT	0-1031450	0944	2
STOUT HORACE E	COL	0-0231846	0954	3
STOUT HOWARD M	1LT	0-0443820	1143	2
STOUT JOSEPH W	MAJ	0-0225553	0150	1
STOUT LEROY	LTC	0-0255363	0159	2
STOUT MARION B	CW4	W-2111955	0554	1
STOUT RICHARD B	MAJ	0-0231373	0945	2
STOUT ROBERT P	COL	0-0137295	0455	3
STOUT STEWART G	CPT	0-0485720	1046	2
STOUT VICTOR H	LTC	0-1644826	0566	1
STOUT WALTER C	CPT	0-0312473	1045	2
STOUTENBURGH ELIOT G	COL	0-0256608	1167	3
STOVALL ANDREW J	CW2	W-2146284	0862	1
STOVALL CARTIER H	LTC	0-0179629	0657	2
STOVALL CLYDE O	CW4	W-2142611	0863	1
STOVALL DAVID P	MAJ	0-0326084	0761	3
STOVALL DONALD A	CW3	W-2147683	0368	1
STOVALL EDWIN A	LTC	0-2204057	0868	1
STOVALL FRANCIS A	CPT	0-0181639	1161	3
STOVALL JAMES J	LTC	0-0362509	1057	2
STOVALL JOE	MAJ	0-0464198	0654	2
STOVALL JONATHAN B	1LT	0-1063051	0346	2
STOVALL ORAN C	COL	0-0349288	0853	2
STOVALL RALPH M	COL	0-0276010	0467	3
STOVALL SID	LTC	0-1546526	0962	1
STOVALL WILLIAM S	CPT	0-2262941	0461	1
STOVALL WILLIAM T	MAJ	0-0453397	1054	1
STOVEN JAMES H	CW3	W-2151706	0262	1
STOVER CHARLES V	CPT	0-0496993	0754	1
STOVER EDWARD C JR	LTC	0-0135632	0353	3
STOVER GEORGE M	LTC	0-0323557	0966	3
STOVER GLEN W	MAJ	0-2027265	1262	1
STOVER HAROLD E	LTC	0-0248183	0165	3
STOVER HENRY A	CW3	W-2147310	0265	1
STOVER JACOB R	LTC	0-1175873	0966	1
STOVER JAMES K	CPT	0-1102074	0547	2
STOVER KENNETH F	LTC	0-0384902	0863	1
STOVER MAYRIALE W	CPT	0-0491517	0259	1
STOVER ORVILLE H	MAJ	0-0450659	0259	1
STOVER ROBERT F	WO1	W-2210152	0160	1
STOVER VERNON R	CW4	W-2143534	0468	1
STOVER WALTER O	MAJ	0-0453260	0954	1
STOVER WILLIAM H	MAJ	0-0274985	1053	3
STOVER WILLIAM H	MAJ	0-1557141	0363	1
STOVIN PHILIP B	LTC	0-0197247	0862	3
STOWE JAMES J	MAJ	0-1013741	1059	1
STOWE NORMAN L	MAJ	0-1923510	0664	1
STOWELL ALVIN C	LTC	0-1895515	0765	3
STOWELL CHARLES W	LTC	0-2046701	0966	1
STOWELL FRED M	LTC	0-1540549	0362	2
STOWELL JAMES F	CW2	W-2211947	0567	1
STOWELL JAMES L	MAJ	0-1926700	1068	1
STOWELL SAMUEL	MAJ	0-0192315	0762	3
STOWER IRVING C	CPT	0-0481515	0245	2
STOWERS DEWEY M	LTC	0-0349256	0862	3
STOWERS JAMES C	COL	0-0245149	0966	3
STOWERS JAMES L	WO1	W-2122763	0845	2
STOWERS JOHN H	B G	0-0176135	0861	3
STOY HAROLD T	CPT	0-0189044	0157	3
STOY HENRY F	MAJ	0-0229699	0245	2
STOYNOFF KARL J	LTC	0-1845354	1065	1
STOZIC NICHOLAS	WO1	W-2106050	0247	2
STRACHAN HARRY L JR	MAJ	0-0490574	1145	2
STRACHAN JOHN M	LTC	0-1282330	0866	1
STRADER BENNIE J	MAJ	0-0488493	0854	1
STRADER RODMAN W	MAJ	0-0371762	0363	1
STRADLEY JOSEPH L	LTC	0-1002843	0966	3
STRAHL JOHN A	1LT	0-1574154	1143	2
STRAIN EARL E	MAJ	0-1950461	0863	1
STRAIN JEROME C	LTC	0-0252702	0146	2
STRAIN PAUL W	LTC	0-1294036	0461	1
STRAIN ROBERT A	LTC	0-1800084	0466	1
STRAIN WILLIAM J	CPT	0-0254974	0867	3
STRAIT ELWIN A	1LT	0-1181475	1145	2
STRAKA JOHN	MAJ	0-1017120	0668	3
STRALLY MICHAEL J	MAJ	0-1644131	0859	1
STRAMAT THOMAS E	CPT	0-0961425	0361	1
STRAMM WILLIAM	CW4	W-2112232	0166	1
STRANATHAN WILLIAM	MAJ	0-0145839	0557	3
STRAND CHARLES O	1LT	0-1535540	0845	2
STRAND HILMA O	CPT	N-0736939	0147	1
STRAND KENNETH E	MAJ	0-0961412	0467	1
STRAND NORMAN V	LTC	0-0326155	0968	3
STRAND ORVILLE M	MAJ	0-0947034	0965	1
STRAND WALTER JR	1LT	0-1044967	1046	2
STRAND WESLEY M	LTC	0-2035898	0363	1
STRANDE ORIN E	LTC	0-0445232	0455	1
STRANG JOSEPH W	COL	0-0456347	0566	1
STRANG TOM B	LTC	0-0377874	0746	2
STRANG WARREN C	MAJ	0-1644132	0158	1
STRANGE BILL M	CW2	W-2115840	0446	2
STRANGE FRANCIS O	1LT	0-2019946	1052	2
STRANGE FRANK L	COL	0-0924330	1063	3
STRANGE FRED A	CPT	0-0496665	0652	2
STRANGE GLEN L	MAJ	0-1011156	0547	2
STRANGE JOHN G	LTC	0-1103956	1167	1
STRANGE JOSEPH L JR	LTC	0-0949454	0667	2
STRANGE LOUIS B	1LT	0-1017424	0845	2
STRANGE ROY C	LTC	0-0251978	1057	1
STRANGE WESLEY R	CW4	W-2112077	0565	1
STRANGEWAYS WILLIAM	LTC	0-1688663	0968	1
STRANLEY OTTO R	LTC	0-0901750	0363	3
STRANO JOHN S	2LT	0-1699960	0652	2
STRANSKY JAMES E	1LT	0-1543846	0445	2
STRASBURGER ALFRED	1LT	0-1577916	1044	2
STRASSBERGER ARUNAH	LTC	0-1002346	0964	1
STRASSBURGER HELLMUT	MAJ	0-0969100	0465	1
STRASSBURGER RICHARD	CW3	W-2147185	0664	2
STRASSER EDWARD J	CW3	W-2205416	0767	1
STRASSER FRANCIS C	MAJ	0-0388940	0959	2
STRASSER JOHN W	LTC	0-1175874	1164	1
STRATER EDWARD H	CPT	0-1555632	0665	1
STRATMOEN MERLIN L	LTC	0-1695700	0268	1
STRATMOEN RALPH D	LTC	0-1703029	0364	1
STRATTE ALF K	LTC	0-0266098	0256	3
STRATTON CLELL T	CPT	0-1645410	1159	1
STRATTON ALBERT G	MAJ	0-1877886	1166	1
STRATTON ARTHUR L	CW3	W-2149947	0364	1
STRATTON DOUGLAS B	1LT	0-0408772	0945	2
STRATTON EDWARD J	1LT	0-0513485	0146	2
STRATTON JOEL H	COL	0-0174751	0761	3
STRATTON JOHN N	LTC	0-0480850	0766	1
STRATTON LAWRENCE	MAJ	0-0406139	0548	2
STRATTON LLOYD W	MAJ	0-0973527	1061	1
STRATTON MARSHALL J	CW2	W-3250493	0467	1
STRATTON REGINALD H	COL	0-0232789	1063	3
STRATTON ROBERT H JR	MAJ	0-0276171	0467	3
STRATTON THOMAS H	LTC	0-0307939	0962	1
STRAUB DELBERT T	CW2	W-2142077	0256	1
STRAUB ELMER F	COL	0-0267270	1054	3
STRAUB GEORGE H	COL	0-0276055	0868	3
STRAUCH IRVING M	2LT	0-1638604	0644	2
STRAUGHAN MILLETT A	1LT	0-0412164	0747	2
STRAUGHN CHARLES E	MAJ	0-2019451	0763	2
STRAUS FRANCIS H	MAJ	0-0445463	0645	2
STRAUS MAURICE L	CPT	0-0319290	0146	2
STRAUSER PEARL H	CW3	V-0700055	0764	1
STRAUSS CHARLES	MAJ	0-1951448	0665	1
STRAUSS DANIEL J	MAJ	0-0478822	1147	1
STRAUSS EMANUEL M	LTC	0-0460005	1062	1
STRAUSS HARRY H	MAJ	0-1321676	0751	1
STRAUSS LEROY J	1LT	0-1341196	0553	2
STRAUSS MACK	LTC	0-1598516	1165	1
STRAUSS ROBERT W	CPT	0-0389216	1146	2
STRAUSS ROGER F	LTC	0-0921189	0164	3
STRAUSSER ELWOOD L	1LT	0-1296285	0544	2
STRAW EDITH N	MAJ	L-1010110	0568	1
STRAW LEO S	LTC	0-0321591	0863	3
STRAW RALSTON	CW4	W-2147676	1167	1
STRAW RAYMOND K JR	MAJ	0-1183199	0263	1
STRAW RICHARD S	LTC	0-0274889	0866	3
STRAW RUTH B	1LT	N-0731780	0246	1
STRAWBRIDGE GEORGE I	LTC	0-1305667	0763	1
STRAWHORN JOHN C	MAJ	0-1686508	1164	2
STRAWN ARTHUR H	CPT	0-0918402	0844	2
STRAWN BUFORD T	LTC	0-0264684	0466	3
STRAWN GEORGE M	LTC	0-0451249	0258	1
STRAWN LEO S	COL	0-0182233	1155	3
STRAWN THOMAS F	LTC	0-0475338	1067	3
STRAWN WILLIS G	MAJ	0-0541234	1063	1
STRAWTHER WILLIAM H	CPT	0-1342129	0561	1
STRAZICICH EMILE J	LTC	0-1165344	1158	1
STREAM CHARLES T	MAJ	0-1684929	0862	1
STREB ROBERT C	MAJ	0-0291099	1066	3
STREBEL FRANK R	CPT	0-1310895	0546	2
STREBIG GLENN K	CW3	W-2141729	1060	1
STRECK EDWIN P	COL	0-0325104	1164	3
STRECK ROYALLE A	MAJ	0-1923562	1263	2
STRECKER EDWARD H	MAJ	0-1037325	0267	1
STRECKER JOHN M	2LT	0-1116425	0245	2
STRECKER WERNER C	COL	0-0211961	0755	3
STREET GLENN M	LTC	0-0330171	0657	3
STREET IRL H	MAJ	0-1299815	0157	1
STREET JOHN E	MAJ	0-0501251	0958	1
STREET LAWRENCE W	LTC	0-0390065	0849	1
STREET PAUL J	CPT	0-2263176	0661	1
STREET PHILIP E	LTC	0-0278552	1063	3
STREET SAMUEL S	LTC	0-0143281	0457	3
STREET WILLIAM A	LTC	0-1001059	0962	1
STREET WILLIAM G	CPT	0-1280361	0646	2
STREETER DANIEL D	LTC	0-0135631	0648	3
STREETER GEORGE A	CPT	0-1577919	1053	1
STREETER MARVIN L	1LT	0-0322801	0861	1
STREETER THEODORE	MAJ	0-0286269	0361	1
STREETMAN WILLIAM J	LTC	0-0450855	0459	2
STREETT ANNE F	MAJ	N-0761593	0266	1
STREETT WILLIAM L	LTC	0-1951563	1166	1
STREHL ROBERT M	1LT	0-1017791	1045	2
STREHLE MALCOLM L	CPT	0-0314598	0162	1
STREHLE WILBUR J	CW3	W-2145084	1057	1
STREHLOW HERMAN F JR	LTC	0-0258884	0964	3
STREHLOW LOUIS H	COL	0-0454819	0163	1
STREIBIG FRANK J JR	COL	0-0206158	0653	2
STREICHER HERMAN J	COL	0-0297955	0147	2
STREICHER WILHELM G	CPT	0-0390653	0746	2
STREIDL WALTER R	MAJ	0-1545418	0958	1
STREITZ CLARENCE E	LTC	0-0370433	0368	3
STREKER CHARLES V JR	LTC	0-1951193	0768	1
STRENNER STEVEN JR	LTC	0-1294555	0560	1
STRETCH GEORGE L	1LT	0-0123972	0253	3
STRETCH JAMES J	LTC	0-1795004	0863	1
STRETCHER JOHN R	MAJ	0-0401426	0447	2
STREUBER DOUGLAS W	CPT	0-1545210	0567	1
STREYCKMANS FELIX B	COL	0-0194449	0663	3
STRIBLING C R JR	LTC	0-0156524	0157	3
STRIBLING FRED D	COL	0-0151654	1154	3
STRIBLING ROSS M	LTC	0-0260466	0767	3
STRIBLING SAM G	LTC	0-0918050	0864	3
STRICK JACOB	CPT	0-1690336	0146	2
STRICKER FRANK W	CW2	W-2143550	0158	1
STRICKER JOSEPH H	CPT	0-0502107	0447	1
STRICKLAND CADE	MAJ	0-1919855	0367	2
STRICKLAND CHARLES S	MAJ	0-1014031	0661	2
STRICKLAND EMMA P	1LT	N-0744851	1045	1
STRICKLAND ERNEST H	CW3	W-2142612	0465	1
STRICKLAND HARRY G	LTC	0-1821928	1060	1
STRICKLAND HENRY H	MAJ	0-0209544	0248	2
STRICKLAND HERMAN L	CW4	W-2145754	1168	1
STRICKLAND HUNTER A	MAJ	0-0238591	0466	3
STRICKLAND JAMES M	CW3	W-2207389	0462	1
STRICKLAND JESSE C	LTC	0-0395661	0764	1
STRICKLAND JOE P	1LT	0-0200607	0257	3
STRICKLAND JOHN H	WO1	W-2121001	0445	2
STRICKLAND MARVIN A	CW2	W-2142905	1057	1
STRICKLAND OLIE A JR	MAJ	0-1055471	0161	1
STRICKLAND ROBERT L	COL	0-0105842	0849	3
STRICKLAND ROBERT T	CPT	0-2017922	1160	1
STRICKLAND ROY W	COL	0-0322401	0152	1
STRICKLAND RUFUS K	LTC	0-1113005	0766	1
STRICKLAND SAMUEL C	CPT	0-0491178	0748	1
STRICKLAND SAMUEL H	COL	0-0274652	0561	3
STRICKLAND SHELLEY T	1LT	0-1304316	0547	2
STRICKLAND TOM E	MAJ	0-0887492	0860	1
STRICKLAND WEYMAN L	MAJ	0-0258694	1063	3
STRICKLER DANIEL B	M G	0-0101918	0557	3
STRICKLER HUGH	MAJ	0-1688830	1163	1
STRICKLER PHILIP A	LTC	0-1292246	0460	1
STRICKLER STAUFFER J	MAJ	0-0348887	1161	1
STRICKLIN HENRY C	1LT	0-1702754	1152	2
STRICKLIN L T	MAJ	0-0531896	0856	1
STRICKLIN SOLOMON F	CW3	W-2146618	0964	1
STRIDER FRANK E	MAJ	0-2026047	0763	1
STRIEBY JAMES N	LTC	0-1552998	0862	1
STRIEPLING JOHN A	2LT	0-1644828	0245	2
STRIGHT ROBERT M	MAJ	0-1054831	0766	1
STRIKE CLARENCE E	MAJ	0-1693106	0762	1
STRIKE WILLIAM J	LTC	0-1798817	0265	1
STRILEY WAYNE A	LTC	0-1646041	0762	1
STRIMPLE GEORGE R	MAJ	0-1643375	0357	1
STRINE CHARLES W	LTC	0-0273702	1066	3
STRINGER HENRY H	WO1	W-2146285	1056	1
STRINGER JOHN L	LTC	0-0439327	0262	1
STRINGER RALPH E	LTC	0-0120357	1055	3
STRINGER SYDNEY W	COL	0-0265784	0968	3
STRINGFELLOW BERTIE	MAJ	0-0368222	0960	1
STRINGFIELD WILLIAM	MAJ	0-1699972	0461	1
STRINGHAM DONALD R	LTC	0-0232559	1156	3
STRIPLING JOHN L	LTC	0-1042179	0564	1
STRIPLING LEWIS	WO1	W-2108970	0165	1
STRITMAN HARRY R	MAJ	0-0290694	0668	3
STRITZLER CONRAD	MAJ	0-1689856	0147	2
STROBEL ALICE C	2LT	N-0725744	1044	1
STROBEL LAWRENCE A	COL	0-0253033	0566	3
STROBEL RUDOLPH W	LTC	0-0322053	0566	3
STROBEL WILLIAM J	CW3	W-2204982	0167	1
STROBL CATHERINE	LTC	L-0711954	0566	1
STROBL WALTER M	MAJ	0-1322658	0960	1
STROBLE CHARLES P JR	CPT	0-0390702	0146	2
STROBLE CHARLES R	MAJ	0-1926332	1064	1
STROCK ALEX	1LT	0-0963304	0354	2
STROCK MOSES S	COL	0-0423087	1161	3
STRODE EDWARD M	COL	0-0294610	1157	2
STRODERD WILBERT J	CW3	W-2153011	0463	1
STROEBEL GEORGE J	MAJ	0-0957652	0962	2
STROEBELE HERMAN A	LTC	0-0518513	0763	1
STROH JOSEPH	LTC	0-1101233	0667	3
STROH OSCAR H	LTC	0-0332252	0268	3
STROHBEHM DOUGLAS W	1LT	0-1030424	0246	2
STROHECKER SAMUEL	COL	0-0238936	1060	3
STROHM JOHN G	COL	0-0141335	0648	3
STROHN ALBERT L	LTC	0-0355077	1060	1

NAME	GRADE	SVC NO	DATE RET MO YR	RET CODE
STROHSCHEIN CARL	1LT	0-1695511	1046	2
STROLLO MARIO G	1LT	0-1174159	0153	2
STROM CARL J	1LT	0-1317576	0645	2
STROM CHARLES H	1LT	0-1315235	0346	2
STROM ELMER A	COL	0-0222150	0463	3
STROM FRANK I	LTC	0-0251021	0368	3
STROM HJALMER R	LTC	0-0277773	0151	1
STROM VICTOR F	LTC	0-1293163	0461	2
STROMBERG DONALD C	MAJ	0-1105212	0347	2
STROMBERG SVEN G	LTC	0-0301544	1168	3
STROMGREN LLOYD W	LTC	0-1106516	0461	1
STROMME RUDOLPH K	LTC	0-1304814	0867	3
STROMMEN ARTHUR K	LTC	0-0274690	0664	3
STROMMEN THEODORE A	CPT	0-0265745	0146	2
STROMSTED ARTHUR R	CW2	W-2108729	0553	1
STRONG BERKELEY J	LTC	0-1695719	0668	1
STRONG BILLY E	MAJ	0-1296503	0661	1
STRONG CHESTER A	CW4	W-2102437	0755	1
STRONG CHESTER F	CW2	W-2142293	1155	1
STRONG CLARA C	1LT	N-0726601	0146	1
STRONG CLAUDE W	LTC	0-0401996	0560	1
STRONG DAVID A	MAJ	0-2017143	0465	1
STRONG EARLE B	CPT	0-0111776	0558	3
STRONG GILES H	MAJ	0-0218309	1152	3
STRONG HAROLD E	LTC	0-1178639	0868	1
STRONG HENRY JR	WO1	W-2142232	1055	1
STRONG JAMES F	COL	0-0275668	0459	1
STRONG JOHN E	COL	0-0285131	0668	3
STRONG JOY H	LTC	0-0254314	0657	1
STRONG OTTIS	MAJ	0-0450479	1067	2
STRONG RALPH M	CPT	0-1042720	0561	1
STRONG ROBERT H	COL	0-0230343	1162	3
STRONG WARD R	COL	0-0257217	0763	3
STRONG WILLIAM G	CW3	W-2147519	0664	1
STROOBAND CHARLES E	LTC	0-1169356	0363	1
STROOTMAN RALPH E	LTC	0-0420586	0865	1
STROSNIDER GEORGE U	LTC	0-0454669	1162	1
STROSS WALTER [illegible]	2LT	0-0492722	1144	2
STROTHER RALPH D	CW2	W-2106598	0960	2
STROUBE ESTHER F	WO1	W-21[illegible]766	1050	2
STROUD DAVID V	MAJ	0-0933062	0164	1
STROUD GEORGE H	LTC	0-0147174	0358	3
STROUD JOSEPH D	MAJ	0-1856140	0856	1
STROUD MARVIN E	CW2	W-2147116	0956	2
STROUD ROBERT F	LTC	0-1302226	0962	1
STROUD ROBERT L	MAJ	0-0333587	1059	3
STROUD ROGER C	MAJ	0-0305402	0567	3
STROUD ROLAND R	LTC	0-1169357	0861	2
STROUDE GILBERT M	MAJ	0-0993384	0266	1
STROUP CECIL H	LTC	0-0239210	0564	3
STROUP CLARENCE S	LTC	0-0188524	0455	3
STROUP DONALD G	CPT	0-1534873	1047	2
STROUP JONATHAN	CW3	W-2206372	1267	1
STROUPE HOWARD E	1LT	0-0544148	1045	2
STROUSE CARL H	LTC	0-1171383	0962	1
STROUSE ROBERT L	MAJ	0-1062084	0864	1
STRUB DANIEL F	MAJ	0-1924099	0964	1
STRUB HARRY	CW2	W-2152840	0961	1
STRUBEL CLARENCE	2LT	0-1877302	0359	2
STRUBEL WAYNE A	2LT	0-2049407	0545	2
STRUBEL WILLIAM E	LTC	0-1316794	0764	1
STRUBILLA VICTOR S	CW2	W-2149373	1059	2
STRUBLE CLARENCE E	CPT	0-1636713	0158	1
STRUBLE GILBERT C	COL	0-0275359	1266	3
STRUCEL BERT J	LTC	0-1329766	0167	1
STRUCK CAROLINE K	2LT	N-0700182	0239	1
STRUCK FREDERICK	CPT	0-1165049	0446	2
STRUCKMEYER F C JR	1LT	0-1293352	0945	2
STRUEWING WILFRED H	MAJ	0-1342402	0763	1
STRUM WILLIE C	COL	0-0275531	0859	3
STRUNESKI JOSEPH F	MAJ	0-1636714	0859	1
STRUSINSKI NICHOLA	LTC	0-0491240	1045	2
STRUTH JOSEPH F	CW4	W-2143057	0361	1
STRUYK ARIE P	2LT	0-1311939	1044	2
STRUZENSKI JOHN F	CPT	0-0201773	1156	3

NAME	GRADE	SVC NO	DATE RET MO YR	RET CODE
STRYKER HARRY R	LTC	0-0266440	0861	3
STUART BROOKS S	LTC	0-0227704	0664	3
STUART CHARLES C	MAJ	0-1549385	1160	2
STUART CHARLES P	MAJ	0-1183426	1158	1
STUART DONALD C	COL	0-0167636	1046	2
STUART DOROTHY A	2LT	N-0783290	0445	1
STUART FREDRIC W	MAJ	0-0283353	0361	3
STUART GEORGE D	MAJ	0-0170751	0956	3
STUART GILBERT K	MAJ	0-0955275	0366	1
STUART HARRY A	LTC	0-1638618	0667	1
STUART HARRY M	WO1	W-2129948	0753	1
STUART HUGH L	MAJ	0-2008253	0865	1
STUART JACK F	CW3	W-2152937	1163	1
STUART JOE V	MAJ	0-0475960	0348	1
STUART JOHN A	CPT	0-0277925	0161	3
STUART JOHN B	MAJ	0-0751573	1064	1
STUART MARCUS C JR	LTC	0-1583732	0168	3
STUART NORMAN C	CW3	W-2206385	1064	1
STUART OMAR G	LTC	0-0294904	0967	3
STUART PAUL W	LTC	0-0350105	0661	1
STUART PERCY E	LTC	0-1824530	0463	2
STUART ROBERT F	CPT	0-0552796	1047	2
STUART ROBERT I	LTC	0-0261959	0167	3
STUART ROBERT M	MAJ	0-0989606	1267	1
STUART ROBERT M	LTC	0-1289006	0363	1
STUART ROBERT T	MAJ	0-0334243	1061	1
STUART RUSSELL W	MAJ	0-0324952	0165	3
STUART SAMUEL F	COL	0-0308074	0268	3
STUART THOMAS F	MAJ	0-1824935	0962	1
STUART WENDELL A	CPT	0-1057281	0960	1
STUART WILBERT E	1LT	0-0394899	1143	2
STUART WILLIAM P	LTC	0-1598873	1167	1
STUART WILLOUGHBY	COL	0-0266233	0466	3
STUART-OUBERG J C	1LT	0-0495707	0944	2
STUBBLEBINE BEULAH	MAJ	N-0901994	0566	2
STUBBLEFIELD H I	COL	0-0216105	0757	3
STUBBLEFIELD JAMES P	CPT	0-0924877	0844	2
STUBBS ARCHIE F	LTC	0-0351605	0467	1
STUBBS BEVERLY W	MAJ	0-2706008	0466	1
STUBBS CHARLES A	LTC	0-0263207	1163	3
STUBBS CHARLES F	CW2	RW-2150620	0763	1
STUBBS DANIEL W	MAJ	0-0370544	0661	1
STUBBS DONALD W A	MAJ	0-1636715	1057	1
STUBBS JAMES R	MAJ	0-0355933	1044	2
STUBBS JOHN H	LTC	0-1003050	0662	1
STUBBS JOSEPH J	LTC	0-0177270	0560	3
STUBBS WILLIAM E	LTC	0-0198057	0455	3
STUBE CHARLES K	CPT	0-1301707	0946	2
STUBENRAD WILLIAM G	MAJ	0-2010482	1062	1
STUBER JUNIOR W	MAJ	0-1014934	1264	1
STUBERT CLARENCE E	1LT	0-1998470	1046	2
STUBLER JOHN N	LTC	0-0205383	0858	3
STUCK SANFORD W	MAJ	0-0263996	0668	3
STUCK VERNON M	MAJ	0-1950935	0963	1
STUCKART JOAN M	2LT	N-0755949	0545	1
STUCKART PAUL G	MAJ	0-1638619	0561	1
STUCKEY AL H	LTC	0-0350057	0462	1
STUCKEY ALEXANDER	CW2	RW-2141088	0565	1
STUCKEY IRA H	MAJ	0-0304749	1167	3
STUCKEY LYLE E	LTC	0-0235372	0760	3
STUCKI FREDERICK	CW4	W-2201146	0168	1
STUCKMEYER WILLIAM	LTC	0-1030192	0361	1
STUCKWISCH LEONHARDT	MAJ	0-0524248	0466	3
STUDDARD WOODROW	CW3	W-2144318	1159	1
STUDEBAKER GEORGE W	COL	0-0198737	0154	1
STUDER BERTRAM J	1LT	0-2263491	0554	2
STUDER JAMES E	LTC	0-0996221	0268	1
STUDER JOHN F	LTC	0-0153010	1156	3
STUDER MAGNUS P	MAJ	0-1897744	0360	1
STUDER WESLEY P	1LT	0-0452476	1043	2
STUDLEY FRED M	LTC	0-0508462	0766	1
STUDWELL JOHN R	COL	0-0180413	0756	3
STUDY EARL H	COL	0-0444897	0865	3
STUEBE ALBERT J	MAJ	0-1175748	0868	3
STUEBE LOUIS F	B G	0-0170245	1059	3

NAME	GRADE	SVC NO	DATE RET MO YR	RET CODE
STUEBEN EDMUND A	CPT	0-0409627	1045	2
STUELKE THERON R	LTC	0-0290520	0446	2
STUESSY EUGENE F	CPT	0-1038497	0846	2
STUFFLEBEAM WILBUR H	LTC	0-0291744	0161	1
STUFFLEBEAN JOHN H	1LT	0-0445866	1143	2
STUHRMAN JERRY	LTC	0-1313320	0865	1
STUK BETTY L	MAJ	L-1010309	1068	1
STUKEY RAYMOND G	CPT	0-1824246	0347	2
STULL AINSLEE J	CW2	W-2207204	0759	2
STULL CHARLES W	LTC	0-1550064	0561	1
STULL HAROLD C	LTC	0-0199102	0648	3
STULL RAYMOND L	MAJ	0-1049938	1160	1
STULL ROBERT A	CPT	0-0176744	0355	3
STULL ROBERT K	LTC	0-0388759	0966	1
STULTS ROBERT L	CW4	W-2146286	0967	1
STULTS ROY	CW2	W-2106164	0464	1
STULTZ BAILEY G JR	MAJ	0-1583734	0660	1
STULTZ JOSEPH B	CW2	W-2148419	0557	1
STULTZ NORMAN F	COL	0-0302758	1267	3
STULTZ OLIVER V	WO1	W-2123036	0152	1
STUMBAUGH LEO A	MAJ	0-1016316	0762	1
STUMBAUGH LYLE H	1LT	0-1178357	1145	2
STUMP CLAUD W	MAJ	0-0222502	1047	2
STUMP EDWARD H	CW2	W-2147520	0263	1
STUMP LEROY C	MAJ	0-0370117	0761	1
STUMP ROBERT J	CW3	W-2210687	1168	1
STUMP ROBERT M	COL	0-0263852	0662	3
STUMP WILLIAM B	LTC	0-1598703	0166	1
STUMPF ANDREW	CW3	W-2143649	0364	1
STUMPO GAETANO J	CW3	W-2144633	0562	1
STUPAKEWICZ HENRY W	LTC	0-1559535	0668	1
STUPPLE ALFRED F	1LT	0-1923564	1057	2
STURDIVANT C W	LTC	0-0376912	0246	2
STURDIVANT WILLIS P	CPT	0-0497751	1046	1
STURGEON JAMES H JR	CPT	0-1322505	0746	2
STURGEON ROBERT C	LTC	0-0266550	0861	3
STURGES EDWARD F	2LT	0-1586291	0544	2
STURGILL DORAN R	CW2	W-2139636	0455	1
STURGIS DUDLEY C JR	MAJ	0-0341292	0647	2
STURGIS FLORENCE M	1LT	N-0726921	0546	1
STURGIS JAMES F JR	LTC	0-0974119	0766	2
STURGIS JOHN E	LTC	0-0243941	0165	3
STURGIS NORMAN R JR	CPT	0-1142270	0947	2
STURKEN FRANK	MAJ	0-0464830	0246	2
STURM CHARLES F	LTC	0-0424989	0966	1
STURM EMET L	1LT	0-0252440	0356	3
STURM JOSEPH M	MAJ	0-1556810	1154	1
STURM LOUIS P	CPT	0-0505665	0154	1
STURMAN HARRY H	1LT	0-0522782	0445	2
STURMAN OLIVE M H	1LT	N-0735890	0646	1
STURMAN ROLAND B	COL	0-0378886	0762	1
STURNIOLO JAMES C	LTC	0-1825076	0268	1
STURROCK ALAN L	1LT	0-1583735	0444	2
STURTEVANT LEVI W JR	MAJ	0-1649720	0461	1
STURTEVANT ROSS H	CPT	0-2042956	0762	2
STURZL BUDO F	LTC	0-1157243	0760	1
STUTEVILLE CLYDE D	CPT	0-0517426	1146	2
STUTEVOSS JAMES F	LTC	0-0141878	1053	2
STUTMAN LOUIS E	LTC	0-1311549	0562	1
STUTMAN MARTIN H	1LT	0-1294929	0852	2
STUTSMAN WILLIAM D	1LT	0-1582180	0247	2
STUTTS JOHN R	LTC	0-0346386	0960	1
STUTTS ROBERT T	MAJ	0-0240082	0167	3
STUTZ RUDOLPH R	CPT	0-1555478	0659	1
STUTZ SHERWOOD S	MAJ	0-1685521	0961	1
STUTZMAN FLETCHER JR	MAJ	0-0958140	0667	1
STUURMANS ANNA	CPT	L-0902781	1263	1
STYLE KENNETH S	MAJ	0-1643378	0862	1
STYLER MICHAEL	MAJ	0-2055481	0367	3
STYRON DAVID F	2LT	0-1595856	0545	2
STYRON JAMES C	M G	0-0177742	0658	3
SUAREZ JOHN H	CW2	W-2122038	1046	1
SUAREZ JOHN M	CW2	W-2205379	1262	1
SUBERS SPENCER C	LTC	0-0269981	0667	3
SUCH JOSEPH F	CPT	0-0499447	0744	1

NAME	GRADE	SVC NO	DATE RET MO YR	RET CODE
SUCHANEK JOHN A	MAJ	0-0913300	0363	1
SUCHARA THADDEUS W	LTC	0-1309434	0660	1
SUCHIER OSCAR A	LTC	0-1287617	0261	1
SUCHMINSKI JOHN C	MAJ	0-0139877	0257	3
SUCHY RAYMOND W	2LT	0-0503716	1045	2
SUDDATH PAUL R	MAJ	0-1300103	0962	1
SUDDERTH JAMES A	LTC	0-1310947	0766	1
SUDDETH VERNON T	MAJ	0-0194279	0956	3
SUDERMAN BERYL D	CPT	0-1102075	0549	2
SUDERS MARY A	MAJ	N-0799597	0468	1
SUDMAN EMIL W	CPT	0-0252637	1059	3
SUDMAN GLENN F	LTC	0-0916308	0546	2
SUDNICK NORMAN E	CPT	0-1536512	0365	2
SUE JULIAN D	LTC	0-0394831	0860	1
SUEIRO-RIOS HUGO	CPT	0-2325669	0868	2
SUENKEL WILLIAM J	LTC	0-1019292	0765	1
SUESS HERBERT R	LTC	0-1580391	0662	1
SUESZ ROBERT W	CW3	W-2146493	0863	1
SUFFECOOL WILSON L	LTC	0-1641002	0361	1
SUFFIELD VANCE P	1LT	0-0431747	0244	2
SUFKA ANDREW P	LTC	0-1326783	0264	1
SUGARMAN JOSEPH R	LTC	0-0336633	0545	2
SUGARS RICHARD H	LTC	0-1288325	0367	1
SUGARS WILLIAM J	CPT	0-2033812	0656	2
SUGEL WILLIAM J	MAJ	0-1324296	0756	1
SUGG ANDREW I	CPT	0-0232579	0-51	3
SUGGS JOHN P	CPT	0-0548810	0264	1
SUGGS ROBERT E	MAJ	0-1293146	0561	1
SUGIYAMA YONE J	MAJ	0-1338151	0261	1
SUGRUE JON J	LTC	0-2020693	0868	1
SUHAR JOHN	MAJ	0-1286029	1047	2
SUHAR STANLEY	LTC	0-0265683	0666	3
SUHR ARNOLD W	CPT	0-0344700	1045	2
SUHR JEROME W	LTC	0-0327158	0460	1
SUHRE MAURICE E	LTC	0-0280057	0764	3
SUHRUSKE JOHN J	MAJ	0-1298150	0758	1
SUIT PAUL C	MAJ	0-0975806	0961	1
SUITER LEO F	MAJ	0-2097014	0964	1
SUITER LUTHER	CPT	0-0333936	1046	2
SUITS WINFORD	MAJ	0-0236919	0252	3
SUITT THOMAS N	MAJ	0-1015302	1263	1
SUKIENNIK STAZY J	LTC	0-0354479	0160	2
SULAK STANLEY A	CPT	0-1171003	1264	1
SULEK ARTHUR E	LTC	0-0345073	0448	2
SULKOWSKI MARY A	2LT	N-0764576	1145	1
SULKOWSKY JOSEPH F	COL	0-1312819	1068	1
SULLENGER WILBUR C	1LT	0-1296931	0845	2
SULLEY WILLIAM F	CW2	W-2149720	0359	1
SULLINGER CARL O	LTC	0-1044690	1262	1
SULLIVAN ADAM	LTC	0-0326750	0754	1
SULLIVAN AGNES P	1LT	N-0731417	0445	1
SULLIVAN AMBROSE J	MAJ	0-0359647	0145	2
SULLIVAN ANN M	2LT	N-0754360	0946	1
SULLIVAN ANNE KITEC	2LT	N-0721059	1144	1
SULLIVAN AUGUSTINE	CW2	W-2101104	0146	2
SULLIVAN BARRY A	CPT	0-1010241	0561	2
SULLIVAN BENJAMIN E	COL	0-0357950	0963	3
SULLIVAN CAMILLUS C	LTC	0-0206688	0661	3
SULLIVAN CARL D	MAJ	0-1798083	1060	1
SULLIVAN CHARLES M	MAJ	0-0253694	0157	3
SULLIVAN CHARLES M	1LT	0-5242094	0968	2
SULLIVAN CLARKE JR	MAJ	0-1283868	0954	2
SULLIVAN CORNELIUS	MAJ	0-1922502	0862	1
SULLIVAN DANIEL E JR	LTC	0-1055168	0763	1
SULLIVAN DANIEL F	COL	0-0337466	0468	3
SULLIVAN DANIEL L JR	LTC	0-1051404	0261	1
SULLIVAN DANIEL M	LTC	0-0202343	0862	3
SULLIVAN DANIEL P	MAJ	0-1014129	0662	1
SULLIVAN DANIEL P	MAJ	0-2262100	0864	1
SULLIVAN DAVID H	MAJ	0-1924899	0166	1
SULLIVAN DAZZEL E	MAJ	0-1555916	1160	1
SULLIVAN DEMPSEY O	MAJ	0-1581406	0665	1
SULLIVAN DENNIS P	LTC	0-0184004	0453	3
SULLIVAN DONALD T	CPT	0-1177202	0248	2
SULLIVAN DORIS M	2LT	N-0733881	0345	1

NAME	GRADE	SVC NO	DATE RET MO YR	RET CODE
SULLIVAN DOUGLAS E	2LT	0-1011360	0844	2
SULLIVAN EDMUND C	LTC	0-0422339	1263	1
SULLIVAN EDSON T	CPT	0-0512091	0153	1
SULLIVAN EDWARD P	MAJ	0-0426252	0546	2
SULLIVAN EDWIN W	LTC	0-0419213	0161	1
SULLIVAN ELIZABETH	2LT	N-0768948	0946	2
SULLIVAN ELMER	LTC	0-0267591	0565	3
SULLIVAN EUGENE F	1LT	0-2036256	114N	2
SULLIVAN FORREST K	CPT	0-1014123	0547	2
SULLIVAN FRANCIS C	MAJ	0-0194813	0862	3
SULLIVAN FRANCIS D	CPT	0-0468389	0747	1
SULLIVAN FRANCIS J	MAJ	0-0421441	0863	1
SULLIVAN FRANCIS K	1LT	0-0925572	0745	2
SULLIVAN FRANK T	MAJ	0-0198927	1054	3
SULLIVAN FREDERICK	MAJ	0-1794879	0161	1
SULLIVAN GEORGE C	COL	0-0112334	1056	3
SULLIVAN GEORGE H	1LT	0-1040158	0544	2
SULLIVAN GERALD P	COL	0-0267260	1164	3
SULLIVAN GOODRICH M	COL	0-0342431	0864	3
SULLIVAN HARRY F	CW3	W-2153271	0965	1
SULLIVAN HARRY L	CPT	0-1037328	0745	2
SULLIVAN HARVEY G	LTC	0-0341698	0550	1
SULLIVAN HENRY	LTC	0-1549125	0361	2
SULLIVAN HENRY C	LTC	0-0547203	1165	1
SULLIVAN HENRY C	LTC	0-1687471	1266	3
SULLIVAN HENRY M	MAJ	0-1280073	0460	1
SULLIVAN HOBERT G	CW2	W-2213623	0767	1
SULLIVAN JAMES A	LTC	0-0283842	1060	1
SULLIVAN JAMES A	CW3	W-2206370	1067	1
SULLIVAN JAMES E	CPT	0-0422558	1046	2
SULLIVAN JAMES F	LTC	0-1172304	0561	1
SULLIVAN JAMES H	MAJ	0-0526406	0856	1
SULLIVAN JAMES J	LTC	0-0240639	0562	3
SULLIVAN JAMES W	CPT	0-1956518	0147	2
SULLIVAN JESSE A	LTC	0-0505100	1152	1
SULLIVAN JOHN B JR	LTC	0-0395051	1067	3
SULLIVAN JOHN C	LTC	0-0356656	0546	2
SULLIVAN JOHN D	LTC	0-0402933	0161	1
SULLIVAN JOHN E	MAJ	0-1103960	0561	1
SULLIVAN JOHN F	MAJ	0-2262830	0563	1
SULLIVAN JOHN F JR	MAJ	0-0324398	0148	1
SULLIVAN JOHN H A	MAJ	0-0344301	1046	2
SULLIVAN JOHN J	2LT	0-0447819	0944	2
SULLIVAN JOHN J	2LT	0-1876116	0454	2
SULLIVAN JOHN J	LTC	0-2030585	0165	1
SULLIVAN JOHN J M C	CPT	0-0498516	1045	2
SULLIVAN JOHN J S	LTC	0-0502920	1060	1
SULLIVAN JOHN L	LTC	0-0343949	0560	1
SULLIVAN JOHN L	2LT	0-1324228	0545	2
SULLIVAN JOHN M	CW4	W-2111151	0858	1
SULLIVAN JOHN P	2LT	0-1000077	0743	2
SULLIVAN JOHN T	MAJ	0-2210050	1166	1
SULLIVAN JOSEPH C	MAJ	0-0429551	0347	2
SULLIVAN JOSEPH D	2LT	0-1310320	0445	2
SULLIVAN JOSEPH F	2LT	0-1999078	1045	2
SULLIVAN JOSEPH J	LTC	0-0388793	0546	2
SULLIVAN JOSEPH J	2LT	0-1111383	0145	2
SULLIVAN JOSEPH L	LTC	0-0259839	0865	3
SULLIVAN KENNETH H	MAJ	0-1110913	1055	1
SULLIVAN LAVERN E	WO1	W-2109000	0757	2
SULLIVAN LEO B	MAJ	0-0472357	0662	1
SULLIVAN LEONARD P	LTC	0-1296287	0865	1
SULLIVAN LOFTON D	CPT	0-0397275	0843	2
SULLIVAN LOREN W	LTC	0-0411447	0960	1
SULLIVAN MARTIN W	COL	0-0280424	1059	1
SULLIVAN MARY D V	1LT	N-0722781	0548	1
SULLIVAN MELVIN T	LTC	0-0330089	0567	3
SULLIVAN MICHAEL F	LTC	0-1575208	0462	1
SULLIVAN MICHAEL J	1LT	0-1914092	1135	1
SULLIVAN MICHAEL J	1LT	0-5331677	0768	2
SULLIVAN OLIVER J L	CW3	W-2151342	0163	1
SULLIVAN PATRICK D	MAJ	0-1638625	1060	1
SULLIVAN PATRICK R	LTC	0-0439165	1147	2
SULLIVAN PHILIP V	LTC	0-0931873	0665	1
SULLIVAN RALPH R	COL	0-0463035	1265	3
SULLIVAN RAYMOND J	1LT	0-0517030	0745	2
SULLIVAN RICHARD J	MAJ	0-0518527	0557	1
SULLIVAN RICHARD M	2LT	0-1575209	0145	2
SULLIVAN RICHARD P	LTC	0-0399856	0546	2
SULLIVAN ROBERT H	CPT	0-0493530	0647	1
SULLIVAN ROBERT J	1LT	0-0278450	0348	2
SULLIVAN ROBERT M	LTC	0-1100786	0962	1
SULLIVAN ROBERT T	MAJ	0-2004186	1168	1
SULLIVAN ROBERT W	LTC	0-1550933	0363	1
SULLIVAN SAMUEL T	LTC	0-1081181	0665	1
SULLIVAN STANLEY L	LTC	0-0212137	0450	2
SULLIVAN THOMAS D	CW3	W-2141793	0158	1
SULLIVAN THOMAS E	CW3	W-2207110	0767	1
SULLIVAN THOMAS E	CW2	W-3151334	0868	1
SULLIVAN THOMAS F	LTC	0-1011898	0966	1
SULLIVAN THOMAS R	CW2	W-3000418	0768	1
SULLIVAN VINCENT J	MAJ	0-1044119	1060	1
SULLIVAN WALTER A	MAJ	0-1948839	0261	2
SULLIVAN WALTER M E	COL	0-0233344	0553	2
SULLIVAN WILBER H	MAJ	0-0300728	0245	2
SULLIVAN WILLIAM B	MAJ	0-1635391	0361	1
SULLIVAN WILLIAM E	CW2	W-2151733	0264	1
SULLIVAN WILLIAM F	LTC	0-0243365	0566	3
SULLIVAN WILLIAM F	MAJ	0-1183203	1164	1
SULLIVAN WILLIAM H	CPT	0-0963659	0759	1
SULLIVAN WILLIAM J	LTC	0-1012504	1262	1
SULLIVAN WILLIAM M	LTC	0-1103430	0767	1
SULLIVAN WILLIAM P	1LT	0-1310648	1145	2
SULLIVAN WILLIAM W	LTC	0-0384485	0966	3
SULLIVAN WILSON T JR	CW3	W-2119883	1263	1
SULOFF SIDNEY E	LTC	0-0168868	0444	2
SULT EDWARD T	CW4	W-2114212	1154	1
SULTAN ERNEST H	CPT	0-0464071	0744	2
SULTZER MORTON	COL	0-0135636	0749	3
SULZBACH WILBUR R	MAJ	0-0240433	0165	3
SUMAN HERBERT A	LTC	0-0276178	0950	3
SUMARAGA ERNESTO	1LT	0-1896913	1161	2
SUMBRY 3RD AUSTIN	WO1	W-2142433	0952	2
SUMEK EDWARD J	MAJ	0-0837220	1266	1
SUMM ALVIN L	MAJ	0-1589644	1160	1
SUMMARELL RUFUS R	LTC	0-1580393	0967	1
SUMMER DAVID	MAJ	0-0339072	104N	2
SUMMER ELBY H	CW2	W-2147300	0755	2
SUMMER ROGER W	CW3	W-2141919	1057	1
SUMMER WILLIAM C	COL	0-0251775	0762	3
SUMMERFIELD MAX H	LTC	0-0127231	0754	3
SUMMERHAYS JOHN W	LTC	0-0290468	0750	3
SUMMERHILL ROBERT J	CW3	W-2145518	0859	1
SUMMERILL C W L	MAJ	0-0298740	1144	2
SUMMERLOT ROBERT L	MAJ	0-1317352	0663	1
SUMMERS BYRON P	MAJ	0-1533208	0157	1
SUMMERS CHARLES A	LTC	0-0247454	0664	3
SUMMERS CHARLES F	MAJ	0-2263085	0767	1
SUMMERS CHARLES F	CW3	W-2152690	0665	1
SUMMERS FRANKLIN L	COL	0-0118096	0652	2
SUMMERS GEORGE	CW3	W-2149782	0161	1
SUMMERS GEORGE C	LTC	0-0369800	1165	3
SUMMERS GEORGE E JR	MAJ	0-1643379	1060	1
SUMMERS HARRISON C	2LT	0-0887964	1045	2
SUMMERS JOHN B	1LT	0-1304286	0646	2
SUMMERS LEONARD JR	CPT	0-0527866	0846	2
SUMMERS NELLIE G	1LT	N-0780393	0148	1
SUMMERS ROBERT E	MAJ	0-2019389	0765	1
SUMMEY JAMES C	LTC	0-0450658	0255	1
SUMMITT BUREN L	2LT	0-0496797	0645	1
SUMMITT KENNETH A	1LT	0-1032053	0645	2
SUMNER F S JR	MAJ	0-1586257	0547	2
SUMNER HANSFORD A	CW2	W-2152329	0161	1
SUMNER HARRIS C	COL	0-0382490	1060	1
SUMNER JOSEPH G	LTC	0-2037102	1165	1
SUMNER MARK	COL	0-0228995	0464	3
SUMNER RAYMOND A	CW2	W-2205304	1063	1
SUMNER WILLIAM F	MAJ	0-1876412	0268	1
SUMNERS RAY H	1LT	0-1031979	0459	1
SUMPTER LEE R JR	LTC	0-0364477	0660	1
SUMRALL EDDIE F	CPT	0-2287191	0862	1
SUNDAHL ALBERT H	CPT	0-0156191	0744	2
SUNDAL EDNA M	1LT	N-0730094	1147	1
SUNDAY HENRY V	MAJ	0-1179641	0361	1
SUNDAY IRA E	LTC	0-0451343	0757	1
SUNDAY JANE W	2LT	N-0769745	1046	1
SUNDBERG DERWIN C	CW3	W-2207304	1267	1
SUNDBERG JOHN L	COL	0-0265455	0768	3
SUNDBERG LYNDON A	LTC	0-0380787	0757	1
SUNDE EIVEN	MAJ	0-0981442	0662	1
SUNDELL ROYAL D	MAJ	0-0117761	0452	3
SUNDERLAGE WILLIAM E	MAJ	0-0958662	0764	1
SUNDERLAND JOSEPH L	2LT	0-1325531	1044	2
SUNDERMAN GEORGE H	COL	0-0221825	0648	3
SUNDERMAN JACK J	LTC	0-1100359	1163	1
SUNDET LYLE J	LTC	0-0342301	0858	2
SUNDHEIMER THOMAS A	1LT	0-1318588	1045	2
SUNDINE SEVERT L	CW4	W-2145028	0368	1
SUNDSTROM VINCENT B	LTC	0-0446130	0466	3
SUNDT MARTIN C	CPT	0-0170419	0555	3
SUNDWALL EDWARD N	2LT	0-1320978	0945	2
SUNDY ROBERT C	LTC	0-0505177	0357	1
SUNNER CURTIS L	CW2	W-2136720	0963	1
SUNSERI ANTHONY J	1LT	0-1302227	0450	2
SUOJANEN ANNE A	2LT	N-0759430	0345	1
SUPENSKY JOHN A	COL	0-0173637	0859	1
SUPERNAW NOEL R	1LT	0-0485269	0453	1
SUPLEMENTO JEROME D	1LT	0-2032109	0450	2
SUPONCIC JOSEPH P	CW4	W-2127888	0658	1
SUPPLE BERNARD P	MAJ	0-2097024	0766	1
SUPPLE LEO E	MAJ	0-0190662	0154	3
SUPPLEE CHARLES L	COL	0-0101241	0855	3
SURACI ALFRED J	LTC	0-0346092	1046	2
SURDYNSKI JOSEPH S	CPT	0-0978475	0262	1
SURGNER STANLEY G	LTC	0-0277543	0858	3
SURINE CLYDE J	CW4	W-2119650	1054	1
SURINGTON CYRIL T	COL	0-0319011	0167	3
SURKEIN ROBERT J	MAJ	0-1951261	0161	1
SURKIN NORMAN	LTC	0-2050370	0166	1
SURLES RICHARD H SR	MAJ	0-2202206	1265	1
SURLS JOSEPH K	COL	0-0199524	0546	2
SURMAIN ANDRE	1LT	0-1320198	C545	2
SURPRISE CHESTER P	1LT	0-1634383	0146	2
SURRATT CLELON M	LTC	0-1534396	0558	1
SURRATT ETHAN R	MAJ	0-0290095	1146	1
SUSBILLA FRANCISCO	1LT	0-1896706	0662	1
SUSHKO ALBERT R	LTC	0-1996705	0268	1
SUSKIN SAMUEL	CPT	0-0349158	0344	2
SUSKO MICHAEL J	MAJ	0-0474785	0647	1
SUSS IRVING D	CPT	0-1018896	0347	2
SUSSE JOHN E	COL	0-0264343	0957	3
SUSSELL SANFORD P	COL	0-0452364	1163	2
SUSSKIND GILBERT D	COL	0-0344533	0565	1
SUSSKY JOSEPH J	CW2	W-2148534	0558	1
SUSSMEIER RICHARD	CW2	W-2214630	0767	1
SUTER HORACE B	2LT	0-1309436	0744	2
SUTER JAMES E	CW2	RW-3430020	0466	1
SUTER WILLIAM R	CPT	0-1321072	0649	2
SUTERA SALVATORE	LTC	0-0302896	0264	1
SUTFIN JUANITA G	MAJ	L-0401076	0467	1
SUTFIN SOCRATES D	CW2	W-2215080	0968	1
SUTHER JOHN H	LTC	0-0281630	0168	3
SUTHERLAND ARTHUR E	COL	0-0237530	0362	3
SUTHERLAND CARL T	M G	0-0258676	0265	3
SUTHERLAND CHARLIE T	MAJ	0-0943863	1262	1
SUTHERLAND DOUGLAS G	LTC	0-0273427	0968	3
SUTHERLAND FRANK E	LTC	0-1323757	1062	1
SUTHERLAND GERTRUD	CPT	N-0755582	0348	1
SUTHERLAND HAROLD M	COL	0-0162545	0654	3
SUTHERLAND HAROLD W	CW2	W-2144320	1154	1
SUTHERLAND HENRY A	LTC	0-0265641	0466	3
SUTHERLAND JAMES D	MAJ	0-0241437	0265	3
SUTHERLAND JOHN A	LTC	0-0291264	0960	3
SUTHERLAND JOHN E	COL	0-1697880	1268	2
SUTHERLAND JOHN G	MAJ	0-1315529	1161	1
SUTHERLAND JOHN H	CPT	0-1289162	0661	1
SUTHERLAND JOSEPH E	CW4	W-2115850	0355	1
SUTHERLAND KENNETH R	LTC	0-1030842	1065	1
SUTHERLAND PAUL F	COL	0-0137350	0256	3
SUTHERLAND ROLAND W	1LT	0-0543146	0646	2
SUTHERLAND RUSSELL E	CPT	0-1030527	1153	2
SUTHERLAND WILLIAM B	LTC	0-1035237	1266	1
SUTHERLAND WILLIAM M	2LT	0-1109048	0544	2
SUTHERLIN LEE	COL	0-0115686	0749	3
SUTLEY ALFRED W	LTC	0-2208445	1067	1
SUTLIFF DONALD A	CW2	W-2109239	1052	2
SUTLIFF EDWARD H	MAJ	0-0137435	0250	3
SUTOR FRANK J	MAJ	0-1329410	0164	1
SUTORIK GEORGE J	LTC	0-1645417	0666	1
SUTPHIN HERMAN T	LTC	0-0498642	0954	1
SUTPHIN LEONA G	CPT	N-0703010	0545	1
SUTTER ERNEST M	1LT	0-0416968	0145	2
SUTTER MARTHA M	2LT	N-0700599	0637	1
SUTTER ROBERT L	1LT	0-0524362	1045	2
SUTTERFIELD W R	CPT	0-1294038	0556	1
SUTTERLIN FRANK W	MAJ	0-0530732	0846	2
SUTTLE JOHN F	CPT	0-0485162	0646	2
SUTTLE REID O	CW4	W-2136648	0865	1
SUTTLES JAMES C	LTC	0-1573610	0557	1
SUTTON ALBERT T JR	MAJ	0-0492766	0465	1
SUTTON ARTHUR M	CPT	0-0483986	0144	2
SUTTON CECILE A	1LT	N-0752632	0248	1
SUTTON EDWARD L	CPT	0-0362970	0746	2
SUTTON EVERETT G	LTC	0-1182469	1066	1
SUTTON FRANCIS D	CPT	0-1998036	0756	1
SUTTON FRANK W	LTC	0-0123037	0756	3
SUTTON GEORGE J	MAJ	0-1102974	0360	1
SUTTON GRANGER G	LTC	0-0185405	1162	3
SUTTON HAZEL D	CPT	N-0703319	0945	1
SUTTON JACK D	CPT	0-0383561	1145	2
SUTTON JAMES C	LTC	0-0188699	0657	3
SUTTON JAMES H	MAJ	0-1291194	0161	1
SUTTON JAMES H	MAJ	0-1308019	1159	1
SUTTON JEFF W	CPT	0-0499114	0954	1
SUTTON JOHN M	CPT	0-1944610	0947	2
SUTTON JOSEPH A	COL	0-0147980	1152	3
SUTTON KENNETH L	1LT	0-0444961	0445	2
SUTTON LEONARD	CPT	0-1309437	0646	2
SUTTON LEVI W	1LT	0-1701921	0145	2
SUTTON OLIVER W	CW3	W-2152857	0763	1
SUTTON RICHARD L JR	MAJ	0-0511361	0146	2
SUTTON ROBERT F	MAJ	0-1925986	0966	1
SUTTON ROBERT H	MAJ	0-1595071	0262	1
SUTTON SEARS G	MAJ	0-1303411	0159	1
SUTTON SHERMAN L	CW3	W-2141794	1061	1
SUTTON SHERWOOD A	MAJ	0-0467828	0446	2
SUTTON WILLIAM	CPT	0-0505631	0145	1
SUTTON WILLIAM R JR	MAJ	0-1341922	1266	1
SUYDAM JAMES H	COL	0-0304896	0947	2
SUYDAM JOHN H	LTC	0-1056568	1262	1
SUZUKAWA FRED F	MAJ	0-2030605	0464	1
SUZUKI TARO	MAJ	0-0242011	1146	2
SUZUKI TOSHIO T	MAJ	0-0942999	0264	1
SVEC JOSEPH R	LTC	0-0486224	0754	1
SVELA JACOB	1LT	0-0381763	0952	1
SVENDSEN GUSTAV	COL	0-0319319	0764	3
SVENSON HULDA	2LT	N-0700197	0737	1
SVERDLIN ABE A	LTC	0-0335194	0646	2
SVERDRUP LEIF J	M G	0-0129029	0358	3
SVEUN LYNN M	1LT	0-1181479	0846	2
SVIEN MYRON B	LTC	0-1081103	0467	1
SVIGALS FRED	LTC	0-0335535	1160	3
SVIRSKY HERMAN H	1LT	0-2102932	0664	2
SVITAK WILLIAM J	CW2	W-2205162	0461	2
SVITAVSKY LEO E	1LT	0-1288139	1144	2
SVITZER DOROTHY W	2LT	N-0798897	0847	1
SVOBODA ALBERT A	COL	0-0103869	0746	2
SVOBODA CHARLES V	CW4	W-2148417	0556	1
SVOBODA GEORGE W	COL	0-0313625	0167	1
SVOBODA HENRY	CW3	W-2146287	0157	1

NAME	GRADE	SVC NO	DATE RET MO YR	RET CODE
SVOBODA LLOYD J	1LT	0-0550514	0146	2
SWABB FRED C	MAJ	0-1647747	0258	1
SWABEY WILLIAM A	CPT	0-0147979	1157	3
SWABON JOHN J JR	MAJ	0-1917941	0965	1
SWACK HARRY J	LTC	0-0282080	1153	1
SWAD CHARLES E	MAJ	0-1917820	0865	1
SWAFFORD EDWIN G	LTC	0-0207279	0862	3
SWAFFORD FRED G	LTC	0-0271962	0260	3
SWAFFORD PAUL C	COL	0-0229966	0660	1
SWAGERTY F CECONIA	1LT	N-0779101	0845	1
SWAGGERT REX J	CW2	W-2112140	0447	1
SWAGLER RUDYARD M	CPT	0-0428614	0746	2
SWAILS ARMSTRONG	CPT	0-0327127	0845	2
SWAILS FLOYD P	COL	0-0383550	0162	1
SWAIM JAMES C	1LT	0-1110279	0346	2
SWAIM LEBERT F	CPT	0-0359593	0745	2
SWAIM RALPH	2LT	0-1933558	0254	2
SWAIM WAYLAND A	1LT	0-0887611	0348	2
SWAIN EARL R	1LT	0-1579193	1058	1
SWAIN FRANK	CPT	0-1037329	0761	1
SWAIN FRANK R JR	LTC	0-0234068	1263	3
SWAIN GEORGE F	CPT	0-0986501	1060	1
SWAIN JAMES C	COL	0-1167245	0868	1
SWAIN JAMES W	LTC	0-1051795	1063	1
SWAIN MILES JR	CW3	W-2144932	0462	1
SWAIN NELLIS C	MAJ	0-1649514	0755	1
SWAIN WILLIAM H	1LT	0-1559265	0847	2
SWALLOW JAMES F	CPT	0-1049364	1060	1
SWALLWELL JAMES	CW2	W-2152405	0760	1
SWAN EDWARD H	LTC	0-1013047	0467	1
SWAN ERVIN D JR	MAJ	0-0185109	0446	1
SWAN FORREST	LTC	0-1110838	1262	2
SWAN GARTH V	2LT	0-0393943	1043	2
SWAN GEORGE E	CPT	0-1577925	1065	1
SWAN GEORGE F	LTC	0-1313317	1062	1
SWAN HARRY E	2LT	0-1314740	0744	2
SWAN HENRY T	COL	0-0241428	0159	3
SWAN JAMES E JR	LTC	0-0239290	0665	3
SWAN PARK P	MAJ	0-1135694	0361	1
SWAN ULMONT	COL	0-0207388	1055	3
SWAN VERNER M	CPT	0-1756922	0849	2
SWAN VICTOR B	MAJ	0-1555638	1263	1
SWAN WILLIAM H	MAJ	0-0364014	1047	2
SWANBERG CHARLES M	CW3	W-2143694	1163	1
SWANBERG F C	MAJ	0-0350890	0446	2
SWANBOM ELMER E	MAJ	0-0129770	0553	3
SWANCARA ARNOLD L	CPT	0-0482507	0647	2
SWANEY ACY L	CPT	0-1684949	0161	1
SWANGO JOHN V	COL	0-1307326	1067	1
SWANK CHARLES W	LTC	0-0308472	0358	1
SWANK CHESTER L	MAJ	0-0503954	1047	2
SWANK CLARENCE F	1LT	0-1592642	0553	1
SWANKE CHRIST A	LTC	0-0493545	0657	1
SWANN EDGAR A	1LT	0-1287433	0344	2
SWANN EDMOND J	MAJ	0-0179166	0850	3
SWANN ERWIN L	CW4	W-2018795	1154	1
SWANN JEFFERSON	LTC	0-1179221	1062	1
SWANN LEONARD V JR	CPT	0-1061788	0361	1
SWANNER ORBY	MAJ	0-2206135	1266	1
SWANO ANTHONY G	CPT	0-0524467	0767	3
SWANSON ARTHUR	CPT	0-0504806	0845	2
SWANSON AUSTIN L	LTC	0-0347429	0860	1
SWANSON CARL E	LTC	0-0252185	0266	3
SWANSON CECIL V	MAJ	0-1646045	1263	1
SWANSON CHARLES E	LTC	0-0406354	0861	1
SWANSON DALE V	COL	0-0240321	1164	3
SWANSON EARL H	LTC	0-0133521	0656	3
SWANSON EDWIN E	CPT	0-0212680	0352	3
SWANSON EDWIN E	MAJ	0-0230013	0744	2
SWANSON EVERETT A	LTC	0-0213087	0761	3
SWANSON EVERETT M	MAJ	0-0224155	0345	2
SWANSON FRANK J C	MAJ	0-0276571	0156	3
SWANSON FREDERICK	COL	0-0119685	0648	3
SWANSON FREDERICK	LTC	0-0238356	0961	3
SWANSON GEORGE S	COL	0-0301519	0355	1

NAME	GRADE	SVC NO	DATE RET MO YR	RET CODE
SWANSON GEORGE W E	CPT	0-1185833	0860	1
SWANSON GREGORY H	MAJ	0-1557098	0962	1
SWANSON HAROLD A	LTC	0-1105218	0767	3
SWANSON HARRY W	CW4	W-2124077	1154	1
SWANSON HENRY J	MAJ	0-2053964	0855	1
SWANSON HERBERT S	LTC	0-0279134	0855	3
SWANSON JOHN L	MAJ	0-1794880	1060	1
SWANSON KARL J	CW2	W-2146401	0158	1
SWANSON LAURENCE C	LTC	0-0370434	0368	3
SWANSON LEONARD E	CPT	0-0188659	0458	3
SWANSON LEONARD E	LTC	0-0240885	0858	3
SWANSON PAUL H	LTC	0-0174273	1160	3
SWANSON RAYMOND J	CPT	0-0281270	0663	3
SWANSON RAYMOND J	1LT	0-2262579	0654	2
SWANSON RICHARD	COL	0-0255972	0156	3
SWANSON RUDOLPH	LTC	0-0309009	0954	1
SWANSON STEWART	CPT	0-2046470	0955	1
SWANSON THEODORE R	1LT	0-1173103	1059	1
SWANSON WILFRED D	LTC	0-1576714	0561	1
SWANSON WILLIAM T	COL	0-0275162	0648	3
SWANTEK MARJORIE A	2LT	N-0773032	0345	1
SWANWICK EVA P M	MAJ	N-0759190	1262	1
SWANWICK WILLIAM J	CW3	W-2103505	0963	1
SWANZ GEORGE J	CW2	W-2150763	0456	1
SWARBERG JOHN F	MAJ	0-1535542	0966	1
SWARNER JOHN L	LTC	0-0296843	0167	3
SWARRINGIM HOWARD W	1LT	0-2005316	1055	1
SWART MALCOLM R	CPT	0-0521097	1153	2
SWART MURL F	LTC	0-0284026	0957	3
SWARTHOUT GERARD SR	LTC	0-0267451	0556	3
SWARTHOUT JOSEPHINE	MAJ	N-0793982	0466	1
SWARTHOUT ROBERT E	MAJ	0-1688441	0665	1
SWARTHOUT WALTER E	LTC	0-0298624	0462	3
SWARTS CHARLES A	1LT	0-0233460	0648	3
SWARTSEL CHARLES V	MAJ	0-1165578	0954	1
SWARTZ CARLYLE D	LTC	0-1103962	0261	1
SWARTZ GEORGE J	MAJ	0-2032134	0263	1
SWARTZ GLENN E	LTC	0-0165651	0245	2
SWARTZ JOHN L	CW3	W-2152631	0164	1
SWARTZ JOSEPH W	CPT	0-1643381	0746	2
SWARTZ MORRIS	LTC	0-0526299	0657	1
SWARTZ OLIVER H	LTC	0-0258497	1062	3
SWARTZ PETER W	CPT	0-0194302	0648	3
SWARTZ RALPH A	MAJ	0-1110839	0466	3
SWARTZ RICHARD F	1LT	0-1056906	1145	2
SWARTZ RONALD R	MAJ	0-0408235	0957	1
SWARTZ SPENCER D	MAJ	0-0211881	0648	3
SWARTZ THOMAS S	MAJ	0-1118512	0960	1
SWARTZ WILEY R	1LT	0-1288326	1045	2
SWARTZELL CHARLES A	CPT	0-0957598	1160	1
SWASICK MAX F	LTC	0-1100789	0766	1
SWAST JOHN J	MAJ	0-1294218	0446	2
SWATEK MATHEW J	MAJ	0-0235227	0454	3
SWATKO MICHAEL R	LTC	0-1171789	1061	1
SWATOSH ROBERT B	LTC	0-0363057	0860	1
SWATSZEL WILLIAM H	LTC	0-0284219	0568	3
SWATTS ROBERT W	COL	0-0108006	0256	3
SWAVELY CHARLES A	MAJ	0-1107170	1160	1
SWAVELY STANLEY L	CW3	W-2143972	0464	1
SWAYZE KENNETH W	LTC	0-1175596	0763	1
SWAZEY VAUGHN R	MAJ	0-0452982	0758	1
SWEANY WILLIAM F	LTC	0-1001913	0268	1
SWEARENGIN HENRY F	WO1	W-2121018	1046	1
SWEARINGEN LLOYD E	COL	0-0192378	0857	3
SWEARINGEN ROBERT W	LTC	0-0492998	0665	2
SWEARINGEN WARREN W	MAJ	0-1593328	0557	1
SWEARINGEN WILLARD P	COL	0-0311312	1061	2
SWEARINGER HARRY P	CW3	W-2147459	0167	1
SWEASEY ARCHIE W	LTC	0-0166786	0157	3
SWEAT ARNOLD D	LTC	0-1924943	1068	1
SWEAT ERNEST L	LTC	0-0400004	0960	1
SWEAT WESLEY A	COL	0-0259536	1167	3
SWECKER EDWIN E	2LT	0-0929093	0645	2
SWEDBERG ARTHUR V	COL	0-0123924	0454	3
SWEDBERG CLARENCE H	LTC	0-0453154	0261	1

NAME	GRADE	SVC NO	DATE RET MO YR	RET CODE
SWEDBERG WILLIAM A	CPT	0-0425850	0443	2
SWEDE ALLEN G	COL	0-0139385	0757	3
SWEE JOHN R	LTC	0-1051797	1167	1
SWEELEY WILLIAM J	LTC	0-0309558	0760	3
SWEELY JOE W	LTC	0-1109053	0365	1
SWEEN ALFRED M	LTC	0-0359307	1152	3
SWEENEY ALAN F	CPT	0-1859672	0861	2
SWEENEY ASHER W	LTC	0-1334516	0468	1
SWEENEY BERNARD J	MAJ	0-1638631	1150	2
SWEENEY CHARLES F	MAJ	0-1924857	0968	1
SWEENEY CLAIR R	CPT	0-1797745	0164	2
SWEENEY DANIEL C	CPT	0-0243023	0458	3
SWEENEY EDWARD A	LTC	0-1101693	1061	1
SWEENEY FRANCIS C	COL	0-0261448	0467	3
SWEENEY FRANCIS E	COL	0-0252682	0860	3
SWEENEY FRANCIS R	COL	0-0203012	0846	2
SWEENEY FRANK E	1LT	0-1181160	0745	2
SWEENEY FRANK J	LTC	0-0118090	0658	3
SWEENEY HARRY D	1LT	0-1313919	0945	2
SWEENEY HUGH A	1LT	0-1321842	0647	2
SWEENEY JAMES A JR	MAJ	0-0371828	0963	3
SWEENEY JAMES R	COL	0-0368456	1263	1
SWEENEY JAMES S	COL	0-0484302	1045	2
SWEENEY JEROME K	LTC	0-1647298	1165	1
SWEENEY JOHN J	MAJ	0-0359286	0745	2
SWEENEY JOHN P	LTC	0-0396321	0546	2
SWEENEY JOHN S	2LT	0-1039240	0944	2
SWEENEY JOSEPH T	CW3	W-2147005	1153	1
SWEENEY LEO P A	COL	0-0243503	1159	3
SWEENEY MERCER W	LTC	0-0239744	0262	3
SWEENEY MICHAEL K	2LT	0-1950652	0346	2
SWEENEY MICHAEL M	CPT	0-1285661	0660	1
SWEENEY RALPH C	COL	0-0108393	0156	3
SWEENEY ROBERT J	MAJ	0-0346931	0546	2
SWEENEY ROBERT L	LTC	0-1285137	0361	1
SWEENEY RUSSELL W	MAJ	0-1307878	0861	1
SWEENEY SAMUEL P	MAJ	0-1796728	0459	1
SWEENEY WILLIAM A	MAJ	0-2002551	1061	1
SWEENEY WILLIAM H	CW2	W-2215069	1266	1
SWEENEY WILLIAM R	CPT	0-0415385	0750	2
SWEET ALVAN A JR	CW4	W-2129118	0656	1
SWEET ARTHUR J	COL	0-0287442	0162	3
SWEET CHARLES T	MAJ	0-0962543	1263	1
SWEET FRANCIS R	MAJ	0-0939681	0762	1
SWEET FREDERICK	LTC	0-2018241	1067	2
SWEET GUSTAF	LTC	0-0380913	0145	2
SWEET HOWARD J	CW3	W-2205340	0166	1
SWEET JOHN J JR	MAJ	0-1300571	0653	1
SWEET LEROY W	MAJ	0-0506512	0357	1
SWEET ROBERT D	LTC	0-0467529	1264	1
SWEET ROSS B	CPT	0-1541588	0245	2
SWEET STUART G	LTC	0-1011970	0166	3
SWEET WILLIAM B	LTC	0-1313934	0762	1
SWEETEN GLEN D	CPT	0-1822482	0446	2
SWEETEN GOMER A	COL	0-0370036	0766	1
SWEETEN WILBUR A	COL	0-0460366	0654	1
SWEETEN WILLIAM L	CPT	0-2056116	0856	1
SWEETING ESTELLA W	1LT	N-0797751	1147	1
SWEETING GEORGE D	MAJ	0-2262791	1265	1
SWEETLAND RUSSELL A	MAJ	0-2034617	0661	1
SWEETMAN HAROLD W	LTC	0-1039941	1062	1
SWEEZEY RAYMON J JR	MAJ	0-0677316	0561	1
SWEGER ARTHUR S SR	1LT	0-1165300	0446	1
SWEIER GEORGE O JR	CPT	0-0493180	0145	2
SWEIGART BERT A	MAJ	0-0205821	0553	3
SWEIGART EARL S	LTC	0-1292085	0961	1
SWEIGART MARION D	MAJ	N-0760482	0368	1
SWEM GILBERT S	MAJ	0-1030193	1051	2
SWENDA STEVE	WO1	W-2123326	0349	1
SWENEY LOWRY H	LTC	0-0147168	0157	3
SWENIE DENIS J	LTC	0-1030194	0866	3
SWENSEN GEORGE M	COL	0-0323975	0561	1
SWENSON ARNOLD	LTC	0-1548320	1055	1
SWENSON DONALD D	MAJ	0-1317701	0259	1
SWENSON EARL W	COL	0-0327344	1060	3

NAME	GRADE	SVC NO	DATE RET MO YR	RET CODE
SWENSON GEORGE K	1LT	0-2035984	1045	2
SWENSON GUSTAVE P	MAJ	0-2202213	1163	1
SWENSON HAROLD V	LTC	0-0285453	0568	3
SWENSON JOHN W	CPT	0-0387201	0343	2
SWENSON OLIVER L	CW2	W-2149056	0865	1
SWENSON PAUL A	1LT	0-1542164	1145	2
SWENSON WILTON G	CPT	0-1333021	0959	1
SWENTY JOHN D	CPT	0-1292086	0261	1
SWEROLIN GEORGE D	MAJ	0-2020482	0263	1
SWEROLOFF GEORGE	LTC	0-0425118	1065	1
SWERYDA JOHN	MAJ	0-0423014	0358	1
SWESNIK ROBERT M	CPT	0-0353894	0144	2
SWETNAM JOHN M	CPT	0-1304289	0545	2
SWETNAM MICHAEL N	CW2	W-2208212	0361	1
SWETT ARTHUR J	LTC	0-0217038	0844	2
SWETT STANTON L	LTC	0-0192420	0661	3
SWETZ CHARLES	1LT	0-1557799	0746	2
SWEZEY CHARLES M	COL	0-0101701	0948	3
SWEZEY ROBERT H	CW3	W-2136530	0965	1
SWIATEK STANLEY E	LTC	0-1299961	1064	2
SWIBEL MORRIS	2LT	0-1320608	0544	1
SWICEGOOD HARRY L	COL	0-0232806	0862	3
SWICK GREGORY H	LTC	0-2030155	1158	2
SWICK LOYAL B	LTC	0-0305015	1262	1
SWICK WILLIARD R	LTC	0-0278514	1059	1
SWICKERATH CARL	CPT	0-1287265	0145	2
SWIDELSKY JOHN E	MAJ	0-1641006	1166	1
SWIDERSKI FRED J	MAJ	0-1333022	0361	1
SWIECA BRUNO J	CPT	0-1303571	0848	2
SWIECKOWSKI S A	MAJ	0-1016223	0258	1
SWIEKATOWSKI S J	MAJ	0-0164755	1146	1
SWIETZER HUGH A	CPT	0-0491208	0857	1
SWIFT ALLAN M	MAJ	0-0367720	0745	2
SWIFT CLARENCE E	CW2	W-2109857	1044	2
SWIFT COE T	CPT	0-0506644	0246	2
SWIFT DAVID W	LTC	0-0310923	0456	1
SWIFT FRANCIS L	2LT	0-0557699	0146	2
SWIFT GEORGE T	LTC	0-1176211	0261	1
SWIFT GEORGE W	LTC	0-1306764	0162	1
SWIFT HARLEY L	COL	0-0147172	0154	3
SWIFT HARRY R	LTC	0-2017299	0563	1
SWIFT HERBERT B	CPT	0-0359749	0966	3
SWIFT HOWELL A	CW3	W-2147026	1163	1
SWIFT IVAN W	MAJ	0-0418101	1149	1
SWIFT JAMES P	MAJ	0-0522364	0954	1
SWIFT JOHN D	WO1	W-2120979	0865	3
SWIFT NEIL K	CPT	0-0416198	104N	2
SWIFT ROBERT G	COL	0-0239858	0946	2
SWIFT TEDDY E	MAJ	0-1933355	0168	1
SWIFT VAUGHN F	LTC	0-1312068	1164	1
SWIFT WILLIAM R	LTC	0-1179223	0767	1
SWIGART KENNETH E	LTC	0-1533925	0662	1
SWIGERT CAMILLE B	LTC	L-0500193	1162	1
SWIGERT VERNE W	MAJ	0-1821214	0146	2
SWIHART DONALD W	COL	0-0240322	0265	3
SWIM BRUCE E	CPT	0-0953908	1161	1
SWIM CHARLES H	MAJ	0-2014588	0164	1
SWIMM FRANKLIN A	WO1	W-2111632	114N	2
SWINDALL VERNON	LTC	0-0408431	0661	1
SWINDELL GEORGE B JR	LTC	0-0324959	0962	1
SWINDELL MYRTLE N	MAJ	N-0727309	0762	1
SWINDELLS JOEL W	LTC	0-0338083	0465	3
SWINDEN ANNA M	2LT	N-0722118	0443	1
SWINDLE DUANE R	1LT	0-1113470	1045	2
SWINDLE JAMES T	MAJ	0-0417870	1146	2
SWINDLER THOMAS H	CPT	0-1642634	1064	2
SWINDON CLIFFORD W	MAJ	0-1309438	1060	1
SWINEHART BILLY J	2LT	0-0519427	0745	2
SWINFORD CECIL	LTC	0-1331782	0768	1
SWING ANDREW L	MAJ	0-1886436	0168	1
SWING ROBERT L	LTC	0-2014774	0868	1
SWINGLE ERNEST A	LTC	0-0257406	0648	3
SWINHOE WALTER A	COL	0-0494594	0656	1
SWINK DONALD D	1LT	0-1638639	1050	2
SWINK LLOYD J	LTC	0-1170217	1060	1

332-811 O - 69 - 23

NAME	GRADE	SVC NO	DATE RET MO YR	RET CODE
SWINK PAUL L JR	MAJ	0-2001124	0960	1
SWINNY BUEV	COL	0-0245221	0959	3
SWIONTKOWSKI S O	CPT	0-0317991	1044	2
SWIPES LEONARD E	2LT	0-1294387	1059	1
SWISHER EDWIN S	2LT	0-1321848	C244	2
SWISHER FLOYD E	CW2	W-2210845	0263	1
SWISHER KEATH M	LTC	0-0258491	1059	3
SWISHER ROBERT M	MAJ	0-0451423	1047	2
SWITKES HERMAN I	COL	0-0485445	0866	3
SWITZ FRED	2LT	0-1315625	0844	2
SWITZER FRANK C	LTC	0-0255470	0359	3
SWITZER GUY P JR	LTC	0-1101236	0368	3
SWITZER HENRY C	COL	0-0109587	0955	3
SWITZER HERBERT E	CW3	W-2210996	0868	1
SWITZER HUGH E	LTC	0-2033583	0866	1
SWITZER LEE P	LTC	0-0455834	0263	1
SWITZER MARION A	1LT	N-0743117	0846	1
SWITZER MARK E	COL	0-1107711	0764	1
SWITZER ROBERT L	1LT	0-1307589	0644	2
SWITZER W HOMER	COL	0-0343821	0162	1
SWOBODA LEO A	COL	0-0193542	0558	3
SWOBODA ROBERT C	LTC	0-1315636	1064	1
SWOFFORD JOSEPH A	MAJ	0-0919552	1163	2
SWOFFORD PERRY	MAJ	0-0395851	0768	3
SWOFFORD ROBERT T JR	CPT	0-0257040	1155	3
SWOISH WILLIAM G	CPT	0-1318589	0647	2
SWOISKIN BERNARD L	CPT	0-0399452	1044	2
SWOKLA STANLEY	MAJ	0-1287084	0855	1
SWONGER HARRY G	CPT	0-0338609	0548	1
SWOPE CHARLES L	LTC	0-1298153	0763	1
SWOPE IANTHE	MAJ	N-0744248	0567	1
SWOPE JOHN H JR	MAJ	0-0910167	0446	2
SWOPE LAWRENCE E	COL	0-0387457	1147	2
SWOPE ROBERT S	MAJ	0-1550934	1160	1
SWOPE WALTER F	CW2	W-2149964	0357	1
SWOPE WILLIAM F	MAJ	0-0402870	0960	1
SWORD CATHERINE	1LT	N-0787264	0945	2
SWORD JOHN W	CPT	0-0108496	1037	2
SWORDS LARRY G JR	CW2	W-2151031	0161	1
SWOYER GROVER E	CPT	0-0141361	0849	3
SWYGERT LUTHER L	LTC	0-0417218	0965	3
SWYHART CARL A	MAJ	0-0331635	1154	1
SWYTAK WALTER	CPT	0-1081761	0462	2
SYDORKO MICHAEL	MAJ	0-0452639	1057	1
SYKES ALFRED JR	LTC	0-1306493	1266	1
SYKES ARTHUR G	1LT	0-0419409	0345	2
SYKES FLOYD L	MAJ	0-1598534	0164	1
SYKES JOY V	CPT	0-1693038	0145	2
SYKES MAURICE C	CPT	0-1877865	0865	1
SYKES WALTER E	MAJ	0-1183981	1262	1
SYKES WILLIAM E	MAJ	0-1289831	0365	1
SYLCE HARRY R	LTC	0-1286206	0161	1
SYLVAN DAVID L	2LT	0-0109381	0337	1
SYLVANDER EGIL H	MAJ	0-0273560	0368	3
SYLVANOWICZ S F	2LT	0-1081254	0845	2
SYLVEST TRUMAN W	1LT	0-1010905	1045	2
SYLVESTER ATHOL R JR	CPT	0-0376982	0942	2
SYLVESTER CAL R	CPT	0-0431738	1046	2
SYLVESTER CHARLES M	2LT	0-1327902	0446	2
SYLVESTER ELLIS P	COL	0-0238293	1165	3
SYLVESTER ELMER	LTC	0-0296693	0667	3
SYLVESTER GEORGE E	LTC	0-0364687	1060	1
SYLVESTER ROBERT E	1LT	0-1874892	1062	2
SYLVIA ALBERT K	1LT	0-0925266	0645	2
SYMANSKI BERNARD F	LTC	0-2008092	0268	1
SYMANSKI THEODORE V	LTC	0-0240723	0858	3
SYMCZYK WALTER J	MAJ	0-1305498	0460	1
SYME WILLIAM M	1LT	0-0391350	0945	2
SYMMES FREDERICK	LTC	0-0359490	1165	1
SYMNS ROBERT V	LTC	0-0924538	0863	1
SYMON ROBERT	1LT	0-1169362	1045	2
SYMONDS GEORGE C	LTC	0-0275939	1049	3
SYMONDS MARY K	1LT	N-0762171	1045	1
SYMONDS N W JR	2LT	0-1311448	0845	2
SYMONS JOHN H	CPT	0-1046663	0646	2
SYMS ZELLA F	1LT	N-0735884	0945	1
SYNHORST STANLEY H	CPT	0-0356419	0645	2
SYNOWSKI ALEXANDER	LTC	0-0451507	0158	1
SYNOWSKY JOHN	MAJ	0-1310172	0561	1
SYRAN ARTHUR G	COL	0-0223286	0764	3
SYRUJO MICHAEL	MAJ	0-2263185	0762	1
SZABO ALEXANDER	MAJ	0-1690907	1059	1
SZARES JOHN W	LTC	0-1306169	0363	1
SZCZECH EDWARD T	CW3	W-2146865	1061	1
SZCZEPANIK STANLEY J	CW2	W-2145520	0860	1
SZCZEPANSKI JOHN J	MAJ	0-2033173	0762	1
SZCZOTKA LEO A	CPT	0-1302229	1045	2
SZCZUDLIK JOSEPH A	CPT	0-0414505	1145	2
SZEFLINSKI CHESTER C	CPT	0-2262630	0364	1
SZEMCSAK STEPHEN T	MAJ	0-0980091	0763	1
SZEPI JOSEPH	CW2	W-2213527	0968	1
SZILVASY GEORGE A	MAJ	0-1308878	0361	1
SZLICHTA STANLEY K	MAJ	0-1296288	1061	2
SZMARA WALTER	1LT	0-1016162	0146	2
SZOBOTA STEVE	CPT	0-2025563	0557	1
SZOKE CHARLES V	CW3	W-2126215	1154	1
SZORADY ANTHONY E	LTC	0-1100790	0266	1
SZPEINSKI WENCEL	CPT	0-0467338	0452	1
SZUBA CHARLES H	CPT	0-0540837	0752	2
SZUKALSKI JOSEPH P	LTC	0-0226106	0760	3
SZUMACHOWSKI VICTOR	CW2	W-2145029	0260	1
SZUSZITZKY VELOON P	CPT	0-0232720	1161	3
SZWABO EARL M	CW2	W-2150367	1060	1
SZWAJER THADDEUS X	MAJ	0-1643384	0461	1
SZWALEK STANLEY J	1LT	0-0504831	0448	2
SZYMANSKI JAMES	CPT	0-1675258	0958	3
SZYMANSKI JOHN V	MAJ	0-2262341	1161	2
SZYMANSKI MARCELL	1LT	0-1319680	0847	2
SZYMCZAK EMIL T	MAJ	0-1997176	0959	1
SZYMCZAK NORBERT S	CW3	W-2143527	0161	1
SZYMKIEWICZ JOSEPH	LTC	0-0484353	0156	1
SZYMKOWICZ FRANK J	MAJ	0-1288463	0857	2
TAAFEL FRANK O	LTC	0-0243168	0758	3
TABB THOMAS R	MAJ	0-1540861	0263	1
TABBERT EVAN T	LTC	0-0972164	0468	1
TABELON EMILIANO	1LT	0-2032089	0655	1
TABER AUGUSTUS K JR	MAJ	0-0933917	1165	1
TABER BEACH E	MAJ	0-0206867	0648	3
TABER CLARENCE B	CW3	W-2150757	1064	1
TABER DAVID T	LTC	0-0396771	0160	1
TABER DONALD E	CPT	0-2287218	0767	1
TABER GERALD F	CW2	W-2208484	0761	1
TABER HARRY A	2LT	0-1913953	0631	1
TABER IRVING J	LTC	0-0214555	1046	2
TABINO SANTIAGO	1LT	0-1896456	0558	1
TABOCK JACK	1LT	0-1039943	1147	2
TABOR CARL P	MAJ	0-0367281	1153	1
TABOR CLIFFORD C	LTC	0-0279164	0667	3
TABOR EDWARD F	CPT	0-0956707	0960	1
TABOR JOSEPH H	1LT	0-0422063	1043	2
TABOR RALPH A	1LT	0-0325966	0245	2
TABORA BENIGNO G	CPT	0-0890528	0968	1
TACEY ROBERT F	MAJ	0-2039490	1161	1
TACHOIR ROBERT E	LTC	0-1634388	0561	1
TACKER HUSTON J JR	CW4	W-2143235	1265	1
TACKER LOYAL W	LTC	0-1934708	0356	2
TACKETT CHARLES L	LTC	0-1703757	0257	1
TACKETT DONALD H	MAJ	0-1825282	0265	1
TACKETT LITTLE D	CPT	0-1540902	1159	1
TACKETT LOUIS L JR	CW2	W-2210089	0465	1
TACKLIND FLOYD O	COL	0-0301735	0360	1
TADINI FRED A	LTC	0-1551316	0861	1
TADLOCK AUD L	MAJ	0-1325174	0959	1
TADLOCK MARION C	COL	0-0194384	0358	1
TADTMAN EMERSON L	MAJ	0-0961192	1061	1
TAFEEN JACK H	1LT	0-1177205	1045	2
TAFF ANTHONY	CPT	0-0505989	0347	1
TAFFE RICHARD P	LTC	0-1283694	0366	1
TAFS WILLIAM D	LTC	0-1543384	0760	1
TAFT FORREST D	LTC	0-1289648	0563	1
TAFT JESSE A	LTC	0-0367394	0868	3
TAFT JOHN L	MAJ	0-1336837	0763	1
TAFT THOMAS G	LTC	0-1046293	0764	1
TAFT WILLARD C	CPT	0-0346727	0264	1
TAGAMI KAN	MAJ	0-2010011	0361	1
TAGER BENJAMIN N	MAJ	0-0507999	0146	2
TAGER ROBERT F	MAJ	0-1876890	0365	1
TAGGART GORDON E	LTC	0-0966378	0763	1
TAGGART RICHARD L	LTC	0-0451424	0953	1
TAGGART ROBERT M	MAJ	0-0956935	C865	1
TAGGART ROBERT M	LTC	0-1314690	0562	1
TAGGART SAMUEL R	COL	0-0253156	0563	3
TAGLIAFERRO JAMES J	1LT	0-2012579	1046	2
TAGLIARINO V A	CPT	0-1685141	1144	2
TAGUE HARRY R	CPT	0-1931286	0765	1
TAGUE JACK L	1LT	0-0437144	0346	2
TAIMI THOMAS T	CPT	0-1114774	1047	2
TAINTER WILLIS K	CPT	0-0274252	0863	3
TAIPALE TAUNO A	MAJ	0-1291724	C748	2
TAIT ARTHUR F	MAJ	0-0294671	0760	1
TAIT EDWARD J	MAJ	0-1043907	1159	1
TAIT HAROLD G	MAJ	0-1647751	0462	1
TAIT LAWRENCE	MAJ	0-2035395	1060	1
TAITTE NEIL	LTC	0-0463019	1152	1
TAKACS WILLIAM J	LTC	0-1172689	1060	1
TAKAHASHI SADAO	MAJ	0-2030787	0461	1
TAKAHASHI TERRY Y	LTC	0-2038042	0364	1
TAKAI ROY T	LTC	0-2010035	0466	1
TAKANO SEIJI	MAJ	0-1337103	0661	1
TALAMBAS SPIRO A	1LT	0-1317117	0646	2
TALAMINI ANTHONY G	LTC	0-0964118	1066	1
TALAN CHARLES J	2LT	0-0455164	0643	2
TALBERG DONALD H	CW4	W-2145912	1068	1
TALBERT CHARLES F	MAJ	0-1580398	1060	1
TALBERT JOHN N	MAJ	0-0377429	0747	2
TALBERT JOHNNIE B	COL	0-0193337	0160	1
TALBERT WILLIAM R	LTC	0-0438976	0168	3
TALBERT WILLIAM R	LTC	0-1945068	1162	1
TALBOT ALFRED H	LTC	0-2033745	0568	1
TALBOT CHARLES H	LTC	0-0442884	1162	2
TALBOT CHARLIE F	COL	0-0302361	0966	3
TALBOT DANIEL G	COL	0-0233595	0965	3
TALBOT GEOFFREY W	MAJ	0-0179877	0648	3
TALBOT GEORGE K	COL	0-0189730	0753	3
TALBOT MANNY J	1LT	0-1946398	0658	1
TALBOT RAYMOND S	CW4	W-2144654	0167	1
TALBOT VINCENT A	MAJ	0-1596822	0363	1
TALBOTT DONALD C	LTC	0-0888418	C866	1
TALBOTT ELLEN P	LTC	L-0308128	0668	1
TALBOTT HOWARD M	2LT	0-0515629	0845	2
TALBOTT JOHN R JR	CPT	0-0389365	0545	2
TALBOTT WALLACE T	LTC	0-1011704	1163	1
TALBOTT WILLIAM A	CW3	W-2150781	0358	1
TALCOTT JAMES R	2LT	0-2034959	0845	2
TALCOTT LEONARD D	1LT	0-1305854	0146	2
TALCOTT ROBERT V	MAJ	0-0342564	0846	2
TALIAFERRO HENRY G	CPT	0-1018445	0646	2
TALIAFERRO LAUREL M	MAJ	0-0133266	0656	3
TALIAFERRO WILLIAM C	LTC	0-1577933	0364	1
TALL LUTHER S	CPT	0-0168790	0560	3
TALLAU HOWARD G	1LT	0-1030844	0145	2
TALLENT JAMES E	LTC	0-1301053	0761	1
TALLENT LOYD	LTC	0-1288813	1060	1
TALLEY BOLIVER E JR	MAJ	0-1920052	1166	1
TALLEY CARTHAL M	MAJ	0-1289504	1060	1
TALLEY CLIFTON P	COL	0-0335970	0854	1
TALLEY CLURON O	CW3	W-2144882	0662	1
TALLEY DAVID	LTC	0-0234052	1163	3
TALLEY DWIGHT M	LTC	0-0253675	0665	3
TALLEY ELDRED J	COL	0-1592647	0467	1
TALLEY EVANS F	MAJ	0-0468118	0246	2
TALLEY FRANK T	LTC	0-0358587	0861	1
TALLEY HAROLD H	CPT	0-2018944	0456	1
TALLEY HELEN BELK	2LT	N-0727852	1145	1
TALLEY JAMES W	LTC	0-0557193	0565	1
TALLEY JAMES W	LTC	0-1036053	0463	1
TALLEY LOUIS	MAJ	0-1111943	0858	2
TALLEY WILLIAM H	LTC	0-0450495	1046	2
TALLICHET RENE I	LTC	0-0328071	0861	2
TALLMAN FRANK L	LTC	0-1010415	1063	1
TALLMAN HAROLD L	1LT	0-1287266	0246	2
TALLMAN JOHN O	LTC	0-2048795	1064	1
TALLMAN MAMIE B	MAJ	N-0778075	0665	1
TALLMAN RAYMOND L	MAJ	0-1181483	0759	1
TALLMAN SAMUEL V	COL	0-0292990	0867	3
TALLON CHARLES F	1LT	0-1945503	0756	1
TALMADGE DANIEL W	CPT	0-0516130	0147	2
TALMADGE JACK A	LTC	0-0451250	1060	1
TALMAGE RALPH H	COL	0-0234452	0460	3
TALMAGE WILLIAM G	MAJ	0-0281619	0246	2
TALPIS STANLEY I	2LT	0-0524422	0444	2
TALSEY WILLIAM C	MAJ	0-0163661	1056	3
TALUBAN REDDORO M	CW2	W-2149848	0862	1
TAM HUNG E	MAJ	0-0309368	1063	3
TAMAMIAN LEO	COL	0-0334408	0464	1
TAMANINI FRANK D	CW2	W-2206692	0664	1
TAMASHIRO ERNEST S	CW2	W-3151438	0968	1
TAMASI JOSEPH J	MAJ	0-0384811	0545	2
TAMAYO FREDERIC	MAJ	0-2027371	0657	1
TAMBLYN GORDON D	LTC	0-1950290	0566	1
TAMER ABRAHAM F	1LT	0-1554982	0256	2
TAMINOSIAN GEORGE R	CPT	0-0275312	1166	3
TAMMARO ALFONSO	LTC	0-0261431	0962	3
TAMMARO MILLIE M	2LT	N-0763367	0146	1
TAMMARO RALPH F	CW2	W-2109833	1044	2
TAMPKE HOMER A	CW4	W-2100006	0966	1
TAMPLIN JACK D	MAJ	0-2023845	0760	1
TAMRAZ JOHN P	MAJ	0-1341131	0865	1
TAMSE SIDNEY	MAJ	0-0467579	0246	2
TANAKA PAUL A	CW2	W-2209804	1165	1
TANAKA WALTER	MAJ	0-2030569	0661	1
TANBERG LUCILLE A	2LT	N-0737079	0944	1
TANBERG MONROE N	MAJ	0-1948063	0862	1
TANCREDI LOUIS	WO1	W-2141093	0259	2
TANDY FRANK G	COL	0-0266303	0758	1
TANGHE ALBERT L F	MAJ	0-1081038	0961	1
TANI MATT A	CW3	W-2152253	0462	1
TANIMURA JOHN M	CPT	0-0214630	0362	3
TANK HAROLD J JR	CPT	0-1919233	0263	1
TANKERSLEY JOHN H	CPT	0-0949620	0760	1
TANKERSLEY RICHARD E	LTC	0-0450922	0962	1
TANKERSLEY WILLIAM C	LTC	0-0312636	0967	3
TANKSLEY CARL B	2LT	0-1328854	0246	2
TANN LEO	CPT	0-0500856	0646	2
TANNASCOLI ROCCO P	LTC	0-1175336	0960	1
TANNEHILL E H	CPT	0-0543630	0546	2
TANNEHILL GEORGE L	CPT	0-0358776	1044	2
TANNER ALVIN L	CPT	0-0267877	0463	1
TANNER AVON W	CPT	0-0230464	0747	1
TANNER CECIL	MAJ	0-2263018	1061	1
TANNER CLAUDE E JR	1LT	0-1306658	0645	2
TANNER DELBERT M	COL	0-0371337	0960	1
TANNER GLENN A	LTC	0-1633590	1264	1
TANNER HERBERT E	MAJ	0-0946629	0664	1
TANNER HOMER W	CPT	0-0496909	0449	1
TANNER JANE M	MAJ	L-0302573	1046	2
TANNER JOSEPH J	LTC	0-1168942	0763	1
TANNER MALCOLM Z	LTC	0-1306765	0766	1
TANNER MERTON W	LTC	0-0419645	1065	3
TANNER MICHAEL A	LTC	0-1924518	0868	1
TANNER PAUL	LTC	0-0171808	0652	3
TANNER ROBERT A	CW2	W-3430139	0368	1
TANNER SAM D JR	LTC	0-0962329	1267	2
TANNER WILKINS E	2LT	0-0401400	0441	2
TANNER WILLIAM F	LTC	0-1288464	0367	1
TANNERY FRED M	LTC	0-0410280	0761	1
TANNEY WILLIAM H	CPT	0-0129040	0156	3
TANNHEIMER J A R	1LT	0-0439475	0945	2
TANNO AL	MAJ	0-1332434	0365	1
TANSIL GEORGE D	MAJ	0-1317998	0266	1

NAME	GRADE	SVC NO	DATE RET MO YR	RET CODE
TANSKI WILLIAM V SR	LTC	0-1595860	0467	1
TANSLEY MAYNARD S	LTC	0-2042952	0963	1
TANTON L M	MAJ	0-1288814	1156	1
TANZER VELMA M	2LT	N-0737096	0745	1
TAPIA JOHN R	MAJ	0-0947809	1065	1
TAPIE ANTHONY W	LTC	0-1166323	0765	1
TAPLEY HOWARD A	MAJ	0-0920169	0547	2
TAPLIN RICHARD D	CPT	0-1894601	0846	2
TAPLIN SABIN C	LTC	0-0400438	0561	2
TAPOVATZ WEB W	1LT	0-1897797	0649	2
TAPP ERNEST M	COL	0-0272390	0664	3
TAPP FELIX C	LTC	0-0275592	1264	3
TAPP GUS M	CPT	0-1822483	0760	1
TAPPA ALBERT	CW4	W-2142406	0266	1
TAPPAN WILLIAM B JR	MAJ	0-1171776	1066	1
TAPPEN DOROTHY R	1LT	N-0797360	0947	1
TAPSCOTT JO J	COL	0-0248035	0855	3
TARA DAVID M JR	MAJ	0-0383251	0960	2
TARA MARGARET W	1LT	N-0703599	0945	1
TARACKO ADAM I	MAJ	0-2026233	0764	1
TARALLO FRANK J	LTC	0-0365992	0463	1
TARALLO GUERRINO J	LTC	0-1104416	0163	1
TARANTO MORRIS B	1LT	0-0548352	1145	2
TARBETT LEWIS N	CPT	0-0377361	0964	1
TARBI SUE K	2LT	N-0738909	1043	1
TARBOX CHARLES H II	1LT	0-0297914	0165	3
TARBOX GEORGE D	CPT	0-0365912	1043	2
TARBOX HENRY A	COL	0-0454142	0567	2
TARBUTTON EDMUND H	LTC	0-1329179	0466	1
TARCY PAUL	LTC	0-0438711	1166	3
TARDIF LEO J	CW2	W-2206277	0363	1
TARDIFF ROLAND A	MAJ	0-0266473	0960	3
TARDY JAMES N	MAJ	0-0153087	1157	3
TARKINGTON CHARTER F	CPT	0-1318486	0667	3
TARKINGTON KENNETH E	1LT	0-1165052	0544	2
TARLAU MILTON	MAJ	0-1690161	0446	2
TARLETON GEORGE W	CPT	0-1103764	1058	1
TARLOW CHARLES M	MAJ	0-0276825	1057	3
TARNO WARREN E	LTC	0-1016560	0267	1
TARONNA ANTHONY P	MAJ	0-0913188	0768	3
TARPAY CHARLES M	MAJ	0-0506741	0157	1
TARPENING JOHN D	MAJ	0-0393604	1145	2
TARPENNING ROBERT A	MAJ	0-0999672	0167	1
TARPLEY CHARLES D	LTC	0-1548569	0363	1
TARPLEY MELVIN	CW2	W-2210484	0364	1
TARPLEY SELDEN A	CPT	0-0184000	1056	3
TARPLEY TROY F	CW2	W-2123066	0556	1
TARR CLARENCE W	CPT	0-0940629	0761	2
TARR FLOYD H	LTC	0-1579198	1055	1
TARR ROBERT M	LTC	0-0363699	0257	1
TARR WILLIAM M	LTC	0-1552809	0867	1
TARRALL ELMER	CPT	0-1594523	0746	2
TARRANCE WILLIAM N	LTC	0-0358963	0466	3
TARRANT ALBERT F	COL	0-0308405	0765	3
TARRANT HOWARD G	MAJ	0-0961239	0361	1
TARRANT MARION B JR	MAJ	0-2262971	0961	1
TART EARL F	CW2	W-2146288	0559	1
TART GUY A	LTC	0-1055746	0165	1
TARTER CLYDE S	LTC	0-0174768	0845	2
TARTER MARVIN N	MAJ	0-2023966	0764	2
TARTER ORAL	1LT	0-0497796	0346	1
TARTT ROY L	MAJ	0-1031766	0859	1
TARVER ROBERT L	LTC	0-0490516	1162	1
TARVER WILLIAM S	LTC	0-0240124	0466	3
TARVES HARRY J	MAJ	0-0371065	0463	1
TARZON FRANCIS D	MAJ	0-2023560	0656	1
TASCHNER LESLIE E	MAJ	0-0462069	0165	3
TASHJIAN LEVON D	CPT	0-5217675	0763	2
TASK LEON	1LT	0-0234512	0345	2
TASKE MEYER	CPT	0-0228361	1056	3
TASKER LEIGHTON E	LTC	0-0410374	1059	1
TASLOV HELEN M	2LT	N-0772432	0745	1
TASSANI PETER R	LTC	0-1182974	0668	1
TASSI LAWRENCE A	LTC	0-1558347	0166	3
TATAR DAVID	COL	0-1945290	0868	3

NAME	GRADE	SVC NO	DATE RET MO YR	RET CODE
TATE ANDREW L	CPT	0-2012703	0657	1
TATE CURVIN F	CPT	0-1556812	1047	2
TATE EUGENE R	LTC	0-1320199	1062	1
TATE GUY M JR	COL	0-0258549	1068	3
TATE HAROLD S	LTC	0-0213446	0164	3
TATE HARRY A SR	CPT	0-0180839	1055	3
TATE JACOB F	CW3	W-2148132	0261	1
TATE JOHN B	WO1	W-2152781	1164	1
TATE JOHN C	LTC	0-0477022	1046	2
TATE JOHN H	2LT	0-1301054	0745	2
TATE LINWOOD C	2LT	0-1824817	1045	2
TATE MELVIN O	LTC	0-0534538	0368	1
TATE PERRY L	LTC	0-0554581	0763	1
TATE ROBERT C	1LT	0-0980309	0762	1
TATE ROBERT L	CPT	0-0495784	0648	1
TATE SIDNEY F JR	COL	0-0391746	1060	1
TATE SOLON H	MAJ	0-2001438	0763	1
TATE WILLIS O	MAJ	0-0289021	0353	2
TATEM EARL W	1LT	0-1306172	0147	2
TATES EDWARD W	CPT	0-4013553	0464	1
TATOM HENRY G	LTC	0-0204383	0862	3
TATUM DAVE H	MAJ	0-0414504	0161	1
TATUM ED	CW3	W-2145701	0860	1
TATUM FRANK J	MAJ	0-0279335	1167	3
TATUM GROVER C JR	CPT	0-0390724	0546	2
TATUM HERBERT M	LTC	0-0215677	0364	3
TATUM HORACE B	1LT	0-1181777	1045	2
TATUM JAMES B	MAJ	0-1298953	0163	1
TATUM JOHN M	COL	0-0255534	0655	3
TATUM JOSEPH C	COL	0-0309262	0465	3
TATUM REUBEN L	COL	0-0267233	0952	2
TATUM VICTOR E	COL	0-0102140	0954	3
TAUBAKI KIYOTO	LTC	0-0275618	1068	3
TAUBE HARRY J	1LT	0-1575202	0745	2
TAUBER MAX	CPT	0-0350330	0346	2
TAUBER RAYMOND L	2LT	0-1178360	0744	2
TAULBEE CHARLES P	LTC	0-1047407	0264	1
TAUS MAURICE R	LTC	0-0309220	0859	1
TAUSCH NORMAN F	MAJ	0-0452055	0561	1
TAUSCHER WALTER E	MAJ	0-0967873	0661	1
TAUSEK THEODORE S	MAJ	0-1797385	0563	1
TAUSEND STANLEIGH	CPT	0-0242252	0346	2
TAUSER LOUIS G	LTC	0-0470980	0357	1
TAUTFEST BENJAMIN M	CW2	W-2119081	0645	2
TAVENNER JOHN L	CPT	0-1821210	1045	2
TAVERNER WILLIAM G	LTC	0-0232696	0147	1
TAVES TAPP S	CPT	0-0478759	1045	2
TAVILLE WILBERT L	MAJ	0-0469604	0263	1
TAVIS VICTOR L	CW4	W-2136693	1164	2
TAVOIAN LAMAR A	MAJ	0-0402094	0459	1
TAVORMINA IGNATIUS J	MAJ	0-0292427	0162	1
TAW RICHARD L	CPT	0-0448626	1145	2
TAWES ROBERT L	CPT	0-1290334	0546	2
TAKSAR MEYER J	1LT	0-1291195	0444	2
TAYE ARNOLD C	CPT	0-0297539	0145	2
TAYLOE HENRY G JR	LTC	0-0339543	0467	1
TAYLOR ABNER U	COL	0-0300457	1057	3
TAYLOR ALBERT W JR	2LT	0-1060666	0445	2
TAYLOR ALFRED L	LTC	0-0235059	0961	3
TAYLOR ALLEN L	LTC	0-1547177	1166	1
TAYLOR ALVIN C	LTC	0-2034862	0861	1
TAYLOR ALVIS M	MAJ	0-1945292	1059	1
TAYLOR AMYTH H	CW4	W-2003641	0265	1
TAYLOR ANDREW J	CPT	0-1640060	0465	1
TAYLOR ARCH K	CPT	0-1598883	0459	1
TAYLOR ARNOLD D	CW3	W-2153328	0965	1
TAYLOR AUBREY A	1LT	0-0501607	0644	2
TAYLOR BAILEY E	1LT	0-0507131	0745	2
TAYLOR BARNEY B	CPT	0-1323045	0346	2
TAYLOR BENJAMIN F	MAJ	0-0250326	1164	3
TAYLOR BENJAMIN G	CPT	0-2262689	0461	1
TAYLOR BERNICE A	CPT	0-1298462	0148	1
TAYLOR BILLY R	MAJ	0-2266171	0767	1
TAYLOR BORDEN E	LTC	0-1296935	1265	3
TAYLOR BRUCE S	1LT	0-1795994	0546	2

NAME	GRADE	SVC NO	DATE RET MO YR	RET CODE
TAYLOR BUFORD C	2LT	0-1826177	1145	2
TAYLOR BURNLEY W	MAJ	0-0[illegible]95219	0863	1
TAYLOR BYRL D	LTC	0-0438831	0867	1
TAYLOR CARL L	MAJ	0-1013529	0456	1
TAYLOR CAROLYN F	1LT	N-0763825	0646	1
TAYLOR CHARLES	LTC	0-0344549	1166	3
TAYLOR CHARLES C	LTC	0-1951548	0766	1
TAYLOR CHARLES E	CPT	0-0239015	0862	3
TAYLOR CHARLES E	MAJ	0-0323174	0768	3
TAYLOR CHARLES F	LTC	0-1183775	0260	1
TAYLOR CHARLES F JR	1LT	0-2049118	0945	2
TAYLOR CHARLES L	CW2	W-2116967	0554	1
TAYLOR CHARLES O JR	MAJ	0-2018435	0962	1
TAYLOR CHARLES S	CPT	0-1576726	0345	2
TAYLOR CHARLES W	1LT	0-2047518	0147	1
TAYLOR CHARLEY S	2LT	0-0451425	1043	2
TAYLOR CHESTER A	LTC	0-0260611	0253	3
TAYLOR CLARA F	2LT	N-0763471	0344	1
TAYLOR CLARENCE W	COL	0-0248331	1063	3
TAYLOR CLARENCE W	CW2	W-2205496	0560	1
TAYLOR CLARK L	MAJ	0-0347762	0847	2
TAYLOR CLAYTON M	MAJ	0-1823371	1060	1
TAYLOR CLIFFORD C	LTC	0-0268335	1162	3
TAYLOR CLYDE A	CPT	0-1178361	1158	1
TAYLOR CLYDE E	CW3	W-2140035	1262	1
TAYLOR CLYDE H JR	LTC	0-1168489	1062	1
TAYLOR DANIEL H	LTC	0-1036054	1166	2
TAYLOR DAVID F JR	COL	0-0192115	0163	3
TAYLOR DELBERT H	MAJ	0-0288844	0568	3
TAYLOR DELOS C	LTC	0-0212849	1059	3
TAYLOR DEWEY	CPT	0-0349041	0750	1
TAYLOR DEWEY	CPT	0-0492203	0749	1
TAYLOR DONALD	MAJ	0-1825322	0261	1
TAYLOR DONALD A	MAJ	0-0373924	0663	1
TAYLOR DUARD F	MAJ	0-2262767	1266	1
TAYLOR EARNEST E SR	MAJ	0-0251272	0549	1
TAYLOR EDGAR L	CPT	0-1591474	0647	2
TAYLOR EDITH C	MAJ	M-0002404	0867	2
TAYLOR EDWARD A	1LT	0-0954927	1053	2
TAYLOR ELBERT R	LTC	0-0281884	0568	3
TAYLOR ELIZABETH	MAJ	N-0741047	1067	1
TAYLOR ELLSWORTH	CW3	W-2152834	0662	1
TAYLOR ETHEL E	2LT	N-0700672	0539	1
TAYLOR EUGENE E	MAJ	0-0480691	1045	2
TAYLOR EVAN J	MAJ	0-0961375	0766	1
TAYLOR FLOYD A	CPT	0-0107839	0648	3
TAYLOR FLOYD W	CW3	W-2146631	0263	1
TAYLOR FRANCES M	MAJ	N-0752227	0867	3
TAYLOR FRANK A	MAJ	0-0245067	0463	3
TAYLOR FRANK G	MAJ	0-0364647	0147	2
TAYLOR FRANK R	MAJ	0-1577936	1157	2
TAYLOR FRED	CPT	0-1998111	0353	2
TAYLOR FREDERICK	MAJ	0-0125064	0544	2
TAYLOR GEORGE A	CPT	0-0707416	1060	1
TAYLOR GEORGE D	MAJ	0-1042965	0457	1
TAYLOR GEORGE E	LTC	0-0386157	0657	1
TAYLOR GEORGE E	CPT	0-2262201	1060	1
TAYLOR GEORGE F	LTC	0-0237117	0262	3
TAYLOR GEORGE G	MAJ	0-1256113	0447	2
TAYLOR GEORGE H	COL	0-0173617	0361	3
TAYLOR GEORGE L	LTC	0-0382663	1164	1
TAYLOR GEORGE M	MAJ	0-1338413	1264	1
TAYLOR GERALD W	LTC	0-0917549	1266	3
TAYLOR GILBERT H	CW3	W-2109018	0655	1
TAYLOR GLENN S	1LT	0-0925589	0145	2
TAYLOR GUY	CPT	0-0487857	0548	1
TAYLOR HAFFRED N	1LT	0-0450496	1044	2
TAYLOR HAROLD A	COL	0-0100236	0454	3
TAYLOR HAROLD E	MAJ	0-1302067	0761	1
TAYLOR HAROLD G	CPT	0-1845253	0359	1
TAYLOR HARRY A	2LT	0-1303414	0644	2
TAYLOR HARRY F	LTC	0-0179254	0151	3
TAYLOR HARRY F	CPT	0-0499653	0754	1
TAYLOR HARRY F	CPT	0-1105856	0147	2
TAYLOR HARRY M	CPT	0-0315700	0966	3

NAME	GRADE	SVC NO	DATE RET MO YR	RET CODE
TAYLOR HARVEY D	COL	0-0187459	0347	2
TAYLOR HENRY B	2LT	0-1323989	0745	2
TAYLOR HENRY H	CPT	0-0101714	0851	3
TAYLOR HENRY L	COL	0-0153581	1056	3
TAYLOR HENRY L	LTC	0-0278432	1160	3
TAYLOR HENRY M	COL	0-0156284	0255	3
TAYLOR HENRY W JR	1LT	0-1174984	0145	2
TAYLOR HERBERT C	COL	0-0190078	0556	3
TAYLOR HERBERT J	MAJ	0-1684969	1262	1
TAYLOR HORACE M	COL	0-0435367	0668	3
TAYLOR HOWARD M	1LT	0-0511013	0352	1
TAYLOR HOWARD W	LTC	0-0450923	0563	2
TAYLOR HOWELL	CW2	W-2120776	0354	1
TAYLOR HUGH	CPT	0-0313450	0866	3
TAYLOR HUGH B	CPT	0-0282324	0845	2
TAYLOR JACK R	LTC	0-1577937	0168	3
TAYLOR JACOB W	CPT	0-2007257	0857	1
TAYLOR JAMES A	MAJ	0-0511776	1044	2
TAYLOR JAMES B	COL	0-0463474	0456	1
TAYLOR JAMES R	MAJ	0-2263487	0763	1
TAYLOR JAMES D	COL	0-0330155	0846	2
TAYLOR JAMES D	MAJ	0-1947101	0163	1
TAYLOR JAMES E	LTC	0-0278146	0561	3
TAYLOR JAMES F	MG	0-0376731	0766	3
TAYLOR JAMES F	MAJ	0-2021229	1066	1
TAYLOR JAMES L	COL	0-0211915	0258	3
TAYLOR JAMES L	MAJ	0-0486646	0954	1
TAYLOR JAMES L	MAJ	0-1547475	1161	1
TAYLOR JAMES L JR	LTC	0-0141342	0648	3
TAYLOR JAMES O JR	CW2	W-2146843	1162	1
TAYLOR JAMES P JR	MAJ	0-1917671	0666	1
TAYLOR JAMES W	1LT	0-0923832	0145	2
TAYLOR JAMES W	CW3	W-2146289	1058	1
TAYLOR JEROME F	MAJ	0-1037930	1164	1
TAYLOR JESSE W	MAJ	0-0424192	0665	1
TAYLOR JIM	CPT	0-0496902	0153	1
TAYLOR JOE G	WO1	W-2127719	1051	1
TAYLOR JOHN A	MAJ	0-1579204	0257	1
TAYLOR JOHN B	COL	0-0197248	0463	3
TAYLOR JOHN B	LTC	0-0377276	1066	3
TAYLOR JOHN B	1LT	0-1639721	0746	2
TAYLOR JOHN C	LTC	0-0437659	0155	2
TAYLOR JOHN F	LTC	0-0297779	0565	3
TAYLOR JOHN F	COL	0-0477260	0754	1
TAYLOR JOHN G	LTC	0-0164265	0549	3
TAYLOR JOHN G	LTC	0-1294040	1057	1
TAYLOR JOHN G JR	LTC	0-0886401	0764	1
TAYLOR JOHN L	MAJ	0-1004047	1154	1
TAYLOR JOHN M	LTC	0-0292290	0667	3
TAYLOR JOHN M	1LT	0-0562886	0163	2
TAYLOR JOHN P	CPT	0-0508869	1046	1
TAYLOR JOHN R	MAJ	0-1046981	0466	1
TAYLOR JOHN W	CPT	0-0368766	0745	2
TAYLOR JOHN W	CPT	0-0451251	0960	1
TAYLOR JOHN W	1LT	0-0511455	0760	1
TAYLOR JOHN W	MAJ	0-1685019	1165	1
TAYLOR JOHNNY H	CW3	W-2150331	1062	1
TAYLOR JOSEPH K	MAJ	0-0997956	0364	1
TAYLOR JOSEPH W	CW4	W-2127155	0555	1
TAYLOR KATHRYN O	1LT	N-0755407	0746	1
TAYLOR KENNETH K	MAJ	0-0959550	0366	1
TAYLOR LAMAR W	LTC	0-0453151	1264	1
TAYLOR LANE F	LTC	0-1556225	1266	3
TAYLOR LEE E	LTC	0-0386654	0760	1
TAYLOR LEON W	CPT	0-0526191	0147	2
TAYLOR LEWIS	MAJ	0-0334879	1057	3
TAYLOR LEWIS A JR	COL	0-1766094	0968	1
TAYLOR LLOYD K	CPT	0-0987842	0361	1
TAYLOR LONNIE P	2LT	0-2010992	0646	2
TAYLOR LORENZO J	LTC	0-1534166	0461	1
TAYLOR LOUIS	1LT	0-1010291	0845	2
TAYLOR LOUIS J	MAJ	0-1949948	0367	1
TAYLOR LYMAN J JR	LTC	0-1636728	1062	1
TAYLOR LYNN C	MAJ	0-0277330	0362	3
TAYLOR MALCOLM I	CPT	0-1004529	1157	1

NAME	GRADE	SVC NO	DATE RET MO YR	RET CODE
TAYLOR MANUEL J	MAJ	0-1685507	0263	1
TAYLOR MARSHALL F	CPT	0-2026341	1057	1
TAYLOR MARTIN L	COL	0-0295756	0368	3
TAYLOR MARY L	MAJ	N-0754267	0665	1
TAYLOR MATHILDA W	CPT	N-0783059	0546	1
TAYLOR MAURICE F	CPT	0-0541784	0448	2
TAYLOR MELVIN B	MAJ	0-1996406	1060	1
TAYLOR MERLE V	MAJ	0-1056944	1262	1
TAYLOR MINOR T	CW4	W-2143567	0266	1
TAYLOR MORRIS B	LTC	0-2005979	0562	1
TAYLOR MORRIS N	1LT	0-0367897	0944	2
TAYLOR MYRON D	1LT	0-1030739	0146	2
TAYLOR NOEL L	CW2	W-2145875	0562	1
TAYLOR OLIN A	2LT	0-1177660	1144	2
TAYLOR ORDIL P JR	LTC	0-1030516	1061	2
TAYLOR PATRICK H	MAJ	0-2014521	1168	1
TAYLOR PAUL W	LTC	0-0171003	0648	3
TAYLOR PHILIP H	COL	0-0192419	0462	3
TAYLOR PHILLIP F	LTC	0-0272916	1263	3
TAYLOR POWELL P	1LT	0-0495730	1146	1
TAYLOR RALPH	CPT	0-1583755	0658	1
TAYLOR RALPH L	LTC	0-0227332	0560	3
TAYLOR RALPH L JR	CW3	W-2144325	0862	1
TAYLOR RAY L	MAJ	0-1043822	0660	1
TAYLOR RAYMOND A	LTC	0-0283782	0146	2
TAYLOR RAYMOND T	CW3	W-2113884	0461	1
TAYLOR REX A	CPT	0-1291725	1046	1
TAYLOR RICHARD E	COL	0-0336358	0356	1
TAYLOR RICHARD F	LTC	0-0408680	0161	1
TAYLOR RICHARD P	MAJ	0-0348103	0568	3
TAYLOR RICHARD S	CPT	0-2030456	0861	1
TAYLOR ROBERT	CW3	W-2148993	0962	1
TAYLOR ROBERT H	1LT	0-1583757	0546	2
TAYLOR ROBERT B	CPT	0-1874747	0262	1
TAYLOR ROBERT G	LTC	0-1574162	0361	1
TAYLOR ROBERT I JR	CPT	0-0538302	0646	2
TAYLOR ROBERT J	MAJ	0-1332654	0962	1
TAYLOR ROBERT L	COL	0-0321031	0767	3
TAYLOR ROBERT L	COL	0-0346564	0467	3
TAYLOR ROBERT L JR	2LT	0-1054137	0444	2
TAYLOR ROBERT M	LTC	0-0263872	0446	2
TAYLOR ROBERT M	CW4	W-2142664	0563	1
TAYLOR ROBERT R JR	MAJ	0-1550937	0660	1
TAYLOR ROBERT S	COL	0-0297309	0668	3
TAYLOR ROBERT W	CPT	0-1016601	1267	1
TAYLOR RONALD V JR	2LT	0-1297983	1044	2
TAYLOR ROSS G	MAJ	0-0466852	1262	1
TAYLOR ROSS H	MAJ	0-1651316	0162	1
TAYLOR ROY D	CPT	0-0989977	1060	1
TAYLOR ROYCE R JR	LTC	0-0449421	0662	1
TAYLOR RUSSELL B	CPT	0-1309075	1046	2
TAYLOR RUSSELL P	MAJ	0-0921993	1162	1
TAYLOR RUTH F	LTC	L-0200580	0168	1
TAYLOR SAM H	LTC	0-0375817	0963	1
TAYLOR SAMUEL C	WO1	W-2152484	0464	2
TAYLOR SETH	CW2	W-2143627	1055	1
TAYLOR SIGISMUND	MAJ	0-1109707	0363	2
TAYLOR TALBERT L JR	CPT	0-1553741	0961	1
TAYLOR THEODORE	LTC	0-0280370	0648	3
TAYLOR THERON J	LTC	0-0171239	0952	3
TAYLOR THOMAS B	LTC	0-1574352	0268	1
TAYLOR THOMAS H	1LT	0-0386545	0944	2
TAYLOR THOMAS H	LTC	0-1646650	0168	1
TAYLOR THOMAS L	MAJ	0-2020980	0765	1
TAYLOR THOMAS F JR	LTC	0-1173484	0364	1
TAYLOR THURMAN M	CPT	0-1997976	0258	1
TAYLOR TOM L	LTC	0-0243988	0554	3
TAYLOR UTRHA D	1LT	N-0721538	104N	1
TAYLOR V D	WO1	W-2146523	0659	1
TAYLOR VICTOR R	LTC	0-0279266	0561	1
TAYLOR VIRGIL F	CW2	W-2113569	1053	1
TAYLOR WAIGHTS M	LTC	0-0316954	0765	1
TAYLOR WALTER L	CW4	W-2142907	0167	1
TAYLOR WARREN F	CPT	0-1012521	1047	2
TAYLOR WESLEY B	LTC	0-0318763	0764	1

NAME	GRADE	SVC NO	DATE RET MO YR	RET CODE
TAYLOR WILLARD J	MAJ	0-0886485	0568	1
TAYLOR WILLIAM A	CW3	W-2147345	0863	1
TAYLOR WILLIAM B	CPT	0-0137065	0648	3
TAYLOR WILLIAM B	LTC	0-1039242	0966	1
TAYLOR WILLIAM D	COL	0-0396127	0966	1
TAYLOR WILLIAM E	LTC	0-1042724	0161	1
TAYLOR WILLIAM G	LTC	0-0351146	0468	3
TAYLOR WILLIAM H	MAJ	0-0177339	1045	2
TAYLOR WILLIAM H	LTC	0-0422833	0663	1
TAYLOR WILLIAM H	1LT	0-0978137	1058	1
TAYLOR WILLIAM L	LTC	0-0542590	0163	1
TAYLOR WILLIAM L	CW3	W-2145709	0363	1
TAYLOR WILLIAM N	MAJ	0-1557802	1064	1
TAYLOR WILLIAM W	LTC	0-0123190	0648	3
TAYLOR WOFFORD L	CW3	W-2147328	1264	1
TAYLOR WYMAN D	LTC	0-0251286	0358	3
TAYS EUGENE	LTC	0-0111971	0549	3
TAYS JAMES H	MAJ	0-0181624	1145	1
TCHAKIRIDES HARRY	LTC	0-1172309	1264	2
TEAGUE CHARLES M	MAJ	0-2046404	0258	1
TEAGUE CHARLES O	MAJ	0-1310526	0764	1
TEAGUE NORRIS M JR	MAJ	0-1294219	0760	1
TEAGUE OLIN E	COL	0-0294931	1146	2
TEAGUE SEMON L	CW3	W-2142742	0766	1
TEAGUE TERRELL A	MAJ	0-1920172	0965	1
TEAGUE WALTER D JR	MAJ	0-1587673	0961	1
TEAGUE WALTER E	MAJ	0-1533692	0859	1
TEAGUE WELDON W	LTC	0-2046700	1267	1
TEAGUE WILLIAM A	2LT	0-1914328	0422	2
TEAL HORACE O	MAJ	0-1298621	0954	1
TEAL WILLIAM H	LTC	0-0525187	0568	1
TEALEY EARL H	LTC	0-0298009	0266	3
TEANEY DARREL F	1LT	0-1825285	0646	2
TEANEY ROBERT J	CW2	W-2151734	1164	1
TEAS HOWARD J	MAJ	0-0208872	0754	3
TEASLEY GERALD H	COL	0-0309897	0767	3
TEASLEY RICHARD JR	CW4	W-2124106	0660	1
TEATER MARGARET E	2LT	N-0786297	0346	1
TEBBETTS HENRY M	CW2	W-2209542	1161	1
TEBBY ERNEST H	2LT	0-1108361	1143	2
TEBERG ERNEST J	COL	0-0176783	0553	3
TEBO BEN C	MAJ	0-0336679	0953	2
TEBO FRANK A	LTC	0-0252229	0365	3
TEBOREK JAMES J	LTC	0-0211242	0258	3
TEBOW ERIC T	COL	0-0225794	0363	3
TEBOW HENRY J	LTC	0-0272743	0868	3
TECLER WILLIAM	LTC	0-0294332	0246	2
TEDU ROBERT N	MAJ	0-1182471	1262	2
TEDESCHI JOSEPH E	LTC	0-1104419	0966	1
TEDESCO JAMES	MAJ	0-1288645	0648	1
TEDFORD CHARLES H	LTC	0-0441373	0663	3
TEDROWE JOHN P JR	MAJ	0-1032252	0461	1
TEEBKEN GEORGE O	CPT	0-0498136	1051	1
TEECE JOSEPH A	M G	0-0242853	0459	3
TEED CHARLES O	MAJ	0-0261702	0665	3
TEED WILLIAM H II	LTC	0-0436443	0568	3
TEEFEY FRANCIS J	CPT	0-1306661	0147	2
TEEGARDEN JACK E	CW3	W-2149356	1267	1
TEEHAN RICHARD J	LTC	0-1339488	0866	1
TEEHEE ROBERT	1LT	0-0403677	1045	2
TEEL EDWARD M	LTC	0-0888590	0657	1
TEEM MARTIN V B	CPT	0-0309710	1044	2
TEEMS THOMAS B	CPT	0-0499652	0247	1
TEEPE SUZANNA F	1LT	N-0729375	1045	1
TEER JAMES B	MAJ	0-1292421	0757	1
TEESE HARRY F	COL	0-0220292	0455	3
TEETER EARL R	MAJ	0-1582199	0854	1
TEETER RUSSELL V	LTC	0-1000482	0462	1
TEETER WALTER W	LTC	0-0358748	0768	3
TEETERS CHARLES A	MAJ	0-0348992	1262	3
TEETERS HIRAM L	WO1	W-2104523	0645	2
TEETSEL WILLIAM J	CPT	0-0289212	114N	2
TEFFT ROGER F	LTC	0-1342015	0867	1
TEFT DONALD E	LTC	0-2053981	0166	1
TEGGE GLENN A	LTC	0-1317443	0667	2

NAME	GRADE	SVC NO	DATE RET MO YR	RET CODE
TEICH DAVID F	MAJ	0-2014574	0963	1
TEICHART ALVIN F	LTC	0-0280347	1044	2
TEICHERT JOHN	MAJ	0-1550849	0662	1
TEICHMAN JAMES A	CPT	0-1305670	0457	1
TEICHMAN LAWRENCE I	CPT	0-2025797	0750	2
TEIEN ROBERT E	MAJ	0-0744517	0365	1
TEIKA ERNEST	CW3	RW-2209723	0566	1
TEINERT JOHN G	LTC	0-1581415	1163	1
TEITELBAUM JACK	1LT	0-1288646	0145	2
TEITLER MAX H	CPT	0-0498147	1043	2
TEIXEIRA FRANK L	MAJ	0-1287086	0154	1
TEJA RAY	CPT	0-1253675	0862	1
TEKULVE ELMER P	1LT	0-1319681	0546	2
TELCHIK LEO	MAJ	0-1688755	0763	1
TELESE ALPHONSE R	LTC	0-1013345	0765	2
TELFER WALDO B	CPT	0-0242812	0858	3
TELFORD DONALD M	LTC	0-1036767	0361	1
TELFORD EDWARD T	COL	0-0241594	0359	3
TELFORD ELBRIDGE W	LTC	0-0236793	1062	3
TELFORD JOHN C	MAJ	0-1534169	0164	1
TELFORD WILLIAM E	1LT	0-2032859	0852	1
TELL JOHN A	LTC	0-1555918	0863	1
TELLEJOHN BENJAMIN H	MAJ	0-0471952	1041	1
TELLER HAROLD R	CW2	W-2148820	1061	1
TELLMAN RALPH L	MAJ	0-0243615	0666	3
TELMAN HARRY	MAJ	0-0570496	0463	1
TEMBRINA PASCUAL C	1LT	0-1896806	1052	1
TEMPERTON LEON E	CPT	0-1951194	0358	1
TEMPINSKI JULIA M	MAJ	N-0754340	0565	1
TEMPLE EDGAR W	1LT	0-1684922	0944	2
TEMPLE EDISON M	LTC	0-1185903	0667	1
TEMPLE ELWOOD L	LTC	0-0469167	0165	1
TEMPLE HARRY G	CPT	0-0288899	0467	3
TEMPLE HENRY E	1LT	0-1017292	0152	2
TEMPLE JOHN W	MAJ	0-0397836	1047	2
TEMPLE LANNIS W	MAJ	0-1002138	0656	1
TEMPLE LESLIE W JR	CPT	0-0296360	0465	3
TEMPLE LONNIE C	LTC	0-1636729	1060	1
TEMPLE RALPH R	COL	0-0523284	0966	3
TEMPLE ROBERT C	WO1	W-2142502	0352	2
TEMPLE RUSSEL E	CW2	W-2141466	1154	1
TEMPLE THOMAS E	CPT	0-1796884	0246	2
TEMPLER ROBERT C	LTC	0-1053839	0165	1
TEMPLETON CECIL C	LTC	0-0904009	0167	3
TEMPLETON CONRAD C	LTC	0-0333997	0566	3
TEMPLETON DICK C	CW3	W-2152562	0462	1
TEMPLETON DONALD E	1LT	0-1323187	0646	2
TEMPLETON HALL R	2LT	0-1045278	0745	2
TEMPLETON JACK C	MAJ	0-0958531	0467	1
TEMPLETON JOHN J	LTC	0-1799396	0866	1
TEMPLETON RAY M	LTC	0-0921051	0263	1
TEMPLETON ROBERT L	LTC	0-0372632	0759	1
TEMPLETON STOKES S	2LT	0-1018478	0547	2
TEMPLETON WILLIAM F	MAJ	0-0240969	1065	3
TEMPLIN FRED M	CW4	W-2132789	0366	1
TEMPLIN PAUL W	LTC	0-0488188	0966	3
TEMPLIN WALLACE W	CW4	W-2104522	1058	1
TEN EYCK JOHN J	2LT	0-1302386	0245	2
TENANT CLARK H	MAJ	0-1017371	1163	1
TENBERG CLIFTON D	MAJ	0-5301921	0568	1
TENBORG HARRY R	MAJ	0-0332190	0144	2
TENCH FREDERICK	MAJ	0-0421425	0164	1
TENEROWICZ STANLEY A	2LT	0-1549618	1044	2
TENNANT DON L	1LT	0-1795008	0345	2
TENNANT ROBERT O	CW4	W-2008576	0665	3
TENNANT ROY I JR	LTC	0-1542672	1061	1
TENNANT WALTER F	MAJ	0-1303796	0561	2
TENNER ROBERT J	LTC	0-0356768	0246	2
TENNERY JAMES S	COL	0-0270129	0568	3
TENNERY RICHARD F	LTC	0-1316867	0267	3
TENNEY EDWARD S	LTC	0-0310699	0360	1
TENNEY PHILLIP H	MAJ	0-1757087	0758	2
TENNEY ROBERT I	CPT	0-1316238	0446	2
TENNEY ROCKWELL C	COL	0-0170846	0554	3
TENNIS CHARLES H	LTC	0-1297451	0461	1

NAME	GRADE	SVC NO	DATE RET MO YR	RET CODE
TENNIS MILTON C	CW4	W-2004892	0866	3
TENNISON CLARA H	MAJ	L-0800284	0766	1
TENNISON GUY	CW4	W-2148386	0456	1
TENORE FRANCIS A	LTC	0-1796183	1060	1
TENTLER HAROLD A	MAJ	0-4074754	1068	1
TENWINKEL HERBERT F	LTC	0-1040315	1057	1
TEPE PAUL L	LTC	0-0338342	0160	1
TEPERSON HYMAN I	COL	0-0162713	0253	3
TEPLE LAWRENCE S	CPT	0-0367835	1045	2
TEPP LOUIS E	MAJ	0-0244241	0251	3
TEPPER SOL H	1LT	0-1291930	0546	2
TERAKAWA ROBERT H	MAJ	0-1924807	1166	1
TERAZAWA TOKIO G	MAJ	0-2030812	0562	1
TERBORG NORMAN R	2LT	0-1643391	0744	2
TERCERO ISMAEL A	CW3	W-2144143	0466	1
TERCY FRANK J	LTC	0-1584994	1161	1
TERESHINSKI THOMAS J	CPT	0-0557231	1047	2
TERESHKO HELEN M	1LT	N-0725406	0946	1
TERESHUK LOUIS	MAJ	0-1111946	0859	1
TERGERSON AULDY	MAJ	0-0329930	1045	2
TERHUNE ALMA W	2LT	L-0811704	0744	2
TERHUNE JOHN W	MAJ	0-2012354	0262	1
TERHUNE SAMUEL R	COL	0-0302300	0767	3
TERLAP MARTIN W	MAJ	0-0497038	1053	1
TERLECKI WILLIAM J	LTC	0-1178363	1062	2
TERLIZZI BRUNO C	LTC	0-1298954	0862	1
TERNEY GEORGE E	1LT	0-1112474	0145	2
TERNOSKY MICHAEL A	MAJ	0-0401473	1047	2
TERPENING ROBERT J	LTC	0-0353819	0661	1
TERRA FRANCIS J	MAJ	0-0156243	0-51	3
TERRALL THOMAS A	1LT	0-1288142	1145	2
TERRAZAS PAUL A	CW4	W-2142665	0765	1
TERRELL CHARLES F	MAJ	0-0318178	0268	3
TERRELL HERMAN B	CW2	W-2144148	1060	1
TERRELL HERSCHEL H	1LT	0-1294220	0344	2
TERRELL HOMER	COL	0-0481134	0154	1
TERRELL JOHN F	COL	0-0280081	0167	3
TERRELL KENNETH D	CPT	0-0422871	0246	2
TERRELL RALPH P JR	LTC	0-2204085	0767	1
TERRELL RUFUS H	MAJ	0-0251489	0645	2
TERRELL SAMMIE	CPT	0-1293495	0762	1
TERRELL WILLIAM S	LTC	0-0351549	1159	1
TERRIAN GERALD J	CW3	W-2210921	0768	1
TERRILL DUDLEY R	LTC	0-0906173	0765	3
TERRY AGNES G	2LT	N-0788507	0445	1
TERRY ALLEN L	LTC	0-0293677	1058	1
TERRY ARCHIE JR	CW2	W-2209282	1262	1
TERRY CHARLES H	MAJ	0-0202712	0648	3
TERRY CHESTER W	COL	0-0216763	0961	3
TERRY CLARENCE	MAJ	0-2043111	0361	1
TERRY EDMUND F	MAJ	0-0502103	1155	1
TERRY EDWARD A	LTC	0-0100425	0660	3
TERRY ELMER E	CW3	W-2114186	0255	1
TERRY EVERETT C	MAJ	0-1109059	1061	1
TERRY FOCH P	MAJ	0-1016280	1262	1
TERRY FORD M	LTC	0-0203948	0553	3
TERRY FRANK E	LTC	0-0388747	0358	1
TERRY FREDERICK	LTC	0-0427394	0660	1
TERRY GEORGE R	COL	0-0232804	0164	3
TERRY GLENN E	1LT	0-1998069	0347	2
TERRY HARRY W	COL	0-0159765	0648	3
TERRY I C HAROLD	MAJ	0-1297807	1062	1
TERRY JAMES H	LTC	0-0417592	0261	1
TERRY JOHN H	MAJ	0-0384627	0546	2
TERRY JOSEPHINE	2LT	N-0753228	1045	2
TERRY LAWRENCE O	LTC	0-0453069	1060	1
TERRY LEON F	CW3	RW-2150685	0463	1
TERRY LEROY B	CW3	W-2147964	0863	1
TERRY LESLIE C JR	MAJ	0-1290842	0960	1
TERRY MARJORIE D	CPT	N-0763462	0547	1
TERRY PAUL L	MAJ	0-0451917	0657	1
TERRY RAY	CW3	W-2148769	0761	1
TERRY RICHARD R	1LT	0-1314074	1144	2
TERRY ROBERT T	MAJ	0-0308075	0946	2
TERRY ROSE VONA	1LT	N-0756803	0446	1

NAME	GRADE	SVC NO	DATE RET MO YR	RET CODE
TERRY ROY H JR	CPT	0-0405712	0448	2
TERRY ROY K	COL	0-0141266	0949	3
TERRY SHIRL L	MAJ	0-1558213	0659	2
TERRY THOMAS E	COL	0-0239153	1053	3
TERRY WALLACE C	MAJ	0-1542679	0855	1
TERRY WILLIAM E	LTC	0-0555841	0765	1
TERRY WILLIAM H	MAJ	0-1041459	0464	1
TERRY WOODROW	LTC	0-1633655	1057	1
TERRYLL GRANT V	CW3	W-2147838	0964	1
TERSCHUREN ALLAN R	CPT	0-1541955	0646	2
TERSTEGGE JOHN F	LTC	0-0369510	0550	2
TERWELP ROME A JR	LTC	0-1545844	0767	1
TERWILLEGAR ROBERT E	LTC	0-0273626	0667	3
TERWILLIGER CHARLES	MAJ	0-0957110	0865	1
TERWILLIGER F WELLS	CPT	0-0358627	0846	2
TERWILLIGER LELAND H	LTC	0-1080076	0361	1
TERWILLIGER RICHARD	LTC	0-2275430	0264	1
TERZELLA JOHN C	MAJ	0-0324501	1047	2
TESALLA ERNESTO	1LT	0-1876482	0849	1
TESCH KENNETH R	MAJ	0-0957156	0568	1
TESCHAN ERHARD G	COL	0-0151773	1049	3
TESCHE WALTER C	MAJ	0-1055476	0662	1
TESCHEL WILLIAM R	MAJ	0-1304291	0747	2
TESCHENDORF ELIZABET	MAJ	N-0767026	0168	1
TESDALE THOR L	CW4	W-2143137	0766	1
TESENEER CHARLES W	2LT	0-2003411	0554	2
TESKE BERNARD A	CPT	0-0234710	0357	3
TESKE CLYDE L	MAJ	0-0850450	1057	1
TESSIER ADRIAN J	CPT	0-0887599	0346	2
TESSIER ALBERT E	CPT	0-0501235	0645	2
TESSIER AMOS F JR	1LT	0-1296450	0445	2
TESSIER ERNEST W	MAJ	0-2055118	0160	1
TESSLER ARTHUR D	CPT	0-0484807	0345	2
TESSMER LLOYD M	CPT	0-2011102	1158	1
TEST CARL W	LTC	0-0306270	0868	3
TESTA JOHN F	MAJ	0-0336303	0561	1
TESTER JAMES L	LTC	0-1551318	1061	1
TESTER JOSEPH J	CW3	W-2136729	0655	1
TESTERMAN ROBERT H	CW3	W-2149064	0263	1
TESTI EDO[illegible]	MAJ	0-1036406	0560	2
TETA ANTHONY R	2LT	0-0111114	0254	3
TETER ELMER P	2LT	0-1551531	0943	2
TETER HOWARD G	CW2	W-2114147	0350	2
TETLEY OWEN P	LTC	0-1291355	0761	1
TETOR PAUL S	MAJ	0-1339776	0265	1
TETRAULT EDWARD J	CPT	0-1945504	0454	1
TETRAULT LEONARD R	LTC	0-1326942	0862	1
TETREAULT GEORGE R	CW2	W-2213500	1068	1
TETREAULT NELSON J	CW4	W-2147292	0868	1
TETROO WILLIAM H	LTC	0-0320989	0467	3
TETSCHNER CARROL J	MAJ	0-2293420	1068	1
TETU ROBERT G	COL	0-0403961	0968	1
TEUKE GILBERT A	CPT	0-1287087	0946	2
TEVAULT RONALD E	MAJ	0-0979011	0966	1
TEWALT JAMES A	1LT	0-1174726	0244	2
TEWMEY BRUCE F	MAJ	0-1340715	0665	1
TEWS ROBERT J	LTC	0-1685606	0768	1
TEWSON RONALD E	LTC	0-0269327	1266	3
TEXTER KENNETH G	1LT	0-0405198	0743	2
TEYSSIER ROGER J	LTC	0-0398234	0562	1
TEZAK JOHN	LTC	0-0464941	0762	1
THACHER CHARLES S	MAJ	0-1576736	0661	1
THACKABERRY SAMUEL J	LTC	0-0471534	0966	3
THACKER CHARLES A	LTC	0-2067592	0968	1
THACKER LOKE C	LTC	0-0250081	0866	3
THACKER ROWENA R	2LT	N-0726292	0844	1
THACKER WILLIAM A	LTC	0-0355600	0646	2
THACKERY ROGER L	CPT	0-0982495	0361	1
THACKREY SAMUEL I	COL	0-0107681	0547	2
THACKSTON JOHN A	MAJ	0-1285138	0147	2
THACKSTON THOMAS W	LTC	0-1337364	1267	1
THADEN HERBERT V	MAJ	0-0127296	0258	3
THALER CLARK M	LTC	0-0363693	0859	1
THAMES HENRY S	CW2	W-2207058	0464	1
THAMES JAMES P	MAJ	0-1289339	1060	1
THAMES JAMES R	CPT	0-1874281	0762	1
THANE GEORGE JR	1LT	W-2200186	0666	3
THARP CHARLES M	LTC	0-0510783	0463	3
THARP KATHLEEN N	1LT	N-0795071	0847	1
THARP MARVEL M	MAJ	L-0701925	1063	1
THARPE LUTHER	2LT	0-0496805	0453	1
THATCHER CARL V	CW2	W-2132064	0450	2
THATCHER DONALD D	1LT	0-1946190	0646	2
THATCHER MOSES JR	COL	0-0306149	0766	3
THATCHER ROBERT L	CPT	0-0678976	1147	2
THAU AUGUST D	LTC	0-0262421	1266	3
THAXTON EMMETT	CPT	0-0219674	1150	3
THAXTON HUGH R	1LT	0-0357485	0144	2
THAXTON MARVIN L	LTC	0-2275045	0462	1
THAXTON WILLIAM O	CPT	0-0966359	0657	1
THAYER ALBERT M	MAJ	0-2033543	0163	1
THAYER EDWARD A JR	CPT	0-0538140	0846	2
THAYER EDWIN B	CPT	0-0396974	1045	2
THAYER GEORGE E	CPT	0-0252155	0367	3
THAYER JOHN F	LTC	0-1285518	1061	1
THAYER JOHN M	LTC	0-0239240	0359	2
THAYER LEROY F	MAJ	0-0321506	0455	1
THAYER MELVIN R	LTC	0-2014541	1067	1
THAYER PHILLIPS O	MAJ	0-0200817	0458	3
THAYER PHILLIPS L	LTC	0-0420196	0963	3
THEAMAN FRANK J JR	MAJ	0-1922883	0868	1
THEBAUD DELPHIN E JR	LTC	0-0420711	0268	1
THEBERT FREDERICK	CPT	0-1105862	0347	2
THEBERT LEO W	CPT	0-0507852	0450	1
THEDOS JACK V	MAJ	0-0455098	0161	1
THEIL LEON S	CPT	0-1995014	0246	2
THEIS ETHEL J	CPT	R-0000627	1163	1
THEIS JOHN F	LTC	0-0272311	0167	3
THEISEN EUGENE C	2LT	0-1327302	0146	2
THEISS HENRY D	MAJ	0-0312435	0363	3
THEISS JOHN S	MAJ	0-0244139	1165	3
THEISS RONALD T	MAJ	0-2028453	1267	1
THELEN LEO A JR	1LT	0-1044401	1145	2
THEN JOHN V	LTC	0-0358290	0957	1
THEO ERNEST	MAJ	0-0270405	0865	3
THEOBALD HERBERT P	LTC	0-1166632	0163	1
THEOBALD JOHN W	LTC	0-0557567	1163	1
THEODORE NICHOLAS P	MAJ	0-1001062	1267	2
THEODORE NORBERT A	COL	0-0358294	0762	3
THEODORE RAYMOND M	LTC	0-0288991	1067	3
THEOPHILUS RALPH H	LTC	0-0276025	1267	3
THERIAULT GERALD E	LTC	0-1306173	0861	2
THEROUX KENNETH J	CW3	W-2205588	0666	1
THEROUX LEO B JR	MAJ	0-1913413	0967	1
THEUS FRANK P JR	MAJ	0-1020130	0461	1
THEUS JAMES T	LTC	0-0439237	0862	1
THEWLIS LEONARD L	MAJ	0-1057910	0163	1
THIBAUDEAU PHILIP A	MAJ	0-0255809	1259	3
THIBAULT GILBERT A	LTC	0-0549035	0965	1
THIBAULT HOWARD W	CPT	0-0889230	0558	1
THIBEAU ROY S	LTC	0-0331229	1059	1
THIBEAULT RAYMOND E	LTC	0-1174985	0865	1
THIBEAUX LOUIS A SR	2LT	0-1950807	1046	2
THIBODEAU FRANK W	CW3	W-2143143	1061	1
THIBODEAU GEORGE E	MAJ	0-1314349	1263	1
THIBODEAU WILLIAM J	COL	0-0286837	0853	3
THIBODEAUX JASON J	MAJ	0-0966629	1066	1
THIBODEAUX SIDNEY J	CPT	0-1319358	0358	1
THIEBAUTH CHARLES K	LTC	0-1052997	0567	1
THIEL CLIFFORD P	CW3	W-2142069	0662	1
THIEL LESLIE C	MAJ	0-0236957	0165	3
THIEL NORMAN E	MAJ	0-1691226	0346	2
THIEL RAYMOND M	2LT	0-1310785	0545	2
THIEL ROBERT A	CPT	0-1107175	0747	2
THIEL ROBERT L	LTC	0-1182977	1162	1
THIEL WILFRED E	CW3	W-2205114	0364	1
THIELE WALTHER H	COL	0-0333816	1165	3
THIELEN RAYMOND J	MAJ	0-0564462	0162	1
THIELER GEORGE	LTC	0-0220328	1156	3
THIEMAN LIONEL D	CW3	W-2147186	0967	1
THIEMANN VINCENT A	MAJ	0-0212369	0464	3
THIEME EARL L	MAJ	0-1882412	1167	1
THIEME HOWARD T	1LT	0-1109061	0345	2
THIEROLF DWIGHT R	CPT	0-2262907	0661	1
THIEROLF LEROY F	CW4	W-2143547	0165	1
THIERRY JOHN H	1LT	0-1316240	0347	2
THIERS WENDELL H	CW3	W-2144197	0261	1
THIES FLOYD L	MAJ	0-1824098	0757	1
THIES LAWRENCE H	CPT	0-1042966	0757	1
THIESS WILLIAM J	2LT	0-1285139	0244	2
THIGPEN OSWALD C	MAJ	0-0249206	0965	3
THIGPIN ROBERT L	CPT	0-0314943	0468	3
THILL LEONARD C	MAJ	0-0245030	1061	3
THISLER JOHN C	LTC	0-1302550	0662	1
THISTED MOSES N	LTC	0-0108277	0856	3
THISTLE THOMAS L	LTC	0-0214990	0354	3
THISTLE ZACHARY T	LTC	0-0967840	0968	1
THIXTON JAMES D	CPT	0-1287088	0161	1
THODE EVERETT W	CPT	0-0542985	0947	2
THODE HARRY W	COL	0-1055994	0966	1
THOE REUBEN S	1LT	0-1315638	0346	2
THOEMKE GEORGE W	MAJ	0-1322486	0763	1
THOENEN CLARENCE A	CW3	RW-2147327	1265	1
THOIN PHILIP P	COL	0-0301605	0266	3
THOLEN HARRY J	LTC	0-1045954	1161	1
THOLL ERWIN F JR	MAJ	0-2033789	1265	1
THOM CHARLES H JR	CPT	0-0434340	0240	2
THOM ERNEST P	MAJ	0-0145231	0952	3
THOM GEORGE R	CW3	W-2123283	0661	1
THOM HAROLD H	MAJ	0-0133069	0648	3
THOM VICTOR L SR	LTC	0-0334635	0760	1
THOMA DANIEL R	LTC	0-0315001	1159	1
THOMA HARRY C	LTC	0-0250444	0965	3
THOMA JOSEPH L	CPT	0-1535093	1046	2
THOMA WILLIAM F	LTC	0-1043615	0368	1
THOMAN KENNETH R	LTC	0-0231494	0561	3
THOMAN ROBERT J	COL	0-0194669	0761	3
THOMAS ALBERT I	MAJ	0-1540612	0558	1
THOMAS ALBERT S JR	CPT	0-0315668	1045	2
THOMAS ALLEN R	LTC	0-1595464	0967	3
THOMAS ALVIN	LTC	0-1341378	0868	1
THOMAS AMBROSE R	2LT	0-1031615	1045	2
THOMAS ANNA N	CPT	N-0727624	0846	1
THOMAS ANTHONY	MAJ	0-1643187	0457	1
THOMAS ARLENE M	MAJ	N-0757351	0665	1
THOMAS ARTHUR B	COL	0-0263899	0258	3
THOMAS ARTHUR H	COL	0-0326452	0966	3
THOMAS ARTHUR S	CW3	W-2145594	0466	2
THOMAS AUBREY L JR	LTC	0-1004836	0268	1
THOMAS AUSTIN M	CPT	0-1950808	1064	1
THOMAS BENJAMIN F	MAJ	0-0172248	0254	3
THOMAS BERT S	COL	0-0222926	1054	3
THOMAS BRENNAN S	LTC	0-0252575	1044	2
THOMAS BROWER R	LTC	0-0918293	0666	3
THOMAS CARL L	CPT	0-0949987	0158	1
THOMAS CASSIUS L	MAJ	0-1287434	0860	1
THOMAS CHARLES A JR	2LT	0-1091183	0844	2
THOMAS CHARLES E	CPT	0-5326496	0868	2
THOMAS CHARLES F	LTC	0-0576479	0968	2
THOMAS CHARLES H	CW4	W-2103522	0260	2
THOMAS CHARLES L	1LT	0-1102501	0146	2
THOMAS CHARLES L	MAJ	0-1824391	0847	2
THOMAS CHARLES W	LTC	0-0275604	0246	2
THOMAS CHESTER A	MAJ	0-1593884	0761	1
THOMAS CHESTER R	LTC	0-1948235	0663	1
THOMAS CLARENCE F	CPT	0-1315237	1058	1
THOMAS CLARENCE H	CW2	W-2143422	1060	1
THOMAS CLAUDE W JR	LTC	0-0374527	0368	3
THOMAS CLIFFORD A	CW3	W-2205550	0766	1
THOMAS COYL B	LTC	0-0257950	0666	3
THOMAS DALE F	LTC	0-0289757	0557	1
THOMAS DALLAS D	MAJ	0-1289650	1058	1
THOMAS DANIEL C	MAJ	0-0359418	0963	1
THOMAS DANIEL C	LTC	0-1179719	0962	1
THOMAS DANIEL L	MAJ	0-0422582	1059	1
THOMAS DANIEL M	CPT	0-1307099	0662	1
THOMAS DELMUS D	MAJ	0-1306910	0857	1
THOMAS DONALD J	MAJ	0-1285847	0563	1
THOMAS DOUGLAS S	LTC	0-2047523	0762	1
THOMAS EARLE L	LTC	0-0124160	0754	3
THOMAS EDGAR L	CW2	W-2148384	1060	1
THOMAS EDWARD A	LTC	0-1924764	0568	1
THOMAS EDWARD C O	COL	0-0107795	0152	3
THOMAS EDWARD H	CPT	0-0122363	0152	3
THOMAS EDWARD W	2LT	0-1334777	0863	2
THOMAS EDWIN	MAJ	0-0425750	1161	1
THOMAS EDWIN M	COL	0-0368710	0964	3
THOMAS ELMER S	MAJ	0-0475091	0148	1
THOMAS ELZY A	CW3	W-2152254	0666	1
THOMAS ERNEST R	CPT	0-0314915	0259	3
THOMAS EUGENE	1LT	0-0990125	0862	1
THOMAS EUGENE	MAJ	0-1182281	0657	1
THOMAS EVERETT A	LTC	0-0260439	0567	3
THOMAS FRANCES	MAJ	N-0742828	0365	1
THOMAS FRANCIS L	MAJ	0-2034074	0963	1
THOMAS FRANK	CW4	W-2101061	0155	1
THOMAS FRANK H	CW3	W-2152752	0466	1
THOMAS FRANK J	LTC	0-1035382	1263	1
THOMAS FRANK N	LTC	0-0264525	0266	3
THOMAS FRANK P	1LT	0-1291543	0745	2
THOMAS FRANK W	COL	0-0283187	1068	3
THOMAS FRED C	CPT	0-0498999	0448	1
THOMAS FRED E	LTC	0-0450909	0762	1
THOMAS FRED J	MAJ	0-1797905	0857	1
THOMAS FREDERICK	MAJ	0-0113762	0449	3
THOMAS FREDERICK	LTC	0-0229855	0755	3
THOMAS G CLARE	MAJ	0-0402885	0546	2
THOMAS GARRY C	CW2	W-2117530	0957	1
THOMAS GEORGE H	LTC	0-0260523	1060	3
THOMAS GEORGE H SR	MAJ	0-1947274	0761	1
THOMAS GEORGE J	MAJ	0-1338657	0163	2
THOMAS GEORGE R	LTC	0-1325533	0163	1
THOMAS GEORGE S	CPT	0-0542329	0548	2
THOMAS GILBERT L	MAJ	0-1339408	1264	1
THOMAS GLADYS H	COL	N-0741070	0668	3
THOMAS GORDON C	LTC	0-0343988	0146	2
THOMAS GORDON E	COL	0-0241198	0466	3
THOMAS GORDON W	CPT	0-0428586	0946	2
THOMAS GROVER E	MAJ	0-0456679	0258	1
THOMAS HAROLD H	MAJ	0-1693568	0245	2
THOMAS HAROLD C	COL	0-0167043	0547	2
THOMAS HAROLD E	LTC	0-0243748	0766	3
THOMAS HAROLD F	MAJ	0-2036893	0459	1
THOMAS HAROLD H	LTC	0-1286394	1060	1
THOMAS HAROLD P	COL	0-0160353	0156	3
THOMAS HAROLD W	COL	0-0237795	0562	3
THOMAS HARRY A	1LT	0-0497824	0646	2
THOMAS HARVEY P	CPT	0-1641854	0357	1
THOMAS HENRY A	CW2	W-2147316	0361	1
THOMAS HENRY E	MAJ	0-1329294	0161	1
THOMAS HIRAM	CPT	0-0497212	0546	2
THOMAS HUBERT M JR	LTC	0-1181782	0565	1
THOMAS J T	LTC	0-0353895	1060	1
THOMAS JACK N	CW2	W-2148889	0260	1
THOMAS JACK W	MAJ	0-1540862	1063	2
THOMAS JACKSON C	CPT	0-0888920	1054	1
THOMAS JAMES A	2LT	0-0108993	0234	2
THOMAS JAMES E	COL	0-0246179	0353	2
THOMAS JAMES E	CPT	0-0450576	0952	1
THOMAS JAMES H	CPT	0-1295642	0446	2
THOMAS JAMES M	CW4	W-2113571	0260	1
THOMAS JAMES P	1LT	0-1998039	1047	2
THOMAS JAMES T	CPT	0-0920228	0346	2
THOMAS JAMES T	LTC	0-1651662	0966	1
THOMAS JAMES W	LTC	0-0370278	0763	3
THOMAS JANIE	CPT	N-0789316	0747	1
THOMAS JERRY	MAJ	0-0455947	0457	1
THOMAS JESSE D	MAJ	0-1951637	0561	1
THOMAS JEWELL A	MAJ	N-0720397	0761	1
THOMAS JOE	COL	0-0165098	0859	3

NAME	GRADE	SVC NO	DATE RET MO YR	RET CODE
THOMAS JOHN A	LTC	0-1393561	1262	1
THOMAS JOHN B	MAJ	0-0955559	0463	1
THOMAS JOHN C JR	MAJ	0-2020774	0968	1
THOMAS JOHN H	LTC	0-0261707	0464	3
THOMAS JOHN H J	CPT	0-1243483	0545	2
THOMAS JOHN P	MAJ	0-0456411	0746	2
THOMAS JOHN P JR	LTC	0-1058136	0864	1
THOMAS JOHN R	LTC	0-0234615	1065	3
THOMAS JOHN W	COL	0-0286097	0562	1
THOMAS JOHN W	1LT	0-0373044	1149	1
THOMAS JOHN W	2LT	0-1336295	0247	2
THOMAS JOSEPH C	MAJ	0-0973461	0163	1
THOMAS JOSEPH M	LTC	0-0259875	0466	3
THOMAS JOSEPH P	MAJ	0-1172633	0660	1
THOMAS KARL W	MAJ	0-2055860	1060	1
THOMAS KENNETH E	LTC	0-0414481	0556	2
THOMAS KENNETH L	MAJ	0-1293676	0157	1
THOMAS KENNETH R	1LT	0-1286395	0346	2
THOMAS KENNETH W	LTC	0-1644949	0161	1
THOMAS LAWRENCE W	MAJ	0-1746294	0261	2
THOMAS LEANDER K	CW4	W-2110469	1154	1
THOMAS LEO E	MAJ	0-1306768	0864	1
THOMAS LEON A	MAJ	0-1540926	0663	1
THOMAS LEONARD M	1LT	0-0496048	0447	1
THOMAS LEROY	LTC	0-0347893	0560	1
THOMAS LEROY	MAJ	0-2008523	0763	1
THOMAS LESTER C	MAJ	0-2009388	0158	1
THOMAS LESTER H	2LT	0-2033234	1055	1
THOMAS LLOYD T	CW3	W-2204970	0167	1
THOMAS LUTHER M	LTC	0-1314972	0962	1
THOMAS MANLY J	CW4	W-2142526	0667	1
THOMAS MARK E	LTC	0-0230045	0765	3
THOMAS MARTIN A	LTC	0-0360664	1056	1
THOMAS MARVIN J	CW3	W-2150365	0863	1
THOMAS MICHAEL R	MAJ	0-1947026	0766	1
THOMAS MORRIS C	COL	0-0278489	1065	3
THOMAS MORTIMER B	2LT	0-1324675	1144	2
THOMAS NEIL O	COL	0-0229753	0261	3
THOMAS NELSON A	LTC	0-0511194	0565	3
THOMAS OCTAVE F V	LTC	0-0406207	0465	1
THOMAS OTAWAY M	LTC	0-1042728	1158	2
THOMAS PAUL H	1LT	0-1315639	0346	2
THOMAS PETER	CPT	0-1796378	0762	1
THOMAS PETER H JR	MAJ	0-1688656	0166	1
THOMAS PHILIP B	LTC	0-0199922	0461	3
THOMAS PHILIP E	1LT	0-1181165	0945	2
THOMAS RALPH L	MAJ	0-0902876	1045	2
THOMAS RAMON	LTC	0-0331923	0560	1
THOMAS RAY C	COL	0-0168157	1058	3
THOMAS RAY C	MAJ	0-1166849	0157	2
THOMAS RAY S	LTC	0-1590851	0863	1
THOMAS RAYMOND B	CPT	0-1725977	0154	2
THOMAS RAYMOND H	CW4	W-2136753	0862	1
THOMAS REBECCA	1LT	N-0727687	0149	2
THOMAS RICHARD C	2LT	0-1594526	0744	2
THOMAS RICHARD H	MAJ	0-1056588	0761	1
THOMAS RICHARD S	MAJ	0-0966015	0866	1
THOMAS ROBERT C	CPT	0-1043812	0359	1
THOMAS ROBERT C	CPT	0-2210220	0166	1
THOMAS ROBERT D	MAJ	0-0221390	0763	3
THOMAS ROBERT F	1LT	0-0475908	0747	2
THOMAS ROBERT E	COL	0-1340951	0768	1
THOMAS ROBERT J	LTC	0-0564468	0661	1
THOMAS ROBERT O	LTC	0-1044127	0563	1
THOMAS ROBERT R	LTC	0-0175415	0359	3
THOMAS ROBERT R	LTC	0-1305698	0556	1
THOMAS ROBERT S	LTC	0-0278623	0462	1
THOMAS ROBERT T	CPT	0-2019673	0461	1
THOMAS RODGER L	MAJ	0-0249955	0544	2
THOMAS ROGER W	2LT	0-1181485	0145	2
THOMAS ROLEN E	CW4	W-2113691	0657	1
THOMAS ROLLIN P	MAJ	0-2096903	0666	1
THOMAS RONALD E	LTC	0-0256720	0960	1
THOMAS ROSCOE	1LT	0-1305133	0246	2
THOMAS ROY C	LTC	0-1765231	0864	1
THOMAS ROY G	2LT	0-1300885	0845	2
THOMAS RUFUS P	CW3	RW-2142908	0562	1
THOMAS SAMUEL J	CW2	W-3100594	0468	1
THOMAS SAMUEL M	H G	0-0230963	0164	3
THOMAS SAMUEL M	1LT	0-0372941	0745	2
THOMAS SARAH F	1LT	N-0725211	1146	1
THOMAS SHIPLEY	COL	0-0103241	1052	3
THOMAS SHIPLEY J	MAJ	0-1013588	0662	1
THOMAS TATUM L	LTC	0-0282919	0267	3
THOMAS THOMAS J	LTC	0-0312154	0562	2
THOMAS TOM E JR	LTC	0-1177663	1161	1
THOMAS VERLIN E	CW2	W-2214727	0868	1
THOMAS VESSIE H	MAJ	0-0472659	1045	2
THOMAS VICTOR G	MAJ	0-1173810	0657	1
THOMAS VIRGINIA E	2LT	N-0773396	0346	1
THOMAS WALTER D	COL	0-0151724	0655	1
THOMAS WALTER E	LTC	0-1797906	0261	1
THOMAS WALTER J	MAJ	0-0398265	0856	1
THOMAS WALTER M	LTC	0-0309216	0964	3
THOMAS WESLEY F	LTC	0-1114310	0463	1
THOMAS WILLARD J	1LT	0-0397815	0946	2
THOMAS WILLIAM C	CW3	W-2141468	0161	1
THOMAS WILLIAM F	MAJ	0-0924653	0451	2
THOMAS WILLIAM E	LTC	0-1300551	0261	1
THOMAS WILLIAM G	LTC	0-0110422	0150	3
THOMAS WILLIAM H	LTC	0-0814842	0265	1
THOMAS WILLIAM H	CW2	W-2211868	0164	1
THOMAS WILLIAM J	MAJ	0-0266080	0956	3
THOMAS WILLIAM J	CW3	W-2141469	0161	1
THOMAS WILLIAM J JR	CW2	W-2148941	0162	1
THOMAS WILLIAM JR	CPT	0-1052639	0161	1
THOMAS WILLIAM L	LTC	0-1166398	1160	1
THOMAS WILLIAM L	CPT	0-1923529	0764	1
THOMAS WILLIAM L	MAJ	0-1923565	0267	1
THOMAS WILLIAM P	LTC	0-0316931	0146	2
THOMAS WILSON	LTC	0-0234021	0657	3
THOMAS WINTHROP A	LTC	0-0191050	0163	3
THOMASON EDWARD A	LTC	0-0236362	1263	3
THOMASON GEORGE W	CW2	W-2101046	1061	1
THOMASON HENRY I	MAJ	0-0222927	0358	3
THOMASON JOHN R	CW2	W-3200474	0867	1
THOMASON LEO B	1LT	0-1301560	1045	2
THOMASON MAX D	LTC	0-0304088	0268	3
THOMASON WILLIAM J	1LT	0-5323654	0567	2
THOMASSEN THOMAS T	MAJ	0-1549391	1164	1
THOMASSON EARL L SR	CW3	W-2120845	0760	1
THOMASSON HAROLD	MAJ	0-0226166	0164	3
THOMASSON JAMES F	MAJ	0-1642647	0461	1
THOMASSON JOHN O	CW2	W-2147342	0764	1
THOMAS WILLIAM H	1LT	0-1573626	0662	1
THOME LEONARD J	LTC	0-0285626	0552	2
THOME MARVIN T	LTC	0-0361761	0668	3
THOMLEY VESTER G	LTC	0-1313324	0360	1
THOMPSON ALBERT A	CW2	W-2131808	0653	2
THOMPSON ALBERT C	CW3	W-2146771	1064	1
THOMPSON ALFRED W	CW3	W-2205361	0367	1
THOMPSON ALLEN T	CPT	0-1895402	1059	1
THOMPSON ARTHUR B	CPT	0-0425561	0247	2
THOMPSON ARTHUR L	WO1	W-2123093	0946	2
THOMPSON BEAUFORD A	CPT	0-0493966	1047	2
THOMPSON BENJAMIN H	LTC	0-2027053	0366	1
THOMPSON BERNICE G	1LT	N-0763272	0246	1
THOMPSON CARL R	1LT	0-1635406	1046	2
THOMPSON CARLETON K	CW4	W-2113624	0659	1
THOMPSON CARROLL B	LTC	0-1320375	0962	1
THOMPSON CARROLL I	LTC	0-1555641	0462	1
THOMPSON CHARLES	CPT	0-1014884	0147	2
THOMPSON CHARLES A	2LT	0-0438044	0545	2
THOMPSON CHARLES B	LTC	0-0390046	0147	2
THOMPSON CHARLES F	LTC	0-0275880	1160	3
THOMPSON CHARLES F	CPT	0-0465798	0447	2
THOMPSON CHARLES H	CPT	0-0499491	0356	3
THOMPSON CHARLES J	LTC	0-1289165	0761	1
THOMPSON CHARLES R	LTC	0-0153270	0956	3
THOMPSON CHARLES R	LTC	0-1641016	1061	1
THOMPSON CLARENCE F	MAJ	0-0345477	0955	1
THOMPSON CLAUDE W	LTC	0-1178008	1160	1
THOMPSON CLAUDE S	LTC	0-0215950	0962	3
THOMPSON CLAUDE V	COL	0-0200713	0255	3
THOMPSON CLAYTON E	LTC	0-1646655	0163	1
THOMPSON CLAYTON P	CW2	W-2211099	0666	1
THOMPSON CLYDE F	CPT	0-1545750	0546	2
THOMPSON CLYDE R	MAJ	0-0929620	0747	2
THOMPSON CLYDE S	CW4	W-2117298	0865	1
THOMPSON CORNELIUS	MAJ	0-1280713	1160	1
THOMPSON COURTENAY	CPT	0-0918446	1045	2
THOMPSON DALCOURTE	CPT	0-0890124	0454	2
THOMPSON DAVID L	MAJ	0-1846078	1157	1
THOMPSON DAVID O	MAJ	0-1684073	0546	2
THOMPSON DEWITT	COL	0-0441693	0954	1
THOMPSON DONALD C	MAJ	0-1017737	0758	1
THOMPSON DONALD H	WO1	W-3430001	0261	1
THOMPSON DONALD O	CPT	0-1325580	0559	1
THOMPSON DONALD O	CPT	0-2017302	0958	1
THOMPSON EARL R	CPT	0-0271609	0458	3
THOMPSON EARLE A	CPT	0-0213447	0462	3
THOMPSON EDMUND G	MAJ	0-1063054	1263	1
THOMPSON EDWARD A	LTC	0-0423237	0161	2
THOMPSON EDWARD J	COL	0-0272780	1264	3
THOMPSON EDWARD K	CPT	0-0288995	0561	3
THOMPSON EDWARD L	CW3	W-2148771	0955	1
THOMPSON ELBERT J	1LT	0-1041661	0145	2
THOMPSON ELDON A	LTC	0-1280608	0165	3
THOMPSON ELI A	CPT	0-0496773	0657	1
THOMPSON ELMER B	CPT	0-1103438	0246	2
THOMPSON ELMYRA	2LT	N-0763794	0446	1
THOMPSON EMMETT W	LTC	0-0414552	0161	1
THOMPSON ERIC D	CPT	0-1717465	0446	2
THOMPSON ERNEST F	MAJ	0-1550514	0449	2
THOMPSON EUGENE E	CPT	0-0252703	1054	3
THOMPSON F L JR	MAJ	0-0399648	0448	2
THOMPSON FLOYD A	LTC	0-0300088	1066	3
THOMPSON FRANCIS A	MAJ	0-0175635	0959	3
THOMPSON FRANCIS G	LTC	0-0454496	0758	1
THOMPSON FRANCIS J	1LT	0-1797042	0845	2
THOMPSON FRANK B	COL	0-0180801	0755	3
THOMPSON FRANK G	MAJ	0-0397747	0660	1
THOMPSON FRANK L	1LT	0-0456255	0946	2
THOMPSON FRANKLIN B	LTC	0-0147502	0854	3
THOMPSON FRED F	MAJ	0-0182453	1057	3
THOMPSON FREDERICK	CPT	0-0388924	1045	2
THOMPSON GEORGE H	MAJ	0-0212990	0860	3
THOMPSON GEORGE O	LTC	0-0261681	0761	3
THOMPSON GEORGE V	LTC	0-0922540	0363	3
THOMPSON GEORGE W	MAJ	0-0212992	0363	3
THOMPSON GEORGE W	CPT	0-1173486	0158	1
THOMPSON GERALD W	LTC	0-1168491	0962	1
THOMPSON GILBERT	LTC	0-0443923	0453	1
THOMPSON GILBERT	CPT	0-2275904	0857	2
THOMPSON GILBERT T	MAJ	0-1166196	0847	2
THOMPSON GLEN D	MAJ	0-0216009	0655	3
THOMPSON GLENN E JR	LTC	0-1917764	1268	1
THOMPSON HAROLD C	COL	0-0114272	0457	3
THOMPSON HAROLD H	CW3	W-2145522	0461	1
THOMPSON HAROLD W	LTC	0-0161500	0955	3
THOMPSON HARRY G	CPT	0-1937564	0466	1
THOMPSON HARRY W	LTC	0-0234514	0757	3
THOMPSON HARVEY R	CW4	W-2142615	0657	1
THOMPSON HASKELL L	LTC	0-0530315	1265	1
THOMPSON HENRY C	CPT	0-0969252	1161	1
THOMPSON HENRY C	MAJ	0-0973495	0464	1
THOMPSON HERBERT W	MAJ	0-1316241	0649	2
THOMPSON HOLGER H	LTC	0-1332436	0668	1
THOMPSON HOMER E	LTC	0-0283157	1167	3
THOMPSON HOMER W	LTC	0-0460273	1064	3
THOMPSON HOWARD E	LTC	0-0406120	0764	1
THOMPSON HOWARD W	LTC	0-0509183	0257	1
THOMPSON HUBERT A JR	MAJ	0-1306175	0161	1
THOMPSON HUGH J	MAJ	0-0993164	0963	1
THOMPSON IRA B	LTC	0-0169496	0649	3
THOMPSON JACK	MAJ	0-0297254	1047	2
THOMPSON JACK	CPT	0-1648518	0349	2
THOMPSON JACK H	MAJ	0-1648733	1162	1
THOMPSON JAMES A	CPT	0-0971747	0761	1
THOMPSON JAMES C	CPT	0-0437655	0855	1
THOMPSON JAMES D	MAJ	0-0574081	1061	1
THOMPSON JAMES E	1LT	0-0413515	0644	2
THOMPSON JAMES F	WO1	W-2145913	1053	1
THOMPSON JAMES H	LTC	0-0272412	1062	1
THOMPSON JAMES H	CPT	0-0553878	0361	1
THOMPSON JAMES L	MAJ	0-0478783	0650	2
THOMPSON JAMES O	LTC	0-0406197	0664	1
THOMPSON JAMES P	MAJ	0-0272221	1165	3
THOMPSON JAMES R	CPT	0-1924065	1165	1
THOMPSON JAY F	MAJ	0-0206729	[illegible]	3
THOMPSON JEROME F	COL	0-0113633	1155	3
THOMPSON JERRY J	2LT	0-0536044	0845	2
THOMPSON JERRY N	2LT	0-1638658	0344	2
THOMPSON JESSE C	CW2	W-2206316	0963	1
THOMPSON JESSE D	LTC	0-0349146	0268	3
THOMPSON JOE A	CW3	W-2208308	0866	1
THOMPSON JOHN B	CPT	0-1684084	1143	2
THOMPSON JOHN C	LTC	0-0260184	0268	3
THOMPSON JOHN C	COL	0-0273883	0661	3
THOMPSON JOHN C	MAJ	0-1589543	1162	1
THOMPSON JOHN H	2LT	0-1185202	0145	2
THOMPSON JOHN J	MAJ	0-2036588	0461	1
THOMPSON JOHN R	COL	0-0111140	0648	3
THOMPSON JOHN R	1LT	0-0532287	0447	2
THOMPSON JOHN R	CPT	0-1302389	0546	2
THOMPSON JOHN R	CW3	W-2148362	1262	1
THOMPSON JOHN W	1LT	0-0268581	0653	1
THOMPSON JOHN W	LTC	0-0460008	0762	1
THOMPSON JOSEPH G	MAJ	0-0922926	0946	2
THOMPSON JOSEPH H	CPT	0-1587681	0157	1
THOMPSON JOSEPH M	LTC	0-0298343	0845	2
THOMPSON JOSEPH P	LTC	0-0262883	0567	3
THOMPSON KARL B	LTC	0-0452951	0756	1
THOMPSON KENNETH E	1LT	0-1303575	0845	2
THOMPSON KENNETH F	CW3	W-2144161	0667	1
THOMPSON KENNETH W	MAJ	0-0112375	1053	3
THOMPSON LARGENT C	MAJ	0-0497491	0154	1
THOMPSON LARRY C	1LT	0-0425628	0445	2
THOMPSON LAVERNE F	CPT	0-1947369	0259	1
THOMPSON LAWRENCE L	CPT	0-0974118	0662	1
THOMPSON LEE B	COL	0-0213541	0546	2
THOMPSON LEIGH	LTC	0-0451500	0860	1
THOMPSON LELAND W	CW4	W-2105725	0662	1
THOMPSON LEON G	1LT	0-0109838	1034	1
THOMPSON LEONARD A	1LT	0-1822212	0246	2
THOMPSON LEONARD R	CPT	0-1589017	0860	1
THOMPSON LESLIE B	LTC	0-0450654	0657	1
THOMPSON LLEWELLYN	LTC	0-1928261	0262	2
THOMPSON LLOYD J	1LT	0-0483696	0645	2
THOMPSON LLOYD L JR	CPT	0-1685148	1045	2
THOMPSON LOREN B	COL	0-0288152	0568	3
THOMPSON LOUIS G JR	MAJ	0-1822652	0867	1
THOMPSON LOUIS P	LTC	0-0216585	0364	3
THOMPSON LOYD	MAJ	0-0259045	0867	3
THOMPSON LOYD B	MAJ	0-0432909	1158	1
THOMPSON MARSHALL F	LTC	0-2053894	0357	1
THOMPSON MCDUFFIE	CW2	W-2209108	0261	1
THOMPSON MELVIN E	CW2	W-2103527	0867	1
THOMPSON MELVIN O	MAJ	0-2262562	0868	1
THOMPSON MERON J	1LT	0-2008403	0547	2
THOMPSON MERRILL R	CPT	0-0177404	1059	3
THOMPSON MIKE	CPT	0-1013661	0550	1
THOMPSON MILTON E	CW4	W-2144482	0167	1
THOMPSON MYRON M	MAJ	0-1575226	0263	1
THOMPSON N B JR	MAJ	0-0167846	0950	3
THOMPSON NATHAN P	LTC	0-0350077	0660	1
THOMPSON NORMAN E	1LT	0-1018463	0857	1
THOMPSON NORMAN F	CPT	0-0486010	1046	1
THOMPSON NORMAN L	COL	0-0189013	0857	1
THOMPSON NORMAN R	MAJ	0-1011964	0860	1

NAME	GRADE	SVC NO	DATE RET MO YR	RET CODE
THOMPSON NORMAN R S	LTC	0-0125389	0154	3
THOMPSON OLE F	LTC	0-0251771	0545	2
THOMPSON ORAL H	2LT	N-0736546	0845	1
THOMPSON ORVILLE H	MAJ	0-0196842	0256	1
THOMPSON ORVILLE J	CW4	W-2000608	0461	2
THOMPSON PATRICK H	1LT	0-1018618	0845	2
THOMPSON PAUL M	LTC	0-0489923	1054	1
THOMPSON PAUL M	MAJ	0-1285519	1065	1
THOMPSON PAUL W	2LT	0-2000984	1045	2
THOMPSON PHILIP G JR	LTC	0-1042185	0268	1
THOMPSON RALPH S	MAJ	0-1019356	0261	1
THOMPSON RAYMOND O	MAJ	0-1591479	1162	1
THOMPSON RHEAGA R	CW4	W-2003069	0568	3
THOMPSON RICHARD G	MAJ	0-1291196	1165	1
THOMPSON RICHARD J	CPT	0-0548316	0548	2
THOMPSON ROBERT A	1LT	0-1924691	0555	2
THOMPSON ROBERT C	LTC	0-1320981	0167	1
THOMPSON ROBERT E	COL	0-0298882	1061	3
THOMPSON ROBERT H	COL	0-0247431	0263	3
THOMPSON ROBERT H	LTC	0-1323875	0361	1
THOMPSON ROBERT J	CW2	W-2214056	0667	1
THOMPSON ROBERT L	LTC	0-0259621	0668	3
THOMPSON ROBERT W	LTC	0-1946624	1066	1
THOMPSON ROGER M	MAJ	0-1287786	1055	1
THOMPSON ROSCOE P	CPT	0-1120786	1060	1
THOMPSON ROY B	CW3	W-2142666	0359	1
THOMPSON ROY E	1LT	0-0449405	0145	2
THOMPSON ROY H	COL	0-0297221	0167	3
THOMPSON RUSSELL F	COL	0-0260292	0766	3
THOMPSON RUSSELL J	LTC	0-1031767	0766	1
THOMPSON RUTH E	1LT	N-0730929	1045	1
THOMPSON STERLING R	MAJ	0-0990044	1168	1
THOMPSON TAYLOR F	LTC	0-0403231	0354	2
THOMPSON TAZEWELL F	COL	0-0259944	0168	3
THOMPSON THEARON E	CW4	W-2203281	0556	1
THOMPSON THEODORE A	MAJ	0-1292255	0261	2
THOMPSON THOMAS F	1LT	0-1845801	1045	2
THOMPSON THOMAS M	LTC	0-0371989	0561	1
THOMPSON TOMMY	MAJ	0-0222068	1046	1
THOMPSON TRACY L	MAJ	0-2262146	1164	1
THOMPSON VELORIS O	CPT	0-1017788	0261	1
THOMPSON VERNON C	MAJ	0-1639730	0863	1
THOMPSON VICTOR L	LTC	0-0213361	0962	3
THOMPSON VIRGIL G	CW2	W-2150699	1056	1
THOMPSON WALTER	LTC	0-0232161	0560	1
THOMPSON WALTER B	CPT	0-0499651	1053	1
THOMPSON WALTER B	LTC	0-2055487	0261	1
THOMPSON WARREN	CW2	W-3150191	1062	1
THOMPSON WAYNE W	MAJ	0-0958665	0563	1
THOMPSON WILLARD O	CPT	0-2029565	1057	1
THOMPSON WILLARD N	LTC	0-1582579	1062	1
THOMPSON WILLARD O	1LT	0-0974697	0457	1
THOMPSON WILLIAM A	LTC	0-1166401	0566	1
THOMPSON WILLIAM A	CW3	W-2208863	0168	1
THOMPSON WILLIAM E	COL	0-0240636	1163	3
THOMPSON WILLIAM E	COL	0-0308509	0257	1
THOMPSON WILLIAM G	LTC	0-0400848	0760	1
THOMPSON WILLIAM H	LTC	0-0421680	0663	1
THOMPSON WILLIAM K	LTC	0-0259220	0168	3
THOMPSON WILLIAM N	MAJ	0-0251804	0467	3
THOMPSON WILLIAM P	CW3	W-2150790	0165	1
THOMPSON WILLIAM R	LTC	0-1100364	0763	1
THOMPSON WILLIAM R	CPT	0-1796546	0564	1
THOMPSON WILLIAM T	CPT	0-0505212	0356	1
THOMPSON WILLIE E	1LT	0-2042859	0451	1
THOMPSON WINSTON C	CW3	W-2151721	0562	1
THOMPSON WOODBERRY	MAJ	0-0885769	1054	1
THOMPSON-BOWERS IAN	MAJ	0-0321865	0253	1
THOMS FORREST	MAJ	0-1046668	0562	1
THOMSON CLINTON	MAJ	0-1302069	0656	1
THOMSON DONALD B	LTC	0-1041250	0562	1
THOMSON EARL W	COL	0-0124147	1053	3
THOMSON HENRY S	LTC	0-0263530	0749	3
THOMSON ISAAC L	LTC	0-0147508	1154	3
THOMSON JAMES C	CPT	0-0253925	0268	3

NAME	GRADE	SVC NO	DATE RET MO YR	RET CODE
THOMSON JAMES L	CPT	0-1300732	0846	2
THOMSON JAMES R	CW2	W-3150896	0267	1
THOMSON JOHN W	MAJ	0-1575227	0859	2
THOMSON LEONARD S	CPT	0-1182473	0347	2
THOMSON RANDOLPH M	1LT	0-1178010	0646	2
THOMSON ROBERT B	MAJ	0-0935689	0262	1
THOMSON ROBERT JR	COL	0-0253717	0860	1
THOMSON ROBERT L	1LT	0-1286736	0146	2
THOMSON ROBERT T	LTC	0-2279947	0668	1
THOMSON WILLIAM H	MAJ	0-0253423	0152	3
THOMY GEORGE A	1LT	0-1315389	0445	2
THOR ROSE M	MAJ	N-0731335	0863	3
THORARINSON GERALD O	MAJ	0-1822653	0461	1
THORESEN LESLIE B	LTC	0-1551971	0765	1
THORESEN TRYGVE	2LT	0-1936816	0754	2
THORESON CARL H	MAJ	0-2097404	0467	1
THORESON WILBUR A	1LT	0-1322732	0845	2
THORLEY IRA O JR	COL	0-0248948	1064	3
THORLIN REGINALD	LTC	0-0468834	0760	2
THORMAN BENJAMIN W	MAJ	0-0221647	1056	3
THORMAN JAMES G	CW3	W-2203481	0967	1
THORN EILAND H	CW2	W-2147839	0961	2
THORN HOWARD W	CPT	0-2000649	0954	2
THORN MARVIN O	MAJ	0-1795751	0165	3
THORN WILLIAM T	MAJ	0-1798315	0657	1
THORNAL REUBEN B	LTC	0-0286804	1058	1
THORNBER MERRILL S	CPT	0-0377505	0245	2
THORNBERRY HALBERT H	CPT	0-0215769	0163	3
THORNBERRY JOHN H	LTC	0-0500921	0463	3
THORNBOFOUGH WILLIAM	MAJ	0-0232967	0563	3
THORNBRUE CARL N	CPT	0-0496119	0754	1
THORNBURG CYRIL F	LTC	0-131C'74	1062	1
THORNBURG HAROLD C	CPT	0-0286334	0259	3
THORNBURG MARGARET S	1LT	N-0760989	0746	1
THORNBURG THOMAS W	2LT	0-1932520	0753	2
THORNBURGH CONWAY O	1LT	0-1032317	0347	2
THORNBURGH MARY G	1LT	N-0784673	0548	1
THORNDIKE AUGUSTUS	COL	0-0226573	0356	3
THORNE ALBERT J	LTC	0-1646656	0866	1
THORNE BAILEY M	CW4	W-2102469	0564	3
THORNE ENNIS P	LTC	0-0429549	1261	3
THORNE JAMES H	CPT	0-0969679	1060	1
THORNE JOE E	CW2	W-2141871	0659	1
THORNE JOHN C	COL	0-0366083	0960	1
THORNE LEWIS W	MAJ	0-0539313	0965	1
THORNE RONALD B	CW3	W-2151004	0764	1
THORNE VIRGIL A	CW2	W-2104530	0246	2
THORNE WILLIAM A	WO1	W-2124227	1146	1
THORNE WILLIAM D	LTC	0-1030617	0361	2
THORNE WILLIAM E	LTC	0-0276407	1057	1
THORNHILL JOHN B	COL	0-0172900	0546	2
THORNLEY BERT L JR	2LT	0-1555405	0646	2
THORNLEY CLARENCE E	CPT	0-0527869	1047	2
THORNLEY JOHN O	CPT	0-0941959	1059	1
THORNSVARD HARRY C	LTC	0-1582208	1167	1
THORNTON BARRIE M	MAJ	0-0407198	0860	1
THORNTON CHARLES S	CW2	W-2104531	0565	1
THORNTON CRATE T	COL	0-0325514	0968	3
THORNTON DELMAR O	MAJ	0-1103973	0548	2
THORNTON DONALD S	LTC	0-0270555	0668	3
THORNTON EARLE D JR	COL	0-0307494	0960	1
THORNTON EUGENE A	MAJ	0-1945070	0759	1
THORNTON EVANS C	MAJ	0-1283168	0446	2
THORNTON FRANK B	CPT	0-1315238	0246	2
THORNTON FRANK S	CPT	0-0221945	0751	3
THORNTON HORACE E	1LT	0-1544459	0757	3
THORNTON HOWARD L	CW2	W-2210724	1065	1
THORNTON JAMES M	LTC	0-0382983	0363	1
THORNTON JOHN R	CW3	W-2209718	0867	1
THORNTON JOHN S	LTC	0-0369600	0367	3
THORNTON LESLIE B	1LT	0-1299651	1145	2
THORNTON LOUIS M	CW2	W-2147170	1065	2
THORNTON LOUISE G	2LT	N-0763903	1044	1
THORNTON OSCEOLA T	LTC	0-0331267	1166	1
THORNTON RALPH E	LTC	0-0210081	0563	3

NAME	GRADE	SVC NO	DATE RET MO YR	RET CODE
THORNTON RAYMOND A	CPT	0-2262709	0361	1
THORNTON ROBERT F	COL	0-0483573	0862	1
THORNTON ROBERT F	1LT	0-1311994	0844	2
THORNTON RONALD G	CPT	0-5328025	0768	2
THORNTON ROZIER L	MAJ	0-1042968	0460	1
THORNTON THOMAS F	LTC	0-0384354	0358	1
THORNTON WALTER J	CW2	W-2152407	0861	1
THORNTON WILLIAM D	MAJ	0-0160619	0151	3
THORNTON WILLIAM M	MAJ	0-2204075	0366	1
THORNTON WILLIAM S	CW2	W-2145523	0559	1
THORP EDWARD G	LTC	0-0125952	0164	3
THORP ELLIS H	LTC	0-1011236	0767	1
THORP KENNETH F	LTC	0-0334669	0268	3
THORP PAUL I	MAJ	0-0270232	0151	1
THORPE CHARLES E	CPT	0-1047808	0657	2
THORPE EDITH	MAJ	N-0721896	1262	1
THORPE KENNETH W	1LT	0-1586973	1045	2
THORPE KNUTE F K	LTC	0-1171799	1268	1
THORPE MELVIN J	1LT	0-1304293	0268	3
THORPE PAUL H	LTC	0-0784802	0868	3
THORPE ROBERT J	CW2	W-3151068	0968	1
THORPE THOMAS D	CPT	0-2032883	0956	1
THORPE THOMAS W JR	LTC	0-0452360	0966	1
THORSEN ARNOLD M	1LT	0-0545050	0445	2
THORSEN THEODORE R	WO1	W-2151177	0463	2
THORSEN THORWALD	MAJ	0-0178950	1144	2
THORSEN WILLIAM L	2LT	0-1824536	0844	2
THORSON AUSTIN T	COL	0-0288305	0668	3
THORSTAD JOHN E	MAJ	0-1822337	0261	1
THORSTED EDWARD L	LTC	0-1294563	0566	1
THORSTENSEN ROY F	MAJ	0-1182980	0561	1
THORWALD WALTER E	1LT	0-1323047	0745	2
THRAILKILL FRED W	CW4	W-2127512	0461	1
THRALL GENTRY H	CW2	W-2152255	1157	1
THRALL WILMA E	MAJ	N-0737298	0962	2
THRALLS HAROLD L	MAJ	0-0966088	0663	1
THRAMS GUY E SR	1LT	0-0016873	0567	3
THRAN CLAIRE N	MAJ	0-1342018	0561	1
THRAP RALPH E	CPT	0-1168108	0753	1
THRASH KENNETH M	COL	0-0252051	1166	3
THRASH MAURICE C	CW2	W-2149952	0857	1
THRASH THOMAS A	COL	0-0119072	0755	3
THRASHER BELIAS L	MAJ	0-1018303	1263	1
THRASHER JAMES W	2LT	0-1113017	0345	2
THRASHER LAWRENCE E	LTC	0-0256004	0967	3
THRASHER LEONARD R	LTC	0-0369844	0762	1
THRASHER WILLARD D	CW2	W-2149469	0761	1
THREAJER WILFRED G	LTC	0-0111873	0950	3
THREET WEBB	LTC	0-1169766	0965	3
THRESHER WILLIAM A	CW3	W-2143144	0361	1
THRIFT CHESTER B	LTC	0-0259159	0367	3
THRIFT GEORGE N	LTC	0-0237323	0965	3
THRIFT HENRY S	LTC	0-0407688	1060	1
THRISTINO FRANK L	2LT	0-1294564	0944	2
THROCKMORTON C O	CPT	0-0201031	0155	3
THROCKMORTON JAMES F	MAJ	0-0216929	0760	3
THROGMORTON JAMES H	CPT	0-1877232	0165	1
THRONE LAWRENCE D	LTC	0-1166197	0263	1
THRONE THOMAS	MAJ	0-2027352	0761	1
THRONEBERRY MARVIN L	CW3	W-2152256	1163	1
THRONTVEIT CARL P	MAJ	0-1998342	0662	1
THROOP J C	CW4	W-2141685	0962	1
THROOP WILLARD L JR	1LT	0-1287435	0145	2
THROWER CLELLAN C	MAJ	0-1328651	0866	1
THROWER EARL C	COL	0-0246088	1054	1
THROWER JAMES H JR	CW3	W-2205272	0868	1
THROWER JOHN H	CPT	0-0246272	0342	2
THROWER MAXWELL O	COL	0-0240504	0753	1
THROWER WEBB A	LTC	0-1560082	0368	3
THRUN FRED M	COL	0-0171721	0756	3
THRUSH WILLIAM C	CPT	0-1549140	1057	1
THUES RAYMOND L	LTC	0-0947570	0567	1
THULIEN HAROLD B	CPT	0-1038869	1059	1
THUM OTTO F	LTC	0-0469021	0762	1
THUN JACK K	MAJ	0-2263164	0563	1

NAME	GRADE	SVC NO	DATE RET MO YR	RET CODE
THURBER CHARLES R	CPT	0-0975982	0356	1
THURBER GEORGE H	COL	0-0309626	0664	3
THURBER GEORGE L	1LT	0-1324962	0346	2
THURBER RAYMOND D	LTC	0-0299861	0565	3
THURESON JOHN D	LTC	0-1581424	0561	1
THURLOW HENRY P	MAJ	0-0153272	0549	3
THURLOW JERRY J	CW3	RW-2145756	0763	1
THURLOW MADALINE V	MAJ	N-0760761	0663	1
THURMAN ARTHUR P	2LT	0-1549853	0743	2
THURMAN DAVID D	LTC	0-1586279	0761	1
THURMAN GEORGE C	MAJ	0-0269742	0645	2
THURMAN RUFUS S	LTC	0-0310885	0656	1
THURMAN SOLOMON	CW4	W-2108641	0358	1
THURMAN WILLIAM R	CPT	0-1288973	0559	1
THURMOND GRANVIL C	CW3	W-3150545	0768	2
THURMOND JAMES S	M G	0-0191221	0163	3
THURMOND WILLIAM L	MAJ	0-2035077	0467	2
THURSTON HENRY E	LTC	0-0913970	1068	3
THURSTON IRA L	MAJ	0-0195239	0861	3
THURSTON IRVING	LTC	0-0176535	1055	3
THURSTON JOSEPH D	CW4	W-2103531	1058	1
THURSTON KATHERINE	2LT	N-0730391	0845	1
THURSTON VERNON L	MAJ	0-1286737	0261	1
THURSTON WILLIAM A	LTC	0-0545785	0365	1
THURTLE GEORGE S	MAJ	0-0391113	0547	2
THUSS ELMER E	MAJ	0-0286627	0362	3
THWEATT CARROLL P	MAJ	0-0127863	0349	3
THYSELL PHILIP W	CPT	0-1017918	1054	1
TIBBE WILLIAM	MAJ	0-0450147	0755	1
TIBBETS ROY R	CPT	0-1540653	1147	2
TIBBETT RALPH W	MAJ	0-1113018	0666	2
TIBBETTS GEORGE E	MAJ	0-1550939	1158	1
TIBBETTS JAMES D	LTC	0-1309442	1162	1
TIBBETTS JOSEPH W	CW2	W-2106419	0847	2
TIBBETTS LESTER K	LTC	0-1113019	0664	2
TIBBETTS STANLEY B	LTC	0-0280046	0364	3
TIBBITS JOHN M	2LT	0-1823086	0645	2
TIBBITT JOHN H	CW3	W-2144251	0363	1
TIBBITTS GORDON C	LTC	0-0203492	0350	2
TIBBS LUTHER W	CW3	W-2149987	0465	1
TIBERI JOHN V	1LT	0-1294752	0745	2
TICARIC NICHOLAS	CPT	0-1014345	0562	1
TICE ALBERT K	MAJ	0-0324939	0546	2
TICE CARL E	MAJ	0-0948740	1062	1
TICE FLETCHER F	MAJ	0-0260410	0166	3
TICE GORDON M	1LT	0-1590856	0844	2
TICE JOHN L	LTC	0-0360265	0863	3
TICHELI LEO P	LTC	0-1044129	0860	2
TICHENOR HILTON R	MAJ	0-0415890	0665	1
TICK JEAN Q	2LT	0-0406605	1144	2
TIDBALL PAUL B	CPT	0-0286117	0562	3
TIDD CHARLES A	CPT	0-0413631	0459	1
TIDD LUZERNE M	COL	0-0122873	0756	3
TIDERMAN ROBERT R	LTC	0-0888198	0164	1
TIDMORE CARL C	MAJ	0-1878220	0868	1
TIDMORE WILLIAM E	LTC	0-0276311	0560	3
TIDWELL DON	MAJ	0-1688827	1264	1
TIDWELL EDGAR L	COL	0-0399970	0764	1
TIDWELL JESSE M JR	MAJ	0-1295625	0760	1
TIDWELL JOHN S	COL	0-0361594	1168	1
TIDWELL SAM E SR	CW2	W-2214458	0768	1
TIEDE JOSEPH W	COL	0-0231315	0159	3
TIEDEMAN LEROY E	CPT	0-0253304	1155	3
TIEDEMANN ELEANDRE H	CPT	L-0204388	1046	2
TIEDGEN ARNO R	CW4	W-2121959	0860	1
TIEFENBRUN ALFONS J	COL	0-0280056	0968	3
TIEGS GEORGE E	MAJ	0-0450498	0747	2
TIEMAN LEON O	LTC	0-1922511	0968	1
TIEMAN MILTON C	MAJ	0-0943626	0666	1
TIEMANN NORBERT T	2LT	0-0955879	0252	2
TIEMANN PHILIP W	COL	0-0173656	0760	3
TIEMEYER CHARLOTTE	1LT	N-0728894	0446	2
TIENKEN WILLIAM II	LTC	0-1177213	0763	2
TIERNAN CHARLES M	MAJ	0-1167671	0861	1
TIERNAN JAMES T	CW3	W-2132953	0461	1

NAME	GRADE	SVC NO	DATE RET MO YR	RET CODE
TIERNAN ROBERT W SR	MAJ	0-1168493	0661	1
TIERNAN WILFRED H	MAJ	0-0178972	[illegible]	3
TIERNEY GARY J	CPT	0-5420426	1268	2
TIERNEY JAMES E	MAJ	0-0954978	0767	1
TIERNEY RICHARD J	CPT	0-0277940	0863	3
TIERNEY ROBERT J	CW3	W-2151629	1265	1
TIESING BERTHOLD U	CPT	0-0367480	0460	1
TIETJEN EDWARD H	CPT	0-1305674	0553	2
TIETJEN OTTOMAR H	COL	0-0514981	0767	1
TIETKE ERNEST A	LTC	0-2070443	0968	1
TIFFANY CHARLES A	1LT	0-0469095	1145	2
TIFFANY FREEMAN R	MAJ	0-2020596	0763	2
TIFFANY HOWARD H	LTC	0-0371699	0756	1
TIFFANY JOHN L	MAJ	0-1313935	0866	1
TIFFANY WILLIAM A	LTC	0-1030428	0557	1
TIGER DAVID	LTC	0-0109159	1046	2
TIGER KENNETH R	LTC	0-2036033	1067	1
TIGERT CLAUDE A JR	CPT	0-3557265	1047	2
TIGH LOUIS M	MAJ	0-0888270	1046	2
TIGHE EDWARD J	MAJ	0-1307479	1160	1
TIGHE JAMES J	MAJ	0-1052999	0762	1
TIGHE JOHN G	LTC	0-0507589	0167	3
TIGHE JOHN J	LTC	0-1638666	0161	1
TIGHE OWEN E	CPT	0-0494822	0649	1
TIGHE ROGER J	COL	0-0218320	0547	2
TIGNER ARMON R	CW2	W-2151908	0863	1
TIGNER OSCAR C	LTC	0-0235775	0166	3
TIGNER VERNON M	CW3	W-2150309	1061	1
TIGNO BENNETT S	2LT	0-1896568	0364	1
TILDEN JOHN	LTC	0-0183115	0552	3
TILEY PAUL L	CPT	0-2262131	1060	1
TILFORD ATLAS B	1LT	0-1301714	1144	2
TILGHMAN ELWAYNE E	MAJ	0-1174727	0562	1
TILKE EDWARD T	MAJ	0-1317054	0159	1
TILKER GEORGE J	LTC	0-0353062	0460	1
TILL FRED N	MAJ	0-2028898	0962	1
TILL SHELTON C JR	LTC	0-0441637	0257	2
TILL WOODROW J	LTC	0-1548324	0563	1
TILLACK RAYMOND L	LTC	0-0505540	0667	1
TILLEMANS DONALD L	MAJ	0-1010530	0959	1
TILLER HOWARD B	MAJ	0-1683948	0446	2
TILLER JACK M SR	LTC	0-1335081	1168	1
TILLERY JAMES P	MAJ	0-1288974	0259	1
TILLERY JOHN L	COL	0-0281792	0847	2
TILLERY SAMUEL E JR	LTC	0-0958215	0768	1
TILLERY SAMUEL H	MAJ	0-0298092	0864	3
TILLES ALBERT	1LT	0-2049744	0847	2
TILLETT SCOTT E	MAJ	0-1684940	1262	1
TILLEY HARRY F	MAJ	0-1825082	0960	1
TILLEY RALPH C	LTC	0-0202145	0756	3
TILLEY WILLIAM H	CPT	0-0286183	0357	3
TILLINGHAST THEOSE E	MAJ	0-0266423	0553	3
TILLMAN CLARENCE C	LTC	0-0329205	0860	1
TILLMAN JAMES C	CW2	W-2206085	1160	1
TILLMAN JEAN P	CPT	0-0389077	0263	1
TILLMAN JOHN	LTC	0-0282625	0247	2
TILLMAN JOHN G	MAJ	0-0410989	0361	1
TILLMAN OLIVER C	CW2	W-2146402	1159	1
TILLMAN RICHARD G	LTC	0-2204110	0767	1
TILLMAN ROBERT	CW2	W-2205782	1159	1
TILLMAN ROBERT L	MAJ	0-0540635	0863	1
TILLMAN SAMUEL C	WO1	W-2120008	1045	2
TILLMAN STEPHEN F	COL	0-0171470	1060	3
TILLMAN THOMAS B	LTC	0-0363320	0265	3
TILLOTSON ROY	LTC	0-1285520	1060	1
TILLOTSON WILLIAM B	MAJ	0-1170582	0157	1
TILLQUIST DAVID E	1LT	0-0266967	0461	3
TILLSON ROGER K	1LT	0-1016152	0246	2
TILSON CHARLES V JR	1LT	0-1297616	0145	2
TILSON GEORGE H	COL	0-0205300	1163	3
TILSON LEMUEL G	MAJ	0-2000059	0862	1
TILTON JOHN E	COL	0-0243793	0666	3
TILTON JOHN F	LTC	0-0406839	0161	1
TILTON NORMAN L	1LT	0-1062088	1045	2
TIMBERLAKE R E JR	LTC	0-0351990	0161	1
TIMBERLAKE TEDSAN S	MAJ	0-0573588	0861	1
TIMBOE ARTHUR C	COL	0-0262939	0160	1
TIMBRELL JOHN Q	LTC	0-0266463	0766	3
TIMEWELL SHIRLEY R	LTC	N-0783160	0665	2
TIMMERMAN FRED	COL	0-0238688	0954	2
TIMMERMAN WILFRED R	MAJ	0-0995961	0765	1
TIMMERMAN WILLIAM H	1LT	0-1306176	0745	2
TIMMINS MERRILL S JR	MAJ	0-0364590	0568	3
TIMMINS RICHARD H	CPT	0-0954854	0954	2
TIMMINS WESLEY D	LTC	0-2047861	0866	1
TIMMONS JOHN E	MAJ	0-0293630	0560	3
TIMMONS MARION	CW2	W-2145846	1057	1
TIMMONS PAUL E	MAJ	0-1340594	0665	1
TIMMONS THADDEUS A	LTC	0-0250105	0946	2
TIMNEY CHARLES J	LTC	0-1641863	0766	1
TIMPANO ANGELO J	CPT	0-0938015	0959	1
TIMSON HORACE W	MAJ	0-1168495	0854	1
TINCHER HARRY R	MAJ	0-1688727	0968	1
TINDALL ALBERT W	1LT	0-1999831	0748	2
TINDALL EDWIN L	LTC	0-0259411	1164	3
TINDALL JOHN R	LTC	0-0188045	1060	3
TINDALL MORRIS H	MAJ	0-0337893	0945	2
TINDALL WALTER L JR	COL	0-0268942	0368	3
TINDER FLOYD S	LTC	0-0902818	0664	3
TINER EDGAR A	MAJ	0-0311812	1047	1
TINETTI ERNEST F	CPT	0-1687271	1145	2
TINGLE EDGAR J	LTC	0-0368374	1160	1
TINGLE JACK K	LTC	0-0100429	1145	2
TINGLEY OSCAR N	CPT	0-1305675	1145	2
TINKER ALLAN M	COL	0-0206542	0259	3
TINKER HAROLD E	CW4	W-2144198	1066	1
TINKER JOHN G	LTC	0-0268328	1064	1
TINKER LEE E	MAJ	0-1326435	0261	1
TINKHAM CHARLES J	COL	0-0291115	1159	1
TINKHAM ERNEST R	LTC	0-0509796	1064	3
TINKHAM LEROY B	MAJ	0-1297810	0246	2
TINNEL OLEN L	MAJ	0-1178011	1160	1
TINNEN HASKELL L	CW3	W-2145524	0761	1
TINNEY JOE R	MAJ	0-1920255	0365	1
TINNIN ALVIS L	2LT	0-1334231	0246	2
TINNIN JOHN V	LTC	0-0482926	1054	2
TINSLEY ERNEST J	LTC	0-1037934	0868	1
TINSLEY EVELYN H	1LT	N-0763513	0546	1
TINSLEY JAMES H	MAJ	0-0493215	0352	2
TINSLEY JOHN N	MAJ	0-0974674	0862	1
TINSLEY K C	LTC	0-0316077	1066	3
TINSLEY LEE F	CPT	0-0332322	1059	3
TINT HERMAN	CPT	0-0297502	0343	2
TINTARY PERLEF W	MAJ	0-2028640	0167	1
TIPA MICHAEL	LTC	0-1323876	0764	1
TIPP VICTOR L	MAJ	0-1311450	0563	1
TIPPETS DARRELL R	CPT	0-0928679	0859	1
TIPPETT ROBERT G JR	LTC	0-1050116	0261	1
TIPPINS EUGENE A	CW3	W-2142684	0163	1
TIPPINS WILLIAM C	COL	0-0196759	0962	3
TIPPIT JAMES H	CW2	W-2147671	0860	1
TIPPIT MATTHEW L	LTC	0-1555481	0562	1
TIPPIT WILSON C	WO1	W-2144735	0657	1
TIPPIT WYLIE A	CPT	0-0179939	0746	2
TIPPLE ALBERT M	MAJ	0-0318073	0646	2
TIPS CHARLES R	COL	0-0157014	0652	3
TIPSWORD JOHN F	CW3	W-2205387	0468	1
TIPTON CARL M	MAJ	0-1588922	1157	1
TIPTON JOHN B	COL	0-0119037	0757	3
TIPTON JOHN H	COL	0-0335118	0757	3
TIPTON LLOYD P	LTC	0-1647304	1262	1
TIPTON MARY E	CPT	N-2310456	0166	2
TIPTON ROY E JR	MAJ	0-1317577	1059	1
TIPTON ROYAL N	MAJ	0-1646967	0363	1
TIPTON WILLIAM L JR	MAJ	0-2288849	0962	1
TIPTON WILLIAM W	MAJ	0-0450190	0358	1
TIRADO PEDRO W	MAJ	0-0953913	0161	1
TIRRELL LORING V	LTC	0-0127009	0956	3
TISCHBIN ROBERT M	1LT	0-1102089	1045	2
TISCHER PHILIP A	MAJ	0-1299963	0861	2
TISCHLER CHARLES	LTC	0-1556815	0761	1
TISCHLER LOUIS N	LTC	0-0300051	0667	3
TISDALE ALBERT A	LTC	0-0357776	0167	3
TISDALE DONALD A	MAJ	0-1044408	0359	1
TISDALE GLENN W	LTC	0-0137974	0753	3
TISDALE JAMES R	MAJ	0-0379489	1045	2
TISDALE JOHN F JR	MAJ	0-2034926	0164	1
TISDALE LEONARD I	MAJ	0-0974555	1163	1
TISDALE WILLIAM G	MAJ	0-0410786	0746	2
TISDALE WILLIAM J	LTC	0-1038502	0467	1
TISDELL NORMAN A	LTC	0-0369231	0667	3
TISHMAN PETER	1LT	0-1597298	0346	2
TISON GERALD J	COL	0-0328107	0358	1
TISSUE JOHN W	CPT	0-1799498	0356	1
TITCHENER FREDERICK	LTC	0-0169245	0646	2
TITEL FRED C	LTC	0-0151232	0253	3
TITERA LADIMIR V	LTC	0-0242282	0962	3
TITKO ANDREW	MAJ	0-0455502	0558	1
TITLEMAN MYER R	CPT	0-1703232	0545	2
TITONE BENEDICT B	LTC	0-1579218	0868	3
TITTLE JAMES I	MAJ	0-2204078	0267	1
TITTLE MORGAN L	MAJ	0-1593887	0563	1
TITUS ANDREW P JR	LTC	0-0339335	1161	1
TITUS CLIFF K	COL	0-0331312	0750	3
TITUS EDGAR F	MAJ	0-0884936	0163	1
TITUS ELROY W	CW3	W-2148772	0666	1
TITUS FRANK G	CW2	W-2152101	0762	1
TITUS FRANK L	LTC	0-0425885	0966	3
TITUS JAMES C	LTC	0-0405663	1165	1
TITUS JOHN B	MAJ	0-0208033	1145	2
TITUS PAUL F	MAJ	0-1885895	0468	1
TITUS ROBERT L JR	1LT	0-0354668	0545	2
TIVENAN JOHN J	MAJ	0-0324972	0959	3
TKACIK JOHN	CPT	0-0109207	0535	2
TOBEY JAMES A	COL	0-0235426	0754	3
TOBEY MILTON K	LTC	0-0489216	0257	1
TOBIAS CARL A	CPT	0-0511156	1145	2
TOBIAS EDWIN R	MAJ	0-1105868	1266	1
TOBIAS HARRY C	CW3	W-2152408	0461	1
TOBIAS HENRY H	CPT	0-1320914	0548	2
TOBIAS HERBERT J	MAJ	0-1055996	0567	3
TOBIAS JOSEPH M	LTC	0-1308561	0168	3
TOBIAS RICHARD E	CW3	W-2150869	0963	1
TOBIAS WALTER A	MAJ	0-1945071	0157	1
TOBIASON REBA Z	1LT	N-0734426	0452	2
TOBIE LOUIS J	CW2	W-2114240	1066	3
TOBIN BERNARD F	LTC	0-0966504	0468	1
TOBIN CHARLEY B	CPT	0-2053960	0449	1
TOBIN CLEMENT J	MAJ	0-0110734	1054	3
TOBIN DAVID I	CW2	W-2143942	0364	1
TOBIN DAVID P	LTC	0-1000293	0858	2
TOBIN EDWARD G	LTC	0-1175604	0862	2
TOBIN EDWARD H	LTC	0-1182284	1262	1
TOBIN FRANK L	MAJ	0-1947536	0966	1
TOBIN JAMES M	CPT	0-2000902	1060	2
TOBIN JERRY P	MAJ	0-0231046	0565	3
TOBIN JOHN E	COL	0-1588329	0868	3
TOBIN MARY W	1LT	N-0701263	0732	1
TOBIN ROBERT P	LTC	0-0294151	1047	2
TOBIN THOMAS R	2LT	0-1322184	0245	2
TOBIN WALTER E	CW3	W-2207469	0167	1
TOCCI JOSEPH A	MAJ	0-1917545	1164	1
TOCCO JOSEPH J	MAJ	0-1030198	0351	1
TOCKS LEO V	LTC	0-0295996	0268	3
TOD CARREL I	LTC	0-1001919	0265	3
TODARO PAUL	CPT	0-0901678	0345	2
TODD BRUCE J	1LT	0-1018304	1045	2
TODD CHARLES E	MAJ	0-1340595	1060	1
TODD CHARLES M	MAJ	0-1321587	1161	1
TODD CHARLES W	1LT	0-1285140	0944	2
TODD CLYDE D	CPT	0-1031277	0455	1
TODD COLEMAN B	COL	0-0185486	0551	3
TODD DANA L	MAJ	0-0151769	0655	3
TODD DAVID B JR	LTC	0-0114810	1154	3
TODD DIMITRI W	LTC	0-1824393	1262	1
TODD DONALD A	1LT	0-1106365	0544	2
TODD EDWARD F JR	LTC	0-0222032	1062	3
TODD EUGENE E	MAJ	0-1013758	0661	1
TODD FREDERICK	COL	0-0264384	0564	3
TODD GEORGE	CW2	W-2120647	1046	1
TODD GROVER C JR	LTC	0-1558217	0865	1
TODD HARRISON T	COL	0-0238134	0665	3
TODD HARRY E	MAJ	0-0553070	1163	1
TODD HOWARD P	CW4	W-2145011	0766	1
TODD IVAN U	CW3	W-2104535	1057	1
TODD JACK R	COL	0-0405963	0461	1
TODD JAMES C	LTC	0-0182564	0854	1
TODD JAMES D	LTC	0-0178421	0753	3
TODD JESS D	CW2	W-2214790	0667	1
TODD JOHN A	LTC	0-0315923	0146	2
TODD JOHN E	CPT	0-1926572	0264	1
TODD JOSEPH W JR	LTC	0-0957243	0667	1
TODD MARTILLUS	COL	0-0205534	0251	3
TODD MYRON G	MAJ	0-1535097	0461	1
TODD RALPH L	LTC	0-0327459	0757	1
TODD ROBERT E	1LT	0-0416007	0644	2
TODD ROLAND H	COL	0-0117203	0648	3
TODD RONALD E	MAJ	0-2021197	0767	1
TODD SAMUEL P	COL	0-0168693	0648	3
TODD WILLIAM B	CPT	0-0387816	1045	2
TODD WILLIAM J	LTC	0-1336452	1266	1
TODD WILLIAM M SR	MAJ	0-1300416	0957	2
TODD WILLIAM S	MAJ	0-0981612	1064	1
TODISH FRANK O	CW2	W-2114629	0948	2
TODOROFF ALEXANDER	LTC	0-0450601	1058	1
TOEPFER ELVERA L	CPT	N-0758292	1048	2
TOEWE CLINTON H	CPT	0-1695816	1145	2
TOEWS HELENA	1LT	N-0743929	0548	1
TOFFT LEROY E	MAJ	0-0476898	0954	1
TOGERSON ROBERT F	COL	0-0451427	0763	1
TOHER PAUL V	MAJ	0-0507243	0754	1
TOHILL DON O	MAJ	0-1822339	1059	2
TOIA MATTHEW J	COL	0-0323034	0163	1
TOIVANEN WAYNE T	LTC	0-1945968	0167	3
TOKER JOHN R	MAJ	0-1314853	0461	1
TOKLE ALF S	LTC	0-1011438	0164	1
TOKUDA SEIKO	MAJ	0-1923048	1166	1
TOKUSHIGE WILLIAM T	MAJ	0-2262213	0865	1
TOLAN HAROLD J	LTC	0-0488616	0865	3
TOLAR DOUGLAS S	1LT	0-0407751	0644	2
TOLAR FREDERICK	CPT	0-0242331	0346	2
TOLAR GRAY W	LTC	0-1575600	1055	1
TOLAR JAMES W	MAJ	0-1291727	0760	1
TOLAR WILLIAM F	COL	0-0264286	0160	3
TOLBERT CHARLES C	LTC	0-1043243	0461	1
TOLBERT MARTHA S	LTC	L-0402344	0967	1
TOLBERT SANTFORD C	CW2	W-2206301	1160	1
TOLBERT THOMAS N	CW3	W-3150546	1067	1
TOLCES FRANCIS T	LTC	0-1797748	0367	3
TOLCH WIENAND A	CPT	0-1845804	0864	1
TOLEDO HENRY A	CW2	W-2209092	1165	1
TOLENTINO LUCIO	2LT	0-1896728	1048	2
TOLER CARLYN G	MAJ	0-1797909	0260	1
TOLER JAMES P JR	LTC	0-0143319	0957	3
TOLER MELVYN C	CPT	0-1312095	1166	2
TOLER WILLIAM A	1LT	0-1318723	0345	2
TOLIN HAROLD C	CW2	W-2210430	0366	1
TOLIN ROY W	LTC	0-0240325	0465	3
TOLIN WILLIAM G	CW3	W-2147992	1264	2
TOLINE CLARENCE A	MAJ	0-0192917	0356	3
TOLINS RICHARD B	1LT	0-1176526	0945	2
TOLIVER CHARLES A	COL	0-0411630	1060	1
TOLIVER EMERY H	CPT	0-2262296	1159	1
TOLIVER JAMES T	LTC	0-0363225	0261	1
TOLL ROBERT M	COL	0-0367898	0764	1
TOLLE BONNIE E	MAJ	N-0727745	1163	3
TOLLE CECIL E	LTC	0-0335688	0648	3
TOLLE JOHN F	MAJ	0-0225470	0363	3
TOLLE ROBERT E	LTC	0-1290500	0561	1
TOLLEFSON ALVIN G	2LT	0-1825083	0745	2

ARMY OF THE UNITED STATES RETIRED LIST

NAME	GRADE	SVC NO	DATE RET MO YR	RET CODE
TOLLEFSON CHARLES I	LTC	0-1169768	0561	1
TOLLEFSON GEORGE F	1LT	0-1291356	0445	2
TOLLEFSON JOHN L	1LT	0-5700277	0362	2
TOLLEFSON MAYNARD	CPT	0-0295757	0945	2
TOLLEFSON WILLIAM G	COL	0-0455427	0960	1
TOLLER VIRGIL C	COL	0-0267887	0364	3
TOLLETT H T EARL JR	MAJ	0-2014686	0465	1
TOLLEY WAYNE	LTC	0-0279905	0268	3
TOLLISON CHARLES H	CPT	0-2006514	0558	1
TOLLISON FRANK J	LTC	0-1541004	0157	1
TOLMAN HUGH H	COL	0-0137477	1048	3
TOLMAN KENNETH W	CPT	0-0510486	0557	1
TOLMAN WILLIAM J	MAJ	0-1330985	1263	1
TOLNAS OLAF J	LTC	0-0106233	0450	3
TOLOCKA FRANK J	LTC	0-1303431	0367	1
TOLSON CARL L	1LT	0-1325607	0959	1
TOLSON CHARLES G	LTC	0-0272040	1164	3
TOLTZIEN FRITZ J	MAJ	0-1181168	1162	1
TOM CLYDE F	MAJ	0-0247828	1155	3
TOM HENRY K	COL	0-0256386	0567	3
TOM KIUNG F	LTC	0-0383866	0964	3
TOMA JOHN J	LTC	0-0349907	0146	2
TOMAJA ALFREDO	1LT	0-0935647	1148	1
TOMAN GEORGE J	LTC	0-0326240	0146	2
TOMAN JOHN J	COL	0-0359426	0560	1
TOMAN WILLIE A	CW2	W-2149680	0957	1
TOMANEK JOSEPH J	MAJ	0-0333292	0968	3
TOMARCHIO JOHN A	1LT	0-1318236	0146	2
TOMASEK CHARLES A	CPT	0-0161260	0648	3
TOMASELLO THERON R	1LT	0-1304819	1145	2
TOMASIK EDMUND J	COL	0-0373015	1162	1
TOMASINI SILVIO R	CW3	W-2148613	0763	1
TOMASKO JOHN M	CW2	W-2146533	0562	1
TOMASKO ROBERT L	CW2	W-3430314	0268	1
TOMASKY STANLEY	CPT	0-1041039	1064	1
TOMASOLO MICHAEL A	MAJ	0-1041251	0960	1
TOMAW DELLIE W	LTC	0-1055173	0462	2
TOMAYKO VAL A	COL	0-0933950	0468	1
TOMBERG JOSEPH J	CPT	0-1167673	0147	2
TOMBERLIN KNAPP A	MAJ	0-1588923	0361	1
TOMBERLIN WILLIAM P	MAJ	0-2204453	0366	1
TOMEI VINCENT C	LTC	0-1796186	1059	1
TOMER ABRAHAM	CW3	W-2149310	0161	1
TOMES GEORGE J	CW2	W-2119294	0857	1
TOMES JAMES B	MAJ	0-1926939	0268	1
TOMES ROBERT L JR	1LT	0-0442619	0945	2
TOMEY JACK P	CW4	W-2146556	0467	1
TOMHAVE ALFRED W	CW4	W-2145758	0868	1
TOMICH JOHN J	CPT	0-1593890	0246	2
TOMKIES DOUGLAS C	LTC	0-0157263	1056	3
TOMKINSON ROBERT L	LTC	0-0375590	0263	1
TOMLIN JACK L	MAJ	0-1252256	0856	1
TOMLIN MERRILL	CW4	W-2003327	1065	3
TOMLINSON CHARLES H	LTC	0-1038871	1164	1
TOMLINSON FLEET	1LT	0-0214013	0842	2
TOMLINSON FLOYD L	MAJ	0-1050957	1164	1
TOMLINSON GILBERT E	CPT	0-1177462	0162	3
TOMLINSON GORDON L	CPT	0-1535545	0947	2
TOMLINSON HOWARD J	LTC	0-0326706	0961	3
TOMLINSON LYNN C	MAJ	0-1295796	1157	1
TOMLINSON SAMUEL A J	LTC	0-0916145	0464	3
TOMLINSON WALDO B	CW3	W-2205993	0566	1
TOMLINSON WALTER G	MAJ	0-0178660	0949	1
TOMPKINS CHARLES E	COL	0-0423211	1053	1
TOMPKINS CLARK W	2LT	0-1013733	0344	2
TOMPKINS CLINTON S	LTC	0-0279740	0968	3
TOMPKINS GEORGE H	LTC	0-0239096	1264	3
TOMPKINS HARVEY J	COL	0-0312806	0766	3
TOMPKINS JOHN W	CW4	W-2144000	0568	2
TOMPKINS L L	CPT	0-0971328	0261	1
TOMPKINS LELAND V	MAJ	0-1549854	0266	1
TOMPKINS MAURICE F	MAJ	0-1333564	0363	1
TOMPKINS ROBERT O	1LT	0-1312731	1045	2
TOMPKINS SMITH H	LTC	0-0260103	1045	2
TOMPLAIT BENNET J	WO1	W-2116977	0245	2

NAME	GRADE	SVC NO	DATE RET MO YR	RET CODE
TOMPSETT ELLIOT W	MAJ	0-0270092	1267	3
TOMS RAYMOND W	LTC	0-0284870	0960	3
TOMS ROBERT W C	CPT	0-1544898	0954	1
TOMS ROYCE I	CPT	0-2034767	0464	1
TOMSU EDWARD M	MAJ	0-0570552	0861	2
TONDERYS WILLIAM F	MAJ	0-1994862	0361	1
TONDRO LYMAN W	LTC	0-0353134	0846	2
TONER JAMES I	LTC	0-1639736	0558	1
TONER JOSEPH P	1LT	0-1688626	0854	2
TONETTI SERGE	LTC	0-1035059	0262	1
TONEY AUDY E	MAJ	0-0238353	1063	3
TONEY ROBERT M	COL	0-0263101	0967	3
TONG WONG K	1LT	0-1596833	1045	2
TONGE MANER L	MAJ	0-0218315	0446	2
TONGE RAPHAEL F	CPT	0-0341699	0544	2
TONJES FREDERICK	MAJ	0-1042972	0258	1
TONKIN WARREN G	CPT	0-1012499	0947	2
TONKS PAUL B	COL	0-0393770	1060	1
TONSING ERNEST F	LTC	0-0527549	0868	3
TONSING FREDERICK	MAJ	0-1932138	1068	1
TOOHEY JAMES W	CW3	W-2147139	1063	1
TOOHEY JOHN T	CW3	W-2132954	0762	1
TOOHY JOHN P	1LT	0-0464428	1142	2
TOOKE AUTHEP D	CW3	W-2146718	0160	1
TOOLE DON P	MAJ	0-0168350	0145	2
TOOLE MACK	LTC	0-1633598	1263	1
TOOLE THOMAS E	CPT	0-0307086	1044	2
TOOLEY FRANCIS L JR	1LT	0-1032771	0146	2
TOOLEY ROY	CW4	W-2107879	1157	1
TOOLIN EDWARD V	MAJ	0-0998395	0363	1
TOOLIN JOSEPH P	LTC	0-0305594	0968	3
TOOLIN PAUL V	COL	0-0249900	0864	3
TOOMER FRANK	CPT	0-0421454	0447	1
TOOMEY HENRY J	COL	0-0102043	0553	3
TOOMEY SAMUEL K JR	COL	0-0306071	0264	1
TOOMEY WILLIAM F	CPT	0-0384007	0644	2
TOOMOTH FREDRIC B	CPT	0-1575230	0859	1
TOON JAMES A	COL	0-0139744	1154	3
TOONE FERD E	LTC	0-0201371	0763	3
TOOTHACKER WILLIAM S	LTC	0-0271889	0967	3
TOOTHAKER GILBERT E	MAJ	0-1636743	0960	1
TOOZE LAMAR	M G	0-0107927	0257	3
TOOZE VICTOR A	MAJ	0-0264902	0547	2
TOPACIO CONRADO S	LTC	0-0500448	1262	1
TOPCHIK ALFRED	MAJ	0-1545295	0762	1
TOPCIK HARRY A	LTC	0-0296635	0963	3
TOPE BILLY J	LTC	0-1055482	0567	1
TOPE GEORGE W	WO1	W-2110012	0561	2
TOPE HENRY P	CPT	0-0502406	0349	1
TOPFER KIMMETT	MAJ	0-2002553	1060	1
TOPHAM VERNON C	1LT	0-1323759	1159	1
TOPIC GEORGE L	MAJ	0-1341600	0566	1
TOPLEY EARL J	CPT	0-1103976	0663	3
TOPOLOSKY HARRY W	1LT	0-0494804	1043	2
TOPP JOHN S JR	1LT	0-1285665	0146	2
TOPP WILLIAM F	CPT	0-1894968	0240	2
TOPPEN ROBERT P	1LT	0-1288819	0245	2
TOPPER FREDRICK B	LTC	0-1294935	0661	1
TOPPER GEORGE E	CW2	W-2102747	1055	1
TOPPING FRANCIS E JR	1LT	0-1314693	0945	2
TOPPING WALTER A	COL	0-0168191	0859	3
TOPPING WALTER S	MAJ	0-1297278	1047	2
TORBERSON CHRISTIAN	MAJ	0-0221317	0648	3
TORBERT ALFRED S	CW4	W-2136651	0865	1
TORBERT MAX H	LTC	0-0266002	0449	1
TORBETT DAVID S	2LT	0-4005383	0254	2
TORCELLINI L J	CPT	0-1311099	0-48	2
TOREN OSCAR F	2LT	0-1635414	0944	2
TORGAN EMERSON A	CPT	0-0336416	1044	2
TORGERSON BLAIR H	1LT	0-0350893	0545	2
TORGERSON ELIZABET	1LT	N-0790753	0947	1
TORGERSON JAMES E	LTC	0-1018782	0163	1
TORGERSON JEROME H	LTC	0-1823521	0361	1
TORGERSON LEO C	LTC	0-2007606	0968	1
TORGERSON WALLACE O	MAJ	0-1633599	0963	1

NAME	GRADE	SVC NO	DATE RET MO YR	RET CODE
TORIE ALEX D	LTC	0-0189423	1157	3
TORKELSON GLEN R	MAJ	0-1315240	0165	1
TORMEY JACK C	2LT	0-0413807	0343	2
TORMEY LOUIS P	MAJ	0-0304162	0668	3
TORMEY PAUL W	CPT	0-0286243	1168	3
TORMEY THOMAS J	2LT	0-1997637	0246	2
TORN ELMORE R	LTC	0-0249441	0766	3
TORNABENE ANTHONY J	CW2	W-2214542	1168	1
TORO-PEREZ JUAN E JR	CW2	W-2213447	1067	1
TORJIAN EDWARD	MAJ	0-0886439	1158	1
TORQUATI ROBERT	CW3	W-2206885	0766	1
TORR ALBERT E	CPT	0-1309444	0447	2
TORRANCE CHARLES C	MAJ	0-0222521	0444	2
TORRANCE HUGH F	LTC	0-0454432	1063	1
TORRE FRANCIS V	LTC	0-1554651	1262	1
TORRES ARCADIO	MAJ	0-0276773	0567	3
TORRES ERASMO	1LT	0-2263228	0657	1
TORRES JOSE M	1LT	0-0217523	0841	1
TORRES LOUIS J	MAJ	0-0986711	0968	1
TORRES MANUEL	1LT	0-1293677	0350	1
TORRES MIGUEL A	CW4	W-2102475	0656	1
TORRES PABLO P	MAJ	0-1115133	0660	1
TORRES SIFREDC	LTC	0-0183916	0260	3
TORRES WALTER	COL	0-0414841	0664	3
TORRES-RODRIGUE CON	MAJ	0-1328773	1063	1
TORRES-RODRIGUE WEN	CW2	W-2007831	1166	1
TORREY JIM A	MAJ	0-0299057	0766	3
TORREY MELVIN L	MAJ	0-0961819	0266	1
TORRUELLA JUAN N JR	MAJ	0-0240635	0444	2
TORSANI GUIDO P	LTC	0-0985674	0668	1
TORSON HAROLD L	LTC	0-0947277	1267	1
TORTORELLA SALVATORE	MAJ	0-1585013	0565	1
TORTORICE RICHARD J	CW2	W-3154096	1267	2
TORWICK OLIVER F	2LT	0-1577964	0444	2
TOSCANO GLADYCE A	CPT	N-0783207	0546	1
TOSCO WILLIAM	MAJ	0-1312361	0662	1
TOSH VERNIE D	MAJ	0-1332887	1062	2
TOSONOTTI EDWARD H	2LT	0-1695619	0146	2
TOSSY PAUL G	LTC	0-0219070	0462	3
TOTH DAVID JR	LTC	0-1053895	1162	1
TOTH JULIUS J	COL	0-0450328	0761	1
TOTH LOUIS L	LTC	0-1288468	0960	1
TOTH VICTOR N	MAJ	0-1112480	0964	1
TOTH WILLIAM A	MAJ	0-0139684	0450	1
TOTHACER AUSTIN J	COL	0-0395453	0864	1
TOTMAN OTTO L	COL	0-0123891	1054	3
TOTOLO CHRISTOPHE	MAJ	0-1107724	0662	1
TOTTEN HAROLD K	1LT	0-1109715	0146	2
TOTTEN HENRY R	LTC	0-0170883	1152	3
TOTTEN JOHN E	LTC	0-1303576	1267	1
TOTTEN LAWRENCE E	LTC	0-0262046	0965	3
TOTTEN SAMUEL A	1LT	0-0291456	0945	2
TOTZ BEVERLY	CPT	N-0767816	0947	1
TOUCHET ALBERT W	MAJ	0-0481930	0154	1
TOUCHETTE ALCIDE A	CPT	0-0341173	0144	1
TOUEY JAMES A	LTC	0-1011485	0758	1
TOUGH TRACY N	LTC	0-0278171	0663	3
TOUKATLIAN VICTORIA	CPT	N-0724441	0961	2
TOUNGE HARRY G	CPT	0-1685358	1045	2
TOUPS ARTHUR L	LTC	0-0473235	0350	1
TOUPS JOSEPH C	LTC	0-1045615	0263	1
TOURTLOTT DERLESS J	CW2	W-2149242	1162	2
TOURVILLE BERNARD J	LTC	0-1000189	0658	1
TOURVILLE CLARENCE W	LTC	0-0287013	0166	3
TOURVILLE HENRY M	COL	0-0260613	0166	3
TOURVILLE KENNETH H	CPT	0-0291566	1052	2
TOURVILLE LESLIE M	1LT	0-1324856	0546	2
TOUSEY BERTLAND J	LTC	0-0280792	0568	3
TOUSEY THOMAS F	1LT	0-1914365	1022	2
TOUSSAINT ROBERT C	1LT	0-1591483	1148	2
TOW ANNABELLE	CPT	N-0737625	0947	1
TOWARD PERCY	COL	0-0278175	1056	3
TOWBER PAUL Z	MAJ	0-1822341	1058	1
TOWE LONNIE E	CW2	W-2152632	0461	1
TOWELL ANNE M	1LT	L-0125010	0845	2

NAME	GRADE	SVC NO	DATE RET MO YR	RET CODE
TOWER HERBERT E	1LT	0-1325949	0146	2
TOWER MARCUS P	1LT	0-1686183	0446	2
TOWER MERLE J	MAJ	0-0347476	0662	3
TOWERS EDWARD J	COL	0-0102160	0648	3
TOWERS JOSEPH A	CPT	0-1167674	0546	2
TOWERS WILBUR E	CW2	W-2122314	1045	2
TOWERY EUGENE S JR	CPT	0-0420107	0545	2
TOWERY LUTHER E	LTC	0-1168952	0560	1
TOWEY ANN E	MAJ	N-0775834	0449	2
TOWEY REX W	1LT	0-1110299	0146	2
TOWLE GEORGE	MAJ	0-0402882	1046	2
TOWLE RICHARD B	CW3	W-2105804	0560	1
TOWLE VICTOR M	MAJ	0-0511537	0446	2
TOWLER BERTHA E	2LT	N-0702665	0539	1
TOWLER WILLIAM A JR	CPT	0-0293439	1067	3
TOWLES ALTON M	MAJ	0-0215479	0863	3
TOWLES FREDDIE B	CPT	0-1300233	1048	2
TOWN CARLES H	MAJ	0-1179652	0161	1
TOWN EDWARD A	MAJ	0-0197900	0261	3
TOWN LEE E	CPT	0-1013859	1058	1
TOWNE CEDRIC C	MAJ	0-1040628	0760	1
TOWNE CHARLES E	COL	0-0371706	0766	3
TOWNE EUGENE M	LTC	0-0556742	0766	1
TOWNE MAURICE H JR	LTC	0-0938197	0866	1
TOWNE VERL E	MAJ	0-1181171	0959	1
TOWNLEY CLYDE W	1LT	0-1285141	0947	2
TOWNLEY GEOFFREY J	CPT	0-0363239	1143	2
TOWNLEY PAUL	2LT	0-1996629	0757	1
TOWNS EDWARD B	COL	0-0161739	0855	3
TOWNSAN NICHOLAS R	LTC	0-1557382	0866	1
TOWNSEND AARON E	CW3	W-2154672	1159	1
TOWNSEND ALAN C	CW4	W-2145759	0857	1
TOWNSEND ALBERT S	COL	0-0162429	0951	3
TOWNSEND ARTHUR M	CPT	0-2263798	0762	1
TOWNSEND BENJAMIN O	LTC	0-0988100	0868	1
TOWNSEND C A JR	MAJ	0-0374692	0460	1
TOWNSEND CLIFFORD	LTC	0-1000190	0157	1
TOWNSEND CLIFFORD O	CW2	W-2123330	1054	1
TOWNSEND DARRELL J	MAJ	0-1641018	1160	1
TOWNSEND DAVID W	MAJ	0-0121732	0-49	3
TOWNSEND FRANCIS M	CPT	0-0449253	0447	2
TOWNSEND GEORGE F JR	LTC	0-1036411	0864	1
TOWNSEND HAROLD L	LTC	0-0168943	1056	2
TOWNSEND HENRY J	LTC	0-0331846	0166	3
TOWNSEND JACK H	1LT	0-0423531	1044	2
TOWNSEND JAMES H	LTC	0-0401418	0346	2
TOWNSEND JAMES L	LTC	0-1180369	0360	1
TOWNSEND JAMES N	CW3	W-2206048	1166	1
TOWNSEND JAMES R	CW3	W-2203545	0765	1
TOWNSEND JAMES S	LTC	0-1030847	1162	1
TOWNSEND JAMES S	1LT	0-1302235	0546	2
TOWNSEND JAMES V	MAJ	0-2288313	1160	1
TOWNSEND JAY G	COL	0-0175043	0254	3
TOWNSEND JOHN L	MAJ	0-1946628	0255	1
TOWNSEND JOHN O	1LT	0-0914712	0546	2
TOWNSEND KEITH E	1LT	0-1634408	0246	2
TOWNSEND LINCOLN H	LTC	0-1550940	0164	1
TOWNSEND LLOYD W	WO1	W-2003833	0252	2
TOWNSEND OSCAR B	LTC	0-0917937	1064	3
TOWNSEND RAYMOND B	MAJ	0-0270661	0861	3
TOWNSEND ROBERT	MAJ	0-0225498	0644	2
TOWNSEND SHERWOOD M	2LT	0-1081039	0344	2
TOWNSEND THOMAS H	LTC	0-1583776	0563	2
TOWNSEND WAYNE W	LTC	0-0279609	0457	3
TOWNSEND WILSON L	COL	0-0201238	1150	3
TOWNSON KENNETH C	B G	0-0163716	0949	3
TOWSON FRANCES A	MAJ	L-0600259	0567	1
TOWSON JAMES R	MAJ	0-0966081	0163	1
TOY JOSEPH C	COL	0-0300023	0560	1
TOY WILLIAM K	LTC	0-1298587	1160	1
TOYAMA NOBUYOSHI	MAJ	0-2263462	0666	1
TOYE JOSEPH J	MAJ	0-0468543	0446	2
TOYN WILSON O	CW3	W-2120536	0754	1
TOYNBEE CHARLES M	COL	0-0240002	1157	3
TOYODA SUSUMU	MAJ	0-2023656	1262	1

NAME	GRADE	SVC NO	DATE RET MO YR	RET CODE
TOZER EDWARD J	LTC	0-2262889	0368	1
TOZIER ALLAN W	LTC	0-1309629	1166	1
TOZIER GEORGE O	MAJ	0-1592664	0761	1
TOZZI GEORGE A	MAJ	0-1107726	0562	1
TRABER EUGENE F	CPT	0-0341822	0868	3
TRACEY DAVID J	MAJ	0-1305136	1058	2
TRACEY JACK M	CW4	W-2004325	1063	3
TRACEY JOHN C	COL	0-0206883	1057	3
TRACEY THOMAS H	COL	0-0121871	0254	3
TRACEY WILLIAM F	CPT	0-1689767	0564	2
TRACH BENEDICT	CPT	0-1700855	1044	2
TRACHSEL DAVID	CW2	W-2150628	0359	1
TRACHTENBERG ISRAEL	CPT	0-1690398	0546	2
TRACHTENBERG L	1LT	0-1046671	0744	2
TRACY ALFRED H	LTC	0-0263208	0263	3
TRACY CHARLES G	LTC	0-0263372	0867	3
TRACY DONALD E	CPT	0-1053849	0546	2
TRACY DONALD J	LTC	0-0958085	0868	1
TRACY ELMER E	CW3	W-2005857	0266	1
TRACY EUGENE R	MAJ	0-0943386	0665	1
TRACY FRANK L	LTC	0-0331874	0864	3
TRACY GEORGE T	MAJ	0-4010777	1167	1
TRACY HORTON H JR	LTC	0-0249542	1166	3
TRACY JAMES K	1LT	0-1323632	1045	2
TRACY JIM E	LTC	0-1013293	0563	1
TRACY JOHN	CPT	0-0428253	0754	1
TRACY JOHN F	LTC	0-1050119	0667	1
TRACY JOHN F	MAJ	0-1303798	1165	1
TRACY JULIA R	MAJ	N-0755045	0365	3
TRACY NATHAN B	CPT	0-0450600	0556	1
TRACY NEAL H	1LT	0-1194318	0147	2
TRACY NORMAN S	LTC	0-1319683	0663	1
TRACY RICHARD L	CW3	W-2147575	1264	1
TRACY ROBERT W	LTC	0-1286035	0860	1
TRACY WARREN	CPT	0-1116322	0346	2
TRACY WINTON G	LTC	0-0332318	0363	3
TRADER PAUL F	MAJ	0-1999973	1060	1
TRADUP EARL E	CW3	W-2209042	0368	1
TRAEGER CARL F	LTC	0-1577967	0961	1
TRAFFORD GEORGE H	LTC	0-1285142	0658	2
TRAFTON STANLEY M	CW3	W-2208655	0867	1
TRAGER LAWRENCE	2LT	0-2008445	0246	2
TRAGESER PAUL J	1LT	0-2040915	1045	2
TRAGESSER JAMES E	LTC	0-1342019	1068	1
TRAGLE HENRY I	LTC	0-1012511	0264	1
TRAHAN JOSEPH E R	CPT	0-1575233	1156	1
TRAIL DURAN E	CW3	W-2142909	1059	2
TRAIN J LEWIS	COL	0-0301080	1064	3
TRAINA PHILIP	COL	0-0499622	1066	1
TRAINER TREVLYN	LTC	0-0285730	0459	1
TRAINOR CHARLES E JR	1LT	0-1302552	0246	2
TRAINOR CHARLES F	LTC	0-0259537	1167	3
TRAINOR CHARLES F	CW2	W-2152409	0661	1
TRAINOR JAMES F	LTC	0-0207741	1153	3
TRAINOR JOHN T	CW3	W-2147592	0567	1
TRAINOR KATHLEEN M	MAJ	L-0116546	0565	3
TRAINOR PAUL W	MAJ	0-1917722	1163	1
TRAINOR PETER J	CW3	W-2148539	0765	1
TRAMMELL CLAUDE W	2LT	0-1566977	0645	2
TRAMMELL JACK R	1LT	0-2268000	0556	2
TRAMMELL JOHN M	MAJ	0-2016567	0562	1
TRAMMELL JOSEPH E	CW4	W-2003371	1265	1
TRAMMELL WILLIAM H	COL	0-0311646	0546	2
TRAMONTI ALBERT	1LT	0-0298377	0561	3
TRANBERGER CARL	CPT	0-0161742	0648	3
TRANK DAVID	CPT	0-0491227	0449	1
TRANTER CHARLES J	LTC	0-1041462	0861	1
TRAPANI ALPHONSO M	CW2	W-2119733	0946	2
TRAPMAN MIKE A	COL	0-0255282	1265	3
TRAPNELL ERNEST L	LTC	0-1062748	1163	1
TRAPP FRITZ C	1LT	0-0551222	0945	2
TRAPP VERN F	2LT	0-1308023	0744	2
TRAPP WALTER S	LTC	0-1550714	0764	1
TRAPP WILLIAM E	LTC	0-1923038	1268	1
TRASHER JOSEPH E	CW2	W-2142207	0756	1
TRASK BURTON W	LTC	0-0307510	0564	3
TRASK EVERETT P	CPT	0-0981985	0261	1
TRASK FLORENCE	MAJ	M-0000663	0263	3
TRASK ROBERT W	1LT	0-1018157	1148	2
TRASK SAMUEL G	LTC	0-0307542	0360	1
TRASK VICTOR M	LTC	0-0218152	0163	3
TRASTER HARRY B	CPT	0-0523244	1046	2
TRATHEN ROBERT O	LTC	0-1035385	1057	1
TRATZ ROBERT F	MAJ	0-1551973	0561	1
TRAUB JOHN L	MAJ	0-0256225	1066	3
TRAUBE LIONEL JR	2LT	0-1821653	0843	2
TRAUBE MARTIN H	CW4	W-2110599	0364	3
TRAUCHT FRANK J	MAJ	0-0336191	0166	3
TRAUGOTT EDGAR H	LTC	0-1324301	0767	1
TRAUPANE PHILIP E	MAJ	0-0970834	0866	1
TRAURIG MAX R	COL	0-0309452	0558	3
TRAUSNECK WILLIAM M	CPT	0-1046971	0446	2
TRAUTMAN FRANK J	MAJ	0-0287539	0260	3
TRAUTMAN FRANK W	CW3	W-2101103	1054	1
TRAUTMAN JEAN E	MAJ	0-1638681	1057	2
TRAUTMAN RAY L	COL	0-0281135	0867	3
TRAUTMANN PHYLLIS F	MAJ	N-0730049	0367	3
TRAVELSTEAD CLYDE	LTC	0-0238627	1061	3
TRAVER GEORGE C	COL	0-0209945	0849	3
TRAVER HAROLD E	CW3	W-2152185	0663	2
TRAVER JAMES R	CW3	W-2209821	0168	2
TRAVER PERRY C	COL	0-0121873	1045	2
TRAVER WALLACE H JR	LTC	0-0750892	0967	1
TRAVERS HAROLD C	LTC	0-0188986	0359	3
TRAVERS JOHN H JR	COL	0-0258655	0747	2
TRAVERS JOSEPH H	COL	0-0181934	0360	3
TRAVERS MILTON P	MAJ	0-0485782	0746	2
TRAVERS WILLIAM J	MAJ	0-2048177	0461	1
TRAVINSKI ROBERT W	1LT	0-5219654	0665	2
TRAVIS ARTHUR L	LTC	0-1168953	0761	1
TRAVIS DONALD A	MAJ	0-2053939	1054	1
TRAVIS ELDRED G	2LT	0-1312363	1144	2
TRAVIS ELROY W	1LT	0-1325340	0246	2
TRAVIS FRANCIS J	WO1	W-2108869	0868	2
TRAVIS GEORGE M	2LT	0-1317057	0245	2
TRAVIS JAMES E	LTC	0-0257604	0560	3
TRAVIS JOHN W	CPT	0-1641868	0146	2
TRAVIS MARY H	1LT	N-0773273	0146	2
TRAVIS PAUL W	CPT	0-0360820	0746	2
TRAVIS ROBERT H	CPT	0-0186633	0555	3
TRAVIS SAMUEL H	CW3	W-2144679	1262	1
TRAVIS SIDNEY E	LTC	0-1574549	0558	1
TRAVIS STANLEY E	LTC	0-0281855	0964	3
TRAWEEK WALTER W	1LT	0-1017049	0446	2
TRAWICK HENRY E	CPT	0-0959336	0161	1
TRAXLER DENVER W	COL	0-0220427	0262	3
TRAXLER ROBERT M	LTC	0-0343767	0955	1
TRAYLOR BOBBIE O	CW3	W-2208414	0267	1
TRAYLOR FRED R	1LT	0-1297617	0645	2
TRAYLOR PASCHAL E	CW3	W-2141472	1059	1
TRAYNER JOSEPH E	CPT	0-0276761	1267	3
TRAYNOR ANDREW F	MAJ	0-2050984	0557	1
TRAYNOR ARCHIE R SR	LTC	0-0359878	0157	1
TRAYNOR ARTHUR R	CPT	0-1015904	0953	2
TRAYNOR BOYD K	CW3	W-2118411	1154	1
TRAYNOR CLIFFORD J	LTC	0-1100802	0663	1
TRAYNOR JAMES A	LTC	0-0481239	0946	2
TRAYNOR PATRICK E	MAJ	0-1549146	0952	1
TRCALEK BENNIE F	2LT	0-1184319	0945	2
TREACY ANDREW J	CPT	0-0377306	1065	3
TREADAWAY STEPHEN T	MAJ	0-0962236	0861	1
TREADO BEN	LTC	0-0212071	0852	3
TREADO CLARENCE E	CPT	0-1951720	0260	2
TREADWAY CHARLES L	MAJ	0-1310788	0258	1
TREADWAY FRANK L	LTC	0-0901976	1068	3
TREADWAY RAYMOND R	MAJ	0-1036773	0459	1
TREADWAY WILLIAM E	COL	0-0286528	0162	3
TREADWELL BILL V	1LT	0-2212040	0852	2
TREADWELL CLEO A	LTC	0-0352823	0362	3
TREADWELL EDWIN H	2LT	0-1101693	1143	2
TREADWELL FRANCIS A	MAJ	0-2201439	0562	1
TREADWELL FRANK L	MAJ	0-0985487	1167	1
TREADWELL JAMES H W	LTC	0-0377467	0461	1
TREANOR JAMES J	MAJ	0-0910260	0246	2
TREANOR ROBERT L	1LT	0-1336843	0148	2
TREAS EARL W	CPT	0-0172537	0852	3
TREASH RICHARD B	LTC	0-0453106	1165	1
TREAT DONALD E	MAJ	0-2014520	1066	1
TREBBE CHARLES F JR	LTC	0-0967524	0967	1
TREBILCOCK GEORGE R	LTC	0-1316246	0863	1
TRECK ANTHONY S	CW4	W-2120921	0157	1
TREDE ARDO C	LTC	0-1054144	0263	1
TREDE NORMAN H	LTC	0-0958068	0868	1
TREDWAY WILLIAM H	CW3	W-2148774	0165	1
TREECE FRANCIS O	1LT	0-0370545	1046	2
TREECE LAWRENCE G	B G	0-0291041	1265	3
TREES HOWARD J	COL	0-0242717	0265	3
TREFETHEN HAROLD P	COL	0-0347385	0264	3
TREFFINGER GLENN R	LTC	0-0336469	0562	3
TREFFRY HARRY R	LTC	0-1289652	0463	1
TREGO LAWRENCE O	2LT	0-1597150	0851	2
TREIBER KENNETH L	LTC	0-0299711	0668	3
TREIBLE JOHN F	MAJ	0-0980410	0166	1
TREITLER PAUL	CPT	0-1002845	1047	2
TRELOGGEN CLYDE H	MAJ	0-0475013	0748	1
TRELSTAD BERTRAM L	MAJ	0-0326090	0146	2
TREMAINE MYRON J	B G	0-0336516	1066	3
TREMARELLO JOSEPH	MAJ	0-0266472	0757	1
TREMAYNE ROTH L	1LT	N-0785599	1048	2
TREMBATH WILLIAM R	CW4	W-2000509	1059	3
TREMBLAY DONALD A	MAJ	0-2200006	0766	1
TREMBLAY HENRY C	MAJ	0-0227002	0245	2
TREMBLAY JOHN F JR	MAJ	0-1080249	0561	1
TREMBLAY LEO A	CW3	W-2144278	0660	1
TREMBLAY TELESPHOR	1LT	0-2005942	0857	1
TREMOLADA SERGIO J	LTC	0-1590226	1162	1
TREMPER CHARLES E	MAJ	0-0476265	0761	1
TRENAM ARTHUR L	MAJ	0-0885512	1158	1
TRENAM MILTON E	CPT	0-0258028	1065	3
TRENARY HORACE I	MAJ	0-0196121	0163	3
TRENT GALE SR	MAJ	0-2033235	0161	1
TRENT RACHEL F	1LT	N-0757715	0546	1
TRENT RALPH W	LTC	0-0276420	0465	3
TRENT ROBERT L	MAJ	0-0352656	1160	1
TRENT ROBERT L	MAJ	0-0969627	1262	1
TRENT THEODORE R	MAJ	0-1120224	0167	1
TRENTINE ARTHUR J	CW2	W-2145259	1061	1
TREPPARD CHARLES E	WO1	W-2125442	1044	2
TRESCA WILLIAM W	CPT	0-0420492	0546	2
TRESEDER DONALD W	LTC	0-0264617	0768	3
TRESENTE JOHN J	1LT	0-1046673	0545	2
TREU WILLIAM L	LTC	0-0180997	1060	3
TREUTEL ALFRED A	MAJ	0-0155713	1153	3
TREVERTON WARD R	COL	0-0280655	1168	3
TREVERTON WILLIAM M	MAJ	0-0250497	0367	3
TREVINO VICTOR O	CPT	0-1105872	0965	2
TREVOR EDWIN F	LTC	0-0246358	0365	3
TREVOR GLENN A	CPT	0-0198022	1044	2
TREVOR THOMAS W JR	1LT	0-1293678	1146	2
TREW RALPH L	LTC	0-1342314	0768	1
TREXLER CHARLES D	COL	0-0245135	0648	3
TREZISE EVERETT A	CPT	0-1341601	0860	1
TRIBBETT WILLIAM A	CW3	W-2203275	0261	1
TRIBBEY BURL P	MAJ	0-0251178	1145	2
TRIBBLE EDWIN	LTC	0-0917569	1046	2
TRIBBLE JAMES M	COL	0-0114844	0850	3
TRIBBLE WALTER W	2LT	0-0510149	0152	2
TRIBBY CHARLES H	LTC	0-1016438	0762	1
TRIBOO SHERWOOD G	LTC	0-0350613	0965	3
TRICE HERMAN M	LTC	0-1640084	0567	1
TRICE JAMES C	MAJ	0-2212094	0763	1
TRICE PETER A JR	CPT	0-1735706	0848	2
TRICE WILLIAM A JR	LTC	0-0408363	0363	1
TRICKETT CHARLES P	MAJ	0-2017306	0263	1
TRICKEY JOHN C	CPT	0-1913483	0462	1
TRICKLE LENOX E	COL	0-0181467	0556	3
TRICOMI JOSEPH N	MAJ	0-1553922	0761	1
TRIER LESTER A	MAJ	0-1041252	0146	2
TRIER OTIS M	LTC	0-1037936	0867	1
TRIESCH GUSTAVE M	COL	0-0252640	1153	3
TRIFILO SANTO S	1LT	0-0890305	0448	2
TRIGG WILLIAM G	LTC	0-1047811	1161	1
TRIGGER NORMAN	CPT	0-0478164	1048	1
TRIGGS WAYNE I	MAJ	0-2088138	0666	1
TRIGILIO RICHARD D	MAJ	0-2002555	0167	1
TRILLANCES BERNARDIN	CPT	0-1696513	0859	1
TRIM LEONARD H	CW2	W-2115203	0246	2
TRIM LOUIE H	MAJ	0-2018952	0760	1
TRIMBLE CARL E	LTC	0-0378628	0447	2
TRIMBLE FLOYD	LTC	0-0280521	0167	3
TRIMBLE GEORGE C	CW3	W-2206250	0966	1
TRIMBLE HARRY H	MAJ	0-1110302	0562	1
TRIMBLE HENRY J JR	CPT	0-0312127	0448	2
TRIMBLE HENRY W	LTC	0-0468146	0457	1
TRIMBLE HENRY W JR	1LT	0-0443921	0145	2
TRIMBLE KIRK F	1LT	0-1325175	0746	2
TRIMBLE MADISON E	LTC	0-0289567	1057	3
TRIMBLE WALTER E	CPT	0-0450928	0244	2
TRIMBLE WEBB W	LTC	0-0286228	0466	3
TRIMBY JAMES E	MAJ	0-1951721	1263	1
TRIMMER ROY J	MAJ	0-1555145	0461	1
TRIMPI ALLAN W	CPT	0-0527290	0854	2
TRINDAL GLEN W	LTC	0-0155591	0155	1
TRINDLE JOSEPH W	1LT	0-0426060	0346	2
TRINER JOSEPH	COL	0-0185724	1054	3
TRINGHESE DOMINECK C	CW2	W-2143975	0454	2
TRINIDAD JOSE M	CPT	0-0959393	0162	2
TRINKLEIN EUGENE F	LTC	0-2008875	1267	1
TRINKNER HENRY G	MAJ	0-2035899	1163	1
TRIPLETT CHARLES L	CW2	W-3430555	0468	1
TRIPLETT HARRY J	1LT	0-0964094	0453	2
TRIPLETT SAMUEL D JR	MAJ	0-0239639	0264	3
TRIPLETT VERLON D	MAJ	0-2262636	0262	1
TRIPLETT WILLIAM H	COL	0-0180128	0445	2
TRIPLETT WILLIAM J	LTC	0-0311841	1066	3
TRIPLETT WILLIAM J	MAJ	0-1876992	0565	1
TRIPLETT WILLOUGHBY	LTC	0-1165371	0962	1
TRIPLIT FRANK C	1LT	0-0885859	0553	1
TRIPODI ANTONIO	COL	0-0117927	0948	3
TRIPP BEVERLY H	LTC	0-1795996	1160	1
TRIPP CHARLIE C	1LT	0-1553766	0945	2
TRIPP EVERETT G	CPT	0-0121991	0653	3
TRIPP GEORGE W	COL	0-0299996	0157	3
TRIPP LOWELL O	LTC	0-1102508	0966	1
TRIPP NORTON M	MAJ	0-1799400	0564	1
TRIPP WILLIAM F	LTC	0-0252751	0365	3
TRIPP WILLIAM R	LTC	0-1651334	0963	1
TRIPPE JAMES E	LTC	0-0295918	0357	3
TRISKET ROBERT G	MAJ	0-1559859	1266	1
TRITLE ROBERT C	MAJ	0-0268154	1161	3
TRITSCH ARTHUR A JR	MAJ	0-1030528	1166	1
TRITSCHLER JOSEPH E	LTC	0-0267718	0868	3
TRITT EARL F	COL	0-0249325	0262	3
TRITTEN JOHN S	LTC	0-0228624	0564	3
TRITTENBACH EDWARD V	CW3	W-2145314	0166	1
TRITTON FRANK	LTC	0-1994542	0259	3
TRIVELLA MARIANO L	CW4	W-2120637	1265	1
TRIVIN ARSENIO R	MAJ	0-2204873	1268	1
TRODERMAN FRANK F	LTC	0-0465036	0463	3
TRODICK HARRY C	MAJ	0-2035446	0860	1
TROEGER FERDINAND	CPT	0-0278204	0355	3
TROESTER JOSEPH	CW3	W-2152919	0562	1
TROGDON DOROTHY L	MAJ	N-0765284	0565	1
TROHMAN JACOB R	CPT	0-1172698	0746	2
TROIA JOSEPH	LTC	0-2048510	0263	1
TROLAN WILLIAM A JR	COL	0-0282959	0658	3
TROLAND THOMAS E	B G	0-0115989	0153	3
TROLINGER RALPH M	LTC	0-0918664	0565	3
TROLINGER W P JR	2LT	0-0485048	0545	2
TROLLMAN JOHN JR	LTC	0-0304139	0667	3

NAME	GRADE	SVC NO	DATE RET MO YR	RET CODE
TROMBLE ANDREW R	CW4	W-2117940	1054	1
TROMBLEY FREDERICK	COL	0-1823671	1168	2
TROMBLEY GEORGE L	LTC	0-1056925	0268	3
TROMINSKI WALTER	COL	0-0320813	0763	3
TROMLEY CHESTER O	CW3	W-2119294	1054	1
TROMMETTER CHARLES F	1LT	0-1304820	1051	2
TRONIK JOSEPH	CW2	W-2110611	0353	1
TRONSETH CLIFFORD A	1LT	0-1577968	1044	2
TRONSON WILLIAM R	CPT	0-0410879	1145	2
TROOLIN WALTER	LTC	0-1280035	0854	1
TROP WILLIAM	LTC	0-0198539	1160	3
TROSETH PAUL E	CW4	W-2118132	0967	1
TROSKA ADAM	LTC	0-1057285	1266	1
TROSKE THEODORE R	CW3	W-2147465	0865	1
TROSSEN KENNETH F	MAJ	0-0420998	0361	1
TROST LAWRENCE J	1LT	0-2046644	1147	2
TROST LOUIS F	LTC	0-0324807	0265	3
TROSTER OLIVER J	COL	0-0133628	0854	3
TROSTLE CHARLES H	CPT	0-1284429	0445	2
TROSTLE KENNETH L	CPT	0-1041040	0746	2
TROTH PAUL H JR	LTC	0-0275055	0768	3
TROTT EMMETT O	MAJ	0-0225117	0648	3
TROTT HAROLD W	CPT	0-0926987	0148	2
TROTT LEROY F	LTC	0-1634411	1060	1
TROTT WILLIAM O	LTC	0-0281136	0465	3
TROTTER CLARENCE E	LTC	0-0280690	0450	3
TROTTER CLARENCE R	LTC	0-0246233	0162	3
TROTTER DORSET B	MAJ	0-0968262	0563	1
TROTTER ISHAM E	CW4	W-2141687	0167	1
TROTTER JO	1LT	0-2018607	0165	1
TROTTER MENCIE B	2LT	N-0755108	0445	1
TROTTER WILLIAM O	CW2	W-2210076	0160	1
TROTTIER EDMUND J	CPT	0-0218709	0547	1
TROUP ARTHUR B	LTC	0-0333196	0662	1
TROUP KENNETH F	CW2	W-2153014	1157	1
TROUPE HAROLD F	LTC	0-1560084	0967	1
TROUSDALE GEORGE W	M G	0-0189048	0361	3
TROUT EDWIN F	MAJ	0-2203783	0568	1
TROUT GEORGE H	CW3	W-2144373	0161	1
TROUT GEORGE W	LTC	0-0210732	0258	3
TROUT JAMES R	CPT	0-2331036	1168	2
TROUT LESTER	LTC	0-0194345	1055	3
TROUT STEWARD R	MAJ	0-0508139	0746	2
TROUTMAN FRANK H	MAJ	0-1179233	1059	1
TROUTMAN WILLIAM J	CPT	0-1049374	0745	2
TROW MARION	MAJ	L-1010062	1263	1
TROWBRIDGE HARVEY M	1LT	0-0432463	0744	2
TROWBRIDGE IRVIN	COL	0-0208450	1055	3
TROWBRIDGE LEON E	CPT	0-1558352	0859	1
TROWBRIDGE ROBERT L	CW2	W-2207041	0164	1
TROXEL RICHARD E	1LT	0-0987627	0158	1
TROXELL ALEXANDER	LTC	0-0239794	0653	2
TROXELL NOLAN	COL	0-0302498	0855	1
TROY CAJETAN J	LTC	0-0498555	0167	1
TROY THOMAS J	MAJ	0-1638690	1163	1
TROY WILLIAM	COL	0-0319818	0655	1
TROY WILLIAM G	2LT	0-1012552	0445	2
TROY WILLIAM G	CW4	W-2101320	0163	1
TROYER ORVE J	2LT	0-2055083	0251	2
TRUAX ALFRED F	LTC	0-0108806	0137	1
TRUAX CHARLES M	MAJ	0-1030199	0657	1
TRUAX DOROTHY B	1LT	N-0741728	1045	1
TRUAX IRENE G	2LT	N-0700876	0741	1
TRUAX NOAH H	LTC	0-0224064	0462	3
TRUAX VERNON H	LTC	0-2007224	0968	3
TRUB MATHIAS C	COL	0-0326725	0860	1
TRUBEY RAYMOND C	LTC	0-1176527	0463	1
TRUBEY ROBERT N	1LT	0-0958590	0252	2
TRUBY GEORGE E	1LT	0-0221122	0543	2
TRUDE ORVIS J	MAJ	0-0980709	1163	1
TRUDEAU DONALD D	CW2	W-2210087	0666	1
TRUDEAU FLOYD H	MAJ	0-0720618	0267	1
TRUDEAU FRANCIS H	MAJ	0-1166199	1059	1
TRUDEAU HUBERT F	CPT	0-0502299	1046	2
TRUDELL HERBERT A	MAJ	0-0200315	0256	3
TRUDELL JOHN N	MAJ	0-1648740	0661	1
TRUE CLYDE I	MAJ	0-0326879	1166	3
TRUE HOWARD R	COL	0-0292246	0965	3
TRUE WILBUR N	CPT	0-1922694	1262	1
TRUE WILLIAM H	CPT	0-0228156	0664	3
TRUEBGER HAROLD M	MAJ	0-0462511	1146	2
TRUEBLOOD LAUREL E	CPT	0-0258619	0766	3
TRUEBLOOD NORMAN N	MAJ	0-0507439	0547	2
TRUEBLOOD ROGER L	LTC	0-0279984	1161	3
TRUEMAN KENNETH E	CW2	W-2214671	0867	1
TRUESDALE HORTEN H	MAJ	0-0976877	0962	1
TRUESDELL ARTHUR J	WO1	W-2146524	0167	3
TRUETT RANDLE B	LTC	0-0225934	0463	3
TRUETT SAM W	CPT	0-0488803	0856	1
TRUEX CUTHBERT M	MAJ	0-2207028	0965	1
TRUEX LESTER S	MAJ	0-2035903	0862	1
TRUFANT ROBERT H	CW4	W-2142008	0659	1
TRUHON ANDREW R	CW3	W-2110128	1054	1
TRUITT AVERY D	LTC	0-1113487	0662	1
TRUITT CECIL A	LTC	0-1636745	0166	1
TRUITT JAMES G	COL	0-0157022	1155	3
TRUITT JOHN	LTC	0-0141597	0648	3
TRUITT LEONARD G	LTC	0-0299875	1267	3
TRUITT RAY A	LTC	0-0519818	0765	3
TRUJILLO GENE B	MAJ	0-0959355	0764	1
TRUJILLO JESSE	CPT	0-1053400	0261	1
TRUJILLO MARIE O	2LT	N-0777876	0348	1
TRUJILLO WILLIAM A	MAJ	0-1287965	0758	1
TRULOVE DENNIS K	CW2	W-2142015	1154	1
TRULUCK JOHN G	CW2	W-2209776	0966	1
TRUMAN GEORGE C	MAJ	0-0292439	0842	2
TRUMAN HARRY S	COL	0-0129869	0153	3
TRUMBLE JOHN W	LTC	0-0408655	0962	1
TRUMBLE LORAN R B	1LT	0-2262657	0164	2
TRUMBLE MANLEY H	MAJ	0-1047814	0557	1
TRUMBO GEORGE H	CPT	0-0452042	0144	2
TRUMBORE JACOB S	MAJ	0-1062793	0264	1
TRUMBULL ALBERT H	COL	0-0240871	0366	3
TRUMBULL DENE	CW2	W-2214314	0968	1
TRUMM BRUCE F	1LT	0-0455910	1044	2
TRUMP VIRGINIA E	2LT	N-0728943	1043	1
TRUMPF FREDERICK	MAJ	0-0415745	1060	1
TRUNCELLITO EDWARD	LTC	0-1588331	0866	1
TRUNDLE GEORGE H	LTC	0-0123996	0455	3
TRUNK DONALD E	CPT	0-1111952	0663	1
TRUOG CLARENCE P	MAJ	0-0497065	1143	2
TRUPP GARRISON G	CPT	0-1685478	0646	2
TRUSCOTT JAMES	COL	0-0263802	0962	3
TRUSCOTT JOHN P	MAJ	0-0178806	0361	3
TRUSDELL WARREN N	LTC	0-0308688	0965	3
TRUSH JOHN	LTC	0-0167119	1038	2
TRUSKO JOSEPH P	MAJ	0-1546867	0559	1
TRUSSELL ALBERT R	MAJ	0-1043244	1060	1
TRUSSELL ERNEST H	LTC	0-1046674	0667	1
TRUSSELL GEORGE O	CW2	W-2106026	0547	1
TRUTOR JOHN	LTC	0-1036064	0457	1
TRUX WILLIAM N	MAJ	0-0986280	0667	1
TRYBALSKI THADDEUS J	CPT	0-1165092	0856	1
TRYGGVI CARL B	LTC	0-0338094	0862	3
TRYTTEN GINA	MAJ	N-0743799	0365	3
TRZECIAK JOSEPH J	CPT	0-1332109	0455	1
TSCHIRHART PETE L	1LT	0-0153236	0156	3
TSCHUDIN HANS W	COL	0-0233928	0956	3
TSHUDY ROBERT E	MAJ	0-2263109	0764	1
TSIMPDES ANDREW G	2LT	0-1030850	0545	2
TSUBOTA SHIGERU	LTC	0-0386483	0264	1
TSUKUNO HARUNOBU	1LT	0-1998666	0647	2
TUBBESING RICHARD F	CPT	0-5536590	1168	2
TUBBS HAZEL L	2LT	N-0775679	1045	1
TUBBS JOE S	MAJ	0-0401703	1060	1
TUBBS LAWRENCE D	LTC	0-1579233	0455	1
TUBBS MARJORIE M	2LT	N-0736050	0345	1
TUBBS MARSHALL A	CW4	W-2115730	0959	1
TUBBS WALTER E	MAJ	0-0402973	0960	1
TUBBS WARREN JR	CPT	0-0334564	0147	2
TUBBS WILLIAM C	MAJ	0-1109719	0164	1
TUBRIDY FRANK J	LTC	0-0235910	0166	3
TUCCINARDI THOMAS E	1LT	0-1639745	1144	2
TUCHMAN JOSEPH N	1LT	0-1323501	0845	2
TUCK ALBERT C	CPT	0-0506662	0545	2
TUCK JOSEPH R	CPT	0-0403454	0246	2
TUCK LELAND H	2LT	0-1324592	0445	2
TUCK THADDEUS	CPT	0-0382820	0546	2
TUCK WILLIAM A	LTC	0-0506050	0668	3
TUCKER ALLEN L	LTC	0-0350617	0555	1
TUCKER ANDREW L	LTC	0-0151059	0555	3
TUCKER BETTY E	MAJ	L-1010304	0365	1
TUCKER BILL L	1LT	0-1111398	0945	2
TUCKER BILLY J SR	CPT	0-2017616	0961	1
TUCKER BROWN C	CW2	W-2114698	0444	2
TUCKER CARL L	CPT	0-1553373	0263	1
TUCKER CLEO W	CW2	W-2143621	0363	1
TUCKER COLIN R	CPT	0-1582223	0546	2
TUCKER CORA L	MAJ	N-0793263	0365	1
TUCKER DALE C	MAJ	0-2102979	0868	1
TUCKER DAVEY L	CW3	W-2211133	0868	1
TUCKER DAVID J	MAJ	0-1323633	0161	1
TUCKER DONALD D	MAJ	0-4010825	0468	1
TUCKER DWIGHT W	CW4	W-2141473	0467	1
TUCKER EDWARD N	LTC	0-1032402	0168	1
TUCKER EDWARD W	WO1	W-2126351	1051	1
TUCKER EDWIN L	COL	0-0229779	0157	1
TUCKER ERNEST R	MAJ	0-0970661	0165	1
TUCKER FLOYD J	CPT	0-0231913	0558	3
TUCKER FRANCIS M	CPT	0-0264063	0745	2
TUCKER FRED D	LTC	0-1311831	0768	1
TUCKER GEORGE E	2LT	0-1308732	0644	2
TUCKER GEORGE T	LTC	0-0179716	0956	3
TUCKER GORDON E	CPT	0-2033236	0364	1
TUCKER GROVER G	COL	0-0250679	0764	3
TUCKER GUY L	LTC	0-1284964	0261	1
TUCKER HELEN F	MAJ	N-0720212	1047	1
TUCKER HERBERT L	LTC	0-1109069	0661	1
TUCKER JACK G	MAJ	0-1534404	0562	2
TUCKER JACK W	CPT	0-0365370	0845	2
TUCKER JAMES R	1LT	0-0515590	0545	2
TUCKER JOHN C	LTC	0-1045617	1063	1
TUCKER JOHN H JR	COL	0-0123913	0251	3
TUCKER JOHN M	LTC	0-1109070	0862	1
TUCKER JOHN S	CW2	W-2142454	0757	1
TUCKER JOSEPH C	CW2	W-2214036	0368	1
TUCKER JOSEPH F	2LT	0-1540716	1050	1
TUCKER JOSEPH S	MAJ	0-2000521	0859	1
TUCKER JULIAN P	LTC	0-0452145	0161	1
TUCKER LEE H	COL	0-0167645	0555	3
TUCKER LEE W	CPT	0-1113489	0247	2
TUCKER LESLIE E	1LT	0-1318591	1045	2
TUCKER LESTER M	MAJ	0-2023336	0265	1
TUCKER LLOYD H	1LT	0-0372379	0861	1
TUCKER MATTHEW	CPT	0-0387934	0845	2
TUCKER ROBERT C	CPT	0-0414194	0545	2
TUCKER ROBERT C	1LT	0-1325243	0945	2
TUCKER ROBERT E	CW2	W-2144100	0762	1
TUCKER ROLLIN S JR	LTC	0-1114786	0955	2
TUCKER ROY J	CPT	0-0481340	1146	1
TUCKER SAM H	1LT	0-2005270	1047	2
TUCKER WILLIAM B	CPT	0-1931990	0264	1
TUCKER WILLIAM G	LTC	0-1591489	0864	1
TUCKER WILLIAM H	CPT	0-0514173	0257	1
TUCKER WILLIS O	MAJ	0-1796733	0257	1
TUCKER WOODSON C JR	LTC	0-0266953	0968	3
TUCKERMAN ALFRED G	M G	0-0181648	1061	3
TUCKERMAN CHESTER W	LTC	0-1825992	0966	1
TUCKETT ROBERT L	MAJ	0-0254485	0665	3
TUCKEY ROBERT L	COL	0-0523849	0766	3
TUCKMAN FLORENCE	2LT	N-0758513	0945	1
TUDHOPE ARTHUR K	LTC	0-0231616	0859	1
TUDOR ARTHUR J	1LT	0-1286925	0746	2
TUDOR JOHN S	LTC	0-0206011	0949	1
TUDOR ROY	CPT	0-0503657	0747	1
TUEGEL WILLIAM C	CPT	0-1341602	1060	1
TUELL CHARLES H	CW3	W-2102483	0356	1
TUERFFS ALBERT M	1LT	0-1549148	0545	2
TUFAROLO LIBERINO	1LT	0-0397052	0144	2
TUFFNER MICHAEL	CW3	W-2141475	0760	1
TUFTE CHESTER O	LTC	0-1044978	0662	1
TUFTE EDWARD E	CPT	0-0382253	0146	2
TUFTE OLIVIA C	2LT	N-0733992	0345	1
TUFTS BEN L	LTC	0-1011126	0963	1
TUFTS JOSEPH E	MAJ	0-0165942	0857	3
TUFTS MELVIN J	MAJ	0-1924590	0863	1
TUGGLE ALFRED A	CPT	0-0511300	0750	1
TUGGLE CLARENCE A	MAJ	0-1017707	0662	1
TUGGLE HAROLD O	LTC	0-1318489	1061	1
TUHUS MELVIL O	LTC	0-0156246	0954	3
TUIN HERMAN	CW3	W-2148994	0963	1
TUINSMA FRIEDA Z	2LT	N-0702202	1031	1
TULIBACKI BERNARD F	MAJ	0-1885438	0568	1
TULISZEWSKI VICTOR J	LTC	0-1080158	0961	1
TULL ELVON L	LTC	0-0291047	0648	3
TULL FISHER A	MAJ	0-0240345	1044	2
TULLBANE JOHN E	MAJ	0-1323877	0359	1
TULLER ALFRED J	CPT	0-1321560	0146	2
TULLER DALE K	COL	0-0181698	0456	3
TULLEY JOHN N	MAJ	0-0336083	1166	3
TULLEY METHOD T	MAJ	0-0965505	0961	1
TULLIS ELONZO A	CW2	W-2110134	1150	2
TULLIS JOHN H	CPT	0-1996421	0761	1
TULLOCH JAMES L JR	LTC	0-1303612	1161	2
TULLOCH JOHN C	MAJ	0-0139772	0560	3
TULLY CHARLEY W	CW3	W-2144933	1060	1
TULLY GEORGE P JR	LTC	0-0976484	0668	1
TULLY GORDON R	LTC	0-0274147	0660	1
TULLY JAMES J	CW2	W-2107997	1146	2
TULLY MARTIN J	2LT	0-1182287	1044	2
TULLY THOMAS H	MAJ	0-0169390	0460	3
TULLY THOMAS N	CPT	0-0384176	1065	3
TUMA HARRY L	LTC	0-2016977	0565	1
TUMAN GEORGE D	MAJ	0-1117765	1066	3
TUMAN JAMES F	MAJ	0-0953852	0865	1
TUMAN WILLIAM G	MAJ	0-0238641	0364	3
TUMINELLA SAMUEL	MAJ	0-0533110	0457	1
TUNING DALLAS D	MAJ	0-1647307	0261	1
TUNISON JAMES S W	1LT	0-0205394	0358	3
TUNISON MERLE E	MAJ	0-1557103	0258	1
TUNNELL BEN F JR	LTC	0-1556671	1066	1
TUNSTALL JAMES F	CPT	0-0487489	1145	2
TUNSTALL WILLIAM C	1LT	0-1319457	0746	2
TUNTLAND JOHN D	WO1	W-2123424	0844	2
TUNTLAND MARTELL F	1LT	0-0504935	0945	2
TUOHY EDWARD L	LTC	0-0273471	0460	2
TUPPER BETTY L	1LT	N-0743222	0146	1
TUPPER EARNEST H	LTC	0-1119002	0564	1
TUPPER NORMAN C	MAJ	0-1297812	1165	1
TUPPER WILLIAM R	CPT	0-0315151	0346	2
TURACEK RACHEL B	MAJ	N-0723707	0266	3
TURBEVILLE WILLIE B	CPT	0-0478163	1046	1
TURBISH JOHN	LTC	0-0887441	0168	1
TURBYFILL EARL L	LTC	0-0237646	0161	3
TURCEK JOSEPH	MAJ	0-1320202	0757	1
TURCK HENRY C	MAJ	0-1059087	0260	2
TURCOTTE EVARISTE	CPT	0-1639747	0954	1
TURCOTTE RICHARD L	LTC	0-0570578	0366	1
TUREK ANNA A	MAJ	N-0793264	0667	1
TUREK EDWIN V	COL	0-0242456	0862	3
TUREMAN GARNET R JR	1LT	0-1725992	0745	2
TURGEON ADELARD L	LTC	0-1554656	0567	3
TURGEON ROY W	MAJ	0-1309445	1060	1
TURINA JOSEPH F	CPT	0-0978474	1060	1
TURISH ANDREW J	LTC	0-1036413	0167	3
TURK EDWARD M	LTC	0-1287792	0663	1
TURK FRED	MAJ	0-1182020	0162	1
TURK JOHN H	CPT	0-0170073	0959	3
TURK LESTER	2LT	0-1176218	0545	2
TURK MERVYN R	LTC	0-0199257	1152	3

NAME	GRADE	SVC NO	DATE RET MO YR	RET CODE
TURKEL [illegible] W	CPT	[illegible]	0647	2
TURK[illegible] WILLIAM A	CPT	[illegible]	0663	2
TURLEY [illegible]	LTC	0-1107741	1062	1
TURLEY [illegible]	MAJ	0-1183535	1262	1
TURLEY [illegible] A JR	CW4	W-[illegible]	0268	1
TURLEY [illegible]	CPT	[illegible]	0245	2
TURLEY ROBERT S	1LT	0-3437412	0350	1
TURLEY [illegible] W	LTC	0-129[illegible]	1166	1
TURLEY THOMAS W	MAJ	0-0396452	0557	1
TURLINGTON RICHARD C	CPT	0-0210524	0264	3
TURMAN [illegible] M	LTC	0-1638627	0366	1
TURMAN JAMES A	1LT	0-1556817	0147	2
TURNBULL CHARLES R	MAJ	0-0978320	0762	1
TURNBULL DAVID L	MAJ	0-0267199	0967	1
TURNBULL FRANKLIN M	LTC	0-0497528	0962	1
TURNBULL GEORGE C	COL	0-0256783	0956	3
TURNBULL JAMES L	LTC	0-2225550	0264	3
TURNBULL JAMES W	LTC	0-0471866	0268	3
TURNBULL NORMAN A	LTC	0-0288343	0962	1
TURNBULL RICHARD G	1LT	0-1316607	0146	2
TURNBULL RODERIC F	LTC	0-2041065	1164	1
TURNBULL WILLIAM G	LTC	0-0255102	1055	1
TURNBULL WILLIAM L	LTC	0-1288998	0264	1
TURNELL LLOYD Y	MAJ	0-0173587	0950	3
TURNELLO ANTHONY R	LTC	0-0358546	1068	3
TURNER ADLAI S	COL	0-0162939	0350	3
TURNER ALICE J	1LT	N-0783311	0446	1
TURNER AMOS	CW3	W-2141476	1163	1
TURNER ARCH	1LT	0-0331109	0561	1
TURNER ART	COL	0-0253009	0665	3
TURNER ARTHUR E	CW3	W-2145876	0267	1
TURNER BENNIE A	MAJ	0-0453621	0657	1
TURNER CARL M	MAJ	0-0332207	0367	3
TURNER CARL R	LTC	0-0252001	0965	3
TURNER CARLOS L	CPT	0-0381400	0445	2
TURNER CARRELL D	LTC	0-0262974	0465	3
TURNER CECIL R	2LT	0-1332551	0247	2
TURNER CHARLES B JR	COL	0-0281228	0368	3
TURNER CHARLES E	LTC	0-0229780	0463	3
TURNER CHARLES G	LTC	0-0385856	0765	2
TURNER CHARLES N	MAJ	0-1647764	1063	2
TURNER CHARLES T	1LT	0-0540848	1044	2
TURNER CLARENCE	CW4	W-2109361	0857	1
TURNER CLEVELAND	MAJ	0-1173112	1061	1
TURNER CLYDE M	MAJ	0-1303231	1059	1
TURNER DAVID F	1LT	0-0313029	0844	2
TURNER DAVID M	WO1	W-2145760	0458	2
TURNER DEAN W	CW2	W-2152989	0559	1
TURNER DONALD W	MAJ	0-1053855	0463	1
TURNER EARL A	2LT	0-1002346	0544	2
TURNER EARL A	LTC	0-1175888	0865	1
TURNER EARL A	LTC	0-2012751	0464	1
TURNER EDWARD F	MAJ	0-0973554	0167	1
TURNER EDWARD F JR	1LT	0-1319907	1145	2
TURNER EDWARD T JR	WO1	W-2006861	0468	3
TURNER EDWIN R	CPT	0-0988208	0561	1
TURNER EDYTHE	COL	N-0726939	1062	1
TURNER ELBERT P	MAJ	0-1013713	0761	1
TURNER EMMETT L	MAJ	0-0426229	0657	1
TURNER EMMONS H JR	MAJ	0-0408578	0246	2
TURNER FORREST D	LTC	0-0267834	1266	3
TURNER FRANCIS J	LTC	0-1636748	1065	1
TURNER FRANK H	CPT	0-1284430	0356	1
TURNER FRED A	LTC	0-1280398	0462	1
TURNER FREDERIC P	MAJ	0-1633606	0755	1
TURNER FREDERICK	COL	0-0518668	0268	1
TURNER GEORGE F	CW2	W-2107978	0645	2
TURNER GEORGE H	COL	0-0258031	0962	3
TURNER GLENN F	COL	0-0266841	0855	1
TURNER GLYN M	1LT	0-1307329	0645	2
TURNER GRADY T	MAJ	0-0175832	1054	3
TURNER HARMON M	MAJ	0-0267825	0256	3
TURNER HENRY C	CPT	0-0245285	0553	3
TURNER HENRY F	LTC	0-0365164	0662	1
TURNER HENRY F JR	LTC	0-1253680	0661	1
TURNER HENRY P SR	CW4	W-2004748	1062	3
TURNER HERBERT A JR	MAJ	0-0927194	1164	1
TURNER HOWARD L	CPT	0-2037808	0456	1
TURNER HOWARD V	CPT	0-0445598	0147	2
TURNER JACK H	MAJ	0-1298788	0357	1
TURNER JACKSON A	CW3	W-2147008	1063	2
TURNER JAMES A JR	MAJ	0-0407004	0348	2
TURNER JAMES C	MAJ	0-2266239	0466	1
TURNER JAMES E	CW3	W-2152362	1265	1
TURNER JAMES F	MAJ	0-4009931	0966	1
TURNER JAMES J	MAJ	0-2262113	0164	1
TURNER JESSE H	COL	0-0251259	0666	3
TURNER JESSE R JR	LTC	0-0366523	0166	1
TURNER JOE F	MAJ	0-1823958	0762	1
TURNER JOEL L	CPT	0-2262205	1060	1
TURNER JOHN C	MAJ	0-4010329	0568	1
TURNER JOHN F	1LT	0-1294566	0845	2
TURNER JOHN F	MAJ	0-4000070	0367	1
TURNER JOHN G	LTC	0-0245492	0764	3
TURNER JOHN H C	CW3	W-2152061	0964	1
TURNER JOHN J	CW3	W-2209911	0466	2
TURNER JOHN L	MAJ	0-0184791	1056	3
TURNER JOHN P	CPT	0-0908981	0449	2
TURNER JOHN S	MAJ	0-1688392	0563	2
TURNER JOHN W	LTC	0-0958213	1068	1
TURNER JOSEPH N	LTC	0-0298275	0568	3
TURNER JOSEPH R	CPT	0-1177529	0354	2
TURNER JULIAN J	LTC	0-0237557	0364	3
TURNER LEON B	LTC	0-0197643	1061	3
TURNER LINTON L JR	MAJ	0-1593350	0759	1
TURNER MARGARET C	1LT	N-0742053	0346	1
TURNER MARGARET E	2LT	N-0760397	0545	1
TURNER MARY F	1LT	N-0728581	0846	1
TURNER MAX H	COL	0-0399490	0662	1
TURNER MELVIN L	CW2	W-2210383	0262	1
TURNER MILO M	1LT	0-0407556	0144	2
TURNER NELSON T	LTC	0-0379986	1065	3
TURNER NICHOLAS F	1LT	0-1642667	0246	2
TURNER NORMAN	CW3	W-2205512	0366	1
TURNER ODILLION C	CPT	0-0263808	0855	3
TURNER PHILIP M	LTC	0-0370241	0860	1
TURNER RALPH S	MAJ	0-0246880	0248	2
TURNER RALPH S	MAJ	0-1037345	0561	1
TURNER RAY	LTC	0-0196337	1160	3
TURNER RAY F	CW3	W-2142333	0760	1
TURNER RICHARD	CW2	W-3151355	0967	1
TURNER RICHARD C	MAJ	0-1295628	0947	2
TURNER ROBERT A	CW2	W-2115793	0556	1
TURNER ROBERT B	MAJ	0-4006939	0167	1
TURNER SHERMAN F JR	LTC	0-1825512	0163	1
TURNER THOMAS D JR	COL	0-0233648	0454	2
TURNER THOMAS F	CW3	W-2121095	0561	1
TURNER THOMAS K JR	MAJ	0-1996400	0562	1
TURNER THOMAS K	CW2	W-3430189	0966	1
TURNER TOM W	LTC	0-1323366	0962	1
TURNER VIRGINIA H	1LT	N-0731650	0445	1
TURNER VIVIAN C	MAJ	0-0955314	0567	1
TURNER WALKER M	CPT	0-0478676	0346	2
TURNER WEAVER A	MAJ	0-2036895	1060	1
TURNER WESLEY S	MAJ	0-2033879	1165	1
TURNER WILBUR D	LTC	0-1057287	1162	1
TURNER WILLIAM R JR	2LT	0-1012260	0544	2
TURNER WILLIAM H	MAJ	0-2043315	0162	1
TURNER WILLIAM J	COL	0-0100202	0954	3
TURNER WILLIAM L	CPT	0-0416096	1050	1
TURNER WILLIAM L	LTC	0-1105875	1061	1
TURNER WILLIAM M	LTC	0-0304093	0265	1
TURNER WINSTON V	LTC	0-2021268	1068	1
TURNER WYLIE C	COL	0-0333737	0654	3
TURNEY ALFRED W	LTC	0-1102513	0663	1
TURNEY EARL B	WO1	W-2127649	0753	1
TURNEY EVERETT G	MAJ	0-1341924	0862	1
TURNEY FORREST N	LTC	0-0356843	0465	3
TURNEY ROBERT C	MAJ	0-0548754	1163	1
TURNEY VALE P	CW4	W-2141901	0566	1
TURNEY WILFRED R	MAJ	0-1542572	0646	2
TURNEYHIGH HARRY H	COL	0-0264748	0259	3
TURNIPSEED JESSE D	LTC	0-1299146	0363	1
TURPIN CHARLES H	MAJ	0-0141645	0755	3
TURPIN CLAYTON R	MAJ	0-0555435	0864	1
TURPIN DORIS J	MAJ	0-0382276	1167	3
TURPIN HERMAN L	CW4	W-2149910	1267	1
TURPIN HERMAN R	CW2	W-2209187	1263	1
TURPIN LEONARD J	CW2	W-2150305	0760	1
TURQUEZA ARSENIO A	MAJ	0-2262264	1164	1
TURRELL DONALD B	LTC	0-1822748	1066	1
TURSI MARTIN D	CPT	0-2262860	0361	1
TURUNEN LUCIA E	LTC	N-0772028	0566	1
TURVENE HORACE V	COL	0-0141259	1054	1
TUSA JOSEPHINE	1LT	N-0726764	0648	2
TUSING WILLIAM C	CW2	W-2147716	0854	1
TUSTISON ALBERT P	LTC	0-0279315	0764	3
TUTAK LAWRENCE A JR	LTC	0-1596836	0163	1
TUTEN CHARLES	CW2	W-2118071	0853	1
TUTEN JAMES M JR	2LT	0-1341726	0949	2
TUTHILL FRANK S	2LT	0-1056582	1044	2
TUTHILL HOWARD E	MAJ	0-2038903	0463	1
TUTLIS STANLEY J	LTC	0-0376490	0655	1
TUTRONE DAVID A	MAJ	0-0367955	0746	2
TUTT GARVIN A	LTC	0-1685674	0268	1
TUTTEROW EDWIN B	WO1	W-2120712	0544	2
TUTTLE ARTHUR W	CPT	0-1633608	0345	2
TUTTLE BLAINE E	CPT	0-0334473	0743	2
TUTTLE CHARLES F JR	LTC	0-1080590	0663	1
TUTTLE ELBERT R	BG	0-0135785	0757	3
TUTTLE GEORGE I	CPT	0-0259160	0967	3
TUTTLE HARRY W	CPT	0-0252597	0648	3
TUTTLE JACOB A	MAJ	0-1596837	0856	1
TUTTLE JAMES H	CPT	0-0141633	0358	3
TUTTLE LAWRENCE W	MAJ	0-0349434	0545	2
TUTTLE LEO E	CPT	0-0496120	0147	1
TUTTLE LESLIE F	LTC	0-1293336	0861	1
TUTTLE LOWELL K	LTC	0-0370952	1059	1
TUTTLE PAUL R	LTC	0-0377144	0161	1
TUTTLE RICHARD F	LTC	0-0946477	0867	1
TUTTLE RICHARD P	MAJ	0-1300552	0161	1
TUTTLE WILJAN R	LTC	0-0338614	0467	3
TUTTLE WILLIAM O JR	CW2	W-2212188	0267	1
TUXBURY CLARENCE W	LTC	0-2283836	1264	2
TUXBURY GEORGE P	LTC	0-0907594	0762	1
TUXWORTH FRANK E JR	LTC	0-0257904	0467	3
TVEDT CHESTER G	MAJ	0-0214004	0853	3
TVEDT HAROLD B	MAJ	0-0544393	0568	1
TWARDZIAK ANTHONY J	MAJ	0-1558353	0759	1
TWEDDELL RICHARD	1LT	0-0443954	0745	2
TWEED JENNIE M	1LT	N-0729705	1145	1
TWEEDIE OLAF H	CW3	W-2139999	0367	2
TWEEDLE THOMAS L	MAJ	0-0262423	1267	3
TWEEDY ROBERT W	LTC	0-0385453	0560	1
TWEEDY WALTER K	COL	0-0220575	0862	3
TWEEDY WILLIAM H	COL	0-0291378	0460	1
TWEET IRENE J	2LT	N-0775832	0345	1
TWEIT PHYLLIS E	MAJ	N-0772724	1264	1
TWELMEYER THEODORE A	LTC	0-0355058	0958	1
TWENTIER MAX E	1LT	0-1312459	0145	2
TWENTYMAN CHESTER H	LTC	0-0403791	0558	1
TWICHELL ALAN F	MAJ	0-1060316	0461	1
TWIFORD JOHN R	MAJ	0-0117665	0155	3
TWIGG RICHARD B	2LT	0-1551327	0744	2
TWILLA ROBERT E	CW3	W-2153108	0466	1
TWILLEAGER JOHN W	CW2	W-2214857	0866	1
TWINEM LINN K	LTC	0-0262103	0767	3
TWINING ELIZABETH	MAJ	N-0758012	0764	1
TWISS RAYMOND L	CW3	W-2151044	1057	1
TWIST JACK B	CPT	0-0312680	0844	2
TWIST RICHARD H	CPT	0-1302392	0767	1
TWIST WILLIAM J	LTC	0-1575608	1062	1
TWITCHELL RICHARD M	LTC	0-0355026	0460	1
TWITTY 3RD WILLIAM C	1LT	0-0523321	1045	2
TWOHY DANIEL W JR	COL	0-0289744	0965	3
TWOMBLY EDWARD H	LTC	0-0145045	0251	3
TWOMBLY JOSEPH G	MAJ	0-1015533	0962	1
TWOMBLY MAYNARD C	CW2	W-2152587	0562	1
TWOMEY CHARLES F	COL	0-0263984	0553	3
TWOMEY JAMES C	MAJ	0-0255342	1066	3
TWOREK GEORGE J	MAJ	0-2262461	1064	1
TWYMAN FREDERICK	CPT	0-1030851	1160	1
TYACK WILLIAM R	MAJ	0-1182730	0564	1
TYBROSKI MAX M	1LT	0-2263006	0366	1
TYE RENNIE V JR	CPT	0-0414095	0246	2
TYE THOMAS H	LTC	0-0199616	0648	3
TYE WILLIAM H	2LT	0-1998329	0446	2
TYER DONALD H JR	MAJ	0-1646076	0258	1
TYER LLOYD	CW2	W-2151097	1057	1
TYER ROBERT H	MAJ	0-1595232	0357	1
TYERYAR JOSEPHINE	MAJ	N-0724816	0662	1
TYERYAR THOMAS L	MAJ	0-2033074	0361	1
TYGER LOUIS E	CW4	W-2146647	0968	1
TYLENDA JOSEPH	CW2	W-2150745	1059	1
TYLER ALFRED R	MAJ	0-2007169	0461	1
TYLER CARL H	MAJ	0-0332297	0146	2
TYLER CATLIN E	COL	0-0280335	0768	3
TYLER CLEMENT	1LT	0-1642668	0745	2
TYLER DAVID G	LTC	0-0207398	0459	3
TYLER DEROY	CW3	W-2142275	0659	1
TYLER EDWARD J	CPT	0-0453520	0147	2
TYLER FRANKLIN A	LTC	0-0155613	0854	3
TYLER GEORGE A	LTC	0-0212325	0162	3
TYLER GERALD R	COL	0-0170590	0755	1
TYLER HARRY W	LTC	0-0499487	0954	1
TYLER HERMAN H	MAJ	0-0992001	1063	1
TYLER HUNTER W JR	LTC	0-1946401	0163	1
TYLER JACK A	MAJ	0-2019743	1060	1
TYLER JACK R	MAJ	0-1937232	0568	1
TYLER JOE C	LTC	0-0245562	0259	1
TYLER JOHN A	1LT	0-1010741	0746	2
TYLER JOHN JR	MAJ	0-0339502	0446	2
TYLER JOHN N	MAJ	0-0189214	0662	3
TYLER KEITH W	1LT	0-0507603	0844	2
TYLER KENNETH A	MAJ	0-1179658	0762	1
TYLER LUCIUS C	CW4	W-2118085	0157	1
TYLER MARK V JR	LTC	0-1636751	1264	1
TYLER NATHAN I	MAJ	0-0240850	0566	3
TYLER OLIN C	LTC	0-0323021	0967	3
TYLER RALPH A	MAJ	0-0213532	0862	3
TYLER RAYMOND C	COL	0-1312625	1268	1
TYLER RICHARD O	1LT	0-0536742	0146	2
TYLER ROBERT E	2LT	0-1320674	1044	2
TYLER STANLEY W	COL	0-0306960	0368	1
TYMNIAK WALTER	MAJ	0-0388497	0861	1
TYNDALL ANDREW	MAJ	0-1703894	0859	1
TYNDALL JOSEPH V	LTC	0-0408225	0563	1
TYNDALL LYNWOOD H	CW3	W-2143779	0963	1
TYNDALL PAUL E	COL	0-0203432	1046	2
TYNDALL PLATO	WO1	W-2124701	0747	1
TYNDALL ROBERT O	LTC	0-1337511	0966	1
TYNER CLARENCE E JR	MAJ	0-1120567	0865	1
TYNER ERNEST C	WO1	W-2109430	0545	2
TYNER FURMAN H	COL	0-0221676	0559	3
TYNER LEE R JR	MAJ	0-1897722	0463	2
TYNER ROY H	CW2	W-2145068	0457	1
TYNER TED H	CPT	0-1824708	0261	1
TYNES ROBERT M	CW3	W-2205116	0365	1
TYNES SEDGIE B	LTC	0-1302669	0657	1
TYREE CLARENCE	1LT	0-0486565	0949	1
TYREE FRANK L JR	COL	0-0149688	0-52	3
TYREE HERMAN E	LTC	0-1541057	0761	1
TYREE JAMES H	MAJ	0-1053404	1063	1
TYREE LAWRENCE H	LTC	0-0418526	1060	1
TYREE PAUL W	CW2	RW-2149462	1262	1
TYRONE MARCUS L	LTC	0-0469753	0666	3
TYRRELL HUBERT L	MAJ	0-0321153	0468	3
TYRRELL STANLEY C	MAJ	0-1304296	0960	1
TYRRELL WILLIAM L	LTC	0-0201330	0758	3
TYSKOWSKI THEODORE E	MAJ	0-1597659	0762	1

NAME	GRADE	SVC NO	DATE RET MO YR	RET CODE
TYSON ARTHUR W	CW4	W-2122867	0161	1
TYSON DAVA K	COL	0-0286279	1262	3
TYSON EDWARD B	MAJ	0-1688058	0946	2
TYSON FREDERICK	MAJ	0-1795036	0455	1
TYSON HARRY D	COL	0-0216107	0950	2
TYSON JAMES B	MAJ	0-2001798	1167	1
TYSON JOHN W	LTC	0-0200183	0648	3
TYTUS JOHN B	CPT	0-1017082	0246	2
TYUS WELMON T	1LT	0-0539653	0645	2
TYVAND RAYMOND E	LTC	0-0278405	1263	3
UBARRO PATRICIO	CPT	0-0359964	0260	1
UBL JOSEPH L	COL	0-0186997	1053	2
UCHIC NELLIE M	MAJ	N-0770149	0965	1
UCHMAN EDWARD	2LT	0-1550077	1143	2
UDALL JESSE A	LTC	0-0237228	0653	3
UDBYE PAUL	LTC	0-0231146	0657	3
UDELL GEORGE	LTC	0-0393254	0466	3
UDELL GERALD S	MAJ	0-0286045	0362	2
UDOUJ HENRY J	1LT	0-1314975	0446	2
UFFNER RAPHAEL L	CPT	0-0335420	0545	2
UFFORD JOHN H	CPT	0-1330127	0868	1
UGLAND NILS F	LTC	0-1315392	0962	1
UGLICK GEORGE V	1LT	0-1318346	0463	1
UGLUM HELMER J	LTC	0-0450146	0454	1
UGRO JOSEPH V	MAJ	0-1639752	0658	1
UHAZI GEORGE	MAJ	0-2014777	1164	1
UHER JERMONE M	CW2	W-2150366	0858	1
UHL AUGUST F	MAJ	0-0191639	0640	2
UHLAND CATHERINE	1LT	N-0724247	1048	1
UHLAND RAY G	MAJ	0-0547792	0264	1
UHLENBERG JOSEPH A	1LT	0-1313472	0246	2
UHLER DAVID M	LTC	0-1646665	1057	1
UHLER EARL G	LTC	0-0220076	0-53	3
UHLER ROMAYNE T	COL	0-0176496	0553	2
UHLER WALTER V	LTC	0-0246381	0461	3
UHLFELDER ALVIN R	1LT	0-1169375	1145	2
UHLICH WILFRED D	LTC	0-0329470	1167	3
UHLS WILLIAM C	CPT	0-1179659	1064	2
UHRICH CARL M	2LT	0-1873798	0845	2
UHRICH GERARD I	COL	0-0355936	1167	3
UIBERALL ERNEST P	LTC	0-1334781	0366	1
UITTI WILLIAM L	LTC	0-0276357	0169	3
UITZ JACOB H	CPT	0-1111401	0447	2
ULAN ALFRED A	CPT	0-1037347	0858	1
ULAN LEWIS A	CPT	0-0526089	0446	2
ULAND IVAN C	LTC	0-0396219	0465	3
ULANDER ROLAND J JR	MAJ	0-0966120	0866	1
ULEKOWSKI WALTER J	CW3	W-2208807	0667	1
ULERICH WILLIAM H	CPT	0-1171400	0746	2
ULERY CLARENCE	COL	0-0166831	0746	2
ULERY JOHN W	LTC	0-0281810	0360	3
ULIASZ JOHN T	MAJ	0-1690721	0260	1
ULICNY FRANK S	1LT	0-1944612	0245	2
ULLENBRUCH WILLIAM J	MAJ	0-0179750	0759	3
ULLERY WILLIAM G	LTC	0-1295964	0367	1
ULLESTAD ROLF J	LTC	0-0200925	0159	3
ULLMAN BERNARD F	LTC	0-1641893	0463	1
ULLMANN KARL H	CPT	0-2053822	0757	3
ULLOM ROBERT F	COL	0-1057230	0768	1
ULLRICH WILLIAM L	COL	0-0293871	0968	3
ULM GERALD K	CPT	0-0411899	0945	2
ULMER BOSWELL R JR	COL	0-0339119	0463	1
ULMER WALTER F	COL	0-0264359	0363	3
ULRICH FREDERICH	MAJ	0-2205764	0964	1
ULRICH FREDERICK	MAJ	0-1641884	0666	1
ULRICH FREDRICK W	LTC	0-1341836	1167	1
ULRICH GEORGE M	CPT	0-2265176	0359	2
ULRICH GEORGE P	CW2	W-3430246	0867	1
ULRICH JOHN L	1LT	0-1049678	1145	2
ULRICH KARL A	1LT	0-2035399	0246	2
ULRICH RICHARD W	LTC	0-0416041	0366	1
ULRICH RODGER K	MAJ	0-0430618	1046	2
ULRICH SAMUEL C	MAJ	0-1013772	0554	1
ULSAKER LAWRENCE T	COL	0-0267556	0557	1
ULSAKER ANDREW G	2LT	0-1176830	0245	2
ULVENES HOWARD K	MAJ	0-0383293	0966	3
UMAN GEORGE L	CPT	0-0909965	0546	2
UMANOFF LEONARD	LTC	0-0320283	1159	1
UMBARGER JOHN N	LTC	0-0269004	1167	3
UMIKER HENRY G	CW2	W-2215782	0967	1
UMLAND LESLIE W	CW2	W-3200347	0766	1
UMLANG EMIL F	LTC	0-0238521	0266	3
UMPHREY SAMUEL B	LTC	0-0491826	1067	3
UMPLEBY CLIFFORD R	CPT	0-0119026	0948	3
UMPREY JOHN W	LTC	0-0420894	0453	1
UNCIANO ISAAC F	CPT	0-1102098	0661	1
UNDEN RAGNAR	CPT	0-0260293	0659	3
UNDERDONK ROBERT J	CW3	W-2142208	0660	1
UNDERDUE BRUCE	CW2	W-2105425	1060	1
UNDERHILL MARION H	COL	0-0382295	0467	1
UNDERWOOD CLARENCE L	LTC	0-0156954	0745	2
UNDERWOOD CLARENCE L	LTC	0-0189788	0748	2
UNDERWOOD CLARENCE S	LTC	0-0384568	0568	3
UNDERWOOD CLYDE G	MAJ	0-1635430	1060	1
UNDERWOOD EARL F	MAJ	0-0953880	1062	1
UNDERWOOD EARL G	MAJ	0-2204154	0663	1
UNDERWOOD EDWARD B	COL	0-0325112	0364	3
UNDERWOOD ERVIN E	MAJ	0-1165683	1146	2
UNDERWOOD EUGENE T	LTC	0-0178233	0648	3
UNDERWOOD IRENE L	1LT	N-0752131	0845	1
UNDERWOOD JAMES A JR	MAJ	0-0559420	0457	1
UNDERWOOD JOHN C	COL	0-0192676	0963	3
UNDERWOOD JOHN C	LTC	0-1639754	0458	2
UNDERWOOD JOSEPH L	MAJ	0-0489845	0257	1
UNDERWOOD LAURENCE E	MAJ	0-0195757	1046	2
UNDERWOOD MURRIE	CPT	0-0497502	1057	1
UNDERWOOD ORIAN A	MAJ	0-1030942	0956	1
UNDERWOOD RALPH	LTC	0-1168960	0664	1
UNDERWOOD RICHARD M	LTC	0-1113492	0463	1
UNDERWOOD ROBERT F	CPT	0-0527393	0645	2
UNDERWOOD VERNON L	MAJ	0-1080972	0563	1
UNDERWOOD W T W	LTC	0-0127122	0648	3
UNDERWOOD WILLIAM D	MAJ	0-1015285	0861	1
UNDERWOOD WILLIAM H	MAJ	0-1299320	0261	1
UNDERWOOD WILLIAM W	COL	0-0417675	0767	1
UNGAR HENRY P	CW3	W-2152724	0563	1
UNGER ARTHUR F	2LT	0-1823091	0144	2
UNGER ARTHUR W	LTC	0-1307105	0157	1
UNGER CHARLES J	CPT	0-1594539	0148	1
UNGER EARL B	COL	0-0399142	1063	1
UNGER GEORGE N	LTC	0-0100454	0255	3
UNGER JEROME F	CW3	W-2153186	1265	1
UNGER JOHN E	1LT	0-1016032	0353	2
UNGER JOSEPH	LTC	0-0450931	0152	2
UNGER JOSEPH M	LTC	0-0227737	0665	3
UNGER LOUIS	LTC	0-1291548	0455	1
UNGER OSCAR W	CW3	W-2203841	1265	1
UNGER RALPH G	COL	0-0276280	0165	3
UNGER SAMUEL	LTC	0-0910782	0466	3
UNGER THOMAS H	LTC	0-0184382	0462	3
UNGVARY ROBERT L	1LT	0-0509337	0945	2
UNLEY WALTER W	COL	0-0305286	0167	3
UNO HOWARD Y	CW3	W-2144266	0163	1
UNRATH WALTER J	MAJ	0-1052188	0658	1
UNREIN GERARD A	LTC	0-0441663	0762	1
UNTALAN PEDRO	MAJ	0-1896917	0762	2
UNTCH ALBERT M	MAJ	0-0337218	1267	3
UNTHANK EDGAR	LTC	0-1323188	0867	1
UNTIET CHARLES J	1LT	0-1304462	0847	2
UNVERDORBEN MARY E	MAJ	N-0725158	0967	1
UNVERSAW WALTER H	COL	0-0171574	0648	3
UNWIN JOSEPH D JR	COL	0-0380028	0165	1
UPDEGRAFF JOHN R	CW4	W-2134061	0559	1
UPCHURCH BARHEE F	CW3	W-3150214	0767	1
UPCHURCH C W JR	1LT	0-0554170	0847	2
UPCHURCH FRED	MAJ	0-0377145	1047	2
UPDEGRAFT KENNETH E	MAJ	0-2015722	0259	2
UPDYKE HARLEY W	CW2	W-3150715	0566	1
UPDYKE RANDALL E	1LT	0-0544029	0546	2
UPHAM FRANCIS B	COL	0-0180207	0553	3
UPHAM JACK W	MAJ	0-0463452	0757	2
UPHAM WILLIAM E	CPT	0-0257249	0865	3
UPHOFF MILTON M	CW3	W-2142910	1061	1
UPHOUSE WILLIAM R	LTC	0-0544642	0966	2
UPP WALDEEN	LTC	0-1047819	0565	1
UPPERCO MARTIN T	2LT	0-1306772	0451	2
UPSHAW ELBERT R	1LT	0-1306685	0845	2
UPSHAW JACKSON E	CPT	0-0522959	0346	2
UPSHUR JAMES M	MAJ	0-0949265	1162	1
UPSON EDITH M	1LT	N-0734994	0945	1
UPSON NEVILLE U	MAJ	0-0396968	0860	1
UPTAIN ARLIN A	MAJ	0-1923753	1068	1
UPTON BADGER V JR	CPT	0-0959103	0759	2
UPTON CALVIN W	COL	0-0450932	0656	1
UPTON GEORGE E	LTC	0-1585022	1163	1
UPTON JOHN F	MAJ	0-1295120	0563	1
UPTON RAYMOND V	LTC	0-1318593	0862	1
UPTON THOMAS F	LTC	0-1541946	0768	3
UPTON THOMAS H	COL	0-0299867	0361	3
UPTON WILLIAM F JR	LTC	0-0124014	1055	3
URATSU MASAJI G	MAJ	0-2030815	0562	1
URBACH RUDOLF	LTC	0-1845529	0960	1
URBAITIS JOHN C	LTC	0-0271801	1066	3
URBAN ALBERT C	LTC	0-0285548	1263	3
URBAN CHARLES H SR	LTC	0-0421005	0254	2
URBAN CLARENCE W	1LT	0-0157958	0949	3
URBAN EDWARD J	LTC	0-0348041	1067	3
URBAN GEORGE H	MAJ	0-0964802	0963	2
URBAN MATTY	LTC	0-0416199	0246	2
URBAN RUSS D	WO1	W-2126024	1145	2
URBAN RUSSELL L	COL	0-0147941	1056	3
URBAN STANLEY J	LTC	0-1165352	0148	1
URBAN WILLARD F	MAJ	0-0279848	1062	1
URBANEK ANN P	2LT	N-0723872	0545	1
URBANICK CHESLAR	LTC	0-1534885	0759	1
URBANSKI EDWARD	MAJ	0-1638704	0361	1
URBANSKI JULIA M	CPT	N-0732058	1047	1
URBANSKI STEVEN M	LTC	0-1642670	1163	1
URBANTKE IRWIN A	LTC	0-1823373	0357	2
URBINA GEORGE S	CPT	0-1686276	1060	1
URBOM OSCAR W	LTC	0-0149713	0648	3
URDANETA MARIO	LTC	0-2025185	0768	1
URECH FRED M	1LT	0-0497845	1153	1
URENSON BERTHA	1LT	N-0755714	1146	1
URETTE SAMUEL S	LTC	0-0278859	1158	1
URIAN RICHARD H	MAJ	0-1800086	0761	1
URIE EDWIN A	CPT	0-0300812	0465	3
URISH GEORGE T	MAJ	0-0949542	0368	1
URIU TADASHI	CW3	W-2135972	0762	1
URLING WENDELL P	1LT	0-0518427	1045	2
URQUHART HUGH G	MAJ	0-0914414	0762	2
URSERY JESSE	MAJ	0-0450933	1150	2
URSICH CHARLES C	CPT	0-0319451	1046	2
URSPRUNG ALLEN J	LTC	0-0451498	0259	1
URSPRUNG RUDOLPH S	COL	0-0162588	0851	3
URSTEIN HARRY	CPT	0-0507117	0246	2
URTES JOHN N	LTC	0-1054146	0863	1
URWILLER CLIFFORD S	COL	0-0180676	1054	1
URY JOSEPH	CW2	W-2149969	0361	1
USHER HERMAN A	LTC	0-0258822	0168	3
USHER JOHN W	MAJ	0-1041667	0966	1
USHER THOMAS J	LTC	0-1315744	1160	1
USI EUGENIO B	1LT	0-1896615	0750	1
USINGER EDWARD M	LTC	0-1558447	0166	1
USSERY JOHN E	LTC	0-1546459	0667	1
USSERY WILLIAM T	LTC	0-0509332	0457	1
USTACH STANLEY F	MAJ	0-0346351	0651	1
USTRUCK MICHAEL F	CPT	0-0295777	0345	2
UTKE RAYMOND F	CPT	0-1307481	0248	2
UTLEY EUGENE F	COL	0-0445223	0364	1
UTLEY HAROLD C	LTC	0-1048625	0466	1
UTLEY JOHN H	LTC	0-0227420	0265	3
UTLEY KENNETH D	CW2	W-2203821	0260	1
UTLEY THOMAS E	CW4	W-2142068	0462	1
UTTER FLOYD J	COL	0-0284382	0266	3
UTTER JOSEPH W	COL	0-0167798	0959	3
UTTERBACK ALVIN P JR	LTC	0-0380479	1046	2
UTTERBACK GENE I	LTC	0-0277104	0361	1
UTTERBACK ORVAL N	1LT	0-0499650	0655	1
UTTERBACK ROBERT L	CW3	W-2129156	0760	1
UYEDA MASAO B	MAJ	0-0956827	1264	2
UYEYAMA KAHN	LTC	0-0317636	0347	2
UZARAVITZ EDWARD T	MAJ	0-0479699	0953	1
UZZELL THOMAS M	LTC	0-0402796	0163	3
VACCA JOHN V	LTC	0-0332094	1060	2
VACCA PETER	LTC	0-0289334	1160	3
VACCARO FRANK T	MAJ	0-1543884	0563	1
VACCARO WILLIAM	LTC	0-0427386	0461	1
VACEK JOHN E	LTC	0-0198053	0558	3
VACHA HELEN E	MAJ	N-0726329	0847	1
VACHER EUGENE D	CW3	W-2146734	0765	1
VACINEK ROBERT D	CW3	W-2146942	0665	1
VACURA HAROLD J	MAJ	0-0418412	0960	1
VADA ALBERT J	LTC	0-1016107	1262	1
VADEN ANDREW C	1LT	0-0378885	0446	2
VADEN DAVID J	CPT	0-0506935	0649	1
VADEN FLOYD L	LTC	0-1293681	1163	1
VADEN FRANK S JR	COL	0-0254623	0566	3
VADEN SAMUEL A	MAJ	0-1060673	0467	1
VADEN THOMAS H	LTC	0-0174869	0760	3
VADNAIS ARTHUR A	CW2	W-2109482	0946	1
VADNER LAWRENCE S	MAJ	0-0102330	0158	3
VADNEY EVELYN F	1LT	N-0720746	0945	1
VAESSEN CORNELIUS	LTC	0-1105879	0166	1
VAGUSKI JOSEPH	CW4	W-2148344	1157	1
VAIL DAVID B	LTC	0-1638707	0165	1
VAIL RALPH	MAJ	0-0922657	0745	2
VAILATI LOUIS T	CPT	0-2012320	0657	1
VAILLANCOURT MARY M	1LT	N-0720299	0546	1
VAILLANCOURT OLIVER	MAJ	0-1824101	0762	1
VAILLANCOURT SIDNEY	CW2	W-2151833	0260	1
VAILLANCOURT VINCENT	CW3	W-2153272	0762	1
VAIRA JACK A	LTC	0-1111402	1062	1
VAITONIS ANTON F	CPT	0-1323189	0251	2
VAITONIS MARJORIE P	CPT	N-0773789	1052	2
VALDEPENAS NUMERIA	2LT	0-0888116	0850	2
VALDEZ ISIDRO S JR	LTC	0-1997748	1262	1
VALDEZ LIBRADO P	MAJ	0-1924997	0965	1
VALDEZ PETRONILO	1LT	0-0890552	1054	1
VALDEZ WALTER E	2LT	0-1329536	1145	2
VALE CHARLES F	MAJ	0-1644861	0758	1
VALE RAMON	LTC	0-0423251	0162	1
VALENCIA LUIS	MAJ	0-0982273	0762	2
VALENTA MARCUS A	LTC	0-0305250	0865	3
VALENTEEN THOMAS W	LTC	0-1178651	0768	1
VALENTI CHARLES N	MAJ	0-0976921	1062	1
VALENTI JOHN S	LTC	0-1638709	1265	1
VALENTIC JOHN A	MAJ	0-1875552	0765	1
VALENTINE ALICE	MAJ	M-0000975	0364	1
VALENTINE APLIE J	COL	0-0444966	0663	3
VALENTINE EDWARD A	MAJ	0-0158984	0853	3
VALENTINE EDWARD R	MAJ	0-0191904	0854	3
VALENTINE JOHN J	LTC	0-1322385	0462	1
VALENTINE JOHN W	MAJ	0-2051729	0359	1
VALENTINE KENNETH B	CPT	0-0123106	0855	3
VALENTINE MAURICE L	LTC	0-1639756	0865	1
VALENTINE PAUL F	COL	0-0917238	1163	3
VALENTINE RALPH N	LTC	0-0287162	0668	3
VALENTINE WILLIAM F	2LT	0-1638710	1143	2
VALENTINI EVELYN E	LTC	0-0100530	0648	3
VALENTINO FILOMENA A	MAJ	N-0722170	1161	1
VALENZUELA CECIL R	CPT	0-1896382	1063	2
VALENZUELA EDWARD J	MAJ	0-2028756	0964	1
VALENZUELA RAOUL P	LTC	0-1549153	0661	1
VALERA MARIANO	1LT	0-0890504	0849	2
VALERIC CHARLES E	CW3	W-2146682	0363	1
VALES JAMES R	LTC	0-0330754	0367	3
VALESKA DONALD G	MAJ	0-1018862	0761	1
VALIGORSKY N M	CW2	W-2146291	0360	1
VALKO ANDREW A	CPT	0-1559131	0156	1

NAME	GRADE	SVC NO	DATE RET MO YR	RET CODE
VALLACHER THEODORE L	CPT	0-0765872	0945	2
VALLANDINGHAM CLINTO	CW2	W-2211082	0164	1
VALLANDINGHAM JOHN T	MAJ	0-0122973	0648	3
VALLARIO RUDOLPH A	LTC	0-1047821	0765	1
VALLAZZA WILLIAM J	LTC	0-1550079	0260	2
VALLE PETER M	LTC	0-0408693	0860	1
VALLEDOR SID [illegible]	2LT	0-1896873	0459	1
VALLEJO MARY E	2LT	N-0771755	0544	1
VALLEJO ROY J	MAJ	0-1543240	0366	1
VALLERY JERRY	LTC	0-1113030	0263	1
VALLESE MARIO J	MAJ	0-1234682	0964	1
VALLEY GEORGE A	MAJ	0-2017676	1160	2
VALLIERE JOSEPH R	LTC	0-0451256	0955	1
VALLO JULIA M	2LT	N-0730626	0743	1
VALLO SEBASTIAN	MAJ	0-0345842	0646	2
VALLOS JOHN C	LTC	0-0373460	0661	1
VALLOW HERBERT P	MAJ	0-1796551	0859	1
VALOIS DOUGLAS J	1LT	0-1647767	0646	2
VALTON EDWARD T	CPT	0-1796199	0557	2
VALVERDE MARIO F	MAJ	0-0350115	0146	2
VAN AUKER EMIL A	CW2	W-2148133	0657	1
VAN AKEN CHETWOOD G	CPT	0-1311950	0461	1
VAN ALLEN ALFRED	LTC	0-1004711	0263	1
VAN AMBURGH PAUL E	MAJ	0-0265948	0943	2
VAN ANDEL ALBERT E	CPT	0-0501748	0750	2
VAN ANDEL SHERMAN L	CW2	W-2214858	0966	1
VAN ANROY OSCAR J	CW4	W-2004563	0164	3
VAN ANTWERP ELMER D	CPT	0-0282298	0662	3
VAN ANTWERP MAURICE	LTC	0-0223431	0964	3
VAN ANTWERP WILLIAM	COL	0-0197205	1159	1
VAN ARNAM WILLIAM D	MAJ	0-0189138	0858	1
VAN ARSDALE FRANK W	CW2	W-2141688	0463	1
VAN ARSDALE WALTON S	COL	0-0303931	0968	3
VAN ARSDALE WILLIA	LTC	0-0204940	0359	3
VAN ATTA ALLEN M	LTC	0-0491665	0868	3
VAN ATTA FREDERICK	COL	0-0267544	0960	3
VAN AUKEN CYNTHIA J	MAJ	L-0705126	0568	1
VAN AUKEN KENNETH R	CW2	W-2143306	0564	1
VAN BEBER BILL E	LTC	0-0962065	0868	1
VAN BESIAN GEORGE J	MAJ	0-0372367	0846	2
VAN BIBBER AMES M	MAJ	0-1936734	0868	1
VAN BORKUM ARNOLD J	COL	0-0337438	0662	2
VAN BUREN GEORGE R	MAJ	0-1548330	1061	1
VAN BUREN HENRY T	CPT	0-0465198	0546	2
VAN BUREN MARTIN E	CPT	0-0514431	0547	2
VAN BUSKIRK ADELBE	CPT	0-0276504	0146	2
VAN BUSKIRK ELLIS C	COL	0-1595404	0968	1
VAN BUSKIRK WILLIAM	LTC	0-1798819	1064	1
VAN CAMPEN JIM A	CW2	W-2208325	0164	1
VAN CAMPEN RICHARD J	LTC	0-1101249	1160	1
VAN CISE PHILIP S	COL	0-0203825	0648	3
VAN CLEAVE DANIEL R	MAJ	0-1297620	0356	1
VAN CLEAVE HOWARD J	LTC	0-0270914	0868	3
VAN COOK ARTHUR F	LTC	0-1172702	0664	1
VAN COURTLAND W R	2LT	0-1633613	0944	2
VAN DAM DON H	LTC	0-0306074	0167	3
VAN DAM JOHN H	MAJ	0-1633028	0253	2
VAN DE CARR FRANCIS	LTC	0-0282208	1161	2
VAN DE GRAAFF WILL	LTC	0-0245236	0354	2
VAN DE MARK DANIEL	1LT	0-0383793	0346	2
VAN DE WALKER WILLIA	LTC	0-0979631	0568	1
VAN DEE ROBERT F	CPT	0-5400073	0468	2
VAN DELLEN CLARENC	MAJ	0-1299148	0554	2
VAN DER WALL HAROLD	1LT	0-0977402	1055	1
VAN DERHOEF FLOYD C	LTC	0-1300108	1060	1
VAN DERLICK EARLE V	MAJ	0-1949960	0767	3
VAN DERRIPE W S	LTC	0-0910330	1060	3
VAN DEUSEN GEORGE W	LTC	0-0290051	0762	3
VAN DEVENTER WILLIAM	COL	0-0330757	0265	3
VAN DIVIER JAMES M	LTC	0-0323660	0468	3
VAN DOORN FREDERIC A	LTC	0-0925105	0963	1
VAN DORN LLOYD S	MAJ	0-0195979	0458	3
VAN DORPE JOHN H	1LT	0-1315453	0446	2
VAN DUSEN CHARLES R	CW4	W-2110390	0660	1
VAN DUSEN CLARENCE R	LTC	0-0288037	1267	3
VAN DUSEN DANIEL	LTC	0-0232318	1060	3
VAN DUSER DAMON E	CPT	0-2012262	0258	1
VAN DUYN JACK H	CPT	0-0355104	0246	2
VAN DUYN ROGER C	COL	0-0387179	1262	1
VAN DUYNE GARDNER	CPT	0-0915646	1046	2
VAN DUYNE RICHARD	CPT	0-1169753	1147	2
VAN DUZEE CHARLES W	CW4	W-2146857	0968	1
VAN DYCK JOHN F	LTC	0-1183212	0162	1
VAN DYKE GEORGE S	LTC	0-1543868	1164	1
VAN DYKE SETH H	LTC	0-0275530	1054	3
VAN DYNE JOSEPH R	MAJ	0-0439064	0746	2
VAN EGEREN ROBERT J	CPT	0-0445447	0146	2
VAN ELZAKKER JOHN S	2LT	0-1314205	0445	2
VAN EMST JAMES H	LTC	0-1592676	0263	1
VAN EPPS JOHN A	LTC	0-0451723	0361	1
VAN ES ERNST A	COL	0-0913166	1161	3
VAN ESSO ANDREW E	COL	0-0241739	0965	3
VAN ETTEN GLEN G	CPT	0-1108383	0646	2
VAN FLEET GEORGE L	LTC	0-1325682	0865	1
VAN FLEET JAMES K	LTC	0-1307107	0366	1
VAN GOETHEM CYRIL C	CW4	W-2141832	0966	1
VAN GORDEN ARCHIE H	CPT	0-0393255	0144	2
VAN GORDEN CLINTON	CPT	0-1341728	0757	1
VAN HAAFTEN EDWARD C	LTC	0-0274122	0754	3
VAN HALE LAURENCE A	MAJ	0-0319403	0246	2
VAN HARDEVELD JACO	COL	0-0274580	0558	1
VAN HAUSEN WILLIS H	CPT	0-1555312	0463	1
VAN HEUCKEROTH ARTHU	LTC	0-0321874	1264	3
VAN HISE EDWARD P	MAJ	0-0110496	0856	3
VAN HOLLEN RUSSELL L	COL	0-0274096	0661	3
VAN HOLSBAKE LEON A	MAJ	0-1031983	0962	1
VAN HOOGEN ANDRE B	1LT	0-0994432	0655	2
VAN HOOK ELMER E	LTC	0-0442611	0846	2
VAN HOOK GEORGE J	CW3	W-2152288	0764	1
VAN HOOK SAMUEL M	MAJ	0-1110858	0458	2
VAN HOOK WARREN B	LTC	0-0372263	1060	1
VAN HOOK WILLIAM Y	LTC	0-0394260	0666	1
VAN HOOMISSEN F H	2LT	N-0736371	1043	1
VAN HOOREBEKE D H	CPT	0-0976430	0261	1
VAN HOOSER HOMER U	MAJ	0-0953765	0862	1
VAN HOOZER FRED Q	LTC	0-0422760	0563	1
VAN HORN EUGENE G	MAJ	0-2007089	0264	1
VAN HORN HAROLD	CPT	0-4011089	0963	1
VAN HORN JOSEPH B	MAJ	0-1030620	0261	1
VAN HORN MAURICE W	LTC	0-0338944	1059	1
VAN HORN WILBOR B	CW3	W-2148271	0463	1
VAN HOUSEN CHARLES	CPT	0-2021883	0464	1
VAN HOUTEN LOUIS M	LTC	0-0378991	1067	3
VAN HOUTEN ROBERT A	LTC	0-0317116	0760	1
VAN HOY LOUIE R	LTC	0-1301227	0461	1
VAN HOY WILLIAM L	LTC	0-0292283	0361	1
VAN HUSS CARL W	MAJ	0-1923509	0765	1
VAN HUSS LYLE J	CW3	W-2150226	0264	1
VAN KAN HUBERT J	LTC	0-1633614	0366	1
VAN KEUREN GERALD M	LTC	0-1548577	0865	1
VAN KIRK JAY K	CPT	0-2028356	0857	2
VAN KIRK JOHN C	CPT	0-0335578	0845	2
VAN KRIEKEN JOHN	CPT	0-1284434	0957	1
VAN KOREN HARRY O	LTC	0-1551136	0367	3
VAN LEEUWEN CHARLES	MAJ	0-0410371	0762	1
VAN LENTEN WILBUR	MAJ	0-0513038	0763	1
VAN LOO WILTON E	MAJ	0-2020597	0865	1
VAN LUVENDER WESLEY	CW3	W-2145212	0364	1
VAN MAASTRICHT PETER	MAJ	0-1175605	1160	1
VAN MAMEREN JOHN A	LTC	0-1042975	0164	1
VAN METER ALBERT R	LTC	0-0445059	0457	1
VAN METER DONALD S	LTC	0-0501011	1163	1
VAN METER JEROME R	1LT	0-1052189	1045	2
VAN METER WHITAM K	COL	0-0233248	0959	1
VAN NATTA MILES C	CPT	0-0385589	0757	1
VAN NESS NOBLE	LTC	0-0294303	0357	3
VAN NESS SHERMAN M	CW2	RW-2209782	0961	1
VAN NEST ARDEN L	MAJ	0-0249545	1266	3
VAN NOPPEN THOMAS P	COL	0-0255988	0368	3
VAN NORMAN GARNETT L	MAJ	0-0208762	1047	1
VAN NOSDALE FREDERIC	MAJ	0-1686597	0664	1
VAN NOSTRAND MANNI	1LT	0-0483697	0943	2
VAN NOTE HARRY T JR	LTC	0-0385205	1161	1
VAN NOTE LEROY J	LTC	0-0281590	0459	3
VAN NOY LESLIE N	LTC	0-0328043	0546	2
VAN OOSTREL FRANK	MAJ	0-0368457	0861	1
VAN ORDEN HAZEL W	LTC	0-0300154	1263	3
VAN ORMAN CHESTER W	MAJ	0-2212096	0862	1
VAN ORMAN GEORGE A	MAJ	0-0450114	0357	1
VAN OS SEYMOUR	COL	0-0123018	0-53	3
VAN OSDEL RICHARD L	CW2	W-2150590	0363	1
VAN PATTEN MAX M	1LT	0-1012801	0245	2
VAN PELT CLARENCE O	CW2	W-2102494	0956	1
VAN PELT CLIFFORD A	CW4	W-2132094	1060	1
VAN PELT ERNEST A	CW2	W-2146946	0855	1
VAN PELT GERALD D	LTC	0-0258805	0866	3
VAN PELT JOHN C	CW4	W-2001933	0466	3
VAN PELT THEODORE L	CW2	W-2206304	0661	1
VAN POPERING ALDEN	MAJ	0-1634424	1062	1
VAN POYCK WALTER S	MAJ	0-1283345	1046	2
VAN PRAAG SAUL	2LT	0-1298622	0845	2
VAN RAALTE ARNOLD B	MAJ	0-0171093	0648	3
VAN RAALTE DERK B K	CPT	0-1313000	0547	2
VAN RAVENSWAAY O P	2LT	N-0759602	0545	1
VAN REED JOHN C	MAJ	0-1290849	0361	1
VAN REET LEO	CW3	W-2147427	1064	1
VAN RIPER ROBERT F	1LT	0-1304593	0447	2
VAN RIPER WENDELL J	LTC	0-2036453	0960	1
VAN RODEN EDWARD L	COL	0-0139956	0652	3
VAN SADERS LEONARD R	MAJ	0-1552611	0866	1
VAN SANT DANIEL M	1LT	0-0551032	1045	2
VAN SANT ELLANOR B	MAJ	N-0721201	0967	1
VAN SANT ELWOOD W	CW3	W-2149132	0559	1
VAN SANT GEORGE A	CPT	0-1645452	0556	1
VAN SANT JOHN E	LTC	0-0386321	0860	1
VAN SANT JOHN W	CPT	0-0494336	0747	1
VAN SANTEN JOHN H JR	LTC	0-2023014	1266	1
VAN SAUN ARTHUR C	MAJ	0-0191121	0644	2
VAN SCHOICK RICHAR	CPT	0-0346295	0648	1
VAN SCIVER HARRY B	COL	0-0321824	0648	3
VAN SCOYOC MELWOOD W	CPT	0-0233201	0763	3
VAN SICKLE ALBERT K	1LT	0-0497771	0845	2
VAN SICKLE MERRILL F	LTC	0-0375354	0562	1
VAN SICKLE ROGER E	MAJ	0-1597846	0867	3
VAN SICKLE VERNON L	CW2	W-2144624	1060	1
VAN SISE FREDERICK	2LT	0-1050495	1050	2
VAN SLYKE GORDON F	1LT	0-1638718	0648	2
VAN SLYKE HELEN L	2LT	N-0721039	0345	2
VAN SLYKE LELAND P	CPT	0-1280177	0144	2
VAN SLYKE STUART O	LTC	0-0392195	0765	1
VAN SLYKE VADER H	LTC	0-0225153	1264	3
VAN SMITH HERBERT C	LTC	0-0131370	1154	3
VAN STOCKUM ANTON W	LTC	0-0253935	0650	3
VAN STORY JOE JR	CW2	W-2212695	1167	1
VAN STUCK W	COL	0-0903193	1165	3
VAN SWARINGEN R L	LTC	0-0411448	0960	1
VAN SWEARINGEN JOS	CPT	0-0923953	0647	2
VAN TASSEL GERALD K	COL	0-0374248	0862	2
VAN TASSEL GORDON E	2LT	0-0451631	0444	2
VAN TASSEL REX	CW2	W-2147983	0261	1
VAN TILL JOHN H	CPT	0-0486654	0451	1
VAN TREESE CHARLES D	1LT	0-1166855	0545	2
VAN TUYL PAUL	COL	0-0253641	0159	3
VAN VALKENBURG GUY A	1LT	0-1287969	1045	2
VAN VALKENBURG KENNE	CPT	0-0370540	0867	3
VAN VALKENBURGH DALE	CPT	0-1825204	1263	1
VAN VELZOR JAMES O	CPT	0-1306204	1047	2
VAN VLECK MARVIN E	2LT	0-1055178	0944	2
VAN VLIET SYLVESTE	MAJ	0-1167684	0155	2
VAN VOAST H S JR	LTC	0-0234941	0361	3
VAN VOORIES ROBERT	CPT	0-0342514	0146	2
VAN VOSSEN NORMAN	2LT	0-1317707	1144	2
VAN VRANKEN RALPH	MAJ	0-0190329	0955	3
VAN WAGENEN JAMES H	LTC	0-0265568	0164	3
VAN WART ROBERT J	1LT	0-1031280	0746	2
VAN WERT HAROLD J	MAJ	0-1286929	0747	2
VAN WERT WAYNE W	LTC	0-1575240	0561	1
VAN WEY CARL C	CPT	0-0488375	0648	1
VAN WICKLE CHARLES O	CPT	0-0262799	0467	3
VAN WINKLE SPENCER	WO1	W-2135062	1045	2
VAN WINKLE THOMAS	1LT	0-1583789	1047	2
VAN WINKLE WILSON W	LTC	0-0392715	1058	1
VAN WOERKOM JOHN W	LTC	0-1100809	0767	1
VAN WYCK WILLIAM O	2LT	0-0390649	0544	2
VAN WYCKHOUSE ROBERT	CW4	W-2143436	0766	1
VAN WYK FRANK J	COL	0-0267019	0163	3
VAN YSSELDYK JACOB L	CPT	0-1011261	0553	1
VAN ZANDT ARNOLD C	COL	0-0164959	0948	3
VAN ZANDT FRANKLIN K	CPT	0-0230181	1263	3
VAN ZANDT GILBERT F	CPT	0-1184964	0159	1
VAN ZANDT JOHN P	CPT	0-0228415	0554	3
VAN ZANT ELMER L	MAJ	0-0496559	1156	1
VAN ZANT HERBERT	LTC	0-0366661	0160	1
VAN ZANTE HOWARD H	MAJ	0-2210163	0468	1
VANGOE&BOGART A A	2LT	0-1010837	0745	2
VANGOE&KAMP ARTHUR H	1LT	0-1168961	0745	2
VANGOE&VENTER DALE	WO1	W-2144548	1053	1
VANGOE&WALKER LYLE E	1LT	0-1168499	0646	2
VANGOFR&LUGT PETER	COL	0-0194414	0452	3
VAN-DEN-HEUVEL STAN	2LT	0-0388038	1043	2
VANAKER BERNARD S	MAJ	0-1540753	0561	1
VANAMAN ROBERT B	MAJ	0-1643405	0258	1
VANASKY JOHN	1LT	0-1575248	0445	2
VANASSE BEATRICE M	1LT	N-0754204	0850	2
VANATTA HARRY W	LTC	0-1580442	1264	1
VANCE ARLINGTON	CW4	W-2141478	0965	1
VANCE BRUCE B	COL	0-0335432	0361	3
VANCE CHARLES S	COL	0-0118125	0155	1
VANCE HAROLD R	MAJ	0-0315469	1047	2
VANCE HARVEY C	MAJ	0-1031279	0854	1
VANCE HEBER G	CPT	0-0343451	1046	2
VANCE HOMER P	MAJ	0-1593354	0361	1
VANCE JAMES D	COL	0-0304390	0861	1
VANCE JAMES W	MAJ	0-1541135	1055	1
VANCE JOHN E	B G	0-0229832	0665	3
VANCE LUTHER J	1LT	0-2018440	0161	1
VANCE ROBERT C C	1LT	0-1001922	0945	2
VANCE ROBERT S H	MAJ	0-0288124	0468	3
VANCE ROBERT T JR	CPT	0-5240020	1068	2
VANCE STEWART H	LTC	0-1846373	1062	1
VANCE TED	LTC	0-2262150	0868	1
VANCE WENDEL F	CPT	0-0450202	0746	2
VANCE WILLIAM M	COL	0-0141733	0357	2
VANCE WILLIAM T	MAJ	0-2030997	1167	1
VANCIL FRANCE E	MAJ	0-0425241	0565	1
VANDAHL HENRY C	MAJ	0-0485078	0945	2
VANDE VEGT JOSEP	MAJ	0-1287624	1160	1
VANDE-WATER CLAREN	CPT	0-1287794	0353	2
VANDEBRAKE CLARENCE	1LT	0-2034709	0946	2
VANDECAVEYE GEORGE R	CW2	W-2214460	0667	1
VANDEGRIFT GEORGE E	MAJ	0-1081679	0265	1
VANDENBERG GERALD	MAJ	0-0241586	1264	3
VANDENBERG MILTON H	CPT	0-0516128	0346	2
VANDENBERG ROBERT L	2LT	0-1320675	0644	2
VANDENBERG ROBERT W	CPT	0-1302236	0645	2
VANDENBOSCH HELEN F	LTC	N-0790506	0768	2
VANDER HEYDEN DON	MAJ	0-0948741	0363	1
VANDER HEYDEN RAL	MAJ	0-0976045	1064	1
VANDER VEER FRANC	LTC	0-0281681	1263	3
VANDER VEER HOWARD J	COL	0-0270549	0868	3
VANDER VLIET A	CPT	0-0262174	0957	1
VANDER VLIET ANTH	CPT	0-2262174	0957	1
VANDER ZWIEP P J	COL	0-0287932	0161	1
VANDER&VOORT DALE G	1LT	0-0552206	0346	2
VANDER-HEIDE IRWIN C	LTC	0-0486305	0266	3
VANDER-LINDEN WILLIA	1LT	0-0485920	0248	2
VANDER-STOLP WILLA	1LT	0-1303439	0845	2
VANDERBERG JOHN H	2LT	0-1014816	0645	2
VANDERBURG ALBERT L	MAJ	0-0455752	0159	1
VANDERBURG JACK R	LTC	0-1643406	0667	1

NAME	GRADE	SVC NO	DATE RET MO YR	RET CODE
VANDERBURGH ARNOTT K	LTC	0-0382493	0154	1
VANDERBURGH LESTER B	MAJ	0-0487636	0553	1
VANDERBURGH WARREN M	MAJ	0-0385163	0762	1
VANDERFORD HAROLD J	MAJ	0-0267072	0966	3
VANDERFORD JOHN H	1LT	0-1320877	0752	2
VANDERGOOT WILBUR	WO1	W-2105949	0947	2
VANDERGRIFF RAYMOND	CW3	W-2147399	0462	1
VANDERHOFF JAMES R	MAJ	0-2038830	0460	1
VANDERHOFF JESS K	LTC	0-0276491	0966	3
VANDERHOFF MALCOLM J	MAJ	0-1688415	1164	1
VANDERKAMP BERNARD J	1LT	0-1012543	0445	2
VANDERLIP ARTHUR N	LTC	0-0250931	0861	3
VANDERLIP CHARLES B	MAJ	0-5301719	0268	1
VANDERPOOL JOSEPH G	1LT	0-0887588	0762	1
VANDERPOOL LEROY J	CPT	0-1951671	1263	1
VANDERPOOL WILLIAM F	MAJ	0-1582229	0161	1
VANDERVOORT WILLIAM	LTC	0-0297358	0663	1
VANDERVORT CHARLES E	LTC	0-1048627	0361	1
VANDERWILT BERT	COL	0-0139961	0953	3
VANDERZALM THEODORE	COL	0-0324515	0853	3
VANDEVENTER JEROME J	MAJ	0-0278043	1059	3
VANDEVER JAMES M	COL	0-0485620	1268	2
VANDEWATER REGINAL	COL	0-0238948	0648	3
VANDISH ARTHUR J	LTC	0-0255590	1146	1
VANDIVER COMER L	COL	0-0250020	1264	3
VANDIVER DAN D	CW2	W-2208430	1064	1
VANDIVER THOMAS C	MAJ	0-0261558	1167	3
VANDOVER JOHN T	COL	0-0335528	0468	3
VANDREUIL RAYMOND L	LTC	0-1032124	0962	1
VANEK VACLAV H	COL	0-0358545	1064	1
VANGE SIMON C	1LT	0-1040632	1148	1
VANGEN TERRANCE A	LTC	0-1283873	0259	1
VANGENE KERMIT E	LTC	0-0415058	1160	1
VANHOUK JOHNIE L	CW3	W-2141479	0460	1
VANKIRK TRAVIS L	CW3	W-2150603	0559	1
VANN JAMES R	LTC	0-0504344	1154	1
VANN LUTHER R	LTC	0-0345112	0362	3
VANN THAD	COL	0-0347290	1067	3
VANN WILLIAM F	LTC	0-1180077	0563	1
VANNEY JOSEPH J	1LT	0-1283874	1145	2
VANNI LOUIS J	1LT	0-1643408	0345	2
VANNONI VASILLI P	CW2	W-2214892	0866	1
VANNORDSTRAND PAUL A	LTC	0-0408635	0960	1
VANNOY GARNETT R	CW2	W-2145170	0956	1
VANNOY THOMAS H	CPT	0-0335661	0756	1
VANNUCCI ALBERT O	1LT	0-1555645	1045	2
VANOSDOL PERRY H	1LT	0-0468055	0845	2
VANSANT ALLEN S	LTC	0-0277962	0565	3
VANSICKLE JAMES A	MAJ	0-1882257	0967	1
VANSTON AUGUST R	LTC	0-1115442	1064	3
VANSTON PAUL J	1LT	0-1295297	1145	2
VANUCCI FRANK	CPT	0-0308447	1045	2
VANZANDT BILLY J	CW3	RW-2145598	0665	1
VANZANT CHARLES V	MAJ	0-1014996	0961	1
VARA JOSEPH J JR	MAJ	0-2204111	0466	1
VARDEN HARRY J	LTC	0-1573649	0556	1
VARELA OSMUND L	LTC	0-0175462	0348	2
VARELLI FRANCIS P	CPT	0-0959337	0562	1
VARETONI RAYMOND	MAJ	0-1635437	0358	1
VARGA ANTHONY A	CW2	W-2149271	1262	2
VARGA WILLIAM	CW3	W-2118536	1157	1
VARGO JOHN C	MAJ	0-2055492	0854	1
VARGO JOSEPH P	MAJ	0-0472126	0854	1
VARGO WILLIAM J	MAJ	0-1823374	0859	1
VARIAN JESSE W	LTC	0-0206858	0556	1
VARIAN JOHN F	B G	0-0259878	0368	3
VARLAND ARTHUR Z JR	CPT	0-0380130	0143	2
VARLEY JOHN W	CPT	0-0340363	1147	2
VARLEY NOLAND	LTC	0-0238522	0965	3
VARNADO HUGH R JR	CPT	0-1046306	0547	2
VARNADO NORMAN L	2LT	0-0557747	1045	2
VARNER DWIGHT S	MAJ	0-0402879	0245	2
VARNER GRAYSON K	CPT	0-0365424	1067	3
VARNER LAURENCE W	COL	0-0198797	0954	1
VARNEY AUSTIN A	LTC	0-1169376	0261	1

NAME	GRADE	SVC NO	DATE RET MO YR	RET CODE
VARNEY EARLE L	CW2	W-2145273	0561	1
VARNEY EWERT	WO1	W-2150057	1060	1
VARNEY GEORGE C	CPT	0-0532796	1145	2
VARNEY HARLEY R	MAJ	0-1821112	1045	2
VARNEY IRVIN J	LTC	0-0309832	0764	1
VARNEY KENNETH A	LTC	0-0251218	0764	3
VARNEY LINWOOD I JR	MAJ	0-1550287	0358	1
VARNEY LYMAN O	COL	0-0209137	0254	3
VARNEY RODERIC A	LTC	0-1080975	1164	1
VARNEY THEODORE R	LTC	0-0248162	0466	3
VARNI JOSEPH C	CPT	0-2027804	0456	1
VARNUM HARVEY C	1LT	0-1306664	0844	2
VARON FRANK A	CW4	W-2147922	0968	2
VARRAVETO MILDRED F	MAJ	N-0785444	0365	1
VARRELMANN GALE L	1LT	0-0540547	0346	2
VARZALY EUGENE	MAJ	0-1582812	0161	1
VASEY JOHNNIE E	CPT	0-2014849	0460	1
VASIL LEON N	MAJ	0-1044415	0756	1
VASILAKE JOHN G	CPT	0-1289169	0562	2
VASILOU GEORGE	CW3	W-2143058	0861	1
VASKO JOHN R	COL	0-0235205	1061	3
VASS ERNEST A JR	MAJ	0-1043823	1159	1
VASS FREDERICK	MAJ	0-1945512	0967	3
VASS GEORGE T	1LT	0-0462665	0146	2
VASSALLO ANTHONY L	LTC	0-0453357	0856	1
VASSALOTTI FRANK J	COL	0-0352433	1168	1
VASSAR CHARLES T	1LT	0-0504035	0645	2
VASSAR WILLIAM F	LTC	0-0389152	0766	1
VASSEL WILLIAM D	LTC	0-1325843	1264	2
VASSER ROY	LTC	0-1102100	0557	1
VASTINE JOHN R	CPT	0-0490688	0944	2
VASU CLAUDE F	1LT	0-1323207	1045	2
VATER FREDERICK	LTC	0-0183774	0648	3
VATH CHARLES H	LTC	0-0267627	0861	3
VAUDRY JAMES W	MAJ	0-0381305	0246	2
VAUGHAN ALVIN A	CPT	0-0502462	0546	2
VAUGHAN BERNICE L	MAJ	0-0974675	0768	1
VAUGHAN CARL E	WO1	W-2110578	1044	2
VAUGHAN CHARLES C	LTC	0-0906227	0266	3
VAUGHAN CONAN W JR	COL	0-0237325	0566	3
VAUGHAN DANIEL V	CPT	0-1823241	0761	1
VAUGHAN DONALD G	LTC	0-0222573	1061	3
VAUGHAN ELLIS F	LTC	0-0259197	0868	3
VAUGHAN EUGENE L	2LT	0-1032608	0744	2
VAUGHAN FREDERICK	MAJ	0-0308140	0262	3
VAUGHAN GEORGE	1LT	0-1036776	0246	2
VAUGHAN HARRY H	M G	0-0205101	0153	2
VAUGHAN HENRY S	1LT	0-1328425	0746	2
VAUGHAN HERMAN A	CW2	W-2118257	1048	1
VAUGHAN JAMES F	MAJ	0-0508945	0756	1
VAUGHAN JAMES H JR	COL	0-0412094	0267	1
VAUGHAN LEWIS C	LTC	0-1283093	1062	1
VAUGHAN MARY S	2LT	N-0794356	1046	1
VAUGHAN MYRON C	MAJ	0-1557386	0863	1
VAUGHAN PERRY A	CPT	0-1043247	0745	2
VAUGHAN ROBERT	LTC	0-0453290	1265	1
VAUGHAN ROBERT B	MAJ	0-1283699	1158	1
VAUGHAN ROBERT W	MAJ	0-0969526	0663	1
VAUGHAN RUFUS E	COL	0-0246417	0954	3
VAUGHAN SAMUEL E	COL	0-0177348	0461	3
VAUGHAN TURNER J JR	CW3	W-2144199	0861	1
VAUGHAN WALES	MAJ	0-0418813	0366	1
VAUGHAN WILLIAM H	MAJ	0-1182985	0861	1
VAUGHN CHARLES E	CPT	0-1108386	1051	2
VAUGHN CHARLES H	1LT	0-1543620	1153	1
VAUGHN ERNEST A	MAJ	0-1542667	0555	1
VAUGHN FRED H	COL	0-0122925	0648	3
VAUGHN GEORGE A JR	LTC	0-0139465	0557	3
VAUGHN GUY V	CPT	0-2001663	1057	1
VAUGHN JAMES A	CPT	0-1586307	0559	1
VAUGHN JAMES F	MAJ	0-1874889	1266	1
VAUGHN JIMMIE D	MAJ	0-0889717	0860	1
VAUGHN JOE D	MAJ	0-0239474	0666	3
VAUGHN JOHN H	LTC	0-2011631	0567	1
VAUGHN JOHN L	CPT	0-0501747	0347	1

NAME	GRADE	SVC NO	DATE RET MO YR	RET CODE
VAUGHN MAURICE B	MAJ	0-1010196	1060	1
VAUGHN MILTON S	LTC	0-1048629	0662	1
VAUGHN RALPH W	COL	0-0237884	0865	3
VAUGHN ROBERT L	CW3	W-2007112	1067	2
VAUGHN VIRGIL E	LTC	0-1014362	0656	1
VAUGHN WALTER R	2LT	0-2010677	0446	2
VAUGHN WILBERT F	CPT	0-2036086	0257	2
VAUGHN WILLIS C	LTC	0-1558357	0958	1
VAUGHN WINFRED E	CPT	0-0389767	1045	2
VAUGHT LESLIE L	CPT	0-0282785	0945	2
VAUPEL ROBERT V	MAJ	0-0302942	0350	2
VAUTRAIN PAUL A	CPT	0-0488169	0853	2
VAUX JOSEPH JR	CW2	W-3411014	1166	1
VAZQUEZ ANGELICO	MAJ	0-1302420	1053	1
VAZQUEZ GENEROSO	COL	0-0331489	0756	3
VAZQUEZ JUAN	CPT	0-0190387	0146	1
VAZQUEZ RICARDO V	MAJ	0-1285342	1060	1
VAZQUEZ ROBERTO	CW3	W-2005790	0965	1
VAZQUEZ SAMUEL C	MAJ	0-1340597	0866	1
VAZQUEZ WILLIAM	CW3	W-2005312	1266	1
VAZQUEZ&MILAN HIRAM	1LT	0-1727087	0345	2
VAZQUEZ-GARCIA V	MAJ	0-2014803	0566	1
VAZZANA WILLIAM E	LTC	0-1295967	0661	1
VEACH ROBERT T	CPT	0-2000646	0657	1
VEADER JOHN F	CW3	W-2152330	0764	1
VEAHMAN PHILLIP H	CW2	W-2211429	0567	1
VEAL CURTIS	MAJ	0-0293588	0846	2
VEAL HORACE	CPT	0-1299821	0954	1
VEAL WILLIE D	COL	0-0246815	0658	1
VEATCH CHARLES K	LTC	0-0297075	0561	1
VEATCH ROBERT W	CPT	0-0296963	1046	2
VEAZEY HAROLD A	COL	0-0236615	0260	1
VEAZEY MYRTLE E	1LT	L-0408607	0149	2
VECCHIO ALEXANDER	MAJ	0-2036284	0258	1
VECCHIOLA CHARLES	1LT	0-1995017	0845	2
VECCHIOLLA FRANK L	LTC	0-0347524	0564	3
VECQUERAY EDWARD F	MAJ	0-4009657	0367	1
VEDELER RICHARDS G	LTC	0-0120969	0360	3
VEDELL HOWARD L	LTC	0-1328654	1167	1
VEECH JAMES E	CPT	0-1550082	0250	1
VEEDER ARTHUR K	1LT	0-0444670	1043	2
VEENSTRA ROBERT J	LTC	0-0337632	1162	2
VEESER LEO W	MAJ	0-0219010	1154	3
VEGA PEDRO A	LTC	0-0368718	0560	1
VEGA VICTOR J	MAJ	0-1101252	1046	2
VEGH MARGARET A	1LT	N-0729005	0546	1
VEGIARD ELSWORTH N	CPT	0-0311786	0743	2
VEGO JOSEPH V	MAJ	0-1322106	0765	1
VEHRS HERMAN F	MAJ	0-0471565	0947	2
VEITCH ALBERT H	LTC	0-0222735	0964	3
VELASQUEZ PERFECTO J	1LT	0-2027805	0854	1
VELAZQUEZ JUSTO P	CW2	W-2005791	0858	2
VELEZ JOBINO	2LT	0-0277618	1050	1
VELISANO GABRIEL	1LT	0-2030126	0149	1
VELONIS STAMATIS G	COL	0-0357366	0966	3
VELTRI SANTO	MAJ	0-0501346	0453	2
VENABLE CLARENCE H	MAJ	0-1917915	0164	1
VENABLE HORACE J JR	MAJ	0-2262492	0365	1
VENABLE MARVIN C	LTC	0-1533698	0662	1
VENABLE ROY M	MAJ	0-1317946	0462	1
VENARD THOMAS W	CW2	W-3350144	0763	1
VENCELIK ROSEMARY	CPT	N-0785062	1156	2
VENDETTI MICHAEL O	CPT	0-5324723	0568	2
VENDITTI EDD G	CPT	0-1046977	0755	1
VENDLEY CLARENCE F	COL	0-0216482	1162	3
VENDOLA LOUIS A	MAJ	0-0969269	1162	1
VENEGAS FRED C	MAJ	0-0195767	0546	1
VENEZIA JOSEPH P	LTC	0-0363814	0462	1
VENN CHARLES F	MAJ	0-0158274	1148	3
VENN EUGENE C	1LT	0-1319237	0745	2
VENN ROLLO E	COL	0-0225772	1162	3
VENNE RICHARD J	1LT	0-1109387	0350	1
VENOR DANIEL A	CPT	0-1917604	0363	1
VENSEL HARRY R	COL	0-0137225	0651	3
VENSEL LESLIE K	LTC	0-1305681	0968	2

NAME	GRADE	SVC NO	DATE RET MO YR	RET CODE
VENSKUS ISADORE E	CPT	0-1282393	0557	1
VENTERS ANDREW L	LTC	0-1047823	0764	1
VENTIMIGLIA VITO	CW3	W-2145238	0761	1
VENTRESCO THERESA A	1LT	N-0805433	0153	2
VENTURA JAMES P	MAJ	0-1594542	0960	1
VENTURO RALPH C	MAJ	0-0462068	0646	2
VER BEEK JOHN	CW3	W-2149833	0766	1
VER MEULEN PET	MAJ	0-0127653	0649	3
VERACRUZ JUAN N	2LT	0-1896948	1148	1
VERAGE FAYE C	MAJ	N-0731579	0966	1
VERBOSH GEORGE	MAJ	0-1924559	0866	1
VERBOSH MICHAEL	LTC	0-0451257	1157	1
VERBURG KEITH B	MAJ	0-2038049	0361	1
VERBURG MITCHELL R	LTC	0-1284965	1264	1
VERCOE SAM G	LTC	0-0257602	0162	1
VERDERBER FRANK J	LTC	0-1011426	0861	1
VEREEN DAVID H	MAJ	0-2030853	0668	2
VEREEN HELEN L	MAJ	N-0727584	0565	1
VERGA FRANK A	COL	0-0376552	0965	3
VERGA SALVATORE	LTC	0-1040162	1060	1
VERGAGNI ROLAND E	MAJ	0-0993810	1163	1
VERGEER SHIRLEY	MAJ	N-0789739	0164	1
VERGHIS GEORGE W	LTC	0-1287970	0167	1
VERHAEGHE GEORGE M	1LT	0-1322496	1045	2
VERHAGE MARTIN D	CPT	0-1686882	0945	2
VERHEYEN KATHRYN J	1LT	N-0772537	0248	1
VERHULST GEORGE J	CPT	0-0972470	1062	1
VERIS HOWARD F	CW3	W-2148821	0767	1
VERITY FRED V L	CPT	0-0184674	0150	3
VERMES EDWARD D	LTC	0-1111407	0865	1
VERMETTE ALBERT L	CW4	W-2142209	0659	1
VERMETTE LAFAYETTE	2LT	0-1800120	0256	1
VERMETTE MARCEL P	LTC	0-0408692	0361	1
VERMEUL JACK E	MAJ	0-1047378	0867	1
VERMILLION PAUL E	MAJ	0-0303249	0146	2
VERMILLION WAYNE D	MAJ	0-1648536	1167	3
VERMONT ROLAND	2LT	0-0301065	0557	3
VERMUELLEN EMMA F	1LT	N-0789078	0846	1
VERNA FRANK P	LTC	0-1795014	0266	1
VERNARELLI ARNOLD F	LTC	0-1288331	0561	1
VERNER PAUL E	CW3	W-2142667	1160	1
VERNER THOMAS	CPT	0-2037753	1156	1
VERNEY ADOLPH A	LTC	0-1111957	0463	1
VERNEY BERNARD	LTC	0-0913165	0967	3
VERNIEL JACOB	CPT	0-1050496	0358	1
VERNON ALBERT E JR	LTC	0-1035390	0867	2
VERNON CLINTON M	LTC	0-0215931	0163	3
VERNON DODO	MAJ	0-1311236	0447	2
VERNON EDWARD C	MAJ	0-1634428	0857	1
VERNON ELWIN A	COL	0-1634429	0868	1
VERNON GORDON L	MAJ	0-0991506	0667	1
VERNON HENRY L	2LT	0-1894577	0344	2
VERNON RALPH R	LTC	0-0263893	0656	2
VERNON RALPH W	LTC	0-1306025	0166	1
VERNON RICHARD P	MAJ	0-1051424	0960	1
VERNON THOMAS D	2LT	0-1914005	0837	1
VERNOSKY HYMAN LTCO	LTC	0-0451546	0258	1
VERRALL RALPH W JR	CW3	W-2152170	1060	1
VERRAN ALMA R	2LT	N-0700289	0338	1
VERREY JOHN P	MAJ	0-0971795	1060	1
VERRILL HERBERT S	1LT	0-0552113	0946	2
VERRILL WILLIAM R	1LT	0-5339296	0868	2
VERSCHOOR BASTIAN C	MAJ	0-0512346	0346	2
VERSCHOYLE HUBERT H	2LT	0-0533510	0745	2
VERSEN HARLIS L	1LT	0-1296947	1045	2
VERSTEEG MARSAILLES	LTC	0-0283563	1263	3
VERTNER WALTER E	CW2	W-2112565	0446	2
VERTREES ALVIN M	MAJ	0-0961905	0164	1
VERVAET ARTHUR W	1LT	0-1326785	0746	2
VERZI LINUS A	MAJ	0-0963647	0468	3
VERZI MARTIN A	LTC	0-1544147	0862	2
VESCE LEILA P	2LT	N-0752341	0345	1
VESCIO PHILLIP L	CW3	W-2147118	0865	1
VESELOVEC STEPHEN	MAJ	0-2046691	0356	1
VESS JAMES A	2LT	0-2019532	0858	1

NAME	GRADE	SVC NO	DATE RET MO YR	RET CODE
VESSELL [illegible] R	CW4	W-2110043	0355	1
VESSELS LEE	LTC	0-0958564	0668	1
VESSER WILLIAM	CW2	W-2141691	1060	1
VEST MAURICE O	COL	0-1701060	0267	3
VEST WILLIAM M	CPT	0-1703464	0565	2
VESTAL HERMAN H	LTC	0-0250381	0364	3
VESTAL MYRON J	MAJ	0-0243116	0368	3
VESTER HERMAN K	LTC	0-2036187	0565	1
VESTERBY VORIS P	CPT	0-1312733	1046	2
VESTNER ELIOT N	LTC	0-0219677	0256	1
VETRANO VICTOR J	2LT	0-1038881	1145	2
VETTER ANDREW G	LTC	0-0209137	0146	2
VETTER ERICH F	CPT	0-1306212	1152	2
VETTER FRANCIS J	CW3	W-2148827	0958	1
VETTERLING HERMAN M	CPT	0-0504420	1048	1
VEXLER CLARENCE J	COL	0-0137137	0354	3
VEZINA CLARA A	MAJ	N-0742451	0562	1
VEZINA GEORGE T	LTC	0-0309255	0867	3
VEZINA LEO J	CW3	W-2142668	0659	1
VEZIS WILFORD J	MAJ	0-0976920	0365	1
VEZZA VINCENT	LTC	0-1944613	0462	1
VEZZETTI HAROLD B	MAJ	0-1634430	0557	1
VEZZOLI DANTE	LTC	0-1549582	0961	1
VIA GEORGE T	WO1	W-2148060	1153	2
VIAJAR CESAR	2LT	0-0395499	0959	1
VIAL LESTER J	2LT	0-1798692	1144	2
VIAL RICHARD J JR	MAJ	0-0265984	0868	3
VIALL OTIS O	LTC	0-0447303	1162	1
VIANI BRUNO R	CPT	0-1307492	1145	2
VIANI HARRY J	LTC	0-1131175	0867	1
VIARENGO LIVIO	CW3	W-2145528	0366	1
VICENTE ELISIO F	LTC	0-0373140	0164	3
VICK ALFRED T	LTC	0-0272220	0868	3
VICK ARTHUR P	CPT	0-1181176	0460	1
VICK DONALD N	MAJ	0-1885224	1266	1
VICK GILBERT M	MAJ	0-0260385	0365	3
VICK J E JR	COL	0-1101253	0261	1
VICK KENNETH S	CW3	W-2102496	0852	2
VICK MAYNARD O	CPT	0-0347725	0161	1
VICK PHARES G	MAJ	0-1113034	0467	1
VICK WARREN A	LTC	0-0465227	0863	1
VICK WILLIAM J JR	MAJ	0-0983474	0664	1
VICKER WILLIAM L	WO1	W-2116726	0445	2
VICKERMAN CHARLES E	LTC	0-0251047	0966	3
VICKERS ELVIN C	CW4	W-2144777	1160	1
VICKERS LAWRENCE H	1LT	0-0436248	1045	2
VICKERS MARION W	LTC	0-1292965	1161	1
VICKERS PAUL A	LTC	0-1102519	0760	1
VICKERS RICHARD H	CPT	0-0378781	0244	2
VICKERS WILBUR N	CPT	0-2029123	0158	1
VICKERS WILLIAM O	LTC	0-1553896	0263	1
VICKERY CHARLES P	MAJ	0-1948537	0764	1
VICKERY CHESTER H	COL	0-1032254	1167	1
VICKERY GRADY M	CPT	0-1959810	0960	1
VICKERY HIRAM K	CW4	W-2146621	0464	1
VICKERY JOE B	1LT	0-0414430	0346	2
VICKERY JOE F	CPT	0-1583796	1154	2
VICKERY PHILIP M	1LT	0-0453779	1143	2
VICKNAIR ROBERT F	CW2	W-2210034	0965	1
VICKREY WILLIAM W	COL	0-0100299	0949	3
VICKSELL ROBERT	CW2	W-2000623	0854	3
VICTOR BERT A	CPT	0-0486379	0747	2
VICTOR CHARLES L	MAJ	0-1284437	0360	1
VICTOR THOMAS M	CPT	0-1324068	1145	2
VIDA GEORGE	LTC	0-0542465	1061	2
VIDA JOSEPH J	CW3	W-2144873	0955	1
VIDALLON WILLIAM A	1LT	0-1896569	0557	1
VIDAURRI ROBERTO F	MAJ	0-2050155	0866	1
VIDEOCK WILFORD F	LTC	0-0498537	0363	1
VIDRA JOHN J	MAJ	0-0499458	1149	1
VIEAU VINCENT K	CPT	0-1295300	0546	2
VIEIRA JOHN	CW3	W-2209820	1068	1
VIELE HOWARD J	CPT	0-0395487	1143	2
VIERGUTZ GEORGE J	1LT	0-2029187	1151	1
VIERLING RAYMOND A	CW3	W-2206125	0567	1
VIERS RAYMOND L	MAJ	0-4030860	0867	1
VIERS WESLEY L	LTC	0-0397745	0860	1
VIERTEL GEORGE F	MAJ	0-1633029	0456	1
VIESTENZ RALPH J	MAJ	0-0972665	0465	1
VIETS LLOYD D	CPT	0-1548584	0867	1
VIEWEG HERMANN F	COL	0-0190439	1060	3
VIEWEGER ARTHUR L	LTC	0-0237950	0664	3
VIGEANT BERTRUM A	LTC	0-1312366	0265	1
VIGEL CARL V	MAJ	0-1691033	0357	1
VIGIL FRED	LTC	0-1798629	0461	1
VIGNEAU ROBERT A	2LT	0-1105447	0145	2
VIGNERON EUGENE M	LTC	0-0168042	0754	3
VIGNOVICH DEMETRE	LTC	0-1011247	0662	1
VIGOR WILLIAM N	MAJ	0-0781585	0146	2
VIGORITO JOSEPH P	1LT	0-0449490	0845	2
VIGUS VICTOR E	LTC	0-1323049	0267	3
VIK CHESTER F	1LT	0-1317959	0546	2
VIKSTROM ARVO J	LTC	0-0985344	1168	2
VILAR CARLOS M	CPT	0-0395492	0844	2
VILDA WILLIAM S	1LT	0-1011561	0745	2
VILE LEARNARD A	CW2	W-2115831	0456	1
VILES VOLER V	LTC	0-1845806	0968	1
VILLA FRANK B	LTC	0-1945970	0960	1
VILLA HAZELETT V	1LT	0-2262912	1154	1
VILLA ROMULO S	1LT	0-1896570	0762	1
VILLADEMOROS JOSEP	CPT	0-0452041	0345	2
VILLADOR EDMUND	1LT	0-1897005	0565	1
VILLADOR RAYMOND	1LT	0-1896411	1058	1
VILLAESCUSA FRANK A	LTC	0-0516280	0956	1
VILLAFANE JUAN A	LTC	0-0934492	0667	1
VILLAFLOR GREGORY P	LTC	0-0357357	0958	2
VILLANORF JAMES F	CPT	0-1540593	0258	1
VILLANO RALPH	MAJ	0-1644180	0664	1
VILLANTI MARIO T	COL	0-0427369	0767	1
VILLAROMAN ISABELO R	1LT	0-0515107	0845	2
VILLEGAS PAUL	2LT	0-2055188	1044	2
VILLEMEZ CLARENCE L	LTC	0-1104429	0860	1
VILLEMEZ CLYDE J	LTC	0-1101255	0960	1
VILLENEUVE ALFRED J	LTC	0-0309278	1067	3
VILLEPIGUE WILLIAM J	CPT	0-0179531	0849	1
VILLEY STEVE	2LT	0-1896530	0149	1
VILLINES AUBREY T	LTC	0-1596843	0766	1
VILLOTT LOUIS P	MAJ	0-1299497	0761	1
VILMUR WALTER M	CW2	W-2108577	1148	1
VILNES MAGNUS	CW4	W-2134449	1154	1
VINAL VICTOR E	CW4	W-2110986	1054	1
VINARDI JOSEPH J	MAJ	0-0266826	0768	3
VINCE JULIUS	CW3	W-2142539	0659	1
VINCENT ARTHUR T	1LT	0-1691490	1045	2
VINCENT CLYDE D	MAJ	0-2016493	0464	1
VINCENT DOYLE C	MAJ	0-1010309	0658	1
VINCENT DWIGHT W	LTC	0-1010591	1160	1
VINCENT EDWARD	MAJ	0-1547817	1262	1
VINCENT FLORENCE	2LT	N-0700486	0640	1
VINCENT HENRY	MAJ	0-0155901	0850	3
VINCENT JOHN L	MAJ	0-0278674	0863	3
VINCENT JOSEPH E	MAJ	0-0319855	0954	2
VINCENT LEE P	LTC	0-1017876	0363	1
VINCENT RUSSELL	LTC	0-0241014	0348	2
VINCENT RUSSIE H	MAJ	0-0263515	0160	3
VINCENT STANLEY J	MAJ	0-1334653	0662	1
VINCENT VARD V	MAJ	0-1543629	0955	1
VINCENT VICTOR K	LTC	0-1639775	0861	1
VINCENT WALTER K	1LT	0-0477578	0643	2
VINCENT WILLIAM G	LTC	0-0449561	0863	1
VINCENT WILLIS E	COL	0-0145364	1054	3
VINCENTI WILFREDO	MAJ	0-1044139	0463	1
VINCETT ERNEST M	MAJ	0-1919315	1165	1
VINCIGUERRA ARMANDO	LTC	0-0505618	0358	3
VINCIGUERRA L	CPT	0-1302393	0157	1
VINCIUS SAMUEL A	CPT	0-0164958	0-49	3
VINCOLI VINCENT	CW2	W-2144517	0656	1
VINDING RANDOLPH H	COL	0-0474952	0361	1
VINER RICHARD A	MAJ	0-0509679	0445	2
VINES HERBERT M	MAJ	0-0394173	0647	2
VINES THELBERT D	CW2	W-2142742	0655	1
VINEYARD COLEMAN W	LTC	0-1175345	0366	1
VINEYARD HENRY C JR	MAJ	0-1182326	0358	1
VINIER CHARLES C	LTC	0-0145397	0648	3
VINING CHARLIE R	CPT	0-2046434	0947	1
VINING WILLIAM F	CW3	W-2143322	1065	2
VINK DONALD R	1LT	0-1298156	1145	2
VINSON BILLY E	MAJ	0-1100378	0857	2
VINSON GEORGE M	CW3	W-2205000	0267	2
VINSON KERMIT J	2LT	0-2005484	1050	1
VINSON MERRILL R	LTC	0-0920791	0260	3
VINSON WILBUR J	MAJ	0-1299347	1057	1
VINTON HAROLD W	CW2	W-2205382	0959	1
VIOLA PETER L	MAJ	0-0171599	0547	1
VIOLETTE ADRIAN J	LTC	0-1298623	0467	1
VIOLYN ROMAN P	CPT	0-0499347	1145	2
VIOX FRANCIS J	LTC	0-0372942	0667	1
VIRAG ALFRED	COL	0-0244080	0866	3
VIRANT LEO B	LTC	0-0202182	0965	1
VIRDEN EMERSON H	LTC	0-0141036	0557	3
VIRDIN JOSEPH O	LTC	0-0176469	0262	3
VIRGIL MAX P	LTC	0-0954773	0766	1
VIRGILIO JOSEPH C	LTC	0-0460868	1061	3
VIROK ARTHUR S	MAJ	0-0975010	0266	1
VIRTS NELLIE M	MAJ	N-0724633	0264	1
VIRTUE JAMES R	LTC	0-0275927	0960	3
VISAGGI JOHN G	CW2	W-2213698	1068	1
VISCO RALPH A	COL	0-0258361	0457	1
VISCONTI CHARLES E	LTC	0-0373094	1163	3
VISCONTI SAMUEL	CW2	W-2214859	0866	1
VISCONTI VINCENT P	WO1	W-2103566	0952	1
VISEL GEORGE V	LTC	0-0501510	0657	1
VISPERAS JUAN	1LT	0-2030579	0250	1
VISTI IVA M	2LT	N-0728494	0246	2
VITACCO ALFRED G	LTC	0-2034592	1165	1
VITEK JOHN R JR	LTC	0-0450143	0658	1
VITIKAS HELEN L	1LT	N-0786892	0750	2
VITO FRANK P	CW2	W-2208667	0460	2
VITRIKAS HAROLD L	CW3	W-2110319	0358	1
VITT GUSTAVE F	LTC	0-0451451	0455	1
VITULLO GEORGE V	1LT	0-1322288	0945	2
VITULLO ORLANDO E	MAJ	0-1014609	0361	1
VITULLO THEODORE L	LTC	0-1042197	0261	1
VIVIANO CLEO L	LTC	0-1312367	1163	2
VIVONA WILLIAM	CPT	0-1289999	0856	1
VLACK JOSEPH B	COL	0-0173569	0561	3
VLAHOS PETER	MAJ	0-0129485	0453	3
VLAMING JOSEPH H	LTC	0-2012086	1065	1
VLASAK FRANK S	LTC	0-2011099	0166	1
VLASICH WILLIAM P	COL	0-0505219	0764	3
VLAZNY ADALBERT L	CPT	0-1684361	0645	2
VLIET RICHARD S	LTC	0-1644185	0763	1
VOBEYDA LUMIR F	CPT	0-0290701	0246	2
VODREY JAMES R JR	CPT	0-1115139	1161	2
VOEGELE WILLIAM C	MAJ	0-1102101	0862	1
VOEHL CHARLES A	LTC	0-1041043	1266	3
VOELKER EDWARD C	COL	0-0239208	0157	3
VOELKER JOACHIM F	LTC	0-0255214	1163	3
VOELKLE PAUL H	CPT	0-2025238	0756	1
VOELKLI HUGO H	CW4	W-2114636	0367	3
VOELTER THEODORE F	COL	0-0171503	1053	3
VOET EUGENE O	LTC	0-2208515	0168	1
VOETBERG HENRY G	LTC	0-0284629	1065	3
VOGAL JACK L	LTC	0-1312071	0863	1
VOGEL ALBERT T JR	CPT	0-1326143	1146	2
VOGEL ALVIN T	1LT	0-1796000	0945	2
VOGEL CARLOS F JR	MAJ	0-0949668	1265	1
VOGEL CLARENCE F	COL	0-0133508	1047	2
VOGEL EDWARD F	1LT	0-1184746	0546	2
VOGEL EDWARD J	MAJ	0-0135146	0648	3
VOGEL FRANCIS D	MAJ	0-0298269	0964	3
VOGEL GEORGE F	1LT	0-1100810	1145	2
VOGEL JOHN H	MAJ	0-1634435	0362	2
VOGEL NELSON W	MAJ	0-0979107	0665	1
VOGEL PHILIP J	MAJ	0-0400522	0146	2
VOGEL ROBERT A	MAJ	0-1861568	1168	1
VOGEL ROBERT H	2LT	0-1171405	1044	2
VOGEL VICTOR H	LTC	0-0305586	0755	1
VOGEL WALTER	CPT	0-0518801	0245	2
VOGELGANG LEWIS O	COL	0-0240140	0262	3
VOGELSTEIN HENRY	2LT	0-1577999	0845	2
VOGES FREMONT	LTC	0-1444871	0868	1
VOGHT WILLIAM A	LTC	0-1876944	1267	1
VOGL OSCAR J	LTC	0-0351971	0759	1
VOGLE VERNON V	CW3	W-2147982	0162	1
VOGLER GEORGE L	MAJ	0-1170234	0865	1
VOGLER HENRY J	MAJ	0-0395088	0760	1
VOGT ERIC A	LTC	0-1313001	0965	3
VOGT FRED K	COL	0-0352870	0267	1
VOGT GEORGE P	LTC	0-1583800	0563	1
VOGT HAROLD M	1LT	0-0970173	0557	1
VOGT HERBERT G	MAJ	0-1011559	1165	1
VOGT JEROME F	LTC	0-0259410	0566	3
VOGT JOHN F	CW2	W-2111167	0645	2
VOGT LLOYD W	LTC	0-0297359	0161	1
VOGT MAX C JR	LTC	0-1796553	1062	2
VOGT ROBERT G	CPT	0-0411336	0645	2
VOGT WILLIAM	2LT	0-2009263	0146	2
VOGT WILLIAM N	2LT	0-1913993	0240	1
VOHL WILLIAM H	LTC	0-0201493	0251	2
VOIGHT MICHAEL F	LTC	0-0338060	0850	2
VOIGT ADOLPH F JR	LTC	0-2007133	1067	1
VOIGT HERMAN O	LTC	0-0363065	0657	1
VOIGT LORENZO G	LTC	0-0211082	1163	3
VOIT OTTO W JR	LTC	0-1186782	0766	1
VOL JANIN DANIEL	LTC	0-0408482	0960	1
VOLO CARL H	1LT	0-0365634	0842	2
VOLO STERLING R	MAJ	0-1312652	0363	2
VOLIN MELDEN E	MAJ	0-0304638	0566	3
VOLK FLOYD F	COL	0-0156396	0953	3
VOLK ROBERT	1LT	0-1307892	0658	1
VOLKER FLORENCE E	1LT	N-0771623	0146	1
VOLKL LESTER E	1LT	0-1293337	1044	2
VOLKOBER JOHN A	CPT	0-1304975	1146	2
VOLKRINGER JOSEPH A	LTC	0-1282069	1263	1
VOLLBRACHT ROY J	1LT	0-0957504	0853	2
VOLLENTINE JOHN T	LTC	0-0411157	0961	1
VOLLMAN NICK W	MAJ	0-4006647	0267	1
VOLLMER EMIL G	CW3	W-2209223	0768	1
VOLLMER FREDERICK	LTC	0-0249950	1068	3
VOLLRATH BERNARD H	COL	0-0242168	0662	3
VOLPE ALBERT J	CW2	W-2143192	0460	1
VOLPE PETER A	MAJ	0-0282079	1146	2
VOLPE WILLIAM M	MAJ	0-1703918	0754	2
VOLSEN ARTHUR J	1LT	0-1288332	0346	2
VOLTZ HENRY E	1LT	0-1290000	0745	2
VOLUNGIS LOUIS V	CPT	0-0977459	0959	2
VOLZ FRED E	CW3	W-2103567	0859	1
VOLZ JOHN G	LTC	0-0320232	0962	3
VOLZ LEONARD F	CPT	0-1950476	0464	1
VON BARGEN GERALD C	LTC	0-1640097	0867	1
VON BERGEN EDWARD F	LTC	0-0336763	0662	1
VON BREMEN DANIEL W	MAJ	0-0910142	0446	2
VON DAACKE FRED J	COL	0-0175836	0660	3
VON DEESTEN ARTHUR P	LTC	0-0219238	0952	3
VON DETTE ALLEN E	LTC	0-2042737	0756	1
VON DOLTEREN CHARLES	MAJ	0-1638729	0761	1
VON ELM HENRY W	CPT	0-1549157	114N	2
VON ESCH ROBERT A JR	1LT	0-2016980	1051	2
VON ESSEN THEODOR	CW2	W-2146940	1055	1
VON HAAM EMMERICH	COL	0-0400460	0963	3
VON HALBAN GEORGE R	COL	0-1031529	0462	1
VON HOFF GODFREY	CPT	0-0206181	0757	3
VON HUSEN FREDERICK	LTC	0-0494857	0668	3
VON KELLER NIKOLAI A	MAJ	0-0385613	1046	2
VON LEHR FREDERIC	MAJ	0-2049423	1160	1
VON MILLER CORWIN C	LTC	0-1558106	0766	1
VON NESSEN HAROLD W	LTC	0-1799806	0762	1
VON NUNES CHARLES S	LTC	0-0492690	0854	1
VON NUNES JESSIE M	2LT	N-0787751	0345	1

NAME	GRADE	SVC NO	DATE RET MO YR	RET CODE
VON SABO THEODORE J	COL	0-0270674	0867	3
VON SCHILLING LEOPOL	LTC	0-0234470	1065	3
VON SEETH EDWARD H	COL	0-0239674	0366	3
VON SETH WILLIAM J	CPT	0-2033527	0457	1
VON TOM GEORGE E	LTC	0-1313596	0265	1
VON VOIGTLANDER KARL	COL	0-0293547	0163	1
VON WEIEN BERYL B	2LT	N-0721447	1144	1
VONDERBRUEGGE CHARLE	MAJ	0-2051572	0868	3
VONDRACEK FELIX J	LTC	0-0175597	1061	3
VONLAND GEORGE O	COL	0-0185776	0157	3
VONTAGEN WILLIAM E	1LT	0-1172703	1044	2
VOORHEES DONALD L	MAJ	0-1551768	0561	1
VOORHEES MALCOLM D	COL	0-0183441	0559	3
VOORHEES NELSON A	LTC	0-0141081	1055	3
VOORHEES WILLIAM D	CPT	0-1725305	0748	2
VOORHEIS CLAUDE H	LTC	0-0930260	0268	3
VOORHIES COERTE A SR	CW4	W-2122881	0268	3
VOORHIES OTTO G	CW4	W-2143204	0268	1
VOORHIS CHARLES C	LTC	0-0415569	0646	2
VOORHIS THOMAS K	MAJ	0-1049005	0261	1
VOORTMEYER WILLIAM B	LTC	0-0384540	0563	1
VOPATEK JOHN A	LTC	0-1108393	0868	3
VORHIES JAMES H	COL	0-1000685	1167	1
VORICK ALBERT R	MAJ	0-2200116	0764	1
VORISEK ELMER A	COL	0-0304941	1060	3
VORLANDER CARL C	LTC	0-0319304	0563	1
VOROBYOFF ALEXANDER	LTC	0-2212067	1268	1
VORPAHL ADOLPH F	LTC	0-0258364	0846	2
VORTRIEDE HARRY M	MAJ	0-1178023	0261	1
VOS OSBORNE R	1LT	0-0884237	1045	2
VOSBURGH STEPHEN E	LTC	0-2049135	0767	1
VOSE CHARLES S	CPT	0-1290507	0345	2
VOSE HAROLD L	MAJ	0-2023454	0362	2
VOSE WILLIAM C	CPT	0-5325509	0768	2
VOSS CLINTON E	MAJ	0-2033091	0865	1
VOSS EDDIE P	CPT	0-0370142	0944	2
VOSS ERNEST F	COL	0-0165135	0755	2
VOSS HAROLD J	CW3	W-2143019	0361	1
VOSS JOHN B	CPT	0-1302086	0447	2
VOSS JOHN C	LTC	0-0344530	0561	1
VOSS LOUIS A	MAJ	0-0173335	0652	3
VOSS LYLE G	CW3	W-2147558	0762	1
VOSS MARION	CW2	W-3430204	0468	1
VOSS ROBERT F	1LT	0-1057923	0946	2
VOSS VERNON V	MAJ	0-0990143	0761	1
VOSS WARREN H	MAJ	0-1103987	0561	1
VOSSBRINCK KARL R	2LT	0-1048631	1044	2
VOTAW FLOYD C	LTC	0-0508443	0862	1
VOTAW GEORGE J	MAJ	0-0339609	0246	2
VOTE CLARENCE E	CPT	0-1295632	1147	2
VOTRUBA FRANCIS J	MAJ	0-0320481	0347	2
VOTYPKA JOSEPH A	MAJ	0-0388534	0346	2
VOUTE REINIER E	CPT	0-5403088	0663	2
VOWELL EDITH	MAJ	N-0726307	1263	1
VOWELL FLETCHER W	CPT	0-0281159	0645	2
VOWELL ROBERT L	MAJ	0-1552200	0959	1
VOYCE VERONICA B	MAJ	N-0796242	0267	1
VOYER ALFRED J	LTC	0-1167261	1163	1
VOYLES MARTHA A	LTC	L-1010115	1068	1
VRABEL VICTOR T	MAJ	0-0354794	0163	1
VRABLIK SAMUEL JR	LTC	0-1001925	1061	1
VRACARICH LAZARETH	MAJ	0-1109726	1161	1
VRADENBURG BRADY J	LTC	0-1945732	0662	1
VREDENBURGH FLETCHER	LTC	0-0414980	0761	1
VREELAND ALBERT L	COL	0-0298640	0861	3
VREELAND ANDREW B	CW4	W-2122828	1163	1
VRNAK FRANK L	CPT	0-1295633	0646	2
VROMAN ALBERT H	2LT	0-1181177	0644	2
VROMAN VERDON	LTC	0-0266176	0256	3
VROOM LAWRENCE M	LTC	0-1045294	0265	1
VROOMAN ROSEMARY A	2LT	N-0779066	0146	1
VUCINOVICH THOMAS H	1LT	0-1547837	0145	2
VUKASIN MILOS N	LTC	0-1340139	0767	1
VYN KENNETH L	MAJ	0-1307628	0262	1
WAARA LEROY J	CW3	W-2152869	0866	1

NAME	GRADE	SVC NO	DATE RET MO YR	RET CODE
WACH EDWIN F	CW3	W-2113122	0959	1
WACHHOLZ PAUL F	LTC	0-0451259	0961	1
WACHS ADAM R	MAJ	0-0122754	0648	3
WACHSMITH JOHN W	1LT	0-0985651	1153	2
WACHSMUTH JOHN E	LTC	0-0517680	0463	1
WACHTELL CHARLES W	CPT	0-0581312	0863	1
WACHTER FRANK J JR	LTC	0-0974418	0268	1
WACHTER FREDERICK	1LT	0-1319102	1045	2
WACHTLER PETER J	CPT	0-1170236	1046	2
WACHTMAN JACOB C	LTC	0-0297911	0962	3
WACKER CHARLES P	CW2	W-2116376	0847	2
WACKER GEORGE P	CPT	0-0504421	0945	2
WACKOWICZ HELEN	MAJ	N-0901269	0866	2
WACKYM MITCHELL A	MAJ	0-0260415	0265	3
WADDEL KENNETH L	LTC	0-0257763	0567	3
WADDELL ALEX W	1LT	0-1317060	0145	2
WADDELL DONALD H	CW2	W-2214945	0567	1
WADDELL HAROLD G	MAJ	0-1691915	0762	1
WADDELL HENRY G	COL	0-0102456	0545	2
WADDELL HUBERT E	CPT	0-2289239	1263	1
WADDELL JOHN C	1LT	0-1822343	1045	2
WADDELL ROBERT G	MAJ	0-1318725	0962	1
WADDELL THOMAS J	1LT	0-1116818	0446	2
WADDEN VINCENT R	COL	0-0178039	1050	3
WADDING ELEANOR M	1LT	N-0794445	0747	1
WADDINGHAM FRANCIS	MAJ	0-0358854	0962	3
WADDLE JAMES B JR	CW2	W-3200346	0868	1
WADDLE SAMUEL W	COL	0-0226273	0963	3
WADDY EDWARD P	MAJ	0-0387721	0461	1
WADDY WILLIAM H	CPT	0-1003063	0766	3
WADE ARTHUR W SR	MAJ	0-1288978	0862	1
WADE BATTAILLE	LTC	0-0221288	0363	3
WADE CECIL C	LTC	0-0205244	0763	3
WADE DELMER T	CW3	W-2152570	0666	1
WADE DONALD M	LTC	0-0517978	0867	3
WADE EDWIN W	LTC	0-1552817	1267	3
WADE ELLIS M	MAJ	0-0329920	0846	2
WADE FRANCIS M	1LT	0-1317212	0547	2
WADE FREDERICK	CW2	W-2122112	0948	1
WADE HOBERT B	CPT	0-1290852	1050	1
WADE JAMES L	1LT	0-1105243	1059	1
WADE JOHN C JR	1LT	0-1115141	0746	2
WADE JOSEPH F	CW2	W-3100503	0968	1
WADE JOSEPH W	COL	0-0251984	0467	3
WADE LEROY F	LTC	0-0296587	0759	1
WADE MARGARET	CPT	L-0115876	1053	2
WADE MARGARET C	1LT	M-0000575	0145	1
WADE NOBLE F	MAJ	0-0163349	1054	3
WADE PIERCE H	1LT	0-2031912	0945	2
WADE RALPH E	MAJ	0-0173147	0352	3
WADE RALPH M	COL	0-0173499	1059	3
WADE RALPH M	CPT	0-0540979	0750	2
WADE RICHARD H	CPT	0-1554991	0749	2
WADE ROBERT	MAJ	0-0109857	0238	1
WADE ROBERT L	CW2	W-2205669	0862	1
WADE ROBERT M	CPT	0-2262524	1062	1
WADE SYDNEY L	CPT	0-0308373	1145	2
WADE WALTER H JR	1LT	0-0447908	1044	2
WADE WALTER D	LTC	0-1010834	0757	1
WADE WALTER R	MAJ	0-0416102	0651	1
WADE WARREN C	MAJ	0-0127589	0648	3
WADE WILLIAM I	MAJ	0-0287293	0245	2
WADE WILLIAM I	MAJ	0-2036285	0259	1
WADELL PAUL M	CPT	0-0274278	0645	2
WADELL VERNA M	MAJ	N-0787440	0665	3
WADELTON EDWIN F	LTC	0-0336831	0267	3
WADHAM LESTER B	LTC	0-0346652	0662	3
WADIAK JOSEPH	MAJ	0-1704140	0563	1
WADLEY BURR P	MAJ	0-0486703	0448	2
WADLINGTON W J JR	COL	0-0343295	1058	3
WADLOW GEORGE J	1LT	0-1050977	0258	1
WADLOW REGINALD C	2LT	0-1698084	0145	2
WADSWORTH AGNES C	2LT	N-0726426	0744	1
WADSWORTH CORWIN Q	LTC	0-0401999	0361	1
WADSWORTH DURANT	CW4	W-2005494	1264	1

NAME	GRADE	SVC NO	DATE RET MO YR	RET CODE
WADSWORTH GEORGE E	CW2	W-2104554	1059	1
WADSWORTH JULIUS	LTC	0-0217986	0662	3
WADSWORTH LOUIE C	B G	0-0260016	0666	3
WAELDE DEWITT C	LTC	0-1633620	0461	1
WAFFLE ROBERT L	COL	0-0331110	0767	3
WAFUL GLENN H	1LT	0-1108394	0545	2
WAGAMAN RAY D	MAJ	0-0958800	0765	1
WAGEMAN JAY J	LTC	0-0347922	0255	1
WAGENBRETH PETER P	LTC	0-1586314	0163	1
WAGENER ALBERT H	MAJ	0-1050978	0461	1
WAGENHALS RUPERT S	CPT	0-0368158	0946	2
WAGER LEONARD F	CPT	0-1294941	0561	1
WAGERS ISAAC S	MAJ	0-0504607	0157	1
WAGES COLEMAN	MAJ	0-1545176	0157	1
WAGES J R	CW3	RW-2151129	1066	1
WAGGAMAN ROY D	MAJ	0-0488921	0153	1
WAGGONER CECIL C	MAJ	0-2017479	0361	1
WAGGONER CLARA L	CW4	V-0708181	0465	1
WAGGONER EDWIN P JR	COL	0-0231929	0566	3
WAGGONER HARRY N	COL	0-0372603	0566	3
WAGGONER PARKE H	COL	0-0201111	0157	3
WAGNER ARTHUR M	LTC	0-0284463	0864	3
WAGNER BYRON W	LTC	0-1185993	0668	1
WAGNER CHARLES B	CPT	0-1342315	0957	1
WAGNER CHARLES H	LTC	0-0448437	1164	3
WAGNER CHARLES M	CW3	W-2145190	1262	1
WAGNER CHARLES R	LTC	0-0272356	0868	3
WAGNER CHARLES S	LTC	0-1109727	1167	1
WAGNER CHESTER S	COL	0-0236321	0163	3
WAGNER DAVID H	1LT	0-0311909	0160	1
WAGNER DONALD J	MAJ	0-4005531	0665	1
WAGNER DONALD L	MAJ	0-1174464	1060	1
WAGNER DONN H	LTC	0-1107202	0463	1
WAGNER EDWARD W	1LT	0-1298625	0446	2
WAGNER EDWARD W	1LT	0-1794887	0244	2
WAGNER ERNEST W JR	MAJ	0-1552201	0459	1
WAGNER FLOYD F	1LT	0-1111410	0753	2
WAGNER FLOYD F	LTC	0-1553747	0863	1
WAGNER FRANCIS E	MAJ	0-0237932	0744	2
WAGNER FRANK W	CW4	W-2131517	0257	1
WAGNER GEORGE E	MAJ	0-1799808	1263	2
WAGNER GEORGE E	CW2	W-2208167	0567	1
WAGNER GERALD A	LTC	0-1634438	0566	1
WAGNER HAROLD C	MAJ	0-1081257	0359	1
WAGNER HAROLD M	MAJ	0-0383685	1145	2
WAGNER HAROLD S	LTC	0-0248792	0565	3
WAGNER HENRY T	LTC	0-1044986	0765	1
WAGNER HENRY W	LTC	0-0261847	0662	1
WAGNER HERMAN H	COL	0-0226947	0365	3
WAGNER HOWARD	MAJ	0-1001268	0559	1
WAGNER HOWARD	CW2	W-2115589	0547	2
WAGNER HUNTER T JR	1LT	0-1056591	0146	2
WAGNER IRA G JR	COL	0-0283786	0866	3
WAGNER JACK W	CW2	W-2148998	0261	1
WAGNER JAMES W	LTC	0-1332445	0768	1
WAGNER JOHN C	CW4	W-2145244	0267	1
WAGNER JOHN F	CW3	W-2202330	1067	3
WAGNER JOHN G	2LT	0-1014446	0644	2
WAGNER JOHN J	LTC	0-2000195	0965	1
WAGNER JULIUS	LTC	0-0335742	1160	3
WAGNER JULIUS W	COL	0-0231047	0962	3
WAGNER LADDIE S	COL	0-0272587	0366	3
WAGNER LARKIN L	MAJ	0-0488227	0157	1
WAGNER LEONARD A	LTC	0-0338636	1062	1
WAGNER MARGUARITE	1LT	N-0736816	0846	1
WAGNER MAX L	CW4	W-2004037	0568	1
WAGNER OSCAR S	MAJ	0-1684008	1058	1
WAGNER OTTO C	COL	0-0296720	1267	3
WAGNER RALPH P	MAJ	0-0191104	0853	3
WAGNER RAY H	LTC	0-1307894	0863	1
WAGNER RAYMOND N	MAJ	0-0965644	0566	1
WAGNER RICHARD B	LTC	0-0248100	0865	3
WAGNER ROBERT A	LTC	0-1309992	0766	1
WAGNER ROBERT A	MAJ	0-1311452	1158	1
WAGNER ROBERT H	LTC	0-1001269	0167	1

NAME	GRADE	SVC NO	DATE RET MO YR	RET CODE
WAGNER ROBERT S	LTC	0-0750899	0167	1
WAGNER ROBERT W	CPT	0-1116024	1166	2
WAGNER ROY A	2LT	0-1299498	0745	2
WAGNER ROY J	COL	0-0139622	0456	3
WAGNER RUDOLPH R	LTC	0-0108177	0133	1
WAGNER STANLEY A JR	1LT	0-1310020	0146	2
WAGNER STUART M	CPT	0-1797566	0462	1
WAGNER THEODORE S	CPT	0-1056592	0247	2
WAGNER VERNON L	MAJ	0-0957396	0761	1
WAGNER WILLIAM J	MAJ	0-1575247	1263	1
WAGNITZ MILTON F	LTC	0-0200269	0854	3
WAGNON PRESH A	LTC	0-1583803	0368	2
WAGO CHARLES T	CW4	W-2136059	0368	1
WAGONER ALBERT E	CW2	W-2141483	0457	1
WAGONER EDGAR W	MAJ	0-1879107	0266	1
WAGONER GEORGE E	MAJ	0-1824541	0462	1
WAGSTAFF GLADYS I	MAJ	N-0736796	0365	3
WAGUESPACK FENWICK E	MAJ	0-1289172	0554	1
WAHL CARL G	COL	0-0267785	0758	2
WAHL CORNELIUS	CW4	W-2110488	0264	1
WAHL EDWARD R	COL	0-0310430	0258	1
WAHL JAMES F SR	COL	0-0173054	0861	3
WAHLBERG ELMER R	LTC	0-1535104	0862	1
WAHLBOM ERNEST T	LTC	0-0223491	0547	2
WAHLBOM PHILIP C	COL	0-0246763	0646	2
WAHLE CLARENCE W	LTC	0-0160812	0258	3
WAHLE GEORGE F JR	1LT	0-1011925	0845	2
WAHLE LEROY L	LTC	0-0178377	0662	3
WAHLGREN NELSON C	LTC	0-0314861	0660	1
WAHLQUIST JOHN A	CPT	0-0408631	0146	2
WAID FRANCES T	MAJ	R-0001346	0265	1
WAID SAMUEL T	LTC	0-0521878	0165	1
WAIDLICH WILLIAM G	LTC	0-1040838	1055	1
WAIKSNIS JOHN P	CPT	0-1645463	1166	2
WAIN JACK O	WO1	W-2120058	0344	2
WAINER ALEX M	MAJ	0-0910452	1046	2
WAINHOUSE EDWARD R	LTC	0-1044717	1262	1
WAINRIGHT CHARLES R	COL	0-0355591	1060	1
WAINWRIGHT CLINTON	MAJ	0-1174185	1159	1
WAINWRIGHT MAX V	LTC	0-1686535	1065	1
WAIT RUE S	CPT	0-0482709	0146	2
WAITE ALPHONSE A	LTC	0-0296694	1266	3
WAITE BURREL V	LTC	0-0503599	0658	1
WAITE CLEMENT F	COL	0-0139656	0649	3
WAITE DAN J	CPT	0-0343796	0544	2
WAITE EMMETT P	LTC	0-0252069	0866	3
WAITE FRANK I	1LT	0-0927573	0549	1
WAITE GILBERT A	LTC	0-0319965	0260	1
WAITE HERALD B	CW3	W-2143168	0659	1
WAITE LOREN A	LTC	0-1012163	0457	1
WAITE MORRISON P	CW2	W-2211991	0267	1
WAITSMAN NATHAN	MAJ	0-0335206	1054	1
WAITT CLAUDE B	LTC	0-1011528	0565	1
WAKEFIELD ELLIS P JR	CPT	0-4010398	0868	1
WAKEFIELD HAROLD F	LTC	0-0156322	0351	3
WAKEFIELD JOHN W	LTC	0-0283110	0968	3
WAKEFIELD LESTER E	CPT	0-1946882	1057	1
WAKEFIELD PAUL W	MAJ	0-0979153	1160	1
WAKEFIELD ROBERT C	COL	0-0238525	0865	3
WAKEHAM ALBERT R	CPT	0-0301937	0548	2
WAKELY GLEN	LTC	0-0293101	0266	3
WAKEM BERTRAND C	CW3	W-2212300	1068	1
WAKEMAN MAURICE M	LTC	0-0169805	0660	3
WAKEN DOROTHY L	CPT	J-2291665	1066	2
WALAS THOMAS S	1LT	0-2005651	0747	2
WALBERT JOHN S	CPT	0-0173570	1162	3
WALBORN CHARLES F	MAJ	0-0240872	1165	3
WALBORN ROBERT A	CPT	0-0309177	1145	2
WALCH JAMES W	MAJ	0-1032125	0366	1
WALCH ROBERT L JR	1LT	0-0524629	0346	2
WALCH RUSSELL	1LT	0-0507304	0450	1
WALCHAK GEORGE A	1LT	0-0886893	0147	2
WALCHER EVERETT E	LTC	0-0248229	0364	3
WALCOTT THEODORE E	CW3	W-2008267	0167	3
WALCZAK CHARLES J	MAJ	0-1042199	1163	1

332-811 O - 69 - 24

NAME	GRADE	SVC NO	DATE RET MO YR	RET CODE
WALD HORACE A	1LT	0-0495376	0144	2
WALDBART RICHARD H	CPT	0-1321369	0549	2
WALDEN BETTY J	CPT	N-2289582	0162	2
WALDEN CHANEY E	CW3	W-2203254	1265	1
WALDEN FARRIS O	CPT	0-0441383	0650	1
WALDEN HENRY E	COL	0-0256674	0751	3
WALDEN LEONARD L	CW3	W-2149093	0764	1
WALDEN LOUIS M	COL	0-0295552	1053	2
WALDEN MARK C	CW2	W-2210068	0264	1
WALDEN PHILIP S	1LT	0-1015350	0846	2
WALDEN RALPH C	MAJ	0-2263709	0867	1
WALDEN REUBEN L	MAJ	0-0401487	0947	2
WALDEN TALMAGE	CPT	0-1319364	0654	2
WALDER HARRY L	LTC	0-1184600	0662	1
WALDER J O	CPT	0-2262947	0461	1
WALDER JOHN A	MAJ	0-0530298	0853	1
WALDINE STEPHEN M	LTC	0-0484583	1155	1
WALDING MALCOLM M	COL	0-0232550	0861	3
WALDMAN CHARLES V	MAJ	0-1303802	0760	1
WALDMAN MURRY R	WO1	W-2127048	0947	2
WALDMAN ROBERT G	CW3	W-2146729	0566	1
WALDMANN JOHN R	LTC	0-0302505	0568	3
WALDO GREGG L	LTC	0-1107204	0664	1
WALDO JESS W	CW3	W-2150666	0463	1
WALDO LYNN L	MAJ	0-0309103	1166	3
WALDOCK JAMES L	MAJ	0-0347358	1044	2
WALDORF FRANCIS E	LTC	0-1648538	0866	1
WALDREP DEUWARD S	LTC	0-0296191	0566	3
WALDRIP MONTGOMERY	CW3	W-2152412	0659	1
WALDRON DALE W	1LT	0-0885768	0347	1
WALDRON ELDRIGE L	CW2	W-2152258	0861	1
WALDRON HAZLE M	LTC	0-0520585	0465	3
WALDRON JACK F	CPT	0-1703919	0855	1
WALDRON JOSEPH H	CPT	0-1639780	1055	2
WALDRON NELLO B	LTC	0-0368703	0967	3
WALDROP HENRY D	CW4	W-2146164	0266	1
WALDROP JOHN J	CW2	W-2119317	0150	1
WALDROP LOUIS G	CW4	W-2141693	0860	1
WALDROP MELVIN T	CW2	W-2208521	1061	1
WALDROP WILFRED E	MAJ	0-0237885	0561	1
WALEA ALFRED S	MAJ	0-0490899	1047	2
WALEN JOHN	MAJ	0-1554298	0855	1
WALENGA RICHARD A	1LT	0-0531216	0646	2
WALES ROBERT F	LTC	0-0249736	0662	1
WALGREN SYLVAN P	MAJ	0-1181179	0761	1
WALINSKI ERWIN F	LTC	0-1551141	0964	1
WALK GENEVIEVE	LTC	N-0741869	0862	1
WALKE JOHN T	LTC	0-0387981	0346	2
WALKEMEYER WILLIAM	LTC	0-0109271	1047	1
WALKER AB O	LTC	0-0305764	0148	2
WALKER ALBERT E	CPT	0-1103990	0346	2
WALKER ALFRED P	COL	0-0162611	1160	3
WALKER ALLEN	CPT	0-1182735	0146	2
WALKER ALLEN J	CW3	W-2152102	0861	1
WALKER ANSIL L	MAJ	0-1303971	0259	1
WALKER ARGYLL E	MAJ	0-1580465	0657	1
WALKER ARTHUR H	LTC	0-0240756	1264	3
WALKER AUSTIN E	COL	0-1010661	1047	2
WALKER BAILEY T	CW4	W-2121153	0858	1
WALKER BARTON F	LTC	0-0122147	0655	3
WALKER BRUCE	LTC	0-1109082	0667	1
WALKER CALVIT L	MAJ	0-1642689	0363	1
WALKER CARL F	1LT	0-0558063	0246	2
WALKER CECIL P	MAJ	0-1937876	0566	1
WALKER CHARLES O	MAJ	0-1035140	0662	1
WALKER CHARLES E	COL	0-0402763	1268	1
WALKER CHARLES E	CW2	W-2213853	0266	1
WALKER CHARLES M	MAJ	0-1012401	0158	2
WALKER CHARLES R	MAJ	0-1303417	0661	1
WALKER CHARLES W	LTC	0-0442455	0367	1
WALKER CHARLES W	CW3	W-2148823	0663	1
WALKER CHARLES W	CW2	W-2212214	0168	1
WALKER CHARLES W JR	CW4	W-2118212	0161	1
WALKER CLAUDIUS J	MAJ	0-0306381	1167	3
WALKER DARWYN E	LTC	0-1307895	0666	1
WALKER DAVID M	MAJ	0-1298322	0757	1
WALKER DEAN C	CPT	0-0480218	0347	2
WALKER DEAN H	1LT	0-1015837	0446	2
WALKER DONALD D	LTC	0-1697942	0961	1
WALKER DOYLE T	CW3	W-2144265	0263	1
WALKER EARL	LTC	0-0333930	0155	1
WALKER EARL E	MAJ	0-1309188	1160	1
WALKER EARL J	MAJ	0-1105247	0461	2
WALKER EDGAR T	1LT	0-1047379	0444	2
WALKER EDWARD	CPT	0-1307483	0845	2
WALKER EDWARD H	MAJ	0-0309326	1167	3
WALKER EDWARD L	COL	0-0241473	0254	3
WALKER EDWARD T	MAJ	0-0264378	0463	3
WALKER EDWIN M	LTC	0-0481180	0266	3
WALKER ELLEN H	CPT	N-0733164	0547	1
WALKER ELMER	CW3	W-2150877	1063	1
WALKER EMORY C JR	1LT	0-1882526	1055	2
WALKER ENOS G	COL	0-0263429	0159	3
WALKER ERNEST L	CPT	0-1575616	0546	2
WALKER ERSAL D	MAJ	0-0887630	1160	1
WALKER ERWIN R JR	LTC	0-0321632	0753	2
WALKER FORREST A	LTC	0-1825515	0163	1
WALKER FRANK H	CPT	0-1319687	1157	1
WALKER FRANK N	CPT	0-1311550	1060	1
WALKER FRED A JR	LTC	0-0531614	0567	1
WALKER GARLAND R	1LT	0-0518133	0346	2
WALKER GEORGE	1LT	0-2000621	1049	1
WALKER GERALD B	LTC	0-1058146	0267	1
WALKER GILBERT P	LTC	0-0122144	0155	3
WALKER HAMILTON T	COL	0-0145820	0657	3
WALKER HARRY C	LTC	0-025..?96	0864	3
WALKER HARRY E	MAJ	0-0294865	0444	2
WALKER HARRY L	MAJ	0-1948675	0357	1
WALKER HARVEY	LTC	0-0267242	0360	3
WALKER HENRY P	LTC	0-0307984	0560	1
WALKER HERBERT C	MAJ	0-1586995	0961	1
WALKER HOMER D	MAJ	0-0228974	0365	3
WALKER HORACE L	CPT	0-1166639	0348	1
WALKER HOWARD O JR	CW2	W-2144133	0659	1
WALKER HOWARD T	CPT	0-1338534	0159	1
WALKER IRA H	CW4	W-2112237	0659	1
WALKER IVAN W	MAJ	0-2000080	0565	1
WALKER J P	MAJ	0-2050993	1059	1
WALKER JAMES	MAJ	0-1895490	0855	1
WALKER JAMES A	LTC	0-0259138	0466	3
WALKER JAMES C	LTC	0-1001070	0658	1
WALKER JAMES L	LTC	0-1287442	1060	1
WALKER JAMES M	LTC	0-0171632	0756	3
WALKER JAMES P	CW3	W-2147896	0864	2
WALKER JAMES S	MAJ	0-0352211	0546	2
WALKER JESSE S	MAJ	0-0289651	0956	3
WALKER JOHN A	LTC	0-0921183	0166	3
WALKER JOHN C	1LT	0-1050980	0944	2
WALKER JOHN E	CPT	0-1056935	1055	1
WALKER JOHN E	CPT	0-1596536	0548	2
WALKER JOHN F JR	MAJ	0-1825291	0663	1
WALKER JOHN F SR	LTC	0-0167479	0648	3
WALKER JOHN H	LTC	0-0268569	0960	1
WALKER JOHN J	CW3	W-2152441	0464	1
WALKER JOHN L	CW2	W-2146985	0860	1
WALKER JOHN M	1LT	0-1102107	0345	2
WALKER JOHN Q	CPT	0-0502658	0859	1
WALKER JOHN R JR	MAJ	0-0407583	0563	1
WALKER JOHN R JR	LTC	0-0915148	0663	1
WALKER JOHN S	MAJ	0-0240184	0861	3
WALKER JOHN W	LTC	0-0462167	1262	2
WALKER JOSEPH A	LTC	0-0450331	0455	1
WALKER JOSEPH J	COL	0-0217502	0751	3
WALKER KATHLEEN W	1LT	N-0756891	0546	1
WALKER LOUIS C	1LT	0-0224034	0145	2
WALKER MARCELLUS	COL	0-0264537	0867	3
WALKER MARK C	CPT	0-0329645	0344	2
WALKER NEAL G JR	2LT	0-1594320	1044	2
WALKER NEWPORT H	LTC	0-0216870	1161	3
WALKER NORMAN R	COL	0-0438053	0154	1
WALKER OPAL	MAJ	N-0723496	1164	1
WALKER PAUL G JR	MAJ	0-1168965	0268	1
WALKER PAUL P SR	MAJ	0-0949010	1160	1
WALKER PAUL S	LTC	0-2202507	0968	1
WALKER RANSOM O	WO1	W-2125690	0647	2
WALKER RAYMOND	LTC	0-1647002	0663	1
WALKER RAYMOND A	LTC	0-0222132	0964	3
WALKER RAYMOND E	LTC	0-0274835	0860	3
WALKER RAYMOND E	WO1	W-2120504	0547	2
WALKER RAYMOND G	CW3	W-2102509	1154	1
WALKER RAYMOND W	LTC	0-0510815	1066	3
WALKER RENJ R	LTC	0-0230528	0365	3
WALKER RICHARD C	MAJ	0-2026539	0163	1
WALKER RICHARD D	1LT	0-1311708	0246	2
WALKER RICHARD H	CPT	0-0389441	0254	1
WALKER RICHARD S	LTC	0-1165216	1165	1
WALKER ROBERT B	MAJ	0-0359181	0749	1
WALKER ROBERT H	CPT	0-0346480	0558	3
WALKER ROBERT J	MAJ	0-1012383	0764	1
WALKER ROBERT L	2LT	0-0858025	0750	2
WALKER ROBERT W	LTC	0-1292619	0457	1
WALKER ROBERT W	WO1	W-2148667	0155	1
WALKER ROBERT W	CW2	W-2207094	0363	1
WALKER ROY F	LTC	0-0100110	1054	3
WALKER ROY S	MAJ	0-0906458	0546	2
WALKER RUBYE E	MAJ	N-0763730	1063	1
WALKER RUSSELL	CPT	0-1599116	1058	1
WALKER RUSSELL A	CPT	0-0294612	0345	2
WALKER SAMUEL A	LTC	0-0334975	0468	3
WALKER SAMUEL E	1LT	0-1292263	0845	2
WALKER SIDNEY R	MAJ	0-0268723	1167	3
WALKER SIMS H	LTC	0-1105889	0463	1
WALKER SOLOMON	CPT	0-1284611	0268	1
WALKER STANLEY M	LTC	0-0336913	0461	1
WALKER STERLING A	CPT	0-0359094	1043	2
WALKER STEVE F	COL	0-0265202	0367	3
WALKER STEWART J	1LT	0-0388455	0245	2
WALKER THEODORE J	LTC	0-0274770	1064	3
WALKER THOMAS A	CW4	W-2146799	0268	1
WALKER THOMAS E	1LT	0-1016792	0446	2
WALKER THOMAS H	MAJ	0-0248861	0145	2
WALKER TROY A	CPT	0-0498519	1051	1
WALKER TROY D	LTC	0-0285890	1159	1
WALKER VERNON O	CW3	W-2144874	0457	1
WALKER VICTOR L	LTC	0-1332761	1062	1
WALKER VIRGIL R	LTC	0-0254723	0766	3
WALKER WALDO L	CPT	0-1287627	0647	2
WALKER WILFORD A	COL	0-0127094	0455	3
WALKER WILLIAM B	CW2	W-2150000	0960	1
WALKER WILLIAM H	COL	0-0292802	1158	3
WALKER WILLIAM J	CW2	W-2150894	0460	1
WALKER WILLIAM P	LTC	0-0275402	0863	3
WALKER WILLIAM R	LTC	0-0118185	0257	3
WALKER WILLIAM S	LTC	0-0364548	0461	1
WALKER WILLIAM S	2LT	0-2036972	1144	2
WALKER ZACK T	CW3	W-2150755	0763	1
WALKUP KENNETH	1LT	0-1308567	1045	2
WALKUP RICHARD W	LTC	0-1550289	1060	1
WALKUP SAM H JR	CPT	0-0557108	0847	2
WALKUW STANLEY L	LTC	0-1177226	0761	1
WALL ARCHIE C	LTC	0-0220337	0545	2
WALL ARNOLD R	LTC	0-0299942	0647	2
WALL CARL H	LTC	0-0374366	0859	1
WALL CHARLES H	CW4	W-2145601	1268	1
WALL CHARLEY K	MAJ	0-0114756	0252	3
WALL EDWARD A	1LT	0-1321355	0349	2
WALL EDWARD C	MAJ	0-0357792	0346	2
WALL FRANCIS T	MAJ	0-0987987	0265	1
WALL HAROLD C	COL	0-0246907	0966	1
WALL HERMAN V	MAJ	0-0475985	0146	2
WALL IRA E JR	CW2	W-2210950	0266	1
WALL JACK C SR	CPT	0-1826116	0862	1
WALL JAMES L	CPT	0-0221960	0949	3
WALL JAMES R JR	CPT	0-0324339	1046	2
WALL JAMES T	CW3	W-2149684	1265	2
WALL JAMES W	MAJ	0-1645465	0963	1
WALL JEFF C	CPT	0-1168508	0858	1
WALL JOHN C	COL	0-0249775	0962	1
WALL JOHN C	MAJ	0-0991825	1063	1
WALL JOHN E	LTC	0-1011607	1061	1
WALL JOHN R	MAJ	0-1295801	0866	1
WALL LARRY O	MAJ	0-1335866	1062	1
WALL LEOLUS L	LTC	0-0414117	1060	1
WALL PERCY L	COL	0-0180746	0258	2
WALL RAYMOND D	MAJ	0-1305683	0161	1
WALL ROBERT B	CPT	0-1313937	0246	2
WALL ROBERT R	MAJ	0-2263397	1166	1
WALL RUSSELL V JR	CW3	W-2143415	0659	1
WALL SAMUEL H	CPT	0-0967806	1160	1
WALL THOMAS W	CW4	W-2005004	1263	3
WALL W L	1LT	0-1292264	104N	2
WALL WILFRED W	WO1	W-2146403	0956	1
WALL WILLIAM E	LTC	0-1585036	0468	1
WALL WILLIAM F	CPT	0-1316610	1046	2
WALL WILLIAM S	LTC	0-0416008	0761	1
WALLA WILLIAM M	LTC	0-0357399	0265	3
WALLACE BUD	LTC	0-1919039	0768	1
WALLACE CHARLES A	MAJ	0-1110867	1160	1
WALLACE CHARLES H	MAJ	0-1553574	0561	1
WALLACE CRISBY D	LTC	0-0450937	0256	1
WALLACE DARREL R	CW2	W-2120106	0653	1
WALLACE DONALD L	MAJ	0-1925857	1167	1
WALLACE EARLE	1LT	0-1013883	0546	2
WALLACE EDWIN F	CPT	0-0499745	0645	1
WALLACE EDWIN R	CPT	0-0265858	0-53	3
WALLACE ELBERT C	LTC	0-0450651	0954	1
WALLACE ELENSWORTH	LTC	0-0270062	1161	3
WALLACE EUGENE W	COL	0-0499950	0168	3
WALLACE FRANCES E	2LT	N-0734579	1042	1
WALLACE FRANK M	LTC	0-0274085	0961	3
WALLACE GEORGE F	MAJ	0-0486213	0954	1
WALLACE GEORGE S	LTC	0-0280031	0253	3
WALLACE GEORGE W	MAJ	0-1695196	0568	1
WALLACE GLEN P	MAJ	0-0166080	0455	3
WALLACE GUY D	1LT	0-1292966	0645	2
WALLACE HARRY E E	CW3	W-2208263	0667	1
WALLACE J M TOLBER	LTC	0-1581438	1262	1
WALLACE JACK JR	LTC	0-0392477	0562	2
WALLACE JAMES G	MAJ	0-1643422	0161	1
WALLACE JAMES J	MAJ	0-2028454	0264	1
WALLACE JAMES M JR	LTC	0-0262803	0264	3
WALLACE JOHN J JR	LTC	0-1049379	0565	1
WALLACE JOHN S	1LT	0-1312254	1045	2
WALLACE JOSEPH F	LTC	0-1648858	0867	1
WALLACE KARL E	COL	0-0149824	0856	3
WALLACE LAWRENCE	CPT	0-0371467	0559	1
WALLACE LENORE S	1LT	N-0723987	1145	1
WALLACE LEO N	1LT	0-1996602	1046	2
WALLACE LEONARD A	LTC	0-0450483	0656	1
WALLACE LYNN D	COL	0-1938498	0665	3
WALLACE MARGARET G	1LT	N-0702989	0646	1
WALLACE MARION S	CPT	0-0227547	0463	3
WALLACE MARK V	2LT	0-1310655	0844	2
WALLACE MARY C	1LT	N-0726525	0646	1
WALLACE MORGAN M	M G	0-0275387	0260	3
WALLACE NEWELL G	CPT	0-0346423	0845	2
WALLACE NORMAN A	MAJ	0-1977934	0962	1
WALLACE ORVAL O	MAJ	0-1554494	0662	1
WALLACE PERC A	2LT	0-1017341	0247	2
WALLACE RALPH	LTC	0-1041672	0566	3
WALLACE RICARDO F	LTC	0-0232184	1058	3
WALLACE RICHARD H	CW3	RW-2208965	0567	1
WALLACE RICHARD T	MAJ	0-1996658	0663	1
WALLACE ROBERT E	COL	0-0318767	0567	1
WALLACE ROBERT E	COL	0-0358519	1158	1
WALLACE ROBERT E	LTC	0-1945734	0966	1
WALLACE ROBERT F	LTC	0-0455907	0264	1
WALLACE RUSSELL G	LTC	0-0249883	0666	3
WALLACE SAMUEL D	LTC	0-0232725	0261	3
WALLACE SAMUEL T	B G	0-0331327	0565	3

NAME	GRADE	SVC NO	DATE RET MO YR	RET CODE
WALLACE TED	MAJ	0-1046679	1157	1
WALLACE THEODORE I	2LT	0-1304466	1146	2
WALLACE THEODORE R	1LT	0-1552819	0446	2
WALLACE VERNON R	CW2	W-2143196	1159	1
WALLACE VINCENT E	CPT	0-0362499	1046	2
WALLACE WALTER W	MAJ	0-1553748	0459	1
WALLACE WASHINGTON	LTC	0-1003064	0755	1
WALLACE WILEY H	CW2	W-2142117	0357	1
WALLACE WILLIAM A	COL	0-0227456	0160	3
WALLACE WILLIAM A	CW4	W-2125212	0461	1
WALLACE WILLIAM C	LTC	0-1309632	0763	1
WALLACE WILLIAM C	CW3	W-2208416	0166	1
WALLACE WILLIAM J	LTC	0-1056265	1062	1
WALLACE WILLIAM O	MAJ	0-0522449	1154	1
WALLACE WOODROW W	LTC	0-0382175	0656	1
WALLACH DONALD M JR	MAJ	0-1342407	1162	1
WALLACH EUGENE	WO1	W-2122801	0745	2
WALLACH FREDERICK	MAJ	0-1997971	0168	3
WALLACH GEORGE E	CPT	0-0482307	0145	2
WALLACH MARTIN A	CW2	W-2212259	1164	1
WALLAR BETTY J	1LT	N-0798121	0747	1
WALLAT EDWIN M	WO1	W-2122812	1052	1
WALLEN ELMER G	MAJ	0-0289689	1158	3
WALLENBERG ALICE G	MAJ	N-0723298	0867	1
WALLENBORN LESLIE T	MAJ	0-1309994	1158	1
WALLENSTEIN WALTER	MAJ	0-0529476	0548	1
WALLER ALVIN L	CPT	0-0493457	0347	2
WALLER EDWARD C	MAJ	0-1824943	0760	2
WALLER LOUIS O	CW2	W-2150872	0361	1
WALLER MACK P	CPT	0-1287093	0450	2
WALLER NATHANIEL	MAJ	0-0294072	0944	2
WALLER R J	CW2	W-3430538	1068	1
WALLER ROBERT R 3	CPT	0-0345618	0947	2
WALLER ROBERT O	COL	0-0259450	0666	3
WALLESCH HUBERT G	CPT	0-2023696	0856	1
WALLEY ROMAN J	LTC	0-1756149	0867	2
WALLIHAN GORDON G	CW4	W-2146612	0568	1
WALLIN FRANK A	CW3	W-2148686	0757	1
WALLIN JAMES W	CW4	W-2105768	0859	1
WALLIN RICHARD A	1LT	0-1552414	0145	2
WALLING MELLES O	CW4	W-2142338	1068	1
WALLING PERCY L	1LT	0-0166663	0554	3
WALLING RAYMOND V	LTC	0-1946199	0867	3
WALLINGFORD MAC L	LTC	0-0279505	0767	3
WALLINGFORD MELVIN D	2LT	0-1014820	0845	2
WALLINGFORD WILBERT	LTC	0-1110319	1265	1
WALLIS CECIL W	CW3	W-2110992	0157	1
WALLIS GALE A	CPT	0-1294575	0564	1
WALLIS GLENN D	CW2	W-2143100	0965	1
WALLIS JOHN P	LTC	0-0289482	0864	3
WALLIS LYNN R	LTC	0-0234560	0850	2
WALLIS MARTIN J	CW3	W-2103575	1155	1
WALLIS RICHARD L	LTC	0-2036034	0562	1
WALLIS WILLIAM R	MAJ	0-0280408	0367	3
WALLK SILAS	1LT	0-0936992	0449	2
WALLNER JOSEPH J	MAJ	0-1100380	0157	1
WALLRATH MAURICE	LTC	0-0221268	1062	3
WALLS CECIL V	CPT	0-1822495	0157	1
WALLS FRANKLYN H	MAJ	0-0257267	1045	2
WALLS JESS W	COL	0-0450332	0666	1
WALLS JOHNNIE R	CPT	0-2263065	0265	1
WALLS JOSEPHINE	MAJ	N-0727198	0468	1
WALLS RAYMOND G	MAJ	0-0231372	1058	3
WALLS WALTER S	COL	0-0284829	0865	3
WALLS WILLIAM R	1LT	0-1590875	0460	1
WALMER BERMOD K	MAJ	0-1685555	0164	1
WALMER HILLARD W	LTC	0-0170864	1043	2
WALMER RICHARD	LTC	0-0334773	0656	1
WALMER ROBERT F	MAJ	0-1556517	0764	1
WALMSLEY PHILIP M	CPT	0-1296772	0347	2
WALNES ROBERT U	LTC	0-2009725	0467	1
WALPER WILLIAM	LTC	0-0441446	0847	2
WALQUIST RAYMOND C	CPT	0-0208660	0755	3
WALRATH CLIFFORD B	LTC	0-2047879	0163	1
WALRATH RICHARD M	LTC	0-0297785	0763	3

NAME	GRADE	SVC NO	DATE RET MO YR	RET CODE
WALSER BOBBY J	CPT	0-1932436	0565	1
WALSER HAROLD W	LTC	0-0312451	0762	1
WALSH ALEXANDER	LTC	0-0245113	0464	3
WALSH ALICE V	2LT	N-0722978	0545	1
WALSH ALOYSIUS J	MAJ	0-0172031	0-53	3
WALSH BERNARD W	2LT	0-0421919	0545	2
WALSH CHARLES C	MAJ	0-1285343	0461	1
WALSH CHARLES J	1LT	0-1290510	0446	2
WALSH CHARLES J	CW2	W-2111847	0246	2
WALSH CHARLOTTE	2LT	N-0724244	0543	1
WALSH CLARENCE H	COL	0-0198803	1056	3
WALSH CLARENCE H JR	MAJ	0-1635458	0560	1
WALSH DAVID J	LTC	0-0420892	0346	2
WALSH DAVID J JR	LTC	0-1556966	0463	1
WALSH DENA G	CPT	N-0702020	0845	1
WALSH EARL F	COL	0-0172523	0752	3
WALSH EDMUND C JR	LTC	0-0302105	0762	1
WALSH EDWARD F	MAJ	0-1061016	0561	1
WALSH EDWARD G	CPT	0-1325610	0662	1
WALSH EDWARD J	LTC	0-0281502	0558	3
WALSH EDWARD T	LTC	0-0451544	0465	1
WALSH ELLARD A	M G	0-0158385	0648	3
WALSH ELLWYN C	CW4	W-2142416	1068	1
WALSH FRANCIS C JR	CW3	RW-2206455	0965	1
WALSH FRANK J	COL	0-0347710	1059	2
WALSH FRANK O JR	LTC	0-0195336	0363	3
WALSH FRANKLIN J	LTC	0-0982123	0568	1
WALSH FRED H JR	LTC	0-0401747	0347	2
WALSH GEORGE C	MAJ	0-1185206	0566	1
WALSH GEORGE T	CW3	W-2146186	0663	1
WALSH GERALD C	LTC	0-2200365	0968	1
WALSH GILBERT C	CPT	0-0448189	0944	2
WALSH GLENN F	1LT	0-0465121	0745	2
WALSH JAMES J	CPT	0-1313043	0963	1
WALSH JAMES P	COL	0-0115438	0556	1
WALSH JAMES T	COL	0-0211659	0962	3
WALSH JOACHIM E	1LT	0-0525316	0344	2
WALSH JOHN A	CW3	W-2142914	0559	1
WALSH JOHN E	M G	0-0256059	0758	3
WALSH JOHN J JR	LTC	0-2047880	1066	1
WALSH JOHN P	1LT	0-1308053	0945	2
WALSH JOHN R	CPT	0-0242958	0656	3
WALSH JOHN R	1LT	0-1174466	0745	2
WALSH JOSEPH D	CPT	0-1108400	0257	1
WALSH JOSEPH G	MAJ	0-0519817	0356	1
WALSH JOSEPH L	1LT	0-0430067	0345	2
WALSH JOSEPH T	LTC	0-1543186	1060	1
WALSH KENNETH M	MAJ	0-1558222	0862	1
WALSH MARTIN T JR	CPT	0-1300421	0248	2
WALSH MARY E	1LT	N-0751302	0946	1
WALSH MARY F	LTC	N-0756719	0468	1
WALSH PAUL R	MAJ	0-1917783	1064	1
WALSH RAYMOND J	LTC	0-1590877	0167	3
WALSH RAYMOND V	LTC	0-1845659	0368	1
WALSH RICHARD J	MAJ	0-2262899	0763	1
WALSH RICHARD M JR	CPT	0-0353797	1143	2
WALSH RITA H	CPT	N-0756393	1047	1
WALSH ROBERT J JR	LTC	0-0236276	0166	3
WALSH ROBERT J JR	MAJ	0-0982679	0365	1
WALSH THOMAS J	LTC	0-0230797	0261	3
WALSH THOMAS J	COL	0-0266012	1061	3
WALSH THOMAS J	CW4	W-2004860	1165	1
WALSH THOMAS P JR	LTC	0-1585041	0264	1
WALSH THOMAS R	1LT	0-1314236	0746	2
WALSH WILLIAM E	COL	0-1169380	0966	1
WALSH WILLIAM J	COL	0-0189957	0758	3
WALSH WILLIAM J	1LT	0-1169784	0845	2
WALSH WILLIAM J	MAJ	0-4074759	0968	1
WALSKI FRANCIS L	LTC	0-0364190	0446	2
WALSTON CECIL D	LTC	0-1017342	1063	1
WALSTON KINDLE	MAJ	0-1703755	1053	2
WALTEMATH CLARENCE	CPT	0-1308736	0746	2
WALTER ARTHUR C	LTC	0-0506570	1265	3
WALTER BERNARD W	LTC	0-0683357	1166	1
WALTER BILLY H	MAJ	0-1800087	0161	1

NAME	GRADE	SVC NO	DATE RET MO YR	RET CODE
WALTER CHARLES K	MAJ	0-0196335	0762	3
WALTER CHARLES S	LTC	0-1535106	0662	1
WALTER EDWIN A	CPT	0-2018797	0356	1
WALTER EDWIN J	MAJ	0-0232546	0363	3
WALTER ELMER J	2LT	0-1913999	0734	1
WALTER FLORENCE A	MAJ	N-0723361	0763	1
WALTER FRANK M	LTC	0-0499317	1166	3
WALTER FREDERICK	LTC	0-1650382	1066	1
WALTER FREDERICK	CW3	RW-2142738	0661	1
WALTER GEORGE H JR	LTC	0-0918262	0263	1
WALTER HENRY M	LTC	0-0194950	0263	3
WALTER IAN	CPT	0-1289348	0465	1
WALTER JOSEPH R	MAJ	0-0227548	0761	3
WALTER LLOYD D	LTC	0-0171799	0648	3
WALTER MORLEY C	LTC	0-0127742	0-51	3
WALTER ROBERT	LTC	0-0336290	0868	3
WALTER ROBERT H	LTC	0-0973563	0867	1
WALTER ROY F	CW3	W-2143287	0262	1
WALTER RUDOLPH L	CPT	0-1290689	0546	2
WALTER WILLIAM F	MAJ	0-1824256	0557	1
WALTER WILLIAM J	MAJ	0-1688394	0961	1
WALTERS AGNES T	MAJ	N-0760452	1266	3
WALTERS ARTHUR M	LTC	0-1110870	0862	1
WALTERS CARL C	2LT	0-1882528	0753	2
WALTERS DALE E	1LT	0-2051574	0647	2
WALTERS DOLF W	LTC	0-1288147	0962	1
WALTERS DOUGLAS W	CW3	W-2145191	0263	1
WALTERS ELMER	LTC	0-1576769	0461	1
WALTERS ERNEST G	1LT	0-1288827	1045	2
WALTERS EUGENE P	COL	0-0145895	0355	3
WALTERS GENE H	CW3	W-2208396	1266	1
WALTERS GERALD A	1LT	0-1316250	0764	2
WALTERS GORDON G	LTC	0-0343297	0854	1
WALTERS HARRIS F	MAJ	0-1589647	1159	1
WALTERS HARRY E	CW2	W-2152726	0558	1
WALTERS HARRY G JR	LTC	0-2014411	0668	1
WALTERS HENRY O	MAJ	0-0109303	0247	1
WALTERS HOWARD C	COL	0-0338343	0364	3
WALTERS HURLIE A	CPT	0-0208697	0554	3
WALTERS JAMES E	CW4	W-2201593	1167	1
WALTERS JAMES H	1LT	0-1302558	0745	2
WALTERS JAMES H	MAJ	0-2262867	0961	1
WALTERS JAMES R	MAJ	0-0481079	0958	1
WALTERS JOHN B	CPT	0-0240482	0265	3
WALTERS JOSEPH M JR	COL	0-0389277	0868	2
WALTERS LEONARD C	CW4	W-2115967	1163	1
WALTERS LOUIS V	LTC	0-0514064	1164	3
WALTERS MARCUS R	MAJ	0-2263231	1061	1
WALTERS MURRAY M	CPT	0-0501328	0446	2
WALTERS NORMAN P	CPT	0-1825723	0947	2
WALTERS PAUL W	MAJ	0-0965040	0963	1
WALTERS PETER	CW3	W-2150722	0864	1
WALTERS RAIMON G	COL	0-0122813	0454	3
WALTERS RALPH	MAJ	0-2030957	1060	1
WALTERS ROBERT E	MAJ	0-1330611	0463	1
WALTERS ROBERT L	1LT	0-1302099	1047	2
WALTERS ROBERT O JR	MAJ	0-1996856	0462	1
WALTERS ROY W	LTC	0-0145893	1153	3
WALTERS RUSSELL B	CW2	W-3400201	0568	1
WALTERS THURMOND L	COL	0-0352241	1160	1
WALTERS TYRE G	1LT	0-0423463	0965	3
WALTERS WAYNE D	LTC	0-1250339	1060	1
WALTERS WAYNE W	LTC	0-1101263	0756	1
WALTERS WILLIAM E	LTC	0-0450650	0657	1
WALTERS WILLIAM F	CW3	W-2149685	0865	1
WALTERS WILLIAM G	LTC	0-0403453	1165	1
WALTERS WILLIAM H	MAJ	0-1321588	0668	2
WALTERS WILLIAM J	CW4	W-2146712	0767	1
WALTERS WILLIAM J	CW2	W-2148999	1157	1
WALTERS WINTHROP F	CPT	0-1184437	0847	2
WALTHALL JAMES W	CPT	0-1296301	0347	2
WALTHALL MELVIN C	MAJ	0-0972979	0963	1
WALTHER RICHARD L	LTC	0-1032562	0763	1
WALTHER WILLIAM C	LTC	0-0237517	0761	1
WALTHERS GEORGE F	LTC	0-1640102	0163	1

NAME	GRADE	SVC NO	DATE RET MO YR	RET CODE
WALTHERS HARRY V	1LT	0-0264278	0254	3
WALTHEW ROBERT F	LTC	0-0914284	0268	3
WALTMAN CLARENCE J	MAJ	0-0309485	0768	3
WALTMAN JAMES R	LTC	0-0123813	0850	3
WALTMAN KENNETH D	CW2	W-2208216	0864	1
WALTMAN LEE R	CW3	W-2146480	0561	2
WALTMAN RICHARD	CPT	0-1689590	0845	2
WALTON ABBOTT B	COL	0-0361106	0466	2
WALTON CHARLES F	LTC	0-2042979	0962	1
WALTON CHARLES J	CW3	W-2147808	0562	1
WALTON CHARLES W	MAJ	0-1576771	0861	1
WALTON CLARENCE M	LTC	0-0511529	1266	1
WALTON CLAYTON J	LTC	0-1550291	0168	1
WALTON CORWIN T	LTC	0-1555316	0666	1
WALTON CURTIS R JR	LTC	0-1180374	0461	1
WALTON DELBERT P	MAJ	0-0359688	0744	2
WALTON EUGENE R	MAJ	0-1648280	0961	1
WALTON FRANK W	CW4	W-2005946	0762	3
WALTON FRANKLIN E	COL	0-0238874	0446	2
WALTON HAROLD C	LTC	0-0394033	0760	1
WALTON JAMES K	LTC	0-1105537	0268	1
WALTON JAMES PHIL	2LT	0-1644198	0351	2
WALTON JOHN E	CPT	0-1697679	0345	2
WALTON JOHN W	COL	0-0232842	0765	3
WALTON JOSEPH F	1LT	0-0528686	0246	2
WALTON JOSEPH P	MAJ	0-1019082	0361	1
WALTON LAWRENCE E	1LT	0-1879232	1054	2
WALTON MARION M	LTC	0-0271297	1066	3
WALTON NORMAN L	MAJ	0-0491184	0747	1
WALTON RALPH E	MAJ	0-1315877	1060	1
WALTON RICHARD T	MAJ	0-0283709	0258	3
WALTON ROLAND L	1LT	0-1821941	1044	2
WALTON SAMUEL E JR	LTC	0-1288653	0363	2
WALTON VERN N	MAJ	0-0145361	0-50	3
WALTON WAYNE A	1LT	0-0412492	1143	2
WALTON WILLIAM A	1LT	0-0496529	0256	1
WALTON WILLIAM S	MAJ	0-1110871	0760	1
WALTON WILLIAM W	CPT	0-0957506	0560	1
WALTRIP JESSE R	MAJ	0-0330526	0545	2
WALTRIP TERRY D	CPT	0-0339121	0145	2
WALTZ DAVID C	CPT	0-1822925	0960	1
WALTZ JACK L	LTC	0-1184438	0567	1
WALTZ WILLIAM E	MAJ	0-1313938	0862	1
WALTZINGER AUGUST F	MAJ	0-1169382	0962	1
WALUSH FRANCIS J	LTC	0-1639788	0262	1
WALWORTH ALLEN C	LTC	0-1591509	0262	1
WALWORTH THOMAS K	CW4	W-2136501	0865	1
WALZ AUGUST F	LTC	0-0251425	0264	3
WAMMACK ROBERT F	1LT	0-1294046	0145	2
WAMPLER JOHN J	CPT	0-2262453	1060	1
WAMPLER RAY M	LTC	0-0329564	0666	3
WAMPLER ROBERT L	1LT	0-1861925	0553	2
WAMPOLE JOHN M	LTC	0-1046680	0363	1
WAMSLEY JAMES G	LTC	0-1176839	1061	1
WANAT JOHN T	LTC	0-0471610	0753	1
WANCHECK JOSEPH N	CW3	W-2142788	0460	1
WANCIO JOSEPH	CPT	0-1289841	1262	1
WANDELL WILBUR H	LTC	0-0223747	1054	1
WANDREY ALFRED F	1LT	0-1313044	0745	2
WANEK HAROLD E	MAJ	0-0318605	0961	1
WANG MALVIN P	COL	0-0226855	0665	3
WANGDAHL ERLAND J	MAJ	0-0502713	1263	3
WANGEMAN CLAYTON P	LTC	0-0302566	0346	2
WANGLER AMBROSE J	CPT	0-0890040	1045	2
WANITSHKA CHARLES F	CPT	0-1555151	0858	1
WANKEN LELAND G	MAJ	0-1886431	0267	1
WANN HENRY S	LTC	0-0488520	0164	1
WANN ROBERT A	MAJ	0-1303235	0761	1
WANNAMAKER A J M	COL	0-0202346	0252	2
WANNAMAKER GEORGE W	COL	0-0145360	0446	2
WANNAMAKER THERON R	LTC	0-0270872	0468	3
WANNAN CHARLES W JR	1LT	0-0418355	0145	2
WANNEBO JOSEPH T	CW2	W-2149721	0963	1
WANT VIRGIL D	LTC	0-0301312	0868	3
WANTUCK LOUIS B	LTC	0-0305273	0361	1

NAME	GRADE	SVC NO	DATE RET MO YR	RET CODE
WANTZ RAYMOND F	LTC	O-1032183	0861	1
WAPENSKY VLADIMIR A	CW3	W-2151148	0465	1
WAPINSKI STANLEY W	LTC	O-1324685	0163	1
WAPLE GEORGE H	CPT	O-0963868	0662	1
WAPNER JOSEPH A	1LT	O-1306667	0146	2
WARACK JOHN L	LTC	O-0301513	0660	1
WARAKSA PETER J	CW2	W-2107263	1047	2
WARBURG FREDERICK	COL	O-0161510	1057	3
WARBURTON JOHN H	LTC	O-1059093	0563	1
WARCHOLIK VICTOR	LTC	O-0393793	0357	1
WARD AARON L	LTC	O-0311528	0761	3
WARD ALBERT	1LT	O-1996396	0347	1
WARD ARTHUR T	MAJ	O-0887631	1059	1
WARD ARTHUR W	2LT	O-1825454	0851	2
WARD BEVERLY M	LTC	O-0525113	1064	1
WARD BILLY E	MAJ	O-2265545	0766	2
WARD BYRON G	LTC	O-1309451	0762	1
WARD CHARLES A	CW3	W-2136393	0563	1
WARD CHARLES A JR	MAJ	O-4074644	1068	1
WARD CHARLES C	CW2	W-2147687	0563	1
WARD CHARLES D	LTC	O-0394876	0965	3
WARD CHARLES F	COL	O-0354064	0747	2
WARD CHARLES F	MAJ	O-1924659	0966	1
WARD CHARLES S	COL	O-0444518	0954	1
WARD CHARLOTTE	2LT	N-0736099	1145	1
WARD CHESTER J	MAJ	O-0279298	0765	3
WARD CLETUS O	MAJ	O-2036455	0954	1
WARD CLIFFORD F	MAJ	O-1049011	1161	2
WARD DELLA A	CPT	N-0702101	0246	1
WARD DELMAR E	MAJ	O-1011343	0951	2
WARD DENNIS P	LTC	O-0346653	1059	1
WARD DOYLE P	LTC	O-0231542	0255	3
WARD EARL E	MAJ	O-0488296	0350	2
WARD EDWARD J	LTC	O-0301833	0847	2
WARD EUGENE A	LTC	O-0271442	0367	3
WARD FLOYD R	CPT	O-1999124	0864	1
WARD FRANK T	CW3	W-2151935	0965	1
WARD GENE G	CW3	W-2142434	1059	1
WARD GEORGE F	CPT	O-0252362	0266	3
WARD GEORGE W	LTC	O-1554659	0968	1
WARD GEROGE A	1LT	O-0402520	1144	2
WARD GILBERT J	2LT	O-2012589	0946	2
WARD GLEN F	CPT	O-2252783	0557	1
WARD HAROLD M	MAJ	O-1119007	0461	1
WARD HAROLD T	LTC	O-0333763	0556	1
WARD HARRISON F	LTC	O-0242676	0752	3
WARD HARRY H	1LT	O-1648220	0845	2
WARD HELEN G	MAJ	N-0720304	0964	3
WARD HENRY P	COL	O-0266401	1262	1
WARD J B	MAJ	O-0302266	1144	2
WARD JACK SR	1LT	O-1575620	0157	1
WARD JAMES A JR	LTC	O-0360407	0460	1
WARD JAMES A SR	CW2	W-2107952	0857	1
WARD JAMES H	CPT	O-0286682	0365	3
WARD JAMES W	MAJ	O-2205311	0667	1
WARD JESSE R	LTC	O-1166203	0361	1
WARD JOHN A	CW4	W-2109613	0360	1
WARD JOHN J	MAJ	O-1044417	1062	1
WARD JOHN T	MAJ	O-1926337	0266	1
WARD JOSEPH L	CPT	O-2006327	0361	1
WARD JULIAN H	CPT	O-1030946	0656	1
WARD KENNEDY G	MAJ	O-2007202	0461	1
WARD KENNETH D	MAJ	O-0300288	0262	3
WARD KENNETH L	1LT	O-1101703	0645	2
WARD KENNON J	CPT	O-0256428	1161	2
WARD LEE R	WO1	W-2114187	0145	2
WARD LEE R G	LTC	O-0107976	1047	1
WARD LEROY J	1LT	O-1634442	0445	2
WARD LEWIS J JR	1LT	O-0540225	0646	2
WARD LYCURGOS B	CPT	O-0366086	0947	2
WARD MARSHALL M	CPT	O-0164056	1045	2
WARD MARY R	MAJ	N-0756508	1063	2
WARD NORMAN J	LTC	O-0748287	0365	1
WARD PARMELEE	LTC	O-0286916	1265	3
WARD PAUL C	LTC	O-1558827	0466	2
WARD PAUL S	MAJ	O-0289063	0568	3
WARD PHILIP J JR	COL	O-0291955	1061	3
WARD RALPH B	LTC	O-0165883	1156	3
WARD RALPH B	CW4	W-2113652	0553	1
WARD RALPH D	1LT	O-0518732	1144	2
WARD RALPH L	LTC	O-0492391	0863	3
WARD RICHARD C	LTC	O-0918569	0664	3
WARD RICHARD C	LTC	O-1574175	0266	1
WARD ROBERT B JR	MAJ	O-2032123	0866	1
WARD ROBERT D	1LT	O-0921332	0245	2
WARD ROBERT L	1LT	O-1103994	1045	2
WARD ROBERT L	LTC	O-1583814	0562	1
WARD ROBERT S	MAJ	O-0968127	0563	1
WARD ROBERT W	LTC	O-0301051	0260	1
WARD ROY M	1LT	O-0903812	0644	2
WARD STANLEY A	LTC	O-0243825	0266	3
WARD STEPHEN A	CPT	O-0340775	1046	2
WARD STEWART H	LTC	O-0281708	0667	3
WARD THEODORE B	LTC	O-0492960	0959	1
WARD THOMAS A	COL	O-0267345	1161	1
WARD THOMAS C	LTC	O-0474575	0257	1
WARD THOMAS P	COL	O-0249982	0557	3
WARD THOMAS R	MAJ	O-1553011	0561	1
WARD THOMAS W	CPT	O-1168969	0647	2
WARD THURMAN L	LTC	O-0355203	0762	1
WARD VERNON	CW4	W-2007068	0567	1
WARD VIRGIL J JR	CW3	W-2152307	0163	1
WARD VIRGIL L	MAJ	O-2262102	0765	1
WARD WALTER J	MAJ	O-1173498	0367	1
WARD WALTER R	CPT	O-0302842	1057	1
WARD WILLIAM B	LTC	O-0235871	0166	3
WARD WILLIAM E	LTC	O-1549163	0661	1
WARD WILLIAM L SR	CPT	O-0476718	0862	1
WARD WILLIAM R JR	CPT	O-0541196	0446	2
WARD WILLIAM W	COL	O-0257323	0761	3
WARD WILMA B	2LT	N-0736047	1143	1
WARDELL CECIL J	LTC	O-1165583	1061	1
WARDELL LLOYD L	LTC	O-0108800	0247	1
WARDEN EDWARD A	LTC	O-1323370	0764	1
WARDEN JOHN B	COL	O-0147395	0656	3
WARDEN LEO W	MAJ	O-1179669	0864	1
WARDEN LEON N	LTC	O-1043533	1066	3
WARDER FREDERIC B JR	LTC	O-0516127	0767	1
WARDIN HERBERT B	CPT	O-0133400	0454	3
WARDLAW JOSEPH G	LTC	O-0170949	1161	3
WARDLE CLARENCE J	LTC	O-0278984	1055	1
WARDLOW HILDA A	1LT	N-0760491	1045	1
WARDLOW LOUIS M	CW3	W-2144364	1064	1
WARDLOW THEODORE G	LTC	O-1166642	0258	1
WARDNER WALTER C	LTC	O-0196191	0961	3
WARDROP HARVEY R	MAJ	O-1103453	0658	1
WARDROP ROBERT W	LTC	O-0331851	0862	1
WARDWELL HILLIARE R	MAJ	O-0291100	1045	2
WARE CHARLES W	LTC	O-0355495	1058	1
WARE DEWEY E	2LT	O-1308028	0744	2
WARE EDWARD R	COL	O-0219533	0452	3
WARE EDWARD V	1LT	O-0445216	0746	2
WARE GEORGE L	CPT	O-0446760	0445	2
WARE GEORGE W	MAJ	O-0196290	0163	3
WARE HERBERT M	CPT	O-0373097	1148	2
WARE IVAN H	MAJ	O-0162349	0258	3
WARE JAMES M	1LT	O-1293500	1045	2
WARE JUSTIN J	CPT	O-1286933	0446	2
WARE MARVIN K	CW4	W-2144450	1166	1
WARE MAURICE L	1LT	O-1295303	0645	2
WARE MAX E	COL	O-0380743	0360	1
WARE ROBERT B	CPT	O-0494143	0450	1
WARE ROBERT E	COL	O-0214782	0663	3
WARE ROBERT L	LTC	O-0226569	0264	3
WARE ROSWELL C	MAJ	O-2026176	1265	1
WARE RUFUS L	1LT	O-1296949	0745	2
WARE RUSSELL H	CPT	O-0149470	0756	3
WARE SAMUEL J	1LT	O-0125463	1051	3
WARE STEPHEN C	COL	O-0270302	0266	3
WARE WILLETT JR	LTC	O-0278722	0663	1
WARE WILLIAM L	CPT	O-2033241	0460	1
WARE WILSON P	CPT	O-1317847	0546	2
WARFEL CHARLES O	COL	O-0118903	0648	3
WARFIELD DAVID K JR	LTC	O-1330014	0964	1
WARFIELD HARRY R	COL	O-0252363	0964	3
WARFIELD PAUL E	B G	O-0246401	1162	3
WARFIELD THOMAS P	LTC	O-0258316	0368	3
WARFIELD WILLIAM K	CW2	W-2205155	1262	1
WARFORD GEORGE F	MAJ	O-1639789	0662	1
WARG ELLEN B	1LT	N-0743802	0346	1
WARGA ANNA H	CPT	N-0751980	1048	2
WARGA CHARLES J	CPT	O-1307899	0246	2
WARGACKI RICHARD T	CPT	O-1573976	1051	2
WARHEIT HARRY G	CPT	O-2011009	0556	1
WARHURST WILBUR L	CW3	W-2147046	0461	1
WARING CLARK D	MAJ	O-0151079	0657	3
WARING FRANK S	COL	O-0200996	0260	1
WARING THOMAS L	COL	O-0248758	0564	3
WARK GEORGE H	B G	O-0183827	0648	3
WARK JOHN T	1LT	O-1310535	0151	2
WARKER PETER F	MAJ	O-0172314	0156	3
WARLEY EXLEY H	MAJ	O-0512378	0147	2
WARLICK G W	1LT	O-0449256	0347	2
WARLICK GEORGE C	CPT	O-0208462	0954	3
WARLICK JOHN L	WO1	W-2118165	0666	1
WARLICK WILLIAM A	LTC	O-1167265	0262	1
WARMAN CLARENCE S	MAJ	O-1102110	1060	1
WARMAN ERNEST E	CPT	O-4074345	0868	1
WARMOUTH LOUIS A	MAJ	O-1308438	0263	1
WARMUTH IVAN J	CPT	O-1180375	0862	1
WARNACK JOSEPH E	MAJ	O-2295022	1267	1
WARNDOF CHARLES R	COL	O-0153058	1159	3
WARNECKE ADOLPH F	LTC	O-0887976	0564	1
WARNEK OLEG V	MAJ	O-2210266	0664	1
WARNER ARTHUR H	COL	O-0198052	0953	3
WARNER CARL J	MAJ	O-2046391	1057	1
WARNER CHARLES J	MAJ	O-0389839	0457	1
WARNER DANIEL E	1LT	O-1105594	1045	2
WARNER DAVID J	1LT	O-1895622	0745	2
WARNER ETHEL C	MAJ	L-1010116	0564	1
WARNER FLOYD N	COL	O-0273409	0356	2
WARNER FRANCIS L	MAJ	O-1293502	0267	1
WARNER FRANK T	LTC	O-0184390	0154	3
WARNER GEORGE B	MAJ	O-0321293	0767	3
WARNER HAROLD C	COL	O-0333870	0861	3
WARNER HAROLD J	MAJ	O-0145890	1043	2
WARNER HAROLD P	1LT	O-0394483	0643	2
WARNER JARED	1LT	O-0450517	0345	2
WARNER JOHN E	1LT	O-0314549	0544	2
WARNER JOHN H	CPT	O-1284061	0745	2
WARNER JOHN W	MAJ	O-0276046	0865	3
WARNER LAURENCE P	MAJ	O-0159404	0860	3
WARNER LORING K	LTC	O-0143898	0648	3
WARNER LYNN J	CPT	O-1183644	0646	2
WARNER MARK T	COL	O-0237614	0249	3
WARNER MORRIS T	COL	O-0156562	1059	3
WARNER OLIVER M	LTC	O-0452369	1055	3
WARNER RAYMOND	CW3	W-2149000	0163	1
WARNER ROBERT E L	CPT	O-0487184	0351	1
WARNER ROY C	CPT	O-2046854	0157	1
WARNER ROY D	MAJ	O-0996924	0863	1
WARNER ROY F	COL	O-0257605	1066	3
WARNER VICTOR E JR	LTC	O-0326147	0957	1
WARNER WALTER H	CPT	O-1296773	0547	2
WARNER WILLIAM M	CPT	O-0206934	0647	1
WARNER WOODREW W	MAJ	O-1580476	0959	1
WARNKE CLIFFORD	CW2	W-2144208	0358	1
WARNKEN MICHAEL P	CPT	O-0395388	0444	2
WARNOCK BRUCE B	1LT	O-1054167	1046	2
WARNOCK NORMAN M	LTC	O-1585050	0865	1
WARREN ALAN D	CW2	W-2215578	0868	1
WARREN ALBERT E	MAJ	O-0156563	0-52	3
WARREN ARBER J	CPT	O-0234128	0747	1
WARREN ARCHIE A	CW3	W-2146767	0465	1
WARREN ARTHUR	MAJ	O-1996734	0960	1
WARREN CLYDE B	MAJ	O-0925374	0859	3
WARREN CLYDE R	MAJ	O-1895023	0560	1
WARREN CULLEN	CW3	W-2146557	0365	1
WARREN DONALD H	LTC	O-1544343	0464	1
WARREN EDWIN H	CPT	O-2036717	0746	2
WARREN FRANCES A	MAJ	N-0727422	0862	1
WARREN FREDERICK	M G	O-0266247	0963	3
WARREN GEORGE B JR	LTC	O-1038509	0365	2
WARREN GEORGE C JR	LTC	O-0352182	0161	1
WARREN GEORGE D	CW3	W-2143976	0862	1
WARREN GEORGE M	CPT	O-2046519	0952	1
WARREN GORDON R	MAJ	O-1341837	0164	1
WARREN HAROLD C	CW3	W-2142277	0463	1
WARREN HAROLD F	LTC	O-0450941	0859	1
WARREN HARRIS B	1LT	O-1321971	0845	2
WARREN HOWARD J	CW2	W-2104569	0746	2
WARREN JACK A	1LT	O-1291552	0644	2
WARREN JAMES A JR	COL	O-0227551	0366	3
WARREN JAMES W	WO1	T-0066402	0563	2
WARREN JOHN	COL	O-0307693	1167	3
WARREN JOHN B	WO1	W-2117531	1152	1
WARREN JOHN R	LTC	O-1699942	0665	1
WARREN KEITH L	LTC	O-2039165	0766	1
WARREN KENNETH D	LTC	O-0885755	0655	1
WARREN LAWRENCE	CPT	O-0272697	0466	3
WARREN LEONARD P	LTC	O-0225695	0165	3
WARREN LYNN R	1LT	O-0519657	1145	2
WARREN MALCOLM S	1LT	O-0271417	1142	2
WARREN MAX A	MAJ	O-2210333	0866	1
WARREN MERL R	COL	O-0189660	0256	3
WARREN MORRILL T	1LT	O-1012396	0750	2
WARREN RAT R	LTC	O-0258108	1058	3
WARREN RAUL N	LTC	O-0478103	0255	1
WARREN RALPH F	MAJ	O-1110326	0857	1
WARREN RALPH M	CW2	W-2150932	0461	1
WARREN RICHARD	CW2	W-2112909	1053	1
WARREN RICHARD A	CPT	O-0461107	0647	2
WARREN RICHARD K	CW2	W-3430201	1167	1
WARREN ROBERT C	LTC	O-0298125	0158	2
WARREN ROBERT E	LTC	O-0260739	0468	3
WARREN ROBERT F	MAJ	O-0496567	0945	2
WARREN ROBERT K	MAJ	O-1019848	0962	1
WARREN ROBERT L	MAJ	O-1341926	0266	1
WARREN RUFUS C	LTC	O-0277111	1060	3
WARREN SAMUEL G	LTC	O-0299782	0168	3
WARREN SAMUEL H	LTC	O-1285344	0263	1
WARREN STANLEY D	MAJ	O-0288761	0267	3
WARREN THOMAS L	CPT	O-0245526	0454	3
WARREN TRUMAN A	WO1	W-2105047	0859	1
WARREN VIRGINIA L	1LT	N-0727205	1047	1
WARREN WILLIAM H	MAJ	O-0299230	0364	3
WARREN WILLIAM H	MAJ	O-1289176	0161	1
WARREN WILLIAM J	LTC	O-0392492	0356	2
WARREN WILLIS B	1LT	O-1319803	0247	2
WARREN WOODROW	COL	O-0423367	0767	1
WARREN WOODROW W	CW3	W-2204957	1065	1
WARRENBURG CLARENCE	LTC	O-0280986	0765	3
WARRICK HAROLD L	1LT	O-1945308	0146	2
WARRICK JAMES R JR	LTC	O-1289516	1161	1
WARRICK JAMES W	LTC	O-1102992	0557	1
WARRICK JOHN L	MAJ	O-0174021	0760	3
WARRICK WILLIAM H	COL	O-0330450	0368	3
WARRING WILLARD B	COL	O-0251461	0562	3
WARROW LEWIS W	MAJ	O-1111419	0261	1
WARSAW EUGENE	CPT	O-0494379	1145	2
WARSHALL ALEXANDER	LTC	O-1324471	0866	1
WARSHAW ISADDRE	1LT	O-1326952	1146	2
WARSHAWSKY EUGENE	CW2	W-2151350	0661	1
WARTERS CHARLES J	MAJ	O-1170912	1166	1
WARTNER ALOYS JR	COL	O-0258881	1166	3
WARTSKY MUNDELL	1LT	O-1044720	0546	2
WARWICK CECIL T	MAJ	O-0921205	1047	2
WARWICK CLARENCE E	MAJ	O-0299470	1043	2
WARWICK HENRY	CW4	W-2103580	1057	1
WARZECHA EDWARD M	LTC	O-0683513	0468	1

NAME	GRADE	SVC NO	DATE RET MO YR	RET CODE
WASCAK ANDREW	CPT	0-1306778	0546	2
WASECKA STEPHEN	LTC	0-1295466	0166	1
WASELEWSKY STANLEY	MAJ	0-1582248	1057	2
WASER WILLIAM B JR	CW3	W-2148776	0762	1
WASH GEORGE M	MAJ	0-2040845	0261	1
WASHBOURNE KYLE V	LTC	0-1044143	1163	1
WASHBURN ARTHUR M	COL	0-0209127	0450	3
WASHBURN ARTHUR S JR	COL	0-0341430	0163	1
WASHBURN CARLYLE	1LT	0-1103996	1045	2
WASHBURN CHARLES E	CPT	0-0181359	0648	3
WASHBURN DULAN R	1LT	0-0886910	1047	1
WASHBURN FRANK E	LTC	0-0182767	1149	3
WASHBURN GEORGE T JR	CW2	W-2145163	1056	2
WASHBURN GEORGE W JR	MAJ	0-1301728	0660	1
WASHBURN GERALD M	2LT	0-1048233	0245	2
WASHBURN GORDON G	LTC	0-1182298	0865	1
WASHBURN LESTER L	LTC	0-0253063	1166	3
WASHBURN PERLEY A	LTC	0-0151946	0157	1
WASHBURN RICHARD P	MAJ	0-2265548	0566	1
WASHBURN SHERMAN S	LTC	0-1043252	0266	1
WASHBURN WILLIAM E	CPT	0-0212487	0648	3
WASHBURN WILLIAM H	MAJ	0-0252546	0964	3
WASHBURN WILLIAM H	MAJ	0-1646094	0161	1
WASHBURNE CLAUDE B	COL	0-0145461	0752	3
WASHER PHINEAS	LTC	0-0232611	0162	3
WASHINGTON ALBERT F	LTC	0-1895064	0961	1
WASHINGTON CHARLES A	CPT	0-0976924	0361	1
WASHINGTON CHARLES W	MAJ	0-1917631	0163	1
WASHINGTON CLARA G	LTC	N-0700232	0146	1
WASHINGTON JOHN H	LTC	0-1575255	0561	1
WASHINGTON JOHN P	CW3	W-2143068	0765	1
WASHINGTON RICHARD B	LTC	0-0394906	0262	1
WASHINGTON ROBBIN E	LTC	0-1165261	0861	1
WASHINGTON WILLIAM D	CPT	0-0232672	1062	3
WASHINGTON WILLIAM H	MAJ	0-0122961	0753	3
WASHLICK MATTHEW E	LTC	0-1557924	0463	1
WASHNOK ROBERT L	LTC	0-0291829	1265	1
WASILEWSKI ADAM J	CPT	0-1331350	0755	1
WASKE LEONARD	CW2	W-2109621	0647	2
WASKO THEODORE E	MAJ	0-1649975	0767	1
WASKOM GEORGE F	CW2	W-2150013	0461	1
WASKOW HARRY N	MAJ	0-1300422	0360	1
WASNETSKY JOHN	CW3	W-2152259	1062	1
WASON ALEXANDER	1LT	0-1595384	0746	2
WASON ALFRED P	LTC	0-0127100	0757	3
WASON GEORGE F	LTC	0-0174209	0958	3
WASON THOMAS H	LTC	0-0314343	0646	2
WASS JOHN R JR	LTC	0-0419534	0657	1
WASSERMAN ISIDORE	1LT	0-0526210	0245	2
WASSERMAN JULIAN	1LT	0-1342023	0852	2
WASSERMAN NATHAN	LTC	0-0341700	0266	3
WASSON CLARENCE C	CPT	0-1844773	0159	2
WASSON EARL D	MAJ	0-1042735	0162	2
WASSON LAWRENCE	CW3	W-2203263	0564	1
WASSON LELAND H	MAJ	0-0180078	0351	3
WASSON ROY C	LTC	0-1179570	1156	1
WASSON WILLIAM A	COL	0-0370156	0157	1
WASSON WILLIAM O	MAJ	0-1825206	0962	1
WASSUM ROBERT A	MAJ	0-1685223	0446	2
WATANABE LLOYD K	CW3	W-2152753	0265	1
WATCKE HENRY S	MAJ	0-0556411	0863	1
WATERBURY JOSEPH W	LTC	0-1341382	0668	1
WATERHOUSE CARMACK	LTC	0-0903869	1168	3
WATERHOUSE EDWARD J	MAJ	0-0169886	0259	3
WATERHOUSE GEORGE T	CPT	0-1043534	0944	2
WATERHOUSE ROBERT L	MAJ	0-1304977	0859	1
WATERHOUSE WILLIAM H	CPT	0-1758630	0554	2
WATERMAN BENJAMIN D	LTC	0-0971830	1168	2
WATERMAN ERNEST A	LTC	0-0336896	0261	3
WATERMAN JEROME A	LTC	0-0171660	0648	3
WATERMAN JOSEPH M	MAJ	0-0406963	0747	2
WATERMAN LEONARD E	MAJ	0-0502548	1147	2
WATERMAN MARCUS M	1LT	0-0922118	1046	2
WATERMAN MEREDITH T	CPT	0-0224576	0144	2
WATERS ARTHUR C	LTC	0-0173813	0256	3

NAME	GRADE	SVC NO	DATE RET MO YR	RET CODE
WATERS BRUCE C	2LT	0-1822752	0344	2
WATERS FRANK H	LTC	0-0240085	1161	1
WATERS FRED O	LTC	0-0414882	1160	1
WATERS GEORGE L	COL	0-0385817	0566	1
WATERS GEORGE M	LTC	0-0435933	0447	2
WATERS HARGET D	MAJ	0-0982453	0764	1
WATERS HARRY D	MAJ	0-0321947	0860	1
WATERS JACK T	MAJ	0-4011094	0967	1
WATERS JAMES F	COL	0-0248463	0766	3
WATERS JAMES M	MAJ	0-2200444	0666	1
WATERS JAMES T	LTC	0-1995019	0766	1
WATERS JOHN R	LTC	0-1544331	0268	2
WATERS JOHN T	2LT	0-1014242	0744	2
WATERS JOSEPH B	2LT	0-1585055	0245	2
WATERS JULIAN H	CW3	W-2149865	0863	1
WATERS LAUGHLIN E	CPT	0-0363553	1145	2
WATERS LEE E	MAJ	0-0383149	0945	2
WATERS LEE T	LTC	0-1588948	0463	1
WATERS MARTIN H	LTC	0-0331609	0461	3
WATERS MARY I	CPT	N-0731549	0447	1
WATERS MELVIN C	LTC	0-1001490	0548	2
WATERS PATTISON A	COL	0-0189546	0453	3
WATERS PAUL E	LTC	0-1105619	0768	1
WATERS RICHARD W	LTC	0-0330745	0960	1
WATERS ROBERT L	MAJ	0-0977371	1164	1
WATERS ROBERT P	LTC	0-0143404	0648	3
WATERS ROBERT W	MAJ	0-0888217	0963	1
WATERS VERLON E	2LT	0-0987691	1051	2
WATERS WALTER C	MAJ	0-4030855	0968	1
WATERS WILLIAM P	CPT	0-1597319	0747	2
WATERS 3RD JOHN S	CPT	0-0456055	0746	2
WATERSTREET KENNET	1LT	0-0924395	1044	2
WATFORD FRANKIE H	CW4	W-2148135	1068	1
WATFORD RAYMOND E SR	CW3	W-2147314	0765	1
WATHEN BENJAMIN S	LTC	0-0271298	1068	3
WATHEN BUELL S	2LT	0-0206409	0640	1
WATKINS ANNABEL	MAJ	R-0010033	0366	1
WATKINS AVIS M	MAJ	L-0115648	0963	1
WATKINS BAZZ	WO1	W-2118351	0550	1
WATKINS BRYAN J	LTC	0-0350818	0868	3
WATKINS CHARLES B	COL	0-0264198	0151	3
WATKINS CLARENCE C	LTC	0-0332454	0658	3
WATKINS CRAIG C	COL	0-1640106	1066	3
WATKINS DACY P	LTC	0-0268246	0660	3
WATKINS DAVIS	LTC	0-0271143	0267	3
WATKINS EDWARD W	LTC	0-0243292	0964	3
WATKINS ELLIS H	2LT	0-2035170	0845	2
WATKINS ELLIS S	LTC	0-1296886	0561	1
WATKINS EUNICE R	MAJ	N-0741719	1165	3
WATKINS EVERETT C	WO1	W-2106280	0548	1
WATKINS EVERETT W	LTC	0-0227495	0963	3
WATKINS FLOYD R	2LT	0-2053914	0645	2
WATKINS GEORGE E	MAJ	0-0122834	0353	3
WATKINS GLENN O	1LT	0-1311240	0745	2
WATKINS GUY H JR	LTC	0-1557692	0368	3
WATKINS HARRY	1LT	0-0205531	0953	3
WATKINS HARRY G	CPT	0-2002564	0457	1
WATKINS HENRY F	1LT	0-0308015	0343	2
WATKINS HERRICK C JR	MAJ	0-0192481	1060	3
WATKINS JAMES C	MAJ	0-2024284	0961	1
WATKINS JAMES C	CW2	W-3350357	1168	1
WATKINS JOHN B	COL	0-0233324	0659	3
WATKINS JOHN H	MAJ	0-0199643	0746	1
WATKINS JOHN O JR	LTC	0-0476121	0646	2
WATKINS JOHN R	MAJ	0-1552822	0859	1
WATKINS MARGARET	MAJ	N-0727719	1267	1
WATKINS MARION H	CPT	0-1590249	0959	1
WATKINS MARTIN O JR	CPT	0-0460013	0747	2
WATKINS PERRY R JR	MAJ	0-2266061	0267	1
WATKINS PERSHING V	LTC	0-1303581	0365	1
WATKINS PETER F	LTC	0-0408687	1060	1
WATKINS RAYMOND	COL	0-0243351	0662	3
WATKINS REGINALD G	LTC	0-0410785	0161	1
WATKINS ROBERT A JR	1LT	0-1289177	1056	1
WATKINS ROBERT B	1LT	0-0467830	0545	2

NAME	GRADE	SVC NO	DATE RET MO YR	RET CODE
WATKINS ROBERT H	LTC	0-0213592	0956	3
WATKINS ROBERT M	CPT	0-0492788	0246	2
WATKINS THELMA C	1LT	N-0764036	0146	1
WATKINS THOMAS H	COL	0-0233013	1061	1
WATKINS THOMAS J	MAJ	0-1051444	0157	1
WATKINS THOMAS R	LTC	0-0432755	0962	1
WATKINS ULYSSES W SR	LTC	0-1824945	0968	3
WATKINS VERNON L	COL	0-0220134	0359	2
WATKINS VICTOR	CW2	W-2148526	1161	2
WATKINS WALLACE	CW4	W-2109484	0456	1
WATKINS WATT	WO1	W-2131465	0344	2
WATLAND LLOYD A	MAJ	0-0541517	0765	1
WATLINGTON JUNIUS A	LTC	0-2025241	0168	1
WATROUS WILLIAM L	MAJ	0-2008074	0462	1
WATSON ALAN M	COL	0-0163882	0160	3
WATSON ALBERT P	MAJ	0-2028761	0864	1
WATSON ALFRED F	CPT	0-1308223	1147	2
WATSON ALFRED W	MAJ	0-1108405	0561	1
WATSON ALLEN J	MAJ	0-0283678	0846	2
WATSON ALMYRA M	MAJ	N-0726087	0963	1
WATSON ARCHIE A	CPT	0-0248454	0945	2
WATSON BARTON H	LTC	0-1822088	0164	1
WATSON BEN D	1LT	0-1030431	0455	1
WATSON BILLY P	2LT	0-2006220	0264	2
WATSON BURTON L	CPT	0-0192143	1054	2
WATSON CHARLES D	WO1	W-2119689	0644	2
WATSON CHARLES G	LTC	0-0545523	0664	1
WATSON CHARLES L	1LT	0-0804007	0865	1
WATSON CHARLES P	LTC	0-0122425	0549	3
WATSON CLARENCE R	CPT	0-1371092	0555	1
WATSON CLIFFORD A	1LT	0-4048864	0959	2
WATSON COMER D	1LT	0-1648546	0456	1
WATSON COVINGTON	MAJ	0-2019256	0260	1
WATSON CULLUM B	COL	0-0422204	0561	1
WATSON DALE I	MAJ	0-2262554	0765	1
WATSON DANIEL G	LTC	0-0332173	1046	1
WATSON DEANE C	1LT	0-0537623	1145	2
WATSON DEWARD H	MAJ	0-1120699	0161	1
WATSON DON R	MAJ	0-1056008	0866	1
WATSON DONALD M	MAJ	0-2006962	1063	1
WATSON DORSEY J	CPT	0-0471802	0448	1
WATSON DURWARD L	CW4	W-2143623	0657	1
WATSON EDWARD L	LTC	0-0443787	0347	2
WATSON ELMER S	COL	0-0264495	0945	2
WATSON FELTON L	LTC	0-0250530	0664	3
WATSON FRANCIS M	LTC	0-0297702	0246	2
WATSON FRANK	CPT	0-0479094	1053	1
WATSON FRANK J	CPT	0-1304830	0254	2
WATSON FRANK P	MAJ	0-1540909	1061	1
WATSON GALE A	LTC	0-1050986	0962	1
WATSON GEORGE	LTC	0-1015601	0363	2
WATSON GEORGE A	LTC	0-1341608	1168	1
WATSON GEORGE O	MAJ	0-2017154	0461	1
WATSON GEORGE P JR	CW2	W-2214143	0668	1
WATSON GEORGE R	LTC	0-0252211	1265	3
WATSON GEORGE S	COL	0-0272590	0863	1
WATSON GEORGIA B	MAJ	L-0402018	0146	2
WATSON GUY M	MAJ	0-0970140	0962	1
WATSON HARRY B	CPT	0-1052613	0963	1
WATSON HARRY H	LTC	0-0157479	0833	1
WATSON HARRY T JR	1LT	0-0300729	0145	2
WATSON HENRY B	LTC	0-0288336	0557	1
WATSON HENRY L	LTC	0-0953869	0466	1
WATSON HENRY P	MAJ	0-1535326	0751	2
WATSON HERBERT R	COL	0-0212179	0754	3
WATSON HUGH F	MAJ	0-1319367	0261	1
WATSON ISABEL M	1LT	N-0734024	1045	1
WATSON JAMES O	MAJ	0-0438873	0246	2
WATSON JAMES E JR	COL	0-0333577	1067	3
WATSON JAMES G	1LT	0-1301062	0945	2
WATSON JAMES R	LTC	0-1686674	0168	1
WATSON JOHN L	CPT	0-1284249	0945	2
WATSON JOHN M	CW2	W-2149723	0764	1
WATSON JOHN T	COL	0-1311241	0768	3
WATSON JOHN W	COL	0-0278228	0663	3

NAME	GRADE	SVC NO	DATE RET MO YR	RET CODE
WATSON JOHNNY J	LTC	0-1040481	1160	1
WATSON JOSEPH	LTC	0-1304624	0666	1
WATSON JOSEPH D	MAJ	0-2204344	0367	1
WATSON JOSEPH L	CW2	W-2208446	0962	1
WATSON JOSEPH M JR	LTC	0-0280685	1067	3
WATSON JOSEPH W	COL	0-0255847	0647	2
WATSON LEASON K	LTC	0-1101707	1060	1
WATSON LESLIE L JR	1LT	0-1575250	1045	2
WATSON LEWIS T	CW2	W-2118188	0149	1
WATSON MARION T	COL	0-0143872	0857	3
WATSON MELVIN L	CW4	W-2149887	0965	1
WATSON MILLARD F	2LT	0-0887708	0253	1
WATSON OLIVER P	MAJ	0-1316799	0360	1
WATSON PARDON D	COL	0-0218727	1047	2
WATSON PAUL R	CPT	0-0362996	0645	2
WATSON RANDOLPH C	CPT	0-1297627	0745	2
WATSON RAY E	COL	0-0323388	0-51	3
WATSON RAYMOND C	CPT	0-0232934	0165	3
WATSON RICHARD E	MAJ	0-0949663	0468	1
WATSON ROBERT F	CW2	W-2209544	1263	1
WATSON ROBERT G	1LT	0-0493778	0549	1
WATSON ROBERT J	MAJ	0-1319368	0663	1
WATSON ROBERT R	CW2	W-2152882	1161	1
WATSON ROE D	MAJ	0-1285345	0346	2
WATSON ROGER L	CW3	W-2149401	0464	1
WATSON ROYAL A	CPT	0-0525310	0347	2
WATSON RUSSELL C	CW3	W-2115996	0559	1
WATSON SHIRLEY P	2LT	N-0743419	0845	1
WATSON STEPHEN B	MAJ	0-1328858	0666	1
WATSON SYLVIA A	MAJ	N-0773802	0167	1
WATSON THOMAS E	COL	0-0398329	1160	1
WATSON THOMAS V	1LT	0-1324711	0846	2
WATSON WALTER L	CW2	W-2119573	0648	1
WATSON WHITE C JR	CPT	0-1946202	0551	2
WATSON WILFRD H	2LT	0-1052221	1044	2
WATSON WILLIAM C	MAJ	0-1336983	0867	1
WATSON WILLIAM E	MAJ	0-1555317	1062	1
WATSON WILLIAM F	MAJ	0-1588950	1060	2
WATSON WILLIAM F JR	COL	0-0143102	1057	3
WATSON WILLIAM J	LTC	0-0321427	0646	2
WATSON WILLIAM J	LTC	0-1573657	0757	1
WATSON WILLIAM L	MAJ	0-0965072	0866	1
WATSON WILLIAM L	CPT	0-1309998	1046	2
WATSON WILLIAM W JR	CPT	0-0523236	0946	2
WATT ALEX S	LTC	0-0213349	0963	3
WATT ALEXIS	MAJ	0-0359869	ß357	1
WATT HUGH C	CPT	0-0889475	0455	1
WATT JAMES F	COL	0-0300555	0157	1
WATT JEWELL K	COL	0-0191406	1059	1
WATT JOHN R	CPT	0-0488396	0149	1
WATT LLOYD A	MAJ	0-0272723	0668	3
WATT RAYMOND	B G	0-0209364	1262	3
WATTERBERG JOHN P	1LT	0-0494776	1145	2
WATTERS CURTISS W	MAJ	0-0415060	0261	1
WATTERS GEORGE W	1LT	0-0466501	0345	2
WATTERS JAMES J	WO1	W-2109173	0651	2
WATTERS JOHN	LTC	0-0298364	0462	3
WATTERS KEIRAN J	CW3	W-2205727	0265	1
WATTERS WALTER P SR	MAJ	0-1592688	0855	2
WATTERSON EULA R	MAJ	N-0759865	0563	1
WATTERSON JOSEPH V	COL	0-0538485	1168	1
WATTERSON ROBERT S	LTC	0-0265288	0865	3
WATTERSON ROBERT T	CW2	W-2212447	0868	1
WATTIE ARNOLD H	1LT	0-2055143	0848	1
WATTIGNY CHARLES C	MAJ	0-1293157	0561	1
WATTS ARTHUR P	COL	0-0300016	0565	3
WATTS AUGUSTUS A	LTC	0-0293197	0260	1
WATTS CECIL E	LTC	0-0129028	0446	2
WATTS CHARLES W	MAJ	0-1642699	0357	2
WATTS CLARENCE B	MAJ	0-0358911	0661	1
WATTS CLYDE J	M G	0-0269820	0168	3
WATTS EDGAR L	CPT	0-2262159	0461	1
WATTS FLOYD J	1LT	0-0427223	1043	2
WATTS HENRY C JR	LTC	0-0989076	1268	1
WATTS HOLWAY D	COL	0-0292772	1161	3

NAME	GRADE	SVC NO	DATE RET MO YR	RET CODE
WATTS HOWARD E	LTC	0-0297654	0958	3
WATTS JACK E	WO1	W-2114353	0158	1
WATTS JACK J	LTC	0-0375604	0867	1
WATTS JAMES A	LTC	0-0291213	0759	1
WATTS JAMES E	WO1	W-2148444	1068	2
WATTS JAMES L	LTC	0-0294535	0858	1
WATTS JAMES P JR	MAJ	0-0961421	1163	1
WATTS JOHN A	CW3	W-2145602	0358	1
WATTS JOHN H	MAJ	0-0726525	0664	1
WATTS JOSEPH C	LTC	0-0242432	1064	3
WATTS JOSEPH C JR	MAJ	0-2263315	0564	1
WATTS JOSEPH R JR	LTC	0-0504140	0559	2
WATTS JOSEPH W	LTC	0-1111422	0762	1
WATTS KENNETH B	MAJ	0-1061577	0758	1
WATTS LAVAUGHN F	MAJ	0-1004057	0561	1
WATTS MONROE H	MAJ	0-2010714	0662	1
WATTS OWEN J	COL	0-0103652	0455	3
WATTS RAY A	CPT	0-2026558	1157	1
WATTS RICHARD W	LTC	0-0967257	0668	1
WATTS ROBERT A	LTC	0-1171824	1267	3
WATTS ROBERT C	MAJ	0-2018615	0164	1
WATTS RUSSELL G	MAJ	0-1643427	0760	1
WATTS SEWELL S JR	MAJ	0-0241735	0564	3
WATTS STANLEY E	MAJ	0-1328953	0763	1
WATTS THEODORE F	LTC	0-0101829	1048	3
WATTS THOMAS N	CW3	W-2205626	1267	1
WATTS ULYSSES V	LTC	0-0450141	0652	1
WATTS WALTER C	MAJ	0-1315989	0457	1
WATTS WILLIAM L	LTC	0-1552205	0863	1
WATZ EARL R	CPT	0-0304004	0646	2
WAUGH ALBERT A	MAJ	0-0420040	1067	3
WAUGH KENNETH B	LTC	0-1551142	0762	1
WAVREK GORDON J	LTC	0-1549165	0166	1
WAWREJKO THAO J	LTC	0-1293857	0561	1
WAXMUTH WILLIAM	MAJ	0-0169803	1058	3
WAY JACOB E JR	2LT	0-1329428	0846	2
WAY LLOYD G	MAJ	0-0972021	0861	1
WAY PAUL P	1LT	0-1257628	0647	2
WAY POWELL E JR	MAJ	0-1056938	0463	1
WAYBURN GATES J	1LT	0-0475483	0750	2
WAYCOTT WILFRED H	LTC	0-1646158	0666	3
WAYLAN ZULETTA M	MAJ	N-0736778	0665	3
WAYMAN JOHN R	CW3	W-3150509	1068	1
WAYMAN LEON H	LTC	0-0135240	0156	3
WAYMAN LUCIUS A	COL	0-0244745	0565	3
WAYMAN LYNFORD A	CW4	W-2117220	1262	1
WAYMENT HAROLD S	MAJ	0-2262726	0664	1
WAYMOTH HARRY K	CPT	0-0398847	0857	1
WAYNE BESSE M	1LT	N-0760446	0346	1
WAYNE FRANK R	MAJ	0-2040904	0561	1
WAYNE FREDERICK	CPT	0-0298972	0860	3
WAYNE WILFORD	CW2	W-2205726	0358	2
WAYT MURL R	CW2	W-2142118	1154	1
WEADER RICHARD J	LTC	0-0356456	0858	1
WEADOCK LEO V	LTC	0-1105256	1064	1
WEAKLAND PAUL A	MAJ	0-1822843	0962	1
WEAKLEY CHARLES L	LTC	0-0174655	0361	3
WEAKLEY KENNETH C	MAJ	0-0254749	0666	3
WEAND WILLIAM H	LTC	0-2019258	1068	1
WEARPA RUEBEN A	MAJ	0-1544280	1059	1
WEAR JOHN E	2LT	0-1042202	1144	2
WEAR THEODORE G JR	LTC	0-0219206	1062	3
WEARE BUEL F	COL	0-0321667	0163	3
WEARE HAROLD G	LTC	0-0294864	1167	3
WEARLEY DAVID A	LTC	0-1304469	0967	1
WEARS HENRY J	MAJ	0-0330525	0157	1
WEASE ARMON E	MAJ	0-0347233	0746	2
WEASNER NELSON	2LT	0-1317711	1044	2
WEATHERBEE CLIFFORD	CW2	W-2151522	0764	1
WEATHERFORD EDWARD E	COL	0-1575251	0464	1
WEATHERFORD VENUS L	MAJ	0-0380149	0346	2
WEATHERFORD WILLIA	CPT	0-1687879	1145	2
WEATHERLEY JOSHUA W	CPT	0-0402450	1043	2
WEATHERLY CARROLL O	MAJ	0-0498143	0645	2
WEATHERLY ROBERT L	MAJ	0-2000143	0267	1
WEATHERS ARTHUR F JR	MAJ	0-0958797	0264	1
WEATHERS DON R	1LT	0-0378211	0244	2
WEATHERS NED S	MAJ	0-0914257	0155	2
WEATHERS ROBERT M	LTC	0-1001272	0161	1
WEATHERS ROY L	CW2	W-2210033	0164	1
WEATHERS UDELL H	2LT	0-0977238	0251	2
WEAVER ALVIN C	CW2	W-3100499	1067	1
WEAVER ARTHUR F	LTC	0-0179380	0652	2
WEAVER ARTHUR T	LTC	0-1650796	0866	1
WEAVER BARRETT M	MAJ	0-1286574	0557	1
WEAVER BURR S	MAJ	0-0127585	0949	3
WEAVER CARL H	MAJ	0-0483541	0650	1
WEAVER CECIL H	2LT	0-1823805	0145	2
WEAVER DAVID E	MAJ	0-0513306	0163	1
WEAVER DAVID K	CW4	W-2141696	0756	1
WEAVER DIXON N	CW3	W-2147568	1162	1
WEAVER EDWARD K	1LT	0-0576630	0746	2
WEAVER EDWIN M	MAJ	0-0984973	0164	1
WEAVER ELLSWORTH	LTC	0-0275446	0863	3
WEAVER FLOYD A	MAJ	0-1686525	1060	1
WEAVER FLOYD E	MAJ	0-1172705	1054	1
WEAVER FOREST K	MAJ	0-2033075	1062	1
WEAVER FRANK M	COL	0-0236358	0266	3
WEAVER GENE A	CPT	0-1309633	0647	2
WEAVER GEORGE E	LTC	0-0922371	0862	3
WEAVER HARRY L	LTC	0-0419958	1060	1
WEAVER HEBRON T	MAJ	0-1167270	0557	1
WEAVER HENRY F	LTC	0-1826034	0868	3
WEAVER HENRY P	CPT	0-0520853	0844	2
WEAVER HOWARD E	MAJ	0-2001793	1064	1
WEAVER JACKSON B	MAJ	0-1116360	0868	3
WEAVER JAMES H	COL	0-0302379	0267	3
WEAVER JAMES H	CW3	W-2144863	0661	1
WEAVER JAMES P	1LT	0-0919447	1045	2
WEAVER JEROME M	1LT	0-1876619	1057	2
WEAVER JOHN H	LTC	0-1105258	0559	1
WEAVER JOHN H	LTC	0-1648903	1266	1
WEAVER JOHN N	1LT	0-0455174	0847	2
WEAVER JOHN W	CPT	0-1597189	0862	2
WEAVER JOSEPH R	LTC	0-0271299	0868	3
WEAVER KENNETH R	2LT	0-1013182	1044	2
WEAVER LUTHER F	LTC	0-2015644	0868	1
WEAVER LUTHER T	WO1	W-2123124	1050	2
WEAVER MALCOLM	1LT	0-1109735	1045	2
WEAVER MARY A	CPT	N-0757887	0247	1
WEAVER RALPH E	LTC	0-1165262	1061	1
WEAVER RAYMOND J	1LT	0-1323882	0845	2
WEAVER REX W	MAJ	0-0427632	1045	2
WEAVER RICHARD W	LTC	0-0423877	0256	2
WEAVER ROBERT J	CPT	0-1302396	0448	2
WEAVER RUSSELL W	CW3	W-2143731	0163	1
WEAVER STANLEY C	1LT	0-1030432	0445	2
WEAVER THOMAS D	LTC	0-0221667	0950	3
WEAVER WALTER L	MAJ	0-0452959	0361	1
WEAVER WILLIAM A	COL	0-0346620	0767	3
WEAVER WILLIAM G	COL	0-0156430	0560	3
WEAVER WILLIAM G JR	CPT	0-0547051	0763	1
WEAVER WILLIAM L	CPT	0-1109736	0352	2
WEAVER WILLIAM N	LTC	0-0423308	0767	3
WEAVER WILLIAM T	LTC	0-0271300	0467	3
WEAVER WILLIAM W	MAJ	0-1050130	0361	1
WEAVER WILLIAM W	CW3	W-2150031	0964	1
WEAVERLING M ELIZA	2LT	N-0700109	0141	1
WEBB AARON	MAJ	0-2021598	1168	2
WEBB ALBERT E	1LT	0-0374609	1043	2
WEBB ARCHIBALD	LTC	0-0368668	0967	3
WEBB CARL E	CW4	W-2143581	1068	1
WEBB CARL F	CPT	0-1046984	0346	2
WEBB CHARLES B	CW2	W-2211074	0867	1
WEBB CHARLES H	LTC	0-0288797	0167	3
WEBB CHARLES J	MAJ	0-1011990	0761	1
WEBB CHARLES M JR	COL	0-0195539	0762	3
WEBB CHARLES W	MAJ	0-0979361	0663	1
WEBB CLARENCE S	MAJ	0-1309635	0867	1
WEBB CLIFFORD G	1LT	0-1821659	0964	1
WEBB DENNIS	LTC	0-1288981	0861	1
WEBB EARL M	CPT	0-0524470	0750	1
WEBB EZRA S	CPT	0-0270934	0968	3
WEBB FAIN E	1LT	0-0302063	0643	2
WEBB FRANK M	LTC	0-1553196	0762	1
WEBB HAROLD C	MAJ	0-1003069	0557	1
WEBB HARRY J	COL	0-0253525	0365	3
WEBB HENRY L	LTC	0-0334211	0262	1
WEBB HERBERT E	1LT	0-1578017	0845	2
WEBB HOLLIS D	WO1	W-2151995	1264	1
WEBB HOMER C JR	MAJ	0-1016442	1064	1
WEBB JACKSON S	CPT	0-1320081	0146	2
WEBB JAMES A	COL	0-0185637	1152	3
WEBB JAMES B	COL	0-0243564	1265	3
WEBB JAMES F	2LT	0-1012635	0451	2
WEBB JAMES H	CW3	W-2210035	0868	1
WEBB JAMES H	CW2	RW-2205402	1263	1
WEBB JOHN B	B G	0-0244400	0264	3
WEBB JOHN B	LTC	0-0374127	0165	1
WEBB JOHN F C	CPT	0-0505021	0161	1
WEBB JYLES L	1LT	0-0991291	0954	2
WEBB LAWRENCE G	CW3	W-2105433	1057	1
WEBB LESTER F	COL	0-0336719	1166	3
WEBB LOYD E	MAJ	0-1947850	0457	1
WEBB MILBURNE	COL	0-0917129	0564	3
WEBB NANCY S	2LT	N-0734968	0945	1
WEBB OSWALD W	LTC	0-1548590	0162	1
WEBB PAUL L	COL	0-0234849	0859	1
WEBB RALPH L	COL	0-0287714	1059	2
WEBB RAYMOND E	CPT	0-0385322	1155	1
WEBB ROBERT D	2LT	0-2035171	0445	2
WEBB ROBERT E	CPT	0-1999386	0948	1
WEBB ROBERT H	MAJ	0-0963232	0566	1
WEBB ROBERT O	LTC	0-0286110	1167	3
WEBB ROY JR	CPT	0-1317061	0552	2
WEBB THOMAS M	2LT	0-1168512	0245	2
WEBB THOMAS W JR	LTC	0-0379233	0867	1
WEBB WALTER J	1LT	0-0109253	0542	1
WEBB WARREN H	CPT	0-4031022	1067	1
WEBB WAYNE S	1LT	0-0514049	0445	2
WEBB WILLARD	B G	0-0341298	1163	3
WEBB WILLIAM C JR	MAJ	0-0334571	0160	1
WEBB WILLIAM M	LTC	0-0415782	0766	1
WEBB WILLIAM M	MAJ	0-1289842	1060	1
WEBB WILLIAM V	MAJ	0-0503635	0954	1
WEBBEN JAMES H	1LT	0-1016173	0745	2
WEBBER BERT W	LTC	0-1339680	1167	1
WEBBER CHARLES C	COL	0-0245223	1059	3
WEBBER FRANK R	MAJ	0-0464230	1148	1
WEBBER GEORGE L	LTC	0-0235375	0646	2
WEBBER HAROLD W	CW4	W-2102522	0659	1
WEBBER JAMES E	MAJ	0-1579277	0557	1
WEBBER JAMES M	CW3	W-2107069	0359	1
WEBBER JOHN B	2LT	0-1308412	1144	2
WEBBER PAUL A	LTC	0-2021225	0468	1
WEBBER PAUL L	CPT	0-0969256	1057	1
WEBBER ROBERT M	CPT	0-0343087	1045	2
WEBBERE GEORGE A	LTC	0-1045965	0962	1
WEBBLEY FREDERICK	COL	0-0202624	0658	3
WEBER ALBERT	MAJ	0-1299501	0457	1
WEBER ALBERT F 3	MAJ	0-1057303	0164	1
WEBER ALVAN J	LTC	0-1183444	1265	1
WEBER ALVIN E	LTC	0-1575253	0563	1
WEBER AMOS S	MAJ	0-1799017	0668	3
WEBER ARTHUR J	LTC	0-1844498	1162	1
WEBER CHARLES H	1LT	0-1015172	0846	2
WEBER CORNELIUS	CPT	0-1319044	0547	2
WEBER DANIEL T	LTC	0-1557850	1168	1
WEBER DAVID E	LTC	0-0262492	0661	3
WEBER EDMUND	MAJ	0-1000297	0756	1
WEBER EDMUND W	LTC	0-0312161	0659	3
WEBER EDWARD T	LTC	0-1011916	0864	1
WEBER ELDRED E	LTC	0-2026431	0868	1
WEBER EMILE O	CW3	W-2146748	0565	1
WEBER ETHEL H	CPT	N-0736721	0356	2
WEBER GENE W	CW2	W-2213422	0968	1
WEBER GEORGE E	CPT	0-2263690	0862	1
WEBER GORDON P	LTC	0-0289996	0967	3
WEBER HAROLD T	B G	0-0171181	1153	3
WEBER HARRY R JR	LTC	0-0309428	0965	3
WEBER HENRY P	LTC	0-1821794	0666	1
WEBER HERMAN J	LTC	0-0135688	0648	3
WEBER JACOB B	CPT	0-0521494	0950	1
WEBER JAMES L	CPT	0-2055475	0647	2
WEBER JOHN	LTC	0-1543549	0364	1
WEBER JOSEPH J	CW2	W-2151826	0356	1
WEBER KALMAN E	CPT	0-1284795	0947	2
WEBER KARL T	MAJ	0-1560395	0761	1
WEBER KENNETH A	LTC	0-1894720	1165	1
WEBER KENNETH J	LTC	0-1588354	1066	1
WEBER LEONARD J	MAJ	0-1119780	1162	1
WEBER LEROY E	COL	0-0266441	0255	2
WEBER LOUIS S	LTC	0-0370821	0166	3
WEBER LYNN C	LTC	0-1558224	0662	1
WEBER REGINALD T	COL	0-0346214	0557	1
WEBER RICHARD H	LTC	0-1105673	0661	1
WEBER RICHARD M	CPT	0-0215630	0342	2
WEBER ROBERT F	COL	0-0484423	0968	1
WEBER STANLEY R	MAJ	0-1642703	0659	1
WEBER WALTER C	LTC	0-0168194	0660	3
WEBER WAYNE V	CW3	W-2153661	1265	1
WEBER WILFRED H	COL	0-0205528	1058	3
WEBER WILLIAM H	CW2	W-2000912	0444	2
WEBERT ALTON J	2LT	0-5704553	0761	2
WEBSTER ALBERT A	MAJ	0-1533467	0953	1
WEBSTER ALFRED D	LTC	0-0374495	0960	1
WEBSTER ARTHUR C	MAJ	0-0215309	0461	3
WEBSTER ASBURY JR	CW2	W-3200341	0666	1
WEBSTER BELTON O	CW3	W-2119407	0762	1
WEBSTER CARLOS G JR	COL	0-0246882	1158	3
WEBSTER DONALD M	LTC	0-0315405	0662	3
WEBSTER DORSEY L JR	CPT	0-0315091	0845	2
WEBSTER EDWARD S	MAJ	0-0203954	0257	3
WEBSTER ELBERT M	LTC	0-0156291	0150	3
WEBSTER ELIOT C	LTC	0-0366908	0668	3
WEBSTER EMORY B	MAJ	0-1924897	0368	1
WEBSTER FORREST U	LTC	0-0174536	0356	3
WEBSTER FREDERICK	MAJ	0-0370294	0946	2
WEBSTER GEORGE M	LTC	0-0512238	0463	3
WEBSTER GLEN M	COL	0-0104557	0459	3
WEBSTER GLENN R	MAJ	0-2008085	0461	1
WEBSTER HAROLD G	1LT	0-1305140	0547	2
WEBSTER HENRY W	CW3	W-2203864	0166	1
WEBSTER HERSHELL F	CW2	W-3350125	1060	1
WEBSTER JACK M	CPT	0-1285153	0246	2
WEBSTER JACKSON O	CPT	0-0519984	0147	2
WEBSTER JOSEPH A JR	1LT	0-1284616	0745	2
WEBSTER LAURENCE A	MAJ	0-1014153	1264	1
WEBSTER LAWRENCE B	LTC	0-0450518	1155	1
WEBSTER LEONARD E	COL	0-0256186	0560	3
WEBSTER MAURICE W	LTC	0-1311833	0862	1
WEBSTER NOEL E	MAJ	0-1101266	0358	1
WEBSTER NORMAN A	MAJ	0-0263319	0845	2
WEBSTER REMINGTON	LTC	0-1101711	1162	1
WEBSTER ROBERT B	CPT	0-1307112	0147	2
WEBSTER ROBERT W	LTC	0-0387216	0860	1
WEBSTER THEODORE J	CPT	0-1294398	0559	2
WEBSTER WILBUR R	LTC	0-1685706	0768	1
WEBSTER WILLIAM B	LTC	0-1111425	0664	1
WEBSTER WILLIAM H	LTC	0-0403992	0546	2
WEBSTER WILLIAM M	LTC	0-0272377	0568	3
WEBSTER WILLIAM R	LTC	0-0418835	0767	1
WEBSTER WILLIAM V	LTC	0-0260528	0456	3
WECHSLER GEORGE J	1LT	0-1321563	1044	2
WECHSLER LOUIS J	CPT	0-0109044	0127	1
WECKER JOHN F	MAJ	0-0962160	0163	1
WEDDLE CHARLES O	CPT	0-0487820	0845	2
WEDDLE LEROY R	CPT	0-0409304	1045	2
WEDDLE PAUL A	LTC	0-0965089	0368	1
WEDDUM FOLMER	1LT	0-2055850	1044	2

NAME	GRADE	SVC NO	DATE RET MO YR	RET CODE
WEDGE CHARLES D	CPT	0-2019537	0761	1
WEDMORE ARTHUR R	1LT	0-0503912	1053	2
WEEBER RICHARD P	LTC	0-0338955	0662	3
WEED CHARLES A	MAJ	0-1285524	1047	2
WEED JOHN H	MAJ	0-1848621	0863	1
WEED MAHLON S	B G	0-0231252	1159	3
WEEDEN JACK W	MAJ	0-1290691	0261	1
WEEDMAN GEORGE C	MAJ	0-2262701	0463	1
WEEDON HUGH H	LTC	0-0918574	0255	2
WEEKES LEROY R	MAJ	0-0331270	0447	2
WEEKES WILLIAM E	CPT	0-0480553	0755	1
WEEKLEY CHARLES F	WO1	W-2125238	0246	2
WEEKLEY ROBERT O	2LT	0-0136459	0646	2
WEEKLY HERBERT S III	CPT	0-1307336	0547	2
WEEKS ARTHUR E	LTC	0-0966105	0766	1
WEEKS BENJAMIN J	1LT	0-1586997	0262	1
WEEKS BILLY J	CW3	W-2206514	0666	1
WEEKS CARL A	LTC	0-1054960	0964	1
WEEKS CARL G	CPT	0-0384979	0348	2
WEEKS CLYDE F	MAJ	0-0212904	1043	2
WEEKS ELBERT W JR	LTC	0-0110712	1043	2
WEEKS FRANK O JR	MAJ	0-1650387	0463	1
WEEKS GEORGE W	COL	0-0345668	1264	3
WEEKS HENRY M III	LTC	0-0255893	1067	3
WEEKS HOWARD L	LTC	0-0371516	0361	1
WEEKS HUBERT	LTC	0-0215475	0564	3
WEEKS JAMES F	CPT	0-0961057	0564	2
WEEKS JOHN S	COL	0-0268074	0864	3
WEEKS JOSEPH W	CPT	0-2263133	0367	1
WEEKS LEE R	CPT	0-1331580	0154	2
WEEKS MALVIN H JR	CPT	0-0923749	0147	2
WEEKS MARVIN F	CPT	0-1574362	0749	1
WEEKS MARVIN L	CPT	0-1014595	0946	2
WEEKS PAUL A	1LT	0-1299329	0146	2
WEEKS RICHARD B	COL	0-0247099	0962	3
WEEKS ROBERT R	MAJ	0-1548591	1060	1
WEEKS ROLAND L	LTC	0-1058685	0263	1
WEEKS STEPHEN J	1LT	0-5339696	1168	2
WEEKS THEODORE W JR	CPT	0-0435181	0246	2
WEEKS WALLACE W	CPT	0-0339408	0944	2
WEEKS WILL D	2LT	0-1056941	0545	2
WEEKS WILLIAM W	LTC	0-1557392	0463	1
WEELDREYER CARL J	LTC	0-0452153	0358	1
WEEMS DAVID A	1LT	0-0476883	1044	2
WEEMS MALLORY P	CPT	0-1685103	1046	2
WEEMS TROY E	LTC	0-0240552	0747	1
WEEMS WARREN B	CW2	W-2143134	0863	1
WEES DALE R	LTC	0-0777880	0966	1
WEESE CHARLES H	CPT	0-0405946	0749	1
WEESE JACK	MAJ	0-0256706	0353	3
WEESE LAWRENCE L	CPT	0-1939079	1264	1
WEESE MABEL O	1LT	N-0730489	0645	1
WEEST HARRY W	COL	0-0171630	1154	3
WEETMAN HAROLD R	COL	0-0300344	0761	1
WEFEL ROBERT L	CW3	W-2148943	0665	1
WEFLER JOHN O	MAJ	0-1920252	0165	1
WEGE HANS F	LTC	0-0275181	1060	1
WEGEMANN LUDWIG	MAJ	0-4010539	0668	1
WEGERSKI MYRON A	CPT	0-1306500	1058	2
WEGHORST RICHARD H	CPT	0-0914985	0647	2
WEGLOSKI ADAM F	LTC	0-1642706	0163	1
WEGMOLLER JACOB P	LTC	0-0275795	1065	3
WEGNER ELMER L C	LTC	0-0243811	0645	2
WEGNER ELMER R	LTC	0-1040636	1161	1
WEGNER FRANKLIN J	LTC	0-1646693	0466	1
WEGNER WILLIAM A	MAJ	0-0274704	0354	3
WEHLING MARTIN P	COL	0-0242785	0-53	1
WEHRER FRANK E	CPT	0-1300558	1046	1
WEHRHEIN JAMES A	1LT	0-0422202	0446	2
WEHRLI FLORENCE C	LTC	N-0756252	0767	3
WEIBELT AUBREY J JR	CW3	W-2206515	1165	1
WEIBY EDWIN O	1LT	0-1113044	0454	2
WEICHEL FREDERICK	LTC	0-1288334	1060	1
WEICHSELDORFER W H	CPT	0-2008532	0257	1
WEICKERT HAROLD N	LTC	0-0169153	1060	3

NAME	GRADE	SVC NO	DATE RET MO YR	RET CODE
WEIDEMAN FRANK A	CPT	0-1579280	0845	2
WEIDENHAMER JOHN P	CPT	0-0506834	0544	2
WEIDERHOLD FRED E	LTC	0-2036718	0867	1
WEIDHORN EDITH W	2LT	N-0751275	1044	1
WEIDIG RICHARD G	COL	0-0260508	0368	3
WEIDMAN HARVEY D	MAJ	0-0890422	0846	2
WEIDMAN JAY G	CPT	0-0550041	0946	2
WEIDNER JOHN J	CPT	0-2097003	0667	1
WEIDNER JOHN M	LTC	0-0309356	0861	3
WEIDNER WARREN W	LTC	0-0277385	0857	3
WEIDNER WILLIAM J	1LT	0-0491462	0344	1
WEIDT GEORGE W	LTC	0-1015590	1064	1
WEIGEL HENRY S	MAJ	0-0194492	0662	3
WEIGEL WILMER F	CPT	0-1647324	0846	2
WEIGELE HAROLD A	LTC	0-0423567	0866	3
WEIGHTMAN LLOYD E	LTC	0-0289917	1060	3
WEIGHTMAN RICHARD H	LTC	0-0363409	0866	1
WEIGHTMAN WILLIAM R	COL	0-0188217	0858	3
WEIGLE GERALD V	COL	0-0364468	1047	2
WEIGLEY WAYNE M	CW4	W-2119276	0655	1
WEIH HANS	CPT	0-1891188	0463	1
WEIHE MARVIN A	MAJ	0-0317762	0445	2
WEIHING GEORGE J	1LT	0-0515800	0645	2
WEIHRAUCH OTHMAR H	LTC	0-1291202	1064	1
WEIKEL IVAN W	MAJ	0-0304190	1146	2
WEIKEL THOMAS E	CPT	0-2262411	0161	1
WEIKEL WALTER D	COL	0-0253296	0663	3
WEIKER CARL	CW4	W-2006659	0862	3
WEIL ALBERT H	LTC	0-0244859	0866	3
WEIL ANDRE F	2LT	0-1031985	0245	2
WEIL CHARLES F	LTC	0-0230998	0665	3
WEIL CHARLES F	CW3	W-21 7925	0363	1
WEIL JAMES M	MAJ	0-0486214	0353	2
WEIL LEONARD L	CPT	0-0480187	0845	2
WEIL LESTER H	CPT	0-0507076	0257	3
WEIL LUDWIG J	CW4	W-2127588	0461	1
WEIL MONROE J	1LT	0-1580484	0645	2
WEIL SOL B JR	CPT	0-0463209	1143	2
WEILAND HERMAN G	CPT	0-1634451	0345	2
WEILAND THOMAS	MAJ	0-1922706	1166	1
WEILAND THOMAS J	MAJ	0-0450942	0363	1
WEILENMAN RUSSELL A	COL	0-0292805	1167	3
WEILENMANN CHARLES	CPT	0-0510068	0846	1
WEILER GEORGE W	1LT	0-1319045	0844	2
WEILER NORBERT E	CPT	0-1288148	0545	2
WEILER RICHARD P	CPT	0-1015104	0446	2
WEILER ROBERT J	LTC	0-1548160	0561	1
WEILER WILLIAM F	B G	0-0237255	0256	3
WEIMAN JOHN R	CW3	W-2209399	1266	1
WEIMANN GUSTAVE H	COL	0-0387741	1160	1
WEIMAR EARL E	LTC	0-0191894	1045	2
WEIMAR WILLIAM C	MAJ	0-1644205	0243	1
WEIMER ROBERT G	CW2	W-2210581	0366	1
WEIN ARTHUR B	CPT	0-0416532	0246	2
WEIN JOHN A	CW3	RW-2145119	0763	1
WEINARD EARL R	MAJ	0-1181499	0265	1
WEINBERG JEROME	MAJ	0-2035183	0455	1
WEINBERG JOSEPH A	MAJ	0-0206467	1145	2
WEINBERG MORRIS L	1LT	0-1308738	0246	2
WEINBERG SYDNEY G	LTC	0-0354790	0865	3
WEINBERG WILLIAM J	CPT	0-0350842	0545	2
WEINBERGER HOWARD J	MAJ	0-0416505	0146	2
WEINBERGER MARTIN I	1LT	0-0538970	0546	2
WEINBERGER SIDNEY	2LT	0-1998345	1045	2
WEINBRENNER BILLIE M	MAJ	L-0800255	0864	1
WEINER BERTRAM T	LTC	0-1698119	0966	1
WEINER ELI	1LT	0-1105261	0945	2
WEINER HARRY H	MAJ	0-0247325	0544	2
WEINER JACOB	1LT	0-0497566	0644	2
WEINER JOSHUA H	CPT	0-0419458	0346	2
WEINER LEON	1LT	0-0529190	0745	2
WEINER SAM F	CPT	0-0418464	1145	2
WEINER SAMUEL O	1LT	0-1325611	0246	2
WEINER STANLEY	LTC	0-0416200	1046	2
WEINER WOLFORD H	1LT	0-1575627	0745	2

NAME	GRADE	SVC NO	DATE RET MO YR	RET CODE
WEINFELD JOSEPH S	LTC	0-0391647	0167	3
WEINFIELD ALLAN	LTC	0-1012022	1061	1
WEINGAR WILLIAM H	LTC	0-0234327	0648	3
WEINGART ROBERT A	CPT	0-1825517	0664	2
WEINGARTEN F W	MAJ	0-0345764	1144	2
WEINGARTNER VICTOR J	CPT	0-1307901	0249	2
WEINGAST HARRY	1LT	0-1321006	0245	2
WEINHEIMER HOWARD E	LTC	0-1166646	0667	1
WEINMEISTER OSCAR K	CW4	W-2142540	0265	1
WEINRICH ARTHUR J	MAJ	0-2016981	1061	1
WEINRICH ROBERT J	1LT	0-0309206	0144	2
WEINSCHEL GEORGE	CPT	0-1557234	1045	2
WEINSHELBAUM SAMUEL	MAJ	0-0966692	1161	1
WEINSTEIN BARNETT	COL	0-0265620	1166	3
WEINSTEIN EDWARD A	1LT	0-1052207	1157	1
WEINSTEIN HYMAN W	CPT	0-0503424	1045	2
WEINSTEIN ISRAEL	LTC	0-0214277	0546	2
WEINSTEIN LEO	1LT	0-1307902	0645	2
WEINSTEIN LEO S	CPT	0-1691146	0845	2
WEINSTEIN LEWIS H	COL	0-0507912	0565	3
WEINSTEIN LOUIS J	COL	0-0324753	0767	3
WEINSTEIN MAX V	1LT	0-0545360	0545	2
WEINSTEIN MAXWELL	CPT	0-0508044	1049	1
WEINSTEIN MORRIS J	1LT	0-1574281	0545	2
WEINSTEIN ROBERT	2LT	0-1118675	0245	2
WEINSTEIN SAMUEL H	CPT	0-1301731	0546	2
WEINSTEIN STANLEY	CPT	0-1697039	0545	2
WEINSTOCK CHESTER E	LTC	0-1557108	1264	1
WEINTRAUB ARTHUR	MAJ	0-0494195	0947	2
WEINTRAUB HENRY J	MAJ	0-0368312	0750	2
WEINTRAUB I IRVING	MAJ	0-0421436	0950	2
WEINTRAUB SOLOMON	COL	0-0249911	0459	3
WEINTRUB JOSEPH	LTC	0-0907032	0163	3
WEIR BROCK M	1LT	0-1300735	0145	2
WEIR DICK B	MAJ	0-0307290	1048	1
WEIR EDWARD R	LTC	0-1556849	0665	3
WEIR JAMES A	LTC	0-1586340	0862	1
WEIR NORMAN L	MAJ	0-0371589	0760	1
WEIR ROBERT L	MAJ	0-0351444	0646	2
WEIR RUSSELL R	MAJ	0-0242124	0964	3
WEIR THOMAS L	CW4	W-2127000	0665	3
WEIR THOMAS J	LTC	0-0476994	0756	1
WEIR TRUETT	LTC	0-1551986	1165	1
WEIR WILLIAM L	MAJ	0-0283530	0668	3
WEIR WILLIAM H	COL	0-0197948	0561	3
WEIRICH ALFRED F	COL	0-0261534	0358	1
WEIRICH COLIN R JR	WO1	W-2149001	1059	1
WEIS JOSEPH F	CPT	0-1184440	0248	2
WEISBERG HERBERT	LTC	0-0454551	0465	2
WEISBERG SAM	CW4	W-2145347	0368	1
WEISBLUM JOSEPH	LTC	0-0338149	0767	3
WEISENBERG JOSEPH	MAJ	0-0231144	0148	1
WEISENBERGER ROYCE S	LTC	0-0360251	0168	3
WEISENFELD ANDREW H	LTC	0-2102626	0768	1
WEISENHORN PAUL G	COL	0-0122063	0452	3
WEISER CONRAD W	CPT	0-0466558	0245	1
WEISER JOSEPH	LTC	0-0331492	1162	2
WEISER LEMOINE D	MAJ	0-0334671	0945	2
WEISERT WILSON G	1LT	0-0447308	0745	2
WEISFELD JOSEPH J	1LT	0-0541378	0745	2
WEISGERBER ADOLPH F	1LT	0-0233737	1148	3
WEISHAUPT ROSEMARY F	1LT	N-0743020	0546	1
WEISHEIT ARTHUR J	LTC	0-1109740	0854	1
WEISHEIT LENAS G	MAJ	0-2023757	0661	1
WEISKIRCHER ERNEST H	MAJ	0-0218153	0461	3
WEISLER HERMAN L	COL	0-0482613	0367	3
WEISLER JOHN C	LTC	0-0502723	0256	1
WEISLO EDMOND	2LT	0-1298467	1043	2
WEISMAN EDWIN	MAJ	0-1102995	0248	2
WEISMAN HERMAN F	LTC	0-0308398	1267	3
WEISMAN IRVING	2LT	0-1595254	0544	2
WEISMAN JACOB I	CPT	0-0382637	0143	2
WEISMAN PAUL G	LTC	0-0235318	0750	3
WEISMAN SAMUEL A	MAJ	0-0169539	0544	2
WEISS ALBERT C	1LT	0-1316265	0851	2

NAME	GRADE	SVC NO	DATE RET MO YR	RET CODE
WEISS ALEXANDER	LTC	0-0371726	1068	3
WEISS ANGELA D	CPT	N-0756113	0746	1
WEISS ARTHUR M	LTC	0-0234465	0759	3
WEISS BARRY E	2LT	0-4038648	0157	2
WEISS BERNARD	LTC	0-0399746	1061	2
WEISS DAVID	MAJ	0-0319528	0546	2
WEISS GEORGE A	LTC	0-0481080	0365	3
WEISS GEORGE H	LTC	0-0454620	0364	1
WEISS HAROLD W	COL	0-0288394	0161	1
WEISS HARRY	MAJ	0-1690493	0246	2
WEISS HERMAN S	MAJ	0-1312368	0261	1
WEISS HORTON C	MAJ	0-1053010	0859	1
WEISS JAMES E	MAJ	0-0355663	0346	2
WEISS JOHN F	1LT	0-1597957	0352	2
WEISS JULIUS E	2LT	0-1310905	1045	2
WEISS LOUIS R	COL	0-0309633	0566	3
WEISS MALCOLM P	CPT	0-0467298	0447	2
WEISS MARY I P	2LT	N-0736784	0845	1
WEISS PEARL	LTC	L-0200126	1162	1
WEISS PHILIP H	2LT	0-1165820	0144	2
WEISS RICHARD J	LTC	0-0291748	0861	1
WEISS SAMUEL	LTC	0-0463023	0450	1
WEISS SHELDON	1LT	0-0542204	0946	2
WEISS THOMAS G	LTC	0-0920384	1265	3
WEISS THOMAS W	LTC	0-1280036	1057	1
WEISS VICTOR R	LTC	0-0317137	0851	1
WEISS WILLIAM D	MAJ	0-0495046	1146	2
WEISSELBERGER DAVID	1LT	0-0543770	0945	2
WEISSENBURGER LAWREN	LTC	0-1822222	0866	1
WEISSER LILLIAN	2LT	N-0723868	0346	1
WEISSHAUS STANLEY Z	LTC	0-0333750	0562	3
WEISSKOPF RAYMOND	LTC	0-1541513	0361	1
WEISSMAN JOSEPH I	LTC	0-0167200	0656	2
WEISSMAN PAUL	1LT	0-1945075	0345	2
WEISSMAN PHILIP	1LT	0-1648229	0346	2
WEISSMANN HARRY M	CW4	W-2106717	0660	1
WEIST CLAYTON A	COL	0-0330578	0968	3
WEISZ WALTER S	CPT	0-0446228	0344	2
WEITHLE PAUL L	COL	0-0238527	0760	3
WEITZ MARTIN E	MAJ	0-0238991	0447	2
WEITZEL BERNARD J	CPT	0-1690891	1055	1
WEITZEL GLADYS T	1LT	N-0736497	1046	1
WEITZEL THEODORE B	MAJ	0-0492213	1154	1
WEITZEL WILLIAM A	LTC	0-0215457	1060	3
WEITZMAN LEONARD	1LT	0-0541746	0547	2
WEITZMANN ALBERT M	CPT	0-1575288	0745	2
WEIX JEROME J	MAJ	0-0991361	0163	1
WEIZER ERNEST A	COL	0-0336906	0968	3
WEKALL OLIVER C	COL	0-0350326	0867	3
WEKER MEYER	LTC	0-1798631	0866	3
WELBORN DOROTHY	2LT	N-0755239	0744	1
WELBORN JAMES H	1LT	0-1324378	1045	2
WELBORN ROBERT T	MAJ	0-0156633	0254	3
WELBOURN ROY E	CPT	0-1821795	0960	2
WELCH BRENT A	MAJ	0-0300645	0545	2
WELCH CARROLL	LTC	0-1546709	0857	1
WELCH CHARLES E	MAJ	0-0913710	0164	3
WELCH CHARLES E	MAJ	0-1053868	0265	1
WELCH CLARENCE W	LTC	0-0445749	0763	1
WELCH CLAUDE L	MAJ	0-0306217	0945	2
WELCH DAVID J	LTC	0-0222288	1156	3
WELCH EDWARD W	CPT	0-1284254	1051	2
WELCH EMMETT J	LTC	0-0404522	0162	1
WELCH ERNEST R	COL	0-0223425	1164	3
WELCH FELIX P	MAJ	0-0259583	0966	3
WELCH FRANCIS W JR	MAJ	0-1081540	0759	1
WELCH FREDERICK	MAJ	0-0964063	0464	1
WELCH FREDERICK	1LT	0-1331582	0152	2
WELCH GARY R	CPT	0-4062023	0467	2
WELCH HAROLD A	CW3	W-2149850	0161	1
WELCH HAROLD E	LTC	0-0453937	0562	1
WELCH HARRY E JR	2LT	0-1996372	0745	2
WELCH HERBERT E	COL	0-0280425	0368	3
WELCH ISABELLE E	MAJ	L-0603794	1065	1
WELCH JAMES L	CPT	0-1319690	0647	2

NAME	GRADE	SVC NO	DATE RET MO YR	RET CODE
WELCH JAMES M	CW3	W-3150311	0768	1
WELCH JAMES R	LTC	0-0364338	0468	3
WELCH JAMES W	CW2	W-2213792	0966	1
WELCH JOHN	LTC	0-1011887	0465	1
WELCH JOHN A	LTC	0-0264032	1166	3
WELCH JOHN G	MAJ	0-0954066	0264	1
WELCH JOHN J	MAJ	0-0390211	0456	1
WELCH JOHN M	COL	0-0220140	0664	3
WELCH JOHN W	MAJ	0-0269329	0367	3
WELCH LEO J	LTC	0-0807371	1067	1
WELCH LEROY L	MAJ	0-1305356	0556	2
WELCH LESTER C	LTC	0-0491158	0457	1
WELCH MARY A	2LT	N-0773545	0645	1
WELCH MARY L	MAJ	N-0756005	0566	1
WELCH NED W	MAJ	0-1110335	0861	1
WELCH NORBERT E	LTC	0-1590255	1167	3
WELCH PARRIS L	MAJ	0-1171296	0361	1
WELCH RAYMOND	LTC	0-1301393	0158	1
WELCH REX M	CPT	0-1686610	0560	1
WELCH RICHARD D	LTC	0-0273052	0155	2
WELCH RICHARD F	COL	0-0225556	1056	3
WELCH ROBERT E L	LTC	0-0269200	0568	3
WELCH ROBERT Z	MAJ	0-1180089	1159	1
WELCH ROGER M	LTC	0-1585068	0162	1
WELCH THOMAS C	MAJ	0-0321915	1064	1
WELCH WALLACE C	MAJ	0-0450140	1160	1
WELCH WILFORD W JR	MAJ	0-1656774	0964	1
WELCH WILLIAM E	COL	0-0246762	0760	1
WELCH WILLIAM H JR	MAJ	0-0411642	1147	2
WELCH WILLIAM I	COL	0-0321778	0755	1
WELCHER ALEXANDER	LTC	0-0355496	1063	1
WELCHER CLARENCE G	MAJ	0-1634455	0457	1
WELCHER ROBERT E	MAJ	0-0966684	0967	1
WELCHMAN PHILIP J	LTC	0-1588955	0962	1
WELCOME EARL H	COL	0-0176655	0648	3
WELD GEORGE S	MAJ	0-0125880	0159	3
WELD STEPHEN M	MAJ	0-0178368	0162	3
WELDEN JAMES W	MAJ	0-1181186	1061	1
WELDON CHARLES N	CPT	0-0492162	0260	3
WELDON GEROLD W	CW2	W-2144712	1159	1
WELDON JOSEPH D	CW2	W-3430091	1066	1
WELDON MARCUS D	LTC	0-0228649	1060	3
WELDY MAX W	1LT	0-0359495	1042	2
WELGE LOUIS A	1LT	0-0914329	0946	2
WELGEHAUSEN KURT A	LTC	0-0260882	1266	3
WELK EDWARD	1LT	0-0509497	0646	1
WELKENER CLARENCE H	LTC	0-0990609	1168	2
WELKER HAROLD L	1LT	0-1305507	0246	2
WELKER JOHN H	WO1	W-2105321	0645	2
WELKER RUSSELL J	2LT	0-2030204	1046	2
WELKER WINIFRED S	2LT	N-0703317	1144	1
WELL JULIUS W	MAJ	0-0518752	0346	2
WELLEN CLYDE W	LTC	0-0153627	1052	3
WELLENS ALBERT G	1LT	0-0395641	0446	2
WELLER FREDERICK	LTC	0-0789998	1068	1
WELLER GEORGE M	CPT	0-0211192	0855	3
WELLER MALCOLM R	MAJ	0-0330579	1266	3
WELLER MILFORD F	1LT	0-1320677	0845	2
WELLER NELLE B	2LT	N-0728541	0244	1
WELLER VICTOR C	1LT	0-1057305	0446	2
WELLES CHARLES B	COL	0-0197204	0961	3
WELLES EDWARD M	1LT	0-1534657	1144	2
WELLES GUY B	LTC	0-0250490	1052	3
WELLHAUSEN FRED C	LTC	0-1110336	0462	1
WELLHOUSE WILLIAM T	2LT	0-0461274	1043	2
WELLING ARTHUR L	MAJ	0-0195154	1047	1
WELLING ARTHUR W	CPT	0-0355155	1144	2
WELLING GRANT M	LTC	0-1648868	0367	1
WELLING HOWARD C	COL	0-0286765	1159	1
WELLINGTON L C	CPT	0-0517304	1144	2
WELLIVER DELBERT C	CPT	0-1795829	1060	1
WELLMAN CLARA J	2LT	N-0703219	1042	1
WELLMAN JOHN M	COL	0-0240354	0466	3
WELLMAN ROY W	MAJ	0-0286457	0454	2
WELLMAN WALTER J	COL	0-0321450	0960	1

NAME	GRADE	SVC NO	DATE RET MO YR	RET CODE
WELLONS JOHN F	LTC	0-1018826	1267	1
WELLS ADDISON E II	COL	0-0268175	1161	3
WELLS ALBERT W JR	CPT	0-1285154	0861	1
WELLS ARLAND R	MAJ	0-0294256	1145	2
WELLS AUSTIN L	COL	0-0505505	0866	3
WELLS BILLY G	MAJ	0-1882262	0867	1
WELLS CARL D	COL	0-0371591	0765	1
WELLS CATHERINE	CPT	N-0751715	0547	1
WELLS CECIL A	1LT	0-2042849	0357	1
WELLS CECIL E	CW2	W-2120774	0244	2
WELLS CHARLES	MAJ	0-0479113	0748	1
WELLS CHARLES A	MAJ	0-1306781	1063	1
WELLS CHARLES G	CPT	0-0233803	0860	3
WELLS CLARENCE R	MAJ	0-0454181	1145	2
WELLS CLYDE E	CW2	W-2207382	0661	1
WELLS COYE L	1LT	0-1315991	1145	2
WELLS DAMON	CW2	W-2148136	0361	1
WELLS DANIEL W	2LT	0-1550087	0945	2
WELLS DON L	COL	0-0113702	0650	3
WELLS EBEN N	COL	0-0261502	0166	3
WELLS EDMOND J	CPT	0-0986721	0761	1
WELLS EDMUND L	COL	0-1045625	1068	1
WELLS EDWARD S	LTC	0-1030435	1164	1
WELLS ELBERT E	LTC	0-0360730	0655	1
WELLS ERNEST L	CW3	W-3150768	0668	1
WELLS EUGENE O	COL	0-0116586	0348	2
WELLS FLOYD J	LTC	0-0486875	0657	1
WELLS GAREY M	LTC	0-0494525	0159	1
WELLS GEORGE	MAJ	0-0279450	0359	3
WELLS GEORGE A	1LT	0-5420295	0268	2
WELLS GEORGE H	COL	0-0310267	0367	3
WELLS GEORGE I III	CW2	W-2210956	0567	1
WELLS GEORGE T	CPT	0-0489925	0855	1
WELLS GERALDINE	MAJ	N-0763791	1168	1
WELLS HARVEY E	MAJ	0-1013975	0761	1
WELLS HARVIE L	1LT	0-0490202	1054	1
WELLS HERBERT B	LTC	0-0270704	0866	3
WELLS JACKSON H	2LT	0-1686335	0745	2
WELLS JAMES A	COL	0-0264061	0766	3
WELLS JAMES C	CPT	0-0220753	0751	3
WELLS JAMES C	CPT	0-1795018	0953	2
WELLS JAMES E	MAJ	0-0956787	0867	1
WELLS JAMES E	MAJ	0-1107226	1147	2
WELLS JAMES H	CPT	0-0212794	0646	2
WELLS JAMES P	LTC	0-1284439	1061	1
WELLS JAMES R	COL	0-0190401	1050	3
WELLS JAMES R	CPT	0-0890028	0846	2
WELLS JAMES T	CPT	0-1301732	0747	2
WELLS JEANNE A	1LT	N-0730791	0845	1
WELLS JOHN A	LTC	0-0296073	1267	3
WELLS JOHN W JR	LTC	0-1010863	0661	1
WELLS JOSEPH L	COL	0-0224442	0360	3
WELLS LEONARD A	MAJ	0-1797398	0657	1
WELLS LESLIE S	COL	0-0272769	1266	3
WELLS LLOYD P III	1LT	0-5424803	0968	2
WELLS LOUIS R	MAJ	0-1824828	0260	1
WELLS LOUISE E	LTC	N-0724264	0963	1
WELLS PAUL D	MAJ	0-1824543	0265	1
WELLS PAUL I	LTC	0-0415386	1060	1
WELLS PAUL K	LTC	0-0558290	0867	1
WELLS RALPH H	LTC	0-0250504	0546	2
WELLS RAY A	MAJ	0-2024268	0959	1
WELLS RICHARD C	COL	0-0355119	1063	3
WELLS RICHARD L	1LT	0-1284617	0144	2
WELLS ROBERT A	CPT	0-0402762	0145	2
WELLS ROBERT S	CW2	W-2152990	1064	1
WELLS ROYCE V	CPT	0-1012154	0663	1
WELLS RUDOLPH G	CPT	0-1922556	0365	1
WELLS RUSSELL L	LTC	0-1055499	0564	1
WELLS SHELDON B	LTC	0-1013185	1166	1
WELLS SIDNEY J	MAJ	0-0900452	0845	2
WELLS SOPHIA G	1LT	N-0799575	0949	2
WELLS THEODORE H	MAJ	0-1704141	0962	1
WELLS THOMAS F	LTC	0-1315650	0667	1
WELLS THOMAS H	CW2	W-2141489	0955	1

NAME	GRADE	SVC NO	DATE RET MO YR	RET CODE
WELLS THORNLEY F	LTC	0-0243829	0861	3
WELLS WELDON B	LTC	0-0349739	0854	1
WELLS WILLIAM C	LTC	0-0961422	0568	1
WELLS WILLIAM H	CW2	W-2144727	0457	1
WELMS LOUIS C	CW3	W-2151817	0665	1
WELSBY ALBERT	1LT	0-1295804	0946	2
WELSCH CATHERINE	1LT	N-0767247	0845	1
WELSCH CHARLES C	LTC	0-0215389	0562	3
WELSCH GLENN A	MAJ	0-0450743	0446	2
WELSCH HAROLD T	COL	0-0302603	0964	3
WELSCH HENRY	CW3	W-2114809	1053	1
WELSCH JULIAN	LTC	0-0324764	0463	3
WELSH ALBERT C	COL	0-0256622	1058	3
WELSH CHARLES H	MAJ	0-1312612	0761	1
WELSH DON M	MAJ	0-0102502	0844	2
WELSH FRANCIS E	CW3	W-2208788	0467	1
WELSH GEORGE B	LTC	0-0333512	0863	3
WELSH JOHN H	MAJ	0-0100852	1053	3
WELSH JOHN L	LTC	0-1339784	0168	1
WELSH LOIS C	MAJ	L-0900048	0962	1
WELSH MAYME R	MAJ	N-0756904	0465	1
WELSH RAYMOND E	CW3	W-2210084	0168	1
WELSH ROBERT F	1LT	0-1313704	0247	2
WELSH SPURGEON F	COL	0-0269623	1166	3
WELSH STEPHEN S	MAJ	0-0451199	1057	1
WELSH WALTER	LTC	0-0495216	1054	1
WELSH WILLIAM W	LTC	0-0214175	1162	3
WELSHANS ALBERT H	CW3	W-2149002	0566	1
WELSON MORRIS L	1LT	0-0166367	0255	3
WELTE EUGENE J	COL	0-0206300	0661	3
WELTER VALERIAN	CW3	W-2006753	0967	3
WELTMER WILLIAM E	CPT	0-0109839	0735	1
WELTON CURTIS C	CW4	W-2124507	0968	1
WELTON THEODORE M	1LT	0-0391171	0246	2
WELTSCH LEO D	MAJ	0-0970536	1166	1
WELTY CHARLES L JR	LTC	0-0257308	1267	3
WELTY ELMER E	COL	0-0246986	1066	3
WELTY JOHN A	CPT	0-0540844	0347	2
WELTY KENNETH D	CPT	0-0506753	0145	2
WELTZIN CLARENCE W	MAJ	0-0133156	0-51	3
WELZBACHER DAMPTHA N	1LT	N-0772422	1045	1
WEMPA ROBERT F	1LT	0-4045022	065	2
WEMPLE JOHN P	COL	0-0177564	1061	3
WENBORNE ARTHUR S	LTC	0-0386037	0566	1
WENDEL ALFRED W	MAJ	0-1301394	0461	1
WENDEL DAVID O	COL	0-0167763	0859	3
WENDELIN CARL G	LTC	0-0267329	1065	3
WENDELKEN HERBERT	COL	0-0324420	0767	3
WENDELL ARNOLD H	CPT	0-1574178	0946	2
WENDELL LEWIS C JR	MAJ	0-2020092	0162	1
WENDLAND RICHARD H	LTC	0-1291363	0766	1
WENDLE CORNELIUS	MAJ	0-0331601	1145	2
WENDLING EDGAR C	CW3	W-2143538	0860	1
WENDLING ROBERT L	CPT	0-1284066	1045	2
WENDLINGER HAROLD M	LTC	0-2208505	0667	1
WENDORF DENVER F JR	1LT	0-1327064	0447	2
WENDT CHARLES F	1LT	0-1579291	0346	2
WENDT REINHOLD C	CPT	0-0309409	0668	3
WENGER EDWARD J	LTC	0-0920483	0466	3
WENGER RENE L	LTC	0-0285555	0960	3
WENGERT ROBERT R	MAJ	0-1544612	0863	1
WENIG BERNARD	2LT	0-1894486	1144	2
WENIG HERBERT E	COL	0-0272876	0268	3
WENK FREDERICK	CPT	0-0141368	0358	3
WENK FREDERICK	LTC	0-2008019	1167	1
WENNER ARTHUR M	1LT	0-1291204	0145	2
WENNER CHARLES	MAJ	0-1549172	0157	1
WENNERGREN VIRGIL J	LTC	0-1017396	0664	1
WENNERHOLM NORMAN J	1LT	0-1596542	0250	1
WENNINGER GEORGE L	LTC	0-0918510	0866	3
WENRICH JAMES R	LTC	0-0902044	0663	3
WENRICH JOHN W	LTC	0-1950667	0564	1
WENRICH RALPH C	LTC	0-0283639	0668	3
WENT JAMES T	1LT	0-1013061	0450	2
WENTHOLD RALPH J	MAJ	0-1691932	0860	1

NAME	GRADE	SVC NO	DATE RET MO YR	RET CODE
WENTWORTH EDWARD T	COL	0-0190620	0648	3
WENTWORTH HARRY P	MAJ	0-0385169	0561	1
WENTWORTH N N JR	CPT	0-0361487	0745	2
WENTWORTH RICHARD D	MAJ	0-1886591	0766	1
WENTWORTH-ROHR R J	MAJ	0-0472305	0146	2
WENTZ ARTHUR F	1LT	0-1794890	0145	2
WENTZ CHARLES J	LTC	0-1018922	1262	1
WENTZ ISABEL M	1LT	N-0725629	0945	1
WENTZ JOHN H	CW3	W-2209873	1267	1
WENTZ LUTHER A	WO1	W-2134018	0645	2
WENTZ RALPH C	1LT	0-1031600	0947	2
WENTZ RAYMOND D	MAJ	0-0887544	1063	1
WENTZ WILLIAM G	LTC	0-0444404	0556	1
WENZEL CARL L	CPT	0-4005865	1066	2
WENZEL ROBERT J	1LT	0-1014456	0556	1
WENZEL RUSSELL A	LTC	0-0368786	0254	2
WENZEL WALTER J	LTC	0-0278743	0457	3
WENZLER RAYMOND E	MAJ	0-2262407	1163	1
WERBA DANIEL P	LTC	0-0233870	0159	3
WERBLOW SOL C	CPT	0-1683858	1145	2
WERDER ROBERT E	1LT	0-1324076	0146	2
WERES JAMES	CPT	0-1696119	0146	2
WERLINGER LOUIS J	MAJ	0-0422588	0854	1
WERLY EMIL F	LTC	0-0258156	1064	3
WERMINE CARL F H	CPT	0-0382174	1055	2
WERMUTH FLOYD	CPT	0-0938000	1156	2
WERNDLE FRANK G	MAJ	0-2033276	0464	2
WERNE JOHN L	MAJ	0-1686275	0261	1
WERNENTIN EDWIN G	LTC	0-0202129	0962	3
WERNER ADRIAN F	COL	0-0127786	0255	3
WERNER ARNOLD B	CW3	W-2150034	0762	1
WERNER CLARENCE W	MAJ	0-1311836	1068	3
WERNER DONALD E	CPT	0-1049693	0656	1
WERNER DWAYNE M	2LT	0-1308739	0366	1
WERNER EDWARD A	LTC	0-1638770	0663	1
WERNER EMILE W	CPT	0-1324307	0248	2
WERNER ERNEST J	CW4	W-2002451	0965	3
WERNER FRANCIS J	MAJ	0-1580493	0247	2
WERNER FRED A	LTC	0-0340185	0562	1
WERNER HAROLD C	LTC	0-1336461	0665	1
WERNER HAROLD W	MAJ	0-1885663	0567	1
WERNER HARRY	CW3	W-2104578	0161	1
WERNER HARRY E	COL	0-0407582	0660	1
WERNER JOHN	MAJ	0-0510888	0954	1
WERNER JOHN A	MAJ	0-1049017	0361	1
WERNER LAWRENCE C	CPT	0-1557996	0446	2
WERNER MAX	CPT	0-0496424	1045	2
WERNER RICHARD J	COL	0-0219225	0246	2
WERNER ROBERT M	LTC	0-0990809	0266	1
WERNER WILLIAM M	MAJ	0-0978450	0867	1
WERNER WILLIAM P	LTC	0-1320575	0962	1
WERNSMAN LAWRENCE J	MAJ	0-1297816	0263	1
WERONECKI STANLEY A	1LT	0-1301065	0745	2
WERP JOSEPH	LTC	0-0404351	0960	1
WERRELL ANGUS J	COL	0-0201549	0754	3
WERRLEIN WILLIAM J	1LT	0-1823734	0747	2
WERSCHLER WALTER F	CPT	0-0942970	0658	1
WERSING RICHARD F	LTC	0-0538484	0567	1
WERSKEY PAUL F	MAJ	0-1686551	0160	1
WERTH CLARA J	CPT	N-0730200	0746	1
WERTHEIMER HAROLD L	LTC	0-0965092	0368	3
WERTHEIMER PHILIP	LTC	0-0261535	0567	3
WERTS MERRILL H	1LT	0-0552126	0346	2
WERTZ CLYDE E	LTC	0-1045968	0361	1
WERTZ THOMAS E	CW4	W-2145176	1068	1
WERTZ WILLIAM J	COL	0-0338413	1056	3
WERTZBERGER JAMES C	CPT	0-1311716	0465	1
WESCOTT MARVIN C	CW2	W-2143979	0855	1
WESELEY LOUIS J	CPT	0-1689399	0650	2
WESLEY EARLIN	CPT	0-4005166	0563	1
WESLEY FELIX J	COL	0-0250894	1166	3
WESLEY JOSEPH G	2LT	0-1012450	0650	2
WESLIN NORMAN U	LTC	0-1924634	0968	1
WESNER CHARLES T	MAJ	0-0276309	0267	3
WESNER DEAN C	MAJ	0-1886498	0967	1

NAME	GRADE	SVC NO	DATE RET MO YR	RET CODE
WESNER IRENE R	1LT	N-0724437	0646	1
WESNER JAMES E	CW2	W-2214867	0866	1
WESNOUSKY WILLIAM	MAJ	0-2262770	0262	1
WESOLOWSKI JOSEPH A	LTC	0-0367458	1057	1
WESSA EDWIN L	CPT	0-0203451	0159	3
WESSLING ALFRED L	MAJ	0-0131345	0648	3
WESSLING ANDREW L JR	LTC	0-1032664	0562	1
WESSMAN PHILIP H	MAJ	0-2210216	0964	1
WESSMANN MARGARET Y	1LT	N-0724764	0146	2
WESSON BILLY H	MAJ	0-1998394	1160	1
WESSON HAROLD L	CW2	W-2215368	1266	1
WESSON NATHANIEL	CW2	W-2144084	1159	1
WESSON ROY A	LTC	0-0281887	1265	3
WESSON RUFUS	COL	0-0341835	1146	2
WESSON WILLIAM T	CPT	0-0394485	0447	2
WEST ALDERMAN C JR	WO1	W-2131582	0162	1
WEST ALFRED C	MAJ	0-0921511	1145	2
WEST ALTHEA L	2LT	N-0736202	0245	1
WEST BAIRD F	LTC	0-0239916	0165	3
WEST CARLTON V JR	MAJ	0-0989599	1168	1
WEST CLARENCE	CPT	0-1046686	0863	2
WEST CLYDE G	MAJ	0-1030947	0161	1
WEST DON L	1LT	0-1010866	0645	2
WEST DOROTHY A	LTC	L-0304599	0163	1
WEST EARL W	CW3	W-2146798	1064	1
WEST EDWARD JR	CPT	0-1015537	0546	2
WEST ELMER J	LTC	0-0290082	0959	3
WEST EUGENE N	CPT	0-0440798	0445	2
WEST FLOYD H	MAJ	0-2046523	0254	1
WEST FRANCIS C	LTC	0-0486722	1054	1
WEST FRANK H	MAJ	0-0257572	0155	3
WEST FRANK J	LTC	0-1269179	0954	1
WEST GEORGE A	MAJ	0-0547972	1068	1
WEST GEORGE B	COL	0-0239114	1047	2
WEST GEORGE G	COL	0-0125872	1059	3
WEST GEORGE J JR	CPT	0-1573662	0945	2
WEST GERALD V	CPT	0-2289279	0462	1
WEST GILBERT E	MAJ	0-0252452	0166	3
WEST GORDON H	1LT	0-1011715	0545	2
WEST HARLEY B	M G	0-0268317	0463	3
WEST HAROLD R	CW4	W-2115175	0756	1
WEST HENRY C JR	MAJ	0-0971597	1267	1
WEST HENRY D JR	1LT	0-0460016	0545	2
WEST HENRY E	MAJ	0-2019826	1262	1
WEST HERBERT JR	CW3	W-2143980	1262	1
WEST HUBERT O	LTC	0-1332017	1267	1
WEST HUGH S	LTC	0-0264197	0145	2
WEST JAMES B	CW2	W-2141920	0561	1
WEST JAMES B JR	1LT	0-1303065	0745	2
WEST JAMES E	LTC	0-0909618	1264	3
WEST JAMES F	LTC	0-1166207	0164	1
WEST JESSE W	LTC	0-0430960	0756	1
WEST JOHN L	MAJ	0-1044147	0959	1
WEST JOHN P	LTC	0-0186415	0352	3
WEST JOHN V	CPT	0-1011517	0650	2
WEST JOHN W	CPT	0-0373964	0646	2
WEST JOHN W	MAJ	0-1895516	0156	1
WEST JOSEPH W	B G	0-0235499	0853	3
WEST JUDSON H	COL	0-0586976	1068	3
WEST KEITH L	MAJ	0-0974117	0266	1
WEST KENNETH	CPT	0-2033039	0958	1
WEST KENNETH B	MAJ	0-0956698	0261	1
WEST KENNETH L	LTC	0-0372363	1164	1
WEST KENNETH O	MAJ	0-1032406	0462	1
WEST KENT W	MAJ	0-1107228	0863	1
WEST LAWRENCE E	MAJ	0-1951565	0762	1
WEST LEO E	LTC	0-1310356	0762	1
WEST LEO K	CW4	RW-2122647	0163	1
WEST LISLE C	MAJ	0-2023951	1064	1
WEST LUKE H	LTC	0-1038319	1061	1
WEST MADELINE L	1LT	N-0744516	0646	2
WEST MARGARET N	2LT	N-0760155	0944	1
WEST MARTIN J	MAJ	0-0982476	1268	1
WEST MELVIN E JR	CW2	W-2206948	1062	1
WEST MITCHELL	CW4	W-2142557	1262	1

NAME	GRADE	SVC NO	DATE RET MO YR	RET CODE
WEST NELLIE R	CW3	V-0400063	1162	1
WEST NORMAN E	CW2	W-2151653	0662	1
WEST ORLY F	CPT	0-0500133	0157	1
WEST PAUL O	WO1	W-2104579	1043	2
WEST PERCY L	LTC	0-0342829	0263	3
WEST PERRY JR	LTC	0-1177694	0762	1
WEST RALEIGH B	1LT	0-1017462	0246	2
WEST RAYMOND I	COL	0-0335490	0465	3
WEST ROBERT W	CW4	W-2005589	0968	1
WEST ROLAND D JR	LTC	0-1327909	1166	1
WEST THEODORE M	LTC	0-1283885	0667	1
WEST THOMAS R	LTC	0-0488555	0947	2
WEST WARREN K	CW3	W-2152754	1164	1
WEST WAYNE G	COL	0-0281804	0858	1
WEST WILBUR M	2LT	0-1173828	0545	2
WEST WILLIAM J	CW2	W-2210469	0865	1
WEST WILLIAM R	CW2	W-2145848	0959	1
WEST WILLIAM S	CPT	0-0381589	0246	2
WEST WILLIE B	CW3	W-2143546	0859	1
WEST WILLIE JR	MAJ	0-2021144	0868	2
WEST WILLIE P	2LT	0-1047386	0746	2
WESTALL THAD E	CW3	W-2150258	0664	1
WESTALL WALTER S	LTC	0-0278818	1157	3
WESTBERG ALVIN L	CW2	W-2147057	0363	1
WESTBERRY K F JR	1LT	0-0315253	0346	2
WESTBERRY MCGLOHON	WO1	W-2139975	0745	2
WESTBROCK CHARLES C	CPT	0-0314260	1145	2
WESTBROOK BERTELLA C	2LT	N-0723335	0844	1
WESTBROOK CHARLES W	MAJ	0-1114802	0862	1
WESTBROOK JAMES A	MAJ	0-0271488	0246	2
WESTBROOK JOSEPH W	LTC	0-0295756	0667	3
WESTBROOK MILDRED D	1LT	L-0405057	0650	2
WESTBROOK WILLIAM G	LTC	0-1051440	0762	1
WESTBROOKE WILLIAM E	LTC	0-0510106	0557	1
WESTBURY JOSEPH E	COL	0-0292227	0562	1
WESTBURY JOSEPH K	LTC	0-1876281	1168	1
WESTBY GEORGE R	CPT	0-1281433	0246	2
WESTCOTT EDWIN T	MAJ	0-2262766	0465	1
WESTCOTT GARDNER W	CW3	W-2151933	1162	1
WESTENBERGER RALPH G	CW3	W-2142784	0761	1
WESTENBROEK AREL B	CW4	W-2151085	0556	1
WESTER BILLY I	CW3	W-2152522	0565	1
WESTER JOHN A	COL	0-0336806	0762	1
WESTER JOHN D	MAJ	0-0924929	0146	2
WESTER JOHN W	LTC	0-0147805	0852	3
WESTERDAHL ANDREW W	LTC	0-1015065	1262	2
WESTERFIELD CHARLES	MAJ	0-2014525	0367	1
WESTERFIELD JAMES P	LTC	0-0214002	0155	3
WESTERFIELD ROY A	MAJ	0-0163350	0648	3
WESTERGARD PAUL J	CPT	0-0245185	0656	3
WESTERHOLM HAROLD S	MAJ	0-1685533	0963	1
WESTERMAN EDWARD J	LTC	0-0267607	0751	1
WESTERMAN FRANCIS H	COL	0-0246765	1162	3
WESTERMAN FRANK C	MAJ	0-1917987	1264	1
WESTERMAN GEORGE F	1LT	0-0334302	0245	2
WESTERMAN MYRON P	LTC	0-2206200	0766	1
WESTERVELT MARCUS W	COL	0-0544986	0568	3
WESTFALL LACY R	COL	0-0365908	1065	3
WESTFALL RUDOLPH E	LTC	0-0317566	0564	3
WESTFALL THEODORE R	MAJ	0-0223504	0348	2
WESTFALL WILLIAM M	LTC	0-0205588	1163	3
WESTHALL HAROLD G	LTC	0-1102997	0464	1
WESTHEIMER SAMUEL	LTC	0-1313004	1166	3
WESTHOLM ROBERT L	LTC	0-1555997	0466	1
WESTLAKE EDGAR A	MAJ	0-2262227	0668	1
WESTMAN GEORGE E	LTC	0-0225940	1156	3
WESTMORE HAL G	1LT	0-1307596	1163	1
WESTMORELAND GRADY W	MAJ	0-0145740	0356	3
WESTMORELAND JAMES B	LTC	0-0315677	0660	1
WESTMORELAND JAMES R	CPT	0-0540403	1147	2
WESTMORELAND JOHN D	MAJ	0-2018962	1063	1
WESTMORELAND JOHN F	LTC	0-1294227	0861	1
WESTNEDGE JOSEPH S	2LT	0-0425942	1043	2
WESTON CLARENCE E	2LT	0-1574553	0643	2
WESTON FRED S	LTC	0-1039259	0763	1

NAME	GRADE	SVC NO	DATE RET MO YR	RET CODE
WESTON FREDERICK	COL	0-0298844	1067	3
WESTON GIFFORD L	COL	0-0242563	1160	1
WESTON GILBERT B	1LT	0-1286217	0944	2
WESTON HARRY B	CPT	0-0204446	0251	3
WESTON JAMES F	1LT	0-2012602	1157	1
WESTON JEROME C	CW3	W-2143981	0562	1
WESTON JOHNSTON W	1LT	0-1287096	0747	2
WESTON JULIAN B	COL	0-0197888	0263	3
WESTON LEON G	LTC	0-2036348	0463	1
WESTON LOGAN E	COL	0-1795021	0968	1
WESTON MARION E	1LT	0-0945876	0351	2
WESTON MICHAEL E	LTC	0-0307690	0667	3
WESTON ROBERT T	1LT	0-0286027	0647	1
WESTON STANLEY A	CW3	W-2148272	0660	1
WESTON STANLEY J	CPT	0-0325530	0146	2
WESTON WILLIAM A	MAJ	0-0975494	0764	1
WESTON WILLIAM J	LTC	0-0256198	0962	3
WESTPHAL JOHN P	LTC	0-1053869	0968	1
WESTPHAL RICHARD O	MAJ	0-1103461	1166	1
WESTPHAL WILLIAM A	1LT	0-1017141	0546	2
WESTRICK ALFRED A	COL	0-0266467	0964	3
WESTWOOD RAYMOND S	LTC	0-1293687	1165	1
WETHERBEE LOWELL A	MAJ	0-0959340	0165	1
WETHERED THEODORE J	MAJ	0-1304154	0264	1
WETHERELL WINTON W	LTC	0-0183677	0360	3
WETHERHOLT JOHN P	COL	0-0159828	1056	3
WETHERINGTON C J	CPT	0-1280391	1053	2
WETHERINGTON LONNIE	LTC	0-1798093	0463	1
WETHINGTON RAYMOND L	LTC	0-1176847	1264	1
WETHINGTON THOMAS H	CW3	W-2142669	0659	1
WETTERAU JOHN A	CPT	0-0505633	0946	1
WETTERAUER DONALD G	LTC	0-0240928	1264	3
WETTIG PAUL R	LTC	0-0129699	0648	3
WETTLAUFER JULES L	COL	0-0427825	0853	2
WETZEL EDWARD G	LTC	0-0262426	0167	3
WETZEL GEORGE L	CPT	0-0314064	0747	2
WETZEL HAROLD B	MAJ	0-1553753	0361	1
WETZEL HAROLD E	LTC	0-0337882	1045	2
WETZEL JAMES J	CW3	W-2205725	1166	1
WETZEL JAMES W	LTC	0-0475484	0564	3
WETZLER BENJAMIN	COL	0-1548336	0268	3
WETZLER HAROLD J	LTC	0-0988613	0968	1
WETZSTEIN ARNOLD L	CPT	0-0975471	1058	1
WEXLER CHARLES	LTC	0-0923008	0866	3
WEXLER MONROE L	LTC	0-0384343	1064	3
WEYAND FOSTER H	COL	0-0214177	0259	1
WEYAND JAMES O	LTC	0-0504569	0367	3
WEYAND MELVIN J	2LT	0-1288476	0445	2
WEYENETH NORRIS E	1LT	0-1175359	1046	2
WEYER GEORGE S JR	LTC	0-1105910	1059	1
WEYHE WILLIAM L	CPT	0-0257619	0357	3
WEYMANN COVERT	LTC	0-0204363	0253	3
WEYRICK JOSEPH B	1LT	0-1288477	0664	1
WHAITE GILBERT G	WO1	W-2149512	1059	1
WHALEN CHANDLER M	CW3	W-2142729	0161	1
WHALEN CHARLES J	CPT	0-1292098	0358	1
WHALEN DONALD H	LTC	0-2055212	0863	1
WHALEN EMMETT M	CPT	0-1052626	0448	2
WHALEN HERBERT W	CPT	0-0249548	0465	3
WHALEN JAMES J	1LT	0-1300425	0646	2
WHALEN JOHN A	CW3	W-2144795	0164	1
WHALEN JOHN J	MAJ	0-0396617	1147	2
WHALEN PAUL	MAJ	0-1120523	0163	1
WHALEN ROBERT J	CPT	0-1549632	1044	2
WHALEN THOMAS F	LTC	0-1294947	0165	1
WHALEN THOMAS J	LTC	0-0242224	0255	3
WHALEN WILLIAM L	COL	0-2052273	1166	1
WHALEY HARRY E	LTC	0-0156740	0452	3
WHALEY JAMES L	COL	0-0223887	0859	3
WHALEY ROBERT S	CPT	0-0977461	1060	1
WHALEY THOMAS F	MAJ	0-1995189	1057	1
WHANG JAMES H S	CPT	0-1640118	0562	1
WHARFIELD ALBERT M	LTC	0-0272698	0668	3
WHARTON JAMES H	CPT	0-0463950	0245	2
WHARTON JUDSON K	MAJ	0-2008336	0662	1

NAME	GRADE	SVC NO	DATE RET MO YR	RET CODE
WHARTON RAEBURN J	COL	0-0137202	0952	3
WHARTON THOMAS	MAJ	0-0319324	1047	1
WHARTON THOMAS J	CPT	0-0313114	0447	2
WHARTON WALTER W	CW4	W-2105882	0459	1
WHARTON WILLIAM G	COL	0-0918375	0158	3
WHATES JOHN	CPT	0-1692585	0455	1
WHATLEY JACK W	CPT	0-2204435	0664	1
WHATLEY JOHN C	MAJ	0-0281161	1166	3
WHATLEY MARGARET I	CPT	L-0403211	1048	2
WHATLEY MELVIN M	LTC	0-1337909	0868	1
WHATLEY THOMAS B	LTC	0-0481137	0953	2
WHATLEY WILLIAM W	LTC	0-1108414	0961	2
WHATTON RICHARD T	MAJ	0-1321974	0261	1
WHEAT ELLIS F	1LT	0-1318730	0845	2
WHEAT GEORGE F R	CPT	0-0143206	1154	3
WHEAT JAMES D	CPT	0-5408586	0763	2
WHEAT JOHN D	CPT	0-1544441	0346	2
WHEAT JOHN R	LTC	0-1013066	1163	1
WHEAT LLOYD F	2LT	0-0531147	0844	2
WHEAT OSCAR G	LTC	0-0213350	1262	3
WHEAT RALPH M	CPT	0-1324966	0746	2
WHEAT ROBERT L	MAJ	0-1634460	0258	1
WHEAT WILLIAM T	2LT	0-0921451	0144	2
WHEATCROFT JOHN A	MAJ	0-1303973	0567	3
WHEATLAND FERN R	CPT	0-0289007	0462	1
WHEATLEY CHARLES W	MAJ	0-4030963	0367	1
WHEATLEY JEFFERSON	WO1	W-2115442	0254	1
WHEATLEY JOHN H	MAJ	0-0239212	0466	3
WHEATLEY TERRENCE P	CW3	W-2136682	1059	1
WHEATLY LEONARD S	MAJ	0-1313836	0664	1
WHEATON HARRY M JR	2LT	0-1002150	1043	2
WHEATON RODRICK K	COL	0-0370694	0861	1
WHEATON SIDNEY L	COL	0-0132548	0656	3
WHEELDON MILO	MAJ	0-0259685	0158	3
WHEELDON ROBERT H JR	LTC	0-0372526	0857	1
WHEELER ALLEN C	WO1	W-2147386	0260	1
WHEELER ARCHIE L	LTC	0-0376738	0268	3
WHEELER ARTHUR L	MAJ	0-0378602	1046	2
WHEELER BURDETTE J	LTC	0-1002749	1062	1
WHEELER CALVIN W	CPT	0-0528927	1046	2
WHEELER CARL D	CW3	W-2145535	0163	1
WHEELER CARLTON L	MAJ	0-0122895	0648	3
WHEELER CHARLES R	CPT	0-0401742	0144	2
WHEELER CHESTER L	2LT	0-0448776	0445	2
WHEELER DONALD O	CW2	W-2125210	0148	1
WHEELER DRUID E JR	MAJ	0-1328956	0168	1
WHEELER DUANE E	CPT	0-2263033	0464	1
WHEELER EARL W	LTC	0-0320145	0868	3
WHEELER EDGAR W	LTC	0-0309112	0659	3
WHEELER EDWARD W JR	MAJ	0-0395322	0158	1
WHEELER ELDEN L	LTC	0-0228626	0265	3
WHEELER EWELL N	LTC	0-0420855	0666	1
WHEELER FRANCIS R	MAJ	0-1055505	0865	1
WHEELER FRANK I JR	MAJ	0-0133050	0750	3
WHEELER FRED K	CPT	0-1551776	1055	2
WHEELER HAROLD F	CW3	W-2141490	0761	1
WHEELER HARRY M	COL	0-0245838	0563	3
WHEELER ISHAM C	1LT	0-0198723	0657	3
WHEELER JACK J	CW3	W-2205623	0464	1
WHEELER JAMES E	1LT	0-1300426	114N	2
WHEELER JAMES F	CW3	W-2209935	1267	1
WHEELER JAMES H	LTC	0-0421404	1060	1
WHEELER JAMES H	1LT	0-1785551	0545	2
WHEELER JAMES M	CW4	W-2121028	1154	1
WHEELER JOHN	LTC	0-1644898	1163	1
WHEELER JOHN F	CPT	0-1015325	0546	2
WHEELER JOHN P	CPT	0-1285861	0347	2
WHEELER JOHN P JR	CW3	W-2143679	0862	1
WHEELER JOHN R	MAJ	0-1031695	0564	1
WHEELER JOHN W	COL	0-0118291	0553	3
WHEELER JOSEPH G	COL	0-1299158	1268	1
WHEELER JOSEPH J	MAJ	0-1588363	0262	1
WHEELER JUSTUS B	CPT	0-0389153	1145	2
WHEELER LELAND E	LTC	0-0184471	0755	3
WHEELER LEO G	CPT	0-0473185	0245	2

NAME	GRADE	SVC NO	DATE RET MO YR	RET CODE
WHEELER LUTHER C	MAJ	0-0330922	0756	1
WHEELER MAURICE A	LTC	0-0439261	0968	3
WHEELER MYRON E	MAJ	0-1580497	0465	1
WHEELER NICHOLAS A	MAJ	0-0464175	0246	2
WHEELER OLIVER R	CW2	W-3200274	0167	1
WHEELER ORVILLE R	1LT	0-1328779	0248	2
WHEELER PAUL A	MAJ	0-3756757	0862	1
WHEELER RAYMOND G	2LT	0-1305205	0864	3
WHEELER RAYMOND R	CPT	0-0492934	0847	1
WHEELER RICHARD F	CW3	W-2144205	1058	1
WHEELER ROBERT M	MAJ	0-0408739	1061	1
WHEELER RUFUS H JR	MAJ	0-1946646	0460	1
WHEELER THOMAS R	COL	0-1294367	0966	1
WHEELER WALTER L	MAJ	0-1338766	1164	1
WHEELER WILBUR B	CW3	W-2153282	0665	1
WHEELER WILLIAM C JR	LTC	0-1107230	1060	1
WHEELER WILLIAM F	1LT	0-1313359	0454	1
WHEELER WILLIAM R	MAJ	0-1169390	1160	1
WHEELER WILLIAM W	LTC	0-0104054	0850	2
WHEELOCK JACK R	MAJ	0-0293554	0568	3
WHEELOCK WILLIAM N	CPT	0-0261247	1059	3
WHEELWRIGHT EDMUND M	MAJ	0-1053870	1060	1
WHEELWRIGHT MARTHA	1LT	N-0727443	0745	2
WHEETING LAWRENCE C	LTC	0-0180342	0356	3
WHEIR IONE M	CW3	V-0912088	0763	1
WHELAN JAMES R	LTC	0-0200631	0546	2
WHELAN JOHN F	LTC	0-1823808	0766	1
WHELAN JOSEPH A	LTC	0-0210479	0560	3
WHELAN JOSEPH A	COL	0-0309072	0766	3
WHELAN THOMAS A	LTC	0-0247577	0366	3
WHELAN THOMAS J	1LT	0-1003652	0246	2
WHELDON MAURICE A	LTC	0-0281788	0854	2
WHELESS JAMES A	LTC	0-0326732	0461	3
WHELESS JOHN R	CPT	0-0488699	1049	1
WHERLEY CHARLES W	1LT	0-1014625	1045	2
WHERLEY RICHARD D	2LT	0-2006312	1145	2
WHERRETT WILLIAM V	MAJ	0-0165208	0649	1
WHERRY BYRON T	MAJ	0-0115679	0648	3
WHERRY RALPH A	1LT	0-1289521	0345	1
WHETHAM MAURICE F	1LT	0-1288331	1045	2
WHETSEL ROBERT C	MAJ	0-1796390	1060	1
WHETSELL JACOB W	CW4	W-2146099	0159	1
WHETSTINE CHARLES E	MAJ	0-1877802	1163	1
WHETZEL JOSHUA C	MAJ	0-0151674	0653	3
WHICHARD WILLIS K	LTC	0-0475267	0955	1
WHICHER AGNES S	2LT	N-0700117	0337	1
WHIDDEN JAMES J	MAJ	0-2263160	1061	1
WHIDDEN RALEIGH J JR	CW3	W-2206013	0764	1
WHIDDON ERNEST C	1LT	0-1043833	0645	2
WHILDEN ALBERT F	LTC	0-1111979	1062	1
WHILDEN HARRIS JR	CW2	W-2152663	0962	1
WHIPP LEO A	2LT	0-1317713	0944	2
WHIPPEN LEONARD S	CPT	0-0133053	0850	3
WHIPPLE FLOYD M	MAJ	0-1550088	0461	1
WHIPPLE FREDERICK	LTC	0-1183216	0564	1
WHIPPLE IVAN C	COL	0-0412327	0857	2
WHIPPLE JAMES F	WO1	W-2107187	1048	1
WHIPPLE JAMES G	LTC	0-0402076	0263	1
WHIPPLE KENNETH E	CW2	W-3150185	1165	1
WHIPPLE LESTER S	LTC	0-0156606	0256	3
WHIPPLE ROBERT A	LTC	0-2018805	0566	1
WHIPPLE ROBERT S	LTC	0-0241811	0560	3
WHIPPLE THEODORE W	CW3	W-2152571	0263	1
WHIPPS GILBERT F	CPT	0-0415202	0546	2
WHISENANT JAMES H	LTC	0-1056943	1165	1
WHISENANT WILLIAM L	LTC	0-1596224	0967	1
WHISENHUNT HOWELL C	1LT	0-1252969	0345	2
WHISENHUNT JOHN M	LTC	0-1548595	0261	1
WHISLER NELD I	1LT	0-0495920	0249	1
WHISNANT STEWART	CW3	W-3150479	0968	1
WHISONANT FRANK	1LT	0-1540697	0346	2
WHISTLER CLARK S	LTC	0-0508807	0468	1
WHISTLER JOHN K	MAJ	0-0312973	0859	1
WHITACRE ESTON J	LTC	0-0398326	0760	1
WHITAKER CHARLES E	1LT	0-0423296	0946	2

NAME	GRADE	SVC NO	DATE RET MO YR	RET CODE
WHITAKER CLIFFORD W	COL	0-0222761	0159	3
WHITAKER DONALD D	LTC	0-1173116	0255	1
WHITAKER EUGENE G	CPT	0-0512038	0844	2
WHITAKER FRANK	MAJ	0-1420208	0759	1
WHITAKER HERBERT E	MAJ	0-0178479	1057	3
WHITAKER JOHN W JR	1LT	0-1291733	0545	2
WHITAKER JOSEPH M	COL	0-0243178	0263	3
WHITAKER LLOYD D JR	CPT	0-0386870	0460	1
WHITAKER LLOYD R	MAJ	0-1693136	0864	1
WHITAKER LYNN D	COL	0-0208925	0155	3
WHITAKER MILLARD H	WO1	W-2128829	1147	1
WHITAKER PAUL R	LTC	0-0348163	1165	1
WHITAKER WALTER L	LTC	0-1583831	0957	1
WHITAKER WARREN E	CW4	W-2145307	0559	1
WHITAKER WARREN S	MAJ	0-1590258	0265	1
WHITAKER WILLIAM	WO1	W-2124585	0745	2
WHITAKER WILLIS F	LTC	0-0141548	0757	3
WHITBECK PHILIP F	CPT	0-0292936	0945	2
WHITBREAD WALTER W	MAJ	0-1059681	0365	1
WHITBURN FANCHER K	COL	0-0280204	0961	1
WHITBY GERTHA L JR	CW4	W-2143780	0865	1
WHITCANACK JAMES A	MAJ	0-1318241	0358	1
WHITCHURCH THOMAS W	LTC	0-1104446	1164	1
WHITCOMB ARTHUR JR	2LT	0-2007752	1145	2
WHITCOMB CECIL B	B G	0-0190131	0359	3
WHITCOMB CHARLES A	COL	0-0348387	1162	1
WHITCOMB CHARLES K	LTC	0-0303556	0662	1
WHITCOMB FRANCIS C	MAJ	0-1171831	0263	1
WHITCOMB HERBERT L	LTC	0-0121988	0250	3
WHITCOMB LAURA M	CPT	N-0754671	0459	2
WHITCOMB RICHARD S	B G	0-0164276	1054	3
WHITCOMB ROBERT J	MAJ	0-1042463	1160	1
WHITCOMB RUTH	MAJ	N-0751626	1164	1
WHITCOMB WILMER R	CW3	W-2206396	0866	1
WHITE ADAMS R	CPT	0-0197907	0544	2
WHITE AILEEN D	1LT	N-0723853	1046	1
WHITE ALFRED C	LTC	0-1105701	1262	1
WHITE ALFRED C	CPT	0-1295331	1046	2
WHITE ALLIE E	CW4	W-2148824	1068	1
WHITE ALVIN A	CW2	W-2147840	1061	1
WHITE ALVIN O JR	LTC	0-1054867	0665	1
WHITE AMA M	1LT	0-1333912	0467	1
WHITE ARCHIE B	CPT	0-0509893	0460	1
WHITE ARCHIE M	LTC	0-0386506	0954	1
WHITE ARTHUR J	MAJ	0-1685638	1060	1
WHITE BENJAMIN F JR	1LT	0-1173830	0551	2
WHITE BERTRAM H	LTC	0-0366004	0546	2
WHITE BEVERLY G	CPT	0-1292621	0246	2
WHITE BOYCE J	CW4	W-2109448	1059	1
WHITE BURL V	LTC	0-2035024	1263	1
WHITE CARL D	2LT	0-2263210	0354	2
WHITE CATHERINE	2LT	N-0760169	1045	1
WHITE CECIL A	CW4	W-2144562	1068	1
WHITE CECIL B	LTC	0-0450127	1057	1
WHITE CHARLES C	MAJ	0-1053016	0761	1
WHITE CHARLES E	MAJ	0-0967550	1062	1
WHITE CHARLES E	LTC	0-1302243	0264	2
WHITE CHARLES F	B G	0-0285841	1059	3
WHITE CHARLES F	1LT	0-0374028	0246	2
WHITE CHARLES J	CPT	0-0243309	1262	3
WHITE CHARLES J	LTC	0-1541270	0461	1
WHITE CHARLES L	CPT	0-0505486	0547	2
WHITE CHARLES R	LTC	0-1796391	0262	1
WHITE CHARLES R	CW3	W-2143078	1162	1
WHITE CHARLES SR	CW3	W-2144686	0263	1
WHITE CLARENCE H	LTC	0-0119370	0655	2
WHITE CLARENCE L	MAJ	0-1105704	0662	1
WHITE CLAUDE W	LTC	0-0044029	1060	1
WHITE CLAUDE W	LTC	0-1038896	0963	2
WHITE CLEMMENSE	COL	0-0190079	0853	3
WHITE CLIFTON L	1LT	0-1595260	0647	2
WHITE CLYDE H	LTC	0-0384103	0760	1
WHITE CLYDE W	MAJ	0-1595078	0368	1
WHITE DAVID A	1LT	0-1301734	0645	2
WHITE DEE M	COL	0-0271312	0155	3

NAME	GRADE	SVC NO	DATE RET MO YR	RET CODE
WHITE DELMAS L	LTC	0-0425961	1058	1
WHITE DONALD D	1LT	0-0515293	0645	2
WHITE DONALD J	MAJ	0-4032693	0966	1
WHITE DONALD M JR	COL	0-0271082	0267	3
WHITE DOROTHY C	1LT	N-0720593	1045	1
WHITE DOUGLAS A	COL	0-0298955	0953	3
WHITE DOYLE	CW2	W-2150245	1057	1
WHITE EARL L	MAJ	0-0383244	0346	2
WHITE EDWARD A	MAJ	0-0524540	1054	1
WHITE EDWARD C	LTC	0-0962631	0667	1
WHITE EDWARD J	MAJ	0-0224173	0257	3
WHITE EDWIN D	1LT	0-1925141	0554	2
WHITE ENNIS L	COL	0-1001275	0767	1
WHITE EUGENE H	LTC	0-0994328	0968	1
WHITE EVERETT R	CPT	0-0942965	0859	1
WHITE FRANK A	LTC	0-0904039	1064	1
WHITE FRANK C	CW3	W-2150627	0957	1
WHITE FRANK E	MAJ	0-1575205	0261	1
WHITE FRANK G	LTC	0-0257636	0262	3
WHITE FRANK P	COL	0-0314416	0168	3
WHITE FRED R	CPT	0-1302399	0159	1
WHITE FREDERICK	LTC	0-0297497	0954	2
WHITE FREDERICK	MAJ	0-1312854	0365	1
WHITE GARVASE N	MAJ	0-0973190	0263	1
WHITE GEORGE C	1LT	0-1045424	1044	2
WHITE GEORGE L	1LT	0-0113681	1055	3
WHITE GEORGE L	LTC	0-1574365	0955	1
WHITE GEORGE S	1LT	0-0353540	0944	2
WHITE GILBERT L	CPT	0-0168730	0861	2
WHITE GRADY D	LTC	0-2274560	1065	1
WHITE GRADY T JR	CW3	W-3150769	0668	1
WHITE HARRY B	MAJ	0-1287811	0257	1
WHITE HARRY C	LTC	0-0363614	0762	1
WHITE HARRY C	CW2	W-2147612	0964	1
WHITE HARRY H	CPT	0-0194186	1045	2
WHITE HARRY J	LTC	0-1797401	1062	1
WHITE HARRY L	COL	0-0133576	1148	2
WHITE HARRY V	CPT	0-0538862	1051	2
WHITE HARVEY E	MAJ	0-0345260	0246	2
WHITE HARVEY L	COL	0-0216796	0256	3
WHITE HENRY E	LTC	0-1533230	1057	3
WHITE HENRY G	LTC	0-0143462	0552	3
WHITE HENRY L	MAJ	0-0131657	0864	1
WHITE HENRY L	MAJ	0-1557238	1266	2
WHITE HENRY M	CW2	W-2141491	0561	1
WHITE HERBERT F	WO1	W-2109485	0547	2
WHITE HOMER	CW3	W-2143151	0263	1
WHITE HOMER H	MAJ	0-1185351	0258	1
WHITE HOWELL S	MAJ	0-0102372	1057	3
WHITE HUGH L JR	LTC	0-1194755	0867	1
WHITE IRVIN	MAJ	0-1295970	0261	1
WHITE ISAAC E	CW3	W-2152938	0563	1
WHITE IVAN JR	LTC	0-0314865	0847	2
WHITE IVAN M	CW3	W-2205811	0766	1
WHITE J D	LTC	0-1296130	0761	1
WHITE JACK	LTC	0-0450944	1054	1
WHITE JACK	MAJ	0-1119732	1060	2
WHITE JACK E	MAJ	0-1636817	0961	1
WHITE JACK H	1LT	0-0375327	0246	2
WHITE JAMES A	MAJ	0-0252999	0447	1
WHITE JAMES A	LTC	0-0302034	0959	1
WHITE JAMES A	MAJ	0-1340044	0663	1
WHITE JAMES E	1LT	0-0378461	0546	2
WHITE JAMES E	CPT	0-0492007	0746	2
WHITE JAMES L	CPT	0-1878591	0665	2
WHITE JAMES M	COL	0-0251611	1065	3
WHITE JAMES O	CPT	0-1994721	0157	1
WHITE JAMES P	CW4	W-2107128	0859	1
WHITE JAMES R	MAJ	0-0450337	0357	1
WHITE JAMES V	MAJ	0-1825725	0455	1
WHITE JAMES W	CW2	W-2150145	0662	1
WHITE JESSE F	CPT	0-1824947	0957	1
WHITE JESSE H	LTC	0-0168539	0648	3
WHITE JEWEL C	LTC	0-0252540	0560	1
WHITE JOE L	LTC	0-0291292	0859	1

NAME	GRADE	SVC NO	DATE RET MO YR	RET CODE
WHITE JOHN	COL	0-0480770	0962	1
WHITE JOHN	CW4	W-2105058	1060	3
WHITE JOHN A	COL	0-0296590	0958	1
WHITE JOHN B	COL	0-0246676	1158	2
WHITE JOHN B	CW2	W-2142123	0156	1
WHITE JOHN B JR	LTC	0-0386289	0864	1
WHITE JOHN C	LTC	0-1042464	0563	1
WHITE JOHN C	CPT	0-2036458	0367	3
WHITE JOHN F	LTC	0-0227708	0165	3
WHITE JOHN F	CPT	0-0488612	0249	1
WHITE JOHN F	MAJ	0-0504521	0446	1
WHITE JOHN G	1LT	0-1056270	1145	2
WHITE JOHN J JR	LTC	0-1310537	0467	3
WHITE JOHN L	COL	0-0204144	0-51	3
WHITE JOHN M	CPT	0-0189422	1043	2
WHITE JOHN M	COL	0-0331102	0561	1
WHITE JOHN N	MAJ	0-0278137	0658	3
WHITE JOHN P	2LT	0-1590259	1044	2
WHITE JOHN Q	CW3	W-2151059	0164	1
WHITE JOHN R	COL	0-0238771	0763	1
WHITE JOHN W	LTC	0-1047841	0166	1
WHITE JOSEPH A	MAJ	0-0135225	0249	2
WHITE JOSEPH A	MAJ	0-1289660	0660	1
WHITE JOSEPH C	CW3	RW-2151807	0563	1
WHITE JOSEPH G	CW3	W-2136734	0255	1
WHITE JOSEPH L	CW4	W-2123427	1053	1
WHITE JOSEPH S	LTC	0-0182546	1156	3
WHITE KATHERINE	MAJ	L-0117476	0666	3
WHITE KENNETH E	MAJ	0-0967899	0861	1
WHITE KENNETH J	LTC	0-0490846	0457	1
WHITE KENNETH S	COL	0-0181287	0157	3
WHITE KENNETH S	LTC	0-0275639	0257	1
WHITE LAWRENCE M	CW3	W-2147949	0263	1
WHITE LEO A	MAJ	0-1304157	0960	1
WHITE LEONARD R	CW3	W-2151081	0264	1
WHITE LEROY M	1LT	0-2017786	0167	2
WHITE LLOYD A	CPT	0-2049757	0757	1
WHITE LOUIS A	LTC	0-0439297	0764	1
WHITE LOUIS A	CW4	W-2145099	0466	1
WHITE LOUIS J	LTC	0-0493006	1062	3
WHITE LOUIS L	MAJ	0-0490807	0447	2
WHITE LOUIS P	MAJ	0-0533085	0846	2
WHITE LYLE B	LTC	0-1995021	0461	1
WHITE LYLE E	2LT	0-0157266	0847	1
WHITE LYMAN G	LTC	0-0337690	0557	2
WHITE MALCOLM B	1LT	0-0395176	1042	1
WHITE MASTIN G	COL	0-0334078	0261	3
WHITE MERRILL M	WO1	W-2146472	0854	1
WHITE MILLER G	M G	0-0286638	0155	2
WHITE MORTON	LTC	0-0290479	1165	3
WHITE NEWELL O	MAJ	0-0314949	0545	2
WHITE NEWMAN W	LTC	0-0306523	0345	2
WHITE ORVAL V	1LT	0-1307598	0246	2
WHITE OWEN M	CW3	W-2149272	0762	1
WHITE PAUL A	MAJ	0-1284968	0654	1
WHITE PAUL E	MAJ	0-2014736	1167	1
WHITE PAUL H	LTC	0-0123670	0158	3
WHITE PAUL H	MAJ	0-0124016	0458	3
WHITE PAUL JR	LTC	0-1286049	0661	1
WHITE PAUL L	COL	0-0268447	0663	3
WHITE PAUL R	COL	0-0248827	0962	1
WHITE PAUL R	LTC	0-1040858	0964	1
WHITE QUITMAN T	CPT	0-2037108	1058	1
WHITE RALPH H	1LT	0-1308440	1257	1
WHITE RAY C	CPT	0-2289278	0867	1
WHITE RAYMOND E	1LT	0-2006589	1049	2
WHITE RAYMOND F	CPT	0-1846240	1267	2
WHITE RAYMOND F	CW4	RW-2113883	0363	1
WHITE RAYMOND L	MAJ	0-0399018	0944	2
WHITE RAYMOND M	LTC	0-2023955	0568	1
WHITE REX D	LTC	0-0923787	0265	1
WHITE RICHARD J	WO1	W-2118246	0352	1
WHITE RICHARD J JR	MAJ	0-0124017	0450	3
WHITE RICHARD K	LTC	0-0463533	1265	3
WHITE RICHARD M	LTC	0-1645488	0168	1

NAME	GRADE	SVC NO	DATE RET MO YR	RET CODE
WHITE ROBERT	CW2	W-2112178	0645	2
WHITE ROBERT A	CPT	O-1050513	0363	1
WHITE ROBERT E	MAJ	O-1917603	1068	2
WHITE ROBERT E	LTC	O-2019682	0968	1
WHITE ROBERT F	LTC	O-1101273	0963	1
WHITE ROBERT G	B G	O-0171250	0360	3
WHITE ROBERT G	CW2	W-2150618	1166	1
WHITE ROBERT H	LTC	O-1702671	0763	2
WHITE RONALD B	CW3	W-3150692	0467	2
WHITE ROSS	1LT	O-1318947	0246	2
WHITE RUBEN G	CPT	O-1825584	1055	1
WHITE RUSSELL E	CPT	O-1107231	0545	2
WHITE RUSSELL E	CW3	W-2147484	0966	1
WHITE RUSSELL G	COL	O-0231817	1263	3
WHITE SAMUEL E	LTC	O-1036084	0767	1
WHITE SHELBY L JR	CPT	O-0422490	0945	2
WHITE SHIRLEY L	2LT	N-0788971	0245	1
WHITE SIDNEY C	COL	O-0204868	0359	3
WHITE SILAS H JR	WO1	W-2126877	0851	2
WHITE STANLEY E	CPT	O-1315454	0251	2
WHITE SYLVIA E	MAJ	N-2297656	0867	2
WHITE TED L	LTC	O-1304159	0264	1
WHITE TED L	MAJ	O-1797402	0661	1
WHITE THADDEUS H	CPT	O-0472440	0646	2
WHITE THEO L	LTC	O-0224632	0460	2
WHITE THOMAS A	MAJ	O-0193384	0654	3
WHITE THOMAS C	1LT	O-1315884	1045	2
WHITE THOMAS J	LTC	O-0225011	0956	3
WHITE THOMAS J	COL	O-0317498	0446	2
WHITE THOMAS J	1LT	O-1288150	0346	2
WHITE THOMAS M	LTC	O-0451263	0258	1
WHITE TURNER O	MAJ	O-0264083	0263	1
WHITE URVEN V	COL	O-0361890	0361	3
WHITE VAN R	COL	O-0230557	0457	1
WHITE WALLACE R	LTC	O-0933082	0968	1
WHITE WALTER D	CW2	W-2210085	C361	1
WHITE WALTER J	CW3	W-2149724	0366	1
WHITE WALTER JR	LTC	O-1284441	0859	1
WHITE WALTER R	MAJ	O-0540952	1166	2
WHITE WALTER P	CPT	O-2288467	0562	1
WHITE WALTER R	CW3	W-2148825	0862	1
WHITE WARREN N	2LT	O-0528108	0545	2
WHITE WAYNE F	LTC	O-0376216	0667	3
WHITE WILLARD S	MAJ	O-2036722	0563	1
WHITE WILLIAM A	LTC	O-0226499	0945	2
WHITE WILLIAM A	MAJ	O-0301874	0144	2
WHITE WILLIAM A	MAJ	O-0978088	0765	1
WHITE WILLIAM B	CPT	O-0492546	1147	1
WHITE WILLIAM B SR	CW2	W-2146923	1061	1
WHITE WILLIAM C JR	LTC	O-0302967	0868	3
WHITE WILLIAM G	LTC	O-1294255	0557	2
WHITE WILLIAM H	LTC	O-2055285	0268	1
WHITE WILLIAM H	CPT	O-4074348	0668	1
WHITE WILLIAM H	CW3	W-2206845	0268	1
WHITE WILLIAM J	LTC	O-0276291	0966	3
WHITE WILLIAM P	1LT	O-1116433	0546	2
WHITE WORTH O	LTC	O-1286939	0960	1
WHITEAKER ATHA B	CPT	O-1031688	1060	1
WHITEBROOK MAXWELL M	CPT	O-0288448	0850	2
WHITECAR ROBERT W	MAJ	O-0974719	1162	1
WHITED BOWMAN T	COL	O-0304395	0465	1
WHITED NORMAN W	LTC	O-0207138	0848	3
WHITEFIELD LYTLE B J	LTC	O-0396606	0965	1
WHITEFOOT HILDA R	1LT	N-0771693	0346	1
WHITEHAIR ELMER V	LTC	O-1641058	0366	2
WHITEHAIR RAYMOND F	1LT	O-1533944	0945	2
WHITEHEAD ARTHUR V	COL	O-0408662	1060	1
WHITEHEAD CLAUDE E	COL	O-0315309	0661	3
WHITEHEAD CORNELIUS	CW3	W-2208506	0568	1
WHITEHEAD DEWIE	CW3	W-2117987	0259	1
WHITEHEAD DONALD F	CW2	W-2104586	0845	2
WHITEHEAD EDWARD L	LTC	O-1292970	0966	1
WHITEHEAD EDWARD Z	CW2	W-3430513	0867	1
WHITEHEAD FRED P SR	LTC	O-0381253	1161	1
WHITEHEAD IRA L	1LT	O-0438830	0246	2

NAME	GRADE	SVC NO	DATE RET MO YR	RET CODE
WHITEHEAD JACK	CW3	W-2136705	0261	1
WHITEHEAD JOSEPH A	MAJ	O-0428616	1146	2
WHITEHEAD ORAN R	LTC	O-1313481	0365	1
WHITEHEAD RICHARD S	LTC	O-0273280	0867	3
WHITEHEAD THOMAS H	COL	O-0223410	1064	3
WHITEHEAD VEARL G	1LT	O-1318109	1045	2
WHITEHEAD WALTER J	CW3	W-2142417	0861	1
WHITEHEAD WILLIAM G	COL	O-0190636	0757	3
WHITEHEAD WILLIAM S	COL	O-0920532	0667	3
WHITEHILL HARVEY H	LTC	O-1045627	0762	1
WHITEHOUSE FRANK H	LTC	O-0234643	0465	3
WHITEHOUSE HARVEY J	LTC	O-1103001	0161	1
WHITEHOUSE RICHARD K	LTC	O-0726532	0166	1
WHITEHURST EDWARD R	COL	O-0278131	0755	1
WHITEHURST WILLIAM W	CPT	O-4032531	0264	2
WHITEKNACT JOHN E	LTC	O-1576808	0662	1
WHITELEGG RUDOLPH F	COL	O-0185722	0654	3
WHITELEY BRAINARD A	MAJ	O-1553014	1263	1
WHITELEY ELI L	CPT	O-1310907	0546	2
WHITELEY JAMES E	CW4	W-2113358	0166	1
WHITELEY PHILIP W	COL	O-0223947	0955	3
WHITEMAN VERN O	LTC	O-0267868	0966	3
WHITEMAN WAYNE W	CPT	O-2009620	0261	1
WHITEMORE ARTHUR C	LTC	O-0268852	0657	1
WHITENER JOHN	CW3	RW-2207976	0868	1
WHITENER PAUL R	CPT	O-0248849	0545	2
WHITESIDE JAMES E	MAJ	O-1336579	1064	1
WHITESIDE PAUL W	1LT	O-0948171	0853	2
WHITESIDE RAYMOND E	LTC	O-0505654	0968	3
WHITESIDE WILLIAM H	MAJ	O-2212057	1064	1
WHITESIDES JOE E	COL	O-0342617	1267	1
WHITESIDES LAWSON E	LTC	O-0299531	0446	2
WHITETREE MAX R	CPT	O-1305145	0246	2
WHITETURKEY RAY L	MAJ	O-1115153	1162	1
WHITFIELD AUBEY J	CPT	O-1877310	1162	1
WHITFIELD CLAUDE	MAJ	O-1635475	0457	1
WHITFIELD HARVEY J	MAJ	O-0353919	0745	2
WHITFIELD ROBERT W	CW2	W-2149814	0857	1
WHITFIELD SAMUEL D	MAJ	O-1934874	0768	1
WHITFIELD WILLIAM A	CPT	O-0485891	1155	1
WHITFORD ANITA B C	2LT	N-0785706	0746	1
WHITFORD MATTHEW C	MAJ	O-1113055	1061	1
WHITFORD ORRIS C	MAJ	O-1290860	0954	1
WHITHAM KEITH W	LTC	O-1342223	0767	1
WHITIN GEORGE W	1LT	O-1050134	0446	2
WHITING CHESTER E	LTC	O-0936552	1060	1
WHITING DAVID D	MAJ	O-1825388	1060	1
WHITING DONALD J	2LT	O-1030627	0545	2
WHITING EBEN S	MAJ	O-0359969	0945	2
WHITING FRANCIS S	MAJ	O-0954034	0166	1
WHITING FRED N	COL	O-0233075	0464	3
WHITING HARVEY A	CW3	W-2146710	0761	1
WHITING HERBERT S	LTC	O-0327170	0266	3
WHITING MARSHALL	LTC	O-1303066	0467	1
WHITING MURRAY D	MAJ	O-1314237	1058	1
WHITING NORMAN O	LTC	O-0236965	1045	2
WHITING ROYAL G JR	1LT	O-1169829	104N	2
WHITING WILLARD W	LTC	O-1170438	0966	1
WHITKER RICHARD P	COL	O-0921199	0267	3
WHITLAW NATHANIEL	COL	O-0292663	0857	1
WHITLEDGE ALVAH O	MAJ	O-0967094	0962	1
WHITLEDGE OSCAR L	CW2	W-2147428	0861	1
WHITLEY CLIFTON M	CPT	O-1649104	0856	1
WHITLEY EDWARD D	LTC	O-0450129	0557	1
WHITLEY FREDERIC N	LTC	O-0240062	0466	3
WHITLEY GEORGE D	CPT	O-0309870	1144	2
WHITLEY GEORGE H	CW2	W-2118674	0453	1
WHITLEY JAMES V	MAJ	O-0302434	1144	2
WHITLEY PHILIP R	LTC	O-0232981	0865	3
WHITLEY ROBERT O	CW3	W-2205153	0565	1
WHITLOCK ARTHUR	CPT	O-0461185	0347	1
WHITLOCK FRED W	LTC	O-0251171	0264	3
WHITLOCK JAMES R	CPT	O-1546284	0156	1
WHITLOCK JOHN A	LTC	O-0261061	0867	3
WHITLOCK JOHN L	1LT	O-1105915	0346	2

NAME	GRADE	SVC NO	DATE RET MO YR	RET CODE
WHITLOCK MAURICE B	WO1	W-2139778	0946	2
WHITLOCK ROBERT S	MAJ	O-1049392	1263	1
WHITLOCK WILLIAM A	1LT	O-1038517	1045	2
WHITLOCK WILLIAM H	CW3	W-2150014	0364	1
WHITLOW FLOYD C	LTC	O-1280114	0657	1
WHITMAN CHARLES R	LTC	O-0461077	0365	3
WHITMAN HAROLD W	CPT	O-0461772	1146	1
WHITMAN JOHN A	1LT	O-0254761	0564	3
WHITMAN JOHN H	MAJ	O-1554112	1063	1
WHITMAN JOHN R	CPT	O-1109746	0952	2
WHITMAN JOSEPH J	MAJ	O-0262277	0765	3
WHITMAN LESTER J	CW3	W-2149312	1061	1
WHITMAN ORLANDO O	LTC	O-1170248	0357	1
WHITMAN ROBERT F	CPT	O-1002152	0857	1
WHITMAN RUSSELL S	WO1	W-2152755	1054	1
WHITMAN STANLEY J	CPT	O-1295805	0158	1
WHITMAN WILLIAM H	LTC	O-0384325	0858	1
WHITMARSH CARYL L	MAJ	O-0262131	0757	3
WHITMER GERALD L	MAJ	O-0959663	1167	1
WHITMER HUBERT F	MAJ	O-1937456	0966	1
WHITMEYER GEORGE L	LTC	O-1315747	1265	1
WHITMIRE ELBERT N JR	MAJ	O-0348581	0446	2
WHITMIRE HANKINS N	MAJ	O-0494339	0855	1
WHITMIRE ROBERT A	MAJ	O-1090497	0258	1
WHITMIRE THOMAS O	LTC	O-0542427	0264	1
WHITMORE EARL H	LTC	O-0299815	C657	1
WHITMORE GARLAND W	MAJ	O-2002571	0262	1
WHITMORE GEORGE I	LTC	O-1015930	0865	1
WHITMORE JAMES M	CW4	W-2139559	1060	1
WHITMORE LUCIAN R	CPT	O-0668170	0159	1
WHITMORE MORRIS T	COL	O-0162929	0455	3
WHITMORE RALPH L	LTC	O-0422201	0960	1
WHITMORE RUSSELL O	LTC	O-1019712	1066	1
WHITMORE SHIRLEY H	CW3	W-2122916	1162	2
WHITMORE WAYNE E	MAJ	O-0450946	1154	1
WHITMORE WILLIAM B	CPT	O-2262209	0261	1
WHITMORE YOTT F	MAJ	O-2016087	0762	1
WHITNEY ALDEN J	MAJ	O-1280261	1162	1
WHITNEY CARL E JR	LTC	O-0398275	0661	1
WHITNEY CLARENCE A	LTC	O-0123737	0850	3
WHITNEY CLARENCE E	LTC	O-0129717	1053	3
WHITNEY COURTNEY	M G	O-0398227	0551	1
WHITNEY EDWIN F	COL	O-0347225	C660	1
WHITNEY ERNEST L	MAJ	O-2262475	0365	1
WHITNEY FRANCES S	1LT	L-0302504	0545	2
WHITNEY FRANK A JR	1LT	O-1014393	0345	2
WHITNEY GEORGE E	MAJ	O-2210051	0968	1
WHITNEY GEORGE H	CPT	O-0501505	0854	1
WHITNEY HARRY P	1LT	O-2055205	1047	1
WHITNEY HERBERT W	LTC	O-0260840	0466	3
WHITNEY HUGH L	1LT	O-0494047	1148	1
WHITNEY JAMES H	CPT	O-0480122	0346	2
WHITNEY JOHN C	1LT	O-2007055	0147	2
WHITNEY LELAND A	LTC	O-1598724	0367	1
WHITNEY MAURICE	COL	O-0214963	0852	3
WHITNEY WILLIAM R	LTC	O-1289180	0558	1
WHITNEY WILLIAM J	CW3	W-2151007	1060	1
WHITPAN HOWARD G	COL	O-0278067	0448	2
WHITSELL FAY M	MAJ	O-0501563	0445	2
WHITSIT ROBERT J	COL	O-0418880	0761	1
WHITSON JAMES F	MAJ	O-2026839	1060	1
WHITSTON LAVAUGHN V	CW3	W-2151799	0562	1
WHITT BUFORD M	LTC	O-0330070	0264	3
WHITT HOWARD O	CPT	O-0509830	0346	1
WHITT JOHN H	CPT	O-0534572	0146	2
WHITT OLLIE B	CPT	O-0123768	0553	3
WHITT WILLIAM W	CW2	W-2149244	1060	1
WHITTAKER CHARLES E	CW3	W-2205154	C165	1
WHITTAKER EDGAR P	CW3	W-2150886	1164	1
WHITTAKER HENRY F	LTC	O-0196453	0454	3
WHITTAKER JAMES A	1LT	O-0454834	0844	2
WHITTAKER JOHN G	LTC	O-1183447	0768	1
WHITTAKER LEE	MAJ	O-1931677	0366	1
WHITTAKER ROBERT L	CW3	W-2148893	0766	1
WHITTAKER WOODROW M	CPT	O-2049150	0348	2

NAME	GRADE	SVC NO	DATE RET MO YR	RET CODE
WHITTED HAROLD H	CPT	O-0279783	0145	2
WHITTED LLOYD M	MAJ	O-1593915	1060	1
WHITTEMORE FORREST J	LTC	O-0127331	0351	3
WHITTEMORE HERBERT	MAJ	O-0208168	1044	2
WHITTEMORE IRVING C	COL	O-0125862	1155	3
WHITTEMORE JOHN G	LTC	O-0935343	0867	1
WHITTEN BEN H	MAJ	O-1576858	0756	1
WHITTEN CARSON D JR	MAJ	O-2289718	0763	1
WHITTEN ELLWOOD T	CPT	O-1920263	0962	1
WHITTEN GEORGE F	1LT	O-2007039	1048	2
WHITTEN JAMES F	CPT	O-1685989	0245	2
WHITTEN JOE W	LTC	O-0228115	0364	3
WHITTEN MARION E	COL	O-0260817	0268	3
WHITTEN RICHARD C	LTC	O-1046319	0662	1
WHITTEN WILLIAM J	CW3	W-2151679	0766	1
WHITTENBERG KENNETH	CW2	W-2215327	0568	1
WHITTIER FLORENCE E	MAJ	N-0785800	0565	1
WHITTIER GEORGE E	LTC	O-0450925	0859	1
WHITTIER LEON W	1LT	O-2049429	1055	1
WHITTINGHAM EDWARD R	COL	O-0166332	0951	3
WHITTINGHILL C L	CPT	O-0353073	0945	2
WHITTINGSTALL CHARLE	MAJ	O-0983813	0263	1
WHITTINGTON GORLEY M	CW3	W-2206374	0168	1
WHITTINGTON HULON B	MAJ	O-0954831	0363	2
WHITTINGTON JACK E	LTC	O-1314700	0161	1
WHITTINGTON JOHN P	MAJ	O-1302423	1263	1
WHITTINGTON JOHN R	MAJ	O-1582912	0667	3
WHITTINGTON JOSEPH M	MAJ	O-1300242	0261	1
WHITTINGTON PAUL E	MAJ	O-0275498	1067	3
WHITTLE ALBERT O	MAJ	O-0504317	0653	1
WHITTLE CHARLES B	COL	O-0347667	0358	1
WHITTLE CHARLES E	2LT	O-1003349	1044	2
WHITTLE VERNON L	CW3	W-2147536	0767	1
WHITTLE WILLIAM O	MAJ	O-0973924	0963	1
WHITTLESEY FRED L	COL	O-0257789	1265	3
WHITTLESEY MAX M SR	MAJ	O-2014538	0363	1
WHITTON CHARLIE M	CW2	W-2209225	0364	1
WHITTON MARGARET J	MAJ	N-0731768	0661	2
WHITTON TEEL D	LTC	O-0327227	1048	1
WHITTON TRUMAN W	CW2	W-2106924	0650	1
WHITTY PAUL X	CW3	W-2153137	1165	1
WHITWELL OMER D	1LT	O-0550527	0447	2
WHITWORTH ROBERT F	COL	O-0273160	0968	3
WHOLLEY SALLY J	CPT	N-0720382	0446	1
WHORTON BLAINE H	1LT	O-1107757	1045	2
WHORTON HAROLD	MAJ	O-1060683	0761	1
WHORTON ROBERT J	1LT	O-0487001	1144	2
WHYBREW ROBERT E	LTC	O-1102544	1164	1
WHYTENA JOHN F	CW2	W-2151883	1057	2
WIACEK JOSEPH J	MAJ	O-1040163	0159	1
WIARD DEHART C	LTC	O-0372541	0157	1
WIARD LAURENCE E JR	CW2	W-2147143	1060	1
WIARD SETH	COL	O-0163906	0754	3
WIATROWSKI HILLARD F	LTC	O-1543519	0768	1
WIBERG MORRIS C	1LT	O-1294948	0845	2
WIBLE JOHN	MAJ	O-0108260	0848	2
WICHAS JOHN J	CPT	O-1298472	0860	1
WICHERT HOWARD C	MAJ	O-1650441	0464	1
WICHMAN THEODORE O	MAJ	O-1311458	0562	1
WICHMANN CARL B JR	CW2	W-2152782	1264	1
WICHROWSKI BCL	LTC	O-0382173	1166	3
WICHTERMAN ROY F	CPT	O-0263062	0765	3
WICK CATHERINE	2LT	N-0700587	0538	1
WICK ELMER L	MAJ	O-1799491	0662	1
WICK ROBERT L	LTC	O-0238661	0765	3
WICKA ANTHONY J	CPT	O-0885738	0546	2
WICKE DICK	1LT	O-0400850	0146	2
WICKE MARGARET K	1LT	N-0729649	0346	1
WICKER EDMOND L	MAJ	O-1113058	0859	1
WICKER GLENES E	LTC	O-0412414	0661	1
WICKER HOMER F	COL	O-0156655	0957	3
WICKER JAMES C	CW3	W-2143732	0663	1
WICKER WORTH	LTC	O-0336096	0246	2
WICKERSHAM GEORGE L	MAJ	O-0363060	0462	1
WICKERSHAM WYMAN	LTC	O-0275346	1168	3

NAME	GRADE	SVC NO	DATE RET MO YR	RET CODE
WICKERT DONALD J	1LT	O-0335221	1267	3
WICKESSER ROBERT A	MAJ	O-1549177	0847	2
WICKHAM HERBERT F	COL	O-0264034	0467	3
WICKHAM JOHN A	LTC	O-0147307	0452	2
WICKHAM ROBERT E	CW2	RW-2209379	0862	1
WICKLAND DONALD J	MAJ	O-1000494	0457	1
WICKLAND LYNN R	LTC	O-1107235	1066	3
WICKLANDER GRANT H	CW4	W-2110307	0360	1
WICKLIFFE KEITH V	LTC	O-0411088	1160	1
WICKLING HARRY F	LTC	O-1641062	1164	3
WICKLUND DAGNE O	MAJ	N-0736590	0365	3
WICKMAN IRVING G	LTC	O-0216975	0455	3
WICKMAN PAUL D	CW3	W-2205724	0368	1
WICKMAN ROBERT E	CPT	O-1688834	0959	2
WICKORD THEODORE F	COL	O-0345291	1146	2
WICKOREN CLARENCE M	MAJ	O-2008801	1062	1
WICKS ARTHUR J	LTC	O-0131669	0648	3
WICKS EARL N	LTC	O-1053017	1062	1
WICKS HERBERT N	MAJ	O-0392499	0146	2
WIDDEN HOWARD J	LTC	O-1002556	0868	3
WIDDIFIELD GLENN R	CW3	W-2151827	0164	1
WIDDOWSON WILLIAM W	COL	O-0363117	0966	3
WIDINCAMP JOHN S	CW4	W-2103602	1160	1
WIDING HARRY F	MAJ	O-2036724	0961	1
WIDING WILLIAM F JR	MAJ	O-1296955	1161	1
WIDMAN DAVID F	CPT	O-0396976	0847	2
WIDMANN ERWIN	COL	O-0319808	1165	3
WIDMAYER LAWRENCE A	CPT	O-0516380	0948	2
WIDMER ALBERT J	LTC	O-1287632	0161	1
WIDMER ERHARDT F	1LT	O-0923312	0744	2
WIDMOYER FRED B	LTC	O-0147311	0655	3
WIDMYER EARL G	LTC	O-0328516	1153	2
WIDMYER IRVING C	MAJ	O-0918338	0747	2
WIDRICH JACK	CPT	O-1693462	1145	2
WIEBE ALVIN F	CPT	O-1045632	0845	2
WIEBEN CLARENCE P	CPT	O-1557239	0962	1
WIEBER PAUL A	1LT	O-1331689	0746	2
WIEBKING WALTER R	MAJ	O-1547366	1160	1
WIEBUSCH ROBERT G	LTC	O-1845125	0161	1
WIECHMAN FRED H	COL	O-0252240	0562	3
WIECK ARTHUR M	COL	O-0324824	0760	1
WIEDELMAN LAWRENCE W	COL	O-0299575	0965	3
WIEDEMER EDWARD C	MAJ	O-1885952	0368	1
WIEDMAN CLARENCE J	COL	O-0267799	1059	1
WIEDRICK WALTER W	CW2	W-2101110	0246	2
WIEGAND FREDERICK	COL	O-0184142	0158	3
WIEGAND VINCENT A	CPT	O-0949230	0659	1
WIEGANDT MARVIN R	2LT	O-0555199	0745	2
WIEGERS ROBERT M	CPT	O-1291364	1047	2
WIEGREFFE JOHN L	LTC	O-0259449	0267	3
WIEHENKAMP PAUL H	LTC	O-0415643	1060	1
WIEK NORMAN E	1LT	O-1016252	0845	2
WIELAND CHARLES C	MAJ	O-1175011	1165	1
WIELAND HERMAN	LTC	O-0266940	0354	3
WIELAND JOHN F	LTC	O-1758968	0468	3
WIEMEYER GEORGE A	MAJ	O-0492969	0864	3
WIENAND JOHN H JR	LTC	O-0261552	0865	3
WIENCEK VINCENT	CPT	O-0451455	0559	1
WIENEKE CARTER H	1LT	O-0549664	0245	2
WIENER FREDERICK	COL	O-0338743	0766	3
WIENER JEAN	LTC	L-0304087	0855	2
WIENER MORRIS F	LTC	O-0264174	0465	3
WIENERT RAYMEN C	LTC	O-0259012	0566	3
WIENTJES CHARLES N	MAJ	O-1317456	0459	1
WIEPKING HERBERT R	CW2	W-2118975	0745	2
WIER CHESTER	1LT	O-1014361	0745	2
WIER DONALD G	CPT	O-1296459	0261	1
WIER HERBERT I	CPT	O-1290862	0745	2
WIER JOHN J	2LT	O-1333150	1046	2
WIER JOHN S	COL	O-0238876	1061	3
WIERMAN JOHN P	CPT	O-1554113	0946	2
WIERSEMA HENRY	LTC	O-0119336	0556	3
WIERSEMA MATTHEW J	CPT	O-1171834	0847	2
WIERTS PAUL H	1LT	O-1558625	1046	2
WIES CARL H	COL	O-0245036	0966	3

NAME	GRADE	SVC NO	DATE RET MO YR	RET CODE
WIESE FRED W	COL	O-0167351	1053	1
WIESE GLENN L	MAJ	O-1546248	0766	3
WIESE JOHN H	LTC	O-1635480	1166	1
WIESEL LEON L	CPT	O-0476773	0246	2
WIESEN JOHN R	2LT	O-1303974	0844	2
WIESEN SEYMOUR A	MAJ	O-0455147	0157	1
WIESENBERG HERBERT	CPT	O-1944430	0546	2
WIESENBURGER WALTER	CW2	W-2149917	0258	1
WIESENTHAL SAM	MAJ	O-0487743	0247	2
WIESNER JEROME J	1LT	O-1775767	0247	2
WIESS CHARLES R II	LTC	O-1317457	1162	2
WIESSNER WALTER H	LTC	O-1105270	0263	1
WIEST ALBERT F	COL	O-0401874	1064	1
WIESTER HARRY B	LTC	O-0207537	0954	1
WIETHORN GUS D	MAJ	O-0289301	0460	1
WIETZ GENEVIEVE	2LT	N-0789082	0944	1
WIGEN DONALD M	CW3	W-2144140	0563	1
WIGGANS CLARENCE E	LTC	O-0249273	0366	3
WIGGER ELMER C	MAJ	O-2262369	0465	1
WIGGER GEORGE F	COL	O-0299724	1157	1
WIGGERS GERALD J	1LT	O-1012582	0347	2
WIGGIN ARNOLD T	MAJ	O-0260239	0567	3
WIGGIN FRANKLIN W	CPT	O-1649005	1166	3
WIGGIN MORRILL	COL	O-0547185	0646	2
WIGGIN WILLIAM B	CPT	O-0202652	0644	2
WIGGINS ARTHUR E	CPT	O-1316353	0557	1
WIGGINS CHARLES E JR	LTC	O-1338890	1268	1
WIGGINS CHARLES S	CPT	O-0333830	0668	3
WIGGINS EARL L	1LT	O-0527876	1145	2
WIGGINS EDGAR C	COL	O-0174125	0361	3
WIGGINS FREDERIC G	LTC	O-0392350	0262	1
WIGGINS FREDERICK	LTC	O-0188657	0750	3
WIGGINS GILBERT N	COL	O-0204034	0858	3
WIGGINS HENRY	MAJ	O-1913491	0963	1
WIGGINS HOYT A	LTC	O-0249201	1265	3
WIGGINS IRIS E B	1LT	N-0774105	0247	1
WIGGINS JOHN L JR	1LT	O-1016431	1145	2
WIGGINS JOSEPH H	MAJ	O-0480104	0549	2
WIGGINS RALPH C	CPT	O-0270876	0668	3
WIGGINS ROSALIE H	MAJ	N-0733432	1163	1
WIGGINS STANLEY B	COL	O-0141500	0648	3
WIGGINS THOMAS A	MAJ	O-1288834	0258	1
WIGGINTON JAMES G	LTC	O-0382831	0768	3
WIGGS JOHN H	COL	O-0380512	1162	1
WIGGS NORMAN S	COL	O-0184590	0152	3
WIGGS W N	WO1	W-2126207	0647	2
WIGHT ANNA D	2LT	N-0700566	0336	1
WIGHT ARTHUR E	CPT	O-0240549	0862	3
WIGHT HEWITT G	CPT	O-0534142	0847	2
WIGHTMAN VINCENT H	MAJ	O-0270486	1267	3
WIGHTMAN WILFRED V	COL	O-0218565	0464	3
WIGHTMAN WILLIAM W	LTC	O-0251855	0346	2
WIGIM TRUEMAN H	LTC	O-2035509	0562	1
WIGINGTON LETCHER JR	MAJ	O-0407808	0546	2
WIGLE CHARLES L	CW2	W-2214563	0868	1
WIGLEY JEREMIAH J	MAJ	O-1103005	0658	1
WIGLEY LAWRENCE J	CW3	W-2142011	1060	1
WIGMORE CHARLES O	CPT	O-1822844	0564	1
WIHR NORMAN L	COL	O-0287931	0266	3
WIHTOL KARL F	LTC	O-0284959	0459	3
WIIG PAUL O	1LT	O-0273250	1042	2
WIKE DAVID W SR	CPT	O-1636822	0256	1
WIKE RALPH A	CPT	O-0217115	1045	2
WIKER BERNARD	CPT	O-2045152	1047	2
WIKLE ROBERT M JR	MAJ	O-1293507	0261	1
WIKNER ERIC F	LTC	O-0337240	0757	1
WIKOFF LOWELL C	MAJ	O-2016010	0562	1
WIKSTROM HOLGAR A	MAJ	O-0423901	0845	2
WILBANKS REX A	LTC	O-0340635	0365	1
WILBANKS SCURLOCK W	CW2	W-2145762	1060	1
WILBANKS THOMAS O	LTC	O-0255309	0162	3
WILBER CHARLES O	CW2	W-2150280	0862	1
WILBER GEORGE E B	1LT	O-1012794	0445	2
WILBER HAROLD A JR	2LT	O-1284798	0844	2
WILBER MARLIN A	CPT	O-1702796	1044	2

NAME	GRADE	SVC NO	DATE RET MO YR	RET CODE
WILBER MORTIMER D	LTC	O-1318845	0264	1
WILBERGER CALVIN L	LTC	O-1331898	0863	1
WILBERGER EVERETT O	MAJ	O-0233603	0857	3
WILBORN EARL A	CW3	W-2151640	0862	1
WILBORN MESSER	1LT	O-0109205	1037	1
WILBUR EDWARD L	COL	O-0129740	1156	3
WILBUR JOHN F	LTC	O-1300736	0865	1
WILBURN CLYDE A	LTC	O-0358196	0560	1
WILBURN JOSHUA M	CPT	O-1587019	0761	1
WILBURN LEON	MAJ	O-1540851	0563	1
WILBURN LUKE J	MAJ	O-0115139	0356	3
WILBURN MURREL O	LTC	O-0276299	1063	3
WILCE JOSEPH M	1LT	O-1545745	0154	1
WILCH CLETUS E	LTC	O-0484828	1165	1
WILCKE HAROLD L	LTC	O-0244972	0966	3
WILCOX ALBERT M JR	LTC	O-0341998	1062	2
WILCOX BERNARD A	LTC	O-0262239	0464	3
WILCOX CHARLES L	CW3	W-2148038	0361	1
WILCOX ELEANOR D	2LT	N-0756223	0245	1
WILCOX ELLIS J	MAJ	O-0248314	0167	3
WILCOX G NEIL	COL	O-0472010	1065	1
WILCOX HARVEY L	CPT	O-1302400	1264	2
WILCOX HOWARD J	CW2	W-2110303	0648	2
WILCOX JERRA	LTC	O-0259021	0564	3
WILCOX LAWRENCE G	2LT	O-1112519	0545	2
WILCOX LELAND F	MAJ	O-0281725	0446	2
WILCOX MILLARD W	LTC	O-0322788	1167	3
WILCOX PAUL K	CPT	O-1032665	0947	2
WILCOX PAUL V	LTC	O-0183707	0260	3
WILCOX PERRY O	MAJ	O-2300992	0765	1
WILCOX ROBERT D	LTC	O-0555557	1167	1
WILCOX ROBERT T	CW2	W-3440011	0667	1
WILCOX THEODORE R	LTC	O-0359663	0363	3
WILCOX WALTER	MAJ	O-0418944	0346	2
WILCOX WALTER J	MAJ	O-0980527	0662	1
WILCOX WESLEY J	CW2	W-3430791	0568	2
WILCOX WILFRED W	COL	O-0282692	0563	3
WILCOX WILLARD S	2LT	O-0256439	0258	3
WILCOXSON CHARLES L	CW3	W-2102547	0354	1
WILCOXSON THOMAS R	CPT	O-1001707	0754	1
WILCUTTS HELEN D	1LT	L-0304117	0946	2
WILD HAROLD A	MAJ	O-1053432	0865	3
WILD JAMES M	COL	O-0312935	0246	2
WILDAY CEDRIC A	CW3	W-2109039	0653	1
WILDE CHARLES F JR	1LT	O-0512557	0345	2
WILDE JOHN J	WO1	W-2111750	0646	2
WILDEBUSH JOSEPH F	MAJ	O-0301706	1143	2
WILDEN SAMUEL J	MAJ	O-0319367	1045	2
WILDER ALLEN S	COL	O-0281051	0665	1
WILDER CHARLES	1LT	O-1311075	1045	2
WILDER DELORES AL	1LT	N-0726091	1045	1
WILDER EUGENE H	LTC	O-0372766	0567	3
WILDER FRANK A	LTC	O-0298301	1045	2
WILDER GEORGE E	MAJ	O-1636825	0748	1
WILDER GUY B	LTC	O-0267259	1061	3
WILDER HARLIS T	MAJ	O-1319460	1160	1
WILDER HARRY	MAJ	O-2018622	0166	1
WILDER JILES C	CPT	O-0459797	1049	1
WILDER LUTHER V	CW2	W-2150697	1157	1
WILDER OMER D	LTC	O-0401343	0860	1
WILDER OSCAR JR	LTC	O-0450347	0656	1
WILDER THOMAS P	MAJ	O-0375231	1047	2
WILDER WILLIAM M	COL	O-0118147	0648	3
WILDER WILLIAM S	MAJ	O-0318069	1166	3
WILDERMUTH HERMAN C	MAJ	O-0273573	0368	3
WILDEROM MORRIS	MAJ	O-1693566	0146	2
WILDHABER FERDINAND	CPT	O-0153587	0144	1
WILDMAN ALBERT C	COL	O-0196638	1260	1
WILDMAN HARRY J	2LT	O-1321723	0245	2
WILDMAN JOHN T	CW3	W-3150217	0368	1
WILDMAN PAUL W	LTC	O-1918930	1168	1
WILDMAN ROBBINS L	CPT	O-2208730	0859	1
WILDMAN VERNON	LTC	O-0475024	0249	1
WILDS WILLIAM	LTC	O-0106459	0648	3
WILEMAN RICHARD D	MAJ	O-1019644	0661	2

NAME	GRADE	SVC NO	DATE RET MO YR	RET CODE
WILES FRED F	CW4	W-2143642	0556	1
WILES HAROLD J	CW3	W-2150562	0763	1
WILES RONALD P	CW4	W-2117938	0960	1
WILES WILLIAM G	COL	O-0305383	0362	3
WILEY ALBERT	LTC	O-0253245	0565	3
WILEY AUDREY M	1LT	N-0744141	0146	1
WILEY BELL I	COL	O-0922753	0266	3
WILEY BERT C	CPT	O-4002020	1154	2
WILEY CHARLES A	CW3	W-2144375	0461	1
WILEY CHARLES D	1LT	O-1103006	0644	2
WILEY CHARLES O	WO1	W-2006587	0763	3
WILEY CLARENCE B	MAJ	O-1039618	0557	1
WILEY CORNELIUS	LTC	O-0450338	0652	2
WILEY GARETH W	MAJ	O-1826117	1059	1
WILEY HAROLD	CW2	W-2150553	0757	1
WILEY HARRY K	CPT	O-1319136	0546	2
WILEY JOHN C	COL	O-0188177	0852	3
WILEY PAUL C	LTC	O-1306922	0561	2
WILEY ROBERT L	CW3	W-2120027	0456	1
WILEY STEPHEN J	MAJ	O-1320703	0157	1
WILEY THEODORE	1LT	O-1011162	1045	2
WILFLEY JOHN S	COL	O-0252578	0562	3
WILFONG ALBERT E	B G	O-0147726	0545	2
WILFONG WILLIAM T	MAJ	O-0174698	1147	2
WILFORD WILLIAM C	LTC	O-1000495	0858	1
WILGEN CHARLES H	LTC	O-0327332	0161	1
WILGUS JOHN E	LTC	O-1112521	1068	3
WILHELM CECELIA W	MAJ	N-0796863	0267	3
WILHELM CHARLES P	MAJ	O-0123952	0642	2
WILHELM DAVID W	LTC	O-0281645	1167	3
WILHELM ROBERT H	LTC	O-0358409	0564	3
WILHELM WARREN	CPT	O-1172337	1146	2
WILHELMI ROY A	CW3	W-2151201	0165	1
WILHELMSON BERNARD W	1LT	O-1299970	0146	2
WILHITE CARL M	MAJ	O-1922594	0367	1
WILHITE RICHARD D	LTC	O-0247490	0466	3
WILHOUR RICHARD O	MAJ	O-1114004	1059	1
WILIE JIM B	MAJ	O-2200004	0762	1
WILJANEN MARTIN V	2LT	O-1826404	0854	1
WILK JOHN S	1LT	O-2037110	0446	2
WILKE CHARLES H	CPT	O-1823529	1163	1
WILKE DONALD E	LTC	O-1913477	1268	1
WILKE GILBERT C	CW2	W-2114652	0965	3
WILKE HARLAN A	CW3	W-2152063	0564	1
WILKEN HAROLD W	MAJ	O-1649667	0357	1
WILKER RICHARD T	LTC	O-1287108	0264	1
WILKERSON BURFORD	LTC	O-0335079	1267	3
WILKERSON CARL F	MAJ	O-1175360	0760	1
WILKERSON CHARLES E	LTC	O-0381164	0846	2
WILKERSON ENOCH H	LTC	O-0178135	1058	3
WILKERSON JAMES R	2LT	O-1825456	0745	2
WILKERSON JOHN C	COL	O-0284077	1060	1
WILKERSON JOHN W	MAJ	O-0509838	0158	2
WILKERSON LYNDAL E	LTC	O-0210221	0664	1
WILKERSON RALPH L	CPT	O-0160465	0459	3
WILKERSON ROY D	CPT	O-0993710	0361	1
WILKERSON WALTER E	MAJ	O-0985121	0864	1
WILKERSON WILLIAM H	1LT	O-1293158	0346	2
WILKES EARL C	CPT	O-1303420	0447	1
WILKES JAMES G	CW3	W-2152633	0360	1
WILKES JOHN V	MAJ	O-2032983	0563	1
WILKES KENNETH G	COL	O-0306296	0547	2
WILKES THOMAS M	LTC	O-0280816	0545	2
WILKES WILLIAM C	LTC	O-0114899	0358	3
WILKIE EDWARD H JR	COL	O-0334862	0363	1
WILKIE JAMES R	MAJ	O-1320494	0862	1
WILKIN FREDERICK	MAJ	O-1013551	0549	2
WILKINS ARTHUR F	CW3	W-2208510	0968	1
WILKINS AUGUSTUS R	CPT	O-0481240	0844	2
WILKINS AUSTIN M	LTC	O-1303599	0263	1
WILKINS CHARLIE S	COL	O-0288599	0465	3
WILKINS EDWIN A	MAJ	O-2018082	0761	1
WILKINS ELMER L	CPT	O-1051828	1054	1
WILKINS FRANK M	COL	O-0319184	0163	1
WILKINS GEORGE F	MAJ	O-2271228	0866	1

NAME	GRADE	SVC NO	DATE RET MO YR	RET CODE
WILKINS HARRY L JR	CPT	0-1293159	1057	2
WILKINS JAMES E	COL	0-0175634	0958	1
WILKINS JAMES P	COL	0-0382964	0557	1
WILKINS JESSIE T	COL	0-0200095	0253	2
WILKINS JOHN F JR	CPT	0-1642724	0745	2
WILKINS JOSEPH P	1LT	0-1320576	0146	2
WILKINS MARION K	LTC	0-0249240	0466	3
WILKINS PAUL F	MAJ	0-0180935	0261	3
WILKINS RAYMOND A	MAJ	0-0195234	0761	3
WILKINS THOMAS C JR	LTC	0-2003402	1168	1
WILKINS WILLIAM A	MAJ	0-0354538	0163	1
WILKINSON ALTON P	COL	0-0266599	0246	2
WILKINSON CARL C	LTC	0-0330904	0960	3
WILKINSON CECIL	CW2	W-2214923	1266	1
WILKINSON CHARLES E	MAJ	0-1307904	0564	1
WILKINSON EARL H	MAJ	0-0386367	0246	2
WILKINSON EDWARD W	MAJ	0-0253214	0356	3
WILKINSON GEORGE G	2LT	0-1046321	0544	2
WILKINSON GORDON J	CPT	0-1059978	0747	2
WILKINSON HAROLD B	2LT	0-0928580	0451	2
WILKINSON HARRY J	MAJ	0-0294766	0550	2
WILKINSON HARRY R JR	CW2	W-2207350	0161	1
WILKINSON HENRY E	CPT	0-0409452	0240	2
WILKINSON HORACE N	CPT	0-0321751	0551	3
WILKINSON JACK W	LTC	0-1326959	0265	1
WILKINSON JAMES G	CPT	0-0186898	0753	3
WILKINSON JAMES W JR	CW3	W-2206769	0668	1
WILKINSON JOHN J	LTC	0-2012330	0562	1
WILKINSON JOSEPH B	COL	0-0261672	0262	3
WILKINSON NEO A	CW3	W-2149970	0962	1
WILKINSON PAUL R	1LT	0-1554998	0163	3
WILKINSON ROBERT E	1LT	0-2021031	1163	2
WILKINSON ROBERT W	CPT	0-0255420	0744	2
WILKINSON STANLEY S	1LT	0-0399960	0846	2
WILKINSON THOMAS C	COL	0-0332142	1059	3
WILKINSON THOMAS E	LTC	0-1300562	0163	1
WILKINSON VERNON R	CW3	W-2142993	0561	1
WILKINSON WALTER R	CPT	0-0492281	0545	2
WILKINSON WILLIAM	1LT	0-0554175	0946	2
WILKINSON WILLIAM S	COL	0-0184689	0255	3
WILKIRSON EUGENE P	MAJ	0-0168058	0654	3
WILKOF ERVIN	1LT	0-1295309	1045	2
WILKOWSKI VICTOR	LTC	0-0550622	0667	1
WILKS BEN	CPT	0-1177248	1047	2
WILKS LESTER W	MAJ	0-0450339	0662	1
WILKS PAUL A	COL	0-0127625	1155	3
WILL CLARENCE A	LTC	0-0143499	0648	3
WILL JOSEPH C	LTC	0-2012257	1068	2
WILLAR MARY C	2LT	N-0777559	0146	1
WILLARD CHARLES W	LTC	0-1182742	1067	1
WILLARD EUGENE L	MAJ	0-0522249	0246	2
WILLARD FRANCIS J	LTC	0-0987299	1268	1
WILLARD FRANK A	LTC	0-0187812	1053	3
WILLARD GEORGE W	CPT	0-0462807	0246	2
WILLARD GORDON W	MAJ	0-2014444	0663	1
WILLARD JOHN H	LTC	0-0316551	1063	1
WILLARD JOSEPH P	CW2	W-2147512	1157	1
WILLARD PIERCE M	LTC	0-0169340	0958	3
WILLARD ROBERT A	CPT	0-0491447	0955	1
WILLARD ROBERT S	CPT	0-1081261	0454	2
WILLARD WILLIAM W	CW2	W-2104848	0260	1
WILLCOX HUGH L	LTC	0-0335926	0965	3
WILLCOX JAMES E	MAJ	0-1290694	0460	1
WILLCUT CLARE F	CW3	W-2145528	0464	2
WILLECKE EDWARD C	LTC	0-0467899	0962	1
WILLEMS FRANCIS M JR	MAJ	0-0959283	0164	1
WILLENS ANTHONY T	MAJ	0-1649239	0557	1
WILLESS HERSEL F	CPT	0-0372042	0843	2
WILLETS DAVID B	COL	0-0245460	0966	3
WILLETT HUBERT T	1LT	0-1301079	0850	2
WILLETT JAMES F	LTC	0-0240069	0146	2
WILLETT MARION L	CPT	0-1011255	0745	2
WILLETT PRENTICE A	LTC	0-0257703	1263	3
WILLETTE HENRY J	WO1	W-2139596	0148	1
WILLETTE WILLIAM L	CW3	W-2211464	0968	1

NAME	GRADE	SVC NO	DATE RET MO YR	RET CODE
WILLEY CLARENCE F	LTC	0-0931308	0168	3
WILLEY EDWARD P JR	CPT	0-0273789	1045	2
WILLEY EVERETT M	LTC	0-1558626	0864	3
WILLEY JAMES B	MAJ	0-0246254	1264	3
WILLEY JOSEPH G	MAJ	0-2005304	0664	1
WILLEY NORMAN D	COL	0-0324432	1262	1
WILLEY RALPH E	COL	0-0213781	0460	3
WILLEY SEAVER A	CW4	W-2108695	0161	1
WILLEY WILLIAM W	LTC	0-0290347	0367	3
WILLEY WINSTON E	LTC	0-0295134	0462	1
WILLHOIT THOMAS D	LTC	0-1115848	0663	1
WILLIAMS ADRIAN H	COL	0-0233204	0365	3
WILLIAMS ALAMANCA L	LTC	0-1288984	0861	1
WILLIAMS ALBERT C	CW2	RW-2151858	0961	1
WILLIAMS ALFRED A	MAJ	0-0220900	0660	3
WILLIAMS ALFRED E	LTC	0-1877794	1068	1
WILLIAMS ALFRED H JR	CPT	0-1016166	0146	2
WILLIAMS ALFRED L	LTC	0-0313377	1047	1
WILLIAMS ALLEN H	COL	0-0501099	1057	3
WILLIAMS ALLEN H	1LT	0-1541344	0651	2
WILLIAMS ALTON P	LTC	0-1101278	0661	1
WILLIAMS ANGEL E	CW2	W-2150259	0561	1
WILLIAMS ANDREW A	CW2	W-2150756	0263	1
WILLIAMS ANDREW J	CPT	0-0494538	0653	1
WILLIAMS ARBERY R	LTC	0-0325045	0759	1
WILLIAMS ARCHIBALD	MAJ	0-0180481	0644	2
WILLIAMS ARTHUR M	CPT	0-1167282	0645	2
WILLIAMS ARTHUR V	COL	0-0250035	0160	2
WILLIAMS ARTIS D	2LT	0-2009747	0257	1
WILLIAMS AUBREY L	LTC	0-1031040	1164	1
WILLIAMS AVERY D	1LT	0-2014995	0152	2
WILLIAMS BEN	CW3	W-2115796	0804	1
WILLIAMS BENJAMIN H	CPT	0-0277957	0861	3
WILLIAMS BENJAMIN S	CW2	W-2152085	0559	1
WILLIAMS BENNIE M	MAJ	0-1341737	0266	1
WILLIAMS BERNARD E	MAJ	0-1639816	0160	1
WILLIAMS BERNARD O	MAJ	0-0976596	1061	1
WILLIAMS BERT A JR	1LT	0-0414884	0545	2
WILLIAMS BERT C	MAJ	0-1182304	1060	1
WILLIAMS BEULAH O	2LT	N-0744421	0645	1
WILLIAMS BRISTOL W	MAJ	0-1549179	1157	1
WILLIAMS BURTON T	1LT	0-0133399	0658	3
WILLIAMS CADINE M	CPT	N-0735039	1148	2
WILLIAMS CARL	CPT	0-1324213	1146	2
WILLIAMS CARL E	LTC	0-2040985	1263	1
WILLIAMS CARL M	2LT	0-0516682	0943	2
WILLIAMS CARLYLE R	LTC	0-0382454	0560	1
WILLIAMS CATHERINE	2LT	N-0772398	0945	1
WILLIAMS CECIL R	CW3	W-2150348	0465	1
WILLIAMS CHARLES A	LTC	0-0363613	0759	1
WILLIAMS CHARLES A	CPT	0-0419076	0944	2
WILLIAMS CHARLES C	CW2	W-2145608	0755	1
WILLIAMS CHARLES E	1LT	0-1594558	0945	2
WILLIAMS CHARLES E	MAJ	0-2096705	0764	1
WILLIAMS CHARLES H	LTC	0-0249952	0966	3
WILLIAMS CHARLES H	CW2	W-2146986	0359	1
WILLIAMS CHARLES L	MAJ	0-1684999	0464	1
WILLIAMS CHARLES R	COL	0-0255895	0261	3
WILLIAMS CHARLES R	LTC	0-0452537	1056	1
WILLIAMS CHARLES S	LTC	0-0431190	0868	3
WILLIAMS CHARLES T	1LT	0-1317458	1046	1
WILLIAMS CHESTER A	LTC	0-0454184	0857	1
WILLIAMS CHESTER A	CW2	W-2104594	0845	2
WILLIAMS CLARENCE V	MAJ	0-0165331	0648	3
WILLIAMS CLARK E	CPT	0-1109753	1047	2
WILLIAMS CLAUDE A	MAJ	0-2262611	0765	1
WILLIAMS CLIFFORD J	CPT	0-1286220	1051	2
WILLIAMS CLYDE J	CPT	0-0108580	0540	1
WILLIAMS CORAN L JR	MAJ	0-1116488	0760	1
WILLIAMS CRAMER L	LTC	0-1824948	1268	2
WILLIAMS CURTIS F	MAJ	0-2035745	0456	1
WILLIAMS DALE E	LTC	0-1289661	0960	1
WILLIAMS DALE V	CW2	W-2151403	0556	1
WILLIAMS DAN	MAJ	0-1017251	0757	1
WILLIAMS DAN W	MAJ	0-1690915	0361	1

NAME	GRADE	SVC NO	DATE RET MO YR	RET CODE
WILLIAMS DANIEL C	MAJ	0-2018451	0563	1
WILLIAMS DARRELL A	MAJ	0-0371765	0768	3
WILLIAMS DAVIC	CPT	0-?323376	0848	2
WILLIAMS DAVIC C	MAJ	0-2263691	1165	1
WILLIAMS DAVID F	MAJ	0-0318838	0446	2
WILLIAMS DAVIC E	CW4	W-2143345	1266	1
WILLIAMS DAVID J JR	LTC	0-0174178	0944	2
WILLIAMS DAVIC T	CPT	0-1311459	0266	1
WILLIAMS DENNIS S	WO1	W-2109767	1046	1
WILLIAMS DEXTER B	LTC	0-0906689	0863	3
WILLIAMS DON C	CW2	W-3200431	0868	1
WILLIAMS DON L	MAJ	0-0269693	1067	3
WILLIAMS DONALD B	CPT	0-0227935	0862	3
WILLIAMS DONALD D	CPT	0-1694391	1045	2
WILLIAMS DONALD V	WO1	W-2105356	0958	1
WILLIAMS DONALD W	COL	0-0302100	0761	1
WILLIAMS DORIS H	1LT	N-0720391	0244	1
WILLIAMS DUDLEY	LTC	0-0127865	0158	1
WILLIAMS DUDLEY M	COL	0-2047541	0865	3
WILLIAMS DWIGHT L	LTC	0-0130732	0753	3
WILLIAMS EARL E	MAJ	0-1107759	0946	2
WILLIAMS EARL J	CW3	W-2203307	0965	1
WILLIAMS EARL R	LTC	0-0383356	0461	1
WILLIAMS EARL T	LTC	0-1541339	0461	1
WILLIAMS EARLE B	COL	0-0244570	0962	3
WILLIAMS EDWARD	CPT	0-0110937	0454	3
WILLIAMS EDWARD B	1LT	0-1012182	0846	2
WILLIAMS EDWARD D	CPT	0-0997090	0467	2
WILLIAMS EDWARD E	LTC	0-0206932	0157	3
WILLIAMS EDWARD F JR	CPT	0-1917790	0764	1
WILLIAMS EDWARD H	MAJ	0-2263394	0263	1
WILLIAMS EDWIN E	MAJ	0-0968265	1062	1
WILLIAMS EDWIN L	CW3	W-2203336	1167	1
WILLIAMS EFFIE F	CPT	N-0764109	1047	1
WILLIAMS ELBERT B SR	CW4	W-2142213	0462	1
WILLIAMS ELLIOTTE J	COL	0-1533233	0568	1
WILLIAMS ELTON V	1LT	0-1647332	1061	1
WILLIAMS ELWOOD E	CPT	0-1003350	0660	1
WILLIAMS EMORY L	MAJ	0-0330802	1056	1
WILLIAMS ERNEST E	CW2	W-2150107	0164	1
WILLIAMS ERNEST E	CW2	W-2205549	0161	1
WILLIAMS ERNEST F JR	MAJ	0-1874753	0466	1
WILLIAMS ERNEST M	LTC	0-1310328	1268	2
WILLIAMS EUGENE H	CPT	0-1999120	0763	2
WILLIAMS EUGENE V	MAJ	0-1331124	1064	1
WILLIAMS EVAN A JR	CPT	0-1040066	0661	1
WILLIAMS EZRA M	LTC	0-0375357	0761	1
WILLIAMS FRANCIS H	MAJ	0-0259131	0668	3
WILLIAMS FRANCIS R	LTC	0-1645705	0566	1
WILLIAMS FRANK E	2LT	0-1297630	1144	2
WILLIAMS FRANK F	MAJ	0-2017319	0665	1
WILLIAMS FRANK M	MAJ	0-0114505	0152	3
WILLIAMS FRANK M	LTC	0-0265083	0364	3
WILLIAMS FRANK M	MAJ	0-0276754	0258	3
WILLIAMS FRANK M	CPT	0-1305360	0947	1
WILLIAMS FRED E	2LT	0-1286750	0145	2
WILLIAMS FREDDIE M	CPT	0-1540898	0259	1
WILLIAMS FREDERICK	MAJ	0-0465613	0645	2
WILLIAMS FREDERICK	MAJ	0-1646111	1154	1
WILLIAMS FREDERICK	CW3	W-2142619	0363	1
WILLIAMS GARLAND H	COL	0-0197966	0264	3
WILLIAMS GARNET C	LTC	0-0289398	1040	2
WILLIAMS GARVIN D	LTC	0-0222596	0149	3
WILLIAMS GEORGE C	MAJ	0-2263283	1061	1
WILLIAMS GEORGE E	CPT	0-0497416	0447	2
WILLIAMS GEORGE F	CPT	0-1186963	0657	1
WILLIAMS GEORGE F	1LT	0-1298327	0347	2
WILLIAMS GEORGE H	LTC	0-1580505	0761	1
WILLIAMS GEORGE H JR	LTC	0-0450506	0758	1
WILLIAMS GEORGE J	COL	0-0261070	0462	1
WILLIAMS GEORGE JR	MAJ	0-0502387	0954	1
WILLIAMS GEORGE JR	LTC	0-1548164	0561	1
WILLIAMS GEORGE K	CPT	0-2035997	0460	1
WILLIAMS GEORGE L	MAJ	0-1590265	1064	1
WILLIAMS GEORGE T	MAJ	0-0488365	0156	1

NAME	GRADE	SVC NO	DATE RET MO YR	RET CODE
WILLIAMS GEORGE W	CPT	0-0538231	0646	2
WILLIAMS GEORGE W	MAJ	0-0974553	0962	1
WILLIAMS GERALD O	MAJ	0-1165054	1046	2
WILLIAMS GIBSON	MAJ	0-2265111	0366	1
WILLIAMS GILBERT M	2LT	0-1587732	0345	2
WILLIAMS GILBERT W	MAJ	0-0232790	0546	2
WILLIAMS GLENN B	MAJ	0-0259487	0964	3
WILLIAMS GLENN C	COL	0-0100386	0552	3
WILLIAMS GLYNN W	CPT	0-1304299	0263	2
WILLIAMS GORDON E	LTC	0-1638795	0768	3
WILLIAMS GOVIE L	1LT	0-0460021	0845	2
WILLIAMS GUS	1LT	0-1913981	0327	1
WILLIAMS GUSS E	LTC	0-1172338	1167	1
WILLIAMS GUY M	COL	0-0145910	0857	3
WILLIAMS GWENDOLYN	MAJ	L-0402041	0168	1
WILLIAMS HAROLD B	LTC	0-1294401	0857	1
WILLIAMS HAROLD D	1LT	0-0381847	1044	2
WILLIAMS HAROLD E	LTC	0-1031852	0166	1
WILLIAMS HAROLD E	2LT	0-2006852	0846	2
WILLIAMS HAROLD F	CPT	0-1555156	0965	1
WILLIAMS HAROLD F	CW3	W-2148670	1065	1
WILLIAMS HAROLD H	MAJ	0-0501708	0349	1
WILLIAMS HAROLD L	CPT	0-0500660	1145	2
WILLIAMS HAROLD L	MAJ	0-0967658	0664	2
WILLIAMS HAROLD O	LTC	0-0257497	0262	3
WILLIAMS HAROLD T	LTC	0-0261979	0866	3
WILLIAMS HARRY G	COL	0-0253746	0153	3
WILLIAMS HARRY K	CPT	0-0548872	1046	2
WILLIAMS HARRY L	CPT	0-0500284	0550	1
WILLIAMS HARRY L	1LT	0-1053877	1045	2
WILLIAMS HARRY M	CPT	0-1341611	0456	1
WILLIAMS HARRY N	CW3	W-2144864	0961	1
WILLIAMS HARVEY J	MAJ	0-0283208	1067	3
WILLIAMS HARVEY V	LTC	0-0137291	1051	3
WILLIAMS HASKELL G	MAJ	0-2014554	1263	1
WILLIAMS HENRY D	COL	0-0362695	0861	1
WILLIAMS HENRY E E	CW3	RW-2151937	1064	1
WILLIAMS HENRY E JR	LTC	0-0258612	1267	3
WILLIAMS HENRY W	COL	0-0232072	1163	3
WILLIAMS HERBERT A	CW2	W-2143487	0360	1
WILLIAMS HERBERT L	MAJ	0-1105724	0266	1
WILLIAMS HERBERT M	MAJ	0-1636831	0364	1
WILLIAMS HIRAM W	CW4	W-2119760	0261	1
WILLIAMS HOMER A	CPT	0-0301573	0450	1
WILLIAMS HOMER O	CW3	W-2146622	0263	1
WILLIAMS HOMER P	CW4	W-2145858	1061	1
WILLIAMS HORACE S	CPT	0-1999764	1053	1
WILLIAMS HOWARD	COL	0-0275383	0764	3
WILLIAMS HOWARD B	CW4	W-2108980	1154	1
WILLIAMS HOWARD F	LTC	0-0286065	1061	3
WILLIAMS HOWARD K	MAJ	0-2035844	0363	1
WILLIAMS HOWARD M	COL	0-1280117	1067	3
WILLIAMS HOWARD W	CW2	W-2148423	1060	1
WILLIAMS HUBERT H	CPT	0-1796892	0755	1
WILLIAMS HUBERT M	CPT	0-1541956	0349	2
WILLIAMS HUGH R	CPT	0-0218997	0347	1
WILLIAMS IRA	CW4	W-2123198	0363	1
WILLIAMS IRENE R	MAJ	N-0702342	0560	1
WILLIAMS IRWIN T	CW2	W-2205952	0363	1
WILLIAMS J C S	CW3	W-2147593	0965	1
WILLIAMS J O	CW2	W-2148401	0559	1
WILLIAMS J STEWART	MAJ	0-0456046	0546	2
WILLIAMS JACK	LTC	0-0452725	1058	1
WILLIAMS JACK A	1LT	0-1030538	0745	2
WILLIAMS JACK B	LTC	0-0918692	0768	3
WILLIAMS JACK C	LTC	0-0450521	0657	1
WILLIAMS JACK G	CPT	0-1574559	1045	2
WILLIAMS JACK L	LTC	0-1050140	0865	1
WILLIAMS JAMES	CPT	0-1824261	0658	2
WILLIAMS JAMES B	2LT	0-1319696	0244	2
WILLIAMS JAMES B	MAJ	0-2024438	1059	1
WILLIAMS JAMES C	LTC	0-0301105	0665	3
WILLIAMS JAMES C	MAJ	0-0886899	1159	1
WILLIAMS JAMES C	MAJ	0-1329654	0157	1
WILLIAMS JAMES O	LTC	0-0366830	0263	1

NAME	GRADE	SVC NO	DATE RET MO YR	RET CODE
WILLIAMS JAMES D	LTC	0-1324215	1062	1
WILLIAMS JAMES E	CPT	0-0250083	0865	3
WILLIAMS JAMES H	MAJ	0-1799925	1262	1
WILLIAMS JAMES H	LTC	0-1949249	0164	1
WILLIAMS JAMES H	MAJ	0-2047541	1162	1
WILLIAMS JAMES J	MAJ	0-1919071	0868	1
WILLIAMS JAMES M	2LT	0-1823678	0966	2
WILLIAMS JAMES R	MAJ	0-1703924	1054	1
WILLIAMS JAMES R	MAJ	0-1920289	1165	1
WILLIAMS JAMES S	COL	0-0163259	0256	3
WILLIAMS JAMES T	MAJ	0-0970837	1161	1
WILLIAMS JAMES T	CPT	0-1287801	0950	2
WILLIAMS JEFFERSON	CPT	0-1288986	1045	2
WILLIAMS JESSIE E	LTC	0-1115156	0762	1
WILLIAMS JOEL L	CPT	0-1945979	0448	2
WILLIAMS JOHN	CPT	0-0502355	1045	2
WILLIAMS JOHN	MAJ	0-1926821	0567	1
WILLIAMS JOHN H	CW2	W-2122222	0647	1
WILLIAMS JOHN C	COL	0-0239922	0263	3
WILLIAMS JOHN C	MAJ	0-0283591	0350	1
WILLIAMS JOHN C	1LT	0-1596856	1045	2
WILLIAMS JOHN C JR	CW4	W-2145851	0868	1
WILLIAMS JOHN D	LTC	0-0285983	0967	3
WILLIAMS JOHN F	COL	0-0172422	1060	3
WILLIAMS JOHN F	COL	0-0143669	0154	3
WILLIAMS JOHN F	LTC	0-1165263	0566	2
WILLIAMS JOHN F	LTC	0-1946639	0264	1
WILLIAMS JOHN J	COL	0-0201995	1146	2
WILLIAMS JOHN M	MAJ	0-1575638	0-48	2
WILLIAMS JOHN R	1LT	0-1292435	0445	2
WILLIAMS JOHN T	WO1	W-2115679	0547	1
WILLIAMS JOHN W	CPT	0-0355041	0945	2
WILLIAMS JOSEPH B	MAJ	0-1578047	0953	1
WILLIAMS JOSEPH H	MAJ	0-2055206	0358	1
WILLIAMS JOSEPH J	2LT	0-1329547	0446	2
WILLIAMS JOSLYN J JR	1LT	0-1884102	0154	2
WILLIAMS KATHRYN L	1LT	N-0770044	0747	1
WILLIAMS KENDALL E	CW3	W-2153273	0464	2
WILLIAMS KENNETH	MAJ	0-1313334	0962	1
WILLIAMS KENNETH L	MAJ	0-1534190	1057	1
WILLIAMS KERMIT C	CPT	0-1595271	0457	1
WILLIAMS KRESS R	COL	0-0254933	1166	3
WILLIAMS L J JR	LTC	0-1541184	0161	1
WILLIAMS L J	2LT	0-1914121	0548	1
WILLIAMS L KEMPER	B G	0-0125140	0648	3
WILLIAMS LELAND H	LTC	0-0357205	0960	1
WILLIAMS LEO C	WO1	W-2119341	0349	1
WILLIAMS LEONARD B	LTC	0-1310935	0668	1
WILLIAMS LEONARD E	CPT	0-1031284	0546	2
WILLIAMS LEONARD L	CPT	0-1305149	0747	2
WILLIAMS LEROY	1LT	0-1001276	0145	2
WILLIAMS LESLIE E	COL	0-0245097	0164	3
WILLIAMS LESTER B	LTC	0-0343425	0461	1
WILLIAMS LEWIS H	LTC	0-1949979	0166	1
WILLIAMS LEWIS O	LTC	0-0905629	1061	3
WILLIAMS LEWIS S	LTC	0-0137946	0-53	3
WILLIAMS LLOYD A	MAJ	0-0453070	1062	1
WILLIAMS LLOYD J	CPT	0-2262558	0762	2
WILLIAMS LONNIE B	LTC	0-0430190	1149	1
WILLIAMS LOREN L	MAJ	0-0231519	0159	3
WILLIAMS LOUGENE	CW2	W-2209371	1263	1
WILLIAMS LOUIE L	LTC	0-1635483	0358	1
WILLIAMS LOUIS F	LTC	0-0453832	0761	1
WILLIAMS LOWELL C	CW4	W-2006362	0365	3
WILLIAMS LOWELL E	MAJ	0-1053884	0761	1
WILLIAMS MARCELLIUS	1LT	0-1894955	0568	1
WILLIAMS MARK F	MAJ	0-0309986	0446	2
WILLIAMS MARTIN J	LTC	0-1946640	0161	1
WILLIAMS MARY E	1LT	N-0751174	0945	1
WILLIAMS MASON L JR	LTC	0-1045640	1065	1
WILLIAMS MAURICE M	LTC	0-1080760	0763	1
WILLIAMS MAX D	CW2	W-3100524	0967	1
WILLIAMS MAXWELL L	MAJ	0-1552420	0858	1
WILLIAMS MILLARD J	LTC	0-0242209	0766	3
WILLIAMS MORRIS C	MAJ	0-1016954	0566	1
WILLIAMS MORRIS F	MAJ	0-2026340	1061	1
WILLIAMS MYRON E	MAJ	0-0336046	0661	1
WILLIAMS NELLIE K	MAJ	L-0904015	1063	3
WILLIAMS NELSON B	CPT	0-1290169	1045	2
WILLIAMS NEWTON A	MAJ	0-0369335	0555	1
WILLIAMS NORMAN W	1LT	0-1324607	0248	2
WILLIAMS ODELL D	COL	0-1100395	0761	1
WILLIAMS OK G	MAJ	0-1169793	1160	1
WILLIAMS OLIVER D	COL	0-0258258	0258	1
WILLIAMS OMER E	LTC	0-1798429	0966	1
WILLIAMS ONIE O	MAJ	0-0284702	0645	2
WILLIAMS OSCAR A JR	CPT	0-0520144	0147	2
WILLIAMS PALMER C	LTC	0-0171836	1054	3
WILLIAMS PAUL L	CPT	0-0530455	0546	2
WILLIAMS PAUL S	CW3	W-2148894	1162	1
WILLIAMS PHILLIP E	COL	0-0235418	0465	3
WILLIAMS PHYLLIS J	2LT	N-0771595	0944	1
WILLIAMS PRESTON A	1LT	0-0509881	1050	1
WILLIAMS PRICE W	MAJ	0-0149605	0950	3
WILLIAMS QUINTON A	1LT	0-2007366	0353	2
WILLIAMS RALPH C	LTC	0-0336515	1061	3
WILLIAMS RALPH C	1LT	0-1311953	0350	1
WILLIAMS RALPH D	MAJ	0-0988683	1162	1
WILLIAMS RAY E	LTC	0-0238228	0161	3
WILLIAMS RAYMOND E	LTC	0-0241369	0756	3
WILLIAMS RAYMOND J	1LT	0-1798537	0655	1
WILLIAMS RAYMOND J	CW3	W-2210723	0868	1
WILLIAMS RAYMOND L	1LT	0-2025187	0247	2
WILLIAMS REIMAN K	MAJ	0-1594427	0767	1
WILLIAMS RICHARD H	CPT	0-0233212	1159	3
WILLIAMS RICHARD O	1LT	0-1913996	0738	1
WILLIAMS ROBERT	LTC	0-2008363	0767	1
WILLIAMS ROBERT C	LTC	0-0259678	1064	3
WILLIAMS ROBERT C	LTC	0-0947674	0867	1
WILLIAMS ROBERT C	CPT	0-1798538	0353	2
WILLIAMS ROBERT C	CW2	W-2145006	1159	1
WILLIAMS ROBERT C JR	MAJ	0-1540895	1264	1
WILLIAMS ROBERT D	MAJ	0-0987374	0565	1
WILLIAMS ROBERT O	CPT	0-1313006	0146	2
WILLIAMS ROBERT D	CW2	W-2210746	0766	1
WILLIAMS ROBERT F	COL	0-0157739	0357	3
WILLIAMS ROBERT H	LTC	0-0362706	1164	1
WILLIAMS ROBERT H	MAJ	0-1301738	0562	1
WILLIAMS ROBERT J	MAJ	0-1014096	1163	1
WILLIAMS ROBERT K	LTC	0-1101719	1162	1
WILLIAMS ROBERT L	1LT	0-1042743	0144	2
WILLIAMS ROBERT L	CW3	W-3150363	0767	1
WILLIAMS ROBERT M	2LT	0-1016082	0145	2
WILLIAMS ROBERT M	CPT	0-1110347	0645	2
WILLIAMS ROBERT W	LTC	0-0398417	0660	1
WILLIAMS ROBERT W	CPT	0-1700202	0845	2
WILLIAMS ROGER B	LTC	0-0157861	0857	3
WILLIAMS ROGER D	COL	0-0216449	1163	3
WILLIAMS ROY E	MAJ	0-0990942	0368	1
WILLIAMS ROY F	CPT	0-0450522	0358	1
WILLIAMS RUFUS E	CW4	W-2115085	0153	1
WILLIAMS RUPERT E	LTC	0-0129457	0450	3
WILLIAMS RUSSELL H	MAJ	0-1926098	0768	1
WILLIAMS SAMUEL E	LTC	0-0291835	1164	3
WILLIAMS SAMUEL H	LTC	0-0219982	0645	2
WILLIAMS SHEDRICK M	WO1	W-2144460	0856	1
WILLIAMS SHRABLE D	LTC	0-0445033	0663	1
WILLIAMS SIDNEY A	COL	0-0354313	1263	3
WILLIAMS SIDNEY J	MAJ	0-2208466	0965	1
WILLIAMS STANLEY E	MAJ	0-1821947	0261	1
WILLIAMS STANLEY M	CW2	W-2149144	0762	1
WILLIAMS STARLIN I	1LT	0-1995539	1147	2
WILLIAMS STELLA E	2LT	N-0700804	1038	1
WILLIAMS THADDEUS E	CPT	0-0486429	1045	2
WILLIAMS THELMA B	MAJ	N-0762460	0864	1
WILLIAMS THOMAS A	CPT	0-2050695	0856	1
WILLIAMS THOMAS C	MAJ	0-1100396	0853	2
WILLIAMS THOMAS C	CW2	W-2147202	0755	1
WILLIAMS THOMAS C JR	LTC	0-1296461	1163	2
WILLIAMS THOMAS D	CW4	W-2109193	1057	1
WILLIAMS THOMAS E	MAJ	0-1587023	0459	1
WILLIAMS THOMAS J	CPT	0-0387003	0845	2
WILLIAMS THOMAS J	1LT	0-0965988	0558	1
WILLIAMS THOMAS M	LTC	0-0235053	0457	1
WILLIAMS THOMAS M	LTC	0-0252153	0166	3
WILLIAMS THOMAS M	LTC	0-0289485	0361	2
WILLIAMS THOMAS M JR	LTC	0-1330994	1068	1
WILLIAMS TRACY	MAJ	0-0506976	0457	1
WILLIAMS TROY	WO1	W-2144513	0760	1
WILLIAMS TROY	CW2	W-2147145	0459	2
WILLIAMS TURNER N	1LT	0-0429111	0546	2
WILLIAMS VERNARD F	CW3	W-2114473	0457	2
WILLIAMS VERNON S	MAJ	0-1105273	0264	1
WILLIAMS VIRGIL B	COL	0-0194139	0-51	3
WILLIAMS VIRGIL C	LTC	0-0394262	0660	1
WILLIAMS VIRGIL E	CW2	W-2145046	0762	1
WILLIAMS VIRGIL H	COL	0-0244104	0458	1
WILLIAMS W R JR	CPT	0-0354069	1059	1
WILLIAMS WALTER	LTC	0-0351052	0759	1
WILLIAMS WALTER A	LTC	0-0235693	0358	3
WILLIAMS WALTER B	LTC	0-0288682	1158	3
WILLIAMS WALTER D	LTC	0-2036846	0566	1
WILLIAMS WALTER H	CPT	0-1314356	0747	2
WILLIAMS WALTER M	COL	0-0286775	0247	2
WILLIAMS WALTER W	CW2	W-3200275	1165	1
WILLIAMS WENTWORTH	COL	0-0124936	0955	3
WILLIAMS WESLEY E	LTC	0-0452313	0461	1
WILLIAMS WILBURN	CW3	W-2152363	1262	1
WILLIAMS WILEY W JR	CW2	W-2211694	0867	1
WILLIAMS WILL J	MAJ	0-0453389	0-53	1
WILLIAMS WILLARD C	1LT	0-1031216	0445	2
WILLIAMS WILLIAM A	LTC	0-0403292	0962	1
WILLIAMS WILLIAM A	LTC	0-1648244	0268	1
WILLIAMS WILLIAM B	CPT	0-0379493	0446	2
WILLIAMS WILLIAM E	COL	0-0266046	1054	3
WILLIAMS WILLIAM E	2LT	0-1593396	0545	2
WILLIAMS WILLIAM F	LTC	0-0342517	0359	1
WILLIAMS WILLIAM F	LTC	0-0480721	0262	1
WILLIAMS WILLIAM G	CPT	0-0547402		2
WILLIAMS WILLIAM H	COL	0-0335927	0556	3
WILLIAMS WILLIAM H	MAJ	0-1179247	0462	1
WILLIAMS WILLIAM H	MAJ	0-2265920	1268	1
WILLIAMS WILLIAM J	MAJ	0-1874870	0963	1
WILLIAMS WILLIAM J	CW3	W-2207637	0966	1
WILLIAMS WILLIAM L	LTC	0-0259448	1264	3
WILLIAMS WILLIAM O	LTC	0-1001277	0658	1
WILLIAMS WILLIAM T	COL	0-0386097	0768	3
WILLIAMS WILLIAM T	CW4	W-2142620	0267	1
WILLIAMS WILLIE	1LT	0-1178670	0546	2
WILLIAMS WILLIE C	CW2	W-2145263	1154	1
WILLIAMS WILLIE F	2LT	0-1651256	0552	1
WILLIAMS WILLIE L	CW3	W-2148630	0863	1
WILLIAMS WILSON C	COL	0-0213651	1058	3
WILLIAMS WINFORD N	CW2	W-3151383	1067	1
WILLIAMS WINTHROP W	LTC	0-0119434	0560	3
WILLIAMS ZACK R JR	MAJ	0-1294053	0464	1
WILLIAMSON ADRIAN	COL	0-0103062	0554	3
WILLIAMSON ADRIAN P	CPT	0-2102784	0862	2
WILLIAMSON ALFRED S	LTC	0-0145840	0655	3
WILLIAMSON ALFRED S	1LT	0-1695661	0560	1
WILLIAMSON ARTHUR M	MAJ	0-1116194	0763	2
WILLIAMSON BUEL A SR	LTC	0-0268458	0555	2
WILLIAMSON CARMEN A	LTC	0-0406592	0662	1
WILLIAMSON CHESTER B	2LT	0-0494652	0145	2
WILLIAMSON CLARENCE	LTC	0-0327883	0346	2
WILLIAMSON CLARENCE	CW3	W-2149803	0963	1
WILLIAMSON CYRUS M	1LT	0-0547403	1045	2
WILLIAMSON DALE F	CW4	W-2151755	0863	1
WILLIAMSON DANNIE A	CPT	0-5420362	0868	2
WILLIAMSON DOW E	2LT	0-1294585	0544	2
WILLIAMSON EARL	CW2	W-2141874	0559	1
WILLIAMSON EDWARD J	LTC	0-0384916	0864	1
WILLIAMSON EDWIN A	MAJ	0-0378213	0848	2
WILLIAMSON ELVIN G	LTC	0-0487590	0858	1
WILLIAMSON EUGENE R	LTC	0-1049024	0662	1
WILLIAMSON FORREST R	CW3	W-2151032	0559	1
WILLIAMSON GEORGE P	MAJ	0-1305362	0165	1
WILLIAMSON GEORGE W	CW2	W-2148424	0766	1
WILLIAMSON GLYNN E	LTC	0-0281189	1067	3
WILLIAMSON HARRY H	MAJ	0-0504477	0350	1
WILLIAMSON HAZEL R	1LT	N-0763532	0546	1
WILLIAMSON HENRY B	WO1	W-2108606	0646	1
WILLIAMSON HOWELL E	LTC	0-2000966	0766	1
WILLIAMSON J C	1LT	0-1703055	0245	2
WILLIAMSON J C	WO1	W-2129525	1157	2
WILLIAMSON JAMES C	MAJ	0-1588373	0363	1
WILLIAMSON JOE E	CW4	W-2144577	0364	1
WILLIAMSON JOHN E	MAJ	0-1332555	0865	1
WILLIAMSON JOHN L	LTC	0-0483117	0252	2
WILLIAMSON JOSEPH F	LTC	0-0188164	0953	3
WILLIAMSON JULIAN S	MAJ	0-0371233	0267	3
WILLIAMSON LINDSAY	LTC	0-1845845	0766	3
WILLIAMSON MARION	B G	0-0196761	0762	3
WILLIAMSON MARION A	MAJ	N-0751313	0563	2
WILLIAMSON MAURICE	CPT	0-0274597	1144	2
WILLIAMSON MELVIN J	1LT	0-1030539	1045	2
WILLIAMSON MORTON T	MAJ	0-0359514	0545	2
WILLIAMSON NORMAN J	MAJ	0-0454936	0962	1
WILLIAMSON NORMAN L	LTC	0-0551554	0368	1
WILLIAMSON ROBERT C	LTC	0-1548339	0757	1
WILLIAMSON ROBERT C	MAJ	0-2040717	0756	1
WILLIAMSON ROBERT E	1LT	0-0386223	1144	2
WILLIAMSON ROBERT E	LTC	0-0445061	1053	2
WILLIAMSON ROBERT N	MAJ	0-1049032	1160	1
WILLIAMSON ROLAND F	MAJ	0-0275328	0965	3
WILLIAMSON ROSCOE E	LTC	0-0283698	1266	3
WILLIAMSON RUFUS S	LTC	0-0151735	0757	3
WILLIAMSON S E	CW2	W-2152086	0555	1
WILLIAMSON SAMUEL D	CW3	W-2205437	0861	1
WILLIAMSON SHIRLEY E	2LT	0-1010723	0544	2
WILLIAMSON STEPHEN A	LTC	0-0102077	0656	1
WILLIAMSON STEPHEN E	2LT	0-1327067	1145	2
WILLIAMSON SYLVESTER	MAJ	0-0425738	1262	1
WILLIAMSON THOMAS	CPT	0-0449019	0347	2
WILLIAMSON THOMAS L	LTC	0-0202612	0153	3
WILLIAMSON THOMAS S	LTC	0-1000890	0862	1
WILLIAMSON WARD W	MAJ	0-2036459	0260	1
WILLIAMSON WAYNE C	LTC	0-0331120	0261	1
WILLIAMSON WILLIAM A	LTC	0-1308743	0466	3
WILLIAMSON WILLIAM E	1LT	0-1554116	0850	2
WILLIAMSON WILLIAM G	LTC	0-0402560	0760	1
WILLIAMSON WILLIAM P	CW2	W-2210136	0365	1
WILLIAMSTON HOMER	CW3	W-2141494	0461	1
WILLIARD WILLIAM C	LTC	0-1175010	0561	1
WILLIBY IVOR J	LTC	0-0336371	0948	2
WILLIE LEON A	MAJ	0-1287635	1160	1
WILLIE WALTER G	CPT	0-0922080	0845	2
WILLIFORD HENRY N	LTC	0-0450523	1056	1
WILLIFORD ROBERT B	COL	0-0354302	1264	3
WILLIG SAMUEL	LTC	0-1945980	1063	3
WILLIMON WALTER E JR	1LT	0-1306348	0545	2
WILLING CARL H C	MAJ	0-1302579	0361	1
WILLINGHAM ALBERT J	CW3	W-2141495	0960	1
WILLINGHAM BURTON A	CW3	W-2149138	0567	1
WILLINGHAM OSCAR B	CPT	0-0378834	0246	2
WILLINGHAM T R	CW3	W-2109073	0556	1
WILLIS ALLEN H	CPT	0-1040328	0647	2
WILLIS ALVIE P	CPT	0-0479704	1048	1
WILLIS AUBREY O	CW2	W-2210995	0765	1
WILLIS BILLY R	CW3	W-2149687	0964	1
WILLIS BURTON D	COL	0-0256871	1057	3
WILLIS CARL P	MAJ	0-2024432	0759	2
WILLIS CHARLES A	B G	0-0357988	0766	3
WILLIS CHARLES A	MAJ	0-4074764	0468	1
WILLIS CHARLES D	CPT	0-1310007	0948	2
WILLIS CHARLES E	MAJ	0-1303978	1062	1
WILLIS CHARLES G	1LT	0-0478881	0946	1
WILLIS CHARLES R	MAJ	0-2033243	0564	1
WILLIS DEWEY J	LTC	0-0250729	0659	3
WILLIS DILLARD L	CPT	0-1289844	0846	1

NAME	GRADE	SVC NO	DATE RET MO YR	RET CODE
WILLIS DOLMAN W	1LT	O-0100725	0257	3
WILLIS EUGENE	LTC	O-0313225	1162	1
WILLIS FRED L	LTC	O-0468913	1167	3
WILLIS GEORGE	CPT	O-1001708	0457	1
WILLIS GEORGE C JR	MAJ	O-1054453	0650	1
WILLIS GEORGE W	CW2	RW-2210422	0262	1
WILLIS HARRY R	1LT	O-0108408	0137	1
WILLIS HENRY J	LTC	O-0375009	1160	1
WILLIS HETTIE F	MAJ	N-0727793	0164	2
WILLIS HOMER A	CW2	W-2104600	0554	1
WILLIS HOUSTON P	MAJ	O-1551338	0760	1
WILLIS HOWARD L	CW3	W-2206475	1065	1
WILLIS JACK H	CW2	W-2151884	0563	1
WILLIS JAMES B	CPT	O-0386214	0844	2
WILLIS JAMES E	MAJ	O-1050518	0766	1
WILLIS JAMES E	MAJ	O-1114807	0959	1
WILLIS JAMES E	CW2	W-2214046	0568	1
WILLIS JESSE M	CPT	O-0299097	0145	2
WILLIS JOE C	CPT	O-2263663	0562	1
WILLIS JOHN A	LTC	O-0665494	0567	1
WILLIS JOHN C JR	LTC	O-1651230	0866	1
WILLIS MERRITT M	1LT	O-0391135	0945	2
WILLIS NEWCOMB M	WO1	W-2135955	0260	1
WILLIS OSCAR W	LTC	O-2020456	0468	1
WILLIS PAUL W	CPT	O-1036800	0648	2
WILLIS RALPH M	CPT	O-1542125	0446	2
WILLIS RAY R	2LT	O-0545831	0545	2
WILLIS RAYMOND F	MAJ	O-1174744	0159	1
WILLIS ROBERT	WO1	W-2120621	0944	2
WILLIS ROBERT E	MAJ	O-0483842	0253	2
WILLIS THOMAS L JR	CW2	W-2210123	0864	2
WILLIS WALDO	COL	O-0173333	0852	3
WILLIS WESTON H	M G	O-0289949	0367	3
WILLIS WILLIAM E	COL	O-0291451	0366	1
WILLIS WILLIAM H	COL	O-0238355	0565	3
WILLIS WOODROW	CW2	W-2147974	1158	2
WILLISTON EDWARD M	2LT	O-0396090	1144	2
WILLISTON JOHN D	LTC	O-0410792	0762	1
WILLITT VICTOR C	LTC	O-1638801	0667	3
WILLMAN WALTER K	LTC	O-0127861	0556	3
WILLMORE CARL	LTC	O-0362685	1264	3
WILLMS HENRY C	1LT	O-0443106	0646	2
WILLNER EDDIE H	MAJ	O-1894096	0568	1
WILLOUGHBY CHARLES W	LTC	O-0348936	0260	1
WILLOUGHBY CLEO M	LTC	O-1039803	0763	1
WILLOUGHBY FRANCIS A	CPT	O-1296778	0447	2
WILLOUGHBY FREDERICK	LTC	O-1314861	0662	1
WILLOUGHBY GERALD F	CW3	W-2148225	0764	1
WILLOUGHBY HAROLD J	1LT	O-1290363	1045	2
WILLOUGHBY KENNETH D	COL	O-0252722	0663	3
WILLOUGHBY ROSCOE R	CPT	O-0189302	0454	3
WILLOUGHBY WILLIAM G	MAJ	O-1936380	0966	1
WILLS ALEXANDER	LTC	O-0339090	1265	3
WILLS DAVID H	CPT	O-0937349	0757	1
WILLS DAVID H	MAJ	O-0959282	0965	1
WILLS GERALD J	CW3	W-2209942	1267	1
WILLS HARLAN J	LTC	O-0451195	1160	1
WILLS HAROLD P	LTC	O-0225865	0659	1
WILLS HAROLD P	LTC	O-0269626	0767	3
WILLS HOWARD	LTC	O-1542635	0963	1
WILLS HOWARD C	1LT	O-0297969	0945	2
WILLS MARGARET	1LT	L-0220183	0146	2
WILLS MERLIN V	LTC	O-0237780	0165	3
WILLS OLIVER T	MAJ	O-1686739	0765	1
WILLS RICHARD H	LTC	O-0260219	0368	3
WILLS WILLIAM H	MAJ	O-0888243	0463	1
WILLS WILLIAM L	CPT	O-2263045	0662	1
WILLSON ALLEN F JR	MAJ	O-2202030	0466	1
WILLSON FOY T	CPT	O-1047844	0258	1
WILLSON HARRY S	COL	O-0125434	0556	3
WILLSON STANLEY G	CW3	W-2150228	1161	1
WILLSON VIRGIL A	LTC	O-0173594	0959	3
WILLSON WESLEY W	LTC	O-0232038	1056	3
WILLUMITIS CHARLES M	CW3	W-2200023	0867	3
WILMARTH CARL R	CPT	O-0336755	1045	2
WILMER FREDERIC P	LTC	O-0163200	0961	3
WILMER RICHARD H	COL	O-0114573	1152	3
WILMETH ELWOOD E	LTC	O-1045637	0663	1
WILMORE ALLEN E	LTC	O-1947615	0163	1
WILMORE CHARLES W	COL	O-0288746	0367	3
WILMORE RALPH C	1LT	O-0487829	1144	2
WILMOT BASIL A	1LT	O-2055173	0446	2
WILMOTH LUTHER H	COL	O-0287765	0660	3
WILMUTH GLEN F	2LT	O-0420932	0544	2
WILNER JULIAN P	2LT	O-1543358	0844	2
WILROY WILLIAM E	COL	O-0274705	1068	3
WILSEY LEONARD L	MAJ	O-1996644	1062	1
WILSON A VINCENT	COL	O-0103700	0952	3
WILSON ADA E	1LT	N-0764582	0746	1
WILSON AGNES G	1LT	N-0775183	1045	1
WILSON ALBERT A	COL	O-0411572	1164	2
WILSON ALBERT W	LTC	O-0530759	1166	2
WILSON ALEXANDER	1LT	O-1032256	0148	2
WILSON ALEXANDER	1LT	O-1895024	1045	2
WILSON ALFRED J P	COL	O-0255186	0661	3
WILSON ALLAN C	LTC	O-1050995	1067	1
WILSON ALPHUS	LTC	O-0239227	1163	3
WILSON ALVA H	COL	O-0236076	0266	3
WILSON AMOS P	CPT	O-1765122	0746	2
WILSON ANDREW J	LTC	O-0499710	0556	1
WILSON ARCHIE T	CPT	O-1003351	0946	2
WILSON ARDEN R	MAJ	O-1105274	0656	1
WILSON ARNOLD W	CPT	O-1785266	0754	2
WILSON ARTHUR J	CPT	O-0475278	0749	1
WILSON ARTHUR K	LTC	O-1303979	0962	1
WILSON ARTHUR L	CPT	O-0974419	1060	1
WILSON ARTHUR M III	LTC	O-0222844	1065	3
WILSON ARTHUR N	MAJ	O-1292624	1057	1
WILSON ARTHUR S	1LT	O-1178984	0345	2
WILSON AUBREY A	COL	O-0298288	0159	3
WILSON AUGUSTUS T	LTC	O-0286516	1168	3
WILSON BARLE O	1LT	O-1287099	0256	1
WILSON BENJAMIN F	MAJ	O-1179250	1060	1
WILSON BERT E	LTC	O-1554999	1262	1
WILSON BEVERLEY L	LTC	O-0291568	1068	3
WILSON BOYD T SR	COL	O-1321977	0967	1
WILSON BRYANT	MAJ	O-0113103	0648	3
WILSON BRYON C	WO1	W-2101013	0551	1
WILSON BURGESS R	LTC	O-1303980	0862	1
WILSON C B JR	LTC	O-0372123	1262	2
WILSON CARL A	MAJ	O-0222944	1061	3
WILSON CARL J	MAJ	O-1017940	0561	1
WILSON CARNOT H	CW2	W-2142671	1163	1
WILSON CATO	COL	O-0229150	1164	3
WILSON CHALMERS R JR	COL	O-0270650	0165	3
WILSON CHANDLER W	MAJ	O-0990943	1163	2
WILSON CHARLES A	1LT	O-1543992	0445	2
WILSON CHARLES E	MAJ	O-2018083	0861	1
WILSON CHARLES H	MAJ	O-0275110	0145	2
WILSON CHARLES H	1LT	O-1298474	0462	1
WILSON CHARLES H	CW3	W-2210067	0568	1
WILSON CHARLES J	MAJ	O-0328474	1052	1
WILSON CHARLES JR	1LT	O-1292806	0845	2
WILSON CHARLES L	LTC	O-0414440	0166	1
WILSON CHARLES M	MAJ	O-0982314	0365	1
WILSON CHARLES M	1LT	O-1014948	0346	2
WILSON CHARLES M	CPT	O-1336581	0365	1
WILSON CHARLES N	LTC	O-0387887	0968	3
WILSON CHARLES T	CPT	O-2262923	1063	1
WILSON CHARLES W JR	CPT	O-2016210	1056	1
WILSON CHARLES W SR	LTC	O-2046863	1167	1
WILSON CHARLEY F	MAJ	O-0485079	0949	1
WILSON CHESTER S	MAJ	O-0127619	0648	3
WILSON CHRIS	LTC	O-0317485	0263	3
WILSON CLARENCE C	1LT	O-1823098	0546	2
WILSON CLAUDE	MAJ	O-0969106	0165	1
WILSON CLETUS L	CW3	W-2150125	0562	1
WILSON CLYDE F	CPT	O-0407987	0945	2
WILSON CLYDE P	MAJ	O-4031281	1068	1
WILSON CLYDE P	CW2	W-2210338	0564	1
WILSON CLYDE S	COL	O-0115861	0-51	3
WILSON CLYDE W	LTC	O-1690701	1161	1
WILSON COLWELL P	1LT	O-1949494	0852	2
WILSON CONSON C	COL	O-0147583	0754	3
WILSON COYE M	CPT	O-1002754	0947	2
WILSON DANIEL O JR	LTC	O-1101285	0155	1
WILSON DAVID A	MAJ	O-1535434	0863	1
WILSON DAVID G	LTC	O-0227271	0157	1
WILSON DAWSON P	LTC	O-0257508	0168	3
WILSON DEAN F	MAJ	O-1931598	0666	1
WILSON DEANEL B	MAJ	O-1996514	1059	1
WILSON DELMAR G	LTC	O-0342809	0155	2
WILSON DENNIS R SR	CW2	W-2147576	0861	1
WILSON DENVER W	COL	O-0278007	0158	2
WILSON DEWEY M	1LT	O-0500071	0548	1
WILSON DONALD E	CW2	W-2208648	0864	1
WILSON DONALD J	COL	O-0235927	0259	3
WILSON DONALD R	COL	O-0334668	0368	3
WILSON DONNELL L	MAJ	O-0959341	0665	1
WILSON DOROTHY J	1LT	N-0776763	0549	2
WILSON DOUGLAS	CW3	W-2152076	0763	1
WILSON DUANE C	COL	O-0304346	0860	1
WILSON EARL F	LTC	O-0404551	0761	1
WILSON EARL G	CW2	W-2217328	1268	1
WILSON EARL J	LTC	O-1180772	1061	1
WILSON EARL R	CW3	W-2209432	1067	1
WILSON EARL S	MAJ	O-0157593	0961	3
WILSON EARL S	MAJ	O-1111988	0859	1
WILSON EDGAR H	CW2	W-2142743	0856	1
WILSON EDWARD F	CPT	O-0450950	0146	2
WILSON EDWARD L JR	MAJ	O-1897786	1262	1
WILSON EDWARD S	CPT	O-0251495	0866	3
WILSON EDWARD T	LTC	O-0263707	1166	3
WILSON EDWIN D	CPT	O-0242959	0857	3
WILSON EDWIN W	1LT	O-2018967	0859	1
WILSON EDYTHE E	MAJ	N-0733438	1262	1
WILSON ELEANOR B	MAJ	L-0600290	0163	1
WILSON ELMER L	1LT	O-0493573	0451	1
WILSON ELYMO	LTC	O-1951723	0766	1
WILSON EMBREY E	2LT	O-1895931	0945	2
WILSON ERLING E	LTC	O-0444172	1154	2
WILSON ERNEST P	LTC	O-1090335	1153	1
WILSON EUGENE A	LTC	O-2045156	0963	1
WILSON EUGENE V	CPT	O-1917747	0563	1
WILSON FLAVIUS K	CPT	O-0264090	0464	3
WILSON FLOYD C JR	LTC	O-1184970	0263	1
WILSON FORREST R	MAJ	O-1913394	1065	1
WILSON FOSTER M	MAJ	O-1685111	1044	2
WILSON FRANCIS C	MAJ	O-1103469	1061	1
WILSON FRANCIS K	LTC	O-0190948	0162	3
WILSON FRANK	CW2	W-2112259	0345	2
WILSON FRANK A	LTC	O-0496633	1262	1
WILSON FRANK B	CPT	O-0182660	0255	3
WILSON FRANKLIN B	LTC	O-0505822	1054	1
WILSON FRANKLIN E	1LT	O-1585089	1167	1
WILSON FRED E	CPT	O-0125432	0358	3
WILSON FRED F	COL	O-0253991	0460	1
WILSON FRED E	CW2	W-2115989	0859	2
WILSON FRED T	MAJ	O-0450495	0854	1
WILSON FREDERICK	WO1	W-2109936	0749	1
WILSON GEORGE D	LTC	O-1554500	0662	2
WILSON GEORGE F	MAJ	O-0323897	0246	2
WILSON GEORGE H	COL	O-0311484	0965	3
WILSON GEORGE H	LTC	O-1573309	1266	1
WILSON GEORGE L	COL	O-0302338	0364	1
WILSON GEORGE L	LTC	O-1182489	0467	3
WILSON GEORGE M	CW4	W-2114269	1154	1
WILSON GEORGE O JR	CPT	O-0351495	0145	2
WILSON GEORGE T	MAJ	O-0354233	0960	1
WILSON GEORGE W	1LT	O-1012790	0146	2
WILSON GERARD F	LTC	O-1646710	0967	1
WILSON GLEASON W	LTC	O-1101297	1263	1
WILSON GLENN H	LTC	O-1048646	1265	1
WILSON GLENN O	1LT	O-1320211	0645	2
WILSON GLYN	CPT	O-1307172	0347	2
WILSON GRANT P	CW3	W-2153304	1066	1
WILSON GROVER	COL	O-0267613	0768	3
WILSON HARDY D	CW2	W-2211686	0167	1
WILSON HAROLD A	CPT	O-0503280	0447	1
WILSON HAROLD G	LTC	O-0286681	0260	1
WILSON HAROLD L	LTC	O-0289841	1160	1
WILSON HAROLD P	CPT	O-1845126	0656	1
WILSON HARRY M	COL	O-1685355	0765	3
WILSON HARRY W	CW2	W-2144225	0557	1
WILSON HARTWELL T	1LT	O-1324382	0546	2
WILSON HARVEY E	COL	O-0223362	0756	2
WILSON HARVEY W	CW3	W-2149997	0659	1
WILSON HENRY	MAJ	O-1283707	0257	1
WILSON HENRY	LTC	O-1543256	0161	1
WILSON HENRY R	LTC	O-0358139	0765	1
WILSON HERBERT R	CPT	O-0428959	0944	2
WILSON HERBERT T	LTC	O-0349994	0762	3
WILSON HILLEARD	MAJ	O-0494633	0550	2
WILSON HORACE H	LTC	O-0226529	0365	3
WILSON HOWARD C	1LT	O-1288728	0945	2
WILSON HOWARD E	MAJ	O-1335870	0866	1
WILSON HOWARD W	MAJ	O-1547503	1161	1
WILSON HOYT G	MAJ	O-1639822	0359	1
WILSON HUGH R	MAJ	O-0169070	0460	3
WILSON ISAAC R JR	MAJ	O-0294575	1165	3
WILSON JACK P	CW3	W-2145011	1060	1
WILSON JACK R	CPT	O-2033016	0960	1
WILSON JACQUES H	CPT	O-2034069	0464	1
WILSON JAMES	1LT	O-0503681	0747	1
WILSON JAMES	MAJ	O-1688511	1165	1
WILSON JAMES A	COL	O-0119351	0449	3
WILSON JAMES A	COL	O-0355091	0960	1
WILSON JAMES A	MAJ	O-0359427	1166	3
WILSON JAMES C	MAJ	O-1040250	0759	1
WILSON JAMES D	LTC	O-0349616	0168	3
WILSON JAMES E	COL	O-0190100	1157	3
WILSON JAMES E	MAJ	O-1553387	0265	1
WILSON JAMES E	CW2	W-2145926	0660	1
WILSON JAMES F	LTC	O-0494172	0666	3
WILSON JAMES H	CW2	W-2203367	0461	1
WILSON JAMES L	CW3	W-2142918	0757	1
WILSON JAMES M	CPT	O-0494509	0448	1
WILSON JAMES P	LTC	O-0382479	0457	1
WILSON JAMES R	MAJ	O-0990203	0967	1
WILSON JAMES S	MAJ	O-0251084	0466	3
WILSON JAMES W	LTC	O-1102120	0363	1
WILSON JAMES W	MAJ	O-1919091	0164	1
WILSON JAMES W	MAJ	O-2019113	0162	2
WILSON JAMES W	CW4	W-2112143	1057	1
WILSON JANE E	2LT	N-0700547	0537	1
WILSON JEAN T	2LT	O-0537924	0645	2
WILSON JIM L	2LT	O-0545607	0945	2
WILSON JOHN	CW2	W-2150544	1162	1
WILSON JOHN A	CPT	O-0445375	0246	2
WILSON JOHN A	MAJ	O-1327596	0364	1
WILSON JOHN A JR	LTC	O-0163756	0245	2
WILSON JOHN B	LTC	O-1104452	0869	3
WILSON JOHN C	M G	O-0291915	0365	3
WILSON JOHN D	LTC	O-0238633	0356	3
WILSON JOHN D	MAJ	O-0967342	0563	1
WILSON JOHN E	CPT	O-0173273	0648	3
WILSON JOHN E	1LT	O-0450951	0443	2
WILSON JOHN F	MAJ	O-1541983	1060	1
WILSON JOHN H	CW3	W-2146931	1263	1
WILSON JOHN JR	COL	O-0333868	0865	3
WILSON JOHN K JR	LTC	O-0263632	0859	3
WILSON JOHN M	LTC	O-1534662	1265	1
WILSON JOHN R	LTC	O-0233360	0865	3
WILSON JOHN S JR	LTC	O-1646712	0561	1
WILSON JOHN T	LTC	O-0504428	0157	1
WILSON JOHN T	1LT	O-1169835	114N	2
WILSON JOSEPH C	1LT	O-0445100	0450	2
WILSON JOSEPH E	MAJ	O-0480334	0954	1
WILSON JOSEPH P	2LT	O-1044428	0244	2
WILSON JOSEPH W	COL	O-1100829	0261	1

NAME	GRADE	SVC NO	DATE RET MO YR	RET CODE
WILSON JOSEPH W	CW2	W-2149944	0961	1
WILSON JULIAN C	CW2	W-2209090	0860	1
WILSON KEENE N	COL	0-1290464	0768	1
WILSON KENNETH W	1LT	0-1296094	0346	2
WILSON KENT R	MAJ	0-0177543	0455	3
WILSON LAURENCE F	LTC	0-0192480	0559	3
WILSON LAWRENCE F	2LT	0-1325050	0357	1
WILSON LAWRENCE C	CW4	W-2142732	0666	1
WILSON LAWRENCE D	MAJ	0-1314702	0966	1
WILSON LAWRENCE R	LTC	0-0422641	0161	1
WILSON LEROY L	MAJ	0-0487447	0367	3
WILSON LESTER R	COL	0-0249109	0959	3
WILSON LEWIS B	CPT	0-0415364	0846	2
WILSON LEWIS D	LTC	0-0405772	0860	1
WILSON LEWIS G	LTC	0-0234752	0665	3
WILSON LLOYD A	MAJ	0-0324988	0347	2
WILSON LLOYD A	MAJ	0-0390060	1163	1
WILSON LOGAN E	MAJ	0-1552828	1057	1
WILSON LOUIS C	CPT	0-2018807	0862	1
WILSON MAURICE R	LTC	0-1043841	0161	1
WILSON MARGARET M	1LT	N-0786682	0348	2
WILSON MARION J	MAJ	0-0221689	0860	3
WILSON MARK L	LTC	0-1555324	0967	1
WILSON MARK S	COL	0-1580509	1167	1
WILSON MARLYN C	MAJ	0-1590896	0760	1
WILSON MASSEY F	COL	0-0298295	0260	2
WILSON MCCULLOCH	MAJ	0-0162945	0648	3
WILSON MCCULLOCH	MAJ	0-0950227	0663	1
WILSON MERLE F	CPT	0-0232230	0950	3
WILSON MERLE E	LTC	0-0307252	1164	3
WILSON MERLE G	LTC	0-1340145	0268	1
WILSON MILLARD H	1LT	0-1300427	0857	1
WILSON MYLDRED R	CPT	N-0787566	0347	1
WILSON MYRON R	MAJ	0-2021134	1066	1
WILSON NAT J	LTC	0-0315099	0264	3
WILSON NED I	CPT	0-5304085	0668	1
WILSON NEIL S JR	CW2	W-2206394	0661	1
WILSON OLIVER F	1LT	0-1080428	0555	1
WILSON OLIVER W	1LT	0-0245752	0363	3
WILSON OLLIE J	COL	0-0359154	1045	2
WILSON OMER B JR	MAJ	0-1313844	0857	1
WILSON OWEN D	LTC	0-1543631	0560	1
WILSON OZZIE L	CPT	0-0503847	0849	1
WILSON PERRY B JR	1LT	0-1175906	0845	2
WILSON PERRY J	CW2	W-2148619	0160	2
WILSON PHILIP	COL	0-0127939	0357	3
WILSON PHILIP	COL	0-0266106	1161	3
WILSON PHILIP M	COL	0-1056947	0464	1
WILSON PRINCESS L	LTC	N-0729172	0365	3
WILSON RAMEY F	LTC	0-1179682	0962	1
WILSON RANDALL R	LTC	0-0300476	0144	2
WILSON RAY M JR	CPT	0-1547637	0755	2
WILSON RAYMOND C	MAJ	0-0455146	1058	1
WILSON RAYMOND E	1LT	0-1013633	0846	2
WILSON RAYMOND H	CW3	W-2121928	0157	1
WILSON RAYMOND R	MAJ	0-1685621	0761	1
WILSON REGINALD S	MAJ	0-1111990	0361	1
WILSON ROBERT	MAJ	0-1329303	0265	1
WILSON ROBERT B	MAJ	0-0106049	0250	3
WILSON ROBERT D	LTC	0-1111445	0864	1
WILSON ROBERT E	MAJ	0-0994430	0367	1
WILSON ROBERT F	1LT	0-0463430	0447	2
WILSON ROBERT F	CW3	W-2144856	0363	1
WILSON ROBERT J	COL	0-0445449	0755	2
WILSON ROBERT L	CW2	W-2205599	0264	1
WILSON ROBERT L JR	COL	0-0191327	0762	3
WILSON ROBERT M	1LT	0-1297822	1045	2
WILSON ROBERT P	COL	0-0304025	0959	1
WILSON ROBERT R	COL	0-0189532	0961	3
WILSON ROBERT T	MAJ	0-1178985	1161	1
WILSON ROBERT W	M G	0-0233644	0-53	3
WILSON ROBERT W	COL	0-0925319	0250	3
WILSON ROSS E	LTC	0-0181303	0955	3
WILSON ROYAL C	LTC	0-0246510	1159	1
WILSON SAM T	LTC	0-0356845	0156	2

NAME	GRADE	SVC NO	DATE RET MO YR	RET CODE
WILSON SAM T	LTC	0-1281547	1064	1
WILSON SEWARD S	MAJ	0-1401069	0660	1
WILSON SHORIA G	1LT	0-0521876	0246	2
WILSON SIDNEY A	CW2	W-2102563	0247	1
WILSON STANFORD R	MAJ	0-1925472	0866	1
WILSON STEPHEN F	2LT	0-1941632	1055	2
WILSON SUMNER S	MAJ	0-1038521	0265	1
WILSON THEODORE	MAJ	0-4006226	0967	1
WILSON THERON D	MAJ	0-0289685	1057	3
WILSON THOMAS C	1LT	0-0154229	1045	2
WILSON THOMAS E	CPT	0-0910099	0745	2
WILSON THOMAS F	CPT	0-1995540	0352	2
WILSON THOMAS G	CW3	W-2206958	0167	1
WILSON THOMAS H JR	LTC	0-1333290	1266	1
WILSON THOMAS I	LTC	0-0384501	1066	3
WILSON THOMAS S	MAJ	0-0370990	0660	1
WILSON THOMAS W	LTC	0-0347684	1266	1
WILSON THOMAS W	LTC	0-1551990	0167	1
WILSON THOMAS W	LTC	0-1796197	1058	1
WILSON TILDEN D	CPT	0-0482715	0746	2
WILSON VERNON A	MAJ	0-1111991	0765	1
WILSON VERNON C	LTC	0-0913795	1166	3
WILSON WALLACE E	COL	0-0145536	0655	3
WILSON WALLACE P	MAJ	0-0398743	0657	1
WILSON WALTER W	MAJ	0-0141015	0753	3
WILSON WARREN A	1LT	0-0527881	0346	2
WILSON WARREN H	CPT	0-1301070	1059	1
WILSON WENDELL P	LTC	0-0177336	1061	3
WILSON WENDELL W	CW2	W-2152332	0157	1
WILSON WILBUR A	LTC	0-0989313	0168	2
WILSON WILBUR C	MAJ	0-0247942	1264	3
WILSON WILLIAM A	MAJ	0-2048523	0765	2
WILSON WILLIAM C	CPT	0-2015822	0652	2
WILSON WILLIAM D	MAJ	0-0452814	0546	2
WILSON WILLIAM E	MAJ	0-0321794	0847	2
WILSON WILLIAM E	CW3	W-2150533	0666	1
WILSON WILLIAM F	WO1	W-2126910	0749	1
WILSON WILLIAM H	MAJ	0-2005939	0561	1
WILSON WILLIAM H	MAJ	0-2010875	0862	1
WILSON WILLIAM H JR	CW2	W-2208886	0965	1
WILSON WILLIAM J	WO1	W-2105249	1047	1
WILSON WILLIAM L	MAJ	0-0414601	0865	1
WILSON WILLIAM L JR	1LT	0-0384035	0544	2
WILSON WILLIAM M JR	CPT	0-0259943	0967	3
WILSON WILLIAM C	1LT	0-0383445	0447	2
WILSON WILLIAM O	LTC	0-0983690	0768	1
WILSON WILLIAM P	COL	0-0324307	0247	2
WILSON WILLIAM P	MAJ	0-0383604	0868	3
WILSON WILLIAM P JR	LTC	0-1167698	0246	2
WILSON WILLIAM R	MAJ	0-0340445	0966	1
WILSON WILLIAM W	LTC	0-1325615	1265	3
WILSON WILLIE M	LTC	0-0450131	0556	1
WILSON WOODROW L	CW2	W-2208378	0764	1
WILSON WOODROW P	MAJ	0-0326125	1147	2
WILSON WOODROW T	LTC	0-0332213	0562	1
WILSON ZELMER C	CW4	W-2146299	0559	1
WILSON 3RD ROBERT C	CPT	0-0464766	1147	2
WILT CHARLES H	CW2	W-2148570	1060	1
WILT ROBERT H	LTC	0-0119506	0-53	3
WILTON DONALD C	LTC	0-1635486	0960	1
WILTON ELLA A	LTC	L-0220109	1164	1
WILTON OTIS N JR	MAJ	0-2028765	0667	1
WILTRAKIS GEORGE A	COL	0-0278953	0465	3
WILTSE HARRY W JR	MAJ	0-2045017	0562	1
WILTSEE DONALD L	MAJ	0-0214750	0664	3
WILTSHIRE MALCOLM	CPT	0-1315653	1047	2
WILVERT HURLEY T	LTC	0-1111446	0963	1
WIMBERLY FRED N	COL	0-0229660	0657	1
WIMBERLY LUCILLE H	CPT	L-0903074	1151	2
WIMBERLY PAUL F	MAJ	0-0296201	0868	3
WIMBERLY VERNON L	LTC	0-0289543	0446	2
WIMBERLY VERNON M	MAJ	0-0206543	0645	2
WIMER FRANK C	MAJ	0-0157268	0255	3
WIMMER VERNON C	LTC	0-1556825	0766	1
WIMMER WILLIAM K	LTC	0-1317856	0465	1

NAME	GRADE	SVC NO	DATE RET MO YR	RET CODE
WIMPLEBERG AUGUST	LTC	0-0263806	0152	3
WINAND KATHRYN F	2LT	N-0703653	1044	1
WINANS CHARLES F	1LT	0-0256646	1263	3
WINANS DOUGLAS K	MAJ	0-1557857	0464	1
WINANS HERMAN L	MAJ	0-2262483	0266	1
WINBURN CLAUDE D	COL	0-0287999	1064	3
WINBURN THOMAS A JR	1LT	0-0476713	0445	2
WINBURN DON C	CW2	W-2147273	0259	1
WINBURN HARRY W	LTC	0-0313152	0660	2
WINBURN HERBERT L	1LT	0-1301739	0845	2
WINCH AL R	CPT	0-2034597	0867	3
WINCH NORMAN M	LTC	0-0461488	1166	3
WINCH STANTON G	LTC	0-0249947	0365	3
WINCHESTER LEROY A	CW4	W-2005136	1066	1
WINCHESTER WILLARD P	MAJ	0-0286037	0661	3
WINDAUGH CARL F	MAJ	0-1017277	0557	1
WINDEBANK EDWARD A	LTC	0-1822135	0264	1
WINDHAM ALFORD P	CW4	W-2103617	0955	1
WINDHAM JOSEPH C	LTC	0-2033305	0868	1
WINDHAM JOSEPH P	COL	0-0248431	0862	2
WINDHAM RAY K	LTC	0-0252840	0364	3
WINDHAM WILLIAM R	MAJ	0-1314862	0960	1
WINDHAM WILLIE H	CW3	W-2153101	0568	1
WINDISCH HERMAN G	CPT	0-1165467	0659	1
WINDISCH ROBERT F	MAJ	0-1579315	0459	1
WINDISH JOHN J JR	1LT	0-1031691	0645	2
WINDMOELLER HENRY F	LTC	0-1581465	0461	1
WINDOM LOREN G	M G	0-0275591	0965	3
WINDOM RALPH	CPT	0-1877906	1062	2
WINDOM RUTH O	2LT	N-0726117	1146	1
WINDORFER JOHN H	1LT	0-1765892	1145	2
WINDSOR ALTON S JR	1LT	0-1861726	0554	2
WINDSOR BUFORD L	CW2	W-2147295	0960	1
WINDSOR JACK JR	MAJ	0-1595273	0461	1
WINDSOR KENNETH H	MAJ	0-1588966	1060	1
WINDSOR MERRILL C	LTC	0-0166027	0260	1
WINE WILLIAM C	COL	0-0312019	1263	2
WINEBERG CHARLES T	WO1	W-2150688	0361	2
WINEBRENNER VICTOR M	LTC	0-1334940	0864	1
WINEBURGH JACOB J	CPT	0-0486881	0245	2
WINEGARD CHARLES I	COL	0-0449520	0954	1
WINEGARDNER JAY H	1LT	0-1168981	0545	2
WINER HAROLD	MAJ	0-0294229	1046	2
WINER JULIUS H	CPT	0-0338856	1146	2
WINER MEYER	MAJ	0-0158246	0150	3
WINES CARROLL F	MAJ	0-2016986	0762	1
WINFREE ROBERT N	LTC	0-0153408	0959	3
WINFREY WILL P	COL	0-1574369	0861	2
WING DUNCAN	CPT	0-0109431	0934	1
WING EDWARD A JR	CPT	0-5301670	1068	1
WING HAROLD M	CW3	W-2206185	0965	1
WING KENNETH A	LTC	0-0254821	0165	3
WING LEONARD A	LTC	0-0272471	0766	3
WING LUBERT	MAJ	0-1919398	0965	1
WING MARY G	CPT	N-0752893	0147	1
WING ROBERT B	COL	0-0275785	0767	3
WING WALLACE C	CW2	W-2152728	0261	1
WINGARD BARRINGER	COL	0-0249100	0666	3
WINGARD JOSEPH E	MAJ	0-1825296	0258	1
WINGATE GARNETT W	LTC	0-2263255	0868	1
WINGATE HARVEY P	LTC	0-0167382	1057	3
WINGATE WILLIAM L	CW2	W-2147200	0961	1
WINGEBACH CHARLES F	CPT	0-0203754	0462	3
WINGERT DONALD G	MAJ	0-0287797	0166	3
WINGFIELD CONRAD B	LTC	0-1583851	0765	1
WINGFIELD DONALD W	CW3	W-2145088	0361	1
WINGFIELD HENRY R	1LT	0-0365442	0146	2
WINGFIELD SAM A	CPT	0-0980887	1166	1
WINGO BURLEY M	CPT	0-2001822	1055	1
WINGO BURREL W	MAJ	0-2024337	0264	1
WINGO CHARLES M JR	MAJ	0-0344421	0945	2
WINGO GEORGE N	CW2	W-2153197	1160	1
WINGO GERALD E	LTC	0-1291367	0765	1
WINGO JESSE M	MAJ	0-1284620	0846	2
WINGO JOHN W	LTC	0-0397752	0168	3

NAME	GRADE	SVC NO	DATE RET MO YR	RET CODE
WINGROVE CHARLES D	CW2	W-2214634	0868	1
WINGROVE JOSEPH F	CPT	0-0149419	0556	3
WINGROVE MARVIN V	CW3	W-2142012	0669	1
WINGROVE WILLIAM H	1LT	0-0511521	0648	1
WINIKER DICK R	CPT	0-0890218	1045	2
WININGER ALBERT J	CW2	W-2110120	0648	1
WININGER DESCO C	CW4	W-2144587	0268	1
WINK EUGENE A	LTC	0-0247027	0854	3
WINK JOSEPH C SR	LTC	0-0330576	0165	1
WINK PETER	1LT	0-1946892	0557	1
WINK ROBERT J	CPT	0-1877698	0565	1
WINKEL ROBERT C	LTC	0-1291555	0966	1
WINKENWERDER R H	LTC	0-0412127	0760	1
WINKLER EARL C	LTC	0-0385218	0960	1
WINKLER FRANK C	LTC	0-0109002	0846	2
WINKLER HERBERT W	MAJ	0-0924804	1163	1
WINKLER IRVEN G	MAJ	0-1037782	0760	1
WINKLER PATRICK J	LTC	0-0918868	0165	3
WINKLER PROVINCE M	MAJ	0-0338281	0246	2
WINKLER ROBERT B	CPT	0-1015623	1054	2
WINLAW CLINTON K	MAJ	0-0335846	1068	3
WINLAW JOHN P	2LT	0-0393612	0142	2
WINLOCK WILLIAM C	MAJ	0-2209717	1068	1
WINN ARVEY S	MAJ	0-1844568	0457	1
WINN CHARLES	MAJ	0-2018626	0166	1
WINN CHARLES F	LTC	0-0276483	0761	1
WINN DALE	WO1	W-2003776	0564	3
WINN FREDERICKS	LTC	0-0236574	0365	3
WINN HENRY JR	CPT	0-2040918	0160	1
WINN HERBERT P	COL	0-0353361	0966	3
WINN LOUIS E	CPT	0-0464281	0949	1
WINN MARK	LTC	0-1042746	0961	1
WINN MONROE G	CPT	0-1030318	1054	2
WINN PERCY E JR	LTC	0-1179251	0363	1
WINN RICHARD J III	MAJ	0-1333291	1263	1
WINN ROY H	1LT	0-1056603	0654	1
WINN WARREN R	COL	0-0265305	0845	2
WINN WILLIAM B	2LT	0-2027752	0246	2
WINNER EDWARD C	1LT	0-1032496	0546	2
WINNER THOMAS A	CPT	0-1320683	1047	2
WINNIE CHARLES D	CW2	W-2150267	0859	2
WINNING WALTER B	1LT	0-1580518	0961	3
WINNINGHAM RICHARD B	LTC	0-1293342	0661	1
WINOGRAD ALVIN M	CPT	0-1684283	0546	2
WINOGRAD SAMUEL	LTC	0-2271005	0468	1
WINSAUER LESLIE R	CPT	0-0285584	1044	2
WINSHIP WILLIAM H	MAJ	0-1795026	1161	1
WINSKOWSKI SIGMUND J	MAJ	0-2035599	1061	1
WINSKY STANLEY G	MAJ	0-1997648	0163	1
WINSLADE HAZEL L	1LT	N-0703289	1144	1
WINSLETT EDMUND J	LTC	0-0103458	0657	3
WINSLETT JIM H	CW4	W-2144796	0666	1
WINSLOW BERRY O	LTC	0-0503062	0657	1
WINSLOW CECIL H	MAJ	0-0153537	0858	3
WINSLOW FRANK JR	1LT	0-1325428	0853	1
WINSLOW HUGH W	COL	0-0414909	1053	1
WINSLOW JOHN W	CPT	0-0319666	0746	1
WINSLOW LYNWOOD A	LTC	0-0491944	0755	1
WINSLOW MARTIN L	CPT	0-1012138	0648	1
WINSMAN LOUIS JR	LTC	0-0980769	0668	1
WINSOR CARLTON W	MAJ	0-0320924	0944	2
WINSOR EDWARD F	MAJ	0-1297461	0261	1
WINSOR MILTON G	LTC	0-0359848	0157	1
WINSOR PAUL B	CPT	0-0272042	1167	3
WINSOR RICHARD R	MAJ	0-1633644	0358	1
WINSTEAD AMBLER W	MAJ	0-0971829	1061	1
WINSTEAD ELTON D	LTC	0-0354444	1057	1
WINSTEAD FREDERICK	MAJ	0-1799412	1264	1
WINSTEAD RICHARD B	CW4	W-2005311	0665	1
WINSTON CARL A	CW3	W-2207750	0466	1
WINSTON CLARENCE N	COL	0-0176512	1054	3
WINSTON DALE L	CPT	0-1336852	0657	1
WINSTON EDWARD J	CW4	W-2002017	0863	3
WINSTON GEORGE E	CW3	W-2126390	0562	1
WINSTON WALDON C	COL	0-0259814	1157	1

NAME	GRADE	SVC NO	DATE RET MO YR	RET CODE
WINTER ALAN W	LTC	0-0352016	0646	2
WINTER CECIL L	MAJ	0-0116057	0654	3
WINTER EARL C	LTC	0-1691798	0862	1
WINTER ELBERT R	MAJ	0-1542234	0561	1
WINTER ERNEST H JR	COL	0-1169403	1068	1
WINTER FRANK S	CW2	W-2205305	1168	2
WINTER FRANKLIN I	MAJ	0-0111255	0648	3
WINTER HAL F	COL	0-0317888	0349	2
WINTER HERBERT A	MAJ	0-1115459	0861	1
WINTER JOHN H	1LT	0-1590900	1045	2
WINTER JOHN W	COL	0-0289160	0546	2
WINTER MARVIN M	MAJ	0-0137127	0853	1
WINTER ROBERT G	LTC	0-1109117	0467	1
WINTER ROBERT H	MAJ	0-0965105	1265	1
WINTER ROBERT L	MAJ	0-2263016	0464	1
WINTER STANLEY T	LTC	0-0250047	0365	3
WINTER WALDO J W	COL	0-0270460	0248	2
WINTER WILLIAM A	WO1	W-2132642	0546	2
WINTER WILLIS G	LTC	0-0277838	0755	1
WINTERBOTTOM JAMES E	LTC	0-1585095	1059	2
WINTERBURG DON E	LTC	0-0193809	0364	3
WINTERHALTER ARTHUR	2LT	0-1011807	1043	2
WINTERHOFF WALTER J	LTC	0-0346948	0247	2
WINTERMUTE EARL C	COL	0-0464875	0765	1
WINTERROTH EDWARD G	1LT	0-1691764	0745	2
WINTERS EARL R	MAJ	0-0965329	0964	1
WINTERS GEORGE J	CPT	0-0447986	1146	1
WINTERS HENRY S	MAJ	0-4011100	0767	1
WINTERS JAMES E	CPT	0-0170861	0844	2
WINTERS JERALD T	CW3	W-2210716	1268	1
WINTERS JOHN P	CW4	W-2111987	1160	1
WINTERS JOHN R	MAJ	0-0739159	0365	1
WINTERS JOHN R	CW3	W-2201758	0268	3
WINTERS LESLIE C	LTC	0-0240731	0366	3
WINTERS RAYMOND F	2LT	0-1547210	1044	2
WINTERS RICHARD D	CW2	W-2150762	0561	1
WINTERS THOMAS H	LTC	0-0265271	1044	1
WINTERS WALTER F	COL	0-0245132	0860	3
WINTERS WILLIAM P	LTC	0-1567027	0656	1
WINTERS WILLIAM R	1LT	0-1182746	0845	2
WINTERS WILLIAM W	LTC	0-1043838	0764	1
WINTERS WILLIS H	2LT	0-1314989	0246	2
WINTERSTEIN WILLIAM	LTC	0-1553756	0157	1
WINTRISS GEORGE	MAJ	0-0349770	0445	2
WINTRUDE ROLLIN V	CW3	W-2151861	0265	1
WINZELER PHYLLIS J	MAJ	N-0729621	0468	1
WINZENREAD WILLIAM H	LTC	0-1645116	1163	1
WIPF WILLIAM	LTC	0-0250732	1154	1
WIPPERMAN RUDOLPH P	LTC	0-0944760	0267	3
WIRE DAVID B	1LT	0-0491275	0646	2
WIREBAUGH FRED W	MAJ	0-0166384	0-52	3
WIREY CARL O	CPT	0-0464108	1045	2
WIRSCHING THOMAS M	2LT	0-0427347	0544	2
WIRSING GORDON E	CW3	W-2149395	0868	1
WIRTH DAVID K	1LT	0-1312031	1145	2
WIRTH EARL A	LTC	0-0967142	0762	1
WIRTH GUSTAVE J	LTC	0-1041060	1168	1
WIRTH HAROLD C	CPT	0-2026492	0257	1
WISAKOWSKY EMIL E	MAJ	0-0442277	1060	1
WISBY HERMAN H	MAJ	0-0510519	0246	2
WISCH LEONA M	CPT	N-0727898	0847	1
WISCHER FRANCIS M	CW4	W-2127501	0658	1
WISCOWITCH GUSTAVO	2LT	0-2050699	0246	2
WISDOM CHARLES L	MAJ	0-0386584	1144	2
WISDOM GEORGE B	WO1	W-2131926	1051	2
WISDOM WILLIAM F	CPT	0-1824262	0659	1
WISE ALBERT J	1LT	0-1825900	0146	2
WISE BERNARD O	LTC	0-0505783	1046	2
WISE ERNEST E	MAJ	0-0130125	0546	2
WISE EUGENE W	LTC	0-0278063	0461	3
WISE FRANCIS J	CPT	0-0504908	1148	1
WISE FRANK J	CPT	0-0247166	0455	3
WISE GEORGE E	COL	0-0361407	0561	1
WISE HAROLD L	CPT	0-2265694	0665	1
WISE HARRIET M	MAJ	L-0504451	0363	1

NAME	GRADE	SVC NO	DATE RET MO YR	RET CODE
WISE JACK III	CPT	0-1288338	1266	3
WISE JACK N	CPT	0-1690998	0765	1
WISE JAMES I	1LT	0-0229262	1262	3
WISE JAY N	CW2	W-2141812	0666	1
WISE JEFF	CPT	0-0445224	1046	1
WISE JOHN E	LTC	0-1032666	0561	1
WISE JOHN H	MAJ	0-0979268	1164	1
WISE JOHN K	LTC	0-1590269	0163	1
WISE JOHN W	CW4	W-2148778	1263	1
WISE LESLIE J	1LT	0-1014543	0348	2
WISE LLOYD H	LTC	0-2035904	1068	1
WISE LOUIS J	COL	0-0100671	0352	3
WISE PAUL F	CPT	0-0518545	0453	1
WISE PRENTICE L	COL	0-0359340	1060	2
WISE RICHARD K	MAJ	0-1534192	0953	1
WISE RICHARD P	1LT	0-1882645	0856	2
WISE ROBERT H	LTC	0-1319372	1062	1
WISE ROBERT M	LTC	0-0394958	1265	1
WISE STANLEY C	CPT	0-1322112	0249	2
WISE WALTER A	1LT	0-1327792	0147	2
WISE WARREN R	1LT	0-1844538	1044	2
WISE WHITBY F JR	2LT	0-0395966	0543	2
WISE WILLARD W	MAJ	0-1316355	0862	1
WISEHEART JOHN W	LTC	0-0202138	0660	2
WISEMAN DELTER B	LTC	0-0946763	0868	1
WISEMAN HAROLD C	WO1	W-2125817	0758	1
WISEMAN JAMES A	MAJ	0-1688785	0267	1
WISEMAN JOHN T	CW4	W-2142672	1158	1
WISEMAN RICHARD A	MAJ	0-0571694	0266	1
WISEMAN T J	CW4	W-2136024	0863	1
WISEMAN WILLIAM R	LTC	0-1037369	1061	1
WISENBAKER WILLIAM C	LTC	0-1949247	0368	1
WISER MERLE F	CPT	0-1289526	0246	2
WISHART ANDREW J	MAJ	0-0571297	0960	1
WISHART JOHN C	LTC	0-1105786	0462	1
WISHNEFSKY PHILIP	2LT	0-1328207	0546	2
WISHNICK SEYMOUR D	CPT	0-0534234	0846	2
WISLER ROY A	COL	0-0153549	0-53	1
WISMAN CALVIN S	COL	0-0390304	0564	1
WISMANN JOHN A	CW3	W-2145171	0862	1
WISMER RAYMOND J	COL	0-0250400	1062	3
WISNEFSKI JOSEPH W	1LT	0-1690486	0943	2
WISNER CLIFFORD W	CW3	W-2141921	0756	1
WISNER JOHN H	2LT	0-1560173	0146	2
WISNESKI EDWARD V	MAJ	0-0963604	1163	1
WISNESKI EMILIA	CPT	N-0735715	0547	1
WISNIEWSKI BERNARD	WO1	W-2114989	0744	2
WISNIEWSKI STANLEY A	MAJ	0-1019842	1265	1
WISOR ROBERT L	LTC	0-1314380	0861	1
WISSE WILLIAM	CPT	0-1299342	1047	2
WISSENBURGER C E	LTC	0-1636803	1160	1
WISSINGER HELEN G	1LT	N-0759182	1145	2
WISSLER ALFRED E	COL	0-0301746	0157	3
WISTAIN LINCOLN D	LTC	0-0196536	1261	3
WISTERMAN JESSE H	CPT	0-0503641	0757	2
WITCHER EARL E	MAJ	0-4074765	0868	1
WITCOSKY JOHN W	CPT	0-1288991	1046	2
WITEK JOHN J	MAJ	0-1705339	0848	2
WITHAM FRANK R	MAJ	0-0173128	0961	3
WITHEREL MURVEN J	1LT	0-1305152	1045	2
WITHERELL LEONARD D	MAJ	0-0262878	1046	2
WITHERELL MAYNARD O	LTC	0-0264361	1168	3
WITHEROW ELMER	CW3	W-2147112	0264	2
WITHERS ARNOLD M	LTC	0-1592718	0163	1
WITHERS CARTER B	LTC	0-0292137	1267	3
WITHERS WILLIAM B	LTC	0-0238594	0963	3
WITHERS WINSTON R	MAJ	0-0102693	0555	3
WITHERSPOON JOHN F	COL	0-0354514	0861	1
WITHERSPOON SHIRLEY	LTC	0-0256863	1266	3
WITHERSTINE EDWARD J	1LT	0-0116646	0851	3
WITHERUP EMMA C	2LT	N-0700526	0738	1
WITHINGTON ALBERT F	MAJ	0-1314864	0863	1
WITHINGTON GILES B	COL	0-0423776	1168	1
WITHINGTON HARRY O	COL	0-0237837	0648	3
WITHINGTON JOSEPH S	COL	0-0219047	1157	1

NAME	GRADE	SVC NO	DATE RET MO YR	RET CODE
WITHINGTON WILLIAM J	CW3	W-2147787	0863	1
WITHINGTON WILLIAM M	2LT	0-1184336	0744	2
WITHROW BERNARD O	LTC	0-1171846	0967	1
WITHROW FRED	MAJ	0-1931437	0567	1
WITHROW JOHN W	1LT	0-1306034	0952	2
WITKOSKIE JAMES A	CPT	0-0544470	0353	2
WITKOWSKI HENRY J	MAJ	0-1822932	0665	1
WITMAN JOSEPH W	1LT	0-1799495	0546	2
WITMER CHARLES R	2LT	0-1295469	1043	2
WITMER JOHN H	LTC	0-0488273	0755	1
WITMER MAX D	LTC	0-0334428	0955	3
WITMER RICHARD L	CPT	0-1040307	0845	2
WITMER SANDS G	LTC	0-0275536	1068	3
WITSCH JOHN E	MAJ	0-0972831	0765	1
WITT CHARLES R	LTC	0-1013278	1061	1
WITT DUANE M	COL	0-1283181	1066	1
WITT EDWARD R	MAJ	0-0493183	0457	1
WITT EUGENE M	LTC	0-0389188	0760	1
WITT FRITZ	CPT	0-0278605	0364	3
WITT HARLEY A	MAJ	0-1177698	0362	2
WITT HARRY	1LT	0-0399297	0744	2
WITT JAMES N	CPT	0-2048198	0347	2
WITT JAMES O JR	MAJ	0-0448107	0747	2
WITT JAMES W	MAJ	0-1648248	0859	1
WITT JAMES W	MAJ	0-2009705	0461	1
WITT KENNETH G	MAJ	0-1794892	0461	1
WITT LESLIE L	MAJ	0-1294055	0658	1
WITT MILTON W	COL	0-0279314	0659	1
WITT PLEASANT B	CW4	W-2107063	0859	1
WITT RAE A	2LT	N-0779593	1046	1
WITT SCOTT J	1LT	0-0554362	0446	2
WITT VINCENT E	MAJ	0-2000980	0959	1
WITT WALTER H JR	2LT	0-0435048	0445	2
WITT WANDAL D	LTC	0-0505498	0863	2
WITTA FRED JR	LTC	0-0404280	0365	1
WITTE ALFRED F	LTC	0-0235990	0754	3
WITTE ARTHUR W	1LT	0-1012534	1045	2
WITTE GRANT L	1LT	0-0386374	0445	2
WITTE HERBERT J	COL	0-0258995	0954	1
WITTEKIND EUGENE C	MAJ	0-1183220	1063	1
WITTEKIND HAROLD H	LTC	0-0415612	0165	1
WITTEN GEORGE W B	LTC	0-0220368	0745	2
WITTEN HAROLD R	LTC	0-0345847	0567	3
WITTEN NASH A	CPT	0-0121201	0949	3
WITTEN WILLIAM W JR	LTC	0-1557998	0762	1
WITTENBERG SHELDON F	CPT	0-1644920	0457	1
WITTER JOSEPH A	MAJ	0-1686873	1045	2
WITTIG DONALD A	MAJ	0-0390075	0546	2
WITTKE ROBERT E	MAJ	0-1651259	1265	1
WITTKOP GEORGE F	CPT	0-1534415	0656	1
WITTKOPP LELAND A	1LT	0-0555983	0646	2
WITTKOWER LOUIS O JR	LTC	0-0398417	0161	1
WITTLAKE OSCAR D	LTC	0-0253343	0763	3
WITTLER JACOB F	LTC	0-0292814	1057	1
WITTMAACK CHARLES C	CW2	W-2152893	1163	1
WITTMANN JOHN G JR	LTC	0-0234644	1062	3
WITTMUS WALDEMAR A	LTC	0-0343633	0859	1
WITTNEBEL ROBERT L	LTC	0-1913466	1268	1
WITTNER DAVID G	MAJ	0-1885863	1267	1
WITTROCK JACK E	LTC	0-0353758	0264	1
WITTSTROM MARTIN D	MAJ	0-1059347	1060	1
WITTWER GLADE S	LTC	0-1101289	0361	1
WITTY STUART E	MAJ	0-1166419	0261	1
WITWICKE JOHN	CW3	W-2142279	1059	2
WITZEL EWALD L	CPT	0-0137273	1054	3
WITZEL TERRENCE P	CPT	0-5709862	0568	2
WITZEL VERNA G	2LT	N-0769717	0546	1
WITZIGMAN FREDERICK	MAJ	0-0344984	0866	3
WITZLEBEN EUGENE A	CW3	W-2141109	0563	1
WIWI PAUL J	CPT	0-1297462	1046	2
WIXSEY EARL B	COL	0-0147921	0258	3
WLADKOWSKI JOSEPH A	CW2	W-3350148	0266	1
WNEK HENRY A	CPT	0-1307606	0348	2
WNEK RUSSELL J	LTC	0-1292104	1061	1
WOEHNER LISLE C	COL	0-0264890	0663	3

NAME	GRADE	SVC NO	DATE RET MO YR	RET CODE
WOCKENFUSS ROLAND C	1LT	0-0384573	1144	2
WODA CHESTER J	CW3	W-2205735	0966	2
WODARCZAK HUBERT T	CW3	W-2143986	1060	1
WOODROP WILLIAM H	CPT	0-2032877	1157	1
WOERLEIN THOMAS J	MAJ	0-1173510	0461	1
WOERPEL CHARLES W	MAJ	0-0451702	1160	2
WOFFORD MONTIE W	MAJ	0-0450467	0658	1
WOGAN MAURICE	MAJ	0-0478786	0147	2
WOGSLAND WALTER	CPT	0-0490324	0145	2
WOHLFERD LEO A	MAJ	0-1895966	0467	3
WOHLFORD EARL G	LTC	0-1036810	0867	1
WOHLGEMUTH GEORGE F	LTC	0-0245922	0259	3
WOHLGEMUTH STEPHEN H	CW4	W-2004201	1056	3
WOHLTMAN ROBERT M	MAJ	0-0274682	0763	3
WOICK FRED H	LTC	0-0506556	0262	3
WOIDA LOUIS D	CW4	W-2146620	0560	1
WOITH MELVIN P	CW2	W-2209809	0863	1
WOITT SOLOMON F	MAJ	0-1581467	1060	1
WOJACK WALTER L	2LT	0-2034712	0845	2
WOJAHN GEORGE W	MAJ	0-1316968	0567	3
WOJAHN HAROLD F	MAJ	0-1924541	1167	1
WOJCIECHOWICZ J C	CW2	W-2206854	0760	1
WOJTAL EDWARD S JR	1LT	0-1289846	1045	2
WOJTANOWSKI HENRY P	MAJ	0-2008762	0365	1
WOJTASZEK JOSEPH H	MAJ	0-0256309	0665	3
WOKULICH JOHN	CW3	W-2143987	1162	1
WOLANGE NELLIE M	MAJ	N-0721273	0264	2
WOLBERT ROBERT E	LTC	0-1183453	0864	1
WOLCHICK MICHAEL T	1LT	0-1050521	1154	1
WOLCOTT LORENE M	MAJ	L-0400509	0845	2
WOLCZYK STANLEY J	1LT	0-0413315	0444	2
WOLD HAROLD	1LT	0-1311257	0845	2
WOLD ROBERT M	COL	0-0230400	0462	3
WOLDER MURRAY P	1LT	0-1301742	0345	2
WOLENBERG HOWARD O	LTC	0-1592723	0862	1
WOLEVER STANLEY E	LTC	0-1169404	0861	1
WOLF ALFRED H	1LT	0-0478976	0847	2
WOLF ARTHUR E	LTC	0-1309466	0468	1
WOLF CHARLES F JR	LTC	0-0761488	0568	2
WOLF DEWITT G	LTC	0-1017467	0766	1
WOLF EARL E	COL	0-0425188	1061	2
WOLF EDWARD D	M G	0-0298530	1064	3
WOLF EDWARD T	LTC	0-0177363	0845	2
WOLF EDWIN J	COL	0-0910396	0667	3
WOLF EUGENE F	LTC	0-0380689	0160	1
WOLF EUGENE H	CPT	0-0299533	0668	3
WOLF GEORGE R	MAJ	0-0222438	0865	3
WOLF GORDON J	COL	0-0225015	0265	3
WOLF HENRY A	CPT	0-0242223	0648	3
WOLF HENRY N	LTC	0-1882647	1268	1
WOLF IRVING	2LT	0-1004263	0245	2
WOLF JOHN S	LTC	0-0386692	0645	2
WOLF KARL R	LTC	0-0251043	1265	3
WOLF MAURICE A	COL	0-0165989	0751	3
WOLF MELVIN E	MAJ	0-1688473	0665	1
WOLF PAUL V	CPT	0-1044429	0855	1
WOLF RALPH L	LTC	0-0256288	0359	3
WOLF RICHARD D JR	MAJ	0-1336013	0765	1
WOLF ROBERT H	CPT	0-1062457	0947	2
WOLF RUSSELL T	MAJ	0-0987001	0168	3
WOLF SHELDON L	CPT	0-0488395	0745	2
WOLF VINCENT E	2LT	0-1308284	0644	2
WOLF WALTER C	CPT	0-0446121	0849	1
WOLFBERG EDGAR H	MAJ	0-0133603	1053	3
WOLFBERG JOHN M	1LT	0-1015865	0945	2
WOLFE ALBERT	CW4	W-2112432	0162	2
WOLFE ALBERT E	CW2	W-2152634	0662	1
WOLFE ALFRED J	LTC	0-0711574	1267	1
WOLFE BURTON A	LTC	0-0451564	0860	1
WOLFE CARL L	LTC	0-0356280	0461	1
WOLFE CHARLES H	CPT	0-1592278	0546	2
WOLFE CHESTER W	COL	0-0277596	1047	2
WOLFE CLAY W	1LT	0-0494342	0947	1
WOLFE CLEMENT V	CPT	0-0213381	1045	2
WOLFE CURTIS N	LTC	0-1642737	0162	1

332-811 O - 69 - 25

ARMY OF THE UNITED STATES RETIRED LIST

NAME	GRADE	SVC NO	DATE RET MO YR	RET CODE
WOLFE DALE H	CW3	W-2209875	1066	1
WOLFE EDGAR W	MAJ	O-0272410	0168	3
WOLFE ESTILL	CPT	O-0488558	0545	2
WOLFE EUGENE	LTC	O-0210932	0-53	1
WOLFE FRANK E	CW2	W-2151171	1058	2
WOLFE FREDERIC S	1LT	O-0320496	0743	2
WOLFE GARLAND H	COL	O-0248759	0560	3
WOLFE GEORGE A JR	CPT	O-0359649	1065	3
WOLFE GEORGE W	1LT	O-0357700	0646	2
WOLFE HAROLD	1LT	O-1320704	0446	2
WOLFE HARRY P	COL	O-0363931	0268	3
WOLFE HENRY M	LTC	O-0135654	0549	3
WOLFE HILREY W	CPT	O-0969412	0861	2
WOLFE IRA G	MAJ	O-0268770	0255	3
WOLFE JAMES W	2LT	O-1824719	0344	2
WOLFE JOHN H	LTC	O-1598383	0462	1
WOLFE JOSEPH	MAJ	O-0225944	0246	2
WOLFE JOSEPH D	1LT	O-0381830	0443	2
WOLFE JOSEPH H	MAJ	O-1947123	0463	1
WOLFE MARTIN C	LTC	O-0193796	1263	3
WOLFE MARTIN P	1LT	O-0312854	0345	2
WOLFE MIRIAM D	2LT	N-0735227	0545	1
WOLFE NED R	1LT	O-1547507	0745	2
WOLFE ORIN K	CW4	W-2104609	0659	1
WOLFE PETER F	MAJ	O-1103474	0555	1
WOLFE RAVALD M	LTC	O-0505943	0267	3
WOLFE RAYMOND D	LTC	O-1286404	0661	1
WOLFE RUSSELL S	COL	O-0147600	0751	3
WOLFE STANLEY	COL	O-0167395	0453	3
WOLFE THOMAS J	LTC	O-0454186	0364	1
WOLFE THOMAS L	COL	O-0242177	1054	3
WOLFE THOMAS P	LTC	O-0255759	0561	3
WOLFE VICTOR	MAJ	O-1633648	0348	2
WOLFELD SIDNEY S	LTC	O-1646124	1062	1
WOLFER FREDERIC F	COL	O-0275670	0159	1
WOLFERT EDWARD C	LTC	O-1050148	1168	1
WOLFF BERNARD P	LTC	O-0397967	1145	2
WOLFF CHARLES R	1LT	O-1649671	0347	2
WOLFF EDWARD L	COL	O-0357616	0466	1
WOLFF HAROLD J	MAJ	O-1286052	0266	1
WOLFF HEINZ O L	CPT	O-0538414	0646	2
WOLFF JAMES A	MAJ	O-0551079	1065	1
WOLFF JOHN	LTC	O-2052086	0566	3
WOLFF LUTHER H	LTC	O-0296324	1167	3
WOLFF MAXWELL J	MAJ	O-0493762	0645	2
WOLFF MILDRED M	CPT	N-0783853	0148	1
WOLFF MORTIMER	LTC	O-0395916	0966	3
WOLFF RAYMOND R	CW3	W-2143139	0962	1
WOLFF ROBERT H	MAJ	O-1330244	0665	1
WOLFF WALTER L	MAJ	O-1333578	0762	1
WOLFINGER WILLIAM F	LTC	O-1590314	0763	2
WOLFMAN AVE	1LT	N-0758465	0846	1
WOLFMAN MILTON	MAJ	O-1192042	0763	1
WOLFORD JOHN P	CW2	W-2208951	0862	1
WOLFORD ROY A	COL	O-0233446	0854	3
WOLFORD SAMUEL H	MAJ	O-0489317	0854	1
WOLFORTH WILLIAM A	LTC	O-1314365	1162	1
WOLFRAM KENNETH G	MAJ	O-1300111	0758	1
WOLFSKILL CLIFFORD L	LTC	O-1824549	1062	1
WOLFSON HENRY	MAJ	O-0137148	0949	3
WOLFSON IRVING	LTC	O-0272187	0866	3
WOLFSON MELVIN L	CPT	O-1041062	1044	2
WOLFSON SARAH A	MAJ	N-0725641	0663	1
WOLFSON SIDNEY H	MAJ	O-1585099	0261	1
WOLGAMOTT MURRAY W	1LT	O-2055324	0556	1
WOLICKI MARCELLI A	CW2	W-2143815	0859	1
WOLICKI WALTER J	CW3	W-2150329	0762	1
WOLINSKY WILLIAM	LTC	O-1796894	1067	3
WOLK GEORGE	2LT	O-1589014	0744	2
WOLK HAROLD	1LT	O-1043258	1045	2
WOLKEN LEO B	MAJ	O-0948742	0763	1
WOLKONSKY PETER N	LTC	O-0954833	0968	1
WOLKUM SAM J	MAJ	O-0494088	0654	1
WOLKOWSKY MELVIN	1LT	O-1736448	0104	2
WOLLAK THEODORE	CPT	O-0252625	1043	2

NAME	GRADE	SVC NO	DATE RET MO YR	RET CODE
WOLLENBERG C H	LTC	O-0238747	0559	3
WOLLENMAN MAX J	LTC	O-0245740	0661	3
WOLLMER CHARLES A	CPT	O-1011429	0546	2
WOLLNER FRANK E	CW3	W-2148895	0864	1
WOLOTIRA ROBERT J	CPT	O-1283182	0845	2
WOLPE LEONARD	CPT	O-1012559	0446	2
WOLPERS JOHN A	1LT	O-1288154	0344	2
WOLPERT GEORGE S	LTC	O-1573679	1067	3
WOLPERT HOWARD A	MAJ	O-0971722	0562	1
WOLPIN ALVIN W	2LT	O-1177701	0644	2
WOLTER FRED W	COL	O-0208721	1156	3
WOLTER FRED W	1LT	O-0695397	1043	2
WOLTER HERBERT H JR	MAJ	O-2046638	1060	1
WOLTJER THEODORIKD	CW2	W-2213472	0568	1
WOMAC JAMES D	LTC	O-1290170	0860	1
WOMACK CHARLES T JR	CPT	O-1293164	0946	2
WOMACK DAVID C	MAJ	O-2041141	0964	1
WOMACK HORACE O	MAJ	O-1914031	0636	1
WOMACK IRVING F	MAJ	O-1823533	0868	1
WOMACK LAWRENCE F	CW3	W-2146731	0962	1
WOMACK LEHMAN E	CW3	W-2144636	0461	1
WOMACK LEONARD D	CPT	O-2040769	0858	1
WOMACK WILLIAM J	COL	O-1102553	0763	1
WOMBLE LYNDELL E	CW3	W-2207502	1166	1
WOMBLE WALTER E	COL	O-0270467	0460	1
WOMELDORFF VIRGIL L	COL	O-0222880	0964	3
WONDER GORDON F	1LT	O-0267723	1042	2
WONDERS GLENN D	LTC	O-1546853	0966	1
WONDRACK ARTHUR J	CPT	O-0261538	0367	3
WONDRASEK STEPHEN M	MAJ	O-1039270	0657	1
WONG GILBERT L	LTC	O-0277929	1060	1
WONG JAMES S F	LTC	O-0259392	0965	3
WONG ROBERT W Y	CW4	W-2135991	0466	1
WONKOVICH SAM	MAJ	O-1846545	0368	3
WONNENBERG RAYMOND H	LTC	O-0132880	0150	3
WOOD ALBERT W	CPT	O-0383965	0446	2
WOOD ALONZO E	COL	O-0171619	1058	1
WOOD ALVIN	CPT	O-0388285	0344	2
WOOD ALVYN P	LTC	O-2006903	1163	1
WOOD ANDREW L	CW3	W-2150041	0862	2
WOOD ARCHIE N	LTC	O-0262141	0357	3
WOOD ARTHUR B	LTC	O-0839444	0768	1
WOOD ARTHUR C	LTC	O-0199792	0254	2
WOOD AUGUST R	LTC	O-0269763	0363	1
WOOD BARLOW L	1LT	O-1310658	0345	2
WOOD BASIL A	COL	O-0212522	0857	2
WOOD BENNETT R	CPT	O-0226110	1059	3
WOOD BERNARD P	LTC	O-0267124	0366	3
WOOD BILLY	LTC	O-0552589	0663	1
WOOD BILLY A	CW2	W-2150682	0961	1
WOOD BILLY B	CPT	O-1643469	1147	2
WOOD BILLY J	CW2	W-3000415	1067	1
WOOD BRENNAN C	CPT	O-1285683	0945	2
WOOD BRUCE T	CW3	W-2208509	0568	1
WOOD BURTON M JR	1LT	O-1294760	0245	2
WOOD CECIL H	COL	O-0288922	0662	1
WOOD CHARLES C	CPT	O-0147226	1055	3
WOOD CHARLES D JR	1LT	O-1300895	1045	2
WOOD CHARLES G	MAJ	O-2028460	0465	1
WOOD CHARLES J	LTC	O-0396204	0861	1
WOOD CHARLES R	MAJ	O-1640139	0961	1
WOOD CHARLES S JR	LTC	O-0316216	0862	1
WOOD CHARLES T	MAJ	O-0218679	0646	2
WOOD CHARLES W	MAJ	O-1598882	0166	1
WOOD CLARENCE A	MAJ	O-0163816	1151	3
WOOD CLYDE C	CPT	O-0224757	0447	1
WOOD CLYNER M	CW3	W-2149167	1060	1
WOOD CONNIE C	CW2	W-2102569	0949	1
WOOD CORDELLE A	LTC	O-0236842	0858	3
WOOD DAVID B	1LT	O-0970839	0454	2
WOOD DAVID L	COL	O-0276956	1062	1
WOOD DEAN K	CPT	O-0336712	0549	2
WOOD DON R	CW3	W-2122834	0167	1
WOOD DONALD F	MAJ	O-2014473	0765	1
WOOD DONALD K	CW2	W-2206985	1163	1

NAME	GRADE	SVC NO	DATE RET MO YR	RET CODE
WOOD DONALD L	LTC	O-0122157	0144	2
WOOD DONALD M	2LT	O-1311724	0344	2
WOOD EARL L	COL	O-0174912	1054	3
WOOD EARL S	MAJ	O-1923672	0367	1
WOOD EDWARD J	CW4	W-2142673	0758	1
WOOD EDWARD L	1LT	O-0304223	0742	2
WOOD EDWARD M	CW3	W-2142919	0157	1
WOOD EDWARD S	LTC	O-0390059	0660	2
WOOD EDWARD W	LTC	O-0239431	0259	3
WOOD EDWIN C	1LT	O-1183797	0946	2
WOOD ELDON G	MAJ	O-0276422	1060	1
WOOD ELMER D	MAJ	O-0227198	0546	2
WOOD ERNEST	CPT	O-0109628	0931	1
WOOD ERNEST L	LTC	O-1635492	0259	1
WOOD FENTON M	COL	O-0166365	0955	2
WOOD FRANK B	LTC	O-0228190	1163	3
WOOD FRANK C JR	LTC	O-0105418	1051	3
WOOD FRANK D	LTC	O-0182911	1060	2
WOOD GEORGE F	LTC	O-1175364	0563	1
WOOD GEORGE W	MAJ	O-0207267	0554	3
WOOD GEORGE W	COL	O-0257822	0565	3
WOOD GILBERT F	COL	O-0451533	1060	1
WOOD GLEN B	COL	O-0256692	0159	3
WOOD HAROLD N	COL	O-0392351	0467	1
WOOD HAROLD S	CW4	W-2117645	0959	1
WOOD HARRY A JR	1LT	O-5513350	0264	2
WOOD HARRY C	MAJ	O-1181806	0457	1
WOOD HERFERD M	COL	O-0323741	0546	2
WOOD HERMAN A	LTC	O-0412077	0162	1
WOOD HERMAN V	MAJ	O-2292488	0168	1
WOOD HOLLIS O	CW3	W-2141500	0159	1
WOOD HOMER L	MAJ	O-1796592	1266	3
WOOD HORACE	CW4	W-2118293	1154	1
WOOD HORACE M	COL	O-0259447	0963	1
WOOD HOWARD D	LTC	O-1796395	1061	1
WOOD HOWARD S	1LT	O-2049768	0846	2
WOOD JACK H	CPT	O-0520437	0546	2
WOOD JACK N	CW2	W-2152664	0361	1
WOOD JAMES A	COL	O-0111569	0648	3
WOOD JAMES C	CPT	O-0991588	0757	2
WOOD JAMES E	COL	O-0203813	0954	1
WOOD JAMES E	LTC	O-0471423	0955	1
WOOD JAMES E	CW3	W-2144202	0961	1
WOOD JAMES I	CW2	W-3250454	0567	1
WOOD JAMES W	CW4	W-2131026	0668	1
WOOD JASON G	CPT	O-1701733	1044	2
WOOD JEFFREY F	1LT	O-5238604	0368	2
WOOD JOE T	LTC	O-0509574	1054	1
WOOD JOEL S	LTC	O-0341756	0459	1
WOOD JOHN B	1LT	O-1322389	0846	2
WOOD JOHN H	MAJ	O-0965804	1162	1
WOOD JOHN H	1LT	O-1551993	0451	1
WOOD JOHN H	MAJ	O-2263051	1164	1
WOOD JOHN M	1LT	O-1311461	0846	2
WOOD JOHN O	LTC	O-1172344	1160	1
WOOD JOHN P	CPT	O-1016397	1262	1
WOOD JOHN R	1LT	O-1306936	0660	1
WOOD JOHN V	CW3	W-2149032	0557	1
WOOD JOSEPH	LTC	O-1543746	0361	1
WOOD JOSEPH D	MAJ	O-0975532	0267	1
WOOD JOSEPH F	LTC	O-0248315	1163	3
WOOD JUSTIN A	LTC	O-0185060	0855	3
WOOD KENNETH A	MAJ	O-0204550	0154	3
WOOD LAWRENCE F	CPT	O-0346206	0544	2
WOOD LEONARD B	MAJ	O-1342144	0866	1
WOOD LEONARD F	LTC	O-1185325	1163	1
WOOD LESLIE C	LTC	O-0294452	1061	1
WOOD LESLIE E	CW4	W-2118342	0559	1
WOOD LOUIS F	1LT	O-1796198	0551	2
WOOD MARK A	MAJ	O-1589594	0264	3
WOOD MASON H	1LT	O-1030733	0245	2
WOOD MORRIS B	CPT	O-0505524	1146	1
WOOD MORTON JR	1LT	O-0549684	0952	2
WOOD NEWELL C	1LT	O-0432524	0444	2
WOOD NEWTON B	MAJ	O-0281260	1168	3

NAME	GRADE	SVC NO	DATE RET MO YR	RET CODE
WOOD PAUL W	CPT	O-0122443	0656	3
WOOD PENMAN J	CPT	O-0145901	0853	3
WOOD PHILIP A	CPT	O-0392493	0944	2
WOOD RALPH H	CPT	O-0968635	1157	1
WOOD RAYMOND F	CPT	O-1298476	0346	2
WOOD REED D	CPT	O-1826044	0647	2
WOOD REGINALD H	COL	O-0173485	0550	3
WOOD RHYS C	LTC	O-1081044	0767	1
WOOD RICHARD A	LTC	O-1640140	0561	1
WOOD RICHARD H	COL	O-0397972	1045	2
WOOD RICHARD S	MAJ	O-1895674	1262	1
WOOD ROBERT B	COL	O-0345737	0161	1
WOOD ROBERT E	2LT	O-0234038	0255	3
WOOD ROBERT J	CPT	O-1878634	0264	2
WOOD ROBERT L	MAJ	O-1037952	0464	1
WOOD ROBERT W JR	LTC	O-0257561	0168	3
WOOD ROLAND M JR	LTC	O-0451518	0960	1
WOOD ROY S	LTC	O-0115564	0755	3
WOOD RYAN L	LTC	O-0180607	0361	3
WOOD SAMUEL S	LTC	O-0339123	0659	1
WOOD THOMAS C	1LT	O-0335056	0264	3
WOOD THOMAS L	LTC	O-0284118	0264	3
WOOD THOMAS S	MAJ	O-0221314	1059	3
WOOD THOMAS W	LTC	O-0302898	0859	2
WOOD THORNTON H	LTC	O-0243587	0757	3
WOOD VIBERT F	LTC	O-0923735	1157	1
WOOD VICTOR H	LTC	O-1556827	1167	1
WOOD WALTER A	LTC	O-0236618	1263	3
WOOD WALTER J	LTC	O-0525578	1165	3
WOOD WARREN C	M G	O-0295588	0768	3
WOOD WARREN W	CW2	W-2004756	0760	2
WOOD WEBSTER D	1LT	O-0443966	0146	2
WOOD WILLIAM A	LTC	O-0202134	0252	3
WOOD WILLIAM A	COL	O-0361652	0147	2
WOOD WILLIAM A	MAJ	O-0397852	1060	1
WOOD WILLIAM A	LTC	O-0499027	0763	3
WOOD WILLIAM B	2LT	O-0920370	1043	2
WOOD WILLIAM E	LTC	O-0304597	0662	1
WOOD WILLIAM F	MAJ	O-1948855	1065	1
WOOD WILLIAM E JR	MAJ	O-1042747	0159	1
WOOD WILLIAM J	LTC	O-1166872	0858	1
WOOD WILLIAM K	COL	O-0287119	0357	1
WOOD WILLIAM L	CW3	W-2125856	0457	2
WOOD WILLIAM N	LTC	O-0483195	0655	1
WOOD WILLIAM O	CPT	O-1651075	0557	1
WOOD WILLIAM S	B G	O-0273707	0658	3
WOOD WILSON B	COL	O-0185638	0158	3
WOOD WOODROW W	2LT	O-1315250	0845	2
WOOD WYATT B	CPT	O-1180778	1068	2
WOOD WYATT R	MAJ	O-1013202	0361	1
WOODALL CHARLES W	LTC	O-0171501	0648	3
WOODALL EMERY L	1LT	O-0919068	0943	2
WOODALL JOHN B	MAJ	O-1328208	0762	1
WOODALL JOHN F	MAJ	O-1688624	0563	1
WOODALL PAUL F	CPT	O-0995951	0861	1
WOODALL RALPH G	CPT	O-0281139	0146	2
WOODARD ALVIN H	CW4	W-2106066	0555	1
WOODARD CARLETON R	CW2	W-3430172	1166	1
WOODARD CHARLES C	1LT	O-0552060	0346	2
WOODARD CHARLES W	LTC	O-0368622	1168	3
WOODARD DONALD S	1LT	O-1011636	0445	2
WOODARD JOHN C	CPT	O-0314815	0845	2
WOODARD RANDLE	CW2	W-2146147	0659	1
WOODARD ROBERT G	CPT	O-1045003	0446	2
WOODARD WILFRIO H	CW3	W-2111435	0255	1
WOODARD WILLIAM O	MAJ	O-1015063	0757	1
WOODARD WILLIAM R	MAJ	O-0400062	0646	2
WOODBECK CAROL E	CW2	RW-2210166	0965	1
WOODBERRY JAMES W	LTC	O-0373443	0260	2
WOODBRIDGE MULFORD	MAJ	O-1560466	0666	1
WOODBRIDGE WILLIAM W	LTC	O-0297893	0246	2
WOODBURN JOHN C	LTC	O-0317889	0263	1
WOODBURN ROBERT L	MAJ	O-1289848	0750	2
WOODBURNE ARTHUR R	COL	O-0263888	1261	3
WOODBURY CLARENCE C	MAJ	O-0157577	1047	1

NAME	GRADE	SVC NO	DATE RET MO YR	RET CODE
WOODBURY CORYTON M	B G	0-0252344	0766	3
WOODBURY EDWARD L	LTC	0-1105935	1161	1
WOODBURY JOSEPH L	CPT	0-0273400	0154	1
WOODBURY LYNN W	CW2	W-2206049	0163	1
WOODBURY ROLISTON S	1LT	0-0178109	0755	3
WOODCOCK DON H	1LT	0-1108429	1144	2
WOODDELL JOSEPH S	LTC	0-1845128	0665	3
WOODELL CARLTON D	LTC	0-1015847	0364	1
WOODEN LEVY K	CPT	0-1053023	0662	1
WOODEND ELMER E	COL	0-0284210	0662	3
WOODFIELD JAMES F	CW3	W-2147812	0465	1
WOODFIN HOWEL W	CPT	0-1545549	0447	2
WOODFORD MARION J	CPT	0-0245441	1064	3
WOODFORD WILLIAM H	COL	0-0326586	0962	1
WOODFORD WILLIAM I	LTC	0-0406587	0364	3
WOODHAM GRADY H	CPT	0-1041262	0157	1
WOODHOUSE HANS C	CPT	0-0446576	0245	2
WOODHOUSE MILTON E	LTC	0-0332916	0661	3
WOODHOUSE THOMAS J	CW2	W-2149314	1060	1
WOODILLA JOHN F	MAJ	0-0244571	1048	2
WOODIN KNOWLTON M	LTC	0-0174413	0259	3
WOODIN WILLIS E	MAJ	0-0290047	0853	3
WOODLAND PAUL S	MAJ	0-0990218	1056	1
WOODLEY FORREST L	CPT	0-0265681	0464	3
WOODLEY GERALD A B	COL	0-0254770	1266	3
WOODLEY LOREN G	1LT	0-1585104	1047	2
WOODLEY TOLLEY O JR	LTC	0-1018005	0566	1
WOODMAN ARNOLD J	LTC	0-0196069	1158	3
WOODMAN ARTHUR P	LTC	0-0274662	0354	3
WOODMAN DONALD H	CPT	0-0302943	0246	2
WOODMAN HAROLD	MAJ	0-5301332	0468	1
WOODMAN KARL W	LTC	0-0402976	0659	1
WOODRING JOSEPH H JR	MAJ	0-0955914	0364	1
WOODRING ORVILLE W	CW2	W-2151116	1059	1
WOODRING RAYMOND B	1LT	0-1190097	0546	2
WOODROME MITCHELL	CPT	0-0475333	0654	1
WOODROW CHARLES W	COL	0-0168444	1060	3
WOODROW FITZ W M	COL	0-0113801	0551	3
WOODROW JACK H	2LT	0-1051339	0745	2
WOODROW JAMES Y	MAJ	0-0910731	0964	3
WOODRUFF BERTRAM F	MAJ	0-0490572	1052	1
WOODRUFF BYRON E	1LT	0-1293369	1144	2
WOODRUFF CHARLES W	COL	0-0193767	0856	3
WOODRUFF DEMA F	MAJ	N-0734115	0265	1
WOODRUFF EDITH M	CPT	L-0521506	0447	2
WOODRUFF FRANCIS R	MAJ	0-0180530	1155	3
WOODRUFF GERALD G	COL	0-0247769	1154	3
WOODRUFF HIRAM G	1LT	0-0236702	1165	3
WOODRUFF JAMES M	WO1	W-2124534	0257	1
WOODRUFF MARION W	LTC	0-0262446	0165	3
WOODRUFF NORBERT A	CW3	W-2205589	0167	1
WOODRUFF REID J	CW3	W-2207139	0666	1
WOODRUFF WARREN V	COL	0-0303501	0662	1
WOODRUFF WILLIAM H	CW3	W-2151769	0959	1
WOODRUFF WILLIAM L	COL	0-0263203	0446	2
WOODRUFF WILLIAM L	LTC	0-0447622	0657	1
WOODRUM RICHARD B	2LT	0-2025698	0153	2
WOODS BEN H	MAJ	0-1341612	0861	1
WOODS CHARLES A JR	MAJ	0-0215583	0763	3
WOODS CHARLES H JR	LTC	0-0201336	0857	3
WOODS CHESTER A	CPT	0-0464231	0855	1
WOODS CLAIR L	CW4	W-2141963	0766	1
WOODS CLELL L	1LT	0-1294057	0346	2
WOODS DON E	LTC	0-0216140	1060	3
WOODS DOYLE F	CW2	W-2215959	1068	1
WOODS EDWARD M JR	LTC	0-0208344	0263	3
WOODS EDWIN R	MAJ	0-0979087	1164	1
WOODS ERNEST J	MAJ	0-0267177	1057	3
WOODS FOLEY O	CPT	0-0503864	0755	1
WOODS FORREST M	1LT	0-1999483	1049	1
WOODS FRANCIS J	MAJ	0-1302312	1065	1
WOODS FRANCIS L	LTC	0-0290753	0765	3
WOODS FRANK N	MAJ	0-0196537	0260	3
WOODS GEORGE E	CW2	W-2151055	0658	1
WOODS HARRY L	CW2	W-2148896	0760	1

NAME	GRADE	SVC NO	DATE RET MO YR	RET CODE
WOODS IVAN F	1LT	0-0455327	0445	2
WOODS JACOB C	LTC	0-1548598	0661	1
WOODS JAMES J	LTC	0-0180590	0649	3
WOODS JAMES R	LTC	0-1110898	0163	1
WOODS JAMES S	1LT	0-1062752	0346	2
WOODS JOE W	CW2	W-2114070	1159	1
WOODS JOE W	CW2	W-2144857	0755	1
WOODS JOHN I	MAJ	0-1799497	0562	1
WOODS JOHN L	MAJ	0-1016860	0457	1
WOODS JOHN T	CW2	W-2210692	0364	1
WOODS JOSEPH M	CPT	0-0176226	1057	3
WOODS KENNETH M	LTC	0-1551344	0263	1
WOODS LEE I	CPT	0-2262871	0361	1
WOODS LELAND L	MAJ	0-1683469	1060	1
WOODS LESTER K	LTC	0-0251235	0265	3
WOODS LIZZIE O	MAJ	N-0734366	0661	1
WOODS MARJORIE E	CPT	N-0767256	1146	1
WOODS MARY	MAJ	N-0721733	0768	1
WOODS NOEL A	CPT	0-0435830	1045	2
WOODS NORMAN T	LTC	0-0422278	0162	1
WOODS ONEIL	CW3	W-2146104	0959	1
WOODS OREN L	WO1	W-2146913	0161	1
WOODS PATRICK	MAJ	0-1314216	0657	1
WOODS PERRY L	LTC	0-0234095	0654	3
WOODS RALPH E	CW4	W-2152015	1266	1
WOODS ROBERT E	LTC	0-1168983	0764	1
WOODS ROBERT F	LTC	0-0347957	0660	1
WOODS SAMUEL H	MAJ	0-1575645	0446	2
WOODS THOMAS	CW4	W-2102574	0955	1
WOODS WILLIAM J	CPT	0-1825390	0946	2
WOODS WILLIAM M	CW4	W-2117251	1154	1
WOODS WOODROW F	CPT	0-2263555	0463	2
WOODSIDE ALBERT	CW4	W-2142418	0865	1
WOODSIDE ARTHUR L	LTC	0-0309050	1045	2
WOODSIDE CHARLES L	1LT	0-0232866	0665	3
WOODSIDE JAMES P	CPT	0-0327139	0651	2
WOODSIDE ROBERT B	MAJ	0-1639833	0957	1
WOODSON BOB M	CPT	0-1045316	0860	1
WOODSON LEWIS E	CPT	0-0954782	1058	1
WOODSON ROBERT S	LTC	0-0246805	1054	3
WOODSON WALTON W	CPT	0-1550732	0946	2
WOODWARD CALVIN L	CW3	W-2206100	0464	1
WOODWARD DOUGLAS C	CPT	0-2205215	1266	2
WOODWARD EARL B	CPT	0-1173130	0655	1
WOODWARD EDWIN D	LTC	0-0145903	0256	3
WOODWARD FRANCES L	1LT	N-0732030	0746	1
WOODWARD FRANK A	MAJ	0-0188525	0648	3
WOODWARD FRANK L	COL	0-0364937	0863	3
WOODWARD FRED H	CW3	W-2143306	0265	1
WOODWARD FRED W	CPT	0-0309942	1061	3
WOODWARD GETTA	CPT	0-0176541	0932	1
WOODWARD HAROLD S	LTC	0-0196711	0961	3
WOODWARD HERBERT E	CW3	W-2144033	0661	2
WOODWARD JABISH H JR	MAJ	0-0118972	0849	3
WOODWARD JESSE A JR	CW3	W-2142920	0659	1
WOODWARD JOHN W	MAJ	0-1824951	0961	1
WOODWARD LEWIS M	LTC	0-0265559	0665	3
WOODWARD MORTIMER H	CPT	0-0287256	0967	3
WOODWARD RAY O	MAJ	0-1105937	0553	1
WOODWARD ROBERT E	COL	0-0175949	1056	3
WOODWARD ROBERT M	COL	0-0266777	1158	3
WOODWARD STANLEY	CPT	0-0279596	0351	1
WOODWARD THEODORE E	LTC	0-0368004	1046	2
WOODWARD THOMAS O	LTC	0-0270688	0168	3
WOODWARD TIMOTHY F	LTC	0-1041689	0264	2
WOODWARD WALLACE W	MAJ	0-0333009	0246	2
WOODWARD WALTER H	LTC	0-0488840	0457	1
WOODWARD WILLIAM S	CW3	W-2003752	0767	1
WOODWORTH GILBERT J	CW4	W-2006333	0168	3
WOODWORTH HAROLD A	1LT	0-1303244	0645	2
WOODWORTH MARION D	COL	0-0334887	0557	3
WOODWORTH PHILIP S	CPT	0-1946895	1050	2
WOODWORTH THOMAS L	MAJ	0-0285675	0368	3
WOODWORTH VALORUS C	LTC	0-1646130	0864	1
WOODWORTH WALTER R	LTC	0-1947124	0867	1

NAME	GRADE	SVC NO	DATE RET MO YR	RET CODE
WOODWORTH WAYNE O	CPT	0-2262944	0866	2
WOODY CLARENCE W	1LT	0-0197846	0648	3
WOODY MONTFORD H	MAJ	0-0193719	0843	2
WOODY RONAL E JR	MAJ	0-1309642	0446	2
WOODY THOMAS W	MAJ	0-0304279	0446	2
WOODYARD WILLARD A	COL	0-0351013	0860	1
WOOG AUDREY J	2LT	N-0772367	0845	1
WOOLARD BERL L	1LT	0-1030438	0645	2
WOOLAVER CECIL G	CPT	0-1080593	1044	2
WOOLDRIDGE GLEN E	CPT	0-0491453	0953	1
WOOLDRIDGE JOHN P	LTC	0-0410067	0960	1
WOOLDRIDGE KERMIT D	LTC	0-0451748	0258	1
WOOLDRIDGE LUKE C	CPT	0-0314926	0366	3
WOOLDRIDGE TROY T	CW3	W-2146789	0763	1
WOOLDRIDGE WILLIAM F	COL	0-0184631	1053	1
WOOLERY BRUCE A	1LT	0-1825582	1045	2
WOOLEVER NEIL F	LTC	0-1177252	0663	1
WOOLEY KEITH F	CW2	W-2215296	0668	2
WOOLEY MYRTIS N	LTC	N-0743351	1062	1
WOOLF DONALD D	CPT	0-0105903	0258	3
WOOLF EMERSON C	CPT	0-0143265	0648	3
WOOLF HAROLD F	LTC	0-0904984	0562	1
WOOLF MARTIN P	CPT	0-0512972	1045	2
WOOLFORD FRANK R	LTC	0-0195368	0961	3
WOOLFORD LEON M JR	CW3	W-2143394	0762	1
WOOLFORD SAMUEL P	MAJ	0-0261768	0368	3
WOOLHEATER ELWOOD J	CW2	W-2146466	0766	2
WOOLHEATER RAYMOND H	CW3	W-2207057	0665	1
WOOLLETT WILLIAM JR	1LT	0-1862271	0254	2
WOOLLEY ARTHUR H	LTC	0-1283708	0860	1
WOOLLEY EARL K	MAJ	0-2014809	0663	1
WOOLLEY FRED K	LTC	0-0271568	0867	3
WOOLLEY GEORGE R	LTC	0-0257307	0663	3
WOOLLEY MAURICE W	MAJ	0-0489936	0247	1
WOOLPERT WALTER R	COL	0-0906790	1053	2
WOOLRIDGE REGINALD H	MAJ	0-1173514	0265	1
WOOLSEY ERNEST L	MAJ	0-0278634	0560	3
WOOLSEY GEORGE C	COL	0-0385954	0661	1
WOOLSEY HOWARD H	CW4	W-2148197	0368	1
WOOLSEY ROBERT J	MAJ	0-0260158	0267	3
WOOLSEY WILLIAM P	CPT	0-1180098	0746	2
WOOLSTENCROFT W R	1LT	0-1101722	0843	2
WOOLUMS ALBERT B	COL	0-0109586	0753	3
WOOLUMS CHARLES N	CPT	0-0402189	0763	1
WOOLVERTON WILLIAM H	MAJ	0-0192761	0553	3
WOOSLEY FRANK P	1LT	0-0438365	0245	2
WOOSTER CHARLES L	CPT	0-0341072	0967	3
WOOSTER FRANCIS E	MAJ	0-1878714	0968	1
WOOSTER JAMES F	LTC	0-0253883	0562	3
WOOSTER MALLERY O	LTC	0-0236441	0165	3
WOOTAN EDWARD C	CPT	0-1102124	0562	1
WOOTEN BOYD W	CW2	W-2148911	0464	1
WOOTEN JAMES A	LTC	0-1297464	0565	1
WOOTEN LOWELL C	MAJ	0-0981844	1264	1
WOOTEN WOOTEN	MAJ	0-0351014	0760	2
WOOTERS PERCIVAL C	COL	0-0304428	1158	1
WOOTON JAMES E	CPT	0-1312831	0965	1
WOOTRESS JOHN A	CW2	W-3440031	0868	1
WORCOTT ARTHUR J	COL	0-0166470	0151	3
WORD FRED L	MAJ	0-1100402	0959	1
WORD KARL H	MAJ	0-0245792	0966	3
WORD SAMUEL B	COL	0-0380389	0168	3
WORDEN BRUCE L	1LT	0-2017322	0747	2
WORDEN GEORGE F	MAJ	0-0961537	0163	1
WORDEN ROBERT P	MAJ	0-0407816	0446	2
WORDEN WILLIAM G	LTC	0-0492796	1262	1
WORDLEY CARL E	LTC	0-1288838	0954	1
WORDLEY STANLEY C	COL	0-1534422	1263	1
WORF GEORGE H	LTC	0-1307608	0763	1
WORHUCK GEORGE W	CW4	W-2120910	0155	1
WORK ARTHUR L	CW4	W-2119872	1154	1
WORK EDGAR A	COL	0-0251985	1066	3
WORK HERMAN	COL	0-0145782	0848	3
WORK JAMES E	LTC	0-0433317	0665	1
WORK RALPH H	LTC	0-0501738	0158	1

NAME	GRADE	SVC NO	DATE RET MO YR	RET CODE
WORKING JESSE D	MAJ	0-0133434	1050	3
WORKMAN JOHN H	1LT	0-1041266	0345	2
WORKMAN WARNER G	LTC	0-0127873	0648	3
WORKMAN WILLIAM V	CPT	0-0419528	0545	2
WORKS FORREST E	LTC	0-2014646	0168	1
WORKS ROY C	CPT	0-2033323	1058	1
WORLAND WILFRID V	COL	0-0270095	0667	3
WORLEIN FRANCIS L	CW2	W-2151819	0262	1
WORLEY BERNICE	LTC	N-0728217	0661	1
WORLEY CHARLES D	LTC	0-1648564	1267	1
WORLEY DELMA A	MAJ	N-0760611	0663	1
WORLEY HORACE D	LTC	0-1533952	0656	1
WORLEY JAMES M	CW3	W-2205365	0168	1
WORLEY JESSIE E	1LT	N-0759688	0546	1
WORLEY OLIVER N JR	LTC	0-1580528	0562	1
WORLEY STEWART E	LTC	0-0248550	1165	3
WORLUND CARL R	CPT	0-0987298	1161	1
WORMAN BENJAMIN	1LT	0-1303985	0246	2
WORMSER YESNER M	LTC	0-1287641	1164	1
WORMSLEY CLAUDE U	CW2	W-2149852	0361	1
WORONIECKI JOHN	MAJ	0-0999017	0165	1
WORRALL C L	CPT	0-0417768	1145	2
WORRALL JAY W JR	LTC	0-1633652	0766	1
WORRALL KENNETH R	LTC	0-1583863	1164	1
WORRALL WILLIAM E	LTC	0-0455111	1160	1
WORRELL DENVER	WO1	W-2118088	0149	1
WORRELL EDGAR V	COL	0-0461071	0954	1
WORRELL JAMES B	LTC	0-0482670	1054	1
WORRELL JAMES H	LTC	0-2004022	1068	1
WORRELL THOMAS A	LTC	0-1044732	0162	1
WORSECK PAUL J	LTC	0-0347126	0968	3
WORSHAM WALLACE V	CW4	W-2106098	0960	1
WORSLEY JOSEPH E	1LT	0-0439385	0444	2
WORST HAROLD J	LTC	0-0286161	1059	3
WORTH AMOS R	LTC	0-1045005	0966	1
WORTH APLINE E	1LT	N-0761844	1145	1
WORTH GEORGE A	MAJ	0-1114815	1159	1
WORTH JACK L	MAJ	0-0787224	0865	1
WORTH LEWIS B	LTC	0-0485510	0450	2
WORTH RAYMOND J SR	CPT	0-0535210	1165	1
WORTHAM HOWARD F	COL	0-0133815	0152	3
WORTHAM SAMUEL S JR	CPT	0-0450135	0146	2
WORTHEM DAIL R	CW2	W-2152756	0163	1
WORTHEN FRANK P	LTC	0-1168984	0960	1
WORTHEN LEE V	LTC	0-0945676	0667	1
WORTHING KENNETH E	COL	0-0250447	0265	3
WORTHINGTON CHARLE	COL	0-0418299	1154	1
WORTHINGTON CHARLIE	MAJ	0-0475362	0753	1
WORTHINGTON ELIZABET	MAJ	N-0759585	0866	3
WORTHINGTON FRED	LTC	0-0471418	0853	1
WORTHINGTON FRED H	MAJ	0-0290231	1045	2
WORTHINGTON GEORGE E	CPT	0-0135525	0648	3
WORTHINGTON NEAL	MAJ	0-1638827	0760	1
WORTHINGTON SETH	CPT	0-1285163	0146	2
WORTHLEY PAUL L	LTC	0-1823680	0163	1
WORTHY LYNWOOD N	CPT	0-1878180	0867	2
WORTMAN HUGH M	CPT	0-0204358	0856	3
WOTHERSPOON GEORGE N	LTC	0-0451795	0965	1
WOTHERSPOON HUGH	MAJ	0-1824164	0666	1
WOTHERSPOON MATTHEW	MAJ	0-0993770	0664	1
WOTHERSPOON SAMUEL G	MAJ	0-2103057	0568	1
WOTRING DONALD R	CW3	W-2153274	0161	1
WOTRING ELLSWORTH	CPT	0-0276168	1068	3
WOTRING MARGARETN	2LT	N-0729636	1144	1
WOTT ALFRED	1LT	0-0289052	0843	2
WOTTLIN WILLIAM D	CPT	0-0404295	1044	2
WOYTON HENRY T	MAJ	0-0224574	1161	3
WOZENCRAFT JAMES P	MAJ	0-1885920	1166	1
WOZENSKI JOSEPH P	LTC	0-0407474	0464	1
WOZNEY MICHAEL J	COL	0-0308754	0362	2
WOZNIAK JOHN	MAJ	0-2005690	0366	1
WOZNIAK JOSEPH J	CW4	W-2111356	1165	2
WRANG ARVIE L	MAJ	0-2006844	0166	1
WRATCHFORD DORCEY H	LTC	0-1284621	0456	1
WRAY ANDREW F	MAJ	0-0174129	0462	3

NAME	GRADE	SVC NO	DATE RET MO YR	RET CODE
WRAY CHARLES V	CPT	0-0390664	0245	2
WRAY FRANCIS M	LTC	0-0174992	0651	2
WRAY GEORGE W	COL	0-0214701	0863	3
WRAY JOHN J	MAJ	0-0114002	0648	3
WRAY LINCOLN A	LTC	0-1017937	0563	1
WRAY SAMUEL S JR	LTC	0-0511092	0564	1
WRAY WALTER N	CPT	0-0160290	1145	2
WREN CLOVIS H	1LT	0-2025393	0949	1
WREN J T	LTC	0-1103839	0359	1
WREN JAMES T	LTC	0-2274783	1265	1
WREN WILLIAM F JR	LTC	0-0196854	0958	1
WRENN LAWRENCE W	LTC	0-1586380	1165	1
WRENN OSCAR I	B G	0-0221793	0364	3
WREVER JACK	1LT	0-0886898	0550	1
WREYFORD LOUIE M	MAJ	0-1589598	0568	3
WRIGHT ALBERT H	COL	0-1307609	1263	3
WRIGHT ALBERT J	LTC	0-2046304	0657	1
WRIGHT ALFRED C	CW3	W-2129247	1058	1
WRIGHT ALONZO W	CPT	0-1685214	0545	2
WRIGHT ANITA W	MAJ	N-0753077	0964	1
WRIGHT ARTHUR	CW3	W-2143758	0365	2
WRIGHT AUBREY B	2LT	0-0210775	0245	1
WRIGHT BEN	WO1	W-2113834	0862	2
WRIGHT BERTRAM C	LTC	0-0282988	0860	1
WRIGHT BRUTUS L	CW2	W-2213000	0567	1
WRIGHT BURCHARD E	COL	0-0294378	0668	3
WRIGHT BYRON C	MAJ	0-0278572	0752	3
WRIGHT CARL J JR	MAJ	0-1040640	1160	1
WRIGHT CARROLL	COL	0-0284216	1163	3
WRIGHT CHARLES A	LTC	0-0247581	0466	3
WRIGHT CHARLES F	COL	0-0245379	0966	3
WRIGHT CHARLES E JR	LTC	0-0543492	1063	1
WRIGHT CHARLES H	WO1	W-2122484	0247	1
WRIGHT CHAUNCEY J	1LT	0-0506641	1263	1
WRIGHT CHESTER F	COL	0-0106003	0752	3
WRIGHT CHESTER M	1LT	0-1011907	0660	1
WRIGHT CLARENCE J	CPT	0-1042990	0755	1
WRIGHT CLEO J	1LT	0-0378499	1045	2
WRIGHT CLIFTON A	LTC	0-1303586	1262	1
WRIGHT DANA M	LTC	0-0165588	1051	3
WRIGHT DANIEL P	1LT	0-0405379	0960	1
WRIGHT DAVID F	MAJ	0-2024320	0662	1
WRIGHT DAVID J	LTC	0-0961237	1068	3
WRIGHT DAVID J	MAJ	0-2001069	1060	1
WRIGHT DEWITT	LTC	0-1288155	0457	1
WRIGHT DONALD G	CPT	0-2033613	0657	1
WRIGHT DOUGLAS O	CPT	0-1282388	0157	1
WRIGHT DURWARD O	COL	0-0372751	0546	2
WRIGHT EARL R	CPT	0-0526401	0653	1
WRIGHT EDWARD S	CW3	W-2205647	1064	1
WRIGHT EDWIN C	CW2	W-2146105	0559	1
WRIGHT ELBERT J	CW2	W-2206574	1059	1
WRIGHT ELIZABETH	1LT	N-0751726	0346	1
WRIGHT ELWOOD J	LTC	0-1573690	1053	1
WRIGHT EMORY L	1LT	0-1296959	1045	2
WRIGHT ERNEST C	1LT	0-1320213	1045	2
WRIGHT EUGENE O	2LT	0-1330996	0346	2
WRIGHT EUGENE L	LTC	0-1597222	0166	3
WRIGHT FRANCIS L	CW2	W-2209222	0851	1
WRIGHT FRANK B JR	MAJ	0-0818082	0867	1
WRIGHT FRANK H	COL	0-0113001	0860	1
WRIGHT FRANKLIN B	CPT	0-1114336	0261	1
WRIGHT FRED A	MAJ	0-0103871	1151	3
WRIGHT FRED A	LTC	0-0122535	1050	3
WRIGHT FRED L	1LT	0-0490676	0452	1
WRIGHT FREDERICK	MAJ	0-0371119	0751	2
WRIGHT FREDERICK	CW2	W-2151399	0660	1
WRIGHT GABRIEL N JR	LTC	0-1101296	1066	3
WRIGHT GARVIN D	2LT	0-1596549	0145	2
WRIGHT GEORGE E	MAJ	0-1179257	0765	1
WRIGHT GEORGE E	COL	0-1284259	0962	1
WRIGHT GEORGE H	MAJ	0-2018624	0661	1
WRIGHT GEORGE R	LTC	0-0332975	0441	2
WRIGHT GEORGE T	COL	0-0919957	0764	3
WRIGHT GEORGE W	LTC	0-0273935	0462	3
WRIGHT GEORGE W	MAJ	0-1102557	1160	1
WRIGHT GROVER L	MAJ	0-1646719	0556	1
WRIGHT HAL D	LTC	0-0310212	0666	3
WRIGHT HARLAN P JR	LTC	0-0216348	0760	3
WRIGHT HAROLD C	LTC	0-1003656	0962	1
WRIGHT HAROLD E	CPT	0-1328862	0161	1
WRIGHT HAROLD D	CW2	W-2119565	0252	2
WRIGHT HARRY J	LTC	0-1310330	0962	1
WRIGHT HAZELLE L	2LT	N-0743443	0944	1
WRIGHT HENRY J	LTC	0-0903820	1065	3
WRIGHT HERBERT M	CPT	0-1316116	0646	2
WRIGHT HERSEY L	LTC	0-0321520	0954	1
WRIGHT HOMER A	MAJ	0-0553223	0664	1
WRIGHT HOMER D	COL	0-0180725	0656	3
WRIGHT HOMER E	LTC	0-0402666	0762	1
WRIGHT HORACE E	LTC	0-1166218	0157	1
WRIGHT HOWARD E	CPT	0-2041857	1062	1
WRIGHT HOWARD H	CPT	0-0471025	1044	2
WRIGHT IRA L	MAJ	0-0122534	0150	3
WRIGHT IRVIN W	MAJ	0-1296140	0864	1
WRIGHT JACK H	WO1	W-2129684	0245	2
WRIGHT JACK R	2LT	0-1325347	0845	2
WRIGHT JACK W	LTC	0-1050149	0864	1
WRIGHT JAMES A	MAJ	0-1576831	1061	1
WRIGHT JAMES B	MAJ	0-1996341	0861	1
WRIGHT JAMES C	COL	0-0250021	0346	2
WRIGHT JAMES C JR	MAJ	0-1913268	0468	1
WRIGHT JAMES F	1LT	0-0447055	0352	2
WRIGHT JAMES H	COL	0-0285378	0964	3
WRIGHT JAMES P	1LT	0-2035511	1045	2
WRIGHT JAMES T	MAJ	0-1558991	0961	1
WRIGHT JASPER K	COL	0-0125046	1054	3
WRIGHT JEFF D	CPT	0-0411C[illegible]	0761	1
WRIGHT JESSE	CPT	0-0493442	0145	1
WRIGHT JESSE J	MAJ	0-2102955	0765	1
WRIGHT JOE O	1LT	0-1724521	0246	2
WRIGHT JOHN A	CW3	W-2149273	1062	1
WRIGHT JOHN H	2LT	0-0550528	0146	2
WRIGHT JOHN L	LTC	0-0228687	0344	2
WRIGHT JOHN S	MAJ	0-0299726	1164	3
WRIGHT JOHN T	2LT	0-1598733	0446	2
WRIGHT JOHN W	CPT	0-0464212	0547	1
WRIGHT JOHN W	MAJ	0-1309682	0863	1
WRIGHT JONES T	1LT	0-1554121	0245	2
WRIGHT JOSEPH	LTC	0-0453661	0356	1
WRIGHT JOSEPH E	MAJ	0-0122044	0457	3
WRIGHT JOSEPH H	COL	0-0267842	1265	3
WRIGHT JOSEPH H JR	LTC	0-0450132	0357	1
WRIGHT KATHLEEN D	CPT	N-0722885	0348	1
WRIGHT KENNETH A	MAJ	0-1594575	0357	1
WRIGHT KENNETH A	MAJ	0-1890595	0667	2
WRIGHT LAWRENCE H	LTC	0-0430370	1262	1
WRIGHT LEE W	LTC	0-1549186	0262	1
WRIGHT LEIGH O	LTC	0-0274816	0354	3
WRIGHT LENN	LTC	0-1588387	0167	1
WRIGHT MARTHA G	MAJ	N-0770124	1065	2
WRIGHT MAURICE K	COL	0-0273897	0860	1
WRIGHT MERFOITH S JR	CW3	W-2149496	0664	1
WRIGHT MORGAN J	MAJ	0-0451576	0163	1
WRIGHT OLIVER A	MAJ	0-1540297	1162	1
WRIGHT OWEN O	MAJ	0-1032130	0562	1
WRIGHT PATRICK N	CW2	W-2110347	0567	3
WRIGHT PAUL	LTC	0-0922516	1163	3
WRIGHT PAUL G	COL	0-0275419	0146	2
WRIGHT QUENTIN E	CPT	0-1017993	0746	2
WRIGHT RANDOLPH S	MAJ	0-1574372	0568	3
WRIGHT RAPHAEL G	MAJ	0-0292823	1162	3
WRIGHT RAYMOND H	MAJ	0-0122005	1055	3
WRIGHT RAYMOND L	MAJ	0-1876433	0367	2
WRIGHT RICHARD A	MAJ	0-1886372	0465	1
WRIGHT RICHARD H	CW3	W-2205187	1164	1
WRIGHT RICHARD P	LTC	0-1176859	1163	1
WRIGHT ROBERT A	LTC	0-0903811	0762	1
WRIGHT ROBERT A JR	COL	0-0295059	1057	1
WRIGHT ROBERT F JR	CPT	0-1826038	0567	1
WRIGHT ROBERT H	MAJ	0-1639335	0757	1
WRIGHT ROBERT J	MAJ	0-1639336	0460	1
WRIGHT ROBERT J	MAJ	0-1696627	0162	1
WRIGHT ROBERT R JR	LTC	0-0397060	0862	1
WRIGHT ROGER F	LTC	0-0355314	0263	1
WRIGHT ROSE B	2LT	N-0725469	0944	1
WRIGHT RUSSELL A	1LT	0-1545252	0346	2
WRIGHT SAMUEL P	LTC	0-0510276	0657	1
WRIGHT THERESA A	1LT	N-0774033	0449	2
WRIGHT THOMAS E	MAJ	0-1549190	0461	1
WRIGHT THOMAS H	LTC	0-0337060	0463	1
WRIGHT THOMAS H	LTC	0-0921557	0263	3
WRIGHT THOMAS H	2LT	0-1258329	1043	2
WRIGHT TIOY F	WO1	W-2105906	0146	2
WRIGHT VERL A	CW2	W-0219149	0445	2
WRIGHT VERNON L	LTC	0-1287642	0568	3
WRIGHT WALLACE D	LTC	0-0250022	0367	3
WRIGHT WALTER B	CPT	0-0447724	1145	2
WRIGHT WALTER H	LTC	0-0334300	1068	3
WRIGHT WALTER W	CW2	W-2146139	0658	1
WRIGHT WARREN K	2LT	0-1003078	0844	2
WRIGHT WAYNE W	CPT	0-1012954	1047	2
WRIGHT WILBUR W	LTC	0-1635495	0961	1
WRIGHT WILLIAM A	CW2	W-2152693	0659	1
WRIGHT WILLIAM B	1LT	0-0325753	0345	2
WRIGHT WILLIAM C	COL	0-0106356	0956	3
WRIGHT WILLIAM E	CPT	0-1703306	0246	2
WRIGHT WILLIAM E JR	LTC	0-1290171	1066	1
WRIGHT WILLIAM F	MAJ	0-0272177	0157	3
WRIGHT WILLIAM G	LTC	0-0902127	0347	2
WRIGHT WILLIAM H	CW2	W-2206974	1262	1
WRIGHT WILLIAM P	CW3	W-2145880	0167	1
WRIGHT WILMER R	LTC	0-0249389	0865	3
WRIGHTMAN ERNEST R	MAJ	0-2041220	0765	1
WRIGLEY EDMUND J SR	LTC	0-0904334	0954	3
WRIGLEY HAROLD J	CPT	0-0241005	1060	3
WRIGLEY WILLIAM S	1LT	0-1314218	0747	2
WROBEL THEODORE	CW3	W-2141501	0656	1
WROBLESKI ALBERT L	MAJ	0-1043541	0462	1
WROBLEWSKI FRED J	2LT	0-1639837	0844	2
WROBLEWSKI RAYMOND J	CW3	W-2152729	1165	1
WROE DUGGINS M	MAJ	0-1540885	0766	1
WRONA THEODORE W	2LT	0-1305515	0545	2
WRONKOSKI JOHN F	2LT	0-1299972	0445	2
WROTEN CECIL H	MAJ	0-0417215	1066	3
WROTEN CHARLES W	1LT	0-1796398	0356	1
WROTEN JENNINGS W	LTC	0-0278619	0957	3
WROTNOWSKI WANDA B	MAJ	N-0900417	0962	2
WUBKER ROBERT E	MAJ	0-0295581	0467	3
WUCHER ROBERT JR	COL	0-0336351	0861	1
WUCHTER DONALD H	LTC	0-1597971	0463	1
WUDARSKI EDWARD	LTC	0-1290006	0163	1
WUEPPER ROBERT C	LTC	0-1183003	1162	1
WUERMLI JOSEPH C	LTC	0-1316117	0967	1
WUETHRICH EMMETT H	CW2	W-2147256	0560	1
WULF HORACE F	COL	0-0234413	0156	3
WULF WILLIAM F	COL	0-0245000	0863	3
WULFF EDWIN T	MAJ	0-0447377	0845	2
WULFF MARCUS W	1LT	0-0389011	0444	2
WULFTANGE JOHN A	1LT	0-1014150	0546	2
WULK WALTER H	LTC	0-0169527	0948	2
WULSIN LUCIEN	1LT	0-1113531	1045	2
WUNDER BERNARD J	CPT	0-1303636	0366	2
WUNDERLICH ALBERT M	LTC	0-0256296	0260	1
WUNDERLICH EDWARD H	CPT	0-0529318	0745	2
WUNDERLICH EDWARD JR	1LT	0-1324450	1045	2
WUNDERLICH ERNEST G	MAJ	0-0137222	0453	3
WUNDERLICH FRED J	MAJ	0-1534194	0346	2
WUNSCH CHARLES L	COL	0-0345088	0166	3
WUNSCH VALENTINE	WO1	W-2118541	0146	2
WURDEMAN ROBERT M	MAJ	0-1293345	0361	1
WURDEMANN WILLIAM	LTC	0-0425930	0359	1
WURM JAMES F	2LT	0-0513846	0145	2
WURMSTICH ARTHUR P J	1LT	0-1287805	0546	2
WURTH CHARLES	LTC	0-0402971	0760	1
WURTH JACK F	LTC	0-0966527	0768	1
WURTZ JOHN G JR	CPT	0-0352702	0844	2
WURTZ ROBERT H	LTC	0-1311079	0363	1
WURZBACH FREDERICK	CPT	0-0502711	1057	1
WURZBACH WILLIAM A	LTC	0-0216792	0464	3
WUSTERBARTH H J JR	1LT	0-1327915	0347	2
WUTZKE ALVIN C	MAJ	0-1646722	1060	1
WYANDT LOREN H	LTC	0-0274115	0355	3
WYANT CHARLES W	LTC	0-0919437	0568	3
WYANT PEARL E	CPT	0-0973207	0758	2
WYANT VICTOR R	MAJ	0-1821677	0161	1
WYANT WALTER M	1LT	0-1582286	0346	2
WYATT ANNIE L	1LT	N-0727093	0446	1
WYATT CARL F	LTC	0-0346527	1067	3
WYATT CECILLE B	1LT	N-0734913	0646	2
WYATT CHARLES N	COL	0-0249117	0264	3
WYATT CLIFFORD C	CW2	W-2143276	1155	1
WYATT DOROTHY M	MAJ	N-0733894	0747	1
WYATT FINIS Q	CPT	0-0490068	0343	2
WYATT GLENN E	MAJ	0-1821800	0557	1
WYATT JAMES I	LTC	0-1876298	0968	1
WYATT JOSEPH A	LTC	0-0492397	0764	3
WYATT JOSEPH R	1LT	0-0543427	1145	2
WYATT LEONARD N JR	CW2	W-2208884	0264	1
WYATT LEONARD O	CPT	0-0274844	1047	1
WYATT MASON L	CW2	W-2141875	0556	1
WYATT ROBERT T	CW3	W-2142505	0959	1
WYATT ROBERT W	MAJ	0-0974514	0764	1
WYATT WILLIAM J	CW3	W-2144765	0960	1
WYBENGA SIMON W	LTC	0-1058156	1063	1
WYBORSKI ALOYSIUS S	1LT	0-1292974	0445	2
WYCHE ALBERTA M	2LT	N-0797416	0246	1
WYCHE MURRAY F	LTC	0-0227573	0664	3
WYCKOFF GEORGE C	CPT	0-0491411	0745	2
WYCKOFF GEORGE F	LTC	0-1641084	0662	1
WYCKOFF JOHN H	LTC	0-1109127	0364	1
WYCKOFF JOHN W	LTC	0-0265127	0957	3
WYCKOFF LOWELL A	CPT	0-1291207	0361	1
WYCOFF SAMUEL N	CPT	0-0282922	1059	2
WYERS RALPH L	CW2	W-2152489	1059	1
WYGAL WILLIAM T	MAJ	0-1684971	0964	1
WYGLE JACK M	LTC	0-1169802	1057	1
WYKERT GEORGE C	CW4	W-2122282	0456	1
WYKES THOMAS V	1LT	0-1322611	0346	2
WYKOFF NORMAN F	LTC	0-0212180	0648	3
WYKOWSKI LEONARD A	LTC	0-1042749	0768	3
WYLIE BALDWIN	LTC	0-0249204	0548	2
WYLIE DONALD P	COL	0-0243898	0766	3
WYLIE FRANK B JR	MAJ	0-0357323	0547	2
WYLIE JEROME T	1LT	0-4023943	0656	2
WYLIE JOHN B	LTC	0-1179259	0462	1
WYLIE ROBERT B	LTC	0-0488646	1168	3
WYLIE ROSS	LTC	0-0906607	0566	3
WYLIE WILLIAM A	2LT	0-1057943	1044	2
WYLIE WILLIAM B	1LT	0-1043543	1045	2
WYLLIE JAMES J	CPT	0-0461420	0348	2
WYLLIE JOHN S	MAJ	0-0946715	0166	1
WYLLIE ROBERT	LTC	0-1062105	0962	1
WYMAN GEORGE G JR	LTC	0-1032321	0768	1
WYMAN JEAN M	1LT	N-0757498	1045	1
WYMAN JOHN F	CPT	0-0275225	0661	3
WYMAN JOHN H	LTC	0-0179495	0848	3
WYMAN MARION H	COL	0-0211631	0648	3
WYMAN OLIVER C	COL	0-0113100	0648	3
WYMAN RALPH J	LTC	0-0335971	0556	2
WYMAN VAUGHN L	MAJ	0-1047001	0863	1
WYMAN WILLARD F	CW4	W-2115876	0660	1
WYMER OTTO U	CPT	0-0105714	1043	2
WYMER ROBERT W	CW3	W-2147051	1163	2
WYMORE DONALD H	1LT	0-0355805	0840	2
WYNALDA MARTIN	CPT	0-1309644	0646	2
WYNANT RALPH E	MAJ	0-0518327	1048	2
WYNDHAM JOHN H	CW2	W-2151676	0659	1
WYNER ALEXANDER	1LT	0-0218795	1161	3
WYNN ELLISON C	MAJ	0-1303423	1163	1

ARMY OF THE UNITED STATES RETIRED LIST

NAME	GRADE	SVC NO	DATE RET MO YR	RET CODE
WYNN JOE MONROE	CPT	0-0347183	0468	2
WYNN KAY W	LTC	0-1825458	0962	1
WYNN NORMAN	CPT	0-0277898	1044	1
WYNN THOMAS A	2LT	0-1323765	0368	2
WYNN VERNON	CW2	W-2102583	0250	1
WYNN WILLIAM F	MAJ	0-1112537	1062	1
WYNNE HAHN	LTC	0-1044259	0562	1
WYNNE JAMES F	MAJ	0-1195564	1266	1
WYNNE JAMESON H	MAJ	L-0400253	0268	3
WYNNE JOHN T	COL	0-0414506	0865	1
WYNNE MICHAEL A	LTC	0-0205967	0961	3
WYNNE THOMAS E	LTC	0-0483425	1265	3
WYON REGINALD F	LTC	0-0915369	0967	3
WYRE HARRY W	LTC	0-1114337	0561	1
WYRICK GEORGE B	CPT	0-0103095	0452	2
WYROCHOWSKI EDWARD P	LTC	0-0202691	0648	2
WYSE RALPH M	LTC	0-0451866	0657	1
WYSOCKI BARBARA K	2LT	N-0720961	1144	1
WYSOCKI JOSEPH J	1LT	0-0509520	0260	1
WYSOCKI LOUIS C JR	CW3	W-2205453	0265	1
WYSOCKI PETER W	MAJ	0-1012904	0847	2
WYSOCKY LAWRENCE C	MAJ	0-1010607	0348	2
WYSONG KENNETH W	LTC	0-0265141	0565	3
WYSZYNSKI JOHN	CPT	0-1923568	1262	1
WYSZYNSKI WALTER P	1LT	0-0482848	0744	2
WYTON ROBERT O	1LT	0-1303245	0146	2
WYTTENBACH JOHN F	COL	0-0278330	0561	3
WYVELL HARVEY P	1LT	0-0301367	0744	2
WYZGA MICHAEL A	LTC	0-0451428	1046	2
WZIONTKA STANLEY	CPT	0-0960916	1060	1
XANTHOPOULOS JOHN S	1LT	0-1183004	1046	2
YABE DONALD T	CPT	0-1899436	0865	1
YABLON ABRAHAM	1LT	0-1688073	1044	2
YACHELSON SAMUEL	LTC	0-1894941	0665	3
YACHNIN SAMUEL C	COL	0-0337002	1264	3
YACONO JOSEPH	CW3	W-2208290	0468	1
YADEN LYNN B	LTC	0-0297729	0448	2
YADRICH JOHN H	1LT	0-1310957	0546	2
YAEGER PHILIP E	MAJ	0-1549187	0661	1
YAFFE SOL	CPT	0-1590278	0346	2
YAGER GEORGE E	MAJ	0-1319910	0461	1
YAGER IRVIN I	CPT	0-0352727	0246	2
YAGER JESSE A	1LT	0-1299165	1145	2
YAGER LESLIE JR	MAJ	0-0207431	0452	3
YAGGI HARRY G	LTC	0-0516237	0864	3
YAISLE KARL R	2LT	0-0233738	1158	3
YAKELY HAROLD E	LTC	0-0167419	0258	3
YAKERSON ROBERT	MAJ	0-0411056	1060	1
YALOVITZ MARVIN S	CPT	0-1735222	1045	2
YAMADA SUSUMU	MAJ	0-1998659	0261	1
YAMAKI BILL S	LTC	0-2037914	0965	1
YAMAMOTO STEVE S	LTC	0-0888916	0861	1
YAMAT FEDERICO N	2LT	0-1896376	0957	2
YAMAUCHI JOHN K	MAJ	0-1899404	0364	1
YAMAZAKI ALFRED A	LTC	0-1339499	0267	1
YAMBAO FORTUNATO	1LT	0-1895718	0952	2
YAMBAO FRANCISCO	1LT	0-1896675	0349	1
YAMBOR STEVE P	CPT	0-2055843	0461	1
YANAJSCH ALBERT J	CPT	0-0241261	0662	3
YANCEY DANIEL L JR	COL	0-0268567	0863	3
YANCEY ERNEST V	1LT	0-4010190	0358	2
YANCEY ROBERT C	LTC	0-1588389	0363	2
YANCEY ROBERT C	WO1	W-2113187	0244	2
YANCEY STEPHEN	CPT	0-0492954	0353	1
YANCEY THEODORE F	LTC	0-0233502	0865	3
YANCEY WILLIAM H	CPT	0-0259082	1066	3
YANCOFSKI LEONARD	CW3	W-2143090	1160	1
YANG SUNG CHAI	CW3	W-2149465	0865	1
YANKOFF BORIS E	CPT	0-0934445	0554	1
YANKOSKY JAMES G	MAJ	0-1179691	0363	1
YANKOVICH MATTHEW J	MAJ	0-0454441	0358	1
YANT JAMES H	COL	0-0490500	0367	3
YANT JOHN F	MAJ	0-1318242	0565	1
YANT JOHN T	MAJ	0-2289697	1166	1
YANTZ THOMAS J	MAJ	0-1317361	0263	1

NAME	GRADE	SVC NO	DATE RET MO YR	RET CODE
YANZ HERMAN H	MAJ	0-0502098	0247	2
YAPIT FELIX	1LT	0-1896868	0653	1
YAPP JAMES R	CW2	W-2113722	0948	1
YARBER CHARLES H JR	MAJ	0-2055948	0457	1
YARBER RUTH M	2LT	N-0767165	1044	1
YARBOROUGH ARTHUR P	MAJ	0-1924653	0864	1
YARBOROUGH JOHN M	CPT	0-0264518	0444	2
YARBOROUGH MARVIN D	LTC	0-1041268	0962	2
YARBOROUGH NEILL A	COL	0-0410004	0863	1
YARBOROUGH OWEN H	1LT	0-1300112	0347	2
YARBOROUGH RICHARD L	MAJ	0-2016990	0263	1
YARBROUGH CHARLES L	MAJ	0-1312616	1060	1
YARBROUGH CHARLIE F	CPT	0-0451646	0745	2
YARBROUGH DONALD R	MAJ	0-0972251	0667	1
YARBROUGH EDWIN S JR	LTC	0-0901410	0168	3
YARBROUGH HERMAN F	1LT	0-1556828	1045	2
YARBROUGH JACK B	CW4	W-2146690	0666	1
YARBROUGH JAMES A	MAJ	0-1918956	1166	1
YARBROUGH JOHN M	LTC	0-2007907	0565	1
YARBROUGH JOHN S III	LTC	0-0507967	0268	2
YARBROUGH LUCIEN B	LTC	0-0269535	0964	3
YARBROUGH RICHARD T	MAJ	0-0974500	0163	1
YARBROUGH RUPERT H	LTC	0-0371450	0760	1
YARD ARTHUR J	MAJ	0-0928224	0767	1
YARDLEY FRANK	LTC	0-0509662	1051	1
YARDLEY RALPH B	CPT	0-0388045	1045	2
YARFITZ LEO J	CPT	0-1636853	0845	2
YARMAN CLIFFORD L	MAJ	0-2050706	1059	1
YARNALL DANIEL F	WO1	W-2125219	0450	1
YARNELL RAY A	MAJ	0-0327775	0347	2
YAROSH WASEL	LTC	0-1580533	1061	1
YARTER MAURICE A	CPT	0-1824218	1047	2
YASINOW AARON B	CPT	0-0147043	1145	2
YASKIN PETER P	COL	0-1103482	1068	1
YASKONISH JACOB	CW3	W-2129927	0361	2
YASUNA ALVIN D	MAJ	0-0267120	1068	3
YASVIN RUTH L	MAJ	N-0799489	0765	1
YATES ANDY D	COL	0-0190310	0855	3
YATES ARTHUR T	CPT	0-0450134	0457	1
YATES CLAUD F	CPT	0-0482910	1147	2
YATES CORNELIUS JR	MAJ	0-0252698	1162	3
YATES EARL J	COL	0-0110662	0955	1
YATES EDWARD W	1LT	0-1015086	0945	2
YATES FRANK I	CW2	W-2102585	0953	1
YATES FRANKLIN W	CW2	W-2110000	0245	2
YATES HARRY	CPT	0-0172515	1156	3
YATES HIAWATHA	CPT	0-0502918	1047	1
YATES HUISH F	LTC	0-0373748	0963	1
YATES JOHN A	LTC	0-0885894	0155	1
YATES JUSTIN J	LTC	0-0298488	0566	3
YATES KENNETH	CPT	0-1081115	1147	2
YATES ONA B	LTC	N-0757609	0367	3
YATES RALPH J	MAJ	0-1300431	1146	2
YATES ROBERT B	LTC	0-0285173	0746	2
YATES THOMAS F	COL	0-0304112	1068	3
YATES VINCENT A	COL	0-0265680	0163	3
YATES WILLIAM E	LTC	0-0352560	0358	1
YATES WILLIAM H	LTC	0-1102559	1067	1
YAUGER AARON J	MAJ	0-0177735	0361	3
YAUGER KENYON F	COL	0-0310655	0768	3
YAUKEY JAMES V	CPT	0-0212610	0546	2
YAVELAK WILLIAM	LTC	0-1291557	0657	1
YAVELOW ISSACHER	MAJ	0-0519131	1046	2
YAVNER MAX	MAJ	0-0127266	1052	3
YAWORSKY JOHN	MAJ	0-1824181	0157	1
YAZELL RAYMOND M	LTC	0-0558122	1268	1
YDEEN BROOKS C	LTC	0-1640146	0863	1
YEAGER ABE H	CPT	0-0156230	0648	3
YEAGER CHARLES	CW3	W-2142291	0261	1
YEAGER CHARLES C	MAJ	0-1549419	0765	1
YEAGER GEORGE F	CW2	W-3420020	0467	1
YEAGER KENNETH G	LTC	0-1575646	1061	1
YEAGER LAWRY H	MAJ	0-0969276	0263	2
YEAGER MARY R	MAJ	N-0755864	0667	1
YEAGER ULYSSES B	LTC	0-0229965	0762	3

NAME	GRADE	SVC NO	DATE RET MO YR	RET CODE
YEAGLE LAWRENCE C	MAJ	0-0450526	1058	1
YEAKEL HAROLD J	CW2	W-2911656	1265	1
YEAKLEY HARRY C	CPT	0-2035998	0646	2
YEARGUS GLENN	LTC	0-0182566	1045	2
YEARWOOD IRVING O	LTC	0-1591548	1163	1
YEARY MICHAEL	1LT	0-1053444	0147	1
YEASLEY ROBERT J	LTC	0-0520171	1166	2
YEATES HARRIS S	CW2	W-2104618	0361	1
YEATS ROBERT H	MAJ	0-0542501	1163	1
YEISER WILLIAM C	LTC	0-0338025	0258	1
YELDELL THOMAS J	LTC	0-1045985	0767	1
YELDERMAN ROBERT L	1LT	0-0441435	0844	2
YELLAND WILFRED J	MAJ	0-2026542	0168	2
YELLEN HIRAM S	COL	0-0137335	0146	2
YELLEN MILTON	CPT	0-0482612	1044	2
YELLOWFISH EDWARD	CW4	W-2147167	0868	1
YELVERTON IRA A	CPT	0-1295973	0746	2
YELVERTON JOHN A	2LT	0-1298477	0444	2
YELVERTON JOHN V	MAJ	0-1995025	0662	1
YENCHAR JOHN C	LTC	0-0135639	0155	3
YENCHO JOHN K	MAJ	0-1081045	0658	1
YENNE WALTER D	MAJ	0-2080592	0666	1
YENS OTTO C	COL	0-0194582	0661	2
YENSAN ALBERT F	CPT	0-1313151	0158	1
YENSUS VINCENT T	MAJ	0-1295313	1055	1
YENTER RAYMOND A	B G	0-0120313	0648	3
YEO CHARLES R	COL	0-1180389	1166	1
YEOKUM GEORGE H	1LT	0-0160264	0953	3
YEOMAN DALE A	MAJ	0-0318775	0446	2
YERBY MARION L	MAJ	0-1643474	0159	1
YEREGA WILLIAM	1LT	0-1184340	1145	2
YERKA JAY H	CPT	0-1304477	0661	1
YERKES PAUL F	LTC	0-0395896	0157	2
YERKEY ROY R	LTC	0-0262218	0965	3
YERKS RAYMOND A	LTC	0-1894881	1067	3
YERMAN JESSE	CW4	W-2142785	0563	1
YESKAWICH MICHAEL J	CW2	W-2211922	0967	1
YETSCHKE CLARENCE	MAJ	0-0237415	0956	3
YETTER CHARLES W JR	CW2	W-2152783	0357	2
YETTER JOSEPH F JR	LTC	0-1549743	0162	1
YETTER RUSSELL J	LTC	0-0218585	0254	2
YETWIN ISIDORE J	LTC	0-0946172	0868	3
YLINEN JOHN S	LTC	0-1051846	0662	1
YOAST SAMUEL H JR	MAJ	0-1114338	0761	1
YOCIS JEROME C	CPT	0-1101725	0646	2
YOCKEY CONWAY E	LTC	0-0172882	0159	3
YOCOM GEORGE F	MAJ	0-0504061	0447	2
YOCUM ALVIN L	MAJ	0-2262887	1163	1
YOCUM DOROTHY E	MAJ	N-0769762	0765	1
YOCUM HORACE C	LTC	0-0135570	1054	3
YOCUM HOWARD R	COL	0-0287082	0265	3
YOCUM MAUDE M	2LT	N-0731030	1044	1
YODER ALVIN B	LTC	0-0296369	1047	2
YODER RUSSELL F	LTC	0-0924401	0667	3
YODER THOMAS W	MAJ	0-1701656	0564	1
YOE WILLIAM S	LTC	0-1324601	0263	1
YOES RALPH	1LT	0-1288665	0345	2
YOFFA ALLAN M	1LT	0-0384261	0745	2
YOHALEM MORTON	CPT	0-1689231	0843	2
YOHANNAN JOHN D	CPT	0-0475956	0451	1
YOHE CARL J JR	LTC	0-0316150	0759	2
YOHE CLAIR F	LTC	0-0478282	0464	3
YOHE PERCE P	COL	0-0104439	0153	3
YOHMAN JOSEPH A	1LT	0-0520540	0945	2
YOHN ROBERT A	CW4	W-2108359	0957	1
YOHO ARNOLD J	LTC	0-1012157	0764	1
YOKE NORRIS H	WO1	W-2184564	0155	1
YOKELEY GILBERT W	LTC	0-0461744	0265	3
YOKLEY WILLIAM R	MAJ	0-0137461	0648	3
YOKOE YUKIO	LTC	0-2263049	0868	1
YOKSAS ALBERT C	LTC	0-1573696	0461	1
YOLDA JAMES J	LTC	0-1647814	0268	1
YONAN NORMAN J	1LT	0-1321079	0646	2
YONKER GEORGE H JR	1LT	0-1318504	0557	2
YONKERS ARTHUR J F	CPT	0-1172349	1164	2

NAME	GRADE	SVC NO	DATE RET MO YR	RET CODE
YONKERS DURWARD W	LTC	0-0291521	0664	3
YONKERS LEO E	CPT	0-1321981	0946	2
YONTS ROBERT W	MAJ	0-0517491	0863	1
YONTZ WELDON J	LTC	0-1012964	0761	1
YOQUELET RAY A	MAJ	0-1323644	1057	1
YORDAN JOAQUIN	MAJ	0-1337258	0863	1
YORDE JOHN J	MAJ	0-2212092	0863	1
YORICHI ALEX N	MAJ	0-2033620	0263	1
YORK BEN H	MAJ	0-2016620	0960	1
YORK BROWER V	LTC	0-0163916	0258	3
YORK CHARLES A	LTC	0-0124075	0551	3
YORK EDWARD	CPT	0-0109453	1137	1
YORK FRANCIS L	CPT	0-1018796	0951	2
YORK FRANK E	MAJ	0-2005309	0961	1
YORK GUSTER R	CPT	0-0491454	0953	1
YORK JAMES	LTC	0-0503626	0457	1
YORK JAMES A	CPT	0-0395894	0246	2
YORK JAMES H	MAJ	0-1108436	0158	1
YORK JAMES H	LTC	0-1306190	0857	1
YORK JAMES L	CW2	W-3200389	1167	1
YORK JAMES O	CW3	W-2152260	0159	1
YORK JOHN S	MAJ	0-2212021	0661	1
YORK OTIS E	CPT	0-0450502	1044	2
YORK SAMUEL W	CW3	W-2141723	0858	1
YORK THOMAS D	LTC	0-0196416	0459	3
YORK VINCENT H	MAJ	0-2000086	1060	1
YORK WALTER R	COL	0-0901981	0762	3
YORK WILMA	LTC	N-0783387	1068	3
YORKE ELEANOR E	MAJ	N-0793254	0465	1
YOSHIHASHI TARO	MAJ	W-2135073	0868	1
YOSHIMURA NOBORU	MAJ	0-2030581	0562	1
YOSKIT HARRY	MAJ	0-0162061	0152	3
YOST CHARLES L	LTC	0-0145638	1055	3
YOST CLIFFORD W	MAJ	0-0498456	0856	1
YOST DENZEL M	WO1	W-2116785	0644	2
YOST JAMES F	LTC	0-1688339	0966	1
YOST JORIER H	CPT	0-1284445	0448	2
YOST LELAND J	1LT	0-0113806	0258	3
YOST LIGHT B	COL	0-0288323	0867	3
YOST RICHARD W	CPT	0-0921284	1044	2
YOSTE FLORIAN H	CPT	0-1290699	1045	2
YOTIVE SIMON P	CPT	0-1794860	0346	2
YOUMAN GEORGE L	LTC	0-0429548	0562	1
YOUMANS BENJAMIN L	MAJ	0-0261583	0268	3
YOUMANS CORREN P	COL	0-0234659	1052	3
YOUMANS ROSS C	MAJ	0-0289687	0558	3
YOUNCE JACK H	LTC	0-1915468	1268	1
YOUNDT ALBERT J	COL	0-0287672	0160	1
YOUNG ALBERT	CPT	0-1297466	0251	2
YOUNG ALEXANDER	COL	0-0212480	0663	3
YOUNG ALFRED A	2LT	0-1081499	1144	2
YOUNG ALFRED G	CW3	W-2146929	0160	1
YOUNG ALFRED H	LTC	0-0193997	0860	3
YOUNG ALGERNON G	1LT	0-0398273	0146	2
YOUNG ALLEN B JR	2LT	0-1647345	0645	2
YOUNG ALPHE B	LTC	0-0181100	1156	3
YOUNG AMOS C	LTC	0-0294285	0168	3
YOUNG ARNOLD R	LTC	0-1295814	1167	1
YOUNG ARTHUR F	COL	0-0335928	0658	3
YOUNG BENJAMIN W	CW2	W-2104853	0664	1
YOUNG BLAINE E	MAJ	0-1080981	0258	1
YOUNG C K BOB	CPT	0-0583017	0450	2
YOUNG CALVIN	CW3	W-2145031	0758	1
YOUNG CAREY M	LTC	0-0528163	1156	2
YOUNG CARLETON S	LTC	0-0570890	1165	3
YOUNG CECIL L	CW3	W-2144757	0960	1
YOUNG CHAPMAN JR	CPT	0-1296961	0146	2
YOUNG CHARLES A	COL	0-0183595	0862	3
YOUNG CHARLES D	LTC	0-0337505	0668	3
YOUNG CHARLES E	LTC	0-0166206	0361	3
YOUNG CHARLES L	MAJ	0-0189140	1055	1
YOUNG CHARLES M	MAJ	0-1103021	1060	1
YOUNG CHARLES R	CW2	W-2150182	1158	2
YOUNG CHESTER R	LTC	0-1289184	0767	1
YOUNG CLAIR F	2LT	0-1320495	0145	2

NAME	GRADE	SVC NO	DATE RET MO YR	RET CODE
YOUNG CLARK	COL	0-0224496	0855	2
YOUNG CLAUDE E	LTC	0-1583871	0467	3
YOUNG CLIFFORD L	MAJ	0-0330099	0567	3
YOUNG CLIFTON H	LTC	0-0339053	0660	1
YOUNG CLYDE B	CPT	0-0462133	0245	2
YOUNG DAVID R	LTC	0-0979824	0468	1
YOUNG DEEL E	MAJ	0-0491991	0154	1
YOUNG DEWITT C	LTC	0-0118996	0146	2
YOUNG EDDIE M	LTC	0-0250992	0164	3
YOUNG EDITH L	MAJ	N-0779118	0768	3
YOUNG EDWARD C	1LT	0-1181516	1145	2
YOUNG EDWARD M JR	1LT	0-1578073	0453	1
YOUNG EDWARD S	CPT	0-1053025	0166	1
YOUNG EDWIN L	LTC	0-1582288	0762	1
YOUNG EDWIN S	CPT	0-0450321	1063	3
YOUNG EMERSON J	MAJ	0-0503739	0657	1
YOUNG EMITTE E	MAJ	0-1300902	0959	1
YOUNG EVERETT L	LTC	0-0177450	0261	3
YOUNG FLOYD L	1LT	0-1175454	1045	2
YOUNG FORD E JR	COL	0-0311305	0568	3
YOUNG FOSTER J	LTC	0-0213323	0660	3
YOUNG FRANCIS A JR	CW3	W-2147993	1062	1
YOUNG FRANCIS H	LTC	0-0121223	0653	3
YOUNG FRANCIS J	2LT	0-0888228	0145	2
YOUNG FRANCIS T	LTC	0-1186527	0667	1
YOUNG FRANK E JR	COL	0-0271577	0567	3
YOUNG FRANK G	MAJ	0-0251356	0744	2
YOUNG FRANK H	LTC	0-0888453	0263	1
YOUNG FRANK R	1LT	0-0519986	0945	2
YOUNG FRANKLIN R	MAJ	0-2002382	0355	1
YOUNG FRED I	CPT	0-1914157	0933	1
YOUNG FREDERICK	LTC	0-1284622	0167	1
YOUNG FREDERICK JR	MAJ	0-1926004	0666	1
YOUNG GAIL K H	1LT	N-0789694	1045	1
YOUNG GEORGE F	LTC	0-0251986	1259	3
YOUNG GUILFORD E	CPT	0-0258615	0945	2
YOUNG HAROLD E	CPT	0-1103484	0146	2
YOUNG HAROLD E	LTC	0-1167704	0263	1
YOUNG HAROLD L	2LT	0-1062554	0544	2
YOUNG HARRISON E	CPT	0-1702513	0945	2
YOUNG HARRY C	LTC	0-1010306	1060	1
YOUNG HENRY E	MAJ	0-1646725	0655	1
YOUNG HERBERT	CPT	0-0501624	0747	1
YOUNG HIRAM D	MAJ	0-0319334	1153	1
YOUNG HOMER D	CW4	W-2111120	0454	1
YOUNG HORACE A	WO1	W-2135685	0659	1
YOUNG HOWARD G	LTC	0-0337704	0868	3
YOUNG IVA C	MAJ	L-0900064	0862	1
YOUNG JACK	1LT	0-1301744	0745	2
YOUNG JACK G	1LT	0-2096994	0259	2
YOUNG JACK T	COL	0-0889127	0668	1
YOUNG JAKE K	1LT	0-2055192	0246	2
YOUNG JAMES C	MAJ	0-1315655	0263	1
YOUNG JAMES D	MAJ	0-0263353	0665	3
YOUNG JAMES D	1LT	0-1296310	0544	2
YOUNG JAMES E	LTC	0-0164200	1136	1
YOUNG JAMES F	LTC	0-0282902	0959	1
YOUNG JAMES J	2LT	0-1306352	0145	2
YOUNG JAMES K	1LT	0-1322500	0746	2
YOUNG JAMES L	MAJ	0-0450955	0356	1
YOUNG JAMES V	LTC	0-2206414	1067	1
YOUNG JAN B	1LT	0-1053445	0744	2
YOUNG JOHN L	CW2	W-2206302	0862	1
YOUNG JOHN L H	COL	0-0239396	0965	3
YOUNG JOHN R	CW2	W-2152172	0761	1
YOUNG JOHN T	MAJ	0-1533714	0657	1
YOUNG JOHN T	2LT	0-2025614	1045	2
YOUNG JOHN W	LTC	0-0214134	1060	3
YOUNG JOHN W	1LT	0-1294059	0646	2
YOUNG JOSEPH E	MAJ	0-0183071	1044	2
YOUNG JOSEPH E	CW2	W-2142621	1159	1
YOUNG JOSEPH L	LTC	0-0229783	0565	3
YOUNG JULIUS C	MAJ	0-0386489	0562	1
YOUNG KATHERINE	2LT	N-0702799	1041	1
YOUNG KENNETH E	COL	0-0236400	0159	1
YOUNG KENNETH E	MAJ	0-1695639	1061	1
YOUNG KERMIT E	CW2	W-3100505	1167	1
YOUNG KIRBY L	CPT	0-5325518	1168	2
YOUNG LENWOOD W	MAJ	0-0537671	0758	1
YOUNG LEO A	MAJ	0-0286772	0458	3
YOUNG LEROY J	LTC	0-0243363	0666	3
YOUNG LEWIS A	WO1	W-2128045	0563	1
YOUNG LOUIS D JR	MAJ	0-1919072	1063	1
YOUNG LUCIUS E	LTC	0-0303909	0261	1
YOUNG MARVIN	COL	0-0178541	0661	3
YOUNG MAURICE	CPT	0-1585113	0844	2
YOUNG MAX E	1LT	0-0532758	0546	2
YOUNG MAX E	LTC	0-0887816	0466	1
YOUNG MAX P	LTC	0-0416047	1061	2
YOUNG MILDRED J	2LT	N-0727586	1044	1
YOUNG MILTON E	LTC	0-2030854	0368	1
YOUNG NATHANIEL	LTC	0-0393611	0646	2
YOUNG OLIVER F	CPT	0-2013942	0754	2
YOUNG RALPH A	LTC	0-1011572	0557	1
YOUNG RALPH H	COL	0-0260795	0268	3
YOUNG RALPH M	MAJ	0-0291063	0346	2
YOUNG RALPH W	1LT	0-2000081	0547	2
YOUNG RANDOLPH M	CW2	W-2209093	0964	1
YOUNG RAY C	MAJ	0-0143775	0455	3
YOUNG RAYMOND B JR	2LT	0-1648568	0146	2
YOUNG RICHARD A	LTC	0-0178734	0534	1
YOUNG RICHARD D	LTC	0-0918723	0467	3
YOUNG RICHARD E	LTC	0-1557401	1163	1
YOUNG ROBERT A	1LT	0-1549420	1144	2
YOUNG ROBERT A	CW3	W-2111642	1263	2
YOUNG ROBERT C	CPT	0-0693540	1051	2
YOUNG ROBERT E	LTC	0-0422516	0462	1
YOUNG ROBERT G	MAJ	0-1100845	1046	2
YOUNG ROBERT H	LTC	0-0310084	0668	3
YOUNG ROBERT H	CPT	0-0885770	0946	2
YOUNG ROBERT L	CW3	W-2149155	0662	1
YOUNG ROBERT N	1LT	0-1315750	0846	2
YOUNG ROBERT S	2LT	0-1031043	0445	2
YOUNG ROBERT S JR	CW2	W-2211917	0367	1
YOUNG ROGER L	COL	0-0344979	0265	1
YOUNG RONALD L	LTC	0-0397854	0261	1
YOUNG ROY A	CW2	W-3440032	1267	1
YOUNG RUBYE B	MAJ	N-0764460	0764	1
YOUNG RUTH A	1LT	N-0720990	1050	2
YOUNG RUTH V	1LT	N-0752064	1145	1
YOUNG SAMUEL G	LTC	0-0165444	1149	3
YOUNG THOMAS E	LTC	0-1169409	0561	1
YOUNG THOMAS H	WO1	W-2125093	0356	2
YOUNG VERNON D	1LT	0-1102140	1045	2
YOUNG VIRGIL A D	CW4	W-2127968	1155	1
YOUNG VIRGIL J	MAJ	0-1582828	1062	1
YOUNG WARREN H	MAJ	0-1545991	0960	1
YOUNG WARREN J	2LT	0-1112000	0444	2
YOUNG WAYNE B	COL	0-0345021	0561	1
YOUNG WHITNEY L	CPT	0-0248482	0662	1
YOUNG WILBUR R	LTC	0-0292069	0761	1
YOUNG WILEY R	1LT	0-0452120	0346	2
YOUNG WILL	CW3	W-2141502	1058	1
YOUNG WILLIAM A	CPT	0-1166655	0767	1
YOUNG WILLIAM A	CW3	W-2148150	0762	1
YOUNG WILLIAM A JR	LTC	0-1876904	1268	1
YOUNG WILLIAM A JR	CW3	W-2204999	0266	1
YOUNG WILLIAM E	LTC	0-1542443	0865	1
YOUNG WILLIAM F	MAJ	0-2016370	0363	1
YOUNG WILLIAM H JR	LTC	0-2263182	1068	1
YOUNG WILLIAM M	COL	0-0201144	0858	3
YOUNG WILLIAM M	CPT	0-0319839	0549	2
YOUNG WILLIAM N	LTC	0-0308657	0660	3
YOUNG WILLIAM P	LTC	0-1167292	1066	1
YOUNG WILLIAM R	MAJ	0-0967548	0468	1
YOUNG WILLIAM T JR	CW3	W-2141705	0159	2
YOUNG WILLIAM W	COL	0-0258557	0860	1
YOUNGBLOOD CLOVIS H	1LT	0-1323642	0146	2
YOUNGBLOOD JACK A	LTC	0-0934750	1166	1
YOUNGBLOOD JAMES C	2LT	0-1597335	1045	2
YOUNGDAHL ELLIS U	LTC	0-0275212	1046	2
YOUNGDAHL HERBERT M	CPT	0-0978108	1061	1
YOUNGER EVERETT W	CPT	0-1107249	0647	2
YOUNGER GEORGE A JR	CW3	W-2152490	0264	1
YOUNGER HARRY H	CW3	W-2205911	0168	1
YOUNGER JAMES L	CPT	0-1298798	0147	2
YOUNGER WILLIAM C	2LT	0-0985435	0451	2
YOUNGFLESH STANLEY F	LTC	0-0204505	0963	3
YOUNGKAMP JOSEPH G	COL	0-0358557	1264	3
YOUNGQUIST REUBEN C	LTC	0-0251343	0366	3
YOUNGREEN DONALD R	MAJ	0-0273004	0666	3
YOUNGREN HARRISON	LTC	0-0341322	0762	1
YOUNGREN RALPH L	MAJ	0-0179606	0644	2
YOUNGS CALVIN J	LTC	0-1017324	0661	1
YOUNGS GILBERT A	LTC	0-0245984	0667	3
YOUNGS JOHN B	LTC	0-0401607	0960	1
YOUNGS LYMAN G	LTC	0-0283930	0568	3
YOUNGS MARCUS L JR	1LT	0-0512159	0645	2
YOUNGS THURSTON B	CW3	W-2152364	0566	1
YOUNGS WALTER C JR	LTC	0-0246495	0764	3
YOUNGSON WILLIAM F	MAJ	0-2006127	0165	1
YOUNK WALTER A	MAJ	0-0979913	1062	1
YOUNKE ALBERT E	CW2	W-2214789	1068	2
YOUNKMAN ESTHER G	1LT	N-0776267	0645	1
YOUNT BURTON T	CPT	0-2033134	0960	1
YOUNT CLARENCE E JR	LTC	0-0252931	0166	3
YOUNT HAROLD J	CPT	0-0920122	0245	2
YOUNT JOHN B	MAJ	0-1286223	0161	1
YOUNT LEWIS L	2LT	0-1314867	0444	2
YOUNT MARCUS C	LTC	0-0133418	1052	3
YOUNT RICHARD H	MAJ	0-1648875	1162	1
YOUNTS PAUL P	COL	0-0185367	0159	3
YOUTS CLAUDE D	CPT	0-1549192	0945	2
YUVAN GEORGE JR	2LT	0-1309143	0444	2
YOWELL BENJAMIN W	COL	0-0285661	0159	1
YRI KENNETH F	2LT	0-1309470	0644	2
YRI WILLIAM	LTC	0-1032410	0662	1
YSMAEL ARTHUR R	1LT	0-0890322	0754	1
YSMAEL BARTOLOME	2LT	0-2027372	1047	1
YU HICO DELFI	CPT	0-0888175	0648	2
YUCKMAN WILLIAM	COL	0-0324747	0163	3
YUEN ALEXANDER	LTC	0-0365845	0863	3
YUEN JUAN H	MAJ	0-0253189	0746	2
YUHAS JOHN	CPT	0-0361950	0159	1
YUHAS JOHN J	CW4	W-2132981	0361	3
YUHOSS JOSEPH JR	CW3	W-2144685	1263	1
YUILL RALPH W	MAJ	0-0227512	0858	3
YUILLE NINIAN L	B G	0-0270933	0666	3
YUKE BENJAMIN J	MAJ	0-0479832	0746	2
YUKNIS LEONARD B	LTC	0-1698134	0566	1
YULIANO EUGENE M	LTC	0-0305154	0368	3
YUNG GEORGE P	LTC	0-0450322	0657	1
YUNKER LEO J	1LT	0-0463010	0144	2
YUNKER ROBERT J	LTC	0-1946899	0664	1
YUNQUE MARCIAL	MAJ	0-1301745	0560	1
YURASEK CECELIA A	MAJ	N-0755457	0165	1
YURCHEK FRANK S	MAJ	0-1545203	1162	1
YURCHISIN MICHAEL	CPT	0-1283353	0245	2
YURICK EDWARD A	LTC	0-0252778	0265	3
YURICK GEORGE	CPT	0-0509346	0650	2
YUSKANICH ANDREW E	1LT	0-0466776	1143	2
YUSKIS ANTHONY J	MAJ	0-1947280	0457	1
YUTUC RICARDO R	1LT	0-1896716	0166	1
YUTZY SCOTT G	CW2	W-2143990	0464	1
ZABALDANO FRANK C	LTC	0-1171854	0167	1
ZABEL HERMAN J	LTC	0-0235039	0654	3
ZABELLE VICTOR F	MAJ	0-2263628	0966	1
ZABIN ALEXANDER	COL	0-0302467	0567	3
ZABLACKAS KASTON R	MAJ	0-1120641	0364	1
ZABLOCKI STANLEY	LTC	0-1592741	0363	1
ZABOVNIK RICHARD J	MAJ	0-2026543	1161	1
ZABUSKI ZIGMOND A	CPT	0-1306927	0463	1
ZACH JOHN M	MAJ	0-0375380	0161	1
ZACHARIAS WILLMAN O	LTC	0-0184436	0952	3
ZACHARY OTIS O	MAJ	0-1293695	0656	1
ZACHARY ZENO N	1LT	0-1031145	0944	2
ZACHMAN ERNEST J	MAJ	0-4005870	0368	1
ZACHOW LAWRENCE E	LTC	0-0324006	0461	1
ZACHRY ABNER T	2LT	0-2006533	0146	2
ZACK LEO R	LTC	0-0342034	0865	3
ZACKED NICHOLAS T	MAJ	0-1328866	1161	1
ZACKEY SAMUEL A JR	CW2	W-2208804	0863	1
ZACOUR JAMES N	WO1	W-2005802	0651	2
ZACUR MAURICE M	1LT	0-1302745	0945	2
ZADNIK ANTON F	1LT	0-1285870	1145	2
ZADRA ROBERT F	LTC	0-1110907	0663	1
ZADROZNY ALICE C	MAJ	N-0752243	0659	2
ZAFFY JOSEPH P	CPT	0-1598735	0647	2
ZAGAMI NATALE R	LTC	0-0349502	0860	1
ZAGATA CHARLES A	MAJ	0-1312370	0760	1
ZAGORSKI WALTER E	CPT	0-0489206	0544	2
ZAGRAPAN CYRIL M	1LT	0-1290868	1056	1
ZAGRODZKY WILLIAM D	MAJ	0-1019600	1061	1
ZAHARA MIKE B	CPT	0-0447238	1048	2
ZAHARIA EDGAR A	LTC	0-1329193	0768	1
ZAHARKO JOSEPH	MAJ	0-1306928	0358	1
ZAHAROFF STEVEN	CW3	W-2149274	0760	1
ZAHL JOHN A	LTC	0-1045988	1167	1
ZAHLER JAMES W	MAJ	0-1996328	0266	1
ZAHN CARL J	1LT	0-0929539	1147	2
ZAHORIAN ELMER	CW3	W-2148780	0966	1
ZAHRN GILBERT E	CPT	0-1287982	0154	1
ZAIA THOMAS F	LTC	0-1178996	0268	3
ZAINO COSTANTINO	COL	0-0324036	0666	3
ZAIS CARL G	LTC	0-1042468	0357	1
ZAJ EDWARD A	LTC	0-0340500	0858	1
ZAJAC WALTER L	2LT	0-1797408	0144	2
ZAJICEK JAMES C	CW4	W-2114360	0960	1
ZAK FELIX	MAJ	0-1586677	0757	1
ZAK FREDERICK	COL	0-0238463	0765	3
ZAKBY ABDALLAH K	LTC	0-0365513	0959	1
ZAKOTA JOHN J JR	LTC	0-0354649	0163	1
ZAKRZEWSKI THEODORE	1LT	0-1105945	0761	1
ZAKULA MICHAEL	1LT	0-1766382	0446	2
ZALAZNIK EDWARD G	CW3	W-2141933	0659	1
ZALDO WILLIAM T JR	LTC	0-0290588	0960	1
ZALDUONDO FERNANDO	2LT	0-5826439	1064	2
ZALEGOWSKI FRANK S	MAJ	0-1796835	1057	1
ZALESKI OLEG Z	MAJ	0-0450780	0358	1
ZALESKI THADDEUS J	MAJ	0-1318603	1061	1
ZALESKY LEWIS E	LTC	0-0292088	0462	1
ZALESKY RICHARD C	COL	0-0038682	1060	1
ZALFA NORMAN G	CW2	W-2211916	0766	1
ZALLES REGINALD G	1LT	0-1303988	0746	2
ZALUSKI EDWARD L	1LT	0-1289187	0844	2
ZAMBA PETER	LTC	0-0298383	0761	3
ZAMBRANA EFRAIN	MAJ	0-0972347	0463	2
ZAMECNIK CHARLES	MAJ	0-1308578	0360	1
ZAMMARELLA LOUIS J	MAJ	0-0948932	0765	1
ZAMMMER EARL R	CW3	W-2144236	0863	1
ZAMORA LAMBERTINI	MAJ	N-0736015	1062	1
ZAMORA PEDRO J	CPT	0-0156628	1152	3
ZAMORA UBALDO JR	CW3	W-2209345	0767	1
ZAMPELL ROGER J	LTC	0-0296799	1068	3
ZAMPELLA ALBERT A	LTC	0-0330813	0267	3
ZANDER ALBERT A	CPT	0-1102563	0944	2
ZANECCHIA ARMANDO L	LTC	0-1994872	0361	1
ZANETTE ALFRED A	CPT	0-0502910	0445	2
ZANETTI JOAQUIN E	COL	0-0177195	0648	3
ZANG CHARLES W	LTC	0-1036443	0568	2
ZANG JOHN L	LTC	0-1011091	0557	1
ZANOLINI ALBERT S	MAJ	0-1112002	0261	1
ZANON LENA M	2LT	N-0743937	0844	1
ZANS JAMES E	CW3	W-2208377	0367	1
ZANT ROYCE O	LTC	0-1556376	0664	1
ZAPALSKI DANIEL J	MAJ	0-1999268	1063	1
ZAPF MICHAEL	MAJ	0-0971958	0364	1
ZAPOTOCKY FRANK E	CPT	0-0503919	0348	1
ZAREMBA EDWARD J	CW3	W-2150230	0765	1
ZAREMSKI ANTHONY J	MAJ	0-2011934	0564	1

ARMY OF THE UNITED STATES RETIRED LIST

NAME	GRADE	SVC NO	DATE RET MO YR	RET CODE
ZARIK HARRY	1LT	0-1555498	0846	2
ZARIT JOHN I	MAJ	0-0498354	0745	2
ZARLENGO ERNEST P	CPT	0-0468575	0744	2
ZARLING KENNETH A	MAJ	0-1081838	0955	1
ZATKOWSKI STANLEY E	2LT	0-1325144	0345	2
ZAUCHE ROY R	MAJ	0-2033967	0968	1
ZAUGG FELIX R	1LT	0-0157099	1153	3
ZAVALICK JOSEPH J	CW4	W-2115923	0659	1
ZAVELOFF ABRAHAM	MAJ	0-0202238	0955	3
ZAVITZ BURDETT N	1LT	0-2040771	0246	2
ZAVOD WILLIAM A	MAJ	0-0501527	0346	2
ZAVOYIANIS SAVAS	MAJ	0-0496190	1046	2
ZAWADSKI ALFONSO S	LTC	0-1012233	0757	1
ZAWALSKI VIOLET	1LT	N-0755841	1045	1
ZAWATSON PAUL J	MAJ	0-1823248	0163	1
ZAWORA EDWARD A	LTC	0-1061914	0466	1
ZAYAS ANGEL R	CW2	W-2141706	1159	1
ZAZZI MELVIN A	COL	0-0289481	0665	3
ZBIKOWSKI EUGENE F	CW2	W-3150186	0666	1
ZBORALSKE FLORIAN F	CPT	0-0553689	0245	2
ZBUDOWSKI ALEXANDE	CPT	0-1687148	0745	2
ZBYLUT ALEXANDER	1LT	0-0885735	1046	2
ZOEB THOMAS J	CW3	W-2151074	1165	2
ZDRAVECKY STEPHEN F	LTC	0-0454198	0757	1
ZDUNCZYK HARRY J SR	CPT	0-1169806	0862	2
ZDUNEK MARCELL J	WO1	W-2141143	1048	1
ZEABLE VICTOR C	LTC	0-0489332	0363	2
ZEBAL FRANCIS T	MAJ	0-1117561	0960	1
ZEBBS FRANCIS L	LTC	0-0321015	0668	3
ZEBELEAN THEODORE	MAJ	0-2262994	0363	1
ZEBLEY JOSEPH T	LTC	0-1324084	0166	1
ZEBLEY JOSEPH W JR	MAJ	0-1573700	0763	1
ZEBLEY ROBERT P JR	CPT	0-0282659	0258	1
ZEBROSKI CHESTER C	MAJ	0-1593929	0565	1
ZEBROWSKI JULIAN J	MAJ	0-1649993	0657	1
ZEBROWSKI VICTOR J	CPT	0-1045646	1160	1
ZECCHIN MALACHI A	CPT	0-1061596	0750	2
ZEEFF BERT	LTC	0-0274291	1057	1
ZEGOLIS GEORGE M D	COL	0-0287619	1161	1
ZEHALA MICHAEL A	LTC	0-0530314	0761	1
ZEHFUSS PAUL E	COL	0-0217201	0768	3
ZEHLER CHARLES R	CW3	W-2203812	0267	1
ZEHNER JOHN M	LTC	0-2049203	0466	1
ZEHNER WILLIAM B	2LT	0-1584979	1043	2
ZEHR ROGER D	CW2	W-2215916	0668	1
ZEIDMAN SIDNEY E	MAJ	0-0977297	1064	1
ZEIEN HENRY	COL	0-0321828	0457	1
ZEIER FRANCIS G	MAJ	0-0370783	0646	2
ZEIGER ARTHUR	1LT	0-1081730	0646	2
ZEIGER MICHAEL R	MAJ	0-0310386	0945	2
ZEIGLER ELWOOD W	CW4	W-2147813	0968	1
ZEIGLER MARTIN L	1LT	0-0536051	1045	2
ZEIGLER ROLAND L	LTC	0-1135370	0962	1
ZEIS DONALD M	LTC	0-0226914	0863	1
ZEISZLER ERNEST E	LTC	0-0455634	0157	1
ZEITLER EDGAR A	MAJ	0-1014566	1059	1
ZEITLER PHYLLIS S	MAJ	N-0756441	0167	3
ZEITLER WOODROW W	1LT	0-1286410	0750	2
ZEITZ AUGUST H	MAJ	0-1542452	0761	1
ZEITZ SIDNEY J	LTC	0-0274472	0863	3
ZEKAN PAUL R	LTC	0-1340730	0967	1
ZELAZNY JOSEPH J JR	LTC	0-1109774	0263	1
ZELEK STANLEY M	2LT	0-1018656	0645	2
ZELENKA LOUIS G	MAJ	0-0260564	0966	3
ZELENKO TONY	MAJ	0-1052642	1065	1
ZELEPSKY STANLEY D	1LT	0-1294235	0647	2
ZELEZNIK LAWRENCE E	1LT	0-1298157	1045	2
ZELINSKAS HELEN	2LT	N-0728354	0845	1
ZELINSKY ROBERT L	MAJ	0-1080680	0464	1
ZELL NORMAN H	CW2	W-2142994	0358	1
ZELL WILLIAM B	CPT	0-1309144	0246	2
ZELLER DONALD F	MAJ	0-0573865	1156	1
ZELLER FRANK J	LTC	0-0971301	0368	1
ZELLER GEORGE W	LTC	0-1013428	0364	1
ZELLER STANLEY A	CPT	0-2006837	0255	1
ZELLER WILLIAM B	COL	0-0220215	0162	3
ZELLERMAYER JACOB	MAJ	0-0341345	1046	2
ZELLERS WOODROW W	CW2	W-2208696	0365	1
ZELLNER NORMAN O	1LT	0-0555596	0646	2
ZELNICK BERNARD	1LT	0-0471718	0245	2
ZELNICKER EDWIN A	MAJ	0-0193304	0857	3
ZELTMAN CHARLES F	LTC	0-0910301	0364	1
ZEMAN ALOIS	CW2	W-2142995	0155	1
ZEMBAS PHILIP	CW3	W-2147058	0363	1
ZEMKE ERHART E	CPT	0-0263435	0145	2
ZEMLA STEPHEN G	CPT	0-1894776	0461	1
ZEMO HARRY	CW4	W-2147927	1266	1
ZEMOTEL JOHN	1LT	0-1554672	1046	2
ZEMSKY DAVID W	CPT	0-0524934	0647	2
ZENDT JAMES E	LTC	0-0213935	0564	3
ZENER FRANCIS B	LTC	0-0214878	0346	2
ZENI ANGELO M	MAJ	0-0961920	1067	1
ZENIZO GERALD H	1LT	0-1031286	1045	2
ZENKER CHARLES W	1LT	0-0129080	0653	3
ZENO TULIO N	LTC	0-0264560	0663	3
ZENSEN GILBERT D	MAJ	0-0508024	0954	1
ZENTNER MILTON C	LTC	0-1934701	0658	2
ZEPER PHILIP	LTC	0-0513039	0765	1
ZEPPENFELD BERNARD M	LTC	0-1178046	0468	1
ZERANSKI HENRY E	MAJ	0-1533716	1058	1
ZERBACH EARL C	LTC	0-0487174	0561	1
ZERBI LOUIS	CPT	0-1303246	1047	2
ZERBY RAYMOND D	CW2	W-2144981	0357	1
ZERDA VINCENT M	MAJ	0-1299973	0665	3
ZERDY ALFONCE W	CPT	0-1695229	0245	2
ZERGER CARL R	2LT	0-1313941	1044	2
ZERMUEHLEN HERMAN W	COL	0-0250459	0466	3
ZERNIA MYRON A	MAJ	0-0317986	0764	3
ZETLAU WALTER S	MAJ	0-1699961	1061	1
ZETTERHOLM MAURICE F	COL	0-0180767	0353	3
ZETTERMAN FRED V	CPT	0-1295315	0446	2
ZEVITAS ERNEST J	LTC	0-2038891	0367	1
ZIAYA JOSEPH J	CPT	0-1171020	0346	2
ZICK LILLIAN E	2LT	N-0794873	0846	1
ZICKEFOOSE MARBLE L	LTC	0-0331428	0967	3
ZIO FRANK A	LTC	0-1574186	0461	1
ZIDJUNAS FRANK E	CPT	0-1322503	0347	2
ZIEBARTH CHARLES F	LTC	0-0299773	0359	3
ZIEBE OTTO E	LTC	0-0237399	1065	3
ZIEBELL MILTON F	COL	0-0246219	0562	3
ZIEBER FRED H	LTC	0-0320416	0465	3
ZIEG DONALD E	MAJ	0-0405240	0662	1
ZIEGFELD JACOB J	2LT	0-1016330	1044	2
ZIEGLER BERNARD L	CW4	W-2144275	0868	1
ZIEGLER EDWARD E	1LT	0-1112003	0747	2
ZIEGLER EDWIN A	COL	0-0141223	0648	3
ZIEGLER EDWIN G	MAJ	0-0174720	0648	3
ZIEGLER FRANCIS A	COL	0-0206925	0863	3
ZIEGLER GERALD F	1LT	0-0263817	0653	2
ZIEGLER HARRY E	MAJ	0-1175019	1065	1
ZIEGLER JAMES D	CW4	W-2141444	1166	1
ZIEGLER LEO E	LTC	0-1294236	0261	1
ZIEGLER MAURICE S	CPT	0-1168535	0546	2
ZIEGLER RAY A	MAJ	0-1894399	0357	1
ZIEGLER THEODORE F	MAJ	0-1319996	0263	1
ZIEGLER WILFRED D	CPT	0-1103487	0645	2
ZIEHM RUDOLPH H	LTC	0-0184391	0159	1
ZIEL MAX G	MAJ	0-0139609	0352	3
ZIELINSKI ANTHONY F	MAJ	0-1019286	0860	1
ZIELINSKI JOSEPH A	LTC	0-0163681	0149	3
ZIELINSKI JOSEPH T	MAJ	0-1557113	0162	1
ZIELSDORF ARTHUR H	CW3	W-2119358	1057	1
ZIEMBA THOMAS P	MAJ	0-1053446	0162	2
ZIEMSKI FRANK J	LTC	0-1057945	1263	1
ZIENK ANTHONY E	CW2	W-2143296	0658	1
ZIERDT WILLIAM H	COL	0-0167999	0648	3
ZIERDT WILLIAM H JR	LTC	0-0346173	0161	1
ZIES FREDERICK	COL	0-0219955	1063	3
ZIESING BENEDICT V	LTC	0-1578079	1058	1
ZIESKE IRENE C R	MAJ	N-0775179	0468	1
ZIEV BENJAMIN	CW2	W-2116388	0644	2
ZIFCAK MICHAEL G	MAJ	0-0983402	0165	1
ZIFCAK MICHAEL J	COL	0-0436569	1266	1
ZIGLAR HORACE W	LTC	0-1167711	1054	1
ZIGLINSKI JOSEPH H	LTC	0-1635504	0962	1
ZIKE FERMA L	CW2	W-3350164	0864	1
ZIKOWITZ ROBERT F	MAJ	0-0955407	0762	1
ZILE GLEN E	LTC	0-1175570	0966	1
ZILINSKAS ANTHONY F	MAJ	0-1894722	0261	1
ZILKIE AUGUST A JR	LTC	0-1320685	0961	1
ZILLMAN BERL G	CW2	W-2215525	0868	1
ZILSKE KARL L	LTC	0-1550305	0364	1
ZIMA PAUL D	1LT	0-5338372	0868	2
ZIMET JOHN J	COL	0-0474609	1065	1
ZIMMEK HENRY C	CPT	0-0477541	1148	1
ZIMMER GEORGE E JR	CPT	0-2014418	1059	1
ZIMMER JOHN	CPT	0-0496181	0665	3
ZIMMER JOHN W	LTC	0-2035513	0761	1
ZIMMER JOSEPH E	LTC	0-0244846	0763	3
ZIMMER RALPH W	LTC	0-1105949	0462	1
ZIMMER ROBERT A	CW3	W-2205813	1067	1
ZIMMER WILLIAM K	MAJ	0-2016197	0663	1
ZIMMERMAN AUGUST A	MAJ	0-1583879	0549	2
ZIMMERMAN AUGUST J	MAJ	0-0199402	0351	3
ZIMMERMAN BARBARA M	2LT	N-0722872	0445	1
ZIMMERMAN CARL C	2LT	0-2007184	1145	2
ZIMMERMAN CARLE C	MAJ	0-0267572	0557	3
ZIMMERMAN CECIL J	LTC	0-0315982	0259	3
ZIMMERMAN COLER	CPT	0-0283788	0446	2
ZIMMERMAN EDGAR	LTC	0-0359876	0757	1
ZIMMERMAN EDWARD E	LTC	0-1104463	0560	1
ZIMMERMAN FRED R	LTC	0-0202798	0944	2
ZIMMERMAN GEORGE G	1LT	0-1012493	0645	2
ZIMMERMAN GRACE I	1LT	N-0760903	0646	1
ZIMMERMAN HENRY G	1LT	0-1052644	0245	2
ZIMMERMAN HENRY H	LTC	0-1304303	0164	1
ZIMMERMAN HORACE S	LTC	0-0336705	1162	1
ZIMMERMAN IRVING M	CPT	0-1590913	0665	2
ZIMMERMAN JAMES A	COL	0-0352534	0766	1
ZIMMERMAN JEAN R	CPT	N-0732805	0347	1
ZIMMERMAN JOHN M	LTC	0-1576849	0461	1
ZIMMERMAN JOSEPH	1LT	0-1327998	0546	2
ZIMMERMAN JUAN M	MAJ	0-2021041	0164	1
ZIMMERMAN KARL	LTC	0-0251857	1163	3
ZIMMERMAN LEO W	MAJ	0-0474245	0745	2
ZIMMERMAN PAUL J	LTC	0-0258216	1067	3
ZIMMERMAN ROBERT F	LTC	0-1185511	0967	1
ZIMMERMAN RUBIN	LTC	0-0512542	0965	3
ZIMMERMAN STANLEY G	LTC	0-1015360	1265	1
ZIMMERMAN WILBUR F	LTC	0-1319461	1166	3
ZIMMERMAN WILLARD P	1LT	0-0516687	0645	2
ZIMMERMAN WILLIAM C	CPT	0-1291210	0561	1
ZIMMERMAN WOODROW	LTC	0-1822464	0664	1
ZIMNOSKI JOSEPH E	CPT	0-1596981	0954	1
ZIMNOWSKI ANTHONY F	1LT	0-1115438	0745	2
ZIMONT LEONARD J	2LT	0-1109778	0345	2
ZIMRIN HENRY L	CPT	0-1312073	0546	2
ZIMRING ALLAN J	MAJ	0-1821142	0246	2
ZIMRING ROBERT H	2LT	0-1294953	0744	2
ZIMRING WILLIAM J	CPT	0-1821159	0546	2
ZINGA ANDREW S	1LT	0-1014423	0146	2
ZINGERELLA PETER A	1LT	0-1559644	1147	1
ZINGLER CLIFFORD F	MAJ	0-0333660	0846	2
ZINK DONALD C	MAJ	0-1595289	0163	1
ZINK HAROLD L	MAJ	0-1686616	0162	1
ZINK HARRY G	CPT	0-0510331	1044	1
ZINK JACK D	1LT	0-1013026	1046	2
ZINK OTTO A JR	CPT	0-1181812	0546	2
ZINK WILLIAM S	LTC	0-0263256	0262	3
ZINN BENNIE A	LTC	0-0231642	0964	3
ZINN JOHN B JR	LTC	0-0407041	1168	1
ZINN JOHNNIE P	LTC	0-1587747	0966	1
ZINN LUCILLE E	MAJ	N-0799201	0965	1
ZINN ROBERT W	LTC	0-1061598	0966	1
ZINNAMON DAVID R	COL	0-0251294	1057	1
ZINSKI ALEX A	1LT	0-1308405	1147	2
ZINTEK SYLVESTER	COL	0-0211723	1058	3
ZINTER REINHOLD H	LTC	0-0502075	0565	3
ZINZ FLORENCE	1LT	N-0759813	0346	1
ZIOMEK EDWARD S	MAJ	0-1062839	0462	1
ZION WALTER S	MAJ	0-0255737	0949	2
ZIPEN JOSEPH L	CPT	0-0497277	1145	2
ZIPF JAMES L	MAJ	0-0327593	1058	1
ZIPP CHARLES C	MAJ	0-1334802	1163	1
ZIPPLE KARL G	1LT	0-0381004	0245	2
ZIRBEL JOSEPH	CW2	W-2211081	0765	1
ZIRJACKS HAMILTON	LTC	0-0450958	0660	1
ZIRKLE PAUL J	LTC	0-1633169	0361	1
ZISCHKAU WILLIAM C	CPT	0-0268989	0857	3
ZISKA CLARENCE W	COL	0-0263499	0657	3
ZISKIND JOSEPH	COL	0-0488926	0467	3
ZITELLI THOMAS S	MAJ	0-1285167	0262	1
ZITKOVICH ROSE P	2LT	N-0731810	1045	1
ZITKUS JOSEPH E	CW3	W-2149999	0166	1
ZITO ANTHONY J	CPT	0-1003871	0256	1
ZITO JOHN	MAJ	0-1559926	0359	1
ZITO JOSEPH	CW4	W-2148363	1264	1
ZITO MICHAEL R	CPT	0-0267240	0158	3
ZITTEL GEORGE H JR	MAJ	0-2033094	0561	1
ZITTEL HAROLD E	COL	0-0219855	0859	3
ZITTELMAN ROY G	LTC	0-1165694	0464	1
ZITTRAUER SIMON D	CPT	0-0887330	0357	1
ZIVICH GEORGE J	COL	0-0377903	0867	1
ZLOTNIK MEYER	WO1	W-2127609	0945	2
ZOBEL RUDOLPH D	COL	0-0245610	0847	2
ZOBEL SIDNEY	COL	0-0112816	0352	3
ZOBERSKI RAY	MAJ	0-1305364	0961	1
ZOBKIW BOHDAN	1LT	0-1100407	0264	2
ZOBROSKY CLARENCE F	CW3	W-2152499	0163	1
ZODER WALLACE L	LTC	0-0240193	0964	3
ZOELLIG PAUL H	1LT	0-1947544	0546	2
ZOELLNER MAX N	CW2	W-2154673	0256	1
ZOELLNER WALTER J	LTC	0-0337269	0760	1
ZOLADZ ALFRED E	CW3	W-2146295	0168	1
ZOLLINGER DON R	MAJ	0-1544733	0664	1
ZOLLO ERNEST G	CW2	W-2214459	0368	1
ZOLNINGER LAMAR	CW2	W-2212499	1066	1
ZOLTY JOHN S	CPT	0-0941983	0261	1
ZONGKER LEONARD E	COL	0-0299732	1068	3
ZOOGMAN MORRIS W	LTC	0-1580545	0868	3
ZOOK HERBERT D	MAJ	0-1690745	0962	1
ZOOK JOHN C	LTC	0-0348903	1059	2
ZOOLE ASHER	LTC	0-0333570	0267	3
ZOPFI JOHN C	MAJ	0-0949047	0763	1
ZOPPI ANTHONY G	2LT	0-1588394	0445	2
ZORN HARVEY A	COL	0-0264983	0765	3
ZORN JOSEPH F JR	LTC	0-0324706	1060	1
ZORNEK JOSEPH F	LTC	0-1106549	0164	1
ZOSCHAK MARY	MAJ	N-0755823	0363	1
ZOUKIS CHRISTO S	LTC	0-0550755	0968	1
ZRALKA ALBERT J	1LT	0-1325145	0845	2
ZSCHACH KARL G	LTC	0-1576850	0765	1
ZSCHAU ERNEST	LTC	0-0173620	0161	3
ZSCHOKKE WALTER J	CW4	W-2146535	1060	1
ZSIPAY GEORGE	CW3	W-2200596	1067	3
ZUBER ANTONE C	CPT	0-2262431	0755	1
ZUBER MARION	LTC	0-1541075	0761	1
ZUBROD JOSEPH A	CW3	W-2152738	0263	1
ZUCCA ANTHONY C	MAJ	0-0983029	0667	1
ZUCCO GAETAN M	COL	0-0924268	1065	3
ZUCK ANTHONY B	CPT	0-1574567	0444	2
ZUCKER MARTIN M	1LT	0-1895180	0545	2
ZUCKER MILTON O	MAJ	0-0475491	0946	2
ZUCKERBROD MORRIS	MAJ	0-0471215	0746	2
ZUCKERMAN HERMAN	LTC	0-0242704	0665	3
ZUCKERMAN LOUIS	LTC	0-0250936	0150	1
ZUCKERMAN SARA	CPT	N-0728593	0547	1
ZUCKERMAN WILLIAM	LTC	0-0273415	1052	3
ZUCKERNICK SAUL	2LT	0-1913547	0838	1
ZUERLEIN EDWARD G	CPT	0-1590915	0857	1

NAME	GRADE	SVC NO	DATE RET MO YR	RET CODE
ZUFELT FRED	CW2	W-2205359	0358	1
ZUG RICHARD V	LTC	O-0917059	0967	3
ZUGSCHWERDT WERNER H	COL	O-0265828	0865	3
ZUIDEMA HENRY B	LTC	O-0454611	1262	1
ZUK CHARLES R	MAJ	O-1303588	0962	1
ZUKOSKI JOSEPH J	CPT	O-1695140	0545	2
ZUKOWSKI EDWARD	1LT	O-1304986	0845	2
ZUMALT ROBERT E	CW2	W-2150149	0860	1
ZUMBRUNN NORMAN J	LTC	O-0155229	0762	3
ZUMWALT DERYL B	CPT	O-0888324	1045	2
ZUMWALT ELMO R	COL	O-0238616	1053	3
ZUMWALT RALPH H	LTC	O-0492907	1162	1
ZUNO JOSEPH K	MAJ	O-0260190	0160	3
ZUNDEL PAUL BAUH	MAJ	O-1296143	0447	2
ZUNICH MICHAEL	CW4	W-2153329	0662	1
ZUNIS GEORGE P	LTC	O-0456662	1065	1
ZUPAN JOSEPH J	CPT	O-2263139	0761	1
ZUPI LOUIS M	MAJ	O-2043300	0765	1
ZUPKO MICHAEL E	COL	O-0262998	0666	3
ZURBRUGG MARY E	1LT	N-0730380	0746	1
ZURETTI ERNEST V	LTC	O-1058708	0867	1
ZURFLUH MILTON G	CPT	O-0310467	1263	1
ZURIAN GEORGE	CW2	W-2205441	0957	1
ZURLO PASCHAL L	CW2	W-2214851	0467	1
ZURN HAROLD W	LTC	O-0382138	0760	1
ZUSSMAN IRVING W	LTC	O-1587045	0462	1
ZUSSMAN LESSER	LTC	O-1586399	0668	3
ZUTAVERN NORMAN E	CW3	W-2106809	0761	1
ZUVER PAUL E	COL	O-0017373	0157	2
ZUZULO FRANCIS X	CPT	O-0353189	0644	2
ZWART CORNELIUS	LTC	O-1642756	1062	1
ZWART EDWARD A	CPT	O-0414946	0351	2
ZWART JOE G	LTC	O-0330468	0566	3
ZWECKER ROBERT G	MAJ	O-4009309	0366	1
ZWELLING HERBERT W	2LT	O-1579337	0245	2
ZWERDLING JOSEPH	1LT	O-2052517	0146	2
ZWERLING SAMUEL	LTC	O-0137242	1054	3
ZWERMANN CARL H	COL	O-0280002	0868	3
ZWICK WALTER H	LTC	O-0295287	1264	3
ZWICKER LEON	LTC	O-0461682	0754	1
ZWIRBLE EDWARD A	MAJ	O-1338770	0661	1
ZWIRNBAUM ABRAHAM M	MAJ	O-0452585	0456	1
ZWIRNER ARTHUR P JR	MAJ	O-0983327	0765	1
ZWITZER MARTIN N	COL	O-1000303	0855	1
ZYCH LLOYD D	MAJ	O-2002112	0962	1
ZYMBOLY JOHN	CW2	W-2113661	0853	1
ZYSK JOHN W	MAJ	O-0989708	0766	1
ZYSKOWSKI ZIGMUND	CPT	O-1323643	0855	1
ZYVITH EDWARD J	MAJ	O-1543590	1160	1
ZYWASKI CHARLES M	COL	O-0280241	0751	1

SECTION 3

TEMPORARY DISABILITY RETIRED LIST

The Temporary Disability Retired List is composed of officers and warrant officers placed on the Temporary Disability Retired List under Title 10, USC, Sections 1202 and 1205 (formerly Section 402, Career Compensation Act of 1949) for physical disability which may be of a permanent nature.

NAME	GRADE	SVC NO	DATE RET MO YR	RET CODE
ABAGIS KENNETH M	LTC	0-0071433	1068	4
ABBOTT JOHN E	LTC	0-0989464	1168	4
ABEL JAMES A	CPT	0-5418419	0668	4
ABEL STEPHEN R	WO1	W-3159072	1168	4
ADDINGTON ALLISON R	MAJ	0-0964938	0165	4
ADEN CHALMER V	COL	0-1596244	0968	4
AKEROYO JOSEPH H	COL	0-0519883	0963	4
ALBERICO KENNETH D	LTC	0-1684958	1068	4
ALLEN DONIVAN D	CW3	W-2205874	1067	4
ALLEN HUGH A JR	COL	0-0032622	0668	4
ALLINSON CELIA	MAJ	N-0721800	0363	4
AMES WARWICK M	CPT	0-1824422	0959	4
ANGOTTI ARTHUR A	1LT	0-5537875	0768	4
ANTONIELLO KATE G	MAJ	N-0051121	0466	4
ARCHER JESSE F	CW2	W-3154521	1268	4
ARCHER RUBYE W	LTC	N-0001634	0567	4
ARENA DANIEL A	1LT	0-5337642	0468	4
ARMSTRONG FRANK M	CW2	W-2105700	1267	4
ARNETT EDWIN W	CPT	0-1596252	0463	4
ARNOLD THOMAS S J	COL	0-0032040	1267	4
ARNOLD WARREN C	CW2	W-2210044	0462	4
ARSENA NINO	1LT	0-5419195	0567	4
ASCHENBACH JULIUS O	CPT	0-0957777	0267	4
ATROCHIN PAUL A	MAJ	0-1634961	0466	4
AULTMAN JOHN L	CPT	0-2204082	0163	4
AUSTIN PAUL	CPT	0-5330093	0868	4
AYERS EDITH A	MAJ	L-0000099	0159	4
BABBITT PAUL E	MAJ	0-4031337	0567	4
BABCOCK JACK E	B G	0-0021413	0368	4
BACON RICHARD H	LTC	0-0028656	0867	4
BAILEY JOSEPH III	2LT	0-5230100	0568	4
BALES ARTHUR W JR	CW4	W-2118074	1166	4
BALLENTINE GEORGE D	LTC	0-1172366	0666	4
BARBER ANDREW G JR	MAJ	0-2263456	0567	4
BARD HARRY E	LTC	0-1119026	0268	4
BARDENHAGEN CHRISTOP	MAJ	0-1004444	1158	4
BARKER GEORGE E	MAJ	0-0245636	0360	4
BARNES CLENN G	CPT	0-1938748	0467	4
BARNES LAWRENCE G	WO1	W-3152383	0866	4
BARROW GEORGE R	LTC	0-0059480	0768	4
BARTELS SANDRA A	CPT	N-5520058	0968	4
BARTKO DONALD A	MAJ	0-1931912	0768	4
BARWICK ALBERT F JR	MAJ	0-1878085	0967	4
BAST ADELBERT C	CW4	W-2142686	0261	4
BATES MICHAEL L	CPT	0-5423995	0968	4
BAUCOM DONALD C	CPT	0-5304293	0467	4
BAUR CHARLES K	CW2	W-3440050	0567	4
BAUZA MIGUEL B	CW4	W-2154863	1168	4
BAZEMORE ROBERT E	CPT	0-2262397	0757	4
BEAM KEITH J	CPT	0-5301020	0764	4
BEAM ROBERT E	MAJ	0-4022967	0668	4
BECHTOLD KENNETH I	LTC	0-1038165	0767	4
BEHANNON HOLLIS P	CPT	0-0086994	1064	4
BELFRY DAVID M	CPT	0-5326359	0768	4
BENNETT EDWARD A	MAJ	0-2263170	1062	4
BENNETT REBECCA L	MAJ	L-0302612	0667	4
BENNETT WILLIAM H	CPT	0-5317220	0568	4
BENSON ANDREW S	1LT	0-5710817	0767	4
BENSON WALTER R JR	LTC	0-0039180	0167	4
BERGMAN PHILIP A	COL	0-0022772	1066	4
BERGSTROM WAYNE A	CPT	0-5525537	1066	4
BERRY ALICE E	MAJ	N-0001882	0460	4
BERRY AUBREY M	CW3	W-2153020	1268	4
BERRY EVA I	CW4	V-0414874	0765	4
BERRY HENRY N JR	CPT	0-1885159	0463	4
BERRY MARY R	MAJ	N-0795854	0868	4
BETTINGER RONALD G	CPT	0-5217638	0267	4
BETZENBERGER CHARLES	CW2	W-3100922	0368	4
BEVEL BOB B	1LT	0-0890182	0463	4
BICKFORD ROSS P	MAJ	0-1893078	0867	4
BIELOT EDWIN S	LTC	0-2053869	1167	4
BIERIE ELWYN L	COL	0-0530286	1068	4
BILLINGS EUGENE D	LTC	0-0030816	1264	4
BILLINGSLEA CHARLES	M G	0-0020367	0766	4
BILLINGSLEY MURRY J	CW2	W-3153358	0468	4
BIRD SAMUEL R	MAJ	0-0092334	0368	4
BIXBY GEORGE W	COL	0-0021056	0868	4
BLACKMORE ROBERT P	CPT	0-0059473	1060	4
BLACKWELL CLYDE G	MAJ	0-0997026	0168	4
BLEVINS ROBERT E	CW3	W-3100256	0968	4
BLIZZARD JOHN G	CW4	W-2123113	0667	4
BLOUNT ROBERT E	M G	0-0019612	0868	4
BLUM ANDREW J	MAJ	RW-2148273	0862	4
BODEEN JERRIE W	CPT	0-5517520	0367	4
BOND VAN H	M G	0-0018601	0966	4
BONIFAY ISAAC F	COL	0-0040061	1166	4
BOONE GEORGE M JR	LTC	0-0060335	0368	4
BOSWORTH FRANK H	CPT	0-5304413	0768	4
BOWLES ROY A	CPT	0-1584022	1168	4
BOXER JOEL M	1LT	0-5247799	1268	4
BOYCE FRANCIS J	LTC	0-1588128	0567	4
BOYD BOBBY	CW2	W-2206478	0663	4
BOYD CHARLES A	MAJ	0-2206264	0267	4
BOYETT JAMES C JR	CW3	W-2206660	1065	4
BOYLE JOHN J	CW3	W-2152087	0565	4
BRACK JOSEPH L	COL	0-0051746	0566	4
BRACKEN GLENN A	MAJ	0-0084956	0767	4
BRADLEY SUE T	LTC	L-0000188	0565	4
BRADY RAYMOND E	CPT	0-1933690	1166	4
BRANDT RITA I	MAJ	L-0903239	1167	4
BRANDT ROBERT I	CPT	0-5706179	0767	4
BRANIGAN GEORGE H JR	LTC	0-1650019	1166	4
BRICE EMMETT T	LTC	0-0088589	0367	4
BRIGMAN LANEAU M JR	MAJ	0-0082147	0465	4
BROWN ALBERT S JR	CPT	0-5318461	1268	4
BROWN ARCHIE J	CPT	0-C401101	0367	4
BROWN CHARLES W	CPT	0-1030124	0767	4
BROWN HARVEY L	CPT	0-0093589	0965	4
BROWN STANLEY W JR	1LT	0-5007631	0965	4
BROWNFIELD LEE B II	COL	0-0036135	0368	4
BRUHNS LOWELL	MAJ	0-0692475	0963	4
BUNDREN ELMO L	LTC	0-1825586	0266	4
BURKE EDMUND J JR	1LT	0-5327171	0267	4
BURLESON PHILIP E	LTC	0-0979938	0968	4
BUSH ROBERT B	COL	0-0030692	1166	4
BUTLER BILLIE D	CPT	0-1999465	1057	4
BYERS BEN A	LTC	0-C946872	0868	4
BYRD DAVID R	WO1	W-3200669	0866	4
BYTHEWAY MARGARET G	LTC	N-0761686	0968	4
CAGLE DANIEL B	1LT	0-5331866	0368	4
CALLAWAY CHARLES V	LTC	0-1018067	1167	4
CALLAWAY ROBERT L	WO1	W-2150586	0765	4
CAMPBELL BRADLEY S	1LT	0-5323679	0167	4
CANNEFAX ROBERT W	CPT	0-0076C03	1068	4
CANNON JOHN C	LTC	0-1997676	0766	4
CAPLINGER CARL B	LTC	0-0094055	1168	4
CARGEN ALFRED J	CW3	W-2206091	0668	4
CARPER FRANK E	CW3	W-2206040	0468	4
CARREIRA-MAS BENIGNO	CW4	W-2002627	1068	4
CARROLL ROBERT E	LTC	0-1798647	0667	4
CARSON JAMES E	LTC	0-0041206	1068	4
CARSON KENNETH A	COL	0-0042030	0562	4
CASSIDY BERNARD J	CPT	0-1037552	0266	4
CAVANAUGH DOROTHY W	LTC	N-0002384	0964	4
CAYTON BUELAH S	CW4	V-0600065	0666	4
CEHRS BERNICE J	COL	0-C029220	0961	4
CHADWICK CLYDE C	LTC	0-2033900	0368	4
CHANDLER HOMER B JR	COL	0-0022982	0868	4
CHAPONIS ANASTASIA	MAJ	N-0001805	0764	4
CHERRY RONALD V	2LT	0-5343460	0268	4
CHRISTENSEN DONALD P	COL	0-0020257	0161	4
CHRISTENSEN HERBERT	LTC	0-0067557	0268	4
CHRISTIANSON J MILTO	LTC	0-0065965	0966	4
CHURCH CHARLES T	LTC	0-0414559	0463	4
CICERO RAYMOND F	LTC	0-C078761	0868	4
CIVELLO ADOLPH J	CW3	W-2209610	0967	4
CLARK CHARLES E	MAJ	0-1633755	0267	4
CLARK CHARLES J	CPT	0-5325542	0768	4
CLARK FELIX G JR	MAJ	0-2203403	0465	4
CLARK HARRY A JR	COL	0-0033937	0768	4
CLARK MILDRED I	COL	N-0000608	1067	4
CLARK ROBERT S	CW3	W-2147709	0267	4
CLARK SAM J	COL	0-0040064	1166	4
CLARK WARREN M	LTC	0-0065294	0967	4
CLARK WILLIS H	LTC	0-0050686	1264	4
CLAY ANTHONY H	2LT	OF-0104674	0566	4
CLICK RALPH M	COL	0-0039188	0265	4
CLIFTON JOSEPH M	CPT	0-1289392	0564	4
CLIFTON WILBURN A	LTC	0-0989689	0668	4
CLINTON ROY J	COL	0-0023774	1068	4
COLBY JOHN R	CPT	0-4074460	0366	4
COLES CLARENCE J	LTC	0-0060432	0768	4
COMBS MARY L	CPT	M-2313256	0467	4
COMITO SALVATORE	1LT	0-5013743	1265	4
COMM EDWARD D	COL	0-0031484	0567	4
CONRAD MARY C	MAJ	L-1000105	0963	4
CONROY GEORGE L	LTC	0-1050607	0966	4
COOCH JOSEPH W	COL	0-0063707	0867	4
COOK JONATHAN L	1LT	0-5321759	0466	4
COOPER SAMUEL	CW4	W-2152943	0868	4
COPELAND KENNETH W	COL	0-0040177	0867	4
COREY WAYNE D	2LT	0-5250233	0168	4
COUCH SIDNEY A	LTC	0-0068090	0968	4
COULD KENNETH	MAJ	0-1556587	0456	4
CRONIN DANIEL W	MAJ	0-0071333	0765	4
CROUCHER JAMES W	LTC	0-1041120	0668	4
CROWDEN EUGENE E JR	COL	0-1286613	0268	4
CROWDER THOMAS H JR	COL	0-0062178	0868	4
CRUZ GLORIA J P	CPT	N-5315804	0966	4
CUMMINS BILLY J	LTC	0-0555574	1168	4
CURRY MARTIN F	CW2	W-3155229	0568	4
CURTIS WILLIAM B	LTC	0-1557434	1167	4
CZELUSNIAK JOHN L	1LT	0-5015982	0965	4
DAMAN MARION L	COL	0-0040496	1068	4
DAMRILL GEORGE W	1LT	0-5340852	1268	4
DANYLCHUK PETER R	CPT	OF-0101403	0868	4
DARLEY GEORGE L	COL	0-0029693	0362	4
DAVANZO LOUIS T	LTC	0-1323668	1167	4
DAVIDSON NORTON A	1LT	0-5329160	0768	4
DAVIS CHARLES L	LTC	0-0044317	0266	4
DAVIS HENRY S	CW4	W-2144816	1068	4
DAVIS JULIA A	MAJ	N-0761082	0465	4
DAVIS MICHAEL A	1LT	0-5253217	1168	4
DAVIS WILLIAM R	MAJ	OF-0105374	0868	4
DAWSON EMMETT C JR	LTC	0-1895009	0567	4
DAY NORMAN C	CPT	0-2014509	0264	4
DE GREEF LEO H	CPT	0-4070744	0768	4
DE LA GARZA CARLOS G	CPT	0-2263552	0363	4
DE MOSS EDWARD L	CW4	W-2003605	0767	4
DE SPAIN LA MAR A	LTC	0-0032587	0966	4
DEAL WILLIAM H JR	2LT	0-5413878	0364	4
DEAN GERALD M	MAJ	0-2014441	0465	4
DECK PATRICK A	1LT	0-5017756	0166	4
DECKER JAMES W	LTC	0-0078791	1265	4
DELANEY JOSEPH J	LTC	0-0033048	1268	4
DEUSCHLE LAWRENCE W	1LT	0-5424295	0968	4
DEVLIN PAUL L	1LT	0-5335781	0968	4
DIAL EVELYN E	MAJ	N-0002444	0564	4
DIAMOND NEAL O	MAJ	0-1106092	0865	4
DICKSON DONALD J	1LT	0-5018852	0767	4
DILLARD MONDELL	MAJ	0-2206054	0467	4
DIRCK FLOYD C	CW3	W-2149694	0166	4
DOBSON JOEL G	COL	0-1283043	1267	4
DOMINGOS MANUEL P	CPT	0-0099155	0768	4
DOWER FRANK J	LTC	0-0956840	1167	4
DOWLING WILLIAM L	1LT	0-1845875	0968	4
DOWSETT PETER J	CPT	0-5712891	0467	4
DREHER MELVIN M	CPT	0-1637326	0764	4
DUBYK ANN T	MAJ	N-0788680	0868	4
DUGAN DONALD C	LTC	0-1305025	0466	4
DUKE WILLIAM G	COL	0-0366484	0166	4
DULEY CLARA M	LTC	N-0001637	0660	4
DUMLAO ALEX P	1LT	0-5427040	1268	4
DUNCAN MILDRED	MAJ	N-0002621	0167	4
DUNGAN JAMES A	CW3	W-0904108	0863	4
DUNN JAMES S	COL	0-0040173	C867	4
DUNN STEPHEN F	LTC	0-1105399	1167	4
DUREN THOMAS R	CW3	W-3440022	1068	4
EASTLAKE ROGER W	2LT	0-1951683	0968	4
EAVES WILLIAM H JR	1LT	0-5339758	1268	4
EDWARDS EMERSON W JR	CW3	W-2149043	0464	4
EDWARDS RALPH	LTC	0-0062827	0268	4
EDWARDS WESLEY B	COL	0-0031848	0468	4
EFFENGHAM ESTHER M	LTC	L-0000324	1167	4
EGGSTAFF CHARLES M	LTC	0-1995247	0764	4
EKBERG HELEN I	MAJ	N-0002757	0568	4
ELLIS HAROLD J	CPT	OF-0102323	1067	4
ELMORE VINCENT M JR	COL	0-0021086	0868	4
EMERSON JAMES W	MAJ	0-0997324	0366	4
EMERY JOHN E	MAJ	0-1311750	0267	4
ENGEL TIBOR	CPT	0-5219989	0967	4
ENGLER JEAN H	CPT	0-0087101	1265	4
ENGLISH WILLIAM W	CW2	W-2001825	0867	4
ERLANDSON KENNETH W	CW3	W-2205523	0566	4
EVANS GILBERT R JR	CW2	W-3100413	0267	4
EZELL JOSEPH J	MAJ	0-1884172	0767	4
FAGG WILLIAM L JR	1LT	0-0083218	1059	4
FAHEY NICHOLAS F	LTC	0-1032584	0464	4
FALCHETTA STEPHEN L	CPT	OF-0101812	0567	4
FALK DONALD G	CW2	W-3400117	0867	4
FANNIN CLYDE	WO1	W-2119951	0366	4
FARRELL JOSEPH E	LTC	0-1307387	0167	4
FEIN JACOB M	CW4	W-2144489	0467	4
FERRIS CHARLES J	CPT	0-2308323	0967	4
FIGGE GRACE H	MAJ	L-1010018	0364	4
FINESINGER JOSEPH	CPT	0-5224005	0765	4
FISHER MARSHALL U	MAJ	0-1327828	0764	4
FITZGERALD FRANCIS X	1LT	0-1598372	0367	4
FITZGERALD JOHN J	CPT	0-5324915	0368	4
FLANAGAN ANDREW P	COL	0-0030609	0466	4
FLANAGAN JAMES A	MAJ	0-0953542	0365	4
FLANAGAN JAMES M	CPT	0-5317362	1067	4
FLEMING EDDY W	1LT	0-5538209	0168	4
FLETCHER AARON J	CPT	0-5209176	0466	4
FOSSA ARISTIDE B	CW3	W-2148608	0168	4
FOSTER JAY W	LTC	0-0084316	1262	4
FOSTER PAUL E JR	1LT	0-5021125	0868	4
FOSTER WILLIAM J	MAJ	0-2306603	1168	4
FOUKE JOSEPH F	CPT	0-2103089	0667	4
FOX ELMER W JR	LTC	0-0052318	0967	4
FRANCISCO HERBERT A	1LT	0-5709875	0468	4
FRANK ARTHUR L	CW2	W-2212526	0365	4
FRANKLIN OLIVER W	CPT	0-0408234	0365	4
FRANKS WILLIAM A	COL	0-0043301	0365	4
FRAZIER WALTER K	MAJ	0-4010496	0167	4
FREEMAN RAYMOND R	1LT	0-5000499	0360	4
FRYE RAYMOND E JR	CPT	0-5210933	0967	4
FUERST LOUIS P	LTC	0-2034967	0766	4
GAFNER RICHARD L SR	CPT	0-0073331	0365	4
GAGNON WILFRED E	CPT	0-1589211	1166	4
GALLAGHER JAMES P	MAJ	0-0960276	1268	4
GALLAHER GLENDALE D	LTC	0-0043925	1067	4
GALLO JOSEPH A JR	1LT	0-5023446	0568	4
GALLOWAY HENRY T	CW3	W-3350267	0667	4
GAMBLE ROBERT D	LTC	0-1994604	0266	4
GANNS RALPH R	COL	0-0020184	0762	4
GARDNER RAY	LTC	0-1112727	0467	4
GAUDREAU LAWRENCE J	1LT	0-5322081	0867	4
GEIST THOMAS O	LTC	0-2036507	0468	4
GENTRY GEORGE T JR	1LT	0-5334064	0368	4
GENTRY ROY C	MAJ	0-0074989	1066	4
GERETY JOHN S	COL	0-0043605	1268	4
GERHARDT HARRISON A	M G	0-C018697	0567	4
GERWITZ RALPH F	CW4	W-0903141	1068	4
GETTYS GEORGE F	CPT	0-5701469	0431	4
GIBSON JOHN R	COL	0-0063454	0667	4
GIBSON JOYCE W	1LT	N-C902131	0356	4
GIESECKE CARL G	COL	0-0063469	0468	4
GIGLIERANO ALFRED	MAJ	0-1999380	0667	4
GILLMAN WILLIAM D	2LT	0-1929498	0255	4

NAME	GRADE	SVC NO	DATE RET MO YR	RET CODE
GILLOTTE DONALD	1LT	0-5340538	0568	4
GILMAN ANNE L	1LT	R-5417218	1167	4
GILMER MAX	LTC	0-0484827	0268	4
GITTES HYMAN R	LTC	0-1037002	0663	4
GLEASON JOSEPH L	MAJ	0-1172463	0965	4
GOFF RICHARD C	CW3	W-2215291	0768	4
GONZALEZ GUSTAVO A	CW3	W-2004329	0268	4
GOODHAND D GLENN	B G	0-0051511	0664	4
GORDON DONALD B	COL	0-0032573	0367	4
GORDON MATTHEW E	CPT	0-2203405	0766	4
GOTTLIEB ABRAHAM M	LTC	0-0963263	0868	4
GRAHAM ALEXANDER	CCL	0-0018688	0862	4
GRAHAM JACKIE C	CPT	0-1936662	0766	4
GRAHAM JACKSON	M G	0-0020553	0367	4
GRANT EDWARD R	2LT	0-2318709	0766	4
GRANTHAM DOUGLAS D	2LT	0-5318502	1164	4
GRAY DAVID W	M G	0-0018988	0768	4
GRAY JAMES E JR	LTC	0-1951687	0468	4
GRAY WALTER A	COL	0-0038939	1068	4
GREEN VICTOR D	LTC	0-0050445	0567	4
GREENE QUENTIN R	CPT	0-2017838	0567	4
GREENGLASS HERMAN A	MAJ	0F-0103525	1266	4
GREENWALT PAUL E	1LT	0-5334390	1068	4
GRIFFIN ROBERT W	COL	0-0080810	0868	4
GRIFFITHS AARON C JR	LTC	0-1289905	0167	4
GUERDRUM THORVALD J	LTC	0-0043829	0861	4
GUSTAFSON PAULINE	MAJ	N-0002148	0162	4
GUTHRIE SIDNEY C	MAJ	0-0057451	0765	4
GUZNICZAK JOSEPH P	CPT	0-2262108	1168	4
HAKEREM NANCY K	CPT	N-2321271	1167	4
HALE JAMES L	CPT	0-5530736	0867	4
HALL ROBERT E	COL	0-0031747	0862	4
HALL THOMAS J JR	CPT	0-1059799	0668	4
HAMILTON LAURENCE G	2LT	0-5013885	0964	4
HAMLETT BARKSDALE	GEN	0-0018143	0964	4
HAMMACK WILLIAM M JR	CW3	W-2209508	1267	4
HAMMOND JAMES P	LTC	0-1582359	0565	4
HAMNER SHIRLEY D	CW2	W-3430580	0867	4
HANLEY JOHN F	LTC	0-0486866	0168	4
HANNAN PHILLIP R	CW2	W-3152364	1167	4
HANNON LAURENCE K	LTC	0-0058915	0268	4
HARDING CLARENCE E	CPT	0-0084339	0668	4
HARRIGAN WILLIAM F	COL	0-0036438	0667	4
HARRINGTON JOHN W	MAJ	0-0974548	0567	4
HARRIS ARTHUR C JR	LTC	0-0020874	0665	4
HARRIS BRADY R	LTC	0-0061563	0167	4
HARRIS GIDEON J	MAJ	0-0964149	1265	4
HARRISON WALTER R JR	LTC	0-0057433	0666	4
HART WILLIAM F	LTC	0-2028590	1268	4
HATFIELD ROGER L	1LT	0-5320167	0965	4
HAYLOW HELEN R	LTC	N-0776391	0268	4
HAYNES HAYTER W	CPT	0-5226121	1167	4
HAYWARD JAMES F JR	LTC	0-1318038	1168	4
HEALEY DERMDT T	CPT	0-0094044	1167	4
HEALEY JAMES P JR	COL	0-0042906	0267	4
HEARD CHARLES C	CPT	0-5325748	0967	4
HEATON LEONARD D	LTG	0-0016960	1166	4
HENDERSON TONY S	LTC	0-0039279	0767	4
HENNESSEY RAYMOND E	MAJ	0-1795901	1067	4
HERBERT SELMA A	MAJ	L-0000047	0264	4
HERTZLER JOHN M	1LT	0-5327070	1167	4
HICKEY PATRICK F	1LT	0-5221311	0468	4
HICKS WILFRED R	1LT	0-1584357	0467	4
HIGBY SUSAN J	CPT	L-2313816	0368	4
HILDEBRAND EDWARD W	LTC	0-1326753	0568	4
HILL GARRETT L	COL	0-0033941	0666	4
HILL MAURICE H	CW4	W-2113881	0864	4
HILL WOODROW W	WO1	W-2126951	1267	4
HODSON EDMUND R	COL	0-0349568	0765	4
HOENSCHEID MILO J	2LT	0-2297227	0362	4
HOFFMAN ALAN C	MAJ	0-0088101	0564	4
HOFFMAN EARL W	LTC	0-1291276	0968	4
HOFFMAN MICHAEL E	1LT	0-5019219	0367	4
HOKANSON WILLIAM E	CPT	0-5534889	0968	4
HOLLINGSWORTH LINDY	CPT	0-4076117	0966	4
HOLLOWELL FREDDIE D	CPT	0-4077704	0468	4
HOLMES JAMES E	1LT	0-5339580	0968	4
HOLMES ROBERT B	LTC	0-1311774	0167	4
HOLZENTHALER M L	MAJ	L-0220092	0267	4
HOOKS WALTER A	LTC	0-0080877	0665	4
HOOPER GARNER J	LTC	0-2204342	1068	4
HOWDESHELL HARMON M	COL	0-0039973	0765	4
HOWES RICHARD H	MAJ	0-0075623	1166	4
HOYT RAYMOND E	1LT	0-5240771	1168	4
HUMPHREY HAROLD W	LTC	0-0069691	0765	4
HUMPHREYS JOHN W	LTC	0-1913459	0468	4
HUSS THEODORE G	1LT	0-0980085	0768	4
HUTSON THOMAS M	MAJ	0-1922902	1166	4
IMMEL ROBERT G	CPT	0-5242147	1168	4
IMWALLE FRANK E	CW3	W-2148077	1167	4
INGRAM JAMES L	COL	0-0031201	0968	4
INGRAM SAMUEL T	CPT	0-0085578	0666	4
INNES WILLIAM H	COL	0-0043867	0866	4
IRVINE FREDERIC H II	MAJ	0-0981776	1066	4
IVY MARION R	MAJ	0-2265861	0367	4
JACKSON MARSHALL D	LTC	0-0037625	0466	4
JACOBS JAMES A	CPT	0-5327838	1068	4
JACOBSON BERNARD	COL	0-4022544	0866	4
JAHN DUANE R	1LT	0-5336503	1268	4
JAMESON MALCOLM M	COL	0-0080905	0468	4
JAN LLOYD V	MAJ	0-0075377	1268	4
JEANETTE ROBERT J	1LT	0-5016225	1166	4
JENSEN EMILIE K	COL	N-0000060	1164	4
JOHNAKIN EVANDER L	1LT	0F-0104138	0567	4
JOHNSON FREDERICK	1LT	0-5428539	1168	4
JOHNSON HAROLD K	GEN	0-0019187	0768	4
JOHNSON JOSEPH A JR	CPT	0-5402483	0966	4
JOHNSON LEWIS C	LTC	0-1597692	1166	4
JOHNSON RICHARD C	CPT	0-5303641	0366	4
JONES DONALD E	CW4	W-2146428	0168	4
JONES GEORGE E JR	LTC	0-0080430	1268	4
JONES JAMES W	MAJ	0-2204417	1266	4
JORDAN ARTHUR C	LTC	0-1573314	0467	4
JORDAN PAUL M	LTC	0-0063125	0168	4
JULIAN HOWARD D	LTC	0-2000783	1268	4
KADISON JOSEPH J	MAJ	0-4011138	0168	4
KAMINSKY NEAL S	1LT	0-5710429	0866	4
KANADY CLAUDE V	CW4	W-2106189	1068	4
KARPE HENRY Z	LTC	0-1002039	0467	4
KAUFMANN MICHAEL M	1LT	0-5012052	1264	4
KAYS LEE G	LTC	0-0032750	0868	4
KEATING GEOFFREY J	CPT	0-5006677	0567	4
KELLER PERCY A	CW3	W-2207292	1166	4
KELLER STANISLAUS	CPT	0-2276566	0964	4
KELSEY JOHN E	B G	0-0021061	0868	4
KENYUN GILBERT A	1LT	0-1823458	1164	4
KEOUGH THOMAS F	MAJ	0-2203039	0667	4
KERCHEVAL BENJAMIN B	COL	0-0023933	0667	4
KING ARTHUR N II	2LT	0-5255191	0568	4
KING EVERETT G	COL	0-0061170	0467	4
KING JAMES A	CPT	0-2308565	0964	4
KINTER KENNETH E	MAJ	0-2005940	0365	4
KLAR LAWRENCE R	COL	0-0084553	1167	4
KLAUSNER DAVID A	CPT	0-5219341	0868	4
KLIGEL ROBERT J	2LT	0F-0113035	0968	4
KNOBLAUCH FREDERICK	COL	0-0021672	0667	4
KNOX RAYMOND A	LTC	0-0051921	0765	4
KOCH WILLIAM H	CPT	0-5711556	0168	4
KOLSTER JIM H	LTC	0-0065265	0867	4
KOPOLL RICHARD A	CW2	W-2207081	0265	4
KONITZER KENNETH R	CW2	W-3430406	0467	4
KOONTZ JOSEPH J	COL	0-0060254	0468	4
KOSZAIKA JULIA E	LTC	N-0001562	0168	4
KOTCHIN STANLEY P	LTC	0-0083554	0868	4
KRAFTSOW MORTON	LTC	0-1036236	1168	4
KRAMER ELDON L	MAJ	0-2029632	0165	4
KRESSE TIFFIN J	CW2	W-2210817	1268	4
KUBALAK RAYMOND R	1LT	0-5222033	1265	4
KUHN GEORGE A	B G	0-0084813	0868	4
KUNZ HENRY F	2LT	0F-0113040	1068	4
LA FLAMME ERNEST H	COL	0-0020781	0163	4
LACEY RALPH W	CW4	W-2146871	1068	4
LAETARE ARLA R	1LT	N-5417401	0567	4
LAIN JAMES L	COL	0-0032967	0768	4
LAMB CARROLL G	1LT	0-5220753	1167	4
LAMBERT JOE C	M G	0-0030033	0968	4
LAMMERS MARVIN E	CPT	0-2266731	0465	4
LANE GEORGE H JR	MAJ	0-0089240	0967	4
LANGSTON JOE V	COL	0-0024182	0367	4
LARRABEE PHILIP A	2LT	0-5347141	1268	4
LARSEN PHILIP J	1LT	0-5537002	0768	4
LAVIGNE JACK E	MAJ	0-0397837	0566	4
LAWLESS MATTHEW T	CW2	W-3156253	1168	4
LAWRENCE ROBERT G JR	COL	0-0561477	0768	4
LAYCOCK JEANNE G	MAJ	N-5003312	0265	4
LEACH HARRY V	CW4	W-2146171	1267	4
LEE ROBERT E	CW2	W-3200481	1068	4
LEEPER DONALD G	COL	0-0455727	0968	4
LEIDHOLT ERNEST B	COL	0-0079712	0768	4
LEONARD LAWRENCE M	LTC	0-0076335	0767	4
LERG ROBERT F	COL	0-0364323	0968	4
LIDDELL RAYMOND N	LTC	0-0468155	1267	4
LIEBOWITZ ETHEL	MAJ	N-0001852	0768	4
LILLY WARREN D	1LT	0-5243129	1068	4
LINCOLN LAWRENCE J	LTG	0-0018968	0868	4
LINDER ROGER M	2LT	0-5346617	0768	4
LINDLEY ROGER M	COL	0-0410141	0266	4
LINDSEY JESSIE E	CW4	W-2143677	0967	4
LINROTHE ROBERT N	LTC	0-0080976	0767	4
LITTLE JAMES V	LTC	0-2042915	0568	4
LITTLE MYRON W	LTC	0-0541651	1268	4
LITTLETON EARL P	1LT	0-1176410	0966	4
LITWAK PHILIP	1LT	0-5519931	0366	4
LIVERMONT CHARLES R	CW2	W-3155939	0868	4
LOMBARDO RICCARDO J	CW3	W-3150498	0467	4
LONG JAMES E	MAJ	0-0097150	1166	4
LONG LUTHER F	COL	0-0355271	0366	4
LORD FORREST F	MAJ	N-0732513	0168	4
LOUIE LOUISE	CPT	N-2302310	0667	4
LOVE RICHARD L	CPT	0F-0109211	1068	4
LOVELL BUDDY	MAJ	0-4006957	1166	4
LUTHMAN CARL R	CPT	0-5023689	1268	4
LYNCH JOHN C	1LT	0-2008045	0864	4
LYNCH WILLIAM F	COL	0-0040182	1167	4
LYTTLE RICHARD N	MAJ	0-2013861	0967	4
MADDEN RAYMOND H	COL	0-0030950	0468	4
MADIGAN FRANCIS L	LTC	0-2010028	0866	4
MAGINESS LATIMER H	CPT	0-5222400	1168	4
MAGUIRE RALPH E	LTC	0-1115684	0965	4
MAIXNER HAROLD V	COL	0-0024439	1068	4
MALKOW DERRYL D	MAJ	0-0431729	0861	4
MANHART ASHTON H	LTG	0-0018773	0867	4
MANY EDWARD M	1LT	0-5228110	0168	4
MANZO FRANK A	1LT	0-5020268	0167	4
MARANGER GEORGE J	LTC	0-0069525	0667	4
MARDICK CLINTON H	LTC	0-1031108	0365	4
MARQUEZ HERNAN G	CPT	0-5015141	0766	4
MARR JOHN E	CPT	0-5211616	0467	4
MARTIN WILLIAM J	LTC	0-0439254	0968	4
MARVIN SIDNEY L	COL	0-0057063	0867	4
MASICK CHARLES V	CPT	0-5020092	0368	4
MASSEY BASTON C	MAJ	0-1541020	0554	4
MASSINGILL GERALDINE	MAJ	N-0001158	0565	4
MATSUZAKI MASAKO	CPT	N-0901484	1065	4
MAYS ROBERT G	LTC	0-0402061	0463	4
MAYWALD STEPHEN W	2LT	0-5351856	0768	4
MC CABE EDWARD F	COL	0-0025926	1168	4
MC CARTHY ROBERT T	CPT	0-1924223	0968	4
MC CLELLAND ELLIS F	MAJ	0-0094772	1066	4
MC CLURE RICHARD B	1LT	0-5009386	0964	4
MC CONNELL WAYNE D	COL	0-0043457	1066	4
MC CORMACK J GORDON	MAJ	0-0072148	0466	4
MC CORMICK OTTO L	CPT	0-0066049	0460	4
MC CUNE RAY D	CW3	W-2150849	0568	4
MC DERMOTT ARTHUR R	LTC	0-0399306	0367	4
MC DEVITT LEO P	MAJ	0-4031411	0368	4
MC EWAN ROBERT C JR	CPT	0-5330644	1168	4
MC FEE HAROLD F	LTC	0-1280615	0867	4
MC GINN ROBERT E JR	1LT	0-5427909	1068	4
MC HUGH FRANCIS J	CW2	W-2120857	1167	4
MC INTYRE MICHAEL J	1LT	0-0098833	0565	4
MC KEE EDGAR S	COL	0-0021182	1268	4
MC LEOD WALTER G	LTC	0-0060748	1055	4
MC LUSTER LENORA E	CPT	N-2308088	1268	4
MC MAHON DANIEL J JR	MAJ	0-1997576	0268	4
MC MAHON JOSEPH M JR	CPT	0-0064848	0466	4
MC MAHON RICHARD J	MAJ	0-1874291	0165	4
MC MANUS MYLES M	LTC	0-1292383	0666	4
MC NUTT JAMES N	MAJ	0-0385784	0866	4
MC SHEA ROYAL E	COL	0-0051881	0667	4
MEAD CHARLES E	LTC	0-0036314	0265	4
MEADOR MAURICE A	COL	0-0030835	1164	4
MEDRICK JOSEPH R	1LT	0-5251766	1268	4
MEIS RAYMOND C	LTC	0-1290975	0967	4
MEISER ROBERT F	LTC	0-1331649	1068	4
MELLON DANIEL R	CPT	0F-0101977	1068	4
MELODY PHILIP B	COL	0-0038782	0964	4
MENDENHALL ROBERT T	LTC	0-2015767	0968	4
MERRITTS ARLINGTON	CPT	0-0966388	0767	4
METZKER JEFF J	MAJ	0-1924856	0864	4
MEYER HARRIET R	LTC	M-0000660	1167	4
MEYERS IRA R	LTC	0-1796669	1166	4
MEYERS JAY M	LTC	0-1337462	0467	4
MICHEL NORA W	CPT	N-2297702	0165	4
MIEZIO DONALD S	CPT	0-5525857	1166	4
MILETICH MILTON M	COL	0-0032546	0168	4
MILLER BLAINE L	MAJ	0-1924981	0764	4
MILLER CAROLE A	CPT	N-5411519	1068	4
MILLER DAVID A	CW2	W-3250215	1064	4
MILLER FRANK L	COL	0-0057564	0866	4
MILLER FRANK L	LTC	0-0979486	0268	4
MILLER KATHLEEN F	MAJ	N-0001253	1268	4
MILLER RAY L	COL	0-0063827	1168	4
MILLER RUFUS J	MAJ	0-0978218	0268	4
MILLER SAMUEL D	MAJ	0-1019274	0267	4
MILLER WALTER L JR	LTC	0-0024495	0161	4
MILLIKEN CHARLES E	MAJ	0-4022784	1067	4
MINCKLER REX D	LTC	0-0025581	1065	4
MISSIK BERNARD	MAJ	0-1575472	0864	4
MITCHELL JOAN L	MAJ	N-0736250	0568	4
MIZE EDWARD M	COL	0-0461638	1265	4
MOBLEY WILLIAM A	MAJ	0-2283755	0667	4
MOCK CHARLES	CW3	W-2144124	0168	4
MOLLISON DOUGLAS A	LTC	0-0062213	0468	4
MONTESI STEVEN G	1LT	0-5419388	0767	4
MONTGOMERY DAVID G	2LT	MR-2326548	0668	4
MOON HOWARD H JR	1LT	0-5516745	0665	4
MOON RANDALL W	2LT	0F-0111750	0568	4
MOORE GENE D	COL	0-0063280	1167	4
MOORE ORVEN D	COL	0-0043581	1268	4
MOORE ROY N	CPT	0-5405083	0265	4
MOORE RUSSELL E	LTC	0-0060615	1268	4
MORDUE NORMAN A	CPT	0F-0108795	1268	4
MORGAN JAMES S	1LT	0-5326444	0667	4
MORRIS PAUL W	1LT	0-5338687	0868	4
MORROW JACK G	LTC	0-0067730	0866	4
MORT KENNETH H	CPT	0-5320201	1067	4
MUELLER EDMUND L	B G	0-0034292	1167	4
MUELLER ROBERT A	CPT	0-5525811	0966	4
MULLINS DEMPSEY F	MAJ	0-2046353	1158	4
MUNDY JAMES C III	MAJ	0-1055396	1167	4
MUNSON LEONARD M	LTC	0-2046764	0568	4
MURPHY JOHN A	MAJ	0-0075723	0768	4
MURRAY BILL M	CPT	0-5410269	0567	4
MURRAY JAMES H JR	1LT	0-2327867	0768	4
NAPIER ALFRED N	CPT	0-0954543	0668	4
NASH DANE P	CPT	0-5406152	0868	4
NAUS LEO	CW4	W-2150604	0564	4
NELSON DOUGLAS A	CPT	0-4056040	0968	4
NELSON EDGAR L JR	1LT	0-2032932	1268	4

TEMPORARY DISABILITY RETIRED LIST

NAME	GRADE	SVC NO	DATE RET MO YR	RET CODE
NELSON ORVILLE W	CPT	0-2279614	0165	4
NEWARK HENRY G	CW3	W-2149021	0166	4
NEWBOLD WILLIAM G	MAJ	0-2037084	0667	4
NEWMAN SAMUEL H JR	CPT	0-5405029	0565	4
NEWPORT HENRY S	MAJ	0-5002806	1068	4
NEWSOM CHARLES L III	CPT	OF-0109252	0568	4
NEWSOM SAMUEL J	COL	0-0057042	1064	4
NICK HENRY J	CW	W-2149135	0667	4
NICODEMUS ROBERT E	LTC	0-1011046	0865	4
NIDA GLENN E	COL	0-0030140	0764	4
NIEHOFF JOHN JR	LTC	0-1055926	1165	4
NIERLING DON D	1LT	0-5013715	0765	4
NOLAN WILLIAM A JR	LTC	0-1052904	0168	4
NORBERG EDWARD J JR	CPT	0-5220510	0868	4
NORTH ROBERT L	1LT	OF-0101634	0766	4
NORTH THOMAS	M G	0-0011879	0553	4
NORTON HENRY C	CW3	W-3150336	1166	4
NOVOTNEY STEPHEN F	CW2	W-2146636	0868	4
NOWAK AMBROSE J	MAJ	0-1316316	0168	4
NUTT SAMUEL C	CPT	0-0093864	1167	4
NYSEWANDER CARLETON	CW3	W-2207996	0268	4
OBRYAN JAMES M	CPT	OF-0100998	0367	4
OCONNOR HENRY J	MAJ	0-1936456	0568	4
OEDING ERNST C	COL	0-0043259	0868	4
OHARA JOHN J JR	LTC	0-2048734	0767	4
OKEEFE JOHN A	CPT	0-5713329	1268	4
OLSEN EARL R	CPT	0-0093483	0564	4
OLSON LESTER K	COL	0-0030640	0166	4
ORGANEK RONALD W	CPT	0-5010284	1068	4
ORTIZ-SUAREZ HUMBERT	CPT	0-5826809	1168	4
OSBORNE PATRICIA J	CPT	N-2313636	0966	4
OSHAY DON K	LTC	0-0966453	0768	4
OSZCZAKIEWICZ WALTER	CW4	W-0903644	0767	4
OTT DELBERT J	MAJ	0-0988873	1068	4
OTTENBACHER RUDOLPH	LTC	0-1326210	0868	4
OTTO THOMAS W	COL	0-0030799	0866	4
OWEN ETHEL	MAJ	N-0752149	0266	4
OWENS DAVID R	CPT	0-5019665	1168	4
OWENS FLOYD E	LTC	0-1177125	0166	4
OWENS WARREN R	CPT	0-0069259	0864	4
OXX LAWRENCE M	LTC	0-0548340	0664	4
PADGETT REUBEN P III	CPT	0-5317329	0268	4
PALM IRA A	COL	0-0040245	0466	4
PANITZ DAVID S	MAJ	0-2029141	0268	4
PARADIS CLARENCE E	1LT	0-4011062	0767	4
PARKER DAVID B	M G	0-0020571	1167	4
PARMLEY LOREN F JR	COL	0-0052087	0868	4
PARSONS DON R	LTC	0-1588218	0767	4
PASSARELLI EUGENE	LTC	0-1638225	0666	4
PATE CONLEY D	LTC	0-0958251	0764	4
PATERNO BARRY R	1LT	0-5342106	1168	4
PATRICK PETER W	CPT	0-5709363	1168	4
PATTESON HARVEY L	COL	0-0043439	0868	4
PAULI FORREST S	LTC	0-1039505	1167	4
PAUS FRANK L	LTC	0-1951031	0168	4
PEACOCK JAMES F	1LT	0-5340937	1268	4
PEARSON MILTON H	CW3	W-2205869	0665	4
PEENE AVA L	LTC	N-0000663	0966	4
PELHAM ALFRED M JR	1LT	0-5532692	0967	4
PERCIACCANTO PETER P	LTC	0-1324738	1064	4
PETRIK VERNON F	MAJ	0-0092113	0567	4
PETRY FRANK JR	CW4	W-2144570	0967	4
PETTET JOSEPH D	CPT	0-0072196	0664	4
PHILLIPS EUGENE F SR	1LT	0-1057566	0566	4
PHILP JOHN M	CPT	0-5315543	0368	4
PICKERING JOE K	CPT	0-1308698	1268	4
PIERCE WILLIAM H	CPT	0-0984583	0861	4
PIERSOL WILBER S	MAJ	0-1012424	0664	4
PINNER JOHN E	2LT	0-1884204	0868	4
PIZANIS STEVE T	MAJ	0-0980436	1267	4
PLEMONS HARRY F	MAJ	0-0967241	0163	4
PLOTNICK STEPHEN L	CPT	0-5021140	0868	4
POE CUPID R	CPT	0-5540188	0967	4
POLANCIC JOSEPH C	1LT	0-1173745	1064	4
POMEROY DEANE A	WO1	W-3200585	0564	4
POMEY ALBERT H SR	CW4	W-2147294	1167	4
PONDER CHARLES A	CPT	OF-0107347	0768	4
PONIKISKI MITCHELL S	LTC	0-2048116	1065	4
POOL RUSSELL F	MAJ	0-0088474	1268	4
PORTER DONALD A JR	CPT	0-5415498	0567	4
PORTER FRED B	COL	0-0040477	0768	4
PORTER RALPH R	LTC	0-1553720	1167	4
POTEET HARRY H	COL	0-0305532	0161	4
POWELL FREDERICK	1LT	0-1315481	1166	4
POWELL JOHN C JR	LTC	0-0068395	1168	4
POWELL ROBERT E	CPT	0-4011931	0966	4
POWELL ROSS F	LTC	0-0033980	0565	4
POWELL VELMA L	MAJ	N-0002495	0864	4
POWER GEORGE W	M G	0-0018691	0867	4
POWERS NORMAN W	CPT	0-5525088	1066	4
PROVENCE EDWARD L	LTC	0-1917806	0768	4
PSAKI RAOULC JR	COL	0-0026467	0968	4
QUINN GENE	COL	0-0030839	0365	4
QUINN JOHN T	CPT	0-0099961	0866	4
RADER RICHARD C II	1LT	0-5222816	0268	4
RAFFERTY ARTHUR J	MAJ	0-0058566	0768	4
RAIMI MORTON D	CW2	W-3156613	0668	4
RAKE CLIFFORD O	WO1	W-2127006	0564	4
RANKIN ROBERT B	LTC	0-0079963	0368	4
RAY ERNEST E JR	LTC	0-1554074	0366	4
RAY WILLIAM K JR	LTC	0-0980104	0867	4
RAYMOND HELEN V	MAJ	N-0723267	0768	4
RECTOR HARRY L	1LT	0-5336382	0868	4
REECE WILLIAM F	CW3	W-2209993	0667	4
REED OLIE B	MAJ	N-0001723	0964	4
REES KENNETH R	CPT	0-0059875	0963	4
REGISTER JAMES C	CW4	W-2149136	1068	4
REID WILLIAM M	CPT	0-5314872	0566	4
REID WILLIAM S	MAJ	0-1054843	0865	4
REILAND NICHOLAS J	CW2	W-2212839	0166	4
REINECKE PAUL S JR	COL	0-0023284	0168	4
REYNOLDS JAMES B	1LT	0-5326787	1167	4
RHEA ROBERT L JR	B G	0-0029285	0868	4
RIALS GRADY F	COL	0-0044022	0768	4
RICCITELLI MARY A	CPT	N-2318306	0867	4
RIDER ROBINSON B JR	2LT	0-5233879	0667	4
RIORDAN MICHAEL W JR	CPT	0-0083442	0463	4
RIOS ALBERT J	MAJ	0-0084508	0267	4
ROACH ARMAND O JR	CPT	0-0089281	0865	4
ROBERTS JAMES J 3D	CPT	0-0093913	0667	4
ROBERTSON MARY N	MAJ	N-0002432	0865	4
ROBINSON BILLY L	LTC	0-0539095	1265	4
ROBINSON MICHAEL S	1LT	0-5339874	0568	4
ROCK MICHAEL B	1LT	0-5536802	1168	4
RODERMUND KARL A	LTC	0-1582088	0666	4
ROGERS JON V	1LT	0-5336384	0768	4
ROGERS LEE F	MAJ	0-0091368	0967	4
ROLLE RUFUS M	CPT	0-5306013	1166	4
ROLLINS ALFRED G	MAJ	0-1595328	1068	4
ROMEO PHILIP J	2LT	0-5019142	1264	4
ROSCOE RICHARD D	1LT	0-5534804	1166	4
ROSEN STEPHEN G	CPT	0-5315916	0765	4
ROW HENRY C JR	LTC	0-0060433	0866	4
RULONG BERNARD C	LTC	0-2288107	0767	4
SALADIN THOMAS A	CPT	0-5246640	1268	4
SALERNO RONALD A	2LT	0-5347727	0868	4
SALLING ROBERT W	COL	0-1645966	0868	4
SALONICK JOSEPH L	COL	0-0040266	0868	4
SALOPEK MARY A	MAJ	N-0760121	1065	4
SAMPLES JAMES C	MAJ	0-1919354	1165	4
SARGENT KENDALL S	MAJ	N-0801262	0268	4
SATTLER WALTER W	1LT	0-2043295	0564	4
SAURER HAROLD D	WO1	W-3155363	0567	4
SAVAGE CHARLES R	MAJ	0-0979490	1267	4
SCHARN EDWARD O	LTC	0-1642545	0665	4
SCHERBERGER FREDERIC	LTC	0-0053918	1167	4
SCHIRMER HARRY C	CPT	0-0305296	1267	4
SCHNEIDER ELEANOR T	MAJ	N-0792322	0367	4
SCHOFIELD DAVID M	CPT	OF-0107944	0868	4
SCHOFIELD JAMES H JR	COL	0-0025754	1267	4
SCHROEDER MARTIN O F	LTC	0-2275928	0868	4
SCHUBERT OSCAR F	MAJ	0-0969102	1067	4
SCHULER JACK A	LTC	0-1913415	0568	4
SCHWARTZ MILTON B	COL	0-0521637	0168	4
SCOGINS BYRON A	CPT	0-5325169	0168	4
SCOTT RAYMOND L	CPT	0-4049262	0464	4
SEITZ JOHN A	B G	0-0030137	1067	4
SELLMAN GARY K	CPT	0-5532369	1168	4
SEVIER JOSEPH H	COL	0-0043464	0568	4
SEXTON HERBERT M	1LT	0-1342125	0566	4
SHANKLIN WILLIAM S	1LT	0-5800365	1065	4
SHARBER STEPHEN B	1LT	0-5234484	0268	4
SHELTON GERALD F	CPT	0-0097780	1168	4
SHERIDAN MARK E	CPT	OF-0105014	1068	4
SHIPMAN FRANKLIN D	CPT	0-2315662	1067	4
SHIRK PAUL R	LTC	0-0064613	0968	4
SHIRLEY ALFRED S	CPT	0-0974546	0466	4
SHULL JAMES M	1LT	0-5715139	1268	4
SIMONE VINCENT A	CPT	0-5525171	1066	4
SINGLETON EVELYN D	CPT	N-5411642	0168	4
SMELLOW SAMUEL JR	1LT	0-5419824	0168	4
SMITH ADRIAN P	CW3	W-2210210	0468	4
SMITH EARL L	MAJ	0-1019464	0966	4
SMITH ELBRIDGE A	LTC	0-0080188	1166	4
SMITH ELSIE L	MAJ	N-0002543	1267	4
SMITH LINDA G	2LT	N-5520492	0267	4
SMITH MARLO E	LTC	0-0056924	1060	4
SMITH MICHAEL A	LTC	0-2208594	1167	4
SMITH STEPHEN K	1LT	0-5021033	1268	4
SMITH VONNIE C	CPT	0-0452589	0566	4
SOUTHARD WILLIAM W	COL	0-0037465	1167	4
SPAIN CHESTER A	CW2	W-2110692	0268	4
SPARKS AARON C	1LT	0-5315153	0865	4
SPAULDING DONALD S	COL	0-1280359	0965	4
SPRAGUE GEORGE R	CPT	MN-3125318	0967	4
SPURGERS ROY K	CPT	0-0076660	0868	4
SPURLOCK ROBERT N	LTC	0-0346460	0266	4
STACKHOUSE EARL L	LTC	0-1296598	1167	4
STAHLER JOHN F	CPT	0-5712677	1068	4
STARKEY JAMES H	MAJ	0-2016211	0666	4
STEADMAN DONALD J	CPT	0-0959677	0866	4
STEIN HERMAN J	CPT	0-5242347	1068	4
STEVENS JOHN R JR	1LT	0-5320719	0568	4
STIDHAM ROBERT J	CPT	0-0098968	0667	4
STOKES JAMES R	MAJ	0-0966089	0564	4
STONE WILLIAM B	LTC	0-1174722	1164	4
STOUGHTON TOM R	M G	0-0018156	0667	4
STRANG TOM H	LTC	0-1115118	0565	4
STRANGE ROBERT O	CPT	0-1941844	0968	4
STRUNCK JACK	MAJ	0-0997715	0964	4
STRUNK STANLEY W	CPT	0-5708414	0766	4
STUART CLARK D	CPT	0-2299848	1065	4
STUART DAVID M	CPT	0-4315841	1265	4
STURIES CHARLES R	2LT	0-5543081	1068	4
SUMNER GEORGE	LTC	0-1045270	0866	4
SUPERAK NORMA J	CPT	N-2322888	0668	4
SWALM OLIVER E	CPT	0-4055949	0565	4
SWEENEY PATRICK C	1LT	0-5017536	0766	4
TAYLOR H B	CW2	W-3350258	0467	4
TAYLOR RAYMOND E	1LT	0-5425459	1268	4
TEMME GEORGE H	LTC	0-0084044	1167	4
TENNYSON WILLIAM W	COL	0-0301437	1266	4
TERRELL CHAILLE H	MAJ	0-1167250	0965	4
TERRY MILTON O	MAJ	0-1045279	0964	4
THOMAS CURTIS R	LTC	0-1184312	1065	4
THOMAS EMMETT N JR	MAJ	0-0967149	1064	4
THOMPSON ROBERT L	CPT	0-2208701	0868	4
TIGERTT WILLIAM D	B G	0-0026412	0968	4
TINDALL EDWARD F	MAJ	0-1044974	1268	4
TIPPINS BEDELL A JR	LTC	0-0065479	0665	4
TKACIK JOHN J	LTC	0-0026590	0665	4
TOM RAYMOND	CPT	0-5708988	0266	4
TOMLINSON AMOS P	WO1	W-2143448	0268	4
TOUCHETTE NORBERT E	LTC	0-0081873	0767	4
TOWNROE FREDERICK	MAJ	0-0063395	0866	4
TOWNSEND THEODORE H	MAJ	0-4030848	1166	4
TRAUL JAMES H	COL	0-1110853	0565	4
TRIM CARL J	LTC	0-0094147	0268	4
TRUAX HARRY D	WO1	W-2146984	0866	4
TRUJILLO MARY A	1LT	N-5417316	1166	4
TRUSSELL ARTHUR S	CW2	W-2213114	0467	4
TULLY CHARLES R	COL	0-0357917	1068	4
TUNNICLIFF ROBERT F	CW3	W-2210209	0568	4
ULERY JULIA A	1LT	N-5245286	0868	4
ULLIAN JOHN R	LTC	0-1039781	1068	4
URLING JOHN M	CPT	0-5420356	0668	4
VALLANDINGHAM MARGAR	MAJ	N-0725155	0667	4
VALLEE GERALD E	CPT	0-5239224	0968	4
VAN FLEET RAYMOND	COL	0-0051801	0866	4
VANLANDINGHAM PAUL C	1LT	0-5423183	1168	4
VERNON HELENA M	MAJ	N-0002987	0168	4
VETTER GERHARDT R	LTC	0-1595235	1163	4
VICKERS ROBERT F	MAJ	0-1685625	0465	4
VIEHMANN FRANCIS L	CPT	0-5322030	0767	4
VILLAS FRANK J	CPT	0-5900094	1268	4
VOGEL MELVIN D	MAJ	0-5712793	1068	4
WAGONER GERALD A	2LT	0-5255434	0568	4
WAGSTAFF MILLIE K	LTC	0-1592678	0367	4
WAKEFORD MARY W	MAJ	L-0402047	0555	4
WALKER ADA M	MAJ	N-0002480	0564	4
WALKER WILLIAM L	CPT	0-0095735	1068	4
WALL J V	LTC	0-1316249	1066	4
WALLACE MILTON I	LTC	0-0021467	1066	4
WALLS DAVID L	CPT	0-5712794	0867	4
WALSH DONALD M	CW3	W-2211700	0968	4
WALSH NORBERT W	LTC	0-1169783	0766	4
WALSH PAUL J	LTC	0-1035616	0567	4
WALTER MERCER C	M G	0-0017151	0764	4
WARD ROBERT J	LTC	0-0035689	1063	4
WARD STEPHEN R	1LT	0-5018077	0965	4
WARDINSKI WALTER I	MAJ	0-1926813	0966	4
WARNER CARL L	1LT	0-0089635	0863	4
WARNER CHESTER D	CW4	W-2142082	0368	4
WARNER GEORGE P	B G	0-0032462	1166	4
WARREN DONALD F	CPT	OF-0104574	0768	4
WATERS FRED B JR	LTC	0-0025449	0265	4
WATERS LAWRENCE E	CPT	0-0096267	0768	4
WATSON ANN M	MAJ	N-0771777	1065	4
WEATHERFORD ROY C	CPT	0-5416375	0268	4
WEAVER CHARLES O	CPT	0-2315038	1266	4
WEBER ROBERT D	1LT	0-5531185	0166	4
WELCH CHARLES R	WO1	T-0005935	0664	4
WENTZ RODNEY D	1LT	0-5535555	1167	4
WENZEL GEORGE H	COL	0-1170245	0368	4
WERTZ MILTON E	COL	0-0313535	0667	4
WEST ARTHUR L JR	M G	0-0025269	0867	4
WHALEN LOUISE A	LTC	N-0001586	0568	4
WHEELER JARVIS A	CW2	W-3430231	0266	4
WHITE CHARLES	LTC	0-1183791	1166	4
WHITE JOSEPH A	CPT	0-1313839	0965	4
WHITE ROBERT T	2LT	0-1996655	1066	4
WHITE VALMORE W JR	MAJ	0-2275061	0568	4
WHITESIDES ALAN B	LTC	0-2210067	0467	4
WHITTED DANIEL D	1LT	0-1112514	0968	4
WILCOX ALVIN J	CPT	0-1285676	0467	4
WILKINSON PAUL	LTC	0-1994722	0665	4
WILLEY HUGH W	COL	0-1554306	1167	4
WILLIAMS CECIL W	CW3	W-2203430	0968	4
WILLIAMS ERNEST E	MAJ	0-1931517	0967	4
WILLIAMS JACK L	COL	0-0042800	0265	4
WILLIAMS JUANITA M	MAJ	N-0761223	0467	4
WILLIAMS LOUIS F JR	CPT	0-0071428	0365	4
WILLIAMS WILLIAM JR	CW3	W-3150229	0768	4
WILLIAMS WILLIAM R	MAJ	0-0068176	0266	4
WILLIAMSON IVAN E SR	MAJ	0-2034015	0567	4
WILSON ARVIL L	CW2	W-2149982	1268	4
WILSON DAVID J	COL	0-0364425	0568	4
WILSON HARRY	CW4	W-2144936	1268	4
WOLCZIK WALTER	CPT	0-1646716	0664	4
WOODBURY HARRY G JR	B G	0-0021432	0568	4

NAME	GRADE	SVC NO	DATE RET MO YR	RET CODE
WOODBURY LEROY B JR	COL	O-0030598	0266	4
WOODWARD JOSEPH G	LTC	O-0039101	0867	4
WOODWARD MARIE F	MAJ	N-0722363	0367	4
WREIDT NIEL M	LTC	O-0034753	0667	4
WRIGHT JAMES F JR	COL	O-0040580	0868	4
WRIGHT WILLIAM P	COL	O-0083574	0567	4
WUBBENA PAUL F JR	MAJ	O-5707315	0268	4
WYANKSI ROBERT A	LTC	O-1595918	0168	4
YEAST DENTON W	1LT	O-1176232	1264	4
YORK ELVA M	MAJ	N-0001765	0768	4
YORMAN WILLIAM H	LTC	O-1995026	0767	4
YOUNG JAMES B	CPT	O-5327151	0968	4
ZEIGLER CLYDE C	COL	O-0019720	0265	4
ZIELKIEWICZ ANTHONY	MAJ	O-1823249	0366	4
ZUELLA HARRY J	CPT	O-5021008	1168	4

SECTION 4
EMERGENCY OFFICERS RETIRED LIST

The Emergency Officers Retired List is composed of officers, other than Regular Army officers, who incurred physical disability in line of duty while in the service of the United States during World War I.

EMERGENCY OFFICERS RETIRED LIST

NAME	GRADE	SVC NO	DATE RET MO YR	RET CODE
ABERNATHY CHARLES	2LT		1028	5
ACKLEY JOHN F	CPT		0528	5
ADAMS DANIEL W	LTC		0628	5
ADAMS JOHN J	1LT		0528	5
ADAMSON DOVA W	1LT		0628	5
ADDISON JOHN D	1LT		0628	5
ADKINS EUGENE M	1LT		0728	5
AFFHOLDER IRVIN E	2LT		0429	5
AFFOLTER GEORGE R	1LT		0529	5
ALE JOHN H	1LT		0528	5
ALLEN CHARLES B	2LT		0628	5
ALLEN GROVER C	2LT		0628	5
ALLEY WILLIAM L	1LT		0728	5
AMET HERBERT P	1LT		0628	5
ANDERSON CECIL H	CPT		0628	5
ANDERSON CLIFTON B	2LT		0628	5
ANDERSON HANSON H	1LT		0329	5
ANDERSON JAMES W	2LT		0628	5
ANDREWS BENJAMIN T	2LT		0628	5
ANDREWS LAWRENCE G	2LT		0628	5
ANGOVE CLARENCE V	2LT		1128	5
APGAR GEORGE L	1LT		0528	5
APPERSON JOHN W	2LT		0628	5
ASHMUN LOUIS H	1LT		0928	5
BACHELDER FRANK F	MAJ		0828	5
BAGALEY EDWARD T	1LT		0828	5
BAIL FRANK W	1LT		0628	5
BAILEY GEORGE T	2LT		0628	5
BAILEY PAUL F	2LT		0628	5
BAILEY SAMUEL T	1LT		0628	5
BAISDEN ROY T JR	2LT		0928	5
BAKER HORACE	CPT		0628	5
BAKER RICHARD R JR	2LT		0828	5
BALL LOGAN M	2LT		0228	5
BANKS THOMAS G	CPT		0628	5
BARCAS VICTOR	CPT		1028	5
BARLOW ALFRED M	1LT		0628	5
BARNES GERALD C	1LT		0728	5
BARNES HARRY D	2LT		0429	5
BARR JESSE W	1LT		0728	5
BARTON CHARLES W	2LT		0628	5
BARTRAM ALFRED J	1LT		0628	5
BASH HENRY E	1LT		0628	5
BATES VERNON F	1LT		0528	5
BEAN HERBERT S	2LT		0528	5
BECK THEODORE	1LT		0628	5
BENNERS ALLEN C	1LT		0728	5
BENNETT CLARENCE W	2LT		1028	5
BERG ELMER W	1LT		0628	5
BERGLUND CLYDE V	CPT		0628	5
BERNARD MARCUS A	2LT		0628	5
BIDDLE JUSTICE M	2LT		0628	5
BILL ROSWELL H	2LT		0129	5
BILLINGS EARL K	2LT		0529	5
BIRKMAN FREDERICK	2LT		0828	5
BITTNER EARL R	2LT		0528	5
BLAIN WEST E	CPT		0528	5
BLAIR GEORGE A	CPT		0528	5
BLANCHARD HOWARD E	CPT		0628	5
BLAND ARTHUR V	1LT		0628	5
BLATHERWICK EDWIN	1LT		1028	5
BLECKAZ JOHN W	1LT		0429	5
BLOCK EDGAR N	CPT		0828	5
BOBST FRANK T	1LT		0628	5
BOCHER LAWRENCE C	2LT		0528	5
BODDY ELIAS M	2LT		0728	5
BOERKE EDISON M	1LT		0628	5
BOLDRIDGE CHAUNCEY	CPT		0229	5
BOLIN FRANK E	CPT		0429	5
BORST FENTON F	1LT		0728	5
BOSTER HAROLD A	1LT		0828	5
BOTJER HENRY G	1LT		0628	5
BOYD CLARENCE E	1LT		0628	5
BOYD LEONARD C	1LT		0628	5
BOYD ROBERT S	1LT		0528	5

NAME	GRADE	SVC NO	DATE RET MO YR	RET CODE
BOYD THEODORE F	2LT		0628	5
BOYD WILLIS M	1LT		0728	5
BOYES ANDREW M C	1LT		0628	5
BRADBURY WILLIAM E	2LT		0628	5
BRADFORD LEONARD G	2LT		0740	5
BRADLEY GLADE T	CPT		1128	5
BRADLEY THOMAS R	1LT		0429	5
BREEN FREDERICK	1LT		0928	5
BREEN VINCENT C	CPT		0628	5
BRENNAN LENNOX C	CPT		0529	5
BROCHE ARTHUR T	1LT		0429	5
BROCK RAYMOND D	2LT		0628	5
BROCKMEYER EDWIN J	2LT		0329	5
BROOKS LOUIS J JR	CPT		0628	5
BROUGHTON AVERELL	1LT		0528	5
BROWN CLARENCE S	MAJ		0628	5
BROWN EMMETT W	CPT		0728	5
BROWN HARRY D	CPT		0529	5
BROWN JOHN D	1LT		0628	5
BROWN MORROW D	CPT		0628	5
BROWN VAN LEONAR	1LT		0728	5
BROWN WILLIAM H JR	1LT		0628	5
BROWNING HERBERT E	2LT		0840	5
BROWNING JOHN W	CPT		0528	5
BROYLES WATKINS A	2LT		0928	5
BRUCE WALTER H	LTC		1028	5
BRUENN JOHN J	2LT		1028	5
BRYANT DONALD R	2LT		0229	5
BRYANT FRED S	CPT		0828	5
BRYANT JOHN L	2LT		0529	5
BUCKLES WALTER A	CPT		0928	5
BUGGY FRANK R	CPT		0528	5
BUIE RODERICK M	CPT		0728	5
BUNGE ROBERT C	CPT		0528	5
BURNLEY EDWIN R	2LT		0129	5
BURNS ELLIS P	CPT		0429	5
BURNS JAMES F	CPT		0529	5
BURNS WILLIAM E	1LT		0628	5
BURR BENJAMIN E	1LT		0628	5
BUSH MARTIN M	1LT		0740	5
BUSH WALTER L	1LT		0528	5
BUTLER STANLEY C	1LT		0628	5
BUTT KIRK	2LT		0628	5
BYERS JAMES E	1LT		0628	5
BYRD JOHN H	1LT		0828	5
CAFFERTY EDMUND J	1LT		0628	5
CALLAHAN FRANCIS X	2LT		0329	5
CAMMER CLAUDE R	1LT		0628	5
CAMP EARL F	2LT		0528	5
CANN WILLIAM G	1LT		0529	5
CARDWELL FOWLER H	2LT		0940	5
CARLISLE JOHN G	1LT		0628	5
CARLSON GEORGE N	CPT		0628	5
CARLSON JOHN R	1LT		0628	5
CARNEY JAMES J	2LT		0628	5
CARPENTER CLARK B	1LT		0728	5
CARROLL DANIEL B	1LT		0628	5
CASEY WILLIAM F JR	2LT		0628	5
CATALA ARTURO	2LT		0828	5
CAVANAGH JOHN	CPT		0528	5
CHAFFEE CHARLES L	CPT		0840	5
CHAPMAN RALPH D C	1LT		0628	5
CHASE CLIFFORD E	MAJ		0528	5
CHAUDRON PERCY D	LTC		0628	5
CHEATHAM CLEMENT A	1LT		0828	5
CHEEK OVID H	1LT		0529	5
CHESHIRE JAMES W	1LT		0628	5
CHRISTENSEN WALTER	CPT		0329	5
CLARKE CECIL A	1LT		0628	5
CLEARY JOHN J	2LT		1028	5
CLEWORTH CLARENCE	2LT		1028	5
CLIFFORD JOHN J	CPT		0529	5
CLOWER CLIFFORD	1LT		0628	5
COATES ARTHUR E	2LT		0928	5
COFFMAN FRANK	2LT		0628	5

NAME	GRADE	SVC NO	DATE RET MO YR	RET CODE
COGHLAN CHARLES C	2LT		1028	5
COLBERT JOHN W	MAJ		0828	5
COLE ARTHUR C	1LT		0840	5
COLLINS LAWRENCE D	CPT		1128	5
COMERFORD JOHN T	CPT		0628	5
CONEY MASON C	1LT		0928	5
CONLIN ALAN B	2LT		0628	5
COOK MORTIMER P	1LT		0329	5
COOLEY BEAMON S	1LT		0828	5
COOVER MERLE F	1LT		0628	5
COPSEY FAY M	2LT		1028	5
CORCORAN WILLIAM W	1LT		0528	5
CORMIER JOSEPH A	2LT		0528	5
CORT THOMAS L	CPT		0928	5
COSGROVE LOUIS C	CPT		0928	5
COSTELLO JOHN T	CPT		0528	5
COSTLOW GLENN C	1LT		0628	5
COTCHER EDWARD H	CPT		0740	5
COURTWRIGHT BENJAM	MAJ		0828	5
COX HARVEY B	1LT		0628	5
COX WILLIAM M	CPT		0728	5
CRADDOCK ABRAM P J	CPT		0329	5
CRAIG HENRY H	CPT		0929	5
CRANDELL HERBERT R	2LT		0840	5
CRAWFORD HILARY H	1LT		0828	5
CRAWFORD LEWIS C	1LT		0628	5
CROCHERON HAL H	2LT		0728	5
CROSBY GASTON E	2LT		0628	5
CROSBY JAMES H	1LT		0628	5
CROSS JAMES	2LT		0628	5
CROW FLOYD A	2LT		0828	5
CULLEN FREDERICK	MAJ		0828	5
CUMMINS RUSCOE D	1LT		0740	5
CUNNINGHAM PETER P	2LT		0628	5
CURLEY HARRY D	CPT		0628	5
CUSHING JOHN B	1LT		1028	5
CZASKOS EDMUND T	CPT		0529	5
DABBS CHARLES H	CPT		0828	5
DALE PHILIP M	CPT		0828	5
DANIELS CHARLES L	CPT		0628	5
DARBY EARL M	1LT		0628	5
DASHIELL WILLIAM A	1LT		0528	5
DAVIS ARTHUR M	2LT		1028	5
DAVIS FREDERIC W	1LT		0728	5
DAVIS HARWELL G	MAJ		1028	5
DAVIS JOHN P	2LT		0628	5
DAVIS JOSEPH A	2LT		0628	5
DAVY JESSE J	CPT		0728	5
DAY WALLACE C	1LT		0828	5
DEAN WILLIAM K	1LT		0628	5
DELKER JOSEPH S	2LT		0828	5
DEERING PRENTISS C	1LT		0728	5
DEGRUMMOND HENRY C	1LT		0728	5
DELANCEY CLINTON C	CPT		0728	5
DEMALIGNON FRANCIS	2LT		0728	5
DEVINE JOSEPH J	2LT		0628	5
DILLARD ROBERT B	CPT		0628	5
DIXON FRANK M	2LT		0229	5
DODD WILLIAM A	1LT		0728	5
DODGE WILLIAM W JR	2LT		0628	5
DOEN RALPH W	CPT		0628	5
DOLAN JAMES H	1LT		1028	5
DORRIS BENJAMIN F	1LT		0628	5
DOUGLAS RICHARD	CPT		0528	5
DOW JULIAN N	CPT		0329	5
DOWNES JOSEPH W	2LT		0129	5
DOZLER JAMES C	1LT		0529	5
DRAYTON FREDERICK	CPT		0628	5
DRUGG WALTER C	2LT		0628	5
DRUMMOND FRANK C P	2LT		0628	5
DUNAGIN GEORGE A	1LT		0528	5
DYSON HENRY B	1LT		0628	5
EASTHAM GRANVILLE	1LT		0628	5
EBY ALLEN D	2LT		0529	5
ECK GUSTAVE E	CPT		0728	5

NAME	GRADE	SVC NO	DATE RET MO YR	RET CODE
EDDY EMMETT W	CPT		0529	5
EDENS NELSON W	1LT		0940	5
EDISON SAMUEL H	CPT		0628	5
EDMISTON ANDREW JR	2LT		0329	5
EDWARDS BRYANT B	1LT		0628	5
EDWARDS HARRY D	1LT		0528	5
EDWARDS RICHARD	2LT		0728	5
EDWARDS WILL E	1LT		0728	5
EGGLETON WILLIAM J	CPT		0628	5
ELLIOTT WELLWOOD C	1LT		1028	5
ELLIS EDWARD K	CPT		0628	5
EMBRY TALTON H	2LT		0528	5
EMERSON JOHN E	2LT		0728	5
EMISON JAMES W	1LT		0740	5
ENSIGN CHESTER O	1LT		0628	5
EPPERSON CARRICK H	2LT		0628	5
ERICSSON RALPH B	1LT		0628	5
EUBANK ALBIA L	2LT		0529	5
EVERETT LEROY	1LT		0129	5
EWELL NATHANIEL	CPT		0628	5
FAIRCHILD HOXIE N	2LT		0529	5
FARRAR BENJAMIN O	2LT		0628	5
FELDENHEIMER ROY	2LT		0628	5
FELFOLDY EDMOND	2LT		0129	5
FENNER FRED A	2LT		0628	5
FERGUSON DAVID MCG	2LT		0628	5
FERRIER WILLIAM H	CPT		0628	5
FESSELMEYER W T	2LT		0429	5
FICKLE MELVIN F	2LT		0628	5
FIECHTER WALTER	1LT		0928	5
FIREY FRANK P	1LT		0628	5
FISHER TUNIS H	2LT		0628	5
FITTS BURON R	2LT		0828	5
FITZHUGH EDWARD J	2LT		0529	5
FLEMING JOHN A	1LT		0828	5
FLICK FRED S	2LT		0529	5
FLOOD JOHN V	2LT		0628	5
FLOOD PETER H A	CPT		0840	5
FLYNN BERNARD A	1LT		0628	5
FLYNN FRANK S	CPT		0628	5
FOGERTY CLEMENT A	COL		0129	5
FOLEY THOMAS F	MAJ		0628	5
FOLKEDAHL JOSEPH R	2LT		0628	5
FOOTE ALFRED F	LTC		0828	5
FOREMAN EVAN H	CPT		0329	5
FOREMAN HERBERT S	1LT		0828	5
FOX ROBERT M	CPT		0728	5
FOX WILLIAM S	1LT		0628	5
FRANKLIN RICHARD	2LT		0840	5
FRARY LEWIS S	2LT		0628	5
FRASER CHARLES E	CPT		0528	5
FRASER DONALD W	2LT		0628	5
FRAZIER WILLIAM	CPT		0628	5
FREDEN GUSTAF E N	2LT		0628	5
FREEMAN JOHN I	CPT		0129	5
FREY NEWT	1LT		0628	5
FULLER HENRY C	2LT		0628	5
FULMER ROLAND H	CPT		0628	5
FUSS JOHN C	CPT		0728	5
GALLISHAW JOHN	2LT		0529	5
GAMBLE CLARK R	1LT		0840	5
GANFIELD ROY W	1LT		0628	5
GARDNER GEORGE W	1LT		0628	5
GARDNER WILLIAM J	CPT		1028	5
GARRETTE EDWIN C	2LT		0628	5
GARRISON DAVID M	1LT		0628	5
GARRY JAMES J	2LT		0728	5
GARVEY PHIL F	2LT		0628	5
GATTERDAM EUGENE A	1LT		0928	5
GEER CLARENCE W	CPT		0728	5
GEIS CARL E	CPT		0841	5
GELLERSTEDT ROBERT	1LT		0429	5
GENTNER JOHN M	CPT		0529	5
GERARD FRED L	1LT		0129	5
GERSTENKORN ROY E	1LT		0628	5

333-811 O - 69 - 26

EMERGENCY OFFICERS RETIRED LIST

NAME	GRADE	SVC NO	DATE RET MO YR	RET CODE
GESELL WALTER B	2LT		0928	5
GETTINGS JAMES A	CPT		0628	5
GIFT LYLE H	CPT		0628	5
GILBERT ROY D	2LT		0628	5
GILLICK OWEN P	1LT		0628	5
GILLIS FREDERICK	1LT		0128	5
GILLIS JOHN A	2LT		0628	5
GILMOUR FREDERICK	CPT		0628	5
GIVENS FRED G	CPT		0529	5
GJELLUM ARTHUR B	CPT		0628	5
GLIDDEN BURT P	2LT		0628	5
GOLDMAN ABRAHAM S	2LT		0628	5
GOODMAN ALLEN L	1LT		0628	5
GOODSPEED EARL L	1LT		0628	5
GORE VERNON	2LT		0628	5
GOSSETT ECKLEY G	CPT		0728	5
GOULD JAMES R JR	1LT		1028	5
GRAHAM STUART D	2LT		0628	5
GRANT JAMES L	2LT		0628	5
GRAUPNER ADOLPHUS	CPT		0528	5
GRAVES HAROLD F	2LT		0529	5
GRAY GEORGE F	CPT		0728	5
GRAY JESSY F	1LT		0628	5
GRAY LOWELL H	2LT		0529	5
GRAYSON THOMAS J	COL		1028	5
GREEMAN NELSON W L	1LT		0129	5
GREENE ALBERT V N	2LT		0528	5
GREENE PAUL C	1LT		0728	5
GRIESEMER ZADOC L	MAJ		0628	5
GRIMES EUSTIS R	2LT		0728	5
GROAH EDWARD H	1LT		0628	5
GUICE JOHN I	1LT		0429	5
GUNDERSON SOPHUS D	2LT		1028	5
GUY THOMAS J	2LT		0628	5
HAAN ALBERT F	CPT		0528	5
HAIGHT WALTER L	CPT		0628	5
HAIR ARTHUR J	1LT		0828	5
HALL EDWARD F	2LT		0529	5
HALL KENNETH C	2LT		0628	5
HALL WILLIAM D	1LT		0628	5
HALLEY JAMES M	2LT		0628	5
HALVERSON HENRY F	CPT		0429	5
HAMILL ROBERT M	2LT		0628	5
HAMPSHIRE CLAUDE C	1LT		0628	5
HANABERGH FRANK J	MAJ		0628	5
HANDLY LUCIUS L	1LT		0728	5
HANSEN JOHN C	CPT		0329	5
HARNED POMEROY	1LT		0628	5
HARRIS ARTHUR C	1LT		0628	5
HARRIS EMORY L	CPT		0928	5
HARRIS RUFUS C	1LT		0828	5
HARTNETT CORNELIUS	2LT		0728	5
HARWOOD MANTON E	1LT		0628	5
HATCH CARL T	2LT		0529	5
HATCH ROSCOE C	1LT		0229	5
HATCHER WILLIAM B	1LT		0628	5
HAUBOLD EGON G	CPT		0728	5
HAUSER SIMEON F	2LT		0528	5
HAVERSTICK FRANK W	CPT		0229	5
HAYS HARLAND R	2LT		1128	5
HAYS VERNE	1LT		0628	5
HEALEY PATRICK F	1LT		0728	5
HEARN GUILFORD C	1LT		0528	5
HECK MAURICE F	CPT		0828	5
HELMER PHIL F	2LT		0628	5
HEMPSTONE FRANK W	1LT		0529	5
HENDERSON JAMES A	2LT		0628	5
HENDLER ULLMANN C	CPT		0429	5
HENNESSEY CARLETON	1LT		0429	5
HENRY ROBERT H	2LT		0628	5
HENRY THOMAS J JR	1LT		0628	5
HENSKE GODFREY W	1LT		0728	5
HERRICK MYRON C	2LT		0728	5
HEWITT JOHN E	MAJ		0628	5
HEYMAN FRED G	2LT		1028	5
HICKS JACOB L	CPT		0628	5
HICKS SAMUEL C	1LT		0840	5
HILL CHARLES A	CPT		0740	5
HILL EDWARD D	CPT		0620	5
HILLIARD CLAUDE P	2LT		0529	5
HINCHMAN EDWARD M	1LT		0529	5
HITZ ALEX M	1LT		0628	5
HOCKRIDGE RICHARD	1LT		0628	5
HODGSON HAROLD B	2LT		1040	5
HOENSTINE FLOYD G	2LT		0628	5
HOFFMAN ARTHUR B	1LT		0628	5
HOGAN CICERO F	CPT		0628	5
HOLMAN WILLIAM S	MAJ		0628	5
HOOK JAMES P	1LT		0628	5
HOPKINS WAYNE L	2LT		0628	5
HOUCHIN ERVIN W	2LT		0628	5
HOUSTON CLARENCE P	CPT		0628	5
HOWARD WILLIAM H	1LT		0628	5
HOYT FRANK W	2LT		0429	5
HOYT HOWARD C	1LT		0229	5
HUDGENS ROBERT W	CPT		0628	5
HUEBNER ALBERT F	CPT		0628	5
HUGHEY GEORGE H	1LT		0628	5
HUGHSTON JAMES B	2LT		0628	5
HULL RICHARD M	1LT		0628	5
HUNT HERBERT P	1LT		0628	5
HUNT WILLIAM C	2LT		0628	5
HUNTER DAVID JR	CPT		0529	5
HUNTER GILBERT M	1LT		0628	5
HUNTER WILLIAM G	CPT		0628	5
HUTCHESON ROBERT S	2LT		0529	5
HUTCHINSON ALVA R	2LT		0628	5
HUTCHISON FRANCIS	CPT		0628	5
HYNDS ARTHUR A	2LT		0628	5
INCE EDWARD G	CPT		0528	5
INMAN GILBERT P	1LT		0728	5
IRELAND WALTER M	1LT		0229	5
IRION EDWIN C	1LT		0447	5
JACOB CLYDE H	1LT		0628	5
JACOBS JOHN M	2LT		0628	5
JACOBUS JESSE J	1LT		0429	5
JAMES ALLEN M	2LT		0628	5
JEFFERS GEORGE L	2LT		0628	5
JELLUM KRISTEN	1LT		0129	5
JERVEY FRANK J	CPT		0528	5
JOHNSON CORTLAND A	2LT		0429	5
JOHNSON WILLIAM B	1LT		0728	5
JONES ALBERT F B	2LT		0429	5
JONES CASEY M	1LT		0628	5
JONES CHARLES H	1LT		0628	5
JONES FRED A	2LT		0628	5
JONES HENRY R	1LT		0628	5
JONES HUBERT B	CPT		0628	5
JONES JAMES W	CPT		1028	5
JONES RAY W	2LT		0628	5
JONES WILLIAM W	1LT		1028	5
JOSEPHSON MAURICE	1LT		0629	5
JULIEN CARL T	2LT		0628	5
KAMINSKI THEOPHILE	2LT		1028	5
KAMPMEIER ARTHUR J	1LT		1028	5
KANE JACK F	2LT		0740	5
KEARNS THOMAS W	1LT		0928	5
KEATH HOWARD B	2LT		0628	5
KEENAN BARRY	1LT		0429	5
KEIM THURMAN E	CPT		0429	5
KELLEY HENRY E	1LT		0429	5
KELLEY JAMES	2LT		0628	5
KELLEY JAMES R	2LT		0628	5
KELLEY RALPH R	1LT		0329	5
KELLIS JOHN H	1LT		0628	5
KELLY HARRY F	2LT		0628	5
KELLY RICHARD B JR	CPT		0528	5
KEMMAN HUGO A	2LT		0628	5
KENNEDY HARVEY J	2LT		0628	5
KERNS SAMUEL M	MAJ		0828	5
KERR JAMES	2LT		0928	5
KESKEY CHARLES A	1LT		0628	5
KESTNBAUM MEYER	2LT		0429	5
KEYSER GEORGE A	1LT		0840	5
KIBBE GORDON M	1LT		0628	5
KILLIKELLY C	CPT		0528	5
KIMBALL GEORGE P	1LT		0628	5
KING EDWARD	1LT		1028	5
KING SAMUEL L JR	2LT		0528	5
KIRBY THOMAS	CPT		0429	5
KIRK GEORGE B	1LT		0828	5
KIRKPATRICK LESTER	1LT		0628	5
KIVLIN ALFRED P	2LT		0628	5
KNAUTH FELIX W	1LT		0628	5
KNEEBONE JOHN H	2LT		0529	5
KNIGHT CHANDLER S	1LT		0728	5
KNIGHT LAURENCE E	1LT		0628	5
KNOBLOCK CECIL C	2LT		0529	5
KNOX LEROY J	2LT		0828	5
KOENNE EDWARD A	2LT		0429	5
KOLPIEN KENNETH H	2LT		0628	5
KRAUSE ROBERT S	1LT		0628	5
KRICHEL JOSEPH H	1LT		0329	5
KRIECHBAUM ROY R	CPT		0628	5
KUEHNE ALBERT W	1LT		1028	5
KVETON PATRICK H	CPT		0628	5
LA PAZE PERCY W	2LT		0628	5
LACEWELL ALEXANDER	2LT		0628	5
LAING DEWITT B	1LT		0628	5
LAMB ORIN R	1LT		0129	5
LANDRUM MARVIN M	1LT		0828	5
LANSDALE GEORGE L	CPT		0628	5
LANSDEN DAVID S	2LT		0628	5
LASSITER JOHN H	CPT		0828	5
LAUER KURVIN W	2LT		1028	5
LAUX THOMAS C	2LT		0628	5
LAWSON EDWIN L	1LT		0528	5
LAWSON HENRY G	CPT		0740	5
LEDFORD JOHN	1LT		0228	5
LEE HENRY D	2LT		0629	5
LEE THOMAS H	1LT		0528	5
LEFFLER ROBERT W	1LT		0628	5
LEFTWICH SNOWDEN M	CPT		0629	5
LEGG HENRY F	1LT		0129	5
LEHARDY FRANK M	2LT		0229	5
LEISNER PAUL W	2LT		0528	5
LEMBKE CHARLES H	1LT		0728	5
LEMON ANDREW M	2LT		0528	5
LERSCH JOSEPH F	2LT		0728	5
LEWIS RAYMOND P	2LT		0429	5
LIGGETT HARRY B	2LT		0728	5
LITTLE LOWELL	CPT		0628	5
LITTY JOHN C	2LT		0628	5
LIVELY CARLOS J	2LT		0928	5
LOGAN ELMER E	2LT		0628	5
LONGFELLOW HAROLD	2LT		0841	5
LOOMIS WALTER O	2LT		0528	5
LOPEZ ENRIQUE	2LT		0328	5
LOTZ TRUMAN L	2LT		0628	5
LOW HAROLD W	1LT		0629	5
LOYE HARRY A	2LT		0628	5
LUCK EVERETT J	1LT		0628	5
LUNDBLAD WALTER E	CPT		0429	5
LUNSTEAD EUGENE L	2LT		0728	5
LUTZ JAMES A JR	1LT		0628	5
LYKSETT ALBERT J	1LT		0928	5
MAC DOUGALL DANIEL	2LT		0728	5
MAC MURPHY ALLEN B	2LT		1028	5
MAC NUTT CECIL C	2LT		0628	5
MAGUIRE EDWARD B	1LT		0728	5
MALONE BENJAMIN F	2LT		0329	5
MANARD HARDIN B	1LT		0253	5
MANLY JETHRO	CPT		0728	5
MANN CHARLES H	MAJ		0628	5
MANN EARL W	1LT		0628	5
MARCUS SAMUEL M	CPT		0429	5
MARINE JAMES S	1LT		1164	5
MARKUS NORBERT W	2LT		0628	5
MARQUISS CHARLES R	1LT		0628	5
MARSHALL CLYDE M	2LT		0528	5
MARSHALL FOSTER	2LT		0528	5
MARSHALL THOMAS B	1LT		0628	5
MARTIN WILLIAM G	2LT		0728	5
MARX ROBERTS S	CPT		0628	5
MARXMILLER HARRY G	MAJ		0628	5
MASON CLINTON C	CPT		0628	5
MASON JAMES P O	1LT		0628	5
MATHIS ALLEN W	1LT		0628	5
MAYVILLE EDWARD M	CPT		0728	5
MC BRAUN JAMES B	2LT		0728	5
MC CALL GEORGE T	1LT		0628	5
MC CANN JAMES S	1LT		0529	5
MC CARTY WILLIAM H	2LT		0628	5
MC CAWLEY HARRISON B	1LT		0946	5
MC CLELLAND FRANK A	1LT		0628	5
MC CLUER EDWIN A	1LT		0628	5
MC COLLOM FRANCIS B	CPT		0840	5
MC CUE EARL N	MAJ		0628	5
MC CUNE MURRAY M	2LT		0628	5
MC DANIEL WINFRED P	CPT		0628	5
MC DONALD F H	1LT		0728	5
MC DONALD GEORGE T	1LT		0329	5
MC DONOUGH HUBERT B	2LT		0529	5
MC DONOUGH JAMES P	1LT		1029	5
MC DOWELL STEWART A	2LT		1140	5
MC ELROY JOSEPH E	CPT		0628	5
MC GUIRE JAMES A	1LT		0628	5
MC INTYRE HARRY J	2LT		1028	5
MC KAY ARTHUR J	2LT		0628	5
MC KAY JAMES D	1LT		0628	5
MC KENNEY HARRY	2LT		0628	5
MC KENZIE GEORGE S	2LT		0628	5
MC KILLIPS C E	1LT		0741	5
MC LEAN CHARLES E	1LT		0129	5
MC LEOD HOWARD L	1LT		0628	5
MC MANIGAL JOHN W	1LT		0628	5
MC NEIL HARRY O	1LT		1128	5
MC NERNEY JOSEPH D	1LT		0628	5
MC QUEEN JOE W	CPT		0628	5
MC TAGGART ERNEST	1LT		0728	5
MC VEY ERIC A	CPT		0628	5
MEADE RAY	1LT		0828	5
MEEHAN EDWARD J	LTC		1128	5
MELLEN CHASE JR	2LT		0129	5
MENEFEE MARVIN J	1LT		0329	5
MERRILL GEORGE B	1LT		1028	5
MERRILL HENRY M	2LT		1128	5
MERRILL ROBERT A	MAJ		0828	5
MESS GEORGE B	2LT		0429	5
METZROTH CARL F	1LT		0628	5
MEYERING WILLIAM D	CPT		0628	5
MEYERS WILLIAM H	LTC		0129	5
MIDDLETON ULYSSES G	1LT		0528	5
MILLBERRY MARK A	CPT		0429	5
MILLER BENJAMIN W	1LT		0728	5
MILLER BOYCE F	CPT		0728	5
MILLER CLARENCE L	1LT		0928	5
MILLER DAVID B	1LT		0528	5
MILLER EARL G	CPT		0628	5
MILLER EDWIN E	CPT		0628	5
MILLER FRANCIS L	2LT		0628	5
MILLER FRANKLIN L	MAJ		0528	5
MILLER GEORGE H	2LT		1028	5
MILLER HAYDOCK H	1LT		0628	5
MILLER JESSE C	2LT		0628	5
MILLER LOUIS L	1LT		0229	5
MILLER WALTER J	1LT		0628	5
MILLER WARREN J	2LT		1028	5
MILLIS JOHN M	2LT		0329	5
MILLSAP CHARLES H	1LT		1040	5

EMERGENCY OFFICERS RETIRED LIST

NAME	GRADE	SVC NO	DATE RET MO YR	RET CODE
MILUM VERN G	2LT		0628	5
MITCHELL FRANK M	1LT		0528	5
MOLONEY HERBERT W	1LT		0628	5
MOORE JOHN R	2LT		0628	5
MOORE WILLIAM A	2LT		0828	5
MOORE WILLIAM B	2LT		0928	5
MORGAN GEORGE H	2LT		0528	5
MORGAN LEWIS R	CPT		0628	5
MORGENSTERN A H	1LT		0229	5
MORRIS GRAYDON L	2LT		0840	5
MORRIS HAROLD P	2LT		0728	5
MORRISON LEWIS R	2LT		0728	5
MOSER ELMER B	1LT		0728	5
MOSES ANDREW	1LT		0628	5
MOSES ROBERT L	1LT		0628	5
MOUSER MERRILL K	1LT		0628	5
MULLER JULIUS	1LT		1028	5
MURDOCK JAMES D	CPT		0129	5
MURPHY EWELL F	2LT		0728	5
MURREY JOSEPH H	1LT		0728	5
MURTHA WILLIAM H	2LT		0628	5
MYERS JAY H	1LT		0528	5
MYRLAND EIEL H	1LT		0529	5
NANCE ALEXANDER	1LT		0628	5
NASH JOSEPH E	2LT		0828	5
NEWELL JAMES K	1LT		0928	5
NEWHALL RICHARD A	2LT		0628	5
NEWSOM ERLE T	CPT		0728	5
NEWTON ROY C	2LT		0129	5
NICHOLLS MELVIN H	2LT		0628	5
NICOL ALEXANDER	1LT		0628	5
NIMS FREDERICK JR	2LT		0429	5
NOBLE GEORGE B	1LT		0229	5
NOWLIN JOSEPH C JR	1LT		0628	5
NOYES EDWIN M	2LT		0740	5
OBERSCHMIDT LEON P	2LT		0529	5
OBRIEN JAMES F	2LT		0628	5
OBRIEN MARTIN A	1LT		0429	5
OBRIEN PATRICK F	1LT		0628	5
OBRIEN RAYMOND J	1LT		0628	5
OHMART WALTER A	1LT		0628	5
OKELLEY LAWRENCE L	2LT		0429	5
OLDHAM RALPH W	2LT		0628	5
OLEARY EDWIN O	2LT		1128	5
OLIVER FRED N	MAJ		0528	5
ONEIL FRANK P	CPT		0628	5
ONEILL EDWARD G	2LT		0329	5
ORRELL EUGENE D	1LT		0628	5
OSBORN MORSE F	CPT		0728	5
OWENS JOHN J	CPT		0528	5
PAGE MARION W	CPT		0628	5
PARK DURWARD B	CPT		0529	5
PARKER EMERSON F	2LT		0129	5
PARKS PAUL B	2LT		0728	5
PARRISH EARL T	1LT		0628	5
PATTEN MORGAN H	1LT		0828	5
PAUL CHARLES H	1LT		0840	5
PAUL EDWARD R	1LT		0628	5
PEACOCK ELI J JR	MAJ		0628	5
PEARSALL FRANCIS S	2LT		0628	5
PECKHAM HOWARD D	CPT		0628	5
PEEL DAVID W JR	1LT		0628	5
PEISTRUP EDWARD C	1LT		0329	5
PELTON HAROLD P	CPT		0628	5
PENNINGTON EDGAR J	2LT		0628	5
PERRY HAROLD C	2LT		0828	5
PERRY OWEN H	1LT		0728	5
PERRY RUFUS A	2LT		0542	5
PETTY WALLACE S	CPT		0628	5
PHELPS FRANCIS M	1LT		0629	5
PHELPS JOSEPH S	1LT		0328	5
PHILLIPS GEORGE W	2LT		0628	5
PHILLIPS WENDEL J	1LT		0628	5
PIERZYNSKI T S	1LT		0728	5
PINNEY NORMAN W	2LT		0728	5
PINTO RENE W	2LT		0628	5
PLANT GEORGE F	CPT		0329	5
PORTMANN MILTON C	MAJ		0529	5
POST FREDERICK	CPT		0129	5
POTTER WILLIAM J	MAJ		0628	5
POWELL ALFRED T	CPT		0628	5
POWELL HERBERT J	1LT		0728	5
POWELL MATHEW J	2LT		0928	5
POWER HERMAN	1LT		0628	5
PRICE EDWARD H	1LT		0628	5
PRITCHARD GEORGE L	1LT		0728	5
PROSISE ALAN B	1LT		0728	5
PRUETT EUGENE F	2LT		0628	5
PULLIS STEPHEN E	CPT		0628	5
PYLES HARRY H	2LT		0629	5
RADEMACHER FRED M	CPT		0840	5
RAEDER WILLIAM J	1LT		0628	5
RALPH KENDRICK J	1LT		0628	5
RANLETT LOUIS F	2LT		0628	5
RAY LECIL S	2LT		0528	5
READ WILLIAM S	2LT		1128	5
REARDON TIMOTHY J	2LT		1128	5
REBUCK WALTER E	2LT		0628	5
REED CHARLES S	2LT		0329	5
REEVES FRANK H	1LT		1028	5
REILLY JOSEPH J	CPT		0628	5
RENSHAWE CLARENCE W	1LT		0828	5
REPASS MERLE M	2LT		0728	5
RICE HAROLD E	2LT		0628	5
RICE MAX	2LT		0628	5
RICHARDSON HARRY F	CPT		0628	5
RICKETTS JOSEPH W	CPT		1128	5
RIDER CARROLL A	2LT		0628	5
RIECKE HENRY A	CPT		0628	5
RIEHL LOUIS A	2LT		0429	5
RILEY FRANKLIN G	CPT		0628	5
RITCHIE WILLIAM JR	CPT		0728	5
ROBB GEORGE S	1LT		0141	5
ROBERT JAMES J	MAJ		1028	5
ROBERTS WILLIAM J	CPT		0628	5
ROBINSON ARTHUR	2LT		0628	5
ROBINSON FRANK C	MAJ		0628	5
ROBINSON GUY T	1LT		0928	5
ROBISON EDWARD M	CPT		0528	5
ROEMER LEON F	2LT		0529	5
ROGERS ALAN	2LT		0828	5
ROGERS GEORGE B	1LT		0628	5
ROGERS JOHN A	2LT		0528	5
ROLLER FRANCIS O	2LT		1028	5
ROSBOROUGH WILLIAM M	1LT		0429	5
ROSENFIELD MILTON S	2LT		0628	5
ROSS JOHN J W	CPT		0229	5
ROWAN WALTER F	2LT		0329	5
ROWELL JAMES T	1LT		0628	5
RUFF HORACE E	MAJ		0528	5
RUHNKA ROY	CPT		0628	5
RYALL ERNEST V	2LT		0529	5
RYAN CHARLES C	1LT		1040	5
RYAN EDWARD L	1LT		0329	5
RYAN THOMAS A	CPT		1028	5
RYLANDER WILBER E	2LT		0628	5
SALADINE JOHN W	1LT		0840	5
SAMS FERROL A	CPT		0129	5
SANCHEZ GILBERT J	2LT		1128	5
SANDERS JAMES L	2LT		0529	5
SAUNDERS WILLIAM H	2LT		0628	5
SAVAGE JAMES A	2LT		0728	5
SAWHILL DONALD V	2LT		0229	5
SAYRES ARTHUR R	1LT		0628	5
SCARBOROUGH C C	1LT		0628	5
SCARLES HERBERT L	1LT		0229	5
SCHAEFFER JOHN A	1LT		0429	5
SCHARDT ARLIE A	LTC		0352	5
SCHAUFELBERGER H S	2LT		0529	5
SCHELLER LOUIS	1LT		0628	5
SCHELTER LOUIS J	CPT		0828	5
SCHIDE CLARENCE C	2LT		0628	5
SCHLESINGER ALBERT L	2LT		1128	5
SCHNECK MAXIMILIAN	2LT		0628	5
SCHOENBERG LOUIS	2LT		0528	5
SCHUH CARL A	1LT		0728	5
SCHULTZ WILLIAM J	1LT		0628	5
SCHUMACHER CLARK P	1LT		0628	5
SCHUMACHER JOHN F	1LT		0628	5
SCHUSTER GEORGE A R	2LT		1028	5
SCOTT BYRON R	2LT		1128	5
SCOTT JOHN W	2LT		0628	5
SCOTT SAMUEL H	1LT		0728	5
SCOTT THOMAS W	1LT		0529	5
SCOTT WILLIAM R	CPT		0628	5
SCRAFTON WALLACE T	1LT		0628	5
SEAGRAVES CHARLES	1LT		0628	5
SEE MART	MAJ		0728	5
SERGEANT FLOYD A	2LT		0628	5
SEVIER HENRY C	2LT		0828	5
SHAMBURGER LACY L	1LT		0429	5
SHARKEY RALPH L	1LT		0628	5
SHARP ROY F	2LT		0628	5
SHARTLE ALBERT J	1LT		0628	5
SHAUGHNESSY PAUL F	CPT		0528	5
SHEA MARTIN C	2LT		0828	5
SHEEHAN EDWARD B	CPT		0628	5
SHEEHAN WALTER R	1LT		0628	5
SHERIDAN LEO D	2LT		0628	5
SHERIDAN WALTER D	2LT		0628	5
SHERWOOD GEORGE W	2LT		0728	5
SHEWALTER GEORGE M	1LT		0529	5
SHINKEL JACOB M	1LT		0628	5
SHISLER GEORGE	2LT		0628	5
SHOEMAKER GEORGE J	2LT		0728	5
SHOEMAKER PHILIP C	1LT		0628	5
SHOLES EBER C	2LT		0628	5
SHRIVER ALFRED W	1LT		0329	5
SHRIVER RAY D	1LT		0429	5
SHUSTER WILLIAM H JR	1LT		0229	5
SIMMONS BENJAMIN F	2LT		0529	5
SIMPKINS WILLARD S	1LT		0728	5
SIMPSON CHARLES P	2LT		0841	5
SLYH DONALD M	1LT		0628	5
SMEAD BURTON A	LTC		0628	5
SMEALLIE JAMES D	1LT		0628	5
SMITH BERT L	CPT		0229	5
SMITH CLARENCE P	1LT		0628	5
SMITH DANIEL T JR	2LT		0429	5
SMITH EDWARD P	2LT		0628	5
SMITH EMMETT P	CPT		0528	5
SMITH ERNEST D	1LT		0529	5
SMITH HAROLD F	1LT		1028	5
SMITH HOWARD G	1LT		0628	5
SMITH IRVING D	1LT		0528	5
SMITH JOHN H	1LT		1140	5
SMITH ROBERT L	CPT		0528	5
SMITH SAMUEL T	1LT		0529	5
SMITH SHIRLEY S	1LT		0628	5
SMITH TAYLOR B	1LT		0628	5
SMITH WILLIAM D	CPT		0329	5
SMITH WINGATE	2LT		0728	5
SNIDER ROBERT J	CPT		0628	5
SNOWDEN FRANK B	1LT		0728	5
SOUTHARD EARL	1LT		0628	5
SOUTHARD WILLIAM E	LTC		1028	5
SPALDING OLIVER R	1LT		0429	5
SPARKS DENTON H	2LT		0828	5
SPENCER C R JR	2LT		0628	5
SPILLYARDS HENRY H	1LT		0628	5
SPONY ALBERT	1LT		0628	5
SPRINGER MARK D	CPT		1028	5
SQUIER LOWELL W	2LT		0628	5
STAGGERS WILLIAM L	1LT		0528	5
STEARNS CAREY S	2LT		0628	5
STEFFY JOHN L	1LT		0628	5
STEIDLE EDWARD	CPT		0528	5
STEINBERGER OTTO C	CPT		0628	5
STELLING SIDNEY J	1LT		0628	5
STEPHENS CLARENCE C	1LT		0628	5
STEUART EDWARD P	2LT		0329	5
STEVENS GEORGE P JR	1LT		0628	5
STEVENSON MAURICE S	1LT		0528	5
STEWART HOWARD B	2LT		0628	5
STEWART JOHN A	CPT		0628	5
STICKNEY GEORGE L	CPT		0740	5
STILLWELL RICHARD C	2LT		0528	5
STOUT FRANCIS R	2LT		0628	5
STOUT WILLIAM	CPT		0528	5
STOWBRIDGE R W JR	1LT		0628	5
STRATTON JOHN M	1LT		0528	5
STRAYER ELMER C	1LT		0628	5
STROLE GLENN F	2LT		0141	5
STRONG ELBERT	1LT		0728	5
STROTHER CARL B	1LT		1128	5
STRYKER WILLIAM L	CPT		0229	5
SULLIVAN DANIEL J	CPT		0740	5
SULLIVAN LESTER E	2LT		0928	5
SULLIVAN WALTER J	CPT		0628	5
SUMNER CHARLES F	CPT		1040	5
SUTTON DANIEL F	1LT		0728	5
SWEENEY JAMES L	2LT		1028	5
SWOPE JOHN O	2LT		0329	5
SYMES CLARENCE D	CPT		0528	5
TALLMADGE F A	CPT		0828	5
TAYLOR BEN B	2LT		0728	5
TAYLOR BRADLEY	2LT		0822	5
TAYLOR NORMAN B	CPT		1028	5
TENNEY GERALD E	CPT		0728	5
TERRALL RALPH E	1LT		0928	5
THAANUM DEAN C	2LT		0728	5
THACKER EDWARD C	2LT		0728	5
THAYER WAYNE	1LT		0628	5
THETFORD ALPHONSO	1LT		0528	5
THICKSTUN DORSEY W	LTC		0628	5
THOMAS JOHN W M	2LT		0628	5
THOMAS LAWRENCE G	1LT		0429	5
THOMPSON DAYTON B	2LT		0840	5
THOMPSON DONALD R	1LT		0728	5
THOMPSON GEORGE	2LT		0828	5
THOMPSON HERBERT L	CPT		0628	5
THOMPSON HERMAN W	CPT		0628	5
THOMPSON JOHN B	2LT		0728	5
THOMPSON JOHN H	1LT		0728	5
THOMPSON JOSIAH D	CPT		0529	5
THORNBURG ZEBULON B	1LT		0528	5
TILDEN JOHN A	1LT		0628	5
TILGHMAN GEORGE O	1LT		0528	5
TITTMANN EUGENE C	1LT		0728	5
TOLLEY CHARLES S JR	1LT		0628	5
TONGATE JAMES M	2LT		1128	5
TRAUT FRED G	1LT		0628	5
TRAVERS WILLIAM A	2LT		0728	5
TUCKER CLAUDE C	1LT		0628	5
TURCK RAYMOND C	COL		0329	5
TURNER WALTER L JR	2LT		0628	5
TWITCHELL F M	2LT		0628	5
TWOMEY THOMAS A	1LT		0529	5
TYLER CLYDE L	1LT		0529	5
TYSON ALFRED	1LT		0728	5
TYSON JOHN T	CPT		0628	5
UPTON FORD J	1LT		0628	5
VINCENT JAMES A	CPT		0628	5
VOGES JOHN C	2LT		0628	5
VOLL BERNARD J	1LT		0628	5
VOLLENWEIDER W F	2LT		0628	5
VOLLMER WILLIAM S	2LT		0928	5
WALE GARLAND B	1LT		0628	5
WALKER JOHN H	2LT		0628	5
WALKER NEWTON W	2LT		0628	5

NAME	GRADE	SVC NO	DATE RET MO YR	RET CODE
WALLACE GEORGE L	1LT		0628	5
WALLER LUTHER H	1LT		0329	5
WALSH FRANCIS W	1LT		0728	5
WALSH MALCOLM	1LT		0429	5
WALTMIRE C A JP	2LT		1040	5
WALTON JAMES C	1LT		1128	5
WARE THOMAS G	2LT		0628	5
WARNER ROSSELL A	1LT		0528	5
WARREN EDWARD R	1LT		0528	5
WASSON CLYDE H	1LT		0529	5
WAYBOR R3BERT R	1LT		0529	5
WEATHERFORD ZADOC L	1LT		0628	5
WEAVER ROBERT H	2LT		0628	5
WEBB BYFORD H	1LT		0429	5
WEBSTER GEORGE D	CPT		0628	5
WEED LEE H	2LT		0728	5
WELLS LEROY T	2LT		0628	5
WENDE JOHN A	1LT		0628	5
WERTZ HAROLD B	1LT		0828	5
WESTPHAL FREDERICK	2LT		0828	5
WESTRATE WILLIAM	1LT		0628	5
WHALEY HARRY R	2LT		0628	5
WHEELER EDGAF L	2LT		0928	5
WHITAKER LEE W	1LT		0628	5
WHITE DAVID L	1LT		0628	5
WHITE EDMOND G	2LT		0529	5
WHITE JOHN R	LTC		0728	5
WHITE RICHARD G	1LT		0628	5
WHITEHEAD JOSEPH L	2LT		0628	5
WHITTHORNE HAPPY S	CPT		0628	5
WIDMANN JESSE F	1LT		0728	5
WIGGINS WILLIAM F	1LT		0528	5
WILD CHARLES A	CPT		0628	5
WILLIAMS EDWARD J	CPT		0628	5
WILLIAMS ROBERTS	1LT		0628	5
WILLIAMS THOMAS C	2LT		0928	5
WILLIAMSON PHILIP H	1LT		0828	5
WILSON CHAUNCEY G	2LT		0828	5
WILSON HARVEY W	2LT		0628	5
WILSON JAMES M	CPT		0429	5
WILSON RICHARC T	1LT		0828	5
WILSON ROSKO J	1LT		0628	5
WILSON WILBE R	1LT		0528	5
WILSON WILLIAM V	1LT		0628	5
WILTSHIRE TURNER H	MAJ		0928	5
WINSLOW CHARLES S	2LT		0529	5
WINSLOW GUY H	1LT		0728	5
WIRTHS CARL W	1LT		0628	5
WISE CHARLES F JR	CPT		0329	5
WISE EARL G	1LT		0628	5
WISE JOHN B	1LT		0429	5
WITTHAUK HENRY F	2LT		0628	5
WOLCOTT LESTER D	1LT		0528	5
WOOD EVANS B	1LT		0628	5
WOOD RAIFORD J	2LT		0529	5
WOODLEY SAMUEL S	2LT		0728	5
WOODRUFF ERNEST W	1LT		0628	5
WOODS PHILIP H	CPT		0528	5
WOODSON HYLAN H	1LT		0628	5
WOOLFORD AUSTIN W	2LT		0628	5
WORNALL FRANCIS	2LT		0628	5
WORTHINGTON LELAND G	1LT		0129	5
WRIGHT JOHN F	2LT		0628	5
YAEGER ROBERT F	2LT		0628	5
YOUNG CHARLES F	1LT		0628	5
YOUNG HARRY P	2LT		0628	5
YOUNG JESSE F	1LT		0329	5
ZACHARIAS JOHN A	CPT		0529	5
ZACHER VERNON B A	1LT		0329	5

SECTION 5

LOSSES TO THE RETIRED LISTS

This section is composed of officer and warrant officer losses to all of the retired lists.

LOSSES TO THE RETIRED LIST

NAME	GRADE	SVC NO	DATE LOSS MO YR
AABEL BERNARD	COL	0-0029239	0268
ABBOTT ARGYLE C	LTC	0-0241145	0768
ACEY RAYMOND F	LTC	0-0288814	
ACKERMAN LOUIS	CPT	0-0367861	0568
ACKLIN CHRISTOPHE	CPT	0-0384301	1068
ACTKINSON ARNOLD R	1LT	0-1303085	1068
ADAMS ALONZO R	MAJ	0-0120767	0368
ADAMS DAVID W	2LT	0-1913598	
ADAMS EMORY S	M G	0-0001731	
ADAMS HARRY L	MAJ	0-0109989	0868
ADAMS LUTHER	MAJ	0-0335706	0868
ADAMS MELVIN F	LTC	0-0504256	0368
ADAMS WALDEMAR R	COL	0-0123409	
AHERN DENNIS J	LTC	0-1636904	0868
AHIN GEORGE A	CPT	0-0230734	0268
ALBERS HELEN J	1LT	N-0756605	0668
ALDEN SAM E	LTC	0-1104033	0668
ALDRIDGE RUSSELL C	2LT	0-0232741	0968
ALEXANDER LAWRENCE J	COL	0-0269667	0768
ALFORD CHARLES F	CPT	0-0920106	0868
ALFORD RICHARD H	CPT	0-0921923	0868
ALLEN ERNEST M	LTC	0-0239658	0468
ALLEN FRED	CPT	0-0502568	1168
ALLEN HERMAN R	MAJ	0-0278897	0468
ALLEN IRVIN L	B G	0-0029810	1168
ALLEN SAMUEL H	1LT	0-0340963	
ALLEN VIRGIL G	COL	0-0011126	0268
ALLEN WILBURN D	MAJ	0-1109959	0668
ALLEN WILLIAM E	LTC	0-0330188	0268
ALLISON DON D	LTC	0-0319349	0268
ALTEE VINCENT J	LTC	0-0115182	0968
ALTER DINSMORE	COL	0-0107645	0968
ALTON CHARLES	MAJ	0-0487988	0168
AMBROSE FORREST E	COL	0-0007974	0668
AMES HARRY T	MAJ	0-0126997	1068
AMIDON DONALD A	LTC	0-2048543	0668
AMMONS EMMETT L	CW3	W-2107867	0568
ANDERSON CHARLES	1LT	0-1914090	
ANDERSON DORSEY B	MAJ	0-1826087	1068
ANDERSON EDWARD K	LTC	0-0193078	0168
ANDERSON FRED T	MAJ	0-0206746	
ANDERSON GUSTAV A N	COL	0-0005685	1168
ANDERSON JAMES B	COL	0-0005008	
ANDERSON JOHN B	1LT	0-0328517	0963
ANDERSON JOSEPH F	LTC	0-0245517	0465
ANDERSON LEROY	CW3	W-2151856	
ANDERSON NELSON J	LTC	0-0173435	1168
ANDERSON ROBERT	1LT	0-0164144	0668
ANDREWS LELAND E JR	MAJ	0-1881299	0968
ANDRUS CLIFT	M G	0-0003266	0968
ANGLIN THOMAS W SR	MAJ	0-1534421	
ANGROS ANDREW G	CPT	0-0255837	1068
APONTE EMILIO E	MAJ	0-1913438	0768
APPLEGATE LAWRENCE W	CPT	0-0501365	C968
ARBENZ HERMAN L	CPT	0-0407634	0668
ARBOGAST MEAD S	LTC	0-1643184	0368
ARCHER KERMIT C	COL	0-0277679	1168
ARETZ LAWRENCE I	CPT	0-0188419	1053
ARLEDGE R F DEACON	COL	0-2051797	0668
ARMITAGE ARTHUR N	MAJ	0-0224598	
ARMSTRONG GERARD T	MAJ	0-1845077	0468
ARMSTRONG LEE	CPT	0-1311277	0668
ARNOLD GILBERT V	LTC	0-1824792	0368
ARRINGTON CLIFTON W	LTC	0-0058032	0768
ARTHUR FRANK M	COL	0-0032290	0268
ARTHUR JAMES F	LTC	0-0186409	0568
ASHER L D	LTC	0-0416861	0668
ASHMORE CLIFFORD G	CPT	0-0507890	0868
ASKINE IRVIN	MAJ	0-0232812	0568
ATWOOD LAURENCE C	COL	0-0196293	0968
AUSTIN VERNE	COL	0-0184808	0368
BABBITT RICHARD C	COL	0-0012128	1268
BACHMAN EDWARD A	MAJ	0-0273663	0668
BACK ALBERT W	1LT	0-1643636	0468
BAGLEY THOMAS B	COL	0-0357805	1068
BAILEY JOHN W	LTC	0-0128510	
BAILEY WILBERT L	LTC	0-0507707	
BAILLY FLORENCE M	1LT	N-0700094	0768
BAISH CHARLES F	COL	0-0009309	0868
BAKER FRANCIS J	LTC	0-0085467	0568
BAKER FRAYNE	B G	0-0134923	0868
BAKER MAURICE	CPT	0-0289658	
BAKER MENTER G	MAJ	0-0241914	0668
BAKER RAYMOND J	LTC	0-1633433	
BAKER THOMAS D	COL	0-0005381	0268
BALDRIDGE JAMES D	LTC	0-0420440	0768
BALDWIN ELLIOTT N	COL	0-0178861	0668
BALDWIN FREDERICK	LTC	0-0238997	1067
BALLENGER JOHN F	MAJ	0-0111519	0268
BANISTER JOHN R	COL	0-0159280	0268
BANKS CLYDE G	COL	0-0011646	0668
BARCLAY HUGH	B G	0-0402854	0768
BARE JOHN W	CPT	0-0190669	0768
BARKER HAROLD R	B G	0-0148571	0565
BARNABY KENNETH T	COL	0-0044385	1068
BARNARD THOMAS W	CPT	0-0007735	0568
BARNES CHARLES N JR	LTC	0-0225232	0668
BARNES FRANK J	1LT	0-1321279	
BARNES HENRY C	CPT	0-0495962	0268
BARNES LESTER H	LTC	0-0197228	0868
BARNES MYRON C	LTC	0-0283592	
BARNES PATRICK H	COL	0-0193656	
BARNEY PHYLLIS W	MAJ	N-0001019	
BARNWELL FRANK H	COL	0-0150052	0468
BARNWELL HOWARD B	MAJ	0-0545747	
BARR WILLIAM L	CW4	W-2149248	0968
BARRY EDWIN J	COL	0-0115260	0968
BARTHOLOMEW EDWARD A	MAJ	0-0509895	0868
BARTHOLOW HOWARD P	CW4	W-2118094	0468
BARTLETT FLOYD H	CW4	W-2113703	0268
BARTMAN KENNETH E	CPT	0-0306655	0768
BATTLE WILLIAM P	MAJ	0-0198696	0168
BAUGHN HERMAN C	COL	0-0225418	0868
BAYLIES ALFRED L	COL	0-0005874	
BAYNHAM ROBERT	1LT	0-0280555	0768
BAZILUS JUSTIN W JR	2LT	0-1302104	0668
BEAM JAMES C	MAJ	0-1290532	0568
BEAM JOHN A	1LT	0-0108242	0968
BEAN WALTER A	COL	0-0221804	1068
BEAUCHAMP ROBERT N	MAJ	0-1685548	0468
BECKER HORACE G	LTC	0-0506202	0368
BEDINGER SAMUEL D	COL	0-0005603	
BEDLE CRAIG R	LTC	0-0308401	
BEECH GEORGE R	LTC	0-0220790	1068
BEER CARL A D	LTC	0-0200874	0168
BEESON WILLIAM M	1LT	0-1642877	1268
BEHERS BERNARD L JR	LTC	0-1633659	0768
BEISEL LEON W	LTC	0-0201448	0968
BELISLE FRED	LTC	0-0215123	
BELL CLIFTON	LTC	0-0320035	0268
BELL FRANK F	B G	0-0173171	0968
BELL LEIGH	COL	0-0005114	0468
BELL MARY S	LTC	L-0702010	0768
BELL VERNE R	MAJ	0-0002189	
BELLIS CHARLES W	MAJ	0-0166790	
BELT CARLE H	COL	0-0172533	0568
BEMONT RICHARD L	LTC	0-1100015	0568
BENOKOWSKI JOSEF J	LTC	0-0376549	0968
BENN FREDERICK	CPT	0-1578161	0368
BENNETT OSCAR	2LT	0-0506853	
BENSON GEORGE W	LTC	0-1547232	
BERL WILLIAM JR	COL	0-0112559	0968
BERNSTROM HARRY D	CPT	0-0160801	0468
BERRIGAN DONALD B	LTC	0-0028960	
BERRY CHARLES W JR	COL	0-0255057	
BETTENBURG PHILIP C	M G	0-0171936	0368
BEWLEY LYLBURN H III	MAJ	0-0364123	0668
BEYETTE HUBERT W	B G	0-0008146	0768
BICKFORD ROBERT J	COL	0-1797936	0568
BIGGS GEORGE N	MAJ	0-0230806	0868
BINKS GEORGE A	MAJ	0-0199312	0668
BIRKHOLZ CARL R	CPT	0-0254890	0965
BISHOP HERBERT C	LTC	0-0290764	1068
BISHOP JESSE F	COL	0-0222952	0368
BISSELL HARRY H	LTC	0-0001986	0768
BLACK HENRY B	1LT	0-1543613	
BLACK IRA W	COL	0-0010113	0368
BLACK LAWRENCE F	COL	0-0295676	0968
BLACK RAYLSTON N	CW2	W-2147789	0768
BLACKBURN BUD	CPT	0-0490861	1267
BLACKFORD ERNEST J	MAJ	0-0403055	0568
BLACKSHEAR JOHN P	LTC	0-0019994	
BLACKWELL WILKIE D	CPT	0-2056261	1068
BLAIR BOB E	MAJ	0-2011746	0768
BLAIR HENRY H	LTC	0-0498442	0368
BLAIR HENRY T	COL	0-0135056	
BLAKNEY HERMAN D	CW3	W-2141200	
BLANCO JUAN R	COL	0-0109959	0668
BLANDING JOHN W	LTC	0-0187055	0468
BLANKENHORN ROBERT D	COL	0-0372063	1068
BLATT JOHN F	COL	0-0018925	
BLENKINSOP F W	LTC	0-0246069	0468
BLISS ARTHUR P	CPT	0-0110253	0868
BLISS BENJAMIN	COL	0-0268578	
BLOGG AINSWORTH	COL	0-0174763	0368
BLOOD IVAN L	CPT	0-1797939	
BLOOM FRED H	CW2	W-0901599	1268
BLOOM PHILLIP	1LT	0-0451079	0868
BLUETHGEN ERNEST F	MAJ	0-0245044	1168
BLUMENSTIEL MONROE A	MAJ	0-0215635	0967
BODINE CHARLES L	LTC	0-0206474	0868
BODINE ROBERT N	COL	0-0003375	1168
BOHLIN OSCAR C	LTC	0-0170806	0668
BOLT ROBERT A	LTC	0-1303624	1068
BOLTON JAMES E	COL	0-0411772	0768
BONAGUIDI JOHN	LTC	0-1594049	0868
BONS JILLES T	2LT	0-1176892	0368
BOOTH GEORGE L	CPT	0-0320750	0968
BOOTH ROBERT	COL	0-0186477	
BOOTHE JOHN E JR	LTC	0-0052533	0868
BORING JAMES W	LTC	0-1317753	
BOSTOCK THOMAS J	CPT	0-0479535	0768
BOSTOCK THOMAS J	2LT	0-1037403	0668
BOUGHTON LLOYD L	1LT	0-0014408	
BOUMENDT BERRO	CPT	0-0442386	0268
BOURNE WILLIAM D	MAJ	0-0179400	
BOUSH JAMES E	COL	0-0010525	
BOWDEN EDWIN T	COL	0-0007164	0768
BOWLES HOWARD G JR	LTC	0-0425237	0968
BOWMAN LESLIE E	MAJ	0-0008433	0668
BOWMAN ORVILLE D	1LT	0-1913557	0268
BOYD LEON H	MAJ	0-0282810	0868
BOYOSTON JAMES E	LTC	0-0475237	
BOYKIN LEMUEL W JR	LTC	0-0317858	
BOYLE JAMES J	MAJ	0-2263237	1068
BRADFORD WILLIAM S	WO1	W-0901144	0468
BRADLEY WILLIAM C	MAJ	0-1167326	
BRADLEY WILLIAM R	COL	0-0011752	0668
BRADY CECIL C	MAJ	0-0280680	
BRADY JOHN J JR	2LT	0-1302768	0368
BRAND TOM S	COL	0-0007123	0368
BRANDON HOMER B	WO1	W-2143874	0268
BRANNAN FRANCIS M	COL	0-0003721	
BRANNAN JOHN E	COL	0-0007170	
BRANNAN LEE R	LTC	0-0287811	0368
BRANNIFF EARL C	LTC	0-0254917	0168
BRANNON MARGARET N	MAJ	N-0000103	
BRAY ELBERT W	1LT	0-0400895	0268
BRAZIER NESTER H	CPT	0-1100891	1068
BREIDENBACH GEORGE F	MAJ	0-0218594	
BREWSTER EDWIN S JR	COL	0-0010620	0468
BREYLA FREDERICK	CW3	W-2129887	0868
BRICE LAWRENCE S	CPT	0-0060867	0568
BRICKLES FRANKLIN R	COL	0-0030278	0368
BRIEGEL GEORGE F	WO1	W-2209292	0568
BRIGHAM CLAUDE E	M G	0-0001356	0768
BRIGHTWELL ROBERT L	COL	0-0179432	
BRINER CHARLES C	MAJ	0-0494417	0468
BRISCOE ALBERT H	CPT	0-0142623	0468
BRISTOL MATT C	COL	0-0001559	0268
BROBERG JOHN A	CPT	0-0107870	0668
BROCKMAN KARL W	LTC	0-0162397	1068
BROKAW ALBERT R	MAJ	0-1996456	0768
BROMLEY CHARLES D	COL	0-0193429	0168
BRONSON RALPH P	COL	0-0438320	0968
BROOKE ELTON O	CPT	0-1306372	0168
BROOKS LOREN R	COL	0-0158349	
BROOKS PAUL K	CW2	W-2118437	0368
BROOKS WILLIAM J	WO1	W-2131124	1168
BROSNAN JOHN R	CPT	0-0192443	1168
BROUSE KARL M	LTC	0-0140345	0868
BROWER JAMES F	MAJ	0-0112698	0168
BROWN ANTHONY J	CPT	0-0889011	1068
BROWN BERNARD W	CW3	W-2205584	0868
BROWN BRYAN B	MAJ	0-0211600	1068
BROWN CHARLES D JR	MAJ	0-1548660	0468
BROWN ERNEST J	COL	0-0503731	0868
BROWN HAROLD	LTC	0-0192645	
BROWN HUBERT L	MAJ	0-0471765	
BROWN IRVEN S	LTC	0-1798113	0368
BROWN JOSEPH B E	CPT	0-0305061	0368
BROWN KERMIT K	CPT	0-0410809	
BROWN LOREN E	2LT	0-1058454	1068
BROWN PAUL H	COL	0-0005324	
BROWN RALPH E	LTC	0-0268135	0168
BROWN ROY F	COL	0-0006374	
BROWNE ROBERT E JR	MAJ	0-0150006	1267
BROWNE THOMAS R	COL	0-0253097	0768
BROWNE WILLIAM C	COL	0-0144123	
BRUCE ROBERT D	LTC	0-0284589	
BRUNKHURST HENRY G	LTC	0-0267342	0968
BRUNNER EDWARD A JR	LTC	0-0383519	0668
BRYANT EVERETT C	1LT	0-1291774	0368
BRYANT HARRY F	MAJ	0-0176932	1068
BRYANT OLNEY H	1LT	0-0274813	
BUCH JOHN E	LTC	0-0150026	
BUCHHOLZ GEORGE H	WO1	W-0900939	1068
BUCHLY WALTER E	COL	0-0004617	0868
BUCK WILLIAM E	1LT	0-0164367	0768
BUCKLEY JOHN J	LTC	0-0324481	0668
BUDDEMEYER HOMER J	1LT	0-1106618	
BUFFINGTON JOHN F	CPT	0-0130521	
BULL NEWTON M	MAJ	0-0253840	0368
BULMER JOHN C	LTC	0-0450567	0768
BUNTING WILLIAM L	LTC	0-0196377	0268
BUNYARD CLAYTON L	WO1	W-2149331	0668
BURGESS THOMAS B	COL	0-0005139	1268
BURNETT LEWIS H	MAJ	0-0229675	1168
BURNS CLAUDE C	CPT	0-0107337	
BURRIS HARRISON L	LTC	0-0118843	0668
BURRITT HAROLD E	LTC	0-0213278	0868
BURROWS STUART S JR	CW2	W-2212346	0568
BURSON MAURICE E	MAJ	0-0298305	0768
BURTON FRANK E	CW3	W-2002969	1168
BUSSE MABEL K	CPT	L-0600080	
BUSWELL JOHN W	COL	0-0270353	0468
BYRD EDWIN L	CW4	W-0902797	1268
CABLE DONALD E	MAJ	0-0231464	0668
CALDWELL ARTHUR N	LTC	0-0347708	0568
CALDWELL JOHN C	LTC	0-0480390	1168
CALDWELL WILL H	LTC	0-0216731	
CALDWELL WILLIAM B	COL	0-0008754	0568
CALHOUN WILLIAM L	B G	0-0042664	0768
CAMPBELL EARL A	CW4	W-0902867	1068
CAMPBELL ERNEST H	1LT	0-1100903	1168
CANTY DANIEL J	CPT	0-0005999	
CAPERTON ROY J	COL	0-0011548	
CARIE JOSEPH	MAJ	0-0172045	
CARLIN CLARA D	1LT	N-0731089	0468
CARLSON LAURANCE S	COL	0-0238101	1068

NAME	GRADE	SVC NO	DATE LOSS MO YR
CARLSON ROLAND P	COL	0-0031456	
CARLTON MAURICE B	MAJ	0-0258148	0368
CARNES THOMAS E	CPT	0-5218143	0468
CARPENTER CARL H	WO1	W-2127496	1268
CARR AMOS J	CPT	0-1914590	0568
CARR MINNIE L	MAJ	N-0000143	0668
CARROLL HERBERT D	MAJ	0-1045693	0768
CARROS COSTAS J	LTC	0-0487672	0468
CARTER CARROLL S	LTC	0-0181198	0468
CARTER JOE K	MAJ	0-0472361	
CASE NORMAN S	COL	0-0166501	
CASE ROBERT A	COL	0-0009758	1068
CASE ROY B	COL	0-0140042	0568
CASH GEORGE L	CPT	0-1058470	0568
CASON GEORGE A	MAJ	0-1545242	1068
CASSIDY GEORGE E JR	LTC	0-1285609	1268
CASSILL GEORGE F	LTC	0-0030464	
CASSODAY JOHN B	LTC	0-0296262	1168
CATES CHARLES G	CPT	0-0255832	0867
CATTE JOSEPH P	MAJ	0-0015033	0968
CAVE WILLIAM H	CPT	0-0268178	
CAVENDER DONALD E	LTC	0-0525255	0668
CAWTHORNE TED H	LTC	0-0006559	
CERRONE LUKE J	MAJ	0-0497467	0368
CHAMBERLAIN HUGH D	CPT	0-0138067	0668
CHAMBERS ANDREW JR	CPT	0-1165595	0268
CHAMP CLIFFORD L	CW3	W-2108922	
CHAPLIN SAXBY	COL	0-0185031	0668
CHAPMAN CARL F	MAJ	0-0118692	0268
CHAPMAN JOHN C	CPT	0-0146420	0868
CHAPPELLE VERGNE	COL	0-0142481	0368
CHASE JOHN A	COL	0-0007966	0368
CHASTAIN CARL W	1LT	0-0527780	0268
CHEAR ROBERT M	LTC	0-0018613	0268
CHEESEMAN EVANS P	LTC	0-0113174	
CHESNUTT NORWOOD B	LTC	0-0168297	0268
CHISHOLM JAMES H	CPT	0-0060343	
CHRISTENSEN W BLAKE	CPT	0-0474980	
CHURCH HENRY H	LTC	0-0486468	0868
CHURCHILL JAMES M	COL	0-0001854	0868
CLARK DEWITT H	MAJ	0-0183658	0868
CLARK ROBERT E JR	CW4	W-2125936	0968
CLARK RUSSELL A	COL	0-0199467	0368
CLARK WILLIAM A	MAJ	0-0422680	
CLARKE FRED M JR	COL	0-0242389	0868
CLARKE GEORGE S	COL	0-0004613	0768
CLEMENTS ALBERT B	MAJ	0-2016850	0268
CLENDINNING JOHN JR	MAJ	0-0136081	1068
COATES JOSEPH A	1LT	0-1303671	
COATES THEODORE P	COL	0-0041480	0968
COBBS NICHOLAS H	B G	0-0008237	
COBLE FRANCES J	LTC	N-0002253	0568
COCKRILL JAMES M	1LT	0-0104699	0668
COESTER EMIL H	COL	0-0215149	0468
COGGS THEODORE W	1LT	0-1302460	0668
COGLEY JOHN P	LTC	0-0487780	0366
COHEN MAXWELL	MAJ	0-0220121	0368
COLBERT JAMES E	COL	0-0186720	0468
COLBY IRVING H	LTC	0-0285273	0668
COLE CLIFFORD B	COL	0-0007601	1068
COLE VICTOR C	COL	0-0483161	0968
COLE WILLIAM JR	MAJ	0-0396979	
COLEMAN FRANK P	LTC	0-1696423	0568
COLEMAN JAMES A	LTC	0-0122417	
COLEMAN V GLENN	1LT	N-0759009	0368
COLLEY MARTIN H	COL	0-0034982	0168
COMER REUBEN H	1LT	0-0115477	
COMPTON EARL C	COL	0-0021703	1268
CONAWAY COY M	MAJ	0-1685637	0958
CONAWAY THOMAS W	MAJ	0-5205633	
CONKLIN GLENN G	CPT	0-2056241	0568
CONLEY FRANK J	COL	0-0334739	0368
CONN GARY R	CW2	W-2117989	0268
CONNER GEORGE F	COL	0-0017777	0668
CONNOLLY PHILIP B	LTC	0-0003296	0768
CONNORS MICHAEL J	MAJ	0-0488847	0868
CONSOLETTI BENJAMIN	MAJ	0-0303533	1068
CONTOIS LEO A	CW2	W-2113705	
CONTOIS PAUL S	MAJ	0-1324911	0568
COOK BUFORD	CW4	W-2144212	
COOK CLARENCE J	MAJ	0-0134985	
COOK LEWIS C	LTC	0-0262912	0168
COOKE JOSEPH C	LTC	0-0473962	0768
COOLEY EDWIN P	COL	0-0051770	1068
COOPER EDGAR G	MAJ	0-0007723	0668
COOPER THOMAS B	MAJ	0-0266049	
COPELAND ARTHUR J	COL	0-0289654	0668
COPEMAN ALBERT B	MAJ	0-1650051	
CORTHRONE WILLIAM A	COL	0-0003544	0768
CORBIN FREDERICK	COL	0-0020972	0668
CORONER CHARLES D	LTC	0-0253721	0468
CORNWELL HAROLD J	MAJ	0-1581622	0968
CORRY JOHN E	1LT	0-2002252	0868
CORZINE JAMES E	2LT	0-1949077	0668
COTTIER WEBSTER J	LTC	0-0262987	
COULBOURN WILLIAM C	COL	0-0301299	0868
COULTER JOHN W	COL	0-0100282	
COURTENAY FRANK A	LTC	0-0192691	0668
COURTER GLEN D	CW4	W-2125874	1268
COURTNEY MARTIN	2LT	0-0112630	0368
COWGILL RALPH P	COL	0-0142305	
COWLEY ARCHIBALD	COL	0-0003127	0668
COX CARLISLE B	COL	0-0005798	0468
COX ROY H	LTC	0-0167220	
COYLE MARVIN J	COL	0-0018602	0768
CRAFT LEE J	MAJ	0-0450116	0666
CRAFT MARTIN M	CPT	0-0473923	
CRAIG PAUL E	CPT	0-0493698	
CRANE DOUGLAS LE	COL	0-0007064	
CRANE JAMES L	LTC	0-0468978	0268
CRASSON SAMUEL L	CPT	0-0210607	
CRAWFORD GEORGE O	CPT	0-0188965	0568
CRAWFORD JOHN A	COL	0-0325261	0768
CRICE MILTON M	LTC	0-0271740	0768
CRINKLEY FRANCIS D	MAJ	0-0029669	0468
CRISP MELVIN L	1LT	0-0157546	
CROFT CLAUDIA K	2LT	N-0761845	0568
CROOK ROWLAND D	1LT	0-0265542	0968
CROSSETT WILLIAM A	2LT	0-1308927	0268
CROWL ALLEN L	CPT	0-0510899	0868
CRUMP WILLIAM W	LTC	0-0173986	0368
CRUMP WILLIAM E JR	LTC	0-0031983	0468
CRUZ ENRIQUE E	1LT	0-0888097	1267
CUBBISON DONALD C	M G	0-0001931	1268
CULBERT WILLIAM	COL	0-0348384	0268
CULBERTSON EUAL W	COL	0-0042263	1068
CULIN FRANK L JR	M G	0-0004717	
CULLEN JOSEPH W	CW3	W-2147911	0668
CUNNINGHAM EUGENE M	LTC	0-0244594	0668
CUNNINGHAM WILLIAM A	COL	0-0007863	0968
CURREY CLAUDE H	CPT	0-1947186	
CURTIN CHARLES J	MAJ	0-0344484	1068
CURTIS FRANK H	COL	0-0011956	0568
CUSACK GORDON K	COL	0-0018414	0968
DAIGER WILLIAM H	LTC	0-0252359	0568
DALE IRVING H	COL	0-0251271	0468
DALE LEROY	CW3	W-2143715	0668
DALEY GEORGE F	1LT	0-1846412	0768
DANCAK EDWARD J	1LT	0-0507751	
DANCE LEE I	MAJ	0-0463471	0368
DANIEL EARNEST J	MAJ	0-1894843	
DANIEL RALPH	1LT	0-0504181	0368
DANIEL RALPH C	MAJ	0-1303679	1168
DANIELS HENRY	COL	0-0136778	1068
DANIELS REX O	LTC	0-0336245	0268
DARCY THOMAS F JR	CPT	0-0020471	0568
DARKEY KARL L	LTC	0-0343377	0668
DARRAGH JOHN C	CW3	W-2101587	1068
DASHER CHARLES L	M G	0-0015634	1168
DATOC QUARDALOPE	1LT	0-2023827	0968
DAUGHERTY CHARLES B	LTC	0-0182240	0868
DAUGHERTY JOSEPH P	CPT	0-0101002	
DAUGHERTY SIMPSON B	COL	0-0254361	0668
DAVEY ROBERT C	LTC	0-0364316	0768
DAVIDSON L B JR	COL	0-0244408	0468
DAVIDSON FRANK F	MAJ	0-1552655	0768
DAVIDSON FRED	LTC	0-2044531	0468
DAVIDSON HERBERT L	COL	0-0256521	
DAVIDSON WALLACE N	COL	0-0193015	
DAVIES JOHN F	CW2	W-2117964	0468
DAVIS ADDISON D	B G	0-0002651	0665
DAVIS ALEXANDER	LTC	0-0251780	
DAVIS BENJAMIN H	CPT	0-0116175	0168
DAVIS GEORGE	MAJ	0-0200818	0668
DAVIS GEORGE A	B G	0-0144767	0368
DAVIS GLEN M	MAJ	0-2051433	1068
DAVIS LESTER M	LTC	0-0164070	
DAVIS MELVIN C	MAJ	0-0410796	
DAVIS MERLE H	B G	0-0009832	
DAVIS UNNER O	COL	0-0132675	0768
DAVIS STUART W	COL	0-0041593	0568
DAVISON ROBERT H	CPT	0-1574411	
DAVISSON ALEXANDER	COL	0-0298589	0368
DAY JOHN B	LTC	0-0005619	0368
DE ASIS CESAREO	LTC	0-0204431	1067
DE BLOIS ERNEST E	LTC	0-0921309	1267
DE FOREST CARL R	MAJ	0-0174059	0868
DE JARNETT ELLIOTT H	LTC	0-0310667	0368
DE LUCA JOSEPH M	MAJ	0-1106087	
DE MILHAU LOUIS J	LTC	0-0161523	
DE VEAUX JOHN A	COL	0-0021470	0368
DE VILLE JOSEPH I	COL	0-0244492	0268
DEALE DANIEL G	MAJ	0-0500389	0768
DEANE HERBERT O	CPT	0-0277272	0668
DECKER RICHARD F	LTC	0-1309156	1168
DEFLON ERIC G	CPT	0-0472900	0168
DEIBER HARRY M	COL	0-0003916	0368
DELA CONCEPCION R	1LT	0-1896388	0768
DELA PERRIERE JOHN J	MAJ	0-0236221	0368
DELAHUNTY JOSEPH P	CW2	W-2117061	0867
DELANY ARTHUR G	LTC	0-1791111	1068
DEMPSEY JOSEPH E	MAJ	0-0464779	
DEMPSEY MARVIN F	MAJ	0-0931058	0868
DENEAU RUTH S	CPT	L-0304002	0768
DENIS HOWARD I	LTC	0-0164454	0668
DENNIS EDWARD W	COL	0-0108892	0268
DENTON DWIGHT O	CPT	0-0361989	0468
DENTREMONT EARL J	COL	0-0924650	0168
DEPPE ARLINGTON	MAJ	0-0109616	0867
DERMIT LEE A	MAJ	0-0491283	1168
DERSHIMER ALEXANDER	LTC	0-0009248	0468
DESOVIER MARIE J	MAJ	N-0784464	0268
DEVENISH GEORGE B	MAJ	0-0188469	
DEW JOSEPH D	CPT	0-0314464	
DIAZ VINCENT N	COL	0-0004842	1268
DICKMAN LOUIS	LTC	0-0389087	0268
DICKSON LOUIS A	CW3	W-2145925	
DICKSON MERWIN C	MAJ	0-0335121	
DIEMER CARL A	MAJ	0-0221920	0768
DIETER OTTO A	LTC	0-0347065	
DIETZ CHARLES W	COL	0-0009642	0568
DILBECK HENRY L	CW2	W-2146590	0568
DILLON GOMER S	LTC	0-0247889	0868
DINERMAN BENJAMIN	LTC	0-0227279	0868
DIONNE GEORGE A	CW4	W-2115161	0768
DISMUKES RUPERT Z	LTC	0-0362299	1068
DODDRIDGE PHILIP	COL	0-0009051	0468
DODGE FLOYD	WO1	W-0901305	0568
DODGE WARREN A	LTC	0-0262692	0668
DODGE WILBUR L	WO1	W-2125232	0157
DOERING CALVIN J	1LT	0-2030427	0468
DOGGETT DENZIL	LTC	0-0107255	0968
DOHM EDWARD C	COL	0-0175076	0768
DOLITSKY MORRIS M	LTC	0-0450003	0868
DOLL GEORGE J	LTC	0-0206736	
DONAHUE DONALD L	CPT	0-1297693	
DONLON VINCENT G	CPT	0-1950334	0768
DONNELLY JOHN A	MAJ	0-0481225	0868
DOOLEY HARRY J	COL	0-0911813	0268
DORSEY FRANCIS L	2LT	0-1013107	0968
DOTY DAVID B JR	MAJ	0-0007565	1068
DOUBLE JOSEPH F	CW4	W-2119903	0668
DOUGLAS GELLERT A	MAJ	0-0017311	0968
DOUGLAS MALCOLM	COL	0-0154234	1168
DOVELL CHAUNCEY E	COL	0-0008810	0368
DRACOTIS BURT A	CPT	0-1547279	
DRAPER ROBERT F	1LT	0-0050857	
DRENNAN GUY	LTC	0-1297331	0468
DREWRY FLAG A	CPT	0-0011170	
DRINKARD JOHN E	LTC	0-0365282	0868
DRISCOLL ROBERT E	CPT	0-0542757	
DRODDY PRUELLA H	MAJ	N-0700373	
DROWNE HENRY P JR	B G	0-0136725	0468
DRURY JOHN D	COL	0-0170024	
DUCHEK CHARLES F	WO1	W-2106721	0968
DUDLEY HARRY E	COL	0-0235619	
DUFF LOGAN	1LT	0-0109736	0968
DUFORT GERALD E	COL	0-0130169	0868
DUGGAN JAPSER T	MAJ	0-0184277	0968
DUKE JACK W	LTC	0-0033662	
DUKE JOHN H	CPT	0-1647858	0168
DULANEY EARL	MAJ	0-0312910	0368
DUNBAR RICHARD A	COL	0-0192667	1168
DUNCAN HARRY L	LTC	0-1290049	
DUNCAN RAY H	1LT	0-0157438	0168
DUNCANSON DONALD D	LTC	0-0144737	0968
DUNN WILLIAM	1LT	0-0506567	
DUNSON DAVID A	CW3	W-2146364	1168
DUNSTER ALBERT E	1LT	0-0178131	0368
DURHAM JAMES R	CW2	W-0903050	0968
DUROCHER RAYMOND E	CPT	0-1687335	0368
DUSINA ROBERT A	1LT	0-4042252	0368
DUSSEAU RALPH E JR	CW4	W-0906710	0868
DUVALL MEARLE D	2LT	0-0463918	1068
DYKHOUSE JAY	COL	0-0178814	0268
DYSART NELSON C	COL	0-0146128	
EARLY JOHN W	COL	0-0201816	
EASTER CHARLES E	CW2	W-2143764	0268
EBERT JOHN A	1LT	0-1580894	0368
EDDY RICHARD T	LTC	0-0122404	0668
EDGAR HAROLD H	CPT	0-0114096	0368
EDGAR PERCY F	CPT	0-0142524	0968
EDWARDS GEORGE M	COL	0-0002771	0868
EDWARDS WILLIAM J	LTC	0-0474704	0568
EGGLER HENRY J	MAJ	0-0297047	1068
EISNITZ SHELDON R	LTC	0-2041008	0768
ELAM GEORGE T	LTC	0-0387715	0468
ELDER EUGENE V	B G	0-0011681	0668
ELDER JACK K	MAJ	0-1010843	0668
ELIASON RAYMOND O	COL	0-0222283	0568
ELKINS DENNIE	CPT	0-0164001	0568
ELLIOTT CROSBY N	COL	0-0005513	
ELLIOTT HOWARD M	COL	0-0051072	0668
ELLIS WALTER C	COL	0-0008192	0168
EMBREE FELIX V	MAJ	0-0155016	0568
EMERSON FITZHUGH L	MAJ	0-1585414	0268
ENGELHART GEORGE K	COL	0-0114578	
ENGLE BYRON E	CPT	0-0466118	0968
ENGLISH ANTHONY G	1LT	0-1535166	0568
ENNIS WILLIAM P	B G	0-0001331	0768
ENSIGN PAUL R	COL	0-0218423	0468
ENTWISTLE GEORGE H	CPT	0-0221547	0968
ERICKSON EDGAR L	CPT	0-0181071	0368
ERICKSON JOSEPH L	LTC	0-0010573	0468
ERICKSON LOUIS	2LT	0-0195096	
ERICKSON OLIVER G	MAJ	0-0220106	0168
ERNST JOSEPH L	COL	0-0190729	1068
ERSIN HUBERT J	CPT	0-1175425	0768
ERWIN JAMES E	LTC	0-0382282	0568
ERWIN ROY M	2LT	0-0339358	

NAME	GRADE	SVC NO	DATE LOSS MO YR
ERWIN WILLIAM B	COL	0-0453426	0368
ESTES LOREN C	MAJ	0-1797106	1068
ESTES WALTER	MAJ	0-0505288	0368
EUBANKS GEORGE W	LTC	0-0323079	0468
EVANS CATHERINE	MAJ	N-0771437	0968
EVANS GEORGE G	COL	0-0150734	
EVANS JOHN W	CPT	0-2050223	0268
EVANS JOSEPH K	COL	0-0010413	1068
EVANS MARVIN J	B G	0-1100975	0468
EVERSOLE GARDNER S	CPT	0-0315735	0368
EWING EDWARD T	MAJ	0-1293740	0468
EWING HARRY G	CPT	0-1920107	0868
FAGONE FRANCIS A	COL	0-0265395	0468
FAIRCHILD JOHN C	COL	0-0347067	1268
FALK DAVID B	COL	0-0003569	1068
FANT JOHN F	LTC	0-0172942	0668
FARMER FRAMPTON W	CPT	0-0324387	0668
FARQUHARSON CHARLES	WO1	W-2140391	0568
FARR RICHARD	COL	0-0033737	0368
FARRAR FLOYD R	LTC	0-0202773	0968
FARRELL FRANCIS D	CW2	W-2211772	0968
FARRINGTON FERRELL	MAJ	0-0262509	0768
FARRIS DONALD M	COL	0-0220760	0668
FAUSEY FRANCIS S	ILT	0-2024907	0368
FAWCETT THOMAS F	MAJ	0-0114642	0368
FEDERSPIEL FRANK J	CPT	0-0210162	1068
FEE DARWIN D	LTC	0-1165287	0568
FEENEY CLINTON	LTC	0-0288652	0768
FEGERT CARL R	LTC	0-0477519	
FEIKE LAWRENCE V	LTC	0-0176930	0368
FELDMAN THEODORE E	2LT	0-2009596	0368
FELDT OTTO F	LTC	0-0220307	0868
FENTON JOEL V	CW2	W-2146237	0968
FERGUSON HARLEY B	M G	0-0000540	0868
FESSENDEN BRADLEY M	LTC	0-0322255	
FETTERS OSCAR M	MAJ	0-0274783	0468
FEW ARTHUR N	MAJ	0-0256020	0968
FIBICH MICHAEL J	COL	0-0178052	0368
FICKLIN MORTIMER T	ILT	0-0414322	
FIDDES EDWIN A	CPT	0-0301577	0868
FIERO LOE E	COL	0-0126405	
FINCH HENRY A	COL	0-0002119	0368
FINK EMIL A	MAJ	0-0198404	0568
FISCHER CARL B	CPT	0-0413762	0268
FISCHER LOUIS F	2LT	0-0370414	1068
FISHER BYRON J	LTC	0-0365454	0668
FISHER EARL J	COL	0-0270652	1168
FISHER LYNWOOD W	COL	0-0243118	
FISHER NELSON L	MAJ	0-0200768	
FISHER THOMAS R	LTC	0-0180195	
FISHER VIRGIL S	CW2	W-2146705	1168
FITCH DAVID G	COL	0-0286551	0368
FITZGERALD HUGH J	COL	0-0006719	1168
FITZPATRICK JAMES E	CPT	0-0983215	0268
FIX HERMAN M	MAJ	0-0263901	0868
FLATT FRANCIS L	COL	0-0051180	0268
FLECK JAMES M	LTC	0-0548609	0668
FLEET RUSSELL T	LTC	0-0441098	
FLEGEL EARL C	COL	0-0006800	0268
FLEMIG ERNEST A	LTC	0-0340164	0268
FLEMING JOSEPH P	LTC	0-0128336	1068
FLYNN FREEMAN J	LTC	0-0330795	0368
FLYNN HENRY L	COL	0-0003387	0468
FLYNN HERBERT L	LTC	0-0265235	0168
FLYNN JOSEPH S	CPT	0-0110099	
FOE GLEN H	LTC	0-0206471	1168
FOGEL SYDNEY M	CPT	0-0500316	0768
FOLTZ FREDERICK	COL	0-0147177	1068
FONT-CARRION JACINTO	CPT	0-5826808	0468
FORBES THOMAS M	CW2	W-2005415	0268
FORCE ROBERT C	ILT	0-0293203	0868
FORD DONALD A	CPT	0-1100542	0468
FORDYCE LESTER J	MAJ	0-0235301	0768
FORREST EDWARD F	ILT	0-2026569	
FORSDICK WILFRED F	LTC	0-0108178	0468

NAME	GRADE	SVC NO	DATE LOSS MO YR
FOSS ELMER T	COL	0-0006184	
FOSS HAROLD D	MAJ	0-0221926	0768
FOSTER HERBERT B JR	LTC	0-0280205	1068
FOSTER HERBERT M	MAJ	0-0222094	
FOSTER JOHN E	2LT	0-1913693	
FOSTER PAUL A	ILT	0-0507607	0968
FOWLKES OTHO G	2LT	0-1913695	0668
FOX EUGENE C	MAJ	0-0128092	0868
FOX HENRY H SR	MAJ	0-0232127	0468
FOX JAMES C	2LT	0-1323820	0668
FOX RICHARD J	CPT	0-0338123	0868
FOX ROY E	COL	0-0004063	0468
FRANCIS HORACE M	COL	0-0142728	
FRANK SIMON C	MAJ	0-0344264	0568
FRANKLIN HERBERT L	CPT	0-1173952	
FRAZEE HARRY W	MAJ	0-0178837	0268
FREDRICKSEN ARTHUR	MAJ	0-1825797	0768
FREEMAN GEORGE D JR	COL	0-0000827	0368
FREEMAN NATHAN	LTC	0-0302011	1068
FRIEMOTH AMEDEUS J	LTC	0-0263075	1267
FRISBY CARL F	LTC	0-1633013	0768
FRITSCHLER JOHN C	COL	0-0253788	0768
FRONK CLARENCE E	COL	0-0176571	0268
FRYE ROBERT	COL	0-0243061	
FULLER HOWARD R	LTC	0-0198677	0468
FULLERTON RALPH D	MAJ	0-0305279	1068
FULTON ROBERT L	COL	0-0171351	
FUNK THOMAS S	2LT	0-0904982	0168
FURBEE BENJAMIN W	ILT	0-0192610	0668
FURMAN ARTHUR E	CPT	0-0481888	
GAECKLE WILLIAM H	COL	0-0041905	1068
GAGE JOHN N	COL	0-0005359	0568
GAHAN JOHN J	COL	0-0010857	
GALBRAITH WILLIAM J	LTC	0-0152179	0768
GALE JOHN J	ILT	0-1592206	0268
GALLAGHER PATRICK J	LTC	0-0328002	0568
GALVIN JACK P	MAJ	0-1010312	0468
GAMBLE WILLIAM D JR	MAJ	0-0237366	
GARBETT JOSEPH E	2LT	0-1914111	1267
GARCIN FREDERICK	COL	0-0002905	0568
GARDNER JESSE J	LTC	0-0186174	
GARLINER JACOB	CPT	0-0302903	1068
GARNETT EARL E	CW3	W-2205982	0768
GARRISON WILLIAM H	CW2	W-2146583	1068
GASSER JAMES L	CPT	0-1113218	0168
GATES WALTER E	MAJ	0-0480568	
GAUMER OSCAR C	LTC	0-0235154	
GAUPER EMMETT G	MAJ	0-0477927	
GAUSE THOMAS W	ILT	0-1295700	0568
GAUTIER THOMAS B	CPT	0-0904370	0368
GAYLE WILLIAM T	COL	0-0229087	0668
GAYNES SEYMOUR S	CW2	W-2111543	1267
GEBERT CHARLES A	COL	0-0148119	0268
GEIGER HARMON P	MAJ	0-0504365	0868
GENTLE HJALMAR T	LTC	0-0259471	0868
GEORGE ERNEST R	ILT	0-1013500	0368
GEORGE PAUL W	MAJ	0-0011225	0768
GERAGHTY MICHAEL J	COL	0-0016263	0468
GERVIN JACK E	CPT	0-1293036	1168
GESTER JOHN L	CW3	W-2205501	0368
GETCHELL JOHN S	LTC	0-0339149	
GIBB FREDERICK	M G	0-0019222	0968
GIBNEY JESSE L	COL	0-0012216	
GIBSON ROY S	COL	0-0006520	0568
GIECK WILLIAM H	CPT	0-0398223	0868
GILCHRIST JACK C	CPT	0-0390853	0868
GILFILLAN WILLIAM F	LTC	0-1042576	0968
GILLESPIE JACK D JR	CPT	0-1299033	0368
GILMAN EDWARD H	LTC	0-0171927	0868
GILMER CARL E	LTC	0-1175719	
GILSON CLAIRE E	MAJ	N-0002874	0968
GINDER PHILIP D	M G	0-0016904	1168
GINNAVEN WILBUR D	MAJ	0-0183864	0468
GIRARD BERNARD J	CPT	0-2032312	0368
GIST JULIAN H	COL	0-0007914	0868

NAME	GRADE	SVC NO	DATE LOSS MO YR
GIST LANDON E	LTC	0-0151128	
GIUFFRE MATTHEW R	LTC	0-0040425	0868
GLADYSZ JOSEPH	CW4	W-2000112	0268
GLASS GEORGE F	LTC	0-0041790	
GLASSBURN ROBERT P	COL	0-0002221	0668
GLEASON GEORGE L	MAJ	0-0333999	
GLEASON JOHN R	LTC	0-0476202	0768
GOCHENOUR FRANK O	CPT	0-1645998	
GODLOVE RONALD L	CW4	W-0903160	1268
GOERL MARTIN	COL	0-0231327	
GOLDMAN FREDERICK	COL	0-0105435	0968
GOMORY GUSTAVE E	LTC	0-1291805	0868
GONZALEZ PRUDENCIO	CPT	0-0337555	
GOOD BERNARD S	ILT	0-0360124	0268
GOOD ROBERT E	MAJ	0-0059995	0368
GORDON KENNETH S	MAJ	0-0220754	
GOSSARD THOMAS E	CPT	0-1322914	0368
GOTTSCHALK TELESPHOR	COL	0-0002338	
GOULD HAROLD G	MAJ	0-0234749	1268
GOULD JAMES A	LTC	0-0153260	
GUVERNALE SAMUEL L	MAJ	0-0274710	0568
GRAHAM EDWARD D	COL	0-0293590	
GRAHAM JAMES M	COL	0-0000665	0768
GRANBERRY JAMES W	MAJ	0-1012536	0468
GRANNIS JOHN D JR	COL	0-0198656	
GRANT 3RD ULYSSES S	M G	0-0001790	0868
GRAVES LEON	MAJ	0-0451111	1068
GRAY HAROLD T	COL	0-0146572	0468
GRAY MALCOLM G	MAJ	0-0351589	0768
GRAY WHITFIELD	CPT	0-0136452	
GREATHOUSE JACK M	CPT	0-0510697	0768
GREEN BENJAMIN	ILT	0-0441662	0668
GREEN CARSON H	CW2	W-2208376	0568
GREEN DANIEL M	LTC	0-0291385	0368
GREEN ELMER G	LTC	0-1289240	0868
GREEN LOYD W	LTC	0-0349120	0868
GREENE HAROLD F	ILT	0-0011982	0268
GREENE THOMAS G	LTC	0-0177347	0268
GREENWOOD GEORGE E	CPT	0-0489918	
GREER ANDREW K	ILT	0-2206420	0768
GREY CALVIN	MAJ	0-1895125	
GRIDER ROSCOE R	CPT	0-0502701	1068
GRIFFIN CHARLES W	MAJ	0-0110401	0768
GRIFFIN HERSCHEL R	COL	0-0166893	0768
GRIFFITH EDWIN G	LTC	0-0017579	0868
GRIFFITHS AARON C	LTC	0-1289902	
GRIMALDI MICHAEL	COL	0-0182849	0568
GRIMM JACK R	LTC	0-1104799	0868
GRIST OLIVER E	LTC	0-0922590	
GROSS BENJAMIN	CW2	W-2123050	0368
GUENTHER FRANK J	COL	0-0213585	0668
GUEST WESLEY T	B G	0-0014654	
GUITERAS GEORGE G	MAJ	0-0019321	
GUNTER LAWRENCE R	CPT	0-0493509	0868
GWINN HUBERT E	ILT	0-1956364	
HAAKENSEN NOBLE T	COL	0-0016589	1068
HAAS LOUIS M	COL	0-0183372	1068
HACKETT JOHN M	LTC	0-1016124	0968
HACKRADT OTTO A	CPT	0-0229756	0268
HAFFORD JOHN L	ILT	0-0399369	0568
HAGEN DUIN M	CPT	0-0494381	0368
HAGGARD ROY S	LTC	0-0185163	
HAISLEY CHESTER D	COL	0-0010175	
HALE THURMAN A	LTC	0-0030275	0668
HALE WILLIAM A	LTC	0-0009238	0268
HALL JOHN	LTC	0-0009384	1168
HALL NOPHLEN R	2LT	0-0108378	0968
HALLENBECK RALPH S	MAJ	0-0256663	1167
HALSTEAD WILLIAM H	COL	0-0005203	0768
HAMILTON ALLEN K	LTC	0-0218161	0868
HAMILTON CHARLES S	COL	0-0001759	0668
HAMILTON FRED L	COL	0-0012716	
HAMILTON HAROLD L	LTC	0-0276390	0468
HAMMOND JOHN W JR	CPT	0-0246942	0668
HAMMOND MATTHEW J	CW3	W-2004231	

NAME	GRADE	SVC NO	DATE LOSS MO YR
HAMMOND PAUL W	LTC	0-0262837	0668
HANDWERK ALLEN S	WO1	W-2134484	0668
HANDZLIK LEON L	CW2	W-2000911	
HANKENSON JOHN A	LTC	0-0920326	1068
HANKINS HENRY E	CW3	W-2142394	
HANKS DALE L	CW2	W-2146664	
HANLY EDWIN C	COL	0-0507918	
HANNAH ROBERT W	MAJ	0-0207245	0568
HANNER KENNETH H	CPT	0-0329688	1168
HANNIGAN FRANCIS	MAJ	0-0279438	1268
HANSELL HAYWOOD S	COL	0-0001453	0168
HANSEN GERHART H	MAJ	0-0134565	0868
HANSON KENNETH E	CPT	0-0954900	0468
HANSON MERLE H	MAJ	0-1797463	1068
HANSON PAUL P	2LT	0-0015336	0468
HARDIN KENNETH E	LTC	0-1317786	1268
HARDIN THOMAS L	MAJ	0-0112116	0768
HARDISON WALTER M	CPT	0-0489914	
HARDY EDWARD J	LTC	0-0104779	
HAREN CHARLES G	MAJ	0-0243006	
HARLEMAN BERMAN C	MAJ	0-1647485	1168
HARMON HOYT H	LTC	0-0110459	0368
HARRINGTON ARTHUR V	COL	0-0170114	0268
HARRINGTON JOHN J	LTC	0-1542675	0268
HARRINGTON ROBERTS	MAJ	0-0231037	0868
HARRIS ARTHUR R	B G	0-0003676	0368
HARRIS AUGUST W	LTC	0-0189202	0168
HARRIS JOSEPH A	MAJ	0-1298223	0168
HARRIS SIDNEY B	MAJ	0-0163044	
HARRISON GEORGE R	LTC	0-0022152	1068
HARRISON LESTER G	ILT	0-0108538	0468
HARRISON LOUIS H	CW3	W-2204981	1168
HARRISON LUCIEN E	LTC	0-0196650	1068
HARRISON RICHARD L	MAJ	0-0286936	0768
HART FRED L	LTC	0-1535190	
HART HARRY	ILT	0-0208048	0468
HART NORMAN E	LTC	0-0180132	
HARTMAN GEORGE E	B G	0-0006538	0768
HARVEY ALLEN P JR	ILT	0-1012148	
HARVEY CHARLES S	LTC	0-0955562	0468
HASKELL LOUIS W	COL	0-0015226	0968
HASKIN JAY R	MAJ	0-0011044	
HATCHER FREDERICK	LTC	0-0144743	0568
HATHAWAY WALTER H	COL	0-0251950	1168
HAUBTMAN SYDNEY C	MAJ	0-0114422	
HAUSER JOHN N	COL	0-0003358	
HAW JOSEPH C	COL	0-0003826	0868
HAWKINS HUGH J	CPT	0-0395588	0668
HAWLEY RALPH S	COL	0-0153090	0868
HEAD ARNOLD T	LTC	0-0967637	0768
HEDGE GEORGE R	COL	0-0006458	0368
HEEN MYLO L	LTC	0-0022208	0868
HEFLEY ROGER E	2LT	0-0109220	0468
HEFLIN RANKIN W	LTC	0-0384868	
HEITMEYER PAUL R	MAJ	0-0368742	0868
HELLEWELL JOSEPH S	COL	0-0314285	0468
HELLMIG RALPH E	LTC	0-1290751	0868
HELMRATH NORMAN K	LTC	0-0307732	0368
HENDERSON DONALD A	COL	0-0236352	0868
HENDERSON JAMES R	2LT	0-0109274	0368
HENDERSON ROLAND S	COL	0-0011665	0468
HENDRICKSON BARNEY G	CPT	0-0353775	
HENDRIX RICHARD W	COL	0-0337136	0968
HENKLE HARRY L	COL	0-0008090	0968
HENLEY STEPHEN C	CPT	0-0474510	0268
HENNING BERTHEL H	COL	0-0240602	
HENRICH MELVIN C	LTC	0-0317569	0868
HENRY GUY V	M G	0-0000605	
HENSLEY ARTHUR L	MAJ	0-0172797	0768
HENSON JAMES L	MAJ	0-1581175	0468
HERNDOBLER JOHN W	LTC	0-1646246	0968
HERREL GORDON K	CPT	0-1285938	
HERRING TULLIE S	MAJ	0-0885818	0368
HERRON AUSTIN R	MAJ	0-0116911	0268
HERSEY RALPH G	LTC	0-0173211	0767

NAME	GRADE	SVC NO	DATE LOSS MO YR
HESLER ALGY F	COL	0-0119209	0468
HESS CLARENCE L	CW4	W-0902123	0468
HIBBARD GEORGE	MAJ	0-0470607	1068
HIBBARD KEZIAH	CPT	N-0701458	0268
HICKERSON CHARLES W	1LT	0-2004014	
HICKEY JOHN C	CW2	W-0901573	0868
HICKLEIN ALLEN H	COL	0-0010222	
HICKS CLAUD M	1LT	0-1044242	1068
HICKS LEONARD D	1LT	0-5334082	0868
HIGGINS CHARLES C	COL	0-0015348	0368
HIGGINS OWEN W	CW2	W-2208892	0468
HILDRETH GLENN W	LTC	0-0264502	1068
HILL CHESTER E	LTC	0-0408913	0568
HILL RONALD E	1LT	0-5417975	0168
HILL SAMUEL T	COL	0-0041680	0568
HILL WILLIAM H	MAJ	0-0247043	0368
HILLIARD LEONARD L	LTC	0-0015046	0368
HILLMANN FREDERICK	CPT	0-0238972	0468
HIMEBAUGH WILLIAM K	MAJ	0-0235749	0468
HINES JOHN L	GEN	0-0000023	1068
HINTON JONATHAN C	LTC	0-0147197	
HIRSCHFELDER CHESTER	COL	0-0006124	0868
HITCHCOCK LOUIS M	MAJ	0-0006376	0468
HLUHANICH ALEXY M	2LT	0-1642187	0368
HOCHSTADT JACK	MAJ	0-1637684	
HODGES CHARLES C	CPT	0-0495496	0468
HODGES DEAN W	LTC	0-0491083	0168
HOEBEKE ADRIAN L	COL	0-0019334	0768
HOGAN H LEON	LTC	0-0008762	1068
HOILMAN LLOYD R	MAJ	0-0264792	0268
HOLCOMB JOSEPH W	LTC	0-1822699	0968
HOLCOMBE ROLAND N	COL	0-0187588	
HOLDERBY ROBERT A P	COL	0-0184413	1067
HOLLENBACH ALBERT M	COL	0-0029240	
HOLLIDAY MILTON G	COL	0-0001572	0468
HOLLINGSWORTH T G	MAJ	0-0355067	
HOLLOMAN JOSEPH P	CPT	0-0492985	
HOLLOWAY JOHN W	MAJ	0-0521908	0768
HOLMES CLAUDE D	COL	0-0004217	0268
HOLMGREN REINOLD A	2LT	0-0106638	1068
HOMAN CLARENCE A	LTC	0-0173539	
HOOD JOHN D	COL	0-0005332	
HOOVER PHILLIP F	COL	0-0381163	
HOPKINS IRVING G	LTC	0-0141956	
HORN WILLIAM G	CPT	0-2263668	0268
HORNER BERNARD J	COL	0-0152843	0968
HORSFALL GEORGE	COL	0-0017827	0968
HOSTETLER ERWIN C	M G	0-0336226	0568
HOUCK JOSEPH F	COL	0-0029162	0368
HOUK EARL T	LTC	0-0333207	0968
HOUTZ JOHN W	LTC	0-0063326	0868
HOWARD JOSEPH F	CW2	W-2152158	0468
HOWE HAROLL M	COL	0-0150698	0468
HOWE RALPH B	COL	0-0116682	0468
HOWELL FRANKLIN H	MAJ	0-0235125	0668
HOWELL HAROLD K	COL	0-0021421	0768
HOYT GEORGE H	CPT	0-1010555	
HUBBARD DOUGLAS G	LTC	0-0132162	
HUBBARD EDMUND J	CW3	W-0904249	0968
HUBBARD FRANK G	LTC	0-0052430	0768
HUBBARD GILES R	LTC	0-0912672	1068
HUDDLESTON ARTHUR N	COL	0-0221102	0268
HUDDLESTON THOMAS	CPT	0-0919473	1168
HUDDY JAMES JR	CPT	0-0255720	
HUDSON PAUL R	LTC	0-0005482	0768
HUEBSCHWERLEN A S	MAJ	0-0493769	0368
HUFF DUANE E	CPT	0-5405247	
HUFFINGTON JOHN H	MAJ	0-1037545	0868
HUGHES HERBERT T	LTC	0-0247381	0868
HUGHETT GALEN A	MAJ	0-1265057	0868
HUGHLETT LANDON C	MAJ	0-1285946	
HUKINS HARRY W	CPT	0-0137927	0968
HUME HOWARD	COL	0-0004327	0668
HUMMELL LUMAN A	MAJ	0-0126899	0368
HUMPHREY CHARLES F	B G	0-0000668	

NAME	GRADE	SVC NO	DATE LOSS MO YR
HUMPHREY EDWARD L	MAJ	0-0414463	0968
HUMPHREY FREDERIC G	CPT	0-0442403	0368
HUMPHREY HAROLD S	MAJ	0-0192037	0768
HUMPHRIES F M	COL	0-0019012	0568
HUNGATE JAMES W JR	LTC	0-0039951	
HUNT ADAM L	CPT	0-0209344	0768
HUNTER JOHN W JR	CPT	0-0364085	0468
HUREWITZ MORTON M	CPT	0-0471806	1168
HUTCHINS THOMAS M	2LT	0-1914114	1068
HUTCHINSON JOHN A	CPT	0-0278373	
HUTCHINSON THOMAS H	LTC	0-1585658	
HYMAN BERNARD	MAJ	0-0278331	
HYSMITH PRICE E	1LT	0-1308647	0368
INGALLS PHINEAS H	2LT	0-0224802	0868
INGRAM CHARLES L	WO1	W-2149116	1068
IOTT DONALD E	LTC	0-1294136	0768
IRVIN GEORGE A	COL	0-0264007	
IRVIN JOHN W	CW2	W-2117963	0568
IRVING BENJAMIN B	LTC	0-0140673	
IRVING JOHN A	MAJ	0-0260452	0368
JACKSON GEORGE S	CPT	0-1298871	0968
JACKSON ROBERT W	COL	0-0255320	
JACKSON WILLIAM D	LTC	0-0483483	0368
JACOBS JAMES H	MAJ	0-1331053	0568
JACOBS ROY M	MAJ	0-1322034	0368
JACOBS WOODROW W	1LT	0-1300972	0968
JAMES ERNEST H	COL	0-0309493	
JAMES JOE JR	2LT	0-2027403	1068
JAMES JOSEPH H	COL	0-1172085	
JANSEN RAYMOND T	CPT	0-1329010	0968
JEFFERS ULIE H	CW2	W-0800230	
JEFFERSON HARRY F	MAJ	0-0451642	
JEFFREY JACK C	COL	0-0030763	0868
JEFFREY ROSS C	LTC	0-0340195	0768
JEFFREY-SMITH C W	CPT	0-0450965	
JENKINS ARTHUR L	CW2	W-2152219	1267
JENKINS FRANKLIN M	CW3	W-2152229	0668
JENNINGS CHARLES J	2LT	0-1641433	0868
JENNINGS JACK H	CPT	0-0336604	0868
JENSEN ALFRED	CPT	0-0138844	0968
JENSEN JENS B	MAJ	0-0494757	0868
JENSEN MARTIN E	LTC	0-0235549	0368
JOHNS CAROL N	CPT	0-0063061	1168
JOHNSON ALBERT S	LTC	0-0239733	0768
JOHNSON BERT	CPT	0-0188802	0568
JOHNSON BYRON T	CPT	0-0152788	0568
JOHNSON CLARENCE E	MAJ	0-0237942	
JOHNSON CLIFFORD L	CPT	0-0125755	0768
JOHNSON HENRY N	CPT	0-0178691	0468
JOHNSON HUGH C	COL	0-0015345	0568
JOHNSON JOHN J	COL	0-0205340	0668
JOHNSON JOHN S B	COL	0-0269112	1068
JOHNSON MAX	M G	0-0016745	
JOHNSON MELVIN W	LTC	0-0286688	0468
JOHNSON RAYMOND C	LTC	0-0346705	0468
JOHNSON ROWE	MAJ	0-0237897	
JOHNSON WALTER A	MAJ	0-0511241	0468
JOHNSON WILLIAM C	CPT	0-0249411	
JOHNSON WILLIAM G	MAJ	0-1167049	1068
JOHNSTON RUSSELL S	COL	0-0195202	0968
JONES CHILION V	2LT	0-1914308	0768
JONES CLARENCE M	LTC	0-0256801	
JONES CLEMENT R JR	LTC	0-0295192	
JONES EARL A	WO1	W-2116006	0268
JONES EARL W	COL	0-0185108	0868
JONES EDWIN C	LTC	0-0902272	0968
JONES GROVER N	CW2	W-2214880	0568
JONES WILLIAM H	COL	0-0003578	0768
JUCHNIK BOGUMIL F	LTC	0-1644468	
JOZEK HARRY J	COL	0-0009467	0768
KAHANAMOKU DAVID P	CPT	0-0248958	0867
KAHN MYER E	1LT	0-1308343	1068
KAISER ELIAS N	LTC	0-0426502	0868
KAITZ ROBERT	CPT	0-1578680	0868
KALINOWSKA CZESLAW	CW2	W-2149957	0968

NAME	GRADE	SVC NO	DATE LOSS MO YR
KALLOCH PARKER C JR	COL	0-0449004	
KAMINSKY AARON L	LTC	0-0023593	
KAMMERLING DONALD	LTC	0-0252760	0668
KANUZA BERNARD	2LT	0-1033486	
KARGER ALFRED G	COL	0-0265810	0968
KASS CHARLES	MAJ	0-2042741	1168
KEANE THOMAS R	LTC	0-1184092	0768
KEARNEY JOHN W	LTC	0-0474175	0668
KEASLER JAMES L	COL	0-0012234	1168
KEIGHER CLINTON T	LTC	0-0243356	0968
KELLEHER PAUL R	CW4	W-2001894	0368
KELLER EDWARD B	1LT	0-0017117	0268
KELLEY CHARLES F	COL	0-0278931	0568
KELLEY EDGAR C	LTC	0-0202515	0568
KELLY JESSE T	MAJ	0-0220695	0768
KELLY JOHN D	COL	0-0003407	0768
KELLY JOSEPH J	1LT	0-1543479	0868
KELLY WILLIAM H	LTC	0-0222000	0968
KENDALL FREDERICK	B G	0-0051236	0668
KENNEDY LIONEL J	CW2	W-2000117	
KENNEDY REUBEN J JR	CW3	W-2104198	0668
KENNEDY STANLEY Y	LTC	0-0005898	
KERBER JOHN R	CPT	0-0301907	0968
KESSLER ARTHUR G	LTC	0-1183332	0368
KESSLER FRANKLIN L	CPT	0-1689572	0268
KEY PERCY N	CPT	0-0572260	
KEY ROMULUS S	CPT	0-0480749	
KIEWIK JOHN W	WO1	W-2151307	0968
KILCH CHARLES W	1LT	0-1311902	0268
KILMORE JOHN H	CPT	0-0330801	0368
KIMBERLY ALLEN	COL	0-0002206	0668
KING JAMES E	WO1	W-2109365	0368
KING PAUL R	MAJ	0-0009482	0468
KING ROBERT C	LTC	0-1997256	0568
KING THOMAS F	CW2	W-2115954	0768
KINNEY LODIE E JR	MAJ	0-0061828	0468
KIRKPATRICK GRAHAM	LTC	0-0233899	0268
KITTRELL WILBURN H	LTC	0-0192686	0268
KLIE HARRY K	LTC	0-0047792	0568
KLOSS ELIZABETH	MAJ	N-0725935	
KNAPP LAWRENCE M	COL	0-0041942	
KNIGHT BUTLER L	MAJ	0-0007725	1068
KOBBE HERMAN	COL	0-0002463	0468
KOCH WALTER D	COL	0-0107918	1168
KOEHN GEORGE L	MAJ	0-0146365	0368
KOENIG FRANK J	LTC	0-0320229	0768
KOKE OSCAR I	LTC	0-0111083	0468
KOOPS FREDERICK JR	LTC	0-0330021	0368
KOSOLAVAGE ADOLPH A	MAJ	0-1649422	0868
KOTOLAN ADOLPH	CPT	0-0277794	1168
KOTZEBUE LEON L	COL	0-0009700	0968
KOZIATEK THEODORE S	LTC	0-0197303	0468
KRAMER FRANK M	1LT	0-0277680	0568
KRASOWSKI REINHOLD C	CPT	0-0109446	1068
KRATZ GOLDEN P	COL	0-0203702	0468
KRIZ JACK J	1LT	0-0409187	0868
KRODEL WILLIAM J	2LT	0-1035041	0868
KRONCKE ADELINE H	MAJ	N-0731978	
KUHAR STEVEN P	MAJ	0-1295037	
KUNKEL RUDOLPH F	COL	0-0275635	
KUNZ ROBERT N	COL	0-0005293	
KURZDORFER PERCE E	MAJ	0-1534065	0468
KUTZ RICHARD H	2LT	0-1002467	
KVITEK FRANCIS A	COL	0-0292062	0368
LA BROAD RALPH G	LTC	0-0471419	0768
LA CONTE LEONARD	COL	0-0287695	
LA FAVE KENNETH M	CW3	W-2150971	0768
LA PLANTE FREDERICK	CPT	0-0993251	0168
LABBE NORRIS M	COL	0-0197452	0768
LACK NORMAN M	B G	0-0163445	0468
LAFIELD WILLIAM C	COL	0-0159255	0468
LAKE WILLARD	LTC	0-0189306	0868
LAMBERTON WILBUR H	LTC	0-0183263	
LANDERS ALLAN R	LTC	0-0494158	
LANDERS HARVEY J	1LT	0-1058292	0968

NAME	GRADE	SVC NO	DATE LOSS MO YR
LANE ALTON L	CPT	0-1040965	0568
LANE CHARLES C	MAJ	0-0154798	
LANGHAM HARAULD D	LTC	0-0032518	0968
LANKER STANLEY	CPT	0-0495428	
LANKFORD CLINTON C	LTC	0-0921433	0568
LANKFORD LELAND O	1LT	0-1031255	1068
LANSING DUDLEY W	MAJ	0-0166361	0668
LAPLANTE FRANCIS J	LTC	0-0237418	0368
LAREW ISAAC L	LTC	0-1112273	
LAREW RUFUS W	1LT	0-1310266	1068
LARKIN THOMAS B	LTG	0-0003785	1068
LASATER MERLE L	MAJ	0-2206201	1068
LASKO DONALD R	MAJ	0-1703450	0968
LASSER CHARLES	CPT	0-0495129	0568
LAUFERSKI STANLEY R	LTC	0-0183841	0768
LAUGHTER PAUL E	CPT	0-0372383	0868
LAUKAITIS ADAM B	LTC	0-1045802	0568
LAUTERBACH HERBERT G	COL	0-0199098	0868
LAWLOR JOHN E	COL	0-0233976	1068
LAWRENCE GERALD P	COL	0-0142275	
LAWRENCE JOHN D	MAJ	0-0242799	0568
LAWRENCE PAUL H	COL	0-0041420	0768
LAY RUIL C	CW3	W-2144284	
LAZURE ALBERT C	COL	0-0287958	0968
LEARY MARY E	MAJ	N-0751228	0468
LEASE STANLEY E	LTC	0-0355449	0568
LEAVITT LEE R	2LT	0-2007032	1267
LEAVITT RAY M	MAJ	0-1648686	0668
LEE CLAUDE F	LTC	0-2034751	0668
LEE FRANK	CW3	W-2143939	0768
LEE JOHN C	CPT	0-0544834	0668
LEEHEY DONALD J	COL	0-0012673	0468
LEFFINGWELL ROBERT B	MAJ	0-0494119	0968
LEHMAN EMORY V	LTC	0-0289562	0668
LEIBERT JULIUS A	LTC	0-0153418	1168
LEIBSLE ROY W	COL	0-0119574	1168
LENARD LEO L	1LT	0-0106291	0468
LENTZ HAROLD T	COL	0-0028766	0868
LEONARD RICHARD A	1LT	0-0813532	1068
LEPAGE FELIX	CPT	0-0208838	0568
LEVEY SAMUEL	MAJ	0-0277993	0668
LEWEN HERBERT E	CW2	W-2000223	0568
LEWIS EUGENE W	COL	0-0010847	0868
LEWIS JOSEPH H	B G	0-0182597	1068
LEWIS MERIWETHER	LTC	0-0252677	0168
LEWIS RAY H	COL	0-0005238	
LEWIS RICHARD L	COL	0-0042224	0768
LIHBERT CORNELIUS	COL	0-0120527	0668
LINDAUER BERNARD J	1LT	0-1293075	0968
LINDSAY HAROLD E	CPT	0-0179948	0768
LINDSEY JOHN T	CPT	0-0450531	
LINGELBACH DALE N	1LT	0-0526278	
LINK JOHN B JR	CPT	0-0277030	1068
LINTH FRANK A	LTC	0-1636227	
LISSNER HENRY H	COL	0-0102510	0168
LITKE WILLIAM E	COL	0-0244608	0568
LITTLE FREDERICK	MAJ	0-1555424	0468
LLANETA NORBERTO	1LT	0-1865863	1168
LLORENTE FLORENCIO	2LT	0-2030663	
LOCKE FREDERICK	1LT	0-0109173	
LOFLAND ROBERT B	1LT	0-1285612	
LOGAN WILBUR B	MAJ	0-0334329	0568
LOGAN WILLIAM R	1LT	0-1315703	0368
LONG ROBERT N	CPT	0-0171920	0468
LONGFELLOW DON	B G	0-0016708	0268
LONGLEY WILLIAM L	COL	0-0020274	0468
LOPEZ ANDRES	COL	0-0004843	0268
LOTT DOYLE W	MAJ	0-1584535	0268
LOVELL JOSEPH M	LTC	0-0017649	1068
LOWELL JOHN H	LTC	0-0198524	
LOWENBERG MILTON A	COL	0-0196410	0568
LOWRY KENNETH F	LTC	0-0490246	0868
LUCAS CHARLES F	CPT	0-0008908	0968
LUCAS CLARENCE P	2LT	0-1106914	0768
LUCAS JAMES A	CPT	0-0348110	0568

LOSSES TO THE RETIRED LIST

NAME	GRADE	SVC NO	DATE LOSS MO YR
LOCEY JOHN F	LTC	0-0042054	
LUEBKERT WILLIAM C	CPT	0-0299555	0268
LUMPKIN OLIN H	COL	0-0279808	0968
LUNDY WALTER D	COL	0-0258302	0268
LUNN VERLE N	LTC	0-0257388	0768
LUTH WILLIAM L	CPT	0-0014409	0368
LUTZ JOHN E	COL	0-0312083	0568
LUTZ RALPH H	CPT	0-0112789	0468
LYCETT WAYNE L	LTC	0-1000407	1268
LYNCH CHARLES P	COL	0-0008247	
LYNCH FRANK J	MAJ	0-0480325	0968
LYNGE WILBUR J	MAJ	0-0354677	0668
LYON WINSLOW	COL	0-0140516	0868
LYONS JOHN F R	COL	0-0225316	0968
MAC DONALD FLORENCE	LTC	N-0700335	0268
MAC DONALD KENNETH J	LTC	0-0358984	0768
MAC FARLANE WILLIAM	LTC	0-0036949	0668
MAC LEOD GEORGE I	LTC	0-0410869	0868
MAC LEOD HAROLD P	LTC	0-0224112	0268
MAC NIDER HANFORD	LTG	0-0109101	0268
MACE RECTOR T	COL	0-0234399	0568
MACKENZIE DOUGLAS C	COL	0-0169135	0568
MACKLIN JACOB J	MAJ	0-0475853	0468
MACKOWEC JOHN P	COL	0-0274989	0568
MADDEN ARTHUR R	LTC	0-0491698	1267
MAGE JACK O	COL	0-0023971	0568
MAGEE FRANCIS J	COL	0-0172920	0868
MAGUIRE CEDRIC F	MAJ	0-0004932	0768
MAHER ROBERT C	CW3	W-2133813	
MAHONEY PAUL H	COL	0-0015022	0968
MAILMAN EUGENE W	COL	0-0283924	0768
MALCOLM DON J	COL	0-0162499	
MALCOLM ROBERT	MAJ	0-0009442	0868
MALONE CHARLES R	LTC	0-0199910	0368
MALONEY TED W	CPT	0-1326213	
MALTBA NEWT P	CW2	W-2114215	0168
MALUMPHY CHARLES P	COL	0-0029131	
MANEES JAMES R	COL	0-0011664	1068
MANKE FRED	CPT	0-0109133	1068
MANNEN LESLIE E	MAJ	0-0267637	0268
MANNING JAMES P	CW4	W-2113649	0668
MANSKER JOSEPH S	LTC	0-0332721	0968
MARCH JOSEPH H	LTC	0-1556106	0968
MARKEIM CHARLES H	2LT	0-1016461	0368
MARKEL NATHANIEL	CPT	0-1302839	0768
MARKER DANIEL I	LTC	0-0256149	0468
MARKER LOUIS W JR	1LT	0-1298420	0668
MARKHAM EDWARD D	LTC	0-0331570	0268
MARKS EDWIN H	B G	0-0002579	
MARLAND JAMES R	MAJ	0-0039145	0868
MARSHALL BENJAMIN F	COL	0-0103512	0368
MARSHALL SCHUYLER C	1LT	0-0999218	0867
MARTENS EARL W	MAJ	0-0504763	0468
MARTIN ALVIN W	MAJ	0-1031499	0768
MARTIN CHARLES F	COL	0-0279593	0268
MARTIN EDWARD H	COL	0-0016359	
MARTIN LAURIE C	LTC	0-0350155	
MARTIN LAWRENCE A	COL	0-0043665	0668
MARTIN LEWIS F	LTC	0-0330785	0268
MARTIN WILLIAM C	CPT	0-0242781	0668
MASON BEN A	MAJ	0-0005182	0368
MASON CARLE W	LTC	0-0229016	0268
MASON DAVID P	MAJ	0-1292553	1068
MATHENY ARTHUR J	LTC	0-0383435	0968
MATHEWS OSCAR K	CW2	W-2210717	1068
MATTAK JAMES C	CPT	0-0506751	1068
MATTHEWS ALLEN L	MAJ	0-0304454	1068
MATTHEWS FRANCIS R	LTC	0-0480726	0568
MATTSON OSCAR	CW2	W-0800212	0468
MAXWELL RUSSELL L	M G	0-0003350	1168
MAY HERBERT D	COL	0-0156348	0368
MAYO JOSH H	1LT	0-0408869	0668
MAYS WILLIAM L	COL	0-0009054	0468
MC BRAYER CHARLES E	LTC	0-0003048	
MC BRIDE DOROTHY	MAJ	N-0002004	

NAME	GRADE	SVC NO	DATE LOSS MO YR
MC CABE FRANK T	COL	0-0003315	1068
MC CALL EDWARD D	COL	0-0274810	1068
MC CARTY JUSTIN J	LTC	0-1646401	0568
MC CLAIN SYLVESTER	MAJ	0-1035933	0968
MC CLARY GEORGE R	LTC	0-0348192	0468
MC CLELLEN CECIL R	CW2	W-2206355	0368
MC CLINTIC KENNETH	MAJ	0-0278554	0468
MC CLOSKEY JOHN	CW3	W-2146023	0568
MC CLOSKEY SHARON	COL	0-0145859	
MC CLUNG MARGARET W	MAJ	M-0010075	0868
MC CLURE EDWARD J	CW2	W-2147479	0368
MC CLURE FREEMAN C	COL	0-0352901	1268
MC COLLUM JEFFERSON	MAJ	0-1311668	1168
MC CONEGHY JOHN K	LTC	0-0009582	
MC CONVILLE THOMAS P	CW2	W-2150843	0568
MC CORMICK LEIGHTON	LTC	0-0284663	0668
MC COY JOHN T	LTC	0-2021022	
MC COY JOSEPH	LTC	0-0081028	0368
MC CUSKEY JOHN M	MAJ	0-0262280	
MC DANIEL EMORY	CPT	0-0316926	
MC DERMOTT FRANCIS D	WO1	W-2129264	0268
MC DEVITT FREDERICK	CPT	0-0918401	
MC DONALD RALPH M	CPT	0-1684861	0368
MC DONALD WILLIAM W	LTC	0-1323386	
MC DONOUGH JOSEPH A	COL	0-0168267	
MC DONOUGH WILLIAM P	CW2	W-2149299	0368
MC DOWELL JAMES W	1LT	0-1119805	0868
MC ELHANNON JAMES E	1LT	0-0445775	1068
MC ELHENNY WILLIAM S	COL	0-0035025	0268
MC GARR ROBERT L	WO1	W-2108903	0368
MC GINN GEORGE F	COL	0-0145960	0868
MC GINNESS JOHN A	MAJ	0-0520277	1068
MC GINNIS WILLIAM H	CPT	0-0323291	0568
MC GRATH MAURICE N	MAJ	0-0386563	0768
MC HUGH PATRICK H	CPT	0-0504833	
MC INNIS WILFRED C	MAJ	0-0358425	0368
MC KAY FRANCIS J	COL	0-1105668	1068
MC KEAN STERLING J	COL	0-0079924	0968
MC KEE WILLIAM A	LTC	0-0152409	0868
MC KENNA WALTER D	LTC	0-0135589	0368
MC KEON ELISHA J	LTC	0-0262459	1068
MC KEON KATHRYN R	2LT	N-0793717	0868
MC KINLEY HAROLD C	LTC	0-0476682	
MC LAIN VOIL C	CW2	W-2150800	
MC LEELAND W S JR	CW3	W-0903525	
MC LEOD PRENTISS R	CPT	0-0364793	0368
MC MAHAN GEORGE T	COL	0-0249314	
MC MATH MERCER B	LTC	0-0213246	0767
MC MURRAY TOM	COL	0-0183082	0768
MC NAIR JAMES B	MAJ	0-0111191	1267
MC NAIR JOHN W	LTC	0-0153686	0568
MC NALLY EDWARD J	B G	0-0017629	0768
MC NAMARA THOMAS	LTC	0-0153183	0168
MC NEILL NORMAN	COL	0-0008631	0668
MC NULTY WAYNE J	LTC	0-1686244	0868
MC PHAUL JOHN A	CPT	0-0275513	0268
MC QUEEN FRANK T	MAJ	0-0162167	1067
MC SWEEN WHITT P	1LT	0-1011010	0967
MC VICAR JOSEPH K	LTC	0-0245551	
MCKINLEY GEORGE R	CPT	0-1030591	0168
MEACHEN LORREN H	MAJ	0-0186499	0768
MEADOWS MARSHALL D	MAJ	0-0330102	0568
MEALEY FRED T	CPT	0-0487155	0968
MEDLAR WILLIAM P	CPT	0-0014272	0568
MEHAFFEY JAMES L	MAJ	0-1293086	
MEHOLIN JOSEPH W	CPT	0-0247284	0368
MELBERG REINOLD	COL	0-0003812	0768
MELHORN WILLIAM H	LTC	0-0051557	1068
MELLIN CLIFFORD O	LTC	0-0280448	0368
MELLIN LEVI R	CPT	0-0121372	0568
MELOAN JOHN H	COL	0-0145054	
MELOY GUY S JR	GEN	0-0016892	1268
MELSON GRESHAM E	CPT	0-0971971	0768
MENAPACE ROBERT B	COL	0-0169581	0968
MENDENHALL EDWIN L	CPT	0-1683501	

NAME	GRADE	SVC NO	DATE LOSS MO YR
MEREDITH LAWRENCE B	CW4	W-0903539	0868
MEREDITH WILLIAM P	COL	0-0323047	0668
MERICLE HAROLD F	LTC	0-0194266	0868
MERRILL HAMILTON	COL	0-0162202	1068
METHVEN ALBERT E	MAJ	0-1040776	
METTLER CHARLES G	COL	0-0002123	0868
METZE ALBERT	CPT	0-0108796	
MEYER HENRY S	MAJ	0-0267402	0868
MEYERS MELVIN C	LTC	0-2035130	
MICKLE ROSS T	COL	0-0368548	
MIDDLEBROOKS RICHARD	COL	0-0028704	0268
MIHALEK JOHN C	1LT	0-0470853	0268
MILLER CHARLES R	LTC	0-2042949	
MILLER EDWARD T	COL	0-0124344	
MILLER HAROLD D	LTC	0-0140933	0268
MILLER HENRY S	MAJ	0-0137605	0867
MILLER JAMES P	COL	0-0904954	0368
MILLER JOSEPH	CPT	0-0147425	0568
MILLER MARY M	2LT	N-0736129	0668
MILLER PHILIP A	MAJ	0-1549334	0768
MILLER RAYMOND W	CPT	0-0487982	0668
MILLER ROLLAND E	LTC	0-0228961	0868
MILLER ROY W	2LT	0-1914181	1168
MILLER VIRGIL R	COL	0-0015847	0868
MILLER WILLIAM M	COL	0-0209920	1168
MILLS WILLIAM J	LTC	0-0215828	1268
MILNER PAUL	WO1	W-2121035	0468
MILTENBERGER EDWIN J	LTC	0-0914200	0368
MINERLEY ROBERT R	CW4	W-2120726	
MITCHELL HUDON A	LTC	0-1577580	
MITCHELL STEVE F	LTC	0-0116404	0568
MIX PERNIER A	MAJ	0-0008499	1068
MOLNAR LUDWIG S	CPT	0-0159676	1068
MONEYHAM DONALD R	CPT	0-1892081	0468
MONICA LEILA J	1LT	N-0721548	
MONIHAN RICHARD J	1LT	0-1014753	0268
MONTGOMERY CHARLES B	MAJ	0-0390838	
MOODY RAYMOND F	WO1	W-2145828	0468
MOONEY CHARLES P JR	MAJ	0-0270117	0268
MOORE LEWIS F	COL	0-0126834	
MOORE ORVILLE M	COL	0-0004904	
MOORE RAY C	2LT	0-1646352	
MOORE WALTER S	LTC	0-0894101	
MOORHEAD ROBERT L	COL	0-0123658	0368
MOORMAN CHAPMAN S	MAJ	0-0245764	0568
MORGAN JACK E	LTC	0-0358023	0868
MORGAN JOSEPH H	MAJ	0-0475017	0568
MORRIS THOMAS B	COL	0-0100744	
MORRISON READ W	LTC	0-0495407	0668
MORTON LENA M	CPT	L-0514194	0668
MOSELEY JAMES L	MAJ	0-1340308	0268
MOSES PERCIVAL S	COL	0-0111551	0468
MOSLEY WASHINHTON	MAJ	0-0163783	0368
MOSS CHESTER A	COL	0-0294265	0568
MOSS FRANK H	LTC	0-0421004	0968
MOSS WALTER J	CW3	W-2142025	0868
MOTE WILLIAM H	MAJ	0-0192506	0968
MOTT HAROLD W	COL	0-0374190	0468
MOUK ROBERT M	COL	0-0042369	0768
MOUNSEY CARY E	MAJ	0-0107234	1167
MOURHESS BERTRAND L	CPT	0-0198401	
MOZIAN GERARD H	MAJ	0-1573888	0568
MOZLEY JAMES H JR	MAJ	0-0103449	
MUELLER WALTER	1LT	0-1948646	1168
MUELLER WILLIAM G	CPT	0-0109311	
MULLEN JOHN J JR	1LT	0-1320340	0568
MULLER WALTER J	M G	0-0012224	
MULLINGS JOHN J	CPT	0-1030272	0968
MULLINS WALTER F	COL	0-0006944	0468
MULRAIN CHRISTOPHE	MAJ	0-0275511	
MUMBY WILLIAM E	CPT	0-0155952	0468
MUNSON CHARLES H	CPT	0-0139338	0968
MURPHY CHARLES V	CPT	0-0505548	
MURPHY EDGAR J	LTC	0-0226951	0668
MURPHY FRANK E	1LT	0-0443795	0867

NAME	GRADE	SVC NO	DATE LOSS MO YR
MURPHY GUY H	COL	0-0285904	
MURPHY JOHN T	LTC	0-0036776	0668
MURPHY MATTHEW F	COL	0-0170752	
MURPHY PAUL J R	COL	0-0202186	0868
MURRELL POWELL G	LTC	0-0901893	
MYERS C B	LTC	0-1289612	0968
MYERS FRANK R	MAJ	0-0219515	0268
MYERS RAYMOND H	LTC	0-0471712	0968
MYERS WALTER E	MAJ	0-0191549	0468
NARDELLA CHARLES S	MAJ	0-1108195	0768
NASH ELMER N	MAJ	0-1120667	0368
NAYLON JOHN T	COL	0-0223921	0868
NEFF SAMUEL W	MAJ	0-0275199	
NEIDIG DESMOND E JR	MAJ	0-0370862	
NELSON EDWIN	MAJ	0-0286836	0868
NELSON JAMES T SR	MAJ	0-0191468	0868
NELSON MELVIN E	CPT	0-1583435	
NELSON RALPH T	M G	0-0017309	1068
NELSON WOODFORD O	LTC	0-0255755	0368
NEWBERRY ROY W	CW3	W-2152335	0468
NEWELL ALBERT C	LTC	0-0151682	0668
NEWMAN EARL W	CPT	0-0167669	0568
NEWNAN HERMAN R	LTC	0-0205930	1068
NEWSOME CHARLES H	MAJ	0-1547414	0468
NEWTON JAMES S	LTC	0-0322597	
NEWTON PERCY W	LTC	0-0198442	
NG-MUN-TAYNE HELEN B	CW3	V-0906970	
NIBLACK CHARLES K	COL	0-0174889	1068
NICHOLLS JOHN F	CPT	0-0141007	0368
NICHOLS GEORGE F	COL	0-0011875	0268
NICKELS DONALD R	LTC	0-1315353	
NICOLAI NORMAN A	COL	0-0199943	0168
NIMMER RAYMOND F	2LT	0-1797339	0368
NIXON BRYAN W	MAJ	0-0220827	1068
NOLAN WALTER H	MAJ	0-0127776	0468
NORCROSS ORION	LTC	0-0189875	
NORDMANN OLAF	CPT	0-1825435	0368
NORRIS BENJAMIN	COL	0-0004084	0768
NORRIS DON R	COL	0-0006500	0268
NORTH EVERETT K	MAJ	0-1576446	0468
NORTON JOHN F	MAJ	0-0476615	1267
NOWELL ALVIN H	1LT	0-0236223	0168
NOWELL JOHN M III	MAJ	0-1995314	
NOXON JAMES A	LTC	0-0165962	0968
NUNNERY OLVIE J	1LT	0-1691944	0668
OCONNELL RICHARD C	COL	0-0182430	1068
OCONNOR FRANCIS B	MAJ	0-0301814	0668
OCONNOR JAMES	CPT	0-1913897	
OCONNOR JOHN J	LTC	0-1015830	0668
OCONNOR MARIE I	MAJ	N-0759115	
ODEEN CARL H	COL	0-0008020	0768
ODONNELL ROBERT W	LTC	0-0181399	
OGARA HERRICK J	LTC	0-0501250	0968
OGDEN CHARLES W	CPT	0-0006612	0368
OHANLON JAMES F	LTC	0-0217676	0568
OHARA CHRISTOPHE	COL	0-0403390	0468
OHARE JAMES P	LTC	0-1825972	0768
OHEARN WILLIAM J	COL	0-0192519	0668
OHMAN CARL S	CPT	0-0495057	0668
OHMER ROBERT F	COL	0-0160347	0868
OLSH JOHN Z	CPT	0-0324144	0868
OLSON SIGURD	LTC	0-2046324	0268
ONEAL HARLLEE R	LTC	0-0042163	0668
ORBESEN CLIFFORD E	LTC	0-0312925	0868
OSLER RALPH	MAJ	0-0991484	0668
OSMUN JOHN B	LTC	0-0247235	
OSTERMAN ARTHUR H	MAJ	0-0965555	0968
OUSTAD CARL A	LTC	0-0194898	
OVENSHINE ENGLEBERT	COL	0-0000627	
OVERBY CARL L	CW2	W-2121439	
OWEN CHARLES R	LTC	0-0371227	0868
OWEN RICHARD W	LTC	0-0205494	0468
OWENS ROBERT H	LTC	0-0336821	0868
OZDOWSKI FRANK C	CPT	0-0384987	
PACKARD EDWARD N	COL	0-0202025	1168

NAME	GRADE	SVC NO	DATE LOSS MO YR
PADEN JOHN A	LTC	0-0210629	0368
PAGE DAVID E	CPT	0-0497616	1068
PAGE JOHN E	CPT	0-0515866	1168
PAGTER AMOS	LTC	0-0127827	0268
PALLASCH PAUL V	CPT	0-0117746	1167
PALMER ARTHUR C	LTC	0-0271736	0768
PALMER HARRY D	CW2	W-2205164	0768
PANETTIERE BARTHOLOM	LTC	0-1592496	
PANGLE HAROLD J	COL	0-0418496	
PARKER GEORGE M JR	M G	0-0002783	1068
PARKER HENRY H	COL	0-0004694	
PARKETT HENRY F	ILT	0-1913898	
PARSHALL FRED N	MAJ	0-1643204	0268
PARSONS CLAIRE K	CW4	W-2109815	0968
PARTIN IRA	LTC	0-0157539	0368
PATERSON JAMES R	MAJ	0-1798608	0568
PATTERSON ARTHUR S	LTC	0-0285834	0868
PATTERSON JAMES C	COL	0-0008185	
PATTON DOUGLAS J	CPT	0-0336341	0868
PATTON EDWARD C	COL	0-0239564	0368
PATTON JOHN W JR	COL	0-0256699	0568
PATTON ROBERT L	CPT	0-0153810	0568
PAULETTE DAVID W	COL	0-0302871	0368
PAVELKA STANLEY G	CPT	0-1549278	
PAWL WALTER F	CW4	W-2146909	1068
PAYNE SAMUEL C	CPT	0-0009392	0468
PEARCE KENNETH E	LTC	0-0280669	
PEARSON MADISON	B G	0-0003607	0768
PEARSON THOMAS J	LTC	0-0133562	
PENHALLOW DAVID P	LTC	0-0227802	
PENNINGTON JOHN M	CPT	0-1289131	0368
PENROSE ARTHUR W	COL	0-0007913	0868
PERE HENRY J	CPT	0-0219598	0468
PERILLOUX FELIX F	WO1	W-2109111	
PERRONE VICTOR E	MAJ	0-4021477	0368
PERRY WILLIAM K	COL	0-0443840	0868
PERSON JOHN L	B G	0-0017517	1068
PERSONETT CHESTER A	CW2	W-2118131	0868
PETERSEN ALLEN L	CW3	RW-2146807	0368
PETRANEK CHARLES W	MAJ	0-0228402	0468
PETTEE JOHN T	MAJ	0-0325109	0967
PETZOLDT ROBERT W	MAJ	0-0239005	0268
PEYTON ALBERT H	COL	0-0005021	0568
PEZAKAT EDGAR T	MAJ	0-1824226	
PHELPS HORACE F	MAJ	0-0165344	1068
PHILLIPS ELI K	ILT	0-1036680	1068
PILLIVANT RAY A	COL	0-0019761	
PINGER ROLAND W	COL	0-0002966	
PIPPIN FRANK J	LTC	0-0300607	0668
PITTMAN JOSEPH M	COL	0-0019121	
PITTS ATWOOD H	MAJ	0-0237664	0568
PLANK MAURICE D	CPT	0-0304048	0368
POE TEDDY	LTC	0-0285772	
POMEROY ERNEST T	CW2	W-2103322	0968
POMEROY JOHN W	LTC	0-0325004	0668
POOLE GEORGE R	COL	0-0287053	0468
POOLE WILLIAM L SR	LTC	0-0178913	0268
PORTER JOHN M	MAJ	0-0209479	0868
PORTER PECK J	ILT	0-0220767	0568
POSEY ORLANDO J	COL	0-0006550	0768
POSSIEL RAKENIUS J	COL	0-0218218	0768
POTEET BRITTAIN JR	LTC	0-0210910	1168
POTTS ADAM E	COL	0-0003723	1068
POTTS RALPH E	MAJ	0-0121037	0468
POURRON JOSEPH F	MAJ	0-0109280	
POWELL GRAYSON C	COL	0-0306403	
POWELL JOHN C	CPT	0-0103123	
POWELL JOSEPH R	MAJ	0-1590111	0768
POWELL WAYNE E	ILT	0-1925357	0968
POWERS EMORY S	CW3	W-0906959	0468
PRATHER HUGH L	COL	0-0017810	0168
PRATT DONALD E	COL	0-1309962	0468
PREBLE THEODORE L	COL	0-0139903	0868
PREVILLE MARTIN W	MAJ	0-1638300	0668
PRICE ARCHIE A	MAJ	0-0207076	1168

NAME	GRADE	SVC NO	DATE LOSS MO YR
PRICE MILTON I	CPT	0-1689693	0867
PRICE RALPH L	CW2	W-2106650	
PRICE TERRILL F	COL	0-0004627	
PRONDZINSKI AARON G	LTC	0-0362079	0568
PROFFITT FLOON A	LTC	0-0237901	0468
PUGH JOHN F	MAJ	0-0507748	0368
PURDIN WILLIAM H	LTC	0-0039504	0468
PUSZYNSKI JOSEPH M	LTC	0-0288335	
PUTMAN CLINT H	LTC	0-0452935	0968
PUTNAM RUFUS W	COL	0-0900404	0468
PUTNAN DOUGLAS G	LTC	0-0451415	
PUTNEY EDWARD W	COL	0-0002349	0568
QUINLAN JOSEPH A	LTC	0-1590741	0967
QUINN FRANCES S JR	ILT	0-1175549	0568
QUINTO EMILIO F	MAJ	0-0888442	0768
QUINTON ALFRED @ JR	M G	0-0003451	0968
RAAEN JOHN C	COL	0-0012373	0668
RAASCH URBAN C	CPT	0-1001443	0668
RADLEY PETE	ILT	0-1324787	
RAMEE PER	COL	0-0002758	0268
RAMON ADOLPH L	COL	0-0263857	
RAMSAY GEORGE W	CPT	0-0980253	0568
RANDALL JIM F	CPT	0-0484382	
RANDALL PHILIP M	MAJ	0-0186771	1068
RANDALL RAYMOND	COL	0-0009548	0368
RANSOM WILLIAM B	LTC	0-0255790	0568
RAREY ERNEST G	COL	0-0141483	0568
RASMERS FRANZ E	MAJ	0-0107553	0468
RASMUSSEN RAYMOND R	MAJ	0-1583542	
RATHKE LOUIS H	MAJ	0-0153410	1267
RAU JAMES J	WO1	W-2108336	1267
RAWLS LUCIAN R	MAJ	0-0176122	0968
RAWSON HENRY P	LTC	0-0137346	0368
READ FLOYD B	CPT	0-0493638	
READ ROBERT E	CPT	0-0370515	0268
REAM WILLIAM M	COL	0-0030905	0468
REED CHARLES B	COL	0-0030193	
REED CLAUDE V	COL	0-0129338	0868
REESE KENNETH W	CW3	W-2152011	0468
REESMAN WALTER L	COL	0-0003976	0968
REGAN HARRY C	CPT	0-0322672	0568
REGAN MICHAEL C	ILT	0-0108903	
REID ALFRED J	MAJ	0-0256482	
REID AUSTIN P	MAJ	0-0474367	0468
REINERT JOSEPH C	MAJ	0-0127562	
REISER PAUL	MAJ	0-0323876	0368
RESTA FRANCIS E	LTC	TM-0001000	0868
RETZER EARL E	MAJ	0-0105135	1267
REYES EVARISTO	ILT	0-0256855	0768
REYNOLDS DAVID M	CPT	0-2262350	0468
REYNOLDS EARL R	MAJ	0-0005111	1267
REYNOLDS NORMAN C	CPT	0-0357479	1168
RHODES MARTIN C	COL	0-0191090	
RHYNE LUADAN V	2LT	0-0109016	0568
RICE JOSEPH R	CW2	W-2102268	
RICHARDSON ELMER M	LTC	0-0245708	
RICHARDSON JEROME M	WO1	W-2116047	0868
RICHARDSON JIM W	LTC	0-0181277	
RICHARDSON RUPERT F	MAJ	0-1579014	0768
RICHEY THURBER G	COL	0-0104977	1168
RICHIE RICHARD F	LTC	0-0239878	0968
RICKETTS WILLIAM A	CPT	0-0997949	0568
RIDGLEY ARTHUR G	MAJ	0-0507301	0168
RIEDINGER ALBERT A	LTC	0-0338994	
RILEY FLETCHER S	ILT	0-0014387	
RILEY WILLIAM E	ILT	0-1015653	
RISTAU GUSTAV A	CPT	0-0245552	
ROAMER JAMES M	COL	0-0008406	1068
ROBAK CHESTER L	MAJ	0-0160714	0268
ROBBINS EARLE	LTC	0-0008729	
ROBBINS MORTON J	LTC	0-0493480	0668
ROBERTS GORDON M	COL	0-0239665	0668
ROBERTS HENRY G	MAJ	0-0133682	0867
ROBERTS LEE	CPT	0-1945258	1168
ROBERTS THERON E	COL	0-0385537	1168

NAME	GRADE	SVC NO	DATE LOSS MO YR
ROBERTS WILLIAM F	ILT	0-0014342	0368
ROBERTS WILLIAM L	B G	0-0003597	1168
ROBERTSON GEORGE J	CPT	0-0322947	0968
ROBERTSON KATHLEEN	ILT	L-0130275	0968
ROBERTSON RUSSEL A	LTC	0-0319789	0268
ROBINET ALEX J	COL	0-0358288	
ROBINETTE WILLIAM R	COL	0-0029539	0668
ROBINS CLYDE A	ILT	0-1914058	
ROBINSON JAMES L	MAJ	0-0480688	0568
ROBINSON KARL	COL	0-0041857	0468
ROBINSON LIONEL F	COL	0-0248029	0368
ROBINSON OTTO A	MAJ	0-0441103	0168
ROBSON ANDREW S	LTC	0-1823062	
RODMAN BILLY R	2LT	N-0703066	
ROGERS ARTHUR H	B G	0-0006206	0568
ROGERS JOHN B JR	MAJ	0-0270857	0268
ROGERS MAX L	MAJ	0-1176176	
ROGERS RICHARD S	MAJ	0-0228648	0468
ROGERS THOMAS D	B G	0-0019351	0368
ROGERS THOMAS S	MAJ	0-0193781	0868
ROMANO MICHAEL J	CPT	0-0270102	
ROMANOW DAVID	CPT	0-1685918	0368
RONEY CALVIN R	CW2	W-2141432	1168
RONEY JOHN W	MAJ	0-1286896	0968
ROSE EDWARD C	COL	0-0003408	
ROSE GEORGE W	LTC	0-0347276	
ROSE ROBERT A	LTC	0-0231180	
ROSE SAMUEL A	CPT	0-0468160	0768
ROSEBERRY ROBERT C	MAJ	0-0503901	0968
ROSENTHAL LEONARD G	MAJ	0-0314204	1168
ROSIER EUGENE R	CW2	W-2146315	0268
ROSING WILLIS S	CPT	0-0129261	0968
ROSS HERMAN M	2LT	0-1825186	
ROSS OGDEN J	B G	0-0235302	1068
ROSS PAUL S	ILT	0-0524163	
ROSSIE WILLIAM L	LTC	0-0274802	0968
ROTEN CHARLES T	CPT	0-0397252	1068
ROTH IRWIN	LTC	0-1647247	1168
ROTHAUSER HARRY	MAJ	0-0488940	0668
ROUNTREE ELLERY L	LTC	0-0468629	0968
ROUSE MARY A	2LT	N-0756058	1167
ROWE JOHN	CPT	0-0102540	0568
ROWE THOMAS W	MAJ	0-0315813	
ROWLAND THOMAS H	MAJ	0-0109382	1168
ROY EARL P	LTC	0-0171234	0468
RUCH OMAR J	COL	0-0145323	0468
RUCKER HARRY E	COL	0-0041381	1068
RUCKMAN ALBERT	CW4	W-2141435	0968
RUDD AUGUSTIN G	COL	0-0014160	1268
RUDDER MARSHALL C	CPT	0-2051537	
RUHAN KATHRYN L	LTC	N-0700189	0568
RUNYON CARROLL R	MAJ	0-0921533	0368
RUPERT GEORGE S	CPT	0-0473925	1068
RUPP PAUL B	COL	0-0009511	
RUPPANNER PAUL W JR	2LT	0-0290341	
RUTLEDGE CECIL E	COL	0-0007298	0968
RUVIO FRANK	CPT	0-0481053	0768
RYALL WILLIAM J	MAJ	0-1896088	0668
RYAN JOSEPH G	ILT	0-0504228	0168
RYDER FREDERICK	COL	0-0005548	
RYSER ROBERT L	WO1	W-2146090	0768
SAEGER WILLIAM R	CW2	W-2109376	0868
SAFFORD JAMES D	COL	0-0125633	
SALLING MINNIS H	CPT	0-2262563	
SALMON STUART H	LTC	0-0299772	0568
SALYER RAMEY	LTC	0-2014724	0368
SAMONI WILLIAM F	MAJ	0-1338860	0768
SAMPSON EARL F	CW3	W-2150643	1068
SAMSON CLYDE D	MAJ	0-1638418	0268
SANDERS JOHN C	2LT	0-1913915	0768
SANDERS JOHN H	ILT	0-0384914	
SANGER EDWIN E	COL	0-0213816	0468
SARGENT LESTER L	LTC	0-0505613	
SARGENT WINTHROP J	COL	0-0149026	0768
SAVAGE JOSEPH	ILT	0-0164216	0268

NAME	GRADE	SVC NO	DATE LOSS MO YR
SAYERS CHARLES F	LTC	0-0445172	1068
SCALES HOWARD N	LTC	0-0005055	
SCHABACKER C H	B G	0-0012714	1068
SCHAFER CHARLES W	MAJ	0-0194703	
SCHAFER NORMAN H	MAJ	0-0271122	0368
SCHMIDT JOSEPH J	COL	0-0007681	1068
SCHMIDT LELAH M	ILT	N-0743837	0468
SCHMITT ROBERT J	LTC	0-0451065	0368
SCHMITTDIEL HENRY A	ILT	0-1580284	0568
SCHNEIDER RAYMOND F	LTC	0-0237550	0568
SCHOCHET SYDNEY S	MAJ	0-0114730	0568
SCHROEDER HENRY J	COL	0-0005231	0468
SCHULL HERMAN W	B G	0-0000758	0268
SCHULZ GEORGE J	COL	0-0294340	1068
SCHUMACHER CLAIR E	COL	0-0176631	0968
SCHUMANN HEINRICH G	COL	0-0039991	1068
SCHUYLER JAMES T	MAJ	0-0123248	
SCHUYLER ROY L	COL	0-0005875	0968
SCHWARTZ JACK W	M G	0-0017823	0568
SCOBEE ELMER D	CW3	W-2148267	0468
SCOFIELD FRANK C	COL	0-0004499	1168
SCOTT JAMES H	MAJ	0-2102622	1168
SCOTT JOSEPH S	CPT	0-1320970	
SCOTT LEONARD E	MAJ	0-1294542	0468
SCOTT ORVEL M	ILT	0-0235935	
SEBASTIAN EDDIE G	ILT	0-1897003	0268
SECHRIST LEROY E	CPT	0-0283613	0368
SECREST HORACE G	MAJ	0-0226846	
SEELEY BURTON A	COL	0-0004407	1068
SEGUR GERALD H	MAJ	0-0114951	0568
SEIDEL RICHARD H	MAJ	0-1825933	0568
SEMEGA BERNARD P	MAJ	0-1303041	
SEMUTA MICHAEL	CW3	W-2129953	
SEWELL GAINES E	MAJ	0-0186723	0768
SEYMOUR PERCY W	ILT	0-0010242	0868
SHAEFFER CRAWFORD C	CPT	0-0483410	
SHANNON ROSCOE W	MAJ	0-0141146	1068
SHAPO DALTON J	COL	0-0243516	1068
SHARBAUGH JOHN J	CPT	0-0422619	0268
SHARER DONALD V	CPT	0-1300402	0668
SHARPLESS FRANK E	COL	0-0005110	
SHAW HOWARD K	LTC	0-0184547	0468
SHAW JAMES L	CW4	W-0906987	
SHAW JOHN A	COL	0-0007720	0368
SHAW RANDOLPH C	COL	0-0111116	0768
SHAW RONALD M	COL	0-0016103	0568
SHEDOUDY EMIL J	CPT	0-0300020	
SHEEHY JOHN J	LTC	0-1294733	0668
SHEERIN JOSEPH G	2LT	0-0425389	
SHEETS ARTHUR M	COL	0-0008028	0568
SHEETS WILLIAM M	MAJ	0-0199193	
SHEPHERD ELMORE	WO1	W-2110969	0768
SHEPHERD REGINALD W	ILT	0-0386566	0768
SHERBURNE EDWARD G	COL	0-0003849	0668
SHERLOCK JOHN V	LTC	0-0080366	0768
SHERMAN DONALD E	CPT	0-1575156	1168
SHERMAN EARLE D	MAJ	0-0302359	0368
SHERMAN FOREST A	CPT	0-0509890	
SHERMAN HERBERT J	CPT	0-1106463	
SHERMAN ROY	CPT	0-1845245	0468
SHERRILL DON D	CPT	0-0203195	1068
SHERWOOD WALTER L	CPT	0-0509499	
SHIER CYRIL W	LTC	0-0297341	1267
SHOEFFSTALL ELVIN H	CPT	0-0287812	
SHORE ALLEN W	CW4	W-2110727	0968
SHREVE HAROLD E	MAJ	0-0982148	0768
SHREWSBURY CHARLES E	CPT	0-0472121	0168
SHUBERT OSCAR A	CW2	W-0901213	0668
SHULTICE ROBERT W	CPT	0-1593275	0668
SHUTTLEWORTH W S	COL	0-0008898	1168
SIBLEY CLELAND C	B G	0-0015671	0368
SIBLEY WALTER C	ILT	0-1043498	0368
SIBSON WALTER W	2LT	0-1535620	
SIGOUIN ROLAND G	CW3	W-2153355	0868
SIGOURNEY DAVID R	LTC	0-0159339	0768

LOSSES TO THE RETIRED LIST

NAME	GRADE	SVC NO	DATE LOSS MO YR
SILVER HARRY J	MAJ	0-0475397	
SILVERS CHESTER D	COL	0-0039564	
SIMCOX LAWRENCE S	COL	0-0030602	0968
SIMMONS CHESTER H	LTC	0-0277853	
SIMON CHARLES J	MAJ	0-0206254	1168
SIMONSON JOE A	LTC	0-0245595	0568
SIMPSON EVERETT W	LTC	0-0114382	0468
SIMPSON WILLIAM E	COL	0-0339393	0868
SIROIS EDWARD D	M G	0-0174746	0268
SISKEL MAURICE	MAJ	0-0275361	0968
SKIDMORE FRANCIS J	COL	0-0309004	0768
SKINNER JOHN T	MAJ	0-0981567	0668
SKINNER THOMAS F	LTC	0-1110805	0968
SLACK JOHN M	CPT	0-0190138	0268
SLACK JULIUS F	B G	0-0012271	0568
SLAUGHTER PAGE H	COL	0-0030250	0868
SLIPAKOFF SAMUEL A	LTC	0-0267778	
SLONE AUGUSTUS D	CPT	0-0482511	0968
SMITH ELLIS E JR	CPT	0-1103335	0568
SMITH FRANCIS M	COL	0-0100084	0368
SMITH FRANK L	LTC	0-0326245	
SMITH GEORGE S	M G	0-0015308	0968
SMITH HARRY B	LTC	0-0006342	0868
SMITH HAZEL F	MAJ	N-0726722	0568
SMITH HENRY T	2LT	0-1913932	0668
SMITH HERBERT T	1LT	0-1103411	
SMITH IRVIN T	LTC	0-1181764	
SMITH JOHN	LTC	0-0184905	0868
SMITH JOSEPH	2LT	0-1016638	0268
SMITH JOSEPH F	1LT	0-1298145	0568
SMITH KARL W	LTC	0-1174146	0668
SMITH LEROY J	1LT	0-1175583	0968
SMITH LOUIS G	COL	0-0105917	
SMITH MILTON T	CPT	0-0249236	0468
SMITH WALDON T	1LT	0-1318339	
SMITH WALTER S	CW2	W-2146679	
SMITH WILLIAM A	MAJ	0-0330509	0768
SMITH WILLIAM W	MAJ	0-0502405	0668
SMITHSON CHARLES E	LTC	0-0185767	0568
SMOLCZYNSKI STEPHEN	LTC	0-0309194	1268
SMUIN JOHN W	CPT	0-0444435	0968
SMYTHE LESTER A	MAJ	0-0474365	0968
SNEAD BENJAMIN F	CPT	0-0221908	
SNOOK JESSE	CPT	0-0520958	0768
SNYDER CLARENCE J	MAJ	0-1057903	
SNYDER ELWYD C	LTC	0-0237124	0868
SODERBERG CHARLES A	1LT	0-0074512	
SOISSONS ALFRED F	COL	0-0483746	1068
SOLODOVNICK JACOB S	CPT	0-0532565	
SOUTHWORTH MAYNARD N	CPT	0-0291444	0768
SPALDING ALBA C	COL	0-0014938	
SPARKS LEONARD C	COL	0-0002466	0468
SPERRY HIRAM	COL	0-0263799	
SPILLER ERNEST M	CPT	0-0208465	0268
SPINKS LESLIE	COL	0-0029012	0368
SPOONER CHARLES E	MAJ	0-0300382	0968
SPRINGER ROBERT W	COL	0-0152015	0568
SQUIER BASIL G	MAJ	0-0164225	0868
SQUIRES CHARLES D	LTC	0-0490594	0168
SQUIRES HAROLD R	COL	0-0119291	0768
STAFFORD WILLIS L	CPT	0-0475510	0368
STALIONS KENNETH W	CW2	W-2144431	0868
STARK ALEXANDER JR	B G	0-0005000	0768
STARKEY ERNEST	CPT	0-0143948	1168
STEELE JOSEPH R	COL	0-0268338	
STEFFEN FREDERICK	COL	0-0118940	0968
STEIGLER ROBERT L	1LT	0-0223742	
STEIGER WALLACE C	COL	0-0008196	
STENSLIE ARNE	LTC	0-0203696	0268
STEPHEN ANNA E B P	CPT	N-0797749	
STEPHENS JAMES R	MAJ	0-0400881	0568
STEPHENSON ALBAN J	1LT	0-1169350	
STEVENS HARRY L	WO1	W-2110420	
STEVENS ROBERT L	CPT	0-0268269	0868
STEWART JOHN W	MAJ	0-0149146	0368
STEWART RALPH B	COL	0-0009527	
STEWART ROY E	CW3	W-2141792	
STEWART WILLIAM B	MAJ	0-0283969	0368
STICKMAN WILLIAM R	COL	0-0006595	0168
STIERLE WILLIAM R	1LT	0-2035867	0268
STITES HENRY J	COL	0-0183202	0468
STOCKDON WALLACE I	LTC	0-0171571	0568
STOCKTON WILLIAM H	1LT	0-1046288	0768
STOCKWELL ROY	LTC	0-0153336	
STOKES BENJAMIN F	MAJ	0-0131351	0468
STOKES JAMES H	CPT	0-0525511	0968
STOKES JOHN H JR	M G	0-0012181	1168
STOLZ ALFRED A	LTC	0-0379850	0368
STOUT JAMES M	CW3	W-2205789	1068
STOUT JAY N	LTC	0-1554643	0468
STRANG ARTHUR L	LTC	0-1165151	0768
STRANGE WILLIAM C	CPT	0-1846225	0568
STRASH VICTOR C	1LT	0-0253950	0868
STRASSBURG HARRY E	MAJ	0-0250836	
STREET HAROLD L JR	LTC	0-0081263	0868
STRIBLING ANDREW C	MAJ	0-0201298	0468
STRICKLAND FRANK Z	LTC	0-0491595	
STRICKLEN WILLIAM A	COL	0-0031473	0568
STRICKLER JOHN C	COL	0-0016445	1068
STRIEGEL JOHN L	LTC	0-1319676	0468
STROM EDWARD T	CPT	0-0921605	
STROME GRANT U	CPT	0-0119786	0168
STROMWALL EDGAR A	CPT	0-0127722	
STRYJEWSKI JOSEPH S	MAJ	0-1550276	0268
STUBBS ROBERT E	MAJ	0-0385721	0568
STYLES ALBERT W	1LT	0-1319678	
SULLIVAN EDWIN J	1LT	0-1297116	
SULLIVAN FRANCIS J	LTC	0-0039507	
SULLIVAN FREDERICK	LTC	0-0312389	0168
SULLIVAN WILLIAM T	MAJ	0-0311998	1068
SUMMERS LILLIE C	MAJ	N-0758727	
SUMRALL HENDRI A	MAJ	0-1876967	0468
SUTFIN HARRY F	WO1	W-2106811	0368
SUTTON STOWE T	COL	0-0011165	
SWADELL ERIC E	LTC	0-0514896	0468
SWARTZ HARRY C	LTC	0-0333986	0568
SWARTZ RALPH R	MAJ	0-0290046	0468
SWETT TREVOR W	COL	0-0007010	
SYLVESTER ETHEL M	MAJ	N-0002157	0168
SYPOLE FLOYD T	MAJ	0-0251755	0968
TABOR LYLIA H	2LT	L-0611361	0268
TAFT MARSHALL F	1LT	0-1036052	
TAGGART ROY M	LTC	0-0280919	0368
TALBOT LYMAN P	COL	0-0268085	0368
TARVIN EARL W	CW2	W-2208143	1168
TATOM LOUIS J	COL	0-0014694	0568
TAYLOR ALBERT L	MAJ	0-0354971	
TAYLOR CHARLES M	COL	0-0004012	1168
TAYLOR EARL A	COL	0-0171126	0368
TAYLOR FRANK	CW2	W-2152225	1168
TAYLOR GEORGE R	LTC	0-0346790	1068
TAYLOR HAROLD A	COL	0-0228432	0768
TAYLOR HERBERT E	COL	0-0003147	0568
TAYLOR INGRAM C	LTC	0-0484881	0968
TAYLOR OZIER C	1LT	0-1297117	
TERKOSKI SYLVESTER	MAJ	0-1545442	0668
TESLAR MICHAEL J	WO1	W-2120947	0768
THACH HENRY C	LTC	0-1295794	0768
THACHER JAMES S	1LT	0-2292648	0668
THOMAS WALTER JR	COL	0-0344189	0368
THOMPSON ALBERT	MAJ	0-0243643	0668
THOMPSON AYLMER S N	CPT	0-0139598	0868
THOMPSON EARL G	MAJ	0-0279615	1068
THOMPSON ERNEST B	COL	0-0015242	1168
THOMPSON JESSIE C	2LT	N-0700557	0568
THOMPSON LESTER E	LTC	0-0188229	0268
THORN HAMILTON	COL	0-0006877	0168
THORNHILL CLYDE M	LTC	0-0321627	1068
THORNTON EARL L	COL	0-0117632	
THRALL C BURTON	COL	0-0277965	0968
THWAITS PRIOR	MAJ	0-0890154	0668
TILLI OLIVER F	LTC	0-0661897	0468
TILLINGHAST LEWIS G	LTC	0-1555143	
TILTON EUGENE H	CPT	0-0007394	0268
TIMMONS JOSEPH W	MAJ	0-0009543	1268
TISDALE HENRY E	COL	0-0007968	1068
TOLENTINO PETE L	CPT	0-1896705	0368
TOLLIS DAVID P	LTC	0-1117336	0468
TOMANENG MAGDALEND	LTC	0-1302234	1168
TOMPKINS ARTHUR F	CPT	0-0347969	
TOOLE WILLIAM F	COL	0-0181823	0468
TOPFER ARTHUR O	1LT	0-0496776	
TOPPING FREDERICK	COL	0-0005882	0368
TORNELL CLAUS A	COL	0-0279012	0368
TOSTON WILLIAM L	CPT	0-0484082	1168
TOWNSEND FRANK C	CPT	0-0201155	0268
TOWNSEND MAURICE L	COL	0-0163280	0368
TRABER OSCAR W	COL	0-0171224	
TRACY JOSEPH P	LTC	0-0252209	0968
TRAMELL JOE P	MAJ	0-1330986	0268
TRAMMELL ADMIRAL B	COL	0-0041501	0268
TRASK CARLTON F	LTC	0-1553744	0668
TRAVIS HARRY F	LTC	0-0145807	
TRAYNOR OWEN J	CPT	0-0501746	
TREANOR ROBERT A	2LT	0-2297638	
TRECARTIN CYRUS S	MAJ	0-0496924	0968
TRIMBLE DONALD F	MAJ	0-0404408	1068
TROTT MAYNARD J JR	LTC	0-1170229	0468
TUCKER DELMAR E	CW4	W-2114330	
TUCKER HYMAN	LTC	0-0219779	
TUCKER ROYAL K	LTC	0-0107440	
TURLEY ROBERT E JR	COL	0-0004722	
TURNER ARCHIBALD	LTC	0-0109938	0468
TURNER CLIFFORD H	CPT	0-1552409	0268
TURNER JOHN H	LTC	0-0271206	0468
TUTTON ROBERT L	CW2	W-2144515	0968
TWAY THOMAS D	COL	0-0145374	0768
TWINING HAROLD C	LTC	0-0334085	0568
TWIST FRANK F	LTC	0-0265653	0468
TYLER PETER C	CPT	0-1914329	
TYNER ROBERT R	MAJ	0-0687168	0468
ULMER JOSEPH J	CW4	W-2101321	1068
UNDERDOWN C M	CPT	N-0000036	0568
UNRUH CHARLES L	LTC	0-0301048	1168
URICH RUSSELL	1LT	0-0509849	
USHAKOFF MICHAEL M	MAJ	0-0253933	0468
UZZEL NORRIS H	MAJ	0-0963524	0468
VALENTINE HENRY D	CPT	0-0189431	
VALIMAKI TAUNO E	MAJ	0-1339828	
VAN AUKEN WILLIAM B	COL	0-0006972	0268
VAN BERNUM FRED	2LT	0-1032606	0468
VAN DEVENTER ROY W	COL	0-0199582	0868
VAN MARTER JAMES H	LTC	0-0182654	1068
VAN OOSTEN JOHN	LTC	0-1287090	
VAN PRAAG DAVID B	1LT	0-4063766	
VANHOLME FLORIMOND	COL	0-0393321	0268
VANNIER EDWARD S	MAJ	0-0212533	0568
VARGO MARGARET M	LTC	N-0728070	0368
VARNEY FRED W	MAJ	0-0953161	1068
VARNEY WILLIAM E	MAJ	0-1636765	0968
VARS DONALD D	LTC	0-0019432	0168
VELTRO FRANK E	MAJ	0-0230065	0368
VERA JOSE JR	CPT	0-1684927	
VERMILYEA HARVEY C	MAJ	0-0191210	0768
VICTORY ARMEL T	MAJ	0-0137135	0168
VIDAL LAWRENCE F	LTC	0-0166163	
VIGLIERO JOHN A	MAJ	0-0183319	0168
VILLAPANDO PRIMITI	1LT	0-1856898	1068
VIOLANTE ANDRE L	COL	0-0010280	0568
VITT EDWARD A	LTC	0-0223282	
VOCKERY WILLIAM	MAJ	0-0450500	
VOLCHOK ROBERT J	1LT	0-1039606	0368
VOSMEIER LEONARD H	MAJ	0-0122696	0768
WAGNER CHESTER T	LTC	0-0285803	0368
WAINWRIGHT WILLIAM H	CPT	0-1292426	0668
WALES HOMER L	CPT	0-0243224	0168
WALKER GLEN	LTC	0-1549159	0968
WALKER JOHN T	LTC	0-0278849	0668
WALL WILLIAM E	LTC	0-0922610	0868
WALLACE BRENTON G	B G	0-0185391	0668
WALLACE ELSIE H	2LT	N-0726446	0668
WALLAR HOMER R	COL	0-0051196	1168
WALSH CHARLES E JR	COL	0-0263555	1267
WALTON PETER W	MAJ	0-1546249	0668
WALTON RUFUS R	CPT	0-0283721	0568
WALTZ STANLEY G	COL	0-0286747	0368
WANGERIEN WILLIAM F	LTC	0-1041939	0668
WARD ARTHUR J	LTC	0-0365879	
WARD CHARLES R	CPT	0-0275031	0468
WARNER LEWIS W	COL	0-0122136	0268
WARNER MILO J	CPT	0-0014373	0168
WARREN CHARLES H	LTC	0-0175366	
WASSER ALFRED	MAJ	0-0250895	0568
WASSERSTEIN JACK J	LTC	0-0204043	
WATERS ARCHIE C	LTC	0-0206833	0568
WATERS PHILEMON B	LTC	0-0168702	1068
WATERS WILLIAM A	CPT	0-0172885	
WATKINS CLIFFORD W	MAJ	0-0207184	
WATKINS ELLIOTT	COL	0-0012214	0668
WATKINS HERBERT E	COL	0-0005867	1268
WATKINS JAMES G	COL	0-0007249	
WATKINS ROBERT L	B G	0-0244532	0767
WATROUS CHARLES A	LTC	0-0105814	0468
WATROUS LIVINGSTON	COL	0-0003176	
WATSON ARTHUR B	LTC	0-0115393	0168
WATSON HARRY L	COL	0-0012933	0468
WATSON JOHN L	LTC	0-0220478	0468
WATTS NATHAN E	CPT	0-0398324	1068
WEAR GEORGE S	COL	0-0007337	0868
WEATHERRED PRESTON A	B G	0-0170749	
WEAVER JAMES L	CPT	0-1544268	0868
WEAVER JOHN H	MAJ	0-0249200	
WEAVER LOGAN M	COL	0-0006368	0768
WEBB IRA V	MAJ	0-0164232	
WELGE CARL J	COL	0-0057041	0268
WELLS HANSEL P	1LT	0-0359470	0968
WENDELL CHARLES A	COL	0-0288189	0868
WENZEL VICTOR	CW2	W-2001980	
WERSICK WILLIAM K	CPT	0-0504834	0768
WEST HORACE W	MAJ	0-2005251	0768
WEST LIONEL M	LTC	0-0262769	0768
WEST ROBERT	MAJ	0-2055793	0468
WEST ROLAND P	LTC	0-0034208	0368
WESTERMAN ACES M	CPT	0-1293686	
WETHERBY LOREN A	COL	0-0007038	1168
WEYRICK LEROY	COL	0-0165766	
WHALEY WILLIAM B	CPT	0-0491438	0668
WHEELER HOWARD J	LTC	0-0922438	0568
WHEELER JOHN S	COL	0-0296955	0468
WHEELER JOSEPH	2LT	0-1913998	0268
WHEELER WILLIAM E	MAJ	0-0143845	
WHIDDON FRANK M	LTC	0-0189750	0568
WHITCHURCH ROY B	CPT	0-0488394	0268
WHITE CECIL B	2LT	0-0323745	
WHITE MAC P	CPT	0-1055509	1068
WHITE MARY P	CW4	V-0609154	1268
WHITE ROBERT L	CW2	W-2105000	0568
WHITEFORD ROGER S	COL	0-0244043	1168
WHITLOCK DEAN R	MAJ	0-1638784	0768
WHITLOCK HOMER N	CPT	0-0995735	
WHITNEY NORMAN E	COL	0-0185440	0268
WHITTEN HAROLD F	1LT	0-1553199	0968
WHITTON JAMES R	LTC	0-0349771	0568
WICKERSHAM C W	B G	0-0147303	0168
WIDDOWSON LYLE E	LTC	0-0368657	0968
WIEDEMER GEORGE J	LTC	0-1019576	0568
WIER ROBERT W	CPT	0-1534187	0968
WIESE WALTER C	CW3	W-2144603	0368
WIGGINS THOMAS H	1LT	0-1104008	0768
WIGHTMAN RICHARD O	CW4	W-0904019	0868

NAME	GRADE	SVC NO	DATE LOSS MO YR
WILCOX BERNHARD B	LTC	0-0204354	0668
WILCOX HERBERT B	COL	0-0012763	0368
WILCOX RUSSELL J	LTC	0-0359452	0268
WILDMAN STANLEY F	LTC	0-0205860	0468
WILEMON WILLIAM N	COL	0-0029060	1068
WILES ELMER J	LTC	0-0232831	
WILKERSON JAMES ?	COL	0-0345240	0368
WILKES GILBERT V	COL	0-0037581	0968
WILKINSON CHARLES T	COL	0-0327487	1068
WILL CAMERON ?	CPT	0-0154599	0468
WILL GEORGE	ILT	0-1895314	
WILLETT BYRON ?	MAJ	0-0322864	1068
WILLIAMS EDWIN M	CPT	0-0942979	0968
WILLIAMS GRANT J	LTC	0-0365852	0268
WILLIAMS HARRY S	MAJ	0-0946721	0767
WILLIAMS HENRY C	CW2	W-2149357	
WILLIAMS JAMES J	MAJ	0-1640125	1068
WILLIAMS JAMES T	LTC	0-0491045	
WILLIAMS RALPH T	CPT	0-1039799	1068
WILLIAMS ROBERT P	B G	0-0003924	
WILLIAMSON JOHN	COL	0-0137446	
WILLKIE ROBERT T	COL	0-0361092	0468
WILMOTH EDWARD M	LTC	0-0182225	0468
WILSON ERNEST H	MAJ	0-0016160	0368
WILSON EUGENE	LTC	0-1575280	0368
WILSON GEORGE A	MAJ	0-0133593	
WILSON HARRY B	CW3	W-2153040	0368
WILSON JAMES J	MAJ	0-0065703	0968
WILSON KENNETH A	CPT	0-0180202	
WILSON MELVIN T	LTC	0-0470923	0768
WILSON VERNON A	MAJ	0-0370516	0468
WIMBERLY JAMES F	LTC	0-0271304	0568
WINDHAM JAMES B	LTC	0-0450952	0868
WINDLE WILLIAM B	COL	0-0157976	0468
WING CHARLES K	COL	0-0002423	1168
WINKING CYRIL H	MAJ	0-1533474	0368
WINN JOHN J JR	LTC	0-0458400	0368
WINSTON NORMAN L	MAJ	0-1107764	
WIRRICK ROY F	CW3	W-2145852	0968
WISE CHARLES S	ILT	0-1650300	
WISHART FRANCIS E	COL	0-0326749	0468
WITHERS ROBERT L	MAJ	0-0137281	0768
WITKOWSKI THOMAS E	LTC	0-1305687	
WITTE JAMES ?	LTC	0-0349178	1068
WITTKOPF PHILIP W	CPT	0-1313007	
WOERNER GARY C	CPT	0-2313065	0168
WOGAN JOHN B	M G	0-0003834	0968
WOLFE HOWARD ?	MAJ	0-0114173	
WOLFE NORMAN B	ILT	0-1062658	0968
WOLFF JOHN P	LTC	0-0291219	
WOLFF 3RD CHARLES	COL	0-0287042	0668
WOOD CHARLES A JR	COL	0-0241851	
WOOD GASTON M	COL	0-0216671	1068
WOOD RUSSELL H	MAJ	0-0233487	0468
WOOD THOMAS C JR	COL	0-0015946	0868
WOOD WILLARD W	MAJ	0-0277113	0668
WOODALL RAY T	LTC	0-0298793	0968
WOODARD LYLE E	WO1	W-2126094	
WOODBURY WILLIAM W	ILT	0-1283183	0568
WOODMAN NED H	COL	0-0029622	
WOODRUFF HALBERT E	LTC	0-0238295	
WOODYARD ELMER A	CPT	0-0493948	0868
WOOFTER CLARENCE J	CPT	0-0473121	0168
WOOLDRIDGE SYLVANUS	LTC	0-1688546	0768
WOOLDRIDGE WARD	MAJ	0-0924784	0568
WOOLFSON ALBERT	MAJ	0-0529207	0868
WORKS JOHN M	COL	0-0012449	
WRIGHT BESSIE F	ILT	0-0309137	0168
WRIGHT EDWARD F	LTC	0-0266172	0468
WRIGHT EUGENE J	CW3	W-2145611	0468
WRIGHT HOWARD	COL	0-0172676	0568
WRIGHT ROBERT C	LTC	0-1579324	
WRIGHT WILBUR T	MAJ	0-0101331	
WUEST WILLIAM J	COL	0-0029026	1068
WUNDERLICH F P	COL	0-0003999	

NAME	GRADE	SVC NO	DATE LOSS MO YR
WYLIE WILLIAM J	2LT	0-1110355	0968
WYMORE PERDUE A	CPT	0-0482476	
YANCY BENJAMIN A	MAJ	0-0004493	0368
YANCY EARL B	CW4	W-2119895	1168
YARIAN LESTER D	MAJ	0-0118995	0468
YEAKEY LEON L	LTC	0-0192365	0968
YERBANCE ALEXANDER	MAJ	0-0189608	0968
YINGST PARKE D	MAJ	0-0270553	
YORK NORMAN J	CW4	W-2110388	
YOTT GEORGE F	MAJ	0-0217095	0668
YOUNG CHARLES C	MAJ	0-0110878	0468
YOUNG DONALD C	LTC	0-1588391	
YOUNG MALCOLM E	ILT	0-1180783	
YOUNG MARION L	LTC	0-0006516	1068
YOUNG STEWART	ILT	0-1914025	0368
ZADYLAK FRANK V	ILT	0-1316477	0668
ZARTARIAN SARKIS M	COL	0-0171485	
ZIEHNERT JULIAN F	MAJ	0-1048263	0968
ZIMMERMAN MORRIS L	LTC	0-0204275	0268
ZION JACOB J	MAJ	0-1003597	0668
ZOLLO CHARLES A	COL	0-0190218	

NAME	GRADE	SVC NO	DATE LOSS MO YR

NAME	GRADE	SVC NO	DATE LOSS MO YR

U. S. GOVERNMENT PRINTING OFFICE : 1969 O - 332-811

Lightning Source UK Ltd.
Milton Keynes UK
UKHW031213050720
366059UK00010B/494